THE
Oxford
American
Dictionary
and
Language
Guide

THE
Oxford American Dictionary and Language Guide

New York   Oxford
Oxford University Press
1999

Oxford University Press

New York   Oxford

Athens   Auckland   Bangkok   Bogotá
Buenos Aires   Calcutta   Cape Town   Chennai   Dar es Salaam
Delhi   Florence   Hong Kong   Instanbul   Karachi
Kuala Lumpur   Madrid   Melbourne
Mexico City   Mumbai   Nairobi   Paris   São Paulo   Singapore
Taipei   Tokyo   Toronto   Warsaw

and associated companies in
Berlin   Ibadan

Published by Oxford University Press, Inc.,
198 Madison Avenue, New York, New York 10016

ISBN 0-19-513449-4

3 5 7 9 8 6 4 2
Printed in the United States of America
on acid free paper

Contents

Project staff

Editor-in-Chief:
Frank R. Abate

Managing Editor:
Elizabeth J. Jewell

Associate Editors:
Christine A. Lindberg
Andrea R. Nagy
Laurie H. Ongley

Assistant Editors:
John Bollard
Linda Costa
Archie Hobson
Mark LaFlaur
Nancy LaRoche
Joseph M. Patwell
Katherine C. Sietsema
Dawn Thornton

Pronunciation Editor:
Rima McKinzey

Special Features Editor:
Sue Ellen Thompson

Art Editor:
Deborah Argosy

Illustrators:
Marta Cone
Elizabeth Gaus
Mark Maglio
Mike Malkovas
Susan Van Winkle

Editorial Assistants:
Alexandra Abate
Karen Fisher
Maurice Lee

Data Entry:
Elaine Cirillo
Kimberly Roberts

Preface

The Oxford American Dictionary and Language Guide covers an extensive range of contemporary American English vocabulary. The text was specially compiled for this edition by Oxford's U.S. Dictionaries Program, in keeping with the renowned lexicographic tradition of Oxford University Press. Oxford's unrivaled language research, including the North American Reading Program (NARP), constantly monitors growth and change in American English. Using computerized search-and-analysis tools developed originally for the 20-volume *Oxford English Dictionary,* our American lexicographers can quickly explore more than 45 million words of citation text collected by NARP, and consult many other massive English language databases. The result is a more sharply refined picture of the language of today, elucidating many complex aspects of meaning, grammar, and usage.

This dictionary reflects the scholarly guidance of Oxford's academic advisors, as well as the experience of specialist consultants in many fields of endeavor. And with the Internet and the World Wide Web, Oxford lexicographers are now able to stay in daily contact with expert sources worldwide, receiving answers to their queries almost instantly.

The text is accompanied by hundreds of examples, illustrations, and usage notes that clarify definitions and provide guidance on the subtleties of appropriate usage. Special boxed features highlight word histories and language tools such as synonym, pronunciation, spelling, and punctuation tips. The extensive Language Guide in the middle of the book (following page 594) provides clear, practical advice on how to improve language skills. Biographical and geographical sections in the back of the book offer essential information on the key people and places of the world, with more than 170 maps highlighting countries of the world. Finally, special reference appendices provide quick-reference information for a variety of subjects that are of frequent interest.

The Oxford American Dictionary and Language Guide is an excellent choice for business people, students, and all those who wish to use English with clarity and style. With its attention to accuracy, currency, and thoroughness, this new American dictionary builds on the tradition of Oxford—the world's most trusted name in dictionaries.

Frank R. Abate
Editor in Chief, U.S. Dictionaries
Oxford University Press, Inc.

How to Use This Dictionary

Below is a complete explanation of the features in the *Oxford American Dictionary and Language Guide*. In addition to information on how to use the dictionary entries themselves, please note the discussion of the various elements of the "Language Guide":

- Language tips that accompany certain entries (as boxed features)
- the Language Guide section itself, at the middle of the dictionary (see the gray-tinted pages following the entries for letter L), with a wealth of useful information on how to use language clearly, correctly, and elegantly.

❶ Main entries

A typical entry and its features is as follows:

> **ad•vo•cate** *n. & v.* ●*n.* /ádvəkət/ **1** (foll. by *of*) a person who supports or speaks in favor. **2** a person who pleads for another. **3** a professional pleader in a court of justice. ●*v.tr.* /ádvəkayt/ **1** recommend or support by argument (a cause, policy, etc.). **2** plead for; defend. □□ **ad•vo•cate•ship** *n.* **ad•voc•a•to•ry** /advókətáwree, ádvəkə–, ádvəkaytəree/ *adj.* [ME f. OF *avocat* f. L *advocatus* past part. of *advocare* (as AD–, *vocare* call)]

Main entries are in bold roman type and are arranged in letter-by-letter alphabetical order. Syllables are indicated by the centered dots in main entries and derivatives; the dots mark acceptable places for word division. Different words that are spelled the same way (homographs) are distinguished by raised numerals:

> **boom**¹ /boom/ *n. & v.* ●*n.* a deep resonant sound. ●*v.intr.* make or speak with a boom. [imit.]
> **boom**² /boom/ *n. & v.* ●*n.* a period of prosperity or sudden activity in commerce, etc. ●*v.intr.* (esp. of commercial ventures) be suddenly prosperous or successful. □□ **boom•let** *n.* [19th-c. US word, perhaps f. BOOM¹ (cf. *make things hum*)]

❷ Pronunciation

Guidance on the pronunciation of a main entry will be found in most cases immediately following the main entry, enclosed in oblique strokes / /. In some cases, more than one pronunciation is given: that given first is the more frequent or preferred pronunciation. When pronunciation is different for different parts of speech, as for **advocate** above, each part of speech label carries its appropriate pronunciation. Guidance on the pronunciation of derivatives of the main entry is limited to cases in which the main entry pronunciation would be of no help in establishing the correct pronunciation of the derivative. The dictionary uses a simple respelling system to represent pronunciation. This is meant to be self-explanatory and easily readable by the lay person without constant recourse to a table of special characters.

For details on the pronunciation symbols, see the "Key to Pronunciation" below.

❸ Part of speech

The grammatical identity of words as noun, verb, adjective, and so on, is given for all main entries and their derivatives. The same part-of-speech labeling is used for groups of more than one word when the group has the function of a particular part of speech, e.g., *ad hoc; vacuum cleaner.* When a main entry has more than one part of speech, a list is given at the beginning of the entry, and the treatment of the successive parts of speech is introduced by a bullet in each case.

The standard part-of-speech names are used, and the following additional explanations should be noted:

- Nouns used attributively are designated *attrib.* when their function does not include predicative use (e.g., *model* in a *model student;* but *the student is very model* is not acceptable usage; see also at "Adjectives," next).
- Adjectives are labeled *attrib.* (= attributive) when they are normally placed before the word they modify (e.g., *acting* in *acting manager*), and *predic.* (= predicative) when they normally occur (usually after a verb) in the predicate of a sentence (e.g., *afraid* in *he was afraid*). When an adjective can occur either attributively or predicatively, the simple designation *adj.* is used.
- The designation *absol.* (= absolute) refers to uses of transitive verbs with an object implied but not stated (as in *smoking kills* and *let me explain*).
- The designation "in *comb.*" (= in combination), or "also in *comb.*," refers to uses of words (especially adjectives and nouns) as an element joined by a hyphen to another word, as with *crested* (which often appears in forms such as *red-crested, large-crested*) or *footer* (as in *six-footer*).

❹ Variants

Variant spellings are given before the definition; in all such cases the form given as the main entry is the preferred form. Variant forms are also given at their own places in the dictionary when these are three or more entries away from the main form.

Variant spellings given at the beginning of an entry normally apply to the whole entry, including any phrases and undefined derivatives. When variants apply only to certain functions or senses of a word, these are given in parentheses at the relevant point in the entry.

Variant British spellings are indicated by the designation *Brit.* These variants are often found in British use in addition to or instead of the main forms given.

Pronunciation of variants is given when it differs significantly from the pronunciation of the main entry.

❺ Inflected forms

Inflected forms of words (i.e., plurals of nouns, past tenses of verbs, etc.) are given after the part of speech concerned:

> **broad•cast** /bráwdkast/ *v., n., adj., & adv.* ● *v.* (*past* **broad•cast** or **broad•cast•ed**; *past part.* **broad•cast**) **1** *tr.* **a** transmit (programs or information) by radio or television. **b** disseminate (information) widely. **2** *intr.* undertake or take part in a radio or television transmission. **3** *tr.* scatter (seed, etc.) over a large area, esp. by hand. ● *n.* a radio or television program or transmission. ● *adj.* **1** transmitted by radio or television. **2 a** scattered widely. **b** (of information, etc.) widely disseminated. ● *adv.* over a large area. □□ **broad•cast•er** *n.* **broad•cast•ing** *n.* [BROAD + CAST *past part.*]

The forms given are normally those in use in American English. Pronunciation of inflected forms is given when it differs significantly from the pronunciation of the main entry. The designation "*pronunc.* same" denotes that the pronunciation, despite a change of form, is the same as that of the main entry. In general, the inflection of nouns, verbs, adjectives, and adverbs is given when it is irregular (as described further below) or when, though regular, it causes difficulty (as with forms such as *budgeted, coos,* and *taxis*).

Plurals of nouns

Nouns that form their plural regularly by adding *-s* (or *-es* when they end in *-s, -x, -z, -sh,* or soft *-ch*) receive no comment. Other plural forms are given, notably in cases where the singular is a noun that:

- ends in *-i* or *-o*.
- ends in *-y*.
- is a Latinate form ending in *-a* or *-um*, etc.
- has more than one plural form, e.g., *fish* and *aquarium*.
- has a plural involving a change in the stem, e.g., *foot, feet*.
- has a plural form identical to the singular form, e.g., *sheep*.
- ends in *-ful*, e.g., *handful*.

Forms of verbs

The following verb forms are regarded as regular:

- third person singular present tense forms adding *-s* to the stem, or *-es* to stems ending in *-s, -x, -z, -sh,* or soft *-ch* (e.g., *bite/bites; pass/passes*)
- past tenses and past participles adding *-ed* to the stem, dropping a final silent *-e* (e.g., *changed; danced*).
- present participles adding *-ing* to the stem, dropping a final silent *-e* (e.g., *changing; dancing*).

Other forms are given, notably those that involve:

- doubling of a final consonant, e.g., *bat, batted, batting*.
- strong and irregular forms involving a change in the stem, e.g., *come, came, come,* and *go, went, gone*.
- irregular inflections of borrowed words, e.g., *polka'd*.

Comparative and superlative of adjectives and adverbs

Words of one syllable adding *-er* or *-est* and those ending in silent *-e* dropping the *-e* (e.g., *braver, bravest*) are regarded as regular. Most one-syllable words have these forms, but participial adjectives (e.g., *pleased*) do not. Those that double a final consonant (e.g., *hot, hotter, hottest*) are given, as are two-syllable words that have comparative and superlative forms in *-er* and *-est* (of which very many are forms ending in *-y*, e.g., *lucky, luckier, luckiest*), and their negative forms (e.g., *unluckier, unluckiest*). It should be noted that specification of these forms indicates only that they are available; it is usually also possible to form comparatives with *more* and superlatives with *most* (as in *more lucky, most unlucky*), which is the standard way of proceeding with adjectives and adverbs that are not regularly inflected.

Adjectives in -able formed from transitive verbs

These are given as derivatives when there is sufficient evidence of their currency; in general they are formed as follows:

- verbs drop silent final *-e* except after *c* and *g* (e.g., *movable* but *changeable*).
- verbs of more than one syllable ending in *-y* (preceded by a consonant or *qu*) change *y* to *i* (e.g., *enviable, undeniable*).
- a final consonant is often doubled as in normal inflection (e.g., *conferrable, regrettable*).

❻ Definition

Definitions are listed in a numbered sequence in order of relative familiarity and importance, with the most current and important senses given first. They are subdivided into lettered senses (**a**, **b**, etc.) when these are closely related or call for collective treatment.

❼ Syntax notes

Some definitions are accompanied by explanations in parentheses of syntax, that is, how the word or phrase in question is used in certain typical contexts. Often, the comment refers to words that usually follow ("foll. by") or precede ("prec. by") the word being explained:

The formula ("foll. by *to* + infin.") means that the word is followed by a normal infinitive with *to*, as after *want* in *wanted to leave* and after *ready* in *ready to burst*. The formula ("foll. by *that* + clause") indicates the routine addition of a clause with *that*, as after *say* in *said that it was late* or after *warn* in *warned him that he was late too often*. The formulas "*pres. part.*" and "*verbal noun*" denote verbal forms in *-ing* that function as adjectives and nouns respectively, as in *set him laughing* and *tired of asking*.

❽ Illustrative examples

Examples of words used in context are given to support or clarify many of the definitions. These appear in italics following the definition, enclosed in parentheses. They are meant to amplify meaning and (especially when following a grammatical point) illustrate how the word is actually used in a phrase or sentence.

❾ Labels

If the use of a word is limited in any way, this is indicated by one of several labels printed in italics, as explained in the following.

Geographical labels

US indicates that the use is found chiefly in American English (often including Canada), but not in British English except as a conscious Americanism.

Brit. indicates that the use is found chiefly in British English (and often also in Australian and New Zealand English, and in other parts of the British Commonwealth), but not typically in American English.

Other geographical labels (e.g., *Austral.*, *NZ*, *S. Afr.*) indicate that usage is largely restricted to the areas designated.

These labels should be distinguished from comments of the type "(in the UK)" preceding definitions, which denote that the thing defined is associated with the country named. For example, *Parliament* is a British institution, but the term is not restricted to British English.

Register labels

Levels of usage, or registers, are indicated as follows:

- *formal* indicates uses that are normally restricted to formal (esp. written) English, e.g., *commence*.
- *colloq.* (= colloquial) indicates a use that is normally restricted to informal (esp. spoken) English.
- *sl.* (= slang) indicates an informal use (typically a word that is equivalent in meaning to a "standard" word), unsuited to written English and often restricted to a particular social group, while *coarse sl.* is used to show that an expression is regarded as vulgar or unacceptable even in spoken use in most social contexts.
- *archaic* indicates a word that is obsolete in general use and is restricted to special contexts such as legal or religious use, or is used for special effect.
- *literary* indicates a word or use that is found chiefly in literature.
- *poet.* (= poetic) indicates uses confined to poetry or other similar contexts.
- *joc.* (= jocular) indicates uses that are intended to be humorous or playful.
- *derog.* (= derogatory) denotes uses that are intentionally disparaging.
- *offens.* (= offensive) denotes uses that cause offense, whether intentionally or not.
- *disp.* (= disputed) indicates a use that is disputed or controversial. When further explanation is needed a usage note (see below) is given as well or instead.
- *hist.* (= historical) denotes a word or use that is confined to historical reference, normally because the thing referred to no longer exists.
- *Trademark* denotes a term that is asserted to have the status of a trademark (see the note on proprietary status, p. iv).

Subject labels

Subject labels, e.g., *Law, Math., Naut.*, show that a word or sense is used in a particular field of activity, and is not in widespread general use.

⑩ Phrases and idioms

These are listed (together with compounds) in alphabetical order after the treatment of the main senses and introduced by the symbol □. The words *a*, *the*, *one*, and *person* do not count for purposes of alphabetical order. They are normally defined under the first key word in the phrase, except when a later word is more clearly the key word or is the common word in a phrase with variants.

⑪ Derivatives

Words formed by adding a standard suffix to another word are in many cases listed at the end of the entry for the main word, introduced by the symbol □ □. These are not defined since they can be understood from the sense of the main entry plus that of the suffix concerned. When further definition is called for they are given main entries in their own right (e.g., *changeable*).

⑫ Prefixes, suffixes, and combining forms

A large selection of these is given in the main body of the text; prefixes are given in the form **ex-**, **re-**, etc., and suffixes in the form **-ion**, **-ness**, etc. These entries should be consulted to explain the many routinely formed derivatives given at the end of entries (see 11 above). Combining forms (e.g., *bio-*, *-graphy*) are semantically significant elements that can be attached to words or elements as explained at the entry for *combining form*.

⑬ Etymology

A brief account of the etymology or origin of words is given in square brackets at the end of entries. It is not given for compound words of obvious formation (such as *bathroom* and *jellyfish*), for routinely formed derivatives (such as *changeable*, *muddy*, and *seller*), or for words consisting of clearly identified elements already explained (such as *Anglo-Saxon*, *overrun*, and many words in *-in*, *re-*, *un-*, etc.). It is not always given for every word of a set sharing the same basic origin (such as the group *proprietary* to *propriety*). The immediate source language is given first. Forms in other languages are not given if they are exactly or nearly the same as the English form given in the headword. Words of Germanic origin are described as "f. Gmc" or "f. WG" (West Germanic) as appropriate; unrecorded or postulated forms are not normally given. OE (Old English) is used for words that are known to have been used before AD 1150, and ME (Middle English) for words traceable to the period 1150–1500 (no distinction being made between early and late Middle English). Words of Romance origin are referred to their immediate source, usually F (French) or OF (Old French before 1400), and then to earlier sources when known. AF (Anglo-French) denotes a variety of French current in England in the Middle Ages after the Norman Conquest. Rmc (Romance) denotes the vernacular descendants of Latin that are the source of French, Spanish, Italian, etc. Romanic forms are almost always of the "unrecorded" or "postulated" kind, and are not specified except to clarify a significant change of form. Often the formula "ult.f.L" (ultimately from Latin) is used to indicate that the route from Latin is via Romanic forms. L (Latin) denotes classical Latin up to about AD 200; OL (Old Latin) Latin before about 75 BC; LL (Late Latin) Latin of about 200–600; med.L (medieval Latin) Latin of about 600–1500; mod.L (modern Latin) Latin in use (mainly for technical purposes) since about 1500. Similar divisions for "late," "medieval," and "modern" are made for Greek. Many English words have corresponding forms in both French and Latin, and it cannot always be established which was the immediate source. In such cases the formula "F or L" is used (e.g., *section* . . . F *section* or L *sectio*); in these cases the Latin form is the source of the French word and (either directly or indirectly) of the English word. Some words are derived from languages that are not in wide enough use for them to be included as entries in the dictionary. These languages are listed below by regions; further information about them can be found in encyclopedias and other reference books.

- Those spoken in **America** are Surinam Negro (a Creole based on English) and the following Native American languages: Araucan, Aymará, Galibi, Miskito, Nootka, Renape, and Taino.
- Those spoken in **Africa** are Bangi, Fiot, Foulah, Khoisan, Kongo, Lingala, Mandingo, Mbuba, Mende, Nguni, Temne, and Twi.
- Those spoken in **Asia** are Ambonese (spoken in Indonesia), Assamese (in India), Batti (in Tibet), Maldive (in the Maldive Islands), Mishmi (in India), Sundanese (in Indonesia), and Tungus (in Siberia).
- Tongan is a Polynesian language.

When the origin of a word cannot be reliably established, the forms "orig. unkn." (= origin unknown) and "orig. uncert." (= origin uncertain) are used, even if frequently canvassed speculative derivations exist (as with *gremlin* and *gloat*). In these cases the century of the first recorded occurrence of the word in English is given. An equals sign (=) precedes words in other languages that are parallel formations from a common source (cognates) rather than sources of the English word.

⑭ Usage Notes

Usage notes give additional information not central to the definition, and explain points of grammar and style. The purpose of these notes is not to prescribe usage, but to alert the user to a difficulty or controversy associated with particular words. Usage notes follow the entry immediately, introduced by ¶.

⑮ Language Tips

In addition to the usage notes themselves, throughout the text of the dictionary are language tips that accompany particular entries, giving background information or guidance on various additional aspects of usage. These notes appear as boxed features following the appropriate entry. There are language tips of the following kinds, each explained below:

- Spelling Tip
- Pronunciation Tip
- Punctuation Tip
- Grammar Tip
- Synonym Tip
- Word History

Spelling tips

These generally give a mnemonic, that is, a phrase that may help to remember how to spell a word that causes problems for many people. For example, at the entry for **separate**, the mnemonic "There's *a rat* in separate" is given, pointing out that the word is to be spelled with the letters "ARAT" in it.

Pronunciation tips

These provide brief guidance on preferred pronunciations, dialectal or regional variants, and other situations where one may wish to proceed carefully with a pronunciation.

Punctuation tips

Use of punctuation is frequently a cause of concern in writing. At the entry for each common punctuation mark (period, comma, semicolon, etc.) a concise set of rules is given, offering guidance for usage that conforms with conventional American practice.

Grammar tips

These provide a quick review of key points of English grammar, and serve as a refresher or reminder of how to apply basic rules and principles.

Synonym tips

These brief paragraphs offer an analytical treatment of the nuances of meaning that distinguish a set of closely related synonyms.

Word histories

Brief paragraphs following certain entries explain the origin of a word. Generally speaking, these word histories tell a particularly interesting story about how a word originated or developed its modern meaning, and are often helpful in understanding and remembering the meaning.

⑯ Cross references

Cross references appear in small capitals if the reference is to a main entry, and in italics if the reference is to an idiom or phrase within an entry. Italic cross references refer to the first word in the expression, unless another word is specified.

Abbreviations

Listed below are abbreviations that occur within the text of entries, except for those in general use (such as *etc.* and *i.e.*), which have their own entries in the dictionary itself. Some abbreviations (especially of language names) occur only in etymologies. Others may appear in italics.

abbr.	abbreviation	Ch.	Church
ablat.	ablative	Chem.	Chemistry
absol.	absolute(ly)	Chin.	Chinese
acc.	according	Cinematog.	Cinematography
accus.	accusative	class.	classical
adj.	adjective	coarse sl.	coarse slang
adv.	adverb	cogn.	cognate
Aeron.	Aeronautics	collect.	collective(ly)
AF	Anglo-French	colloq.	colloquial(ly)
Afr.	Africa; African	comb.	combination; combining
Afrik.	Afrikaans	compar.	comparative
Akkad.	Akkadian	compl.	complement
AL	Anglo-Latin	Conchol.	Conchology
alt.	alteration	conj.	conjunction
Amer.	America; American	conn.	connected
Anat.	Anatomy	constr.	construction
anc.	ancient	contr.	contraction
Anglo-Ind.	Anglo-Indian	Corn.	Cornish
Anthropol.	Anthropology	corresp.	corresponding
Antiq.	Antiquities; Antiquity	corrupt.	corruption
app.	apparently	Criminol.	Criminology
Arab.	Arabic	Crystallog.	Crystallography
Aram.	Aramaic		
arbitr.	arbitrary; arbitrarily	Da.	Danish
Archaeol.	Archaeology	decl.	declension
Archit.	Architecture	def.	definite
Arith.	Arithmetic	Demog.	Demography
assim.	assimilated	demons.	demonstrative
assoc.	associated; association	demons.adj.	demonstrative adjective
Assyr.	Assyrian	demons.pron.	demonstrative pronoun
Astrol.	Astrology	deriv.	derivative
Astron.	Astronomy	derog.	derogatory
Astronaut.	Astronautics	dial.	dialect
Attrib.	attributive(ly)	different.	differentiated
attrib.adj.	attributive adjective	dimin.	diminutive
augment.	augmentative	disp.	disputed (use or pronunciation)
Austral.	Australia; Australian	dissim.	dissimilated
aux.	auxiliary	distrib.	distributive
		Du.	Dutch
back-form.	back-formation		
Bibl.	Biblical	E	English
Bibliog.	Bibliography	Eccl.	Ecclesiastical
Biochem.	Biochemistry	Ecol.	Ecology
Biol.	Biology	Econ.	Economics
Bot.	Botany	EFris	East Frisian
Braz.	Brazil; Brazilian	Egypt.	Egyptian
Bret.	Breton	E.Ind.	East Indian; of the East Indies
Brit.	British	Electr.	Electricity
Bulg.	Bulgarian	elem.	elementary
Burm.	Burmese	ellipt.	elliptical(ly)
Byz.	Byzantine	emphat.	emphatic(ally)
		Engin.	Engineering
c.	century	Engl.	England; English
c.	*circa*	Entomol.	Entomology
Can.	Canada; Canadian	erron.	erroneous(ly)
Cat.	Catalan	esp.	especial(ly)
Celt.	Celtic	etym.	etymology

euphem.	euphemism
Eur.	Europe; European
ex.	example
exc.	except
exclam.	exclamation
F	French
f.	from
fam.	familiar
fem.	feminine
fig.	figurative(ly)
Finn.	Finnish
fl.	flourished
Flem.	Flemish
foll.	followed; following
form.	formation
Fr.	French
Frank.	Frankish
frequent.	frequentative(ly)
G	German
Gael.	Gaelic
Gallo-Rom.	Gallo-Roman
gen.	general
genit.	genitive
Geog.	Geography
Geol.	Geology
Geom.	Geometry
Ger.	German
Gk	Greek
Gk Hist.	Greek History
Gmc	Germanic
Goth.	Gothic
Gram.	Grammar
Heb.	Hebrew
Hind.	Hindustani
Hist.	History
hist.	with historical reference
Horol.	Horology
Hort.	Horticulture
Hung.	Hungarian
Icel.	Icelandic
IE	Indo-European
illit.	illiterate
imit.	imitative
immed.	immediate(ly)
imper.	imperative
impers.	impersonal
incept.	inceptive
incl.	including; inclusive
Ind.	of the subcontinent comprising India, Pakistan, and Bangladesh
ind.	indirect
indecl.	indeclinable
indef.	indefinite
infin.	infinitive
infl.	influence(d)
instr.	instrumental (case)
int.	interjection
interrog.	interrogative(ly)
interrog.adj.	interrogative adjective
interrog.pron.	interrogative pronoun
intr.	intransitive
Ir.	Irish (language or usage)
iron.	ironical(ly)
irreg.	irregular(ly)
It.	Italian
Jap.	Japan; Japanese
Jav.	Javanese
joc.	jocular(ly)
L	Latin
lang.	language
LG	Low German
LHeb.	Late Hebrew
lit.	literal(ly)
LL	Late Latin
M	Middle (with languages)
masc.	masculine
Math.	Mathematics
MDa.	Middle Danish
MDu.	Middle Dutch
ME	Middle English
Mech.	Mechanics
Med.	Medicine
med.	medieval
med.L	medieval Latin
metaph.	metaphorical
metath.	metathesis
Meteorol.	Meteorology
Mex.	Mexican
MFlem.	Middle Flemish
MHG	Middle High German
Mil.	Military
Mineral.	Mineralogy
mistransl.	mistranslation
MLG	Middle Low German
mod.	modern
mod.L	modern Latin
MSw.	Middle Swedish
Mus.	Music
Mythol.	Mythology
n.	noun
N.Amer.	North America; North American
Nat.	National
Naut.	Nautical
neg.	negative(ly)
neut.	neuter
N.Engl.	New England
No. of Engl.	North of England
Norm.	Norman
north.	northern
Norw.	Norwegian
n.pl.	noun plural
num.	numeral
NZ	New Zealand
O	Old (with languages)
obj.	object; objective
OBret.	Old Breton
OBrit.	Old British
obs.	obsolete
Obstet.	Obstetrics

OBulg.	Old Bulgarian	prep.	preposition
occas.	occasional(ly)	pres.part.	present participle
OCelt.	Old Celtic	prob.	probable; probably
ODa.	Old Danish	pron.	pronoun
ODu.	Old Dutch	pronunc.	pronunciation
OE	Old English	propr.	proprietary term
OF	Old French	Prov.	Provencal
offens.	offensive	Psychol.	Psychology
OFrank.	Old Frankish		
OFris.	Old Frisian	RC Ch.	Roman Catholic Church
OGael.	Old Gaelic	redupl.	reduplicated
OHG	Old High German	ref.	reference
OIcel.	Old Icelandic	refl.	reflexive(ly)
OIr.	Old Irish	rel.	related; relative
OIt.	Old Italian	rel.adj.	relative adjective
OL	Old Latin	Relig.	Religion
OLG	Old Low German	rel.pron.	relative pronoun
ON	Old Norse	repr.	representing
ONF	Old Norman French	Rhet.	Rhetoric
ONorw.	Old Norwegian	rhet.	rhetorical(ly)
OPers.	Old Persian	Rmc	Romanic
OPort.	Old Portuguese	Rom.	Roman
opp.	(as) opposed (to); opposite (of)	Rom.Hist.	Roman History
OProv.	Old Provencal	Russ.	Russian
orig.	origin; original(ly)		
Ornithol.	Ornithology		
OS	Old Saxon	S.Afr.	South Africa; South African
OScand.	Old Scandinavian	S.Amer.	South America; South American
OSlav.	Old Slavonic	Sc.	Scottish
OSp.	Old Spanish	Scand.	Scandinavia; Scandinavian
OSw.	Old Swedish	Sci.	Science
		Shakesp.	Shakespeare
		sing.	singular
Paleog.	Palaeography	Sinh.	Sinhalese
Parl.	Parliament; Parliamentary	Skr.	Sanskrit
part.	participle	sl.	slang
past part.	past participle	Slav.	Slavic; Slavonic
Pathol.	Pathology	Sociol.	Sociology
pejor.	pejorative	Sp.	Spanish
perf.	perfect (tense)	spec.	special(ly)
perh.	perhaps	Stock Exch.	Stock Exchange
Pers.	Persian	subj.	subject; subjunctive
pers.	person(al)	superl.	superlative
Peruv.	Peruvian	Sw.	Swedish
Pharm	Pharmacy; Pharmacology	syll.	syllable
Philol.	Philology	symb.	symbol
Philos.	Philosophy	syn.	synonym
Phoen.	Phoenician		
Phonet.	Phonetics		
Photog.	Photography	techn.	technical(ly)
phr.	phrase	Telev.	Television
Phrenol.	Phrenology	Teut.	Teutonic
Physiol.	Physiology	Theatr.	Theater; Theatrical
pl.	plural	Theol.	Theology
poet.	poetical	tr.	transitive
Pol.	Polish	transf.	in transferred sense
Polit.	Politics	transl.	translation
pop.	popular, not technical	Turk.	Turkish
pop.L.	popular Latin, informal spoken Latin	Typog.	Typography
Port.	Portuguese		
poss.	possessive	ult.	ultimate(ly)
poss.pron.	possessive pronoun	uncert.	uncertain
prec.	preceded; preceding	unexpl.	unexplained
predic.	predicate; predicative(ly)	univ.	university
predic.adj.	predicative adjective	unkn.	unknown

US	American; in use in the United States	v.refl.	reflexive verb
usu.	usual(ly)	v.tr.	transitive verb
		WFris.	West Frisian
v.	verb	WG	West Germanic
var.	variant(s)	W.Ind.	West Indian; of the West Indies
v.aux.	auxiliary verb	WS	West Saxon
Vet.	Veterinary	WSlav.	West Slavonic
v.intr.	intransitive verb		
voc.	vocative	Zool.	Zoology

Large-format Illustrations

Key to Pronunciation

This dictionary uses a simple respelling system to show how entries are pronounced, using the following symbols:

a, á	*as in*	**pat** /pat/, **fasten** /fásən/
aa, áa	*as in*	**father** /fáaTHər/, **barnyard** /báarnyaard/
air, áir	*as in*	**fair** /fair/, **share** /shair/, **heir** /air/
aw, áw	*as in*	**law** /law/, **caught** /kawt/, **thought** /thawt/
ay, áy	*as in*	**day** /day/, **raid** /rayd/, **made** /mayd/, **prey** /pray/
ch	*as in*	**church** /chərch/, **picture** /píkchər/
e, é	*as in*	**men** /men/, **said** /sed/
ee, ée	*as in*	**feet** /feet/, **receive** /riséev/
ə	*as in*	**along** /əlóng/, **soda** /sṓdə/, **civil** /sívəl/
ər, ə́r	*as in*	**parade** /pəráyd/, **bitter** /bítər/, **person** /pə́rsən/
g	*as in*	**get** /get/, **exhaust** /igzáwst/, **egg** /eg/
i, í	*as in*	**pin** /pin/, **guild** /gild/, **women** /wímin/
ī, ī́	*as in*	**time** /tīm/, **fight** /fīt/, **guide** /gīd/
īr, ī́r	*as in*	**fire** /fīr/, **desire** /dizī́r/
j	*as in*	**judge** /juj/, **carriage** /kárij/
<u>KH</u>	*as in*	**loch** /loKH/, **Bach** /baaKH/
N	*as in*	**en route** /oN root/ (preceding vowel is nasalized)
ng	*as in*	**sing** /sing/, **anger** /ánggər/
o, ó	*as in*	**rob** /rob/, **pocket** /pókit/
ō, ṓ	*as in*	**go** /gō/, **promote** /prəmṓt/
ö, ö́	*as in*	**jeu** /ZHö/, **schön** /shön/
o͞o, ó͞o	*as in*	**wood** /wo͞od/, **football** /fó͞otbawl/
o͞o, ó͞o	*as in*	**food** /fo͞od/, **music** /myó͞osik/
ow, ów	*as in*	**mouse** /mows/, **coward** /kówərd/
oy, óy	*as in*	**boy** /boy/, **noisy** /nóyzee/
r	*as in*	**run** /run/, **fur** /fər/, **spirit** /spírit/
sh	*as in*	**shut** /shut/, **social** /sṓshəl/, **action** /ákshən/
th	*as in*	**thin** /thin/, **truth** /tro͞oth/
<u>TH</u>	*as in*	**then** /THen/, **mother** /mútHər/
u, ú	*as in*	**cut** /kut/, **blood** /blud/, **enough** /inúf/
y	*as in*	**yet** /yet/, **accuse** /əkyo͞óz/
Y	*as in*	**mot juste** /mō ZHYst/
<u>ZH</u>	*as in*	**measure** /méZHər/, **vision** /víZHən/

    More than one acceptable pronunciation may be given, with commas between the variants; for example:

news /no͞oz, nyo͞oz/

    If the pronunciations of a word differ only in part, then the syllable or syllables affected are shown as follows:

bedroom /bédro͞om, -ro͞om/, **forest** /fáwrist, fór-/

The same principle applies to derivative forms that are given within the main entry; for example:

complete /kəmpleét/, **completion** /-pleéshən/

Stress The mark that appears over the vowel symbol in words of more than one syllable indicates the part of the word that carries the stress. Where a word has two or more stress markers then the main stress may vary according to the context in which a word is used; for example:

afternoon /áftərno͞on/

In the phrase "afternoon tea" the main stress falls on the first syllable /áftər/, but in the phrase "all afternoon" the main stress falls on the last syllable /no͞on/.

THE
Oxford
American
Dictionary
and
Language
Guide

A

A¹ /ay/ *n.* (also **a**) (*pl.* **As** or **A's**) **1** the first letter of the alphabet. **2** *Mus.* the sixth note of the diatonic scale of C major. **3** the first hypothetical person or example. **4** the highest class or category (of academic grades, etc.). **5** (usu. **a**) *Algebra* the first known quantity. **6** a human blood type of the ABO system. □ **A1** /áy wún/ *n. Naut.* a first-class vessel, esp. in Lloyd's Register of Shipping. ● *adj.* **1** *Naut.* (of a ship) first-class. **2** *colloq.* excellent; first-class. **from A to B** from one place to another (*a means of getting from A to B*). **from A to Z** over the entire range; completely.

A² /ay/ *abbr.* (also **A.**) **1** ampere(s). **2** answer. **3** Associate of. **4** atomic (energy, etc.).

a¹ /ə, ay/ *adj.* (also **an** before a vowel) (called the indefinite article) **1** (as an unemphatic substitute) one; some; any. **2** one like (*a Judas*). **3** one single (*not a thing in sight*). **4** the same (*all of a size*). **5** in, to, or for each (*twice a year*; *$20 a person*; *seven a side*). [weakening of OE *ān* one; sense 5 orig. = A²]

a² /ə/ *prep.* (usu. as *prefix*) **1** to; toward (*ashore*; *aside*). **2** (with verb in pres. part. or infin.) in the process of; in a specified state (*a-hunting*; *a-wandering*; *abuzz*; *aflutter*). **3** on (*afire*; *afoot*). **4** in (*nowadays*). [weakening of OE prep. *an, on* (see ON)]

a³ *abbr.* atto-.

Å *abbr.* ångström(s).

a-¹ /ay, a/ *prefix* not; without (*amoral*; *agnostic*; *apetalous*). [Gk *a-*, or L f. Gk, or F f. L f. Gk]

a-² /ə/ *prefix* implying motion onward or away, adding intensity to verbs of motion (*arise*; *awake*). [OE *a-*, orig. *ar-*]

a-³ /ə/ *prefix* to, at, or into a state (*adroit*; *agree*; *amass*; *avenge*). [ME *a-* (= OF prefix *a-*), (f. F) f. L *ad-* to, at]

a-⁴ /ə/ *prefix* **1** from; away (*abridge*). **2** of (*akin*; *anew*). **3** out; utterly (*abash*; *affray*). **4** in, on, engaged in, etc. (see A²). [sense 1 f. ME *a-*, OF *a-*, f. L *ab*; sense 2 f. ME a- f. OE *of* prep.; sense 3 f. ME, AF *a-* = OF *e-*, *es-* f. L *ex*]

a-⁵ /ə, a/ *prefix* assim. form of AD- before *sc, sp, st.*

-a¹ /ə/ *suffix* forming nouns from Greek, Latin, and Romance feminine singular, esp.: **1** ancient or Latinized modern names of animals and plants (*amoeba*; *campanula*). **2** oxides (*alumina*). **3** geographical names (*Africa*). **4** ancient or Latinized modern feminine names (*Lydia*; *Hilda*).

-a² /ə/ *suffix* forming plural nouns from Greek and Latin neuter plural, esp. names (often from modern Latin) of zoological groups (*phenomena*; *Carnivora*).

-a³ /ə/ *suffix colloq.* **1** of (*kinda*; *coupla*). **2** have (*mighta*; *coulda*). **3** to (*oughta*).

AA *abbr.* **1** Alcoholics Anonymous. **2** Associate of Arts. **3** *Mil.* antiaircraft.

AAA *abbr.* **1** American Automobile Association. **2** Amateur Athletic Association. **3** antiaircraft artillery.

A. & M. *abbr.* **1** Agricultural and Mechanical (college or university). **2** (Hymns) Ancient and Modern.

A. & R. *abbr.* **1** artists and recording. **2** artists and repertoire.

aard•vark /áardvaark/ *n.* a nocturnal mammal of southern Africa, *Orycteropus afer*, with a tubular snout and a long extensible tongue, that feeds on termites. Also called **ant bear.** [Afrik. f. *aarde* earth + *vark* pig]

aard•wolf /áardwŏolf/ *n.* (*pl.* **aardwolves** /–wŏolvz/) an African mammal, *Proteles cristatus*, of the hyena family, with gray fur and black stripes, that feeds on insects. [Afrik. f. *aarde* earth + *wolf* wolf]

Aar•on's beard /áirənz, ár–/ *n.* any of several plants, esp. rose of Sharon (*Hypericum calycinum*). [ref. to Ps. 133:2]

Aar•on's rod /áirən, ár–/ *n.* any of several tall plants, esp. goldenrod or mullein. [ref. to Num. 17:8]

AAU *abbr.* Amateur Athletic Union.

AB¹ /áybeé/ *n.* a human blood type of the ABO system.

AB² *abbr.* **1** able seaman. **2** Bachelor of Arts. [sense 1 f. able-bodied; sense 2 f. L *Artium Baccalaureus*]

ab- /əb, ab/ *prefix* off; away; from (*abduct*; *abnormal*; *abuse*). [F or L]

a•ba /əbaá, aábə/ *n.* (also **abba, abaya** /əbáy-yə, əbíyə/) a sleeveless outer garment worn by Arabs. [Arab. `*abā'*]

a•ba•ca /əbəkaá/ *n.* **1** Manila hemp. **2** the plant, *Musa textilis*, yielding this. [Sp. *abacá*]

a•back /əbák/ *adv.* **1** *archaic* backward; behind. **2** *Naut.* (of a sail) pressed against the mast by a head wind. □ **take aback 1** surprise; disconcert (*your request took me aback*; *I was greatly taken aback by the news*). **2** (as **taken aback**) (of a ship) with the sails pressed against the mast by a head wind. [OE *on bæc* (as A², BACK)]

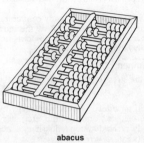

abacus

ab•a•cus /ábəkəs, əbákəs/ *n.* (*pl.* **abacuses**) **1** an oblong frame with rows of wires or grooves along which beads are slid, used for calculating. **2** *Archit.* the flat slab on top of a capital, supporting the architrave. [L f. Gk *abax abakos* slab, drawing board, f. Heb. '*ābāk* dust]

A•bad•don /əbád'n/ *n.* **1** hell. **2** the Devil (Rev. 9:11). [Heb., = destruction]

a•baft /əbáft/ *adv. & prep. Naut.* ● *adv.* in the stern half of a ship. ● *prep.* nearer the stern than; aft of. [A² + –*baft* f. OE *bæftan* f. *be* BY + *æftan* behind]

ab•a•lo•ne /ábəlōnee/ *n.* any mollusk of the genus *Haliotis*, with a shallow ear-shaped shell having respiratory holes, and lined with mother-of-pearl, e.g., the ormer. [Amer. Sp. *abulón*]

a•ban•don /əbándən/ *v. & n.* ● *v.tr.* **1** give up completely or before completion (*abandoned hope*; *abandoned the game*). **2 a** forsake or desert (a person or a post of responsibility). **b** leave or desert (a motor vehicle, ship, building, etc.). **3 a** give up to another's control or mercy. **b** *refl.* yield oneself completely to a passion or impulse. ● *n.* lack of inhibition or restraint; reckless freedom of manner. □□ **a•ban•don•er** *n.* **a•ban•don•ment** *n.* [ME f. OF *abandoner* f. *àbandon* under control ult. f. LL *bannus*, –*um* BAN]

a•ban•doned /əbándənd/ *adj.* **1 a** (of a person or animal) deserted; forsaken (*an abandoned child*). **b** (of a building, vehicle, etc.) left empty or unused (*an abandoned cottage*; *an abandoned ship*). **2** (of a person or behavior) unrestrained; profligate.

a•base /əbáys/ *v.tr. & refl.* humiliate or degrade (another person or oneself). □□ **a•base•ment** *n.* [ME f. OF *abaissier* (as A-³, *baissier* to lower ult. f. LL *bassus* short of stature): infl. by BASE²]

a•bash /əbásh/ *v.tr.* (usu. as **abashed** *adj.*) embarrass; disconcert. □□ **a•bash•ment** *n.* [ME f. OF *esbaïr* (es- = A-⁴ 3, *baïr* astound or *baer* yawn)]

a•bate /əbáyt/ *v.* **1** *tr. & intr.* make or become less strong, severe, intense, etc. **2** *tr. Law* a quash (a writ or action). **b** put an end to (a nuisance). □□ **a•bate•ment** *n.* [ME f. OF *abatre* f. Rmc (as A-³, L *batt(u)ere* beat)]

ab•a•tis /ábətis/ *n.* (also **abattis** /əbátis/) (*pl.* same or **abatises, abattises**) *hist.* a defense made of felled trees with the sharpened branches pointing outward. □□ **ab•a•tised** *adj.* [F f. *abatre* fell: see ABATE]

ab•at•toir /ábətwaar/ *n.* a slaughterhouse. [F (as ABATIS, –ORY¹)]

ab•ax•i•al /abákseeəl/ *adj. Bot.* facing away from the stem of a plant, esp. of the lower surface of a leaf (cf. ADAXIAL). [AB- + AXIAL]

a•bay•a (also **ab•ba**) var. of ABA.

ab•ba•cy /ábəsee/ *n.* (*pl.* **-cies**) the office, jurisdiction, or period of office of an abbot or abbess. [ME f. eccl.L *abbacia* f. *abbat-* ABBOT]

Ab•bas•id /əbásid, ábəsid/ *n. & adj.* ● *n.* a member of a dynasty of caliphs ruling in Baghdad 750–1258. ● *adj.* of this dynasty. [*Abbas*, Muhammad's uncle d. 652]

ab•ba•tial /əbáyshəl/ *adj.* of an abbey, abbot, or abbess. [F *abbatial* or med.L *abbatialis* (as ABBOT)]

ab•bé /abáy, ábay/ *n.* (in France) an abbot; a man entitled to wear ecclesiastical dress. [F f. eccl.L *abbas abbatis* ABBOT]

ab•bess /ábis/ *n.* a woman who is the head of certain communities of nuns. [ME f. OF *abbesse* f. eccl.L *abbatissa* (as ABBOT)]

Abbe•vill•i•an /abvíleeən, abə–/ *n. & adj.* ● *n.* the culture of the earliest Paleolithic period in Europe. ● *adj.* of this culture. [F *Abbevillien* f. *Abbeville* in N. France]

ab•bey /ábee/ *n.* (*pl.* **-beys**) **1** the building(s) occupied by a community of monks or nuns. **2** the community itself. **3** a church or house that was once an abbey. [ME f. OF *abbeie*, etc., f. med.L *abbatia* ABBACY]

ab•bot /ábət/ *n.* a man who is the head of an abbey of monks. □□ **ab•bot•ship** *n.* [OE *abbod* f. eccl.L *abbas –atis* f. Gk *abbas* father f. Aram. '*abbā*]

abbr. *abbr.* (also **abbrev.**) abbreviation.

ab•bre•vi•ate /əbreévee-ayt/ *v.tr.* shorten, esp. represent (a word, etc.) by a part of it. [ME f. LL *abbreviare* shorten f. *brevis* short: cf. ABRIDGE]

ab·bre·vi·a·tion /əbreevee-áyshən/ n. **1** an abbreviated form, esp. a shortened form of a word or phrase. **2** the process or result of abbreviating.

ABC[1] /áybeeseé/ n. **1** the alphabet. **2** the rudiments of any subject. **3** an alphabetical guide.

ABC[2] abbr. American Broadcasting Company.

ab·di·cate /ábdikayt/ v.tr. **1** (usu. absol.) give up or renounce (a throne). **2** renounce (a responsibility, duty, etc.). □□ **ab·di·ca·tion** /-káyshən/ n. **ab·di·ca·tor** n. [L abdicare abdicat- (as AB-, dicare declare)]

ab·do·men /ábdəmən, abdō-/ n. **1** the part of the body containing the stomach, bowels, reproductive organs, etc. **2** Zool. the hind part of an insect, crustacean, spider, etc. □□ **ab·dom·i·nal** /abdóminəl/ adj. **ab·dom·i·nal·ly** /abdóminəlee/ adv. [L]

> **PRONUNCIATION TIP** abdomen
>
> Pronouncing this word with the stress on the first syllable (AB-do-min) is fully acceptable.

ab·duct /əbdúkt/ v.tr. **1** carry off or kidnap (a person) illegally by force or deception. **2** (of a muscle, etc.) draw (a limb, etc.) away from the middle line of the body. □□ **ab·duc·tion** /-dúkshən/ n. **ab·duc·tor** n. [L abducere abduct- (as AB-, ducere draw)]

a·beam /əbeém/ adv. **1** on a line at right angles to a ship's or an aircraft's length. **2** (foll. by of) opposite the middle of (a ship, etc.). [A² + BEAM]

a·bed /əbéd/ adv. archaic in bed. [OE as A², BED]

a·bele /əbeél, áybəl/ n. the white poplar, Populus alba. [Du. abeel f. OF abel, aubel ult. f. L albus white]

a·be·li·a /əbeéleeə/ n. any shrub of the genus Abelia, esp. A. grandiflora. [Clarke Abel, Engl. botanist d. 1826]

A·be·na·ki /abənáakee/ n. (also **Ab·na·ki** /abnáakee/) **1 a** a N. American people native to northern New England and adjoining parts of Quebec. **b** a member of this people. **2** either of the two languages of this people.

Ab·er·deen An·gus /ábərdeen ánggəs/ n. **1** an animal of a Scottish breed of hornless black beef cattle. **2** this breed. [Aberdeen in Scotland, Angus former Scottish county]

ab·er·rant /əbérənt, ábə-/ adj. **1** esp. Biol. diverging from the normal type. **2** departing from an accepted standard. □□ **ab·er·rance** /-rəns/ n. **ab·er·ran·cy** n. [L aberrare aberrant- (as AB-, errare stray)]

> **PRONUNCIATION TIP** aberrant
>
> The traditional pronunciation of this word places the stress on the second syllable (a-BER-ent). A newer pronunciation places the stress on the first syllable, probably because of its similarity to the word aberration. Both are well-established, and both are now considered acceptable.

ab·er·ra·tion /ábəráyshən/ n. **1** a departure from what is normal or accepted or regarded as right. **2** a moral or mental lapse. **3** Biol. deviation from a normal type. **4** Optics the failure of rays to converge at one focus because of a defect in a lens or mirror. **5** Astron. the apparent displacement of a celestial body, meteor, etc., caused by the observer's velocity. □□ **ab·er·ra·tion·al** adj. [L aberratio (as ABERRANT)]

a·bet /əbét/ v.tr. (**a·bet·ted**, **a·bet·ting**) (usu. in **aid and abet**) encourage or assist (an offender or offense). □□ **a·bet·ment** n. [ME f. OF abeter f. à to + beter BAIT¹]

a·bet·tor /əbétər/ n. (also **a·bet·ter**) one who abets.

a·bey·ance /əbáyəns/ n. (usu. prec. by in, into) a state of temporary disuse or suspension. □□ **a·bey·ant** /-ənt/ adj. [AF abeiance f. OF abeer f. à to + beer f. med.L batare gape]

ab·hor /əbháwr/ v.tr. (**abhorred**, **abhorring**) detest; regard with disgust and hatred. □□ **ab·hor·rer** n. [ME f. F abhorrer or f. L abhorrēre (as AB-, horrēre shudder)]

ab·hor·rence /əbháwrəns, -hór-/ n. **1** disgust; detestation. **2** a detested thing.

ab·hor·rent /əbháwrənt, -hór-/ adj. **1** (often foll. by to) (of conduct, etc.) inspiring disgust; repugnant; hateful; detestable. **2** (foll. by to) not in accordance with; strongly conflicting with (abhorrent to the spirit of the law). **3** archaic (foll. by from) inconsistent with.

a·bide /əbíd/ v. (past **abode** /əbṓd/ or **abided**) **1** tr. (usu. in neg. or interrog.) tolerate; endure (can't abide him). **2** intr. (foll. by by) **a** act in accordance with (abide by the rules). **b** remain faithful to (a promise). **3** intr. archaic **a** remain; continue. **b** dwell. **4** tr. archaic sustain; endure. □□ **a·bid·ance** n. [OE ābīdan (as A-², bidan BIDE)]

a·bid·ing /əbíding/ adj. enduring; permanent (an abiding sense of loss). □□ **a·bid·ing·ly** adv.

a·bil·i·ty /əbílitee/ n. (pl. **·ties**) **1** (often foll. by to + infin.) capacity or power (has the ability to write songs). **2** cleverness; talent; mental power (a person of great ability; has many abilities). [ME f. OF ablete f. L habilitas –tatis f. habilis able]

-ability /əbílitee/ suffix forming nouns of quality from, or correspond-

ing to, adjectives in –able (capability; vulnerability). [F –abilité or L –abilitas: cf. –ITY]

ab in·i·ti·o /áb inísheeṓ/ adv. from the beginning. [L]

a·bi·o·gen·e·sis /áybīōjénisis/ n. **1** the formation of living organisms from inanimate substances. **2** the supposed spontaneous generation of living organisms. □□ **a·bi·o·gen·ic** /–jénik/ adj. [A-¹ + Gk bios life + GENESIS]

ab·ject /ábjekt, abjékt/ adj. **1** miserable; wretched. **2** degraded; self-abasing; humble. **3** despicable. □□ **ab·ject·ly** adv. **ab·ject·ness** n. [ME f. L abjectus past part. of abicere (as AB-, jacere throw)]

ab·jec·tion /əbjékshən/ n. a state of misery or degradation. [ME f. OF abjection or L abjectio (as ABJECT)]

ab·jure /əbjŏŏr/ v.tr. **1** renounce under oath (an opinion, cause, claim, etc.). **2** swear perpetual absence from (one's country, etc.). □□ **ab·ju·ra·tion** /–ráyshən/ n. [L abjurare (as AB-, jurare swear)]

ab·la·tion /abláyshən/ n. **1** the surgical removal of body tissue. **2** Geol. the wasting or erosion of a glacier, iceberg, or rock by melting, evaporation, or the action of water. **3** Astronaut. the evaporation or melting of part of the outer surface of a spacecraft through heating by friction with the atmosphere. □□ **ab·late** v.tr. [F ablation or LL ablatio f. L ablat- (as AB-, lat- past part. stem of ferre carry)]

ab·la·tive /áblətiv/ n. & adj. Gram. ●n. the case (esp. in Latin) of nouns and pronouns (and words in grammatical agreement with them) indicating an agent, instrument, or location. ● adj. of or in the ablative. [ME f. OF ablatif –ive or L ablativus (as ABLATION)]

ab·la·tive ab·so·lute n. an absolute construction in Latin with a noun and participle or adjective in the ablative case (see ABSOLUTE).

ab·laut /áblowt/ n. a change of vowel in related words or forms, esp. in Indo-European languages, arising from differences of accent and stress in the parent language, e.g., in sing, sang, sung. [G]

a·blaze /əbláyz/ predic.adj. & adv. **1** on fire (set it ablaze; the house was ablaze). **2** (often foll. by with) glittering; glowing; radiant. **3** (often foll. by with) greatly excited.

a·ble /áybəl/ adj. (**abler**, **ablest**) **1** (often foll. by to + infin.; used esp. in is able, will be able, was able, etc., replacing tenses of can) having the capacity or power (was not able to come). **2** having great ability; clever; skillful. [ME f. OF hable, able f. L habilis handy f. habēre to hold]

-able /əbəl/ suffix forming adjectives meaning: **1** that may or must be (eatable; forgivable; payable). **2** that can be made the subject of (dutiable; objectionable). **3** that is relevant to or in accordance with (fashionable; seasonable). **4** (with active sense, in earlier word formations) that may (comfortable; suitable). [F –able or L –abilis forming verbal adjectives f. verbs of first conjugation]

a·ble-bod·ied /áybəl-bódeed/ adj. fit; healthy.

a·ble-bod·ied sea·man n. Naut. one able to perform all duties.

a·bled /áybəld/ adj. having a full range of physical and mental abilities; able-bodied. □ **differently abled** euphem. disabled.

a·ble·ism /áybəlizəm/ n. (also **ablism**, **a·ble·bod·ied·ism**) discrimination in favor of the able-bodied.

a·bloom /əblŏŏm/ predic.adj. blooming; in flower.

a·blush /əblúsh/ predic.adj. blushing.

ab·lu·tion /əblŏŏshən/ n. (usu. in pl.) **1** the ceremonial washing of parts of the body or sacred vessels, etc. **2** colloq. the ordinary washing of the body. **3** Brit. a building containing toilet or bathing facilities, etc., in a military camp, ship, etc. □□ **ab·lu·tion·ar·y** adj. [ME f. OF ablution or L ablutio (as AB-, lutio f. luere lut- wash)]

a·bly /áyblee/ adv. capably; cleverly; competently.

-ably /əblee/ suffix forming adverbs corresponding to adjectives in –able.

ABM abbr. antiballistic missile.

ab·ne·gate /ábnigayt/ v.tr. **1** give up or deny oneself (a pleasure, etc.). **2** renounce or reject (a right or belief). □□ **ab·ne·ga·tor** n. [L abnegare abnegat- (as AB-, negare deny)]

ab·ne·ga·tion /ábnigáyshən/ n. **1** denial; the rejection or renunciation of a doctrine. **2** = SELF-ABNEGATION. [OF abnegation or LL abnegatio (as ABNEGATE)]

ab·nor·mal /abnáwrməl/ adj. **1** deviating from what is normal or usual; exceptional. **2** relating to or dealing with what is abnormal (abnormal psychology). □□ **ab·nor·mal·ly** adv. [earlier and F anormal, anomal f. Gk anōmalos ANOMALOUS, assoc. with L abnormis: see ABNORMITY]

ab·nor·mal·i·ty /ábnawrmálitee/ n. (pl. **·ties**) **1 a** an abnormal quality, occurrence, etc. **b** the state of being abnormal. **2** a physical irregularity.

ab·nor·mi·ty /abnáwrmitee/ n. (pl. **·ties**) an abnormality or irregularity. [L abnormis (as AB-, normis f. norma rule)]

A·bo /ábō/ n. & adj. (also **abo**) Austral. offens. sl. ●n. (pl. **Abos**) an Aborigine. ● adj. Aboriginal. [abbr.]

a·board /əbáwrd/ adv. & prep. **1** on or into (a ship, aircraft, train, etc.). **2** alongside. □ **all aboard!** a call that warns of the imminent departure of a ship, train, etc. [ME f. A² + BOARD & F àbord]

a·bode[1] /əbṓd/ n. **1** a dwelling; one's home. **2** archaic a stay or sojourn. [verbal noun of ABIDE: cf. ride, rode, road]

a·bode[2] past of ABIDE.

a·bol·ish /əbólish/ v.tr. put an end to the existence or practice of (esp. a custom or institution). □□ **a·bol·ish·a·ble** *adj.* **a·bol·ish·er** *n.* **a·bol·ish·ment** *n.* [ME f. F *abolir* f. L *abolēre* destroy]

ab·o·li·tion /ábəlíshən/ *n.* **1** the act or process of abolishing or being abolished. **2** an instance of this. [F *abolition* or L *abolitio* (as ABOLISH)]

ab·o·li·tion·ist /ábəlíshənist/ *n.* one who favors the abolition of a practice or institution, esp. of capital punishment or slavery. □□ **ab·o·li·tion·ism** *n.*

ab·o·ma·sum /ábəmáysəm/ *n.* (*pl.* **abomasa** /–sə/) the fourth stomach of a ruminant. [mod.L f. AB- + OMASUM]

A-bomb /áybom/ *n.* = ATOM BOMB. [*A* (for ATOMIC) + BOMB]

a·bom·i·na·ble /əbóminəbəl/ *adj.* **1** detestable; loathsome; morally reprehensible. **2** *colloq.* very bad or unpleasant (*abominable weather*). □□ **a·bom·i·na·bly** *adv.* [ME f. OF f. L *abominabilis* f. *abominari* deprecate (as AB-, *ominari* f. OMEN)]

a·bom·i·na·ble snow·man *n.* an unidentified humanoid or bearlike animal said to exist in the Himalayas; a yeti.

a·bom·i·nate /əbóminayt/ *v.tr.* detest; loathe. □□ **a·bom·i·na·tor** *n.* [L *abominari* (as ABOMINABLE)]

a·bom·i·na·tion /əbómináyshən/ *n.* **1** loathing. **2** an odious or degrading habit or act. **3** (often foll. by *to*) an object of disgust. [ME f. OF (as ABOMINATE)]

ab·o·ral /abáwrəl/ *adj.* away from or opposite the mouth. [AB- + ORAL]

ab·o·rig·i·nal /ábəríjinəl/ *adj. & n.* ● *adj.* **1** (of peoples and natural phenomena) inhabiting or existing in a land from the earliest times or from before the arrival of colonists. **2** (usu. **Aboriginal**) of the Australian Aborigines. ● *n.* **1** an aboriginal inhabitant. **2** (usu. **Aboriginal**) an aboriginal inhabitant of Australia. □□ **Ab·o·rig·i·nal·i·ty** /–nálitee/ *n.* **ab·o·rig·i·nal·ly** *adv.* [as ABORIGINE + –AL]

ab·o·rig·i·ne /ábəríjinee/ *n.* (usu. in *pl.*) **1** an aboriginal inhabitant. **2** (usu. **Aborigine**) an aboriginal inhabitant of Australia. **3** an aboriginal plant or animal. [back-form. f. pl. *aborigines* f. L, prob. f. phr. *ab origine* from the beginning]

a·bort /əbáwrt/ *v. & n.* ● *v.* **1** *intr.* **a** (of a woman) undergo abortion; miscarry. **b** (of a fetus) undergo abortion. **2** *tr.* **a** effect the abortion of (a fetus). **b** effect abortion in (a mother). **3 a** *tr.* cause to end fruitlessly or prematurely; stop in the early stages. **b** *intr.* end unsuccessfully or prematurely. **4 a** *tr.* abandon or terminate (a space flight or other technical project) before its completion, usu. because of a fault. **b** *intr.* terminate or fail to complete such an undertaking. **5** *Biol.* **a** *intr.* (of an organism) remain undeveloped; shrink away. **b** *tr.* cause to do this. ● *n.* **1** a prematurely terminated space flight or other undertaking. **2** the termination of such an undertaking. [L *aboriri* miscarry (as AB-, *oriri ort-* be born)]

a·bor·ti·fa·cient /əbáwrtifáyshənt/ *adj. & n.* ● *adj.* effecting abortion. ● *n.* a drug or other agent that effects abortion.

a·bor·tion /əbáwrshən/ *n.* **1** the expulsion of a fetus (naturally or esp. by medical induction) from the womb before it is able to survive independently, esp. in the first 28 weeks of a human pregnancy. **2** a stunted or deformed creature or thing. **3** the failure of a project or an action. **4** *Biol.* the arrest of the development of an organ. [L *abortio* (as ABORT)]

a·bor·tion·ist /əbáwrshənist/ *n.* a person who carries out abortions, esp. illegally.

a·bor·tive /əbáwrtiv/ *adj.* **1** fruitless; unsuccessful; unfinished. **2** resulting in abortion. **3** *Biol.* (of an organ, etc.) rudimentary; arrested in development. □□ **a·bor·tive·ly** *adv.* [ME f. OF *abortif –ive* f. L *abortivus* (as ABORT)]

ABO sys·tem /áybee-ó/ *n.* a system of four types (A, AB, B, and O) by which human blood may be classified, based on the presence or absence of certain inherited antigens.

a·bou·li·a var. of ABULIA.

a·bound /əbównd/ *v.intr.* **1** be plentiful. **2** (foll. by *in*, *with*) be rich; teem or be infested. [ME f. OF *abunder*, etc., f. L *abundare* overflow (as AB-, *undare* f. *unda* wave)]

a·bout /əbówt/ *prep. & adv.* ● *prep.* **1 a** on the subject of; in connection with (*a book about birds*; *what are you talking about?*; *argued about money*). **b** relating to (*something funny about this*). **c** in relation to (*symmetry about a plane*). **d** so as to affect (*can do nothing about it*; *what are you going to do about it?*). **2** at a time near to (*come about four*). **3 a** in; around; surrounding (*wandered about the town*; *a scarf about her neck*). **b** all around from a center (*look about you*). **4** here and there in; at points throughout (*toys lying about the house*). **5** at a point or points near to (*fighting going on about us*). ● *adv.* **1 a** approximately (*costs about a dollar*; *is about right*). **b** *colloq.* used to indicate understatement (*just about had enough*; *it's about time they came*). **2** here and there; at points nearby (*a lot of flu about*; *I've seen him about recently*). **3** all around; in every direction (*look about*; *wandered about*; *scattered all about*). **4** on the move; in action (*out and about*). **5** in partial rotation or alteration from a given position (*the wrong way about*). **6** in rotation or succession (*turn and turn about*). **7** *Naut.* on or to the opposite tack (*go about*; *put about*). □ **be about to** be on the point of (doing something) (*was about to laugh*). [OE *onbūtan* (*on* = A[2], *būtan* BUT[1])]

a·bout-face /əbówtfáys/ *n., v., & int.* ● *n.* **1** a turn made so as to face the opposite direction. **2** a change of opinion or policy, etc. ● *v.intr.*

make an about-face. ● *int.* *Mil.* a command to make an about-face. [orig. as *int.*]

a·bout-turn /əbówt-túrn/ *n., v., & int.* *Brit.* = ABOUT-FACE.

a·bove /əbúv/ *prep., adv., adj., & n.* ● *prep.* **1** over; on the top of; higher (vertically, up a slope or stream, etc.) than; over the surface of (*head above water*; *above the din*). **2** more than (*above average*). **3** higher in rank, position, importance, etc., than (*thwarted by those above him*). **4 a** too great or good for (*above one's station*; *is not above cheating at cards*). **b** beyond the reach of; not affected by (*above my understanding*; *above suspicion*). **5** *archaic* to an earlier time than (*not traced above the third century*). ● *adv.* **1** at or to a higher point; overhead (*the floor above*; *the clouds above*). **2 a** upstairs (*lives above*). **b** esp. *Brit.* upstream. **3** (of a text reference) further back on a page or in a book (*as noted above*). **4** on the upper side (*looks similar above and below*). **5** in addition (*over and above*). **6** *rhet.* in heaven (*Lord above!*). ● *adj.* mentioned earlier; preceding (*the above argument*). ● *n.* (prec. by *the*) what is mentioned above (*the above shows*). □ **above all** most of all; more than anything else. **above one's head** see HEAD. **above oneself** conceited; arrogant. [A[2] + OE *bufan* f. *be* = BY + *ufan* above]

a·bove·board /əbúvbawrd/ *adj. & adv.* without concealment; fair or fairly; open or openly.

a·bove·ground /əbúvgrownd/ **1** alive. **2** not secret or underground.

ab o·vo /ab óvō/ *adv.* from the very beginning. [L, = from the egg]

Abp. *abbr.* Archbishop.

ab·ra·ca·dab·ra /ábrəkədábrə/ *int. & n.* ● *int.* a supposedly magic word used by magicians in performing a trick. ● *n.* **1** a spell or charm. **2** jargon or gibberish. [a mystical word engraved and used as a charm: L f. Gk]

a·brade /əbráyd/ *v.tr.* scrape or wear away (skin, rock, etc.) by rubbing. □□ **a·brad·er** *n.* [L f. *radere ras-* scrape]

a·bra·sion /əbráyzhən/ *n.* **1** the scraping or wearing away (of skin, rock, etc.). **2** a damaged area resulting from this. [L *abrasio* (as ABRADE)]

a·bra·sive /əbráysiv/ *adj. & n.* ● *adj.* **1 a** tending to rub or abrade. **b** capable of polishing by rubbing or grinding. **2** harsh or hurtful in manner. ● *n.* an abrasive substance. [as ABRADE + –IVE]

ab·re·act /ábreeákt/ *v.tr.* *Psychol.* release (an emotion) by abreaction. [back-form. f. ABREACTION]

ab·re·ac·tion /ábreeákshən/ *n.* *Psychol.* the free expression and consequent release of a previously repressed emotion. □□ **ab·re·ac·tive** *adj.* [AB- + REACTION after G *Abreagierung*]

a·breast /əbrést/ *adv.* **1** side by side and facing the same way. **2 a** (often foll. by *with*) up to date. **b** (foll. by *of*) well-informed (*abreast of all the changes*). [ME f. A[2] + BREAST]

a·bridge /əbríj/ *v.tr.* **1** shorten (a book, movie, etc.) by using fewer words or making deletions. **2** curtail (liberty). □□ **a·bridg·a·ble** or **a·bridge·a·ble** *adj.* **a·bridg·er** *n.* [ME f. OF *abreg(i)er* f. LL *abbreviare* ABBREVIATE]

a·bridg·ment /əbríjmənt/ *n.* (also **a·bridge·ment**) **1 a** a shortened version, esp. of a book; an abstract. **b** the process of producing this. **2** a curtailment (of rights). [F *abrégement* (as ABRIDGE)]

a·broad /əbráwd/ *adv.* **1** in or to a foreign country or countries. **2** over a wide area; in different directions; everywhere (*scatter abroad*). **3** at large; freely moving about; in circulation (*there is a rumor abroad*). **4** in or into the open; out of doors. **5** *archaic* wide of the mark; erring. □ **from abroad** from another country. [ME f. A[2] + BROAD]

ab·ro·gate /ábrəgayt/ *v.tr.* repeal, annul, or abolish (a law or custom). □□ **ab·ro·ga·tion** /–gáyshən/ *n.* **ab·ro·ga·tor** *n.* [L *abrogare* (as AB-, *rogare* propose a law)]

ab·rupt /əbrúpt/ *adj.* **1** sudden and unexpected; hasty (*his abrupt departure*). **2** (of speech, manner, etc.) uneven; lacking continuity; curt. **3** steep; precipitous. **4** *Bot.* truncated. **5** *Geol.* (of strata) suddenly appearing at the surface. □□ **ab·rupt·ly** *adv.* **ab·rupt·ness** *n.* [L *abruptus* past part. of *abrumpere* (as AB-, *rumpere* break)]

ABS *abbr.* antilock brake (or braking) system.

abs- /əbs, əbs/ *prefix* var. of L *ab-* used before *c*, *q*, *t*]

ab·scess /ábses/ *n.* a swollen area accumulating pus within a body tissue. □□ **ab·scessed** *adj.* [L *abscessus* a going away (as AB-, *cedere cess-* go)]

ab·scis·ic ac·id /ábsízik/ *n.* a plant hormone which promotes leaf detachment and bud dormancy and inhibits germination. [L *abscis-* past part. stem of *abscindere* (as AB-, *scindere* to cut)]

ab·scis·sa /əbsísə/ *n.* (*pl.* **abscissae** /–ee/ or **abscissas**) *Math.* **1** (in a system of coordinates) the shortest distance from a point to the vertical or *y*-axis, measured parallel to the

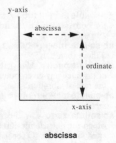

abscissa

horizontal or *x*–axis; the Cartesian *x*–coordinate of a point (cf. OR-DINATE). **2** the part of a line between a fixed point on it and an ordinate drawn to it from any other point. [mod.L *abscissa (linea)* fem. past part. of *abscindere absciss-* (as AB-, *scindere* cut)]

ab·scis·sion /əbsízhən/ *n.* **1** the act or an instance of cutting off. **2** *Bot.* the natural detachment of leaves, branches, flowers, etc. [L *abscissio* (as ABSCISSA)]

ab·scond /əbskónd/ *v.intr.* depart hurriedly and furtively, esp. unlawfully or to avoid arrest. □□ **ab·scond·er** *n.* [L *abscondere* (as AB-, *condere* stow)]

ab·seil /áapzil, ábsayl/ esp. *Brit.* = RAPPEL.

ab·sence /ábsəns/ *n.* **1** the state of being away from a place or person. **2** the time or duration of being away. **3** (foll. by *of*) the nonexistence or lack of. □ **absence of mind** inattentiveness. [ME f. OF f. L *absentia* (as ABSENT)]

ab·sent *adj. & v.* • *adj.* /ábsənt/ **1 a** not present. **b** (foll. by *from*) not present at or in. **2** not existing. **3** inattentive to the matter in hand. • *v.refl.* /absént/ **1** stay away. **2** withdraw. □□ **ab·sent·ly** *adv.* (in sense 3 of *adj.*). [ME ult. f. L *absent-* pres. part. of *abesse* be absent]

ab·sen·tee /ábsəntée/ *n.* a person not present, esp. one who is absent from work or school.

ab·sen·tee bal·lot *n.* a ballot, usu. returned by mail, for a voter who cannot be present at the polls.

ab·sen·tee·ism /ábsəntéeizəm/ *n.* the practice of absenting oneself from work or school, etc., esp. frequently or illicitly.

ab·sen·tee land·lord *n.* a landlord who rents out a property while living elsewhere.

ab·sent·mind·ed /ábsəntmíndid/ *adj.* habitually forgetful or inattentive; with one's mind on other things. □□ **ab·sent·mind·ed·ly** *adv.* **ab·sent·mind·ed·ness** *n.*

ab·sinthe /ábsinth/ *n.* (also **ab·sinth**) **1** a shrubby plant, *Artemisia absinthium*, or its essence. Also called **wormwood**. **2** a green aniseed flavored potent liqueur based on wormwood and turning milky when water is added. [F *absinthe* f. L *absinthium* f. Gk *apsinthion*]

ab·so·lute /ábsəlōōt/ *adj. & n.* • *adj.* **1** complete; utter; perfect (*an absolute fool; absolute bliss*). **2** unconditional; unlimited (*absolute authority*). **3** despotic; ruling arbitrarily or with unrestricted power (*an absolute monarch*). **4** (of a standard or other concept) universally valid; not admitting exceptions; not relative or comparative. **5** *Gram.* **a** (of a construction) syntactically independent of the rest of the sentence, as in *dinner being over, we left the table; let us toss for it, loser to pay.* **b** (of an adjective or transitive verb) used or usable without an expressed noun or object (e.g., *the deaf; guns kill*). **6** (of a legal decree, etc.) final. • *n. Philos.* **1** a value, standard, etc., which is objective and universally valid; not subjective or relative. **2** (prec. by *the*) **a** *Philos.* that which can exist without being related to anything else. **b** *Theol.* ultimate reality; God. □□ **ab·so·lute·ness** *n.* [ME f. L *absolutus* past part.: see ABSOLVE]

ab·so·lute al·co·hol *n. Chem.* ethanol free from water or other impurities.

ab·so·lute·ly /ábsəlōōtlee/ *adv.* **1** completely; utterly; perfectly (*absolutely marvelous; he absolutely denies it*). **2** independently; in an absolute sense. **3** (foll. by *neg.*) (no or none) at all (*absolutely no chance of winning; absolutely nowhere*). **4** *colloq.* in actual fact; positively (*it absolutely exploded*). **5** *Gram.* in an absolute way, esp. (of a verb) without a stated object. **6** *colloq.* (used in reply) quite so; yes.

ab·so·lute mag·ni·tude *n.* the magnitude, i.e., brightness, of a celestial body as seen at a standard distance of 10 parsecs (opp. APPARENT MAGNITUDE).

ab·so·lute ma·jor·i·ty *n.* **1** a majority over all others combined. **2** more than half.

ab·so·lute pitch *n. Mus.* **1** the ability to recognize the pitch of a note or produce any given note. **2** a fixed standard of pitch defined by the rate of vibration.

ab·so·lute tem·per·a·ture *n.* a temperature measured from absolute zero.

ab·so·lute ze·ro *n.* a theoretical lowest possible temperature, at which the particle motion that constitutes heat is minimal, calculated as −273.15 °C (or 0 °K).

ab·so·lu·tion /ábsəlōōshən/ *n.* **1** a formal release from guilt, obligation, or punishment. **2** an ecclesiastical declaration of forgiveness

of sins. **3** a remission of penance. **4** forgiveness. [ME f. OF f. L *absolutio –onis* (as ABSOLVE)]

ab·so·lut·ism /ábsəlōōtizəm/ *n.* the acceptance of or belief in absolute principles in political, philosophical, ethical, or theological matters. □□ **ab·so·lut·ist** *n. & adj.*

ab·solve /əbzólv, –sólv/ *v.tr.* **1** (often foll. by *from, of*) **a** set or pronounce free from blame or obligation, etc. **b** acquit; pronounce not guilty. **2** pardon or give absolution for (a sin, etc.). □□ **ab·solv·er** *n.* [L *absolvere* (as AB-, *solvere solut-* loosen)]

ab·sorb /əbsáwrb, –záwrb/ *v.tr.* **1** include or incorporate as part of itself or oneself (*the country successfully absorbed its immigrants*). **2** take in; suck up (liquid, heat, knowledge, etc.) (*she quickly absorbed all she was taught*). **3** reduce the effect or intensity of; deal easily with (an impact, sound, difficulty, etc.). **4** consume (income, time, resources, etc.) (*his debts absorbed half his income*). **5** engross the attention of (*television absorbs them completely*). □□ **ab·sorb·a·ble** *adj.* **ab·sorb·a·bil·i·ty** /–bəbílitee/ *n.* **ab·sorb·er** *n.* [ME f. F *absorber* or L *absorbēre absorpt-* (as AB-, *sorbēre* suck in)]

ab·sorbed /əbsáwrbd, –záwrbd/ *adj.* intensely engaged or interested (*he was absorbed in his work*). □□ **ab·sorb·ed·ly** /–bidlee/ *adv.*

ab·sorb·ent /əbsáwrbənt, –záwr–/ *adj. & n.* • *adj.* having a tendency to absorb (esp. liquids). • *n.* **1** an absorbent substance. **2** any of the vessels in plants and animals (e.g., root tips) that absorb nutriment. □□ **ab·sorb·en·cy** /–bənsee/ *n.* [L *absorbent-* f. *absorbēre* ABSORB]

ab·sorb·ing /əbsáwrbing, –záwr–/ *adj.* engrossing; intensely interesting. □□ **ab·sorb·ing·ly** *adv.*

ab·sorp·tion /əbsáwrpshən, –záwrp–/ *n.* **1** the process or action of absorbing or being absorbed. **2** disappearance through incorporation into something else. **3** mental engrossment. □□ **ab·sorp·tive** *adj.* [L *absorptio* (as ABSORB)]

ab·stain /əbstáyn/ *v.intr.* **1 a** (usu. foll. by *from*) restrain oneself; refrain from indulging in (*abstained from cake and candy; abstained from mentioning it*). **b** refrain from drinking alcohol. **2** formally decline to use one's vote. □□ **ab·stain·er** *n.* [ME f. AF *astener* f. OF *abstenir* f. L *abstinēre abstent-* (as AB-, *tenēre* hold)]

ab·ste·mi·ous /əbsteémeeəs/ *adj.* (of a person, habit, etc.) moderate, not self-indulgent, esp. in eating and drinking. □□ **ab·ste·mi·ous·ly** *adv.* **ab·ste·mi·ous·ness** *n.* [L *abstemius* (as AB-, *temetum* strong drink)]

ab·sten·tion /əbsténshən/ *n.* the act or an instance of abstaining, esp. from voting. [F *abstention* or LL *abstentio –onis* (as ABSTAIN)]

ab·sti·nence /ábstinəns/ *n.* **1** the act of abstaining, esp. from food, alcohol, or sexual relations. **2** the habit of abstaining from pleasure, food, etc. [ME f. OF f. L *abstinentia* (as ABSTINENT)]

ab·sti·nent /ábstinənt/ *adj.* practicing abstinence. □□ **ab·sti·nent·ly** *adv.* [ME f. OF f. L (as ABSTAIN)]

ab·stract *adj., v., & n.* /ábstrakt/ **1 a** to do with or existing in thought rather than matter, or in theory rather than practice; not tangible or concrete (*abstract questions rarely concerned him*). **b** (of a word, esp. a noun) denoting a quality or condition or intangible thing rather than a concrete object. **2** (of art) achieving its effect by grouping shapes and colors in satisfying patterns rather than by the recognizable representation of physical reality. • *v.* /əbstrákt/ **1** *tr.* (often foll. by *from*) take out of; extract; remove. **2 a** *tr.* summarize (an article, book, etc.). **b** *intr.* do this as an occupation. **3** *tr. & refl.* (often foll. by *from*) disengage (a person's attention, etc.); distract. **4** *tr.* (foll. by *from*) consider abstractly or separately from

ABNEGATION, ABSTEMIOUSNESS, CONTINENCE, FORBEARANCE, MODERATION, TEMPERANCE. **Abstinence** implies voluntary self-denial and is usually associated with the non-indulgence of an appetite (*total abstinence from cigarettes and alcohol*). **Abstemiousness** is the quality or habit of being abstinent; an abstemious person would be one who is moderate when it comes to eating and drinking. **Continence, temperance,** and **moderation** all imply various forms of self-restraint or self-denial: *moderation* is the avoidance of extremes or excesses (*he drank in moderation*); *temperance* is habitual moderation, or even total abstinence, particularly with regard to alcohol (*the 19th century temperance movement*); and *continence* (in this regard) refers to self-restraint with regard to sexual activity. **Forbearance** is self-control, the patient endurance that characterizes deliberately holding back from action or response. **Abnegation** is the rejection or renunciation of something that is generally held in high esteem (*abnegation of the Christian Church*), although it can also mean to refuse or deny oneself a particular right, claim, or convenience (*abnegation of worldly goods*).

something else. **5** *tr. euphem.* steal. • *n.* /ábstrakt/ **1** a summary or statement of the contents of a book, scholarly paper, etc. **2** an abstract work of art. **3** an abstraction or abstract term. □ **in the abstract** in theory rather than in practice. □□ **ab·stract·ly** *adv.* **ab·stract·or** *n.* (in sense 2 of *v.*). [ME f. OF *abstract* or L *abstractus* past part. of *abstrahere* (as AB-, *trahere* draw)]

Abstract nouns are nouns made by adding suffixes such as *-ance, -ation,* and *-ment* to nouns like *solicit, govern, enhance,* and *improve.* Writers who overuse them in an attempt to sound more impressive usually end up being less clear. It is better to say, *Soliciting neighbors for contributions will not enhance your relationships in the neighborhood* rather than *Solicitation of neighbors will not lead to the enhancement of relationships in the neighborhood.*

ab·stract·ed /əbstráktid/ *adj.* inattentive to the matter at hand; preoccupied. □□ **ab·stract·ed·ly** *adv.*

ab·stract ex·pres·sion·ism *n.* a development of abstract art which aims at a subjective emotional expression of an ideal rather than a picture of a physical object.

ab·strac·tion /əbstrákshən/ *n.* **1** the act or an instance of abstracting or taking away. **2 a** an abstract or visionary idea. **b** the formation of abstract ideas. **3 a** abstract qualities (esp. in art). **b** an abstract work of art. **4** absentmindedness. [F *abstraction* or L *abstractio* (as ABSTRACT)]

ab·strac·tion·ism /əbstrákshənizəm/ *n.* **1** the principles and practice of abstract art. **2** the pursuit or cult of abstract ideas. □□ **ab·strac·tion·ist** *n.*

ab·struse /əbstrōos/ *adj.* hard to understand; obscure; profound. □□ **ab·struse·ly** *adv.* **ab·struse·ness** *n.* [F *abstruse* or L *abstrusus* (as AB-, *trusus* past part. of *trudere* push)]

ab·surd /əbsərd/ *adj.* **1** (of an idea, suggestion, etc.) wildly unreasonable, illogical, or inappropriate. **2** (of a person) unreasonable or ridiculous in manner. **3** (of a thing) ludicrous; incongruous (*an absurd hat; the situation was becoming absurd*). □□ **ab·surd·ly** *adv.* **ab·surd·ness** *n.* [F *absurde* or L *absurdus* (as AB-, *surdus* deaf, dull)]

FOOLISH, LUDICROUS, PREPOSTEROUS, RIDICULOUS, UNREASONABLE. We call something **absurd** when it is utterly inconsistent with what common sense or experience tells us (*she found herself in the absurd position of having to defend the intelligence of a cockroach*). **Ludicrous** applies to whatever is so incongruous that it provokes laughter or scorn (*a ludicrous suggestion that he might escape unnoticed if he dressed up as a woman*), and **ridiculous** implies that ridicule or mockery is the only appropriate response (*she tried to look younger, but succeeded only in making herself look ridiculous*). **Foolish** behavior shows a lack of intelligence or good judgment (*it was foolish to keep that much money under a mattress*), while **unreasonable** behavior implies that the person has intentionally acted contrary to good sense (*his response was totally unreasonable in view of the fact that he'd asked for his honest opinion*). **Preposterous** should be reserved for those acts or situations that are glaringly absurd or ludicrous. For example, it might be *unreasonable* to judge an entire nation on the basis of one tourist's experience and *foolish* to turn down an opportunity to visit that country on those grounds alone, but it would be *preposterous* to suggest that everyone who comes to the United States will be robbed at gunpoint.

ab·surd·ism /əbsərdizm/ *n.* a philosophical belief that the universe is without meaning or rationality and that humankind exists in isolation.

ab·surd·i·ty /əbsərditee/ *n.* (*pl.* **·ties**) **1** wild inappropriateness or incongruity. **2** extreme unreasonableness. **3** an absurd statement or act. [F *absurdité* or LL *absurditas* (as ABSURD)]

a·bu·li·a /əbōōleeə/ *n.* (also **a·bou·li·a**) the loss of willpower as a mental disorder. □□ **a·bu·lic** /–bōōlik/ *adj.* [Gk *a–* not + *boulē* will]

a·bun·dance /əbúndəns/ *n.* **1** a very great quantity, usu. considered to be more than enough. **2** wealth; affluence. **3** wealth of emotion (*abundance of heart*). **4** a call in solo whist undertaking to make nine tricks. [ME f. OF *abundance* f. L *abundantia* (as ABUNDANT)]

a·bun·dant /əbúndənt/ *adj.* **1** existing or available in large quantities; plentiful. **2** (foll. by *in*) having an abundance of (*a country abundant in fruit*). □□ **a·bun·dant·ly** *adv.* [ME f. L (as ABOUND)]

a·buse *v. & n.* • *v.tr.* /əbyōōz/ **1 a** use to bad effect or for a bad purpose; misuse (*abused his position of power*). **b** take (a drug) for a purpose other than a therapeutic one; be addicted to (a substance). **2** insult verbally. **3** maltreat; assault (esp. sexually). • *n.* /əbyōōs/ **1** a incorrect or improper use (*the abuse of power*). **b** an instance of this. **2** insulting language (*a torrent of abuse*). **3** unjust or corrupt practice. **4** maltreatment of a person (*child abuse*). □□ **a·bused** /əbyōōzd/ *adj.* **a·bus·er** /əbyōōzər/ *n.* [ME f. OF *abus* (n.), *abuser* (v.) f. L *abusus, abuti* (as AB-, *uti us–* USE)]

a·bu·sive /əbyōōsiv/ *adj.* **1** using or containing insulting language. **2** (of language) insulting. **3** involving or given to physical abuse. □□ **a·bu·sive·ly** *adv.* **a·bu·sive·ness** *n.*

a·but /əbút/ *v.* (**a·but·ted, a·but·ting**) **1** *intr.* (foll. by *on*) (of land, countries, etc.) adjoin (another). **2** *intr.* (foll. by *on, against*) (of part of a building) touch or lean on (another) with a projecting end or point (*the shed abutted on the side of the house*). **3** *tr.* abut on. [OF *abouter* (BUTT[1]) and AL *abuttare* f. OF *but* end]

a·but·ment /əbútmənt/ *n.* **1** the lateral supporting structure of a bridge, arch, etc. **2** the point of junction between such a support and the thing supported.

a·but·ter /əbútər/ *n.* *Law* the owner of an adjoining property.

a·buzz /əbúz/ *adv. & adj.* in a 'buzz' (see BUZZ *n.* 3); in a state of excitement or activity.

a·bys·mal /əbízməl/ *adj.* **1** *colloq.* extremely bad (*abysmal weather; the standard is abysmal*). **2** profound; utter (*abysmal ignorance*). □□ **a·bys·mal·ly** *adv.* [archaic or poet. *abysm* = ABYSS, f. OF *abi(s)me* f. med.L *abysmus*]

a·byss /əbís/ *n.* **1** a deep or seemingly bottomless chasm. **2 a** an immeasurable depth (*abyss of despair*). **b** a catastrophic situation as contemplated or feared (*his loss brought him a step nearer the abyss*). **3** (prec. by *the*) primal chaos; hell. [ME f. LL *abyssus* f. Gk *abussos* bottomless (as A-[1], *bussos* depth)]

a·byss·al /əbísəl/ *adj.* **1** at or of the ocean depths or floor. **2** *Geol.* plutonic.

AC *abbr.* **1** (also **ac**) alternating current. **2** air conditioning. **3** before Christ. **4** *Brit.* aircraftman. [sense 3 f. L *ante Christum*]

Ac *symb. Chem.* the element actinium.

a/c *abbr.* account. [*account current:* see ACCOUNT *n.* 2, 3]

ac- /ək/ *prefix* assim. form of AD- before *c, k, q.*

-ac /ak/ *suffix* forming adjectives which are often also (or only) used as nouns (*cardiac; maniac*) (see also –ACAL). [F –*aque* or L –*acus* or Gk –*akos* adj. suffix]

a·ca·cia /əkáyshə/ *n.* **1** any tree of the genus *Acacia,* with yellow or white flowers, esp. *A. senegal,* yielding gum arabic. **2** (also **false a·ca·cia**) the locust tree, *Robinia pseudoacacia,* grown for ornament. [L f. Gk *akakia*]

ac·a·deme /ákədeem/ *n.* **1 a** the world of learning. **b** universities collectively. **c** the academic community in general. **2** *literary* a college or university. □ **grove** (or **groves**) **of Academe** a university environment. [Gk *Akadēmos* (see ACADEMY): used by Shakesp. (*Love's Labour's Lost* I.i.13) and Milton (*Paradise Regained* iv. 244)]

ac·a·de·mi·a /ákədeemeeə/ *n.* the academic world; scholastic life. [mod.L: see ACADEMY]

ac·a·dem·ic /ákədémik/ *adj. & n.* • *adj.* **1 a** scholarly; to do with learning. **b** of or relating to a scholarly institution (*academic dress*). **2** abstract; theoretical; not of practical relevance. **3** *Art* conventional; overly formal. **4 a** of or concerning Plato's philosophy. **b** skeptical. • *n.* a teacher or scholar in a university or institute of higher education. □□ **ac·a·dem·i·cal·ly** *adv.* [F *académique* or L *academicus* (as ACADEMY)]

ac·a·dem·i·cal /ákədémikəl/ *adj. & n.* • *adj.* belonging to a college or university. • *n.* (in *pl.*) academic costume.

ac·a·de·mi·cian /ákədəmíshən, əkádə–/ *n.* **1** a member of an Academy. **2** = ACADEMIC. [F *académicien* (as ACADEMIC)]

ac·a·dem·i·cism /ákədémisizəm/ *n.* (also **a·cad·e·mism** /əkádəmizəm/) academic principles or their application in art.

ac·a·dem·ic year *n.* **1** the customary period of instruction in schools, colleges, and universities, usu. from September to June. **2** *Brit.* a period of nearly a year reckoned usu. from the beginning of the autumn term to the end of the summer term.

a·cad·e·my /əkádəmee/ *n.* (*pl.* **·mies**) **1 a** a place of study or training in a special field (*military academy; academy of dance*). **b** *hist.* a place of study. **2** (usu. **Academy**) a society or institution of distinguished scholars, artists, scientists, etc. (*Royal Academy*). **3** a secondary school, esp. one that is private. **4** the community of scholars, academe. **5 a** Plato's followers or philosophical system. **b** the garden near Athens where Plato taught. [F *académie* or L *academia* f. Gk *akadēmeia* f. *Akadēmos* the hero after whom Plato's garden was named]

A·ca·di·an /əkáydeeən/ *n. & adj.* ● *n.* **1** a native or inhabitant of Acadia in Nova Scotia, esp. a French-speaking descendant of the early French settlers in Canada. **2** a descendant of French-speaking Nova Scotian immigrants in Louisiana. ● *adj.* of or relating to Acadians. [F *Acadie* Nova Scotia]

-acal /əkəl/ *suffix* forming adjectives, often used to distinguish them from nouns in *−ac* (*heliacal*; *maniacal*).

a·can·thus /əkánthəs/ *n.* **1** any herbaceous plant or shrub of the genus *Acanthus*, with spiny leaves. **2** *Archit.* a conventionalized representation of an acanthus leaf, used esp. as a decoration for Corinthian column capitals. [L f. Gk *akanthos* f. *akantha* thorn perh. f. *akē* sharp point]

a cap·pel·la /áakəpélə/ *adj. & adv.* (also **al·la cap·pel·la** /álə/) *Mus.* (of choral music) unaccompanied. [It., = in church style]

a·car·i·cide /əkárisīd/ *n.* a preparation for destroying mites.

ac·a·rid /ákərid/ *n.* any small arachnid of the order Acarina, including mites and ticks. [mod.L *acarida* f. *acarus* f. Gk *akari* mite]

a·car·pous /əkáarpəs/ *adj. Bot.* (of a plant, etc.) without fruit or that does not produce fruit. [A⁻¹ + Gk *karpos* fruit]

Ac·ca·di·an var. of AKKADIAN.

ac·cede /akseéd/ *v.intr.* (often foll. by *to*) **1** assent or agree (*acceded to the proposal*). **2** take office, esp. become monarch. **3** (foll. by *to*) formally subscribe to a treaty or other agreement. [ME f. L *accedere* (as AC-, *cedere cess-* go)]

ac·cel·er·an·do /əksélərándō, aachéləráan-/ *adv., adj., & n. Mus.* ● *adv. & adj.* with a gradual increase of speed. ● *n.* (*pl.* **ac·cel·er·an·dos** or **ac·cel·er·an·di** /–dee/) a passage performed accelerando. [It.]

ac·cel·er·ate /əksélərayt/ *v.* **1** *intr.* **a** (of a moving body) move or begin to move more quickly; increase speed. **b** (of a process) happen or reach completion more quickly. **2** *tr.* **a** cause to increase speed. **b** cause (a process) to happen more quickly. [L *accelerare* (as AC-, *celerare* f. *celer* swift)]

ac·cel·er·a·tion /əkséləráyshən/ *n.* **1** the process or act of accelerating or being accelerated. **2** an instance of this. **3** (of a vehicle, etc.) the capacity to gain speed (*the car has good acceleration*). **4** *Physics* the rate of change of velocity measured in terms of a unit of time. [F *accélération* or L *acceleratio* (as ACCELERATE)]

ac·cel·er·a·tive /əkséləraytiv, –ərətiv/ *adj.* tending to increase speed; quickening.

ac·cel·er·a·tor /əkséləraytər/ *n.* **1** a device for increasing speed, esp. the pedal that controls the speed of a vehicle's engine. **2** *Physics* an apparatus for imparting high speeds to charged particles. **3** *Chem.* a substance that speeds up a chemical reaction.

ac·cel·er·om·e·ter /əksélərómitər/ *n.* an instrument for measuring acceleration. [ACCELERATE + −METER]

ac·cent *n. & v.* ● *n.* /áksent/ **1** a particular mode of pronunciation, esp. one associated with a particular region or group (*Boston accent*; *German accent*; *upper-crust accent*). **2** prominence given to a syllable by stress or pitch. **3** a mark on a letter or word to indicate pitch, stress, or the quality of a vowel. **4** a distinctive feature or emphasis (*an accent on comfort*). **5** *Mus.* emphasis on a particular note or chord. ● *v.tr.* /aksént/ **1** pronounce with an accent; emphasize (a word or syllable). **2** write or print accents on (words, etc.). **3** accentuate. **4** *Mus.* play (a note, etc.) with an accent. □□ **ac·cen·tu·al** /akséncho͞oəl/ *adj.* [L *accentus* (as AC-, *cantus* song) repr. Gk *prosōidia* (PROSODY), or through F *accent, accenter*]

ac·cen·tor /akséntər/ *n.* any bird of the genus *Prunella*, e.g., the hedge sparrow. [med.L *accentor* f. L *ad* to + *cantor* singer]

ac·cen·tu·ate /akséncho͞oayt/ *v.tr.* emphasize; make prominent. □□ **ac·cen·tu·a·tion** /–áyshən/ *n.* [med.L *accentuare accentuat-* (as ACCENT)]

ac·cept /aksépt/ *v.tr.* **1** (also *absol.*) consent to receive (a thing offered). **2** (also *absol.*) give an affirmative answer to (an offer or proposal). **3** regard favorably; treat as welcome (*her mother-in-law never accepted her*). **4 a** believe; receive (an opinion, explanation, etc.) as adequate or valid. **b** be prepared to subscribe to (a belief, philosophy, etc.). **5** receive as suitable (*the hotel accepts traveler's checks; the machine only accepts tokens*). **6 a** tolerate; submit to (*accepted the umpire's decision*). **b** (often foll. by *that* + clause) be willing to believe (*we accept that you meant well*). **7** undertake (an office or responsibility). **8** agree to meet (an obligation) or pay (a bill of exchange, etc.). □ **accepted opinion** one generally held to be correct. □□ **ac·cept·er** *n.* [ME f. OF *accepter* or L *acceptare* f. *accipere* (as AC-, *capere* take)]

▶Accept, which means 'to take that which is offered,' may be confused with the verb **except,** which means 'to exclude.' Thus: *I accept the terms of your offer, but I wish to except the clause calling for repayment of the deposit.*

ac·cept·a·ble /ákséptəbəl/ *adj.* **1 a** worthy of being accepted. **b** pleasing; welcome. **2** adequate; satisfactory. **3** tolerable (*an acceptable risk*). □□ **ac·cept·a·bil·i·ty** /–bílitee/ *n.* **ac·cept·a·ble·ness** *n.* **ac·cept·a·bly** *adv.* [ME f. OF f. LL *acceptabilis* (as ACCEPT)]

ac·cept·ance /ákséptəns/ *n.* **1** willingness to receive (a gift, payment, duty, etc.). **2** an affirmative answer to an invitation or proposal. **3** (often foll. by *of*) a willingness to accept (conditions, a circumstance, etc.). **4 a** approval; belief (*found wide acceptance*). **b** willingness or ability to tolerate. **5 a** agreement to meet a bill of exchange. **b** a bill so accepted. [F f. *accepter* (as ACCEPT)]

ac·cept·ant /ákséptənt/ *adj.* (foll. by *of*) willingly accepting. [F (as ACCEPTANCE)]

ac·cep·ta·tion /ákséptáyshən/ *n.* a particular sense, or the generally recognized meaning, of a word or phrase. [ME f. OF f. med.L *acceptatio* (as ACCEPT)]

ac·cep·tor /ákséptər/ *n.* **1** *Commerce* a person who accepts a bill. **2** *Physics* an atom or molecule able to receive an extra electron, esp. an impurity in a semiconductor. **3** *Chem.* a molecule or ion, etc., to which electrons are donated in the formation of a bond. **4** *Electr.* a circuit able to accept a given frequency.

ac·cess /ákses/ *n. & v.* ● *n.* **1** a way of approaching or reaching or entering (*a building with rear access*). **2 a** (often foll. by *to*) the right or opportunity to reach or use or visit; admittance (*has access to secret files; was granted access to the prisoner*). **b** the condition of being readily approached; accessibility. **3** (often foll. by *of*) an attack or outburst (*an access of anger*). **4** (*attrib.*) (of broadcasting) allowed to special interest groups to undertake (*community access*). ● *v.tr.* **1** *Computing* gain access to (data, a file, etc.). **2** accession. [ME f. OF *acces* or L *accessus* f. *accedere* (as AC-, *cedere cess-* go)]

ac·ces·sa·ry var. of ACCESSORY.

ac·ces·si·ble /aksésibəl/ *adj.* (often foll. by *to*) **1** that can readily be reached, entered, or used. **2** (of a person) readily available (esp. to subordinates). **3** (in a form) easy to understand. □□ **ac·ces·si·bil·i·ty** /–bílitee/ *n.* **ac·ces·si·bly** *adv.* [F *accessible* or LL *accessibilis* (as ACCEDE)]

ac·ces·sion /akséshən/ *n. & v.* ● *n.* **1** entering upon an office (esp. the throne) or a condition (as adulthood). **2** (often foll. by *to*) a thing added (e.g., a book to a library); increase; addition. **3** *Law* the incorporation of one item of property into another. **4** assent; the formal acceptance of a treaty, etc. ● *v.tr.* record the addition of (a new item) to a library or museum. [F *accession* or L *accessio −onis* (as ACCEDE)]

ac·ces·so·rize /aksésərīz/ *v.tr.* provide (clothing, etc.) with accessories.

ac·ces·so·ry /aksésəree/ *n. & adj.* (also **ac·ces·sa·ry**) ● *n.* (*pl.* **·ries**) **1** an additional or extra thing. **2** (usu. in *pl.*) **a** a small attachment or fitting. **b** a small item of (esp. a woman's) dress (e.g., shoes, gloves, belt, etc.). **3** (often foll. by *to*) a person who helps in or knows the details of an (esp. illegal) act, without taking part in it. ● *adj.* additional; contributing or aiding in a minor way; dispensable. □ **accessory before** (or **after**) **the fact** a person who incites (or assists) another to commit a crime. □□ **ac·ces·so·ri·al** /áksesáwreeəl/ *adj.* [med.L *accessorius* (as ACCEDE)]

ac·cess road *n.* **1** a road giving access to a highway. **2** a road giving access only to the properties along it.

ac·cess time *n. Computing* the time taken to retrieve data from storage.

ac·ciac·ca·tu·ra /əchaakəto͞orə/ *n. Mus.* a grace note performed as quickly as possible before an essential note of a chord or melody. [It.]

ac·ci·dence /áksidəns/ *n.* the part of grammar that deals with the variable parts or inflections of words. [med.L sense of L *accidentia* (transl. Gk *parepomena*) neut. pl. of *accidens* (as ACCIDENT)]

ac·ci·dent /áksidənt/ *n.* **1** an event that is without apparent cause, or is unexpected (*their early arrival was just an accident*). **2** an unfortunate event, esp. one causing physical harm or damage, brought about unintentionally. **3** occurrence of things by chance; the working of fortune (*accident accounts for much in life*). **4** *colloq.* an occurrence of involuntary urination or defecation. **5** an irregularity in structure. □ **by accident** unintentionally. [ME f. OF f. LL *accidens* f. L *accidere* (as AC-, *cadere* fall)]

ac·ci·den·tal /áksidént'l/ *adj. & n.* ● *adj.* **1** happening by chance, unintentionally, or unexpectedly. **2** not essential to a conception; subsidiary. ● *n.* **1** *Mus.* a sign indicating a momentary departure from the key signature by raising or lowering a note. **2** something not essential to a conception. □□ **ac·ci·den·tal·ly** *adv.* [ME f. LL *accidentalis* (as ACCIDENT)]

ADVENTITIOUS, CASUAL, CONTINGENT, FORTUITOUS, INCIDENTAL. Things don't always go as planned, but there are many ways to describe the role that chance plays. **Accidental** applies to events that occur entirely by chance (*an accidental encounter with the candidate outside the men's room*); but it is so strongly influenced by the noun "accident" that it carries connotations of undesirable or possibly disastrous results (*an accidental miscalculation of the distance he had to jump*). A **casual** act or event is one that is unpremeditated (*a casual conversation with her son's teacher in the grocery store*), in which the role that chance plays is not always clear. Something that is **incidental** may or may not involve chance; it typically refers to what is secondary or non-essential (*incidental expenses in the budget*) or what occurs without design or regularity (*incidental lighting throughout the garden*). **Adventitious** also implies the lack of an essential relationship, referring to something that is a mere random occurrence (*adventitious circumstances that led to victory*). In contrast, **contingent** points to something that is entirely dependent on an uncertain event for its existence or occurrence (*travel plans that are contingent upon the weather*). **Fortuitous** refers to chance events of a fortunate nature; it is about as far as one can get from *accidental* (*a fortuitous meeting with the candidate outside the men's room just before the press conference*).

ac·ci·dent-prone *n.* (of a person) subject to frequent accidents.
ac·ci·die /áksidee/ var of ACEDIA.
ac·claim /əkláym/ *v. & v. tr.* **1** welcome or applaud enthusiastically; praise publicly. **2** (foll. by compl.) hail as (*acclaimed him king; was acclaimed the winner*). ● *n.* **1** applause; welcome; public praise. **2** a shout of acclaim. □□ **ac·claim·er** *n.* [ME f. L *acclamare* (as AC-, *clamare* shout: spelling assim. to *claim*)]
ac·cla·ma·tion /ákləmáyshən/ *n.* **1** loud and eager assent to a proposal. **2** (usu. in *pl.*) shouting in a person's honor. **3** the act or process of acclaiming. □ **by acclamation** *Polit.* (elected or enacted) by overwhelming vocal approval and not formal ballot. [L *acclamatio* (as ACCLAIM)]
ac·cli·mate /áklimayt, əklímit/ *v. tr.* acclimatize. [F *acclimater* f. *à to* + *climat* CLIMATE]
ac·cli·ma·tion /ákləmáyshən/ *n.* acclimatization. [irreg. f. ACCLIMATE]
ac·cli·ma·tize /əklímətīz/ *v.* **1** *tr.* accustom to a new climate or to new conditions. **2** *intr.* become acclimatized. □□ **ac·cli·ma·ti·za·tion** /-tizáyshən/ *n.* [F *acclimater*: see ACCLIMATE]
ac·cliv·i·ty /əklívitee/ *n.* (*pl.* **·ties**) an upward slope. □□ **ac·cliv·i·tous** *adj.* [L *acclivitas* f. *acclivis* (as AC-, *clivis* f. *clivus* slope)]
ac·co·lade /ákəláyd/ *n.* **1** the awarding of praise; an acknowledgment of merit. **2** a touch made with a sword at the bestowing of a knighthood. [F f. Prov. *acolada* (as AC-, L *collum* neck)]
ac·com·mo·date /əkómədayt/ *v. tr.* **1** provide lodging or room for (*the apartment accommodates three people*). **2** adapt; harmonize; reconcile (*must accommodate ourselves to new surroundings; cannot accommodate your needs to mine*). **3 a** do a service or favor to; oblige (a person). **b** (foll. by *with*) supply (a person) with. [L *accommodare* (as AC-, *commodus* fitting)]
ac·com·mo·dat·ing /əkómədayting/ *adj.* obliging; compliant. □□ **ac·com·mo·dat·ing·ly** *adv.*
ac·com·mo·da·tion /əkómədáyshən/ *n.* **1** (in *pl.*) **a** lodgings; a place to live. **b** room and board. **2 a** an adjustment or adaptation to suit a special or different purpose. **b** a convenient arrangement; a settlement or compromise. **3** the act or process of accommodating or being accommodated. **4** (in *pl.*) a seat, berth, or other facilities or services provided for a passenger of a public vehicle. [F *accommodation* or L *accommodatio –onis* (as ACCOMMODATE)]
ac·com·mo·da·tion lad·der *n.* a ladder up the side of a ship for access to or from a small boat.
ac·com·pa·ni·ment /əkúmpənimənt/ *n.* **1** *Mus.* an instrumental or orchestral part supporting or partnering a solo instrument, voice, or group. **2** an accompanying thing; an appendage. [F *accompagnement* (as ACCOMPANY)]
ac·com·pa·nist /əkúmpənist/ *n.* (also **ac·com·pa·ny·ist** /–nee-ist/) a person who provides a musical accompaniment.
ac·com·pa·ny /əkúmpənee/ *v. tr.* (**·nies, ·nied**) **1** go with; escort; attend. **2** (usu. in *passive*; foll. by *with, by*) **a** be done or found with;

supplement (*speech accompanied with gestures*). **b** have as a result (*pills accompanied by side-effects*). **3** *Mus.* support or partner with accompaniment. [ME f. F *accompagner* f. *à* to + OF *compaing* COMPANION[1]: assim. to COMPANY]
ac·com·plice /əkómplis, əkúm–/ *n.* a partner or helper, esp. in a crime or wrongdoing.

Mid-16th cent.: alteration (probably by association with ACCOMPANY) of Middle English *complice* 'an associate,' via Old French from late Latin *complex, complic-* 'allied,' from *com-* 'together' + the root of *plicare* 'to fold.'

ac·com·plish /əkómplish/ *v. tr.* perform; complete; succeed in doing. □□ **ac·com·plish·a·ble** *adj.* [ME f. OF *acomplir* f. L *complēre* COMPLETE]
ac·com·plished /əkómplisht/ *adj.* clever; skilled; well trained or educated.
ac·com·plish·ment /əkómplishmənt/ *n.* **1** the fulfillment or completion (of a task, etc.). **2** an acquired skill, esp. a social one. **3** a thing done or achieved.
ac·cord /əkáwrd/ *v. & n.* ● *v.* **1** *intr.* (often foll. by *with*) (esp. of a thing) be in harmony; be consistent. **2** *tr.* **a** grant (permission, a request, etc.). **b** give (a welcome, etc.). ● *n.* **1** agreement; consent. **2** harmony or harmonious correspondence in pitch, tone, color, etc. **3** a formal treaty or agreement. □ **in accord** of one mind; united; in harmony. **of one's own accord** on one's own initiative; voluntarily. **with one accord** unanimously; in a united way. [ME f. OF *acord, acorder* f. L *cor cordis* heart]
ac·cord·ance /əkáwrd'ns/ *n.* harmony; agreement. □ **in accordance with** in a manner corresponding to (*we acted in accordance with your wishes*). [ME f. OF *acordance* (as ACCORD)]
ac·cord·ant /əkáwrd'nt/ *adj.* (often foll. by *with*) in tune; agreeing. □□ **ac·cord·ant·ly** *adv.* [ME f. OF *acordant* (as ACCORD)]
ac·cord·ing /əkáwrding/ *adv.* **1** (foll. by *to*) **a** as stated by or in (*according to my sister; according to their statement*). **b** in a manner corresponding to; in proportion to (*he lives according to his principles*). **2** (foll. by *as* + clause) in a manner or to a degree that varies as (*he pays according as he is able*).
ac·cord·ing·ly /əkáwrdinglee/ *adv.* **1** as suggested or required by the (stated) circumstances (*silence is vital so please act accordingly*). **2** consequently; therefore (*accordingly, he left the room*).
ac·cor·di·on /əkáwrdeeən/ *n.* a portable musical instrument with reeds blown by bellows and played by means of keys and buttons. □□ **ac·cor·di·on·ist** *n.* [G *Akkordion* f. It. *accordare* to tune]

ac·cost /əkáwst, əkóst/ *v. tr.* **1** approach and address (a person), esp. boldly. **2** (of a prostitute) solicit. [F *accoster* f. It. *accostare* ult. f. L *costa* rib: see COAST]
ac·couche·ment /ákooshmón/ *n.* **1** childbirth. **2** the period of childbirth. [F f. *accoucher* act as midwife]
ac·cou·cheur /ákooshő́r/ *n.* one, esp. a doctor, who assists at childbirth. [F (as ACCOUCHEMENT)]

accordion

ac·count /əkównt/ *n. & v.* ● *n.* **1** a narration or description (*gave a long account of the ordeal*). **2 a** an arrangement or facility at a bank, etc., for commercial or financial transactions, esp. for depositing and withdrawing money (*opened an account*). **b** the assets credited by such an arrangement (*has a large account; paid the money into her account*). **c** an arrangement at a store for buying goods on credit (*has an account at the hardware store*). **3 a** (often in *pl.*) a record or statement of money, goods, or services received or expended, with the balance (*firms must keep detailed accounts*). **b** (in *pl.*) the practice of accounting or reckoning (*is good at accounts*). **4** a statement of the administration of money in trust (*demand an account*). **5** *Brit.* the period during which transactions take place on a stock exchange; the period from one account day to the next. **6** counting; reckoning. **7** estimation; importance; consideration. ● *v. tr.* (foll. by *to be* or compl.) consider; regard as (*account it a misfortune; account him wise; account him to be guilty*). □ **account for 1** serve as or provide an explanation or reason for (*that accounts for their misbehavior*). **2 a** give a reckoning of or answer for (money, etc., entrusted). **b** answer for (one's conduct). **3** succeed in killing, destroying, disposing of, or defeating. **4** supply or make up a specified amount or proportion of (*rent accounts for 50% of expenditures*). **by all accounts** in everyone's opinion. **call to account** require an explanation from (a person). **give a good** (or **bad**) **account of oneself** make a favorable (or unfavorable) impression; be successful (or unsuccessful). **keep account of** keep a record of; follow closely. **leave out of account** fail or decline to consider. **money of account** denominations of money used in reckoning, but not necessarily in circulation, as coins or paper money. **of no account** unimportant. **of some account** important. **on account 1** (of goods or services) to be paid for later. **2** (of money) in part payment. **on account of** because of. **on no account** under no circumstances; certainly not. **on one's own account** for one's own purposes; at one's own risk. **settle (or square) accounts with 1** receive or pay money, etc., owed to. **2** have revenge on. **take account of** (or **take into account**) consider along with other factors (*took their age into account*). **turn to account** (or **good account**) turn to one's advantage. [ME f. OF *acont, aconter* (as AC-, *conter* COUNT¹)]

▶Use with *as* (*we accounted him as wise*) is considered incorrect.

ac•count•a•ble /əkówntəbəl/ *adj.* **1** responsible; required to account for (one's conduct) (*accountable for one's actions*). **2** explicable, understandable. □□ **ac•count•a•bil•i•ty** /–bílitee/ *n.* **ac•count•a•ble•ness** *n.* **ac•count•a•bly** *adv.*

ac•count•an•cy /əkównt'nsee/ *n.* the profession or duties of an accountant.

ac•count•ant /əkównt'nt/ *n.* a professional keeper or inspector of accounts. [legal F f. pres. part. of OF *aconter* ACCOUNT]

ac•count•ing /əkównting/ *n.* **1** the process of or skill in keeping and verifying accounts. **2** in senses of ACCOUNT *v.*

ac•cou•ter /əkóŏtər/ *v.tr.* (also **ac•cou•tre**) (usu. as **accoutred** *adj.*) attire, equip, esp. with a special costume. [F *accoutrer* f. OF *acoustrer* (as A-³, *cousture* sewing: cf. SUTURE)]

ac•cou•ter•ment /əkóŏtərmənt/ *n.* (also **ac•cou•tre•ment**/–trəmənt/) (usu. in *pl.*) **1** equipment; trappings. **2** *Mil.* a soldier's outfit other than weapons and garments. [F (as ACCOUTRE)]

PRONUNCIATION TIP   accouterment

In British English, this word is spelled *accoutrement* and pronounced in a way reflecting this (a-KOO-tri-ment), closer to the original French. In American English, however, the accepted spelling is *accouterment*, pronounced "a-KOO-ter-ment".

---

ac•cred•it /əkrédit/ *v.tr.* (**accredited, accrediting**) **1** (foll. by *to*) attribute (a saying, etc.) to (a person). **2** (foll. by *with*) credit (a person) with (a saying, etc.). **3** (usu. foll. by *to* or *at*) send (an ambassador, etc.) with credentials; recommend by documents as an envoy (*was accredited to the president*). **4** gain belief or influence for or make credible (an adviser, a statement, etc.). **5** certify (esp. an educational institution) as maintaining professional standards. □□ **ac•cred•i•ta•tion** /–táyshən/ *n.* [F *accréditer* (as AC-, *crédit* CREDIT)]

ac•cred•it•ed /əkréditid/ *adj.* **1 a** (of a person or organization) officially recognized. **b** (of an educational institution) having credentials that indicate the maintenance of professional standards. **2** (of a belief) generally accepted; orthodox. **3** (of cattle, milk, etc.) having guaranteed quality.

ac•crete /əkréet/ *v.* **1** *intr.* grow together or into one. **2** *intr.* (often foll. by *to*) form around or on, as around a nucleus. **3** *tr.* attract (such additions). [L *accrescere* (as AC-, *crescere cret-* grow)]

ac•cre•tion /əkréeshən/ *n.* **1** growth by organic enlargement. **2 a** the growing of separate things into one. **b** the product of such growing. **3 a** extraneous matter added to anything. **b** the adhesion of this. **4** *Law* **a** = ACCESSION. **b** the increase of a legacy, etc., by the share of a failing co-legatee. □□ **ac•cre•tive** *adj.* [L *accretio* (as AC-CRETE)]

ac•crue /əkróŏ/ *v.intr.* (**accrues, accrued, accruing**) (often foll. by *to*) come as a natural increase or advantage, esp. financial. □□ **ac•cru•al** *n.* **ac•crued** *adj.* **ac•crue•ment** *n.* [ME f. AF *acru(e)*, past part. of *acreistre* increase f. L *accrescere* ACCRETE]

acct. *abbr.* **1** account. **2** accountant.

ac•cul•tur•ate /əkúlchərayt/ *v.* **1** *intr.* adapt to or adopt a different culture. **2** *tr.* cause to do this. □□ **ac•cul•tur•a•tion** /–ráyshən/ *n.* **ac•cul•tur•a•tive** /–rətiv/ *adj.*

ac•cu•mu•late /əkyóŏmyəlayt/ *v.* **1** *tr.* **a** acquire an increasing number or quantity of; heap up. **b** produce or acquire (a resulting whole) in this way. **2** *intr.* grow numerous or considerable; form an increasing mass or quantity. [L *accumulare* (as AC-, *cumulus* heap)]

ac•cu•mu•la•tion /əkyóŏmyəláyshən/ *n.* **1** the act or process of accumulating or being accumulated. **2** an accumulated mass. **3** the growth of capital by continued interest. [L *accumulatio* (as ACCUMULATE)]

ac•cu•mu•la•tive /əkyóŏmyəlaytiv, –lətiv/ *adj.* **1** arising from accumulation; cumulative (*accumulative evidence*). **2** arranged so as to accumulate. **3** acquisitive; given to hoarding. □□ **ac•cu•mu•la•tive•ly** *adv.*

ac•cu•mu•la•tor /əkyóŏmyəlaytər/ *n.* **1** a person who accumulates things. **2** a register in a computer used to contain the results of an operation. **3** *Brit.* a storage battery. **4** *Brit.* a bet placed on a se-

quence of events, the winnings and stake from each being placed on the next.

ac•cu•ra•cy /ákyərəsee/ *n.* exactness or precision, esp. arising from careful effort.

ac•cu•rate /ákyərət/ *adj.* **1** careful; precise; lacking errors. **2** conforming exactly with a qualitative standard, physical or quantitative target, etc. □□ **ac•cu•rate•ly** *adv.* **ac•cu•rate•ness** *n.* [L *accuratus* done carefully, past part. of *accurare* (as AC-, *cura* care)]

ac•curs•ed /əkórsid, əkórst/ *adj.* (*archaic* **accurst** /əkúrst/) **1** being under a curse; ill-fated. **2** *colloq.* detestable; annoying. [past part. of *accurse*, f. A-² + CURSE]

ac•cu•sal /əkyóŏzəl/ *n.* accusation.

ac•cu•sa•tion /ákyəzáyshən/ *n.* **1** the act or process of accusing or being accused. **2** a statement charging a person with an offense or crime. [ME f. OF f. L *accusatio –onis* (as ACCUSE)]

ac•cu•sa•tive /əkyóŏzətiv/ *n. & adj. Gram.* ●*n.* the case of nouns, pronouns, and adjectives expressing the object of an action or the goal of motion. ●*adj.* of or in this case. □□ **ac•cu•sa•ti•val** /–tívəl/ *adj.* **ac•cu•sa•tive•ly** *adv.* [ME f. OF *accusatif –ive* or L (*casus*) *accusativus*, transl. Gk (*ptōsis*) *aitiatikē*]

ac•cu•sa•to•ri•al /əkyóŏzətáwreeəl/ *adj. Law* (of proceedings) involving accusation by a prosecutor and a verdict reached by an impartial judge or jury (opp. INQUISITORIAL). [L *accusatorius* (as AC-CUSE)]

ac•cu•sa•to•ry /əkyóŏzətawree/ *adj.* (of language, manner, etc.) of or implying accusation.

ac•cuse /əkyóŏz/ *v.tr.* **1** (foll. by *of*) charge (a person, etc.) with a fault or crime; indict (*accused them of murder; was accused of stealing a car*). **2** lay the blame on. □ **the accused** the person or persons charged with a crime. □□ **ac•cus•er** *n.* **ac•cus•ing•ly** *adv.* [ME *acuse* f. OF *ac(c)user* f. L *accusare* (as AC-, CAUSE)]

ac•cus•tom /əkústəm/ *v.tr. & refl.* (foll. by *to*) make (a person or thing or oneself) used to (*the army accustomed him to discipline; was accustomed to their strange ways*). [ME f. OF *acostumer* (as AD-, *costume* CUSTOM)]

ac•cus•tomed /əkústəmd/ *adj.* **1** (usu. foll. by *to*) used to (*accustomed to hard work*). **2** customary; usual.

ace /ays/ *n. & adj.* ●*n.* **1 a** a playing card, domino, etc., with a single spot and generally having the value ``one'' or in card games the highest value in each suit. **b** a single spot on a playing card, etc. **2 a** a person who excels in some activity. **b** *Mil.* a pilot who has shot down many enemy aircraft. **3 a** (in tennis) a service too good for the opponent to touch. **b** a point scored in this way. **4** *Golf* a hole in one. ●*adj. sl.* excellent. □ **ace up one's sleeve** (*or* **in the hole**) something effective kept in reserve. **play one's ace** use one's best resource. **within an ace of** on the verge of. [ME f. OF f. L *as* unity, AS²]

-acea /áyshə/ *suffix* forming the plural names of orders and classes of animals (*Crustacea*) (cf. –ACEAN). [neut. pl. of L adj. suffix –*aceus* of the nature of]

-aceae /áysi-ee/ *suffix* forming the plural names of families of plants (*Rosaceae*). [fem. pl. of L adj. suffix –*aceus* of the nature of]

-acean /áyshən/ *suffix* **1** forming adjectives, = –ACEOUS. **2** forming nouns as the sing. of names in –*acea* (crustacean). [L –*aceus*: see –ACEA]

a•ce•di•a /əseediə/ *n.* laziness; sloth; apathy. [LL *acedia* f. Gk *akēdia* listlessness]

a•cel•lu•lar /aysélyoolər/ *adj. Biol.* **1** having no cells; not consisting of cells. **2** (esp. of protozoa) consisting of one cell only; unicellular.

-aceous /áyshəs/ *suffix* forming adjectives, esp. from nouns in –*acea*, –*aceae* (herbaceous; rosaceous). [L –*aceus*: see –ACEA]

a•ceph•a•lous /əséfələs, əkéf–/ *adj.* **1** headless. **2** having no chief. **3** *Zool.* having no part of the body specially organized as a head. **4** *Bot.* with a head aborted or cut off. **5** *Prosody* lacking a syllable or syllables in the first foot. [med.L *acephalus* f. Gk *akephalos* headless (as A-¹, *kephalē* head)]

a•cerb /əsérb/ *adj.* = ACERBIC.

a•cer•bic /əsérbik/ *adj.* **1** astringently sour; harsh-tasting. **2** bitter in speech, manner, or temper. □□ **a•cer•bi•cal•ly** *adv.* **a•cer•bi•ty** *n.* (*pl.* **•ties**). [L *acerbus* sour-tasting]

ac•e•tab•u•lum /ásitábyooləm/ *n.* (*pl.* **acetabulums** or **acetabula** /–lə/) *Zool.* **1** the socket for the head of the thighbone, or of the leg in insects. **2** a cup-shaped sucker of various organisms, including tapeworms and cuttlefish. [ME f. L, = vinegar cup f. *acetum* vinegar + –*abulum* dimin. of –*abrum* holder]

ac•e•tal /ásital/ *n. Chem.* any of a class of organic compounds formed by the condensation of two alcohol molecules with an aldehyde molecule. [as ACETIC + –AL]

ac•et•al•de•hyde /ásitáldihid/ *n.* a colorless volatile liquid aldehyde. Also called **ethanal**. ¶ Chem. formula: CH_3CHO. [ACETIC + ALDEHYDE]

a•ce•ta•min•o•phen /əseetəmínəfən/ *n.* a crystalline substance, $C_8H_9NO_2$, that is used medically to reduce fever and relieve pain. [*acet* + *amino* + *phenol*]

ac•e•tate /ásitayt/ *n.* **1** a salt or ester of acetic acid, esp. the cellulose ester used to make textiles, phonograph records, etc. **2** a fabric made from cellulose acetate. [ACETIC + -ATE[1] 2]

ac•e•tate fi•ber *n.* (also **ac•e•tate silk**) fiber (or silk) made artificially from cellulose acetate.

a•ce•tic /əse͡etik/ *adj.* of or like vinegar. [F *acétique* f. L *acetum* vinegar]

ace•tic ac•id *n.* the clear liquid acid that gives vinegar its characteristic taste. ¶ Chem. formula: CH_3COOH.

aceto- /ásitō/ *comb. form Chem.* acetic, acetyl.

ac•e•tone /ásitōn/ *n.* a colorless, volatile liquid ketone valuable as a solvent of organic compounds, esp. paints, varnishes, etc. Also called **propanone**. ¶ Chem. formula: CH_3COCH_3. [ACETO- + -ONE]

a•ce•tous /ásitəs, əse͡e-/ *adj.* **1** having the qualities of vinegar. **2** producing vinegar. **3** sour. [LL *acetosus* sour (as ACETIC)]

a•ce•tyl /ásitil, -tĭl/ *n. Chem.* the univalent radical of acetic acid. ¶ Chem. formula: CH_3CO-. [ACETIC + -YL]

a•ce•tyl•cho•line /ásitilkṓleen, ásitil-/ *n.* a compound serving to transmit impulses from nerve fibers. [ACETYL + CHOLINE]

a•cet•y•lene /əsétileen/ *n.* a colorless hydrocarbon gas, burning with a bright flame, used esp. in welding and formerly in lighting. ¶ Chem. formula: C_2H_2. [ACETIC + -YL + -ENE]

a•ce•ty•lide /əsétilīd/ *n.* any of a class of salts formed from acetylene and a metal.

a•ce•tyl•sal•i•cyl•ic ac•id /ásitilsálisílik/ *n.* = ASPIRIN. [ACETYL + SALICYLIC ACID]

A•chae•an /əke͡eən/ *adj. & n.* ● *adj.* **1** of or relating to Achaea in ancient Greece. **2** *literary* (esp. in Homeric contexts) Greek. ● *n.* **1** an inhabitant of Achaea. **2** *literary* (usu. in *pl.*) a Greek. [L *Achaeus* f. Gk *Akhaios*]

A•chae•me•nid /əke͡eəmənid/ *adj. & n.* (also **Achaemenian** /ákime͡eneeən/) ● *adj.* of or relating to the dynasty ruling in Persia from Cyrus I to Darius III (553–330 BC). ● *n.* a member of this dynasty. [L *Achaemenius* f. Gk *Akhaimenēs*, ancestor of the dynasty]

a•char•ne•ment /áshaarnmóN/ *n.* **1** bloodthirsty fury; ferocity. **2** gusto. [F]

ache /ayk/ *n. & v.* ● *n.* **1** a continuous or prolonged dull pain. **2** mental distress. ● *v.intr.* **1** suffer from or be the source of an ache (*I ached all over; my left leg ached*). **2** (foll. by *to* + infin.) desire greatly (*we ached to be at home again*). □□ **ach•ing•ly** *adv.*

WORD HISTORY   ache

Old English *æce* (noun), *acan* (verb). In Middle and early modern English the noun was spelled *atche* and pronounced so as to rhyme with 'batch,' the verb was spelled and pronounced as it is today. The noun began to be pronounced like the verb around 1700. The modern spelling is largely due to Dr. Johnson, who mistakenly assumed its derivation to be from Greek *akhos* 'pain.'

a•chene /əke͡en/ *n. Bot.* a small, dry, one-seeded fruit that does not open to liberate the seed (e.g., a strawberry pip). [mod.L *achaenium* f. Gk *khainō* gape)]

A•cheu•li•an /əshoo͡liən/ *adj. & n.* (also **A•cheu•le•an**) ● *adj.* of the Paleolithic period in Europe, etc., following the Abbevillian and preceding the Mousterian. ● *n.* the culture of this period. [F *acheuléen* f. St-*Acheul* in N. France, where remains of it were found]

a•chieve /əche͡ev/ *v.tr.* **1 a** reach or attain by effort (*achieved victory*). **b** acquire; gain; earn (*achieved notoriety*). **2** accomplish or carry out (a feat or task). **3** *absol.* be successful; attain a desired level of performance. □□ **a•chiev•a•ble** *adj.* **a•chiev•er** *n.* [ME f. OF *achever* f. *chief* to a head]

a•chieve•ment /əche͡evmənt/ *n.* **1** something achieved; an instance of achieving. **2** the act or process of achieving. **3** *Psychol.* performance in a standardized test. **4** *Heraldry* **a** an escutcheon with adjuncts, or bearing, esp. in memory of a distinguished feat. **b** = HATCHMENT.

ach•il•le•a /ákile͡eə, əkil-/ *n.* any plant of the genus *Achillea*, comprising hardy perennial, usu. aromatic plants with flower heads (often white or yellow) usu. in corymbs. [L f. Gk *Akhilleia* a plant supposed to have been used medicinally by Achilles]

A•chil•les heel /əke͡elez/ *n.* a person's weak or vulnerable point. [L *Achilles* f. Gk *Akhilleus*, a hero in the *Iliad*, invulnerable except in the heel]

A•chil•les ten•don /əke͡elez/ *n.* the tendon connecting the heel with the calf muscles.

a•chi•ral /áykírəl/ *adj. Chem.* (of a crystal or molecule) not chiral.

ach•ro•mat /ákrōmat/ *n.* a lens made achromatic by correction.

ach•ro•mat•ic /ákrōmátik/ *adj. Optics* **1** that transmits light without separating it into constituent colors (*achromatic lens*). **2** without color (*achromatic gloom*). □□ **ach•ro•mat•i•cal•ly** *adv.* **ach•ro•ma•tic•i•ty** / əkrṓmətísitee/ *n.* **a•chro•ma•tism** /əkrṓmətizəm/ *n.* [F *achromatique* f. Gk *akhromatos* (as A-[1], CHROMATIC)]

ach•y /áykee/ *adj.* (**achier, achiest**) full of or suffering from aches.

ac•id /ásid/ *n. & adj.* ● *n.* **1** *Chem.* **a** any of a class of substances that liberate hydrogen ions in water, are usu. sour and corrosive, turn litmus red, and have a pH of less than 7. **b** any compound or at-

om donating protons. **2** (in general use) any sour substance. **3** *sl.* the drug LSD. ● *adj.* **1** sharp-tasting; sour. **2** biting; sharp (*an acid wit*). **3** *Chem.* having the essential properties of an acid. **4** *Geol.* containing much silica. **5** (of a color) intense; bright. □ **put the acid on** *Austral. sl.* seek to extract a loan or favor, etc., from. □□ **a•cid•ic** /əsídik/ *adj.* □□ **ac•id•ly** *adv.* **ac•id•ness** *n.* [F *acide* or L *acidus* f. *acēre* be sour]

ac•id•head /ásidhed/ *n. sl.* a user of the drug LSD.

a•cid•i•fy /əsídifī/ *v.tr. & intr.* (**•fies, •fied**) make or become acid. □□ **a•cid•i•fi•ca•tion** /–fikáyshən/ *n.*

ac•i•dim•e•ter /ásidímitər/ *n.* a device for measuring the strengths of acids in a solution. □□ **ac•i•dim•e•try** /ásidímitree/ *n.*

a•cid•i•ty /əsíditee/ *n.* (*pl.* **•ties**) an acid quality or state, esp. an excessively acid condition of the stomach.

ac•i•do•sis /ásidósis/ *n.* an overacid condition of the body fluids or tissues. □□ **ac•i•dot•ic** /–dótik/ *adj.*

ac•id rad•i•cal *n. Chem.* a radical formed by the removal of hydrogen ions from an acid.

ac•id rain *n.* rainfall made sufficiently acidic by atmospheric pollution that it causes environmental harm.

ac•id test *n.* **1** a severe or conclusive test. **2** a test in which acid is used to test for gold, etc.

a•cid•u•late /əsídyoolayt/ *v.tr.* make somewhat acid. □□ **a•cid•u•la•tion** /–láyshən/ *n.* [L *acidulus* dimin. of *acidus* sour]

a•cid•u•lous /əsídyooləs/ *adj.* somewhat acid.

ac•i•nus /ásinəs/ *n.* (*pl.* **acini** /–nī/) **1** any of the small elements that make up a compound fruit of the blackberry, raspberry, etc. **2** the seed of a grape or berry. **3** *Anat.* **a** any multicellular gland with saclike secreting ducts. **b** the terminus of a duct in such a gland. [L, = berry, kernel]

-acious /áyshəs/ *suffix* forming adjectives meaning 'inclined to, full of' (*vivacious; pugnacious; voracious; capacious*). [L *-ax -acis*, added chiefly to verbal stems to form adjectives + -OUS]

-acity /ásitee/ *suffix* forming nouns of quality or state corresponding to adjectives in *-acious*. [F *-acité* or L *-acitas -tatis*]

ack-ack /ákák/ *adj. & n. colloq.* ● *adj.* antiaircraft. ● *n.* an antiaircraft gun, etc. [formerly Brit. signalmen's name for the letters *AA*]

ac•kee var. of AKEE.

ac•knowl•edge /əknólij/ *v.tr.* **1 a** recognize; accept; admit the truth of (*acknowledged the failure of the plan*). **b** (often foll. by *to be* + compl.) recognize as (*acknowledged it to be a great success*). **c** (often foll. by *that* + clause or *to* + infin.) admit that something is so (*acknowledged that he was wrong; acknowledged him to be wrong*). **2** confirm the receipt of (*acknowledged her letter*). **3 a** show that one has noticed (*acknowledged my arrival with a grunt*). **b** express appreciation of (a service, etc.). **4** own; recognize the validity of (*the acknowledged king*). □□ **ac•knowl•edge•a•ble** *adj.* [obs. KNOWLEDGE *v.* after obs. *acknow* (as A-[4], KNOW), or f. obs. noun *acknowledge*]

SPELLING TIP   acknowledgeable

Think of *able* + *acknowledge* when you spell this word. If you spell it wrong, it will end with *-gable*.

ac•knowl•edg•ment /əknólijmənt/ *n.* (also **ac•knowl•edge•ment**) **1** the act or an instance of acknowledging. **2 a** a thing given or done in return for a service, etc. **b** a letter confirming receipt of something. **3** (usu. in *pl.*) an author's statement of indebtedness to others.

a•clin•ic line /əklínik/ *n.* = MAGNETIC EQUATOR. [Gk *aklinēs* (as A-[1], *klinō* bend)]

ACLU *abbr.* American Civil Liberties Union.

ac•me /ákmee/ *n.* the highest point or period (of achievement, success, etc.); the peak of perfection (*displayed the acme of good taste*). [Gk, = highest point]

ac•ne /áknee/ *n.* a skin condition, usu. of the face, characterized by red pimples. □□ **ac•ned** *adj.* [mod.L f. erron. Gk *aknas* for *akmas* accus. pl. of *akmē* facial eruption: cf. ACME]

ac•o•lyte /ákəlīt/ *n.* **1** a person assisting a priest in a service or procession; an altar boy or girl. **2** an assistant; a beginner. [ME f. OF *acolyt* or eccl.L *acolytus* f. Gk *akolouthos* follower]

ac•o•nite /ákənīt/ *n.* **1 a** any poisonous plant of the genus *Aconitum*, esp. monkshood or wolfsbane. **b** the drug obtained from this. Also called **aconitine**. **2** (in full **winter aconite**) any ranunculaceous plant of the genus *Eranthis*, with yellow flowers. □□ **ac•o•nit•ic** /–nítik/ *adj.* [F *aconit* or L *aconitum* f. Gk *akoniton*]

ac•o•ni•tine /əkóniteen/ *n. Pharm.* a poisonous alkaloid obtained from the aconite plant.

a•corn /áykorn/ *n.* the fruit of the oak, with a smooth nut in a rough cuplike base. [OE *æcern*, rel. to *æcer* ACRE, later assoc. with OAK and CORN[1]]

acorn

a•corn bar•na•cle *n.* a multivalve marine cirriped, Balanus balanoides, living on rocks.

a•corn worm *n.* any marine wormlike animal of the phylum Hemichordata, having a proboscis and gill slits, and inhabiting seashores.

a•cot•y•le•don /əkótileéd'n/ *n.* a plant with no distinct seed leaves. □□ a•cot•y•le•don•ous *adj.* [mod.L *acotyledones* pl. (as A-¹, COTYLEDON)]

a•cous•tic /əkóฺostik/ *adj. & n.* ● *adj.* 1 relating to sound or the sense of hearing. 2 (of a musical instrument, phonograph, or recording) not having electrical amplification (*acoustic guitar*). 3 (of building materials) used for soundproofing or modifying sound. 4 *Mil.* (of a mine) that can be exploded by sound waves transmitted under water. ● *n.* 1 (usu. in *pl.*) the properties or qualities (esp. of a room or hall, etc.) in transmitting sound (*good acoustics; a poor acoustic*). 2 (in *pl.*; usu. treated as *sing.*) the science of sound (*acoustics is not widely taught*). □□ a•cous•ti•cal *adj.* a•cous•ti•cal•ly *adv.* [Gk *akoustikos* f. *akouō* hear]

a•cous•tic cou•pler *n.Computing* a modem that converts digital signals into audible signals and vice versa, so that the former can be transmitted and received over telephone lines.

ac•ous•ti•cian /ákoostíshən/ *n.* an expert in acoustics.

ac•quaint /əkwáynt/ *v.tr. & refl.* (usu. foll. by *with*) make (a person or oneself) aware of or familiar with (*acquaint me with the facts*). □ be acquainted with have personal knowledge of (a person or thing); have made the acquaintance of (a person). [ME f. OF *acointier* f. LL *accognitare* (as AC-, *cognoscere cognit-* come to know)]

ac•quaint•ance /əkwáyntəns/ *n.* 1 (usu. foll. by *with*) slight knowledge (of a person or thing). 2 the fact or process of being acquainted (*our acquaintance lasted a year*). 3 a person one knows slightly. □ make a person's acquaintance first meet or introduce oneself to another person; come to know. □□ ac•quaint•ance•ship *n.* [ME f. OF *acointance* (as ACQUAINT)]

ac•qui•esce /ákwee-és/ *v.intr.* 1 agree, esp. tacitly. 2 raise no objection. 3 (foll. by *in*) accept (an arrangement, etc.). □□ ac•qui•es•cence *n.* ac•qui•es•cent *adj.* [L *acquiescere* (as AC-, *quiescere* rest)]

ac•quire /əkwíir/ *v.tr.* 1 gain by and for oneself; obtain. 2 come into possession of (*acquired fame; acquired much property*). □□ ac•quir•a•ble *adj.* [ME f. OF *aquerre* ult. f. L *acquirere* (as AC-, *quaerere* seek)]

ac•quired char•ac•ter•is•tic *n. Biol.* a characteristic caused by the environment, not inherited.

ac•quired im•mune de•fi•cien•cy syn•drome *n. Med.* see AIDS.

ac•quired taste *n.* 1 a liking gained by experience. 2 the object of such a liking.

ac•quire•ment /əkwíirmənt/ *n.* 1 something acquired, esp. a mental attainment. 2 the act or an instance of acquiring.

ac•qui•si•tion /ákwizíshən/ *n.* 1 something acquired, esp. if regarded as useful. 2 the act or an instance of acquiring. [L *acquisitio* (as ACQUIRE)]

ac•quis•i•tive /əkwízitiv/ *adj.* eager to acquire things; avaricious; materialistic. □□ ac•quis•i•tive•ly *adv.* ac•quis•i•tive•ness *n.* [F *acquisitive* or LL *acquisitivus* (as ACQUIRE)]

ac•quit /əkwít/ *v.* (acquitted, acquitting) 1 *tr.* (often foll. by *of*) declare (a person) not guilty (*were acquitted of the offense*). 2 *refl.* a conduct oneself or perform in a specified way (*we acquitted ourselves well*). b (foll. by *of*) discharge (a duty or responsibility). [ME f. OF *aquiter* f. med.L *acquitare* pay a debt (as AC-, QUIT)]

ac•quit•tal /əkwít'l/ *n.* 1 the process of freeing or being freed from a charge, esp. by a judgment of not guilty. 2 performance of a duty.

ac•quit•tance /əkwít'ns/ *n.* 1 payment of or release from a debt. 2 a written receipt attesting settlement of a debt. [ME f. OF *aquitance* (as ACQUIT)]

a•cre /áykər/ *n.* 1 a measure of land, 4,840 sq. yds., 4047 sq. m. 2 *archaic* a piece of land; a field. 3 (in *pl.*) a large area. □□ a•cred *adj.* (also in *comb.*).

WORD HISTORY acre

Old English *æcer* (denoting the amount of land a yoke of oxen could plow in a day), of Germanic origin; related to Dutch *akker* and German *Acker* 'field,' from an Indo-European root shared by Sanskrit *ajra* 'field,' Latin *ager*, and Greek *agros*.

a•cre•age /áykərij, áykrij/ *n.* 1 a number of acres. 2 an extent of land.

ac•rid /ákrid/ *adj.* 1 bitterly pungent; irritating; corrosive. 2 bitter in temper or manner. □□ a•crid•i•ty /–ríditee/ *n.* ac•rid•ly *adv.* [irreg. f. L *acer acris* keen + –ID¹; prob. after *acid*]

ac•ri•dine /ákrideen/ *n.* a colorless crystalline compound used in the manufacture of dyes and drugs. [ACRID + –INE⁴]

ac•ri•fla•vine /ákrifláyvin, –veen/ *n.* a reddish powder used as an antiseptic. [irreg. f. ACRIDINE + FLAVINE]

ac•ri•mo•ni•ous /ákrimóneeəs/ *adj.* bitter in manner or temper. □□ ac•ri•mo•ni•ous•ly *adv.* [F *acrimonieux, –euse* f. med.L *acrimoniosus* f. L *acrimonia* ACRIMONY]

ac•ri•mo•ny /ákrimōnee/ *n.* (*pl.* •nies) bitterness of temper or manner; ill feeling. [F *acrimonie* or L *acrimonia* pungency (as ACRID)]

ac•ro•bat /ákrəbat/ *n.* 1 a performer of spectacular gymnastic feats. 2 a person noted for constant change of mind, allegiance, etc. □□ ac•ro•bat•ic /–bátik/ *adj.* ac•ro•bat•i•cal•ly *adv.* [F *acrobate* f. Gk *akrobatēs* f. *akron* summit + *bainō* walk]

ac•ro•bat•ics /ákrəbátiks/ *n.pl.* 1 acrobatic feats. 2 (as *sing.*) the art of performing these. 3 a skill requiring ingenuity (*mental acrobatics*).

ac•ro•gen /ákrəjən/ *n. Bot.* any nonflowering plant having a perennial stem with the growing point at its apex, e.g., a fern or moss. □□ a•crog•e•nous /əkrójinəs/ *adj.* [Gk *akron* tip + –GEN]

ac•ro•meg•a•ly /ákrəmégəlee/ *n. Med.* the abnormal growth of the hands, feet, and face, caused by excessive activity of the pituitary gland. □□ ac•ro•me•gal•ic /–migálik/ *adj.* [F *acromégalie* f. Gk *akron* extremity + *megas megal-* great]

ac•ro•nym /ákrənim/ *n.* a word, usu. pronounced as such, formed from the initial letters of other words (e.g., *laser, NATO*). [Gk *akron* end + *–onum- = onoma* name]

a•crop•e•tal /əkrópit'l/ *adj. Bot.* developing from below upwards. □□ a•crop•e•tal•ly *adv.* [Gk *akron* tip + L *petere* seek]

ac•ro•pho•bi•a /ákrəfóbeeə/ *n. Psychol.* an abnormal dread of heights. □□ ac•ro•pho•bic /–fóbik/ *adj.* [Gk *akron* peak + –PHOBIA]

a•crop•o•lis /əkrópəlis/ *n.* 1 a citadel or upper fortified part of esp. an ancient Greek city. 2 (**Acropolis**) the ancient citadel at Athens. [Gk *akropolis* f. *akron* summit + *polis* city]

a•cross /əkráws, əkrós/ *prep. & adv.* ● *prep.* 1 to or on the other side of (*walked across the road; lives across the river*). 2 from one side to another side of (*the cover stretched across the opening; a bridge across the river*). 3 at or forming an angle (esp. a right angle) with (*deep cuts across his legs*). ● *adv.* 1 to or on the other side (*ran across; shall soon be across*). 2 from one side to another (*a blanket stretched across*). 3 forming a cross (*with cuts across*). 4 (of a crossword clue or answer) read horizontally (*cannot do nine across*). □ across the board general; generally; applying to all. [ME f. OF *a croix, en croix*, later regarded as f. A² + CROSS]

a•cros•tic /əkráwstik, əkrós–/ *n.* 1 a poem or other composition in which certain letters in each line form a word or words. 2 a word puzzle constructed in this way. [F *acrostiche* or Gk *akrostikhis* f. *akron* end + *stikhos* row, line of verse, assim. to –IC]

a•cryl•ic /əkrílik/ *adj. & n.* ● *adj.* 1 of material made with a synthetic polymer derived from acrylic acid. 2 *Chem.* of or derived from acrylic acid. ● *n.* an acrylic fiber. □ acrylic acid a pungent liquid organic acid. ¶ Chem. formula: $C_3H_4O_2$. [*acrolein* f. L *acer acris* pungent + *olēre* to smell + –IN + –YL + –IC]

a•cryl•ic res•in *n.* any of various transparent colorless polymers of acrylic acid.

ACT *abbr.* 1 American College Test. 2 Australian Capital Territory.

act /akt/ *n. & v.* ● *n.* 1 something done; a deed; an action. 2 the process of doing something (*caught in the act*). 3 a a piece of entertainment, usu. one of a series in a program. b the performer(s) of this. 4 a pretense; behavior intended to deceive or impress (*it was all an act*). 5 a main division of a play or opera. 6 a a written ordinance of a legislature or other legislative body. b a document attesting a legal transaction. 7 (often in *pl.*) the recorded decisions or proceedings of a committee, an academic body, etc. 8 (**Acts**) (in full **Acts of the Apostles**) the New Testament book relating the growth of the early Church. ● *v.* 1 *intr.* behave (*see how they act under stress*). 2 *intr.* perform actions or functions; operate effectively; take action (*act as referee; we must act quickly*). 3 *intr.* (also foll. by *on*) exert energy or influence (*the medicine soon began to act; alcohol acts on the brain*). 4 *intr.* a perform a part in a play, movie, etc. b pretend. 5 *tr.* a perform the part of (*acted Othello; acts the fool*). b perform (a play, etc.). c portray (an incident) by actions. d feign (*we acted indifference*). □ act for be the (*Brit.*, esp. legal) representative of. act on (or upon) perform or carry out; put into operation (*acted on my advice*). act out 1 translate (ideas, etc.) into action. 2 *Psychol.* represent (one's subconscious desires, etc.) in action. 3 perform (a drama). act up *colloq.* misbehave; give trouble (*my car is acting up again*). get one's act together *sl.* become properly organized; make preparations for an undertaking, etc. **get into** (or **in on**) **the act** *sl.* become a participant (esp. for profit). **put on an act** *colloq.* carry out a pretense. □□ **act•a•ble** *adj.* (in sense 5 of *v.*). **act•a•bil•i•ty** /áktəbílitee/ *n.* (in sense 5 of *v.*). [ME ult. f. L *agere* act- do]

ACTH *abbr. Med.* adrenocorticotrophic hormone.

act•ing /ákting/ *n. & attrib. adj.* ● *n.* **1** the art or occupation of performing parts in plays, movies, etc. **2** in senses of ACT *v.* ● *attrib.adj.* serving temporarily or on behalf of another or others (*acting manager; Acting President*).

ac•tin•i•a /aktíneeə/ *n.* (*pl.* **actiniae** /–nee-ee/) any sea anemone, esp. of the genus *Actinia*. [mod.L f. Gk *aktis –inos* ray]

ac•ti•nide /áktinīd/ *n. Chem.* any of the series of 15 radioactive elements having increasing atomic numbers from actinium to lawrencium. [ACTINIUM + –IDE as in *lanthanide*]

ac•tin•ism /áktinizəm/ *n.* the property of shortwave radiation that produces chemical changes, as in photography. □□ **ac•tin•ic** /aktínik/ *adj.* [Gk *aktis –inos* ray]

ac•tin•i•um /aktíneeəm/ *n. Chem.* a radioactive metallic element of the actinide series, occurring naturally in pitchblende. ¶ Symb.: **Ac.**

ac•ti•nom•e•ter /áktinómitər/ *n.* an instrument for measuring the intensity of radiation, esp. ultraviolet radiation. [Gk *aktis –tinos* ray + –METER]

ac•tin•o•mor•phic /áktinəmáwrfik/ *adj. Biol.* radially symmetrical. [as ACTINOMETER + Gk *morphē* form]

ac•tin•o•my•cete /áktinōmíseet, –mīseét/ *n.* any of the usu. nonmotile filamentous anerobic bacteria of the order Actinomycetales. [as ACTINOMORPHIC + –*mycetes* f. Gk *mukēs –ētos* mushroom]

ac•tion /ákshən/ *n. & v.* ● *n.* **1** the fact or process of doing or acting (*demanded action; put ideas into action*). **2** forcefulness or energy as a characteristic (*a woman of action*). **3** the exertion of energy or influence (*the action of acid on metal*). **4** something done; a deed or act (*not aware of his own actions*). **5 a** a series of events represented in a story, play, etc. **b** *sl.* exciting activity (*arrived late and missed the action; want some action*). **6 a** armed conflict; fighting (*killed in action*). **b** an occurrence of this, esp. a minor military engagement. **7 a** the way in which a machine, instrument, etc., works (*explain the action of an air pump*). **b** the mechanism that makes a machine, instrument, etc. (e.g., a musical instrument, a gun, etc.), work. **c** the mode or style of movement of an animal or human (usu. described in some way) (*a runner with good action*). **8** a legal process; a lawsuit (*bring an action*). **9** (in *imper.*) a word of command to begin, esp. used by a film director, etc. ● *v.tr.* bring a legal action against. □ **go into action** start work. **out of action** not working. **take action** begin to act (esp. energetically in protest). [ME f. OF f. L *actio –onis* (as ACT)]

ac•tion•a•ble /ákshənəbəl/ *adj.* giving cause for legal action. □□ **ac•tion•a•bly** *adv.*

ac•tion com•mit•tee *n.* (also **ac•tion group**) a group formed to campaign politically, typically on a particular issue.

ac•tion-packed *adj.* full of action or excitement.

ac•tion paint•ing *n.* an aspect of abstract expressionism with paint applied by the artist's random or spontaneous gestures.

ac•ti•vate /áktivayt/ *v.tr.* **1** make active; bring into action. **2** *Chem.* cause reaction in; excite (a substance, molecules, etc.). **3** *Physics* make radioactive. □□ **ac•ti•va•tion** /–váyshən/ *n.* **ac•ti•va•tor** *n.*

ac•ti•vat•ed car•bon *n.* (also **ac•ti•vat•ed char•coal**) carbon, esp. charcoal, treated to increase its adsorptive power.

ac•ti•vat•ed sludge *n.* aerated sewage containing aerobic bacteria.

ac•tive /áktiv/ *adj. & n.* ● *adj.* **1 a** consisting in or marked by action; energetic; diligent (*leads an active life; an active helper*). **b** able to move about or accomplish practical tasks (*infirmity made him less active*). **2** working; operative (*an active volcano*). **3** originating action; not merely passive or inert (*active support; active ingredients*). **4** radioactive. **5** *Gram.* designating the voice that attributes the action of a verb to the person or thing from which it logically proceeds (e.g., of the verbs in *guns kill; we saw him*). ● *n. Gram.* the active form or voice of a verb. □□ **ac•tive•ly** *adv.* **ac•tive•ness** *n.* [ME f. OF *actif –ive* or L *activus* (as ACT *v.*)]

ac•tive list *n.Mil.* a list of officers available for service.

ac•tive serv•ice *n.* service in the armed forces during a war.

ac•tiv•ism /áktivizəm/ *n.* a policy of vigorous action in a cause, esp. in politics. □□ **ac•tiv•ist** *n.*

ac•tiv•i•ty /aktívitee/ *n.* (*pl.* **•ties**) **1 a** the condition of being active or moving about. **b** the exertion of energy; vigorous action. **2** (often in *pl.*) a particular occupation or pursuit (*outdoor activities*). **3** = RADIOACTIVITY. [F *activité* or LL *activitas* (as ACTIVE)]

act of God *n.* the operation of uncontrollable natural forces.

act of grace *n.* a privilege or concession that cannot be claimed as a right.

ac•tor /áktər/ *n.* **1** the performer of a part in a play, movie, etc. **2** a person whose profession is performing such parts. [L, = doer, actor (as ACT, –OR¹)]

Ac•tors' Eq•ui•ty As•so•ci•a•tion *n.* stage actors' labor union.

ac•tress /áktris/ *n.* a female actor.

ac•tu•al /ákchōōəl/ *adj.* (usu. *attrib.*) **1** existing in fact; real (often as distinct from ideal). **2** existing now; current. □□ **ac•tu•al•ize** *v.tr.* **ac-**

tu•al•i•za•tion /–lizáyshən/ *n.* [ME f. OF *actuel* f. LL *actualis* f. *agere* ACT]

▶Redundant use, as in *tell me the actual facts*, is disputed, but common.

ac•tu•al•i•ty /ákchōō-álitee/ *n.* (*pl.* **•ties**) **1** reality; what is the case. **2** (in *pl.*) existing conditions. [ME f. OF *actualité* entity or med.L *actualitas* (as ACTUAL)]

ac•tu•al•ly /ákchōōəlee/ *adv.* **1** as a fact; really (*I asked for ten, but actually got nine*). **2** as a matter of fact; even (strange as it may seem) (*he actually refused!*). **3** at present; for the time being.

ac•tu•ar•y /ákchōōeree/ *n.* (*pl.* **•ies**) an expert in statistics, esp. one who calculates insurance risks and premiums. □□ **ac•tu•ar•i•al** /–chōōáireeəl/ *adj.* **ac•tu•ar•i•al•ly** *adv.* [L *actuarius* bookkeeper f. *actus* past part. of *agere* ACT]

ac•tu•ate /ákchōō-ayt/ *v.tr.* **1** communicate motion to (a machine, etc.). **2** cause the operation of (an electrical device, etc.). **3** cause (a person) to act. □□ **ac•tu•a•tion** /–áyshən/ *n.* **ac•tu•a•tor** *n.* [med.L *actuare* f. L *actus*: see ACTUAL]

a•cu•i•ty /əkyōōitee/ *n.* sharpness; acuteness (of a needle, senses, understanding). [F *acuité* or med.L *acuitas* f. *acuere* sharpen: see ACUTE]

a•cu•le•ate /əkyōōleeət, –ayt/ *adj.* **1** *Zool.* having a sting. **2** *Bot.* prickly. **3** pointed; incisive. [L *aculeatus* f. *aculeus* sting, dimin. of *acus* needle]

a•cu•men /ákyəmən, əkyōō–/ *n.* keen insight or discernment; penetration. [L *acumen –minis* anything sharp f. *acuere* sharpen: see ACUTE]

a•cu•mi•nate /əkyōōminət, –nayt/ *adj. Biol.* tapering to a point. [L *acuminatus* pointed (as ACUMEN)]

ac•u•pres•sure /ákyəpreshər/ *n.* a form of therapy in which symptoms are relieved by applying pressure with the thumbs or fingers to specific points on the body. [alt. of ACUPUNCTURE]

ac•u•punc•ture /ákyəpungkchər/ *n.* a method (orig. Chinese) of treating various conditions by pricking the skin or tissues with needles. □□ **ac•u•punc•tur•ist** *n.* [L *acu* with a needle + PUNCTURE]

a•cu•tance /əkyōōt'ns/ *n.* sharpness of a photographic or printed image; a measure of this. [ACUTE + –ANCE]

a•cute /əkyōōt/ *adj. & n.* ● *adj.* **1 a** (of senses, etc.) keen; penetrating. **b** (of pain) intense; severe; sharp or stabbing rather than dull, aching, or throbbing. **2** shrewd; perceptive (*an acute critic*). **3** (of a disease) coming sharply to a crisis; severe, not chronic. **4** (of a difficulty or controversy) critical; serious. **5 a** (of an angle) less than 90°. **b** sharp; pointed. **6** (of a sound) high; shrill. ● *n.* = ACUTE ACCENT. □□ **a•cute•ly** *adv.* **a•cute•ness** *n.* [L *acutus* past part. of *acuere* sharpen f. *acus* needle]

a•cute ac•cent *n.* a mark (´) placed over letters in some languages to show quality, vowel length, pronunciation (e.g., maté), etc.

-acy /əsee/ *suffix* forming nouns of state or quality (*accuracy, piracy; supremacy*), or an instance of it (*conspiracy; fallacy*) (see also –CRACY). [a back-form. of the suffix –CY from or after F –*acie* or L –*acia* or –*atia* or Gk –*ateia*]

ac•yl /ásil/ *n. Chem.* the univalent radical of an organic acid. [G (as ACID, –YL)]

AD *abbr.* (of a date) of the Christian era. [*Anno Domini*, 'in the year of the Lord']

▶Strictly, AD should precede a date (e.g., AD 410), but uses such as *the tenth century AD* are well established.

ad /ad/ *n. colloq.* an advertisement. [abbr.]

ad- /əd, ad/ *prefix* (also **a-** before *sc*, *sp*, *st*, **ac-** before *c*, *k*, *q*, **af-** before *f*, **ag-** before *g*, **al-** before *l*, **an-** before *n*, **ap-** before *p*, **ar-** before *r*, **as-** before *s*, **at-** before *t*) **1** with the sense of motion or direction to, reduction or change into, addition, adherence, increase, or intensification. **2** formed by assimilation of other prefixes (*accurse; admiral; advance; affray*). [(sense 1) (through OF *a-*) f. L *ad* to: (sense 2) *a-* repr. various prefixes other than *ad–*]

-ad¹ /əd, ad/ *suffix* forming nouns: **1** in collective numerals (*myriad; triad*). **2** in fem. patronymics (*Dryad*). **3** in names of poems and similar compositions (*Iliad; Dunciad; jeremiad*). [Gk –*as* –*ada*]

-ad² /əd/ *suffix* forming nouns (*ballad; salad*) (cf. –ADE¹). [F –*ade*]

ad•age /ádij/ *n.* a traditional maxim; a proverb. [F f. L *adagium* (as AD-, root of *aio* say)]

a•da•gio /ədáazheeō/ *adv., adj., & n. Mus.* ● *adv. & adj.* in slow time. ● *n.* (*pl.* **•gios**) an adagio movement or passage. [It.]

Ad•am¹ /ádəm/ *n.* the first man, in the biblical and Koranic traditions. □ **not know a person from Adam** be unable to recognize the person in question. [Heb. *ādām* man]

Ad•am² /ádəm/ *adj.* of the style of architecture, furniture, and design created by the Scottish brothers Robert and James Adam (18th c.).

ad•a•mant /ádəmənt/ *adj. & n.* ● *adj.* stubbornly resolute; resistant to persuasion. ● *n.* archaic diamond or other hard substance. □□ **ad•a•mance** *n.* **ad•a•man•tine** /–mántin/ *adj.* **ad•a•mant•ly** *adv.* [OF *adamaunt* f. L *adamas adamant-* untamable f. Gk (as A-¹, *damaō* to tame)]

Ad·am's ale *n.* water.

Ad·am's ap·ple *n.* a projection of the thyroid cartilage of the larynx, esp. as prominent in men.

a·dapt /ədápt/ *v.* **1** *tr.* **a** (foll. by *to*) fit; adjust (one thing to another). **b** (foll. by *to, for*) make suitable for a purpose. **c** alter or modify (esp. a text). **d** arrange for broadcasting, etc. **2** *intr. & refl.* (usu. foll. by *to*) become adjusted to new conditions. □□ **a·dap·tive** *adj.* **a·dap·tive·ly** *adv.* [F *adapter* f. L *adaptare* (as AD-, *aptare* f. *aptus* fit)]

▶Avoid confusing **adapt** with **adopt**. Trouble sometimes arises because in *adapting* to new conditions an animal or plant can be said to *adopt* something—e.g., a new color or behavior pattern.

a·dapt·a·ble /ədáptəbəl/ *adj.* **1** able to adapt oneself to new conditions. **2** that can be adapted. □□ **a·dapt·a·bil·i·ty** /–bílitee/ *n.* **adapt·ably** *adv.*

ad·ap·ta·tion /ádaptáyshən/ *n.* **1** the act or process of adapting or being adapted. **2** a thing that has been adapted. **3** *Biol.* the process by which an organism or species becomes suited to its environment. [F f. LL adaptatio –onis (as ADAPT)]

a·dapt·er /ədáptər/ *n.* (also **a·dap·tor**) **1** a device for making equipment compatible. **2** *Brit.* a device for connecting several electrical plugs to one socket. **3** a person who adapts.

ad·ax·i·al /adákseeəl/ *adj. Bot.* facing toward the stem of a plant, esp. of the upper side of a leaf (cf. ABAXIAL). [AD- + AXIAL]

ADD *abbr.* attention deficit disorder.

add /ad/ *v.tr.* **1** join (one thing to another) as an increase or supplement (*add your efforts to mine; add insult to injury*). **2** put together (two or more numbers) to find a number denoting their combined value. **3** say in addition (*added a remark; added that I was wrong; "What's more, I don't like it," he added*). □ **add in** include. **add to** increase; be a further item among (*this adds to our difficulties*). **add up 1** find the total of. **2** (foll. by *to*) amount to; constitute (*adds up to a disaster*). **3** *colloq.* make sense; be understandable. □□ **add·ed** *adj.* [ME f. L *addere* (as AD-, *dare* put)]

ad·dax /ádaks/ *n.* a large antelope, *Addax nasomaculatus*, of North Africa, with twisted horns. [L f. an African word]

ad·den·dum /ədéndəm/ *n.* (*pl.* **addenda** /–də/) **1** a thing (usu. something omitted) to be added, esp. (in *pl.*) as additional matter at the end of a book. **2** an appendix; an addition. [L, gerundive of *addere* ADD]

ad·der /ádər/ *n.* **1** any of various small venomous snakes, esp. the common European viper, *Vipera berus*. **2** any of various small N. American snakes similar to the viper. [OE *nædre*: *n* lost in ME by wrong division of *a naddre*: cf. APRON, AUGER, UMPIRE]

ad·der's tongue *n.* any fern of the genus Ophioglossum.

ad·dict *v. & n.* ● *v.tr. & refl.* /ədíkt/ (usu. foll. by *to*) devote or apply habitually or compulsively; make addicted. ● *n.* /ádikt/ **1** a person addicted to a habit, esp. one dependent on a (specified) drug (*drug addict; heroin addict*). **2** *colloq.* an enthusiastic devotee of a sport or pastime (*movie addict*). [L *addicere* assign (as AD-, *dicere dict-* say)]

ad·dict·ed /ədíktid/ *adj.* (foll. by *to*) **1** dependent on as a habit; unable to do without (*addicted to heroin; addicted to smoking*). **2** devoted (*addicted to football*).

ad·dic·tion /ədíkshən/ *n.* the fact or process of being addicted, esp. the condition of taking a drug habitually and being unable to give it up without incurring adverse effects. [L *addictio*: see ADDICT]

ad·dic·tive /ədíktiv/ *adj.* (of a drug, habit, etc.) causing addiction or dependence.

Ad·di·son's dis·ease /ádisənz/ *n.* a disease characterized by progressive anemia and debility and brown discoloration of the skin. [T. *Addison*, Engl. physician d. 1860, who first recognized it]

ad·di·tion /ədíshən/ *n.* **1** the act or process of adding or being added. **2** a person or thing added (*a useful addition to the team*). □ **in addition** moreover; furthermore; as well. **in addition to** as well as; as something added to. [ME f. OF *addition* or L *additio* (as ADD)]

ad·di·tion·al /ədíshənəl/ *adj.* added; extra; supplementary. □□ **ad·di·tion·al·ly** *adv.*

ad·di·tive /áditiv/ *n. & adj.* ● *n.* a thing added, esp. a substance added to another so as to give it specific qualities (*food additive*). ● *adj.* **1** characterized by addition (*additive process*). **2** to be added. [LL *additivus* (as ADD)]

ad·dle /ád'l/ *v. & adj.* ● *v.* **1** *tr.* muddle; confuse. **2** *intr.* (of an egg) become addled. ● *adj.* **1** muddled; unsound (*addlebrained*). **2** empty; vain. **3** (of an egg) addled. [OE *adela* filth, used as adj., then as verb]

ad·dled /ád'ld/ *adj.* **1** (of an egg) rotten, producing no chick. **2** muddled. [ADDLE adj., assim. to past part. form]

addn. *abbr.* addition.

add-on *n.* something added to an existing object or quantity.

ad·dress /ədrés/ *n. & v.* ● *n.* **1** (also /ádres/) **a** the place where a person lives or an organization is situated. **b** particulars of this, esp. for postal purposes. **c** *Computing* the location of an item of stored information. **2** a discourse delivered to an audience. **3** skill; dexterity; readiness. **4** (in *pl.*) a courteous approach; courtship (*pay one's addresses to*). **5** *archaic* manner in conversation. ● *v.tr.* **1** write directions for delivery (esp. the name and postal location of the intended recipient) on (an envelope, package, etc.). **2** direct in speech or writing (remarks, a protest, etc.). **3** speak or write to, esp. formally (*addressed the audience; asked me how to address the ambassador*). **4** direct one's attention to. **5** *Golf* take aim at or prepare to hit (the ball). □ **address oneself to 1** speak or write to. **2** attend to. □□ **ad·dress·er** *n.* [ME f. OF *adresser* ult. f. L (as AD-, *directus* DIRECT): (n.) perh. f. F *adresse*]

ad·dress·ee /ádresée/ *n.* the person to whom something (esp. a letter) is addressed.

Ad·dres·so·graph /ədrésəgraf/ *n. Trademark* a machine for printing addresses on envelopes.

ad·duce /ədōōs, ədyōōs/ *v.tr.* cite as an instance or as proof or evidence. □□ **ad·duc·i·ble** *adj.* [L *adducere adduct-* (as AD-, *ducere* lead)]

ad·duct /ədúkt/ *v.tr.* draw toward a middle line, esp. draw (a limb) toward the middle line of the body. □□ **ad·duc·tion** /–dúkshən/ *n.*

ad·duc·tor /ədúktər/ *n.* (in full **adductor muscle**) any muscle that moves one part of the body toward another or toward the middle line of the body.

-ade¹ /ayd/ *suffix* forming nouns: **1** an action done (*blockade; tirade*). **2** the body concerned in an action or process (*cavalcade*). **3** the product or result of a material or action (*arcade; lemonade; masquerade*). [from or after F *–ade* f. Prov., Sp., or Port. *–ada* or It. *–ata* f. L *–ata* fem. sing. past part. of verbs in *–are*]

-ade² /ayd/ *suffix* forming nouns (*decade*) (cf. –AD¹). [F *–ade* f. Gk *–as –ada*]

-ade³ /ayd/ *suffix* forming nouns: **1** = –ADE¹ (*brocade*). **2** a person concerned (*renegade*). [Sp. or Port. *–ado*, masc. form of *–ada*: see –ADE¹]

ad·e·nine /ád'neen, –in/ *n.* a purine derivative found in all living tissue as a component base of DNA or RNA. [G *Adenin* formed as ADENOIDS: see –INE⁴]

ad·e·noids /ád'noydz/ *n.pl. Med.* a mass of enlarged lymphatic tissue between the back of the nose and the throat, often hindering speaking and breathing in the young. □□ **ad·e·noi·dal** /–nóyd'l/ *adj.*

ad·e·noi·dal·ly *adv.* [Gk *adēn –enos* gland + –OID]

ad·e·no·ma /ád'nómə/ *n.* (*pl.* **adenomas** or **adenomata** /–mətə/) a glandlike benign tumor. [mod.L f. Gk *adēn* gland + –OMA]

a·den·o·sine /ədénəseen/ *n.* a nucleoside of adenine and ribose present in all living tissue in a combined form (see ADP, AMP, ATP). [ADENINE + RIBOSE]

a·dept *adj. & n.* ● *adj.* /ədépt/ (foll. by *at, in*) thoroughly proficient. ● *n.* /ádept/ a skilled performer; an expert. □□ **a·dept·ly** *adv.* **a·dept·ness** *n.* [L *adeptus* past part. of *adipisci* attain]

ad·e·quate /ádikwət/ *adj.* **1** sufficient; satisfactory. **2** (foll. by *to*) proportionate. **3** barely sufficient. □□ **ad·e·qua·cy** *n.* **ad·e·quate·ly** *adv.* [L *adaequatus* past part. of *adaequare* make equal (as AD-, *aequus* equal)]

à deux /aa dö́/ *adv. & adj.* **1** for two. **2** between two. [F]

ad fin. /ad fin/ *abbr.* at or near the end. [L *ad finem*]

ADHD *abbr.* attention deficit hyperactivity disorder.

ad·here /ədheér/ *v.intr.* **1** (usu. foll. by *to*) (of a substance) stick fast to a surface, another substance, etc. **2** (foll. by *to*) behave according to; follow in detail (*adhered to our plan*). **3** (foll. by *to*) give support or allegiance. [F *adhérer* or L *adhaerēre* (as AD-, *haerēre haes-* stick)]

ad·her·ent /ədheérənt, –hér–/ *n. & adj.* ● *n.* **1** a supporter of a party, person, etc. **2** a devotee of an activity. ● *adj.* **1** (foll. by *to*) faithfully observing a rule, etc. **2** (often foll. by *to*) (of a substance) sticking fast. □□ **ad·her·ence** /–rəns/ *n.* [F *adhérent* (as ADHERE)]

ad·he·sion /ədheézhən/ *n.* **1** the act or process of adhering. **2** the capacity of a substance to stick fast. **3** *Med.* an unnatural union of surfaces due to inflammation. **4** the maintenance of contact between the wheels of a vehicle and the road. **5** the giving of support or allegiance. [F *adhésion* or L *adhaesio* (as ADHERE)]

▶**Adhesion** is more commonly used in physical senses (e.g., *the glue has good adhesion*), with **adherence** used in abstract senses (e.g., *adherence to principles*).

ad·he·sive /ədheésiv, –ziv/ *adj. & n.* ● *adj.* sticky; enabling surfaces or substances to adhere to one another. ● *n.* an adhesive substance, esp. one used to stick other substances together. □□ **ad·he·sive·ly** *adv.* **ad·he·sive·ness** *n.* [F *adhésif –ive* (as ADHERE)]

ad·hib·it /ədhíbit/ *v.tr.* (**ad·hib·it·ed, ad·hib·it·ing**) **1** affix. **2** apply or administer (a remedy). □□ **ad·hi·bi·tion** /ádhibíshən/ *n.* [L *adhibēre adhibit-* (as AD-, *habēre* have)]

ad hoc /ád hók/ *adv. & adj.* for a particular (usu. exclusive) purpose (*an ad hoc appointment*). [L, = to this]

ad ho·mi·nem /ad hóminem, hó–/ *adv. & adj.* **1** relating to or associated with a particular person. **2** (of an argument) appealing to the emotions and not to reason. [L, = to the person]

ad·i·a·bat·ic /ádeeəbátik, áydiə–/ *adj. & n. Physics* ● *adj.* **1** impassable to heat. **2** occurring without heat entering or leaving the system. ● *n.* a curve or formula for adiabatic phenomena. □□ **ad·i·a·bat·i·cal·ly** *adv.* [Gk *adiabatos* impassable (as A-¹, *diabainō* pass)]

ad·i·an·tum /ádeeántəm/ *n.* **1** any fern of the genus *Adiantum*, e.g., maidenhair. **2** (in general use) a spleenwort. [L f. Gk *adianton* maidenhair (as A-¹, *diantos* wettable)]

a·dieu /ədyŏŏ, ədŏŏ/ *int. & n.* ● *int.* good-bye. ● *n.* (*pl.* **adieus** or **adieux** /ədyŏŏz, ədŏŏz/) a good-bye. [ME f. OF f. *à* to + *Dieu* God]

ad in·fi·ni·tum /ad ínfinítəm/ *adv.* without limit; forever. [L]

ad in·te·rim /ad íntərim/ *adv. & adj.* for the meantime. [L]

ad·i·os /áadee-ŏs, ádee–/ *int.* good-bye. [Sp. *adiós* f. *a* to + *Dios* God]

ad·i·po·cere /ádipōseér/ *n.* a grayish fatty or soapy substance generated in dead bodies subjected to moisture. [F *adipocire* f. L *adeps adipis* fat + F *cire* wax f. L *cera*]

ad·i·pose /ádipōs/ *adj.* of or characterized by fat; fatty. □□ **ad·i·pos·i·ty** /–pósitee/ *n.* [mod.L *adiposus* f. *adeps adipis* fat]

ad·i·pose tis·sue *n.* fatty connective tissue in animals.

ad·it /ádit/ *n.* **1** a horizontal entrance or passage in a mine. **2** a means of approach. [L *aditus* (as AD-, *itus* f. *ire it-* go)]

ad·ja·cent /əjáysənt/ *adj.* (often foll. by *to*) lying near or adjoining. □□ **ad·ja·cen·cy** /–sənsee/ *n.* [ME f. L *adjacēre* (as AD-, *jacēre* lie)]

ad·jec·tive /ájiktiv/ *n. & adj.* ● *n.* a word or phrase naming an attribute, added to or grammatically related to a noun to modify it or describe it. ● *adj.* additional; not standing by itself; dependent. □□ **ad·jec·ti·val** /ájiktívəl/ *adj.* **ad·jec·ti·val·ly** *adv.* [ME f. OF *adjectif –ive* ult. f. L *adjicere adject-* (as AD-, *jacere* throw)]

GRAMMAR TIP adjectives

An *old* man; a *black* cat; a *long* bill. *Old*, *black*, and *long* are adjectives. Each is used to modify, or to give an added quality or description to, a noun. It is not just any man, it is an *old* man; it is not just any cat, it is a *black* cat; it is not just any bill, it is a *long* bill.

Descriptive adjectives describe a quality or condition of a noun: a *short* stick, a *sad* girl, a *grassy* slope. Limiting adjectives single out the object talked about or indicate quantity: *this* book, *that* ring, *two* words. Notice that some limiting adjectives are regularly used as pronouns (*that*, *these*, *this*, *those*). *A*, *an*, and *the*, also limiting adjectives, are sometimes called articles.

Phrases and clauses may also serve as adjectives: "The man *with the green hat* saw me." In addition to modifying nouns, adjectives modify a word or group of words that is acting as a noun: "*Going to school* (noun) is *necessary* (adjective)."

---

ad·join /əjóyn/ *v.tr.* **1** (often as **adjoining** *adj.*) be next to and joined with. **2** *archaic* = ADD 1. [ME f. OF *ajoindre, ajoign-* f. L *adjungere adjunct-* (as AD-, *jungere* join)]

ad·journ /əjə́rn/ *v.* **1** *tr.* a put off; postpone. **b** break off (a meeting, discussion, etc.) with the intention of resuming later. **2** *intr.* of persons at a meeting: **a** break off proceedings and disperse. **b** (foll. by *to*) transfer the meeting to another place. [ME f. OF *ajorner* (as AD-, *jorn* day ult. f. L *diurnus* DIURNAL): cf. JOURNAL, JOURNEY]

ad·journ·ment /əjə́rnmənt/ *n.* adjourning or being adjourned.

ad·judge /əjúj/ *v.tr.* **1** adjudicate (a matter). **2** (often foll. by *that* + clause, or *to* + infin.) pronounce judicially. **3** (foll. by *to*) award judicially. **4** *archaic* condemn. [ME f. OF *ajuger* f. L *adjudicare*: see ADJUDICATE]

ad·ju·di·cate /əjŏŏdikayt/ *v.* **1** *intr.* act as judge in a competition, court, tribunal, etc. **2** *tr.* **a** decide judicially regarding (a claim, etc.). **b** (foll. by *to be* + compl.) pronounce (*was adjudicated to be bankrupt*). □□ **ad·ju·di·ca·tion** /–dikáyshən/ *n.* **ad·ju·di·ca·tive** *adj.* **ad·ju·di·ca·tor** *n.* [L *adjudicare* (as AD-, *judicare* f. *judex –icis* judge)]

ad·junct /ájungkt/ *n.* **1** (foll. by *to, of*) a subordinate or incidental thing. **2** an assistant; a subordinate person, esp. one with temporary appointment only. **3** *Gram.* a word or phrase used to explain or amplify the predicate, subject, etc. □□ **ad·junc·tive** /əjúngktiv/ *adj.* **ad·junc·tive·ly** /əjúngktivlee/ *adv.* [L *adjunctus*: see ADJOIN]

ad·jure /əjŏŏr/ *v.tr.* (usu. foll. by *to* + infin.) charge or request (a person) solemnly or earnestly, esp. under oath. □□ **ad·ju·ra·tion** /ájŏŏráyshən/ *n.* **ad·jur·a·to·ry** /–rətawree/ *adj.* [ME f. L *adjurare* (as AD-, *jurare* swear) in LL sense 'put a person to an oath']

ad·just /əjúst/ *v.* **1** *tr.* **a** arrange; put in the correct order or position. **b** regulate, esp. by a small amount. **2** *tr.* (usu. foll. by *to*) make suitable. **3** *tr.* harmonize (discrepancies). **4** *tr.* assess (loss or damages). **5** *intr.* (usu. foll. by *to*) make oneself suited to; become familiar with (*adjust to one's surroundings*). □□ **ad·just·a·ble** *adj.* **ad·just·a·bil·i·ty** /əjústəbilitee/ *n.* **ad·just·er** *n.* **ad·just·ment** *n.* [F *adjuster* f. OF *ajoster* ult. f. L *juxta* near]

ad·ju·tant /ájət'nt/ *n.* **1** *Mil.* an officer who assists superior officers by communicating orders, conducting correspondence, etc. **2** an assistant. □□ **ad·ju·tan·cy** /–t'nsee/ *n.* [L *adjutare* frequent. of *adjuvare*: see ADJUVANT]

Ad·ju·tant Gen·er·al *n.* **1** the chief administrative officer in the U.S. Army. **2** a high-ranking administrative officer in the British army.

ad·ju·tant stork *n.* (also **ad·ju·tant bird**) a large Indian stork, *Leptoptilus dubius*, with a massive bill and a bare head and neck.

ad·ju·vant /ájəvənt/ *adj. & n.* ● *adj.* helpful; auxiliary. ● *n.* an adjuvant person or thing. [F *adjuvant* or L *adjuvare* (as AD-, *juvare jut-* help)]

Ad·le·ri·an /adleéreeən/ *adj.* of or relating to A. Adler, Austrian psychologist d. 1937, or his system of psychology.

ad lib /ád líb/ *v., adj., adv., & n.* ● *v.intr.* (**ad libbed, ad libbing**) speak or perform without formal preparation; improvise. ● *adj.* improvised. ● *adv.* as one pleases; to any desired extent. ● *n.* something spoken or played extempore. [abbr. of AD LIBITUM]

ad lib·i·tum /ad líbitəm/ *adv.* = AD LIB *adv.* [L, = according to pleasure]

ad li·tem /ad lítem/ *adj.* (of a guardian, etc.) appointed for a lawsuit. [L]

ad loc *abbr.* to or at that place. [L *ad locum*]

Adm. *abbr.* (preceding a name) Admiral.

ad·man /ádman/ *n.* (*pl.* **admen**) *colloq.* a person who produces advertisements commercially.

ad·mass /ádmas/ *n.* esp. Brit. the section of the community that is regarded as readily influenced by advertising and mass communication.

ad·meas·ure /admézhər/ *v.tr.* apportion; assign in due shares. □□ **ad·meas·ure·ment** *n.* [ME f. OF *amesurer* f. med.L *admensurare* (as AD-, MEASURE)]

ad·min /ádmin/ *n.* Brit. *colloq.* administration. [abbr.]

ad·min·i·cle /ədmínikəl/ *n.* **1** a thing that helps. **2** (in Scottish law) collateral evidence of the contents of a missing document. □□ **ad·mi·nic·u·lar** /ádminíkyŏŏlər/ *adj.* [L *adminiculum* prop]

ad·min·is·ter /ədmínistər/ *v.* **1** *tr.* attend to the running of (business affairs, etc.); manage. **2** *tr.* **a** be responsible for the implementation of (the law, justice, punishment, etc.). **b** *Eccl.* give out, or perform the rites of (a sacrament). **c** (usu. foll. by *to*) direct the taking of (an oath). **3** *tr.* **a** provide; apply (a remedy). **b** give; deliver (a rebuke). **4** *intr.* act as administrator. □□ **ad·min·is·tra·ble** *adj.* [ME f. OF *aministrer* f. L *administrare* (as AD-, MINISTER)]

ad·min·is·trate /ədmínistrayt/ *v.tr. & intr.* administer (esp. business affairs); act as an administrator. [L *administrare* (as ADMINISTER)]

ad·min·is·tra·tion /ədmínistráyshən/ *n.* **1** management of a business. **2** the management of public affairs; government. **3** the government in power. **4 a** a President's period of office. **b** a President's advisers, cabinet officials, and their subordinates. **5** *Law* the management of another person's estate. **6** (foll. by *of*) **a** the administering of justice, an oath, etc. **b** application of remedies. [ME f. OF *administration* or L *administratio* (as ADMINISTER)]

ad·min·is·tra·tive /ədmínistráytiv, –trətiv/ *adj.* concerning or relating to the management of affairs. □□ **ad·min·is·tra·tive·ly** *adv.* [F *administratif –ive* or L *administrativus* (as ADMINISTRATION)]

ad·min·is·tra·tor /ədmínistraytər/ *n.* (*fem.* **administratrix**) **1** a person who administers a business or public affairs. **2** a person capable of organizing (*is no administrator*). **3** *Law* a person appointed to manage the estate of a person who has died intestate. **4** a person who performs official duties in some sphere, e.g., in religion. □□ **ad·min·is·tra·tor·ship** *n.* [L (as ADMINISTER)]

ad·mi·ra·ble /ádmərəbəl/ *adj.* **1** deserving admiration. **2** excellent. □□ **ad·mi·ra·bly** *adv.* [F f. L *admirabilis* (as ADMIRE)]

ad·mi·ral /ádmərəl/ *n.* **1 a** the commander in chief of a country's navy. **b** a naval officer of high rank, the commander of a fleet or squadron. **2** any of various butterflies (*red admiral; white admiral*). □□ **ad·mi·ral·ship** *n.*

WORD HISTORY admiral

Middle English (denoting an emir or Saracen commander): from Old French *amiral, admirail*, via medieval Latin from Arabic *'amīr* 'commander' (from *'amara* 'to command'). The ending *-al* was from Arabic *-al-* in the sense 'of the' used in forming titles (e.g. *'amīr-al-'umarā* 'ruler of rulers'), later assimilated to the familiar Latinate suffix -AL.

Ad·mi·ral of the Fleet *n.* an admiral of the highest rank in the British navy.

Ad·mi·ral·ty /ádmərəltee/ *n.* (*pl.* **·ties**) **1** (*hist.* except in titles) (in the UK) the department administering the Royal Navy. **2** (**admiralty**) *Law* trial and decision of maritime questions and offenses. [ME f. OF *admiral(i)té* (as ADMIRAL)]

ad·mi·ra·tion /ádmiráyshən/ *n.* **1** pleased contemplation. **2** respect; warm approval. **3** an object of this (*was the admiration of the whole town*). [F *admiration* or L *admiratio* (as ADMIRE)]

ad·mire /ədmír/ *v.tr.* **1** regard with approval, respect, or satisfaction. **2** express one's admiration of. [F *admirer* or L *admirari* (as AD-, *mirari* wonder at)]

ad·mir·er /ədmírər/ *n.* **1** a woman's suitor. **2** a person who admires, esp. a fan of a famous person.

ad·mir·ing /ədmíring/ *adj.* showing or feeling admiration (*an admiring follower; admiring glances*). □□ **ad·mir·ing·ly** *adv.*

ad·mis·si·ble /ədmísibəl/ *adj.* **1** (of an idea or plan) worth accepting or considering. **2** *Law* allowable as evidence. **3** (foll. by *to*) capable of being admitted. □□ **ad·mis·si·bil·i·ty** /–bílitee/ *n.* [F *admissible* or med.L *admissibilis* (as ADMIT)]

ad·mis·sion /ədmíshən/ *n.* **1** an acknowledgment (*admission of error*; *admission that he was wrong*). **2 a** the process or right of entering or being admitted. **b** a charge for this (*admission is $5*). **3** a person admitted to a hospital. [ME f. L *admissio* (as ADMIT)]
▶ **Admission** traditionally referred to the price paid for entry or the right to enter: *Admission was $5.* **Admittance** more often referred to physical entry: *We were denied admittance by a large man with a forbidding scowl.* In the sense of 'permission or right to enter,' these words have become almost interchangeable, although **admittance** is more formal and technical.

ad·mit /ədmít/ *v.* (**admitted, admitting**) **1** *tr.* **a** (often foll. by *to be*, or *that* + clause) acknowledge; recognize as true. **b** accept as valid or true. **2** *intr.* **a** (foll. by *to*) acknowledge responsibility for (a deed, fault, etc.). **b** (foll. by *of*) allow for something to exist, have influence, etc. **3** *tr.* **a** allow (a person) entrance or access. **b** allow (a person) to be a member of (a class, group, etc.) or to share in (a privilege, etc.). **c** (of a hospital, etc.) bring in (a person) for inpatient treatment. **4** *tr.* (of an enclosed space) have room for; accommodate. **5** *intr.* (foll. by *of*) allow as possible. □□ **ad·mit·ta·ble** *adj.* [ME f. L *admittere admiss-* (as AD-, *mittere* send)]

ad·mit·tance /ədmít'ns/ *n.* **1** the right or process of admitting or being admitted, usu. to a place (*no admittance except on business*). **2** *Electr.* the reciprocal of impedance.
▶ See note at ADMISSION.

ad·mit·ted·ly /ədmítidlee/ *adv.* as an acknowledged fact (*admittedly there are problems*).

ad·mix /admíks/ *v.* **1** *tr. & intr.* (foll. by *with*) mingle. **2** *tr.* add as an ingredient.

ad·mix·ture /admíkschər/ *n.* **1** a thing added, esp. a minor ingredient. **2** the act of adding this. [L *admixtus* past part. of *admiscēre* (as AD-, *miscēre* mix)]

ad·mon·ish /ədmónish/ *v.tr.* **1** reprove. **2** (foll. by *to* + infin., or *that* + clause) urge. **3** give earnest advice to. **4** (foll. by *of*) warn. □□ **ad·mon·ish·ment** *n.* **ad·mo·ni·tion** /ádməníshən/ *n.* **ad·mon·i·to·ry** *adj.* [ME f. OF *amonester* ult. f. L *admonēre* (as AD-, *monēre monit-* warn)]

ad nau·se·am /ad náwzeeəm/ *adv.* to an excessive or disgusting degree. [L, = to sickness]

ad·nom·i·nal /adnóminəl/ *adj. Gram.* attached to a noun. [L *adnomen –minis* (added name)]

a·do /ədōo̅/ *n.* (*pl.* **ados**) fuss; busy activity; trouble; difficulty. □ **without more** (or **further**) **ado** immediately. [orig. in *much ado* = much to do, f. north. ME *at do* (= to do) f. ON *at* AT as sign of infin. + DO¹]

-ado /aádō/ *suffix* forming nouns (*desperado*) (cf. –ADE³). [Sp. or Port. *–ado* f. L *-atus* past part. of verbs in *–are*]

a·do·be /ədṓbee/ *n.* **1** a sun-dried brick of clay and straw. **2** the clay used for making such bricks. **3** a structure of such bricks. [Sp. f. Arab.]

ad·o·les·cent /ádəlésənt/ *adj. & n.* • *adj.* between childhood and adulthood. • *n.* an adolescent person. □□ **ad·o·les·cence** /–səns/ *n.* [ME f. OF f. L *adolescere* grow up]

A·don·is /ədónis, ədṓ–/ *n.* a handsome young man. [the name of a youth loved by Venus: L f. Gk f. Phoen. *adōn* lord]

A·don·is blue *n.* a kind of butterfly, *Lysandra bellargus*.

a·dopt /ədópt/ *v.tr.* **1** take (a person) into a relationship, esp. another's child as one's own. **2** choose to follow (a course of action, etc.). **3** take over (a name, idea, etc.) and use as one's own. **4** *Brit.* choose as a candidate for office. **5** esp. *Brit.* (of a local authority) accept responsibility for the maintenance of (a road, etc.). **6** accept; formally approve (a report, accounts, etc.). □□ **a·dop·tion** /–dópshən/ *n.* [F *adopter* or L *adoptare* (as AD-, *optare* choose)]
▶ See note at ADAPT.

a·dop·tive /ədóptiv/ *adj.* due to adoption (*adoptive son*; *adoptive father*). □□ **a·dop·tive·ly** *adv.* [ME f. OF *adoptif –ive* f. L *adoptivus* (as ADOPT)]

a·dor·a·ble /ədáwrəbəl/ *adj.* **1** deserving adoration. **2** *colloq.* delightful; charming. □□ **a·dor·a·bly** *adv.* [F f. L *adorabilis* (as ADORE)]

a·dore /ədáwr/ *v.tr.* **1** regard with honor and deep affection. **2 a** worship as divine. **b** *RC Ch.* offer reverence to. **3** *colloq.* like very much. □□ **ad·o·ra·tion** /ádəráyshən/ *n.* **a·dor·ing** *adj.* **a·dor·ing·ly** *adv.* [ME f. OF *aourer* f. L *adorare* worship (as AD-, *orare* speak, pray)]

a·dor·er /ədáwrər/ *n.* **1** a worshiper. **2** an ardent admirer.

a·dorn /ədáwrn/ *v.tr.* **1** add beauty or luster to; be an ornament to. **2** furnish with ornaments; decorate. □□ **a·dorn·ment** *n.* [ME f. OF *ao(u)rner* f. L *adornare* (as AD-, *ornare* furnish, deck)]

ADP *abbr.* **1** adenosine diphosphate. **2** automatic data processing.

ad rem /ad rém/ *adv. & adj.* to the point; to the purpose. [L, = to the matter]

ad·re·nal /ədreénəl/ *adj. & n.* • *adj.* **1** at or near the kidneys. **2** of the adrenal glands. • *n.* (in full **adrenal gland**) either of two ductless glands above the kidneys, secreting adrenaline. [AD- + RENAL]

a·dren·a·line /ədrénəlin/ *n.* = EPINEPHRINE.

a·dre·no·cor·ti·co·trop·hic hor·mone /ədreénōkáwrtikōtrófik, –trófik/ *n.* (also **a·dre·no·cor·ti·co·trop·ic** /–trópik, –trṓ–/) a hormone secreted by the pituitary gland and stimulating the adrenal glands. ¶ Abbr.: **ACTH**. [ADRENAL + CORTEX + –TROPHIC, –TROPIC]

a·dre·no·cor·ti·co·troph·in /ədreénōkáwrtikōtrófin, –trófin/ *n.* (also **a·dre·no·cor·ti·co·trop·in** /–trópin, –trṓ–/) = ADRENOCORTICOTROPHIC HORMONE. [ADRENOCORTICOTROPHIC (HORMONE) + –IN]

a·drift /ədríft/ *adv. & predic.adj.* **1** drifting. **2** at the mercy of circumstances. **3** *Brit. colloq.* **a** unfastened. **b** out of touch. **c** absent without leave. **d** (often foll. by *of*) failing to reach a target. **e** out of order. **f** ill-informed. [A² + DRIFT]

a·droit /ədróyt/ *adj.* dexterous; skillful. □□ **a·droit·ly** *adv.* **a·droit·ness** *n.* [F f. *àdroit* according to right]

ad·sorb /adsáwrb, –záwrb/ *v.tr.* (usu. of a solid) hold (molecules of a gas or liquid or solute) to its surface, causing a thin film to form. □□ **ad·sorb·a·ble** *adj.* **ad·sorb·ent** *adj. & n.* **ad·sorp·tion** *n.* (also **ad·sorb·tion**). [AD-, after ABSORB]

ad·sorb·ate /adsáwrbayt, –bit, –záwr–/ *n.* a substance adsorbed.

ad·su·ki var. of ADZUKI.

ad·u·late /ájəlayt/ *v.tr.* flatter obsequiously. □□ **ad·u·la·tion** /–láyshən/ *n.* **ad·u·la·tor** *n.* **ad·u·la·to·ry** /–lətáwree/ *adj.* [L *adulari adulat-* fawn on]

a·dult /ədúlt, ádult/ *adj. & n.* • *adj.* **1** mature; grown-up. **2 a** of or for adults (*adult education*). **b** *euphem.* sexually explicit; indecent (*adult films*). • *n.* **1** an adult person. **2** *Law* a person who has reached the age of majority. □□ **a·dult·hood** *n.* **a·dult·ly** *adv.* [L *adultus* past part. of *adolescere* grow up: cf. ADOLESCENT]

a·dul·ter·ant /ədúltərənt/ *adj. & n.* • *adj.* used in adulterating. • *n.* an adulterant substance.

a·dul·ter·ate *v. & adj.* • *v.tr.* /ədúltərayt/ debase (esp. foods) by adding other or inferior substances. • *adj.* /ədúltərət/ spurious; debased; counterfeit. □□ **a·dul·ter·a·tion** /–ráyshən/ *n.* **a·dul·ter·a·tor** *n.* [L *adulterare adulterat-* corrupt]

a·dul·ter·er /ədúltərər/ *n.* (*fem.* **a·dul·ter·ess** /–təris/) a person who commits adultery. [obs. *adulter* (v.) f. OF *avoutrer* f. L *adulterare*: see ADULTERATE]

a·dul·ter·ine /ədúltərīn, –reen/ *adj.* **1** illegal; unlicensed. **2** spurious. **3** born of adultery. [L *adulterinus* f. *adulter*: see ADULTERY]

a·dul·ter·ous /ədúltərəs/ *adj.* of or involved in adultery. □□ **a·dul·ter·ous·ly** *adv.* [ME f. *adulter*: see ADULTERER]

a·dul·ter·y /ədúltəree/ *n.* voluntary sexual intercourse between a married person and a person (married or not) other than his or her spouse. [ME f. OF *avoutrie*, etc., f. *avoutre* adulterer f. L *adulter*, assim. to L *adulterium*]

ad·um·brate /ádumbrayt/ *v.tr.* **1** indicate faintly. **2** represent in outline. **3** foreshadow; typify. **4** overshadow. □□ **ad·um·bra·tion** /–bráyshən/ *n.* **ad·um·bra·tive** /ədúmbrətiv/ *adj.* [L *adumbrare* (as AD-, *umbrare* f. *umbra* shade)]

ad va·lo·rem /ád valáwrəm/ *adv. & adj.* (of taxes) in proportion to the estimated value of the goods concerned. [L, = according to the value]

ad·vance /ədváns/ *v., n., & adj.* • *v.* **1** *tr. & intr.* move or put forward. **2** *intr.* make progress. **3** *tr.* **a** pay (money) before it is due. **b** lend (money). **4** *tr.* give active support to; promote (a person, cause, or plan). **5** *tr.* put forward (a claim or suggestion). **6** *tr.* cause (an event) to occur at an earlier date (*advanced the meeting three hours*). **7** *tr.* raise (a price). **8** *intr.* rise (in price). **9** *tr.* (as **advanced** *adj.*) **a** far on in progress (*the work is well advanced*). **b** ahead of the times (*advanced ideas*). • *n.* **1** an act of going forward. **2** progress. **3** a payment made before the due time. **4** a loan. **5** (esp. in *pl.*; often foll. by *to*) an amorous or friendly approach. **6** a rise in price. • *attrib.adj.* done or supplied beforehand (*advance warning*; *advance copy*). □ **advance on** approach threateningly. **in advance** ahead in place or time. □□ **ad·vanc·er** *n.* [ME f. OF *avancer* f. LL *abante* in front f. L *ab* away + *ante* before: (n.) partly through F *avance*]

ad·vance guard *n.* a body of soldiers preceding the main body of an army.

ad·vance·ment /ədvánsmənt/ *n.* the promotion of a person, cause, or plan. [ME f. F *avancement* f. *avancer* (as ADVANCE)]

ad·van·tage /ədvántij/ *n. & v.* • *n.* **1** a beneficial feature; a favorable circumstance. **2** benefit; profit (*is not to your advantage*). **3** (often foll. by *over*) a better position; superiority in a particular respect. **4** (in tennis) the next point won after deuce. • *v.tr.* **1** be beneficial or favorable to. **2** further; promote. □ **have the advantage of** be in a better position in some respect than. **take advantage of 1** make good use of (a favorable circumstance). **2** exploit or outwit (a person), esp. unfairly. **3** *euphem.* seduce. **to advantage** in a way which exhibits the merits (*was seen to advantage*). **turn to advantage** benefit from. □□ **ad·van·ta·geous** /ádvəntáyjəs/ *adj.* **ad·van·ta·geous·ly** *adv.* [ME f. OF *avantage, avantager f. avant* in front f. LL *abante*: see ADVANCE]

ad·vec·tion /ədvékshən/ *n.* **1** *Meteorol.* transfer of heat by the horizontal flow of air. **2** horizontal flow of air or water. □□ **ad•vec•tive** *adj.* [L *advectio* f. *advehere* (as AD-, *vehere vect-* carry)]

Ad•vent /ádvent/ *n.* **1** the season before Christmas, including the four preceding Sundays. **2** the coming or second coming of Christ. **3** (**advent**) the arrival, esp. of an important person or thing. [OE f. OF *advent, auvent* f. L *adventus* arrival f. *advenire* (as AD-, *venire vent-* come)]

Ad•vent cal•en•dar *n.* a calendar for Advent, usu. of cardboard with flaps to open each day revealing a picture or scene.

Ad•vent•ist /ádvéntist/ *n.* a member of a Christian sect that believes in the imminent second coming of Christ. □□ **Ad•vent•ism** *n.*

ad•ven•ti•tious /ádventíshəs/ *adj.* **1** accidental; casual. **2** added from outside. **3** *Biol.* formed accidentally or under unusual conditions. **4** *Law* (of property) coming from a stranger or by collateral succession rather than directly. □□ **ad•ven•ti•tious•ly** *adv.* [L *adventicius* (as ADVENT)]

Ad•vent Sun•day *n.* the first Sunday in Advent.

ad•ven•ture /ədvénchər/ *n. & v.* • *n.* **1** an unusual and exciting experience. **2** a daring enterprise; a hazardous activity. **3** enterprise (*the spirit of adventure*). **4** a commercial speculation. • *v.intr.* **1** (often foll. by *into, upon*) dare to go or come. **2** (foll. by *on, upon*) dare to undertake. **3** incur risk; engage in adventure. □□ **ad•ven•ture•some** *adj.* [ME f. OF *aventure, aventurer* f. L *adventurus* about to happen (as ADVENT)]

ad•ven•tur•er /ədvénchərər/ *n.* (*fem.* **adventuress** /–chəris/) **1** a person who seeks adventure, esp. for personal gain or enjoyment. **2** a financial speculator. [F *aventurier* (as ADVENTURE)]

ad•ven•tur•ism /ədvénchərizəm/ *n.* a tendency to take risks, esp. in foreign policy. □□ **ad•ven•tur•ist** *n.*

ad•ven•tur•ous /ədvénchərəs/ *adj.* **1** rash; venturesome; enterprising. **2** characterized by adventures. □□ **ad•ven•tur•ous•ly** *adv.* **ad•ven•tur•ous•ness** *n.* [ME f. OF *aventuros* (as ADVENTURE)]

ad•verb /ádvərb/ *n.* a word or phrase that modifies or qualifies another word (esp. an adjective, verb, or other adverb) or a group of words, expressing a relation of place, time, circumstance, manner, cause, degree, etc. (e.g., *gently, quite, then, there*). □□ **ad•ver•bi•al** /ədvə́rbeeəl/ *adj.* [F *adverbe* or L *adverbium* (as AD-, VERB)]

GRAMMAR TIP adverbs

Adverbs, like adjectives, give an additional quality or description to other words. Adverbs modify verbs, adjectives, other adverbs, entire sentences, or clauses. "The boat was *absolutely* waterproof." (adverb modifying adjective) "The radio worked *unusually* well." (adverb modifying adverb) "I went to school *yesterday.*" (adverb modifying sentence)

An adverb *usually* answers the questions: How? When? Where? or To what extent? "He ran *quickly* down the road." (How?) "She went to school *today.*" (When?) "She dropped the ball *there.*" (Where?) "John sang *loudly.*" (To what extent?)

Interrogative adverbs ask questions. "*Where* did she go?" "*Why* did she go?" Other common interrogative adverbs are *when* and *how*.

Conjunctive adverbs appear between clauses and serve the double function of connecting the two clauses and modifying one of them. "You signed a contract; *therefore,* we demand payment." Other conjunctive adverbs are *however, moreover, nevertheless, otherwise,* and *still*.

Words commonly used as adverbs are *almost, fast, very,* and most words ending in *-ly: badly, sorely*.

---

ad•ver•sar•i•al /ádvərsáireeəl/ *adj.* **1** involving conflict or opposition. **2** opposed; hostile. [ADVERSARY + –IAL]

ad•ver•sar•y /ádvərseree/ *n. & adj.* • *n.* (*pl.* **·ies**) **1** an enemy. **2** an opponent in a sport or game; an antagonist. • *adj.* opposed; antagonistic. [ME f. OF *adversarie* f. L *adversarius* f. *adversus*: see ADVERSE]

ad•ver•sa•tive /ədvə́rsətiv/ *adj.* (of words, etc.) expressing opposition or antithesis. □□ **ad•ver•sa•tive•ly** *adv.* [F *adversatif –ive* or LL *adversativus* f. *adversari* oppose (as *adversus*: see ADVERSE]

ad•verse /advə́rs, ád–/ *adj.* (often foll. by *to*) **1** contrary; hostile. **2** harmful; injurious. □□ **ad•verse•ly** *adv.* **ad•verse•ness** *n.* [ME f. OF *advers* f. L *adversus* past part. of *advertere* (as AD-, *vertere* vers-turn)]

▶**Adverse** means 'hostile, unfavorable, opposed,' and is usually applied to situations, conditions, or events, not people, e.g., *The dry weather has had an adverse effect on the garden.* **Averse** is related in origin and also has the sense of 'opposed,' but is usually employed to describe a person's attitude, e.g., *I would not be averse to making the repairs myself.* A way to remember the spelling of *averse* is with the mnemonic, "*A verse* of bad poetry makes you feel *averse* to poetry in general."

ad•ver•si•ty /ədvə́rsitee/ *n.* (*pl.* **·ties**) **1** the condition of adverse fortune. **2** a misfortune. [ME f. OF *adversité* f. L *adversitas –tatis* (as ADVERSE)]

ad•vert¹ /ədvə́rt/ *v.intr.* (foll. by *to*) *literary* refer in speaking or writing. [ME f. OF *avertir* f. L *advertere*: see ADVERSE]

ad•vert² /ádvərt/ *n. Brit. colloq.* an advertisement. [abbr.]

ad•ver•tise /ádvərtiz/ (also **ad•ver•tize**) *v.* **1** *tr.* draw attention to or describe favorably (goods or services) in a public medium to promote sales. **2** *tr.* make generally or publicly known. **3** *intr.* (foll. by *for*) seek by public notice, esp. in a newspaper. **4** *tr.* (usu. foll. by *that* + clause) notify. □□ **ad•ver•tis•er** *n.* [ME f. OF *avertir* (stem *advertiss-*): see ADVERT²]

ad•ver•tise•ment /ádvərtízmənt, ədvə́rtis–, –tiz–/ *n.* **1** a public notice or announcement, esp. one advertising goods or services in newspapers, on posters, or in broadcasts. **2** the act or process of advertising. **3** *archaic* a notice to readers in a book, etc. [earlier *avert-* f. F *avertissement* (as ADVERTISE)]

ad•vice /ədvís/ *n.* **1** words given or offered as an opinion or recommendation about future action or behavior. **2** information given; news. **3** formal notice of a transaction. **4** (in *pl.*) communications from a distance. □ **take advice** act according to advice given. [ME f. OF *avis* f. L *ad* to + *visum* past part. of *vidēre* see]

ad•vis•a•ble /ədvízəbəl/ *adj.* **1** (of a course of action, etc.) to be recommended. **2** expedient. □□ **ad•vis•a•bil•i•ty** /–bílitee/ *n.* **ad•vis•a•bly** *adv.*

ad•vise /ədvíz/ *v.* **1** *tr.* (also *absol.*) give advice to. **2** *tr.* recommend; offer as advice (*they advise caution; advised me to rest*). **3** *tr.* (usu. foll. by *of,* or *that* + clause) inform; notify. **4** *intr.* **a** (foll. by *with*) consult. **b** offer advice. [ME f. OF *aviser* f. L *ad* to + *visare* frequent. of *vidēre* see]

ad•vised /ədvízd/ *adj.* **1** judicious (*well-advised*). **2** deliberate; considered. □□ **ad•vis•ed•ly** /–zidlee/ *adv.*

ad•vis•er /ədvízər/ *n.* (also **ad•vi•sor**) **1** a person who advises, esp. one appointed to do so and regularly consulted. **2** a person who advises students on education, careers, etc.

▶Either spelling of the word is acceptable, although **adviser** may be seen as less formal, while **advisor** suggests an official position.

ad•vi•so•ry /ədvízəree/ *adj. & n.* • *adj.* **1** giving advice; constituted to give advice (*an advisory body*). **2** consisting in giving advice. • *n.* (*pl.* **·ries**) an advisory statement, esp. a warning about bad weather, potential danger, etc.

ad•vo•caat /ádvəkaat/ *n.* a liqueur of eggs, sugar, and brandy. [Du., = ADVOCATE (being orig. an advocate's drink)]

ad•vo•ca•cy /ádvəkəsee/ *n.* **1** (usu. foll. by *of*) verbal support or argument for a cause, policy, etc. **2** the function of an advocate. [ME f. OF *a(d)vocacie* f. med.L *advocatia* (as ADVOCATE)]

ad•vo•cate *n. & v.* • *n.* /ádvəkət/ **1** (foll. by *of*) a person who supports or speaks in favor. **2** a person who pleads for another. **3** a professional pleader in a court of justice. • *v.tr.* /ádvəkayt/ **1** recommend or support by argument (a cause, policy, etc.). **2** plead for; defend. □□ **ad•vo•cate•ship** *n.* **ad•vo•ca•to•ry** /advókətáwree, ádvəkə–, ádvəkaytəree/ *adj.* [ME f. OF *avocat* f. L *advocatus* past part. of *advocare* (as AD-, *vocare* call)]

ad•vow•son /ədvówzən/ *n. Brit. Eccl.* (in ecclesiastical law) the right of recommending a member of the clergy for a vacant benefice, or of making the appointment. [ME f. AF *a(d) voweson* f. OF *avoeson* f. L *advocatio –onis* (as ADVOCATE)]

advt. *abbr.* advertisement.

ad•y•tum /áditəm/ *n.* (*pl.* **adyta** /–tə/) the innermost part of an ancient temple. [L f. Gk *aduton* neut. of *adutos* impenetrable (as A-¹, *duō* enter)]

adze /adz/ *n. & v.* (also **adz**) • *n.* a tool for cutting away the surface of wood, like an axe with an arched blade at right angles to the handle. • *v.tr.* dress or cut with an adze. [OE *adesa*]

ad•zu•ki /ədzóõkee/ *n.* (also **adsuki**, **azuki**) **1** an annual leguminous plant, *Vigna angularis*, native to China and Japan. **2** the small round dark red edible bean of this plant. [Jap. *azuki*]

-ae /ee/ *suffix* forming plural nouns, used in names of animal and plant families, tribes, etc., (*Felidae; Rosaceae*) and instead of *–as* in the plural of many nonnaturalized or unfamiliar nouns in *–a* derived from Latin or Greek (*larvae; actiniae*). [pl. *–ae* of L nouns in *–a* or pl. *–ai* of some Gk nouns]

ae•dile /éėdīl/ *n.* either of a pair of Roman magistrates who administered public works, maintenance of roads, public games, the grain supply, etc. □□ **ae•dile•ship** *n.* [L *aedilis* concerned with buildings f. *aedes* building]

ae•gis /éejis/ *n.* a protection; an impregnable defense. □ **under the aegis of** under the auspices of. [L f. Gk *aigis* mythical shield of Zeus or Athene]

ae•gro•tat /éėgrōtat/ *n. Brit.* **1** a certificate that a university student is too ill to attend an examination. **2** an examination pass awarded in such circumstances. [L, = is sick f. *aeger* sick]

-aemia esp. *Brit.* var. of –EMIA.

ae•o•li•an /éėōleeən/ *Brit.* = EOLIAN. [L *Aeolius* f. *Aeolus* god of the winds f. Gk *Aiolos*]

ae•o•li•an harp *n.* a stringed instrument or toy that produces musical sounds when the wind passes through it.

Ae•o•li•an mode /eeóleeən/ n. Mus. the mode represented by the natural diatonic scale A–A. [L Aeolius f. Aeolis in Asia Minor f. Gk Aiolis]

ae•on var. of EON.

aer•ate /áirayt/ v.tr. 1 expose to the mechanical or chemical action of the air. 2 oxygenate, esp. the blood. 3 Brit. = CARBONATE. □□ **aer•a•tion** /-ráyshən/ n. **aer•a•tor** n. [L aer AIR + −ATE³, after F aérer]

aer•en•chy•ma /aréngkəmə/ n. Bot. a soft plant tissue containing air spaces found esp. in many aquatic plants. [Gk aēr air + egkhuma infusion]

aer•i•al /áireeəl/ n. & adj. • n. = ANTENNA. • adj. 1 by or from or involving aircraft (aerial navigation; aerial photography). 2 a existing, moving, or happening in the air. b of or in the atmosphere, atmospheric. 3 operated or powered by elevated cables or rails (aerial ski lift). 4 a thin as air; ethereal. b immaterial; imaginary. c of air; gaseous. □□ **aer•i•al•i•ty** /-reeálitee/ n. **aer•i•al•ly** adv. [L aerius f. Gk aerios f. aēr air]

aer•i•al•ist /áireeəlist/ n. a high-wire or trapeze artist.

aer•ie /áiree, áree/ n. (also **ey•rie**) 1 a nest of a bird of prey, esp. an eagle, built high up. 2 a house, etc., perched high up. [med. L. aeria, aerea, etc., prob. f. OF aire lair ult. f. L agrum piece of ground]

aer•i•form /áirifawrm/ adj. 1 of the form of air; gaseous. 2 unsubstantial; unreal. [L aer AIR + −FORM]

aero- /áirō/ comb. form 1 air. 2 aircraft. [Gk aero- f. aēr air]

aer•o•bat•ics /áirəbátiks/ n.pl. 1 feats of expert and usu. spectacular flying and maneuvering of aircraft. 2 (as sing.) a performance of these. [AERO- + ACROBATICS]

aer•obe /áirōb/ n. a microorganism usu. growing in the presence of oxygen, or needing oxygen for growth. [F aérobie (as AERO-, Gk bios life)]

aer•o•bic /airōbik/ adj. 1 existing or active only in the presence of oxygen. 2 of or relating to aerobes. 3 of or relating to aerobics.

aer•o•bics /airóbiks/ n.pl. vigorous exercises designed to increase the body's heart rate and oxygen intake.

aer•o•bi•ol•o•gy /áirōbíōləjee/ n. the study of airborne microorganisms, pollen, spores, etc., esp. as agents of infection.

aer•o•drome /áirədrōm/ n. Brit. a small airport or airfield.

aer•o•dy•nam•ics /áirōdīnámiks/ n.pl. (usu. treated as sing.) the study of the interaction between the air and solid bodies moving through it. □□ **aer•o•dy•nam•ic** adj. **aer•o•dy•nam•i•cal•ly** adv. **aer•o•dy•nam•i•cist** /-misist/ n.

aer•o•em•bo•lism /áirōémbəlizəm/ n. a condition caused by the sudden lowering of air pressure and formation of bubbles in the blood. Also called **caisson disease**, **decompression sickness**, or the **bends** (see BEND¹ n. 4).

aer•o•en•gine /áirōenjin/ n. Brit. an engine used to power an aircraft.

aer•o•foil esp. Brit. var. of AIRFOIL.

aer•o•gram /áirəgram/ n. (also **aerogramme**) an air letter in the form of a single sheet that is folded and sealed.

aer•o•lite /áirəlīt/ n. a stony meteorite.

aer•ol•o•gy /airóləjee/ n. the study of the upper levels of the atmosphere. □□ **aer•o•log•i•cal** /áirəlójikəl/ adj.

aer•o•nau•tics /áirənáwtiks/ n.pl. (usu. treated as sing.) the science or practice of motion or travel in the air. □□ **aer•o•nau•tic** adj. **aer•o•nau•ti•cal** adj. [mod.L aeronautica (as AERO-, NAUTICAL)]

aer•on•o•my /airónəmee/ n. the science, esp. the physics and chemistry, of the upper atmosphere.

aer•o•plane esp. Brit. var. of AIRPLANE.

aer•o•sol /áirəsawl, −sol/ n. 1 a a container used to hold a substance packed under pressure with a device for releasing it as a fine spray. b the releasing device. c the substance contained in an aerosol. 2 a system of colloidal particles dispersed in a gas (e.g., fog or smoke). [AERO- + SOL²]

aer•o•space /áirōspays/ n. 1 the earth's atmosphere and outer space. 2 the technology of aviation in this region.

aer•o•train /áirōtrayn/ n. an experimental train that is supported on an air cushion and guided by a track. [F aérotrain (as AERO-, TRAIN)]

ae•ru•gi•nous /iróōjinəs/ adj. of the nature or color of verdigris. [L aeruginosus f. aerugo −inis verdigris f. aes aeris bronze]

Aes•cu•la•pi•an /éskyəláypeeən/ adj. of or relating to medicine or physicians. [L Aesculapius f. Gk Asklēpios god of medicine]

aes•thete /és-theet/ n. (also **es•thete**) a person who has or professes to have a special appreciation of beauty. [Gk aisthētēs one who perceives, or f. AESTHETIC]

aes•thet•ic /es-thétik/ adj. & n. (also **es•thet•ic**) • adj. 1 concerned with beauty or the appreciation of beauty. 2 having such appreciation; sensitive to beauty. 3 in accordance with the principles of good taste. • n. 1 (in pl.) the philosophy of the beautiful, esp. in art. 2 a set of principles of good taste and the appreciation of beauty. □□ **aes•thet•i•cal•ly** adv. **aes•thet•i•cism** /-tisizəm/ n.

aes•ti•val esp. Brit. var. of ESTIVAL.

aes•ti•vate esp. Brit. var. of ESTIVATE.

aes•ti•va•tion esp. Brit. var. of ESTIVATION.

aet. abbr. (also **aetat.**) aetatis.

ae•ta•tis /ītaátis, eetáy−/ adj. of or at the age of.

ae•ther var. of ETHER 2, 3.

ae•ti•ol•o•gy esp. Brit. var. of ETIOLOGY.

AF abbr. 1 Air Force. 2 audio frequency.

af- /əf/ prefix assim. form of AD- before f.

a•far /əfaár/ adv. at or to a distance. □ **from afar** from a distance. [ME f. A-², A-⁴ + FAR]

AFB abbr. Air Force Base.

AFC abbr. 1 American Football Conference. 2 Brit. Association Football Club.

af•fa•ble /áfəbəl/ adj. 1 (of a person) approachable and friendly. 2 kind and courteous. □□ **af•fa•bil•i•ty** /−bílitee/ n. **af•fa•bly** adv. [F f. L affabilis f. affari (as AD-, fari speak)]

af•fair /əfáir/ n. 1 a concern; a business; a matter to be attended to (that is my affair). 2 a a celebrated or notorious happening or sequence of events. b colloq. a noteworthy thing or event (was a puzzling affair). 3 = LOVE AFFAIR. 4 (in pl.) a ordinary pursuits of life. b business dealings. c public matters (current affairs). [ME f. AF afere f. OF afaire f. àfaire to do: cf. ADO]

af•faire /afáir/ n. (also **affaire de cœur** /afáir də kŏr/) a love affair. [F]

af•fect¹ /əfékt/ v.tr. 1 a produce an effect on. b (of a disease, etc.) attack (his liver is affected). 2 move; touch the feelings of (affected me deeply). □□ **af•fect•ing** adj. **af•fect•ing•ly** adv. [F affecter or L afficere affect- influence (as AD-, facere do)]

▶Both affect and effect are both verbs and nouns, but only effect is common as a noun, usually meaning 'a result, consequence, impression, etc.,' e.g., My father's warnings had no effect on my adventurousness. As verbs they are used differently. Affect means 'to produce an effect upon,' e.g., Smoking during pregnancy can affect the baby's development. Effect means 'to bring about,' e.g., The negotiators effected an agreement despite many difficulties.

af•fect² /əfékt/ v.tr. 1 pretend to have or feel (affected indifference). 2 (foll. by to + infin.) pretend. 3 assume the character or manner of; pose as (affect the freethinker). 4 make a show of liking or using (she affects fancy hats). [F affecter or L affectare aim at, frequent. of afficere (as AFFECT¹)]

af•fect³ /áfekt/ n. Psychol. a feeling, emotion, or desire, esp. as leading to action. [G Affekt f. L affectus disposition f. afficere (as AFFECT¹)]

af•fec•ta•tion /áfektáyshən/ n. 1 an assumed or contrived manner of behavior, esp. in order to impress. 2 (foll. by of) a studied display. 3 pretense. [F affectation or L affectatio (as AFFECT²)]

af•fect•ed /əféktid/ adj. 1 in senses of AFFECT¹, AFFECT². 2 artificially assumed or displayed; pretended (an affected air of innocence). 3 (of a person) full of affectation; artificial. 4 (prec. by adv.; often foll. by toward) disposed, inclined. □□ **af•fect•ed•ly** adv. **af•fect•ed•ness** n.

af•fec•tion /əfékshən/ n. 1 (often foll. by for, toward) goodwill; fond or tender feeling. 2 a disease; a diseased condition. 3 a mental state; an emotion. 4 a mental disposition. 5 the act or process of affecting or being affected. □□ **af•fec•tion•al** adj. (in sense 3). **af•fec•tion•al•ly** adv. [ME f. OF f. L affectio −onis (as AFFECT¹)]

af•fec•tion•ate /əfékshənət/ adj. loving; tender; showing love or tenderness. □□ **af•fec•tion•ate•ly** adv. [F affectionné or med.L affectionatus (as AFFECTION)]

af•fec•tive /əféktiv/ adj. 1 concerning the affections; emotional. 2 Psychol. relating to affects. □□ **af•fec•tiv•i•ty** /áfektivitee/ n. [F affectif −ive f. LL affectivus (as AFFECT¹)]

af•fen•pin•scher /áfənpinshər/ n. 1 a dog of a small breed resembling the griffon. 2 this breed. [G f. Affe monkey + Pinscher terrier]

af•fer•ent /áfərənt/ adj. Physiol. conducting inwards or toward (afferent nerves; afferent vessels) (opp. EFFERENT). [L afferre (as AD-, ferre bring)]

af•fi•ance /əffəns/ v.tr. (usu. in passive) literary promise solemnly to give (a person) in marriage. [ME f. OF afiancer f. med.L affidare (as AD-, fidus trusty)]

af•fi•da•vit /áfidáyvit/ n. a written statement confirmed under oath, for use as evidence in court. [med.L, = has stated on oath, f. affidare: see AFFIANCE]

af•fil•i•ate v. & n. • v. /əfíleeayt/ 1 tr. (usu. in passive; foll. by to, with) attach or connect (a person or society) with a larger organization. 2 tr. (of an institution) adopt (persons as members, societies as branches, etc.). 3 intr. a (foll. by to) associate oneself with a society. b (foll. by with) associate oneself with a political party. • n. /əfíleeət, −leeayt/ an affiliated person or organization. [med.L affiliare adopt (as AD-, filius son)]

WORD HISTORY aesthetic

Late 18th cent. (in the sense 'relating to perception by the senses'): from Greek aisthētikos, from aisthēta 'perceptible things,' from aisthesthai 'perceive.' The sense 'concerned with beauty' was coined in German in the mid-18th cent. and adopted into English in the early 19th cent., but its use was controversial until much later in the century.

af·fil·i·a·tion /əfileeáyshən/ n. the act or process of affiliating or being affiliated. [F f. med.L *affiliatio* f. *affiliare*: see AFFILIATE]

af·fined /əfínd/ adj. related; connected. [*affine* (adj.) f. L *affinis* related: see AFFINITY]

af·fin·i·ty /əfínitee/ n. (pl. **·ties**) **1** (often foll. by *between*, or *disp. to*, *for*) a spontaneous or natural liking for or attraction to a person or thing. **2** relationship, esp. by marriage. **3** resemblance in structure between animals, plants, or languages. **4** a similarity of character suggesting a relationship. **5** *Chem.* the tendency of certain substances to combine with others. [ME f. OF *afinité* f. L *affinitas –tatis* f. *affinis* related, lit. bordering on (as AD- + *finis* border)]

af·firm /əfərm/ v. **1** tr. assert strongly; state as a fact. **2** intr. **a** *Law* make an affirmation. **b** make a formal declaration. **3** tr. *Law* confirm; ratify (a judgment). □□ **af·firm·a·to·ry** adj. **af·firm·er** n. [ME f. OF *afermer* f. L *affirmare* (as AD-, *firmus* strong)]

af·fir·ma·tion /áfərmáyshən/ n. **1** the act or process of affirming or being affirmed. **2** *Law* a solemn declaration by a person who conscientiously declines to take an oath. [F *affirmation* or L *affirmatio* (as AFFIRM)]

af·firm·a·tive /əfərmətiv/ adj. & n. • adj. **1** affirming; asserting that a thing is so. **2** (of a vote) expressing approval. • n. **1** an affirmative statement, reply, or word. **2** (prec. by *the*) a positive or affirming position. □ **in the affirmative** with affirmative effect; so as to accept or agree to a proposal; yes (*the answer was in the affirmative*). □□ **af·firm·a·tive·ly** adv. [ME f. OF *affirmatif –ive* f. LL *affirmativus* (as AFFIRM)]

af·firm·a·tive ac·tion n. action favoring those who often suffer or have previously suffered from discrimination.

af·fix v. & n. • v.tr. /əfíks/ **1** (usu. foll. by *to*, *on*) attach; fasten. **2** add in writing (a signature or postscript). **3** impress (a seal or stamp). • n. /áfiks/ **1** an appendage; an addition. **2** *Gram.* an addition or element placed at the beginning (*prefix*) or end (*suffix*) of a root, stem, or word, or in the body of a word (*infix*), to modify its meaning. □□ **af·fix·al** or **af·fix·i·al** adj. **af·fix·a·tion** /áfiksáyshən/ n. **af·fix·ture** /əfiks-chər/ n. [F *affixer*, *affixe* or med.L *affixare* frequent. of L *affigere* (as AD-, *figere* fix- fix)]

af·fla·tus /əfláytəs/ n. a divine creative impulse; inspiration. [L f. *afflare* (as AD-, *flare* flat- to blow)]

af·flict /əflíkt/ v.tr. inflict bodily or mental suffering on. □ **afflicted with** suffering from. □□ **af·flic·tive** adj. [ME f. L *afflictare*, or *afflict-* past part. stem of *affligere* (as AD-, *fligere* flict- dash)]

af·flic·tion /əflíkshən/ n. **1** physical or mental distress, esp. pain or illness. **2** a cause of this. [ME f. OF f. L *afflictio –onis* (as AFFLICT)]

af·flu·ence /áflōoəns/ n. an abundant supply of money, commodities, etc.; wealth. [ME f. F f. L *affluentia* f. *affluere*: see AFFLUENT]

af·flu·ent /áflōoənt/ adj. & n. • adj. **1** wealthy; rich. **2** abundant. **3** flowing freely or copiously. • n. a tributary stream. □□ **af·flu·ent·ly** adv. [ME f. OF f. L *affluere* (as AD-, *fluere flux-* flow)]

> **PRONUNCIATION TIP** affluent/affluence
>
> Most people pronounce *affluent* and *affluence* with the stress on the first syllable (AF-loo-ent, AF-loo-ens). Putting the stress on the second syllable (a-FLOO-ent) is a newer pronunciation in American English that is avoided by careful speakers.

af·flu·ent so·ci·e·ty n. a society in which material wealth is widely distributed.

af·flux /áfluks/ n. a flow toward a point; an influx. [med.L *affluxus* f. L *affluere*: see AFFLUENT]

af·ford /əfáwrd/ v.tr. **1** (prec. by *can* or *be able to*; often foll. by *to* + infin.) **a** have enough money, means, time, etc., for; be able to spare (*can afford $50; could not afford a vacation; can we afford to buy a new television?*). **b** be in a position to do something (esp. without risk of adverse consequences) (*can't afford to let him think so*). **2** yield a supply of. **3** provide (*affords a view of the sea*). □□ **af·ford·a·ble** adj. **af·ford·a·bil·i·ty** n. [ME f. OE *geforthian* promote (as Y-, FORTH), assim. to words in AF-]

af·for·est /əfáwrist, əfór–/ v.tr. **1** convert into forest. **2** plant with trees. □□ **af·for·est·a·tion** /–stáyshən/ n. [med.L *afforestare* (as AD-, *foresta* FOREST)]

af·fran·chise /əfránchīz/ v.tr. release from servitude or an obligation. [OF *afranchir* (as ENFRANCHISE, with prefix A-³)]

af·fray /əfráy/ n. a breach of the peace by fighting or rioting in public. [ME f. AF *afrayer* (v.) f. OF *esfreer* f. Rmc]

af·fri·cate /áfrikət/ n. *Phonet.* a combination of a stop, or plosive, with an immediately following fricative or spirant, e.g., *ch.* [L *affricare* (as AD-, *fricare* rub)]

af·front /əfrúnt/ n. & v. • n. an open insult (*feel it an affront; offer an affront to*). • v.tr. **1** insult openly. **2** offend the modesty or self respect of. **3** face, confront. [ME f. OF *afronter* slap in the face; insult, ult. f. L *frons frontis* face]

Af·ghan /áfgan/ n. & adj. • n. **1 a** a native or inhabitant of Afghanistan. **b** a person of Afghan descent. **2** the official language of Afghanistan (also called **Pashto**). **3** (**afghan**) a knitted or crocheted and sewn woolen blanket or shawl. **4** *Brit.* (in full **Afghan coat**) a kind of sheepskin coat with the skin outside and usu. with a shag-

gy border. • adj. of or relating to Afghanistan or its people or language. [Pashto *afghānī*]

Af·ghan hound n. a tall hunting dog with long silky hair.

a·fi·cio·na·do /əfisheeənaáadō, əfisee–/ n. (pl. **·dos**) a devotee of a sport or pastime (orig. of bullfighting). [Sp.]

a·field /əfeéld/ adv. **1** away from home; to or at a distance (esp. far afield). **2** in the field. [OE (as A², FIELD)]

a·fire /əfír/ adv. & predic.adj. **1** on fire. **2** intensely roused or excited.

a·flame /əfláym/ adv. & predic.adj. **1** in flames. **2** = AFIRE 2.

af·la·tox·in /áflətóksin/ n. *Chem.* any of several related toxic compounds produced by the fungus *Aspergillus flavus*, which cause tissue damage and cancer. [*Aspergillus* + *flavus* + TOXIN]

a·float /əflót/ adv. & predic.adj. **1** floating in water or on air. **2** at sea; on board ship. **3** out of debt or difficulty. **4** in general circulation; current. **5** full of or covered with a liquid. **6** in full swing. [OE (as A², FLOAT)]

a·foot /əfŏŏt/ adv. & predic.adj. **1** in operation; progressing. **2** astir; on the move.

a·fore /əfáwr/ prep. & adv. archaic & dial. before; previously; in front (of). [OE *onforan* (as A², FORE)]

afore- /əfáwr/ comb. form before; previously (*aforementioned; aforesaid*).

a·fore·thought /əfáwrthawt/ adj. premeditated (following a noun: *malice aforethought*).

a for·ti·o·ri /aáfawrtiáwrī/ adv. & adj. with a yet stronger reason (than a conclusion already accepted); more conclusively. [L]

a·foul /əfówl/ adv. foul. □ **run afoul of** come into conflict with.

a·fraid /əfráyd/ predic.adj. **1** (often foll. by *of*, or *that* or *lest* + clause) alarmed; frightened. **2** (foll. by *to* + infin.) unwilling or reluctant for fear of the consequences (*was afraid to go in*). □ **be afraid** (foll. by *that* + clause) *colloq.* admit or declare with (real or politely simulated) regret (*I'm afraid there's none left*). [ME, past part. of obs. *affray* (v.) f. AF *afrayer* f. OF *esfreer*]

af·reet /áfreet/ n. (also **af·rit**) a demon in Muslim or Arabic mythology. [Arab. *'ifrīt*]

a·fresh /əfrésh/ adv. anew; with a fresh beginning. [A-² + FRESH]

Af·ri·can /áfrikən/ n. & adj. • n. **1** a native of Africa (esp. a black person). **2** a person of African descent. • adj. of or relating to Africa. [L *Africanus*]

Af·ri·ca·na /áfrikaánə/ n.pl. things connected with Africa.

Af·ri·can-A·mer·i·can n. & adj. • n. an American citizen of African origin or descent, esp. a black American. • adj. of or relating to American blacks or their culture.
►See note at BLACK.

Af·ri·can·der /áfrikándər/ n. (also **Afrikander**) one of a S. African breed of sheep or longhorn cattle. [frik. *Afrikaander* alt. of Du. *Afrikaner* after *Hollander*, etc.]

Af·ri·can el·e·phant n. the elephant *Loxodonta africana* of Africa, which is larger than the Indian elephant.

Af·ri·can vi·o·let n. a tropical plant, *Saintpaulia ionantha*, with heart-shaped velvety leaves and blue, purple, or pink flowers.

Af·ri·kaans /áfrikaáns/ n. the language of the Afrikaner people developed from Cape Dutch, an official language of the Republic of South Africa. [Du., = African]

Af·ri·kan·der var. of AFRICANDER.

Af·ri·ka·ner /áfrikaánər/ n. **1** an Afrikaans-speaking white person in S. Africa, esp. one of Dutch descent. **2** *Bot.* a S. African species of *Gladiolus* or *Homoglossum*. [Afrik., formed as AFRICANDER]

af·rit var. of AFREET.

Af·ro /áfrō/ adj. & n. • adj. (of a hairstyle) full and bushy, as naturally grown originally by blacks. • n. (pl. **·ros**) an Afro hairstyle. [AFRO-, or abbr. of AFRICAN]

Afro- /áfrō/ comb. form African (*Afro-Asian*) . [L *Afer Afr-* African]

Af·ro-A·mer·i·can /áfrōōmérikən/ adj. & n. = AFRICAN-AMERICAN.
►See note at BLACK.

Af·ro-Car·ib·be·an /áfrōkáribeéən, –kəríbeeən/ n. & adj. • n. a person of African descent in or from the Caribbean. • adj. of or relating to the Afro-Caribbeans or their culture.

af·ror·mo·si·a /áfrawrmózeeə, –zhə/ n. **1** an African tree, *Pericopsis* (formerly *Afrormosia*) *elata*, yielding a hard wood resembling teak and used for furniture. **2** this wood. [mod.L f. AFRO- + *Ormosia* genus of trees]

aft /aft/ adv. *Naut.* & *Aeron.* at or toward the stern or tail. [prob. f. ME *baft*: see ABAFT]

af·ter /áftər/ prep., conj., adv., & adj. • prep. **1 a** following in time; later than (*after six months; after midnight; day after day*). **b** in specifying time (*a quarter after eight*). **2** (with causal force) in view of (something that happened shortly before) (*after your behavior tonight what do you expect?*). **3** (with concessive force) in spite of (*after all my efforts I'm no better off*). **4** behind (*shut the door after you*). **5** in pursuit or quest of (*run after them; inquire after him; hanker after it; is* *after a job).* **6** about; concerning (*asked after her; asked after her health*). **7** in allusion to (*named him William after his uncle*). **8** in imitation of (a person, word, etc.) (*a painting after Rubens*). **9** next in importance to (*the best book on the subject after mine*). **10** according to (*after a fashion*). • *conj.* in or at a time later than that when (*left after we arrived*). • *adv.* **1** later in time (*soon after; a week after*). **2** behind in place (*followed on after*). • *adj.* **1** later; following (*in after years*). **2** *Naut.* nearer the stern (*after cabins; after mast*). □ **after all 1** in spite of all that has happened or has been said, etc. (*after all, what does it matter?*). **2** in spite of one's exertions, expectations, etc. (*they tried for an hour and failed after all; so you have come after all!*). **after one's own heart** see HEART. **after you** a formula used in offering precedence. [OE *æfter* f. Gmc]

af·ter·birth /áftərbərth/ *n. Med.* the placenta and fetal membranes discharged from the womb after childbirth.

af·ter·burn·er /áftərbərnər/ *n.* an auxiliary burner in a jet engine to increase thrust.

af·ter·care /áftərkair, –ker/ *n.* care of a patient after a stay in the hospital or of a person on release from prison.

af·ter·damp /áftərdamp/ *n.* choking gas left after an explosion of firedamp in a mine.

af·ter·ef·fect /áftərəfékt/ *n.* an effect that follows after an interval or after the primary action of something.

af·ter·glow /áftərglō/ *n.* a light or radiance remaining after its source has disappeared or been removed.

af·ter·im·age /áftərímij/ *n.* an image retained by a sense organ, esp. the eye, and producing a sensation after the cessation of the stimulus.

af·ter·life /áftərlif/ *n.* **1** life after death. **2** life at a later time.

af·ter·mar·ket /áftərmaarkit/ *n.* **1** a market in spare parts and components. **2** *Stock Exch.* a market in shares after their original issue.

af·ter·math /áftərmath/ *n.* **1** consequences; aftereffects (*the aftermath of war*). **2** new grass growing after mowing or after a harvest. [AFTER *adj.* + *math* mowing f. OE *mæth* f. Gmc]

af·ter·most /áftərmōst/ *adj.* **1** last. **2** *Naut.* farthest aft. [AFTER *adj.* + –MOST]

af·ter·noon /áftərnóon/ *n. & int.* • *n.* **1** the time from noon or lunchtime to evening (*this afternoon; during the afternoon*). **2** this time spent in a particular way (*had a lazy afternoon*). **3** a time compared with this, esp. the later part of something (*the afternoon of life*). • *int.* = *good afternoon* (see GOOD *adj.* 14).

af·ter·pains /áftərpaynz/ *n.pl.* pains caused by contraction of the womb after childbirth.

af·ters /áftərz/ *n.pl. Brit. colloq.* the course following the main course of a meal.

af·ter·shave /áftərshayv/ *n.* an astringent lotion for use after shaving.

af·ter·shock /áftərshok/ *n.* a lesser shock following the main shock of an earthquake.

af·ter·taste /áftərtáyst/ *n.* a taste remaining or recurring after eating or drinking.

af·ter·tax /áftərtáks/ *adj.* (of income) after the deduction of taxes.

af·ter·thought /áftərthawt/ *n.* an item or thing that is thought of or added later.

af·ter·ward /áftərwórd/ *adv.* (also **af·ter·wards**) later; subsequently. [OE *æftanwearde adv.* f. *æftan* AFT + –WARD]

af·ter·word /áftərwərd/ *n.* concluding remarks in a book, esp. by a person other than its author.

Ag *symb. Chem.* the element silver. [L *argentum*]

ag- /əg/ *prefix* assim. form of AD- before *g.*

a·ga /áagə/ *n.* (in Muslim countries) a commander; a chief. [Turk. *ağa* master]

a·gain /əgén/ *adv.* **1** another time; once more. **2** as in a previous position or condition (*back again; home again; healthy again*). **3** in addition (*as much again; half as many again*). **4** further; besides (*again, what about the children?*). **5** on the other hand (*I might, and again I might not*). □ **again and again** repeatedly. [orig. a northern form of ME *ayen,* etc., f. OE *ongēan, ongægn,* etc., f. Gmc]

a·gainst /əgénst/ *prep.* **1** in opposition to (*fight against the invaders; arson is against the law*). **2** into collision or contact with (*ran against a rock; lean against the wall; up against a problem*). **3** to the disadvantage of (*his age is against him*). **4** in contrast to (*against a dark background; 99 as against 102 yesterday*). **5** in anticipation of or preparation for (*against his coming; against a rainy day; protected against the cold; warned against pickpockets*). **6** as a compensating factor to (*income against expenditure*). **7** in return for (*issued against a later payment*). □ **against the clock** see CLOCK[1] 3. **against the grain** see GRAIN. **against time** see TIME. [ME *ayenes,* etc., f. *ayen* AGAIN + –*t* as in *amongst:* see AMONG]

A·ga Khan *n.* the spiritual leader of the Ismaili Muslims.

ag·a·ma /ágəmə, əgáy–/ *n.* any Old World lizard of the genus *Agama.* [Carib]

ag·am·ic /əgámik/ *adj.* characterized by the absence of asexual reproduction. [as AGAMOUS + –IC]

ag·a·mo·gen·e·sis /əgáməjénisis, ágəmō–/ *n. Biol.* asexual reproduction. □□ **ag·a·mo·gen·e·tic** /–jinétik/ *adj.* [as AGAMOUS + Gk *genesis* birth]

ag·a·mous /ágəməs/ *adj. Biol.* without (distinguishable) sexual organs. [LL *agamus* f. Gk *agamos* (as A-[1], *gamos* marriage)]

ag·a·pan·thus /ágəpánthəs/ *n.* any African plant of the genus *Agapanthus,* esp. the ornamental African lily, with blue or white flowers. [mod.L f. Gk *agapē* love + *anthos* flower]

a·gape[1] /əgáyp/ *adv. & predic.adj.* gaping, openmouthed, esp. with wonder or expectation.

a·gape[2] /əgáapay, ágə–/ *n.* **1** a Christian feast in token of fellowship, esp. one held by early Christians in commemoration of the Last Supper. **2** love for one's fellow humans, esp. as distinct from erotic love. [Gk, = brotherly love]

a·gar /áygaar/ *n.* (also **a·gar-a·gar** /áygaaráygaar/) a gelatinous substance obtained from any of various kinds of red seaweed and used in food, microbiological media, etc. [Malay]

ag·a·ric /ágərik, əgár–/ *n.* any fungus of the family Agaricaceae, with cap and stalk, including the common edible mushroom. [L *agaricum* f. Gk *agarikon*]

ag·ate /ágət/ *n.* **1** any of several varieties of hard usu. streaked chalcedony. **2** a colored toy marble resembling this. [F *agate, –the,* f. L *achates* f. Gk *akhatēs*]

a·ga·ve /əgáavee, əgáy–/ *n.* any plant of the genus *Agave,* with rosettes of narrow spiny leaves and tall inflorescences, e.g., the aloe. [L f. Gk *Agauē,* proper name in myth f. *agauos* illustrious]

a·gaze /əgáyz/ *adv.* gazing.

age /ayj/ *n. & v.* • *n.* **1 a** the length of time that a person or thing has existed or is likely to exist. **b** a particular point in or part of one's life, often as a qualification (*old age; voting age*). **2 a** *colloq.* (often in *pl.*) a long time (*took an age to answer; have been waiting for ages*). **b** a distinct period of the past (*golden age; Bronze age; Middle Ages*). **c** *Geol.* a period of time. **d** a generation. **3** the latter part of life; old age (*the infirmity of age*). • *v.* (*pres. part.* **ag·ing, age·ing**) **1** *intr.* show signs of advancing age (*has aged a lot recently*). **2** *intr.* grow old. **3** *intr.* mature. **4** *tr.* cause or allow to age. □ **come of age** reach adult status. **of age** old enough; of adult status. [ME f. OF ult. f. L *aetas –atis* age]

-age /ij/ *suffix* forming nouns denoting: **1** an action (*breakage; spillage*). **2** a condition or function (*bondage*). **3** an aggregate or number of (*coverage; acreage*). **4** fees payable for; the cost of using (*postage*). **5** the product of an action (*dosage; wreckage*). **6** a place; an abode (*anchorage; orphanage; parsonage*). [OF ult. f. L –*aticum* neut. of adj. suffix –*aticus* –ATIC]

aged *adj.* **1** /ayjd/ **a** of the age of (*aged ten*). **b** that has been subjected to aging. **c** (of a horse) over six years old. **d** allowed to reach maturity or ripeness in storage (*aged cheese*). **2** /áyjid/ having lived long; old.

age·ism /áyjizəm/ *n.* (also **ag·ism**) prejudice or discrimination on the grounds of age. □□ **age·ist** *adj. & n.* (also **ag·ist**).

age·less /áyjlis/ *adj.* **1** never growing or appearing old or outmoded. **2** eternal; timeless.

age·long /áyjlong/ *adj.* lasting for a very long time.

a·gen·cy /áyjənsee/ *n.* (*pl.* **-cies**) **1 a** the business or establishment of an agent (*employment agency*). **b** the function of an agent. **2 a** active operation; action. **b** intervening action; means (*fertilized by the agency of insects*). **c** action personified (*an invisible agency*). **3** a specialized department, as of a government. [med.L *agentia* f. L *agere* do]

a·gen·da /əjéndə/ *n.* **1** (*pl.* **a·gen·das**) **a** a list of items of business to be considered at a meeting. **b** a series of things to be done. **2** (as *pl.*) **a** items to be considered. **b** things to be done. **3** an ideology or underlying motivation. [L, neut. pl. of gerundive of *agere* do]
▶ Although **agenda** is the plural of the Latin word *agendum,* in standard modern English it is a normal singular noun with a normal plural form (**agendas**). See also notes at DATA and MEDIUM.

a·gent /áyjənt/ *n.* **1 a** a person who acts for another in business, politics, etc. (*insurance agent*). **b** a spy. **2 a** a person or thing that exerts power or produces an effect. **b** the cause of a natural force or effect on matter (*oxidizing agent*). **c** such a force or effect. □□ **a·gen·tial** /əjénshəl/ *adj.* [L *agent-* part. stem of *agere* do]

a·gent-gen·er·al *n.* a representative of an Australian state or Canadian province, usu. in England.

A·gent Or·ange *n.* a dioxin-containing herbicide used as a defoliant by the US during the Vietnam War; so-called from the orange stripe on storage drums.

a·gent pro·vo·ca·teur /áazhon prəvókətór/ *n.* (*pl.* **agents provocateurs** *pronunc.* same) a person employed to detect suspected offenders by tempting them to overt self-incriminating action. [F, = provocative agent]

age of con·sent *n.* the age at which consent to sexual intercourse is valid in law.

age of dis·cre·tion *n.* the esp. legal age at which a person is able to manage his or her own affairs.

age-old *adj.* having existed for a very long time.

ag·glom·er·ate *v., n., & adj.* • *v.tr. & intr.* /əglómərayt/ **1** collect into a mass. **2** accumulate in a disorderly way. ● *n.* /əglómərət/ **1** a mass or collection of things. **2** *Geol.* a mass of large volcanic fragments bonded under heat (cf. CONGLOMERATE). ● *adj.* /əglómərət/ collected into a mass. □□ **ag·glom·er·a·tion** /–ráyshən/ *n.* **ag·glom·er·a·tive** /əglómərətiv, –raytiv/ *adj.* [L *agglomerare* (as AD–, *glomer-are* f. *glomus –meris* ball)]

ag·glu·ti·nate /əglóot'nayt/ *v.* **1** *tr.* unite as with glue. **2** *tr. & intr. Biol.* cause or undergo adhesion (of bacteria, erythrocytes, etc.). **3** *tr.* (of language) combine (simple words) without change of form to express compound ideas. □□ **ag·glu·ti·na·tion** /–náyshən/ *n.* **ag·glu·ti·na·tive** /əglóot'nətiv, –aytiv/ *adj.* [L *agglutinare* (as AD–, *glutinare* f. *gluten –tinis* glue)]

ag·glu·ti·nin /əglóot'nin/ *n. Biol.* a substance or antibody causing agglutination. [AGGLUTINATE + –IN]

ag·gran·dize /əgrándīz/ *v.tr.* **1** increase the power, rank, or wealth of (a person or nation). **2** cause to appear greater than is the case. □□ **ag·gran·dize·ment** /–dizmənt/ *n.* **ag·gran·diz·er** *n.* [F *agrandir* (stem *agrandiss-*), prob. f. It. *aggrandire* f. L *grandis* large: assim. to verbs in –IZE]

ag·gra·vate /ágrəvayt/ *v.tr.* **1** increase the seriousness of (an illness, offense, etc.). **2** *disp.* annoy; exasperate (a person). □□ **ag·gra·va·tion** /–váyshən/ *n.* [L *aggravare aggravat-* make heavy f. *gravis* heavy]

ag·gre·gate *n., adj., & v.* ● *n.* /ágrigət/ **1** a collection of, or the total of, disparate elements. **2** pieces of crushed stone, gravel, etc., used in making concrete. **3 a** *Geol.* a mass of minerals formed into solid rock. **b** a mass of particles. ● *adj.* /ágrigət/ **1** (of disparate elements) collected into one mass. **2** constituted by the collection of many units into one body. **3** *Bot.* **a** (of fruit) formed from several carpels derived from the same flower (e.g., raspberry). **b** (of a species) closely related. ● *v.* /ágrigayt/ **1** *tr. & intr.* collect together; combine into one mass. **2** *tr. colloq.* amount to (a specified total). **3** *tr. Brit.* unite (*was aggregated to the group*). □ **in the aggregate** as a whole. □□ **ag·gre·ga·tion** /–gáyshən/ *n.* **ag·gre·ga·tive** /–gáytiv/ *adj.* [L *aggregare aggregat-* herd together (as AD–, *grex gregis* flock)]

ag·gres·sion /əgréshən/ *n.* **1** the act or practice of attacking without provocation, esp. beginning a fight or war. **2** an unprovoked attack. **3** self-assertiveness; forcefulness. **4** *Psychol.* hostile or destructive tendency or behavior. [F *agression* or L *aggressio* attack f. *aggredi aggress-* (as AD–, *gradi* walk)]

ag·gres·sive /əgrésiv/ *adj.* **1** of a person: **a** given to aggression; openly hostile. **b** forceful; self-assertive. **2** (of an act) offensive; hostile. **3** of aggression. □□ **ag·gres·sive·ly** *adv.* **ag·gres·sive·ness** *n.*

ag·gres·sor /əgrésər/ *n.* a person who attacks without provocation. [L (as AGGRESSION)]

ag·grieved /əgréevd/ *adj.* having a grievance. □□ **ag·griev·ed·ly** /–vidlee/ *adv.* [ME, past part. of *aggrieve* f. OF *agrever* make heavier (as AD–, GRIEVE[1])]

ag·gro /ágrō/ *n. Brit. sl.* **1** aggressive troublemaking. **2** trouble; difficulty. [abbr. of *aggravation* (see AGGRAVATE) or AGGRESSION]

a·ghast /əgást/ *adj.* (usu. *predic.*; often foll. by *at*) filled with dismay, shock, or consternation.

WORD HISTORY aghast
Late Middle English: past participle of the obsolete verb *agast*, *gast* 'frighten,' from Old English *gǣsten*. The spelling with *gh* (originally Scots) became general by about 1700, probably influenced by GHOST; compare with GHASTLY.

ag·ile /ájəl, ájil/ *adj.* quick-moving; nimble; active. □□ **ag·ile·ly** *adv.* **a·gil·i·ty** /əjílitee/ *n.* [F f. L *agilis* f. *agere* do]

a·gin /əgín/ *prep. colloq.* or *dial.* against. [corrupt. of AGAINST or synonymous *again* obs. prep.]

ag·ing /áyjing/ *n.* (also **age·ing**) **1** growing old. **2** giving the appearance of advancing age. **3** a change of properties occurring in some metals after heat treatment or cold working.

agism var. of AGEISM.

ag·i·tate /ájitayt/ *v.* **1** *tr.* (often as **agitated** *adj.*) disturb or excite (a person or feelings). **2** *intr.* (often foll. by *for, against*) stir up interest or concern, esp. publicly (*agitated for tax reform*). **3** *tr.* shake or move, esp. briskly. □□ **ag·i·tat·ed·ly** *adv.* **ag·i·ta·tive** *adj.* [L *agitare agitat-* frequent. of *agere* drive]

ag·i·ta·tion /ájitáyshən/ *n.* **1** the act or process of agitating or being agitated. **2** mental anxiety or concern. [F *agitation* or L *agitatio* (as AGITATE)]

a·gi·ta·to /ájitáÁtō/ *adv. & adj. Mus.* in an agitated manner. [It.]

ag·i·ta·tor /ájitaytər/ *n.* **1** a person who agitates, esp. publicly for a cause, etc. **2** an apparatus for shaking or mixing liquid, etc. [L (as AGITATE)]

ag·it·prop /ájitprop/ *n.* the dissemination of Communist political propaganda, esp. in plays, movies, books, etc. [Russ. (as AGITATION, PROPAGANDA)]

ag·let /áglit/ *n.* **1** a metal or plastic tag attached to each end of a shoelace, etc. **2** = AIGUILLETTE. [ME f. F *aiguillette* small needle, ult. f. L *acus* needle]

a·gley /əgláy, əgleé/ *adv. Sc.* askew; awry. [A[2] + Sc. *gley* squint]

a·glow /əglō/ *adv. & adj.* ● *adv.* glowingly. ● *predic.adj.* glowing.

ag·ma /ágmə/ *n.* **1** the sound represented by the pronunciation /ng/. **2** a symbol (ŋ) used for this sound. [Gk, lit. 'fragment']

ag·nail /ágnayl/ = HANGNAIL.

ag·nate /ágnayt/ *adj. & n.* ● *adj.* **1** descended esp. by male line from the same male ancestor (cf. COGNATE). **2** descended from the same forefather; of the same clan or nation. **3** of the same nature; akin. ● *n.* one who is descended, esp. by male line, from the same male ancestor. □□ **ag·nat·ic** /–nátik/ *adj.* **ag·na·tion** /–náyshən/ *n.* [L *agnatus* f. *ad* to + *gnasci* be born f. stem *gen-* beget]

ag·no·sia /agnṓzhə/ *n. Med.* the loss of the ability to interpret sensations. [mod.L f. Gk *agnōsia* ignorance]

ag·nos·tic /agnóstik/ *n. & adj.* ● *n.* a person who believes that nothing is known, or can be known, of the existence or nature of God or a god or of anything beyond material phenomena. ● *adj.* of or relating to agnostics. □□ **ag·nos·ti·cism** *n.* [A–[1] + GNOSTIC]

Ag·nus De·i /ágnəs dáyee, deé-ī, aányoōs/ *n.* **1** a figure of a lamb bearing a cross or flag, as an emblem of Christ. **2** the prayer in the Mass beginning with the words "Lamb of God." [L, = lamb of God]

a·go /əgó/ *adv.* earlier; before the present (*ten years ago; long ago*). [ME (*ago, agone*), past part. of obs. *ago* (v.) (as A–[2], GO[1])]

a·gog /əgóg/ *adv. & adj.* ● *adv.* eagerly; expectantly. ● *predic.adj.* eager; expectant. [F *en gogues* f. *en* in + pl. of *gogue* fun]

à go·go /əgógō/ *adv.* in abundance (*whiskey à gogo*). [F]

a·gon·ic /əgónik/ *adj.* having or forming no angle. [Gk *agōnios* without angle (as A–[1], *gōnia* angle)]

a·gon·ic line *n.* a line passing through the two poles, along which a magnetic needle points directly north or south.

ag·o·nis·tic /ágənístik/ *adj.* polemical; combative. □□ **ag·o·nis·ti·cal·ly** *adv.* [LL *agonisticus* f. Gk *agōnistikos* f. *agōnistēs* contestant f. *agōn* contest]

ag·o·nize /ágəniz/ *v.* **1** *intr.* (often foll. by *over*) undergo (esp. mental) anguish; suffer agony. **2** *tr.* (often as **agonizing** *adj.*) cause agony or mental anguish to. **3** *tr.* (as **agonized** *adj.*) expressing agony (*an agonized look*). **4** *intr.* struggle; contend. □□ **ag·o·niz·ing·ly** *adv.* [F *agoniser* or LL *agonizare* f. Gk *agōnizomai* contend f. *agōn* contest]

ag·o·ny /ágənee/ *n.* (*pl.* **·nies**) **1** extreme mental or physical suffering. **2** a severe struggle. [ME f. OF *agonie* or LL f. Gk *agōnia* f. *agōn* contest]

ag·o·ny col·umn *n. colloq.* **1** *Brit.* a column in a newspaper or magazine offering personal advice to readers who write in. **2** = PERSONAL COLUMN.

ag·o·ra·phobe /ágərəfōb/ *n.* a person who suffers from agoraphobia.

ag·o·ra·pho·bi·a /ágərəfṓbeeə/ *n. Psychol.* an abnormal fear of open spaces or public places. □□ **ag·o·ra·pho·bic** *adj. & n.* [mod.L f. Gk *agora* place of assembly, marketplace + –PHOBIA]

a·gou·ti /əgoōtee/ *n.* (also **a·gu·ti**) (*pl.* **agoutis**) any burrowing rodent of the genus *Dasyprocta* or *Myoprocta* of Central and S. America, related to the guinea pig. [F *agouti* or Sp. *aguti* f. Tupi *aguti*]

a·grar·i·an /əgráireeən/ *adj. & n.* ● *adj.* **1** of or relating to the land or its cultivation. **2** relating to the ownership of land. ● *n.* a person who advocates a redistribution of land ownership. [L *agrarius* f. *ager agri* field]

a·gree /əgreé/ *v.* (**a·grees, a·greed, a·gree·ing**) **1** *intr.* hold a similar opinion (*I agree with you about that; they agreed that it would rain*). **2** *intr.* (often foll. by *to*, or *to* + infin.) consent (*agreed to the arrangement; agreed to go*). **3** *intr.* (often foll. by *with*) **a** become or be in harmony. **b** suit; be good for (*caviar didn't agree with him*). **c** *Gram.* have the same number, gender, case, or person as. **4** *tr. Brit.* reach agreement about (*agreed a price*). **5** *tr. Brit.* consent to or approve of (terms, a proposal, etc.). **6** *tr. Brit.* bring (things, esp. accounts) into harmony. **7** *intr.* (often foll. by *on*) decide by mutual consent (*agreed on a compromise*). □ **agree to differ** leave a difference of opinion, etc., unresolved. **be agreed** have reached the same opinion. [ME f. OF *agreer* ult. f. L *gratus* pleasing]
▶Note the distinction between *agreeing to* something like a plan, scheme, or project; and *agreeing with* somebody: *I agree to the repayment schedule suggested. Danielle agrees with Eric that we should all go hiking on Saturday. Humid weather does not agree with me. Agree with* is also used regarding two things that go together: *That story does not agree with the facts.* The verb must agree with the noun in person and number.

a·gree·a·ble /əgreéəbəl/ *adj.* **1** (often foll. by *to*) pleasing. **2** (often foll. by *to*) (of a person) willing to agree (*was agreeable to going*). **3** (foll. by *to*) conformable; consonant with. □□ **a·gree·a·bil·i·ty** /–bílitee/ *n.* **a·gree·a·ble·ness** *n.* **a·gree·a·bly** *adv.* [ME f. OF *agreable* f. *agreer* AGREE]

a·gree·ment /əgreémənt/ *n.* **1** the act of agreeing; the holding of the same opinion. **2** mutual understanding. **3** an arrangement between parties as to a course of action, etc. **4** *Gram.* having the same number, gender, case, or person. **5** mutual conformity of things; harmony. [ME f. OF (as AGREE)]

ag·ri·busi·ness /ágribiznis/ *n.* **1** agriculture conducted on strictly commercial principles, esp. using advanced technology. **2** an organization engaged in this. **3** the group of industries dealing with the produce of, and services to, farming. □□ **ag·ri·busi·ness·man** *n.* (*pl.* ·men; *fem.* **agribusinesswoman**, *pl.* -women). [AGRICULTURE + BUSINESS]

ag·ri·cul·ture /ágrikulchər/ *n.* the science or practice of cultivating the soil, raising crops, and rearing animals. □□ **ag·ri·cul·tur·al** /-kúlchərəl/ *adj.* **ag·ri·cul·tur·al·ist** *n.* **ag·ri·cul·tur·al·ly** *adv.* **ag·ri·cul·tur·ist** *n.* [F *agriculture* or L *agricultura* f. *ager agri* field + *cultura* CULTURE]

ag·ri·mo·ny /ágrimōnee/ *n.* (*pl.* ·**nies**) any perennial plant of the genus *Agrimonia*, esp. *A. eupatoria* with small yellow flowers. [ME f. OF *aigremoine* f. L *agrimonia* alt. of *argemonia* f. Gk *argemōnē* poppy]

agro- /ágrō/ *comb. form* agricultural (*agrochemical*; *agro-ecological*). [Gk *agros* field]

ag·ro·chem·i·cal /ágrōkémikəl/ *n.* a chemical used in agriculture, esp. an insecticide or herbicide.

a·gron·o·my /əgrónəmee/ *n.* the science of soil management and crop production. □□ **ag·ro·nom·ic** /ágrənómik/ *adj.* **ag·ro·nom·i·cal** *adj.* **ag·ro·nom·i·cal·ly** *adv.* **a·gron·o·mist** /-grón-/ *n.* [F *agronomie* f. *agronome* agriculturist f. Gk *agros* field + *−nomos* f. *nemō* arrange]

a·ground /əgrównd/ *predic.adj. & adv.* (of a ship) on or on to the bottom of shallow water (*be aground*; *run aground*). [ME f. A[2] + GROUND[1]]

a·gue /áygyōō/ *n.* **1** *hist.* a malarial fever, with cold, hot, and sweating stages. **2** a shivering fit. □□ **a·gued** *adj.* **a·gu·ish** *adj.* [ME f. OF f. med.L *acuta* (*febris*) acute (fever)]

a·gu·ti var. of AGOUTI.

AH *abbr.* in the year of the Hegira (AD 622); of the Muslim era. [L *anno Hegirae*]

ah /aa/ *int.* expressing surprise, pleasure, sudden realization, resignation, etc. [ME f. OF *a*]
▶The sense depends a great deal on intonation.

a·ha /aahaá, əhaá/ *int.* expressing surprise, triumph, mockery, irony, etc. [ME f. AH + HA[1]]
▶The sense depends a great deal on intonation.

a·head /əhéd/ *adv.* **1** further forward in space or time. **2** in the lead; further advanced (*ahead on points*). **3** in the line of one's forward motion (*road construction ahead*). **4** straight forward. □ **ahead of 1** further forward or advanced than. **2** in the line of the forward motion of. **3** prior to. [orig. *Naut.*, f. A[2] + HEAD]

a·hem /əhém/ *int.* (not usu. clearly articulated) *int.* used to attract attention, gain time, or express disapproval. [lengthened form of HEM[2]]

a·him·sa /əhímsaa/ *n.* (in the Hindu, Buddhist, and Jainist tradition) respect for all living things and avoidance of violence toward others both in thought and deed. [Skr. f. *a* without + *himsa* injury]

-aholic /əhólik/ *suffix* (also **–oholic**) denoting one addicted to or compulsively in need of what is specified in the initial element (*workaholic*, *chocoholic*). [extracted f. *alcoholic*]

a·hoy /əhóy/ *int. Naut.* a call used in hailing. [AH + HOY[1]]

AI *abbr.* **1** artificial insemination. **2** artificial intelligence.

ai /aá-ee/ *n.* (*pl.* **ais**) the three-toed sloth of S. America, of the genus *Bradypus*. [Tupi *ai*, repr. its cry]

AID *abbr.* **1** Agency for International Development. **2** *Brit.* artificial insemination by donor.

aid /ayd/ *n. & v.* ●*n.* **1** help. **2** financial or material help, esp. given by one country to another. **3** a material source of help (*teaching aid*). **4** a person or thing that helps. **5** *hist.* a grant of subsidy or tax to a king. ●*v.tr.* **1** (often foll. by *to* + infin.) help. **2** promote or encourage (*sleep will aid recovery*). □ **in aid of** in support of. **what's this** (or **all this**) **in aid of?** *Brit. colloq.* what is the purpose of this? [ME f. OF *aide, aïdier*, ult. f. L *adjuvare* (as AD-, *juvare jut-* help)]

-aid /ayd/ *comb. form* esp. *Brit.* denoting an organization or event that raises money for charity (*school aid*). [20th c.: orig. in *Band Aid*, rock musicians campaigning for famine relief]

aide /ayd/ *n.* **1** an aide-de-camp. **2** an assistant. **3** an unqualified assistant to a social worker, teacher, etc. [abbr.]

aide-de-camp /áyd-dəkámp/ *n.* (*pl.* **aides-de-camp** *pronunc.* same) an officer acting as a confidential assistant to a senior officer. [F]

aide-mé·moire /áydmemwaár/ *n.* (*pl.* **aides-mémoire** *pronunc.* same) **1 a** an aid to the memory. **b** a book or document meant to aid the memory. **2** *Diplomacy* a memorandum. [F f. *aider* to help + *mémoire* memory]

AIDS /aydz/ *n.* acquired immune deficiency syndrome, a fatal disorder caused by a virus transmitted in the blood and other bodily fluids, marked by severe loss of resistance to infection. [abbr.]

AIDS-re·lat·ed com·plex *n.* the symptoms of a person affected with the AIDS virus who has not developed the disease.

ai·grette /áygret, aygrét/ *n.* **1** a tuft of feathers or hair, esp. the plume of an egret. **2** a spray of gems or similar ornament. [F]

ai·guille /aygwéel/ *n.* a sharp peak of rock, esp. in the Alps. [F: see AGLET]

ai·guil·lette /áygwilét/ *n.* a tagged braid or cord hanging from the shoulder on the breast of some uniforms. [F: see AGLET]

ai·ki·do /íkeedō/ *n.* a Japanese form of self-defense making use of the attacker's own movements without causing injury. [Jap. f. *ai* mutual + *ki* mind + *dō* way]

ail /ayl/ *v.* **1** *tr. archaic* (only in 3rd person interrog. or indefinite constructions) trouble or afflict in mind or body (*what ails him?*). **2** *intr.* (usu. **be ailing**) be ill. [OE *egl(i)an* f. *egle* troublesome]

ai·lan·thus /aylánthəs/ *n.* a tall deciduous tree of the genus *Ailanthus*, esp. *A. altissima*, native to China and Australasia. [mod.L *ailantus* f. Ambonese *aylanto*]

ai·ler·on /áyləron/ *n.* a hinged surface in the trailing edge of an airplane wing, used to control lateral balance and to initiate banking for turns, etc. [F, dimin. of *aile* wing f. L *ala*]

aileron

ail·ing /áyling/ *adj.* **1** ill, esp. chronically. **2** in poor condition.

ail·ment /áylmənt/ *n.* an illness, esp. a minor or chronic one.

aim /aym/ *v. & n.* ●*v.* **1** *intr.* (foll. by *at* + verbal noun, or *to* + infin.) intend or try (*aim at winning*; *aim to win*). **2** *tr.* (usu. foll. by *at*) direct or point (a weapon, remark, etc.). **3** *intr.* take aim. **4** *intr.* (foll. by *at*, *for*) seek to attain or achieve. ●*n.* **1** a purpose; a design; an object aimed at. **2** the directing of a weapon, missile, etc., at an object. □ **take aim** direct a weapon, etc., at an object. [ME f. OF ult. f. L *aestimare* reckon]

aim·less /áymlis/ *adj.* without aim or purpose. □□ **aim·less·ly** *adv.* **aim·less·ness** *n.*

ain't /aynt/ *contr. colloq.* **1** am not; are not; is not (*you ain't doing it right*; *she ain't nice*). **2** has not; have not (*we ain't seen him*). [contr. of *are not*]
▶Although this form has been used for hundreds of years, it is generally thought incorrect, and should be avoided in formal contexts.

air /air/ *n. & v.* ●*n.* **1** an invisible gaseous substance surrounding the earth, a mixture mainly of oxygen and nitrogen. **2 a** the earth's atmosphere. **b** the free or unconfined space in the atmosphere (*birds of the air*; *in the open air*). **c** the atmosphere as a place where aircraft operate. **3 a** a distinctive impression or characteristic (*an air of absurdity*). **b** one's manner or bearing, esp. a confident one (*with a triumphant air*; *does things with an air*). **c** (esp. in *pl.*) an affected manner; pretentiousness (*gave himself airs*; *airs and graces*). **4** *Mus.* a tune or melody; a melodious composition. **5** a breeze or light wind. ●*v.tr.* **1** esp. *Brit.* warm (washed laundry) to dry, esp. at a fire or in a heated closet. **2** expose (a room, etc.) to the open air; ventilate. **3** express publicly (an opinion, grievance, etc.). **4** parade; show ostentatiously (esp. qualities). **5** broadcast, esp. a radio or television program. **6** *refl.* go out in the fresh air. □ **by air** by aircraft; in an aircraft. **in the air** (of opinions, feelings, etc.) prevalent; gaining currency. **on** (or **off**) **the air** in (or not in) the process of broadcasting. **take the air** go outdoors. **up in the air** (of projects, etc.) uncertain; not decided. **walk** (or **tread**) **on air** feel elated. [ME f. F and L f. Gk *aēr*]

air bag *n.* a safety device that fills with nitrogen on impact to protect the occupants of a vehicle in a collision.

air base /áir bays/ *n.* a base for the operation of military aircraft.

air bed *n.* = AIR MATTRESS.

air blad·der *n.* a bladder or sac filled with air in fish or some plants (cf. SWIM BLADDER).

air·borne /áirbawrn/ *adj.* **1** transported by air. **2** (of aircraft) in the air after taking off.

air brake *n.* **1** a brake worked by air pressure. **2** a movable flap or spoiler on an aircraft to reduce its speed.

air brick *n.* a brick perforated with small holes for ventilation.

air·brush /áirbrush/ *n. & v.* ●*n.* an artist's device for spraying paint by means of compressed air. ●*v.tr.* paint with an airbrush.

Air·bus /áirbus/ *n.* (also **airbus**) *Trademark* a passenger aircraft serving routes of relatively short distance.

air-con·di·tion·ing *n.* **1** a system for regulating the humidity, ventilation, and temperature in a building. **2** the apparatus for this. □□ **air-con·di·tioned** *adj.* **air con·di·tion·er** *n.*

air-cooled *adj.* cooled by means of a current of air.

air cor·ri·dor *n.* = CORRIDOR 4.

air·craft /áirkraft/ *n.* (*pl.* same) a machine capable of flight, esp. an airplane or helicopter.

air·craft car·ri·er *n.* a warship that carries and serves as a base for airplanes.

air·crew /áirkrōō/ *n.* **1** the crew manning an aircraft. **2** (*pl.* **air·crew**) a member of such a crew.

air cush•ion *n.* **1** an inflatable cushion. **2** the layer of air supporting a hovercraft or similar vehicle.

Aire•dale /áirdayl/ *n.* **1** a large terrier of a rough-coated breed. **2** this breed. [*Airedale* in Yorkshire, England]

air•er /áirər/ *n. Brit.* a frame or stand for airing or drying clothes, etc.

air•fare /áirfair/ *n.* the price of a passenger ticket for travel by aircraft.

air•field /áirfeeld/ *n.* an area of land where aircraft take off and land, are maintained, etc.

air•foil /áirfoyl/ *n.* a structure with curved surfaces (e.g., a wing, fin, or horizontal stabilizer) designed to give lift in flight. [AIR + FOIL²]

air force *n.* a branch of the armed forces concerned with fighting or defense in the air.

air•frame /áirfraym/ *n.* the body of an aircraft as distinct from its engine(s).

air•freight /áirfrayt/ *n. & v. • n.* cargo carried by an aircraft. *• v.tr.* transport by air.

air•glow /áirglō/ *n.* radiation from the upper atmosphere, detectable at night.

air gun *n.* a gun using compressed air to propel pellets.

air•head /áirhed/ *n.* **1** *Mil.* a forward base for aircraft in enemy territory. **2** *sl.* a silly or stupid person.

air•ing /áiring/ *n.* **1** exposure to fresh air, esp. for exercise or an excursion. **2** esp. *Brit.* exposure (of laundry, etc.) to warm air. **3** public expression of an opinion, etc. (*the idea will get an airing at tomorrow's meeting*). **4** a broadcast, esp. of a radio or television program.

air lane *n.* a path or course regularly used by aircraft (cf. LANE 4).

air•less /áirlis/ *adj.* **1** stuffy; not ventilated. **2** without wind or breeze; still. □□ **air•less•ness** *n.*

air let•ter *n.* a sheet of light paper forming a letter for sending by airmail.

air•lift /áirlift/ *n. & v. • n.* the transport of troops, supplies, or passengers by air, esp. in a blockade or other emergency. *• v.tr.* transport in this way.

air line *n.* a pipe or tube supplying air, esp. to a diver.

air•line /áirlīn/ *n.* an organization providing a regular public service of air transport on one or more routes.

air•lin•er /áirlīnər/ *n.* a passenger aircraft, esp. a large one.

air•lock /áirlok/ *n.* **1** a stoppage of the flow in a pump or pipe, caused by an air bubble. **2** a compartment with controlled pressure and parallel sets of doors, to permit movement between areas at different pressures.

air•mail /áirmayl/ *n. & v. • n.* **1** a system of transporting mail by air. **2** mail carried by air. *• v.tr.* send by airmail.

air•man /áirmən/ *n.* (*pl.* **•men**) **1** a pilot or member of the crew of an aircraft. **2** a member of the USAF or RAF below commissioned rank.

air mat•tress *n.* an inflatable mattress.

air•miss /áirmis/ *n. Brit.* a circumstance in which two or more aircraft in flight on different routes are less than a prescribed distance apart.

air•mo•bile /áirmóbəl, –beel, –bil/ *adj.* (of troops) that can be moved about by air.

air•plane /áirplayn/ *n.* a powered heavier-than-air flying vehicle with fixed wings. [F *aéroplane* (as AERO-, PLANE¹)]

air plant *n.* a plant growing naturally without soil, esp. an epiphyte.

air•play /áirplay/ *n.* broadcasting (of recorded music).

air pock•et *n.* an apparent downdraft in the air causing an aircraft to drop suddenly.

air•port /áirpawrt/ *n.* a complex of runways and buildings for the takeoff, landing, and maintenance of civil aircraft, with facilities for passengers.

air pow•er *n.* the ability to defend and attack by means of aircraft, missiles, etc.

air pump *n.* a device for pumping air into or out of a vessel.

air raid *n.* an attack by aircraft.

air ri•fle *n.* a rifle using compressed air to propel pellets.

air sac *n.* an extension of the lungs in birds or the tracheae in insects.

air•screw /áirskrōō/ *n. Brit.* an aircraft propeller.

air-sea res•cue *n.* rescue from the sea by aircraft.

air•ship /áirship/ *n.* a power-driven aircraft that is lighter than air.

air•sick /áirsik/ *adj.* affected with nausea due to travel in an aircraft. □□ **air•sick•ness** *n.*

air•space /áirspays/ *n.* the air available to aircraft to fly in, esp. the part subject to the jurisdiction of a particular country.

airship (dirigible)

air•speed /áirspeed/ *n.* the speed of an aircraft relative to the air through which it is moving.

air•strip /áirstrip/ *n.* a strip of ground suitable for the takeoff and landing of aircraft but usu. without other facilities.

air•tight /áirtīt/ *adj.* **1** not allowing air to pass through. **2** having no visible or apparent weaknesses (*an airtight alibi*).

air•time /áirtīm/ *n.* time allotted for a broadcast.

air-to-air *adj.* directed or operating from one aircraft to another in flight (*air-to-air communication*).

air-traf•fic con•trol•ler *n.* an airport official who controls air traffic by giving radio instructions to pilots concerning route, altitude, takeoff, and landing.

air•waves /áirwayvz/ *n.pl. colloq.* radio waves used in broadcasting.

air•way /áirway/ *n.* **1 a** a recognized route followed by aircraft. **b** (often in *pl.*) = AIRLINE. **2** a ventilating passage in a mine. **3** *Med.* (often in *pl.*) the passage(s) through which air passes into the lungs.

air•wom•an /áirwŏŏmən/ *n.* (*pl.* **•women**) **1** a woman pilot or member of the crew of an aircraft. **2** a member of the USAF or WRAF below commissioned rank.

air•wor•thy /áirwərthee/ *adj.* (of an aircraft) fit to fly.

air•y /áiree/ *adj.* (**airier, airiest**) **1** well ventilated; breezy. **2** flippant; superficial. **3 a** light as air. **b** graceful; delicate. **4** insubstantial; ethereal; immaterial. □□ **air•i•ly** *adv.* **air•i•ness** *n.*

air•y-fair•y *adj. colloq.* unrealistic; impractical; foolishly idealistic.

aisle /īl/ *n.* **1** part of a church, esp. one parallel to and divided by pillars from the nave, choir, or transept. **2** a passage between rows of pews, seats, etc. **3** a passageway in a supermarket, department store, etc. □□ **aisled** *adj.* [ME *ele, ile* f. OF *ele* f. L *ala* wing: confused with *island* and F *aile* wing]

ait /ayt/ *n.* a small island, esp. in a river. [OE *iggath,* etc. f. *īeg* ISLAND + dimin. suffix]

aitch /aych/ *n.* the name of the letter H. □ **drop one's aitches** esp. *Brit.* fail to pronounce the initial *h* in words. [ME f. OF *ache*]

aitch•bone /áychbōn/ *n.* **1** the buttock or rump bone. **2** a cut of beef lying over this. [ME *nage-, nache-bone* buttock, ult. f. L *natis, –es* buttock(s): for loss of *n* cf. ADDER, APRON]

a•jar¹ /əjáar/ *adv. & predic.adj.* (of a door) slightly open. [A² + obs. *char* f. OE *cerr* a turn]

a•jar² /əjáar/ *adv.* out of harmony. [A² + JAR²]

AK *abbr.* Alaska (in official postal use).

a.k.a. *abbr.* also known as.

AKC *abbr.* American Kennel Club.

a•kee /əkée/ *n.* (also **ac•kee**) **1** a tropical tree, *Blighia sapida.* **2** its fruit, edible when cooked. [Kru *ākee*]

a•ke•la /əkéélə, aakáylə/ *n.* the adult leader of a group of Cub Scouts. [name of the leader of a wolf pack in Kipling's *Jungle Book*]

a•kim•bo /əkímbō/ *adv.* (of the arms) with hands on the hips and elbows turned outwards. [ME in *kenebowe,* prob. f. ON]

a•kin /əkín/ *predic.adj.* **1** related by blood. **2** (often foll. by *to*) of similar or kindred character. [A-⁴ + KIN]

Ak•ka•di•an /əkáydeeən/ (also **Ac•ca•di•an**) *adj. & n. hist. • adj.* of Akkad in ancient Babylonia. *• n.* **1** the Semitic language of Akkad. **2** an inhabitant of Akkad.

ak•va•vit var. of AQUAVIT.

AL *abbr.* Alabama (in official postal use).

Al *symb. Chem.* the element aluminum.

al- /al, əl/ *prefix* assim. form of AD- before –*l.*

-al /əl/ *suffix* **1** forming adjectives meaning 'relating to; of the kind of': **a** from Latin or Greek words (*central; regimental; colossal; tropical*) (cf. –IAL, –ICAL). **b** from English nouns (*tidal*). **2** forming nouns, esp. of verbal action (*animal; rival; arrival; proposal; trial*). [sense 1 f. F –*el* or L –*alis* adj. suffix rel. to –*aris* (-AR¹); sense 2 f. F –*aille* or f. (or after) L –*alis,* etc., used as noun]

Ala. *abbr.* Alabama.

à la /aá laa/ *prep.* after the manner of (*à la russe*). [F, f. À LA MODE]

al•a•bas•ter /áləbastər/ *n. & adj. • n.* a translucent usu. white form of gypsum, often carved into ornaments. *• adj.* **1** of alabaster. **2** like alabaster in whiteness or smoothness. □□ **al•a•bas•trine** /–bástrin/ *adj.* [ME f. OF *alabastre* f. L *alabaster, –trum,* f. Gk *alabast(r)os*]

à la carte /aá laa kaárt/ *adv. & adj.* ordered as separately priced item(s) from a menu, not as part of a set meal. [F]

a•lack /əlák/ *int.* (also **a•lack-a-day** /əlákəday/) *archaic* an expression of regret or surprise. [prob. f. AH + LACK]

a•lac•ri•ty /əlákritee/ *n.* briskness or cheerful readiness. [L *alacritas* f. *alacer* brisk]

A•lad•din's cave /əlád'nz/ *n.* a place of great riches. [*Aladdin* in the *Arabian Nights' Entertainments*]

A•lad•din's lamp *n.* a talisman enabling its holder to gratify any wish.

à la mode /aá laa mód/ *adv. & adj.* **1** in fashion; fashionable. **2 a** served with ice cream. **b** (of beef) braised in wine. [F, = in the fashion]

a•lar /áylər/ *adj.* **1** relating to wings. **2** winglike or wing-shaped. **3** axillary. [L *alaris* f. *ala* wing]

a•larm /əláarm/ *n. & v. • n.* **1** a warning of danger, etc. (*gave the alarm*). **2 a** a warning sound or device (*the burglar alarm was set off* *accidentally).* **b** = ALARM CLOCK. **3** frightened expectation of danger or difficulty (*were filled with alarm*). ● *v.tr.* **1** frighten or disturb. **2** arouse to a sense of danger. [ME f. OF *alarme* f. It. *allarme* f. *all'arme!* to arms]

a•larm clock *n.* a clock with a device that can be made to sound at a time set in advance.

a•larm•ing /əláarming/ *adj.* disturbing; frightening. □□ **a•larm•ing•ly** *adv.*

a•larm•ist /əláarmist/ *n. & adj.* ● *n.* a person given to spreading needless alarm. ● *adj.* creating needless alarm. □□ **a•larm•ism** *n.*

a•lar•um /əláarəm/ *n. archaic* = ALARM.

a•lar•ums and ex•cur•sions *n.* confused noise and activity.

Alas. *abbr.* Alaska.

a•las /əlás/ *int.* an expression of grief, pity, or concern. [ME f. OF *a las*(*se*) f. *a* ah + *las*(*se*) f. L *lassus* weary]

a•late /áylayt/ *adj.* having wings or winglike appendages. [L *alatus* f. *ala* wing]

alb /alb/ *n.* a usu. white vestment reaching to the feet, worn by some Christian priests at church ceremonies. [OE *albe* f. eccl.L *alba* fem. of L *albus* white]

al•ba•core /álbəkawr/ *n.* **1** a long-finned tuna, *Thunnus alalunga.* **2** any of various other related fish. [Port. *albacor*, –*cora*, f. Arab. *al* the + *bakr* young camel or *bakūr* premature, precocious]

Al•ba•ni•an /albáyneeən, awl–/ *n. & adj.* ● *n.* **1 a** a native or inhabitant of Albania in SE Europe. **b** a person of Albanian descent. **2** the language of Albania. ● *adj.* of or relating to Albania or its people or language.

al•ba•ta /albáatə/ *n. Brit.* German silver; an alloy of nickel, copper, and zinc. [L *albata* whitened f. *albus* white]

al•ba•tross /álbətraws, –tros/ *n.* **1 a** any long-winged stout-bodied bird of the family Diomedeidae related to petrels, inhabiting the Pacific Ocean. **b** a source of frustration or guilt; an encumbrance. **2** *Brit. Golf* = DOUBLE EAGLE 2.

WORD HISTORY   albatross

Late 17th cent.: alteration (influenced by Latin *albus* 'white') of 16th-cent. *alcatras*, applied to various seabirds including the frigate bird and pelican, from Spanish and Portuguese *alcatraz*, from Arabic *al-ġaṭṭās* 'the diver.'

al•be•do /albeedō/ *n.* (*pl.* •**dos**) the proportion of light or radiation reflected by a surface, esp. of a planet or moon. [eccl.L, = whiteness, f. L *albus* white]

al•be•it /áwlbeeit/ *conj. formal* though (*he tried, albeit without success*).

al•bes•cent /albésənt/ *adj.* growing or shading into white. [L *albescere albescent-* f. *albus* white]

Al•bi•gen•ses /álbijénseez/ *n.pl.* the members of a heretic sect in S. France in the 12th–13th c. □□ **Al•bi•gen•si•an** *adj.* [L f. *Albi* in S. France]

al•bi•no /albínō/ *n.* (*pl.* •**nos**) **1** a person or animal having a congenital absence of pigment in the skin and hair (which are white), and the eyes (which are usu. pink). **2** a plant lacking normal coloring. □□ **al•bi•nism** /álbinizəm/ *n.* [Sp. &Port. f. *albo* L f. *albus* white + –*ino* = –INE¹]

Al•bi•on /álbeeən/ *n. literary* (also **per•fid•i•ous Al•bi•on**) Britain or England. [OE f. L f. Celt. *Albio* (unrecorded): F *la perfide Albion* with ref. to alleged treachery to other nations]

al•bite /álbīt/ *n. Mineral.* a feldspar, usu. white, rich in sodium. [L *albus* white + –ITE¹]

al•bum /álbəm/ *n.* **1** a blank book for the insertion of photographs, stamps, etc. **2 a** a long-playing phonograph, audio cassette, or compact disc recording. **b** a set of these. [L, = a blank tablet, neut. of *albus* white]

al•bu•men /albyōómin/ *n.* **1** egg white. **2** *Bot.* the substance found between the skin and embryo of many seeds, usu. the edible part; = ENDOSPERM. [L *albumen* –*minis* white of egg f. *albus* white]

al•bu•min /albyōómin/ *n.* any of a class of water-soluble proteins found in egg white, milk, blood, etc. □□ **al•bu•mi•nous** *adj.* [F *albumine* f. L *albumin*-: see ALBUMEN]

al•bu•mi•noid /albyōóminoyd/ *n.* = SCLEROPROTEIN.

al•bu•mi•nu•ri•a /albyōóminōóreeə, –nyōór–/ *n.* the presence of albumin in the urine, usu. as a symptom of kidney disease.

al•bur•num /albə́rnəm/ *n.* = SAPWOOD. [L f. *albus* white]

al•ca•hest var. of ALKAHEST.

al•ca•ic /alkáyik/ *adj. & n.* ● *adj.* of the verse meter invented by Alcaeus, lyric poet of Mytilene *c.*600 BC, occurring in four line stanzas. ● *n.* (in *pl.*) alcaic verses. [LL *alcaicus* f. Gk *alkaikos* f. *Alkaios* Alcaeus]

al•cal•de /aalkáalday/ *n.* a magistrate or mayor in a Spanish, Portuguese, or Latin American town. [Sp. f. Arab. *al-kāḍī* the judge: see CADI]

al•che•my /álkəmee/ *n.* (*pl.* •**mies**) **1** the medieval forerunner of chemistry, esp. seeking to turn base metals into gold or silver. **2** a miraculous transformation or the means of achieving this. □□ **al•**

chem•ic /alkémik/ *adj.* **al•chem•i•cal** /–kémikəl/ *adj.* **al•che•mist** *n.* **al•che•mize** *v.tr.* [ME f. OF *alkemie, alkamie* f. med.L *alchimia*, –*emia*, f. Arab. *alkīmiyā'* f. *al* the + *kīmiyā'* f. Gk *khēmia*, –*meia* art of transmuting metals]

al•che•rin•ga /álchəríngga/ *n.* (in the mythology of some Australian Aboriginals) the "golden age" when the first ancestors were created. [Aboriginal, = dreamtime]

al•co•hol /álkəhawl, –hol/ *n.* **1** (in full **ethyl alcohol**) a colorless volatile flammable liquid forming the intoxicating element in wine, beer, liquor, etc., and also used as a solvent, as fuel, etc. Also called **ethanol.** ¶ Chem. formula: C_2H_5OH. **2** any liquor containing this. **3** *Chem.* any of a large class of organic compounds that contain one or more hydroxyl groups attached to carbon atoms.

WORD HISTORY   alcohol

Mid-16th cent.: French (earlier form of *alcool*), or from medieval Latin, from Arabic *al-kuḥl* 'the kohl.' In early use the term denoted powders, specifically kohl, and especially those obtained by sublimation; later 'a distilled or rectified spirit' (mid-17th cent).

al•co•hol•ic /álkəháwlik, –hól–/ *adj. & n.* ● *adj.* of, relating to, containing, or caused by alcohol. ● *n.* a person suffering from alcoholism.

al•co•hol•ism /álkəhawlízəm, –ho–/ *n.* **1** an addiction to the consumption of alcoholic liquor. **2** the diseased condition resulting from this. [mod.L *alcoholismus* (as ALCOHOL)]

al•co•hol•om•e•ter /álkəhawlómitər, –ho–/ *n.* an instrument for measuring alcoholic concentration in a liquid. □□ **al•co•hol•om•e•try** *n.*

al•cove /álkōv/ *n.* a recess, esp. in the wall of a room or of a garden. [F f. Sp. *alcoba* f. Arab. *al-kubba* f. *al* the + *kubba* vault]

al•de•hyde /áldihīd/ *n. Chem.* any of a class of compounds formed by the oxidation of alcohols (and containing the group –CHO). □□ **al•de•hy•dic** /áldihídik/ *adj.* [abbr. of mod.L *alcohol dehydrogenatum* alcohol deprived of hydrogen]

al den•te /aal déntay, al déntee/ *adj.* (of pasta, etc.) cooked so as to be still firm when bitten. [It., lit. 'to the tooth']

al•der /áwldər/ *n.* any tree of the genus *Alnus*, related to the birch, with catkins and toothed leaves. [OE *alor, aler*, rel. to L *alnus*, with euphonic *d*]

al•der buck•thorn *n.* a shrub, Frangula alnus, related to the buckthorn.

al•der•man /áwldərmən/ *n.* (*pl.* •**men**; *fem.* **alderwoman**, *pl.* -**women**) **1** an elected municipal official serving on the governing council of a city. **2** esp. *hist.* a co-opted member of an English county or borough council, next in dignity to the mayor. □□ **al•der•man•ic** /–mánik/ *adj.* **al•der•man•ship** *n.* [OE *aldor* patriarch f. *ald* old + MAN]

al•drin /áwldrin/ *n.* a white crystalline chlorinated hydrocarbon used as an insecticide. [K. *Alder*, Ger. chemist d. 1958 + –IN]

ale /ayl/ *n.* **1** beer. **2** a similar beverage with a more pronounced, often bitter taste. [OE *alu*, = old *öl*]

a•le•a•tor•ic /áyleeətáwrik, –tór–/ *adj.* **1** depending on the throw of a die or on chance. **2** *Mus. & Art* involving random choice by a performer or artist; improvisational. [L *aleatorius aleator* dice player f. *alea* die]

a•le•a•to•ry /áyleeətawree/ *adj.* = ALEATORIC. [as ALEATORIC]

al•ec /álik/ *n.* (also **al•eck**) *Austral. sl.* a stupid person. [shortening of SMART ALEC]

a•lee /əlée/ *adv. & predic.adj.* **1** on the lee or sheltered side of a ship. **2** to leeward. [ME, f. A² + LEE]

ale•house /áylhows/ *n.* a tavern.

a•lem•bic /əlémbik/ *n.* **1** *hist.* an apparatus formerly used in distilling. **2** a means of refining or extracting. [ME f. OF f. med.L *alembicus* f. Arab. *al-'anbīk* f. *al* the + '*anbīk* still f. Gk *ambix*, –*ikos* cup, cap of a still]

a•leph /áalif/ *n.* the first letter of the Hebrew alphabet. [Heb. '*ālep*, lit. 'ox']

a•lert /ələ́rt/ *adj., n., & v.* ● *adj.* **1** watchful or vigilant; ready to take action. **2** quick (esp. of mental faculties); attentive. ● *n.* **1** a warning call or alarm. **2 a** a warning of an air raid, weather emergency, etc. **b** the duration of this. ● *v.tr.* (often foll. by *to*) make alert; warn (*were alerted to the danger*). □ **on the alert** on the lookout against danger or attack. □□ **a•lert•ly** *adv.* **a•lert•ness** *n.* [F *alerte* f. It. *all' erta* to the watchtower]

-ales /áyleez/ *suffix* forming the plural names of orders of plants (*Rosales*). [pl. of L adj. suffix –*alis*: see –AL]

al•eu•rone /áalyōrōn/ *n.* (also **aleuron** /–ron/) *Biochem.* a protein found as granules in the seeds of plants, etc. [Gk *aleuron* flour]

Al•eut /aleeōót, əlōót/ *n.* **1 a** a N. American people native to the Aleutian Islands and the western Alaskan Peninsula. **b** a member of this people. **2** the language of this people. □□ **A•leu•tian** *adj.*

ale•wife /áylwīf/ *n.* (*pl.* **alewives**) any of several species of fish related to the herring. [corrupt. of 17th-c. *aloofe*: orig. uncert.]

al•ex•an•ders /áligzándərz/ *n.* **1** an umbelliferous plant, *Smyrnium* *olusatrum*, with yellow flowers formerly used in salads. **2** a white-flowered tall plant, *Angelica atropurpurea*, of the parsley family. [OE f. med.L *alexandrum*]

Al•ex•an•dri•an /áligzándreeən/ *adj.* **1** of or characteristic of Alexandria in Egypt. **2 a** belonging to or akin to the schools of literature and philosophy of Alexandria. **b** (of a writer) derivative or imitative; fond of recondite learning.

al•ex•an•drine /áligzándrin, –dreen/ *adj. & n.* ● *adj.* (of a line of verse) having six iambic feet. ● *n.* an alexandrine line. [F *alexandrin* f. *Alexandre* Alexander (the Great), the subject of an Old French poem in this meter]

al•ex•an•drite /áligzándrīt/ *n. Mineral.* a green variety of chrysoberyl. [Tsar *Alexander* I of Russia + –ITE[1]]

a•lex•i•a /əlékseeə/ *n.* the inability to see words or to read, caused by a condition of the brain. [mod.L A-[1] + Gk *lexis* speech f. *legein* to speak, confused with L *legere* to read]

al•fal•fa /alfálfə/ *n.* a leguminous plant, *Medicago sativa*, with clover-like leaves and flowers used for fodder. Also called **lucerne**. [Sp. f. Arab. *al-fasfaṣa*, a green fodder]

al•fres•co /alfréskō/ *adv. & adj.* in the open air (*we lunched alfresco; an alfresco lunch*). [It. *al fresco* in the fresh (air)]

al•ga /álgə/ *n.* (*pl.* **algae** /áljee/ also **algas**) (usu. in *pl.*) a nonflowering stemless water plant, esp. seaweed and phytoplankton. □□ **al•gal** *adj.* **al•goid** *adj.* [L]

al•ge•bra /áljibrə/ *n.* **1** the branch of mathematics that uses letters and other general symbols to represent numbers and quantities in formulae and equations. **2** a system of this based on given axioms (*linear algebra; the algebra of logic*). □□ **al•ge•bra•ic** /áljibráyik/ *adj.* **al•ge•bra•i•cal** *adj.* **al•ge•bra•i•cal•ly** *adv.* **al•ge•bra•ist** *n.*

WORD HISTORY algebra

Late Middle English: from Italian, Spanish, and medieval Latin, from Arabic *al-jabr* 'the reunion of broken parts,' 'bone-setting,' from *jabara* 'reunite, restore.' The original sense, 'the surgical treatment of fractures,' probably came via Spanish, in which it survives; the mathematical sense comes from the title of a book, *'ilm al-jabr wa'l-muḳābala* 'The Science of Restoring What Is Missing and Equating Like with Like,' by the mathematician al-Kwārizmī (see ALGORITHM).

-algia /áljə/ *comb. form Med.* denoting pain in a part specified by the first element (*neuralgia*). □□ **–algic** *comb. form* forming adjectives. [Gk f. *algos* pain]

al•gi•cide /áljisīd/ *n.* a preparation for destroying algae.

al•gid /áljid/ *adj. Med.* cold; chilly. □□ **al•gid•i•ty** /aljíditee/ *n.* [L *algidus* f. *algēre* be cold]

al•gi•nate /áljinayt/ *n.* a salt or ester of alginic acid. [ALGA + –IN + –ATE[1]]

al•gin•ic ac•id /aljínik/ *n.* an insoluble carbohydrate found (chiefly as salts) in many brown seaweeds. [ALGA + –IN + –IC]

al•goid see ALGA.

Al•gol /álgawl, –gol/ *n.* (also **ALGOL**) a high-level computer programming language. [*algorithmic* (see ALGORITHM) + LANGUAGE]

al•go•lag•ni•a /álgolágneeə/ *n.* sexual pleasure derived from inflicting pain on oneself or others; masochism or sadism. □□ **al•go•lag•nic** *adj. & n.* [mod.L f. G *Algolagnie* f. Gk *algos* pain + *lagneia* lust]

al•gol•o•gy /algóləjee/ *n.* the study of algae. □□ **al•go•log•i•cal** /–lójikəl/ *adj.* **al•gol•o•gist** *n.*

Al•gon•qui•an /algóngkweeən/ *n.* any of the languages or dialects used by the Algonquin peoples.

Al•gon•quin /algóngkwən/ *n.* **1** a N. American people native to the Ottawa River valley and the northern St. Lawrence River valley. **2** a member of this people.

al•go•rithm /álgərithəm/ *n.* **1** *Math.* a process or set of rules used for calculation or problem-solving, esp. with a computer. **2** (also **al•go•rism** /álgərizəm/) the Arabic or decimal notation of numbers. □□ **al•go•rith•mic** /álgəríthmik/ *adj.* [*algorism* ME ult. f. Pers. *al-Kuwārizmī* 9th-c. mathematician: *algorithm* infl. by Gk *arithmos* number (cf. F *algorithme*)]

al•gua•cil /álgwəsil/ *n.* (also **al•gua•zil** /–zíl/) **1** a mounted official at a bullfight. **2** a constable or an officer of justice in Spain or Spanish-speaking countries. [Sp. f. Arab. *al-wazīr* f. *al* the + *wazir*: see VIZIER]

a•li•as /áyleeəs/ *adv. & n.* ● *adv.* also named or known as. ● *n.* a false or assumed name. [L, = at another time, otherwise]

al•i•bi /álibī/ *n. & v.* (*pl.* **al•i•bis**) ● *n.* **1** a claim, or the evidence supporting it, that when an alleged act took place one was elsewhere. **2** an excuse of any kind; a pretext or justification. ● *v.* (**al•i•bis, al•i•bied, al•i•bi•ing**) *colloq.* **1** *tr.* provide an alibi or offer an excuse for (a person). **2** *intr.* provide an alibi. [L, = elsewhere]
▶The chief meaning of this Latin word is 'evidence that when something took place one was elsewhere, ' e.g., *He has no alibi for the evening in question*. It is also used informally, however, to mean 'an excuse, pretext, or justification'; many consider this incorrect.

al•i•cy•clic /álisíklik, –síklik/ *adj. Chem.* of, denoting, or relating to organic compounds combining a cyclic structure with aliphatic properties, e.g., cyclohexane. [G *alicyclisch* (as ALIPHATIC, CYCLIC)]

al•i•dade /álidayd/ *n. Surveying & Astron.* an instrument for determining directions or measuring angles. [F f. med.L f. Arab. *al-'iḍāda* the revolving radius f. *'aḍud* upper arm]

al•ien /áyleeən/ *adj. & n.* ● *adj.* **1 a** (often foll. by *to*) unfamiliar; not in accordance or harmony; unfriendly; hostile; unacceptable or repugnant (*army discipline was alien to him; struck an alien note*). **b** (often foll. by *to* or *from*) different or separated. **2** foreign; from a foreign country. **3** of or relating to beings supposedly from other worlds. **4** *Bot.* (of a plant) introduced from elsewhere and naturalized in its new home. ● *n.* **1** a foreigner, esp. one who is not a naturalized citizen of the country where he or she is living. **2** a being supposedly from another world. **3** *Bot.* an alien plant. □□ **al•ien•ness** *n.* [ME f. OF f. L *alienus* belonging to another (*alius*)]

al•ien•a•ble /áyleeənəbəl/ *adj. Law* able to be transferred to new ownership. □□ **al•ien•a•bil•i•ty** /–bílitee/ *n.*

al•ien•age /áyleeənij/ *n.* the state or condition of being an alien.

al•ien•ate /áyleeənayt/ *v.tr.* **1 a** cause (a person) to become unfriendly or hostile. **b** (often foll. by *from*) cause (a person) to feel isolated or estranged from (friends, society, etc.). **2** transfer ownership of (property) to another person, etc. □□ **al•ien•a•tor** *n.* [ME f. L *alienare alienat-* (as ALIEN)]

al•ien•a•tion /áyleeənáyshən/ *n.* **1** the act or result of alienating. **2** (*Theatr.* **al•ien•a•tion ef•fect**) a theatrical effect whereby an audience remains objective, not identifying with the characters or action of a play.

al•ien•ist /áyleeənist/ *n.* a psychiatrist, esp. a legal adviser on psychiatric problems. [F *aliéniste* (as ALIEN)]

al•i•form /áylifawrm/ *adj.* wing-shaped. [mod.L *aliformis* f. L *ala* wing: see –FORM]

a•light[1] /əlít/ *v.intr.* **1** esp. *Brit.* **a** (often foll. by *from*) descend from a vehicle. **b** dismount from a horse. **2** descend and settle; come to earth from the air. **3** (foll. by *on*) find by chance; notice. [OE *ālīhtan* (as A-[2], *līhtan* LIGHT[2] *v.*)]

a•light[2] /əlít/ *predic.adj.* **1** on fire; burning (*they set the old shed alight; is the fire still alight?*). **2** lighted up; excited (*eyes alight with expectation*). [ME, prob. f. phr. *on a light* (= lighted) *fire*]

a•lign /əlín/ *v.tr.* (also **a•line**) **1** put in a straight line or bring into line (*three books were neatly aligned on the shelf*). **2** esp. *Polit.* (usu. foll. by *with*) bring (oneself, etc.) into agreement or alliance with (a cause, policy, political party, etc.). □□ **a•lign•ment** *n.* [F *aligner* f. phr. *àligne* into line: see LINE[1]]

a•like /əlík/ *adj. & adv.* ● *adj.* (usu. *predic.*) similar; like one another; indistinguishable. ● *adv.* in a similar way or manner (*all were treated alike*) . [ME f. OE *gelīc* and ON *glíkr* (LIKE[1])]

al•i•ment /álimənt/ *n. formal* **1** food. **2** support or mental sustenance. □□ **al•i•men•tal** /áliment'l/ *adj.* [ME f. F *aliment* or L *alimentum* f. *alere* nourish]

al•i•men•ta•ry /áliméntəree/ *adj.* of, relating to, or providing nourishment or sustenance. [L *alimentarius* (as ALIMENT)]

al•i•men•ta•ry ca•nal *n. Anat.* the passage along which food is passed from the mouth to the anus during digestion, including the esophagus, stomach, and intestines.

al•i•men•ta•tion /álimentáyshən/ *n.* **1** nourishment; feeding. **2** maintenance; support; supplying with the necessities of life. [F *alimentation* or med.L *alimentatio* f. *alimentare* (as ALIMENT)]

al•i•mo•ny /álimōnee/ *n.* the money payable by a man to his wife or former wife or by a woman to her husband or former husband after they are separated or divorced. [L *alimonia* nutriment f. *alere* nourish]

A-line /áylīn/ *adj.* (of a garment) having a narrow waist or shoulders and somewhat flared skirt.

al•i•phat•ic /álifátik/ *adj. Chem.* of, denoting, or relating to organic compounds in which carbon atoms form open chains, not aromatic rings. [Gk *aleiphar –atos* fat]

al•i•quot /álikwot/ *adj. & n.* ● *adj.* (of a part or portion) contained by the whole an integral or whole number of times (*4 is an aliquot part of 12*). ● *n.* **1** an aliquot part; an integral factor. **2** (in general use) any known fraction of a whole; a sample. [F *aliquote* f. L *aliquot* some, so many]

a•live /əlív/ *adj.* (usu. *predic.*) **1** (of a person, animal, plant, etc.) living; not dead. **2 a** (of a thing) existing; continuing; in operation or action (*kept his interest alive*). **b** under discussion; provoking interest (*the topic is still very much alive today*). **3** (of a person or animal) lively; active. **4** charged with an electric current; connected to a source of electricity. **5** (foll. by *to*) aware of; alert or responsive to. **6** (foll. by *with*) **a** swarming or teeming with. **b** full of. □ **alive and kicking** *colloq.* very active; lively. **alive and well** still alive or ac-

See page xx for the **Key to Pronunciation**.

SYNONYM TIP alive

ANIMATE, ANIMATED, LIVING, VITAL. Dead is dead, but one can be **alive** to varying degrees. The broadest of these terms describing what has life or shows signs of having it, *alive* can refer to what barely exists (*he was unconscious but still alive when they found him*) as well as to what is bursting with (literal or figurative) life (*her face was alive with excitement and anticipation*). **Living**, on the other hand, is more limited in scope and implies the condition of not being dead (*at 92, she was the oldest living member of the family*) or a state of continued existence or activity (*America's greatest living historian*). **Animate** has fewer connotations than *living* or *alive*; though rare, it is used to distinguish living organisms as opposed to dead ones (*one of the few animate creatures after the devastating explosion*). **Animated**, on the other hand, is used to describe inanimate things to which life or the appearance of life has been given (*an animated cartoon*), or things that are vigorous and lively (*an animated debate on the death penalty*). Anything that is essential to life is **vital** (*vital functions; vital organs*), but it can also be used to describe the energy, activity, and alertness of living things (*an aging but vital member of the historical society*).

tive (esp. despite contrary assumptions or rumors). □□ **a·live·ness** *n.* [OE *on līfe* (as A², LIFE)]

a·liz·a·rin /əlízərin/ *n.* **1** a red coloring matter of madder root, used in dyeing. **2** (*attrib.*) (of a dye) derived from or similar to this pigment. [F *alizarine* f. *alizari* madder f. Arab. *al-'iṣara* pressed juice f. 'aṣara *to press fruit*]

al·ka·hest /álkəhest/ *n.* (also **al·ca·hest**) the universal solvent sought by alchemists. [sham Arab., prob. invented by Paracelsus]

al·ka·li /álkəli/ *n.* (*pl.* **alkalis**) **1 a** any of a class of substances that liberate hydroxide ions in water, usu. form caustic or corrosive solutions, turn litmus blue, and have a pH of more than 7, e.g., sodium hydroxide. **b** any other substance with similar but weaker properties, e.g., sodium carbonate. **2** *Chem.* any substance that reacts with or neutralizes hydrogen ions. □□ **al·ka·lim·e·ter** /álkəlímitər/ *n.* **al·ka·lim·e·try** /álkəlímitree/ *n.* [ME f. med.L, f. Arab. *al- ḳalī* calcined ashes f. *ḳala* fry]

al·ka·li met·als *n.* any of the univalent group of metals, lithium, sodium, potassium, rubidium, and cesium, whose hydroxides are alkalis.

al·ka·line /álkəlin/ *adj.* of, relating to, or having the nature of an alkali; rich in alkali. □□ **al·ka·lin·i·ty** /álkəlínitee/ *n.*

al·ka·line earth *n.* (also **al·ka·line earth met·al**) **1** any of the bivalent group of metals, beryllium, magnesium, calcium, strontium, barium, and radium. **2** an oxide of the lime group.

al·ka·loid /álkəloyd/ *n.* any of a series of nitrogenous organic compounds of plant origin, many of which are used as drugs, e.g., morphine, quinine. [G (as ALKALI)]

al·ka·lo·sis /álkəlósis/ *n.* *Med.* an excessive alkaline condition of the body fluids or tissues.

al·kane /álkayn/ *n.* *Chem.* any of a series of saturated aliphatic hydrocarbons having the general formula C_nH_{2n+2}, including methane, ethane, and propane. [ALKYL + –ANE²]

al·ka·net /álkənet/ *n.* **1 a** any plant of the genus *Alkanna*, esp. *A. tinctoria*, yielding a red dye from its roots. **b** the dye itself. **2** any of various similar plants. [ME f. Sp. *alcaneta* dimin. of *alcana* f. Arab. *al-ḥinnā'* the henna shrub]

al·kene /álkeen/ *n.* *Chem.* any of a series of unsaturated aliphatic hydrocarbons containing a double bond and having the general formula C_nH_{2n}, including ethylene. [ALKYL + –ENE]

al·kyd /álkid/ *n.* any of the group of synthetic resins derived from various alcohols and acids. [ALKYL + ACID]

al·kyl /álkil/ *n.* (in full **alkyl radical**) *Chem.* any radical derived from an alkane by the removal of a hydrogen atom. [G *Alkohol* ALCOHOL + –YL]

al·kyl·ate /álkilayt/ *v.tr. Chem.* introduce an alkyl radical into (a compound).

al·kyne /álkin/ *n.* *Chem.* any of a series of unsaturated aliphatic hydrocarbons containing a triple bond and having the general formula C_nH_{2n-2}, including acetylene. [ALKYL + –YNE]

all /awl/ *adj., n., & adv.* ● *adj.* **1 a** the whole amount, quantity, or extent of (*waited all day; all his life; we all know why; take it all*). **b** (with *pl.*) the entire number of (*all the others left; all ten men; the children are all boys; movie stars all*). **2** any whatever (*beyond all doubt*). **3** greatest possible (*with all speed*). **4** *dial.* consumed; entirely finished. ● *n.* **1 a** all the persons or things concerned (*all were present; all were thrown away*). **b** everything (*all is lost; that is all*). **2** (foll. by *of*) **a** the whole of (*take all of it*). **b** every one of (*all of us*). **c** *colloq.* as much as (*all of six feet tall*). **d** *colloq.* affected by; in a state of (*all of a dither*). **3** one's whole strength or resources (*gave it by my, your, etc.*). **4** (in games) on both sides (*the score was two all*). ● *adv.* **1 a** entirely; quite (*dressed all in black; all around the room; the all-important thing*). **b** as an intensifier (*a book all about ships; stop all this grum-*

bling). **2** *colloq.* very (*went all shy*). **3** (foll. by *the* + compar.) **a** by so much; to that extent (*if they go, all the better*). **b** in the full degree to be expected (*that makes it all the worse*). □ **all along** all the time (*he was joking all along*). **all and sundry** everyone. **all but** very nearly (*it was all but impossible; he was all but drowned*). **all for** *colloq.* strongly in favor of. **all in** *colloq.* exhausted. **all in all** everything considered. **all-in wrestling** esp. *Brit.* wrestling with few or no restrictions. **all manner of** see MANNER. **all of a sudden** see SUDDEN. **all one** (or **the same**) (usu. foll. by *to*) a matter of indifference (*it's all one to me*). **all over 1** completely finished. **2** in or on all parts of (esp. the body) (*went hot and cold all over; mud all over the carpet*). **3** *colloq.* typically (*that is you all over*). **4** *sl.* effusively attentive to (a person). **all the same** nevertheless, in spite of this (*he was innocent but was punished all the same*). **all set** *colloq.* ready to start. **all there** *colloq.* mentally alert. **all the time** see TIME. **all together** all at once; all in one place or in a group (*they came all together*) (cf. ALTOGETHER). **all told** in all. **all very well** *colloq.* an expression used to reject or to imply skepticism about a favorable or consoling remark. **all the way** the whole distance; completely. **at all** (with *neg.* or *interrog.*) in any way; to any extent (*did not swim at all; did you like it at all?*). **in all** in total number; altogether (*there were 10 people in all*). **on all fours** see FOUR. **one and all** everyone. [OE *all, eall*, prob. f. Gmc]

al·la bre·ve /álə brév, áalaa brévay/ *n. Mus.* a time signature indicating 2 or 4 half note beats in a bar. [It., = at the BREVE]

al·la cap·pel·la var. of A CAPPELLA.

Al·lah /álə, áalaa/ *n.* the name of God in Islam. [Arab. 'allāh contr. of *al-'ilāh* f. *al* the + *ilāh* god]

all-A·mer·i·can *adj. & n.* ● *adj.* **1** representing the whole of (or only) America or the US. **2** truly American (*all-American boy*). **3** *Sports* recognized as one of the best in a particular sport. ● *n.* a sportsperson honored as one of the best amateurs in the US.

al·lan·to·is /əlántōis/ *n.* (*pl.* **al·lan·to·ides** /álontō-ideez/) *Zool.* one of several membranes that develop in embryonic reptiles, birds, or mammals. □□ **al·lan·to·ic** /álontō-ik/ *adj.* [mod.L f. Gk *allantoeidēs* sausage-shaped]

all-a·round *adj. & adv.* ● *adj.* (of a person) versatile. ● *adv.* (usu. **all around**) **1** in all respects (*a good performance all-around*). **2** for each person (*he bought drinks all-around*).

al·lay /əláy/ *v.tr.* **1** diminish (fear, suspicion, etc.). **2** relieve or alleviate (pain, hunger, etc.) . [OE *ālecgan* (as A-², LAY¹)]

all clear *n.* a signal that danger or difficulty is over.

all com·ers *n.* any applicants (with reference to a position, or esp. a challenge to a champion, that is unrestricted in entry).

al·le·ga·tion /áligáyshən/ *n.* **1** an assertion, esp. an unproved one. **2** the act or an instance of alleging. [ME f. F *allégation* or L *allegatio* f. *allegare* allege]

al·lege /əléj/ *v.tr.* **1** (often foll. by *that* + clause, or *to* + infin.) declare to be the case, esp. without proof. **2** advance as an argument or excuse. □□ **al·leged** *adj.* [ME f. AF *alegier*, OF *esligier* clear at law; confused in sense with L *allegare*: see ALLEGATION]

al·leg·ed·ly /əléjidlee/ *adv.* as is alleged or said to be the case.

al·le·giance /əléejəns/ *n.* **1** loyalty (to a person or cause, etc.). **2** the duty of a subject to his or her sovereign or government. [ME f. AF f. OF *ligeance* (as LIEGE): perh. assoc. with ALLIANCE]

al·le·gor·i·cal /áligáwrikəl, –gór–/ *adj.* (also **al·le·gor·ic** /–rik/) consisting of or relating to allegory; by means of allegory. □□ **al·le·gor·i·cal·ly** *adv.*

al·le·go·rize /áligəriz/ *v.tr.* treat as or by means of an allegory. □□ **al·le·go·ri·za·tion** /–rizáyshən/ *n.*

al·le·go·ry /áligawree/ *n.* (*pl.* **-ries**) **1** a story, play, poem, picture, etc., in which the meaning or message is represented symbolically. **2** the use of such symbols. **3** a symbol. □□ **al·le·go·rist** *n.* [ME f. OF *allegorie* f. L *allegoria* f. Gk *allēgoria* f. *allos* other + –*agoria* speaking]

al·le·gret·to /áligrétō/ *adv., adj., & n. Mus.* ● *adv. & adj.* in a fairly brisk tempo. ● *n.* (*pl.* **·tos**) an allegretto passage or movement. [It., dimin. of ALLEGRO]

al·le·gro /əléggrō, əláy–/ *adv., adj., & n. Mus.* ● *adv. & adj.* in a brisk tempo. ● *n.* (*pl.* **·gros**) an allegro passage or movement. [It., = lively]

al·lele /əleel/ *n.* one of the (usu. two) alternative forms of a gene. □□ **al·lel·ic** /əleélik/ *adj.* [G *Allel*, abbr. of ALLELOMORPH]

al·le·lo·morph /əleeləmawrf, əlél–/ *n.* = ALLELE. □□ **al·le·lo·mor·phic** /–mórfik/ *adj.* [Gk *allēl-* one another + *morphē* form]

al·le·lu·ia /álilóoyə/ *int. & n.* (also **al·le·lu·ya, hal·le·lu·jah** /hál–/) ● *int.* God be praised. ● *n.* **1** praise to God. **2** a song of praise to God. **3** *RC Ch.* the part of the mass including this. [ME f. eccl.L f. (Septuagint) Gk *allēlouia* f. Heb. *hallᵉlūyāh* praise ye the Lord]

al·le·mande /álemánd, –maánd/ *n.* **1** a figure in a country dance. **2 a** the name of several German dances. **b** the music for any of these, esp. as a movement of a suite. [F, = German (dance)]

Al·len screw /álən/ *n.* a screw with a hexagonal socket in the head.

Al·len wrench /álən/ *n.* a hexagonal wrench designed to fit into and turn an Allen screw. [*Allen*, name of the manufacturer]

al·ler·gen /álərjən/ *n.* any substance that causes an allergic reaction. □□ **al·ler·gen·ic** /–jénik/ *adj.* [ALLERGY + –GEN]

al•ler•gic /əlɔ́rjik/ *adj.* **1** (foll. by *to*) **a** having an allergy to. **b** *colloq.* having a strong dislike for (a person or thing). **2** caused by or relating to an allergy.

al•ler•gy /álərjee/ *n.* (*pl.* **•gies**) **1** *Med.* a condition of reacting adversely to certain substances, esp. particular foods, pollen, fur, or dust. **2** *colloq.* an antipathy or dislike. □□ **al•ler•gist** *n.* [G *Allergie*, after *Energie* ENERGY, f. Gk *allos* other]

al•le•vi•ate /əleéveeayt/ *v.tr.* lessen or make less severe (pain, suffering, etc.). □□ **al•le•vi•a•tion** /-áyshən/ *n.* **al•le•vi•a•tive** *adj.* **al•le•vi•a•tor** *n.* **al•le•vi•a•to•ry** /–veeətáwree/ *adj.* [LL *alleviare* lighten f. L *allevare* (as AD-, *levare* raise)]

SYNONYM TIP   **alleviate**

ABATE, ALLAY, ASSUAGE, MITIGATE, RELIEVE, TEMPER. To **alleviate** is to make something easier to endure (*alleviate the pain following surgery*); **allay** is often used interchangeably, but it also means to put to rest, to quiet or calm (*to allay their suspicions*). **Assuage** and *allay* both suggest the calming or satisfying of a desire or appetite, but *assuage* implies a more complete or permanent satisfaction (*we allay our hunger by nibbling hors d'oeuvres, but a huge dinner assuages our appetite*). To **relieve** implies reducing the misery or discomfort to the point where something is bearable (*relieve the monotony of the cross-country bus trip*) and **mitigate**, which comes from a Latin word meaning to soften, usually means to lessen in force or intensity (*mitigate the storm's impact*). **Abate** suggests a progressive lessening in degree or intensity (*her fever was abating*). To **temper** is to soften or moderate (*to temper justice with mercy*), but it can also mean the exact opposite: to harden or toughen something (*tempering steel; a body tempered by lifting weights*).

---

al•ley¹ /álee/ *n.* (*pl.* **•leys**) **1** (also **al•ley•way**) **a** a narrow street. **b** a narrow passageway, esp. between or behind buildings. **2** a path or walk in a park or garden. **3** an enclosure for bowling, etc. **4** (in tennis) either of the two side strips of a doubles court. □ **up** (or **right up**) **one's alley** (or **street**) *colloq.* **1** within a person's range of interest or knowledge. **2** to a person's liking. [ME f. OF *alee* walking, passage f. *aler* go f. L *ambulare* walk]

al•ley² /álee/ *n.* (also **ally**) (*pl.* **•leys** or **•lies**) a choice playing marble made of marble, alabaster, or glass. [perh. dimin. of ALABASTER]

al•ley cat *n.* a stray cat often mangy or half wild.

All Fools' Day *n.* esp. *Brit.* April 1.

All•hal•lows *n.* All Saints' Day, Nov. 1.

al•li•a•ceous /álee-áyshəs/ *adj.* **1** of or relating to the genus Allium. **2** tasting or smelling like onion or garlic. [mod.L alliaceus f. L allium garlic]

al•li•ance /əlíəns/ *n.* **1 a** a union or agreement to cooperate, esp. of nations by treaty or families by marriage. **b** the parties involved. **2** (Alliance) a political party formed by the allying of separate parties. **3** a relationship resulting from an affinity in nature or qualities, etc. (*the old alliance between logic and metaphysics*). **4** *Bot.* a group of allied families. [ME f. OF aliance (as ALLY¹)]

al•lied /əlíd, álid/ *adj.* **1 a** united or associated in an alliance. **b** (**Allied**) of or relating to the US and its allies in World War I and World War II. **2** connected or related (*studied medicine and allied subjects*).

al•li•ga•tor /áligaytər/ *n.* **1** a large reptile of the crocodile family native to the Americas and China, with upper teeth that lie outside the lower teeth and a head broader and shorter than that of the crocodile. **2** (in general use) any of several large members of the crocodile family. **3 a** the skin of such an animal or material resembling it. **b** (in *pl.*) shoes of this. [Sp. *el lagarto* the lizard f. L *lacerta*]

al•li•ga•tor clip *n.* a clip with teeth for gripping.

al•li•ga•tor pear *n.* an avocado.

al•li•ga•tor snap•per *n.* (also **alligator snapping turtle**) a large American freshwater snapping turtle, *Macroclemys temmincki*.

all-im•por•tant *adj.* crucial; vitally important.

alligator clip

al•lit•er•ate /əlítərayt/ *v.* **1** *intr.* **a** contain alliteration. **b** use alliteration in speech or writing. **2** *tr.* **a** construct (a phrase, etc.) with alliteration. **b** speak or pronounce with alliteration. □□ **al•lit•er•a•tive** /əlítəraytiv, –rətiv/ *adj.* [back-form. f. ALLITERATION]

al•lit•er•a•tion /əlítəráyshən/ *n.* the occurrence of the same letter or sound at the beginning of adjacent or closely connected words (e.g., *calm, cool, and collected*). [mod.L alliteratio (as AD-, *littera* letter)]

al•li•um /áleeəm/ *n.* any plant of the genus *Allium*, usu. bulbous and strong smelling, e.g., onion and garlic. [L, = garlic]

allo- /álō, əlō/ *comb. form* other (*allophone; allogamy*). [Gk *allos* other]

al•lo•cate /áləkayt/ *v.tr.* (usu. foll. by *to*) assign, apportion, or devote to (a purpose, person, or place). □□ **al•lo•ca•ble** /–kəbəl/ *adj.* **al•lo•ca•tion** /–káyshən/ *n.* **al•lo•ca•tor** *n.* [med.L allocare f. *locus* place]

al•lo•cu•tion /áləkyōōshən/ *n.* formal or hortatory speech or manner of address. [L *allocutio* f. *alloqui allocut-* speak to]

al•log•a•my /əlógəmee/ *n. Bot.* cross-fertilization in plants. [ALLO- + Gk *–gamia* f. *gamos* marriage]

al•lo•morph /áləmawrf/ *n. Linguistics* any of two or more alternative forms of a morpheme. □□ **al•lo•mor•phic** *adj.* [ALLO- + MORPHEME]

al•lo•path /áləpath/ *n.* one who practices allopathy. [F *allopathe* back-form. f. *allopathie* = ALLOPATHY]

al•lop•a•thy /əlópəthee/ *n.* the treatment of disease with drugs or other agents having opposite effects to the symptoms (cf. HOMEOPATHY). □□ **al•lo•path•ic** /áləpáthik/ *adj.* **al•lop•a•thist** *n.* [G *Allopathie* (as ALLO-, –PATHY)]

al•lo•phone /áləfōn/ *n. Linguistics* any of the variant sounds forming a single phoneme. □□ **al•lo•phon•ic** /–fónik/ *adj.* [ALLO- + PHONEME]

al•lot /əlót/ *v.tr.* (**al•lot•ted, al•lot•ting**) **1** give or apportion to (a person) as a share or task; distribute officially to (*they allotted us each a pair of boots; the men were allotted duties*). **2** (foll. by *to*) give or distribute officially (*a sum was allotted to each charity*). [OF *aloter* f. *a* to + LOT]

▶See note at LOT.

al•lot•ment /əlótmənt/ *n.* **1** a share allotted. **2** *Brit.* a small piece of land rented (usu. from a local authority) for cultivation. **3** the action of allotting.

al•lo•trope /álətrōp/ *n.* any of two or more different physical forms in which an element can exist (*graphite, charcoal, and diamond are all allotropes of carbon*). [back-form. f. ALLOTROPY]

al•lot•ro•py /əlótrəpee/ *n.* the existence of two or more different physical forms of a chemical element. □□ **al•lo•trop•ic** /álətrópik/ *adj.* **al•lo•trop•i•cal** /–kəl/ *adj.* [Gk *allotropos* of another form f. *allos* different + *tropos* manner f. *trepō* to turn]

al•lot•tee /əlotée/ *n.* a person to whom something is allotted.

all-out *adj.* involving all one's strength; at full speed (*an all-out effort*).

al•low /əlów/ *v.* **1** *tr.* permit (a practice, a person to do something, a thing to happen, etc.) (*smoking is not allowed; we allowed them to speak*). **2** *tr.* give or provide; permit (a person) to have (a limited quantity or sum) (*we were allowed $500 a year*). **3** *tr.* provide or set aside for a purpose; add or deduct in consideration of something (*allow 10% for inflation*). **4** *tr.* **a** admit; agree; concede (*he allowed that it was so; "You know best," he allowed*). **b** assert; be of the opinion. **5** *refl.* permit oneself; indulge oneself in (conduct) (*allowed herself to be persuaded; allowed myself a few angry words*). **6** *intr.* (foll. by *of*) admit of. **7** *intr.* (foll. by *for*) take into consideration or account; make addition or deduction corresponding to (*allowing for waste*). □□ **al•low•a•ble** *adj.* **al•low•a•bly** *adv.* [ME, orig. = 'praise', f. OF *alouer* f. L *allaudare* to praise, and med.L *allocare* to place]

al•low•ance /əlówəns/ *n. & v.* • *n.* **1** an amount or sum allowed to a person, esp. regularly for a stated purpose. **2** an amount allowed in reckoning. **3** (foll. by *of*) a deduction or discount. **4** (foll. by *of*) tolerance of. • *v.tr.* **1** make an allowance to (a person). **2** supply in limited quantities. □ **make allowances** (often foll. by *for*) **1** take into consideration (mitigating circumstances) (*made allowances for his demented state*). **2** look with tolerance upon; make excuses for (a person, bad behavior, etc.). [ME f. OF alouance (as ALLOW)]

al•low•ed•ly /əlówidlee/ *adv.* as is generally allowed or acknowledged.

al•loy /áloy, əlóy/ *n. & v.* • *n.* **1** a mixture of two or more chemical elements, at least one of which is a metal, e.g., brass (a mixture of copper and zinc). **2** an inferior metal mixed esp. with gold or silver. • *v.tr.* **1** mix (metals). **2** debase (a pure substance) by admixture. **3** moderate. [F *aloi* (n.), *aloyer* (v.) f. OF *aloier, aleier* combine f. L *alligare* bind]

all-pur•pose *adj.* suitable for many uses.

all right *adj., adv., & int.* • *adj.* (*predic.*) satisfactory; safe and sound; in good condition. • *adv.* satisfactorily; as desired (*it worked out all right*). • *int.* **1** expressing consent or assent to a proposal or order. **2** used to express how certain one is about something (*that's the one all right*).

▶Although found widely, **alright** remains nonstandard, even where standard spelling leads to awkwardness, e.g., *I wanted to make sure it was all all right.*

all-right *attrib. adj. colloq.* fine; acceptable (*an all-right guy*).

all round *adj.* (also **all-round**) *Brit.* = ALL-AROUND.

All Saints' Day *n.* a Christian festival in honor of all the saints, held (in the Western Church) on Nov. 1.

All Souls' Day *n.* a festival in some Christian churches with prayers for the souls of the dead, held on Nov. 2.

all•spice /áwlspīs/ *n.* **1** the aromatic spice obtained from the ground berry of the pimento plant, *Pimenta dioica*. **2** the berry of this. **3** any of various other aromatic shrubs.

all-time *adj.* (of a record, etc.) hitherto unsurpassed.

al•lude /əlōōd/ *v.intr.* (foll. by *to*) **1** refer, esp. indirectly, covertly, or briefly to. **2** mention. [L *alludere* (as AD-, *ludere lus-* play)]

al•lure /əlōōr/ *v. & n.* ● *v.tr.* attract, charm, or fascinate. ● *n.* attractiveness; personal charm; fascination. □□ **al•lure•ment** *n.* **al•lur•ing** *adj.* **al•lur•ing•ly** *adv.* [ME f. OF *alurer* attract (as AD-, *luere* LURE *v.* 1)]

al•lu•sion /əl ōōzhən/ *n.* (often foll. by *to*) a reference, esp. a covert, passing, or indirect one. [F *allusion* or LL *allusio* (as ALLUDE)]
▶Because of the similarity in their pronunciation and spelling, **allusion**, **illusion**, and **elusion** are easily confused. An *allusion* is an indirect or passing reference to something without actually naming it. An *illusion* is a false dream, an unrealistic idea, or the perception of something that is not real. *Elusion* is the noun form of the verb *to elude*, and it refers to a deception or evasion.

al•lu•sive /əlōōsiv/ *adj.* **1** (often foll. by *to*) containing an allusion. **2** containing many allusions. □□ **al•lu•sive•ly** *adv.* **al•lu•sive•ness** *n.*

al•lu•vi•al /əlōōveeəl/ *adj. & n.* ● *adj.* of or relating to alluvium. ● *n.* alluvium, esp. containing a precious metal.

al•lu•vi•on /əlōōveeən/ *n.* **1** the wash of the sea against the shore, or of a river against its banks. **2 a** a large overflow of water. **b** matter deposited by this, esp. alluvium. **3** the formation of new land by the movement of the sea or of a river. [F f. L *alluvio –onis* f. *luere* wash]

al•lu•vi•um /əlōōveeəm/ *n.* (*pl.* **alluviums** or **alluvia** /–ə/) a deposit of usu. fine fertile soil left during a time of flood, esp. in a river valley or delta. [L neut. of *alluvius* adj. f. *luere* wash]

al•ly[1] /álī/ *n. & v.* ● *n.* (*pl.* **-lies**) **1** a government formally cooperating or united with another for a special purpose, esp. by a treaty. **2** a person or organization that cooperates with or helps another. ● *v.tr.* also /əlī/ (**-lies, -lied**) (often foll. by *with*) combine or unite in alliance. [ME f. OF *al(e) ier* f. L *alligare* bind: cf. ALLOY]

PRONUNCIATION TIP   **ally**[1]

The main stress in this word, both as a noun and as a verb, was originally on the second syllable. But the stress has now shifted to the first syllable when it is used as a noun. The adjective *allied* is also stressed on the first syllable when it precedes a noun (*the Allied forces*); otherwise the stress falls on the second syllable, as in *we were allied with our neighbor.*

---

al•ly[2] var. of ALLEY[2].

-ally /əlee/ *suffix* forming adverbs from adjectives in *–al* (cf. –AL, –LY[2], –ICALLY).

al•lyl /álil/ *n. Chem.* the unsaturated univalent radical $CH_2{=}CH{-}CH_2$. [L *allium* garlic + –YL]

al•ma ma•ter /áalmə máatər, álmə máytər/ *n.* (also **Al•ma Ma•ter**) **1** the university, school, or college one attends or attended. **2** the official anthem or song of a university, school, or college. [L, = bounteous mother]

al•ma•nac /áwlmənak, ál–/ *n.* an annual calendar of months and days, usu. with astronomical data and other information. [ME f. med.L *almanac(h)* f. Gk *almenikhiaka*]

al•man•dine /álməndeen, –dīn/ *n.* (also **almandite** /–dīt/) a kind of garnet with a violet tint. [F, alt. of obs. *alabandine* f. med.L *alabandina* f. *Alabanda*, ancient city in Asia Minor]

al•might•y /áwlmītee/ *adj. & adv.* ● *adj.* **1** having complete power; omnipotent. **2** (**the Almighty**) God. **3** *sl.* very great (*an almighty crash*). ● *adv. sl.* extremely; very much. [OE *ælmihtig* (as ALL, MIGHTY)]

al•mond /áamənd, ám–/ *n.* **1** the oval nutlike seed (kernel) of the fruit from the tree *Prunus dulcis*, of which there are sweet and bitter varieties. **2** the tree itself, of the rose family and related to the peach and plum. [ME f. OF *alemande*, etc. f. med.L *amandula* f. L *amygdala* f. Gk *amugdalē*: assoc. with words in AL-]

al•mond eyes *n.* narrow almond-shaped eyes.

al•mond oil *n.* the oil expressed from the seed (esp. the bitter variety), used for cosmetic preparations, flavoring, and medicinal purposes.

al•mon•er /áamənər, álmə–/ *n.* **1** *Brit.* a social worker attached to a hospital. **2** *hist.* an official distributor of alms. [ME f. AF *aumoner*, OF *aumonier*, ult. f. med.L *eleēmosynarius* (as ALMS)]
▶Now usually called *medical social worker*.

al•most /áwlmōst/ *adv.* all but; very nearly. [OE *ælmæst* for the most part (as ALL, MOST)]

alms /aamz/ *n.pl. hist.* the charitable donation of money or food to the poor. [OE *ælmysse, –messe*, f. Gmc ult. f. Gk *eleēmosunē* compassionateness f. *eleēmōn* (adj.) f. *eleos* compassion]

alms•house /áamz-hows/ *n.* esp. *Brit. hist.* a house founded by charity for the poor.

al•oe /álō/ *n.* **1** any plant of the genus *Aloe*, usu. having toothed fleshy leaves. **2** (in *pl.*) (in full **bitter aloes**) a strong laxative obtained from the bitter juice of various species of aloe. **3** (also **A•mer•i•can al•oe**) an agave native to Central America. **4** (also **aloe vera**) a spe-

cies of aloe whose leaves yield an emollient juice. [OE *al(e)we* f. L *aloē* f. Gk]

al•o•et•ic /álō-étik/ *adj. & n.* ● *adj.* of or relating to an aloe. ● *n.* a medicine containing aloes. [Gk *aloē* aloe, on the false analogy of *diuretic*, etc.]

a•loft /əláwft, əlóft/ *predic.adj. & adv.* **1** high up; overhead. **2** upwards. [ME f. ON *álopt(i)* f. *áin*, on, to + *lopt* air: cf. LIFT, LOFT]

a•log•i•cal /áylójikəl/ *adj.* **1** not logical. **2** opposed to logic.

a•lo•ha /əlóhaa, aa–/ *int.* a Hawaiian salutation at meeting or parting. [Hawaiian, *aloha* love]

a•lone /əlón/ *predic.adj. & adv.* **1 a** without others present (*they wanted to be alone; the tree stood alone*). **b** without others' help (*succeeded alone*). **c** lonely and isolated (*felt alone*). **d** (often foll. by *in*) standing by oneself in an opinion, quality, etc. (*was alone in thinking this*). **3** only; exclusively (*you alone can help me*). □ **go it alone** act by oneself without assistance. □□ **a•lone•ness** *n.* [ME f. ALL + ONE]

a•long /əláwng, əlóng/ *prep. & adv.* ● *prep.* **1** from one end to the other end of (*a handkerchief with lace along the edge*). **2** on or through any part of the length of (*was walking along the road*). **3** beside or through the length of (*shelves stood along the wall*). ● *adv.* **1** onward; into a more advanced state (*come along; getting along nicely*). **2** at or to a particular place or time; arriving (*I'll be along soon*). **3** in company with a person, esp. oneself (*bring a book along*). **4** beside or through part or the whole length of a thing. □ **along with** in addition to; together with. [OE *andlang* f. WG, rel. to LONG[1]]

a•long•shore /əláwngsháwr, əlóng–/ *adv.* along or by the shore.

a•long•side /əláwngsíd, əlóng–/ *adv. & prep.* ● *adv.* at or to the side (of a ship, pier, etc.). ● *prep.* close to the side of; next to. □ **alongside of** side by side with; together or simultaneously with.

a•loof /əlōōf/ *adj. & adv.* ● *adj.* distant; unsympathetic. ● *adv.* away; apart (*he kept aloof from his colleagues*). □□ **a•loof•ly** *adv.* **a•loof•ness** *n.* [orig. Naut., f. A[2] + LUFF]

al•o•pe•ci•a /áləpéeshə/ *n. Med.* the absence (complete or partial) of hair from areas of the body where it normally grows; baldness. [L f. Gk *alōpekia* fox mange f. *alōpēx* fox]

a•loud /əlówd/ *adv.* **1** audibly; not silently or in a whisper. **2** *archaic* loudly. [A[2] + LOUD]

a•low /əló/ *adv. & predic.adj. Naut.* in or into the lower part of a ship. [A[2] + LOW[1]]

alp /alp/ *n.* **1 a** a high mountain. **b** (**the Alps**) the high range of mountains in Switzerland and adjoining countries. **2** (in Switzerland) pastureland on a mountainside. [orig. pl., f. F f. L *Alpes* f. Gk *Alpeis*]

al•pac•a /alpákə/ *n.* **1** a S. American mammal, *Lama pacos*, related to the llama, with long shaggy hair. **2** the wool from the animal. **3** fabric made from the wool, with or without other fibers. [Sp. f. Aymará or Quechua]

al•pen•horn /álpənhawrn/ *n.* a long wooden horn used by Alpine herdsmen to call their cattle. [G, = Alp horn]

al•pen•stock /álpənstok/ *n.* a long iron-tipped staff used in hiking and mountain climbing. [G, = Alp stick]

al•pha /álfə/ *n.* **1** the first letter of the Greek alphabet (A, α). **2** a beginning; something that is primary or first. **3** *Brit.* a first-class mark given for a piece of work or on an examination. **4** *Astron.* the chief star in a constellation. [ME f. L f. Gk]

al•pha and o•me•ga *n.* the beginning and the end; the most important features.

al•pha•bet /álfəbet/ *n.* **1** the set of letters used in writing a language (*the Cyrillic alphabet*). **2** a set of symbols or signs representing letters. [L *alphabetum* f. Gk *alpha*, *bēta*, the first two letters of the alphabet]

al•pha-be•ta brass /álfəbaytə brás/ *n.* = MUNTZ METAL.

al•pha•bet•i•cal /álfəbétikəl/ *adj.* (also **al•pha•bet•ic** /–bétik/) **1** of or relating to an alphabet. **2** in the order of the letters of the alphabet. □□ **al•pha•bet•i•cal•ly** *adv.*

al•pha•bet•ize /álfəbətīz/ *v.tr.* arrange (words, names, etc.) in alphabetical order. □□ **al•pha•bet•i•za•tion** /–izáyshən/ *n.*

al•pha•nu•mer•ic /álfənōōmérik, –nyōō–/ *adj.* (also **al•pha•mer•ic** /álfəmérik/, **al•pha•nu•mer•i•cal**) containing both alphabetical and numerical symbols. [*alphabetic* (see ALPHABETICAL) + NUMERICAL]

al•pha par•ti•cle *n.* (also **al•pha ray**) a helium nucleus emitted by a radioactive substance, orig. regarded as a ray.

al•pine /álpīn/ *adj. & n.* ● *adj.* **1 a** of or relating to high mountains. **b** growing or found on high mountains. **2** (**Alpine**) of or relating to the Alps. ● *n.* a plant native or suited to a high mountain habitat. [L *Alpinus*: see ALP]

Al•pin•ist /álpinist/ *n.* (also **alpinist**) a climber of high mountains, esp. the Alps. [F *alpiniste* (as ALPINE; see –IST)]

al•read•y /áwlrédee/ *adv.* **1** before the time in question (*I knew that already*). **2** as early or as soon as this (*already at the age of six*). [ALL *adv.* + READY]
▶Already is an adverb meaning 'previously' (*she had already left by the time we got there*). **All ready** means 'fully prepared' and is always written as two words (*"Are you ready?" he asked. "We're all ready," we replied*).

al•right /áwlrít/ *adj., adv., & int. disp.* = ALL RIGHT.
▶See note at ALL RIGHT.

ALS *abbr.* AMYOTROPHIC LATERAL SCLEROSIS.

Al·sa·tian /alsáyshən/ *n.* **1** a native of Alsace, a region of E. France. **2** esp. *Brit.* = GERMAN SHEPHERD. [*Alsatia* (= Alsace) + –AN]

al·sike /álsik/ *n.* a European species of clover, *Trifolium hybridum.* [*Alsike* in Sweden]

al·so /áwlsō/ *adv.* in addition; likewise; besides. [OE *alswā* (as ALL *adv.*, SO¹)]

al·so-ran *n.* **1** a horse or dog, etc., not among the winners in a race. **2** one who does not win a competition. **3** an undistinguished person.

alt. *abbr.* **1** alternate. **2** altimeter. **3** altitude.

Alta. *abbr.* Alberta.

al·tar /áwltər/ *n.* **1** a table or flat-topped block, often of stone, for sacrifice or offering to a deity. **2** a raised surface or table at which a Christian service, esp. the Eucharist, is celebrated. [OE *altar –er*, Gmc adoption of LL *altar, altarium* f. L *altaria* (pl.) burnt offerings, altar, prob. rel. to *adolēre* burn in sacrifice]

al·tar boy *n.* (also **al·tar girl**) a child who serves as a priest's assistant in a service.

al·tar·piece /áwltərpees/ *n.* a piece of art, esp. a painting, set above or behind an altar.

alt·az·i·muth /altázimǝth/ *n.* a telescope or other instrument mounted so as to allow both vertical and horizontal movement, esp. one used for measuring the altitude and azimuth of celestial bodies. [ALTITUDE + AZIMUTH]

al·ter /áwltər/ *v.* **1** *tr. & intr.* make or become different; change. **2** *tr.* castrate or spay. □□ **al·ter·a·ble** *adj.* **al·ter·a·tion** /–ráyshən/ *n.* [ME f. OF *alterer* f. LL *alterare* f. L *alter* other]

al·ter·a·tive /áwltǝráytiv, –rǝtiv/ *adj. & n.* ● *adj.* **1** tending to alter. **2** (of a medicine) that alters bodily processes. ● *n.* an alterative medicine or treatment. [ME f. med.L *alterativus* (as ALTER)]

al·ter·cate /áwltərkayt/ *v.intr.* (often foll. by *with*) dispute hotly; wrangle. □□ **al·ter·ca·tion** /–káyshən/ *n.* [L *altercari altercat–*]

al·ter e·go /áwltǝr eégō, égō/ *n.* (*pl.* **alter egos**) **1** an intimate and trusted friend. **2** a person's secondary or alternative personality. [L, = other self]

al·ter·nate *v., adj., & n.* ● *v.* /áwltərnayt, ál–/ **1** *intr.* (often foll. by *with*) (of two things) succeed each other by turns (*rain and sunshine alternated; elation alternated with depression*). **2** *intr.* (foll. by *between*) change repeatedly (between two conditions) (*the patient alternated between hot and cold fevers*). **3** *tr.* (often foll. by *with*) cause (two things) to succeed each other by turns (*the band alternated fast and slow tunes; we alternated criticism with reassurance*). ● *adj.* /áwltǝrnǝt, ál–/ **1** (with noun in *pl.*) every other (*comes on alternate days*). **2** (of things of two kinds) each following and succeeded by one of the other kind (*alternate joy and misery*). **3** (of a sequence, etc.) consisting of alternate things. **4** *Bot.* (of leaves, etc.) placed alternately on the two sides of the stem. **5** = ALTERNATIVE. ● *n.* /áwltǝrnǝt, ál–/ something or someone that is an alternative; a deputy or substitute. □□ **al·ter·nate·ly** *adv.* [L *alternatus* past part. of *alternare* do things by turns f. *alternus* every other f. *alter* other]

▶In both American and British English **alternate** means 'every other,' e.g., *There will be a dance on alternate Saturdays*, and **alternative** means 'available as another choice,' e.g., *an alternative route.* In American usage, however, **alternate** can also be used to mean 'available as another choice,' e.g., *An alternate plan called for construction to begin immediately rather than waiting for spring.*

al·ter·nate an·gles *n.* two angles, not adjoining one another, that are formed on opposite sides of a line that intersects two other lines.

al·ter·nat·ing cur·rent *n.* an electric current that reverses its direction at regular intervals.

al·ter·na·tion /áwltǝrnáyshǝn, ál–/ *n.* the action or result of alternating.

al·ter·na·tion of gen·er·a·tions *n.* reproduction occurring in the life cycle of some lower plants and invertebrates, involving a regular alternation between two distinct forms, e.g., sexual and asexual.

al·ter·na·tive /awltɔ́rnǝtiv, ál–/ *adj. & n.* ● *adj.* **1** (of one or more things) available or usable instead of another (*an alternative route*). **2** (of two things) mutually exclusive. **3** of or relating to practices that offer a substitute for established or conventional ones (*alternative medicine; alternative theater*). ● *n.* **1** any of two or more possibilities. **2** the freedom or opportunity to choose between two or more things (*I had no alternative but to go*). □□ **al·ter·na·tive·ly** *adv.* [F *alternatif –ive* or med.L *alternativus* (as ALTERNATE)]

▶Use with reference to more than two options (*many alternative methods*) is common and acceptable. See also note at ALTERNATE.

al·ter·na·tive med·i·cine *n.* any of a range of medical therapies that are not regarded as orthodox by the medical profession, such as herbalism, homeopathy, and acupuncture.

al·ter·na·tive so·ci·e·ty *n.* a group of people dissociating themselves from conventional society and its values.

al·ter·na·tor /áwltǝrnaytǝr, ál–/ *n.* a generator that produces an alternating current.

alt·horn /ált-hawrn/ *n. Mus.* an instrument of the saxhorn family, esp. the alto or tenor saxhorn in E flat. [G f. *alt* high f. L *altus* + HORN]

al·though /awlthố/ *conj.* = THOUGH *conj.* 1–3. [ME f. ALL *adv.* + THOUGH]

al·tim·e·ter /altīmitǝr, áltmeetǝr/ *n.* an instrument for showing height above sea or ground level, esp. one fitted in an aircraft. [L *altus>o? high* + –METER]

al·ti·tude /áltitōod, –tyōōd/ *n.* **1** the height of an object in relation to a given point, esp. sea level or the horizon. **2** *Geom.* the length of the perpendicular from a vertex to the opposite side of a figure. **3** a high or exalted position (*a social altitude*). □□ **al·ti·tu·di·nal** /–tōódin'l, –tyōo–/ *adj.* [ME f. L *altitudo* f. *altus* high]

al·ti·tude sick·ness *n.* a sickness experienced at high altitudes due to a lack of oxygen.

al·to /áltō/ *n.* (*pl.* **·tos**) **1** = CONTRALTO. **2** = COUNTERTENOR. **3 a** (*attrib.*) denoting the member of a family of instruments pitched next below a soprano of its type. **b** an alto instrument. [It. *alto* (*canto*) high (singing)]

al·to clef *n.* a clef placing middle C on the middle line of the staff, used chiefly for viola music.

al·to·cu·mu·lus /áltōkyōómyǝlǝs/ *n.* (*pl.* **altocumuli** /–lī/) *Meteorol.* a cloud formation at medium altitude consisting of rounded masses with a level base. [mod.L f. L *altus* high + CUMULUS]

al·to·geth·er /áwltǝgéthǝr/ *adv.* **1** totally; completely (*you are altogether wrong*). **2** on the whole (*altogether it had been a good day*). **3** in total (*there are six bedrooms altogether*). □ **in the altogether** *colloq.* naked. [ME f. ALL + TOGETHER]

▶**Altogether** and **all together** are used in different contexts. **Altogether** means 'in total,' e.g., *The hotel has twenty rooms altogether. Altogether, I spent five years on the island.* **All together** means 'all at once' or 'all in one place or in one group,' e.g., *The packages arrived all together. We managed to get three bedrooms all together* (i.e., near each other).

al·to-re·lie·vo /áltōrileévō/ *n.* (also **al·to·ri·lie·vo** /áltōrilyáyvō/) (*pl.* **·vos**) *Sculpture* **1** a form of relief in which the sculptured shapes stand out from the background to at least half their actual depth. **2** a sculpture characterized by this. [ALTO + RELIEVO]

al·to·stra·tus /áltōstráytǝs, –strátǝs/ *n.* (*pl.* **altostrati** /–tī/) a continuous and uniformly flat cloud formation at medium altitude. [mod.L f. L *altus* high + STRATUS]

al·tri·cial /altríshǝl/ *adj. & n.* ● *adj.* (esp. of a bird) whose young require care and feeding by the parents after hatching or birth. ● *n.* an altricial bird or animal (cf. PRECOCIAL). [L *altrix altricis* (fem.) nourisher f. *altor* f. *alere altus* nourish]

al·tru·ism /áltrōoizǝm/ *n.* **1** regard for others as a principle of action. **2** unselfishness; concern for other people. □□ **al·tru·ist** *n.* **al·tru·is·tic** /–ístik/ *adj.* **al·tru·is·ti·cal·ly** *adv.* [F *altruisme* f. It. *altrui* somebody else (infl. by L *alter* other)]

al·um /álǝm/ *n.* **1** a double sulfate of aluminum and potassium. **2** any of a group of compounds of double sulfates of a monovalent metal (or group) and a trivalent metal. [ME f. OF f. L *alumen aluminis*]

a·lu·mi·na /ǝlōomǝnǝ/ *n.* the compound aluminum oxide occurring naturally as corundum and emery. [L *alumen* alum, after *soda*, etc.]

a·lu·mi·nize /ǝlōominīz/ *v.tr.* coat with aluminum. □□ **a·lu·mi·ni·za·tion** /–izáyshǝn/ *n.*

a·lu·mi·num /ǝlōominǝm/ *n.* (*Brit.* **aluminium** /ályǝmíneeǝm/) a silvery light and malleable metallic element resistant to tarnishing by air. ¶ Symb.: Al. □ **aluminum bronze** an alloy of copper and aluminum. [earlier *aluminum* f. ALUM + –IUM]

a·lum·nus /ǝlúmnǝs/ *n.* (*pl.* **alumni** /–nī/; *fem.* **alumna**, *pl.* **alumnae** /–nee, nī/) a former pupil or student of a particular school, college, or university. [L, = nursling, pupil f. *alere* nourish]

al·ve·o·lar /alvéeǝlǝr/ *adj.* **1** of an alveolus. **2** *Phonet.* (of a consonant) pronounced with the tip of the tongue in contact with the ridge of the upper teeth, e.g., *n, s, t.* [ALVEOLUS + –AR¹]

al·ve·o·lus /alvéeǝlǝs/ *n.* (*pl.* **alveoli** /–lī/) **1** a small cavity, pit, or hollow. **2** any of the many tiny air sacs of the lungs which allow for rapid gaseous exchange. **3** the bony socket for the root of a tooth. **4** the cell of a honeycomb. □□ **al·ve·o·late** *adj.* [L dimin. of *alveus* cavity]

al·ways /áwlwayz/ *adv.* **1** at all times; on all occasions (*they are always late*). **2** whatever the circumstances (*I can always sleep on the floor*). **3** repeatedly; often (*they are always complaining*). **4** for ever; for all time (*I am with you always*). [ME, prob. distrib. genit. f. ALL + WAY + –'s¹]

a·lys·sum /álisǝm/ *n.* any plant of the genus *Alyssum*, widely cultivated and usu. having yellow or white flowers. [L f. Gk *alusson*]

Alz·hei·mer's dis·ease /áalts-hímǝrz, álts–, áwlts–, áwlz–/ *n.* a serious disorder of the brain manifesting itself in premature senility. [A. *Alzheimer*, Ger. neurologist d. 1915]

AM *abbr.* **1** amplitude modulation. **2** Master of Arts. **3** Member of the Order of Australia. [(sense 2) L *artium Magister*]

Am *symb. Chem.* the element americium.

am *1st person sing. present* of BE.

a.m. *abbr.* (also **A.M.** or **AM**) between midnight and noon. [L *ante meridiem*]

AMA *abbr.* American Medical Association.

am•a•dou /ámədoō/ *n.* a spongy and combustible tinder prepared from dry fungi. [F f. mod.Prov., lit. = lover (because quickly kindled) f. L (as AMATEUR)]

a•mah /aámə, aámaa/ *n.* (in Asia) a nursemaid or maid. [Port. *ama* nurse]

a•mal•gam /əmálgəm/ *n.* **1** a mixture or blend. **2** an alloy of mercury with one or more other metals, used esp. in dentistry. [ME f. F *amalgame* or med.L *amalgama* f. Gk *malagma* an emollient]

a•mal•ga•mate /əmálgəmayt/ *v.* **1** *tr. & intr.* combine or unite to form one structure, organization, etc. **2** *tr.* (of metals) alloy with mercury. □□ **a•mal•ga•ma•tion** /–máyshən/ *n.* [med.L *amalgamare amalgamat–* (as AMALGAM)]

a•man•u•en•sis /əmányoō-énsis/ *n.* (*pl.* **amanuenses** /–seez/) **1** a person who writes from dictation or copies manuscripts. **2** a literary assistant. [L f. (*servus*) *a manu* secretary + –*ensis* belonging to]

am•a•ranth /áməranth/ *n.* **1** any plant of the genus *Amaranthus*, usu. having small green, red, or purple tinted flowers, e.g., prince's feather and pigweed. **2** an imaginary flower that never fades. **3** a purple color. □□ **am•a•ran•thine** /–ránthin, –thin/ *adj.* [F *amarante* or mod.L *amaranthus* f. L f. Gk *amarantos* everlasting f. *a-* not + *marainō* wither, alt. after *polyanthus*, etc.]

am•a•ret•to /ámərétō/ *n.* an almond-flavored liqueur. [It. dimin. of *amaro* bitter f. L *amarus*]

am•a•ryl•lis /ámərílis/ *n.* **1** a plant genus with a single species, *Amaryllis belladonna*, a bulbous lilylike plant native to S. Africa with white, pink, or red flowers (also called **belladonna lily**). **2** any of various related plants formerly of this genus now transferred to other genera, notably *Hippeastrum*. [L f. Gk *Amarullis*, name of a country girl]

a•mass /əmás/ *v.tr.* **1** gather or heap together. **2** accumulate (esp. riches). □□ **a•mass•er** *n.* **a•mass•ment** *n.* [F *amasser* or med.L *amassare* ult. f. L *massa* MASS[1]]

am•a•teur /áməchoōr, –chər, –tər, –tŏr/ *n. & adj.* •*n.* **1 a** a person who engages in a pursuit (e.g., an art or sport) as a pastime rather than a profession. **b** *derog.* a person who does something unskillfully, in the manner of an amateur rather than a professional. **2** (foll. by *of*) a person who is fond of (a thing). •*adj.* for or done by amateurs; amateurish; unskillful (*amateur athletics; did an amateur job*). □□ **am•a•teur•ism** *n.* [F f. It. *amatore* f. L *amator –oris* lover f. *amare* love]

am•a•teur•ish /áməchoōr, –chərish, tər–, –tŏr/ *adj.* characteristic of an amateur, esp. unskillful or inexperienced. □□ **am•a•teur•ish•ly** *adv.* **am•a•teur•ish•ness** *n.*

am•a•to•ry /ámətawree/ *adj.* of or relating to sexual love or desire. [L *amatorius* f. *amare* love]

am•au•ro•sis /ámərósis/ *n.* the partial or total loss of sight, from disease of the optic nerve, retina, spinal cord, or brain. □□ **am•au•rot•ic** /–rótik/ *adj.* [mod.L f. Gk f. *amauroō* darken f. *amauros* dim]

a•maze /əmáyz/ *v.tr.* (often foll. by *at*, or *that* + clause, or *to* + infin.) surprise greatly; overwhelm with wonder (*am amazed at your indifference; was amazed to find them alive*). □□ **a•maze•ment** *n.* **a•maz•ing** *adj.* **a•maz•ing•ly** *adv.* **a•maz•ing•ness** *n.* [ME f. OE *āmasod* past part. of *āmasian*, of uncert. orig.]

Am•a•zon /áməzon, –zən/ *n.* **1** a member of a mythical race of female warriors in Scythia and elsewhere. **2** (**amazon**) a very tall, strong, or athletic woman. □□ **Am•a•zo•ni•an** /–zóneeən/ *adj.* [ME f. L f. Gk: expl. by the Greeks as 'breastless' (as if A-[1] + *mazos* breast), but prob. of foreign orig.]

am•bas•sa•dor /ambásədər, –dawr/ *n.* **1** an accredited diplomat sent by a nation on a mission to, or as its permanent representative in, a foreign country. **2** a representative or promoter of a specified thing (*an ambassador of peace*). □□ **am•bas•sa•do•ri•al** /–dáwreeəl/ *adj.* **am•bas•sa•dor•ship** *n.* [ME f. F *ambassadeur* f. It. *ambasciator*, ult. f. L *ambactus* servant]

am•bas•sa•dor-at-large *n.* an ambassador with special duties, not appointed to a particular country.

am•bas•sa•dress /ambásədris/ *n.* **1** a female ambassador. **2** an ambassador's wife.

am•batch /ámbach/ *n.* an African tree, *Aeschynomene elaphroxylon*, with very light spongy wood. [Ethiopic]

am•ber /ámbər/ *n. & adj.* •*n.* **1 a** a yellowish translucent fossilized resin deriving from extinct (esp. coniferous) trees and used in jewelry. **b** the honey-yellow color of this. **2** a yellow traffic signal meaning caution, showing between red for "stop" and green for "go." •*adj.* made of or colored like amber. [ME f. OF *ambre* f. Arab. '*anbar* ambergris, amber]

am•ber•gris /ámbərgris, –grees/ *n.* a strong-smelling waxlike secretion of the intestine of the sperm whale, found floating in tropical seas and used in perfume manufacture. [ME f. OF *ambre gris* gray AMBER]

am•ber•jack /ámbərjak/ *n.* any large brightly-colored marine fish of the genus *Seriola* found in tropical and subtropical Atlantic waters.

am•bi•ance var. of AMBIENCE.

am•bi•dex•trous /ámbidékstrəs/ *adj.* (*Brit.* also **ambidexterous**) **1** able to use the right and left hands equally well. **2** working skillfully in more than one medium. □□ **am•bi•dex•ter•i•ty** /–stéritee/ *n.* **am•bi•dex•trous•ly** *adv.* **am•bi•dex•trous•ness** *n.* [LL *ambidexter* f. *ambi-* on both sides + *dexter* right-handed]

am•bi•ence /ámbeeəns, aanbeeaáns/ *n.* (also **am•bi•ance**) the surroundings or atmosphere of a place. [AMBIENT + –ENCE or F *ambiance*]

PRONUNCIATION TIP ambience

Although many English speakers pronounce this word in a manner reflective of its French origins (AHM-bee-ahns), the American pronunciation AM-bee-ens is also widely used. It is sometimes spelled *ambiance*.

---

am•bi•ent /ámbeeənt/ *adj.* surrounding. [F *ambiant* or L *ambiens –entis* pres. part. of *ambire* go round]

am•bi•gu•i•ty /ámbigyoōitee/ *n.* (*pl.* •**ties**) **1 a** a double meaning which is either deliberate or caused by inexactness of expression. **b** an example of this. **2** an expression able to be interpreted in more than one way (e.g., *fighting dogs should be avoided*). [ME f. OF *ambiguité* or L *ambiguitas* (as AMBIGUOUS)]

am•big•u•ous /ambígyoōəs/ *adj.* **1** having an obscure or double meaning. **2** difficult to classify. □□ **am•big•u•ous•ly** *adv.* **am•big•u•ous•ness** *n.* [L *ambiguus* doubtful f. *ambigere* f. *ambi-* both ways + *agere* drive]

am•bit /ámbit/ *n.* **1** the scope, extent, or bounds of something. **2** precincts or environs. [ME f. L *ambitus* circuit f. *ambire*: see AMBIENT]

am•bi•tion /ambíshən/ *n.* **1** (often foll. by *to* + infin.) the determination to achieve success or distinction, usu. in a chosen field. **2** the object of this determination. **3** energy; interest in activity, etc. **4** aggressive self-centeredness. [ME f. OF f. L *ambitio –onis* f. *ambire ambit-* canvass for votes: see AMBIENT]

am•bi•tious /ambíshəs/ *adj.* **1 a** full of ambition. **b** showing ambition (*an ambitious attempt*). **2** (foll. by *of*, or *to* + infin.) strongly determined. □□ **am•bi•tious•ly** *adv.* **am•bi•tious•ness** *n.* [ME f. OF *ambitieux* f. L *ambitiosus* (as AMBITION)]

am•biv•a•lence /ambívələns/ *n.* (also **ambivalency** /–lənsee/) **1** the coexistence in one person's mind of opposing feelings, esp. love and hate, in a single context. **2** uncertainty over a course of action or decision. □□ **am•biv•a•lent** *adj.* **am•biv•a•lent•ly** *adv.* [G *Ambivalenz* f. L *ambo* both, after *equivalence, –ency*]

am•bi•vert /ámbivert/ *n. Psychol.* a person who fluctuates between being an introvert and an extrovert. □□ **am•bi•ver•sion** /–vérzhən/ *n.* [L *ambi-* on both sides + –*vert* f. L *vertere* to turn, after EXTROVERT, INTROVERT]

am•ble /ámbəl/ *v. & n.* •*v.intr.* **1** move at an easy pace, in a way suggesting an ambling horse. **2** (of a horse, etc.) move by lifting the two feet on one side together. **3** ride an ambling horse; ride at an easy pace. •*n.* an easy pace; the gait of an ambling horse. [ME f. OF *ambler* f. L *ambulare* walk]

am•bly•o•pi•a /ámbleeópeeə/ *n.* dimness of vision without obvious defect or change in the eye. □□ **am•bly•op•ic** /–leeópik/ *adj.* [Gk f. *ambluōpos* (adj.) f. *amblus* dull + *ōps, ōpos* eye]

am•bo /ámbō/ *n.* (*pl.* **bos** or **ambones** /–bóneez/) a stand for reading lessons in an early Christian church, etc. [med.L f. Gk *ambōn* rim (in med.Gk = pulpit)]

am•boy•na /ambóynə/ *n.* the decorative wood of the SE Asian tree *Pterocarpus indicus*. [*Amboyna* Island in Indonesia]

am•bro•sia /ambrózhə/ *n.* **1** (in Greek and Roman mythology) the food of the gods; the elixir of life. **2** anything very pleasing to taste or smell. **3** the food of certain bees and beetles. □□ **am•bro•sial** *adj.* **am•bro•sian** *adj.* [L f. Gk, = elixir of life f. *ambrotos* immortal]

am•bry var. of AUMBRY.

am•bu•lance /ámbyələns/ *n.* **1** a vehicle specially equipped for conveying the sick or injured to and from a hospital, esp. in emergencies. **2** *hist.* a mobile hospital following an army. [F (as AMBULANT)]

am•bu•lant /ámbyələnt/ *adj. Med.* **1** (of a patient) able to walk about; not confined to bed. **2** (of treatment) not confining a patient to bed. [L *ambulare ambulant-* walk]

am•bu•la•to•ry /ámbyələtawree/ *adj. & n.* •*adj.* **1** = AMBULANT. **2** of or adapted for walking. **3 a** movable. **b** not permanent. •*n.* (*pl.* •**ries**) a place for walking, esp. an aisle or cloister in a church or monastery. [L *ambulatorius* f. *ambulare* walk]

am•bus•cade /ámbəskáyd/ *n. & v.* •*n.* an ambush. •*v.* **1** *tr.* attack by means of an ambush. **2** *intr.* lie in ambush. **3** *tr.* conceal in an ambush. [F *embuscade* f. It. *imboscata* or Sp. *emboscada* f. L *imboscare*: see AMBUSH, –ADE[1]]

am•bush /ámboŏsh/ *n. & v.* •*n.* **1** a surprise attack by persons (e.g., troops) in a concealed position. **2 a** the concealment of troops, etc., to make such an attack. **b** the place where they are concealed. **c** the troops, etc., concealed. • *v.tr.* **1** attack by means of an ambush. **2** lie in wait for. [ME f. OF *embusche, embuschier*, f. a Rmc form = 'put in a wood': rel. to BUSH[1]]

a·me·ba var. of AMOEBA.

a·meer var. of EMIR.

a·mel·io·rate /əméelyərayt/ *v.tr. & intr.* make or become better; improve. □□ **a·mel·io·ra·tion** /-ráyshən/ *n.* **a·mel·io·ra·tive** *adj.* **a·mel·io·ra·tor** *n.* [alt. of MELIORATE after F *améliorer*]

a·men /aámén, áy-/ *int. & n.* • *int.* **1** uttered at the end of a prayer or hymn, etc., meaning 'so be it.' **2** (foll. by *to*) expressing agreement or assent (*amen to that*). • *n.* an utterance of 'amen' (sense 1). [ME f. eccl.L f. Gk f. Heb. 'āmēn certainly]

a·me·na·ble /əméenəbəl, əmén-/ *adj.* **1** responsive; tractable. **2** (often foll. by *to*) (of a person) responsible to law. **3** (foll. by *to*) (of a thing) subject or liable. □□ **a·me·na·bil·i·ty** /-bílitee/ *n.* **a·me·na·ble·ness** *n.* **a·me·na·bly** *adv.* [AF (Law) f. F *amener* bring to f. *a*- to + *mener* bring f. LL *minare* drive animals f. L *minari* threaten]

a·mend /əménd/ *v.tr.* **1** make minor improvements in (a text or a written proposal). **2** correct an error or errors in (a document). **3** make better; improve. **4** modify formally, as a legal document or legislative bill. □□ **a·mend·a·ble** *adj.* **a·mend·er** *n.* [ME f. OF *amender* ult. f. L *emendare* EMEND]

▶Amend is often confused with emend, which is a more technical word used in the context of textual correction.

a·mende ho·no·ra·ble /əménd ónərəbəl, amaáNd awnawraáblə/ *n.* (*pl.* **amendes honorables** *pronunc.* same) a public or open apology, often with some form of reparation. [F, = honorable reparation]

a·mend·ment /əméndmənt/ *n.* **1** a minor change in a document (esp. a legal or statutory one). **2** an article added to the US Constitution. [AMEND + -MENT]

a·mends /əméndz/ *n.* □ **make amends** (often foll. by *for*) compensate or make up (for). [ME f. OF *amendes* penalties, fine, pl. of *amende* reparation f. *amender* AMEND]

a·men·i·ty /əménitee, əmée-/ *n.* (*pl.* **·ties**) **1** (usu. in *pl.*) a pleasant or useful feature. **2** pleasantness (of a place, person, etc.). [ME f. OF *amenité* or L *amoenitas* f. *amoenus* pleasant]

a·men·or·rhe·a /aymếnəréeə/ *n.* (*Brit.* **amenorrhoea**) *Med.* an abnormal absence of menstruation. [A-[1] + MENO- + Gk -*rrhoia* f. *rheō* flow]

a·ment /əmént/ *n.* (also **amentum** /-təm/) (*pl.* **aments** or **amenta** /-tə/) a catkin. [L, = thong]

a·men·tia /əménshə/ *n. Med.* severe congenital mental deficiency. [L f. *amens ament-* mad (as A-[1],*mens* mind)]

Am·er·a·sian /aməráyzhən/ *n.* a person of American and Asian descent.

a·merce /əmə́rs/ *v.tr.* **1** *Law* punish by fine. **2** punish arbitrarily. □□ **a·merce·ment** *n.* **a·merce·a·ble** *adj.* [ME *amercy* f. AF *amercier* f. *a* at + *merci* MERCY]

A·mer·i·can /əmérikən/ *adj. & n.* • *adj.* **1** of, relating to, or characteristic of the United States or its inhabitants. **2** (usu. in *comb.*) of or relating to the continents of America (*Latin-American*). • *n.* **1** a native or citizen of the United States. **2** (usu. in *comb.*) a native or inhabitant of the continents of America (*North Americans*). **3** (also **A·mer·i·can Eng·lish**) the English language as it is used in the United States. [mod.L *Americanus* f. *America* f. Latinized name of *Amerigo* Vespucci, It. navigator d. 1512]

A·mer·i·ca·na /əmérikánə, -kaánə, -káynə/ *n.pl.* things connected with America, esp. with the United States.

A·mer·i·can dream *n.* the traditional social ideals of the American people, such as equality, democracy, and material prosperity.

A·mer·i·can In·di·an *n.* a member of the aboriginal peoples of America or their descendants.

▶See note at INDIAN.

A·mer·i·can·ism /əmérikənizəm/ *n.* **1 a** a word, sense, or phrase peculiar to or originating from the United States. **b** a thing or feature characteristic of or peculiar to the United States. **2** attachment to or sympathy for the United States.

A·mer·i·can·ize /əmérikənīz/ *v.* **1** *tr.* **a** make American in character. **b** naturalize as an American. **2** *intr.* become American in character. □□ **A·mer·i·can·i·za·tion** /-nizáyshən/ *n.*

A·mer·i·can Le·gion *n.* an association of US ex-servicemen formed in 1919.

am·er·i·ci·um /ámərísheeəm/ *n. Chem.* an artificially made transuranic radioactive metallic element. ¶ Symb.: Am. [*America* (where first made) + -IUM]

Am·er·in·di·an /áməríndeeən/ *adj. & n.* (also **Am·er·ind** /ámərínd/) = AMERICAN INDIAN. □□ **Am·er·in·dic** /-ríndik/ *adj.* [portmanteau word]

am·e·thyst /ámithist/ *n.* a precious stone of a violet or purple variety of quartz. □□ **am·e·thys·tine** /-thísteen/ *adj.* [ME f. OF *ametiste* f. L *amethystus* f. Gk *amethustos* not drunken, the stone being supposed to prevent intoxication]

Am·har·ic /amhárik/ *n. & adj.* • *n.* the official and commercial lan-

guage of Ethiopia. • *adj.* of this language. [*Amhara*, Ethiopian province + -IC]

a·mi·a·ble /áymeeəbəl/ *adj.* friendly and pleasant in temperament; likable. □□ **a·mi·a·bil·i·ty** /-bílitee/ *n.* **a·mi·a·ble·ness** *n.* **a·mi·a·bly** *adv.*

WORD HISTORY amiable

Late Middle English (originally in the senses 'kind,' and 'lovely, lovable'): via Old French from late Latin *amicabilis* 'amicable.' The current sense, influenced by modern French *aimable* 'trying to please,' dates from the mid-18th cent.

am·i·an·thus /ámee-ánthəs/ *n.* (also **amiantus** /-təs/) any fine silky-fibered variety of asbestos. [L f. Gk *amiantos* undefiled f. *a*- not + *miainō* defile, i.e. purified by fire, being incombustible: for -*h*- cf. AMARANTH]

am·i·ca·ble /ámikəbəl/ *adj.* showing or done in a friendly spirit (*an amicable meeting*). □□ **am·i·ca·bil·i·ty** /-bílitee/ *n.* **am·i·ca·ble·ness** *n.* **am·i·ca·bly** *adv.* [LL *amicabilis* f. *amicus* friend]

am·ice[1] /ámis/ *n.* a white linen cloth worn on the neck and shoulders by a priest celebrating the Eucharist. [ME f. med.L *amicia*, -*sia* (earlier *amit* f. OF), f. L *amictus* outer garment]

am·ice[2] /ámis/ *n.* a cap, hood, or cape worn by members of certain religious orders. [ME f. OF *aumusse* f. med.L *almucia*, etc., of unkn. orig.]

a·mi·cus cu·ri·ae /ameékəs kyə́oree-ee, kyə́oree-ī/ *n.* (*pl.* **amici curiae** /ameéki, -kee/) *Law* an impartial adviser in a court of law. [mod.L, = friend of the court]

a·mid /əmíd/ *prep.* **1** in the middle of. **2** in the course of. [ME *amidde(s)* f. OE *on* ON + MID[1]]

a·mide /áymīd, ám-/ *n. Chem.* a compound formed from ammonia by replacement of one (or sometimes more than one) hydrogen atom by a metal or an acyl radical. [AMMONIA + -IDE]

a·mid·ships /əmídships/ *adv.* (also **a·mid·ship**) in or into the middle of a ship. [MIDSHIP after AMID]

a·midst var. of AMID.

a·mi·go /əmeégō/ *n.* (*pl.* **·gos**) (often as a form of address) a friend or comrade, esp. in Spanish-speaking areas. [Sp.]

a·mine /əméen, ámeen/ *n. Chem.* a compound formed from ammonia by replacement of one or more hydrogen atoms by an organic radical or radicals. [AMMONIA + -INE[4]]

a·mi·no /əméenō/ *n.* (*attrib.*) *Chem.* of, relating to, or containing the monovalent group -NH_2. [AMINE]

a·mi·no ac·id /əméenō/ *n. Biochem.* any of a group of organic compounds containing both the carboxyl (COOH) and amino (NH_2) groups, occurring naturally in plant and animal tissues and forming the basic constituents of proteins. [AMINE + ACID]

a·mir var. of EMIR.

A·mish /aámish, ám-/ *adj. & n.* • *adj.* belonging to a strict Mennonite sect in the US. • *n.* a follower of this sect. [prob. f. G *Amisch* f. J. *Amen* 17th-c. Swiss preacher]

a·miss /əmís/ *predic.adj. & adv.* • *predic.adj.* wrong; out of order; faulty (*knew something was amiss*). • *adv.* wrong; wrongly; inappropriately (*everything went amiss*). □ **take amiss** be offended by (*took my words amiss*). [ME prob. f. ON *àmiss* so as to miss f. *àon* + *mis* rel. to MISS[1]]

am·i·to·sis /ámitósis/ *n. Biol.* a form of nuclear division that does not involve mitosis. [A-[1] + MITOSIS]

am·i·trip·ty·line /ámitríptileen/ *n. Pharm.* an antidepressant drug that has a mild tranquilizing action. [AMINE + TRI- + *heptyl* (see HEPTANE) + -INE[4]]

am·i·ty /ámitee/ *n.* friendship; friendly relations. [ME f. OF *amitié* ult. f. L *amicus* friend]

am·me·ter /ám-meetər/ *n.* an instrument for measuring electric current in amperes. [AMPERE + -METER]

am·mo /ámō/ *n. colloq.* ammunition. [abbr.]

am·mo·nia /əmónyə/ *n.* **1** a colorless strongly alkaline gas with a characteristic pungent smell. ¶ *Chem.* formula: NH_3. **2** (in full **ammonia water**) (in general use) a solution of ammonia gas in water. [mod.L f. SAL AMMONIAC]

am·mo·ni·a·cal /ámənīəkəl/ *adj.* of, relating to, or containing ammonia or sal ammoniac. [ME *ammoniac* f. OF (*arm-, amm-*) f. L f. Gk *ammōniakos* of Ammon (cf. SAL AMMONIAC) + -AL]

am·mo·ni·at·ed /əmóneeaytid/ *adj.* combined or treated with ammonia.

am·mo·nite /ámənīt/ *n.* any extinct cephalopod mollusk of the order Ammonoidea, with a flat coiled spiral shell found as a fossil. [mod.L *ammonites*, after med.L *cornu Ammonis*, = L *Ammonis cornu* (Pliny), horn of (Jupiter) Ammon]

am·mo·ni·um /əmóneeəm/ *n.* the univalent ion NH_4^+, formed from ammonia. [mod.L (as AMMONIA)]

am·mu·ni·tion /ámyəníshən/ *n.* **1** a supply of projectiles (esp. bullets, shells, and grenades). **2** points used or usable to advantage in an argument. [obs. F *amunition*, corrupt. of (*la*) *munition* (the) MUNITION]

am·ne·sia /amneeézhə/ *n.* a partial or total loss of memory. □□ **am·ne·si·ac** /–zeeak, –zheeak/ *n.* **am·ne·sic** *adj.* & *n.* [mod.L f. Gk, = forgetfulness]

am·nes·ty /ámnistee/ *n. & v.* ● *n.* (*pl.* **·ties**) a general pardon, esp. for political offenses. ● *v.tr.* (**·ties, ·tied**) grant an amnesty to. [F *amnestie* or L f. Gk *amnēstia* oblivion]

Am·nes·ty In·ter·na·tion·al *n.* an independent international organization in support of human rights, esp. for prisoners of conscience.

am·ni·o·cen·te·sis /ámneeōsenteésis/ *n.* (*pl.* **amniocenteses** /–seez/) *Med.* the sampling of amniotic fluid by insertion of a hollow needle to determine the sex of or certain abnormalities in an embryo. [AMNION + Gk *kentēsis* pricking f. *kentō* to prick]

am·ni·on /ámneeən/ *n.* (*pl.* **amnia**) *Zool. & Physiol.* the innermost membrane that encloses the embryo of a reptile, bird, or mammal. □□ **am·ni·ot·ic** /ámneeótik/ *adj.* [Gk, = caul (dimin. of *amnos* lamb)]

a·moe·ba /əmeébə/ *n.* (also **a·me·ba**) (*pl.* **amoebas** or **amoebae** /–bee/) any usu. aquatic protozoan of the genus *Amoeba*, esp. *A. proteus*, capable of changing shape. □□ **a·moe·bic** *adj.* **a·moe·boid** *adj.* [mod.L f. Gk *amoibē* change]

a·mok /əmúk, əmók/ *adv.* (also **a·muck** /əmúk/) □ **run amok** run about wildly in an uncontrollable violent rage. [Malay *amok* rushing in a frenzy]

a·mong /əmúng/ *prep.* (also esp. *Brit.* **amongst** /əmúngst/) **1** surrounded by; in the company of (*lived among the trees; be among friends*). **2** in the number of (*among us were those who disagreed*). **3** an example of; in the class or category of (*is among the richest men alive*). **4 a** between; within the limits of (collectively or distributively); shared by (*had $5 among us; divide it among you*). **b** by the joint action or from the joint resources of (*among us we can manage it*). **5** with one another; by the reciprocal action of (*was decided among the participants; talked among themselves*). **6** as distinguished from; preeminent in the category of (*she is one among many*). [OE *ongemang* f. ON *on* + *gemang* assemblage (cf. MINGLE): –*st* = adverbial genitive –*s* + –*t* as in AGAINST]
▶ See note at BETWEEN.

a·mon·til·la·do /əmóntiláadō, –tee-áadō/ *n.* (*pl.* **·dos**) a medium dry sherry. [Sp. f. *Montilla* in Spain + –*ado* = –ATE²]

a·mor·al /áymáwrəl, –mór–/ *adj.* **1** not concerned with or outside the scope of morality. **2** having no moral principles. □□ **a·mor·al·ism** *n.* **a·mor·al·ist** *n.* **a·mor·al·i·ty** /–rálitee/ *n.*
▶ See note at IMMORAL.

am·o·ret·to /ámərétō/ *n.* (*pl.* **amoretti** /–tee/) a Cupid. [It., dimin. of *amore* love f. L (as AMOUR)]

am·o·rist /ámərist/ *n.* a person who professes or writes of (esp. sexual) love. [L *amor* or F *amour* + –IST]

a·mo·ro·so¹ /ámərōsō/ *adv. & adj. Mus.* in a loving or tender manner. [It.]

a·mo·ro·so² /áamərōsō/ *n.* (*pl.* **·sos**) a full rich type of sherry. [Sp., = amorous]

am·o·rous /ámərəs/ *adj.* **1** showing, feeling, or inclined to sexual love. **2** of or relating to sexual love. □□ **am·o·rous·ly** *adv.* **am·o·rous·ness** *n.* [ME f. OF f. med.L *amorosus* f. L *amor* love]

a·mor·phous /əmáwrfəs/ *adj.* **1** shapeless. **2** vague; ill-organized; unclassifiable. **3** *Mineral. & Chem.* noncrystalline; having neither definite form nor structure. □□ **a·mor·phous·ly** *adv.* **a·mor·phous·ness** *n.* [med.L *amorphus* f. Gk *amorphos* shapeless f. *a*- not + *morphē* form]

am·or·tize /ámərtīz, əmáwr–/ *v.tr. Commerce* **1** gradually extinguish (a debt) by money regularly put aside. **2** gradually write off the initial cost of (assets). **3** transfer (land) to a corporation in mortmain. □□ **am·or·ti·za·tion** /–tizáyshən/ *n.* [ME f. OF *amortir* (stem *amortiss-*) ult. f. L *ad* to + *mors mort-* death]

a·mount /əmównt/ *n. & v.* ● *n.* **1** a quantity, esp. the total of a thing or things in number, size, value, extent, etc. (*a large amount of money; came to a considerable amount*). **2** the full effect or significance. ● *v.intr.* (foll. by *to*) **1** be equivalent to in number, size, significance, etc. (*amounted to $100; amounted to a disaster*). **2** (of a person) develop into; become (*might one day amount to something*). □ **any amount of** a great deal of. **no amount of** not even the greatest possible amount of. [ME f. OF *amunter* f. *amont* upward, lit. uphill, f. L *ad montem*]
▶ Use **amount** when talking about things that cannot be counted (*the recipe called for a large amount of sugar*). Use **number** when referring to things that can be counted (*he made a huge number of mistakes on his exam*).

a·mour /əmōōr/ *n.* a love affair, esp. a secret one. [F, = love, f. L *amor amoris*]

a·mour-pro·pre /áamōōrr práwprə/ *n.* self-respect. [F]

AMP *abbr.* adenosine monophosphate.

amp¹ /amp/ *n. Electr.* an ampere. [abbr.]

---

amp² /amp/ *n. colloq.* an amplifier. [abbr.]

am·pe·lop·sis /ámpilópsis/ *n.* (*pl.* same) any plant of the genus *Ampelopsis* or *Parthenocissus*, usu. a climber supporting itself by twining tendrils, e.g., Virginia creeper. [mod.L f. Gk *ampelos* vine + *opsis* appearance]

am·per·age /ámpərij/ *n. Electr.* the strength of an electric current in amperes.

am·pere /ámpeer/ *n. Electr.* the SI base unit of electric current. ¶ Symb.: A. [A. M. *Ampère*, Fr. physicist d. 1836]

am·per·sand /ámpərsand/ *n.* the sign & (= *and*). [corrupt. of *and per se and* ('&' by itself is 'and')]

am·phet·a·mine /amfétəmeen, –min/ *n.* a synthetic drug used esp. as a stimulant. [abbr. of chemical name *alpha methyl phenethylamine*]

amphi- /ámfee/ *comb. form* **1** both. **2** of both kinds. **3** on both sides. **4** around. [Gk]

am·phib·i·an /amfíbeeən/ *adj. & n.* ● *adj.* **1** living both on land and in water. **2** *Zool.* of or relating to the class Amphibia. **3** (of a vehicle) able to operate on land and water. ● *n.* **1** *Zool.* any vertebrate of the class Amphibia, with a life history of an aquatic gill-breathing larval stage followed by a terrestrial lung-breathing adult stage, including frogs, toads, newts, and salamanders. **2** (in general use) a creature living both on land and in water. **3** an amphibian vehicle.

WORD HISTORY   amphibian

Mid-17th cent. (in the sense 'having two modes of existence or of doubtful nature'): from modern Latin *amphibium* 'an amphibian,' from Greek *amphibion* (noun use of *amphibios* 'living both in water and on land,' from *amphi* 'both' + *bios* 'life').

am·phib·i·ous /amfíbeeəs/ *adj.* **1** living both on land and in water. **2** of or relating to or suited for both land and water. **3** *Mil.* **a** (of a military operation) involving forces landed from the sea. **b** (of forces) trained for such operations. **4** having a twofold nature; occupying two positions. □□ **am·phib·i·ous·ly** *adv.*

am·phi·bol·o·gy /ámfibóləjee/ *n.* (*pl.* **·gies**) **1** a quibble. **2** an ambiguous wording. [ME f. OF *amphibologie* f. LL *amphibologia* for L f. Gk *amphibolia* ambiguity]

am·phi·mix·is /ámfimíksis/ *n. Biol.* true sexual reproduction with the fusion of gametes from two individuals (cf. APOMIXIS). □□ **am·phi·mic·tic** /–míktik/ *adj.* [mod.L, formed as AMPHI- + Gk *mixis* mingling]

am·phi·ox·us /ámfeeóksəs/ *n.* any lancelet of the genus *Branchiostoma* (formerly *Amphioxus*). [mod.L, formed as AMPHI- + Gk *oxus* sharp]

am·phi·path·ic /ámfipáthik/ *adj. Chem.* **1** of a substance or molecule that has both a hydrophilic and a hydrophobic part. **2** consisting of such parts. [AMPHI- Gk *pathikos* (as PATHOS)]

am·phi·pod /ámfipod/ *n.* any crustacean of the largely marine order Amphipoda, having a laterally compressed abdomen with two kinds of limb, e.g., the freshwater shrimp (*Gammarus pulex*). [AMPHI- + Gk *pous podos* foot]

am·phi·pro·style /amfíprəstīl, amfipró–/ *n. & adj.* ● *n.* a classical building with a portico at each end. ● *adj.* of or in this style. [L *amphiprostylus* f. Gk *amphiprostulos* (as AMPHI-, *prostulos* PRO-² STYLE)]

am·phis·bae·na /ámfisbeénə/ *n.* **1** *Mythol. & poet.* a mythical serpent with a head at each end. **2** *Zool.* any burrowing wormlike lizard of the family Amphisbaena, having no apparent division of head from body, making both ends look similar. [ME f. L f. Gk *amphisbaina* f. *amphis* both ways + *bainō* go]

am·phi·the·a·ter /ámfitheeətər/ *n.* **1** a round, usu. unroofed building with tiers of seats surrounding a central space. **2** a semicircular gallery in a theater. **3** a large circular hollow. **4** the scene of a contest. [L *amphitheatrum* f. Gk *amphitheatron* (as AMPHI-, THEATER)]

am·pho·ra /ámfərə/ *n.* (*pl.* **amphorae** /–ree/ or **amphoras**) a Greek or Roman vessel with two handles and a narrow neck. [L f. Gk *amphoreus*]

am·pho·ter·ic /ámfətérik/ *adj. Chem.* able to react as a base and an acid. [Gk *amphoteros* compar. of *amphō* both]

am·pi·cil·lin /ámpisílin/ *n. Pharm.* a semisynthetic penicillin used esp. in treating infections of the urinary and respiratory tracts. [*amino* + *penicillin*]

am·ple /ámpəl/ *adj.* (**ampler, amplest**) **1 a** plentiful; abundant; extensive. **b** *euphem.* (esp. of a person) large; stout. **2** enough or more than enough. □□ **am·ple·ness** *n.* **am·ply** *adv.* [F f. L *amplus*]

am·pli·fi·er /ámplifīər/ *n.* an electronic device for increasing the strength of electrical signals, esp. for conversion into sound in radio, etc., equipment.

am·pli·fy /ámplifī/ *v.* (**·fies, ·fied**) **1** *tr.* increase the volume or strength of (sound, electrical signals, etc.). **2** *tr.* enlarge upon or add detail to (a story, etc.). **3** *intr.* expand what is said or written. □□ **am·pli·fi·ca·tion** /–fikáyshən/ *n.* [ME f. OF *amplifier* f. L *amplificare* (as AMPLE, –FY)]

am·pli·tude /ámplitōōd, –tyōōd/ *n.* **1 a** *Physics* the maximum extent of a vibration or oscillation from the position of equilibrium.

b *Electr.* the maximum departure of the value of an alternating current or wave from the average value. **2 a** spaciousness; breadth; wide range. **b** abundance. [F *amplitude* or L *amplitudo* (as AMPLE)]

am·pli·tude mod·u·la·tion *n.Electr.* **1** the modulation of a wave by variation of its amplitude. **2** the system using such modulation.

am·poule /ámpyōōl, –pōōl/ *n.* (also **am·pule** or **am·pul**) a small capsule in which measured quantities of liquids or solids, esp. for injecting, are sealed ready for use. [F f. L AMPULLA]

amp·ster /ámstər/ *n.* (also **amster**) *Austral. sl.* the accomplice of a sideshow operator who acts as a purchaser in an attempt to persuade others to follow his example. [f. *Amsterdam*, rhyming sl. for RAM *n.* 6]

am·pul·la /ampóōlə/ *n.* (*pl.* **ampullae** /–ee/) **1 a** a Roman globular flask with two handles. **b** a vessel for sacred uses. **2** *Anat.* the dilated end of a vessel or duct. [L]

am·pu·tate /ámpyətayt/ *v.tr.* cut off by surgical operation (a part of the body, esp. a limb), usu. because of injury or disease. □□ **am·pu·ta·tion** /–táyshən/ *n.* **am·pu·ta·tor** *n.* [L *amputare* f. *amb-* about + *putare* prune]

am·pu·tee /ámpyətée/ *n.* a person who has lost a limb, etc., by amputation.

am·trac /ámtrak/ *n.* (also **am·track**) an amphibious tracked vehicle used for landing assault troops on a shore. [*amphibious* + *tractor*]

Am·trak /ámtrak/ *n. Trademark* US passenger railroad system.

amu *abbr.* atomic mass unit.

a·muck var. of AMOK.

am·u·let /ámyəlit/ *n.* **1** an ornament or small piece of jewelry worn as a charm against evil. **2** something which is thought to give such protection. [L *amuletum*, of unkn. orig.]

a·muse /əmyóōz/ *v.* **1** *tr.* cause (a person) to laugh or smile. **2** *tr.* & *refl.* (often foll. by *with*, *by*) interest or occupy; keep (a person) entertained. □□ **a·mus·ing** *adj.* **a·mus·ing·ly** *adv.* [ME f. OF *amuser* cause to muse (see MUSE²) f. causal *a* to + *muser* stare]

a·muse·ment /əmyóōzmənt/ *n.* **1** something that amuses, esp. a pleasant diversion, game, or pastime. **2 a** the state of being amused. **b** the act of amusing. **3** *Brit.* a mechanical device (e.g., a merry-go-round) for entertainment at a fairground, etc. [F f. *amuser*: see AMUSE, –MENT]

a·muse·ment park *n.* a park with rides such as a merry-go-round, Ferris wheel, roller coaster, etc., and usu. booths with games of chance or skill, foods, etc.

a·myg·da·loid /əmígdəloyd/ *adj.* shaped like an almond. [L *amygdala* f. Gk *amugdalē* almond]

am·yl /ámil/ *n.* (used *attrib.*) *Chem.* the monovalent group C_5H_{11}–, derived from pentane. Also called **pentyl**. [L *amylum* starch, from which oil containing it was distilled]

am·yl·ase /ámilays, –layz/ *n. Biochem.* any of several enzymes that convert starch and glycogen into simple sugars. [AMYL + –ASE]

am·y·lop·sin /ámilópsin/ *n. Biochem.* an enzyme of the pancreas that converts starch into maltose. [AMYL after *pepsin*]

a·my·o·troph·ic lat·er·al scle·ro·sis /aymīətrófik, –tró–/ *n.* an incurable degenerative disease of the nervous system marked by increasing muscle weakness and eventual paralysis. Also called **Lou Gehrig's disease.** [A-¹ + MYO- + –TROPHIC]

Am·y·tal /ámitawl, –tal/ *n. Trademark* a trade name for amobarbital, a barbiturate drug used as a sedative and a hypnotic. [chem. name *amylethyl barbituric acid*]

an /an, ən/ *adj.* the form of the indefinite article (see A¹) used before words beginning with a vowel sound (*an egg*; *an hour*).
►Now less often used before aspirated words beginning with *h* and stressed on a syllable other than the first (so *a hotel*, not *an hotel*).

an-¹ /ən, an/ *prefix* not; without (*anarchy*) (cf. A-¹). [Gk *an-*]

an-² /ən, an/ assim. form of AD- before *n*.

-an /ən/ *suffix* (also **–ean**, **–ian**) forming adjectives and nouns, esp. from names of places, systems, zoological classes or orders, and founders (*Mexican*; *Anglican*; *crustacean*; *European*; *Lutheran*; *Georgian*; *theologian*). [ult. f. L adj. endings –(*i*)*anus*, *–aeus*: cf. Gk *–aios*, *–eios*]

an·a /áanə/ *n.* **1** (as *pl.*) anecdotes or literary gossip about a person. **2** (as *sing.*) a collection of a person's memorable sayings. [= –ANA]

ana- /ánə/ *prefix* (usu. **an-** before a vowel) **1** up (*anadromous*). **2** back (*anamnesis*). **3** again (*anabaptism*). [Gk *ana* up]

-ana /áanə, aánə, áynə/ *suffix* forming plural nouns meaning 'things associated with' (*Victoriana*; *Americana*). [neut. pl. of L adj. ending –*anus*]

An·a·bap·tism /ánəbáptizəm/ *n.* the doctrine that baptism should only be administered to believing adults. □□ **An·a·bap·tist** *n.* [eccl.L *anabaptismus* f. Gk *anabaptismos* (as ANA-, BAPTISM)]

an·a·bas /ánəbas/ *n.* any of the freshwater fish of the climbing perch family native to Asia and Africa, esp. the genus *Anabas*, able to breathe air and move on land. [mod.L f. Gk past part. of *anabainō* walk up]

a·nab·a·sis /ənábəsis/ *n.* (*pl.* **anabases** /–seez/) **1** a march from a coast into the interior, as that of the younger Cyrus into Asia in 401 BC narrated by Xenophon in his work *Anabasis*. **2** a military advance. [Gk, = ascent f. *anabainō* (as ANA-, *bainō* go)]

an·a·bat·ic /ánəbátik/ *adj. Meteorol.* (of a wind) caused by air flowing upwards (cf. KATABATIC). [Gk *anabatikos* ascending (as ANABASIS)]

an·a·bi·o·sis /ánəbīósis/ *n.* (*pl.* **anabioses** /–seez/) revival after apparent death. □□ **an·a·bi·ot·ic** /–bīótik/ *adj.* [med.L f. Gk *anabiōsis* f. *anabioō* return to life]

an·a·bol·ic /ánəbólik/ *adj. Biochem.* of or relating to anabolism.

an·a·bol·ic ste·roid *n.* any of a group of synthetic steroid hormones used to increase muscle size.

a·nab·o·lism /ənábəlizəm/ *n. Biochem.* the synthesis of complex molecules in living organisms from simpler ones together with the storage of energy; constructive metabolism (opp. CATABOLISM). [Gk *anabolē* ascent (as ANA-, *ballō* throw)]

an·a·branch /ánəbranch/ *n.* a stream that leaves a river and reenters it lower down. [ANASTOMOSE + BRANCH]

an·a·chron·ic /ánəkrónik/ *adj.* **1** out of date. **2** involving anachronism. [ANACHRONISM after *synchronic*, etc.]

a·nach·ro·nism /ənákrənizəm/ *n.* **1 a** the attribution of a custom, event, etc., to a period to which it does not belong. **b** a thing attributed in this way. **2 a** anything out of harmony with its period. **b** an old-fashioned or out-of-date person or thing. □□ **a·nach·ro·nis·tic** /–nístik/ *adj.* **a·nach·ro·nis·ti·cal·ly** *adv.* [F *anachronisme* or Gk *anakhronismos* (as ANA-, *khronos* time)]

an·a·co·lu·thon /ánəkəlóōthon/ *n.* (*pl.* **anacolutha** /–thə/) a sentence or construction that lacks grammatical sequence (e.g., *while in the garden the door banged shut*). □□ **an·a·co·lu·thic** *adj.* [LL f. Gk *anakolouthon* (as AN-¹, *akolouthos* following)]

an·a·con·da /ánəkóndə/ *n.* a large nonpoisonous snake living mainly in water or in trees that kills its prey by constriction. [alt. of *anacondaia* f. Sinh. *henakandayā* whipsnake f. *hena* lightning + *kanda* stem: orig. of a snake in Sri Lanka]

a·nac·re·on·tic /ənákree-óntik/ *n. & adj.* ● *n.* a poem written after the manner of Anacreon, a Greek lyric poet (d. 478 BC). ● *adj.* **1** after the manner of Anacreon. **2** convivial and amatory in tone. [LL *anacreonticus* f. Gk *Anakreōn*]

an·a·cru·sis /ánəkróōsis/ *n.* (*pl.* **anacruses** /–seez/) **1** (in poetry) an unstressed syllable at the beginning of a verse. **2** *Mus.* an unstressed note or notes before the first bar line. [Gk *anakrousis* (as ANA-, *krousis* f. *krouō* strike)]

a·nad·ro·mous /ənádrəməs/ *adj.* (of a fish, e.g., the salmon) that swims up a river from the sea to spawn (opp. CATADROMOUS). [Gk *anadromos* (as ANA-, *dromos* running)]

an·aer·obe /ánərōb, anáirōb/ *n.* an organism that grows without air, or requires oxygen-free conditions to live. □□ **an·aer·o·bic** *adj.* [F *anaérobie* formed as AN-¹ + AEROBE]

an·aes·the·sia *Brit.* var. of ANESTHESIA.

an·aes·thet·ic *Brit.* var. of ANESTHETIC.

an·aes·the·tist *Brit.* var. of ANESTHETIST.

an·aes·the·tize *Brit.* var. of ANESTHETIZE.

an·a·glyph /ánəglif/ *n.* **1** *Photog.* a composite stereoscopic photograph printed in superimposed complementary colors. **2** an embossed object cut in low relief. □□ **an·a·glyph·ic** /–glifik/ *adj.* [Gk *anagluphē* (as ANA-, f. *gluphō* carve)]

an·a·gram /ánəgram/ *n.* a word or phrase formed by transposing the letters of another word or phrase. □□ **an·a·gram·mat·ic** /–mátik/ *adj.* **an·a·gram·mat·i·cal** *adj.* **an·a·gram·ma·tize** /–grámətiz/ *v.tr.* [F *anagramme* or mod.L *anagramma* f. Gk ANA- + *gramma* –*atos* letter: cf. –GRAM]

a·nal /áynəl/ *adj.* **1** relating to or situated near the anus. **2** = ANAL RETENTIVE. □□ **a·nal·ly** *adv.* [mod.L *analis* (as ANUS)]

an·a·lects /ánəlekts/ *n.pl.* (also **analecta** /ánəléktə/) a collection of short literary extracts. [L f. Gk *analekta* things gathered f. *analegō* pick up]

an·a·lep·tic /ánəléptik/ *adj. & n.* ● *adj.* (of a drug, etc.) restorative; stimulating the central nervous system. ● *n.* a restorative medicine or drug. [Gk *analēptikos* f. *analambanō* take back]

an·al·ge·si·a /ánəljeezeeə, –seeə/ *n.* the absence or relief of pain. [mod.L f. Gk, = painlessness]

an·al·ge·sic /ánəljeezik, –sik/ *adj. & n.* ● *adj.* relieving pain. ● *n.* an analgesic drug.

an·a·log /ánəlog/ *n.* **1** an analogous or parallel thing. **2** (*attrib.*) (of a computer or electronic process) using physical variables, e.g., voltage, weight, or length, to represent numbers (cf. DIGITAL). [F f. Gk *analogon* neut. adj.: see ANALOGOUS]

a·nal·o·gize /ənáləjīz/ *v.* **1** *tr.* represent or explain by analogy. **2** *intr.* use analogy.

a·nal·o·gous /ənáləgəs/ *adj.* (usu. foll. by *to*) partially similar or parallel; showing analogy. □□ **a·nal·o·gous·ly** *adv.* [L *analogus* f. Gk *analogos* proportionate]

an·a·logue var. of ANALOG.

a·nal·o·gy /ənáləjee/ *n.* (*pl.* **·gies**) **1** (usu. foll. by *to*, *with*, *between*) correspondence or partial similarity. **2** *Logic* a process of arguing from similarity in known respects to similarity in other respects. **3** *Philol.* the imitation of existing words in forming inflections or constructions of others, without the existence of corresponding intermediate stages. **4** *Biol.* the resemblance of function between organs essentially different. **5 =** ANALOG 1. □□ **an‧a‧log‧i‧cal** /ánəlójikəl/ *adj.* **an‧a‧log‧i‧cal‧ly** *adv.* [F *analogie* or L *analogia* proportion f. Gk (as ANALOGOUS)]

a‧nal re‧ten‧tive *adj.* (of a person) excessively orderly and fussy (supposedly owing to aspects of toilet training in infancy).

a‧nal‧y‧sand /ənálisand/ *n.* a person undergoing psychoanalysis.

an‧a‧lyse *Brit.* var. of ANALYZE.

a‧nal‧y‧sis /ənálisis/ *n.* (*pl.* **analyses** /–seez/) **1 a** a detailed examination of the elements or structure of a substance, etc. **b** a statement of the result of this. **2 a** *Chem.* the determination of the constituent parts of a mixture or compound. **b** the act or process of breaking something down into its constituent parts. **3** psychoanalysis. **4** *Math.* the use of algebra and calculus in problem solving. □ **in the final** (or **last** or **ultimate**) **analysis** after all due consideration; in the end. [med.L f. Gk *analusis* (as ANA-, *luō* set free)]

an‧a‧lyst /ánəlist/ *n.* **1** a person skilled in (esp. chemical) analysis. **2** a psychoanalyst. [F *analyste*]

an‧a‧lyt‧ic /ánəlítik/ *adj.* **1** of or relating to analysis. **2** *Philol.* analytical. **3** *Logic* (of a statement, etc.) such that its denial is self-contradictory; true by definition (see SYNTHETIC). [LL f. Gk *analutikos* (as ANALYSIS)]

an‧a‧lyt‧i‧cal /ánəlítikəl/ *adj.* **1** using analytic methods. **2** *Philol.* using separate words instead of inflections (cf. SYNTHETIC). □ **analytical geometry** geometry using coordinates. □□ **an‧a‧lyt‧i‧cal‧ly** *adv.*

an‧a‧lyze /ánəlīz/ *v.tr.* **1** examine in detail the constitution or structure of. **2 a** *Chem.* ascertain the constituents of (a sample of a mixture or compound). **b** take apart; break (something) down into its constituent parts. **3** find or show the essence or structure of (a book, music, etc.). **4** *Gram.* resolve (a sentence) into its grammatical elements. **5** psychoanalyze. □□ **an‧a‧lyz‧a‧ble** *adj.* **an‧a‧lyz‧er** *n.* [obs. *analyse* (n.) or F *analyser* f. *analyse* (n.) f. med.L ANALYSIS]

an‧am‧ne‧sis /ánəmneésis/ *n.* (*pl.* **amnamneses** /–seez/) **1** recollection (esp. of a supposed previous existence). **2** a patient's account of his or her medical history. **3** *Eccl.* the part of the anaphora recalling the Passion, Resurrection, and Ascension of Christ. [Gk, = remembrance]

an‧an‧drous /ənándrəs/ *adj. Bot.* having no stamens. [Gk *anandros* without males f. *an-* not + *anēr andros* male]

A‧nan‧gu /áanaangoo/ *n.* (*pl.* **same**) *Austral.* an Aborigine, esp. one from Central Australia. [Western Desert language, = person]

an‧a‧pest /ánəpest/ *n. Prosody* a foot consisting of two short or unstressed syllables followed by one long or stressed syllable. □□ **an‧a‧pes‧tic** /–péstik/ *adj.* [L *anapaestus* f. Gk *anapaistos* reversed (because the reverse of a dactyl)]

an‧a‧phase /ánəfayz/ *n. Biol.* the stage of meiotic or mitotic cell division when the chromosomes move away from one another to opposite poles of the spindle. [ANA- + PHASE]

a‧naph‧o‧ra /ənáfərə/ *n.* **1** *Rhet.* the repetition of a word or phrase at the beginning of successive clauses. **2** *Gram.* the use of a word referring to or replacing a word used earlier in a sentence, to avoid repetition (e.g., *do* in *I like it and so do they*). **3** *Eccl.* the part of the Eucharist which contains the consecration, anamnesis, and communion. □□ **an‧a‧phor‧ic** /ánəfórik/ *adj.* [L f. Gk, = repetition (as ANA-, *pherō* to bear)]

an‧aph‧ro‧dis‧i‧ac /ánáfrədeézeeak, –díz–/ *adj. & n.* ● *adj.* tending to reduce sexual desire. ● *n.* an anaphrodisiac drug.

an‧a‧phy‧lax‧is /ánəfiláksis/ *n.* (*pl.* **anaphylaxes** /–seez/) *Med.* hypersensitivity of tissues to a dose of antigen, as a reaction against a previous dose. □□ **an‧a‧phy‧lac‧tic** /–láktik/ *adj.* [mod.L f. F *anaphylaxie* (as ANA- + Gk *phulaxis* guarding)]

an‧ap‧tyx‧is /ánəptíksis/ *n.* (*pl.* **anaptyxes** /–seez/) *Phonet.* the insertion of a vowel between two consonants to aid pronunciation (as in *went thataway*). □□ **an‧ap‧tyc‧tic** /–tíktik/ *adj.* [mod.L f. Gk *anaptuxis* (as ANA-, *ptussō* fold)]

an‧ar‧chism /ánərkizəm/ *n.* the doctrine that all government should be abolished. [F *anarchisme* (as ANARCHY)]

an‧ar‧chist /ánərkist/ *n.* an advocate of anarchism or of political disorder. □□ **an‧ar‧chis‧tic** *adj.* [F *anarchiste* (as ANARCHY)]

an‧ar‧chy /ánərkee/ *n.* **1** disorder, esp. political or social. **2** lack of government in a society. □□ **an‧ar‧chic** /ənáarkik/ *adj.* **an‧ar‧chi‧cal** *adj.* **an‧ar‧chi‧cal‧ly** *adv.* [med.L f. Gk *anarkhia* (as AN-[1], *arkhē* rule)]

A‧na‧sa‧zi /onəsáazee/ *n.* **1 a** a prehistoric N. American people native to the southwestern US. **b** a member of this people. **2** the language of this people.

an‧as‧tig‧mat /ənástigmat/ *n.* a lens or system of lenses made free from astigmatism by correction. [G f. *anastigmatisch* ANASTIGMATIC]

an‧as‧tig‧mat‧ic /ánəstigmátik/ *adj.* free from astigmatism.

a‧nas‧to‧mose /ənástəmōz, –mōs/ *v.intr.* link by anastomosis. [F *anastomoser* (as ANASTOMOSIS)]

a‧nas‧to‧mo‧sis /ənástəmósis/ *n.* (*pl.* **anastomoses** /–seez/) a cross-connection of arteries, branches, rivers, etc. [mod.L f. Gk f. *anastomoō* furnish with a mouth (as ANA-, *stoma* mouth)]

a‧nas‧tro‧phe /ənástrəfee/ *n. Rhet.* the inversion of the usual order of words or clauses. [Gk *anastrophē* turning back (as ANA-, *strephō* to turn)]

anat. *abbr.* **1** anatomical. **2** anatomy.

a‧nath‧e‧ma /ənáthəmə/ *n.* (*pl.* **anathemas**) **1** a detested thing or person (*is anathema to me*). **2 a** an ecclesiastical curse, excommunicating a person or denouncing a doctrine. **b** a cursed thing or person. **c** a strong curse. [eccl.L, = excommunicated person, excommunication, f. Gk *anathema* thing devoted, (later) accursed thing, f. *anatithēmi* set up]

a‧nath‧e‧ma‧tize /ənáthəmətīz/ *v.tr. & intr.* curse. [F *anathématiser* f. L *anathematīzāre* f. Gk *anathematizo* (as ANATHEMA)]

an‧a‧tom‧i‧cal /ánətómikəl/ *adj.* **1** of or relating to anatomy. **2** structural. □□ **an‧a‧tom‧i‧cal‧ly** *adv.* [F *anatomique* or LL *anatomicus* (as ANATOMY)]

a‧nat‧o‧mist /ənátəmist/ *n.* a person skilled in anatomy. [F *anatomiste* or med.L *anatomista* (as ANATOMIZE)]

a‧nat‧o‧mize /ənátəmīz/ *v.tr.* **1** examine in detail. **2** dissect. [F *anatomiser* or med.L *anatomizare* f. *anatomia* (as ANATOMY)]

a‧nat‧o‧my /ənátəmee/ *n.* (*pl.* **‧mies**) **1** the science of the bodily structure of animals and plants. **2** this structure. **3** *colloq.* a human body. **4** analysis. **5** the dissection of the human body, animals, or plants. [F *anatomie* or LL *anatomia* f. Gk (as ANA-, –TOMY)]

a‧nat‧ta (also **a‧nat‧to**) var. of ANNATTO.

ANC *abbr.* African National Congress.

-ance /əns/ *suffix* forming nouns expressing: **1** a quality or state or an instance of one (*arrogance; protuberance; relevance; resemblance*). **2** an action (*assistance; furtherance; penance*). [from or after F *–ance* f. L *–antia, –entia* (cf. *–*ENCE) f. pres. part. stem *–ant-, –ent–*]

an‧ces‧tor /ánsestər/ *n.* (*fem.* **ancestress** /–stris/) **1** any (esp. remote) person from whom one is descended. **2** an early type of animal or plant from which others have evolved. **3** an early prototype or forerunner (*ancestor of the computer*). [ME f. OF *ancestre* f. L *antecessor –oris* f. *antecedere* (as ANTE-, *cedere cess-* go)]

an‧ces‧tral /anséstrəl/ *adj.* belonging to or inherited from one's ancestors. [F *ancestrel* (as ANCESTOR)]

an‧ces‧try /ánsestree/ *n.* (*pl.* **‧tries**) **1** one's (esp. remote) family descent. **2** one's ancestors collectively. [ME alt. of OF *ancesserie* (as ANCESTOR)]

an‧chor /ángkər/ *n. & v.* ● *n.* **1** a heavy metal weight used to moor a ship to the seafloor or a balloon to the ground. **2 a** a thing affording stability. **3** a source of confidence. **4** (in full **anchorman, anchorperson, anchorwoman**) **a** a person who plays a vital part, as the end member of a tug-of-war team, the last member of a relay team, etc. **b** a news broadcaster who introduces segments and reads the main portion of the news. ● *v.* **1** *tr.* secure (a ship or balloon) by means of an anchor. **2** *tr.* fix firmly. **3** *intr.* cast anchor. **4** *intr.* be moored by means of an anchor. □ **at anchor** moored by means of an anchor. **cast** (or **come to**) **anchor** let the anchor down. **weigh anchor** take the anchor up. [OE *ancor* f. L *anchora* f. Gk *agkura*]

anchor with arm and flukes   mushroom anchor

anchor, 1

an‧chor‧age /ángkərij/ *n.* **1** a place where a ship may be anchored. **2** the act of anchoring or lying at anchor. **3** anything dependable.

an‧cho‧rite /ángkərīt/ *n.* (also **anchoret** /–rit/) (*fem.* **an‧cho‧ress** /–ris/) **1** a hermit; a religious recluse. **2** a person of secluded habits. □□ **an‧cho‧ret‧ic** /–rétik/ *adj.* **an‧cho‧rit‧ic** /–rítik/ *adj.* [ME f. med.L *anc(h) orita,* eccl.L *anchoreta* f. eccl.Gk *anakhōrētēs* f. *anakhōreō* retire]

an‧chor light *n.* a light shown by a ship at anchor.

an‧chor‧man /ángkərmən/ *n.* (*pl.* **‧men**) = ANCHOR *n.* 4.

an‧cho‧vet‧a /ánchəvétə/ *n.* (also **anchoveta**) a small Pacific anchovy caught for use as bait or to make fishmeal. [Sp., dimin. of *anchova*: cf. ANCHOVY]

an‧cho‧vy /ánchóvee/ *n.* (*pl.* **‧vies**) any of various small silvery fish of the herring family usu. preserved in salt and oil and having a strong taste. [Sp. &Port. *ancho(v)a*, of uncert. orig.]

an•cho•vy pear *n.* a W. Indian fruit like a mango.

an•chu•sa /ankyŏoz, anchŏoz/ *n.* any plant of the genus *Anchusa*, akin to borage. [L f. Gk *agkhousa*]

an•chy•lose var. of ANKYLOSE.

an•chy•lo•sis var. of ANKYLOSIS.

an•cien ré•gime /onsyán rezheém/ *n.* (*pl.* **anciens régimes** pronunc. same) **1** the political and social system in France before the Revolution of 1789. **2** any superseded regime. [F, = old rule]

an•cient[1] /áynshənt/ *adj. & n.* ● *adj.* **1** of long ago. **2** having lived or existed long. ● *n. archaic* **1** an old man. **2** (**ancients**) the people of ancient civilizations and cultures, esp. those of ancient Greece and Rome. □□ **an•cient•ness** *n.* [ME f. AF *auncien* f. OF *ancien*, ult. f. L *ante* before]

an•cient[2] /áynshənt/ *n. archaic* = ENSIGN. [corrupt. of form *ensyne*, etc., by assoc. with *ancien* = ANCIENT[1]]

an•cient his•to•ry *n.* **1** the history of the ancient civilizations of the Mediterranean area and the Near East before the fall of the Western Roman Empire in A.D. 476. **2** something already long familiar.

an•cient•ly /áynshəntlee/ *adv.* long ago.

an•cil•lar•y /ánsəleree/ *adj. & n.* ● *adj.* **1** (of a person, activity, or service) providing essential support to a central service or industry, esp. the medical service. **2** (often foll. by *to*) subordinate; subservient. ● *n.* (*pl.* **-ies**) **1** an ancillary worker. **2** something which is ancillary; an auxiliary or accessory. [L *ancillaris* f. *ancilla* maidservant]

an•con /ángkən/ *n.* (*pl.* **-nes** /angkóneez/) *Archit.* **1** a console, usu. of two volutes, supporting or appearing to support a cornice. **2** each of a pair of projections on either side of a block of stone, etc., for lifting or repositioning. [L f. Gk *agkōn* elbow]

-ancy /ənsee/ *suffix* forming nouns denoting a quality (*constancy; relevancy*) or state (*expectancy; infancy*) (cf. –ANCE). [from or after L *-antia*: cf. –ENCY]

and /and, ənd/ *conj.* **1 a** connecting words, clauses, or sentences, that are to be taken jointly (*cakes and pastries; white and brown bread; buy and sell; two hundred and forty*). **b** implying progression (*better and better*). **c** implying causation (*do that and I'll hit you; she hit him and he cried*). **d** implying great duration (*he cried and cried*). **e** implying a great number (*miles and miles*). **f** implying addition (*two and two are four*). **g** implying variety (*there are books and books*). **h** implying succession (*walking two and two*). **2** *colloq.* to (*try and open it*). **3** in relation to (*Britain and the US*). [OE *and*]

-and /and/ *suffix* forming nouns meaning 'a person or thing to be treated in a specified way' (*ordinand*). [L gerundive ending *-andus*]

an•dan•te /aandáantay, andánté/ *adv., adj., & n. Mus.* ● *adv. & adj.* in a moderately slow tempo. ● *n.* an andante passage or movement. [It., part. of *andare* go]

an•dan•ti•no /áandaanteénō, ándan–/ *adv., adj., & n. Mus.* ● *adv. & adj.* somewhat quicker (orig. slower) than andante. ● *n.* (*pl.* **-nos**) an andantino passage or movement. [It., dimin. of ANDANTE]

an•des•ite /ándizít/ *n.* a fine-grained brown or grayish intermediate volcanic rock. [*Andes* mountain chain in S. America + –ITE[1]]

and•i•ron /ándīrn/ *n.* a metal stand (usu. one of a pair) for supporting burning wood in a fireplace; a firedog. [ME f. OF *andier*, of unkn. orig.: assim. to IRON]

and/or *conj.* either or both of two stated possibilities (usually restricted to legal and commercial use).

an•droe•ci•um /andreéseeəm/ *n.* (*pl.* **androecia** –seeə/) *Bot.* the stamens taken collectively. [mod.L f. Gk *andro-* male + *oikion* house]

andirons

an•dro•gen /ándrəjən/ *n.* a male sex hormone or other substance capable of developing and maintaining certain male sexual characteristics. □□ **an•dro•gen•ic** /–jénik/ *adj.* [Gk *andro-* male + –GEN]

an•dro•gyne /ándrəjīn/ *adj. & n.* ● *adj.* hermaphrodite. ● *n.* a hermaphroditic person. [OF *androgyne* or L *androgynus* f. Gk *androgunos* (*anēr andros* male, *gunē* woman)]

an•drog•y•nous /andrójinəs/ *adj.* **1** hermaphroditic. **2** not clearly male or female; exhibiting the appearance or attributes of both sexes. **3** *Bot.* with stamens and pistils in the same flower or inflorescence.

an•drog•y•ny /andrójinee/ *n.* hermaphroditism.

an•droid /ándroyd/ *n.* a robot with a human form or appearance. [Gk *andro-* male, man + –OID]

-androus /ándrəs/ *comb. form Bot.* forming adjectives meaning 'having specified male organs or stamens' (*monandrous*). [mod.L f. Gk *–andros* f. *anēr andros* male + –OUS]

-ane[1] /ayn/ *suffix* var. of –AN; usu. with distinction of sense (*germane; humane; urbane*) but sometimes with no corresponding form in *-an* (*mundane*).

-ane[2] /ayn/ *suffix Chem.* forming names of saturated hydrocarbons (*methane; propane*). [after *-ene, -ine*, etc.]

an•ec•dot•age /ánikdótij/ *n.* **1** *joc.* garrulous old age. **2** anecdotes. [ANECDOTE + –AGE: sense 1 after DOTAGE]

an•ec•dote /ánikdōt/ *n.* a short account (or painting, etc.) of an entertaining or interesting incident. □□ **an•ec•do•tal** /–dōt'l/ *adj.* **an•ec•do•tal•ist** /–dōt'list/ *n.* **an•ec•dot•ic** /–dótik/ *adj.* **an•ec•dot•ist** *n.* [F *anecdote* or mod.L f. Gk *anekdota* things unpublished (as AN-[1], *ekdotos* f. *ekdidōmi* publish)]

an•e•cho•ic /ánikóik/ *adj.* free from echo.

a•ne•mi•a /əneémeeə/ *n.* a deficiency in the blood, usu. of red cells or their hemoglobin, resulting in pallor and weariness. [mod.L f. Gk *anaimia* (as AN-[1], –AEMIA)]

a•ne•mic /əneémik/ *adj.* **1** relating to or suffering from anemia. **2** pale; lacking in vitality.

a•nem•o•graph /ənéməgraf/ *n.* an instrument for recording on paper the direction and force of the wind. □□ **a•nem•o•graph•ic** /–gráfik/ *adj.* [Gk *anemos* wind + –GRAPH]

an•e•mom•e•ter /ánimómitər/ *n.* an instrument for measuring the force of the wind. [Gk *anemos* wind + –METER]

an•e•mom•e•try /ánimómitree/ *n.* the measurement of the force, direction, etc., of the wind. □□ **an•e•mo•met•ric** /–məmétrik/ *adj.* [Gk *anemos* wind + –METRY]

a•nem•o•ne /ənémənee/ *n.* **1** any plant of the genus *Anemone*, akin to the buttercup, with flowers of various vivid colors. **2** = PASQUEFLOWER. [L f. Gk *anemōnē* wind flower f. *anemos* wind]

a•ne•moph•i•lous /ánimófiləs/ *adj.* wind-pollinated. [Gk *anemos* wind + –*philous* (see –PHILIA)]

a•nent /ənént/ *prep.* concerning. [OE *on efen* on a level with]

-aneous /áyneeəs/ *suffix* forming adjectives (*cutaneous; miscellaneous*). [L *–aneus* + –OUS]

an•er•oid /ánəroyd/ *adj. & n.* ● *adj.* (of a barometer) that measures air pressure by its action on the elastic lid of an evacuated box, not by the height of a column of fluid. ● *n.* an aneroid barometer. [F *anéroïde* f. Gk *a-* not + *nēros* water]

an•es•the•sia /ánis-theézhə/ *n.* the absence of sensation, esp. artificially induced insensitivity to pain usu. achieved by the administration of gases or the injection of drugs. □□ **an•es•the•si•ol•o•gy** /–zeeóləjee/ *n.* [mod.L f. Gk *anaisthēsia* (as AN-[1], *aisthēsis* sensation)]

an•es•thet•ic /ánis-thétik/ *adj. & n.* ● *n.* a substance that produces insensibility to pain, etc. ● *adj.* producing partial or complete insensibility to pain, etc. [Gk *anaisthētos* insensible (as ANESTHESIA)]

an•es•the•tist /ənés-thətist/ *n.* a specialist in the administration of anesthetics.

an•es•the•tize /ənés-thətīz/ *v.tr.* **1** administer an anesthetic to. **2** deprive of physical or mental sensation. □□ **an•es•the•ti•za•tion** /–tizáyshən/ *n.*

an•eu•rin /ányərin/ *n.* = THIAMINE. [*anti* + poly*neur*itis + vitam*in*]

an•eu•rysm /ányərizəm/ *n.* (also **an•eu•rism**) an excessive localized enlargement of an artery. □□ **an•eu•rys•mal** /–rízməl/ *adj.* (also **an•eu•ris•mal**). [Gk *aneurusma* f. *aneurunō* widen out f. *eurus* wide]

a•new /ənŏo, ənyŏo/ *adv.* **1** again. **2** in a different way. [ME, f. A-[4] + NEW]

an•frac•tu•os•i•ty /anfrákchŏo-ósitee/ *n.* **1** circuitousness. **2** intricacy. [F *anfractuosité* f. LL *anfractuosus* f. L *anfractus* a bending]

an•frac•tu•ous /anfrákchŏoəs/ *adj.* winding; sinuous; roundabout; circuitous. [f. late L *anfractuosus*, f. L *anfractus* a bending]

an•ga•ry /ánggəree/ *n. Law* the right of a belligerent (subject to compensation for loss) to seize or destroy neutral property under military necessity. [F *angarie* ult. f. Gk *aggareia* f. *aggaros* courier]

an•gel /áynjəl/ *n.* **1 a** an attendant or messenger of God. **b** a conventional representation of this in human form with wings. **c** an attendant spirit (*evil angel; guardian angel*). **d** a member of the lowest order of the ninefold celestial hierarchy (see ORDER). **2 a** a very virtuous person. **b** an obliging person (*be an angel and answer the door*). **3** *Brit.* an old English coin bearing the figure of the archangel Michael piercing the dragon. **4** *sl.* a financial backer of an enterprise, esp. in the theater. **5** an unexplained radar echo. [ME f. OF *angele* f. eccl.L *angelus* f. Gk *aggelos* messenger]

an•gel dust *n. sl.* the hallucinogenic drug phencyclidine hydrochloride.

an•gel•fish /áynjəlfish/ *n.* any of various fish, esp. *Pterophyllum scalare*, with large dorsal and ventral fins.

an•gel food cake *n.* (also *Brit.* **angel cake**) a very light sponge cake.

an•gel•ic /anjélik/ *adj.* **1** like or relating to angels. **2** having characteristics attributed to angels, esp. sublime beauty or innocence. □□ **an•gel•i•cal** *adj.* **an•gel•i•cal•ly** *adv.* [ME f. F *angélique* or LL *angelicus* f. Gk *aggelikos* (as ANGEL)]

an•gel•i•ca /anjélikə/ *n.* **1** an aromatic umbelliferous plant, *Angelica archangelica*, used in cooking and medicine. **2** its candied stalks. [med.L (*herba*) *angelica* angelic herb]

an•gel shark *n.* a bottom-dwelling cartilaginous fish of the genus *Squatina*, with broad winglike pectoral fins.

an•ge•lus /ánjiləs/ *n.* **1** a Roman Catholic devotion commemorating the Incarnation, said at morning, noon, and sunset. **2** a bell rung to announce this. [opening words *Angelus domini* (L, = the angel of the Lord)]

an•ger /ánggər/ *n. & v.* ● *n.* extreme or passionate displeasure. ● *v.tr.* make angry; enrage. [ME f. ON *angr* grief, *angra* vex]

An•ge•vin /ánjivin/ *n. & adj.* ● *n.* **1** a native or inhabitant of the Anjou region of France. **2** a Plantagenet, esp. any of the English kings from Henry II to John. ● *adj.* **1** of Anjou. **2** of the Plantagenets. [F]

an•gi•na /anjínə, ánjənə/ *n.* **1** an attack of intense constricting pain often causing suffocation. **2** (in full **angina pectoris** /péktəris/) pain in the chest brought on by exertion, owing to an inadequate blood supply to the heart. [L, = spasm of the chest f. *angina* quinsy f. Gk *agkhonē* strangling]

an•gi•o•gram /ánjeəgram/ *n.* an X-ray taken by angiography. [Gk *aggeion* vessel + –GRAM]

an•gi•og•ra•phy /anjeeágrəfee/ *n.* the visualization by X-ray of blood vessels following injection with a substance that is radiopaque. [Gk *aggeion* vessel + –GRAPHY]

an•gi•o•ma /ánjeeómə/ *n.* (*pl.* **angiomata** /–mətə/) a tumor produced by the dilatation or new formation of blood vessels. [mod.L f. Gk *aggeion* vessel]

an•gi•o•plas•ty /ánjeeəplastee/ *n.* surgical repair or unblocking of a blood vessel, especially a coronary artery.

an•gi•o•sperm /ánjeeəspərm/ *n.* any plant producing flowers and reproducing by seeds enclosed within a carpel, including herbaceous plants, herbs, shrubs, grasses, and most trees (opp. GYMNOSPERM). □□ **an•gi•o•sper•mous** /–spɔ́rməs/ *adj.* [Gk *aggeion* vessel + *sperma* seed]

An•gle /ánggəl/ *n.* (usu. in *pl.*) a member of a tribe from Schleswig, Germany, that settled in Eastern Britain in the 5th c. □□ **An•gli•an** *adj.* [L *Anglus* f. Gmc (OE *Engle*: cf. ENGLISH) f. *Angul* a district of Schleswig (now in N. Germany) (as ANGLE²)]

an•gle¹ /ánggəl/ *n. & v.* ● *n.* **1 a** the space between two meeting lines or surfaces. **b** the inclination of two lines or surfaces to each other. **2 a** a corner. **b** a sharp projection. **3 a** the direction from which a photograph, etc., is taken. **b** the aspect from which a matter is considered. **c** an approach, technique, etc. ● *v.* **1** *tr. & intr.* move or place obliquely; point in a particular direction. **2** *tr.* present (information) from a particular point of view (*was angled in favor of the victim*). [ME f. OF *angle* or f. L *angulus*]

an•gle² /ánggəl/ *v. & n.* ● *v.intr.* **1** (often foll. by *for*) fish with hook and line. **2** (foll. by *for*) seek an objective by devious or calculated means (*angled for a pay raise*). ● *n. archaic* a fishhook. [OE *angul*]

an•gle brack•ets *n.* brackets in the form < > (see BRACKET *n.* 3).

an•gled /ánggəld/ *adj.* **1** placed at an angle to something else. **2** presented to suit a particular point of view. **3** having an angle.

an•gle i•ron *n.* a piece of iron or steel with an L-shaped cross section, used to strengthen a framework.

acute

right

obtuse

angles

an•gle of in•ci•dence *n.* the angle which an incident line, ray, etc., makes with the perpendicular to the surface at the point of incidence.

an•gle of re•flec•tion *n. Physics* the angle made by a reflected ray with a perpendicular to the reflecting surface.

an•gle of re•frac•tion *n.* the angle made by a refracted ray with the perpendicular to the refracting surface.

an•gle of re•pose *n.* the angle beyond which an inclined body will not support another on its surface by friction.

an•gler /ánggl̇ər/ *n.* **1** a person who fishes with a hook and line. **2** = ANGLERFISH.

an•gler•fish /ánggl̇ərfish/ *n.* any of various fishes that prey upon small fish, attracting them by filaments arising from the dorsal fin. Also called **frogfish**.

An•gli•can /ánggl̇ikən/ *adj. & n.* ● *adj.* of or relating to the Church of England or any Church in communion with it. ● *n.* a member of an Anglican Church. □□ **An•gli•can•ism** *n.* [med.L *Anglicanus* (Magna Carta) f. *Anglicus* (Bede) f. *Anglus* ANGLE]

an•gli•ce /ángglisee/ *adv.* in English. [med.L]

An•gli•cism /ángglisizəm/ *n.* **1** a peculiarly English word or custom. **2** Englishness. **3** preference for what is English. [L *Anglicus* (see ANGLICAN) + –ISM]

An•gli•cist /ángglɔsist/ *n.* a student of or scholar in English language or literature. □□ **Ang•lis•tics** /angglístiks/ *n.* [G f. L *Anglus* English]

An•gli•cize /ángglisīz/ *v.tr.* **1** make English in form or character. **2** (**anglicize**) adopt (a foreign word) into English.

An•glist /ángglist/ var. of ANGLICIST.

An•glo /ánggl̇ō/ *n.* (*pl.* **–glos**) **1** a person of British or northern European origin. **2** a white, English-speaking person not of Hispanic descent. [abbr. of ANGLO-SAXON]

Anglo- /ánggl̇ō/ *comb. form* **1** English (*Anglo-Catholic*). **2** of English origin (*an Anglo-American*). **3** English or British and (*an Anglo-American agreement*). [f. mod.L f. L *Anglus* English]

An•glo-Cath•o•lic /ánggl̇ōkáthəlik, –káthlik/ *adj. & n.* ● *adj.* of a High Church Anglican group that emphasizes its Roman Catholic tradition. ● *n.* a member of this group.

An•glo•cen•tric /ánggl̇ōséntrik/ *adj.* centered on or considered in terms of England.

An•glo-French /ánggl̇ōfrénch/ *adj. & n.* ● *adj.* **1** English (or British) and French. **2** of Anglo-French. ● *n.* the French language as retained and separately developed in England after the Norman Conquest.

An•glo-In•di•an /ánggl̇ō-índeeən/ *adj. & n.* ● *adj.* **1** of or relating to England and India. **2 a** of British descent or birth but living or having lived long in India. **b** of mixed British and Indian parentage. **3** (of a word) adopted into English from an Indian language. ● *n.* an Anglo-Indian person.

An•glo-Lat•in /ánggl̇ōlát'n/ *adj. & n.* ● *adj.* of Latin as used in medieval England. ● *n.* this form of Latin.

An•glo•ma•ni•a /ánggl̇ōmáyneeə/ *n.* excessive admiration of English customs.

An•glo-Nor•man /ánggl̇ōnáwrmən/ *adj. & n.* ● *adj.* **1** English and Norman. **2** of the Normans in England after the Norman Conquest. **3** of the dialect of French used by them. ● *n.* the Anglo-Norman dialect.

An•glo•phile /ánggl̇əfīl/ *n. & adj.* (also **An•glo•phil** /–fil/) ● *n.* a person who is fond of or greatly admires England or the English. ● *adj.* being or characteristic of an Anglophile.

An•glo•phobe /ánggl̇əfōb/ *n. & adj.* ● *n.* a person who greatly hates or fears England or the English. ● *adj.* being or characteristic of an Anglophobe.

An•glo•pho•bi•a /ánggl̇əfóbeeə/ *n.* intense hatred or fear of England or the English.

an•glo•phone /ánggl̇əfōn/ *adj. & n.* ● *adj.* English-speaking. ● *n.* an English-speaking person. [ANGLO-, after FRANCOPHONE]

An•glo-Sax•on /ánggl̇ōsáksən/ *adj. & n.* ● *adj.* **1** of the English Saxons (as distinct from the Old Saxons of the European continent, and from the Angles) before the Norman Conquest. **2** of the Old English people as a whole before the Norman Conquest. **3** of English descent. ● *n.* **1** an Anglo-saxon person. **2** the Old English language. **3** *colloq.* plain (esp. crude) English. [mod.L *Anglo-Saxones*, med.L *Angli Saxones* after OE *Angulseaxe*, *–an*]

an•go•ra /anggáwrə/ *n.* **1** a fabric made from the hair of the angora goat or rabbit. **2** a long-haired variety of cat, goat, or rabbit. [*Angora* (Ankara) in Turkey]

an•go•ra wool *n.* a mixture of sheep's wool and angora rabbit hair.

an•gos•tu•ra /ánggəstŏŏrə, –styŏŏrə/ *n.* (in full **angostura bark**) an aromatic bitter bark used as a flavoring, and formerly used as a medicinal tonic and to reduce fever. [*Angostura*, a town in Venezuela on the Orinoco, now Ciudad Bolívar]

An•gos•tu•ra Bit•ters *n. Trademark* a kind of tonic first made in Angostura.

an•gry /ánggree/ *adj.* (**angrier, angriest**) **1** feeling or showing anger; extremely displeased or resentful. **2** (of a wound, sore, etc.) inflamed; painful. **3** suggesting or seeming to show anger (*an angry sky*). □□ **an•gri•ly** *adv.* [ME, f. ANGER + –Y¹]

angst /aangkst/ *n.* **1** anxiety. **2** a feeling of guilt or remorse. [G]

ang•strom /ángstrəm/ *n.* (also **ång•ström** /áwngstrŏm/) a unit of length equal to 10⁻¹⁰ meter. ¶ Symb.: Å. [A.J. *Ångström*, Swedish physicist d. 1874]

an•guine /ánggwin/ *adj.* of or resembling a snake. [L *anguinus* f. *anguis* snake]

an•guish /ánggwish/ *n. & v.* ● *n.* severe misery or mental suffering. ● *v.tr.* (often as **anguished** *adj.*) cause to suffer physical or mental pain. [ME f. OF *anguisse* choking f. L *angustia* tightness f. *angustus* narrow]

an•guished /ánggwisht/ *adj.* suffering or expressing anguish. [past part. of *anguish* (v.) f. OF *anguissier* f. eccl.L *angustiare* to distress, formed as ANGUISH]

an•gu•lar /ánggyəlr/ *adj.* **1 a** having angles or sharp corners. **b** (of a person) having sharp features; lean and bony. **c** awkward in manner. **2** forming an angle. **3** measured by angle (*angular distance*). □□ **an•gu•lar•i•ty** /–láritee/ *n.* **an•gu•lar•ly** *adv.* [L *angularis* f. *angulus* ANGLE¹]

an·gu·lar mo·men·tum *n.* the quantity of rotation of a body, the product of its moment of inertia and angular velocity.

an·gu·lar ve·loc·i·ty *n.* the rate of change of angular position of a rotating body.

an·he·dral /anheˊedrəl/ *n. & adj. Aeron.* ● *n.* the angle between the wing and horizontal when the wing is inclined downwards. ● *adj.* of or having an anhedral. [AN-¹ + –*hedral* (see –HEDRON)]

an·hy·dride /anhídrid/ *n. Chem.* a substance obtained by removing the elements of water from a compound, esp. from an acid. [as AN-HYDROUS + –IDE]

an·hy·drite /anhídrīt/ *n.* a naturally occurring usu. rock-forming anhydrous mineral form of calcium sulfate. [as ANHYDROUS + –ITE¹ 2]

an·hy·drous /anhídrəs/ *adj. Chem.* without water, esp. water of crystallization. [Gk *anudros* (as AN-¹, *hudōr* water)]

an·i·line /ánillin, –lin/ *n.* a colorless oily liquid, used in the manufacture of dyes, drugs, and plastics. [G *Anilin* f. *Anil* indigo (from which it was orig. obtained), ult. f. Arab. *an-nīl*]

an·i·line dye *n.* **1** any of numerous dyes made from aniline. **2** any synthetic dye.

an·i·ma /ánimə/ *n. Psychol.* **1** the inner personality (opp. PERSONA). **2** Jung's term for the feminine part of a man's personality (opp. ANIMUS). [L, = mind, soul]

an·i·mad·vert /ánimadvért/ *v.intr.* (foll. by *on*) criticize; censure (conduct, a fault, etc.). □□ **an·i·mad·ver·sion** /–vórzhən/ *n.* [L *animadvertere* f. *animus* mind + *advertere* (as AD-, *vertere* vers- turn)]

an·i·mal /ánimal/ *n. & adj.* ● *n.* **1** a living organism which feeds on organic matter, usu. one with specialized sense organs and a nervous system, and able to respond rapidly to stimuli. **2** such an organism other than human beings. **3** a brutish or uncivilized person. **4** *colloq.* a person or thing of any kind (*there is no such animal*). ● *adj.* **1** characteristic of animals. **2** of animals as distinct from vegetables (*animal charcoal*). **3** characteristic of the physical needs of animals; carnal; sensual. [L f. *animale* neut. of *animalis* having breath f. *anima* breath]

an·i·mal·cule /ánimálkyōol/ *n.* a microscopic animal. □□ **an·i·mal·cu·lar** *adj.* [mod.L *animalculum* (as ANIMAL, –CULE)]

an·i·mal hus·band·ry *n.* the science of breeding and caring for farm animals.

an·i·mal·ism /ániməlizəm/ *n.* **1** the nature and activity of animals. **2** the belief that humans are not superior to other animals. **3** concern with physical matters; sensuality.

an·i·mal·i·ty /ánimálitee/ *n.* **1** the animal world. **2** the nature or behavior of animals. [F *animalité* f. *animal* (adj.)]

an·i·mal·ize /ánimǝlīz/ *v.tr.* **1** make (a person) bestial; sensualize. **2** convert to animal substance. □□ **an·i·mal·i·za·tion** /–lizáyshǝn/ *n.*

an·i·mal mag·net·ism *n.* **1** *hist.* mesmerism. **2** sex appeal.

an·i·mal rights *n.* (a movement upholding) the natural right of animals to live free from human exploitation.

an·i·mal spir·its *n.* natural exuberance.

an·i·mate *adj. & v.* ● *adj.* /ánimǝt/ **1** having life. **2** lively. ● *v.tr.* /ánimayt/ **1** enliven; make lively. **2** give life to. **3** inspire; actuate. **4** encourage. **5** produce using animation. [L *animatus* past part. of *animare* give life to f. *anima* life, soul]

an·i·mat·ed /ánimaytid/ *adj.* **1** lively; vigorous. **2** having life. **3** (of a movie, etc.) using techniques of animation. □□ **an·i·mat·ed·ly** *adv.* **an·i·ma·tor** *n.* (in sense 3).

an·i·ma·tion /ánimáyshǝn/ *n.* **1** vivacity; ardor. **2** the state of being alive. **3** *Cinematog.* the technique of filming successive drawings or positions of puppets, etc., to create an illusion of movement when the film is shown as a sequence.

an·i·mé /ánimay/ *n.* any of various resins, esp. a W. Indian resin used in making varnish. [F, of uncert. orig.]

an·i·mism /ánimizəm/ *n.* **1** the attribution of a living soul to plants, inanimate objects, and natural phenomena. **2** the belief in a supernatural power that organizes and animates the material universe. □□ **an·i·mist** *n.* **an·i·mis·tic** /–místik/ *adj.* [L *anima* life, soul + –ISM]

an·i·mos·i·ty /ánimósitee/ *n.* (*pl.* **-ties**) a spirit or feeling of strong hostility. [ME f. OF *animosité* or LL *animositas* f. *animosus* spirited, formed as ANIMUS]

an·i·mus /ánimǝs/ *n.* **1** a display of animosity. **2** ill feeling. **3** a motivating spirit or feeling. **4** *Psychol.* Jung's term for the masculine part of a woman's personality (opp. ANIMA). [L, = spirit, mind]

an·i·on /ánion/ *n.* a negatively charged ion; an ion that is attracted to the anode in electrolysis (opp. CATION). [ANA- + ION]

an·i·on·ic /ániónik/ *adj.* **1** of an anion or anions. **2** having an active anion.

an·ise /ánis/ *n.* an umbelliferous plant, *Pimpinella anisum,* having aromatic seeds (see ANISEED). [ME f. OF *anis* f. L f. Gk *anison* anise, dill]

an·i·seed /ániseed/ *n.* the seed of the anise, used to flavor liqueurs and candy. [ME f. ANISE + SEED]

an·i·sette /ánisét, –zét/ *n.* a liqueur flavored with aniseed. [F, dimin. of *anis* anise]

an·i·so·trop·ic /ánīsǝtrópik, –trō–/ *adj.* having physical properties that are different in different directions, e.g., the strength of wood along the grain differing from that across the grain (opp. ISOTROP-

IC). □□ **an·i·so·trop·i·cal·ly** *adv.* **an·i·sot·ro·py** /–sótrǝpee/ *n.* [AN-¹ + ISOTROPIC]

ankh /angk/ *n.* a device consisting of a looped bar with a shorter crossbar, used in ancient Egypt as a symbol of life. [Egypt., = life, soul]

an·kle /ángkǝl/ *n. & v.* ● *n.* **1** the joint connecting the foot with the leg. **2** the part of the leg between this and the calf. ● *v.intr. Brit. sl.* walk. [ME f. ON *ankul-* (unrecorded) f. Gmc: rel. to ANGLE¹]

an·kle-bit·er *n. colloq.* a child.

an·kle·bone /ángkǝlbōn/ *n.* a bone forming the ankle.

an·kle sock *n.* esp. *Brit.* = ANKLET 2.

an·klet /ángklit/ *n.* **1** an ornament or fetter worn around the ankle. **2** a short sock just covering the ankle. [ANKLE + –LET, after BRACELET]

ankh

an·ky·lose /ángkilōs/ *v.tr. & intr.* (also **an·chy·lose**) (of bones or a joint) stiffen or unite by ankylosis. [back-form. f. ANKYLOSIS after *anastomose,* etc.]

an·ky·lo·sis /ángkilósis/ *n.* (also **an·chy·lo·sis**) **1** the abnormal stiffening and immobility of a joint by fusion of the bones. **2** such fusion. □□ **an·ky·lot·ic** /–lótik/ *adj.* [mod.L f. Gk *agkulōsis* f. *agkuloō* crook]

an·na /áanə/ *n.* a former monetary unit of India and Pakistan, one-sixteenth of a rupee. [Hind. *ānā*]

an·nal /ánǝl/ *n.* **1** the annals of one year. **2** a record of one item in a chronicle. [back-form. f. ANNALS]

an·nal·ist /ánǝlist/ *n.* a writer of annals. □□ **an·nal·is·tic** /–lístik/ *adj.* **an·nal·is·ti·cal·ly** /–lístikǝlee/ *adv.*

an·nals /ánǝlz/ *n.pl.* **1** a narrative of events year by year. **2** historical records. [F *annales* or L *annales* (*libri*) yearly (books) f. *annus* year]

an·nat·to /ǝnátó/ *n.* (also **an·at·ta** /–tǝ/, **a·nat·to**) an orangish red dye from the pulp of a tropical fruit, used for coloring foods. [Carib name of the fruit tree]

an·neal /ǝneél/ *v. & n.* ● *v.tr.* **1** heat (metal or glass) and allow it to cool slowly, esp. to toughen it. **2** toughen. ● *n.* treatment by annealing. □□ **an·neal·er** *n.* [OE *onǣlan* f. *on* + *ǣlan* burn, bake f. *āl* fire]

an·nec·tent /ǝnéktǝnt/ *adj. Biol.* connecting (*annectent link*). [L *annectere annectent-* bind (as ANNEX)]

an·ne·lid /án'lid/ *n.* any segmented worm of the phylum Annelida, e.g., earthworms, lugworms, etc. [F *annélide* or mod.L *annelida* (pl.) f. F *annelés* ringed animals f. OF *anel* ring f. L *anellus* dimin. of *anulus* ring]

an·nel·i·dan /ǝnélid'n/ *adj. & n.* ● *adj.* of the annelids. ● *n.* an annelid.

an·nex *v. & n.* /anéks, áneks/ ● *v.tr.* **1 a** add as a subordinate part. **b** (often foll. by *to*) append to a book, etc. **2** incorporate (territory of another) into one's own. **3** add as a condition or consequence. **4** *colloq.* take without right. ● *n.* (*Brit.* also **annexe** /áneks, ániks/) **1** a separate or added building, esp. for extra accommodation. **2** an addition to a document. □□ **an·nex·a·tion** /–sáyshǝn/ *n.* [ME f. OF *annexer* f. L *annectere* (as AN-², *nectere nex-* bind)]

an·ni·hi·late /ǝníǝlayt/ *v.tr.* **1** completely destroy. **2** defeat utterly; make insignificant or powerless. □□ **an·ni·hi·la·tor** *n.* [LL *annihilare* (as AN-², *nihil* nothing)]

an·ni·hi·la·tion /ǝníǝláyshǝn/ *n.* **1** the act or process of annihilating. **2** *Physics* the conversion of a particle and an antiparticle into radiation. [F *annihilation* or L *annihilatio* (as ANNIHILATE)]

an·ni·ver·sa·ry /ánivérsǝree/ *n.* (*pl.* **-ries**) **1** the date on which an event took place in a previous year. **2** the celebration of this. [ME f. L *anniversarius* f. *annus* year + *versus* turned]

An·no Dom·i·ni /ánō dóminī, –nee/ *adv. & n.* ● *adv.* in the year of our Lord; in the year of the Christian era. ● *n. Brit. colloq.* advancing age (*suffering from Anno Domini*). [L, = in the year of the Lord]

an·no·tate /ánōtayt/ *v.tr.* add explanatory notes to (a book, document, etc.). □□ **an·no·tat·a·ble** *adj.* **an·no·ta·tion** /–táyshǝn/ *n.* **an·no·ta·tive** *adj.* **an·no·ta·tor** *n.* [L *annotare* (as AD-, *nota* mark)]

an·nounce /ǝnówns/ *v.* **1** *tr.* (often foll. by *that*) make publicly known. **2** *tr.* make known the arrival or imminence of (a guest, dinner, etc.). **3** *intr.* declare one's candidacy for office. **4** *tr.* make known (without words) to the senses or the mind; be a sign of. [ME f. OF *annoncer* f. L *annuntiare* (as AD-, *nuntius* messenger)]

SYNONYM TIP announce

BLAZON, PUBLISH, PROCLAIM, DECLARE, PROMULGATE. When you **announce** something, you communicate it in a formal and public manner, often for the first time (*to announce the arrival of the guest of honor*). But just how you go about announcing something

See page xx for the **Key to Pronunciation**.

depends on what you're trying to convey. If you want to make sure no one misses your message, use **blazon** (*signs along the highway blazoned the local farmers' complaints*). If you plan to make your views known to the general public through the medium of writing, use **publish** (*to publish a story on drunk driving in the local newspaper*). Use **proclaim** if you have something of great importance that you want to announce very formally and officially (*proclaim a national day of mourning*). Although **declare** also implies a very formal announcement (*declare war*), it can refer to any clear and explicit statement (*declare one's love*). **Promulgate** is usually associated with the communication of a creed, doctrine, or law (*promulgate the views of the Democratic Party*).

an•nounce•ment /ənównsmənt/ *n.* **1** the action of announcing; something announced. **2** an official communication or statement. **3** an advertisement or other piece of promotional material.

an•nounc•er /ənównsər/ *n.* a person who announces, esp. introducing programs or describing sports events in broadcasting.

an•noy /ənóy/ *v.tr.* **1** cause slight anger or mental distress to. **2** (in *passive*) be somewhat angry (*am annoyed with you; was annoyed at my remarks*). **3** molest; harass repeatedly. □□ **an•noy•er** *n.* **an•noy•ing** *adj.* [ME f. OF *anuier, anui, anoi,* etc., ult. f. L *in odio* hateful]

an•noy•ance /ənóyəns/ *n.* **1** the action of annoying or the state of being annoyed; irritation; vexation. **2** something that annoys; a nuisance.

an•nu•al /ányōoəl/ *adj. & n.* ● *adj.* **1** reckoned by the year. **2** occurring every year. **3** living or lasting for one year. ● *n.* **1** a book, etc., published once a year; a yearbook. **2** a plant that lives only for a year or less. □□ **an•nu•al•ly** *adv.* [ME f. OF *annuel* f. LL *annualis* f. L *annalis* f. *annus* year]

an•nu•al•ized /ányōoəlīzd/ *adj.* (of rates of interest, inflation, etc.) calculated on an annual basis, as a projection from figures obtained for a shorter period.

an•nu•al meet•ing *n.* a yearly meeting of members or shareholders, esp. for holding elections and reporting on the year's events.

an•nu•al ring *n.* a ring in the cross section of a plant, esp. a tree, produced by one year's growth.

an•nu•i•tant /ənóoit'nt, ənyóo–/ *n.* a person who holds or receives an annuity. [ANNUITY + –ANT, by assim. to *accountant,* etc.]

an•nu•i•ty /ənóoitee, ənyóo–/ *n.* (*pl.* **•ties**) **1** a yearly grant or allowance. **2** an investment of money entitling the investor to a series of equal annual sums. **3** a sum payable in respect of a particular year. [ME f. F *annuité* f. med.L *annuitas –tatis* f. L *annuus* yearly (as ANNUAL)]

an•nul /ənúl/ *v.tr.* (**annulled, annulling**) **1** declare (a marriage, etc.) invalid. **2** cancel; abolish. □□ **an•nul•ment** *n.* [ME f. OF *anuller* f. LL *annullare* (as AD–, *nullus* none)]

an•nu•lar /ányələr/ *adj.* ring-shaped; forming a ring. □□ **an•nu•lar•ly** *adv.* [F *annulaire* or L *annularis* f. *an(n)ulus* ring]

an•nu•lar e•clipse *n.* an eclipse of the sun in which the moon leaves a ring of sunlight visible around it.

an•nu•late /ányələt, –layt/ *adj.* having rings; marked with or formed of rings. □□ **an•nu•la•tion** /–láyshən/ *n.* [L *annulatus* (as ANNULUS)]

an•nu•let /ányəlit/ *n.* **1** *Archit.* a small fillet or band encircling a column. **2** a small ring. [L *annulus* ring + –ET[1]]

an•nu•lus /ányələs/ *n.* (*pl.* **annuli** /–lī/) esp. *Math. & Biol.* a ring. [L *an(n)ulus*]

an•nun•ci•ate /ənúnseeayt/ *v.tr.* **1** proclaim. **2** indicate as coming or ready. [LL *annunciare* f. L *annuntiare annuntiat-* announce]

an•nun•ci•a•tion /ənúnseeáyshən/ *n.* **1** (**Annunciation**) **a** the announcing of the Incarnation, made by the angel Gabriel to Mary, related in Luke 1:26-38. **b** the festival commemorating this on March 25. **2 a** the act or process of announcing. **b** an announcement. [ME f. OF *annonciation* f. LL *annuntiatio –onis* (as ANNUNCIATE)]

an•nun•ci•a•tor /ənúnseeaytər/ *n.* **1** a device giving an audible or visible indication of which of several electrical circuits has been activated, of the position of a train, etc. **2** an announcer. [LL *annuntiator* (as ANNUNCIATE)]

an•nus mi•ra•bi•lis /ánəs mirábilis/ *n.* a remarkable or auspicious year. [mod.L, = wonderful year]

a•no•a /ənóə/ *n.* any of several small deerlike water buffalo of the genus *Bubalus,* native to Sulawesi. [name in Sulawesi]

an•ode /ánōd/ *n. Electr.* **1** the positive electrode in an electrolytic cell or electronic tube. **2** the negative terminal of a primary cell such as a battery (opp. CATHODE). □□ **an•o•dal** *adj.* **an•od•ic** /ənódik/ *adj.* [Gk *anodos* way up f. *ana* up + *hodos* way]

an•ode ray *n.* a beam of particles emitted from the anode of a high vacuum tube.

an•o•dize /ánədiz/ *v.tr.* coat (a metal, esp. aluminum) with a protective oxide layer by electrolysis. □□ **an•o•diz•er** *n.* [ANODE + –IZE]

an•o•dyne /ánədin/ *adj. & n.* ● *adj.* **1** able to relieve pain. **2** mentally soothing. ● *n.* an anodyne drug or medicine. [L *anodynus* f. Gk *anōdunos* painless (as AN–[1], *odunē* pain)]

an•o•e•sis /ánō-eésis/ *n. Psychol.* consciousness with sensation but without thought. □□ **an•o•et•ic** /–étik/ *adj.* [A–[1] + Gk *noēsis* understanding]

a•noint /ənóynt/ *v.tr.* **1** apply oil or ointment to, esp. as a religious ceremony (e.g., at baptism, or the consecration of a priest or king, or in ministering to the sick). **2** (usu. foll. by *with*) smear; rub. □□ **a•noint•er** *n.* [ME f. AF *anoint* (adj.) f. OF *enoint* past part. of *enoindre* f. L *inungere* (as IN–[2], *ungere unct-* smear with oil)]

SPELLING TIP anoint

Use "an oil" to *anoint* someone; there is a single *n* before the *o*.

---

a•nom•a•lis•tic /ənóməlístik/ *adj. Astron.* of the anomaly or angular distance of a planet from its perihelion.

a•nom•a•lis•tic month *n.* a month measured between successive perigees of the moon.

a•nom•a•lis•tic year *n.* a year measured between successive perihelia of the earth.

a•nom•a•lous /ənómələs/ *adj.* having an irregular or deviant feature; abnormal. □□ **a•nom•a•lous•ly** *adv.* **a•nom•a•lous•ness** *n.* [LL *anomalus* f. Gk *anōmalos* (as AN–[1], *homalos* even)]

a•nom•a•ly /ənóməlee/ *n.* (*pl.* **•lies**) **1** an anomalous circumstance or thing; an irregularity. **2** irregularity of motion, behavior, etc. **3** *Astron.* the angular distance of a planet or satellite from its last perihelion or perigee. [L f. Gk *anōmalia* f. *anōmalos* ANOMALOUS]

an•o•mie /ánəmee/ *n.* (also **an•o•my**) lack of the usual social or ethical standards in an individual or group. □□ **a•nom•ic** /ənómik/ *adj.* [Gk *anomia* f. *anomos* lawless: *–ie* f. F]

a•non /ənón/ *adv.* archaic or *literary* soon; shortly (*will say more of this anon*). [OE *on ān* into one, *on āne* in one]

anon. /ənón/ *abbr.* anonymous; an anonymous author.

an•o•nym /ánənim/ *n.* **1** an anonymous person or publication. **2** a pseudonym. [F *anonyme* f. Gk *anōnumos*: see ANONYMOUS]

a•non•y•mous /ənóniməs/ *adj.* **1** of unknown name. **2** of unknown or undeclared source or authorship. **3** without character; featureless; impersonal. □□ **an•o•nym•i•ty** /ánənímitee/ *n.* **a•non•y•mous•ly** *adv.* [LL *anonymus* f. Gk *anōnumos* nameless (as AN–[1], *onoma* name)]

a•noph•e•les /ənófileez/ *n.* any of various mosquitoes of the genus *Anopheles,* many of which are carriers of the malarial parasite. [mod.L f. Gk *anōphelēs* unprofitable]

an•o•rak /ánərak/ *n.* a waterproof jacket of cloth or synthetic material, usu. with a hood, of a kind orig. used in polar regions; a parka. [Greenland Eskimo *anoraq*]

an•o•rec•tic var. of ANOREXIC.

an•o•rex•i•a /ánəreksee-ə/ *n.* **1** a lack or loss of appetite for food. **2** (in full **anorexia nervosa** /nərvósə/) a psychological illness, esp. in young women, characterized by an obsessive desire to lose weight by refusing to eat. [LL f. Gk f. *an-* not + *orexis* appetite]

an•o•rex•ic /ánəréksik/ *adj. & n.* (also **an•o•rec•tic** /–réktik/) ● *adj.* **1** involving, producing, or characterized by a lack of appetite, esp. in anorexia nervosa. **2** *colloq.* extremely thin. ● *n.* **1** an anorexic agent. **2** a person with anorexia. [F *anoréxique; anorectic* f. Gk *anorektos* without appetite (as ANOREXIA)]

an•os•mi•a /ánózmeeə/ *n.* the loss of the sense of smell. □□ **an•os•mic** *adj.* [LL f. Gk f. *an-* not + *osmē* smell]

an•oth•er /ənúthər/ *adj. & pron.* ● *adj.* **1** an additional; one more (*have another piece of cake; after another six months*). **2** a person like or comparable to (*another Lincoln*). **3** a different (*quite another matter*). **4** some or any other (*will not do another person's work*). ● *pron.* **1** an additional one (*have another*). **2** a different one (*take this book away and bring me another*). **3** some or any other one (*I love another*). **4** *Brit.* an unnamed additional party to a legal action (*X versus Y and another*). **5** *Brit.* (also **A. N. Other** /áy en úthər/) a player unnamed or not yet selected. □ **such another** another of the same sort. [ME f. AN + OTHER]

an•ov•u•lant /anóvyələnt/ *n. & adj. Pharm.* ● *n.* a drug preventing ovulation. ● *adj.* preventing ovulation. [AN–[1] + *ovulation* (see OVULATE) + –ANT]

an•ox•i•a /ənókseeə/ *n. Med.* an absence or deficiency of oxygen reaching the tissues; severe hypoxia. □□ **an•ox•ic** *adj.* [mod.L, formed as AN–[1] + OXYGEN + –IA[1]]

an•schluss /áanshlōos/ *n.* a unification, esp. the annexation of Austria by Germany in 1938. [G f. *anschliessen* join]

an•ser•ine /ánsərin, –rin/ *adj.* **1** of or like a goose. **2** silly. [L *anserinus* f. *anser* goose]

an•swer /ánsər/ *n. & v.* ● *n.* **1** something said or done to deal with or in reaction to a question, statement, or circumstance. **2** the solution to a problem. ● *v.* **1** *tr.* make an answer to (*answer me; answer my question*). **2** *intr.* (often foll. by *to*) make an answer. **3** *tr.* respond to the summons or signal of (*answer the door, answer the telephone*). **4** *tr.* be satisfactory for (a purpose or need). **5** *intr.* **a** (foll. by *for, to*) be responsible (*you will answer to me for your conduct*). **b** (foll. by *for*) vouch (for a person, conduct, etc.). **6** *intr.* (foll. by *to*) correspond, esp. to a description. **7** *intr.* be satisfactory or successful. □ **answer back** answer a rebuke, etc., impudently. **answer to the name of** be called. [OE *andswaru, andswarian* f. Gmc, = swear against (charge)]

an·swer·a·ble /ánsərəbəl/ *adj.* **1** (usu. foll. by *to*, *for*) responsible (*answerable to them for any accident*). **2** that can be answered. □□ **an·swer·a·bil·i·ty** /–bílitee/ *n.*

an·swer·ing ma·chine *n.* a tape recorder which supplies a recorded answer to a telephone call and usu. records incoming messages.

an·swer·ing serv·ice *n.* a business that receives and answers telephone calls for its clients.

ant /ant/ *n.* any small insect of a widely distributed hymenopterous family, living in complex social colonies, wingless (except for adults in the mating season), and proverbial for industry. □ **have ants in one's pants** *colloq.* be fidgety; be restless. [OE *ǣmet(t)e, ēmete* (see EMMET) f. WG]

ant- /ant/ *assim.* form of ANTI- before a vowel or *h* (*Antarctic*).

-ant /ənt/ *suffix* **1** forming adjectives denoting attribution of an action (*pendant; repentant*) or state (*arrogant; expectant*). **2** forming nouns denoting an agent (*assistant; celebrant; deodorant*). [F *-ant* or L *–ant-*, *-ent-*, pres. part. stem of verbs: cf. –ENT]

ant·ac·id /antásid/ *n. & adj.* ● *n.* a substance that prevents or corrects acidity, esp. in the stomach. ● *adj.* having these properties.

an·tag·o·nism /antágənizəm/ *n.* active opposition or hostility. [F *antagonisme* (as ANTAGONIST)]

an·tag·o·nist /antágənist/ *n.* **1** an opponent or adversary. **2** *Biol.* a substance, muscle, or organ that partially or completely opposes the action of another. □□ **an·tag·o·nis·tic** *adj.* **an·tag·o·nis·ti·cal·ly** *adv.* [F *antagoniste* or LL *antagonista* f. Gk *antagōnistēs* (as ANTAGONIZE)]

an·tag·o·nize /antágəniz/ *v.tr.* **1** evoke hostility or opposition or enmity in. **2** (of one force, etc.) counteract or tend to neutralize (another). □□ **an·tag·o·ni·za·tion** /–nizáyshən/ *n.* [Gk *antagōnizomai* (as ANTI-, *agōnizomai* f. *agōn* contest)]

ant·al·ka·li /antálkəli/ *n.* (*pl.* **antalkalis**) any substance that counteracts an alkali.

Ant·arc·tic /antáarktik/ *adj. & n.* ● *adj.* of the south polar regions. ● *n.* this region. [ME f. OF *antartique* or L *antarcticus* f. Gk *antarktikos* (as ANTI-, *arktikos* ARCTIC)]

PRONUNCIATION TIP Antarctic

See note at ARCTIC.

Ant·arc·tic Cir·cle *n.* the parallel of latitude 66° 32 S., forming an imaginary line around this region.

ant bear *n.* = AARDVARK.

an·te /ántee/ *n. & v.* ● *n.* **1** a stake put up by a player in poker, etc., before receiving cards. **2** an amount to be paid in advance. ● *v.tr.* (**antes, anted**) **1** put up as an ante. **2 a** bet; stake. **b** (foll. by *up*) pay. [L, = before]

ante- /ántee/ *prefix* forming nouns and adjectives meaning 'before; preceding' (*anteroom; antenatal*). [L *ante* (prep. &adv.), = before]

ant·eat·er /ánteetər/ *n.* any of various mammals feeding on ants and termites, e.g., a tamandua.

an·te·bel·lum /ánteebéləm/ *adj.* occurring or existing before a particular war, esp. the US Civil War. [L f. *ante* before + *bellum* war]

anteater

an·te·ced·ent /ántiseéd'nt/ *n. & adj.* ● *n.* **1** a preceding thing or circumstance. **2** *Gram.* a word, phrase, clause, or sentence, to which another word (esp. a relative pronoun, usu. following) refers. **3** (in *pl.*) past history, esp. of a person. **4** *Logic* the statement contained in the 'if' clause of a conditional proposition. ● *adj.* **1** (often foll. by *to*) previous. **2** presumptive; a priori. □□ **an·te·ced·ence** /–d'ns/ *n.* **an·te·ced·ent·ly** *adv.* [ME f. F *antecedent* or L *antecedere* (as ANTE-, *cedere* go)]

GRAMMAR TIP antecedent

Pronouns and their antecedents. An **antecedent** is the noun or pronoun to which a pronoun refers. For example, if you say, *Bob worked hard on his speech all afternoon*, "Bob" is the antecedent of "his." Usually an antecedent comes before its pronoun, but not always. In the sentence, *Although she knew she didn't have a chance, Emily applied for the scholarship*, "Emily" is the antecedent for "she." A pronoun must agree with its antecedent in number gender, and person. For example: *The Smiths are having dinner at their house tonight* (both *Smiths* and *their* are third person plural). *She should check her room upon returning* (*she* agrees with *her*; both are third person feminine singular). *Jack stood by his son, just as we stood by ours* (*Jack* agrees with *his* [third person singular; *we* agrees with *ours* [first person plural]).

---

an·te·cham·ber /ánteechaymbər/ *n.* a small room leading to a main one. [earlier *anti–*, f. F *antichambre* f. It. *anticamera* (as ANTE-, CHAMBER)]

an·te·chap·el /ánteechapəl/ *n.* an anteroom to a church or chapel.

an·te·date /ántidáyt/ *v. & n.* ● *v.tr.* **1** exist or occur at a date earlier than. **2** assign an earlier date to (a document, event, etc.), esp.

---

one earlier than its actual date. ● *n.* a date earlier than the actual one.

an·te·di·lu·vi·an /ánteedilóoveeən/ *adj.* **1** of or belonging to the time before the biblical flood. **2** *colloq.* very old or out of date. [ANTE- + L *diluvium* DELUGE + –AN]

an·te·lope /ántilōp/ *n.* (*pl.* same or **antelopes**) **1 a** any of various deerlike ruminants of the family Bovidae, esp. abundant in Africa and typically tall, slender, graceful, and swift-moving with smooth hair and upward-pointing horns, e.g., gazelles, gnus, kudus, and impala. **b** a pronghorn. **2** leather made from the skin of any of these. [ME f. OF *antelop* or f. med.L *ant(h)alopus* f. late Gk *antholops*, of unkn. orig.]

an·te·na·tal /ánteenáyt'l/ *adj.* **1** existing or occurring before birth; prenatal. **2** relating to the period of pregnancy.

an·ten·na /antén ə/ *n.* (*pl.* **antennae** /–ee/) **1** *Zool.* one of a pair of mobile appendages on the heads of insects, crustaceans, etc., sensitive to touch and taste; a feeler. **2** (*pl.* **antennas**) a metal rod, wire, or other structure by which signals are transmitted or received as part of a radio or television transmission or receiving system. □□ **an·ten·nal** *adj.* (in sense 1). **an·ten·na·ry** *adj.* (in sense 1). [L, = sail yard]

an·te·nup·tial /ánteenúpshəl/ *adj.* = PRENUPTIAL.

an·te·pen·di·um /ánteepéndeeəm/ *n.* (*pl.* **antependia** /–deeə/) a veil or hanging for the front of an altar, podium, etc. [med.L (as ANTE-, *pendēre* hang)]

an·te·pe·nult /ánteepinúlt/ *n.* the last syllable but two in a word as ``te'' in ``antepenult.'' [abbr. of LL *antepaenultimus* (as ANTE-, *paenultimus* PENULT)]

an·te·pe·nul·ti·mate /ánteepinúltimət/ *adj. & n.* ● *adj.* last but two; third from the end. ● *n.* anything that is last but two.

an·te·ri·or /anteéreeər/ *adj.* **1** nearer the front. **2** (often foll. by *to*) earlier; prior. □□ **an·te·ri·or·i·ty** /–reeáwritee/ *n.* **an·te·ri·or·ly** *adv.* [F *antérieur* or L *anterior* f. *ante* before]

an·te·room /ánteeróom, –róom/ *n.* a small room leading to a main one.

ant·heap /ánt-heep/ *n.* = ANTHILL.

ant·he·li·on /ant-héeleeən, anthée–/ *n.* (*pl.* **anthelia** /–liə/) a luminous halo projected on a cloud or fog bank opposite to the sun. [Gk, neut. of *anthēlios* opposite to the sun (as ANTI-, *hēlios* sun)]

ant·hel·min·tic /ánt-helmíntik, ánthel–/ (also **ant·hel·min·thic** /–thik/) *n. & adj.* ● *n.* any drug or agent used to destroy parasitic, esp. intestinal, worms, e.g., tapeworms, roundworms, and flukes. ● *adj.* having the power to eliminate or destroy parasitic worms. [ANTI- + Gk *helmins helminthos* worm]

an·them /ánthəm/ *n.* **1** an elaborate choral composition usu. based on a passage of scripture for church use. **2** a solemn hymn of praise, etc., esp. = NATIONAL ANTHEM. **3** a composition sung antiphonally. [OE *antefn, antifne* f. LL *antiphona* ANTIPHON]

an·the·mi·on /anthée meeən/ *n.* (*pl.* **anthemia** /–meeə/) a flowerlike ornament used in art. [Gk, = flower]

an·ther /ánthər/ *n. Bot.* the apical portion of a stamen containing pollen. □□ **an·ther·al** *adj.* [F *anthère* or mod.L *anthera*, in L 'medicine extracted from flowers' f. Gk *anthēra* flowery, fem. adj. f. *anthos* flower]

an·ther·id·i·um /ánthərídeeəm/ *n.* (*pl.* **antheridia** /–deeə/) *Bot.* the male sex organ of algae, mosses, ferns, etc. [mod.L f. *anthera* (as ANTHER) + Gk *–idion* dimin. suffix]

ant·hill /ánt-hil/ *n.* **1** a moundlike nest built by ants or termites. **2** a community teeming with people.

an·thol·o·gize /anthóləjiz/ *v.tr. & intr.* compile or include in an anthology.

an·thol·o·gy /anthóləjee/ *n.* (*pl.* **-gies**) a published collection of passages from literature, songs, reproductions of paintings, etc. □□ **an·thol·o·gist** *n.*

WORD HISTORY anthology

Mid-17th cent.: via French or medieval Latin from Greek *anthologia*, from *anthos* 'flower' + *-logia* 'collection' (from *legein* 'gather'). In Greek, the word originally denoted a collection of the 'flowers' of verse, i.e. small choice poems or epigrams, by various authors.

---

an·tho·zo·an /ánthəzóən/ *n. & adj.* ● *n.* any of the sessile marine coelenterates of the class Anthozoa, including sea anemones and corals. ● *adj.* of or relating to this class. [mod.L *Anthozoa* f. Gk *anthos* flower + *zōia* animals]

an·thra·cene /ánthrəseen/ *n.* a colorless crystalline aromatic hydrocarbon obtained by the distillation of crude oils and used in the manufacture of chemicals. [Gk *anthrax –akos* coal + –ENE]

an·thra·cite /ánthrəsit/ *n.* coal of a hard variety burning with little flame and smoke. □□ **an·thra·cit·ic** /–sítik/ *adj.* [Gk *anthrakitis* a kind of coal (as ANTHRACENE)]

See page xx for the **Key to Pronunciation**.

an·thrax /ánthraks/ *n.* a disease of sheep and cattle transmissible to humans. [LL f. Gk, = carbuncle]

anthropo- /ánthrəpō/ *comb. form* human; humankind. [Gk *anthrŏpos* human being]

an·thro·po·cen·tric /ánthrəpōséntrik/ *adj.* regarding humankind as the center of existence. □□ **an·thro·po·cen·tri·cal·ly** *adv.* **an·thro·po·cen·trism** *n.*

an·thro·po·gen·e·sis /ánthrəpōjénisis/ *n.* = ANTHROPOGENY.

an·thro·pog·e·ny /ánthrəpójinee/ *n.* the study of the origin of humans. □□ **an·thro·po·gen·ic** /ánthrəpōjénik/ *adj.*

an·thro·poid /ánthrəpoyd/ *adj. & n.* • *adj.* **1** resembling a human being in form. **2** *colloq.* (of a person) apelike. • *n.* a being that is human in form only, esp. an anthropoid ape. [Gk *anthrŏpoeidēs* (as ANTHROPO-, –OID)]

an·thro·pol·o·gy /ánthrəpólajee/ *n.* **1** the study of humankind, esp. of its societies and customs. **2** the study of the structure and evolution of human beings as animals. □□ **an·thro·po·log·i·cal** /–pəlójikəl/ *adj.* **an·thro·pol·o·gist** *n.*

an·thro·pom·e·try /ánthrəpómitree/ *n.* the scientific study of the measurements of the human body. □□ **an·thro·po·met·ric** /–pəmétrik/ *adj.*

an·thro·po·mor·phic /ánthrəpōmáwrfik/ *adj.* of or characterized by anthropomorphism. □□ **an·thro·po·mor·phi·cal·ly** *adv.* [as ANTHROPOMORPHOUS + –IC]

an·thro·po·mor·phism /ánthrəpōmáwrfizəm/ *n.* the attribution of a human form or personality to a god, animal, or thing. □□ **an·thro·po·mor·phize** *v.tr.*

an·thro·po·mor·phous /ánthrəpōmáwrfəs/ *adj.* human in form. [Gk *anthrŏpomorphos* (as ANTHROPO-, *morphē* form)]

an·thro·pon·y·my /ánthrəpónimee/ *n.* the study of personal names. [ANTHROPO- + Gk *ōnumia* f. *onoma* name: cf. TOPONYMY]

an·thro·poph·a·gy /ánthrəpófəjee/ *n.* cannibalism. □□ **an·thro·poph·a·gous** *adj.* [Gk *anthrŏpophagia* (as ANTHROPO-, *phagō* eat)]

an·thro·pos·o·phy /ánthrəpósəfee/ *n.* a movement inaugurated by Rudolf Steiner (1861–1925) to develop the faculty of cognition and the realization of spiritual reality. [ANTHROPO- + Gk *sophia* wisdom f. *sophos* wise]

an·ti /ántee, –tī/ *prep. & n.* • *prep.* (also *absol.*) opposed to (*is anti everything; seems to be rather anti*). • *n.* (*pl.* **antis**) a person opposed to a particular policy, etc. [ANTI-]

anti- /ántee/ *prefix* (also **ant-** before a vowel or *h*) forming nouns and adjectives meaning: **1** opposed to; against (*antivivisectionism*). **2** preventing (*antiscorbutic*). **3** the opposite of (*anticlimax*). **4** rival (*antipope*). **5** unlike the conventional form (*antihero; antinovel*). **6** *Physics* the antiparticle of a specified particle (*antineutrino; antiproton*). [from or after Gk *anti-* against]

an·ti·a·bor·tion /ánteeəbáwrshən, ántī–/ *adj.* opposing abortion. □□ **an·ti·a·bor·tion·ist** *n.*

an·ti·air·craft /ánteeáirkraft, ántī–/ *adj.* (of a gun, missile, etc.) used to attack enemy aircraft.

an·ti·ar /ánteeaar/ *n.* = UPAS 1a, 2. [Jav. *antjar*]

an·ti·bal·lis·tic mis·sile /ánteebəlístik, ántī–/ *n.* a missile designed for intercepting and destroying a ballistic missile while in flight.

an·ti·bi·o·sis /ánteebīósis, ántī–/ *n.* an antagonistic association between two organisms (esp. microorganisms), in which one is adversely affected (cf. SYMBIOSIS). [mod.L f. F *antibiose* (as ANTI-, SYMBIOSIS)]

an·ti·bi·ot·ic /ántibīótik, ántī–/ *n. & adj. Pharm.* • *n.* any of various substances (e.g., penicillin) produced by microorganisms or made synthetically, that can inhibit or destroy susceptible microorganisms. • *adj.* functioning as an antibiotic. [F *antibiotique* (as ANTI-, Gk *biŏtikos* fit for life f. *bios* life)]

an·ti·bod·y /ántibodee, ántī–/ *n.* (*pl.* **·ies**) any of various blood proteins produced in response to and then counteracting antigens. [transl. of G *Antikörper* (as ANTI-, *Körper* body)]

an·tic /ántik/ *n. & adj.* • *n.* **1** (usu. in *pl.*) absurd or foolish behavior. **2** an absurd or silly action; a prank. • *adj. archaic* grotesque; bizarre. [It. *antico* ANTIQUE, used as = grotesque]

an·ti·cath·ode /ánteekáthōd, ántī–/ *n.* the target (or anode) of an X-ray tube on which the electrons from the cathode impinge and from which X-rays are emitted.

An·ti·christ /ánteekrīst, ántī–/ *n.* **1** an archenemy of Christ. **2** a postulated personal opponent of Christ expected by some denominations of the Christian church to appear before the end of the world. [ME f. OF *antecrist* f. eccl.L *antichristus* f. Gk *antikhristos* (as ANTI-, *Khristos* CHRIST)]

an·ti·chris·tian /ánteekríschən, ántī–/ *adj.* **1** opposed to Christianity. **2** concerning the Antichrist.

an·tic·i·pate /antísipayt/ *v.tr.* **1** deal with or use before the proper time. **2** *disp.* expect; foresee; regard as probable (*did not anticipate any difficulty*). **3** forestall (a person or thing). **4** look forward to. □□ **an·tic·i·pa·tive** *adj.* **an·tic·i·pa·tor** *n.* **an·tic·i·pa·to·ry** *adj.* [L *anticipare* f. *anti-* for ANTE- + –*cipare* f. *capere* take]

▶Anticipate in the sense 'expect, foresee' is well-established in in-

formal use (e.g., *He anticipated a restless night*), but is regarded as incorrect by some people. The formal sense, 'deal with or use before the proper time,' is illustrated by the sentence *The doctor anticipated the possibility of a relapse by prescribing new medications.*

an·tic·i·pa·tion /antísipáyshən/ *n.* **1** the act or process of anticipating. **2** *Mus.* the introduction beforehand of part of a chord which is about to follow. [F *anticipation* or L *anticipatio* (as ANTICIPATE)]

an·ti·cler·i·cal /ánteeklérikəl, ántī–/ *adj. & n.* • *adj.* opposed to the influence of the clergy, esp. in politics. • *n.* an anticlerical person. □□ **an·ti·cler·i·cal·ism** *n.*

an·ti·cli·max /ánteeklímaks, ántī–/ *n.* a trivial conclusion to something significant or impressive, esp. where a climax was expected. □□ **an·ti·cli·mac·tic** /–máktik/ *adj.* **an·ti·cli·mac·ti·cal·ly** *adv.*

an·ti·cline /ántiklīn/ *n. Geol.* a ridge or fold of stratified rock in which the strata slope down from the crest (opp. SYNCLINE). □□ **an·ti·cli·nal** *adj.* [ANTI- + Gk *klinō* lean, after INCLINE]

an·ti·clock·wise /ánteeklókwīz, ántī–/ *adv. & adj. Brit.* = COUNTERCLOCKWISE.

an·ti·co·ag·u·lant /ánteekō-ágyələnt, ántī–/ *n. & adj.* • *n.* any drug or agent that retards or inhibits coagulation, esp. of the blood. • *adj.* retarding or inhibiting coagulation.

an·ti·co·don /ánteekódon, ántī–/ *n. Biochem.* a sequence of three nucleotides forming a unit of genetic code in a transfer RNA molecule that corresponds to a complementary codon in messenger RNA.

an·ti·con·vul·sant /ánteekənvúlsənt, ántī–/ *n. & adj.* • *n.* any drug or agent that prevents or reduces the severity of convulsions, esp. as in epilepsy. • *adj.* preventing or reducing convulsions.

an·ti·cy·clone /ánteesíklōn, ántī–/ *n.* a system of winds rotating outwards from an area of high barometric pressure, clockwise in the Northern hemisphere and counterclockwise in the Southern hemisphere. □□ **an·ti·cy·clon·ic** /–klónik/ *adj.*

an·ti·de·pres·sant /ánteediprésənt, ántī–/ *n. & adj.* • *n.* any drug or agent that alleviates depression. • *adj.* alleviating depression.

an·ti·di·u·ret·ic hor·mone /ánteedíyərétik, ántī–/ *n.* = VASOPRESSIN. [ANTI- + DIURETIC]

an·ti·dote /ántidōt/ *n.* **1** a medicine, etc., taken or given to counteract poison. **2** anything that counteracts something unpleasant or evil. □□ **an·ti·dot·al** *adj.* [F *antidote* or L *antidotum* f. Gk *antidoton* neut. of *antidotos* given against (as ANTI- + stem of *didonai* give)]

SPELLING TIP antidote

An *antidote* is a remedy that is used against a poison; that is, it is *anti*-poison.

---

an·ti·freeze /ántifreez, ántee–/ *n.* a substance (usu. ethylene glycol) added to water to lower its freezing point, esp. in the radiator of a motor vehicle.

an·ti·gen /ántijən/ *n.* a foreign substance (e.g., toxin) that causes the body to produce antibodies. □□ **an·ti·gen·ic** /–jénik/ *adj.* [G (as ANTIBODY, –GEN)]

an·ti·grav·i·ty /ánteegrávitee, ántī–/ *n. Physics* a hypothetical force opposing gravity.

an·ti·he·ro /ánteeheerō, ántī–/ *n.* (*pl.* **·roes**) a central character in a story or drama who noticeably lacks conventional heroic attributes.

an·ti·his·ta·mine /ánteehístəmin, –meen, ántī–/ *n.* a substance that counteracts the effects of histamine, used esp. in the treatment of allergies.

an·ti·in·flam·ma·to·ry /anteeinflámətōree, ántī–/ *adj. & n.* • *adj.* reducing or counteracting inflammation (*aspirin is an anti-inflammatory drug*). • *n.* (*pl.* **·ries**) an anti-inflammatory medication.

an·ti·knock /ánteenók, ántī–/ *n.* a substance added to motor fuel to prevent premature combustion.

an·ti·lock /ánteelók, ántī–/ *n. & attrib. adj.* (of brakes) designed so as to prevent locking and skidding when applied suddenly.

an·ti·log /ánteelawg, –log, ántī–/ *n. colloq.* = ANTILOGARITHM. [abbr.]

an·ti·log·a·rithm /ánteelắwgərithəm, –lóg–, ántī–/ *n.* the number to which a logarithm belongs (*100 is the common antilogarithm of 2*).

an·til·o·gy /ántiləjee/ *n.* (*pl.* **·gies**) a contradiction in terms. [F *antilogie* f. Gk *antilogia* (as ANTI-, –LOGY)]

an·ti·ma·cas·sar /ánteeməkásər/ *n.* a covering put over furniture, esp. over the back of a chair as protection or as an ornament. [ANTI- + MACASSAR]

an·ti·mat·ter /ánteematər, ántī–/ *n. Physics* matter composed solely of antiparticles.

an·ti·me·tab·o·lite /ánteemitábəlīt, ántī–/ *n. Pharm.* a drug that interferes with the normal metabolic processes within cells, usu. by combining with enzymes.

an·ti·mo·ny /ántimōnee/ *n. Chem.* a brittle silvery white metallic element used esp. in alloys. ¶ Symb.: **Sb**. □□ **an·ti·mo·ni·al** /–mōneeəl/ *adj.* **an·ti·mo·nic** *adj.* **an·ti·mo·ni·ous** /–mōneeəs/ *adj.* [ME f. med.L *antimonium* (11th c.), of unkn. orig.]

an·ti·node /ánteenōd, ántī–/ *n. Physics* the position of maximum displacement in a standing wave system.

an·ti·no·mi·an /ántinṓmeeən/ *adj. & n.* ● *adj.* of or relating to the view that Christians are released from the obligation of observing the moral law. ● *n.* (**Antinomian**) *hist.* a person who holds this view. □□ **an·ti·no·mi·an·ism** *n.* [med.L *Antinomi*, name of a sect in Germany (1535) alleged to hold this view (as ANTI-, Gk *nomos* law)]

an·tin·o·my /antínəmee/ *n.* (*pl.* **·mies**) **1** a contradiction between two beliefs or conclusions that are in themselves reasonable; a paradox. **2** a conflict between two laws or authorities. [L *antinomia* f. Gk (as ANTI-, *nomos* law)]

an·ti·nov·el /ánteenovəl, ántī-/ *n.* a novel in which the conventions of the form are studiously avoided.

an·ti·nu·cle·ar /ánteenóōkleeər, –nyóō–, ántī-/ *adj.* opposed to the development of nuclear weapons or nuclear power.

an·ti·ox·i·dant /ántee-óksid'nt, ántī-/ *n.* an agent that inhibits oxidation, esp. used to reduce deterioration of products stored in air.

an·ti·par·ti·cle /ánteepaartikəl, ántī-/ *n. Physics* an elementary particle having the same mass as a given particle but opposite electric or magnetic properties.

an·ti·pas·to /ánteepaástō/ *n.* (*pl.* **·tos** or **antipasti** /–tee/) an hors d'oeuvre, esp. in an Italian meal. [It.]

an·ti·pa·thet·ic /antípəthétik/ *adj.* (usu. foll. by *to*) having a strong aversion or natural opposition. □□ **an·ti·pa·thet·i·cal** *adj.* **an·ti·pa·thet·i·cal·ly** *adv.* [as ANTIPATHY after PATHETIC]

an·ti·path·ic /ántipáthik/ *adj.* of a contrary nature or character.

an·tip·a·thy /antípəthee/ *n.* (*pl.* **·thies**) (often foll. by *to, for, between*) a strong or deep-seated aversion or dislike. [F *antipathie* or L *antipathia* f. Gk *antipatheia* f. *antipathēs* opposed in feeling (as ANTI-, *pathos –eos* feeling)]

an·ti·per·son·nel /ánteepérsənél, ántī-/ *adj.* (of a bomb, mine, etc.) designed to kill or injure people rather than to damage buildings or equipment.

an·ti·per·spi·rant /ánteepérspirənt, ántī-/ *n. & adj.* ● *n.* a substance applied to the skin to prevent or reduce perspiration. ● *adj.* that acts as an antiperspirant.

an·ti·phlo·gis·tic /ánteefləjístik, ántī-/ *n. & adj.* ● *n.* any drug or agent that alleviates or reduces inflammation. ● *adj.* alleviating or reducing inflammation.

an·ti·phon /ántifon/ *n.* **1** a hymn or psalm, the parts of which are sung or recited alternately by two groups. **2** a versicle or phrase from this. **3** a sentence sung or recited before or after a psalm or canticle. **4** a response. [eccl.L *antiphona* f. Gk (as ANTI-, *phōnē* sound)]

an·tiph·o·nal /antífənəl/ *adj. & n.* ● *adj.* **1** sung or recited alternately by two groups. **2** responsive; answering. ● *n.* a collection of antiphons. □□ **an·tiph·o·nal·ly** *adv.*

an·tiph·o·nar·y /antífənéree/ *n.* (*pl.* **·ies**) a book of antiphons. [eccl.L *antiphonarium* (as ANTIPHON)]

an·tiph·o·ny /antífənee/ *n.* (*pl.* **·nies**) **1** antiphonal singing or chanting. **2** a response or echo.

an·ti·pode /ántipōd/ *n.* (usu. foll. by *of, to*) the exact opposite. [see ANTIPODES]

an·tip·o·des /antípədeez/ *n.pl.* **1 a** (also **Antipodes**) a place diametrically opposite another, esp. Australasia as the region on the opposite side of the earth from Europe. **b** places diametrically opposite each other. **2** (usu. foll. by *of, to*) the exact opposite. □□ **an·tip·o·dal** *adj.* **an·tip·o·de·an** /–deéən/ *adj. & n.* [F or LL f. Gk *antipodes* having the feet opposite (as ANTI-, *pous podos* foot)]

an·ti·pole /ántipōl/ *n.* **1** the direct opposite. **2** the opposite pole.

an·ti·pope /ánteepōp, ántī-/ *n.* a person set up as pope in opposition to one (held by others to be) canonically chosen. [F *antipape* f. med.L *antipapa*, assim. to POPE[1]]

an·ti·pro·ton /ánteeprṓton, ántī-/ *n. Physics* the negatively charged antiparticle of a proton.

an·ti·pru·rit·ic /ánteeprōōrítik, ántī-/ *adj. & n.* ● *adj.* relieving itching. ● *n.* an antipruritic drug or agent. [ANTI- + PRURITUS + –IC]

an·ti·py·ret·ic /ánteepīrétik, ántī-/ *adj. & n.* ● *adj.* preventing or reducing fever. ● *n.* an antipyretic drug or agent.

an·ti·quar·i·an /ántikwáireeən/ *adj. & n.* ● *adj.* **1** of or dealing in antiques or rare books. **2** of the study of antiquities. ● *n.* an antiquary. □□ **an·ti·quar·i·an·ism** *n.* [see ANTIQUARY]

an·ti·quar·y /ántikweree/ *n.* (*pl.* **·ies**) a student or collector of antiques or antiquities. [L *antiquarius* f. *antiquus* ancient]

an·ti·quat·ed /ántikwaytid/ *adj.* old-fashioned; out of date. [eccl.L *antiquare antiquat-* make old]

an·tique /anteék/ *n., adj., & v.* ● *n.* an object of considerable age, esp. an item of furniture or the decorative arts having a high value. ● *adj.* **1** of or existing from an early date. **2** old-fashioned; archaic. **3** of ancient times. ● *v.tr.* (**antiques, antiqued, antiquing**) give an antique appearance to (furniture, etc.) by artificial means. [F *antique* or L *antiquus, anticus* former, ancient f. *ante* before]

an·tiq·ui·ty /antíkwitee/ *n.* (*pl.* **·ties**) **1** ancient times, esp. the period before the Middle Ages. **2** great age (*a city of great antiquity*). **3** (usu. in *pl.*) physical remains or relics from ancient times, esp. buildings and works of art. **4** (in *pl.*) customs, events, etc., of ancient times.

5 the people of ancient times regarded collectively. [ME f. OF *antiquité* f. L *antiquitas –tatis* f. *antiquus*: see ANTIQUE]

an·ti·ra·cism /ánteeráysizəm, ántī-/ *n.* the policy or practice of opposing racism and promoting racial tolerance. □□ **an·ti·ra·cist** *n. & adj.*

an·tir·rhi·num /ántirínəm/ *n.* any plant of the genus *Antirrhinum*, esp. the snapdragon. [L f. Gk *antirrhinon* f. *anti* counterfeiting + *rhis rhinos* nose (from the resemblance of the flower to an animal's snout)]

an·ti·scor·bu·tic /ánteeskawrbyóōtik, ántī-/ *adj. & n.* ● *adj.* preventing or curing scurvy. ● *n.* an antiscorbutic agent or drug.

an·ti-Sem·i·tism /–sémitizəm/ *n.* hostility to or prejudice against Jews. □□ **an·ti-Sem·ite** *n. & adj.* **an·ti-Se·mit·ic** /–simítik/ *adj.*

an·ti·sep·sis /antisépsis/ *n.* the process of using antiseptics to eliminate undesirable microorganisms such as bacteria, viruses, and fungi that cause disease. [mod.L (as ANTI-, SEPSIS)]

an·ti·sep·tic /antiséptik/ *adj. & n.* ● *adj.* **1** counteracting sepsis, esp. by preventing the growth of disease-causing microorganisms. **2** sterile or free from contamination. **3** lacking character. ● *n.* an antiseptic agent. □□ **an·ti·sep·ti·cal·ly** *adv.*

an·ti·se·rum /ántiseerəm/ *n.* (*pl.* **antisera** /–rə/) a blood serum containing antibodies against specific antigens, injected to treat or protect against specific diseases.

an·ti·so·cial /ánteesṓshəl, ántī-/ *adj.* **1** opposed or contrary to normal social instincts or practices. **2** not sociable. **3** opposed or harmful to the existing social order.

an·ti·stat·ic /ánteestátik, ántī-/ *adj.* that counteracts the effects of static electricity.

an·tis·tro·phe /antístrəfee/ *n.* the second section of an ancient Greek choral ode or of one division of it (see STROPHE). [LL f. Gk *antistrophē* f. *antistrephō* turn against]

an·tith·e·sis /antíthisis/ *n.* (*pl.* **antitheses** /–seez/) **1** (foll. by *of, to*) the direct opposite. **2** (usu. foll. by *of, between*) contrast or opposition between two things. **3** a contrast of ideas expressed by parallelism of strongly contrasted words. [LL f. Gk *antitithēmi* set against (as ANTI-, *tithēmi* place)]

an·ti·thet·i·cal /ántithétikəl/ *adj.* (also **an·ti·thet·ic**) **1** contrasted; opposite. **2** connected with, containing, or using antithesis. □□ **an·ti·thet·i·cal·ly** *adv.* [Gk *antithetikos* (as ANTITHESIS)]

an·ti·tox·in /ánteetóksin/ *n.* an antibody that counteracts a toxin. □□ **an·ti·tox·ic** *adj.*

an·ti·trades /ántitráydz/ *n.pl.* winds that blow in the opposite direction to (and usu. above) a trade wind.

an·ti·trust /ánteetrúst, ántī-/ *adj.* (of a law, etc.) opposed to or controlling trusts or other monopolies.

an·ti·type /ánteetíp/ *n.* **1** that which is represented by a type or symbol. **2** a person or thing of the opposite type. □□ **an·ti·typ·i·cal** /–típikəl/ *adj.* [Gk *antitupos* corresponding as an impression to the die (as ANTI-, *tupos* stamp)]

an·ti·ven·in /ánteevénin, ántī-/ *n.* an antiserum containing antibodies against specific poisons in the venom of esp. snakes, spiders, scorpions, etc. [ANTI- + VENOM.]

an·ti·vi·ral /ánteevírəl, ántī-/ *adj.* effective against viruses.

an·ti·viv·i·sec·tion·ism /ánteevívisékshənizəm, ántī-/ *n.* opposition to vivisection. □□ **an·ti·viv·i·sec·tion·ist** *n.*

ant·ler /ántlər/ *n.* **1** each of the branched horns of a stag or other (usu. male) deer. **2** a branch of this. □□ **ant·lered** *adj.* [ME f. AF, var. of OF *antoillier*, of unkn. orig.]

ant li·on *n.* any of various dragonflylike insects, the larvae of which dig pits in which to trap ants and other insects for food.

an·to·no·ma·sia /ántənəmáyzhə/ *n.* **1** the substitution of an epithet or title, etc., for a proper name (e.g., *the Maid of Orleans* for Joan of Arc). **2** the use of a proper name to express a general idea (e.g., *a Scrooge* for a miser). [L f. Gk f. *antonomazō* name instead (as ANTI-, + *onoma* name)]

antlers

an·to·nym /ántənim/ *n.* a word opposite in meaning to another in the same language (e.g., *bad* and *good*) (opp. SYNONYM). □□ **an·ton·y·mous** /antóniməs/ *adj.* [F *antonyme* (as ANTI-, SYNONYM)]

an·trum /ántrəm/ *n.* (*pl.* **antra** /–trə/) *Anat.* a natural chamber or cavity in the body, esp. in a bone. □□ **an·tral** *adj.* [L f. Gk *antron* cave]

ants·y /ántsee/ *adj. colloq.* irritated; impatient; fidgety; restless. [*ants*, pl. of ANT + –Y[1]]

an·u·ran /ənóōrən, ənyóōr–/ *n. & adj.* ● *n.* any tailless amphibian of the order Anura, including frogs and toads. ● *adj.* of or relating to this order. [mod.L *Anura* (AN-[1] + Gk *oura* tail)]

a·nus /áynəs/ *n. Anat.* the excretory opening at the end of the alimentary canal. [L]

an•vil /ánvil/ n. 1 a block (usu. of iron) with a flat top, concave sides, and often a pointed end, on which metals are worked in forging. 2 Anat. a bone of the ear; the incus. [OE anfilte, etc.]

anvil

anx•i•e•ty /angzíotee/ n. (pl. •ties) 1 the state of being anxious. 2 concern about an imminent danger, difficulty, etc. 3 (foll. by for, or to + infin.) anxious desire. 4 a thing that causes anxiety. 5 Psychol. a nervous disorder characterized by a state of excessive uneasiness. [F anxiété or L anxietas –tatis (as ANXIOUS)]

anx•ious /ángkshəs/ adj. 1 troubled; uneasy in the mind. 2 causing or marked by anxiety (an anxious moment). 3 (foll. by for, or to + infin.) earnestly or uneasily wanting or trying (anxious to please; anxious for you to succeed). □□ anx•ious•ly adv. anx•ious•ness n. [L anxius f. angere choke]

▶Anxious and eager both mean 'looking forward to something,' but they have different connotations. Eager suggests enthusiasm about something, a positive outlook: I'm eager to get started on my vacation. Anxious implies worry about something: I'm anxious to get started before it rains.

an•y /énee/ adj., pron., & adv. ● adj. 1 (with interrog., neg., or conditional expressed or implied) a one, no matter which, of several (cannot find any answer). b some, no matter how much or many or of what sort (if any books arrive; have you any sugar?). 2 a minimal amount of (hardly any difference). 3 whichever is chosen (any fool knows that). 4 a an appreciable or significant (did not stay for any length of time). b a very large (has any amount of money). ● pron. 1 any one (did not know any of them). 2 any number (are any of them yours?). 3 any amount (is there any left?). ● adv. (usu. with neg. or interrog.) at all; in some degree (is that any good?; do not make it any larger; without being any the wiser). **any time** (or **day** or **minute**, etc.) now colloq. at any time in the near future. **not having any** colloq. unwilling to participate. [OE ǽnig f. Gmc (as ONE, –Y¹)]

an•y•bod•y /éneebudee, –bodee/ n. & pron. 1 a person, no matter who. b a person of any kind. c whatever person is chosen. 2 a person of importance (are you anybody?). □ **anybody's** (of a contest) evenly balanced (it was anybody's game). **anybody's guess** see GUESS.

an•y•how /éneehow/ adv. 1 anyway. 2 in a disorderly manner or state (does his work anyhow).

an•y•more /eneemáwr/ adv. to any further extent (don't like you anymore).

an•y•one /éneewun/ pron. anybody.

▶Anyone is written as two words only to emphasize singularity, e.g., Any one of us could do the job. Otherwise it is written as one word (e.g., Anyone who wants to come is welcome).

an•y•place /éneeplays/ adv. anywhere.

an•y•thing /éneething/ pron. 1 a thing, no matter which. 2 a thing of any kind. 3 whatever thing is chosen. □ **anything but** not at all (was anything but honest). **like anything** colloq. with great vigor, intensity, etc.

an•y•time /éneetim/ adv. colloq. at any time.

an•y•way /éneeway/ adv. (also dial. **anyways** /éneewayz/) 1 in any way or manner. 2 at any rate. 3 in any case. 4 to resume (anyway, as I was saying).

▶The word anyways is considered dialectal. Never add an s to anywhere, everywhere, or nowhere, either.

an•y•where /éneehwair, –wair/ adv. & pron. ● adv. in or to any place. ● pron. any place (anywhere will do).

▶See note at ANYWAY.

an•y•wise /éneewiz/ adv. in any manner. [OE on ǽnige wīsan in any wise]

An•zac /ánzak/ n. 1 a soldier in the Australian and New Zealand Army Corps (1914–18). 2 any person, esp. a member of the armed services, from Australia or New Zealand. [acronym]

An•zac Day n. April 25, commemorating the Anzac landing at Gallipoli in 1915.

An•zus /ánzəs/ n. (also **ANZUS**) Australia, New Zealand, and the US, as an alliance for the Pacific area.

A-OK abbr. colloq. excellent; in good order. [all systems OK]

a•o•rist /áyərist/ n. & adj. Gram. ● n. an unqualified past tense of a verb (esp. in Greek), without reference to duration or completion. ● adj. of or designating this tense. □□ **a•o•ris•tic** adj. [Gk aoristos indefinite f. a- not + horizō define, limit]

a•or•ta /ayáwrtə/ n. (pl. **aortas**) the main artery, giving rise to the arterial network through which oxygenated blood is supplied to the body from the heart. □□ **a•or•tic** adj. [Gk aortē f. a(e)irō raise]

à ou•trance /aa ootróns/ adv. 1 to the death. 2 to the bitter end. [F, = to the utmost]

ap-¹ /ap/ prefix assim. form of AD- before p.

ap-² /ap/ prefix assim. form of APO- before a vowel or h.

a•pace /əpáys/ adv. literary swiftly; quickly. [OF àpas at (a considerable) pace]

A•pach•e /əpáchee/ n. 1 a member of a N. American Indian tribe of the southwestern US. 2 (**apache**) (/əpásh/) a violent street ruffian, orig. in Paris. [Mex. Sp.]

ap•a•nage var. of APPANAGE.

a•part /əpáart/ adv. 1 separately; not together (stand apart from the crowd). 2 into pieces (came apart in my hands). 3 a to or on one side. b out of consideration (placed after noun: joking apart). 4 to or at a distance. □ **apart from** 1 excepting; not considering. 2 in addition to (apart from roses we grow irises). [ME f. OF f. à to + part side]

a•part•heid /əpáart-hayt, –hīt/ n. 1 (esp. as formerly in S. Africa) a policy or system of segregation or discrimination on grounds of race. 2 segregation in other contexts. [Afrik. (as APART, –HOOD)]

a•part•ment /əpáartmənt/ n. 1 a set of rooms, usu. on one floor, used as a residence. 2 (in pl.) a suite of rooms, usu. rented. [F appartement f. It. appartamento f. appartare to separate f. a parte apart]

a•part•ment build•ing n. (also **a•part•ment house**) a building containing a number of separate apartments.

ap•a•thet•ic /ápəthétik/ adj. having or showing no emotion or interest. □□ **ap•a•thet•i•cal•ly** adv. [APATHY, after PATHETIC]

ap•a•thy /ápəthee/ n. (often foll. by toward) lack of interest or feeling; indifference. [F apathie f. L apathia f. Gk apatheia f. apathēs without feeling f. a- not + pathos suffering]

ap•a•tite /ápətīt/ n. a naturally occurring crystalline mineral of calcium phosphate and fluoride, used in the manufacture of fertilizers. [G Apatit f. Gk apatē deceit (from its deceptive forms)]

ap•a•to•sau•rus /əpátəsáwrəs/ n. a large herbivorous dinosaur of the late Jurassic period, with a long neck and tail. Formerly called **brontosaurus.**

ape /ayp/ n. & v. ● n. 1 any of the various primates of the family Pongidae characterized by the absence of a tail, e.g., the gorilla, chimpanzee, orangutan, or gibbon. 2 (in general use) any monkey. 3 a an imitator. b an apelike person. ● v.tr. imitate; mimic. □ **go ape** sl. 1 become crazy. 2 be emotional or enthusiastic. [OE apa f. Gmc]

ape-man n. (pl. •men) any of various apelike primates held to be forerunners of present-day human beings.

a•per•çu /aapersý/ n. 1 a summary or survey. 2 an insight. [F, past part. of apercevoir perceive]

a•per•i•ent /əpéereeənt/ adj. & n. ● adj. laxative. ● n. a laxative medicine. [L aperire aperient- to open]

a•pe•ri•od•ic /áypeereeódik/ adj. 1 not periodic; irregular. 2 Physics (of a potentially oscillating or vibrating system, e.g., an instrument with a pointer) that is adequately damped to prevent oscillation or vibration. 3 (of an oscillation or vibration) without a regular period. □□ **a•pe•ri•o•dic•i•ty** /–reeədísitee/ n.

a•pe•ri•tif /əpériteéf/ n. an alcoholic drink taken before a meal to stimulate the appetite. [F apéritif f. med.L aperitivus f. L aperire to open]

ap•er•ture /ápərchər/ n. 1 an opening; a gap. 2 a space through which light passes in an optical or photographic instrument, esp. a variable space in a camera. [L apertura f. APERITIF]

ap•er•y /áypəree/ n. (pl. •ies) 1 mimicry. 2 a prank or trick.

a•pet•al•ous /aypét'ləs/ adj. Bot. (of flowers) having no petals. [mod.L apetalus f. Gk apetalos leafless f. a- not + petalon leaf]

A•pex /áypeks/ n. (also **APEX**) (often attrib.) a system of reduced fares for scheduled airline flights when paid for before a certain period in advance of departure. [Advance Purchase Excursion]

a•pex /áypeks/ n. (pl. **apexes** or **apices** /áypiseez/) 1 the highest point. 2 a climax; a high point of achievement, etc. 3 the vertex of a triangle or cone. 4 a tip or pointed end. [L, = peak, tip]

a•phaer•e•sis /əférisis/ n. (also **apheresis**) (pl. **aphaereses, aphereses** /–seez/) the omission of a letter or syllable at the beginning of a word as a morphological development (e.g., in the derivation of adder from naddre). [LL f. Gk aphairesis (as APO-, haireō take)]

a•pha•sia /əfáyzhə/ n. Med. the loss of ability to understand or express speech, owing to brain damage. □□ **a•pha•sic** /–zik/ adj. & n. [mod.L f. Gk f. aphatos speechless f. a- not + pha- speak]

a•phe•li•on /əfeéleeən, ap-heéleeən/ n. (pl. **aphelia**) the point in a body's orbit where it is furthest from the sun (opp. PERIHELION). ¶ Symb.: **Q.** [f. mod.L aphelium f. Gk aph' hēliou from the sun]

aph•e•sis /áfisis/ n. (pl. **apheses** /–seez/) the gradual loss of an unstressed vowel at the beginning of a word (e.g., of e from esquire to form squire). □□ **a•phet•ic** /əfétik/ adj. **a•phet•i•cal•ly** adv. [Gk, = letting go (as APO-, hiēmi send)]

a•phid /áyfid/ n. any small homopterous insect which feeds by sucking sap from leaves, stems, or roots of plants; a plant louse. [back-form. f. aphides: see APHIS]

a•phis /áyfis, áfis/ n. (pl. **aphides** /áyfideez/) an aphid, esp. of the genus Aphis including the greenfly. [mod.L (Linnaeus) f. Gk (1523), perh. a misreading of koris bug]

a•pho•ni•a /ayfóneeə/ n. (also **aphony** /áfənee/) Med. the loss or absence of the voice through a disease of the larynx or mouth. [mod.L aphonia f. Gk f. aphōnos voiceless f. a- not + phōnē voice]

aph•o•rism /áfərizəm/ n. 1 a short pithy maxim. 2 a brief statement of a principle. □□ **aph•o•rist** n. **aph•o•ris•tic** adj. **aph•o•ris•ti•cal•ly**

adv. **aph•o•rize** *v.intr.* [F *aphorisme* or LL f. Gk *aphorismos* definition f. *aphorizō* (as APO-, *horos* boundary)]

aph•ro•dis•i•ac /áfrədéézeeak,–díz–/ *adj. & n.* ● *adj.* that arouses sexual desire. ● *n.* an aphrodisiac drug. [Gk *aphrodisiakos* f. *aphrodisios* f. *Aphroditē* Gk goddess of love]

a•phyl•lous /ayfíləs/ *adj. Bot.* (of plants) having no leaves. [mod.L f. Gk *aphullos* f. *a-* not + *phullon* leaf]

a•pi•an /áypeeən/ *adj.* of or relating to bees. [L *apianus* f. *apis* bee]

a•pi•ar•y /áypee-eree/ *n.* (*pl.* -ies) a place where bees are kept. □□ a•pi•a•rist *n.* [L *apiarium* f. *apis* bee]

a•pi•cal /áypikəl, áp–/ *adj.* of, at, or forming an apex. □□ a•pi•cal•ly *adv.* [L *apex apicis*: see APEX]

a•pi•ces *pl.* of APEX.

a•pi•cul•ture /áypikulchər/ *n.* beekeeping. □□ a•pi•cul•tur•al /–kúlchərəl/ *adj.* a•pi•cul•tur•ist *n.* [L *apis* bee, after AGRICULTURE]

a•piece /əpées/ *adv.* for each one; severally; individually (*had five dollars apiece*). [A² + PIECE]

ap•ish /áypish/ *adj.* 1 of or like an ape. 2 silly; affected. □□ ap•ish•ly *adv.* ap•ish•ness *n.*

ap•la•nat /áplənat/ *n.* a reflecting or refracting surface made aplanatic by correction. [G]

ap•la•nat•ic /áplənátik/ *adj.* (of a reflecting or refracting surface) free from spherical aberration. [Gk *aplanētos* free from error f. *a-* not + *planaō* wander]

a•pla•sia /əpláyzhə/ *n. Med.* total or partial failure of development of an organ or tissue. □□ a•plas•tic /əplástik/ *adj.* [mod.L f. Gk f. *a-* not + *plasis* formation]

a•plen•ty /əpléntee/ *adv.* in plenty.

a•plomb /əplóm, əplúm/ *n.* assurance; self-confidence. [F, = perpendicularity, f. *àplomb* according to a plummet]

ap•ne•a /ápneeə, apnéeə/ *n. Med.* a temporary cessation of breathing. [mod.L f. Gk *apnoia* f. *apnous* breathless]

APO *abbr.* US Army post office.

apo– /ápó/ *prefix* 1 away from (*apogee*). 2 separate (*apocarpous*). [Gk *apo* from, away, un–, quite]

Apoc. *abbr.* 1 Apocalypse (New Testament). 2 Apocrypha.

a•poc•a•lypse /əpókəlips/ *n.* 1 (**the Apocalypse**) Revelation, the last book of the New Testament, recounting a divine revelation to St John. 2 a revelation, esp. of the end of the world. 3 a grand or violent event resembling those described in the Apocalypse. [ME f. OF ult. f. Gk *apokalupsis* f. *apokaluptō* uncover, reveal]

a•poc•a•lyp•tic /əpókəlíptik/ *adj.* 1 of or resembling the Apocalypse. 2 revelatory; prophetic. □□ a•poc•a•lyp•ti•cal•ly *adv.* [Gk *apokaluptikos* (as APOCALYPSE)]

ap•o•car•pous /ápəkáarpəs/ *adj. Bot.* (of ovaries) having distinct carpels not joined together (opp. SYNCARPOUS). [APO- + Gk *karpos* fruit]

ap•o•chro•mat /ápəkrōmát/ *n.* a lens or lens system that reduces spherical and chromatic aberrations. □□ ap•o•chro•mat•ic *adj.* [APO- + CHROMATIC]

a•poc•o•pe /əpókəpee/ *n.* the omission of a letter or letters at the end of a word as a morphological development (e.g., in the derivation of *curio* from *curiosity*). [LL f. Gk *apokopē* (as APO-, *koptō* cut)]

Apocr. *abbr.* Apocrypha.

ap•o•crine /ápəkrin, –krīn/ *adj. Biol.* (of a multicellular gland, e.g., the mammary gland) releasing some cytoplasm when secreting. [APO- + Gk *krinō* to separate]

A•poc•ry•pha /əpókrifə/ *n.pl.* 1 the books included in the Septuagint and Vulgate versions of the Old Testament but not in the Hebrew Bible. 2 (**apocrypha**) writings or reports not considered genuine. [ME f. eccl.L *apocrypha* (*scripta*) hidden writings f. Gk *apokruphos* f. *apokruptō* hide away]

▶Modern Bibles sometimes include these books (sense 1) in the Old Testament or as an appendix, and sometimes omit them.

a•poc•ry•phal /əpókrifəl/ *adj.* 1 of doubtful authenticity. 2 invented; mythical (*an apocryphal story*). 3 of or belonging to the Apocrypha.

ap•o•dal /ápəd'l/ *adj.* 1 without (or with undeveloped) feet. 2 (of fish) without ventral fins. [Gk *apous* apodal creature f. Gk *apous* footless f. *a-* not + *pous podos* foot]

ap•o•dic•tic /ápədíktik/ *adj.* (also **apodeictic** /–díktik/) 1 clearly established. 2 of clear demonstration. [L *apodicticus* f. Gk *apodeiktikos* (as APO-, *deiknumi* show)]

a•pod•o•sis /əpódəsis/ *n.* (*pl.* **apodoses** /–seez/) the main (consequent) clause of a conditional sentence (e.g., *I would agree* in *if you asked me I would agree*). [LL f. Gk f. *apodidōmi* give back (as APO-, *didōmi* give)]

ap•o•gee /ápəjee/ *n.* 1 a the point in a celestial body's orbit where it is farthest from the earth (opp. PERIGEE). b the point in a celestial body's orbit where it is farthest from the body being orbited. 2 the most distant or highest point. □□ ap•o•ge•an /ápəjéeən/ *adj.* [F *apogée* or mod.L *apogaeum* f. Gk *apogeion* away from earth (as APO-, *gē* earth)]

a•po•lit•i•cal /áypəlítikəl/ *adj.* not interested in or concerned with politics.

A•pol•lo•ni•an /ápəlōneeən/ *adj.* 1 of or relating to Apollo, the Greek

and Roman sun god, patron of music and poetry. 2 orderly; rational; self-disciplined. [L *Apollonius* f. Gk *Apollōnios*]

a•pol•o•get•ic /əpólójétik/ *adj. & n.* ● *adj.* 1 regretfully acknowledging or excusing an offense or failure. 2 diffident. 3 of reasoned defense or vindication. ● *n.* (usu. in *pl.*) a reasoned defense, esp. of Christianity. □□ a•pol•o•get•i•cal•ly *adv.* [F *apologétique* f. LL *apologeticus* f. Gk *apologētikos* f. *apologeomai* speak in defense]

a•po•lo•gi•a /ápəlójeeə/ *n.* a formal defense of one's opinions or conduct. [L: see APOLOGY]

a•pol•o•gist /əpóləjist/ *n.* a person who defends something by argument. [F *apologiste* f. Gk *apologizomai* render account f. *apologos* account]

a•pol•o•gize /əpólójīz/ *v.intr.* 1 (often foll. by *for*) make an apology for an offense or failure; express regret. 2 (foll by *for*) seek to explain or justify. [Gk *apologizomai*: see APOLOGIST]

ap•o•logue /ápəlawg, –log/ *n.* a moral fable. [F *apologue* or L *apologus* f. Gk *apologos* story (as APO-, *logos* discourse)]

a•pol•o•gy /əpóləjee/ *n.* (*pl.* **-gies**) 1 a regretful acknowledgement of an offense or failure. 2 an assurance that no offense was intended. 3 an explanation or defense. 4 (foll. by *for*) a poor or scanty specimen of (*this apology for a letter*). [F *apologie* or LL *apologia* f. Gk (as APOLOGETIC)]

ap•o•lune /ápəlōōn/ *n.* the point in a body's lunar orbit where it is furthest from the moon's center (opp. PERILUNE). [APO-+ L *luna* moon, after *apogee*]

ap•o•mix•is /ápəmíksis/ *n.* (*pl.* **apomixes** /–seez/) *Biol.* a form of asexual reproduction (cf. AMPHIMIXIS). □□ ap•o•mic•tic /–míktik/ *adj.* [mod.L, formed as APO- + Gk *mixis* mingling]

ap•o•plec•tic /ápəpléktik/ *adj.* 1 of, causing, suffering, or liable to apoplexy. 2 *colloq.* enraged. □□ ap•o•plec•ti•cal•ly *adv.* [F *apoplectique* or LL *apoplecticus* f. Gk *apoplēktikos* f. *apoplēssō* strike completely (as APO-, *plēssō* strike)]

ap•o•plex•y /ápəpleksee/ *n.* a sudden loss of consciousness, voluntary movement, and sensation caused by blockage or rupture of a brain artery; a stroke. [ME f. OF *apoplexie* f. LL *apoplexia* f. Gk *apoplēxia* (as APOPLECTIC)]

ap•o•se•mat•ic /ápəsimátik/ *adj. Zool.* (of coloration, markings, etc.) serving to warn or repel. [APO- + Gk *sēma sēmatos* sign]

a•pos•ta•sy /əpóstəsee/ *n.* (*pl.* **-sies**) 1 renunciation of a belief or faith, esp. religious. 2 abandonment of principles or of a party. 3 an instance of apostasy. [ME f. eccl.L f. NT Gk *apostasia* f. *apostasis* defection (as APO-, *stat-* stand)]

a•pos•tate /əpóstayt/ *n. & adj.* ● *n.* a person who renounces a former belief, adherence, etc. ● *adj.* engaged in apostasy. □□ ap•o•stat•i•cal /ápəstátikəl/ *adj.* [ME f. OF *apostate* or eccl.L *apostata* f. Gk *apostatēs* deserter (as APOSTASY)]

a•pos•ta•tize /əpóstətiz/ *v.intr.* renounce a former belief, adherence, etc. [med.L *apostatizare* f. *apostata*: see APOSTATE]

a pos•te•ri•o•ri /áy posteéree-áwree, –áwri/ *adj. & adv.* ● *adj.* (of reasoning) inductive; empirical; proceeding from effects to causes. ● *adv.* inductively; empirically; from effects to causes (opp. A PRIORI). [L, = from what comes after]

a•pos•tle /əpósəl/ *n.* 1 (**Apostle**) a any of the chosen twelve first sent out to preach the Christian Gospel. b the first successful Christian missionary in a country or to a people. 2 a leader or outstanding figure, esp. of a reform movement (*apostle of temperance*). 3 a messenger or representative. □□ a•pos•tle•ship *n.* [OE *apostol* f. eccl.L *apostolus* f. Gk *apostolos* messenger (as APO-, *stellō* send forth)]

a•pos•tle bird *n.* any of various Australian birds, forming flocks of about a dozen.

A•pos•tles' Creed *n.* an early statement of the Christian creed, ascribed to the Apostles.

a•pos•to•late /əpóstələt, –layt/ *n.* 1 the position or authority of an Apostle. 2 leadership in reform. [eccl.L *apostolatus* (as APOSTLE)]

ap•os•tol•ic /ápəstólik/ *adj.* 1 of or relating to the Apostles. 2 of the Pope regarded as the successor of St. Peter. 3 of the character of an Apostle. [F *apostolique* or eccl.L *apostolicus* f. Gk *apostolikos* (as APOSTLE)]

Ap•os•tol•ic Fa•thers *n.* the Christian leaders immediately succeeding the Apostles.

ap•os•tol•ic suc•ces•sion *n.* the uninterrupted transmission of spiritual authority from the Apostles through successive popes and bishops.

a•pos•tro•phe[1] /əpóstrəfee/ *n.* a punctuation mark used to indicate: 1 the omission of letters or numbers (e.g., *can't*; *he's*; *Class of '92*). 2 the possessive case (e.g., *Harry's book*; *boys' coats*). [F *apostrophe* or LL *apostrophus* f. Gk *apostrophos* accent of elision f. *apostrephō* turn away (as APO-, *strephō* turn)]

▶The apostrophe is used 1.to indicate missing letters or numbers: *Hallowe'en, the summer of '63*; 2. in forming some possessives; see note at POSSESSIVE; 3. in forming some plurals; see note at PLURAL.

a•pos•tro•phe[2] /əpóstrəfee/ *n.* an exclamatory passage in a speech or poem, addressed to a person (often dead or absent) or thing (often personified). □□ **a·pos·tro·phize** *v.tr. & intr.* [L f. Gk, lit. 'turning away' (as APOSTROPHE[1])]

a·poth·e·car·ies' meas·ure *n.* (also **a·poth·e·car·ies' weight**) system of weights formerly used in dispensing drugs.

a·poth·e·car·y /əpóthəkeree/ *n.* (*pl.* **-ies**) *archaic* a pharmacist or pharmacy licensed to dispense medicines and drugs. [ME f. OF *apotecaire* f. LL *apothecarius* f. L *apotheca* f. Gk *apothēkē* storehouse]

ap·o·thegm /ápəthem/ *a* terse saying or maxim; an aphorism. □□ **ap·o·theg·mat·ic** /–thegmátik/ *adj.* [F *apophthegme* or mod.L *apothegma* f. Gk *apophthegma –matos* f. *apophtheggomai* speak out]

ap·o·them /ápəthem/ *n. Geom.* a line from the center of a regular polygon at right angles to any of its sides. [Gk *apotithēmi* put aside (as APO-, *tithēmi* place)]

a·poth·e·o·sis /əpóthee-ósis/ *n.* (*pl.* **apotheoses** /–seez/) **1** elevation to divine status; deification. **2** a glorification of a thing; a sublime example (*apotheosis of the dance*). **3** a deified ideal. [eccl.L f. Gk *apotheoō* make a god of (as APO-, *theos* god)]

a·poth·e·o·size /əpótheeəsīz/ *v.tr.* **1** make divine; deify. **2** idealize; glorify.

ap·o·tro·pa·ic /ápətrōpáyik/ *adj.* supposedly having the power to avert an evil influence or bad luck. [Gk *apotropaios* (as APO-, *trepō* turn)]

ap·pall /əpáwl/ *v.tr.* (also **ap·pal**) (**ap·palled, ap·pall·ing**) **1** greatly dismay or horrify. **2** (as **appalling** *adj.*) *colloq.* shocking; unpleasant; bad. □□ **ap·pall·ing·ly** *adv.* [ME f. OF *apalir* grow pale]

Ap·pa·loo·sa /ápəlōōsə/ *n.* **1** a horse of a N. American breed having dark spots on a light background. **2** this breed. [*Opelousa* in Louisiana, or *Palouse*, a river in Idaho]

ap·pa·nage /ápənij/ *n.* (also **apanage**) **1** government provision for the maintenance of members of a royal family, etc. **2** a perquisite. **3** a natural accompaniment or attribute. [F ult. f. med.L *appanare* endow with the means of subsistence (as APO-, *panis* bread)]

ap·pa·rat /ápərát, áápəráat/ *n.* the administrative system of a political party, esp. of a Communist party in a Communist country. [Russ. f. G, = apparatus]

ap·pa·rat·chik /áapəráatchik/ *n.* (*pl.* **apparatchiks** or *Russ.* **apparatchiki** /–kee/) **1 a** a member of a Communist apparat. **b** a Communist agent or spy. **2 a** a member of a political party in any country who blindly executes policy; a zealous functionary. **b** an official of a public or private organization. [Russ.: see APPARAT]

ap·pa·rat·us /ápərátəs, –ráytəs/ *n.* **1** the equipment needed for a particular purpose or function, esp. scientific or technical. **2** a political or other complex organization. **3** *Anat.* the organs used to perform a particular process. **4** (in full **apparatus criticus**) a collection of variants and annotations accompanying a printed text and usu. appearing below it. [L f. *apparare apparat-* make ready for]

ap·par·el /əpárəl/ *n. & v.* ● *n.* **1** clothing; dress. **2** embroidered ornamentation on some ecclesiastical vestments. ● *v.tr.* (**appareled, appareling** or **apparelled, apparelling**) clothe. [ME *aparailen* (v.) f. OF *apareillier* f. Rmc *appariculare* (unrecorded) make equal or fit, ult. f. L *par* equal]

ap·par·ent /əpárənt/ *adj.* **1** readily visible or perceivable. **2** seeming. □□ **ap·par·ent·ly** *adv.* [ME f. OF *aparant* f. L (as APPEAR)]

ap·par·ent mag·ni·tude *n.* the magnitude, i.e., brightness, of a celestial body as seen from the earth (opp. ABSOLUTE MAGNITUDE).

ap·par·ent time *n.* solar time (see SOLAR *adj.*).

ap·pa·ri·tion /ápəríshən/ *n.* a sudden or dramatic appearance, esp. of a ghost or phantom; a visible ghost. [ME f. F *apparition* or f. L *apparitio* attendance (as APPEAR)]

ap·peal /əpeel/ *v. & n.* ● *v.* **1** *intr.* make an earnest or formal request; plead (*appealed for calm; appealed to us not to leave*). **2** *intr.* (usu. foll. by *to*) be attractive or of interest; be pleasing. **3** *intr.* (foll. by *to*) resort to or cite for support. **4** *Law* a *intr.* (often foll. by *to*) apply (to a higher court) for a reconsideration of the decision of a lower court. **b** *tr.* refer to a higher court to review (a case). **c** *intr.* (foll. by *against*) apply to a higher court to reconsider (a verdict or sentence). **5** *intr. Sports* call on an umpire or referee to reverse a decision. ● *n.* **1** the act or an instance of appealing. **2** a formal or urgent request for public support, esp. financial, for a cause. **3** *Law* the referral of a case to a higher court. **4** attractiveness; appealing quality (*sex appeal*). □□ **ap·peal·er** *n.* [ME f. OF *apel, apeler* f. L *appellare* to address]

ap·peal·a·ble /əpeeləbəl/ *adj. Law* (of a case) that can be referred to a higher court for review.

ap·peal·ing /əpeeling/ *adj.* attractive; likable. □□ **ap·peal·ing·ly** *adv.*

ap·pear /əpeer/ *v.intr.* **1** become or be visible. **2** be evident (*a new problem then appeared*). **3** seem; have the appearance of being (*appeared unwell; you appear to be right*). **4** present oneself publicly or formally, esp. on stage or as the accused or counsel in a court of law. **5** be published (*it appeared in the papers; a new edition will appear*). [ME f. OF *apareir* f. L *apparēre apparit-* come in sight]

ap·pear·ance /əpeerəns/ *n.* **1** the act or an instance of appearing. **2** an outward form as perceived (whether correctly or not), esp.

visually (*neaten up one's appearance; gives the appearance of trying hard*). **3** a semblance. □ **keep up appearances** maintain an impression or pretense of virtue, affluence, etc. **make** (or **put in**) **an appearance** be present, esp. briefly. **to all appearances** as far as can be seen; apparently. [ME f. OF *aparance, –ence* f. LL *apparentia* (as APPEAR, –ENCE)]

ap·pease /əpeez/ *v.tr.* **1** make calm or quiet, esp. conciliate (a potential aggressor) by making concessions. **2** satisfy (an appetite, scruples). □□ **ap·pease·ment** *n.* **ap·peas·er** *n.* [ME f. AF *apeser*, OF *apaisier* f. *à* to + *pais* PEACE]

ap·pel·lant /əpélənt/ *n. Law* a person who appeals to a higher court. [ME f. F (as APPEAL, –ANT)]

ap·pel·late /əpélət/ *adj. Law* (esp. of a court) concerned with or dealing with appeals. [L *appellatus* (as APPEAL, –ATE[2])]

ap·pel·la·tion /ápəláyshən/ *n. formal* a name or title; nomenclature. [ME f. OF f. L *appellatio –onis* (as APPEAL, –ATION)]

ap·pel·la·tive /əpélətiv/ *adj.* **1** naming. **2** *Gram.* (of a noun) that designates a class; common. [LL *appellativus* (as APPEAL, –ATIVE)]

ap·pend /əpénd/ *v.tr.* (usu. foll. by *to*) attach, affix, add, esp. to a written document, etc. [L *appendere* hang]

ap·pend·age /əpéndij/ *n.* **1** something attached; an addition. **2** *Zool.* a limb or other projecting part of a body.

ap·pend·ant /əpéndənt/ *adj. & n.* ● *adj.* (usu. foll. by *to*) attached in a subordinate capacity. ● *n.* an appendant person or thing. [OF *apendant* f. *apendre* formed as APPEND, –ANT]

ap·pen·dec·to·my /ápəndéktəmee/ *n.* (also **ap·pen·di·cec·to·my** /–diséktəmee/) (*pl.* **-mies**) the surgical removal of the appendix. [APPENDIX + –ECTOMY]

ap·pen·di·ci·tis /əpéndisítis/ *n.* inflammation of the appendix. [APPENDIX + –ITIS]

ap·pen·dix /əpéndiks/ *n.* (*pl.* **appendices** /–diseez/; **appendixes**) **1** (in full **vermiform appendix**) *Anat.* a small outgrowth of tissue forming a tube-shaped sac attached to the lower end of the large intestine. **2** subsidiary matter at the end of a book or document. [L *appendix –icis* f. *appendere* APPEND]

ap·per·ceive /ápərseev/ *v.tr.* **1** be conscious of perceiving. **2** *Psychol.* compare (a perception) to previously held ideas so as to extract meaning from it. □□ **ap·per·cep·tion** /–sépshən/ *n.* **ap·per·cep·tive** *adj.* [ME (in obs. sense 'observe') f. OF *aperceveir* ult. f. L *percipere* PERCEIVE]

ap·per·tain /ápərtáyn/ *v.intr.* (foll. by *to*) **1** relate. **2** belong as a possession or right. **3** be appropriate. [ME f. OF *apertenir* f. LL *appertinēre* f. *pertinēre* PERTAIN]

ap·pe·tence /ápitəns/ *n.* (also **appetency** /–tənsee/) (foll. by *for*) longing or desire. [F *appétence* or L *appetentia* f. *appetere* seek after]

ap·pe·tite /ápitīt/ *n.* **1** a natural desire to satisfy bodily needs, esp. for food or sexual activity. **2** (usu. foll. by *for*) an inclination or desire. □□ **ap·pe·ti·tive** /ápitítiv/ *adj.* [ME f. OF *apetit* f. L *appetitus* f. *appetere* seek after]

ap·pe·tiz·er /ápitīzər/ *n.* a small amount, esp. of food or drink served before a meal, to stimulate an appetite. [appetize (back-form. f. APPETIZING)]

ap·pe·tiz·ing /ápitīzing/ *adj.* stimulating an appetite, esp. for food. □□ **ap·pe·tiz·ing·ly** *adv.* [F *appétissant* irreg. f. *appétit*, formed as APPETITE]

ap·plaud /əpláwd/ *v.* **1** *intr.* express strong approval or praise, esp. by clapping. **2** *tr.* express approval of (a person or action). [L *aapplaudere applaus-* clap hands]

ap·plause /əpláwz/ *n.* **1** an expression of approbation, esp. from an audience, etc., by clapping. **2** emphatic approval. [med.L *applausus* (as APPLAUD)]

ap·ple /ápəl/ *n.* **1** the fruit of a tree of the genus *Malus*, rounded in form and with a crisp flesh. **2** the tree bearing this. □ **apple of one's eye** a cherished person or thing. **she's apples** *Austral. sl.* everything is fine. **upset the applecart** spoil careful plans. [OE *æppel* f. Gmc]

ap·ple·jack /ápəljak/ *n.* an alcoholic beverage made by distilling or freezing fermented apple cider. [APPLE + JACK[1]]

ap·ple-pie bed *n.* a bed made (as a joke) with the sheets folded short, so that the legs cannot be accommodated.

ap·ple-pie or·der *n.* perfect order; extreme neatness.

ap·pli·ance /əplíəns/ *n.* a device or piece of equipment used for a specific task, esp. a household device for washing, drying, cooking, etc. [APPLY + –ANCE]

ap·pli·ca·ble /áplikəbəl, əplíkə–/ *adj.* (often foll. by *to*) **1** that may be applied. **2** having reference; appropriate. □□ **ap·pli·ca·bil·i·ty** *n.* **ap·pli·ca·bly** *adv.* [OF *applicable* or med.L *applicabilis* (as APPLY, –ABLE)]

PRONUNCIATION TIP applicable

The older pronunciation of this word places the stress on the first syllable, but it is fully acceptable to place the stress on the second syllable.

ap·pli·cant /áplikənt/ *n.* a person who applies for something, esp. a job. [APPLICATION + –ANT]

ap·pli·ca·tion /áplikáyshən/ n. **1** the act or an instance of applying. **2** a formal request, usu. in writing, for employment, membership, etc. **3 a** relevance. **b** the use to which something can or should be put. **4** sustained or concentrated effort; diligence. [ME f. F f. L *applicatio –onis* (as APPLY, –ATION)]

ap·pli·ca·tor /áplikaytər/ n. a device for applying a substance to a surface. [APPLICATION + –OR[1]]

ap·plied /əplíd/ adj. (of a subject of study) put to practical use as opposed to being theoretical (cf. PURE adj. 10). □ **applied mathematics** see MATHEMATICS.

ap·pli·qué /áplikáy/ n., adj., & v. ● n. ornamental work in which fabric is cut out and attached, usu. sewn, to the surface of another fabric to form pictures or patterns. ● adj. executed in appliqué. ● v.tr. (**appliqués, appliquéd, appliquéing**) decorate with appliqué; make using appliqué technique. [F, past part. of *appliquer* apply f. L *applicare*: see APPLY]

ap·ply /əplí/ v. (**·plies, ·plied**) **1** intr. (often foll. by *for, to,* or *to* + infin.) make a formal request for something to be done, given, etc. (*apply for a job; apply for help to the governors; applied to be sent overseas*). **2** intr. have relevance (*does not apply in this case*). **3** tr. **a** make use of as relevant or suitable; employ (*apply the rules*). **b** operate (*apply the hand brake*). **4** tr. (often foll. by *to*) **a** put or spread on (*applied the ointment to the cut*). **b** administer (*applied the remedy; applied common sense to the problem*). **5** refl. (often foll. by *to*) devote oneself (*applied myself to the task*). □□ **ap·pli·er** n. [ME f. OF *aplier* f. L *applicare* fold, fasten to]

ap·pog·gia·tu·ra /əpój ətóŏrə/ n. *Mus.* a grace note performed before an essential note of a melody and normally taking half or less than half its time value. [It.]

ap·point /əpóynt/ v.tr. **1** assign a post or office to (*appoint him governor; appoint her to govern; appointed to the post*). **2** (often foll. by *for*) fix; decide on (a time, place, etc.) (*Wednesday was appointed for the meeting; 8:30 was the appointed time*). **3** prescribe; ordain. **4** *Law* **a** (also *absol.*) declare the destination of (property, etc.). **b** declare (a person) as having an interest in property, etc. (*Jones was appointed in the will*). **5** (as **appointed** adj.) equipped; furnished (*a badly appointed hotel*). □□ **ap·point·ee** /–teé/ n. **ap·point·er** n. **ap·poin·tor** adj. [ME f. OF *apointer* f. *à point* to a point]

ap·point·ment /əpóyntmənt/ n. **1** an arrangement to meet at a specific time and place. **2 a** a post or office, esp. one available for applicants, or recently filled (*took up the appointment on Monday*). **b** a person appointed. **c** the act or an instance of appointing, esp. to a post. **3** (usu. in *pl.*) **a** furniture; fittings. **b** equipment. [ME f. OF *apointement* (as APPOINT, –MENT)]

ap·por·tion /əpáwrshən/ v.tr. (often foll. by *to*) share out; assign as a share. □□ **ap·por·tion·a·ble** adj. **ap·por·tion·ment** n. [F *apportionner* or f. med.L *apportionare* (as AD-, PORTION)]

ap·po·site /ápəzit/ adj. (often foll. by *to*) apt; well chosen. **2** well expressed. □□ **ap·po·site·ly** adv. **ap·po·site·ness** n. [L *appositus* past part. of *apponere* (as AD-, *ponere* put)]

ap·po·si·tion /ápəzíshən/ n. **1** placing side by side; juxtaposition. **2** *Gram.* the placing of a word next to another, esp. the addition of one noun to another, in order to qualify or explain the first (e.g., *William the Conqueror; my friend Sue*). □□ **ap·po·si·tion·al** adj. [ME f. F *apposition* or f. LL *appositio* (as APPOSITE, –ITION)]

ap·pos·i·tive /əpózitiv/ n. a word or phrase placed in apposition to another.

ap·prais·al /əpráyzəl/ n. the act or an instance of appraising.

ap·praise /əpráyz/ v.tr. **1** estimate the value or quality of (*appraised her skills*). **2** (esp. officially or expertly) set a price on; value. □□ **ap·prais·a·ble** adj. **ap·prais·er** n. **ap·prais·ive** adj. [APPRIZE by assim. to PRAISE]

▶Appraise, meaning 'evaluate,' should not be confused with **apprise**, which means 'inform': *The painting was appraised at $3 million. They gasped when apprised of this valuation.*

ap·pre·ci·a·ble /əpréeshəbəl/ adj. large enough to be noticed; significant; considerable (*appreciable progress has been made*). □□ **ap·pre·ci·a·bly** adv. [F f. *apprécier* (as APPRECIATE)]

ap·pre·ci·ate /əpréeshee-áyt/ v. **1** tr. **a** esteem highly; value. **b** be grateful for (*we appreciate your sympathy*). **c** be sensitive to (*appreciate the nuances*). **2** tr. (often foll. by *that* + clause) understand; recognize (*I appreciate that I may be wrong*). **3 a** intr. (of property, etc.) rise in value. **b** tr. raise in value. □□ **ap·pre·cia·tive** /–shətiv, –shee-áytiv/ adj. **ap·pre·cia·tive·ly** adv. **ap·pre·cia·tive·ness** n. **ap·pre·ci·a·tor** n. **ap·pre·ci·a·to·ry** /–sheeətáwree/ adj. [LL *appretiare* appraise (as AD-, *pretium* price)]

ap·pre·ci·a·tion /əpreéshee-áyshən/ n. **1** favorable or grateful

recognition. **2** an estimation or judgment; sensitive understanding of or reaction to (*a quick appreciation of the problem*). **3** an increase in value. **4** a (usu. favorable) review of a book, movie, etc. [F f. LL *appretiatio –onis* (as APPRECIATE, –ATION)]

ap·pre·hend /áprihénd/ v.tr. **1** understand; perceive (*apprehend your meaning*). **2** seize; arrest (*apprehended the criminal*). **3** anticipate with uneasiness or fear (*apprehending the results*). [F *appréhender* or L *apprehendere* (as AD-, *prehendere prehens-* lay hold of)]

ap·pre·hen·si·ble /áprihénsibəl/ adj. capable of being apprehended by the senses or the intellect (*an apprehensible theory; an apprehensible change in her expression*). □□ **ap·pre·hen·si·bil·i·ty** /–bilitee/ n. [LL *apprehensibilis* (as APPREHEND, –IBLE)]

ap·pre·hen·sion /áprihénshən/ n. **1** uneasiness; dread. **2** understanding; perception. **3** arrest; capture (*apprehension of the suspect*). **4** an idea; a conception. [F *appréhension* or LL *apprehensio* (as APPREHEND, –ION)]

ap·pre·hen·sive /áprihénsiv/ adj. **1** (often foll. by *of, for, over, about*) uneasily fearful; dreading. **2** relating to perception by the senses or the intellect. **3** perceptive; intelligent. □□ **ap·pre·hen·sive·ly** adv. **ap·pre·hen·sive·ness** n. [F *appréhensif* or med.L *apprehensivus* (as APPREHEND, –IVE)]

ap·pren·tice /əpréntis/ n. & v. ● n. **1** a person who is learning a trade by being employed in it for an agreed period usu. at low wages. **2** a beginner; a novice. ● v.tr. (usu. foll. by *to*) engage or bind as an apprentice (*was apprenticed to a builder*). □□ **ap·pren·tice·ship** n. [ME f. OF *aprentis* f. *apprendre* learn (as APPREHEND), after words in –*tis*, –*tif*, f. L –*tivus*: see –IVE]

ap·prise /əpríz/ v.tr. inform. □ **be apprised of** be aware of. [F *appris –ise* past part. of *apprendre* learn, teach (as APPREHEND)]
▶See note at APPRAISE.

ap·prize /əpríz/ v.tr. **1** esteem highly. **2** appraise. [ME f. OF *aprisier* f. *à* to + *pris* PRICE]

ap·pro /áprō/ n. *Brit. colloq.* □ **on appro** = *on approval* (see APPROVAL). [abbr. of *approval* or *approbation*]

ap·proach /əprō ch/ v. & n. ● v. **1** tr. come near or nearer to (a place or time). **2** intr. come near or nearer in space or time (*the hour approaches*). **3** tr. make a tentative proposal or suggestion to (*approached me about a loan*). **4** tr. **a** be similar in character, quality, etc., to (*doesn't approach her for artistic skill*). **b** approximate to (*a population approaching 5 million*). **5** tr. attempt to influence or bribe. **6** tr. set about, tackle (a task, etc.). **7** intr. *Golf* play an approach shot. **8** intr. *Aeron.* prepare to land. **9** tr. *archaic* bring near. ● n. **1** an act or means of approaching (*made an approach; an approach lined with trees*). **2** an approximation (*an approach to an apology*). **3** a way of dealing with a person or thing (*needs a new approach*). **4** (usu. in *pl.*) a sexual advance. **5** *Golf* a stroke from the fairway to the green. **6** *Aeron.* the final descent of a flight before landing. **7** *Bridge* a bidding method with a gradual advance to a final contract. [ME f. OF *aproch(i) er* f. eccl.L *appropiare* draw near (as AD-, *propius* compar. of *prope* near)]

ap·proach·a·ble /əprṓchəbəl/ adj. **1** friendly; easy to talk to. **2** able to be approached. □□ **ap·proach·a·bil·i·ty** /–bilitee/ n.

ap·pro·bate /áprəbayt/ v.tr. approve formally; sanction. [ME f. L *approbare* (as AD-, *probare* test f. *probus* good)]

ap·pro·ba·tion /áprəbáyshən/ n. approval; consent. □□ **ap·pro·ba·tive** adj. **ap·pro·ba·to·ry** /áprṓbətawree/ adj. [ME f. OF f. L *approbatio –onis* (as APPROBATE, –ATION)]

ap·pro·pri·ate adj. & v. ● adj. /əprṓpreeət/ (often foll. by *to, for*) **1** suitable or proper. **2** belonging or particular to. ● v.tr. /əprṓpreeayt/ **1** take possession of, esp. without authority. **2** devote (money, etc.) to special purposes. □□ **ap·pro·pri·ate·ly** adv. **ap·pro·pri·ate·ness** n. **ap·pro·pri·a·tor** n. [LL *appropriatus* past part. of *appropriare* (as AD-, *proprius* own)]

ap·pro·pri·a·tion /əprṓpreeáyshən/ n. **1** an act or instance of appropriating. **2** something appropriated, as money officially set aside for a specific use.

ap·prov·al /əprṓŏvəl/ n. **1** the act of approving. **2** an instance of this; consent; a favorable opinion (*with your approval; looked at him with approval*). □ **on approval** (of goods supplied) to be returned if not satisfactory.

ap·prove /əprṓŏv/ v. **1** tr. confirm; sanction (*approved her application*). **2** intr. give or have a favorable opinion. **3** tr. commend (*approved the new hat*). **4** tr. *archaic* (usu. *refl.*) demonstrate oneself to be (*approved himself a coward*). □ **approve of 1** pronounce or consider good or satisfactory; commend. **2** agree to. □□ **ap·prov·er** n. **ap·prov·ing·ly** adv. [ME f. OF *aprover* f. L (as APPROBATE)]

technical agreement (*to approve the plan*) to enthusiastic support (*she was quick to approve her son's decision to marry*). **Endorse** implies a more public and official expression of support and is used primarily in reference to things that require promotion or publicity (*endorse a political candidate*), while **commend** is to make a formal and usually public statement of approval or congratulation (*he was commended for his heroism*). **Sanction, certify,** and **ratify** imply that approval is not only official but that it makes something legal. To *sanction* is not only to *approve* but to authorize (*school authorities would not sanction the wearing of hats in class*), while *certify* implies conformity with certain standards (*certified to teach in the State of New York*). *Ratify* is usually confined to only the most official and authoritative settings. For example, an employer might *sanction* the idea of hiring a woman to perform a job that only men have performed in the past, and the woman in question might have to *certify* that she possesses the necessary training and qualifications. But to *ratify* a constitutional amendment granting equal rights to women requires a lengthy set of legislative procedures.

ap•proved school *n. Brit. hist.* a residential school for delinquents.
approx. *abbr.* **1** approximate. **2** approximately.
ap•prox•i•mate *adj. & v.* • *adj.* /əpr óksimət/ **1** fairly correct or accurate; near to the actual (*the approximate time of arrival; an approximate guess*). **2** near or next to (*your approximate neighbor*). • *v. tr. & intr.* /əpróksimayt/ bring or come near (esp. in quality, number, etc.), but not exactly (*approximates to the truth; approximates the amount required*). □□ **ap•prox•i•mate•ly** /-mətlee/ *adv.* **ap•prox•i•ma•tion** /-máyshən/ *n.* [LL *approximatus* past part. of *approximare* (as AD-, *proximus* very near)]
ap•pur•te•nance /əpərt'nəns/ *n.* (usu. in *pl.*) a belonging; an appendage; an accessory. [ME f. AF *apurtenaunce*, OF *apertenance* (as APPERTAIN, −ANCE)]
ap•pur•te•nant /əpərt'nənt/ *adj.* (often foll. by *to*) belonging or appertaining; pertinent. [ME f. OF *apartenant* pres. part. (as APPERTAIN)]
APR *abbr.* annual or annualized percentage rate (esp. of interest on loans or credit).
Apr. *abbr.* April.
a•près-ski /áprayskée, áapray−/ *n. & adj.* • *n.* the evening, esp. its social activities, following a day's skiing. • *attrib. adj.* (of clothes, drinks, etc.) appropriate to social activities following skiing. [F]
ap•ri•cot /áprikot, áypri−/ *n. & adj.* • *n.* **1 a** a juicy soft fruit, smaller than a peach, of an orange-yellow color. **b** the tree, *Prunus armeniaca*, bearing it. **2** the ripe fruit's orange-yellow color. • *adj.* orange-yellow (*apricot dress*). [Port. *albricoque* or Sp. *albaricoque* f. Arab. *al* the + *barkuk* f. late Gk *praikokion* f. L *praecoquum* var. of *praecox* early ripe: *apri-* after L *apricus* ripe, −*cot* by assim. to F *abricot*]
A•pril /áypril/ *n.* the fourth month of the year. [ME f. L *Aprilis*]
A•pril fool *n.* a person successfully tricked on April 1.
A•pril Fool's Day *n.* (also **April Fools' Day**) April 1, traditionally an occasion for playing tricks on people in many Western countries.
a pri•o•ri /áa pree-áwree, áy prī-áwrī ī/ *adj. & adv.* • *adj.* **1** (of reasoning) deductive; proceeding from causes to effects (opp. A POSTERIORI). **2** (of concepts, knowledge, etc.) logically independent of experience; not derived from experience (opp. EMPIRICAL). **3** not submitted to critical investigation (*an a priori conjecture*). • *adv.* **1** in an a priori manner. **2** as far as one knows; presumptively. □□ **a•pri•o•rism** /áypríoriz əm/ *n.* [L, = from what is before]
a•pron /áyprən/ *n.* **1 a** a garment covering and protecting the front of a person's clothes, either from chest or waist level, and tied at the back. **b** official clothing of this kind. **c** anything resembling an apron in shape or function. **2** *Theatr.* the part of a stage in front of the curtain. **3** the paved area of an airfield used for maneuvering or loading aircraft. **4** an endless conveyor belt. □□ **a•proned** *adj.*
a•pron•ful *n.* (*pl.* **-fuls**). [ME *naperon* etc., f. OF dimin. of *nape* tablecloth f. L *mappa*: for loss of *n* cf. ADDER]
a•pron strings *n.* ties for fastening an apron around one's body. □ **tied to a person's apron strings** dominated by or dependent on that person (usu. a woman).
ap•ro•pos /áprəpó/ *adj., adv., & prep.* • *adj.* to the point or purpose; appropriate (*his comment was apropos*). • *adv.* **1** appropriately (*spoke apropos*). **2** (*absol.*) by the way; incidentally (*apropos, she's not going*). • *prep.* (foll. by *of*) in respect to; concerning. [F *à propos* f. *à* to + *propos* PURPOSE]
apse /aps/ *n.* **1** a large semicircular or polygonal recess, arched or with a domed roof, esp. at the eastern end of a church. **2** = APSIS. □□ **ap•si•dal** /ápsid'l/ *adj.* [L APSIS]
ap•sis /ápsis/ *n.* (*pl.* **apsides** /-sideez/) either of two points in the orbit of a planet or satellite that are nearest to or farthest from the body around which it moves. □□ **ap•si•dal** /ápsid'l/ *adj.* [L f. Gk (*h*)*apsis, −idos* arch, vault]
apt /apt/ *adj.* **1** appropriate; suitable. **2** (foll. by *to* + infin.) having a

tendency (*apt to lose his temper*). **3** clever; quick to learn (*an apt pupil; apt at the work*). □□ **apt•ly** *adv.* **apt•ness** *n.* [ME f. L *aptus* fitted, past part. of *apere* fasten]
apt. *abbr.* **1** apartment. **2** aptitude.
ap•ter•ous /áptərəs/ *adj.* **1** *Zool.* (of insects) without wings. **2** *Bot.* (of seeds or fruits) having no winglike expansions. [Gk *apteros* f. *a-* not + *pteron* wing]
ap•ter•yx /áptəriks/ *n.* = KIWI. [mod.L f. Gk *a-* not + *pterux* wing]
ap•ti•tude /áptitōōd, −tyōōd/ *n.* **1** a natural propensity or talent (*shows an aptitude for drawing*). **2** ability or suitability, esp. to acquire a particular skill. [F f. LL *aptitudo −inis* (as APT, −TUDE)]
aq•ua /ákwə, áakwə/ *n.* the color aquamarine. [abbr.]
aq•ua•cul•ture /ákwəkulchər, áakwə−/ *n.* (also **aquiculture**) the cultivation or rearing of aquatic plants or animals. □□ **aq•ua•cul•tur•al** *adj.* **aq•ua•cul•tur•ist** *n.* [L *aqua* water + CULTURE, after *agriculture*]
aq•ua for•tis /ákwə fáwrtis, áakwə/ *n. Chem.* nitric acid. [L, = strong water]
Aq•ua-Lung /ákwəlung, áakwə−/ *n. & v. Trademark* (*Brit.* **aqualung**) • *n.* a portable breathing apparatus for divers, consisting of cylinders of compressed air strapped on the back, feeding air automatically through a mask or mouthpiece. • *v. intr.* use an Aqua-Lung. [L *aqua* water + LUNG]
aq•ua•ma•rine /ákwəmərée̅n, áakwə−/ *n.* **1** a light bluish green beryl. **2** its color. [L *aqua marina* sea water]
aq•ua•naut /ákwənawt, áakwə−/ *n.* an underwater swimmer or explorer. [L *aqua* water + Gk *nautēs* sailor]
aq•ua•plane /ákwəplayn, áakwə−/ *n. & v.* • *n.* a board for riding on the water, pulled by a speedboat. • *v. intr.* **1** ride on an aquaplane. **2** *Brit.* = HYDROPLANE *v.* 2 [L *aqua* water + PLANE[1]]
aq•ua re•gi•a /ákwə reéjeeə, reéjə, áakwə/ *n. Chem.* a mixture of concentrated nitric and hydrochloric acids, a highly corrosive liquid attacking many substances unaffected by other reagents. [L, = royal water]
aq•ua•relle /ákwərél/ *n.* a painting in thin, usu. transparent watercolors. [F f. It. *acquarella* watercolor, dimin. of *acqua* f. L *aqua* water]
a•quar•i•um /əkwáireeəm/ *n.* (*pl.* **aquariums** or **aquaria** /−reeə/) **1** an artificial environment designed for keeping live aquatic plants and animals for study or exhibition, esp. a tank of water with transparent sides. **2** an institution in which live aquatic plants and animals are kept for study and exhibition. [neut. of L *aquarius* of water (*aqua*) after *vivarium*]
A•quar•i•us /əkwáireeəs/ *n.* **1** a constellation, traditionally regarded as portraying the figure of a water carrier. **2 a** the eleventh sign of the zodiac (the Water Carrier). **b** a person born when the sun is in this sign. □□ **A•quar•i•an** *adj. & n.* [ME f. L (as AQUARIUM)]
a•quat•ic /əkwátik, əkwótik/ *adj. & n.* • *adj.* **1** growing or living in or near water. **2** (of sport) played in or on water. • *n.* **1** an aquatic plant or animal. **2** (in *pl.*) aquatic sports. [ME f. F *aquatique* or L *aquaticus* f. *aqua* water]
aq•ua•tint /ákwətint, áakwə−/ *n.* **1** a print resembling a watercolor, produced from a copper plate etched with nitric acid. **2** the process of producing this. [F *aquatinte* f. It. *acqua tinta* colored water]
aq•ua•vit /áakwəveet, ákwə−/ *n.* (also **ak•va•vit** /ákvə−/) an alcoholic liquor made from potatoes, etc., and usu. flavored with caraway seeds. [Scand.]
aq•ua vi•tae /áakwə vítee, veé−/ *n.* a strong alcoholic liquor, esp. brandy. [L = water of life]
aq•ue•duct /ákwidukt/ *n.* **1** an artificial channel for conveying water, esp. in the form of a bridge supported by tall columns across a valley. **2** *Physiol.* a small canal or passage for liquids in the body. [L *aquae ductus* conduit f. *aqua* water + *ducere duct-* to lead]
a•que•ous /áykweeəs, ák−/ *adj.* **1** of, containing, or like water. **2** *Geol.* produced by water (*aqueous rocks*). [med.L *aqueus* f. L *aqua* water]
a•que•ous hu•mor *n. Anat.* the clear fluid in the eye between the lens and the cornea.
aq•ui•fer /ákwifər/ *n. Geol.* a layer of rock or soil able to hold or transmit much water. [L *aqui-* f. *aqua* water + −*fer* bearing f. *ferre* bear]
aq•ui•le•gi•a /ákwileéjə/ *n.* any (often blue-flowered) plant of the genus *Aquilegia*. Also called **columbine.** [mod. use of a med.L word: orig. unkn.]
aq•ui•line /ákwilīn/ *adj.* **1** of or like an eagle. **2** (of a nose) curved like an eagle's beak. [L *aquilinus* f. *aquila* eagle]
AR *abbr.* Arkansas (in official postal use).
Ar *symb. Chem.* the element argon.
ar- /ər/ *prefix* assim. form of AD- before *r*.
-ar[1] /ər/ *suffix* **1** forming adjectives (*angular; linear; nuclear; titular*). **2** forming nouns (*scholar*). [OF −*aire* or −*ier* or L −*aris*]
-ar[2] /ər/ *suffix* forming nouns (*pillar*). [F −*er* or L −*ar*, −*are*, neut. of −*aris*]
-ar[3] /ər/ *suffix* forming nouns (*bursar; exemplar; mortar; vicar*). [OF −*aire* or −*ier* or L −*arius*, −*arium*]
-ar[4] /ər/ *suffix* assim. form of −ER[1], −OR[1] (*liar; beggar*).
Ar•ab /árəb/ *n. & adj.* • *n.* **1** a member of a Semitic people inhabiting originally Saudi Arabia and the neighboring countries, now the Middle East generally. **2** = ARABIAN 2. • *adj.* of Arabia or the

Arabs (esp. with ethnic reference). [F *Arabe* f. L *Arabs Arabis* f. Gk *Araps –abos* f. Arab. 'arab]

ar·a·besque /árəbésk/ *n.* **1** *Ballet* a posture with one leg extended horizontally backward, torso extended forward, and arms outstretched. **2** a design of intertwined leaves, scrolls, etc. **3** *Mus.* a florid melodic section or composition. **4** an elaborate, florid, or intricate design. [F f. It. *arabesco* f. *arabo* Arab]

arabesque

A·ra·bi·an /əráybeeən/ *adj. & n.* • *adj.* of or relating to Arabia (esp. with geographical reference) (*the Arabian desert*). • *n.* **1** a native of Arabia. **2** (in full **Arabian horse**) a horse of a breed orig. native to Arabia. [ME f. OF *arabi* prob. f. Arab. 'arabī, or f. L *Arabus, Arabius* f. Gk *Arabios*]

▶Arab is now generally used in reference to people; the use of **Arabian** in sense 1 of the noun is historical.

A·ra·bi·an cam·el *n.* a domesticated camel, *Camelus dromedarius*, native to the deserts of N. Africa and the Near East, with one hump. Also called **dromedary**.

Ar·a·bic /árəbik/ *n. & adj.* • *n.* the Semitic language of the Arabs, now spoken in much of N. Africa and the Middle East. • *adj.* of or relating to Arabia (esp. with reference to language or literature). [ME f. OF *arabic* f. L *arabicus* f. Gk *arabikos*]

Ar·a·bic nu·mer·al *n.* any of the numerals 0, 1, 2, 3, 4, 5, 6, 7, 8, and 9 (cf. ROMAN NUMERAL).

Ar·ab·ist /árəbist/ *n.* **1** a student of Arabic civilization, language, etc. **2** an advocate of Arabic interests, etc.

ar·a·ble /árəbəl/ *adj. & n.* • *adj.* **1** (of land) plowed, or suitable for plowing and crop production. **2** (of crops) that can be grown on arable land. • *n. Brit.* arable land or crops. [F *arable* or L *arabilis* f. *arare* to plow]

Ar·a·by /árəbee/ *n. poet.* Arabia. [OF *Arabie* f. L *Arabia* f. Gk]

a·rach·nid /əráknid/ *n.* any arthropod of the class Arachnida, having four pairs of walking legs and characterized by simple eyes, e.g., scorpions, spiders, mites, and ticks. □□ **a·rach·nid** *adj.* **a·rach·ni·dan** *adj. & n.* [F *arachnide* or mod.L *arachnida* f. Gk *arakhnē* spider]

a·rach·noid /əráknoyd/ *n. & adj.* • *n. Anat.* (in full **arachnoid membrane**) one of the three membranes (see MENINX) that surround the brain and spinal cord of vertebrates. • *adj. Bot.* covered with long cobweblike hairs. [mod.L *arachnoides* f. Gk *arakhnoeidēs* like a cobweb f. *arakhnē*: see ARACHNID]

a·rach·no·pho·bi·a /əráknəfóbeeə/ *n.* an abnormal fear of spiders. □□ **a·rach·no·phobe** /əráknəfób/ *n.* [mod. L. f. Gk *arakhnē* spider + –PHOBIA]

ar·ak var. of ARRACK.

Ar·a·ma·ic /árəmáyik/ *n. & adj.* • *n.* a branch of the Semitic family of languages, esp. the language of Syria used as a lingua franca in the Near East from the sixth century BC, later dividing into varieties one of which included Syriac and Mandaean. • *adj.* of or in Aramaic. [L *Aramaeus* f. Gk *Aramaios* of Aram (bibl. name of Syria)]

A·rap·a·ho /ərápəhō/ *n.* **1 a** a N. American people native to the central plains of Canada and the US. **b** a member of this people. **2** the language of this people.

a·ra·tion·al /áyráshənəl/ *adj.* that does not purport to be rational.

ar·au·car·i·a /árawkáreeə/ *n.* any evergreen conifer of the genus *Araucaria*, e.g., the monkey puzzle tree. [mod.L f. *Arauco*, name of a province in Chile]

arb /aarb/ *n. colloq.* = ARBITRAGEUR.

ar·ba·lest /áarbəlest/ *n.* (also **arbalist** or *Brit.* **arblast** /áarblast/) *hist.* a crossbow with a mechanism for drawing the string. [OE arblast f. OF *arbaleste* f. LL *arcubalista* f. *arcus* bow + BALLISTA]

ar·bi·ter /áarbitər/ *n.* **1 a** an arbitrator in a dispute. **b** a judge; an authority (*arbiter of taste*). **2** (often foll. by *of*) a person who has entire control of something. [L]

ar·bi·ter e·le·gan·ti·a·rum /élegaánteeáarəm/ *n.* (also **arbiter e·le·gan·ti·ae** /élegaánshee-ee/) a judge of artistic or social taste and etiquette.

ar·bi·trage /áarbitraazh, –trij/ *n.* the buying and selling of stocks or bills of exchange to take advantage of varying prices in different markets. [F f. *arbitrer* (as ARBITRATE)]

ar·bi·tra·geur /áarbitraazhőr/ *n.* (also **ar·bi·trag·er** /áarbitraazhər/) a person who engages in arbitrage. [F]

ar·bi·tral /áarbitrəl/ *adj.* concerning arbitration. [F *arbitral* or LL *arbitralis*: see ARBITER]

ar·bit·ra·ment /aarbitrəmənt/ *n.* **1** the deciding of a dispute by an arbiter. **2** an authoritative decision made by an arbiter. [ME f. OF *arbitrement* f. med.L *arbitramentum* (as ARBITRATE, –MENT)]

ar·bi·trar·y /áarbitreree/ *adj.* **1** based on or derived from uninformed opinion or random choice; capricious. **2** despotic. □□ **ar·bi·trar·i·ly** *adv.* **ar·bi·trar·i·ness** *n.* [L *arbitrarius* or F *arbitraire* (as ARBITER, –ARY[1])]

---

ar·bi·trate /áarbitrayt/ *v.tr. & intr.* decide by arbitration. [L *arbitrari* judge]

ar·bi·tra·tion /áarbitráyshən/ *n.* the settlement of a dispute by an arbitrator. [ME f. OF f. L *arbitratio –onis* (as ARBITER, –ATION)]

ar·bi·tra·tor /áarbitraytər/ *n.* a person appointed to settle a dispute; an arbiter. □□ **ar·bi·tra·tor·ship** *n.* [ME f. LL (as ARBITRATION, –OR[1])]

ar·blast var. of ARBALEST.

ar·bor[1] /áarbər/ *n.* **1** an axle or spindle on which something revolves. **2** a device holding a tool in a lathe, etc. [F *arbre* tree, axis, f. L *arbor*: refashioned on L]

ar·bor[2] /áarbər/ *n.* a shady alcove with the sides and roof formed by trees or climbing plants; a bower. □□ **ar·bored** *adj.* [ME f. AF *erber* f. OF *erbier* f. *erbe* herb f. L *herba*: phonetic change to *ar*- assisted by assoc. with L *arbor* tree]

ar·bo·ra·ceous /áarbəráyshəs/ *adj.* **1** treelike. **2** wooded. [L *arbor* tree + –ACEOUS]

Ar·bor Day /áarbər/ *n.* a day dedicated annually to tree planting in the US, Australia, and other countries. [L *arbor* tree]

ar·bo·re·al /aarbáwreeəl/ *adj.* of, living in, or connected with trees. [L *arboreus* f. *arbor* tree]

ar·bo·re·ous /aarbáwreeəs/ *adj.* **1** wooded. **2** arboreal.

ar·bo·res·cent /áarbərésənt/ *adj.* treelike in growth or general appearance. □□ **ar·bo·res·cence** *n.* [L *arborescere* grow into a tree (*arbor*)]

ar·bo·re·tum /áarbəréetəm/ *n.* (*pl.* **arboretums** or **arboreta** /–tə/) a botanical garden devoted to trees, shrubs, etc. [L f. *arbor* tree]

ar·bor·i·cul·ture /áarbərikúlchər, aarbáwri–/ *n.* the cultivation of trees and shrubs. □□ **ar·bor·i·cul·tur·al** *adj.* **ar·bor·i·cul·tur·ist** *n.* [L *arbor –oris* tree, after *agriculture*]

ar·bor·i·za·tion /áarbərizáyshən/ *n.* a treelike arrangement, esp. in anatomy.

ar·bor vi·tae /áarbər vítee/ *n.* any of the evergreen conifers of the genus *Thuja*, native to N. Asia and N. America, usu. of pyramidal shape with flattened shoots bearing scale-leaves. [L, = tree of life]

ar·bour *Brit.* var. of ARBOR[2].

ar·bu·tus /aarbyőotəs/ *n.* **1** any evergreen ericaceous tree or shrub of the genus *Arbutus*, having white or pink clusters of flowers and strawberrylike berries. Also called STRAWBERRY TREE. **2** = TRAILING ARBUTUS. [L]

ARC *abbr.* AIDS-related complex.

arc /aark/ *n. & v.* • *n.* **1** part of the circumference of a circle or any other curve. **2** *Electr.* a luminous discharge between two electrodes. • *v.intr.* (**arced** /aarkt/; **arcing** /áarking/) form an arc or follow an arc-shaped trajectory. [ME f. OF f. L *arcus* bow, curve]

ar·cade /aarkáyd/ *n.* **1** a passage with an arched roof. **2** any covered walk, esp. with shops along one or both sides. **3** *Archit.* a series of arches supporting or set along a wall. **4** an entertainment establishment with coin-operated games, etc. □□ **ar·cad·ed** *adj.* [F f. Prov. *arcada* or It. *arcata* f. Rmc: rel. to ARCH[1]]

Ar·ca·di·an /aarkáydeeən/ *n. & adj.* • *n.* an idealized peasant or country dweller, esp. in poetry. • *adj.* simple and poetically rural. □□ **Ar·ca·di·an·ism** *n.* [L *Arcadius* f. Gk *Arkadia* mountain district in Peloponnese]

Ar·ca·dy /áarkədee/ *n.* (also **Arcadia** /aarkáydeeə/) *poet.* an ideal rustic paradise. [Gk *Arkadia*: see ARCADIAN]

ar·cane /aarkáyn/ *adj.* mysterious; secret; understood by few. □□ **ar·cane·ly** *adv.* [F *arcane* or L *arcanus* f. *arcēre* shut up f. *arca* chest]

ar·ca·num /aarkáynəm/ *n.* (*pl.* **arcana** /–nə/) (usu. in *pl.*) a mystery; a profound secret. [L neut. of *arcanus*: see ARCANE]

arch[1] /aarch/ *n. & v.* • *n.* **1 a** a curved structure as an opening or a support for a bridge, roof, floor, etc. **b** an arch used in building as an ornament. **2** any arch-shaped curve, e.g., as on the inner side of the foot, the eyebrows, etc. • *v.* **1** provide with or form into an arch. **2** *tr.* span like an arch. **3** *intr.* form an arch. [ME f. OF *arche* ult. f. L *arcus* arc]

arch[2] /aarch/ *adj.* self-consciously or affectedly playful or teasing. □□ **arch·ly** *adv.* **arch·ness** *n.* [ARCH-, orig. in *arch rogue*, etc.]

arch

arch- /aarch/ *comb. form* **1** chief; superior (*archbishop*; *archduke*). **2** preeminent of its kind (esp. in unfavorable senses) (*archenemy*). [OE *arce*- or OF *arche*-, ult. f. Gk *arkhos* chief]

ar·chae·ol·o·gy /áarkee-óləjee/ *n.* (also **ar·che·ol·o·gy**) the study of human history and prehistory through the excavation of sites and the analysis of physical remains. □□ **ar·chae·o·log·ic** /–keeəlójik/ *adj.* **ar·chae·o·log·i·cal** *adj.* **ar·chae·ol·o·gist** *n.* **ar·chae·ol·o·gize**

v.intr. [mod.L *archaeologia* f. Gk *arkhaiologia* ancient history (as ARCHEAN, –LOGY)]

ar·chae·op·ter·yx /aárkee-óptəriks/ *n.* the oldest known fossil bird, *Archaeopteryx lithographica*, with teeth, feathers, and a reptilian tail. [Gk *arkhaios* ancient + *pteryx* wing]

ar·cha·ic /aarkáyik/ *adj.* **1 a** antiquated. **b** (of a word, etc.) no longer in ordinary use, though retained for special purposes. **2** primitive. **3** of an early period of art or culture, esp. the 7th–6th c. BC in Greece. □□ **ar·cha·i·cal·ly** *adv.* [F *archaïque* f. Gk *arkhaïkos* (as ARCHEAN)]

ar·cha·ism /aárkeeizəm, –kay–/ *n.* **1** the retention or imitation of the old or obsolete, esp. in language or art. **2** an archaic word or expression. □□ **ar·cha·ist** *n.* **ar·cha·is·tic** *adj.* [mod.L f. Gk *arkhaïsmos* f. *arkhaïzō* (as ARCHAIZE, –ISM)]

ar·cha·ize /aárkeeiz, –kay–/ *v.* **1** *intr.* imitate the archaic. **2** *tr.* make (a work of art, literature, etc.) imitate the archaic. [Gk *arkhaïzō* be old-fashioned f. *arkhaios* ancient]

arch·an·gel /aárkaynjəl/ *n.* **1** an angel of the highest rank. **2** a member of the eighth order of the nine ranks of heavenly beings (see ORDER). □□ **arch·an·gel·ic** /–anjélik/ *adj.* [OE f. AF *archangele* f. eccl.L *archangelus* f. eccl.Gk *arkhaggelos* (as ARCH–, ANGEL)]

arch·bish·op /aárchbíshəp/ *n.* the chief bishop of a province. [OE (as ARCH–, BISHOP)]

arch·bish·op·ric /aárchbíshəprik/ *n.* the office or diocese of an archbishop. [OE (as ARCH–, BISHOPRIC)]

arch·dea·con /aárchdeékən/ *n.* a cleric in various churches ranking below a bishop. □□ **arch·dea·con·ry** *n.* (*pl.* **·ries**). **arch·dea·con·ship** *n.* [OE *arce-, ercediacon*, f. eccl.L *archidiaconus* f. eccl.Gk *arkhidiakonos* (as ARCH–, DEACON)]

arch·di·o·cese /aárchdíəsis, –sees, –seez/ *n.* the diocese of an archbishop. □□ **arch·di·oc·e·san** /aárchdíósisən/ *adj.*

arch·duke /aárchdoók, –dyoók/ *n.* (*fem.* **archduchess** /–dúchis/) *hist.* the chief duke (esp. as the title of a son of the Emperor of Austria). □□ **arch·du·cal** *adj.* **arch·duch·y** /–dúchee/ *n.* (*pl.* **·ies**). [OF *archeduc* f. med.L *archidux –ducis* (as ARCH–, DUKE)]

Ar·che·an /aarkeéən/ *adj. & n.* **1** *adj.* of or relating to the earlier part of the Precambrian era. ● *n.* this time. [Gk *arkhaios* ancient f. *arkhē* beginning]

ar·che·go·ni·um /aárkigóneeəm/ *n.* (*pl.* **archegonia** /–eeə/) *Bot.* the female sex organ in mosses, ferns, conifers, etc. [L, dimin. of Gk *arkhegonos* f. *arkhe-* chief + *gonos* race]

arch·en·e·my /aárchénəmee/ *n.* (*pl.* **·mies**) **1** a chief enemy. **2** the Devil.

ar·che·ol·o·gy var. of ARCHAEOLOGY.

arch·er /aárchər/ *n.* **1** a person who shoots with a bow and arrows. **2** (**the Archer**) the zodiacal sign or constellation Sagittarius. [AF f. OF *archier* ult. f. L *arcus* bow]

ar·cher·fish /árchərfish/ a SE Asian fish that catches flying insects by shooting water at them from its mouth.

ar·cher·y /aárchəree/ *n.* shooting with a bow and arrows, esp. as a sport. [OF *archerie* f. *archier* (as ARCHER, –ERY)]

ar·che·type /aárkitīp/ *n.* **1 a** an original model; a prototype. **b** a typical specimen. **2** (in Jungian psychology) a primitive mental image inherited from man's earliest ancestors, and supposed to be present in the collective unconscious. **3** a recurrent symbol or motif in literature, art, etc. □□ **ar·che·typ·al** *adj.* **ar·che·typ·i·cal** /–típikəl/ *adj.* [L *archetypum* f. Gk *arkhetupos* (as ARCH–, *tupos* stamp)]

ar·chi·di·ac·o·nal /aárkidiákənəl/ *adj.* of or relating to an archdeacon. □□ **ar·chi·di·ac·o·nate** /–nət, –nayt/ *n.* [med.L *archidiaconalis* (as ARCH–, DIACONAL)]

ar·chi·e·pis·co·pal /aárkee-ipískəpəl/ *adj.* of or relating to an archbishop. □□ **ar·chi·e·pis·co·pate** /–pət, –payt/ *n.* [eccl.L *archiepiscopus* f. Gk *arkhiepiskopos* archbishop]

ar·chil var. of ORCHIL.

ar·chi·man·drite /aárkimándrīt/ *n.* **1** the superior of a large monastery or group of monasteries in the Orthodox Church. **2** an honorary title given to a monastic priest. [F *archimandrite* or eccl.L *archimandrita* f. eccl. Gk *arkhimandrites* (as ARCH–, *mandra* monastery)]

Ar·chi·me·de·an /aárkimeédeeən/ *adj.* of or associated with the Greek mathematician Archimedes (d. 212 BC).

Ar·chi·me·de·an screw *n.* a device of ancient origin for raising water by means of a spiral inside a tube.

Ar·chi·me·des' prin·ci·ple /aárkimeédeez/ *n.* the law that a body totally or partially immersed in a fluid is subject to an upward force equal in magnitude to the weight of fluid it displaces.

ar·chi·pel·a·go /aárkipéləgō/ *n.* (*pl.* **·gos** or **·goes**) **1** a group of islands. **2** a sea with many islands. [It. *arcipelago* f. Gk *arkhi-* chief + *pelagos* sea (orig. = the Aegean Sea)]

ar·chi·tect /aárkitekt/ *n.* **1** a designer who prepares plans for buildings, ships, etc., and supervises their construction. **2** (foll. by *of*) a person who brings about a specified thing (*the architect of the tax reform bill*). [F *architecte* f. It. *architetto*, or L *architectus* f. Gk *arkhitektōn* (as ARCH–, *tektōn* builder)]

ar·chi·tec·ton·ic /aárkitektónik/ *adj. & n.* ● *adj.* **1** of or relating to architecture or architects. **2** of or relating to the systematization of knowledge. ● *n.* (in *pl.*; usu. treated as *sing.*) **1** the scientific study of architecture. **2** the study of the systematization of knowledge. [L *architectonicus* f. Gk *arkhitektonikos* (as ARCHITECT)]

ar·chi·tec·ture /aárkitekchər/ *n.* **1** the art or science of designing and constructing buildings. **2** the style of a building as regards design and construction. **3** buildings or other structures collectively. □□ **ar·chi·tec·tur·al** /–tékchərəl/ *adj.* **ar·chi·tec·tur·al·ly** *adv.* [F *architecture* or L *architectura* f. *architectus* (as ARCHITECT)]

ar·chi·trave /aárkitrayv/ *n.* **1** (in classical architecture) a main beam resting across the tops of columns. **2** the molded frame around a doorway or window. **3** a molding around the exterior of an arch. [F f. It. (as ARCH–, *trave* f. L *trabs trabis* beam)]

ar·chive /aárkiv/ *n. & v.* ● *n.* (usu. in *pl.*) **1** a collection of esp. public or corporate documents or records. **2** the place where these are kept. ● *v.tr.* **1** place or store in an archive. **2** *Computing* transfer (data) to a less frequently used file or less easily accessible medium, e.g., from disk to tape. □□ **ar·chi·val** /aárkivəl/ *adj.* [F *archives* (pl.) f. L *archi(υ)a* f. Gk *arkheia* public records f. *arkhē* government]

ar·chi·vist /aárkivist, aárkī–/ *n.* a person who maintains and is in charge of archives.

ar·chi·volt /aárkivōlt/ *n.* **1** a band of moldings around the lower curve of an arch. **2** the lower curve itself from impost to impost of the columns. [F *archivolte* or It. *archivolto* (as ARC, VAULT)]

arch·lute /aárchloōt/ *n.* a bass lute with an extended neck and unstopped bass strings. [F *archiluth* (as ARCH–, LUTE[1])]

ar·chon /aárkon, –kən/ *n.* each of the nine chief magistrates in ancient Athens. □□ **ar·chon·ship** *n.* [Gk *arkhōn* ruler, = pres. part. of *arkhō* rule]

arch·way /aárchway/ *n.* **1** a vaulted passage. **2** an arched entrance.

arc lamp *n.* (also **arc light**) a light source using an electric arc.

Arc·tic /aárktik, aártik/ *adj. & n.* ● *adj.* **1** of the north polar regions. **2** (**arctic**) *colloq.* (esp. of weather) very cold. ● *n.* **1** the Arctic regions. **2** (**arctic**) a thick waterproof overshoe. [ME f. OF *artique* f. L *ar(c)ticus* f. Gk *arktikos* f. *arktos* bear, Ursa Major]

PRONUNCIATION TIP   **Arctic**

Both *Arctic* and *Antarctic* were once spelled without the first *c*, which was reintroduced at the beginning of the 17th century to make the English words conform etymologically to the original Greek spelling. The spelling with the *c* following the *r* is now the only acceptable one, but both words may be pronounced either with the *c* sounded (ARK-tik, ant-ARK-tik) or without it (AR-tik, ant-AR-tik).

Arc·tic Cir·cle *n.* the parallel of latitude 66° 33 N, forming an imaginary line around this region.

ar·cu·ate /aárkyooət, –ayt/ *adj.* shaped like a bow; curved. [L *arcuatus* past part. of *arcuare* curve f. *arcus* bow, curve]

ar·cus se·ni·lis /aárkəs sənílis/ *n.* a narrow opaque band commonly encircling the cornea in old age. [L, lit. 'senile bow']

arc weld·ing *n.* a method of using an electric arc to melt metals to be welded.

-ard /ərd/ *suffix* **1** forming nouns in depreciatory senses (*drunkard*; *sluggard*). **2** forming nouns in other senses (*Spaniard*; *wizard*). [ME & OF f. G *–hard* hardy (in proper names)]

ar·dent /aárd'nt/ *adj.* **1** eager; zealous; (of persons or feelings) fervent; passionate. **2** burning. □□ **ar·den·cy** /–d'nsee/ *n.* **ar·dent·ly** *adv.* [ME f. OF *ardant* f. L *ardens –entis* f. *ardēre* burn]

ar·dor /aárdər/ *n.* zeal; burning enthusiasm; passion. [ME f. OF f. L *ardor –oris* f. *ardēre* burn]

ar·du·ous /aárjooəs/ *adj.* **1** (of a task, etc.) hard to achieve or overcome; difficult; laborious. **2** (of an action, etc.) energetic; strenuous. □□ **ar·du·ous·ly** *adv.* **ar·du·ous·ness** *n.* [L *arduus* steep, difficult]

are[1] *2nd sing. present & 1st, 2nd, 3rd pl. present* of BE.

are[2] /aar/ *n.* a metric unit of measure, equal to 100 square meters. [F f. L AREA]

ar·e·a /áireeə/ *n.* **1** the extent or measure of a surface (*over a large area*; *3 acres in area*; *the area of a triangle*). **2** a region or tract (*the southern area*). **3** a space allocated for a specific purpose (*dining area*; *camping area*). **4** the scope or range of an activity or study. **5** = AREAWAY. □□ **ar·e·al** *adj.* [L, = vacant piece of level ground]

ar·e·a code *n.* a three-digit number that identifies one of the telephone service regions into which the US, Canada, etc., are divided and which is dialed when calling from one area to another.

ar·e·a·way /áireeəway/ *n.* a space below ground level in front of the basement of a building.

a·re·ca /əreékə, áríkə/ *n.* any tropical palm of the genus *Areca*, native to Asia. [Port. f. Malayalam *ádekka*]

a·re·ca nut *n.* the astringent seed of a species of areca, *A. catechu*. Also called **betel nut**.

a·re·na /əreénə/ *n.* **1** the central part of an amphitheater, etc., where contests take place. **2** a scene of conflict; a sphere of action or discussion. [L (*h*) *arena* sand, sand-strewn place of combat]

ar·e·na·ceous /árináyshəs/ *adj.* **1** (of rocks) containing sand; having a sandy texture. **2** sandlike. **3** (of plants) growing in sand. [L *arenaceus* (as ARENA, –ACEOUS)]

ar·e·na the·a·ter *n.* (also **ar·e·na stage**) a stage situated with the audience all around it.

aren't /aarnt, áarənt/ *contr.* **1** are not. **2** (in *interrog.*) am not (*aren't I coming too?*).

a·re·o·la /əréeələ/ *n.* (*pl.* **areolae** /–lee/) **1** *Anat.* a circular pigmented area, esp. that surrounding a nipple. **2** any of the spaces between lines on a surface, e.g., of a leaf or an insect's wing. □□ **a·re·o·lar** *adj.* [L, dimin. of *area* AREA]

a·rête /əráyt/ *n.* a sharp mountain ridge. [F f. L *arista* ear of wheat, fishbone, spine]

ar·ga·li /áargəlee/ *n.* (*pl.* same) a large Asiatic wild sheep, *Ovis ammon*, with massive horns. [Mongol]

ar·gent /áarjənt/ *n. & adj. Heraldry* silver; silvery white. [F f. L *argentum*]

ar·gen·tif·er·ous /aárjəntífərəs/ *adj.* containing natural deposits of silver. [L *argentum* + –FEROUS]

Ar·gen·tine /áarjənteen, –tin/ *adj. & n.* (also **Ar·gen·tin·i·an** /–tíneeən/) ● *adj.* of or relating to Argentina in S. America. ● *n.* **1** a native or citizen of Argentina. **2** a person of Argentine descent. **3** (**the Argentine**) Argentina. [Sp. *Argentina* (as ARGENTINE)]

ar·gen·tine /áarjəntin, –teen/ *adj.* of silver; silvery. [F *argentin* f. *argent* silver]

ar·gil /áarjil/ *n.* clay, esp. that used in pottery. □□ **ar·gil·la·ceous** /–jiláyshəs/ *adj.* [F *argille* f. L *argilla* f. Gk *argillos* f. *argos* white]

ar·gi·nine /áarjineen/ *n.* an amino acid present in many animal proteins and an essential nutrient in the vertebrate diet. [G *Arginin*, of uncert. orig.]

Ar·give /áargiv/ *adj. & n.* ● *adj.* **1** of Argos in ancient Greece. **2** *literary* (esp. in Homeric contexts) Greek. ● *n.* **1** a citizen of Argos. **2** *literary* (usu. in *pl.*) a Greek. [L *Argivus* f. Gk *Argeios*]

ar·gol /áargawl/ *n.* crude potassium hydrogen tartar. [ME f. AF *argoile*, of unkn. orig.]

ar·gon /áargon/ *n. Chem.* an inert gaseous element, of the noble gas group and forming almost 1% of the earth's atmosphere. ¶ Symb.: **Ar.** [Gk, neut. of *argos* idle f. a– not + *ergon* work]

ar·go·sy /áargəsee/ *n.* (*pl.* **·sies**) *poet.* **1** a large merchant ship, orig. esp. from Ragusa (now Dubrovnik) or Venice. **2** an opulent or abundant supply. [prob. It. *Ragusea* (*nave*) Ragusan (vessel)]

ar·got /áargō, –gət/ *n.* the jargon of a group or class, formerly esp. of criminals. [F: orig. unkn.]

ar·gu·a·ble /áargyōōəbəl/ *adj.* **1** that may be argued; open to dispute. **2** reasonable; supported by argument. □□ **ar·gu·a·bly** *adv.*

ar·gue /áargyōō/ *v.* (**argues, argued, arguing**) **1** *intr.* (often foll. by *with, about*, etc.) exchange views or opinions, especially heatedly or contentiously (with a person). **2** *tr. & intr.* (often foll. by *that* + clause) indicate; maintain by reasoning. **3** *intr.* (foll. by *for, against*) reason (*argued against joining*). **4** *tr.* treat by reasoning (*argue the point*). **5** *tr.* (foll. by *into, out of*) persuade (*argued me into going*). □ **argue the toss** *Brit. colloq.* dispute a decision or choice already made. □□ **ar·gu·er** *n.* [ME f. OF *arguer* f. L *argutari* prattle, frequent. of *arguere* make clear, prove, accuse]

ar·gu·fy /áargyəfi/ *v.intr.* (**·fies, ·fied**) *colloq.* argue excessively or tediously. [fanciful f. ARGUE: cf. SPEECHIFY]

ar·gu·ment /áargyəmənt/ *n.* **1** an exchange of views, esp. a contentious or prolonged one. **2** (often foll. by *for, against*) a reason advanced; a reasoning process (*an argument for abolition*). **3** a summary of the subject matter or line of reasoning of a book. **4** *Math.* an independent variable determining the value of a function. [ME f. OF f. L *argumentum* f. *arguere* (as ARGUE, –MENT)]

ar·gu·men·ta·tion /aárgyəméntáyshən/ *n.* **1** methodical reasoning. **2** debate or argument. [F f. L *argumentatio* f. *argumentari* (as ARGUMENT, –ATION)]

ar·gu·men·ta·tive /aárgyəméntətiv/ *adj.* **1** fond of arguing; quarrelsome. **2** using methodical reasoning. □□ **ar·gu·men·ta·tive·ly** *adv.* **ar·gu·men·ta·tive·ness** *n.* [F *argumentatif* –*ive* or LL *argumentativus* (as ARGUMENT, –ATIVE)]

Ar·gus /áargəs/ *n.* **1** a watchful guardian. **2** an Asiatic pheasant having markings on its tail resembling eyes. **3** a butterfly having markings resembling eyes. [ME f. L f. Gk *Argos* mythical person with a hundred eyes]

Ar·gus-eyed *n.* vigilant.

ar·gy-bar·gy /áarjeebaárjee/ *n. & v. Brit. joc.* ● *n.* (*pl.* **·gies**) a dispute or wrangle. ● *v.intr.* (**·gies, ·gied**) quarrel, esp. loudly. [orig. Sc.]

a·ri·a /áareeə/ *n. Mus.* a long accompanied song for solo voice in an opera, oratorio, etc. [It.]

Ar·i·an /áireeən/ *adj. & n.* ● *n.* an adherent of the doctrine of Arius of Alexandria (4th c.), who denied the divinity of Christ. ● *adj.* of or concerning this doctrine. □□ **Ar·i·an·ism** *n.*

-arian /áireeən/ *suffix* forming adjectives and nouns meaning '(one) concerned with or believing in' (*agrarian; antiquarian; humanitarian; vegetarian*). [L –*arius* (see –ARY[1])]

ar·id /árid/ *adj.* **1 a** (of ground, climate, etc.) dry; parched. **b** too dry to support vegetation; barren. **2** uninteresting (*arid verse*). □□ **a·rid·i·ty** /əríditee/ *n.* **ar·id·ly** *adv.* **ar·id·ness** *n.* [F *aride* or L *aridus* f. *arēre* be dry]

Ar·ies /áireez/ *n.* (*pl.* same) **1** a constellation, traditionally regarded as portraying the figure of a ram. **2 a** the first sign of the zodiac (the Ram). **b** a person born when the sun is in this sign. □□ **Ar·i·an** /–reeən/ *adj. & n.* [ME f. L, = ram]

a·right /ərít/ *adv.* rightly. [OE (as A[2], RIGHT)]

ar·il /áril/ *n. Bot.* an extra seed covering, often colored and hairy or fleshy, e.g., the red fleshy cup around a yew seed. □□ **ar·il·late** *adj.* [mod.L *arillus*: cf. med.L *arilli* dried grape stones]

-arious /áireeəs/ *suffix* forming adjectives (*gregarious; vicarious*). [L –*arius* (see –ARY[1]) + –OUS]

a·rise /əríz/ *v.intr.* (*past* **arose** /əróz/; *past part.* **arisen** /ərízən/) **1** begin to exist; originate. **2** (usu. foll. by *from, out of*) result (*accidents can arise from carelessness*). **3** come to one's notice; emerge (*the question of payment arose*). **4** rise. [OE *ārīsan* (as A–[2], RISE)]

ar·is·toc·ra·cy /árístókrəsee/ *n.* (*pl.* **·cies**) **1 a** the highest class in society; the nobility. **b** the nobility as a ruling class. **2 a** a government by a privileged group. **b** a nation governed in this way. **3** (often foll. by *of*) those considered to be the best representatives or upper echelons (*aristocracy of intellect; aristocracy of labor*). [F *aristocratie* f. Gk *aristokratia* f. *aristos* best + *kratia* (as –CRACY)]

▶ **Aristocracy, oligarchy,** and **plutocracy** are sometimes confused. All mean some form of rule by a small elite. **Aristocracy** is rule by a traditional elite, held to be made up of 'the best' people, and is usually hereditary. **Oligarchy** is literally rule by a few. **Plutocracy** is rule by the (necessarily few) very rich.

a·ris·to·crat /ərístəkrat, áris–/ *n.* **1** a member of the aristocracy. **2** something believed to be the best of its kind. [F *aristocrate* (as ARISTOCRATIC)]

a·ris·to·crat·ic /ərístəkrátik/ *adj.* **1** of or relating to the aristocracy. **2 a** distinguished in manners or bearing. **b** grand; stylish. □□ **a·ris·to·crat·i·cal·ly** *adv.* [F *aristocratique* f. Gk *aristokratikos* (as ARISTOCRACY)]

Ar·is·to·te·lian /árístətéeleeən, əris–/ *n. & adj.* ● *n.* a disciple or student of the Greek philosopher Aristotle (d. 322 BC). ● *adj.* of or concerning Aristotle or his ideas.

A·ri·ta /əréetə/ *n.* (usu. *attrib.*) a type of Japanese porcelain characterized by asymmetric decoration. [*Arita* in Japan]

a·rith·me·tic *n. & adj.* ● *n.* /əríthmətik/ **1 a** the science of numbers. **b** esp. *Brit.* one's knowledge of this (*have improved my arithmetic*). **2** the use of numbers; computation (*a problem involving arithmetic*). ● *adj.* /árithmétik/ (also **ar·ith·met·i·cal** /–métikəl/) of or concerning arithmetic. □□ **a·rith·me·ti·cian** /əríthmətíshən/ *n.* [ME f. OF *arismetique* f. L *arithmetica* f. Gk *arithmētikē* (*tekhnē*) art of counting f. *arithmos* number]

ar·ith·met·i·cal se·ries *n.* (also **ge·o·met·ric·al se·ries**) a series in arithmetical (or geometrical) progression.

a·rith·me·tic mean *n.* an average calculated by adding quantities and dividing the total by the number of quantities.

a·rith·me·tic pro·gres·sion *n.* **1** an increase or decrease by a constant quantity (e.g., 1, 2, 3, 4, etc., 9, 7, 5, 3, etc.). **2** a sequence of numbers showing this.

-arium /áireeəm/ *suffix* forming nouns usu. denoting a place (*aquarium; planetarium*). [L, neut. of adjs. in –*arius*: see –ARY[1]]

Ariz. *abbr.* Arizona.

Ark. *abbr.* Arkansas.

ark /aark/ *n.* **1** = NOAH'S ARK 1. **2** *archaic* a chest or box. **3** a refuge. □ **out of the ark** *colloq.* very antiquated. [OE *ærc* f. L *arca* chest]

Ark of the Cov·e·nant *n.* a chest or box containing the tablets of the Ten Commandments, kept in the Temple at Jerusalem until the destruction of the Temple.

arm[1] /aarm/ *n.* **1** each of the upper limbs of the human body from the shoulder to the hand. **2 a** the forelimb of an animal. **b** the flexible limb of an invertebrate animal (e.g., an octopus). **3 a** the sleeve of a garment. **b** the side part of a chair, etc., used to support a sitter's arm. **c** a thing resembling an arm in branching from a main stem (*an arm of the sea*). **d** a large branch of a tree. **4** a control; a means of reaching (*arm of the law*). **5** a branch or division of a larger group (*the pacifist arm of the movement*). □ **an arm and a leg** a large sum of money. **arm in arm** (of two or more persons) with arms linked. **as long as your** (or **my**) **arm** *colloq.* very long. **at arm's length 1** as far as an arm can reach. **2** far enough to avoid undue familiarity. **in arms** (of a baby) too young to walk. **in a person's arms** embraced. **on one's arm** supported by one's arm. **under one's arm** between the arm and the body. **within arm's reach** reachable without moving one's position. **with open arms** cordially. □□ **arm·ful** *n.* (*pl.* **·fuls**). **arm·less** *adj.* [OE f. Gmc]

arm[2] /aarm/ *n. & v.* ● *n.* **1** (usu. in *pl.*) **a** a weapon. **b** = FIREARM. **2** (in *pl.*) the military profession. **3** a branch of the military (e.g., infantry, cavalry, artillery, etc.). **4** (in *pl.*) heraldic devices (*coat of arms*).

• *v. tr. & refl.* **1** supply with weapons. **2** supply with tools or other requisites or advantages (*armed with the truth*). **3** make (a bomb, etc.) able to explode. □ **in arms** armed. **lay down one's arms** cease fighting. **take up arms** begin fighting. **under arms** ready for war or battle. **up in arms** (usu. foll. by *against*, *about*) actively rebelling. □□ **arm•less** *adj.* [ME f. OF *armes* (pl.), *armer*, f. L *arma* arms, fittings]

ar•ma•da /aarmaáadǝ/ *n.* a fleet of warships, esp. those sent by Spain against England in 1588. [Sp. f. Rmc *armata* army]

ar•ma•dil•lo /aarmǝdílō/ *n.* (*pl.* **-los**) a nocturnal insect-eating mammal of the family Dasypodidae, native to Central and S. America and spreading into the southern US, with large claws for digging and a body covered in bony plates. [Sp. dimin. of *armado* armed man f. L *armatus* past part. of *armare* ARM²]

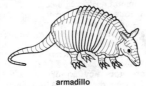

armadillo

Ar•ma•ged•don /aarmǝgéd'n/ *n.* **1 a** (in the New Testament) the last battle between good and evil before the Day of Judgment. **b** the place where this will be fought. **2** a bloody battle or struggle on a huge scale. [Gk f. Heb. *har megiddōn* hill of Megiddo: see Rev. 16:16]

ar•ma•ment /aarmǝmǝnt/ *n.* **1** (often in *pl.*) military weapons and equipment, esp. guns on a warship. **2** the process of equipping for war. **3** a force equipped for war. [L *armamentum* (as ARM², –MENT)]

ar•ma•men•tar•i•um /aarmǝmentáireeǝm/ *n.* (*pl.* **armamentaria** /–reeǝ/) **1** a set of medical equipment or drugs. **2** the resources available to a person engaged in a task. [L, = arsenal]

ar•ma•ture /aarmǝchoŏr/ *n.* **1 a** the rotating coil or coils of a generator or electric motor. **b** any moving part of an electrical machine in which a voltage is induced by a magnetic field. **2** a piece of soft iron placed in contact with the poles of a horseshoe magnet to preserve its power. Also called **keeper**. **3** *Biol.* the protective covering of an animal or plant. **4** a metal framework on which a sculpture is molded with clay or similar material. **5** *archaic* arms; armor. [F f. L *armatura* armor (as ARM², –URE)]

arm•band /aarmband/ *n.* a band worn around the upper arm to hold up a shirtsleeve or as a form of identification, etc.

arm•chair /aarmcháir/ *n.* **1** a comfortable, usu. upholstered, chair with side supports for the arms. **2** (*attrib.*) theoretical rather than active or practical (*an armchair critic*).

Ar•me•ni•an /aarmeéneeǝn/ *n. & adj.* • *n.* **1 a** a native of Armenia, an ancient kingdom corresponding to an area in modern Armenia, Turkey, and Iran. **b** a person of Armenian descent. **2** the language of Armenia. • *adj.* of or relating to Armenia, its language, or the Christian Church established there *c.*300.

arm•hole /aarmhōl/ *n.* each of two holes in a garment through which the arms are put, usu. into a sleeve.

ar•mi•ger /aarmijǝr/ *n.* a person entitled to heraldic arms. □□ **ar•mig•er•ous** /–míjǝrǝs/ *adj.* [L, = bearing arms, f. *arma* arms + *gerere* bear]

ar•mil•lar•y /aarmíleree/ *adj.* relating to bracelets. [mod.L *armillaris* f. L *armilla* bracelet]

ar•mil•lar•y sphere *n. hist.* a representation of the celestial globe constructed from metal rings and showing the celestial equator, the celestial tropics, etc.

Ar•min•i•an /aarmíneeǝn/ *adj. & n.* • *adj.* relating to the doctrine of Arminius, a Dutch Protestant theologian (d. 1609), who opposed the views of Calvin, esp. on predestination. • *n.* an adherent of this doctrine. □□ **Ar•min•i•an•ism** *n.*

ar•mi•stice /aarmistis/ *n.* a stopping of hostilities by common agreement of the opposing sides; a truce. [F *armistice* or mod.L *armistitium*, f. *arma* arms (ARM²) + *–stitium* stoppage]

Ar•mi•stice Day *n.* former name of Veterans Day, the anniversary of the World War I armistice of Nov. 11, 1918.

arm•let /aarmlit/ *n.* **1** a band worn around the arm. **2** a small inlet of the sea, or branch of a river.

ar•moire /aarmwaár/ *n.* a tall, upright, often ornate cupboard or wardrobe. [F, f. L *armarium* chest]

ar•mor *n.* /aarmǝr/ *n. & v.* **1** a defensive covering, usu. of metal, formerly worn to protect the body in fighting. **2 a** (in full **armor plate**) a protective metal covering for an armed vehicle, ship, etc. **b** armored fighting vehicles collectively. **3** a protective covering or shell on certain animals and plants. **4** heraldic devices. • *v. tr.* (usu. as **armored** *adj.*) provide with a protective covering, and often with guns (*armored car, armored train*) . [ME f. OF *armure* f. L *armatura*: see ARMATURE]

ar•mor•er *n.* /aarmǝrǝr/ *n.* **1** a maker or repairer of arms or armor. **2** an official in charge of a ship's or a regiment's arms. [AF *armurer*, OF *–urier* (as ARMOR, –ER⁵)]

ar•mor•y¹ /aarmǝree/ *n.* (*pl.* **-ies**) **1 a** a place where arms are kept; an arsenal. **b** a place where military reservists are trained or head-

quartered. **2** an array of weapons, defensive resources, usable material, etc. **3** a place where arms are manufactured. [ME f. OF *armoirie, armoierie* f. *armoier* to blazon f. *arme* ARM²: assim. to ARMOR]

ar•mor•y² /aarmǝree/ *n.* (*pl.* **-ies**) heraldry. □□ **ar•mo•ri•al** /aarmóreeǝl/ *adj.* [OF *armoierie*: see ARMORY¹]

arm•pit /aarmpit/ *n.* **1** the hollow under the arm at the shoulder. **2** *colloq.* a place or part considered disgusting or contemptible (*the armpit of the world*).

arm•rest /aarmrest/ *n.* = ARM¹ 3b.

arms con•trol *n.* international disarmament or arms limitation, esp. by mutual agreement.

arms race *n.* a contest for superiority, esp. in nuclear weapons between the US and the former Soviet Union.

arm-twist•ing *n. colloq.* (persuasion by) the use of physical force or moral pressure.

arm wres•tling *n.* a trial of strength in which each party tries to force the other's arm down onto a table on which their elbows rest.

ar•my /aarmee/ *n.* (*pl.* **-mies**) **1** an organized force armed for fighting on land. **2** (prec. by *the*) the military profession. **3** (often foll. by *of*) a very large number (*an army of locusts; an army of helpers*). **4** an organized body regarded as working for a particular cause. [ME f. OF *armee* f. Rmc *armata* fem. past part. of *armare* arm]

ar•my ant *n.* any ant of the subfamily Dorylinae, foraging in large groups.

ar•my•worm /aarmeewǝrm/ *n.* any of various moth or fly larvae occurring in destructive swarms.

ar•ni•ca /aarnikǝ/ *n.* **1** any composite plant of the genus *Arnica*, having erect stems bearing yellow daisylike flower heads. **2** a medicine prepared from this, used for bruises, etc. [mod.L: orig. unkn.]

ar•oid /áiroyd/ *adj.* of or relating to the family Araceae, including arums. [ARUM + –OID]

a•ro•ma /ǝrōmǝ/ *n.* **1** a fragrance; a distinctive and pleasing smell, often of food. **2** a subtle pervasive quality. [L f. Gk *arōma* –*atos* spice]

a•ro•ma•ther•a•py /ǝrōmǝthérǝpee/ *n.* the use of plant extracts and essential oils in massage. □□ **a•ro•ma•ther•a•peu•tic** /–pyoŏtik/ *adj.* **a•ro•ma•ther•a•pist** *n.*

ar•o•mat•ic /árǝmátik/ *adj. & n.* • *adj.* **1** fragrant; (of a smell) pleasantly pungent. **2** *Chem.* of organic compounds having an unsaturated ring, esp. containing a benzene ring. • *n.* an aromatic substance. □□ **ar•o•mat•i•cal•ly** *adv.* **ar•o•ma•tic•i•ty** /árǝmǝtísitee/ *n.* [ME f. OF *aromatique* f. LL *aromaticus* f. Gk *arōmatikos* (as AROMA, –IC)]

a•ro•ma•tize /ǝrōmǝtiz/ *v. tr. Chem.* convert (a compound) into an aromatic structure. □□ **a•ro•ma•ti•za•tion** /–tizáyshǝn/ *n.*

a•rose *past* of ARISE.

a•round /ǝrównd/ *adv. & prep.* • *adv.* **1** on every side; on all sides. **2** in various places; here and there; at random (*fool around; shop around*). **3** *colloq.* **a** in existence; available (*has been around for weeks*). **b** near at hand (*it's good to have you around*). **4** approximately (*around 400 people attended*). **5** with circular motion (*wheels go around*). **6** with return to the starting point or an earlier state (*summer soon comes around*). **7 a** with rotation, or change to an opposite position (*he turned around to look*). **b** with change to an opposite opinion, etc. (*they were angry but I soon won them around*). **8** to, at, or affecting all or many points of a circumference or an area or the members of a company, etc. (*tea was then handed around; may I look around?*). **9** in every direction from a center or within a radius (*spread destruction around; everyone for a mile around*). **10** by a circuitous way (*will you jump over or go around?; go a long way around*). **11 a** to a person's house, etc. (*ask him around; will be around soon*). **b** to a more prominent or convenient position (*brought the car around*). **12** measuring a (specified distance) in girth. • *prep.* **1** on or along the circuit of. **2** on every side of; enveloping. **3** here and there; in or near (*chairs around the room*). **4** (of amount, time, etc.) about; at a time near to (*come around four o'clock; happened around June*). **5** so as to encircle or enclose (*tour around the world; has a blanket around him*). **6** at or to points on the circumference of (*sat around the table*). **7** with successive visits to (*hawks them around the cafés*). **8** in various directions from or with regard to (*towns around; shells bursting around them*). **9** having as an axis of revolution or as a central point (*turns around its center of gravity; write a book around an event*). **10 a** so as to double or pass in a curved course (*go around the corner*). **b** having passed in this way (*be around the corner*). **c** in the position that would result from this (*find them around the corner*). **11** so as to come close from various sides but not into contact. **12** at various places in or around (*had lots of clocks around the house to always know the time*). • □ **around the bend** see BEND¹. **have been around** *colloq.* be widely experienced. [A² + ROUND]

a•rouse /ǝrówz/ *v. tr.* **1** induce; call into existence (esp. a feeling, emotion, etc.). **2** awake from sleep. **3** stir into activity. **4** stimulate sexually. □□ **a•rous•a•ble** *adj.* **a•rous•al** *n.* **a•rous•er** *n.* [A–² + ROUSE]

ar•peg•gi•o /aarpéjeeō/ *n.* (*pl.* **-os**) *Mus.* the notes of a chord played in succession, either ascending or descending. [It. f. *arpeggiare* play the harp f. *arpa* harp]

ar•que•bus var. of HARQUEBUS.

arr. *abbr.* **1** *Mus.* arranged by. **2** arrives.

ar•rack /árək/ *n.* (also **arak** /árák/) an alcoholic liquor, esp. distilled from coco sap or rice. [Arab. *'arak* sweat, alcoholic liquor from grapes or dates]

ar•raign /əráyn/ *v.tr.* **1** indict before a court; formally accuse. **2** find fault with; call into question (an action or statement). □□ **ar•raign•ment** *n.* [ME f. AF *arainer* f. OF *araisnier* (ult. as AD-, L *ratio −onis* reason, discourse)]

ar•range /əráynj/ *v.* **1** *tr.* put into the required or suitable order; classify. **2** *tr.* plan or provide for; cause to occur (*arranged a meeting*). **3** *tr.* settle beforehand the order or manner of. **4** *intr.* take measures; make plans; give instructions (*arrange to be there at eight; arranged for a taxi to come*). **5** *intr.* come to an agreement (*arranged with her to meet later*). **6** *tr.* **a** *Mus.* adapt (a composition) for performance with instruments or voices other than those originally specified. **b** *Brit.* adapt (a play, etc.) for broadcasting. **7** *tr.* settle (a dispute, etc.). □□ **ar•range•a•ble** *adj.* **ar•rang•er** *n.* (esp. in sense 6). [ME f. OF *arangier* f. *à* to + *rangier* RANGE]

ar•range•ment /əráynjmənt/ *n.* **1** the act or process of arranging or being arranged. **2** the condition of being arranged; the manner in which a thing is arranged. **3** something arranged. **4** (in *pl.*) plans; preparations (*make your own arrangements*). **5** *Mus.* a composition arranged for performance by different instruments or voices (see ARRANGE 6a). **6** settlement of a dispute, etc. [F (as ARRANGE, −MENT)]

ar•rant /árənt/ *attrib.adj.* downright; utter; notorious (*arrant liar; arrant nonsense*). □□ **ar•rant•ly** *adv.* [ME, var. of ERRANT, orig. in phrases like *arrant* (= outlawed, roving) *thief*]

ar•ras /árəs/ *n. hist.* a rich tapestry, often hung on the walls of a room, or to conceal an alcove. [*Arras*, a town in NE France famous for the fabric]

ar•ray /əráy/ *n. & v.* ● *n.* **1** an imposing or well-ordered series or display. **2** an ordered arrangement, esp. of troops (*battle array*). **3** an outfit or dress (*in fine array*). **4 a** *Math.* an arrangement of quantities or symbols in rows and columns; a matrix. **b** *Computing* an ordered set of related elements. **5** *Law* a list of jurors impaneled. ● *v.tr.* **1** deck; adorn. **2** set in order; marshal (forces). **3** *Law* impanel (a jury). [ME f. AF *araier*, OF *areer* ult. f. a Gmc root; = prepare]

ar•rears /əreérz/ *n.pl.* an amount still outstanding or uncompleted, esp. work undone or a debt unpaid. □ **in arrears** (or **arrear**) behindhand, esp. in payment. □□ **ar•rear•age** *n.* [ME (orig. as adv.) f. OF *arere* f. med.L *adretro* (as AD-, *retro* backward): first used in phr. *in arrear*]

ar•rest /ərést/ *v. & n.* ● *v.tr.* **1 a** seize (a person) and take into custody, esp. by legal authority. **b** seize (a ship) by legal authority. **2** stop or check (esp. a process or moving thing). **3 a** attract (a person's attention). **b** attract the attention of (a person). ● *n.* **1** the act of arresting or being arrested, esp. the legal seizure of a person. **2** a stoppage or check (*cardiac arrest*). □ **under arrest** in custody; deprived of liberty. □□ **ar•rest•ing** *adj.* **ar•rest•ing•ly** *adv.* **ar•rest•ment** *n.* [ME f. OF *arester* ult. f. L *restare* remain, stop]

ar•rest•a•ble /əréstəbəl/ *adj.* **1** susceptible to arrest. **2** *Brit. Law* (esp. of an offense) such that the offender may be arrested without a warrant.

ar•ri•ère-pen•sée /áryairpONsáy/ *n.* **1** an undisclosed motive. **2** a mental reservation. [F, = behind thought]

ar•ris /áris/ *n. Archit.* a sharp edge formed by the meeting of two flat or curved surfaces. [corrupt. f. F *areste*, mod. ARÊTE]

ar•ri•val /ərívəl/ *n.* **1 a** the act of arriving. **b** an appearance on the scene. **2** a person or thing that has arrived. □ **new arrival** *colloq.* a newborn child. [ME f. AF *arrivaille* (as ARRIVE, −AL)]

ar•rive /ərív/ *v.intr.* (often foll. by *at, in*) **1** reach a destination; come to the end of a journey or a specified part of a journey (*arrived in Tibet; arrived at the station; arrived late*). **2** (foll. by *at*) reach (a conclusion, decision, etc.). **3** *colloq.* establish one's reputation or position. **4** *colloq.* (of a child) be born. **5** (of a thing) be brought (*the flowers have arrived*). **6** (of a time) come (*her birthday arrived at last*). [ME f. OF *ariver*, ult. as AD- + L *ripa* shore]

ar•ri•vism /árəvízəm/ *n.* the behavior and condition of an arriviste.

ar•ri•viste /áreevéest/ *n.* **1** an ambitious or ruthlessly self-seeking person. **2** a person who is newly arrived in social status, wealth, etc. [F f. *arriver* f. OF (as ARRIVE, −IST)]

ar•ro•gant /árəgənt/ *adj.* (of a person, attitude, etc.) aggressively assertive or presumptuous; overbearing. □□ **ar•ro•gance** *n.* **ar•ro•gant•ly** *adv.* [ME f. OF (as ARROGATE, −ANT)]

ar•ro•gate /árəgayt/ *v.tr.* **1** (often foll. by *to* oneself) claim (power, responsibility, etc.) without justification. **2** (often foll. by *to*) attribute unjustly (to a person). □□ **ar•ro•ga•tion** /−gáyshən/ *n.* [L *arrogare arrogat-* (as AD-, *rogare* ask)]

ar•ron•disse•ment /arÓNdeesmón/ *n.* **1** a subdivision of a French department, for local government administration purposes. **2** an administrative district of a large city, esp. Paris. [F]

ar•row /árō/ *n.* **1** a sharp pointed wooden or metal stick shot from a bow as a weapon. **2** a drawn or printed, etc., representation of an arrow indicating a direction; a pointer. □□ **ar•row•y** *adj.* [OE *ar(e)we* f. ON *ör* f. Gmc]

ar•row•head /árōhed/ *n.* **1** the pointed end of an arrow. **2** an aquatic plant, *Sagittaria sagittaria*, with arrow-shaped leaves. **3** a decorative device resembling an arrowhead.

ar•row•root /árōrōōt, −rŏŏt/ *n.* a plant of the family Marantaceae from which a starch is prepared and used for nutritional and medicinal purposes.

ar•row•worm /árōwərm/ *n.* = CHAETOGNATH.

ar•roy•o /əróyō/ *n.* (*pl.* **•os**) **1** a brook or stream, esp. in an arid region. **2** a gully. [Sp.]

arse esp. *Brit.* var. of ASS².

ar•se•nal /áarsənəl/ *n.* **1** a store of weapons. **2** a government establishment for the storage and manufacture of weapons and ammunition. **3** resources regarded collectively. [obs. F *arsenal* or It. *arzanale* f. Arab. *dārṣinā'a* f. *dār* house + *sinā'a* art, industry f. *ṣana'a* fabricate]

ar•se•nic *n. & adj.* ● *n.* /áarsənik/ **1** a nonscientific name for arsenic trioxide, a highly poisonous white powdery substance used in weed killers, rat poison, etc. **2** *Chem.* a brittle semimetallic element, used in semiconductors and alloys. ¶ Symb.: **As**. ● *adj.* /aarsénik/ **1** of or concerning arsenic. **2** *Chem.* containing arsenic with a valence of five. □□ **ar•se•ni•ous** /aarseéniəs/ *adj.* [ME f. OF f. L *arsenicum* f. Gk *arsenikon* yellow orpiment, identified with *arsenikos* male, but in fact f. Arab. *al* the + *zarnīk* f. al the + *zarnīk* orpiment f. Pers. f. *zar* gold]

ar•sen•i•cal /aarsénikəl/ *adj. & n.* ● *adj.* of or containing arsenic. ● *n.* a drug containing arsenic.

ar•sine /áarseen/ *n. Chem.* arsenic trihydride, a colorless poisonous gas smelling slightly of garlic. [ARSENIC after *amine*]

ar•sis /áarsis/ *n.* (*pl.* **arses** /−seez/) a stressed syllable or part of a metrical foot in Greek or Latin verse (opp. THESIS). [ME f. LL f. Gk, = lifting f. *airō* raise]

ar•son /áarsən/ *n.* the act of maliciously setting fire to property. □□ **ar•son•ist** *n.* [legal AF, OF, f. med.L *arsio −onis* f. L *ardēre arsburn*]

ars•phen•a•mine /aarsfénəmeen/ *n.* a drug formerly used in the treatment of syphilis and parasitic diseases. [ARSENIC + PHENYL + AMINE]

art¹ /aart/ *n.* **1 a** human creative skill or its application. **b** work exhibiting this. **2 a** (in *pl.*; prec. by *the*) the various branches of creative activity concerned with the production of imaginative designs, sounds, or ideas, e.g., painting, music, writing, considered collectively. **b** any one of these branches. **3** creative activity, esp. painting and drawing, resulting in visual representation (*interested in music but not art*). **4** human skill or workmanship as opposed to the work of nature (*art and nature had combined to make her a great beauty*). **5** (often foll. by *of*) a skill, aptitude, or knack (*the art of writing clearly; keeping people happy is quite an art*). **6** (in *pl.*; usu. prec. by *the*) those branches of learning (esp. languages, literature, and history) associated with creative skill as opposed to scientific, technical, or vocational skills. **7** crafty or wily behavior; an instance of this. [ME f. OF f. L *ars artis*]

art² /aart/ *archaic* or *dial. 2nd sing. present* of BE.

art. /aart/ *abbr.* article.

art and mys•ter•y *n. Brit.* any of the special skills or techniques in a specified area.

art dec•o *n.* /dékō/ the predominant decorative art style of the period 1910–30, characterized by precise and boldly delineated geometric motifs, shapes, and strong colors.

ar•te•fact *Brit.* var. of ARTIFACT.

ar•tel /aartél/ *n.* an association of craftsmen, peasants, etc., in the former USSR. [Russ.]

ar•te•ri•al /aarteéreeəl/ *adj.* **1** of or relating to an artery (*arterial blood*). **2** (esp. of a road) main, important, esp. linking large cities or towns. [F *artériel* f. *artère* artery]

ar•te•ri•al•ize /aarteéreeəlīz/ *v.tr.* **1** convert venous into arterial (blood) by reoxygenation esp. in the lungs. **2** provide with an arterial system. □□ **ar•te•ri•al•i•za•tion** *n.*

ar•te•ri•ole /aarteéreeōl/ *n.* a small branch of an artery leading into capillaries. [F *artériole*, dimin. of *artère* ARTERY]

ar•te•ri•o•scle•ro•sis /aarteéreeōsklərósis/ *n.* the loss of elasticity and thickening of the walls of the arteries, esp. in old age; hardening of the arteries. □□ **ar•te•ri•o•scle•rot•ic** /−rótik/ *adj.* [ARTERY + SCLEROSIS]

ar•ter•y /áartəree/ *n.* (*pl.* **•ies**) **1** any of the muscular-walled tubes forming part of the blood circulation system of the body, carrying oxygen-enriched blood from the heart (cf. VEIN). **2** a main road or railroad line. □□ **ar•te•ri•tis** /−rítis/ *n.* [ME f. L *arteria* f. Gk *artēria* prob. f. *airō* raise]

ar•te•sian well /aartéezhən/ *n.* a well bored perpendicularly, esp. through rock, into water-bearing strata lying at an angle, so that natural pressure produces a constant supply of water with little or no pumping. [F. *artésien* f. Artois, an old French province]

art form *n.* **1** any medium of artistic expression. **2** an established form of composition (e.g., the novel, sonata, sonnet, etc.).

art·ful /aártfŏol/ *adj.* **1** (of a person or action) crafty; deceitful. **2** skillful; clever. □□ **art·ful·ly** *adv.* **art·ful·ness** *n.*

ar·thri·tis /aarthrítis/ *n.* inflammation of a joint or joints. □□ **ar·thrit·ic** /-thrítik/ *adj. & n.* [L f. Gk f. *arthron* joint]

ar·thro·pod /aárthrəpod/ *n. Zool.* any invertebrate animal of the phylum Arthropoda, with a segmented body, jointed limbs, and an external skeleton, e.g., an insect, spider, or crustacean. [Gk *arthron* joint + *pous podos* foot]

ar·thro·scope /árthrəskōp/ *n.* an endoscope for viewing the interior of a joint, as the knee. □□ **ar·thro·scop·ic** *adj.* **ar·thros·co·py** *n.* [Gk *arthron* joint + –SCOPE]

Ar·thu·ri·an /aarthŏoreeən/ *adj.* relating to or associated with King Arthur, the legendary British ruler, or his court.

ar·ti·choke /aártichōk/ *n.* **1** a European plant, *Cynara scolymus,* allied to the thistle. **2** (in full **globe artichoke**) the flower head of the artichoke, the bracts of which have edible bases **3** = JERUSALEM ARTICHOKE. [It. *articiocco* f. Arab. *al-karšúfa*]

artichoke

ar·ti·cle /aártikəl/ *n. & v.* ● *n.* **1** (often in *pl.*) an item or commodity, usu. not further distinguished (*a collection of odd articles*). **2** a nonfictional essay, esp. one included with others in a newspaper, magazine, journal, etc. **3 a** a particular part (*an article of faith*). **b** a separate clause or portion of any document (*articles of apprenticeship*). **4** *Gram.* the definite or indefinite article. ● *v.tr.* bind by articles of apprenticeship. [ME f. OF f. L *articulus* dimin. of *artus* joint]

ar·ti·cles of a·gree·ment *n.* the terms on which seamen take service on a ship.

ar·tic·u·lar /aartíkyələr/ *adj.* of or relating to the joints. [ME f. L *articularis* (as ARTICLE, –AR¹)]

ar·tic·u·late *adj. & v.* ● *adj.* /aartíkyələt/ **1** able to speak fluently and coherently. **2** (of sound or speech) having clearly distinguishable parts. **3** having joints. ● *v.* /aartíkyəlayt/ **1** *tr.* **a** pronounce (words, syllables, etc.) clearly and distinctly. **b** express (an idea, etc.) coherently. **2** *intr.* speak distinctly (*was quite unable to articulate*). **3** *tr.* (usu. in *passive*) connect by joints. **4** *tr.* mark with apparent joints. **5** *intr.* (often foll. by *with*) form a joint. □□ **ar·tic·u·la·cy** *n.* **ar·tic·u·late·ly** *adv.* **ar·tic·u·late·ness** *n.* **ar·tic·u·la·tor** *n.* [L *articulatus* (as ARTICLE, –ATE²)]

ar·tic·u·la·tion /aartíkyəláyshən/ *n.* **1 a** the act of speaking. **b** articulate utterance; speech. **2 a** the act or a mode of jointing. **b** a joint. [F *articulation* or L *articulatio* f. *articulare* joint (as ARTICLE, –ATION)]

ar·ti·fact /aártifakt/ *n.* (*Brit.* **artefact**) **1** a product of human art and workmanship. **2** *Archaeol.* a product of prehistoric or aboriginal workmanship as distinguished from a similar object naturally produced. **3** *Biol.,* etc., a feature not naturally present, introduced during preparation or investigation (e.g., as in the preparation of a slide). □□ **ar·ti·fac·tu·al** /-fákchŏoəl/ *adj.* (in senses 1 and 2). [L *arte* (ablat. of *ars* art) + *factum* (neut. past part. of *facere* make)]

ar·ti·fice /aártifis/ *n.* **1** a clever device; a contrivance. **2 a** cunning. **b** an instance of this. **3** skill; dexterity. **4** the products of human skill; man-made objects. [F f. L *artificium* f. *ars artis* art, –*ficium* making f. *facere* make]

ar·tif·i·cer /aartífisər/ *n.* **1** an inventor. **2** a craftsman. [ME f. AF, prob. alt. of OF *artificien*]

ar·ti·fi·cial /aártifíshəl/ *adj.* **1** produced by human art or effort rather than originating naturally (*an artificial lake*). **2** not real; imitation; fake (*artificial flowers*). **3** affected; insincere (*an artificial smile*). □□ **ar·ti·fi·ci·al·i·ty** /-sheeálitee/ *n.* **ar·ti·fi·cial·ly** *adv.* [ME f. OF *artificiel* or L *artificialis* (as ARTIFICE, –AL)]

ar·ti·fi·cial in·sem·i·na·tion *n.* the injection of semen into the vagina or uterus other than by sexual intercourse.

ar·ti·fi·cial in·tel·li·gence *n.* the application of computers to areas normally regarded as requiring human intelligence.

ar·ti·fi·cial kid·ney *n.* an apparatus that performs the functions of the human kidney (outside the body), when one or both organs are damaged.

ar·ti·fi·cial res·pi·ra·tion *n.* the restoration or initiation of breathing by manual or mechanical or mouth-to-mouth methods.

ar·til·ler·y /aartíləree/ *n.* (*pl.* **-ies**) **1** large-caliber guns used in warfare on land. **2** a branch of the armed forces that uses these. □□ **ar·til·ler·ist** *n.* [ME f. OF *artillerie* f. *artiller* alt. of *atillier, atirier* equip, arm]

ar·til·ler·y·man /aartíləreeman/ *n.* (*pl.* **·men**) a member of the artillery.

ar·ti·san /aártizən, –sən/ *n.* **1** a skilled, esp. manual, worker or craftsman. **2** *Brit.* a mechanic. □□ **ar·ti·san·ship** *n.* [F f. It. *artigiano,* ult. f. L *artitus* past part. of *artire* instruct in the arts]

art·ist /aártist/ *n.* **1** a painter. **2** a person who practices any of the arts. **3** a professional performer, esp. a singer or dancer. **4** a person who works with the dedication and attributes associated with an artist (*an artist in crime*). **5** *colloq.* a devotee; a habitual or skillful practicer of a specified activity (*con artist*). □□ **art·ist·ry** *n.* [F *artiste* f. It. *artista* (as ART¹, –IST)]

ar·tiste /aarteést/ *n.* esp. *Brit.* n. = ARTIST 3.

ar·tis·tic /aartístik/ *adj.* **1** having natural skill in art. **2** made or done with art. **3** of art or artists. □□ **ar·tis·ti·cal·ly** *adv.*

art·less /aártlis/ *adj.* **1** guileless; ingenuous. **2** not resulting from or displaying art. **3** clumsy. □□ **art·less·ly** *adv.* **art·less·ness** *n.*

art nou·veau *n.* /áart nŏovṓ/ an art style of the late 19th century characterized by flowing lines and natural organic forms.

art of war *n.* the strategy, tactics, and techniques of combat.

arts and crafts *n.* decorative design and handcrafts.

art·sy-craft·sy /ártsee-kráftsee/ *adj.* quaintly artistic; (of furniture, etc.) seeking stylistic effect rather than usefulness or comfort.

art·work /aártwərk/ *n.* **1** an artistic work, esp. in the visual arts. **2** the illustrations in a printed work.

art·y /aártee/ *adj.* (**artier, artiest**) *colloq.* pretentiously or affectedly artistic. □□ **art·i·ness** *n.*

ar·um /áirəm/ *n.* any plant of the genus *Arum,* usu. stemless with arrow-shaped leaves. [L f. Gk *aron*]

ar·um lil·y *n.* = CALLA 1.

ar·vo /aárvō/ *n. Austral. sl.* afternoon. [abbr.]

-ary¹ /eree/ *suffix* **1** forming adjectives (*budgetary; contrary; primary; unitary*). **2** forming nouns (*dictionary; fritillary; granary; January*). [F –*aire* or L –*arius* 'connected with']

-ary² /eree/ *suffix* forming adjectives (*military*). [F –*aire* or f. L –*aris* 'belonging to']

Ar·y·an /áireeən/ *n. & adj.* ● *n.* **1** a member of the peoples speaking any of the languages of the Indo-European (esp. Indo-Iranian) family. **2** the parent language of this family. **3** *improperly* (in Nazi ideology) a Caucasian not of Jewish descent. ● *adj.* of or relating to Aryan or the Aryans. [Skr. *āryas* noble]

ar·yl /áril/ *n. Chem.* any radical derived from or related to an aromatic hydrocarbon by removal of a hydrogen atom. [G *Aryl* (as AROMATIC, –YL)]

AS *abbr.* **1** Anglo-Saxon. **2** American Samoa (in official postal usu).

As *symb. Chem.* the element arsenic.

as¹ /az, *unstressed* əz/ *adv., conj., & pron.* ● *adv. & conj.* (*adv.* as antecedent in main sentence; *conj.* in relative clause expressed or implied) . . . to the extent to which . . . is or does, etc. (*I am as tall as he; am as tall as he is; am not so tall as he;* (*colloq.*) *am as tall as him; as many as six; as recently as last week; it is not as easy as you think*). ● *conj.* (with relative clause expressed or implied) **1** (with antecedent *so*) expressing result or purpose (*came early so as to meet us; we so arranged matters as to avoid a long wait; so good as to exceed all hopes*). **2** (with antecedent adverb omitted) having concessive force (*good as it is* = although it is good; *try as he might* = although he might try). **3** (without antecedent adverb) in the manner in which (*do as you like; was regarded as a mistake; they rose as one*). **b** in the capacity or form of (*I speak as your friend; Olivier as Hamlet; as a matter of fact*). **c** during or at the time that (*came up as I was speaking; fell just as I reached the door*). **d** for the reason that; seeing that (*as you are here, we can talk*). **e** for instance (*composers, as Monteverdi*). ● *rel.pron.* (with verb of relative clause expressed or implied) **1** that; who; which (*I had the same trouble as you; he is a writer, as his wife; such money as you have; such countries as France*). **2** (with sentence as antecedent) a fact that (*he lost, as you know*). □ **as and when** to the extent and at the time that (*I'll do it as and when I want to*). **as for** with regard to (*as for you, I think you are wrong*). **as from** esp. *Brit.* = *as of 1.* **as if** (or **though**) as would be the case if (*acts as if she were in charge; as if you didn't know!; looks as though we've won*). **as it is** (or **as is**) in the existing circumstances or state. **as it were** in a way; to a certain extent (*he is, as it were, infatuated*). **as long as** see LONG¹. **as much** see MUCH. **as of 1** on and after (a specified date). **2** as at (a specified time). **as per** see PER. **as regards** see REGARD. **as soon as** see SOON. **as such** see SUCH. **as though** see *as if.* **as to** with respect to; concerning (*said nothing as to money; as to you, I think you are wrong*). **as was** in the previously existing circumstances or state. **as well** see WELL¹. **as yet** until now or a particular time in the past (usu. with *neg.* and with implied reserve about the future: *have received no news as yet*). [reduced form of OE *alswá* ALSO]

▶See note at LIKE¹.

as² /as/ *n.* (*pl.* **asses**) a Roman copper coin. [L]

as- /əs/ *prefix* assim. form of AD- before *s.*

as·a·fet·i·da /ásəfétidə /*n.* (also **asafoetida**) a resinous plant gum with a fetid ammoniac smell, formerly used in medicine, now as an herbal remedy and in Indian cooking. [ME f. med.L f. *asa* f. Pers. *azā* mastic + *fetida* (as FETID)]

a.s.a.p. *abbr.* (also **ASAP**) as soon as possible.

as·bes·tos /asbéstəs, az–/ *n.* **1** a fibrous silicate mineral that is not flammable. **2** this used as a heat-resistant or insulating material. □□ **as·bes·tine** /-tin/ *adj.* [ME f. OF *albeston,* ult. f. Gk *asbestos* unquenchable f. *a-* not + *sbestos* f. *sbennumi* quench]

as·bes·to·sis /àsbestósis, áz–/ n. a lung disease resulting from the inhalation of asbestos particles.

as·ca·rid /áskərid/ n. (also **ascaris** /–ris/) a parasitic nematode worm of the genus *Ascaris*, e.g., the intestinal roundworm of humans and other vertebrates. [mod.L *ascaris* f. Gk *askaris*]

as·cend /əsénd/ v. **1** intr. move upward; rise. **2** intr. a slope upward. **b** lie along an ascending slope. **3** tr. climb; go up. **4** intr. rise in rank or status. **5** tr. mount upon. **6** intr. (of sound) rise in pitch. **7** tr. go along (a river) to its source. **8** intr. *Printing* (of a letter) have part projecting upward. □ **ascend the throne** become king or queen. [ME f. L *ascendere* (as AD–, *scandere* climb)]

as·cend·an·cy /əséndənsee/ n. (also **as·cend·en·cy**) (often foll. by *over*) a superior or dominant condition or position.

as·cend·ant /əséndənt/ adj. & n. ● adj. **1** rising. **2** *Astron.* rising toward the zenith. **3** *Astrol.* just above the eastern horizon. **4** predominant. ● n. *Astrol.* the point of the sun's apparent path that is ascendant at a given time. □ **in the ascendant 1** supreme or dominating. **2** rising; gaining power or authority. [ME f. OF f. L (as ASCEND, –ANT)]

as·cend·er /əséndər/ n. **1 a** a part of a letter that extends above the main part (as in *b* and *d*). **b** a letter having this. **2** a person or thing that ascends.

ascenders and descenders

as·cen·sion /əsénshən/ n. **1** the act or an instance of ascending. **2** (**Ascension**) the ascent of Christ into heaven on the fortieth day after the Resurrection. □□ **as·cen·sion·al** adj. [ME f. OF f. L *ascensio –onis* (as ASCEND, –ION)]

As·cen·sion Day n. the fortieth day after Easter, on which Christ's Ascension is celebrated in the Christian Church. Also called **Holy Thursday**.

as·cent /əsént/ n. **1** the act or an instance of ascending. **2 a** an upward movement or rise. **b** advancement or progress (*the ascent of mammals*). **3** a way by which one may ascend; an upward slope. [ASCEND, after *descent*]

as·cer·tain /ásərtáyn/ v.tr. **1** find out as a definite fact. **2** get to know. □□ **as·cer·tain·a·ble** adj. **as·cer·tain·ment** n. [ME f. OF *acertener*, stem *acertain-* f. *à to* + CERTAIN]

as·ce·sis /əseésis/ n. the practice of self-discipline. [Gk *askēsis* training f. *askeō* exercise]

as·cet·ic /əsétik/ n. & adj. ● n. a person who practices severe self-discipline and abstains from all forms of pleasure, esp. for religious or spiritual reasons. ● adj. relating to or characteristic of ascetics or asceticism; abstaining from pleasure. □□ **as·cet·i·cal·ly** adv. **as·cet·i·cism** /–tisizəm/ n. [med.L *asceticus* or Gk *askētikos* f. *askētēs* monk f. *askeō* exercise]

as·cid·i·an /əsídeeən/ n. *Zool.* any tunicate animal of the class Ascidiacea, often found in colonies, the adults sedentary on rocks or seaweeds, e.g., the sea squirt. [mod.L *Ascidia* f. Gk *askidion* dimin. of *askos* wineskin]

ASCII /áskee/ abbr. *Computing* American Standard Code for Information Interchange.

as·ci·tes /əsíteez/ n. (pl. same) *Med.* the accumulation of fluid in the abdominal cavity, causing swelling. [ME f. LL f. Gk f. *askitēs* f. *askos* wineskin]

a·scor·bic ac·id /əskáwrbik/ n. a vitamin found in citrus fruits and green vegetables, essential in maintaining healthy connective tissue, a deficiency of which results in scurvy. Also called **vitamin C**.

as·cot /áskot, –kət/ n. a scarflike item of neckwear with broad ends worn looped to lie flat one over the other against the chest. [f. its being worn traditionally by men attending the races at Ascot, England]

as·cribe /əskríb/ v.tr. (usu. foll. by *to*) **1** attribute or impute (*ascribes his well-being to a sound constitution*). **2** regard as belonging. □□ **a·scrib·a·ble** adj. [ME f. L *ascribere* (as AD–, *scribere* script- write)]

as·crip·tion /əskrípshən/ n. **1** the act or an instance of ascribing. **2** a preacher's words ascribing praise to God at the end of a sermon. [L *ascriptio –onis* (as ASCRIBE)]

ascot

asdic /ázdik/ n. = SONAR. [initials of *Allied Submarine Detection Investigation Committee*]

-ase /ays/ suffix *Biochem.* forming the name of an enzyme (*amylase*). [DIASTASE]

ASEAN /áseeən/ abbr. Association of South East Asian Nations.

a·sep·sis /aysépsis/ n. **1** the absence of harmful bacteria, viruses, or other microorganisms. **2** a method of achieving asepsis in surgery.

a·sep·tic /ayséptik/ adj. **1** free from contamination caused by harmful bacteria, viruses, or other microorganisms. **2** (of a wound, instrument, or dressing) surgically sterile or sterilized. **3** (of a surgical method, etc.) aiming at the elimination of harmful microorganisms, rather than counteraction (cf. ANTISEPTIC).

a·sex·u·al /aysékshōōəl/ adj. *Biol.* **1** without sex or sexual organs. **2** (of reproduction) not involving the fusion of gametes. **3** without sexuality. □□ **a·sex·u·al·i·ty** /–shōōálitee/ n. **a·sex·u·al·ly** adv.

ash[1] /ash/ n. **1** (often in pl.) the powdery residue left after the burning of any substance. **2** (pl.) the remains of the human body after cremation or disintegration. **3** ashlike material thrown out by a volcano. [OE *æsce*]

ash[2] /ash/ n. **1** any tree of the genus *Fraxinus*, with silvery-gray bark, compound leaves, and hard, tough, pale wood. **2** its wood. **3** an Old English runic letter, = æ (named from a word of which it was the first letter). [OE *æsc* f. Gmc]

a·shamed /əsháymd/ adj. (usu. predic.) **1** (often foll. by *of* (= with regard to), *for* (= on account of), or *to* + infin.) embarrassed or disconcerted by shame (*ashamed of his aunt; ashamed of having lied; ashamed for you; ashamed to be seen with him*). **2** (foll. by *to* + infin.) hesitant; reluctant (but usu. not actually refusing or declining) (*am ashamed to admit that I was wrong*). □□ **a·sham·ed·ly** /–midlee/ adv. [OE *āscamod* past part. of *āscamian* feel shame (as A–[2], SHAME)]

ash·bin /áshbin/ n. *Brit.* a receptacle for the disposal of ashes.

ash blond n. (also **ash blonde**) **1** a very pale blond color. **2** a person with hair of this color.

ash can /áshkan/ n. a container for household trash.

ash·en[1] /áshən/ adj. **1** of or resembling ashes. **2** ash colored; gray or pale.

ash·en[2] /áshən/ adj. **1** of or relating to the ash tree. **2** *archaic* made of ash wood.

Ash·ke·naz·i /àashkənáazee/ n. (pl. **Ashkenazim** /–zim/) **1** an eastern European Jew. **2** a Jew of eastern European ancestry (cf. SEPHARDI). □□ **Ash·ke·naz·ic** adj. [mod.Heb., f. *Ashkenaz* (Gen. 10:3)]

ash·lar /áshlər/ n. **1** a large square-cut stone used in building. **2** masonry made of ashlars. **3** such masonry used as a facing on a rough rubble or brick wall. [ME f. OF *aisselier* f. L *axilla* dimin. of *axis* board]

ash·lar·ing /áshləring/ n. **1** ashlar masonry. **2** the short upright boarding in a garret which cuts off the acute angle between the roof and the floor.

a·shore /əsháwr/ adv. toward or on the shore or land (*sailed ashore; stayed ashore*).

ash·ram /áashrəm/ n. *Ind.* a place of religious retreat for Hindus; a hermitage. [Skr. *āshrama* hermitage]

ash·tray /áshtray/ n. a small receptacle for cigarette ashes, butts, etc.

Ash Wednes·day n. the first day of Lent (from the custom of marking the foreheads of penitents with ashes on that day).

ash·y /áshee/ adj. (**ashier, ashiest**) **1** = ASHEN[1]. **2** covered with ashes.

A·sian /áyzhən, –shən/ n. & adj. ● n. **1** a native of Asia. **2** a person of Asian descent. ● adj. of or relating to Asia or its people, customs, or languages. [L *Asianus* f. Gk *Asianos* f. *Asia*]
▶ See note at ORIENTAL.

A·si·at·ic /áyzheeátik, –shee–, –zee–/ n. & adj. ● n. offens. an Asian. ● adj. Asian. [L *Asiaticus* f. Gk *Asiatikos*]

A-side /áysīd/ n. the side of a phonograph record regarded as the main one.

a·side /əsíd/ adv. & n. ● adv. **1** to or on one side; away. **2** out of consideration (placed after noun: *joking aside*). ● n. **1** words spoken in a play for the audience to hear, but supposed not to be heard by the other characters. **2** an incidental remark. □ **aside from** apart from. **set aside 1** put to one side. **2** keep for a special purpose or future use. **3** reject or disregard. **4** annul. **5** remove (land) from agricultural production for fallow, forestry, or other use. **take aside** engage (a person) esp. in a private conversation. [orig. *on side*: see A[2]]

as·i·nine /ásinīn/ adj. **1** stupid. **2** of or concerning asses; like an ass. □□ **as·i·nin·i·ty** /–nínitee/ n. [L *asininus* f. *asinus* ass]

-asis /əsis/ suffix (usu. as **–iasis**) forming the names of diseases (*psoriasis; satyriasis*). [L f. Gk *–asis* in nouns of state f. verbs in *–aō*]

ask /ask/ v. **1** tr. call for an answer to or about (*ask her about it; ask him his name; ask a question of him*). **2** tr. seek to obtain from another person (*ask a favor of; ask to be allowed*). **3** tr. (usu. foll. by *out* or *over*, or *to* (a function, etc.)) invite; request the company of (*must ask them over; asked her to dinner*). **4** intr. (foll. by *for*) **a** seek to obtain, meet, or be directed to (*ask for a donation; ask for the post office; asking for you*). **b** invite; provoke (trouble, etc.) by one's behavior; bring upon oneself (*they were asking for all they got*). **5** tr. archaic require (a thing). □ **ask after** inquire about (esp. a person). **ask for**

it *sl.* invite trouble. **ask me another** *colloq.* I do not know. **for the asking** (obtainable) for nothing. **I ask you!** an exclamation of disgust, surprise, etc. **if you ask me** *colloq.* in my opinion. □□ **ask•er** *n.* [OE *āscian*, etc. f. WG]

a•skance /əskáns/ *adv.* (also **askant** /–skánt/) sideways or squinting. □ **look askance at** regard with suspicion or disapproval. [16th c.: orig. unkn.]

as•ka•ri /askaáree/ *n.* (*pl.* same or **askaris**) an East African soldier or policeman. [Arab. 'askarī soldier]

a•skew /əskyo͞o/ *adv. & predic.adj.* ● *adv.* obliquely; awry. ● *predic.adj.* oblique; awry. [A[2] + SKEW]

ask•ing price *n.* the price of an object set by the seller.

a•slant /əslánt/ *adv. & prep.* ● *adv.* obliquely or at a slant. ● *prep.* obliquely across (*lay aslant the path*).

a•sleep /əsleép/ *predic.adj. & adv.* **1 a** in or into a state of sleep (*he fell asleep*). **b** inactive; inattentive (*the nation is asleep*). **2** (of a limb, etc.) numb. **3** *euphem.* dead.

a•slope /əslóp/ *adv. & predic.adj.* sloping; crosswise. [ME: orig. uncert.]

ASM *abbr.* air-to-surface missile.

a•so•cial /áysóshəl/ *adj.* **1** not social; antisocial. **2** *colloq.* inconsiderate of or hostile to others.

asp /asp/ *n.* **1** a small viper, *Vipera aspis*, native to southern Europe, resembling the adder. **2** a small venomous snake, *Naja haje*, native to North Africa and Arabia. [ME f. OF *aspe* or L *aspis* f. Gk]

as•par•a•gus /əspárəgəs/ *n.* **1** any plant of the genus *Asparagus*. **2** one species of this, *A. officinalis*, with edible young shoots and leaves; this as food. [L f. Gk *asparagos*]

as•par•a•gus fern *n.* a decorative plant, Asparagus setaceus.

as•par•tame /əspaártaym/ *n.* a very sweet, low-calorie substance used as a sweetener instead of sugar or saccharin. [chem. name 1-- methyl N-L-aspartyl-L-phenylalanine, f. aspartic acid (invented name)]

as•pect /áspekt/ *n.* **1 a** a particular component or feature of a matter (*only one aspect of the problem*). **b** a particular way in which a matter may be considered. **2 a** a facial expression; a look (*a cheerful aspect*). **b** the appearance of a person or thing, esp. as presented to the mind of the viewer (*has a frightening aspect*). **3** the side of a building or location facing a particular direction (*southern aspect*). **4** *Gram.* a verbal category or form expressing inception, duration, or completion. **5** *Astrol.* the relative position of planets, etc., measured by angular distance. □□ **as•pec•tu•al** /áspékcho͞oəl/ *adj.* (in sense 4). [ME f. L *aspectus* f. *adspicere adspect-* look at (as AD-, *specere* look)]

as•pect ra•tio *n.* **1** *Aeron.* the ratio of the span to the mean chord of an airfoil. **2** *Telev.* the ratio of picture width to height.

as•pen /áspən/ *n.* a poplar tree, *Populus tremula*, with especially tremulous leaves. [earlier name *asp* f. OE *æspe* + –EN[2] forming adj. taken as noun]

as•per•i•ty /əspéritee/ *n.* (*pl.* **•ties**) **1** harshness or sharpness of temper or tone. **2** roughness. **3** a rough excrescence. [ME f. OF *asperité* or L *asperitas* f. *asper* rough]

as•perse /əspérs/ *v.tr.* (often foll. by *with*) attack the reputation of; calumniate. □□ **as•per•sive** *adj.* [ME, = besprinkle, f. L *aspergere aspers-* (as AD-, *spargere* sprinkle)]

as•per•sion /əspérzhən/ *n.* a slander; a false insinuation. □ **cast aspersions on** attack the reputation or integrity of. [L *aspersio* (as ASPERSE, –ION)]

as•phalt /ásfalt/ *n. & v.* ● *n.* **1** a dark bituminous pitch occurring naturally or made from petroleum. **2** a mixture of this with sand, gravel, etc., for surfacing roads, etc. ● *v.tr.* surface with asphalt. □□ **as•phalt•er** *n.* **as•phal•tic** /–fáltik/ *adj.* [ME, ult. f. LL asphalton, –um, f. Gk asphalton]

as•pho•del /ásfədel/ *n.* **1** any plant of the genus *Asphodelus*, of the lily family. **2** *poet.* an immortal flower growing in Elysium. [L *asphodelus* f. Gk *asphodelos*: cf. DAFFODIL]

as•phyx•i•a /asfíkseeə/ *n.* a lack of oxygen in the blood, causing unconsciousness or death; suffocation. □□ **as•phyx•i•al** *adj.* **as•phyx•i•ant** *adj. & n.* [mod.L f. Gk asphuxia f. a- not + sphuxis pulse]

as•phyx•i•ate /asfíkseeayt/ *v.tr.* cause (a person) to have asphyxia; suffocate. □□ **as•phyx•i•a•tion** /–áyshən/ *n.* **as•phyx•i•a•tor** *n.*

as•pic /áspik/ *n.* a savory meat jelly used as a garnish or to contain game, eggs, etc. [F, = ASP, from the colors of the jelly (compared to those of the asp)]

as•pi•dis•tra /áspidístrə/ *n.* a foliage plant of the genus *Aspidistra*, with broad tapering leaves, often grown as a houseplant. [mod.L f. Gk aspis –idos shield (from the shape of the leaves)]

as•pir•ant /áspirənt, əspírənt/ *adj. & n.* (usu. foll. by *to, after, for*) ● *adj.* aspiring. ● *n.* a person who aspires. [F *aspirant* or f. L *aspirant-* (as ASPIRE, –ANT)]

as•pi•rate /áspir ət/ *adj., n., & v.* Phonet. ● *adj.* **1** pronounced with an exhalation of breath. **2** blended with the sound of *h*. ● *n.* **1** a consonant pronounced in this way. **2** the sound of *h*. ● *v.* also /áspiráyt/ **1 a** *tr.* pronounce with a breath. **b** *intr.* make the sound of *h*. **2** *tr.*

draw (fluid) by suction from a vessel or cavity. **3** *tr.* draw (air, fluid, etc.) into the lungs, as by breathing. [L *aspiratus* past part. of *aspirare*: see ASPIRE]

as•pi•ra•tion /áspiráyshən/ *n.* **1** a strong desire to achieve an end; an ambition. **2** the act or process of drawing breath. **3** the action of aspirating. [ME f. OF *aspiration* or L *aspiratio* (as ASPIRE, –ATION)]

as•pi•ra•tor /áspiraytər/ *n.* an apparatus for aspirating fluid. [L *aspirare* (as ASPIRE, –OR[1])]

as•pire /əspír/ *v.intr.* (usu. foll. by *to* or *after*, or *to* + infin.) **1** have ambition or strong desire. **2** *poet.* rise high. [ME f. F *aspirer* or L *aspirare* f. *ad* to + *spirare* breathe]

as•pi•rin /ásprin/ *n.* (*pl.* same or **aspirins**) **1** a white powder, acetylsalicylic acid, used to relieve pain and reduce fever. **2** a tablet of this. [G, formed as ACETYL + *spiraeic* (= salicylic) *acid* + –IN]

a•squint /əskwínt/ *predic.adj. & adv.* (usu. *look asquint*). **1** to one side; from the corner of an eye. **2** with a squint. [ME perh. f. Du. *schuinte* slant]

ass[1] /as/ *n.* **1 a** either of two kinds of four-legged long-eared mammals of the horse genus *Equus*, *E. africanus* of Africa and *E. hemionus* of Asia. **b** (in general use) a donkey. **2** a stupid person. □ **make an ass of** make (a person) look absurd or foolish. [OE *assa* thr. OCelt. f. L *asinus*]

ass[2] /as/ *n. & v.* (*Brit.* **arse** /aars/) *coarse sl.* ● *n.* **1** the buttocks. **2** the anus. ● *v.intr.* (usu. foll. by *about, around*) play the fool. [OE *ærs*]

as•sa•gai var. of ASSEGAI.

as•sa•i /así/ *adv. Mus.* very (*adagio assai*). [It.]

as•sail /əsáyl/ *v.tr.* **1** make a strong or concerted attack on. **2** make a resolute start on (a task). **3** make a strong or constant verbal attack on (*was assailed with angry questions*). □□ **as•sail•a•ble** *adj.* [ME f. OF *asaill-* stressed stem of *asalir* f. med.L *assalire* f. L *assilire* (as AD-, *salire salt-* leap)]

as•sail•ant /əsáylənt/ *n.* a person who attacks another physically or verbally. [F (as ASSAIL)]

as•sas•sin /əsásin/ *n.* **1** a killer, esp. of a political or religious leader. **2** *hist.* any of a group of Muslim fanatics sent on murder missions in the time of the Crusades. [F *assassin* or f. med.L *assassinus* f. Arab. *ḥaššāš* hashish eater]

as•sas•si•nate /əsásinayt/ *v.tr.* kill (esp. a political or religious leader) for political, fanatical, or religious motives. □□ **as•sas•si•na•tion** /–náyshən/ *n.* **as•sas•si•na•tor** *n.* [med.L *assassinare* f. *assassinus*: see ASSASSIN]

as•sault /əsáwlt/ *n. & v.* ● *n.* **1** a violent physical or verbal attack. **2 a** *Law* an act that threatens physical harm to a person (whether or not actual harm is done). **b** *euphem.* an act of rape. **3** (*attrib.*) relating to or used in an assault (*assault craft; assault troops*). **4** a vigorous start made to a lengthy or difficult task. **5** a final rush on a fortified place, esp. at the end of a prolonged attack. ● *v.tr.* **1** make an assault on. **2** *euphem.* rape. □□ **as•sault•er** *n.* **as•saul•tive** *adj.* [ME f. OF *asaut*, *assauter* ult. f. L (*salire salt-* leap)]

as•sault and bat•ter•y *n.Law* a threatening act that results in physical harm done to a person.

as•sault course *n.* esp. *Brit.* an obstacle course used in training soldiers, etc.

as•say /əsáy, ásay/ *n. & v.* ● *n.* **1** the testing of a metal or ore to determine its ingredients and quality. **2** *Chem.*, etc., the determination of the content or strength of a substance. ● *v.* **1** *tr.* make an assay of (a metal or ore). **2** *tr. Chem.* etc., perform a concentration on (a substance). **3** *tr.* show (content) on being assayed. **4** *intr.* make an assay. **5** *tr. archaic* attempt. □□ **as•say•er** *n.* [ME f. OF *assaier*, *assai*, var. of *essayer*, *essai*: see ESSAY]

as•say of•fice *n.* an establishment which assays and registers prospecters' claims, gold sales, etc.

as•se•gai /ásigí/ *n.* (also **as•sa•gai** /ásəgí/) a slender iron-tipped spear of hard wood, esp. as used by S. African peoples. [obs. F *azagaie* or Port. *azagaia* f. Arab. *az-zaḡāyah* f. *al* the + *zaḡāyah* spear]

as•sem•blage /əsémblij/ *n.* **1** the act or an instance of bringing or coming together. **2** a collection of things or gathering of people. **3 a** the act or an instance of fitting together. **b** an object made of pieces fitted together. **4** a work of art made by grouping found or unrelated objects.

as•sem•ble /əsémbəl/ *v.* **1** *tr. & intr.* gather together; collect. **2** *tr.* arrange in order. **3** *tr.* esp. *Mech.* fit together the parts of. [ME f. OF *asembler* ult. f. L *ad* + *simul* together]

as•sem•bler /əsémblər/ *n.* **1** a person who assembles a machine or its parts. **2** *Computing* **a** a program for converting instructions written in low-level symbolic code into machine code. **b** the low-level symbolic code itself; an assembly language.

as•sem•bly /əsémblee/ *n.* (*pl.* **•blies**) **1** the act or an instance of assembling or gathering together. **2 a** a group of persons gathered together, esp. as a deliberative or legislative body. **b** a gathering of the entire membership of a school. **3** the assembling of a machine or structure or its parts. **4** *Mil.* a call to assemble, given by drum or bugle. [ME f. OF *asemblee* fem. past part. of *asembler*: see ASSEMBLE]

as•sem•bly lan•guage *n. Computing* the low-level symbolic code converted by an assembler.

as·sem·bly line *n.* machinery arranged in stages by which a product is progressively assembled.

as·sem·bly room *n.* (also **as·sem·bly shop**) a place where a machine or its components are assembled.

as·sent /əsént/ *v. & n.* ● *v.intr.* (usu. foll. by *to*) **1** express agreement (*assented to my view*). **2** consent (*assented to my request*). ● *n.* **1** mental or inward acceptance or agreement (*a nod of assent*). **2** consent or sanction, esp. official. □ **royal assent** *Brit.* assent of the sovereign to a bill passed by Parliament. □□ **as·sen·tor** *n.* (also **assenter**). [ME f. OF *asenter, as(s)ente* ult. f. L *assentari* (*ad* to, *sentire* think)]

as·sert /əsə́rt/ *v.* **1** *tr.* declare; state clearly (*assert one's beliefs; assert that it is so*). **2** *refl.* insist on one's rights or opinions; demand recognition. **3** *tr.* vindicate a claim to (*assert one's rights*). □□ **as·ser·tor** *n.* [L *asserere* (as AD-, *serere sert-* join)]

as·ser·tion /əsə́rshən/ *n.* **1** a declaration; a forthright statement. **2** the act or an instance of asserting. **3** (also **self-assertion**) insistence on the recognition of one's rights or claims. [ME f. F *assertion* or L *assertio* (as ASSERT, –ION)]

as·ser·tive /əsə́rtiv/ *adj.* **1** tending to assert oneself; forthright; positive. **2** dogmatic. □□ **as·ser·tive·ly** *adv.* **as·ser·tive·ness** *n.*

as·ses *pl.* of AS[2], ASS[1], ASS[2].

asses' bridge *n.* = PONS ASINORUM.

as·sess /əsés/ *v.tr.* **1 a** estimate the size or quality of. **b** estimate the value of (a property) for taxation. **2 a** (usu. foll. by *on*) fix the amount of (a tax, etc.) and impose it on a person or community. **b** (usu. foll. by *in, at*) fine or tax (a person, community, etc.) in or at a specific amount (*assessed them at $100*). □□ **as·sess·a·ble** *adj.* **as·sess·ment** *n.* [ME f. F *assesser* f. L *assidēre* (as AD-, *sedēre* sit)]

as·ses·sor /əsésər/ *n.* **1** a person who assesses taxes or estimates the value of property for taxation purposes. **2** a person called upon to advise a judge, committee of inquiry, etc., on technical questions. □□ **as·ses·so·ri·al** /ásesáwreeəl/ *adj.* [ME f. OF *assessour* f. L *assessor –oris* assistant judge (as ASSESS, –OR[1]): sense 1 f. med.L]

as·set /áset/ *n.* **1 a** a useful or valuable quality. **b** a person or thing possessing such a quality or qualities (*is an asset to the firm*). **2** (usu. in *pl.*) **a** property and possessions, esp. regarded as having value in meeting debts, commitments, etc. **b** any possession having value. [*assets* (taken as pl.), f. AF *asetz* f. OF *asez* enough, ult. f. L *ad* to + *satis* enough]

as·set strip·ping *n. Commerce* the practice of taking over a company and selling off its assets to make a profit.

as·sev·er·ate /əsévərayt/ *v.tr.* declare solemnly. □□ **as·sev·er·a·tion** /–ráyshən/ *n.* **as·sev·er·a·tive** /–rətiv/ *adj.* [L *asseverare* (as AD-, *severus* serious)]

ass·hole /ás-hōl/ *n.* **1** the anus. **2** *offens.* a term of contempt for a person.

as·sib·i·late /əsíbilayt/ *v.tr. Phonet.* **1** pronounce (a sound) as a sibilant or affricate ending in a sibilant. **2** alter (a syllable) to become this. □□ **as·sib·i·la·tion** /–láyshən/ *n.* [L *assibilare* (as AD-, *sibilare* hiss)]

as·si·du·i·ty /ásidóoitee, –dyóo–/ *n.* (*pl.* **·ties**) **1** constant or close attention to what one is doing. **2** (usu. in *pl.*) constant attentions to another person. [L *assiduitas* (as ASSIDUOUS, –ITY)]

as·sid·u·ous /əsíjəəs/ *adj.* **1** persevering; hardworking. **2** attending closely. □□ **as·sid·u·ous·ly** *adv.* **as·sid·u·ous·ness** *n.* [L *assiduus* (as ASSESS)]

as·sign /əsín/ *v. & n.* ● *v.tr.* **1** (usu. foll. by *to*) **a** allot as a share, task, or responsibility. **b** appoint to a position, task, etc. **2** fix (a time, place, etc.) for a specific purpose. **3** (foll. by *to*) ascribe or refer to (a reason, date, etc.) (*assigned the manuscript to 1832*). **4** (foll. by *to*) transfer formally (esp. personal property) to (another). ● *n.* a person to whom property or rights are legally transferred. □□ **as·sign·a·ble** *adj.* **as·sign·er** *n.* **as·sign·or** *n.* (in sense 4 of *v.*). [ME f. OF *asi(g)ner* f. L *assignare* mark out to (as AD-, *signum* sign)]

as·sig·na·tion /ásignáyshən/ *n.* **1 a** an appointment to meet. **b** a secret appointment, esp. between illicit lovers. **2** the act or an instance of assigning or being assigned. [ME f. OF f. L *assignatio –onis* (as ASSIGN, –ATION)]

as·sign·ee /ásineé/ *n.* **1** a person appointed to act for another. **2** an assign. [ME f. OF *assigné* past part. of *assigner* ASSIGN]

as·sign·ment /əsínmənt/ *n.* **1** something assigned, esp. a task allotted to a person. **2** the act or an instance of assigning or being assigned. **3 a** a legal transfer. **b** the document effecting this. [ME f. OF *assignement* f. med.L *assignamentum* (as ASSIGN, –MENT)]

as·sim·i·late /əsímilayt/ *v.* **1** *tr.* **a** absorb and digest (food, etc.) into the body. **b** absorb (information, etc.) into the mind. **c** absorb (people) into a larger group. **2** *tr.* (usu. foll. by *to, with*) make like; cause to resemble. **3** *tr. Phonet.* make (a sound) more like another in the same or next word. **4** *intr.* be absorbed into the body, mind, or a larger group. □□ **as·sim·i·la·ble** /əsíməlbəl/ *adj.* **as·sim·i·la·tion** /–láyshən/ *n.* **as·sim·i·la·tive** *adj.* **as·sim·i·la·tor** *n.* **as·sim·i·la·to·ry** /–lətáwree/ *adj.* [ME f. L *assimilare* (as AD-, *similis* like)]

As·sin·i·boin /əsínəboyn/ *n.* **1 a** a N. American people native to northeastern Montana and adjoining parts of Canada. **b** a member of this people. **2** the language of this people.

as·sist /əsíst/ *v. & n.* ● *v.* **1** *tr.* (often foll. by *in* + verbal noun) help (a person, process, etc.) (*assisted them in running the playgroup*). **2** *intr.* (often foll. by *in, at*) attend or be present (*assisted in the ceremony*). ● *n.* **1** an act of helping. **2** *Sports* a player's action of helping a teammate to put out a runner (as in baseball) or score (as in basketball). □□ **as·sis·tance** *n.* **as·sist·er** *n.* [ME f. F *assister* f. L *assistere* take one's stand by (as AD-, *sistere* take one's stand)]

as·sis·tant /əsístənt/ *n.* **1** a helper. **2** (often *attrib.*) a person who assists, esp. as a subordinate in a particular job or role. **3** *Brit.* = SHOP ASSISTANT. [ME *assistent* f. med.L *assistens assistent-* present (as ASSIST, –ANT, –ENT)]

as·size /əsíz/ *n.* (usu. in *pl.*) *Brit. hist.* a court sitting at intervals in each county of England and Wales to administer the civil and criminal law. [ME f. OF *as(s)ise*, fem. past part. of *aseeir* sit at, f. L *assidēre*: cf. ASSESS]

ass-kiss·ing *n. vulgar sl.* the use of compliments, flattery, or other obsequious behavior in order to gain favor. □□ **ass-kiss·er** *n.*

assn. *abbr.* association.

Assoc. *abbr.* (as part of a title) Association.

as·so·ci·a·ble /əsóshəbəl/ *adj.* (usu. foll. by *with*) capable of being connected in thought. □□ **as·so·ci·a·bil·i·ty** *n.* [F f. *associer* (as ASSOCIATE, –ABLE)]

as·so·ci·ate *v., n., & adj.* ● *v.* /əsósheeayt, –see–/ **1** *tr.* connect in the mind (*associate fireworks with Independence Day*). **2** *tr.* join or combine. **3** *refl.* make oneself a partner; declare oneself in agreement (*associate myself in your endeavor; did not want to associate ourselves with the plan*). **4** *intr.* combine for a common purpose. **5** *intr.* (usu. foll. by *with*) meet frequently or have dealings; be friends. ● *n.* /əsósheeət, –see–/ **1** a business partner or colleague. **2** a friend or companion. **3** a subordinate member of a body, institute, etc. **4** a thing connected with another. ● *adj.* /əsóshiət, əsósee–/ **1** joined in companionship, function, or dignity. **2** allied; in the same group or category. **3** of less than full status (*associate member*). □□ **as·so·ci·ate·ship** *n. adj.* [E f. L *associatus* past part. of *associare* (as AD-, *socius* sharing, allied)]

as·so·ci·a·tion /əsóseeáyshən/ *n.* **1** a group of people organized for a joint purpose; a society. **2** the act or an instance of associating. **3** fellowship; human contact or cooperation. **4** a mental connection between ideas. **5** *Chem.* a loose aggregation of molecules. **6** *Ecol.* a group of associated plants. □□ **as·so·ci·a·tion·al** *adj.* [F *association* or med.L *associatio* (as ASSOCIATE, –ATION)]

As·so·ci·a·tion Foot·ball *n. Brit.* = SOCCER.

as·so·ci·a·tive /əsósheeətiv, –see–/ *adj.* **1** of or involving association. **2** *Math. & Computing* involving the condition that a group of quantities connected by operators (see OPERATOR 4) gives the same result whatever their grouping, as long as their order remains the same, e.g., $(a \times b) \times c = a \times (b \times c)$.

as·so·nance /ásənəns/ *n.* the resemblance of sound between two syllables in nearby words, arising from the rhyming of two or more accented vowels, but not consonants, or the use of identical consonants with different vowels, e.g., *sonnet, porridge,* and *killed, cold, culled.* □□ **as·so·nant** *adj.* **as·so·nate** /–nayt/ *v.intr.* [F f. L *assonare* respond to (as AD-, *sonus* sound)]

as·sort /əsáwrt/ *v.* **1** *tr.* (usu. foll. by *with*) classify or arrange in groups. **2** *intr.* suit; fit into; harmonize with (*assort well with*). [OF *assorter* f. *à* to + *sorte* SORT]

as·sort·a·tive /əsáwrtətiv/ *adj.* assorting.

as·sort·a·tive mat·ing *n. Biol.* selective mating based on the similarity of the partners' characteristics, etc.

as·sort·ed /əsáwrtid/ *adj.* **1** of various kinds put together; miscellaneous. **2** sorted into groups. **3** matched (*ill-assorted; poorly assorted*).

as·sort·ment /əsáwrtmənt/ *n.* a set of various kinds of things or people put together; a mixed collection.

ASSR *abbr. hist.* Autonomous Soviet Socialist Republic.

Asst. *abbr.* Assistant.

as·suage /əswáyj/ *v.tr.* **1** calm or soothe (a person, pain, etc.). **2** appease or relieve (an appetite or desire). □□ **as·suage·ment** *n.* **as·suag·er** *n.* [ME f. OF *as(s)ouagier* ult. f. L *suavis* sweet]

as·sume /əsóōm/ *v.tr.* **1** (usu. foll. by *that* + clause) take or accept as being true, without proof, for the purpose of argument or action. **2** simulate or pretend (ignorance, etc.). **3** undertake (an office or duty). **4** take or put on oneself or itself (an aspect, attribute, debt, etc.) (*the problem assumed immense proportions*). **5** (usu. foll. by *to*) arrogate, usurp, or seize (credit, power, etc.) (*assumed to himself the right of veto*). □□ **as·sum·a·ble** *adj.* **as·sum·ed·ly** /–midlee/ *adv.* [ME f. L *assumere* (as AD-, *sumere sumpt-* take)]

as·sumed /əsóōmd/ *adj.* **1** false; adopted (*went under an assumed name*). **2** supposed; accepted (*assumed income*).

as·sum·ing /əsóōming/ *adj.* (of a person) taking too much for granted; arrogant; presumptuous.

as·sump·tion /əsúmpshən/ *n.* **1** the act or an instance of assuming. **2 a** the act or an instance of accepting without proof. **b** a thing assumed in this way. **3** arrogance. **4** (**Assumption**) **a** the reception of the Virgin Mary bodily into heaven, according to Roman Catholic and Orthodox Christian belief. **b** the feast in honor of this (August 15) . [ME f. OF *asompsion* or L *assumptio* (as ASSUME, –ION)]

as·sump·tive /əsúmptiv/ *adj.* **1** taken for granted. **2** arrogant. [L *assumptivus* (as ASSUME, –IVE)]

as·sur·ance /əshoŏrəns/ *n.* **1** a positive declaration that a thing is true. **2** a solemn promise or guarantee. **3** esp. *Brit.* insurance, esp. life insurance. **4** certainty. **5 a** self-confidence. **b** impudence. [ME f. OF *aseürance* f. *aseürer* (as ASSURE, –ANCE)]

as·sure /əshoŏr/ *v.tr.* **1** (often foll. by *of*) **a** make (a person) sure; convince (*assured him of my sincerity*). **b** tell (a person) confidently (*assured him the bus went to Baltimore*). **2 a** make certain of; ensure the happening, etc., of (*will assure her success*). **b** make safe (against overthrow, etc.). **3** confirm; encourage. **4** *Brit.* insure (esp. a life). **5** (as **assured** *adj.*) **a** guaranteed. **b** self-confident. □ **rest assured** remain confident. □□ **as·sur·a·ble** *adj.* **as·sur·er** *n.* [ME f. OF *aseürer* ult. f. L *securus* safe, SECURE]

▶See note at INSURE.

as·sur·ed·ly /əshoŏridlee/ *adv.* certainly.

as·sur·ed·ness /əshoŏridnis/ *n.* certainty; (self-)assurance.

As·syr·i·an /əsíreeən/ *n. & adj. hist.* ● *n.* **1** an inhabitant of Assyria, an ancient kingdom in Mesopotamia. **2** the Semitic language of Assyria. ● *adj.* of or relating to Assyria. [L *Assyrius* f. Gk *Assurios* of Assyria]

As·syr·i·ol·o·gy /əsíreeólǝjee/ *n.* the study of the language, history, and antiquities of Assyria. □□ **As·syr·i·ol·o·gist** *n.*

AST *abbr.* Atlantic Standard Time.

a·stat·ic /áystátik/ *adj.* **1** not static; unstable or unsteady. **2** *Physics* not tending to keep one position or direction. [Gk *astatos* unstable f. *a-* not + *sta-* stand]

as·ta·tine /ástǝteen, –tin/ *n. Chem.* a radioactive element, the heaviest of the halogens, which occurs naturally and can be artificially made by nuclear bombardment of bismuth. ¶ Symb.: **At**. [formed as ASTATIC + –INE[4]]

as·ter /ástǝr/ *n.* any composite plant of the genus *Aster*, with bright daisylike flowers, e.g., the Michaelmas daisy. [L f. Gk *astēr* star]

-aster /ástǝr/ *suffix* **1** forming nouns denoting poor quality (*criticaster; poetaster*). **2** *Bot.* denoting incomplete resemblance (*oleaster; pinaster*). [L]

as·ter·isk /ástǝrisk/ *n. & v.* ● *n.* a symbol (*) used in printing and writing to mark words, etc., for reference, to stand for omitted matter, to signify a hypothetical linguistic form, etc. ● *v.tr.* mark with an asterisk. [ME f. LL *asteriscus* f. Gk *asteriskos* dimin. (as ASTER)]

> **PRONUNCIATION TIP**   asterisk
>
> Many speakers seem to have difficulty with the final syllable of this word, which they pronounce "-riks." Care should be taken to pronounce this syllable just as in the word *risk*.

as·ter·ism /ástǝrizǝm/ *n.* **1** a cluster of stars. **2** a group of three asterisks (*⁂*) calling attention to following text. [Gk *asterismos* (as ASTER, –ISM)]

a·stern /əstɚn/ *adv. Naut. & Aeron.* (often foll. by *of*) **1** aft; away to the rear. **2** backward. [A[2] + STERN[2]]

as·ter·oid /ástǝroyd/ *n.* **1** any of the small celestial bodies revolving around the sun, mainly between the orbits of Mars and Jupiter. **2** *Zool.* a starfish. □□ **as·ter·oi·dal** /ástǝróyd'l/ *adj.* [Gk *asteroeidēs* (as ASTER, –OID)]

as·the·ni·a /asthéeneeə/ *n. Med.* loss of strength; debility. [mod.L f. Gk *astheneia* f. *asthenēs* weak]

as·then·ic /asthénik/ *adj. & n.* ● *adj.* **1** of a lean or long-limbed build; ectomorphic. **2** *Med.* of or characterized by asthenia. ● *n.* a lean long-limbed person; an ectomorph.

asth·ma /ázmǝ, ás–/ *n.* a usu. allergic respiratory disease, often with paroxysms of difficult breathing. [ME f. Gk *asthma* –*matos* f. *azō* breathe hard]

asth·mat·ic /azmátik, as–/ *adj. & n.* ● *adj.* relating to or suffering from asthma. ● *n.* a person suffering from asthma. □□ **asth·mat·i·cal·ly** *adv.* [L *asthmaticus* f. Gk *asthmatikos* (as ASTHMA, –IC)]

As·ti /áastee/ *n.* (*pl.* **Astis**) an Italian white wine. [*Asti* in Piedmont]

a·stig·ma·tism /əstígmǝtizǝm/ *n.* a defect in the eye or in a lens resulting in distorted images, as light rays are prevented from meeting at a common focus. □□ **as·tig·mat·ic** /ástigmátik/ *adj.* [A–[1] + Gk *stigma* –*matos* point]

a·stil·be /əstílbee/ *n.* any plant of the genus *Astilbe*, with plumelike heads of tiny white or red flowers. [mod.L f. Gk *a-* not + *stilbē* fem. of *stilbos* glittering, from the inconspicuous (individual) flowers]

a·stir /əstɚr/ *predic.adj. & adv.* **1** in motion. **2** awake and out of bed (*astir early; already astir*). **3** excited. [A[2] + STIR[1] *n.*]

as·ton·ish /əstónish/ *v.tr.* amaze; surprise greatly. □□ **as·ton·ish·ing** *adj.* **as·ton·ish·ing·ly** *adv.* **as·ton·ish·ment** *n.* [obs. *astone* f. OF *estoner* f. Gallo-Roman: see –ISH[2]]

as·tound /əstównd/ *v.tr.* shock with alarm or surprise; amaze. □□ **as·**

---

a·strad·dle /əstrád'l/ *adv. & predic.adj.* in a straddling position.

as·tra·gal /ástrǝgǝl/ *n. Archit.* a small semicircular molding around the top or bottom of a column. [ASTRAGALUS]

as·trag·a·lus /əstrágǝlǝs/ *n.* (*pl.* **·li** /–lī/) **1** *Anat.* = TALUS[1]. **2** *Bot.* a leguminous plant of the genus *Astragalus*, e.g., the milk vetch. [L f. Gk *astragalos* ankle bone, molding, a plant]

as·tra·khan /ástrǝkán/ *n.* **1** the dark curly fleece of young lambs from Astrakhan. **2** a cloth imitating astrakhan. [*Astrakhan* in Russia]

as·tral /ástrǝl/ *adj.* **1** of or connected with the stars. **2** consisting of stars; starry. **3** *Theosophy* relating to or arising from a supposed ethereal existence, esp. of a counterpart of the body, associated with oneself in life and surviving after death. [LL *astralis* f. *astrum* star]

a·stray /əstráy/ *adv. & predic.adj.* **1** in or into error or morally questionable behavior (esp. *lead astray*). **2** away from the correct path or direction. □ **go astray** become lost or mislaid. [ME f. OF *estraié* past part. of *estraier* ult. f. L *extra* out of bounds + *vagari* wander]

a·stride /əstríd/ *adv. & prep.* ● *adv.* **1** (often foll. by *of*) with a leg on each side. **2** with legs apart. ● *prep.* with a leg on each side of; extending across.

as·trin·gent /əstrínjǝnt/ *adj. & n.* ● *adj.* **1** causing the contraction of body tissues. **2** checking bleeding. **3** severe; austere. ● *n.* an astringent substance or drug. □□ **as·trin·gen·cy** /–jǝnsee/ *n.* **as·trin·gent·ly** *adv.* [F f. L *astringere* (as AD–, *stringere* bind)]

astro- /ástrō/ *comb. form* **1** relating to the stars or celestial bodies. **2** relating to outer space. [Gk f. *astron* star]

as·tro·chem·is·try /ástrōkémistree/ *n.* the study of molecules and radicals in interstellar space.

as·tro·dome /ástrǝdōm/ *n.* a domed window in an aircraft for astronomical observations.

as·tro·hatch /ástrǝhach/ *n.* = ASTRODOME.

as·tro·labe /ástrǝlayb/ *n.* an instrument, usu. consisting of a disk and pointer, formerly used to make astronomical measurements, esp. of the altitudes of celestial bodies, and as an aid in navigation. [ME f. OF *astrelabe* f. med.L *astrolabium* f. Gk *astrolabon*, neut. of *astrolabos* star taking]

as·trol·o·gy /əstrólǝjee/ *n.* the study of the movements and relative positions of celestial bodies interpreted as an influence on human affairs. □□ **as·trol·o·ger** *n.* **as·tro·log·i·cal** /ástrǝlójikǝl/ *adj.* **as·trol·o·gist** *n.* [ME f. OF *astrologie* f. L *astrologia* f. Gk (as ASTRO–, –LOGY)]

as·tro·naut /ástrǝnawt/ *n.* a person who is trained to travel in a spacecraft. □□ **as·tro·nau·ti·cal** /–náwtikǝl/ *adj.* [ASTRO–, after *aeronaut*]

as·tro·nau·tics /ástrǝnáwtiks/ *n.* the science of space travel.

as·tro·nom·i·cal /ástrǝnómikǝl/ *adj.* (also **as·tro·nom·ic**) **1** of or relating to astronomy. **2** extremely large; too large to contemplate. □□ **as·tro·nom·i·cal·ly** *adv.* [L *astronomicus* f. Gk *astronomikos*]

as·tro·nom·i·cal u·nit *n.* a unit of measurement in astronomy equal to the mean distance from the center of the earth to the center of the sun, 1.496 x 10[11] meters or 92.9 million miles.

as·tro·nom·i·cal year *n.* see YEAR *n.* 1.

as·tron·o·my /əstrónǝmee/ *n.* the scientific study of celestial bodies and other matter beyond earth's atmosphere. □□ **as·tron·o·mer** *n.* [ME f. OF *astronomie* f. L f. Gk *astronomia* f. *astronomos* (adj.) star arranging f. *nemō* arrange]

as·tro·phys·ics /ástrōfiziks/ *n.* a branch of astronomy concerned with the physics and chemistry of celestial bodies and phenomena. □□ **as·tro·phys·i·cal** *adj.* **as·tro·phys·i·cist** /–zisist/ *n.*

As·tro·turf /ástrōtɚrf/ *n. Trademark* an artificial grass surface, esp. for sports fields. [*Astrodome*, name of a sports stadium in Texas where it as first used, + TURF]

as·tute /əstoŏt, əstyoŏt/ *adj.* **1** shrewd; sagacious. **2** crafty. □□ **as·tute·ly** *adv.* **as·tute·ness** *n.* [obs. F *astut* or L *astutus* f. *astus* craft]

a·sun·der /əsúndǝr/ *adv. literary* apart. [OE *on sundran* into pieces: cf. SUNDER]

a·sy·lum /əsílǝm/ *n.* **1** sanctuary; protection, esp. for those pursued by the law (*seek asylum*). **2** *hist.* any of various kinds of institution offering shelter and support to distressed or destitute individuals, esp. the mentally ill. [ME f. L f. Gk *asulon* refuge f. *a-* not + *sulon* right of seizure]

a·sym·me·try /aysímitree/ *n.* lack of symmetry. □□ **a·sym·met·ric** /–métrik/ *adj.* **a·sym·met·ri·cal** *adj.* **a·sym·met·ri·cal·ly** /–métrikǝlee/ *adv.* [Gk *asummetria* (as A–[1], SYMMETRY)]

a·symp·to·mat·ic /áysimptǝmátik/ *adj.* producing or showing no symptoms.

as·ymp·tote /ásimptōt/ *n. Math* a line that continually approaches a given curve but does not meet it at a finite distance. □□ **as·ymp·tot·ic** /–tótik/ *adj.* **as·ymp·tot·i·cal·ly** *adv.* [mod.L *asymptota* (linea line) f. Gk *asumptōtos* not falling together f. *a-* not + *sun* together + *ptōtos* falling f. *piptō* fall]

a·syn·chro·nous /aysíngkrǝnǝs/ *adj.* not synchronous. □□ **a·syn·chro·nous·ly** *adv.*

a·syn·de·ton /əsínditǝn/ *n.* (*pl.* **a·syn·de·ta** /–tǝ/) the omission of a conjunction. □□ **as·yn·det·ic** /ásindétik/ *adj.* [mod.L f. Gk *asundeton* (neut. adj.) f. *a-* not + *sundetos* bound together]

At *symb. Chem.* the element astatine.

at /at, *unstressed* ət/ *prep.* **1** expressing position, exact or approximate (*wait at the corner; at the top of the hill; is at school; at a distance*). **2** expressing a point in time (*see you at three; went at dawn*). **3** expressing a point in a scale or range (*at boiling point; at his best*). **4** expressing engagement or concern in a state or activity (*at war; at work; at odds*). **5** expressing a value or rate (*sell at $10 each*). **6 a** with or with reference to; in terms of (*at a disadvantage; annoyed at losing; good at soccer; play at fighting; sick at heart; came at a run; at short notice; work at it*). **b** by means of (*starts at a touch; drank it at a gulp*). **7** expressing: **a** motion toward (*arrived at the station; went at them*). **b** aim toward or pursuit of (physically or conceptually) (*aim at the target; work at a solution; guess at the truth; laughed at us; has been at the milk again*). □ **at all** see ALL. **at hand** see HAND. **at home** see HOME. **at it 1** engaged in an activity; working hard. **2** *colloq.* repeating a habitual (usu. disapproved of) activity (*found them at it again*). **at once** see ONCE. **at that** moreover (*found one, and a good one at that*). **at times** see TIME. [OE *æt*, rel. to L *ad* to]

at- /ət/ *prefix* assim. form of AD- before *t*.

At·a·brine /átəbreen/ *n.* (also **At·e·brin** /-brin/) *Trademark* = QUINACRINE. [-ATE[1] 2 + BRINE]

at·a·rac·tic /átəráktik/ *adj. & n.* (also **ataraxic** /-ráksik/) ● *adj.* calming or tranquilizing. ● *n.* a tranquilizing drug. [Gk *ataraktos* calm: cf. ATARAXY]

at·a·rax·y /átəraksee/ *n.* (also **ataraxia** /-rákseeə/) calmness or tranquility; imperturbability. [F *ataraxie* f. Gk *ataraxia* impassiveness]

at·a·vism /átəvizəm/ *n.* **1** a resemblance to remote ancestors rather than to parents in plants or animals. **2** reversion to an earlier type. □□ **at·a·vis·tic** *adj.* **at·a·vis·ti·cal·ly** *adv.* [F *atavisme* f. L *atavus* great-grandfather's grandfather]

a·tax·i·a /ətákseeə/ *n.* (also **a·tax·y** /-see/) *Med.* the loss of full control of bodily movements. □□ **a·tax·ic** *adj.* [mod.L *ataxia* f. Gk f. *a-* not + *taxis* order]

ATC *abbr.* **1** air traffic control. **2** Air Training Corps.

ate *past of* EAT.

-ate[1] /ət, ayt/ *suffix* **1** forming nouns denoting: **a** status or office (*doctorate; episcopate*). **b** state or function (*curate; magistrate; mandate*). **2** *Chem.* forming nouns denoting the salt of an acid with a corresponding name ending in *-ic* (*chlorate; nitrate*). **3** forming nouns denoting a group (*electorate*). **4** *Chem.* forming nouns denoting a product (*condensate; filtrate*). [from or after OF *-at* or *é(e)* or f. L *-atus* noun or past part.: cf. -ATE[2]]

-ate[2] /ət, ayt/ *suffix* **1** forming adjectives and nouns (*associate; delegate; duplicate; separate*). **2** forming adjectives from Latin or English nouns and adjectives (*cordate; insensate; Italianate*). [from or after (F *-é* f.) L *-atus* past part. of verbs in *-are*]

-ate[3] /ayt/ *suffix* forming verbs (*associate; duplicate; fascinate; hyphenate; separate*). [from or after (F *-er* f.) L *-are* (past part. *-atus*): cf. -ATE[2]]

At·e·brin var. of ATABRINE.

at·el·ier /átəlyáy/ *n.* a workshop or studio, esp. of an artist or designer. [F]

a tem·po /aa témpō/ *adv. Mus.* in the previous tempo. [It., lit. 'in time']

Ath·a·na·sian Creed /áthənáyzhən/ *n.* an affirmation of Christian faith formerly thought to have been drawn up by Athanasius, bishop of Alexandria d. 373.

a·the·ism /áytheeizəm/ *n.* the theory or belief that God does not exist. □□ **a·the·ist** *n.* **a·the·is·tic** *adj.* **a·the·is·ti·cal** *adj.* [F *athéisme* f. Gk *atheos* without God f. *a-* not + *theos* god]

ath·el·ing /áthəling/ *n. hist.* a prince or nobleman in Anglo-Saxon England. [OE *ætheling* = OHG *ediling* f. WG: see -ING[3]]

a·the·mat·ic /áytheemátik/ *adj.* **1** *Mus.* not based on the use of themes. **2** *Gram.* (of a verb form) having a suffix attached to the stem without a correcting (thematic) vowel.

ath·e·nae·um /áthineéəm/ *n.* (also **atheneum**) **1** an institution for literary or scientific study. **2** a library. [LL *Athenaeum* f. Gk *Athēnaion* temple of Athene (used as a place of teaching)]

A·the·ni·an /ətheéneeən/ *n. & adj.* ● *n.* a native or inhabitant of ancient or modern Athens. ● *adj.* of or relating to Athens. [L *Atheniensis* f. *Athenae* f. Gk *Athēnai* Athens, principal city of Greece]

ath·er·o·scle·ro·sis /áthərōsklərósis/ *n.* a form of arteriosclerosis characterized by the degeneration of the arteries because of a build-up of fatty deposits. □□ **ath·er·o·scle·rot·ic** /-rótik/ *adj.* [G *Atherosklerose* f. Gk *athērē* gruel + SCLEROSIS]

a·thirst /əthúrst/ *predic.adj. poet.* **1** (usu. foll. by *for*) eager (*athirst for knowledge*). **2** thirsty. [OE *ofthyrst* for *ofthyrsted* past part. of *ofthyrstan* be thirsty]

ath·lete /áthleet/ *n.* **1** a skilled performer in sports and physical activities, esp. *Brit.* in track and field events. **2** a person with natural athletic ability. [L *athleta* f. Gk *athlētēs* f. *athleō* contend for a prize (*athlon*)]

ath·lete's foot *n.* a fungal foot condition affecting esp. the skin between the toes.

ath·let·ic /áthlétik/ *adj.* **1** of or relating to athletes or athletics (*an athletic competition*). **2** muscular or physically powerful. □□ **ath·let·**

i·cal·ly *adv.* **ath·let·i·cism** /-tisizəm/ *n.* [F *athlétique* or L *athleticus* f. Gk *athlētikos* (as ATHLETE, -IC)]

PRONUNCIATION TIP | athletic

Don't put a fourth syllable in this word. Pronounce it exactly as it is spelled (ath-LEH-tik).

ath·let·ics /áthlétiks/ *n.pl.* (usu. treated as *sing.*) **1 a** physical exercises, esp. *Brit.* track and field events. **b** the practice of these. **2** physical sports and games of any kind.

a·thwart /əthwáwrt/ *adv. & prep.* ● *adv.* **1** across from side to side (usu. obliquely). **2** perversely or in opposition. ● *prep.* **1** from side to side of. **2** in opposition to. [A[2] + THWART]

-atic /átik/ *suffix* forming adjectives and nouns (*aquatic; fanatic; idiomatic*). [F *-atique* or L *-aticus*, often ult. f. Gk *-atikos*]

a·tilt /ətilt/ *adv.* tilted and nearly falling. [A[2] + TILT]

-ation /áyshən/ *suffix* **1** forming nouns denoting an action or an instance of it (*alteration; flirtation; hesitation*). **2** forming nouns denoting a result or product of action (*plantation; starvation; vexation*) (see also -FICATION). [from or after F *-ation* or L *-atio* *-ationis* f. verbs in *-are: see* -ION]

-ative /ətiv, aytiv/ *suffix* forming adjectives denoting a characteristic or propensity (*authoritative; imitative; pejorative; qualitative; talkative*). [from or after F *-atif* *-ative* or f. L *-ativus* f. past part. stem *-at-* of verbs in *-are* + *-ivus* (see -IVE): cf. -ATIC]

At·lan·te·an /ətlánteeən/ *adj. literary* of or like Atlas, esp. in physical strength. [L *Atlanteus* (as ATLAS)]

at·lan·tes /ətlánteez/ *n.pl. Archit.* male figures carved in stone and used as columns to support the entablature of a Greek or Greek-style building. Also called **telamon**. [Gk, pl. of *Atlas*: see ATLAS]

At·lan·tic /ətlántik/ *n. & adj.* ● *n.* the ocean between Europe and Africa to the east, and North and South America to the west. ● *adj.* of or adjoining the Atlantic. [ME f. L *Atlanticus* f. Gk *Atlantikos* (as ATLAS, -IC): orig. of the Atlas Mountains, then of the sea near the W. African coast]

At·lan·tic Time *n.* the standard time used in the most eastern parts of Canada and in parts of the Caribbean.

at·las /átləs/ *n.* **1** a book of maps or charts. **2** *Anat.* the cervical vertebra of the backbone articulating with the skull at the neck. [L f. Gk *Atlas* *-antos* a Titan who held up the pillars of the universe, whose picture appeared at the beginning of early atlases]

ATM *abbr.* automated teller machine.

atm *abbr. Physics* atmosphere(s).

at·man /áatmən/ *n. Hinduism* **1** the real self. **2** the supreme spiritual principle. [Skr. *ātmán* essence, breath]

at·mos·phere /átməsfeer/ *n.* **1 a** the envelope of gases surrounding the earth, any other planet, or any substance. **b** the air in any particular place, esp. if unpleasant. **2 a** the pervading tone or mood of a place or situation, esp. with reference to the feelings or emotions evoked. **b** the feelings or emotions evoked by a work of art, a piece of music, etc. **3** *Physics* a unit of pressure equal to mean atmospheric pressure at sea level, 101,325 pascals or 14.7 pounds per square inch. ¶ Abbr.: **atm**. □□ **at·mos·pher·ic** /-férik, -feér-/ *adj.* **at·mos·pher·i·cal** *adj.* **at·mos·pher·i·cal·ly** *adv.* [mod.L *atmosphaera* f. Gk *atmos* vapor: see SPHERE]

at·mos·pher·ics /átməsfériks, -feér-/ *n.pl.* **1** electrical disturbance in the atmosphere, esp. caused by lightning. **2** interference with telecommunications caused by this.

at·oll /átawl, átol, áy-/ *n.* a ring-shaped coral reef enclosing a lagoon. [Maldive *atolu*]

at·om /átəm/ *n.* **1 a** the smallest particle of a chemical element that can take part in a chemical reaction. **b** this particle as a source of nuclear energy. **2** (usu. with *neg.*) the least portion of a thing or quality (*not an atom of pity*). [ME f. OF *atome* f. L *atomus* f. Gk *atomos* indivisible]

at·om bomb *n.* a bomb involving the release of energy by nuclear fission = *fission bomb*.

a·tom·ic /ətómik/ *adj.* **1** concerned with or using atomic energy or atomic bombs. **2** of or relating to an atom or atoms. □ **atomic structure** the structure of an atom as being a central positively charged nucleus surrounded by negatively charged orbiting electrons. □□ **a·tom·i·cal·ly** *adv.* [mod.L *atomicus* (as ATOM, -IC)]

a·tom·ic bomb *n.* = ATOM BOMB.

a·tom·ic clock *n.* a clock in which the periodic process (time scale) is regulated by the vibrations of an atomic or molecular system, such as cesium or ammonia.

a·tom·ic en·er·gy *n.* nuclear energy.

at·o·mic·i·ty /átəmísitee/ *n.* **1** the number of atoms in the molecules of an element. **2** the state or fact of being composed of atoms.

a·tom·ic mass *n.* the mass of an atom measured in atomic mass units.

a·tom·ic mass u·nit *n.* a unit of mass used to express atomic and molecular weights that is equal to one twelfth of the mass of an atom of carbon-12. ¶ Abbr.: **amu**.

a·tom·ic num·ber *n.* the number of protons in the nucleus of an atom, which is characteristic of a chemical element and determines its place in the periodic table. ¶ Symb.: **Z**.

a·tom·ic par·ti·cle *n.* any one of the particles of which an atom is constituted.

a·tom·ic phys·ics *n.* the branch of physics concerned with the structure of the atom and the characteristics of the elementary particles of which it is composed.

a·tom·ic pile *n.* a nuclear reactor.

a·tom·ic pow·er *n.* nuclear power.

a·tom·ic spec·trum *n.* the emission or absorption spectrum arising from electron transitions inside an atom and characteristic of the element.

a·tom·ic the·o·ry *n.* **1** the concept of an atom as being composed of elementary particles. **2** the theory that all matter is made up of small indivisible particles called atoms, and that the atoms of any one element are identical in all respects but differ from those of other elements and only unite to form compounds in fixed proportions. **3** *Philos.* atomism.

a·tom·ic weight *n.* the ratio of the average mass of one atom of an element to one twelfth of the mass of an atom of carbon-12. Also called **relative atomic mass**.

at·om·ism /átəmizəm/ *n. Philos.* **1** the theory that all matter consists of tiny individual particles. **2** *Psychol.* the theory that mental states are made up of elementary units. □□ **at·om·ist** *n.* **at·om·is·tic** /–místik/ *adj.*

at·om·ize /átəmíz/ *v.tr.* **1** reduce to atoms or fine particles. **2** fragment or divide into small units. □□ **at·om·i·za·tion** *n.*

at·om·iz·er /átəmīzər/ *n.* an instrument for emitting liquids as a fine spray.

at·om smash·er *n. colloq.* = ACCELERATOR 2.

at·o·my /átəmee/ *n.* (*pl.* **-mies**) *archaic* **1** a skeleton. **2** an emaciated body. [ANATOMY taken as *an atomy*]

a·ton·al /áytón'l/ *adj. Mus.* not written in any key or mode. □□ **a·to·nal·i·ty** /–nálitee/ *n.*

a·tone /ətón/ *v.intr.* (usu. foll. by *for*) make amends; expiate for (a wrong). [back-form. f. ATONEMENT]

a·tone·ment /ətónmənt/ *n.* **1** expiation; reparation for a wrong or injury. **2** (in Christianity) the reconciliation of God and humans. **3** (**the Atonement**) the expiation by Christ of humankind's sin. □ **Day of Atonement** the most solemn religious fast of the Jewish year, eight days after the Jewish New Year. [*at one* + –MENT, after med.L *adunamentum* and earlier *onement* f. obs. *one* (v.) unite]

a·ton·ic /ətónik/ *adj.* **1** without accent or stress. **2** *Med.* lacking bodily tone. □□ **at·o·ny** /átənee/ *n.*

a·top /ətóp/ *adv. & prep.* • *adv.* (often foll. by *of*) on the top. • *prep.* on the top of.

-ator /áytər/ *suffix* forming agent nouns, usu. from Latin words (sometimes via French) (*agitator; creator; equator; escalator*). See also –OR¹. [L –*ator*]

-atory /ətáwree/ *suffix* forming adjectives meaning 'relating to or involving (a verbal action)' (*amatory; explanatory; predatory*). See also –ORY². [L –*atorius*]

ATP *abbr.* adenosine triphosphate.

at·ra·bil·ious /átrəbílyəs/ *adj.* melancholy; ill-tempered. [L *atra bilis* black bile, transl. Gk *melakgholia* MELANCHOLY]

a·tri·um /áytreeəm/ *n.* (*pl.* **atriums** or **atria** /–treeə/) **1 a** the central court of an ancient Roman house. **b** a usu. skylit central court rising through several stories with galleries and rooms opening off at each level. **c** (in a modern house) a central hall or courtyard with rooms opening off it. **2** *Anat.* a cavity in the body, esp. one of the two upper cavities of the heart, receiving blood from the veins. □□ **a·tri·al** *adj.* [L]

a·tro·cious /ətróshəs/ *adj.* **1** very bad or unpleasant (*atrocious weather; their manners were atrocious*). **2** extremely savage or wicked (*atrocious cruelty*). □□ **a·tro·cious·ly** *adv.* **a·tro·cious·ness** *n.* [L *atrox –ocis* cruel]

a·troc·i·ty /ətrósitee/ *n.* (*pl.* **-ties**) **1** an extremely evil or cruel act, esp. one involving physical violence or injury. **2** extreme wickedness. [F *atrocité* or L *atrocitas* (as ATROCIOUS, –ITY)]

at·ro·phy /átrəfee/ *v. & n.* • *v.* (**-phies**, **-phied**) **1** *intr.* waste away through undernourishment, aging, or lack of use; become emaciated. **2** *tr.* cause to atrophy. • *n.* the process of atrophying; emaciation. [F *atrophie* or LL *atrophia* f. Gk f. *a-* not + *trophē* food]

at·ro·pine /átrəpeen, –pin/ *n.* a poisonous alkaloid found in deadly nightshade, used in medicine to treat renal and biliary colic, etc. [mod.L *Atropa belladonna* deadly nightshade f. Gk *Atropos* inflexible, the name of one of the Fates]

at·tach /ətách/ *v.* **1** *tr.* fasten; affix; join. **2** *tr.* (in *passive*; foll. by *to*) be very fond of or devoted to (*am deeply attached to her*). **3** *tr.* attribute; assign (some function, quality, or characteristic) (*can you attach a name to it?; attaches great importance to it*). **4 a** *tr.* include;

enclose (*attach no conditions to the agreement; attach particulars*). **b** *intr.* (foll. by *to*) be an attribute or characteristic (*great prestige attaches to the job*). **5** *refl.* (usu. foll. by *to*) (of a thing) adhere; (of a person) join; take part (*the sticky stamps attached themselves to his fingers; climbers attached themselves to the expedition*). **6** *tr.* appoint for special or temporary duties. **7** *tr.* seize (as ATTACH, –MENT) erty) by legal authority. □□ **at·tach·a·ble** *adj.* **at·tach·er** *n.* [ME f. OF *estachier* fasten f. Gmc: in Law sense thr. OF *atachier*]

at·ta·ché /átasháy/ *n.* a person appointed to an ambassador's staff, usu. with a special sphere of activity (*military attaché; press attaché*). [F, past part. of *attacher*: see ATTACH]

at·ta·ché case *n.* a small flat rectangular case for carrying documents, etc.

at·tached /ətácht/ *adj.* **1** fixed; connected; enclosed. **2** (of a person) involved in a long-term relationship, esp. engagement or marriage.

at·tach·ment /ətáchmənt/ *n.* **1** a thing attached or to be attached, esp. to a machine, device, etc., for a special function. **2** affection; devotion. **3** a means of attaching. **4** the act of attaching or the state of being attached. **5** legal seizure. **6** a temporary position in an organization. [ME f. F *attachement* f. *attacher* (as ATTACH, –MENT)]

at·tack /əták/ *v. & n.* • *v.* **1** *tr.* act against with (esp. armed) force. **2** *tr.* seek to hurt or defeat. **3** *tr.* criticize adversely. **4** *tr.* act harmfully upon (*a virus attacking the nervous system*). **5** *tr.* vigorously apply oneself to; begin work on (*attacked his meal with gusto*). **6** *intr.* make an attack. **7** *intr.* be in a mode of attack. • *n.* **1** the act or process of attacking. **2 a** an offensive operation or mode of behavior. **b** severe criticism. **3** *Mus.* the action or manner of beginning a piece, passage, etc. **4** gusto; vigor. **5** a sudden occurrence of an illness. **6** a player or players seeking to score goals, etc.; offensive players. □□ **at·tack·er** *n.* [F *attaque, attaquer* f. It. *attacco* attack, *attaccare* ATTACK]

ASSAIL, ASSAULT, BESET, BESIEGE, BOMBARD, CHARGE, MOLEST, STORM. There is no shortage of 'fighting words.' **Attack** is the most general verb, meaning to set upon someone or something in a violent, forceful, or aggressive way (*the rebels attacked at dawn*); but it can also be used figuratively (*attack the government's policy*). **Assault** implies a greater degree of violence or viciousness and the infliction of more damage. As part of the legal term "assault and battery," it suggests an attempt or threat to injure someone physically. **Molest** is another word meaning to *attack* and is used today almost exclusively of sexual molestation (*she had been molested as a child*). **Charge** and **storm** are primarily military words, both suggesting a forceful assault on a fixed position. To *charge* is to make a violent onslaught (*the infantry charged the enemy camp*) and is often used as a command (*"Charge!" the general cried*). To *storm* means to take by force, with all the momentum and fury of a storm (*after days of planning, the soldiers stormed the castle*), but there is often the suggestion of a last-ditch, all-out effort to end a long siege or avoid defeat. To **assail** is to attack with repeated thrusts or blows, implying that victory depends not so much on force as on persistence. To **bombard** is to assail continuously with bombs or shells (*they bombarded the city without mercy for days*). **Besiege** means to surround with an armed force (*to besiege the capital city*). When used figuratively, its meaning comes close to that of *assail*, but with an emphasis on being hemmed in and enclosed rather than punished repeatedly (*besieged with fears*). **Beset** also means to attack on all sides (*beset by enemies*), but it is also used frequently in other contexts to mean set or placed upon (*a bracelet beset with diamonds*).

at·tain /ətáyn/ *v.* **1** *tr.* arrive at; reach (a goal, etc.). **2** *tr.* gain; accomplish (an aim, distinction, etc.). **3** *intr.* (foll. by *to*) arrive at by conscious development or effort. □□ **at·tain·a·ble** *adj.* **at·tain·a·bil·i·ty** *n.* **at·tain·a·ble·ness** *n.* [ME f. AF *atain-, atein-*, OF *ataign-* stem of *ataindre* f. L *attingere* (as AD-, *tangere* touch)]

at·tain·der /ətáyndər/ *n. hist.* the forfeiture of land and civil rights suffered as a consequence of a sentence of death for treason or felony. [ME f. AF, = OF *ateindre* ATTAIN used as noun: see –ER⁶]

at·tain·ment /ətáynmənt/ *n.* **1** (often in *pl.*) something attained or achieved; an accomplishment. **2** the act or an instance of attaining.

at·taint /ətáynt/ *v.tr.* **1** *hist.* subject to attainder. **2 a** (of disease, etc.) strike; affect. **b** *archaic* taint. [ME f. obs. *attaint* (adj.) f. OF *ataint, ateint* past part. formed as ATTAIN: confused in meaning with TAINT]

at·tar /átaar/ *n.* (also **ot·to** /ótō/) a fragrant essential oil, esp. from rose petals. [Pers. ʻ*atar* f. Arab. f. ʻ*iṭr* perfume]

at·tempt /ətémpt/ *v. & n.* • *v.tr.* (often foll. by *to* + infin.) seek to achieve, complete, or master (a task, action, challenge, etc.) (*attempted the exercise; attempted to explain; attempted Everest*). • *n.* (often foll. by *at, on*, or *to* + infin.) an act of attempting; an endeavor (*made an attempt at winning; an attempt to succeed; an attempt on his life*). □ **attempt the life of** *archaic* try to kill. □□ **at·tempt·a·ble** *adj.* [OF *attempter* f. L *attemptare* (as AD-, *temptare* TEMPT)]

at·tend /əténd/ *v.* **1** *tr.* **a** be present at (*attended the meeting*). **b** go regularly to (*attends the local school*). **2** *intr.* **a** be present (*many mem-*

bers failed to attend). **b** be present in a serving capacity; wait on. **3 a** *tr.* escort; accompany (*the king was attended by soldiers*). **b** *intr.* (foll. by *on*) wait on; serve. **4** *intr.* **a** (usu. foll. by *to*) turn or apply one's mind; focus one's attention (*attend to what I am saying; was not attending*). **b** (foll. by *to*) deal with; take care of (*shall attend to the matter myself; attend to the older people*). **5** *tr.* (usu. in *passive*) follow as a result from (*the error was attended by serious consequences*). □□ **at•tend•er** *n.* [ME f. OF *atendre* f. L *attendere* (as AD-, *tendere* *tent*- stretch)]

at•tend•ance /ǝténdǝns/ *n.* **1** the act of attending or being present. **2** the number of people present (*a high attendance*). □ **in attendance** on hand; available for service. [ME f. OF *atendance* (as AT-TEND, -ANCE)]

at•tend•ant /ǝténdǝnt/ *n. & adj.* ● *n.* a person employed to wait on others or provide a service (*cloakroom attendant; museum attendant*). ● *adj.* **1** accompanying (*attendant circumstances*). **2** waiting on; serving (*ladies attendant on the queen*). [ME f. OF (as ATTEND, -ANT)]

at•tend•ee /átendeé/ *n.* a person who attends (a meeting, etc.).

at•ten•tion /ǝténshǝn/ *n. & int.* ● *n.* **1** the act or faculty of applying one's mind (*give me your attention; attract his attention*). **2 a** consideration (*give attention to the problem*). **b** care (*give special attention to your handwriting*). **c** notice; publicity (*only needs a bit of attention; labeled an attention seeker*). **3** (in *pl.*) **a** ceremonious politeness (*he paid his attentions to her*). **b** wooing; courting (*he was the subject of her attentions*). **4** *Mil.* an erect attitude of readiness (*stand at attention*). ● *int.* (in full **stand to attention!**) an order to assume an attitude of attention. [ME f. L *attentio* (as ATTEND, -ION)]

at•ten•tion def•i•cit dis•or•der *n.* (also **at•ten•tion def•i•cit hy•per•ac•tiv•i•ty dis•or•der**) any of a range of behavioral disorders occurring primarily in children, including such symptoms as poor concentration, hyperactivity, and learning difficulties. ¶ *Abbr.:* **ADD** or **ADHD**.

at•ten•tive /ǝténtiv/ *adj.* **1** concentrating; paying attention. **2** assiduously polite. **3** heedful. □□ **at•ten•tive•ly** *adv.* **at•ten•tive•ness** *n.* [ME f. F *attentif* *–ive* f. *attente*, OF *atente*, fem. past part. of *atendre* ATTEND]

at•ten•u•ate *v. & adj.* ● *v.tr.* /ǝtényooayt/ **1** make thin. **2** reduce in force, value, or virulence. **3** *Electr.* reduce the amplitude of (a signal or current). ● *adj.* /ǝtényooǝt/ **1** slender. **2** tapering gradually. **3** rarefied. □□ **at•ten•u•at•ed** *adj.* **at•ten•u•a•tion** /–áyshǝn/ *n.* **at•ten•u•a•tor** *n.* [L *attenuare* (as AD-, *tenuis* thin)]

at•test /ǝtést/ *v.* **1** *tr.* certify the validity of. **2** *tr. Brit.* enroll (a recruit) for military service. **3** *intr.* (foll. by *to*) bear witness to. **4** *intr. Brit.* enroll oneself for military service. □□ **at•test•a•ble** *adj.* **at•tes•tor** *n.* [F *attester* f. L *attestari* (as AD-, *testis* witness)]

at•tes•ta•tion /átestáyshǝn/ *n.* **1** the act of attesting. **2** a testimony. [F attestation (as ATTEST, –ATION)]

At•tic /átik/ *adj. & n.* ● *adj.* of ancient Athens or Attica, or the form of Greek spoken there. ● *n.* the form of Greek used by the ancient Athenians. [L *Atticus* f. Gk *Attikos*]

at•tic /átik/ *n.* **1** the uppermost story in a house, usu. under the roof. **2** a room in the attic area. [F *attique*, as ATTIC: orig. (Archit.) a small order above a taller one]

At•ti•cism /átisizǝm/ *n.* **1** extreme elegance of speech. **2** an instance of this. [Gk *Attikismos* (as ATTIC, –ISM)]

At•tic salt *n.* (also **At•tic wit**) refined or dry wit.

at•tire /ǝtír/ *v. & n. formal* ● *v.tr.* dress, esp. in fine clothes or formal wear. ● *n.* clothes, esp. fine or formal. [ME f. OF atir(i)er equip f. à tire in order, of unkn. orig.]

at•ti•tude /átitood, –tyood/ *n.* **1 a** a settled opinion or way of thinking. **b** behavior reflecting this (*I don't like his attitude*). **2 a** a bodily posture. **b** a pose adopted in a painting or a play, esp. for dramatic effect (*strike an attitude*). **3** the position of an aircraft, spacecraft, etc., in relation to specified directions. □□ **at•ti•tu•di•nal** /–tood'nǝl, –tyood–/ *adj.* [F f. It. *attitudine* fitness, posture, f. LL *aptitudo* *–dinis* f. *aptus* fit]

at•ti•tu•di•nize /átitood'nīz, –tyood–/ *v.intr.* **1** practice or adopt attitudes, esp. for effect. **2** speak, write, or behave affectedly. [It. *attitudine* f. LL (as ATTITUDE) + –IZE]

attn. *abbr.* **1** attention. **2** for the attention of.

atto- /átō/ *comb. form Math.* denoting a factor of 10^{-18} (*attometer*). [Da. or Norw. *atten* eighteen + –o–]

at•tor•ney /ǝtórnee/ *n.* (*pl.* **-neys**) **1** a person, esp. a lawyer, appointed to act for another in business or legal matters. **2** a qualified lawyer, esp. one representing a client in a court of law. □□ **at•tor•ney•ship** *n.* [ME f. OF *atorné* past part. of *atorner* assign f. *à* to + *torner* turn]

at•tor•ney gen•er•al *n.* the chief legal officer in the US, England, and other countries.

at•tract /ǝtrákt/ *v.tr.* **1** (also *absol.*) draw or bring to oneself or itself (*attracts many admirers; attracts attention*). **2** be attractive to; fascinate. **3** (of a magnet, gravity, etc.) exert a pull on (an object). □□ **at•tract•a•ble** *adj.* **at•trac•tor** *n.* [L *attrahere* (as AD-, *trahere tract*- draw)]

at•tract•ant /ǝtráktǝnt/ *n. & adj.* ● *n.* a substance which attracts (esp. insects). ● *adj.* attracting.

at•trac•tion /ǝtrákshǝn/ *n.* **1 a** the act or power of attracting (*the attraction of foreign travel*). **b** a person or thing that attracts by arousing interest (*the fair is a big attraction*). **2** *Physics* the force by which bodies attract or approach each other (opp. REPULSION). **3** *Gram.* the influence exerted by one word on another which causes it to change to an incorrect form, e.g., *the wages of sin is death*. [F *attraction* or L *attractio* (as ATTRACT, –ION)]

at•trac•tive /ǝtráktiv/ *adj.* **1** attracting or capable of attracting; interesting (*an attractive proposition*). **2** aesthetically pleasing or appealing. □□ **at•trac•tive•ly** *adv.* **at•trac•tive•ness** *n.* [F *attractif –ive* f. LL *attractivus* (as ATTRACT, –IVE)]

at•trib•ute *v. & n.* ● *v.tr.* /ǝtríbyoot/ (usu. foll. by *to*) **1** regard as belonging or appropriate (*a poem attributed to Shakespeare*). **2** ascribe; regard as the effect of a stated cause (*the delays were attributed to the heavy traffic*). ● *n.* /átribyoot/ **1 a** a quality ascribed to a person or thing. **b** a characteristic quality. **2** a material object recognized as appropriate to a person, office, or status (*a large car is an attribute of seniority*). **3** *Gram.* an attributive adjective or noun. □□ **at•trib•ut•a•ble** /ǝtríbyootǝbǝl/ *adj.* **at•tri•bu•tion** /–byooshǝn/ *n.* [ME f. L *attribuere attribut-* (as AD-, *tribuere* assign): (n.) f. OF *attribut* or L *attributum*]

at•trib•u•tive /ǝtríbyǝtiv/ *adj. Gram.* (of an adjective or noun) preceding the word described and expressing an attribute, as *old* in *the old dog* (but not in *the dog is old*) and *expiration* in *expiration date* (opp. PREDICATIVE). □□ **at•trib•u•tive•ly** *adv.* [F *attributif –ive* (as ATTRIBUTE, –IVE)]

at•trit /ǝtrit/ *v.tr. colloq.* wear (an enemy or opponent) down by attrition. [back-form. f. ATTRITION]

at•tri•tion /ǝtríshǝn/ *n.* **1 a** the act or process of gradually wearing out, esp. by friction. **b** abrasion. **2** a gradual reduction, as by retirement, etc., in a work force. **3** *Theol.* sorrow for sin, falling short of contrition. □□ **at•tri•tion•al** *adj.* [ME f. LL *attritio* f. *atterere attrit-* rub]

at•tune /ǝtoon, ǝtyoon/ *v.tr.* **1** (usu. foll. by *to*) adjust (a person or thing) to a situation. **2** bring (an orchestra, instrument, etc.) into musical accord. [AT- + TUNE]

atty. *abbr.* attorney.

Atty. Gen. *abbr.* Attorney General.

ATV *abbr.* all-terrain vehicle.

a•typ•i•cal /áytípikǝl/ *adj.* not typical; not conforming to a type. □□ **a•typ•i•cal•ly** *adv.*

AU *abbr.* **1** (also **au.**) astronomical unit. **2** ångström unit.

Au *symb. Chem.* the element gold. [L *aurum*]

au•bade /ōbaád/ *n.* a poem or piece of music appropriate to the dawn or early morning. [F f. Sp. *albada* f. *alba* dawn]

au•berge /ōbáirzh/ *n.* an inn. [F]

au•ber•gine /ṓbǝrzheen/ *n. esp. Brit.* = EGGPLANT. [F f. Cat. *alberginia* f. Arab. *al-bādinjān* f. Pers. *bādingān* f. Skr. *vātimgaṇa*]

au•burn /áwbǝrn/ *adj.* reddish brown (usu. of a person's hair).

WORD HISTORY   **auburn**

late Middle English: from Old French *auborne, alborne*, from Latin *alburnus* 'whitish,' from *albus* 'white.' The original sense was 'yellowish white,' but the word became associated with *brown* because in the 16th and 17th centuries it was often written *abrune* or *abroun*.

AUC *abbr.* (of a date) from the foundation of the city (of Rome). [L *ab urbe condita*]

au cou•rant /ṓkooróN/ *predic.adj.* (usu. foll. by *with, of*) knowing what is going on; well-informed. [F, = in the (regular) course]

auc•tion /áwkshǝn/ *n. & v.* ● *n.* **1** a sale of goods, usu. in public, in which articles are sold to the highest bidder. **2** the sequence of bids made in auction bridge or other card games. ● *v.tr.* sell at auction. [L *auctio* increase, auction f. *augēre auct*- increase]

auc•tion bridge *n.* a form of bridge in which players bid for the right to name trump.

auc•tion•eer /áwkshǝneér/ *n.* a person who conducts auctions professionally, by calling for bids and declaring goods sold. □□ **auc•tion•eer•ing** *n.*

au•da•cious /awdáyshǝs/ *adj.* **1** daring; bold. **2** impudent. □□ **au•da•cious•ly** *adv.* **au•da•cious•ness** *n.* **au•dac•i•ty** /awdásitee/ *n.* [L *audax –acis* f. *audēre* dare]

au•di•ble /áwdibǝl/ *adj.* capable of being heard. □□ **au•di•bil•i•ty** *n.* **au•di•ble•ness** *n.* **au•di•bly** *adv.* [LL *audibilis* f. *audire* hear]

au•di•ence /áwdeeǝns/ *n.* **1 a** the assembled listeners or spectators at an event, esp. a stage performance, concert, etc. **b** the people addressed by a movie, book, play, etc. **2** a formal interview with a person in authority. **3** *archaic* a hearing (*give audience to my plea*). [ME f. OF f. L *audientia* f. *audire* hear]

au•dile /áwdil/ *adj.* of or referring to the sense of hearing. [irreg. f. L *audire* hear, after *tactile*]

au·di·o /áwdeeō/ *n.* (usu. *attrib.*) sound or the reproduction of sound. [AUDIO-]

audio- /áwdeeō/ *comb. form* hearing or sound. [L *audire* hear + –o-]

au·di·o·cas·sette /áwdeeōkəsét/ *n.* an audiotape enclosed within a cassette.

au·di·o fre·quen·cy *n.* a frequency capable of being perceived by the human ear.

au·di·ol·o·gy /áwdeeóləjee/ *n.* the science of hearing. □□ **au·di·ol·o·gist** *n.*

au·di·om·e·ter /áwdeeómitər/ *n.* an instrument for testing hearing.

au·di·o·phile /áwdeeōfīl/ *n.* a high-fidelity sound enthusiast.

au·di·o·tape /áwdeeōtayp/ *n. & v.* ● *n.* **1 a** magnetic tape on which sound can be recorded. **b** a length of this. **2** a sound recording on tape. ● *v.tr.* record (sound, speech, etc.) on tape.

au·di·o·vis·u·al /áwdeeōvízhyōōəl/ *adj.* (esp. of teaching methods) using both sight and sound.

au·dit /áwdit/ *n. & v.* ● *n.* an official examination of accounts. ● *v.tr.* (**audited, auditing**) **1** conduct an audit of. **2** attend (a class) informally, without working for a grade or credit. [ME f. L *auditus* hearing f. *audire* audit- hear]

au·di·tion /awdíshən/ *n. & v.* ● *n.* **1** an interview for a role as a singer, actor, dancer, etc., consisting of a practical demonstration of suitability. **2** the power of hearing or listening. ● *v.* **1** *tr.* interview (a candidate at an audition). **2** *intr.* be interviewed at an audition. [F *audition* or L *auditio* f. *audire* audit- hear]

au·di·tive /áwditiv/ *adj.* concerned with hearing. [F *auditif* –ive (as AUDITION, –IVE)]

au·di·tor /áwditər/ *n.* **1** a person who audits accounts. **2** a person who audits a class. **3** a listener. □□ **au·di·to·ri·al** /–táwreeəl/ *adj.* [ME f. AF *auditour* f. L *auditor* –oris (as AUDITIVE, –OR¹)]

au·di·to·ri·um /áwditáwreeəm/ *n.* (*pl.* **auditoriums** or **auditoria** /–reeə/) **1** a large room or building for meetings, etc. **2** the part of a theater, etc., in which the audience sits. [L neut. of *auditorius* (adj.): see AUDITORY, –ORIUM]

au·di·to·ry /áwditawree/ *adj.* **1** concerned with hearing. **2** received by the ear. [L *auditorius* (as AUDITOR, –ORY²)]

au fait /ōfáy/ *predic.adj.* (usu. foll. by *with*) having current knowledge; conversant (*fully au fait with the arrangements*). □ **put** (or **make**) **au fait** with esp. *Brit.* instruct in. [F]

au fond /ōfáwN/ *adv.* basically; at bottom. [F]

Aug. *abbr.* August.

Au·ge·an /awjéeən/ *adj.* **1** filthy; extremely dirty. **2** extremely difficult and unpleasant. [L *Augeas* f. Gk *Augeias* (in Gk mythology, the owner of stables cleaned by Hercules by diverting a river through them)]

au·ger /áwgər/ *n.* **1** a tool resembling a large corkscrew, for boring holes in wood. **2** a similar larger tool for boring holes in the ground. [OE *nafogār* f. *nafu* NAVE², + *gār* pierce: for loss of *n* cf. ADDER]

auger

aught¹ /awt/ *n.* (also **ought**) *archaic* (usu. implying *neg.*) anything at all. [OE *āwiht* f. Gmc]

aught² /awt/ *n.* (also **ought**) *colloq.* a figure denoting nothing; zero. [perh. f. *an aught* for a NAUGHT]

au·gite /áwjīt/ *n. Mineral.* a complex calcium magnesium aluminous silicate occurring in many igneous rocks. [L *augites* f. Gk *augitēs* f. *augē* luster]

aug·ment *v. & n.* ● *v.tr. & intr.* /awgmént/ **1** make or become greater; increase. **2** add to; supplement. ● *n.* /áwgment/ *Gram.* a vowel prefixed to the past tenses in the older Indo-European languages. □□ **aug·ment·er** *n.* [ME f. OF *augment* (n.), F *augmenter* (v.), or LL *augmentum*, *augmentare* f. L *augēre* increase]

aug·men·ta·tion /áwgmentáyshən/ *n.* **1** enlargement; growth; increase. **2** *Mus.* the lengthening of the time values of notes in melodic parts. [ME f. F f. LL *augmentatio –onis* f. *augmentare* (as AUGMENT)]

aug·men·ta·tive /awgméntətiv/ *adj.* **1** having the property of increasing. **2** *Gram.* (of an affix or derived word) reinforcing the idea of the original word. [F *augmentatif –ive* or med.L *augmentativus* (as AUGMENT)]

au grat·in /ōgrátáN/ *adj. Cooking* cooked with a crisp brown crust, usu. of breadcrumbs or melted cheese. [F f. *gratter*, = by grating, f. GRATE¹]

au·gur /áwgər/ *v. & n.* ● *v.* **1** *intr.* **a** (of an event, circumstance, etc.) suggest a specified outcome (usu. *augur well* (or *ill*). **b** portend; bode (*all augured well for our success*). **2** *tr.* **a** foresee; predict. **b** portend. ● *n.* an ancient Roman religious official who observed natural signs, esp. the behavior of birds, interpreting these as an indication of divine approval or disapproval of a proposed action. □□ **au·gu·ral** *adj.* [L]

au·gu·ry /áwgyəree/ *n.* (*pl.* **·ries**) **1** an omen; a portent. **2** the work

of an augur; the interpretation of omens. [ME f. OF *augurie* or L *augurium* f. AUGUR]

Au·gust /áwgəst/ *n.* the eighth month of the year. [OE f. L *Augustus* Caesar, the first Roman emperor]

au·gust /awgúst/ *adj.* inspiring reverence and admiration; venerable; impressive. □□ **au·gust·ly** *adv.* **au·gust·ness** *n.* [F *auguste* or L *augustus* consecrated, venerable]

Au·gus·tan /awgústən/ *adj. & n.* ● *adj.* **1** connected with, occurring during, or influenced by the reign of the Roman emperor Augustus, esp. as an outstanding period of Latin literature. **2** (of a nation's literature) refined and classical in style (as the literature of the 17th–18th c. in England). ● *n.* a writer of the Augustan age of any literature. [L *Augustanus* f. *Augustus*]

Au·gus·tine /awgústeen/ *n.* an Augustinian friar. [ME f. OF *augustin* f. L *Augustinus*: see AUGUSTINIAN]

Au·gus·tin·i·an /áwgəstíneeən/ *adj. & n.* ● *adj.* **1** of or relating to St. Augustine, a Doctor of the Church (d. 430), or his doctrines. **2** belonging to a religious order observing a rule derived from St. Augustine's writings. ● *n.* **1** an adherent of the doctrines of St. Augustine. **2** one of the order of Augustinian friars. [L *Augustinus* Augustine]

auk /awk/ *n.* any sea diving bird of the family Alcidae, with heavy body, short wings, and black and white plumage, e.g., the guillemot, puffin, and razorbill. [ON *álka*]

auld /awld/ *adj. Sc.* old. [OE *ald*, Anglian form of OLD]

auld lang syne /áwld lang zīn, sín/ *n.* times long past. [Sc., = old long since: also as the title and refrain of a song]

aum·bry /áwmbree/ *n.* (also **ambry** /ámbree/) (*pl.* **·bries**) **1** a small recess in the wall of a church. **2** *Brit. hist.* a small cupboard. [ME f. OF *almarie*, *armarie* f. L *armarium* closet, chest f. *arma* utensils]

au na·tu·rel /ōnáchərél/ *predic.adj. & adv. Cooking* uncooked; (cooked) in the most natural or simplest way. **2** naked. [F, = in the natural state]

aunt /ant, aant/ *n.* **1** the sister of one's father or mother. **2** an uncle's wife. **3** *colloq.* an unrelated woman friend of a child or children. □ **my** (or **my sainted**, etc.) **aunt** esp. *Brit. sl.* an exclamation of surprise, disbelief, etc. [ME f. AF *aunte*, OF *ante*, f. L *amita*]

PRONUNCIATION TIP   **aunt**

The typical British English pronunciation of this word (also heard in certain American dialects) rhymes with *font*, while the more widely used American English pronunciation rhymes with *pant*. Both are considered acceptable, although it is useful to be aware of the variation and individual preferences.

---

aunt·ie /ántee, aántee/ *n.* (also **aunt·y**) (*pl.* **·ies**) *colloq.* **1** = AUNT. **2** *Brit.* (**Auntie**) an institution considered to be conservative or cautious, esp. the BBC.

Aunt Sal·ly *n. Brit.* **1** a game in which players throw sticks or balls at a wooden dummy. **2** the object of an unreasonable attack.

au pair /ōpáir/ *n.* a young foreign person, esp. a woman, helping with housework, etc., in exchange for room, board, and pocket money, esp. as a means of learning a language. [F]

au·ra /áwrə/ *n.* (*pl.* **aurae** /–ree/ or **auras**) **1** the distinctive atmosphere diffused by or attending a person, place, etc. **2** (in mystic or spiritualistic use) a supposed subtle emanation, visible as a sphere of white or colored light, surrounding the body of a living creature. **3** a subtle emanation or aroma from flowers, etc. **4** *Med.* premonitory symptom(s) in epilepsy, etc. [ME f. L f. Gk, = breeze, breath]

au·ral¹ /áwrəl/ *adj.* of or relating to or received by the ear. □□ **au·ral·ly** *adv.* [L *auris* ear]

au·ral² /áwrəl/ *adj.* of, relating to, or resembling an aura; atmospheric. [as AURA]

au·re·ate /áwreeət/ *adj.* **1** golden, gold colored. **2** resplendent. **3** (of a language) highly ornamented. [ME f. LL *aureatus* f. L *aureus* golden f. *aurum* gold]

au·re·ole /áwreeōl/ *n.* (also **au·re·o·la** /awréeōlə/) **1** a halo or circle of light, esp. around the head or body of a portrayed religious figure. **2** a corona around the sun or moon. [ME f. L *aureola* (*corona*), = golden (crown), fem. of *aureolus* f. *aureus* f. *aurum* gold: *aureole* f. OF f. L *aureola*]

Au·re·o·my·cin /áwreeōmísin/ *n. Trademark* an antibiotic used esp. in lung diseases. [L *aureus* golden + Gk *mukēs* fungus + –IN]

au re·voir /órəvwáár/ *int. & n.* good-bye (until we meet again). [F]

au·ric¹ /áwrik/ *adj.* of or relating to trivalent gold. [L *aurum* gold]

au·ric² /áwrik/ *adj.* = AURAL².

au·ri·cle /áwrikəl/ *n. Anat.* **1 a** a small muscular pouch on the surface of each atrium of the heart. **b** the atrium itself. **2** the external ear of animals. Also called **pinna**. **3** an appendage shaped like the ear. [AURICULA]

au·ric·u·la /awríkyələ/ *n.* a primrose, *Primula auricula*, with leaves shaped like bears' ears. [L, dimin. of *auris* ear]

au·ric·u·lar /awríkyələr/ *adj.* **1** of or relating to the ear or hearing. **2** of or relating to the auricle of the heart. **3** shaped like an auricle. □□ **au·ric·u·lar·ly** *adv.* [LL *auricularis* (as AURICULA)]

au•ric•u•late /awríkyələt, –layt/ *adj.* having one or more auricles or ear-shaped appendages. [L]

au•rif•er•ous /awrífərəs/ *adj.* naturally bearing gold. [L *aurifer* f. *aurum* gold]

Au•ri•gna•cian /áwrignáyshən/ *n. & adj.* ● *n.* a flint culture of the Paleolithic period in Europe following the Mousterian and preceding the Solutrean. ● *adj.* of this culture. [F *Aurignacien* f. *Aurignac* in SW France, where remains of it were found]

au•rochs /áwroks, ówroks/ *n.* (*pl.* same) an extinct wild ox, *Bos primigenius*, ancestor of domestic cattle and formerly native to many parts of the world. Also called **urus**. [G f. OHG *ūrohso* f. *ūr-* urus + *ohso* ox]

au•ro•ra /awráwrə/ *n.* (*pl.* **auroras** or **aurorae** /–ree/) **1** a luminous electrical atmospheric phenomenon, usu. of streamers of light in the sky above the northern or southern magnetic pole. **2** *poet.* the dawn. □□ **au•ro•ral** *adj.* **au•ro•re•an** *adj.* [L, = dawn, goddess of dawn]

au•ro•ra aus•tra•lis *n.* /awstráylis/ a southern occurrence of aurora.

au•ro•ra bo•re•al•is *n.* /báwree-ális/ a northern occurrence of aurora.

aus•cul•ta•tion /áwskəltáyshən/ *n.* the act of listening, esp. to sounds from the heart, lungs, etc., as a part of medical diagnosis. □□ **aus•cul•ta•to•ry** /–kúltətawree/ *adj.* [L *auscultatio* f. *auscultare* listen to]

aus•pice /áwspis/ *n.* **1** (in *pl.*) patronage (esp. under the auspices of). **2** a forecast. [orig. 'observation of bird flight in divination': F *auspice* or L *auspicium* f. *auspex* observer of birds f. *avis* bird]

aus•pi•cious /awspíshəs/ *adj.* **1** of good omen; favorable. **2** prosperous. □□ **aus•pi•cious•ly** *adv.* **aus•pi•cious•ness** *n.* [AUSPICE + –OUS]

Aus•sie /áwsee, –zee/ *n. & adj.* (also **Os•sie, Oz•zie**) *colloq.* ● *n.* **1** an Australian. **2** Australia. ● *adj.* Australian. [abbr.]

aus•tere /awstéer/ *adj.* (**austerer, austerest**) **1** severely simple. **2** morally strict. **3** harsh; stern. □□ **aus•tere•ly** *adv.* [ME f. OF f. L *austerus* f. Gk *austēros* severe]

aus•ter•i•ty /awstéritee/ *n.* (*pl.* **-ties**) **1** sternness; moral severity. **2** severe simplicity, e.g., of economies. **3** (esp. in *pl.*) an austere practice (*the austerities of a monk's life*).

Aus•tin /áwstin/ *n.* = AUGUSTINIAN. [contr. of AUGUSTINE]

aus•tral /áwstrəl/ *adj.* **1** southern. **2** (**Austral**) of Australia or Australasia (*Austral English*). [ME f. L *australis* f. *Auster* south wind]

Aus•tral•a•sian /áwstrəláyzhən, –shən/ *adj.* of or relating to Australasia, a region consisting of Australia and islands of the SW Pacific. [*Australasia* f. F *Australasie*, formed as *Australia* + *Asia*]

Aus•tral•ian /awstráylyən/ *n. & adj.* ● *n.* **1** a native or inhabitant of Australia. **2** a person of Australian descent. **3** any of the aboriginal languages of Australia. ● *adj.* of or relating to Australia. □□ **Aus•tral•ian•ism** *n.* **Aus•tral•ian•ize** *v.* [F *australien* f. L (as AUSTRAL)]

Aus•tra•li•a•na /awstráyleeánə, –áánə/ *n. pl.* objects relating to or characteristic of Australia.

Aus•tral•ian Rules Foot•ball *n.* a form of football played with a rugby ball by teams of 18.

Aus•tral•ian ter•ri•er *n.* a wirehaired Australian breed of terrier.

Aus•tra•loid /áwstrəloyd/ *adj.* of the ethnological type of the Australian aborigines.

aus•tra•lo•pith•e•cus /áwstrəlōpíthikəs/ *n.* any extinct bipedal primate of the genus *Australopithecus* having apelike and human characteristics, or its fossilized remains. □□ **aus•tra•lo•pith•e•cine** /–píthiseen/ *n. & adj.* [mod.L f. L *australis* southern + Gk *pithēkos* ape]

Austro- /áwstrō/ *comb. form* Austrian; Austrian and (*Austro-Hungarian*).

au•tar•chy /áwtaarkee/ *n.* (*pl.* **-chies**) **1** absolute sovereignty. **2** despotism. **3** an autarchic country or society. □□ **au•tar•chic** /–táárkik/ *adj.* **au•tar•chi•cal** *adj.* [mod.L *autarchia* (as AUTO-, Gk –*arkhia* f. *arkhō* rule)]

au•tar•ky /áwtaarkee/ *n.* (*pl.* **-kies**) **1** self-sufficiency, esp. as an economic system. **2** a government, etc., run according to such a system. □□ **au•tar•kic** /–táárkik/ *adj.* **au•tar•ki•cal** *adj.* **au•tar•kist** *n.* [Gk *autarkeia* (as AUTO-, *arkeō* suf fice)]

auth. *abbr.* **1** authentic. **2** author. **3** authority. **4** authorized.

au•then•tic /awthéntik/ *adj.* **1 a** of undisputed origin; genuine. **b** reliable or trustworthy. **2** *Mus.* (of a mode) containing notes between the final and an octave higher (cf. PLAGAL). □□ **au•then•ti•cal•ly** *adv.* **au•then•tic•i•ty** /áwthentísitee/ *n.* [ME f. OF *autentique* f. LL *authenticus* f. Gk *authentikos* principal, genuine]

au•then•ti•cate /awthéntikayt/ *v.tr.* **1** establish the truth or genuineness of. **2** validate. □□ **au•then•ti•ca•tion** /–káyshən/ *n.* **au•then•ti•ca•tor** *n.* [med.L *authenticare* f. LL *authenticus*: see AUTHENTIC]

au•thor /áwthər/ *n. & v.* ● *n.* (*fem.* **authoress** /áwthris, áwthərés/) **1** a writer, esp. of books. **2** the originator of an event, a condition, etc. (*the author of all my woes*). ● *v.tr.* be the author of (a book, the universe, a child, etc.). □□ **au•tho•ri•al** /awtháwriəl/ *adj.*

au•thor•i•tar•i•an /ətháwritáireeən, əthór–/ *n. & adj.* ● *adj.* **1** favoring, encouraging, or enforcing strict obedience to authority, as opposed to individual freedom. **2** tyrannical or domineering. ● *n.* a person favoring absolute obedience to a constituted authority. □□ **au•thor•i•tar•i•an•ism** *n.*

au•thor•i•ta•tive /ətháwritáytiv, əthór–/ *adj.* **1** being recognized as true or dependable. **2** (of a person, behavior, etc.) commanding or self-confident. **3** official; supported by authority (*an authoritative document*). **4** having or claiming influence through recognized knowledge or expertise. □□ **au•thor•i•ta•tive•ly** *adv.* **au•thor•i•ta•tive•ness** *n.*

au•thor•i•ty /ətháwritee, əthór–/ *n.* (*pl.* **-ties**) **1 a** the power or right to enforce obedience. **b** (often foll. by *for*, or *to* + infin.) delegated power. **2** (esp. in *pl.*) a person or body having authority, esp. political or administrative. **3 a** an influence exerted on opinion because of recognized knowledge or expertise. **b** such an influence expressed in a book, quotation, etc. (*an authority on vintage cars*). **c** a person whose opinion is accepted, esp. an expert in a subject. **4** the weight of evidence. [ME f. OF *autorité* f. L *auctoritas* f. *auctor*: see AUTHOR]

au•thor•ize /áwthərīz/ *v.tr.* **1** sanction. **2** (foll. by *to* + infin.) **a** give authority. **b** commission (a person or body) (*authorized to trade*). □□ **au•thor•i•za•tion** /–rizáyshən/ *n.* [ME f. OF *autoriser* f. med.L *auctorizare* f. *auctor*: see AUTHOR]

Au•thor•ized Ver•sion *n.* an English translation of the Bible made in 1611 and used in Protestant worship. Also called **King James Version**.

au•thor•ship /áwthərship/ *n.* **1** the origin of a book or other written work (*of unknown authorship*). **2** the occupation of writing.

au•tism /áwtizəm/ *n. Psychol.* a mental condition, usu. present from childhood, characterized by complete self-absorption and a reduced ability to respond to or communicate with the outside world. □□ **au•tis•tic** /awtístik/ *adj.* [mod.L *autismus* (as AUTO-, –ISM)]

au•to /áwtō/ *n.* (*pl.* **-tos**) *colloq.* an automobile. [abbr. of AUTOMOBILE]

auto- /áwtō/ *comb. form* (usu. **aut-** before a vowel) **1** self (*autism*). **2** one's own (*autobiography*). **3** by oneself or spontaneous (*autosuggestion*). **4** by itself or automatic (*automobile*). [from or after Gk *auto-* f. *autos* self]

au•to•bahn /áwtōbaan/ *n.* (*pl.* **autobahns** or **autobahnen** /–nən/) a German, Austrian, or Swiss highway. [G f. *Auto* car + *Bahn* path, road]

au•to•bi•og•ra•phy /áwtōbīógrəfee/ *n.* (*pl.* **-phies**) **1** a personal account of one's own life, esp. for publication. **2** this as a process or literary form. □□ **au•to•bi•og•ra•pher** *n.* **au•to•bi•o•graph•ic** /–bíəgráfik/ *adj.* **au•to•bi•o•graph•i•cal** *adj.*

au•to•ceph•a•lous /áwtōséfələs/ *adj.* **1** (esp. of an Eastern church) appointing its own head. **2** (of a bishop, church, etc.) independent. [Gk *autokephalos* (as AUTO-, *kephalē* head)]

au•toch•thon /awtókthən/ *n.* (*pl.* **autochthons** or **autochthones** /–thəneez/) (in *pl.*) the original or earliest known inhabitants of a country; aboriginals. □□ **au•toch•tho•nal** *adj.* **au•toch•thon•ic** /–thónik/ *adj.* **au•toch•tho•nous** *adj.* [Gk, = sprung from the earth (as AUTO-, *khthōn*, –*onos* earth)]

au•to•clave /áwtōklayv/ *n.* **1** a strong vessel used for chemical reactions at high pressures and temperatures. **2** a sterilizer using high pressure steam. [AUTO- + L *clavus* nail or *clavis* key]

au•toc•ra•cy /awtókrəsee/ *n.* (*pl.* **-cies**) **1** absolute government by one person. **2** the power exercised by such a person. **3** an autocratic country or society. [Gk *autokrateia* (as AUTOCRAT)]

au•to•crat /áwtōkrat/ *n.* **1** an absolute ruler. **2** a dictatorial person. □□ **au•to•crat•ic** /–krátik/ *adj.* **au•to•crat•i•cal•ly** *adv.* [F *autocrate* f. Gk *autokratēs* (as AUTO-, *kratos* power)]

au•to•cross /áwtōkraws, –kros/ *n.* automobile racing across country or on unpaved roads or to display driving skill. [AUTOMOBILE + CROSS- 1]

Au•to•cue /áwtōkyōō/ *n. Brit. Trademark* a device, unseen by the audience, displaying a television script to a speaker or performer as an aid to memory (cf. TELEPROMPTER).

au•to•da•fé /áwtōdaafáy/ *n.* (*pl.* **autos-da-fé** /áwtōz–/) **1** a sentence of punishment by the Spanish Inquisition. **2** the execution of such a sentence, esp. the burning of a heretic. [Port., = act of the faith]

au•to•di•dact /áwtōdídakt, –dákt/ *n.* a self-taught person. □□ **au•to•di•dac•tic** /–dáktik/ *adj.* [AUTO- + *didact* as DIDACTIC]

au•to•er•o•tism /áwtō-érətizəm/ *n.* (also **au•to•e•rot•i•cism** /–irótisizəm/) *Psychol.* sexual excitement generated by stimulating one's own body; masturbation. □□ **au•to•e•rot•ic** /–irótik/ *adj.*

au•to•fo•cus /áwtōfókəs/ *n.* a device for focusing a camera, etc., automatically.

WORD HISTORY author

Middle English (in the sense 'a person who invents or causes something'): from Old French *autor*, from Latin *auctor*, from *augere* 'increase, originate, promote.' The spelling with *th* arose in the 15th cent., and perhaps became established under the influence of *authentic*.

See page xx for the **Key to Pronunciation**.

au·tog·a·my /awtógəmee/ *n. Bot.* self-fertilization in plants. □□ **au·tog·a·mous** *adj.* [AUTO- + Gk *–gamia* f. *gamos* marriage]

au·tog·e·nous /awtójinəs/ *adj.* self-produced. □ **autogenous welding** a process of joining metal by melting the edges together without adding material.

au·to·gi·ro /áwtōjírō/ *n.* (also **autogyro**) (*pl. ·ros*) an early form of helicopter with freely rotating horizontal vanes and a propeller. [Sp. (as AUTO-, *giro* gyration)]

au·to·graft /áwtōgraft/ *n. Surgery* a graft of tissue from one point to another of the same person's body.

au·to·graph /áwtəgraf/ *n. & v.* ● *n.* **1 a** a signature, esp. that of a celebrity. **b** handwriting. **2** a manuscript in an author's own handwriting. **3** a document signed by its author. ● *v.tr.* **1** sign (a photograph, autograph album, etc.). **2** write (a letter, etc.) by hand. [F *autographe* or LL *autographum* f. Gk *autographon* neut. of *autographos* (as AUTO-, –GRAPH)]

au·tog·ra·phy /awtógrəfee/ *n.* **1** writing done with one's own hand. **2** the facsimile reproduction of writing or illustration. □□ **au·to·graph·ic** /–təgráfik/ *adj.*

au·to·gy·ro var. of AUTOGIRO.

Au·to·harp /áwtōhaarp/ *n. Trademark* a kind of zither with a mechanical device to allow the playing of chords.

au·to·im·mune /áwtōimyóõn/ *adj. Med.* (of a disease) caused by antibodies produced against substances naturally present in the body. □□ **au·to·im·mu·ni·ty** *n.*

au·to·in·tox·i·ca·tion /áwtōintóksikáyshən/ *n. Med.* poisoning by a toxin formed within the body itself.

au·tol·y·sis /awtólisis/ *n.* the destruction of cells by their own enzymes. □□ **au·to·lyt·ic** /áwtəlítik/ *adj.* [G *Autolyse* (as AUTO-, –LYSIS)]

Au·to·mat /áwtəmat/ *n. Trademark* a cafeteria containing coin-operated machines dispensing food and drink. [G f. F *automate*, formed as AUTOMATION]

au·to·mate /áwtəmayt/ *v.tr.* convert to or operate by automation (*the ticket office has been automated*). [back-form. f. AUTOMATION]

au·to·mat·ed tel·ler ma·chine *n.* electronic machine that allows customers to insert a card, punch in an identification number, and then perform banking transactions such as depositing or withdrawing funds, etc. ¶ Abbr.: **ATM.**

au·to·mat·ic /áwtəmátik/ *adj. & n.* ● *adj.* **1** (of a machine, device, etc., or its function) working by itself, without direct human intervention. **2 a** done spontaneously; without conscious thought or intention (*an automatic reaction*). **b** necessary and inevitable (*an automatic penalty*). **3** *Psychol.* performed unconsciously or subconsciously. **4** (of a firearm) that continues firing until the ammunition is exhausted or the pressure on the trigger is released. **5** (of a motor vehicle or its transmission) using gears that change automatically according to speed and acceleration. ● *n.* **1** an automatic device, esp. a gun or transmission. **2** *colloq.* a vehicle with automatic transmission. □□ **au·to·mat·i·cal·ly** *adv.* **au·to·ma·tic·i·ty** /áwtəmətísitee/ *n.* [formed as AUTOMATON + –IC]

au·to·mat·ic pi·lot *n.* an electronic device for keeping an aircraft on a set course.

au·to·mat·ic tel·ler ma·chine *n.* = AUTOMATED TELLER MACHINE.

au·to·ma·tion /áwtəmáyshən/ *n.* **1** the use of automatic equipment to save mental and manual labor. **2** the automatic control of the manufacture of a product through its successive stages. [irreg. f. AUTOMATIC + –ATION]

au·tom·a·tism /awtómətizəm/ *n.* **1** *Psychol.* the performance of actions unconsciously or subconsciously; such action. **2** involuntary action. **3** unthinking routine. [F *automatisme* f. *automate* AUTOMATON]

au·tom·a·tize /awtómətīz/ *v.tr.* **1** make (a process, etc.) automatic. **2** subject (a business, enterprise, etc.) to automation. □□ **au·tom·a·ti·za·tion** *n.* [AUTOMATIC + –IZE]

au·tom·a·ton /awtómətən, –ton/ *n.* (*pl.* **automata** /–tə/ or **automatons**) **1** an automated device with concealed motive power; a robot. **2** a person who behaves in a mechanical or unemotional way. [L f. Gk, neut. of *automatos* acting of itself: see AUTO-]

au·to·mo·bile /áwtəməbeel/ *n.* a motor vehicle for road use with an enclosed passenger compartment; a car. [F (as AUTO-, MOBILE)]

au·to·mo·tive /áwtəmótiv/ *adj.* concerned with motor vehicles.

au·to·nom·ic /áwtənómik/ *adj.* esp. *Physiol.* functioning involuntarily. [AUTONOMY + –IC]

au·to·nom·ic nerv·ous sys·tem *n.* the part of the nervous system responsible for control of the bodily functions not consciously directed, e.g., heartbeat.

au·ton·o·mous /awtónəməs/ *adj.* **1** having self-government. **2** acting independently or having the freedom to do so. □□ **au·ton·o·mous·ly** *adv.* [Gk *autonomos* (as AUTONOMY)]

au·ton·o·my /awtónəmee/ *n.* (*pl.* **·mies**) **1** the right of self-government. **2** personal freedom. **3** freedom of will. **4** a self-governing community. □□ **au·ton·o·mist** *n.* [Gk *autonomia* f. *autos* self + *nomos* law]

au·to·pi·lot /áwtōpīlət/ *n.* an automatic pilot. [abbr.]

au·top·sy /áwtopsee/ *n.* (*pl.* **·sies**) **1** a postmortem examination to determine cause of death, etc. **2** any critical analysis. **3** a personal inspection. [F *autopsie* or mod.L *autopsia* f. Gk f. *autoptēs* eyewitness]

au·to·ra·di·o·graph /áwtōráydeeəgraf/ *n.* a photograph of an object, produced by radiation from radioactive material in the object. □□ **au·to·ra·di·o·graph·ic** *adj.* **au·to·ra·di·og·ra·phy** /áwtōráydiógrəfee/ *n.*

au·to·sug·ges·tion /áwtōsəgjéschən/ *n.* a hypnotic or subconscious suggestion made by a person to himself or herself and affecting behavior.

au·to·tel·ic /áwtōtélik/ *adj.* having or being a purpose in itself. [AUTO- + Gk *telos* end]

au·tot·o·my /awtótəmee/ *n. Zool.* the casting off of a part of the body when threatened, e.g., the tail of a lizard.

au·to·tox·in /áwtótóksin/ *n.* a poisonous substance originating within an organism. □□ **au·to·tox·ic** *adj.*

au·to·troph·ic /áwtətrófik, –trō–/ *adj. Biol.* able to form complex nutritional organic substances from simple inorganic substances such as carbon dioxide (cf. HETEROTROPHIC). [AUTO- + Gk *trophos* feeder]

au·to·type /áwtōtīp/ *n.* **1** a facsimile. **2 a** a photographic printing process for monochrome reproduction. **b** a print made by this process.

au·tox·i·da·tion /awtóksidáyshən/ *n. Chem.* oxidation by exposure to air at room temperature.

au·tumn /áwtəm/ *n.* **1** the third season of the year, when crops and fruits are gathered, and leaves fall, in the N. hemisphere from September to November and in the S. hemisphere from March to May. Also called **fall. 2** *Astron.* the period from the autumnal equinox to the winter solstice. **3** a time of maturity or incipient decay. [ME f. OF *autompne* f. L *autumnus*]

au·tum·nal /awtúmnəl/ *adj.* **1** of, characteristic of, or appropriate to autumn (*autumnal colors*). **2** occurring in autumn (*autumnal equinox*). **3** maturing or blooming in autumn. **4** past the prime of life. [L *autumnalis* (as AUTUMN, –AL)]

au·tum·nal e·qui·nox *n.* see EQUINOX.

au·tumn cro·cus *n.* any plant of the genus *Colchicum*, esp. meadow saffron, of the lily family and unrelated to the true crocus.

aux·il·ia·ry /awgzílyəree/ *adj. & n.* ● *adj.* **1** (of a person or thing) that gives help. **2** (of services or equipment) subsidiary; additional. ● *n.* (*pl.* **·ries**) **1** an auxiliary person or thing. **2** (in *pl.*) *Mil.* auxiliary troops. **3** *Gram.* an auxiliary verb. [L *auxiliarius* f. *auxilium* help]

> ### PRONUNCIATION TIP　auxiliary
>
> Be careful to pronounce the *ia* in this word (awks-IL-ya-ree). Many people have a tendency to lose the sound of the second *i*.

aux·il·ia·ry troops *n. Mil.* foreign or allied troops in a belligerent nation's service.

aux·il·ia·ry verb *n. Gram.* a verb used in forming tenses, moods, and voices of other verbs.

> ### GRAMMAR TIP　auxiliary verbs
>
> **Auxiliary verbs** are "helping verbs": they are used with other verb forms to complete the meaning and show the tense of main verbs. The most common auxiliary verbs are from the verb *to be* (*We are working as hard as we can*) and *to have* (*She had been a grandmother for several years*). A main verb can have up to three auxiliary verbs (*was coughing; should have known; will have been waiting*). The verb *to be* can function as both a main verb and a helping verb in the same sentence: *The puppy was being a pest again.*

aux·in /áwksin/ *n.* a plant hormone that regulates growth. [G f. Gk *auxō* increase + –IN]

AV *abbr.* **1** audiovisual (teaching aids, etc.). **2** Authorized Version (of the Bible).

a·vail /əváyl/ *v. & n.* ● *v.* **1** *tr.* help; benefit. **2** *refl.* (foll. by *of*) profit by; take advantage of. **3** *intr.* **a** provide help. **b** be of use, value, or profit. ● *n.* (usu. in *neg.* or *interrog.* phrases) use; profit (*to no avail; without avail; of what avail?*). [ME f. obs. *vail* (v.) f. OF *valoir* be worth f. L *valēre*]

a·vail·a·ble /əváyləbəl/ *adj.* (often foll. by *to, for*) **1** capable of being used; at one's disposal. **2** within one's reach. **3** (of a person) **a** free. **b** able to be contacted. □□ **a·vail·a·bil·i·ty** *n.* **a·vail·a·ble·ness** *n.* **a·vail·a·bly** *adv.* [ME f. AVAIL + –ABLE]

av·a·lanche /ávəlanch/ *n. & v.* ● *n.* **1** a mass of snow and ice tumbling rapidly down a mountain. **2** a sudden appearance or arrival of anything in large quantities (*faced with an avalanche of work*). ● *v.* **1** *intr.* descend like an avalanche. **2** *tr.* carry down like an avalanche. [F, alt. of dial. *lavanche* after *avaler* descend]

a·vant-garde /avón-gáard/ *n. & adj.* ● *n.* pioneers or innovators, esp. in art and literature. ● *adj.* (of ideas, etc.) new; progressive. □□ **a·vant-gard·ism** *n.* **a·vant-gard·ist** *n.* [F, = vanguard]

av·a·rice /ávəris/ *n.* extreme greed for money or gain; cupidity. □□ **av·**

a·ri·cious /–ríshəs/ *adj.* **av·a·ri·cious·ly** *adv.* **av·a·ri·cious·ness** /–ríshəsnis/ *n.* [ME f. OF f. L *avaritia* f. *avarus* greedy]

a·vast /əvást/ *int. Naut.* stop; cease. [Du. *houd vast* hold fast]

av·a·tar /ávətaar/ *n.* **1** (in Hindu mythology) the descent of a deity or released soul to earth in bodily form. **2** incarnation; manifestation. **3** a manifestation or phase. [Skr. *avatāra* descent f. *áva* down + *ṭṛ-* pass over]

a·vaunt /əváwnt, əváant/ *int. archaic* begone. [ME f. AF f. OF *avant* ult. f. L *ab* from + *ante* before]

Ave. *abbr.* Avenue.

ave /aavay/ *int. & n.* ● *int.* **1** welcome. **2** farewell. ● *n.* **1** (in full **Ave Maria**) a prayer to the Virgin Mary, the opening line from Luke 1:28. Also called **Hail Mary**. **2** a shout of welcome or farewell. [ME f. L, 2nd sing. imper. of *avēre* fare well]

a·venge /əvénj/ *v.tr.* **1** inflict retribution on behalf of (a person, a violated right, etc.). **2** take vengeance for (an injury). □ **be avenged** avenge oneself. □□ **a·veng·er** *n.* [ME f. OF *avengier* f. *à* to + *vengier* f. L *vindicare* vindicate]

av·ens /ávənz/ *n.* any of various plants of the genus *Geum.* [ME f. OF *avence* (med.L *avencia*) of unkn. orig.]

a·ven·tu·rine /əvénchəreen, –rin/ *n. Mineral.* **1** brownish glass or mineral containing sparkling gold colored particles usu. of copper or gold. **2** a variety of spangled quartz resembling this. [F f. It. *avventurino* f. *avventura* chance (because of its accidental discovery)]

av·e·nue /ávənōō, –nyōō/ *n.* **1 a** a broad road or street, often with trees at regular intervals along its sides. **b** esp. *Brit.* a tree-lined approach to a country house. **2** a way of approaching or dealing with something (*explored every avenue to find an answer*). [F, fem. past part. of *avenir* f. L *advenire* come to]

a·ver /əvór/ *v.tr.* (**averred**, **averring**) *formal* assert; affirm. [ME f. OF *averer* (as AD-, L *verus* true)]

av·er·age /ávərij, ávrij/ *n., adj., & v.* ● *n.* **1 a** the usual amount, extent, or rate. **b** the ordinary standard. **2** an amount obtained by dividing the total of given amounts by the number of amounts in the set. **3** *Law* the distribution of loss resulting from damage to a ship or cargo. ● *adj.* **1 a** usual; typical. **b** mediocre; undistinguished. **2** estimated or calculated by average. ● *v.tr.* **1** amount on average to (*the sale of the product averaged one hundred a day*). **2** do on average (*averages six hours' work a day*). **3 a** estimate or calculate the average of. **b** estimate the general standard of. □ **average out** result in an average. **average out at** result in an average of. **on** (or **on an**) **average** as an average rate or estimate. □□ **av·er·age·ly** *adv.* ▶See note at MEAN³.

WORD HISTORY average

Late 15th cent.: from French *avarie* 'damage to ship or cargo,' earlier 'customs duty,' from Italian *avaria*, from Arabic *'awār* 'damage to goods'; the suffix *-age* is on the pattern of *damage*. Originally denoting a charge or customs duty payable by the owner of goods to be shipped, the term later denoted the financial liability from goods lost or damaged at sea, and specifically the equitable apportionment of this between the owners of the vessel and the cargo (late 16th cent.); this gave rise to the general sense of the equalizing out of gains and losses by calculating the mean (mid-18th cent.).

---

a·ver·ment /əvórmənt/ *n.* a positive statement; an affirmation, esp. *Law* one with an offer of proof. [ME f. AF, OF *aver(r) ement* (as AVER, –MENT)]

a·verse /əvórs/ *predic.adj.* (usu. foll. by *to*; also foll. by *from*) opposed; disinclined (*was not averse to helping me*). [L *aversus* (as AVERT)] ▶See note at ADVERSE.

a·ver·sion /əvórzhən, –shən/ *n.* **1** (usu. foll. by *to, from, for*) a strong dislike or disinclination (*has an aversion to hard work*). **2** someone or something that arouses such feelings. [F *aversion* or L *aversio* (as AVERT, –ION)]

a·ver·sion ther·a·py *n.* psychiatric therapy designed to make a patient give up an undesirable habit by causing him or her to associate it with an unpleasant effect.

a·vert /əvórt/ *v.tr.* (often foll. by *from*) **1** turn away (one's eyes or thoughts). **2** prevent or ward off (an undesirable occurrence). □□ **a·vert·a·ble**, **a·vert·i·ble** *adj.* [ME f. L *avertere* (as AB-, *vertere* versturn): partly f. OF *avertir* f. Rmc]

A·ves·ta /əvéstə/ *n.* (usu. prec. by *the*) the sacred writings of Zoroastrianism (cf. ZEND). [Pers.]

A·ves·tan /əvéstən/ *adj. & n.* ● *adj.* of or relating to the Avesta. ● *n.* the ancient Iranian language of the Avesta.

avg. *abbr.* average.

a·vi·an /áyveeən/ *adj.* of or relating to birds. [L *avis* bird]

a·vi·ar·y /áyvee–eree/ *n.* (pl. **·ies**) a large enclosure or building for keeping birds. [L *aviarium* (as AVIAN, –ARY¹)]

a·vi·ate /áyveeayt/ *v.* **1** *intr.* fly in an airplane. **2** *tr.* pilot (an airplane). [back-form. f. AVIATION]

a·vi·a·tion /áyveeáyshən/ *n.* **1** the skill or practice of operating aircraft. **2** aircraft manufacture. [F f. L *avis* bird]

a·vi·a·tor /áyveeaytər/ *n.* (fem. **aviatrix** /áyveeáytriks/) a person who pilots an aircraft. [F *aviateur* f. L *avis* bird]

a·vi·cul·ture /áyvikulchər/ *n.* the rearing and keeping of birds. □□ **a·vi·cul·tur·ist** /–kúlchərist/ *n.* [L *avis* bird, after AGRICULTURE]

av·id /ávid/ *adj.* (usu. foll. by *of, for*) having or showing a keen interest in or enthusiasm for something (*an avid reader of science fiction*). □□ **a·vid·i·ty** /əvíditee/ *n.* **av·id·ly** *adv.* [F *avide* or L *avidus* f. *avēre* crave]

a·vi·fau·na /áyvifawnə/ *n.* birds of a region or country collectively. [L *avis* bird + FAUNA]

a·vi·on·ics /áyveeóniks/ *n.pl.* (treated as *sing.*) electronics as applied to aviation.

a·vi·ta·min·o·sis /ayvítəminósis/ *n. Med.* a condition resulting from a deficiency of one or more vitamins.

a·viz·an·dum /ávizándəm/ *n. Sc. Law* a period of time for further consideration of a judgment. [med.L, gerund of *avizare* consider (as ADVISE)]

av·o·ca·do /ávəkaádō, aávə–/ *n.* (pl. **·dos**) **1** (in full **avocado pear**) a pear-shaped fruit with rough leathery skin, a smooth oily edible flesh, and a large stone. **2** the tropical evergreen tree, *Persea americana*, native to Central America, bearing this fruit. Also called **alligator pear. 3** the light green color of the flesh of this fruit. [Sp., = advocate (substituted for Aztec *ahuacatl*)]

av·o·ca·tion /ávōkáyshən/ *n.* **1** a minor occupation. **2** *colloq.* a vocation or calling. [L *avocatio* f. *avocare* call away]

av·o·cet /ávəset/ *n.* any wading bird of the genus *Recurvirostra* with long legs and a long slender upward-curved bill and usu. black and white plumage. [F *avocette* f. It. *avosetta*]

A·vo·ga·dro's con·stant /ávōgaádrōz, aávō–/ *n.* (also **Avogadro's number**) *Physics* the number of atoms or molecules in one mole of a substance; 6.02 ;ts 10²³. [A. *Avogadro*, It. physicist d. 1856]

A·vo·ga·dro's law /ávōgaádrōz, aávō–/ *n. Physics* the law that equal volumes of all gases at the same temperature and pressure contain the same number of molecules.

a·void /əvóyd/ *v.tr.* **1** refrain or keep away from (a thing, person, or action). **2** escape; evade. **3** *Law* **a** nullify (a decree or contract). **b** quash (a sentence). □□ **a·void·a·ble** *adj.* **a·void·a·bly** *adv.* **a·void·ance** *n.* **a·void·er** *n.* [AF *avoider*, OF *evuider* clear out, get quit of, f. *vuide* empty, VOID]

av·oir·du·pois /ávərdəpóyz/ *n.* (in full **avoirdupois weight**) **1** a system of weights based on a pound of 16 ounces or 7,000 grains. **2** weight; heaviness. [ME f. OF *aveir de peis* goods of weight f. *aveir* f. L *habēre* have + *peis* (see POISE¹)]

a·vouch /əvówch/ *v.tr. & intr.* guarantee; affirm; confess. □□ **a·vouch·ment** *n.* [ME f. OF *avochier* f. L *advocare* (as AD-, *vocare* call)]

a·vow /əvów/ *v.tr.* **1** admit; confess. **2 a** admit that one is (*avowed himself the author*). **b** (as **avowed** *adj.*) admitted (*the avowed author*). □□ **a·vow·al** *n.* **a·vow·ed·ly** /əvówidlee/ *adv.* [ME f. OF *avouer* acknowledge f. L *advocare* (as AD-, *vocare* call)]

a·vul·sion /əvúlshən/ *n.* **1** a tearing away. **2** *Law* a sudden removal of land by a flood, etc., to another person's property. [F *avulsion* or L *avulsio* f. *avellere avuls-* pluck away]

a·vun·cu·lar /əvúngkyələr/ *adj.* like or of an uncle; kind and friendly, esp. toward a younger person. [L *avunculus* maternal uncle, dimin. of *avus* grandfather]

AWACS /áywaks/ *n.* a long-range radar system for detecting enemy aircraft. [abbr. of *airborne warning and control system*]

a·wait /əwáyt/ *v.tr.* **1** wait for. **2** (of an event or thing) be in store for (*a surprise awaits you*). [ME f. AF *awaitier*, OF *aguaitier* (as AD-, *waitier* WAIT)]

a·wake /əwáyk/ *v. & adj.* ● *v.* (past **awoke** /əwṓk/; past part. **awoken** /əwṓkən/) **1** *intr.* **a** cease to sleep. **b** become active. **2** *intr.* (foll. by *to*) become aware of. **3** *tr.* rouse, esp. from sleep. ● *predic.adj.* **1 a** not asleep. **b** vigilant. **2** (foll. by *to*) aware of. [OE *āwæcnan*, *āwacian* (as A-², WAKE¹)]

a·wak·en /əwáykən/ *v.tr. & intr.* **1** = AWAKE *v.* **2** *tr.* (often foll. by *to*) make aware. [OE *onwæcnan*, etc. (as A-², WAKEN)]

a·ward /əwáwrd/ *v. & n.* ● *v.tr.* **1** give or order to be given as a payment, compensation, or prize (*awarded her a scholarship; was awarded damages*). **2** grant; assign. ● *n.* **1 a** a payment, compensation, or prize awarded. **b** the act or process of awarding. **2** a judicial decision. □□ **a·ward·er** *n.* [ME f. AF *awarder*, ult. f. Gmc: see WARD]

a·ware /əwáir/ *predic.adj.* **1** (often foll. by *of*, or *that* + clause) conscious; not ignorant; having knowledge. **2** well-informed. □□ **a·ware·ness** *n.* [OE *gewær*] ▶The use of **aware** attributively, as in *a very aware person* is considered incorrect by some.

a·wash /əwósh, əwáwsh/ *predic.adj.* **1** level with the surface of water, so that it just washes over. **2** carried or washed by the waves; flooded or as if flooded.

a·way /əwáy/ *adv., adj., & n.* ● *adv.* **1** to or at a distance from the place, person, or thing in question (*go away; give away; look away;*

they are away; 5 miles away). **2** toward or into nonexistence (*sounds die away; explain it away; idled their time away*). **3** constantly; persistently; continuously (*work away; laugh away*). **4** without delay (*ask away*). ● *adj.* **1** *Sports* played at an opponent's field, etc. (*away game; away win*). **2** absent or distant. **3** *Baseball* out. ● *n. Sports* an away game or win. □ **away with** (as *imper.*) take away; let us be rid of. [OE *onweg, aweg* on one's way f. A[2] + WAY]

awe /aw/ *n. & v.* ● *n.* reverential fear or wonder (*stand in awe of*). ● *v.tr.* inspire with awe. [ME *age* f. ON *agi* f. Gmc]

a·wea·ry /əweeree/ *predic.adj. poet.* (often foll. by *of*) weary. [aphetic *a* + WEARY]

a·weigh /əwáy/ *predic.adj. Naut.* (of an anchor) clear of the sea or river bed; hanging. [A[2] + WEIGH[1]]

awe-in·spir·ing *adj.* causing awe or wonder; amazing; magnificent. □□ **awe-in·spir·ing·ly** *adv.*

awe·some /áwsəm/ *adj.* **1** inspiring awe. **2** *sl.* excellent; superb. □□ **awe·some·ly** *adv.* **awe·some·ness** *n.* [AWE + –SOME[1]]

awe·strick·en /áwstrikən/ *adj.* (also **awe·struck** /–struk/) struck or affected by awe.

aw·ful /áwfŏŏl/ *adj.* **1** *colloq.* **a** unpleasant or horrible (*awful weather*). **b** poor in quality; very bad (*has awful writing*). **c** (*attrib.*) excessive; remarkably large (*an awful lot of money*). **2** *poet.* inspiring awe. □□ **aw·ful·ness** *n.* [AWE + –FUL]

aw·ful·ly /áwfəlee, –flee/ *adv.* **1** *colloq.* in an unpleasant, bad, or horrible way (*he played awfully*). **2** *colloq.* very (*she's awfully pleased*). **3** *poet.* reverently.

a·while /əhwíl, əwíl/ *adv.* for a short time. [OE *āne hwīle* a while]

awk·ward /áwkwərd/ *adj.* **1** ill-adapted for use; causing difficulty in use. **2** clumsy or bungling. **3 a** embarrassed (*felt awkward about it*). **b** embarrassing (*an awkward situation*). **4** difficult to deal with (*an awkward customer*). □□ **awk·ward·ly** *adv.* **awk·ward·ness** *n.* [obs. *awk* backhanded, untoward (ME f. ON *afugr* turned the wrong way) + –WARD]

awk·ward age *n.* adolescence.

awl /awl/ *n.* a small pointed tool used for piercing holes, esp. in leather. [OE *æl*]

awn /awn/ *n.* a stiff bristle growing from the grain sheath of grasses, or terminating a leaf, etc. □□ **awned** *adj.* [ME f. ON *ǫgn*]

awn·ing /áwning/ *n.* a sheet of canvas or similar material stretched on a frame and used to shade a window, doorway, ship's deck, or other area from the sun or rain. [17th c. (Naut.): orig. uncert.]

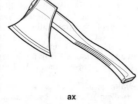

awl

a·woke *past* of AWAKE.

a·wo·ken *past part.* of AWAKE.

AWOL /áywawl/ *abbr.* absent without leave.

a·wry /ərí/ *adv. & adj.* ● *adv.* **1** crookedly or askew. **2** improperly or amiss. ● *predic.adj.* crooked; deviant or unsound (*his theory is awry*). □ **go awry** go or do wrong. [ME f. A[2] + WRY]

ax /aks/ *n. & v.* (also **axe**) ● *n.* **1** a chopping tool, usu. of iron with a steel edge at a right angle to a wooden handle. **2** the drastic cutting or elimination of expenditure, staff, etc. ● *v.tr.* (**axing**) **1** use an ax. **2** cut (esp. costs or services) drastically. **3** remove or dismiss. □ **an ax to grind** private or selfish purpose to serve. [OE *æx* f. Gmc]

ax

ax·el /áksəl/ *n.* a jumping movement in skating, similar to a loop (see LOOP *n.* 7) but from one foot to the other. [*Axel* R. Paulsen, Norw. skater d. 1938]

ax·es *pl.* of AXIS[1].

ax·i·al /ákseeəl/ *adj.* **1** forming or belonging to an axis. **2** around or along an axis (*axial rotation; axial symmetry*). □□ **ax·i·al·i·ty** /–seeáli-tee/ *n.* **ax·i·al·ly** *adv.*

ax·il /áksil/ *n.* the upper angle between a leaf and the stem it springs from, or between a branch and the trunk. [L *axilla*: see AXILLA]

ax·il·la /aksílə/ *n.* (*pl.* **axillae** /–ee/) **1** *Anat.* the armpit. **2** an axil. [L, = armpit, dimin. of *ala* wing]

ax·il·lar·y /áksiléree/ *adj.* **1** *Anat.* of or relating to the armpit. **2** *Bot.* in or growing from the axil.

ax·i·om /ákseeəm/ *n.* **1** an established or widely accepted principle. **2** esp. *Geom.* a self-evident truth. [F *axiome* or L *axioma* f. Gk *axiōma axiōmat-* f. *axios* worthy]

ax·i·o·mat·ic /ákseeəmátik/ *adj.* **1** self-evident. **2** relating to or con-

axil

taining axioms. □□ **ax·i·o·mat·i·cal·ly** *adv.* [Gk *axiōmatikos* (as AXIOM)]

ax·is[1] /áksis/ *n.* (*pl.* **ax·es** /–seez/) **1 a** an imaginary line about which a body rotates or about which a plane figure is conceived as generating a solid. **b** a line that divides a regular figure symmetrically. **2** *Math.* a fixed reference line for the measurement of coordinates, etc. **3** *Bot.* the central column of an inflorescence or other growth. **4** *Anat.* the second cervical vertebra. **5** *Physiol.* the central part of an organ or organism. **6 a** an agreement or alliance between two or more countries forming a center for an eventual larger grouping of nations sharing an ideal or objective. **b** (**the Axis**) the alliance of Germany and Italy formed before and during World War II, later extended to include Japan and other countries; these countries as a group. [L, = axle, pivot]

ax·is[2] /áksis/ *n.* a white spotted deer, *Cervus axis*, of S. Asia. Also called **chital**. [L]

ax·le /áksəl/ *n.* a rod or spindle (either fixed or rotating) on which a wheel or group of wheels is fixed. [orig. *axletree* f. ME *axeltre>o?* f. ON öxulltré]

Ax·min·ster /áksminstər/ *n.* (in full **Axminster carpet**) a kind of machine-woven patterned carpet with a cut pile. [*Axminster* in S. England]

ax·o·lotl /áksəlot'l/ *n.* an aquatic newtlike salamander, *Ambystoma mexicanum*, from Mexico, which in natural conditions retains its larval form for life but is able to breed. [Nahuatl f. *atl* water + *xolotl* servant]

ax·on /ákson/ *n. Anat. & Zool.* a long threadlike part of a nerve cell, conducting impulses from the cell body. [mod.L f. Gk *axōn* axis]

ay var. of AYE.

a·yah /íə/ *n.* a native nurse or maidservant, esp. in India and other former British overseas territories. [Anglo-Ind. f. Port. *aia* nurse]

a·ya·tol·lah /íətŏlə/ *n.* a Shiite religious leader in Iran. [Pers. f. Arab., = token of God]

aye[1] /ī/ *adv. & n.* (also **ay**) ● *adv.* **1** *archaic* or *dial.* yes. **2** (in voting) I assent. **3** (as **aye aye**) *Naut.* a response accepting an order. ● *n.* an affirmative answer or assent, esp. in voting. □ **the ayes have it** the affirmative votes are in the majority. [16th c.: prob. f. first pers. personal pron. expressing assent]

aye[2] /ay/ *adv.* (also **ay**) *archaic* ever; always. [ME f. ON *ei, ey* f. Gmc]

aye-aye /í-í/ *n.* an arboreal nocturnal lemur, *Daubentonia madagascariensis*, native to Madagascar. [F f. Malagasy *aiay*]

Ayles·bur·y /áylzbəree/ *n.* (*pl.* **Aylesburys**) **1** a bird of a breed of large white domestic ducks. **2** this breed. [*Aylesbury* in S. England]

Ayr·shire /áirshər, –sheer/ *n.* **1** one of a mainly white breed of dairy cattle. **2** this breed. [name of a former Scottish county]

AZ *abbr.* Arizona (in official postal use).

a·zal·ea /əzáylyə/ *n.* any of various flowering deciduous shrubs of the genus *Rhododendron*, with large pink, purple, white, or yellow flowers. [mod.L f. Gk, fem. of *azaleos* dry (from the dry soil in which it was believed to flourish)]

a·ze·o·trope /əzeeətrŏp, áyzee–/ *n. Chem.* a mixture of liquids in which the boiling point remains constant during distillation at a given pressure, without change in composition. □□ **a·ze·o·trop·ic** /əzeeətrópik/ *adj.* [A-[1] + Gk *zeō* boil + *tropos* turning]

az·ide /áyzīd/ *n. Chem.* any compound containing the radical N[3].

A·zil·ian /əzíleeən/ *n. & adj. Archaeol.* ● *n.* the transitional culture between the Paleolithic and neolithic ages in Europe. ● *adj.* of or relating to this culture. [Mas d'*Azil* in the French Pyrenees, where remains of it were found]

az·i·muth /áziməth/ *n.* **1** the angular distance from a north or south point of the horizon to the intersection with the horizon of a vertical circle passing through a given celestial body. **2** the horizontal angle or direction of a compass bearing. □□ **az·i·muth·al** /–múthəl/ *adj.* [ME f. OF *azimut* f. Arab. *as-sumūt* f. *al* the + *sumūt* pl. of *samt* way, direction]

az·ine /ázeen, áy–/ *n. Chem.* any organic compound with two or more nitrogen atoms in a six atom ring. [AZO- + –INE[4]]

azo- /ázŏ, áy–/ *prefix Chem.* containing two adjacent nitrogen atoms between carbon atoms. [F *azote* nitrogen f. Gk *azōos* without life]

a·zo·ic /ayzóik/ *adj.* **1** having no trace of life. **2** *Geol.* (of an age, etc.) having left no organic remains. [Gk *azōos* without life]

AZT *n.* a drug used against the AIDS virus. [chem. name *azidothymidine*]

Az·tec /áztek/ *n. & adj.* ● *n.* **1** a member of the native people dominant in Mexico before the Spanish conquest of the 16th century. **2** the language of the Aztecs. ● *adj.* of the Aztecs or their language (see also NAHUATL). [F *Aztèque* or Sp. *Azteca* f. Nahuatl *aztecatl* men of the north]

a·zu·ki var. of ADZUKI.

az·ure /ázhər/ *n. & adj.* ● *n.* **1 a** a deep sky-blue color. **b** *Heraldry* blue. **2** *poet.* the clear sky. ● *adj.* **1 a** of the color azure. **b** *Heraldry* blue. **2** serene; untroubled. [ME f. OF *asur, azur,* f. med.L *azzurum, azolum* f. Arab. *al* the + *lāzaward* f. Pers. *lāžward* lapis lazuli]

az·y·gous /ayzígəs/ *adj. & n. Anat.* ● *adj.* (of any organic structure) single; not existing in pairs. ● *n.* an organic structure occurring singly. [Gk *azugos* unyoked f. a- not + *zugon* yoke]

B

B¹ /bee/ *n.* (also **b**) (*pl.* **Bs** or **B's**) **1** the second letter of the alphabet. **2** *Mus.* the seventh note of the diatonic scale of C major. **3** the second hypothetical person or example. **4** the second highest class or category (of roads, academic marks, etc.). **5** *Algebra* (usu. **b**) the second known quantity. **6** a human blood type of the ABO system.

B² *symb.* **1** *Chem.* the element boron. **2** *Physics* magnetic flux density.

B³ *abbr.* (also **B.**) **1** Bachelor. **2** bel(s). **3** bishop. **4** black (pencil lead). **5** Blessed. **6** *Baseball* base; baseman.

b *symb. Physics* barn.

b. *abbr.* **1** born. **2** billion.

BA *abbr.* **1** Bachelor of Arts. **2** British Academy. **3** British Airways. **4** batting average.

Ba *symb. Chem.* the element barium.

BAA *abbr.* Bachelor of Applied Arts.

baa /baa/ *v. & n.* ● *v.intr.* (**baas, baaed** or **baa'd**) (esp. of a sheep) bleat. ● *n.* (*pl.* **baas**) the cry of a sheep or lamb. [imit.]

baas /baas/ *n. S.Afr.* boss; master (often as a form of address). [Du.: cf. BOSS¹]

ba·ba /baabaa/ *n.* (in full **baba au rhum** /ō rúm/) a small rich sponge cake, usu. soaked in rum syrup. [F f. Pol.]

ba·ba·coo·te /baábəkoֿot/ *n.* = INDRI. [Malagasy *babakoto*]

Bab·bitt¹ /bábit/ *n.* (also **bab·bitt**) **1** (in full **Babbitt metal**) any of a group of soft alloys of tin, antimony, copper, and usu. lead, used for lining bearings, etc., to diminish friction. **2** (**babbitt**) a bearing lining made of this. [I. *Babbitt*, Amer. inventor d. 1862]

Bab·bitt² /bábit/ *n.* a materialistic, complacent businessman. □□ **Bab·bitt·ry** *n.* [George *Babbitt*, a character in the novel *Babbitt* (1922) by S. Lewis]

bab·ble /bábəl/ *v. & n.* ● *v.* **1** *intr.* **a** talk in an inarticulate or incoherent manner. **b** chatter excessively or irrelevantly. **c** (of a stream, etc.) murmur; trickle. **2** *tr.* repeat foolishly; divulge through chatter. ● *n.* **1 a** incoherent speech. **b** foolish, idle, or childish talk. **2** the murmur of voices, water, etc. **3** *Teleph.* background disturbance caused by interference from conversations on other lines. □□ **bab·ble·ment** *n.* [ME f. MLG *babbelen*, or imit.]

bab·bler /báblər/ *n.* **1** a chatterer. **2** a person who reveals secrets. **3** any of a large group of passerine birds with loud chattering voices.

babe /bayb/ *n.* **1** esp. *literary* a baby. **2** an innocent or helpless person (*babes in the wood*). **3** sometimes *derog. sl.* a young woman (often as a form of address). [ME: imit. of child's *ba, ba*]

ba·bel /báybəl, báb–/ *n.* **1** a confused noise, esp. of voices. **2** a noisy assembly. **3** a scene of confusion. [ME f. Heb. *Bābel* Babylon f. Akkad. *bab ili* gate of god (with ref. to the biblical account of the tower that was built to reach heaven but ended in chaos when God confused the builders' speech: see Gen. 11)]

Bab·ist /bábis/ *n.* a member of a Persian eclectic sect founded in 1844 whose doctrine includes Muslim, Christian, Jewish, and Zoroastrian elements. □□ **Bab·ism** *n.* [Pers. *Bab*-ed-Din, gate (= intermediary) of the Faith]

ba·boon /baboֿon/ *n.* **1** any of various large Old World monkeys of the genus *Papio*, having a long doglike snout, large teeth, and naked callosities on the buttocks. **2** an ugly or uncouth person. [ME f. OF *babuin* or med.L *babewynus*, of unkn. orig.]

ba·bu /baaboֿo/ *n.* (also **ba·boo**) *Ind.* **1** a title of respect, esp. to Hindus. **2** *derog.* formerly, an English-writing Indian clerk. [Hindi *bābū*]

ba·bush·ka /bəboֿoshkə/ *n.* **1** a headscarf tied under the chin. **2** an elderly or grandmotherly Russian woman. [Russ., = grandmother]

ba·by /báybee/ *n. & v.* ● *n.* (*pl.* **-bies**) **1** a very young child or infant, esp. one not yet able to walk. **2** an unduly childish person (*is a baby about injections*). **3** the youngest member of a family, team, etc. **4** (often *attrib.*) **a** a young or newly born animal. **b** a thing that is small of its kind (*baby car; baby rose*). **5** *sl.* a young woman; a sweetheart (often as a form of address). **6** *sl.* a person or thing regarded with affection or familiarity. **7** one's own responsibility, invention, concern, achievement, etc., regarded in a personal way. ● *v.tr.* (**-bies, -bied**) **1** treat like a baby. **2** pamper. ● **carry** (or **hold**) **the baby** bear unwelcome responsibility. **throw out the baby with the bath water** reject the essential with the inessential. □□ **ba·by·hood** *n.* [ME, formed as BABE, –Y²]

ba·by boom *n. colloq.* a temporary marked increase in the birthrate.

ba·by boom·er *n.* a person born during a baby boom, esp. the one after World War II.

ba·by car·riage *n.* a four-wheeled carriage for a baby, pushed by a person on foot.

ba·by grand *n.* the smallest size of grand piano.

Ba·by·gro /báybeegrō/ *n.* (*pl.* **-gros**) *Brit. Trademark* a kind of all-in-one stretch garment for babies. [BABY + GROW]

ba·by·ish /báybeeish/ *adj.* **1** childish; simple. **2** immature. □□ **ba·by·ish·ly** *adv.*

Bab·y·lo·ni·an /bábilóneeən/ *n. & adj.* ● *n.* an inhabitant of Babylon, an ancient city and kingdom in Mesopotamia. ● *adj.* of or relating to Babylon. [L *Babylonius* f. Gk *Babulonios* f. *Babulon* f. Heb. *Bābel*]

ba·by·sit /báybee-sit/ *v.* look after a child or children while the parents are out. □□ **ba·by·sit·ter** *n.*

ba·by talk *n.* childish talk used by or to young children.

Ba·car·di /bəkaárdee/ *n.* (*pl.* **Ba·car·dis**) *Trademark* a West Indian rum produced orig. in Cuba. [name of the company producing it]

bac·ca·lau·re·ate /bákələáwreeət/ *n.* **1** the college or university degree of bachelor. **2** an examination intended to qualify successful candidates for higher education. **3** a religious service held for a graduating class. [F *baccalauréat* or med.L *baccalaureatus* f. *baccalaureus* bachelor]

bac·ca·rat /baakəraá, bá–/ *n.* a gambling card game played against the dealer. [F]

bac·cate /bákayt/ *adj. Bot.* **1** bearing berries. **2** of or like a berry. [L *baccatus* berried f. *bacca* berry]

bac·cha·nal /bákənál, bákənəl/ *n. & adj.* ● *n.* **1** a wild and drunken revelry. **2** a drunken reveler. **3** a priest, worshiper, or follower of Bacchus. ● *adj.* **1** of or like Bacchus, the Greek or Roman god of wine, or his rites. **2** riotous; roistering. [L *bacchanalis* f. *Bacchus* god of wine f. Gk *Bakkhos*]

Bac·cha·na·li·a /bákənáylyə/ *n.pl.* **1** the Roman festival of Bacchus. **2** (**bacchanalia**) a drunken revelry. □□ **Bac·cha·na·li·an** *adj. & n.* [L, neut. pl. of *bacchanalis*: see BACCHANAL]

bac·chant /bəkánt, –kaánt, bákənt/ *n. & adj.* ● *n.* (*pl.* **bac·chants** or **bac·chan·tes** /bəkánteez/; *fem.* **bac·chan·te** /bəkántee, –kaánt–/) **1** a priest, worshiper, or follower of Bacchus. **2** a drunken reveler. ● *adj.* **1** of or like Bacchus or his rites. **2** riotous; roistering. □□ **bac·chan·tic** *adj.* [F *bacchante* f. L *bacchari* celebrate Bacchanal rites]

Bac·chic /bákik/ *adj.* = BACCHANAL *adj.* [L *bacchicus* f. Gk *bakkhikos* of Bacchus]

bac·cy /bákee/ *n.* (*pl.* **-cies**) *Brit. colloq.* tobacco. [abbr.]

bach·e·lor /báchələr, báchlər/ *n.* **1** an unmarried man. **2** a man or woman who has taken the degree of Bachelor of Arts or Science, etc. **3** *hist.* a young knight serving under another's banner. □□ **bach·e·lor·hood** *n.* **bach·e·lor·ship** *n.* [ME & OF *bacheler* aspirant to knighthood, of uncert. orig.]

bach·e·lor girl *n.* an independent unmarried young woman.

bach·e·lor's but·tons *n.* any of various ornamental plants which bear small, round flowerheads, esp. the cornflower.

bac·il·lar·y /básəleree, bəsíləree/ *adj.* relating to or caused by bacilli.

ba·cil·li·form /bəsílifawrm/ *adj.* rod-shaped.

ba·cil·lus /bəsíləs/ *n.* (*pl.* **ba·cil·li** /–lī/) **1** any rod-shaped bacterium. **2** (usu. in *pl.*) any pathogenic bacterium. [LL, dimin. of L *baculus* stick]

back /bak/ *n., adv., v., & adj.* ● *n.* **1 a** the rear surface of the human body from the shoulders to the hips. **b** the corresponding upper surface of an animal's body. **c** the spine (*fell and broke his back*). **d** the keel of a ship. **2** any surface regarded as corresponding to the human back, e.g., of the head or hand, or of a chair. **b** the part of a garment that covers the back. **3 a** the less active or visible or important part of something functional, e.g., of a knife or a piece of paper (*write it on the back*). **b** the side or part normally away from the spectator or the direction of motion or attention, e.g., of a car, house, or room (*stood at the back*). **4 a** a defensive player in some games. **b** this position. ● *adv.* **1** to the rear; away from what is considered to be the front (*go back a little; ran off without looking back*). **2 a** in or into an earlier or normal position or condition (*came back late; went back home; ran back to the car; put it back on the shelf*). **b** in return (*pay back*). **3** in or into the past (*back in June; three years back*). **4** at a distance (*stand back from the road*). **5** in check (*hold him back*). **6** (foll. by *of*) behind (*was back of the house*). ● *v.* **1** *tr.* a help with moral or financial support. **b** bet on the success of (a horse, etc.). **2** *tr. & intr.* move, or cause (a vehicle, etc.) to move, backward. **3** *tr.* **a** put or serve as a back, background, or support to. **b** *Mus.* accompany. **4** *tr.* lie at the back of (*a beach backed by steep cliffs*). **5** *intr.* (of the wind) move around to a counterclockwise direction. ●*adj.* **1** situated behind, esp. as remote or subsidiary (*back street; back teeth; back entrance*). **2** of or relating to the past; not current (*back pay; back issue*). **3** reversed (*back flow*). □ **at a person's back** in pursuit or support. **at the back of one's mind** remembered but not consciously thought of. **back and forth** to and fro. **back down** withdraw one's claim or point of view, etc.; concede defeat in an argument, etc. **back off 1** draw back; retreat. **2** abandon one's intention, stand, etc. **back on to** have its back adjacent to (*the house backs on to a field*). **back out** (often foll. by *of*) withdraw from a commitment. **back up 1** give (esp. moral) support to. **2** *Computing* make a spare copy of (data, a disk, etc.). **3** (of running water) accumulate behind an obstruction. **4** reverse (a vehicle) into a desired position. **5** form a line or mass of vehicles, etc., esp. in congested traffic. **back water** reverse a boat's forward motion using oars. **get** (or **put**) **a person's back up** annoy or anger a person. **get off a person's back** stop troubling a person. **go back on** fail to honor (a promise or commitment). **know like the back of one's hand** be entirely familiar with. **on one's back** injured or ill in bed. **on the back burner** see BURNER. **put one's back into** approach (a task, etc.) with vigor. **see the back of** see SEE[1]. **turn one's back on 1** abandon. **2** disregard; ignore. **with one's back to** (or **up against) the wall** in a desperate situation; hard-pressed. □□ **back•er** *n.* (in sense 1 of *v.*). **back•less** *adj.* [OE *bæc* f. Gmc]

back•ache /bákayk/ *n.* a (usu. prolonged) pain in one's back.
back•bite /bákbīt/ *v.tr.* slander; speak badly of. □□ **back•bit•er** *n.*
back•blocks /bákbloks/ *n.pl. Austral. & NZ* land in the remote and sparsely inhabited interior. □□ **back•block•er** *n.*
back•board /bákbawrd/ *n.* **1 a** a board worn to support or straighten the back. **2 a** a board placed at or forming the back of anything. **b** *Basketball* the board behind the basket.
back•bone /bákbōn/ *n.* **1** the spine. **2** the main support of a structure. **3** firmness of character. **4** the spine of a book.
back•break•ing /bákbrayking/ *adj.* (esp. of manual work) extremely hard.
back•chat /bákchat/ *n. Brit.* = BACK TALK.
back•cloth /bák-klawth, -kloth/ *n. Brit.* = BACKDROP.
back•coun•try /bák-kuntree/ *n.* an area away from settled districts.
back•crawl /bák-krawl/ *n.*
back•cross /bák-kraws/ *v. & n. Biol.* ●*v.tr.* cross a hybrid with one of its parents. ●*n.* an instance or the product of this.
back•date /bákdáyt/ *v.tr.* **1** put an earlier date on (an agreement, etc.) than the actual one. **2** *Brit.* make retrospectively valid.
back•door /bákdáwr/ *adj.* (of an activity) clandestine; underhand (*backdoor deal*).
back door *n.* a secret or ingenious means of gaining an objective.
back•drop /bákdrop/ *n. Theatr.* a painted cloth at the back of the stage as a main part of the scenery.
back•fill /bákfil/ *v.tr. & intr.* refill an excavated hole with the material dug out of it.
back•fire /bákfīr/ *v. & n.* ●*v.intr.* **1** undergo a mistimed explosion in the cylinder or exhaust of an internal combustion engine. **2** (of a plan, etc.) rebound adversely on the originator; have the opposite effect to what was intended. ●*n.* an instance of backfiring.
back•for•ma•tion /bák-fawrmáyshən/ *n.* **1** the formation of a word from its seeming derivative (e.g., *laze* from *lazy*). **2** a word formed in this way.
back•gam•mon /bákgámən/ *n.* **1** a game for two played on a board with pieces moved according to throws of the dice. **2** the most complete form of win in this. [BACK + GAMMON[2]]

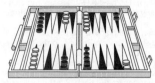

backgammon board

back•ground /bákgrownd/ *n.* **1** part of a scene, picture, or description that serves as a setting to the chief figures or objects and foreground. **2** an inconspicuous or obscure position (*kept in the background*). **3 a** person's education, knowledge, or social circumstances. **4** explanatory or contributory information or circumstances. **5** *Physics* low intensity ambient radiation from radioisotopes present in the natural environment. **6** *Electronics* unwanted signals, such as noise in the reception or recording of sound.
back•ground mu•sic *n.* music intended as an unobtrusive accompaniment to some activity, or to provide atmosphere in a movie, etc.
back•hand /bák-hand/ *n. Tennis*, etc. **1** a stroke played with the back

of the hand turned toward the opponent. **2** (*attrib.*) of or made with a backhand (*backhand volley*).
back•hand•ed /bák-hándid/ *adj.* **1** (of a blow, etc.) delivered with the back of the hand, or in a direction opposite to the usual one. **2** indirect; ambiguous (*a backhanded compliment*). **3** = BACKHAND *attrib.*
back•hand•er /bák-hándər/ *n.* **1 a** a backhand stroke. **b** a backhanded blow. **2** *colloq.* an indirect attack. **3** *Brit. sl.* a bribe.
back•ing /báking/ *n.* **1 a** a support. **b** a body of supporters. **c** material used to form a back or support. **2** musical accompaniment, esp. to a singer; backup.
back•lash /báklash/ *n.* **1** an excessive or marked adverse reaction. **2 a** a sudden recoil or reaction between parts of a mechanism. **b** excessive play between such parts.
back•list /báklist/ *n.* a publisher's list of books published before the current season and still in print.
back•lit /báklit/ *adj.* (esp. in photography) illuminated from behind.
back•log /báklawg, -lóg/ *n.* **1** accumulation of uncompleted work, etc. **2** a reserve; reserves (*a backlog of goodwill*).
back•mark•er /bákmaarkər/ *n. Brit.* a competitor who has the least favorable handicap in a race, etc.
back•most /bákmōst/ *adj.* furthest back.
back num•ber *n.* **1** an issue of a periodical earlier than the current one. **2** *sl.* an out-of-date person or thing.
back of be•yond *n.* a very remote or inaccessible place.
back•pack /bákpak/ *n. & v.* ●*n.* a bag slung by straps from both shoulders and resting on the back. ●*v.intr.* travel or hike with a backpack. □□ **back•pack•er** *n.*
back•ped•al /bákped'l/ *v.* (**•ped•aled, •ped•al•ing**) **1** pedal backward on a bicycle, etc. **2** reverse one's previous action or opinion.
back pro•jec•tion *n.* the projection of a picture from behind a translucent screen for viewing or filming.
back•rest /bákrest/ *n.* a support for the back.
back room *n.* (often, with hyphen, *attrib.*) a place where secret work is done.
back•scat•ter /bákskatər/ *n.* the scattering of radiation in a reverse direction.
back•scratch•er /bákskrachər/ *n.* **1** a rod terminating in a clawed hand for scratching one's own back. **2** a person who performs mutual services with another for gain.
back•seat /bákseet/ *n.* **1** a seat in the rear. **2** an inferior position or status.
back•seat driv•er *n.* a person who is eager to advise without responsibility (orig. of a passenger in a car, etc.).
back•sheesh var. of BAKSHEESH.
back•side /báksíd/ *n. colloq.* the buttocks.
back•sight /báksīt/ *n.* **1** the sight of a rifle, etc., that is nearer the stock. **2** *Surveying* a sight or reading taken backward or toward the point of starting.
back slang *n.* slang using words spelled backward (e.g., *yob*).
back•slap•ping /bákslaping/ *adj.* vigorously hearty.
back•slash /bákslash/ *n.* a backward-sloping diagonal line; a reverse slash (\).
back•slide /bákslīd/ *v.intr.* (*past* **•slid** /-slid/; *past part.* **•slid** or **•slid•den** /-slid'n/) relapse into bad ways or error. □□ **back•slid•er** *n.*
back•space /bákspays/ *v.intr.* move a typewriter carriage, computer cursor, etc., back one or more spaces.
back•spin /bákspin/ *n.* a backward spin imparted to a ball causing it to fly off at an angle on hitting a surface.
back•stage /bákstáyj/ *adv. & adj.* ●*adv.* **1** *Theatr.* out of view of the audience, esp. in the wings or dressing rooms. **2** not known to the public. ●*adj.* that is backstage; concealed.
back•stairs /bákstairz/ *n.pl.* **1** stairs at the back or side of a building. **2** (also **back•stair**) (*attrib.*) denoting underhand or clandestine activity.
back•stay /bákstay/ *n.* a rope, etc., leading downward and aft from the top of a mast.
back•stitch /bákstich/ *n. & v.* ●*n.* a stitch bringing the thread back to the preceding stitch. ●*v.tr. & intr.* sew using backstitch.
back•stop /bákstaap/ *n.* **1** *Baseball.* a fence or screen positioned behind home plate. **2** something that provides support or reinforcement.
back•street *n. & adj.* ●*n.* a street in a quiet part of a town, away from the main streets. ●*adj.* denoting illicit, secretive, or illegal activity (*a backstreet drug deal*).
back•stroke /bákstrōk/ *n.* a swimming stroke performed on the back with the arms lifted alternately out of the water in a backward circular motion and the legs extended in a kicking action.
back talk *n. colloq.* rude or impertinent remarks made in reply to someone in authority.
back to back *adv.* with backs adjacent and opposite each other (*we stood back to back*). □□ **back-to-back** *adj.*
back to front *adv.* **1** with the back at the front and the front at the back. **2** in disorder.
back-to-na•ture *adj.* (usu. *attrib.*) applied to a movement or enthusiast for the reversion to a simpler way of life.

back•track /báktrak/ *v.intr.* **1** retrace one's steps. **2** reverse one's previous action or opinion.

back•up /bákup/ *n.* **1** moral or technical support (*called for extra backup*). **2** a reserve. **3** *Computing* (often *attrib.*) **a** the procedure for making security copies of data (*backup facilities*). **b** the copy itself (*made a backup*). **4** a line or mass of vehicles, etc., esp. in congested traffic. **5** musical accompaniment.

back•up light *n.* a white light at the rear of a vehicle operated when the vehicle is in reverse gear.

back•veld /bákvelt/ *n. S.Afr.* remote country districts, esp. those strongly conservative. □□ **back•veld•er** *n.*

back•ward /bákwərd/ *adv. & adj.* • *adv.* (also **back•wards**) **1** away from one's front (*lean backward; look backward*). **2 a** with the back foremost (*walk backward*). **b** in reverse of the usual way (*count backward; spell backward*). **3 a** into a worse state (*new policies are taking us backward*). **b** into the past (*looked backward over the years*). **c** (of a thing's motion) back toward the starting point (*rolled backward*). • *adj.* **1** directed to the rear or starting point (*a backward look*). **2** reversed. **3 a** mentally retarded or slow. **b** slow to progress; late. **4** reluctant; shy; unassertive. □ **backward and forward** in both directions alternately; to and fro. **bend** (or **fall** or **lean**) **over backward** (often foll. by *to* + infin.) *colloq.* make every effort, esp. to be fair or helpful. **know backward and forward** be entirely familiar with. □□ **back•ward•ness** *n.* [earlier *abackward*, assoc. with BACK]

back•wash /bákwosh, –wawsh/ *n.* **1 a** receding waves created by the motion of a ship, etc. **b** a backward current of air created by a moving aircraft. **2** repercussions.

back•wa•ter /bákwawtər, –wotər/ *n.* **1** a place or condition remote from the center of activity or thought. **2** stagnant water or water not fed by a main current.

back•woods /bákwŏŏdz/ *n.pl.* **1** remote uncleared forest land. **2** any remote or sparsely inhabited region.

back•woods•man /bakwŏŏdzmən/ *n.* (*pl.* **•men**) **1** an inhabitant of backwoods. **2** an uncouth person.

back•yard /bakyaárd/ *n.* a yard at the back of a house, etc. □ **in one's own backyard** *colloq.* near at hand.

ba•cla•va var. of BAKLAVA.

ba•con /báykən/ *n.* cured meat from the back or sides of a pig. □ **bring home the bacon** *colloq.* **1** succeed in one's undertaking. **2** supply material provision or support. [ME f. OF f. Frank. *bako* = OHG *bahho* ham, flitch]

Ba•co•ni•an /baykóneeən/ *adj. & n.* • *adj.* of or relating to the English philosopher Sir Francis Bacon (d. 1626), or to his inductive method of reasoning and philosophy. • *n.* **1** a supporter of the view that Bacon was the author of Shakespeare's plays. **2** a follower of Bacon.

bac•te•ri•a *pl.* of BACTERIUM.

bac•te•ri•cide /baktéerisíd/ *n.* a substance capable of destroying bacteria. □□ **bac•te•ri•cid•al** /–risíd'l/ *adj.*

bac•te•ri•ol•o•gy /bákteereeóləjee/ *n.* the study of bacteria. □□ **bac•te•ri•o•log•i•cal** /–reeəlójikəl/ *adj.* **bac•te•ri•o•log•i•cal•ly** *adv.* **bac•te•ri•o•gist** /–óləjist/ *n.*

bac•te•ri•ol•y•sis /bakteereeólisis/ *n.* the rupture or destruction of bacterial cells.

bac•te•ri•o•lyt•ic /bakteereeəlítik/ *adj.* capable of rupturing bacteria.

bac•te•ri•o•phage /bakteereeəfayj/ *n.* a virus parasitic on a bacterium. [BACTERIUM + Gk *phagein* eat]

bac•te•ri•o•sta•sis /bakteereeóstáysis/ *n.* the inhibition of the growth of bacteria without destroying them. □□ **bac•te•ri•o•stat•ic** /–státik/ *adj.*

bac•te•ri•um /bakteereeəm/ *n.* (*pl.* **bac•te•ri•a** /–reeə/) a member of a large group of unicellular microorganisms lacking organelles and an organized nucleus, some of which can cause disease. □□ **bac•te•ri•al** *adj.* [mod.L f. Gk *baktērion* dimin. of *baktron* stick]

Bac•tri•an /báktreeən/ *adj.* of or relating to Bactria in central Asia. [L *Bactrianus* f. Gk *Baktrianos*]

Bac•tri•an cam•el *n.* /báktree-ən káməl/ a camel, *Camelus bactrianus*, native to central Asia, with two humps.

bad /bad/ *adj., n., & adv.* • *adj.* (**worse** /wərs/, **worst** /wərst/) **1** inferior; inadequate; defective (*bad work; a bad driver; bad light*). **2 a** unpleasant; unwelcome (*bad weather; bad news*). **b** unsatisfactory; unfortunate (*bad business*). **3** harmful (*is bad for you*). **4 a** (of food) decayed; putrid. **b** polluted (*bad air*). **5** ill; injured (*am feeling bad today; a bad leg*). **6** *colloq.* regretful; guilty; ashamed (*feels bad about it*). **7** (of an unwelcome thing) serious; severe (*a bad headache; a bad mistake*). **8 a** morally unsound or offensive (*a bad man; bad language*). **b** disobedient; badly behaved (*a bad child*). **9** worthless; not valid (*a bad check*).

Bactrian camel

10 (**bad•der**, **bad•dest**) *sl.* good; excellent. • *n.* **1 a** ill fortune (*take the bad with the good*). **b** ruin; a degenerate condition (*go to the bad*). **2** the debit side of an account (*$500 to the bad*). **3** (as *pl.*; prec. by *the*) bad or wicked people. • *adv. colloq.* badly (*took it bad*). □ **from bad to worse** into an even worse state. **in a bad way** ill; in trouble (*looked in a bad way*). **not** (or **not so**) **bad** *colloq.* fairly good. **too bad** *colloq.* (of circumstances, etc.) regrettable but now beyond retrieval. □□ **bad•dish** *adj.* **bad•ness** *n.* [ME, perh. f. OE *bæddel* hermaphrodite, womanish man: for loss of *l* cf. MUCH, WENCH]
▶Confusion in the use of **bad** and **good** vs. **badly** and **well** usually has to do with verbs called copulas, such as **feel** or **seem**: Thus, standard usage calls for *I feel bad* and *I feel well*, but *I feel badly*, to a precise speaker or writer, means 'I do not have a good sense of touch.' See note at GOOD.

bad blood *n.* ill feeling.

bad break *n. colloq.* **1** a piece of bad luck. **2** a mistake or blunder.

bad breath *n.* unpleasant smelling breath.

bad debt *n.* a debt that is not recoverable.

bad•die /bádee/ *n.* (also **bad•dy**) (*pl.* **•dies**) *colloq.* a villain or criminal, esp. in a story, movie, etc.

bade see BID.

bad egg *n.* an unreliable or dishonest person.

bad faith *n.* insincerity or dishonesty, intent to deceive.

bad form *n.* an offense against current social conventions.

badge /baj/ *n.* **1** a distinctive emblem worn as a mark of office, membership, achievement, licensed employment, etc. **2** any feature or sign which reveals a characteristic condition or quality. [ME: orig. unkn.]

badg•er /bájər/ *n. & v.* • *n.* **1** an omnivorous gray-coated nocturnal mammal of the family Mustelidae with a white stripe flanked by black stripes on its head, which lives in sets. **2** a fishing fly, brush, etc., made of its hair. • *v.tr.* pester; harass; tease. [16th c.: perh. f. BADGE, with ref. to its white forehead mark]

badger

bad•i•nage /bád'naázh/ *n.* humorous or playful ridicule. [F f. *badiner* to joke]

bad•lands /bádlandz/ *n.* extensive uncultivable eroded tracts in arid areas. [transl. F *mauvaises terres*]

bad lot *n.* a person of bad character.

bad•ly /bádlee/ *adv.* (**worse** /wərs/; **worst** /wərst/) **1** in a bad manner (*works badly*). **2** *colloq.* very much (*wants it badly*). **3** severely (*was badly defeated*).

bad•min•ton /bádmint'n/ *n.* **1** a game with rackets in which a shuttlecock is volleyed back and forth across a net. **2** *Brit.* a summer drink of claret, soda, and sugar. [*Badminton* in S. England]

SPELLING TIP   **badminton**

Remember the *t* in this word with the mnemonic, "Your racket must be in *mint* condition to play *badminton*."

---

bad-mouth *v.tr.* subject to malicious gossip or criticism.

bad news *n. colloq.* an unpleasant or troublesome person or thing.

bad-tem•pered /bádtémpərd/ *adj.* having a bad temper; irritable; easily annoyed. □□ **bad-tem•pered•ly** *adv.*

Bae•de•ker /báydikər/ *n.* any of various travel guidebooks published by the firm founded by the German Karl *Baedeker* (d. 1859).

baf•fle /báfəl/ *v. & n.* • *v.tr.* **1** confuse or perplex (a person, one's faculties, etc.). **2 a** frustrate or hinder (plans, etc.). **b** restrain or regulate the progress of (fluids, sounds, etc.). • *n.* (also **baf•fle-board**, **baf•fle-plate**) a device used to restrain or deflect the flow of fluid, gas, sound, etc., often found in microphones, loudspeakers, etc., to regulate spreading or the emission of sound. □□ **baf•fle•ment** *n.* **baf•fling** *adj.* **baf•fling•ly** *adv.* [perh. rel. to F *bafouer* ridicule, OF *beffer* mock]

baf•fler /báflər/ *n.* = BAFFLE *n.*

bag /bag/ *n. & v.* • *n.* **1** a receptacle of flexible material with an opening at the top. **2 a** (usu. in *pl.*) a piece of luggage (*put the bags in the trunk*). **b** a woman's handbag. **3** (in *pl.*; usu. foll. by *of*) *colloq.* a large amount; plenty (*bags of money*). **4** (in *pl.*) *Brit. colloq.* trousers. **5** *sl. derog.* a woman, esp. regarded as unattractive or unpleasant. **6** an animal's sac containing poison, honey, etc. **7** an amount of game shot or allowed. **8** (usu. in *pl.*) baggy folds of skin under the eyes. **9** *sl.* a person's particular interest or preoccupation (*his bag is baroque music*). • *v.* (**bagged**, **bag•ging**) **1** *tr.* put in a bag. **2** *colloq. tr.* **a** secure; get hold of (*bagged the best seat*). **b** *colloq.* steal. **c** shoot (game). **d** (often in phr. **bags I**) *Brit. colloq.* claim on grounds of being the first to do so (*bagged first go; bags I go first*). **3** *a intr.* hang loosely; bulge; swell. **b** *tr.* cause to do this. **4** *tr. Austral. sl.* criticize; disparage. □ **bag and baggage** with all one's belongings. **bag** (or **whole bag**) **of tricks** *colloq.* everything; the whole lot. **in the bag** *colloq.* achieved; as good as secured. □□ **bagful** *n.* (*pl.* **-fuls**). [ME, perh. f. ON *baggi*]

ba·gasse /bəgás/ *n.* the dry pulpy residue left after the extraction of juice from sugar cane, usable as fuel or to make paper, etc. [F f. Sp. *bagazo*]

bag·a·telle /bágətél/ *n.* **1** a game in which small balls are struck into numbered holes on a board, with pins as obstructions. **2** a mere trifle; a negligible amount. **3** *Mus.* a short piece of music, esp. for the piano. [F f. It. *bagatella* dimin., perh. f. *baga* BAGGAGE]

ba·gel /báygəl/ *n.* a hard bread roll in the shape of a ring. [Yiddish *beygel*]

bag·gage /bágij/ *n.* **1** everyday belongings packed up in suitcases, etc., for traveling; luggage. **2** the portable equipment of an army. [ME f. OF *bagage* f. *baguer* tie up or *bagues* bundles: perh. rel. to BAG]

bag·gage car *n.* a car on a passenger train used for luggage, etc.

bag·gy /bágee/ *adj.* (**bag·gi·er, bag·gi·est**) **1** hanging in loose folds. **2** puffed out. □□ **bag·gi·ly** *adv.* **bag·gi·ness** *n.*

bag la·dy *n.* a homeless woman who carries her possessions around in shopping bags.

bag·man /bágmən/ *n.* (*pl.* **-men**) **1** *sl.* an agent who collects or distributes illicitly gained money. **2** *Brit. sl.* a traveling salesman. **3** *Austral.* a tramp.

bagn·io /baányō/ *n.* (*pl.* **-os**) **1** a brothel. **2** *hist.* a prison in the Orient. [It. *bagno* f. L *balneum* bath]

bag·pipe /bágpīp/ *n.* (usu. in *pl.*) a musical instrument consisting of a windbag connected to two kinds of reeded pipes: drone pipes which produce single sustained notes and a fingered melody pipe or 'chanter'. □□ **bag·pip·er** *n.*

ba·guette /bagét/ *n.* **1** a long narrow French loaf. **2** a gem cut in a long rectangular shape. **3** *Archit.* a small molding, semicircular in section. [F f. It. *bacchetto* dimin. of *bacchio* f. L *baculum* staff]

bah /baa/ *int.* an expression of contempt or disbelief. [prob. F]

Ba·ha'i /bəhaá-ee, –hí/ *n.* (*pl.* **Ba·ha'is**) a member of a monotheistic religion founded in 1863 as a branch of Babism (see BABIST), emphasizing religious unity and world peace. □□ **Ba·ha'ism** *n.* [Pers. *bahá* splendor]

bagpipes

Ba·ha·mi·an /bəháymeeən, –haá–/ *n. & adj.* • *n.* **1** a native or inhabitant of the Bahamas in the W. Indies. **2** a person of Bahamian descent. • *adj.* of or relating to the Bahamas.

Ba·ha·sa In·do·ne·sia /baaháasə índəneézhə/ *n.* the official language of Indonesia. [Indonesian *bahasa* language f. Skr. *bhāṣā* f. *bhāṣate* he speaks: see INDONESIAN]

bail[1] /bayl/ *n. & v.* • *n.* **1** money, etc., required as security for the temporary release of a prisoner pending trial. **2** a person or persons giving such security. • *v.tr.* (usu. foll. by *out*) **1** release or secure the release of (a prisoner) on payment of bail. **2** release from a difficulty; come to the rescue of. □ **forfeit** (*colloq.* **jump**) **bail** fail to appear for trial after being released on bail. **go** (or **stand**) **bail** (often foll. by *for*) act as or provide surety (for an accused person). □□ **bail·a·ble** *adj.* [ME f. OF *bail* custody, *bailler* take charge of, f. L *bajulare* bear a burden]

bail[2] /bayl/ *n. & v.* • *n.* **1** the bar on a typewriter holding the paper against the platen. **2** *Cricket* either of the two crosspieces bridging the stumps. **3** an arched usu. wire handle, as of a pail. **4** a bar separating horses in an open stable. **5** *Austral. & NZ* a framework for securing the head of a cow during milking. • *v.tr. Austral. & NZ* (usu. foll. by *up*) **1** *tr.* secure (a cow) during milking. **2 a** *tr.* make (a person) hold up his or her arms to be robbed. **b** *intr.* surrender by throwing up one's arms. **c** *tr.* buttonhole (a person). [ME f. OF *bail(e)*, perh. f. *bailler* enclose]

bail[3] /bayl/ *v.tr.* **1** (usu. foll. by *out*) scoop water out of (a boat, etc.). **2** scoop (water, etc.) out. □ **bail out** (of a pilot, etc.) make an emergency parachute descent from an aircraft. □□ **bail·er** *n.* [obs. *bail* (n.) bucket. F *baille* ult. f. L *bajulus* carrier]

bail·ee /baylée/ *n. Law* a person or party to whom goods are committed for a purpose, e.g., custody or repair, without transfer of ownership. [BAIL[1] + –EE]

bai·ley /báylee/ *n.* (*pl.* **-leys**) **1** the outer wall of a castle. **2** a court enclosed by it. [ME, var. of BAIL[2]]

Bai·ley bridge /báylee/ *n.* a temporary bridge of lattice steel designed for rapid assembly from prefabricated standard parts, used esp. in military operations. [Sir D. *Bailey* (d. 1985), its designer]

bail·ie /báylee/ *n. esp. hist.* a municipal officer and magistrate in Scotland. [ME, f. OF *bailli(s)* BAILIFF]

bail·iff /báylif/ *n.* **1** an official in a court of law who keeps order, looks after prisoners, etc. **2** esp. *Brit.* a sheriff's officer who executes writs

and processes and carries out distraints and arrests. **3** *Brit.* the agent or steward of a landlord. **4** *Brit.* (*hist.* except in formal titles) the sovereign's representative in a district, esp. the chief officer of a hundred. **5** *Brit.* the first civil officer in the Channel Islands. [ME f. OF *baillif* ult. f. L *bajulus* carrier, manager]

bail·i·wick /báyliwik/ *n.* **1** *Law* the district or jurisdiction of a bailie or bailiff. **2** *joc.* a person's sphere of operations or particular area of interest. [BAILIE + WICK[2]]

bail·ment /báylmənt/ *n.* the act of delivering goods, etc., for a (usu. specified) purpose.

bail·or /báylor/ *n. Law* a person or party that entrusts goods to a bailee. [BAIL[1] + –OR]

bail·out /báylowt/ *n.* a rescue from a dire situation (*a financial bailout for an ailing company*).

bails·man /báylzmən/ *n.* (*pl.* **-men**) a person who stands bail for another. [BAIL[1] + MAN]

bain-ma·rie /báNmareé/ *n.* (*pl.* **bains-ma·rie** *pronunc.* same) **1** a cooking utensil consisting of a vessel of hot water in which a receptacle containing a sauce, etc., can be slowly and gently heated. **2** esp. *Brit.* a double boiler. [F, transl. med.L *balneum Mariae* bath of Maria (an alleged Jewish alchemist)]

bairn /bairn/ *n. Sc. & No. of Engl.* a child. [OE *bearn*]

bait[1] /bayt/ *n. & v.* • *n.* **1** food used to entice a prey, esp. a fish or an animal. **2** an allurement; something intended to tempt or entice. **3** *archaic* a halt on a journey for refreshment or a rest. **4** = BATE[2]. • *v.* **1** *tr.* **a** harass or annoy (a person). **b** torment (a chained animal). **2** *tr.* put bait on (a hook, trap, etc.) to entice a prey. **3** *archaic* **a** *tr.* give food to (horses on a journey). **b** *intr.* stop on a journey to take food or a rest. [ME f. ON *beita* hunt or chase]

bait[2] var. of BATE[2].

baize /bayz/ *n.* a coarse usu. green woolen material resembling felt used as a covering or lining, esp. on the tops of billiard and card tables. [F *baies* (pl.) fem. of *bai* chestnut colored (BAY[4]), treated as sing.: cf. BODICE]

bake /bayk/ *v. & n.* • *v.* **1** *tr.* cook (food) by dry heat in an oven or on a hot surface, without direct exposure to a flame. **b** *intr.* undergo the process of being baked. **2** *intr. colloq.* **a** (usu. as **be baking**) (of weather, etc.) be very hot. **b** (of a person) become hot. **3 a** *tr.* harden (clay, etc.) by heat. **b** *intr.* (of clay, etc.) be hardened by heat. **4 a** *tr.* (of the sun) affect by its heat, e.g., ripen (fruit). **b** *intr.* (e.g., of fruit) be affected by the sun's heat. • *n.* **1** the act or an instance of baking. **2** a batch of baking. **3** a social gathering at which baked food is eaten. [OE *bacan*]

baked A·las·ka *n.* sponge cake and ice cream with a meringue covering browned in an oven.

bake·house /báyk-hows/ *n.* = BAKERY.

Ba·ke·lite /báykəlit, báyklit/ *n. Trademark* any of various thermosetting resins or plastics made from formaldehyde and phenol and used for cables, buttons, plates, etc. [G *Bakelit* f. L.H. *Baekeland* its Belgian-born inventor d. 1944]

bak·er /báykər/ *n.* a person who bakes and sells bread, cakes, etc., esp. professionally. [OE *bæcere*]

bak·er's doz·en *n.* thirteen (so called from the former bakers' custom of adding an extra loaf to a dozen sold; the exact reason for this is unclear).

bak·er·y /báykəree/ *n.* (*pl.* **-ies**) a place where bread and cakes are made or sold.

bak·ing pow·der *n.* a mixture of sodium bicarbonate, cream of tartar, etc., used instead of yeast in baking.

bak·ing so·da *n.* sodium bicarbonate.

ba·kla·va /baáklə́vaá/ *n.* (also **ba·cla·va**) a rich dessert of flaky pastry, honey, and nuts. [Turk.]

bak·sheesh /báksheesh/ *n.* (also **back·sheesh**) (in some eastern countries) a small sum of money given as a gratuity or as alms. [ult. f. Pers. *bakšīš* f. *bakšīdan* give]

bal·a·cla·va /báləklaávə/ *n.* (in full **bala·clava helmet**) a tight woolen garment covering the whole head and neck except for parts of the face, worn orig. by soldiers on active service in the Crimean War. [*Balaclava* in the Crimea, the site of a battle in 1854]

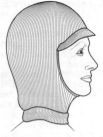

balaclava

bal·a·lai·ka /báləlíkə/ *n.* a guitarlike musical instrument having a triangular body and 2–4 strings, popular in Russia and other Slavic countries. [Russ.]

bal·ance /báləns/ *n. & v.* • *n.* **1** an apparatus for weighing, esp. one with a central pivot, beam, and two scales. **2 a** a counteracting weight or force. **b** (in full **balance wheel**) the regulating device in a clock, etc. **3 a** an

balalaika

even distribution of weight or amount. **b** stability of body or mind (*regained his balance*). **4** a preponderating weight or amount (*the balance of opinion*). **5 a** an agreement between or the difference between credits and debits in an account. **b** the difference between an amount due and an amount paid (*will pay the balance next week*). **c** an amount

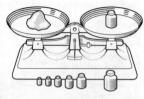

balance (scales)

left over; the rest. **6 a** *Art* harmony of design and proportion. **b** *Mus.* the relative volume of various sources of sound (*bad balance between violins and trumpets*). **c** proportion. **7** (**the Balance**) the zodiacal sign or constellation Libra. ● *v.* **1** *tr.* (foll. by *with*, *against*) offset or compare (one thing) with another (*must balance the advantages with the disadvantages*). **2** *tr.* counteract, equal, or neutralize the weight or importance of. **3 a** *tr.* bring into or keep in equilibrium (*balanced a book on her head*). **b** *intr.* be in equilibrium (*balanced on one leg*). **4** *tr.* (usu. as **balanced** *adj.*) establish equal or appropriate proportions of elements in (*a balanced diet*; *balanced opinion*). **5** *tr.* weigh (arguments, etc.) against each other. **6 a** *tr.* compare and esp. equalize debits and credits of (an account). **b** *intr.* (of an account) have credits and debits equal. □ **in the balance** uncertain; at a critical stage. **on balance** all things considered. **strike a balance** choose a moderate course or compromise. □□ **bal·ance·a·ble** *adj.* **bal·anc·er** *n.* [ME f. OF, ult. f. LL (*libra*) *bilanx bilancis* two-scaled (balance)]

bal·ance of pay·ments *n.* the difference in value between payments into and out of a country.

bal·ance of pow·er *n.* **1** a situation in which the chief nations of the world have roughly equal power. **2** the power held by a small group when larger groups are of equal strength.

bal·ance of trade *n.* the difference in value between imports and exports.

bal·ance sheet *n.* a statement giving the balance of an account.

ba·la·ta /bəlótə/ *n.* **1** any of several latex-yielding trees of Central America, esp. *Manilkara bidentata*. **2** the dried sap of this used as a substitute for gutta-percha. [ult. f. Carib]

bal·brig·gan /balbrígən/ *n.* a knitted cotton fabric used for underwear, etc. [*Balbriggan* in Ireland, where it was orig. made]

bal·co·ny /bálkənee/ *n.* (*pl.* **-nies**) **1 a** a usu. balustraded platform on the outside of a building, with access from an upper floor window or door. **b** such a balustraded platform inside a building; a gallery. **2 a** a tier of seats in a gallery in a theater, etc. **b** the upstairs seats in a movie theater, etc. □□ **bal·co·nied** *adj.* [It. *balcone*]

bald /bawld/ *adj.* **1** (of a person) with the scalp wholly or partly lacking hair. **2** (of an animal, plant, etc.) not covered by the usual hair, feathers, leaves, etc. **3** *colloq.* with the surface worn away (*a bald tire*). **4 a** blunt; unelaborated (*a bald statement*). **b** undisguised (*the bald effrontery*). **5** meager or dull (*a bald style*). **6** marked with white, esp. on the face (*a bald horse*). □□ **bald·ing** *adj.* (in senses 1–3). **bald·ish** *adj.* **bald·ly** *adv.* (in sense 4). **bald·ness** *n.* [ME *ballede*, orig. 'having a white blaze,' prob. f. an OE root *ball-* 'white patch']

bal·da·chin /báwldəkin/ *n.* (also **bal·da·chi·no** /-kéenō/, **bal·da·quin**) **1** a ceremonial canopy over an altar, throne, etc. **2** a rich brocade. [It. *baldacchino* f. *Baldacco* Baghdad, its place of origin]

bald ea·gle *n.* a white-headed eagle (*Haliaeetus leucocephalus*), used as the emblem of the United States.

bal·der·dash /báwldərdash/ *n.* senseless talk or writing; nonsense. [earlier = 'mixture of drinks': orig. unkn.]

bald·head /báwldhed/ *n.* a person with a bald head.

bal·dric /báwldrik/ *n. hist.* a belt for a sword, bugle, etc., hung from the shoulder across the body to the opposite hip. [ME *baudry* f. OF *baudré* cf. MHG *balderich*, of unkn. orig.]

bale[1] /bayl/ *n. & v.* ● *n.* **1** a bundle of merchandise or hay, etc., tightly wrapped and bound with cords or hoops. **2** the quantity in a bale as a measure, esp. 500 lb. of cotton. ● *v.tr.* make up into bales. [ME prob. f. MDu., ult. identical with BALL[1]]

bale[2] /bayl/ *n. archaic* or *poet.* evil; destruction; woe; pain; misery. [OE *b(e)alu*]

ba·leen /bəléen/ *n.* whalebone. [ME f. OF *baleine* f. L *balaena* whale]

ba·leen whale *n.* any of various whales of the suborder Mysticeti, having plates of baleen fringed with bristles for straining plankton from the water.

bale·ful /báylfŏŏl/ *adj.* **1** (esp. of a manner, look, etc.) gloomy; menacing. **2** harmful; malignant; destructive. □□ **bale·ful·ly** *adv.* **bale·ful·ness** *n.* [BALE[2] + -FUL]

bal·er /báylər/ *n.* a machine for making bales of hay, straw, metal, etc.

Ba·li·nese /baalineéz/ *n. & adj.* ● *n.* (*pl.* same) **1** a native of Bali, an island in Indonesia. **2** the language of Bali. ● *adj.* of or relating to Bali or its people or language.

balk /bawk/ *v. & n.* ● *v.* **1** *intr.* **a** refuse to go on. **b** (often foll. by *at*) hesitate. **2** *tr.* **a** thwart; hinder. **b** disappoint. **3** *tr.* **a** miss; let slip

(a chance, etc.). **b** ignore; shirk. ● *n.* **1 a** a hindrance; a stumbling block. **2 a** a roughly-squared timber beam. **b** a tie beam of a house. **3** *Billiards*, etc., the area on a billiard table from which a player begins a game. **4** *Baseball* an illegal action made by a pitcher. **5** a ridge left unplowed between furrows. □□ **balk·er** *n.* [OE *balc* f. ON *bálkr* f. Gmc]

Bal·kan /báwlkən/ *adj. & n.* ● *adj.* **1** of or relating to the region of SE Europe bounded by the Adriatic, the Aegean, and the Black Sea. **2** of or relating to its peoples or countries. ● *n.* (**the Balkans**) the Balkan countries. [Turk.]

balk·y /báwkee/ *adj.* (**balk·i·er**, **balk·i·est**) reluctant; perverse. □□ **balk·i·ness** *n.* [BALK + -Y[1]]

ball[1] /bawl/ *n. & v.* ● *n.* **1 a** a solid or hollow sphere, esp. for use in a game. **b** a game played with such a sphere. **2 a** a ball-shaped object; material forming the shape of a ball (*ball of snow*; *ball of wool*; *rolled himself into a ball*). **b** a rounded part of the body (*ball of the foot*). **3** a solid nonexplosive missile for a cannon, etc. **4** a single delivery of a ball in cricket, etc., or passing of a ball in soccer. **5** *Baseball* a pitched ball that is not swung at by the batter and that does not pass through the strike zone. **6** (in *pl.*) *coarse sl.* **a** the testicles. **b** *Brit.* (usu. as an exclam. of contempt) nonsense; rubbish. **c** *Brit.* = *balls up.* **d** courage; guts. ● *v.* **1** *tr.* squeeze or wind into a ball. **2** *intr.* form or gather into a ball or balls. **3** *tr. & intr. coarse sl.* have sexual intercourse. □ **the ball is in your**, etc., **court** you, etc., must be next to act. **balls** (or **ball**) **up** *Brit. coarse sl.* bungle; make a mess of. **have the ball at one's feet** *Brit.* have one's best opportunity. **keep the ball rolling** maintain the momentum of an activity. **on the ball** *colloq.* alert. **play ball 1** start or continue a ballgame. **2** *colloq.* cooperate. **start**, etc., **the ball rolling** set an activity in motion; make a start. [ME f. ON *böllr* f. Gmc]

▶ Sense 6 of the noun is usually considered a taboo use.

ball[2] /bawl/ *n.* **1** a formal social gathering for dancing. **2** *sl.* an enjoyable time (esp. have a ball). [F *bal* f. LL=20 *ballare* to dance]

bal·lad /báləd/ *n.* **1** a poem or song narrating a popular story. **2** a slow sentimental or romantic song.

WORD HISTORY ballad

Late 15th century (denoting a light, simple song): from Old French *balade*, from Provençal *balada* 'dance, song to dance to,' from *balar* 'to dance,' from late Latin *ballare*, from Greek *ballizein* 'to dance.' The sense 'narrative poem' dates from the mid-18th century.

bal·lade /balaád/ *n.* **1** a poem of one or more triplets of stanzas with a repeated refrain and an envoy. **2** *Mus.* a short lyrical piece, esp. for piano. [earlier spelling and pronunc. of BALLAD]

bal·lad·eer /báladéer/ *n.* a singer or composer of ballads.

bal·lad·ry /bálədree/ *n.* ballad poetry.

bal·lad stan·za *n.* (also **bal·lad meter**) esp. *Brit.* = COMMON MEASURE.

ball-and-sock·et joint *n. Anat.* a joint in which a rounded end lies in a concave cup or socket, allowing freedom of movement.

bal·last /báləst/ *n. & v.* ● *n.* **1** any heavy material placed in a ship or the basket of a balloon, etc., to secure stability. **2** coarse stone, etc., used to form the bed of a railroad track or road. **3** *Electr.* any device used to stabilize the current in a circuit. **4** anything that affords stability or permanence. ● *v.tr.* **1** provide with ballast. **2** afford stability or weight to. [16th c.: f. LG or Scand., of uncert. orig.]

ball bear·ing *n.* **1** a bearing in which the two halves are separated by a ring of small metal balls which reduce friction. **2** one of these balls.

ball·boy /báwlboy/ *n.* (*fem.* **ball·girl** /-gərl/) a boy or girl who retrieves balls that go out of play during a game.

ball cock *n.* a floating ball on a hinged arm, whose movement up and down controls the water level in a cistern, etc.

bal·le·ri·na /báləreénə/ *n.* a female ballet dancer. [It., fem. of *ballerino* dancing master f. *ballare* dance f. LL: see BALL[2]]

bal·let /baláy, bálay/ *n.* **1 a** a dramatic or representational style of dancing and mime, using set steps and techniques and usu. (esp. in classical ballet) accompanied by music. **b** a particular piece or performance of ballet. **c** the music for this. **2** a company performing ballet. □□ **bal·let·ic** /balétik/ *adj.* [F f. It. *balletto* dimin. of *ballo* BALL[2]]

bal·let danc·er *n.* a dancer who specializes in ballet.

bal·let·o·mane /balétəmayn/ *n.* a devotee of ballet. □□ **bal·let·o·ma·ni·a** /-máyneeə/ *n.*

ball game *n.* **1** any game played with a ball, esp. a game of baseball. **2** *colloq.* a particular affair or concern (*a whole new ball game*).

bal·lis·ta /bəlístə/ *n.* (*pl.* **bal·lis·tae** /-stee/) a catapult used in ancient warfare for hurling large stones, etc. [L f. Gk *balló* throw]

bal·lis·tic /bəlístik/ *adj.* **1** of or relating to projectiles. **2** moving under the force of gravity only. □ **go ballistic** *colloq.* become frantically overwrought or furiously angry. □□ **bal·lis·ti·cal·ly** *adv.* [BALLISTA + -IC]

bal·lis·tic mis·sile *n.* a missile which is initially powered and guided but falls under gravity on its target.

bal·lis·tics /bəlístiks/ *n.pl.* (usu. treated as *sing.*) the science of projectiles and firearms.

ball light·ning *n.* a rare kind of lightning having the form of a moving globe of light.

bal·locks var. of BOLLOCKS.

bal·loon /bəlóōn/ *n. & v.* ● *n.* **1** a small inflatable rubber pouch with a neck, used as a child's toy or as decoration. **2** a large usu. round bag inflatable with hot air or gas to make it rise in the air, often carrying a basket for passengers. **3** a balloon shape enclosing the words or thoughts of characters in a comic strip or cartoon. **4** a large globular drinking glass, usu. for brandy. ● *v.* **1** *intr. & tr.* swell out or cause to swell out like a balloon. **2** *intr.* travel by balloon. **3** *tr. Brit.* hit or kick (a ball, etc.) high in the air. □ **when the balloon goes up** *colloq.* when the action or trouble starts. □□ **bal·loon·ist** *n.* [F *ballon* or It. *ballone* large ball]

bal·lot /bál ət/ *n. & v.* ● *n.* **1** a process of voting, in writing and usu. secret. **2** the total of votes recorded in a ballot. **3** the drawing of lots. **4** a paper or ticket, etc., used in voting. **5** the right to vote. ● *v.* (**bal·lot·ed, bal·lot·ing**) **1** *intr.* (usu. foll. by *for*) a hold a ballot; give a vote. **b** draw lots for precedence, etc. **2** *tr.* take a ballot of (*the union balloted its members*). [It. *ballotta* dimin. of *balla* BALL[1]]

bal·lot box *n.* a sealed box into which voters put completed ballot papers.

bal·lot pa·per *n.* a slip of paper used to register a vote.

ball·park /báwlpaark/ *n.* **1** a baseball field. **2** (*attrib.*) *colloq.* approximate; rough (*a ballpark figure*). □ **in the (right) ballpark** *colloq.* close to one's objective; approximately correct.

ball·point /báwlpoint/ *n.* (in full **ball·point pen**) a pen with a tiny ball as its writing point.

ball·room /báwlrōōm, –rŏŏm/ *n.* a large room or hall for dancing.

ball·room danc·ing *n.* formal social dancing as a recreation.

bal·ly /bálee/ *adj. & adv. Brit. sl.* a mild form of *bloody* (see BLOODY *adj.* 3) (*took the bally lot*). [alt. of BLOODY]

bal·ly·hoo /báleehŏŏ/ *n.* **1** a loud noise or fuss; a confused state or commotion. **2** extravagant or sensational publicity. [19th or 20th c.: orig. unkn.]

bal·ly·rag var. of BULLYRAG.

balm /baam/ *n.* **1** an aromatic ointment for anointing, soothing, or healing. **2** a fragrant and medicinal exudation from certain trees and plants. **3** a healing or soothing influence or consolation. **4** an Asian and N. African tree yielding balm. **5** any aromatic herb, esp. one of the genus *Melissa.* **6** a pleasant perfume or fragrance. [ME f. OF *ba(s)me* f. L *balsamum* BALSAM]

balm of Gil·e·ad *n.* **1 a** a fragrant resin formerly much used as an unguent. **b** a plant of the genus *Commiphora* yielding such resin. **2** the balsam fir or poplar.

bal·mor·al /balmáwrəl, –mór–/ *n.* **1** a type of brimless boat-shaped cocked hat with a cockade or ribbons attached, usu. worn by certain Scottish regiments. **2** a heavy leather walking shoe with laces up the front. [*Balmoral* Castle in Scotland]

balm·y /báamee/ *adj.* (**balm·i·er, balm·i·est**) **1** mild and fragrant; soothing. **2** yielding balm. **3** crazy; stupid. □□ **balm·i·ly** *adv.* **balm·i·ness** *n.*

bal·ne·ol·o·gy /bálneeóləjee/ *n.* the scientific study of bathing and medicinal springs. □□ **bal·ne·o·log·i·cal** /–neeəlójikəl/ *adj.* **bal·ne·ol·o·gist** *n.* [L *balneum* bath + –LOGY]

ba·lo·ney /bəlónee/ *n.* (also **bo·lo·ney**) (*pl.* **·neys**) *sl.* **1** humbug; nonsense. **2** = BOLOGNA. [20th c.: alt. of BOLOGNA]

bal·sa /báwlsə/ *n.* **1** (in full **balsa wood**) a type of tough lightweight wood used for making models, etc. **2** the tropical American tree, *Ochroma lagopus,* from which it comes. [Sp., = raft]

bal·sam /báwlsəm/ *n.* **1** any of several aromatic resinous exudations, such as balm, obtained from various trees and shrubs and used as a base for certain fragrances and medical preparations. **2** an ointment, esp. one composed of a substance dissolved in oil or turpentine. **3** any of various trees or shrubs which yield balsam. **4** any of several flowering plants of the genus *Impatiens.* **5** a healing or soothing agency. □□ **bal·sam·ic** /–sámik/ *adj.* [OE f. L *balsamum*]

bal·sam ap·ple *n.* any of various gourdlike plants of the genus *Momordica,* having warty orange-yellow fruits.

bal·sam fir *n.* a N. American tree (*Abies balsamea*) which yields pulpwood and balsam.

bal·sam pop·lar *n.* any of various N. American poplars, esp. *Populus balsamifera,* yielding balsam.

Bal·tic /báwltik/ *n. & adj.* ● *n.* **1** (**the Baltic**) **a** an almost landlocked sea of NE Europe. **b** the nations bordering this sea. **2** an Indo-European branch of languages comprising Old Prussian, Lithuanian, and Latvian. ● *adj.* of or relating to the Baltic or the Baltic

branch of languages. [med.L *Balticus* f. LL *Balthae* dwellers near the Baltic Sea]

bal·us·ter /báləstər/ *n.* each of a series of often ornamental short posts or pillars supporting a rail or coping, etc.
▶Often confused with *banister.*

bal·us·trade /báləstráyd/ *n.* a railing supported by balusters, esp. forming an ornamental parapet to a balcony, bridge, or terrace. [F (as BALUSTER)]

ba·ma /báámə, páámə/ *n.* (also **pa·ma**) *Austral.* an Aboriginal person, esp. one from northern Queensland. [f. many north Qld. languages *bama* person or man]

bam·bi·no /bambeénō/ *n.* (*pl.* **bam·bi·ni** /–nee/) *colloq.* **1** a young child. **2** an image of the Christ child. [It., dimin. of *bambo* silly]

bam·boo /bambōō/ *n.* **1** a mainly tropical giant woody grass of the subfamily Bambusidae. **2** its hollow jointed stem, used as a stick or to make furniture, etc. [Du. *bamboes* f. Port. *mambu* f. Malay]

balustrade

bam·boo·zle /bambōōzəl/ *v.tr. colloq.* cheat; hoax; mystify. □□ **bam·boo·zle·ment** *n.* **bam·boo·zler** *n.* [c.1700: prob. of cant orig.]

ban /ban/ *v. & n.* ● *v.tr.* (**banned, banning**) forbid; prohibit (an action, etc.), esp. formally; refuse admittance to (a person). ● *n.* **1** a formal or authoritative prohibition (*a ban on smoking*). **2** a tacit prohibition by public opinion. **3** *hist.* a sentence of outlawry. **4** *archaic* a curse or execration. [OE *bannan* summon f. Gmc]

ba·nal /bənál, báynəl, bənaál/ *adj.* trite; feeble; commonplace. □□ **ba·nal·i·ty** /–nálitee/ *n.* (*pl.* **·ties**). **ba·nal·ly** *adv.* [orig. in sense 'compulsory,' hence 'common to all,' f. F f. *ban* (as BAN)]

bamboo

ba·nan·a /bənánə/ *n.* **1** a long curved fruit with soft pulpy flesh and yellow skin when ripe, growing in clusters. **2** (in full **banana tree**) the tropical and subtropical treelike plant, *Musa sapientum,* bearing this. □ **go bananas** *sl.* become crazy or angry. [Port. or Sp., f. a name in Guinea]

ba·nan·a re·pub·lic *n. derog.* a small nation, esp. in Central America, dependent on one crop or the influx of foreign capital.

ba·nan·a split *n.* a dessert made with split bananas, ice cream, sauce, whipped cream, etc.

ba·nau·sic /bənáwsik/ *adj.* usu. *derog.* **1 a** uncultivated. **b** materialistic. **2** utilitarian. [Gk *banausikos* for artisans]

banc /bangk/ *n.* a judge's seat in court. □ **in banc** *Law* sitting as a full court. [AF (= bench) f. med.L (as BANK[2])]

band[1] /band/ *n. & v.* ● *n.* **1** a flat, thin strip or loop of material (e.g., paper, metal, or cloth) put around something esp. to hold it together or decorate it (*headband; rubber band*). **2 a** a strip of material forming part of a garment (*hatband; waistband*). **b** a stripe of a different color or material in or on an object. **3 a** a range of frequencies or wavelengths in a spectrum (esp. of radio frequencies). **b** a range of values within a series. **4** a plain or simple ring, esp. without a gem, etc. **5** *Mech.* a belt connecting wheels or pulleys. **6** (in *pl.*) a collar having two hanging strips, worn by some lawyers, ministers, and academics in formal dress. **7** *archaic* a thing that restrains, binds, connects, or unites; a bond. ● *v.tr.* **1** put a band on. **2 a** mark with stripes. **b** (as **banded** *adj.*) *Bot. & Zool.* marked with colored bands or stripes. [ME f. OF *bande, bende* (sense 7 f. ON *band*) f. Gmc]

band[2] /band/ *n. & v.* ● *n.* **1** an organized group of people having a common object, esp. of a criminal nature (*band of cutthroats*). **2 a** a group of musicians, esp. playing wind instruments and percussion (*brass band; military band*). **b** a group of musicians playing jazz, pop, or dance music. **c** *colloq.* an orchestra. **3** a herd or flock. ● *v.tr.*

& intr. form into a group for a purpose (*band together for mutual protection*). [ME f. OF *bande, bander,* med.L *banda,* prob. of Gmc orig.]

band•age /bándij/ *n. & v.* ● *n.* **1** a strip of material for binding up a wound, etc. **2** a piece of material used as a blindfold. ● *v.tr.* bind (a wound, etc.) with a bandage. [F f. *bande* (as BAND¹)]

Band-Aid /bándayd/ *n.* **1** *Trademark* an adhesive bandage with a gauze pad in the center for covering minor wounds. **2** (**band-aid**) a stopgap solution to a problem.

ban•dan•na /bandánə/ *n.* a large handkerchief or neckerchief, usu. of silk or cotton, and often having a colorful pattern. [prob. Port. f. Hindi]

b. & b. *abbr.* (also **B & B**) bed and breakfast.

band•box /bándboks/ *n.* a usu. circular cardboard box for carrying hats. □ **out of a bandbox** extremely neat. [BAND¹ + BOX¹]

ban•deau /bandó/ *n.* (*pl.* **ban•deaux** /–dōz/) **1** a narrow band worn around the head. **2** a narrow covering for the breasts. [F]

band•ed ant•eat•er *n.* = NUMBAT.

ban•de•ril•la /bándəreéə, –rílyə/ *n.* a decorated dart thrust into a bull's neck or shoulders during a bullfight. [Sp.]

ban•de•role /bándəról/ *n.* (also **ban•de•rol**) **1 a** a long narrow flag with a cleft end, flown at a masthead. **b** an ornamental streamer on a knight's lance. **2 a** a ribbonlike scroll. **b** a stone band resembling a banderole, bearing an inscription. [F *banderole* f. It. *banderuola* dimin. of *bandiera* BANNER]

ban•di•coot /bándikōot/ *n.* **1** any of the insect- and plant-eating marsupials of the family Peramelidae. **2** (in full **bandicoot rat**) *Ind.* a destructive rat, *Bandicota benegalensis.* [Telugu *pandikokku* pig-rat]

ban•dit /bándit/ *n.* (*pl.* **ban•dits** or **ban•dit•ti** /–ditee/) **1** a robber or murderer, esp. a member of a band. **2** an outlaw. □□ **ban•dit•ry** *n.* [It. *bandito* (pl. –*iti*), past part. of *bandire* ban, = med.L *bannire* proclaim: see BANISH]

band•mas•ter /bándmastər/ *n.* the conductor of a (esp. military or brass) band. [BAND² + MASTER]

ban•do•lier /bándəleéer/ *n.* (also **ban•do•leer**) a shoulder belt with loops or pockets for cartridges. [Du. *bandelier* or F *bandoulière,* prob. formed as BANDEROLE]

band saw *n.* a mechanical saw with a blade formed by an endless toothed band.

bands•man /bándzmən/ *n.* (*pl.* **•men**) a player in a (esp. military or brass) band.

band•stand /bándstand/ *n.* a covered outdoor platform for a band to play on, usu. in a park.

band•wag•on /bándwagən/ *n.* a wagon used for carrying a band in a parade, etc. □ **climb** (or **jump**) **on the bandwagon** join a party, cause, or group that seems likely to succeed.

bandolier

bandolier

band•width /bándwidth, –with/ *n.* the range of frequencies within a given band (see BAND¹ *n.* 3a).

ban•dy¹ /bándee/ *adj.* (**ban•di•er, ban•di•est**) **1** (of the legs) curved so as to be wide apart at the knees. **2** (also **ban•dy-leg•ged** /–légəd, –legd/) (of a person) having bandy legs. [perh. f. obs. *bandy* curved stick]

ban•dy² /bándee/ *v.tr.* (**•dies, •died**) **1** (often foll. by *about*) **a** pass (a story, rumor, etc.) to and fro. **b** throw or pass (a ball, etc.) to and fro. **2** (often foll. by *about*) discuss disparagingly (*bandied his name about*). **3** (often foll. by *with*) exchange (blows, insults, etc.) (*don't bandy words with me*). [perh. f. F *bander* take sides f. *bande* BAND²]

bane /bayn/ *n.* **1** the cause of ruin or trouble; the curse (esp. the bane of one's life). **2** ruin; woe. **3** *archaic* (except in *comb.*) poison (*ratsbane*). □□ **bane•ful** *adj.* **bane•ful•ly** *adv.* [OE *bana* f. Gmc]

bane•ber•ry /báynberee/ *n.* (*pl.* **•ries**) **1** a plant of the genus *Actaea.* **2** the bitter poisonous berry of this plant.

bang /bang/ *n., v., & adv.* ● *n.* **1 a** a loud short sound. **b** an explosion. **c** the report of a gun. **2 a** a sharp blow. **b** the sound of this. **3** (esp. in *ital.*) a fringe of hair cut straight across the forehead. **4** *coarse sl.* **a** an act of sexual intercourse. **b** a partner in sexual intercourse. **5** *sl.* a drug injection (cf. BHANG). **6** *sl.* a thrill (*got a bang from going fast*). ● *v.* **1** *tr. & intr.* strike or shut noisily (*banged the door shut; banged on the table*). **2** *tr. & intr.* make or cause to make the sound of a blow or an explosion. **3** *tr.* cut (hair) in bangs. **4** *coarse sl.* **a** *intr.* have sexual intercourse. **b** *tr.* have sexual intercourse with. ● *adv.* **1** with a bang or sudden impact. **2** esp. *Brit. colloq.* exactly (*bang in the middle*). □ **bang off** *Brit. sl.* immediately. **bang on** *Brit. colloq.* exactly right. **bang up 1** damage. **2** *Brit. sl.* lock up; imprison. **go bang 1** (of a door, etc.) shut noisily. **2** explode. **3** *colloq.* be suddenly destroyed (*bang went their chances*). **go with a bang** go successfully. [16th c.: perh. f. Scand.]

bang•er /bángər/ *n. Brit.* **1** *sl.* a sausage. **2** *sl.* an old car, esp. a noisy one. **3** a loud firework.

ban•gle /bánggəl/ *n.* a rigid ornamental band worn around the arm or occas. the ankle. [Hindi *bangri* glass bracelet]

bang•tail /bángtayl/ *n. & v.* ● *n.* a horse, esp. with its tail cut short and straight across. ● *v.tr. Austral.* cut the tails of (horses or cattle) as an aid to counting or identification.

bang•tail mus•ter *n. Austral.* the counting of cattle involving cutting across the tufts at the tail ends as each is counted.

bang-up *adj. sl.* first-class, excellent (esp. bang-up job).

ban•ian var. of BANYAN.

ban•ish /bánish/ *v.tr.* **1** formally expel (a person), esp. from a country. **2** dismiss from one's presence or mind. □□ **ban•ish•ment** *n.* [ME f. OE *banir* ult. f. Gmc]

ban•is•ter /bánistər/ *n.* (also **ban•nis•ter**) **1** the uprights and handrail at the side of a staircase. **2** an upright supporting a handrail. [earlier *barrister,* corrupt. of BALUSTER]
▶Often confused with *baluster.*

ban•jo /bánjō/ *n.* (*pl.* **•jos** or **•joes**) a stringed musical instrument with a neck and head like a guitar and an open-backed body consisting of parchment stretched over a metal hoop. □□ **ban•jo•ist** *n.* [prob. ult. of African origin, akin to Kimbundu (a Banta language) *mbanza* a similar stringed instrument]

bank¹ /bangk/ *n. & v.* ● *n.* **1 a** the sloping edge of land by a river. **b** the area of ground alongside a river (*had a picnic on the bank*). **2** a raised shelf of ground; a slope. **3** an elevation in the sea or a river bed. **4** the artificial slope of a road, etc., enabling vehicles to maintain speed around a curve. **5** a mass of cloud, fog, snow, etc. **6** the edge of a hollow place (e.g., the top of a mine shaft). ● *v.* **1** *tr. & intr.* (often foll. by *up*) heap or rise into banks. **2** *tr.* heap up (a fire) tightly so that it burns slowly. **3 a** *intr.* (of a vehicle or aircraft or its occupant) travel with one side higher than the other in rounding a curve. **b** *tr.* cause (a vehicle or aircraft) to do this. **4** *tr.* contain or confine within a bank or banks. **5** *tr.* build (a road, etc.) higher at the outer edge of a bend to enable fast cornering. [ME f. Gmc f. ON *banki* (unrecorded: cf. OIcel. *bakki*): rel. to BENCH]

bank² /bangk/ *n. & v.* ● *n.* **1 a** a financial establishment which uses money deposited by customers for investment, pays it out when required, makes loans at interest, exchanges currency, etc. **b** a building in which this business takes place. **2** = PIGGY BANK. **3 a** the money or tokens held by the banker in some gambling games. **b** the banker in such games. **4** a place for storing anything for future use (*blood bank; data bank*). ● *v.* **1** *tr.* deposit (money or valuables) in a bank. **2** *intr.* engage in business as a banker. **3** *intr.* (often foll. by *at, with*) keep money (at a bank). **4** *intr.* act as banker in some gambling games. □ **bank on** rely on (*I'm banking on your help*). [F *banque* or It. *banca* f. med.L *banca, bancus,* f. Gmc: rel. to BANK¹]

bank³ /bangk/ *n.* **1** a row of similar objects, esp. of keys, lights, or switches. **2** a tier of oars. **3** a row or set of elevators, pay telephones, etc. [ME f. OF *banc* f. Gmc: rel. to BANK¹, BENCH]

bank•a•ble /bángkəbəl/ *adj.* **1** acceptable at a bank. **2** reliable (a *bankable reputation*). **3** certain to bring profit; good for the box office (*Hollywood's most bankable stars*).

bank bal•ance *n.* the amount of money held in a bank account at a given moment.

bank bill *n.* **1** *Brit.* a bill drawn by one bank on another. **2** = BANKNOTE.

bank•book /bángkbōok/ *n.* = PASSBOOK.

bank•card /bángk-kard/ *n.* a bank-issued credit card or automatic teller machine card.

bank•er¹ /bángkər/ *n.* **1** a person who manages or owns a bank or group of banks. **2 a** a keeper of the bank or dealer in some gambling games. **b** a card game involving gambling. **3** *Brit.* a result forecast identically (while other forecasts differ) in several soccer pool entries on one coupon. [F *banquier* f. *banque* BANK²]

bank•er² /bángkər/ *n.* **1 a** a fishing boat off Newfoundland. **b** a Newfoundland fisherman. **2** *Austral. colloq.* a river flooded to the top of its banks. [BANK¹ + –ER¹]

bank hol•i•day *n.* a day on which banks are officially closed (in the UK), usu. kept as a public holiday.

bank•ing /bángking/ *n.* the business transactions of a bank.

bank•note /bángknōt/ *n.* a banker's promissory note, esp. from a central bank, payable to the bearer on demand, and serving as money.

Bank of Eng•land *n.* the central bank of England and Wales, issuing banknotes and having the government as its main customer.

bank•roll /bángkról/ *n. & v.* ● *n.* **1** a roll of paper currency. **2** funds. ● *v.tr. colloq.* support financially.

bank•rupt /bángkrupt/ *adj., n., & v.* ● *adj.* **1 a** insolvent; declared in law unable to pay debts. **b** undergoing the legal process resulting from this. **2** (often foll. by *of*) exhausted or drained (of some quality, etc.); deficient; lacking. ● *n.* **1 a** an insolvent person whose estate is administered and disposed of for the benefit of the creditors. **b** an insolvent debtor. **2** a person exhausted of or deficient in a certain attribute (*a moral bankrupt*). ● *v.tr.* make bankrupt.

□□ **bank•rupt•cy** /–ruptsee/ *n.* (*pl.* **•cies**). [16th c.: f. It *banca rotta* broken bench (as BANK², L *rumpere rupt-* break), assim. to L]

bank•sia /bángkseeə/ *n.* any evergreen flowering shrub of the genus *Banksia*, native to Australia. [Sir J. *Banks*, Engl. naturalist d. 1820]

bank•sia rose *n.* a Chinese climbing rose with small flowers.

bank state•ment *n.* a printed statement of transactions and balance issued periodically to the holder of a bank account.

bank swal•low *n.* a swallowlike bird, *Riparia riparia*, nesting in the side of a sandy bank, etc.

ban•ner /bánər/ *n.* **1 a** a large rectangular sign bearing a slogan or design and usu. carried on two side poles or a crossbar in a demonstration or procession. **b** a long strip of cloth, etc., hung across a street or along the front of a building, etc., and bearing a slogan. **2** a flag on a pole used as the standard of a king, knight, etc., esp. in battle. **3** (*attrib.*) excellent; outstanding (*a banner year in sales*). □ **join** (or **follow**) **the banner of** adhere to the cause of. **under the banner of** associated with the cause of, esp. by the use of the same slogans as, adherence to the same principles as, etc. □□ **ban•nered** *adj.* [ME f. AF *banere*, OF *baniere* f. Rmc ult. f. Gmc]

ban•ner•et /bánəret/ *n.* **1** a small banner. **2** (also /–rit/) *hist.* a knight who commanded his own troops in battle under his own banner. **3** *hist.* a knighthood given on the battlefield for courage. [ME & OF *baneret* f. *baniere* BANNER + *-et* as –ATE¹]

ban•ner head•line *n.* a large newspaper headline, esp. one across the top of the front page.

ban•nis•ter var. of BANISTER.

ban•nock /bánək/ *n. Sc.* & *No. of Engl.* a round flat griddle cake, usu. unleavened. [OE *bannuc*, perh. f. Celt.]

banns /banz/ *n.pl.* a notice read out, esp. on three successive Sundays in a parish church, announcing an intended marriage and giving the opportunity for objections. □ **forbid the banns** raise an objection to an intended marriage, esp. in church following the reading of the banns. [pl. of BAN]

ban•quet /bángkwit/ *n. & v.* ●*n.* **1** an elaborate usu. extensive feast. **2** a dinner for many people followed by speeches in favor of a cause or in celebration of an event. ●*v.* (**banqueted, banqueting**) **1** *intr.* hold a banquet; feast. **2** *tr.* entertain with a banquet. □□ **ban•quet•er** *n.* [F, dimin. of *banc* bench, BANK²]

ban•quette /bangkét/ *n.* **1** an upholstered bench along a wall, esp. in a restaurant or bar. **2** a raised step behind a rampart. [F f. It. *banchetta* dimin. of *banca* bench, BANK²]

ban•shee /bánshee, –shée/ *n.* a female spirit whose wailing warns of a death in a house. [Ir. *bean sídhe* f. OIr. *ben síde* woman of the fairies]

ban•tam /bántəm/ *n.* **1** any of several small breeds of domestic fowl, of which the male is very aggressive. **2** a small but aggressive person. [app. f. *Banten* in Java, although the fowl is not native there]

ban•tam•weight /bántəmwayt/ *n.* **1** a weight in certain sports intermediate between flyweight and featherweight. **2** a sportsman of this weight.

ban•ter /bántər/ *n. & v.* ●*n.* good-humored teasing. ●*v.* **1** *tr.* ridicule in a good-humored way. **2** *intr.* talk humorously or teasingly. □□ **ban•ter•er** *n.* [17th c.: orig. unkn.]

Ban•tu /bántōō/ *n. & adj.* ●*n.* (*pl.* same or **Bantus**) **1** often *offens.* **a** a large group of Negroid peoples of central and southern Africa. **b** a member of any of these peoples. **2** the group of languages spoken by them. ●*adj.* of or relating to these peoples or languages. [Bantu, = people]

Ban•tu•stan /bántōōstan/ *n. S.Afr. hist.* often *offens.* any of several partially self-governing areas formerly reserved for black South Africans (see also HOMELAND). [BANTU + *-stan* as in *Hindustan*]

ban•yan /bányən/ *n.* (also **ban•ian**) **1** an Indian fig tree, *Ficus benghalensis*, the branches of which hang down and root themselves. **2** a Hindu trader. **3** a loose flannel jacket, shirt, or gown worn in India.

WORD HISTORY banyan

Late 16th century: from Portuguese, from Gujarati *vāṇiyo* 'man of the trading caste,' from Sanskrit. Originally denoting a Hindu trader or merchant, the term was applied by Europeans in the mid-17th century to a particular tree under which such traders had built a pagoda.

ban•zai /baanzí/ *int.* **1** a Japanese battle cry. **2** a form of greeting used to the Japanese emperor. [Jap., = ten thousand years (of life to you)]

ba•o•bab /báyōbab, baa–/ *n.* an African tree, *Adansonia digitata*, with an enormously thick trunk and large fruit containing edible pulp. [L (1592), prob. f. an Afr. lang.]

bap /bap/ *n. Brit.* a soft flattish bread roll. [16th c.: orig. unkn.]

bap•tism /báptizəm/ *n.* **1 a** the religious rite, symbolizing admission to the Christian Church, of sprinkling the forehead with water, or (usu. only with adults) by immersion, generally accompanied by name giving. **b** the act of baptizing or being baptized. **2** any similar non-Christian rite. **3** an initiation, e.g., into battle. **4** the naming of ships, church bells, etc. □□ **bap•tis•mal** /–tízməl/ *adj.* [ME f. OF *ba(p)te(s)me* f. eccl.L *baptismus* f. eccl.Gk *baptismos* f. *baptizō* BAPTIZE]

bap•tism of fire *n.* **1** initiation into battle. **2** a painful new undertaking or experience.

bap•tist /báptist/ *n.* **1** a person who baptizes, esp. John the Baptist. **2** (**Baptist**) a Christian advocating baptism by total immersion, esp. of adults, as a symbol of membership of and initiation into the Church. [ME f. OF *baptiste* f. eccl.L *baptista* f. eccl.Gk *baptistēs* f. *baptizō* BAPTIZE]

bap•tis•ter•y /báptistree/ *n.* (also **bap•tis•try**) (*pl.* **•ies**) **1 a** the part of a church used for baptism. **b** *hist.* a building next to a church, used for baptism. **2** (in a Baptist chapel) a sunken receptacle used for total immersion. [ME f. OF *baptisterie* f. eccl.L *baptisterium* f. eccl.Gk *baptistērion* bathing place f. *baptizō* BAPTIZE]

bap•tize /báptíz/ *v.tr.* **1** (also *absol.*) administer baptism to. **2** give a name or nickname to; christen. [ME f. OF *baptiser* f. eccl.L *baptizare* f. Gk *baptizō* immerse, baptize]

bar¹ /baar/ *n., v., & prep.* ●*n.* **1 a** a long rod or piece of rigid wood, metal, etc., esp. used as an obstruction, confinement, fastening, weapon, etc. **2 a** something resembling a bar in being (thought of as) straight, narrow, and rigid (*bar of soap; bar of chocolate*). **b** a band of color or light, esp. on a flat surface. **c** the heating element of an electric heater. **d** = CROSSBAR. **e** *Brit.* a metal strip below the clasp of a medal, awarded as an extra distinction. **f** a sandbank or shoal as at the mouth of a harbor or an estuary. **g** *Brit.* a rail marking the end of each chamber in the Houses of Parliament. **h** *Heraldry* a narrow horizontal stripe across a shield. **3 a** a barrier of any shape. **b** a restriction (*color bar; a bar to promotion*). **4 a** a counter in a restaurant, etc., across which alcohol or refreshments are served. **b** a room in which alcohol is served and customers may sit and drink. **c** an establishment selling alcoholic drinks to be consumed on the premises. **d** a small store or stall serving refreshments (*snack bar*). **5 a** an enclosure in which a defendant stands in a court of law. **b** a public standard of acceptability, before which a person is said to be tried (*bar of conscience*). **c** a plea arresting an action or claim in a law case. **d** a particular court of law. **6** *Mus.* **a** any of the sections of usu. equal time value into which a musical composition is divided by vertical lines across the staff. **b** = BAR LINE. **7** (**the Bar**) *Law* **a** lawyers collectively. **b** the profession of lawyers. ●*v.tr.* (**barred, barring**) **1 a** fasten (a door, window, etc.) with a bar or bars. **b** (usu. foll. by *in, out*) shut or keep in or out (*barred him in*). **2** obstruct; prevent (*bar his progress*). **3 a** (usu. foll. by *from*) prohibit; exclude (*bar them from attending*). **b** exclude from consideration (cf. BARRING). **4** mark with stripes. **5** *Law* prevent or delay (an action) by objection. ●*prep.* **1** except (*all were there bar a few*). **2** *Brit. Racing* except (the horses indicated: used in stating the odds, indicating the number of horses excluded) (*33–1 bar three*). □ **bar none** with no exceptions. **be called to the Bar** be admitted as a lawyer or barrister. **behind bars** in prison. [ME f. OF *barre, barrer,* f. Rmc]

bar² /baar/ *n.* esp. Meteorol. a unit of pressure, 10^5 newtons per square meter, approx. one atmosphere. [Gk *baros* weight]

bar•a•the•a /bárəthéeə/ *n.* a fine woolen cloth, sometimes mixed with silk or cotton, used esp. for coats, suits, etc. [19th c.: orig. unkn.]

barb /baarb/ *n. & v.* ●*n.* **1** a secondary, backward facing projection from an arrow, fishhook, etc., angled to make extraction difficult. **2** a deliberately hurtful remark. **3** a beardlike filament at the mouth of some fish, e.g., barbel and catfish. **4** any one of the fine hairlike filaments growing from the shaft of a feather, forming the vane. ●*v.tr.* **1** provide (an arrow, a fishhook, etc.) with a barb or barbs. **2** (as **barbed** *adj.*) (of a remark, etc.) deliberately hurtful. [ME f. OF *barbe* f. L *barba* beard]

Bar•ba•di•an /baarbáydeeən/ *n. & adj.* ●*n.* **1** a native or inhabitant of Barbados in the W. Indies. **2** a person of Barbadian descent. ●*adj.* of or relating to Barbados or its people.

bar•bar•i•an /baarbáireeən/ *n. & adj.* ●*n.* **1** an uncultured or brutish person; a lout. **2** a member of a primitive community or tribe. ●*adj.* **1** rough and uncultured. **2** uncivilized. [orig. of any foreigner with a different language or customs: F *barbarien* f. *barbare* (as BARBAROUS)]

bar•bar•ic /baarbárik/ *adj.* **1** brutal; cruel (*flogging is a barbaric punishment*). **2** rough and uncultured; unrestrained. **3** of or like barbarians and their art or taste; primitive. □□ **bar•bar•i•cal•ly** *adv.* [ME f. OF *barbarique* or L *barbaricus* f. Gk *barbarikos* f. *barbaros* foreign]

bar•ba•rism /baárbərizəm/ *n.* **1 a** the absence of culture and civilized standards; ignorance and rudeness. **b** an example of this. **2 a** word or expression not considered correct; a solecism. **3** anything considered to be in bad taste. [F *barbarisme* f. L *barbarismus* f. Gk *barbarismos* f. *barbarizō* speak like a foreigner f. *barbaros* foreign]

bar•bar•i•ty /baarbáritee/ *n.* (*pl.* **•ties**) **1** savage cruelty. **2** an example of this.

bar•ba•rize /baárbəriz/ *v.tr. & intr.* make or become barbarous. □□ **bar•ba•ri•za•tion** *n.*

bar•ba•rous /baárbərəs/ *adj.* **1** uncivilized. **2** cruel. **3** coarse and unrefined. □□ **bar•ba•rous•ly** *adv.* **bar•ba•rous•ness** *n.* [orig. of any foreign language or people: f. L f. Gk *barbaros* foreign]

Bar·ba·ry ape /baárbəree/ n. a macaque, *Macaca sylvanus*, of N. Africa and Gibraltar. [*Barbary*, an old name of the western part of N. Africa, ult. f. Arab. *barbar* BERBER]

barb bolt n. a bolt with barbs to keep it tight when it has been driven in.

bar·be·cue /baárbikyōō/ n. & v. ●n. **1 a** a meal cooked on an open fire out of doors, esp. meat grilled on a metal appliance. **b** a party at which such a meal is cooked and eaten. **c** marinated or seasoned meat prepared for cooking as such a meal. **2 a** the metal appliance used for the preparation of a barbecue. **b** a fireplace, usu. of brick, containing such an appliance. ●*v.tr.* (**bar·be·cues, bar·be·cued, bar·be·cu·ing**) cook (esp. meat) on a barbecue.

WORD HISTORY barbecue

Mid-17th century: from Spanish *barbacoa*, perhaps from Arawak *barbacoa* 'wooden frame on posts.' The original sense was 'wooden framework for sleeping on, or for storing meat or fish to be dried.'

bar·be·cue sauce n. a highly seasoned sauce, usu. containing chilies, in which meat, etc., may be cooked.

barbed wire n. wire bearing sharp pointed spikes close together and used in fencing, or in warfare as an obstruction.

bar·bel /baárbəl/ n. **1** any large European freshwater fish of the genus *Barbus*, with fleshy filaments hanging from its mouth. **2** such a filament growing from the mouth of any fish. [ME f. OF f. LL *barbellus* dimin. of *barbus* barbel f. *barba* beard]

bar·bell /baárbel/ n. an iron bar with a series of weighted disks at each end, used for weightlifting exercises. [BAR¹ + BELL¹]

bar·ber /baárbər/ n. & v. ●n. a person who cuts men's hair and shaves or trims beards as an occupation; a men's hairdresser. ●*v.tr.* **1** cut the hair, shave or trim the beard of. **2** cut or trim closely (*barbered the grass*). [ME & AF f. OF *barbeor* f. med.L *barbator –oris* f. *barba* beard]

bar·ber pole n. a spirally painted striped red and white pole hung outside barbers' shops as a business sign.

bar·ber·ry /baárberee/ n. (pl. **·ries**) **1** any shrub of the genus *Berberis*, with spiny shoots, yellow flowers, and ovoid red berries, often grown as hedges. **2** its berry. [ME f. OF *berberis*, of unkn. orig.: assim. to BERRY]

bar·ber·shop /bárbərshop/ n. a barber's place of business.

bar·ber·shop quar·tet n. a popular style of close harmony singing for four male voices.

bar·bet /baárbit/ n. any small brightly colored tropical bird of the family Capitonidae, with bristles at the base of its beak. [F f. *barbe* beard]

bar·bette /baárbét/ n. a platform in a fort or ship from which guns can be fired over a parapet, etc., without an embrasure. [F, dimin. of *barbe* beard]

bar·bi·can /baárbikən/ n. the outer defense of a city, castle, etc., esp. a double tower above a gate or drawbridge. [ME f. OF *barbacane*, of unkn. orig.]

bar·bie /baárbee/ n. *Austral. colloq.* a barbecue. [abbr.]

bar·bi·tal /baárbitawl, –tal/ n. (*Brit.* **bar·bi·tone** /baárbitōn/) a sedative drug. [as BARBITURIC ACID + –al as in *veronal*]

bar·bi·tu·rate /baarbítchərət, –rayt/ n. any derivative of barbituric acid used in the preparation of sedative and sleep-inducing drugs. [BARBITURIC + –ATE¹]

bar·bi·tu·ric ac·id /baárbitoŏrik, –tyoŏr–/ n. *Chem.* an organic acid from which various sedatives and sleep-inducing drugs are derived. [F *barbiturique* f. G *Barbitursäure* (*Säure* acid) f. the name *Barbara*]

bar·bule /baárbyōōl/ n. a minute filament projecting from the barb of a feather. [L *barbula*, dimin. of *barba* beard]

barb·wire /baárbwír/ n. = BARBED WIRE.

bar·ca·role /baárkərōl/ n. (also **bar·ca·rolle**) **1** a song sung by Venetian gondoliers. **2** music in imitation of this. [F *barcarolle* f. Venetian It. *barcarola* boatman's song f. *barca* boat]

bar chart n. a chart using bars to represent quantity.

bar code n. a machine-readable code in the form of a pattern of stripes printed on and identifying a commodity, used esp. for inventory control.

Bar·coo /baarkōō/ adj. *Austral.* of or relating to a remote area of the country. [river in W. Qld.]

Bard n. (also the **Bard of Avon**) Shakespeare.

bard¹ /baard/ n. **1 a** *hist.* a Celtic minstrel. **b** the winner of a prize for Welsh verse at an Eisteddfod. **2** a poet, esp. one treating heroic themes. **3** a composer or singer of epic poetry. □□ **bard·ic** adj. [Gael. & Ir. *bárd*, Welsh *bard*, f. OCelt.]

bard² /baard/ n. & v. ●n. a strip of fat placed on meat or game before roasting. ●*v.tr.* cover (meat, etc.) with bards. [F *barde*, orig. = horse's breastplate, ult. f. Arab.]

bare /bair/ adj. & v. ●adj. **1** (esp. of part of the body) unclothed or uncovered (*with bare head*). **2** without appropriate covering or contents: **a** (of a tree) leafless. **b** unfurnished; empty (*bare rooms*; *the cupboard was bare*). **c** (of a floor) uncarpeted. **3 a** undisguised (*the bare truth*). **b** unadorned (*bare facts*). **4** (attrib.) **a** scanty (*a bare majority*). **b** mere (*bare necessities*). ●*v.tr.* **1** uncover; unsheathe

(*bared his teeth*). **2** reveal (*bared his soul*). □ **bare of** without. **with one's bare hands** without using tools or weapons. □□ **bare·ness** n. [OE *bær, barian* f. Gmc]

bare·back /báirbak/ adj. & adv. on an unsaddled horse, donkey, etc.

bare bones n. the minimum essential facts, ingredients, etc.

bare·faced /báirfáyst/ adj. undisguised; impudent (*barefaced lie*). □□ **bare·fac·ed·ly** /–fáysidlee/ adv. **bare·fac·ed·ness** n.

bare·foot /báirfŏŏt/ adj. & adv. (also **bare·foot·ed** /–fŏŏtid/) with nothing on the feet.

bare·foot doc·tor n. a paramedical worker with basic medical training, esp. in China.

ba·rège /bərézh/ n. a silky gauze made from wool or other material. [F f. *Barèges* in SW France, where it was orig. made]

bare·head·ed /báirhédid/ adj. & adv. without a covering for the head.

bare·ly /báirlee/ adv. **1** only just; scarcely (*barely escaped*). **2** scantily (*barely furnished*). **3** *archaic* openly; explicitly.

barf /baarf/ v. & n. *sl.* ●*v.intr.* vomit or retch. ●n. vomit. [20th c.: orig. unkn.]

bar·fly /baárflí/ n. (pl. **·flies**) *colloq.* a person who frequents bars.

bar·gain /baárgin/ n. & v. ●n. **1 a** an agreement on the terms of a transaction or sale. **b** this seen from the buyer's viewpoint (*a bad bargain*). **2** something acquired or offered cheaply. ●*v.intr.* (often foll. by *with, for*) discuss the terms of a transaction (*expected him to bargain, but he paid up; bargained with her; bargained for the table*). □ **bargain away** part with for something worthless (*had bargained away the estate*). **bargain for** (or *colloq.* **on**) (usu. with *neg.* actual or implied) be prepared for; expect (*didn't bargain for bad weather; more than I bargained for*). **bargain on** rely on. **drive a hard bargain** pursue one's own profit in a transaction keenly. **in** (also *into*) **the bargain** moreover; in addition to what was expected. **make** (or **strike**) **a bargain** agree to or on a transaction. □□ **bar·gain·er** n. [ME f. OF *bargaine, bargaignier*, prob. f. Gmc]

bar·gain base·ment n. (also *attrib.*) the basement of a store where bargains are displayed.

barge /baarj/ n. & v. ●n. **1** a long flat-bottomed boat for carrying freight on canals, rivers, etc. **2 a** long ornamental boat used for pleasure or ceremony. **3** a boat used by the chief officers of a flagship, etc. ●*v.intr.* **1** (often foll. by *around*) lurch or rush clumsily about. **2** (foll. by *in, into*) **a** intrude or interrupt rudely or awkwardly (*barged in while we were kissing*). **b** collide with (*barged into her*). [ME f. OF perh. f. med.L *barica* f. Gk *baris* Egyptian boat]

barge·board /baárjbawrd/ n. a board (often ornamental) fixed to the gable end of a roof to hide the ends of the roof timbers. [perh. f. med.L *bargus* gallows]

barg·ee /baarjeé/ n. *Brit.* a person in charge of or working on a barge.

barge·pole /baárjpōl/ n. a long pole used for punting barges, etc., and for fending off obstacles. □ **would not touch with a bargepole** *Brit.* refuse to be associated or concerned with (a person or thing).

ba·ril·la /bərée·ə, –rílə/ n. **1** any plant of the genus *Salsola* found chiefly in Spain and Sicily. **2** an impure alkali made by burning either this or kelp. [Sp.]

bar·ite /báirít, bár–/ n. a mineral form of barium sulfate. [Gk *barus* heavy, partly assim. to mineral names in –*ite*]

bar·i·tone /báritōn/ n. & adj. ●n. **1 a** the second-lowest adult male singing voice. **b** a singer with this voice. **c** a part written for it. **2 a** an instrument that is second-lowest in pitch in its family. **b** its player. ●adj. of the second-lowest range. [It. *baritono* f. Gk *barutonos* f. *barus* heavy + *tonos* TONE]

bar·i·um /báireeəm, bár–/ n. *Chem.* a white reactive soft metallic element of the alkaline earth group. ¶ Symb.: **Ba**. [BARYTA + –IUM]

bar·i·um meal n. (also **bar·i·um enema**) a mixture of barium sulfate and water, which is opaque to X-rays, and is given to patients requiring radiological examination of the stomach and intestines.

bark¹ /baark/ n. & v. ●n. **1** the sharp explosive cry of a dog, fox, etc. **2** a sound resembling this cry. ●v. **1** *intr.* (of a dog, fox, etc.) give a bark. **2** *tr. & intr.* speak or utter sharply or brusquely. **3** *intr.* cough fiercely. **4** *tr.* sell or advertise publicly by calling out. □ **one's bark is worse than one's bite** one is not as ferocious as one appears. **bark up the wrong tree** be on the wrong track; make an effort in the wrong direction. [OE *beorcan*]

bark² /baark/ n. & v. ●n. **1** the tough protective outer sheath of the trunks, branches, and twigs of trees or woody shrubs. **2** this material used for tanning leather or dyeing material. ●*v.tr.* **1** graze or scrape (one's shin, etc.). **2** strip bark from (a tree, etc.). **3** tan or dye (leather, etc.) using the tannins found in bark. [ME f. OIcel. *börkr bark-*: perh. rel. to BIRCH]

bark³ /baark/ n. a ship or boat. [= BARQUE]

bar·keep·er /baárkeepər/ n. (also **bar·keep**) a person who owns or serves drinks in a bar.

bark·en·tine /baárkənteen/ n. (also **bar·quen·tine, bar·quan·tine**) a sailing ship with the foremast square-rigged and the remaining (usu. two) masts fore-and-aft rigged. [BARQUE after *brigantine*]

See page xx for the **Key to Pronunciation**.

bark·er /baárkər/ *n.* a person at an auction, sideshow, etc., who calls out to passersby for advertisement. [BARK¹ + –ER¹]

bar·ley /baárlee/ *n.* **1** any of various hardy awned cereals of the genus *Hordeum* widely used as food and in malt liquors and spirits such as whiskey. **2** the grain produced from this (cf. PEARL BARLEY). [OE *bærlic* (adj.) f. *bære, bere* barley]

bar·ley·corn /baárleekawrn/ *n.* **1** the grain of barley. **2** a former unit of measure (about a third of an inch) based on the length of a grain of barley.

bar·ley sug·ar *n.* an amber-colored candy made of boiled sugar, traditionally shaped as a twisted stick.

bar·ley wa·ter *n.* a drink made from water and a boiled barley mixture.

bar line *n. Mus.* a vertical line used to mark divisions between bars.

barm /baarm/ *n.* **1** the froth on fermenting malt liquor. **2** *archaic* or *dial.* yeast or leaven. [OE *beorma*]

bar·maid /baármayd/ *n.* a woman serving drinks in a bar, restaurant, etc.

bar·man /baármən/ *n.* (*pl.* **·men**) esp. *Brit.* = BARTENDER.

Bar·me·cide /baármisīd/ *adj. & n.* (also **Bar·me·cid·al** /–sīd'l/) • *adj.* illusory; imaginary; such as to disappoint. • *n.* a giver of benefits that are illusory or disappointing. [the name of a wealthy man in the *Arabian Nights' Entertainments* who gave a beggar a feast consisting of ornate but empty dishes]

bar mitz·vah /baar mítsvə/ *n.* **1** the religious initiation ceremony of a Jewish boy who has reached the age of 13. **2** the boy undergoing this ceremony. □□ **bar mitz·vah** *v.* [Heb., = 'son of the commandment']

barm·y /baármee/ *adj.* (**barm·i·er, barm·i·est**) **1** frothy; foamy. **2** esp. *Brit. sl.* = BALMY 3. □□ **barm·i·ly** *adv.* **barm·i·ness** *n.* [earlier = frothy, f. BARM]

barn¹ /baarn/ *n.* **1** a large farm building for storing grain, housing livestock, etc. **2** a large plain or unattractive building. **3** a large shed for storing road or railroad vehicles, etc. [OE *bern, beren* f. *bere* barley + *ern, ærn* house]

barn² /baarn/ *n. Physics* a unit of area, 10^{-28} square meters, used esp. in particle physics. ¶ Symb.: **b**. [perh. f. phrase 'as big as a barn']

bar·na·cle /baárnəkəl/ *n.* **1** any of various species of small marine crustaceans of the class Cirripedia which in adult form cling to rocks, ships' hulls, etc. **2** a tenacious attendant or follower who cannot easily be shaken off. □□ **bar·na·cled** *adj.* [ME *bernak* (= med.L *bernaca*), of unkn. orig.]

bar·na·cle goose *n.* an Arctic goose, *Branta leucopsis.*

barn burn·er *n.* (also **barn·burn·er**) *colloq.* something or someone that has a sensational effect or stirs excited interest.

barn dance *n.* **1** an informal social gathering for country dancing, orig. in a barn. **2** a dance for a number of couples forming a line or circle, with couples moving along it in turn.

bar·ney /baárnee/ *n.* (*pl.* **·neys**) esp. *Brit. colloq.* a noisy quarrel. [perh. dial.]

barn owl *n.* a kind of owl, *Tyto alba*, frequenting barns.

barn·storm /baárnstawrm/ *v.intr.* **1** tour rural districts giving theatrical performances (formerly often in barns). **2** make a rapid tour esp. for political meetings. **3** *Aeron.* give informal flying exhibitions; do stunt flying. □□ **barn·storm·er** *n.*

barn·yard /baárnyaard/ *n.* the area around a barn.

bar·o·graph /bárəgraf/ *n.* a barometer equipped to record its readings. [Gk *baros* weight + –GRAPH]

ba·rom·e·ter /bərómitər/ *n.* **1** an instrument measuring atmospheric pressure, esp. in forecasting the weather and determining altitude. **2** anything which reflects changes in circumstances, opinions, etc. □□ **bar·o·met·ric** /bárəmétrik/ *adj.* **bar·o·met·ri·cal** /bárəmétrikəl/ *adj.* **ba·rom·e·try** *n.*

bar·on /báron/ *n.* **1 a** a member of the lowest order of the British nobility. **b** a similar member of a foreign nobility. **2** an important businessman or other powerful or influential person (*sugar baron; newspaper baron*). **3** *hist.* a person who held lands or property from the sovereign or a powerful overlord. [ME f. AF *barun*, OF *baron* f. med.L *baro, –onis* man, of unkn. orig.]

bar·on·age /bárənij/ *n.* **1** barons or nobles collectively. **2** an annotated list of barons or peers. [ME f. OF *barnage* (as BARON)]

bar·on·ess /báronis/ *n.* **1** a woman holding the rank of baron. **2** the wife or widow of a baron. [ME f. OF *baronesse* (as BARON)]

bar·on·et /báronit, –nét/ *n.* a member of the lowest hereditary titled British order. [ME f. AL *baronettus* (as BARON)]

bar·on·et·age /báronitij, –nét–/ *n.* **1** baronets collectively. **2** an annotated list of baronets.

bar·on·et·cy /báronitsee, –nét–/ *n.* (*pl.* **·cies**) the domain, rank, or tenure of a baronet.

ba·ro·ni·al /bəróneeəl/ *adj.* of, relating to, or befitting barons.

bar·on of beef *n.* chiefly *Brit.* a double sirloin cut of beef.

bar·o·ny /bárónee/ *n.* (*pl.* **·nies**) **1** the domain, rank, or tenure of a baron. **2** (in Ireland) a division of a county. **3** (in Scotland) a large manor or estate. [ME f. OF *baronie* (as BARON)]

ba·roque /bərók/ *adj. & n.* • *adj.* **1** highly ornate and extravagant in style, esp. of European art, architecture, and music of the 17th and 18th c. **2** of or relating to this period. • *n.* **1** the baroque style. **2** baroque art collectively. [F (orig. = 'irregular pearl') f. Port. *barroco,* of unkn. orig.]

ba·rouche /bəróosh/ *n.* a horse-drawn carriage with four wheels and a collapsible hood over the rear half, used esp. in the 19th c. [G (dial.) *Barutsche* f. It. *baroccio* ult. f. L *birotus* two-wheeled]

barque /baark/ *n.* (also **bark**) **1** a sailing ship with the rear mast fore-and-aft rigged and the remaining (usu. two) masts squarerigged. **2** *poet.* any boat. [ME f. F prob. f. Prov. *barca* f. L *barca* ship's boat]

bar·quen·tine var. of BARKENTINE.

bar·rack¹ /bárək/ *n. & v.* • *n.* (usu. in *pl.*, often treated as *sing.*) **1** a building or building complex used to house soldiers. **2** any building used to accommodate large numbers of people. **3** a large building of a bleak or plain appearance. • *v.tr.* place (soldiers, etc.) in barracks. [F *baraque* f. It. *baracca* or Sp. *barraca* soldier's tent, of unkn. orig.]

bar·rack² /bárək/ *v. Brit.* **1** *tr.* shout or jeer at (players in a game, a performer, speaker, etc.). **2** *intr.* (of spectators at games, etc.) shout or jeer. [app. f. BORAK]

bar·ra·cou·ta /bárəkóotə/ *n.* (*pl.* same or **bar·ra·cou·tas**) **1** a long slender fish, *Thyrsites atun*, usu. found in southern oceans. **2** *NZ* a small narrow loaf of bread. [var. of BARRACUDA]

bar·ra·cu·da /bárəkóodə/ *n.* (*pl.* same or **bar·ra·cu·das**) a large and voracious tropical marine fish of the family Sphyraenidae. [Amer. Sp. *barracuda*]

bar·rage /bəraázh/ *n.* **1** a concentrated artillery bombardment over a wide area. **2** a rapid succession of questions or criticisms. **3** /baárij/ an artificial barrier, esp. in a river. [F f. *barrer* (as BAR¹)]

bar·rage bal·loon *n.* a large anchored balloon, often with netting suspended from it, used (usu. as one of a series) as a defense against low-flying aircraft.

bar·ra·mun·di /bárəmúndee/ *n.* (*pl.* same or **bar·ra·mun·dis**) any of various Australian freshwater fishes, esp. *Lates calcarifer*, used as food. [Aboriginal]

bar·ra·tor /bárətər/ *n.* **1** a malicious person causing discord. **2** one who commits barratry. [ME f. AF *baratour*, OF *barateor* trickster, f. *barat* deceit]

bar·ra·try /bárətree/ *n.* **1** fraud or gross negligence of a ship's master or crew at the expense of its owners or users. **2** frivolous or groundless litigation or incitement to it. **3** *hist.* trade in the sale of church or state appointments. □□ **bar·ra·trous** *adj.* [ME f. OF *baraterie* (as BARRATOR)]

barre /baar/ *n.* a horizontal bar at waist level used in dance exercises. [F]

bar·ré /baaráy/ *n. Mus.* a method of playing a chord on the guitar, etc., with a finger laid across the strings at a particular fret, raising their pitch. [F, past part. of *barrer* bar]

bar·rel /bárəl/ *n. & v.* • *n.* **1** a cylindrical container usu. bulging out in the middle, traditionally made of wooden staves with metal hoops around them. **2** the contents of this. **3** a measure of capacity, usu. varying from 30 to 40 gallons. **4** a cylindrical tube forming part of an object such as a gun or a pen. **5** the trunk of a four-legged animal, e.g., a horse. • *v.* (**bar·reled, bar·rel·ing** or **bar·relled, bar·rel·ling**) **1** *tr.* put into a barrel or barrels. **2** *intr. sl.* drive or move fast. □ **over a barrel** *colloq.* in a helpless or awkward position; at a person's mercy. [ME f. OF *baril* perh. f. Rmc.: rel to BAR¹]

bar·rel-chest·ed *adj.* having a large rounded chest.

bar·rel or·gan *n.* a mechanical musical instrument in which a rotating pin-studded cylinder acts on a series of pipe valves, strings, or metal tongues.

bar·rel roll *n.* an aerobatic maneuver in which an aircraft follows a single turn of a spiral while rolling once about its longitudinal axis.

bar·rel vault *n. Archit.* a vault forming a half cylinder.

bar·ren /báron/ *adj. & n.* • *adj.* (**bar·ren·er, bar·ren·est**) **1 a** unable to bear young. **b** unable to produce fruit or vegetation. **c** devoid of vegetation or other signs of life. **2** meager; unprofitable. **3** dull; unstimulating. **4** (foll. by *of*) lacking in (*barren of wit*). • *n.* (also in *pl.*) a barren tract or tracts of land. □□ **bar·ren·ly** *adv.* **bar·ren·ness** *n.* [ME f. AF *barai(g)ne*, OF *barhaine*, etc., of unkn. orig.]

bar·rette /bərét/ *n.* a typically bar-shaped clip or ornament for the hair. [F, dimin. of *barre* bar]

bar·ri·cade /bárikáyd/ *n. & v.* • *n.* a barrier, esp. one improvised across a street, etc. • *v.tr.* block or defend with a barricade. [F *barrique* cask f. Sp. *barrica*, rel. to BARREL]

bar·ri·er /báreeər/ *n.* **1** a fence, mountain range, or other obstacle that bars advance or access. **2** an obstacle or circumstance that keeps people or things apart, or prevents communication (*class barriers; a language barrier*). **3** anything that prevents progress or success. **4** a gate at a parking lot, toll booth, etc., that controls access. **5** *colloq.* = SOUND BARRIER. [ME f. AF *barrere*, OF *barriere*]

bar·ri·er is·land *n.* a sandy island running parallel to shore and protecting it from storms, etc.

bar·ri·er reef *n.* a coral reef separated from the shore by a broad deep channel.

bar·ring /baaring/ *prep.* except; not including. [BAR¹ + –ING²]

bar·ri·o /baareeō, bár–/ *n.* (*pl.* **·os**) **1** (in Spanish-speaking countries) a division or district of a city or town. **2** (in the US) the Spanish-speaking quarter or neighborhood of a town or city. [Sp., = district of a town]

bar·ris·ter /báristər/ *n.* (in full **barrister-at-law**) **1** *Brit.* a person called to the bar and entitled to practice as an advocate in the higher courts. **2** a lawyer. [16th c.: f. BAR¹, perh. after *minister*]

bar·room /bároōm, –roōm/ *n.* an establishment specializing in serving alcoholic drinks.

bar·row¹ /bárō/ *n.* **1** a ▭▭▭▭ ▭ame with two wheels used for transporting luggage, etc. **2** = WHEELBARROW. **3** *Brit.* a two-wheeled handcart used esp. by street vendors. [OE *bearwe* f. Gmc]

bar·row² /bárō/ *n. Archaeol.* an ancient grave mound or tumulus. [OE *beorg* f. Gmc]

bar·row boy *n. Brit.* a boy who sells wares from a barrow.

bar sin·is·ter *n.* = *bend sinister* (see BEND²).

Bart. /baart/ *abbr.* Baronet.

bar·tend·er /báartendər/ *n.* a person serving behind the bar of a tavern, bar, etc.

bar·ter /báartər/ *v. & n.* ● *v.* **1** *tr.* exchange (goods or services) without using money. **2** *intr.* make such an exchange. ● *n.* trade by exchange of goods. □□ **bar·ter·er** *n.* [prob. OF *barater*: see BARRATOR]

bar·ti·zan /báartizən, –zán/ *n. Archit.* a battlemented parapet or an overhanging corner turret at the top of a castle or church tower. □□ **bar·ti·zaned** *adj.* [var. of *bertisene*, erron. spelling of *bratticing*: see BRATTICE]

bar·y·on /báreeon/ *n. Physics* an elementary particle that is of equal mass to or greater mass than a proton (i.e., is a nucleon or a hyperon). □□ **bar·y·on·ic** /–ónik/ *adj.* [Gk *barus* heavy + –ON]

bar·y·sphere /bárisfeer/ *n.* the dense interior of the earth, including the mantle and core, enclosed by the lithosphere. [Gk *barus* heavy + *sphaira* sphere]

bar·y·ta /bərítə/ *n.* barium oxide or hydroxide. □□ **bar·yt·ic** /–rítik/ *adj.* [BARYTES, after *soda*, etc.]

bar·y·tes /bəríteez/ *n. Brit.* = BARITE.

ba·sal /báysəl, –zəl/ *adj.* **1** of, at, or forming a base. **2** fundamental. [BASE¹ + –AL]

ba·sal me·tab·o·lism *n.* the chemical processes occurring in an organism at complete rest.

ba·salt /bəsáwlt, báysawlt/ *n.* **1** a dark basic volcanic rock whose strata sometimes form columns. **2** a kind of black stoneware resembling basalt. □□ **ba·sal·tic** /–sáwltik/ *adj.* [L *basaltes* var. of *basanites* f. Gk f. *basanos* touchstone]

bas·cule bridge /báskyoōl/ *n.* a type of drawbridge that is raised and lowered using counterweights. [F, earlier *bacule* seesaw f. *battre* bump + *cul* buttocks]

base¹ /bays/ *n. & v.* ● *n.* **1 a** a part that supports from beneath or serves as a foundation for an object or structure. **b** a notional structure or entity on which something draws or depends (*power base*). **2** a principle or starting point; a basis. **3** esp. *Mil.* a place from which an operation or activity is directed. **4 a** a main or important ingredient of a mixture. **b** a substance, e.g., water, in combination with which pigment forms paint, etc. **5** a substance used as a foundation for makeup. **6** *Chem.* a substance capable of combining with an acid to form a salt and water and usu. producing hydroxide ions when dissolved in water. **7** *Math.* a number in terms of which other numbers or logarithms are expressed (see RADIX). **8** *Archit.* the part of a column between the shaft and pedestal or pavement. **9** *Geom.* a line or surface on which a figure is regarded as standing. **10** *Surveying* a known line used as a geometrical base for trigonometry. **11** *Electronics* the middle part of a transistor separating the emitter from the collector. **12** *Linguistics* a root or stem as the origin of a word or a derivative. **13** *Baseball*, etc. one of the four stations that must be reached in turn to score a run. **14** *Bot. & Zool.* the end at which an organ is attached to the trunk. **15** *Heraldry* the lowest part of a shield. ● *v.tr.* **1** (usu. foll. by *on, upon*) found or establish (*a theory based on speculation; his opinion was soundly based*). **2** (foll. by *at, in,* etc.) station (*troops were based in Malta*). [F *base* or L *basis* stepping f. Gk]

base² /bays/ *adj.* **1** lacking moral worth; cowardly; despicable. **2** menial. **3** not pure; alloyed (*base coin*). **4** (of a metal) low in value (opp. NOBLE, PRECIOUS). **5** cheap; shoddy. **6** mean; degraded. □□ **base·ly** *adv.* **base·ness** *n.* [ME in sense 'of small height,' f. F *bas* f. med.L *bassus* short (in L as a cognomen)]

base·ball /báysbawl/ *n.* **1** a game played with two teams of nine, a bat and ball, and a circuit of four bases that must be completed to score. **2** the ball used in this game.

base·board /báysbawrd/ *n.* a narrow board, etc., along the bottom of the wall of a room.

base hit *n. Baseball* a fair ball that enables the batter to get on base without benefit of an opponent's error and without forcing out another player already on base.

base hos·pi·tal *n.* a military hospital situated at some distance from the area of active operations during a war.

---

base·less /báyslis/ *adj.* unfounded; groundless. □□ **base·less·ly** *adv.* **base·less·ness** *n.*

base·line /báyslīn/ *n.* **1** a line used as a base or starting point. **2** (in tennis, basketball, etc.) the line marking each end of a court. **3** *Baseball* either of the lines leading from home plate and determining the boundaries of fair territory.

base·load /báyslōd/ *n. Brit. Electr.* the permanent load on power supplies, etc.

base·man /báysmən/ *n.* (*pl.* **·men**) *Baseball* a fielder stationed near a base.

base·ment /báysmənt/ *n.* the lowest floor of a building, usu. at least partly below ground level. [prob. Du., perh. f. It. *basamento* column base]

base on balls *n. Baseball* advancement to first base by a player who has been pitched four balls while at bat.

base pair·ing *n. Biochem.* complementary binding by means of hydrogen bonds of a purine to a pyrimidine base in opposite strands of nucleic acids.

ba·ses *pl.* of BASE¹, BASIS.

base u·nit *n.* a unit that is defined arbitrarily and not by combinations of other units.

bash /bash/ *v. & n.* ● *v.* **1** *tr.* **a** strike bluntly or heavily. **b** (often foll. by *up*) *colloq.* attack or criticize violently. **c** (often foll. by *down, in,* etc.) damage or break by striking forcibly. **2** *intr.* (foll. by *into*) collide with. ● *n.* **1** a heavy blow. **2** *Brit. sl.* an attempt (*had a bash at painting*). **3** *sl.* a party or social event. □□ **bash·er** *n.* [imit., perh. f. *bang, smash, dash,* etc.]

bash·ful /báshfoōl/ *adj.* **1** shy; diffident; self-conscious. **2** sheepish. □□ **bash·ful·ly** *adv.* **bash·ful·ness** *n.* [obs. *bash* (v.), = ABASH]

BASIC /báysik/ *n.* a computer programming language using familiar English words and designed for beginners. [Beginner's All-purpose Symbolic Instruction Code]

ba·sic /báysik/ *adj. & n.* ● *adj.* **1** forming or serving as a base. **2** fundamental. **3 a** simplest or lowest in level (*basic pay; basic requirements*). **b** vulgar (*basic humor*). **4** *Chem.* having the properties of or containing a base. **5** *Geol.* (of volcanic rocks, etc.) having less than 50 percent silica. **6** *Metallurgy* of or produced in a furnace, etc., which is made of a basic material. ● *n.* (usu. in *pl.*) the fundamental facts or principles. □□ **ba·si·cal·ly** *adv.* [BASE¹ + –IC]

ba·sic dye *n.* a dye consisting of salts of organic bases.

Ba·sic Eng·lish *n.* a simplified form of English limited to 850 selected words intended for international communication.

ba·sic in·dus·try *n.* an industry of fundamental economic importance.

ba·sic·i·ty /baysísitee/ *n. Chem.* the number of protons with which a base will combine.

ba·sic slag *n.* fertilizer containing phosphates formed as a byproduct during steel manufacture.

ba·sid·i·um /bəsídeeəm/ *n.* (*pl.* **ba·sid·i·a** /–deeə/) a microscopic spore-bearing structure produced by certain fungi. [mod.L f. Gk *basidion* dimin. of BASIS]

bas·il /bázəl, báyzəl/ *n.* an aromatic herb of the genus *Ocimum*, esp. *O. basilicum* (in full **sweet basil**), whose leaves are used as a flavoring in cooking. [ME f. OF *basile* f. med.L *basilicus* f. Gk *basilikos* royal]

bas·i·lar /básilər/ *adj.* of or at the base (esp. of the skull). [mod.L *basilaris* (as BASIS)]

ba·sil·i·ca /bəsílikə/ *n.* **1** an ancient Roman public hall with an apse and colonnades, used as a court of law and place of assembly. **2** a similar building used as a Christian church. **3** a church having special privileges from the Pope. □□ **ba·sil·i·can** *adj.* [L f. Gk *basilikē* (*oikia, stoa*) royal (house, portico) f. *basileus* king]

bas·i·lisk /básilisk, báz–/ *n.* **1** a mythical reptile with a lethal breath and look. **2** any small American lizard of the genus *Basiliscus*, with a crest from its back to its tail. **3** *Heraldry* a cockatrice. [ME f. L *basiliscus* f. Gk *basiliskos* kinglet, serpent]

ba·sin /báysən/ *n.* **1** a wide, shallow, open container, esp. a fixed one for holding water. **2** a hollow, rounded depression. **3** any sheltered area of water where boats can moor safely. **4** a round valley. **5** an area drained by rivers and tributaries. **6** *Geol.* **a** a rock formation where the strata dip toward the center. **b** an accumulation of rock strata formed in this dip as a result of subsidence and sedimentation. □□ **ba·sin·ful** *n.* (*pl.* **·fuls**). [ME f. OF *bacin* f. med.L *ba(s)cinus*, perh. f. Gaulish]

ba·sip·e·tal /baysípit'l/ *adj. Bot.* (of each new part produced) developing nearer the base than the previous one did. □□ **ba·sip·e·tal·ly** *adv.* [BASIS + L *petere* seek]

ba·sis /báysis/ *n.* (*pl.* **ba·ses** /–seez/) **1** the foundation or support of something, esp. an idea or argument. **2** the main or determining principle or ingredient (*on a purely friendly basis*). **3** the starting point for a discussion, etc. [L f. Gk, = BASE¹]

bask /bask/ *v.intr.* **1** sit or lie back lazily in warmth and light (*bask-*

ing in the sun). **2** (foll. by *in*) derive great pleasure (from) (*basking in glory*). [ME, app. f. ON: rel. to BATHE]

bas·ket /báskit/ *n.* **1** a container made of interwoven cane, etc. **2** a container resembling this. **3** the amount held by a basket. **4** the goal in basketball, or a goal scored. **5** *Econ.* a group or range of currencies). **6** *Brit. euphem. colloq.* bastard. □□ **bas·ket·ful** *n.* (*pl.* **fuls**). [AF & OF *basket*, AL *baskettum*, of unkn. orig.]

bas·ket·ball /báskitbawl/ *n.* **1** a game between two teams, usu. of five, in which points are scored by making the ball drop through hooped nets fixed high up at each end of the court. **2** the ball used in this game.

bas·ket case *n.* **1** a person who cannot function because of tension, stress, etc. **2** *offensive* a person who has had all four limbs amputated. [early 20th c. slang for a soldier who had lost all four limbs]

bas·ket·ry /báskitree/ *n.* **1** the art of making baskets. **2** baskets collectively.

bas·ket weave *n.* a weave resembling that of a basket.

bas·ket·work /báskitwərk/ *n.* **1** material woven in the style of a basket. **2** the art of making baskets.

bask·ing shark *n.* a very large shark, *Cetorhinus maximus*, which often lies near the surface.

bas·ma·ti /baasmáatee/ *n.* (in full **bas·ma·ti rice**) a long-grained aromatic kind of Indian rice. [Hindi, = fragrant]

bas mitz·vah /bas mítsvə/ *n.* var. of BAT MITZVAH.

Basque /bask/ *n. & adj.* ● *n.* **1** a member of a people of the Western Pyrenees. **2** the language of this people. ● *adj.* of or relating to the Basques or their language. [F f. L *Vasco –onis*]

basque /bask/ *n.* a close-fitting bodice extending from the shoulders to the waist and often with a short continuation below waist level. [BASQUE]

bas-re·lief /baá-rileéf, bás-/ *n.* (Also **low re·lief**) sculpture or carving in which the figures project slightly from the background. [earlier *basse relieve* f. It. *basso rilievo* low relief: later altered to F form]

bass[1] /bays/ *n. & adj.* ● *n.* **1 a** the lowest adult male singing voice. **b** a singer with this voice. **c** a part written for it. **2** the lowest part in harmonized music. **3 a** an instrument that is the lowest in pitch in its family. **b** its player. **4** *colloq.* **a** a bass guitar or double bass. **b** its player. **5** the low-frequency output of a radio, CD player, turntable, etc., corresponding to the bass in music. ● *adj.* **1** lowest in musical pitch. **2** deep sounding. □□ **bass·ist** *n.* (in sense 4b). [alt. of BASE[2] after It. *basso*]

bass[2] /bas/ *n.* (*pl.* same or **bass·es**) any of various edible fishes including the common European perch and several N. American marine and freshwater fishes, esp. *Morone saxatilis* and *Micropterus salmoides*. [earlier *barse* f. OE *bærs*]

bass[3] /bas/ *n.* = BAST. [alt. f. BAST]

bass clef *n.* a clef placing F below middle C on the second highest line of the staff.

bas·set /básit/ *n.* (in full **basset hound**) **1** a sturdy hunting dog of a breed with a long body, short legs, and big ears. **2** this breed. [F, dimin. of *bas basse* low: see *base*]

basset hound

bas·set horn /básit hawrn/ *n.* an alto clarinet in F. [G, transl. of F *cor de bassette* f. It. *corno di bassetto* f. *corno* horn + *bassetto* dimin. of *basso* BASE[2]]

bas·si·net /básinét/ *n.* a child's wicker cradle, usu. with a hood. [F, dimin. of *bassin* BASIN]

bas·so /báso, baá–/ *n.* (*pl.* **·sos** or **bas·si** /–see/) a singer with a bass voice. [It., = BASS[1]; *profondo* deep]

bas·soon /bəsoón/ *n.* **1 a** a bass instrument of the oboe family, with a double reed. **b** its player. **2** an organ stop with the quality of a bassoon. □□ **bas·soon·ist** *n.* (in sense 1b). [F *basson* f. *bas* BASS[1]]

bas·so pro·fun·do /prōfoóndō/ *n.* a bass singer with an exceptionally low range.

bas·so-re·lie·vo /báso-rileévō/ *n.* (also **bas·so-ri·lie·vo** /báso-reelyáyvō/) (*pl.* **·vos**) = BAS-RELIEF. [It. *basso-rilievo* = BAS-RELIEF]

bass vi·ol *n.* **1 a** a viola da gamba. **b** its player. **2** a double bass.

bass·wood /báswŏod/ *n.* **1** the American linden, *Tilia americana*. **2** the wood of this tree. [BASS[3] + WOOD]

bast /bast/ *n.* the inner bark of linden, or other flexible fibrous bark, used as fiber in matting, etc. [OE *bæst* f. Gmc]

bas·tard /bástərd/ *n. & adj.* ● *n.* **1** a person born of parents not married to each other. **2** *sl.* **a** an unpleasant or despicable person. **b** a

person of a specified kind (*poor bastard; lucky bastard*). **3** *sl.* a difficult or awkward thing, undertaking, etc. ● *adj.* **1** born of parents not married to each other; illegitimate. **2** (of things): **a** unauthorized; counterfeit. **b** hybrid. □□ **bas·tar·dy** *n.* (in sense 1 of *n.*).

▶In the past the word **bastard** was the standard term in both legal and non-legal use for 'an illegitimate child.' Today, however, it has little importance as a legal term and is retained in this older sense only as a term of abuse.

bas·tard·ize /bástərdīz/ *v.tr.* **1** declare (a person) illegitimate. **2** corrupt, debase. □□ **bas·tard·i·za·tion** *n.*

baste[1] /bayst/ *v.tr.* moisten (meat) with gravy or melted fat during cooking. [16th c.: orig. unkn.]

baste[2] /bayst/ *v.tr.* stitch loosely together in preparation for sewing; tack. [ME f. OF *bastir* sew lightly, ult. f. Gmc]

baste[3] /bayst/ *v.tr.* beat soundly; thrash. [perh. figurative use of BASTE[1]]

bas·tille /basteél/ *n. hist.* a fortress or prison. [ME f. OF *bastille* f. Prov. *bastir* build: orig. of the fortress and prison in Paris, destroyed in 1789]

bas·ti·na·do /bástináydō, –naá–/ *n. & v.* ● *n.* punishment by beating with a stick on the soles of the feet. ● *v.tr.* (**·does**, **·doed**) punish (a person) in this way. [Sp. *bastonada* f. *baston* BATON]

bas·tion /báschən, –teeən/ *n.* **1** a projecting part of a fortification built at an angle of, or against the line of, a wall. **2** a thing regarded as protecting (*bastion of freedom*). **3** a natural rock formation resembling a bastion. [F f. It. *bastione* f. *bastire* build]

ba·su·co /bəsoókō/ *n.* a cheap impure form of cocaine smoked for its stimulating effect. [Colombian Sp.]

bat[1] /bat/ *n. & v.* ● *n.* **1** an implement with a handle, usu. of wood and with a flat or curved surface, used for hitting balls in games. **2** *Cricket* a turn at using this. **3** a batsman, esp. in cricket, etc., usu. described in some way (*an excellent bat*). **4** (usu. in *pl.*) an object like a table tennis paddle used to guide aircraft when taxiing. ● *v.* (**bat·ted, bat·ting**) **1** *tr.* hit with or as with a bat. **2** *intr.* take a turn at batting. **3** have a batting average of. □ **bat around 1** *sl.* drift or putter aimlessly. **2** discuss (an idea or proposal). **3** *Baseball* have each player in a lineup bat in the course of a single inning. **off one's own bat** *Brit.* unprompted; unaided. **right off the bat** immediately. [ME f. OE *batt* club, perh. partly f. OF *batte* club f. *battre* strike]

bat[2] /bat/ *n.* any mouselike nocturnal mammal of the order Chiroptera, capable of flight by means of membranous wings extending from its forelimbs. □ **have bats in the belfry** be eccentric or crazy. **like a bat out of hell** very fast. [16th c., alt. of ME *bakke* f. Scand.]

leaf-nosed bat

bat[3] /bat/ *v.tr.* (**bat·ted, bat·ting**) wink (one's eye) (now usu. in phr.). □ **not** (or **never**) **bat an eye** *colloq.* show no reaction or emotion. [var. of obs. *bate* flutter]

batch /bach/ *n. & v.* ● *n.* **1** a number of things or persons forming a group or dealt with together. **2** an installment (*have sent off the latest batch*). **3** the loaves produced at one baking. **4** (*attrib.*) using or dealt with in batches, not as a continuous flow (*batch production*). **5** *Computing* a group of records processed as a single unit. ● *v.tr.* arrange or deal with in batches. [ME f. OE *bæcce* f. *bacan* BAKE]

bate[1] /bayt/ *v.* **1** *tr.* moderate; restrain. **2** *tr.* diminish; deduct. **3** *intr.* diminish; abate.

bate[2] /bayt/ *n.* (also **bait**) *Brit. sl.* a rage; a cross mood (*is in an awful bate*). [BAIT[1] = state of baited person]

ba·teau /bató/ *n.* (*pl.* **ba·teaux** /–tōz/) a light riverboat, esp. of the flat-bottomed kind used in Canada and the southern US. [F = boat]

bat·ed /báytid/ *adj.* □ **with bated breath** very anxiously. [past part. of obs. *bate* (v.) restrain, f. ABATE]

ba·te·leur /bátəlŏr/ *n.* a short-tailed African eagle, *Terathopius ecaudatus*. [F, = juggler]

bath /bath/ *n. & v.* ● *n.* (*pl.* **baths** /bathz, baths/) **1 a** = BATHTUB. **b** a bathtub with its contents (*your bath is ready*). **2** the act or process of immersing the body for washing or therapy (*take a bath*). **3 a** a vessel containing liquid in which something is immersed, e.g., a film for developing, for controlling temperature, etc. **b** this with its contents. **4** *esp. Brit.* (usu. in *pl.*) a building with baths or a swimming pool, usu. open to the public. ● *v. Brit.* **1** *tr.* wash (esp. a person) in a bath. **2** *intr.* take a bath. □ **take a bath** *sl.* suffer a large financial loss. [OE *bæth* f. Gmc]

Bath bun /bath/ *n. Brit.* a round spiced kind of sweet bun with currants, often with icing. [*Bath* in S. England, named from its hot springs]

Bath chair /bath/ *n.* esp. *Brit.* a wheelchair for invalids.

bathe /bayth/ *v. & n.* ● *v.* **1** *intr.* immerse oneself in water, esp. (*Brit.*) to swim or wash oneself. **2** *tr.* immerse in or wash or treat with liquid, esp. for cleansing or medicinal purposes. **3** *tr.* (of sunlight, etc.) suffuse or envelop with. ● *n. Brit.* an immersion in liquid, esp. to swim. [OE *bathian* f. Gmc]

bath•er /báythər/ *n.* **1** a person who bathes. **2** (in *pl.*) *Austral.* a bathing suit.

bath•house /báth-hows/ *n.* **1** a building with baths for public use. **2** a building with changing rooms, as at the beach.

bath•ing suit *n.* a garment worn for swimming.

bath•o•lith /báthəlith/ *n.* a dome of igneous rock extending inward to an unknown depth. [G f. Gk *bathos* depth + –LITH]

ba•thom•e•ter /bəthómitər/ *n.* an instrument used to measure the depth of water. [Gk *bathos* depth + –METER]

ba•thos /báythaws, –thos/ *n.* (esp. in a work of literature) an unintentional lapse in mood from the sublime to the absurd or trivial; a commonplace or ridiculous feature offsetting an otherwise sublime situation; an anticlimax. □□ **ba•thet•ic** /bəthétik/ *adj.* **ba•thot•ic** /bəthótik/ *adj.* [Gk, = depth]

bath•robe /báthrōb/ *n.* a loose robe or dressing gown, worn before and after taking a bath or for lounging.

bath•room /báthrōōm, –rŏŏm/ *n.* **1** a room containing a toilet. **2** a room containing a bath and usu. other washing facilities.

bath salts *n.* soluble salts used for softening or scenting bathwater.

bath•tub /báthtəb/ *n.* a tub, usu. installed in a bathroom, used for immersing and washing the body.

bath•y•scaphe /báthiskaf/ *n.* a manned vessel controlled by ballast for deep-sea diving. [Gk *bathus* deep + *skaphos* ship]

bath•y•sphere /báthisfeer/ *n.* a spherical vessel connected to a surface vessel by cables, used for deep-sea observation. [Gk *bathus* deep + SPHERE]

ba•tik /bəteék, bátik/ *n.* a method (orig. used in Indonesia) of producing colored designs on textiles by applying wax to the parts to be left uncolored; a piece of cloth treated in this way. [Jav., = painted]

ba•tiste /bateést/ *n. & adj.* ● *n.* a fine linen or cotton cloth. ● *adj.* made of batiste. [F (earlier *batiche*), perh. rel. to *battre* BATTER[1]]

bat•man /bátmən/ *n.* (*pl.* •men) *Brit. Mil.* an attendant serving an officer. [OF *bat, bast* f. med.L *bastum* packsaddle + MAN]

bat mitz•vah /bat mítsvə/ (also **bas mitz•vah**) **1** an initiation ceremony for a Jewish girl who has reached the age of 12 or 13 and is ready to assume adult religious responsibilities. **2** a girl confirmed by this ceremony [Heb. *bath miṣwāh*, lit. daughter of the divine law]

ba•ton /bətón, ba–, bát'n/ *n.* **1** a thin stick used by a conductor to direct an orchestra, choir, etc. **2** *Sports* a short stick or tube carried and passed on by the runners in a relay race. **3** a long stick carried and twirled by a drum major. **4** a staff of office or authority, esp. (*Brit.*) a field marshal's. **5** esp. *Brit.* a policeman's truncheon. **6** *Heraldry* a narrow truncated bend. **7** *Horol.* a short bar replacing some figures on dials. [F *bâton, baston* ult. f. LL *bastum* stick]

ba•tra•chi•an /bətráykeeən/ *n. & adj.* ● *n.* any of the amphibians that discard gills and tails, esp. the frog and toad. ● *adj.* of or relating to the batrachians. [Gk *batrakhos* frog]

bats /bats/ *predic.adj. sl.* crazy. [f. phr. (*have*) *bats in the belfry*: see BAT[2]]

bats•man /bátsmən/ *n.* (*pl.* •men) **1** a person who bats or is batting, esp. in cricket. **2** esp. *Brit.* a signaler using bats to guide aircraft on the ground. □□ **bats•man•ship** *n.* (in sense 1).

bat•tal•ion /bətályən/ *n.* **1** a large body of men ready for battle, esp. an infantry unit forming part of a brigade. **2** a large group of people pursuing a common aim or sharing a major undertaking. [F *battaillon* f. It. *battaglione* f. *battaglia* BATTLE]

bat•ten[1] /bát'n/ *n. & v.* ● *n.* **1** a long flat strip of squared lumber or metal, esp. used to hold something in place or as a fastening against a wall, etc. **2** a strip of wood used for clamping the boards of a door, etc. **3** *Naut.* a strip of wood or metal for securing a tarpaulin over a ship's hatchway. ● *v.tr.* strengthen or fasten with battens. □ **batten down the hatches 1** *Naut.* secure a ship's tarpaulins. **2** prepare for a difficulty or crisis. [OF *batant* part. of *batre* beat f. L *battuere*]

bat•ten[2] /bát'n/ *v.intr.* (foll. by *on*) thrive or prosper at another's expense. [ON *batna* f. *bati* advantage]

bat•ter[1] /bátər/ *v.* **1 a** *tr.* strike repeatedly with hard blows, esp. so as to cause visible damage. **b** *intr.* (often foll. by *against, at,* etc.) strike repeated blows; pound heavily and insistently (*batter at the door*). **2** *tr.* (often in *passive*) **a** handle roughly, esp. over a long period. **b** censure or criticize severely. □□ **bat•ter•er** *n.* **bat•ter•ing** *n.* [ME f. AF *baterer* f. OF *batre* beat f. L *battuere*]

bat•ter[2] /bátər/ *n.* **1** a fluid mixture of flour, egg, and milk or water, used in cooking, esp. for cakes, etc., and for coating food before frying. **2** *Printing* an area of damaged type. [ME f. AF *batour* f. OF *bateüre* f. *batre*: see BATTER[1]]

bat•ter[3] /bátər/ *n. Sports* a player batting, esp. in baseball.

bat•ter[4] /bátər/ *n. & v.* ● *n.* **1** a wall, etc., with a sloping face. **2** a receding slope. ● *v.intr.* have a receding slope. [ME: orig. unkn.]

bat•tered /bátərd/ *adj.* injured by repeated blows or punishment.

bat•ter•ing ram *n. hist.* a heavy beam, orig. with an end in the form of a carved ram's head, used in breaching fortifications.

bat•ter•y /bátəree/ *n.* (*pl.* •ies) **1** a usu. portable container of a cell or cells carrying an electric charge, as a source of current. **2** (often *attrib.*) esp. *Brit.* a series of cages for the intensive breeding and rearing of poultry or cattle. **3** a set of similar units of equipment, esp. connected. **4** a series of tests, esp. psychological. **5 a** a fortified emplacement for heavy guns. **b** an artillery unit of guns, soldiers, and vehicles. **6** *Law* an act inflicting unlawful personal violence on another (see ASSAULT). **7** *Baseball* the pitcher and the catcher. [F *batterie* f. *batre, battre* strike f. L *battuere*]

bat•ting /báting/ *n.* **1** the action of hitting with a bat. **2** cotton wadding prepared in sheets for use in quilts, etc.

bat•ting av•er•age *n.* **1** *Baseball* a batter's safe hits per official times at bat. **2** *Cricket* a batsman's runs scored per completed innings.

bat•ting or•der *n.* the order in which people act or take their turn, esp. of batters in baseball.

bat•tle /bát'l/ *n. & v.* ● *n.* **1 a** a prolonged fight between large organized armed forces. **b** a fight between two individuals. **2** a contest; a prolonged or difficult struggle (*life is a constant battle; a battle of wits*). ● *v.* **1** *intr.* struggle; fight persistently (*battled against the elements; battled for women's rights*). **2** *tr.* fight (one's way, etc.). **3** *tr.* engage in battle with. □ **half the battle** the key to the success of an undertaking. □□ **bat•tler** *n.* [ME f. OF *bataille* ult. f. LL *battualia* gladiatorial exercises f. L *battuere* beat]

bat•tle-ax *n.* **1** a large ax used in ancient warfare. **2** *colloq.* a formidable or domineering older woman.

bat•tle cruis•er *n.* a heavily armed ship faster and more lightly armored than a battleship.

bat•tle cry *n.* a cry or slogan of participants in a battle or contest.

bat•tle•dore /bát'ldawr/ *n. hist.* **1 a** (in full **battledore and shuttlecock**) a game similar to badminton played with a shuttlecock and rackets. **b** the racket used in this. **2** a kind of wooden utensil like a paddle, formerly used in washing, baking, etc. [15th c., perh. f. Prov. *batedor* beater f. *batre* beat]

bat•tle dress *n.* the field uniform of a soldier, often camouflaged.

bat•tle fa•tigue *n.* a mental disorder caused by stress in wartime combat. Also called **combat fatigue.**

bat•tle•field *n.* (also **bat•tle•ground** /–grownd/) the piece of ground on which a battle is or was fought.

bat•tle•ment /bát'lmənt/ *n.* (usu. in *pl.*) **1 a** a parapet with recesses along the top of a wall, as part of a fortification. **2** a section of roof enclosed by this (*walking on the battlements*). □□ **bat•tle•ment•ed** *adj.* [OF *bataillier* furnish with ramparts + –MENT]

bat•tle roy•al *n.* **1** a battle in which several combatants or all available forces engage; a free fight. **2** a heated argument.

bat•tle•ship /bát'lship/ *n.* a warship with the heaviest armor and the largest guns.

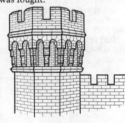

battlement

bat•tue /batoó, –tyoó/ *n.* **1 a** the driving of game toward hunters by beaters. **b** a hunt arranged in this way. **2** wholesale slaughter. [F, fem. past part. of *battre* beat f. L *battuere*]

bat•ty /bátee/ *adj.* (**bat•ti•er, bat•ti•est**) *sl.* crazy. □□ **bat•ti•ly** *adv.* **bat•ti•ness** *n.* [BAT[2] + –Y[1]]

bat•wing /bátwing/ *adj.* (esp. of a sleeve or a flame) shaped like the wing of a bat.

bat•wom•an /bátwŏŏmən/ *n.* (*pl.* •wom•en) *Brit.* a female attendant serving an officer in the women's services. [as BATMAN + WOMAN]

bau•ble /báwbəl/ *n.* **1** a showy trinket or toy of little value. **2** a baton formerly used as an emblem by jesters. [ME f. OF *ba(u)bel* child's toy, of unkn. orig.]

baud /bawd/ *n.* (*pl.* same or **bauds**) *Computing*, etc. **1** a unit used to express the speed of electronic code signals, corresponding to one information unit per second. **2** (loosely) a unit of data transmission speed of one bit per second. [J. M. E. *Baudot*, Fr. engineer d. 1903]

Bau•haus /bówhows/ *n.* **1** a German school of architectural design (1919–33). **2** its principles, based on functionalism and development of existing skills. [G f. *Bau* building + *Haus* house]

baux•ite /báwksīt/ *n.* a claylike mineral containing varying proportions of alumina, the chief source of aluminum. □□ **baux•it•ic** /–sítik/ *adj.* [F f. *Les Baux* near Arles in S. France + –ITE[1]]

bawd /bawd/ *n.* a woman who runs a brothel. [ME *bawdstrot* f. OF *baudetrot, baudestroyt* procuress]

bawd·y /báwdee/ *adj. & n.* ● *adj.* (**bawd·i·er, bawd·i·est**) (esp. humorously) indecent; raunchy. ● *n.* bawdy talk or writing. □□ **bawd·i·ly** *adv.* **bawd·i·ness** *n.* [BAWD + -Y¹]

bawd·y house *n.* a brothel.

bawl /bawl/ *v.* **1** *tr.* speak or call out noisily. **2** *intr.* weep loudly. □ **bawl out** *colloq.* reprimand angrily. □□ **bawl·er** *n.* [imit.: cf. med.L *baulare* bark, Icel. *baula* (Sw. *böla*) to low]

bay¹ /bay/ *n.* **1** a broad inlet of the sea where the land curves inward. **2** a recess in a mountain range. [ME f. OF *baie* f. OSp. *bahia*]

bay² /bay/ *n.* **1** (in full **bay laurel**) a laurel, *Laurus nobilis,* having deep green leaves and purple berries. Also called **sweet bay. 2** (in *pl.*) a wreath made of bay leaves, for a victor or poet. [OF *baie* f. L *baca* berry]

bay³ /bay/ *n.* **1** a space created by a window line projecting outwards from a wall. **2** a recess; a section of wall between buttresses or columns, esp. in the nave of a church, etc. **3** a compartment (*bomb bay*). **4** an area specially allocated or marked off (*sick bay; loading bay*). **5** *Brit.* the terminus of a branch line at a railroad station also having through lines, usu. at the side of an outer platform. [ME f. OF *baie* f. *ba(y)er* gape f. med.L *batare*]

bay⁴ /bay/ *adj. & n.* ● *adj.* (esp. of a horse) dark reddish brown. ● *n.* a bay horse with a black mane and tail. [OF *bai* f. L *badius*]

bay⁵ /bay/ *v. & n.* ● *v.* **1** *intr.* (esp. of a large dog) bark or howl loudly and plaintively. **2** *tr.* bay at. ● *n.* the sound of baying, esp. in chorus from hounds in close pursuit. □ **at bay 1** cornered; apparently unable to escape. **2** in a desperate situation. **bring to bay** gain on in pursuit; trap. **hold** (or **keep**) **at bay** hold off (a pursuer). **stand at bay** turn to face one's pursuers. [ME f. OF *bai, baiier* bark f. It. *baiare,* of imit. orig.]

bay·ber·ry /báyberee/ *n.* (*pl.* **-ries**) any of various N. American plants of the genus *Myrica,* having aromatic leaves and bearing berries covered in a wax coating. [BAY² + BERRY]

bay leaf *n.* the aromatic (usu. dried) leaf of the bay tree, used in cooking.

bay·o·net /báyǝnét/ *n. & v.* ● *n.* **1** a stabbing blade attachable to the muzzle of a rifle. **2** an electrical or other fitting engaged by being pushed into a socket and twisted. ● *v.tr.* (**bay·o·net·ed, bay·o·net·ing**) stab with a bayonet. [F *baïonnette,* perh. f. *Bayonne* in SW France, where they were first made]

bay·ou /bí-oō/ *n.* a marshy offshoot of a river, etc., in the southern US. [Amer. F: cf. Choctaw *bayuk*]

bay rum *n.* a perfume, esp. for the hair, distilled orig. from bayberry leaves in rum.

bay win·dow *n.* a window built to project outward from an outside wall.

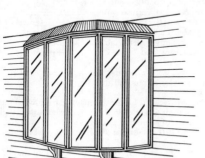

bayonet

bay window

ba·zaar /bǝzáar/ *n.* **1** a market in an Eastern or Middle Eastern country. **2** a fund-raising sale of goods, esp. for charity. **3** a large store selling fancy goods, etc.; a department store. [Pers. *bāzār,* prob. through Turk. and It.]

ba·zoo·ka /bǝzoōkǝ/ *n.* **1** a tubular short-range rocket launcher used against tanks. **2** a crude trombonelike musical instrument. [app. f. *bazoo* mouth, of unkn. orig.]

BB *abbr.* **1** a shot pellet about .18 inch in diameter, for use in a BB gun or air gun. **2** *Brit.* double-black (pencil lead).

bazooka

BBC *abbr.* British Broadcasting Corporation.

BBC Eng·lish *n.* a form of standard spoken English associated with BBC announcers.

bbl. *abbr.* barrels (esp. of oil).

BC *abbr.* **1** (of a date) before Christ. **2** British Columbia.

BCD /béeseedée/ *n. Computing* a code representing decimal numbers as a string of binary digits. [abbr. for binary coded decimal]

BCE *abbr.* (of a date) before the Common Era.

BCG *abbr.* Bacillus Calmette-Guérin, an anti-tuberculosis vaccine.

BD *abbr.* Bachelor of Divinity.

Bde *abbr.* Brigade.

bdel·li·um /déleeǝm/ *n.* **1** any of various trees, esp. of the genus *Commiphora,* yielding resin. **2** this fragrant resin used in perfumes. [L f. Gk *bdellion* f. Heb. *bᵉdhōlaḥ*]

bdrm. *abbr.* bedroom.

BE *abbr.* **1** Bachelor of Education. **2** Bachelor of Engineering. **3** bill of exchange.

Be *symb. Chem.* the element beryllium.

be /bee/ *v. & v.aux.* (*sing. present* **am** /am, ǝm/; **are** /aar, ǝr/; **is** /iz/; *pl. present* **are**; *1st and 3rd sing. past* **was** /wuz, woz, wǝz/; *2nd sing. past and pl. past* **were** /wǝr/; *present subj.* **be**; *past subj.* **were**; *pres. part.* **being**; *past part.* **been** /bin/) ● *v.intr.* **1** (often prec. by *there*) exist; live (*I think, therefore I am; there is a house on the corner; there is no God*). **2 a** occur; take place (*dinner is at eight*). **b** occupy a position in space (*he is in the garden; have you been to Paris?*). **3** remain; continue (*let it be*). **4** linking subject and predicate, expressing: **a** identity (*she is the person; today is Thursday*). **b** condition (*he is ill today*). **c** state or quality (*he is very kind; they are my friends*). **d** opinion (*I am against hanging*). **e** total (*two and two are four*). **f** cost or significance (*it is $5 to enter; it is nothing to me*). ● *v.aux.* **1** with a past participle to form the passive mood (*it was done; it is said; we shall be helped*). **2** with a present participle to form continuous tenses (*we are coming; it is being cleaned*). **3** with an infinitive to express duty or commitment, intention, possibility, destiny, or hypothesis (*I am to tell you; we are to wait here; he is to come at four; it was not to be found; they were never to meet again; if I were to die*). **4** *archaic* with the past participle of intransitive verbs to form perfect tenses (*the sun is set; Babylon is fallen*). □ **be about** occupy oneself with (*is about his business*). **be at** occupy oneself with (*mice have been at the food*). **been** (or **been and gone**) and esp. *Brit. sl.* an expression of protest or surprise (*he's been and taken my car!*). **be off** *colloq.* go away; leave. **be that as it may** see MAY. **–to-be** of the future (in *comb.*: *bride-to-be*). [OE *beo(m), (e)am, is, (e)aron;* past f. OE *wæs* f. *wesan* to be; there are numerous Gmc cognates]

be- /bee/ *prefix* forming verbs: **1** (from transitive verbs) **a** all over; all around (*beset; besmear*). **b** thoroughly; excessively (*begrudge; belabor*). **2** (from intransitive verbs) expressing transitive action (*bemoan; bestride*). **3** (from adjectives and nouns) expressing transitive action (*befool; befoul*). **4** (from nouns) **a** affect with (*befog*). **b** treat as (*befriend*). **c** (forming adjectives in *-ed*) having; covered with (*bejeweled; bespectacled*). [OE *be-,* weak form of *bī* BY as in *bygone, byword,* etc.]

beach /beech/ *n. & v.* ● *n.* a pebbly or sandy shore esp. of the sea between high- and low-water marks. ● *v.tr.* run or haul up (a boat, etc.) on to a beach. [16th c.: orig. unkn.]

beach ball *n.* a large inflated ball for games on the beach.

beach bug·gy *n.* esp. *Brit.* = dune buggy.

beach·comb·er /béechkōmǝr/ *n.* **1** a vagrant who lives by searching beaches for articles of value. **2** a long wave rolling in from the sea.

beach·head /béech-hed/ *n. Mil.* a fortified position established on a beach by landing forces. [after *bridgehead*]

Beach-la-mar /béechlǝmáar/ *n. Brit.* an English-based Creole language spoken in the W. Pacific. [corrupt. f. Port. *bicho do mar* BÊCHE-DE-MER]

beach plum *n.* **1** a maritime N. American shrub, *Prunus maritima.* **2** its edible fruit.

bea·con /béekǝn/ *n.* **1 a** a fire or light set up in a high or prominent position as a warning, etc. **b** *Brit.* (now often in place-names) a hill suitable for this. **2** a visible warning or guiding point or device (e.g., a lighthouse, navigation buoy, etc.). **3** a radio transmitter whose signal helps fix the position of a ship or aircraft. [OE *bēacn* f. WG]

bead /beed/ *n. & v.* ● *n.* **1 a** a small usu. rounded and perforated piece of glass, stone, etc., for threading with others to make jewelry, or sewing on to fabric, etc. **b** (in *pl.*) a string of beads; a rosary. **2** a drop of liquid; a bubble. **3** a small knob in the foresight of a gun. **4** the inner edge of a pneumatic tire that grips the rim of the wheel. **5** *Archit.* **a** a molding like a series of beads. **b** a narrow molding with a semicircular cross section. ● *v.* **1** *tr.* furnish or decorate with beads. **2** *tr.* string together. **3** *intr.* form or grow into beads. □ **draw a bead on** take aim at. **tell one's beads** use the beads of a rosary, etc., in counting prayers. □□ **bead·ed** *adj.* [orig. = 'prayer' (for which the earliest use of beads arose): OE *gebed* f. Gmc, rel. to BID]

bead·ing /béeding/ *n.* **1** decoration in the form of or resembling a row of beads, esp. lacelike looped edging. **2** *Archit.* a bead molding. **3** the bead of a tire.

bea·dle /béed'l/ *n.* **1** *Brit.* a ceremonial officer of a church, college,

cardinal

heavy, triangular beak
for cracking seeds

red-tailed hawk

strong, sharp, hooked beak
for tearing flesh

great blue heron

long, daggerlike beak for spearing
and seizing fish and frogs

ruby-throated hummingbird

needlelike beak for
collecting nectar

mallard

wide bill for scooping and sifting
vegetation and insects from water's surface

white pelican

long, flat bill with throat pouch for
scooping and swallowing fish

roseate spoonbill

spatulate bill that sweeps through the
water to scoop up crustaceans and fish

tree swallow

short, wide-opening beak for
catching flying insects

red-bellied woodpecker

tapered beak for boring
into wood for insects

beaks and bills

---

etc. **2** *Sc.* a church officer attending on the minister. **3** *Brit. hist.* a minor parish officer dealing with petty offenders, etc. □□ **bea·dle·ship** *n.* [ME f. OF *bedel* ult. f. Gmc]

beads·man /beedzmən/ *n.* (*pl.* **·men**) *hist.* **1** a pensioner provided for by a benefactor in return for prayers. **2** an inmate of an almshouse.

bead·y /beedee/ *adj.* (**bead·i·er, bead·i·est**) **1** (of the eyes) small, round, and bright. **2** covered with beads or drops. □□ **bead·i·ly** *adv.* **bead·i·ness** *n.*

bead·y-eyed *adj.* with beady eyes.

bea·gle /beegəl/ *n. & v.* • *n.* **1 a** a small hound of a breed with a short coat, orig. used for hunting hares. **b** this breed. **2** *hist.* an informer or spy; a constable. • *v.intr.* (often as **beagling** *n.*) esp. *Brit.* hunt with beagles. □□ **bea·gler** *n.* [ME f. OF *beegueule* noisy person, prob. f. *beer* open wide + *gueule* throat]

beak[1] /beek/ *n.* **1 a** a bird's horny projecting jaws; a bill. **b** the similar projecting jaw of other animals, e.g., a turtle. **2** *sl.* a hooked nose. **3** *Naut. hist.* the projection at the prow of a warship. **4** a spout. □□ **beaked** *adj.* **beak·y** *adj.* [ME f. OF *bec* f. L *beccus*, of Celt. orig.]

beak[2] /beek/ *n. Brit. sl.* **1** a magistrate. **2** a schoolmaster. [19th c.: prob. f. thieves' cant]

beak·er /beekər/ *n.* **1 a** tall drinking vessel, usu. of plastic and tumbler-shaped. **2** a lipped cylindrical glass vessel for scientific experiments. **3** *archaic* or *literary* a large drinking vessel with a wide mouth. [ME f. ON *bikarr*, perh. f. Gk *bikos* drinking bowl]

Beak·er folk *n. Archaeol.* a people thought to have come to Britain from Central Europe in the early Bronze Age, named after beaker-shaped pottery found in their graves.

be-all and end-all *n. colloq.* the feature of an activity or way of life that is of greater importance than any other.

beam /beem/ *n. & v.* • *n.* **1** a long sturdy piece of squared timber or metal spanning an opening or room, usu. to support the structure above. **2 a** a ray or shaft of light. **b** a directional flow of particles or radiation. **3** a bright look or smile. **4 a** a series of radio or radar signals as a guide to a ship or aircraft. **b** the course indicated by this (*off beam*). **5** the crossbar of a balance. **6 a** a ship's breadth at its widest point. **b** the width of a person's hips (esp. *broad in the beam*). **7** (in *pl.*) the horizontal cross-timbers of a ship supporting the deck and joining the sides. **8** the side of a ship (*land on the port beam*).

9 the chief timber of a plow. **10** the cylinder in a loom on which the warp or cloth is wound. **11** the main stem of a stag's antlers. **12** the lever in an engine connecting the piston rod and crank. **13** the shank of an anchor. • *v.* **1** *tr.* emit or direct (light, radio waves, etc.). **2** *intr.* **a** shine. **b** look or smile radiantly. □ **a beam in one's eye** a fault that is greater in oneself than in the person one is finding fault with (see Matt. 7:3). **off** (*or* **off the**) **beam** *colloq.* mistaken. **on the beam** *colloq.* on the right track. **on the beam-ends** (of a ship) on its side; almost capsizing. **on one's beam-ends** near the end of one's resources. [OE *bēam* tree f. WG]

beam com·pass *n.* (also **beam com·pass·es**) a drawing compass consisting of a horizontal rod or beam connected by sliding sockets to two vertical legs, used for drawing large circles.

beam·er /beemər/ *n. Cricket colloq.* a ball bowled at a batsman's head.

beam·y /beemee/ *adj.* (of a ship) broad-beamed.

bean /been/ *n. & v.* • *n.* **1 a** any kind of leguminous plant with edible usu. kidney-shaped seeds in long pods. **b** one of these seeds. **2** a similar seed of coffee and other plants. **3** *sl.* the head, esp. as a source of common sense. **4** (in *pl.*; with *neg.*) *sl.* anything at all (*doesn't know beans about it*). • *v.tr. sl.* hit on the head. □ **full of beans** *colloq.* **1** lively; in high spirits. **2** mistaken. **not a bean** *Brit. sl.* no money. **spill the beans** see SPILL. [OE *bēan* f. Gmc]

bean·bag /beenbag/ *n.* **1** a small bag filled with dried beans and used esp. in children's games. **2** (in full **beanbag chair**) a large cushion filled usu. with polystyrene beads and used as a seat.

bean count·er *n.* a person, esp. an accountant, who is regarded as concerned with financial details to the exclusion of other factors.

bean curd *n.* soft cheeselike cake or paste made from soybeans, used esp. in Asian cooking.

bean·er·y /beenəree/ *n.* (*pl.* **·ies**) *sl.* a cheap restaurant.

bean·feast /beenfeest/ *n. Brit.* **1** *colloq.* a celebration; a merry time. **2** an employer's annual dinner given to employees. [BEAN + FEAST, beans and bacon being regarded as an indispensable dish]

bean·ie /beenee/ *n.* a small close-fitting cap worn on the back of the head. [perh. f. BEAN 'head' + –IE]

bean·o /beenō/ *n.* (*pl.* **·os**) **1** bingo. **2** *Brit. sl.* a celebration; a party. [abbr. of BEANFEAST]

See page xx for the **Key to Pronunciation**.

bean•pole /beénpōl/ n. 1 a stick for supporting bean plants. 2 colloq. a tall thin person.

bean sprout n. a sprout of a bean seed, esp. of the mung bean, used as food.

bean•stalk /beénstawk/ n. the stem of a bean plant.

bear[1] /bair/ v. (past **bore** /bor/; past part. **borne, born** /bawrn/) 1 tr. carry, bring, or take (esp. visibly) (bear gifts). 2 tr. show; be marked by; have as an attribute or characteristic (bear marks of violence; bears no relation to the case; bore no name). 3 tr. a produce; yield (fruit, etc.). b give birth to (has borne a son; was born last week). 4 tr. a sustain (a weight, responsibility, cost, etc.). b stand; endure (an ordeal, difficulty, etc.). 5 tr. (usu. with neg. or interrog.) a tolerate; put up with (can't bear him; how can you bear it?). b admit of; be fit for (does not bear thinking about). 6 tr. carry in thought or memory (bear a grudge). 7 intr. veer in a given direction (bear left). 8 tr. bring or provide (something needed) (bear him company). 9 refl. behave (in a certain way). □ **bear arms 1** carry weapons; serve as a soldier. 2 Brit. wear or display heraldic devices. **bear away** (or **off**) win (a prize, etc.). **bear down** exert downward pressure. **bear down on** approach rapidly or purposefully. **bear fruit** have results. **bear hard on** oppress. **bear in mind** remember and take into account. **bear on** (or **upon**) be relevant to. **bear out** support or confirm (an account or the person giving it). **bear repeating** be worth repetition. **bear up 1** raise one's spirits; not despair. **2** (often foll. by against, under) endure; survive. **bear with** treat forbearingly; tolerate patiently. **bear witness** testify. [OE beran f. Gmc]
▶See note at BORN.

bear[2] /bair/ n. & v. ● n. 1 any large heavy mammal of the family Ursidae, having thick fur and walking on its soles. 2 a rough, unmannerly, or uncouth person. 3 Stock Exch. a person who sells shares hoping to buy them back later at a lower price. 4 = TEDDY. 5 (the Bear) colloq. Russia. ● v. Stock Exch. 1 intr. speculate for a fall in price. 2 tr. produce a fall in the price of (stocks, etc.). □ **like a bear with a sore head** Brit. colloq. very irritable. [OE bera f. WG]

bear•a•ble /báirəbəl/ adj. that may be endured or tolerated. □□ **bear•a•bil•i•ty** /–bílitee/ n. **bear•a•ble•ness** n. **bear•a•bly** adv.

bear•bait•ing /báirbayting/ n. hist. an entertainment involving setting dogs to attack a captive bear.

beard /beerd/ n. & v. ● n. 1 hair growing on the chin and lower cheeks of the face. 2 a similar tuft or part on an animal (esp. a goat). 3 the awn of a grass, sheath of barley, etc. ● v.tr. oppose openly; defy. □□ **beard•ed** adj. **beard•less** adj. [OE f. WG]

bear•er /báirər/ n. 1 a person or thing that bears, carries, or brings. 2 a carrier of equipment on an expedition, etc. 3 a person who presents a check or other order to pay money. 4 (attrib.) payable to the possessor (bearer stock). 5 hist. (in India, etc.) a personal servant.

bear•gar•den /báirgaard'n/ n. a rowdy or noisy scene.

bear hug n. a tight embrace.

bear•ing /báiring/ n. 1 a person's bodily attitude or outward behavior. 2 (foll. by on, upon) relation or relevance to (his comments have no bearing on the subject). 3 endurability (beyond bearing). 4 a part of a machine that supports a rotating or other moving part. 5 direction or position relative to a fixed point, measured esp. in degrees. 6 (in pl.) a one's position relative to one's surroundings. b awareness of this; a sense of one's orientation (get one's bearings; lose one's bearings). 7 Heraldry a device or charge. 8 = BALL BEARING.

bear•ing rein n. a fixed rein from bit to saddle that forces a horse to arch its neck.

bear•ish /báirish/ adj. 1 like a bear, esp. in temper. 2 Stock Exch. causing or associated with a fall in prices.

bear mar•ket n. Stock Exch. a market with falling prices.

Béar•naise sauce /báirnáyz/ n. a rich sauce thickened with egg yolks and flavored with tarragon. [F, fem. of béarnais of Béarn in SW France]

bear's breech n. a kind of acanthus, Acanthus mollis.

bear's ear n. auricula.

bear's foot n. a hellebore, Helleborus fetidus.

bear•skin /báirskin/ n. 1 a the skin of a bear. b a wrap, etc., made of this. 2 a tall furry hat worn ceremonially by some regiments.

beast /beest/ n. 1 an animal other than a human being, esp. a wild quadruped. 2 a a brutal person. b colloq. an objectionable or unpleasant person or thing (a beast of a problem). 3 (prec. by the) a human being's brutish or uncivilized characteristics (saw the beast in him). [ME f. OF beste f. Rmc besta f. L bestia]

beast•ie /beéstee/ n. a small animal.

beast•ly /beéstlee/ adj. & adv. ● adj. (**beast•li•er, beast•li•est**) 1 colloq. objectionable; unpleasant. 2 like a beast; brutal. ● adv. Brit. colloq. very; extremely. □□ **beast•li•ness** n.

beast of bur•den n. an animal, e.g., an ox, used for carrying or pulling loads.

beast of prey n. (also **bird of prey**) an animal (or bird) that hunts animals for food.

beat[2] /beet/ v., n., & adj. ● v. (past **beat**; past part. **beat•en** /beét'n/)

1 tr. a strike (a person or animal) persistently or repeatedly, esp. to harm or punish. b strike (a thing) repeatedly, e.g., to remove dust from (a carpet, etc.), or to sound (a drum, etc.). 2 intr. (foll. by against, at, on, etc.) a pound or knock repeatedly (waves beat against the shore; beat at the door). b = beat down 3. 3 tr. a overcome; surpass; win a victory over. b complete an activity before (another person, etc.). c be too hard for; perplex. 4 tr. (often foll. by up) stir (eggs, etc.) vigorously into a frothy mixture. 5 tr. (often foll. by out) fashion or shape (metal, etc.) by blows. 6 intr. (of the heart, a drum, etc.) pulsate rhythmically. 7 tr. (often foll. by out) a indicate (a tempo or rhythm) by gestures, tapping, etc. b sound (a signal, etc.) by striking a drum or other means (beat a tattoo). 8 a intr. (of a bird's wings) move up and down. b tr. cause (wings) to move in this way. 9 tr. make (a path, etc.) by trampling. 10 tr. strike (bushes, etc.) to rouse game. 11 intr. Naut. sail in the direction from which the wind is blowing. ● n. 1 a main accent or rhythmic unit in music or verse (three beats to the bar; missed a beat and came in early). b the indication of rhythm by a conductor's movements (watch the beat). c the tempo or rhythm of a piece of music as indicated by the repeated fall of the main beat. d (in popular music) a strong rhythm. e (attrib.) characterized by a strong rhythm (beat music). 2 a a stroke or blow (e.g., on a drum). b a measured sequence of strokes (the beat of the waves on the rocks). c a throbbing movement or sound (the beat of his heart). 3 a a route or area allocated to a police officer, etc. b a person's habitual round. 4 Physics a pulsation due to the combination of two sounds or electric currents of similar but not equivalent frequencies. 5 colloq. = BEATNIK. 6 Naut. an instance of beating. ● adj. 1 (predic.) sl. exhausted; tired out. 2 (attrib.) of the beat generation or its philosophy. □ **beat about** (often foll. by for) search (for an excuse, etc.). **beat around** (or **about**) **the bush** discuss a matter without coming to the point. **beat the bounds** Brit. mark parish boundaries by striking certain points with rods. **beat one's breast** strike one's chest in anguish or sorrow. **beat the clock** complete a task within a stated time. **beat down 1** a bargain with (a seller) to lower the price. b cause a seller to lower (the price). 2 strike (a resisting object) until it falls (beat the door down). 3 (of the sun, rain, etc.) radiate heat or fall continuously and vigorously. **beat the drum for** publicize; promote. **beaten at the post** defeated at the last moment. **beat in** crush. **beat it** sl. go away. **beat off** drive back (an attack, etc.). **beat a retreat** withdraw; abandon an undertaking. **beat time** indicate or follow a musical tempo with a baton or other means. **beat a person to it** arrive or achieve something before another person. **beat up** give a beating to, esp. with punches and kicks. **it beats me** I do not understand (it). □□ **beat•a•ble** adj. [OE bēatan f. Gmc]

beat•en /beét'n/ adj. 1 outwitted; defeated. 2 exhausted; dejected. 3 (of gold or any other metal) shaped by a hammer. 4 (of a path, etc.) well-trodden; much used. □ **off the beaten track** (or **path**) 1 in or into an isolated place. 2 unusual. [past part. of BEAT]

beat•er /beétər/ n. 1 a person employed to rouse game for shooting. 2 an implement used for beating (esp. a carpet or eggs). 3 a person who beats metal.

beat gen•er•a•tion n. the members of a movement of young people esp. in the 1950s who rejected conventional society in their dress, habits, and beliefs (see BEATNIK).

be•a•tif•ic /beéətífik/ adj. 1 colloq. blissful (a beatific smile). 2 a of or relating to blessedness. b making blessed. □□ **be•a•tif•i•cal•ly** adv. [F béatifique or L beatificus f. beatus blessed]

be•at•i•fi•ca•tion /beeátifikáyshən/ n. 1 RC Ch. the act of formally declaring a dead person "blessed," often a step toward canonization. 2 making or being blessed. [F béatification or eccl.L beatificatio (as BEATIFY)]

be•at•i•fy /beeátifi/ v.tr. (**-fies, -fied**) 1 RC Ch. announce the beatification of. 2 make happy. [F béatifier or eccl.L beatificare f. L beatus blessed]

beat•ing /beéting/ n. 1 a physical punishment or assault. 2 a defeat. □ **take some** (or **a lot of**) **beating** be difficult to surpass.

be•at•i•tude /beeátitood, –tyood/ n. 1 blessedness. 2 (in pl.) the declarations of blessedness in Matt. 5:3–11. 3 a title given to patriarchs in the Orthodox Church. [F béatitude or L beatitudo f. beatus blessed]

beat•nik /beétnik/ n. a member of the beat generation. [BEAT + –nik after sputnik, perh. infl. by US use of Yiddish –nik agent suffix]

beat-up adj. colloq. dilapidated; in a state of disrepair.

beau /bō/ n. (pl. **beaux** or **beaus** /bōz, bō/) 1 an admirer; a boyfriend. 2 a fop; a dandy. [F, = handsome, f. L bellus]

Beau•fort scale /bófərt/ n. a scale of wind speed ranging from 0 (calm) to 12 (hurricane). [Sir F. Beaufort, Engl. admiral d. 1857]

beau geste /bō zhést/ n. (pl. **beaux gestes** pronunc. same) a generous or gracious act. [F, = splendid gesture]

beau i•de•al /bō ĭdeéəl/ n. (pl. **beaux i•de•als** /bóz ĭdeéəlz/) the highest type of excellence or beauty. [F beau idéal = ideal beauty: see BEAU, IDEAL]

Beau•jo•lais /bózhəlay/ n. a red or white burgundy wine from the Beaujolais district of France.

Beau·jo·lais nou·veau /nōōvṓ/ *n.* Beaujolais wine sold in the first year of a vintage.

beau monde /bō mónd, máwNd/ *n.* fashionable society. [F]

beaut /byōōt/ *n. & adj. sl.* ● *n.* an excellent or beautiful person or thing. ● *adj. Austral. & NZ* excellent; beautiful. [abbr. of BEAUTY]

beau·te·ous /byōōteeəs/ *adj. poet.* beautiful. [ME f. BEAUTY + –OUS, after *bounteous, plenteous*]

beau·ti·cian /byōōtíshən/ *n.* **1** a person who gives beauty treatment. **2** a person who runs or owns a beauty salon.

beau·ti·ful /byōōtifōōl/ *adj.* **1** delighting the aesthetic senses (*a beautiful voice*). **2** pleasant; enjoyable (*had a beautiful time*). **3** excellent (*a beautiful specimen*). □□ **beau·ti·ful·ly** *adv.*

beau·ti·fy /byōōtifī/ *v.tr.* (**·fies, ·fied**) make beautiful; adorn. □□ **beau·ti·fi·ca·tion** /–fikáyshən/ *n.* **beau·ti·fi·er** /–fīər/ *n.*

beau·ty /byōōtee/ *n.* (*pl.* **·ties**) **1 a** a combination of qualities such as shape, color, etc., that pleases the aesthetic senses, esp. the sight. **b** a combination of qualities that pleases the intellect or moral sense (*the beauty of the argument*). **2** *colloq.* **a** an excellent specimen (*what a beauty!*). **b** an attractive feature; an advantage (*that's the beauty of it!*). **3** a beautiful woman. □ **beauty is only skin-deep** a pleasing appearance is not a guide to character. [ME f. AF *beuté,* OF *bealté, beauté,* ult. f. L (as BEAU)]

beau·ty par·lor *n.* (also **beau·ty sa·lon**) an establishment in which hairdressing, manicures, makeup, etc., are offered to women.

beau·ty queen *n.* the woman judged most beautiful in a competition.

beau·ty sleep *n.* **1** sleep before midnight, supposed to be healthgiving. **2** any sleep, esp. extra sleep.

beau·ty spot *n.* **1** a place known for its beauty. **2** a small natural or artificial mark such as a mole on the face, considered to enhance another feature.

beaux *pl.* of BEAU.

beaux arts /bōz áar/ *n.pl.* **1** fine arts. **2** (*attrib.*) relating to the rules and conventions of the École des Beaux-Arts in Paris (later called Académie des Beaux Arts). [F *beaux-arts*]

bea·ver[1] /béevər/ *n. & v.* ● *n.* (*pl.* same or **bea·vers**) **1 a** any large amphibious broad-tailed rodent of the genus *Castor,* native to N. America, Europe, and Asia, and able to cut down trees and build dams. **b** its soft light-brown fur. **c** a hat of this. **2** (in full **beaver cloth**) a heavy woolen cloth like beaver fur. ● *v.intr. Brit. colloq.* (usu. foll. by *away*) work hard. [OE *be(o)for* f. Gmc]

bea·ver[2] /béevər/ *n. hist.* the lower face-guard of a helmet. [OF *baviere* bib f. *baver* slaver f. *beve* saliva f. Rmc]

bea·ver[3] /béevər/ *n. Brit. sl.* a bearded man. [20th c.: orig. uncert.]

Bea·ver·board /béevərbawrd/ *n. Trademark* a kind of fiberboard. [BEAVER[1] + BOARD]

be·bop /béebop/ *n.* a type of jazz originating in the 1940s and characterized by complex harmony and rhythms. □□ **be·bop·per** *n.* [imit. of the typical rhythm]

be·calm /bikáam/ *v.tr.* (usu. in *passive*) deprive (a ship) of wind.

be·came *past* of BECOME.

be·cause /bikáwz, –kúz/ *conj.* for the reason that; since. □ **because of** on account of; by reason of. [ME f. BY *prep.* + CAUSE, after OF *par cause de* by reason of]

GRAMMAR TIP because

Starting a Sentence with *Because*. American students are taught never to begin a sentence with the word *because.* As a conjunction, *because* introduces dependent clauses, and these are not, by themselves, complete sentences. Still, a dependent clause can begin a sentence, hence so can *because* (*Because you are my best friend, I will tell you exactly what I'm thinking*). What teachers are really trying to say is that one should write and speak in full sentences and not sentence fragments. The same rule holds true for starting a sentence with *and* or *but*—good writers do it all the time. Just make sure that what follows is a complete sentence.

---

bé·cha·mel /béshəmel/ *n.* a kind of thick white sauce. [invented by the Marquis de *Béchamel,* Fr. courtier d. 1703]

bêche-de-mer /béshdəmáir/ *n.* (*pl.* same or **bêches-de-mer** *pronunc.* same) **1** = TREPANG. **2** = BEACH-LA-MAR. [F, alt. of *biche de mer* f. Port. *bicho do mar* sea worm]

beck[1] /bek/ *n. No. of Engl.* a brook; a mountain stream. [ME f. ON *bekkr* f. Gmc]

beck[2] /bek/ *n.* a gesture requesting attention, e.g., a nod, wave, etc. □ **at a person's beck and call** having constantly to obey a person's orders. [*beck* (v.) f. BECKON]

beck·et /békit/ *n. Naut.* a contrivance such as a hook, bracket, or rope loop, for securing loose ropes, tackle, or spars. [18th c.: orig. unkn.]

beck·on /békən/ *v.* **1** *tr.* attract the attention of; summon by gesture. **2** *intr.* (usu. foll. by *to*) make a signal to attract a person's attention; summon a person by doing this. [OE *bīecnan, bēcnan* ult. f. WG *baukna* BEACON]

be·cloud /biklówd/ *v.tr.* **1** obscure (*becloud the argument*). **2** cover with clouds.

be·come /bikúm/ *v.* (*past* **be·came** /bikáym/; *past part.* **be·come**) **1** *intr.* (foll. by *compl.*) begin to be; come to be; turn into (*became president; will become famous; tadpoles become frogs*). **2** *tr.* **a** look well on; suit (*blue becomes him*). **b** befit (*it ill becomes you to complain*). **3** *intr.* (as **becoming** *adj.*) **a** flattering the appearance. **b** suitable; decorous. □ **become of** happen to (*what will become of me?*). □□ **be·com·ing·ly** *adj.* **be·com·ing·ness** *n.* [OE *becuman* f. Gmc: cf. BE-, COME]

B.Ed. *abbr.* Bachelor of Education.

bed /bed/ *n. & v.* ● *n.* **1 a** a piece of furniture used for sleeping on, usu. a framework with a mattress and coverings. **b** such a mattress, with or without coverings. **2** any place used by a person or animal for sleep or rest; a litter. **3 a** a garden plot, esp. one used for planting flowers. **b** a place where other things may be grown (*osier bed*). **4** the use of a bed: **a** *colloq.* for sexual intercourse. **b** for rest. **5** something flat, forming a support or base as in: **a** the bottom of the sea or a river. **b** the foundations of a road or railroad. **c** the slates, etc., on a billiard table. **6** a stratum, such as a layer of oysters, etc. ● *v.* (**bed·ded, bed·ding**) **1** *tr. & intr.* (usu. foll. by *down*) put or go to bed. **2** *tr. colloq.* have sexual intercourse with. **3** *tr.* (usu. foll. by *out*) plant in a garden bed. **4** *tr.* cover up or fix firmly in something. **5 a** *tr.* arrange as a layer. **b** *intr.* be or form a layer. □ **brought to bed** (often foll. by *of*) *archaic* delivered of a child. **get out of bed on the wrong side** be bad-tempered all day long. **go to bed 1** retire for the night. **2** have sexual intercourse. **3** (of a newspaper) go to press. **keep one's bed** *Brit.* stay in bed because of illness. **make the bed** arrange the bed for use. **make one's bed and lie in it** accept the consequences of one's acts. **put to bed 1** cause to go to bed. **2** make (a newspaper) ready for press. **take to one's bed** stay in bed because of illness. [OE *bed(d), beddian* f. Gmc]

be·dab·ble /bidábəl/ *v.tr.* stain or splash with dirty liquid, blood, etc.

bed and board *n.* **1** lodging and food. **2** marital relations.

bed and break·fast *n.* **1** one night's lodging and breakfast in a hotel, etc. **2** an establishment that provides this.

be·daub /bidáwb/ *v.tr.* smear or daub with paint, etc.; decorate gaudily.

be·daz·zle /bidázəl/ *v.tr.* **1** dazzle. **2** confuse (a person). □□ **be·daz·zle·ment** *n.*

bed·bug /bédbug/ *n.* a flat, wingless, bloodsucking insect, *Cimex lectularius,* infesting beds and houses.

bed·cham·ber /bédchaymbər/ *n. archaic* a bedroom.

bed·clothes /bédklōthz, –klōz/ *n.pl.* coverings for a bed, such as sheets, blankets, etc.

bed·da·ble /bédəbəl/ *adj. colloq.* sexually attractive; able to be seduced. [BED + –ABLE]

bed·der /bédər/ *n.* **1** a plant suitable for a garden bed. **2** a bedmaker.

bed·ding /béding/ *n.* **1** a mattress and bedclothes. **2** litter for cattle, horses, etc. **3** a bottom layer. **4** *Geol.* the stratification of rocks, esp. when clearly visible.

bed·ding plant *n.* a plant suitable for a garden bed.

be·deck /bidék/ *v.tr.* adorn.

bed·e·guar /bédigaar/ *n.* a mosslike growth on rose bushes produced by a gall wasp. [F *bédegar* f. Pers. *bād-āwar* wind brought]

be·del /béed'l, bidél/ *n.* (also **be·dell**) *Brit.* a university official with chiefly processional duties. [= BEADLE]

be·dev·il /bidévəl/ *v.tr.* (**be·dev·iled, be·dev·il·ing**) **1** plague; afflict. **2** confound; confuse. **3** possess as if with a devil; bewitch. **4** treat with diabolical violence or abuse. □□ **be·dev·il·ment** *n.*

be·dew /bidōō, –dyōō/ *v.tr.* **1** cover or sprinkle with dew or drops of water. **2** *poet.* sprinkle with tears.

bed·fel·low /bédfelō/ *n.* **1** a person who shares a bed. **2** an associate.

Bed·ford cord /bédfərd/ *n.* a tough woven fabric having prominent ridges, similar to corduroy. [*Bedford* in S. England]

be·dight /bidít/ *adj. archaic* arrayed; adorned. [ME past part. of *bedight* (v.) (as BE-, DIGHT)]

be·dim /bidím/ *v.tr.* (**be·dimmed, be·dim·ming**) *poet.* make (the eyes, mind, etc.) dim.

be·di·zen /bidízən, –dízən/ *v.tr. poet.* deck out gaudily. [BE- + obs. *dizen* deck out]

bed·jack·et /bédjakit/ *n.* a jacket worn when sitting up in bed.

bed·lam /bédləm/ *n.* **1** a scene of uproar and confusion. **2** *archaic* a madhouse; an asylum. [hospital of St. Mary of *Bethlehem* in London]

bed lin·en *n.* sheets and pillowcases.

Bed·ling·ton ter·ri·er /bédlingtən/ *n.* **1** a terrier of a breed with narrow head, long legs, and curly gray hair. **2** this breed. [*Bedlington* in Northumberland]

bed·mak·er /bédmaykər/ *n.* **1** a person who makes beds. **2** *Brit.* a person employed to clean students' rooms in a college.

bed of ros·es *n.* a life of ease.

Bed·ou·in /bédōōin/ *n. & adj.* (also **Bed·u·in**) (*pl.* same) ● *n.* **1** a nomadic Arab of the desert. **2** a wanderer; a nomad. ● *adj.* **1** of or re-

See page xx for the **Key to Pronunciation.**

lating to the Bedouin. **2** wandering; nomadic. [ME f. OF *beduin* ult. f. Arab. *badwiyyīn* (oblique case) dwellers in the desert f. *badw* desert]

bed·pan /bédpan/ *n.* a receptacle used by a bedridden patient for urine and feces.

bed·plate /bédplayt/ *n.* a metal plate forming the base of a machine, etc.

bed·post /bédpōst/ *n.* any of the four upright supports of a bedstead. □ **between you and me and the bedpost** *colloq.* in strict confidence.

be·drag·gled /bidrágəld/ *adj.* **1** wet and soiled from rain or mud. **2** dirty and disheveled (*bedraggled refugees*). [BE- + DRAGGLE]

bed rest *n.* confinement of an invalid to bed.

bed·rid·den /bédrid'n/ *adj.* **1** confined to bed by infirmity. **2** decrepit. [OE *bedreda* f. *ridan* ride]

bed·rock /bédrok/ *n.* **1** solid rock underlying alluvial deposits, etc. **2** the underlying principles or facts of a theory, character, etc.

bed·roll /bédrōl/ *n.* portable bedding rolled into a bundle, esp. a sleeping bag.

bed·room /bédrōōm, –rŏŏm/ *n.* **1** a room for sleeping in. **2** (*attrib.*) of or referring to sexual relations (*bedroom comedy*).

bed·side /bédsīd/ *n.* **1** the space beside esp. a patient's bed. **2** (*attrib.*) of or relating to the side of a bed (*bedside lamp*).

bed·side man·ner *n.* (of a doctor) an approach or attitude to a patient.

bed·sit·ter /bédsítər/ *n.* (also **bed·sit**) *Brit. colloq.* = BEDSITTING ROOM. [contr.]

bed·sit·ting room /bédsíting/ *n. Brit.* a one-room unit of accommodation usu. consisting of combined bedroom and sitting room with cooking facilities.

bed·sock /bédsok/ *n.* each of a pair of thick socks worn in bed.

bed·sore /bédsawr/ *n.* a sore developed by an invalid because of pressure caused by lying in bed.

bed·spread /bédspred/ *n.* an often decorative cloth used to cover a bed when not in use.

bed·stead /bédsted/ *n.* the framework of a bed.

bed·straw /bédstraw/ *n.* **1** any herbaceous plant of the genus *Galium*, once used as straw for bedding. **2** (in full **Our Lady's bedstraw**) a bedstraw, *G. verum*, with yellow flowers.

bed ta·ble *n.* a portable table or tray with legs used by a person sitting up in bed.

bed·time /bédtīm/ *n.* **1** the usual time for going to bed. **2** (*attrib.*) of or relating to bedtime (*bedtime story*).

Bed·u·in var. of BEDOUIN.

bed·wet·ting /bédweting/ *n.* involuntary urination during the night.

bee /bee/ *n.* **1** any four-winged insect of the superfamily Apoidea which collects nectar and pollen, produces wax and honey, and lives in large communities. **2** any insect of a similar type. **3** (usu. **busy bee**) a busy person. **4** a meeting for communal work or amusement. □ **a bee in one's bonnet** an obsession. **the bee's knees** *old-fashioned sl.* something outstandingly good (*thinks he's the bee's knees*). [OE *bēo* f. Gmc]

bee·bread /bébred/ *n.* honey or pollen used as food by bees.

beech /beech/ *n.* **1** any large forest tree of the genus *Fagus*, having smooth gray bark and glossy leaves. **2** (also **beech·wood**) its wood. **3** *Austral.* any of various similar trees in Australia. □□ **beech·y** *adj.* [OE *bēce* f. Gmc]

beech fern *n.* one of two ferns, *Thelypteris phagopteris* and *T. hexagonoptera*, found in damp woods.

beech mar·ten *n.* a white-breasted marten, *Martes foina*, of S. Europe and Asia.

beech mast *n.* the small rough-skinned fruit of the beech tree.

bee dance *n.* a series of movements performed by worker bees to inform the colony of the location of food.

bee-eat·er *n.* any brightly plumaged insect-eating bird of the family Meropidae with a long slender curved bill.

beef /beef/ *n. & v.* • *n.* **1** the flesh of the ox, bull, or cow for eating. **2** *colloq.* well-developed male muscle. **3** (*pl.* **beeves** /beevz/ or **beefs**) a cow, bull, or ox fattened for beef; its carcass. **4** (*pl.* **beefs**) *sl.* a complaint; a protest. • *v.intr. sl.* complain. □ **beef up** *sl.* strengthen; reinforce; augment. [ME f. AF, OF *boef* f. L *bos bovis* ox]

beef·burg·er /béefbərgər/ *n.* = HAMBURGER.

beef·cake /béefkayk/ *n. sl.* well-developed male muscles, esp. when photographed and displayed for admiration.

beef·eat·er /béefeetər/ *n.* a warder in the Tower of London; a Yeoman of the Guard. [f. obs. sense 'well-fed menial']

beef·steak /béefstáyk/ *n.* a thick slice of lean beef, esp. from the rump, usu. for grilling or frying.

beef·steak fun·gus *n.* a red edible fungus, *Fistulina hepatica*, resembling beef.

beef tea *n.* esp. *Brit.* boiled extract of beef, given to invalids.

beef·wood /béfwŏŏd/ *n.* **1** any of various Australian and W. Indian hardwood trees. **2** the close-grained red timber of these.

beef·y /béefee/ *adj.* (**beef·i·er**, **beef·i·est**) **1** like beef. **2** solid; muscular. □□ **beef·i·ly** *adv.* **beef·i·ness** *n.*

bee·hive /béehīv/ *n.* **1** an artificial habitation for bees. **2** a busy place. **3** anything resembling a wicker beehive in being domed.

bee·keep·er /békeepər/ *n.* a keeper of bees.

bee·keep·ing /békeeping/ *n.* the occupation of keeping bees.

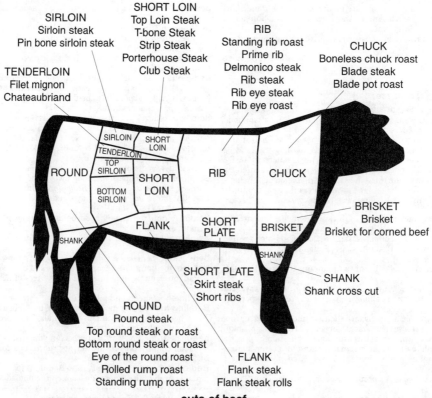

SHORT LOIN
Top Loin Steak
T-bone Steak
Strip Steak
Porterhouse Steak
Club Steak

SIRLOIN
Sirloin steak
Pin bone sirloin steak

TENDERLOIN
Filet mignon
Chateaubriand

RIB
Standing rib roast
Prime rib
Delmonico steak
Rib steak
Rib eye steak
Rib eye roast

CHUCK
Boneless chuck roast
Blade steak
Blade pot roast

BRISKET
Brisket
Brisket for corned beef

SHANK
Shank cross cut

SHORT PLATE
Skirt steak
Short ribs

ROUND
Round steak
Top round steak or roast
Bottom round steak or roast
Eye of the round roast
Rolled rump roast
Standing rump roast

FLANK
Flank steak
Flank steak rolls

cuts of beef

bee•line /beelin/ n. a straight line between two places. □ **make a bee-line for** hurry directly to.

Be•el•ze•bub /bee-élzibub/ n. the Devil. [OE f. L f. Gk *beelzeboub* & Heb. *ba'al zᵉbûb* lord of the flies, name of a Philistine god]

been *past part.* of BE.

bee or•chid n. a kind of European orchid, *Ophrys apifera*, with bee-shaped flowers.

beep /beep/ n. & v. •n. **1** the sound of an automobile horn. **2** any similar high-pitched noise. •v.intr. emit a beep. [imit.]

beep•er /beepər/ n. an electronic device that receives signals and emits a beep to summon the person carrying it to the telephone, etc.

beer /beer/ n. **1 a** an alcoholic drink made from yeast-fermented malt, etc., flavored with hops. **b** a glass, can, or bottle of this, esp. (*Brit.*) a pint or half-pint. **2** any of several other fermented drinks, e.g., ginger beer, birch beer. [OE *bēor* f. LL *biber* drink f. L *bibere*]

beer and skit•tles n. *Brit.* amusement (*life is not all beer and skittles*).

beer-cel•lar n. **1** an underground room for storing beer. **2** a basement or cellar for selling or drinking beer.

beer gar•den n. a garden or outdoor bar where beer is sold and drunk.

beer hall n. a large room where beer is sold and drunk.

beer•house /beerhows/ n. *Brit.* a bar licensed to sell beer, ale, etc., but not hard liquor.

beer pump n. a machine that draws up beer from a barrel or keg.

beer•y /beeree/ adj. (**beer•i•er, beer•i•est**) **1** showing the influence of drink in one's appearance or behavior. **2** smelling or tasting of beer. □□ **beer•i•ly** adv. **beer•i•ness** n.

bee•stings /beestingz/ n.pl. (also treated as *sing.*) the first milk (esp. of a cow) after giving birth. [OE *bēsting* (implied by *bēost*), of unkn. orig.]

bees•wax /beezwaks/ n. & v. •n. **1** the wax secreted by bees to make honeycombs. **2** this wax refined and used to polish wood. •v.tr. polish (furniture, etc.) with beeswax.

bees•wing /beezwing/ n. a filmy second crust on old port.

beet /beet/ n. any plant of the genus *Beta* with an edible root (see BEETROOT, *sugar beet*). [OE *bēte* f. L *beta*, perh. of Celt. orig.]

bee•tle¹ /beetl/ n. & v. •n. **1** any insect of the order Coleoptera, with modified front wings forming hard protective cases closing over the back wings. **2** *colloq.* any similar, usu. black, insect. **3** *sl.* a type of compact round-ed Volkswagen car. •v.intr. *colloq.* (foll. by *about, away*, etc.) *Brit.* hurry; scurry. [OE *bitula* biter f. *bītan* BITE]

beetle (gold bug)

bee•tle² /beetl/ n. & v. •n. **1** a tool with a heavy head and a handle, used for ramming, crushing, driving wedges, etc. **2** a machine used for heightening the luster of cloth by pressure from rollers. •v.tr. **1** ram, crush, drive, etc., with a beetle. **2** finish (cloth) with a beet-le. [OE *bētel* f. Gmc]

bee•tle³ /beetl/ adj. & v. •adj. (esp. of the eyebrows) projecting; shaggy; scowling. •v.intr. (usu. as **beetling** adj.) (of brows, cliffs, etc.) projecting; overhanging threateningly. [ME: orig. unkn.]

bee•tle-browed adj. with shaggy, projecting, or scowling eyebrows.

beet•root /beetroot, –root/ n. esp. *Brit.* **1** a beet, *Beta vulgaris*, with an edible spherical dark red root. **2** this root used as a vegetable.

beeves pl. of BEEF.

BEF abbr. hist. British Expeditionary Force.

be•fall /bifáwl/ v. (*past* **be•fell** /bifél/; *past part.* **be•fall•en** /bifáwlən/) *poet.* **1** *intr.* happen (*so it befell*). **2** *tr.* happen to (a person, etc.) (*what has befallen her?*). [OE *befeallan* (as BE-, *feallan* FALL)]

be•fit /bifit/ v.tr. (**be•fit•ted, be•fit•ting**) **1** be fitted or appropriate for; suit. **2** be incumbent on. □□ **be•fit•ting** adj. **be•fit•ting•ly** adv.

be•fog /bifawg, –fóg/ v.tr. (**be•fogged, be•fog•ging**) **1** confuse; obscure. **2** envelop in fog.

be•fool /bifool/ v.tr. make a fool of; delude.

be•fore /bifáwr/ conj., prep., & adv. •conj. **1** earlier than the time when (*crawled before he walked*). **2** rather than that (*would starve before he stole*). •prep. **1 a** in front of (*before her in the queue*). **b** ahead of (*crossed the line before him*). **c** under the impulse of (*recoil before the attack*). **d** awaiting (*the future before them*). **2** earlier than; preceding (*Lent comes before Easter*). **3** rather than (*death before dishonor*). **4 a** in the presence of (*appear before the judge*). **b** for the attention of (*a plan put before the committee*). •adv. **1 a** earlier than the time in question; already (*heard it before*). **b** in the past (*happened long before*). **2** ahead (*go before*). **3** on the front (*hit before and behind*). □ **before God** a solemn oath meaning 'as God sees me'. **before time** see TIME. [OE *beforan* f. Gmc]

Be•fore Christ adv. (of a date) reckoned backward from the birth of Christ.

be•fore•hand /bifáwrhand/ adv. in anticipation; in advance; in readiness (*had prepared the meal beforehand*). □ **be beforehand with** anticipate; forestall. [ME f. BEFORE + HAND: cf. AF *avant main*]

be•foul /bifówl/ v.tr. *poet.* **1** make foul or dirty. **2** degrade; defile.

---

be•friend /bifrénd/ v.tr. act as a friend to; help.

be•fud•dle /bifúd'l/ v.tr. **1** make drunk. **2** confuse. □□ **be•fud•dle•ment** n.

beg /beg/ v. (**begged, beg•ging**) **1 a** intr. (usu. foll. by *for*) ask for (esp. food, money, etc.) (*begged for alms*). **b** tr. ask for (food, money, etc.) as a gift. **c** intr. live by begging. **2** tr. & intr. (usu. foll. by *for*, or *to* + infin.) ask earnestly or humbly (*begged for forgiveness; begged to be allowed out; please, I beg of you; beg your indulgence for a time*). **3** tr. ask formally for (*beg leave*). **4** intr. (of a dog, etc.) sit up with the front paws raised expectantly. **5** tr. take or ask leave (to do something) (*I beg to differ; beg to enclose*). □ **beg one's bread** live by begging. **beg off 1** decline to take part in or attend. **2** get (a person) excused from a penalty, etc. **beg pardon** see PARDON. **beg the question 1** assume the truth of an argument or proposition to be proved, without arguing it. **2** *disp.* pose the question. **3** *colloq.* evade a difficulty. **go begging** (or *Brit.* **a-begging**) (of a chance or a thing) not be taken; be unwanted. [ME prob. f. OE *bedecian* f. Gmc: rel. to BID]

be•gad /bigád/ int. archaic colloq. by God! [corrupt.: cf. GAD²]

be•gan past of BEGIN.

be•gat archaic past of BEGET.

be•get /bigét/ v.tr. (**be•get•ting**; *past* **be•got** /bigót/; *archaic* **be•gat** /bigát/; *past part.* **be•got•ten** /bigót'n/) *literary* **1** (usu. of a father, sometimes of a father and mother) procreate. **2** give rise to; cause (*beget strife*). □□ **be•get•ter** n. [OE *begietan*, formed as BE- + GET = procreate]

beg•gar /bégər/ n. & v. •n. **1** a person who begs, esp. one who lives by begging. **2** a poor person. **3** *colloq.* a person; a fellow (*poor beggar*). •v.tr. **1** reduce to poverty. **2** *Brit.* outshine. **3** exhaust the resources of (*beggar description*). □ **beggars cannot** (or **must not**) **be choosers** those without other resources must take what is offered. [ME f. BEG + –AR³]

beg•gar•ly /bégərlee/ adj. **1** poverty-stricken; needy. **2** intellectually poor. **3** mean; sordid. **4** ungenerous. □□ **beg•gar•li•ness** n.

beg•gar-my-neigh•bor n. (also **beg•gar-your-neigh•bor**) **1** a card game in which a player seeks to capture an opponent's cards. **2** (*attrib.*) (esp. of national policy) self-aggrandizing at the expense of competitors.

beg•gar•y /bégəree/ n. extreme poverty.

beg•ging bowl n. **1** a bowl, etc., held out for food or alms. **2** an earnest appeal for help.

be•gin /bigín/ v. (**be•gin•ning**; *past* **be•gan** /bigán/; *past part.* **be•gun** /bigún/) **1** tr. perform the first part of; start (*begin work; begin crying; begin to understand*). **2** intr. come into being; arise: **a** in time (*the season began last week*). **b** in space (*your jurisdiction begins beyond the river*). **3** intr. (foll. by *to* + infin.) start at a certain time (*then began to feel ill*). **4** intr. be begun (*the meeting will begin at 7*). **5** intr. **a** start speaking (*'No,' he began*). **b** take the first step; be the first to do something (*who wants to begin?*). **6** intr. *colloq.* (usu. with *neg.*) show any attempt or likelihood (*can't begin to compete*). □ **be-gin at** start from. **begin on** (or **upon**) set to work at. **begin school** attend school for the first time. **begin with** take (a subject, task, etc.) first or as a starting point. **to begin with** in the first place; as the first thing. [OE *beginnan* f. Gmc]

be•gin•ner /bigínər/ n. a person just beginning to learn a skill, etc.

beginner's luck n. good luck supposed to attend a beginner at games, etc.

be•gin•ning /bigíning/ n. **1** the time or place at which anything begins. **2** a source or origin. **3** the first part. □ **the beginning of the end** the first clear sign of a final result.

be•gone /bigáwn, –gón/ int. poet. go away at once!

be•go•nia /bigónyə/ n. any plant of the genus *Begonia* with brightly colored sepals and no petals, and often having brilliant glossy foliage. [M. *Bégon*, Fr. patron of science d. 1710]

be•gor•ra /bigáwrə, –górə/ *int. Ir.* by God! [corrupt.]

be•got *past* of BEGET.

be•got•ten *past part.* of BEGET.

be•grime /bigrím/ *v.tr.* make grimy.

be•grudge /bigrúj/ *v.tr.* **1** resent; be dissatisfied at. **2** envy (a person) the possession of. **3** be reluctant or unwilling to give (a thing to a person). □□ **be•grudg•ing•ly** *adv.*

be•guile /bigíl/ *v.tr.* **1** charm; amuse. **2** divert attention pleasantly from (work, etc.). **3** (often foll. by *of*, *out of*, or *into* + verbal noun) delude; cheat (*beguiled him into paying*). □□ **be•guile•ment** *n.* **be•guil•er** *n.* **be•guil•ing** *adj.* **be•guil•ing•ly** *adv.* [BE- + obs. *guile* to deceive]

be•guine /bigeén/ *n.* **1** a popular dance of W. Indian origin. **2** its rhythm. [Amer. F f. F *béguin* infatuation]

be•gum /báygəm/ *n.* on the Indian subcontinent: **1** a Muslim lady of high rank. **2** (**Begum**) the title of a married Muslim woman, equivalent to Mrs. [Urdu *begam* f. E.Turk. *bīgam* princess, fem. of *big* prince: cf. BEY]

be•gun *past part.* of BEGIN.

be•half /biháf/ *n.* □ **on** (also **in**) **behalf of** (or **on a person's behalf**) **1** in the interests of (a person, principle, etc.). **2** as representative of (*acting on behalf of my client*). [mixture of earlier phrases *on his halve* and *bihalve him*, both = on his side: see BY, HALF]

be•have /biháyv/ *v.* **1** *intr.* **a** act or react (in a specified way) (*behaved well*). **b** (esp. to or of a child) conduct oneself properly. **c** (of a machine, etc.) work well (or in a specified way) (*the computer is not behaving today*). **2** *refl.* (esp. of or to a child) show good manners (*behaved herself*). □ **behave toward** treat (in a specified way). [BE- + HAVE]

be•hav•ior /biháyvyər/ *n.* **1 a** the way one conducts oneself; manners. **b** the treatment of others; moral conduct. **2** the way in which a ship, machine, chemical substance, etc., acts or works. **3** *Psychol.* the response (of a person, animal, etc.) to a stimulus. □ **be on one's good** (or **best**) **behavior** behave well when being observed. [BEHAVE after *demeanor* and obs. *haviour* f. *have*]

be•hav•ior•al /biháyvyərəl/ *adj.* of or relating to behavior. □□ **be•hav•ior•al•ist** *n.*

be•hav•ior•al sci•ence *n.* the scientific study of human behavior (see BEHAVIORISM).

be•hav•ior•ism /biháyvyərizəm/ *n. Psychol.* **1** the theory that human behavior is determined by conditioning rather than by thoughts or feelings, and that psychological disorders are best treated by altering behavior patterns. **2** such study and treatment in practice. □□ **be•hav•ior•ist** *n.* **be•hav•ior•is•tic** /–rístik/ *adj.*

be•hav•ior ther•a•py *n.* the treatment of neurotic symptoms by training the patient's reactions (see BEHAVIORISM).

be•head /bihéd/ *v.tr.* **1** cut off the head of (a person), esp. as a form of execution. **2** kill by beheading. [OE *behēafdian* (as BE-, *hēafod* HEAD)]

be•held *past* and *past part.* of BEHOLD.

be•he•moth /bihéeməth, beéə–/ *n.* an enormous creature or thing. [ME f. Heb. *bᵉhēmōt* intensive pl. of *bᵉhēmāh* beast, perh. f. Egyptian *p-ehe-mau* water ox]

be•hest /bihést/ *n.* literary a command; an entreaty (*went at his behest*). [OE *behǣs* f. Gmc]

be•hind /bihínd/ *prep., adv., & n.* • *prep.* **1 a** in, toward, or to the rear of. **b** on the farther side of (*behind the bush*). **c** hidden by (*something behind that remark*). **2 a** in the past in relation to (*trouble is behind me now*). **b** late in relation to (*behind schedule*). **3** inferior to; weaker than (*behind the others in math*). **4 a** in support of (*she's right behind us*). **b** responsible for; giving rise to (*the person behind the project; the reasons behind his resignation*). **5** in the tracks of; following. • *adv.* **1 a** in or to or toward the rear; farther back (*the street behind; glance behind*). **b** on the farther side (*a high wall with a field behind*). **2** remaining after departure (*leave behind; stay behind*). **3** (usu. foll. by *with*) **a** in arrears (*behind with the rent*). **b** late in accomplishing a task, etc. (*working too slowly and getting behind*). **4** in a weak position; backward (*behind in Latin*). • *n.* **1** *colloq.* the buttocks. **2** (in Australian Rules Football) a kick, etc., scoring one point. □ **behind a person's back** without a person's knowledge. **behind the scenes** see SCENE. **behind time** late. **behind the times** old-fashioned; antiquated. **come from behind** win after being behind in scoring. **fall** (or **lag**) **behind** see FALL. **put behind one 1** refuse to consider. **2** get over (an unhappy experience, etc.). [OE *behindan, bihindan* f. *bi* BY + *hindan* from behind, *hinder* below]

be•hind•hand /bihíndhand/ *adv. & predic.adj.* **1** (usu. foll. by *with, in*) late (in discharging a duty, paying a debt, etc.). **2** slow; backwards. [BEHIND + HAND: cf. BEFOREHAND]

behind-the-scenes *adj.* (*attrib.*) secret, using secret information (*a behind-the-scenes investigation*).

be•hold /bihóld/ *v.tr.* (*past & past part.* **be•held** /bihéld/) literary (esp.

in *imper.*) see; observe. □□ **be•hold•er** *n.* [OE *bihaldan* (as BE-, *haldan* hold)]

be•hold•en /bihóldən/ *predic.adj.* (usu. foll. by *to*) under obligation. [past part. (obs. except in this use) of BEHOLD, = bound]

be•hoof /bihóof/ *n. archaic* (prec. by *to, for, on*; foll. by *of*) benefit; advantage. [OE *behōf*]

be•hoove /bihóov/ *v.tr.* (*Brit.* **be•hove** /–hóv/) (prec. by *it* as subject; foll. by *to* + infin.) **1** be incumbent on. **2** (usu. with *neg.*) befit (*ill behooves him to protest*). [OE *behōfian* f. *behōf*: see BEHOOF]

beige /bayzh/ *n. & adj.* • *n.* a pale sandy fawn color. • *adj.* of this color. [F: orig. unkn.]

be•ing /beéing/ *n.* **1** existence. **2** the nature or essence (of a person, etc.) (*his whole being revolted*). **3** a human being. **4** anything that exists or is imagined. □ **in being** existing.

be•ja•bers /bijáybərz/ *int.* (also **be•jab•bers** /–jábərz/) *Ir.* by Jesus! [corrupt.]

be•jew•eled /bijóoəld/ *adj.* adorned with jewels.

bel /bel/ *n.* a unit used in the comparison of power levels in electrical communication or intensities of sound, corresponding to an intensity ratio of 10 to 1 (cf. DECIBEL). [A. G. *Bell*, inventor of telephone d. 1922]

be•la•bor /bilaybər/ *v.tr.* **1 a** thrash; beat. **b** attack verbally. **2** argue or elaborate (a subject) in excessive detail. [BE- + LABOR = exert one's strength]

be•lat•ed /biláytid/ *adj.* **1** coming late or too late. **2** *archaic* overtaken by darkness. □□ **be•lat•ed•ly** *adv.* **be•lat•ed•ness** *n.* [past part. of obs. *belate* delay (as BE-, LATE)]

be•lay /bilay/ *v. & n.* • *v.* **1** *tr.* fix (a running rope) around a cleat, pin, rock, etc., to secure it. **2** *tr. & intr.* (usu. in *imper.*) *Naut. sl.* stop; enough! (esp. belay there!) . • *n.* **1** an act of belaying. **2** a spike of rock, etc., used for belaying.

be•lay•ing pin *n.* a fixed wooden or iron pin used for fastening a rope around. [Du. *beleggen*]

bel can•to /bel kántō, kaán–/ *n.* **1** a lyrical style of operatic singing using a full rich broad tone and smooth phrasing. **2** (*attrib.*) (of a type of aria or voice) characterized by this type of singing. [It., = fine song]

belch /belch/ *v. & n.* • *v.* **1** *intr.* emit wind noisily from the stomach through the mouth. **2** *tr.* **a** (of a chimney, volcano, gun, etc.) send (smoke, etc.) out or up. **b** utter forcibly. • *n.* an act of belching. [OE *belcettan*]

bel•dam /béldəm, –dam/ *n.* (also **bel•dame**) *archaic* **1** an old woman; a hag. **2** a virago. [ME & OF *bel* beautiful + DAM², DAME]

be•lea•guer /bileégər/ *v.tr.* **1** besiege. **2** vex; harass. [Du. *belegeren* camp around (as BE-, *leger* a camp)]

bel•em•nite /béləmnīt/ *n.* any extinct cephalopod of the order Belemnoidea, having a bullet-shaped internal shell often found in fossilized form. [mod.L *belemnites* f. Gk *belemnon* dart + –ITE¹]

bel es•prit /bél espreé/ *n.* (*pl.* **beaux es•prits** /bóz espreé/) a witty person. [F, lit. fine mind]

bel•fry /bélfree/ *n.* (*pl.* **–fries**) **1** a bell tower or steeple housing bells, esp. forming part of a church. **2** a space for hanging bells in a church tower. □ **bats in the belfry** see BAT². [ME f. OF *berfrei* f. Frank.: altered by assoc. with *bell*]

Bel•gian /béljən/ *n. & adj.* • *n.* **1** a native or inhabitant of Belgium in W. Europe. **2** a person of Belgian descent. • *adj.* of or relating to Belgium.

Bel•gian hare *n.* a dark red long-eared breed of domestic rabbit.

Bel•gic /béljik/ *adj.* **1** of the ancient Belgae of N. Gaul. **2** of the Low Countries. [L *Belgicus* f. *Belgae*]

Be•li•al /beéleeəl/ *n.* the Devil. [Heb. *bᵉliyya'al* worthless]

be•lie /bilí/ *v.tr.* (**be•ly•ing**) **1** give a false notion of; fail to corroborate (*its appearance belies its age*). **2 a** fail to fulfill (a promise, etc.). **b** fail to justify (a hope, etc.). [OE *belēogan* (as BE-, *lēogan* LIE²)]

be•lief /bileéf/ *n.* **1 a** a person's religion; religious conviction (*has no belief*). **b** a firm opinion (*my belief is that he did it*). **c** an acceptance (of a thing, fact, statement, etc.) (*belief in the afterlife*). **2** (usu. foll. by *in*) trust or confidence. □ **beyond belief** incredible. **to the best of my belief** in my genuine opinion. [ME f. OE *gelēafa* (as BELIEVE)]

be•lieve /bileév/ *v.* **1** *tr.* accept as true or as conveying the truth (*I believe it; don't believe him; believes what he is told*). **2** *tr.* think; suppose (*I believe it's raining; Mr. Smith, I believe?*). **3** *intr.* (foll. by *in*) **a** have faith in the existence of (*believes in ghosts*). **b** have confidence in (a remedy, a person, etc.) (*believes in alternative medicine*). **c** have trust in the advisability of (*believes in telling the truth*). **4** *intr.* have (esp. religious) faith. □ **believe one's ears** (or **eyes**) accept that what one apparently hears or sees, etc., is true. **believe it or not** *colloq.* it is true though surprising. **make believe** (often foll. by *that* + clause, or *to* + infin.) pretend (*let's make believe that we're young*

SPELLING TIP believe

Aside from the "i before e" rule, remember the correct spelling of this common word with the mnemonic, "You can't believe a lie, but there is a *lie* in *believe*."

again). **would you believe it?** *colloq.* = *believe it or not.* [OE *belȳfan*, *belēfan*, with change of prefix f. *gelēfan* f. Gmc: rel. to LIEF]

be·liev·a·ble /bilēevəbəl/ *adj.* **1** (of an account or the person relating it) able to be believed; credible. **2** (of a fictional character or situation) convincing or realistic. □□ **be·liev·a·bil·i·ty** /–lēevəbílitee/ *n.*

be·liev·er /bilēevər/ *n.* **1** an adherent of a specified religion. **2** a person who believes, esp. in the efficacy of something (*a great believer in exercise*).

be·lit·tle /bilít'l/ *v.tr.* **1** disparage; depreciate. **2** make small; dwarf. □□ **be·lit·tle·ment** *n.* **be·lit·tler** *n.*

bell¹ /bel/ *n. & v.* ● *n.* **1** a hollow usu. metal object in the shape of a deep upturned cup usu. widening at the lip, made to sound a clear musical note when struck (either externally or by means of a clapper inside). **2 a** a sound or stroke of a bell, esp. as a signal. **b** (prec. by a numeral) *Naut.* the time as indicated every half hour of a watch by the striking of the ship's bell one to eight times. **3** anything that sounds like or functions as a bell, esp. an electronic device that rings, etc., as a signal. **4 a** any bell-shaped object or part, e.g., of a musical instrument. **b** the corolla of a flower when bell-shaped. **5** (in *pl.*) *Mus.* a set of cylindrical metal tubes of different lengths, suspended in a frame and played by being struck with a hammer. ● *v.tr.* **1** provide with a bell or bells; attach a bell to. **2** (foll. by *out*) form into the shape of the lip of a bell. □ **bell the cat** perform a daring feat. **clear** (or **sound**) **as a bell** perfectly clear or sound. **give a person a bell** *Brit. colloq.* telephone a person. **ring a bell** *colloq.* revive a distant recollection; sound familiar. **saved by the bell 1** *Boxing* spared a knockout or further blows by the ringing of the bell signaling the end of a round. **2** spared trouble, an unwanted task, etc., by another claim on one's attention. **with bells on** eagerly and prepared for enjoyment (*I'll be there with bells on*). [OE *belle*: perh. rel. to BELL²]

bell² /bel/ *n. & v.* ● *n.* the cry of a stag or buck at rutting time. ● *v.intr.* make this cry. [OE *bellan* bark, bellow]

bel·la·don·na /béladóna/ *n.* **1** *Bot.* a poisonous plant, *Atropa belladonna*, with purple flowers and purple-black berries. Also called **deadly nightshade**. **2** *Med.* a drug prepared from this. [mod.L f. It., = fair lady, perh. from its use as a cosmetic]

bel·la·don·na lil·y *n.* a S. African amaryllis with white or pink flowers, *Amaryllis belladonna*.

bell·bird /bélbərd/ *n.* any of various birds with a bell-like song, esp. any Central or S. American bird of the genus *Procnias*, a New Zealand honey eater, *Anthornis melanura*, and an Australian bird, *Oreoica gutturalis*.

bell-bot·tom *n.* **1** a marked flare below the knee (of a pants leg). **2** (in *pl.*) pants with bell-bottoms. □□ **bell-bot·tomed** *adj.*

bell·boy /bélboy/ *n. Brit.* = BELLHOP.

bell bu·oy *n.* a buoy equipped with a warning bell rung by the motion of the sea.

belle /bel/ *n.* **1** a beautiful woman. **2** a woman recognized as the most beautiful or most charming (*the belle of the ball*). [F f. L *bella* fem. of *bellus* beautiful]

belle é·poque /bél epúk/ *n.* the period of settled and comfortable life preceding World War I. [F, = fine period]

belles let·tres /bel-létrə/ *n.pl.* (also treated as *sing.*) essays, particularly of literary and artistic criticism, written and read primarily for for their aesthetic effect. □□ **bel·let·rism** /bel-létrizəm/ *n.* **bel·let·rist** /bel-létrist/ *n.* **bel·let·ris·tic** /bél-letrístik/ *adj.* [F, = fine letters]

bell·flow·er /bélflowr/ *n.* = CAMPANULA.

bell found·er *n.* a person who casts large bells in a foundry.

bell glass *n.* a bell-shaped glass cover for plants.

bell·hop /bélhop/ *n.* a person who carries luggage, runs errands, etc., in a hotel or club.

bel·li·cose /bélikōs/ *adj.* eager to fight; warlike. □□ **bel·li·cos·i·ty** /–kósitee/ *n.* [ME f. L *bellicosus* f. *bellum* war]

bel·lig·er·ence /bilíjərəns/ *n.* (also **bel·lig·er·en·cy** /–rənsee/) **1** aggressive or warlike behavior. **2** the status of a belligerent.

bel·lig·er·ent /bilíjərənt/ *adj. & n.* ● *adj.* **1** engaged in war or conflict. **2** given to constant fighting; pugnacious. ● *n.* a nation or person engaged in war or conflict. □□ **bel·lig·er·ent·ly** *adv.* [L *belligerare* wage war f. *bellum* war + *gerere* wage]

bell jar *n.* a bell-shaped glass cover or container for use in a laboratory.

bell·man /bélmən/ *n.* (*pl.* **·men**) *hist.* a town crier.

bell met·al *n.* an alloy of copper and tin for making bells (the tin content being greater than in bronze).

bel·low /bélō/ *v. & n.* ● *v.* **1** *intr.* **a** emit a deep loud roar. **b** cry or shout with pain. **2** *tr.* utter loudly and usu. angrily. ● *n.* a bellowing sound. [ME: perh. rel. to BELL²]

bel·lows /bélōz/ *n.pl.* (also treated as *sing.*) **1** a device with an air bag that emits a stream of air when squeezed, esp.: **a** (in full **pair of bellows**) a kind with two handles used for blowing air onto a fire. **b** a kind used in a harmonium or small organ. **2** an expandable component, e.g., joining the lens to the body of a camera. [ME prob. f. OE *belga* pl. of *belig* belly]

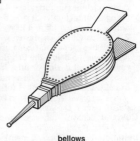
bellows

bell pep·per *n.* a sweet pepper of the genus *Capsicum*, with a bell shape.

bell·pull /bélpool/ *n.* a cord or handle which rings a bell when pulled.

bell push *n.* a button that operates an electric bell when pushed.

bells and whis·tles *n. colloq.* attractive but unnecessary additional features added to a product.

bell·weth·er /bélwethər/ *n.* **1** the leading sheep of a flock, with a bell on its neck. **2** a ringleader.

bel·ly /bélee/ *n. & v.* ● *n.* (*pl.* **·lies**) **1** the part of the human body below the chest, containing the stomach and bowels. **2** the stomach, esp. representing the body's need for food. **3** the front of the body from the waist to the groin. **4** the underside of a four-legged animal. **5 a** a cavity or bulging part of anything. **b** the surface of an instrument of the violin family, across which the strings are placed. ● *v.tr. & intr.* (**·lies, ·lied**) (often foll. by *out*) swell or cause to swell; bulge. □ **go belly up** *colloq.* fail financially. [OE *belig* (orig. = bag) f. Gmc]

bel·ly·ache /béleeayk/ *n. & v.* ● *n. colloq.* a stomach pain. ● *v.intr. sl.* complain noisily or persistently. □□ **bel·ly·ach·er** *n.*

bel·ly·band /béleeband/ *n.* a band placed around a horse's belly, holding the shafts of a cart, etc.

bel·ly but·ton *n. colloq.* the navel.

bel·ly dance *n.* a Middle Eastern dance performed by a woman, involving voluptuous movements of the belly. □□ **bel·ly danc·er** *n.* a woman who performs belly dances, esp. professionally. **bel·ly danc·ing** *n.* the performance of belly dances.

bel·ly·flop /béleeflop/ *n. & v. colloq.* ● *n.* a dive into water in which the body lands with the belly flat on the water. ● *v.intr.* (**·flopped, ·flop·ping**) perform this dive.

bel·ly·ful /béleefool/ *n.* (*pl.* **·fuls**) **1** enough to eat. **2** *colloq.* enough or more than enough of anything (esp. unwelcome).

bel·ly land·ing *n.* a crash-landing of an aircraft on the underside of the fuselage, without lowering the undercarriage.

bel·ly laugh *n.* a loud unrestrained laugh.

be·long /bilawng, –lóng/ *v.intr.* **1** (foll. by *to*) **a** be the property of. **b** be rightly assigned to as a duty, right, part, member, characteristic, etc. **c** be a member of (a club, family, group, etc.). **2** have the right personal or social qualities to be a member of a particular group (*he's nice but just doesn't belong*). **3** (foll. by *in, under*) **a** be rightly placed or classified. **b** fit a particular environment. □□ **be·long·ing·ness** *n.* [ME f. intensive BE- + *longen* belong f. OE *langian* (*gelang* at hand)]

be·long·ing /biláwnging, –lóng–/ *n.* **1** (in *pl.*) one's movable possessions or luggage. **2** membership; relationship; esp. a person's membership of, and acceptance by, a group or society.

Be·lo·rus·sian /bélōrúshən/ *n. & adj.* (also **Bye·lo·rus·sian** /byélō–/) ● *n.* **1** a native of Belorussia, now officially the Republic of Belarus. **2** the East Slavonic language of Belorussia. ● *adj.* of or relating to Belorussia or its people or language. [Russ. *Belorussiya* f. *belyi* white + *Russiya* Russia]

be·lov·ed /bilúvid, –lúvd/ *adj. & n.* ● *adj.* much loved. ● *n.* a much loved person. [obs. *belove* (v.)]

be·low /bilṓ/ *prep. & adv.* ● *prep.* **1** lower in position (vertically, down a slope or stream, etc.) than. **b** (from the map position) south of. **2** beneath the surface of; at or to a greater depth than (*head be-*

low water; below 500 feet). **3** lower or less than in amount or degree (below freezing). **4** lower in rank, position, or importance than. **5** unworthy of. • adv. **1** at or to a lower point or level. **2 a** downstairs (lives below). **b** downstream. **3** (of a text reference) further forward on a page or in a book (as noted below). **4** on the lower side (looks similar above and below). **5** rhet. on earth; in hell. **6** below zero; esp. below freezing. [BE- + LOW[1]]

Bel Pa·e·se /bél paa-áyzay/ n. Trademark a rich white mild creamy cheese of a kind orig. made in Italy. [It., = fair country]

belt /belt/ n. & v. • n. **1** a strip of leather or other material worn around the waist or across the chest, esp. to retain or support clothes or to carry weapons or as a safety belt. **2** a belt worn as a sign of rank or achievement. **3 a** a circular band of material used as a driving medium in machinery. **b** a conveyor belt. **c** flexible strip carrying machine gun cartridges. **4** a strip of color or texture, etc., differing from that on each side. **5** a distinct region or extent (cotton belt; commuter belt). **6** sl. a heavy blow. • v. **1** tr. put a belt around. **2** tr. (often foll. by on) fasten with a belt. **3** tr. **a** beat with a belt. **b** sl. hit hard. **4** intr. sl. rush; hurry (usu. with compl.: belted along; belted home). □ **below the belt** unfair or unfairly; disregarding the rules. **belt out** sl. sing or utter loudly and forcibly. **belt up 1** Brit. sl. be quiet. **2** colloq. put on a seat belt. **tighten one's belt** live more frugally. **under one's belt 1** (of food) eaten. **2** securely acquired (has a degree under her belt). □□ **belt·er** n. (esp. in sense of belt out). [OE f. Gmc f. L balteus]

Bel·tane /béltayn, –tən/ n. an ancient Celtic festival celebrated on May Day. [Gael. bealltainn]

belt·man /béltman/ n. (pl. ·men) Austral. a member of a lifesaving team of surfers; a lifeguard.

belt·way /béltway/ n. **1** a highway skirting a metropolitan region. **2** (**the Beltway**) the highway skirting Washington DC, viewed as encompassing a parochial, self-interested world of federal politics.

be·lu·ga /bəlоógə/ n. **1 a** a large kind of sturgeon, Huso huso. **b** caviar obtained from it. **2** a white whale. [Russ. beluga f. belyi white]

bel·ve·dere /bélvideer/ n. a summerhouse or open-sided gallery, usu. at rooftop level. [It. f. bel beautiful + vedere see]

be·ly·ing pres. part. of BELIE.

BEM abbr. British Empire Medal.

be·mire /bimír/ v.tr. **1** cover or stain with mud. **2** (in passive) be stuck in mud. [BE- + MIRE]

be·moan /bimón/ v.tr. **1** express regret or sorrow over; lament. **2** complain about. [OE]

be·muse /bimyoóz/ v.tr. stupefy or bewilder (a person). □□ **be·mus·ed·ly** /–zidlee/ adv. **be·muse·ment** n. [BE- + MUSE[2]]

ben[1] /ben/ n. Sc. a high mountain or mountain peak, esp. in names (Ben Nevis). [Gael. beann]

ben[2] /ben/ n. Sc. an inner room, esp. of a two-room cottage. [ellipt. use of ben (adv.), = within (OE binnan)]

bench /bench/ n. & v. • n. **1** a long seat of wood or stone for seating several people. **2** a worktable, e.g., for a carpenter, mechanic, or scientist. **3** (prec. by the) **a** the office of judge or magistrate. **b** a judge's seat in a court of law. **c** a court of law. **d** judges and magistrates collectively. **4** Sports **a** an area to the side of a field with seating where coaches and players not taking part can watch the game. **b** those players not taking part in a game. **5** Brit. Parl. a seat appropriated as specified (front bench). **6** a level ledge in masonry or an earthwork, on a hillside, etc. • v.tr. **1** exhibit (a dog) at a show. **2** Sports **a** keep (a player) on the bench. **b** withdraw (a player) from the field to the bench or court. □ **on the bench** appointed a judge or magistrate. [OE benc f. Gmc]

bench·er /bénchər/ n. Brit. **1** Law a senior member of any of the Inns of Court. **2** (in comb.) Parl. an occupant of a specified bench (backbencher).

bench·mark /bénchmaark/ n. & v. • n. **1** a surveyor's mark cut in a wall, pillar, building, etc., used as a reference point in measuring altitudes. **2** a standard or point of reference against which things may be compared or assessed. **3** a means of testing a computer, usu. by a set of programs run on a series of different machines to compare their performance. • v.tr. evaluate (a computer) by a benchmark.

bench test n. & v. • n. esp. Computing a test made by benchmarking. • v.tr. run a series of tests on (a computer, etc.) before its use.

bend[1] /bend/ v. & n. • v. (past bent; past part. bent exc. in bended knee) **1 a** tr. force or adapt (something straight) into a curve or angle. **b** intr. (of an object) be altered in this way. **2** intr. move or stretch in a curved course (the road bends to the left). **3** intr. & tr. (often foll. by down, over, etc.) incline or cause to incline from the vertical (bent down to pick it up). **4** tr. interpret or modify (a rule) to suit oneself. **5** tr. & refl. (foll. by to, on) direct or devote (oneself or one's attention, energies, etc.). **6** tr. turn (one's steps or eyes) in a new direction. **7** tr. (in passive; foll. by on) have firmly decided; be determined (was bent on selling; on pleasure bent). **8 a** intr. stoop or submit (bent before his master). **b** tr. force to submit. **9** tr. Naut. attach (a sail or cable) with a knot. • n. **1** a curve

in a road, stream, etc. **2** a departure from a straight course. **3** a bent part of anything. **4** (in pl.; prec. by the) colloq. sickness due to too rapid decompression underwater. □ **around the bend** colloq. crazy; insane. **bend over backward** see BACKWARD. □□ **bend·a·ble** adj. [OE bendan f. Gmc]

bend[2] /bend/ n. **1** Naut. any of various knots for tying ropes (fisherman's bend). **2** Heraldry **a** a diagonal stripe from top right to bottom left of a shield. **b** (in full **bend sinister**) a diagonal stripe from top left to bottom right, as a sign of bastardy. [OE bend band, bond f. Gmc]

bend·er /béndər/ n. sl. a wild drinking spree. [BEND[1] + –ER[1]]

bend·y /béndee/ adj. (**bend·i·er**, **bend·i·est**) colloq. capable of bending; soft and flexible. □□ **ben·di·ness** n.

be·neath /bineéth/ prep. & adv. • prep. **1** not worthy of; too demeaning for (it was beneath him to reply). **2** below; under. • adv. below; under; underneath. □ **beneath contempt** see CONTEMPT. [OE binithan, bineothan f. bi BY + nithan, etc., below f. Gmc]

ben·e·di·ci·te /bénidísitee/ n. a blessing, esp. a grace said at table in religious communities. [ME f. L, = bless ye: see BENEDICTION]

Ben·e·dic·tine /bénidíktin, (in sense 2) –teen/ n. & adj. • n. **1** a monk or nun of an order following the rule of St. Benedict established c.540. **2** Trademark a liqueur based on brandy, orig. made by Benedictines in France. • adj. of St. Benedict or the Benedictines. [F bénédictine or mod.L benedictinus f. Benedictus Benedict]

ben·e·dic·tion /bénidíkshən/ n. **1** the utterance of a blessing, esp. at the end of a religious service or as a special church service. **2** the state of being blessed. [ME f. OF f. L benedictio –onis f. benedicere –dict- bless]

ben·e·dic·to·ry /bénidíktəree/ adj. of or expressing benediction. [L benedictorius (as BENEDICTION)]

Ben·e·dic·tus /bénidíktəs/ n. **1** the section of the Latin Mass beginning Benedictus qui venit in nomine Domini (Blessed is he who comes in the name of the Lord). **2** a canticle beginning Benedictus Dominus Deus (Blessed be the Lord God) from Luke 1:68–79. [L, = blessed: see BENEDICTION]

ben·e·fac·tion /bénifákshən/ n. **1** a donation or gift. **2** an act of giving or doing good. [LL benefactio (as BENEFIT)]

ben·e·fac·tor /bénifaktər/ n. (fem. **ben·e·fac·tress** /–tris/) a person who gives support (esp. financial) to a person or cause. [ME f. LL (as BENEFIT)]

ben·e·fice /bénifis/ n. **1** an income from a church office. **2** the property attached to a church office, esp. that bestowed on a cleric. □□ **ben·e·ficed** adj. [ME f. OF f. L beneficium favor f. bene well + facere do]

be·nef·i·cent /binéfisənt/ adj. doing good; generous; actively kind. □□ **be·nef·i·cence** /–səns/ n. **be·nef·i·cent·ly** adv. [L beneficent- (as BENEFICE)]

ben·e·fi·cial /bénifíshəl/ adj. **1** advantageous; having benefits. **2** Law relating to the use or benefit of property; having rights to this use or benefit. □□ **ben·e·fi·cial·ly** adv. [ME f. F bénéficial or LL beneficialis (as BENEFICE)]

ben·e·fi·ci·ar·y /bénifishee-e-ree, –fishəree/ n. (pl. ·**ies**) **1** a person who receives benefits, esp. under a person's will, insurance policy, etc. **2** a holder of a benefice. [L beneficiarius (as BENEFICE)]

ben·e·fit /bénifit/ n. & v. • n. **1** a favorable or helpful factor or circumstance; advantage; profit. **2** (often in pl.) payment made under insurance, social security, welfare, etc. **3** a public performance or game of which the proceeds go to a particular charitable cause. • v. (**ben·e·fit·ed**, **ben·e·fit·ing**; also **ben·e·fit·ted**, **ben·e·fit·ting**) **1** tr. do good to; bring advantage to. **2** intr. (often foll. by from, by) receive an advantage or gain. □ **the benefit of the doubt** a concession that a person is innocent, correct, etc., although doubt exists. [ME f. AF benfet, OF bienfet, f. L benefactum f. bene facere do well]

benefit of cler·gy n. **1** hist. exemption of the English tonsured clergy and nuns from the jurisdiction of the ordinary civil courts. **2** ecclesiastical sanction or approval (marriage without benefit of clergy).

Ben·e·lux /béniluks/ n. Belgium, the Netherlands, and Luxembourg in association as a regional economic group. [Belgium + Netherlands + Luxembourg]

be·nev·o·lent /binévələnt/ adj. **1** wishing to do good; actively friendly and helpful. **2** charitable (benevolent fund; benevolent society). □□ **be·nev·o·lence** /–ləns/ n. **be·nev·o·lent·ly** adv. [ME f. OF benivolent f. L bene volens –entis well wishing f. velle wish]

Ben·ga·li /benggáwlee, –gáalee/ n. & adj. • n. **1** a native of Bengal, a former Indian province now consisting of Bangladesh and the Indian state of W. Bengal. **2** the language of this people. • adj. of or relating to Bengal or its people or language.

Ben·gal light /benggáwl, bénggəl/ n. a kind of flare giving off a blue flame, used for signals.

be·night·ed /binítid/ adj. **1** intellectually or morally ignorant. **2** overtaken by darkness. □□ **be·night·ed·ness** n. [obs. benight (v.)]

be·nign /binín/ adj. **1** gentle; mild; kind **2** fortunate; salutary. **3** (of the climate, soil, etc.) mild; favorable. **4** Med. (of a disease, tumor, etc.) not malignant. □□ **be·nign·ly** adv. [ME f. OF benigne f. L benignus f. bene well + –genus born]

be·nig·nant /binígnənt/ adj. **1** kindly, esp. to inferiors. **2** salutary;

beneficial. **3** *Med.* = BENIGN **4.** □□ **be·nig·nan·cy** /–nənsee/ *n.* **be·nig·nant·ly** *adv.* [f. BENIGN or L *benignus*, after *malignant*]

be·nig·ni·ty /binígnitee/ *n.* (*pl.* **·ties**) **1** kindliness. **2** *archaic* an act of kindness. [ME f. OF *benignité* or L *benignitas* (as BENIGN)]

ben·i·son /bénizən, –sən/ *n.* a blessing. [ME f. OF *beneiçun* f. L *benedictio –onis*]

bent[1] /bent/ *past* and *past part.* of BEND[1] *v.* ● *adj.* **1** curved or having an angle. **2** *Brit. sl.* dishonest; illicit. **3** esp. *Brit. sl.* **a** sexually deviant. **b** strange; weird; warped. **4** (foll. by *on*) determined to do or have. ● *n.* **1** an inclination or bias. **2** (foll. by *for*) a talent for something specified (*a bent for mimicry*).

bent[2] /bent/ *n.* **1 a** any stiff grass of the genus *Agrostis*. **b** any of various grasslike reeds, rushes, or sedges. **2** a stiff stalk of a grass usu. with a flexible base. **3** esp. *Brit. archaic* or *dial.* a heath or unenclosed pasture. [ME repr. OE *beonet-* (in place-names), f. Gmc]

Ben·tham·ism /bénthəmizəm/ *n.* the utilitarian philosophy of Jeremy Bentham, Engl. philosopher d. 1832. □□ **Ben·tham·ite** *n. & adj.*

ben·thos /bénthos/ *n.* the flora and fauna found at the bottom of a sea or lake. □□ **ben·thic** /–thik/ *adj.* [Gk, = depth of the sea]

ben·ton·ite /béntənīt/ *n.* a kind of absorbent clay used esp. as a filler. [Fort *Benton* in Montana]

ben tro·va·to /bén trōváatō/ *adj.* **1** well invented. **2** characteristic if not true. [It., = well found]

bent·wood /béntwŏŏd/ *n.* wood that is artificially shaped for use in making furniture.

be·numb /binúm/ *v.tr.* **1** make numb; deaden. **2** paralyze (the mind or feelings). [orig. = deprived, as past part. of ME *benimen* f. OE *beniman* (as BE-, *niman* take)]

Ben·ze·drine /bénzidreen/ *n. Trademark* amphetamine. [BENZOIC + EPHEDRINE]

ben·zene /bénzeen/ *n.* a colorless carcinogenic volatile liquid found in coal tar, petroleum, etc., and used as a solvent and in the manufacture of plastics, etc. ¶ *Chem.* formula: C_6H_6. □□ **ben·ze·noid** /–zənoyd/ *adj.* [BENZOIC + -ENE]

ben·zene ring *n.* the hexagonal unsaturated ring of six carbon atoms in the benzene molecule.

ben·zine /bénzeen/ *n.* (also **ben·zin** /–zin/) a mixture of liquid hydrocarbons obtained from petroleum. [BENZOIN + -INE[4]]

ben·zo·ic /benzóik/ *adj.* containing or derived from benzoin or benzoic acid. [BENZOIN + -IC]

ben·zo·ic ac·id *n.* a white crystalline substance used as a food preservative. ¶ *Chem.* formula: $C_7H_6O_2$

ben·zo·in /bénzōin/ *n.* **1** a fragrant gum resin obtained from various E. Asian trees of the genus *Styrax*, and used in the manufacture of perfumes and incense. **2** the white crystalline constituent of this. Also called **gum benjamin**. [earlier *benjoin* ult. f. Arab. *lubān jāwī* incense of Java]

ben·zol /bénzawl, –zol/ *n.* (also **ben·zole** /–zōl/) benzene, esp. unrefined and used as a fuel.

ben·zo·yl /bénzōil/ *n.* (usu. *attrib.*) *Chem.* the radical C_6H_5CO.

ben·zo·yl per·ox·ide *n.* a white crystalline compound, $C_{14}H_{10}O_4$, used as a bleaching agent and medicinally for acne.

ben·zyl /bénzil, –zeel/ *n.* (usu. *attrib.*) *Chem.* the radical $C_6H_5CH_2$.

be·queath /bikwéeth, –kwéeth/ *v.tr.* **1** leave (a personal estate) to a person by a will. **2** hand down to posterity. □□ **be·queath·al** *n.* **be·queath·er** *n.* [OE *becwethan* (as BE-, *cwethan* say: cf. QUOTH)]

be·quest /bikwést/ *n.* **1** the act or an instance of bequeathing. **2** a thing bequeathed. [ME f. BE- + obs. *quiste* f. OE *–cwiss, cwide* saying]

be·rate /biráyt/ *v.tr.* scold; rebuke. [BE- + RATE[2]]

Ber·ber /bɔ́rbər/ *n. & adj.* ● *n.* **1** a member of the indigenous mainly Muslim peoples of N. Africa. **2** the language of these peoples. ● *adj.* of the Berbers or their language. [Arab. *barbar*]

ber·ber·is /bɔ́rbəris/ *n.* = BARBERRY. [med.L & OF, of unkn. orig.]

ber·ceuse /báirsɔ́z/ *n.* (*pl.* **ber·ceuses** *pronunc.* same) **1** a lullaby. **2** an instrumental piece in the style of a lullaby. [F]

be·reave /biréev/ *v.tr.* (esp. as **bereaved** *adj.*) (foll. by *of*) deprive of a relation, friend, etc., esp. by death. □□ **be·reave·ment** *n.* [OE *berēafian* (as BE-, REAVE)]

be·reft /biréft/ *adj.* (foll. by *of*) deprived (esp. of a non-material asset) (*bereft of hope*). [past part. of BEREAVE]

be·ret /bəráy/ *n.* a round flattish visorless cap of felt or cloth. [F *béret* Basque cap f. Prov. *berret*]

berg[1] /bɔrg/ *n.* = ICEBERG. [abbr.]

berg[2] /bɔrg/ *n. S.Afr.* a mountain or hill. [Afrik. f. Du.]

ber·ga·mot[1] /bɔ́rgəmot/ *n.* **1** an aromatic herb, esp. *Mentha citrata*. **2** an oily perfume extracted from the rind of the fruit of the citrus tree *Citrus bergamia*, a dwarf variety of the Seville orange tree. **3** the tree itself. [*Bergamo* in N. Italy]

ber·ga·mot[2] /bɔ́rgəmot/ *n.* a variety of fine pear. [F *bergamotte* f. It. *bergamotta* f. Turk. *begarmüdi* prince's pear f. *beg* prince + *armudi* pear]

berg·schrund /báirkshrŏŏnt/ *n.* a crevasse or gap at the head of a glacier or névé. [G]

berg wind *n.* a hot dry northerly wind blowing from the interior to coastal districts.

ber·i·ber·i /béreebéree/ *n.* a disease causing inflammation of the nerves due to a deficiency of vitamin B_1. [Sinh., f. *beri* weakness]

berk /bɔrk/ *n.* (also **burk**) *Brit. sl.* a fool; a stupid person. [abbr. of *Berkeley* or *Berkshire Hunt*, rhyming sl. for *cunt*] ▶Usually this slang term is not considered offensive despite the etymology.

ber·ke·li·um /bɔrkéeleeəm, bɔ́rkleeəm/ *n. Chem.* a transuranic radioactive metallic element produced by bombardment of americium. ¶ Symb.: **Bk**. [mod.L f. *Berkeley*, California (where first made) + –IUM]

Ber·li·ner /bɔrlínər/ *n.* a native or citizen of Berlin in Germany. [G]

berm /bɔrm/ *n.* **1** a narrow path or grass strip beside a road, canal, etc. **2** a narrow ledge, esp. in a fortification between a ditch and the base of a parapet. [F *berme* f. Du. *berm*]

Ber·mu·da on·ion /bərmyŏŏdə/ *n.* a large, yellow-skinned onion with a mild flavor.

Ber·mu·da shorts /bɔrmyŏŏdə/ *n.pl.* (also **Ber·mu·das**) shorts reaching almost to the knees. [*Bermuda* in the W. Atlantic]

Ber·mu·da tri·an·gle *n.* an area of the western Atlantic where ships and aircraft are reported to have disappeared without a trace.

ber·ry /béree/ *n. & v.* ● *n.* (*pl.* **·ries**) **1** any small roundish juicy fruit without a stone. **2** *Bot.* a fruit with its seeds enclosed in a pulp (e.g., a banana, tomato, etc.). **3** any of various kernels or seeds (e.g., coffee bean, etc.). **4** a fish egg or roe of a lobster, etc. ● *v.intr.* (**·ries**, **·ried**) **1** (usu. as **berrying** *n.*) go gathering berries. **2** form a berry; bear berries. □□ **ber·ried** *adj.* (also in *comb.*). [OE *berie* f. Gmc]

ber·serk /bɔrsɔ́rk, –zɔ́rk/ *adj. & n.* ● *adj.* (esp. in **go berserk**) wild; frenzied; in a violent rage. ● *n.* (also **ber·serk·er** /–kər/) an ancient Norse warrior who fought with a wild frenzy. [Icel. *berserkr* (n.) prob. f. *bern-* BEAR[2] + *serkr* coat]

berth /bɔrth/ *n. & v.* ● *n.* **1** a fixed bunk on a ship, train, etc., for sleeping in. **2** a ship's place at a wharf. **3** room for a ship to swing at anchor. **4** adequate sea room. **5** *colloq.* a situation or appointment. **6** the proper function for anything. ● *v.* **1** *tr.* moor (a ship) in its berth. **2** *tr.* provide a sleeping place for. **3** *intr.* (of a ship) come to its mooring place. □ **give a wide berth to** stay away from. [prob. f. naut. use of BEAR[1] + –TH[2]]

ber·tha /bɔ́rthə/ *n.* **1** a deep falling collar often of lace. **2** a small cape on a dress. [F *berthe* f. *Berthe* Bertha (the name)]

ber·yl /béril/ *n.* **1** a kind of transparent precious stone, esp. pale green, blue, or yellow, and consisting of beryllium aluminum silicate in a hexagonal form. **2** a mineral species which includes this, emerald, and aquamarine. [ME f. OF f. L *beryllus* f. Gk *bērullos*]

be·ryl·li·um /bəríleeəm/ *n. Chem.* a hard white metallic element used in the manufacture of light corrosion-resistant alloys. ¶ Symb.: **Be**. [BERYL + –IUM]

be·seech /biséech/ *v.tr.* (*past* and *past part.* **be·sought** /–sáwt/ or **be·seeched**) **1** (foll. by *for*, or *to* + infin.) entreat. **2** ask earnestly for. □□ **be·seech·ing** *adj.* [ME f. BE- + *secan* SEEK]

be·set /bisét/ *v.tr.* (**be·set·ting**; *past* and *past part.* **be·set**) **1** attack or harass persistently (*beset by worries*). **2** surround or hem in (a person, etc.). **3** *archaic* cover with (*beset with pearls*). □□ **be·set·ment** *n.* [OE *besettan* f. Gmc]

be·set·ting sin *n.* the sin that especially or most frequently tempts one.

be·side /bisíd/ *prep.* **1** at the side of; near. **2** compared with. **3** irrelevant to (*beside the point*). **4** = BESIDES. □ **beside oneself** overcome with worry, anger, etc. [OE *be sīdan* (as BY, SIDE)]

be·sides /bisídz/ *prep. & adv.* ● *prep.* in addition to; apart from. ● *adv.* also; as well; moreover.

be·siege /biséej/ *v.tr.* **1** lay siege to. **2** crowd around oppressively. **3** harass with requests. □□ **be·sieg·er** *n.* [ME f. *assiege* by substitution of BE-, f. OF *asegier* f. Rmc]

be·smear /bisméer/ *v.tr.* **1** smear with greasy or sticky stuff. **2** sully (a reputation, etc.). [OE *bismierwan* (as BE-, SMEAR)]

be·smirch /bismɔ́rch/ *v.tr.* **1** soil; discolor. **2** dishonor; sully the reputation or name of. [BE- + SMIRCH]

be·som /béezəm/ *n.* a broom made of twigs tied round a stick. [OE *besema*]

be·sot·ted /bisótid/ *adj.* **1** intoxicated; stupefied. **2** foolish; confused. **3** infatuated. [*besot* (v.) (as BE-, SOT)]

be·sought *past* and *past part.* of BESEECH.

be·span·gle /bispánggəl/ *v.tr.* adorn with spangles.

be·spat·ter /bispátər/ *v.tr.* **1** spatter (an object) all over. **2** spatter (liquid, etc.). **3** overwhelm with abuse, slander, etc.

be·speak /bispéek/ *v.tr.* (*past* **be·spoke** /–spók/; *past part.* **be·spoken** /–spókən/ or as *adj.* **be·spoke**) **1** engage in advance. **2** order (goods). **3** suggest; be evidence of (*his gift bespeaks a kind heart*). **4** *literary* speak to. [OE *bisprecan* (as BE-, SPEAK)]

be·spec·ta·cled /bispéktəkəld/ *adj.* wearing eyeglasses.

be•spoke *past* and *past part.* of BESPEAK.● *adj. Brit.* **1** (of goods, esp. clothing) made to order. **2** (of a tradesman) making goods to order.

be•spo•ken *past part.* of BESPEAK.

be•sprin•kle /bispríngkəl/ *v.tr.* sprinkle or strew all over with liquid, etc. [ME f. BE- + *sprengen* in the same sense]

Bes•se•mer con•vert•er /bésimər/ *n.* a special furnace used to purify pig iron using the Bessemer process. [Sir H. *Bessemer*, Engl. engineer d. 1898]

Bes•se•mer proc•ess /bésimər/ *n.* a process once widely used, in which air is blown through molten pig iron to remove carbon, silicon, and other impurities in order to render it suitable for making steel.

best /best/ *adj., adv., n., & v.* ● *adj. (superl.* of GOOD) of the most excellent or outstanding or desirable kind (*my best work; the best solution; the best thing to do would be to confess*). ● *adv. (superl.* of WELL[1]). **1** in the best manner (*does it best*). **2** to the greatest degree (*like it best*). **3** most usefully (*is best ignored*). ● *n.* **1** that which is best (*the best is yet to come*). **2** the chief merit or advantage; the best aspect or side; a person's best performance, achievement, etc. (*brings out the best in him; gave their best to the task*). **3** (foll. by *of*) a winning majority of (a certain number of games, etc., played) (*the best of five*). **4** = SUNDAY BEST. ● *v.tr. colloq.* defeat, outwit, outbid, etc. □ **all the best** an expression used to wish a person good fortune. **as best one can** (or **may**) as effectively as possible under the circumstances. **at best** on the most optimistic view. **at one's best** in peak condition, etc. **at the best of times** even in the most favorable circumstances. **be for** (or **all for**) the best be desirable in the end. **the best part of** most of. **do one's best** do all one can. **get the best of** defeat; outwit. **give a person the best** *Brit.* admit the superiority of that person. **had best** would find it wisest to. **make the best of** derive what limited advantage one can from (something unsatisfactory or unwelcome); put up with. **to the best of one's ability, knowledge,** etc., as far as one can do, know, etc. **with the best of them** as well as anyone. [OE *betest* (adj.), *bet(o)st* (adv.), f. Gmc]

best boy *n.* the assistant to the chief electrician of a movie crew.

bes•tial /béschəl, bées–/ *adj.* **1** brutish; cruel; savage. **2** sexually depraved; lustful. **3** of or like a beast. □□ **bes•tial•ize** *v.tr.* **bes•tial•ly** *adv.* [ME f. OF f. LL *bestialis* f. *bestia* beast]

bes•ti•al•i•ty /béscheeálitee, bées–/ *n. (pl.* **·ties**) **1** bestial behavior or an instance of this. **2** sexual intercourse between a person and an animal. [F *bestialité* (as BESTIAL)]

bes•ti•ar•y /béschee-eree, bées–/ *n. (pl.* **·ies**) a moralizing medieval treatise on real and imaginary beasts. [med.L *bestiarium* f. L *bestia* beast]

be•stir /bistér/ *v.refl.* (**be•stirred, be•stir•ring**) exert or rouse (oneself).

best man *n.* the bridegroom's chief attendant at a wedding.

be•stow /bistő/ *v.tr.* **1** (foll. by *on, upon*) confer (a gift, right, etc.). **2** deposit. □□ **be•stow•al** *n.* [ME f. BE- + OE *stow* a place]

be•strew /bistróő/ *v.tr. (past part.* **be•strewed** or **be•strewn** /–stróőn/) **1** (foll. by *with*) cover or partly cover (a surface). **2** scatter (things) about. **3** lie scattered over. [OE *bestrēowian* (as BE-, STREW)]

be•stride /bistríd/ *v.tr. (past* **be•strode** /–stród/; *past part.* **be•strid•den** /–stríd'n/) **1** sit astride on. **2** stand astride over. **3** dominate. [OE *bestrīdan*]

best sell•er *n.* **1** a book or other item that has sold in large numbers. **2** esp. *Brit.* the author of such a book.

bet /bet/ *v. & n.* ● *v.* (**bet•ting;** *past* and *past part.* **bet** or **bet•ted**) **1** *intr.* (foll. by *on* or *against* with ref. to the outcome) risk a sum of money, etc., against another's on the basis of the outcome of an unpredictable event (esp. the result of a race, game, etc., or the outcome in a game of chance). **2** *tr.* risk (an amount) on such an outcome or result (*bet $10 on a horse*). **3** *tr.* risk a sum of money against (a person). **4** *tr. colloq.* feel sure (*bet they've forgotten it*). ● *n.* **1** the act of betting (*make a bet*). **2** the money, etc., staked (*put a bet on*). **3** *colloq.* an opinion, esp. a quickly formed or spontaneous one (*my bet is that he won't come*). **4** *colloq.* a choice or course of action (*she's our best bet*). □ **you bet** *colloq.* you may be sure. [16th c.: perh. a shortened form of ABET]

bet. *abbr.* between.

be•ta /báytə, bée–/ *n.* **1** the second letter of the Greek alphabet (Β, β). **2** *Brit.* a second-class grade given for a piece of work or in an examination. **3** *Astron.* the second brightest star in a constellation. **4** the second member of a series. [ME f. L f. Gk]

be•ta-block•er *n. Pharm.* a drug that prevents the stimulation of increased cardiac action, used to treat angina and reduce high blood pressure.

be•take /bitáyk/ *v.refl. (past* **be•took** /bitóők/; *past part.* **be•tak•en** /bitáykən/) (foll. by *to*) go to (a place or person).

be•ta par•ti•cle *n.* (also **be•ta ray**) a fast-moving electron emitted by radioactive decay of substances (orig. regarded as rays).

be•ta•tron /báytətron, bée–/ *n. Physics* an apparatus for accelerating electrons in a circular path by magnetic induction. [BETA + –TRON]

be•tel /bée't'l/ *n.* the leaf of the Asian evergreen climbing plant *Piper betle,* chewed in parts of Asia with parings of the areca nut. [Port. f. Malayalam *veṭṭila*]

be•tel nut *n.* the areca nut.

bête noire /bet nwáar/ *n. (pl.* **bêtes noires** *pronunc.* same) a person or thing one particularly dislikes or fears. [F, = black beast]

be•think /bithíngk/ *v.refl. (past* and *past part.* **be•thought** /–tháwt/) (foll. by *of, how,* or *that* + clause) *formal* **1** reflect; stop to think. **2** be reminded by reflection. [OE *bithencan* f. Gmc (as BE-, THINK)]

be•tide /bitíd/ *v. poet.* (only in infin. and 3rd sing. subj.) **1** *tr.* happen to (*woe betide him*). **2** *intr.* happen (*whate'er may betide*). [ME f. obs. *tide* befall f. OE *tīdan*]

be•times /bitímz/ *adv. literary* **1** early; in good time. **2** occasionally. [ME f. obs. *betime* (as BY, TIME)]

bê•tise /baytéez/ *n.* **1** a foolish or ill-timed remark or action. **2** a piece of folly. [F]

be•to•ken /bitókən/ *v.tr.* **1** be a sign of; indicate. **2** augur. [OE (as BE-, *tācnian* signify: see TOKEN)]

bet•o•ny /bét'nee/ *n.* **1** a purple-flowered plant, *Stachys officinalis.* **2** any of various similar plants. [ME f. OF *betoine* f. L *betonica*]

be•took *past* of BETAKE.

be•tray /bitráy/ *v.tr.* **1** place (a person, one's country, etc.) in the hands or power of an enemy. **2** be disloyal to (another person, a person's trust, etc.). **3** reveal involuntarily or treacherously; be evidence of (*his shaking hand betrayed his fear*). **4** lead astray or into error. □□ **be•tray•al** *n.* **be•tray•er** *n.* [ME f. obs. *tray,* ult. f. L *tradere* hand over]

be•troth /bitróth, –tráwth/ *v.tr.* (usu. as **betrothed** *adj.*) bind with a promise to marry. □□ **be•troth•al** *n.* [ME f. BE- + *trouthe, treuthe* TRUTH, later assim. to TROTH]

bet•ter[1] /bétər/ *adj., adv., n., & v.* ● *adj. (compar.* of GOOD). **1** of a more excellent or outstanding or desirable kind (*a better product; it would be better to go home*). **2** partly or fully recovered from illness (*feeling better*). ● *adv. (compar.* of WELL[1]). **1** in a better manner (*she sings better*). **2** to a greater degree; more (*like it better; took us better than an hour to finish*). **3** more usefully or advantageously (*is better forgotten*). ● *n.* **1** that which is better (*the better of the two; had the better of me*). **2** (usu. in *pl.;* prec. by *my,* etc.) one's superior in ability or rank (*take notice of your betters*). ● *v.* **1** *tr.* improve on; surpass (*I can better his offer*). **2** *tr.* make better; improve. **3** *refl.* improve one's position, etc. **4** *intr.* become better; improve. □ **better off** in a better (esp. financial) position. **the better part of** most of. **for better or for worse** on terms accepting all results; whatever the outcome. **get the better of** defeat; outwit; win an advantage over. **go one better 1** outbid, etc., by one. **2** (*go one better than*) outdo another person. **had better** would find it wiser to. [OE *betera* f. Gmc]

bet•ter[2] var. of BETTOR.

bet•ter half *n. colloq.* one's wife or husband.

bet•ter•ment /bétərmənt/ *n.* **1** making better; improvement. **2** *Econ.* enhanced value (of real property) arising from local improvements.

bet•ting /béting/ *n.* **1** gambling by risking money on an unpredictable outcome. **2** the odds offered in this. □ **what's the betting?** *Brit. colloq.* it is likely or to be expected (*what's the betting he'll be late?*).

bet•ting shop *n. Brit.* a bookmaker's shop or office.

bet•tor /bétər/ *n.* (also **bet•ter**) a person who bets.

be•tween /bitwée'n/ *prep. & adv.* ● *prep.* **1 a** at or to a point in the area or interval bounded by two or more other points in space, time, etc. (*broke down between Boston and Providence; we must meet between now and Friday*). **b** along the extent of such an area or interval (*there are five shops between here and the main road; works best between five and six; the numbers between 10 and 20*). **2** separating, physically or conceptually (*the distance between here and the moon; the difference between right and wrong*). **3 a** by combining the resources of (*great potential between them; between us we could afford it*). **b** shared by; as the joint resources of (*$5 between them*). **c** by joint or reciprocal action (*an agreement between us; sorted it out between themselves*). **4** to and from (*runs between New York and Philadelphia*). **5** taking one and rejecting the other of (*decide between eating here and going out*). ● *adv.* (also **in be•tween**) at a point or in the area bounded by two or more other points in space, time, sequence, etc. (*not fat or thin but in between*). □ **between ourselves** (or **you and me**) in confidence. [OE *betwēonum* f. Gmc (as BY, TWO)]

▶ **1. Between** is used in speaking of only two things, people, etc.: *We must choose between two equally unattractive alternatives.* **Among** is used when more than two are involved: *Agreement on landscaping was reached among all the neighbors.* But where there are more than two parties involved, **between** may be proper to emphasize the relationship of pairs within the group or the sense 'shared by': *There is close friendship between the members of the club; relations between the United States, Canada, and Mexico.* **2.** *Between you and I, between you and he,* etc., are incorrect; **between** should be followed only by the objective case: *me, her, him, them.*

be•tween times *n.* in the intervals between other actions; occasionally.

be•twixt /bitwíkst/ *prep. & adv. archaic* between. □ **betwixt and be–**

tween *colloq.* neither one thing nor the other. [ME f. OE *betwēox* f. Gmc: cf. AGAINST]

BeV *abbr.* a billion (=10⁹) electronvolts. Also called **GeV**.

bev·a·tron /bévətron/ *n.* a synchrotron used to accelerate protons to energies in the billion electron-volt range. [BeV + –TRON]

bev·el /bévəl/ *n. & v.* • *n.* **1** a slope from the horizontal or vertical in carpentry and stonework; a sloping surface or edge. **2** (in full **bevel square**) a tool for marking angles in carpentry and stonework. • *v.* (**bev·eled, bev·el·ing** or **bev·elled, bev·el·ling**) **1** *tr.* reduce (a square edge) to a sloping edge. **2** *intr.* slope at an angle; slant. [OF *bevel* (unrecorded) f. *baïf* f. *baer* gape]

bev·el gear *n.* a gear working another gear at an angle to it by means of bevel wheels.

bev·el wheel *n.* a toothed wheel whose working face is oblique to the axis.

bev·er·age /bévərij, bévrij/ *n.* a drink (*hot beverage; alcoholic beverage*). [ME f. OF *be(u)vrage*, ult. f. L *bibere* drink]

bev·vy /bévee/ *n.* (also **bev·y**) *Brit. sl.* (a) drink, esp. (of) beer or another alcoholic beverage. [shortened f. BEVERAGE]

bev·y /bévee/ *n.* (*pl.* **·ies**) **1** a flock of quails or larks. **2** a company or group (orig. of women). [15th c.: orig. unkn.]

be·wail /biwáyl/ *v.tr.* **1** greatly regret or lament. **2** wail over; mourn for. □□ **be·wail·er** *n.*

be·ware /biwáir/ *v.* (only in *imper.* or *infin.*) **1** *intr.* (often foll. by *of*, or *that, lest*, etc. + clause) be cautious; take heed (*beware of the dog; told us to beware; beware that you don't fall*). **2** *tr.* be cautious of (*beware the Ides of March*). [BE + WARE³]

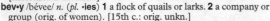
bevel gears

bi·cam·er·al /bíkámərəl/ adj. (of a parliament or legislative body) having two chambers. □□ **bi·cam·er·al·ism** n. [BI- + L camera chamber]

bi·carb /bikaárb/ n. colloq. = BICARBONATE 2. [abbr.]

bi·car·bo·nate /bikaárbənit/ n. 1 Chem. any acid salt of carbonic acid. 2 (in full **bicarbonate of soda**) sodium bicarbonate used as an antacid or in baking powder.

bice /bis/ n. Brit. 1 any of various pigments made from blue or green basic copper carbonate. 2 any similar pigment made from smalt. 3 a shade of blue or green given by these. [orig. = brownish gray, f. OF bis dark gray, of unkn. orig.]

bi·cen·ten·ar·y /bísenténəree, biséntəneree/ n. & adj. esp. Brit. = BICENTENNIAL.

bi·cen·ten·ni·al /bísenténeeəl/ n. & adj. esp. US ● n. 1 a two-hundredth anniversary. 2 a celebration of this. ● adj. 1 lasting two hundred years or occurring every two hundred years. 2 of or concerning a bicentennial.

bi·ceph·a·lous /bíséfələs/ adj. having two heads.

bi·ceps /bíseps/ n. a muscle having two heads or attachments, esp. the one which bends the elbow. [L, = two-headed, formed as BI- + −ceps f. caput head]

bick·er /bíkər/ v.intr. 1 quarrel pettily; wrangle. 2 poet. a (of a stream, rain, etc.) patter (over stones, etc.). b (of a flame, light, etc.) flash; flicker. □□ **bick·er·er** n. [ME biker, beker, of unkn. orig.]

bick·ie /bíkee/ n. (also **bik·kie**) Brit. & Austral. colloq. a biscuit. □ **big bickies** Austral. colloq. a large sum of money. [abbr.]

bi·col·or /bíkúlər/ adj. & n. ● adj. having two colors. ● n. a bicolor blossom or animal.

bi·con·cave /bíkónkayv, bíkonkáyv/ adj. (esp. of a lens) concave on both sides.

bi·con·vex /bíkónveks, bíkonvéks/ adj. (esp. of a lens) convex on both sides.

bi·cul·tur·al /bíkúlchərəl/ adj. having or combining two cultures.

bi·cus·pid /bíkúspid/ adj. & n. ● adj. having two cusps or points. ● n. 1 the premolar tooth in humans. 2 a tooth with two cusps. □□ **bi·cus·pi·date** adj. [BI- + L cuspis −idis sharp point]

bi·cy·cle /bísikəl, −síkəl/ n. & v. ● n. a vehicle of two wheels held in a frame one behind the other, propelled by pedals and steered with handlebars attached to the front wheel. ● v.intr. ride a bicycle. □□ **bi·cy·cler** n. **bi·cy·clist** /−klist/ n. [F f. BI- + Gk kuklos wheel]

bi·cy·cle chain n. a chain transmitting power from the bicycle pedals to the wheels.

bi·cy·cle clip n. either of two metal clips used to confine a cyclist's pants at the ankle.

bi·cy·cle pump n. a portable pump for inflating bicycle tires.

bid /bid/ v. & n. ● v. (**bid·ding**; past **bid**, archaic **bade** /bayd, bad/; past part. **bid**, archaic **bid·den** /bíd'n/) 1 tr. & intr. (past and past part. **bid**) (often foll. by for, against) a (esp. at an auction) offer (a certain price) (did not bid for the vase; bid against the dealer; bid $20). b offer to do work, etc., for a stated price. 2 tr. archaic or literary a command; order (bid the soldiers to shoot). b invite (bade her to start). 3 tr. archaic or literary a utter (greeting or farewell) to (I bade him welcome). b proclaim (defiance, etc.). 4 (past and past part. **bid**) Cards a intr. state before play how many tricks one intends to make. b tr. state (one's intended number of tricks). ● n. 1 a (esp. at an auction) an offer (of a price) (a bid of $5). b an offer (to do work, supply goods, etc.) at a stated price; a tender. 2 Cards a statement of the number of tricks a player proposes to make. 3 an attempt; an effort (a bid for power). □ **bid fair to** seem likely to. **make a bid for** try to gain (made a bid for freedom). □□ **bid·der** n. [OE biddan ask f. Gmc, & OE bēodan offer, command]

bid·da·ble /bídəbəl/ adj. 1 obedient. 2 Cards (of a hand or suit) suitable for being bid. □□ **bid·da·bil·i·ty** n.

bid·den archaic past part. of BID.

bid·ding /bíding/ n. 1 the offers at an auction. 2 Cards the act of making a bid or bids. 3 a command, request, or invitation.

bid·ding prayer n. Anglican Ch. one inviting the congregation to join in.

bid·dy /bídee/ n. (pl. **·dies**) sl. derog. a woman (esp. old biddy). [pet form of the name Bridget]

bide /bid/ v.intr. archaic or dial. remain; stay. □ **bide one's time** await one's best opportunity. [OE bīdan f. Gmc]

bi·det /beedáy/ n. a low oval basinlike bathroom fixture used esp. for washing the genital area. [F, = pony]

Bie·der·mei·er /beedərmiər/ attrib.adj. 1 (of styles, furnishings, etc.) characteristic of the period 1815–48 in Germany. 2 derog. conventional; bourgeois. [Biedermaier a fictitious German poet (1854)]

bi·en·ni·al /bí-éneeəl/ adj. & n. ● adj. 1 lasting two years. 2 recurring every two years (cf. BIANNUAL). ● n. 1 Bot. a plant that takes two years to grow from seed to fruition and die (cf. ANNUAL, PERENNIAL). 2 an event celebrated or taking place every two years. □□ **bi·en·ni·al·ly** adv. [L biennis (as BI-, annus year)]

▶Biennial means 'lasting or occurring every two years': Congressional elections are a biennial phenomenon. A biennial plant is one that

lives a two-year cycle, flowering and producing seed in the second year. **Biannual** means 'twice a year': The solstice is a biannual event.

bi·en·ni·um /bí-éneeəm/ n. (pl. **bi·en·ni·ums** or **bi·en·ni·a** /−neeə/) a period of two years. [L (as BIENNIAL)]

bier /beer/ n. a movable frame on which a coffin or a corpse is placed, or taken to a grave. [OE bēr f. Gmc]

biff /bif/ n. & v. sl. ● n. a sharp blow. ● v.tr. strike (a person). [imit.]

bif·fin /bífin/ n. Brit. a deep-red cooking apple. [= beefing f. BEEF + −ING[1], with ref. to the color]

bi·fid /bífid/ adj. divided by a deep cleft into two parts. [L bifidus (as BI-, fidus f. stem of findere cleave)]

bi·fo·cal /bífókəl/ adj. & n. ● adj. having two focuses, esp. of a lens with a part for distant vision and a part for near vision. ● n. (in pl.) bifocal eyeglasses.

bi·fur·cate /bífərkayt/ v. & adj. ● v.tr. & intr. divide into two branches; fork. ● adj. forked; branched. [med.L bifurcare f. L bifurcus two-forked (as BI-, furca fork)]

bi·fur·ca·tion /bífərkáyshən/ n. 1 a a division into two branches. b either or both of such branches. 2 the point of such a division.

big /big/ adj. & adv. ● adj. (**big·ger, big·gest**) 1 a of considerable size, amount, intensity, etc. (a big mistake; a big helping). b of a large or the largest size (big toe; big drum). c (of a letter) capital, uppercase. 2 a important; significant; outstanding (the big race; my big chance). b colloq. (of a person) famous, important, esp. in a named field. 3 a grown up (a big boy now). b elder (big sister). 4 colloq. a boastful (big words). b often iron. generous (big of him). c ambitious (big ideas). d popular (when disco was big). 5 (usu. foll. by with) advanced in pregnancy; fecund (big with child; big with consequences). ● adv. colloq. in a big manner, esp.: 1 effectively (went over big). 2 boastfully (talk big). 3 ambitiously (think big). □ **come** (or **go**) **over big** make a great effect. **in a big way** on a large scale. 2 colloq. with great enthusiasm, display, etc. **talk big** boast. **think big** be ambitious. **too big for one's boots** (or **breeches**) sl. conceited. □□ **big·gish** adj. **big·ness** n. [ME: orig. unkn.]

big·a·my /bígəmee/ n. (pl. **·mies**) the crime of marrying when one is lawfully married to another person. □□ **big·a·mist** n. **big·a·mous** adj. [ME f. OF bigamie f. bigame bigamous f. LL bigamus (as BI-, Gk gamos marriage)]

Big Ap·ple n. sl. New York City.

big band n. a large jazz or swing orchestra.

ordinary (1880s)

ladies' safety bicycle (1890s)

mountain bike

racing bike

tandem　　　　　recumbent

bicycles

big bang the•ory *n.* the theory that the universe began with the explosion of dense matter.

Big Ben *n.* the great clock tower of the Houses of Parliament in London and its bell.

Big Board *n. colloq.* the New York Stock Exchange.

Big Broth•er *n.* an all-powerful supposedly benevolent dictator (as in Orwell's *1984*).

big bud *n.* a plant disease caused by the gall mite.

big busi•ness *n.* large-scale financial dealings and the businesses involved in them.

Big Dad•dy *n.* (also **Big Chief**) *sl.* = BIGWIG.

big deal *n. sl.* **1** a thing considered to be important or impressive (*he's a big deal in the art world*). **2** *iron.* used to express one's scorn (*we got a nickel raise – big deal!*).

Big Dip•per *n.* a constellation of seven bright stars in Ursa Major in the shape of a dipper.

big end *n.* (in a motor vehicle) the end of the connecting rod that encircles the crankpin.

Big•foot /bígfŏot/ *n.* = SASQUATCH.

big game *n.* large animals hunted for sport.

big gun *n. sl.* = BIGWIG.

big•head /bíghed/ *n. colloq.* a conceited person. □□ **big•head•ed** *adj.* **big•head•ed•ness** *n.*

big•heart•ed /bíghártid/ *adj.* generous.

big•horn /bíghawrn/ *n.* (in full **bighorn sheep**) an American sheep, *Ovis canadensis,* esp. native to the Rocky Mountains.

big house *n.* **1** *sl.* a prison. **2** esp. *Brit.* the principal house in a village, etc.

bight /bīt/ *n.* **1** a curve or recess in a coastline, river, etc. **2** a loop of rope. [OE *byht*, MLG *bucht* f. Gmc: see BOW²]

big i•de•a *n.* often *iron.* a clever or important intention or scheme (*OK, what's the big idea?*).

big lie *n.* (also **Big Lie**) a gross distortion of the truth promulgated blatantly despite its falsity, esp. as propaganda.

big mon•ey *n.* large amounts; high profit; high pay.

big•mouth /bígmowth/ *n. colloq.* a boastful or talkative person; a gossipmonger.

big name *n.* a famous person.

big noise *n.* (also **big shot**) *colloq.* = BIGWIG.

big•ot /bígət/ *n.* an obstinate and intolerant believer in a religion, political theory, etc. □□ **big•ot•ry** *n.* [16th c. f. F: orig. unkn.]

big•ot•ed /bígətid/ *adj.* unreasonably prejudiced and intolerant.

big smoke *n. Brit. sl.* **1** London. **2** any large town.

big stick *n.* a display of force.

Big Three *n.* (also **Big Four**, etc.) the predominant few.

big time *n. sl.* success in a profession, esp. show business.

big-tim•er /bíg-tímər/ *n. sl.* a person who achieves success.

big top *n.* the main tent in a circus.

big tree *n.* a giant evergreen conifer, *Sequoiadendron giganteum,* usu. with a trunk of large girth.

big wheel *n.* **1** a Ferris wheel. **2** *sl.* = BIGWIG.

big•wig /bígwig/ *n. colloq.* an important person.

bi•jou /beézhōo/ *n. & adj.* ● *n.* (*pl.* **bi•joux** *pronunc.* same) a jewel; a trinket. ● *attrib.adj.* small and elegant. [F]

bi•jou•te•rie /beezhōotəree/ *n.* jewelry; trinkets. [F (as BIJOU, –ERY)]

bike /bīk/ *n. & v.* ● *n. colloq.* a bicycle or motorcycle. ● *v.intr.* ride a bicycle or motorcycle. [abbr.]

bik•er /bíkər/ *n.* a cyclist, esp. a motorcyclist.

bik•ie /bíkee/ *n. Austral. colloq.* a member of a gang of motorcyclists.

bi•ki•ni /bikeénee/ *n.* a two-piece swimsuit for women.

WORD HISTORY   bikini

1940s: named after Bikini atoll in the Pacific, where an atom bomb was tested in 1946 (because of the supposed "explosive" effect created by the garment).

bi•ki•ni briefs *n.* men's or women's scanty briefs.

bi•la•bi•al /bíláybeeəl/ *adj. Phonet.* (of a sound, etc.) made with closed or nearly closed lips.

bi•lat•er•al /bílátərəl/ *adj.* **1** of, on, or with two sides. **2** affecting or between two parties, countries, etc. (*bilateral negotiations*). □□ **bi•lat•er•al•ly** *adv.*

bi•lat•er•al sym•me•try *n.* the property of being divisible into symmetrical halves on either side of a unique plane.

bil•ber•ry /bílberee/ *n.* (*pl.* **•ries**) **1** a hardy dwarf shrub, *Vaccinium myrtillus,* of N. Europe, growing on heaths and mountains, and having red drooping flowers and dark blue berries. **2** the small blue edible berry of this species. **3** any of various shrubs of the genus *Vaccinium* having dark blue berries. [orig. uncert.: cf. Da. *bøllebær*]

bil•bo /bílbō/ *n.* (*pl.* **•bos** or **•boes**) *hist.* a sword noted for the temper and elasticity of its blade. [*Bilboa* = Bilbao in Spain]

bil•boes /bílbōz/ *n.pl. hist.* an iron bar with sliding shackles for a prisoner's ankles. [16th c.: orig. unkn.]

Bil•dungs•ro•man /bíldŏongzrōmaán/ *n.* a novel dealing with one person's early life and development. [Gf. *Bildung* formation + *Roman* novel]

bile /bīl/ *n.* **1** a bitter greenish brown alkaline fluid which aids digestion and is secreted by the liver and stored in the gallbladder. **2** bad temper; peevish anger. [F f. L *bilis*]

bile duct *n.* the duct which conveys bile from the liver and the gallbladder to the duodenum.

bilge /bilj/ *n. & v.* ● *n.* **1 a** the almost flat part of a ship's bottom, inside or out. **b** (in full **bilgewater**) filthy water that collects inside the bilge. **2** *sl.* nonsense; worthless ideas (*don't talk bilge*). ● *v.* **1** *tr.* stave in the bilge of (a ship). **2** *intr.* spring a leak in the bilge. **3** *intr.* swell out; bulge. [prob. var. of BULGE]

bilge keel *n.* a plate or timber fastened under the bilge to prevent rolling.

bil•har•zi•a /bilhaártzeeə/ *n.* **1** a tropical flatworm of the genus *Schistosoma* (formerly *Bilharzia*) which is parasitic in blood vessels in the human pelvic region. Also called **schistosome. 2** the chronic tropical disease produced by its presence. Also called **bilharziasis** or **schistosomiasis**. [mod.L f. T. *Bilharz,* Ger. physician d. 1862]

bil•har•zi•a•sis /bílhaarzíəsis/ *n.* the disease of bilharzia. Also called **schistosomiasis**.

bil•i•ar•y /bílee-eree/ *adj.* of the bile. [F *biliaire:* see BILE, –ARY²]

bi•lin•gual /bílínggwəl/ *adj. & n.* ● *adj.* **1** able to speak two languages, esp. fluently. **2** spoken or written in two languages. ● *n.* a bilingual person. □□ **bi•lin•gual•ism** *n.* [L *bilinguis* (as BI-, *lingua* tongue)]

bil•ious /bílyəs/ *adj.* **1** affected by a disorder of the bile. **2** bad-tempered. □□ **bil•ious•ly** *adv.* **bil•ious•ness** *n.* [L *biliosus* f. *bilis* bile]

bil•i•ru•bin /bíleerŏobin/ *n.* the orangish yellow pigment occurring in bile and causing jaundice when accumulated in blood. [G f. L *bilis* BILE + *ruber* red]

bilk /bilk/ *v.tr. sl.* **1** cheat. **2** give the slip to. **3** avoid paying (a creditor or debt). □□ **bilk•er** *n.* [orig. uncert., perh. = BALK: earliest use (17th c.) in cribbage, = spoil one's opponent's score]

bill¹ /bil/ *n. & v.* ● *n.* **1 a** a printed or written statement of charges for goods supplied or services rendered. **b** the amount owed (*ran up a bill of $300*). **2 a** a draft of a proposed law. **3 a** a poster; a placard. **b** = HANDBILL. **4 a** a printed list, esp. a theater program. **b** the entertainment itself (*top of the bill*). **5** a piece of paper money, esp. of a specified value (*ten dollar bill*). **6** *sl.* one hundred dollars. ● *v.tr.* **1** put in the program; announce. **2** (foll. by *as*) advertise. **3** send a note of charges to (*billed him for the books*). □□ **bill•a•ble** *adj.* [ME f. AF *bille,* AL *billa,* prob. alt. of med.L *bulla* seal, sealed documents, BULL²]

bill² /bil/ *n. & v.* ● *n.* **1** the beak of a bird, esp. when it is slender, flattened, or weak, or belongs to a web-footed bird or a bird of the pigeon family. **2** the muzzle of a platypus. **3** a narrow promontory. **4** the point of an anchor fluke. **5** the visor of a cap. ● *v.intr.* (of doves, etc.) stroke bill with bill during courtship. □ **bill and coo** exchange caresses. □□ **billed** *adj.* (usu. in *comb.*). [OE *bile,* of unkn. orig.]

bill³ /bil/ *n.* **1** *hist.* a weapon like a halberd with a hook instead of a blade. **2** = BILLHOOK. [OE *bil,* ult. f. Gmc]

bil•la•bong /bíləbawng, –bong/ *n. Austral.* **1** a branch of a river forming a backwater or a stagnant pool. **2** a watercourse holding water only seasonally. [Aboriginal *Billibang* Bell River f. *billa* water]

bill•board /bílbawrd/ *n.* a large outdoor board for advertisements, etc.

bil•let¹ /bílit/ *n. & v.* ● *n.* **1 a** a place where troops, etc., are lodged, usu. with civilians. **b** a written order requiring a householder to lodge the bearer, usu. a soldier. **2** *colloq.* a situation; a job. ● *v.tr.* (**bil•let•ed, bil•let•ing**) **1** (usu. foll. by *on, in, at*) quarter (soldiers, etc.). **2** (of a householder) provide (a soldier, etc.) with board and lodging. □□ **bil•let•ee** /–teé/ *n.* **bil•let•er** *n.* [ME f. AF *billette,* AL *billetta,* dimin. of *billa* BILL¹]

bil•let² /bílit/ *n.* **1** a thick piece of firewood. **2** a small metal bar. **3** *Archit.* each of a series of short rolls inserted at intervals in some decorative moldings. [ME f. F *billette* small log, ult. prob. of Celtic orig.]

bil•let-doux /bílaydŏo/ *n.* (*pl.* **bil•lets-doux** /–dŏoz/) often *joc.* a love letter. [F, = sweet note]

bill•fold /bílfōld/ *n.* a wallet for keeping paper money.

bill•head /bílhed/ *n.* a printed account form.

bill•hook /bílhŏok/ *n.* a sickle-shaped tool with a sharp inner edge, used for pruning, lopping, etc.

bil•liards /bílyərdz/ *n.* **1** any of several games played on an oblong cloth-covered table, esp. one with three balls struck with cues into pockets around the edge of the table. **2** (**billiard**) (in *comb.*) used in billiards (*billiard ball; billiard table*). [orig. pl., f. F *billard* billiards, cue, dimin. of *bille* log: see BILLET²]

bil•lion /bílyən/ *n. & adj.* ● *n.* (*pl.* same or (in sense 3) **bil•lions**) (in *sing.* prec. by *a* or *one*) **1** a thousand million (1,000,000,000 or 10⁹). **2** *Brit.* a million million (1,000,000,000,000 or 10¹²). **3** (in *pl.*) *colloq.* a very large number (*billions of years*). ● *adj.* that amount to a billion. □□ **bil•lionth** *adj. & n.* [F (as BI-, MILLION)]

bil·lion·aire /bílyənáir/ *n.* a person possessing over a billion dollars, pounds, etc. [after MILLIONAIRE]

bill of at·tain·der *n.* an act of legislation inflicting attainder without judicial process.

bill of ex·change *n. Econ.* a written order to pay a sum of money on a given date to the drawer or to a named payee.

bill of fare *n.* 1 a menu. 2 a program (for a theatrical event).

bill of goods *n.* 1 a shipment of merchandise, often for resale. 2 *colloq.* an article that is misrepresented, fraudulent, etc. (*at first it seemed a bargain, but we were being sold a bill of goods*).

bill of health *n.* 1 *Naut.* a certificate regarding the state of infectious disease on a ship or in a port at the time of sailing. 2 (**clean bill of health**) **a** such a certificate stating that there is no disease. **b** a declaration that a person or thing examined has been found to be free of illness or in good condition.

bill of in·dict·ment *n.* a written accusation as presented to a grand jury.

bill of lad·ing *n. Naut.* 1 a shipmaster's detailed list of the ship's cargo. 2 = WAYBILL.

Bill of Rights *n.* 1 *Law* (in the US) the original constitutional amendments of 1791, affirming basic civil rights. 2 *Law* the English constitutional settlement of 1689. 3 a statement of the rights of a class of people.

bill of sale *n. Econ.* a certificate of transfer of personal property, esp. as a security against debt.

bil·lon /bílən/ *n.* an alloy of gold or silver with a predominating admixture of a base metal. [F f. *bille* BILLET²]

bil·low /bíló/ *n. & v.* • *n.* 1 a wave. 2 a soft upward-curving flow. 3 any large soft mass. • *v.intr.* move, swell, or build up in billows. □□ **bil·low·y** *adj.* [ON *bylgja* f. Gmc]

bill·post·er /bílpōstər/ *n.* (also **bill·stick·er** /–stíkər/) a person who pastes up advertisements. □□ **bill·post·ing** *n.*

bil·ly¹ /bílee/ *n.* (*pl.* **·lies**) (in full **billycan**) esp. *Austral.* a tin or enamel pot with a lid and wire handle, for use in cooking outdoors. [perh. f. Aboriginal *billa* water]

bil·ly² /bílee/ *n.* (*pl.* **·lies**) 1 = BILLY GOAT. 2 (in full **billy club**) a bludgeon.

bil·ly goat /bíligōt/ *n.* a male goat. [*Billy*, pet form of the name *William*]

bil·ly-oh /bíleeó/ *n. Brit.* □ **like billy-oh** *sl.* very much, hard, strongly, etc. (*raining like billy-oh*). [19th c.: orig. unkn.]

bi·lo·bate /bílōbayt/ *adj.* (also **bi·lobed** /–lōbd/) having or consisting of two lobes.

bil·tong /bíltong/ *n. S.Afr.* boneless meat salted and dried in strips. [Afrik., of uncert. orig.]

bi·man·u·al /bímányooəl/ *adj.* performed with both hands.

bim·bo /bímbō/ *n.* (*pl.* **·bos** or **·boes**) *sl.* usu. *derog.* 1 a person. 2 a woman, esp. a young empty-headed one. 3 a promiscuous woman. [It., = little child]

bi·me·tal·lic /bímitálik/ *adj.* 1 made of two metals. 2 of or relating to bimetallism. [F *bimétallique* (as BI-, METALLIC)]

bi·me·tal·lic strip *n.* a sensitive element in some thermostats made of two bands of different metals that expand at different rates when heated, causing the strip to bend.

bi·met·al·lism /bímét'lizəm/ *n.* a system of allowing the unrestricted currency of two metals (e.g., gold and silver) at a fixed ratio to each other, as coined money. □□ **bi·met·al·list** *n.*

bi·mil·le·nar·y /bímíləneree, –mílénəree/ *adj. & n.* (also **bi·mil·le·ni·al** /–léneeəl/) • *adj.* of or relating to a two-thousandth anniversary. • *n.* (*pl.* **·naries**) a bimillenary year or festival.

bi·month·ly /bímúnthlee/ *adj., adv., & n.* • *adj.* occurring twice a month or every two months. • *adv.* twice a month or every two months. • *n.* (*pl.* **·lies**) a periodical produced bimonthly.

▶Often avoided, because of the ambiguity of meaning, in favor of *every two months* and *twice a month*.

bin /bin/ *n. & v.* • *n.* a large receptacle for storage or for depositing trash, garbage, etc. • *v.tr. colloq.* (**binned, bin·ning**) store or put in a bin. □ **bin-liner** *Brit.* a bag (usu. of plastic) for lining a garbage can. [OE *bin(n), binne*]

bin- /bin, bīn/ *prefix* var. of BI- before a vowel.

bi·na·ry /bíneree/ *adj. & n.* • *adj.* 1 **a** dual. **b** of or involving pairs. 2 of the arithmetical system using 2 as a base. • *n.* (*pl.* **·ries**) 1 something having two parts. 2 a binary number. 3 a binary star. [LL *binarius* f. *bini* two together]

bi·na·ry code *n. Computing* a coding system using the binary digits 0 and 1 to represent a letter, digit, or other character in a computer.

bi·na·ry com·pound *n. Chem.* a compound having two elements or radicals.

bi·na·ry fis·sion *n.* the division of a cell or organism into two parts.

bi·na·ry num·ber *n.* (also **bi·na·ry dig·it**) one of two digits (usu. 0 or 1) in a binary system of notation.

bi·na·ry star *n.* a system of two stars orbiting each other.

bi·na·ry sys·tem *n.* a system in which information can be expressed by combinations of the digits 0 and 1 (corresponding to 'off' and 'on' in computing).

bi·na·ry tree *n.* a data structure in which a record is branched to the left when greater and to the right when less than the previous record.

bi·nate /bínayt/ *adj. Bot.* 1 growing in pairs. 2 composed of two equal parts. [mod.L *binatus* f. L *bini* two together]

bin·au·ral /bínáwrəl/ *adj.* 1 of or used with both ears. 2 (of sound) recorded using two microphones and usu. transmitted separately to the two ears.

bind /bīnd/ *v. & n.* • *v.* (*past* and *past part.* **bound** /bownd/) (see also BOUNDEN). 1 *tr.* (often foll. by *to, on, together*) tie or fasten tightly. 2 *tr.* a restrain; put in bonds. **b** (as **–bound** *adj.*) obstructed (*snowbound*). 3 *tr.* esp. *Cooking* cause (ingredients) to cohere using another ingredient. 4 *tr.* fasten or hold together as a single mass. 5 *tr.* compel; impose an obligation or duty on. 6 *tr.* **a** edge (fabric, etc.) with braid, etc. **b** fix together and fasten (the pages of a book) in a cover. 7 *tr.* constipate. 8 *tr.* ratify (a bargain, agreement, etc.). 9 *tr.* (in *passive*) be required by an obligation or duty (*am bound to answer*). 10 *tr.* (often foll. by *up*) **a** put a bandage or other covering around. **b** fix together with something put around (*bound her hair*). 11 *tr.* indenture as an apprentice. 12 *intr.* (of snow, etc.) cohere; stick. 13 *intr.* be prevented from moving freely. 14 *intr. Brit. sl.* complain. • *n.* 1 *colloq.* **a** a nuisance; a restriction. **b** a tight or difficult situation. 2 an act or instance of being bound. 3 = BINE. □ **be bound up with** be closely associated with. **bind over** *Law* order (a person) to do something, esp. keep the peace. **bind up** bandage. **I'll be bound** a statement of assurance, or guaranteeing the truth of something. [OE *bindan*]

bind·er /bíndər/ *n.* 1 a cover for sheets of paper, for a book, etc. 2 a substance that acts cohesively. 3 a reaping machine that binds grain into sheaves. 4 a bookbinder. 5 a temporary agreement providing insurance coverage until a policy is issued.

bind·er·y /bíndəree/ *n.* (*pl.* **·er·ies**) a workshop or factory for binding books.

bind·ing /bínding/ *n. & adj.* • *n.* something that binds, esp. the covers, glue, etc., of a book. • *adj.* (often foll. by *on*) obligatory.

bind·weed /bíndweed/ *n.* 1 convolvulus. 2 any of various species of climbing plants such as honeysuckle.

bine /bīn/ *n.* 1 the twisting stem of a climbing plant, esp. the hop. 2 a flexible shoot. [orig. a dial. form of BIND]

Bi·net-Si·mon test /bínaysímən/ *adj.* (also **Bi·net test scale**) *Psychol.* a test used to measure intelligence, esp. of children. [A. *Binet* d. 1911 and T. *Simon* d. 1961, Fr. psychologists]

binge /binj/ *n. & v. sl.* • *n.* a spree; a period of uncontrolled eating, drinking, etc. • *v.intr.* go on a spree; indulge in uncontrolled eating, drinking, etc. [prob. orig. dial., = soak]

bin·gle /bínggəl/ *n. Austral. colloq.* a collision. [Brit. dial. *bing* thump, blow]

bin·go /bínggō/ *n. & int.* • *n.* a game for any number of players, each having a card of squares with numbers which are marked off as numbers are randomly drawn by a caller. • *int.* 1 expressing sudden surprise, satisfaction, etc., as in winning at bingo. 2 expressing confirmation, esp. of another's guess or speculation. [prob. imit.: cf. dial. *bing* 'with a bang']

bin·gy /bínjee/ *n.* (also **bin·gie**) *Austral. colloq.* the stomach; the belly. [Dharuk *bindhi* belly]

bin·man /bínman/ *n.* (*pl.* **·men**) *Brit. colloq.* a garbage collector.

bin·na·cle /bínəkəl/ *n.* a built-in housing for a ship's compass. [earlier *bittacle*, ult. f. L *habitaculum* habitation f. *habitare* inhabit]

bin·oc·u·lar /bínókyələr/ *adj.* adapted for or using both eyes. [BIN- + L *oculus* eye]

bin·oc·u·lars /bínókyələrz/ *n.pl.* an optical instrument with a lens for each eye, for viewing distant objects.

bi·no·mi·al /bīnómeeəl/ *n. & adj.* • *n.* 1 an algebraic expression of the sum or the difference of two terms. 2 a two-part name, esp. in taxonomy. • *adj.* consisting of two terms. □□ **bi·no·mi·al·ly** *adv.* [F *binôme* or mod.L *binomium* (as BI-, Gk *nomos* part, portion)]

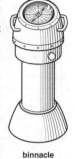

binnacle

bi·no·mi·al dis·tri·bu·tion *n.* a frequency distribution of the possible number of successful outcomes in a given number of trials in each of which there is the same probability of success.

bi·no·mi·al no·men·cla·ture *n.* a system of nomenclature using two terms, the first one indicating the genus and the second the species.

bi·no·mi·al the·o·rem *n.* a formula for finding any power of a binomial without multiplying at length.

bint /bint/ *n. Brit. sl. offens.* a girl or woman. [Arab., = daughter, girl]

bin·tu·rong /bíntoórawng, –rong/ *n.* a civet, *Arctictis binturong*, of S. Asia, with a shaggy black coat and a prehensile tail. [Malay]

bi·o /bí-ō/ *n. & adj.* • *n.* 1 biology. 2 (*pl.* **bios**) biography. • *adj.* biological. [abbr.]

bio- /bí-ō/ *comb. form* **1** life (*biography*). **2** biological (*biomathematics*). **3** of living beings (*biophysics*). [Gk *bios* (course of) human life]

bi•o•chem•is•try /bí-ōkémistree/ *n.* the study of the chemical and physicochemical processes of living organisms. □□ **bi•o•chem•i•cal** *adj.* **bi•o•chem•ist** *n.*

bi•o•ce•no•sis /bí-ōseenósis/ *n.* (also **bi•o•coe•no•sis**) (*pl.* •no•ses /-seez/) **1** an association of different organisms forming a community. **2** the relationship existing between such organisms. □□ **ce•no•lo•gy** /–nólejee/ *n.* **bi•o•ce•not•ic** /–nótik/ *adj.* [mod.L f. BIO- + Gk *koinōsis* sharing f. *koinos* common]

bi•o•de•grad•a•ble /bí-ōdigráydəbəl/ *adj.* capable of being decomposed by bacteria or other living organisms. □□ **bi•o•de•grad•a•bil•i•ty** *n.* **bi•o•deg•ra•da•tion** /bí-ōdégrədáyshən/ *n.*

bi•o•di•ver•si•ty /bí-ōdivórsitee, -dī-/ *n.* the variety of plant and animal species found within a specified geographic area.

bi•o•en•gi•neer•ing /bí-ō-énjineéring/ *n.* **1** the application of engineering techniques to biological processes. **2** the use of artificial tissues, organs, or organ components to replace damaged or absent parts of the body, e.g., artificial limbs, heart pacemakers, etc. □□ **bi•o•en•gi•neer** *n. & v.*

bi•o•eth•ics /bí-ō-éthiks/ *n.pl.* (treated as *sing.*) the ethics of medical and biological research. □□ **bi•o•eth•i•cist** *n.*

bi•o•feed•back /bí-ōfeédbak/ *n.* the use of electronic monitoring of a normally automatic bodily function in order to train someone to acquire voluntary control of that function.

bi•o•fla•vo•noid /bí-ōfláyvənoyd/ *n.* = CITRIN. [BIO- + *flavonoid* f. FLAVINE + −OID]

biog. *abbr.* **1** biographer. **2** biographical. **3** biography.

bi•o•gen•e•sis /bí-ōjénisis/ *n.* **1** the synthesis of substances by living organisms. **2** the hypothesis that a living organism arises only from another similar living organism. □□ **bi•o•ge•net•ic** /–jinétik/ *adj.*

bi•o•gen•ic /bí-ōjénik/ *adj.* produced by living organisms.

bi•o•ge•og•ra•phy /bí-ōjeeeógrəfee/ *n.* the scientific study of the geographical distribution of plants and animals. □□ **bi•o•ge•o•graph•i•cal** /–jeeəgráfikəl/ *adj.*

bi•og•ra•phy /bīógrəfee/ *n.* (*pl.* •phies) **1 a** a written account of a person's life, usu. by another. **b** such writing as a branch of literature. **2** the course of a living (usu. human) being's life. □□ **bi•og•ra•pher** *n.* **bi•o•graph•ic** /bíəgráfik/ *adj.* **bi•o•graph•i•cal** *adj.* [F *biographie* or mod.L *biographia* f. med.Gk]

biol. *abbr.* **1** biologic. **2** biological. **3** biologist. **4** biology.

bi•o•log•i•cal /bíəlójikəl/ *adj.* **1** of or relating to biology or living organisms. **2** related genetically, not by marriage, adoption, etc. □□ **bi•o•log•i•cal•ly** *adv.*

bi•o•log•i•cal clock *n.* an innate mechanism controlling the rhythmic physiological activities of an organism.

bi•o•log•i•cal con•trol *n.* the control of a pest by the introduction of a natural enemy.

bi•o•log•i•cal war•fare *n.* warfare involving the use of toxins or microorganisms.

bi•ol•o•gy /bíóləjee/ *n.* **1** the study of living organisms. **2** the plants and animals of a particular area. □□ **bi•ol•o•gist** *n.* [F *biologie* f. G *Biologie* (as BIO-, –LOGY)]

bi•o•lu•mi•nes•cence /bí-ōlōōminésəns/ *n.* the emission of light by living organisms such as the firefly and glowworm. □□ **bi•o•lu•mi•nes•cent** *adj.*

bi•o•mass /bí-ōmas/ *n.* the total quantity or weight of organisms in a given area or volume. [BIO- + MASS[1]]

bi•o•math•e•mat•ics /bí-ōmáthimátiks/ *n.* the science of the application of mathematics to biology.

bi•ome /bí-ōm/ *n.* **1** a large naturally occurring community of flora and fauna adapted to the particular conditions in which they occur, e.g., tundra. **2** the geographical region containing such a community. [BIO- + −OME]

bi•o•me•chan•ics /bí-ōmikániks/ *n.* the study of the mechanical laws relating to the movement or structure of living organisms.

bi•om•e•try /bíómitree/ *n.* (also **bi•o•met•rics** /bí-ōmétriks/) the application of statistical analysis to biological data. □□ **bi•o•met•ric** /bí-əmétrik/ *adj.* **bi•o•met•ri•cal** *adj.* **bi•o•me•tri•cian** /bí-ōmitríshən/ *n.*

bi•o•morph /bí-ōmawrf/ *n.* a decorative form based on a living organism. □□ **bi•o•mor•phic** /–əmáwrfik/ *adj.* [BIO- + Gk *morphē* form]

bi•on•ic /bíónik/ *adj.* **1** having artificial body parts or the superhuman powers resulting from these. **2** relating to bionics. □□ **bi•on•i•cal•ly** *adv.* [BIO- after ELECTRONIC]

bi•on•ics /bíóniks/ *n.pl.* (treated as *sing.*) the study of mechanical systems that function like living organisms or parts of living organisms.

bi•o•nom•ics /bíənómiks/ *n.pl.* (treated as *sing.*) the study of the mode of life of organisms in their natural habitat and their adaptations to their surroundings; ecology. □□ **bi•o•nom•ic** *adj.* [BIO- after ECONOMICS]

bi•o•phys•ics /bí-ōfíziks/ *n.pl.* (treated as *sing.*) the science of the application of the laws of physics to biological phenomena. □□ **bi•o•phys•i•cal** *adj.* **bi•o•phys•i•cist** *n.*

bi•op•sy /bíopsee/ *n.* (*pl.* •sies) the examination of tissue removed from a living body to discover the presence, cause, or extent of a disease. [F *biopsie* f. Gk *bios* life + *opsis* sight, after *necropsy*]

bi•o•rhythm /bí-ōríthəm/ *n.* **1** any of the recurring cycles of biological processes thought to affect a person's emotional, intellectual, and physical activity. **2** any periodic change in the behavior or physiology of an organism. □□ **bi•o•rhyth•mic** /–ərithmik/ *adj.* **bi•o•rhyth•mi•cal•ly** *adv.*

bi•o•scope /bí-ōskōp/ *n. S.Afr. sl.* a movie theater.

bi•o•sphere /bí-ōsfeer/ *n.* the regions of the earth's crust and atmosphere occupied by living organisms. [G *Biosphäre* (as BIO-, SPHERE)]

bi•o•syn•the•sis /bí-ōsínthisis/ *n.* the production of organic molecules by living organisms. □□ **bi•o•syn•thet•ic** /–thétik/ *adj.*

bi•o•ta /bí-ōtə/ *n.* the animal and plant life of a region. [mod.L: cf. Gk *biotē* life]

bi•o•tech•nol•o•gy /bí-ōteknóləjee/ *n.* the exploitation of biological processes for industrial and other purposes, esp. genetic manipulation of microorganisms (for the production of antibiotics, hormones, etc.).

bi•ot•ic /bíótik/ *adj.* **1** relating to life or to living things. **2** of biological origin. [F *biotique* or LL *bioticus* f. Gk *biōtikos* f. *bios* life]

bi•o•tin /bíətin/ *n.* a vitamin of the B complex, found in egg yolk, liver, and yeast, and involved in the metabolism of carbohydrates, fats, and proteins. [G f. Gk *bios* life + −IN]

bi•o•tite /bíətīt/ *n. Mineral.* a black, dark brown, or green micaceous mineral occurring as a constituent of metamorphic and igneous rocks. [J. B. *Biot*, Fr. physicist d. 1862]

bi•par•ti•san /bīpáartizən, –sən/ *adj.* of or involving two (esp. political) parties. □□ **bi•par•ti•san•ship** *n.*

bi•par•tite /bípáartīt/ *adj.* **1** consisting of two parts. **2** shared by or involving two parties. **3** *Law* (of a contract, treaty, etc.) drawn up in two corresponding parts or between two parties. [L *bipartitus* f. *bipartire* (as BI-, *partire* PART)]

bi•ped /bíped/ *n. & adj.* ● *n.* a two-footed animal. ● *adj.* two-footed. □□ **bi•ped•al** *adj.* [L *bipes −edis* (as BI-, *pes pedis* foot)]

bi•pin•nate /bīpínayt/ *adj.* (of a pinnate leaf) having leaflets that are further subdivided in a pinnate arrangement.

bi•plane /bíplayn/ *n.* a type of airplane having two sets of wings, one above the other.

bi•po•lar /bīpólər/ *adj.* having two poles or extremities. □□ **bi•po•lar•i•ty** /–láritee/ *n.*

bi•po•lar dis•or•der *n. Psychol.* a disorder characterized by alternating periods of mania and depression.

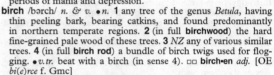

biplane

birch /bərch/ *n. & v.* ● *n.* **1** any tree of the genus *Betula*, having thin peeling bark, bearing catkins, and found predominantly in northern temperate regions. **2** (in full **birchwood**) the hard fine-grained pale wood of these trees. **3** *NZ* any of various similar trees. **4** (in full **birch rod**) a bundle of birch twigs used for flogging. ● *v.tr.* beat with a birch (in sense 4). □□ **birch•en** *adj.* [OE *bi(e)rce* f. Gmc]

birch bark *n.* **1** the bark of *Betula papyrifera* used to make canoes. **2** such a canoe.

bird /bərd/ *n.* **1** a feathered vertebrate with a beak, two wings, and two feet, egg-laying and usu. able to fly. **2** a game bird. **3** *Brit. sl.* a young woman. **4** *colloq.* a person (*a wily old bird*). **5** *Brit. sl.* **a** a prison. **b** *rhyming sl.* a prison sentence (short for *birdlime* = time). □ **a bird in the hand** something secured or certain. **the bird is** (or **has**) **flown** the prisoner, quarry, etc., has escaped. **the birds and the bees** *euphem.* sexual activity and reproduction. **birds of a feather** people of like character. **for** (or **strictly for**) **the birds** *colloq.* trivial; uninteresting. **get the bird** *Brit. sl.* **1** be dismissed. **2** be hissed at or booed. **like a bird** without difficulty or hesitation. **a little bird** an unnamed informant. [OE *brid*, of unkn. orig.]

bird•bath /bórdbath/ *n.* a basin in a garden, etc., with water for birds to bathe in.

bird•brain /bórdbrayn/ *n. colloq.* a stupid or flighty person. □□ **bird•brained** *adj.*

bird•cage /bórdkayj/ *n.* **1** a cage for birds usu. made of wire or cane. **2** an object of a similar design.

bird call *n.* **1** a bird's natural call. **2** an instrument imitating this.

bird cher•ry *n.* a wild cherry *Prunus padus*.

bird•er /bórdər/ *n.* a bird-watcher. □□ **bird•ing** *n.*

bird•ie /bórdee/ *n. & v.* ● *n.* **1** *colloq.* a little bird. **2** *Golf* a score of one stroke less than par at any hole. ● *v.tr.* (**bird•ies, bird•ied, bird•y•ing**) *Golf* play (a hole) in a birdie.

bird•lime /bórdlīm/ *n.* sticky material painted on twigs to trap small birds.

See page xx for the **Key to Pronunciation**.

bird·nest·ing /bŕd-nésting/ n. (also **birds'-nest·ing**) hunting for birds' nests, usu. to get eggs.

bird of par·a·dise n. any bird of the family Paradiseidae found chiefly in New Guinea, the males having very beautiful brilliantly colored plumage.

bird of pas·sage n. **1** a migrant. **2** any transient visitor.

bird of prey n. a predatory bird, distinguished by a hooked bill and sharp talons.

bird·seed /bŕdseed/ n. a blend of seed for feeding caged or wild birds.

bird's-eye /bŕdz-ī/ n. & adj. • n. **1** any of several plants having small bright round flowers, such as the germander speedwell. **2** a pattern with many small spots. • adj. of or having small bright round flowers (bird's-eye primrose).

bird's-eye view n. a general view from above.

bird's-foot n. (pl. **bird's-foots**) any plant like the foot of a bird, esp. of the genus Lotus, having claw-shaped pods.

bird's nest soup n. soup made (esp. in Chinese cooking) from the dried gelatinous coating of the nests of swifts and other birds.

bird·song /bŕdsawng, –song/ n. the musical cry of a bird or birds.

bird-strike /bŕd-strīk/ n. a collision between a bird and an aircraft.

bird-watch·er /bŕd-wóchər/ n. a person who observes birds in their natural surroundings. □□ **bird-watch·ing** n.

bi·re·frin·gent /bírifrinjənt/ adj. Physics having two different refractive indices. □□ **bi·re·frin·gence** /–jəns/ n.

bi·reme /bíreem/ n. hist. an ancient Greek warship, with two banks of oarsmen on each side. [L biremis (as BI–, remus oar)]

bi·ret·ta /biréta/ n. a square usu. black cap with three flat projections on top, worn by (esp. Roman Catholic) clergymen. [It. berretta or Sp. birreta f. LL birrus cape]

bi·ri·an·i var. of BIRYANI.

Bi·ro /bírō/ n. (pl. **·ros**) Brit. Trademark a kind of ballpoint pen. [L. Biró, Hung. inventor d. 1985]

birth /bŕth/ n. & v. • n. **1** the emergence of a (usu. fully developed) infant or other young from the body of its mother. **2** rhet. the beginning or coming into existence of something (the birth of civilization; the birth of socialism). **3 a** origin; descent; ancestry (of noble birth). **b** high or noble birth; inherited position. • v.tr. colloq. **1** to give birth to. **2** to assist (a woman) to give birth. □ **give birth** bear a child, etc. **give birth to 1** produce (young) from the womb. **2** cause to begin; found. [ME f. ON byrth f. Gmc: see BEAR¹, –TH²]

birth cer·tif·i·cate n. an official document identifying a person by name, place, date of birth, and parentage.

birth con·trol n. the control of the number of children one conceives, esp. by contraception.

birth con·trol pill n. a contraceptive pill usu. containing the hormones estrogen and progesterone, that inhibits ovulation.

birth·day /bŕthday/ n. **1** the day on which a person, etc., was born. **2** the anniversary of this. □ **in one's birthday suit** joc. naked.

birth·day hon·ors n. Brit. titles, etc., given on a sovereign's official birthday.

birth de·fect n. a physical, mental, or biochemical abnormality present at birth.

birth·mark /bŕthmaark/ n. an unusual brown or red mark on one's body at or from birth.

birth·place /bŕthplays/ n. the place where a person was born.

birth rate n. the number of live births per thousand of population per year.

birth·right /bŕthrīt/ n. a right of possession or privilege one has from birth.

birth·stone /bŕthstōn/ n. a gemstone popularly associated with the month of one's birth.

bir·y·a·ni /biree-áanee/ n. (also **bi·ri·a·ni**) an Indian dish made with highly seasoned rice, and meat or fish, etc. [Urdu]

bis·cuit /bískit/ n. & adj. • n. **1** a small bread or cake leavened with baking soda or baking powder. **2** Brit. **a** = COOKIE. **b** = CRACKER. **3** fired unglazed pottery. **4** a light brown color. • adj. biscuit colored.

> **WORD HISTORY** biscuit
>
> Middle English: from Old French bescuit, based on Latin bis 'twice' + coctus, past participle of coquere 'to cook' (so named because originally biscuits were cooked in a twofold process: first baked and then dried out in a slow oven so that they would keep).

bi·sect /bísékt/ v.tr. divide into two (equal) parts. □□ **bi·sec·tion** /–sékshən/ n. **bi·sec·tor** n. [BI– + L secare sect- cut]

bi·sex·u·al /bísékshōōəl/ adj. & n. • adj. **1** sexually attracted to persons of both sexes. **2** Biol. having characteristics of both sexes. **3** of or concerning both sexes. • n. a bisexual person. □□ **bi·sex·u·al·i·ty** /–sékshoo-álitee, –séksyoo-álitee/ n.

bish /bish/ n. Brit. sl. a mistake. [20th c.: orig. uncert.]

bish·op /bíshəp/ n. **1** a senior member of the Christian clergy usu. in charge of a diocese, and empowered to confer holy orders. **2** a chess piece with the top sometimes shaped like a miter. **3** mulled and spiced wine. [OE biscop, ult. f. Gk episkopos overseer (as EPI–, –skopos –looking)]

bish·op·ric /bíshəprik/ n. **1** the office of a bishop. **2** a diocese. [OE bisceoprīce (as BISHOP, rīce realm)]

bis·muth /bízməth/ n. Chem. **1** a brittle reddish white metallic element, occurring naturally and used in alloys. ¶ Symb.: Bi. **2** any compound of this element used medicinally. [mod.L bisemutum, Latinization of G Wismut, of unkn. orig.]

bi·son /bísən/ n. (pl. same) either of two wild humpbacked shaggy-haired oxen of the genus Bison, native to N. America (B. bison) or Europe (B. bonasus). [ME f. L f. Gmc]

bisque¹ /bisk/ n. a rich shellfish soup, made esp. from lobster. [F]

bisque² /bisk/ n. Tennis, Croquet, & Golf an advantage of scoring one free point, or taking an extra turn or stroke. [F]

bisque³ /bisk/ n. = BISCUIT 3.

bi·sta·ble /bístáybəl/ adj. (of an electrical circuit, etc.) having two s-table states.

bis·ter /bístər/ n. & adj. (Brit. **bis·tre**) • n. **1** a brownish pigment made from the soot of burned wood. **2** the brownish color of this. • adj. of this color. [F, of unkn. orig.]

bis·tort /bístawrt/ n. an herb, Polygonum bistorta, with a twisted root and a cylindrical spike of flesh-colored flowers. [F bistorte or med.L bistorta f. bis twice + torta fem. past part. of torquēre twist]

bis·tou·ry /bístəree/ n. (pl. **·ries**) a surgical scalpel. [F bistouri, bistorie, orig. = dagger, of unkn. orig.]

bis·tro /béestrō, bís–/ n. (pl. **·tros**) a small restaurant. [F]

bi·sul·fate /bisúlfayt/ n. Chem. a salt or ester of sulfuric acid.

bit¹ /bit/ n. **1** a small piece or quantity (a bit of cheese; give me another bit; that bit is too small). **2** (prec. by a) a fair amount (sold quite a bit; needed a bit of persuading). **b** colloq. somewhat (am a bit tired). **c** (foll. by of) colloq. rather (a bit of an idiot). **d** (foll. by of) colloq. only a little; a mere (a bit of a boy). **3** a short time or distance (wait a bit; move up a bit). **4** sl. an amount equal to 12½ cents (esp. in the phrase two bits). □ **bit by bit** gradually. **bit of all right** Brit. sl. a pleasing person or thing, esp. a woman. **bit of fluff** (or **skirt** or **stuff**) see FLUFF, SKIRT, STUFF. **bit on the side** sl. an extramarital sexual relationship. **bits and pieces** (or Brit. **bobs**) an assortment of small items. **do one's bit** colloq. make a useful contribution to an effort or cause. **every bit as** see EVERY. **not a bit** (or Brit. **not a bit of it**) not at all. **to bits** into pieces. [OE bita f. Gmc, rel. to BITE]

bit² past of BITE.

bit³ /bit/ n. & v. • n. **1** a metal mouthpiece on a bridle, used to control a horse. **2** a (usu. metal) tool or piece for boring or drilling. **3** the cutting or gripping part of a plane, pliers, etc. **4** the part of a key that engages with the bolt. **5** the copper head of a soldering iron. • v.tr. **1** put a bit into the mouth of (a horse). **2** restrain. □ **take the bit between one's teeth 1** take decisive personal action. **2** escape from control. [OE bite f. Gmc, rel. to BITE]

bit⁴ /bit/ n. Computing a unit of information expressed as a choice between two possibilities; a 0 or 1 in binary notation. [BINARY + DIGIT]

bitch /bich/ n. & v. • n. **1** a female dog or other canine animal. **2** sl. offens. a malicious or spiteful woman. **3** sl. a very unpleasant or difficult thing or situation. • v. colloq. **1** intr. (often foll. by about) **a** speak scathingly. **b** complain. **2** tr. be spiteful or unfair to. **3** tr. spoil; botch. [OE bicce]

bitch·y /bíchee/ adj. (**bitch·i·er**, **bitch·i·est**) sl. spiteful; bad-tempered. □□ **bitch·i·ly** adv. **bitch·i·ness** n.

bite /bīt/ v. & n. • v. (past **bit** /bit/; past part. **bit·ten** /bít'n/) **1** tr. cut or puncture using the teeth. **2** tr. (often foll. by off, etc.) detach with the teeth. **3** tr. (of an insect, snake, etc.) wound with a sting, fangs, etc. **4** intr. (of a wheel, screw, etc.) grip; penetrate. **5** intr. accept bait or an inducement. **6** intr. have a (desired) adverse effect. **7** tr. (in passive) take in; swindle. **b** (foll. by by, with, etc.) be infected by (enthusiasm, etc.). **8** tr. (as bitten adj.) cause a glowing or smarting pain to (frostbitten). **9** intr. (foll. by at) snap at. • n. **1** an act of biting. **2** a wound or sore made by biting. **3 a** a mouthful of food. **b** a snack or light meal. **4** the taking of bait by a fish. **5** pungency (esp. of flavor). **6** incisiveness; sharpness. **7** = OCCLUSION 3. □ **bite back** restrain (one's speech, etc.) by or as if by biting the lips. **bite (or Brit. bite on) the bullet** sl. behave bravely or stoically. **bite the dust** sl. **1** die. **2** fail; break down. **bite the hand that feeds one** hurt or offend a benefactor. **bite a person's head off** colloq. respond fiercely or angrily. **bite one's lip** see LIP. **bite off more than one can chew** take on a commitment one cannot fulfill. **once bitten twice shy** an unpleasant experience induces caution. **put the bite on** sl. borrow or extort money from. **what's biting you?** Brit. sl. what is worrying you? □□ **bit·er** n. [OE bītan f. Gmc]

bit·ing /bíting/ adj. **1** stinging; intensely cold (a biting wind). **2** sharp; effective (biting wit; biting sarcasm). □□ **bit·ing·ly** adv.

bit part n. a minor part in a play or a movie.

bit·ten past part. of BITE.

bit·ter /bítər/ adj. & n. • adj. **1** having a sharp pungent taste; not sweet. **2 a** caused by or showing mental pain or resentment (bitter memories; bitter rejoinder). **b** painful or difficult to accept (bitter dis-

appointment). **3 a** harsh; virulent (*bitter animosity*). **b** piercingly cold. • *n.* 1 *Brit.* beer strongly flavored with hops and having a bitter taste. **2** (in *pl.*) liquor with a bitter flavor used as an additive in cocktails. □ **to the bitter end** to the very end in spite of difficulties. □□ **bit·ter·ly** *adv.* **bit·ter·ness** *n.* [OE *biter* prob. f. Gmc: *to the bitter end* may be assoc. with a Naut. word *bitter* = 'last part of a cable': see BITTS]

bit·ter ap·ple *n.* = COLOCYNTH.

bit·ter·ling /bítərling/ *n.* a small brightly colored freshwater fish, *Rhodeus amarus*, from Central Europe. [BITTER + –LING¹]

bit·tern /bítərn/ *n.* **1** any of a group of wading birds of the heron family, esp. of the genus *Botaurus* with a distinctive booming call. **2** *Chem.* the liquid remaining after the crystallization of common salt from sea water. [ME f. OF *butor* ult. f. L *butio* bittern + *taurus* bull; –*n* perh. f. assoc. with HERON]

bit·ter or·ange *n.* = SEVILLE ORANGE.

bit·ter pill *n.* something unpleasant that has to be accepted.

bit·ter·sweet /bítərswēt/ *adj. & n.* • *adj.* **1** sweet with a bitter aftertaste. **2** arousing pleasure tinged with pain or sorrow. • *n.* **1 a** sweetness with a bitter aftertaste. **b** pleasure tinged with pain or sorrow. **2 a** = *woody nightshade* (see NIGHTSHADE). **b** a climbing plant, *Celastrus scandens*, of N. America having red seeds contained in orange capsules.

bitts /bits/ *n.pl. Naut.* a pair of posts on the deck of a ship, for fastening cables, etc. [ME prob. f. LG: cf. LG & Du. *beting*]

bit·ty /bítee/ *adj.* **1** *colloq.* tiny. **2** *Brit.* (**bit·ti·er**, **bit·ti·est**) made up of unrelated bits; scrappy. □□ **bit·ti·ly** *adv.* **bit·ti·ness** *n.*

bi·tu·men /bítŏŏmin, –tyŏŏ–, bi–/ *n.* **1** any of various tarlike mixtures of hydrocarbons derived from petroleum naturally or by distillation and used for road surfacing and roofing. **2** *Austral. colloq.* an asphalt road. [L *bitumen –minis*]

bi·tu·mi·nize /bítŏŏminīz, -tyŏŏ–, bi–/ *v.tr.* convert into, impregnate with, or cover with bitumen. □□ **bi·tu·mi·ni·za·tion** /–izáyshən/ *n.*

bi·tu·mi·nous /bítŏŏminəs, -tyŏŏ–, bi–/ *adj.* of, relating to, or containing bitumen.

bi·tu·mi·nous coal *n.* a form of coal burning with a smoky flame.

bit·zer /bítsər/ *n.* (also **bit·ser**) *Austral. colloq.* **1** a contraption made from previously unrelated parts. **2** a mongrel dog. [prob. abbr. of *bits and pieces*]

bi·va·lent /bīváylənt/ *adj. & n.* • *adj.* **1** *Chem.* having a valence of two. **2** *Biol.* (of homologous chromosomes) associated in pairs. • *n. Biol.* any pair of homologous chromosomes. □□ **bi·va·lence** /–ləns/ *n.* **bi·va·len·cy** *n.* [BI– + *valent*- pres. part. stem formed as VALENCE¹]

bi·valve /bīvalv/ *n. & adj.* • *n.* any of a group of aquatic mollusks of the class Bivalvia, with laterally compressed bodies enclosed within two hinged shells, e.g., oysters, mussels, etc. • *adj.* **1** with a hinged double shell. **2** *Biol.* having two valves, e.g., of a peapod.

biv·ou·ac /bívŏŏ-ak, bívwak/ *n. & v.* • *n.* a temporary open encampment without tents, esp. of soldiers. • *v.intr.* (**biv·ou·acked, biv·ou·ack·ing**) camp in a bivouac, esp. overnight. [F, prob. f. Swiss G *Beiwacht* additional guard at night]

bi·week·ly /bīwéeklee/ *adv., adj., & n.* • *adv.* **1** every two weeks. **2** twice a week. • *adj.* produced or occurring biweekly. • *n.* (*pl.* · **lies**) a biweekly periodical.
▶ See the note at *bimonthly.*

bi·year·ly /bíyéerlee/ *adv. & adj.* • *adv.* **1** every two years. **2** twice a year. • *adj.* produced or occurring biyearly.
▶ See the note at *bimonthly.*

biz /biz/ *n. colloq.* business. [abbr.]

bi·zarre /bizáar/ *adj.* strange in appearance or effect; eccentric; grotesque. □□ **bi·zarre·ly** *adv.* **bi·zarre·ness** *n.* [F, = handsome, brave, f. Sp. & Port. *bizarro* f. Basque *bizarra* beard]

bi·zar·re·rie /bizaárərəree/ *n.* a bizarre quality; bizarreness. [F]

Bk *symb. Chem.* the element berkelium.

bk. *abbr.* book.

BL *abbr.* **1** Bachelor of Law. **2** Bachelor of Letters. **3** British Library. **4** bill of lading.

bl. *abbr.* **1** barrel. **2** black. **3** block. **4** blue.

blab /blab/ *v. & n.* • *v.* (**blabbed, blab·bing**) **1** *intr.* **a** talk foolishly or indiscreetly. **b** reveal secrets. **2** *tr.* reveal (a secret, etc.) by indiscreet talk. • *n.* a person who blabs. [ME prob. f. Gmc]

blab·ber /blábər/ *n. & v.* • *n.* (also **blab·ber·mouth** /blábərmowth/) a person who blabs. • *v.intr.* (often foll. by *on*) talk foolishly or inconsequentially, esp. at length.

black /blak/ *adj., n., & v.* • *adj.* **1** very dark; having no color from the absorption of all or nearly all incident light (like coal or soot). **2** completely dark from the absence of a source of light (*black night*). **3 a** of the human group having dark-colored skin, esp. of African or Aboriginal descent. **b** of or relating to black people (*black rights; historically black colleges*). **4** (of the sky, a cloud, etc.) dusky; heavily overcast. **5** angry; threatening (*a black look*). **6** implying disgrace or condemnation (*in his black books*). **7** wicked; sinister; deadly (-*black-hearted*). **8** gloomy; depressed; sullen (*a black mood*). **9** portending trouble or difficulty (*things looked black*). **10** (of hands, clothes, etc.) dirty; soiled. **11** (of humor or its representation) sinister or macabre, as well as comic, import (*black comedy*). **12** (of

coffee or tea) without milk. **13** *Brit.* **a** (of industrial labor or its products) boycotted, esp. by a trade union, in an industrial dispute. **b** (of a person) doing work or handling goods that have been boycotted. **14** dark in color as distinguished from a lighter variety (*black bear; black pine*). • *n.* **1** a black color or pigment. **2** black clothes or material (*dressed in black*). **3 a** (in a game or sport) a black piece, ball, etc. **b** the player using such pieces. **4** the credit side of an account (*in the black*). **5** a member of a dark-skinned race, esp. one of African or Aboriginal descent. • *v.tr.* **1** make black (*blacked his face*). **2** polish with blacking. **3** *Brit.* declare (goods, etc.) 'black'. □ **beyond the black stump** *Austral. colloq.* in the remote outback. **black in the face** livid with strangulation, exertion, or passion. **black out 1 a** effect a blackout on. **b** undergo a blackout. **2** obscure windows, etc., or extinguish all lights for protection esp. against an air attack. □□ **black·ish** *adj.* **black·ly** *adv.* **black·ness** *n.* [OE *blæc*]

▶**Black,** designating Americans of African heritage, became the most widely used and accepted term in the 1960s and 1970s, replacing **Negro.** It is not usually capitalized: *black Americans.* Through the 1980s, the more formal **African-American** replaced **black** in much usage, but both are now generally acceptable. **Afro-American,** an earlier alternative to **black,** is heard mostly in anthropological and cultural contexts. "Colored people", common earlier in the twentieth century, is now usually regarded as derogatory, although the phrase survives in the full name of the NAACP. An inversion, "people of color" has gained some favor, but is also used for all non-white ethnic groups: *a gathering spot for African-Americans and other people of color interested in reading about their cultures.*

Black Af·ri·ca *n.* the area of Africa, generally south of the Sahara, where blacks predominate.

black·a·moor /blákəmŏŏr/ *n. archaic* a dark-skinned person, esp. a black person. [BLACK + MOOR]

black and blue *n.* discolored by bruises.

Black and Tans *n.* an armed force recruited to fight Sinn Fein in Ireland in 1921, wearing a mixture of military and constabulary uniforms.

black and white *n.* **1** recorded in writing or print (*down in black and white*). **2** (of film, etc.) not in color. **3** consisting of extremes only; oversimplified (*interpreted the problem in black and white terms*).

black art *n.* = BLACK MAGIC.

black·ball /blákbawl/ *v.tr.* **1** reject (a candidate) in a ballot (orig. by voting with a black ball). **2** exclude; ostracize.

black bee·tle *n. Brit.* the common cockroach, *Blatta orientalis.*

black belt *n.* **1** a black belt worn by an expert in judo, karate, etc. **2** a person qualified to wear this.

black·ber·ry /blákberee/ *n. & v.* • *n.* (*pl.* **·ries**) **1** a climbing thorny rosaceous shrub, *Rubus fruticosus*, bearing white or pink flowers. Also called **bramble.** **2** a black fleshy edible fruit of this plant. • *v.intr.* (**·ries, ·ried**) gather blackberries.

black·bird /blákbərd/ *n.* **1** a common Eurasian thrush, *Turdus merula*, of which the male is black with an orange beak. **2** any of various birds, esp. a grackle, with black plumage. **3** *hist.* a kidnapped African or Polynesian on a slave ship.

black·board /blákbawrd/ *n.* a board with a smooth usu. dark surface for writing on with chalk.

black·bod·y /blákbaádē/ *n. Physics* a hypothetical perfect absorber and radiator of energy, with no reflecting power.

black box *n.* **1** a flight recorder in an aircraft. **2** any complex piece of equipment, usu. a unit in an electronic system, with contents which are mysterious to the user.

black·boy /blákboy/ *n.* any tree of the genus *Xanthorrhea*, native to Australia, with a thick dark trunk and a head of grasslike leaves. Also called **grass tree.**

black bread *n.* a coarse dark-colored type of rye bread.

black bry·o·ny *n.* a rooted climber, *Tamus communis*, with clusters of poisonous red berries.

black buck *n.* a small Indian gazelle, *Antilope cervicapra*, with a black back and white underbelly. Also called **sasin.**

black·cap /blák-kap/ *n.* **1** a small European warbler, *Sylvia atricapilla*, the male of which has a black-topped head. **2** a chickadee.

black·cur·rant /blák-kə́rənt, –kúr–/ *n.* **1** a widely cultivated shrub, *Ribes nigrum*, bearing flowers in racemes. **2** the small dark edible berry of this plant.

black damp *n.* = CHOKEDAMP.

Black Death *n.* (usu. prec. by *the*) a widespread epidemic of bubonic plague in Europe in the 14th c.

black dia·mond *n.* (in *pl.*) coal.

black disk *n. Brit.* a long-playing phonograph record, as distinct from a compact disc.

black e·con·o·my *n.* unrecorded, unofficial economic activity.

black·en /blákən/ *v.* **1** *tr. & intr.* make or become black or dark. **2** *tr.* speak evil of; defame (*blacken someone's character*).

black Eng·lish *n.* the form of English spoken by many African-Americans, esp. as an urban dialect of the US.

black eye *n.* bruised skin around the eye resulting from a blow.

black-eyed pea *n.* (or *Brit.* **black-eye bean**) a variety of bean, *Vigna sinensis*, with seeds often dried and stored prior to eating (so called from its black hilum).

black-eyed Su·san *n.* any of several flowers, esp. of the genus *Rudbeckia*, with yellow colored petals and a dark center.

black·face /blákfays/ *n.* **1** a variety of sheep with a black face. **2** the makeup used by a non-black performer playing a black role.

black·fel·low /blákfelō/ *n.* offens. an Australian Aboriginal.

black·fish /blákfish/ *n.* **1** any of several species of dark-colored fish. **2** any of several dark whales of the genus *Globicephala*.

black flag *n.* **1** *hist.* a pirate's ensign, usually with a white skull and crossbones on a black background. **2** *hist.* a black flag hoisted outside a prison to announce an execution. **3** a black flag used to signal to a automobile racing driver that he must stop.

black·fly /blákfʊt/ *n.* (*pl.* **·flies**) **1** any of various small biting flies of the family Simuliidae. **2** any of various thrips or aphids, esp. *Aphis fabae*, infesting plants.

Black·foot /blákfʊt/ *n.* **1 a** a N. American people native to Montana and adjoining parts of Canada. **b** a member of this people. **2** the language of this people.

black for·est cake *n.* a chocolate cake with layers of morello cherries or cherry jam and whipped cream and topped with chocolate icing, orig. from S. Germany.

Black Fri·ar *n.* a Dominican friar.

black frost *n.* intense cold that blackens vegetation without a visible frost.

black grouse *n.* (or *Brit.* **black game**) a European grouse, *Lyrurus tetrix*.

black gin·ger *n.* unscraped root of ginger.

black·guard /blágaard, –ərd/ *n.* & *v.* ●*n.* a villain; a scoundrel; an unscrupulous, unprincipled person. ●*v.tr.* abuse scurrilously. □□ **black·guard·ly** *adj.* [BLACK + GUARD: orig. applied collectively to menials, etc.]

PRONUNCIATION TIP   **blackguard**

This word dates back to the 16th century, when it was probably pronounced as two distinct words. By the 18th century the two words were either hyphenated or spelled as a compound. As the two parts of the compound lost their distinct meanings, they also lost their separate pronunciations. The correct pronunciation in American English is BLAG-erd.

---

black·head /blák-hed/ *n.* a black-topped pimple on the skin.

black hole *n.* **1** a region of space possessing a strong gravitational field from which matter and radiation cannot escape. **2** a place of confinement for punishment, esp. in the armed services.

black ice *n.* thin hard transparent ice, esp. on a road surface.

black·ing /bláking/ *n.* any black paste or polish, esp. for shoes.

black·jack[1] /blákjak/ *n.* **1** a card game in which players try to acquire cards with a face value totaling 21 and no more. **2** *US* a flexible, usu. lead-filled bludgeon. **3** a pirates' black flag. **4** a tar-coated leather vessel for beer, ale, etc. [BLACK + JACK[1]]

black·lead /blákled/ *n.* & *v.* esp. *Brit.* ●*n.* graphite. ●*v.tr.* polish with graphite.

black·leg /blákleg/ *n.* an infectious, usu. fatal disease of young cattle and sheep caused by the soil bacterium Clostridium chauvoei.

black leop·ard *n.* = PANTHER.

black let·ter *n.* an early, ornate, bold typeface.

black light *n. Physics* the invisible ultraviolet or infrared radiations of the electromagnetic spectrum.

black·list /bláklist/ *n.* & *v.* ●*n.* a list of persons under suspicion, in disfavor, etc. ●*v.tr.* put the name of (a person) on a blacklist.

black lung *n.* a chronic lung disease caused by the inhalation of coal dust.

black mag·ic *n.* magic involving supposed invocation of evil spirits.

black·mail /blákmayl/ *n.* & *v.* ●*n.* **1 a** an extortion of payment in return for not disclosing discreditable information, a secret, etc. **b** any payment extorted in this way. **2** the use of threats or moral pressure. ●*v.tr.* **1** extort or try to extort money, etc., from (a person) by blackmail. **2** threaten; coerce. □□ **black·mail·er** *n.* [BLACK + obs. *mail* rent, OE *māl* f. ON *mál* agreement]

Black Ma·ri·a *n. sl.* a police vehicle for transporting prisoners.

black mark *n.* an indication of disfavor or discredit (*an arrest will be a black mark on your record*).

black mar·ket *n.* an illicit traffic in officially controlled or scarce commodities. □□ **black mar·ke·teer** *n.*

Black Mass *n.* a travesty of the Roman Catholic Mass allegedly in worship of Satan.

Black Monk *n.* a Benedictine monk.

Black Mus·lim *n.* a member of an exclusively African-American Islamic sect proposing a separate African-American community.

Black Na·tion·al·ism *n.* advocacy of civil rights and separatism for African-Americans and occas. blacks in other countries.

black night·shade *n.* see NIGHTSHADE.

black·out /blákowt/ *n.* **1** a temporary or complete loss of vision, consciousness, or memory. **2** a temporary loss of power, radio reception, etc. **3** a compulsory period of darkness as a precaution against air raids. **4** a temporary suppression of the release of information, esp. from police or government sources. **5** a sudden darkening of a theater stage.

Black Pan·ther *n.* one of a group of extremist activists for African-American civil rights in the US, active during the late 1960s and early 1970s.

black pep·per *n.* pepper made by grinding the whole dried berry, including the husk, of the pepper plant, *Piper nigrum*.

Black Pow·er *n.* a movement in support of rights and political power for blacks in various Western countries.

black pud·ding *n.* a black sausage containing pork, dried pig's blood, suet, etc.

black rasp·ber·ry *n.* **1** a N. American shrub, *Rubus occidentalis*. **2** the edible fruit of this shrub.

Black Rod *n. Brit.* the principal usher of the Lord Chamberlain's department, House of Lords, etc.

black sal·si·fy *n.* scorzonera.

black sheep *n. colloq.* an unsatisfactory or disreputable member of a family, group, etc.; a scoundrel.

black·shirt /blákshərt/ *n.* a member of a fascist organization. [f. the color of the It. Fascist uniform]

black·smith /bláksmith/ *n.* a smith who works in iron.

black stump *n. Austral. colloq.* a mythical marker of distance in the outback.

black swan *n. Brit.* **1** something extremely rare. **2** an Australian swan, *Cygnus atratus*, with black plumage.

black tea *n.* tea that is fully fermented before drying.

black·thorn /blákthawrn/ *n.* **1** a thorny rosaceous shrub, *Prunus spinosa*, bearing white flowers before small blue-black fruits. Also called **sloe**. **2** a cudgel or walking stick made from its wood.

black tie *n.* **1** a black bow tie worn with a dinner jacket. **2** *colloq.* formal evening dress.

black·top /bláktop/ *n.* a type of surfacing material for roads.

black vel·vet *n.* a drink made from stout and champagne.

Black Watch *n.* (usu. prec. by *the*) (in the UK) the Royal Highland Regiment (so called from its dark tartan uniform).

black·wa·ter fe·ver /blákwawtər/ *n.* a complication of malaria in which blood cells are rapidly destroyed, resulting in dark urine.

black wid·ow *n.* a venomous spider, *Latrodectus mactans*, of which the female has an hourglass-shaped red mark on her abdomen.

blad·der /bládər/ *n.* **1 a** any of various membranous sacs in some animals, containing urine (**urinary bladder**), bile (**gallbladder**), or air (**swim bladder**). **b** this or part of it or a similar object prepared for various uses. **2** an inflated pericarp or vesicle in various plants. **3** anything inflated and hollow. [OE *blǣdre* f. Gmc]

blad·der·wort /bládərwərt, –wawrt/ *n.* any insectivorous aquatic plant of the genus *Utricularia*, with leaves having small bladders for trapping insects.

blad·der wrack /bládərak/ *n.* a common brown seaweed, *Fucus vesiculosus*, with fronds containing air bladders which give buoyancy to the plant.

blade /blayd/ *n.* **1 a** the flat part of a knife, chisel, etc., that forms the cutting edge. **b** a flat piece of metal with a sharp edge or edges used in a razor. **2** the flattened functional part of an oar, spade, propeller, skate, snowplow, etc. **3** a the flat, narrow, usu. pointed leaf of grass and cereals. **b** the whole of such plants before the ear is formed (*in the blade*). **c** *Bot.* the broad thin part of a leaf apart from the petiole. **4** (in full **bladebone**) a flat bone, e.g., in the shoulder. **5** *Archaeol.* a long narrow flake (see FLAKE[1] 3). **6** *poet.* a sword. **7** *colloq.* (usu. *archaic*) a carefree young fellow. □□ **blad·ed** *adj.* (also in *comb.*). [OE *blæd* f. Gmc]

blae·ber·ry /bláyberee/ *n.* (*pl.* **·ries**) *Brit.* = BILBERRY. [ME f. *blae* (Sc. and No. of Engl. dial. f. ME *blo* f. ON *blár* f. Gmc: see BLUE[1]) + BERRY]

blah /blaa/ *n.* & *adj. colloq.* ●*n.* **1** (also **blah-blah-blah**) pretentious nonsense. **2** (**the blahs**) a lethargic, depressing feeling of malaise. ●*adj.* insipid; dull. [imit.]

blain /blayn/ *n.* an inflamed swelling or sore on the skin. [OE *blegen* f. WG]

blame /blaym/ *v.* & *n.* ●*v.tr.* **1** assign fault or responsibility to. **2** (foll. by *on*) assign the responsibility for (an error or wrong) to a person, etc. (*blamed his death on a poor diet*). ●*n.* **1** responsibility for a bad result; culpability (*shared the blame equally; put the blame on the bad weather*). **2** the act of blaming or attributing responsibility; censure (*she got all the blame*). □ **be to blame** (often foll. by *for*) be responsible; deserve censure (*she is not to blame for the accident*). **have only oneself to blame** be solely responsible (for something one suffers). **I don't blame you**, etc. I think your, etc., action was justifiable. □□ **blam·a·ble** or **blame·a·ble** *adj.* [ME f. OF *bla(s)mer* (v.), *blame* (n.) f. pop.L *blastemare* f. eccl.L *blasphemare* reproach f. Gk *blasphēmeō* blaspheme]

blame·ful /bláymfŏŏl/ *adj.* deserving blame; guilty. □□ **blame·ful·ly** *adv.*

blame·less /bláymlis/ *adj.* innocent; free from blame. □□ **blame·less·ly** *adv.* **blame·less·ness** *n.*

blame·wor·thy /bláymwərthee/ *adj.* deserving blame. □□ **blame·wor·thi·ness** *n.*

blanch /blanch/ *v.* **1** *tr.* make white or pale by extracting color. **2** *intr. & tr.* grow or make pale from shock, fear, etc. **3** *tr. Cooking* **a** peel (almonds, etc.) by scalding. **b** immerse (vegetables or meat) briefly in boiling water. **4** *tr.* whiten (a plant) by depriving it of light. □ **blanch over** give a deceptively good impression of (a fault, etc.) by misrepresentation. [ME f. OF *blanchir* f. *blanc* white, BLANK]

blanc·mange /bləmáanj/ *n.* a sweet opaque gelatinous dessert made with flavored cornstarch and milk. [ME f. OF *blancmanger* f. *blanc* white, BLANK + *manger* eat f. L *manducare* MANDUCATE]

bland /bland/ *adj.* **1 a** mild; not irritating. **b** tasteless; unstimulating; insipid. **2** gentle in manner; smooth. □□ **bland·ly** *adv.* **bland·ness** *n.* [L *blandus* soft, smooth]

bland·ish /blándish/ *v.tr.* flatter; coax; cajole. [ME f. OF *blandir* (-ISH²) f. L *blandiri* f. *blandus* soft, smooth]

bland·ish·ment /blándishmənt/ *n.* (usu. in *pl.*) flattery; cajolery.

blank /blangk/ *adj., n., & v.* ● *adj.* **1 a** (of paper) not written or printed on. **b** (of a document) with spaces left for a signature or details. **2 a** not filled; empty (*a blank space*). **b** unrelieved; plain; undecorated (*a blank wall*). **3 a** having or showing no interest or expression (*a blank face*). **b** void of incident or result. **c** puzzled; nonplussed. **d** having (temporarily) no knowledge or understanding (*my mind went blank*). **4** (with neg. import) complete; downright (*a blank refusal*; *blank despair*). **5** *euphem.* used in place of an adjective regarded as coarse or abusive. ● *n.* **1 a** a space left to be filled in a document. **b** a document having blank spaces to be filled. **2** (in full **blank cartridge**) a cartridge containing gunpowder but no bullet, used for training, etc. **3** an empty space or period of time. **4 a** a coin disk before stamping. **b** a metal or wooden block before final shaping. **5 a** a dash written instead of a word or letter, esp. instead of an obscenity. **b** *euphem.* used in place of a noun regarded as coarse. **6** a domino with one or both halves blank. **7** a lottery ticket that gains no prize. **8** the white center of the target in archery, etc. ● *v.tr.* **1** (usu. foll. by *off, out*) screen; obscure (*clouds blanked out the sun*). **2** (usu. foll. by *out*) cut (a metal blank). **3** defeat without allowing to score. □ **draw a blank** elicit no response; fail. □□ **blank·ly** *adv.* **blank·ness** *n.* [ME f. OF *blanc* white, ult. f. Gmc]

blank check *n.* **1** a check with the amount left for the payee to fill in. **2** *colloq.* unlimited freedom of action (cf. CARTE BLANCHE).

blan·ket /blángkit/ *n., adj., & v.* ● *n.* **1** a large piece of woolen or other material used esp. as a bed covering or to wrap up a person or an animal for warmth. **2** (usu. foll. by *of*) a thick mass or layer that covers something (*blanket of fog*; *blanket of silence*). **3** *Printing* a rubber surface transferring an impression from a plate to paper, etc., in offset printing. ● *adj.* covering all cases or classes; inclusive (*blanket condemnation*; *blanket agreement*). ● *v.tr.* (**blan·ket·ed, blan·ket·ing**) **1** cover with or as if with a blanket (*snow blanketed the land*). **2** stifle; keep quiet (*blanketed all discussion*). **3** *Naut.* take wind from the sails of (another craft) by passing to windward. □ **born on the wrong side of the blanket** illegitimate. [ME f. OF *blancquet, blanchet* f. *blanc* white, BLANK]

blan·ket stitch *n.* a stitch used to neaten the edges of a blanket or other material too thick for hemming.

blank·e·ty-blank /blángkətee blangk/ *adj. colloq.* used euphemistically to replace a word considered coarse or vulgar (*blankety-blank taxes!*).

blank test *n. Chem.* a scientific test done without a specimen, to verify the absence of the effects of reagents, etc.

blank verse *n.* unrhymed verse, esp. iambic pentameters.

blan·quette /bloNkét/ *n. Cooking* a dish consisting of white meat, e.g., veal, in a white sauce. [F (as BLANKET)]

blare /blair/ *v. & n.* ● *v.* **1** *tr. & intr.* sound or utter loudly. **2** *intr.* make the sound of a trumpet. ● *n.* a loud sound resembling that of a trumpet. [ME f. MDu. *blaren, bleren,* imit.]

blar·ney /bláarnee/ *n. & v.* ● *n.* **1** cajoling talk; flattery. **2** nonsense. ● *v.* (**·neys, ·neyed**) **1** *tr.* flatter (a person) with blarney. **2** *intr.* talk flatteringly. [*Blarney,* an Irish castle near Cork with a stone said to confer a cajoling tongue on whoever kisses it]

bla·sé /blaazáy/ *adj.* **1** unimpressed or indifferent because of overfamiliarity. **2** tired of pleasure; surfeited. [F]

blas·pheme /blasféem, blásfeem/ *v.* **1** *intr.* talk profanely, making use of religious names, etc. **2** *tr.* talk profanely about; revile. □□ **blas·phem·er** *n.* [ME f. OF *blasfemer* f. eccl.L *blasphemare* f. Gk *blasphēmeō*; cf. BLAME]

blas·phe·my /blásfəmee/ *n.* (*pl.* **·mies**) **1** profane talk. **2** an instance of this. □□ **blas·phe·mous** *adj.* **blas·phe·mous·ly** *adv.* [ME f. OF *blasfemie* f. eccl.L f. Gk *blasphēmia* slander, blasphemy]

blast /blast/ *n., v., & int.* ● *n.* **1** a strong gust of wind. **2 a** a destructive wave of highly compressed air spreading outward from an

explosion. **b** such an explosion. **3** the single loud note of a wind instrument, car horn, whistle, etc. **4** *colloq.* a severe reprimand. **5** a strong current of air used in smelting, etc. **6** *sl.* a party; a good time. ● *v.* **1** *tr.* blow up (rocks, etc.) with explosives. **2** *tr.* **a** wither, shrivel, or blight (a plant, animal, limb, etc.) (*blasted oak*). **b** destroy; ruin (*blasted her hopes*). **c** strike with divine anger; curse. **3** *intr. & tr.* make or cause to make a loud or explosive noise (*blasted away on his trumpet*). **4** *tr. colloq.* reprimand severely. **5** *colloq.* **a** *tr.* shoot; shoot at. **b** *intr.* shoot. ● *int. Brit.* expressing annoyance. □ **at full blast** *colloq.* working at maximum speed, etc. **blast off** (of a rocket, etc.) take off from a launching site. [OE *blǣst* f. Gmc]

-blast /blast/ *comb. form Biol.* **1** an embryonic cell (*erythroblast*) (cf. −CYTE). **2** a germ layer of an embryo (*epiblast*). [Gk *blastos* sprout]

blast·ed /blástid/ *adj. & adv.* ● *attrib.adj.* **1** damned; annoying (*that blasted mosquito!*). **2** damaged by or as by a blast. ● *adv. Brit. colloq.* damned; extremely (*it's blasted cold*).

blast·er /blástər/ *n.* **1** in senses of BLAST *v.* **2** *Brit. Golf* a heavy lofted club for playing from a bunker.

blast fur·nace *n.* a smelting furnace into which compressed hot air is driven.

blast hole *n.* a hole containing an explosive charge for blasting.

blast·off /blástawf/ *n.* **1** the launching of a rocket, etc. **2** the initial thrust for this.

blas·tu·la /bláschələ/ *n.* (*pl.* **blas·tu·las** or **blas·tu·lae** /−lee/) *Biol.* an animal embryo at an early stage of development when it is a hollow ball of cells. [mod.L f. Gk *blastos* sprout]

bla·tant /bláyt'nt/ *adj.* **1** flagrant; unashamed (*blatant attempt to steal*). **2** offensively noisy or obtrusive. □□ **bla·tan·cy** /−t'nsee/ *n.* **bla·tant·ly** *adv.* [a word used by Spenser (1596), perh. after Sc. *blatand* = bleating]

blath·er /bláthər/ *n. & v.* (also **bleth·er** /bléthər/) ● *n.* foolish chatter. ● *v.intr.* chatter foolishly. [ME *blather,* Sc. *blether,* f. ON *blathra* talk nonsense f. *blathr* nonsense]

blath·er·skite /bláthərskīt/ (also **bleth·er·skate** /bléthərskayt/) *n.* **1** a person who blathers. **2** = BLATHER *n.* [BLATHER + *skite,* corrupt. of derog. use of SKATE²]

blaze¹ /blayz/ *n. & v.* ● *n.* **1** a bright flame or fire. **2 a** a bright glaring light (*the sun set in a blaze of orange*). **b** a full light (*a blaze of publicity*). **3** a violent outburst (of passion, etc.) (*a blaze of patriotic fervor*). **4 a** a glow of color (*roses were a blaze of scarlet*). **b** a bright display (*a blaze of glory*). ● *v.intr.* **1** burn with a bright flame. **2** be brilliantly lit. **3** be consumed with anger, excitement, etc. **4 a** show bright colors (*blazing with jewels*). **b** emit light (*stars blazing*). □ **blaze away** (often foll. by *at*) **1** fire continuously with rifles, etc. **2** work enthusiastically. **blaze up 1** burst into flame. **2** burst out in anger. **like blazes** *sl.* **1** with great energy. **2** very fast. **what the blazes!** esp. *Brit. sl.* what the hell! □□ **blaz·ing** *adj.* **blaz·ing·ly** *adv.* [OE *blǣse* torch, f. Gmc: ult. rel. to BLAZE²]

blaze² /blayz/ *n. & v.* ● *n.* **1** a white mark on an animal's face. **2** a mark made on a tree by slashing the bark esp. to mark a route. ● *v.tr.* mark (a tree or a path) by chipping bark. □ **blaze a trail 1** mark out a path or route. **2** be the first to do, invent, or study something; pioneer. [17th c.: ult. rel. to BLAZE¹]

blaze³ /blayz/ *v.tr.* proclaim as with a trumpet. □ **blaze abroad** spread (news) about. [ME f. LG or Du. *blāzen* blow, f. Gmc *blǣsan*]

blaz·er /bláyzər/ *n.* **1** a man's or woman's sports jacket not worn with matching trousers. **2** a colored summer jacket worn by schoolchildren, sportsmen, etc., as part of a uniform. [BLAZE¹ + −ER¹]

bla·zon /bláyzən/ *v. & n.* ● *v.tr.* **1** proclaim (esp. blazon abroad). **2** *Heraldry* **a** describe or paint (arms). **b** inscribe or paint (an object) with arms, names, etc. ● *n.* **1** *Heraldry* **a** a shield, coat of arms, bearings, or a banner. **b** a correct description of these. **2** a record or description, esp. of virtues, etc. □□ **bla·zon·er** *n.* **bla·zon·ment** *n.* [ME f. OF *blason* shield, of unkn. orig.; verb also f. BLAZE³]

bla·zon·ry /bláyzənree/ *n. Heraldry* **1 a** the art of describing or painting heraldic devices or armorial bearings. **b** such devices or bearings. **2** brightly colored display.

bldg. *abbr.* building.

bleach /bleech/ *v. & n.* ● *v.tr. & intr.* whiten by exposure to sunlight or by a chemical process. ● *n.* **1** a bleaching substance. **2** the process of bleaching. [OE *blēcan* f. Gmc]

bleach·er /bléechər/ *n.* **1 a** a person who bleaches (esp. textiles). **b** a vessel or chemical used in bleaching. **2** (usu. in *pl.*) a bench seat at a sports field or arena, esp. one in an outdoor uncovered stand usu. arranged in tiers and very cheap.

bleach·ing pow·der *n.* a powder containing calcium hypochlorite used esp. to remove color from materials.

bleak¹ /bleek/ *adj.* **1** bare; exposed; windswept. **2** unpromising; dreary (*bleak prospects*). **3** cold; raw. □□ **bleak·ly** *adv.* **bleak·ness** *n.* [16th c.: rel. to obs. adjs. *bleach, blake* (f. ON *bleikr*) pale, ult. f. Gmc: cf. BLEACH]

bleak² /bleek/ *n.* any of various species of small European river fish, esp. *Alburnus alburnus*. [ME prob. f. ON *bleikja*, OHG *bleicha* f. Gmc]

blear /bleer/ *adj. & v.* ●*adj.* **1** (of the eyes or the mind) dim; dull; filmy. **2** indistinct. ●*v.tr.* make dim or obscure; blur. [ME, of uncert. orig.]

blear•y /bleeree/ *adj.* (**blear•i•er**, **blear•i•est**) **1** (of the eyes or mind) dim; blurred. **2** indistinct. □□ **blear•i•ly** *adv.* **blear•i•ness** *n.*

blear•y-eyed *adj.* having dim sight or wits.

bleat /bleet/ *v. & n.* ●*v.* **1** *intr.* (of a sheep, goat, or calf) make a weak, wavering cry. **2** *intr. & tr.* (often foll. by *out*) speak or say feebly, foolishly, or plaintively. ●*n.* **1** the sound made by a sheep, goat, etc. **2** a weak, plaintive, or foolish cry. □□ **bleat•er** *n.* **bleat•ing•ly** *adv.* [OE *blǣtan* (imit.)]

bleb /bleb/ *n.* **1** esp. Med. a small blister on the skin. **2** a small bubble in glass or on water. [var. of BLOB]

bleed /bleed/ *v. & n.* ●*v.* (*past* and *past part.* **bled** /bled/) **1** *intr.* emit blood. **2** *tr.* draw blood from surgically. **3** a *tr.* extort money from. **b** *intr.* part with money lavishly; suffer extortion. **4** *intr.* (often foll. by *for*) suffer wounds or violent death (*bled for the Revolution*). **5** *intr.* **a** (of a plant) emit sap. **b** (of dye) come out in water. **6** *tr.* **a** allow (fluid or gas) to escape from a closed system through a valve, etc. **b** treat (such a system) in this way. **7** *Printing* **a** *intr.* (of a printed area) be cut into when pages are trimmed. **b** *tr.* cut into the printed area of when trimming. **c** *tr.* extend (an illustration) to the cut edge of a page. ●*n.* an act of bleeding (cf. NOSEBLEED). □ **one's heart bleeds** usu. *iron.* one is very sorrowful. [OE *blēdan* f. Gmc]

bleed•er /bleedər/ *n.* **1** *colloq.* a hemophiliac. **2** *Brit. coarse sl.* a person (esp. as a term of contempt or disrespect) (*you bleeder; lucky bleeder*).

bleed•ing /bleeding/ *adj. & adv. Brit. coarse sl.* expressing annoyance or antipathy (*a bleeding nuisance*).

bleed•ing heart *n.* **1** *colloq.* a dangerously or foolishly soft-hearted person. **2** any of various plants, esp. *Dicentra spectabilis* having heart-shaped dark pink or crimson flowers hanging from an arched stem.

bleep /bleep/ *n. & v.* ●*n.* an intermittent high-pitched sound made electronically. ●*v.intr. & tr.* **1** make or cause to make such a sound, esp. as a signal. **2** alert or summon by a bleep or bleeps. [imit.]

bleep•er /bleepər/ *n. Brit.* = BEEP.

blem•ish /blemish/ *n. & v.* ●*n.* a physical or moral defect; a stain; a flaw (*not a blemish on his character*). ●*v.tr.* spoil the beauty or perfection of; stain (*spots blemished her complexion*). [ME f. OF *ble(s)mir* (-ISH²) make pale, prob. of Gmc orig.]

blench /blench/ *v.intr.* flinch; quail. [ME f. OE *blencan*, ult. f. Gmc]

blend /blend/ *v. & n.* ●*v.* **1** *tr.* **a** mix (esp. sorts or grades) together to produce a desired flavor, etc. **b** produce by this method (*blended whiskey*). **2** *intr.* form a harmonious compound; become one. **3** a *tr. & intr.* (often foll. by *with*) mingle or be mingled (*truth blended with lies; blends well with the locals*). **b** *tr.* (often foll. by *in, with*) mix thoroughly. **4** *intr.* (esp. of colors): **a** pass imperceptibly into each other. **b** go well together; harmonize. ●*n.* **1** a a mixture, esp. of various sorts or grades of a substance. **b** a combination (of different abstract or personal qualities). **2** a portmanteau word. [ME prob. f. ON *blanda* mix]

blende /blend/ *n.* **1** (in full **zinc blende**) = SPHALERITE. **2** any of various other sulfides. [G f. *blenden* deceive, so called because while often resembling galena it yielded no lead]

blend•er /blendər/ *n.* **1** a mixing machine used in food preparation for liquefying, chopping, or puréeing. **2 a** a thing that blends. **b** a person who blends.

Blen•heim /blenim/ *n.* **1** a small spaniel of a red and white breed. **2** this breed. [the Duke of Marlborough's seat at Woodstock in S. England, named after his victory at Blenheim in Bavaria (1704)]

blen•ny /blenee/ *n.* (*pl.* **•nies**) any of a family of small spiny-finned marine fish, esp. of the genus *Blennius*, having scaleless skins. [L *blennius* f. Gk *blennos* mucus, with reference to its mucous coating]

blent /blent/ *poet. past* and *past part.* of BLEND.

bleph•a•ri•tis /blefərítis/ *n.* inflammation of the eyelids. [Gk *blepharon* eyelid + -ITIS]

bles•bok /blesbok/ *n.* (also **bles•buck** /-buk/) a subspecies of bontebok, native to southern Africa, having small lyre-shaped horns. [Afrik. f. *bles* BLAZE², (from the white mark on its forehead) + *bok* goat]

hairy blenny

bless /bles/ *v.tr.* (*past* and *past part.* **blessed**, *poet.* **blest** /blest/) **1** (of a priest, etc.) pronounce words, esp. in a religious rite, asking for divine favor; ask God to look favorably on (*bless this house*). **2 a** consecrate (esp. bread and wine). **b** sanctify by the sign of the cross.

3 call (God) holy; adore. **4** attribute one's good fortune to (an auspicious time, one's fate, etc.); thank (*bless the day I met her; bless my stars*). **5** (usu. in *passive*; often foll. by *with*) **a** make happy or successful (*blessed with children; they were truly blessed*). **b** be endowed with. **6** *euphem.* curse; damn (*bless the boy!*). □ **(God) bless me** (or **my soul**) an exclamation of surprise, pleasure, indignation, etc. **(God) bless you!** **1** an exclamation of endearment, gratitude, etc. **2** an exclamation made to a person who has just sneezed. **I'm** (or **well, I'm**) **blessed** an exclamation of surprise, etc. **not have a penny to bless oneself with** *Brit.* be impoverished.

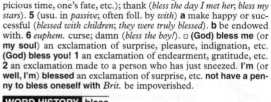

bless•ed /blésid, blest/ *adj.* (also *poet.* **blest**) **1 a** consecrated (*Blessed Sacrament*). **b** revered. **2** /blest/ (usu. foll. by *with*) often *iron.* fortunate (in the possession of) (*blessed with good health; blessed with children*). **3** *euphem.* cursed; damned (*blessed nuisance!*). **4 a** in paradise. **b** *RC Ch.* a title given to a dead person as an acknowledgment of his or her holy life; beatified. **5** bringing happiness; blissful (*blessed ignorance*). □□ **bless•ed•ly** *adv.*

bless•ed•ness /blésidnis/ *n.* **1** happiness. **2** the enjoyment of divine favor. □ **single blessedness** *joc.* the state of being unmarried (perversion of Shakesp. *Midsummer Night's Dream* I. i. 78).

bless•ing /blésing/ *n.* **1** the act of declaring, seeking, or bestowing (esp. divine) favor (*sought God's blessing; mother gave them her blessing*). **2** grace said before or after a meal. **3** a gift of God, nature, etc.; a thing one is glad of (*what a blessing he brought it!*). □ **blessing in disguise** an apparent misfortune that eventually has good results.

blest /blest/ *poet.* var. of BLESSED.

bleth•er var. of BLATHER.

blew *past* of BLOW¹, BLOW³.

blew•its /blóoits/ *n.* any fungus of the genus *Tricholoma*, with edible lilac-stemmed mushrooms. [prob. f BLUE¹]

blight /blit/ *n. & v.* ●*n.* **1** any plant disease caused by mildews, rusts, smuts, fungi, or insects. **2** any insect or parasite causing such a disease. **3** any obscure force which is harmful or destructive. **4** an unsightly or neglected urban area. ●*v.tr.* **1** affect with blight. **2** harm; destroy. **3** spoil. [17th c.: orig. unkn.]

blight•er /blítər/ *n. Brit. colloq.* a person (esp. as a term of contempt or disparagement). [BLIGHT + -ER¹]

Blight•y /blítee/ *n.* (*pl.* **•ies**) *Brit. sl.* (used by soldiers, esp. during World War I) England; home. [Anglo-Ind. corrupt. of Hind. *bilāyatī, wilāyatī* foreign, European]

bli•mey /blímee/ *int.* (also **cor bli•mey** /kawr/) *Brit. sl.* an expression of surprise, contempt, etc. [corrupt. of (*God*) *blind me!*]

blimp /blimp/ *n.* **1 a** a small nonrigid airship. **b** a barrage balloon. **2** *Brit.* (also **(Colonel) Blimp**) a proponent of reactionary establishment opinions. **3** *Brit.* a soundproof cover for a movie camera. **4** *derog. sl.* a fat person. □□ **blimp•er•y** *n.* **blimp•ish** *adj.* [20th. c., of uncert. orig.: in sense 2, a pompous, obese, elderly character invented by cartoonist David Low (d. 1963), and used in anti-German or anti-government drawings before and during World War II]

blind /blind/ *adj., v., n., & adv.* ●*adj.* **1** lacking the power of sight. **2 a** without foresight, discernment, intellectual perception, or adequate information (*blind effort*). **b** (often foll. by *to*) unwilling or unable to appreciate (a factor, circumstance, etc.) (*blind to argument*). **3** not governed by purpose or reason (*blind forces*). **4** reckless (*blind hitting*). **5 a** concealed (*blind ditch*). **b** (of a door, window, etc.) walled up. **c** closed at one end. **6** *Aeron.* (of flying) without direct observation, using instruments only. **7** *Cooking* (of a flan case, pie crust, etc.) baked without a filling. **8** esp. *Brit. sl.* drunk. ●*v.* **1** *tr.* deprive of sight, permanently or temporarily (*blinded by tears*). **2** *tr.* (often foll. by *to*) rob of judgment; deceive (*blinded them to the danger*). **3** *intr. Brit. sl.* go very fast and dangerously, esp. in a motor vehicle. ●*n.* **1 a** a screen for a window, esp. (*Brit.*) on a roller, or with slats (*roller blind; Venetian blind*). **b** *Brit.* an awning over a shop window. **2 a** something designed or used to hide the truth; a pretext. **b** *Brit.* a legitimate business concealing a criminal enterprise (*he's a spy, and his job is just a blind*). **3** any obstruction to sight or light. **4** *Brit.* a heavy drinking bout. **5** *Cards* a stake put up by a poker player before the cards dealt are seen. **6** a camouflaged shelter used for observing wildlife or hunting animals. ●*adv.* blindly (*fly blind; bake it blind*). □ **blind as a bat** completely blind. **blind to** incapable of appreciating. **blind with science** esp. *Brit.* overawe with a display of (often spurious) knowledge. **go it blind** act recklessly or without proper consideration. **not a blind bit of** (or **blind**) *Brit. sl.* not the slightest; not a single (*took not a blind bit of notice; not a blind word out of him*). **turn a** (or **one's**) **blind eye to** pretend not to notice. □□ **blind•ly** *adv.* **blind•ness** *n.* [OE f. Gmc]

blind al·ley n. **1** a cul-de-sac. **2** a course of action leading nowhere.

blind cor·ner n. a corner around which a motorist, etc., cannot see.

blind date n. **1** a social engagement between two people who have not previously met. **2** either of the couple on a blind date.

blind·er /blíndər/ n. colloq. **1** (in pl.) either of a pair of screens or flaps attached to a horse's bridle to prevent it from seeing sideways. **2** Brit. an excellent piece of play in a game.

blind·fold /blíndfōld/ v., n., adj., & adv. • v.tr. **1** deprive (a person) of sight by covering the eyes, esp. with a tied cloth. **2** deprive of understanding; hoodwink. • n. **1** a bandage or cloth used to blindfold. **2** any obstruction to understanding. • adj. & adv. (usu. **blindfolded**) **1** with eyes covered. **2** without care or circumspection (went into it blindfolded). **3** Chess without sight of board and pieces. [replacing (by assoc. with FOLD[1]) ME blindfellen, past part. blindfelled (FELL[1]) strike blind]

blind gut n. the cecum.

blind·ing /blínding/ n. **1** the process of covering a newly made road, etc., with grit to fill cracks. **2** such grit.

blind man's buff n. (also **blind man's bluff**) a game in which a blindfolded player tries to catch others while being pushed around by them.

blind·side /blíndsīd/ v.tr. **1** strike or attack unexpectedly from one's blind side. **2** spring a disagreeable surprise upon.

blind side n. a direction in which one cannot see the approach of danger, etc.

blind spot n. **1** Anat. the point of entry of the optic nerve on the retina, insensitive to light. **2** an area in which a person lacks understanding or impartiality. **3** a point of unusually weak radio reception.

blind stamp·ing n. (also **blind tool·ing**) the embossing of a book cover without the use of color or gold leaf.

blind-stitch n. & v. • n. sewing visible on one side only. • v. sew with this stitch.

blind·worm /blíndwərm/ n. = SLOWWORM.

blink /blingk/ v. & n. • v. **1** intr. shut and open the eyes quickly and usu. involuntarily. **2** intr. (often foll. by at) look with eyes opening and shutting. **3** tr. **a** (often foll. by back) prevent (tears) by blinking. **b** (often foll. by away, from) clear (dust, etc.) from the eyes by blinking. **4** tr. & (foll. by at) intr. shirk consideration of; ignore; condone. **5** intr. **a** shine with an unsteady or intermittent light. **b** cast a momentary gleam. **6** tr. blink with (eyes). • n. **1** an act of blinking. **2** a momentary gleam or glimpse. **3** = ICEBLINK. □ **on the blink** sl. out of order, esp. intermittently. [partly var. of blenk = BLENCH, partly f. MDu. blinken shine]

blink·er /blíngkər/ n. & v. • n. **1** a device that blinks, esp. a vehicle's turn indicator. **2** = BLINDER 1. • v.tr. **1** obscure with blinders. **2** (as **blinkered** adj.) having narrow and prejudiced views.

blink·ing /blíngking/ adj. & adv. Brit. sl. an intensive, esp. expressing disapproval (a blinking idiot; a blinking awful time). [BLINK + –ING[2] (euphem. for BLOODY)]

blip /blip/ n. & v. • n. **1** a quick popping sound, as of dripping water or an electronic device. **2** a small image of an object on a radar screen. **3** a minor deviation or error. • v. (**blipped**, **blip·ping**) **1** intr. make a blip. **2** tr. strike briskly. [imit.]

bliss /blis/ n. **1** a perfect joy or happiness. **b** enjoyment; gladness. **2 a** being in heaven. **b** a state of blessedness. [OE blīths, bliss f. Gmc blīthsjō f. blīthiz BLITHE: sense infl. by BLESS]

bliss·ful /blísfool/ adj. perfectly happy; joyful. □ **blissful ignorance** fortunate unawareness of something unpleasant. □□ **bliss·ful·ly** adv. **bliss·ful·ness** n.

blis·ter /blístər/ n. & v. • n. **1** a small bubble on the skin filled with serum and caused by friction, burning, etc. **2** a similar swelling on any other surface. **3** Med. anything applied to raise a blister. **4** Brit. sl. an annoying person. • v. **1** tr. raise a blister on. **2** intr. come up in a blister or blisters. **3** tr. attack sharply (blistered them with his criticisms). **4** (as **blistering** adj.) causing blisters; severe; hot. □□ **blis·ter·y** adj. [ME perh. f. OF blestre, blo(u)stre swelling, pimple]

blis·ter cop·per n. copper which is almost pure.

blis·ter gas n. a poison gas causing blisters on the skin.

blis·ter pack n. a type of packaging consisting of a transparent plastic material attached to a cardboard backing for containing and displaying a product in a store. Also called **bubble pack**.

blithe /blīth/ adj. **1** poet. gay; joyous. **2** careless; casual (with blithe indifference). □□ **blithe·ly** adv. **blithe·ness** n. **blithe·some** /blíthsəm/ adj. [OE blīthe f. Gmc]

blith·er·ing /blíthəring/ adj. colloq. **1** senselessly talkative. **2 a** (attrib.) utter; hopeless (blithering idiot). **b** contemptible. [blither, var. of BLATHER + –ING[2]]

B.Litt. abbr. Bachelor of Letters. [L Baccalaureus Litterarum]

blitz /blits/ n. & v. colloq. • n. **1 a** an intensive or sudden (esp. aerial) attack. **b** an energetic intensive attack, usu. on a specific task (must have a blitz on this room). **2** (**the Blitz**) the German air raids on London in 1940 during World War II. **3** Football a charge of the quarterback by the defensive linebackers just after the ball is snapped. • v.tr. attack, damage, or destroy by a blitz. [abbr. of BLITZKRIEG]

blitz·krieg /blítskreeg/ n. an intense military campaign intended to bring about a swift victory. [G, = lightning war]

bliz·zard /blízərd/ n. **1** a severe snowstorm with high winds. **2** an overbundance; a deluge. ['violent blow' (1829), 'snowstorm' (1859), perh. imit.]

bloat /blōt/ v. **1** tr. & intr. inflate; swell (wind bloated the sheets; bloated with gas). **2** tr. (as **bloated** adj.) **a** swollen; puffed. **b** puffed up with pride or excessive wealth (bloated plutocrat). **3** tr. cure (a herring) by salting and smoking lightly. [obs. bloat swollen, soft and wet, perh. f. ON blautr soaked, flabby]

bloat·er /blōtər/ n. a herring cured by bloating.

blob /blob/ n. **1** a small roundish mass; a drop of matter. **2** a drop of liquid. **3** a spot of color. [imit.: cf. BLEB]

bloc /blok/ n. a combination of parties, governments, groups, etc., sharing a common purpose. [F, = block]

block /blok/ n., v., & adj. • n. **1** a large solid piece of hard material, esp. rock, stone, or wood, usu. with flat surfaces on each side (block of ice; block of marble). **2** a flat-topped base for chopping food, hammering on, etc. **3** a group of buildings bounded by (usu. four) streets. **4** an obstruction; anything preventing progress or normal working (a block in the pipe). **5** a chock for stopping the motion of a wheel, etc. **6** a pulley or system of pulleys mounted in a case. **7** (in pl.) any of a set of solid cubes, etc., used as a child's toy. **8** Printing a piece of wood or metal engraved for printing on paper or fabric. **9** a head-shaped mold used for shaping hats or wigs. **10** sl. the head (knock his block off). **11 a** the area between streets in a town or suburb. **b** the length of such an area, esp. as a measure of distance (lives three blocks away). **12** a stolid, unimaginative, or hard-hearted person. **13** a large quantity or allocation of things treated as a unit, esp. shares, seats in a theater, etc. **14** esp. Brit. a set of sheets of paper used for writing, or esp. drawing, glued along one edge. **15** Cricket a spot on which a batsman blocks the ball before the wicket, and rests the bat before playing. **16** Track & Field = STARTING BLOCK. **17** Football a blocking action. • v.tr. **1 a** (often foll. by up, off) obstruct (a passage, etc.) (the road was blocked; you are blocking my view). **b** put obstacles in the way of (progress, etc.). **2** restrict the use or conversion of (currency or any other asset). **3** use a block for making (a hat, wig, etc.). **4** emboss or impress a design on (a book cover). **5** Sports stop (a ball, hockey puck, etc.) with a bat, racket, hand, etc., defensively. **6** Football impede the progress of (an opponent) with one's body. **7** Theatr. design or plan the on stage movements of actors in a play, etc. • attrib.adj. treating (many similar things) as one unit (block booking). □ **block in 1** sketch roughly; plan. **2** park one's car in such a way as to prevent another car from moving away. **block out 1 a** shut out (light, noise, etc.). **b** exclude something unpleasant from one's thoughts or memory. **2** sketch roughly; plan. **on the block** being auctioned; for sale. □□ **block·er** n. [ME f. OF bloc, bloquer f. MDu. blok, of unkn. orig.]

block·ade /blokáyd/ n. & v. • n. **1** the surrounding or blocking of a place, esp. a port, by an enemy to prevent entry and exit of supplies, etc. **2** anything that prevents access or progress. • v.tr. **1** subject to a blockade. **2** obstruct (a passage, a view, etc.). □ **run a blockade** enter or leave a blockaded port by evading the blockading force. □□ **block·ad·er** n. [BLOCK + –ADE[1], prob. after ambuscade]

block·ade-run·ner n. **1** a vessel which runs or attempts to run into a blockaded port. **2** the owner, master, or one of the crew of such a vessel.

block·age /blókij/ n. **1** an obstruction. **2** a blocked state.

block and tack·le n. a system of pulleys and ropes, esp. for lifting.

block·bust·er /blókbustər/ n. sl. **1** something of great power or size, esp. an epic or extremely popular movie or a book. **2** a huge bomb capable of destroying a whole block of buildings.

block cap·i·tals n. (also **block let·ters**) letters printed without serifs, or written with each letter separate and in capitals.

block di·a·gram n. a diagram showing the general arrangement of parts of an apparatus.

block·head /blókhed/ n. a stupid person. □□ **block·head·ed** adj.

block·house /blókhows/ n. **1** a reinforced concrete shelter used as an observation point, etc. **2** hist. a one-story timber building with loopholes, used as a fort. **3** a house made of squared logs.

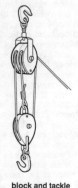

block and tackle

block·ish /blókish/ adj. **1** resembling a block. **2** excessively dull; stupid; obtuse. **3** clumsy; rude; roughly hewn. □□ **block·ish·ly** adv. **block·ish·ness** n.

block moun·tain n. Geol. a mountain formed by natural faults.

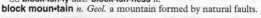

block sys•tem *n.* a system by which no railroad train may enter a section that is not clear.

block tin *n.* refined tin cast in ingots.

block vote *n.* a vote proportional in power to the number of people a delegate represents.

bloc vote *n.* = BLOCK VOTE.

bloke /blōk/ *n. Brit. sl.* a man; a fellow. [Shelta]

blond /blond/ *adj. & n.* ● *adj.* **1** (of hair) light-colored; fair. **2** (of the complexion, esp. as an indication of race) light-colored. **3** (of wood, etc.) light in color or tone. ● *n.* a person with fair hair and skin. □□ **blond•ish** *adj.* **blond•ness** *n.* [ME f. F f. med.L *blondus, blundus* yellow, perh. of Gmc orig.]

▶**Blonde** is still widely used as a noun pertaining to females (*the blonde in the red dress*), although some people object to this distinction and prefer **blond** for persons of both sexes. As an adjective used to describe hair color or complexion, *blond* is more common and can refer to either sex (*a young blond girl, two blond sons*).

blonde /blond/ *adj. & n.* ● *adj.* (of a woman or a woman's hair) blond. ● *n.* a blond-haired woman. [F fem. of *blond*; see BLOND]

▶See note at BLOND

blood /blud/ *n. & v.* ● *n.* **1** a liquid, usually red and circulating in the arteries and veins of vertebrates, that carries oxygen to and carbon dioxide from the tissues of the body. **2** a corresponding fluid in invertebrates. **3** bloodshed, esp. killing. **4** passion; temperament. **5** race; descent; parentage (*of the same blood*). **6** a relationship; relations (*own flesh and blood; blood is thicker than water*). **7** a dandy; a man of fashion. ● *v.tr.* **1** give (a hound) a first taste of blood. **2** initiate (a person) by experience. □ **one's blood is up** one is in a fighting mood. **in one's blood** inherent in one's character. **make a person's blood boil** infuriate. **make a person's blood run cold** horrify. **new** (or **fresh**) **blood** new members admitted to a group, esp. as an invigorating force. **of the blood** esp. *Brit.* royal. **out for a person's blood** set on getting revenge. **taste blood** be stimulated by an early success. **young blood 1** a younger member or members of a group. **2** a rake or fashionable young man. [OE *blōd* f. Gmc]

blood-and-thun•der *n. colloq.* sensationalism; melodrama.

blood bank *n.* a place where supplies of blood or plasma for transfusion are stored.

blood•bath *n.* a massacre.

blood broth•er *n.* a brother by birth or by the ceremonial mingling of blood.

blood count *n.* **1** the counting of the number of corpuscles in a specific amount of blood. **2** the number itself.

blood•cur•dling /blúdkərdling/ *adj.* horrifying.

blood•ed /blúdid/ *adj.* **1** (of horses, etc.) of good pedigree. **2** (in *comb.*) having blood or a disposition of a specified kind (*cold-blooded; red-blooded*).

blood feud *n.* a feud between families involving killing or injury.

blood group *n.* any one of the various types of human blood determining compatibility in transfusion.

blood-heat *n.* the normal body temperature of a healthy human being, on average about 98.6 °F or 37 °C.

blood horse *n.* a thoroughbred.

blood•hound /blúdhownd/ *n.* **1** a large hound of a breed used in tracking and having a very keen sense of smell. **2** this breed.

blood•less /blúdlis/ *adj.* **1** without blood. **2** unemotional; cold. **3** pale. **4** without bloodshed (*a bloodless coup*). **5** feeble; lifeless. □□ **blood•less•ly** *adv.* **blood•less•ness** *n.*

blood•let•ting /blúdleting/ *n.* **1** the surgical removal of some of a patient's blood. **2** bloodshed.

blood•line /blúdlin/ *n.* a line of descent; pedigree; descent.

blood lust *n.* the desire for shedding blood.

blood•mo•bile /blúdmōbeel/ *n.* a van, truck, or bus equipped and staffed to take blood from donors.

blood mon•ey *n.* **1** money paid to the next of kin of a person who has been killed. **2** money paid to a hired murderer. **3** money paid for information about a murder or murderer. **4** money gained through the suffering of others.

blood or•ange *n.* an orange with red or red-streaked pulp.

blood poi•son•ing *n.* a diseased state caused by the presence of microorganisms in the blood.

blood pres•sure *n.* the pressure of the blood in the circulatory system, often measured for diagnosis since it is closely related to the force and rate of the heartbeat and the diameter and elasticity of the arterial walls.

blood red *n.* red as blood.

blood re•la•tion *n.* (also **blood rel•a•tive**) a relative by blood, not by marriage or adoption.

blood roy•al *n.* a royal family.

blood se•rum *n.* see SERUM.

blood•shed /blúdshed/ *n.* **1** the spilling of blood. **2** slaughter.

blood•shot /blúdshot/ *adj.* (of an eyeball) inflamed; tinged with blood.

blood spav•in *n.* a soft swelling of a horse's hock due to distension of the main vein.

blood sport *n.* sport involving the wounding or killing of animals, esp. hunting.

blood•stain /blúdstayn/ *n.* a discoloration caused by blood.

blood•stained /blúdstaynd/ *adj.* **1** stained with blood. **2** guilty of bloodshed.

blood•stock /blúdstok/ *n.* thoroughbred horses.

blood•stone /blúdstōn/ *n.* a type of green chalcedony spotted or streaked with red, often used as a gemstone.

blood•stream /blúdstreem/ *n.* blood in circulation.

blood•suck•er /blúdsukər/ *n.* **1** an animal or insect that sucks blood, esp. a leech. **2** an extortioner. **3** a person who lives off others; a parasite. □□ **blood•suck•ing** *adj.*

blood sug•ar *n.* the amount of glucose in the blood.

blood test *n.* a scientific examination of blood, esp. for diagnosis.

blood•thirst•y /blúdthərstee/ *adj.* (**blood•thirst•i•er, blood•thirst•i•est**) eager for bloodshed. □□ **blood•thirst•i•ly** *adv.* **blood•thirst•i•ness** *n.*

blood trans•fu•sion *n.* the injection of a volume of blood, previously taken from a healthy person, into a patient.

blood type *n.* see BLOOD GROUP.

blood ves•sel *n.* a vein, artery, or capillary carrying blood.

blood•worm /blúdwərm/ *n.* **1** any of a variety of bright red midge larvae. **2** a small tubifex worm used as food for aquarium fish.

blood•y /blúdee/ *adj., adv., & v.* ● *adj.* (**blood•i•er, blood•i•est**) **1 a** of or like blood. **b** running or smeared with blood (*bloody bandage*). **2 a** involving, loving, or resulting from bloodshed (*bloody battle*). **b** sanguinary; cruel (*bloody butcher*). **3** esp. *Brit. coarse sl.* expressing annoyance or antipathy, or as an intensive (*a bloody shame; a bloody sight better; not a bloody chocolate left*). **4** red. ● *adv.* esp. *Brit. coarse sl.* as an intensive (*a bloody good job; I'll bloody pound him*). ● *v.tr.* (**•ies, •ied**) make bloody; stain with blood. □□ **blood•i•ly** *adv.* **blood•i•ness** *n.* [OE *blōdig* (as BLOOD, -Y¹)]

blood•y hand *n. Heraldry* the armorial device of a baronet.

Blood•y Mar•y *n.* a drink composed of vodka and tomato juice.

blood•y-mind•ed *adj. Brit. colloq.* deliberately uncooperative.

bloom¹ /bloom/ *n. & v.* ● *n.* **1 a** a flower, esp. one cultivated for its beauty. **b** the state of flowering (*in bloom*). **2** a state of perfection or loveliness; the prime (*in full bloom*). **3 a** (of the complexion) a flush; a glow. **b** a delicate powdery surface deposit on plums, grapes, leaves, etc., indicating freshness. **c** a cloudiness on a shiny surface. **4** an overgrowth of algae, plankton, etc. ● *v.* **1** *intr.* bear flowers; be in bloom. **2** *intr.* **a** come into; or remain in, full beauty. **b** flourish; be in a healthy, vigorous state. **3** *intr.* become overgrown with algae, plankton, etc. (esp. of a lake or stream). **4** *tr. Photog.* coat (a lens) so as to reduce reflection from its surface. □ **take the bloom off** make stale. [ME f. ON *blóm, blómi*, etc. f. Gmc: cf. BLOSSOM]

bloom² /bloom/ *n. & v.* ● *n.* a mass of puddled iron hammered or squeezed into a thick bar. ● *v.tr.* make into bloom. [OE *blōma*]

bloom•er¹ /bloomər/ *n. Brit. sl.* a blunder. [= BLOOMING error]

bloom•er² /bloomər/ *n. Brit.* an oblong loaf with a rounded diagonally slashed top. [20th c.: orig. uncert.]

bloom•er³ /bloomər/ *n.* a plant or person that blooms (in a specified way) (*early autumn bloomer; late bloomer*).

bloo•mers /bloomərz/ *n.pl.* **1** women's loose almost knee-length underpants. **2** *colloq.* any women's underpants. **3** *hist.* women's loose trousers, gathered at the knee or (orig.) the ankle. [Mrs. A. *Bloomer*, Amer. social reformer d. 1894, who advocated a similar costume]

bloom•er•y /bloomʌree/ *n.* (*pl.* **•ies**) a factory that makes puddled iron into blooms.

bloom•ing /blooming/ *adj. & adv.* ● *adj.* **1** flourishing; healthy. **2** *Brit. sl.* an intensive (*a blooming miracle*). ● *adv. Brit. sl.* an intensive (*was blooming difficult*). [BLOOM¹ + -ING²: euphem. for BLOODY]

Blooms•bur•y /bloomzbəree, –bree/ *n. & adj.* ● *n.* (in full **Bloomsbury Group**) a group of writers, artists, and philosophers living in or associated with Bloomsbury in London in the early 20th c. ● *adj.* **1** associated with or similar to the Bloomsbury Group. **2** intellectual; highbrow.

bloop•er /bloopər/ *n. colloq.* an embarrassing error. [imit. *bloop* + -ER¹]

blos•som /blósəm/ *n. & v.* ● *n.* **1** a flower or a mass of flowers, esp. of a fruit tree. **2** the stage or time of flowering (*the cherry tree in blossom*). **3** a promising stage (*the blossom of youth*). ● *v.intr.* **1** open into flower. **2** reach a promising stage; mature; thrive. □□ **blos•som•y** *adj.* [OE *blōstm(a)* prob. formed as BLOOM¹]

blot /blot/ *n. & v.* ● *n.* **1** a spot or stain esp. of ink, etc. **2** a moral defect in an otherwise good character; a disgraceful act or quality. **3** any disfigurement or blemish. ● *v.* (**blot•ted, blot•ting**) **1 a** *tr.* spot or stain esp. with ink; smudge. **b** *intr.* (of a pen, ink, etc.) make blots. **2** *tr.* **a** use blotting paper or other absorbent material to absorb excess liquid, esp. ink. **b** (of blotting paper, etc.) soak up (esp. ink). **3** *tr.* disgrace (*blotted his reputation*). □ **blot one's copybook** *Brit.* damage one's reputation. **blot on the escutcheon** a disgrace to the family name. **blot out 1 a** obliterate (writing). **b** obscure (a view, sound, etc.). **2** obliterate (from the memory) as too painful. **3** destroy. [ME prob. f. Scand.: cf. Icel. *blettr* spot, stain]

blotch /bloch/ *n. & v.* ● *n.* **1** a discolored or inflamed patch on the skin. **2** an irregular patch of ink or color. ● *v.tr.* cover with blotches. □□ **blotch•y** *adj.* (**blotch•i•er, blotch•i•est**). [17th c.: f. obs. *plotch* and BLOT]

blot•ter /blótər/ *n.* **1** a sheet or sheets of blotting paper, usu. inserted into a frame. **2** a temporary record book, esp. a police charge sheet.

blot•ting pa•per *n.* unsized absorbent paper used for soaking up excess ink.

blot•to /blótō/ *adj. sl.* very drunk, esp. unconscious from drinking. [20th c.: perh. f. BLOT]

blouse /blows, blowz/ *n. & v.* ● *n.* **1 a** a woman's loose, usu. lightweight, upper garment, usu. buttoned and collared. **b** the upper part of a military uniform. **2** a worker's or peasant's loose linen or cotton garment, usu. belted at the waist. ● *v.tr.* make (a shirt, etc.) fall loosely like a blouse. [F, of unkn. orig.]

blous•on /blówson, blóŏzon/ *n.* a short blouse-shaped jacket. [F]

blow¹ /blō/ *v. & v.* ● *v.* (*past* **blew** /blōō/; *past part.* **blown** /blōn/) **1 a** *intr.* (of the wind or air, or impersonally) move along; act as an air current (*it was blowing hard*). **b** *intr.* be driven by an air current (*paper blew along the gutter*). **c** *tr.* drive with an air current (*blew the door open*). **2 a** *tr.* send out (esp. air) by breathing (*blew cigarette smoke; blew a bubble*). **b** *intr.* send a directed air current from the mouth. **3** *tr. & intr.* sound or be sounded by blowing (*the whistle blew; they blew the trumpets*). **4** *tr.* **a** direct an air current at (*blew the embers*). **b** (foll. by *off, away*, etc.) clear of by means of an air current (*blew the dust off*). **5** *tr.* **a** clear (the nose) of mucus by blowing. **b** remove contents from (an egg) by blowing through it. **6 a** *intr.* puff; pant. **b** *tr.* (esp. in *passive*) exhaust of breath. **7** *sl.* **a** *tr.* depart suddenly from (*he blew town yesterday*). **b** *intr.* depart suddenly. **8** *tr.* shatter or send flying by an explosion (*the bomb blew the tiles off the roof; blew them to smithereens*). **9** *tr.* make or shape (glass or a bubble) by blowing air in. **10** *tr. & intr.* melt or cause to melt from overloading (*the fuse has blown*). **11** *intr.* (of a whale) eject air and water through a blowhole. **12** *tr.* break into (a safe, etc.) with explosives. **13** *tr. sl.* **a** squander; spend recklessly (*blew $20 on a meal*). **b** spoil; bungle (an opportunity, etc.) (*he's blown his chances of winning*). **c** reveal (a secret, etc.). **14** *intr.* (of a can of food, gasket, etc.) burst from internal pressure. **15** *tr.* work the bellows of (an organ). **16** *tr.* (of flies) deposit eggs in. **17** *intr. colloq.* boast. ● *n.* **1 a** an act of blowing (e.g., one's nose, a wind instrument). **b** *colloq.* a turn or spell of playing jazz (on any instrument); a musical session. **2 a** a violent wind or storm. **b** a gust of wind or air. **c** exposure to fresh air. **3** = FLYBLOW. □ **blow hot and cold** *colloq.* vacillate. **blow in 1** break inwards by an explosion. **2** *colloq.* arrive unexpectedly. **blow a kiss** kiss one's hand and wave it or blow it toward a distant person. **blow a person's mind** *sl.* impress or affect someone very strongly. **blow off 1** escape or allow (steam, pressure, etc.) to escape forcibly. **2** *sl.* renege on (an obligation) (*I decided to blow off studying so I could go to the party*). **blow out 1 a** extinguish by blowing. **b** send outward by an explosion. **2** (of a tire) burst. **3** (of a fuse, etc.) melt. **blow over** (of trouble, etc.) fade away without serious consequences. **blow one's own trumpet** praise oneself. **blow one's top** (or **stack**) *colloq.* explode in rage. **blow up 1 a** shatter or destroy by an explosion. **b** explode; erupt. **2** *colloq.* lose one's temper. **3** inflate (a tire, etc.). **4** *colloq.* enlarge (a photograph, etc.). **5** exaggerate. **blow the whistle on** see WHISTLE. [OE *blāwan* f. Gmc]

blow² /blō/ *n.* **1** a hard stroke with a hand or weapon. **2** a sudden shock or misfortune. □ **at one blow** by a single stroke; in one operation. **come to blows** end up fighting. **strike a blow for** (or **against**) help (or oppose). [15th c.: orig. unkn.]

blow³ /blō/ *v. & n. archaic* ● *v.intr.* (*past* **blew** /blōō/; *past part.* **blown** /blōn/) burst into or be in flower. ● *n.* blossoming; bloom (*in full blow*). [OE *blōwan* f. Gmc]

blow•ball /blóbawl/ *n.* the globular seed head of a dandelion, etc.

blow-by-blow *adj.* (of a description, etc.) giving all the details in sequence.

blow-dry *v.* arrange (the hair) while drying it with a hand-held dryer.

blow-dry•er *n.* a hand-held electrical dryer that emits a stream of warm air.

blow•er /blóər/ *n.* **1** in senses of BLOW¹ *v.* **2** a device for creating a current of air. **3** esp. *Brit. colloq.* a telephone.

blow•fish /blófish/ *n.* any of several kinds of fish able to inflate their bodies when frightened, etc.

blow•fly /blófli/ *n.* (*pl.* **•flies**) a meat fly; a bluebottle.

blow•gun /blógun/ *n.* a tube used esp. by primitive peoples for propelling arrows or darts by blowing.

blow•hard /blóhaard/ *n. & adj. colloq.* ● *n.* a boastful person. ● *adj.* boastful; blustering.

blow•hole /blóhōl/ *n.* **1** the nostril of a whale or other cetacean, on the top of its head. **2** a hole (esp. in ice) for breathing or fishing through. **3** a vent for air, smoke, etc., in a tunnel, etc.

blow job *n. coarse sl.* fellatio.

blown *past part.* of BLOW¹, BLOW³.

blow-out /blō-owt/ *n. colloq.* **1** a burst tire. **2** a melted fuse. **3** a huge meal. **4** a large party. **5** *Sports* victory by a wide margin.

blow•pipe /blópīp/ *n.* **1** = BLOWGUN. **2** a tube used to intensify the heat of a flame by blowing air or other gas through it at high pressure. **3** a tube used in glass blowing.

blow•torch /blótawrch/ *n.* a portable device with a very hot flame used for burning off paint, soldering, etc.

blow-up /blóup/ *n.* **1** *colloq.* an enlargement (of a photograph, etc.). **2** an explosion.

blow•y /blóee/ *adj.* (**blow•i•er, blow•i•est**) windy; windswept. □□ **blow•i•ness** *n.*

blowz•y /blówzee/ *adj.* (**blowz•i•er, blowz•i•est**) **1** coarse looking; red-faced. **2** disheveled; slovenly. □□ **blowz•i•ly** *adv.* **blowz•i•ness** *n.* [obs. *blowze* beggar's wench, of unkn. orig.]

BLT *abbr.* (*pl.* **BLT's** or **BLTs**) a bacon, lettuce, and tomato sandwich.

blub•ber¹ /blúbər/ *n. & v.* ● *n.* **1 a** whale fat. **b** thick or excessive fat. **2** a spell of weeping. ● *v.* **1** *intr.* sob loudly. **2** *tr.* sob out (words). □□ **blub•ber•er** *n.* **blub•ber•ing•ly** *adv.* **blub•ber•y** *adj.* [ME perh. imit. (obs. meanings 'foaming, bubble')]

blub•ber² /blúbər/ *adj.* (of the lips) swollen; protruding. [earlier *blabber, blobber*, imit.]

blu•chers /blóŏkərz/ *n.pl. hist.* strong leather half boots or high shoes. [G. L. von *Blücher*, Prussian general d. 1819]

bludge /bluj/ *v. & n. Austral. & NZ sl.* ● *v.intr.* avoid work. ● *n.* an easy job or assignment. □ **bludge on** impose on. [back-form. f. BLUDGER]

bludg•eon /blújən/ *n. & v.* ● *n.* a club with a heavy end. ● *v.tr.* **1** beat with a bludgeon. **2** coerce. [18th c.: orig. unkn.]

bludg•er /blújər/ *n. Austral. & NZ sl.* **1** a hanger-on. **2** a loafer. [orig. E sl., = pimp, f. obs. *bludgeoner* f. BLUDGEON]

blue¹ /blōō/ *adj., n., & v.* ● *adj.* **1** having a color like that of a clear sky. **2** sad; depressed; (of a state of affairs) gloomy; dismal (*feel blue; blue times*). **3** indecent; pornographic (*a blue film*). **4** with bluish skin through cold, fear, anger, etc. **5** *Brit.* politically conservative. **6** having blue as a distinguishing color (*blue jay*). ● *n.* **1** a blue color or pigment. **2** blue clothes or material (*dressed in blue*). **3** (usu. **Blue**) **a** a soldier in the Union army in the US Civil War. **b** the Union army. **4** *Brit.* **a** a person who has represented a university in a sport, esp. Oxford or Cambridge. **b** this distinction. **5** *Brit.* a supporter of the Conservative party. **6** any of various small blue-colored butterflies of the family Lycaenidae. **7** = BLUING. **8** *Austral. sl.* an argument or row. **b** (as a nickname) a red-headed person. **9** a blue ball, piece, etc., in a game or sport. **10 a** (prec. by *the*) the clear sky. **b** the sea. ● *v.tr.* (**blues, blued, blu•ing** or **blue•ing**) **1** make or turn blue. **2** treat with laundering blue. □ **blue in the face** in a state of extreme anger or exasperation. **once in a blue moon** very rarely. **out of the blue** unexpectedly. □□ **blue•ness** *n.* [ME f. OF *bleu* f. Gmc]

blue² /blōō/ *v.tr.* (**blues, blued, blu•ing** or **blue•ing**) *Brit. sl.* squander (money). [perh. var. of BLOW¹]

blue ba•by *n.* a baby with a blue complexion from lack of oxygen in the blood due to a congenital defect of the heart or major vessels.

Blue•beard /blóŏbeerd/ *n.* **1** a man who murders several wives in succession. **2** a person with a horrible secret. [a character in a fairy tale told orig. in F (*Barbe-Bleue*) by Perrault]

blue•bell /blóŏbel/ *n.* **1** a liliaceous plant, *Hyacinthoides nonscripta*, with clusters of bell-shaped blue flowers on a stem arising from a rhizome. Also called **wild hyacinth** or **wood hyacinth**. **2** a plant, *Campanula rotundifolia*, with solitary bell-shaped blue flowers on long stalks. Also called **harebell**. **3** any of several plants with blue bell-shaped flowers, as of the genus *Mertensia*.

blue•ber•ry /blóŏberee/ *n.* (*pl.* **•ries**) **1** any of several plants of the genus *Vaccinium*, with an edible fruit. **2** the small blue-black fruit of these plants.

blue bice *n.* a shade of blue between ultramarine and azure derived from smalt.

blue•bird /blóŏbərd/ *n.* any of various N. American songbirds of the thrush family, esp. of the genus *Sialia*, with distinctive blue plumage usu. on the back or head.

blue blood *n.* noble birth. □□ **blue-blood•ed** *adj.*

blue book *n.* **1** a listing of socially prominent people. **2** a blank book used for college examinations. **3** (**Blue Book**) a reference book listing the prices of used cars. **4** (**Blue Book**) **a** a report issued by the government. **b** *Brit.* a report issued by Parliament or the Privy Council.

blue•bot•tle /blóŏbot'l/ *n.* **1** a large buzzing fly, *Calliphora vomitoria*, with a metallic blue body. Also called **blowfly**. **2** *Austral.* a Portuguese man-of-war. **3** a dark blue cornflower. **4** *Brit. colloq.* a policeman.

blue cheese *n.* cheese produced with veins of blue mold, e.g., Stilton and Danish Blue.

blue-chip *adj.* denoting shares of stock considered to be a reliable investment, though less secure than gilt-edged stock.

blue-col·lar *adj.* of workers who wear work clothes or specialized protective clothing, as miners, mechanics, etc.

blue crab *n.* an edible bluish-green crab, *Callinectes sapidus*, of the Atlantic and Gulf coasts.

blue·fish /blóofish/ *n.* a voracious marine fish, *Pomatomus saltatrix*, inhabiting tropical and temperate waters and popular as a game fish.

blue funk *n. sl.* a state of great terror or panic.

blue·grass /blóogras/ *n.* **1** any of several bluish green grasses, esp. Kentucky bluegrass, *Poa pratensis*. **2** a kind of unamplified country music characterized by virtuosic playing of banjos, guitars, etc., and close usu. high harmony.

blue-green al·ga *n.* = CYANOBACTERIUM.

blue ground *n.* = KIMBERLITE.

blue·gum /blóogum/ *n.* any tree of the genus *Eucalyptus*, esp. *E. regnans* with blue-green aromatic leaves.

blue·jack·et /blóojakit/ *n.* a sailor in the navy.

blue jay *n.* a crested jay, *Cyanocitta cristata*, common to N. America, with a blue back and head and a gray breast.

blue jeans *n.* pants made of blue denim.

blue mold *n.* a bluish fungus growing on food and other organic matter.

blue-pen·cil *v.* (·pen·ciled, ·pen·cil·ing; also ·pen·cilled, ·pen·cil·ling) censor or make cuts in (a manuscript, movie, etc.).

Blue Pe·ter *n.* a blue flag with a white square raised on board a ship leaving port.

blue·print /blóoprint/ *n. & v.* **•** *n.* **1** a photographic print of the final stage of engineering or other plans in white on a blue background. **2** a detailed plan, esp. in the early stages of a project or idea. **•** *v.tr.* work out (a program, plan, etc.).

blue rib·bon *n.* **1** a high honor. **2** *Brit.* the ribbon of the Order of the Garter.

blue-rib·bon ju·ry *n.* jury whose members are selected for their education, experience, etc.

blue rinse *n.* a preparation for tinting gray hair.

blue roan *adj. & n.* **•** *adj.* black mixed with white. **•** *n.* a blue roan animal.

blues /blooz/ *n.pl.* **1** (prec. by *the*) a bout of depression (*had a fit of the blues*). **2 a** (prec. by *the*; often treated as *sing.*) melancholic music of African-American folk origin, often in a twelve-bar sequence. **b** (*pl.* same) (as *sing.*) a piece of such music. □□ **blues·y** *adj.* (in sense 2).

blue·stock·ing /blóostoking/ *n.* usu. *derog.* an intellectual or literary woman. [from the (less formal) blue stockings worn by one man at a literary society meeting *c*.1750]

blu·et /blóoit/ *n.* a blue-flowered plant of the genus *Houstonia*.

blue tit *n.* a common European tit, *Parus caeruleus*, with a distinct blue crest on a black and white head.

blue vit·ri·ol *n.* (also *Brit.* **blue stone**) copper sulfate crystals.

blue wa·ter *n.* open sea.

blue whale *n.* a rorqual, *Balaenoptera musculus*, the largest known living mammal.

blue·y /blóoee/ *n.* (*pl.* **·eys**) *Austral. colloq.* **1** a bundle carried by a bushman. **2** = BLUE[1] *n.* 8b.

bluff[1] /bluf/ *v. & n.* **•** *v.* **1** *intr.* make a pretense of strength or confidence to gain an advantage. **2** *tr.* mislead by bluffing, esp. in a card game. **•** *n.* an act of bluffing; a show of confidence or assertiveness intended to deceive. □ **call a person's bluff** challenge a person thought to be bluffing. □□ **bluff·er** *n.* [19th c. (orig. in poker) f. Du. *bluffen* brag]

bluff[2] /bluf/ *adj. & n.* **•** *adj.* **1** (of a cliff, or a ship's bows) having a vertical or steep broad front. **2** (of a person or manner) blunt; frank; hearty. **•** *n.* a steep cliff or headland. □□ **bluff·ly** *adv.* (in sense 2 of *adj.*). **bluff·ness** *n.* (in sense 2 of *adj.*). [17th-c. Naut. word: orig. unkn.]

blu·ing /blóoing/ *n.* (also **blue·ing**) blue powder used to whiten laundry.

blu·ish /blóoish/ (also **blue·ish**) *adj.* somewhat blue.

blun·der /blúndər/ *n. & v.* **•** *n.* a clumsy or foolish mistake, esp. an important one. **•** *v.* **1** *intr.* make a blunder; act clumsily or ineptly. **2** *tr.* deal incompetently with; mismanage. **3** *intr.* move about blindly or clumsily; stumble. □□ **blun·der·er** *n.* **blund·er·ing·ly** *adv.* [ME prob. f. Scand.: cf. MSw *blundra* shut the eyes]

blun·der·buss /blúndərbus/ *n. hist.* a short large-bored gun firing balls or slugs. [alt. of Du. *donderbus* thunder gun, assoc. with BLUNDER]

blunge /blunj/ *v.tr.* (in ceramics, etc.) mix (clay, etc.) with water. □□ **blung·er** *n.* [after *plunge*, blend]

blunt /blunt/ *adj. & v.* **•** *adj.* **1** (of a knife, pencil, etc.) lacking in sharpness; having a worn-down point or edge. **2** (of a person or manner) direct; uncompromising; outspoken. **•** *v.tr.* make blunt or less sharp. □□ **blunt·ly** *adv.* (in sense 2 of *adj.*). **blunt·ness** *n.* [ME perh. f. Scand.: cf. ON *blunda* shut the eyes]

blur /blər/ *v. & n.* **•** *v.* (**blurred, blur·ring**) **1** *tr. & intr.* make or become unclear or less distinct. **2** *tr.* smear; partially efface. **3** *tr.* make (one's memory, perception, etc.) dim or less clear. **•** *n.* something that appears or sounds indistinct or unclear. □□ **blur·ry** *adj.* (**blur·ri·er, blur·ri·est**). [16th c.: perh. rel. to BLEAR]

blurb /blərb/ *n.* a (usu. eulogistic) description of a book, esp. printed on its jacket, as promotion by its publishers. [coined by G. Burgess, Amer. humorist d. 1951]

blurt /blərt/ *v.tr.* (usu. foll. by *out*) utter abruptly, thoughtlessly, or tactlessly. [prob. imit.]

blush /blush/ *v. & n.* **•** *v.intr.* **1 a** develop a pink tinge in the face from embarrassment or shame. **b** (of the face) redden in this way. **2** feel embarrassed or ashamed. **3** be or become red or pink. **•** *n.* **1** the act of blushing. **2** a pink tinge. □ **at first blush** on the first glimpse or impression. **spare a person's blushes** refrain from causing embarrassment esp. by praise. [ME f. OE *blyscan*]

blush·er /blúshər/ *n.* a cosmetic used to give a usu. reddish or pinkish color to the face.

blus·ter /blústər/ *v. & n.* **•** *v.intr.* **1** behave pompously and boisterously; utter empty threats. **2** (of the wind, etc.) blow fiercely. **•** *n.* **1** noisily self-assertive talk. **2** empty threats. □□ **blus·ter·er** *n.* **blus·ter·y** *adj.* [16th c.: ult. imit.]

blvd. *abbr.* boulevard.

BM *abbr.* **1** Bachelor of Medicine. **2** Bachelor of Music. **3** British Museum. **4** basal metabolism. **5** bowel movement.

B.Mus. *abbr.* Bachelor of Music.

BMX /bée-emeks/ *n.* **1** organized bicycle racing on a dirt track, esp. for youngsters. **2** a kind of bicycle used for this. **3** (*attrib.*) of or related to such racing or the equipment used (*BMX gloves*). [abbr. of bicycle *motocross*]

B mov·ie *n.* a supporting, usu. less well-known movie in a theater's program.

Bn. *abbr.* **1** Baron. **2** Battalion.

BO *abbr. colloq.* body odor.

bo·a /bóə/ *n.* **1** any large nonpoisonous snake from tropical America esp. of the genus *Boa*, which kills its prey by crushing and suffocating it in its coils. **2** any snake which is similar in appearance, such as Old World pythons. **3** a long scarf made of feathers or fur. [L]

bo·a con·stric·tor *n.* a large snake, *Boa constrictor*, native to tropical America and the West Indies, which crushes its prey.

boar /bawr/ *n.* **1** (in full **wild boar**) the tusked wild pig, *Sus scrofa*, from which domestic pigs are descended. **2** an uncastrated male pig. **3** its flesh. **4** a male guinea pig, etc. [OE *bār* f. WG]

board /bawrd/ *n. & v.* **•** *n.* **1 a** a flat thin piece of sawn lumber, usu. long and narrow. **b** a piece of material resembling this, made from compressed fibers. **c** a thin slab of wood or a similar substance, often with a covering, used for any of various purposes (*chessboard*; *ironing board*). **d** thick stiff cardboard used in bookbinding. **2** the provision of regular meals, usu. with accommodation, for payment. **3** *archaic* a table spread for a meal. **4** the directors of a company; any other specially constituted administrative body, e.g., a committee or group of councilors, examiners, etc. **5** (in *pl.*) the stage of a theater (cf. *tread the boards*). **6** *Naut.* the side of a ship. **•** *v.* **1** *tr.* a go on board (a ship, train, aircraft, etc.). **b** force one's way on board (a ship, etc.) in attack. **2 a** *intr.* receive regular meals or meals and lodging, for payment. **b** *tr.* esp. *Brit.* (often foll. by *out*) arrange accommodation away from home for (esp. a schoolchild). **c** *tr.* provide (a lodger, etc.) with regular meals. **3** *tr.* (usu. foll. by *up*) cover with boards; seal or close. □ **go by the board** be neglected, omitted, or discarded. **on board** on or on to a ship, aircraft, oil rig, etc. **take on board** esp. *Brit.* consider (a new idea, etc.). [OE *bord* f. Gmc]

board·er /báwrdər/ *n.* **1** a person who boards (see BOARD *v.* 2a), esp. a pupil at a boarding school. **2** a person who boards a ship, esp. an enemy.

board game *n.* a game, such as chess, checkers, or backgammon, that involves moving pieces on a board.

board·ing·house /báwrdinghows/ *n.* an establishment providing board and lodging.

board·ing school /báwrding skool/ *n.* a school where students reside during the school term.

board·room /báwrdroom, –room/ *n.* a room in which a board of directors, etc., meets regularly.

board·sail·ing /báwrdsayling/ *n.* = WINDSURFING. □□ **board·sail·or** *n.*

board·walk /báwrdwawk/ *n.* **1** a wooden walkway across sand, marsh, etc. **2** a promenade, esp. of wooden planks, along a beach.

boart var. of BORT.

boast /bōst/ *v. & n.* **•** *v.* **1** *intr.* declare one's achievements, possessions, or abilities with indulgent pride and satisfaction. **2** *tr.* own or have as something praiseworthy, etc. (*the hotel boasts magnificent views*). **•** *n.* **1** an act of boasting. **2** something one is proud of. □□ **boast·er** *n.* **boast·ing·ly** *adv.* [ME f. AF *bost*, of unkn. orig.]

boast·ful /bóstfool/ *adj.* **1** given to boasting. **2** characterized by boasting (*boastful talk*). □□ **boast·ful·ly** *adv.* **boast·ful·ness** *n.*

boat /bōt/ *n. & v.* **•** *n.* **1** a small vessel propelled on water by an engine, oars, or sails. **2** (in general use) a ship of any size. **3** an elongated boat-shaped jug used for holding sauce, gravy, etc. ● *v.intr.* travel or go in a boat, esp. for pleasure. □ **in the same boat** sharing the same adverse circumstances. **push the boat out** *Brit. colloq.* celebrate lavishly. □□ **boat•ful** *n.* (*pl.* **•fuls**). [OE *bāt* f. Gmc]

boat•er /bótǝr/ *n.* a flat-topped straw hat with a stiff brim.

boat hook *n.* a long pole with a hook and a spike at one end, for moving boats.

boat•house /bót-hows/ *n.* a house or shed at the edge of a river, lake, etc., for housing boats.

boat•ing /bóting/ *n.* rowing or sailing in boats as a sport or form of recreation.

boat•load /bótlōd/ *n.* **1** enough to fill a boat. **2** *colloq.* a large number of people.

boat•man /bótmǝn/ *n.* (*pl.* **•men**) a person who hires out boats or provides transport by boat.

boat peo•ple *n.* refugees who have left a country by sea.

boat train *n.* a train scheduled to meet or go on a boat.

boat•swain /bós'n/ *n.* (also **bo'sun, bo•sun, bo's'n**) a ship's officer in charge of equipment and the crew. [OE *bātswegen* (as BOAT, SWAIN)]

boat•swain's chair *n.* a seat suspended from ropes for work on the side of a ship or building.

bob[1] /bob/ *v.* ● *v.intr.* (**bobbed, bob•bing**) **1** move quickly up and down; dance. **2** (usu. foll. by *back, up*) **a** bounce buoyantly. **b** emerge suddenly; become active or conspicuous again after a defeat, etc. **3** curtsy. **4** (foll. by *for*) try to catch with the mouth alone (an apple, etc., floating or hanging). ● *n.* **1** a jerking or bouncing movement, esp. upward. **2** a curtsy. **3** one of several kinds of change in long peals in bell ringing. [14th c.: prob. imit.]

bob[2] /bob/ *n. & v.* ● *n.* **1** a short hairstyle for women and children. **2 a** a weight on a pendulum, plumb line, or kite tail. **b** a cork or quill on a fishing line as an indicator of a fish biting. **3** = BOBSLED. **4** a horse's docked tail. **5** a short line at or toward the end of a stanza. **6** a knot of hair; a tassel or curl. ● *v.* (**bobbed, bob•bing**) **1** *tr.* cut (a woman's or child's hair) so that it hangs clear of the shoulders. **2** *intr.* ride on a bobsled. [ME: orig. unkn.]

bob[3] /bob/ *n.* (*pl.* same) *Brit. sl.* a former shilling (now = 5 decimal pence). [19th c.: orig. unkn.]

Bob /bob/ *n.* □ **Bob's your uncle** *Brit. sl.* an expression of completion or satisfaction. [pet form of the name *Robert*]

bob•bin /bóbin/ *n.* **1** a cylinder or cone holding thread, yarn, wire, etc., used esp. in weaving and machine sewing. **2** a spool or reel. [F *bobine*]

bob•bi•net /bóbinet/ *n.* machine-made cotton, etc., net (imitating lace made with bobbins on a pillow). [BOBBIN + NET[1]]

bob•bin lace *n.* lace made by hand with thread wound on bobbins.

bob•ble /bóbǝl/ *n.* **1** a small woolly or tufted ball as a decoration or trimming. **2** a fumble, esp. of a baseball or football. [dimin. of BOB[2]]

bob•by[1] /bóbee/ *n.* (*pl.* **•bies**) *Brit. colloq.* a police officer. [Sir *Robert* Peel, Engl. statesman d. 1850, founder of the metropolitan police force]

bob•by[2] /bóbee/ *n.* (*pl.* **•bies**) (in full **bobby calf**) *Austral. & NZ* an unweaned calf slaughtered for veal. [Eng. dial.]

bob•by pin /bóbeepin/ *n.* a flat, closed hairpin. [BOB[2] + -Y[2]]

bob•by socks *n.pl.* (also **bob•by sox**) short socks reaching just above the ankle.

bob•cat /bóbkat/ *n.* a small N. American lynx, *Felix rufus*, with a spotted reddish brown coat and a short tail. [BOB[2] + CAT]

bob•o•link /bóbǝlingk/ *n.* a N. American songbird, *Dolichonyx oryzivorus*. [orig. *Bob* (*o'*) *Lincoln*: imit. of its call]

bob•sled /bóbsled/ (also *Brit.* **bob•sleigh** /bóbslay/) *n. & v.* ● *n.* a mechanically steered and braked sled used for racing down a steep ice-covered run. ● *v.intr.* race in a bobsled. [BOB[2] + SLED]

bob•stay /bóbstay/ *n.* the chain or rope holding down a ship's bowsprit. [prob. BOB[1] + STAY[2]]

bob•tail /bóbtayl/ *n.* a docked tail; a horse or a dog with a bobtail. [BOB[2] + TAIL[1]]

bob•white /bóbhwít, bóbwít/ *n.* an American quail of the genus *Colinus*. [imit. of the bird's call]

Boche /bosh, bawsh/ *n. & adj. sl. derog.* ● *n.* **1** a German, esp. a soldier. **2** (prec. by *the*) Germans, esp. German soldiers, collectively. ● *adj.* German. [F *sl.*, orig. = rascal: applied to Germans in World War I]

bock /bok/ *n.* a strong dark German beer. [F f. G abbr. of *Eimbockbier* f. *Einbeck* in Hanover]

bod /bod/ *n.* **1** *colloq.* a person's physique. **2** *Brit. colloq.* a person. [abbr. of BODY]

bode /bōd/ *v.* **1** *tr.* portend; foreshow. **2** *tr.* foresee; foretell (evil). □ **bode well** (or **ill**) show good (or bad) signs for the future. □□ **bod•ing** *n.* [OE *bodian* f. *boda* messenger]

bo•de•ga /bōdáygǝ/ *n.* **1** a grocery store in a Spanish-speaking neighborhood. **2** a wineshop. [Sp. f. L *apotheca* f. Gk *apothēkē* storehouse]

bo•dhi•satt•va /bódisútvǝ/ *n.* in Mahayana Buddhism, one who is able to reach nirvana but delays doing so through compassion for suffering beings. [Skr., = one whose essence is perfect knowledge]

bod•ice /bódis/ *n.* **1** the part of a woman's dress above the waist. **2** a woman's vest, esp. a laced vest worn as an outer garment. [orig. *pair of bodies* = stays, corsets]

bod•i•less /bódeelis/ *adj.* **1** lacking a body. **2** incorporeal; insubstantial.

bod•i•ly /bód'lee/ *adj. & adv.* ● *adj.* of or concerning the body. ● *adv.* **1** with the whole bulk; as a whole (*threw them bodily*). **2** in the body; as a person.

bod•kin /bódkin/ *n.* **1** a blunt thick needle with a large eye used esp. for drawing tape, etc., through a hem. **2** a long pin for fastening hair. **3** a small pointed instrument for piercing cloth, removing a piece of type for correction, etc. [ME perh. f. Celt.]

bodice

bod•y /bódee/ *n. & v.* ● *n.* (*pl.* **•ies**) **1** the physical structure, including the bones, flesh, and organs, of a person or an animal, whether dead or alive. **2** the trunk apart from the head and the limbs. **3 a** the main or central part of a thing (*body of the car; body of the attack*). **b** the bulk or majority; the aggregate (*body of opinion*). **4 a** a group of persons regarded collectively, esp. as having a corporate function (*governing body*). **b** (usu. foll. by *of*) a collection (*body of facts*). **5** a quantity (*body of water*). **6** a piece of matter (*heavenly body*). **7** *colloq.* a person. **8** a full or substantial quality of flavor, tone, etc., e.g., in wine, musical sounds, etc. ● *v.tr.* (**•ies, •ied**) (usu. foll. by *forth*) give body or substance to. □ **in a body** all together. **keep body and soul together** keep alive, esp. barely. **over my dead body** *colloq.* entirely without my assent. □□ **–bod•ied** *adj.* (in *comb.*) (*able-bodied*). [OE *bodig*, of unkn. orig.]

CHOOSING THE RIGHT WORD body

CADAVER, CARCASS, CORPSE, CREMAINS, REMAINS. The problem of what to call the human **body** after it has departed this life is a delicate one. Although a *body* can be either dead or alive, human or animal, a **corpse** is most definitely a dead human body and a **carcass** is the body of a dead animal. The issue has been confused, of course, by the figurative use of *carcass* as a term of contempt (*"Get your carcass out of bed and come down here!"*). While *carcass* is often used humorously, there's nothing funny about *corpse*, a no-nonsense term for a lifeless physical body (*the battlefield was littered with corpses*). A funeral director is likely to prefer the term **remains**, which is a euphemism for the body of the deceased (*he had his wife's remains shipped home for burial*), or **cremains**, if the body has been cremated. A medical student, on the other hand, is much more likely to use the term **cadaver**, which is a corpse that is dissected in a laboratory for scientific study.

bod•y blow *n.* **1** *Boxing* a blow to the body, esp. the upper torso. **2** a severe setback.

bod•y•build•ing /bódeebílding/ *n.* the practice of strengthening the body, esp. shaping and enlarging the muscles, by exercise.

bod•y check /bódeechek/ *n. & v.* ● *n.* *Sports* a deliberate obstruction of one player by another. ● *v.* (also **bodycheck**) obstruct or impede another player with one's own body.

bod•y clock *n.* an internal biological mechanism that is thought to regulate one's circadian rhythms.

bod•y Eng•lish *n.* a twisting or other movement of one's body in an attempt to control the path of an object, as a ball, that one has thrown, kicked, etc.

bod•y•guard /bódeegaard/ *n.* a person or group of persons escorting and protecting another person (esp. a dignitary).

bod•y lan•guage *n.* the process of communicating through conscious or unconscious gestures and poses.

bod•y o•dor *n.* the smell of the human body, esp. when unpleasant.

bod•y pol•i•tic *n.* the nation or government as a corporate body.

bod•y shop *n.* a workshop where repairs to the bodies of vehicles are carried out.

bod•y stock•ing *n.* a woman's one-piece undergarment which covers the torso and legs.

bod•y•suit /bódeesoot/ *n.* a close-fitting one-piece stretch garment for women that covers the torso.

bod•y•work /bódeewǝrk/ *n.* **1** the outer shell of a vehicle. **2** the repairing of automobile bodies.

Boer /bōr, bawr/ *n. & adj.* ● *n.* a South African of Dutch descent. ● *adj.* of or relating to the Boers. [Du.: see BOOR]

bof•fin /bófin/ *n.* esp. *Brit. colloq.* a person engaged in scientific (esp. military) research. [20th c.: orig. unkn.]

Bo•fors gun /bófǝrz/ *n.* a type of light antiaircraft gun. [*Bofors* in Sweden]

bog /bog, bawg/ *n. & v.* ● *n.* **1 a** a wet spongy ground. **b** a stretch of

See page xx for the **Key to Pronunciation**.

such ground. **2** *Brit. sl.* a toilet. • *v.tr.* (**bogged, bog•ging**) (foll. by *down*; usu. in *passive*) impede (*was bogged down by difficulties*). □□ **bog•gy** *adj.* (**bog•gi•er, bog•gi•est**). **bog•gi•ness** *n.* [Ir. or Gael. *bogach* f. *bog* soft]

bo•gey[1] /bṓgee/ *n. & v. Golf* • *n.* (*pl.* **•geys**) **1** a score of one stroke more than par at any hole. **2** esp. *Brit.* (formerly) a score that a good player should do a hole or course in; par. • *v.tr.* (**•geys, •geyed**) play (a hole) in one stroke more than par. [perh. f. *Bogey* as an imaginary player]

bo•gey[2] /bṓgee/ *n.* (also **bo•gy**) (*pl.* **•geys** or **•gies**) **1** an evil or mischievous spirit; a devil. **2** an awkward thing or circumstance. **3** *Brit. sl.* a piece of dried nasal mucus. [19th c., orig. as a proper name: cf. BOGLE]

bo•gey[3] /bṓgee/ *n. & v.* (also **bo•gie**) *Austral.* • *n.* a swim or bathe; a bath. • *v.intr.* swim; bathe. [Dharuk *bugi* to bathe or dive]

bo•gey•man /bŏŏgeeman, bṓgee-, bŏŏgee-/ *n.* (also **bo•gy•man, boog•ey•man, boog•ie•man**) (*pl.* **•men**) a person (real or imaginary) causing fear or difficulty.

PRONUNCIATION TIP bogeyman

This word is spelled in various ways: *bogeyman, bogyman, boogeyman, boogyman, boogieman, boogerman,* and *buggerman.* Pronunciation options include BO-gee-man, BOO-gee-man, and BUH-gee-man. The form *boogerman* is more popular in the Southern United States, while *boogeyman* prevails in other parts of the country.

bog•gle /bógəl/ *v.intr. colloq.* **1** be startled or baffled (esp. the mind boggles). **2** (usu. foll. by *about, at*) hesitate; demur. [prob. f. dial. *boggle* BOGEY[2]]

bo•gie /bṓgee/ *n.* esp. *Brit.* **1** a wheeled undercarriage pivoted below the end of a rail vehicle. **2** a small cart used for carrying coal, rubble, etc. [19th-c. north. dial. word: orig. unkn.]

bo•gle /bógəl/ *n.* **1** = BOGEY[2]. **2** a phantom. **3** a scarecrow. [orig. Sc. (16th c.), prob. rel. to BOGEY[2]]

bog myr•tle *n.* a deciduous shrub, *Myrica gale,* which grows in damp open places and has short upright catkins and aromatic gray-green leaves. Also called **sweet gale.**

bog oak *n.* ancient oak that has been preserved in peat bogs.

bog spav•in *n.* a soft swelling of the joint capsule of the hock of horses.

bo•gus /bṓgəs/ *adj.* sham; fictitious; spurious. □□ **bo•gus•ly** *adv.* **bo•gus•ness** *n.* [19th-c. US word: orig. unkn.]

bo•gy var. of BOGEY[2].

bo•gy•man var. of BOGEYMAN.

bo•hea /bōhée/ *n.* a black tea, the last crop of the season and usu. regarded as of low quality. [*Bu-i* (Wuyi) Hills in China]

Bo•he•mi•an /bōhéemeeən/ *n. & adj.* • *n.* **1** a native of Bohemia, a former kingdom in central Europe corresponding to part of the modern Czech Republic; Czech. **2** (**bohemian**) a socially unconventional person, esp. an artist or writer. • *adj.* **1** of, relating to, or characteristic of Bohemia or its people. **2** socially unconventional. □□ **bo•he•mi•an•ism** *n.* (in sense 2). [*Bohemia* + -AN: sense 2 f. F *bohémien* gypsy]

boil[1] /boyl/ *v. & n.* • *v.* **1** *intr.* **a** (of a liquid) start to bubble up and turn into vapor; reach a temperature at which this happens. **b** (of a vessel) contain boiling liquid (*the kettle is boiling*). **2 a** *tr.* bring (a liquid or vessel) to a temperature at which it boils. **b** *tr.* cook (food) by boiling. **c** *intr.* (of food) be cooked by boiling. **d** *tr.* subject to the heat of boiling water, e.g., to clean. **3** *intr.* **a** (of the sea, etc.) undulate or seethe like boiling water. **b** (of a person or feelings) be greatly agitated, esp. by anger. **c** *colloq.* (of a person or the weather) be very hot. • *n.* the act or process of boiling; boiling point (*at a boil*). □ **boil down 1** reduce volume by boiling. **2** reduce to essentials. **3** (foll. by *to*) amount to; signify basically. **boil over 1** spill over in boiling. **2** lose one's temper; become overexcited. **make one's blood boil** see BLOOD. [ME f. AF *boiller,* OF *boillir,* f. L *bullire* to bubble f. *bulla* bubble]

boil[2] /boyl/ *n.* an inflamed pus-filled swelling caused by infection of a hair follicle, etc. [OE *bȳl(e)* f. WG]

boiled shirt *n.* a dress shirt with a starched front.

boiled sweet *n. Brit.* a candy made of boiled sugar.

boil•er /bóylər/ *n.* **1** a fuel-burning apparatus for heating a hot water supply. **2** a tank for heating water, esp. for turning it to steam under pressure. **3** *Brit.* a metal tub for boiling laundry, etc. **4** a fowl, vegetable, etc., suitable for cooking only by boiling.

boil•er room *n.* a room with a boiler and other heating equipment, esp. in the basement of a large building.

boil•er suit *n. Brit.* a one-piece suit worn as overalls for heavy manual work.

boil•ing /bóyling/ *adj.* (also **boil•ing hot**) *colloq.* very hot.

boil•ing point /bóyling poynt/ *n.* **1** the temperature at which a liquid starts to boil. **2** high excitement (*feelings reached boiling point*).

bois•ter•ous /bóystərəs/ *adj.* **1** (of a person) rough; noisily exuberant. **2** (of the sea, weather, etc.) stormy; rough. □□ **bois•ter•ous•ly** *adv.* **bois•ter•ous•ness** *n.* [var. of ME *boist(u)ous,* of unkn. orig.]

bok choy /bok chóy/ *n.* a Chinese vegetable resembling cabbage. [f. Chin. *baahk-choi* white cabbage]

bo•ko /bṓkō/ *n. & adj. Austral.* • *n.* an animal or person who is blind in one eye. • *adj.* blind. [perh. f. an Aboriginal language]

bo•las /bṓləs/ *n.* (as *sing.* or *pl.*) (esp. in S. America) a missile consisting of a number of balls connected by strong cord, which when thrown entangles the limbs of the quarry. [Sp. & Port., pl. of *bola* ball]

bold /bōld/ *adj.* **1** confidently assertive; adventurous; courageous. **2** forthright; impudent. **3** vivid; distinct; well-marked (*bold colors; a bold imagination*). **4** *Printing* (in full **boldface** or **–faced**) printed in a thick black typeface. □ **as bold as brass** excessively bold or self-assured. **make** (or **be**) **so bold as to** presume to; venture to. □□ **bold•ly** *adv.* **bold•ness** *n.* [OE *bald* dangerous f. Gmc]

SYNONYM TIP bold

AGGRESSIVE, AUDACIOUS, BUMPTIOUS, BRAZEN, INTREPID, PRESUMPTUOUS. Is walking up to an attractive stranger and asking him or her to have dinner with you tonight a **bold** move or merely an **aggressive** one? Both words suggest assertive, confident behavior that is a little on the shameless side, but *bold* has a wider range of application. It can suggest self-confidence that borders on impudence (*to be so bold as to call the president by his first name*), but it can also be used to describe a daring temperament that is either courageous or defiant (*a bold investigator who would not give up*). *Aggressive* behavior, on the other hand, usually falls within a narrower range, somewhere between menacing (*aggressive attacks on innocent villagers*) and just plain pushy (*an aggressive salesperson*). **Brazen** implies a defiant lack of modesty (*a brazen stare*), and **presumptuous** goes even further, suggesting over-confidence to the point of causing offense (*a presumptuous request for money*). **Bumptious** behavior can also be offensive, but it is usually associated with the kind of cockiness that can't be helped (*a bumptious young upstart*). An **audacious** individual is bold to the point of recklessness (*an audacious explorer*), which brings it very close in meaning to **intrepid**, suggesting fearlessness in the face of the unknown (*intrepid enough to marry someone she'd only known for a week*).

bole[1] /bōl/ *n.* the stem or trunk of a tree. [ME f. ON *bolr,* perh. rel. to BALK]

bole[2] /bōl/ *n.* fine compact earthy clay. [LL BOLUS]

bo•le•ro /bōláirō, bə–/ *n.* (*pl.* **•ros**) **1 a** a Spanish dance in simple triple time. **b** music for or in the time of a bolero. **2** a woman's short open jacket. [Sp.]

boll /bōl/ *n.* a rounded capsule containing seeds, esp. flax or cotton. [ME f. MDu. *bolle:* see BOWL[1]]

bol•lard /bólərd/ *n.* **1** a short post on a wharf or ship for securing a rope. **2** *Brit.* a short metal, concrete, or plastic post in the road, esp. as part of a traffic island. [ME perh. f. ON *bolr* BOLE[1] + –ARD]

bol•lock•ing /bóləking/ *n. Brit. coarse sl.* a severe reprimand.

bol•locks /bóləks/ *n.* (also **bal•locks**) *Brit. coarse sl.* **1** the testicles. **2** (usu. as an exclam. of contempt) nonsense; rubbish. [OE *beallluc,* rel. to BALL[1]]

▶Usually considered a taboo word.

bol•lock•y /bóləkee/ *adj. Austral. sl.* naked.

boll wee•vil *n.* a small American or Mexican weevil, *Anthonomus grandis,* whose larvae destroy cotton bolls.

bo•lo•gna /bəlṓnee, –nyə/ *n.* a large smoked sausage made of beef, veal, pork, and other meats, and sold ready for eating. [*Bologna* in Italy]

bo•lom•e•ter /bōlómitər/ *n.* a sensitive electrical instrument for measuring radiant energy. □□ **bo•lom•e•try** *n.* **bo•lo•met•ric** /bōləmétrik/ *adj.* [Gk *bolē* ray + –METER]

bo•lo•ney var. of BALONEY.

Bol•she•vik /bólshəvik, ból–/ *n. & adj.* • *n.* **1** *hist.* a member of the radical faction of the Russian Social Democratic party, which became the Communist party in 1918. **2** a Russian communist. **3** (in general use) any revolutionary socialist. • *adj.* **1** of, relating to, or characteristic of the Bolsheviks. **2** communist. □□ **Bol•she•vism** *n.* **Bol•she•vist** *n.* [Russ., = a member of the majority, from the fact that this faction formed the majority group of the Russian Social Democratic party in 1903, f. *bol'she* greater]

Bol•shie /bólshee/ *adj. & n.* (also *Brit.* **Bol•shy**) *sl.* • *adj.* (usu. **bolshie**) **1** uncooperative; rebellious; awkward; bad-tempered. **2** left-wing; socialist. • *n.* (*pl.* **•shies**) a Bolshevik. □□ **bolshiness** *n.* (in sense 1 of *adj.*). [abbr.]

bol•ster[1] /bólstər/ *n. & v.* • *n.* **1** a long thick pillow. **2** a pad or support, esp. in a machine. **3** *Building* a short timber cap over a post to increase the bearing of the beams it supports. • *v.tr.* (usu. foll. by *up*) **1** encourage; reinforce (*bolstered our morale*). **2** support with a bolster; prop up. □□ **bol•ster•er** *n.* [OE f. Gmc]

bol•ster[2] /bólstər/ *n.* a chisel for cutting bricks. [20th c.: orig. uncert.]

bolt[1] /bōlt/ *n., v., & adv.* • *n.* **1** a sliding bar and socket used to fasten or lock a door, gate, etc. **2** a large usu. metal pin with a head, usu. riveted or used with a nut, to hold things together. **3** a discharge of lightning. **4** an act of bolting (cf. sense 4 of *v.*); a sudden escape or dash for freedom. **5** *hist.* an arrow for shooting from a crossbow. **6** a roll of fabric, wallpaper, etc. (orig. as a measure). ● *v.* **1** *tr.* fasten or lock with a bolt. **2** *tr.* (foll. by *in, out*) keep (a person, etc.) from leaving or entering by bolting a door. **3** *tr.* fasten together with bolts. **4** *intr.* **a** dash suddenly away, esp. to escape. **b** (of a horse) suddenly gallop out of control. **5** *tr.* gulp down (food) unchewed; eat hurriedly. **6** *intr.* (of a plant) run to seed. ● *adv.* (usu. in **bolt upright**) rigidly; stiffly. □ **a bolt from the blue** a complete surprise. **shoot one's bolt** do all that is in one's power. □□ **bolt** *n.* (in sense 4 of *v.*). [OE *bolt* arrow]

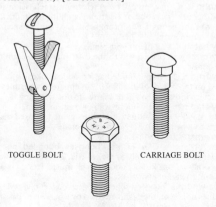

TOGGLE BOLT　　　CARRIAGE BOLT

HEX-HEAD BOLT

bolt¹ 2

bolt² /bōlt/ *v.tr.* sift (flour, etc.). □□ **bolt·er** *n.* [ME f. OF *bulter, buleter,* of unkn. orig.]

bolt-hole *n.* esp. *Brit.* **1** a place of escape, esp. a hole in the ground into which a pursued animal can flee. **2** a secret refuge.

bo·lus /bṓləs/ *n.* (*pl.* **bo·lus·es**) **1** a soft ball, esp. of chewed food. **2** a large pill. [LL f. Gk *bōlos* clod]

bomb /bom/ *n. & v.* ● *n.* **1 a** a container with explosive, incendiary material, smoke, gas, etc., designed to explode on impact or by means of a time mechanism, remote-control device, or lit fuse. **b** an ordinary object fitted with an explosive device (*letter bomb*). **2** (prec. by *the*) the atomic or hydrogen bomb considered as a weapon with supreme destructive power. **3** a small pressurized container that sprays liquid, foam, or gas (*an aerosol bomb*). **4** a mass of solidified lava thrown from a volcano. **5** *colloq.* a failure (esp. a theatrical one). **6** *sl.* an old car. **7** *Football* a long forward pass. **8** *Brit. sl.* a drugged cigarette. **9** *Brit. sl.* a large sum of money (*cost a bomb*). ● *v.* **1** *tr.* attack with bombs; drop bombs on. **2** *tr.* (foll. by *out*) drive (a person, etc.) out of a building or refuge by using bombs. **3** *intr.* throw or drop bombs. **4** *intr. sl.* fail badly. **5** *intr. colloq.* move or go very quickly. **6** *tr. sl.* criticize fiercely. □ **go down a bomb** *Brit. colloq.,* often *iron.* be very well received. **like a bomb** *Brit. colloq.* **1** often *iron.* very successfully. **2** very fast. [F *bombe* f. It. *bomba* f. L *bombus* f. Gk *bombos* hum]

bom·bard /bombärd/ *v.tr.* **1** attack with a number of heavy guns or bombs. **2** (often foll. by *with*) subject to persistent questioning, abuse, etc. **3** *Physics* direct a stream of high-speed particles at (a substance). □□ **bom·bard·ment** *n.* [F *bombarder* f. *bombarde* f. med.L *bombarda* a stone throwing engine: see BOMB]

bom·bar·dier /bómbərdeér/ *n.* **1** a member of a bomber crew responsible for sighting and releasing bombs. **2** *Brit.* a noncommissioned officer in the artillery. [F (as BOMBARD)]

bom·bar·don /bombáardən, bómbərdən/ *n. Mus.* **1** a type of valved bass tuba. **2** an organ stop imitating this. [It. *bombardone* f. *bombardo* bassoon]

bom·ba·sine var. of BOMBAZINE.

bom·bast /bómbast/ *n.* pompous or extravagant language. □□ **bom·bas·tic** /-bástik/ *adj.* **bom·bas·ti·cal·ly** *adv.* [earlier *bombace* cotton wool f. F f. med.L *bombax –acis* alt. f. *bombyx*; see BOMBAZINE]

Bom·bay duck /bómbay dúk/ *n.* a dried fish, esp. bummalo, usu. eaten in Indian cuisine with curried dishes. [corrupt. of *bombil:* see BUMMALO]

bom·ba·zine /bómbəze´en/ *n.* (also **bom·ba·sine**) a twilled dress material of worsted with or without an admixture of silk or cotton, esp., when black, formerly used for mourning. [F *bombasin* f. med.L *bombacinum* f. LL *bombycinus* silken f. *bombyx –ycis* silk or silkworm f. Gk *bombux*]

bomb bay *n.* a compartment in an aircraft used to hold bombs.

bombe /boᴎb/ *n. Cooking* a round or dome-shaped dish or confection, often frozen. [F, = BOMB]

bomb·er /bómər/ *n.* **1** an aircraft equipped to carry and drop bombs. **2** a person using bombs, esp. illegally.

bomb·er jack·et *n.* a short esp. leather jacket tightly gathered at the waist and cuffs.

bomb·bor·a /bombáwrə/ *n. Austral.* a dangerous sea area where waves break over a submerged reef. [Aboriginal]

bomb·proof /bómprōōf/ *adj.* strong enough to resist the effects of blast from a bomb.

bomb·shell /bómshel/ *n.* **1** an overwhelming surprise or disappointment. **2** an artillery bomb. **3** *sl.* a very attractive woman (*blonde bombshell*).

bomb·sight /bómsīt/ *n. Brit.* a device in an aircraft for aiming bombs.

bo·na fide /bṓnə fīd, fīdee, bónə/ *adj. & adv.* ● *adj.* genuine; sincere. ● *adv.* genuinely; sincerely. [L, ablat. sing. of BONA FIDES]

bo·na fi·des /bónaa feédes, fideez, bónə/ *n.* (*esp.* for 2) bṓnə fīdz/ *n.* **1** esp. *Law* an honest intention; sincerity. **2** (as *pl.*) *colloq.* documentary evidence of acceptability (*his bona fides are in order*). [L, = good faith]

bo·nan·za /bənánzə/ *n.* **1** a source of wealth or prosperity. **2** a large output (esp. of a mine). **3** **a** prosperity; good luck. **b** a run of good luck. [orig. US f. Sp., = fair weather, f. L *bonus* good]

bon·bon /bónbon/ *n.* a piece of confectionery; a candy, esp. with a chocolate or fondant coating. [F f. *bon* good f. L *bonus*]

bonce /bons/ *n. Brit.* **1** *sl.* the head. **2** a large playing marble. [19th c.: orig. unkn.]

bond /bond/ *n. & v.* ● *n.* **1 a** a thing that ties another down or together. **b** (usu. in *pl.*) a thing restraining bodily freedom (*broke his bonds*). **2** (often in *pl.*) **a** a uniting force (*sisterly bond*). **b** a restraint; a responsibility (*bonds of duty*). **3** a binding engagement; an agreement (*his word is his bond*). **4** *Commerce* a certificate issued by a government or a public company promising to repay borrowed money at a fixed rate of interest at a specified time; a debenture. **5** adhesiveness. **6** *Law* a deed by which a person is bound to make payment to another. **7** *Chem.* linkage between atoms in a molecule or a solid. **8** *Building* the laying of bricks in one of various patterns in a wall in order to ensure strength (*English bond; Flemish bond*). ● *v.* **1** *tr.* **a** lay (bricks) overlapping. **b** bind together (resin with fibers, etc.). **2** *intr.* adhere; hold together. **3** *tr.* connect with a bond. **4** *tr.* place (goods) in bond. **5** *intr.* become emotionally attached. □ **in bond** (of goods) stored until the importer pays the duty owing. [ME var. of BAND¹]

bond·age /bóndij/ *n.* **1** serfdom; slavery. **2** subjection to constraint, influence, obligation, etc. **3** sadomasochistic practices, including the use of physical restraints or mental enslavement. [ME f. AL *bondagium*: infl. by BOND]

bond·ed /bóndid/ *adj.* **1** (of goods) placed in bond. **2** (of material) reinforced by or cemented to another. **3** (of a debt) secured by bonds.

bond·ed ware·house *n.* a government-controlled warehouse for the retention of imported goods until the duty owed is paid.

bon·di /bóndi/ *n. Austral.* a heavy club with a knob on the end. □ **give a person bondi** attack savagely. [Wiradhuri *bundi*]

bond pa·per *n.* high-quality writing paper.

bonds·man /bóndzmən/ *n.* (also **bond·man**) (*pl.* **·men**) **1** a slave. **2** a person in thrall to another. [var. of *bondman* (f. archaic *bond* in serfdom or slavery) as though f. *bond's* genitive of BOND]

bone /bōn/ *n. & v.* ● *n.* **1** any of the pieces of hard tissue making up the skeleton in vertebrates. **2** (in *pl.*) **a** the skeleton, esp. as remains after death. **b** the body, esp. as a seat of intuitive feeling (*felt it in my bones*). **3 a** the material of which bones consist. **b** a similar substance such as ivory, dentine, or whalebone. **4** a thing made of bone. **5** (in *pl.*) the essential part of a thing (*the bare bones*). **6** (in *pl.*) **a** dice. **b** flat bone or wood clappers held between the fingers and used as a simple rhythm instrument. **7** a strip of stiffening in a corset, etc. ● *v.* **1** *tr.* take out the bones from (meat or fish). **2** *tr.* stiffen (a garment) with bone, etc. □ **bone up** (often foll. by *on*) *colloq.* study (a subject) intensively. **close to** (or **near**) **the bone 1** tactless to the point of offensiveness. **2** destitute; hard up. **have a bone to pick** (usu. foll. by *with*) have a cause for dispute (with another person). **make no bones about 1** admit or allow without fuss. **2** hesitate or scruple. **point the bone** (usu. foll. by *at*) *Austral.* **1** wish bad luck on. **2** cast a spell on in order to kill. **to the bone 1** to the bare minimum. **2** penetratingly. **work one's fingers to the bone** work very hard, esp. thanklessly. □□ **bone·less** *adj.* [OE *bān* f. Gmc]

bone chi·na *n.* fine china made of clay mixed with the ash from bones.

bone-dry *adj.* very dry.

bone of con·ten·tion *n.* a subject or issue over which there is continuing disagreement.

bone spav·in *n.* osteoarthritis of the hock in horses, which may cause swelling and lameness.

bone tired *adj.* extremely weary.

bone·fish /bónfish/ *n.* any of several species of large game fish, esp. *Albula vulpes*, having many small bones.

bone·head /bónhed/ *n. sl.* a stupid person. □□ **bone·head·ed** *adj.*

bone·meal /bónmeel/ *n.* crushed or ground bones used esp. as a fertilizer.

bon·er /bónǝr/ *n. sl.* a stupid mistake. [BONE + -ER¹]

bone·set·ter /bónsetǝr/ *n.* a person who sets broken or dislocated bones, esp. without being a qualified physician.

bon·fire /bónfīr/ *n.* a large open-air fire for burning trash, as part of a celebration, or as a signal. □ **make a bonfire of** destroy by burning. [earlier *bonefire* f. BONE (bones being the chief material formerly used) + FIRE]

Bon·fire Night *n. Brit.* Nov. 5, on which fireworks are displayed and an effigy of Guy Fawkes burned (see GUY¹).

bong /bong, bawng/ *n.* a water pipe for smoking marijuana or the like. [Thai *bhaung*]

bon·go¹ /bónggō/ *n.* (*pl.* **·gos** or **·goes**) either of a pair of small connected drums usu. held between the knees and played with the fingers. [Amer. Sp. *bongó*]

bon·go² /bónggō/ *n.* (*pl.* same or **·gos**) a rare antelope, *Tragelaphus euryceros*, native to the forests of central Africa, having spiraled horns and a chestnut-red coat with narrow white vertical stripes. [cf. Bangi *mbangani*, Lingala *mongu*]

bongos

bon·ho·mie /bónomee/ *n.* geniality; good-natured friendliness. [F f. *bonhomme* good fellow]

bon·ho·mous /bónǝmǝs/ *adj.* full of bonhomie.

bo·ni·to /bǝneétō/ *n.* (*pl.* **·tos**) any of several fish similar to the tuna and striped like mackerel. [Sp.]

bonk /bongk/ *v. & n.* ● *v.* **1** *tr.* hit resoundingly. **2** *intr.* bang; bump. **3** *Brit. coarse sl.* **a** *intr.* have sexual intercourse. **b** *tr.* have sexual intercourse with. ● *n.* an instance of bonking (*a bonk on the head*). □□ **bonk·er** *n.* [imit.: cf. BANG, BUMP, CONK²]

bon·kers /bóngkǝrz/ *adj. sl.* crazy. [20th c.: orig. unkn.]

bon mot /bawN mó/ *n.* (*pl.* **bons mots** *pronunc.* same or /–móz/) a witty saying. [F]

bon·net /bónit/ *n.* **1 a** a woman's or child's hat tied under the chin and usu. with a brim framing the face. **b** a soft round brimless hat like a beret worn by men and boys in Scotland (cf. TAM-O'-SHANTER). **c** *colloq.* any hat. **2** *Brit.* a hinged cover over the engine of a motor vehicle; a hood. **3** the ceremonial feathered headdress of a Native American. **4** the cowl of a chimney, etc. **5** a protective cap in various machines. **6** *Naut.* additional canvas laced to the foot of a sail. □□ **bon·net·ed** *adj.* [ME f. OF *bonet* short for *chapel de bonet* cap of some kind of material (med.L *bonetus*)]

bon·net·head /bónit-hed/ *n.* = SHOVELHEAD.

bon·net mon·key *n.* an Indian macaque, *Macaca radiata*, with a bonnetlike tuft of hair.

bon·ny /bónee/ *adj.* (**bon·ni·er, bon·ni·est**) esp. *Sc. & No. of Engl.* **1 a** physically attractive. **b** healthy looking. **2** good; fine; pleasant. □□ **bon·ni·ly** *adv.* **bon·ni·ness** *n.* [16th c.: perh. f. F *bon* good]

bon·sai /bónsī, –zī/ *n.* (*pl.* same) **1** the art of cultivating ornamental artificially dwarfed varieties of trees and shrubs. **2** a tree or shrub grown by this method. [Jap.]

bon·spiel /bónspeel/ *n.* a curling competition, usu. between two teams. [16th c.: perh. f. LG]

bon·te·bok /bónteebuk/ *n.* (also **bont·bok** /bóntbuk/) (*pl.* same or **·boks**) a large chestnut antelope, *Damaliscus dorcas*, native to southern Africa, having a white tail and a white patch on its head and rump. [Afrik. f. *bont* spotted + *bok* BUCK¹]

bo·nus /bónǝs/ *n.* **1** an unsought or unexpected extra benefit. **2 a** a usu. seasonal gratuity to employees beyond their normal pay. **b** an extra dividend or issue paid to the shareholders of a company. [L *bonus, bonum* good (thing)]

bon vi·vant /báwN veevaáN/ *n.* (*pl.* **bon vi·vants** or **bons vi·vants** *pronunc.* same) a person indulging in good living; a gourmand. [F, lit. good liver f. *vivre* to live]

bon vo·yage /báwN vwaayaázh/ *int. & n.* an expression of good wishes to a departing traveler. [F]

bon·y /bónee/ *adj.* (**bon·i·er, bon·i·est**) **1** (of a person) thin with prominent bones. **2** having many bones. **3** of or like bone. **4** (of a fish) having bones rather than cartilage. □□ **bon·i·ness** *n.*

bonze /bonz/ *n.* a Japanese or Chinese Buddhist monk. [F *bonze* or Port. *bonzo* perh. f. Jap. *bonzō* f. Chin. *fanseng* religious person, or f. Jap. *bō–zi* f. Chin. *fasi* teacher of the law]

bon·zer /bónzǝr/ *adj. Austral. sl.* excellent; first-rate. [perh. f. BONANZA]

boo /boo/ *int., n., & v.* ● *int.* **1** an expression of disapproval or contempt. **2** a sound, made esp. to a child, intended to surprise. ● *n.*

an utterance of *boo,* esp. as an expression of disapproval or contempt made to a performer, etc. ● *v.* (**boos, booed**) **1** *intr.* utter a boo or boos. **2** *tr.* jeer at (a performer, etc.) by booing. □ **can't (or wouldn't) say boo to a goose** is very shy or timid. [imit.]

boob¹ /boob/ *n. sl.* **1** a simpleton. **2** an embarrassing mistake. [abbr. of BOOBY]

boob² /boob/ *n. sl.* a woman's breast. [earlier *bubby, booby,* of uncert. orig.]

boo·boo /bóoboo/ *n. sl.* **1** a mistake. **2** (esp. by or to a child) a minor injury. [BOOB¹]

boo·book /bóobook/ *n. Austral.* a brown spotted owl, *Ninox novaeseelandiae,* native to Australia and New Zealand. [imit. of its call]

boob tube *n. sl.* (usu. prec. by *the*) television; a television set.

boo·by /bóobee/ *n.* (*pl.* **·bies**) **1** a stupid or childish person. **2** a small gannet of the genus *Sula.* [prob. f. Sp. *bobo* (in both senses) f. L *balbus* stammering]

boo·by hatch *n. sl.* a mental hospital.

boo·by prize *n.* a prize given to the least successful competitor in any contest.

boo·by trap *n.* **1** a trap intended as a practical joke, e.g., an object placed on top of a door ajar. **2** *Mil.* an apparently harmless explosive device intended to kill or injure anyone touching it.

boo·by-trap *v.tr.* place a booby trap or traps in or on.

boo·dle /bóod'l/ *n. sl.* money, esp. when gained or used dishonestly, e.g., as a bribe. [Du. *boedel* possessions]

boog·ey·man var. of BOGEYMAN.

boog·ie /bóogee/ *v. & n.* ● *v.intr.* (**boog·ies, boog·ied, boog·y·ing**) *sl.* **1** dance enthusiastically to rock music. **2** leave, esp. quickly. ● *n.* **1** = BOOGIE-WOOGIE. **2** *sl.* a dance to rock music. [BOOGIE-WOOGIE]

boog·ie·man var. of BOGEYMAN.

boog·ie-woog·ie /bóogeewóogee, bóogeewóogee/ *n.* a style of playing blues or jazz on the piano, marked by a persistent bass rhythm. [20th c.: orig. unkn.]

book /book/ *n. & v.* ● *n.* **1 a** a written or printed work consisting of pages glued or sewn together along one side and bound in covers. **b** a literary composition intended for publication (*is working on her book*). **2** a bound set of blank sheets for writing or keeping records in. **3** a set of tickets, stamps, matches, checks, samples of cloth, etc., bound up together. **4** (in *pl.*) a set of records or accounts. **5** a main division of a literary work, or of the Bible (*the Book of Deuteronomy*). **6 a** a libretto, script of a play, etc. **b** a set of rules or regulations. **7** *colloq.* a magazine. **8** a telephone directory (*my number's in the book*). **9** a record of bets made and money paid out at a racetrack by a bookmaker. **10** a set of six tricks collected together in a card game. **11 a** an imaginary record or list (*the book of life*). **b** a source of information or knowledge. ● *v.* **1** *tr.* **a** engage (a seat, etc.) in advance; make a reservation for. **b** engage (a guest, supporter, musical act, etc.) for some occasion. **2** *tr.* **a** take the personal details of (esp. a criminal offender). **b** enter in a book or list. **3** *tr.* issue an airline, etc., ticket to. **4** *intr.* make a reservation (*no need to book*). □ **book in** esp. *Brit.* register one's arrival at a hotel, etc. **book up 1** *Brit.* buy tickets in advance for a theater, concert, vacation, etc. **2** (as **booked up**) with all places reserved. **bring to book** call to account. **go by the book** proceed according to the rules. **in a person's bad (or good) books** in disfavor (or favor) with a person. **know (or read) like a book** know or read (someone or something) completely. **in my book** in my opinion. **make book** take bets and pay out winnings on a race, game, etc. **not in the book** disallowed. **off the books** (of business) conducted on a cash basis, without keeping accounting records. **one for the books** an event worthy of being recorded. **on the books** contained in a list of members, etc. **suits my book** *Brit.* is convenient to me. **take a leaf out of a person's book** imitate a person. **throw the book at** *colloq.* charge or punish to the utmost. [OE *bōc, bōcian,* f. Gmc, usu. taken to be rel. to BEECH (the bark of which was used for writing on)]

book·bind·er /bóokbīndǝr/ *n.* a person who binds books professionally. □□ **book·bind·ing** *n.*

book·case /bóok-kays/ *n.* a set of shelves for books in the form of a cabinet.

book club *n.* an organization that sells selected books to its members usu. through the mail and at a discounted price.

book·end /bóokend/ *n.* a usu. ornamental prop used to keep a row of books upright.

book·ie /bóokee/ *n. colloq.* = BOOKMAKER.

book·ing /bóoking/ *n.* the act or an instance of booking or reserving a seat, a room in a hotel, etc.; a reservation (see BOOK *v.* 1).

book·ing clerk *n. Brit.* an official selling tickets at a railroad station.

book·ish /bóokish/ *adj.* **1** studious; fond of reading. **2** acquiring knowledge from books rather than practical experience. **3** (of a word, language, etc.) literary; not colloquial. □□ **book·ish·ly** *adv.* **book·ish·ness** *n.*

book·keep·er /bóok-keepǝr/ *n.* a person who keeps accounts for a business, etc. □□ **book·keep·ing** *n.*

book learn·ing *n.* theory, as opposed to practical knowledge.

book·let /bóoklit/ *n.* a small book consisting of a few sheets, usu. with paper covers.

book•mak•er /bŏŏkmaykər/ *n.* a person who takes bets, esp. on horse races, calculates odds, and pays out winnings. □□ **book•mak•ing** *n.*

book•man /bŏŏkmən/ *n.* (*pl.* **-men**) a literary person, esp. one involved in the business of books.

book•mark /bŏŏkmaark/ *n.* (also **book•mark•er**) a strip of leather, cardboard, etc., used to mark one's place in a book.

book•mo•bile /bŏŏkmōbēel/ *n.* a mobile library. [after AUTOMOBILE]

book•plate /bŏŏkplayt/ *n.* a decorative label stuck in the front of a book bearing the owner's name.

book•sell•er /bŏŏkselər/ *n.* a dealer in books.

book•store /bŏŏkstawr/ *n.* a store where books are sold.

books•y /bŏŏksee/ *adj.* *Brit.* *colloq.* having literary or bookish pretensions.

book val•ue *n.* the value of a commodity as entered in a company's books (cf. MARKET VALUE).

book•work /bŏŏkwərk/ *n.* the study of books (as opposed to practical work).

book•worm /bŏŏkwərm/ *n.* **1** *colloq.* a person devoted to reading. **2** the larva of a moth or beetle which feeds on the paper and glue used in books.

Bool•e•an /bŏŏleeən/ *adj.* denoting a system of algebraic notation to represent logical propositions. [G. *Boole*, Engl. mathematician d. 1864]

Bool•e•an al•ge•bra *n.* an algebraic system applied to symbolic logic and computer operations.

Bool•e•an log•ic *n.* the use of the logical operators 'and,' 'or,' and 'not' in retrieving information from a computer database.

boom[1] /bŏŏm/ *n. & v.* ●*n.* a deep resonant sound. ●*v.intr.* make or speak with a boom. [imit.]

boom[2] /bŏŏm/ *n. & v.* ●*n.* a period of prosperity or sudden activity in commerce, etc. ●*v.intr.* (esp. of commerce, etc.) be suddenly prosperous or successful. □□ **boom•let** *n.* [19th-c. US word, perhaps f. BOOM[1] (cf. *make things hum*)]

boom[3] /bŏŏm/ *n.* **1** *Naut.* a pivoted spar to which the foot of a sail is attached, allowing the angle of the sail to be changed. **2** a long pole over a movie or television stage set, carrying microphones and other equipment. **3** a floating barrier across the mouth of a harbor or river, or enclosing an oil spill. [Du., = BEAM *n.*]

boom box *n.* *sl.* a large, powerful portable radio, often with a cassette and/or CD player.

boom•er /bŏŏmər/ *n.* **1** a transient construction worker, esp. a bridge builder. **2** a N. American mountain beaver, *Aplodontia rufa*. **3** a large male kangaroo. **4** a large wave.

boo•mer•ang /bŏŏmərang/ *n. & v.* ●*n.* **1** a curved flat hardwood missile orig. used by Australian Aboriginals to kill prey, and often of a kind able to return in flight to the thrower. **2** a plan or scheme that recoils on its originator. ●*v.intr.* **1** act as a boomerang. **2** (of a plan or action) backfire. [Aboriginal name, perh. modified]

boom•slang /bŏŏmslang/ *n.* a large venomous tree snake, *Dispholidus typus*, native to southern Africa. [Afrik. f. *boom* tree + *slang* snake]

boom town *n.* a town undergoing sudden growth due to a boom.

boon[1] /bŏŏn/ *n.* **1** an advantage; a blessing. **2 a** a thing asked for; a request. **b** a gift; a favor. [ME, orig. = prayer, f. ON *bón* f. Gmc]

boon[2] /bŏŏn/ *adj.* close; intimate; favorite (usu. *boon companion*). [ME (orig. = jolly, congenial) f. OF *bon* f. L *bonus* good]

boon•docks /bŏŏndoks/ *n.* *sl.* rough, remote, or isolated country. [Tagalog *bundok* mountain]

boon•dog•gle /bŏŏndogəl, –daw–/ *n. & v.* ●*n.* **1** work or activity that is wasteful or pointless but gives the appearance of having value. **2** a public project of questionable merit that typically involves political patronage and graft. ●*v.intr.* participate in a boondoggle. [f. *boondoggle*, a braided leather cord worn by Boy Scouts]

boong /bŏŏng/ *n.* *Austral.* *sl.* *offens.* an Aborigine. [orig. uncert.]

boon•ies /bŏŏneez/ *n.pl.* (prec. by *the*) *sl.* = BOONDOCKS.

boor /bŏŏr/ *n.* **1** a rude, unmannerly person. **2** a clumsy person. **3** a peasant; a yokel. □□ **boor•ish** *adj.* **boor•ish•ly** *adv.* **boor•ish•ness** *n.* [LG *būr* or Du. *boer* farmer]

boost /bŏŏst/ *v. & n.* *colloq.* ●*v.tr.* **1 a** promote or increase the reputation of (a person, scheme, commodity, etc.) by praise or advertising; push; increase or assist (*boosted his spirits*; *boosted sales*). **b** push from below; assist (*boosted me up into the tree*). **2 a** raise the voltage of (an electric circuit, etc.). **b** amplify (a radio signal). ●*n.* **1** an act, process, or result of boosting; a push (*asked for a boost up the hill*). **2 a** *Brit.* an advertising campaign. **b** the resulting advance in value, reputation, etc. [19th-c. US word: orig. unkn.]

boost•er /bŏŏstər/ *n.* **1** a device for increasing electrical power or voltage. **2** an auxiliary engine or rocket used to give initial acceleration. **3** (also **boost•er shot**) *Med.* a dose of an immunizing agent increasing or renewing the effect of an earlier one. **4** *colloq.* a person who boosts by helping or encouraging.

boost•er ca•bles *n.* = JUMPER CABLES.

boot[1] /bŏŏt/ *n. & v.* ●*n.* **1** an outer covering for the foot, esp. of leather, rubber, etc., reaching above the ankle, often to the knee. **2** a covering or sheath to protect a mechanical connection, etc. **3** *colloq.* a firm kick. **4** (prec. by *the*) *colloq.* dismissal, esp. (*Brit.*) from employment (*gave them the boot*). **5** *Mil.* a navy or marine recruit. **6** (also **Den•ver Boot**) a device attached to the wheel of a parked car that makes it immobile; used by police against those who park illegally, ignore fines, etc. **7** *hist.* an instrument of torture encasing and crushing the foot. **8** *Brit.* the luggage compartment of an automobile; the trunk. ●*v.tr.* **1** kick, esp. hard. **2** (often foll. by *out*) dismiss (a person) forcefully. **3** (usu. foll. by *up*) put (a computer) in a state of readiness (cf. BOOTSTRAP 2). □ **die with one's boots on** (of a soldier, etc.) die fighting. **you bet your boots** *sl.* it is quite certain. □□ **boot•ed** *adj.* [ME f. ON *bóti* or f. OF *bote*, of unkn. orig.]

boot[2] /bŏŏt/ *n.* □ **to boot** as well; to the good; in addition. [orig. = 'advantage': OE *bōt* f. Gmc]

boot•black /bŏŏtblak/ *n.* a person who polishes boots and shoes.

boot camp *n.* *Mil.* a camp for training navy or marine recruits.

boot•ee /bŏŏtee/ *n.* (also **boot•ie**) **1** a soft shoe worn by a baby. **2** a woman's short boot.

booth /bŏŏth/ *n.* (*pl.* **booths** /bŏŏthz, bŏŏths/) **1** a small temporary roofed structure of canvas, wood, etc., used esp. for the sale or display of goods at a market, fair, etc. **2** an enclosure or compartment for various purposes, e.g., telephoning, broadcasting, or voting. **3** a set of a table and benches in a restaurant or bar. [ME f. Scand.]

boot•jack /bŏŏtjak/ *n.* a device for holding a boot by the heel to ease withdrawal of the leg.

boot•lace /bŏŏtlays/ *n.* **1** a cord or leather thong for lacing boots. **2** *Brit.* = SHOELACE.

boot•leg /bŏŏtleg/ *adj. & v.* ●*adj.* (esp. of liquor) smuggled; illicitly sold. ●*v.tr.* (•**legged**, •**leg•ging**) make, distribute, or smuggle (illicit goods, esp. alcohol, computer software, etc.). □□ **boot•leg•ger** *n.* [f. the smugglers' practice of concealing bottles in their boots]

boot•less /bŏŏtlis/ *adj.* unavailing; useless. [OE *bōtlēas* (as BOOT[2], LESS)]

boot•lick•er /bŏŏtlikər/ *n.* *colloq.* a person who behaves obsequiously or servilely; a toady. □□ **boot•lick** *v.intr.* **boot•lick•ing** *n. & adj.*

boots /bŏŏts/ *n.* *Brit.* a hotel employee who cleans boots and shoes, carries luggage, etc.

boot•strap /bŏŏtstrap/ *n.* **1** a loop at the back of a boot used to pull it on. **2** *Computing* a technique of loading a program into a computer by means of a few initial instructions which enable the introduction of the rest of the program from an input device. □ **pull oneself up by one's bootstraps** better oneself by one's own efforts.

boo•ty /bŏŏtee/ *n.* **1** plunder gained esp. in war or by piracy. **2** *colloq.* something gained or won. [ME f. MLG *būte, buite* exchange, of uncert. orig.]

booze /bŏŏz/ *n. & v.* *colloq.* ●*n.* **1** alcohol, esp. hard liquor. **2** the drinking of this (*on the booze*). ●*v.intr.* drink alcohol esp. excessively or habitually. [earlier *bouse, bowse*, f. MDu. *būsen* drink to excess]

booz•er /bŏŏzər/ *n.* *colloq.* **1** a person who drinks alcohol, esp. to excess. **2** *Brit.* a place for drinking; a tavern or bar.

booze-up *n.* esp. *Brit.* *sl.* a drinking bout; a spree.

booz•y /bŏŏzee/ *adj.* (**booz•i•er, booz•i•est**) *colloq.* intoxicated; addicted to drink. □□ **booz•i•ly** *adv.* **booz•i•ness** *n.*

bop[1] /bop/ *n. & v.* *colloq.* ●*n.* **1** = BEBOP. **2** *Brit.* **a** an interval of dancing, esp. to pop music. **b** an organized social occasion for this. ●*v.intr.* (**bopped, bop•ping**) *Brit.* dance, esp. to pop music. □□ **bop•per** *n.* [abbr. of BEBOP]

bop[2] /bop/ *v. & n.* *colloq.* ●*v.tr.* (**bopped, bop•ping**) hit; punch lightly. ●*n.* a light blow or hit. [imit.]

bo-peep /bōpeep/ *n.* = PEEKABOO. [*bo* BOO + *peep*[1]]

bor. *abbr.* borough.

bo•ra[1] /báwrə/ *n.* a strong cold dry NE wind blowing in the upper Adriatic. [It. dial. f. L *boreas* north wind: see BOREAL]

bo•ra[2] /báwrə/ *n.* *Austral.* an Aboriginal rite in which boys are initiated into manhood. [Aboriginal]

bo•rac•ic /bərásik/ *adj.* of borax; containing boron. [med.L *borax –acis*]

bo•rac•ic ac•id *n.* = BORIC ACID.

bor•age /báwrij, bór–/ *n.* any plant of the genus *Borago*, esp. *Borago officinalis*, native to Europe, with bright blue flowers and leaves used as flavoring. [OF *bourrache* f. med.L *borrago* f. Arab. '*abu* '*āraḳ* father of sweat (from its use as a diaphoretic)]

bor•ak /báwrak/ *n.* *Austral.* & *NZ* *sl.* banter; ridicule; nonsense. □ **poke borak at** make fun of. [Aboriginal Austral.]

bo•rane /báwrayn/ *n.* *Chem.* any hydride of boron.

bo•rate /báwrayt/ *n.* a salt or ester of boric acid.

bo•rax /báwraks/ *n.* **1** the mineral salt sodium borate, occurring in alkaline deposits as an efflorescence or as crystals. **2** the purified

boomerang, 1

form of this salt, used in making glass and china, and as an antiseptic. [ME f. OF *boras* f. med.L *borax* f. Arab. *būraḳ* f. Pers. *būrah*]

Bo·ra·zon /báwrəzon/ *n. Trademark* a hard form of boron nitride, resistant to oxidation. [BORON + AZO- nitrogen + *–on*]

bor·bo·ryg·mus /báwrbərígməs/ *n.* (*pl.* **bor·bo·ryg·mi** /–mī/) a rumbling of gas in the intestines. □□ **bor·bo·ryg·mic** *adj.* [mod.L f. Gk]

Bor·deaux /bawrdó/ *n.* (*pl.* same /–dóz/) any of various red, white, or rosé wines from the district of Bordeaux in SW France.

Bor·deaux mix·ture *n.* a fungicide for vines, fruit trees, etc., composed of equal quantities of copper sulfate and calcium oxide in water.

bor·del·lo /bawrdélō/ *n.* (*pl.* **·los**) a brothel. [ME (f. It. *bordello*) f. OF *bordel* small farm, dimin. of *borde* ult. f. Frank.: see BOARD]

bor·der /báwrdər/ *n. & v.* ● *n.* **1** the edge or boundary of anything, or the part near it. **2 a** the line separating two political or geographical areas, esp. countries. **b** the district on each side of this. **3** a distinct edging around anything, esp. for strength or decoration. **4** a long narrow bed of flowers or shrubs in a garden (*herbaceous border*). ● *v.* **1** *tr.* be on or along a border. **2** *tr.* provide with a border. **3** *intr.* (usu. foll. by *on, upon*) **a** adjoin; come close to being. **b** approximate; resemble. [ME f. OF *bordure*: cf. BOARD]

SYNONYM TIP border

BRIM, BRINK, EDGE, MARGIN, RIM, VERGE. A **border** is the part of a surface that is nearest to its boundary (*a rug with a flowered border*)—although it may also refer to the boundary line itself (*the border between Vermont and New Hampshire*). A **margin** is a *border* of a definite width that is usually distinct in appearance from what it encloses; but unlike *border*, it usually refers to the blankness or emptiness that surrounds something (*the margin on a printed page*). While *border* and *margin* usually refer to something that is circumscribed, **edge** may refer to only a part of the perimeter (*the edge of the lawn*) or the line where two planes or surfaces converge (*the edge of the table*). *Edge* can also connote sharpness (*the edge of a knife*) and can be used metaphorically to suggest tension, harshness, or keenness (*there was an edge in her voice; take the edge off their nervousness*). **Verge** may also be used metaphorically to describe the extreme limit of something (*on the verge of a nervous breakdown*), but in a more literal sense, it sometimes is used of the line or narrow space that marks the limit or termination of something (*the verge of a desert or forest*). **Brink** denotes the edge of something very steep or an abrupt division between land and water (*the brink of the river*), or metaphorically the very final limit before an abrupt change (*on the brink of disaster*). **Rim** and **brim** apply only to things that are circular or curving. But while *rim* describes the edge or lip of a rounded or cylindrical shape (*the rim of a glass*), *brim* refers to the inner side of the rim when the container is completely full (*a cup filled to the brim with steaming coffee*). However, when one speaks of the *brim* of a hat, it comes closer to the meaning of *margin* or *border*.

Bor·der col·lie *n.* a common working sheepdog of British origin.

bord·er·er /báwrdərər/ *n.* a person who lives near a border.

bord·er·land /báwrdərland/ *n.* **1 a** the district near a border. **b** the fringes. **2** an intermediate condition between two extremes. **3** an area for debate.

bord·er·line /báwrdərlīn/ *n. & adj.* ● *n.* **1** the line dividing two (often extreme) conditions. **2** a line marking a boundary. ● *adj.* **1** on the borderline. **2** verging on an extreme condition; only just acceptable.

Bord·er ter·ri·er *n.* **1** a small terrier of a breed with rough hair. **2** this breed.

bor·dure /báwrjər/ *n. Heraldry* a border round the edge of a shield. [ME form of BORDER]

bore[1] /bawr/ *v. & n.* ● *v.* **1** *tr.* make a hole in, esp. with a revolving tool. **2** *tr.* hollow out (a tube, etc.). **3** *tr.* **a** make (a hole) by boring or excavation. **b** make (one's way) through a crowd, etc. **4** *intr.* drill a well, mine, etc. ● *n.* **1** the hollow of a firearm barrel or of a cylinder in an internal combustion engine. **2** the diameter of this; the caliber. **3** = BOREHOLE. [OE *borian* f. Gmc]

bore[2] /bawr/ *n. & v.* ● *n.* a tiresome or dull person or thing. ● *v.tr.* weary by tedious talk or dullness. □ **bore a person to tears** weary (a person) in the extreme. [18th c.: orig. unkn.]

bore[3] /bawr/ *n.* a high tidal wave rushing up a narrow estuary. *Brit.* Also called **eagre**. [ME, perh. f. ON *bára* wave]

bore[4] *past* of BEAR[1].

bo·re·al /báwreeəl/ *adj.* **1** of the north or northern regions. **2** of the north wind. [ME f. F *boréal* or LL *borealis* f. L *Boreas* f. Gk *Boreas* god of the north wind]

bore·dom /báwrdəm/ *n.* the state of being bored; ennui.

bore·hole /báwrhōl/ *n.* **1** a deep narrow hole, esp. one made in the earth to find water, oil, etc. **2** *Austral.* a water hole for cattle.

bor·er /báwrər/ *n.* **1** any of several worms, mollusks, insects, or in-

---

sect larvae which bore into wood, other plant material, or rock. **2** a tool for boring.

bo·ric /báwrik/ *adj.* of or containing boron.

bo·ric ac·id *n.* an acid derived from borax, used as a mild antiseptic and in the manufacture of heat-resistant glass and enamels.

bor·ing /báwring/ *adj.* that makes one bored; uninteresting; tedious; dull. □□ **bor·ing·ly** *adv.* **bor·ing·ness** *n.*

born /bawrn/ *adj.* **1** existing as a result of birth. **2 a** being such or likely to become such by natural ability or quality (*a born leader*). **b** (usu. foll. by *to* + infin.) having a specified destiny or prospect (*born lucky; born to lead*). **3** (in *comb.*) of a certain status by birth (-*French-born; well-born*). □ **born and bred** by birth and upbringing. **in all one's born days** *colloq.* in one's life so far. **not born yesterday** *colloq.* not stupid; shrewd. [past part. of BEAR[1]]

▶**Born** refers to birth (e.g., *born in Detroit in 1947*). **Borne**, meaning 'carried,' is used in the expression *borne by* followed by the name of the mother (e.g., *the baby borne by Sarah*), as well as in other senses (e.g., *a litter borne by slaves*).

born-a·gain *adj.* (*attrib.*) converted (esp. to fundamentalist Christianity).

borne /bawrn/ **1** *past part.* of BEAR[1]. **2** (in *comb.*) carried or transported by (*airborne*).

boro- /báwrō/ *comb. form* indicating salts containing boron.

bo·ron /báwron/ *n. Chem.* a nonmetallic yellow crystalline or brown amorphous element extracted from borax and boric acid and mainly used for hardening steel. ¶ Symb.: **B**. [BORAX + *–on* f. *carbon* (which it resembles in some respects)]

bo·ro·sil·i·cate /báwrōsílikit, –kayt/ *n.* any of many substances containing boron, silicon, and oxygen generally used in glazes and enamels and in the production of glass.

bor·ough /bórō, búrō/ *n.* **1** an incorporated municipality in certain states. **2** each of five political divisions of New York City. **3** (in Alaska) a county equivalent. **4** *Brit.* **a** a town represented in the House of Commons. **b** a town or district granted the status of a borough. **5** *Brit. hist.* a town with a municipal corporation and privileges conferred by a royal charter. [OE *burg, burh* f. Gmc: cf. BURGH]

bor·row /bórō, báwrō/ *v.* **1 a** *tr.* acquire temporarily with the promise or intention of returning. **b** *intr.* obtain money in this way. **2** *tr.* use (an idea, invention, etc.) originated by another; plagiarize. □□ **bor·row·er** *n.* **bor·row·ing** *n.* [OE *borgian* give a pledge]

bor·rowed time *n.* an unexpected extension esp. of life.

borscht /bawrsht/ *n.* (also **borsch** /bawrsh, bawrshch/) a highly seasoned Russian or Polish soup made primarily with beets and cabbage and served with sour cream. [Russ. *borshch*]

Bor·stal /báwrstəl/ *n. Brit. hist.* an institution for reforming and training juvenile delinquents. [*Borstal* in S. England, where the first of these was established]

bort /bawrt/ *n.* (also **boart**) **1** an inferior or malformed diamond, used for cutting. **2** fragments of diamonds used in cutting or abrasion. [Du. *boort*]

bor·zoi /báwrzoy/ *n.* **1** a large Russian wolfhound of a breed with a narrow head and silky, usu. white, coat. **2** this breed. [Russ. f. *borzyi* swift]

bos·cage /bóskij/ *n.* (also **bos·kage**) **1** a mass of trees or shrubs. **2** a wood or thicket. [ME f. OF *boscage* f. Gmc: cf. BUSH[1]]

bosh /bosh/ *n. & int. sl.* nonsense; foolish talk. [Turk. *boş* empty]

bosk·y /bóskee/ *adj.* (**bosk·i·er, bosk·i·est**) wooded; bushy. [ME *bosk* thicket]

bo's'n *var.* of BOATSWAIN.

bos·om /boʊzəm/ *n. & adj.* ● *n.* **1 a** a person's breast or chest, esp. a woman's. **b** *colloq.* each of a woman's breasts. **c** the enclosure formed by a person's breast and arms. **2** the seat of the emotions; an emotional center, esp. as the source of an enfolding relationship (*in the bosom of one's family*). **3** the part of a woman's dress covering the breast. ● *adj.* (esp. in **bosom friend**) close; intimate. [OE *bōsm* f. Gmc]

bos·om·y /boʊzəmee/ *adj.* (of a woman) having large breasts.

bo·son /bóson/ *n. Physics* any of several elementary particles obeying the relations stated by Bose and Einstein, with a zero or integral spin, e.g., photons (cf. FERMION). [S. N. Bose, Ind. physicist d. 1974]

boss[1] /baws/ *n. & v.* ● *n.* **1** a person in charge; an employer, manager, or overseer. **2** a person who controls or dominates a political organization. ● *v.tr.* **1** (usu. foll. by *around*) treat domineeringly; give constant peremptory orders to. **2** be the master or manager of. [orig. US: f. Du. *baas* master]

boss[2] /baws/ *n.* **1** a round knob, stud, or other protuberance, esp. in the center of a shield or in ornamental work. **2** *Archit.* a piece of ornamental carving, etc., covering the point where the ribs in a vault or ceiling cross. **3** *Geol.* a large mass of igneous rock. **4** *Mech.* an enlarged part of a shaft. [ME f. OF *boce* f. Rmc]

bos·sa no·va /bósə nóvə, báwsə/ *n.* **1** a dance like the samba, originating in Brazil. **2** a piece of music for this or in its rhythm. [Port., = new flair]

boss-eyed /báwsíd, bós–/ *adj. Brit. colloq.* **1** having only one good eye; cross-eyed. **2** crooked; out of true. [dial. *boss* miss, bungle]

boss-shot /báws-shot, bós–/ *n. Brit. dial. & sl.* **1** a bad shot or aim. **2** an unsuccessful attempt. [as BOSS-EYED]

boss•y /báwsee, bós–/ *adj.* (**boss•i•er, boss•i•est**) *colloq.* domineering; tending to boss. □□ **boss•i•ly** *adv.* **boss•i•ness** *n.*

bos•sy-boots *n. Brit. colloq.* a domineering person.

bo•sun (also **bo'sun**) *var.* of BOATSWAIN.

bot /bot/ *n.* (also **bott**) any of various parasitic larvae of flies of the family Oestridae, infesting horses, sheep, etc. [prob. of LG orig.]

bot. *abbr.* **1** bottle. **2** botanic; botanical; botany. **3** bought.

bot•a•nize /bót'niz/ *v.intr.* study plants, esp. in their habitat.

bot•a•ny /bót'nee/ *n.* **1** the study of the physiology, structure, genetics, ecology, distribution, classification, and economic importance of plants. **2** the plant life of a particular area or time. □□ **bo•tan•ic** /bətánik/ *adj.* **bo•tan•i•cal** *adj.* **bo•tan•i•cal•ly** *adv.* **bot•a•nist** /bót'nist/ *n.* [*botanic* f. F *botanique* or LL *botanicus* f. Gk *botanikos* f. *botanē* plant]

botch /boch/ *v. & n.* (also *Brit.* **bodge**) •*v.tr.* **1** bungle; do badly. **2** patch or repair clumsily. •*n.* bungled or spoiled work (*made a botch of it*). □□ **botch•er** *n.* [ME: orig. unkn.]

bot•fly /bótfli/ *n.* (*pl.* **•flies**) any dipterous fly of the genus *Oestrus*, with stout hairy bodies.

both /bōth/ *adj., pron., & adv.* •*adj. & pron.* the two; not only one (*both boys; both the boys; both of the boys; the boys are both here*). •*adv.* with equal truth in two cases (*both the boy and his sister are here; she is both here and hungry*). □ **have it both ways** alternate between two incompatible points of view to suit the needs of the moment. [ME f. ON *báthir*]

▶Avoid using **both** when you mean **each**: *Q:Would you like vanilla or chocolate? A: May I have a little of each?* (not "of both"); *Each child* (not "Both children") *claimed the toy.*

both•er /bóthər/ *v., n., & int.* **1** *tr.* **a** give trouble to; worry; disturb. **b** *refl.* be anxious or concerned. **2** *intr.* **a** (often foll. by *to* + infin.) worry or trouble oneself (*don't bother about that; didn't bother to tell me*). **b** (foll. by *with*) be concerned. •*n.* **1 a** a person or thing that bothers or causes worry. **b** a minor nuisance. **2** trouble; worry; fuss; a state of worry. •*int.* expressing annoyance or impatience. □ **cannot be bothered** will not make the effort needed. [Ir. *bodhraim* deafen]

both•er•a•tion /bóthəráyshən/ *n. & int. colloq.* = BOTHER *n., int.*

both•er•some /bóthərsəm/ *adj.* causing bother; troublesome.

both•y /bóthee, báw–/ *n.* (also **both•ie**) (*pl.* **•ies**) *Sc.* a small hut or cottage. [18th c.: orig. unkn.: perh. rel. to BOOTH]

bo-tree /bótree/ *n.* the Indian fig tree, *Ficus religiosa*, regarded as sacred by Buddhists. Also called **pipal** or **peepul**. [repr. Sinh. *bogaha* tree of knowledge (Buddha's enlightenment having occurred beneath such a tree)]

bott *var.* of BOT.

bot•tle /bót'l/ *n. & v.* •*n.* **1** a container, usu. of glass or plastic and with a narrow neck, for storing liquid. **2** the amount that will fill a bottle. **3** a container used in feeding a baby (esp. formula or milk). **4** = HOT-WATER BOTTLE. **5** *Brit. sl.* courage; confidence. •*v.tr.* **1** put

into bottles or jars. **2** (foll. by *up*) **a** conceal or restrain for a time (esp. a feeling). **b** keep (an enemy force, etc.) contained or entrapped. **3** *Brit.* preserve (fruit, etc.) in jars. **4** (as **bottled** *adj.*) *Brit. sl.* drunk. □ **hit the bottle** *sl.* drink heavily. **on the bottle** *sl.* drinking (alcohol) heavily. □□ **bot•tle•ful** *n.* (*pl.* **•fuls**). [ME f. OF *botele, botaille* f. med.L *butticula* dimin. of LL *buttis* BUTT[4]]

bot•tle bank *n. Brit.* a place where used bottles may be deposited for recycling.

bot•tle•brush /bót'lbrush/ *n.* **1** a cylindrical brush for cleaning inside bottles. **2** any of various plants with a flower of this shape.

bot•tle-feed *v.tr.* feed (a baby) with milk, formula, etc., by means of a bottle.

bot•tle green *adj.* a dark shade of green.

bot•tle•neck /bót'lnek/ *n.* **1** a point at which the flow of traffic, production, etc., is constricted. **2** a narrow place causing constriction.

bot•tle•nose /bót'lnōz/ *n.* (also **bot•tle•nosed**) a swollen nose.

bot•tle-nosed dol•phin /bót'l-nōzd/ *n.* a dolphin, *Tursiops truncatus*, with a bottle-shaped snout.

bot•tle par•ty *n.* a party to which guests bring their own (esp. alcoholic) drink.

bot•tler /bótlər/ *n.* **1** a person who bottles drinks, etc. **2** *Austral. & NZ sl.* an excellent person or thing.

bot•tle tree *n.* any of various Australian trees of the genus *Brachychiton* with a swollen bottle-shaped trunk.

bot•tom /bótəm/ *n., adj., & v.* •*n.* **1 a** the lowest point or part (*bottom of the stairs*). **b** the part on which a thing rests (*bottom of a frying pan*). **c** the underneath part (*scraped the bottom of the car*). **d** the farthest or innermost part (*bottom of the yard*). **2** *colloq.* **a** the buttocks. **b** the seat of a chair, etc. **3 a** the less honorable, important, or successful end of a table, a class, etc. (*at the bottom of the list of requirements*). **b** a person occupying this place (*he's always the bottom of the class*). **c** *Baseball* the second half of an inning. **4** the ground under the water of a lake, a river, etc. (*swam until she touched the bottom*). **5** the basis; the origin (*he's at the bottom of it*). **6** the essential character; reality. **7** *Naut.* **a** the keel or hull of a ship. **b** a ship, esp. a cargo ship. **8** staying power; endurance. •*adj.* **1** lowest (*bottom button*). **2** last (*got the bottom score*). •*v.* **1** *tr.* put a bottom on (a chair, pot, etc.). **2** *intr.* (of a ship) reach or touch the bottom. **3** *tr.* find the extent or real nature of; work out. **4** *tr.* (usu. foll. by *on*) base (an argument, etc.) (*reasoning bottomed on logic*). **5** *tr.* touch the bottom or lowest point of. □ **at bottom** basically; essentially. **be at the bottom of** have caused. **bet one's bottom dollar** *sl.* stake everything. **bottom falls out** collapse occurs. **bottom out** reach the lowest level. **bottoms up!** a call to drain one's glass. **get to the bottom of** fully investigate and explain. **knock the bottom out of** prove (a thing) worthless. □□ **bot•tom•most** /bótəm-mōst/ *adj.* [OE *botm* f. Gmc]

bot•tom dog *n.* = UNDERDOG.

bot•tom draw•er *n. Brit.* = HOPE CHEST.

bot•tom•less /bótəmlis/ *adj.* **1** without a bottom. **2** (of a supply, etc.) inexhaustible.

bot•tom line *n. colloq.* the underlying or ultimate truth; the ultimate, esp. financial, criterion.

bot•u•lism /bóchəlizəm/ *n.* poisoning caused by a toxin produced by the bacillus *Clostridium botulinum* growing in spoiled food. [G *Botulismus* f. L *botulus* sausage]

bou•clé /bōōkláy/ *n.* **1** a looped or curled yarn (esp. wool). **2** a fabric, esp. knitted, made of this. [F, = buckled, curled]

bou•doir /bōōdwaar/ *n.* a woman's private room or bedroom. [F, lit. sulking place f. *bouder* sulk]

bouf•fant /bōōfaant/ *adj.* (of a dress, hair, etc.) puffed out. [F]

bou•gain•vil•le•a /bōōgənvílyə, –véeə/ *n.* (also **bou•gain•vil•la•ea**) any plant widely cultivated plant of the genus *Bougainvillaea*, with large colored bracts (usu. purple, red, or cream) almost concealing the inconspicuous flowers. [L. A. de *Bougainville*, Fr. navigator d. 1811]

bough /bow/ *n.* a branch of a tree, esp. a main one. [OE *bōg, bōh* f. Gmc]

bought *past* and *past part.* of BUY.

bought•en /báwt'n/ *adj. dial.* bought at a store; not homemade. [var. of past part. of BUY]

bou•gie /bōōzhee/ *n.* **1** *Med.* a thin flexible surgical instrument for exploring, dilating, etc. the passages of the body. **2** a wax candle. [F f. Arab. *Bujiya* Algerian town with a wax trade]

bouil•la•baisse /bōōyəbés, bōōlyəbáys/ *n. Cooking* a rich, spicy fish stew, orig. from Provence. [F]

bouil•lon /bōōlyən, –yon, bōōyóN/ *n.* a clear soup; broth. [F f. *bouillir* to boil]

boul•der /bóldər/ *n.* a large stone worn smooth by erosion. [short for *boulderstone*, ME f. Scand.]

boul•der clay *n. Geol.* a mixture of boulders, etc., formed by depo-

CHAMPAGNE   BORDEAUX   BURGUNDY   CHIANTI ("fiasco")

PORT   RHINE   ALSACE   CÔTES DE PROVENCE

bottle shapes for wine

See page xx for the **Key to Pronunciation.**

sition from massive bodies of melting ice, to give distinctive glacial formations.

boule[1] /bool/ *n.* (also **boules** *pronunc.* same) a French form of lawn bowling, played on rough ground with usu. metal balls. [F, = BOWL[2]]

boule[2] /boolee/ *n.* a legislative body of an ancient Greek city or of modern Greece. [Gk *boulē* senate]

boule[3] var. of BUHL.

boules var. of BOULE[1].

boul·e·vard /boolavaard/ *n.* **1** a broad tree-lined avenue. **2** a broad main road. [F f. G *Bollwerk* BULWARK, orig. of a promenade on a demolished fortification]

boulle var. of BUHL.

boult var. of BOLT[2].

bounce /bowns/ *v. & n.* ●*v.* **1 a** *intr.* (of a ball, etc.) rebound. **b** *tr.* cause to rebound. **c** *tr. & intr.* bounce repeatedly. **2** *intr. sl.* (of a check) be returned by a bank when there are insufficient funds to meet it. **3** *intr.* **a** (foll. by *about*, *up*) (of a person, dog, etc.) jump or spring energetically. **b** (foll. by *in*, *out*, etc.) rush noisily, angrily, enthusiastically, etc. (*bounced into the room*; *bounced out in a temper*). **4** *tr. colloq.* (usu. foll. by *into* + verbal noun) hustle; persuade (*bounced him into signing*). **5** *intr. colloq.* talk boastfully. **6** *tr. sl.* eject forcibly (from a dancehall, club, etc.). ●*n.* **1 a** a rebound. **b** the power of rebounding (*this ball has a good bounce*). **2** *colloq.* **a** swagger; self-confidence (*has a lot of bounce*). **b** liveliness. **c** resilience. **3** *sl.* (often prec. by *the*) dismissal or ejection. □ **bounce back** regain one's good health, spirits, prosperity, etc. [ME *bunsen* beat, thump, (perh. imit.), or f. LG *bunsen*, Du. *bons* thump]

bounc·er /bównsər/ *n.* **1** *sl.* a person employed to eject troublemakers from a dancehall, club, etc. **2** *Cricket* = BUMPER.

bounc·ing /bównsing/ *adj.* **1** (esp. of a baby) big and healthy. **2** boisterous.

bounc·y /bównsee/ *adj.* (**bounc·i·er**, **bounc·i·est**) **1** (of a ball, etc.) that bounces well. **2** cheerful and lively. **3** resilient; springy (*a bouncy sofa*). □□ **bounc·i·ly** *adv.* **bounc·i·ness** *n.*

bound[1] /bownd/ *v. & n.* ●*v.intr.* **1 a** spring; leap (*bounded out of bed*). **b** walk or run with leaping strides. **2** (of a ball, etc.) recoil from a wall or the ground; bounce. ●*n.* **1** a springy movement upward or outward; a leap. **2** a bounce. □ **by leaps and bounds** see LEAP. [F *bond*, *bondir* (orig. of sound) f. LL *bombitare* f. L *bombus* hum]

bound[2] /bownd/ *n. & v.* ●*n.* (usu. in *pl.*) **1** a limitation; a restriction (*beyond the bounds of possibility*). **2** a border of a territory; a boundary. ●*v.tr.* **1** (esp. in *passive*; foll. by *by*) set bounds to; limit (*views bounded by prejudice*). **2** be the boundary of. □ **out of bounds 1 a** outside the part of a school, etc., in which one is allowed to be. **b** *Sports* outside the limits of the court, field, etc. (*the ball was out of bounds*). **2** beyond what is acceptable; forbidden. [ME f. AF *bounde*, OF *bonde*, etc., f. med.L *bodina*, earlier *butina*, of unkn. orig.]

bound[3] /bownd/ *adj.* **1** (usu. foll. by *for*) ready to start or having started (*bound for stardom*). **2** (in *comb.*) moving in a specified direction (*northbound*; *outward bound*). [ME f. ON *búinn* past part. of *búa* get ready: *-d* euphonic, or partly after BIND]

bound[4] /bownd/ *past* and *past part.* of BIND. □ **bound to** certain to (*he's bound to come*).

bound·a·ry /bówndəree, -dree/ *n.* (*pl.* **-ries**) a real or notional line marking the limits of an area, territory, etc.; the limit itself or the area near it (*the fence is the boundary*; *boundary between liberty and license*). [dial. *bounder* f. BOUND[2] + -ER[1] perh. after *limitary*]

bound·a·ry lay·er *n.* *Physics* the fluid immediately surrounding an object that is immersed and moving.

bound·a·ry rid·er *n.* *Austral. & NZ* a person employed to ride around the fences, etc., of a cattle or sheep station and keep them in good order.

bound·en /bówndən/ *adj. archaic* obligatory. [archaic past part. of BIND]

bound·en du·ty *n.* solemn responsibility.

bound·er /bówndər/ *n. Brit. colloq.* or *joc.* a cad; an ill-bred person.

bound·less /bówndlis/ *adj.* unlimited; immense (*boundless enthusiasm*). □□ **bound·less·ly** *adv.* **bound·less·ness** *n.*

boun·te·ous /bównteeəs/ *adj. poet.* **1** generous; liberal. **2** freely given (*bounteous affection*). □□ **boun·te·ous·ly** *adv.* **boun·te·ous·ness** *n.* [ME f. OF *bontif* f. *bonté* BOUNTY after *plenteous*]

boun·ti·ful /bówntifool/ *adj.* **1** = BOUNTEOUS. **2** ample. □□ **boun·ti·ful·ly** *adv.* [BOUNTY + -FUL]

boun·ty /bówntee/ *n.* (*pl.* **-ties**) **1** liberality; generosity. **2** a gift or reward, made usu. by a government, esp.: **a** a sum paid for capturing an outlaw, killing destructive wild animals, etc. **b** a sum paid to encourage a business, etc. **c** a sum paid to army or navy recruits on enlistment. [ME f. OF *bonté* f. L *bonitas* *-tatis* f. *bonus* good]

boun·ty hunt·er *n.* a person who pursues a criminal or seeks an achievement for the sake of the reward.

bou·quet /bookáy, bō-/ *n.* **1** a bunch of flowers, esp. for carrying at a wedding or other ceremony. **2** the scent of wine, etc. **3** a favorable comment; a compliment. [F f. dial. var. of OF *bos*, *bois* wood]

This word was borrowed from French in the 18th century. When used to refer to a bunch of flowers, it can be pronounced as either "bo-KAY" or "boo-KAY" in American English. When referring to an aroma (of wine, for example), it is usually pronounced "boo-KAY."

bou·quet gar·ni *n.* /gaarneé/ *Cooking* a bunch of herbs used for flavoring stews, etc.

bour·bon /bárbən/ *n.* whiskey distilled from corn and rye. [*Bourbon* County, Kentucky, where it was first made]

Bour·bon /boórbən, boobáwN/ *n.* a reactionary, esp. a conservative Southern Democrat. [the Bourbon family, whose descendants founded dynasties in France and Spain]

bour·don /boórdən/ *n. Mus.* **1** a low-pitched stop in an organ, etc. **2** the lowest bell in a peal of bells. **3** the drone pipe of a bagpipe. [F, = bagpipe drone, f. Rmc, imit.]

bour·geois /boorzhwaá/ *adj. & n.* often *derog.* ●*adj.* **1 a** conventionally middle class. **b** humdrum; unimaginative. **c** selfishly materialistic. **2** upholding the interests of the capitalist class; noncommunist. ●*n.* a bourgeois person. [F: see BURGESS]

bour·geoi·sie /boorzhwaazeé/ *n.* **1** the capitalist class. **2** the middle class. [F]

bourn[1] /bawrn, boórn/ *n.* (also **bourne**) a small stream. [ME: S. Engl. var. of BURN[2]]

bourn[2] /bawrn, boórn/ *n.* (also **bourne**) *archaic* **1** a goal; a destination. **2** a limit. [F *borne* f. OF *bodne* BOUND[2]]

bour·rée /booráy/ *n.* **1** a lively French dance like a gavotte. **2** the music for this dance. [F]

bourse /boors/ *n.* **1** a stock exchange, esp. on the European continent. **2** a money market. [F, = purse, f. med.L *bursa*: cf. PURSE]

bou·stro·phe·don /boóstrəfeéd'n, bów-/ *adj. & adv.* (of written words) from right to left and from left to right in alternate lines. [Gk (adv.) = as an ox turns in plowing f. *bous* ox + *-strophos* turning]

bout /bowt/ *n.* (often foll. by *of*) **1 a** a limited period (of intensive work or exercise). **b** a drinking session. **c** a period (of illness) (*a bout of flu*). **2 a** a wrestling or boxing match. **b** a trial of strength. [16th c.: app. the same as obs. *bought* bending]

bou·tique /booteék/ *n.* a small shop or department of a store, esp. one selling fashionable clothes or accessories. [F, = small shop, f. L (as BODEGA)]

bou·ton·niere /boótəneér, -tənyáir/ *n.* (also **bou·ton·nière**) a spray of flowers worn in a buttonhole. [F]

bou·zou·ki /boozoökee/ *n.* a Greek form of mandolin. [mod. Gk]

bo·vate /bóvayt/ *n. hist.* a measure of land, as much as one ox could plow in a year, varying from 10 to 18 acres. [med.L *bovata* f. L *bos bovis* ox]

bo·vine /bóvīn, -veen/ *adj.* **1** of or relating to cattle. **2** stupid; dull. □□ **bo·vine·ly** *adv.* [LL *bovinus* f. L *bos bovis* ox]

bov·ver /bóvər/ *n. Brit. sl.* deliberate troublemaking. [cockney pronunc. of BOTHER]

bow[1] /bō/ *n. & v.* ●*n.* **1 a** a slipknot with a double loop. **b** a ribbon, shoelace, etc., tied with this. **c** a decoration (on clothing, or painted, etc.) in the form of a bow. **2** a device for shooting arrows with a taut string joining the ends of a curved piece of wood, etc. **3 a** a rod with horsehair stretched along its length, used for playing the violin, cello, etc. **b** a single stroke of a bow across the strings. **4 a** a shallow curve or bend. **b** a rainbow. **5** = SADDLEBOW. **6** a metal ring forming the handle of scissors, a key, etc. **7** the sidepiece of an eyeglass frame. **8** *Archery* = BOWMAN[1]. ●*v.tr.* (also *absol.*) use a bow on (a violin, etc.) (*he bowed vigorously*). [OE *boga* f. Gmc: cf. BOW[2]]

bow[2] /bow/ *v. & n.* ●*v.* **1** *intr.* incline the head or trunk, esp. in greeting or assent or acknowledgment of applause. **2** *intr.* submit (*bowed to the inevitable*). **3** *tr.* cause to incline or submit (*bowed his head*; *bowed his will to hers*). **4** *tr.* express (thanks, assent, etc.) by bowing (*bowed agreement to the plan*). **5** *tr.* (foll. by *in*, *out*) usher or escort obsequiously (*bowed us out of the restaurant*). ●*n.* an inclining of the head or body in greeting, assent, or in the acknowledgment of applause, etc. □ **bow and scrape** be obsequious; fawn. **bow down 1** bend or kneel in submission or reverence (*bowed down before the king*). **2** (usu. in *passive*) make stoop; crush (*was bowed down by care*). **bow out 1** make one's exit (esp. formally). **2** retreat; withdraw; retire gracefully. **make one's bow** make a formal exit or entrance. **take a bow** acknowledge applause. [OE *būgan*, f. Gmc: cf. BOW[1]]

bow[3] /bow/ *n. Naut.* **1** the forward end of a boat or ship. **2** = BOWMAN[2]. □ **on the bow** within 45° of the point directly ahead. **a shot across the bows** a warning. [LG *boog*, Du. *boeg*, ship's bow, orig. shoulder: see BOUGH]

bow com·pass *n.* (also **bow com·pass·es**) a compass with jointed legs.

bowd·ler·ize /bówdlərīz/ *v.tr.* expurgate (a book, etc.). □□ **bowd·ler·ism** *n.* **bowd·ler·i·za·tion** /-rizáyshən/ *n.* [T. *Bowdler* (d. 1825), expurgator of Shakespeare.]

bow·el /bówəl/ *n.* **1** the part of the alimentary canal below the stomach; the intestine. **2** (in *pl.*) the depths; the innermost parts (*the bowels of the earth*). [ME f. OF *buel* f. L *botellus* little sausage]

bow·el move·ment *n.* **1** discharge from the bowels; defecation. **2** the feces discharged from the body.

bow·er[1] /bówər/ *n.* **1 a** a secluded place, esp. in a garden, enclosed by foliage; an arbor. **b** a summer house or cottage. **2** *poet.* an inner room; a boudoir. • *v.tr. poet.* embower. □□ **bow·er·y** *adj.* [OE *būr* f. Gmc]

bow·er[2] /bówər/ *n.* (in full **bower anchor**) either of two anchors carried at a ship's bow. [BOW[3] + -ER[1]]

bow·er·bird /bówərbərd/ *n.* **1** any of various birds of the Ptilonorhyncidae family, native to Australia and New Guinea, the males of which construct elaborate bowers of feathers, grasses, shells, etc., during courtship. **2** *Brit.* a person who collects bric-à-brac.

bow·er ca·ble *n.* the cable attached to a bower anchor.

bow·er·y /bówəree, bówree/ *n.* (also **Bow·er·y**) (*pl.* **·ies**) a district known as a neighborhood of drunks and derelicts. [orig. the Bowery, a street in New York City, f. Du. *bouwerij* farm]

bow·fin /bófin/ *n.* a voracious American freshwater fish, *Amia calva*. [BOW[1] + FIN]

bow·head /bóhed/ *n.* an Arctic whale, *Balaena mysticetus*.

bow·ie /bóðee, bó–/ *n.* (in full **bowie knife**) a long knife with a blade double-edged at the point, used as a weapon by American pioneers. [J. *Bowie*, Amer. soldier d. 1836]

bowl[1] /bōl/ *n.* **1 a** a usu. round deep basin used for food or liquid. **b** the quantity (of soup, etc.) a bowl holds. **c** the contents of a bowl. **2 a** any deep-sided container shaped like a bowl (*toilet bowl*). **b** the bowl-shaped part of a tobacco pipe, spoon, balance, etc. **3 a** bowl-shaped region or building, esp. an amphitheater (*Hollywood Bowl*). **4** *Sports* a post-season football game between invited teams or as a championship. □□ **bowl·ful** *n.* (*pl.* **·fuls**). [OE *bolle, bolla,* f. Gmc]

bowl[2] /bōl/ *n. & v.* • *n.* **1 a** a wooden or hard rubber ball, slightly asymmetrical so that it runs on a curved course, used in the game of bowls. **b** a wooden ball or disk used in playing skittles. **c** *Brit.* = BOWLING BALL. **2** esp. *Brit.* (in *pl.*; usu. treated as *sing.*) **a** a game played with bowls (sense 1a) on grass; lawn bowling. **b** *Brit.* tenpin bowling. **c** *Brit.* skittles. **3** a spell or turn of bowling in cricket. • *v.* **1 a** *tr.* roll (a ball, a hoop, etc.) along the ground. **b** *intr.* play bowls or skittles. **2** *intr.* (often foll. by *along*) go along rapidly by revolving, esp. on wheels (*the cart bowled along the road*). **3** *tr.* (also *absol.*) *Cricket,* etc. **a** deliver (a ball, an over, etc.) (*bowled six overs; bowled well*). **b** (often foll. by *out*) dismiss (a batsman) by knocking down the wicket with a ball (*soon bowled him out*). **c** (often foll. by *down*) knock (a wicket, pin, etc.) over. □ **bowl over 1** knock down. **2** *colloq.* **a** impress greatly. **b** overwhelm (*bowled over by her energy*). [ME & F *boule* f. L *bulla* bubble]

bow·leg·ged /bólegid/ *adj.* having legs that curve outward at the knee.

bow·legs /bólegz/ *n.* legs that curve outward at the knee.

bowl·er[1] /bólər/ *n.* **1** a player at bowls or bowling. **2** *Cricket,* etc., a member of the fielding side who bowls or is bowling.

bowl·er[2] /bólər/ *n.* (in full **bowler hat**) a man's hard felt hat with a round dome-shaped crown. [*Bowler,* a hatter, who designed it in 1850]

bow·line /bólin/ *n. Naut.* **1** a rope attaching the weather side of a square sail to the bow. **2** a simple knot for forming a nonslipping loop at the end of a rope. [ME f. MLG *bōlīne* (as BOW[3], LINE[1])]

bowl·ing /bóling/ *n.* the games of tenpins, skittles, or bowls as a sport or recreation.

bowl·ing al·ley *n.* **1** a long, smooth, wooden lane used in bowling. **2** a building containing a number of these.

bowl·ing ball *n.* a hard ball with holes drilled in it for gripping, used in tenpin bowling.

bowl·ing crease *n. Cricket* the line from behind which a bowler delivers the ball.

bowl·ing green *n.* a lawn used for lawn bowling.

bow·man[1] /bómən/ *n.* (*pl.* **·men**) an archer.

bow·man[2] /bówmən/ *n.* (*pl.* **·men**) the rower nearest the bow of esp. a racing boat.

bow saw *n. Carpentry* a narrow saw stretched like a bowstring on a light frame.

bow·shot /bóshot/ *n.* the distance to which a bow can send an arrow.

bow·sprit /bówsprit/ *n. Naut.* a spar running out from a ship's bow to which the forestays are fastened. [ME f. Gmc (as BOW[3], SPRIT)]

Bow Street run·ner /bō/ *n.* (also **Bow Street of·fi·cer**) *hist.* a London policeman. [*Bow Street* in London, containing the chief metropolitan police court]

bow·string /bóstring/ *n. & v.* • *n.* the

bowsprit

string of an archer's bow. • *v.tr.* strangle with a bowstring (a former Turkish method of execution).

bow tie *n.* a necktie in the form of a bow (sense 1).

bow wave *n.* a wave generated at the bow of a moving ship or in front of a body moving in air, caused by the forward motion of the moving body.

bow win·dow *n.* a curved bay window.

bow-wow /bów-wów/ *int. & n.* • *int.* an imitation of a dog's bark. • *n.* **1** *colloq.* a dog. **2** a dog's bark. [imit.]

bow·yer /bó-yər/ *n.* a maker or seller of archers' bows.

box[1] /boks/ *n. & v.* • *n.* **1** a container, usu. with flat sides and of firm material such as wood or cardboard, esp. for holding solids. **2 a** the amount that will fill a box. **b** *Brit.* a gift of a kind formerly given to delivery people, etc., at Christmas. **3** a separate compartment for any of various purposes, e.g., for a small group in a theater, for witnesses in a court, for horses in a stable or vehicle. **4** an enclosure or receptacle for a special purpose (often in *comb.*: *cash box*). **5** a facility at a newspaper office for receiving replies to an advertisement. **6** (prec. by *the*) *colloq.* television; one's television set (*what's on the box?*). **7** an enclosed area or space. **8** a space or area of print on a page, enclosed by a border. **9** *Brit.* a small country house for use when shooting, fishing, or for other sporting activity. **10** a protective casing for a piece of mechanism. **11** *Brit.* a light shield for protecting the genitals in sports. **12** (prec. by *the*) *Soccer colloq.* the penalty area. **13** *Baseball* one of several areas occupied by the batter, catcher, pitcher, and first and third base coaches. **14** a coachman's seat. • *v.tr.* **1** put in or provide with a box. **2** (foll. by *in, up*) confine; restrain from movement. **3** (foll. by *up*) *Austral. & NZ* mix up (different flocks of sheep). □ **box the compass** *Naut.* recite the points of the compass in the correct order. □□ **box·ful** *n.* (*pl.* **·fuls**). **box·like** *adj.* [OE f. LL *buxis* f. L PYXIS]

box[2] /boks/ *v. & n.* • *v.* **1 a** *tr.* fight (an opponent) at boxing. **b** *intr.* practice boxing. **2** slap (esp. a person's ears). • *n.* a slap with the hand, esp. on the ears. [ME: orig. unkn.]

box[3] /boks/ *n.* **1** any small evergreen tree or shrub of the genus *Buxus,* esp. *B. sempervirens,* a slow-growing tree with glossy dark green leaves that is often used in hedging. **2** its wood, used for carving, turning, engraving, etc. **3** any of various trees in Australasia that have similar wood or foliage, esp. those of several species of *Eucalyptus*. [OE f. L *buxus,* Gk *puxos*]

Box and Cox /bóks ənd kóks/ *n. & v. Brit.* • *n.* (often *attrib.*) two persons sharing a room, apartment, etc., and using it at different times. • *v.intr.* share accommodations, duties, etc., by a strictly timed arrangement. [the names of characters in a play (1847) by J. M. Morton]

box cam·er·a *n.* a simple box-shaped hand camera.

box·car /bókskaar/ *n.* an enclosed railroad freight car, usu. with sliding doors on the sides.

box el·der *n.* the American ash-leaved maple, *Acer negundo*.

box·er /bóksər/ *n.* **1** a person who practices boxing, esp. for sport. **2 a** a medium-sized dog of a breed with a smooth brown coat and puglike face. **b** this breed.

Box·er /bóksər/ *n. hist.* a member of a fiercely nationalistic Chinese secret society that flourished in the 19th c. [transl. of Chin. *i ho chuan,* lit. 'righteous harmony fists']

boxer

box·er shorts *n.* men's loose-fitting underpants similar to shorts worn in boxing, with an elastic waist.

box gird·er *n.* a hollow girder square in cross-section.

box·ing /bóksing/ *n.* the practice of fighting with the fists as a sport, esp. with padded gloves.

Box·ing Day /bóksing/ *n.* esp. *Brit.* the first weekday after Christmas. [from the custom of giving delivery people gifts or money: see BOX[1] *n.* 2b]

box·ing glove *n.* each of a pair of heavily padded gloves used in boxing.

box kite *n.* a kite in the form of a long box open at each end.

box lunch *n.* a lunch packed in a box.

box num·ber *n.* a number by which replies are made to a private advertisement in a newspaper.

box of·fice *n.* **1** an office for booking seats and buying tickets at a theater, movie theater, etc. **2** the commercial aspect of the arts and entertainment (often *attrib.*: *a box-office failure*).

box pleat *n.* a pleat consisting of two parallel creases forming a raised band.

box·room /bóksroom, -room/ *n. Brit.* a room or large closet for storing boxes, luggage, etc.

box score *n. Sports* printed information about a game in which players for both teams are listed with statistics about their performances, as goals, assists, errors, etc.

box seat *n.* a seat in a box enclosure, as at a theater, sports arena, etc.

box spring *n.* each of a set of vertical springs housed in a frame, e.g., in a mattress.

box stall *n.* a compartment for a horse, in a stable or vehicle, in which it can move around.

box·wood /bókswŏŏd/ *n.* **1** the wood of the box used esp. by engravers for the fineness of its grain and for its hardness. **2** = BOX³ 1.

box wrench *n.* a wrench with a box-shaped end fitting over the head of a nut.

box·y /bóksee/ *adj.* (**box·i·er, box·i·est**) reminiscent of a box; (of a room or space) very cramped.

boy /boy/ *n. & int.* ● *n.* **1** a male child or youth. **2** a young man, esp. regarded as not yet mature. **3** a male servant, attendant, etc. **4** (**the boys**) *colloq.* a group of men mixing socially. ● *int.* expressing pleasure, surprise, etc. □□ **boy·hood** *n.* **boy·ish** *adj.* **boy·ish·ly** *adv.* **boy·ish·ness** *n.* [ME = servant, perh. ult. f. L *boia* fetter]

bo·yar /bō-yaár/ *n. hist.* a member of the old aristocracy in Russia. [Russ. *boyarin* grandee]

boy·cott /bóykot/ *v. & n.* ● *v.tr.* **1** combine in refusing social or commercial relations with (a person, group, country, etc.) usu. as punishment or coercion. **2** refuse to purchase or handle (goods) to this end. ● *n.* such a refusal. [Capt. C. C. *Boycott*, Irish land agent d. 1897, so treated from 1880]

boy·friend /bóyfrend/ *n.* a person's regular male companion or lover.

Boyle's law /boylz/ *n.* the law that the pressure of a given mass of gas is inversely proportional to its volume at a constant temperature. [Robert *Boyle*, Irish scientist d. 1691]

boy·o /bóyō/ *n.* (*pl.* **·os**) *Welsh & Ir. colloq.* boy; fellow (esp. as a form of address).

boy scout *n.* **1** (also **Boy Scout**) a member of an organization of boys, esp. the Boy Scouts of America, that promotes character, outdoor activities, community service, etc. **2** a boy or man who demonstrates the qualities associated with a Boy Scout.

boy·sen·ber·ry /bóyzənberee/ *n.* (*pl.* **·ries**) **1** a hybrid of several species of bramble. **2** the large red edible fruit of this plant. [R. *Boysen*, 20th-c. Amer. horticulturalist]

boys in blue *n.* esp. *Brit.* policemen.

boy toy *n.* (also esp. *Brit.* **toy boy**) *colloq.* a woman's much younger male lover.

BP *abbr.* **1** boiling point. **2** blood pressure. **3** before the present (era). **4** British Petroleum.

Bp. *abbr.* Bishop.

B.Phil. *abbr.* Bachelor of Philosophy.

bps *abbr.* (also **BPS**) *Computing* bits per second.

Br *symb. Chem.* the element bromine.

Br. *abbr.* **1** British. **2** Brother.

bra /braa/ *n.* (*pl.* **bras**) *colloq.* = BRASSIERE. [abbr.]

brace /brays/ *n. & v.* ● *n.* **1 a** a device that clamps or fastens tightly. **b** a strengthening piece of iron or lumber in building. **2** (in *pl.*) *Brit.* = SUSPENDER 1. **3** (in *pl.*) a wire device for straightening the teeth. **4** (*pl.* same) a pair (esp. of game). **5** a rope attached to the yard of a ship for trimming the sail. **6 a** a connecting mark ({ or }) used in printing. **b** *Mus.* a similar mark connecting staves to be performed at the same time. ● *v.tr.* **1** fasten tightly; give strength to. **2** make steady by supporting. **3** (esp. as **bracing** *adj.*) invigorate; refresh. **4** (often *refl.*) prepare for a difficulty, shock, etc. □□ **brac·ing·ly** *adv.* **brac·ing·ness** *n.* [ME f. OF *brace* two arms, *bracier* embrace, f. L *bra(c)chia* arms]

brace and bit *n.* a revolving tool with a D-shaped central handle for boring.

brace·let /bráyslit/ *n.* **1** an ornamental band, hoop, or chain worn on the wrist or arm. **2** *sl.* a handcuff. [ME f. OF, dimin. of *bracel* f. L *bracchiale* f. *bra(c)chium* arm]

brac·er /bráysər/ *n. colloq.* a tonic, esp. an alcoholic drink.

bra·chi·al /bráykeeəl, brák-/ *adj.* **1** of or relating to the arm (*brachial artery*). **2** like an arm. [L *brachialis* f. *bra(c)chium* arm]

bra·chi·ate /bráykeeit, -ayt, brák-/ *v. & adj.* ● *v.intr.* (of certain apes and monkeys) move by using the arms to swing from branch to branch. ● *adj. Biol.* **1** having arms. **2** having paired branches on alternate sides. □□ **bra·chi·a·tion** /-áyshən/ *n.* **bra·chi·a·tor** *n.* [L *bra(c)chium* arm]

bra·chi·o·pod /bráykeeəpod, brák-/ *n.* any marine invertebrate of the phylum Brachiopoda (esp. a

brace and bit

fossil one) having a bivalved chalky shell and a ciliated feeding arm. [mod.L f. Gk *brakhiōn* arm + *pous podos* foot]

bra·chi·o·sau·rus /bráykeeəsáwrəs, brák–/ *n.* any huge plant-eating dinosaur of the genus *Brachiosaurus* with forelegs longer than its hind legs. [mod.L f. Gk *brakhiōn* arm + *sauros* lizard]

bra·chis·to·chrone /brakístəkrōn/ *n.* a curve between two points along which a body can move in a shorter time than for any other curve. [Gk *brakhistos* shortest + *khronos* time]

brachy- /brákee/ *comb. form* short. [Gk *brakhus* short]

brach·y·ce·phal·ic /brákeesifálik/ *adj.* having a broad short head. □□ **brach·y·ceph·a·lous** /-séfələs/ *adj.* [BRACHY- + Gk *kephalē* head]

bra·chyl·o·gy /brəkílǝjee/ *n.* (*pl.* **·gies**) **1** conciseness of expression. **2** an instance of this.

brack /brak/ *n. Ir.* cake or bread containing dried fruit, etc. [abbr. of *barmbrack* f. Ir. *bairigen breac* speckled cake]

brack·en /brákən/ *n.* **1** any large coarse fern, esp. *Pteridium aquilinum*, abundant in tropical and temperate areas. **2** a mass of such ferns. Also called **brake**. [north. ME f. ON]

brack·et /brákit/ *n. & v.* ● *n.* **1** a right-angled or other support attached to and projecting from a vertical surface. **2** a shelf fixed with such a support to a wall. **3 a** each of a pair of marks [ ] (**square brackets**) or <> (**angle brackets**) used to enclose words or figures. **b** PARENTHESIS 1b. **c** BRACE 6a. **4** a group classified as containing similar elements or falling between given limits (*income bracket*). **5** *Mil.* the distance between two artillery shots fired either side of the target to establish range. ● *v.tr.* (**brack·et·ed, brack·et·ing**) **1 a** combine (names, etc.) within brackets. **b** imply a connection or equality between. **2 a** enclose in brackets as parenthetic or spurious. **b** *Math.* enclose in brackets as having specific relations to what precedes or follows. **c** include in a bracket. **3** *Mil.* establish the range of (a target) by firing two preliminary shots, one short of and the other beyond it. [F *braguette* or Sp. *bragueta* codpiece, dimin. of F *brague* f. Prov. *braga* f. L *braca*, pl. *bracae* breeches]

PUNCTUATION TIP   **brackets**

Brackets are used to set off a writer's comments, particularly within quoted material. For example: *The senator said, "It [Social Security reform] is the most pressing issue we face today."* If there is a spelling error, a questionable fact, or a misused word in a quotation, it is often followed by the Latin word *sic* (meaning 'thus') enclosed in brackets. This indicates that the writer is quoting exactly and is aware of the questionable material or mistake. For example: *He said in his note, "I am seperated [sic] from my wife and family, and nobody cares."*

---

brack·ish /brákish/ *adj.* (of water, etc.) slightly salty. □□ **brack·ish·ness** *n.* [obs. *brack* (adj.) f. MLG, MDu. *brac*]

bract /brakt/ *n.* a modified and often brightly colored leaf, with a flower or an inflorescence in its axil. □□ **brac·te·al** *adj.* **brac·te·ate** /–tee-it, –ayt/ *adj.* [L *bractea* thin plate, gold leaf]

brad /brad/ *n.* a thin flat nail with a head in the form of slight enlargement at the top. [var. of ME *brod* goad, pointed instrument, f. ON *broddr* spike]

brad·awl /brádawl/ *n.* a small tool with a pointed end for boring holes by hand. [BRAD + AWL]

brad·y·car·di·a /brádikaárdeeə/ *n. Med.* abnormally slow heart action. [Gk *bradus* slow + *kardia* heart]

brae /bray/ *n. Sc.* a steep bank or hillside. [ME f. ON *brá* eyelash]

brag /brag/ *v. & n.* ● *v.* (**bragged, brag·ging**) **1** *intr.* talk boastfully. **2** *tr.* boast about. ● *n.* **1** a card game like poker. **2** a boastful statement; boastful talk. □□ **brag·ger** *n.* **brag·ging·ly** *adv.* [ME, orig. adj., = spirited, boastful: orig. unkn.]

brag·ga·do·ci·o /brágədósheeō/ *n.* empty boasting; a boastful manner of speech and behavior. [*Braggadochio*, a braggart in Spenser's *Faerie Queene*, f. BRAG or BRAGGART + It. augment. suffix –*occio*]

brag·gart /brágǝrt/ *n. & adj.* ● *n.* a person given to bragging. ● *adj.* boastful. [F *bragard* f. *braguer* BRAG]

Brah·ma /braámə/ *n.* **1** the Hindu Creator. **2** the supreme divine reality in Hindu belief. [Skr., = creator]

Brah·man¹ /braámən/ *n.* (*pl.* **·mans**) **1** a member of the highest Hindu caste, whose members are traditionally eligible for the priesthood. **2** = BRAHMA 2. □□ **Brah·man·ic** /–mánik/ *adj.* **Brah·man·i·cal** *adj.* **Brah·man·ism** *n.* [Skr. *brāhmaṇas* f. *brahman* priest]

Brah·man² /braámən, braámən/ *n.* (also **brah·man**) a breed of humped, heat-resistant, grayish cattle developed from the Indian Zebu and common in the southern US.

brah·ma·pu·tra /braámǝpŏŏtrǝ/ *n.* (also **brah·ma**) **1** any bird of a large Asian breed of domestic fowl. **2** this breed. [*Brahmaputra* River in India, from where it was brought]

Brah•min /bráamin/ n. 1 = BRAHMAN. 2 (esp. in New England) a socially or culturally superior person. [var. of BRAHMAN]

braid /brayd/ n. & v. •n. 1 a woven band of silk or thread used for edging or trimming. 2 a length of hair, straw, etc. in three or more interlaced strands. •v.tr. 1 weave or intertwine (hair or thread). 2 trim or decorate with braid. □□ braid•er n. [OE bregdan f. Gmc]

braid•ing /bráyding/ n. 1 various types of braid collectively. 2 braided work.

Braille /brayl/ n. & v. •n. a system of writing and printing for the blind, in which characters are represented by patterns of raised dots. •v.tr. print or transcribe in Braille. [L. Braille, Fr. teacher d. 1852, its inventor]

brain /brayn/ n. & v. •n. 1 an organ of soft nervous tissue contained in the skull of vertebrates, functioning as the coordinating center of sensation and of intellectual and nervous activity. 2 (in pl.) the substance of the brain, esp. as food. 3 a a person's intellectual capacity (has a weak brain). b (often in pl.) intelligence; high intellectual capacity (has a brain; has brains). c colloq. a clever person. 4 (in pl.; prec. by the) colloq. a the cleverest person in a group. b a person who originates a complex plan or idea (the brains behind the robbery). 5 an electronic device with functions comparable to those of a brain. •v.tr. 1 dash out the brains of. 2 strike hard on the head. □ on the brain colloq. obsessively in one's thoughts. [OE brægen f. WG]

brain•child /bráynchīld/ n. (pl. •chil•dren) colloq. an idea, plan, or invention regarded as the result of a person's mental effort.

brain-dead adj. suffering from brain death.

brain death n. irreversible brain damage causing the end of independent respiration and a flat electroencephalogram, regarded as indicative of death.

brain drain n. colloq. the loss of skilled personnel by emigration.

brain fe•ver n. inflammation of the brain.

brain•less /bráynlis/ adj. stupid; foolish.

brain•pan /bráynpan/ n. colloq. the skull.

brain•pow•er /bráynpowr/ n. mental ability or intelligence.

brain stem n. the central trunk of the brain, upon which the cerebrum and cerebellum are set, and which continues downward to form the spinal cord.

brain•storm /bráynstawrm/ n. & v. •n. 1 a violent or excited outburst often as a result of a sudden mental disturbance. 2 colloq. mental confusion. 3 a brain wave. 4 a concerted intellectual treatment of a problem by discussing spontaneous ideas about it. •v.intr. 1 discuss ideas spontaneously and openly. 2 tr. discuss (an issue) in this way. □□ brain•storm•ing n. (in sense 4).

brain•teas•er /bráyntēzər/ n. (also brain•twist•er /–twístər/) colloq. a puzzle or problem.

brain trust n. a group of experts, official or unofficial, who advise on policy and strategy.

brain•wash /bráynwosh, –wawsh/ v.tr. subject (a person) to a prolonged process by which ideas other than and at variance with those already held are implanted in the mind. □□ brain•wash•ing n.

brain wave n. 1 (usu. in pl.) an electrical impulse in the brain. 2 colloq. a sudden bright idea; inspiration.

brain•y /bráynee/ adj. (brain•i•er, brain•i•est) intellectually clever or active. □□ brain•i•ly adv. brain•i•ness n.

braise /brayz/ v.tr. fry lightly and then stew slowly with a little liquid in a closed container. [F braiser f. braise live coals]

brake[1] /brayk/ n. & v. •n. 1 (often in pl.) a device for checking the motion of a mechanism, esp. a wheel or vehicle, or for keeping it at rest. 2 anything that has the effect of hindering or impeding (shortage of money was a brake on their enthusiasm). •v. 1 intr. apply a brake. 2 tr. retard or stop with a brake. □□ brake•less adj. [prob. obs. brake in sense 'machine handle, bridle']

brake[2] /brayk/ n. Brit. a large station wagon. [var. of BREAK[2]]

brake[3] /brayk/ n. & v. •n. 1 a toothed instrument used for crushing flax and hemp. 2 (in full brake harrow) a heavy kind of harrow for breaking up large lumps of earth. •v.tr. crush (flax or hemp) by beating it. [ME, rel. to BREAK[1]]

brake[4] /brayk/ n. 1 a thicket. 2 brushwood. [ME f. OF bracu, MLG brake branch, stump]

brake[5] /brayk/ n. bracken. [ME, perh. shortened f. BRACKEN, –en being taken as a pl. ending]

brake[6] archaic past of BREAK[1].

brake drum n. a cylinder attached to a wheel on which the brake shoe presses to brake.

brake flu•id n. fluid used in a hydraulic brake system.

brake horse•pow•er n. the power of an engine reckoned in terms of the force needed to brake it.

brake lin•ing n. a strip of material which increases the friction of the brake shoe.

brake•man /bráykmən/ n. (pl. •men) 1 a railroad worker responsible for maintenance on a journey. 2 a person in charge of brakes. [BRAKE[1] + MAN]

brake shoe n. a long curved block which presses on the brake drum to brake.

brake van n. Brit. a railroad car or vehicle from which the train's brakes can be controlled; a caboose.

bram•ble /brámbəl/ n. 1 any of various thorny shrubs bearing fleshy red or black berries, esp. (Brit.) the blackberry bush, Rubus fruticosus. 2 Brit. the edible berry of these shrubs. 3 any of various other rosaceous bushes with similar foliage, esp. the dog rose (Rosa canina). □□ bram•bly adj. [OE bræmbel (earlier brēmel): see BROOM]

bram•bling /brámbling/ n. the speckled finch, Fringilla montifringilla, native to northern Eurasia, the male having a distinctive red breast. [G Brämling f. WG (cf. BRAMBLE)]

bran /bran/ n. grain husks separated from the flour. [ME f. OF. of unkn. orig.]

branch /branch/ n. & v. •n. 1 a limb extending from a tree or bough. 2 a lateral extension or subdivision, esp. of a river, or railroad. 3 a conceptual extension or subdivision, as of a family, knowledge, etc. 4 a local division or office, etc., of a large business, as of a bank, library, etc. •v.intr. (often foll. by off) 1 diverge from the main part. 2 divide into branches. 3 (of a tree) bear or send out branches. □ branch out extend one's field of interest. □□ branched adj. branch•let n. branch•like adj. branch•y adj. [ME f. OF branche f. LL branca paw]

bran•chi•a /brángkeeə/ n.pl. (also bran•chi•ae /–kee-ee/) gills. □□ bran•chi•al adj. bran•chi•ate /–eeit, –eeayt/ adj. [L branchia, pl. –ae, f. Gk bragkhia pl.]

brand /brand/ n. & v. •n. 1 a a particular make of goods. b an identifying trademark, label, etc. 2 (usu. foll. by of) a special or characteristic kind (brand of humor). 3 an identifying mark burned on livestock or (formerly) prisoners, etc., with a hot iron. 4 an iron used for this. 5 a piece of burning, smoldering, or charred wood. 6 a stigma; a mark of disgrace. 7 poet. a a torch. b a sword. •v.tr. 1 mark with a hot iron. 2 stigmatize; mark with disgrace (they branded him a liar; was branded for life). 3 impress unforgettably on one's mind. 4 assign a trademark or label to. □□ brand•er n. [OE f. Gmc]

brand•ish /brándish/ v.tr. wave or flourish as a threat or in display. □□ brand•ish•er n. [OF brandir ult. f. Gmc, rel. to BRAND]

brand•ling /brándling/ n. a red earthworm, Eisenia foetida, with rings of a brighter color, which is often found in manure and used as bait. [BRAND + –LING[1]]

brand name n. an identifying trademark, label, etc., given by the maker to a product or range of products.

brand-new adj. completely or obviously new.

bran•dy /brándee/ n. (pl. •dies) a strong alcoholic spirit distilled from wine or fermented fruit juice. [earlier brand(e)wine f. Du. brandewijn burned (distilled) wine]

brant /brant/ n. (Brit. brent) a small migratory goose, Branta bernicla. [16th c.: orig. unkn.]

brash[1] /brash/ adj. 1 vulgarly or overly self-assertive. 2 hasty; rash. 3 impudent. □□ brash•ly adv. brash•ness n. [orig. dial., perh. f. RASH[1]]

brash[2] /brash/ n. 1 loose broken rock or ice. 2 clippings from hedges, shrubs, etc. [18th c.: orig. unkn.]

brass /bras/ n. & adj. •n. 1 a yellow alloy of copper and zinc. 2 a an ornament or other decorated piece of brass. b brass objects collectively. 3 Mus. brass wind instruments (including trumpet, horn, trombone) forming a band or a section of an orchestra. 4 Brit. sl. money. 5 (in full top brass) colloq. persons in authority or of high (esp. military) rank. 6 esp. Brit. an inscribed or engraved memorial tablet of brass. 7 colloq. effrontery; gall (then had the brass to demand money). 8 a brass block or die used for making a design on a book binding. •adj. made of brass. □ not have a brass farthing Brit. colloq. have no money or assets at all. [OE bræs, of unkn. orig.]

bras•sard /brəsaárd, brásaard/ n. a band with an identifying mark worn on the sleeve, esp. with a uniform. [F bras arm + –ARD]

brass band n. a group of musicians playing brass instruments, sometimes also with percussion.

bras•se•rie /brásəree/ n. a restaurant, orig. one serving beer with food. [F, = brewery]

brass hat n. colloq. an officer of high rank, usu. one with gold braid on the cap.

bras•si•ca /brásikə/ n. any cruciferous plant of the genus Brassica, having tap roots and erect branched stems, including cabbage, rutabaga, broccoli, brussels sprout, mustard, rape, cauliflower, kohlrabi, kale, and turnip. [L, = cabbage]

brass•ie /brásee/ n. (also brass•y) (pl. •ies) a wooden-headed golf club with a brass sole.

bras•siere /brəzeér/ n. an undergarment worn by women to support the breasts. [F, = child's vest]

brass knuck•les n. a metal guard worn over the knuckles in fighting, esp. to increase the effect of the blows.

brass ring n. sl. an opportunity for wealth or success; a rich prize.

brass-rub•bing n. 1 the rubbing of charcoal, etc., over paper laid

See page xx for the Key to Pronunciation.

on an engraved brass to take an impression of its design. **2** the impression obtained by this.

brass tacks *n. sl.* actual details; real business (*get down to brass tacks*).

brass•y[1] /brásee/ *adj.* (**brass•i•er, brass•i•est**) **1** impudent. **2** pretentious; showy. **3** loud and blaring. **4** of or like brass. □□ **brass•i•ly** *adv.* **brass•i•ness** *n.*

brass•y[2] var. of BRASSIE.

brat /brat/ *n.* usu. *derog.* a child, esp. a badly-behaved one. □□ **brat•ty** *adj.* [perh. abbr. of Sc. *bratchart* hound, or f. *brat* rough garment]

brat pack *n. sl.* a rowdy or ostentatious group of young celebrities, esp. movie stars.

brat•tice /brátis/ *n.* a wooden partition or shaft lining in a mine. [ME ult. f. OE *brittisc* BRITISH]

brat•wurst /brátwərst, –vo͞orst/ *n.* a type of small pork sausage. [G f. *braten* fry, roast + *Wurst* sausage]

bra•va•do /brəvaádō/ *n.* a bold manner or a show of boldness intended to impress. [Sp. *bravata* f. *bravo*: cf. BRAVE, –ADO]

brave /brayv/ *adj., n., & v.* ● *adj.* **1** able or ready to face and endure danger or pain. **2** splendid; spectacular (*make a brave show*). ● *n.* a Native American warrior. ● *v.tr.* defy; encounter bravely. □ **brave it out** behave defiantly under suspicion or blame; see a thing through to the end. □□ **brave•ly** *adv.* **brave•ness** *n.* [ME f. F, ult. f. L *barbarus* BARBAROUS]

brav•er•y /bráyvəree/ *n.* **1** brave conduct. **2** a brave nature. [F *braverie* or It. *braveria* (as BRAVE)]

bra•vo[1] /braávō/ *int. & n.* ● *int.* expressing approval of a performer, etc. ● *n.* (*pl.* **•vos**) a cry of bravo. [F f. It.]

bra•vo[2] /braávō/ *n.* (*pl.* **•voes** or **•vos**) a hired thug or killer. [It.: see BRAVE]

bra•vu•ra /brəvo͞orə, –vyo͞orə/ *n.* (often *attrib.*) **1** a brilliant or ambitious action or display. **2 a** a style of (esp. vocal) music requiring exceptional ability. **b** a passage of this kind. **2** bravado. [It.]

braw /braw/ *adj.* Sc. fine; good. [var. of *brawf* BRAVE]

brawl /brawl/ *n. & v.* ● *n.* a noisy quarrel or fight. ● *v.intr.* **1** quarrel noisily or roughly. **2** (of a stream) run noisily. □□ **brawl•er** *n.* [ME f. OProv., rel. to BRAY[1]]

brawn /brawn/ *n.* **1** muscular strength. **2** muscle; lean flesh. **3** *Brit.* a jellied preparation of the chopped meat from a boiled pig's head. [ME f. AF *braun*, OF *braon* f. Gmc]

brawn•y /bráwnee/ *adj.* (**brawn•i•er, brawn•i•est**) muscular; strong. □□ **brawn•i•ness** *n.*

bray /bray/ *n. & v.* ● *n.* **1** the cry of a donkey. **2** a sound like this cry, e.g., that of a harshly played brass instrument, a laugh, etc. ● *v.* **1** *intr.* make a braying sound. **2** *tr.* utter harshly. [ME f. OF *braire*, perh. ult. f. Celt.]

bray[2] /bray/ *v.tr.* pound or crush to small pieces, esp. with a pestle and mortar. [ME f. AF *braier*, OF *breier* f. Gmc]

braze[1] /brayz/ *v. & n.* ● *v.tr.* solder with an alloy of brass and zinc at a high temperature. ● *n.* **1** a brazed joint. **2** the alloy used for brazing. [F *braser* solder f. *braise* live coals]

braze[2] /brayz/ *v.tr.* **1 a** make of brass. **b** cover or ornament with brass. **2** make hard like brass. [OE *bræsen* f. *bræs* BRASS]

bra•zen /bráyzən/ *adj. & v.* ● *adj.* **1** (also **bra•zen-faced**) flagrant and shameless; insolent. **2** made of brass. **3** of or like brass, esp. in color or or sound. ● *v.tr.* (foll. by *out*) face or undergo defiantly. □ **brazen it out** be defiantly unrepentant esp. under censure. □□ **bra•zen•ly** *adv.* **bra•zen•ness** *n.* [OE *bræsen* f. *bræs* brass]

bra•zier[1] /bráyzhər/ *n.* a portable heater consisting of a pan or stand for holding lighted coals. [F *brasier* f. *braise* hot coals]

bra•zier[2] /bráyzhər/ *n.* a worker in brass. □□ **bra•zier•y** *n.* [ME prob. f. BRASS + –IER, after *glass, glazier*]

Bra•zil /brəzíl/ *n.* **1** a tall tree, *Bertholletia excelsa*, forming large forests in S. America. **2** (in full **Brazil nut**) a large three-sided nut with an edible kernel from this tree. [the name of a S.Amer. country, named from *brazilwood*, ult. f. med.L *brasilium*]

bra•zil•wood /brəzílwo͝od/ *n.* a hard red wood from any tropical tree of the genus *Caesalpina*, that yields dyes.

breach /breech/ *n. & v.* ● *n.* **1** (often foll. by *of*) the breaking of or failure to observe a law, contract, etc. **2 a** a breaking of relations; an estrangement. **b** a quarrel. **3 a** a broken state. **b** a gap in a wall, barrier, or defense, especially one made by an attacking army. ● *v.tr.* **1** break through; make a gap in. **2** break (a law, contract, etc.). □ **stand in the breach** bear the brunt of an attack. **step into the breach** give help in a crisis, esp. by replacing someone who has dropped out. [ME f. OF *breche*, ult. f. Gmc]

breach of prom•ise *n.* the breaking of a promise, esp. a promise to marry.

breach of the peace *n.* an infringement or violation of the public peace by any disturbance or riot, etc.

bread /bred/ *n. & v.* ● *n.* **1** baked dough made of flour usu. leavened with yeast and moistened, eaten as a staple food. **2 a** necessary food. **b** (also **dai•ly bread**) one's livelihood. **3** *sl.* money. ● *v.tr.* coat with breadcrumbs for cooking. □ **cast one's bread upon the waters** do good without expecting gratitude or reward. **know which**

side one's bread is buttered on know where one's advantage lies. take the bread out of a person's mouth take away a person's living, esp. by competition, etc. [OE *brēad* f. Gmc]

bread and but•ter *n.* **1** bread spread with butter. **2 a** one's livelihood. **b** routine work to ensure an income.

bread-and-but•ter letter *n.* a letter of thanks for hospitality.

bread and cir•cus•es *n.* the public provision of subsistence and entertainment, esp. as a palliative to divert attention or avert discontent.

bread and wine *n.* the Eucharist.

bread bas•ket *n.* **1** a basket for bread or rolls. **2** *sl.* the stomach.

bread•board /brédbawrd/ *n.* **1** a board for cutting bread on. **2** a board for making an experimental model of an electric circuit.

bread box *n.* a container for keeping bread in.

bread•crumb /brédkrum/ *n.* **1** a small fragment of bread. **2** (in *pl.*) bread crumbled for use in cooking.

bread•fruit /brédfro͞ot/ *n.* **1** a tropical evergreen tree, *Artocarpus altilis*, bearing edible usu. seedless fruit. **2** the fruit of this tree which when roasted becomes soft like new bread.

bread•line /brédlin/ *n.* a line of people waiting to receive free food from a charity or government agency.

bread mold *n.* any of various molds, esp. *Rhizopus nigricans*, found esp. on bread.

breadth /bredth/ *n.* **1** the distance or measurement from side to side of a thing; broadness. **2** a piece (of cloth, etc.) of standard or full breadth. **3** extent; distance; room. **4** (usu. foll. by *of*) capacity to respect other opinions; freedom from prejudice or intolerance (esp. *breadth of mind* or *view*). **5** *Art* unity of the whole, achieved by the disregard of unnecessary details. □□ **breadth•ways** *adv.* **breadth•wise** *adv.* [obs. *brede*, OE *brǣdu*, f. Gmc, rel. to BROAD]

bread•win•ner /brédwinər/ *n.* a person who earns the money to support a family.

break[1] /brayk/ *v. & n.* ● *v.* (*past* **broke** /brōk/ or *archaic* **brake** /brayk/; *past part.* **broken** /brṓkən/ or *archaic* **broke**) **1** *tr. & intr.* **a** separate into pieces violently, as from a blow or strain; shatter. **b** make or become inoperative, esp. from damage (*the toaster has broken*). **c** break a bone in or dislocate (part of the body). **d** break the skin of (the head or crown). **2 a** *tr.* cause or effect an interruption in (*broke our journey; the spell was broken; broke the silence*). **b** *intr.* have an interval between periods of work (*let's break now; we broke for coffee*). **3** *tr.* fail to observe or keep (a law, promise, etc.). **4 a** *tr. & intr.* make or become subdued or weakened; yield or cause to yield (*broke his spirit; he broke under the strain*). **b** *tr.* weaken the effect of (a fall, blow, etc.). **c** *tr.* tame or discipline (an animal); accustom (a horse) to saddle and bridle, etc. **d** *tr.* defeat; destroy (*broke the enemy's power*). **e** *tr.* defeat the object of (a strike, e.g., by hiring other personnel). **5** *tr.* surpass (a record, time, score, etc.). **6** *intr.* (foll. by *with*) **a** quarrel or cease association with (another person, etc.). **b** repudiate; depart from (a tradition, practice, etc.) **7** *tr.* **a** be no longer subject to (a habit). **b** (foll. by *of*) cause (a person) to be free of a habit (*broke them of their addiction*). **8** *tr. & intr.* reveal or be revealed; (cause to) become known (*broke the news; the story broke on Friday*). **9** *intr.* **a** (of the weather) change suddenly, esp. after a long period without change. **b** (of waves) curl over and dissolve into foam. **c** (of the day) dawn. **d** (of clouds) move apart; show a gap. **e** (of a storm) begin violently. **10** *tr. Electr.* disconnect (a circuit). **11** *intr.* **a** (of the voice) change with emotion. **b** (of a boy's voice) change in register, etc., at puberty. **12** *tr.* **a** (often foll. by *up*) divide (a set, etc.) into parts, e.g., by selling to different buyers. **b** change (a bill, etc.) for coins or smaller denominations. **13** *tr.* ruin (an individual or institution) financially (see also BROKE *adj.*). **14** *tr.* penetrate (e.g., a safe) by force. **15** *tr.* decipher (a code). **16** *tr.* make (a way, path, etc.) by separating obstacles. **17** *intr.* burst forth (*the sun broke through the clouds*). **18** *Mil.* **a** *intr.* (of troops) disperse in confusion. **b** *tr.* make a rupture in (ranks). **19 a** *intr.* (usu. foll. by *free, loose, out*, etc.) escape from constraint by a sudden effort. **b** *tr.* escape or emerge from (prison, cover, etc.). **20** *tr. Tennis*, etc., win a game against (an opponent's service). **21** *intr. Boxing*, etc. (of two fighters, usu. at the referee's command) come out of a clinch. **22** *tr. Mil.* demote (an officer). **23** *intr.* esp. *Stock Exch.* (of prices) fall sharply. **24** *intr.* (of a thrown or bowled ball) change direction abruptly. **25** *intr. Billiards*, etc., disperse the balls at the beginning of a game. **26** *tr.* unfurl (a flag, etc.). **27** *tr. Phonet.* subject (a vowel) to fracture. **28** *tr.* fail to rejoin (one's ship) after absence on leave. **29** *tr.* disprove (an alibi). ● *n.* **1 a** an act or instance of breaking. **b** a point where something is broken; a gap; a split. **2** an interval; an interruption; a pause in work; a vacation. **3** a sudden dash (esp. to escape). **4** *colloq.* **a** a piece of good luck; a fair chance. **b** (also **bad break**) an unfortunate remark or action; a blunder. **c** (in *pl.*, prec. by *the*) fate. **5** a change in direction of a thrown or bowled ball. **6** *Billiards*, etc. **a** a series of points scored during one turn. **b** the opening shot that disperses the balls. **7** *Mus.* (in jazz, etc.) a short unaccompanied passage for a soloist, usu. improvised. **8** *Electr.* a discontinuity in a circuit. □ **break away** make or become free or separate (see also BREAKAWAY). **break the back of 1** do the hardest or greatest part of; crack (a problem, etc.). **2** overburden (a person) physically or mentally; crush; defeat. **break bread** have a meal (with someone). **break down 1 a** fail in mechanical action; cease to function. **b** (of human relationships, etc.) fail; collapse. **c** (of health) fail; deteriorate; (of a person) fail in (esp. mental) health. **d** be overcome by emotion; collapse in tears. **2 a** demolish; destroy. **b** suppress (resistance). **c** force (a person) to yield under pressure. **3** analyze into components (see also BREAKDOWN). **break even** emerge from a transaction, etc., with neither profit nor loss. **break ground** begin construction. **break a person's heart** see HEART. **break the ice 1** begin to overcome formality or shyness, esp. between strangers. **2** make a start. **break in 1** enter premises by force, esp. with criminal intent. **2** interrupt. **3 a** accustom to a habit, etc. **b** wear, etc., until comfortable. **c** = break 4c. **4** Austral. & NZ bring (virgin land) into cultivation. **break in on** disturb; interrupt. **break into 1** enter forcibly or violently. **2 a** suddenly begin; burst forth with (a song, laughter, etc.). **b** suddenly change one's pace for (a faster one) (broke into a gallop). **3** interrupt. **break a leg** Theatr. phrase to wish a performer good luck. **break new ground** innovate; start on something new. **break off 1** detach by breaking. **2** bring to an end. **3** cease talking, etc. **break open** open forcibly. **break out 1** escape by force, esp. from prison. **2** begin suddenly; burst forth (then violence broke out). **3** (foll. by in) become covered in (a rash, etc.). **4** exclaim. **5** unfurl (a flag, etc.). **6 a** open up (a receptacle) and remove its contents. **b** remove (articles) from a place of storage. **break step** get out of step. **break up 1** break into small pieces. **2** disperse; disband. **3** Brit. end the school term. **4 a** terminate a relationship; disband. **b** cause to do this. **5** esp. Brit. (of the weather) change suddenly (esp. after a fine spell). **6 a** upset or be upset. **b** excite or be excited. **c** convulse or be convulsed (see also BREAKUP). **break wind** release gas from the anus.

break² /brayk/ n. **1** a carriage frame without a body, for breaking in young horses. **2** = BRAKE². [perh. = brake framework: 17th c., of unkn. orig.]

break·a·ble /bráykəbəl/ adj. & n. • adj. that may or is apt to be broken easily. • n. (esp. in pl.) a breakable thing.

break·age /bráykij/ n. **1 a** a broken thing. **b** damage or loss caused by breaking. **2** an act or instance of breaking.

break·a·way /bráykəway/ n. **1 a** the act or an instance of breaking away or seceding. **b** Sports the act or instance of moving forward from a group, as in cycling. **2** (attrib.) that breaks away or has broken away; separate.

break danc·ing n. an energetic, acrobatic style of street-dancing, developed by African-Americans.

break·down /bráykdown/ n. **1 a** a mechanical failure. **b** a loss of (esp. mental) health and strength. **2 a** a collapse or disintegration (breakdown of communication). **b** physical or chemical decomposition. **3 a** detailed analysis (of statistics, chemical components, etc.).

break·er /bráykər/ n. **1** a person or thing that breaks something, esp. (Brit.) disused machinery. **2** a person who breaks in a horse. **3** a heavy wave that breaks.

break·fast /brékfəst/ n. & v. • n. the first meal of the day. • v.intr. have breakfast. □□ **break·fast·er** n. [BREAK¹ interrupt + FAST²]

break-in n. an illegal forced entry into premises, esp. with criminal intent.

break·ing and en·ter·ing n. the illegal entering of a building with intent to commit a felony.

break·ing point n. the point of greatest strain, at which a thing breaks or a person gives way.

break line n. Printing the last line of a paragraph (usu. not of full length).

break·neck /bráyknek/ adj. (of speed) dangerously fast.

break of day n. dawn.

break·out /bráykowt/ n. a forcible escape or emergence.

break point n. **1** a place or time at which an interruption or change is made. **2** Computing (usu. breakpoint) a place in a computer program where the sequence of instructions is interrupted, esp. by another program. **3 a** (in tennis) a point which would win the game for the player(s) receiving service. **b** the situation at which the receiver(s) may break service by winning such a point. **4** = BREAKING POINT.

break·through /bráykthroo/ n. **1** a major advance or discovery. **2** an act of breaking through an obstacle, etc.

break·up /bráykup/ n. **1** disintegration; collapse. **2** dispersal.

break·wa·ter /bráykwawtər, -wotər/ n. a barrier built out into the sea to break the force of waves.

bream¹ /breem/ n. (pl. same) **1** a yellowish arch-backed European freshwater fish, Abramis brama. **2** (in full **sea bream**) a similarly shaped marine fish of the family Sparidae. [ME f. OF bre(s)me f. WG]

bream² /breem/ v.tr. Naut. hist. clean (a ship's bottom) by burning and scraping. [prob. f. LG: rel. to BROOM]

breast /brest/ n. & v. • n. **1** either of two milk-secreting organs on the upper front of a woman's body. **b** the corresponding usu. rudimentary part of a man's body. **2 a** the upper front part of a human body; the chest. **b** the corresponding part of an animal. **3** the part of a garment that covers the breast. **4** the breast as a source

of nourishment or emotion. • v.tr. **1** face; meet in full opposition (breast the wind). **2** contend with; face (prepared to breast the difficulties of the journey). **3** climb; reach the top of (a hill). □ **breast the tape** see TAPE. **make a clean breast of** confess fully. □□ **breast·ed** adj. (also in comb.). **breast·less** adj. [OE brēost f. Gmc]

breast·bone /bréstbōn/ n. a thin flat vertical bone and cartilage in the chest connecting the ribs.

breast-feed v.tr. (past and past part. **·fed**) feed (a baby) from the breast.

breast·plate /bréstplayt/ n. a piece of armor covering the breast.

breast·stroke /bréststrōk/ n. a stroke made while swimming face down by extending arms forward and sweeping them back in unison.

breast·sum·mer /brésəmər, -umər/ n. Archit. a beam across a broad opening, sustaining a superstructure. [BREAST + SUMMER²]

breast·work /bréstwərk/ n. a low temporary defense or parapet.

breath /breth/ n. **1 a** the air taken into or expelled from the lungs. **b** one respiration of air. **c** an exhalation of air that can be seen, smelled, or heard (breath steamed in the cold air; bad breath). **2 a** a slight movement of air; a breeze. **b** a whiff of perfume, etc. **3** a whisper; a murmur (esp. of a scandalous nature). **4** the power of breathing; life (is there breath in him?). □ **below** (or **under**) **one's breath** in a whisper. **breath of fresh air 1** a small amount of or a brief time in the fresh air. **2** a refreshing change. **catch one's breath 1** cease breathing momentarily in surprise, suspense, etc. **2** rest after exercise to restore normal breathing. **draw breath** breathe; live. **hold one's breath 1** cease breathing temporarily. **2** colloq. wait in eager anticipation. **in the same breath** (esp. of saying two contradictory things) within a short time. **out of breath** gasping for air, esp. after exercise. **take a person's breath away** astound; surprise; awe; delight. **waste one's breath** talk or give advice without effect. [OE brēth f. Gmc]

Breath·a·lyz·er /bréthəlizər/ n. (also Brit. **Breath·a·lys·er**) Trademark an instrument for measuring the amount of alcohol in the breath (and hence in the blood) of a driver. □□ **breath·a·lyze** v.tr. [BREATH + ANALYZE + -ER¹]

breathe /breeth/ v. **1** intr. take air into and expel it from the lungs. **2** intr. be or seem alive (is she breathing?). **3** tr. a utter; say (esp. quietly) (breathed her forgiveness). **b** express; display (breathed defiance). **4** intr. take a breath; pause. **5** tr. send out or take in (as if) with breathed air (breathed enthusiasm into them; breathed whiskey). **6** intr. (of wine, fabric, etc.) be exposed to fresh air. **7** intr. **a** sound; speak (esp. quietly). **b** (of wind) blow softly. **8** tr. allow (a horse, etc.) to breathe; give rest after exertion. □ **breathe again** (or **freely**) recover from a shock, fear, etc., and be at ease. **breathe down a person's neck** follow or check up on a person, esp. menacingly. **breathe new life into** revitalize; refresh. **breathe one's last** die. **not breathe a word** keep silent about something, keep secret. [ME f. BREATH]

breath·er /bréethər/ n. **1** colloq. **a** a brief pause for rest. **b** a short interval of exercise. **2** a safety vent in the crankcase of a motor vehicle, etc.

breath·ing /bréething/ n. **1** the process of taking air into and expelling it from the lungs. **2** Phonet. a sign in Greek indicating that an initial vowel is aspirated (**rough breathing**) or not aspirated (**smooth breathing**).

breath·ing space n. (also **breath·ing room**) time to breathe; a pause.

breath·less /bréthlis/ adj. **1** panting; out of breath. **2** (as if) holding the breath because of excitement, suspense, etc. (a state of breathless expectancy). **3** unstirred by wind; still. □□ **breath·less·ly** adv. **breath·less·ness** n.

breath·tak·ing /bréthtayking/ adj. astounding; awe-inspiring. □□ **breath·tak·ing·ly** adv.

breath test n. a test of a person's alcohol consumption, using a Breathalyzer.

breath·y /bréthee/ adj. (**breath·i·er**, **breath·i·est**) (of a singing voice, etc.) containing the sound of breathing. □□ **breath·i·ly** adv. **breath·i·ness** n.

brec·ci·a /bréchee-ə/ n. & v. • n. a rock of angular stones, etc., cemented by finer material. • v.tr. form into breccia. □□ **brec·ci·ate** /-eeayt/ v.tr. **brec·ci·a·tion** n. [It., = gravel, f. Gmc, rel. to BREAK¹]

bred /bred/ past and past part. of BREED.

breech /breech/ n. & v. • n. **1 a** the part of a cannon behind the bore. **b** the back part of a rifle or gun barrel. **2** the buttocks. • v.tr. archaic put (a boy) into breeches. [OE brōc, pl. brēc (treated as sing. in ME), f. Gmc]

breech birth n. (also **breech de·liv·er·y**) the delivery of a baby with the buttocks or feet foremost.

breech·block /bréechblok/ n. a metal block that closes the breech aperture in a gun.

breech·es /bríchiz/ n.pl. (also **pair of breech·es** sing.) **1** short trousers, esp. fastened below the knee, now used esp. for riding.

2 *colloq.* any trousers. □ **too big for one's breeches** *colloq.* too assertive or forward for one's status, position, abilities, etc. [pl. of BREECH]

breech·es buoy *n.* a life buoy suspended from a rope which has canvas breeches for the user's legs.

breech·load·er /bréchlōdər/ *n.* a gun loaded at the breech, not through the muzzle.

breech-load·ing *adj.* (of a gun) loaded at the breech, not through the muzzle.

breed /breed/ *v. & n.* ● *v.* (*past* and *past part.* **bred** /bred/) **1** *tr. & intr.* bear; generate (offspring); reproduce. **2** *tr. & intr.* propagate or cause to propagate; raise (livestock). **3** *tr.* **a** yield; produce; result in (*war breeds famine*). **b** spread (*discontent bred by rumor*). **4** *intr.* arise; spread (*disease breeds in poor sanitation*). **5** *tr.* bring up; train (*bred to the law*; *Hollywood breeds stars*). **6** *tr. Physics* create (fissile material) by nuclear reaction. ● *n.* **1** a stock of animals or plants within a species, having a similar appearance, and usu. developed by deliberate selection. **2** a race; a lineage. **3** a sort; a kind. □ **bred and born** = *born and bred.* **bred in the bone** hereditary. **breed in** mate with or marry a close relation. □□ **breed·er** *n.* [OE *brēdan*: rel. to BROOD]

breed·er re·ac·tor *n.* a nuclear reactor that can create more fissile material than it consumes.

breed·ing /breeding/ *n.* **1** the process of developing or propagating (animals, plants, etc.). **2** generation; childbearing. **3** the result of training or education; behavior. **4** good manners (*has no breeding*).

breeks /breeks/ *n.pl. Sc.* var. of BREECHES.

breeze[1] /breez/ *n. & v.* ● *n.* **1** a gentle wind. **2** *Meteorol.* a wind of 4–31 m.p.h. and between force 2 and force 6 on the Beaufort scale. **3** a wind blowing from land at night or sea during the day. **4** *colloq.* an easy task. **5** esp. *Brit. colloq.* a quarrel or display of temper. ● *v.intr.* (foll. by *in, out, along,* etc.) *colloq.* come or go in a casual or lighthearted manner. [prob. f. OSp. & Port. *briza* NE wind]

breeze[2] /breez/ *n.* small cinders. [F *braise* live coals]

breeze[3] /breez/ *n. Brit.* a gadfly or horsefly. [OE *briosa*, of unkn. orig.]

breeze block *n. Brit.* = CINDER BLOCK.

breez·y /bréezee/ *adj.* (**breez·i·er, breez·i·est**) **1 a** windswept. **b** pleasantly windy. **2** *colloq.* lively; jovial. **3** *colloq.* careless (*with breezy indifference*). □□ **breez·i·ly** *adv.* **breez·i·ness** *n.*

brems·strah·lung /brémshtraáləng/ *n. Physics* the electromagnetic radiation produced by the acceleration or esp. the deceleration of a charged particle after passing through the electric and magnetic fields of a nucleus. [G, = braking radiation]

Bren /bren/ *n.* (in full **Bren gun**) a lightweight quick-firing machine gun. [*Br*no in the Czech Republic (where orig. made) + *En*field in England (where later made)]

brent *Brit.* var. of BRANT.

breth·ren see BROTHER.

Bre·ton /brétən, brətáwN/ *n. & adj.* ● *n.* **1** a native of Brittany. **2** the Celtic language of Brittany. ● *adj.* of or relating to Brittany or its people or language. [OF, = BRITON]

breve /brev, breev/ *n.* **1** *Mus.* a note, now rarely used, having the time value of two whole notes. **2** a written or printed mark (˘) indicating a short or unstressed vowel. **3** *hist.* an authoritative letter from a sovereign or pope. [ME var. of BRIEF]

bre·vet /brəvét, brévit/ *n. & v.* ● *n.* (often *attrib.*) a document conferring a privilege from a sovereign or government, esp. a rank in the army, without the appropriate pay (*was promoted by brevet*; *brevet major*). ● *v.tr.* (**bre·vet·ted, bre·vet·ting** or **bre·vet·ed, bre·vet·ing**) confer brevet rank on. [ME f. OF dimin. of *bref* BRIEF]

bre·vi·ar·y /brēevee-eree, brév–/ *n.* (*pl.* **·ies**) *RC Ch.* a book containing the service for each day, to be recited by those in holy orders. [L *breviarium* summary f. *breviare* abridge: see ABBREVIATE]

brev·i·ty /brévitee/ *n.* **1** economy of expression; conciseness. **2** shortness (of time, etc.) (*the brevity of happiness*). [AF *breveté,* OF *brieveté* f. *bref* BRIEF]

brew /broo/ *v. & n.* ● *v.* **1** *tr.* **a** make (beer, etc.) by infusion, boiling, and fermentation. **b** make (tea, coffee, etc.) by infusion or (punch, etc.) by mixture. **2** *intr.* undergo either of these processes (*the tea is brewing*). **3** *intr.* (of trouble, a storm, etc.) gather force; threaten (*mischief was brewing*). **4** *tr.* bring about; set in motion; concoct (*brewed their fiendish scheme*). ● *n.* **1 a** an amount (of beer, etc.) brewed at one time (*this year's brew*). **b** a serving (of beer, etc.). **2** what is brewed (esp. with regard to its quality) (*a good strong brew*). **3** the action or process of brewing. □ **brew up** *Brit.* **1** make tea. **2** = BREW *v.* 2 above. **3** = BREW *v.* 4 above. **brew-up** *n. Brit.* an instance of making tea. □□ **brew·er** *n.* [OE *brēowan* f. Gmc]

brew·er·y /brooəree, brooeree/ *n.* (*pl.* **·ies**) a place where beer, etc., is brewed commercially.

bri·ar[1] var. of BRIER[1].

bri·ar[2] var. of BRIER[2].

bribe /brīb/ *v. & n.* ● *v.tr.* (often foll. by *to* + infin.) persuade (a person, etc.) to act improperly in one's favor by a gift of money, ser-

vices, etc. (*bribed the guard to release the suspect*). ● *n.* money or services offered in the process of bribing. □□ **brib·a·ble** *adj.* **brib·er** *n.* **brib·er·y** *n.* [ME f. OF *briber, brimber* beg, of unkn. orig.]

bric-à-brac /bríkəbrak/ *n.* (also **bric-a-brac, bric·a·brac**) miscellaneous, often odd, ornaments, trinkets, furniture, etc., of no great value. [F f. obs. *à bric et à brac* at random]

brick /brik/ *n., v., & adj.* ● *n.* **1 a** a small, usu. rectangular, block of fired or sun-dried clay, used in building. **b** the material used to make these. **c** a similar block of concrete, etc. **2** a brick-shaped solid object (*a brick of ice cream*). **3** *sl.* a generous or loyal person. **4** *Brit.* a child's toy building block. ● *v.tr.* (foll. by *in, up, over*) close, pave, or block with brickwork. ● *adj.* **1** built of brick (*brick wall*). **2** of a dull red color. □ **bang** (or **knock** or **run**) **one's head against a brick wall** attempt the impossible. **brick red** the color of bricks. **like a load** (or **ton**) **of bricks** *colloq.* with crushing weight, force, or authority. **see through a brick wall** have miraculous insight. □□ **brick·y** *adj.* [ME f. MLG, MDu. *bri(c)ke,* of unkn. orig.]

brick·bat /bríkbat/ *n.* **1** a piece of brick, esp. when used as a missile. **2** an uncomplimentary remark.

brick·field *Brit.* = BRICKYARD.

brick·field·er /bríkfeeldər/ *n. Austral.* a hot, dry north wind.

brick·ie /bríkee/ *n. Brit. sl.* a bricklayer.

brick·lay·er /bríklayər/ *n.* a worker who builds with bricks. □□ **brick·lay·ing** *n.*

brick·work /bríkwərk/ *n.* **1** building in brick. **2** a wall, building, etc., made of brick.

brick·yard /bríkyaard/ *n.* a place where bricks are made.

brid·al /bríd'l/ *adj.* of or concerning a bride or a wedding. □□ **brid·al·ly** *adv.* [orig. as noun, = wedding feast, f. OE *brȳdealu* f. *brȳd* BRIDE + *ealu* ale drinking]

bride /brīd/ *n.* a woman on her wedding day and for some time before and after it. [OE *brȳd* f. Gmc]

bride·groom /brídgroom, –groom/ *n.* a man on his wedding day and for some time before and after it. [OE *brȳdguma* (as BRIDE, *guma* man, assim. to GROOM)]

bride-price *n.* money or goods given to a bride's family in some cultures.

brides·maid /brídzmayd/ *n.* a girl or woman attending a bride on her wedding day. [earlier *bridemaid,* f. BRIDE + MAID]

bride·well /brídwəl, –wel/ *n. Brit. archaic* a prison; a reformatory. [St. *Bride's Well* in London, near which such a building stood]

bridge[1] /brij/ *n. & v.* ● *n.* **1 a** a structure carrying a road, path, railroad, etc., across a stream, ravine, road, railroad, etc. **b** anything providing a connection between different things (*English is a bridge between nations*). **2** the superstructure on a ship from which the captain and officers direct operations. **3** the upper bony part of the nose. **4** *Mus.* an upright piece of wood on a violin, etc., over which the strings are stretched. **5** = BRIDGEWORK. **6** *Billiards,* etc. **a** a long stick with a structure at the end which is used to support a cue for a difficult shot. **b** a support for a cue formed by a raised hand. **7** = LAND BRIDGE. **8** = BRIDGE PASSAGE. ● *v.tr.* **1 a** be a bridge over (*a fallen tree bridges the stream*). **b** make a bridge over; span. **2** span as if with a bridge (*bridged their differences with understanding*). □ **cross a** (or **that**) **bridge when one comes to it** deal with a problem when and if it arises. □□ **bridge·a·ble** *adj.* [OE *brycg* f. Gmc]

bridge[2] /brij/ *n.* a card game derived from whist, in which one player's cards are exposed and are played by his or her partner (cf. AUCTION BRIDGE, CONTRACT BRIDGE). [19th c.: orig. unkn.]

bridge·head /bríjhed/ *n. Mil.* a fortified position held on the enemy's side of a river or other obstacle.

bridge loan *n.* vg(also *Brit.* **bridg·ing loan**) a loan from a bank, etc., to cover the short interval between buying a house, etc., and selling another.

bridge of ass·es *n.* = PONS ASINORUM.

bridge of boats *n.* a bridge formed by mooring boats together abreast across a river, etc.

bridge pas·sage *n. Mus.* a transitional piece between main themes.

bridge roll *n.* a small soft bread roll.

bridge·work /bríjwərk/ *n. Dentistry* a dental structure used to cover a gap, joined to and supported by the teeth on either side.

bri·dle /bríd'l/ *n. & v.* ● *n.* **1 a** the headgear used to control a horse, consisting of buckled leather straps, a metal bit, and reins. **b** a restraining device or influence (*put a bridle on your tongue*). **2** *Naut.* a mooring cable. **3** *Physiol.* a ligament checking the motion of a part. ● *v.* **1** *tr.* put a bridle on (a horse, etc.). **2** *tr.* bring under control; curb. **3** *intr.* (often foll. by *at* or *up at*)

bridle, 1

express offense, resentment, etc., esp. by throwing up the head and drawing in the chin. [OE *brīdel*]

bri•dle path *n.* (also esp. *Brit.* **bri•dle road** or **bri•dle way**) a rough path or road suitable for horseback riding.

Brie /bree/ *n.* a kind of soft ripened cheese. [*Brie* in N. France]

brief /breef/ *adj., n., & v.* •*adj.* 1 of short duration; fleeting. 2 concise in expression. 3 abrupt; brusque (*was rather brief with me*). 4 scanty; lacking in substance (*wearing a brief skirt*). •*n.* 1 (in *pl.*) women's or men's brief underpants. 2 *Law* **a** a summary of the facts and legal points of a case drawn up for the court or counsel. **b** *Brit.* a piece of work for a barrister. 3 instructions given for a task, operation, etc. (orig. a bombing plan given to an aircrew). 4 *RC Ch.* a letter from the Pope to a person or community on a matter of discipline. 5 a short account or summary; a synopsis. •*v.tr.* 1 instruct (an employee, a participant, etc.) in preparation for a task; inform or instruct thoroughly in advance (*briefed him for the interview*) (cf. DEBRIEF). 2 *Brit. Law* instruct (a barrister) by brief. □ **be brief** use few words. **hold a brief for** 1 argue in favor of. 2 *Brit.* be retained as counsel for. **in brief** in short. □□ **brief•ly** *adv.* **brief•ness** *n.* [ME f. AF *bref*, OF *brief*, f. L *brevis* short]

brief•case /breefkays/ *n.* a flat rectangular case for carrying documents, etc.

brief•ing /breefing/ *n.* 1 a meeting for giving information or instructions. 2 the information or instructions given; a brief. 3 the action of informing or instructing.

brief•less /breeflis/ *adj. Brit. Law* (of a barrister) having no clients.

bri•er[1] /brīər/ *n.* (also **bri•ar**) any prickly bush, esp. of a wild rose. □ **brier rose** dog rose. □□ **bri•er•y** *adj.* [OE *brǣr, brēr*, of unkn. orig.]

bri•er[2] /brīər/ *n.* (also **bri•ar**) 1 a white heath, *Erica arborea*, native to S. Europe. 2 a tobacco pipe made from its root. [19th-c. *bruyer* f. F *bruyère* heath]

brig /brig/ *n.* 1 a two-masted square-rigged ship with an additional lower fore-and-aft sail on the gaff and a boom to the mainmast. 2 a prison, esp. in the navy. [abbr. of BRIGANTINE]

Brig. *abbr.* Brigadier.

bri•gade /brigáyd/ *n. & v.* •*n.* 1 *Mil.* **a** a subdivision of an army. **b** an infantry unit consisting usu. of three battalions and forming part of a division. **c** a corresponding armored unit. 2 an organized or uniformed band of workers (*fire brigade*). 3 *colloq.* any group of people with a characteristic in common (*the couldn't-care-less brigade*). •*v.tr.* form into a brigade. [F f. It. *brigata* company f. *brigare* be busy with f. *briga* strife]

brig•a•dier /brígədeer/ *n. Mil.* 1 *Brit.* an officer commanding a brigade. 2 **a** *Brit.* a staff officer of similar standing, above a colonel and below a major general. **b** the titular rank granted to such an officer. [F (as BRIGADE, –IER)]

brig•a•dier gen•er•al *n.* an officer ranking between colonel and major general.

brig•and /brígənd/ *n.* a member of a robber band living by pillage and ransom, usu. in wild terrain. □□ **brig•and•age** *n.* **brig•and•ish** *adj.* **brig•and•ism** *n.* **brig•and•ry** *n.* [ME f. OF f. It. *brigante* f. *brigare*: see BRIGADE]

brig•an•tine /brígənteen/ *n.* a two-masted sailing ship with a square-rigged foremast and a fore-and-aft rigged mainmast. [OF *brigandine* or It. *brigantino* f. *brigante* BRIGAND]

bright /brīt/ *adj. & adv.* •*adj.* 1 emitting or reflecting much light; shining. 2 (of color) intense; vivid. 3 clever; talented; quick-witted

---

SYNONYM TIP *bright*

BRILLIANT, EFFULGENT, LUMINOUS, LUSTROUS, RADIANT, REFULGENT, RESPLENDENT, SHINING. Looking for just the right word to capture the quality of the light on a moonlit night or a summer day? All of these adjectives describe an intense, steady light emanating (or appearing to emanate) from a source. **Bright** is the most general term, applied to something that gives forth, reflects, or is filled with light (*a bright and sunny day; a bright star*). **Brilliant** light is even more intense or dazzling (*the brilliant diamond on her finger*), and **resplendent** is a slightly more formal, even poetic, way of describing a striking brilliance (*the sky was resplendent with stars*). Poets also prefer adjectives like **effulgent** and **refulgent**, both of which can be applied to an intense, pervading light, sometimes from an unseen source (*her effulgent loveliness*); but *refulgent* specifically refers to reflected light (*a chandelier of refulgent crystal pendants*). **Radiant** is used to describe the power of giving off light, either literally or metaphorically (*a radiant June day; the bride's radiant face*); it describes a steady, warm light that is emitted in all directions. Like *radiant*, **luminous** suggests sending forth light, but light of the glow-in-the-dark variety (*the luminous face of the alarm clock*). While diamonds are known for being *brilliant*, fabrics like satin and surfaces like polished wood, which reflect light and take on a gloss or sheen, are often called **lustrous**. If none of these words captures the exact quality of the light you're trying to describe, you can always join the masses and use **shining**, a word that has been overworked to the point of cliché (*my knight in shining armor*).

(*a bright idea; a bright child*). 4 **a** (of a person) cheerful; vivacious. **b** (of prospects, the future, etc.) promising; hopeful. •*adv.* esp. *poet.* brightly (*the moon shone bright*). □ **bright and early** very early in the morning. **the bright lights** the glamour and excitement of the city. **look on the bright side** be optimistic. □□ **bright•ish** *adj.* **bright•ly** *adv.* **bright•ness** *n.* [OE *beorht*, (adv.) *beorhte*, f. Gmc]

bright•en /brīt'n/ *v.tr. & intr.* (often foll. by *up*) 1 make or become brighter. 2 make or become more cheerful or hopeful.

bright-eyed *adj.* □□ **bright-eyed and bushy-tailed** *colloq.* alert and energetic.

Bright's dis•ease /brīts/ *n.* inflammation of the kidney from any of various causes; nephritis. [R. *Bright*, Engl. physician d. 1858]

brill[1] /bril/ *n.* a European flatfish, *Scophthalmus rhombus*, resembling a turbot. [15th c.: orig. unkn.]

brill[2] /bril/ *adj. Brit. colloq.* = BRILLIANT *adj.* 4. [abbr.]

bril•liance /brílyəns/ *n.* (also **bril•lian•cy** /–ənsee/) 1 great brightness; sparkling or radiant quality. 2 outstanding talent or intelligence.

bril•lian•cy var. of BRILLIANCE.

bril•liant /brílyənt/ *adj. & n.* •*adj.* 1 very bright; sparkling. 2 outstandingly talented or intelligent. 3 showy; outwardly impressive. 4 esp. *Brit. colloq.* excellent; superb. •*n.* a diamond of the finest cut with many facets. □□ **bril•liant•ly** *adv.* [F *brillant* part. of *briller* shine f. It. *brillare*, of unkn. orig.]

bril•lian•tine /brílyənteen/ *n.* 1 an oily liquid ointment for making the hair glossy. 2 a lustrous dress fabric. [F *brillantine* (as BRILLIANT)]

brim /brim/ *n. & v.* •*n.* 1 the edge or lip of a cup or other vessel, or of a hollow. 2 the projecting edge of a hat. •*v.tr. & intr.* (**brimmed, brim•ming**) fill or be full to the brim. □ **brim over** overflow. □□ **brim•less** *adj.* **brimmed** *adj.* (usu. in *comb.*). [ME *brimme*, of unkn. orig.]

brim•ful /brímfool/ *adj.* (also **brim•full**) (often foll. by *of*) filled to the brim.

brim•stone /brímston/ *n.* 1 the element sulfur. 2 a butterfly, *Gonepteryx rhamni*, or moth, *Opisthograptis luteolata*, having yellow wings. 3 see FIRE AND BRIMSTONE. [ME prob. f. OE *bryne* burning + STONE]

brin•dled /bríndl'd/ *adj.* (also **brin•dle**) brownish or tawny with streaks of other color(s) (esp. of domestic animals). [earlier *brinded, brended* f. *brend*, perh. of Scand. orig.]

brine /brīn/ *n. & v.* •*n.* 1 water saturated or strongly impregnated with salt. 2 sea water. •*v.tr.* soak in or saturate with brine. [OE *brīne*, of unkn. orig.]

bring /bring/ *v.tr.* (*past* and *past part.* **brought** /brawt/) 1 **a** come conveying esp. by carrying or leading. **b** come with. 2 cause to come or be present (*what brings you here?*). 3 cause or result in (*war brings misery*). 4 be sold for; produce as income. 5 **a** prefer (a charge). **b** initiate (legal action). 6 cause to become or to reach a particular state (*brings me alive; brought them to their senses; cannot bring myself to agree*). 7 adduce (evidence, an argument, etc.). □ **bring about** 1 cause to happen. 2 turn (a ship) around. **bring around** 1 restore to consciousness. 2 persuade. **bring back** call to mind. **bring down** 1 cause to fall. 2 lower (a price). 3 *sl.* make unhappy or less happy. 4 *colloq.* damage the reputation of; demean. **bring forth** 1 give birth to. 2 produce; emit; cause. **bring forward** 1 move to an earlier date or time. 2 transfer from the previous page or account. 3 draw attention to; adduce. **bring home to** cause to realize fully (*brought home to me that I was wrong*). **bring the house down** receive rapturous applause. **bring in** 1 introduce (legislation, a custom, fashion, topic, etc.). 2 yield or earn as income or profit. **bring into play** cause to operate; activate. **bring low** overcome. **bring off** achieve successfully. **bring on** 1 cause to happen or appear. 2 accelerate the progress of. **bring out** 1 emphasize; make evident. 2 publish. **bring over** convert to one's own side. **bring through** aid (a person) through adversity, esp. illness. **bring to** 1 restore to consciousness (*brought him to*). 2 check the motion of. **bring to bear** (usu. foll. by *on*) direct and concentrate (forces). **bring to light** reveal; disclose. **bring to mind** recall; cause one to remember. **bring to pass** cause to happen. **bring under** subdue. **bring up** 1 rear (a child). 2 vomit; regurgitate. 3 call attention to; broach. 4 (*absol.*) stop suddenly. **bring upon oneself** be responsible for (something one suffers). □□ **bring•er** *n.* [OE *bringan* f. Gmc]

►Use **bring** to describe a motion toward the speaker (*please bring me a cup of coffee*). Use **take** to describe a motion away from the speaker (*please take a piece of cake home with you*).

brin•jal /brínjol/ *n.* (in India and Africa) an eggplant. [ult. Port. *berinjela* formed as AUBERGINE]

brink /bringk/ *n.* 1 the extreme edge of land before a precipice, river, etc., esp. when a sudden drop follows. 2 the furthest point before something dangerous or exciting is discovered. □ **on the brink of** about to experience or suffer; in imminent danger of. [ME f. ON: orig. unkn.]

brink•man•ship /bríngkmənship/ *n.* the art or policy of pursuing a dangerous course to the brink of catastrophe before desisting.

See page xx for the **Key to Pronunciation.**

brin·y /brínee/ adj. & n. ● adj. (brin·i·er, brin·i·est) of brine or the sea; salty. ● n. (prec. by the) Brit. sl. the sea. □□ **brin·i·ness** n.

bri·o /bree-ō/ n. dash; vigor; vivacity. [It.]

bri·oche /bree-ōsh, bree-ōsh, –osh/ n. a small rounded sweet roll made with a light yeast dough. [F]

bri·quette /brikét/ n. (also **bri·quet**) a block of compressed coal dust or charcoal used as fuel. [F briquette, dimin. of brique brick]

brisk /brisk/ adj. & v. ● adj. 1 quick; lively (a brisk pace; brisk trade). 2 enlivening; fresh (a brisk wind). 3 curt; peremptory (a brisk manner). ● v.tr. & intr. (often foll. by up) make or grow brisk. □□ **brisk·ly** adv. **brisk·ness** n. [prob. F brusque BRUSQUE]

bris·ket /brískit/ n. an animal's breast, esp. as a cut of meat. [AF f. OF bruschet, perh. f. ON]

bris·ling /brízling, brís–/ n. a small herring or sprat. [Norw. & Da., = sprat]

bris·tle /brísəl/ n. & v. ● n. 1 a short stiff hair, esp. one of those on an animal's back. 2 this, or an artificial substitute, used in clumps to make a brush. ● v. 1 a intr. (of the hair) stand upright, esp. in anger or pride. b tr. make (the hair) do this. 2 intr. show irritation or defensiveness. 3 intr. (usu. foll. by with) be covered or abundant (in). [ME bristel, brestel f. OE byrst]

bris·tle·tail /brísəltayl/ n. = SILVERFISH.

brist·ly /bríslee/ adj. (bris·tli·er, bris·tli·est) full of bristles; rough; prickly.

Bris·tol board /bríst'l/ n. a kind of fine smooth pasteboard for drawing on. [Bristol in S. England]

Bris·tol fash·ion /bríst'l/ n. (functioning as predic.adj.) Brit. (in full **shipshape and Bristol fashion**) orig. Naut. with all in good order.

bris·tols /brístəlz/ n.pl. Brit. coarse sl. a woman's breasts. [rhyming sl. f. Bristol cities = titties]

Brit /brit/ n. colloq. a British person. [abbr.]

Brit. abbr. 1 British. 2 Britain.

Bri·tan·nia /britányə/ n. the personification of Britain, esp. as a helmeted woman with shield and trident. [L f. Gk Brettania f. Brettanoi Britons]

Bri·tan·nia met·al n. a silvery alloy of tin, antimony, and copper.

Bri·tan·nic /británik/ adj. (esp. in His (or Her) Britannic Majesty) of Britain. [L Britannicus (as BRITANNIA)]

Brit·i·cism /brítisizəm/ n. (also **Brit·ish·ism** /–tishizəm/) an idiom used in Britain but not in other English-speaking countries. [BRITISH, after GALLICISM]

Brit·ish /brítish/ adj. & n. ● adj. 1 of or relating to Great Britain or the United Kingdom, or to its people or language. 2 of the British Commonwealth or (formerly) the British Empire (British subject). ● n. 1 (prec. by the; treated as pl.) the British people. 2 = BRITISH ENGLISH. □□ **Brit·ish·ness** n. [OE Brettisc, etc., f. Bret f. L Britto or OCelt.]

Brit·ish Eng·lish n. English as used in Great Britain, as distinct from that used elsewhere.

Brit·ish·er /brítishər/ n. a British subject, esp. of British descent. ▶Not used in British English.

Brit·ish·ism var. of BRITICISM.

Brit·ish ther·mal u·nit n. the amount of heat needed to raise 1 lb. of water at maximum density through one degree Fahrenheit, equivalent to 1.055×10^3 joules. ¶ Abbr: **BTU & B.t.u.**

Brit·on /brítən/ n. 1 one of the people of S. Britain before the Roman conquest. 2 a native or inhabitant of Great Britain or (formerly) of the British Empire. [ME & OF Breton f. L Britto –onis f. OCelt.]

brit·tle /brít'l/ adj. & n. ● adj. 1 hard and fragile; apt to break. 2 frail; weak; unstable. ● n. a brittle confection made from nuts and hardened melted sugar. □□ **brit·tle·ly** adv. **brit·tle·ness** n. **brit·tly** adv. [ME ult. f. a Gmc root rel. to OE brēotan break up]

brit·tle-bone dis·ease n. = OSTEOPOROSIS.

brit·tle star n. an echinoderm of the class Ophiuroidea, with long brittle arms radiating from a small central body.

bro. abbr. brother.

broach /brōch/ v. & n. ● v.tr. 1 raise (a subject) for discussion. 2 pierce (a cask) to draw liquor, etc. 3 open and start using contents of (a box, bale, bottle, etc.). 4 begin drawing (liquor, etc.). ● n. 1 a bit for boring. 2 a roasting spit. [ME f. OF broche (n.), brocher (v.) ult. f. L brocc(h)us projecting]

broach spire n. an octagonal church spire rising from a square tower without a parapet.

broad /brawd/ adj. & n. ● adj. 1 large in extent from one side to the other; wide. 2 (following a measurement) in breadth (2 meters broad). 3 spacious or extensive (broad acres; a broad plain). 4 full and clear (broad daylight). 5 explicit; unmistakable (broad hint). 6 general; not taking account of detail (broad intentions; a broad inquiry; in the broadest sense of the word). 7 chief or principal (the broad facts). 8 tolerant; liberal (take a broad view). 9 somewhat coarse (broad humor). 10 (of speech) markedly regional (broad Brooklyn accent). ● n. 1 the broad part of something (broad of the back). 2 sl. a woman. 3 Brit. (the Broads) large areas of fresh water in E. Anglia, formed where rivers widen. □□ **broad-mind·ed·ly** adv. **broad-**

mind·ed·ness n. **broad·ness** n. **broad·ways** adv. **broad·wise** adv. [OE brād f. Gmc]

broad arrow n. Brit. a mark resembling a broad arrowhead, formerly used on British prison clothing and other government property.

broad bean n. 1 a kind of bean, Vicia faba, with pods containing large edible flat seeds. 2 one of these seeds.

broad·cast /bráwdkast/ v., n., adj., & adv. ● v. (past **broad·cast** or **broad·cast·ed**; past part. **broad·cast**) 1 tr. a transmit (programs or information) by radio or television. b disseminate (information) widely. 2 intr. undertake or take part in a radio or television transmission. 3 tr. scatter (seed, etc.) over a large area, esp. by hand. ● n. a radio or television program or transmission. ● adj. 1 transmitted by radio or television. 2 a scattered widely. b (of information, etc.) widely disseminated. ● adv. over a large area. □□ **broad·cast·er** n. **broad·cast·ing** n. [BROAD + CAST past part.]

Broad Church n. esp. Brit. a group within the Anglican Church favoring a liberal interpretation of doctrine.

broad·cloth /bráwdklawth, –kloth/ n. a fine cloth of wool, cotton, or silk. [orig. with ref. to width and quality]

broad·en /bráwdən/ v.tr. & intr. make or become broader.

broad-gauge n. a railway track with a gauge wider than the standard one.

broad-leaved adj. (of a tree) deciduous and hard-timbered.

broad·loom /bráwdloom/ adj. (esp. of carpet) woven in broad widths.

broad·ly /bráwdlee/ adv. in a broad manner; widely (grinned broadly). □ **broadly speaking** disregarding minor exceptions.

broad-mind·ed adj. tolerant or liberal in one's views. □□ **broad-mind·ed·ly** adv. **broad-mind·ed·ness** n.

broad pen·nant n. a short swallow-tailed pennant distinguishing the commodore's ship in a squadron.

broad·sheet /bráwdsheet/ n. 1 a large sheet of paper printed on one side only, esp. with information. 2 Brit. a newspaper with a large format.

broad·side /bráwdsīd/ n. 1 the firing of all guns from one side of a ship. 2 a vigorous verbal onslaught. 3 the side of a ship above the water between the bow and quarter. 4 = BROADSHEET. □ **broadside on** sideways on.

broad spec·trum adj. (of a medicinal substance) effective against a large variety of microorganisms.

broad·sword /bráwdsawrd/ n. a sword with a broad blade, for cutting rather than thrusting.

broad·tail /bráwdtayl/ n. 1 the karakul sheep. 2 the fleece or wool from its lamb.

broad·way /bráwdway/ n. 1 a large open or main road. 2 (as **Broadway**) a principal thoroughfare in New York City, noted for its theaters, and the center of U.S. commercial theater production.

bro·cade /brōkáyd/ n. & v. ● n. a rich fabric with a silky finish woven with a raised pattern, and often with gold or silver thread. ● v.tr. weave with this design. [Sp. & Port. brocado f. It. broccato f. brocco twisted thread]

broc·co·li /brókəlee/ n. 1 a vegetable related to cabbage with a loose cluster of greenish flower buds. 2 the flower stalk and head used as a vegetable. [It., pl. of broccolo dimin. of brocco sprout]

broch /brok, brokh, brukh/ n. (in Scotland) a prehistoric circular stone tower. [ON borg castle]

bro·chette /brōshét/ n. a skewer on which chunks of meat are cooked, esp. over an open fire. [F, dimin. of broche BROACH]

bro·chure /brōshōōr/ n. a pamphlet or leaflet, esp. one giving descriptive information. [F, lit. 'stitching,' f. brocher stitch]

brock /brok/ n. Brit. (esp. in rural use) a badger. [OE broc(c) f. OBrit. brokkos]

brock·et /brókit/ n. any small deer of the genus Mazama, native to Central and S. America, having short straight antlers. [ME f. AF broque (= broche BROACH)]

brogue[1] /brōg/ n. 1 a strong outdoor shoe with ornamental perforated bands. 2 a rough shoe of untanned leather. [Gael. & Ir. brōg f. ON brók]

brogue[2] /brōg/ n. a marked dialect or accent, esp. Irish. [18th c.: orig. unkn.: perh. allusively f. BROGUE[1]]

broil[1] /broyl/ v. 1 tr. cook (meat) on a rack or a grill. 2 tr. & intr. make or become very hot, esp. from the sun. [ME f. OF bruler burn f. Rmc]

broil[2] /broyl/ n. a brawl; a tumult. [obs. broil to muddle: cf. EMBROIL]

broil·er /bróylər/ n. 1 a young chicken raised for broiling or roasting. 2 a a device or oven setting on a stove for radiating heat downward. b a grill, griddle, etc., for broiling. 3 colloq. a very hot day.

broke /brōk/ past of BREAK[1]. ● predic.adj. colloq. having no money; financially ruined. □ **go for broke** sl. risk everything in a strenuous effort. [(adj.) archaic past part. of BREAK[1]]

bro·ken /brōkən/ past part. of BREAK[1]. ● adj. 1 that has been broken; out of order. 2 (of a person) reduced to despair; beaten. 3 (of a language or of speech) spoken falteringly and with many mistakes, as by a foreigner (broken English). 4 disturbed; interrupted (broken time). 5 uneven (broken ground). 6 (of an animal) trained to obey; tamed. 7 transgressed; not observed (broken rules). □□ **bro·ken·ly** adv. **bro·ken·ness** n.

bro·ken chord *n. Mus.* a chord in which the notes are played successively.

bro·ken-down *adj.* **1** worn out by age, use, or maltreatment. **2** out of order.

bro·ken·heart·ed /brókənháartid/ *adj.* overwhelmed with sorrow or grief. □□ **bro·ken·heart·ed·ness** *n.*

bro·ken home *n.* a family in which the parents are divorced or separated.

bro·ken wind *n.* heaves (see HEAVE *n.* 3).

bro·ken-wind·ed *adj.* (of a horse) disabled by ruptured air cells in the lungs.

bro·ker /brókər/ *n.* **1** an agent who buys and sells for others; an intermediary. **2** a member of the stock exchange dealing in stocks and bonds. **3** *Brit.* an official appointed to sell or appraise distrained goods. [ME f. AF *brocour*, of unkn. orig.]

bro·ker·age /brókərij/ *n.* **1** a broker's fee or commission. **2** a broker's business.

bro·ker·ing /brókəring/ *n.* (also *Brit.* **bro·king** /bróking/) the trade or business of a broker.

brol·ga /brólgə/ *n. Austral.* a large Australian crane, *Grus rubicunda*, with a booming call. [Aboriginal]

brol·ly /brólee/ *n.* (*pl.* **·lies**) *Brit.* **1** *colloq.* an umbrella. **2** *sl.* a parachute. [abbr.]

bro·mate /brómayt/ *n. Chem.* a salt or ester of bromic acid.

brome /bróm/ *n.* (also **brome·grass**) any oatlike grass of the genus *Bromus*, having slender stems with flowering spikes. [mod.L *Bromus* f. Gk *bromos* oat]

bro·me·li·ad /brōmée·leead/ *n.* any plant of the family Bromeliaceae (esp. of the genus *Bromelia*), native to the New World, having short stems with rosettes of stiff usu. spiny leaves, e.g., pineapple. [O. *Bromel,* Sw. botanist d. 1705]

bro·mic /brómik/ *adj. Chem.* of or containing bromine.

bro·mic ac·id *n.* a strong acid used as an oxidizing agent.

bro·mide /brómīd/ *n.* **1** *Chem.* any binary compound of bromine. **2** *Pharm.* a preparation of usu. potassium bromide, used as a sedative. **3** a trite remark.

bro·mide pa·per *n.* a photographic printing paper coated with silver bromide emulsion.

bro·mine /brómeen/ *n. Chem.* a dark fuming liquid element with a choking irritating smell, extracted from bittern and used in the manufacture of chemicals for photography and medicine. ¶ Symb.: **Br.** □□ **bro·mism** *n.* [F *brome* f. Gk *brōmos* stink]

bromo- /brómō/ *comb. form Chem.* bromine.

bronc /brongk/ *n. colloq.* = BRONCO. [abbr.]

bron·chi *pl.* of BRONCHUS.

bron·chi·al /bróngkeeəl/ *adj.* of or relating to the bronchi or bronchioles.

bron·chi·al tree *n.* the branching system of bronchi and bronchioles conducting air from the windpipe to the lungs.

bron·chi·al tube *n.* a bronchus or any tube branching from it.

bron·chi·ole /bróngkeeōl/ *n.* any of the minute divisions of a bronchus. □□ **bron·chi·o·lar** /–ṓlər, –kíə–/ *adj.*

bron·chi·tis /brongkítis/ *n.* inflammation of the mucous membrane in the bronchial tubes. □□ **bron·chit·ic** /–kítik/ *adj. & n.*

broncho- /bróngkō/ *comb. form* bronchi.

bron·cho·cele /bróngkəseel/ *n.* a goiter.

bron·cho·pneu·mo·nia /bróngkōnoomṓnyə, –nyoo–/ *n.* inflammation of the lungs, arising in the bronchi or bronchioles.

bron·cho·scope /bróngkəskōp/ *n.* a fiber-optic instrument for inspecting the bronchi. □□ **bron·chos·co·py** /–kóskəpee/ *n.*

bron·chus /bróngkəs/ *n.* (*pl.* **bronchi** /–kī/) any of the major air passages of the lungs, esp. either of the two main divisions of the windpipe. [LL f. Gk *brogkhos* windpipe]

bron·co /bróngkō/ *n.* (*pl.* **·cos**) a wild or half-tamed horse of western N. America. [Sp., = rough]

bron·co·bus·ter /bróngkōbustər/ *n.* a person who breaks wild horses.

bron·to·sau·rus /bróntəsáwrəs/ *n.* (also **bron·to·saur** /brónt əsawr/) a large plant-eating dinosaur of the genus *Brontosaurus,* with a long whiplike tail and trunklike legs. Now more correctly APATOSAURUS. [Gk *brontē* thunder + *sauros* lizard]

Bronx cheer /brongks/ *n. colloq.* = RASPBERRY 3a. [*Bronx,* a borough of New York City.]

bronze /bronz/ *n., adj., & v.* ● *n.* **1** any alloy of copper and tin. **2** its brownish color. **3** a thing made of bronze, esp. as a work of art. ● *adj.* **1** made of or colored like bronze. ● *v.* **1** *tr.* give a bronzelike surface to. **2** *tr. & intr.* make or become brown; tan. □□ **bronz·y** *adj.* [F f. It. *bronzo,* prob. f. Pers. *birinj* copper]

Bronze Age *n. Archaeol.* the period preceding the Iron Age, when weapons and tools were usu. made of bronze.

bronze med·al *n.* a medal usu. awarded to a competitor who comes in third in a meet, etc.

brooch /brōch, brōoch/ *n.* an ornament fastened to clothing with a hinged pin. [ME *broche* = BROACH *n.*]

brood /brōod/ *n. & v.* ● *n.* **1** the young of an animal (esp. a bird) produced at one hatching or birth. **2** *colloq.* the children in a family.

3 a group of related things. **4** bee or wasp larvae. **5** (*attrib.*) kept for breeding (*broodmare*). ● *v.* **1** *intr.* (often foll. by *on, over,* etc.) worry or ponder (esp. resentfully). **2 a** *intr.* sit as a hen on eggs to hatch them. **b** *tr.* sit on (eggs) to hatch them. **3** *intr.* (usu. foll. by *over*) (of silence, a storm, etc.) hang or hover closely. □□ **brood·ing·ly** *adv.* [OE *brōd* f. Gmc]

brood·er /brōodər/ *n.* **1** a heated house for chicks, piglets, etc. **2** a person who broods.

brood·y /brōodee/ *adj.* (**brood·i·er, brood·i·est**) **1** (of a hen) wanting to brood. **2** sullenly thoughtful or depressed. **3** *Brit. colloq.* (of a woman) wanting to have a baby. □□ **brood·i·ly** *adv.* **brood·i·ness** *n.*

brook[1] /brŏŏk/ *n.* a small stream. □□ **brook·let** /–lət/ *n.* [OE *brōc,* of unkn. orig.]

brook[2] /brŏŏk/ *v.tr.* (usu. with *neg.*) *formal* tolerate; allow. [OE *brūcan* f. Gmc]

brook·lime /brŏŏklīm/ *n.* a kind of speedwell, *Veronica beccabunga,* growing in wet areas.

brook trout *n.* the speckled trout (*Salvelinus fontinalis*), a game fish of N. America.

brook·weed /brŏŏkweed/ *n.* a small herb, *Samolus valerandi,* having slender stems with tiny white flowers and growing in wet places.

broom /brŏŏm, brŏŏm/ *n.* **1** a long-handled brush of bristles, twigs, etc., for sweeping (orig. one made of twigs of broom). **2** any of various shrubs, esp. *Cytisus scoparius* bearing bright yellow flowers. [OE *brōm*]

broom·rape /brŏŏmrayp, brŏŏm–/ *n.* any parasitic plant of the genus *Orobanche,* with tubular flowers on a leafless brown stem, and living on the roots of broom and similar plants. [BROOM + L *rapum* tuber]

broom·stick /brŏŏmstik, brŏŏm–/ *n.* the handle of a broom, esp. as allegedly ridden on through the air by witches.

Bros. *abbr.* Brothers (esp. in the name of a business).

brose /brōz/ *n.* esp. *Sc. Cooking* a dish of oatmeal with boiling water or milk poured on it. [Sc. form of *brewis* broth: ME f. OF *bro(u)ez,* ult. f. Gmc]

broth /brawth, broth/ *n.* **1** *Cooking* **a** a thin soup of meat or fish stock. **b** unclarified meat, fish or vegetable stock. **2** *Biol.* meat stock as a nutrient medium for bacteria. [OE f. Gmc: rel. to BREW]

broth·el /bróthəl/ *n.* a house, etc., where prostitution takes place. [orig. *brothel* house f. ME *brothel* worthless man, prostitute, f. OE *brēothan* go to ruin]

broth·er /brúthər/ *n.* **1** a man or boy in relation to other sons and daughters of his parents. **2 a** (often as a form of address) a close male friend or associate. **b** a male fellow member of a labor union, etc. **3** (*pl.* also **breth·ren** /bréthrin/) **a** a member of a male religious order, esp. a monk. **b** a fellow member of a congregation, a religion, or (formerly) a guild, etc. **4** a fellow human being. □□ **broth·er·less** *adj.* **broth·er·ly** *adj. & adv.* **brother·li·ness** *n.* [OE *brōthor* f. Gmc]

broth·er·hood /brúthərhŏŏd/ *n.* **1 a** the relationship between brothers. **b** brotherly friendliness; companionship. **2 a** an association, society, or community of people linked by a common interest, religion, business, etc. **b** its members collectively. **3** a labor union. **4** community of feeling between all human beings. [ME alt. f. *brotherrede* f. OE *brōthor-rǣden* (cf. KINDRED) after words in –HOOD, –HEAD]

broth·er-in-law *n.* (*pl.* **broth·ers-in-law**) **1** the brother of one's wife or husband. **2** the husband of one's sister. **3** the husband of one's sister-in-law.

brough·am /brŏŏəm, brŏŏm, brŏəm/ *n. hist.* **1** a horse-drawn closed carriage with a driver perched outside in front. **2** an automobile with an open driver's seat. [Lord *Brougham,* d. 1868]

brought *past* and *past part.* of BRING.

brou·ha·ha /brŏŏhaahaa/ *n.* commotion; sensation; hubbub; uproar. [F]

brow /brow/ *n.* **1** the forehead. **2** (usu. in *pl.*) an eyebrow. **3** the summit of a hill or pass. **4** the edge of a cliff, etc. **5** *colloq.* intellectual level. □□ **browed** *adj.* [OE *brū* f. Gmc]

brow·beat /brówbeet/ *v.tr.* (*past* **·beat**; *past part.* **·beat·en**) intimidate with stern looks and words. □□ **brow·beat·er** *n.*

brown /brown/ *adj., n., & v.* ● *adj.* **1** having the color produced by mixing red, yellow, and black, as of dark wood or rich soil. **2** darkskinned or suntanned. **3** (of bread) made from a dark flour such as whole wheat. **4** (of species or varieties) distinguished by brown coloration. ● *n.* **1** a brown color or pigment. **2** brown clothes or material (*dressed in brown*). **3** (in a game or sport) a brown ball, piece, etc. **4** (prec. by *the*) *Brit.* a brown mass of flying game birds. ● *v.tr. & intr.* make or become brown by cooking, sunburn, etc. □ **in a brown study** see STUDY. □□ **brown·ish** *adj.* **brown·ness** *n.* **brown·y** *adj.* [OE *brūn* f. Gmc]

brown ale *n. Brit.* a dark, mild, bottled beer.

brown bag *v.* **1** take one's lunch to work, etc., in a brown paper bag.

2 take one's own liquor, wine etc., into a restaurant that is not licensed to serve alcohol. ▫▫ **brown·bag·ger** *n.* **brown·bag·ging** *n.*

brown bear *n.* a large N. American brown bear, *Ursus arctos.*

brown bread *n.* **1** a bread made with a dark flour, as whole-wheat or rye. **2** a steamed bread made of cornmeal, molasses, flour, etc.

brown coal *n.* = LIGNITE.

brown dwarf *n.* a dark dwarf star with insufficient mass for nuclear fusion.

brown fat *n.* a dark-colored adipose tissue with a rich supply of blood vessels.

brown hol·land *n.* unbleached holland linen..

Brown·i·an mo·tion /brównian/ *n.* (also **Brown·i·an move·ment**) *Physics* the erratic random movement of microscopic particles in a liquid, gas, etc., as a result of continuous bombardment from molecules of the surrounding medium. [R. *Brown*, Sc. botanist d. 1858]

Brown·ie /brównee/ *n.* **1** a member of the junior branch of the Girl Scouts. **2** (**brownie**) *Cooking* **a** a small square of rich, usu. chocolate, cake with nuts. **b** *Austral. & NZ* a sweet currant bread. **3** (**brownie**) a benevolent elf said to haunt houses and do household work secretly.

Brown·ie point *n. colloq.* an imaginary award given to someone who does good deeds or tries to please.

brown·nose /brównnōz/ *v. tr. coarse sl.* ingratiate oneself; be servile.

brown·nos·er /brównnōzər/ *n. coarse sl.* a toady; a yes-man.

brown·out /brównowt/ *n.* a period during which electrical voltage is reduced to avoid a blackout, resulting in lowered illumination.

brown owl *n.* any of various owls, esp. the tawny owl.

brown rat *n.* = NORWAY RAT.

brown rice *n.* unpolished rice with only the husk of the grain removed.

Brown shirt *n.* a Nazi; a member of a fascist organization.

brown·stone /brównstōn/ *n.* **1** a kind of reddish brown sandstone used for building. **2** a building faced with this.

brown sug·ar *n.* unrefined or partially refined sugar.

brown trout *n.* a common trout, *Salmo trutta*, of northern Europe.

browse /browz/ *v. & n.* •*v.* **1** *intr. & tr.* read or survey desultorily. **2** *intr.* (often foll. by *on*) feed (on leaves, twigs, or scanty vegetation). **3** *tr.* crop and eat. •*n.* **1** twigs, young shoots, etc., as fodder for cattle. **2** an act of browsing. ▫▫ **brows·er** *n.* [(n.) f. earlier *brouse* f. OF *brost* young shoot, prob. f. Gmc; (v.) f. F *broster*]

bru·cel·lo·sis /brōōsəlṓsis/ *n.* a disease caused by bacteria of the genus *Brucella*, affecting esp. cattle and causing undulant fever in humans. [*Brucella* f. Sir D. *Bruce*, Sc. physician d. 1931 + –OSIS]

bru·cite /brōōsīt/ *n.* a mineral form of magnesium hydroxide. [A. *Bruce*, US mineralogist d. 1818]

bru·in /brōō-in/ *n.* a bear. [ME f. Du., = BROWN: used as a name in *Reynard the Fox*]

bruise /brōōz/ *n. & v.* •*n.* **1** an injury appearing as an area of discolored skin on a human or animal body, caused by a blow or impact. **2** a similar area of damage on a fruit, etc. •*v.* **1** *tr.* **a** inflict a bruise on. **b** hurt mentally. **2** *intr.* be susceptible to bruising. **3** *tr.* crush or pound. [ME f. OE *brÿsan* crush, reinforced by AF *bruser*, OF *bruisier* break]

bruis·er /brōōzər/ *n. colloq.* **1** a large tough-looking person. **2** *Brit.* a professional boxer.

bruit /brōōt/ *v. & n.* •*v.tr.* (often foll. by *abroad, about*) spread (a report or rumor). •*n. archaic* a report or rumor. [F, = noise f. *bruire* roar]

brum·by /brúmbee/ *n.* (*pl.* **·bies**) *Austral.* a wild or unbroken horse. [19th c.: orig. unkn.]

brume /brōōm/ *n.* mist; fog. [F f. L *bruma* winter]

brum·ma·gem /brúməjəm/ *adj.* **1** cheap and showy (*brummagem goods*). **2** counterfeit. [dial. form of *Birmingham*, England, with ref. to counterfeit coins and plated goods once made there]

brunch /brunch/ *n. & v.* •*n.* a late-morning meal eaten as the first meal of the day. •*v.intr.* eat brunch. [BR(EAKFAST) + (L)UNCH]

bru·nette /brōōnét/ *n. & adj.* (also *masc.* **bru·net**) •*n.* a woman with dark hair. •*adj.* (of a woman) having dark hair. [F, fem. of *brunet*, dimin. of *brun* BROWN]

▶As an adjective describing someone with relatively dark hair, **brunet** is traditionally supposed to refer to males and **brunette** to females. But in fact, men are far more often described as "dark-haired," and both spellings usually refer to females. As a noun, *brunette* is the more common spelling.

brunt /brunt/ *n.* the chief or initial impact of an attack, task, etc. (esp. *bear the brunt of*). [ME: orig. unkn.]

brush /brush/ *n. & v.* •*n.* **1** an implement with bristles, hair, wire, etc., varying in firmness set into a block or projecting from the end of a handle, for any of various purposes, esp. cleaning or scrubbing, painting, arranging the hair, etc. **2** the application of a brush; brushing. **3 a** (usu. foll. by *with*) a short esp. unpleasant encounter (*a brush with the law*). **b** a skirmish. **4 a** the bushy tail of a fox. **b** a brushlike tuft. **5** *Electr.* **a** a piece of carbon or metal serving as

an electrical contact esp. with a moving part. **b** (in full **brush discharge**) a faint brushlike electrical discharge without sparks. **6 a** undergrowth; thicket; small trees and shrubs. **b** such wood cut or broken. **c** land covered with brush. **d** *Austral.* dense forest. **7** *Austral. & NZ sl.* a girl or young woman. •*v.* **1** *tr.* **a** sweep or scrub or put in order with a brush. **b** treat (a surface) with a brush so as to change its nature or appearance. **2** *tr.* **a** remove (dust, etc.) with a brush. **b** apply (a liquid preparation) to a surface with a brush. **3** *tr. & intr.* graze or touch in passing. **4** *intr.* perform a brushing action or motion. ▫ **brush aside** dismiss or dispose of (a person, idea, etc.) curtly or lightly. **brush off** rebuff; dismiss abruptly. **brush over** paint lightly. **brush up 1** (often foll. by *on*) revive one's former knowledge of (a subject). **2** *Brit.* clean up or smarten. ▫▫ **brush·like** *adj.* **brush·y** *adj.* [ME f. OF *brosse*]

brushed a·lu·mi·num *n.* aluminum with a lusterless surface.

brushed fab·ric *n.* fabric brushed so as to raise the nap.

brush·less /brúshlis/ *adj.* not requiring the use of a brush.

brush-off *n.* a rebuff; an abrupt dismissal.

brush tur·key *n. Austral.* a large mound-building bird, *Alectura lathami.*

brush·wood /brúshwŏŏd/ *n.* **1** cut or broken twigs, etc. **2** undergrowth; a thicket.

brush·work /brúshwərk/ *n.* **1** manipulation of the brush in painting. **2** a painter's style in this.

brusque /brusk/ *adj.* abrupt or offhand in manner or speech. ▫▫ **brusque·ly** *adv.* **brusque·ness** *n.* **brus·que·rie** /brüskəree´/ *n.* [F f. It. *brusco* sour]

BLUNT, BLUFF, CURT, GRUFF, SURLY. **Brusque**, which comes from an Italian word meaning rude, describes an abruptness of speech or manner that is not necessarily meant to be rude (*a brusque handshake; a brusque reply*). **Curt** is more deliberately unfriendly, suggesting brevity and coldness of manner (*a curt dismissal*). There's nothing wrong with being **blunt**, although it implies an honesty and directness that can border on tactlessness (*a blunt reply to his question about where the money went*). Someone who is **bluff** is usually more likable, possessing a frank, hearty manner that may be a little too outspoken but is seldom offensive (*a bluff man who rarely minced words*). Exhibiting **gruff** or **surly** behavior will not win friends, since both words suggest bad temper if not rudeness. But *gruff* is used to describe a rough or grouchy disposition and, like *bluff*, is applied more often to a man. Anyone who has had to deal with an overworked store clerk while shopping during the holidays knows the meaning of *surly*, which is worse than *gruff*. It describes not only a sour disposition but an outright hostility toward people, and it can apply to someone of either sex (*that surly woman at the customer service desk*).

Brus·sels car·pet /brúsəlz/ *n.* a carpet with a wool pile and a strong linen back. [*Brussels* in Belgium]

Brus·sels lace /brúsəlz/ *n.* an elaborate needlepoint or pillow lace.

brus·sels sprout /brúsəlz/ *n.* **1** a vegetable related to cabbage with small compact cabbagelike buds borne close together along a tall single stem. **2** any of these buds used as a vegetable.

brut /brōōt/ *adj.* (of wine) very dry; unsweetened. [F]

bru·tal /brōōt'l/ *adj.* **1** savagely or viciously cruel. **2** harsh; merciless. ▫▫ **bru·tal·i·ty** /–tálitee/ *n.* (*pl.* **·ties**) **bru·tal·ly** *adv.* [F *brutal* or med.L *brutalis* f. *brutus* BRUTE]

bru·tal·ism /brōōt'lizəm/ *n.* **1** brutality. **2** a heavy plain style of architecture, etc.

bru·tal·ize /brōōt'līz/ *v.tr.* **1** make brutal. **2** treat brutally. ▫▫ **bru·tal·i·za·tion** /–lizáyshən/ *n.*

Brussels sprouts

brute /brōōt/ *n. & adj.* •*n.* **1 a** a savagely violent person or animal. **b** *colloq.* a cruel, unpleasant, or insensitive person. **2** an animal as opposed to a human being. •*adj.* **1** not possessing the capacity to reason. **2 a** unthinking; merely physical (*brute force*). **b** harsh, fundamental, or inescapable (*brute necessities*). ▫▫ **brut·ish** *adj.* **brut·ish·ly** *adv.* **brut·ish·ness** *n.* [F f. L *brutus* stupid]

brux·ism /brúksizəm/ *n.* the involuntary or habitual grinding or clenching of the teeth. [Gk *brukhein* gnash the teeth]

bry·ol·o·gy /brī-ólajee/ *n.* the study of bryophytes. ▫▫ **bry·o·log·i·cal** /bríəlójikəl/ *adj.* **bry·ol·o·gist** *n.* [Gk *bruon* moss]

bry·o·ny /brîənee/ *n.* (*pl.* **·nies**) any climbing plant of the genus *Bryonia*, esp. *B. dioica* bearing greenish white flowers and red berries. [L *bryonia* f. Gk *bruōnia*]

bry·o·phyte /brîəfīt/ *n.* any plant of the phylum Bryophyta, including mosses and liverworts. ▫▫ **bry·o·phyt·ic** /–fítik/ *adj.* [mod.L *Bryophyta* f. Gk *bruon* moss + *phuton* plant]

bry·o·zo·an /brîəzóən/ *n. & adj.* •*n.* any aquatic invertebrate animal of the phylum Bryozoa, forming colonies attached to rocks, seaweeds, etc. Also called **polyzoan**. ● *adj.* of or relating to the phylum Bryozoa. □□ **bry•o•zo•ol•o•gy** /-zō-ól əjee, -zōō-/ *n.* [Gk *bruon* moss + *zōia* animals]

Bry•thon•ic /brithónik/ *n. & adj.* ●*n.* the language of the Celts of southern Britain and Brittany. ● *adj.* of or relating to this people or their language. [W *Brython* Britons f. OCelt.]

BS *abbr.* **1** Bachelor of Science. **2** Bachelor of Surgery. **3** blessed Sacrament. **4** *coarse sl.* bullshit.

B.Sc. *abbr.* Bachelor of Science.

B-side /beésīd/ *n.* the side of a phonograph record regarded as less important.

BTU *abbr.* (also **B.t.u.**, esp. *Brit.* **B.th.u.**, **B.Th.U.**) British thermal unit(s).

bu. *abbr.* bushel(s).

bub /bub/ *n. colloq.* a boy or a man, often used as a form of address. [earlier *bubby*, perh. a childish form of BROTHER or f. G *Bube* boy]

bu•bal /byoobəl/ *n.* = HARTEBEEST. [L *bubalus* f. Gk *boubalos* oxlike antelope]

bub•ble /búbəl/ *n. & v.* ●*n.* **1 a** a thin sphere of liquid enclosing air, etc. **b** an air-filled cavity in a liquid or a solidified liquid such as glass or amber. **c** (in *pl.*) froth; foam. **2** the sound or appearance of boiling. **3** a semicylindrical or domed cavity or structure. **4** a visionary or unrealistic project or enterprise. ● *v.intr.* **1** rise in or send up bubbles. **2** make the sound of boiling. **3** be lively or cheerful. □ **bubble over** (often foll. by *with*) be exuberant with laughter, excitement, anger, etc. [ME: prob. imit.]

bub•ble bath *n.* **1** a preparation for adding to bath water to make it foam. **2** a bath with this added.

bub•ble cham•ber *n. Physics* an apparatus designed to make the tracks of ionizing particles visible as a row of bubbles in a liquid.

bub•ble gum *n.* chewing gum that can be blown into bubbles.

bub•ble mem•o•ry *n. Computing* a type of memory which stores data as a pattern of magnetized regions in a thin layer of magnetic material.

bub•ble pack *n.* = BLISTER PACK.

bub•ble wrap *n.* clear plastic packaging material in sheets containing numerous small air cushions designed to protect fragile objects in shipping.

bub•bly /búblee/ *adj. & n.* ● *adj.* (**bub•bli•er, bub•bli•est**) **1** having or resembling bubbles. **2** exuberant. ● *n. colloq.* champagne.

bu•bo /byoobō, boo-/ *n.* (*pl.* **-boes**) a swollen inflamed lymph node in the armpit or groin. [med.L *bubo –onis* swelling f. Gk *boubōn* groin]

bu•bon•ic /byoobónik, boo-/ *adj.* relating to or characterized by buboes.

bu•bon•ic plague *n.* a contagious bacterial disease characterized by fever, delirium, and the formation of buboes.

buc•cal /búkəl/ *adj.* **1** of or relating to the cheek. **2** of or in the mouth. [L *bucca* cheek]

buc•ca•neer /búkəneer/ *n. & v.* ●*n.* **1** a pirate, orig. off the American coast in the late 17th c. **2** an unscrupulous adventurer. ● *v.intr.* be a buccaneer. □□ **buc•ca•neer•ing** *n. & adj.* **buc•ca•neer•ish** *adj.* [F *boucanier* f. *boucaner* cure meat on a barbecue f. *boucan* f. Tupi *mukem*]

buc•ci•na•tor /búksinaytər/ *n.* a flat thin cheek muscle. [L f. *buccinare* blow a trumpet (*buccina*)]

buck[1] /buk/ *n. & v.* ●*n.* **1** the male of various animals, esp. the deer, hare, or rabbit. **2** *archaic* a fashionable young man. **3** (*attrib.*) **a** *sl.* male (*buck antelope*). **b** *Mil.* of the lowest rank (*buck private*). ● *v.* **1** *intr.* (of a horse) jump upwards with back arched and feet drawn together. **2** *tr.* **a** (usu. foll. by *off*) throw (a rider or another) in this way. **b** oppose; resist. **3** *tr. & intr.* (usu. foll. by *up*) *colloq.* **a** make or become more cheerful. **b** *Brit.* hurry. **4** *tr.* (as **bucked** *adj.*) *Brit. colloq.* encouraged; elated. □□ **buck•er** *n.* [OE *buc* male deer, *bucca* male goat, f. ON]

buck[2] /buk/ *n. sl.* a dollar. [19th c.: orig. unkn.]

buck[3] /buk/ *n. sl.* an article placed as a reminder before a player whose turn it is to deal at poker. □ **pass the buck** *colloq.* shift responsibility (to another). [19th c.: orig. unkn.]

buck[4] /buk/ *n.* **1** a sawhorse. **2** a vaulting horse. [Du. (*zaag*)*boc*]

buck[5] /buk/ *n.* the body of a cart. [perh. f. obs. *bouk* belly, f. OE *būc* f. Gmc]

buck[6] /buk/ *n. Brit.* conversation; boastful talk. [Hindi *buk buk*]

buck•bean /búkbeen/ *n.* a bog plant, *Menyanthes trifoliata*, with white or pinkish hairy flowers.

buck•board /búkbawrd/ *n.* a horse-drawn vehicle with the body formed by a plank fixed to the axles. [BUCK[5] + BOARD]

buck•et /búkit/ *n. & v.* ●*n.* **1 a** a roughly cylindrical open container, esp. of metal, with a handle, used for carrying, catching, or holding water, etc. **b** the amount contained in this (*need three buckets to fill the tub*). **2** (in *pl.*) large quantities of liquid, esp. rain or tears (*wept buckets*). **3** a compartment on the outer edge of a waterwheel. **4** the scoop of a dredger or a grain elevator. ● *v.* (**buck•et•ed, buck•et•ing**) **1** *intr.* (often foll. by *down*) (of liquid, esp. rain) pour heavily. **2** *intr. & tr.* (often foll. by *along*) *Brit.* move or drive jerkily or

bumpily. □□ **buck•et•ful** *n.* (*pl.* **-fuls**). [ME & AF *buket, buquet*, perh. f. OE *būc* pitcher]

buck•et seat *n.* a seat with a rounded back to fit one person, esp. in a car.

buck•et shop *n.* a brokerage office that sells stocks very aggressively, esp. an illegal or dishonest one.

buck•eye /búkī/ *n.* **a** any shrub of the genus *Aesculus* of the horse chestnut family, with large sticky buds and showy red or white flowers. **b** the shiny brown nutlike seed of this plant.

buck fe•ver *n.* **1** nervousness experienced by novice hunters when they first sight game. **2** nervousness when exposed to a new experience or situation.

buck•horn /búkhawrn/ *n.* horn of a buck as a material for knife handles, etc.

buck•hound /búkhownd/ *n.* a small kind of staghound.

buck•le /búkəl/ *n. & v.* ●*n.* **1** a flat often rectangular frame with a hinged pin, used for joining the ends of a belt, strap, etc. **2** a similarly shaped ornament, esp. on a shoe. ● *v.* **1** *tr.* (often foll. by *up, on*, etc.) fasten with a buckle. **2** *tr. & intr.* give way or cause to give way under longitudinal pressure; crumple. □ **buckle down** make a determined effort. **buckle to** (or **down to**) prepare for; set about (work, etc.). **buckle to** get to work; make a vigorous start. [ME f. OF *boucle* f. L *buccula* cheek strap of a helmet f. *bucca* cheek: sense 2 of *v.* f. F *boucler* bulge]

buck•ler /búklər/ *n.* **1** *hist.* a small round shield held by a handle. **2** *Bot.* any of several ferns of the genus *Dryopteris*, having bucklershaped indusia. Also called **shield fern**. [ME f. OF *bocler* lit. 'having a boss' f. *boucle* BOSS[2]]

Buck•ley's /búkleez/ *n.* (in full **Buckley's chance**) *Austral. & NZ colloq.* little or no chance. [19th c.: orig. uncert.]

buck•o /búkō/ *n. & adj. sl.* ●*n.* (*pl.* **-oes**) a swaggering or domineering fellow. ● *adj.* blustering; swaggering; bullying. [BUCK[1] + -O]

buck•ram /búkrəm/ *n. & adj.* ●*n.* **1** a coarse linen or other cloth stiffened with gum or paste, and used as interfacing or in bookbinding. **2** *archaic* stiffness in manner. ● *adj. archaic* starchy; formal. [ME f. AF *bukeram*, OF *boquerant*, perh. f. *Bokhara* in central Asia]

buck rare•bit *n. Brit.* Welsh rarebit with a poached egg on top.

Bucks. /buks/ *abbr.* Buckinghamshire.

buck•saw /búksaw/ *n.* a two-handed saw set in an H-shaped frame and used for sawing wood.

buck•shee /búkshee/ *adj. & adv. Brit. sl.* free of charge. [corrupt. of BAKSHEESH]

buck•shot /búkshot/ *n.* large-sized lead shot.

buck•skin /búkskin/ *n.* **1 a** the skin of a buck. **b** leather made from a buck's skin. **2** a thick smooth cotton or wool cloth.

buck•thorn /búkthawrn/ *n.* any thorny shrub of the genus *Rhamnus*, esp. *R. cathartica* with berries formerly used as a cathartic.

buck•tooth /búktooth/ *n.* an upper tooth that projects.

buck•wheat /búkhweet, –weet/ *n.* any cereal plant of the genus *Fagopyrum*, esp. *F. esculentum* with seeds used for fodder and for flour to make bread and pancakes. [MDu. *boecweite* beech wheat, its grains being shaped like beechnuts]

bu•col•ic /byookólik/ *adj. & n.* ● *adj.* of or concerning shepherds, the pastoral life, etc.; rural. ●*n.* **1** (usu. in *pl.*) a pastoral poem or poetry. **2** a peasant. □□ **bu•col•i•cal•ly** *adv.* [L *bucolicus* f. Gk *boukolikos* f. *boukolos* herdsman f. *bous* OX]

bud[1] /bud/ *n. & v.* ●*n.* **1 a** an immature knoblike shoot from which a stem, leaf, or flower develops. **b** a flower or leaf that is not fully open. **2** *Biol.* an asexual outgrowth from a parent organism that separates to form a new individual. **3** anything still undeveloped. ● *v.* (**bud•ded, bud•ding**) **1** *intr. Bot. & Zool.* form a bud. **2** *intr.* begin to grow or develop (*a budding violinist*). **3** *tr. Hort.* graft a bud (of a plant) on to another plant. □ **in bud** having newly formed buds. [ME: orig. unkn.]

bud[2] /bud/ *n. colloq.* (as a form of address) = BUDDY. [abbr.]

Bud•dha /bóodə, bóodə/ *n.* **1** a title given to successive teachers of Buddhism, esp. to its founder, Gautama. **2** a statue or picture of the Buddha. [Skr., = enlightened, past part. of *budh* know]

Bud•dhism /bóodizəm, bóod–/ *n.* a widespread Asian religion or philosophy, founded by Gautama Buddha in India in the 5th c. BC, which teaches that elimination of the self and earthly desires is the highest goal (cf. NIRVANA). □□ **Bud•dhist** *n. & adj.* **Bud•dhis•tic** *adj.* **Bud•dhis•ti•cal** *adj.*

bud•dle•ia /búdleeə/ *n.* any shrub of the genus *Buddleia*, with fragrant lilac, yellow, or white flowers attractive to butterflies. [A. *Buddle*, Engl. botanist d. 1715]

bud•dy /búdee/ *n. & v. colloq.* ●*n.* (*pl.* **-dies**) (often as a form of address) a close friend or companion. ● *v.intr.* (**-dies, -died**) (often foll. by *up*) become friendly. [perh. corrupt. of *brother*, or var. of BUTTY[1]]

budge /buj/ *v.* (usu. with *neg.*) **1** *intr.* **a** make the slightest movement. **b** change one's opinion (*he's stubborn, he won't budge*). **2** *tr.* cause or compel to budge (*nothing will budge him*). □ **budge up** (or **over**) *Brit.* make room for another person by moving. [F *bouger* stir ult. f. L *bullire* boil]

budg•er•i•gar /búdʒəreegaar/ *n.* a small green parrot, *Melopsittacus undulatus*, native to Australia, and bred in colored varieties which are often kept as cage birds. [Aboriginal, = good cockatoo]

budg•et /búdʒit/ *n.* ● *n.* **1** the amount of money needed or available (for a specific item, etc.) (*a budget of $200; mustn't exceed the budget*). **2 a** the usu. annual estimate of national revenue and expenditure. **b** an estimate or plan of expenditure in relation to income for a business, etc. **c** a private person's or family's similar estimate. **3** (*attrib.*) inexpensive. **4** *archaic* a quantity of material, etc., esp. written or printed. ● *v. tr. & intr.* (**budg•et•ed, budg•et•ing**) (often foll. by *for*) allow or arrange for in a budget (*have budgeted for a new car; can budget $60*). □ **on a budget** avoiding expense; cheap. □□ **budg•et•ar•y** *adj.* [ME = pouch, f. OF *bougette* dimin. of *bouge* leather bag f. L *bulga* (f. Gaulish) knapsack: cf. BULGE]

budg•et ac•count *n.* (also **budget plan**) a bank account, or account with a utility company, etc., into which one makes regular, usu. monthly, payments to cover bills.

budg•ie /búdʒee/ *n. colloq.* = BUDGERIGAR. [abbr.]

buff /buf/ *adj., n., & v.* ● *adj.* of a yellowish beige color. ● *n.* **1 a** a yellowish beige color. **2** *colloq.* an enthusiast, esp. for a particular hobby (*railroad buff*). **3** *colloq.* the human skin unclothed. **4 a** a velvety dull yellow ox leather. **b** (*attrib.*) (of a garment, etc.) made of this (*buff gloves*). **5** *Brit.* (**the Buffs**) the former East Kent Regiment (from the color of its uniform facings). ● *v. tr.* **1** polish (metal, fingernails, etc.). **2** make (leather) velvety like buff, by removing the surface. □ **in the buff** *colloq.* naked. [orig. sense 'buffalo,' prob. f. F *buffle*; sense 2 of *n.* orig. f. buff uniforms formerly worn by New York volunteer firemen, applied to enthusiastic fire watchers]

buf•fa•lo /búfəlō/ *n.* ● *n.* (*pl.* same or •**loes**) **1** a N. American bison, *Bison bison*. **2** either of two species of ox, *Synceros caffer*, native to Africa, or *Bubalus arnee*, native to Asia with heavy backswept horns. ● *v. tr.* (•**loes,** •**loed**) *sl.* overawe; outwit. [prob. f. Port. *bufalo* f. LL *bufalus* f. L *bubalus* f. Gk *boubalos* antelope, wild ox]

buf•fa•lo grass *n.* **1** a grass, *Buchloe dactyloides*, of the N. American plains. **2** a grass, *Stenotaphrum secundatum*, of Australia and New Zealand.

buf•fa•lo wings *n. pl.* fried chicken wings coated in a hot, spicy sauce and served with blue cheese dressing.

buff•er[1] /búfər/ *n. & v.* ● *n.* **1 a** a device that protects against or reduces the effect of an impact, etc. **b** such a device (usu. one of a pair) on the front and rear of a railroad vehicle or at the end of a track. **2** *Biochem.* a substance that maintains the hydrogen ion concentration of a solution when an acid or alkali is added. **3** *Computing* a temporary memory area or queue for data to aid its transfer between devices or programs operating at different speeds, etc. ● *v. tr.* **1** act as a buffer to. **2** *Biochem.* treat with a buffer. [prob. f. obs. buff (v.), imit. of the sound of a soft body struck]

buff•er[2] /búfər/ *n. Brit. sl.* a silly or incompetent old man (esp. old buffer). [18th c.: prob. formed as BUFFER[1] or with the sense 'stutterer']

buff•er state *n.* a small nation situated between two larger ones potentially hostile to one another and regarded as reducing the likelihood of open hostilities.

buff•er stock *n.* a reserve of commodity to offset price fluctuations.

buff•er zone *n.* **1** a neutral area between two warring groups. **2** any area separating those in conflict.

buf•fet[1] /bəfáy, boo-/ *n.* a meal consisting of several dishes set out on a table from which guests serve themselves (*buffet lunch*). **2** esp. *Brit.* a restaurant or counter where light meals or snacks may be bought (*station buffet*). **3** a sideboard or recessed cupboard for china, etc. [F f. OF *bufet* stool, of unkn. orig.]

buf•fet[2] /búfit/ *v. & n.* ● *v.* (**buf•feted, buf•fet•ing**) **1** *tr.* **a** strike or knock repeatedly (*wind buffeted the trees*). **b** strike, esp. repeatedly, with the hand or fist. **2** *tr.* (of fate, etc.) treat badly (*cheerful though buffeted by misfortune*). **3 a** *intr.* struggle; fight one's way (through difficulties, etc.). **b** *tr.* contend with (waves, etc.). ● *n.* **1** a blow, esp. of the hand or fist. **2** a shock. [ME f. OF dimin. of *bufe* blow]

buf•fet car *n.* /bəfáy, boo-/ a railroad car serving light meals or snacks.

buf•fet•ing /búfiting/ *n.* **1** a beating; repeated blows. **2** *Aeron.* an irregular oscillation, caused by air eddies, of any part of an aircraft.

buf•fle•head /búfəlhed/ *n.* a duck, *Bucephala albeola*, native to N. America, with a head that appears overlarge. [obs. *buffle* buffalo + HEAD]

buf•fo /bóofō/ *n. & adj.* ● *n.* (*pl.* •**fos**) a comic actor, esp. in Italian opera. ● *adj.* comic; burlesque. [It.]

buf•foon /bəfóon/ *n.* **1** a jester; a mocker. **2** a stupid person. □□ **buf•foon•er•y** *n.* **buf•foon•ish** *adj.* [F *bouffon* f. It. *buffone* f. med.L *buffo* clown f. Rmc]

buff stick *n.* a stick covered with buff and used for polishing.

bug /bug/ *n. & v.* ● *n.* **1 a** any of various hemipterous insects with

oval flattened bodies and mouthparts modified for piercing and sucking. **b** *colloq.* any small insect. **2** *sl.* a microorganism, esp. a bacterium, or a disease caused by it. **3** a concealed microphone. **4** *sl.* an error in a computer program or system, etc. **5** *sl.* **a** an obsession, enthusiasm, etc. **b** an enthusiast. ● *v.* (**bugged, bug•ging**) **1** *tr.* conceal a microphone in (esp. a building or room). **2** *tr. sl.* annoy; bother. **3** *intr.* (often foll. by *out*) *sl.* leave quickly. [17th c.: orig. unkn.]

bug•a•boo /búgəboo/ *n.* a bogey (see BOGEY[2]) or bugbear. [prob. f. dial. orig.: cf. Welsh *bwcibo* the Devil, *bwci* hobgoblin]

bug•bear /búgbair/ *n.* **1** a cause of annoyance or anger; a bête noire. **2** an object of baseless fear. **3** *archaic* a sort of hobgoblin or any being invoked to intimidate children. [obs. *bug* + BEAR[2]]

bug-eyed *adj.* with bulging eyes.

bug•ger /búgər/ *n., v., & int. coarse sl.* (except in sense 2 of *n.* and 3 of *v.*) ● *n.* **1** esp. *Brit.* **a** an unpleasant or awkward person or thing (*the bugger won't fit*). **b** a person of a specified kind (*he's a miserable bugger*). **2** a person who commits buggery. ● *v. tr.* **1** as an exclamation of annoyance (*bugger the thing!*). **2** (often foll. by *up*) *Brit.* **a** ruin; spoil (*really buggered it up; no good, it's buggered*). **b** exhaust; tire out. **3** commit buggery with. ● *int.* expressing annoyance. □ **bugger about** (or **around**) *Brit.* **1** (often foll. by *with*) fool around. **2** mislead; persecute; make things awkward for. **bugger off** *Brit.* (often in *imper.*) go away. [ME f. MDu. f. OF *bougre*, orig. 'heretic' f. med.L *Bulgarus* Bulgarian (member of the Greek Church)] ►Usually considered a taboo word.

bug•ger-all *n. Brit.* nothing.

bug•ger•y /búgəree/ *n.* **1** esp. *Brit.* anal intercourse. **2** = BESTIALITY 2. [ME f. MDu. *buggerie* f. OF *bougerie*: see BUGGER]

bug•gy[1] /búgee/ *n.* (*pl.* •**gies**) **1** a light, horse-drawn vehicle for one or two people. **2** a small, sturdy, esp. open, motor vehicle (*beach buggy; dune buggy*). **3** a baby carriage. [18th c.: orig. unkn.]

bug•gy[2] /búgee/ *adj.* (**bug•gi•er, bug•gi•est**) infested with bugs.

bu•gle[1] /byóogəl/ *n. & v.* ● *n.* (also **bu•gle horn**) a brass instrument like a small trumpet, used esp. for military signals. ● *v.* **1** *intr.* sound a bugle. **2** *tr.* sound (a note, a call, etc.) on a bugle. □□ **bu•gler** /byóoglər/ *n.* **bu•glet** /byóoglit/ *n.* [ME, orig. = 'buffalo,' f. OF f. L *buculus* dimin. of *bos* ox]

bu•gle[2] /byóogəl/ *n.* a blue-flowered mat-forming European plant, *Ajuga reptans*. [ME f. LL *bugula*]

bu•gle[3] /byóogəl/ *n.* a tube-shaped bead sewn on a dress, etc., for ornament. [16th c.: orig. unkn.]

bu•gloss /byóoglaws, -glos/ *n.* **1** any of various bristly plants related to borage, esp. of the genus *Anchusa* with bright blue tubular flowers. **2** = VIPER'S BUGLOSS. [F *buglosse* or L *buglossus* f. Gk *bouglōssos* ox-tongued]

buhl /bool/ *n.* (also **boule, boulle**) **1** pieces of brass, tortoiseshell, etc., cut to make a pattern and used as decorative inlays esp. on furniture. **2** work inlaid with buhl. **3** (*attrib.*) inlaid with buhl. [(*buhl* Germanized) f. A. C. *Boule*, Fr. wood carver d. 1732]

build /bild/ *v. & n.* ● *v. tr.* (*past* and *past. part.* **built** /bilt/) **1 a** construct (a house, vehicle, fire, road, model, etc.) by putting parts or material together. **b** commission, finance, and oversee the building of (*the board has built two new schools*). **2 a** (often foll. by *up*) establish, develop, make, or accumulate gradually (*built the business up from nothing*). **b** (often foll. by *on*) base (hopes, theories, etc.) (*ideas built on a false foundation*). **3** (as **built** *adj.*) having a specified build (*sturdily built; brick-built*). ● *n.* **1** the proportions of esp. the human body (*a slim build*). **2** a style of construction; a make. □ **build in** incorporate as part of a structure. **build on** add (an extension, etc.). **build up 1** increase in size or strength. **2** praise; boost. **3** gradually become established. **build up** (or *Brit.* **in** or **round**) surround with houses, etc. **built on sand** unstable. [OE *byldan* f. *bold* dwelling f. Gmc: cf. BOWER[1], BOOTH]

build•er /bíldər/ *n.* **1** a contractor for building houses, etc.; a master builder. **2** a person engaged as a construction worker, etc., on a building site.

build•ing /bílding/ *n.* **1** a permanent fixed structure forming an enclosure and providing protection from the elements, etc. (e.g., a house, school, factory, or stable). **2** the constructing of such structures.

build•ing line *n.* a limit or boundary between a house and a street beyond which the owner may not build.

build•ing site *n.* an area before or during the construction of a house, etc.

build•up /bíldəp/ *n.* **1** a favorable description in advance; publicity. **2** a gradual approach to a climax or maximum (*the buildup was slow but sure*).

built *past* and *past. part.* of BUILD.

built-in *adj.* **1** forming an integral part of a structure or device (*built-in bookshelves*). **2** forming an integral part of a person's character (*built-in integrity*).

built-up *adj.* **1** (of a locality) densely covered by houses, etc. **2** increased in height, etc., by the addition of parts. **3** composed of separately prepared parts.

bulb /bulb/ *n.* **1 a** an underground fleshy-leaved storage organ of some plants (e.g., lily, onion) sending roots downwards and leaves upwards. **b** a plant grown from this, e.g., a daffodil. **2** = LIGHTBULB (see LIGHT¹). **3** any object or part shaped like a bulb. [L *bulbus* f. Gk *bolbos* onion]

bul·bous /búlbəs/ *adj.* **1** shaped like a bulb; fat or bulging. **2** having a bulb or bulbs. **3** (of a plant) growing from a bulb.

bulbul /bŏŏlbŏŏl/ *n.* **1** any songbird of the family Pycnonotidae, of dull plumage with contrasting bright patches. **2** a singer or poet. [Pers. f. Arab., of imit. orig.]

Bul·gar /búlgaar/ *n.* **1** a member of a tribe who settled in what is now Bulgaria in the 7th c. **2** a Bulgarian. [med.L *Bulgarus* f. OBulg. *Blŭgarinŭ*]

bul·gar var. of BULGUR.

Bul·gar·i·an /bulgáireeən/ *n. & adj.* ● *n.* **1 a** a native or inhabitant of Bulgaria. **b** a person of Bulgarian descent. **2** the language of Bulgaria. ● *adj.* of or relating to Bulgaria or its people or language. [med.L *Bulgaria* f. *Bulgarus*: see BULGAR]

bulge /bulj/ *n. & v.* ● *n.* **1 a** a convex part of an otherwise flat or flatter surface. **b** an irregular swelling; a lump. **2** *colloq.* a temporary increase in quantity or number. **3** *Naut.* the bilge of a ship. **4** *Mil.* a salient. ● *v.* **1** *intr.* swell outward. **2** *intr.* be full or replete. **3** *tr.* swell (a bag, cheeks, etc.) by stuffing. □□ **bulg·ing·ly** *adv.* **bulg·y** *adj.* [ME f. OF *boulge, bouge* f. L *bulga*: see BUDGET]

SYNONYM TIP bulge

PROJECT, PROTRUDE, PROTUBERATE. While all of these verbs mean to extend outward, beyond the normal line or surface of something, it is almost impossible not to associate the word **bulge** with the human body (*a stomach that bulges over a waistband, muscles that bulge beneath a shirt*). *Bulge* suggests a swelling out that is quite noticeable or even abnormal, and that may be the result of internal pressure, although a brick wall can *bulge*, as can a bicep muscle. **Protuberate** is a less common word meaning to swell or stick out, but it does not necessarily imply that anything is abnormal or radically wrong (*he was so thin that his knees protuberated*). To **protrude** is to thrust forth in an unexpected way or to stick out in a way that is abnormal or disfiguring (*her eyes protruded from her skull*). **Project** is the least upsetting of all these words, probably because it is used less often with reference to the human body. Anything that juts out abruptly beyond the rest of a surface is said to *project* (*the balcony projected from the south side of the house*).

bul·gur /búlgər/ *n.* (also **bul·gar, bul·ghur**) whole wheat that has been partially boiled then dried. [Turk.]

bu·lim·a·rex·i·a /bŏŏlímərékseeə, –leemə–, byŏŏ–/ *n.* = BULIMIA 2. □□ **bu·lim·a·rex·ic** *adj. & n.* [BULIMIA + ANOREXIA]

bu·lim·i·a /bŏŏleemeeə, –li–, byŏŏ–/ *n. Med.* **1** insatiable overeating. **2** (in full **bulimia nervosa**) an emotional disorder in which bouts of extreme overeating are followed by depression and self-induced vomiting, purging, or fasting. □□ **bu·lim·ic** *adj. & n.* [mod.L f. Gk *boulimia* f. *bous* ox + *limos* hunger]

bulk /bulk/ *n. & v.* ● *n.* **1 a** size; magnitude (esp. large). **b** a large mass. **c** a large quantity. **2** a large shape, body, or person (*jacket barely covered his bulk*). **3** (usu. prec. by *the*; treated as *pl.*) the greater part or number (*the bulk of the applicants are women*). **4** roughage. **5** *Naut.* cargo, esp. unpackaged. ● *v.* **1** *intr.* seem in respect to size or importance (*bulks large in his reckoning*). **2** *tr.* (often foll. by *out*) make (a book, a textile yarn, etc.) seem thicker by suitable treatment (*bulked it with irrelevant stories*). **3** *tr.* combine (consignments, etc.). □ **in bulk 1** in large quantities. **2** (of a cargo) loose, not packaged. [sense 'cargo' f. OIcel. *búlki*; sense 'mass,' etc., perh. alt. f. obs. *bouk* (cf. BUCK³)]

bulk·head /búlk-hed/ *n.* **1** an upright partition separating the compartments in a ship, aircraft, vehicle, etc. **2** an embankment or retaining wall, esp. along a waterfront. [*bulk* stall f. ON *bálkr* + HEAD]

bulk·y /búlkee/ *adj.* (**bulk·i·er, bulk·i·est**) **1** taking up much space; large. **2** awkwardly large; unwieldy. □□ **bulk·i·ly** *adv.* **bulk·i·ness** *n.*

bull¹ /bŏŏl/ *n., adj., & v.* ● *n.* **1 a** an uncastrated male bovine animal. **b** a male of the whale, elephant, and other large animals. **2** (**the Bull**) the zodiacal sign or constellation Taurus. **3** *Brit.* the bull's-eye of a target. **4** *Stock Exch.* a person who buys shares hoping to sell them at a higher price later (cf. BEAR²). ● *adj.* like that of a bull (*bull neck*). ● *v.* **1** *tr. & intr.* act or treat violently. **2** *Stock Exch.* **a** *intr.* speculate for a rise in stock prices. **b** *tr.* raise price of (stocks, etc.). □ **bull at a gate** a hasty or rash person. **bull in a china shop** a reckless or clumsy person. **take the bull by the horns** face danger or challenge boldly. □□ **bull·ish** *adj.* [ME f. ON *boli* = MLG, MDu *bulle*]

bull² /bŏŏl/ *n.* a papal edict. [ME f. OF *bulle* f. L *bulla* rounded object, in med.L 'seal']

bull³ /bŏŏl/ *n.* **1** (also **Irish bull**) an expression containing a contradiction in terms or implying ludicrous inconsistency. **2** *sl.* **a** unnecessary routine tasks or discipline. **b** nonsense. **c** trivial or insincere talk or writing. **d** a bad blunder in speech (cf. BULLSHIT). [17th c.: orig. unkn.]

bul·lace /bŏŏlis/ *n.* a thorny European shrub, *Prunus insititia*, bearing globular yellow or purple-black fruits, of which the damson plum is the cultivated form. [ME f. OF *buloce, beloce*]

bull ant *n. Austral.* = BULLDOG ANT.

bull·dog /bŏŏldawg, –dog/ *n.* **1 a** a dog of a sturdy powerful breed with a large head and smooth hair. **b** this breed. **2** a tenacious and courageous person.

bull·dog ant *n. Austral.* a large ant with a powerful sting.

bull·dog clip *n.* a strong sprung clip for papers.

bull·doze /bŏŏldōz/ *v.tr.* **1** clear with a bulldozer. **2** *colloq.* **a** intimidate. **b** make (one's way) forcibly. [perh. fr. BULL¹ + alter. of DOSE]

bull·doz·er /bŏŏldōzər/ *n.* **1** a powerful tractor with a broad curved vertical blade at the front for clearing ground. **2** a forceful and domineering person.

bulldozer

bul·let /bŏŏlit/ *n.* **1** a small round or cylindrical missile with a pointed end, fired from a rifle, revolver, etc. **2** *Printing* a round black dot used as a marker (●). [F *boulet, boulette* dimin. of *boule* ball f. L *bulla* bubble]

bul·le·tin /bŏŏlitin/ *n.* **1** a short official statement of news. **2** a regular periodical issued by an organization or society.

WORD HISTORY bulletin

Mid-17th century (denoting an official warrant in some European countries) from French, from Italian *bullettino*, diminutive of *bulletta* 'passport,' diminutive of *bulla* 'official seal on a document.'

bul·le·tin board *n.* **1** a board for posting notices, information, etc. **2** *Computing* a public computer file serving the function of a bulletin board.

bul·let·proof /bŏŏlitprŏŏf/ *adj. & v.* ● *adj.* (of a material) designed to resist the penetration of bullets. ● *v.tr.* make bulletproof.

bull fid·dle *n. colloq.* a double bass.

bull·fight /bŏŏlfīt/ *n.* a sport of baiting and (usu.) killing bulls as a public spectacle, esp. in Spain. □□ **bull·fight·er** *n.* **bull·fight·ing** *n.*

bull·finch /bŏŏlfinch/ *n.* a European finch, *Pyrrhula pyrrhula*, with a short stout beak and bright plumage.

bull·frog /bŏŏlfrawg, –frog/ *n.* a large frog, *Rana catesbiana*, native to eastern N. America, with a deep croak.

bull·head /bŏŏlhed/ *n.* any of various marine fishes with large flattened heads.

bull·head·ed /bŏŏlhédid/ *adj.* obstinate; impetuous; blundering. □□ **bull·head·ed·ly** *adv.* **bull·head·ed·ness** *n.*

bull·horn /bŏŏlhawrn/ *n.* an electronic device for amplifying the sound of the voice so it can be heard at a distance.

bul·lion /bŏŏlyən/ *n.* a metal (esp. gold or silver) in bulk before coining, or valued by weight. [AF = mint, var. of OF *bouillon* ult. f. L *bullire* boil]

bull·ish /bŏŏlish/ *adj.* **1** like a bull, esp. in size or temper. **2 a** *Stock Exch.* causing or associated with a rise in prices. **b** optimistic.

bull mar·ket *n.* a market with shares rising in price.

bull nose *adj.* (also **bull nosed**) with rounded end.

bul·lock /bŏŏlək/ *n. & v.* ● *n.* a castrated bull. ● *v.intr.* (often foll. by *at*) *Austral. colloq.* work very hard. [OE *bulluc*, dimin. of BULL¹]

bul·lock·y /bŏŏləkee/ *n. Austral. & NZ colloq.* a bullock driver.

bull pen *n.* (also **bull·pen**) **1** *Baseball* **a** an area in which relief pitchers warm up during a game. **b** the relief pitchers on a team. **2 a** large holding cell for prisoners awaiting court appearances. **3** *colloq.* an open, unpartitioned area for several workers.

bull·ring /bŏŏlring/ *n.* an arena for bullfights.

bull ses·sion *n.* an informal group discussion.

bull's-eye *n.* **1** the center of a target; a shot that hits this. **2** a large hard peppermint-flavored candy. **3** a hemisphere or thick disk of glass in a ship's deck or side to admit light. **4** a small circular window. **5 a** a hemispherical lens. **b** a lantern fitted with this. **6** a boss of glass at the center of a blown glass sheet.

bull·shit /bŏŏlshit/ *n. & v. coarse sl.* ● *n.* **1** (often as *int.*) nonsense; foolish talk. **2** trivial or insincere talk or writing. ● *v.intr.* (·**shit·ted**, ·**shit·ting**) talk nonsense; bluff. □□ **bull·shit·ter** *n.* [BULL³SHIT]

bull ter·ri·er *n.* **1** a short-haired dog of a breed that is a cross between a bulldog and a terrier. **2** this breed.

bull·trout /bŏŏltrowt/ *n. Brit.* a salmon trout.

bul·ly¹ /bŏŏlee/ *n. & v.* ● *n.* (*pl.* ·**lies**) a person who uses strength or power to coerce others by fear. ● *v.tr.* (·**lies**, ·**lied**) **1** persecute or oppress by force or threats. **2** (foll. by *into* + verbal noun) pressure or coerce (a person) to do something (*bullied him into agreeing*). [orig. as a term of endearment, prob. f. MDu. *boele* lover]

bul·ly² /bŏŏlee/ *adj. & int. colloq.* ● *adj.* very good; first-rate. ● *int.*

(foll. by *for*) expressing admiration or approval, or *iron.* (*bully for them!*). [perh. f BULLY¹]

bul•ly³ /bŏolee/ *n. & v.* (in full **bully off**) • *n.* (*pl.* **•lies**) the start of play in field hockey in which two opponents strike each other's sticks or the ground three times and then go for the ball. • *v.intr.* (•**lies, •lied**) start play in this way. [19th c.: perh. f. *bully* scrum in Eton football, of unkn. orig.]

bul•ly⁴ /bŏolee/ *n.* (in full **bully beef**) corned beef. [F *bouilli* boiled beef f. *bouillir* BOIL¹]

bul•ly•boy /bŏoleeboy/ *n.* a hired thug.

bul•ly•rag /bŏoleerag/ *v.tr.* (also **bal•ly•rag** /bál–/) (**•ragged, •rag•ging**) *sl.* play tricks on; intimidate; harass. [18th c.: orig. unkn.]

bul•ly tree /bŏolee/ *n.* = BALATA. [corrupt.]

bul•rush /bŏolrush/ *n.* **1** *Brit.* = CATTAIL. **2** a rushlike water plant, *Scirpus lacustris*, used for weaving. **3** *Bibl.* a papyrus plant. [perh. f. BULL¹ = large, coarse, as in bullfrog, bulltrout, etc.]

bul•wark /bŏolwərk/ *n. & v.* • *n.* **1** a defensive wall, esp. of earth; a rampart; a mole or breakwater. **2** a person, principle, etc., that acts as a defense. **3** (usu. in *pl.*) a ship's side above deck. • *v.tr.* serve as a bulwark to; defend; protect. [ME f. MLG, MDu. *bolwerk*: see BOLE¹, WORK]

bum¹ /bum/ *n.* esp. *Brit. sl.* the buttocks. [ME *bom*, of unkn. orig.]

bum² /bum/ *n., v., & adj. sl.* • *n.* a habitual loafer or tramp; a lazy dissolute person. • *v.* (**bummed, bum•ming**) **1** *intr.* (often foll. by *about, around*) loaf or wander around; be a bum. **2** *tr.* get by begging; cadge. • *attrib.adj.* **1** of poor quality; bad; worthless. **2** false; fabricated. **3** not entirely functional (*bum ankle*). □ **on the bum** vagrant; begging. [prob. abbr. or back-form. f. BUMMER]

bum-bag *n. Brit.* = FANNY PACK.

bum•ble /búmbəl/ *v.intr.* **1** (foll. by *on*) speak in a rambling incoherent way. **2** (often as **bumbling** *adj.*) move or act ineptly; blunder. **3** make a buzz or hum. □□ **bum•bler** *n.* [BOOM¹ + –LE⁴: partly f. *bumble* = blunderer]

bum•ble•bee /búmbəlbee/ *n.* any large loud humming bee of the genus *Bombus*. [as BUMBLE]

bum•boat /búmbōt/ *n.* any small boat selling provisions, etc., to ships.

bumf /bumf/ *n.* (also **bumph**) *Brit. colloq.* **1** usu. *derog.* papers; documents. **2** toilet paper. [abbr. of *bum fodder*]

bum•ma•lo /búmalō/ *n.* (*pl.* same) a small fish, *Harpodon nehereus*, of S. Asian coasts, dried and used as food (see BOMBAY DUCK). [perh. f. Marathi *bombil(a)*]

bum•mer /búmər/ *n. sl.* **1** a bum; a loafer. **2** an unpleasant occurrence. [19th c.: perh. f. G *Bummler*]

bump /bump/ *n., v., & adv.* • *n.* **1** a dull-sounding blow or collision. **2** a swelling or dent caused by this. **3** an uneven patch on a road, field, etc. **4** *Phrenol.* any of various prominences on the skull thought to indicate different mental faculties. **5** *Aeron.* **a** an irregularity in an aircraft's motion. **b** a rising air current causing this. • *v.* **1 a** *tr.* hit or come against with a bump. **b** *intr.* (of two objects) collide. **2** *intr.* (foll. by *against, into*) hit with a bump; collide with. **3** *tr.* (often foll. by *against, on*) hurt or damage by striking (*bumped my head on the ceiling; bumped the car while parking*). **4** *intr.* (usu. foll. by *along*) move or travel with much jolting (*we bumped along the road*). **5** *tr.* displace, esp. by seniority. • *adv.* with a bump; suddenly; violently. □ **bump into** *colloq.* meet by chance. **bump off** *sl.* murder. **bump up** *colloq.* increase (prices, etc.). [16th c., imit.: perh. f. Scand.]

bump•er /búmpər/ *n.* **1** a horizontal bar or strip fixed across the front or back of a vehicle, at the end of a track, etc., to reduce damage in a collision or as a trim. **2** (*attrib.*) an unusually large or fine example (*a bumper crop*). **3** a brimful glass of wine, etc.

bump•er car *n.* each of a number of small electrically-driven cars in an enclosure at an amusement park, driven around and bumped into each other.

bump•er stick•er *n.* a strip of paper backed with adhesive that may be affixed to an automobile bumper, usu. bearing a joke, political slogan, tourism advertisement, etc.

bumph var. of BUMF.

bump•kin /búmpkin/ *n.* a rustic or socially inept person. [perh. Du. *boomken* little tree or MDu. *bommekijn* little barrel]

bump•tious /búmpshəs/ *adj.* offensively self-assertive or conceited. □□ **bump•tious•ly** *adv.* **bump•tious•ness** *n.* [BUMP, after FRACTIOUS]

bump•y /búmpee/ *adj.* (**bump•i•er, bump•i•est**) **1** having many bumps (*a bumpy road*). **2** affected by bumps (*a bumpy ride*). □□ **bump•i•ly** *adv.* **bump•i•ness** *n.*

bum rap *n. sl.* imprisonment on a false charge.

bum's rush *n. sl.* forcible ejection from a place.

bum steer *n.* false information.

bun /bun/ *n.* **1** a small often sweet bread roll, often with dried fruit. **2** *Sc.* a rich fruit cake or currant bread. **3** hair worn in the shape of a bun. **4** (in *pl.*) *sl.* the buttocks. □ **have a bun in the oven** *sl.* be pregnant. [ME: orig. unkn.]

Bu•na /bŏonə, byŏonə/ *n. Trademark* a synthetic rubber made by polymerization of butadiene. [G (as BUTADIENE, *natrium* sodium)]

bunch /bunch/ *n. & v.* • *n.* **1** a cluster of things growing or fastened together (*bunch of grapes; bunch of keys*). **2** a collection; a set or lot (*best of the bunch*). **3** *colloq.* a group; a gang. • *v.* **1** *tr.* make into a bunch or bunches; gather into close folds. **2** *intr.* form into a group or crowd. □□ **bunch•y** *adj.* [ME: orig. unkn.]

bunch grass *n.* a N. American grass that grows in clumps.

bun•co /búngkō/ *n. & v.* (also **bun•ko**) *sl.* • *n.* (*pl.* **•cos**) a swindle, esp. by card sharping or a confidence trick. • *v.tr.* (**•coes, •coed**) swindle; cheat. [perh. f. Sp. *banca* a card game]

bun•combe var. of BUNKUM.

Bun•des•rat /bŏondəsraat/ *n.* the Upper House of Parliament in Germany or in Austria. [G f. *Bund* federation + *Rat* council]

Bun•des•tag /bŏondəstaag/ *n.* the Lower House of Parliament in Germany. [G f. *Bund* federation + *tagen* confer]

bun•dle /búndəl/ *n. & v.* • *n.* **1** a collection of things tied or fastened together. **2** a set of nerve fibers, etc., banded together. **3** *sl.* a large amount of money. • *v.* **1** *tr.* **a** (usu. foll. by *up*) tie in or make into a bundle (*bundled up my exercise things*). **b** sell (a product) together with another one in a single transaction. **2** *tr.* (usu. foll. by *into*) throw or push, esp. quickly or confusedly (*bundled the papers into the drawer*). **3** *tr.* (usu. foll. by *out, off, away*, etc.) send (esp. a person) away hurriedly or unceremoniously (*bundled them off the premises*). **4** *intr. archaic* sleep clothed with another person, esp. a fiancé(e), as a local custom. □ **be a bundle of nerves** (or **prejudices**, etc.) be extremely nervous (or prejudiced, etc.). **bundle up** dress warmly or cumbersomely. **go a bundle on** *Brit. sl.* be very fond of. □□ **bun•dler** *n.* [ME, perh. f. OE *byndelle* a binding, but also f. LG, Du *bundel*]

bung¹ /bung/ *n. & v.* • *n.* a stopper for closing a hole in a container, esp. a cask. • *v.tr.* **1** stop with a bung. **2** *Brit. sl.* throw; toss. □ **bunged up** closed; blocked. [MDu. *bonghe*]

bung² /bung/ *adj. Austral. & NZ sl.* dead; ruined; useless. □ **go bung 1** die. **2** fail; go bankrupt. [Aboriginal]

bun•ga•low /búnggalō/ *n.* a one-storied house. [Gujarati *bangalo* f. Hind. *bangla* belonging to Bengal]

bun•gee /búnjee/ *n.* (in full **bungee cord**) elasticized cord used for securing baggage and in bungee jumping. [20th c.: orig. unkn.]

bun•gee jump•ing *n.* the sport of jumping from a height while secured by a bungee from the ankles or a harness.

bung•hole /búnghōl/ *n.* a hole for filling or emptying a cask, etc.

bun•gle /búnggəl/ *v. & n.* • *v.* **1** *tr.* blunder over, mismanage, or fail at (a task). **2** *intr.* work badly or clumsily. • *n.* a bungled attempt; bungled work. □□ **bun•gler** *n.* [imit.: cf. BUMBLE]

bun•ion /búnyən/ *n.* a swelling on the foot, esp. at the first joint of the big toe. [OF *buignon* f. *buigne* bump on the head]

bunk¹ /bungk/ *n. & v.* • *n.* a sleeping berth, esp. a shelflike bed against a wall, e.g., in a ship. • *v. intr.* **1** sleep in a bunk. **2** share a BUNK BED (*bunked together in the army*). [18th c.: orig. unkn.]

bunk² /bungk/ *n.* □ **do a bunk** *Brit. sl.* leave or abscond hurriedly. [19th c.: orig. unkn.]

bunk³ /bungk/ *n. sl.* nonsense; humbug. [abbr. of BUNKUM]

bunk bed *n.* each of two or more beds one above the other, forming a unit.

bun•ker /búngkər/ *n. & v.* • *n.* **1** a large container or compartment for storing fuel. **2** a reinforced underground shelter, esp. for use in wartime. **3** a hollow filled with sand, used as an obstacle in a golf course. • *v.tr.* **1** fill the fuel bunkers of (a ship, etc.). **2** (usu. in *passive*) **a** trap in a bunker (in sense 3). **b** *Brit.* bring into difficulties. [19th c.: orig. unkn.]

bunk•house /búngkhows/ *n.* a house where workers, ranch hands, etc., are lodged.

bun•kum /búngkəm/ *n.* (also **bun•combe**) nonsense; humbug. [orig. *buncombe* f. *Buncombe* county in N. Carolina, mentioned in a nonsense speech by its congressman, *c.*1820]

bun•ny /búnee/ *n.* (*pl.* **•nies**) **1** a child's name for a rabbit. **2** *Austral.* a victim or dupe. **3** a club hostess, waitress, etc., wearing a skimpy costume with ears and a tail suggestive of a rabbit. [dial. *bun* rabbit]

Bun•sen burn•er /búnsən/ *n.* a small adjustable gas burner used in scientific work as a source of intense heat. [R. W. *Bunsen*, Ger. chemist d. 1899]

bunt¹ /bunt/ *n.* the baggy center of a fishing net, sail, etc. [16th c.: orig. unkn.]

bunt² /bunt/ *n.* a disease of wheat caused by the fungus *Tilletia caries*. [18th c.: orig. unkn.]

bunt³ /bunt/ *v. & n.* • *v.* **1** *tr. & intr.* push with the head or horns; butt. **2** *tr. Baseball* to tap or push (a ball) with the bat without swinging. • *n.* an act of bunting. [19th c.: cf. BUTT¹]

bunt•ing¹ /búnting/ *n.* any of numerous seed-eating birds of the family Emberizidae, related to the finches and sparrows. [ME: orig. unkn.]

bunt•ing² /búnting/ *n.* **1** flags and other decorations. **2** a loosely woven fabric used for these. [18th c.: orig. unkn.]

bunt•ing³ /búnting/ *n.* a baby's hooded sleeping bag made of soft fabric. [prob. f. the term in the nursery rhyme "Bye, baby bunting"]

bunt·line /búntlin, –lin/ *n.* a line for confining the bunt (see BUNT[1]) when furling a sail.

bun·ya /búnyə/ *n.* (also **bun·ya bun·ya**) *Austral.* a tall coniferous tree, *Araucaria bidwillii*, bearing large nutritious cones. [Aboriginal]

bun·yip /búnyip/ *n. Austral.* **1** a fabulous monster inhabiting swamps and lagoons. **2** an impostor. [Aboriginal]

bu·oy /bŏŏ-ee, boy/ *n. & v.* ● *n.* **1** an anchored float serving as a navigation mark or to show reefs, etc. **2** a life buoy. ● *v.tr.* **1** (usu. foll. by *up*) a keep afloat. **b** sustain the courage or spirits of (a person, etc.); uplift; encourage. **2** (often foll. by *out*) mark with a buoy or buoys. [ME prob. f. MDu. *bo(e)ye*, ult. f. L *boia* collar f. Gk *boeiai* ox hides]

buoy·an·cy /bóyənsee/ *n.* **1** the capacity to be or remain buoyant. **2** resilience; recuperative power. **3** cheerfulness.

buoy·ant /bóyənt/ *adj.* **1 a** able or apt to keep afloat or rise to the top of a liquid or gas. **b** (of a liquid or gas) able to keep something afloat. **2** lighthearted; resilient. □□ **buoy·ant·ly** *adv.* [F *buoyant* or Sp. *boyante* part. of *boyar* float f. *boya* BUOY]

bur /bər/ *n.* var. of BURR. [ME: cf. Da. *burre* bur, burdock, Sw. *kardborre* burdock]

bur. *abbr.* bureau.

bur·ble /bórbəl/ *v. & n.* ● *v.intr.* **1** speak ramblingly; make a murmuring noise. **2** *Aeron.* (of an airflow) break up into turbulence. ● *n.* **1** a murmuring noise. **2** rambling speech. □□ **bur·bler** *n.* [19th c.: imit.]

bur·bot /bórbət/ *n.* an eellike, flat-headed, bearded freshwater fish, *Lota lota*. [ME: cf. OF *barbote*]

bur·den /bórdən/ *n. & v.* ● *n.* **1 a** a load, esp. a heavy one. **2** an oppressive duty, obligation, expense, emotion, etc. **3** the bearing of loads (*beast of burden*). **4** (also *archaic* **bur·then** /bórthən/) a ship's carrying capacity; tonnage. **5 a** the refrain or chorus of a song. **b** the chief theme or gist of a speech, book, poem, etc. ● *v.tr.* load with a burden; encumber; oppress. □□ **bur·den·some** *adj.* **bur·den·some·ness** *n.* [OE *byrthen*: rel. to BIRTH]

bur·den of proof *n.* the obligation to prove one's case.

bur·dock /bórdok/ *n.* any plant of the genus *Arctium*, with prickly flowers and docklike leaves. [BUR + DOCK[3]]

bu·reau /byŏŏrō/ *n.* (*pl.* **bu·reaus** or **bu·reaux** /-rōz/) **1 a** a chest of drawers. **b** *Brit.* a writing desk with drawers and usu. an angled top opening downward to form a writing surface. **2 a** an office or department for transacting specific business. **b** a government department. [F, = desk, orig. its baize covering, f. OF *burel* f. *bure*, *buire* dark brown ult. f. Gk *purros* red]

bu·reauc·ra·cy /byŏŏrókrəsee/ *n.* (*pl.* **·cies**) **1 a** a government by central administration. **b** a nation or organization so governed. **2** the officials of such a government, esp. regarded as oppressive and inflexible. **3** conduct typical of such officials. [F *bureaucratie*: see BUREAU]

bu·reau·crat /byŏŏrəkrat/ *n.* **1** an official in a bureaucracy. **2** an inflexible or insensitive administrator. □□ **bu·reau·crat·ic** /–krátik/ *adj.* **bu·reau·crat·i·cal·ly** *adv.* [F *bureaucrate* (as BUREAUCRACY)]

bu·reauc·ra·tize /byŏŏrókrətiz/ *v.tr.* govern by or transform into a bureaucratic system. □□ **bu·reauc·ra·ti·za·tion** /–tizáyshən/ *n.*

bu·rette /byŏŏrét/ *n.* (also **bu·ret**) a graduated glass tube with a stopcock for measuring small volumes of liquid in chemical analysis. [F]

burg /bərg/ *n. colloq.* a town or city. [see BOROUGH]

bur·gage /bórgij/ *n. hist.* (in England and Scotland) tenure of land in a town on a yearly rent. [ME f. med.L *burgagium* f. *burgus* BOROUGH]

bur·gee /bərjée/ *n.* a triangular or swallow-tailed flag bearing the colors or emblem of a yacht club. [18th c.: perh. = (ship)owner, ult. F *bourgeois*: see BURGESS]

bur·geon /bórjən/ *v. & n. literary* ● *v.intr.* **1** begin to grow rapidly; flourish. **2** put forth young shoots; bud. ● *n.* a bud or young shoot. [ME f. OF *bor–*, *burjon* ult. f. LL *burra* wool]

burg·er /bórgər/ *n.* **1** *colloq.* a hamburger. **2** (in *comb.*) a certain kind of hamburger or variation of it (*beefburger*, *veggieburger*). [abbr.]

bur·gess /bórjis/ *n.* **1** *Brit.* an inhabitant of a town or borough, esp. of one with full municipal rights. **2** *Brit. hist.* a Member of Parliament for a borough, corporate town, or university. **3** *hist.* a borough magistrate or legislator in colonial Maryland or Virginia. [ME f. OF *burgeis* ult. f. LL *burgus* BOROUGH]

burgh /bərg, búrə/ *n. hist.* a Scottish borough or chartered town. □□ **burgh·al** /bórgəl/ *adj.* [Sc. form of BOROUGH]

burgh·er /bórgər/ *n.* **1** a citizen or freeman, esp. of a town on the European continent. **2** *S.Afr. hist.* a citizen of a Boer republic. **3** a descendant of a Dutch or Portuguese colonist in Sri Lanka. [G *Burger* or Du. *burger* f. *Burg*, *burg* BOROUGH]

bur·glar /bórglər/ *n.* a person who commits burglary. □□ **bur·glar·i·ous** /–gláireeəs/ *adj.* [legal AF *burgler*, rel. to OF *burgier* pillage]

bur·glar·ize /bórgləriz/ *v.* **1** *tr.* commit burglary against (a building or person). **2** *intr.* commit burglary.

bur·gla·ry /bórgləree/ *n.* (*pl.* **·ries**) **1** entry into a building illegally with intent to commit theft, do bodily harm, or do damage. **2** an instance of this. [legal AF *burglarie*: see BURGLAR]

▶Traditionally (under common law), **burglary** was the crime of breaking into a dwelling with the intent of committing a felony. It was essentially a crime against the security of one's home. Today, common usage and statutes have made burglary the crime of breaking into any building at any time with intent to steal or commit a felony; it is now essentially a crime against property.

bur·gle /bórgəl/ *v.tr. & intr.* = BURGLARIZE. [back-form. f BURGLAR]

bur·go·mas·ter /bórgəmastər/ *n.* the mayor of a Dutch or Flemish town. [Du. *burgemeester* f. *burg* BOROUGH: assim. to MASTER]

bur·grave /bórgrayv/ *n. hist.* the ruler of a town or castle. [G *Burggraf* f. *Burg* BOROUGH + *Graf* COUNT[2]]

bur·gun·dy /bórgəndee/ *n.* (*pl.* **·dies**) **1 a** the wine (usu. red) of Burgundy in E. France. **b** a similar wine from another place. **2** the dark red color of Burgundy wine.

burh·el var. of BHARAL.

bur·i·al /béreeəl/ *n.* **1 a** the burying of a dead body. **b** a funeral. **2** *Archaeol.* a grave or its remains. [ME, erron. formed as sing. of OE *byrgels* f. Gmc: rel. to BURY]

bur·i·al ground *n.* a cemetery.

bu·rin /byŏŏrin, bór–/ *n.* **1** a steel tool for engraving on copper or wood. **2** *Archaeol.* a flint tool with a chisel point. [F]

burk var. of BERK.

bur·ka /bórkə/ *n.* a long enveloping garment worn in public by Muslim women. [Hind. f. Arab. *burka'*]

Bur·kitt's lym·pho·ma /bórkits/ *n. Med.* a malignant tumor of the lymphatic system, esp. affecting children of Central Africa. [D. P. *Burkitt*, Brit. surgeon b. 1911]

burl /bərl/ *n.* **1** a knot or lump in wool or cloth. **2** a rounded knotty growth on a tree. [ME f. OF *bourle* tuft of wool, dimin. of *bourre* coarse wool f. LL *burra* wool]

bur·lap /bórlap/ *n.* **1** coarse canvas esp. of jute used for sacking, etc. **2** a similar lighter material for use in dressmaking or furnishing. [17th c.: orig. unkn.]

bur·lesque /bərlésk/ *n., adj., & v.* ● *n.* **1 a** a comic imitation, esp. in parody of a dramatic or literary work. **b** a performance or work of this kind. **c** bombast; mock-seriousness. **2** a variety show, often including striptease. ● *adj.* of or in the nature of burlesque. ● *v.tr.* (**burlesques, burlesqued, burlesquing**) make or give a burlesque of. □□ **bur·lesqu·er** *n.* [F f. It. *burlesco* f. *burla* mockery]

bur·ly /bórlee/ *adj.* (**bur·li·er, bur·li·est**) of stout sturdy build; big and strong. □□ **bur·li·ness** *n.* [ME *borli* prob. f. an OE form = 'fit for the bower' (BOWER[1])]

Bur·mese /bórmeez/ *n. & adj.* ● *n.* (*pl.* same) **1 a** a native or inhabitant of Burma (also called Myanmar) in SE Asia. **b** a person of Burmese descent. **2** a member of the largest ethnic group of Burma. **3** the language of this group. ● *adj.* of or relating to Burma or its people or language.

burn[1] /bərn/ *v. & n.* ● *v.* (*past* and *past part.* **burned** or **burnt**) **1** *tr. & intr.* be or cause to be consumed or destroyed by fire. **2** *tr.* **a** blaze or glow with fire. **b** be in the state characteristic of fire. **3** *tr. & intr.* be or cause to be injured or damaged by fire or great heat or by radiation. **4** *tr. & intr.* use or be used as a source of heat, light, or other energy. **5** *tr. & intr.* char or scorch in cooking (*burned the vegetables; the vegetables are burning*). **6** *tr.* produce (a hole, a mark, etc.) by fire or heat. **7** *tr.* **a** subject (clay, chalk, etc.) to heat for a purpose. **b** harden (bricks) by fire. **c** make (lime or charcoal) by heat. **8** *tr.* color, tan, or parch with heat or light (*we were burned brown by the sun*). **9** *tr. & intr.* put or be put to death by fire or electrocution. **10** *tr.* **a** cauterize; brand. **b** (foll. by *in*) imprint by burning. **11** *tr. & intr.* make or be hot; give or feel a sensation or pain of or like heat. **12 a** *tr. & intr.* (often foll. by *with*) make or be passionate; feel or cause to feel great emotion (*burn with shame*). **b** *intr.* (usu. foll. by *to* + infin.) desire passionately; long. **13** *intr. sl.* drive fast. **14** *tr. sl.* anger; infuriate. **15** *intr.* (foll. by *into*) (of acid, etc.) gradually penetrate (into) causing disintegration. ● *n.* **1** a mark or injury caused by or as if by burning. **2** the ignition of a rocket engine in flight, giving extra thrust. **3** a forest area cleared by burning. **4** *Brit. sl.* a cigarette. **5** *Brit. sl.* a car race. □ **burn one's bridges** (or *Brit.* **boats**) commit oneself irrevocably. **burn the candle at both ends** exhaust one's strength or resources by undertaking too much. **burn down 1 a** destroy (a building) by burning. **b** (of a building) be destroyed by fire. **2** burn less vigorously as fuel fails. **burn one's fingers** suffer for meddling or rashness. **burn a hole in one's pocket** (of money) be quickly spent. **burn in** darken (part of a photograph) by masking other parts of it and giving more exposure to the unmasked portion during printing. **burn low** (of fire) be nearly out. **burn off** be dissipated by the sun, as fog or mist. **burn the midnight oil** read or work late into the night. **burn out 1** be reduced to nothing by burning. **2** fail or cause to fail by burning. **3** (usu. *refl.*) suffer physical or emotional exhaustion (see BURNED-OUT). **4** consume the contents of by burning. **5** make (a person) homeless by burning his or her house. **burn up 1** get rid of by fire. **2** begin to blaze. **3** *sl.* be or make furious. **have money to burn** have more money than one needs. [OE *birnan, bærnan* f. Gmc]

▶The past and past participle of the verb **burn** is either **burned** or **burnt**. *Burned* is more common as both a transitive and intransitive verb in American English (*I burned the toast; she burned with embarrassment*). *Burnt* is more widely used in British English, especially as an intransitive verb. Either form may be used as a participial adjective (*burned toast* or *burnt toast*). In certain combinations, *burnt* is standard (*burnt offerings; burnt umber*).

CAUTERIZE, CHAR, SCALD, SCORCH, SEAR, SINGE. If you're not an experienced cook, you're likely to **burn** your vegetables, **char** your meat, and, if you put your face too close to the stove, you might even **singe** your eyebrows. All of these verbs mean to injure or bring about a change in something by exposing it to fire or intense heat. *Burn*, which is the most comprehensive term, can mean to change only slightly (*she burned her face by staying out in the sun*) or to destroy completely (*the factory was burned to the ground*). To *char* is to reduce a substance to carbon or charcoal (*the beams in the ceiling were charred by the fire*). Like *char*, **singe** and **scorch** mean to burn only partially or superficially (*scorched the blouse while ironing it; singe the chicken before cooking it*). *Singeing* is often done deliberately to remove the hair, bristles, or feathers from the carcass of an animal or bird. *Scald* refers specifically to burning with, or as if with, a hot liquid or steam (*the cook scalded herself when she spilled the boiling water*); it can also mean to parboil or heat to a temperature just below boiling (*scald the milk to make the sauce*). *Sear* is also a term used in cooking, where it means to brown the outside of a piece of meat by subjecting it briefly to intense heat to seal in the juices. When it's human flesh that's being seared in surgery, the correct verb is **cauterize**, which means to burn for healing purposes (*the doctor cauterized the wound to ward off infection*).

burn[2] /bərn/ *n. Sc.* a small stream. [OE *burna*, etc., f. Gmc]

burned-out *adj.* (also **burnt-out**) physically or emotionally exhausted.

burn·er /bɔ́rnər/ *n.* the part of a gas stove, lamp, etc., that emits and shapes the flame. □ **on the back** (or **front**) **burner** *colloq.* receiving little (or much) attention.

bur·net /bɔ́rnét, bɔ́rnit/ *n.* **1** any rosaceous plant of the genus *Sanguisorba*, with pink or red flowers. **2** any of several diurnal moths of the family Zygaenidae, with crimson spots on greenish black wings. [obs. *burnet* (adj.) dark brown f. OF *burnete*]

burn·ing /bɔ́rning/ *adj.* **1** ardent; intense (*burning desire*). **2** hotly discussed; exciting (*burning question*). **3** flagrant (*burning shame*). **4** that burns; on fire; very hot. □□ **burn·ing·ly** *adv.*

burn·ing bush *n.* **1** any of various shrubs with red fruits or red autumn leaves (with ref. to Exod. 3:2). **2** fraxinella.

burn·ing glass *n.* a lens for concentrating the sun's rays on an object to burn it.

bur·nish /bɔ́rnish/ *v.tr.* polish by rubbing. □□ **bur·nish·er** *n.* [ME f. OF *burnir = brunir* f. *brun* BROWN]

bur·noose /bərnoōs/ *n.* (also **bur·nous**) an Arab or Moorish hooded cloak. [F f. Arab. *burnus* f. Gk *birros* cloak]

burn·out /bɔ́rnowt/ *n.* **1** physical or emotional exhaustion, esp. caused by stress. **2** depression; disillusionment.

burnt see BURN[1].

burnt o·cher *n.* (also **burnt si·en·na, burnt um·ber**) a pigment darkened by burning.

burnt of·fer·ing *n.* **1** an offering burned on an altar as a sacrifice. **2** *joc.* overcooked food.

bur oak *n.* a N. American oak, *Quercus macrocarpa*, with large fringed acorn cups.

burp /bərp/ *v. & n. colloq.* ● *v.* **1** *intr.* belch. **2** *tr.* make (a baby) belch, usu. by patting its back. ● *n.* a belch. [imit.]

burp gun *n. sl.* a lightweight machine gun.

burr /bər/ *n. & v.* ● *n.* **1 a** a whirring sound. **b** a rough sounding of the letter *r.* **2 a** a rough edge left on cut or punched metal or paper. **b** a surgeon's or dentist's small drill. **3 a** a siliceous rock used for millstones. **b** a whetstone. **4 a** a prickly clinging seedcase or flowerhead. **b** any plant producing these. **5** a person hard to shake off. **6** the coronet of a deer's antler. ● *v.* **1** *tr.* pronounce with a burr. **2** *intr.* speak indistinctly. **3** *intr.* make a whirring sound. [var. of BUR]

bur·ri·to /bəreētō/ *n.* (*pl.* **·tos**) a tortilla rolled around a usu. meat or bean filling. [Amer. Sp., dimin. of *burro* BURRO]

bur·ro /bɔ́rō, boŏrō, bɔ́orō/ *n.* (*pl.* **·ros**) a small donkey used as a pack animal. [Sp.]

burnoose

bur·ro's tail *n.* a succulent plant of Mexico *Sedum morganianum*, with plump hanging stems and clustered pale green leaves.

bur·row /bɔ́rō, bɔ́rō/ *n. & v.* ● *n.* a hole or tunnel dug by a small animal, esp. a rabbit, as a dwelling. ● *v.* **1** *intr.* make or live in a burrow. **2** *tr.* make (a hole, etc.) by digging. **3** *intr.* hide oneself. **4** *intr.* (foll. by *into*) investigate; search. □□ **bur·row·er** *n.* [ME, app. var. of BOROUGH]

bur·sa /bɔ́rsə/ *n.* (*pl.* **bur·sae** /-see/ or **bur·sas**) *Anat.* a fluid-filled sac or saclike cavity to lessen friction. □□ **bur·sal** *adj.* [med.L = bag: cf. PURSE]

bur·sar /bɔ́rsər/ *n.* **1** a treasurer, esp. the person in charge of the funds and other property of a college. **2** *Brit.* the holder of a bursary. □□ **bur·sar·ship** *n.* [F *boursier* or (in sense 1) med.L *bursarius* f. *bursa* bag]

bur·sa·ry /bɔ́rsəree/ *n.* (*pl.* **·ries**) **1** the post or room of a bursar. **2** *Brit.* a grant, esp. a scholarship. □□ **bur·sar·i·al** /-sáireeəl/ *adj.* [med.L *bursaria* (as BURSAR)]

bur·si·tis /bərsítis/ *n.* inflammation of a bursa.

burst /bɔrst/ *v. & n.* ● *v.* (*past* and *past part.* **burst**) **1 a** *intr.* break suddenly and violently apart by expansion of contents or internal pressure. **b** *tr.* cause to do this. **c** *tr.* send (a container, etc.) violently apart. **2 a** *tr.* open forcibly. **b** *intr.* come open or be opened forcibly. **3 a** *intr.* (usu. foll. by *in, out*) make one's way suddenly, dramatically, or by force. **b** *tr.* break away from or through (*the river burst its banks*). **4** *tr. & intr.* fill or be full to overflowing. **5** *intr.* appear or come suddenly (*burst into flame; burst upon the scene; sun burst out*). **6** *intr.* (foll. by *into*) suddenly begin to shed or utter (esp. burst into tears or laughter or song). **7** *intr.* be as if about to burst because of effort, excitement, etc. **8** *tr.* suffer bursting of (*burst a blood vessel*). **9** *tr.* separate (continuous stationery) into single sheets. ● *n.* **1** the act of or an instance of bursting; a split. **2** a sudden issuing forth (*burst of flame*). **3** a sudden outbreak (*burst of applause*). **4 a** a short sudden effort; a spurt. **b** a gallop. **5** an explosion. □ **bursting at the seams** being fuller or more crowded than expected. **burst out 1** suddenly begin (*burst out laughing*). **2** exclaim. [OE *berstan* f. Gmc]

bur·then *archaic* var. of BURDEN *n.* 4.

bur·ton[1] /bɔ́rt'n/ *n.* □ **go for a burton** *Brit. sl.* be lost or destroyed or killed. [20th c.: perh. *Burton* ale f. *Burton-on-Trent* in England]

bur·ton[2] /bɔ́rt'n/ *n.* a light two-block tackle for hoisting. [ME *Breton tackles*: see BRETON]

bur·y /béree/ *v.tr.* (**·ies, ·ied**) **1** place (a dead body) in the earth, in a tomb, or in the sea. **2** lose by death (*has buried three husbands*). **3 a** put under ground (*bury alive*). **b** hide (treasure, a bone, etc.) in the earth. **c** cover up; submerge. **4 a** put out of sight (*buried his face in his hands*). **b** consign to obscurity (*the idea was buried after brief discussion*). **c** put away; forget. **5** involve deeply (*buried himself in his work; was buried in a book*). □ **bury the hatchet** cease to quarrel. [OE *byrgan* f. WG: cf. BURIAL]

bur·y·ing bee·tle *n.* a sexton beetle.

bur·y·ing ground *n.* (also **place**) a cemetery.

bus /bus/ *n. & v.* (*pl.* **bus·es** or **bus·ses**) **1** a large passenger vehicle, esp. one serving the public on a fixed route. **2** *colloq.* an automobile, airplane, etc. **3** *Computing* a defined set of conductors carrying data and control signals within a computer. ● *v.* (**bus·es** or **bus·ses, bused, or bussed, bus·ing** or **bus·sing**) **1** *intr.* go by bus. **2** *tr.* transport by bus, esp. children to more distant schools to promote racial integration. [abbr. of OMNIBUS]

bus. *abbr.* business.

bus·bar /búsbaar/ *n. Electr.* a system of conductors in a generating or receiving station on which power is concentrated for distribution.

bus·boy /búsboy/ *n.* an assistant to a restaurant waiter who performs such chores as filling water glasses and removing dirty dishes from diners' tables. [f. *omnibus*]

bus·by /búzbee/ *n.* (*pl.* **·bies**) a tall fur hat worn by some military, esp. British, units. [18th c.: orig. unkn.]

bush[1] /boŏsh/ *n.* **1** a shrub or clump of shrubs with stems of moderate length. **2** a thing resembling this, esp. a clump of hair or fur. **3** (esp. in Australia and Africa) a wild uncultivated or settled district; woodland or forest. **4** *hist.* a bunch of ivy as a vintner's sign. □ **go bush** *Austral.* leave one's usual surroundings; run wild. [ME f. OE & ON, ult. f. Gmc]

bush[2] /boŏsh/ *n. Brit.* = BUSHING. [MDu. *busse* BOX[1]]

bush ba·by *n.* (*pl.* **·bies**) a small African tree-climbing lemur; a galago.

bush ba·sil *n.* a culinary herb, *Ocimum minimum*.

bush·buck /boŏshbuk/ *n.* a small antelope, *Tragelaphus scriptus*, of southern Africa, having a chestnut coat with white stripes. [BUSH[1] + BUCK[1], after Du. *boschbok* f. *bosch* bush]

bushed /boŏsht/ *adj. colloq.* **1** tired out. **2** *Austral. & NZ* **a** lost in the bush. **b** bewildered.

bush·el /boŏshəl/ *n.* a measure of capacity for grain, fruit, etc. (64

busby

pints; *Brit.* 8 gallons, or 36.4 liters). ▫▫ **bush·el·ful** *n.* (*pl.* **·fuls**). [ME f. OF *buissiel*, etc., perh. of Gaulish orig.]

bush·fire /boͦoshfīr/ *n.* esp. *Austral.* a fire in a forest or in scrub often spreading widely.

bu·shi·do /boͦosheedō/ *n.* the code of honor and morals evolved by the Japanese samurai. [Jap., = military knight's way]

bush·ing /boͦoshing/ *n.* **1** a metal lining for a round hole enclosing a revolving shaft, etc. **2** a sleeve providing electrical insulation.

bush jack·et *n.* a belted cotton jacket with patch pockets.

bush law·yer *n.* **1** *Austral.* & *NZ* a person claiming legal knowledge without qualifications for it. **2** *NZ* a bramble.

bush·man /boͦoshmən/ *n.* (*pl.* **·men**) **1** a person who lives or travels in the Australian bush. **2** (**Bushman**) **a** a member of an aboriginal people in S. Africa. **b** the language of this people. [BUSH[1] + MAN: sense 2 after Du. *boschjesman* f. *bosch* bush]

bush·mas·ter /boͦoshmastər/ *n.* a venomous viper, *Lachesis muta*, of Central and S. America. [perh. f. Du. *boschmeester*]

bush pi·lot *n.* a pilot who flies a small plane into remote areas.

bush·rang·er /boͦoshraynjər/ *n.* *hist.* an Australian outlaw living in the bush.

bush sick·ness *n.* a disease of animals due to a lack of cobalt in the soil.

bush tel·e·graph *n.* rapid spreading of information, a rumor, etc.

bush·veld /boͦoshfelt/ *n.* open country consisting largely of bush. [BUSH[1] + VELD, after Afrik. *bosveld*]

bush·whack /boͦosh-hwak, –wak/ *v.* **1** *intr.* **a** clear woods and bush country. **b** live or travel in bush country. **2** *tr.* ambush.

bush·whack·er /boͦosh-hwakər, –wakər/ *n.* **1 a** a person who clears woods and bush country. **b** a person who lives or travels in bush country. **2** a guerrilla fighter (orig. in the American Civil War).

bush·y[1] /boͦoshee/ *adj.* (**bush·i·er, bush·i·est**) **1** growing thickly like a bush. **2** having many bushes. **3** covered with bush. ▫▫ **bush·i·ly** *adv.* **bush·i·ness** *n.*

bush·y[2] /boͦoshee/ *n.* (*pl.* **·ies**) *Austral.* & *NZ colloq.* a person who lives in the bush (as distinct from in a town).

bus·i·ly /bízilee/ *adv.* in a busy manner.

busi·ness /bíznis/ *n.* **1** one's regular occupation, profession, or trade. **2** a thing that is one's concern. **3 a** a task or duty. **b** a reason for coming (*what is your business?*). **4** serious work or activity (*get down to business*). **5** *derog.* an affair; a matter (*sick of the whole business*). **6** a thing or series of things needing to be dealt with (*the business of the day*). **7** business; relations; dealings, esp. of a commercial nature (*good stroke of business*). **8** a commercial house or firm. **9** *Theatr.* action on stage. **10** a difficult matter (*what a business it is!; made a great business of it*). ▫ **has no business to** has no right to. **in business 1** trading or dealing. **2** able to begin operations. **in the business of 1** engaged in. **2** intending to (*we are not in the business of surrendering*). **like nobody's business** *colloq.* extraordinarily. **make it one's business** to undertake to. **mind one's own business** not meddle. **on business** with a definite purpose, esp. one relating to one's regular occupation. **send a person about his or her business** dismiss a person; send a person away. [OE *bisignis* (as BUSY, –NESS)]

---

busi·ness card *n.* a card printed with one's name and professional details.

busi·ness end *n.* *colloq.* the functional part of a tool or device.

busi·ness·like /bíznislik/ *adj.* efficient; systematic; practical.

busi·ness·man /bíznismən/ *n.* (*pl.* **·men**; *fem.* **busi·ness·wom·an**, *pl.* **·wom·en**) a man or woman engaged in business or commerce, esp. at a senior level (see also BUSINESS PERSON).

busi·ness park *n.* an office park or industrial park.

busi·ness per·son *n.* a businessman or businesswoman.

busi·ness re·ply mail *n.* a system of sending business mail in envelopes prepaid by the addressee.

busi·ness stud·ies *n.* training in economics, management, etc.

busi·ness suit *n.* **1** a man's suit consisting of a jacket, trousers, and sometimes a vest. **2** a woman's suit, consisting of a jacket and usu. a skirt.

busk /busk/ *v.intr.* perform (esp. music) for voluntary donations, usu. in the street or in subways. ▫▫ **busk·er** *n.* **busk·ing** *n.* [*busk* peddle, etc. (perh. f. obs. F *busquer* seek)]

bus·kin /búskin/ *n.* **1** either of a pair of thick-soled laced boots worn by an ancient Athenian tragic actor to gain height. **2** (usu. prec. by *the*) tragic drama; its style or spirit. **3** *hist.* either of a pair of calf- or knee-high boots of cloth or leather used in the Middle Ages. ▫▫ **bus·kined** *adj.* [prob. f. OF *bouzequin*, var. of *bro(u)sequin*, of unkn. orig.]

bus lane *n.* a part of a roadway marked off mainly for use by buses.

bus·man /búsmən/ *n.* (*pl.* **·men**) the driver of a bus.

bus·man's hol·i·day *n.* leisure time spent in an activity similar to one's regular work.

buss /bus/ *n.* & *v. colloq.* ●*n.* a kiss. ●*v.tr.* kiss. [earlier *bass* (n. & v.): cf. F *baiser* f. L *basiare*]

bus sta·tion *n.* a center, esp. in a town, where (esp. long-distance) buses depart and arrive.

bus stop *n.* **1** a regular stopping place for a bus. **2** a sign marking this.

bust[1] /bust/ *n.* **1 a** the human chest, esp. that of a woman; the bosom. **b** the circumference of the body at bust level (*a 36-inch bust*). **2** a sculpture of a person's head, shoulders, and chest. [F *buste* f. It. *busto*, of unkn. orig.]

bust[2] /bust/ *v., n., & adj. colloq.* ●*v.* (*past* and *past part.* **bust·ed** or **bust**) **1** *tr.* & *intr.* burst; break. **2** *tr.* reduce (a soldier, etc.) to a lower rank; dismiss. **3** *tr.* **a** raid; search. **b** arrest. ●*n.* **1** a sudden failure; a bankruptcy. **2 a** a police raid. **b** an arrest. **3** a drinking bout. **4** a punch; a hit. **5** a worthless thing. **6** a bad hand at cards. ●*adj.* (also **bust·ed**) **1** broken; burst; collapsed. **2** bankrupt. **3** arrested. ▫ **bust a gut** make every possible effort. **bust up 1** bring or come to collapse; explode. **2** (of esp. a married couple) separate. **go bust** become bankrupt; fail. [orig. a (dial.) pronunc. of BURST]

▶**Busted** meaning 'broken' is best avoided in formal settings.

bus·tard /bústərd/ *n.* any large terrestrial bird of the family Otididae, with long neck, long legs, and stout tapering body. [ME f. OF *bistarde* f. L *avis tarda* slow bird (? = slow on the ground; but possibly a perversion of a foreign word)]

bust·er /bústər/ *n.* **1** *sl.* buddy; fellow (used esp. as a disrespectful form of address). **2** a violent gale.

bus·tier /boͦostyáy, bústeeay/ *n.* a woman's strapless close-fitting bodice, worn alone or under clothing. [F]

bus·tle[1] /búsəl/ *v.* & *n.* ●*v.* **1** *intr.* (often foll. by *about*) **a** work, etc., showily, energetically, and officiously. **b** hasten (*bustled about the kitchen banging saucepans*). **2** *tr.* make (a person) hurry or work hard (*bustled him into his overcoat*). **3** *intr.* (as **bustling** *adj.*) *colloq.* full of activity. ●*n.* excited activity; a fuss. ▫▫ **bus·tler** *n.* [perh. f. *buskle* frequent. of *busk* prepare]

bus·tle[2] /búsəl/ *n.* *hist.* a pad or frame worn under a skirt and puffing it out behind. [18th c.: orig. unkn.]

bust-up *n.* **1** esp. *Brit.* a quarrel. **2** a collapse; a breakup; an explosion.

bust·y /bústee/ *adj.* (**bust·i·er, bust·i·est**) (of a woman) having a prominent bust. ▫▫ **bust·i·ness** *n.*

bus·y /bízee/ *adj.* & *v.* ●*adj.* (**busier, busiest**) **1** (often foll. by *in*, *with*, *at*, or pres. part.) occupied or engaged in work, etc., with the attention concentrated (*busy at their needlework; he was busy packing*). **2** full of activity or detail; fussy (*a busy evening; a picture busy with detail*). **3** employed continuously; unresting (*busy as a bee*). **4** meddlesome; prying. **5** (of a telephone line) in use. ●*v.tr.* (**·ies, ·ied**) (often *refl.*) keep busy; occupy (*the work busied him for many hours; busied herself with the accounts*). ▫▫ **bus·i·ly** /bízilee/ *adv.* **bus·y·ness** /bízeenis/ *n.* (cf. BUSINESS). [OE *bisig*]

---

bus·y·bod·y /bízeebodee, –budee/ *n.* (*pl.* **·ies**) **1** a meddlesome person. **2** a mischief maker.

bus·y sig·nal *n.* an intermittent sound indicating that a telephone line is in use.

but[1] /but, bət/ *conj., prep., adv., pron., n., & v.* ●*conj.* **1 a** nevertheless; however (*tried hard but did not succeed; I am old, but I am not weak*). **b** on the other hand; on the contrary (*I am old but you are young*). **2** (prec. by *can*, etc.; in *neg.* or *interrog.*) except; other than; otherwise than (*cannot choose but do it; what could we do but run?*). **3** without the result that (*it never rains but it pours*). **4** prefixing an interruption to the speaker's train of thought (*the weather is ideal*—

but is that a cloud on the horizon?). ● *prep.* except; apart from; other than (*everyone went but me*; *nothing but trouble*). ● *adv.* **1** only; no more than; only just (*we can but try*; *is but a child*; *had but arrived*; *did it but once*). **2** introducing emphatic repetition; definitely (*wanted to see nobody, but nobody*). **3** *Austral., NZ, & Sc.* though; however (*didn't like it, but*). ● *rel.pron.* who not; that not (*there is not a man but feels pity*). ● *n.* an objection (*ifs and buts*). ● *v.tr.* (in phr. **but me no buts**) do not raise objections. □ **but for** without the help or hindrance, etc., of (*but for you I'd be rich by now*). **but one** (or **two**, etc.) excluding one (or two, etc.) from the number (*next door but one*; *last but one*). **but that** (prec. by *neg.*) that (*I don't deny but that it's true*). **but that** (or *colloq.* **what**) other than that; except that (*who knows but that it is true?*). **but then** (or **yet**) however; on the other hand (*I won, but then the others were beginners*). [OE *be-ūtan, būtan, būta* outside, without]

but² /but/ *n. Sc.* □ **but and ben** the outer and inner rooms of a two-roomed house (see BEN²). [BUT¹ = outside]

bu·ta·di·ene /bŏŏtədíeen/ *n. Chem.* a colorless gaseous hydrocarbon used in the manufacture of synthetic rubbers. ¶ *Chem.* formula: C_4H_6. [BUTANE + DI-² + -ENE: cf. BUNA]

bu·tane /byŏŏtayn/ *n. Chem.* a gaseous hydrocarbon of the alkane series used in liquefied form as fuel. ¶ *Chem.* formula: C_4H_{10}. [BUTYL + -ANE²]

butch /bŏŏch/ *adj. & n. sl.* ● *adj.* masculine; tough-looking. ● *n.* **1** (often *attrib.*) **a** a mannish woman. **b** a mannish lesbian. **2** a tough, usu. muscular, youth or man. [perh. abbr. of BUTCHER]

butch·er /bŏŏchər/ *n. & v.* ● *n.* **1 a** a person whose trade is dealing in meat. **b** a person who slaughters animals for food. **2** a person who kills or has people killed indiscriminately or brutally. ● *v.tr.* **1** slaughter or cut up (an animal) for food. **2** kill (people) wantonly or cruelly. **3** ruin (esp. a job or a musical composition) through incompetence. □ **the butcher, the baker, the candlestick maker** people of all kinds or trades. □□ **butch·er·ly** *adj.* [ME f. OF *bo(u)chier* f. *boc* BUCK¹]

butch·er·bird *n.* a shrike of the genus *Lanius*, native to Australia and New Guinea, with a long hook-tipped bill for catching prey.

butch·er's-broom *n.* a low spiny-leaved evergreen shrub, *Ruscus aculeatus* native to Europe.

butch·er·y /bŏŏchəree/ *n. (pl. ·ies)* **1** needless or cruel slaughter (of people). **2** the butcher's trade. **3** a slaughterhouse. [ME f. OF *boucherie* (as BUTCHER)]

but·le *var. of* BUTTLE.

but·ler /bútlər/ *n.* the principal manservant of a household, usu. in charge of the wine cellar, pantry, etc. [ME f. AF *buteler*, OF *bouteillier*: see BOTTLE]

butt¹ /but/ *v. & n.* ● *v.* **1** *tr. & intr.* push with the head or horns. **2 a** *intr.* (usu. foll. by *against, upon*) place with one end flat against; meet end to end with; abut. **b** *tr.* (usu. foll. by *against*) place (lumber, etc.) with the end flat against a wall, etc. ● *n.* **1 a** a push with the head. **2** a join of two edges. □ **butt in** interrupt; meddle. [ME f. AF *buter*, OF *boter* f. Gmc: infl. by BUTT² and ABUT]

butt² /but/ *n.* **1** (often foll. by *of*) an object (of ridicule, etc.) (*the butt of his jokes*; *made him their butt*). **2 a** a mound behind a target. **b** (in *pl.*) a shooting range. **c** a target. **3** a bird hunter's blind screened by low turf or a stone wall. [ME f. OF *but* goal, of unkn. orig.]

butt³ /but/ *n.* **1** (also **butt end**) the thicker end, esp. of a tool or a weapon (*gun butt*). **2 a** the stub of a cigar or a cigarette. **b** (also **butt end**) a remnant (*the butt of the evening*). **3** *sl.* the buttocks. **4** (also **butt end**) the square end of a plank meeting a similar end. **5** the trunk of a tree, esp. the part just above the ground. [Du. *bot* stumpy]

butt⁴ /but/ *n.* a cask, esp. as a measure of wine or ale. [AL *butta, bota*, AF *but*, f. OF *bo(u)t* f. LL *buttis*]

butt⁵ /but/ *n.* a flatfish (e.g., a sole, plaice, or turbot). [MLG, MDu. *but* flatfish]

butte /byoot/ *n.* a high, isolated, steep-sided hill. [F, = mound]

but·ter /bútər/ *n. & v.* ● *n.* **1 a** a pale yellow edible fatty substance made by churning cream and used as a spread or in cooking. **b** a substance of a similar consistency or appearance (*peanut butter*). **2** excessive flattery. ● *v.tr.* spread, cook, or serve with butter (*butter the bread*; *buttered rum*). □ **butter up** *colloq.* flatter excessively. **look as if butter wouldn't melt in one's mouth** seem demure or innocent, probably deceptively. [OE *butere* f. L *butyrum* f. Gk *bouturon*]

but·ter-and-eggs *n.* any of several plants having two shades of yellow in the flower, e.g., toadflax.

but·ter·ball /bútərbawl/ *n.* **1** a piece of butter shaped into a ball. **2** = BUFFLEHEAD (because it is very fat in autumn). **3** *sl.* a fat person.

but·ter bean *n.* **1** the flat, dried, white lima bean. **2** a yellow-podded bean.

but·ter·bur /bútərbər/ *n.* any of several plants of the genus *Petasites* with large soft leaves, formerly used to wrap butter.

but·ter cream *n.* (also **butter ic·ing**) a mixture of butter, confectioner's sugar, etc., used as a filling or a topping for a cake.

but·ter·cup /bútərkup/ *n.* any common yellow-flowered plant of the genus *Ranunculus*.

but·ter·fat /bútərfat/ *n.* the essential fats of pure butter.

but·ter·fin·gers /bútərfingərz/ *n. colloq.* a clumsy person prone to drop things.

but·ter·fish /bútərfish/ *n.* = GUNNEL¹.

but·ter·fly /bútərflī/ *n. (pl. ·flies)* **1** any diurnal insect of the order Lepidoptera, with knobbed antennae, a long thin body, and four usu. brightly colored wings erect when at rest. **2** a showy or frivolous person. **3** (in *pl.*) *colloq.* a nervous sensation felt in the stomach. [OE *buttor-flēoge* (as BUTTER, FLY²)]

butterfly (swallow tail)

but·ter·fly net *n.* a fine net on a ring attached to a pole, used for catching butterflies.

but·ter·fly nut *n.* a kind of wing nut.

but·ter·fly stroke *n.* a stroke in swimming, with both arms raised out of the water and lifted forward together.

but·ter·fly valve *n.* a valve with hinged semicircular plates.

but·ter knife *n.* a blunt knife used for cutting butter at table.

but·ter·milk /bútərmilk/ *n.* a slightly acid liquid left after churning butter.

but·ter mus·lin *n. Brit.* a thin, loosely woven cloth with a fine mesh, orig. for wrapping butter.

but·ter·nut /bútərnut/ *n.* **1** a N. American tree, *Juglans cinerea*. **2** the oily nut of this tree.

but·ter·scotch /bútərskoch/ *n.* **1** a brittle candy made from butter, brown sugar, etc. **2** this flavor in dessert toppings, puddings, etc. [SCOTCH]

but·ter·wort /bútərwərt, -wawrt/ *n.* any bog plant of the genus *Pinguicula*, esp. *P. vulgaris* with violetlike flowers and fleshy leaves that secrete a fluid to trap small insects for food.

but·ter·y¹ /bútəree/ *n. (pl. ·ies)* **1** *Brit.* a room, esp. in a college, where provisions are kept and supplied to students, etc. **2** a pantry. [ME f. AF *boterie* butt-store (as BUTT⁴)]

but·ter·y² /bútəree/ *adj.* like, containing, or spread with butter. □□ **but·ter·i·ness** *n.*

but·tle /bútəl/ *v.intr.* (also **but·le**) *joc.* work as a butler. [back-form. f. BUTLER]

but·tock /bútək/ *n.* (usu. in *pl.*) **1** each of two fleshy protuberances on the lower rear part of the human trunk. **2** the corresponding part of an animal. [butt ridge + -OCK]

but·ton /bút'n/ *n. & v.* ● *n.* **1 a** a small disk or knob sewn or pinned on to a garment, either to fasten it by being pushed through a buttonhole, or as an ornament or badge. **2** a knob on a piece of esp. electronic equipment which is pressed to operate it. **3 a** a small round object (*chocolate buttons*). **b** (*attrib.*) anything resembling a button (*button nose*). **4 a** a bud. **b** a button mushroom. **5** *Fencing* a terminal knob on a foil making it harmless. ● *v.* **1** *tr. & intr.* = *button up* 1. **2** *tr.* supply with buttons. □ **buttoned up** *colloq.* **1** formal and inhibited in manner. **2** silent. **button one's lip** *sl.* remain silent. **button through** *Brit.* (of a dress) fastened with buttons from neck to hem like a coat. **button up 1** fasten with buttons. **2** *colloq.* complete (a task, etc.) satisfactorily. **3** *colloq.* become silent. **4** fasten or close securely. **not worth a button** *Brit.* worthless. **on the button** *sl.* precisely. □□ **but·toned** *adj.* **but·ton·less** *adj.* **but·ton·y** *adj.* [ME f. OF *bouton*, ult. f. Gmc]

but·ton chry·san·the·mum *n.* a variety of chrysanthemum with small spherical flowers.

but·ton·hole /bút'nhōl/ *n. & v.* ● *n.* **1** a slit made in a garment to receive a button for fastening. **2** *Brit.* a flower or spray worn in a lapel buttonhole; a boutonniere. ● *v.tr.* **1** *colloq.* accost and detain (a reluctant listener). **2** make buttonholes in.

but·ton·hole stitch *n.* a looped stitch used for making buttonholes.

but·ton·hook /bút'nhŏŏk/ *n.* a hook formerly used esp. for pulling the buttons on tight boots, gloves, etc., into place for fastening.

but·ton mush·room *n.* a young unopened mushroom.

but·tons /bút'nz/ *n. Brit. colloq.* a liveried page boy; a bellhop. [from the rows of buttons on his jacket]

but·tress /bútris/ *n. & v.* ● *n.* **1 a** a projecting support of stone or brick, etc., built against a wall. **b** a source of help or encouragement (*she was a buttress to him in his trouble*). **2** a projecting portion of a hill or mountain. ● *v.tr.* (often foll. by *up*) **1** support with a buttress. **2** support by argument, etc. (*claim buttressed by facts*). [ME f. OF (*ars*) *bouterez* thrusting (arch) f. *bouteret* f. *bouter* BUTT¹]

butt weld *n.* a weld in which the pieces are joined end to end.

but·ty¹ /bútee/ *n. (pl. ·ties) Brit.* **1** *colloq.* or *dial.* a friend; a companion. **2** *hist.* a middleman negotiating between a mine owner and the miners. **3** a barge or other craft towed by another. [19th c.: perh. f. BOOTY in phr. *play booty* join in sharing plunder]

but·ty² /bútee/ *n. (pl. ·ties) No. of Engl.* a sandwich (*bacon butty*). **2** a slice of bread and butter. [BUTTER + -Y²]

but·ty-gang *n.* a gang of men contracted to work on a large job and sharing the profits equally.

bu•tyl /býo͞ot'l/ *n. Chem.* the univalent alkyl radical C_4H_9. [BUTYRIC (ACID) + –YL]

bu•tyl rub•ber *n.* a synthetic rubber used in the manufacture of tire inner tubes.

bu•tyr•ic ac•id /byo͞otírik/ *n. Chem.* either of two colorless syrupy liquid organic acids found in rancid butter or arnica oil. □□ **bu•tyr•ate** /byo͞otírayt/ *n.* [L *butyrum* BUTTER + –IC]

bux•om /búksəm/ *adj.* (esp. of a woman) plump and healthy-looking; large and shapely; full-bosomed. □□ **bux•om•ly** *adv.* **bux•om•ness** *n.* [earlier sense *pliant*: ME f. stem of OE *būgan* BOW² + –SOME¹]

buy /bī/ *v. & n.* ● *v.* (**buys, buy•ing**; *past* and *past part.* **bought** /bawt/) **1** *tr.* **a** obtain in exchange for money, etc. **b** (usu. in *neg.*) serve to obtain (*money can't buy happiness*). **2** *tr.* **a** procure (the loyalty, etc.) of a person by bribery, promises, etc. **b** win over (a person) in this way. **3** *tr.* get by sacrifice, great effort, etc. (*dearly bought; bought with our sweat*). **4** *tr. sl.* accept; believe in; approve of (*it's a good scheme, I'll buy it; he bought it, he's so gullible*). **5** *absol.* be a buyer for a store, etc. (*buys for Macy's; are you buying or selling?*). ● *n. colloq.* a purchase (*that sofa was a good buy*). □ **buy the farm** die. **buy in 1** buy a supply of. **2** withdraw (an item) at auction because of failure to reach the reserve price. **buy into** obtain a share in (an enterprise) by payment. **buy it** (usu. in *past*) *sl.* be killed. **buy off** get rid of (a claim, a claimant, a blackmailer) by payment. **buy oneself out** obtain one's release (esp. from the armed services) by payment. **buy out** pay (a person) to give up an ownership, interest, etc. **buy time** delay an event, conclusion, etc., temporarily. **buy up 1** buy as much as possible of. **2** absorb (another business, etc.) by purchase. [OE *bycgan* f. Gmc]

buy•er /bíər/ *n.* **1** a person employed to select and purchase stock for a large store, etc. **2** a purchaser; a customer.

buy•er's mar•ket *n.* (also **buy•ers' mar•ket**) an economic position in which goods are plentiful and cheap and buyers have the advantage.

buy•out /bíowt/ *n.* the purchase of a controlling share in a company, etc.

buzz /buz/ *n. & v.* ● *n.* **1** the hum of a bee, etc. **2** the sound of a buzzer. **3 a** a confused low sound as of people talking; a murmur. **b** a stir; hurried activity (*a buzz of excitement*). **c** *colloq.* a rumor. **4** *sl.* a telephone call. **5** *sl.* a thrill; a euphoric sensation. ● *v.* **1** *intr.* make a humming sound. **2 a** *tr. & intr.* signal or signal to with a buzzer. **b** *tr. sl.* telephone. **3** *intr.* **a** (often foll. by *about*) move or hover busily. **b** (of a place) have an air of excitement or purposeful activity. **4** *tr. colloq.* throw hard. **5** *tr. Aeron. colloq.* fly fast and very close to (another aircraft, the ground, etc.). □ **buzz off** *sl.* go or hurry away. [imit.]

buz•zard /búzərd/ *n.* **1** a turkey vulture. **2** *Brit.* any of a group of predatory birds of the hawk family, esp. of the genus *Butea*, with broad wings well adapted for soaring flight. [ME f. OF *busard*, *buson* f. L *buteo –onis* falcon]

buzz•er /búzər/ *n.* **1** an electrical device, similar to a bell, that makes a buzzing noise. **2** a whistle or siren.

buzz saw *n.* a circular saw.

buzz•word /búzwərd/ *n. sl.* **1** a fashionable piece of esp. technical or computer jargon. **2** a catchword; a slogan.

BVM *abbr.* Blessed Virgin Mary.

bwa•na /bwaánə/ *n. Afr.* master; sir. [Swahili]

BWI *abbr. hist.* British West Indies.

by /bī/ *prep., adv., & n.* ● *prep.* **1** near; beside; in the region of (*stand by the door; sit by me; path by the river*). **2** through the agency, means, instrumentality, or causation of (*by proxy; bought by a millionaire; a poem by Frost; went by bus; succeeded by persisting; divide four by two*). **3** not later than; as soon as (*by next week; by now; by the time he arrives*). **4 a** past; beyond (*drove by the zoo; came by us*). **b** passing through; via (*went by Paris*). **5** in the circumstances of (*by day; by daylight*). **6** to the extent of (*missed by a foot; better by far*). **7** according to; using as a standard or unit (*judge by appearances; paid by the hour*). **8** with the succession of (*worse by the minute; day by day; one by one*). **9** concerning; in respect of (*did our duty by them; Smith by name; all right by me*). **10** used in mild oaths (*orig.* = as surely as one believes in) (*by God; by gum; swear by all that is sacred*). **11** placed between specified lengths in two directions (*three feet by two*). **12** avoiding; ignoring (*pass by him; passed us by*). **13** inclining to (*north by northwest*). ● *adv.* **1** near (*sat by, watching; lives close by*).

2 aside; in reserve (*put $5 by*). **3** past (*they marched by*). ● *n.* = BYE¹. □ **by and by** before long; eventually. **by and large** on the whole; everything considered. **by the by** (or **bye**) incidentally; parenthetically. **by oneself 1 a** unaided. **b** without prompting. **2** alone; without company. [OE *bī, bi, be* f. Gmc]

by- /bī/ *prefix* (also **bye-**) subordinate; incidental; secondary (*by-effect; byroad*).

by-blow /bíblō/ *n.* esp. *Brit.* **1** a side blow not at the main target. **2** an illegitimate child.

bye¹ /bī/ *n.* **1** the status of an unpaired competitor in a sport, who proceeds to the next round as if having won. **2** *Golf* one or more holes remaining unplayed after the match has been decided. □ **by the bye** = *by the by* (see BY). [BY as noun]

bye² /bī/ *int. colloq.* = GOOD-BYE. [abbr.]

bye- *prefix* var. of BY-.

bye-bye¹ /bíbí, bəbí/ *int. colloq.* = GOOD-BYE. [childish corrupt.]

bye-bye² /bíbī/ *n.* (also **bye-byes** /–bīz/) (a child's word for) sleep. [ME, f. the sound used in lullabies]

by-e•lec•tion /bí-ilekshən/ *n. Brit.* the election of an MP in a single constituency to fill a vacancy arising during a government's term of office.

Bye•lo•rus•sian var. of BELORUSSIAN.

by-form /bífawrm/ *n.* a collateral form of a word, etc.

by•gone /bígawn, –gon/ *adj. & n.* ● *adj.* belonging to an earlier time; past (*bygone years*). ● *n.* (in *pl.*) past offenses (*let bygones be bygones*).

by•law /bílaw/ *n.* (also **bye•law**) **1** a regulation made by a local authority or corporation. **2** a rule made by a company or society for its members. [ME prob. f. obs. *byrlaw* local custom (ON *býjar* genitive sing. of *býr* town, but assoc. with BY)]

by•line /bílīn/ *n.* **1** a line in a newspaper, etc., naming the writer of an article. **2** a secondary line of work.

by•name /bínaym/ *n.* a sobriquet; a nickname.

by•pass /bípas/ *n. & v.* ● *n.* **1 a** a road passing around a town or its center to provide an alternative route for through traffic. **2 a** a secondary channel or pipe, etc., to allow a flow when the main one is closed or blocked. **b** an alternative passage for the circulation of blood during a surgical operation on the heart. ● *v.tr.* **1** avoid; go around. **2** provide with a bypass. **3** neglect or intentionally ignore.

by•path /bípath/ *n.* **1** a secluded path. **2** a minor or obscure branch of a subject.

by•play /bíplay/ *n.* a secondary action or sequence of events, esp. in a play.

by-prod•uct /bíprodəkt/ *n.* **1** an incidental product of the manufacture of something else. **2** a secondary often unforeseen result.

byre /bīr/ *n. Brit.* a cowshed. [OE *bȳre*: perh. rel. to BOWER¹]

by•road /bírōd/ *n.* a minor road.

By•ron•ic /bírónik/ *adj.* **1** characteristic of Lord Byron, English poet d. 1824, or his romantic poetry. **2** (of a man) handsomely dark, mysterious, or moody.

bys•si•no•sis /bísinósis/ *n. Med.* a lung disease caused by prolonged inhalation of textile fiber dust. [mod.L f. Gk *bussinos* made of byssus + –OSIS]

bys•sus /bísəs/ *n. hist.* (*pl.* **bys•sus•es** or **bys•si** /–sī/) **1** *hist.* a fine textile fiber and fabric of flax. **2** a tuft of tough silky filaments by which some mollusks adhere to rocks, etc. [ME f. L f. Gk *bussos*]

by•stand•er /bístandər/ *n.* a person who stands by but does not take part; a mere spectator.

byte /bīt/ *n. Computing* a group of eight binary digits, often used to represent one character. [20th c.: perh. based on BIT⁴ and BITE]

by•way /bíway/ *n.* **1** a small seldom-traveled road. **2** a minor activity.

by•word /bíwərd/ *n.* **1** a person or thing cited as a notable example (*is a byword for luxury*). **2** a familiar saying; a proverb.

Byz•an•tine /bízənteen, –tīn, bizántin/ *adj. & n.* ● *adj.* **1** of Byzantium or the E. Roman Empire. **2** (of a political situation, etc.): **a** extremely complicated. **b** inflexible. **c** carried on by underhand methods. **3** *Archit. & Painting* of a highly decorated style developed in the Eastern Empire. ● *n.* a citizen of Byzantium or the E. Roman Empire. □□ **Byz•an•tin•ism** *n.* **Byz•an•tin•ist** *n.* [F *byzantin* or L *Byzantinus* f. *Byzantium*, later Constantinople and now Istanbul]

C

C¹ /see/ *n.* (also **c**) (*pl.* **Cs** or **C's**) **1** the third letter of the alphabet. **2** *Mus.* the first note of the diatonic scale of C major (the major scale having no sharps or flats). **3** the third hypothetical person or example. **4** the third highest class or category (of academic marks, etc.). **5** *Algebra* (usu. **c**) the third known quantity. **6** (as a Roman numeral) 100. **7** (**c**) the speed of light in a vacuum. **8** (also ©) copyright.

C² *symb. Chem.* the element carbon.

C³ *abbr.* (also **C.**) **1** Cape. **2** Conservative. **3** Celsius; centigrade. **4** Coulomb(s); capacitance.

c. *abbr.* **1** century; centuries. **2** chapter. **3** cent(s). **4** cold. **5** cubic. **6** colt. **7** *Baseball* catcher. **8** centi–. **9** circa; about.

CA *abbr.* **1** California (in official postal use). **2** *Sc. & Can.* chartered accountant.

Ca *symb. Chem.* the element calcium.

ca. *abbr.* circa, about.

CAA *abbr.* Civil Aeronautics Administration.

Caa·ba var. of KAABA.

CAB *abbr.* Civil Aeronautics Board.

cab /kab/ *n.* **1** a taxi. **2** the driver's compartment in a truck, train, crane, etc. **3** *hist.* a hackney carriage. [abbr. of CABRIOLET]

ca·bal /kəbál/ *n. & v.* **1** a secret intrigue. **2** a political clique or faction. **3** *hist.* a committee of five ministers under Charles II, whose surnames happened to begin with C, A, B, A, and L. ● *v.intr.* (**ca·balled, ca·bal·ling**) (often foll. by *together, against*) plot; intrigue. [F *cabale* f. med.L *cabala,* CABALA]

cab·a·la /kábələ, kəbáálə/ *n.* (also **cab·ba·la, kab·ba·la**) **1** the Jewish mystical tradition. **2** mystic interpretation; any esoteric doctrine or occult lore. □□ **cab·a·lism** *n.* **cab·a·list** *n.* **cab·a·lis·tic** /–lístik/ *adj.* [med.L f. Rabbinical Heb. *ḳabbālā* tradition]

ca·bal·le·ro /kábəlyáirō, –bəláirō, káabaayáirō/ *n.* (*pl.* **·ros**) a Spanish gentleman. [Sp.: see CAVALIER]

ca·ban·a /kəbánə, –baányə/ *n.* a shelter, bathhouse, etc., at a beach or swimming pool. [Sp. *cabaña* f. LL (as CABIN)]

cab·a·ret /kabəráy/ *n.* **1** an entertainment in a nightclub or restaurant while guests eat or drink at tables. **2** such a nightclub, etc. [F, = wooden structure, tavern]

cab·bage /kábij/ *n.* **1 a** any of several cultivated varieties of *Brassica oleracea,* with thick green or purple leaves forming a round heart or head. **b** this head usu. eaten as a vegetable. **2** *Brit. colloq. derog.* a person who is inactive or lacks interest. □□ **cab·bag·y** *adj.* [earlier *cabache, –oche* f. OF (Picard) *caboche* head, OF *caboce,* of unkn. orig.]

cab·bage palm *n.* a palm tree, *Cordyline australis,* with edible cabbagelike terminal buds.

cab·bage rose *n.* a double rose with a large round compact flower.

cab·bage tree *n.* = CABBAGE PALM.

cab·bage white *n.* a mainly white butterfly, *Pieris brassicae,* whose caterpillars feed on cabbage leaves.

cab·ba·la var. of CABALA.

cab·by /kábee/ *n.* (also **cab·bie**) (*pl.* **·bies**) *colloq.* a cabdriver. [CAB + –Y²]

cab·driv·er /kábdrīvər/ *n.* the driver of a cab.

ca·ber /káybər/ *n.* a roughly trimmed tree trunk used in the Scottish Highland sport of tossing the caber. [Gael. *cabar* pole]

cab·in /kábin/ *n. & v.* ● *n.* **1** a small shelter or house, esp. of wood. **2** a room or compartment in an aircraft or ship for passengers or crew. **3** a driver's cab. ● *v.tr.* (**cab·ined, cab·in·ing**) confine in a small place; cramp. [ME f. OF *cabane* f. Prov. *cabana* f. LL *capanna, cavanna*]

cab·in boy *n.* a boy who waits on a ship's officers or passengers.

cab·in class *n.* the intermediate class of accommodation in a ship.

cab·in crew *n.* the crew members on an airplane attending to passengers and cargo.

cab·in cruis·er *n.* a large motorboat with living accommodations.

cab·i·net /kábinit/ *n.* **1 a** a cupboard or case with drawers, shelves, etc., for storing or displaying articles. **b** a piece of furniture housing a radio or television set, etc. **2** (**Cabinet**) the committee of senior advisers responsible for counseling the head of state on government policy. **3** *archaic* a small private room. [CABIN + –ET¹, infl. by F *cabinet*]

cab·i·net·mak·er /kábinitmáykər/ *n.* a skilled craftsman of wood furniture, etc.

cab·i·net min·is·ter *n.* esp. *Brit.* a member of a government cabinet.

cab·i·net pud·ding *n.* a steamed pudding with dried fruit.

cab·i·net·ry /kábinitree/ *n.* finished woodwork, esp. of professional quality. [CABINET + –RY]

cab·in fe·ver *n.* a state of restlessness and irritability from having been confined or in a remote location for an extended period.

ca·ble /káybəl/ *n. & v.* ● *n.* **1** a thick rope of wire or hemp. **2** an encased group of insulated wires for transmitting electricity or electrical signals. **3** a cablegram. **4** *Naut.* **a** the chain of an anchor. **b** (in full **cable length**) a measure of 720 feet (US Navy) or 608 feet (Brit. Navy). **5** (in full **cable-stitch**) a knitted stitch resembling twisted rope. **6** *Archit.* a rope-shaped ornament. ● *v.* **1 a** *tr.* transmit (a message) by cablegram. **b** *tr.* inform (a person) by cablegram. **c** *intr.* send a cablegram. **2** *tr.* furnish or fasten with a cable or cables. **3** *Archit. tr.* furnish with cables. [ME f. OF *chable,* ult. f. LL *capulum* halter f. Arab. *ḥabl*]

ca·ble car *n.* **1** a transportation system, typically one traveling up and down a mountain, in which cabins are suspended on a continuous moving cable driven by a motor at one end of the route. **2** a vehicle drawn along a cable railway.

ca·ble·gram /káybəlgram/ *n.* a telegraph message sent by undersea cable, etc.

ca·ble-laid *adj.* (of rope) having three triple strands.

ca·ble rail·way *n.* a railroad along which cars are drawn by a continuous cable.

ca·ble-read·y *adj.* (of a TV, VCR, etc.) designed for direct connection to a coaxial cable TV system.

ca·ble tel·e·vi·sion *n.* a broadcasting system with signals transmitted by cable to subscribers' sets.

ca·ble·way /káybəlway/ *n.* a transporting system with a usu. elevated cable.

cab·man /kábmən/ *n.* (*pl.* **·men**) a cabdriver.

cab·o·chon /kábəshon/ *n.* a gem polished but not faceted. [F dimin. of *caboche*: see CABBAGE]

ca·boo·dle /kəbood'l/ *n.* □ **the whole (kit and) caboodle** *sl.* the whole lot (of persons or things). [19th c. US: perh. f. phr. *kit and boodle*]

ca·boose /kəbooss/ *n.* **1** a freight train car for the rail workers, typically attached to the end of the train. **2** esp. *Brit.* a kitchen on a ship's deck. [Du. *cabūse,* of unkn. orig.]

cab·o·tage /kábətaazh, –tij/ *n.* **1** *Naut.* coastal navigation and trade. **2** esp. *Aeron.* the reservation to a country of (esp. air) traffic operation within its territory. [F f. *caboter* to coast, perh. f. Sp. *cabo* CAPE²]

cab·ri·ole /kábreeōl/ *n.* a kind of curved leg characteristic of Queen Anne and Chippendale furniture. [F f. *cabrioler, caprioler* f. It. *capriolare* to leap in the air; from the resemblance to a leaping animal's foreleg: see CAPRIOLE]

cab·ri·o·let /kábreeōláy/ *n.* **1** a light, two-wheeled carriage with a hood, drawn by one horse. **2** an automobile with a folding top. [F f. *cabriole* goat's leap (cf. CAPRIOLE), applied to its motion]

ca'can·ny /kaakánee/ *n. Brit.* **1** the practice of 'going slow' at work; a labor union policy of limiting output. **2** extreme caution. [Sc., = proceed warily]

ca·ca·o /kəkaá-ō, –káyō/ *n.* (*pl.* **·os**) **1** a seed pod from which cocoa and chocolate are made. **2** a small, widely cultivated evergreen tree, *Theobroma cacao,* bearing these. [Sp. f. Nahuatl *cacauatl* (*uatl* tree)]

cach·a·lot /káshəlot, –lō/ *n.* a sperm whale. [F f. Sp. & Port. *cachalote,* of unkn. orig.]

cache /kash/ *n. & v.* ● *n.* **1** a hiding place for treasure, provisions, ammunition, etc. **2** what is hidden in a cache. ● *v.tr.* put in a cache. [F f. *cacher* to hide]

ca·chec·tic /kəkéktik/ *adj.* relating to or having the symptoms of cachexia.

ca·chet /kasháy/ *n.* **1** a distinguishing mark or seal. **2** prestige. **3** *Med.* a flat capsule enclosing a dose of unpleasant-tasting medicine. [F f. *cacher* press ult. f. L *coactare* constrain]

ca·chex·i·a /kəkékseeə/ *n.* (also **ca·chex·y** /–kéksee/) a condition of weakness of body or mind associated with chronic disease. [F *cachexie* or LL *cachexia* f. Gk *kakhexia* f. *kakos* bad + *hexis* habit]

cach·in·nate /kákinayt/ *v.intr. literary* laugh loudly. □□ **cach·in·na·tion** /–náyshən/ *n.* **cach·in·na·to·ry** /–nətáwree/ *adj.* [L *cachinnare cachinnat–*]

ca·chou /káshoo/ *n.* **1** a lozenge to sweeten the breath. **2** var. of CATECHU. [F f. Port. *cachu* f. Malay *kāchu:* cf. CATECHU]

ca·chu·cha /kəchoochə/ *n.* a Spanish solo dance. [Sp.]

ca·cique /kəseek/ *n.* **1** a native tribal chief of the West Indies or

Mexico. **2** a political boss in Spain or Latin America. [Sp., of Carib orig.]

cack·hand·ed /kák-hándid/ *adj. Brit. colloq.* **1** awkward; clumsy. **2** left-handed. □□ **cack·hand·ed·ly** *adv.* **cack·hand·ed·ness** *n.* [dial. *cack* excrement]

cack·le /kákəl/ *n. & v.* ● *n.* **1** a clucking sound as of a hen or a goose. **2** a loud, silly laugh. **3** noisy inconsequential talk. ● *v.* **1** *intr.* emit a cackle. **2** *intr.* talk noisily and inconsequentially. **3** *tr.* utter or express with a cackle. □ **cut the cackle** esp. *Brit. colloq.* stop talking aimlessly and come to the point. [ME prob. f. MLG, MDu. *kākelen* (imit.)]

ca·co·de·mon /kákədeémən/ *n.* (also **cac·o·dae·mon**) **1** an evil spirit. **2** a malignant person. [Gk *kakodaimōn* f. *kakos* bad + *daimōn* spirit]

cac·o·dyl /kákədil/ *n.* a malodorous, toxic, spontaneously flammable liquid, tetramethyldiarsine. □□ **cac·o·dyl·ic** /–dílik/ *adj.* [Gk *kakōdēs* stinking f. *kakos* bad]

cac·o·e·thes /kákō-eétheez/ *n.* an urge to do something inadvisable. [L f. Gk *kakoēthes* neut. adj. f. *kakos* bad + *ēthos* disposition]

ca·cog·ra·phy /kəkógrəfee/ *n.* **1** bad handwriting. **2** bad spelling. □□ **ca·cog·ra·pher** *n.* **cac·o·graph·ic** /kákəgráfik/ *adj.* **cac·o·graph·i·cal** *adj.* [Gk *kakos* bad, after *orthography*]

ca·col·o·gy /kəkóləjee/ *n.* **1** bad choice of words. **2** bad pronunciation. [LL *cacologia* f. Gk *kakologia* vituperation f. *kakos* bad]

cac·o·mis·tle /kákəmisəl/ *n.* any raccoonlike animal of several species of the genus *Bassariscus*, native to Central America, having a dark-ringed tail. [Amer. Sp. *cacomixtle* f. Nahuatl *tlacomiztli*]

ca·coph·o·ny /kəkófənee/ *n.* (*pl.* **·nies**) **1** a harsh discordant mixture of sound. **2** dissonance; discord. □□ **ca·coph·o·nous** *adj.* [F *cacophonie* f. Gk *kakophōnia* f. *kakophōnos* f. *kakos* bad & *phōnē* sound]

cac·tus /káktəs/ *n.* (*pl.* **cac·ti** /–tī/or **cac·tus·es**) any succulent plant of the family Cactaceae, with a thick fleshy stem, usu. spines but no leaves, and brilliantly colored flowers. □□ **cac·ta·ceous** /–táyshəs/ *adj.* [L f. Gk *kaktos* cardoon]

cac·tus dahl·ia *n.* a variety of dahlia with quilled petals resembling a cactus flower.

ca·cu·mi·nal /kakyoˉominəl/ *adj. Phonet.* = RETROFLEX 2. [L *cacuminare* make pointed f. *cacumen –minis* treetop]

CAD /kad/ *abbr.* computer-aided design.

cad /kad/ *n.* a person (esp. a man) who behaves dishonorably. □□ **cad·dish** *adj.* **cad·dish·ly** *adv.* **cad·dish·ness** *n.* [abbr. of CADDIE in sense 'odd-job man']

ca·das·tral /kədástrəl/ *adj.* of or showing the extent, value, and ownership, of land for taxation. [F f. *cadastre* register of property f. Prov. *cadastro* f. It. *catast(r)o*, earlier *catastico* f. late Gk *katastikhon* list, register f. *kata stikhon* line by line]

ca·dav·er /kədávər/ *n.* esp. *Med.* a corpse. □□ **ca·dav·er·ic** /–dávərik/ *adj.* [ME f. L f. *cadere* fall]

ca·dav·er·ous /kədávərəs/ *adj.* **1** corpselike. **2** deathly pale. [L *cadaverosus* (as CADAVER)]

cad·die /kádee/ *n. & v.* (also **cad·dy**) ● *n.* (*pl.* **·dies**) a person who assists a golfer during a match, by carrying clubs, etc. ● *v.intr.* (**cad·dies, cad·died, cad·dy·ing**) act as caddie.

Mid 17th century (originally Scots): from French *cadet*. The original term denoted a gentleman who joined the army without a commission, intending to learn the profession and follow a military career, later coming to mean 'odd-job man.' The current sense dates from the late 18th century.

cad·dis fly /kádisflī/ *n.* (*pl.* **flies**) any small, hairy-winged nocturnal insect of the order Trichoptera, living near water. [17th c.: orig. unkn.]

cad·dis·worm /kádiswərm/ *n.* (also **cad·dis**) a larva of the caddis fly, living in water and making protective cylindrical cases of sticks, leaves, etc., and used as fishing bait. [as CADDIS FLY]

cad·dy¹ /kádee/ *n.* (*pl.* **·dies**) a small container, esp. a box for holding tea. [earlier *catty* weight of 1¹⁄₃ lb., f. Malay *kātī*]

cad·dy² var. of CADDIE.

ca·dence /káyd'ns/ *n.* **1** a fall in pitch of the voice, esp. at the end of a phrase or sentence. **2** intonation; tonal inflection. **3** *Mus.* the close of a musical phrase. **4** rhythm; the measure or beat of sound or movement. □□ **ca·denced** *adj.* [ME f. OF f. It. *cadenza*, ult. f. L *cadere* fall]

ca·den·tial /kədénshəl/ *adj.* of a cadence or cadenza.

ca·den·za /kədénzə/ *n. Mus.* a virtuosic passage for a solo instrument or voice, usu. near the close of a movement of a concerto, sometimes improvised. [It.: see CADENCE]

ca·det /kədét/ *n.* **1** a young trainee in the armed services or police force. **2** a business trainee. **3** a younger son. □□ **ca·det·ship** *n.* [F f. Gascon dial. *capdet*, ult. f. L *caput* head]

cadge /kaj/ *v.* **1** *tr.* get or seek by begging. **2** *intr.* beg. □□ **cadg·er** *n.* [19th c., earlier = ? bind, carry: orig. unkn.]

ca·di /kaádee, káydee/ *n.* (also **ka·di**) (*pl.* **·dis**) a judge in a Muslim country. [Arab. *ḳāḍī* f. *ḳaḍā* to judge]

Cad·me·an /kadmeéən/ *adj.* = PYRRHIC¹. [L *Cadmeus* f. Gk *Kadmeios* f. *Kadmos* Cadmus: see CADMIUM]

cad·mi·um /kádmeeəm/ *n.* a soft, bluish-white metallic element occurring naturally with zinc ores, used in the manufacture of solders and in electroplating. ¶ Symb.: **Cd**. [obs. *cadmia* calamine f. L *cadmia* f. Gk *kadm(e)ia (gē)* Cadmean (earth), f. *Cadmus* legendary founder of Thebes: see –IUM]

cad·mi·um yel·low *n.* an intense yellow pigment containing cadmium sulfide and used in paints, etc.

ca·dre /kádree, kaádray/ *n.* **1** a basic unit, esp. of servicemen, forming a nucleus for expansion when necessary. **2 a** a group of activists in a communist or any revolutionary party. **b** a member of such a group. [F f. It. *quadro* f. L *quadrus* square]

This word, borrowed from French during the 19th century, has a variety of pronunciations. United States military personnel often pronounce it "KAD-ree," although "KAH-dray" is also popular, probably because of its similarity to *padre*. Also in wide use are the pronunciations "KAH-dree" and "KAD-ray."

ca·du·ce·us /kədoˉoˉseeəs, –shəs, –dyoˉoˉ–/ *n.* (*pl.* **ca·du·ce·i** /–see-ī/) **1** an ancient Greek or Roman herald's wand, usu. with two serpents twined around it, carried by the messenger god Hermes or Mercury. **2** this used as a symbol of the medical profession. [L f. Doric Gk *karuk(e)ion* f. *kērux* herald]

ca·du·cous /kədoˉokəs, –dyoˉo–/ *adj. Biol.* (of organs and parts) easily detached or shed at an early stage. □□ **ca·du·ci·ty** /–sitee/ *n.* [L *caducus* falling f. *cadere* fall]

cae·cil·ian /səsíleeən/ *n.* any burrowing wormlike amphibian of the order Gymnophiona, having poorly developed eyes and no limbs. [L *caecilia* kind of lizard]

caduceus

cae·cum *Brit.* var. of CECUM.

Cae·no·zo·ic var. of CENOZOIC.

Caer·phil·ly /kairfilee, kaar–/ *n.* a kind of mild white cheese orig. made in Caerphilly in Wales.

Cae·sar /seézər/ *n.* **1** the title of the Roman emperors, esp. from Augustus to Hadrian. **2** an autocrat. □□ **Cae·sar·e·an, Cae·sar·i·an** /–záireeən/ *adj.* [L, family name of Gaius Julius *Caesar*, Roman statesman d. 44 BC]

Cae·sar·e·an (also **Cae·sar·i·an**) var. of CESAREAN.

cae·si·um *Brit.* var. of CESIUM.

cae·su·ra /sizhoˉoˉrə, –zoˉoˉrə/ *n.* (*pl.* **cae·su·ras** or **cae·su·rae** /–zhoˉoˉree, –zoˉoˉree/) *Prosody* **1** (in Greek and Latin verse) a break between words within a metrical foot. **2** (in modern verse) a pause near the middle of a line. □□ **cae·su·ral** *adj.* [L f. *caedere caes-* cut]

CAF *abbr.* cost and freight.

ca·fé /kafáy/ *n.* (also **ca·fe**) **1** a small coffeehouse; a simple restaurant. **2** a bar. [F, = coffee, coffeehouse]

ca·fé au lait /ōláy/ *n.* **1** coffee with milk. **2** the color of this.

ca·fé noir /nwaar/ *n.* black coffee.

ca·fé so·ci·e·ty *n.* the regular patrons of fashionable restaurants and nightclubs.

caf·e·te·ri·a /káfiteéreeə/ *n.* a restaurant in which customers collect their meals on trays at a counter and usu. pay before sitting down to eat. [Amer. Sp. *cafetería* coffee shop]

The word *cafeteria* comes from French *café*, meaning 'coffee,' and a place where coffee is served.

caf·feine /káfeen, kafeén/ *n.* an alkaloid drug with stimulant action found esp. in tea leaves and coffee beans. [F *caféine* f. *café* coffee]

Caffeine, like *coffee*, has two *f*'s and two *e*'s.

caf·tan /káftan/ *n.* (also **kaf·tan**) **1** a long, usu. belted tunic worn in countries of the Near East. **2 a** a long, loose dress. **b** a loose shirt or top. [Turk. *kaftān*, partly through F *cafetan*]

cage /kayj/ *n. & v.* ● *n.* **1** a structure of bars or wires, esp. for confining animals or birds. **2** any similar open framework, as an enclosed platform for passengers in a freight elevator, etc. **3** *colloq.* a camp for prisoners of war. ● *v.tr.* place or keep in a cage. [ME f. OF f. L *cavea*]

cage bird *n.* a bird of the kind customarily kept in a cage.

cag·ey /káyjee/ *adj.* (also **cag·y**) (**cag·i·er, cag·i·est**) *colloq.* cautious and uncommunicative; wary. □□ **cag·i·ly** *adv.* **cag·i·ness** *n.* (also **cag·ey·ness**). [20th-c. US: orig. unkn.]

ca·hoots /kəhóőts/ *n.pl.* □ **in cahoots** (often foll. by *with*) *sl.* in collusion. [19th c.: orig. uncert.]

CAI *abbr.* computer-assisted (or –aided) instruction.

cai·man /káymən/ *n.* (also **cay·man**) any of various S. American alligatorlike reptilians, esp. of the genus *Caiman*. [Sp. & Port. *caiman*, f. Carib *acayuman*]

Cain /kayn/ *n.* □ **raise Cain** *colloq.* make a disturbance; create trouble. [*Cain*, eldest son of Adam (Gen. 4)]

Cai·no·zo·ic var. of CENOZOIC.

ca·ique /ki-éék/ *n.* 1 a light rowboat on the Bosporus. 2 a Levantine sailing ship. [F f. It. *caicco* f. Turk. *kayik*]

cairn /kairn/ *n.* 1 a mound of rough stones as a monument or landmark. 2 (in full **cairn terrier**) **a** a small terrier of a breed with short legs, a longish body, and a shaggy coat (perhaps so called from its being used to hunt among cairns). **b** this breed. [Gael. *carn*]

cairn·gorm /káirngawrm/ *n.* a yellow or wine-colored semiprecious form of quartz. [found on *Cairngorm*, a mountain in Scotland f. Gael. *carn gorm* blue cairn]

cais·son /káyson, –sən/ *n.* 1 a watertight chamber in which underwater construction work can be done. 2 a floating vessel used as a floodgate in docks. 3 an ammunition chest or wagon. [F (f. It. *cassone*) assim. to *caisse* CASE²]

cais·son dis·ease *n.* = AEROEMBOLISM.

cai·tiff /káytif/ *n. & adj. poet.* or *archaic* ● *n.* a base or despicable person; a coward. ● *adj.* base; despicable; cowardly. [ME f. OF *caitif, chaitif* ult. f. L *captivus* CAPTIVE]

ca·jole /kəjól/ *v.tr.* (often foll. by *into, out of*) persuade by flattery, deceit, etc. □□ **ca·jole·ment** *n.* **ca·jol·er** *n.* **ca·jol·er·y** *n.* [F *cajoler*]

cake /kayk/ *n. & v.* ● *n.* 1 **a** a mixture of flour, butter, eggs, sugar, etc., baked in the oven. **b** a quantity of this baked in a flat round or ornamental shape and often iced and decorated. 2 other food in a flat round shape (*fish cake*). 3 a flattish compact mass (*a cake of soap*). 4 *Sc. & No. of Engl.* thin oaten bread. ● *v.* 1 *tr. & intr.* form into a compact mass. 2 *tr.* (usu. foll. by *with*) cover (with a hard or sticky mass) (*boots caked with mud*). □ **cakes and ale** merrymaking. **have one's cake and eat it too** *colloq.* enjoy both of two mutually exclusive alternatives. **a piece of cake** *colloq.* something easily achieved. **a slice of the cake** esp. *Brit.* participation in benefits. [ME f. ON *kaka*]

cake·walk /káykwawk/ *n.* 1 a dance developed from a black American contest in graceful walking with a cake as a prize. 2 *colloq.* an easy task.

CAL *abbr.* computer-assisted learning.

Cal *abbr.* large calorie(s).

Cal. *abbr.* California.

cal *abbr.* small calorie(s).

Cal·a·bar bean /káləbaar/ *n.* a poisonous seed of the tropical African climbing plant *Physostigma venosum*, yielding a medicinal extract. [*Calabar* in Nigeria]

cal·a·bash /káləbash/ *n.* 1 **a** an evergreen tree, *Crescentia cujete*, native to tropical America, bearing fruit in the form of large gourds. **b** a gourd from this tree. 2 the shell of this or a similar gourd used as a vessel for water, to make a tobacco pipe, etc. [F *calebasse* f. Sp. *calabaza* perh. f. Pers. *karbuz* melon]

cal·a·boose /kálǝboŏs/ *n. sl.* a prison. [black F *calabouse* f. Sp. *calabozo* dungeon]

cal·a·man·co /kálǝmángkō/ *n.* (*pl.* **·coes**) *hist.* a glossy woolen cloth checkered on one side. [16th c.: orig. unkn.]

cal·a·man·der /kálǝmandǝr/ *n.* a fine-grained, red-brown ebony streaked with black, from the Asian tree *Diospyros qualsita*, used in furniture. [19th c.: orig. unkn.: perh. conn. with Sinh. word for the tree *kalu-madīriya*]

ca·la·ma·ri /kaalǝmáaree, ka–/ *n.* (*pl.* **·ries**) any cephalopod mollusk with a long, tapering, penlike horny internal shell, esp. a squid of the genus *Loligo*. [med.L *calamarium* pen case f. L *calamus* pen]

cal·a·mine /kálǝmīn/ *n.* 1 a pink powder consisting of zinc carbonate and ferric oxide used as a lotion or ointment. 2 a zinc mineral usu. zinc carbonate. [ME f. F f. med.L *calamina* alt. f. L *cadmia: see* CADMIUM]

cal·a·mint /kálǝmint/ *n.* any aromatic herb or shrub of the genus *Calamintha*, esp. *C. officinalis* with purple or lilac flowers. [ME f. OF *calament* f. med.L *calamentum* f. LL *calaminthe* f. Gk *kalaminthē*]

ca·lam·i·ty /kəlámitee/ *n.* (*pl.* **·ties**) 1 a disaster, a great misfortune. 2 **a** adversity. **b** deep distress. □□ **ca·lam·i·tous** *adj.* **ca·lam·i·tous·ly** *adv.* [ME f. F *calamité* f. L *calamitas* –*tatis*]

ca·lan·do /kəlaándō/ *adv. Mus.* gradually decreasing in speed and volume. [It., = slackening]

ca·lash /kəlásh/ *n. hist.* 1 **a** a light, low-wheeled carriage with a removable folding hood. **b** the folding hood itself. 2 a two-wheeled, horse-drawn vehicle. 3 a woman's hooped silk hood. [F *calèche* f. G *Kalesche* f. Pol. *kolaska* or Czech *kolesa*]

calc- /kalk/ *comb. form* lime or calcium. [G *Kalk* f. L CALX]

cal·ca·ne·us /kalkáyneeǝs/ *n.* (also **cal·ca·ne·um** /–neeǝm/) (*pl.* **cal·**

ca·ne·i /–nee-ī/ or **cal·ca·ne·a** /–neeǝ/) the bone forming the heel. [L]

cal·car·e·ous /kalkáireeǝs/ *adj.* (also **cal·car·i·ous**) of or containing calcium carbonate; chalky. [L *calcarius* (as CALX)]

cal·ce·o·lar·i·a /kálseeǝláireeǝ/ *n. Bot.* any plant of the genus *Calceolaria*, native to S. America, with slipper-shaped flowers. [mod.L f. L *calceolus* dimin. of *calceus* shoe + –*aria* fem. = –ARY¹]

cal·ce·o·late /kálseeǝlayt/ *adj. Bot.* slipper-shaped.

cal·ces *pl.* of CALX.

cal·cif·er·ol /kalsífǝrōl, –rol/ *n.* one of the D vitamins, routinely added to dairy products, essential for the deposition of calcium in bones. Also called **ergocalciferol** or **vitamin D₂**. [CALCIFEROUS + –OL¹]

cal·cif·er·ous /kalsífǝrǝs/ *adj.* yielding calcium salts, esp. calcium carbonate. [L CALX lime + –FEROUS]

cal·ci·fy /kálsifī/ *v.tr. & intr.* (**·fies, ·fied**) 1 harden or become hardened by deposition of calcium salts; petrify. 2 convert or be converted to calcium carbonate. □□ **cal·cif·ic** /–sífik/ *adj.* **cal·ci·fi·ca·tion** *n.*

cal·cine /kálsīn, –sin/ *v.* 1 *tr.* **a** reduce, oxidize, or desiccate by strong heat. **b** burn to ashes; consume by fire; roast. **c** reduce to calcium oxide by roasting or burning. 2 *tr.* consume or purify as if by fire. 3 *intr.* undergo any of these. □□ **cal·ci·na·tion** /–sináyshǝn/ *n.* [ME f. OF *calciner* or med.L *calcinare* f. LL *calcina* lime f. L CALX]

cal·cite /kálsīt/ *n.* natural crystalline calcium carbonate. [G *Calcit* f. L CALX lime]

cal·ci·um /kálseeǝm/ *n.* a soft, gray metallic element of the alkaline earth group occurring naturally in limestone, marble, chalk, etc., that is important in industry and essential for normal growth in living organisms. ¶ Symb.: **Ca**. [L CALX lime + –IUM]

cal·ci·um car·bide *n.* a grayish compound used in the production of acetylene.

cal·ci·um car·bon·ate *n.* a white, insoluble solid occurring naturally as chalk, limestone, marble, and calcite, and used in the manufacture of lime and cement.

cal·ci·um hy·drox·ide *n.* a white crystalline powder used in the manufacture of plaster and cement; slaked lime.

cal·ci·um ox·ide *n.* a white crystalline solid from which many calcium compounds are manufactured. Also called **lime** or **calx**.

cal·ci·um phos·phate *n.* the main constituent of animal bones, used as bone ash fertilizer.

cal·ci·um sul·fate *n.* a white crystalline solid occurring as anhydrite and gypsum.

calcspar /kálkspaar/ *n.* = CALCITE. [CALC- + SPAR³]

cal·cu·la·ble /kálkyǝlǝbǝl/ *adj.* able to be calculated or estimated. □□ **cal·cu·la·bil·i·ty** *n.* **cal·cu·la·bly** *adv.*

cal·cu·late /kálkyǝlayt/ *v.* 1 *tr.* ascertain or determine beforehand, esp. by mathematics or by reckoning. 2 *tr.* plan deliberately. 3 *intr.* (foll. by *on, upon*) rely on; make an essential part of one's reckoning (*calculated on a quick response*). 4 *tr. dial.* suppose; believe. □□ **cal·cu·la·tive** /–lǝtiv/ *adj.* [LL *calculare* (as CALCULUS)]

cal·cu·lat·ed /kálkyǝlaytid/ *adj.* 1 (of an action) done with awareness of the likely consequences. 2 (foll. by *to* + infin.) designed or suitable; intended. □□ **cal·cu·lat·ed·ly** *adv.*

cal·cu·lat·ing /kálkyǝlayting/ *adj.* (of a person) shrewd; scheming. □□ **cal·cu·lat·ing·ly** *adv.*

cal·cu·la·tion /kálkyǝláyshǝn/ *n.* 1 the act or process of calculating. 2 a result obtained by calculating. 3 a reckoning or forecast. [ME f. OF f. LL *calculatio* (as CALCULATE)]

cal·cu·la·tor /kálkyǝlaytǝr/ *n.* 1 a device (esp. a small electronic one) used for making mathematical calculations. 2 a person or thing that calculates. 3 a set of tables used in calculation. [ME f. L (as CALCULATE)]

cal·cu·lus /kálkyǝlǝs/ *n.* (*pl.* **cal·cu·li** /–lī/ or **cal·cu·lus·es**) 1 *Math.* **a** a particular method of calculation or reasoning (*calculus of probabilities*). **b** the infinitesimal calculi of integration or differentiation (see INTEGRAL CALCULUS, DIFFERENTIAL CALCULUS). 2 *Med.* a stone or concretion of minerals formed within the body. □□ **cal·cu·lous** *adj.* (in sense 2). [L, = small stone used in reckoning on an abacus]

cal·de·ra /kaldáirǝ/ *n.* a large volcanic depression. [Sp. f. LL *caldaria* boiling-pot]

cal·dron var. of CAULDRON.

Cal·e·do·ni·an /kálidóneeǝn/ *adj. & n.* ● *adj.* 1 of or relating to Scotland. 2 *Geol.* of a mountain-forming period in Europe in the Paleozoic era. ● *n.* a Scotsman. [L *Caledonia* northern Britain]

cal·e·fa·cient /kálifáyshǝnt/ *n. & adj. Med.* ● *n.* a substance producing or causing a sensation of warmth. ● *adj.* of this substance. [L *calefacere* f. *calēre* be warm + *facere* make]

cal·en·dar /kálindǝr/ *n. & v.* ● *n.* 1 a system by which the beginning, length, and subdivisions of the year are fixed. 2 a chart or series of pages showing the days, weeks, and months of a particular year, or giving special seasonal information. 3 a timetable or program of appointments, special events, etc. ● *v.tr.* register or enter in a calendar or timetable, etc. □□ **ca•len•dric** /–léndrik/ *adj.* **ca•len•dri•cal** *adj.* [ME f. AF *calender*, OF *calendier* f. L *calendarium* account book (as CALENDS)]

cal•en•dar month *n.* (also **cal•en•dar year**) see MONTH, YEAR.

cal•en•der /kálindər/ *n. & v.* • *n.* a machine in which cloth, paper, etc., is pressed by rollers to glaze or smooth it. • *v.tr.* press in a calender. [F *calendre(r)*, of unkn. orig.]

cal•ends /kálendz/ *n.pl.* (also **kal•ends**) the first of the month in the ancient Roman calendar. [ME f. OF *calendes* f. L *kalendae, calendae*]

ca•len•du•la /kəlénjələ/ *n.* any plant of the genus *Calendula*, with large yellow or orange flowers. [mod.L dimin. of *calendae* (as CALENDS), perh. = little clock]

cal•en•ture /kálenchər/ *n. hist.* a tropical delirium of sailors, who think the sea is green fields. [F f. Sp. *calentura* fever f. *calentar* be hot ult. f. L *calēre* be warm]

calf¹ /kaf/ *n.* (pl. **calves** /kavz/) **1** a young bovine animal, used esp. of domestic cattle. **2** the young of other animals, e.g., elephant, deer, and whale. **3** *Naut.* a floating piece of ice detached from an iceberg. □□ **calf** (of a cow) pregnant. □□ **calf•hood** *n.* **calf•ish** *adj.* **calf•like** *adj.* [OE *cælf* f. WG]

calf² /kaf/ *n.* (pl. **calves** /kavz/) the fleshy hind part of the human leg below the knee. □□ **–calved** /kavd/ *adj.* (in *comb.*). [ME f. ON *kálfi*, of unkn. orig.]

calf-love *n.* = PUPPY LOVE.

calf•skin /káfskin/ *n.* calf leather, esp. in bookbinding and shoemaking.

cal•i•ber /kálibər/ *n.* (*Brit.* **cal•i•bre**) **1 a** the internal diameter of a gun or tube. **b** the diameter of a bullet or shell. **2** strength or quality of character; ability; importance (*we need someone of your caliber*). □□ **cal•i•bered** *adj.* (also in *comb.*). [F *caliber* or It. *calibro*, f. Arab. *ḳālib* mold]

cal•i•brate /kálibrayt/ *v.tr.* **1** mark (a gauge) with a standard scale of readings. **2** correlate the readings of (an instrument) with a standard. **3** determine the caliber of (a gun). **4** determine the correct capacity or value of. □□ **cal•i•bra•tion** /–bráyshən/ *n.* **cal•i•bra•tor** *n.* [CALIBER + –ATE³]

cal•i•bre *Brit.* var. of CALIBER.

ca•li•che /kəleéechee/ *n.* a mineral deposit of gravel, sand, and nitrates, esp. found in Chile and Peru. [Amer. Sp.]

cal•i•co /kálikō/ *n. & adj.* • *n.* (pl. **•coes** or **•cos**) **1** a printed cotton fabric. **2** *Brit.* a cotton cloth, esp. plain white or unbleached. • *adj.* **1** made of calico. **2** multicolored; piebald. [earlier *calicut* f. *Calicut* in India]

Calif. *abbr.* California.

cal•i•for•ni•um /kálifáwrneeəm/ *n. Chem.* a transuranic radioactive metallic element produced artificially from curium. ¶ Symb.: **Cf**. [*California* (where it was first made) + –IUM]

cal•i•per /kálipər/ *n. & v.* • *n.* **1** (in *pl.*) (also **cal•i•per com•pas•ses**) compasses with bowed legs for measuring the diameter of convex bodies, or with out-turned points for measuring internal dimensions. **2** (in full **caliper splint**) a metal splint to support the leg. • *v.tr.* measure with calipers. [app. var. of CALIBER]

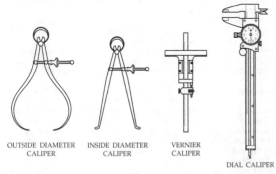

OUTSIDE DIAMETER　　INSIDE DIAMETER　　VERNIER
CALIPER　　　　　　　CALIPER　　　　　　CALIPER

DIAL CALIPER

calipers

ca•liph /káylif, kál–/ *n. esp. hist.* the chief Muslim civil and religious ruler, regarded as the successor to Muhammad. □□ **cal•iph•ate** *n.* [ME f. OF *caliphe* f. Arab. *ḳalīfa* successor]

cal•is•then•ics /kálisthéniks/ *n.pl.* (also *esp. Brit.* **cal•lis•the•nics**) gymnastic exercises to achieve bodily fitness and grace of movement. □□ **cal•is•then•ic** *adj.* [Gk *kallos* beauty + *sthenos* strength]

calk var. of CAULK.

call /kawl/ *v. & n.* • *v.* **1** *intr.* **a** (often foll. by *out*) cry; shout; speak loudly. **b** (of a bird or animal) emit its characteristic note or cry. **2** *tr.* communicate or converse with by telephone or radio. **3** *tr.* **a** bring to one's presence by calling; summon (*will you call the chil-*

dren?). **b** arrange for (a person or thing) to come or be present (*called a taxi*). **4** *intr.* (often foll. by *at, on*) pay a brief visit (*called at the house; come and call on me*). **5** *tr.* **a** order to take place; fix a time for (*called a meeting*). **b** direct to happen; announce (*call a halt*). **6 a** *intr.* require one's attention or consideration (*duty calls*). **b** *tr.* urge; invite; nominate (*call to run for office*). **7** *tr.* name; describe as (*call her Jennifer*). **8** *tr.* consider; regard or estimate as (*I call that silly*). **9** *tr.* rouse from sleep (*call me at 8*). **10** *tr.* guess the outcome of tossing a coin, etc. **11** *intr.* (foll. by *for*) order; require; demand (*called for silence*). **12** *tr.* (foll. by *over*) read out (a list of names to determine those present). **13** *intr.* (foll. by *on, upon*) invoke; appeal to; request or require (*called on us to be quiet*). **14** *tr. Cricket* (of an umpire) disallow a ball from (a bowler). **15** *tr. Cards* specify (a suit or contract) in bidding. **16** *tr. Sc.* drive (an animal, vehicle, etc.). • *n.* **1** a shout or cry; an act of calling. **2 a** the characteristic cry of a bird or animal. **b** an imitation of this. **c** an instrument for imitating it. **3** a brief visit (*paid them a call*). **4 a** an act of telephoning. **b** a telephone conversation. **5 a** an invitation or summons to appear or be present. **b** an appeal or invitation (from a specific source or discerned by a person's conscience, etc.) to follow a certain profession, set of principles, etc. **6** (foll. by *for*, or *to* + infin.) a duty, need, or occasion (*no call to be rude; no call for violence*). **7** (foll. by *for, on*) a demand (*not much call for it these days; a call on one's time*). **8** a signal on a bugle, etc.; a signal. **9** *Stock Exch.* an option of buying stock at a fixed price at a given date. **10** *Cards* a player's right or turn to make a bid. **b** a bid made. □ **at call** = *on call*. **call away** divert; distract. **call down 1** invoke. **2** reprimand. **call forth** elicit. **call in** *tr.* **1** withdraw from circulation. **2** seek the advice or services of. **call in** (or **into**) **question** dispute; doubt the validity of. **call into play** give scope for; make use of. **call a person names** abuse a person verbally. **call off 1** cancel (an arrangement, etc.). **2** order (an attacker or pursuer) to desist. **call out 1** summon (troops, etc.) to action. **2** order (workers) to strike. **call the shots** (or **tune**) be in control; take the initiative. **call to account** see ACCOUNT. **call to mind** recollect; cause one to remember. **call to order** request to be orderly. **2** declare (a meeting) open. **call up 1** reach by telephone. **2** imagine; recollect. **3** summon, esp. to serve on active military duty. **on call 1** (of a doctor, etc.) available if required but not formally on duty. **2** (of money lent) repayable on demand. **within call** near enough to be summoned by calling. [OE *ceallian* f. ON *kalla*]

cal•la /kálə/ *n.* **1** (in full **calla lily**) a tall, lilylike plant, *Zantedeschia aethiopica*, with white spathe and spadix. **2** an aquatic plant, *Calla palustris*. [mod.L]

call•boy /káwlboy/ *n.* **1** a theater attendant who summons actors when needed on stage. **2** a bellhop. **3** (also **call boy**) a male prostitute who accepts appointments by telephone.

call•er /káwlər/ *n.* **1** a person who calls, esp. one who pays a visit or makes a telephone call. **2** *Austral.* a racing or sports commentator.

call girl *n.* a female prostitute who accepts appointments by telephone.

cal•lig•ra•phy /kəlígrəfee/ *n.* **1** handwriting, esp. when fine or pleasing. **2** the art of handwriting. □□ **cal•lig•ra•pher** *n.* **cal•li•graph•ic** /káligráfik/ *adj.* **cal•lig•ra•phist** *n.*

call•ing /káwling/ *n.* **1** a profession or occupation. **2** an inwardly felt call or summons; a vocation.

call•ing card *n.* **1** a card with a person's name, etc., sent or left in lieu of a formal visit. **2** evidence of someone's presence; an identifying mark, etc., left behind (by someone). **3** a card used to charge a telephone call to a number other than that from which the call is placed.

cal•li•o•pe /kəlíəpee/ *n.* a keyboard instrument resembling an organ, with a set of steam whistles producing musical notes. [Gk *Kalliopē* muse of epic poetry (lit. 'beautiful-voiced')]

cal•li•per *Brit.* var. of CALIPER.

cal•lis•then•ics esp. *Brit.* var. of CALISTHENICS.

call of nature *n.* a need to urinate or defecate.

cal•lop /kálop/ *n. Austral.* a gold-colored freshwater fish, *Plectroplites ambiguus*, used as food. Also called **golden perch**. [Aboriginal]

cal•los•i•ty /kəlósitee/ *n.* (pl. **•ties**) a hard, thick area of skin usu. occurring in parts of the body subject to pressure or friction. [F *callosité* or L *callositas* (as CALLOUS)]

cal•lous /káləs/ *adj.* **1** unfeeling; insensitive. **2** (of skin) hardened or hard. □□ **cal•lous•ly** *adv.* (in sense 1). **cal•lous•ness** *n.* [ME f. L *callosus* (as CALLUS) or F *calleux*]

cal·low /kálō/ adj. inexperienced; immature. □□ **cal·low·ly** adv. **cal·low·ness** n. [OE calu]

call sign n. (also **call sig·nal**) a broadcast signal identifying the radio transmitter used.

call-up n. the act or process of calling up (sense 3).

cal·lus /káləs/ n. **1** a hard thick area of skin or tissue. **2** a hard tissue formed around bone ends after a fracture. **3** Bot. a new protective tissue formed over a wound. [L]

SPELLING TIP callus

If you have a painful *callus*, the doctor may ask you to "Call us." See also note at CALLOUS.

calm /kaam/ adj., n., & v. • adj. **1** tranquil; quiet; windless (a calm sea; a calm night). **2** (of a person or disposition) settled; not agitated (remained calm throughout the ordeal). **3** self-assured; confident (his calm assumption that we would wait). • n. **1** a state of being calm; stillness; serenity. **2** a period without wind or storm. • v.tr. & intr. (often foll. by down) make or become calm. □□ **calm·ly** adv. **calm·ness** n. [ME ult. f. LL cauma f. Gk kauma heat]

SYNONYM TIP calm

HALCYON, PEACEFUL, PLACID, SERENE, TRANQUIL. We usually speak of the weather or the sea as **calm**, meaning free from disturbance or storm. When applied to people and their feelings or moods, *calm* implies an unruffled state, often under disturbing conditions (to remain calm in the face of disaster). **Halcyon** is another adjective associated with the weather (the halcyon days of summer); it comes from the name of a mythical bird, usually identified with the kingfisher, that builds its nest on the sea and possesses a magical power to calm the winds and waves. **Peaceful** also suggests a lack of turbulence or disorder, although it is usually applied to situations, scenes, and activities rather than to people (a peaceful gathering of protesters; a peaceful resolution to their problems). **Serene**, **tranquil**, and **placid** are more often used to describe human states of being. *Serene* suggests a lofty and undisturbed calmness (he died with a serene look on his face), while *tranquil* implies an intrinsic calmness (they led a tranquil life in the country). **Placid** usually refers to a prevailing tendency and is sometimes used disparagingly to suggest a lack of responsiveness or a dull complacency (with her placid disposition, she seldom got involved in family arguments).

calm·a·tive /káamətiv, kálm–/ adj. & n. Med. • adj. tending to calm or sedate. • n. a calmative drug, etc.

cal·o·mel /kálomel/ n. a compound of mercury, esp. when used medicinally as a cathartic. [mod.L perh. f. Gk kalos beautiful + melas black]

ca·lor·ic /kəláwrik, –lór–/ adj. & n. • adj. of heat or calories. • n. hist. a supposed material form or cause of heat. [F calorique f. L calor heat]

cal·o·rie /káləree/ n. (also **cal·o·ry**) (pl. **·ries**) a unit of quantity of heat: **1** (in full **small calorie**) the amount needed to raise the temperature of 1 gram of water through 1 °C. ¶ Abbr.: **cal**. **2** (in full **large calorie**) the amount needed to raise the temperature of 1 kilogram of water through 1 °C, often used to measure the energy value of foods. ¶ Abbr.: **Cal**. [F, arbitr. f. L calor heat + –ie]

cal·o·rif·ic /kálərífik/ adj. producing heat. □□ **cal·o·rif·i·cal·ly** adv. [L calorificus f. calor heat]

cal·o·rif·ic val·ue n. the amount of heat produced by a specified quantity of fuel, food, etc.

cal·o·rim·e·ter /kálərímitər/ n. any of various instruments for measuring quantity of heat, esp. to find calorific values. □□ **cal·o·ri·met·ric** /–métrik/ adj. **cal·o·rim·e·try** n. [L calor heat + –METER]

cal·o·ry var. of CALORIE.

calque /kalk/ n. Philol. = LOAN TRANSLATION. [F, = copy, tracing f. calquer trace ult. f. L calcare tread]

cal·trop /káltrəp/ n. (also **cal·trap**) **1** hist. a four-spiked iron ball thrown on the ground to impede cavalry horses. **2** Heraldry a representation of this. **3** any creeping plant of the genus Tribulus, with woody carpels usu. having hard spines. [(sense 3) OE calcatrippe f. med.L calcatrippa (senses 1–2) ME f. OF chauchetrape f. chauchier tread, trappe trap: ult. the same word]

cal·u·met /kályəmét/ n. a Native American ceremonial peace pipe. [F, ult. f. L calamus reed]

ca·lum·ni·ate /kəlúmneeayt/ v.tr. slander. □□ **ca·lum·ni·a·tion** /–neeáyshən/ n. **ca·lum·ni·a·tor** n. **ca·lum·ni·a·to·ry** /–ətáwree/ adj. [L calumniari]

cal·um·ny /káləmnee/ n. & v. • n. (pl. **·nies**) **1** slander; malicious representation. **2** an instance of this. • v.tr. (**·nies**, **·nied**) slander. □□ **ca·lum·ni·ous** /–lúmneeəs/ adj. [L calumnia]

cal·va·dos /kálvədōs/ n. (also **Cal·va·dos**) an apple brandy. [Calvados in France]

calumet

133

Cal·va·ry /kálvəree/ n. the place where Christ was crucified. [ME f. LL calvaria skull, transl. Gk golgotha, Aram. gûlgûltâ (Matt. 27:33)]

calve /kav/ v. **1 a** intr. give birth to a calf. **b** tr. (esp. in passive) give birth to (a calf). **2** tr. (also absol.) (of an iceberg) break off or shed (a mass of ice). [OE calfian]

calves pl. of CALF[1], CALF[2].

Cal·vin·ism /kálvinizəm/ n. the theology of the French theologian J. Calvin (d. 1564) or his followers, in which predestination and justification by faith are important elements. □□ **Cal·vin·ist** n. **Cal·vin·is·tic** adj. **Cal·vin·is·ti·cal** adj. [F calvinisme or mod.L calvinismus]

calx /kalks/ n. (pl. **calx·es** or **cal·ces** /kálseez/) **1** a powdery metallic oxide formed when an ore or mineral has been heated. **2** calcium oxide. [L calx calcis lime prob. f. Gk khalix pebble, limestone]

ca·lyp·so /kəlípsō/ n. (pl. **·sos**) a W. Indian song in African rhythm, usu. improvised on a topical theme. [20th c.: orig. unkn.]

ca·lyx /káyliks, kál–/ n. (pl. **ca·lyx·es** or **cal·y·ces** /–liseez/) **1** Bot. the sepals collectively, forming the protective layer of a flower in bud. **2** Biol. any cuplike cavity or structure. [L f. Gk kalux case of bud, husk: cf. kaluptō hide]

cam /kam/ n. a projection on a rotating part in machinery, shaped to impart reciprocal or variable motion to the part in contact with it. [Du. kam comb: cf. Du. kamrad cogwheel]

ca·ma·ra·de·rie /kaàməraádəree/ n. mutual trust and sociability among friends. [F]

PRONUNCIATION TIP camaraderie

If you pronounce all five syllables of this word clearly, you'll be less likely to misspell it. But it is also acceptable to pronounce it without sounding the second a.

cam·a·ril·la /kámərílə/ n. a cabal or clique. [Sp., dimin. of camara chamber]

Camb. abbr. Cambridge.

cam·ber /kámbər/ n. & v. • n. **1** the slightly convex or arched shape of the surface of a ship's deck, aircraft wing, etc. **2** the slight sideways inclination of the front wheel of a motor vehicle. • v. **1** intr. (of a surface) have a camber. **2** tr. give a camber to; build with a camber. [F cambre arched f. L camurus curved inward]

cam·bi·um /kámbeeəm/ n. (pl. **cam·bi·ums** or **cam·bi·a** /–beeə/) Bot. a cellular plant tissue responsible for the increase in girth of stems and roots. □□ **cam·bi·al** adj. [med.L, = change, exchange]

Cam·bo·di·an /kambódeeən/ n. & adj. • n. **1 a** a native or national of Cambodia (Kampuchea) in SE Asia. **b** a person of Cambodian descent. **2** the language of Cambodia. • adj. **1** of or relating to Cambodia or its people or language. **2** another term for KHMER the language. Also called **Kampuchean**.

Cam·bri·an /kámbreeən/ adj. & n. • adj. **1** Welsh. **2** Geol. of or relating to the first period in the Paleozoic era, marked by the occurrence of many forms of invertebrate life (including trilobites and brachiopods). • n. this period or system. [L Cambria var. of Cumbria f. Welsh Cymry Welshman or Cymru Wales]

cam·bric /kámbrik/ n. a fine white linen or cotton fabric. [Kamerijk, Flem. form of Cambrai in N. France, where it was orig. made]

cam·cord·er /kámkawrdər/ n. a combined video camera and sound recorder. [camera + recorder]

came past of COME.

cam·el /káməl/ n. **1** either of two kinds of large, cud-chewing mammals having slender, cushion-footed legs and one hump (**Arabian camel**, Camelus dromedarius) or two humps (**Bactrian camel**, Camelus bactrianus). **2** a fawn color. **3** an apparatus for providing additional buoyancy to ships, etc.; a pontoon. **4** (in full **camel spin**) an arabesque spin in figure skating. [OE f. L camelus f. Gk kamēlos, of Semitic orig.]

cam·el hair n. (also **cam·el's hair**) **1** a fabric made from the hair of a camel. **2** fine, soft hair from a squirrel's tail, used in artists' brushes.

cam·el·eer /káməleér/ n. a camel driver.

ca·mel·lia /kəméelyə/ n. any evergreen shrub of the genus Camellia, native to E. Asia, with shiny leaves and showy flowers. [J. Camellus or Kamel, 17th-c. Jesuit botanist]

ca·mel·o·pard /kəméləpaard/ n. archaic a giraffe. [L camelopardus f. Gk kamēlopardalis (as CAMEL, PARD)]

cam·el·ry /káməlree/ n. (pl. **·ries**) troops mounted on camels.

Cam·em·bert /káməmbair/ n. a kind of soft, creamy cheese, usu. with a strong flavor. [Camembert in N. France, where it was orig. made]

cam·e·o /kámeeō/ n. (pl. **·os**) **1 a** a small piece of onyx or other hard stone carved in relief with a background of a different color. **b** a similar relief design using other materials. **2 a** a short descriptive literary sketch or acted scene. **b** a small character part in a play or film, usu. brief and played by a distinguished actor. [ME f. OF camahieu and med.L cammaeus]

cam·er·a /kámrə, kámərə/ n. **1** an apparatus for taking photographs, consisting of a lightproof box to hold light-sensitive film, a lens, and a shutter mechanism, either for still photographs or for motion-picture film. **2** *Telev.* a piece of equipment that forms an optical image and converts it into electrical impulses for transmission or storage. □ **in camera 1** *Law* in a judge's private room. **2** privately; not in public. **on camera** (esp. of an actor or actress) being filmed or televised at a particular moment. [orig. = chamber f. L *camera* f. Gk *kamara* vault, etc.]

cam·er·a·man /kámrəmən/ n. (pl. **·men**) a person who operates a camera professionally, esp. in filmmaking or television.

cam·er·a ob·scu·ra n. /obskyóōrə/ an internally darkened box with an aperture for projecting the image of an external object on a screen inside it.

cam·er·a-read·y adj. *Printing* (of copy) in a form suitable for immediate photographic reproduction.

cam·i·knick·ers /kámənikərz/ n.pl. *Brit.* a one-piece close-fitting undergarment formerly worn by women. [CAMISOLE + KNICKERS]

cam·i·sole /kámisōl/ n. a woman's loose-fitting upper-body undergarment, typically held up by shoulder straps and having decorative trimming. [F f. It. *camiciola* or Sp. *camisola*: see CHEMISE]

cam·o·mile var. of CHAMOMILE.

cam·ou·flage /kámɔflaazh/ n., adj., & v. ● n. **1 a** the disguising, by the military, of people, vehicles, aircraft, ships, and installations by painting them or covering them to make them blend with their surroundings. **b** such a disguise. **2** the natural coloring of an animal that enables it to blend in with its surroundings. **3** a misleading or evasive precaution or expedient. ● adj. (usu. of clothing) of a mottled green, brown, etc., pattern similar to military camouflage. ● v.tr. hide or disguise by means of camouflage.

WORD HISTORY camouflage

World War I: from French, from *camoufler* 'to disguise' (originally thieves' slang), from Italian *camuffare* 'disguise, deceive,' perhaps by association with French *camouflet* 'whiff of smoke in the face.'

camp¹ /kamp/ n. & v. ● n. **1 a** a place where troops are lodged or trained. **b** the military life (*court and camp*). **2** temporary overnight lodging in tents, etc., in the open. **3 a** temporary accommodation of various kinds, usu. consisting of huts or tents, for detainees, homeless persons, and other emergency use. **b** a complex of buildings for vacation accommodation, usu. with extensive recreational facilities. **4** the adherents of a particular party or doctrine regarded collectively (*the Conservative camp was jubilant*). **5** *S.Afr.* a portion of veld fenced off for pasture on farms. **6** *Austral. & NZ* an assembly place of sheep or cattle. ● v.intr. **1** set up or spend time in a camp (in senses 1 and 2 of n.). **2** (often foll. by *out*) lodge in temporary quarters or in the open. **3** *Austral. & NZ* (of sheep or cattle) flock together, esp. for rest. □□ **camp·ing** n. [F f. It. *campo* f. L *campus* level ground]

camp² /kamp/ adj., n., & v. colloq. ● adj. **1** done in an exaggerated way for effect. **2** affected; effeminate. ● n. a camp manner or style. ● v.intr. & tr. behave or do in a camp way. □ **camp it up** overact; behave affectedly. □□ **camp·i·er, camp·i·est**) **camp·i·ly** adv. **camp·i·ness** n. [20th c.: orig. uncert.]

cam·paign /kampáyn/ n. & v. ● n. **1** an organized course of action for a particular purpose, esp. to arouse public interest (e.g., before a political election). **2 a** a series of military operations in a definite area or to achieve a particular objective. **b** military service in the field (*on campaign*). ● v.intr. conduct or take part in a campaign. □□ **cam·paign·er** n.

WORD HISTORY campaign

Early 17th century (denoting a tract of open country): from French *campagne* 'open country,' via Italian from late Latin *campania*, from *campus* 'level ground.' The change in sense arose from the army's practice of 'taking the field' (i.e., moving from fortress or town, etc., to open country) at the onset of summer.

cam·pa·ni·le /kámpəneélə, –neél/ n. a bell tower (usu. freestanding), esp. in Italy. [It. f. *campana* bell]

cam·pa·nol·o·gy /kámpənólɔjee/ n. **1** the study of bells. **2** the art or practice of bell ringing. □□ **cam·pa·nol·o·ger** n. **cam·pa·no·log·i·cal** /–nɔlójikəl/ adj. **cam·pa·nol·o·gist** n. [mod.L *campanologia* f. LL *campana* bell]

cam·pan·u·la /kampányɔlə/ n. any plant of the genus *Campanula*, with bell-shaped usu. blue, purple, or white flowers. Also called **bellflower**. [mod.L dimin. of L *campana* bell]

cam·pan·u·late /kampányɔlət, –layt/ adj. *Bot. & Zool.* bell-shaped.

camp bed n. a folding portable bed of a kind used in camping.

Cam·pea·chy wood /kampeéchee/ n. = LOGWOOD. [*Campeche* in Mexico, from where it was first exported]

camp·er /kámpər/ n. **1** a person who camps out or lives temporarily in a tent, hut, etc., esp. for recreation. **2** a large motor vehicle with accommodation for camping out.

camp·fire /kámpfir/ n. an open-air fire in a camp, etc.

camp fol·low·er n. **1** a civilian worker in a military camp. **2** a civilian, esp. a prostitute, who follows or lives near a military camp. **3** a person who is nominally attached to a group but is not fully committed.

cam·phor /kámfər/ n. a white, translucent, crystalline volatile substance with aromatic smell and bitter taste, used to make celluloid and in medicine. □□ **cam·phor·ic** /–fórik/ adj. [ME f. OF *camphore* or med.L *camphora* f. Arab. *kāfūr* f. Skr. *karpūram*]

cam·phor·ate /kámfɔrayt/ v.tr. impregnate or treat with camphor.

cam·pi·on /kámpeeən/ n. **1** any plant of the genus *Silene*, with usu. pink or white notched flowers. **2** any of several similar cultivated plants of the genus *Lychnis*. [perh. f. obs. *campion* f. OF, = CHAMPION: transl. of Gk *lukhnis stephanōmatikē* a plant used for (champions') garlands]

camp·site /kámpsit/ n. a place suitable for camping; a site used by campers.

cam·pus /kámpəs/ n. (pl. **cam·pus·es**) **1** the grounds of a university or college. **2** a college or university, esp. as a teaching institution. **3** the grounds of a school, hospital, or other institution. [L, = field]

cam·shaft /kámshaft/ n. a shaft with one or more cams attached to it.

Can. abbr. Canada; Canadian.

can¹ /kan, kən/ v.aux. (3rd sing. present **can**; past **could** /kōōd/) (foll. by infin. without *to*, or absol.; present and past only in use) **1 a** be able to; know how to (*I can run fast; can he?; can you speak German?*). **b** be practically capable of (*you can do it if you try*). **2** be permitted to (*can we go to the party?*). [OE *cunnan* know]

▶ **Can** is properly used to mean 'be able': *I can solve any problem on this list.* **May** means 'be permitted or have approval': *May I leave now?; You may take anything you like.*

can² /kan/ n. & v. ● n. **1** a metal vessel for liquid. **2** a metal container in which food or drink is hermetically sealed to enable storage over long periods. **3** (prec. by *the*) sl. **a** prison (*sent to the can*). **b** sl. toilet. **4** sl. the buttocks. ● v.tr. (**canned, can·ning**) **1** put or preserve in a can. **2** record on film or tape for future use. □ **in the can** colloq. completed; ready (orig. of filmed or recorded material). □□ **can·ner** n. [OE *canne*]

Ca·naan /káynən/ n. **1** a promised land (orig. that west of the Jordan River, the Promised Land of the Israelites). **2** heaven. [eccl.L f. eccl.Gk *Khanaan* f. Heb. *kena'an*]

Can·a·da bal·sam /kánədə/ n. *Biol.* a yellow resin obtained from the balsam fir and used for mounting preparations on microscope slides (its refractive index being similar to that of glass).

Can·a·da goose n. a wild goose, *Branta canadensis*, of N. America, with a brownish-gray body and white cheeks and breast.

ca·naille /kənaá-ee, –náyl/ n. the rabble; the populace. [F f. It. *canaglia* pack of dogs f. *cane* dog]

ca·nal /kənál/ n. **1** an artificial waterway for inland navigation or irrigation. **2** any of various tubular ducts in a plant or animal, for carrying food, liquid, or air. **3** *Astron.* any of a network of apparent linear markings on the planet Mars. [ME f. OF (earlier *chanel*) f. L *canalis* or It. *canale*]

canal boat n. a long, narrow boat for use on canals.

can·al·ize /kánɔliz/ v.tr. **1** make a canal through. **2** convert (a river) into a canal. **3** provide with canals. **4** give the desired direction or purpose to. □□ **ca·nal·i·za·tion** n. [F *canaliser*: see CANAL]

can·a·pé /kánɔpay, –pee/ n. **1** a small piece of bread or pastry with a savory food on top, often served as an hors d'oeuvre. **2** a sofa. [F]

ca·nard /kənaárd/ n. **1** an unfounded rumor or story. **2** an extra surface attached to an airplane forward of the main lifting surface, for extra stability or control. [F, = duck]

Ca·na·rese var. of KANARESE.

ca·nar·y /kənáiree/ n. (pl. **·ies**) **1** any of various small finches of the genus *Serinus*, esp. *S. canaria*, a songbird native to the Canary Islands, with mainly yellow plumage. **2** hist. a sweet wine from the Canary Islands. [*Canary* Islands f. F *Canarie* f. Sp. & L *Canaria* f. *canis* dog, one of the islands being noted in Roman times for large dogs]

ca·nar·y·bird flow·er /kənáireebərd/ n. a climbing plant, *Tropaeolum peregrinum*, with flowers of bright yellow, deeply toothed petals, which give the appearance of a small bird in flight. Also called **canarybird vine**.

ca·nar·y grass n. a Mediterranean plant *Phalaris canariensis*, grown as a crop plant for birdseed.

ca·nar·y yel·low n. bright yellow.

ca·nas·ta /kənástə/ n. **1** a card game using two packs and resembling rummy, the aim being to collect sets (or melds) of cards. **2** a set of seven cards in this game. [Sp., = basket]

ca·nas·ter /kənástər/ n. tobacco made from coarsely broken dried leaves. [orig. the container: Sp. *canastro* ult. f. Gk *kanastron*]

can·can /kánkan/ n. a lively stage dance with high kicking, performed by women in ruffled skirts and petticoats. [F]

can·cel /kánsəl/ v. & n. •v. (**can·celed, can·cel·ing**; esp. Brit. **can·celled, can·cel·ling**) **1** tr. **a** withdraw or revoke (a previous arrangement). **b** discontinue (an arrangement in progress). **2** tr. obliterate or delete (writing, etc.). **3** tr. mark or pierce (a ticket, stamp, etc.) to invalidate it. **4** tr. annul; make void; abolish. **5** (often foll. by out) **a** tr. (of one factor or circumstance) neutralize or counterbalance (another). **b** intr. (of two factors or circumstances) neutralize each other. **6** tr. Math. strike out (an equal factor) on each side of an equation or from the numerator and denominator of a fraction. •n. **1** a countermand. **2** the cancellation of a postage stamp. **3** Printing a new page or section inserted in a book to replace the original text, usu. to correct an error. □□ **can·cel·er** n. [ME f. F canceller f. L cancellare f. cancelli crossbars, lattice]

can·cel·late /kánsilət, –layt/ adj. (also **can·cel·lat·ed** /–laytid/) Biol. marked with crossing lines. [L cancelli lattice]

can·cel·la·tion /kánsəláyshən/ n. (also **can·cel·a·tion**) **1** the act or an instance of canceling or being canceled. **2** something that has been canceled, esp. a booking or reservation. [L cancellatio (as CANCEL)]

can·cel·lous /kánsiləs/ adj. (of a bone) with pores. [L cancelli lattice]

can·cer /kánsər/ n. **1 a** any malignant growth or tumor from an abnormal and uncontrolled division of body cells. **b** a disease caused by this. **2** an evil influence or corruption spreading uncontrollably. **3** (**Cancer**) **a** a constellation, traditionally regarded as contained in the figure of a crab. **b** the fourth sign of the zodiac (the Crab). **c** a person born when the sun is in this sign. □□ **Can·cer·i·an** /–séreeən/ n. & adj. (in sense 3). **can·cer·ous** adj.

can·cer stick n. sl. a cigarette.

can·croid /kángkroyd/ adj. & n. •adj. **1** crablike. **2** resembling cancer. •n. a disease resembling cancer.

can·de·la /kandeélə, –délə/ n. the SI unit of luminous intensity. ¶ Abbr.: **cd**. [L = candle]

can·de·la·brum /kánd'laábrəm/ n. (also **can·de·la·bra** /–brə/) (pl. **can·de·la·bra, can·de·la·brums, can·de·la·bras**) a large branched candlestick or lamp holder. [L f. candela CANDLE]

can·des·cent /kandésənt/ adj. glowing with or as with white heat. □□ **can·des·cence** n. [L candēre be white]

can·did /kándid/ adj. **1** frank; not hiding one's thoughts. **2** (of a photograph) taken informally, usu. without the subject's knowledge. □□ **can·did·ly** adv. **can·did·ness** n. [F candide or L candidus white]

can·di·da /kándidə/ n. any yeastlike parasitic fungus of the genus Candida, esp. C. albicans causing thrush. [mod.L fem. of L candidus: see CANDID]

can·di·date /kándidət, –dayt/ n. **1** a person who seeks or is nominated for an office, award, etc. **2** a person or thing likely to gain some distinction or position. **3** a person entered for an examination. □□ **can·di·da·cy** /–dəsee/ n. **can·di·da·ture** /–dəchər/ n. Brit. [F candidat or L candidatus white-robed (Roman candidates wearing white)]

can·dle /kánd'l/ n. & v. •n. **1** a cylinder or block of wax or tallow with a central wick, for giving light when burning. **2** = CANDLEPOWER. •v.tr. test (an egg) for freshness by holding it to the light. □ **cannot hold a candle to** cannot be compared with; is much inferior to. **not worth the candle** not justifying the cost or trouble. □□ **can·dler** n. [OE candel f. L candela f. candēre shine]

can·dle·light /kánd'l-lit/ n. **1** light provided by candles. **2** dusk. □□ **can·dle·lit** adj.

Can·dle·mas /kándəlməs/ n. a feast with blessing of candles (Feb. 2), commemorating the Purification of the Virgin Mary and the presentation of Christ in the Temple. [OE Candelmæsse (as CANDLE, MASS²)]

can·dle·pow·er /kánd'lpowr/ n. a unit of luminous intensity.

can·dle·stick /kánd'lstik/ n. a holder for one or more candles.

can·dle·wick /kánd'lwik/ n. **1** a thick soft cotton yarn. **2** material made from this, usu. with a tufted pattern.

can·dor /kándər/ n. (Brit. **can·dour**) candid behavior or action; frankness. [F candeur or L candor whiteness]

C. & W. abbr. COUNTRY AND WESTERN.

can·dy /kándee/ n. & v. •n. (pl. **·dies**) **1** a sweet confection, usu. containing sugar, chocolate, etc. **2** (in full **sugar candy**) sugar crystallized by repeated boiling and slow evaporation. •v.tr. (**·dies, ·died**) (usu. as **candied** adj.) preserve by coating and impregnat-

ing with a sugar syrup (candied fruit). [F sucre candi candied sugar f. Arab. ḳand sugar]

can·dy floss n. Brit. = COTTON CANDY.

can·dy stripe n. a pattern consisting of alternate stripes of white and a color (usu. pink).

can·dy-striped adj. (of fabric) having a pattern of candy stripe.

can·dy strip·er n. a hospital volunteer, esp. a teenager, who wears a candy-striped uniform.

can·dy·tuft /kándeetuft/ n. any of various plants of the genus Iberis, native to W. Europe, with white, pink, or purple flowers in tufts. [obs. Candy (Candia Crete) + TUFT]

cane /kayn/ n. & v. •n. **1 a** the hollow jointed stem of giant reeds or grasses (bamboo cane). **b** the solid stem of slender palms (malacca cane). **2** = SUGAR CANE. **3** a raspberry cane. **4** material of cane used for wickerwork, etc. **5 a** a cane used as a walking stick or a support for a plant or an instrument of punishment. **b** any slender walking stick. •v.tr. **1** beat with a cane. **2** weave cane into (a chair, etc.). □□ **can·er** n. (in sense 2 of v.). **can·ing** n. [ME f. OF f. L canna f. Gk kanna]

cane·brake /káynbrayk/ n. a tract of land overgrown with canes.

cane chair n. a chair with a seat made of woven cane strips.

cane sug·ar n. sugar obtained from sugar cane.

ca·nine /káynin/ adj. & n. •adj. **1** of a dog or dogs. **2** of or belonging to the family Canidae, including dogs, wolves, foxes, etc. •n. **1** a dog. **2** (in full **canine tooth**) a pointed tooth between the incisors and premolars. [ME f. canin –ine or f. L caninus f. canis dog]

can·is·ter /kánistər/ n. **1** a small container, usu. of metal and cylindrical, for storing sugar, etc. **2 a** a cylinder of shot, tear gas, etc., that explodes on impact. **b** such cylinders collectively. [L canistrum f. Gk f. kanna CANE]

can·ker /kángkər/ n. & v. •n. **1 a** a destructive fungus disease of trees and plants. **b** an open wound in the stem of a tree or plant. **2** Zool. an ulcerous ear disease of animals, esp. cats and dogs. **3** Med. an ulceration, esp. of the lips. **4** a corrupting influence. •v.tr. **1** consume with canker. **2** corrupt. **3** (as **cankered** adj.) soured; malignant; crabbed. □□ **can·ker·ous** adj. [OE cancer & ONF cancre, OF chancre f. L cancer crab]

can·ker·worm /kángkərwərm/ n. any caterpillar of various wingless moths that consume the buds and leaves of shade and fruit trees in N. America.

can·na /kánə/ n. any tropical plant of the genus Canna with bright flowers and ornamental leaves. [L: see CANE]

can·na·bis /kánəbis/ n. **1** any hemp plant of the genus Cannabis, esp. Indian hemp. **2** a preparation of parts of this used as a mild intoxicant or hallucinogen; marijuana. [L f. Gk]

can·na·bis res·in n. a sticky product, esp. from the flowering tops of the female cannabis plant.

canned /kand/ adj. **1** prerecorded (canned laughter, canned music). **2** supplied in a can (canned beef). **3** sl. fired from a job.

can·nel /kánəl/ n. (in full **cannel coal**) a bituminous coal burning with a bright flame. [16th c.: orig. No. of Engl.]

can·nel·lo·ni /kánəlónee/ n.pl. tubes or rolls of pasta stuffed with meat or a vegetable mixture. [It. f. cannello stalk]

can·ner·y /kánəree/ n. (pl. **·ies**) a factory where food is canned.

can·ni·bal /kánibəl/ n. & adj. •n. **1** a person who eats human flesh. **2** an animal that feeds on flesh of its own species. •adj. of or like a cannibal. □□ **can·ni·bal·ism** n. **can·ni·bal·is·tic** adj. **can·ni·bal·is·ti·cal·ly** adv. [orig. pl. Canibales f. Sp.: var. of Caribes name of a W.Ind. nation]

can·ni·bal·ize /kánibəliz/ v.tr. use (a machine, etc.) as a source of spare parts for others. □□ **can·ni·bal·i·za·tion** n.

can·ni·kin /kánikin/ n. a small can. [Du. kanneken (as CAN², –KIN)]

can·non /kánən/ n. & v. •n. **1** hist. (pl. same) a large, heavy gun installed on a carriage or mounting. **2** an automatic aircraft gun firing shells. **3** Billiards Brit. CAROM. **4** (in full **cannon bit**) a smooth round bit for a horse. •v.intr. Brit. (usu. foll. by against, into) collide heavily or obliquely. [F canon f. It. cannone large tube f. canna CANE: in Billiards sense f. older CAROM]

cannon 1

can·non·ade /kánənáyd/ n. & v. •n. a period of continuous heavy gunfire. •v.tr. bombard with a cannonade. [F f. It. cannonata]

can·non·ball /kánənbawl/ n., adj., & v. •n. **1** a large, usu. metal ball fired by a cannon. **2** Tennis a very rapid serve. **3** a very fast vehicle, etc., esp. an express train. **4** a jump into water in which the knees are held tight against the chest. •adj. **1** moving at great speed. **2** of

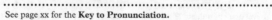

a jump into water in a curled-up position (*a cannonball dive*). • *v.intr.* travel with great force, momentum, and speed.

can•non bone *n.* the tube-shaped bone between the hock and fetlock of a horse.

can•non fod•der *n.* soldiers regarded merely as material to be expended in war.

can•not /kánot, kanót/ *v.aux.* can not.

can•nu•la /kányələ/ *n.* (*pl.* **can•nu•las** or **can•nu•lae** /–lee/) *Surgery* a small tube for inserting into the body to allow fluid to enter or escape. [L, dimin. of *canna* cane]

can•nu•late /kányəlayt/ *v.tr. Surgery* introduce a cannula into.

can•ny /kánee/ *adj.* (**can•ni•er, can•ni•est**) **1 a** shrewd; worldly-wise. **b** thrifty. **c** circumspect. **2** sly; dryly humorous. **3** *Sc. & No. of Engl.* pleasant; agreeable. □□ **can•ni•ly** *adv.* **can•ni•ness** *n.* [CAN[1] (in sense 'know') + -Y[1]]

ca•noe /kəno͞o/ *n. & v.* • *n.* a small, narrow boat with pointed ends usu. propelled by paddling. • *v.intr.* (**ca•noes, ca•noed, ca•noe•ing**) travel in a canoe. □□ **ca•noe•ist** *n.* [Sp. and Haitian *canoa*]

can of worms *n.* *colloq.* a source of unexpected complications.

canoe

can•o•la oil /kəno͞olə/ *n.* a type of cooking oil derived from the seed of a variety of the rape plant. [*Canada* oil low acid]

can•on /kánən/ *n.* **1 a** a general law, rule, principle, or criterion. **b** a church decree or law. **2** (*fem.* **can•on•ess**) **a** a member of a cathedral chapter. **b** a member of certain Roman Catholic orders. **3 a** a collection or list of sacred books, etc., accepted as genuine. **b** the recognized genuine works of a particular author; a list of these. **c** literary works as part of a school or university curriculum. **4** *Eccl.* the part of the Mass containing the words of consecration. **5** *Mus.* a piece with different parts taking up the same theme successively, either at the same or at a different pitch. [OE f. L f. Gk *kanōn*, in ME also f. AF & OF *canun, –on*; in sense 2 ME f. OF *canonie* f. eccl.L *canonicus*: cf. CANONICAL]

ca•non•ic /kənónik/ *adj.* = CANONICAL *adj.* [OE f. OF *canonique* or L *canonicus* f. Gk *kanonikos* (as CANON)]

ca•non•i•cal /kənónikəl/ *adj. & n.* • *adj.* **1 a** according to or ordered by canon law. **b** included in the canon of Scripture. **2** authoritative; standard; accepted. **3** of a cathedral chapter or a member of it. **4** *Mus.* in canon form. • *n.* (in *pl.*) the canonical dress of the clergy. □□ **ca•non•i•cal•ly** *adv.* [med.L *canonicalis* (as CANONIC)]

ca•non•i•cal hours *n. Eccl.* the times fixed for a formal set of prayers or for the celebration of marriage.

can•on•ic•i•ty /kánənísitee/ *n.* the status of being canonical. [L *canonicus* canonical]

can•on•ist /kánənist/ *n.* an expert in canon law. [ME f. F *canoniste* or f. med.L *canonista*: see CANON]

can•on•ize /kánəniz/ *v.tr.* **1 a** declare officially to be a saint, usu. with a ceremony. **b** regard as a saint. **2** admit to the canon of Scripture. **3** sanction by church authority. □□ **can•on•i•za•tion** *n.* [ME f. med.L *canonizare*: see CANON]

can•on law *n.* ecclesiastical law.

can•on reg•u•lar *n.* (also **reg•u•lar can•on**) see REGULAR *adj.* 9b.

can•on•ry /kánənree/ *n.* (*pl.* **-ries**) the office or benefice of a canon.

ca•noo•dle /kəno͞od'l/ *v.intr. colloq.* kiss and cuddle amorously. [-19th-c. US: orig. unkn.]

can o•pen•er *n.* a device for opening cans (in sense 2 of *n.*).

ca•no•pic jar /kənópik, –nóp–/ *n.* (also **ca•no•pic vase**) an urn used for holding the entrails of an embalmed body in an ancient Egyptian burial. [L *Canopicus* f. *Canopus* in ancient Egypt]

can•o•py /kánəpee/ *n. & v.* • *n.* (*pl.* **-pies**) **1 a** a covering hung or held up over a throne, bed, person, etc. **b** the sky. **c** an overhanging shelter. **2** *Archit.* a rooflike projection over a niche, etc. **3** the uppermost layers of foliage, etc., in a forest. **4 a** the expanding part of a parachute. **b** the cover of an aircraft's cockpit. • *v.tr.* (**•pies, •pied**) supply or be a canopy to. [ME f. med.L *canopeum* f. *conopeum* f. Gk *kōnōpeion* couch with mosquito netting f. *kōnōps* gnat]

ca•no•rous /kənáwrəs/ *adj.* melodious; resonant. [L *canorus* f. *canere* sing]

canst /kanst/ *archaic* 2nd person sing. of CAN[1].

Cant. *abbr.* Canticles (Old Testament).

cant[1] /kant/ *n. & v.* • *n.* **1** insincere pious or moral talk. **2** ephemeral or fashionable catchwords. **3** language peculiar to a class, profession, sect, etc.; jargon. • *v.intr.* use cant. [earlier of musical sound, of intonation, and of beggars' whining; perh. from the singing of religious mendicants: prob. f. L *canere* sing]

cant[2] /kant/ *n. & v.* • *n.* **1 a** a slanting surface, e.g., of a bank. **b** a bevel of a crystal, etc. **2** an oblique push or movement that upsets

or partly upsets something. **3** a tilted or sloping position. • *v.* **1** *tr.* push or pitch out of level; tilt. **2** *intr.* take or lie in a slanting position. **3** *tr.* impart a bevel to. **4** *intr. Naut.* swing around. [ME f. MLG *kant, kante,* MDu. *cant,* point, side, edge, ult. f. L *cant(h)us* iron tire]

can't /kant/ *contr.* can not.

Cantab. /kántab/ *abbr.* Cantabrigian; of Cambridge University. [L *Cantabrigiensis*]

can•ta•bi•le /kantaábilay/ *adv., adj., & n. Mus.* • *adv. & adj.* in a smooth singing style. • *n.* a cantabile passage or movement. [It., = singable]

Can•ta•brig•i•an /kántəbríjeeən/ *adj. & n.* • *adj.* of Cambridge (England or Massachusetts) or Cambridge University or Harvard University. • *n.* **1** a student of Cambridge University or Harvard University. **2** a native of Cambridge (England or Massachusetts). [L *Cantabrigia* Cambridge]

can•ta•loupe /kánt'lōp/ *n.* a small, round ribbed variety of melon with orange flesh. [F *cantaloup* f. *Cantaluppi* near Rome, where it was first grown in Europe]

can•tan•ker•ous /kantángkərəs/ *adj.* bad-tempered; quarrelsome. □□ **can•tan•ker•ous•ly** *adv.* **can•tan•ker•ous•ness** *n.* [perh. f. Ir. *cant* outbidding + *rancorous*]

can•ta•ta /kəntaátə/ *n. Mus.* a short narrative or descriptive composition with vocal solos and usu. chorus and orchestral accompaniment. [It. *cantata (aria)* sung (air) f. *cantare* sing]

cant dog *n.* = CANT HOOK.

can•teen /kanteén/ *n.* **1 a** a restaurant for employees in an office or factory, etc. **b** a store selling provisions or liquor in a barracks or camp. **2** *Brit.* a case or box of cutlery. **3** a soldier's or camper's water flask or set of eating or drinking utensils. [F *cantine* f. It. *cantina* cellar]

can•ter /kántər/ *n. & v.* • *n.* a gentle gallop. • *v.* **1** *intr.* (of a horse or its rider) go at a canter. **2** *tr.* make (a horse) canter. [short for *Canterbury pace,* from the supposed easy pace of medieval pilgrims to Canterbury]

can•ter•bur•y /kántərberee/ *n.* (*pl.* **•ies**) a piece of furniture with partitions for holding music, etc. [*Canterbury* in Kent]

Can•ter•bur•y bell /kántərbəree/ *n.* a cultivated campanula with large flowers. [after the bells of Canterbury pilgrims' horses: see CANTER]

can•thar•i•des /kanthárideez/ *n.pl.* a preparation made from dried bodies of a beetle *Lytta vesicatoria,* causing blistering of the skin and formerly used in medicine and as an aphrodisiac. Also called **Spanish fly.** [L f. Gk *kantharis* Spanish fly]

cant hook *n.* an iron hook at the end of a long handle, used for gripping and rolling logs.

can•thus /kánthəs/ *n.* (*pl.* **can•thi** /–thī/) the outer or inner corner of the eye, where the upper and lower lids meet. [L f. Gk *kanthos*]

can•ti•cle /kántikəl/ *n.* **1** a song or chant with a biblical text. **2** (in full **Canticle of Canticles**) the Song of Solomon. [ME f. OF *canticle* (var. of *cantique*) or L *canticulum* dimin. of *canticum* f. *canere* sing]

can•ti•le•na /kánt'leénə/ *n. Mus.* a simple or sustained melody. [It.]

can•ti•le•ver /kánt'leevər, –evər/ *n. & v.* • *n.* **1** a long bracket or beam, etc., projecting from a wall to support a balcony, etc. **2** a beam or girder fixed at only one end. • *v.intr.* **1** project as a cantilever. **2** be supported by cantilevers. [17th c.: orig. unkn.]

can•ti•le•ver bridge *n.* a bridge made of cantilevers projecting from the piers and connected by girders.

can•til•late /kánt'layt/ *v.tr. & intr.* chant or recite with musical tones. □□ **can•til•la•tion** /–láyshən/ *n.* [L *cantillare* sing low: see CHANT]

can•ti•na /kanteénə/ *n.* esp. *SW US* a tavern, bar, etc. [Sp. & It.]

cant•ing arms *n. Heraldry* arms containing an allusion to the name of the bearer.

can•to /kántō/ *n.* (*pl.* **•tos**) a division of a long poem. [It., = song, f. L *cantus*]

can•ton *n. & v.* • *n.* **1** /kánton/ **a** a subdivision of a country. **b** a state of the Swiss confederation. **2** /kántən/ *Heraldry* a square division, less than a quarter, in the upper (usu. dexter) corner of a shield. • *v.tr.* **1** /kántón, –tōn/ *Brit.* put (troops) into quarters. **2** /kántón/ divide into cantons. □□ **can•ton•al** /kánt'nəl, kántónəl/ *adj.* [OF, = corner (see CANT[2]): (v.) also partly f. F *cantonner*]

Can•ton•ese /kántəneéz/ *adj. & n.* • *adj.* of Canton or the Cantonese dialect of Chinese. • *n.* (*pl.* same) **1** a native of Canton. **2** the dialect of Chinese spoken in SE China and Hong Kong. [*Canton* in China]

can•ton•ment /kantónmənt, –tón–/ *n.* a military camp, esp. a permanent military station in British India. [F *cantonnement*: see CANTON]

can•tor /kántər/ *n.* **1** the leader of the singing in church; a precentor. **2** the precentor in a synagogue. [L, = singer f. *canere* sing]

can•to•ri•al /kantáwreeəl/ *adj.* **1** of or relating to the cantor. **2** of the north side of the choir in a church (cf. DECANAL).

can•to•ris /kantáwris/ *adj. Mus.* to be sung by the cantorial side of the choir in antiphonal singing (cf. DECANI). [L, genit. of CANTOR precentor]

can•trip /kántrip/ n. Sc. **1** a witch's trick. **2** esp. Brit. a piece of mischief; a playful act. [18th c.: orig. unkn.]

Ca•nuck /kənúk/ n. & adj. sl. often derog. •n. **1** a Canadian, esp. a French Canadian. **2** a Canadian horse or pony. •adj. Canadian, esp. French Canadian. [app. f. Canada]

can•vas /kánvəs/ n. & v. •n. **1 a** a strong coarse kind of cloth made from hemp or flax or other coarse yarn and used for sails and tents, etc., and as a surface for oil painting. **b** a piece of this. **2** a painting on canvas, esp. in oils. **3** an open kind of canvas used as a basis for tapestry and embroidery. **4** sl. the floor of a boxing or wrestling ring. •v.tr. (**can•vased, can•vas•ing**; esp. Brit. **can•vassed, can•vas•sing**) cover with canvas. □ **under canvas 1** in a tent or tents. **2** with sails spread. [ME & ONF canevas, ult. f. L cannabis hemp]

can•vas•back /kánvəsbak/ n. a wild duck, Aythya valisineria, of N. America, with back feathers the color of unbleached canvas.

can•vass /kánvəs/ v. & n. •v. **1 a** intr. solicit votes. **b** tr. solicit votes from (electors in a constituency). **2** tr. **a** ascertain opinions of. **b** seek business from. **c** discuss thoroughly. **3** tr. Brit. propose (an idea or plan, etc.). •n. the process of or an instance of canvassing, esp. of electors. □□ **can•vass•er** n. [orig. = toss in a sheet, agitate, f. CANVAS]

can•yon /kányən/ n. a deep gorge, often with a stream or river. [Sp. cañón tube, ult. f. L canna CANE]

can•zo•net /kánzənét/ n. **1** a short, light song. **2** a kind of madrigal. [It., dimin. of canzone song f. L cantio –onis f. canere sing]

caou•tchouc /kówchŏŏk/ n. raw rubber. [F f. Carib cahuchu]

CAP abbr. Civil Air Patrol.

cap /kap/ n. & v. •n. **1 a** a covering for the head, often soft and with a visor. **b** a head covering worn in a particular profession (nurse's cap). **c** esp. Brit. a cap awarded as a sign of membership of a sports team. **d** an academic mortarboard or soft hat. **e** a special hat as part of Highland costume. **2 a** a cover like a cap in shape or position (kneecap; toecap). **b** a device to seal a bottle or protect the point of a pen, lens of a camera, etc. **3** = MOBCAP. **4** = PERCUSSION CAP. **5** = CROWN n. 9b. •v.tr. (**capped, cap•ping**) **1 a** put a cap on. **b** cover the top or end of. **c** set a limit to (rate-capping). **2 a** esp. Brit. award a sports cap to. **b** Sc. & NZ confer a university degree on. **3 a** lie on top of; form the cap of. **b** surpass; excel. **c** improve on (a story, quotation, etc.), esp. by producing a better or more apposite one. □ **cap in hand** humbly. **set one's cap for** try to attract as a suitor. □□ **cap•ful** n. (pl. **•fuls**). **cap•ping** n. [OE cæppe f. LL cappa, perh. f. L caput head]

cap. abbr. **1** capital. **2** capital letter. **3** chapter. [L capitulum or caput]

ca•pa•bil•i•ty /káypəbílitee/ n. (pl. **•ties**) **1** (often foll. by of, for, to) ability; power; the condition of being capable. **2** an undeveloped or unused faculty.

ca•pa•ble /káypəbəl/ adj. **1** competent; able; gifted. **2** (foll. by of) **a** having the ability or fitness or necessary quality for. **b** susceptible or admitting of (explanation or improvement, etc.). □□ **ca•pa•bly** adv. [F f. LL capabilis f. L capere hold]

ca•pa•cious /kəpáyshəs/ adj. roomy; able to hold much. □□ **ca•pa•cious•ly** adv. **ca•pa•cious•ness** n. [L capax –acis f. capere hold]

ca•pac•i•tance /kəpásit'ns/ n. Electr. **1** the ability of a system to store an electric charge. **2** the ratio of the change in an electric charge in a system to the corresponding change in its electric potential. ¶ Symb.: **C.** [CAPACITY + –ANCE]

ca•pac•i•tate /kəpásitayt/ v.tr. **1** (usu. foll. by for, or to + infin.) render capable. **2** make legally competent.

ca•pac•i•tor /kəpásitər/ n. Electr. a device of one or more pairs of conductors separated by insulators used to store an electric charge.

ca•pac•i•ty /kəpásitee/ n. (pl. **•ties**) **1 a** the power of containing, receiving, experiencing, or producing (capacity for heat, pain, etc.). **b** the maximum amount that can be contained or produced, etc. **c** the volume, e.g., of the cylinders in an internal combustion engine. **d** (attrib.) fully occupying the available space, resources, etc. (a capacity audience). **2 a** mental power. **b** a faculty or talent. **3 a** position or function (in a civil capacity; in my capacity as a critic). **4** legal competence. **5** Electr. capacitance. □ **to capacity** fully; using all resources (working to capacity). □□ **ca•pac•i•tive** /–táytiv/ adj. (also **ca•pac•i•tive**) (in sense 5). [ME f. F f. L capacitas –tatis (as CAPACIOUS)]

ca•par•i•son /kəpárisən/ n. & v. •n. **1** (usu. in pl.) a horse's trappings. **2** equipment; finery. •v.tr. put caparisons on; adorn richly. [obs. F caparasson f. Sp. caparazón saddlecloth f. capa CAPE¹]

cape¹ /kayp/ n. **1** a sleeveless cloak. **2** a short, sleeveless cloak as a fixed or detachable part of a longer cloak or coat. [F f. Prov. capa f. LL cappa CAP]

cape² /kayp/ n. **1** a headland or promontory. **2** (**the Cape**) **a** the Cape of Good Hope. **b** the S. African province containing it. **c** Cape Cod, Massachusetts. [ME f. OF cap f. Prov. cap ult. f. L caput head]

Cape Dutch n. archaic Afrikaans.

cape goose•ber•ry n. **1** an edible, soft, roundish yellow berry enclosed in a lanternlike husk. **2** the plant, Physalis peruviana, bearing these.

cap•e•lin /kápəlin, káplin/ n. (also **cap•lin** /káplin/) a small smeltlike fish, Mallotus villosus, of the N. Atlantic, used as food and as bait for catching cod, etc. [F f. Prov. capelan: see CHAPLAIN]

ca•per¹ /káypər/ v. & n. •v.intr. jump or run about playfully. •n. **1** a playful jump or leap. **2 a** a fantastic proceeding; a prank. **b** sl. any activity or occupation. □ **cut a caper** (or **capers**) act friskily. □□ **ca•per•er** n. [abbr. of CAPRIOLE]

ca•per² /káypər/ n. **1** a bramblelike S. European shrub, Capparis spinosa. **2** (in pl.) its flower buds cooked and pickled for use as flavoring, esp. for a savory sauce. [ME capres & F câpres f. L capparis f. Gk kapparis, treated as pl.: cf. CHERRY, PEA]

cap•er•cail•lie /kápərkáylee/ n. (also **cap•er•cail•zie** /–káylzee/) a large European grouse, Tetrao urogallus. [Gael. capull coille horse of the wood]

cape•skin /káypskin/ n. a soft leather made from S. African sheepskin.

ca•pi•as /káypeeəs/ n. Law a writ ordering the arrest of the person named. [L, = you are to seize, f. capere take]

cap•il•lar•i•ty /kápiláritee/ n. a phenomenon at liquid boundaries resulting in the rise or depression of liquids in narrow tubes. Also called **capillary action.** [F capillarité (as CAPILLARY)]

cap•il•lar•y /kápəleree/ adj. & n. •adj. **1** of or like a hair. **2** (of a tube) of hairlike internal diameter. **3** of one of the delicate ramified blood vessels intervening between arteries and veins. •n. (pl. **•ies**) **1** a capillary tube. **2** a capillary blood vessel. [L capillaris f. capillus hair]

cap•il•lar•y ac•tion n. = CAPILLARITY.

cap•i•tal¹ /kápit'l/ n., adj., & int. •n. **1** the most important town or city of a country, state, or region, usu. its seat of government and administrative center. **2 a** the money or other assets with which a company starts in business. **b** accumulated wealth, esp. as used in further production. **c** money invested or lent at interest. **3** capitalists generally. **4** a capital letter. •adj. **1 a** principal; most important; leading. **b** colloq. excellent; first-rate. **2 a** involving or punishable by death (capital punishment; a capital offense). **b** (of an error, etc.) vitally harmful; fatal. **3** (of letters of the alphabet) large in size and of the form used to begin sentences and names, etc. •int. expressing approval or satisfaction. □ **make capital out of** use to one's advantage. **with a capital – –** emphatically such (art with a capital A). □□ **cap•i•tal•ly** adv. [ME f. OF f. L capitalis f. caput –itis head]

▶If you're talking about a capital letter, the capital of Ohio, or a capital investment, use the word that ends in -al. If you're talking about the name of the building in Washington, D.C., use Capitol with a capital C. When referring to buildings located in the individual U.S. states, use a lower case c (a model of the new state capitol building).

cap•i•tal² /kápit'l/ n. Archit. the head or cornice of a pillar or column. [ME f. OF capitel f. LL capitellum dimin. of L caput head]

cap•i•tal gain n. a profit from the sale of investments or property.

cap•i•tal goods n. goods, esp. machinery, plant, etc., used or to be used in producing commodities (opp. CONSUMER GOODS).

cap•i•tal•ism /kápit'lizəm/ n. **1 a** an economic system in which the production and distribution of goods depend on invested private capital and profit making. **b** the possession of capital or wealth. **2** Polit. the dominance of private owners of capital and production for profit.

cap•i•tal•ist /kápit'list/ n. & adj. •n. **1** a person using or possessing capital; a rich person. **2** an advocate of capitalism. •adj. of or favoring capitalism. □□ **cap•i•tal•is•tic** adj. **cap•i•tal•is•ti•cal•ly** adv.

cap•i•tal•ize /kápit'līz/ v. **1** tr. **a** convert into or provide with capital. **b** calculate or realize the present value of an income. **c** reckon (the value of an asset) by setting future benefits against the cost of maintenance. **2** tr. **a** write (a letter of the alphabet) as a capital. **b** begin (a word) with a capital letter. **3** intr.

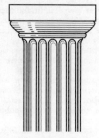

Doric

Ionic

Corinthian

capital²

(foll. by *on*) use to one's advantage; profit from. □□ **cap·i·tal·i·za·tion** *n*. [F *capitaliser* (as CAPITAL[1])]

cap·i·tal lev·y *n*. a tax by means of which the government appropriates a fixed proportion of private wealth.

cap·i·tal sum *n*. a lump sum of money, esp. payable to an insured person.

cap·i·ta·tion /kápitáyshən/ *n*. **1** a tax or fee at a set rate per person. **2** the levying of such a tax or fee. [F *capitation* or LL *capitatio* poll-tax f. *caput* head]

Cap·i·tol /kápit'l/ *n*. **1** the building in Washington, D.C., in which the U.S. Congress meets. **2** (**capitol**) a building in which a state legislature meets.
▶see note at CAPITAL[1].

ca·pit·u·lar /kəpíchələr/ *adj*. **1** of or relating to a cathedral chapter. **2** *Anat*. of or relating to a terminal protuberance of a bone. [LL *capitularis* f. L *capitulum* CHAPTER]

ca·pit·u·lar·y /kəpíchələree/ *n*. (*pl.* ·**ies**) a collection of ordinances, esp. of the Frankish kings. [LL *capitularius* (as CAPITULAR)]

ca·pit·u·late /kəpíchəlayt/ *v.intr.* surrender, esp. on stated conditions. □□ **ca·pit·u·la·tor** *n*. **ca·pit·u·la·to·ry** /–lətáwree/ *adj*. [med.L *capitulare* draw up under headings f. L *caput* head]

ca·pit·u·la·tion /kəpíchələyshən/ *n*. **1** the act of capitulating; surrender. **2** a statement of the main divisions of a subject. **3** an agreement or set of conditions.

ca·pit·u·lum /kəpíchələm/ *n*. (*pl.* **ca·pit·u·la** /–lə/) *Bot*. an inflorescence with flowers clustered together like a head, as in the daisy family. [L, dimin. of *caput* head]

cap·lin var. of CAPELIN.

cap'n /káp'm/ *n. sl.* captain. [contr.]

ca·po /káypō/ *n*. (in full **capotasto** /–tástō/) (*pl.* **ca·pos** or **ca·po·tas·tos**) *Mus*. a device secured across the neck of a fretted instrument to raise equally the tuning of all strings by the required amount. [It. *capo tasto* head stop]

ca·pon /káypon, –pən/ *n*. a domestic cock castrated and fattened for eating. □□ **ca·pon·ize** *v.tr.* [OE f. AF *capun*, OF *capon*, ult. f. L *capo –onis*]

ca·po·nier /kápənéer/ *n*. a covered passage across a ditch around a fort. [Sp. *caponera*, lit. 'capon pen']

ca·pot /kəpót/ *n. & v.* •*n*. (in piquet) the winning of all the tricks by one player. •*v.tr.* (**ca·pot·ted, ca·pot·ting**) score a capot against (an opponent). [F]

ca·pote /kəpót, kapó/ *n. hist.* a long cloak with a hood, formerly worn by soldiers and travelers, etc. [F, dimin. of *cape* CAPE[1]]

cap·puc·ci·no /kápōocheénō/ *n*. (*pl.* ·**nos**) espresso coffee with milk made frothy with pressurized steam. [It., = CAPUCHIN]

ca·pric·ci·o /kəpréecheeō/ *n*. (*pl.* ·**os**) **1** a lively and usu. short musical composition. **2** a painting, etc., representing a fantasy or a mixture of real and imaginary features. [It., = sudden start, orig. 'horror']

ca·pric·ci·o·so /kəpréecheeōsō/ *adv., adj., & n. Mus.* •*adv. & adj.* in a free and impulsive style. •*n*. (*pl.* ·**sos**) a capriccioso passage or movement. [It., = capricious]

ca·price /kəprées/ *n*. **1 a** an unaccountable or whimsical change of mind or conduct. **b** a tendency to this. **2** a work of lively fancy in painting, drawing, or music; a capriccio. [F f. It. CAPRICCIO]

ca·pri·cious /kəpríshəs, -prée-/ *adj*. **1** guided by or given to caprice. **2** irregular; unpredictable. □□ **ca·pri·cious·ly** *adv*. **ca·pri·cious·ness** *n*. [F *capricieux* f. It. CAPRICCIOSO]

Cap·ri·corn /káprikawrn/ *n*. (also **Cap·ri·cor·nus** /–káwrnəs/) **1** a constellation, traditionally regarded as contained in the figure of a goat's horns. **2 a** the tenth sign of the zodiac (the Goat). **b** a person born when the sun is in this sign. □□ **Capricornian** *n. & adj*. [ME f. OF *capricorne* f. L *capricornus* f. *caper –pri* goat + *cornu* horn]

ca·prine /káprin, –rin/ *adj*. of or like a goat. [ME f. L *caprinus* f. *caper –pri* goat]

cap·ri·ole /kápreeōl/ *n. & v.* •*n*. **1** a leap or caper. **2** a trained horse's high leap and kick without advancing. •*v*. **1** *intr*. (of a horse or its rider) perform a capriole. **2** *tr*. make (a horse) capriole. [F f. It. *capriola* leap, ult. f. *caper –pri* goat]

ca·pris /kəpréez/ *n.pl.* (also **ca·pri pants**) women's close-fitting tapered trousers that end above the ankle. [*Capri*, an island in the bay of Naples]

cap rock *n*. a hard rock or stratum overlying a deposit of oil, gas, coal, etc.

caps. *abbr.* capital letters.

Cap·si·an /kápseeən/ *adj. & n.* •*adj*. of or relating to a paleolithic culture of N. Africa and S. Europe. •*n*. this culture. [L *Capsa* = Gafsa in Tunisia]

cap·si·cum /kápsikəm/ *n*. **1** any plant of the genus *Capsicum*, having edible capsular fruits containing many seeds, esp. *C. annuum* yielding several varieties of pepper. **2** the fruit of any of these plants, which vary in size, color, and pungency. [mod.L, perh. f. L *capsa* box]

cap·sid[1] /kápsid/ *n*. any bug of the family Capsidae, esp. one that feeds on plants. [mod.L *Capsus* a genus of them]

cap·sid[2] /kápsid/ *n*. the protein coat or shell of a virus. [F *capside* f. L *capsa* box]

cap·size /kápsīz, –sīz/ *v*. **1** *tr*. upset or overturn (a boat). **2** *intr*. capsized. □□ **cap·siz·al** /–sízəl/ *n*. [*cap-* as in Prov. *capvirar*, F *chavirer*: *–size* unexpl.]

cap sleeve *n*. a sleeve extending only a short distance from the shoulder.

cap·stan /kápstən/ *n*. **1** a thick revolving cylinder with a vertical axis, for winding an anchor cable or a halyard, etc. **2** a revolving spindle on a tape recorder that guides the tape past the head. [Prov. *cabestan*, ult. f. L *capistrum* halter f. *capere* seize]

capstan 1

cap·stone /kápstōn/ *n*. **1** coping; a coping stone. **2** a crowning achievement.

cap·sule /kápsəl, –sōōl/ *n*. **1** a small gelatinous case enclosing a dose of medicine and swallowed with it. **2** a detachable compartment of a spacecraft or nose cone of a rocket. **3** an enclosing membrane in the body. **4 a** a dry fruit that releases its seeds when ripe. **b** the spore-producing part of mosses and liverworts. **5** *Biol.* an enveloping layer surrounding certain bacteria. **6** (*attrib.*) concise; highly condensed (*a capsule history of jazz*). □□ **cap·su·lar** *adj*. **cap·su·late** *adj*. [F f. L *capsula* f. *capsa* CASE[2]]

cap·sul·ize /kápsəlīz, –syōō–/ *v.tr.* put (information, etc.) in compact form.

Capt. *abbr.* Captain.

cap·tain /káptin/ *n. & v.* •*n*. **1 a** a chief or leader. **b** the leader of a team, esp. in sports. **c** a powerful or influential person (*captain of industry*). **2 a** the person in command of a merchant or passenger ship. **b** the pilot of a civil aircraft. **3 a** an army or air force officer next above lieutenant. **b** a navy officer in command of a warship; one ranking below commodore or rear admiral and above commander. **c** a police officer in charge of a precinct, ranking below chief. **4** a supervisor of waiters or bellboys. **5 a** a great soldier or strategist. **b** an experienced commander. •*v.tr.* be captain of; lead. □□ **cap·tain·cy** *n*. (*pl.* ·**cies**). **cap·tain·ship** *n*. [ME & OF *capitain* f. LL *capitaneus* chief f. L *caput capit-* head]

cap·tion /kápshən/ *n. & v.* •*n*. **1** a title or brief explanation appended to an illustration, cartoon, etc. **2** wording appearing on a motion-picture or television screen as part of a movie or broadcast. **3** the heading of a chapter or article, etc. **4** *Law* a certificate attached to or written on a document. •*v.tr.* provide with a caption.

cap·tious /kápshəs/ *adj*. given to finding fault or raising petty objections. □□ **cap·tious·ly** *adv*. **cap·tious·ness** *n*. [ME f. OF *captieux* or L *captiosus* (as CAPTION)]

cap·ti·vate /káptivayt/ *v.tr.* **1** overwhelm with charm or affection. **2** fascinate. □□ **cap·ti·vat·ing** *adj*. **cap·ti·vat·ing·ly** *adv*. **cap·ti·va·tion** /–váyshən/ *n*. [LL *captivare* take captive (as CAPTIVE)]

cap·tive /káptiv/ *n. & adj.* •*n*. a person or animal that has been taken prisoner or confined. •*adj*. **1 a** taken prisoner. **b** kept in confinement or under restraint. **2 a** unable to escape. **b** in a position of having to comply (*captive audience; captive market*). **3** of or like a prisoner (*captive state*). [ME f. L *captivus* f. *capere capt-* take]

cap·tiv·i·ty /kaptívitee/ *n*. (*pl.* ·**ties**) **1 a** the condition or circumstances of being a captive. **b** a period of captivity. **2** (**the Captivity**) the captivity of the Jews in Babylon in the 6th c. BC.

cap·tor /káptər, –tawr/ *n*. a person who captures (a person, place, etc.). [L (as CAPTIVE)]

cap·ture /kápchər/ *v. & n.* •*v.tr.* **1 a** take prisoner; seize as a prize. **b** obtain by force or trickery. **2** portray in permanent form (*could not capture the likeness*). **3** *Physics* absorb (a subatomic particle). **4** (in board games) make a move that secures the removal of (an opposing piece) from the board. **5** (of a stream) divert the upper course of (another stream) by encroaching on its basin. **6** cause (data) to be stored in a computer. •*n*. **1** the act of capturing. **2** a thing or person captured. □□ **cap·tur·er** *n*. [F f. L *captura* f. *capere capt-* take]

cap·u·chin /kápyəchin, –shin, kəpyōō–, kapü–/ *n*. **1** (**Capuchin**) a

Franciscan friar of the new rule of 1529. **2** a cloak and hood formerly worn by women. **3 a** any monkey of the genus *Cebus* of S. America, with cowllike head hair. **b** a variety of pigeon with head and neck feathers resembling a cowl. [F f. It. *cappuccino* f. *cappuccio* cowl f. *cappa* CAPE[1]]

cap·y·ba·ra /kápəbáərə/ *n.* a very large semiaquatic rodent, *Hydrochoerus hydrochaeris*, native to S. America. [Tupi]

car /kaar/ *n.* **1** a road vehicle with an enclosed passenger compartment, powered by an internal combustion engine; an automobile. **2** a vehicle that runs on rails, esp. a railroad car or a streetcar. **3** a railroad car of a specified type (*dining car*). **4** the passenger compartment of an elevator, cable railway, balloon, etc. **5** *poet.* a wheeled vehicle; a chariot. □□ **car·ful** *n.* (*pl.* **·fuls**). [ME f. AF & ONF *carre* ult. f. L *carrum*, *carrus*, of OCelt. orig.]

car·a·bi·neer /kárəbineér/ *n.* (also **car·a·bi·nier**) *hist.* **1** a soldier whose principal weapon is a carbine. **2** (**the Carabineers**) the Royal Scots Dragoon Guards. [F *carabinier* f. *carabine* CARBINE]

car·a·bi·ner /karəbeénər/ *n.* (also *Brit.* **kar·a·bi·ner**) a coupling link with a safety closure, used by rock climbers. [G. lit. *carbine*]

car·a·bi·nie·re /káraabeenyére, károbinyáiree/ *n.* (*pl.* **car·a·bi·nie·ri** *pronunc.* same) an Italian gendarme. [It.]

car·a·cal /kárəkal/ *n.* a lynx, *Felis caracal*, native to N. Africa and SW Asia. [F or Sp. f. Turk. *karakulak* f. *kara* black + *kulak* ear]

car·a·cole /kárəkōl/ *n. & v.* ● *n.* a horse's half turn to the right or left. ● *v.* **1** *intr.* (of a horse or its rider) perform a caracole. **2** *tr.* make (a horse) caracole. [F]

car·a·cul var. of KARAKUL.

ca·rafe /kəráf/ *n.* a glass container for water or wine, esp. at a table or bedside. [F f. It. *caraffa*, ult. f. Arab. *ǧarrāfa* drinking vessel]

ca·ram·bo·la /kárəmbólə/ *n.* **1** a small tree, *Averrhoa carambola*, native to SE Asia, bearing golden-yellow ribbed fruit. **2** this fruit. Also **starfruit**. [Port., prob. of Indian or E. Indian orig.]

car·a·mel /kárəmel, –məl, kaárməl/ *n.* **1 a** sugar or syrup heated until it turns brown, then used as a flavoring or to color spirits, etc. **b** a kind of soft toffee made with sugar, butter, etc., melted and further heated. **2** the light-brown color of caramel. [F f. Sp. *caramelo*]

car·a·mel·ize /kárəməlīz, kaármə–/ *v.* **1 a** *tr.* convert (sugar or syrup) into caramel. **b** *intr.* (of sugar or syrup) be converted into caramel. **2** *tr.* coat or cook (food) with caramelized sugar or syrup. □□ **car·a·mel·i·za·tion** /–lizáyshən/ *n.*

car·a·pace /kárəpays/ *n.* the hard upper shell of a turtle or a crustacean. [F f. Sp. *carapacho*]

car·at /kárət/ *n.* **1** a unit of weight for precious stones, now equivalent to 200 milligrams. **2** *Brit.* var. of KARAT.

WORD HISTORY carat

From French, from Italian *carato*, from Arabic *ḳīrāṭ* (a unit of weight), from Greek *keration* 'fruit of the carob' (also denoting a unit of weight), diminutive of *keras* 'horn,' with reference to the elongated seed pod of the carob.

---

car·a·van /kárəvan/ *n. & v.* ● *n.* **1 a** a covered or enclosed wagon or truck; van. **b** *Brit.* a vehicle equipped for living in and usu. towed by a motor vehicle or a horse; trailer. **2** a company of merchants or pilgrims, etc., traveling together, esp. across a desert in Asia or N. Africa. **3** a covered cart or carriage. ● *v.intr.* (**car·a·vaned**, *or* **car·a·vanned**, **car·a·van·ing**, *or* **car·a·van·ning**) travel or live in a caravan. □□ **car·a·van·ner** *n.* [F *caravane* f. Pers. *kārwān*]

car·a·van·sa·ry /kárəvánsəree, –ri/ *n.* (also **car·a·van·se·rai**) **1 a** Near Eastern inn with a central court where caravans (see CARA-VAN 2) may rest. **2** a hotel. [Pers. *kārwānsarāy* f. *sarāy* palace]

car·a·van site *n.* (also **car·a·van park**) *Brit.* = TRAILER PARK.

car·a·vel /kárəvel/ *n.* (also **car·vel** /kaárvəl/) *hist.* a small, light, fast ship, chiefly Spanish and Portuguese of the 15th–17th c. [F *caravelle* f. Port. *caravela* f. Gk *karabos* horned beetle; light ship]

car·a·way /kárəway/ *n.* an umbelliferous plant of the parsley family, *Carum carvi*, bearing clusters of tiny white flowers. [prob. OSp. *alcarahueya* f. Arab. *alkarāwiyā*, perh. f. Gk *karon*, *kareon* cumin]

car·a·way seed *n.* the seedlike fruit of the caraway plant used as flavoring and as a source of oil.

carb /kaarb/ *n. colloq.* a carburetor. [abbr.]

car·ba·mate /kaárbəmayt/ *n. Chem.* a salt or ester of an amide of carbonic acid. [CARBONIC + AMIDE]

car·bide /kaárbīd/ *n. Chem.* **1** a binary compound of carbon. **2** = CALCIUM CARBIDE.

car·bine /kaárbeen, –bīn/ *n.* a lightweight firearm, usu. a rifle, orig. for cavalry use. [F *carabine* (this form also earlier in Engl.), weapon of the *carabin* mounted musketeer]

carbo- /kaárbō/ *comb. form* carbon (*carbohydrate*; *carbolic*; *carboxyl*).

car·bo·hy·drate /kaárbəhídrayt, –bō–/ *n. Biochem.* any of a large group of energy-producing organic compounds containing carbon, hydrogen, and oxygen, e.g., starch, glucose, and other sugars.

car·bol·ic /kaarbólik/ *n.* (in full **carbolic acid**) phenol, esp. when used as a disinfectant. [CARBO- + -OL[1] + -IC]

car·bol·ic soap *n.* a disinfectant soap containing phenol.

car bomb *n.* a terrorist bomb concealed in or under a parked car.

car·bon /kaárbən/ *n.* **1** a nonmetallic element occurring naturally as diamond, graphite, and charcoal, and in all organic compounds. ¶ Symb.: **C. 2 a** = CARBON COPY. **b** = CARBON PAPER. **3** a rod of carbon in an arc lamp. [F *carbone* f. L *carbo* –*onis* charcoal]

car·bo·na·ceous /kaárbənáyshəs/ *adj.* **1** consisting of or containing carbon. **2** of or like coal or charcoal.

car·bo·na·do /kaárbənáydō/ *n.* (*pl.* **·dos**) a dark opaque or impure kind of diamond used as an abrasive, for drills, etc. [Port.]

car·bo·nate /kaárbənayt/ *n. & v.* ● *n. Chem.* a salt of carbonic acid. ● *v.tr.* **1** impregnate with carbon dioxide; aerate. **2** convert into a carbonate. □□ **car·bo·na·tion** /–náyshən/ *n.* [F *carbonat* f. mod.L *carbonatum* (as CARBON)]

car·bon black *n.* a fine carbon powder made by burning hydrocarbons in insufficient air.

car·bon cop·y *n.* **1** a copy made with carbon paper. **2** a person or thing identical or similar to another (*he is a carbon copy of his father*).

car·bon cy·cle *n. Biol.* the cycle in which carbon compounds are interconverted, usu. by living organisms.

car·bon dat·ing *n.* the determination of the age of an organic object from the ratio of isotopes, which changes as carbon 14 decays.

car·bon di·ox·ide *n.* a colorless, odorless gas occurring naturally in the atmosphere and formed by respiration. ¶ Chem. formula: CO_2.

car·bon di·sul·fide *n.* a colorless liquid used as a solvent. ¶ Chem. formula: CS_2.

car·bon fi·ber *n.* a thin, strong crystalline filament of carbon used as strengthening material in resins, ceramics, etc.

car·bon 14 *n.* a long-lived radioactive carbon isotope of mass 14, used in radiocarbon dating, and as a tracer in biochemistry.

car·bon·ic /kaarbónik/ *adj. Chem.* containing carbon.

car·bon·ic ac·id *n.* a very weak acid formed from carbon dioxide dissolved in water.

car·bon·ic ac·id gas *n. archaic* carbon dioxide.

car·bon·if·er·ous /kaárbənífərəs/ *adj. & n.* ● *adj.* **1** producing coal. **2** (**Carboniferous**) *Geol.* of or relating to the fifth period in the Paleozoic era, with evidence of the first reptiles and extensive coal-forming swamp forests. ● *n.* (**Carboniferous**) *Geol.* this period or system.

car·bon·ize /kaárbənīz/ *v.tr.* **1** convert into carbon by heating. **2** reduce to charcoal or coke. **3** coat with carbon. □□ **car·bon·i·za·tion** /–nizáyshən/ *n.*

car·bon mon·ox·ide *n.* a colorless, odorless toxic gas formed by the incomplete burning of carbon. ¶ Chem. formula: CO.

car·bon pa·per *n.* a thin carbon-coated paper placed between two sheets of paper when writing to make a copy onto the bottom sheet.

car·bon steel *n.* a steel with properties dependent on the percentage of carbon present.

car·bon tet·ra·chlo·ride *n.* a colorless, volatile liquid used as a solvent. ¶ Chem. formula: CCl_4.

car·bon 12 *n.* a carbon isotope of weight 12, used in calculations of atomic weight.

car·bon·yl /kaárbənil/ *n.* (used *attrib.*) *Chem.* the divalent radical CO.

car·bo·run·dum /kaárbərúndəm/ *n.* a compound of carbon and silicon used esp. as an abrasive. [CARBON + CORUNDUM]

car·box·yl /kaarbóksil/ *n. Chem.* the univalent acid radical (-COOH), present in most organic acids. □□ **car·box·yl·ic** /–boksi-lik/ *adj.* [CARBON + OXYGEN + -YL]

car·boy /kaárboy/ *n.* a large bottle often protected by a frame, used for containing liquids. [Pers. *karāba* large glass flagon]

car·bun·cle /kaárbungkəl/ *n.* **1** a severe abscess in the skin. **2** a bright red gem. □□ **car·bun·cu·lar** /–búngkyələr/ *adj.* [ME f. OF *charbucle*, etc. f. L *carbunculus* small coal f. *carbo* coal]

car·bu·ra·tion /kaárbəráyshən, –byə–/ *n.* the process of charging air with a spray of liquid hydrocarbon fuel, esp. in an internal combustion engine. [as CARBURET]

car·bu·ret /kaárbəráyt, –rét, –byə–/ *v.tr.* (**car·bu·ret·ed**, **car·bu·ret·ing**) combine (a gas, etc.) with carbon. [earlier *carbure* f. F f. L *carbo* (as CARBON)]

car·bu·re·tor /kaárbəráytter, –byə–/ *n.* (also **car·bu·ra·tor** an apparatus for carburation of fuel and air in an internal combustion engine. [as CARBURET + -OR[1]]

car·ca·jou /kaárkəjoo, –kəzhoō/ *n.* = WOLVERINE. [F, app. of Algonquian orig.]

car·cass /kaárkəs/ *n.* (also *Brit.* **car·case**) **1** the dead body of an animal, esp. a trunk for cutting up as meat. **2** the bones of a cooked bird. **3** *derog.* the human body, living or dead. **4** the skeleton, framework of a building, ship, etc. **5** worthless remains. [ME f. AF *carcois* (OF *charcois*) & f. F *carcasse*: ult. orig. unkn.]

car·cin·o·gen /kaarsínəjən, kaársinəjen/ *n.* any substance that produces cancer. [as CARCINOMA + -GEN]

car·cin·o·gen·e·sis /kaársinəjénisis/ *n.* the production of cancer.

car·cin·o·gen·ic /kaársinəjénik/ adj. producing cancer. □□ **car·ci·no·ge·nic·i·ty** /–nísitee/ n.

car·ci·no·ma /kaársinṓmə/ n. (pl. **car·ci·no·mas** or **car·ci·no·ma·ta** /–mətə/) a cancer, esp. one arising in epithelial tissue. □□ **car·ci·no·ma·tous** adj. [L f. Gk karkinōma f. karkinos crab]

car coat n. a hip-length coat originally designed for driving a car.

Card. abbr. Cardinal.

card[1] /kaard/ n. & v. ● n. **1** thick, stiff paper or thin pasteboard. **2 a** a flat piece of this, esp. for writing or printing on. **b** = POSTCARD. **c** a card used to send greetings, issue an invitation, etc. (birthday card). **d** = CALLING CARD. **e** = BUSINESS CARD. **f** a ticket of admission or membership. **3 a** = PLAYING CARD. **b** a similar card in a set designed for board games, etc. **c** (in pl.) card playing; a card game. **4** (in pl.) Brit. colloq. an employee's documents, esp. for tax and national insurance, held by the employer. **5 a** a program of events at boxing matches, races, etc. **b** a scorecard. **c** a list of holes on a golf course, on which a player's scores are entered. **6** colloq. a person, esp. an odd or amusing one (what a card!; a knowing card). **7** a plan or expedient (sure card). **8** a printed or written notice, set of rules, etc., for display. **9** a small rectangular piece of plastic issued by a bank, retail establishment, etc., with personal (often machine-readable) data on it, chiefly to obtain cash or credit (credit card; do you have a card?). ● v.tr. **1** fix to a card. **2** write on a card, esp. for indexing. □ ask for proof of age, as at a bar. □ **in the cards** possible or likely. **put** (or **lay**) **one's cards on the table** reveal one's resources, intentions, etc. [ME f. OF carte f. L charta f. Gk khartēs papyrus-leaf]

card[2] /kaard/ n. & v. ● n. a toothed instrument, wire brush, etc., for raising a nap on cloth or for disentangling fibers before spinning. ● v.tr. brush, comb, cleanse, or scratch with a card. □□ **card·er** n. [ME f. OF carde f. Prov. carda f. cardar tease, comb, ult. f. L carere card]

car·da·mom /kaárdəməm/ n. (also **car·da·mum**) **1** an aromatic SE Asian plant, Elettaria cardamomum. **2** the seed capsules of this used as a spice. [L cardamomum or F cardamome f. Gk kardamōmon f. kardamon cress + amōmon a spice plant]

Car·dan joint /kaárd'n/ n. Engin. a universal joint. [G. Cardano, It. mathematician d. 1576]

card·board /kaárdbawrd/ n. & adj. ● n. pasteboard or stiff paper, esp. for making cards or boxes. ● adj. **1** made of cardboard. **2** flimsy; insubstantial.

card-car·ry·ing adj. being a registered member of an organization, esp. a political party or labor union.

card game n. a game in which playing cards are used.

car·di·ac /kaárdeeak/ adj. & n. ● adj. **1** of or relating to the heart. **2** of or relating to the part of the stomach nearest the esophagus. ● n. a person with heart disease. [F cardiaque or L cardiacus f. Gk kardiakos f. kardia heart]

car·di·gan /kaárdigən/ n. a knitted sweater fastening down the front, usu. with long sleeves.

WORD HISTORY   cardigan

Mid-19th century (Crimean War): named after James Thomas Brudenel, 7th Earl of Cardigan (1797–1868), leader of the famous Charge of the Light Brigade; his troops first wore such garments.

---

car·di·nal /kaárd'nəl/ n. & adj. ● n. **1** (as a title **Cardinal**) a leading dignitary of the RC Church, one of the college electing the Pope. **2** any small American songbird of the genus Richmondena, the males of which have scarlet plumage. **3** hist. a woman's cloak, orig. of scarlet cloth with a hood. ● adj. **1** chief; fundamental; on which something hinges. **2** of deep scarlet (like a cardinal's cassock). □□ **car·di·nal·ate** /–nəlayt/ n. (in sense 1 of n.). **car·di·nal·ly** adv. **car·di·nal·ship** n. (in sense 1 of n.). [ME f. OF f. L cardinalis f. cardo –inis hinge: in Eng. first applied to the four virtues on which conduct 'hinges']

Northern cardinal

car·di·nal flow·er n. the scarlet lobelia.

car·di·nal num·ber n. a number expressing quantity (one, two, three, etc.), as opposed to an ordinal number (first, second, third, etc.).

car·di·nal points n. the four main points of the compass (N, S, E, W).

car·di·nal vir·tues n. the chief moral attributes: justice, prudence, temperance, and fortitude.

card in·dex n. an index or file in which each item is entered on a separate card.

cardio- /kaárdeeō/ comb. form heart (cardiogram; cardiology). [Gk kardia heart]

car·di·o·gram /kaárdeeəgram/ n. a record of muscle activity within the heart, made by a cardiograph.

car·di·o·graph /kaárdeeəgraf/ n. an instrument for recording heart muscle activity. □□ **car·di·og·ra·pher** /–deeógrəfər/ n. **car·di·og·ra·phy** n.

car·di·ol·o·gy /kaárdeeóləjee/ n. the branch of medicine concerned with diseases and abnormalities of the heart. □□ **car·di·ol·o·gist** n.

car·di·o·pul·mo·nar·y re·sus·ci·ta·tion /kardeeōpoolmənaree/ n. emergency medical procedures for restoring normal heartbeat and breathing to victims of heart failure, drowning, etc. ¶ Abbr.: **CPR.**

car·di·o·vas·cu·lar /kaárdeeōváskyələr/ adj. of or relating to the heart and blood vessels.

car·doon /kaardoon/ n. a thistlelike plant, Cynara cardunculus, allied to the globe artichoke, with leaves used as a vegetable. [F cardon ult. f. L cardu(u)s thistle]

card·phone /kaárdfōn/ n. Brit. a public telephone operated by the insertion of a prepaid phonecard instead of coins.

card play·er n. a person who plays card games.

card·sharp /kaárdshaarp/ n. (also **card·sharp·er**) a swindler at card games.

card ta·ble n. a lightweight folding table for card playing.

care /kair/ n. & v. ● n. **1** worry; anxiety. **2** an occasion for this. **3** serious attention; heed; caution; pains (assembled with care; handle with care). **4 a** protection; charge. **b** Brit. = CHILD CARE. **5** a thing to be done or seen to. ● v.intr. **1** (usu. foll. by about, for, whether) feel concern or interest. **2** (usu. foll. by for, about) feel liking, affection, regard, or deference (don't care for jazz; she cares for him a great deal). **3** (foll. by to + infin.) wish or be willing (do not care to be seen with him; would you care to try them?). □ **care for** provide for; look after. **care of** at the address of (sent it care of his sister). **for all one cares** colloq. denoting uninterest or unconcern (for all I care they can leave tomorrow; I could be dying for all you care). **I** (etc.) **couldn't** (freq. **could**) **care less** colloq. an expression of complete indifference. **take care 1** be careful. **2** (foll. by to + infin.) not fail nor neglect. **take care of 1** look after; keep safe. **2** deal with. **3** dispose of. [OE caru, carian, f. Gmc]

ca·reen /kəréen/ v. **1** tr. turn (a ship) on one side for cleaning, caulking, or repair. **2 a** intr. tilt; lean over. **b** tr. cause to do this. **3** intr. swerve about; career. □□ **ca·reen·age** n. [earlier as noun, = careened position of ship, f. F carène f. It. carena f. L carina keel]

▶ Sense 3 is infl. by career (v.).

ca·reer /kəréer/ n. & v. ● n. **1 a** one's advancement through life, esp. in a profession. **b** the progress through history of a group or institution. **2** a profession or occupation, esp. as offering advancement. **3** (attrib.) **a** pursuing or wishing to pursue a career (career woman). **b** working permanently in a specified profession (career diplomat). **4** swift course; impetus (in full career). ● v.intr. **1** move or swerve about wildly. **2** go swiftly. [F carrière f. It. carriera ult. f. L carrus CAR]

ca·reer·ist /kəréerist/ n. a person predominantly concerned with personal advancement.

care·free /káirfree/ adj. free from anxiety or responsibility; lighthearted. □□ **care·free·ness** n.

care·ful /káirfool/ adj. **1** painstaking; thorough. **2** cautious. **3** done with care and attention. **4** (usu. foll. by that + clause, or to + infin.) taking care; not neglecting. **5** (foll. by for, of) concerned for; taking care of. □□ **care·ful·ly** adv. **care·ful·ness** n. [OE carful (as CARE, –FUL)]

care·giv·er /káirgivər/ n. a person who provides care for children, the sick, the elderly, etc.

care la·bel n. a label attached to clothing, with instructions for washing, etc.

care·less /káirlis/ adj. **1** not taking care nor paying attention. **2** unthinking; insensitive. **3** done without care; inaccurate. **4** lighthearted. **5** (foll. by of) not concerned about; taking no heed of. **6** effortless; casual. □□ **care·less·ly** adv. **care·less·ness** n. [OE carlēas (as CARE, –LESS)]

ca·ress /kərés/ v. & n. ● v.tr. **1** touch or stroke gently or lovingly; kiss. **2** treat fondly or kindly. ● n. a loving or gentle touch or kiss. [F caresse (n.), caresser (v.), f. It. carezza ult. f. L carus dear]

car·et /kárət/ n. a mark (^) indicating a proposed insertion in printing or writing. [L, = is lacking]

care·tak·er /káirtaykər/ n. **1 a** a person employed to look after something, esp. a house in the owner's absence. **b** Brit. a janitor. **2** (attrib.) exercising temporary authority (caretaker government).

care·worn /káirwawrn/ adj. showing the effects of prolonged worry.

car·fare /kaárfair/ n. a passenger's fare to travel by public transport (orig. streetcar).

car·go /kaárgō/ n. (pl. **·goes** or **·gos**) **1 a** goods carried on a ship or aircraft. **b** a load of such goods. **2 a** goods carried in a motor vehicle. **b** a load of such goods. [Sp. (as CHARGE)]

car·go cult n. (orig. in the Pacific Islands) a belief in the forthcoming arrival of ancestral spirits bringing cargoes of food and other goods.

car·hop /kaárhop/ n. colloq. a waiter at a drive-in restaurant.

car·i·am·a var. of SERIEMA.

Car·ib /kárib/ *n. & adj.* •*n.* **1** an aboriginal inhabitant of the southern W. Indies or the adjacent coasts. **2** the language of this people. •*adj.* of or relating to this people. [Sp. *Caribe* f. Haitian]

Car·ib·be·an /káribéeən, kəríbeeən/ *n. & adj.* •*n.* the part of the Atlantic between the southern W. Indies and Central America. •*adj.* **1** of or relating to this region. **2** of the Caribs or their language or culture.

SPELLING TIP Caribbean

Remember that the name of this popular destination has two *b*'s by thinking of two popular foods that are served there: ri*b*s and *b*eans.

---

car·i·bou /kárib͞oo/ *n.* (*pl.* same) a N. American reindeer.

WORD HISTORY caribou

Mid-17th century: from Canadian French, from Micmac *γalipu*, literally 'snow-shoveler,' because the caribou scrapes away snow to feed on the vegetation underneath.

caribou

---

car·i·ca·ture /kárikəchər, –ch͞oor/ *n. & v. • n.* **1** a grotesque usu. comic representation of a person by exaggeration of characteristic traits, in a picture, writing, or mime. **2** a ridiculously poor or absurd imitation or version. •*v.tr.* make or give a caricature of. □□ **car·i·ca·tur·al** /–ch͞oorəl/ *adj.* **car·i·ca·tur·ist** *n.* [F f. It. *caricatura* f. *caricare* load, exaggerate: see CHARGE]

SYNONYM TIP caricature

BURLESQUE, LAMPOON, MIMICRY, PARODY, TRAVESTY. Skilled writers and artists who want to poke fun at someone or something have a number of weapons at their disposal. An artist might come up with a **caricature**, which is a drawing or written piece that exaggerates its subject's distinguishing features or peculiarities (*the cartoonist's caricature of the presidential candidate*). A **parody** is similar to a caricature in purpose, but is used of written work, or performances that ridicule an author or performer's work by imitating its language and style for comic effect (*a parody of the scene between Romeo and Juliet*). While a *parody* concentrates on distorting the content of the original work, a **travesty** retains the subject matter but imitates the style in a grotesque or absurd way (*their version of the Greek tragedy was a travesty*). A **lampoon** is a strongly satirical piece of writing that attacks or ridicules an individual or an institution; it is more commonly used as a verb (*to lampoon the government in a local newspaper*). While a *caricature*, a *parody*, and a *travesty* must have an original to imitate, a **burlesque** can be an independent creation or composition; it is a comic or satiric imitation, often a theatrical one, that treats a serious subject lightly or a trivial subject with mock seriousness (*the play was a burlesque of Homeric themes*). **Mimicry** is something you don't have to be an artist, a writer, or an actor to be good at. Anyone who successfully imitates another person's speech or gestures is a good mimic or impressionist, whether the intent is playful or mocking (*he showed an early talent for mimicry, entertaining his parents with imitations of their friends*).

---

car·ies /káireez/ *n.* (*pl.* same) decay and crumbling of a tooth or bone. [L]

car·il·lon /kárilon, –lən/ *n.* **1** a set of bells sounded either from a keyboard or mechanically. **2** a tune played on bells. **3** an organ stop imitating a peal of bells. [F f. OF *quarregnon* peal of four bells, alt. of Rmc *quaternio* f. L *quattuor* four]

ca·ri·na /kəréenə/ *n.* (*pl.* **ca·ri·nas** or **ca·ri·nae** /–nee/) *Biol.* a keel-shaped structure, esp. the ridge of a bird's breastbone. □□ **ca·ri·nal** *adj.* [L, = keel]

car·i·nate /kárinayt/ *adj.* (of a bird) having a keeled breastbone (opp. RATITE). [L *carinatus* keeled f. *carina* keel]

car·ing /káiring/ *adj.* **1** compassionate. **2** involving the care of the sick, elderly, or disabled.

car·i·o·ca /káreeókə/ *n.* **1 a** a Brazilian dance like the samba. **b** the music for this. **2** a native of Rio de Janeiro. [Port.]

car·i·o·gen·ic /káireeōjénik/ *adj.* causing caries.

car·i·ole /káreeōl/ *n.* **1** a small open carriage for one. **2** a covered light cart. **3** a Canadian sleigh. [F f. It. *carriuola*, dimin. of *carro* CAR]

car·i·ous /káireeəs/ *adj.* (of bones or teeth) decayed. [L *cariosus*]

car·jack·ing /kárjaking/ *n.* the action of violently stealing an occupied car. □□ **car·jack** *v.* **car·jack·er** *n.*

cark·ing /káarking/ *adj. archaic* burdensome (*carking care*). [part. of obs. *cark* (v.) f. ONF *carkier* f. Rmc, rel. to CHARGE]

---

carl /kaarl/ *n. Sc.* a man; a fellow. [OE f. ON *karl*, rel. to CHURL]

car·line /káarlin/ *n.* any plant of the genus *Carlina*, esp. the thistle-like *C. vulgaris*. [F f. med.L *carlina* perh. for *cardina* (L *carduus* thistle), assoc. with *Carolus Magnus* Charlemagne]

car·load /káarlōd/ *n.* **1** a quantity that can be carried in a car. **2** the minimum quantity of goods for which a lower rate is charged for transport.

Car·lo·vin·gi·an var. of CAROLINGIAN.

Car·mel·ite /káarmilīt/ *n. & adj.* •*n.* **1** a friar of the Order of Our Lady of Mount Carmel, following a rule of extreme asceticism. **2** a nun of a similar order. •*adj.* of or relating to the Carmelites. [F *Carmelite* or med.L *carmelita* f. Mt. *Carmel* in Palestine, where the order was founded in the 12th c.]

car·min·a·tive /kaarmínətiv, káarminaytiv/ *adj. & n.* •*adj.* relieving flatulence. •*n.* a carminative drug. [F *carminatif –ive* or med.L *carminare* heal (by incantation): see CHARM]

car·mine /káarmin, –mīn/ *adj. & n.* •*adj.* of a vivid crimson color. •*n.* **1** this color. **2** a vivid crimson pigment made from cochineal. [F *carmin* or med.L *carminium* perh. f. *carmesinum* crimson + *minium* cinnabar]

car·nage /káarnij/ *n.* great slaughter, esp. of human beings in battle. [F f. It. *carnaggio* f. med.L *carnaticum* f. L *caro carnis* flesh]

car·nal /káarnəl/ *adj.* **1** of the body or flesh; worldly. **2** sensual; sexual. □□ **car·nal·i·ty** /–áalitee/ *n.* **car·nal·ize** *v.tr.* **car·nal·ly** *adv.* [ME f. LL *carnalis* f. *caro carnis* flesh]

car·nal know·ledge *n. Law* sexual intercourse.

car·nas·si·al /kaarnáseeəl/ *adj. & n.* •*adj.* (of a carnivore's upper premolar and lower molar teeth) adapted for shearing flesh. •*n.* such a tooth. Also called **sectorial**. [F *carnassier* carnivorous]

car·na·tion[1] /kaarnáyshən/ *n.* **1** any of several cultivated varieties of clove-scented pink, with variously colored showy flowers (see also CLOVE[1] 2). **2** this flower. [orig. uncert.: in early use varying with *coronation*]

car·na·tion[2] /kaarnáyshən/ *n. & adj.* •*n.* a rosy pink color. •*adj.* of this color. [F f. It. *carnagione* f. L *caro carnis* flesh]

car·nau·ba /kaarnówbə, –náwbə, –n͞oobə/ *n.* **1** a fan palm, *Copernicia cerifera*, native to NE Brazil. **2** (in full **carnauba wax**) the yellowish leaf wax of this tree used as a polish, etc. [Port.]

car·nel·ian /kaarneélyən/ *n.* (also **cor·nel·ian** /kawr–/) **1** a dull red or reddish-white variety of chalcedony. **2** this color. [ME f. OF *corneline*; *car*- after L *caro carnis* flesh]

car·net /kaarnáy/ *n.* **1** a customs permit to take a motor vehicle across an international border for a limited period of time. **2** a permit allowing use of a campsite while traveling abroad. [F, = notebook]

car·ni·val /káarnivəl/ *n.* **1 a** the festivities usual during the period before Lent in Roman Catholic countries. **b** any festivities, esp. those occurring at a regular date. **2** merrymaking; revelry. **3** a traveling fair or circus. [It. *carne-, carnovale* f. med.L *carnelevarium*, etc. Shrovetide f. L *caro carnis* flesh + *levare* put away]

car·ni·vore /káarnivawr/ *n.* **1 a** any mammal of the order Carnivora, with powerful jaws and teeth adapted for stabbing, tearing, and eating flesh. **b** any other flesh-eating mammal. **2** any flesh-eating plant.

car·niv·o·rous /kaarnívərəs/ *adj.* **1** (of an animal) feeding on other animals. **2** (of a plant) digesting trapped insects or other animal substances. **3** of or relating to the order Carnivora. □□ **car·niv·o·rous·ly** *adv.* **car·niv·o·rous·ness** *n.* [L *carnivorus* f. *caro carnis* flesh + –VOROUS]

car·ob /kárəb/ *n.* **1** an evergreen tree, *Ceratonia siliqua*, native to the Mediterranean, bearing edible pods. **2** its bean-shaped edible seed pod sometimes used as a substitute for chocolate. [obs. F *carobe* f. med.L *carrubia*, *–um* f. Arab. *ḵarrūba*]

car·ol /kárəl/ *n. & v.* •*n.* a joyous song, esp. a Christmas hymn. •*v.* (**car·oled, car·ol·ing**; esp. *Brit.* **car·olled, car·ol·ling**) **1** *intr.* sing carols, esp. outdoors at Christmas. **2** *tr. & intr.* sing joyfully. □□ **car·ol·er** *n.* (also esp. *Brit.* **car·ol·ler**). [ME f. OF *carole, caroler*, of unkn. orig.]

Car·o·line /kárəlin/ *adj.* **1** (also **Car·o·lean** /–leéən/) of the time of Charles I or II of England. **2** = CAROLINGIAN *adj.* 2. [L *Carolus* Charles]

Car·o·lin·gi·an /kárəlínjən, –jeeən/ *adj. & n.* (also **Car·lo·vin·gian** /káarləvínjeeən/) •*adj.* **1** of or relating to the second Frankish dynasty, founded by Charlemagne (d. 814). **2** of a style of script developed in France at the time of Charlemagne. •*n.* **1** a member of the Carolingian dynasty. **2** the Carolingian style of script. [F *carlovingien* f. *Karl* Charles after *mérovingien* (see MEROVINGIAN): reformed after L *Carolus*]

car·om /kárəm/ *n. & v. Billiards* •*n.* the hitting of two balls by the one ball on one shot. •*v.intr.* **1** make a carom. **2** (usu. foll. by *off*) strike and rebound. [abbr. of *carambole* f. Sp. *carambola*]

car·o·tene /kárəteen/ *n.* any of several orange-colored plant pigments found in carrots, tomatoes, etc., acting as a source of vitamin A. [G *Carotin* f. L *carota* CARROT]

ca·rot·e·noid /kərót'noyd/ *n.* any of a group of yellow, orange, or brown pigments giving characteristic color to plant organs, e.g., ripe tomatoes, carrots, autumn leaves, etc.

ca·rot·id /kərótid/ *n. & adj.* ● *n.* each of the two main arteries carrying blood to the head and neck. ● *adj.* of or relating to either of these arteries. [F *carotide* or mod.L *carotides* f. Gk *karōtides* (pl.) f. *karoō* stupefy (compression of these arteries being thought to cause stupor)]

ca·rouse /kərówz/ *v. & n.* ● *v.intr.* **1** have a noisy or lively drinking party. **2** drink heavily. ● *n.* a noisy or lively drinking party. □□ **ca·rous·al** *n.* **ca·rous·er** *n.* [orig. as adv. = right out, in phr. *drink carouse* f. G *gar aus trinken*]

car·ou·sel /kárəsél, –zél/ *n.* (also **car·rou·sel**) **1** a merry-go-round. **2** a rotating delivery or conveyor system, esp. for passengers' luggage at an airport. **3** *hist.* a kind of equestrian tournament. [F *carrousel* f. It. *carosello*]

carp[1] /kaarp/ *n.* (*pl.* same) any freshwater fish of the family Cyprinidae, esp. *Cyprinus carpio*, often bred for use as food. [ME f. OF *carpe* f. Prov. or f. LL *carpa*]

carp[2] /kaarp/ *v.intr.* (usu. foll. by *at*) find fault; complain pettily. □□ **carp·er** *n.* [obs. ME senses 'talk, say, sing' f. ON *karpa* to brag: mod. sense (16th c.) from or infl. by L *carpere* pluck at, slander]

car·pal /káarpəl/ *adj. & n.* ● *adj.* of or relating to the bones in the wrist. ● *n.* any of the bones forming the wrist. [CARPUS + –AL]

car·pal tun·nel syn·drome *n.* a condition caused by pressure on a nerve in the wrist, characterized by numbness, tingling, weakness, and pain in the hand.

car park *n.* esp. *Brit.* an area for parking cars.

car·pel /káarpəl/ *n. Bot.* the female reproductive organ of a flower, consisting of a stigma, style, and ovary. □□ **car·pel·lar·y** *adj.* [F *carpelle* or mod.L *carpellum* f. Gk *karpos* fruit]

car·pen·ter /káarpintər/ *n. & v.* ● *n.* a person skilled in woodwork, esp. of a structural kind (cf. JOINER). ● *v.* **1** *intr.* do carpentry. **2** *tr.* make by means of carpentry. **3** *tr.* (often foll. by *together*) construct; fit together.

WORD HISTORY carpenter

Middle English: from Anglo-Norman French, from Old French *carpentier, charpentier,* from late Latin *carpentarius (artifex)* 'carriage(-maker),' from *carpentum* 'wagon,' of Gaulish origin; related to *car*

car·pen·ter ant *n.* any large ant of the genus *Camponotus*, boring into wood to nest.

car·pen·ter bee *n.* any of various solitary bees that bore into wood.

car·pen·try /káarpintree/ *n.* **1** the work or occupation of a carpenter. **2** work constructed by a carpenter. [ME f. OF *carpenterie* f. L *carpentaria*: see CARPENTER]

car·pet /káarpit/ *n. & v.* ● *n.* **1 a** thick fabric for covering a floor or stairs. **b** a piece of this fabric. **2** an expanse or layer resembling a carpet in being smooth, soft, or thick (*carpet of snow*). ● *v.tr.* **1** cover with or as with a carpet. **2** *colloq.* reprimand; reprove. □ **on the carpet 1** *colloq.* being reprimanded. **2** under consideration. **sweep under the carpet** conceal (a problem or difficulty) in the hope that it will be forgotten. [ME f. OF *carpite* or med.L *carpita*, f. obs. It. *carpita* woolen counterpane, ult. f. L *carpere* pluck, pull to pieces]

car·pet·bag /káarpitbag/ *n.* a traveling bag of a kind orig. made of carpetlike material.

car·pet·bag·ger /káarpitbagər/ *n.* **1** a political candidate in an area where the candidate has no local connections (orig. a Northerner in the South after the Civil War). **2** an unscrupulous opportunist, esp. an outsider.

car·pet·ing /káarpiting/ *n.* **1** material for carpets. **2** carpets collectively.

car·pet slip·per *n.* a soft slipper, the upper part of which is made of wool or thick cloth.

car·pet sweep·er *n.* a long-handled, manual household implement used for sweeping carpets, with a revolving brush or brushes and a receptacle for dust and dirt.

car phone *n.* a cellular telephone for use in an automobile.

car·pol·o·gy /kaarpóləjee/ *n.* the study of the structure of fruit and seeds. [Gk *karpos* fruit]

car·pool /káarpool/ *n. & v.* ● *n.* (also **car pool**) **1** an arrangement by which a group of commuters travel to and from their destination in a single vehicle, often with the members taking turns as driver. **2** the commuters taking part in such an arrangement (*there are four people in our carpool*). ● *v.intr.* (also **car-pool**) participate in or organize a carpool.

car·port /káarpawrt/ *n.* a shelter with a roof and open sides for a car, usu. beside a house.

car·pus /káarpəs/ *n.* (*pl.* **car·pi** /–pī/) the small bones between the

forelimb and metacarpus in terrestrial vertebrates, forming the wrist in humans. [mod.L f. Gk *karpos* wrist]

car·rack /kárək/ *n. hist.* a large armed merchant ship. [ME f. F *caraque* f. Sp. *carraca* f. Arab. *karākir*]

car·ra·geen /kárəgeen/ *n.* (also **car·ra·gheen** or **car·ra·geen moss**) an edible red seaweed, *Chondrus crispus*, of the N. hemisphere. Also called **Irish moss**. [orig. uncert.: perh. f. Ir. *cosáinín carraige* carrageen, lit. 'little stem of the rock']

car·ra·geen·an /kárəgeenən/ *n.* a substance extracted from red and purple seaweeds, consisting of a mixture of polysaccharides; used as a thickening or emulsifying agent in food products.

car·rel /kárəl/ *n.* **1** a small cubicle for a reader in a library. **2** *hist.* a small enclosure or study in a cloister. [OF *carole*, med.L *carola*, of unkn. orig.]

car·riage /kárij/ *n.* **1** a wheeled vehicle, esp. one with four wheels and pulled by horses. **2** *Brit.* a railroad passenger coach. **3** *Brit.* **a** the conveying of goods. **b** the cost of this (*carriage paid*). **4** the part of a machine (e.g., a typewriter) that carries other parts into the required position. **5** a gun carriage. **6** a manner of carrying oneself; one's bearing or deportment. [ME f. ONF *cariage* f. *carier* CARRY]

car·riage dog *n.* a dalmatian.

car·riage·way /kárijway/ *n. Brit.* the part of a road intended for vehicles; highway.

car·rick bend /kárik/ *n. Naut.* a kind of knot used to join ropes. [BEND[2]: *carrick* perh. f. CARRACK]

car·ri·er /káreeər/ *n.* **1** a person or thing that carries. **2** a person or company undertaking to convey goods or passengers for payment. **3** = AIRCRAFT CARRIER. **4** a part of a bicycle, etc., for carrying luggage or a passenger. **5** an insurance company. **6** a person or animal that may transmit a disease or a hereditary characteristic without suffering from or displaying it. **7** a substance used to support or convey a pigment, a catalyst, radioactive material, etc. **8** *Physics* a mobile electron or hole that carries a charge in a semiconductor.

car·ri·er pig·eon *n.* a homing pigeon trained to carry messages tied to its neck or leg.

car·ri·er wave *n.* a high-frequency electromagnetic wave modulated in amplitude or frequency to convey a signal.

car·ri·on /káriən/ *n. & adj.* ● *n.* **1** dead putrefying flesh. **2** something vile or filthy. ● *adj.* rotten; loathsome. [ME f. AF & ONF *caroine, –oigne,* OF *charoigne* ult. f. L *caro* flesh]

car·ri·on crow *n.* a black crow, *Corvus corone*, native to Europe, feeding mainly on carrion.

car·ri·on flow·er *n.* = STAPELIA.

car·rot /kárət/ *n.* **1 a** an umbelliferous plant, *Daucus carota*, with a tapering orange-colored root. **b** this root as a vegetable. **2** a means of enticement or persuasion. **3** (in *pl.*) *sl.* a red-haired person. □□ **car·rot·y** *adj.* [F *carotte* f. L *carota* f. Gk *karōton*]

car·rou·sel var. of CAROUSEL.

car·ry /káree/ *v. & n.* ● *v.* (**·ries, ·ried**) **1** *tr.* support or hold up, esp. while moving. **2** *tr.* convey with one from one place to another. **3** *tr.* have on one's person (*carry a watch*). **4** *tr.* conduct or transmit (*pipe carries water; wire carries electric current*). **5** *tr.* take (a process, etc.) to a specified point (*carry into effect; carry a joke too far*). **6** *tr.* (foll. by *to*) continue or prolong (*carry modesty to excess*). **7** *tr.* involve; imply; have as a feature or consequence (*carries a two-year guarantee; principles carry consequences*). **8** *tr.* (in reckoning) transfer (a figure) to a column of higher value. **9** *tr.* hold in a specified way (*carry oneself erect*). **10** *tr.* **a** (of a newspaper or magazine) publish; include in its contents, esp. regularly. **b** (of a radio or television station) broadcast, esp. regularly. **11** *tr.* (of a retailing outlet) keep a regular stock of (particular goods for sale) (*have stopped carrying that brand*). **12** *intr.* **a** (of sound, esp. a voice) be audible at a distance. **b** (of a missile) travel; penetrate. **13** *tr.* (of a gun, etc.) propel to a specified distance. **14** *tr.* **a** win victory or acceptance for (a proposal, etc.). **b** win acceptance from (*carried the audience with them*). **c** win; capture (a prize, a fortress, etc.). **d** gain (a state or district) in an election. **e** *Golf* cause the ball to pass beyond (a bunker, etc.). **15** *tr.* **a** endure the weight of; support (*columns carry the dome*). **b** be the chief cause of the effectiveness of; be the driving force in (*you carry the sales department*). **16** *tr.* be pregnant with (*is carrying twins*). **17** *tr.* **a** (of a motive, money, etc.) cause or enable (a person) to go to a specified place. **b** (of a journey) bring (a person) to a specified point. ● *n.* (*pl.* **·ries**) **1** an act of carrying. **2** *Golf* the distance a ball travels before reaching the ground. **3** a portage between rivers, etc. **4** the range of a gun, etc. □ **carry all before one** succeed; overcome all opposition. **carry away 1** remove. **2** inspire; affect emotionally or spiritually. **3** deprive of self-control (*got carried away*). **4** *Naut.* lose (a mast, etc.) by breakage. **b** break off or away. **carry back** take (a person) back in thought to a past time. **carry conviction** be convincing. **carry the day** be victorious or successful. **carry forward** transfer to a new page or account. **carry it off** (or **carry it off well**) do well under difficulties. **carry off 1** take away, esp. by force. **2** win (a prize). **3** (esp. of a disease) kill. **4** render acceptable or passable. **carry on 1** continue (*carry on eating; carry on, don't mind me*). **2** engage in (a conversation or a business).

3 *colloq.* behave strangely or excitedly. **4** (often foll. by *with*) *Brit. colloq.* flirt or have a love affair. **5** advance (a process) by a stage. **carry out** put (ideas, instructions, etc.) into practice. **carry over 1** = *carry forward*. **2** postpone (work, etc.). **3** *Stock Exch.* keep over to the next settling day. **carry through 1** complete successfully. **2** bring safely out of difficulties. **carry weight** be influential or important. **carry with one** bear in mind. [ME f. AF & ONF *carier* (as CAR)]

car·ry·all /kárēeawl/ *n.* **1** a large bag or case. **2** a light carriage (cf. CARIOLE). **3** a car with seats placed sideways.

car·ry·ing-on *n.* (also **car·ry·ings-on**) *sl.* **1** a state of excitement or fuss. **2** a questionable piece of behavior. **3** a flirtation or love affair.

car·ry·out /kárēeowt/ *n. & adj.* • *n.* **1** food prepared and packaged for consumption elsewhere than the place of sale. **2** an establishment that sells such food. • *adj.* of or designating such foods.

car·ry·over /kárēeōvər/ *n.* **1** something carried over. **2** *Stock Exch.* postponement to the next settling day.

carse /kaars/ *n. Sc.* fertile lowland beside a river. [ME, perh. f. *carrs* swamps]

car·sick /káarsik/ *adj.* affected with nausea caused by the motion of a car. □□ **car·sick·ness** *n.*

cart /kaart/ *n. & v.* • *n.* **1** a strong vehicle with two or four wheels for carrying loads, usu. drawn by a horse. **2** a light vehicle for pulling by hand. **3** a light vehicle with two wheels for driving in, drawn by a single horse. • *v.tr.* **1** convey in or as in a cart. **2** *sl.* carry (esp. a cumbersome thing) with difficulty or over a long distance (*carted it all the way home*). □ **cart off** remove, esp. by force. **put the cart before the horse 1** reverse the proper order or procedure. **2** take an effect for a cause. □□ **cart·er** *n.* **cart·ful** *n.* (*pl.* **·fuls**). [ME f. ON *kartr* cart & OE *cræt*, prob. infl. by AF & ONF *carete* dimin. of *carre* CAR]

cart·age /káartij/ *n.* the price paid for carting.

carte var. of QUART 4.

carte blanche /kaart blónsh, blánch/ *n.* full discretionary power given to a person. [F, = blank paper]

car·tel /kaartél/ *n.* **1** an informal association of manufacturers or suppliers to maintain prices at a high level, and control production, marketing arrangements, etc. **2** a political combination between parties. □□ **car·tel·ize** /káartəlīz/ *v.tr. & intr.* [G *Kartell* f. F *cartel* f. It. *cartello* dimin. of *carta* CARD¹]

Car·te·sian /kaartéezhən/ *adj. & n.* • *adj.* of or relating to R. Descartes, 17th-c. French philosopher and mathematician. • *n.* a follower of Descartes. □□ **Car·te·sian·ism** *n.* [mod.L *Cartesianus* f. *Cartesius*, name of *Descartes*]

Car·te·sian co·or·di·nates *n.* a system for locating a point by reference to its distance from two or three axes intersecting at right angles.

cart horse *n.* a thickset horse suitable for heavy work.

Car·thu·sian /kaarthóōzhən/ *n. & adj.* • *n.* a monk of a contemplative order founded by St. Bruno in 1084. • *adj.* of or relating to this order. [med.L *Carthusianus* f. L *Cart(h)usia* Chartreuse, near Grenoble]

car·ti·lage /káart'lij/ *n.* gristle; a firm flexible connective tissue forming the infant skeleton, which is mainly replaced by bone in adulthood. □□ **car·ti·lag·i·noid** /-lájinoyd/ *adj.* **car·ti·lag·i·nous** /-lájinəs/ *adj.* [F f. L *cartilago –ginis*]

cart·load /káartlōd/ *n.* **1** an amount filling a cart. **2** esp. *Brit.* a large quantity of anything.

car·to·gram /káartəgram/ *n.* a map with diagrammatic statistical information. [F *cartogramme* f. *carte* map, card]

car·tog·ra·phy /kaartógrəfee/ *n.* the science or practice of map drawing. □□ **car·tog·ra·pher** *n.* **car·to·graph·ic** /-təgráfik/ *adj.* **car·to·graph·i·cal** *adj.* [F *cartographie* f. *carte* map, card]

car·to·man·cy /káartəmansee/ *n.* fortune-telling by interpreting a random selection of playing cards. [F *cartomancie* f. *carte* CARD¹]

car·ton /káart'n/ *n.* a light box or container, esp. one made of cardboard. [F (as CARTOON)]

car·toon /kaartóŏn/ *n. & v.* • *n.* **1** a humorous drawing in a newspaper, magazine, etc., esp. as a topical comment. **2** a sequence of drawings, often with speech indicated, telling a story; comic strip. **3** a filmed sequence of drawings using the technique of animation. **4** a full-size drawing as an artist's preliminary design for a painting, tapestry, mosaic, etc. • *v.* **1** *tr.* draw a cartoon of. **2** *intr.* draw cartoons. □□ **car·toon·ist** *n.* [It. *cartone* f. *carta* CARD¹]

car·touche /kaartóŏsh/ *n.* **1** a *Archit.* a scroll-like ornament, e.g., the volute of an Ionic capital. **b** a tablet imitating, or a drawing of, a scroll with rolled-up ends, used ornamentally or bearing an inscription. **c** an ornate frame. **2** *Archaeol.* an oval ring enclosing Egyptian hieroglyphs, usu. representing the name and title of a king. [F, = cartridge, f. It. *cartoccio* f. *carta* CARD¹]

car·tridge /káartrij/ *n.* **1** a case containing a charge of propelling explosive for firearms or blasting, with a bullet or shot if for small arms. **2** a spool of film, magnetic tape, etc., in a sealed container ready for insertion. **3** a component carrying the stylus on the pick-up head of a record player. **4** an ink container for insertion in a pen. [corrupt. of CARTOUCHE (but recorded earlier)]

cartridge belt *n.* a belt with pockets or loops for cartridges (in sense 1).

cart·wheel /káart–hweel, –weel/ *n.* **1** the (usu. spoked) wheel of a cart. **2** a circular sideways handspring with the arms and legs extended.

cart·wright /káartrīt/ *n.* a maker of carts.

car·un·cle /kərúngkəl, kárung–/ *n.* **1** *Zool.* a fleshy excrescence, e.g., a male turkey's wattles or the red prominence at the inner angle of the eye. **2** *Bot.* an outgrowth from a seed near the micropyle. □□ **car·un·cu·lar** /kərúngkyələr/ *adj.* [obs. F f. L *caruncula* f. *caro carnis* flesh]

carve /kaarv/ *v.* **1** *tr.* produce or shape (a statue, representation in relief, etc.) by cutting into a hard material (*carved a figure out of rock; carved it in wood*). **2** *tr.* **a** cut patterns, designs, letters, etc., in (hard material). **b** (foll. by *into*) form a pattern, design, etc., from (*carved it into a bust*). **c** (foll. by *with*) cover or decorate (material) with figures or designs cut in it. **3** *tr.* (*absol.*) cut (meat, etc.) into slices for eating. □ **carve out 1** take from a larger whole. **2** establish (a career, etc.) purposefully (*carved out a name for themselves*). **carve up** divide into several pieces; subdivide (territory, etc.). [OE *ceorfan* cut f. WG]

car·vel /káarvəl/ *n.* var. of CARAVEL. [as CARAVEL]

car·vel-built *n.* (of a boat) made with planks flush, not overlapping (cf. CLINKER-BUILT).

carv·en /káarvən/ *archaic past part.* of CARVE.

Carv·er /káarvər/ *n.* (in full **Carver chair**) a chair with arms, a rush seat, and a back having horizontal and vertical spindles. [J. *Carver*, first governor of Plymouth Colony, d. 1621, for whom a prototype was allegedly made]

car·ver /káarvər/ *n.* **1** a person who carves. **2 a** a carving knife. **b** (in *pl.*) a knife and fork for carving. **3** *Brit.* the principal chair, with arms, in a set of dining chairs, intended for the person who carves. ▶To be distinguished (in sense 3) from *Carver*.

carv·er·y /káarvəree/ *n.* (*pl.* **·ies**) esp. *Brit.* a buffet or restaurant with cuts of meat displayed, and carved as required, in front of customers.

carv·ing /káarving/ *n.* a carved object, esp. as a work of art.

carving knife *n.* a knife with a long blade, for carving meat.

car·y·at·id /kárēeátid/ *n.* (*pl.* **car·y·at·ids** or **car·y·at·ides** /-deez/) *Archit.* a pillar in the form of a draped female figure, supporting an entablature. [F *caryatide* f. It. *cariatide* or L f. Gk *karuatis –idos* priestess at Caryae (*Karuai*) in Laconia]

car·y·op·sis /kárēeópsis/ *n.* (*pl.* **car·y·op·ses** /-seez/) *Bot.* a dry, one-seeded indehiscent fruit, as in wheat and corn. [mod.L f. Gk *karuon* nut + *opsis* appearance]

Cas·a·no·va /kásənōvə/ *n.* a man notorious for seducing women. [G. J. *Casanova* de Seingalt, It. adventurer d. 1798]

Cas·bah /kázbaa, káaz–/ *n.* (also **Kas·bah**) **1** the citadel of a N. African city. **2** an Arab quarter near this. [F *casbah* f. Arab. *Kas(a)ba* citadel]

cas·cade /kaskáyd/ *n. & v.* • *n.* **1** a small waterfall, esp. forming one in a series or part of a large broken waterfall. **2** a succession of electrical devices or stages in a process. **3** a quantity of material, etc., draped in descending folds. • *v.intr.* fall in or like a cascade. [F f. It. *cascata* f. *cascare* to fall ult. f. L *casus*: see CASE¹]

cas·car·a /kaskárə/ *n.* (in full **cascara sagrada** /səgraadə/) the bark of a California buckthorn, *Rhamnus purshiana*, used as a purgative. [Sp., = sacred bark]

case¹ /kays/ *n.* **1** an instance of something occurring. **2** a state of affairs, hypothetical or actual. **3 a** an instance of a person receiving professional guidance, e.g., from a doctor or social worker. **b** this person or the circumstances involved. **4** a matter under official investigation, esp. by the police. **5** *Law* **a** a cause or suit for trial. **b** a statement of the facts in a cause sub judice, drawn up for a higher court's consideration (*judge states a case*). **c** a cause that has been decided and may be cited (*leading case*). **6 a** the sum of the arguments on one side, esp. in a lawsuit (*that is our case*). **b** a set of arguments, esp. in relation to persuasiveness (*have a good case; have a*

GRAMMAR TIP case¹

Case refers to the form a pronoun takes to indicate how it is used grammatically in a sentence. There are three cases in English. The **nominative case** (*I, you, he/she/it, we, they, who*) is used when a pronoun functions as a subject or the complement of a verb (*she sings beautifully; it is we who bear the responsibility*). The **objective case** (*me, you, him/her/it, us, them, whom*) is used when the pronoun is a direct object of a verb (*I encouraged her to write a letter*), an indirect object (*please write them a letter*), or the object of a preposition (*to whom should the letter be addressed?*). The **possessive case** (*my/mine, your/yours, his/hers/its, our/ours, their/theirs, whose*) is used to show ownership or possession (*theirs is the shop that was robbed*).

weak case). **c** a valid set of arguments (*have no case*). **7** *Gram.* **a** the relation of a word to other words in a sentence. **b** a form of a noun, adjective, or pronoun expressing this. **8** *colloq.* a comical person. **9** the position or circumstances in which one is. □ **as the case may be** according to the situation. **in any case** whatever the truth is; whatever may happen. **in case 1** in the event that; if. **2** lest; in provision against a stated or implied possibility (*take an umbrella in case it rains; took it in case*). **in case of** in the event of. **in the case of** as regards. **in no case** under no circumstances. **in that case** if that is true; should that happen. **is** (or **is not**) **the case** is (or is not) so. [ME f. OF *cas* f. L *casus* fall f. *cadere cas-* to fall]

case² /kays/ *n. & v.* ● *n.* **1** a container or covering serving to enclose or contain. **2** a container with its contents. **3** the outer protective covering of a watch, book, seed vessel, sausage, etc. **4** an item of luggage, esp. a suitcase. **5** *Printing* a partitioned receptacle for type. **6** a glass box for showing specimens, curiosities, etc. ● *v.tr.* **1** enclose in a case. **2** (foll. by *with*) surround. **3** *sl.* reconnoiter (a house, etc.), esp. with a view to robbery. [ME f. OF *casse, chasse*, f. L *capsa* f. *capere* hold]

case•book /káysbŏŏk/ *n.* a book containing a record of legal or medical cases.

case•bound /káysbownd/ *adj.* (of a book) in a hard cover.

case-hard•en *n.* **1** harden the surface of, esp. give a steel surface to (iron) by carbonizing. **2** make callous.

case his•to•ry *n.* information about a person for use in professional treatment, e.g., by a doctor.

ca•sein /káyseen, káyseein/ *n.* the main protein in milk, esp. in coagulated form as in cheese. [L *caseus* cheese]

ca•sein•o•gen /kaysínəjən/ *n.* the soluble form of casein as it occurs in milk.

case in point *n.* an instance that is relevant or (prec. by *the*) under consideration.

case knife *n.* a knife carried in a sheath.

case law *n.* the law as established by the outcome of former cases (cf. COMMON LAW, STATUTE LAW).

case•load /káyslōd/ *n.* the cases with which a lawyer, doctor, etc., is concerned at one time.

case•mate /káysmayt/ *n.* **1** a chamber in the thickness of the wall of a fortress, with embrasures. **2** an armored enclosure for guns on a warship. [F *casemate* & It. *casamatta* or Sp. *–mata*, f. *camata*, perh. f. Gk *khasma –atos* gap]

case•ment /káysmənt/ *n.* **1** a window or part of a window hinged vertically to open like a door. **2** *poet.* a window. [ME f. AL *cassimentum* f. *cassa* CASE²]

case of con•science *n.* a matter in which one's conscience has to decide a conflict of principles.

case shot *n.* **1** bullets in an iron case fired from a cannon. **2** shrapnel.

case stud•y *n.* **1** an attempt to understand a person, institution, etc., from collected information. **2** a record of such an attempt. **3** the use of a particular instance as an exemplar of general principles.

case•work /káyswərk/ *n.* social work concerned with individuals, esp. involving understanding of the client's family and background. □□ **case•work•er** *n.*

cash¹ /kash/ *n. & v.* ● *n.* **1** money in coins or bills, as distinct from checks or orders. **2** (also **cash down**) money paid as full payment at the time of purchase, as distinct from credit. **3** *colloq.* wealth. ● *v.tr.* give or obtain cash for (a note, check, etc.). □ **cash in 1** obtain cash for. **2** *colloq.* (usu. foll. by *on*) profit (from); take advantage (of). **3** *Brit.* pay into a bank, etc. **4** (in full **cash in one's chips**) *colloq.* die. **cash up** *Brit.* count and check cash takings at the end of a day's trading. □□ **cash•a•ble** *adj.* **cash•less** *adj.* [obs. F *casse* box or It. *cassa* f. L *capsa* CASE²]

cash² /kash/ *n.* (*pl.* same) *hist.* any of various small coins of China or the E. Indies. [ult. f. Port. *ca(i)xa* f. Tamil *kāsu* f. Skr. *karsha*]

cash and car•ry *n.* **1** a system in which goods are paid for in cash and taken away by the purchaser. **2** a store where this system operates.

cash•book /kashbŏŏk/ *n.* a book in which receipts and payments of cash are recorded.

cash cow *n.* a business, product, etc., generating steady profits that are usu. used to fund other enterprises.

cash crop *n.* a crop produced for sale, not for use as food, etc.

cash•ew /káshŏŏ, kashŏŏ/ *n.* **1** a bushy evergreen tree, *Anacardium occidentale*, native to Central and S. America, bearing kidney-shaped nuts attached to fleshy fruits. **2** (in full **cashew nut**) the edible nut of this tree. [Port. f. Tupi *(a)caju*]

cash•ew ap•ple *n.* the edible fleshy fruit of the cashew tree, from which the cashew nut hangs.

cash flow *n.* the movement of money into and out of a business, as a measure of profitability, or as affecting liquidity.

cash•ier¹ /kasheér/ *n.* a person dealing with cash transactions in a store, bank, etc. [Du. *cassier* or F *caissier* (as CASH¹)]

cash•ier² /kasheér/ *v.tr.* dismiss from service, esp. from the armed forces with disgrace. [Flem. *kasseren* disband, revoke, f. F *casser* f. L *quassare* QUASH]

cash•ier's check *n.* a check drawn by a bank on its own funds and signed by a cashier of the bank.

cash ma•chine *n.* = AUTOMATED TELLER MACHINE.

cash•mere /kázhmeer, kásh–/ *n.* **1** a fine soft wool, esp. that of a Kashmir goat. **2** a material made from this. [*Kashmir* in Asia]

cash on de•liv•er•y *n.* a system of paying the carrier for goods when they are delivered.

cash reg•is•ter *n.* a machine used in places of business that records the amount of each sale, totals receipts, and has a drawer for making change.

cas•ing /káysing/ *n.* **1** a protective or enclosing cover or shell. **2** the material for this.

ca•si•no /kəseénō/ *n.* (*pl.* **-nos**) a public room or building for gambling. [It., dimin. of *casa* house f. L *casa* cottage]

cask /kask/ *n.* **1** a large barrellike container made of wood, metal, or plastic, esp. one for alcoholic liquor. **2** its contents. **3** its capacity. [F *casque* or Sp. *casco* helmet]

cas•ket /káskit/ *n.* **1 a** a coffin, esp. a rectangular one. **b** a small wooden box for cremated ashes. **2** a small, often ornamental box or chest for jewels, letters, etc. [perh. f. AF form of OF *cassette* f. It. *cassetta* dimin. of *cassa* f. L *capsa* CASE²]

casque /kask/ *n.* **1** *hist.* or *poet.* a helmet. **2** *Zool.* a helmetlike structure, e.g., the process on the bill of the cassowary. [F f. Sp. *casco*]

Cas•san•dra /kəsándrə/ *n.* a prophet of disaster, esp. one who is disregarded. [L f. Gk *Kassandra*, daughter of Priam King of Troy: she was condemned by Apollo to prophesy correctly but not be believed]

cas•sa•tion /kasáyshən/ *n. Mus.* an informal instrumental composition of the 18th c., similar to a divertimento and orig. often for outdoor performance. [It. *cassazione*]

cas•sa•va /kəsáavə/ *n.* **1 a** any plant of the genus *Manihot*, esp. the cultivated varieties *M. esculenta* (**bitter cassava**) and *M. dulcis* (**sweet cassava**), having starchy tuberous roots. **b** the roots themselves. **2** a starch or flour obtained from these roots. Also called **tapioca** or **manioc**. [earlier *cas(s)avi*, etc., f. Taino *casavi*, infl. by F *cassave*]

cas•se•role /kásərōl/ *n. & v.* ● *n.* **1** a covered dish, usu. of earthenware or glass, in which food is cooked, esp. slowly in the oven. **2** food cooked in a casserole. ● *v.tr.* cook in a casserole. [F f. *cassole* dimin. of *casse* f. Prov. *casa* f. LL *cattia* ladle, pan f. Gk *kuathion* dimin. of *kuathos* cup]

cas•sette /kəsét, ka–/ *n.* a sealed case containing a length of tape, ribbon, etc., ready for insertion in a machine, esp.: **1** a length of magnetic tape wound on to spools, ready for insertion in a tape recorder. **2** a length of photographic film, ready for insertion in a camera. [F, dimin. of *casse* CASE²]

cas•sia /káshə/ *n.* **1** any tree of the genus *Cassia*, bearing leaves from which senna is prepared. **2** the cinnamonlike bark of this tree used as a spice. [L f. Gk *kasia* f. Heb. *ḳeṣî'āh* bark like cinnamon]

cas•sis /kaseés/ *n.* a syrupy liqueur flavored with black currants and produced mainly in Burgundy. [F, = black currant]

cas•sit•er•ite /kəsítərīt/ *n.* a naturally occurring ore of tin dioxide, from which tin is extracted. Also called **tinstone**. [Gk *kassiteros* tin]

cas•sock /kásək/ *n.* a long, close-fitting, usu. black or red garment worn by clergy, members of choirs, etc. □□ **cas•socked** *adj.* [F *casaque* long coat f. It. *casacca* horseman's coat, prob. f. Turkic: cf. COSSACK]

cas•sou•let /kasŏŏláy/ *n.* a stew of meat and beans. [F, dimin. of dial. *cassolo* stew pan]

cas•so•war•y /kásəwairee/ *n.* (*pl.* **-ies**) any large flightless Australasian bird of the genus *Casuarius*, with heavy body, stout legs, a wattled neck, and a bony crest on its forehead. [Malay *kasuārī, kasavārī*]

cast /kast/ *v. & n.* ● *v.* (*past* and *past part.* **cast**) **1** *tr.* throw, esp. deliberately or forcefully. **2** *tr.* (often foll. by *on, over*) **a** direct or cause to fall (one's eyes, a glance, light, a shadow, a spell). **b** express (doubts, aspersions, etc.). **3** *tr.* throw out (a fishing line) into the water. **4** *tr.* let down (an anchor, etc.). **5** *tr.* **a** throw off, get rid of. **b** shed (skin, etc.); esp. in the process of growth. **c** (of a horse) lose (a shoe). **6** *tr.* record, register, or give (a vote). **7** *tr.* **a** shape (molten metal or plastic material) in a mold. **b** make (a product) in this way. **8** *tr. Printing* make (type). **9** *tr.* **a** (usu. foll. by *as*) assign (an actor) to play a particular character. **b** allocate roles in (a play, motion picture, etc.). **10** *tr.* (foll. by *in, into*) arrange or formulate (facts, etc.) in a specified form. **11** *tr. & intr.* reckon; add up; calculate (accounts or figures). **12** *tr.* calculate and record details of (a horoscope). ● *n.* **1 a** the throwing of a missile, etc. **b** the distance reached by this. **2** a throw or a number thrown at dice. **3** a throw of a net, fishing line, etc. **4** *Fishing* **a** that which is cast, esp. the line with hook and fly. **b** a place for casting (*a good cast*). **5 a** an object of metal, clay, etc., made in a mold. **b** a molded mass of solidified material, esp. plaster protecting a broken limb. **6** the actors taking part in a play, motion picture, etc. **7** form, type, or quality (*cast of* features; cast of mind). **8** a tinge or shade of color. **9 a** (in full **cast in the eye**) a slight squint. **b** a twist or inclination. **10 a** a mass of earth excreted by a worm. **b** a mass of indigestible food thrown up by a hawk, owl, etc. **11** the form into which any work is thrown or arranged. **12 a** a wide area covered by a dog or pack to find a trail. **b** *Austral.* & *NZ* a wide sweep made by a sheepdog in mustering sheep. □ **cast about** (or **around**) make an extensive search (actually or mentally) (*cast about for a solution*). **cast adrift** leave to drift. **cast ashore** (of waves, etc.) throw to the shore. **cast aside** give up using; abandon. **cast away 1** reject. **2** (in *passive*) be shipwrecked (cf. CASTAWAY). **cast one's bread upon the waters** see BREAD. **cast down** depress; deject (cf. DOWNCAST). **cast loose** detach; detach oneself. **cast lots** see LOT. **cast off 1** abandon. **2** *Knitting* take the stitches off the needle by looping each over the next to finish the edge. **3** *Naut.* **a** set a ship free from a mooring, etc. **b** loosen and throw off (rope, etc.). **4** *Printing* estimate the space that will be taken in print by manuscript copy. **cast on** *Knitting* make the first row of loops on the needle. **cast out** expel. **cast up 1** (of the sea) deposit on the shore. **2** add up (figures, etc.). [ME f. ON *kasta*]

cas·ta·net /kástənét/ n. (usu. in *pl.*) a small concave piece of hardwood, ivory, etc., in pairs held in the hands and clicked together by the fingers as a rhythmic accompaniment, esp. by Spanish dancers. [Sp. *castañeta* dimin. of *castaña* f. L *castanea* chestnut]

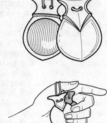

cast·a·way /kástəway/ n. & adj. •n. a shipwrecked person. •adj. **1** shipwrecked. **2** cast aside; rejected.

caste /kast/ n. **1** any of the Hindu hereditary classes, distinguished by relative degrees of purity or pollution, whose members are socially equal with one another and often follow the same occupations. **2** a more or less exclusive social class. **3** a system of such classes. **4** the position it confers. **5** *Zool.* a form of social insect having a particular function. □ **lose caste** descend in the social order.

castanets

[Sp. and Port. *casta* lineage, race, breed, fem. of *casto* pure, CHASTE]
caste·ism /kástizəm/ n. often *derog.* the caste system.
cas·tel·lan /kástələn/ n. *hist.* the governor of a castle. [ME f. ONF *castelain* f. med.L *castellanus*: see CASTLE]
cas·tel·lat·ed /kástəlaytid/ adj. **1** having battlements. **2** castlelike. □□ **cas·tel·la·tion** /-láyshən/ n. [med.L *castellatus*: see CASTLE]
caste mark n. a symbol usu. on the forehead denoting a person's caste.
cast·er /kástər/ n. (also *Brit.* **cas·tor**) **1** a small swiveled wheel (often one of a set) fixed to a leg (or the underside) of a piece of furniture. **2** a small container with holes in the top for sprinkling the contents. **3** a person who casts. **4** a machine for casting type.
cas·ti·gate /kástigayt/ v.tr. rebuke or punish severely. □□ **cas·ti·ga·tion** /-gáyshən/ n. **cas·ti·ga·tor** n. **cas·ti·ga·to·ry** /-gətáwree/ adj. [L *castigare* reprove f. *castus* pure]
cas·tile soap /kasteél/ n. a fine, hard, white or mottled soap made with olive oil and soda. [as CASTILIAN]
Cas·til·ian /kəstílyən/ n. & adj. •n. **1** a native of Castile in Spain. **2** the language of Castile, standard spoken and literary Spanish. •adj. of or relating to Castile.
cast·ing /kásting/ n. an object made by casting, esp. of molten metal.
cast·ing vote n. (also **cast·ing voice**) a deciding vote usu. given by the chairperson when the votes on two sides are equal.
▶From an obsolete sense of *cast* = turn the scale.
cast i·ron n. a hard alloy of iron, carbon, and silicon cast in a mold. □□ **cast-i·ron** adj. **1** made of cast iron. **2** hard; unchallengeable; unchangeable.
cas·tle /kásəl/ n. & v. •n. **1 a** a large fortified building or group of buildings; a stronghold. **b** a formerly fortified mansion. **2** *Chess* = ROOK[2]. •v. *Chess* **1** *intr.* make a special move (once only in a game on each side) in which the king is moved two squares along the back rank and the nearer rook is moved to the square passed over by the king. **2** *tr.* move (the king) by castling. □ **castles in the air** (or **in Spain**) a visionary unattainable scheme; a daydream. □□ **cas·tled** adj. [AF & ONF *castel*, *chastel* f. L *castellum* dimin. of *castrum* fort]
cast·off /kástawf/ adj. & n. •adj. no longer wanted; abandoned or discarded (*a pile of castoff clothes*). •n. something, especially a garment, that is no longer wanted.
cas·tor[1] *Brit.* var. of CASTER.
cas·tor[2] /kástər/ n. **1** an oily substance secreted by beavers and used in medicine and perfumes. **2** a beaver. [F or L f. Gk *kastōr* beaver]
cas·tor oil /kástər/ n. **1** an oil from the seeds of a plant, *Ricinus communis*, used as a purgative and lubricant. **2** (in full **castor-oil plant**) this plant. [18th c.: orig. uncert.: perh. so called as having succeeded CASTOR[2] in the medical sense]

cas·tor-oil bean n. (or **cas·tor bean**) a seed of the castor-oil plant.
cas·trate /kástrayt/ v.tr. **1** remove the testicles of; geld. **2** deprive of vigor. □□ **cas·tra·tion** /-tráyshən/ n. **cas·tra·tor** n. [L *castrare*]
cas·tra·to /kastraáto/ n. (pl. **cas·tra·ti** /-tee/) *hist.* a male singer castrated in boyhood so as to retain a soprano or alto voice. [It., past part. of *castrare*: see CASTRATE]
ca·su·al /kázhōōəl/ adj. & n. •adj. **1** accidental; due to chance. **2** not regular nor permanent; temporary; occasional (*casual work; a casual affair*). **3 a** unconcerned; uninterested (*was very casual about it*). **b** made or done without great care or thought (*a casual remark*). **c** acting carelessly or unmethodically. **4** (of clothes) informal. •n. **1** a casual worker. **2** (usu. in *pl.*) casual clothes or shoes. □□ **cas·u·al·ly** adv. **cas·u·al·ness** n. [ME f. OF *casuel* & L *casualis* f. *casus* CASE[1]]
ca·su·al·ty /kázhōōəltee/ n. (pl. **·ties**) **1** a person killed or injured in a war or accident. **2** a thing lost or destroyed. **3** (in full **casualty department**) *Brit.* a hospital emergency room. **4** an accident, mishap, or disaster. [ME f. med.L *casualitas* (as CASUAL), after ROYALTY, etc.]
ca·su·a·ri·na /kázhōōərínə/ n. any tree of the genus *Casuarina*, native to Australia and SE Asia, having tiny, scalelike leaves on slender, jointed branches, resembling gigantic horsetails. [mod.L *casuarius* cassowary (from the resemblance between branches and feathers)]
cas·u·ist /kázhōōist/ n. **1** a person, esp. a theologian, who resolves problems of conscience, duty, etc., often with clever but false reasoning. **2** a sophist or quibbler. □□ **cas·u·is·tic** adj. **cas·u·is·ti·cal** adj. **cas·u·is·ti·cal·ly** adv. **cas·u·ist·ry** /kázhōōəstree/ n. [F *casuiste* f. Sp. *casuista* f. L *casus* CASE[1]]
ca·sus bel·li /káysəs béli, kaásəs bélee/ n. an act or situation provoking or justifying war. [L]
CAT /kat/ abbr. **1** *Med.* computerized axial tomography. **2** clear-air turbulence.
cat /kat/ n. & v. •n. **1** a small, soft-furred, four-legged domesticated animal, *Felis catus* or *F. domestica*. **2 a** any wild animal of the genus *Felis*, e.g., a lion, tiger, or leopard. **b** = WILDCAT 2. **3** a catlike animal of any other species (*civet cat*). **4** *colloq.* a malicious or spiteful woman. **5 a** *sl.* a jazz enthusiast. **6** *Naut.* = CATHEAD. **7** = CAT-O'-NINE-TAILS. **8** *Brit.* a short, tapered stick in the game of tipcat. •v.tr. (also *absol.*) (**cat·ted**, **cat·ting**) *Naut.* raise (an anchor) from the surface of the water to the cathead. □ **let the cat out of the bag** reveal a secret, esp. involuntarily. **rain cats and dogs** *colloq.* rain very hard. [OE *catt(e)* f. LL *cattus*]
cata- /kátə/ prefix (usu. **cat-** before a vowel or *h*) **1** down; downward (*catadromous*). **2** wrongly; badly (*catachresis*). [Gk *kata* down]
ca·tab·o·lism /kətábəlizəm/ n. *Biochem.* the breakdown of complex molecules in living organisms to form simpler ones with the release of energy; destructive metabolism (opp. ANABOLISM). □□ **cat·a·bol·ic** /kátəbólik/ adj. [Gk *katabolē* descent f. *kata* down + *bolē* f. *ballō* throw]
cat·a·chre·sis /kátəkréesis/ n. (pl. **cat·a·chre·ses** /-seez/) an incorrect use of words. □□ **cat·a·chres·tic** /-kréstik/ adj. [L f. Gk *katakhrēsis* f. *khraomai* use]
cat·a·cla·sis /kátəkláysis/ n. (pl. **cat·a·cla·ses** /-seez/) *Geol.* the natural process of fracture, shearing, or breaking up of rocks. □□ **cat·a·clas·tic** /-klástik/ adj. [mod.L f. Gk *kataklasis* breaking down]
cat·a·clasm /kátəklazəm/ n. a violent break; a disruption. [Gk *kataklasma* (as CATA-, *klaō* to break)]
cat·a·clysm /kátəklizəm/ n. **1 a** a violent, esp. social or political, upheaval or disaster. **b** a great change. **2** a great flood or deluge. □□ **cat·a·clys·mal** /-klízməl/ adj. **cat·a·clys·mic** adj. **cat·a·clys·mi·cal·ly** adv. [F *cataclysme* f. L *cataclysmus* f. Gk *kataklusmos* f. *klusmos* flood f. *kluzō* wash]
cat·a·comb /kátəkōm/ n. (often in *pl.*) **1** an underground cemetery, esp. a Roman subterranean gallery with recesses for tombs. **2** a similar underground construction; a cellar. [F *catacombes* f. LL *catacumbas* (name given in the 5th c. to the cemetery of St. Sebastian near Rome), of unkn. orig.]
ca·tad·ro·mous /kətádrəməs/ adj. (of a fish, e.g., the eel) that swims down rivers to the sea to spawn (cf. ANADROMOUS). [Gk *katadromos* f. *kata* down + *dromos* running]
cat·a·falque /kátəfawk, -fawlk/ n. a decorated wooden framework for supporting the coffin of a distinguished person during a funeral or while lying in state. [F f. It. *catafalco*, of unkn. orig.: cf. SCAFFOLD]
Cat·a·lan /kát'lan/ n. & adj. •n. **1** a native of Catalonia in Spain. **2** the language of Catalonia. •adj. of or relating to Catalonia or its people or language. [F f. Sp.]
cat·a·lase /kát'lays, -layz/ n. *Biochem.* an enzyme that catalyzes the reduction of hydrogen peroxide. [CATALYSIS]
cat·a·lep·sy /kát'lepsee/ n. a state of trance or seizure with loss of sensation and consciousness accompanied by rigidity of the body.

See page xx for the **Key to Pronunciation**.

□□ **cat•a•lep•tic** /–léptik/ adj. & n. [F catalepsie or LL catalepsia f. Gk katalēpsis (as CATA-, lēpsis seizure)]

cat•a•log /kát'lawg, –log/ n. & v. (also **cat•a•logue**) • n. **1** a list of items (e.g., articles for sale, books held by a library), usu. in alphabetical or other systematic order and often with a description of each. **2** an extensive list (a catalog of crimes). **3** a listing of a university's courses, etc. • v.tr. (**cat•a•logs, cat•a•loged, cat•a•log•ing; cat•a•logues, cat•a•logued, cat•a•logu•ing**) **1** make a catalog of. **2** enter in a catalog. □□ **cat•a•log•er** n. (also **cat•a•logu•er**). [F f. LL catalogus f. Gk katalogos f. katalegō enroll (as CATA-, legō choose)]

ca•ta•logue rai•son•né /kát'lawg ráyzənáy, –log/ n. a descriptive catalog with explanations or comments. [F, = explained catalog]

ca•tal•pa /kətálpə/ n. any tree of the genus Catalpa, with heart-shaped leaves, trumpet-shaped flowers, and long pods. [Creek]

cat•a•lyse Brit. var. of CATALYZE.

ca•tal•y•sis /kətálisis/ n. (pl. **ca•tal•y•ses** /–seez/) Chem. & Biochem. the acceleration of a chemical or biochemical reaction by a catalyst. [Gk katalusis dissolution (as CATA-, luō set free)]

cat•a•lyst /kát'list/ n. **1** Chem. a substance that, without itself undergoing any permanent chemical change, increases the rate of a reaction. **2** a person or thing that precipitates a change. [as CATALYSIS after analyst]

cat•a•lyt•ic /kát'lítik/ adj. Chem. relating to or involving catalysis.

cat•a•lyt•ic con•vert•er n. a device incorporated in the exhaust system of a motor vehicle, with a catalyst for converting pollutant gases into harmless products.

cat•a•lyt•ic crack•er n. a device for cracking (see CRACK v. 9) petroleum oils by catalysis.

cat•a•lyze /kátəlīz/ v.tr. (Brit. **cat•a•lyse**) Chem. produce (a reaction) by catalysis. [as CATALYSIS after analyze]

cat•a•ma•ran /kátəmərán/ n. **1** a boat with twin hulls in parallel. **2** a raft of yoked logs or boats. **3** colloq. a quarrelsome woman. [Tamil kaṭṭumaram tied wood]

cat•a•mite /kátəmīt/ n. **1** a boy kept for homosexual practices. **2** the passive partner in sodomy. [L catamitus through Etruscan f. Gk Ganumēdēs Ganymede, cupbearer of Zeus]

cat•a•moun•tain /kátəmowntin/ n. (also **cat-a-moun•tain, cat•a•mount**) a lynx, leopard, puma, or other wild cat. [ME f. cat of the mountain]

catamaran

cat•a•nan•che /kátənángkee/ n. any composite plant of the genus Catananche, with blue or yellow flowers. [mod.L f. L catanancē plant used in love potions f. Gk katanagkē (as CATA-, anagkē compulsion)]

cat-and-dog adj. (of a relationship, etc.) full of quarrels.

cat and mouse n. a series of cunning maneuvers designed to thwart an opponent (played cat and mouse with the cops).

cat•a•plex•y /kátəpleksee/ n. sudden temporary paralysis due to fright, etc. □□ **cat•a•plec•tic** /–pléktik/ adj. [Gk kataplēxis stupefaction]

cat•a•pult /kátəpult, –poolt/ n. & v. • n. **1** a mechanical device for launching a glider, an aircraft from the deck of a ship, etc. **2** hist. a military machine worked by a lever and ropes for hurling large stones, etc. **3** Brit. = SLINGSHOT. • v. **1** tr. **a** hurl from or launch with a catapult. **b** fling forcibly. **2** intr. leap or be hurled forcibly. [F catapulte or L catapulta f. Gk katapeltēs (as CATA-, pallō hurl)]

cat•a•ract /kátərakt/ n. **1 a** a large waterfall or cascade. **b** a downpour; a rush of water. **2** Med. a condition in which the lens of the eye becomes progressively opaque resulting in blurred vision. [L cataracta f. Gk katarrhaktēs downrushing; in med. sense prob. f. obs. sense 'portcullis']

ca•tarrh /kətaár/ n. **1** inflammation of the mucous membrane of the nose, air passages, etc. **2** a watery discharge in the nose or throat due to this. □□ **ca•tarrh•al** adj. [F catarrhe f. LL catarrhus f. Gk katarrhous f. katarrheō flow down]

cat•ar•rhine /kátərīn/ adj. & n. Zool. • adj. (of primates) having nostrils close together, and directed downward, e.g., a baboon, chimpanzee, or human. • n. such an animal (cf. PLATYRRHINE). [CATA- + rhis rhinos nose]

ca•tas•tro•phe /kətástrəfee/ n. **1** a great and usu. sudden disaster. **2** the denouement of a drama. **3** a disastrous end; ruin. **4** an event producing a subversion of the order of things. □□ **ca•ta•stroph•ic** /kátəstrófik/ adj. **cat•a•stroph•i•cal•ly** /kátəstrófikəlee/ adv. [L catastropha f. Gk katastrophē (as CATA-, strophē turning f. strephō turn)]

ca•tas•tro•phism /kətástrəfizəm/ n. Geol. the theory that changes in the earth's crust have occurred in sudden violent and unusual events. □□ **ca•tas•tro•phist** n.

cat•a•to•ni•a /kátətóneeə/ n. **1** schizophrenia with intervals of catalepsy and sometimes violence. **2** catalepsy. □□ **cat•a•ton•ic** /–tónik/ adj. & n. [G Katatonie (as CATA-, TONE)]

Ca•taw•ba /kətáwbə/ n. **1** a variety of grape. **2** a white wine made from it. [Catawba River in S. Carolina, named for a Native American people of the Carolinas]

cat•boat /kátbōt/ n. a sailboat with a single mast placed well forward and carrying only one sail. [perh. f. cat a former type of coaler in NE England, + BOAT]

cat bur•glar n. a burglar who enters by climbing to an upper story.

cat•call /kátkawl/ n. & v. • n. a shrill whistle of disapproval made at sporting events, stage performances, meetings, etc. • v. **1** intr. make a catcall. **2** tr. make a catcall at.

catch /kach/ v. & n. • v. (past and past part. **caught** /kawt/) **1** tr. **a** lay hold of so as to restrain or prevent from escaping; capture in a trap, in one's hands, etc. **b** (also **catch hold of**) get into one's hands so as to retain, operate, etc. (caught hold of the handle). **2** tr. detect or surprise (a person, esp. in a wrongful or embarrassing act) (caught me in the act; caught him smoking). **3** tr. intercept and hold (a moving thing) in the hands, etc. (failed to catch the ball; a bowl to catch the drips). **4** tr. **a** contract (a disease) by infection or contagion. **b** acquire (a quality or feeling) from another's example (caught her enthusiasm). **5** tr. **a** reach in time and board (a train, bus, etc.). **b** be in time to see, etc. (a person or thing about to leave or finish) (if you hurry you'll catch them; caught the end of the performance). **6** tr. **a** apprehend with the senses or the mind (esp. a thing occurring quickly or briefly) (didn't catch what he said). **b** (of an artist, etc.) reproduce faithfully. **7 a** intr. become fixed or entangled; be checked (the bolt began to catch). **b** tr. cause to do this (caught her tights on a nail). **c** tr. (often foll. by on) hit; deal a blow to (caught him on the nose; caught his elbow on the table). **8** tr. draw the attention of; captivate (caught his eye; caught her fancy). **9** intr. begin to burn. **10** tr. (often foll. by up) reach or overtake (a person, etc., ahead). **11** tr. check suddenly (caught his breath). **12** tr. (foll. by at) grasp or try to grasp. • n. **1 a** an act of catching. **b** Baseball a chance or act of catching the ball. **2 a** an amount of a thing caught, esp. of fish. **b** a thing or person caught or worth catching, esp. in marriage. **3 a** a question, trick, etc., intended to deceive, incriminate, etc. **b** an unexpected or hidden difficulty or disadvantage. **4** a device for fastening a door or window, etc. **5** Mus. a round, esp. with words arranged to produce a humorous effect. □ **catch one's death** see DEATH. **catch fire** see FIRE. **catch it** sl. be punished or in trouble. **catch on** colloq. **1** (of a practice, fashion, etc.) become popular. **2** (of a person) understand what is meant. **catch up 1 a** (often foll. by with) reach a person, etc., ahead (he caught up in the end; he caught up with us). **b** (often foll. by with, on) make up arrears (of work, etc.) (must catch up with my correspondence). **2** snatch or pick up hurriedly. **3** (often in passive) entangle (caught up in suspicious dealings). **b** fasten up (hair caught up in a ribbon). □□ **catch•a•ble** adj. [ME f. AF & ONF cachier, OF chacier, ult. f. L captare try to catch]

catch•all /káchawl/ n. (often attrib.) **1** something designed to be all-inclusive. **2** a container for odds and ends.

catch-as-catch-can n. & adj. • n. a style of wrestling with few holds barred. • adj. using any method available (our catch-as-catch-can repair of fences).

catch ba•sin n. **1** a receptacle at the entrance to a sewer designed to catch objects too large to pass through the sewer. **2** a reservoir into which surface water can be drained.

catch crop n. a crop grown between two staple crops (in position or time).

catch•er /káchər/ n. **1** a person or thing that catches. **2** Baseball a fielder positioned behind home plate.

catch•fly /káchflī/ n. (pl. **-flies**) any plant of the genus Silene or Lychnis with a sticky stem.

catch•ing /káching/ adj. **1 a** (of a disease) infectious. **b** (of a practice, habit, etc.) likely to be imitated. **2** attractive; captivating.

catch•line /káchlīn/ n. Printing a short line of type, esp. at the head of copy or as a running headline.

catch•ment /káchmənt/ n. **1** the collection of rainfall. **2** an opening or basin for storm water, etc.

catch•ment ar•e•a n. **1** the area from which rainfall flows into a river, etc. **2** the area served by a school, hospital, etc.

catch•pen•ny /káchpenee/ adj. intended merely to sell quickly; superficially attractive.

catch•phrase /káchfrayz/ n. a phrase in frequent use.

catch-22 /káchtwenteetoo/ n. (often attrib.) colloq. a circumstance that presents a dilemma because of mutually conflicting or dependent conditions. [title of a novel by J. Heller (1961) featuring a dilemma of this kind]

catch•up var. of KETCHUP.

catch•weight /káchwayt/ adj. & n. • adj. unrestricted as regards weight. • n. unrestricted weight, as a weight category in sports.

catch•word /káchwərd/ n. **1** a word or phrase in common (often temporary) use; a topical slogan. **2** a word so placed as to draw attention. **3** Theatr. an actor's cue. **4** Printing the first word of a page given at the foot of the previous one.

catch•y /káchee/ adj. (**catch•i•er, catch•i•est**) **1** (of a tune) easy to remember; attractive. **2** that snares or entraps; deceptive. **3** (of the wind, etc.) fitful; spasmodic. □□ **catch•i•ly** adv. **catch•i•ness** n. [CATCH + −Y¹]

cat door n. a small swinging flap in an outer door, for a cat to pass in and out.

cate /kayt/ n. archaic (usu. in pl.) choice food; delicacies. [obs. acate purchase f. AF acat, OF achat f. acater, achater buy: see CATER]

cat•e•chet•i•cal /kátikétikǝl/ adj. (also **cat•e•chet•ic**) **1** of or by oral teaching. **2** according to the catechism of a church. **3** consisting of or proceeding by question and answer. □□ **cat•e•chet•i•cal•ly** adv. **cat•e•chet•ics** n. [eccl.Gk katēkhētikos f. katēkhētēs oral teacher: see CATECHIZE]

cat•e•chism /kátikizǝm/ n. **1 a** a summary of the principles of a religion in the form of questions and answers. **b** a book containing this. **2** a series of questions put to anyone. □□ **cat•e•chis•mal** /−kízmǝl/ adj. [eccl.L catechismus (as CATECHIZE)]

cat•e•chist /kátikist/ n. a religious teacher, esp. one using a catechism.

cat•e•chize /kátikīz/ v.tr. **1** instruct by means of question and answer, esp. from a catechism. **2** put questions to; examine. □□ **cat•e•chiz•er** n. [LL catechizare f. eccl.Gk katēkhizō f. katēkheō make hear (as CATA-, ēkheō sound)]

cat•e•chu /kátichoō/ n. (also **ca•chou** /káshoō/) gambier or similar vegetable extract, containing tannin. [mod.L f. Malay kachu]

cat•e•chu•men /kátikyoōmǝn/ n. a Christian convert under instruction before baptism. [ME f. OF catechumene or eccl.L catechumenus f. Gk katēkheō: see CATECHIZE]

cat•e•gor•i•cal /kátigáwrikǝl, −gór−/ adj. (also **cat•e•gor•ic**) unconditional; absolute; explicit; direct (a categorical refusal). □□ **cat•e•gor•i•cal•ly** adv. [F catégorique or LL categoricus f. Gk katēgorikos: see CATEGORY]

cat•e•gor•i•cal im•per•a•tive n. Philos. (in the ethical system of Immanuel Kant) an unconditional moral obligation that is binding in all circumstances and is not dependent on a person's inclination or purpose.

cat•e•go•rize /kátigǝrīz/ v.tr. place in a category or categories. □□ **cat•e•go•ri•za•tion** n.

cat•e•go•ry /kátigawree, −goree/ n. (pl. •**ries**) **1** a class or division. **2** Philos. **a** one of a possibly exhaustive set of classes among which all things might be distributed. **b** one of the a priori conceptions applied by the mind to sense-impressions. **c** any relatively fundamental philosophical concept. □□ **cat•e•go•ri•al** /−gáwreeǝl/ adj. [F catégorie or LL categoria f. Gk katēgoria statement f. katēgoros accuser]

ca•te•na /kateénǝ/ n. (pl. **ca•te•nae** /−nee/ or **ca•te•nas**) **1** a connected series of patristic comments on Scripture. **2** a series or chain. [L, = chain: orig. catena patrum chain of the Fathers (of the Church)]

cat•e•nar•y /kát'neree, kǝteénǝree/ n. & adj. • n. (pl. •**ies**) a curve formed by a uniform chain hanging freely from two points not in the same vertical line. • adj. of or resembling such a curve. [L catenarius f. catena chain]

cat•e•nate /kát'nayt/ v.tr. connect like links of a chain. □□ **cat•e•na•tion** /−náyshǝn/ n. [L catenare catenat− (as CATENARY)]

ca•ter /káytǝr/ v. **1 a** intr. (often foll. by for) provide food. **b** tr. provide food and service (cater a party). **2** intr. (foll. by for, to) provide what is desired or needed by. **3** intr. (foll. by to) pander to (esp. low tastes). [obs. noun cater (now caterer), f. acater f. AF acatour buyer f. acater buy f. Rmc]

cat•er•an /kátǝrǝn/ n. Sc. a Highland irregular fighting man; a marauder. [ME f. med.L cateranus & Gael. ceathairne peasantry]

cat•er•cor•nered /kátǝrkáwrnǝrd/ adj. & adv. (also **cat•er•cor•ner**, **cat•ty•cor•nered** /kátee−/, **kit•ty•cor•ner** /kítee−/) • adj. placed or situated diagonally. • adv. diagonally. [dial. adv. cater diagonally (cf. obs. cater the four on dice f. F quatre f. L quattuor four)]

cat•er•er /káytǝrǝr/ n. a person who supplies food for social events, esp. professionally.

ca•ter•ing /káytǝring/ n. the profession or work of a caterer.

cat•er•pil•lar /kátǝrpilǝr/ n. **1 a** the larva of a butterfly or moth. **b** (in general use) any similar larva of various insects. **2** (**Caterpillar**) **a** (in full **Caterpillar track** or **tread**) Trademark a continuous belt of linked pieces passing around the wheels of a

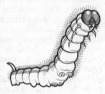

caterpillar 1

tractor, etc., for travel on rough ground. **b** a vehicle with these tracks, e.g., a tractor or tank.

cat•er•waul /kátǝrwawl/ v. & n. • v.intr. make the shrill howl of a cat. • n. a caterwauling noise. [ME f. CAT + −waul, etc. imit.]

cat•fish /kátfish/ n. any of various esp. freshwater fish, usu. having whiskerlike barbels around the mouth.

cat•gut /kátgut/ n. a material used for the strings of musical instruments and surgical sutures, made of the dried twisted intestines of sheep and horses, but not cats.

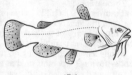

catfish

Cath. abbr. **1** cathedral. **2** Catholic.

Cath•ar /káthaar/ n. (pl. **Cath•ars** or **Cath•a•ri** /−rī/) a member of a medieval sect that sought to achieve great spiritual purity. □□ **Cath•a•rism** n. **Cath•a•rist** n. [med.L Cathari (pl.) f. Gk katharoi pure]

ca•thar•sis /kǝtháarsis/ n. (pl. **ca•thar•ses** /−seez/) **1** an emotional release in drama or art. **2** Psychol. the process of freeing repressed emotion by association with the cause, and elimination by abreaction. **3** Med. purgation. [mod.L f. Gk katharsis f. kathairō cleanse: sense 1 f. Aristotle's Poetics]

ca•thar•tic /kǝtháartik/ adj. & n. • adj. **1** effecting catharsis. **2** purgative. • n. a cathartic drug. □□ **ca•thar•ti•cal•ly** adv. [LL catharticus f. Gk kathartikos (as CATHARSIS)]

Ca•thay /katháy/ n. archaic or poet. the country China. [med.L Cataya]

cat•head /kát-hed/ n. Naut. a horizontal beam from each side of a ship's bow for raising and carrying the anchor.

ca•thec•tic see CATHEXIS.

ca•the•dral /kǝtheédrǝl/ n. the principal church of a diocese, containing the bishop's throne. [ME (as adj.) f. OF cathedral or f. LL cathedralis f. L f. Gk kathedra seat]

Cath•er•ine wheel /káthrin/ n. **1** a firework in the form of a flat coil that spins when fixed and lit. **2** a circular window with radial divisions. [mod.L Catharina f. Gk Aikaterina name of a saint martyred c. 310 on a spiked wheel]

cath•e•ter /káthitǝr/ n. Med. a tube for insertion into a body cavity for introducing or removing fluid. [LL f. Gk kathetēr f. kathiēmi send down]

cath•e•ter•ize /káthitǝrīz/ v.tr. Med. insert a catheter into.

cath•e•tom•e•ter /káthitómitǝr/ n. a telescope mounted on a graduated scale along which it can slide, used for accurate measurement of small vertical distances. [L cathetus f. Gk kathetos perpendicular line (as CATHETER + −METER)]

ca•thex•is /kǝthéksis/ n. (pl. **ca•thex•es** /−seez/) Psychol. concentration of mental energy in one channel. □□ **ca•thec•tic** adj. [Gk kathexis retention]

cath•ode /káthōd/ n. Electr. **1** the negative electrode in an electrolytic cell or electronic valve or tube. **2** the positive terminal of a primary cell such as a battery (opp. ANODE). □□ **cath•o•dal** adj. **cath•o•dic** /kǝthódik/ adj. [Gk kathodos descent f. kata down + hodos way]

cath•ode ray n. a beam of electrons emitted from the cathode of a high-vacuum tube.

cath•ode-ray tube n. a high-vacuum tube in which cathode rays produce a luminous image on a fluorescent screen. ¶ Abbr.: **CRT**.

cath•o•lic /káthǝlik, káthlik/ adj. & n. • adj. **1** of interest or use to all; universal. **2** all-embracing; of wide sympathies or interests (has catholic tastes). **3** (**Catholic**) **a** of the Roman Catholic religion. **b** including all Christians. **c** including all of the Western Church. • n. (**Catholic**) a Roman Catholic. □□ **cath•o•lic•al•ly** /kǝthóliklee/ adv. **Ca•thol•i•cism** /kǝthólisizǝm/ n. **cath•o•lic•i•ty** /káthǝlísitee/ n. **ca•thol•ic•ly** adv. [ME f. OF catholique or LL catholicus f. Gk katholikos universal f. kata in respect of + holos whole]

ca•thol•i•cize /kǝthólisīz/ v.tr. & intr. **1** make or become catholic. **2** (**Catholicize**) make or become a Roman Catholic.

cat•i•on /kátīǝn/ n. a positively charged ion; an ion that is attracted to the cathode in electrolysis (opp. ANION). [CATA- + ION]

cat•i•on•ic /kátiónik/ adj. **1** of a cation or cations. **2** having an active cation.

cat•kin /kátkin/ n. a spike of usu. downy or silky male or female flowers hanging from a willow, hazel, etc. [obs. Du. katteken kitten]

cat•like /kátlīk/ adj. **1** like a cat. **2** stealthy.

cat•nap /kátnap/ n. & v. • n. a short sleep. • v.intr. (•**napped**, •**napping**) have a catnap.

cat•nip /kátnip/ n. a white-flowered plant, Nepeta cataria, having a pungent smell attractive to cats. [CAT + dial. nip catnip, var. of dial. nep]

cat-o'-nine-tails n. hist. a rope whip with nine knotted lashes for flogging sailors, soldiers, or criminals.

WORD HISTORY caterpillar

Late Middle English: perhaps from a variant of Old French chatepelose, literally 'hairy cat,' influenced by obsolete piller 'ravager.' The association with 'cat' is found in other languages, e.g., Swiss teufelskatz (literally 'devil's cat'), Lombard gatta (literally 'cat'). Compare with French chaton, English catkin, resembling hairy caterpillars.

ca·top·tric /kətóptrik/ *adj.* of or relating to a mirror, a reflector, or reflection. □□ **ca·top·trics** *n.* [Gk *katoptrikos* f. *katoptron* mirror]

CAT scan /kat/ *n.* an X-ray image made using computerized axial tomography. □□ **CAT scan·ner** *n.* [*C*omputerized *A*xial *T*omography]

cat's cra·dle *n.* a child's game in which a loop of string is held between the fingers and patterns are formed.

cat's-eye *n.* any of various semiprecious stones, esp. CHRYSOBERYL.

cat's-foot *n.* any small plant of the genus *Antennaria*, having soft woolly leaves and growing on the surface of the ground.

cat's-paw *n.* **1** a person used as a tool by another. **2** a slight breeze rippling the surface of the water.

cat·sup /kátsəp, kéchəp, kách-/ var. of KETCHUP.

cat·tail /kát-tayl/ *n.* any tall, reedlike marsh plant of the genus *Typha*, esp. *T. latifolia*, with long, flat leaves and brown, velvety flower spikes. Also called **bulrush** or **reed mace.**

cat·te·ry /kátəree/ *n.* (*pl.* **·ries**) a place where cats are boarded or bred.

cat·tish /kátish/ *adj.* = CATTY. □□ **cat·tish·ly** *adv.* **cat·tish·ness** *n.*

cat·tle /kát'l/ *n.pl.* **1** bison, buffalo, yaks, or domesticated bovine animals, esp. of the genus *Bos.* **2** *archaic* livestock. [ME & AF *catel* f. OF *chatel* CHATTEL]

cat·tle·duf·fer /kát'ldúfər/ *n. Austral.* a cattle thief.

cat·tle guard *n.* a grid covering a ditch, allowing vehicles to pass over but not cattle, sheep, etc.

cat·tle·man /kát'lmən/ *n.* (*pl.* **·men**) a person who breeds or rears cattle.

cat·tle plague *n.* rinderpest.

cat·tle·ya /kátleeə/ *n.* any epiphytic orchid of the genus *Cattleya*, with handsome violet, pink, or yellow flowers. [mod.L f. W. *Cattley*, Engl. patron of botany d. 1832]

cat·ty /kátee/ *adj.* (**cat·ti·er, cat·ti·est**) **1** sly; spiteful; deliberately hurtful in speech. **2** catlike. □□ **cat·ti·ly** *adv.* **cat·ti·ness** *n.*

cat·ty-cor·nered var. of CATERCORNERED.

CATV *abbr.* community antenna television.

cat·walk /kátwawk/ *n.* **1** a narrow footway along a bridge, above a theater stage, etc. **2** a narrow platform or gangway used in fashion shows, etc.

Cau·ca·sian /kawkáyzhən/ *adj. & n.* ● *adj.* **1** of or relating to the white or light-skinned division of mankind. **2** of or relating to the Caucasus. ● *n.* a Caucasian person. [*Caucasus*, mountains between the Black and Caspian Seas, the supposed place of origin of this people]

Cau·ca·soid /káwkəsoyd/ *adj.* of or relating to the Caucasian division of mankind.

cau·cus /káwkəs/ *n.* **1 a** a meeting of the members of a political party, esp. in a legislature or convention, to decide policy. **b** a bloc of such members. **c** this system as a political force. **2** often *derog.* (esp. in the UK) **a** a usu. secret meeting of a group within a larger organization or party. **b** such a group. [18th-c. US, perh. f. Algonquian *cau'-cau-as'u* adviser]

cau·dal /káwd'l/ *adj.* **1** of or like a tail. **2** of the posterior part of the body. □□ **cau·dal·ly** *adv.* [L *cauda* tail]

cau·date /káwdayt/ *adj.* having a tail. [see CAUDAL]

cau·dil·lo /kawdeélyō, –deéyō, kowtheélyō, –theéyō/ *n.* (*pl.* **·los**) (in Spanish-speaking countries) a military or political leader. [Sp. f. LL *capitellum* dimin. of *caput* head]

caught past and past part. of CATCH.

caul /kawl/ *n.* **1 a** the inner membrane enclosing a fetus. **b** part of this occasionally found on a child's head at birth, thought to bring good luck. **2** *hist.* **a** a woman's close-fitting indoor headdress. **b** the plain back part of a woman's indoor headdress. **3** the omentum. [ME perh. f. OF *cale* small cap]

caul·dron /káwldrən/ *n.* (also **cal·dron**) **1** a large, deep, bowl-shaped vessel for boiling over an open fire. **2** an ornamental vessel resembling this. [ME f. AF & ONF *caudron*, ult. f. L *caldarium* hot bath f. *calidus* hot]

cau·li·flow·er /káwliflowr, kól-/ *n.* **1** a variety of cabbage with a large immature flower head of small usu. creamy-white flower buds. **2** the flower head eaten as a vegetable. [earlier *cole-florie*, etc., f. obs. F *chou fleuri* flowered cabbage, assim. to COLE and FLOWER]

cau·li·flow·er ear *n.* an ear deformed by repeated blows, esp. in boxing.

caulk /kawk/ *v.tr.* (also **calk**) **1** stop up (the seams of a boat, etc.) with oakum, etc., and waterproofing material, or by driving plate junctions together. **2** make (esp. a boat) watertight by this method.

cattail

cauliflower

caulk·er *n.* [OF dial. *cauquer* tread, press with force, f. L *calcare* tread f. *calx* heel]

caus·al /káwzəl/ *adj.* **1** of, forming, or expressing a cause or causes. **2** relating to, or of the nature of, cause and effect. □□ **caus·al·ly** *adv.* [LL *causalis*: see CAUSE]

cau·sal·i·ty /kawzálitee/ *n.* **1** the relation of cause and effect. **2** the principle that everything has a cause.

cau·sa·tion /kawzáyshən/ *n.* **1** the act of causing or producing an effect. **2** = CAUSALITY. [F *causation* or L *causatio* pretext, etc., in med.L the action of causing, f. *causare* CAUSE]

caus·a·tive /káwzətiv/ *adj.* **1** acting as cause. **2** (foll. by *of*) producing; having as effect. **3** *Gram.* expressing cause. □□ **caus·a·tive·ly** *adv.* [ME f. OF *causatif* or f. LL *causativus*: see CAUSATION]

cause /kawz/ *n. & v.* ● *n.* **1 a** that which produces an effect, or gives rise to an action, phenomenon, or condition. **b** a person or thing that occasions something. **c** a reason or motive; a ground that may be held to justify something (*no cause for complaint*). **2** a reason adjudged adequate (*show cause*). **3** a principle, belief, or purpose that is advocated or supported (*faithful to the cause*). **4 a** a matter to be settled at law. **b** an individual's case offered at law (*plead a cause*). **5** the side taken by any party in a dispute. ● *v.tr.* **1** be the cause of; produce; make happen (*caused a commotion*). **2** (foll. by to + infin.) induce (*caused me to smile; caused it to be done*). □ **in the cause of** to maintain, defend, or support (*in the cause of justice*). **make common cause with** join the side of. □□ **caus·a·ble** *adj.* **cause·less** *adj.* **caus·er** *n.* [ME f. OF f. L *causa*]

'cause /kawz, kuz/ *conj. & adv. colloq.* = BECAUSE. [abbr.]

cause cé·lè·bre /káwz selébrə/ *n.* (*pl.* **causes cé·lè·bres** *pronunc.* same) a trial or case that attracts public attention. [F]

cau·se·rie /kōzərée, kōzə–/ *n. (pl.* **cau·se·ries** *pronunc.* same) an informal article or talk, esp. on a literary subject. [F f. *causer* talk]

cause·way /káwzway/ *n.* **1** a raised road or track across low or wet ground or a stretch of water. **2** a raised path by a road. [earlier *cauce, causeway* f. ONF *caucié* ult. f. L CALX lime, limestone]

cau·sey /káwzee/ *n. archaic* or *Brit. dial.* = CAUSEWAY.

caus·tic /káwstik/ *adj. & n.* ● *adj.* **1** that burns or corrodes organic tissue. **2** sarcastic; biting. **3** *Chem.* strongly alkaline. **4** *Physics* formed by the intersection of reflected or refracted parallel rays from a curved surface. ● *n.* **1** a caustic substance. **2** *Physics* a caustic surface or curve. □□ **caus·ti·cal·ly** *adv.* **caus·tic·i·ty** /–tísitee/ *n.* [L *causticus* f. Gk *kaustikos* f. *kaustos* burned f. *kaiō* burn]

caus·tic pot·ash *n.* potassium hydroxide.

caus·tic so·da *n.* sodium hydroxide.

cau·ter·ize /káwtərīz/ *v.tr. Med.* burn or coagulate (tissue) with a heated instrument or caustic substance, esp. to stop bleeding. □□ **cau·ter·i·za·tion** *n.* [F *cautériser* f. LL *cauterizare* f. Gk *kautēriazō* f. *kautērion* branding iron f. *kaiō* burn]

cau·ter·y /káwtəree/ *n.* (*pl.* **·ies**) *Med.* **1** an instrument or caustic for cauterizing. **2** the operation of cauterizing. [L *cauterium* f. Gk *kautērion*: see CAUTERIZE]

cau·tion /káwshən/ *n. & v.* ● *n.* **1** attention to safety; prudence; carefulness. **2 a** esp. *Brit.* a warning, esp. a formal one in law. **b** a formal warning and reprimand. **3** *colloq.* an amusing or surprising person or thing. ● *v.tr.* **1** (often foll. by *against*, or *to* + infin.) warn or admonish. **2** esp. *Brit.* issue a caution to. [ME f. OF f. L *cautio –onis* f. *cavēre caut-* take heed]

cau·tion·ar·y /káwshəneree/ *adj.* that gives or serves as a warning (*a cautionary tale*).

cau·tious /káwshəs/ *adj.* careful; prudent; attentive to safety. □□ **cau·tious·ly** *adv.* **cau·tious·ness** *n.* [ME f. OF f. L: see CAUTION]

cav·al·cade /kávəlkáyd/ *n.* a procession or formal company of riders, motor vehicles, etc. [F f. It. *cavalcata* f. *cavalcare* ride ult. f. L *caballus* packhorse]

cav·a·lier /kávəleér/ *n. & adj.* ● *n.* **1** *hist.* (**Cavalier**) a supporter of Charles I in the English Civil War. **2** a courtly gentleman, esp. as a lady's escort. **3** *archaic* a horseman. ● *adj.* offhand; supercilious; blasé. □□ **cav·a·lier·ly** *adv.* [F f. It. *cavaliere*: see CHEVALIER]

cav·al·ry /kávəlree/ *n.* (*pl.* **·ries**) (usu. treated as *pl.*) soldiers on horseback or in armored vehicles. [F *cavallerie* f. It. *cavalleria* f. *cavallo* horse f. L *caballus*]

cav·al·ry·man /kávəlrimən/ *n.* (*pl.* **·men**) a soldier of a cavalry regiment.

cav·al·ry twill *n.* a strong fabric in a double twill.

cav·a·ti·na /kávəteénə/ *n.* **1** a short simple song. **2** a similar piece of instrumental music, usu. slow and emotional. [It.]

cave /kayv/ *n. & v.* ● *n.* **1** a large hollow in the side of a cliff, hill, etc., or underground. **2** *Brit. hist.* a dissident political group. ● *v.intr.* explore caves, esp. interconnecting or underground. □ **cave in 1 a** (of a wall, earth over a hollow, etc.) subside; collapse. **b** cause (a wall, earth, etc.) to do this. **2** yield or submit under pressure; give up. □□ **cave·like** *adj.* **cav·er** *n.* [ME f. OF f. L *cava* f. *cavus* hollow: *cave in* prob. f. E Anglian dial. *calve in*]

ca·ve·at /kávee-aat, kaá–, –at/ *n.* **1** a warning or proviso. **2** *Law* a process in court to suspend proceedings. [L, = let a person beware]

ca·ve·at emp·tor /émptawr/ *n.* the principle that the buyer alone is responsible if dissatisfied. [L, = let the buyer beware]

cave bear *n.* a large extinct bear of the Pleistocene epoch, whose bones have been found in caves in Europe.

cave dwell•er *n.* **1** = CAVEMAN. **2** *sl.* a person who lives in an apartment building in a big city.

cave-in *n.* **1** a collapse, as of a roof, tunnel or other structure. **2** an instance of yielding or submitting under pressure.

cave•man /káyvman/ *n.* (*pl.* **-men**) **1** a prehistoric human living in a cave. **2** a primitive or crude person, esp. a man who behaves roughly toward women.

cav•ern /kávərn/ *n.* **1** a cave, esp. a large or dark one. **2** a dark, cave-like place, e.g., a room. □□ **cav•ern•ous** *adj.* **cav•ern•ous•ly** *adv.* [ME f. OF *caverne* or f. L *caverna* f. *cavus* hollow]

cav•i•ar /kávee–aár/ *n.* (also **cav•i•are**) the pickled roe of sturgeon or other large fish, eaten as a delicacy. [early forms repr. It. *caviale*, Fr. *caviar*, prob. f. med.Gk *khaviari*]

cav•il /kávil/ *v. & n.* • *v.intr.* (**cav•iled**, **cav•il•ing**; esp. *Brit.* **cav•illed**, **cav•il•ling**) (usu. foll. by *at*, *about*) make petty objections; carp. • *n.* a trivial objection. □□ **cav•il•er** *n.* [F *caviller* f. L *cavillari* f. *cavilla* mockery]

cav•ing /káyving/ *n.* exploring caves as a sport or pastime.

cav•i•ta•tion /kávitáyshən/ *n.* **1** the formation of a cavity in a structure. **2** the formation of bubbles, or of a vacuum, in a liquid.

cav•i•ty /kávitee/ *n.* (*pl.* **-ties**) **1** a hollow within a solid body. **2** a decayed part of a tooth. [F *cavité* or LL *cavitas* f. L *cavus* hollow]

cav•i•ty wall *n.* a wall formed from two thicknesses of masonry with a space between them.

cav•ort /kəváwrt/ *v.intr. sl.* caper excitedly; gambol; prance. [US, perh. f. CURVET]

ca•vy /káyvee/ *n.* (*pl.* **-vies**) any small rodent of the family Caviidae, native to S. America and having a sturdy body and vestigial tail, including guinea pigs. [mod.L *cavia* f. Galibi *cabiai*]

caw /kaw/ *n. & v.* • *n.* the harsh cry of a rook, crow, etc. • *v.intr.* utter this cry. [imit.]

cay /kee, kay/ *n.* a low insular bank or reef of coral, sand, etc. (cf. KEY²). [Sp. *cayo* shoal, reef f. F *quai*: see QUAY]

cay•enne /kī–én, kay–/ *n.* (in full **cayenne pepper**) a pungent red powder obtained from various plants of the genus *Capsicum* and used for seasoning. [Tupi *kyynha* assim. to *Cayenne* capital of French Guiana]

cay•man var. of CAIMAN.

Ca•yu•ga /kayóōgə, kī–/ *n.* **1 a** a N. American people native to New York. **b** a member of this people. **2** the language of this people.

CB *abbr.* **1** citizens' band. **2** (in the UK) Companion of the Order of the Bath.

Cb *symb. Chem.* the element columbium.

CBC *abbr.* **1** Canadian Broadcasting Corporation. **2** complete blood count.

CBE *abbr.* Commander of the Order of the British Empire.

CBI *abbr.* computer-based instruction.

CBS *abbr.* Columbia Broadcasting System.

CC *abbr.* **1** city council. **2** county clerk. **3** circuit court.

cc *abbr.* (also **c.c.**) **1** cubic centimeter(s). **2** (carbon) copy; copies.

CCTV *abbr.* closed-circuit television.

CCU *abbr.* **1** cardiac care unit. **2** coronary care unit. **3** critical care unit.

CD *abbr.* **1** compact disc. **2** certificate of deposit. **3** congressional district. **4** civil defense. **5** diplomatic corps (*corps diplomatique*).

Cd *symb. Chem.* the element cadmium.

cd *abbr.* candela(s).

CDC *abbr.* Centers for Disease Control (and Prevention).

Cdr. *abbr. Mil.* commander.

Cdre. *abbr.* commodore.

CD-ROM /séedeeróm/ *abbr.* compact disc read-only memory, a medium for data storage and distribution.

CDT *abbr.* central daylight time.

CE *abbr.* **1** Church of England. **2** civil engineer. **3** (with dates) Common Era.

Ce *symb. Chem.* the element cerium.

ce•a•no•thus /séeənóthəs/ *n.* any shrub of the genus *Ceanothus*, with small blue or white flowers. [mod.L f. Gk *keanōthos* kind of thistle]

cease /sees/ *v. & n.* • *v.tr. & intr.* stop; bring or come to an end (*ceased breathing*). • *n.* (in *without cease*) unendingly. [ME f. OF *cesser*, L *cessare* frequent. of *cedere cess-* yield]

cease-fire *n.* **1** the order to stop firing. **2** a period of truce; a suspension of hostilities.

cease•less /séeslis/ *adj.* without end; not ceasing. □□ **cease•less•ly** *adv.*

cec•i•tis /sikítis/ *n.* inflammation of the cecum.

ce•cum /séekəm/ *n.* (*Brit.* **cae•cum**) (*pl.* **-ca** /–kə/) a blind-ended pouch at the junction of the small and large intestines. □□ **ce•cal** *adj.* [L for *intestinum caecum* f. *caecus* blind, transl. of Gk *tuphlon enteron*]

ce•dar /séedər/ *n.* **1** any spreading evergreen conifer of the genus *Cedrus*, bearing tufts of small needles and cones of papery scales. **2** any of various similar conifers yielding timber. **3** = CEDARWOOD. □□ **ce•darn** *adj. poet.* [ME f. OF *cedre* f. L *cedrus* f. Gk *kedros*]

ce•dar•wood /séedərwŏŏd/ *n.* the fragrant durable wood of any cedar tree.

cede /seed/ *v.tr.* give up one's rights to or possession of. [F *céder* or L *cedere* yield]

ce•dil•la /sidílə/ *n.* **1** a mark written under the letter *c*, esp. in French, to show that it is sibilant (as in *façade*). **2** a similar mark under *s* in Turkish and other Eastern languages. [Sp. *cedilla* dimin. of *zeda* f. Gk *zēta* letter Z]

cei•lidh /káylee/ *n.* orig. *Ir.* & *Sc.* an informal gathering for conversation, music, dancing, songs, and stories. [Gael.]

ceil•ing /séeling/ *n.* **1 a** the upper interior surface of a room or other similar compartment. **b** the material forming this. **2** an upper limit on prices, wages, performance, etc. **3** *Aeron.* the maximum altitude a given aircraft can reach. **4** *Naut.* the inside planking of a ship's bottom and sides. [ME *celynge, siling*, perh. ult. f. L *caelum* heaven or *celare* hide]

cel•a•don /sélədon/ *n. & adj.* • *n.* **1** a willow-green color. **2** a gray-green glaze used on some pottery. **3** Chinese pottery glazed in this way. • *adj.* of a gray-green color. [F, f. the name of a character in d'Urfé's *L'Astrée* (1607–27)]

cel•an•dine /séləndin, –deen/ *n.* either of two yellow-flowered plants, the greater celandine, *Chelidonium majus*, and the lesser celandine, *Ranunculus ficaria*. [ME and OF *celidoine* ult. f. Gk *khelidōn* swallow: the flowering of the plant was associated with the arrival of swallows]

-cele /seel/ *comb. form* (also **–coele**) *Med.* swelling; hernia (*gastrocele*). [Gk *kēlē* tumor]

ce•leb /siléb/ *n. colloq.* a celebrity; a star.

cel•e•brant /sélibrənt/ *n.* a person who performs a rite, esp. a priest at the Eucharist. [F *célébrant* or L *celebrare celebrant-*: see CELEBRATE]

cel•e•brate /sélibrayt/ *v.* **1** *tr.* mark (a festival or special event) with festivities, etc. **2** *tr.* perform publicly and duly (a religious ceremony, etc.). **3 a** *tr.* officiate at (the Eucharist). **b** *intr.* officiate, esp. at the Eucharist. **4** *intr.* engage in festivities, usu. after a special event, etc. **5** *tr.* (esp. as **celebrated** *adj.*) honor publicly; make widely known. □□ **cel•e•bra•tion** /–bráyshən/ *n.* **cel•e•bra•tor** *n.* **cel•e•bra•to•ry** /–brətáwree, səlébrətáwree/ *adj.* [L *celebrare* f. *celeber –bris* frequented, honored]

ce•leb•ri•ty /silébritee/ *n.* (*pl.* **-ties**) **1** a well-known person. **2** fame. [F *célébrité* or L *celebritas* f. *celeber*: see CELEBRATE]

ce•ler•i•ac /siléereeak, silér–/ *n.* a variety of celery with a swollen turniplike stem base used as a vegetable. [CELERY: *–ac* is unexplained]

ce•ler•i•ty /siléritee/ *n. archaic* or *literary* swiftness (esp. of a living creature). [ME f. F *célérité* f. L *celeritas –tatis* f. *celer* swift]

cel•er•y /séləree/ *n.* an umbelliferous plant, *Apium graveolens*, with closely packed succulent leafstalks used as a vegetable. [F *céleri* f. It. dial. *selleri* f. L *selinum* f. Gk *selinon* parsley]

ce•les•ta /siléstə/ *n. Mus.* a small keyboard instrument resembling a glockenspiel, with hammers striking steel plates suspended over wooden resonators, giving an ethereal bell-like sound. [pseudo-L f. F *céleste*: see CELESTE]

ce•leste /silést/ *n. Mus.* **1** an organ and harmonium stop with a soft tremulous tone. **2** = CELESTA. [F *céleste* heavenly f. L *caelestis* f. *caelum* heaven]

ce•les•tial /siléschəl/ *adj.* **1** heavenly; divinely good or beautiful; sublime. **2 a** of the sky; of the part of the sky commonly observed in astronomy, etc. **b** of heavenly bodies. □□ **ce•les•tial•ly** *adv.* [ME f. OF f. med.L *caelestialis* f. L *caelestis*: see CELESTE]

ce•les•tial e•qua•tor *n.* the great circle of the sky in the plane perpendicular to the earth's axis.

ce•les•tial ho•ri•zon *n.* see HORIZON 1c.

ce•les•tial nav•i•ga•tion *n.* navigation by the stars, etc.

ce•li•ac /séeleeak/ *adj.* (esp. *Brit.* **coe•li•ac**) of or affecting the belly. [L *coeliacus* f. Gk *koiliakos* f. *koilia* belly]

ce•li•ac dis•ease *n.* a digestive disease of the small intestine brought on by contact with dietary gluten.

cel•i•bate /sélibət/ *adj. & n.* • *adj.* **1** committed to abstention from sexual relations and from marriage, esp. for religious reasons. **2** abstaining from sexual relations. • *n.* a celibate person. □□ **cel•i•ba•cy** /–bəsee/ *n.* [F *célibat* or L *caelibatus* unmarried state f. *caelebs –ibis* unmarried]

cell /sel/ *n.* **1** a small room, esp. in a prison or monastery. **2** a small compartment, e.g., in a honeycomb. **3** a small group as a nucleus of political activity, esp. of a subversive kind. **4** *hist.* a small monastery or nunnery dependent on a larger one. **5** *Biol.* **a** the structural and functional usu. microscopic unit of an organism, consisting of cytoplasm and a nucleus enclosed in a membrane. **b** an enclosed cavity in an organism, etc. **6** *Electr.* a vessel for containing electrodes within an electrolyte for current generation or electrolysis. □□ **celled** *adj.* (also in *comb.*). [ME f. OF *celle* or f. L *cella* storeroom, etc.]

cel·lar /sélər/ n. & v. •n. 1 a room below ground level in a house, used for storage, etc. 2 a stock of wine in a cellar (*has a good cellar*). •v.tr. store or put in a cellar. [ME f. AF *celer*, OF *celier* f. LL *cellarium* storehouse]

cel·lar·age /sélərij/ n. 1 cellar space. 2 the charge for the use of a cellar or storehouse.

cel·lar·er /sélərər/ n. a monastic officer in charge of wine.

cel·lar·et /sélərét/ n. a case, cabinet, etc., for holding wine bottles in a dining room.

cel·lo /chélō/ n. (pl. ·los) a bass instrument of the violin family, held upright on the floor between the legs of the seated player. □□ **cel·list** n. [abbr. of VIOLONCELLO]

cel·lo·phane /séləfayn/ n. *formerly Trademark* a thin transparent wrapping material made from viscose. [CELLULOSE + –*phane* (cf. DIAPHANOUS)]

cell·phone /sélfōn/ n. a small, portable radiotelephone having access to a CELLULAR TELEPHONE system.

cel·lu·lar /sélyələr/ adj. 1 of or having small compartments or cavities. 2 of open texture; porous. 3 *Physiol.* of or consisting of cells. □□ **cel·lu·lar·i·ty** /–lárritee/ n. **cel·lu·late** adj. **cel·lu·la·tion** /–láyshən/ n. **cel·lu·lous** adj. [F *cellulaire* f. mod.L *cellularis:* see CELLULE]

cello

cel·lu·lar tel·e·phone n. (also **cel·lu·lar phone**) a system of mobile radiotelephone transmission with an area divided into "cells" each served by its own small transmitter.

cel·lule /sélyōōl/ n. *Biol.* a small cell or cavity. [F *cellule* or L *cellula* dimin. of *cella* CELL]

cel·lu·lite /sélyəlīt/ n. a lumpy form of fat, esp. on the hips and thighs of women, causing puckering of the skin. [F (as CELLULE)]

cel·lu·li·tis /sélyəlítis/ n. inflammation of cellular tissue.

cel·lu·loid /sélyəloyd/ n. 1 a transparent flammable plastic made from camphor and cellulose nitrate. 2 motion-picture film. [irreg. f. CELLULOSE]

cel·lu·lose /sélyəlōs, –lōz/ n. 1 *Biochem.* a carbohydrate forming the main constituent of plant cell walls, used in the production of textile fibers. 2 (in general use) a paint or lacquer consisting of esp. cellulose acetate or nitrate in solution. □□ **cel·lu·lo·sic** /–lōsik/ adj. [F (as CELLULE)]

ce·lom var. of COELOM.

Cel·si·us /sélseeəs/ adj. of or denoting a temperature on the Celsius scale. [A. *Celsius,* Sw. astronomer d. 1744]

Cel·si·us scale n. a scale of temperature on which water freezes at 0° and boils at 100° under standard conditions.

Celt /kelt, selt/ n. (also **Kelt**) a member of a group of W. European peoples, including the pre-Roman inhabitants of Britain and Gaul and their descendants, esp. in Ireland, Wales, Scotland, Cornwall, Brittany, and the Isle of Man. [L *Celtae* (pl.) f. Gk *Keltoi*]

celt /kelt/ n. *Archaeol.* a stone or metal prehistoric implement with a chisel edge. [med.L *celtes* chisel]

Celt·ic /kéltik, séltik/ adj. & n. •adj. of or relating to the Celts. •n. a group of languages spoken by Celtic peoples, including Gaelic, Welsh, Cornish, and Breton. □□ **Celt·i·cism** /–tisizəm/ n. [L *celticus* (as CELT) or F *celtique*]

Celt·ic cross n. a Latin cross with a circle around the center.

cem·ba·lo /chémbəlō/ n. (pl. ·los) a harpsichord. [abbr. of CLAVICEMBALO]

ce·ment /simént/ n. & v. •n. 1 a powdery substance made by calcining lime and clay, mixed with water to form mortar or used in concrete (see also PORTLAND CEMENT). 2 any similar substance that hardens and fastens on setting. 3 a uniting factor or principle. 4 a substance for filling cavities in teeth. 5 (also **ce·men·tum**) *Anat.* a thin layer of bony material that fixes teeth to the jaw. •v.tr. 1 a unite with or as with cement. b establish or strengthen (a friendship, etc.). 2 apply cement to. 3 line or cover with cement. □□ **ce·ment·er** n. [ME f. OF *ciment* f. L *caementum* quarry stone f. *caedere* hew]

ce·men·ta·tion /seeməntáyshən/ n. 1 the act or process of cementing or being cemented. 2 the heating of iron with charcoal powder to form steel.

ce·ment mix·er n. a machine (usu. with a revolving drum) for mixing cement with water.

cem·e·ter·y /sémitəree/ n. (pl. ·ies) a burial ground, esp. one not in a churchyard. [LL *coemeterium* f. Gk *koimētērion* dormitory f. *koimaō* put to sleep]

ce·no·bite /seenəbīt/ n. (esp. *Brit.* **coe·no·bite**) a member of a monastic community. □□ **ce·no·bit·ic** /–bítik/ adj. **ce·no·bit·i·cal** adj. [OF *cenobite* or eccl.L *coenobita* f. LL *coenobium* f. Gk *koinobion* convent f. *koinos* common + *bios* life]

cen·o·taph /sénətaf/ n. a tomblike monument, esp. a war memorial, to a person whose body is elsewhere. [F *cénotaphe* f. LL *cenotaphium* f. Gk *kenos* empty + *taphos* tomb]

Ce·no·zo·ic /seenəzóik, sén–/ (also **Cai·no·zo·ic** /kīnə–/, **Cae·no·zo·ic** /seenə–/) adj. & n. *Geol.* •adj. of or relating to the most recent era of geological time, marked by the evolution and development of mammals, birds, and flowers. •n. this era (cf. MESOZOIC, PALEOZOIC). [Gk *kainos* new + *zōion* animal]

cen·ser /sénsər/ n. a vessel in which incense is burned, esp. during a religious procession or ceremony. [ME f. AF *censer,* OF *censier* aphetic of *encensier* f. *encens* INCENSE[1]]

cen·sor /sénsər/ n. & v. •n. 1 an official authorized to examine printed matter, movies, news, etc., before public release, and to suppress any parts on the grounds of obscenity, a threat to security, etc. 2 *Rom.Hist.* either of two annual magistrates responsible for holding censuses and empowered to supervise public morals. 3 *Psychol.* an impulse that is said to prevent certain ideas and memories from emerging into consciousness. •v.tr. 1 act as a censor of. 2 make deletions or changes in. □□ **cen·so·ri·al** /–sáwreeəl/ adj. **cen·sor·ship** n. [L f. *censēre* assess: in sense 3 mistransl. of G *Zensur* censorship]

▶Both **censor** and **censure** are both verbs and nouns, but **censor** is used to mean 'to cut unacceptable parts out of a book, movie, etc.' or 'a person who does this,' while **censure** means 'to criticize harshly' or 'harsh criticism:' *The censure of her friends caused her to regret her actions.*

cen·so·ri·ous /sensáwreeəs/ adj. severely critical; faultfinding; quick or eager to criticize. □□ **cen·so·ri·ous·ly** adv. **cen·so·ri·ous·ness** n. [L *censorius:* see CENSOR]

cen·sure /sénshər/ v. & n. •v.tr. criticize harshly; reprove. •n. harsh criticism; expression of disapproval. □□ **cen·sur·a·ble** adj. [ME f. OF f. L *censura* f. *censēre* assess]

▶See note at CENSOR.

cen·sus /sénsəs/ n. (pl. **cen·sus·es**) the official count of a population or of a class of things, often with various statistics noted. [L f. *censēre* assess]

cent /sent/ n. 1 a a monetary unit valued at one-hundredth of a dollar or other metric unit. b a coin of this value. 2 *colloq.* a very small sum of money. 3 see PERCENT. [F *cent* or It. *cento* or L *centum* hundred]

cent. abbr. century.

cen·taur /séntawr/ n. a creature in Greek mythology with the head, arms, and torso of a man and the body and legs of a horse. [ME f. L *centaurus* f. Gk *kentauros,* of unkn. orig.]

cen·tau·ry /séntawree/ n. (pl. ·ies) any plant of the genus *Centaurium,* esp. *C. erythraea,* formerly used in medicine. [LL *centaurea* ult. f. Gk *kentauros* CENTAUR: from the legend that it was discovered by the centaur Chiron]

cen·ta·vo /sentaavō/ n. a small coin of Spain, Portugal, and some Latin American countries, worth one-hundredth of the standard unit. [Sp. f. L *centum* hundred]

centaur

cen·te·nar·i·an /séntináireeən/ n. & adj. •n. a person a hundred or more years old. •adj. a hundred or more years old.

cen·ten·ar·y /senténəree, séntəneree/ n. & adj. •n. (pl. ·ies) = CENTENNIAL n. •adj. 1 of or relating to a centenary. 2 occurring every hundred years. [L *centenarius* f. *centeni* a hundred each f. *centum* a hundred]

cen·ten·ni·al /senténeeəl/ adj. & n. •adj. 1 lasting for a hundred years. 2 occurring every hundred years. •n. 1 a hundredth anniversary. 2 a celebration of this. [L *centum* a hundred, after BIENNIAL]

cen·ter /séntər/ n. & v. •n. 1 the middle point, esp. of a line, circle, or sphere, equidistant from the ends or from any point on the circumference or surface. 2 a pivot or axis of rotation. 3 a a place or group of buildings forming a central point in a district, city, etc., or a main area for an activity (*shopping center, town center*). b (with preceding word) a piece or set of equipment for a number of connected functions (*music center*). **4** a point of concentration or dispersion; a nucleus or source. **5** a political party or group holding moderate opinions. **6** the filling in a chocolate, candy, etc. **7** *Sports* **a** the middle player in a line or group in many games. **b** a kick or hit from the side to the center of the playing area. **8** (in a lathe, etc.) a conical adjustable support for the workpiece. **9** (*attrib.*) of or at the center. • *v.* **1** *intr.* (foll. by *in*, *on*; *disp.* foll. by *around*) have as its main center. **2** *tr.* place in the center. **3** *tr.* mark with a center. **4** *tr.* (foll. by *in*, etc.) concentrate. **5** *tr. Sports* kick or hit (the ball) from the side to the center of the playing area. □□ **cen•tered** *adj.* (often in *comb.*). **cen•ter•most** *adj.* **cen•tric** *adj.* **cen•tri•cal** *adj.* **cen•tric•i•ty** /–trísitee/ *n.* [ME f. OF *centre* or L *centrum* f. Gk *kentron* sharp point]

cen•ter bit *n.* a boring tool with a center point and side cutters.

cen•ter•board /séntərbawrd/ *n.* a retractable keel, as for a small sailboat.

cen•ter•fold /séntərfōld/ *n.* a printed and usu. illustrated sheet folded to form the center spread of a magazine, etc.

cen•ter•ing /séntəring/ *n.* a temporary frame used to support an arch, dome, etc., while under construction.

cen•ter of flo•ta•tion *n.* the center of gravity in a floating body.

cen•ter of grav•i•ty *n.* (also **cen•ter mass**) the point at which the weight of a body may be considered to act.

cen•ter of mass *n.* a point representing the mean position of matter in a body or system.

cen•ter•piece /séntərpees/ *n.* **1** an ornament for the middle of a table. **2** a principal item.

cen•ter spread *n.* the two facing middle pages of a newspaper, etc.

cen•tes•i•mal /sentésiməl/ *adj.* reckoning or reckoned by hundredths. □□ **cen•tes•i•mal•ly** *adv.* [L *centesimus* hundredth f. *centum* hundred]

centi- /séntee/ *comb. form* **1** one-hundredth, esp. of a unit in the metric system (*centigram*; *centiliter*). **2** hundred. ¶ Abbr.: **c**. [L *centum* hundred]

cen•ti•grade /séntigrayd/ *adj.* **1** = CELSIUS. **2** having a scale of a hundred degrees. [F f. L *centum* hundred + *gradus* step]
► In sense 1 *Celsius* is usually preferred in technical use.

cen•ti•gram /séntigram/ *n.* a metric unit of mass, equal to one-hundredth of a gram.

cen•ti•li•ter /séntileetər/ *n.* a metric unit of capacity, equal to one-hundredth of a liter.

cen•time /soNteém/ *n.* **1** a monetary unit valued at one-hundredth of a franc. **2** a coin of this value. [F f. L *centum* a hundred]

cen•ti•me•ter /séntimeetər/ *n.* a metric unit of length, equal to one-hundredth of a meter.

cen•ti•me•ter-gram-sec•ond system *n.* a system of measurement using the centimeter, the gram, and the second as basic units of length, mass, and time. ¶ Abbr.: **cgs system**.

cen•ti•pede /séntipeed/ *n.* any arthropod of the class Chilopoda, with a wormlike body of many segments each with a pair of legs. [F *centipède* or L *centipeda* f. *centum* hundred + *pes pedis* foot]

cen•to /séntō/ *n.* (*pl.* **-tos**) a composition made up of quotations from other authors. [L, = patchwork garment]

cen•tral /séntrəl/ *adj.* **1** of, at, or forming the center. **2** from the center. **3** chief; essential; most important. □□ **cen•tral•i•ty** /–trálitee/ *n.* **cen•tral•ly** *adv.* [F *central* or L *centralis* f. *centrum* CENTER]

centipede

Cen•tral A•mer•i•ca *n.* the isthmus joining N. and S. America, usually comprising the countries from Guatemala and Belize south to Panama.

cen•tral bank *n.* a national bank that provides financial services for its country's government and commercial banking system, as well as implementing the government's monetary policy and issuing currency.

cen•tral heat•ing *n.* a method of warming a building by pipes, radiators, etc., fed from a central source of heat.

cen•tral•ism /séntrəlizəm/ *n.* a system that centralizes (esp. an administration) (see also DEMOCRATIC CENTRALISM). □□ **cen•tral•ist** *n.*

cen•tral•ize /séntrəliz/ *v.* **1** *tr. & intr.* bring or come to a center. **2** *tr.* **a** concentrate (administration) at a single center. **b** subject (a government) to this system. □□ **cen•tral•i•za•tion** *n.*

cen•tral nerv•ous sys•tem *n. Anat.* the complex of nerve tissues that controls the activities of the body, in vertebrates the brain and spinal cord.

cen•tral proc•es•sor *n.* (also **cen•tral proc•es•sing u•nit**) the principal operating part of a computer.

cen•tre *Brit.* var. of CENTER.

-centric /séntrik/ *comb. form* forming adjectives with the sense 'having a (specified) center' (*anthropocentric*; *egocentric*). [after *concentric*, etc., f. Gk *kentrikos*: see CENTER]

cen•trif•u•gal /sentrífyəgəl, –trífə–/ *adj.* moving or tending to move from a center (cf. CENTRIPETAL). □□ **cen•trif•u•gal•ly** *adv.* [mod.L *centrifugus* f. L *centrum* center + *fugere* flee]

cen•trif•u•gal force *n.* an apparent outward force that acts on a body moving around a center, arising from the body's inertia.

cen•tri•fuge /séntrifyooj/ *n. & v.* • *n.* a machine with a rapidly rotating device designed to separate liquids from solids or other liquids (e.g., cream from milk). • *v. tr.* **1** subject to the action of a centrifuge. **2** separate by centrifuge. □□ **cen•trif•u•ga•tion** /–fyəgáyshən, –fə–/ *n.*

cen•tri•ole /séntreeōl/ *n. Biol.* a minute organelle usu. within a centrosome involved esp. in the development of spindles in cell division. [med.L *centriolum* dimin. of *centrum* center]

cen•trip•e•tal /sentrípit'l/ *adj.* moving or tending to move toward a center (cf. CENTRIFUGAL). □□ **cen•trip•e•tal•ly** *adv.* [mod.L *centripetus* f. L *centrum* center + *petere* seek]

cen•trip•e•tal force *n.* the force acting on a body causing it to move about a center.

cen•trist /séntrist/ *n. Polit.* often *derog.* a person who holds moderate views. □□ **cen•trism** *n.*

cen•tro•mere /séntrəmeer/ *n. Biol.* the point on a chromosome to which the spindle is attached during cell division. [L *centrum* center + Gk *meros* part]

cen•tro•some /séntrəsōm/ *n. Biol.* a distinct part of the cytoplasm in a cell, usu. near the nucleus, that contains the centriole. [G *Centrosoma* f. L *centrum* center + Gk *sōma* body]

cen•tu•ple /séntəpəl, séntyə–/ *n., adj., & v.* • *n.* a hundredfold amount. • *adj.* increased a hundredfold. • *v. tr.* multiply by a hundred or by a large amount. [F *centuple* or eccl.L *centuplus*, *centuplex* f. L *centum* hundred]

cen•tu•ri•on /sentyŏoreeən, –tyŏor–/ *n.* the commander of a century in the ancient Roman army. [ME f. L *centurio –onis* (as CENTURY)]

cen•tu•ry /sénchəree/ *n.* (*pl.* **-ries**) **1 a** a period of one hundred years. **b** any of the centuries calculated from the birth of Christ (*twentieth century* = 1901–2000; *fifth century* BC = 500–401 BC). **2 a** a score, etc., of a hundred in a sporting event, esp. a hundred runs by one batsman in cricket. **b** a group of a hundred things. **3 a** a company in the ancient Roman army, orig. of 100 men. **b** an ancient Roman political division for voting. [L *centuria* f. *centum* hundred]
► In modern use often calculated as, e.g., 1900–1999.

cen•tu•ry plant *n.* a plant, *Agave americana*, flowering once in many years and yielding sap from which tequila is distilled. Also called **American aloe**.

CEO *abbr.* CHIEF EXECUTIVE OFFICER.

cep /sep/ *n.* an edible mushroom, *Boletus edulis*, with a stout stalk and brown smooth cap. [F *cèpe* f. Gascon *cep* f. L *cippus* stake]

ce•phal•ic /sifálik/ *adj.* of or in the head. [F *céphalique* f. L *cephalicus* f. Gk *kephalikos* f. *kephalē* head]

-cephalic /sifálik/ *comb. form* = -CEPHALOUS.

ce•phal•ic in•dex *n. Anthropol.* a number expressing the ratio of the maximum breadth of a skull to its maximum length.

ceph•a•lo•pod /séfələpod/ *n.* any mollusk of the class Cephalopoda, having a distinct tentacled head, e.g., octopus, squid, and cuttlefish. [Gk *kephalē* head + *pous podos* foot]

ceph•a•lo•tho•rax /séfəlōtháwraks/ *n.* (*pl.* **-tho•rax•es** or **-tho•ra•ces** /–tháwrəseez/) *Anat.* the fused head and thorax of a spider, crab, or other arthropod.

-cephalous /séfələs/ *comb. form* –headed (*brachycephalous*; *dolichocephalic*). [Gk *kephalē* head]

Ce•pheid /seefeeid, séf–/ *n.* (in full **Cepheid variable**) *Astron.* any of a class of variable stars with a regular cycle of brightness that can be used to measure distances. [L *Cepheus* f. Gk *Kēpheus*, a mythical king whose name was given to a constellation]

ce•ram•ic /sirámik/ *adj. & n.* • *adj.* **1** made of (esp.) clay and permanently hardened by heat (*a ceramic bowl*). **2** of or relating to ceramics (*the ceramic arts*). • *n.* **1** a ceramic article or product. **2** a substance, esp. clay, used to make ceramic articles. [Gk *keramikos* f. *keramos* pottery]

ce•ram•ics /sirámiks/ *n.pl.* **1** ceramic products collectively (*exhibition of ceramics*). **2** (usu. treated as *sing.*) the art of making ceramic articles.

ce•ram•ist /sirámist, –sérə/ *n.* a person who makes ceramics.

ce•ras•tes /sirásteez/ *n.* any viper of the genus *Cerastes*, esp. *C. cerastes*, having a sharp, upright spike over each eye and moving forward in a lateral motion. [L f. Gk *kerastēs* f. *keras* horn]

ce•ras•ti•um /sirásteeəm/ *n.* any plant of the genus *Cerastium*, with white flowers and often horn-shaped capsules. [mod.L f. Gk *kerastes* horned f. *keras* horn]

cere /seer/ *n.* a waxy fleshy covering at the base of the upper beak in some birds. [L *cera* wax]

ce•re•al /seereeəl/ *n. & adj.* • *n.* **1** (usu. in *pl.*) **a** any kind of grain used for food. **b** any grass producing this, e.g., wheat, corn, rye, etc. **2** a breakfast food made from roasted grain, typically eaten with milk. • *adj.* of edible grain or products of it. [L *cerealis* f. *Ceres* goddess of agriculture]

cer·e·bel·lum /séribéləm/ n. (pl. **cer·e·bel·lums** or **cer·e·bel·la** /-lə/) the part of the brain at the back of the skull in vertebrates, which coordinates and regulates muscular activity. □□ **cer·e·bel·lar** adj. [L dimin. of CEREBRUM]

ce·re·bral /séribrəl, sərée´-/ adj. **1** of the brain. **2** intellectual rather than emotional. **3** = RETROFLEX. □□ **ce·re·bral·ly** adv. [L cerebrum brain]

PRONUNCIATION TIP   **cerebral**

The older, British English pronunciation of this word places the stress on the first syllable ("SER-e-brul"). Placing the stress on the second syllable with a "long e" ("seh-REE-brul") is common in American English.

ce·re·bral hem·i·sphere n. each of the two halves of the vertebrate cerebrum.

ce·re·bral pal·sy n. Med. a condition marked by impaired muscle coordination and/or other disabilities, typically caused by damage to the brain before or at birth.

cer·e·bra·tion /séribráyshən/ n. working of the brain. □□ **cer·e·brate** /-brayt/ v.intr.

cerebro- /séribrō, sərée´-/ comb. form brain (cerebrospinal).

ce·re·bro·spi·nal /séribrōspínəl, sərée-/ adj. of the brain and spine.

ce·re·bro·vas·cu·lar /séribrōváskyələr, sərée-/ adj. of the brain and its blood vessels.

ce·re·brum /séribrəm, sərée-/ n. (pl. **ce·re·brums** or **ce·re·bra** /-brə/) the principal part of the brain in vertebrates, located in the front area of the skull, which integrates complex sensory and neural functions. [L, = brain]

cere·cloth /séerklawth, -kloth/ n. hist. waxed cloth used as a waterproof covering or (esp.) as a shroud. [earlier cered cloth f. cere to wax f. L cerare f. cera wax]

cere·ment /séermənt/ n. (usu. in pl.) literary graveclothes; cerecloth. [first used by Shakesp. in Hamlet (1602): app. f. CERECLOTH]

cer·e·mo·ni·al /sérimôneeəl/ adj. & n. • adj. **1** with or concerning ritual or ceremony. **2** formal (a ceremonial bow). • n. **1** a system of rites, etc., to be used esp. at a formal or religious occasion. **2** the formalities or behavior proper to any occasion (the ceremonial of a presidential appearance). **3** RC Ch. a book containing an order of ritual. □□ **cer·e·mo·ni·al·ism** n. **cer·e·mo·ni·al·ist** n. **cer·e·mo·ni·al·ly** adv. [LL caerimonialis (as CEREMONY)]

cer·e·mo·ni·ous /sérimôneeəs/ adj. **1** excessively polite; punctilious. **2** having or showing a fondness for ritualistic observance or formality. □□ **cer·e·mo·ni·ous·ly** adv. **cer·e·mo·ni·ous·ness** n. [F cérémonieux or LL caerimoniosus (as CEREMONY)]

cer·e·mo·ny /sérimônee/ n. (pl. **·nies**) **1** a formal religious or public occasion, esp. celebrating a particular event or anniversary. **2** formalities, esp. of an empty or ritualistic kind (ceremony of exchanging compliments). **3** excessively polite behavior (bowed low with great ceremony). □ **stand on ceremony** insist on the observance of formalities. **without ceremony** informally. [ME f. OF ceremonie or L caerimonia religious worship]

Ce·ren·kov ra·di·a·tion /chiréngkawf/ n. (also **Che·ren·kov**) the electromagnetic radiation emitted by particles moving in a medium at speeds faster than that of light in the same medium. [P. A. Cherenkov, Russian physicist b. 1904]

cer·e·sin /sérisin/ n. a hard, whitish wax used with or instead of beeswax. [mod.L ceres f. L cera wax + -IN]

ce·rise /sərées, -réez/ adj. & n. • adj. of a light, clear red. • n. this color. [F, = CHERRY]

ce·ri·um /séereeəm/ n. Chem. a silvery metallic element of the lanthanide series occurring naturally in various minerals and used in the manufacture of lighter flints. ¶ Symb.: **Ce**. [named after the asteroid Ceres, discovered (1801) about the same time as this]

cer·met /sórmet/ n. a heat-resistant material made of ceramic and sintered metal. [ceramic + metal]

CERN /sərn/ abbr. European Organization for Nuclear Research. [F Conseil Européen pour la Recherche Nucléaire, its former title]

cero- /séerō/ comb. form wax (cf. CEROGRAPHY, CEROPLASTIC). [L cera or Gk kēros wax]

ce·rog·ra·phy /seerógrəfee/ n. the technique of engraving or designing on or with wax.

ce·ro·plas·tic /séerōplástik/ adj. **1** modeled in wax. **2** of or concerning wax modeling.

cert. /sərt/ abbr. **1** a certificate. **2** certified.

cer·tain /sórt'n/ adj. & pron. • adj. **1 a** (often foll. by of, or that + clause) confident; convinced (certain that I put it here). **b** (often foll. by that + clause) indisputable; known for sure (it is certain that he is guilty). **2** (often foll. by to + infin.) **a** that may be relied on to happen (it is certain to rain). **b** destined (certain to become a star). **3** definite; unfailing; reliable (a certain indication of the coming storm; his touch is certain). **4** (of a person, place, etc.) that might be specified, but is not (a certain lady; of a certain age). **5** some though not much (a certain reluctance). **6** (of a person, place, etc.) existing, though probably unknown to the reader or hearer (a certain John Smith). • pron. (as pl.) some but not all (certain of them were wounded). □ **for certain** without doubt. **make certain** = make sure (see SURE). [ME f. OF ult. f. L certus settled]

SPELLING TIP   **certain**

Words Spelled with ai and ia. Use a before i when sounded as in certain, villain, captain, chieftain, Britain, and mountain. Use i before a when sounded as "UH" or "YUH," as in civilian, familiar, financial, peculiar, partial, brilliant, genial, beneficial, and auxiliary. Also use i before a when the letters are pronounced separately, as in median, genial, and guardian.

cer·tain·ly /sórt'nlee/ adv. **1** undoubtedly; definitely. **2** confidently. **3** (in affirmative answer to a question or command) yes; by all means.

cer·tain·ty /sórt'ntee/ n. (pl. **·ties**) **1 a** an undoubted fact. **b** a certain prospect (his return is a certainty). **2** (often foll. by of, or that + clause) an absolute conviction (has a certainty of his own worth). **3** (often foll. by to + infin.) a thing or person that may be relied on (a certainty to win the Derby). □ **for a certainty** beyond the possibility of doubt. [ME f. AF certainté, OF -eté (as CERTAIN)]

cer·ti·fi·a·ble /sórtifíəbəl/ adj. **1** able or needing to be certified. **2** colloq. insane.

cer·tif·i·cate n. & v. • n. /sərtífikət/ a formal document attesting a fact, esp. birth, marriage, death, a medical condition, a level of achievement, a fulfillment of requirements, ownership of shares, etc. • v.tr. /sərtífikayt/ (esp. as **certificated** adj.) provide with or license or attest by a certificate. □□ **cer·ti·fi·ca·tion** /sórtifikáyshən/ n. [F certificat or med.L certificatum f. certificare: see CERTIFY]

cer·tif·i·cate of de·pos·it n. a certificate issued by a bank to a depositor, stating the amount of money on deposit, usu. at a specified rate of interest and for a specified time period.

cer·ti·fied check n. a check the validity of which is guaranteed by a bank.

cer·ti·fied mail n. a postal service in which the dispatch and receipt of a letter or package are recorded.

cer·ti·fied milk n. milk guaranteed free from the tuberculosis bacillus.

cer·ti·fied pub·lic ac·count·ant n. a member of an officially accredited professional body of accountants.

cer·ti·fy /sórtifī/ v.tr. (**·fies, ·fied**) **1** make a formal statement of; attest; attest to (certified that he had witnessed the crime). **2** declare by certificate (that a person is qualified or competent) (certified as a trained bookkeeper). **3** officially declare insane (he should be certified). [ME f. OF certifier f. med.L certificare f. L certus certain]

cer·ti·o·ra·ri /sórsheeəráiree, -raírī/ n. Law a writ from a higher court requesting the records of a case tried in a lower court. [LL passive of certiorare inform f. certior compar. of certus certain]

cer·ti·tude /sórtitōōd, -tyōōd/ n. a feeling of absolute certainty or conviction. [ME f. LL certitudo f. certus certain]

ce·ru·le·an /sərōōleeən/ adj. & n. literary • adj. deep blue like a clear sky. • n. this color. [L caeruleus sky blue f. caelum sky]

ce·ru·men /sərōōmen/ n. the yellow waxy substance in the outer ear. □□ **ce·ru·mi·nous** adj. [mod.L f. L cera wax]

ce·ruse /sirōōs, séerōōs/ n. white lead. [ME f. OF f. L cerussa, perh. f. Gk kēros wax]

cer·ve·lat /sórvəlaa, -lat/ n. a kind of smoked pork or beef sausage. [obs. F f. It. cervellata]

cer·vi·cal /sórvikəl/ adj. Anat. **1** of or relating to the neck (cervical vertebrae). **2** of or relating to the cervix. [F cervical or mod.L cervicalis f. L cervix -icis neck]

cer·vi·cal screen·ing n. examination of a large number of apparently healthy women for cervical cancer.

cer·vi·cal smear n. a specimen of cellular material from the neck of the uterus for detection of cancer (see also PAP SMEAR).

cer·vine /sórvin/ adj. of or like a deer. [L cervinus f. cervus deer]

cer·vix /sórviks/ n. (pl. **cer·vices** /-viseez/ or **cer·vix·es**) Anat. **1** the neck. **2** any necklike structure, esp. the neck of the womb. [L]

Ce·sar·e·an /sizáireeən/ adj. & n. (also **Ce·sar·i·an, Cae·sar·e·an, Cae·sar·i·an**) • adj. (of a birth) effected by cesarean section. • n. a cesarean section. [L Caesarianus]

ce·sar·e·an sec·tion n. (also **C-sec·tion**) an operation for delivering a child by cutting through the wall of the abdomen (Julius Caesar supposedly having been born this way).

ce·sar·e·vitch /sizáirivich, -záar-/ n. hist. the eldest son of the emperor of Russia (cf. TSAREVICH). [Russ. tsesarevich]

ce·si·um /séezeeəm/ n. (Brit. **cae·si·um**) a soft, silver-white element of the alkali metal group, occurring naturally in a number of minerals, and used in photoelectric cells. ¶ Symb.: **cs**. [L caesius]

ce·si·um clock n. an atomic clock that uses cesium.

cess[1] /ses/ n. (also **sess**) Sc., Ir., & Ind., etc., a tax; a levy. [properly sess for obs. assess n.: see ASSESS]

cess[2] /ses/ n. Ir. □ **bad cess to** may evil befall (bad cess to their clan). [perh. f. CESS[1]]

ces·sa·tion /sesáyshən/ n. 1 a ceasing (*cessation of the truce*). 2 a pause (*resumed fighting after the cessation*). [ME f. L *cessatio* f. *cessare* CEASE]

ces·sion /séshən/ n. 1 (often foll. by *of*) the ceding or giving up (of rights, property, and esp. of territory by a nation). 2 the territory, etc., so ceded. [ME f. OF *cession* or L *cessio* f. *cedere* cess- go away]

ces·sion·ar·y /séshəneree/ n. (pl. ·ies) *Law* an assignee.

cess·pit /séspit/ n. 1 a pit for the disposal of refuse. 2 = CESSPOOL. [*cess* in CESSPOOL + PIT¹]

cess·pool /séspool/ n. 1 an underground container for the temporary storage of liquid waste or sewage. 2 a center of corruption, depravity, etc. [perh. alt., after POOL¹, f. earlier *cesperalle*, f. *suspiral* vent, water pipe, f. OF *souspirail* air-hole f. L *suspirare* breathe up, sigh (as SUB-, *spirare* breathe)]

ces·tode /séstōd/ n. (also **ces·toid** /séstoyd/) any flatworm of the class Cestoda, including tapeworms. [L *cestus* f. Gk *kestos* girdle]

ce·ta·ce·an /sitáyshən/ n. & adj. ● n. any marine mammal of the order Cetacea with streamlined hairless body and dorsal blowhole for breathing, including whales, dolphins, and porpoises. ● adj. of cetaceans. □□ **ce·ta·ceous** /-táyshəs/ adj. [mod.L *Cetacea* f. L *cetus* f. Gk *kētos* whale]

ce·tane /séetayn/ n. *Chem.* a colorless liquid hydrocarbon of the alkane series used in standardizing ratings of diesel fuel. [f. SPERMACETI after *methane*, etc.]

ce·tane num·ber n. a measure of the ignition properties of diesel fuel.

ce·te·ris pa·ri·bus /sétəris páribəs, káytəres paáriboos/ adv. other things being equal. [L]

Cey·lon moss /silón, say-/ n. a red seaweed, *Gracilaria lichenoides*, from E. India. [*Ceylon*, now Sri Lanka]

Cf *symb. Chem.* the element californium.

cf. *abbr.* compare. [L *confer* imper. of *conferre* compare]

c.f. *abbr.* 1 carried forward. 2 *Baseball* center fielder.

CFA *abbr.* chartered financial analyst.

CFC *abbr. Chem.* chlorofluorocarbon, any of various usu. gaseous compounds of carbon, hydrogen, chlorine, and fluorine, used in refrigerants, aerosol propellants, etc., and thought to be harmful to the ozone layer in the earth's atmosphere.

cfm *abbr.* cubic feet per minute.

cfs *abbr.* cubic feet per second.

cg *abbr.* centigram(s).

cgs *abbr.* centimeter-gram-second.

ch. *abbr.* 1 church. 2 chapter. 3 *Chess* check.

c.h. *abbr.* (also **C.H.**) 1 clearing house. 2 courthouse.

cha var. of CHAR³.

Cha·blis /shablée, sháblee/ n. (pl. same /–leez/) a type of dry white wine. [*Chablis* in E. France]

cha-cha /cháachaa/ (also **cha-cha-cha** /cháachaachaá/) n. & v. ● n. 1 a ballroom dance with a Latin-American rhythm. 2 music for or in the rhythm of a cha-cha. ● v. intr. (**cha-chas, cha-chaed** /–chaad/, **cha-cha·ing** /–chaa-ing/) dance the cha-cha. [Amer. Sp.]

cha·conne /shakáwn, –kón/ n. *Mus.* 1 a musical form consisting of variations on a ground bass. b a musical composition in this style. 2 *hist.* a dance performed to this music. [F f. Sp. *chacona*]

chad·or /chaadáwr/ n. (also **chad·ar, chud·dar**) a large piece of cloth worn in some countries by Muslim women, wrapped around the body to leave only the face exposed. [Pers. *chador*, Hindi *chador*]

chae·tog·nath /keétəgnath/ n. any dart-shaped worm of the phylum Chaetognatha, usu. living among marine plankton, and having a head with external thorny teeth. [mod.L *Chaetognatha* f. Gk *khaitē* long hair + *gnathos* jaw]

chafe /chayf/ v. & n. ● v. 1 tr. & intr. make or become sore or damaged by rubbing. 2 tr. rub (esp. the skin to restore warmth or sensation). 3 tr. & intr. make or become annoyed; fret (*was chafed by the delay*). ● n. 1 a an act of chafing. b a sore resulting from this. 2 a state of annoyance. [ME f. OF *chaufer* ult. f. L *calefacere* f. *calēre* be hot + *facere* make]

chaf·er /cháyfər/ n. any of various large, slow-moving beetles of the family Scarabaeidae, esp. the cockchafer. [OE *ceafor, cefer* f. Gmc]

chaff /chaf/ n. & v. ● n. 1 the husks of grain or other seed separated by winnowing or threshing. 2 chopped hay and straw used as fodder. 3 lighthearted joking; banter. 4 worthless things; rubbish. 5 strips of metal foil released in the atmosphere to obstruct radar detection. ● v. tr. 1 tease; banter. 2 chop (straw, etc.). □ **separate the wheat from the chaff** distinguish good from bad. □□ **chaff·y** adj. [OE *ceaf, cæf* prob. f. Gmc: sense 3 of n. & 1 of v. perh. f. CHAFE]

chaf·fer /cháfər/ v. & n. ● v. intr. haggle; bargain. ● n. bargaining; haggling. □□ **chaf·fer·er** n. [ME f. OE *ceapfaru* f. *ceap* bargain + *faru* journey]

chaf·finch /cháfinch/ n. a common European finch, *Fringilla coelebs*, the male of which has a blue-gray head with pinkish cheeks. [OE *ceaffinc*: see CHAFF, FINCH]

chaf·ing dish /cháyfing/ n. 1 a cooking pot with an outer pan of hot water, used for keeping food warm. 2 a dish with an alcohol lamp, etc., for cooking at table. [obs. sense of CHAFE = warm]

Cha·gas' dis·ease /shaágəs/ (also **Cha·gas's dis·ease**) n. a kind of

---

sleeping sickness caused by a protozoan transmitted by bloodsucking bugs. [C. *Chagas*, Braz. physician d. 1934]

cha·grin /shəgrin/ n. & v. ● n. acute vexation or mortification. ● v. tr. affect with chagrin. [F *chagrin(er)*, of uncert. orig.]

chain /chayn/ n. & v. ● n. 1 a a connected flexible series of esp. metal links as decoration or for a practical purpose. b something resembling this (*formed a human chain*). 2 (in pl.) a fetters used to confine prisoners. b any restraining force. 3 a sequence, series, or set (*chain of events; mountain chain*). 4 a group of associated hotels, shops, newspapers, etc. 5 esp. *Brit.* a badge of office in the form of a chain worn around the neck (*mayoral chain*). 6 a jointed measuring line consisting of linked metal rods. b its length (66 or 100 ft.). 7 *Chem.* a group of (esp. carbon) atoms bonded in sequence in a molecule. 8 a figure in a quadrille or similar dance. 9 (in pl.) *Naut.* channels (see CHANNEL²). 10 (also **chain shot**) *hist.* two cannonballs or half balls joined by a chain and used in sea battles for bringing down a mast, etc. ● v. tr. 1 (often foll. by *up*) secure or confine with a chain. 2 confine or restrict (a person) (*is chained to the office*). [ME f. OF *cha(e)ine* f. L *catena*]

chain bridge n. a suspension bridge supported by chains rather than cables.

chain drive n. a mechanism in which power is transmitted from an engine by means of a moving endless chain.

chain gang n. a team of convicts chained together while working outside the prison.

chain gear n. a gear transmitting motion by means of an endless chain.

chain let·ter n. one of a sequence of letters, the recipient of which is requested to send copies to a specific number of other people.

chain-link adj. made of wire in a diamond-shaped mesh (*chain-link fencing*).

chain mail n. armor made of interlaced rings.

chain re·ac·tion n. 1 *Physics* a self-sustaining nuclear reaction, esp. one in which a neutron from a fission reaction initiates a series of these reactions. 2 *Chem.* a self-sustaining molecular reaction in which intermediate products initiate further reactions. 3 a series of events, each caused by the previous one.

chain saw n. a motor-driven saw with teeth on an endless chain.

chain-smok·er n. a person who smokes continually, esp. one who lights a cigarette, etc., from the stub of the last one smoked.

chain stitch n. an ornamental embroidery or crochet stitch resembling chains.

chain store n. one of a series of stores owned by one company and selling the same kind of goods.

chain-wale n. (also **chain wale**) = CHANNEL².

chain·wheel /cháynwheel, –weel/ n. a wheel transmitting power by a chain fitted to its edges; a sprocket.

chair /chair/ n. & v. ● n. 1 a separate seat for one person, of various forms, usu. having a back and four legs. 2 a a professorship (*offered the chair in physics*). b a seat of authority, esp. on a board of directors. c *Brit.* a mayoralty. 3 a a chairperson. b the seat or office of a chairperson (*will you take the chair?; I'm in the chair*). 4 = ELECTRIC CHAIR. 5 esp. *Brit.* an iron or steel socket holding a railroad rail in place. 6 *hist.* = sedan chair. ● v. tr. 1 act as chairperson of or preside over (a meeting). 2 *Brit.* carry (a person) aloft in a chair or in a sitting position, in triumph. 3 install in a chair, esp. as a position of authority. □ **take a chair** sit down. [ME f. AF *chaere*, OF *chaiere* f. L *cathedra* f. Gk *kathedra*: see CATHEDRAL]

chair bed n. a chair that unfolds into a bed.

chair·borne /cháirbawrn/ adj. 1 (of an administrator) not active. 2 (of military personnel) assigned to a desk job rather than field duty.

chair car n. a railroad car with chairs instead of long seats; a parlor car.

chair·la·dy /cháirlaydee/ n. (pl. ·dies) = chairwoman (see CHAIRMAN).

chair·lift /cháirlift/ n. a series of chairs on an endless cable for carrying passengers up and down a mountain, etc.

chair·man /cháirmən/ n. (pl. ·men; fem. **chair·wom·an**, pl. ·wom·en) 1 a person chosen to preside over a meeting. 2 the permanent president of a committee, a board of directors, (*Brit.*) a firm, etc. 3 the master of ceremonies at an entertainment, etc. 4 *hist.* either of two sedan bearers. □□ **chair·man·ship** n.

chair·per·son /cháirpərsən/ n. a chairman or chairwoman (used as a neutral alternative).

chaise /shayz/ n. 1 esp. *hist.* a horse-drawn carriage for one or two persons, esp. one with an open top and two wheels. 2 = post chaise (see POST²). [F var. of *chaire*, formed as CHAIR]

chaise longue /sháyz lóng, shéz/ n. a reclining chair with a lengthened seat forming a leg rest. [F, lit. long chair]

cha·la·za /kəláyzə/ n. (pl. **cha·la·zae** /–zee/ or **cha·la·zas**) each of two twisted membranous strips joining the yolk to the ends of an egg. [mod.L f. Gk, = hailstone]

chal•ced•o•ny /kalséd'nee/ n. a type of quartz occurring in several different forms, e.g., onyx, agate, tiger's eye, etc. □□ **chal•ce•don•ic** /kálsidónik/ adj. [ME f. L c(h)alcedonius f. Gk khalkēdōn]

chal•co•lith•ic /kálkəlíthik/ adj. Archaeol. of a prehistoric period in which both stone and bronze implements were used. [Gk khalkos copper + lithos stone]

chal•co•py•rite /kálkəpíɾīt/ n. a yellow mineral of copper-iron sulfide, which is the principal ore of copper. [Gk khalkos copper + PYRITE]

Chal•de•an /kaldéeən/ n. & adj. • n. **1 a** a native of ancient Chaldea or Babylonia. **b** the language of the Chaldeans. **2** an astrologer. **3** a member of the Uniat (formerly Nestorian) sect in Iran, etc. • adj. **1** of or relating to ancient Chaldea or its people or language. **2** of or relating to astrology. **3** of or relating to the Uniat sect. [L Chaldaeus f. Gk Khaldaios f. Assyr. Kaldu]

Chal•dee /kaldée/ n. **1** the language of the Chaldeans. **2** a native of ancient Chaldea. **3** the Aramaic language as used in Old Testament books. [ME, repr. L Chaldaei (pl.) (as CHALDEAN)]

cha•let /shaláy, shálay/ n. **1** a small suburban house or bungalow, esp. with an overhanging roof. **2** a small, usu. wooden hut or house at a ski resort, beach, etc. **3** a Swiss cowherd's hut, or wooden cottage, with overhanging eaves. [Swiss F]

chal•ice /chális/ n. **1** a wine cup used in the Communion service. **2** literary a goblet. [ME f. OF f. L calix –icis cup]

chalk /chawk/ n. & v. • n. **1** a white, soft, earthy limestone (calcium carbonate) formed from the skeletal remains of sea creatures. **2 a** a similar substance (calcium sulfate), sometimes colored, used for writing or drawing. **b** a piece of this (a box of chalk). **3** a series of strata consisting mainly of chalk. **4** = FRENCH CHALK. • v.tr. **1** rub, mark, draw, or write with chalk. **2** (foll. by up) **a** write or record with chalk. **b** register (a success, etc.). **c** Brit. charge (to an account). □ **by a long chalk** Brit. by far (from the use of chalk to mark the score in games). **chalk out** sketch or plan a thing to be accomplished. **chalk something up** ascribe something to a particular cause (chalked his defeat up to lack of experience). [OE cealc ult. f. WG f. L CALX]

chalk•board /cháwkbawrd/ n. = BLACKBOARD.

chalk•ie /cháwkee/ n. Austral. colloq. a schoolteacher.

chalk•stone /cháwkstōn/ n. a concretion of urates like chalk in tissues and joints, esp. of hands and feet.

chalk stripe n. a pattern of thin white stripes on a dark background.

chalk-striped adj. having chalk stripes.

chalk•y /cháwkee/ adj. (**chalk•i•er**, **chalk•i•est**) **1 a** abounding in chalk. **b** white as chalk. **2** like or containing chalk stones. □□ **chalk•i•ness** n.

chal•lenge /chálinj/ n. & v. • n. **1 a** a summons to take part in a contest or a trial of strength, etc., esp. to a duel. **b** a summons to prove or justify something. **2** a demanding or difficult task (rose to the challenge of the new job). **3** an act of disputing or denying a statement, claim, etc. **4** Law an objection made to seating a jury member. **5** a call to respond, esp. a sentry's call for a password, etc. **6** an invitation to a sporting contest, esp. one issued to a reigning champion. **7** Med. a test of immunity after immunization treatment. • v.tr. **1** (often foll. by to + infin.) **a** invite to take part in a contest, game, debate, duel, etc. **b** invite to prove or justify something. **2** dispute; deny (I challenge that remark). **3 a** stretch; stimulate (challenges him to produce his best). **b** (as **challenging** adj.) demanding; stimulating; difficult. **4** (of a sentry) call to respond. **5** claim (attention, etc.). **6** Law object to (a jury member, evidence, etc.). **7** Med. test by a challenge. □□ **chal•lenge•a•ble** adj. **chal•leng•er** n. [ME f. OF c(h)alenge, c(h)alenger f. L calumnia calumniari calumny]

chal•lis /shálee/ n. a lightweight, soft clothing fabric. [perh. f. a surname]

cha•lyb•e•ate /kəlíbeeət/ adj. (of mineral water, etc.) impregnated with iron salts. [mod.L chalybeatus f. L chalybs f. Gk khalups –ubos steel]

cham•ae•phyte /kámifit/ n. a plant whose buds are on or near the ground. [Gk khamai on the ground + –PHYTE]

cham•ber /cháymbər/ n. **1 a** a hall used by a legislative or judicial body. **b** the body that meets in it. **c** any of the houses of a legislature (the House chamber). **2** (in pl.) a judge's room used for hearing cases not needing to be taken in court. **3** poet. or archaic a room, esp. a bedroom. **4** Mus. (attrib.) of or for a small group of instruments (chamber orchestra; chamber music). **5** an enclosed space in machinery, etc. (esp. the part of a gun bore that contains the charge). **6 a** a cavity in a plant or in the body of an animal. **b** a compartment in a structure. **7** = CHAMBER POT. [ME f. OF chambre f. L CAMERA]

cham•bered /cháymbərd/ adj. (of a tomb) containing a burial chamber.

cham•ber•lain /cháymbərlin/ n. **1** an officer managing the household of a sovereign or a great noble. **2** Brit. the treasurer of a corporation, etc. □□ **cham•ber•lain•ship** n. [ME f. OF chamberlain, etc., f. Frank. f. L camera CAMERA]

cham•ber•maid /cháymbərmayd/ n. **1** a housemaid at a hotel, etc. **2** a housemaid.

cham•ber of com•merce n. a local association to promote the interests of the business community in a particular place.

cham•ber of hor•rors n. a exhibition containing gruesome objects or scenes (orig. a room of criminals, etc., in Madame Tussaud's waxworks).

cham•ber pot n. a receptacle for urine, etc., used in a bedroom.

Cham•ber•tin /shoNbertáN/ n. a high-quality, dry, red wine. [Gevrey Chambertin region in E. France]

cham•bray /shámbray/ n. a cotton, silk, or linen gingham cloth with a white weft and a colored warp. [irreg. f. Cambrai: see CAMBRIC]

cha•me•le•on /kəmée'lyən/ n. **1** any of a family of small lizards having grasping tails, long tongues, protruding eyes, and the power of changing color. **2** a variable or inconstant person. □□ **cha•me•le•on•ic** /–leeónik/ adj. [ME f. L f. Gk khamaileōn f. khamai on the ground + leōn lion]

cham•fer /chámfər/ v. & n. • v.tr. bevel symmetrically (a right-angled edge or corner). • n. a beveled surface at an edge or corner. [backform. f. chamfering f. F chamfrain f. chant edge (CANT²) + fraint broken f. OF fraindre break f. L frangere]

cham•ois /shámee/ n. (pl. same /–eez/) **1** an agile goat antelope, Rupicapra rupicapra, native to the mountains of Europe and Asia. **2** (in full **chamois leather**) **a** a soft pliable leather from sheep, goats, deer, etc. **b** a piece of this for polishing, etc. [F: cf. Gallo-Roman camox]

cham•o•mile /káməmil, –meel/ n. (also **cam•o•mile**) any aromatic plant of the genus Anthemis or Matricaria, with daisylike flowers, used medicinally and as a tea. [ME f. OF camomille f. LL camomilla or chamomilla f. Gk khamaimēlon earth apple (from the apple smell of its flowers)]

champ¹ /champ/ v. & n. • v. **1** tr. & intr. munch or chew noisily. **2** tr. (of a horse, etc.) work (the bit) noisily between the teeth. **3** intr. fret with impatience (is champing to be away). • n. a chewing noise or motion. □ **champ at the bit** be restlessly impatient. [prob. imit.]

champ² /champ/ n. sl. a champion. [abbr.]

cham•pagne /shampáyn/ n. **1 a** a white sparkling wine from Champagne. **b** a similar wine from elsewhere. **2** a pale cream or straw color. [Champagne, former province in E. France] ▶Use in sense 1 b is technically incorrect.

cham•paign /shampáyn/ n. literary **1** open country. **2** an expanse of open country. [ME f. OF champagne f. LL campania: cf. CAMPAIGN]

cham•pers /shámpɔrz/ n. Brit. sl. champagne.

cham•per•ty /chámpərtee/ n. (pl. **-ties**) Law an illegal agreement in which a person not naturally interested in a lawsuit finances it with a view to sharing the disputed property. □□ **cham•per•tous** adj. [ME f. AF champartie f. OF champart feudal lord's share of produce, f. L campus field + pars part]

cham•pi•on /chámpeeən/ n. & v. • n. **1** (often attrib.) a person (esp. in a sport or game), animal, plant, etc., that has defeated or surpassed all rivals in a competition, etc. **2 a** a person who fights or argues for a cause or on behalf of another person. **b** hist. a knight, etc., who fought in single combat on behalf of a king, etc. • v.tr. support the cause of; defend; argue in favor of. [ME f. OF f. med.L campio –onis fighter f. L campus field]

cham•pi•on•ship /chámpeeənship/ n. **1** (often in pl.) a contest for the position of champion in a sport, etc. **2** the position of champion on over all rivals. **3** the advocacy or defense (of a cause, etc.).

champ•le•vé /shóNləváy/ n. & adj. • n. a type of enamelwork in which hollows made in a metal surface are filled with colored enamels. • adj. of or relating to champlevé (cf. CLOISONNÉ). [F, = raised field]

chance /chans/ n., adj., & v. • n. **1 a** a possibility (just a chance we will catch the train). **b** (often in pl.) probability (the chances are against it). **2** a risk (have to take a chance). **3 a** an undesigned occurrence (just a chance that they met). **b** the absence of design or discoverable cause (here merely because of chance). **4** an opportunity (didn't have a chance to speak to him). **5** the way things happen; fortune; luck (we'll just leave it to chance). **6** (often **Chance**) the course of events regarded as a power; fate (blind Chance rules the universe). • adj. fortuitous; accidental (a chance meeting). • v. **1** tr. colloq. risk (we'll chance it and go). **2** intr. (often foll. by that + clause, or to + infin.) happen without intention (it chanced that I found it; I chanced to find it). □ **by any chance** as it happens; perhaps. **by chance** without design; unintentionally. **chance on** (or **upon**) happen to find, meet, etc. **on the chance** (often foll. by of, or that + clause) in view of the possibility. **stand a chance** have a prospect of success, etc. **take a chance** (or **chances**) behave riskily; risk failure. **take a** (or **one's**) **chance on** (or **with**) consent to take the consequences of; trust to luck. [ME f. AF ch(e)aunce, OF chēance chēoir fall ult. f. L cadere]

chan•cel /chánsəl/ n. the part of a church near the altar, reserved for the clergy, the choir, etc., usu. enclosed by a screen or separated from the nave by steps. [ME f. OF f. L cancelli lattice]

chan•cel•ler•y /chánsələree, chánslə–/ n. (pl. **-ies**) **1 a** the position, office, staff, department, etc., of a chancellor. **b** the official residence of a chancellor. **2** an office attached to an embassy or consulate. [ME f. OF *chancellerie* (as CHANCELLOR)]

chan·cel·lor /chánsələr, chánslər/ *n.* **1** a government official of various kinds; the head of the government in some European countries, e.g., Germany. **2** the president of a chancery court. **3 a** the chief administrator at certain universities. **b** *Brit.* the nonresident honorary head of a university. **4** a bishop's law officer. □□ **chan·cel·lor·ship** *n.* [OE f. AF *c(h)anceler*, OF *–ier* f. LL *cancellarius* porter, secretary, f. *cancelli* lattice]

Chan·cel·lor of the Ex·cheq·uer *n.* the finance minister of the United Kingdom.

chance-med·ley /chánsmédlee/ *n.* (*pl.* **·leys**) **1** *Law* a fight, esp. homicidal, beginning unintentionally. **2** inadvertency. [AF *chance medlee* (see MEDDLE) mixed chance]

chan·cer·y /chánsəree/ *n.* (*pl.* **·ies**) **1** (in full **court of chancery**) a court of equity. **2** the administrative office for a diocese. **3** *Brit.* Law (**Chancery**) the Lord Chancellor's court, a division of the High Court of Justice. **4** *hist.* the records office of an order of knighthood. **5** *hist.* the court of a bishop's chancellor. **6** an office attached to an embassy or consulate. **7** a public record office. □ **in chancery** *sl.* (of a boxer or wrestler) with the head held under the opponent's arm and being pummeled. [ME, contracted f. CHANCELLERY]

chan·cre /shángkər/ *n.* a painless ulcer developing in venereal disease, etc. [F f. L CANCER]

chan·croid /shángkroyd/ *n.* ulceration of lymph nodes in the groin, from venereal disease.

chanc·y /chánsee/ *adj.* (**chanc·i·er**, **chanc·i·est**) subject to chance; uncertain; risky. □□ **chanc·i·ly** *adv.* **chanc·i·ness** *n.*

chan·de·lier /shándəleér/ *n.* an ornamental branched hanging support for several candles or electric lightbulbs. [F (*chandelle* f. as CANDLE)]

chan·dler /chándlər/ *n.* a dealer in candles, oil, soap, paint, groceries, etc. □ **ship** (or **ship's**) **chandler** a dealer in cordage, canvas, etc. [ME f. AF *chaundeler*, OF *chandelier* (as CANDLE)]

chan·dler·y /chándləree/ *n.* **1** the warehouse or store of a chandler. **2** the goods sold by a chandler.

change /chaynj/ *n. & v.* ● *n.* **1 a** the act or an instance of making or becoming different. **b** an alteration or modification (*the change in her expression*). **2 a** money given in exchange for money in larger units or a different currency. **b** money returned as the balance of that given in payment. **c** = SMALL CHANGE. **3** a new experience; variety (*fancied a change; for a change*). **4 a** the substitution of one thing for another; an exchange (*change of scene*). **b** a set of clothes, etc., put on in place of another. **5** (in full **change of life**) *colloq.* the menopause. **6** (usu. in *pl.*) the different orders in which a peal of bells can be rung. **7** (**Change**) (also '**Change**) *Brit. hist.* a place where merchants, etc., met to do business. **8** (of the moon) arrival at a fresh phase, esp. at the new moon. ● *v.* **1** *tr. & intr.* undergo, show, or subject to change; make or become different (*the toupee changed his appearance; changed from an introvert into an extrovert*). **2** *tr.* **a** take or use another instead of; go from one to another (*change one's socks; changed his doctor; changed trains*). **b** (usu. foll. by *for*) give up or get rid of in exchange (*changed the car for a van*). **3** *tr.* **a** give or get change in smaller denominations for (*can you change a ten-dollar bill?*). **b** (foll. by *for*) exchange (a sum of money) for (*changed his dollars for pounds*). **4** *tr. & intr.* put fresh clothes or coverings on (*changed the baby since he was wet; changed into something loose*). **5** *tr.* (often foll. by *with*) give and receive; exchange (*changed places with him*). **6** *intr.* change trains, etc. (*changed at Pennsylvania Station*). **7** *intr.* (of the moon) arrive at a fresh phase, esp. become new. □ **change color** blanch or flush. **change gear** engage a different gear in a vehicle. **change hands 1** pass to a different owner. **2** substitute one hand for another. **change one's mind** adopt a different opinion or plan. **change over** change from one system or situation to another; effect a changeover. **change step** begin to keep step with the opposite leg when marching, etc. **change the subject** begin talking of something different, esp. to avoid embarrassment. **change one's tune 1** voice a different opinion from that expressed previously. **2** change one's style of language or manner, esp. from an insolent to a respectful tone. **ring the changes (on)** vary the ways of expressing, arranging, or doing something. □□ **change·ful** *adj.* **chang·er** *n.* [ME f. AF *chaunge*, OF *change*, *changer* f. LL *cambiare*, L *cambire* barter, prob. of Celt. orig.]

change·a·ble /cháynjəbəl/ *adj.* **1** irregular; inconstant. **2** that can change or be changed. □□ **change·a·bil·i·ty** *n.* **change·a·ble·ness** *n.* **change·a·bly** *adv.* [ME f. OF, formed as CHANGE]

change·less /cháynjlis/ *adj.* unchanging. □□ **change·less·ly** *adv.* **change·less·ness** *n.*

change·ling /cháynjling/ *n.* a child believed to be substituted for another by stealth, esp. an elf child left by fairies.

change of heart *n.* a conversion to a different view.

change of scene (also **change of scen·er·y**) *n.* a variation of surroundings.

change·o·ver /cháynjōvər/ *n.* a change from one system or situation to another.

chan·nel¹ /chánəl/ *n. & v.* ● *n.* **1 a** a length of water wider than a strait, joining two larger areas, esp. seas. **b** (**the Channel**) the English Channel between Britain and France. **2** a medium of communication; an agency for conveying information (*through the usual channels*). **3** *Broadcasting* **a** a band of frequencies used in radio and television transmission, esp. as used by a particular station. **b** a service or station using this. **4** the course in which anything moves; a direction. **5 a** a natural or artificial hollow bed of water. **b** the navigable part of a waterway. **6** a tubular passage for liquid. **7** *Electronics* a lengthwise strip on recording tape, etc. **8** a groove or a flute, esp. in a column. ● *v.tr.* (**chan·neled**, **chan·nel·ing**; esp. *Brit.* **chan·nelled**, **chan·nel·ling**) **1** guide; direct (*channeled them through customs*). **2** form channels in; groove. [ME f. OF *chanel* f. L *canalis* CANAL]

chan·nel² /chánəl/ *n. Naut.* any of the broad thick planks projecting horizontally from a ship's side abreast of the masts, used to widen the basis for the shrouds. [for *chain-wale*: cf. *gunnel* for *gunwale*]

chan·nel·ize /chánəlīz/ *v.tr.* convey in, or as if in, a channel; guide.

chan·son de geste /shoNsáwn də zhést/ *n.* (*pl.* **chan·sons** *pronunc.* same) any of a group of medieval French epic poems. [F, = song of heroic deeds]

chant /chant/ *n. & v.* ● *n.* **1 a** a spoken singsong phrase, esp. one performed in unison by a crowd, etc. **b** a repetitious singsong way of speaking. **2** *Mus.* **a** a short musical passage in two or more phrases used for singing unmetrical words, e.g., psalms, canticles. **b** the psalm or canticle so sung. **c** a song, esp. monotonous or repetitive. **3** a musical recitation, esp. of poetry. ● *v.tr.* **1** talk or repeat monotonously (*a crowd chanting slogans*). **2** sing or intone (a psalm, etc.). [ME (orig. as verb) f. OF *chanter* sing f. L *cantare* frequent. of *canere cant-* sing]

chant·er /chántər/ *n. Mus.* the melody pipe, with finger holes, of a bagpipe.

chan·te·relle /chántərél/ *n.* an edible fungus, *Cantharellus cibarius*, with a yellow, funnel-shaped cap and smelling of apricots. [F f. mod.L *cantharellus* dimin. of *cantharus* f. Gk *kantharos* a kind of drinking vessel]

chan·teuse /shaantőz/ *n.* a female singer of popular songs. [F]

chan·tey /shántee, chán–/ *n.* (also **chant·y**, **shant·y**) (*pl.* **chant·eys**, **·ies**) (in full **sea chantey**) a song with alternating solo and chorus, of a kind orig. sung by sailors while hauling ropes, etc. [prob. F *chantez*, imper. pl. of *chanter* sing: see CHANT]

chan·ti·cleer /chántikleér, shán–/ *n. literary* a name given to a domestic cock, esp. in fairy tales, etc. [ME f. OF *chantecler* (as CHANT, CLEAR), a name in *Reynard the Fox*]

Chan·til·ly /shantílee, shóNteeyée/ *n.* **1** a delicate kind of bobbin lace. **2** sweetened or flavored whipped cream. [*Chantilly* near Paris]

chan·try /chántree/ *n.* (*pl.* **·tries**) **1** an endowment for a priest or priests to celebrate Masses for the founder's soul. **2** the priests, chapel, altar, etc., endowed. [ME f. AF *chaunterie*, OF *chanterie* f. *chanter* CHANT]

chant·y var. of CHANTEY.

Cha·nuk·kah var. of HANUKKAH.

cha·os /káyos/ *n.* **1 a** utter confusion. **b** *Math.* the unpredictable and apparently random behavior of a deterministic system that is extremely sensitive to infinitesimal changes in initial parameters. **2** the formless matter supposed to have existed before the creation of the universe. □□ **cha·ot·ic** /kayótik/ *adj.* **cha·ot·i·cal·ly** *adv.* [F or L f. Gk *khaos*: *–otic* after *erotic*, etc.]

cha·os the·o·ry *n. Math.* the study of the apparently random behavior of deterministic systems.

chap¹ /chap/ *v. & n.* ● *v.* (**chapped**, **chap·ping**) **1** *intr.* (esp. of the skin; also of dry ground, etc.) crack in fissures, esp. because of exposure and dryness. **2** *tr.* (of the wind, cold, etc.) cause to chap. ● *n.* (usu. in *pl.*) **1** a crack in the skin. **2** an open seam. [ME, perh. rel. to MLG, MDu. *kappen* chop off]

chap² /chap/ *n.* esp. *Brit. colloq.* a man; a boy; a fellow. [abbr. of CHAPMAN]

chap³ /chap/ *n.* the lower jaw or half of the cheek, esp. of a pig as food. [16th c.: var. of CHOP², of unkn. orig.]

chap. *abbr.* chapter.

chap·ar·ral /shápərál, cháp–/ *n.* dense, tangled brushwood; undergrowth. [Sp. f. *chaparra* evergreen oak]

chap·ar·ral cock *n.* (also **chap·ar·ral bird**) = ROADRUNNER.

cha·pa·ti /chəpáatee/ *n.* (also **cha·pat·ti**) (*pl.* **·tis**) *Ind.* a flat thin cake of unleavened whole-wheat bread. [Hindi *capāti*]

chap·book /chápbook/ *n. hist.* a small pamphlet containing tales, ballads, tracts, etc., hawked by chapmen. [19th c.: see CHAPMAN]

chape /chayp/ *n.* **1** the metal cap of a scabbard point. **2** the back piece of a buckle attaching it to a strap, etc. **3** a sliding loop on a belt or strap. [ME f. OF, = cope, hood, formed as CAP]

cha·peau bras /shápōbraa/ *n.* (*pl.* **cha·peaux bras** *pronunc.* same) a three-cornered, flat silk hat often carried under the arm. [F f. *chapeau* hat + *bras* arm]

chap•el /chápəl/ n. **1 a** a place for private Christian worship in a large church or esp. a cathedral, with its own altar and dedication. **b** a place of Christian worship attached to a private house or institution. **2** a building or room in which funeral services are held. **3** *Brit.* **a** a place of worship for certain Protestant denominations. **4** an Anglican church subordinate to a parish church. **5** the members or branch of printers' union. **b** a meeting of them. [ME f. OF *chapele* f. med.L *cappella* dimin. of *cappa* cloak: the first chapel was a sanctuary in which St. Martin's sacred cloak (*cappella*) was preserved]

chap•er•on /shápərōn/ n. & v. (also **chap•er•one**) • n. **1** a person, esp. an older woman, who ensures propriety by accompanying a young unmarried woman on social occasions. **2** a person who takes charge of esp. young people in public. • v.tr. act as a chaperon to. □□ **chap•er•on•age** /shápərōnij/ n. [F, = hood, chaperon, dimin. of *chape* cope, formed as CAP]

chap•fall•en /cháp fawlən/ adj. dispirited; dejected (with the lower jaw hanging).

chap•lain /cháplin/ n. a member of the clergy attached to a private chapel, institution, ship, regiment, etc. □□ **chap•lain•cy** n. (pl. **-cies**). [ME f. AF & OF *c(h)apelain* f. med.L *cappellanus*, orig. custodian of the cloak of St. Martin: see CHAPEL]

chap•let /cháplit/ n. **1** a garland or circlet for the head. **2** a string of 55 beads (one-third of the rosary number) for counting prayers, or as a necklace. **3** a bead molding. □□ **chap•let•ed** adj. [ME f. OF *chapelet*, ult. f. LL *cappa* cap]

chap•man /chápmən/ n. (pl. **-men**) *Brit. hist.* a peddler. [OE *cēapman* f. *cēap* barter]

chap•pie /chápee/ n. *Brit. colloq.* = CHAP[2].

chap•py /chápee/ adj. *Brit.* full of chaps; chapped (*chappy knuckles*).

chaps /chaps/ n.pl. a cowboy's leather leggings worn over the trousers as protection for the front of the legs. [Mex. Sp. *chaparejos*]

Chap Stick *Trademark* a cylinder of a cosmetic substance used to prevent chapping of the lips.

chap•ter /cháptər/ n. **1** a main division of a book. **2** a period of time (in a person's life, a nation's history, etc.). **3** a series or sequence (*a chapter of misfortunes*). **4 a** the canons of a cathedral or other religious community or knightly order. **b** a meeting of these. **5** *Brit.* an Act of Parliament numbered as part of a session's proceedings. **6** a local branch of a society. □ **chapter and verse** an exact reference or authority. [ME f. OF *chapitre* f. L *capitulum* dimin. of *caput* –*itis* head]

chap•ter house n. **1** a building used for the meetings of a chapter. **2** the place where a college fraternity or sorority meets.

char[1] /chaar/ v.tr. & intr. (**charred**, **char•ring**) **1** make or become black by burning; scorch. **2** burn or be burned to charcoal. [app. back-form. f. CHARCOAL]

char[2] /chaar/ n. & v. *Brit. colloq.* • n. = CHARWOMAN. • v.intr. (**charred**, **char•ring**) work as a charwoman. [earlier *chare* f. OE *cerr* a turn, *cierran* to turn]

char[3] /chaar/ n. (also **cha** /chaa/) *Brit. sl.* tea. [Chin. *cha*]

char[4] /chaar/ n. (also **charr**) (pl. same) any small troutlike fish of the genus *Salvelinus*. [17th c.: orig. unkn.]

char•a•banc /shárəbang/ n. *Brit. hist.* an early form of tour bus. [F *char à bancs* seated carriage]

char•ac•ter /káriktər/ n. & v. • n. **1** the collective qualities or characteristics, esp. mental and moral, that distinguish a person or thing. **2 a** moral strength (*has a weak character*). **b** reputation, esp. good reputation. **3 a** a person in a novel, play, etc. **b** a part played by an actor; a role. **4** *colloq.* a person, esp. an eccentric or outstanding individual (*he's a real character*). **5 a** a printed or written letter, symbol, or distinctive mark (*Chinese characters*). **b** *Computing* any of a group of symbols representing a letter, etc. **6** a written description of a person's qualities; a testimonial. **7** a characteristic (esp. of a biological species). • v.tr. *archaic* inscribe; describe. □ **in** (or **out of**) **character** consistent (or inconsistent) with a person's character. □□ **char•ac•ter•ful** adj. **char•ac•ter•ful•ly** adv. **char•ac•ter•less** adj. [ME f. OF *caractere* f. L *character* f. Gk *kharaktēr* stamp, impress]

char•ac•ter ac•tor n. an actor who specializes in playing eccentric or unusual persons.

char•ac•ter as•sas•si•na•tion n. a malicious attempt to harm or destroy a person's good reputation.

char•ac•ter•is•tic /káriktərístik/ adj. & n. • adj. typical; distinctive (*with characteristic expertise*). • n. **1** a characteristic feature or quality. **2** *Math.* the whole number or integral part of a logarithm.

□□ **char•ac•ter•is•ti•cal•ly** adv. [F *caractéristique* or med.L *characterizare* f. Gk *kharaktērizō*]

char•ac•ter•is•tic curve n. a graph showing the relationship between two variable but interdependent quantities.

char•ac•ter•is•tic ra•di•a•tion n. radiation the wavelengths of which are peculiar to the element that emits them.

char•ac•ter•ize /káriktərīz/ v.tr. **1 a** describe the character of. **b** (foll. by *as*) describe as. **2** be characteristic of. **3** impart character to. □□ **char•ac•ter•i•za•tion** n. [F *caractériser* or med.L *characterizare* f. Gk *kharaktērizō*]

cha•rade /shəráyd/ n. **1 a** (usu. in pl., treated as *sing.*) a game of guessing a word from a written or acted clue given for each syllable and for the whole. **b** one such clue. **2** an absurd pretense. [F f. mod.Prov. *charrado* conversation f. *charra* chatter]

cha•ras /chaáros/ n. a narcotic resin from the flower heads of hemp; cannabis resin; hashish. [Hindi]

char•coal /chaárkōl/ n. **1 a** an amorphous form of carbon consisting of a porous black residue from partially burned wood, bones, etc. **b** (usu. in pl.) a piece of this used for drawing. **2** a drawing in charcoal. **3** (in full **charcoal gray**) a dark gray color. [ME COAL = charcoal: first element perh. *chare* turn (cf. CHAR[1], CHAR[2])]

chard /chaard/ n. (in full **Swiss chard**) a kind of beet, *Beta vulgaris cicla*, with edible broad, white leafstalks and green leaves. [F *carde*, and *chardon* thistle: cf. CARDOON]

Char•don•nay /shaárd'náy/ n. **1** a variety of white grape used for making champagne and other wines. **2** the vine on which this grape grows. **3** a wine made from Chardonnay grapes. [F]

charge /chaarj/ v. & n. • v. **1** tr. **a** ask (an amount) as a price (*charges $5 a ticket*). **b** ask (a person) for an amount as a price (*you forgot to charge me*). **2** tr. **a** (foll. by *to, up to*) debit the cost of to (a person or account; *charge it to my account; charge it up to me*). **b** debit (a person or an account) (*bought a new car and charged the company*). **3** tr. **a** (often foll. by *with*) accuse (of an offense) (*charged him with theft*). **b** (foll. by *that* + clause) make an accusation that. **4** tr. (foll. by *to* + infin.) instruct or urge. **5** (foll. by *with*) **a** tr. entrust with. **b** *refl.* undertake. **6 a** intr. make a rushing attack; rush headlong. **b** tr. make a rushing attack on; throw oneself against. **7** *Sports* to incur a foul by running, skating, etc., into a player on the opposing team. **8** tr. (often foll. by *up*) **a** give an electric charge to (a body). **b** store energy in (a battery). **9** tr. (often foll. by *with*) load or fill (a vessel, gun, etc.) to the full or proper extent. **10** tr. (usu. as **charged** adj.) **a** (foll. by *with*) saturated with (*air charged with vapor*). **b** (usu. foll. by *with*) pervaded with strong feelings, etc.) (*atmosphere charged with emotion; a charged atmosphere*). • n. **1 a** a price asked for goods or services. **b** a financial liability or commitment. **2** an accusation, esp. against a prisoner brought to trial. **3 a** a task, duty, or commission. **b** care, custody, responsible possession. **c** a person or thing entrusted; a minister's congregation. **4 a** an impetuous rush or attack, esp. in a battle. **b** the signal for this. **5** the appropriate amount of material to be put into a receptacle, mechanism, etc., at one time, esp. of explosive for a gun. **6 a** a property of matter that is a consequence of the interaction between its constituent particles and exists in a positive or negative form, causing electrical phenomena. **b** the quantity of this carried by a body. **c** energy stored chemically for conversion into electricity. **d** the process of charging a battery. **7** an exhortation; directions; orders. **8** a burden or load. **9** *Heraldry* a device; a bearing. □ **free of charge** gratis. **give a person in charge** *Brit.* hand a person over to the police. **in charge** having command. **return to the charge** begin again, esp. in argument. **take charge** (often foll. by *of*) assume control or direction. □□ **charge•a•ble** adj. [ME f. OF *charger* f. LL *car(ri)care* load f. L *carrus* CAR]

charge ac•count n. an account to which goods or services may be charged on credit.

charge card n. an identifying card enabling a customer to purchase goods or services on a charge account.

char•gé d'af•faires /shaarzháy dafáir/ n. (also **char•gé**) (pl. **char•gés** pronunc. same) **1** an ambassador's deputy. **2** an envoy to a minor country. [F, = in charge (of affairs)]

charg•er[1] /chaárjor/ n. **1 a** a cavalry horse. **b** *poet.* any horse. **2** an apparatus for charging a battery. **3** a person or thing that charges.

charg•er[2] /chaárjor/ n. a large, flat dish; a platter. [ME f. AF *chargeour*]

charge-hand n. *Brit.* a worker, ranking below a foreman, in charge of others on a particular job.

charge-sheet n. esp. *Brit.* a record of cases and charges made at a police station.

char•i•ot /cháreeət/ n. & v. • n. **1** *hist.* **a** a two-wheeled vehicle drawn by horses, used in ancient warfare and racing. **b** a four-wheeled carriage with

chariot

back seats only. **2** *poet.* a stately or triumphal vehicle. ● *v.tr. literary* convey in or as in a chariot. [ME f. OF, augment. of *char* CAR]

char·i·ot·eer /cháreeətéer/ *n.* a chariot driver.

cha·ris·ma /kərízmə/ *n.* (*pl.* **cha·ris·ma·ta** /–mətə/) **1 a** the ability to inspire followers with devotion and enthusiasm. **b** an attractive aura; great charm. **2** a divinely conferred power or talent. [eccl.L f. Gk *kharisma* f. *kharis* favor, grace]

char·is·mat·ic /kárizmátik/ *adj.* **1** having charisma; inspiring enthusiasm. **2** (of Christian worship) characterized by spontaneity, ecstatic utterances, etc. □□ **char·is·mat·i·cal·ly** *adv.*

char·is·mat·ic move·ment *n.* a Christian movement emphasizing ecstatic religious experience, speaking in tongues, etc.

char·i·ta·ble /cháritəbəl/ *adj.* **1** generous in giving to those in need. **2** of, relating to, or connected with a charity or charities. **3** apt to judge favorably of persons, acts, and motives. □□ **char·i·ta·ble·ness** *n.* **char·i·ta·bly** *adv.* [ME f. OF f. *charité* CHARITY]

char·i·ty /cháritee/ *n.* (*pl.* **·ties**) **1 a** giving voluntarily to those in need; almsgiving. **b** the help, esp. money, so given. **2** an institution or organization for helping those in need. **3 a** kindness; benevolence. **b** tolerance in judging others. **c** love of one's fellow men. [OE f. OF *charité* f. L *caritas –tatis* f. *carus* dear]

cha·ri·va·ri /shívəreé/ *n.* (also **shiv·a·ree**) **1** a serenade of banging saucepans, etc., to a newly married couple. **2** a medley of sounds; a hubbub. [F, = serenade with pans, trays, etc., to an unpopular person]

char·la·dy /chaárlaydee/ *n.* (*pl.* **·dies**) = CHARWOMAN.

char·la·tan /shaárlətən/ *n.* a person falsely claiming a special knowledge or skill. □□ **char·la·tan·ism** *n.* **char·la·tan·ry** *n.* [F f. It. *ciarlatano* f. *ciarlare* babble]

Charles' Law /chaárlz/ (also **Charles's Law** /chaárlziz/) *n. Chem.* the law stating that the volume of an ideal gas at constant pressure is directly proportional to the absolute temperature. [J. A. C. *Charles*, Fr. scientist d. 1823]

Charles's Wain /chaárlziz wáyn/ *n.* esp. *Brit.* the constellation Ursa Major or its seven bright stars; the *Big Dipper*. Also called (esp. *Brit.*) **Plough**. [OE *Carles wægn* the wain of Carl (Charles the Great, Charlemagne), perh. by assoc. of the star Arcturus with legends of King Arthur and Charlemagne]

Charles·ton /chaárlstən/ *n. & v.* ● *n.* a lively American dance of the 1920s with side kicks from the knee. ● *v.intr.* dance the Charleston. [*Charleston* in S. Carolina]

char·ley horse /chaárlee/ *n. sl.* stiffness or cramp in an arm or leg. [19th c.: orig. uncert.]

char·lock /chaárlok/ *n.* a wild mustard, *Sinapis arvensis*, with yellow flowers. Also called **field mustard**. [OE *cerlic*, of unkn. orig.]

char·lotte /shaárlət/ *n.* a dessert made of stewed fruit with a casing or layers or covering of bread, sponge cake, cookies, or breadcrumbs (*apple charlotte*). [F]

char·lotte russe /roos/ *n.* /roós/ custard, etc., enclosed in sponge cake or a casing of ladyfingers.

charm /chaarm/ *n. & v.* ● *n.* **1 a** the power or quality of giving delight or arousing admiration. **b** fascination; attractiveness. **c** (usu. in *pl.*) an attractive or enticing quality. **2** a trinket on a bracelet, etc. **3 a** an object, act, or word(s) supposedly having occult or magic power; a spell. **b** a thing worn to avert evil, etc.; an amulet. **4** *Physics* a property of matter manifested by some elementary particles. ● *v.tr.* **1** delight; captivate (*charmed by the performance*). **2** influence or protect as if by magic (*leads a charmed life*). **3 a** gain by charm (*charmed agreement out of him*). **b** influence by charm (*charmed her into consenting*). **4** cast a spell on; bewitch. □ **like a charm** perfectly; wonderfully (*worked like a charm; fits like a charm*). □□ **charm·er** *n.* [ME f. OF *charme, charmer* f. L *carmen* song]

charm brace·let *n.* a bracelet hung with small trinkets.

char·meuse /shaarmőz/ *n.* a soft, smooth, silky dress fabric. [F, fem. of *charmeur* (as CHARM)]

charm·ing /chaárming/ *adj.* **1** delightful; attractive; pleasing. **2** (often as *int.*) *iron.* expressing displeasure or disapproval. □□ **charm·ing·ly** *adv.*

charm·less /chaármlis/ *adj.* lacking charm; unattractive. □□ **charm·less·ly** *adv.* **charm·less·ness** *n.*

char·nel house /chaárnəlhows/ *n.* a house or vault in which dead bodies or bones are piled. [ME & OF *charnel* burying place f. med.L *carnale* f. LL *carnalis* CARNAL]

Cha·ro·lais /shárəláy/ *n.* (also **Cha·ro·laise**) (*pl.* same) **1** an animal of a breed of large, white beef cattle. **2** this breed. [Monts du *Charollais* in E. France]

char·poy /chaárpoy/ *n. Ind.* a light bedstead. [Hind. *chārpāi*]

chart /chaart/ *n. & v.* ● *n.* **1** a geographical map or plan, esp. for navigation by sea or air. **2** a sheet of information in the form of a table, graph, or diagram. **3** (usu. in *pl.*) *colloq.* a listing of the currently most popular music recordings. ● *v.tr.* make a chart of, map. [F *charte* f. L *charta* CARD[1]]

chart·bust·er /chaártbustər/ *n. colloq.* a best-selling popular song, recording, etc.

char·ter /chaártər/ *n. & v.* ● *n.* **1 a** a written grant of rights, by the

sovereign or legislature, esp. the creation of a borough, company, university, etc. **b** a written constitution or description of an organization's functions, etc. **2** a contract to hire an aircraft, ship, etc., for a special purpose. **3** (in full **charter party**) a deed between a shipowner and a merchant for the hire of a ship and the delivery of cargo. **4** an aircraft, boat, or bus that is reserved for private use (*he preferred to see the boat sparkling clean before each charter*). ● *v.tr.* **1** grant a charter to. **2** hire (an aircraft, ship, etc.). □□ **char·ter·er** *n.* [ME f. OF *chartre* f. L *chartula* dimin. of *charta* CARD[1]]

char·tered ac·count·ant *n. Brit.* a member of a professional body of accountants that has a royal charter.

char·ter flight *n.* a flight by a chartered aircraft.

char·ter mem·ber *n.* an original member of a society, corporation, etc.

Chart·ism /chaártizəm/ *n. hist.* the principles of the UK Parliamentary reform movement of 1837–48. □□ **Char·tist** *n.* [L *charta* charter + –ISM: name taken from the manifesto 'People's Charter']

char·treuse /shaartrőz, –trōs/ *n.* **1** (**Chartreuse**) a pale green or yellow liqueur of brandy and aromatic herbs, etc. **2** the pale yellow or pale green color of this. [La Grande *Chartreuse* (Carthusian monastery near Grenoble)]

char·wom·an /chaárwoomən/ *n.* (*pl.* **·wom·en**) a woman employed as a cleaner in houses or offices.

char·y /cháiree/ *adj.* (**char·i·er, char·i·est**) **1** cautious; wary (*chary of employing such people*). **2** sparing; ungenerous (*chary of giving praise*). **3** shy. □□ **char·i·ly** *adv.* **char·i·ness** *n.* [OE *cearig*]

Cha·ryb·dis see SCYLLA AND CHARYBDIS.

Chas. *abbr.* Charles.

chase[1] /chays/ *v. & n.* ● *v.* **1** *tr.* pursue in order to catch. **2** *tr.* (foll. by *from, out of, to*, etc.) drive. **3** *intr.* **a** (foll. by *after*) hurry in pursuit of (a person). **b** (foll. by *around*, etc.) *colloq.* act or move about hurriedly. **4** *tr. Brit.* (usu. foll. by *up*) *colloq.* pursue (overdue work, payment, etc., or the person responsible for it). **5** *tr. colloq.* **a** try to attain. **b** court persistently and openly. ● *n.* **1** pursuit. **2** *Brit.* unenclosed hunting land. **3** (prec. by *the*) hunting, esp. as a sport. **4** an animal, etc., that is pursued. **5** = STEEPLECHASE. □ **go and chase oneself** (usu. in *imper.*) *Brit. colloq.* depart. [ME f. OF *chace chacier*, ult. f. L *capere* take]

chase[2] /chays/ *v.tr.* emboss or engrave (metal). [app. f. earlier *enchase* f. F *enchâsser* (as EN-[1], CASE[2])]

chase[3] /chays/ *n. Printing* a metal frame holding composed type. [F *châsse* f. L *capsa* CASE[2]]

chase[4] /chays/ *n.* **1** the part of a gun enclosing the bore. **2** a trench or groove cut to receive a pipe, etc. [F *chas* enclosed space f. Prov. *ca(u)s* f. med.L *capsum* thorax]

chas·er /cháysər/ *n.* **1** a person or thing that chases. **2** a horse for steeplechasing. **3** *colloq.* a drink taken after another of a different kind, e.g., beer after liquor.

chasm /kázəm/ *n.* **1** a deep fissure or opening in the earth, rock, etc. **2** a wide difference of feeling, interests, etc.; a gulf. **3** *archaic* a hiatus. □□ **chas·mic** *adj.* [L *chasma* f. Gk *khasma* gaping hollow]

chas·sé /shasáy/ *n. & v.* ● *n.* a gliding step in dancing. ● *v.intr.* (**chas·séd; chas·sé·ing**) make this step. [F, = chasing]

chas·sis /shásee, chás–/ *n.* (*pl.* same /–siz/) **1** the base frame of a motor vehicle, carriage, etc. **2** a frame to carry radio, etc., components. [F *châssis* ult. f. L *capsa* CASE[2]]

chaste /chayst/ *adj.* **1** abstaining from extramarital, or from all, sexual intercourse. **2** (of behavior, speech, etc.) pure, virtuous, decent. **3** (of artistic, etc., style) simple; unadorned. □□ **chaste·ly** *adv.* **chaste·ness** *n.* [ME f. OF f. L *castus*]

chas·ten /cháysən/ *v.tr.* **1** (esp. as **chastening, chastened** *adjs.*) subdue; restrain (*a chastening experience; chastened by his failure*). **2** discipline; punish. **3** moderate. □□ **chas·ten·er** *n.* [obs. *chaste* (v.) f. OF *chastier* f. L *castigare* CASTIGATE]

chaste tree *n.* an ornamental shrub, *Vitex agnus-castus*, with blue or white flowers.

chas·tise /chastíz, chástiz/ *v.tr.* **1** rebuke or reprimand severely. **2** punish, esp. by beating. □□ **chas·tise·ment** *n.* **chas·tis·er** *n.* [ME, app. irreg. formed f. obs. verbs *chaste, chasty*: see CHASTEN]

chas·ti·ty /chástitee/ *n.* **1** being chaste. **2** sexual abstinence; virginity. **3** simplicity of style or taste. [ME f. OF *chasteté* f. L *castitas –tatis* f. *castus* CHASTE]

chas·ti·ty belt *n. hist.* a garment designed to prevent a woman from having sexual intercourse.

chas·u·ble /cházəbəl, cházyə–, chás–/ *n.* a loose, sleeveless, often outer vestment worn by a priest celebrating Mass or the Eucharist. [ME f. OF *chesible*, later *–uble*, ult. f. L *casula* hooded cloak, little cottage, dimin. of *casa* cottage]

chat[1] /chat/ *v. & n.* ● *v.intr.* (**chat·ted, chat·ting**) talk in a light familiar way. ● *n.* **1** informal conversation or talk. **2** an instance of this. □ **chat up** *Brit. colloq.* chat to, esp. flirtatiously or with an ulterior motive. [ME: shortening of CHATTER]

chat[2] /chat/ *n.* any of various small birds with harsh calls, esp. a stone-chat or yellow–breasted chat. [prob. imit.]

châ·teau /shatō/ *n.* (*pl.* **châ·teaus** or **châ·teaux** /–tōz/) a large French country house or castle, often giving its name to wine made in its neighborhood. [F f. OF *chastel* CASTLE]

cha·teau·bri·and /shatōbreé-ón/ *n.* a thick fillet of beef steak usu. served with a béarnaise sauce. [Vicomte de *Chateaubriand* d. 1848, Fr. writer and statesman]

chat·e·laine /shát'layn/ *n.* **1** the mistress of a large house. **2** *hist.* a set of short chains attached to a woman's belt, for carrying keys, etc. [F *châtelaine*, fem. of *–ain* lord of a castle, f. med.L *castellanus* CASTELLAN]

chat·tel /chát'l/ *n.* (usu. in *pl.*) a moveable possession; any possession or personal property other than real estate. □ **goods and chattels** personal possessions. [ME f. OF *chatel*: see CATTLE]

chat·tel mort·gage *n.* a mortgage on a movable item of property.

chat·ter /chátər/ *v. & n.* ● *v.intr.* **1** talk quickly, incessantly, trivially, or indiscreetly. **2** (of a bird) emit short, quick notes. **3** (of the teeth) click repeatedly together (usu. from cold). **4** (of a tool) clatter from vibration. ● *n.* **1** chattering talk or sounds. **2** the vibration of a tool. □□ **chat·ter·er** *n.* **chat·ter·y** *adj.* [ME: imit.]

chat·ter·box /chátərboks/ *n.* a talkative person.

chat·ty /chátee/ *adj.* (**chat·ti·er**, **chat·ti·est**) **1** fond of chatting; talkative. **2** resembling chat; informal and lively (*a chatty letter*). □□ **chat·ti·ly** *adv.* **chat·ti·ness** *n.*

Chau·ce·ri·an /chawseéreeən/ *adj. & n.* ● *adj.* of or relating to the English poet Chaucer (d. 1400) or his style. ● *n.* a student of Chaucer.

chaud·froid /shōfrwaá/ *n.* a dish of cold cooked meat or fish in jelly or sauce. [F f. *chaud* hot + *froid* cold]

chauf·feur /shōfər, –fōr/ *n. & v.* ● *n.* (*fem.* **chauf·feuse** /–fōz/) a person employed to drive a private or rented automobile or limousine. ● *v.tr.* drive (a car or a person) as a chauffeur. [F, = stoker]

chaul·moo·gra /chawlmoōgrə/ *n.* any tree of the genus *Hydnocarpus*, esp. *H. wightiana*, with seeds yielding an oil formerly used in the treatment of leprosy. [Bengali]

chau·tau·qua /shətáwkwə, chə–/ *n.* (also **Chau·tau·qua**) a cultural and educational program of lectures, performances, etc., usu. held outdoors in the summer. [*Chautauqua* in New York State, where these originated in 1874]

chau·vin·ism /shóvinizəm/ *n.* **1** exaggerated or aggressive patriotism. **2** excessive or prejudiced support or loyalty for one's cause or group or sex (*male chauvinism*). [*Chauvin*, a Napoleonic veteran in the Cogniards' *Cocarde Tricolore* (1831)]

chau·vin·ist /shóvinist/ *n.* **1** a person exhibiting chauvinism. **2** (in full **male chauvinist**) a man showing excessive loyalty to men and prejudice against women. □□ **chau·vin·is·tic** /–nístik/ *adj.* **chau·vin·is·ti·cal·ly** /–nístikəlee/ *adv.*

Ch.E. *abbr.* chemical engineer.

cheap /cheep/ *adj. & adv.* ● *adj.* **1** low in price; worth more than its cost (*a cheap vacation; cheap labor*). **2** charging low prices; offering good value (*a cheap restaurant*). **3** of poor quality; inferior (*cheap housing*). **4 a** costing little effort or acquired by discreditable means and hence of little worth (*cheap popularity; a cheap joke*). **b** contemptible; despicable (*a cheap criminal*). ● *adv.* cheaply (*got it cheap*). □ **feel cheap** feel ashamed or contemptible. **on the cheap** cheaply. □□ **cheap·ish** *adj.* **cheap·ly** *adv.* **cheap·ness** *n.* [obs. phr. *good cheap* f. *cheap* a bargain f. OE *cēap* barter, ult. f. L *caupo* innkeeper]

cheap·en /cheépən/ *v.tr. & intr.* make or become cheap or cheaper; depreciate; degrade.

cheap·jack /cheépjak/ *n. & adj.* ● *n.* a seller of inferior goods at low prices. ● *adj.* inferior; shoddy. [CHEAP + JACK[1]]

cheap·o /cheépō/ *attrib.adj. sl.* cheap.

cheap·skate /cheépskayt/ *n. colloq.* a stingy person.

cheat /cheet/ *v. & n.* ● *v.* **1** *tr.* **a** (often foll. by *into, out of*) deceive or trick (*cheated into parting with his savings*). **b** (foll. by *of*) deprive of (*cheated of a chance to reply*). **2** *intr.* gain unfair advantage by deception or breaking rules, esp. in a game or examination. **3** *tr.* avoid (something undesirable) by luck or skill (*cheated the bad weather*). **4** *tr. archaic* divert attention from; beguile (time, tedium, etc.). ● *n.* **1** a person who cheats. **2** a trick, fraud, or deception. **3** an act of cheating. □ **cheat on** *colloq.* be sexually unfaithful to. □□ **cheat·ing·ly** *adv.* [ME *chete* f. *achete*, var. of ESCHEAT]

cheat·er /cheétər/ *n.* **1** a person who cheats. **2** (in *pl.*) *sl.* eyeglasses.

check[1] /chek/ *v., n., & int.* ● *v.* **1** *tr.* (also *absol.*) **a** examine the accuracy, quality, or condition of. **b** (often foll. by *that* + clause) make sure; verify; establish to one's satisfaction (*checked that the doors were locked; checked the train times*). **2** *tr.* **a** stop or slow the motion of; curb; restrain (*progress was checked by bad weather*). **b** *colloq.* find fault with; rebuke. **3** *tr. Chess* move a piece into a position that directly threatens (the opposing king). **4** *intr.* agree or correspond when compared. **5** *tr.* mark with a check mark, etc. **6** *tr.* deposit (luggage, etc.) for storage or dispatch. **7** *intr.* (of hounds) pause to

ensure or regain scent. ● *n.* **1** a means or act of testing or ensuring accuracy, quality, satisfactory condition, etc. **2 a** a stopping or slowing of motion; a restraint on action. **b** a rebuff or rebuke. **c** a person or thing that restrains. **3** *Chess* (also as *int.*) **a** the exposure of a king to direct attack from an opposing piece. **b** an announcement of this by the attacking player. **4** a bill in a restaurant. **5** a token of identification for left luggage, etc. **6** *Cards* a counter used in various games, esp. a poker chip. **7** a temporary loss of the scent in hunting. **8** a crack or flaw in lumber. **9** = CHECK MARK. ● *int.* expressing assent or agreement. □ **check in** arrive or register at a hotel, airport, etc. **2** record the arrival of. **check into** register one's arrival at (a hotel, etc.). **check off** mark on a list, etc., as having been examined or dealt with. **check on** examine carefully or in detail; ascertain the truth about; keep a watch on (a person, work done, etc.). **check out 1** (often foll. by *of*) leave a hotel, etc., with due formalities. **2** *colloq.* investigate; examine for authenticity or suitability. **check over** examine for errors; verify. **check through** inspect or examine exhaustively; verify successive items of. **check up** ascertain; verify; make sure. **check up on** = *check on.* **in check** under control; restrained. □□ **check·a·ble** *adj.* [ME f. OF *eschequier* play chess, give check to, and OF *eschec*, ult. f. Pers. *šāh* king]

check[2] /chek/ *n.* **1** a pattern of small squares. **2** fabric having this pattern.

check[3] /chek/ *n.* (*Brit.* **cheque**) **1** a written order to a bank to pay the stated sum from the drawer's account. **2** the printed form on which such an order is written. **3** *Austral.* the total sum received by a rural worker at the end of a seasonal contract. [special use of CHECK[1] to mean 'device for checking the amount of an item']

SPELLING TIP check[3]

In American English, the draft written against deposited funds is called a *check*. *Cheque* is the British spelling.

---

check·book /chékbook/ *n.* a book of blank checks with a register for recording checks written.

check·book jour·nal·ism *n.* the payment of large sums for exclusive rights to material for (esp. personal) newspaper stories.

checked /chekt/ *adj.* having a pattern of small squares.

check·er[1] /chékər/ *n.* **1** a person or thing that verifies or examines, esp. in a factory, etc. **2** a cashier in a supermarket, etc.

check·er[2] /chékər/ *n. & v.* (*Brit.* **chequ·er**) ● *n.* **1** (often in *pl.*) a pattern of squares often alternately colored. **2 a** (in *pl.*) a game for two played with 12 pieces each on a checkerboard. **b** each of the usu. red or black disk-shaped playing pieces in a game of checkers. ● *v.tr.* **1** mark with checkers. **2** variegate; break the uniformity of. **3** (as **checkered** *adj.*) with varied fortunes (*a checkered career*). [ME *checker* chessboard]

check·er·ber·ry /chékərberee/ *n.* (*pl.* **·ries**) **1** a wintergreen, *Gaultheria procumbens*. **2** the fruit of this plant. [*checkers* berries of service tree]

check·er·board /chékərbawrd/ *n.* **1** a checkered board, identical to a chessboard, used in the game of checkers. **2** a pattern or design resembling it.

check·in *n.* the act or place of checking in.

check·ing ac·count /chéking/ *n.* an account at a bank against which checks can be drawn by the account depositor. [CHECK[3]]

check·list /chéklist/ *n.* a list for reference and verification.

check mark *n.* a mark (√) to denote correctness, check items in a list, etc.

check·mate /chékmayt/ *n. & v.* ● *n.* **1** (also as *int.*) *Chess* a check from which a king cannot escape. **b** an announcement of this. **2 a** final defeat or deadlock. ● *v.tr.* **1** *Chess* put into checkmate. **2** defeat; frustrate. [ME f. OF *eschec mat* f. Pers. *šāh māt* the king is dead]

check·out /chékowt/ *n.* **1** an act of checking out. **2** a point at which goods are paid for in a supermarket, etc.

check·point /chékpoynt/ *n.* a place, esp. a barrier or manned entrance, where documents, vehicles, etc., are inspected.

check·rein /chékrayn/ *n.* a rein attaching one horse's rein to another's bit, or preventing a horse from lowering its head.

check·room /chékroom, –room/ *n.* **1** a cloakroom in a hotel or theater. **2** an office for left luggage, etc.

check·up /chékup/ *n.* a thorough (esp. medical) examination.

check valve *n.* a valve allowing flow in one direction only.

ched·dar /chédər/ *n.* (in full **cheddar cheese**) a kind of firm smooth cheese orig. made in Cheddar in S. England.

cheek /cheek/ *n. & v.* ● *n.* **1 a** the side of the face below the eye. **b** the sidewall of the mouth. **2** esp. *Brit.* impertinent speech. **b** impertinence; cool confidence (*had the cheek to ask for more*). **3** *sl.* either buttock. **4 a** either of the side posts of a door, etc. **b** either of the jaws of a vise. **c** either of the sidepieces of various parts of machines arranged in lateral pairs. ● *v.tr.* speak impertinently to. □ **cheek by jowl** close together; intimate. **turn the other cheek** accept attack, etc., meekly; refuse to retaliate. [OE *cē(a)ce, cēoce*]

cheek·bone /cheékbōn/ *n.* the bone below the eye.

cheek•y /chéekee/ *adj.* (**cheek•i•er, cheek•i•est**) impertinent; impudent. ▫▫ **cheek•i•ly** *adv.* **cheek•i•ness** *n.*

cheep /cheep/ *n. & v.* • *n.* the weak shrill cry of a young bird. • *v.intr.* make such a cry. [imit.: cf. PEEP[2]]

cheer /cheer/ *n. & v.* • *n.* **1** a shout of encouragement or applause. **2** mood; disposition (*full of good cheer*). **3** cheerfulness; joy. **4** (in *pl.*; as *int.*) *colloq.* **a** expressing good wishes on parting. **b** expressing good wishes before drinking. **c** expressing gratitude. • *v.* **1** *tr.* **a** applaud with shouts. **b** (usu. foll. by *on*) urge or encourage with shouts. **2** *intr.* shout for joy. **3** *tr.* gladden; comfort. ▫ **cheer up** make or become less depressed. [ME f. AF *chere* face, etc., OF *chiere* f. LL *cara* face f. Gk *kara* head]

cheer•ful /chéerfōōl/ *adj.* **1** in good spirits; noticeably happy (*a cheerful disposition*). **2** bright; pleasant (*a cheerful room*). **3** willing; not reluctant. ▫▫ **cheer•ful•ly** *adv.* **cheer•ful•ness** *n.*

cheer•i•o /chíreeó/ *int. Brit. colloq.* expressing good wishes on parting or before drinking.

cheer•lead•er /chéerleedər/ *n.* a person who leads cheers of applause, etc., esp. at a sports event.

cheer•less /chéerlis/ *adj.* gloomy; dreary; miserable. ▫▫ **cheer•less•ly** *adv.* **cheer•less•ness** *n.*

cheer•ly /chéerlee/ *adv. & adj.* • *adv.* esp. *Naut.* heartily; with a will. • *adj. archaic* cheerful.

cheer•y /chéeree/ *adj.* (**cheer•i•er, cheer•i•est**) lively; in good spirits; genial; cheering. ▫▫ **cheer•i•ly** *adv.* **cheer•i•ness** *n.*

cheese[1] /cheez/ *n.* **1 a** a food made from the pressed curds of milk. **b** a complete cake of this with rind. **2** *Brit.* a conserve having the consistency of soft cheese (*lemon cheese*). **3** *Brit.* a round flat object, e.g., the heavy, flat, wooden disk used in skittles. [OE *cēse*, etc. ult. f. L *caseus*]

cheese[2] /cheez/ *v.tr. Brit. sl.* (as **cheesed** *adj.*) (often foll. by *off*) bored; fed up. ▫ **cheese it 1** look out. **2** run away. [19th c.: orig. unkn.]

cheese[3] /cheez/ *n.* (also **big cheese**) *sl.* an important person. [perh. f. Hind. *chīz* thing]

cheese•board /chéezbawrd/ *n.* **1** a board from which cheese is served. **2** a selection of cheeses.

cheese•burg•er /chéezbərgər/ *n.* a hamburger with cheese on it.

cheese•cake /chéezkayk/ *n.* **1** a rich dessert cake made with cream cheese, etc. **2** *sl.* the portrayal of women in a sexually attractive manner.

cheese•cloth /chéezklawth, –kloth/ *n.* thin loosely woven cloth, used orig. for wrapping cheese.

cheese knife *n.* (also **cheese slic•er**) **1** a knife with a broad curved blade. **2** a device for cutting cheese by pulling a wire through it.

cheese•par•ing /chéezpairing/ *adj. & n.* • *adj.* stingy. • *n.* stinginess.

cheese•wood /chéezwōōd/ *n.* **1** an Australian tree of the genus *Pittosporum*. **2** its hard yellowish wood.

chees•y /chéezee/ *adj.* (**chees•i•er, chees•i•est**) **1** like cheese in taste, smell, appearance, etc. **2** *sl.* inferior; cheap and nasty. ▫▫ **chees•i•ness** *n.*

chee•tah /chéetə/ *n.* a swift-running feline, *Acinonyx jubatus*, with a leopardlike spotted coat. [Hindi *cītā*, perh. f. Skr. *citraka* speckled]

chef /shef/ *n.* a cook, esp. the chief cook in a restaurant, etc. [F, = head]

chef d'oeu•vre /shaydóvrə/ *n.* (*pl.* **chefs d'oeu•vre** *pronunc.* same) a masterpiece. [F]

cheiro- *comb. form* var. of CHIRO-.

che•la[1] /kéelə/ *n.* (*pl.* **che•lae** /–lee/) a prehensile claw of crabs, lobsters, scorpions, etc. [mod.L f. L *chele*, or Gk *khēlē* claw]

che•la[2] /cháylə/ *n.* **1** (in esoteric Buddhism) a novice qualifying for initiation. **2** a disciple; a pupil. [Hindi, = servant]

che•late /kéelayt/ *n., adj., & v.* • *n. Chem.* a usu. organometallic compound containing a bonded ring of atoms including a metal atom. • *adj.* **1** *Chem.* of a chelate. **2** *Zool.* & *Anat.* of or having chelae. • *v.intr. Chem.* form a chelate. ▫▫ **che•la•tion** /–láyshən/ *n.*

Chel•le•an /shéleeən/ *adj. Archaeol.* = ABBEVILLIAN. [F *chelléen* f. *Chelles* near Paris]

che•lo•ni•an /kilóneeən/ *n. & adj.* • *n.* any reptile of the order Chelonia, including turtles, terrapins, and tortoises, having a shell of bony plates covered with horny scales. • *adj.* of or relating to this order. [mod.L *Chelonia* f. Gk *khelōnē* tortoise]

chem. *abbr.* **1** chemical. **2** chemist. **3** chemistry.

chemi- *comb. form* var. of CHEMO-.

chem•i•cal /kémikəl/ *adj. & n.* • *adj.* of, made by, or employing chemistry or chemicals. • *n.* a substance obtained or used in chemistry. ▫▫ **chem•i•cal•ly** *adv.* [*chemic* alchemic f. F *chimique* or mod.L *chimicus, chymicus*, f. med.L *alchymicus*: see ALCHEMY]

chem•i•cal bond *n.* the force holding atoms together in a molecule or crystal.

chem•i•cal en•gi•neer *n.* one engaged in chemical engineering, esp. professionally.

chem•i•cal en•gi•neer•ing *n.* the design, manufacture, and operation of industrial chemical plants.

chem•i•cal re•ac•tion *n.* a process that involves change in the structure of atoms, molecules, or ions.

chem•i•cal war•fare *n.* warfare using poison gas and other chemicals.

chemico- /kémikō/ *comb. form* chemical; chemical and (*chemicophysical*).

chem•i•lum•i•nes•cence /kémilōōminésəns/ *n.* the emission of light during a chemical reaction. ▫▫ **chem•i•lu•mi•nes•cent** /–nésənt/ *adj.* [G *Chemilumineszenz* (as CHEMI-, LUMINESCENCE)]

chem•in de fer /shəmáN də fáir/ *n.* a form of baccarat. [F, = railway, lit. road of iron]

che•mise /shəméez/ *n. hist.* a woman's loose-fitting undergarment or dress hanging straight from the shoulders. [ME f. OF f. LL *camisia* shirt]

chem•i•sorp•tion /kémisáwrpshən/ *n.* adsorption by chemical bonding. [CHEMI- + *adsorption* (see ADSORB)]

chem•ist /kémist/ *n.* **1** a person practicing or trained in chemistry. **2** *Brit.* **a** a dealer in medicinal drugs, usu. also selling other medical goods and toiletries. **b** an authorized dispenser of medicines. [earlier *chymist* f. F *chimiste* f. mod.L *chimista* f. *alchimista* alchemist (see ALCHEMY)]

chem•is•try /kémistree/ *n.* (*pl.* **•tries**) **1** the study of the elements and the compounds they form and the reactions they undergo. **2** any complex (esp. emotional) change or process (*the chemistry of fear*). **3** *colloq.* a person's personality or temperament. **4** the emotional or psychological interaction between two people, especially when experienced as a powerful mutual attraction.

chemo- /kéemō/ *comb. form* (also **chemi-** /kémee/) chemical.

che•mo•syn•the•sis /kéemōsínthisis/ *n.* the synthesis of organic compounds by energy derived from chemical reactions.

che•mo•ther•a•py /kéemōthérəpee/ *n.* the treatment of disease, esp. cancer, by use of chemical substances. ▫▫ **che•mo•ther•a•pist** *n.*

chem•ur•gy /kémərjee, kimór–/ *n.* the chemical and industrial use of organic raw materials. ▫▫ **chem•ur•gic** /–órjik/ *adj.* [CHEMO-, after *metallurgy*]

che•nille /shənéel/ *n.* **1** a tufty, velvety cord or yarn, used in trimming furniture, etc. **2** fabric made from this. [F, = hairy caterpillar f. L *canicula* dimin. of *canis* dog]

cheong•sam /chawngsám/ *n.* a Chinese woman's garment with a high neck and slit skirt. [Chin.]

cheongsam

cheque *Brit.* var. of CHECK[3].

SPELLING TIP cheque

See note at CHECK[3].

cheq•uer *Brit.* var. of CHECKER[2].

Che•ren•kov ra•di•a•tion /chiréngkawf/ var. of CERENKOV RADIATION.

cher•ish /chérish/ *v.tr.* **1** protect or tend (a child, plant, etc.) lovingly. **2** hold dear; cling to (hopes, feelings, etc.). [ME f. OF *cherir* f. *cher* f. L *carus* dear]

cher•no•zem /chérnəzem, chírnəzyáwm/ *n.* a fertile, black soil rich in humus, found in temperate regions, esp. S. Russia. Also called **black earth.** [Russ. f. *chernyĭ* black + *zemlya* earth]

Cher•o•kee /chérəkee/ *n. & adj.* • *n.* **1 a** a N. American people formerly inhabiting much of the southern US. **b** an individual of this people. **2** the language of this people. • *adj.* of or relating to the Cherokees or their language. [Cherokee *Tsálăgĭ*]

Cher•o•kee rose *n.* a fragrant white rose, *Rosa laevigata*, of the southern US.

che•root /shərōōt/ *n.* a cigar with both ends open. [F *cheroute* f. Tamil *shuruṭṭu* roll]

cher•ry /chéree/ *n. & adj.* • *n.* (*pl.* **•ries**) **1 a** a small, soft, round stone fruit. **b** any of several trees of the genus *Prunus* bearing this or grown for its ornamental flowers. **2** (in full **cherry wood**) the wood of a cherry. **3** *coarse sl.* **a** hymen. **b** virginity. • *adj.* of a light red color. [ME f. ONF *cherise* (taken as pl.: cf. PEA) f. med.L *ceresia* perh. f. L f. Gk *kerasos*]

cher•ry lau•rel *n. Brit.* a small evergreen tree, *Prunus laurocerasus*, with white flowers and cherrylike fruits.

cher•ry pick•er *n. colloq.* a hydraulic crane with a platform or bucket attached, for raising and lowering people for work on telephone cables, power lines, etc.

cher•ry plum *n.* **1** a tree, *Prunus cerasifera*, native to SW Asia, with solitary white flowers and red fruits. **2** the fruit of this tree.

cher•ry to•ma•to *n.* a miniature tomato.

cher•so•nese /kórsəneez, –nees/ *n.* a peninsula, esp. the Thracian peninsula west of the Hellespont. [L *chersonesus* f. Gk *khersonēsos* f. *khersos* dry + *nēsos* island]

chert /chərt/ n. a flintlike form of quartz composed of chalcedony. □□ **chert·y** adj. [17th c.: orig. unkn.]

cher·ub /chérəb/ n. **1** (pl. **cher·u·bim** /–bim/) an angelic being of the second order of the celestial hierarchy. **2** (pl. usu. **cher·ubs**) **a** a representation of a winged child or the head of a winged child. **b** a beautiful or innocent child. □□ **che·ru·bic** /chiróóbik/ adj. **che·ru·bi·cal·ly** /chiróóbikəlee/ adv. [ME f. OE cherubin and f. Heb. kᵉrūḇ, pl. kᵉrūḇīm]

cher·vil /chórvil/ n. an umbelliferous plant, Anthriscus cerefolium, with small white flowers, used as an herb for flavoring soup, salads, etc. [OE cerfille f. L chaerephylla f. Gk khairephullon]

Chesh·ire /chéshər/ n. (in full **Cheshire cheese**) a kind of firm crumbly cheese, orig. made in Cheshire. □ **like a Cheshire cat** with a broad fixed grin. [Cheshire, a county in England]

chess /ches/ n. a game for two with 16 pieces each, played on a chessboard. [ME f. OF esches pl. of eschec CHECK¹]

chess·board /chésbawrd/ n. a checkered board of 64 squares on which chess and checkers are played.

chess·man /chésman, –mən/ n. (pl. **·men**) any of the 32 pieces with which chess is played.

chest /chest/ n. **1** a large strong box, esp. for storage or transport. **2 a** the part of a human or animal body enclosed by the ribs. **b** the front surface of the body from neck to waist. **3** a small cabinet for medicines, toiletries, etc. **4 a** the treasury or financial resources of an institution. **b** the money available from it. □ **get a thing off one's chest** colloq. disclose a fact, secret, etc., to relieve one's anxiety about it; say what is on one's mind. **play one's cards close to one's chest** colloq. be cautious or secretive about something. □□ **–chest·ed** adj. (in comb.). [OE cest, cyst f. Gmc f. L f. Gk kistē]

ches·ter·field /chéstərfeeld/ n. **1** a sofa with arms and back of the same height and curved outward at the top. **2** (also **Ches·ter·field**) a plain overcoat usu. with a velvet collar. [19th-c. Earl of Chesterfield]

chest·nut /chésnut/ n. & adj. **•**n. **1 a** a glossy, hard, brown edible nut. **b** the tree Castanea sativa, bearing flowers in catkins and nuts enclosed in a spiny fruit. Also called **Spanish chestnut** or **sweet chestnut**. **2** any other tree of the genus Castanea, esp. the American chestnut C. dentata. **3** = HORSE CHESTNUT. **4** (in full **chestnut wood**) the heavy wood of any chestnut tree. **5** a horse of a reddish-brown or yellowish-brown color. **6** colloq. a stale joke or anecdote. **7** a small hard patch on a horse's leg. **8** a reddish-brown color. **•**adj. of the color chestnut. [obs. chesten f. OF chastaine f. L castanea f. Gk kastanea]

chest of drawers n. a piece of furniture consisting of a set of drawers in a frame.

chest·y /chéstee/ adj. (**chest·i·er**, **chest·i·est**) **1** colloq. having a large chest or prominent breasts. **2** sl. arrogant. □□ **chest·i·ly** adv. **chest·i·ness** n.

Chet·nik /chétnik/ n. hist. a member of a guerrilla force in the Balkans, esp. during World Wars I and II. [Serbian četnik f. četa band, troop]

che·val glass /shəválglas/ n. a tall mirror swung on an upright frame. [F cheval horse, frame]

chev·a·lier /shévəleér/ n. **1 a** a member of certain orders of knighthood, and of modern French orders, as the Legion of Honor. **b** archaic or hist. a knight. **2** Brit. hist. the title of James and Charles Stuart, pretenders to the British throne. **3** a chivalrous man; a cavalier. [ME f. AF chevaler, OF chevalier f. med.L caballarius f. L caballus horse]

che·vet /shəváy/ n. the apsidal end of a church, sometimes with an attached group of apses. [F, = pillow, f. L capitium f. caput head]

chev·i·ot /chéveeət, cheév–, shév–/ n. **1** (also **Chev·i·ot**) **a** a large sheep of a breed with short thick wool. **b** this breed. **2** the wool or cloth obtained from this breed. [Cheviot Hills in Northern England and Scotland]

chè·vre /shévrə/ n. a variety of goat cheese. [F, = goat, she-goat]

chev·ron /shévrən/ n. **1** a badge in a V shape on the sleeve of a uniform indicating rank or length of service. **2** Heraldry & Archit. a bent bar of an inverted V shape. **3** any V-shaped line or stripe. [ME f. OF ult. f. L caper goat: cf. L capreoli pair of rafters]

chev·ro·tain /shévrətayn/ (also **chev·ro·tin** /–tin/) n. any small deerlike animal of the family Tragulidae, native to Africa and SE Asia, having small tusks. Also called **mouse deer**. [F, dimin. of OF chevrot dimin. of chèvre goat]

chev·y var. of CHIVVY.

chevron

chew /choo/ v. & n. **•**v.tr. (also absol.) work (food, etc.) between the teeth; crush or indent with the teeth. **•**n. **1** an act of chewing. **2** something for chewing, esp. a chewy candy. □ **chew the cud** reflect; ruminate. **chew the fat** (or **rag**) sl. **1** chat. **2** grumble. **chew on 1** work continuously between the teeth (chewed on a piece of string). **2** think about; meditate on. **chew out** colloq. reprimand. **chew over 1** discuss; talk over. **2** think about; meditate on. □□ **chew·a·ble** adj. **chew·er** n. [OE cēowan]

chew·ing gum n. flavored gum for chewing, typically sold in packets of individually wrapped thin strips.

chew·y /chóoee/ adj. (**chew·i·er**, **chew·i·est**) **1** needing much chewing. **2** suitable for chewing. □□ **chew·i·ness** n.

Chey·enne /shīán, –én/ n. & adj. **•**n. **1 a** a N. American people formerly living between the Missouri and Arkansas rivers. **b** a member of this people. **2** the language of this people. **•**adj. of or relating to the Cheyenne or their language. [Canadian F f. Dakota Sahiyena]

chez /shay/ prep. at the house or home of. [F f. OF chiese f. L casa cottage]

chi /kī/ n. the twenty-second letter of the Greek alphabet (X, χ). [ME f. Gk khi]

chi·ack /chíak/ v. & n. (also **chy·ack**) Austral. & NZ **•**v.tr. jeer; taunt. **•**n. jeering; banter. □□ **chi·ack·ing** n. [19th c.: orig. unkn.]

Chi·an·ti /keeaántee, keeán–/ n. (pl. **Chi·an·tis**) a dry, red Italian wine. [Chianti, an area in Tuscany, Italy]

chi·a·ro·scu·ro /keeaárəskóórō/ n. **1** the treatment of light and shade in drawing and painting. **2** the use of contrast in literature, etc. **3** (attrib.) half-revealed. [It. f. chiaro CLEAR + oscuro dark, OBSCURE]

chi·as·ma /kíazmə/ n. (pl. **chi·as·ma·ta** /–mətə/) Biol. the point at which paired chromosomes remain in contact after crossing over during meiosis. [mod.L f. Gk chiasma a cross-shaped mark]

chi·as·mus /kíazməs/ n. inversion in the second of two parallel phrases of the order followed in the first (e.g., to stop too fearful and too faint to go). □□ **chi·as·tic** /–ástik/ adj. [mod.L f. Gk khiasmos crosswise arrangement f. khiazō mark with letter CHI]

chi·bouk /chibóók, shi–/ n. (also **chi·bouque**) a long Turkish tobacco pipe. [Turk. çubuk tube]

chic /sheek/ adj. & n. **•**adj. (**chic·er**, **chic·est**) stylish; elegant (in dress or appearance). **•**n. stylishness; elegance. □□ **chic·ly** adv. [F]

chi·cane /shikáyn/ n. & v. **•**n. **1** chicanery. **2** an artificial barrier or obstacle on an automobile racecourse. **3** Bridge a hand without trump, or without cards of one suit. **•**v. archaic **1** intr. use chicanery. **2** tr. (usu. foll. by into, out of, etc.) cheat (a person). [F chicane(r) quibble]

chi·can·er·y /shikáynəree/ n. (pl. **·ies**) **1** clever but misleading talk; a false argument. **2** trickery; deception. [F chicanerie (as CHICANE)]

Chi·ca·no /chikáanō/ n. (pl. **·nos**; fem. **chi·ca·na**, pl. **·nas**) an American of Mexican origin. [Sp. mejicano Mexican]

chi·chi /sheéshee/ adj. & n. **•**adj. **1** (of a thing) frilly; showy. **2** (of a person or behavior) fussy; affected. **•**n. **1** overrefinement; pretentiousness; fussiness. **2** a frilly, showy, or pretentious object. [F]

chick¹ /chik/ n. **1 a** a young bird, esp. one newly hatched. **2** sl. **a** a young woman. **b** a child. [ME: shortening of CHICKEN]

chick² /chik/ n. Ind. a screen for a doorway, etc., made from split bamboo and twine. [Hindi chik]

chick·a·dee /chíkədee/ n. any of various small birds of the titmouse family, esp. Parus atricapillus with a distinctive black crown and throat. [imit.]

Chick·a·saw /chíkəsaw/ n. **1 a** a N. American people native to Mississippi and Alabama. **b** a member of this people. **2** the language of this people.

chick·en /chíkin/ n., adj., & v. **•**n. (pl. same or **chick·ens**) **1** a common breed of domestic fowl. **2 a** a domestic fowl prepared as food. **b** its flesh. **3** colloq.

black capped chickadee

a pastime testing courage, usu. recklessly. **•**adj. colloq. cowardly. **•**v.intr. (foll. by out) colloq. withdraw from or fail in some activity through fear or lack of nerve. [OE cīcen, cȳcen f. Gmc]

chick·en-and-egg prob·lem n. (also **chick·en di·lem·ma**, etc.) the unresolved question as to which of two things caused the other.

chick·en chol·er·a n. (also **fowl chol·er·a**) an infectious disease of fowls.

chick·en feed n. **1** food for poultry. **2** colloq. an unimportant amount, esp. of money.

chick·en-heart·ed /chíkinhaartəd/ adj. easily frightened; lacking nerve or courage.

chick·en-liv·ered adj. = CHICKENHEARTED.

chick·en pox n. an infectious disease, esp. of children, with a rash of small blisters. (Also called VARICELLA).

chick·en wire n. a light wire netting with a hexagonal mesh.

chick·pea /chíkpee/ n. **1** a leguminous plant, Cicer arietinum, with short, swollen pods containing yellow, beaked seeds. **2** this seed used as a vegetable. [orig. ciche pease f. L cicer: see PEASE]

chick·weed /chíkweed/ n. any of numerous small plants, esp. Stellaria media, a garden weed with slender stems and tiny white flowers.

chic•le /chíkəl/ n. the milky juice of the sapodilla tree, used in the manufacture of chewing gum. [Amer. Sp. f. Nahuatl *tzietli*]

chic•o•ry /chíkəree/ n. (pl. •ries) 1 a blue-flowered plant, *Cichorium intybus*, cultivated for its salad leaves and its root. 2 its root, roasted and ground for use with or instead of coffee. 3 = ENDIVE. [ME f. obs. F *cicorée* endive f. med.L *cic(h)orea* f. L *cichorium* f. Gk *kikhorion* SUCCORY]

chide /chīd/ v.tr. & intr. (past chid•ed or chid /chid/; past part. chid•ed or chid or chid•den /chíd'n/) archaic or literary scold; rebuke. □□ chid•er n. chid•ing•ly adv. [OE *cīdan*, of unkn. orig.]

chief /cheef/ n. & adj. • n. 1 a a leader or ruler. b the head of a tribe, clan, etc. 2 the head of a department; the highest official. 3 *Heraldry* the upper third of a shield. • adj. (usu. attrib.) 1 first in position, importance, influence, etc. (*chief engineer*). 2 prominent; leading. □ in chief supreme (*commander in chief*). □□ chief•dom n. [ME f. OF *ch(i)ef* ult. f. L *caput* head]

chief ex•ec•u•tive of•fi•cer n. the highest ranking executive in a corporation, organization, etc. ¶ Abbr.: **CEO.**

chief jus•tice n. 1 the presiding judge in a court having several judges. 2 (**Chief Justice of the United States**) the presiding judge of the US Supreme Court.

chief•ly /cheéflee/ adv. above all; mainly but not exclusively.

chief of staff n. the senior staff officer of a service or command.

chief•tain /cheéftən/ n. (fem. chief•tain•ess /–tənis/) the leader of a tribe, clan, etc. □□ chief•tain•cy /–tənsee/ n. (pl. •cies). chief•tain•ship n. [ME f. OF *chevetaine* f. LL *capitaneus* CAPTAIN: assim. to CHIEF]

chiff•chaff /chífchaf/ n. a small European bird, *Phylloscopus collybita*, of the warbler family. [imit.]

chif•fon /shifón, shífon/ n. & adj. • n. a light, diaphanous fabric of silk, nylon, etc. • adj. 1 made of chiffon. 2 (of a pie filling, dessert, etc.) light-textured. [F f. *chiffe* rag]

chif•fo•nier /shífəneer/ n. 1 a tall chest of drawers. 2 a movable low cupboard with a sideboard top. [F *chiffonnier*, –*ière* ragpicker, chest of drawers for odds and ends]

chig•ger /chígər/ n. 1 = CHIGOE. 2 any harvest mite of the genus *Leptotrombidium* with parasitic larvae. [var. of CHIGOE]

chi•gnon /shéenyon, sheenyón/ n. a coil or knot of hair worn at the back of the head. [F, orig. = nape of the neck]

chig•oe /chígō/ n. a tropical flea, *Tunga penetrans*, the females of which burrow beneath the skin causing painful sores. Also called CHIGGER. [Carib]

chi•hua•hua /chiwaáwə/ n. 1 a very small dog of a smooth-haired, large-eyed breed originating in Mexico. 2 this breed. [*Chihuahua* state and city in Mexico]

chil•blain /chílblayn/ n. a painful, itchy swelling of the skin, usu. on a hand, foot, etc., caused by exposure to cold and by poor circulation. □□ chil•blained adj. [CHILL + BLAIN]

chihuahua

child /chīld/ n. (pl. chil•dren /chíldrən/) 1 a a young human being below the age of puberty. b an unborn or newborn human being. 2 one's son or daughter (at any age). 3 (foll. by of) a descendant, follower, adherent, or product of (*children of Israel*; *child of God*; *child of nature*). 4 a childish person. □□ child•less adj. child•less•ness n. [OE *cild*]

child a•buse n. maltreatment of a child, esp. by physical violence or sexual molestation.

child•bear•ing /chíldbairing/ n. the act of giving birth to a child or children.

child•bed /chíldbed/ n. archaic = CHILDBIRTH.

child•birth /chíldbərth/ n. the act of giving birth to a child.

child care n. the care of children, esp. by someone other than a parent, as at a day-care center, etc.

Childe /chīld/ n. archaic a youth of noble birth (*Childe Harold*). [var. of CHILD]

Chil•der•mas /chíldərmas/ n. archaic the feast of the Holy Innocents, Dec. 28. [OE *cildramæsse* f. cildra genit. pl. of cild CHILD + *mæsse* MASS²]

child•hood /chíldhŏŏd/ n. the state or period of being a child. [OE *cildhād*]

child•ish /chíldish/ adj. 1 of, like, or proper to a child. 2 immature, silly. □□ child•ish•ly adv. child•ish•ness n.

child•like /chíldlīk/ adj. having the good qualities of a child as innocence, frankness, etc.

child•mind•er /chíldmīndər/ n. *Brit.* a person who looks after children for payment; baby-sitter.

child•proof /chíldprŏŏf/ adj. & v. • adj. that cannot be damaged, opened, or operated by a child. • v.tr. make inaccessible to children (*childproof those cabinets with safety latches*).

chil•dren pl. of CHILD.

child's play n. an easy task.

Chil•e•an /chíleeən, chiláyən/ n. & adj. • n. 1 a native or national of Chile in S. America. 2 a person of Chilean descent. • adj. of or relating to Chile.

Chil•e pine /chílee, cheélay/ n. a monkey puzzle tree.

Chil•e salt•pe•ter /chílee/ n. (also **Chil•e ni•ter**) naturally occurring sodium nitrate.

chil•i /chílee/ n. (pl. •ies) a small, hot-tasting dried red pod of a capsicum, *Capsicum frutescens*, used as seasoning and in curry powder, cayenne pepper, etc. [Sp. *chile, chili*, f. Aztec *chilli*]

chil•i•ad /kíleead/ n. 1 a thousand. 2 a thousand years. [LL *chilias chiliad-* f. Gk *khilias –ados*]

chil•i•asm /kíleeazəm/ n. the doctrine of or belief in Christ's prophesied reign of 1,000 years on earth (see MILLENNIUM). [Gk *khiliasmos*: see CHILIAD]

chil•i•ast /kíleeast/ n. a believer in chiliasm. □□ chil•i•as•tic /–ástik/ adj. [LL *chiliastes*: see CHILIAD, CHILIASM]

chil•i con car•ne /kon kaárnee/ n. a stew of chili-flavored ground meat and usu. beans.

chil•i pow•der n. a powder made of dried chilies, garlic, herbs, spices, etc., used as a seasoning.

chil•i sauce n. a spicy sauce made with tomatoes, chilies, and spices.

chill /chil/ n., v., & adj. • n. 1 an unpleasant cold sensation; lowered body temperature. b a feverish cold (*catch a chill*). 2 unpleasant coldness (of air, water, etc.). 3 a a depressing influence (*cast a chill over*). b a feeling of fear or dread accompanied by coldness. 4 coldness of manner. • v. 1 tr. & intr. make or become cold. 2 tr. depress; dispirit. 3 tr. cool (food or drink); preserve by cooling. 4 intr. sl. = chill out. 5 tr. harden (molten metal) by contact with cold material. • adj. = CHILLY. □ chill out become calm or less agitated. take the chill off warm slightly. □□ chill•er n. chill•ing•ly adv. chill•ness n. chill•some adj. *literary*. [OE *cele, ciele*, etc.: in mod. use the verb is the oldest (ME), and is of obscure orig.]

chill•y /chílee/ adj. (chill•i•er, chill•i•est) 1 (of the weather or an object) somewhat cold. 2 (of a person or animal) feeling somewhat cold; sensitive to the cold. 3 unfriendly; unemotional. □□ chill•i•ness n.

Chil•tern Hun•dreds /chíltərn/ n.pl. (in the UK) a Crown manor, whose administration is a nominal office for which a member of Parliament applies as a way of resigning from the House of Commons. [*Chiltern* Hills in S. England]

chi•mae•ra var. of CHIMERA.

chime¹ /chīm/ n. & v. • n. 1 a a set of attuned bells. b the series of sounds given by this. c (usu. in pl.) a set of attuned bells as a door bell. 2 agreement; correspondence; harmony. • v. 1 a intr. (of bells) ring. b tr. sound (a bell or chime) by striking. 2 tr. show (the hour) by chiming. 3 intr. (usu. foll. by together, with) be in agreement; harmonize. □ chime in 1 interject a remark. 2 join in harmoniously. 3 (foll. by with) agree with. □□ chim•er n. [ME, prob. f. *chym(b)e* bell f. OE *cimbal* f. L *cymbalum* f. Gk *kumbalon* CYMBAL]

chime² /chīm/ n. (also chimb) the projecting rim at the end of a cask. [ME: cf. MDu., MLG *kimme*]

chi•me•ra /kīmeérə, kee–/ (also chi•mae•ra) n. 1 (in Greek mythology) a fire-breathing female monster with a lion's head, a goat's body, and a serpent's tail. 2 a fantastic or grotesque product of the imagination; a bogey. 3 any fabulous beast with parts taken from various animals. 4 *Biol.* a an organism containing genetically different tissues, formed by grafting, mutation, etc. b a nucleic acid formed by laboratory manipulation. 5 any cartilaginous fish of the family Chimaeridae, usu. having a long tapering caudal fin. □□ chi•mer•ic /–mérik/ adj. chi•mer•i•cal adj. chi•mer•i•cal•ly adv. [L f. Gk *khimaira* she-goat, chimera]

chim•ney /chímnee/ n. (pl. •neys) 1 a vertical channel conducting smoke or combustion gases, etc., up and away from a fire, furnace, etc. 2 the part of this that projects above a roof. 3 a glass tube protecting the flame of a lamp. 4 a narrow vertical crack in a rock face, often used by mountaineers to ascend. [ME f. OF *cheminée* f. LL *caminata* having a fireplace, f. L *caminus* f. Gk *kaminos* oven]

chim•ney breast n. a projecting interior wall surrounding a chimney.

chim•ney•piece /chímneepees/ n. esp. *Brit.* an ornamental structure around an open fireplace; a mantelpiece.

chim•ney pot n. an earthenware or metal pipe at the top of a chimney, narrowing the aperture and increasing the updraft.

chim•ney sweep n. a person whose job is removing soot from inside chimneys.

chimp /chimp/ n. *colloq.* = CHIMPANZEE. [abbr.]

chim•pan•zee /chímpanzeé, chimpánzee/ n. a small African anthropoid ape, *Pan troglodytes*. [F *chimpanzé* f. Kongo]

chin /chin/ n. the front of the lower jaw. □ chin up *colloq.* cheer up. keep one's chin up *colloq.* remain cheerful, esp. in adversity. take on the chin 1 suffer a severe blow from (a misfortune, etc.). 2 endure courageously. □ –chinned adj. (in comb.). [OE *cin(n)* f. Gmc]

china /chínə/ n. & adj. • n. 1 a kind of fine white or translucent ceramic ware, porcelain, etc. **2** things made from ceramic, esp. household tableware. **3** *Brit. rhyming sl.* one's 'mate,' i.e., husband or wife (short for *china plate*). ● *adj.* made of china. [orig. *China ware* (from China in Asia): name f. Pers. *chīnī*]

Chi·na as·ter *n.* a plant, *Callistephus chinensis*, related to the aster and cultivated for its bright and showy flowers.

chi·na clay *n.* kaolin.

Chi·na·graph /chínəgraf/ *n. Trademark* a waxy colored pencil used to write on china, glass, etc.

Chi·na·man /chínəmən/ *n.* (*pl.* ·**men**) *archaic* or *derog.* (now usu. *offens.*) a native of China.

Chi·na tea *n.* smoke-cured tea from a small-leaved tea plant grown in China.

Chi·na·town /chínətown/ *n.* a district of any non-Chinese city in which the population is predominantly Chinese.

chinch /chinch/ *n.* (in full **chinch bug**) **1** a small insect, *Blissus leucopterus*, that destroys the shoots of grasses and grains. **2** a bedbug. [Sp. *chinche* f. L *cimex –icis*]

chin·che·rin·chee /chínchərinchee, chíngkə–/ *n.* a white-flowered bulbous plant, *Ornithogalum thyrsoides*, native to S. Africa. [imit. of the squeaky rubbing of its stalks]

chin·chil·la /chinchílə/ *n.* **1 a** any small rodent of the genus *Chinchilla*, native to S. America, having soft, silver-gray fur and a bushy tail. **b** its highly valued fur. **2** a breed of cat or rabbit. [Sp. prob. f. S. Amer. native name]

chin-chin /chínchín/ *int. Brit. colloq.* a toast; a greeting or farewell. [Chin. *qingqing* (pr. ch-)]

Chindit /chíndit/ *n. hist.* a member of the Allied forces behind the Japanese lines in Burma (now Myanmar) in 1943–45. [Burm. *chinthé*, a mythical creature]

chine[1] /chīn/ *n. & v.* ● *n.* **1 a** a backbone, esp. of an animal. **b** a joint of meat containing all or part of this. **2** a ridge or arête. ● *v. tr.* cut (meat) across or along the backbone. [ME f. OF *eschine* f. L *spina* SPINE]

chine[2] /chīn/ *n. Brit. dial.* a deep, narrow ravine formed by running water. [OE *cinu* chink, etc., f. Gmc]

chine[3] /chīn/ *n.* the joint between the side and the bottom of a ship, etc. [var. of CHIME[2]]

Chi·nese /chíneez/ *adj. & n.* ● *adj.* **a** of or relating to China. **b** of Chinese descent. ● *n.* **1** the Chinese language. **2** (*pl.* same) **a** a native or national of China. **b** a person of Chinese descent.

Chi·nese cab·bage *n.* **1** = BOK CHOY. **2** a lettucelike cabbage, *Brassica chinensis.*

Chi·nese goose·ber·ry *n.* = KIWI FRUIT.

Chi·nese lan·tern *n.* **1** a collapsible paper lantern. **2** a solanaceous plant, *Physalis alkekengi*, bearing white flowers and globular orange fruits enclosed in an orange-red, papery calyx.

Chi·nese puz·zle *n.* a very intricate puzzle or problem.

Chi·nese wa·ter chest·nut *n.* see WATER CHESTNUT 2.

Chi·nese white *n.* zinc oxide as a white pigment.

Chink /chingk/ *n. sl. offens.* a Chinese person. □□ **Chink·y** *adj.* [abbr.]

chink[1] /chingk/ *n.* **1** an unintended crack that admits light or allows an attack; a flaw. **2** a narrow opening; a slit. [16th c.: rel. to CHINE[2]]

Chinese lanterns

chink[2] /chingk/ *v. & n.* ● *v.* **1** *intr.* make a slight ringing sound, as of glasses or coins striking together. **2** *tr.* cause to make this sound. ● *n.* this sound. [imit.]

chin·less /chínlis/ *adj. colloq.* weak or feeble in character.

chin·less won·der *n. Brit.* an ineffectual, esp. upper-class, person.

chi·no /cheenō/ *n.* (*pl.* ·**nos**) **1** a cotton twill fabric, usu. khaki-colored. **2** (in *pl.*) a garment, esp. trousers, made from this. [Amer. Sp., = toasted]

Chino- /chínō/ *comb. form* = SINO-.

chi·nois *n.* a cone-shaped sieve made with closely-woven mesh for straining sauces.

chi·noi·se·rie /sheenwáazəree/ *n.* **1** the imitation of Chinese motifs and techniques in painting and in decorating furniture. **2** an object or objects in this style. [F]

Chi·nook /shənõŏk, chə–/ *n.* **1 a** a N. American people native to the northwestern coast of the US. **b** a member of this people. **2** the language of this people and other nearby peoples. **3** (**chinook**) **a** a warm, dry wind that blows east of the Rocky Mountains. **b** a warm, wet southerly wind west of the Rocky Mountains. □□ **Chi·nook·an**, *adj.*

chinois

chi·nook salm·on *n.* a large salmon, *Oncorhynchus tshawytscha*, of the N. Pacific.

chin strap *n.* a strap for fastening a hat, etc., under the chin.

chintz /chints/ *n. & adj.* ● *n.* a printed, multicolored cotton fabric with a glazed finish. ● *adj.* made from or upholstered with this fabric. [earlier *chints* (pl.) f. Hindi *chīnṭ* f. Skr. *citra* variegated]

chintz·y /chíntsee/ *adj.* (**chintz·i·er, chintz·i·est**) **1** like chintz. **2** gaudy; cheap. **3** characteristic of the decor associated with chintz soft furnishings. □□ **chintz·i·ly** *adv.* **chintz·i·ness** *n.*

chin-up *n.* an exercise in which the chin is raised up to the level of an overhead horizontal bar that one grasps.

chi·o·no·dox·a /kíənədóksə/ *n.* any liliaceous plant of the genus *Chionodoxa*, having early-blooming blue flowers. Also called **glory-of-the-snow**. [mod.L f. Gk *khiōn* snow + *doxa* glory]

chip /chip/ *n. & v.* ● *n.* **1** a small piece removed by or in the course of chopping, cutting, or breaking, esp. from hard material such as wood or stone. **2** the place where such a chip has been made. **3 a** = POTATO CHIP. **b** (*Brit.* usu. in *pl.*) a strip of potato, deep fried (*fish and chips*). **4** a counter used in some gambling games to represent money. **5** *Electronics* = MICROCHIP. **6** *Brit.* **a** a thin strip of wood, straw, etc., used for weaving hats, baskets, etc. **b** a basket made from these. **7** *Soccer & golf*, etc. a short shot, kick, or pass with the ball describing an arc. ● *v.* (**chipped, chip·ping**) **1** *tr.* (often foll. by *off, away*) cut or break (a piece) from a hard material. **2** *intr.* (foll. by *at, away at*) cut pieces off (a hard material) to alter its shape, break it up, etc. **3** *intr.* (of stone, china, etc.) be susceptible to being chipped; be apt to break at the edge (*will chip easily*). **4** *tr.* (also *absol.*) *Soccer & Golf* etc. strike or kick (the ball) with a chip (cf. sense 7 of *n.*). **5** *tr.* (usu. as **chipped** *adj.*) cut into chips. □ **chip in** *colloq.* **1** interrupt or contribute abruptly to a conversation (*chipped in with a reminiscence*). **2** contribute (money or resources). **a chip off the old block** one who resembles a parent, esp. in character. **a chip on one's shoulder** *colloq.* a disposition or inclination to feel resentful or aggrieved. **in the chips** *sl.* moneyed; affluent. **when the chips are down** *colloq.* in times of discouragement or disappointment. [ME f. OE *cipp, cyp* beam]

chip·board /chípbawrd/ *n.* a rigid sheet or panel made from compressed wood chips and resin.

chip·munk /chípmungk/ *n.* any ground squirrel of the genus *Tamias* or *Eutamias*, having alternate light and dark stripes running down the body. [Algonquian]

chipmunk

chip·o·la·ta /chípəláatə/ *n. Brit.* a small, thin sausage. [F f. It. *cipollata* a dish of onions f. *cipolla* onion]

Chip·pen·dale /chípəndayl/ *adj.* **1** (of furniture) designed or made by the English cabinetmaker Thomas Chippendale (d. 1779). **2** in the ornately elegant style of Chippendale's furniture.

chip·per /chípər/ *adj. colloq.* **1** cheerful. **2** smartly dressed. [perh. f. No. of Engl. dial. *kipper* lively]

Chip·pe·wa /chípəwaw, –wə, –waa, –way/ *n.* = OJIBWA.

chip·pie var. of CHIPPY[2].

chip·ping /chíping/ *n. Brit.* **1** a small fragment of stone, wood, etc. **2** (in *pl.*) these used as a surface for roads, roofs, etc.

chip·py[1] /chípee/ *adj.* (**chip·pi·er, chip·pi·est**) marked by belligerence or aggression, esp. in the play of ice hockey.

chip·py[2] /chípee/ *n.* (also **chip·pie**) (*pl.* ·**pies**) **1** *derog.* a promiscuous female; a prostitute. **2** *Brit. colloq.* a fish-and-chip store.

chip shot *n. Soccer*, etc., & *Golf* a short shot, kick, or pass with the ball describing an arc.

chi·ral /kírəl/ *adj. Chem.* (of a crystal, etc.) not superimposable on its mirror image. □□ **chi·ral·i·ty** /–rálitee/ *n.* [Gk *kheir* hand]

Chi-Rho /kí/ *n.* a monogram of chi and rho as the first two letters of Greek *Khristos* Christ.

chiro- /kírō/ (also **cheiro-**) *comb. form* of the hand. [Gk *kheir* hand]

chi·rog·ra·phy /kírógrəfee/ *n.* handwriting; calligraphy.

chi·ro·man·cy /kírəmansee/ *n.* palmistry.

chi·rop·o·dy /kirópədee/ = PODIATRY. □□ **chi·rop·o·dist** *n.* [CHIRO- + Gk *pous podos* foot]

chi·ro·prac·tic /kírəpráktik/ *n.* the diagnosis and manipulative treatment of mechanical disorders of the joints, esp. of the spinal column. □□ **chi·ro·prac·tor** *n.* [CHIRO- + Gk *praktikos*: see PRACTICAL]

chi·rop·ter·an /kíróptərən/ *n.* any member of the order Chiroptera, with membraned limbs serving as wings including bats and flying foxes. □□ **chi·rop·ter·ous** *adj.* [CHIRO- + Gk *pteron* wing]

chirp /chərp/ *v. & n.* ● *v.* **1** *intr.* (usu. of small birds, grasshoppers, etc.) utter a short, sharp, high-pitched note. **2** *tr. & intr.* (esp. of a child) speak or utter in a lively or jolly way. ● *n.* a chirping sound. □□ **chirp·er** *n.* [ME, earlier *chirk, chirt*: imit.]

chirp·y /chɔ́rpee/ *adj. colloq.* (**chirp·i·er, chirp·i·est**) cheerful; lively. □□ **chirp·i·ly** *adv.* **chirp·i·ness** *n.*

chirr /chər/ v. & n. (also **churr**) ● v.intr. (esp. of insects) make a prolonged low trilling sound. ● n. this sound. [imit.]

chir·rup /chírəp/ v. & n. ● v.intr. (**chir·ruped, chir·rup·ing**) (esp. of small birds) chirp, esp. repeatedly; twitter. ● n. a chirruping sound. □□ **chir·rup·y** adj. [trilled form of CHIRP]

chis·el /chízəl/ n. & v. ● n. a hand tool with a squared, beveled blade for shaping wood, stone, or metal. ● v. **1** tr. (**chis·eled, chis·el·ing**; esp. Brit. **chis·elled, chis·el·ling**) cut or shape with a chisel. **2** tr. (as chiseled adj.) (of facial features) clear-cut; fine. **3** tr. & intr. sl. cheat; swindle. □□ **chis·el·er** n. [ME f. ONF ult. f. LL cisorium f. L caedere caes- cut]

chi-square test n. a method of comparing observed and theoretical values in statistics.

chit[1] /chit/ n. **1** derog. or joc. a young, small, or frail girl or woman (esp. a chit of a girl). **2** a young child. [ME, = whelp, cub, kitten, perh. = dial. chit sprout]

chit[2] /chit/ n. **1** a note of requisition; a note of a sum owed, esp. for food or drink. **2** esp. Brit. a note or memorandum. [earlier chitty: Anglo-Ind. f. Hindi ciṭṭhī pass f. Skr. citra mark]

chi·tal /cheétl/ n. = AXIS[2]. [Hindi cītal]

chit·chat /chítchat/ n. & v. colloq. ● n. light conversation; gossip. ● v.intr. (·chat·ted, ·chat·ting) talk informally; gossip. [redupl. of CHAT[1]]

chi·tin /kít'n/ n. Chem. a polysaccharide forming the major constituent in the exoskeleton of arthropods and in the cell walls of fungi. □□ **chi·tin·ous** adj. [F chitine irreg. f. Gk khitōn: see CHITON]

chi·ton /kít'n, –ton/ n. **1** a long, woolen tunic worn by ancient Greeks. **2** any marine mollusk of the class Amphineura, having a shell of overlapping plates. [Gk khitōn tunic]

chit·ter·lings /chítlin/ n. (also **chit·lings, chit·lins**) the small intestines of pigs, etc., esp. as cooked for food. [ME: orig. uncert.]

chiv·al·rous /shívəlrəs/ adj. **1** (usu. of a male) gallant; honorable; courteous. **2** involving or showing chivalry. □□ **chiv·al·rous·ly** adv. [ME f. OF chevalerous: see CHEVALIER]

chiv·al·ry /shívəlree/ n. **1** the medieval knightly system with its religious, moral, and social code. **2** the combination of qualities expected of an ideal knight, esp. courage, honor, courtesy, justice, and readiness to help the weak. **3** a man's courteous behavior, esp. toward women. **4** archaic knights, noblemen, and horsemen collectively. □□ **chiv·al·ric** adj. [ME f. OF chevalerie, etc., f. med.L caballerius for LL caballarius horseman: see CAVALIER]

chive /chiv/ n. a small alliaceous plant, Allium schoenoprasum, having purple-pink flowers and dense tufts of long tubular leaves, which are used as an herb. [ME f. OF cive f. L cepa onion]

chiv·vy /chívee/ v.tr. (·vies, ·vied) (also **chiv·y, chev·y** /chévee/) harass; nag; pursue. [chevy (n. & v.), prob. f. the ballad of Chevy Chase, a place on the Scottish border]

chla·myd·i·a /kləmídeeə/ n. (pl. **chla·myd·i·ae** /–dee-ee/) any parasitic bacterium of the genus Chlamydia, some of which cause diseases such as trachoma, psittacosis, and nonspecific urethritis. [mod.L f. Gk khlamus –udos cloak]

chlam·y·dom·o·nas /klámidəmónəs/ n. any unicellular green freshwater alga of the genus Chlamydomonas. [mod.L (as CHLAMYDIA)]

chlor- var. of CHLORO-.

chlo·ral /kláwrəl/ n. **1** a colorless liquid aldehyde used in making DDT. **2** (in full **chloral hydrate**) Pharm. a colorless crystalline solid made from chloral and used as a sedative. [F f. chlore chlorine + alcool alcohol]

chlo·ram·phen·i·col /kláwramfénikawl, –kol/ n. Pharm. an antibiotic prepared from Streptomyces venezuelae or produced synthetically and used esp. against typhoid fever. [CHLORO- + AMIDE + PHENO- + NITRO- + GLYCOL]

chlo·rate /kláwrayt/ n. Chem. any salt of chloric acid.

chlo·rel·la /klawrélə/ n. any nonmotile, unicellular green alga of the genus Chlorella. [mod.L, dimin. of Gk khlōros green]

chlo·ric ac·id /kláwrik/ n. Chem. a colorless liquid acid with strong oxidizing properties. [CHLORO- + –IC]

chlo·ride /kláwrid/ n. Chem. **1** any compound of chlorine with another element or group. **2** any bleaching agent containing chloride. [CHLORO- + –IDE]

chlo·ri·nate /kláwrinayt/ v.tr. **1** impregnate or treat with chlorine. **2** Chem. cause to react or combine with chlorine. □□ **chlo·ri·na·tor** n.

chlo·ri·na·tion /kláwrináyshən/ n. **1** the treatment of water with chlorine to disinfect it. **2** Chem. a reaction in which chlorine is introduced into a compound.

chlo·rine /kláwreen/ n. Chem. a poisonous, greenish-yellow gaseous element of the halogen group occurring naturally in salt, seawater, rock salt, etc., and used for purifying water, bleaching, and the manufacture of many organic chemicals. ¶ Symb.: **Cl**. [Gk khlōros green + –INE[4]]

chlo·rite /kláwrit/ n. Chem. any salt of chlorous acid. □□ **chlo·rit·ic** /–ritik/ adj.

chloro- /kláwrō/ comb. form (also **chlor-** esp. before a vowel) **1** Bot. & Mineral. green. **2** Chem. chlorine. [Gk khlōros green: in sense 2 f. CHLORINE]

chlo·ro·fluor·o·car·bon see CFC.

chlo·ro·form /kláwrəfawrm/ n. & v. ● n. a colorless, volatile, sweet-smelling liquid used as a solvent and formerly used as a general anesthetic. ¶ Chem. formula: CHCl₃. ● v.tr. render (a person) unconscious with this. [F chloroforme formed as CHLORO- + formyle: see FORMIC(ACID)]

Chlo·ro·my·ce·tin /kláwrōmíseetin/ n. Trademark = CHLORAMPHENICOL. [CHLORO- + Gk mukēs –ētos fungus]

chlo·ro·phyll /kláwrəfil/ n. the green pigment found in most plants, responsible for light absorption to provide energy for photosynthesis. □□ **chlo·ro·phyl·lous** /–filəs/ adj. [F chlorophylle f. Gk phullon leaf: see CHLORO-]

chlo·ro·plast /kláwrōplast/ n. a plastid containing chlorophyll, found in plant cells undergoing photosynthesis. [G: (as CHLORO-, PLASTID)]

chlo·ro·sis /klərósis/ n. **1** hist. a severe form of anemia from iron deficiency esp. in young women, causing a greenish complexion (cf. GREENSICK). **2** Bot. a reduction or loss of the normal green coloration of plants. □□ **chlo·rot·ic** /–rótik/ adj. [CHLORO- + –OSIS]

chlo·rous ac·id /kláwrəs/ n. Chem. a pale yellow liquid acid with oxidizing properties. ¶ Chem. formula: HClO₂. [CHLORO- + –OUS]

chlor·prom·a·zine /klawrpróməzeen/ n. Pharm. a drug used as a sedative and to control nausea and vomiting. [F (as CHLORO-, PROMETHAZINE)]

choc /chok/ n. & adj. Brit. colloq. chocolate. [abbr.]

chock /chok/ n., v., & adv. ● n. a block or wedge of wood to check motion, esp. of a cask or a wheel. ● v.tr. **1** fit or make fast with chocks. **2** (usu. foll. by up) Brit. cram full. ● adv. as closely or tightly as possible. [prob. f. OF çouche, çoche, of unkn. orig.]

chock·a·block /chókəblók/ adj. & adv. crammed close together; crammed full (a street chockablock with cars). [orig. Naut., with ref. to tackle with the two blocks run close together]

chock·er /chókər/ adj. Brit. sl. fed up; disgusted. [CHOCKABLOCK]

chock-full adj. = CHOCKABLOCK (chock-full of rubbish).

choc·o·late /cháwkələt, cháwklət, chók–/ n. & adj. ● n. **1 a** a food preparation in the form of a paste or solid block made from roasted and ground cacao seeds, usually sweetened. **b** a candy made of or coated with this. **c** a drink made with chocolate. **2** a deep brown color. ● adj. **1** made from or of chocolate. **2** chocolate-colored. □□ **choc·o·lat·y** adj. (also **choc·o·lat·ey**).

WORD HISTORY chocolate

Early 17th century (in the sense 'a drink made with chocolate'): from French chocolat or Spanish chocolate, from Nahuatl chocolatl 'food made from cacao seeds,' influenced by unrelated cacauaatl 'drink made from cacao.'

Choc·taw /chóktaw/ n. (pl. same or **Choc·taws**) **1 a** a N. American people orig. from Alabama. **b** an individual of this people. **c** the language of this people. **2** (in skating) a step from one edge of a skate to the other edge of the other skate in the opposite direction. [native name]

choice /choys/ n. & adj. ● n. **1 a** the act or an instance of choosing. **b** a thing or person chosen (not a good choice). **2** a range from which to choose. **3** (usu. foll. by of) the élite; the best. **4** the power or opportunity to choose (what choice have I?). ● adj. of superior quality; carefully chosen. □□ **choice·ly** adv. **choice·ness** n. [ME f. OF chois f. choisir CHOOSE]

choir /kwir/ n. **1** a regular group of singers, esp. taking part in church services. **2** the part of a cathedral or large church between the altar and the nave, used by the choir and clergy. **3** a company of singers, birds, angels, etc. (a heavenly choir). **4** Mus. a group of instruments of one family playing together. [ME f. OF quer f. L chorus: see CHORUS]

choir·boy /kwirboy/ n. a boy who sings in a church or cathedral choir.

choir loft n. a church gallery in which the choir is situated.

choke[1] /chōk/ v. & n. ● v.tr. **1** tr. hinder or impede the breathing of (a person or animal), esp. by constricting the windpipe or (of gas, smoke, etc.) by being unbreathable. **2** intr. suffer a hindrance or stoppage of breath. **3** tr. & intr. make or become speechless from emotion. **4** tr. retard the growth of or kill (esp. plants) by the deprivation of light, air, nourishment, etc. **5** tr. (often foll. by back) suppress (feelings) with difficulty. **6** tr. block or clog (a passage, tube, etc.). **7** tr. (as choked adj.) Brit. colloq. disgusted; disappointed. **8** tr. enrich the fuel mixture in (an internal combustion engine) by reducing the intake of air. ● n. **1** the valve in the carburetor of an internal combustion engine that controls the intake of air, esp. to enrich the fuel mixture. **2** Electr. an inductance coil used to smooth the variations of an alternating current or to alter its phase. □ **choke down** swallow with difficulty. **choke up 1** become overly anxious or emotionally affected (got all choked up over that sad movie). **2** block (a channel, etc.). [ME f. OE ācēocian f. cēoce, cēce CHEEK]

choke² /chōk/ n. the center part of an artichoke. [prob. confusion of the ending of *artichoke* with CHOKE¹]

choke·ber·ry /chōkberee/ n. (pl. ·ries) Bot. **1** any rosaceous shrub of the genus *Aronia*. **2** its scarlet berrylike fruit.

choke chain n. (also **choke col·lar**) a chain formed into a loop by passing one end through a ring on the other, placed around a dog's neck to exert control by causing pressure on its windpipe when the dog pulls.

choke·cher·ry /chōkcheree/ n. (pl. ·ries) an astringent N. American cherry, *Prunus virginiana*.

choke·damp /chōkdamp/ n. carbon dioxide in mines, wells, etc.

chok·er /chōkər/ n. **1** a close-fitting necklace or ornamental neckband. **2** a clerical or other high collar.

chok·y¹ /chōkee/ n. (also **chok·ey**) (pl. ·ies or ·eys) Brit. sl. prison. [orig. Anglo-Ind., f. Hindi *caukī* shed]

chok·y² /chōkee/ adj. (**chok·i·er, chok·i·est**) tending to choke or to cause choking.

cho·lan·gi·og·ra·phy /kōlanjeeógrəfee/ n. Med. X-ray examination of the bile ducts, used to find the site and nature of any obstruction. [CHOLE- + Gk *aggeion* vessel + –GRAPHY]

chole- /kōlee/ comb. form (also **chol-** esp. before a vowel) Med. & Chem. bile. [Gk *kholē* gall, bile]

cho·le·cal·cif·er·ol /kōlikalsífərawl, –rol/ n. one of the D vitamins, produced by the action of sunlight on a cholesterol derivative widely distributed in the skin, a deficiency of which results in rickets in children and osteomalacia in adults. Also called **vitamin D₃**. [CHOLE- + CALCIFEROL]

cho·le·cys·tog·ra·phy /kōlisistógrəfee/ n. Med. X-ray examination of the gallbladder, esp. used to detect the presence of any gallstones. [CHOLE- + CYSTO- + –GRAPHY]

chol·er /kólər/ n. **1** hist. one of the four humors, bile. **2** poet. or archaic anger; irascibility. [ME f. OF *colere* bile, anger f. L *cholera* f. Gk *kholera* diarrhea, in LL = bile, anger, f. Gk *kholē* bile]

chol·er·a /kólərə/ n. Med. an infectious and often fatal disease of the small intestine caused by the bacterium *Vibrio cholerae*, resulting in severe vomiting and diarrhea. □□ **chol·e·ra·ic** /–ráyik/ adj. [ME f. L f. Gk *kholera*: see CHOLER]

chol·er·ic /kólərik, kəlérik/ adj. irascible; angry. □□ **chol·er·i·cal·ly** adv. [ME f. OF *cholerique* f. L *cholericus* f. Gk *kholerikos*: see CHOLER]

PRONUNCIATION TIP choleric

The British English pronunciation of this word places the stress on the first syllable ("KAHL-er-ik"), as in *cholera*. A variant American English pronunciation places the stress on the second syllable ("kah-LEHR-ik").

---

cho·les·ter·ol /kəléstərawl, –rōl/ n. Biochem. a sterol found in most body tissues, including the blood, where high concentrations promote arteriosclerosis. [*cholesterin* f. Gk *kholē* bile + *stereos* stiff]

cho·li /chōlee/ n. (pl. **cho·lis**) a type of short-sleeved bodice worn by Hindu women. [Hindi *colī*]

cho·li·am·bus /kōleeámbəs/ n. Prosody a line of iambic meter with the last foot being a spondee or trochee. □□ **cho·li·am·bic** /–ámbik/ adj. [LL *choliambus* f. Gk *khōliambos* f. *khōlos* lame: see IAMBUS]

cho·line /kōleen/ n. Biochem. a basic nitrogenous organic compound occurring widely in living matter. [G *Cholin* f. Gk *kholē* bile]

chomp /chomp/ v.tr. = CHAMP¹. [imit.]

chon·drite /kóndrīt/ n. a stony meteorite containing small mineral granules. [Gk *chondri* f. Gk *khondros* granule]

chon·dro·cra·ni·um /kóndrōkráyneeəm/ n. Anat. the embryonic skull composed of cartilage and later replaced by bone. [Gk *khondros* grain, cartilage]

choo-choo /chōōchōō/ n. colloq. (esp. as a child's word) a railroad train or locomotive, esp. a steam engine. [imit.]

chook /chōōk/ n. (also **chook·ie**) Austral. & NZ colloq. **1** a chicken or fowl. **2** sl. an older woman. [E dial. *chuck* chicken]

choose /chōōz/ v. (past **chose** /chōz/; past part. **cho·sen** /chōzən/) **1** tr. select out of a greater number. **2** intr. (usu. foll. by *between, from*) take or select one or another. **3** tr. (usu. foll. by *to* + infin.) decide; be determined (*chose to stay behind*). **4** tr. (foll. by complement) select as (*was chosen king*). **5** tr. Theol. (esp. as **chosen** adj.) destine to be saved (*God's chosen people*). □ **cannot choose but** archaic must. **nothing** (or **little**) **to choose between them** they are equivalent. □□ **choos·er** n. [OE *cēosan* f. Gmc]

choos·y /chōōzee/ adj. (**choos·i·er, choos·i·est**) colloq. fastidious. □□ **choos·i·ly** adv. **choos·i·ness** n.

chop¹ /chop/ v. & n. • v.tr. (**chopped, chop·ping**) **1** (usu. foll. by *off, down*, etc.) cut or fell by a blow, usu. with an axe. **2** (often foll. by *up*) cut (esp. meat or vegetables) into small pieces. **3** strike (esp. a ball) with a short heavy edgewise blow. **4** colloq. dispense with; shorten or curtail. • n. **1** a cutting blow, esp. with an axe. **2** a thick slice of meat (esp. pork or lamb) usu. including a rib. **3** a short, sharp, edgewise stroke or blow in tennis, karate, boxing, etc. **4** the

broken motion of water, usu. owing to the action of the wind against the tide. **5** (prec. by *the*) Brit. sl. a dismissal from employment. **b** the action of killing or being killed. [ME, var. of CHAP¹]

chop² /chop/ n. (usu. in pl.) the jaw of an animal, etc. [16th-c. var. (occurring earlier) of CHAP³, of unkn. orig.]

chop³ /chop/ v.intr. (**chopped, chop·ping**) □ **chop and change** Brit. vacillate; change direction frequently. [ME, perh. rel. to *chap* f. OE *cēapian* (as CHEAP)]

chop⁴ /chop/ n. Brit. archaic a trademark; a brand of goods. □ **not much chop** esp. Austral. & NZ no good. [orig. in India & China, f. Hindi *chāp* stamp]

chop-chop /chópchóp/ adv. & int. (pidgin English) quickly; quick. [f. Chin. dial. *k'wâi-k'wâi*]

chop·log·ic /chóplojik/ n. & adj. (also **chop log·ic**) • n. overly pedantic or complicated argument. • adj. (also **chop·log·i·cal**) engaging in or exhibiting such.

chop·per /chópər/ n. **1 a** Brit. a short axe with a large blade. **b** a butcher's cleaver. **2** colloq. a helicopter. **3** a device for regularly interrupting an electric current or light beam. **4** colloq. a type of bicycle or motorcycle with high handlebars. **5** (in pl.) sl. teeth.

chop·py /chópee/ adj. (**chop·pi·er, chop·pi·est**) (of the sea, the weather, etc.) fairly rough. □□ **chop·pi·ly** adv. **chop·pi·ness** n. [CHOP¹ + –Y¹]

chop shop n. colloq. a garage in which stolen cars are dismantled so that the parts can be sold separately.

chop·stick /chópstik/ n. each of a pair of small thin sticks of wood or ivory, etc., held both in one hand as eating utensils by the Chinese, Japanese, etc. [pidgin Engl. f. *chop* = quick + STICK¹ equivalent of Cantonese *k'wâi-tsze* nimble ones]

chopsticks

chop su·ey /chopsŏŏ-ee/ n. (pl. ·eys) a Chinese-style dish of meat stewed and fried with bean sprouts, bamboo shoots, onions, and served with rice. [Cantonese *shap sui* mixed bits]

cho·ral /káwrəl/ adj. of, for, or sung by a choir or chorus. □□ **cho·ral·ly** adv. [med.L *choralis* f. L *chorus*: see CHORUS]

cho·rale /kərál, –rāál/ n. (also **cho·ral**) **1** a stately and simple hymn tune; a harmonized version of this. **2** a choir or choral society. [G *Choral(gesang)* f. med.L *cantus choralis*]

chord¹ /kawrd/ n. Mus. a group of (usu. three or more) notes sounded together, as a basis of harmony. □□ **chord·al** adj. [orig. *cord* f. ACCORD: later confused with CHORD²]

chord² /kawrd/ n. **1** Math. & Aeron., etc., a straight line joining the ends of an arc, the wings of an airplane, etc. **2** Anat. = CORD. **3** poet. the string of a harp, etc. **4** Engin. one of the two principal members, usu. horizontal, of a truss. □ **strike a chord 1** recall something to a person's memory. **2** elicit sympathy. **touch the right chord** appeal skillfully to the emotions. □□ **chord·al** adj. [16th-c. refashioning of CORD after L *chorda*]

chor·date /káwrdayt/ n. & adj. • n. any animal of the phylum Chordata, possessing a notochord at some stage during its development. • adj. of or relating to the chordates. [mod.L *chordata* f. L *chorda* after *Vertebrata*, etc.]

chore /chawr/ n. a tedious or routine task, esp. domestic. [orig. dial. & US form of CHAR²]

cho·re·a /kawréeə/ n. Med. a disorder characterized by jerky involuntary movements affecting esp. the shoulders, hips, and face. [L f. Gk *khoreia* (as CHORUS)]

cho·re·o·graph /káwreeəgraf/ v.tr. compose the choreography for (a ballet, etc.). □□ **cho·re·og·ra·pher** /–reeógrəfər/ n. [back-form. f. CHOREOGRAPHY]

cho·re·og·ra·phy /káwreeógrəfee/ n. **1** the design or arrangement of a ballet or other staged dance. **2** the sequence of steps and movements in dance. **3** the written notation for this. □□ **cho·re·o·graph·ic** /–reeəgráfik/ adj. **cho·re·o·graph·i·cal·ly** adv. [Gk *khoreia* dance + –GRAPHY]

cho·re·ol·o·gy /káwreeóləjee/ n. the study and description of the movements of dancing. □□ **cho·re·ol·o·gist** n.

cho·ri·am·bus /káwreeámbəs/ n. (pl. **cho·ri·am·bi** /–bī/) Prosody a metrical foot consisting of two short (unstressed) syllables between two long (stressed) ones. □□ **cho·ri·am·bic** adj. [LL Gk *khoriambos* f. *khoreios* of the dance + IAMBUS]

cho·ric /káwrik/ adj. of, like, or for a chorus in drama or recitation. [LL *choricus* f. Gk *khorikos* (as CHORUS)]

cho·rine /káwreen/ n. a chorus girl. [CHORUS + –INE³]

cho·ri·on /káwreeən/ n. the outermost membrane surrounding an embryo of a reptile, bird, or mammal. □□ **cho·ri·on·ic** /–reeónik/ adj. [Gk *khorion*]

chor·is·ter /káwristər, kór–/ n. **1** a member of a choir, esp. a choirboy. **2** the leader of a church choir. [ME, ult. f. OF *cueriste* f. *quer* CHOIR]

cho·rog·ra·phy /kərógrəfee/ n. the systematic description of regions or districts. □□ **cho·rog·ra·pher** n. **cho·ro·graph·ic** /káwrəgráfik/ adj. [F *chorographie* or L f. Gk *khōrographia* f. *khōra* region]

cho•roid /káwroyd/ *adj. & n.* • *adj.* like a chorion in shape or vascularity. • *n.* (in full **choroid coat** or **membrane**) a layer of the eyeball between the retina and the sclera. [Gk *khoroeidēs* for *khorioeidēs*: see CHORION]

cho•rol•o•gy /kərólǝjee/ *n.* the study of the geographical distribution of animals and plants. □□ **cho•ro•log•i•cal** /káwrǝlójikǝl/ *adj.* **cho•rol•o•gist** *n.* [Gk *khōra* region + –LOGY]

chor•tle /cháwrt'l/ *v. & n.* • *v.intr. colloq.* chuckle gleefully. • *n.* a gleeful chuckle. [portmanteau word coined by Lewis Carroll, prob. f. CHUCKLE + SNORT]

cho•rus /káwrǝs/ *n. & v.* • *n.* (*pl.* **cho•rus•es**) 1 a group (esp. a large one) of singers; a choir. 2 a piece of music composed for a choir. 3 the refrain or the main part of a popular song. 4 any simultaneous utterance by many persons, etc. (*a chorus of disapproval followed*). 5 a group of singers and dancers performing in concert in a musical comedy, opera, etc. 6 *Gk Antiq.* **a** in Greek tragedy, a group of performers who comment together in voice and movement on the main action. **b** an utterance of the chorus. 7 esp. in Elizabethan drama, a character who speaks the prologue and other linking parts of the play. 8 the part spoken by this character. • *v.tr. & intr.* (of a group) speak or utter simultaneously. □ **in chorus** (uttered) together; in unison. [L f. Gk *khoros*]

cho•rus girl *n.* a young woman who sings or dances in the chorus of a musical comedy, etc.

chose *past* of CHOOSE.

cho•sen *past part.* of CHOOSE.

chough /chuf/ *n.* a European corvine bird of the genus *Pyrrhocorax*, with a glossy, blue-black plumage and red legs. [ME, prob. orig. imit.]

choux pastry /shoo/ *n.* (also **chou**) very light pastry enriched with eggs. [F, pl. of *chou* cabbage, rosette]

chow /chow/ *n.* 1 *sl.* food. 2 *offens.* a Chinese. 3 (in full **chow chow**) **a** a dog of a Chinese breed with long hair and bluish-black tongue. **b** this breed. [shortened f. CHOW-CHOW]

chow•chow /chówchow/ *n.* 1 a Chinese preserve of ginger, orange-peel, etc., in syrup. 2 a mixed vegetable pickle. [pidgin Engl.]

chow•der /chówdǝr/ *n.* a rich soup or stew usu. containing fresh fish, clams, or corn with potatoes, onions, etc. [perh. F *chaudière* pot: see CAULDRON]

chow mein /chów máyn/ *n.* a Chinese-style dish of fried noodles with shredded meat or shrimp, etc., and vegetables. [Chin. *chao mian* fried flour]

Chr. *abbr.* Chronicles (Old Testament).

chres•tom•a•thy /krestómǝthee/ *n.* (*pl.* **•thies**) a selection of passages from an author or authors, designed to help in learning a language. [F *chrestomathie* or Gk *khrēstomatheia* f. *khrēstos* useful + –*matheia* learning]

chrism /krízǝm/ *n.* a consecrated oil or unguent used esp. for anointing in Roman Catholic, Anglican, and Orthodox Christian rites. [OE *crisma* f. eccl.L f. Gk *khrisma* anointing]

chris•om /krízǝm/ *n.* 1 = CHRISM. 2 (in full **chrisom cloth**) *hist.* a white robe put on a child at baptism, and used as its shroud if it died within the month. [ME, as pop. pronunc. of CHRISM]

Christ /krist/ *n. & int.* • *n.* 1 the title, also now treated as a name, given to Jesus of Nazareth, believed by Christians to have fulfilled the Old Testament prophecies of a coming Messiah. 2 the Messiah as prophesied in the Old Testament. 3 an image or picture of Jesus. • *int. sl.* expressing surprise, anger, etc. □□ **Christ•hood** *n.* **Christ•like** *adj.* **Christ•ly** *adj.* [OE *Crīst* f. L *Christus* f. Gk *khristos* anointed one f. *khriō* anoint: transl. of Heb. *māšīah* MESSIAH]

Chris•ta•delph•i•an /krístǝdélfeeǝn/ *n. & adj.* • *n.* a member of a Christian sect rejecting the doctrine of the Trinity and expecting a second coming of Christ on Earth. • *adj.* of or adhering to this sect and its beliefs. [CHRIST + Gk *adelphos* brother]

chris•ten /krísǝn/ *v.tr.* 1 give a Christian name to at baptism as a sign of admission to a Christian church. 2 give a name to anything, esp. formally or with a ceremony. 3 *colloq.* use for the first time. □□ **chris•ten•er** *n.* **chris•ten•ing** *n.* [OE *crīstnian* make Christian]

Chris•ten•dom /krísǝndǝm/ *n.* Christians worldwide, regarded as a collective body. [OE *cristendōm* f. *cristen* CHRISTIAN + –DOM]

Chris•tian /kríschǝn/ *adj. & n.* • *adj.* 1 of Christ's teachings or religion. 2 believing in or following the religion based on the teachings of Jesus Christ. 3 showing the qualities associated with Christ's teachings. 4 *colloq.* (of a person) kind; fair; decent. • *n.* 1 **a** a person who has received Christian baptism. **b** an adherent of Christ's teachings. 2 a person exhibiting Christian qualities. □□ **Christ•tian•ize** *v.tr. & intr.* **Chris•tian•i•za•tion** *n.* **Chris•tian•ly** *adv.* [*Christianus* f. *Christus* CHRIST]

Chris•tian e•ra *n.* the era calculated from the traditional date of Christ's birth.

Chris•ti•an•i•ty /krischeeánitee/ *n.* 1 the Christian religion; its beliefs and practices. 2 being a Christian; Christian quality or character. 3 = CHRISTENDOM. [ME *cristianite* f. OF *crestienté* f. *crestien* CHRISTIAN]

Chris•tian name *n.* a forename, esp. as given at baptism.

Chris•tian Sci•ence *n.* a Christian sect believing in the power of healing by prayer alone. □□ **Chris•tian Sci•en•tist** *n.*

chris•tie /krístee/ *n.* (also **chris•ty**) (*pl.* **•ties**) *Skiing* a sudden turn in which the skis are kept parallel, used for changing direction fast or stopping short. [abbr. of *Christiania* (now Oslo) in Norway]

Christ•mas /krísmǝs/ *n. & int.* • *n.* (*pl.* **Christ•mas•es**) 1 (also **Christ•mas Day**) the annual festival of Christ's birth, celebrated on Dec. 25. 2 the season in which this occurs; the time immediately before and after Dec. 25. • *int. sl.* expressing surprise, dismay, etc. □□ **Christ•mas•sy** *adj.* [OE *Crīstes mæsse* (MASS²)]

Christ•mas card *n.* an ornamental card sent with greetings at Christmas.

Christ•mas club *n.* a savings account into which weekly deposits are made to defray the cost of Christmas gifts.

Christ•mas Eve *n.* the day or the evening before Christmas Day.

Christ•mas pud•ding *n. Brit.* a rich boiled pudding eaten at Christmas, made with flour, suet, dried fruit, etc.

Christ•mas rose *n.* a white-flowered, winter-blooming evergreen, *Helleborus niger.*

Christ•mas tree *n.* an evergreen or artificial tree decorated at Christmas.

Christo- /krístō/ *comb. form* Christ.

Chris•tol•o•gy /kristólǝjee/ *n.* the branch of theology relating to Christ.

chris•ty var. of CHRISTIE. [abbr.]

chro•ma /krōmǝ/ *n.* purity or intensity of color. [Gk *khrōma* color]

chro•mate /krōmayt/ *n. Chem.* a salt or ester of chromic acid.

chro•mat•ic /krōmátik/ *adj.* 1 of or produced by color; in (esp. bright) colors. 2 *Mus.* **a** of or having notes not belonging to a diatonic scale. **b** (of a scale) ascending or descending by semitones. □□ **chro•mat•i•cal•ly** *adv.* **chro•mat•i•cism** /–tisizǝm/ *n.* [F *chromatique* or L *chromaticus* f. Gk *khrōmatikos* f. *khrōma –atos* color]

chro•mat•ic ab•er•ra•tion *n. Optics* the failure of different wavelengths of electromagnetic radiation to come to the same focus after refraction.

chro•ma•tic•i•ty /krōmǝtísitee/ *n.* the quality of color regarded independently of brightness.

chro•ma•tic sem•i•tone *n. Mus.* an interval between a note and its flat or sharp.

chro•ma•tid /krōmǝtid/ *n.* either of two threadlike strands into which a chromosome divides longitudinally during cell division. [Gk *khrōma –atos* color + –ID²]

chro•ma•tin /krōmǝtin/ *n.* the material in a cell nucleus that stains with basic dyes and consists of protein, RNA, and DNA, of which eukaryotic chromosomes are composed. [G: see CHROMATID]

chromato- /krōmǝtō/ *comb. form* (also **chromo-** /krōmō/) color (*chromatopsia*). [Gk *khrōma –atos* color]

chro•ma•tog•ra•phy /krōmǝtógrǝfee/ *n. Chem.* the separation of the components of a mixture by slow passage through or over a material that adsorbs them differently. □□ **chro•mat•o•graph** /–mátǝgraf/ *n.* **chro•mat•o•graph•ic** *adj.* [G *Chromatographie* (as CHROMATO-, –GRAPHY)]

chromatopsia /krōmǝtópseeǝ/ *n. Med.* abnormally colored vision. [CHROMATO- + Gk *–opsia* seeing]

chrome /krōm/ *n.* 1 chromium, esp. as plating. 2 (in full **chrome yellow**) a yellow pigment obtained from lead chromate. [F, = chromium, f. Gk *khrōma* color]

chrome leath•er *n.* leather tanned with chromium salts.

chrome-nick•el *n.* (of stainless steel) containing chromium and nickel.

chrome-plate /krōm–pláyt/ *n. & v.* • *n.* an electrolytically deposited protective coating of chromium. • *v.tr.* 1 coat with this. 2 (as **chrome-plated** *adj.*) pretentiously decorative.

chrome steel *n.* a hard, fine-grained steel containing much chromium and used for tools, etc.

chro•mic /krōmik/ *adj. Chem.* of or containing trivalent chromium.

chro•mic ac•id *n.* an acid that exists only in solution or in the form of chromate salts.

chro•mite /krōmīt/ *n.* 1 *Mineral.* a black mineral of chromium and iron oxides, which is the principal ore of chromium. 2 *Chem.* a salt of bivalent chromium.

chro•mi•um /krōmeeǝm/ *n. Chem.* a hard, white metallic transition element, occurring naturally as chromite and used as a shiny decorative electroplated coating. ¶ Symb.: **Cr.** □ **chro•mi•um steel** = *chrome steel.* [mod.L f. F CHROME]

chromo-¹ /krōmō/ *comb. form Chem.* chromium.

chromo-² *comb. form* var. of CHROMATO-.

chro•mo•lith•o•graph /krōmōlíthǝgraf/ *n. & v.* • *n.* a colored picture printed by lithography. • *v.tr.* print or produce by this process. □□ **chro•mo•li•thog•ra•pher** /–lithǝgrǝfǝr/ *n.* **chro•mo•lith•o•graph•ic** *adj.* **chro•mo•li•thog•ra•phy** /–lithógrǝfee/ *n.*

chro•mo•some /krōmǝsōm/ *n. Biochem.* one of the threadlike structures, usu. found in the cell nucleus, that carry the genetic information in the form of genes. □□ **chro•mo•so•mal** *adj.* [G *Chromosom* (as CHROMO-[2], –SOME[3])]

chro•mo•some map *n.* a plan showing the relative positions of genes along the length of a chromosome.

chro•mo•sphere /krómǝsfeer/ *n.* a gaseous layer of the sun's atmosphere between the photosphere and the corona. □□ **chro•mo•spher•ic** /–sféerik, –sfér–/ *adj.* [CHROMO-[2] + SPHERE]

Chron. *abbr.* Chronicles (Old Testament).

chron•ic /krónik/ *adj.* **1** persisting for a long time (usu. of an illness or a personal or social problem). **2** having a chronic complaint. **3** *colloq. disp.* habitual; inveterate (*a chronic liar*). **4** *Brit. colloq.* very bad; intense; severe. □□ **chron•i•cal•ly** *adv.* **chro•nic•i•ty** /krónísitee/ *n.* [F *chronique* f. L *chronicus* (in LL of disease) f. Gk *khronikos* f. *khronos* time]

▶**Chronic** is often used to mean 'habitual, inveterate,' e.g., *a chronic liar.* Some consider this use incorrect. The precise meaning of **chronic** is 'persisting for a long time' and it is used chiefly of illnesses or other problems, e.g., *More than one million people in the United States have chronic bronchitis.*

chron•i•cle /krónikǝl/ *n. & v.* •*n.* **1** a register of events in order of their occurrence. **2** a narrative; a full account. **3** (**Chronicles**) the name of two of the historical books of the Old Testament or Hebrew bible. •*v.tr.* record (events) in the order of their occurrence. □□ **chron•i•cler** *n.* [ME f. AF *cronicle* ult. f. L *chronica* f. Gk *khronika* annals: see CHRONIC]

chrono- /krónō/ *comb. form* time. [Gk *khronos* time]

chron•o•graph /krónǝgraf, krónǝ–/ *n.* **1** an instrument for recording time with extreme accuracy. **2** a stopwatch. □□ **chron•o•graph•ic** *adj.*

chron•o•log•i•cal /krónǝlójikǝl/ *adj.* **1** (of a number of events) arranged or regarded in the order of their occurrence. **2** of or relating to chronology. □□ **chron•o•log•i•cal•ly** *adv.*

chro•nol•o•gy /krǝnólǝjee/ *n.* (*pl.* **-gies**) **1** the study of historical records to establish the dates of past events. **2 a** the arrangement of events, dates, etc., in the order of their occurrence. **b** a table or document displaying this. □□ **chro•nol•o•gist** *n.* **chro•nol•o•gize** *v.tr.* [mod.L *chronologia* (as CHRONO-, –LOGY)]

chro•nom•e•ter /krǝnómitǝr/ *n.* a time-measuring instrument, esp. one keeping accurate time at all temperatures and used in navigation.

chro•nom•e•try /krǝnómitree/ *n.* the science of accurate time measurement. □□ **chron•o•met•ric** /krónǝmétrik/ *adj.* **chron•o•met•ri•cal** *adj.* **chron•o•met•ri•cal•ly** *adv.*

chrys•a•lis /krísǝlis/ *n.* (also **chrys•a•lid**) (*pl.* **chrys•a•lides** /krísálideez/ or **chrys•a•lis•es**) **1 a** a quiescent pupa of a butterfly or moth. **b** the hard outer case enclosing it. **2** a preparatory or transitional state. [L f. Gk *khrusallis –idos* f. *khrusos* gold]

chry•santh /krisánth/ *n. colloq.* any of the autumn-blooming cultivated varieties of chrysanthemum. [abbr.]

chry•san•the•mum /krisánthǝmǝm/ *n.* any composite plant of the genus *Chrysanthemum,* having brightly colored flowers. [L f. Gk *khrusanthemon* f. *khrusos* gold + *anthemon* flower]

chrys•el•e•phan•tine /kríselifántin, –tīn/ *adj.* (of ancient Greek sculpture) overlaid with gold and ivory. [Gk *khruselephantinos* f. *khrusos* gold + *elephas* ivory]

chrys•o•ber•yl /krísǝbéril/ *n.* a yellowish-green gem consisting of a beryllium salt. [L *chrysoberyllus* f. Gk *khrusos* gold + *bērullos* beryl]

chrys•o•lite /krísǝlīt/ *n.* a precious stone, a yellowish-green or brownish variety of olivine. [ME f. OF *crisolite* f. med.L *crisolitus* f. L *chrysolithus* f. Gk *khrusolithos* f. *khrusos* gold + *lithos* stone]

chrys•o•prase /krísǝprayz/ *n.* **1** an apple-green variety of chalcedony containing nickel and used as a gem. **2** (in the New Testament) prob. a golden-green variety of beryl. [ME f. OF *crisopace* f. L *chrysopassus* var. of L *chrysoprasus* f. Gk *khrusoprasos* f. *khrusos* gold + *prason* leek]

chthon•ic /thónik/ (also **chtho•ni•an** /thóneeǝn/) *adj.* of, relating to, or inhabiting the underworld. [Gk *khthōn* earth]

chub /chub/ *n.* a thick-bodied, coarse-fleshed river fish, *Leuciscus cephalus.* [15th c.: orig. unkn.]

chub•by /chúbee/ *adj.* (**chub•bi•er, chub•bi•est**) plump and rounded (esp. of a person or a part of the body). □□ **chub•bi•ly** *adv.* **chub•bi•ness** *n.* [CHUB]

chuck[1] /chuk/ *v. & n.* •*v.tr.* **1** *colloq.* fling or throw carelessly or with indifference. **2** *colloq.* give up; reject; abandon; jilt (*chucked my job; chucked her boyfriend*). **3** touch playfully, esp. under the chin. •*n.* a playful touch under the chin. □ **the chuck** *Brit. sl.* dismissal (*he got the chuck*). **chuck it** *sl.* stop; desist. **chuck out** *colloq.* **1** expel (a person) from a gathering, etc. **2** get rid of; discard. [16th c., perh. f. F *chuquer, choquer* to knock]

chuck[2] /chuk/ *n. & v.* •*n.* **1** a cut of beef between the neck and the ribs. **2** a device for holding a workpiece in a lathe or a tool in a drill. •*v.tr.* fix (wood, a tool, etc.) to a chuck. [var. of CHOCK]

chuck•le /chúkǝl/ *v. & n.* •*v.intr.* laugh quietly or inwardly. •*n.* a quiet or suppressed laugh. □□ **chuck•ler** *n.* [*chuck* cluck]

chuck•le•head /chúkǝlhed/ *n. colloq.* a stupid person. □□ **chuck•le•head•ed** *adj.* [*chuckle* clumsy, prob. rel. to CHUCK[2]]

chuck wag•on *n.* a wagon with cooking facilities for providing meals outdoors on a ranch, worksite, or campsite.

chud•dar var. of CHADOR.

chuff /chuf/ *v.intr.* (of a steam engine, etc.) work with a regular sharp puffing sound. [imit.]

chuffed /chuft/ *adj. Brit. sl.* delighted. [dial. *chuff* pleased]

chug /chug/ *v. & n.* •*v.intr.* (**chugged, chug•ging**) **1** emit a regular muffled explosive sound, as of an engine running slowly. **2** move with this sound. •*n.* a chugging sound. [imit.]

chu•kar /chukáar/ *n.* a red-legged partridge, *Alectoris chukar,* native to India. [Hindi *cakor*]

chuk•ka boot *n.* an ankle-high leather boot similar to a boot worn by polo players.

chuk•ker /chúkǝr/ *n.* (also **chuk•ka**) each of the periods of play into which a game of polo is divided. [Hindi *cakkar* f. Skr. *cakra* wheel]

chum[1] /chum/ *n. & v.* •*n. colloq.* (esp. among schoolchildren) a close friend. •*v.intr.* (often foll. by *with*) *Brit.* share rooms. □ **chum up** (often foll. by *with*) become a close friend (of). □□ **chum•my** *adj.* (**chum•mi•er, chum•mi•est**). **chum•mi•ly** *adv.* **chum•mi•ness** *n.* [17th c.: prob. short for *chamber-fellow*]

chum[2] /chum/ *n. & v.* •*n.* **1** refuse from fish. **2** chopped fish used as bait. •*v.* **1** *intr.* fish using chum. **2** *tr.* bait (a fishing place) using chum. [19th c.: orig. unkn.]

chump /chump/ *n.* **1 a** *colloq.* a foolish person. **b** an easily deceived person; a sucker. **2** *Brit.* the thick end, esp. of a loin of lamb or mutton (*chump chop*). **3** a short thick block of wood. [18th c.: blend of CHUNK and LUMP[1]]

chun•der /chúndǝr/ *v.intr. & n. Austral. sl.* vomit. [20th c.: orig. unkn.]

chunk /chungk/ *n.* **1** a thick, solid slice or piece of something firm or hard. **2** a substantial amount or piece. [prob. var. of CHUCK[2]]

chunk•y /chúngkee/ *adj.* (**chunk•i•er, chunk•i•est**) **1** containing or consisting of chunks. **2** short and thick; small and sturdy. **3** (of clothes) made of a thick material. □□ **chunk•i•ness** *n.*

Chun•nel /chúnǝl/ *n. colloq.* a tunnel under the English Channel linking England and France. [portmanteau word f. *Channel tunnel*]

chun•ter /chúntǝr/ *v.intr. Brit. colloq.* mutter; grumble. [prob. imit.]

church /chǝrch/ *n. & v.* •*n.* **1** a building for public (usu. Christian) worship. **2** a meeting for public worship in such a building (*go to church; met after church*). **3** (**Church**) the body of all Christians. **4** (**Church**) the clergy or clerical profession (*went into the Church*). **5** (**Church**) an organized Christian group or society of any time, country, or distinct principles of worship (*the Baptist Church; Church of England*). **6** institutionalized religion as a political or social force (*church and state*). •*v.tr.* bring to church for a service of thanksgiving.

WORD HISTORY church

Old English *cir(i)ce, cyr(i)ce,* related to Dutch *kerk* and German *Kirche,* based on medieval Greek *kurikon,* from Greek *kuriakon (dōma)* 'Lord's (house),' from *kurios* 'master or lord.'

---

church•go•er /chǝrchgōǝr/ *n.* a person who goes to church, esp. regularly. □□ **church•go•ing** *n. & adj.*

church•man /chǝrchmǝn/ *n.* (*pl.* **-men**) **1** a member of the clergy or of a church. **2** a supporter of the Church.

Church of England *n.* the English Church, which combines Catholic and Protestant traditions, rejects the Pope's authority, and has the monarch as its titular head.

church school *n.* a private school supported by a church or parish.

Church vis•i•ble *n.* the whole body of professed Christian believers.

church•ward•en /chǝrchwáwrd'n/ *n.* **1** *Anglican Ch.* either of two elected lay representatives of a parish, assisting with routine administration. **2** *Brit.* a long-stemmed clay pipe.

church•wom•an /chǝrchwŏŏmǝn/ *n.* (*pl.* **-wom•en**) **1** a woman member of the clergy or of a church. **2** a woman supporter of the Church.

church•y /chǝrchee/ *adj.* **1** obtrusively or intolerantly devoted to the Church or opposed to religious dissent. **2** like a church. □□ **church•i•ness** *n.*

church•yard /chǝrchyaard/ *n.* the enclosed ground around a church, esp. as used for burials.

chu•rin•ga /chǝrínggǝ/ *n.* (*pl.* same or **chu•rin•gas**) a sacred object, esp. an amulet, among the Australian Aboriginals. [Aboriginal]

churl /chǝrl/ *n.* **1** an ill-bred person. **2** *archaic* a peasant; a person of low birth. **3** *archaic* a surly or mean person. [OE *ceorl* f. a WG root, = man]

churl•ish /chǝrlish/ *adj.* surly; mean. □□ **churl•ish•ly** *adv.* **churl•ish•ness** *n.* [OE *cierlisc, ceorlisc* f. *ceorl* CHURL]

churn /chǝrn/ *n. & v.* •*n.* **1** a machine for making butter by agitating milk or cream. **2** *Brit.* a large milk can. •*v.* **1** *tr.* agitate (milk or cream) in a churn. **2** *tr.* produce (butter) in this way. **3** *tr.* (usu.

foll. by *up*) cause distress to; upset; agitate. **4** *intr.* (of a liquid) seethe; foam violently (*the churning sea*). **5** *tr.* agitate or move (liquid) vigorously, causing it to foam. □ **churn out** produce routinely or mechanically, esp. in large quantities. [OE *cyrin* f. Gmc]

churr var. of CHIRR.

chute¹ /shoot/ *n.* **1** a sloping channel or slide, with or without water, for conveying things to a lower level. **2** a slide into a swimming pool. **3** a cataract or cascade of water; a steep descent in a riverbed producing a swift current. [F *chute* fall (of water, etc.), f. OF *cheoite* fem. past part. of *cheoir* fall f. L *cadere*; in some senses = SHOOT]

chute² /shoot/ *n. colloq.* parachute. □□ **chut·ist** *n.* [abbr.]

chut·ney /chútnee/ *n.* (*pl.* **·neys**) a pungent orig. Indian condiment made of fruits or vegetables, vinegar, spices, sugar, etc. [Hindi *caṭnī*]

chutz·pah /kʰoótspə/ *n.* (also **chutzpa**) *sl.* shameless audacity; gall. [Yiddish]

chy·ack var. of CHIACK.

chyle /kil/ *n.* a milky fluid consisting of lymph and absorbed food materials from the intestine after digestion. □□ **chy·lous** *adj.* [LL *chylus* f. Gk *khulos* juice]

chyme /kim/ *n.* the acidic, semisolid, and partly digested food produced by the action of gastric secretion. □□ **chy·mous** *adj.* [LL *chymus* f. Gk *khumos* juice]

Cl *abbr.* Channel

Ci *abbr.* curie(s).

CIA *abbr.* Central Intelligence Agency.

cia·o /chow/ *int. colloq.* **1** good-bye. **2** hello. [It.]

ci·bo·ri·um /sibáwreeəm/ *n.* (*pl.* **ci·bo·ri·a** /-reeə/) **1** a vessel with an arched cover used to hold the Eucharist. **2** *Archit.* **a** a canopy. **b** a shrine with a canopy. [med.L f. Gk *kibōrion* seed vessel of the water lily, a cup made from it]

ci·ca·da /sikáydə, -kaádə/ *n.* (also **ci·ca·la** /sikaálə/) (*pl.* **ci·ca·das** or **ci·ca·dae** /-dee/) any transparent-winged large insect of the family Cicadidae, the males of which make a loud, rhythmic, chirping sound. [L *cicada*, It. f. L *cicala*, It. *cigala*]

cicada

cic·a·trix /síkətriks, sikáy-/ *n.* (also **cic·a·trice** /síkətris/) (*pl.* **cic·a·tri·ces** /-tríseez/) **1** any mark left by a healed wound; a scar. **2** *Bot.* **a** a mark on a stem, etc., left when a leaf or other part becomes detached. **b** a scar on the bark of a tree. □□ **cic·a·tri·cial** /-tríshəl/ *adj.* [ME f. OF *cicatrice* or L *cicatrix –icis*]

cic·a·trize /síkətriz/ *v.* **1** *tr.* heal (a wound) by scar formation. **2** *intr.* (of a wound) heal by scar formation. □□ **cic·a·tri·za·tion** *n.* [F *cicatriser*: see CICATRIX]

cic·e·ly /sísəlee/ *n.* (*pl.* **·lies**) any of various umbelliferous plants, esp. sweet cicely (see SWEET). [app. f. L *seselis* f. Gk, assim. to the woman's Christian name]

cic·e·ro·ne /chíchərónee, sísə-/ *n.* (*pl.* **cic·e·ro·ni** *pronunc.* same) a guide who gives information about antiquities, places of interest, etc., to sightseers. [It.: see CICERONIAN]

Cic·e·ro·ni·an /sísərōneeən/ *adj.* (of language) eloquent, classical, or rhythmical, in the style of Cicero. [L *Ciceronianus* f. *Cicero –onis* Roman statesman and orator d. 43 BC]

cich·lid /síklid/ *n.* any tropical freshwater fish of the family Cichlidae, esp. the kinds kept in aquariums. [mod.L *Cichlidae* f. Gk *kikhlē* a kind of fish]

CID *abbr.* (in the UK) Criminal Investigation Department.

-cide /sid/ *suffix* forming nouns meaning: **1** a person or substance that kills (*regicide*; *insecticide*). **2** the killing of (*infanticide*; *suicide*). [F f. L *–cida* (sense 1), *–cidium* (sense 2), *caedere* kill]

ci·der /sidər/ *n.* **1** *US* a usu. unfermented drink made from crushed apples. **2** *Brit.* (also **cy·der**) an alcoholic drink made from fermented apple juice. [ME f. OF *sidre*, ult. f. Heb. *šēkār* strong drink]

ci·der press *n.* a press for crushing apples to make cider.

ci·de·vant /seedəvón/ *adj. & adv.* that has been (with person's earlier name or status); former or formerly. [F, = heretofore]

c.i.f. *abbr.* cost, insurance, freight (as being included in a price).

cig /sig/ *n. colloq.* cigarette; cigar. [abbr.]

ci·gar /sigaár/ *n.* a cylinder of tobacco rolled in tobacco leaves for smoking. [F *cigare* or Sp. *cigarro*]

cig·a·rette /sígərét/ *n.* (also **cig·a·ret**) **1** a thin cylinder of finely cut tobacco rolled in paper for smoking. **2** a similar cylinder containing a narcotic or medicated substance. [F, dimin. of *cigare* CIGAR]

cig·a·ril·lo /sígərílō/ *n.* (*pl.* **·los**) a small cigar. [Sp., dimin. of *cigarro* CIGAR]

cig·gy /sígee/ *n.* (*pl.* **·gies**) *colloq.* cigarette. [abbr.]

cil·ice /sílis/ *n.* **1** haircloth. **2** a garment of this. [F f. L *cilicium* f. Gk *kilikion*. *Kilikia* Cilicia in Asia Minor]

cil·i·um /síleeəm/ *n.* (*pl.* **cil·i·a** /-leeə/) **1** a short, minute, hairlike vibrating structure on the surface of some cells, causing currents in the surrounding fluid. **2** an eyelash. □□ **cil·i·ar·y** *adj.* **cil·i·ate** /-ayt, -ət/ *adj.* **cil·i·at·ed** *adj.* **cil·i·a·tion** *n.* [L, = eyelash]

cim·ba·lom var. of CYMBALOM.

C. in C. *abbr.* commander in chief.

cinch /sinch/ *n. & v.* ●*n.* **1** *colloq.* **a** a sure thing; a certainty. **b** an easy task. **2** a firm hold. **3** a girth for a saddle or pack. ●*v.tr.* **1 a** tighten as with a cinch (*cinched at the waist with a belt*). **b** secure a grip on. **2** *sl.* make certain of. **3** put a cinch (sense 3) on. [Sp. *cincha*]

cin·cho·na /singkónə/ *n.* **1 a** any evergreen tree or shrub of the genus *Cinchona*, native to S. America, with fragrant flowers and yielding cinchona bark. **b** the bark of this tree, containing quinine. **2** any drug from this bark formerly used as a tonic and to stimulate the appetite. □□ **cin·cho·nic** /-kónik/ *adj.* **cin·cho·nine** /síngkəneen/ *n.* [mod.L f. Countess of Chinchón d. 1641, introducer of drug into Spain]

cinc·ture /síngkchər/ *n.* **1** *literary* a girdle, belt, or border. **2** *Archit.* a ring at either end of a column shaft. [L *cinctura* f. *cingere cinct-gird*]

cin·der /síndər/ *n.* **a** the residue of coal or wood, etc., that has stopped giving off flames but still has combustible matter in it. **b** slag. **c** (in *pl.*) ashes. □ **burned to a cinder** made useless by burning. □□ **cin·der·y** *adj.* [OE *sinder*, assim. to the unconnected F *cendre* and L *cinis* ashes]

cin·der block *n.* a concrete building block, usu. made from cinders mixed with sand and cement.

Cin·der·el·la /síndəréla/ *n.* **1** a person or thing of unrecognized or disregarded merit or beauty. **2** a neglected or despised member of a group. [the name of a girl in a fairy tale]

cine- /sínə/ *comb. form* pertaining to film or movies (CINEMATOGRAPHY). [abbr.]

cin·e·aste /síneeast/ *n.* (also **cin·e·ast**) **1** a person who makes films, esp. professionally. **2** a movie lover. [F *cinéaste* (as CINE-): cf. ENTHUSIAST]

cin·e·ma /sínəmə/ *n.* **1 a** films collectively. **b** the production of films as an art or industry; cinematography. **2** *Brit.* a theater where motion pictures are shown. [F *cinéma*: see CINEMATOGRAPH]

cin·e·ma·theque /sínəmətek/ *n.* **1** a film library or archive. **2** a small movie theater. [F]

cin·e·mat·ic /sínəmátik/ *adj.* **1** having the qualities characteristic of the cinema. **2** of or relating to motion pictures. □□ **cin·e·mat·i·cal·ly** *adv.*

cin·e·mat·o·graph /sínəmátəgraf/ (also **kin·e·mat·o·graph** /kín-/) *n.* **1** *Brit.* an apparatus for showing movies. **2** a movie camera. [F *cinématographe* f. Gk *kinēma –atos* movement f. *kineō* move]

cin·e·ma·tog·ra·phy /sínəmətógrəfee/ *n.* the art of making motion pictures. □□ **cin·e·ma·tog·ra·pher** *n.* **cin·e·mat·o·graph·ic** /-mátəgráfik/ *adj.* **cin·e·mat·o·graph·i·cal·ly** *adv.*

cin·e·ma ve·ri·té /seénemaá véreetáy/ *n. Cinematog.* **1** the art or process of making realistic (esp. documentary) films that avoid artificiality and artistic effect. **2** such films collectively. [F, = cinema truth]

cin·e·rar·i·a /sínəráireeə/ *n.* any of several varieties of the composite plant, *Cineraria cruentus*, having bright flowers and ash-colored down on its leaves. [mod.L, fem. of L *cinerarius* of ashes f. *cinis –eris* ashes, from the ash-colored down on the leaves]

cin·e·rar·i·um /sínəráireeəm/ *n.* (*pl.* **cin·e·rar·i·a** /-eeə/) a place where a cinerary urn is deposited. [LL, neut. of *cinerarius*: see CINERARIA]

cin·e·rar·y /sínəreree/ *adj.* of ashes. [L *cinerarius*: see CINERARIA]

cin·e·rar·y urn *n.* an urn for holding the ashes after cremation.

ci·ne·re·ous /sineéreeəs/ *adj.* (esp. of a bird or plumage) ash-gray. [L *cinereus* f. *cinis –eris* ashes]

Cin·ga·lese /sínggəleéz/ *adj. & n.* (*pl.* same) *archaic* Sinhalese. [F *cing(h)aiais*: see SINHALESE]

cin·gu·lum /síngyələm/ *n.* (*pl.* **cin·gu·la** /-lə/) *Anat.* a girdle, belt, or analogous structure, esp. a ridge surrounding the base of the crown of a tooth. [L, = belt]

cin·na·bar /sínəbaar/ *n.* **1** a bright red mineral form of mercuric sulfide from which mercury is obtained. **2** vermilion. **3** a moth (*Callimorpha jacobaeae*) with reddish marked wings. [ME f. L *cinnabaris* f. Gk *kinnabari*, of Oriental orig.]

cin·na·mon /sínəmən/ *n.* **1** an aromatic spice from the peeled, dried, and rolled bark of a SE Asian tree. **2** any tree of the genus *Cinnamomum*, esp. *C. zeylanicum* yielding the spice. **3** yellowish-brown. [ME f. OF *cinnamome* f. L *cinnamomum* f. Gk *kinnamōmon*, and L *cinnamon* f. Gk *kinnamon*, f. Semitic (cf. Heb. *ḳinnāmōn*)]

cinque /singk, sangk/ *n.* the five on dice, playing cards, etc. [ME f. OF *cinc*, *cink*, f. L *quinque* five]

cin·que·cen·to /chíngkwichéntō/ *n.* the style of Italian art and literature of the 16th c., with a reversion to classical forms. □□ **cin·que·cen·tist** *n.* [It., = 500, used with ref. to the years 1500–99]

cinque·foil /síngkfoyl/ *n.* **1** any plant of the genus *Potentilla*, with compound leaves of five leaflets. **2** *Archit.* a five-cusped ornament in a circle or arch. [ME f. L *quinquefolium* f. *quinque* five + *folium* leaf]

Cinque Ports /síngk páwrts/ *n.pl.* (in the UK) a group of medieval ports (orig. five only) on the SE coast of England with ancient privileges. [ME f. OF *cink porz*, L *quinque portus* five ports]

ci·on var. of SCION 1.

ci·pher /sífər/ *n. & v.* (*Brit.* **ci·pher** or **cy·pher**) •*n.* **1 a** a secret or disguised way of writing. **b** a thing written in this way. **c** the key to it. **2** the arithmetical symbol (0) denoting no amount but used to occupy a vacant place in decimal, etc., numeration (as in 12.05). **3** a person or thing of no importance. **4** the interlaced initials of a person or company, etc.; a monogram. **5** any Arabic numeral. **6** continuous sounding of an organ pipe, caused by a mechanical defect. •*v.* **1** *tr.* put into secret writing; encipher. **2 a** *tr.* (usu. foll. by *out*) work out by arithmetic; calculate. **b** *intr.* *archaic* do arithmetic. [ME, f. OF *cif(f)re*, ult. f. Arab *ṣifr* ZERO]

cip·o·lin /sípəlin/ *n.* an Italian white and green marble. [F *cipolin* or It. *cipollino* f. *cipolla* onion]

cir. *abbr.* (also **circ.**) **1** circle. **2** circuit. **3** circular. **4** circulation. **5** circumference.

cir·ca /sórkə/ *prep.* (preceding a date) about. [L]

cir·ca·di·an /sərkáydeeən/ *adj.* *Physiol.* occurring or recurring about once per day. [irreg. f. L *circa* about + *dies* day]

Cir·ce /sórsee/ *n.* a dangerously attractive enchantress. [L f. Gk *Kirkē*, an enchantress in Gk mythol.]

cir·ci·nate /sórsinayt/ *adj.* *Bot. & Zool.* rolled up with the apex in the center, e.g., of young fronds of ferns. [L *circinatus* past part. of *circinare* make round f. *circinus* pair of compasses]

cir·cle /sórkəl/ *n. & v.* •*n.* **1 a** a round plane figure whose circumference is everywhere equidistant from its center. **b** the line enclosing a circle. **2** a roundish enclosure or structure. **3** a ring. **4** a curved upper tier of seats in a theater, etc. (*dress circle*). **5** a circular route. **6** *Archaeol.* a group of (usu. large embedded) stones arranged in a circle. **7** persons grouped around a center of interest. **8** a set or class or restricted group (*literary circles*; *not done in the best circles*). **9** a period or cycle (*the circle of the year*). **10** (in full **vicious circle**) **a** an unbroken sequence of reciprocal cause and effect. **b** the fallacy of proving a proposition from another which depends on the first for its own proof. •*v.* **1** *tr.* (often foll. by *around*, *about*) move in a circle. **2** *tr.* **a** revolve around. **b** form a circle around. □ **circle back** move in a wide loop toward the starting point. **come full circle** return to the starting point. **go around in circles** make no progress despite effort. **run around in circles** *colloq.* be fussily busy with little result. □□ **cir·cler** *n.* [ME f. OF *cercle* f. L *circulus* dimin. of *circus* ring]

cir·clet /sórklit/ *n.* **1** a small circle. **2** a circular band, esp. of gold or jeweled, etc., as an ornament.

circs /sórks/ *n.pl.* *Brit. colloq.* circumstances. [abbr.]

cir·cuit /sórkit/ *n.* **1 a** a line or course enclosing an area; the distance around; the circumference. **b** the area enclosed. **2** *Electr.* **a** the path of a current. **b** the apparatus through which a current passes. **3 a** the journey of a judge in a particular district to hold courts. **b** this district. **c** the lawyers following a circuit. **4** a chain of theaters, etc., under a single management. **5** *Brit.* an automobile racing track. **6 a** a sequence of sporting events (*the US tennis circuit*). **b** a sequence of athletic exercises. **7** a roundabout journey. **8 a** a group of local Methodist churches forming a minor administrative unit. **b** the journey of an itinerant minister within this. [ME f. OF, f. L *circuitus* f. CIRCUM- + *ire it-* go]

cir·cuit board *n.* *Electronics* a board of nonconductive material on which integrated circuits, printed circuits, etc., are mounted or etched.

cir·cuit break·er *n.* an automatic device for stopping the flow of current in an electrical circuit as a safety measure.

cir·cu·i·tous /sərkyóo-itəs/ *adj.* **1** indirect (and usu. long). **2** going a long way around. □□ **cir·cu·i·tous·ly** *adv.* **cir·cu·i·tous·ness** *n.* [med.L *circuitosus* f. *circuitus* CIRCUIT]

cir·cuit·ry /sórkitree/ *n.* (*pl.* **·ries**) **1** a system of electric circuits. **2** the equipment forming this.

cir·cu·lar /sórkyələr/ *adj. & n.* •*adj.* **1 a** having the form of a circle. **b** moving or taking place along a circle; indirect; circuitous (*circular route*). **2** *Logic* (of reasoning) depending on a vicious circle. **3** (of a letter or advertisement, etc.) printed for distribution to a large number of people. •*n.* a circular letter, leaflet, etc. □□ **cir·cu·lar·i·ty** /-láritee/ *n.* **cir·cu·lar·ly** *adv.* [ME f. AF *circuler*, OF *circulier*, *cerclier* f. LL *circularis* f. L *circulus* CIRCLE]

cir·cu·lar·ize /sórkyələriz/ *v.tr.* **1** distribute circulars to. **2** seek opinions of (people) by means of a questionnaire. □□ **cir·cu·lar·i·za·tion** *n.*

cir·cu·lar saw *n.* a power saw with a rapidly rotating toothed disk.

cir·cu·late /sórkyəlayt/ *v.* **1** *intr.* go around from one place or person, etc., to the next and so on; be in circulation. **2** *tr.* **a** cause to go around; put into circulation. **b** give currency to (a report, etc.). **c** circularize. **3** *intr.* be actively sociable at a party, gathering, etc.

□□ **cir·cu·la·tive** *adj.* **cir·cu·la·tor** *n.* [L *circulare circulat-* f. *circulus* CIRCLE]

cir·cu·lat·ing li·brar·y *n.* a library with books available for borrowing; a lending library.

cir·cu·lat·ing me·di·um *n.* notes or gold, etc., used in commercial exchange.

cir·cu·la·tion /sórkyəláyshən/ *n.* **1 a** movement to and fro, or from and back to a starting point, esp. of a fluid in a confined area or circuit. **b** the movement of blood from and to the heart. **c** a similar movement of sap, etc. **2 a** the transmission or distribution (of news or information or books, etc.). **b** the number of copies sold, esp. of journals and newspapers. **3 a** currency, coin, etc. **b** the movement or exchange of this in a country, etc. □ **in** (or **out of**) **circulation** participating (or not participating) in activities, etc. [F *circulation* or L *circulatio* f. *circulare* CIRCULATE]

cir·cu·la·to·ry /sórkyələtawree/ *adj.* of or relating to the circulation of blood or sap.

circum- /sórkəm/ *comb. form* about; around; used: **1** adverbially (*circumambient*; *circumfuse*). **2** prepositionally (*circumlunar*, *circumocular*). [from or after L *circum* prep. = around, about]

circum. *abbr.* circumference.

cir·cum·am·bi·ent /sórkəmámbeeənt/ *adj.* (esp. of air or another fluid) surrounding. □□ **cir·cum·am·bi·ence** /–beeəns/ *n.* **cir·cum·am·bi·en·cy** *n.*

cir·cum·am·bu·late /sórkəmámbyəlayt/ *v.tr. & intr.* *formal* walk around or about. □□ **cir·cum·am·bu·la·tion** /–láyshən/ *n.* **cir·cum·am·bu·la·to·ry** /–lətáwree/ *adj.* [CIRCUM- + ambulate f. L *ambulare* walk]

cir·cum·cir·cle /sórkəmsərkəl/ *n.* *Geom.* a circle touching all the vertices of a triangle or polygon.

cir·cum·cise /sórkəmsiz/ *v.tr.* **1** cut off the foreskin, as a Jewish or Muslim rite or a surgical operation. **2** cut off the clitoris (and sometimes the labia), usu. as a religious rite. **3** *Bibl.* purify (the heart, etc.). [ME f. OF f. L *circumcidere circumcis-* (as CIRCUM-, *caedere* cut)]

cir·cum·ci·sion /sórkəmsízhən/ *n.* **1** the act or rite of circumcising or being circumcised. **2** (**Circumcision**) *Eccl.* the feast of the Circumcision of Christ, Jan. 1. [ME f. OF *circoncision* f. LL *circumcisio –onis* (as CIRCUMCISE)]

cir·cum·fer·ence /sərkúmfərəns/ *n.* **1** the enclosing boundary, esp. of a circle or other figure enclosed by a curve. **2** the distance around. □□ **cir·cum·fer·en·tial** /–fərénshəl/ *adj.* **cir·cum·fer·en·tial·ly** *adv.* [ME f. OF *circonference* f. L *circumferentia* (as CIRCUM-, *ferre* bear)]

cir·cum·flex /sórkəmfleks/ *n. & adj.* •*n.* (in full **circumflex accent**) a mark (ˆ) placed over a vowel in some languages to indicate a contraction, length, or a special quality. •*adj.* *Anat.* curved, bending around something else (*circumflex nerve*). [L *circumflexus* (as CIRCUM-, *flectere flex-* bend), transl. of Gk *perispōmenos* drawn around]

cir·cum·flu·ent /sərkúmflōoənt/ *adj.* flowing around, surrounding. □□ **cir·cum·flu·ence** *n.* [L *circumfluere* (as CIRCUM-, *fluere* flow)]

cir·cum·fuse /sórkəmfyóoz/ *v.tr.* pour around or about. [CIRCUM- + L *fundere fus-* pour]

cir·cum·ja·cent /sórkəmjáysənt/ *adj.* situated around. [L *circumjacēre* (as CIRCUM-, *jaceō* lie)]

cir·cum·lo·cu·tion /sórkəmlōkyóoshən/ *n.* **1 a** a roundabout expression. **b** evasive talk. **2** the use of many words where fewer would do; verbosity. □□ **cir·cum·lo·cu·tion·al** *adj.* **cir·cum·lo·cu·tion·ar·y** *adj.* **cir·cum·lo·cu·tion·ist** *n.* **cir·cum·loc·u·to·ry** /–lókyətáwree/ *adj.* [ME f. F *circumlocution* or L *circumlocutio* (as CIRCUM-, LOCUTION), transl. of Gk PERIPHRASIS]

cir·cum·lu·nar /sórkəmlōonər/ *adj.* moving or situated around the moon.

cir·cum·nav·i·gate /sórkəmnávigayt/ *v.tr.* sail around (esp. the world). □□ **cir·cum·nav·i·ga·tion** /–gáyshən/ *n.* **cir·cum·nav·i·ga·tor** *n.* [L *circumnavigare* (as CIRCUM-, NAVIGATE)]

cir·cum·po·lar /sórkəmpólər/ *adj.* **1** *Geog.* around or near one of the earth's poles. **2** *Astron.* (of a star or motion, etc.) above the horizon at all times in a given latitude.

cir·cum·scribe /sórkəmskrib/ *v.tr.* **1** (of a line, etc.) enclose or outline. **2** lay down the limits of; confine; restrict. **3** *Geom.* draw (a figure) around another, touching it at points but not cutting it (cf. INSCRIBE). □□ **cir·cum·scrib·a·ble** *adj.* **cir·cum·scrib·er** *n.* **cir·cum·scrip·tion** /–skrípshən/ *n.* [L *circumscribere* (as CIRCUM-, *scribere script-* write)]

SYNONYM TIP circumscribe

ENCIRCLE, ENCLOSE, ENCOMPASS, ENVELOP, SURROUND. Strictly speaking, to **circumscribe** is to draw a line around something to mark its limits or boundary (*a square circumscribed by a circle*). Beyond the realm of geometry, however, it suggests something that is hemmed in on all sides (*a lake circumscribed by mountains*). **Encompass** is used when something is set within a circle or within limits (*a road that encompassed the grounds of the estate*; *a view that encompassed the harbor*). **Surround** is a less formal word for *circumscribe*, but it can also refer to an undesirable, threatening, or dangerous situation (*surrounded by angry demonstrators*; *surrounded* *by skyscrapers*). **Encircle** is similar to *surround* in meaning, but it suggests a tight or quite circular clustering around a central object (*a bowl of fruit encircled by flowers*) or a deliberate attempt to surround someone or something for a definite reason (*to encircle the enemy camp*). **Envelop** is the right word if something is surrounded to the point where it can barely be seen (*a lonely figure enveloped in fog*) or if it is surrounded by layers or folds of an amorphous material (*enveloped in soft cotton to prevent breakage*). **Enclose** is very similar to *envelop*, but it suggests that something has been especially designed to fit around something else for protection or containment (*a ship model enclosed in a glass case*).

cir·cum·so·lar /sórkəmsólər/ *adj.* moving or situated around or near the sun.

cir·cum·spect /sórkəmspekt/ *adj.* wary; cautious; taking everything into account. □□ **cir·cum·spec·tion** /-spékshən/ *n.* **cir·cum·spect·ly** *adv.* [ME f. L *circumspicere circumspect-* (as CIRCUM-, *specere* spect- look)]

cir·cum·stance /sórkəmstans/ *n.* **1 a** a fact, occurrence, or condition, esp. (in *pl.*) the time, place, manner, cause, occasion, etc., or surroundings of an act or event. **b** (in *pl.*) the external conditions that affect or might affect an action. **2** (often foll. by *that* + clause) an incident, occurrence, or fact, as needing consideration (*the circumstance that he left early*). **3** (in *pl.*) one's state of financial or material welfare (*in reduced circumstances*). **4** ceremony; fuss (*pomp and circumstance*). **5** full detail in a narrative (*told it with much circumstance*). □ **in** (or **under**) **the** (or **these**) **circumstances** the state of affairs being what it is. **in** (or **under**) **no circumstances** not at all; never. □□ **cir·cum·stanced** *adj.* [ME f. OF *circonstance* or L *circumstantia* (as CIRCUM-, *stantia* f. *sto* stand)]

cir·cum·stan·tial /sórkəmstánshəl/ *adj.* **1** given in full detail (*a circumstantial account*). **2** (of evidence, a legal case, etc.) tending to establish a conclusion by inference from known facts hard to explain otherwise. **3 a** depending on circumstances. **b** adventitious; incidental. □□ **cir·cum·stan·ti·al·i·ty** /-sheeálitee/ *n.* **cir·cum·stan·ti·al·ly** *adv.* [L *circumstantia*: see CIRCUMSTANCE]

cir·cum·ter·res·tri·al /sórkəmtəréstreeəl/ *adj.* moving or situated around the earth.

cir·cum·val·late /sórkəmválayt/ *v.tr.* surround with or as with a rampart. [L *circumvallare circumvallat-* (as CIRCUM-, *vallare* f. *vallum* rampart)]

cir·cum·vent /sórkəmvént/ *v.tr.* **1 a** evade (a difficulty); find a way around. **b** baffle; outwit. **2** entrap (an enemy) by surrounding. □□ **cir·cum·ven·tion** /-vénshən/ *n.* [L *circumvenire circumvent-* (as CIRCUM-, *venire* come)]

cir·cum·vo·lu·tion /sórkəmvəlṓshən/ *n.* **1** rotation. **2** the winding of one thing around another. **3** a sinuous movement. [ME f. L *circumvolvere circumvolut-* (as CIRCUM-, *volvere* roll)]

cir·cus /sórkəs/ *n.* (*pl.* **cir·cus·es**) **1** a traveling show of performing animals, acrobats, clowns, etc. **2** *colloq.* **a** a scene of lively action; a disturbance. **b** a group of people in a common activity, esp. sports. **3** *Brit.* an open space in a town or city, where several streets converge (*Piccadilly Circus*). **4** a circular hollow surrounded by hills. **5** *Rom. Antiq.* **a** a rounded or oval arena with tiers of seats, for equestrian and other sports and games. **b** a performance given there (*bread and circuses*). [L, = ring]

ci·ré /siráy/ *n. & adj.* •*n.* a fabric with a smooth shiny surface obtained esp. by waxing and heating. • *adj.* having such a surface. [F, = waxed]

ci·re per·due /seér perdṓ, –dyṓ/ = LOST WAX PROCESS.

cirque /sərk/ *n.* **1** *Geol.* a deep, bowl-shaped hollow at the head of a valley or on a mountainside. **2** *poet.* **a** a ring. **b** an amphitheater or arena. [F f. L CIRCUS]

cir·rho·sis /sirósis/ *n.* a chronic disease of the liver marked by the degeneration of cells and the thickening of surrounding tissues, as a result of alcoholism, hepatitis, etc. □□ **cir·rhot·ic** /sirótik/ *adj.* [mod.L f. Gk *kirrhos* tawny]

cir·ri·ped /síriped/ *n.* (also **cir·ri·pede** /síripeed/) any marine crustacean of the class Cirripedia, having a valved shell and usu. sessile when adult, e.g., a barnacle. [mod.L *Cirripedia* f. L *cirrus* curl (from the form of the legs) + *pes pedis* foot]

cirro- /síró/ *comb. form* cirrus (cloud).

cir·rus /sírəs/ *n.* (*pl.* **cir·ri** /–rī/) **1** *Meteorol.* a form of white wispy cloud, esp. at high altitude. **2** *Bot.* a tendril. **3** *Zool.* a long, slender appendage or filament. □□ **cir·rose** *adj.* **cir·rous** *adj.* [L, = curl]

cis- /sis/ *prefix* (opp. TRANS- or ULTRA-). **1** on this side of; on the side nearer to the speaker or writer (*cisatlantic*). **2** *Rom. Antiq.* on the Roman side of (*cisalpine*). **3** (of time) closer to the present (*cis-Elizabethan*). **4** *Chem.* (of an isomer) having two atoms or groups on the same side of a given plane in the molecule. [L *cis* on this side of]

cis·al·pine /sisálpīn/ *adj.* on the southern side of the Alps.

cis·at·lan·tic /sísətlántik/ *adj.* on this side of the Atlantic.

cis·co /sískō/ *n.* (*pl.* **·coes**) any of various freshwater whitefish of the genus *Coregonus*, native to N. America. [19th c.: orig. unkn.]

cis·lu·nar /sislóonər/ *adj.* between the earth and the moon.

cis·pon·tine /sispóntin/ *adj.* on the north side of the Thames River in London. [CIS- (orig. the better-known side) + L *pons pont-* bridge]

cis·sy esp. *Brit.* var. of SISSY.

cist[1] /sist, kist/ *n.* (also **kist** /kist/) *Archaeol.* a coffin or burial chamber made from stone or a hollowed tree. [Welsh, = CHEST]

cist[2] /sist/ *n.* Gk *Antiq.* a box used for sacred utensils. [L *cista* f. Gk *kistē* box]

Cis·ter·cian /sistŕshən/ *n. & adj.* •*n.* a monk or nun of an order founded in 1098 as a stricter branch of the Benedictines. • *adj.* of the Cistercians. [F *cistercien* f. L *Cistercium* Cîteaux near Dijon in France, where the order was founded]

cis·tern /sístərn/ *n.* **1** a tank or container for storing water, etc. **2** an underground reservoir for rainwater. [ME f. OF *cisterne* f. L *cisterna* (as CIST[2])]

cis·tus /sístəs/ *n.* any shrub of the genus *Cistus*, with large white or red flowers. Also called **rock rose**. [mod.L f. Gk *kistos*]

cit. *abbr.* **1** citation. **2** cited. **3** citizen.

cit·a·del /sítəd'l, –del/ *n.* a fortress, usu. on high ground protecting or dominating a city. [F *citadelle* or It. *citadella*, ult. f. L *civitas –tatis* city]

ci·ta·tion /sītáyshən/ *n.* **1** the citing of a book or other source; a passage cited. **2** a mention in an official dispatch. **3** a note accompanying an award, describing the reasons for it.

cite /sīt/ *v.tr.* **1** adduce as an instance. **2** quote (a passage, book, or author) in support of an argument, etc. **3** mention in an official dispatch. **4** summon to appear in a court of law. □□ **cit·a·ble** *adj.* [ME f. F f. L *citare* f. *ciēre* set moving]

cit·i·fied /sítifīd/ *adj.* (also **cit·y·fied**) usu. *derog.* citylike or urban in appearance or behavior.

cit·i·zen /sítizən/ *n.* **1** a member of a nation or commonwealth, either native or naturalized (*American citizen*). **2** (usu. foll. by *of*) **a** an inhabitant of a city. **b** a freeman of a city. **3** a civilian. □□ **cit·i·zen·hood** *n.* **cit·i·zen·ry** *n.* **cit·i·zen·ship** *n.* [ME f. AF *citesein*, OF *citeain* ult. f. L *civitas –tatis* city: cf. DENIZEN]

cit·i·zen of the world *n.* a person who is at home anywhere; a cosmopolitan.

cit·i·zen's ar·rest *n.* an arrest by an ordinary person without a warrant, allowable in certain cases.

cit·i·zens band *n.* a system of local intercommunication by individuals on special radio frequencies.

cit·ole /sitṓl/ *n.* a small cittern. [ME f. OF: rel. to CITTERN with dimin. suffix]

cit·ric /sítrik/ *adj.* derived from citrus fruit. □□ **cit·rate** *n.* [F *citrique* f. L *citrus* citron]

cit·ric ac·id *n.* a sharp-tasting, water-soluble organic acid found in the juice of lemons and other sour fruits.

cit·rin /sítrin/ *n.* a group of substances occurring mainly in citrus fruits and black currants, and formerly thought to be a vitamin. Also called **bioflavonoid**.

cit·rine /sítreen, sitréen/ *adj. & n.* •*adj.* lemon-colored. •*n.* a transparent yellow variety of quartz. Also called **false topaz**. [ME f. OF *citrin* (as CITRUS)]

cit·ron /sítrən/ *n.* **1** a shrubby tree, *Citrus medica*, bearing large lemonlike fruits with thick fragrant peel. **2** this fruit. [F f. L CITRUS, after *limon* lemon]

cit·ron·el·la /sítrənélə/ *n.* **1** any fragrant grass of the genus *Cymbopogon*, native to S. Asia. **2** the scented oil from these, used in insect repellent, and in perfume and soap manufacture. [mod.L, formed as CITRON + dimin. suffix]

cit·rus /sítrəs/ *n.* **1** any tree of the genus *Citrus*, including citron, lemon, lime, orange, and grapefruit. **2** (also **citrus fruit**) a fruit from such a tree. □□ **cit·rous** *adj.* [L = citron tree]

cit·tern /sítərn/ *n. hist.* a wire-stringed, lutelike instrument usu. played with a plectrum. [L *cithara*, Gk *kithara* a kind of harp, assim. to GITTERN]

cit·y /sítee/ *n.* (*pl.* **·ies**) **1 a** a large town. **b** a state-chartered municipal corporation occupying a definite area. **2** (**the City**) the financial and commercial district of London, England. □□ **cit·y·ward** *adj. & adv.* **cit·y·wards** *adv.*

Middle English: from Old French *cite*, from Latin *civitas*, from *civis* 'citizen.' Originally denoting a town, and often used as a Latin equivalent to Old English *burh* 'borough,' the term was later applied to foreign and ancient cities and to the more important English boroughs. The connection between city and cathedral grew up under the Norman kings, as the episcopal sees (many of which had been established in villages) were removed to the chief borough of the diocese.

Cit·y Com·pa·ny *n.* (in the UK) a corporation descended from an ancient trade guild.

cit·y desk *n.* a department of a newspaper dealing with local news.

cit·y ed·i·tor *n.* a newspaper editor dealing with local news.

cit·y fa·ther *n.* (usu. in *pl.*) a person concerned with or experienced in the administration of a city.

cit·y·fied var. of CITIFIED.

cit·y hall *n.* **1** the administration building and offices of a municipal government. **2** municipal offices or officers collectively; bureaucracy (*he's trying to fight city hall*).

cit·y man·a·ger *n.* (in some US cities) an official directing the administration of a city.

cit·y page *n. Brit.* the part of a newspaper or magazine dealing with the financial and business news.

cit·y·scape /síteeskayp/ *n.* **1** a view of a city (actual or depicted). **2** city scenery.

cit·y slick·er *n.* usu. *derog.* a smart and sophisticated city dweller.

cit·y-state *n.* esp. *hist.* a city that with its surrounding territory forms an independent state.

civ·et /sívit/ *n.* **1** (in full **civet cat**) any catlike animal of the mongoose family, esp. *Civetticis civetta* of Central Africa, having well-developed anal scent glands. **2** a strong musky perfume obtained from the secretions of these scent glands. [F *civette* f. It. *zibetto* f. med.L *zibethum* f. Arab. *azzabād* f. *al* the + *zabād* this perfume]

civ·ic /sívik/ *adj.* **1** of a city; municipal. **2** of or proper to citizens (*civic virtues*). **3** of citizenship; civil. □□ **civ·i·cal·ly** *adv.* [F *civique* or L *civicus* f. *civis* citizen]

civ·ic cen·ter *n.* a municipal building with space for conventions, sports events, theatrical entertainment, etc., often publicly supported.

civ·ics /síviks/ *n.pl.* (usu. treated as *sing.*) the study of the rights and duties of citizenship.

civ·il /sívəl/ *adj.* **1** of or belonging to citizens. **2** of ordinary citizens and their concerns, as distinct from military or naval or ecclesiastical matters. **3** polite; obliging; not rude. **4** *Law* relating to civil law (see below), not criminal or political matters (*civil court; civil lawyer*). **5** (of the length of a day, year, etc.) fixed by custom or law, not natural or astronomical. **6** occurring within a community or among fellow citizens; internal (*civil unrest*). □□ **civ·il·ly** *adv.* [ME f. OF f. L *civilis* f. *civis* citizen]

civ·il a·vi·a·tion *n.* nonmilitary, esp. commercial aviation.

civ·il de·fense *n.* the organization and training of civilians for the protection of lives and property during and after attacks in wartime, natural disasters, emergencies, etc.

civ·il dis·o·be·di·ence *n.* the refusal to comply with certain laws or to pay taxes, etc., as a peaceful form of political protest.

civ·il en·gi·neer *n.* an engineer who designs or maintains roads, bridges, dams, etc. □□ **civ·il en·gi·neer·ing** *n.*

ci·vil·ian /sivílyən/ *n. & adj.* ● *n.* a person not in the armed services or the police force. ● *adj.* of or for civilians.

ci·vil·ian·ize /sivílyəniz/ *v.tr.* make civilian in character or function. □□ **ci·vil·ian·i·za·tion** *n.*

ci·vil·i·ty /sivílitee/ *n.* (*pl.* **·ties**) **1** politeness. **2** an act of politeness. [ME f. OF *civilité* f. L *civilitas –tatis* (as CIVIL)]

civ·i·li·za·tion /síviləzáyshən/ *n.* **1** an advanced stage or system of social development. **2** those peoples of the world regarded as having this. **3** a people or nation (esp. of the past) regarded as an element of social evolution (*ancient civilizations; the Inca civilization*). **4** making or becoming civilized.

civ·i·lize /síviliz/ *v.tr.* **1** bring out of a barbarous or primitive stage of society. **2** enlighten; refine and educate. □□ **civ·i·liz·a·ble** *adj.* **civ·i·liz·er** *n.* [F *civiliser* (as CIVIL)]

civ·il law *n.* **1** law concerning private rights (opp. CRIMINAL LAW). **2** *hist.* Roman or nonecclesiastical law.

civ·il lib·er·tar·i·an *n.* an advocate of increased civil liberty.

civ·il lib·er·ty *n.* (often in *pl.*) freedom of action and speech subject to the law.

civ·il list *n.* (in the UK) an annual allowance voted by Parliament for the royal family's household expenses.

civ·il mar·riage *n.* a marriage solemnized as a civil contract without religious ceremony.

civ·il rights *n.* the rights of citizens to political and social freedom and equality.

civ·il serv·ant *n.* an employee of the civil service.

civ·il serv·ice *n.* the permanent professional branches of governmental administration, excluding military and judicial branches and elected politicians.

civ·il war *n.* a war between citizens of the same country.

civ·il year *n.* see YEAR 2.

civ·vies /síveez/ *n.pl. sl.* civilian clothes, as opposed to a uniform. [abbr.]

CJ *abbr.* Chief Justice.

Cl *symb. Chem.* the element chlorine.

cl *abbr.* **1** centiliter(s). **2** class.

clack /klak/ *v. & n.* ● *v.intr.* **1** make a sharp sound as of boards struck together. **2** chatter; gossip. ● *n.* **1** a clacking sound. **2** clacking talk. □□ **clack·er** *n.* [ME, = to chatter, prob. f. ON *klaka*, of imit. orig.]

clad¹ /klad/ *adj.* **1** clothed. **2** provided with cladding. [past part. of CLOTHE]

clad² /klad/ *v.tr.* (**clad·ding**; *past* and *past part.* **clad·ded** or **clad**) provide with cladding. [app. f. CLAD¹]

clad·ding /kláding/ *n.* a covering or coating on a structure or material, etc.

clade /klayd/ *n. Biol.* a group of organisms evolved from a common ancestor. [Gk *klados* branch]

cla·dis·tics /klədístiks/ *n.pl.* (usu. treated as *sing.*) *Biol.* a method of classification of animals and plants on the basis of shared characteristics, which are assumed to indicate common ancestry. □□ **clad·ism** /kládizəm/ *n.* [as CLADE + –IST + –ICS]

clad·ode /kladōd/ *n.* a flattened, leaflike stem. [Gk *kladōdēs* many-shooted f. *klados* shoot]

claim /klaym/ *v. & n.* ● *v.tr.* **1 a** (often foll. by *that* + clause) demand as one's due or property. **b** (usu. *absol.*) submit a request for payment under an insurance policy. **2 a** represent oneself as having or achieving (*claim victory; claim accuracy*). **b** (foll. by *to* + infin.) profess (*claimed to be the owner*). **c** assert; contend (*claim that one knows*). **3** have as an achievement or a consequence (*could then claim five wins; the fire claimed many victims*). **4** (of a thing) deserve (one's attention, etc.). ● *n.* **1 a** a demand or request for something considered one's due (*lay claim to; put in a claim*). **b** an application for compensation under the terms of an insurance policy. **2** (foll. by *to*, *on*) a right or title to a thing (*his only claim to fame; have many claims on my time*). **3** a contention or assertion. **4** a thing claimed. **5** a statement of the novel features in a patent. **6** *Mining* a piece of land allotted or taken. □□ **claim·a·ble** *adj.* **claim·er** *n.* [ME f. OF *claime* f. *clamer* call out f. L *clamare*]

claim·ant /kláymənt/ *n.* a person making a claim, esp. in a lawsuit or for a government benefit.

claims ad·just·er *n.* an insurance agent who assesses the amount of compensation arising from a loss.

clair·au·di·ence /klairáwrdeeəns/ *n.* the supposed faculty of perceiving, as if by hearing, what is inaudible. □□ **clair·au·di·ent** /–deeənt/ *adj. & n.* [F *clair* CLEAR, + AUDIENCE, after CLAIRVOYANCE]

clair·voy·ance /klairvóyəns/ *n.* **1** the supposed faculty of perceiving things or events in the future or beyond normal sensory contact. **2** exceptional insight. [F *clairvoyance* f. *clair* CLEAR + *voir voy-* see]

clair·voy·ant /klairvóyənt/ *n. & adj.* ● *n.* a person having clairvoyance. ● *adj.* having clairvoyance. □□ **clair·voy·ant·ly** *adv.*

clam /klam/ *n. & v.* ● *n.* **1** any bivalve mollusk, esp. the edible N. American hard or round clam (*Mercenaria mercenaria*) or the soft or long clam (*Mya arenaria*). **2** *colloq.* a shy or withdrawn person. ● *v.intr.* (**clammed**, **clamming**) **1** dig for clams. **2** (foll. by *up*) *colloq.* refuse to talk. [16th c.: app. f. *clam* a clamp]

clam

cla·mant /kláymənt/ *adj. literary* noisy; insistent; urgent. □□ **cla·mant·ly** *adv.* [L *clamare clamant-* cry out]

clam·bake /klámbayk/ *n.* a picnic at the seashore typically featuring clams, lobsters, and ears of corn steamed over hot stones beneath a layer of seaweed.

clam·ber /klámbər/ *v. & n.* ● *v.intr.* climb with hands and feet, esp. with difficulty or laboriously. ● *n.* a difficult climb. [ME, prob. f. *clamb*, obs. past tense of CLIMB]

clam·my /klámee/ *adj.* (**clam·mi·er**, **clam·mi·est**) **1** unpleasantly damp and sticky or slimy. **2** (of weather) cold and damp. □□ **clam·mi·ly** *adv.* **clam·mi·ness** *n.* [ME f. *clam* to daub]

clam·or /klámər/ *n. & v.* ● *n.* **1** loud or vehement shouting or noise. **2** a protest or complaint; an appeal or demand. ● *v.* **1** *intr.* make a clamor. **2** *tr.* utter with a clamor. □□ **clam·or·ous** *adj.* **clam·or·ous·ly** *adv.* **clam·or·ous·ness** *n.* [ME f. OF f. L *clamor –oris* f. *clamare* cry out]

clamp¹ /klamp/ *n. & v.* ● *n.* a device, esp. a brace or band of iron, etc., for strengthening other materials or holding things together. ● *v.tr.* **1** strengthen or fasten with a clamp. **2** place or hold firmly. **3** immobilize (an illegally parked car) by fixing a clamp to one of its wheels. □ **clamp down 1** (often foll. by *on*) be rigid in enforcing a rule, etc. **2** (foll. by *on*) try to suppress. [ME prob. f. MDu., MLG *klamp(e)*]

clamp² /klamp/ *n. Brit.* **1** a heap of potatoes or other root vegetables stored under straw or earth. **2** a pile of bricks for burning. **3** a pile of turf or peat or garden rubbish, etc. [16th c.: prob. f. Du. *klamp* heap (in sense 2 related to CLUMP)]

clamp·down /klámpdown/ *n.* severe restriction or suppression.

clamp¹

clan /klan/ *n.* **1** a group of people with a common ancestor, esp. in the Scottish Highlands. **2** a large family as a social group. **3** a group with a strong common interest. **4 a** a genus, species, or class. **b** a family or group of animals, e.g., elephants. [ME f. Gael. *clann* f. L *planta* sprout]

clan·des·tine /klandéstin/ *adj.* surreptitious; secret. □□ **clan·des·tine·ly** *adv.* **clan·des·tin·i·ty** /–tínitee/ *n.* [F *clandestin* or L *clandestinus* f. *clam* secretly]

clang /klang/ *n. & v.* • *n.* a loud, resonant, metallic sound as of a bell or hammer, etc. • *v.* **1** *intr.* make a clang. **2** *tr.* cause to clang. [imit.: infl. by L *clangere* resound]

clang·er /klángər/ *n. Brit. sl.* a mistake or blunder. □ **drop a clanger** commit a conspicuous indiscretion.

clang·or /klánggər/ *n.* (*Brit.* **clang·our**) **1** a prolonged or repeated clanging noise. **2** an uproar or commotion. □□ **clang·or·ous** *adj.* **clang·or·ous·ly** *adv.* [L *clangor* noise of trumpets, etc.]

clank /klangk/ *n. & v.* • *n.* a sound as of heavy pieces of metal meeting or a chain rattling. • *v.* **1** *intr.* make a clanking sound. **2** *tr.* cause to clank. □□ **clank·ing·ly** *adv.* [imit.: cf. CLANG, CLINK[1], Du. *klank*]

clan·nish /klánish/ *adj.* usu. *derog.* **1** (of a family or group) tending to hold together. **2** of or like a clan. □□ **clan·nish·ly** *adv.* **clan·nish·ness** *n.*

clan·ship /klánship/ *n.* **1** a patriarchal system of clans. **2** loyalty to one's clan.

clans·man /klánzmən/ *n.* (*pl.* **·men**; *fem.* **clans·wom·an**, *pl.* **·wom·en**) a member or fellow member of a clan.

clap[1] /klap/ *v. & n.* • *v.* (**clapped, clap·ping**) **1 a** *intr.* strike the palms of one's hands together as a signal or repeatedly as applause. **b** *tr.* strike (the hands) together in this way. **2** *tr.* **a** *Brit.* applaud or show one's approval of (esp. a person) in this way. **b** slap with the palm of the hand as a sign of approval or encouragement. **3** *tr.* (of a bird) flap (its wings) audibly. **4** *tr.* put or place quickly or with determination (*clapped him in prison*; *clap a tax on whiskey*). • *n.* **1** the act of clapping, esp. as applause. **2** an explosive sound, esp. of thunder. **3** a slap; a pat. □ **clap eyes on** *colloq.* see. **clap on the back** = *slap on the back.* [OE *clappian* throb, beat, of imit. orig.]

clap[2] /klap/ *n. coarse sl.* venereal disease, esp. gonorrhea. [OF *clapoir* venereal bubo]

clap·board /klábərd, klápbawrd/ *n. & v.* • *n.* **1** each of a series of horizontal boards with edges overlapping to keep out the rain, etc., used as a siding esp. of houses. **2** = CLAPPERBOARD. • *v.tr.* fit or supply with clapboards (in sense 1 of *n.*). [Anglicized f. LG *klappholt* cask stave]

clap·per /klápər/ *n.* the tongue or striker of a bell. □ **like the clappers** *Brit. sl.* very fast or hard.

clap·per·board /klápərbawrd/ *n. Cinematog.* a device of hinged boards struck together to synchronize the starting of picture and sound machinery in filming.

clap·trap /kláptrap/ *n.* **1** insincere or pretentious talk; nonsense. **2** language used or feelings expressed only to gain applause. [CLAP[1] + TRAP[1]]

claque /klak/ *n.* a group of people hired to applaud in a theater, etc. [F f. *claquer* to clap]

cla·queur /klakőr/ *n.* a member of a claque. [F (as CLAQUE)]

clar·a·bel·la /klárəbélə/ *n.* an organ stop of flute quality. [fem. forms of L *clarus* clear and *bellus* pretty]

clar·ence /klárəns/ *n. hist.* a four-wheeled closed carriage with seats for four inside and two on the box. [Duke of *Clarence*, afterward William IV]

clar·et /klárət/ *n. & adj.* • *n.* **1** red wine, esp. from Bordeaux. **2** a deep purplish-red. **3** *archaic sl.* blood. • *adj.* claret-colored. [ME f. OF (*vin*) *claret* f. med.L *claratum* (*vinum*) f. L *clarus* clear]

clar·i·fy /klárifī/ *v.* (**·fies, ·fied**) **1** *tr. & intr.* make or become clearer. **2** *tr.* **a** free (liquid, butter, etc.) from impurities. **b** make transparent. **c** purify. □□ **clar·i·fi·ca·tion** *n.* **clar·i·fi·er** *n.* [ME f. OF *clarifier* f. L *clarus* clear]

clar·i·net /klárinét/ *n.* **1 a** a woodwind instrument with a single-reed mouthpiece, a cylindrical tube with a flared end, holes, and keys. **b** its player. **2** an organ stop with a quality resembling a clarinet. □□ **clar·i·net·ist** *n.* (also **clar·i·net·tist**). [F *clarinette*, dimin. of *clarine* a kind of bell]

clar·i·on /kláreeən/ *n. & adj.* • *n.* **1** a clear, rousing sound. **2** *hist.* a shrill, narrow-tubed war trumpet. **3** an organ stop with the quality of a clarion. • *adj.* clear and loud. [ME f. med.L *clario –onis* f. L *clarus* clear]

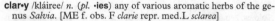

clarinet

clar·i·ty /kláritee/ *n.* the state or quality of being clear, esp. of sound or expression. [ME f. L *claritas* f. *clarus* clear]

clark·i·a /kláarkeeə/ *n.* any plant of the genus *Clarkia*, with showy white, pink, or purple flowers. [mod.L f. W. *Clark*, US explorer d. 1838]

clar·y /kláiree/ *n.* (*pl.* **·ies**) any of various aromatic herbs of the genus *Salvia*. [ME f. obs. F *clarie* repr. med.L *sclarea*]

clash /klash/ *n. & v.* • *n.* **1 a** a loud, jarring sound as of metal objects being struck together. **b** a collision, esp. with force. **2** a conflict or disagreement. **b** a discord of colors, etc. • *v.* **1 a** *intr.* make a clashing sound. **b** *tr.* cause to clash. **2** *intr.* collide; coincide awkwardly. **3** *intr.* (often foll. by *with*) **a** come into conflict or be at variance. **b** (of colors) be discordant. □□ **clash·er** *n.* [imit.: cf. *clack, clang, crack, crash*]

clasp /klasp/ *n. & v.* • *n.* **1 a** a device with interlocking parts for fastening. **b** a buckle or brooch. **c** a metal fastening on a book cover. **2 a** an embrace; a person's reach. **b** a grasp or handshake. **3** a bar of silver on a medal ribbon with the name of the battle, etc., at which the wearer was present. • *v.* **1** *tr.* fasten with or as with a clasp. **2** *tr.* **a** grasp; hold closely. **b** embrace, encircle. **3** *intr.* fasten a clasp. □ **clasp hands** shake hands with fervor or affection. **clasp one's hands** press one's hands together with the fingers interlaced. □□ **clasp·er** *n.* [ME: orig. unkn.]

clasp·er /kláspər/ *n.* (in *pl.*) the appendages of some male fish and insects used to hold the female in copulation.

clasp knife *n.* a folding knife, usu. with a catch holding the blade when open.

class /klas/ *n. & v.* • *n.* **1** any set of persons or things grouped together, or graded or differentiated from others esp. by quality (*first class*; *economy class*). **2 a** a division or order of society (*upper class*; *professional classes*). **b** a caste system; a system of social classes. **c** (**the classes**) *archaic* the rich or educated. **3** *colloq.* distinction or high quality in appearance, behavior, etc.; stylishness. **4 a** a group of students taught together. **b** an occasion when they meet. **c** their course of instruction. **5** all the college or school students of the same standing or graduating in a given year (*the class of 1990*). **6** (in conscripted armies) all the recruits born in a given year (*the 1950 class*). **7** *Brit.* a division of candidates according to merit in an examination. **8** *Biol.* a grouping of organisms, the next major rank below a division or phylum. • *v.tr.* assign to a class or category. □ **in a class of** (or **on**) **its** (or **one's**) **own** unequaled. **no class** *colloq.* a lack of quality or distinction, esp. in behavior. [L *classis* assembly]

class-con·scious *adj.* aware of and reacting to social divisions or one's place in a system of social class. □□ **class-con·scious·ness** *n.*

clas·sic /klásik/ *adj. & n.* • *adj.* **1 a** of the first class; of acknowledged excellence. **b** remarkably and instructively typical (*a classic case*). **c** having enduring worth; timeless. **2 a** of ancient Greek and Latin literature, art, or culture. **b** (of style in art, music, etc.) simple, harmonious, well-proportioned; in accordance with established forms (cf. ROMANTIC). **3** having literary or historic associations (*classic ground*). **4** (of clothes) made in a simple elegant style not much affected by changes in fashion. • *n.* **1** a classic writer, artist, work, or example. **2 a** an ancient Greek or Latin writer. **b** (in *pl.*) the study of ancient Greek and Latin literature and history. **c** *archaic* a scholar of ancient Greek and Latin. **3** a follower of classic models (cf. ROMANTIC). **4** a garment in classic style. **5** (in *pl.*) *Brit.* the classic races. [F *classique* or L *classicus* f. *classis* class]

▶Traditionally, **classic** means 'typical; excellent as an example; timeless' and **classical** means 'of (esp. Greek or Roman) antiquity.' Thus: *John Ford directed many classic Westerns. The museum was built in the classical style.* Great art is considered **classic**, not **classical**, unless it is created in the forms of antiquity. *Classical music*

SYNONYM TIP clarify

CONSTRUE, ELUCIDATE, EXPLAIN, EXPLICATE, INTERPRET. When a biology teacher gets up in front of a class and tries to **explain** how two brown-eyed parents can produce a blue-eyed child, the purpose is to make an entire process or sequence of events understandable. In a less formal sense, to *explain* is to make a verbal attempt to justify certain actions or to make them understood (*she tried to explain why she was so late*). That same teacher might **clarify** a particular exam question that almost everyone in the class got wrong—a word that means to make an earlier event, situation, or statement clear. **Elucidate** is a more formal word meaning to *clarify*, but where the root of the latter refers to clearness, the root of the former refers to light; to *elucidate* is to shed light on something through explanation, illustration, etc. (*the principal's comments were an attempt to elucidate the school's policy on cheating*). A teacher who **explicates** something discusses a complex subject in a point-by-point manner (*to explicate a poem*). If a personal judgment is inserted in making such an explication, the correct word is **interpret** (*to interpret a poem's symbolic meanings*). To **construe** is to make a careful interpretation of something, especially where the meaning is ambiguous. For example, when a class misbehaves in front of a visitor, the teacher is likely to *construe* that behavior as an attempt to cause embarrassment or ridicule.

is formal and sophisticated music adhering to certain stylistic principles, esp. those of the late 18th century, but *a classic folk song* is one that well expresses its culture. A *classical education* exposes a student to *classical* literature, disciplines, and languages (especially Latin and Greek), but the study of Greek and Latin languages and their literature is also referred to as *classics*, as in *he majored in classics at college*.

clas·si·cal /klásikəl/ *adj.* **1 a** of ancient Greek or Latin literature or art. **b** (of language) having the form used by the ancient standard authors (*classical Latin; classical Hebrew*). **c** based on the study of ancient Greek and Latin (*a classical education*). **d** learned in classical studies. **2 a** (of music) serious or conventional; following traditional principles and intended to be of permanent rather than ephemeral value (cf. POPULAR, LIGHT). **b** of the period *c.*1750–1800 (cf. ROMANTIC). **3 a** in or following the restrained style of classical antiquity (cf. ROMANTIC). **b** (of a form or period of art, etc.) representing an exemplary standard; having a long-established worth. **4** *Physics* relating to the concepts that preceded relativity and quantum theory. □□ **clas·si·cal·ism** *n.* **clas·si·cal·ist** *n.* **clas·si·cal·i·ty** /–kálitee/ *n.* **clas·si·cal·ly** *adv.* [L *classicus* (as CLASSIC)]

clas·si·cism /klásisizəm/ *n.* **1** the following of a classic style. **2** a classical scholarship. **b** the advocacy of a classical education. **3** an ancient Greek or Latin idiom. □□ **clas·si·cist** *n.*

clas·si·cize /klásisīz/ *v.* **1** *tr.* make classic. **2** *intr.* imitate a classical style.

clas·si·fied /klásifīd/ *adj.* **1** arranged in classes or categories. **2** (of information, etc.) designated as officially secret. **3** (of newspaper advertisements) arranged in columns according to various categories.

clas·si·fy /klásifī/ *v.tr.* (·**fies**, ·**fied**) **1 a** arrange in classes or categories. **b** assign (a thing) to a class or category. **2** designate as officially secret or not for general disclosure. □□ **clas·si·fi·a·ble** *adj.* **clas·si·fi·ca·tion** *n.* **clas·si·fi·ca·to·ry** /klásifikətáwree, kləsifi–, klásifikáytəree/ *adj.* **clas·si·fi·er** *n.* [back-form. f. *classification* f. F (as CLASS)]

class·less /kláslis/ *adj.* making or showing no distinction of classes (*classless society; classless accent*). □□ **class·less·ness** *n.*

class·mate /klásmayt/ *n.* a fellow member of a class, esp. at school.

class·room /klásroom, –room/ *n.* a room in which a class of students is taught, esp. in a school.

class war *n.* conflict between social classes.

class·y /klásee/ *adj.* (**class·i·er, class·i·est**) *colloq.* superior; stylish. □□ **class·i·ly** *adv.* **class·i·ness** *n.*

clas·tic /klástik/ *adj.* *Geol.* composed of broken pieces of older rocks. [F *clastique* f. Gk *klastos* broken in pieces]

clath·rate /kláthrayt/ *n.* *Chem.* a solid in which one component is enclosed in the structure of another. [L *clathratus* f. *clathri* lattice bars f. Gk *klēthra*]

clat·ter /klátər/ *n. & v.* ● *n.* **1** a rattling sound as of many hard objects struck together. **2** noisy talk. ● *v.* **1** *intr.* **a** make a clatter. **b** fall or move, etc., with a clatter. **2** *tr.* cause (plates, etc.) to clatter. [OE, of imit. orig.]

clau·di·ca·tion /kláwdikáyshən/ *n.* *Med.* a cramping pain, esp. in the leg, caused by arterial obstruction; limping. [L *claudicare* limp f. *claudus* lame]

clause /klawz/ *n.* **1** *Gram.* a distinct part of a sentence, including a subject and predicate. **2** a single statement in a treaty, law, bill, or contract. □□ **claus·al** *adj.* [ME f. OF f. L *clausula* conclusion f. *claudere claus-* shut]

GRAMMAR TIP clause

A **clause** is a group of related words that contains a subject and a verb. An **independent (main) clause** can stand alone as a complete sentence. A **dependent (subordinate) clause** cannot stand alone as a complete sentence, and depends grammatically on a main clause. In the sentence *Because it is so good for health, aerobic exercise should be part of everyone's fitness routine,* the clause starting with "Because" is a dependent clause, while the clause beginning "aerobic exercise" is an independent clause.

---

claus·tral /kláwstrəl/ *adj.* **1** of or associated with the cloister; monastic. **2** narrow-minded. [ME f. LL *claustralis* f. *claustrum* CLOISTER]

claus·tro·pho·bi·a /kláwstrəfóbeeə/ *n.* an abnormal fear of confined places. □□ **claus·tro·phobe** /–rəfōb/ *n.* [mod.L f. L *claustrum*: see CLOISTER]

claus·tro·pho·bic /kláwstrəfóbik/ *adj.* **1** suffering from claustrophobia. **2** inducing claustrophobia. □□ **claus·tro·pho·bi·cal·ly** *adv.*

cla·vate /kláyvayt/ *adj.* *Bot.* club-shaped. [mod.L *clavatus* f. *clava* club]

clave[1] /kláavay/ *n.* *Mus.* a hardwood stick used in pairs to make a hollow sound when struck together. [Amer. Sp. f. Sp., = keystone, f. L *clavis* key]

clave[2] *past* of CLEAVE[2].

clav·i·cem·ba·lo /klávichémbəlō/ *n.* (*pl.* ·**los**) a harpsichord. [It.]

clav·i·chord /klávikawrd/ *n.* a small keyboard instrument with a very soft tone. [ME f. med.L *clavichordium* f. L *clavis* key, *chorda* string: see CHORD[2]]

clav·i·cle /klávikəl/ *n.* the collarbone. □□ **cla·vic·u·lar** /kləvíkyələr/ *adj.* [L *clavicula* dimin. of *clavis* key (from its shape)]

cla·vier /kləveér, kláveeər, kláyveeər/ *n.* *Mus.* **1** any keyboard instrument. **2** its keyboard. [F *clavier* or G *Klavier* f. med.L *claviarius*, orig. = key-bearer, f. L *clavis* key]

clav·i·form /klávifawrm/ *adj.* club-shaped. [L *clava* club]

claw /klaw/ *n. & v.* ● *n.* **1 a** a pointed horny nail on an animal's or bird's foot. **b** a foot armed with claws. **2** the pincers of a shellfish. **3** a device for grappling, holding, etc. ● *v.* **1 a** *tr. & intr.* scratch, maul, or pull (a person or thing) with claws. **b** *intr.* (often foll. by *at*) grasp, clutch, or scrabble at as with claws. **2** *tr. & intr. Sc.* scratch gently. **3** *intr. Naut.* beat to windward. □ **claw back** regain laboriously or gradually. □□ **clawed** *adj.* (also in *comb.*). **claw·er** *n.* **claw·less** *adj.* [OE *clawu, clawian*]

claw ham·mer *n.* a hammer with one side of the head forked for extracting nails.

clay /klay/ *n.* **1** a stiff, sticky earth, used for making bricks, pottery, ceramics, etc. **2** *poet.* the substance of the human body. **3** (in full **clay pipe**) a tobacco pipe made of clay. □□ **clay·ey** *adj.* **clay·ish** *adj.* **clay·like** *adj.* [OE *clæg* f. WG]

clay·more /kláymawr/ *n.* **1** *hist.* **a** a Scottish two-edged broadsword. **b** a broadsword, often with a single edge, having a hilt with a basketwork design. **2** a type of antipersonnel mine. [Gael. *claidheamh mór* great sword]

clay·pan /kláypan/ *n.* **1** hardpan consisting mostly of clay. **2** *Austral.* a natural hollow in clay soil, retaining water after rain.

clay pig·eon *n.* a breakable disk thrown up from a trap as a target for shooting.

-cle /kəl/ *suffix* forming (orig. diminutive) nouns (*article; particle*). [as –CULE]

clean /kleen/ *adj., adv., v., & n.* ● *adj.* **1** (often foll. by *of*) free from dirt or contaminating matter; unsoiled. **2** clear; unused or unpolluted; preserving what is regarded as the original state (*clean air; clean page*). **3** free from obscenity or indecency. **4 a** attentive to personal hygiene and cleanliness. **b** (of animals) house-trained. **5** complete; clear-cut; unobstructed; even. **6 a** (of a ship, aircraft, or car) streamlined; smooth. **b** well-formed; slender and shapely (*clean-limbed*). **7** adroit; skillful (*clean fielding*). **8** (of a nuclear weapon) producing relatively little fallout. **9 a** free from ceremonial defilement or from disease. **b** (of food) not prohibited. **10 a** free from any record of a crime, offense, etc. (*a clean driving record*). **b** *colloq.* (of an alcoholic or drug addict) not possessing or using alcohol or drugs. **c** *sl.* not carrying a weapon or incriminating material; free from suspicion. **11** (of a taste, smell, etc.) sharp; fresh; distinctive. **12** (of lumber) free from knots. ● *adv.* **1** completely; outright; simply (*cut clean through; clean forgot*). **2** in a clean manner. ● *v.* **1** *tr.* (also foll. by *of*) & *intr.* make or become clean. **2** *tr.* eat all the food on (one's plate). **3** *tr. Cookery* remove the innards of (fish or fowl). **4** *intr.* make oneself clean. ● *n.* esp. *Brit.* the act or process of cleaning or being cleaned (*give it a clean*). □ **clean out 1** clean or clear thoroughly. **2** *sl.* empty or deprive (esp. of money). **clean up 1 a** clear (a mess) away. **b** (also *absol.*) make (things) neat. **c** make (oneself) clean. **2** restore order or morality to. **3** *sl.* **a** acquire as gain or profit. **b** make a gain or profit. **come clean** *colloq.* own up; confess everything. **make a clean breast of** see BREAST. **make a clean sweep of** see SWEEP. □□ **clean·a·ble** *adj.* **clean·ish** *adj.* **clean·ness** *n.* [OE *clēne* (adj. & adv.), *clēne* (adv.), f. WG]

clean bill of health *n.* a declaration or confirmation that someone is healthy or that something is in good condition.

clean break *n.* a quick and final separation.

clean-cut *adj.* **1** sharply outlined. **2** neatly groomed.

clean·er /kleénər/ *n.* **1** a person employed to clean the interior of a building. **2** (usu. in *pl.*) a commercial establishment for cleaning clothes. **3** a device or substance for cleaning. □ **take to the cleaners** *sl.* **1** defraud or rob (a person) of all his or her money. **2** criticize severely.

clean hands *n.* freedom from guilt.

clean-liv·ing *n.* of upright character.

clean·ly[1] /kleénlee/ *adv.* **1** in a clean way. **2** efficiently; without difficulty. [OE *clēnlīce*: see CLEAN, –LY[2]]

clean·ly[2] /klénlee/ *adj.* (**clean·li·er, clean·li·est**) habitually clean; with clean habits. □□ **clean·li·ly** *adv.* **clean·li·ness** *n.* [OE *clēnlic*: see CLEAN, –LY[1]]

cleanse /klenz/ *v.tr.* **1** usu. *formal* make clean. **2** (often foll. by *of*) purify from sin or guilt. **3** *archaic* cure (a leper, etc.). [OE *clēnsian* (see CLEAN)]

cleans·er /klénzər/ *n.* **1** one that cleanses. **2** an agent, as a lotion or an abrasive powder, used for cleansing.

clean-shav·en *adj.* without beard, whiskers, or mustache.

cleans·ing cream *n.* cream for removing grease, dirt, and make-up from the skin.

clean·skin /klée'nskin/ *n. Austral.* **1** an unbranded animal. **2** *sl.* a person free from blame, without a police record, etc.

clean slate *n.* freedom from commitments or imputations; the removal of these from one's record.

clean·up /klée'nup/ *n.* **1** an act of cleaning up. **2** *sl.* a huge profit. **3** *Baseball* the fourth position in the batting order.

clear /kleer/ *adj., adv., & v.* ● *adj.* **1** free from dirt or contamination. **2** (of weather, the sky, etc.) not dull or cloudy. **3 a** transparent. **b** lustrous; shining; free from obscurity. **c** (of the complexion) fresh and unblemished. **4** (of soup) not containing solid ingredients. **5** (of a fire) burning with little smoke. **6 a** distinct; easily perceived by the senses. **b** unambiguous; easily understood (*make a thing clear; make oneself clear*). **c** manifest; not confused nor doubtful (*clear evidence*). **7** that discerns or is able to discern readily and accurately (*clear thinking; clear-sighted*). **8** (usu. foll. by *about, on,* or *that* + clause) confident; convinced; certain. **9** (of a conscience) free from guilt. **10** (of a road, etc.) unobstructed; open. **11 a** net; without deduction (*a clear $1,000*). **b** complete (*three days clear*). **12** (often foll. by *of*) free; unhampered; unencumbered by debt, commitments, etc. **13** (foll. by *of*) not obstructed by. ● *adv.* **1** clearly (*speak loud and clear*). **2** completely (*he got clear away*). **3** apart; out of contact (*keep clear; stand clear of the doors*). **4** (foll. by *to*) all the way. ● *v.* **1** *tr. & intr.* make or become clear. **2 a** *tr.* (often foll. by *of*) free from prohibition or obstruction. **b** *tr. & intr.* make or become empty or unobstructed. **c** *tr.* free (land) for cultivation or building by cutting down trees, etc. **d** *tr.* cause people to leave (a room, etc.). **3** *tr.* (often foll. by *of*) show or declare (a person) to be innocent (*cleared them of complicity*). **4** *tr.* approve (a person) for special duty, access to information, etc. **5** *tr.* pass over or by safely or without touching, esp. by jumping. **6** *tr.* make (an amount of money) as a net gain or to balance expenses. **7** *tr. & intr.* pass (a check) through a clearinghouse. **8** *tr.* pass through (a customs office, etc.). **9** *tr.* remove (an obstruction, an unwanted object, etc.) (*clear them out of the way*). **10** *tr.* (also *absol.*) *Sports* send (the ball, puck, etc.) out of one's defensive zone. **11** *intr.* (often foll. by *away, up*) (of physical phenomena) disappear; gradually diminish (*mist cleared by lunchtime; my cold has cleared up*). **12** *tr.* (often foll. by *off*) discharge (a debt). □ **clear the air 1** make the air less sultry. **2** disperse an atmosphere of suspicion, tension, etc. **clear away 1** remove completely. **2** remove the remains of a meal from the table. **clear the decks** prepare for action, esp. fighting. **clear off 1** get rid of. **2** *colloq.* go away. **clear out 1** empty. **2** remove. **3** *colloq.* go away. **clear one's throat** cough slightly to make one's voice clear. **clear up 1** tidy up. **2** solve (a mystery, etc.); remove (a difficulty, etc.). **3** (of weather) become fine. **clear the way 1** remove obstacles. **2** stand aside. **clear a thing with** get approval or authorization for a thing from (a person). **in clear** not in cipher or code. **in the clear** free from suspicion or difficulty. **out of a clear (blue) sky** as a complete surprise. □□ **clear·a·ble** *adj.* **clear·er** *n.* **clear·ly** *adv.* **clear·ness** *n.* [ME f. OF *cler* f. L *clarus*]

clear·ance /klée'rəns/ *n.* **1** the removal of obstructions, etc., esp. removal of buildings, persons, etc., so as to clear land. **2** clear space allowed for the passing of two objects or two parts in machinery, etc. **3** special authorization or permission (esp. for an aircraft to take off or land, or for access to information, etc.). **4 a** the clearing of a person, ship, etc., by customs. **b** a certificate showing this. **5** the clearing of checks. **6** making clear.

clear·ance sale *n.* a sale of goods at reduced prices to get rid of superfluous stock or because the store is closing down.

clear·cole /klée'rkōl/ *n. & v.* ● *n.* a mixture of size and whiting or white lead, used as a primer for distemper. ● *v.tr.* paint with clearcole. [F *claire colle* clear glue]

clear-cut *adj.* sharply defined; easy to perceive or understand; obvious (*we now had a clear-cut objective*).

clear·ing /klée'ring/ *n.* **1** in senses of CLEAR *v.* **2** an area in a forest cleared of trees or foliage.

clear·ing·house /klée'ringhows/ *n.* **1** a bankers' establishment where checks and bills from member banks are exchanged, so that only the balances need be paid in cash. **2** an agency for collecting and distributing information, etc.

clear·sto·ry var. of CLERESTORY.

clear·way /klée'rway/ *n. Brit.* a main road (other than a freeway) on which vehicles are not normally permitted to stop.

cleat /kleet/ *n.* **1** a piece of metal, wood, etc., bolted on for fastening ropes to, or to strengthen woodwork, etc. **2** a projecting piece on a spar, gangway, athletic shoe, etc., to give footing or prevent slipping. **3** a wedge. [OE: cf. CLOT]

cleat 1

cleav·age /klée'vij/ *n.* **1** the hollow between a woman's breasts, esp. as exposed by a low-cut garment. **2** a division or splitting. **3** the splitting of rocks, crystals, etc., in a preferred direction.

cleave¹ /kleev/ *v.* (*past* **cleaved** or **cleft** /kleft/ or **clove** /klōv/; *past part.* **cleaved** or **cleft** or **clo·ven** /klóvən/) *literary* **1 a** *tr.* chop or break apart, split, esp. along the grain or the line of cleavage. **b** *intr.* come apart in this way. **2** *tr.* make one's way through (air or water). □□ **cleav·a·ble** *adj.* [OE *clēofan* f. Gmc]

cleave² /kleev/ *v.intr.* (*past* **cleaved** or **clove** /klōv/ or **clave** /klayv/) (foll. by *to*) *literary* stick fast; adhere. [OE *cleofian, clifian* f. WG: cf. CLAY]

cleav·er /klée'vər/ *n.* **1** a tool for cleaving, esp. a heavy chopping tool used by butchers. **2** a person who cleaves.

cleaver

cleav·ers /klée'vərz/ *n.* (also **cliv·ers** /klívərz/) (treated as *sing.* or *pl.*) a plant, *Galium aparine*, having hooked bristles on its stem that catch on clothes, etc. Also called **goosegrass**. [OE *clife*, formed as CLEAVE²]

clef /klef/ *n. Mus.* any of several symbols placed at the beginning of a staff, indicating the pitch of the notes written on it. [F f. L *clavis* key]

cleft¹ /kleft/ *adj.* split; partly divided. [past part. of CLEAVE¹]

cleft² /kleft/ *n.* a split or fissure; a space or division made by cleaving. [OE (rel. to CLEAVE¹): assim. to CLEFT¹]

cleft lip *n.* (also **cleft pal·ate**) a congenital split in the lip or the roof of the mouth.

cleis·to·gam·ic /klístəgámik/ *adj. Bot.* (of a flower) permanently closed and self-fertilizing. [Gk *kleistos* closed + *gamos* marriage]

clem·a·tis /klémətis, kləmátis/ *n.* any erect or climbing plant of the genus *Clematis*, bearing white, pink, or purple flowers and feathery seeds, e.g., old man's beard. [L f. Gk *klēmatis* f. *klēma* vine branch]

clem·en·cy /klémənsee/ *n.* mercy; lenience (*an appeal for clemency*).

clem·ent /klémənt/ *adj.* **1** mild (*clement weather*). **2** merciful. [ME f. L *clemens −entis*]

clem·en·tine /kléməntin, −teen/ *n.* a small citrus fruit, thought to be a hybrid between a tangerine and sweet orange. [F *clémentine*]

clench /klench/ *v. & n.* ● *v.tr.* **1** close (the teeth or fingers) tightly. **2** grasp firmly. **3** = CLINCH *v.* 4. ● *n.* **1** a clenching action. **2** a clenched state. [OE f. Gmc: cf. CLING]

clep·sy·dra /klépsidrə/ *n.* an ancient time-measuring device worked by a flow of water. [L f. Gk *klepsudra* f. *kleptō* steal + *hudōr* water]

clere·sto·ry /klée'rstawree/ *n.* (also **clear·sto·ry**) (*pl.* **·ries**) **1** an upper row of windows in a cathedral or large church, above the level of the aisle roofs. **2** a raised section of the roof of a railroad car, with windows or ventilators. [ME f. CLEAR + STORY]

cler·gy /klórjee/ *n.* (*pl.* **·gies**) (usu. treated as *pl.*) **1** (usu. prec. by *the*) the body of all persons ordained for religious duties. **2** a number of such persons (*ten clergy were present*). [ME, partly f. OF *clergé* f. eccl.L *clericatus*, partly f. OF *clergie* f. *clerc* CLERK]

cler·gy·man /klórjeemən/ *n.* (*pl.* **·men**; *fem.* **cler·gy·wom·an**, *pl.* **·wom·en**) a member of the clergy.

cler·ic /klérik/ *n.* a member of the clergy. [(orig. adj.) f. eccl.L f. Gk *klērikos* f. *klēros* lot, heritage, as in Acts 1:17]

cler·i·cal /klérikəl/ *adj.* **1** of the clergy or clergymen. **2** of or done by a clerk or clerks. □□ **cler·i·cal·ism** *n.* **cler·i·cal·ist** *n.* **cler·i·cal·ly** *adv.* [eccl.L *clericalis* (as CLERIC)]

cler·i·cal col·lar *n.* a stiff upright white collar fastening at the back, as worn by the clergy in some churches.

cler·i·cal er·ror *n.* an error made in copying or writing out.

cler·i·hew /klérihyōō/ *n.* a short comic or nonsensical verse, usu. in two rhyming couplets with lines of unequal length and referring to a famous person. [E. *Clerihew* Bentley, Engl. writer d. 1956, its inventor]

clerk /klərk/ *n. & v.* ● *n.* **1** a person employed in an office, bank, etc., to keep records, accounts, etc. **2** a secretary, agent, or record keeper of a municipality (*town clerk*), court, etc. **3** a lay officer of a church (*parish clerk*), college chapel, etc. **4** *Brit.* a senior official in Parliament. **5** a person who works at the sales counter of a store, at a hotel desk, etc. **6** *archaic* a clergyman. ● *v.intr.* work as a clerk. □□ **clerk·dom** *n.* **clerk·ish** *adj.* **clerk·ly** *adj.* **clerk·ship** *n.* [OE *cleric, clerc,* & OF *clerc* f. eccl.L *clericus* CLERIC]

clev·er /klévər/ *adj.* (**clev·er·er, clev·er·est**) **1 a** skillful; talented; quick to understand and learn. **b** showing good sense or wisdom; wise. **2** adroit; dextrous. **3** (of the doer or the thing done) ingenious; cunning. □□ **clev·er·ly** *adv.* **clev·er·ness** *n.*

WORD HISTORY   clever

Middle English (in the sense 'quick to catch hold,' only recorded in this period): perhaps of Dutch or Low German origin, and related to CLEAVE². In the late 16th century the term came to mean (probably through dialect use) 'manually skillful'; the sense 'possessing mental agility' dates from the early 18th century.

---

clev·is /klévis/ *n.* **1** a U-shaped piece of metal at the end of a beam for attaching tackle, etc. **2** a connection in which a bolt holds one part that fits between the forked ends of another. [16th c.: rel. to CLEAVE[1]]

clew /kloo/ n. & v. • n. **1** Naut. **a** a lower or after corner of a sail. **b** a set of small cords suspending a hammock. **2** archaic **a** a ball of thread or yarn, esp. with reference to the legend of Theseus and the labyrinth. **b** Brit. = CLUE. • v.tr. Naut. **1** (foll. by up) draw the lower ends of (a sail) to the upper yard or the mast ready for furling. **2** (foll. by down) let down (a sail) by the clews in unfurling. [OE cliwen, cleowen]

cli·an·thus /kleeánthəs/ n. any leguminous plant of the genus Clianthus, native to Australia and New Zealand, bearing drooping clusters of red pealike flowers. [mod.L, app. f. Gk klei-, kleos glory + anthos flower]

cli·ché /kleesháy/ n. (also **cli·che**) **1** a hackneyed phrase or opinion. **2** Brit. a metal casting of a stereotype or electrotype. [F f. clicher to stereotype]

SPELLING TIP cliché

Cliché may be spelled with or without an acute accent over the final e. The past participle clichéd is easier to read and pronounce if it is spelled with the accent.

cli·chéd /kleesháyd/ adj. hackneyed; full of clichés.

click /klik/ n. & v. • n. **1** a slight, sharp sound, as of a switch being operated. **2** a sharp nonvocal suction, used as a speech sound in some languages. **3** a catch in machinery acting with a slight, sharp sound. **4** (of a horse) an action causing a hind foot to touch the shoe of a forefoot. • v. **1 a** intr. make a click. **b** tr. cause (one's tongue, heels, etc.) to click. **2** intr. colloq. **a** become clear or understandable (often prec. by it as subject: when I saw them it all clicked). **b** be successful; secure one's object. **c** (foll. by with) become friendly, esp. with a person of the opposite sex. **d** come to an agreement. □□ **click·er** n. [imit.: cf. Du. klikken, F cliquer]

click bee·tle n. any of a family of beetles (Elateridae) that make a click in recovering from being overturned.

cli·ent /klíənt/ n. **1** a person using the services of a lawyer, architect, social worker, or other professional person. **2** a customer. **3** Rom.Hist. a plebeian under the protection of a patrician. **4** archaic a dependent or hanger-on. □□ **cli·ent·ship** n. [ME f. L cliens −entis f. cluere hear, obey]

cli·en·tele /klíəntél, kleéon−/ n. **1** clients collectively. **2** customers, esp. of a store or restaurant. **3** the patrons of a theater, etc. [L clientela clientship & F clientèle]

cliff /klif/ n. a steep rock face, as at the edge of the sea. □□ **cliff·like** adj. **cliff·y** adj. [OE clif f. Gmc]

cliff·hang·er n. a story, etc., with a strong element of suspense; a suspenseful ending to an episode of a serial. □□ **cliff-hang·ing** adj.

cli·mac·ter·ic /klīmáktərik, klímaktérik/ n. & adj. • n. **1** Med. the period of life when fertility and sexual activity are in decline. **2** a supposed critical period in life (esp. occurring at intervals of seven years). • adj. **1** Med. occurring at the climacteric. **2** constituting a crisis; critical. [F climactérique or L climactericus f. Gk klimaktērikos f. klimaktēr critical period f. klimax −akos ladder]

cli·mac·tic /klīmáktik/ adj. of or forming a climax. □□ **cli·mac·ti·cal·ly** adv. [CLIMAX + −IC, perh. after SYNTACTIC or CLIMACTERIC]

cli·mate /klímit/ n. **1** the prevailing weather conditions of an area. **2** a region with particular weather conditions. **3** the prevailing trend of opinion or public feeling. □□ **cli·mat·ic** /−mátik/ adj. **cli·mat·i·cal** adj. **cli·mat·i·cal·ly** adv. [ME f. OF climat or LL clima climat- f. Gk klima f. klinō slope]

cli·ma·tol·o·gy /klímətóləjee/ n. the scientific study of climate. □□ **cli·ma·to·log·i·cal** /−təlójikəl/ adj. **cli·ma·tol·o·gist** n.

cli·max /klímaks/ n. & v. • n. **1** the event or point of greatest intensity or interest; a culmination or apex. **2** a sexual orgasm. **3** Rhet. **a** a series arranged in order of increasing importance, etc. **b** the last term in such a series. **4** Ecol. a state of equilibrium reached by a plant community. • v.tr. & intr. colloq. bring or come to a climax. [LL f. Gk klimax −akos ladder, climax]

climb /klīm/ v. & n. • v. **1** tr. & intr. (often foll. by up) ascend, mount, go or come up, esp. by using one's hands. **2** intr. (of a plant) grow up a wall, tree, trellis, etc., by clinging with tendrils or by twining. **3** intr. make progress from one's own efforts, esp. in social rank, intellectual or moral strength, etc. **4** intr. (of an aircraft, the sun, etc.) go upward. **5** intr. slope upward. • n. **1** an ascent by climbing. **2 a** a place, esp. a hill, climbed or to be climbed. **b** a recognized route up a mountain, etc. □ **climb down 1** descend with the help of one's hands. **2** withdraw from a stance taken up in argument, negotiation, etc. □□ **climb·a·ble** adj. [OE climban f. WG, rel. to CLEAVE[2]]

climb·er /klímər/ n. **1** a mountaineer. **2** a climbing plant. **3** a person with strong social, etc., aspirations.

climb·ing i·ron n. a set of spikes attachable to a boot, etc., for climbing trees or ice slopes.

clime /klīm/ n. literary **1** a region. **2** a climate. [LL clima: see CLIMATE]

clinch /klinch/ v. & n. • v. **1** tr. confirm or settle (an argument, bargain, etc.) conclusively. **2** intr. Boxing & Wrestling (of participants) become too closely engaged. **3** intr. colloq. embrace. **4** tr. secure (a nail or rivet) by driving the point sideways when through. **5** tr. Naut. fasten (a rope) with a particular half hitch. • n. **1 a** a clinching action. **b** a clinched state. **2** colloq. an (esp. amorous) embrace. **3** Boxing & Wrestling an action or state in which participants become too closely engaged. [16th-c. var. of CLENCH]

clinch·er /klínchər/ n. colloq. a remark or argument that settles a matter conclusively.

clinch·er-built var. of CLINKER-BUILT.

cline /klīn/ n. Biol. the graded sequence of differences within a species, etc. □□ **cli·nal** adj. [Gk klinō to slope]

cling /kling/ v. & n. • v.intr. (past and past part. **clung** /klung/) **1** (foll. by to) adhere, stick, or hold on (by means of stickiness, suction, grasping, or embracing). **2** (foll. by to) remain persistently or stubbornly faithful (to a friend, habit, idea, etc.). **3** maintain one's grasp; keep hold; resist separation. • n. = CLINGSTONE. □ **cling together** remain in one body or in contact. □□ **cling·er** n. **cling·ing·ly** adv. [OE clingan f. Gmc: cf. CLENCH]

cling·stone /klíngstōn/ n. a variety of peach or nectarine in which the flesh adheres to the stone (cf. FREESTONE 2).

cling·y /klíngee/ adj. (**cling·i·er, cling·i·est**) liable to cling. □□ **cling·i·ness** n.

clin·ic /klínik/ n. **1** a private or specialized hospital. **2** a place or occasion for giving specialist medical treatment or advice (eye clinic; fertility clinic). **3** a gathering at a hospital bedside for the teaching of medicine or surgery. **4** a conference or short course on a particular subject (golf clinic). □□ **cli·ni·cian** /kliníshən/ n. [F clinique f. Gk klinikē (tekhnē) clinical, lit. bedside (art)]

clin·i·cal /klínikəl/ adj. **1** Med. of or relating to the observation and treatment of actual patients rather than theoretical or laboratory studies (clinical medicine). **2** efficient and unemotional; coldly detached. □□ **clin·i·cal·ly** adv. [L clinicus f. Gk klinikos f. klinē bed]

clin·i·cal death n. death judged by the medical observation of cessation of vital functions.

clin·i·cal ther·mom·e·ter n. a thermometer with a small range, for measuring body temperature.

clink[1] /klingk/ n. & v. • n. a sharp ringing sound. • v. **1** intr. make a clink. **2** tr. cause (glasses, etc.) to clink. [ME, prob. f. MDu. klinken; cf. CLANG, CLANK]

clink[2] /klingk/ n. (often prec. by in) sl. prison. [16th c.: orig. unkn.]

clink·er[1] /klíngkər/ n. **1** a mass of slag or lava. **2** a stony residue from burned coal. [earlier clincard, etc., f. obs. Du. klinkaerd f. klinken CLINK[1]]

clink·er[2] /klíngkər/ n. **1** sl. a mistake or blunder. **2** Brit. sl. something excellent or outstanding. [CLINK[1] + −ER[1]]

clink·er-built /klíngkərbilt/ adj. (also **clinch·er-built** /klínchərbilt/) (of a boat) having external planks overlapping downward and secured with clinched copper nails. [clink No. of Engl. var. of CLINCH + −ER[1]]

clink·stone /klíngkstōn/ n. a kind of feldspar that rings like iron when struck.

cli·nom·e·ter /klīnómitər/ n. Surveying an instrument for measuring slopes. [Gk klinō to slope + −METER]

cli·o·met·rics /klíəmétriks/ n.pl. (usu. treated as sing.) a method of historical research making much use of statistical information and methods. [Clio, Muse of history + METRIC + −ICS]

clip[1] /klip/ n. & v. • n. **1** a device for holding things together or for attachment to an object as a marker, esp. a paper clip or a device worked by a spring. **2** a piece of jewelry fastened by a clip. **3** a set of attached cartridges for a firearm. • v.tr. (**clipped, clip·ping**) **1** fix with a clip. **2** grip tightly. **3** surround closely. [OE clyppan embrace f. WG]

clip[2] /klip/ v. & n. • v.tr. (**clipped, clip·ping**) **1** cut with shears or scissors, esp. cut short or trim (hair, wool, etc.). **2** trim or remove the hair or wool of (a person or animal). **3** colloq. hit smartly. **4 a** curtail; diminish; cut short. **b** omit (a letter, etc.) from a word; omit letters or syllables of (words pronounced). **5** Brit. remove a small piece of (a ticket) to show that it has been used. **6** cut (an extract) from a newspaper, etc. **7** sl. swindle; rob. **8** pare the edge of (a coin). • n. **1** an act of clipping, esp. shearing or haircutting. **2** colloq. a smart blow, esp. with the hand. **3** a short sequence from a motion picture. **4** the quantity of wool clipped from a sheep, flock, etc. **5** colloq. speed, esp. rapid. □ **clip a person's wings** prevent a person from pursuing ambitions or acting effectively. □□ **clip·pa·ble** adj. [ME f. ON klippa, prob. imit.]

clip·board /klípbawrd/ n. a small board with a spring clip for holding papers, etc., and providing support for writing.

clip-clop /klípklóp/ n. & v. • n. a sound such as the beat of a horse's hooves. • v.intr. (**·clopped, ·clop·ping**) make such a sound. [imit.]

clip joint n. sl. a nightclub or other business that charges exorbitant prices.

clip-on adj. attached by a clip.

clip·per /klípər/ n. **1** (usu. in pl.) any of various instruments for clipping hair, fingernails, hedges, etc. **2** a fast sailing ship, esp. one with raking bows and masts. **3** a fast horse.

clip•pie /klípee/ *n. Brit. colloq.* a female bus conductor.

clip•ping /klíping/ *n.* a piece clipped or cut from something, esp. from a newspaper.

clique /kleek, klik/ *n.* a small exclusive group of people. ▫▫ **cli•quey** *adj.* (**cli•qui•er, cli•qui•est**). **cli•quish** *adj.* **cli•quish•ness** *n.* **cli•quism** *n.* [F f. *cliquer* CLICK]

PRONUNCIATION TIP clique

In British English, the preferred pronunciation of this word is "KLEEK." In American English, "KLICK" is also acceptable.

clit•ic /klítik/ *n.* (often *attrib.*) an enclitic or proclitic.

clit•o•ris /klítəris, klí–/ *n.* a small erectile part of the female genitals at the upper end of the vulva. ▫▫ **clit•o•ral** *adj.* [mod.L f. Gk *kleitoris*]

cliv•ers var. of CLEAVERS.

clo•a•ca /klōáykə/ *n.* (*pl.* **clo•a•cae** /–áysee/) **1** the genital and excretory cavity at the end of the intestinal canal in birds, reptiles, etc. **2** a sewer. ▫▫ **clo•a•cal** *adj.* [L, = sewer]

cloak /klōk/ *n. & v.* • *n.* **1** an outdoor overgarment, usu. sleeveless, hanging loosely from the shoulders. **2** a covering (*cloak of snow*). • *v.tr.* **1** cover with a cloak. **2** conceal; disguise. ▫ **under the cloak of** using as a pretext or for concealment. [ME f. OF *cloke*, dial. var. of *cloche* bell, cloak (from its bell shape) f. med.L *clocca* bell: see CLOCK[1]]

cloak-and-dag•ger *adj.* involving or characteristic of mystery, intrigue, or espionage (*a cloak-and-dagger operation*).

cloak•room /klṓkrōōm, –rŏŏm/ *n.* **1** a room where outdoor clothes or luggage may be left by visitors, clients, etc. **2** *Brit. euphem.* a toilet.

clob•ber[1] /klóbər/ *v.tr. sl.* **1** hit repeatedly; beat up. **2** defeat. **3** criticize severely. [20th c.: orig. unkn.]

clob•ber[2] /klóbər/ *n. Brit. sl.* clothing or personal belongings. [19th c.: orig. unkn.]

cloche /klōsh/ *n.* **1** a small translucent cover for protecting or forcing outdoor plants. **2** (in full **cloche hat**) a woman's close-fitting, bell-shaped hat. [F, = bell, f. med.L *clocca*: see CLOCK[1]]

cloche 2

clock[1] /klok/ *n. & v.* • *n.* **1** an instrument for measuring time, driven mechanically or electrically and indicating hours, minutes, etc., by hands on a dial or by displayed figures. **2 a** any measuring device resembling a clock. **b** *colloq.* a speedometer, taximeter, or stopwatch. **3** time taken as an element in competitive sports, etc. (*ran against the clock*). **4** *Brit. sl.* a person's face. **5** *Brit.* a downy seed head, esp. that of a dandelion. • *v.tr.* **1** *colloq.* **a** (often foll. by *up*) attain or register (a stated time, distance, or speed, esp. in a race). **b** time (a race) with a stopwatch. **2** *sl.* hit, esp. on the head. ▫ **around the clock** all day and (usu.) night. **clock in** (or **on**) register one's arrival at work, esp. by means of an automatic recording clock. **clock off** (or **out**) register one's departure similarly. [ME f. MDu., MLG *klocke* f. med.L *clocca* bell, perh. f. Celt.]

clock[2] /klok/ *n.* an ornamental pattern on the side of a stocking or sock near the ankle. [16th c.: orig. unkn.]

clock golf *n.* a lawn game in which the players putt to a hole in the center of a circle from successive points on its circumference.

clock ra•di•o *n.* a combined radio and alarm clock.

clock-watch•er *n.* one who works while watching the time closely so as not to exceed minimum working hours.

clock•wise /klókwīz/ *adj. & adv.* in a curve corresponding in direction to the movement of the hands of a clock.

clock•work /klókwərk/ *n.* **1** a mechanism like that of a mechanical clock, with a spring and gears. **2** (*attrib.*) **a** driven by clockwork. **b** regular; mechanical. ▫ **like clockwork** smoothly; regularly; automatically.

clod /klod/ *n.* **1** a lump of earth, clay, etc. **2** *sl.* a silly or foolish person. ▫▫ **clod•dy** *adj.* [ME: var. of CLOT]

clod•dish /klódish/ *adj.* loutish; foolish; clumsy. ▫▫ **clod•dish•ly** *adv.* **clod•dish•ness** *n.*

clod•hop•per /klódhopər/ *n.* **1** (usu. in *pl.*) *colloq.* a large heavy shoe. **2** = CLOD 2.

clod•hop•ping /klódhoping/ *adj.* = CLODDISH.

clod•poll /klódpol/ *n. sl.* = CLOD 2.

clog /klawg, klog/ *n. & v.* • *n.* **1** a shoe with a thick wooden sole. **2** *archaic* an encumbrance or impediment. **3** a block of wood to impede an animal's movement. • *v.* (**clogged, clog•ging**) **1** (often foll. by *up*) **a** *tr.* obstruct, esp. by accumulation of glutinous matter. **b** *intr.* become obstructed. **2** *tr.* impede; hamper. **3** *tr. & intr.* (often foll. by *up*) fill with glutinous or choking matter. [ME: orig. unkn.]

clog dance *n.* a dance performed in clogs.

clog•gy /klawgee, klógee/ *adj.* (**clog•gi•er, clog•gi•est**) **1** lumpy; knotty. **2** sticky.

cloi•son•né /klóyzənáy, klwaá–/ *n. & adj.* • *n.* **1** an enamel finish produced by forming areas of different colors separated by strips of wire placed edgeways on a metal backing. **2** this process. • *adj.* (of enamel) made by this process. [F f. *cloison* compartment]

clois•ter /klóystər/ *n. & v.* • *n.* **1** a covered walk, often with a wall on one side and a colonnade open to a quadrangle on the other, esp. in a convent, monastery, college, or cathedral. **2** monastic life or seclusion. **3** a convent or monastery. • *v.tr.* seclude or shut up usu. in a convent or monastery. ▫▫ **clois•tral** *adj.* [ME f. OF *cloistre* f. L *claustrum*, *clostrum* lock, enclosed place f. *claudere claus-* CLOSE[2]]

cloister 1

clois•tered /klóystərd/ *adj.* **1** secluded; sheltered. **2** monastic.

clomp var. of CLUMP *v.* 2.

clone /klōn/ *n. & v.* • *n.* **1 a** a group of organisms produced asexually from one stock or ancestor. **b** one such organism. **2** a person or thing regarded as identical with another. • *v.tr.* propagate as a clone. ▫▫ **clon•al** *adj.* [Gk *klōn* twig, slip]

clonk /klongk, klawngk/ *n. & v.* • *n.* an abrupt heavy sound of impact. • *v.* **1** *intr.* make such a sound. **2** *tr. colloq.* hit. [imit.]

clo•nus /klṓnəs/ *n. Physiol.* a spasm with alternate muscular contractions and relaxations. ▫▫ **clo•nic** *adj.* [Gk *klonos* turmoil]

clop /klop/ *n. & v.* • *n.* the sound made by a horse's hooves. • *v.intr.* (**clopped, clop•ping**) make this sound. [imit.]

clo•que /klōkáy/ *n.* (also **clo•qué**) a fabric with an irregularly raised surface. [F, = blistered]

close[1] /klōs/ *adj., adv., & n.* • *adj.* **1** (often foll. by *to*) situated at only a short distance or interval. **2 a** having a strong or immediate relation or connection (*close friend; close relative*). **b** in intimate friendship or association (*were very close*). **c** corresponding almost exactly (*close resemblance*). **d** fitting tightly (*close cap*). **e** (of hair, etc.) short; near the surface. **3** in or almost in contact (*close combat; close proximity*). **4** dense; compact; with no or only slight intervals (*close texture; close writing; close formation; close thicket*). **5** in which competitors are almost equal (*close contest; close election*). **6** leaving no gaps or weaknesses; rigorous (*close reasoning*). **7** concentrated; searching (*close examination; close attention*). **8** (of air, etc.) stuffy or humid. **9 a** closed; shut. **b** shut up; under secure confinement. **10** limited or restricted to certain persons, etc. (*close corporation; close scholarship*). **11 a** hidden; secret; covered. **b** secretive. **12** (of a danger, etc.) directly threatening; narrowly avoided (*that was close*). **13** niggardly. **14** (of a vowel) pronounced with a relatively narrow opening of the mouth. **15** narrow; confined; contracted. **16** under prohibition. • *adv.* **1** (often foll. by *by, to*) at only a short distance or interval (*they live close by; close to the church*). **2** closely; in a close manner (*shut close*). • *n.* **1** an enclosed space. **2** *Brit.* a street closed at one end. **3** *Brit.* the precinct of a cathedral. **4** *Brit.* a school playing field or playground. **5** *Sc.* an entry from the street to a common stairway or to a court at the back. ▫ **at close quarters** very close together. **close to the wind** see SAIL. **go close** (of a racehorse) win or almost win. ▫▫ **close•ly** *adv.* **close•ness** *n.* **clos•ish** *adj.* [ME f. OF *clos* f. L *clausum* enclosure & *clausus* past part. of *claudere* shut]

close[2] /klōz/ *v. & n.* • *v.* **1 a** *tr.* shut (a lid, box, door, room, house, etc.). **b** *intr.* become shut (*the door closed slowly*). **c** *tr.* block up. **2 a** *tr. & intr.* bring or come to an end. **b** *intr.* finish speaking (*closed with an expression of thanks*). **c** *tr.* settle (a bargain, etc.). **3 a** *intr.* end the day's business. **b** *tr.* end the day's business at (a store, office, etc.). **4** *tr. & intr.* bring or come closer or into contact (*close ranks*). **5** *tr.* make (an electric circuit, etc.) continuous. **6** *intr.* (foll. by *with*) express agreement (with an offer, terms, or the person offering them). **7** *intr.* (often foll. by *with*) come within striking distance; grapple. **8** *intr.* (foll. by *on*) (of a hand, box, etc.) grasp or entrap. • *n.* **1** a conclusion; an end. **2** *Mus.* a cadence. ▫ **close down 1** (of a store, factory, etc.) discontinue business, esp. permanently. **close one's eyes 1** (foll. by *to*) pay no attention. **2** die. **close in 1** enclose. **2** come nearer. **3** (of days) get successively shorter with the approach of the winter solstice. **close off** prevent access to by blocking or sealing the entrance. **close out** discontinue; terminate; dispose of (a business). **close up 1** (often foll. by *to*) move closer. **2** shut, esp. temporarily. **3** block up. **4** (of an aperture) grow smaller. **5** coalesce. ▫▫ **clos•a•ble** *adj.* **clos•er** *n.* [ME f. OF *clos-* stem of *clore* f. L *claudere* shut]

closed /klōzd/ *adj.* **1** not giving access; shut. **2** (of a store, etc.)

having ceased business temporarily. **3** (of a society, system, etc.) self-contained; not communicating with others. **4** (of a sport, etc.) restricted to specified competitors, etc.

closed book *n.* (also **sealed book**) a subject of which one is ignorant.

closed-cap·tioned *adj.* (of a television program) broadcast with captions visible only to viewers with a decoding device attached to their television sets.

closed-cir·cuit *adj.* (of television) transmitted by wires to a restricted set of receivers.

closed-end *adj.* having a predetermined and fixed extent (*a closed-end contract*) (cf. OPEN-ENDED).

closed sea·son *n.* the season when something, esp. the killing of game, etc., is illegal.

closed shop *n.* **1** a place of work, etc., where all employees must belong to an agreed labor union. **2** this system.

closed syl·la·ble *n.* a syllable ending in a consonant.

close-fist·ed /klósfistid/ *adj.* stingy, parsimonious.

close-fit·ting *adj.* (of a garment) fitting close to the body.

close-grained *adj.* without gaps between fibers, etc.

close har·mo·ny *n.* harmony in which the notes of the chord are close together.

close-hauled *adj.* (of a ship) with the sails hauled aft to sail close to the wind.

clos·ing time *n.* the regular time at which a restaurant, bar, or other place closes to the public each day.

close-knit *adj.* tightly bound or interlocked; closely united in friendship.

close·mouthed /klósmówthd/ *adj.* reticent.

close-set *adj.* separated only by a small interval or intervals.

close shave *n. colloq.* a narrow escape.

clos·et /klózit/ *n. & v.* ●*n.* **1** a small or private room. **2** a cupboard or recess. **3** *Brit.* = WATER CLOSET. **4** (*attrib.*) secret; covert (*closet homosexual*). ●*v.tr.* (**clos·et·ed, clos·et·ing**) shut away, esp. in private conference or study. □ **come out of the closet** stop hiding something about oneself, esp. one's homosexuality. [ME f. OF, dimin. of *clos*: see CLOSE[1]]

clos·et dra·ma *n.* a play to be read rather than acted.

close-up *n.* **1** a photograph, movie, or video taken at close range and showing the subject on a large scale. **2** an intimate description.

clo·sure /klózhər/ *n. & v.* ●*n.* **1** the act or process of closing. **2** a closed condition. **3** something that closes or seals, e.g., a cap or tie (cf. CLOTURE) [ME f. OF f. LL *clausura* f. *claudere claus-* CLOSE[2]]

clot /klot/ *n. & v.* ●*n.* **1 a** a thick mass of coagulated liquid, esp. of blood exposed to air. **b** a mass of material stuck together. **2** *Brit. colloq.* a silly or foolish person. ●*v.tr. & intr.* (**clot·ted, clot·ting**) form into clots. [OE *clot(t)* f. WG: cf. CLEAT]

cloth /klawth, kloth/ *n.* (*pl.* **cloths** /kloths, klothz/) **1** woven or felted material. **2** a piece of this. **3** a piece of cloth for a particular purpose; a tablecloth, dishcloth, etc. **4** woolen woven fabric as used for clothes. **5 a** a profession or status, esp. of the clergy, as shown by clothes (*respect due to his cloth*). **b** (prec. by *the*) the clergy. [OE *clāth*, of unkn. orig.]

cloth book *n.* a children's book made out of cloth.

clothe /klōth/ *v.tr.* (*past* and *past part.* **clothed** or *formal* **clad**) **1** put clothes on; provide with clothes. **2** cover as with clothes or a cloth. **3** (foll. by *with*) endue (with qualities, etc.). [OE: rel. to CLOTH]

cloth-eared *adj. colloq.* somewhat deaf.

clothes /klōz, klōthz/ *n.pl.* **1** garments worn to cover the body and limbs. **2** bedclothes. □ **clothes-peg** *Brit.* = CLOTHESPIN. [OE *clāthas* pl. of *clāth* CLOTH]

clothes·horse /klózhawrs, klóthz–/ *n.* **1** a frame for airing washed clothes. **2** *colloq.* a determinedly fashionable person.

clothes·line /klózhawrs, klóthz–/ *n.* a rope or wire, etc., on which washed clothes are hung to dry.

clothes moth *n.* any moth of the family Tineidae, with a larva destructive to wool, fur, etc.

clothes·pin /klózpin, klóthz–/ *n.* a clip or forked device for securing clothes to a clothesline.

cloth·ier /klótheeər/ *n.* a seller of clothes. [ME *clother* f. CLOTH]

cloth·ing /klóthing/ *n.* clothes collectively.

clot·ted cream *n.* esp. *Brit.* thick cream obtained by heating milk slowly and then allowing it to cool while the cream content rises to the top in coagulated lumps.

clo·ture /klóchər/ *n. & v.* ●*n.* the legislative procedure for ending debate and taking a vote. ●*v.tr.* apply cloture. [F *clôture* f. OF CLOSURE]

clou /kloo/ *n.* **1** the point of greatest interest; the chief attraction. **2** the central idea. [F, = nail]

cloud /klowd/ *n. & v.* ●*n.* **1** a visible mass of condensed watery vapor floating in the atmosphere high above the general level of the ground. **2** a mass of smoke or dust. **3** (foll. by *of*) a great number of insects, birds, etc., moving together. **4 a** a state of gloom, trouble, or suspicion. **b** a frowning or depressed look (*a cloud on his brow*). **5** a local dimness or a vague patch of color in or on a liquid or a transparent body. **6** an unsubstantial or fleeting thing. **7** obscurity. ●*v.* **1** *tr.* cover or darken with clouds or gloom or trouble. **2** *intr.* (often foll. by *over, up*) become overcast or gloomy. **3** *tr.* make unclear. **4** *tr.* variegate with vague patches of color. □ **in the clouds 1** unreal; imaginary; mystical. **2** (of a person) abstracted; inattentive. **on cloud nine** (or *Brit.* **seven**) *colloq.* extremely happy. **under a cloud** out of favor, discredited; under suspicion. **with one's head in the clouds** daydreaming; unrealistic. □□ **cloud·less** *adj.* **cloud·less·ly** *adv.* **cloud·let** *n.* [OE *clūd* mass of rock or earth, prob. rel. to CLOD]

cloud·ber·ry /klówdberee/ *n.* (*pl.* **·ries**) a small mountain bramble, *Rubus chamaemorus*, with a white flower and an orange-colored fruit.

cloud·burst /klówdbərst/ *n.* a sudden violent rainstorm.

cloud cham·ber *n.* a device containing vapor for tracking the paths of charged particles, X rays, and gamma rays.

cloud-cuck·oo-land /klowdkóōkoōland, –koōkoō–/ *n.* a fanciful or ideal place. [transl. of Gk *Nephelokokkugia* f. *nephelē* cloud + *kokkux* cuckoo (in Aristophanes' *Birds*)]

cloud·ed leop·ard *n.* a mottled arboreal S. Asian feline, *Neofelis nebulosa.*

cloud·land /klówdland/ *n.* a Utopia or fairyland.

cloud·scape /klówdskayp/ *n.* **1** a picturesque grouping of clouds. **2** a picture or view of clouds. [CLOUD *n.*, after *landscape*]

cloud·y /klówdee/ *adj.* (**cloud·i·er, cloud·i·est**) **1 a** (of the sky) covered with clouds; overcast. **b** (of weather) characterized by clouds. **2** not transparent; unclear. □□ **cloud·i·ly** *adv.* **cloud·i·ness** *n.*

clough /kluf/ *n. dial.* a steep valley usu. with a torrent bed; a ravine. [OE *clōh* f. Gmc]

clout /klowt/ *n. & v.* ●*n.* **1** a heavy blow. **2** *colloq.* influence; power of effective action esp. in politics or business. **3** *dial.* a piece of cloth or clothing (*cast not a clout*). **4** *Archery hist.* a piece of canvas on a frame, used as a mark. **5** a nail with a large, flat head. **6** a patch. ●*v.tr.* **1** hit hard. **2** mend with a patch. [OE *clūt*, rel. to CLEAT, CLOT]

clove[1] /klōv/ *n.* **1 a** a dried flower bud of a tropical plant, *Eugenia aromatica*, used as a pungent aromatic spice. **b** this plant. **2** (in full **clove gillyflower** or **clove pink**) a clove-scented pink, *Dianthus caryophyllus*, the original of the carnation and other double pinks. [ME f. OF *clou* (*de girofle*) nail (of gillyflower), from its shape, GILLYFLOWER being orig. the name of the spice; later applied to the similarly scented pink]

clove[2] /klōv/ *n.* any of the small bulbs making up a compound bulb of garlic, shallot, etc. [OE *clufu*, rel. to CLEAVE[1]]

clove[3] *past* of CLEAVE[1].

clove hitch *n.* a knot by which a rope is secured by passing it twice around a spar or rope that it crosses at right angles. [old past part. of CLEAVE[1], as showing parallel separate lines]

clo·ven /klóv'n/ *adj.* split; partly divided. [past part. of CLEAVE[1]]

clo·ven hoof *n.* (also **clo·ven foot**) the divided hoof of ruminant quadrupeds (e.g., oxen, sheep, goats); also ascribed to the god Pan, and so to the Devil. □ **show the cloven hoof** reveal one's evil nature. □□ **clo·ven-foot·ed** /–foŏtid/ *adj.* **clo·ven-hoofed** /–hoŏft/ *adj.*

clo·ver /klóvər/ *n.* any leguminous fodder plant of the genus *Trifolium*, having dense flower heads and leaves each consisting of usu. three leaflets. □ **in clover** in ease and luxury. [OE *clāfre* f. Gmc]

clo·ver·leaf /klóvərleef/ *n.* a junction of roads intersecting at different levels with connecting sections forming the pattern of a four-leaf clover.

clown /klown/ *n. & v.* ●*n.* **1** a comic entertainer, esp. in a pantomime or circus, usu. with traditional costume and makeup. **2** a silly, foolish, or playful person. **3** *archaic* a rustic. ●*v.* **1** *intr.* (often foll. by *about, around*) behave like a clown; act foolishly or playfully. **2** *tr.* perform (a part, an action, etc.) like a clown. □□ **clown·er·y** *n.* **clown·ish** *adj.* **clown·ish·ly** *adv.* **clown·ish·ness** *n.* [16th c.: perh. of LG orig.]

white clover

cloy /kloy/ *v.tr.* (usu. as *adj.* **cloy·ing**) satiate or sicken with an excess of sweetness, richness, etc. □□ **cloy·ing·ly** *adv.* [ME f. obs. *acloy* f. AF *acloyer*, OF *encloyer* f. Rmc: cf. ENCLAVE]

cloze /klōz/ *n.* the exercise of supplying a word that has been omitted from a passage as a test of readability or comprehension (usu. *attrib.*: *cloze test*). [CLOSURE]

CLU *abbr.* chartered life underwriter.

club /klub/ *n. & v.* ●*n.* **1** a heavy stick with a thick end, used as a weapon, etc. **2** a stick used in a game, esp. a stick with a head used in golf. **3 a** a playing card of a suit denoted by a black trefoil. **b** (in *pl.*) this suit. **4** an association of persons united by a common interest, usu. meeting periodically for a shared activity (*tennis club*; *yacht club*). **5 a** an organization or premises offering members social amenities, meals, and temporary residence, etc. **b** a nightclub. **6** an organization offering subscribers certain benefits (*book club*). **7** a group of persons, nations, etc., having something in common. **8** = CLUBHOUSE. **9** a structure or organ, esp. in a plant, with a knob at the end. ● *v.* (**clubbed, club•bing**) **1** *tr.* beat with or as with a club. **2** *intr.* (foll. by *together, with*) combine for joint action, esp. making up a sum of money for a purpose. **3** *tr.* contribute (money, etc.) to a common stock. □□ **club•ber** *n.* [ME f. ON *klubba* assim. form of *klumba* club, rel. to CLUMP]

club•ba•ble /klúbəbəl/ *adj.* sociable; fit for membership of a club. □□ **club•ba•bil•i•ty** /–bílitee/ *n.* **club•ba•ble•ness** *n.*

club•by /klúbee/ *adj.* (**club•bi•er, club•bi•est**) sociable; friendly.

club•foot /klúbfoot/ *n.* a congenitally deformed foot. □□ **club•foot•ed** *adj.*

club•house /klúbhows/ *n.* the premises used by a club.

club•man /klúbmən, –man/ *n.* (*pl.* •**men;** *fem.* •**wom•an,** *pl.* •**women**) a member of one or more social clubs.

club•moss /klúbmaws, –mos/ *n.* any pteridophyte of the family Lycopodiaceae, bearing upright spikes of spore cases.

club•root /klúbroot/ *n.* a disease of cabbages, etc., with swelling at the base of the stem.

club sand•wich *n.* a sandwich with two layers of filling between three slices of toast or bread.

club so•da *n.* = SODA *n.* 2.

cluck /kluk/ *n. & v.* ● *n.* **1** a guttural cry like that of a hen. **2** *sl.* a silly or foolish person (*dumb cluck*). ● *v.intr.* emit a cluck or clucks. [imit.]

clue /kloō/ *n. & v.* ● *n.* **1** a fact or idea that serves as a guide, or suggests a line of inquiry, in a problem or investigation. **2** a piece of evidence, etc., in the detection of a crime. **3** a verbal formula serving as a hint as to what is to be inserted in a crossword. **4** a thread of a story. **b** a train of thought. ● *v.tr.* (**clues, clued, clue•ing** or **clu•ing**) provide a clue to. □ **clue in** (or *Brit.* **up**) *sl.* inform. **not have a clue** *colloq.* be ignorant or incompetent. [var. of CLEW]

clue•less /kloōlis/ *adj. colloq.* ignorant; stupid. □□ **clue•less•ly** *adv.* **clue•less•ness** *n.*

clump /klump/ *n. & v.* ● *n.* **1** (foll. by *of*) a cluster of plants, esp. trees or shrubs. **2** an agglutinated mass of blood cells, etc. **3** a thick extra sole on a boot or shoe. ● *v.* **1 a** *intr.* form a clump. **b** *tr.* heap or plant together. **2** *intr.* (also **clomp** /klomp/) walk with heavy tread. **3** *tr. colloq.* hit. □□ **clump•y** *adj.* (**clump•i•er, clump•i•est**). [MLG *klumpe,* MDu. *klompe:* see CLUB]

clum•sy /klúmzee/ *adj.* (**clum•si•er, clum•si•est**) **1** awkward in movement or shape; ungainly. **2** difficult to handle or use. **3** tactless. □□ **clum•si•ly** *adv.* **clum•si•ness** *n.* [obs. *clumse* be numb with cold (prob. f. Scand.)]

clung *past* and *past part.* of CLING.

clunk /klungk/ *n. & v.* ● *n.* a dull sound as of thick pieces of metal meeting. ● *v.intr.* make such a sound. [imit.]

clus•ter /klústər/ *n. & v.* ● *n.* **1** a close group or bunch of similar things growing together. **2** a close group or swarm of people, animals, faint stars, gems, etc. **3** a group of successive consonants or vowels. ● *v.* **1** *tr.* bring into a cluster or clusters. **2** *intr.* be or come into a cluster or clusters. **3** *intr.* (foll. by *around*) gather; congregate. [OE *clyster:* cf. CLOT]

clus•ter bomb *n.* an antipersonnel bomb spraying pellets on impact.

clus•tered /klústərd/ *adj.* **1** growing in or brought into a cluster. **2** *Archit.* (of pillars, columns, or shafts) several close together, or disposed around or half detached from a pier.

clus•ter pine *n.* a Mediterranean pine *Pinus pinaster* with clustered cones: Also called **pinaster**.

clutch[1] /kluch/ *n. & v.* ● *v.* **1** *tr.* seize eagerly; grasp tightly. **2** *intr.* (foll. by *at*) snatch suddenly. ● *n.* **1 a** a tight grasp. **b** (foll. by *at*) grasping. **2** (in *pl.*) grasping hands, esp. as representing a cruel or relentless grasp or control. **3 a** (in a motor vehicle) a device for connecting and disconnecting the engine to the transmission. **b** the pedal operating this. **c** an arrangement for connecting or disconnecting working parts of a machine. **4** a critical situation in a game, etc. (*always comes through in the clutch*). [ME *clucche, clicche* f. OE *clyccan* crook, clench, f. Gmc]

clutch[2] /kluch/ *n.* **1** a set of eggs for hatching. **2** a brood of chickens. [18th c.: prob. S.Engl. var. of *cletch* f. *cleck* to hatch f. ON *klekja,* assoc. with CLUTCH[1]]

clutch bag *n.* (also **clutch purse**) a slim, flat handbag without handles.

clut•ter /klútər/ *n. & v.* ● *n.* **1** a crowded and untidy collection of things. **2** an untidy state. ● *v.tr.* (often foll. by *up, with*) crowd untidily; fill with clutter. [partly var. of *clotter* coagulate, partly assoc. with CLUSTER, CLATTER]

Clydes•dale /klídzdayl/ *n.* **1 a** a horse of a heavy powerful breed,

used as draft horses. **b** this breed. **2** a kind of small terrier. [orig. bred near the *Clyde* river in Scotland: see DALE]

clyp•e•us /klípeeəs/ *n.* (*pl.* **clyp•e•i** /–pee-ī/) the hard protective area of an insect's head. □□ **clyp•e•al** *adj.* **clyp•e•ate** *adj.* [L, = round shield]

clys•ter /klístər/ *n. & v. archaic* ● *n.* an enema. ● *v.tr.* treat with an enema. [ME f. OF *clystere* or f. L f. Gk *klustēr* syringe f. *kluzō* wash out]

Cm *symb. Chem.* the element curium.

cm *abbr.* centimeter(s).

Cmdr. *abbr.* commander.

Cmdre. *abbr.* commodore.

CMG *abbr.* (in the UK) Companion (of the Order) of St. Michael and St. George.

cnr. *abbr.* corner.

CNS *abbr.* central nervous system.

CO *abbr.* **1** Colorado (in official postal use). **2** commanding officer. **3** conscientious objector. **4** carbon monoxide.

Co *symb. Chem.* the element cobalt.

Co. *abbr.* **1** company. **2** county. □ **and Co.** /kō/ *Brit. colloq.* and the rest of them; and similar things.

c/o *abbr.* care of.

co- /kō/ *prefix* **1** added to: **a** nouns, with the sense 'joint, mutual, common' (*coauthor, coequality*). **b** adjectives and adverbs, with the sense 'jointly, mutually' (*cobelligerent; coequal; coequally*). **c** verbs, with the sense 'together with another or others' (*cooperate; coauthor*). **2** *Math.* **a** of the complement of an angle (*cosine*). **b** the complement of (*colatitude; coset*). [orig. a form of COM-]

coach /kōch/ *n. & v.* ● *n.* **1** a passenger bus, usu. comfortably equipped for longer journeys. **2** a railroad car. **3** a horse-drawn carriage, usu. closed, esp. a stagecoach. **4** a** an instructor or trainer in sport. **b** a private tutor. **5** economy-class seating in an aircraft. **6** *Austral.* a docile cow or bullock used as a decoy to attract wild cattle. ● *v.* **1** *tr.* **a** train or teach (a pupil, sports team, etc.) as a coach. **b** give hints to; prime with facts. **2** *intr.* travel by stagecoach (*in the old coaching days*). [F *coche* f. Magyar *kocsi* (adj.) f. *Kocs* in Hungary]

coach house *n.* an outbuilding for carriages.

coach•man /kóchmən/ *n.* (*pl.* •**men**) the driver of a horse-drawn carriage.

coach sta•tion *n. Brit.* a stopping place for a number of tour buses, usu. with buildings and amenities.

coach•wood /kóchwood/ *n. Austral.* any tree, esp. *Ceratopetalum apetalum,* with close-grained wood suitable for cabinetmaking.

coach•work /kóchwərk/ *n.* the bodywork of a road or rail vehicle.

co•ad•ju•tor /kō-ájətər, kóəjoō–/ *n.* an assistant, esp. an assistant bishop. [ME f. OF *coadjuteur* f. LL *coadjutor* (as CO-, *adjutor* f. *adjuvare –jut–* help)]

co•ag•u•lant /kō-ágyələnt/ *n.* a substance that produces coagulation.

co•ag•u•late /kō-ágyəlayt/ *v.tr. & intr.* **1** change from a fluid to a solid or semisolid state. **2** clot; curdle. **3** set; solidify. □□ **co•ag•u•la•ble** *adj.* **co•ag•u•la•tive** /–láytiv, –lətiv/ *adj.* **co•ag•u•la•tor** *n.* [ME f. L *coagulare* f. *coagulum* rennet]

co•ag•u•la•tion /kó-agyəláyshən/ *n.* the process by which a liquid changes to a semisolid mass. [as COAGULATE]

co•ag•u•lum /kō-ágyələm/ *n.* (*pl.* **co•ag•u•la** /–lə/ or **co•ag•u•lums**) a mass of coagulated matter. [L: see COAGULATE]

coal /kōl/ *n. & v.* ● *n.* **1 a** a hard black or blackish rock, mainly carbonized plant matter, found in underground seams and used as a fuel and in the manufacture of gas, tar, etc. **b** a piece of this for burning. **2** a red-hot piece of coal, wood, etc., in a fire. ● *v.* **1** *intr.* take in a supply of coal. **2** *tr.* put coal into (an engine, fire, etc.). □ **coals to Newcastle** something brought or sent to a place where it is already plentiful. **haul** (or **rake**) **over the coals** reprimand. □□ **coal•y** *adj.* [OE *col* f. Gmc]

coal-black *adj.* as black as coal; completely black.

coal•er /kólər/ *n.* a ship, etc., transporting coal.

co•a•lesce /kóəlés/ *v.intr.* **1** come together and form one whole. **2** combine in a cohesion. □□ **co•a•les•cence** *n.* **co•a•les•cent** *adj.* [L *coalescere* (as CO-, *alescere alit–* grow f. *alere* nourish)]

coal•face /kólfays/ *n.* an exposed surface of coal in a mine.

coal•field /kólfeeld/ *n.* an extensive area with strata containing coal.

coal-fired *adj.* heated or driven by coal.

coal•fish /kólfish/ *n.* = SAITHE.

coal gas *n.* mixed gases extracted from coal and used for lighting and heating.

coal•hole /kólhōl/ *n.* **1** a hole, as from a sidewalk, leading to a coal bin. **2** *Brit.* (as **coal-hole**) a compartment for storing coal.

co•a•li•tion /kóəlíshən/ *n.* **1** *Polit.* a temporary alliance for combined action, esp. of distinct parties forming a government, or of nations. **2** fusion into one whole. □□ **co•a•li•tion•ist** *n.* [med.L *coalitio* (as COALESCE)]

coal·man /kólmən/ n. (pl. ·men) a person who carries or delivers coal.

coal mea·sures n. Geol. a series of strata of the Carboniferous period, including coal seams.

coal mine n. a mine in which coal is dug.

coal min·er n. a worker in a coal mine.

coal oil n. dated petroleum or kerosene.

Coal·sack /kólsak/ n. Astron. a black patch in the Milky Way, esp. the one near the Southern Cross.

coal scut·tle n. a container for coal to supply a domestic fire.

coal seam n. a stratum of coal suitable for mining.

coal tar n. a thick, black, oily liquid distilled from coal and used as a source of benzene.

coam·ing /kóming/ n. a raised border around the hatches, etc., of a ship to keep out water. [17th c.: orig. unkn.]

coarse /kawrs/ adj. **1 a** rough or loose in texture or grain; made of large particles. **b** (of a person's features) rough or large. **2** lacking refinement or delicacy; crude; obscene (coarse humor). **3** rude; uncivil. **4** inferior; common. □□ **coarse·ly** adv. **coarse·ness** n. **coars·ish** adj. [ME: orig. unkn.]

coars·en /káwrsən/ v.tr. & intr. make or become coarse.

coast /kōst/ n. & v. • n. **1 a** the border of the land near the sea; the seashore. **b** (the Coast) the Pacific coast of the US. **2 a** a run, usu. downhill, on a bicycle without pedaling or in a motor vehicle without using the engine. **b** a toboggan slide or slope. • v.intr. **1** ride or move, usu. downhill, without use of power; freewheel. **2** make progress without much effort. **3** slide down a hill on a toboggan or other sled. **4 a** sail along the coast. **b** trade between ports on the same coast. □ **the coast is clear** there is no danger of being observed or caught. □□ **coast·al** adj. [ME f. OF coste, costeier f. L costa rib, flank, side]

coast·er /kóstər/ n. **1** a ship that travels along the coast from port to port. **2** a small tray or mat for a bottle or glass.

Coast Guard /kōst gaard/ n. the U.S. military service that protects coastal waters, aids shipping and pleasure craft, and enforces maritime laws.

coast·line /kóstlīn/ n. the line of the seashore, esp. with regard to its shape (a rugged coastline).

coast-to-coast adj. all the way across an island or continent (a coast-to-coast journey).

coast·wise /kóstwīz/ adj. & adv. along, following, or connected with the coast.

coat /kōt/ n. & v. • n. **1** an outer garment with sleeves and often extending below the hips; an overcoat or jacket. **2 a** an animal's fur, hair, etc. **b** Physiol. a structure, esp. a membrane, enclosing or lining an organ. **c** a skin, rind, or husk. **d** a layer of a bulb, etc. **3 a** a layer or covering. **b** a covering of paint, etc., laid on a surface at one time. • v.tr. **1** (usu. foll. by with, in) **a** apply a coat of paint, etc., to; provide with a layer or covering. **b** (as coated adj.) covered with. **2** (of paint, etc.) form a covering to. □□ **coat·ed** adj. (also in comb.). [ME f. OF cote f. Rmc f. Frank., of unkn. orig.]

coat ar·mor n. heraldic arms.

coat·dress /kótdres/ n. a woman's tailored dress resembling a coat.

coat hang·er n. see HANGER[1].

co·a·ti /kō-áatee/ n. (pl. **co·a·tis**) any raccoonlike, carnivorous mammal of the genus Nasua, with a long, flexible snout and a long, usu. ringed tail. [Tupi f. cua belt + tim nose]

co·a·ti·mun·di /kó-aateemúndee/ n. (pl. **co·a·ti·mun·dis**) = COATI. [as COATI + Tupi mondi solitary]

coat·ing /kóting/ n. **1** a thin layer or covering of paint, etc. **2** material for making coats.

coat of arms n. the heraldic bearings or shield of a person, family, or corporation.

coat of mail n. a garment covered with or composed of metal rings or plates, serving as armor.

coat·tail /kóttayl/ n. **1** the back flap of a man's jacket or coat. **2** (in pl.) **a** the back skirts of a dress coat, cutaway, etc. **b** Polit. (of a party candidate) popularity such as to attract votes for other party candidates.

co·au·thor /kó-áwthər/ n. & v. • n. a joint author. • v.tr. be a joint author of.

coax /kōks/ v.tr. **1** (usu. foll. by into, or to + infin.) persuade (a person) gradually or by flattery. **2** (foll. by out of) obtain (a thing from a person) by coaxing. **3** manipulate (a thing) carefully or slowly. □□ **coax·er** n. **coax·ing·ly** adv. [16th c.: f. 'make a cokes' f. obs. cokes simpleton, of unkn. orig.]

co·ax·i·al /kō-ákseeəl/ adj. **1** having a common axis. **2** Electr. (of a cable or line) transmitting by means of two concentric conductors separated by an insulator. □□ **co·ax·i·al·ly** adv.

cob[1] /kob/ n. **1** = CORNCOB. **2** a sturdy riding or driving horse with short legs. **3** a male swan. **4** Brit. a roundish lump, loaf of bread, etc. [ME: orig. unkn.]

cob[2] /kob/ n. Brit. a material for walls, made from compressed earth, clay, or chalk reinforced with straw. [17th c.: orig. unkn.]

co·balt /kóbawlt/ n. Chem. a silvery-white, magnetic metallic element occurring naturally as a mineral in combination with sulfur and arsenic, and used in many alloys. ¶ Symb.: Co. □□ **co·bal·tic** /kōbáwltik/ adj. **co·bal·tous** /kōbáwltəs/ adj. [G Kobalt, etc., prob. = KOBOLD in mines]

co·balt blue n. **1** a pigment containing a cobalt salt. **2** the deep-blue color of this.

cob·ber /kóbər/ n. Austral. & NZ colloq. a companion or friend. [19th c.: perh. rel. to E dial. cob take a liking to]

cob·ble[1] /kóbəl/ n. & v. • n. **1** (in full **cobblestone**) a small rounded stone of a size used for paving. **2** (in pl.) Brit. coal in lumps of this size. • v.tr. pave with cobbles. [ME cobel(- ston), f. COB[1]]

cob·ble[2] /kóbəl/ v.tr. **1** mend or patch up (esp. shoes). **2** (often foll. by together) join or assemble roughly. [back-form. f. COBBLER]

cob·bler /kóblər/ n. **1** a person who mends shoes, esp. professionally. **2** an iced drink of wine, etc., sugar, and lemon (sherry cobbler). **3** a fruit pie with a rich, thick biscuit crust usu. only on the top. **4** (in pl.) Brit. sl. nonsense. **5** Austral. & NZ sl. the last sheep to be shorn. [ME, of unkn. orig.: sense 4 f. rhyming sl. cobbler's awls = balls: sense 5 with pun on LAST[3]]

co·bel·lig·er·ent /kóbilíjərənt/ n. & adj. • n. any of two or more nations engaged in war as allies. • adj. of or as a cobelligerent. □□ **co·bel·lig·er·ence** /–rəns/ n. **co·bel·lig·er·en·cy** n.

co·ble /kóbəl/ n. a flat-bottomed fishing boat in Scotland and NE England. [OE, perh. f. Celt.]

COBOL /kóbawl/ n. Computing a programming language designed for use in commerce. [common business oriented language]

co·bra /kóbrə/ n. any venomous snake of the genus Naja, native to Africa and Asia, with a neck dilated like a hood when excited. [Port. f. L colubra snake]

cob·web /kóbweb/ n. **1 a** a fine network of threads spun by a spider from a liquid secreted by it, used to trap insects, etc., **b** the thread of this. **2** anything compared with a cobweb, esp. in flimsiness of texture. **3** a trap or insidious entanglement. **4** (in pl.) a state of languishing; fustiness. □□ **cob·webbed** adj. **cob·web·by** adj. [ME cop(pe)web f. obs. coppe spider]

co·ca /kókə/ n. **1** a S. American shrub, Erythroxylum coca. **2** its dried leaves, chewed as a stimulant. [Sp. f. Quechua cuca]

Co·ca-Co·la /kókəkólə/ n. Trademark a carbonated soft drink flavored with extract of cola nuts.

co·caine /kōkáyn/ n. a drug derived from coca or prepared synthetically, used as a local anesthetic and as a stimulant. [COCA + –INE[4]]

coc·cid·i·o·sis /kóksideeósis/ n. a disease of birds and mammals caused by any of various parasitic protozoa, esp. of the genus Eimeria, affecting the intestine. [coccidium (mod.L f. Gk kokkis dimin. of kokkos berry) + –OSIS]

coc·cus /kókəs/ n. (pl. **coc·ci** /kóksī, kókī/) any spherical or roughly spherical bacterium. □□ **coc·cal** adj. **coc·coid** adj. [mod.L f. Gk kokkos berry]

coc·cyx /kóksiks/ n. (pl. **coc·cy·ges** /–sijeez/ or **coc·cyx·es**) the small triangular bone at the base of the spinal column in humans and some apes. □□ **coc·cyg·e·al** /koksíjeeəl/ adj. [L f. Gk kokkux –ugos cuckoo (from being shaped like its bill)]

Co·chin /kóchin/ n. (in full **Cochin China**) **1** a fowl of an Asian breed with feathery legs. **2** this breed. [Cochin China in Vietnam]

coch·i·neal /kóchineél/ n. **1** a scarlet dye used esp. for coloring food. **2** the dried bodies of the female of the Mexican insect, Dactylopius coccus, yielding this. [F cochenille or Sp. cochinilla f. L coccinus scarlet f. Gk kokkos berry]

coch·le·a /kókleeə/ n. (pl. **coch·le·as** or **coch·le·ae** /–lee-ee/) the spiral cavity of the internal ear. □□ **coch·le·ar** adj. [L, = snail shell, f. Gk kokhlias]

cock[1] /kok/ n. & v. • n. **1** a male bird, esp. of a domestic fowl. **2** coarse sl. the penis. **3** Brit. sl. (usu. old cock as a form of address) a friend; a fellow. **4** Brit. nonsense. **5 a** a firing lever in a gun which can be raised to be released by the trigger. **b** the cocked position of this (at full cock). **6** a tap or valve controlling flow. • v.tr. **1** raise or make upright or erect. **2** turn or move (the eye or ear) attentively or knowingly. **3** set aslant, or turn up the brim of (a hat). **4** raise the cock of (a gun). □ **at half cock** only partly ready. **cock a snook** = thumb one's nose (see THUMB). **cock up** Brit. sl. bungle; make a mess of. **knock into a cocked hat** defeat utterly. [OE cocc and OF coq prob. f. med.L coccus]

▶ In senses 2 and 4 of the noun this is usually considered a taboo word.

cock[2] /kok/ n. & v. • n. a small pile of hay, straw, etc., with vertical sides and a rounded top. • v.tr. pile into cocks. [ME, perh. of Scand. orig.]

cock·ade /kokáyd/ n. a rosette, etc., worn in a hat as a badge of office or party, or as part of a livery. □□ **cock·ad·ed** adj. [F cocarde orig. in bonnet à la coquarde, f. fem. of obs. coquard saucy f. coq COCK[1]]

cock-a-doo·dle-doo n. used to represent the sound made by a cock when it crows.

cock-a-hoop /kókəhōop/ adj. & adv. esp. Brit. • adj. exultant; crowing boastfully. • adv. exultantly. [16th c.: orig. in phr. set cock a hoop denoting some action preliminary to hard drinking] cock·a·leek·ie /kókəleékee/ n. (also cock·y-leek·y /kókee–/) a soup traditionally made in Scotland with boiled chicken and leeks. [COCK¹ + LEEK]

cock·a·lo·rum /kókəláwrəm/ n. colloq. a self-important little person. [18th c.: arbitr. f. COCK¹]

cock-and-bull sto·ry n. an absurd or incredible tale presented as being true.

cock·a·tiel /kókəteél/ n. (also cock·a·teel) a small, delicately colored Australian crested parrot, Nymphicus hollandicus. [Du. kaketielje]

cock·a·too /kókətoő/ n. 1 any of several parrots of the family Cacatuinae, having powerful beaks and erectile crests. 2 colloq. a small farmer. [Du. kaketoe f. Malay kakatua, assim. to COCK¹]

cock·a·trice /kókətris, –trīs/ n. 1 = BASILISK 1. 2 Heraldry a fabulous animal, a cock with a serpent's tail. [ME f. OF cocatris f. L calcare tread, track, rendering Gk ikhneumōn tracker: see ICHNEUMON]

sulfur-crested cockatoo

cock·boat /kókbōt/ n. a small boat, esp. one used as a ship's tender. [obs. cock small boat (f. OF coque) + BOAT]

cock·chaf·er /kókchayfər/ n. a large nocturnal beetle, Melolontha melolontha, which feeds on leaves and whose larva feeds on roots of crops, etc. [perh. f. COCK¹ as expressing size or vigor + CHAFER]

cock·crow /kókkrō/ n. dawn.

cock n. a brimless triangular hat pointed at the front, back, and top. □ knock something into a cocked hat utterly defeat or outdo something

cock·er /kókər/ n. (in full cocker spaniel) 1 a small spaniel of a breed with a silky coat. 2 this breed. [as COCK¹, from use in hunting woodcocks, etc.]

cock·er·el /kókrəl/ n. a young cock. [ME: dimin. of COCK¹]

cock·eyed /kókíd/ adj. colloq. 1 crooked; askew; not level. 2 (of a scheme, etc.) absurd; not practical. 3 drunk. 4 squinting. [19th c.: app. f. COCK¹ + EYE]

cock·fight /kókfit/ n. an arranged fight between cocks, usu. having their legs fitted with metal spurs. □□ cock·fight·ing n.

cock·le¹ /kókəl/ n. 1 a any edible mollusk of the genus Cardium, having a chubby, ribbed bivalve shell. b (in full cockleshell) its shell. 2 (in full cockleshell) a small shallow boat. □ warm the cockles of one's heart make one contented; be satisfying. [ME f. OF coquille shell ult. f. Gk kogkhulion f. kogkhē CONCH]

cock·le² /kókəl/ n. 1 any of various plants, esp. the pink-flowered corn cockle, Agrostemma githago, growing with grain, esp. wheat. 2 a disease of wheat that turns the grains black. [OE coccul, perh. ult. f. LL COCCUS]

cock·le³ /kókəl/ v. & n. •v. 1 intr. pucker; wrinkle. 2 tr. cause to cockle. •n. a pucker or wrinkle in paper, glass, etc. [F coquiller blister (bread in cooking) f. coquille: see COCKLE¹]

cock·ney /kóknee/ n. & adj. •n. (pl. ·neys) 1 a a native of East London, esp. one born within hearing of Bow Bells (or the Bow church in London's East End district). b the dialect or accent typical of this area. 2 Austral. a young snapper fish, Chrysophrys auratus. •adj. of or characteristic of cockneys or their dialect or accent. □□ cock·ney·ism n. [ME cokeney cock's egg, later derog. for 'townsman']

cock-of-the-rock n. a S. American bird, Rupicola rupicola, having a crest and bright orange plumage.

cock of the walk n. a dominant or arrogant person.

cock of the wood n. (also cock of the woods) 1 a capercaillie. 2 a pileated woodpecker.

cock·pit /kókpit/ n. 1 a a compartment for the pilot (or the pilot and crew) of an aircraft or spacecraft. b a similar compartment for the driver in a racing car. c a space for the helmsman in some small yachts. 2 an arena of war or other conflict. 3 a place where cockfights are held. [orig. in sense 3, f. COCK¹ + PIT¹]

cockroach

cock·roach /kókrōch/ n. any of various flat brown insects, esp. Blatta orientalis, infesting kitchens, bathrooms, etc. [Sp. cucaracha, assim. to COCK¹, ROACH¹]

cocks·comb /kókskōm/ n. 1 the crest or comb of a cock. 2 a garden plant, Celosia cristata, with a terminal broad plume of usu. crimson or reddish-purple flowers.

cocks·foot /kóksfoŏt/ n. Brit. any pasture grass of the genus Dactylis, with broad leaves and green or purplish spikes.

cock·shy /kókshī/ n. (pl. ·shies) Brit. 1 a a

cockscomb

---

target for throwing at with sticks, stones, etc. b a throw at this. 2 an object of ridicule or criticism.

cock·sure /kókshoŏr/ adj. 1 presumptuously or arrogantly confident. 2 (foll. by of, about) absolutely sure. □□ cock·sure·ly adv. cock·sure·ness n. [cock = God + SURE]

cock·tail /kóktayl/ n. 1 a usu. alcoholic drink made by mixing various spirits, fruit juices, etc. 2 a dish of mixed ingredients (fruit cocktail; shellfish cocktail). 3 any hybrid mixture. [orig. unkn.: cf. earlier sense 'docked horse' f. COCK¹: the connection is unclear]

cock·tail dress n. a usu. short evening dress suitable for wearing at a cocktail party.

cock·tail party n. a social gathering, usu. in the early evening, at which cocktails and hors d'oeuvres, etc. are served.

cock-up n. Brit. sl. a muddle or mistake.

cock·y¹ /kókee/ adj. (cock·i·er, cock·i·est) 1 conceited; arrogant. 2 saucy; impudent. □□ cock·i·ly adv. cock·i·ness n. [COCK¹ + –Y¹]

cock·y² /kókee/ n. (pl. ·ies) Austral. & NZ colloq. = COCKATOO 2. [abbr.]

cock·y-leek·y var. of COCK-A-LEEKIE.

co·co /kókō/ n. (pl. co·cos) a tall tropical palm tree, Cocos nucifera, bearing coconuts. [Port. & Sp. coco grimace: the base of the shell resembles a face]

co·coa /kókō/ n. 1 a powder made from crushed cacao seeds, often with other ingredients. 2 a hot drink made from this. [alt. of CACAO]

co·coa bean n. a cacao seed.

co·coa but·ter n. a fatty substance obtained from cocoa beans and used esp. in the manufacture of candy and cosmetics.

co·co-de-mer /kókōdəmáir/ n. 1 a tall palm tree, Lodoicea maldivica, native to the Seychelles, that has an immense nut in a hard woody shell, the largest known seed. 2 the large nut of this palm. [F]

co·co·nut /kókənut/ n. (also co·coa·nut) 1 a a large ovate brown seed of the coco, with a hard shell and edible white fleshy lining enclosing a milky juice. b = COCO. c the edible white fleshy lining of a coconut. 2 sl. the human head. [COCO + NUT]

co·co·nut mat·ting n. a matting made of fiber from coconut husks.

co·co·nut oil n. a solid oil obtained from the lining of the coconut, and used in soap, candles, ointment, etc.

co·coon /kəkoőn/ n. & v. •n. 1 a a silky case spun by many insect larvae for protection as pupae. b a similar structure made by other animals. 2 a protective covering, esp. to prevent corrosion of metal equipment. •v. 1 tr. & intr. wrap in or form a cocoon. 2 tr. spray with a protective coating. [F cocon f. mod. Prov. coucoun dimin. of coca shell]

co·cotte /kəkót, kawkáwt/ n. 1 a a small fireproof dish for cooking and serving an individual portion of food. b a deep cooking pot with a tight-fitting lid and handles. 2 archaic a fashionable prostitute. [F]

COD abbr. 1 cash on delivery. 2 collect on delivery.

cod¹ /kod/ n. (pl. same) any large marine fish of the family Gadidae, used as food, esp. Gadus morhua. [ME: orig. unkn.]

cod² /kod/ n. & v. Brit. sl. •n. 1 a parody. 2 a hoax. 3 (attrib.) = MOCK adj. •v. (cod·ded, cod·ding) 1 a intr. perform a hoax. b tr. play a trick on; fool. 2 tr. parody. [19th c.: orig. unkn.]

cod³ /kod/ n. Brit. sl. nonsense. [abbr. of CODSWALLOP]

co·da /kódə/ n. 1 Mus. the concluding passage of a piece or movement, usu. forming an addition to the basic structure. 2 Ballet the concluding section of a dance. 3 a concluding event or series of events. [It. f. L cauda tail]

cod·dle /kód'l/ v.tr. 1 a treat as an invalid; protect attentively. b Brit. (foll. by up) strengthen by feeding. 2 cook (an egg) in water below boiling point. □□ cod·dler n. [prob. dial. var. of caudle invalids' gruel]

code /kōd/ n. & v. •n. 1 a system of words, letters, figures, or symbols, used to represent others for secrecy or brevity. 2 a system of prearranged signals, esp. used to ensure secrecy in transmitting messages. 3 Computing a piece of program text. 4 a a systematic collection of statutes, a body of laws so arranged as to avoid inconsistency and overlapping. b a set of rules on any subject. 5 a the prevailing morality of a society or class (code of honor). b a person's standard of moral behavior. •v.tr. put (a message, program, etc.) into code. □□ cod·er n. [ME f. OF f. L CODEX]

code·book /kódboŏk/ n. a list of symbols, etc., used in a code.

co·deine /kódeen/ n. an alkaloid derived from morphine and used to relieve pain. [Gk kōdeia poppyhead + –INE²]

code name n. (also code num·ber) a word or symbol (or number) used for secrecy or convenience instead of the usual name.

co·de·pend·en·cy /kódipéndənsee/ n. an emotional or psychological reliance on a partner, typically one with an illness or addiction who requires support. □□ co·de·pend·ent /–dənt/ adj. & n. [CO- + DEPENDENCY]

co·de·ter·mi·na·tion /kóditərmináyshən/ n. cooperation between management and workers in decision making. [CO- + DETERMINATION, after G Mitbestimmung]

See page xx for the **Key to Pronunciation.**

co·dex /kṓdeks/ n. (pl. **co·di·ces** /kṓdiseez, kŏd–/) **1** an ancient manuscript text in book form. **2** a collection of pharmaceutical descriptions of drugs, etc. [L, = block of wood, tablet, book]

cod·fish /kŏdfish/ n. = COD[1].

codg·er /kŏjər/ n. (usu. in **old codger**) colloq. a person, esp. an old or strange one. [perh. var. of cadger: see CADGE]

co·di·ces pl. of CODEX.

cod·i·cil /kŏdisil/ n. an addition explaining, modifying, or revoking a will or part of one. □□ **cod·i·cil·la·ry** /kŏdisílŏree/ adj. [L codicillus, dimin. of CODEX]

co·di·col·o·gy /kŏdikŏlŏjee/ n. the study of manuscripts. □□ **codicological** /–kŏlójikəl/ adj. **codicologically** adv. [F codicologie f. L codex codicis: see CODEX]

cod·i·fy /kŏdifī, kŏd–/ v.tr. (·fies, ·fied) arrange (laws, etc.) systematically into a code. □□ **cod·i·fi·ca·tion** /–fikáyshən/ n. **cod·i·fi·er** n.

PRONUNCIATION TIP codify

In American English, this word is usually pronounced with a "short o," rhyming with *modify*. But it is also acceptable to pronounce it with a "long o," as in *notify*.

---

cod·ling[1] /kŏdling/ n. Brit. (also **cod·lin**) **1** any of several varieties of cooking apple, having a long tapering shape. **2** a small moth, *Carpocapsa pomonella*, the larva of which feeds on apples. [ME f. AF quer de lion lion heart]

cod·ling[2] /kŏdling/ n. a small codfish.

cod-liv·er oil n. an oil pressed from the fresh liver of cod, which is rich in vitamins D and A.

co·do·main /kŏdōmayn/ n. Math. a set that includes all the possible expressions of a given function. [CO- 2 + DOMAIN]

co·don /kŏdon/ n. Biochem. a sequence of three nucleotides, forming a unit of genetic code in a DNA or RNA molecule. [CODE + –ON]

cod·piece /kŏdpees/ n. hist. an appendage like a small bag or flap at the front of a man's breeches to cover the genitals. [ME, f. cod scrotum + PIECE]

cod·riv·er /kŏdrívər/ n. a person who shares the driving of a vehicle with another, esp. in a race, rally, etc.

cods·wal·lop /kŏdzwoləp/ n. esp. Brit. sl. nonsense. [20th c.: orig. unkn.]

co·ed /kó-ed, –éd/ n. & adj. colloq. •n. **1** a coeducational system or institution. **2** a female student at a coeducational institution. • adj. coeducational. [abbr.]

co·ed·u·ca·tion /kóejŏŏkáyshən/ n. the education of pupils of both sexes together. □□ **co·ed·u·ca·tion·al** adj.

co·ef·fi·cient /kŏifíshənt/ n. **1** Math. a quantity placed before and multiplying an algebraic expression (e.g., 4 in $4x^y$). **2** Physics a multiplier or factor that measures some property (coefficient of expansion). [mod.L coefficiens (as CO-, EFFICIENT)]

coe·la·canth /seélŏkanth/ n. a large bony marine fish, *Latimeria chalumnae*, formerly thought to be extinct, having a trilobed tail fin and fleshy pectoral fins. [mod.L Coelacanthus f. Gk koilos hollow + akantha spine]

-coele comb. form var. of –CELE.

coe·len·ter·ate /seeléntərayt, –tərit/ n. any marine animal of the phylum Coelenterata with a simple tube-shaped or cup-shaped body, e.g., jellyfish, corals, and sea anemones. [mod.L Coelenterata f. Gk koilos hollow + enteron intestine]

coe·li·ac esp. Brit. var. of CELIAC.

coe·lom /seélŏm/ n. (also **coe·lom**) (pl. ·loms or ·lo·ma·ta /–lṓmətə/) Zool. the principal body cavity in animals, between the intestinal canal and the body wall. □□ **coe·lo·mate** adj. & n. [Gk koilōma cavity]

coe·lo·stat /seélŏstat/ n. Astron. an instrument with a rotating mirror that continuously reflects the light from the same area of sky allowing the path of a celestial body to be monitored. [L caelum sky + –STAT]

coe·no·bite esp. Brit. var. of CENOBITE.

co·en·zyme /kō-énzīm/ n. Biochem. a nonproteinaceous compound that assists in the action of an enzyme.

co·e·qual /kō-eékwəl/ adj. & n. archaic or literary • adj. equal with one another. •n. an equal. □□ **co·e·qual·i·ty** /kŏ-eekwólitee/ n. **co·e·qual·ly** adv. [ME f. L or eccl.L coaequalis (as CO-, EQUAL)]

co·erce /kō-órs/ v.tr. (often foll. by into) persuade or restrain (an unwilling person) by force (coerced you into signing). □□ **co·er·ci·ble** adj. [ME f. L coercēre restrain (as CO-, arcēre restrain)]

co·er·cion /kō-órzhon, –shon/ n. **1** the act or process of coercing. **2** government by force. □□ **co·er·cive** /–siv/ adj. **co·er·cive·ly** adv. **co·er·cive·ness** n. [OF cohercion, –tion f. L coer(c)tio, coercitio –onis (as COERCE)]

Coeur d'A·lene /kórd'lăn/ n. **1 a** a N. American people native to northern Idaho. **b** a member of this people. **2** the language of this people.

co·e·val /kō-eévəl/ adj. & n. • adj. **1** having the same age or date of

origin. **2** living or existing at the same epoch. **3** having the same duration. ●n. a coeval person, a contemporary. □□ **co·e·val·i·ty** /–válitee/ n. **co·e·val·ly** adv. [LL coaevus (as CO-, L aevum age)]

co·ex·ist /kŏigzíst/ v.intr. (often foll. by with) **1** exist together (in time or place). **2** (esp. of nations) exist in mutual tolerance though professing different ideologies, etc. □□ **co·ex·ist·ence** n. **co·ex·ist·ent** adj. [LL coexistere (as CO-, EXIST)]

co·ex·ten·sive /kŏiksténsiv/ adj. extending over the same space or time.

C. of E. abbr. Church of England.

cof·fee /káwfee, kófee/ n. **1 a** a drink made from the roasted and ground beanlike seed of a tropical shrub. **b** a cup of this. **2 a** any shrub of the genus *Coffea*, yielding berries containing one or more seeds. **b** these seeds raw, or roasted and ground. **3** a pale brown color, as of coffee mixed with milk. [ult. f. Turk. kahveh f. Arab. kahwa, the drink]

cof·fee bar n. a bar or café serving coffee and light refreshments from a counter.

cof·fee bean n. the beanlike seeds of the coffee shrub.

cof·fee break n. a short rest from work during which refreshments are usually taken.

cof·fee cake n. a type of cake or sweetened bread, often made with nuts, raisins, or fruit.

cof·fee·house /káwfeehows, kóf–/ n. a place serving coffee and other refreshments, and often providing informal entertainment.

cof·fee mill n. a small machine for grinding roasted coffee beans.

cof·fee shop n. a small informal restaurant, esp. in a hotel or department store.

cof·fee ta·ble n. a long, low table usu. placed in front of a sofa.

cof·fee-ta·ble book n. a large, lavishly illustrated book.

cof·fer /káwfər, kóf–/ n. **1** a box, esp. a large strongbox for valuables. **2** (in pl.) a treasury or store of funds. **3** a sunken panel in a ceiling, etc. □□ **cof·fered** adj. [ME f. OF coffre f. L cophinus f. Gk kophinos basket]

cof·fer·dam /káwfərdam, kóf–/ n. a watertight enclosure pumped dry to permit work below the waterline on building bridges, etc., or for repairing a ship.

cof·fin /káwfin, kóf–/ n. & v. •n. **1** a long, narrow, usu. wooden box in which a corpse is buried or cremated. **2** the part of a horse's hoof below the coronet. • v.tr. (**cof·fined**, **cof·fin·ing**) put in a coffin. [ME f. OF cof(f)in little basket, etc. f. L cophinus: see COFFER]

cof·fin bone n. the terminal bone in a horse's hoof (the distal phalanx).

cof·fin nail n. sl. a cigarette.

cof·fle /káwfəl, kóf–/ n. a line of animals, slaves, etc., fastened together. [Arab. kāfila caravan]

cog /kawg, kog/ n. **1** each of a series of projections on the edge of a wheel or bar transferring motion by engaging with another series. **2** an uncelebrated member of an organization, etc. □□ **cogged** adj. [ME: prob. of Scand. orig.]

co·gent /kójənt/ adj. (of arguments, reasons, etc.) convincing; compelling. □□ **co·gen·cy** /–jənsee/ n. **co·gent·ly** adv. [L cogere compel (as CO-, agere act- drive)]

cog·i·ta·ble /kójitəbəl/ adj. able to be grasped by the mind; conceivable. [L cogitabilis (as COGITATE)]

cog·i·tate /kójitayt/ v.tr. & intr. ponder; meditate. □□ **cog·i·ta·tion** /–táyshən/ n. **cog·i·ta·tive** adj. **cog·i·ta·tor** n. [L cogitare think (as CO-, AGITATE)]

co·gi·to /kṓgitō, kójitō/ n. Philos. the principle establishing the existence of a being from the fact of its thinking or awareness. [L, = I think, in Fr. philosopher Descartes's formula (1641) cogito, ergo sum I think, therefore I exist]

co·gnac /káwnyak, kón–/ n. a high-quality brandy, properly that distilled in Cognac in W. France.

cog·nate /kógnayt/ adj. & n. • adj. **1** related to or descended from a common ancestor (cf. AGNATE). **2** Philol. (of a word) having the same linguistic family or derivation (as another); representing the same original word or root (e.g., English *father*, German *Vater*, Latin *pater*). • n. **1** a relative. **2** a cognate word. □□ **cog·nate·ly** adv. **cog·nate·ness** n. [L cognatus (as CO-, natus born)]

cog·nate ob·ject n. Gram. an object that is related in origin and sense to the verb governing it (as in live a good life).

cog·ni·tion /kogníshən/ n. **1** Philos. knowing, perceiving, or conceiving as an act or faculty distinct from emotion and volition. **2** a result of this; a perception, sensation, notion, or intuition. □□ **cog·ni·tion·al** adj. **cog·ni·tive** /kógnitiv/ adj. [L cognitio (as CO-, gnoscere gnit- apprehend)]

cog·ni·za·ble /kógnizəbəl, kón–, kogní–/ adj. **1** perceptible; recognizable; clearly identifiable. **2** within the jurisdiction of a court. □□ **cog·ni·za·bly** adv. [COGNIZANCE + –ABLE]

cog·ni·zance /kógnizəns/ n. **1** knowledge or awareness; perception; notice. **2** the sphere of one's observation or concern. **3** Law the action of taking judicial notice. **4** Heraldry a distinctive device or mark. □ **have cognizance of** know, esp. officially. **take cognizance of** attend to; take account of. [ME f. OF conoisance ult. f. L cognoscent- f. cognitio: see COGNITION]

cog·ni·zant /kógnizənt/ *adj.* (foll. by *of*) having knowledge or being aware of.

cog·no·men /kognómen/ *n.* **1** a nickname. **2** an ancient Roman's personal name or epithet, as in Marcus Tullius *Cicero*, Publius Cornelius Scipio *Africanus*. [L]

co·gno·scen·ti /kónyəshéntee, kógnə–/ *pl. n.* people who are considered to be especially well informed about a particular subject. [obs. It.]

cog rail·way *n.* a railway with a cogged third rail designed to mesh with a cogwheel on a locomotive to prevent slippage on steep slopes.

cog·wheel /kóghweel, –weel/ *n.* a wheel with cogs.

co·hab·it /kōhábit/ *v.intr.* (also **co·hab·i·tate**) (**co·hab·it·ed**, **co·hab·it·ing**) live together, esp. as husband and wife without being married to one another. □□ **co·hab·i·tant** *n.* **co·hab·i·ta·tion** *n.* **co·hab·i·tee** /–teé/ *n.* **co·hab·i·ter** *n.* [L *cohabitare* (as co-, *habitare* dwell)]

co·here /kōheér/ *v.intr.* **1** (of parts or a whole) stick together; remain united. **2** (of reasoning, etc.) be logical or consistent. [L *cohaerēre cohaes-* (as co-, *haerēre* stick)]

co·her·ent /kōheérənt, –hér–/ *adj.* **1** (of a person) able to speak intelligibly and articulately. **2** (of speech, an argument, etc.) logical and consistent; easily followed. **3** cohering; sticking together. **4** *Physics* (of waves) having a constant phase relationship. □□ **co·her·ence** /–rəns/ *n.* **co·her·en·cy** *n.* **co·her·ent·ly** *adv.* [L *cohaerēre cohaerent-* (as COHERE)]

co·he·sion /kōheézhən/ *n.* **1 a** the act or condition of sticking together. **b** a tendency to cohere. **2** *Chem.* the force with which molecules cohere. □□ **co·he·sive** /–heésiv/ *adj.* **co·he·sive·ly** /–heésivlee/ *adv.* **co·he·sive·ness** /–heésivnis/ *n.* [L *cohaes-* (see COHERE) after *adhesion*]

co·ho /kóhō/ *n.* (also **co·hoe**) (*pl.* same or **·hos** or **·hoes**) a silver salmon, *Oncorhynchus kisutch*, of the N. Pacific coast. [19th c.: orig. unkn.]

co·hort /kóhawrt/ *n.* **1** an ancient Roman military unit, equal to one-tenth of a legion. **2** a band of warriors. **3 a** persons banded or grouped together, esp. in a common cause. **b** a group of persons with a common statistical characteristic. **4** a companion or colleague. [ME f. F *cohorte* or L *cohors cohort-* enclosure, company]

coif /koyf/ *n. hist.* **1** a close-fitting cap, esp. as worn by nuns under a veil. **2** a protective metal skullcap worn under armor. **3** = COIFFURE. [ME f. OF *coife* f. LL *cofia* helmet]

coif·feur /kwaafőr/ *n.* (*fem.* **coif·feuse** /–főz/) a hairdresser. [F]

coif·fure /kwaafyőor/ *n. & v.* ● *n.* (also **coif**) the way hair is arranged; a hairstyle. ● *v.* to provide a coiffure. [F]

coign of van·tage /koyn/ *n.* a favorable position for observation or action. [earlier spelling of COIN in the sense 'cornerstone']

coil[1] /koyl/ *n. & v.* ● *n.* **1** anything arranged in a joined sequence of concentric circles. **2** a length of rope, a spring, etc., arranged in this way. **3** a single turn of something coiled, e.g., a snake. **4** a lock of hair twisted and coiled. **5** an intrauterine contraceptive device in the form of a coil. **6** *Electr.* a device consisting of a coiled wire for converting low voltage to high voltage, esp. for transmission to the spark plugs of an internal combustion engine. **7** a piece of wire, piping, etc., wound in circles or spirals. **8** a roll of postage stamps. ● *v.* **1** *tr.* arrange in a series of concentric loops or rings. **2** *tr. & intr.* twist or be twisted into a circular or spiral shape. **3** *intr.* move sinuously. [OF *coillir* f. L *colligere* COLLECT[1]]

coil[2] /koyl/ *n.* □ **this mortal coil** the difficulties of earthly life (with ref. to Shakesp. *Hamlet* III. i. 67). [16th c.: orig. unkn.]

coin /koyn/ *n. & v.* ● *n.* **1** a piece of flat, usu. round metal stamped and issued by authority as money. **2** (*collect.*) metal money. ● *v.tr.* **1** make (coins) by stamping. **2** make (metal) into coins. **3** invent or devise (esp. a new word or phrase). □ **coin money** make much money quickly. **to coin a phrase** *iron.* introducing a banal remark or cliché. [ME f. OF, = stamping die, f. L *cuneus* wedge]

coin·age /kóynij/ *n.* **1** the act or process of coining. **2 a** coins collectively. **b** a system or type of coins in use (*decimal coinage*; *bronze coinage*). **3** an invention, esp. of a new word or phrase. [ME f. OF *coigniage*]

coin box *n. Brit.* **1** a telephone operated by inserting coins. **2** the receptacle for these.

co·in·cide /kóinsíd/ *v.intr.* **1** occur at or during the same time. **2** occupy the same portion of space. **3** (often foll. by *with*) be in agreement; have the same view. [med.L *coincidere* (as co-, INCIDENT)]

co·in·ci·dence /kō-ínsidəns/ *n.* **1 a** occurring or being together. **b** an instance of this. **2** a remarkable concurrence of events or circumstances without apparent causal connection. **3** *Physics* the presence of ionizing particles, etc., in two or more detectors simultaneously, or of two or more signals simultaneously in a circuit. [med.L *coincidentia* (as COINCIDE)]

co·in·ci·dent /kō-ínsidənt/ *adj.* **1** occurring together in space or time. **2** (foll. by *with*) in agreement; harmonious. □□ **co·in·ci·dent·ly** *adv.*

co·in·ci·den·tal /kō-ínsidént'l/ *adj.* **1** in the nature of or resulting from a coincidence. **2** happening or existing at the same time. □□ **co·in·ci·den·tal·ly** *adv.*

coin·er /kóynər/ *n.* **1** a person who coins money, esp. *Brit.* the maker of counterfeit coin. **2** a person who invents or devises something (esp. a new word or phrase).

coin·op·er·a·ted *adj. & n.* (also **coin-op**) ● *adj.* operated by inserting coins into a slot. ● *n.* **1** a machine that is coin-operated. **2** a place with coin-operated machines, esp. a self-serve laundry.

Coin·treau /kwaántrō/ *n. Trademark* a colorless orange-flavored liqueur. [F]

coir /kóyər/ *n.* fiber from the outer husk of the coconut, used for ropes, matting, etc. [Malayalam *kāyar* cord f. *kāyaru* be twisted]

co·i·tion /kō-íshən/ *n. Med.* = COITUS. [L *coitio* f. *coire coit-* go together]

co·i·tus /kó-itəs, kō-eé–/ *n. Med.* sexual intercourse. □□ **co·i·tal** *adj.* [L (as COITION)]

co·i·tus in·ter·rup·tus /íntərúptəs/ *n.* sexual intercourse in which the penis is withdrawn before ejaculation.

Coke /kōk/ *n. Trademark* Coca-Cola. [abbr.]

coke[1] /kōk/ *n. & v.* ● *n.* **1** a solid substance left after the gases have been extracted from coal. **2** a residue left after the incomplete combustion of gasoline, etc. ● *v.tr.* convert (coal) into coke. [prob. f. N.Engl. dial. *colk* core, of unkn. orig.]

coke[2] /kōk/ *n. sl.* cocaine. [abbr.]

Col. *abbr.* **1** colonel. **2** Colossians (New Testament).

col /kol/ *n.* **1 a** a depression in the summit line of a chain of mountains, generally affording a pass from one slope to another. **2** *Meteorol.* a low-pressure region between anticyclones. [F, = neck, f. L *collum*]

col. *abbr.* column.

col- /kol/ *prefix* assim. form of COM- before *l*.

COLA /kólə/ *abbr.* **1** cost-of-living adjustment. **2** cost-of-living allowance.

co·la /kólə/ *n.* (also **ko·la**) **1** any small tree of the genus *Cola*, native to W. Africa, bearing seeds containing caffeine. **2** a carbonated drink usu. flavored with these seeds. [W.Afr.]

col·an·der /kúləndər, kól–/ *n.* a perforated vessel used to strain off liquid in cooking. [ME, ult. f. L *colare* strain]

co·la nut *n.* (also **ko·la nut**) the seed of the cola tree, which contains caffeine and is chewed or made into a drink.

co·lat·i·tude /kōlátitood, –tyood/ *n. Astron.* the complement of the latitude, the difference between it and 90°.

col·chi·cine /kólchiseen, kól–/ *n.* a yellow alkaloid obtained from colchicum, used in the treatment of gout.

col·chi·cum /kólchikəm, kólkee–/ *n.* **1** any liliaceous plant of the genus *Colchicum*, esp. meadow saffron. **2** its dried corm or seed. Also called **autumn crocus**. [L f. Gk *kolkhikon* of Kolkhis, a region east of the Black Sea]

cold /kōld/ *adj., n., & adv.* ● *adj.* **1** of or at a low or relatively low temperature, esp. when compared with the human body. **2** not heated; cooled after being heated. **3** (of a person) feeling cold. **4** lacking ardor, friendliness, or affection; undemonstrative; apathetic. **5** depressing; dispiriting; uninteresting (*cold facts*). **6 a** dead. **b** *colloq.* unconscious. **7** *colloq.* at one's mercy (*had me cold*). **8** sexually frigid. **9** (of soil) slow to absorb heat. **10** (of a scent in hunting) having become weak. **11** (in children's games) far from finding or guessing what is sought. **12** without preparation or rehearsal. ● *n.* **1 a** the prevalence of a low temperature, esp. in the atmosphere. **b** cold weather; a cold environment (*went out into the cold*). **2** an infection in which the mucous membrane of the nose and throat becomes inflamed, causing running at the nose, sneezing, sore throat, etc. ● *adv.* completely; entirely (*was stopped cold midsentence*). □ **catch a cold 1** become infected with a cold. **2** esp. *Brit.* encounter trouble or difficulties. **in cold blood** without feeling or passion; deliberately; ruthlessly. **out in the cold** ignored; neglected. **throw** (or **pour**) **cold water on** be discouraging or depreciatory about. □□ **cold·ish** *adj.* **cold·ly** *adv.* **cold·ness** *n.* [OE *cald* f. Gmc, rel. to L *gelu* frost]

cold-blood·ed /kóldblúdid/ *adj.* **1** having a body temperature varying with that of the environment (e.g., of fish); poikilothermic. **2 a** callous; deliberately cruel. **b** without excitement or sensibility; dispassionate. □□ **cold-blood·ed·ly** *adv.* **cold-blood·ed·ness** *n.*

cold call *n.* an unsolicited call on (someone) by telephone or in person, in an attempt to sell goods or services. □□ **cold-call** *v.tr.*

cold cath·ode *n.* a cathode that emits electrons without being heated.

cold chis·el *n.* a chisel suitable for cutting metal.

cold com·fort *n.* poor or inadequate consolation.

cold cream *n.* ointment for cleansing and softening the skin.

cold cuts *n.* slices of cold cooked meats.

cold feet *n. colloq.* loss of nerve or confidence.

cold frame *n.* a structure with a glass top in which small plants are grown and protected without artificial heat.

cold front *n.* the forward edge of an advancing mass of cold air.

cold fu·sion *n.* hypothetical nuclear fusion at room temperature esp. as a possible energy source.

cold-heart·ed /kóldhaártid/ *adj.* lacking affection or warmth; unfriendly. □□ **cold-heart·ed·ly** *adv.* **cold-heart·ed·ness** *n.*

cold shoul·der *n.* a show of intentional unfriendliness.

cold-shoul·der *v.tr.* be deliberately unfriendly to; snub.

cold sore *n.* inflammation and blisters in and around the mouth, caused by the herpes simplex virus.

cold steel *n.* weapons such as swords or knives collectively.

cold stor·age *n.* **1** storage in a refrigerator or other cold place for preservation. **2** a state in which something (esp. an idea) is put aside temporarily.

cold sweat *n.* a state of sweating induced by fear or illness.

cold tur·key *n. sl.* the abrupt and complete withdrawal from taking a drug to which one is addicted.

cold war *n.* a state of hostility between nations without actual fighting.

cold wave *n.* **1** a temporary spell of cold weather over a wide area. **2** a kind of permanent wave for the hair using chemicals and without heat.

cole /kōl/ *n.* (usu. in *comb.*) **1** cabbage. **2** = RAPE[2]. [ME f. ON *kál* f. L *caulis* stem, cabbage]

co·le·op·ter·on /kóleeóptərən/ *n.* any insect of the order Coleoptera, with front wings modified into sheaths to protect the hind wings, e.g., a beetle or weevil. □□ **co·le·op·ter·an** *adj.* **co·le·op·ter·ist** *n.* **co·le·op·ter·ous** *adj.* [mod.L *Coleoptera* f. Gk *koleopteros* f. *koleon* sheath + *pteron* wing]

co·le·op·tile /kóleeóptil/ *n. Bot.* a sheath protecting a young shoot tip in grasses. [Gk *koleon* sheath + *ptilon* feather]

cole·seed /kólseed/ *n.* = COLE 2.

cole·slaw /kólslaw/ *n.* a dressed salad of sliced raw cabbage, carrot, onion, etc. [Du. *koolsla*: see COLE, SLAW]

co·le·us /kóleeəs/ *n.* any plant of the genus *Coleus*, having variegated colored leaves. [mod.L f. Gk *koleon* sheath]

col·ic /kólik/ *n.* a severe spasmodic abdominal pain. □□ **col·ick·y** *adj.* [ME f. F *colique* f. LL *colicus*: see COLON[2]]

col·i·se·um /kóliseéəm/ *n.* (also **col·os·se·um**) a large stadium or amphitheater (see COLOSSEUM).

co·li·tis /kəlítis/ *n.* inflammation of the lining of the colon.

coll. *abbr.* **1** collect. **2** collection. **3** collateral. **4** college.

col·lab·o·rate /kəlábərayt/ *v.intr.* (often foll. by *with*) **1** work jointly, esp. in a literary or artistic production. **2** cooperate traitorously with an enemy. □□ **col·lab·o·ra·tion** /–ráyshən/ *n.* **col·lab·o·ra·tion·ist** *n. & adj.* **col·lab·o·ra·tive** /–ráytiv, –rətiv/ *adj.* **col·lab·o·ra·tor** *n.* [L *collaborare collaborat-* (as COM-, *laborare* work)]

SPELLING TIP   **collaborate**

In order to *coll*aborate, you need a *coll*eague.

---

col·lage /kəláazh/ *n.* **1** a form of art in which various materials (e.g., photographs, pieces of paper, matchsticks) are arranged and glued to a backing. **2** a work of art done in this way. **3** a collection of unrelated things. □□ **col·lag·ist** *n.* [F, = gluing]

col·la·gen /kóləjən/ *n.* a protein found in animal connective tissue, yielding gelatin on boiling. [F *collagène* f. Gk *kolla* glue + *–gène* = –GEN]

col·lapse /kəláps/ *n. & v.* ● *n.* **1** the tumbling down or falling in of a structure; folding up; giving way. **2** a sudden failure of a plan, undertaking, etc. **3** a physical or mental breakdown. ● *v.* **1 a** *intr.* undergo or experience a collapse. **b** *tr.* cause to collapse. **2** *intr. colloq.* lie or sit down and relax, esp. after prolonged effort (*collapsed into a chair*). **3 a** *intr.* (of furniture, etc.) be foldable into a small space. **b** *tr.* fold (furniture) in this way. □□ **col·laps·i·ble** *adj.* **col·laps·i·bil·i·ty** /–səbílitee/ *n.* [L *collapsus* past part. of *collabi* (as COM-, *labi* slip)]

col·lar /kólər/ *n. & v.* ● *n.* **1** the part of a shirt, dress, coat, etc., that goes around the neck, either upright or turned over. **2** a band of linen, lace, etc., completing the upper part of a costume. **3** a band of leather or other material put around an animal's (esp. a dog's) neck. **4** a restraining or connecting band, ring, or pipe in machinery. **5** a colored marking resembling a collar around the neck of a bird or animal. **6** *Brit.* a piece of meat rolled up and tied. ● *v.tr.* **1** seize (a person) by the collar or neck. **2** capture; apprehend. **3** *colloq.* accost. **4** *sl.* take, esp. illicitly. □□ **col·lared** *adj.* (also in *comb.*). **col·lar·less** *adj.* [ME f. AF *coler*, OF *colier*, f. L *collare* f. *collum* neck]

col·lar·bone /kólərbōn/ *n.* either of two bones joining the breastbone and the shoulder blades; the clavicle.

col·late /kəláyt, kólayt, kṓ–/ *v.tr.* **1** analyze and compare (texts, statements, etc.) to identify points of agreement and difference. **2 a** arrange (pages) in proper sequence. **b** *Bibliog.* verify the order of (sheets) by their signatures. **3** assemble (information) from different sources. **4** (often foll. by *to*) *Eccl.* appoint (a clergyman) to a benefice. □□ **col·la·tor** *n.* [L *collat-* past part. stem of *conferre* compare]

col·lat·er·al /kəlátərəl/ *n. & adj.* ● *n.* **1** security pledged as a guarantee for repayment of a loan. **2** a person having the same descent as another but by a different line. ● *adj.* **1** descended from the same stock but by a different line. **2** side by side; parallel. **3 a** additional but subordinate. **b** connected but aside from the main subject, course, etc. □□ **col·lat·er·al·i·ty** /–rálitee/ *n.* **col·lat·er·al·ly** *adv.* [ME f. med.L *collateralis* (as COM-, LATERAL)]

col·la·tion /kəláyshən, ko–/ *n.* **1** the act or an instance of collating. **2** *RC Ch.* a light meal allowed during a fast. **3** a light informal meal. [ME f. OF f. L *collatio –onis* (see COLLATE): sense 2 f. Cassian's *Collationes Patrum* (= *Lives of the Fathers*) read by Benedictines and followed by a light meal]

col·league /kóleeg/ *n.* a fellow official or worker, esp. in a profession or business. [F *collègue* f. L *collega* (as COM-, *legare* depute)]

col·lect[1] /kəlékt/ *v., adj., & adv.* ● *v.* **1** *tr. & intr.* bring or come together; assemble; accumulate. **2** *tr.* systematically seek and acquire (books, stamps, etc.), esp. as a continuing hobby. **3 a** *tr.* obtain (taxes, contributions, etc.) from a number of people. **b** *intr. colloq.* receive money. **4** *tr.* call for; fetch (*went to collect the laundry*). **5 a** *refl.* regain control of oneself esp. after a shock. **b** *tr.* concentrate (one's energies, thoughts, etc.). **c** *tr.* (as **collected** *adj.*) calm and cool; not perturbed nor distracted. **6** *tr.* infer; gather; conclude. ● *adj. & adv.* to be paid for by the receiver (of a telephone call, parcel, etc.). □□ **col·lect·a·ble** *adj.* **col·lect·ed·ly** *adv.* [F *collecter* or med.L *collectare* f. L *collectus* past part. of *colligere* (as COM-, *legere* pick)]

col·lect[2] /kólekt, –ikt/ *n.* a short prayer of the Anglican and Roman Catholic churches, esp. one assigned to a particular day or season. [ME f. OF *collecte* f. L *collecta* fem. past part. of *colligere*: see COLLECT[1]]

col·lect·i·ble /kəléktibəl/ *adj. & n.* ● *adj.* worth collecting. ● *n.* an item sought by collectors.

col·lec·tion /kəlékshən/ *n.* **1** the act or process of collecting or being collected. **2** a group of things collected together (e.g., works of art, literary items, or specimens), esp. systematically. **3** (foll. by *of*) an accumulation; a mass or pile (*a collection of dust*). **4 a** the collecting of money, esp. in church or for a charitable cause. **b** the amount collected. **5** the regular removal of mail, esp. from a public mailbox, for dispatch. **6** (in *pl.*) *Brit.* college examinations held at the end of a term, esp. at Oxford University. [ME f. OF f. L *collectio –onis* (as COLLECT[1])]

col·lec·tive /kəléktiv/ *adj. & n.* ● *adj.* **1** formed by or constituting a collection. **2** taken as a whole; aggregate (*our collective opinion*). **3** of or from several or many individuals; common. ● *n.* **1 a** = COLLECTIVE FARM. **b** any cooperative enterprise. **c** its members. **2** = COLLECTIVE NOUN. □□ **col·lec·tive·ly** *adv.* **col·lec·tive·ness** *n.* **col·lec·tiv·i·ty** /kólektívitee/ *n.* [F *collectif* or L *collectivus* (as COLLECT[1])]

col·lec·tive bar·gain·ing *n.* negotiation of wages, etc., by an organized body of employees.

col·lec·tive farm *n.* a jointly operated esp. government-owned amalgamation of several small farms.

col·lec·tive noun *n. Gram.* a noun that is grammatically singular and denotes a collection or number of individuals (e.g., *assembly*, *family*, *troop*).

GRAMMAR TIP   **collective noun**

Subject-Verb Agreement with Collective Nouns. A collective noun names a group of people, animals, or things (e.g., *audience*, *herd*, *batch*). If the group is acting together as a single unit, the collective noun usually takes a singular verb (*a pack of wolves crosses the frozen tundra*). A collective noun sometimes (usually, in British English) takes a plural verb when members of the group are acting as individuals (*the committee were arguing noisily in the next room; the crew were unable to reach a consensus about when they should set sail*).

---

col·lec·tive own·er·ship *n.* ownership of land, means of production, etc., by all for the benefit of all.

col·lec·tive un·con·scious *n. Psychol.* (in Jungian theory) the part of the unconscious mind derived from ancestral memory and experience common to all mankind, as distinct from the personal unconscious.

col·lec·tiv·ism /kóléktivizəm/ *n.* the theory and practice of the collective ownership of land and the means of production. □□ **col·lec·tiv·ist** *n.* **col·lec·tiv·is·tic** /–vístik/ *adj.*

col·lec·ti·vize /kəléktivīz/ *v.tr.* organize on the basis of collective ownership. □□ **col·lec·ti·vi·za·tion** *n.*

col·lec·tor /kəléktər/ *n.* **1** a person who collects, esp. things of interest as a hobby. **2** a person who collects money, esp. due (*tax collector, ticket collector*). **3** *Electronics* the region in a transistor that absorbs carriers of a charge. [ME f. AF *collectour* f. med.L *collector* (as COLLECT[1])]

col·lec·tor's i·tem *n.* (also **col·lec·tor's piece**) a valuable object, esp. one of interest to collectors.

col·leen /koléen/ *n. Ir.* a girl. [Ir. *cailín*, dimin. of *caile* countrywoman]

col•lege /kólij/ n. **1** an establishment for further or higher education, sometimes part of a university. **2** an establishment for specialized professional education (business college; college of music; naval college) . **3** Brit. the buildings or premises of a college (lived in college) . **4** the students and teachers in a college. **5** Brit. a public school. **6** an organized body of persons with shared functions and privileges (electoral college). □□ **col•le•gial** /kəleéjəl/ adj. [ME f. OF college or L collegium f. collega (as COLLEAGUE)]

Col•lege of Arms n. (in the UK) a corporation recording lineage and granting arms.

col•le•gian /kəleéjən/ n. a member of a college. [med.L collegianus (as COLLEGE)]

col•le•giate /kəleéjət/ adj. constituted as or belonging to a college; corporate. □□ **col•le•giate•ly** adv. [LL collegiatus (as COLLEGE)]

col•le•giate church n. **1** a church endowed for a chapter of canons but without a bishop's see. **2** esp. US & Sc. a church or group of churches established under a joint pastorate.

col•len•chy•ma /koléngkimə/ n. Bot. a tissue of cells with thick cellulose cell walls, strengthening young stems, etc. [Gk kolla glue + egkhuma infusion]

Col•les' frac•ture /kólis/ n. a fracture of the lower end of the radius with a backward displacement of the hand. [A. Colles, Ir. surgeon d. 1843]

col•let /kólit/ n. **1** a flange or socket for setting a gem in jewelry. **2** Engin. a segmented band or sleeve put around a shaft or spindle and tightened to grip it. **3** Horol. a small collar to which the inner end of a balance spring is attached. [F, dimin. of COL]

col•lide /kəlíd/ v.intr. (often foll. by with) **1** come into abrupt or violent impact. **2** be in conflict. [L collidere collis- (as COM-, laedere strike, damage)]

col•lie /kólee/ n. **1** a sheepdog orig. of a Scottish breed, with a long pointed nose and usu. dense, long hair. **2** this breed. [perh. f. coll COAL (as being orig. black)]

col•lier /kólyər/ n. **1** a coal miner. **2** a coal-carrying ship. [ME, f. COAL + -IER]

col•lier•y /kólyəree/ n. (pl. -ies) a coal mine and its associated buildings.

col•li•gate /kóligayt/ v.tr. bring into connection (esp. isolated facts by a generalization). □□ **col•li•ga•tion** /-gáyshən/ n. [L colligare colligat- (as COM-, ligare bind)]

col•li•mate /kólimayt/ v.tr. **1** adjust the line of sight of (a telescope, etc.). **2** make (telescopes or rays) accurately parallel. □□ **col•li•ma•tion** /-máyshən/ n. [L collimare, erron. for collineare align (as COM-, linea line)]

col•li•ma•tor /kólimaytər/ n. **1** a device for producing a parallel beam of rays or radiation. **2** a small fixed telescope used for adjusting the line of sight of an astronomical telescope, etc.

col•lin•e•ar /kəlíneeər/ adj. Geom. (of points) lying in the same straight line. □□ **col•lin•e•ar•i•ty** /-neeáiritee/ n. **col•lin•e•ar•ly** adv.

col•lins /kólinz/ n. (also **Col•lins**) an iced drink made of gin or whiskey, etc., with soda water, lemon or lime juice, and sugar. [20th c.: orig. unkn.]

col•li•sion /kəlízhən/ n. **1** a violent impact of a moving body, esp. a vehicle or ship, with another or with a fixed object. **2** the clashing of opposed interests or considerations. **3** Physics the action of particles striking or coming together. □□ **col•li•sion•al** adj. [ME f. LL collisio (as COLLIDE)]

col•li•sion course n. a course or action that is bound to cause a collision or conflict.

col•lo•cate /kólokayt/ v.tr. **1** place together or side by side. **2** arrange; set in a particular place. **3** (often foll. by with) Linguistics juxtapose (a word, etc.) with another. □□ **col•lo•ca•tion** /-káyshən/ n. [L collocare collocat- (as COM-, locare to place)]

col•loc•u•tor /kólokyōōtər, kōlókyətər/ n. a person who takes part in a conversation. [LL f. colloqui (as COM-, loqui locut- talk)]

col•lo•di•on /kəlódeeən/ n. a syrupy solution of cellulose nitrate in a mixture of alcohol and ether, used in photography and surgery. [Gk kollōdēs gluelike f. kolla glue]

col•logue /kəlóg/ v.intr. (**col•logues, col•logued, col•logu•ing**) (foll. by with) talk confidentially. [prob. alt. of obs. colleague conspire, by assoc. with L colloqui converse]

col•loid /kóloyd/ n. **1** Chem. **a** a substance consisting of ultramicroscopic particles. **b** a mixture of such a substance uniformly dispersed through a second substance esp. to form a viscous solution. **2** Med. a substance of a homogeneous gelatinous consistency. □□ **col•loi•dal** /kəlóyd'l/ adj. [Gk kolla glue + -OID]

col•lop /kóləp/ n. a slice, esp. of meat or bacon; an escalope. [ME, = fried bacon and eggs, of Scand. orig.]

col•lo•qui•al /kəlókweeəl/ adj. belonging to or proper to ordinary or familiar conversation, not formal or literary. □□ **col•lo•qui•al•ly** adv. [L colloquium COLLOQUY]

col•lo•qui•al•ism /kəlókweeəlizəm/ n. **1** a colloquial word or phrase. **2** the use of colloquialisms.

col•lo•qui•um /kəlókweeəm/ n. (pl. **col•lo•qui•ums** or **col•lo•qui•a** /-kweeə/) an academic conference or seminar. [L: see COLLOQUY]

col•lo•quy /kóləkwee/ n. (pl. **-quies**) **1** the act of conversing. **2** a

conversation. **3** Eccl. a gathering for discussion of theological questions. [L colloquium (as COM-, loqui speak)]

col•lo•type /kólətīp/ n. Printing **1** a thin sheet of gelatin exposed to light, treated with reagents, and used to make high quality prints by lithography. **2** a print made by this process. [Gk kolla glue + TYPE]

col•lude /kəlóōd/ v.intr. come to an understanding or conspire together, esp. for a fraudulent purpose. □□ **col•lud•er** n. [L colludere collus- (as COM-, ludere lus- play)]

col•lu•sion /kəlóōzhən/ n. **1** a secret understanding, esp. for a fraudulent purpose. **2** Law such an understanding between ostensible opponents in a lawsuit. □□ **col•lu•sive** /-lōōsiv/ adj. **col•lu•sive•ly** adv. [ME f. OF collusion or L collusio (as COLLUDE)]

col•lyr•i•um /kəleéreeəm/ n. (pl. **col•lyr•i•a** /-reeə/ or **col•lyr•i•ums**) a medicated eyewash. [L f. Gk kollurion poultice f. kollura coarse bread roll]

col•ly•wob•bles /kóleewobəlz/ n.pl. colloq. **1** a rumbling or pain in the stomach. **2** a feeling of strong apprehension. [fanciful, f. COLIC + WOBBLE]

Colo. abbr. Colorado.

col•o•bus /kóləbəs/ n. any leaf-eating monkey of the genus Colobus, native to Africa, having shortened thumbs. [mod.L f. Gk kolobos docked]

col•o•cynth /kóləsinth/ n. (also **col•o•quin•ti•da** /kóləkwíntidə/) **1 a** a plant of the gourd family, Citrullus colocynthis, bearing a pulpy fruit. **b** this fruit. **2** a bitter purgative drug obtained from the fruit. [L colocynthis f. Gk kolokunthis]

co•logne /kəlṓn/ n. (in full **cologne water**) eau de cologne or a similar scented toilet water. [abbr.]

co•lon¹ /kólən/ n. a punctuation mark (:), used esp. to introduce a quotation or a list of items or to separate clauses when the second expands or illustrates the first; also between numbers in a statement of proportion (as in 10:1) and in biblical references (as in Exodus 3:2). [L f. Gk kōlon limb, clause]

co•lon² /kólən/ n. Anat. the lower and greater part of the large intestine, from the cecum to the rectum. □□ **co•lon•ic** /kəlónik/ adj. [ME, ult. f. Gk kolon]

colo•nel /kɔ́rnəl/ n. **1** an army, air force, or marine officer, immediately below a brigadier general in rank. **2** = LIEUTENANT COLONEL. □□ **colo•nel•cy** n. (pl. **-cies**).

WORD HISTORY colonel

Mid-16th century: from obsolete French coronel (earlier form of colonel), from Italian colonnello 'column of soldiers,' from colonna 'column,' from Latin columna. The form coronel, the source of the modern pronunciation, was usual until the mid-17th century.

Colo•nel Blimp n. see BLIMP n. 1.

co•lo•ni•al /kəlóneeəl/ adj. & n. • adj. **1** of, relating to, or characteristic of a colony or colonies. **2** (esp. of architecture or furniture) built or designed in, or in a style characteristic of, the period of the British colonies in America before independence. • n. **1** a native or inhabitant of a colony. **2** a house built in colonial style. □□ **co•lo•ni•al•ly** adv.

co•lo•ni•al goose n. Austral. & NZ a boned and stuffed roast leg of mutton.

co•lo•ni•al•ism /kəlóneeəlizəm/ n. **1** a policy of acquiring or maintaining colonies. **2** derog. this policy regarded as the esp. economic exploitation of weak or backward peoples by a larger power. □□ **co•lo•ni•al•ist** n.

co•lo•nist /kólənist/ n. a settler in or inhabitant of a colony.

col•o•nize /kólənīz/ v. **1** tr. **a** establish a colony or colonies in (a country or area). **b** settle as colonists. **2** intr. establish or join a colony. **3** tr. Polit. plant voters in (a district) for party purposes. **4** tr. Biol. (of plants and animals) become established in (an area). □□ **col•o•ni•za•tion** n. **co•lo•niz•er** n.

col•on•nade /kólənáyd/ n. a row of columns, esp. supporting an entablature or roof. □□ **col•on•nad•ed** adj. [F f. colonne COLUMN]

col•o•ny /kólənee/ n. (pl. **-nies**) **1 a** a group of settlers in a new country (whether or not already inhabited) fully or partly subject to the mother country. **b** the settlement or its territory. **2 a** people of one nationality or race or occupation in a city, esp. if living more or less in isolation or in a special quarter. **b** a separate or segregated group (nudist colony). **3** Biol. a collection of animals, plants, etc., connected, in contact, or living close together. [ME f. L colonia f. colonus farmer f. colere cultivate]

co•lo•phon /kóləfon, -fən/ n. **1** a publisher's device or imprint, esp. on the title page. **2** a tailpiece in a manuscript or book, often ornamental, giving the writer's or printer's name, the date, etc. [LL f. Gk kolophōn summit, finishing touch]

col•o•pho•ny /kəlófənee/ n. = ROSIN. [L colophonia (resin) from Colophon in Asia Minor]

col·o·quin·ti·da var. of COLOCYNTH.

col·or /kúlər/ *n. & v.* ● *n.* (*Brit.* **col·our**) **1 a** the sensation produced on the eye by rays of light when resolved as by a prism, selective reflection, etc., into different wavelengths. **b** perception of color; a system of colors. **2** one, or any mixture, of the constituents into which light can be separated as in a spectrum or rainbow, sometimes including (loosely) black and white. **3** a coloring substance, esp. paint. **4** the use of all colors, not only black and white, as in photography and television. **5 a** pigmentation of the skin, esp. when dark. **b** this as a ground for prejudice or discrimination. **6** ruddiness of complexion (*a healthy color*). **7** (in *pl.*) appearance or aspect (*see things in their true colors*). **8** (in *pl.*) **a** *Brit.* a colored ribbon or uniform, etc., worn to signify membership of a school, club, team, etc. **b** the flag of a regiment or ship. **c** a national flag. **9** quality, mood, or variety in music, literature, speech, etc.; distinctive character or timbre. **10** a show of reason; a pretext (*lend color to*; *under color of*). ● *v.* **1** *tr.* apply color to, esp. by painting or dyeing or with colored pens or pencils. **2** *tr.* influence (*an attitude colored by experience*). **3** *tr.* **a** misrepresent, exaggerate, esp. with spurious detail (*a highly colored account*). **b** disguise. **4** *intr.* take on color; blush. □ **show one's true colors** reveal one's true character or intentions. **under false colors** falsely; deceitfully. **with flying colors** see FLYING. [ME f. OF *color, colorer* f. L *color, colorare*]

col·or·a·ble /kúlərəbəl/ *adj.* **1** specious; plausible. **2** counterfeit. □□ **col·or·a·bly** *adv.*

Col·o·rad·o po·ta·to bee·tle /kólərádo,–ráadō/ *n.* a yellow and black striped beetle, *Leptinotarsa decemlineata*, the larva of which is highly destructive to the potato plant. [the state of *Colorado*]

col·or·ant /kúlərənt/ *n.* a coloring substance.

col·or·a·tion /kúləráyshən/ *n.* **1** coloring; a scheme or method of applying color. **2** the natural (esp. variegated) color of living things or animals. [F *coloration* or LL *coloratio* f. *colorare* COLOR]

col·o·ra·tu·ra /kúlərəto͝orə, –tyo͝or–/ *n.* **1** elaborate ornamentation of a vocal melody. **2** a singer (esp. a soprano) skilled in coloratura singing. [It. f. L *coloratura* COLOR]

col·or-blind *adj.* **1** unable to distinguish certain colors. **2** ignoring racial prejudice. □□ **col·or-blind·ness** *n.*

col·or code *n.* a system of marking things with different colors as a means of identification.

col·or-code *v.tr.* mark things with different colors as a means of identification.

col·ored /kúlərd/ *adj. & n.* ● *adj.* **1** having color(s). **2** (also **Colored**) **a** often *offens.* wholly or partly of nonwhite descent. **b** *S.Afr.* of mixed white and nonwhite descent. ● *n.* (also **Colored**) **1** a colored person. **2** *S.Afr.* a person of mixed descent speaking Afrikaans or English as the mother tongue.
▶See note at BLACK.

col·or·fast /kúlərfast/ *adj.* dyed in colors that will not fade nor be washed out. □□ **col·or·fast·ness** *n.*

col·or·ful /kúlərfo͝ol/ *adj.* **1** having much or varied color; bright. **2** full of interest; vivid; lively. □□ **col·or·ful·ly** *adv.* **color·ful·ness** *n.*

col·or·if·ic /kúlərífik/ *adj.* **1** producing color. **2** highly colored. [F *colorifique* or mod.L *colorificus* (as COLOR)]

col·or·im·e·ter /kúlərímitər/ *n.* an instrument for measuring the intensity of color. □□ **col·or·i·met·ric** /–métrik/ *adj.* **col·or·im·e·try** *n.* [L *color* COLOR + –METER]

col·or·ing /kúləring/ *n.* **1** the process of or skill in using color(s). **2** the style in which a thing is colored, or in which an artist uses color. **3** facial complexion.

col·or·ist /kúlərist/ *n.* a person who uses color, esp. in art.

col·or·ize /kúləriz/ *v.tr.* (**col·or·ized, col·or·iz·ing**) add color to (orig. black-and-white movie film) using computer technology.

col·or·less /kúlərlis/ *adj.* **1** without color. **2** lacking character or interest. **3** dull or pale in hue. **4** neutral; impartial; indifferent. □□ **col·or·less·ly** *adv.*

col·or scheme *n.* an arrangement or planned combination of colors esp. in interior design.

col·or ser·geant *n.* the senior sergeant of an infantry company.

co·los·sal /kəlósəl/ *adj.* **1** of immense size; huge, gigantic. **2** *colloq.* remarkable; splendid. **3** *Archit.* (of an order) having more than one story of columns. **4** *Sculpture* (of a statue) about twice life size. □□ **co·los·sal·ly** *adv.* [F f. *colosse* COLOSSUS]

Col·os·se·um /kóləseéəm/ *n.* **1** an ancient Roman amphitheater, built in the first century AD. **2** (**colosseum**) = COLISEUM. [med.L, neut. of *colosseus* gigantic (as COLOSSUS)]

co·los·sus /kəlósəs/ *n.* (*pl.* **co·los·si** /–sī/ or **co·los·sus·es**) **1** a statue much bigger than life size. **2** a gigantic person, animal, building, etc. **3** an imperial power personified. [L f. Gk *kolossos*]

co·los·to·my /kəlóstəmee/ *n.* (*pl.* **·mies**) *Surgery* an operation on the colon to make an opening in the abdominal wall to provide an artificial anus. [as COLON[2] + Gk *stoma* mouth]

co·los·trum /kəlóstrəm/ *n.* the first secretion from the mammary glands occurring after giving birth. [L]

co·lot·o·my /kəlótəmee/ *n.* (*pl.* **·mies**) *Surgery* an incision in the colon. [as COLON[2] + –TOMY]

col·our *Brit.* var. of COLOR.

col·pos·co·py /kolpóskəpee/ *n.* examination of the vagina and the neck of the womb. □□ **col·po·scope** /kólpəskōp/ *n.* [Gk *kolpos* womb + –SCOPY]

colt /kōlt/ *n.* a young, uncastrated male horse, usu. less than four years old. □□ **colt·hood** *n.* **colt·ish** *adj.* **colt·ish·ly** *adv.* **colt·ish·ness** *n.* [OE = young ass or camel]

col·ter /kóltər/ *n.* esp. (*Brit.* **coul·ter**) a vertical cutting blade fixed in front of a plowshare. [OE f. L *culter*]

colts·foot /kóltsfo͝ot/ *n.* (*pl.* **colts·foots**) a wild composite plant, *Tussilago farfara*, with large leaves and yellow flowers.

col·u·brine /kóləbrīn, kólyə–/ *adj.* **1** snakelike. **2** of the subfamily Colubrinae of nonpoisonous snakes. [L *colubrinus* f. *coluber* snake]

Col·um·bine /kóləmbīn/ *n.* the partner of Harlequin in pantomime. [F *Colombine* f. It. *Colombina* f. *colombino* dovelike]

col·um·bine /kóləmbīn/ *n.* any plant of the genus *Aquilegia*, esp. *A. vulgaris*, having purple-blue flowers. Also called **aquilegia**. [ME f. OF *colombine* f. med.L *colombina herba* dovelike plant f. L *columba* dove (from the supposed resemblance of the flower to a cluster of 5 doves)]

co·lum·bite /kəlúmbīt/ *n. Chem.* an ore of iron and niobium found in America. [*Columbia*, a poetic name for America, + –ITE[1]]

co·lum·bi·um /kəlúmbiəm/ *n. Chem.* = NIOBIUM.

col·umn /kóləm/ *n.* **1** *Archit.* an upright cylindrical pillar often slightly tapering and usu. supporting an entablature or arch, or standing alone as a monument. **2** a structure or part shaped like a column. **3** a vertical cylindrical mass of liquid or vapor. **4 a** a vertical division of a page, chart, etc., containing a sequence of figures or words. **b** the figures or words themselves. **5** a part of a newspaper regularly devoted to a particular subject (*gossip column*). **6 a** *Mil.* an arrangement of troops in successive lines, with a narrow front. **b** *Naut.* a similar arrangement of ships. □□ **dodge the column** *Brit. colloq.* shirk one's duty; avoid work. □□ **co·lum·nar** /kəlúmnər/ *adj.* **col·umned** *adj.* [ME f. OF *columpne* & L *columna* pillar]

col·umn inch *n.* a quantity of print (esp. newsprint) occupying a one-inch length of a column.

col·um·nist /kóləmnist, –mist/ *n.* a journalist contributing regularly to a newspaper.

co·lure /kəlo͝or/ *n. Astron.* either of two great circles intersecting at right angles at the celestial poles and passing through the ecliptic at either the equinoxes or the solstices. [ME f. LL *colurus* f. Gk *kolouros* truncated]

col·za /kólzə, kól–/ *n.* = RAPE[2]. [F *kolza(t)* f. LG *kōlsāt* (as COLE, SEED)]

COM *abbr.* computer output on microfilm or microfiche.

com- /kom, kəm, kum/ *prefix* (also **co-, col-, con-, cor-**) with; together; jointly; altogether. [L *com-, cum* with]
▶*Com-* is used before *b, m, p,* and occasionally before vowels and *f; co-* esp. before vowels, *h,* and *gn; col-* before *l, cor-* before *r,* and *con-* before other consonants.

co·ma[1] /kómə/ *n.* (*pl.* **co·mas**) a prolonged deep unconsciousness, caused esp. by severe injury or excessive use of drugs. [med.L f. Gk *kōma* deep sleep]

co·ma[2] /kómə/ *n.* (*pl.* **co·mae** /–mee/) **1** *Astron.* a cloud of gas and dust surrounding the nucleus of a comet. **2** *Bot.* a tuft of silky hairs at the end of some seeds. [L f. Gk *komē* hair of head]

Co·man·che /kəmánchee/ *n.* **1 a** a N. American people native to the western plains. **b** a member of this people. **2** the language of this people.

com·a·tose /kómətōs, kóm–/ *adj.* **1** in a coma. **2** drowsy; sleepy; lethargic.

comb /kōm/ *n. & v.* ● *n.* **1** a toothed strip of rigid material for tidying and arranging the hair, or for keeping it in place. **2** a part of a machine having a similar design or purpose. **3 a** the red, fleshy crest of a fowl, esp. a cock. **b** an analogous growth in other birds. **4** a honeycomb. ● *v.tr.* **1** arrange or tidy (the hair) by drawing a comb through. **2** curry (a horse). **3** dress (wool or flax) with a comb. **4** search (a place) thoroughly. □ **comb out 1** tidy and arrange (hair) with a comb. **2** remove with a comb. **3** search or attack systematically. **4** search out and get rid of (anything unwanted). □□ **combed** *adj.* [OE *camb* f. Gmc]

com·bat *n. & v.* /kómbat, kúm–/ **1** a fight; an armed encounter or conflict; fighting; battle. **2** a struggle, contest, or dispute. ● *v.* /kəmbát, kómbat/ (**com·bat·ed, com·bat·ing**) **1** *intr.* engage in combat. **2** *tr.* engage in combat with. **3** *tr.* oppose; strive against. [F *combat* f. *combattre* f. LL (as COM-, L *batuere* fight)]

com·bat·ant /kəmbát'nt, kómbət'nt/ *n. & adj.* ● *n.* a person engaged in fighting. ● *adj.* **1** fighting. **2** for fighting.

com·bat fa·tigue *n.* = BATTLE FATIGUE.

com·bat·ive /kəmbátiv/ *adj.* ready or eager to fight; pugnacious. □□ **com·bat·ive·ly** *adv.* **com·bat·ive·ness** *n.*

combe var. of COOMB.

comb·er[1] /kómər/ *n.* **1** a person or thing that combs, esp. a machine for combing cotton or wool very fine. **2** a long curling wave; a breaker.

comb·er² /kṓmər/ *n. Brit.* a fish of the perch family, *Serranus cabrilla.* [18th c.: orig. unkn.]

com·bi·na·tion /kómbináyshən/ *n.* **1** the act or an instance of combining; the process of being combined. **2** a combined state (*in combination with*). **3** a combined set of things or people. **4** a sequence of numbers or letters used to open a combination lock. **5** *Brit.* a motorcycle with sidecar attached. **6** (in *pl.*) a single undergarment for the body and legs. **7** a group of things chosen from a larger number without regard to their arrangement. **8 a** united action. **b** *Chess* a coordinated and effective sequence of moves. **9** *Chem.* a union of substances in a compound with new properties. □□ **com·bi·na·tion·al** *adj.* **com·bi·na·tive** /kómbináytiv, kəmbínə–/ *adj.* **com·bi·na·to·ry** /kəmbínətawree/ *adj.* [obs. F *combination* or LL *combinatio* (as COMBINE)]

com·bi·na·tion lock *n.* a lock that is opened by rotating a dial or set of dials marked with letters or numbers, through a specific sequence.

com·bi·na·to·ri·al /kómbinətáwreeəl, kəmbínə–/ *adj. Math.* relating to combinations of items.

com·bine *v. & n.* • *v.* /kəmbín/ **1** *tr. & intr.* join together; unite for a common purpose. **2** *tr.* possess (qualities usually distinct) together (*combines charm and authority*). **3 a** *intr.* coalesce in one substance. **b** *tr.* cause to do this. **c** *intr.* form a chemical compound. **4** *intr.* cooperate. **5** /kómbin/ *tr.* harvest (crops, etc.) by means of a combine harvester. • *n.* /kómbin/ a combination of esp. commercial interests to control prices, etc. □□ **com·bin·a·ble** /kəmbínəbəl/ *adj.* [ME f. OF *combiner* or LL *combinare* (as COM–, L *bini* two)]

com·bine har·ves·ter /kómbin/ *n.* a mobile machine that reaps and threshes in one operation.

comb·ings /kṓmingz/ *n.pl.* hairs removed with a comb.

comb·ing wool *n.* long-stapled wool, suitable for combing and making into worsted.

com·bin·ing form *n. Gram.* a linguistic element used in combination with another element to form a word (e.g., *Anglo–* = English, *bio–* = life, *–graphy* = writing).

▶In this dictionary, *combining form* is used of an element that contributes to the particular sense of words (as with both elements of *biography*), as distinct from a prefix or suffix that adjusts the sense of or determines the function of words (as with *un–*, *–able*, and *–ation*).

GRAMMAR TIP combining forms

Form	Meaning	Example
aero-	atmosphere	aerospace
agro-	field, soil	agrology
ambi-	both	ambidextrous
amphi-	around; on both sides	amphitheater
archaeo-	primitive, ancient	archaeology
astro-	star; heavenly body	astrophysics
atmo-	vapor, steam	atmosphere
auto-	self	autobiography
baro-	atmospheric pressure	barometer
biblio-	books	bibliography
bio-	life; of living things	biochemistry
calci-	lime, calcium	calciferous
cardio-	heart	cardiology
centi-	one hundred	centipede
	one hundredth	centimeter
centro-	center, central	centrobaric
chromato-	color, pigment	chromatology,
chromo-		chromoplast
chrono-	time	chronometer
-cide	killer	insecticide
cosmo-	world, universe	cosmological
counter-	against	counteract
cranio-	skull	craniology
crypto-	hidden, secret	cryptography
cyclo-	circle	cyclotron
cyto-	cell	cytogenesis
deca-	ten	decade
deci-	one tenth	decibel
dextro-	toward the right	dextrorotatory
ecto-	to or on the outside	ectoderm
electro-	electric	electromagnet
endo-	inner	endoderm
equi-	equal	equivalence
ethno-	race, nation	ethnology
ferro-	contains iron	ferronickel
fibro-	fiber, fibrous	fibrovascular
-gamous	marrying, joining	bigamous
-gamy	marriage	polygamy
geo-	earth	geology
giga-	one billion	gigabyte
-gram	something written	telegram
-graph	instrument that writes	seismograph

Form	Meaning	Example
-graphy	to write	biography
-gynous	woman, female	misogynous
gyro-	circle	gyroscope
hecto-	a hundred	hectogram
helio-	the sun	helioscope
hema-, hemo-	blood	hemachrome, hemolymph
hepta-	seven	heptagon
hexa-	six	hexagon
holo-	whole	holocaust
homo-	the same; equal	homogeneous
hydro-	water	hydroplane
hypno-	sleep, hypnosis	hypnology
hypo-	under, below	hypodermic
ideo-	idea	ideograph
iso-	equal, alike	isobar
kilo-	one thousand	kilometer
lacto-	milk	lactoprotein
leuko-	without color, white	leukocyte
levo-	toward the left	levorotatory
litho-	stone, stony	lithography
-logy	science of	biology
macro-	large	macrocosm
mal-	bad, poor	maladjusted
mega-	large	megaphone
	one million	megabyte
-meter	a device for measuring	chronometer
micro-	small	microcosm
	one millionth	microfarad
mid-	middle	midnight
milli-	one thousandth	millimeter
-monger	dealer, seller	fishmonger
mono-	one, single	monorail
multi-	many, much	multiform
nano-	one billionth	nanosecond
neo-	new, recent	neoplasm
neuro-	nerve	neurosurgery
nitro-	nitric acid	nitrocellulose
oct-, octa-, octo-	eight	octet, octachord, octopus
omni-	all, completely	omnipotent
ortho-	straight, correct	orthopedics
paleo-	old, ancient	paleography
pan-	all	Pan-American
-pathy	feeling	antipathy
	disease	psychopathy
pedo-	child, children	pedodontics
penta-	five	pentameter
phil-, philo-	loving; fond of	philanthropy, philobiblic
-phobia	fear, hatred	acrophobia
phon-, phono-	sound	phonics, phonometer
photo-	light	photograph
phyto-	plant	phytochemistry
pico-	one trillionth	picofarad
poly-	many	polynomial
pyro-	having to do with fire	pyromania
quadr-, quadri-	four	quadrangle, quadrilateral
schizo-	split, divided	schizophrenic
sept-	seven	septangular
sex-	six	sexangular
spectro-	spectrum	spectroscope
spermato-	seed, sperm	spermatocyte
sporo-	spore	sporogenesis
-stat	stabilizing instrument	thermostat
stereo-	solid	stereobate
	three dimensional	stereoscopic
tel-, tele-	operating over long distances	telectric, telescope
tera-	one trillion	terabyte
tetra-	four	tetrahedron
theo-	a god or gods	theology
thermo-	heat	thermodynamics
topo-	place	topography
tri-	three	triangle
tricho-	hair, hairlike	trichosis
vaso-	blood vessel	vasoconstrictor
xeno-	stranger	xenophobia
xero-	dry	xeroderma
xylo-	wood, woody	xylophone
zoo-	animal	zoology
zygo-	yoke, paired	zygomorphic

See page xx for the **Key to Pronunciation.**

com•bo /kómbō/ *n.* (*pl.* **•bos**) *sl.* a small jazz or dance band. [abbr. of COMBINATION + –O]

com•bust /kəmbúst/ *v.tr.* subject to combustion. [obs. *combust* (adj.) f. L *combustus* past part. (as COMBUSTION)]

com•bus•ti•ble /kəmbústibəl/ *adj. & n.* • *adj.* **1** capable of or used for burning. **2** excitable; easily irritated. • *n.* a combustible substance. ▫▫ **com•bus•ti•bil•i•ty** /–bílitee/ *n.* [F *combustible* or med.L *combustibilis* (as COMBUSTION)]

com•bus•tion /kəmbúschən/ *n.* **1** burning; consumption by fire. **2** *Chem.* the development of light and heat from the chemical combination of a substance with oxygen. ▫▫ **com•bus•tive** /–bústiv/ *adj.* [ME f. F *combustion* or LL *combustio* f. L *comburere combust-* burn up]

Comdr. *abbr.* commander.

come /kum/ *v. & n.* • *v.intr.* (*past* **came** /kaym/; *past part.* **come**) **1** move, be brought toward, or reach a place thought of as near or familiar to the speaker or hearer (*come and see me; shall we come to your house?; the books have come*). **2** reach or be brought to a specified situation or result (*you'll come to no harm; have come to believe it; has come to be used wrongly; came into prominence*). **3** reach or extend to a specified point (*the road comes within a mile of us*). **4** traverse or accomplish (with compl.: *have come a long way*). **5** occur; happen; become present instead of future (*how did you come to break your leg?*). **6** take or occupy a specified position in space or time (*it comes on the third page; Clinton came after Bush; it does not come within the scope of the inquiry*). **7** become perceptible or known (*the church came into sight; the news comes as a surprise; it will come to me*). **8** be available (*the dress comes in three sizes; this model comes with optional features*). **9** become (with compl.: *the handle has come loose*). **10** (foll. by *of*) **a** be descended from (*comes of a rich family*). **b** be the result of (*that comes of complaining*). **11** *colloq.* play the part of; behave like (with compl.: *don't come the bully with me*). **12** *sl.* have a sexual orgasm. **13** (in *subj.*) *colloq.* when a specified time is reached (*come next month*). **14** (as *int.*) expressing caution or reserve (*come now, it cannot be that bad*). • *n. sl.* semen ejaculated at a sexual orgasm. ▫ **as ... as they come** typically or supremely so (*is as tough as they come*). **come about 1** happen; take place. **2** *Naut.* tack. **come across 1 a** be effective or understood. **b** appear or sound in a specified way (*you came across very well; the ideas came across clearly*). **2** (foll. by *with*) *sl.* hand over what is wanted. **3** meet or find by chance (*came across an old jacket*). **come again** *colloq.* **1** make a further effort. **2** (as *imper.*) what did you say? **come along 1** make progress; move forward. **2** (as *imper.*) hurry up. **come and go 1** pass to and fro; be transitory. **2** pay brief visits. **come apart** fall or break into pieces; disintegrate. **come around 1** pay an informal visit. **2** recover consciousness. **3** be converted to another person's opinion. **4** (of a date or regular occurrence) recur; be imminent again. **come at 1** reach; discover; get access to. **2** attack (*came at me with a knife*). **come away 1** become detached or broken off (*came away in my hands*). **2** (foll. by *with*) be left with a feeling, impression, etc. (*came away with many misgivings*). **come back 1** return. **2** recur to one's memory. **3** become fashionable or popular again. **4** reply; retort. **come before** be dealt with by (a judge, etc.). **come between 1** interfere with the relationship of. **2** separate; prevent contact between. **come by 1** pass; go past. **2** call on a visit (*why not come by tomorrow?*). **3** acquire; obtain; attain (*came by a new bicycle*). **come clean** see CLEAN. **come down 1** come to a place or position regarded as lower. **2** lose position or wealth (*has come down in the world*). **3** be handed down by tradition or inheritance. **4** be reduced; show a downward trend (*prices are coming down*). **5** (foll. by *against, in favor of, on the side of*) reach a decision or recommendation (*the report came down against change*). **6** (foll. by *to*) signify or betoken basically; be dependent on (a factor) (*it comes down to who is willing to go*). **7** (foll. by *on*) criticize harshly; rebuke; punish. **8** (foll. by *with*) begin to suffer from (a disease). **come for 1** come to collect or receive. **2** attack (*came for me with a hammer*). **come forward 1** advance. **2** offer oneself for a task, post, etc. **come in 1** enter a house or room. **2 a** take a specified position in a race, etc. (*came in third*). **b** *colloq.* win. **3** become fashionable or seasonable. **4 a** have a useful role or function. **b** (with compl.) prove to be (*came in very handy*). **c** have a part to play (*where do I come in?*). **5** be received (*more news has just come in*). **6** begin speaking, esp. in radio transmission. **7** be elected; come to power. **8** *Cricket* begin an inning. **9** (foll. by *for*) receive; be the object of (usu. something unwelcome) (*came in for much criticism*). **10** (foll. by *on*) join (an enterprise, etc.). **11** (of a tide) turn to high tide. **12** (of a train, ship, or aircraft) approach its destination. **come into 1** see senses 2, 7 of *v.* **2** receive, esp. as heir. **come near** see NEAR. **come of age** see AGE. **come off 1** *colloq.* (of an action) succeed; be accomplished. **2** (with compl.) fare; turn out (*came off badly; came off the winner*). **3** *Brit. coarse sl.* have a sexual orgasm. **4** be detached or detachable (from). **5** fall (from). **6** be reduced or subtracted from (*$5 came off the price*). **come off it** (as *imper.*) *colloq.* an expression of disbelief or refusal to accept another's opinion, behavior, etc. **come on 1** continue to come. **2 a** advance, esp. to attack. **b** (foll. by *to*) make sexual advances. **3** make progress; thrive (*is really coming on*). **4** (foll. by *to* + infin.) *Brit.* begin (*it came on to rain*). **5** appear on the stage, field of play, etc. **6** be heard or seen on television, on the telephone, etc. **7** arise to be discussed. **8** (as *imper.*) expressing encouragement. **9** = *come upon*. **come out 1 a** emerge; become known (*it came out that he had left*). **b** end; turn out. **2** appear or be published (*comes out every Saturday*). **3 a** declare oneself; make a decision (*came out in favor of joining*). **b** openly declare that one is a homosexual. **4** *Brit.* go on strike. **5 a** be satisfactorily visible in a photograph, etc., or present in a specified way (*the dog didn't come out; he came out badly*). **b** (of a photograph) be produced satisfactorily or in a specified way (*only three have come out; they all came out well*). **6** attain a specified result in an examination, etc. **7** (of a stain, etc.) be removed. **8** make one's début on stage or in society. **9** (foll. by *in*) be covered with (*came out in spots*). **10** (of a problem) be solved. **11** (foll. by *with*) declare openly; disclose. **come over 1** come from some distance or nearer to the speaker (*came over from Paris; come over here a moment*). **2** change sides or one's opinion. **3 a** (of a feeling, etc.) overtake or affect (a person). **b** *Brit. colloq.* feel suddenly (*came over faint*). **4** esp. *Brit.* = *come across* 1 b. **5** affect or influence (*I don't know what came over me*). **come through 1** be successful; survive. **2** be received by telephone. **3** survive or overcome (a difficulty) (*came through the ordeal*). **come to 1** recover consciousness. **2** *Naut.* bring a vessel to a stop. **3** reach in total; amount to. **4** *refl.* **a** recover consciousness. **b** *Brit.* stop being foolish. **5** have as a destiny; reach (*what is the world coming to?*). **6** be a question of (*when it comes to wine, he is an expert*). **come to hand** *Brit.* become available; be recovered. **come to light** see LIGHT[1]. **come to nothing** have no useful result in the end; fail. **come to pass** happen; occur. **come to rest** cease moving. **come to one's senses** see SENSE. **come to that** *colloq.* in fact; if that is the case. **come under 1** be classified as or among. **2** be subject to (influence or authority). **come up 1** come to a place or position regarded as higher. **2** attain wealth or position (*come up in the world*). **3** (of an issue, problem, etc.) arise; present itself; be mentioned or discussed. **4** (often foll. by *to*) **a** approach a person, esp. to talk. **b** (foll. by *to, on*) approach or draw near to a specified time, event, etc. (*is coming up to eight o'clock*). **5** (foll. by *to*) match (a standard, etc.). **6** (foll. by *with*) produce (an idea, etc.), esp. in response to a challenge. **7** (of a plant, etc.) spring up out of the ground. **8** become brighter (e.g., with polishing); shine more brightly. **come up against** be faced with or opposed by. **come upon 1** meet or find by chance. **2** attack by surprise. **come what may** no matter what happens. **have it coming to one** *colloq.* be about to get one's deserts. **how come?** *colloq.* **1** why is that? **2** how did that happen? **if it comes to that** in that case. **to come** future; in the future (*the year to come; many problems were still to come*). [OE *cuman* f. Gmc]

come-at-able /kumátəbəl/ *adj.* reachable; accessible.

come•back /kúmbak/ *n.* **1** a return to a previous (esp. successful) state. **2** *sl.* a retaliation or retort. **3** *Austral.* a sheep bred from crossbred and purebred parents for both wool and meat.

co•me•di•an /kəméedeeən/ *n.* **1** a humorous entertainer on stage, television, etc. **2** an actor in comedy. [F *comédien* f. *comédie* COMEDY]

co•me•di•enne /kəméedee-én/ *n.* a female comedian. [F fem. (as COMEDIAN)]

com•e•dist /kómidist/ *n.* a writer of comedies.

com•e•do /kómidō/ *n.* (*pl.* **com•e•dones** /–dōneez/) *Med.* a blackhead. [L, = glutton f. *comedere* eat up]

come•down /kúmdown/ *n.* **1** a loss of status; decline or degradation. **2** a disappointment.

com•e•dy /kómidee/ *n.* (*pl.* **•dies**) **1 a** a play, film, etc., of an amusing or satirical character, usu. with a happy ending. **b** the dramatic genre consisting of works of this kind (*she excels in comedy*) (cf. TRAGEDY). **2** an amusing or farcical incident or series of incidents in everyday life. **3** humor, esp. in a work of art, etc. ▫▫ **co•me•dic** /kəméedik/ *adj.* [ME f. OF *comedie* f. L *comoedia* f. Gk *kōmōidia* f. *kōmōidos* comic poet f. *kōmos* revel]

com•e•dy of man•ners *n.* satirical portrayal of social behavior, esp. of the upper classes.

come-hith•er *adj. colloq.* (of a look or manner) enticing; flirtatious.

come•ly /kúmlee/ *adj.* (**come•li•er, come•li•est**) pleasant to look at. ▫▫ **come•li•ness** /kúmleenis/ *n.* [ME *cumelich, cumli* prob. f. *becumelich* f. BECOME]

come-on *n. sl.* a lure or enticement.

com•er /kúmər/ *n.* **1** a person who comes, esp. as an applicant, participant, etc. (*offered the job to the first comer*). **2** *colloq.* a person likely to be a success.

co•mes•ti•ble /kəméstibəl/ *n.* (usu. in *pl.*) *formal* or *joc.* food. [ME f. F f. med.L *comestibilis* f. L *comedere comest-* eat up]

com•et /kómit/ *n.* a hazy object usu. with a nucleus of ice and dust surrounded by gas and with a tail pointing away from the sun, moving in an eccentric orbit around the sun. ▫▫ **com•et•ar•y** *adj.* [ME f. OF *comete* f. L *cometa* f. Gk *komētes* long-haired (star)]

come•up•pance /kumúpəns/ *n. colloq.* one's deserved fate or punishment (*got his comeuppance*). [COME + UP + –ANCE]

com·fit /kúmfit/ n. archaic a sweet consisting of a nut, seed, etc., coated in sugar. [ME f. OF confit f. L confectum past part. of conficere prepare: see CONFECTION]

com·fort /kúmfərt/ n. & v. • n. 1 consolation; relief in affliction. 2 a a state of physical well-being; being comfortable (live in comfort). b (usu. in pl.) things that make life easy or pleasant (has all the comforts). 3 a cause of satisfaction (a comfort to me that you are here). 4 a person who consoles or helps one (he's a comfort to her in her old age). • v.tr. 1 soothe in grief; console. 2 make comfortable (comforted by the warmth of the fire). [ME f. OF confort(er) f. LL confortare strengthen (as COM-, L fortis strong)]

com·fort·a·ble /kúmftəbəl, –fərtəbəl/ adj. 1 a such as to avoid hardship or trouble and give comfort or ease (a comfortable pair of shoes). b (of a person) relaxing to be with; congenial. 2 free from discomfort; at ease (I'm quite comfortable, thank you). 3 colloq. having an adequate standard of living; free from financial worry. 4 a having an easy conscience (did not feel comfortable about refusing him). b colloq. complacent; placidly self-satisfied. 5 with a wide margin (a comfortable win). □□ com·fort·a·ble·ness n. com·fort·a·bly adv. [ME f. AF confortable (as COMFORT)]

com·fort·er /kúmfərtər/ n. 1 a person who comforts. 2 a warm quilt. 3 Brit. a baby's pacifier. 4 archaic a woolen scarf. [ME f. AF confortour, OF –ëor (as COMFORT)]

com·fort·less /kúmfərtlis/ adj. 1 dreary, cheerless. 2 without comfort.

com·fort sta·tion n. euphem. a public lavatory.

com·frey /kúmfree/ n. (pl. **·freys**) any of various plants of the genus Symphytum, esp. S. officinale having large, hairy leaves and clusters of usu. white or purple bell-shaped flowers. [ME f. AF cumfrie, ult. f. L conferva (as COM-, fervëre boil)]

com·fy /kúmfee/ adj. (**com·fi·er, com·fi·est**) colloq. comfortable. □□ com·fi·ly adv. com·fi·ness n. [abbr.]

com·ic /kómik/ adj. & n. • adj. 1 (often attrib.) of, or in the style of, comedy (a comic actor; comic opera). 2 causing or meant to cause laughter; funny (comic to see his struggles). • n. 1 a professional comedian. 2 (pl.) section or page of a newspaper featuring several comic strips. [L comicus f. Gk kōmikos f. kōmos revel]

com·i·cal /kómikəl/ adj. funny; causing laughter. □□ com·i·cal·i·ty /–kálitee/ n. com·i·cal·ly adv. [COMIC]

com·ic book n. a magazine in the form of comic strips.

com·ic op·er·a n. 1 an opera with much spoken dialogue, usu. with humorous treatment. 2 this genre of opera.

com·ic strip n. a horizontal series of drawings in a comic book, newspaper, etc., telling a story.

com·ing /kúming/ adj. & n. • attrib.adj. 1 approaching; next (in the coming week; this coming Sunday). 2 of potential importance (a coming man). • n. arrival; approach.

Com·in·tern /kómintərn/ n. the Third International (see INTERNATIONAL n. 2), a communist organization (1919–43). [Russ. Komintern f. Russ. forms of communist, international]

co·mi·tad·ji /kómitájee/ n. (also **ko·mi·tad·ji, ko·mi·ta·ji**) a member of an irregular band of soldiers in the Balkans. [Turk. komitacı, lit. 'member of a (revolutionary) committee']

com·i·ty /kómitee/ n. (pl. **·ties**) 1 courtesy; civility; considerate behavior toward others. 2 an association of nations, etc., for mutual benefit. b (in full comity of nations) the mutual recognition by nations of the laws and customs of others. [L comitas f. comis courteous]

comm. abbr. 1 commerce. 2 commercial. 3 commissioner. 4 commission. 5 committee. 6 common. 7 commonwealth. 8 community.

com·ma /kómə/ n. 1 a punctuation mark (,) indicating a pause between parts of a sentence, or dividing items in a list, string of figures, etc. 2 Mus. a definite minute interval or difference of pitch. [L f. Gk komma clause]

com·ma ba·cil·lus n. a comma-shaped bacillus causing cholera.

com·mand /kəmánd/ v. & n. • v.tr. 1 (also absol.; often foll. by to + infin., or that + clause) give formal order or instructions to (commands us to obey; commands that it be done). 2 (also absol.) have authority or control over. 3 a (often refl.) restrain; master. b gain the use of; have at one's disposal or within reach (skill, resources, etc.) (commands an extensive knowledge of history; commands a salary of $40,000). 4 deserve and get (sympathy, respect, etc.). 5 Mil. dominate (a strategic position) from a superior height; look down over. • n. 1 an authoritative order; an instruction. 2 mastery; control; possession (a good command of languages; has command of the resources). 3 the exercise or tenure of authority, esp. naval or military (has command of this ship). 4 Mil. a a body of troops, etc. (Artillery Command). b a district under a commander (Western Command). 5 Computing a an instruction causing a computer to perform one of its basic functions. b a signal initiating such an operation. □ at command ready to be used at will. at (or by) a person's command in pursuance of a person's bidding. in command of commanding; having under control. under command of commanded by. [ME f. AF comaunder, OF comander f. LL commandare COMMEND]

com·man·dant /kóməndánt, –daánt/ n. a commanding officer, esp.

of a particular force, military academy, etc. □□ com·man·dant·ship n. [F commandant, or It. or Sp. commandante (as COMMAND)]

com·man·deer /kóməndeér/ v.tr. 1 seize (men or goods) for military purposes. 2 take possession of without authority. [S.Afr. Du. kommanderen f. F commander COMMAND]

com·mand·er /kəmándər/ n. 1 a person who commands, esp. a naval officer next in rank below captain. 2 an officer in charge of a London police district. 3 (in full knight commander) a member of a higher class in some orders of knighthood. 4 a large wooden mallet. □□ com·mand·er·ship n. [ME f. OF comandere, –eör f. Rmc (as COMMAND)]

com·mand·er in chief n. the supreme commander, esp. of a nation's forces.

com·mand·ing /kəmánding/ adj. 1 dignified; exalted; impressive. 2 (of a hill or other high point) giving a wide view. 3 (of an advantage, a position, etc.) controlling; superior (has a commanding lead). □□ com·mand·ing·ly adv.

com·mand·ment /kəmándmənt/ n. a divine command. □ the Ten Commandments the divine rules of conduct given by God to Moses on Mount Sinai, according to Exod. 20:1– 17. [ME f. OF comandement (as COMMAND)]

com·mand mod·ule n. the control compartment in a spacecraft.

com·man·do /kəmándō/ n. (pl. **·dos**) Mil. 1 a a unit of amphibious shock troops. b a member of such a unit. 2 a a party of men called out for military service. b a body of troops. 3 (attrib.) of or concerning a commando (a commando operation). [Port. f. commandar COMMAND]

com·mand per·for·mance n. a theatrical or film performance given at the request of a head of state or sovereign.

com·mand post n. the headquarters of a military unit.

comme ci, comme ça /kum seé kum saá/ adv. & adj. so-so; middling or middlingly. [F, = like this, like that]

com·me·dia dell'ar·te /kumáydeeə deláartay/ n. an improvised kind of popular comedy in Italian theaters in the 16th– 18th c., based on stock characters. [It., = comedy of art]

comme il faut /kúm eel fố/ adj. & adv. • predic.adj. (esp. of behavior, etiquette, etc.) proper; correct. • adv. properly; correctly. [F, = as is necessary]

com·mem·o·rate /kəmémərayt/ v.tr. 1 celebrate in speech or writing. 2 a preserve in memory by some celebration. b (of a stone, plaque, etc.) be a memorial of. □□ com·mem·o·ra·tive /–ráytiv, –rətiv/ adj. com·mem·o·ra·tor n. [L commemorare (as COM-, memorare relate f. memor mindful)]

com·mem·o·ra·tion /kəméməráyshən/ n. 1 an act of commemorating. 2 a service or part of a service in memory of a person, an event, etc. [ME f. F commemoration or L commemoratio (as COMMEMORATE)]

com·mence /kəméns/ v.tr. & intr. formal begin. [ME f. OF com(m)encier f. Rmc (as COM-, L initiare INITIATE)]

com·mence·ment /kəménsmənt/ n. formal 1 a beginning. 2 a ceremony of degree conferment. [ME f. OF (as COMMENCE)]

com·mend /kəménd/ v.tr. 1 (often foll. by to) entrust; commit (commends his soul to God). 2 praise (commends her singing voice). 3 recommend (method commends itself). □ commend me to archaic remember me kindly to. highly commended (of a competitor, etc.) just missing the top places. [ME f. L commendare (as COM-, mendare = mandare entrust: see MANDATE)]

com·mend·a·ble /kəméndəbəl/ adj. praiseworthy. □□ com·mend·a·bly adv. [ME f. OF f. L commendabilis (as COMMEND)]

com·men·da·tion /kómendáyshən/ n. 1 an act of commending or recommending (esp. a person to another's favor). 2 praise. [ME f. OF f. L commendatio (as COMMEND)]

com·men·da·to·ry /kəméndətawree/ adj. commending; recommending. [LL commendatorius (as COMMEND)]

com·men·sal /kəménsəl/ adj. & n. • adj. 1 Biol. of, relating to, or exhibiting commensalism. 2 (of a person) eating at the same table as another. • n. 1 Biol. a commensal organism. 2 one who eats at the same table as another. □□ com·men·sal·i·ty /kómənsálitee/ n. [ME f. F commensal or med.L commensalis (in sense 2) (as COM-, mensa table)]

com·men·sal·ism /kəménsəlizəm/ n. Biol. an association between two organisms in which one benefits and the other derives no benefit or harm.

com·men·su·ra·ble /kəménsərəbəl, –shərə–/ adj. 1 (often foll. by with, to) measurable by the same standard. 2 (foll. by to) proportionate to. 3 Math. (of numbers) in a ratio equal to the ratio of integers. □□ com·men·su·ra·bil·i·ty n. com·men·su·ra·bly adv. [LL commensurabilis (as COM-, MEASURE)]

com·men·su·rate /kəménsərət, –shərət/ adj. 1 (usu. foll. by with) having the same size, duration, etc.; coextensive. 2 (often foll. by to, with) proportionate. □□ com·men·su·rate·ly adv. [LL commensuratus (as COM-, MEASURE)]

com·ment /kóment/ n. & v. • n. 1 a a remark, esp. critical; an opinion (*passed a comment on her hat*). **b** commenting; criticism (*his behavior aroused much comment; an hour of news and comment*). **2 a** an explanatory note (e.g., on a written text). **b** written criticism or explanation (e.g., of a text). **3** (of a play, book, etc.) a critical illustration; a parable (*his art is a comment on society*). • *v.intr.* **1** (often foll. by *on, upon,* or *that* + clause) make (esp. critical) remarks (*commented on her choice of friends*). **2** (often foll. by *on, upon*) write explanatory notes. □ **no comment** *colloq.* I decline to answer your question. □□ **com•ment•er** *n.* [ME f. L *commentum* contrivance (in LL also = interpretation), neut. past part. of *comminisci* devise, or F *commenter* (v.)]

com•men•tar•y /kómənteree/ *n.* (*pl.* **•ies**) **1** a set of explanatory or critical notes on a text, etc. **2** a descriptive spoken account (esp. on radio or television) of an event or a performance as it happens. [L *commentarius, –ium* adj. used as noun (as COMMENT)]

com•men•tate /kóməntayt/ *v.intr. disp.* act as a commentator. [backform. f. COMMENTATOR]

com•men•ta•tor /kóməntaytər/ *n.* **1** a person who provides a commentary on an event, etc. **2** the writer of a commentary. **3** a person who writes or speaks on current events. [L f. *commentari* frequent. of *comminisci* devise]

com•merce /kómərs/ *n.* **1** financial transactions, esp. the buying and selling of merchandise, on a large scale. **2** social intercourse (*the daily commerce of gossip and opinion*). **3** *archaic* sexual intercourse. [F *commerce* or L *commercium* (as COM-, *mercium* f. *merx mercis* merchandise)]

com•mer•cial /kəmɔ́rshəl/ *adj. & n.* • *adj.* **1** of, engaged in, or concerned with, commerce. **2** having profit as a primary aim rather than artistic, etc., value; philistine. **3** (of chemicals) supplied in bulk more or less unpurified. • *n.* a television or radio advertisement. □□ **com•mer•cial•ism** *n.* **com•mer•ci•al•i•ty** /–sheeálitee/ *n.* **com•mer•cial•ly** *adv.*

com•mer•cial art *n.* art used in advertising, selling, etc.

com•mer•cial broad•cast•ing *n.* television or radio broadcasting in which programs are financed by advertisements.

com•mer•cial•ize /kəmɔ́rshəliz/ *v.tr.* **1** exploit or spoil for the purpose of gaining profit. **2** make commercial. □□ **com•mer•cial•i•za•tion** *n.*

com•mer•cial ve•hi•cle *n.* a vehicle used for carrying goods or fare-paying passengers.

com•mère /kómair/ *n. Brit.* a female compère. [F, fem. of COMPÈRE]

com•mie /kómee/ *n. sl. derog.* (also **Com•mie**) a Communist. [abbr.]

com•mi•na•tion /kómináyshən/ *n.* **1** the threatening of divine vengeance. **2 a** the recital of divine threats against sinners in the Anglican liturgy for Ash Wednesday. **b** the service that includes this. [ME f. L *comminatio* f. *comminari* threaten]

com•min•a•to•ry /kəmínətawree, kómínə–/ *adj.* threatening; denunciatory. [med.L *comminatorius* (as COMMINATION)]

com•min•gle /kəmínggəl/ *v.tr. & intr. literary* mingle together.

com•mi•nute /kómənoot, –nyoot/ *v.tr.* **1** reduce to small fragments. **2** divide (property) into small portions. □□ **com•mi•nu•tion** /–noóshən, –nyoó–/ *n.* [L *comminuere comminut-* (as COM-, *minuere* lessen)]

com•mi•nut•ed frac•ture *n.* a fracture producing multiple bone splinters.

com•mis /kómee/ *n. Brit.* (*pl.* **com•mis** /komée, komeéz/) a junior waiter or chef. [orig. = deputy, clerk, f. F, past part. of *commettre* entrust (as COMMIT)]

com•mis•er•ate /kəmízərayt/ *v.* **1** *intr.* (usu. foll. by *with*) express or feel pity. **2** *tr. archaic* express or feel pity for (*commiserate you on your loss*). □□ **com•mis•er•a•tion** /–ráyshən/ *n.* **com•mis•er•a•tive** /–ráytiv/ *adj.* **com•mis•er•a•tor** *n.* [L *commiserari* (as COM-, *miserari* pity f. *miser* wretched)]

com•mis•sar /kómisaar/ *n. hist.* **1** an official of the former Soviet Communist party responsible for political education and organization. **2** the head of a government department in the former USSR before 1946. [Russ. *komissar* f. F *commissaire* (as COMMISSARY)]

com•mis•sar•i•at /kómisáireeət/ *n.* **1** esp. *Mil.* **a** a department for the supply of food, etc. **b** the food supplied. **2** *hist.* a government department of the former USSR before 1946. [F *commissariat* & med.L *commissariatus* (as COMMISSARY)]

com•mis•sar•y /kómiseree/ *n.* (*pl.* **•ies**) **1** *Mil.* **a** a store for the supply of food, etc., to soldiers. **b** an officer responsible for the supply of food, etc., to soldiers. **2 a** a restaurant in a movie studio, etc. **b** the food supplied. **3** a deputy or delegate. **4** a representative or deputy of a bishop. □□ **com•mis•sar•i•al** *adj.* **com•mis•sar•y•ship** *n.* [ME f. med.L *commissarius* person in charge (as COMMIT)]

com•mis•sion /kəmíshən/ *n. & v.* • *n.* **1 a** the authority to perform a task or certain duties. **b** a person or group entrusted esp. by a government with such authority (*set up a commission to look into it*). **c** an instruction, command, or duty given to such a group or person (*their commission was to simplify the procedure; my commission was to find him*). **2** an order for something, esp. a work of art, to be produced specially. **3** *Mil.* **a** a warrant conferring the rank of officer in the army, navy, marines, or air force. **b** the rank so conferred. **4 a** the authority to act as agent for a company, etc., in trade. **b** a percentage paid to the agent from the profits of goods, etc., sold, or business obtained (*his wages are low, but he gets 20 percent commission*). **c** the pay of a commissioned agent. **5** the act of committing (a crime, sin, etc.). **6** the office or department of a commissioner. • *v.tr.* **1** authorize or empower by a commission. **2 a** give (an artist, etc.) a commission for a piece of work. **b** order (a work) to be written (*commissioned a new concerto*). **3** *Naut.* **a** give (an officer) the command of a ship. **b** prepare (a ship) for active service. **4** bring (a machine, equipment, etc.) into operation. □ **in commission** (of a warship, etc.) manned, armed, and ready for service. **out of commission** (esp. of a ship) not in service; not in working order. [ME f. OF f. L *commissio –onis* (as COMMIT)]

com•mis•sion a•gent *n. Brit.* a bookmaker.

com•mis•sion•aire /kəmíshənáir/ *n.* esp. *Brit.* a uniformed door attendant at a theater, etc. [F (as COMMISSIONER)]

com•mis•sion•er /kəmíshənər/ *n.* **1** a person appointed by a commission to perform a specific task, e.g., a municipal police commissioner, etc. **2** a person appointed as a member of a government commission (*Civil Service Commissioner*). **3** a representative of the supreme authority in a district, department, etc. [ME f. med.L *commissionarius* (as COMMISSION)]

com•mis•sure /kómishoor/ *n.* **1** a junction, joint, or seam. **2** *Anat.* **a** the joint between two bones. **b** a band of nerve tissue connecting the hemispheres of the brain, the two sides of the spinal cord, etc. **c** the line where the upper and lower lips, or eyelids, meet. **3** *Bot.* any of several joints, etc., between different parts of a plant. □□ **com•mis•su•ral** /–míshərəl/ *adj.* [ME f. L *commissura* junction (as COMMIT)]

com•mit /kəmít/ *v.tr.* (**com•mit•ted, com•mit•ting**) **1** (usu. foll. by *to*) entrust or consign for: **a** safe keeping (*I commit him to your care*). **b** treatment, usu. destruction (*committed the book to the flames*). **c** official custody as a criminal or as insane (*you could be committed for such behavior*). **2** perpetrate, do (esp. a crime, sin, or blunder). **3** pledge, involve, or bind (esp. oneself) to a certain course or policy (*does not like committing herself; committed by the vow he had made*). **4** (as **committed** *adj.*) (often foll. by *to*) **a** morally dedicated or politically aligned (*a committed Christian; committed to the cause; a committed socialist*). **b** obliged (to take certain action) (*felt committed to staying there*). **5** *Polit.* refer (a bill, etc.) to a committee. □ **commit to memory** memorize. **commit to prison** consign officially to custody, esp. on remand. □□ **com•mit•ta•ble** *adj.* **com•mit•ter** *n.* [ME f. L *committere* join, entrust (as COM-, *mittere miss-* send)]

com•mit•ment /kəmítmənt/ *n.* **1** an engagement or (esp. financial) obligation that restricts freedom of action. **2** the process or an instance of committing oneself; a pledge or undertaking. **3** dedication, application.

com•mit•tal /kəmít'l/ *n.* **1** the act of committing a person to an institution, esp. prison or a mental hospital. **2** the burial of a dead body.

com•mit•tee /kəmítee/ *n.* **1 a** a body of persons appointed for a specific function by, and usu. out of, a larger body. **b** such a body appointed by a legislature, etc., to consider the details of proposed legislation. **2** /kómitee/ *Law* a person entrusted with the charge of another person or another person's property. [COMMIT + –EE]

com•mix /kəmíks/ *v.tr. & intr. archaic* or *poet.* mix. □□ **com•mix•ture** *n.* [ME: back-form. f. *commixt* past part. f. L *commixtus* (as COM-, MIXED)]

com•mode /kəmód/ *n.* **1** a chest of drawers. **2 a** = TOILET 1. **b** (also **night com•mode**) a bedside table with a cupboard containing a chamber pot. **3** = CHIFFONIER. [F, adj. (as noun) f. L *commodus* convenient (as COM-, *modus* measure)]

com•mo•di•ous /kəmódeeəs/ *adj.* **1** roomy and comfortable. **2** *archaic* convenient. □□ **com•mo•di•ous•ly** *adv.* **com•mo•di•ous•ness** *n.* [F *commodieux* or f. med.L *commodiosus* f. L *commodus* (as COMMODE)]

com•mod•i•ty /kəmóditee/ *n.* (*pl.* **•ties**) **1** *Commerce* an article or raw material that can be bought and sold, esp. a product as opposed to a service. **2** a useful thing. [ME f. OF *commodité* or f. L *commoditas* (as COMMODE)]

com•mo•dore /kómədawr/ *n.* **1** a naval officer above a captain and below a rear admiral. **2** the commander of a squadron or other division of a fleet. **3** the president of a yacht club. **4** the senior captain of a shipping line. [prob. f. Du. *komandeur* f. F *commandeur* COMMANDER]

com•mon /kómən/ *adj. & n.* • *adj.* (**com•mon•er, com•mon•est**) **1 a** occurring often (*a common mistake*). **b** occurring too frequently; overused; trite. **c** ordinary; of ordinary qualities; without special rank or position (*no common mind; common soldier; the common people*). **2 a** shared by, coming from, or done by, more than one (*common knowledge; by common consent; our common benefit*). **b** belonging to, open to, or affecting, the whole community or the public (*common land*). **3** *derog.* low-class; vulgar; inferior (*a common little man*). **4** of the most familiar type (*common cold; common nightshade*). **5** *Math.* belonging to two or more quantities (*common* denominator; common factor). **6** Gram. (of gender) referring to individuals of either sex (e.g., teacher). **7** Prosody (of a syllable) that may be either short or long. **8** Mus. having two or four beats, esp. four quarter notes, in a bar. **9** Law (of a crime) of lesser importance (cf. GRAND, PETTY). ● n. **1** a piece of open public land, esp. in a village or town. **2** Eccl. a service used for each of a group of occasions. **3** (in full **right of common**) Law a person's right over another's land, e.g., for pasturage. □ **in common 1** in joint use; shared. **2** of joint interest (have little in common). **in common with** in the same way as. **least** (or **lowest**) **common denominator, multiple** see DENOMINATOR, MULTIPLE. □□ **com•mon•ly** adv. **com•mon•ness** n. [ME f. OF comun f. L communis]

com•mon•a•ble /kómənəbəl/ adj. **1** (of an animal) that may be pastured on common land. **2** (of land) that may be held in common. [obs. common to exercise right of common + –ABLE]

com•mon•age /kómənij/ n. **1** = right of common (see COMMON n. 3). **2 a** land held in common. **b** the state of being held in common. **3** the common people; commonalty.

com•mon•al•i•ty /kómənálitee/ n. (pl. •ties) **1** the sharing of an attribute. **2** a common occurrence. **3** = COMMONALTY. [var. of COMMONALTY]

com•mon•al•ty /kómənəltee/ n. (pl. •ties) **1** the common people. **2** the general body (esp. of mankind). **3** a corporate body. [ME f. OF comunalté f. med.L communalitas –tatis (as COMMON)]

com•mon car•ri•er n. a person or firm undertaking to transport any goods or person in a specified category.

com•mon chord n. Mus. any note with its major or minor third and perfect fifth.

com•mon de•nom•i•na•tor n. **1** a common multiple of the denominators of several fractions. **2** a common feature of members of a group.

com•mon•er /kómənər/ n. **1** one of the common people, as opposed to the aristocracy. **2** a person who has the right of common. **3** a student at a British university who does not have a scholarship. [ME f. med.L communarius f. communa (as COMMUNE¹)]

Com•mon E•ra n. the Christian era.

com•mon frac•tion n. a fraction expressed by numerator and denominator, not decimally.

com•mon ground n. a point or argument accepted by both sides in a dispute.

com•mon ju•ry n. a jury with members of no particular social standing (cf. BLUE RIBBON JURY).

com•mon law n. law derived from custom and judicial precedent rather than statutes (cf. case law (see CASE¹), statute law).

com•mon-law hus•band n. (also **common-law wife**) a partner in a marriage recognized by common law, esp. after a period of cohabitation.

com•mon log•a•rithm n. a logarithm to the base 10.

Com•mon Mar•ket n. the European Economic Community.

com•mon meas•ure n. (also **com•mon me•ter**) a hymn stanza of four lines containing eight and six syllable alternately.

com•mon noun n. (also **com•mon name**) Gram. a name denoting a class of objects or a concept as opposed to a particular individual (e.g., boy, chocolate, beauty).

com•mon•place /kómənplays/ adj. & n. ● adj. lacking originality; trite. ● n. **1 a** an everyday saying; a platitude (uttered a commonplace about the weather). **b** an ordinary topic of conversation. **2** anything usual or trite. **3** a notable passage in a book, etc., copied into a commonplace book. □□ **com•mon•place•ness** n. [transl. of L locus communis = Gk koinos topos general theme]

com•mon•place book n. a book into which notable extracts from other works are copied for personal use.

Com•mon Prayer n. the Church of England liturgy orig. set forth in the Book of Common Prayer of Edward VI (1549).

com•mon prop•er•ty n. **1** property held jointly by all members of a community. **2** information known by most people; common knowledge.

com•mon room n. esp. Brit. **1** a room in some colleges, schools, etc., which members may use for relaxation or work. **2** the members who use this.

com•mons /kómənz/ n.pl. **1** a dining hall at a residential school, university, etc. **2** New Eng. a central public park or ground in a town, etc. **3** (**the Commons**) = HOUSE OF COMMONS. **4 a** the common people. **b** (prec. by the) the common people regarded as a part of a political, esp. British, system. [ME pl. of COMMON]

com•mon salt n. see SALT.

com•mon sense n. sound practical sense, esp. in everyday matters.

com•mon•sen•si•cal /kómənsénsikəl/ adj. possessing or marked by common sense. [COMMON SENSE]

com•mon sol•dier n. see SOLDIER.

com•mon stock n. US ordinary shares of stock in a corporation (cf. PREFERRED STOCK).

com•mon va•le•ri•an n. a valerian, Valeriana officinalis, with pink or white flowers, valued medicinally. Also called **setwall**.

com•mon•weal /kómənweel/ n. archaic **1** = COMMON WEAL. **2** = COMMONWEALTH.

---

com•mon weal n. public welfare.

com•mon•wealth /kómənwelth/ n. **1 a** an independent state or community, esp. a democratic republic. **b** such a community or organization of shared interests in a nonpolitical field (the commonwealth of learning). **2** (**the Commonwealth**) **a** (in full **the British Commonwealth of Nations**) an international association consisting of the UK together with nations that were previously part of the British Empire. **b** the republican period of government in Britain 1649–60. **c** a part of the title of Puerto Rico and some of the states of the US. **d** the title of the federated Australian states. [COMMON + WEALTH]

Com•mon•wealth Day n. the second Monday in March, commemorating the British Commonwealth (formerly called Empire Day).

com•mon year n. see YEAR 2.

com•mo•tion /kəmóshən/ n. **1 a** a confused and noisy disturbance or outburst. **b** loud and confusing noise. **2** a civil insurrection. [ME f. OF commotion or L commotio (as COM-, MOTION)]

com•mu•nal /kəmyóonəl, kómyə–/ adj. **1** relating to or benefiting a community; for common use (communal baths). **2** of a commune, esp. the Paris Commune. □□ **com•mu•nal•i•ty** /–nálitee/ n. **com•mu•nal•ly** adv. [F f. LL communalis (as COMMUNE¹)]

com•mu•nal•ism /kəmyóonəlizəm, kómyənə–/ n. **1** a principle of political organization based on federated communes. **2** the principle of communal ownership, etc. □□ **com•mu•nal•ist** n. **com•mu•nal•is•tic** adj.

com•mu•nal•ize /kəmyóonəliz, kómyənə–/ v.tr. make communal. □□ **com•mu•nal•i•za•tion** n.

com•mu•nard /kómyənaard/ n. **1** a member of a commune. **2** (also **Communard**) hist. a supporter of the Paris Commune. [F (as COMMUNE¹)]

com•mune¹ /kómyōon/ n. **1 a** a group of people, not necessarily related, sharing living accommodation, goods, etc., esp. as a political act. **b** a communal settlement esp. for the pursuit of shared interests. **2 a** the smallest French territorial division for administrative purposes. **b** a similar division elsewhere. **3** (**the Commune**) the communalistic government in Paris in 1871. [F f. med.L communia neut. pl. of L communis common]

com•mune² /kəmyóon/ v.intr. **1** (usu. foll. by with) **a** speak confidentially and intimately (communed together about their loss; communed with his heart). **b** feel in close touch (with nature, etc.) (communed with the hills). **2** receive Holy Communion. [ME f. OF comuner share f. comun common]

com•mu•ni•ca•ble /kəmyóonikəbəl/ adj. **1** (esp. of a disease) able to be passed on. **2** archaic communicative. □□ **com•mu•ni•ca•bil•i•ty** n. **com•mu•ni•ca•bly** adv. [ME f. OF communicable or LL communicabilis (as COMMUNICATE)]

com•mu•ni•cant /kəmyóonikənt/ n. **1** a person who receives Holy Communion, esp. regularly. **2** a person who imparts information. [L communicare communicant- (as COMMON)]

com•mu•ni•cate /kəmyóonikayt/ v. **1** tr. **a** transmit or pass on by speaking or writing (communicated his ideas). **b** transmit (heat, motion, etc.). **c** pass on (an infectious illness). **d** impart (feelings, etc.) nonverbally (communicated his affection). **2** intr. (often foll. by with) be in communication; succeed in conveying information, evoking understanding, etc. (she communicates well). **3** intr. (often foll. by with) share a feeling or understanding; relate socially. **4** intr. (often foll. by with) (of a room, etc.) have a common door (my room communicates with yours). **5 a** tr. administer Holy Communion to. **b** intr. receive Holy Communion. □□ **com•mu•ni•ca•tor** n. **com•mu•ni•ca•to•ry** /–nikətáwree/ adj. [L communicare communicat- (as COMMON)]

com•mu•ni•ca•tion /kəmyóonikáyshən/ n. **1 a** the act of imparting, esp. news. **b** an instance of this. **c** the information, etc., communicated. **2** a means of connecting different places, such as a door, passage, road, or railroad. **3** social intercourse (it was difficult to maintain communication in the uproar). **4** (in pl.) the science and practice of transmitting information esp. by electronic or mechanical means. **5** (in pl.) Mil. the means of transport between a base and the front.

com•mu•ni•ca•tion sat•el•lite n. (also **com•mu•ni•ca•tions sat•el•lite**) an artificial satellite used to relay telephone circuits or broadcast programs.

com•mu•ni•ca•tion the•o•ry n. the study of the principles and methods by which information is conveyed.

com•mu•ni•ca•tive /kəmyóonikáytiv, –kətiv/ adj. **1** open; talkative; informative. **2** ready to communicate. □□ **com•mu•ni•ca•tive•ly** adv. [LL communicativus (as COMMUNICATE)]

com•mun•ion /kəmyóonyən/ n. **1** a sharing, esp. of thoughts, etc.; fellowship (their minds were in communion). **2** participation; a sharing in common (communion of interests). **3** (**Communion, Holy Communion**) **a** the Eucharist. **b** participation in the Communion service. **c** (attrib.) of or used in the Communion service (Commun-

ion table; *Communion cloth*; *Communion rail*). **4** fellowship, esp. between branches of the Catholic Church. **5** a body or group within the Christian faith (*the Methodist communion*). [ME f. OF *communion* or L *communio* f. *communis* common]

com•mun•ion of saints *n.* fellowship between Christians living and dead.

com•mu•ni•qué /kəmyŏŏnikáy/ *n.* an official communication, esp. a news report. [F, = communicated]

com•mu•nism /kómyənizəm/ *n.* **1** a political theory derived from Marx, advocating class war and leading to a society in which all property is publicly owned and each person is paid and works according to his or her needs and abilities. **2** (usu. **Communism**) **a** the communistic form of society established in the former USSR and elsewhere. **b** any movement or political doctrine advocating communism. **3** = COMMUNALISM. [F *communisme* f. *commun* COMMON]

com•mu•nist /kómyənist/ *n. & adj.* ●*n.* **1** a person advocating or practicing communism. **2** (**Communist**) a member of a Communist party. ●*adj.* of or relating to communism (*a communist play*). □□ **com•mu•nis•tic** /-nístik/ *adj.* [COMMUNISM]

com•mu•ni•tar•i•an /kəmyŏŏnitáireeən/ *n. & adj.* ●*n.* a member of a communistic community. ●*adj.* of or relating to such a community. [COMMUNITY + –ARIAN after *unitarian*, etc.]

com•mu•ni•ty /kəmyŏŏnitee/ *n.* (pl. **•ties**) **1 a** all the people living in a specific locality. **b** a specific locality, including its inhabitants. **2** a body of people having a religion, a profession, etc., in common (*the immigrant community*). **3** fellowship of interests, etc.; similarity (*community of intellect*). **4** a monastic, socialistic, etc., body practicing common ownership. **5** joint ownership or liability (*community of goods*). **6** (prec. by *the*) the public. **7** a body of nations unified by common interests. **8** *Ecol.* a group of animals or plants living or growing together in the same area. [ME f. OF *comuneté* f. L *communitas –tatis* (as COMMON)]

com•mu•ni•ty cen•ter *n.* a place where people from a particular community can meet for social, educational, or recreational activities.

com•mu•ni•ty col•lege *n.* a nonresidential junior college offering college courses to a local community or region.

com•mu•ni•ty serv•ice *n.* unpaid work performed in service to the community, esp. as part of a criminal sentence.

com•mu•nize /kómyəniz/ *v.tr.* **1** make (land, etc.) common property. **2** make (a person, etc.) communistic. □□ **com•mu•ni•za•tion** *n.* [L *communis* COMMON]

com•mut•a•ble /kəmyŏŏtəbəl/ *adj.* **1** convertible into money; exchangeable. **2** *Law* (of a punishment) able to be commuted. **3** within commuting distance. □□ **com•mut•a•bil•i•ty** *n.* [L *commutabilis* (as COMMUTE)]

com•mu•tate /kómyətayt/ *v.tr. Electr.* **1** regulate the direction of (an alternating current), esp. to make it a direct current. **2** reverse the direction (of an electric current). [L *commutare commutat-* (as COMMUTE)]

com•mu•ta•tion /kómyətáyshən/ *n.* **1** the act or process of commuting or being commuted (in legal and exchange senses). **2** *Electr.* the act or process of commutating or being commutated. **3** *Math.* the reversal of the order of two quantities. [F *commutation* or L *commutatio* (as COMMUTE)]

com•mu•ta•tive /kəmyŏŏtətiv/ *adj.* **1** relating to or involving substitution. **2** *Math.* unchanged in result by the interchange of the order of quantities. [F *commutatif* or med.L *commutativus* (as COMMUTE)]

com•mu•ta•tor /kómyətaytər/ *n.* **1** *Electr.* a device for reversing electric current. **2** an attachment connected with the armature of a dynamo which directs and makes continuous the current produced.

com•mute /kəmyŏŏt/ *v.* **1** *intr.* travel to and from one's daily work, usu. in a city, esp. by car or train. **2** *tr. Law* (usu. foll. by *to*) change (a judicial sentence, etc.) to another less severe. **3** *tr.* (often foll. by *into*, *for*) **a** change (one kind of payment) for another. **b** make a payment, etc., to change (an obligation, etc.) for another. **4** *tr.* **a** exchange; interchange (two things). **b** change (to another thing). **5** *tr. Electr.* commutate. **6** *intr. Math.* have a commutative relation. **7** *intr.* buy and use a season ticket. [L *commutare commutat-* (as COM-, *mutare* change)]

com•mut•er /kəmyŏŏtər/ *n.* a person who travels some distance to work, esp. in a city, usu. by car or train.

co•mose /kómōs/ *adj. Bot.* (of seeds, etc.) having hairs, downy. [L *comosus* (as COMA²)]

comp /komp/ *n. & v. colloq.* ●*n.* **1** compensation. **2** a complimentary item or service. **3** *Brit.* a competition. **4** *Printing* a compositor. **5** *Mus.* an accompaniment. ●*v.* **1** *Mus.* **a** *tr.* accompany. **b** *intr.* play an accompaniment. **2** *Printing* **a** *intr.* work as a compositor. **b** *tr.* work as a composer on. [abbr.]

comp. *abbr.* **1** companion. **2** comparative. **3** compensation. **4** compilation. **5** compiled. **6** compiler. **7** complete. **8** composite. **9** composition. **10** compositor. **11** comprehensive.

com•pact¹ *adj., v., & n.* ●*adj.* /kəmpákt, kóm-/ **1** closely or neatly packed together. **2** (of a piece of equipment, a room, etc.) well-fitted and practical though small. **3** (of style, etc.) condensed; brief. **4** (esp. of the human body) small but well-proportioned. **5** (foll. by *of*) composed or made up of. ●*v.tr.* /kəmpákt/ **1** join or press firmly together. **2** condense. **3** (usu. foll. by *of*) compose; make up. ●*n.* /kómpakt/ **1** a small, flat, usu. decorated, case for face powder, a mirror, etc. **2** an object formed by compacting powder. **3** a medium-sized automobile. □□ **com•pac•tion** /–pákshən/ *n.* **com•pact•ly** *adv.* **com•pact•ness** *n.* **com•pac•tor** *n.* [ME f. L *compingere compact-* (as COM-, *pangere* fasten)]

com•pact² /kómpakt/ *n.* an agreement or contract between two or more parties. [L *compactum* f. *compacisci compact-* (as COM-, *pacisci* covenant): cf. PACT]

com•pact disc /kómpakt/ *n.* a disc on which information or sound is recorded digitally and reproduced by reflection of laser light.

com•pa•ges /kəmpáyjeez/ *n.* (*pl.* same) **1** a framework; a complex structure. **2** something resembling a compages in complexity, etc. [L *compages* (as COM-, *pages* f. *pangere* fasten)]

com•pan•ion¹ /kəmpányən/ *n. & v.* ●*n.* **1 a** (often foll. by *in*, *of*) a person who accompanies, associates with, or shares with, another (*a companion in adversity*; *they were close companions*). **b** a person, esp. an unmarried or widowed woman, employed to live with and assist another. **2** a handbook or reference book on a particular subject (*A Companion to North Wales*). **3** a thing that matches another (*the companion of this bookend is over there*). **4** (**Companion**) a member of the lowest grade of some orders of knighthood (*Companion of the Bath*). **5** *Astron.* a star, etc., that accompanies another. **6** esp. *Brit.* equipment or a piece of equipment that combines several uses. ●*v.* **1** *tr.* accompany. **2** *intr. literary* (often foll. by *with*) be a companion. [ME f. OF *compaignon* ult. f. L *panis* bread]

com•pan•ion² /kəmpányən/ *n. Naut.* **1** a raised frame on a quarterdeck used for lighting the cabins, etc., below. **2** = COMPANIONWAY. [obs. Du. *kompanje* quarterdeck f. OF *compagne* f. It. (*camera della*) *compagna* pantry, prob. ult. rel. to COMPANION¹]

com•pan•ion•a•ble /kəmpányənəbəl/ *adj.* agreeable as a companion; sociable. □□ **com•pan•ion•a•ble•ness** *n.* **com•pan•ion•a•bly** *adv.*

com•pan•ion•ate /kəmpányənit/ *adj.* **1** well-suited; (of clothes) matching. **2** of or like a companion.

com•pan•ion hatch *n.* a wooden covering over a companionway.

com•pan•ion lad•der *n.* a ladder from a ship's deck to a cabin.

com•pan•ion•ship /kəmpányənship/ *n.* good fellowship; friendship.

com•pan•ion•way /kəmpányənway/ *n. Naut.* a staircase or ladder to a ship's cabin.

com•pa•ny /kúmpənee/ *n. & v.* ●*n.* (pl. **•nies**) **1 a** a number of people assembled; a crowd; an audience (*addressed the company*). **b** guests or a guest (*am expecting company*). **2** a state of being a companion or fellow; companionship, esp. of a specific kind (*enjoys low company*; *do not care for his company*). **3 a** a commercial business. **b** (usu. **Co.**) the partner or partners not named in the title of a firm (*Smith and Co.*). **4** a troupe of actors or entertainers. **5** *Mil.* a subdivision of an infantry battalion usu. commanded by a major or a captain. ●*v.* (**•nies**, **•nied**) **1** *tr. archaic* accompany. **2** *intr. literary* (often foll. by *with*) be a companion. □ **be in good company** discover that one's companions, or better people, have done the same as oneself. **in company** not alone. **in company with** together with. **keep company** (often foll. by *with*) associate habitually. **keep** (*archaic* **bear**) **a person company** accompany a person; be sociable. **part company** (often foll. by *with*) cease to associate. [ME f. AF *compainie*, OF *compai(g)nie* f. Rmc (as COMPANION¹)]

com•pa•ny of•fi•cer *n. Mil.* a captain or a lower commissioned officer.

com•pa•ra•ble /kómpərəbəl/ *adj.* **1** (often foll. by *with*) able to be compared. **2** (often foll. by *to*) fit to be compared; worth comparing. □□ **com•pa•ra•bil•i•ty** *n.* **com•pa•ra•ble•ness** *n.* **com•pa•ra•bly** *adv.* [ME f. OF f. L *comparabilis* (as COMPARE)]

▶Use with *to* and *with* corresponds to the senses at *compare*; *to* is more common.

com•par•a•tive /kəmpárətiv/ *adj. & n.* ●*adj.* **1** perceptible by comparison; relative (*in comparative comfort*). **2** estimated by comparison (*the comparative merits of the two ideas*). **3** of or involving comparison (esp. of sciences, etc.). **4** *Gram.* (of an adjective or adverb) expressing a higher degree of a quality, but not the highest possible (e.g., *braver*, *more fiercely*) (cf. POSITIVE, SUPERLATIVE). ●*n. Gram.* **1** the comparative expression or form of an adjective or adverb. **2** a word in the comparative. □□ **com•par•a•tive•ly** *adv.* [ME f. L *comparativus* (as COMPARE)]

com•par•a•tor /kəmpárətər/ *n. Engin.* a device for comparing a product, an output, etc., with a standard, esp. an electronic circuit comparing two signals.

com•pare /kəmpáir/ *v. & n.* ●*v.* **1** *tr.* (usu. foll. by *to*) express similarities in; liken (*compared the landscape to a painting*). **2** *tr.* (often foll. by *to*, *with*) estimate the similarity or dissimilarity of; assess the relation between (*compared radio with television*; *that lacks quality compared to this*). **3** *intr.* (often foll. by *with*) bear comparison (*compares favorably with the rest*). **4** *intr.* (often foll. by *with*) be equal or equivalent to. **5** *tr. Gram.* form the comparative and superlative degrees of (an adjective or an adverb). ● *n. literary* comparison (*beyond compare; without compare; has no compare*). □ **compare notes** exchange ideas or opinions. [ME f. OF *comparer* f. L *comparare* (as COM-, *parare* f. *par* equal)]

▶Traditionally, **compare to** is used when similarities are noted in dissimilar things: *He compares life to a box of chocolates.* To **compare with** is to look for either differences or similarities, usually in similar things: *Let's compare the movie with the book on which it was based.* In practice, however, this distinction is rarely maintained. See also note at **contrast**.

com·par·i·son /kəmpárisən/ *n.* **1** the act or an instance of comparing. **2** a simile or semantic illustration. **3** capacity for being likened; similarity (*there's no comparison*). **4** (in full **degrees of comparison**) *Gram.* the positive, comparative, and superlative forms of adjectives and adverbs. □ **bear** (or **stand**) **comparison** (often foll. by *with*) be able to be compared favorably. **beyond comparison 1** totally different in quality. **2** greatly superior; excellent. **in comparison with** compared to. [ME f. OF *comparesoun* f. L *comparatio –onis* (as COMPARE)]

com·part·ment /kəmpaártmənt/ *n. & v.* ● *n.* **1** a space within a larger space, separated from the rest by partitions, e.g., in a railroad car, wallet, desk, etc. **2** *Naut.* a watertight division of a ship. **3** an area of activity, etc., kept apart from others in a person's mind. ● *v.tr.* put into compartments. □□ **com·part·men·ta·tion** /–mentáyshən/ *n.* [F *compartiment* f. It. *compartimento* f. LL *compartiri* (as COM-, *partiri* share)]

com·part·men·tal /kómpaartmént'l/ *adj.* consisting of or relating to compartments or a compartment. □□ **com·part·men·tal·ly** *adv.*

com·part·men·tal·ize /kómpaartmént'līz, kómpaart–/ *v.tr.* divide into compartments or categories. □□ **com·part·men·tal·i·za·tion** *n.*

com·pass /kúmpəs, kóm–/ *n. & v.* ● *n.* **1** (in full **magnetic compass**) an instrument showing the direction of magnetic north and bearings from it. **2** (often *pl.*) an instrument for taking measurements and describing circles, with two arms connected at one end by a movable joint. **3** a circumference or boundary. **4** area, extent; scope (e.g., of knowledge or experience) (*beyond my compass*). **5** the range of tones of a voice or a musical instrument. ● *v.tr. literary* **1** hem in. **2** grasp mentally. **3** contrive; accomplish. **4** go around. □□ **com·pass·a·ble** *adj.* [ME f. OF *compas* ult. f. L *passus* PACE¹]

com·pass card *n.* a circular rotating card showing the 32 principal bearings, forming the indicator of a magnetic compass.

com·pas·sion /kəmpáshən/ *n.* pity inclining one to help or be merciful. □□ **com·pas·sion·less** *adj.* [ME f. OF f. eccl.L *compassio –onis* f. *compati* (as COM-, *pati* pass- suffer)]

com·pas·sion·ate /kəmpáshənət/ *adj.* sympathetic; pitying. □□ **com·pas·sion·ate·ly** *adv.* [obs. F *compassioné* f. *compassioner* feel pity (as COMPASSION)]

com·pas·sion·ate leave *n. Brit.* a period of absence from work granted to someone as the result of particular personal circumstances, especially the death of a close relative.

com·pass rose *n.* a circle showing the principal directions printed on a map or chart.

com·pass saw *n.* a saw with a narrow blade, for cutting curves.

com·pass win·dow *n.* a bay window with a semicircular curve.

com·pat·i·ble /kəmpátəbəl/ *adj.* **1** (often foll. by *with*) **a** able to coexist; well-suited; mutually tolerant (*a compatible couple*). **b** consistent (*their views are not compatible with their actions*). **2** (of equipment, machinery, etc.) capable of being used in combination. □□ **com·pat·i·bil·i·ty** *n.* **com·pat·i·bly** *adv.* [F f. med.L *compatibilis* (as COMPASSION)]

com·pa·tri·ot /kəmpáytreeət, –ot/ *n.* a fellow countryman. □□ **com·pa·tri·ot·ic** /–reeótik/ *adj.* [F *compatriote* f. LL *compatriota* (as COM-, *patriota* PATRIOT)]

com·peer /kómpeer, –péer/ *n.* **1** an equal; a peer. **2** a comrade. [ME f. OF *comper* (as COM-, PEER²)]

com·pel /kəmpél/ *v.tr.* (**com·pelled, com·pel·ling**) **1** (usu. foll. by *to* + infin.) force, constrain (*compelled them to admit it*). **2** bring about (an action) by force (*compel submission*). **3** (as **compelling** *adj.*) rousing strong interest, attention, conviction, or admiration. **4** *archaic* drive forcibly. □□ **com·pel·la·ble** *adj.* **com·pel·ling·ly** *adv.* [ME f. L *compellere compuls-* (as COM-, *pellere* drive)]

com·pen·di·ous /kəmpéndeeəs/ *adj.* (esp. of a book, etc.) comprehensive but fairly brief. □□ **com·pen·di·ous·ly** *adv.* **com·pen·di·ous·**

ness *n.* [ME f. OF *compendieux* f. L *compendiosus* brief (as COMPENDIUM)]

com·pen·di·um /kəmpéndeeəm/ *n.* (*pl.* **com·pen·di·ums** or **com·pen·di·a** /–deeə/) **1** esp. *Brit.* a usu. one-volume handbook or encyclopedia. **2 a** a summary or abstract of a larger work. **b** an abridgment. **3 a** a collection of games in a box. **b** any collection or mixture. **4** a package of writing paper, envelopes, etc. [L, = what is weighed together, f. *compendere* (as COM-, *pendere* weigh)]

com·pen·sate /kómpənsayt/ *v.* **1** *tr.* (often foll. by *for*) recompense (a person) (*compensated him for his loss*). **2** *intr.* (usu. foll. by *for* a thing, *Brit. to* a person) make amends (*will compensate to her in full*). **3** *tr.* counterbalance. **4** *tr. Mech.* provide (a pendulum, etc.) with extra or less weight, etc., to neutralize the effects of temperature, etc. **5** *intr. Psychol.* offset a disability or frustration by development in another direction. □□ **com·pen·sa·tive** /kəmpénsətiv, kómpənsáytiv/ *adj.* **com·pen·sa·tor** *n.* **com·pen·sa·to·ry** /–pénsətáwree/ *adj.* [L *compensare* (as COM-, *pensare* frequent. of *pendere pens-* weigh)]

com·pen·sa·tion /kómpensáyshən/ *n.* **1 a** the act of compensating. **b** the process of being compensated. **2** something, esp. money, given as a recompense. **3** *Psychol.* **a** an act of compensating. **b** the result of compensating. **4** a salary or wages. □□ **com·pen·sa·tion·al** *adj.* [ME f. OF f. L *compensatio* (as COMPENSATE)]

com·père /kómpair/ *n. & v. Brit.* ● *n.* a person who introduces and links the performers in a variety show, etc.; a master of ceremonies. ● *v.* **1** *tr.* act as a compère to. **2** *intr.* act as compère. [F, = godfather f. Rmc (as COM-, L *pater* father)]

com·pete /kəmpét/ *v.intr.* **1** (often foll. by *with*, *against* a person, *for* a thing) strive for superiority or supremacy (*competed with his brother; compete against the Russians; compete for the victory*). **2** (often foll. by *in*) take part (in a contest, etc.) (*competed in the hurdles*). [L *competere competit–*, in late sense 'strive after or contend for (something)' (as COM-, *petere* seek)]

com·pe·tence /kómpit'ns/ *n.* (also **com·pe·ten·cy** /kómpitənsee/) **1** (often foll. by *for*, or *to* + infin.) ability; the state of being competent. **2** an income large enough to live on, usu. unearned. **3** *Law* the legal capacity (of a court, a magistrate, etc.) to deal with a matter.

com·pe·tent /kómpit'nt/ *adj.* **1 a** (usu. foll. by *to* + infin. or *for*) properly qualified or skilled (*not competent to drive*); adequately capable; satisfactory. **2** *Law* (of a judge, court, or witness) legally qualified or qualifying. □□ **com·pe·tent·ly** *adv.* [ME f. OF *competent* or L *competent–* (as COMPETE)]

com·pe·ti·tion /kómpətíshən/ *n.* **1** (often foll. by *for*) competing, esp. in an examination, in trade, etc. **2** an event or contest in which people compete. **3 a** the people competing against a person. **b** the opposition they represent. [LL *competitio* rivalry (as COMPETITIVE)]

com·pet·i·tive /kəmpétitiv/ *adj.* **1** involving, offered for, or by competition (*competitive contest*). **2** (of prices, etc.) low enough to compare well with those of rival traders. **3** (of a person) having a strong urge to win; keen to compete. □□ **com·pet·i·tive·ly** *adv.* **com·pet·i·tive·ness** *n.* [*competit–*, past part. stem of L *competere* COMPETE]

com·pet·i·tor /kəmpétitər/ *n.* a person who competes; a rival, esp. in business or commerce. [F *compétiteur* or L *competitor* (as COMPETE)]

com·pi·la·tion /kómpiláyshən/ *n.* **1 a** the act of compiling. **b** the process of being compiled. **2** something compiled, esp. a book, etc., composed of separate articles, stories, etc. [ME f. OF f. L *compilatio –onis* (as COMPILE)]

com·pile /kəmpíl/ *v.tr.* **1 a** collect (material) into a list, volume, etc. **b** make up (a volume, etc.) from such material. **2** accumulate (a

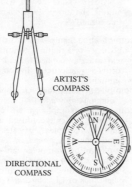

ARTIST'S COMPASS

DIRECTIONAL COMPASS

compasses

CHOOSING THE RIGHT WORD compel

COERCE, CONSTRAIN, FORCE, NECESSITATE, OBLIGE. A parent faced with a rebellious teenager may try to **compel** him to do his homework by threatening to take away his allowance. *Compel* commonly implies the exercise of authority, the exertion of great effort, or the impossibility of doing anything else (*compelled to graduate from high school by her eagerness to leave home*). It typically requires a personal object, although it is possible to *compel* a reaction or response (*she compels admiration*). **Force** is a little stronger, suggesting the exertion of power, energy, or physical strength to accomplish something or to subdue resistance (*his mother forced him to confess that he'd broken the basement window*). **Coerce** can imply the use of force, but often stops short of using it (*she was coerced into obedience by the threat of losing her telephone privileges*). **Constrain** means *compel*, but by means of restriction, confinement, or limitation (*constrained from dating by his parents' strictness*). **Necessitate** and **oblige** make an action necessary by imposing certain conditions that demand a response (*Her mother's illness obliged her to be more cooperative; it also necessitated giving up her social life*).

large number of) (*compiled a score of 160*). **3** *Computing* produce (a machine-coded form of a high-level program). [ME f. OF *compiler* or its apparent source, L *compilare* plunder, plagiarize]

com•pil•er /kəmpílər/ *n.* **1** *Computing* a program for translating a high-level programming language into machine code. **2** a person who compiles.

com•pla•cen•cy /kəmpláysənsee/ *n.* (also **com•pla•cence**) **1** smug self-satisfaction. **2** tranquil pleasure. [med.L *complacentia* f. L *complacēre* (as COM-, *placēre* please)]

com•pla•cent /kəmpláysənt/ *adj.* **1** smugly self-satisfied. **2** calmly content. □□ **com•pla•cent•ly** *adv.* [L *complacēre*: see COMPLACENCY]

►**Complacent** means 'smugly self-satisfied:' *After four consecutive championships, the team became complacent.* **Complaisant,** a much rarer word, means 'deferential, willing to please:' *Once released from the pen, the barking dogs become peaceful and complaisant.*

com•plain /kəmpláyn/ *v.intr.* **1** (often foll. by *about, at,* or *that* + clause) express dissatisfaction (*complained at the state of the room; is always complaining*). **2** (foll. by *of*) **a** announce that one is suffering from (an ailment) (*complained of a headache*). **b** state a grievance concerning (*complained of the delay*). **3** make a mournful sound; groan, creak under a strain. □□ **com•plain•er** *n.* **com•plain•ing•ly** *adv.* [ME f. OF *complaindre* (stem *complaign-*) f. med.L *complangere* bewail (as COM-, *plangere planct-* lament)]

com•plain•ant /kəmpláynənt/ *n. Law* a plaintiff in certain lawsuits.

com•plaint /kəmpláynt/ *n.* **1** an act of complaining. **2** a grievance. **3** an ailment or illness. **4** *Law* the plaintiff's case in a civil action. [ME f. OF *complainte* f. *complaint* past part. of *complaindre*: see COMPLAIN]

com•plai•sant /kəmpláysənt/ *adj.* **1** politely deferential. **2** willing to please; acquiescent. □□ **com•plai•sance** /–səns/ *n.* [F f. *complaire* (stem *complais-*) acquiesce to please, f. L *complacēre*: see COMPLACENCY]

►See note at COMPLACENT.

com•pleat *archaic* var. of COMPLETE.

com•ple•ment *n. & v.* ● *n.* /kómplimənt/ **1 a** something that completes. **b** one of a pair, or one of two things that go together. **2** (often **full complement**) **a** the full number or quantity of something required to make a group complete **b** the number of people required to crew a ship. **3** *Gram.* a word or phrase added to a verb to complete the predicate of a sentence. **4** *Biochem.* a group of proteins in the blood capable of lysing bacteria, etc. **5** *Math.* any element not belonging to a specified set or class. **6** *Geom.* the amount by which an angle is less than 90° (cf. SUPPLEMENT). ● *v.tr.* /kómpliment/ **1** complete. **2** form a complement to (*the scarf complements her dress*). □□ **com•ple•men•tal** /–mént'l/ *adj.* [ME f. L *complementum* (as COMPLETE)]

com•ple•men•tar•i•ty /kómplimentáritee/ *n.* (*pl.* **•ties**) **1** a complementary relationship or situation. **2** *Physics* the concept that a single model may not be adequate to explain atomic systems in different experimental conditions.

com•ple•men•ta•ry /kómpliméntəree/ *adj.* **1** completing; forming a complement. **2** (of two or more things) complementing each other. □□ **com•ple•men•ta•ri•ly** /–táirəlee/ *adv.* **com•ple•men•ta•ri•ness** *n.*

►**Complementary** means 'forming a complement or addition, completing': *I purchased a suit with a complementary tie and handkerchief.* It can be confused with **complimentary,** for which one sense is 'given freely, as a courtesy': *You must pay for the suit, but the tie and handkerchief are complimentary.*

com•ple•men•ta•ry an•gle *n.* either of two angles making up 90°.

com•ple•men•ta•ry col•ors *n.pl.* colors directly opposite each other in the color spectrum, such as red and green or blue and orange, that when combined in right proportions, produce white light. The effect is not the same when mixing paints.

com•ple•men•ta•ry med•i•cine *n.* any of a range of medical therapies, such as acupuncture and osteopathy, that fall beyond the scope of scientific medicine but may be used alongside it in the treatment of disease.

com•plete /kəmpléet/ *adj. & v.* ● *adj.* **1** having all its parts; entire (*the set is complete*). **2** finished (*my task is complete*). **3** of the maximum extent or degree (*a complete surprise; a complete stranger*). **4** (also **com•pleat** after Walton's *Compleat Angler*) *joc.* accomplished (*the complete horseman*). ● *v.tr.* **1** finish. **2 a** make whole or perfect. **b** make up the amount of (*completes the quota*). **3** fill in the answers to (a questionnaire, etc.). **4** (usu. *absol.*) *Law* conclude a sale of property. □ **complete with** having (as an important accessory) (*comes complete with instructions*). □□ **com•plete•ly** *adv.* **com•plete•**

ness *n.* **com•ple•tion** /–pléeshən/ *n.* [ME f. OF *complet* or L *completus* past part. of *complēre* fill up]

com•plex *n. & adj.* ● *n.* /kómpleks/ **1** a building, a series of rooms, a network, etc. made up of related parts (*the arts complex*). **2** *Psychol.* a related group of usu. repressed feelings or thoughts which cause abnormal behavior or mental states (see INFERIORITY COMPLEX, OEDIPUS COMPLEX). **3** (in general use) a preoccupation or obsession (*has a complex about punctuality*). **4** *Chem.* a compound in which molecules or ions form coordinate bonds to a metal atom or ion. ● *adj.* /kompléks, kómpleks/ **1** consisting of related parts; composite. **2** complicated (*a complex problem*). **3** *Math.* containing real and imaginary parts (cf. IMAGINARY). □□ **com•plex•i•ty** /–pléksitee/ *n.* (*pl.* **•ties**). **com•plex•ly** *adv.* [F *complexe* or L *complexus* past part. of *complectere* embrace, assoc. with *complexus* plaited]

com•plex•ion /kəmplékshən/ *n.* **1** the natural color, texture, and appearance, of the skin, esp. of the face. **2** an aspect; a character (*puts a different complexion on the matter*). □□ **com•plex•ioned** *adj.* (also in *comb.*) [ME f. OF f. L *complexio –onis* (as COMPLEX): orig. = combination of supposed qualities determining the nature of a body]

com•plex•ion•less /kəmplékshənlis/ *adj.* pale-skinned.

com•plex sen•tence *n.* a sentence containing a subordinate clause or clauses.

com•pli•ance /kəmplíəns/ *n.* **1** the act or an instance of complying; obedience to a request, command, etc. **2** *Mech.* the capacity to yield under an applied force. **b** the degree of such yielding. **3** unworthy acquiescence. □ **in compliance with** according to (a wish, command, etc.).

com•pli•ant /kəmplíənt/ *adj.* disposed to comply; yielding; obedient. □□ **com•pli•ant•ly** *adv.*

com•pli•cate /kómplikayt/ *v.tr. & intr.* **1** (often foll. by *with*) make or become difficult, confused, intricate, or complex. **2** (as **complicated** *adj.*) complex; intricate. □□ **com•pli•cat•ed•ly** *adv.* **com•pli•cat•ed•ness** *n.* [L *complicare complicat-* (as COM-, *plicare* fold)]

com•pli•ca•tion /kómplikáyshən/ *n.* **1 a** an involved or confused condition or state. **b** a complicating circumstance; a difficulty. **2** *Med.* a secondary disease or condition aggravating a previous one. [F *complication* or LL *complicatio* (as COMPLICATE)]

com•plic•i•ty /kəmplísitee/ *n.* partnership in a crime or wrongdoing. [*complice* (see ACCOMPLICE) + –ITY]

com•pli•ment *n. & v.* ● *n.* /kómplimənt/ **1 a** a spoken or written expression of praise. **b** an act or circumstance implying praise (*their success was a compliment to their efforts*). **2** (in *pl.*) **a** formal greetings, esp. as a written accompaniment to a gift, etc. (*with the compliments of the management*). **b** praise (*my compliments to the cook*). ● *v.tr.* /kómpliment/ **1** (often foll. by *on*) congratulate; praise (*complimented him on his roses*). **2** (often foll. by *with*) present as a mark of courtesy (*complimented her with his attention*). □ **pay a compliment to** praise. **return the compliment 1** give a compliment in return for another. **2** retaliate or recompense in kind. [F *complimenter* f. It. *complimento* ult. f. L (as COMPLEMENT)]

com•pli•men•ta•ry /kómpliméntəree/ *adj.* **1** expressing a compliment; praising. **2** (of a ticket for a play, etc.) given free of charge, esp. as a mark of favor. □□ **com•pli•men•ta•ri•ly** *adv.*

►See note at COMPLEMENTARY.

com•pli•ments of the sea•son *n.* greetings appropriate to the time of year, esp. Christmas.

com•pline /kómplin, –plín/ (also **com•plin**) *n. Eccl.* **1** the last of the canonical hours of prayer. **2** the service taking place during this. [ME f. OF *complie*, fem. past part. of obs. *complir* complete, ult. f. L *complēre* fill up]

com•ply /kəmplí/ *v.intr.* (**•plies, •plied**) (often foll. by *with*) act in accordance (with a wish, command, etc.) (*complied with her expectation; had no choice but to comply*). [It. *complire* f. Cat. *complir*, Sp. *cumplir* f. L *complēre* fill up]

com•po /kómpō/ *n. & adj.* ● *n.* (*pl.* **•pos**) a composition of plaster, etc., e.g., stucco. ● *adj.* = COMPOSITE. [abbr.]

com•po•nent /kəmpónənt/ *n. & adj.* ● *n.* **1** a part of a larger whole, esp. part of a motor vehicle. **2** *Math.* one of two or more vectors equivalent to a given vector. ● *adj.* being part of a larger whole (*as-*

sembled the component parts). □□ **com•po•nen•tial** /kómpənénshəl/ adj. [L componere component- (as COM-, ponere put)]

com•port /kəmpáwrt/ v.refl. literary conduct oneself; behave. □ **comport with** suit; befit. □□ **com•port•ment** n. [L comportare (as COM-, portare carry)]

com•pos var. of COMPOS MENTIS.

com•pose /kəmpóz/ v. **1 a** tr. construct or create (a work of art, esp. literature or music). **b** intr. compose music (gave up composing in 1917). **2** tr. constitute; make up (six tribes which composed the German nation). **3** tr. put together to form a whole, esp. artistically; order; arrange (composed the group for the photographer). **4** tr. **a** (often refl.) calm; settle (compose your expression; composed himself to wait). **b** (as **composed** adj.) calm; settled. **5** tr. settle (a dispute, etc.). **6** tr. Printing **a** set up (type) to form words and blocks of words. **b** set up (a manuscript, etc.) in type. □ **composed of** made up of; consisting of (a flock composed of sheep and goats). □□ **com•pos•ed•ly** /-zidlee/ adv. [F composer, f. L componere (as COM-, ponere put)]

▶Both **compose** and **comprise** can be used to mean 'to constitute or make up' but **compose** is preferred in this sense, e.g., Citizens who have been chosen at random and screened for prejudices compose a jury. **Comprise** is correctly used to mean ' to be composed of, consist of,' e.g., Each crew comprises a commander, a gunner, and a driver. The usage "is comprised of" is avoided by careful speakers and writers.

com•pos•er /kəmpózər/ n. a person who composes (esp. music).

com•pos•ite /kəmpózit/ adj., n., & v. • adj. **1** made up of various parts; blended. **2** (esp. of a synthetic building material) made up of recognizable constituents. **3** Archit. of the fifth classical order of architecture, consisting of elements of the Ionic and Corinthian orders. **4** Bot. of the plant family Compositae. • n. **1** a thing made up of several parts or elements. **2** a synthetic building material. **3** a reconstructed picture of a person (esp. one sought by the police) made by combining images of separate facial features (cf. IDENTI-KIT). **4** Bot. any plant of the family Compositae, having a head of many small flowers forming one bloom, e.g., the daisy or the dandelion. **5** Polit. a resolution composed of two or more related resolutions. • v. tr. Polit. amalgamate (two or more similar resolutions). □□ **com•pos•ite•ly** adv. **com•pos•ite•ness** n. [F f. L compositus past part. of componere (as COM-, ponere posit- put)]

com•po•si•tion /kómpəzíshən/ n. **1 a** the act of putting together; formation or construction. **b** something so composed; a mixture. **c** the constitution of such a mixture; the nature of its ingredients (the composition is two parts oil to one part vinegar). **2 a** a literary or musical work. **b** the act or art of producing such a work. **c** an essay, esp. written by a schoolchild. **d** an artistic arrangement (of parts of a picture, subjects for a photograph, etc.). **3** mental constitution; character (jealousy is not in his composition). **4** (often attrib.) a compound artificial substance, esp. one serving the purpose of a natural one. **5** Printing the setting-up of type. **6** Gram. the formation of words into a compound word. **7** Law **a** a compromise, esp. a legal agreement to pay a sum in lieu of a larger sum, or other obligation (made a composition with his creditors). **b** a sum paid in this way. **8** Math. the combination of functions in a series. □□ **com•po•si•tion•al** adj. **com•po•si•tion•al•ly** adv. [ME f. OF, f. L compositio -onis (as COMPOSITE)]

com•pos•i•tor /kəmpózitər/ n. Printing a person who sets up type for printing. [ME f. AF compositour f. L compositor (as COMPOSITE)]

com•pos men•tis /kómpəs méntis/ adj. (also **com•pos**) having control of one's mind; sane. [L]

com•pos•si•ble /kəmpósibəl/ adj. formal (often foll. by with) able to coexist. [OF f. med.L compossibilis (as COM-, POSSIBLE)]

post /kómpōst/ n. & v. • n. **1 a** mixed manure, esp. of organic origin. **b** a loam soil or other medium with added compost, used for growing plants. **2** a mixture of ingredients (a rich compost of lies and innuendo). • v. tr. **1** treat (soil) with compost. **2** make (manure, vegetable matter, etc.) into compost. [ME f. OF composte f. L compos(i)tum (as COMPOSITE)]

com•post heap n. (also **com•post pile**) a layered structure of garden refuse, soil, etc., which decays to become compost.

com•po•sure /kəmpózhər/ n. a tranquil manner; calmness. [COMPOSE + -URE]

com•pote /kómpōt/ n. fruit preserved or cooked in syrup. [F f. OF composte (as COMPOSITE)]

com•pound[1] n., adj., & v. • n. /kómpownd/ **1** a mixture of two or more things, qualities, etc. **2** (also **com•pound word**) a word made up of two or more existing words. **3** Chem. a substance formed from two or more elements chemically united in fixed proportions. • adj. /kómpownd/ **1 a** made up of several ingredients. **b** consisting of several parts. **2** combined; collective. **3** Zool. consisting of individual organisms. **4** Biol. consisting of several or many parts. • v. /kəmpównd/ **1** tr. mix or combine (ingredients, ideas, motives, etc.) (grief compounded with fear). **2** tr. increase or complicate (difficulties, etc.) (anxiety compounded by discomfort). **3** tr. make up or concoct (a composite whole). **4** tr. (also absol.) settle (a debt, dispute, etc.) by concession or special arrangement. **5** tr. Law a condone (a liability or offense) in exchange for money, etc. **b** forbear

from prosecuting (a felony) from private motives. **6** intr. (usu. foll. by with, for) Law come to terms with a person, for forgoing a claim, etc., for an offense. **7** tr. combine (words or elements) into a word. □□ **com•pound•a•ble** /-pówndəbəl/ adj. [ME compoun(e) f. OF compondre f. L componere (as COM-, ponere put: -d as in expound)]

com•pound[2] /kómpownd/ n. **1** a large open enclosure for housing workers, etc., esp. miners in S. Africa. **2** an enclosure, esp. in India, China, etc., in which a factory or a house stands (cf. KAMPONG). **3** a large enclosed space in a prison or prison camp. **4** = POUND[3]. [Port. campon or Du. kampong f. Malay]

com•pound eye n. an eye consisting of numerous visual units, as found in insects and crustaceans.

com•pound frac•ture n. an injury in which a broken bone pierces the skin, causing a risk of infection.

com•pound in•ter•est n. interest payable on capital and its accumulated interest (cf. SIMPLE INTEREST).

com•pound in•ter•val n. Mus. an interval exceeding one octave.

com•pound leaf n. a leaf of a plant consisting of several or many distinct parts (leaflets) joined to a single stem.

com•pound sen•tence n. a sentence with more than one main, independent clause.

com•pound time n. Mus. music having more than one group of simple-time units in each bar.

com•pra•dor /kómprədáwr/ n. (also **com•pra•dore**) **1** hist. a Chinese business agent of a foreign company. **2** an agent of a foreign power. [Port. comprador buyer f. LL comparator f. L comparare purchase]

com•pre•hend /kómprihénd/ v. tr. **1** grasp mentally; understand (a person or a thing). **2** include; take in. [ME f. OF comprehender or L comprehendere comprehens- (as COM-, prehendere grasp)]

com•pre•hen•si•ble /kómprihénsibəl/ adj. **1** that can be understood; intelligible. **2** that can be included or contained. □□ **com•pre•hen•si•bil•i•ty** /-bilitee/ n. **com•pre•hen•si•bly** adv. [F compréhensible or L comprehensibilis (as COMPREHEND)]

com•pre•hen•sion /kómprihénshən/ n. **1 a** the act or capability of understanding, esp. writing or speech. **b** Brit. an extract from a text set as an examination, with questions designed to test understanding of it. **2** inclusion. **3** Eccl. hist. the inclusion of Nonconformists in the Anglican Church. [F compréhension or L comprehensio (as COMPREHENSIBLE)]

com•pre•hen•sive /kómprihénsiv/ adj. & n. • adj. **1** complete; including all or nearly all elements, aspects, etc. (a comprehensive grasp of the subject). **2** of or relating to understanding (the comprehensive faculty). **3** (of automobile insurance) providing complete protection. • n. (in full **comprehensive school**) Brit. a secondary school catering to children of all abilities from a given area. □□ **com•pre•hen•sive•ly** adv. **com•pre•hen•sive•ness** n. [F compréhensif –ive or LL comprehensivus (as COMPREHENSIBLE)]

com•press v. & n. • v. tr. /kəmprés/ **1** squeeze together. **2** bring into a smaller space or shorter extent. • n. /kómpres/ a pad of cotton, etc., pressed on to part of the body to relieve inflammation, stop bleeding, etc. □□ **com•press•i•ble** /kəmprésəbəl/ adj. **com•press•i•bil•i•ty** n. **com•pres•sive** /kəmprésiv/ adj. [ME f. OF compresser or LL compressare frequent. of L comprimere compress- (as COM-, premere press)]

com•pressed air n. air that has been compressed to a pressure higher than atmospheric pressure.

com·pres·sion /kəmpréshən/ n. **1** the act of compressing or being compressed. **2** the reduction in volume (causing an increase in pressure) of the fuel mixture in an internal combustion engine before ignition. [F f. L *compressio* (as COMPRESS)]

com·pres·sor /kəmprésər/ n. an instrument or device for compressing, esp. a machine used for increasing the pressure of air or other gases.

com·prise /kəmprīz/ v.tr. **1** include; comprehend. **2** consist of; be composed of (*the book comprises 350 pages*). **3** *disp.* make up, compose (*the essays comprise his total work*). □□ **com·pris·a·ble** adj. [ME f. F, fem. past part. of *comprendre* COMPREHEND]
► See note at COMPOSE.

com·pro·mise /kómprəmīz/ n. & v. • n. **1** the settlement of a dispute by mutual concession (*reached a compromise by bargaining*). **2** (often foll. by *between*) an intermediate state between conflicting opinions, actions, etc., reached by mutual concession or modification (*a compromise between ideals and material necessity*). • v. **1 a** intr. settle a dispute by mutual concession (*compromised over the terms*). **b** tr. archaic settle (a dispute) by mutual concession. **2** tr. bring into disrepute or danger esp. by indiscretion or folly. □□ **com·pro·mis·er** n. **com·pro·mis·ing·ly** adv. [ME f. OF *compromis* f. LL *compromissum* neut. past part. of *compromittere* (as COM-, *promittere* PROMISE)]

compte ren·du /káwNt roND;AAY/ n. (pl. **comptes ren·dus** pronunc. same) a report; a review; a statement. [F]

comp·trol·ler /kəntrólər/ n. a controller (used in the title of some financial officers) (*comptroller and auditor general*). [var. of CONTROLLER, by erron. assoc. with COUNT[1], L *computus*]

com·pul·sion /kəmpúlshən/ n. **1** a constraint; an obligation. **2** *Psychol.* an irresistible urge to a form of behavior, esp. against one's conscious wishes. □ **under compulsion** because one is compelled. [ME f. F f. LL *compulsio –onis* (as COMPEL)]

com·pul·sive /kəmpúlsiv/ adj. **1** compelling. **2** resulting or acting from, or as if from, compulsion (*a compulsive gambler*). **3** *Psychol.* resulting or acting from compulsion against one's conscious wishes. **4** irresistible (*compulsive viewing*). □□ **com·pul·sive·ly** adv. **com·pul·sive·ness** n. [med.L *compulsivus* (as COMPEL)]

com·pul·so·ry /kəmpúlsəree/ adj. **1** required by law or a rule (*it is compulsory to keep dogs on leashes*). **2** essential; necessary. □□ **com·pul·so·ri·ly** adv. **com·pul·so·ri·ness** n. [med.L *compulsorius* (as COMPEL)]

com·punc·tion /kəmpúngkshən/ n. (usu. with *neg.*) **1** the pricking of the conscience. **2** a slight regret; a scruple (*without compunction; have no compunction in refusing her*). □□ **com·punc·tious** /–shəs/ adj. **com·punc·tious·ly** /–shəslee/ adv. [ME f. OF *componction* f. eccl.L *compunctio –onis* f. L *compungere compunct-* (as COM-, *pungere* prick)]

com·pur·ga·tion /kómpərgáyshən/ n. *Law hist.* an acquittal from a charge or accusation obtained by the oaths of witnesses. □□ **com·pur·ga·to·ry** /kəmpórgətáwree/ adj. [med.L *compurgatio* f. L *compurgare* (as COM-, *purgare* purify)]

com·pur·ga·tor /kómpərgaytər/ n. *Law hist.* a witness who swore to the innocence or good character of an accused person.

com·pute /kəmpyóōt/ v. **1** tr. (often foll. by *that* + clause) reckon or calculate (a number, an amount, etc.). **2** intr. make a reckoning, esp. using a computer. □□ **com·put·a·bil·i·ty** /–təbílitee/ n. **com·put·a·ble** adj. **com·pu·ta·tion** /kompyōōtáyshən/ n. **com·pu·ta·tion·al** adj. [F *computer* or L *computare* (as COM-, *putare* reckon)]

com·put·er /kəmpyóōtər/ n. **1** a usu. electronic device for storing and processing data (usu. in binary form), according to instructions given to it in a variable program. **2** a person who computes or makes calculations.

com·put·er·ize /kəmpyóōtərīz/ v.tr. **1** equip with a computer; install a computer in. **2** store, perform, or produce by computer. □□ **com·put·er·i·za·tion** n.

com·put·er·lit·er·ate n. able to use computers; familiar with the operation of computers.

com·put·er sci·ence n. the study of the principles and use of computers.

com·put·er vi·rus n. a hidden code within a computer program intended to corrupt a system or destroy data stored in it.

com·rade /kómrad, –rid/ n. **1** (also **com·rade in arms**) **a** (usu. of males) a coworker, friend, or companion. **b** fellow soldier, etc. **2** *Polit.* a fellow socialist or communist (often as a form of address). □□ **com·rade·ly** adj. **com·rade·ship** n. [earlier *cama- camerade* f. F

camerade, camarade (orig. fem.) f. Sp. *camarada* roommate (as CHAMBER)]

con[1] /kon/ n. & v. sl. • n. a confidence trick. • v.tr. (**conned, con·ning**) swindle; deceive (*conned him into thinking he had won*). [abbr.]

con[2] /kon/ n., prep., & adv. • n. (usu. in pl.) a reason against. • prep. & adv. against (cf. PRO[2]). [L *contra* against]

con[3] /kon/ n. sl. a convict. [abbr.]

con[4] *Brit.* var. of CONN.

con[5] /kon/ v.tr. (**conned, con·ning**) archaic (often foll. by *over*) study; learn by heart (*conned his part well*). [ME *cunn-, con*, forms of CAN[1]]

con- /kon, kən/ prefix assim. form of COM- before *c, d, f, g, j, n, q, s, t, v*, and sometimes before vowels.

con a·mo·re /kón amáwree, káwn aamáwray/ adv. **1** with devotion or zeal. **2** *Mus.* tenderly. [It., = with love]

co·na·tion /kōnáyshən/ n. *Philos.* & *Psychol.* **1** the desire to perform an action. **2** voluntary action; volition. □□ **con·a·tive** /kónətiv, kó–/ adj. [L *conatio* f. *conari* try]

con bri·o /kón brée-ō, káwn/ adv. *Mus.* with vigor. [It.]

con·cat·e·nate /konkát'nayt/ v. & adj. • v.tr. link together (a chain of events, things, etc.). • adj. joined; linked. □□ **con·cat·e·na·tion** /–náyshən/ n. [LL *concatenare* (as COM-, *catenare* f. *catena* chain)]

con·cave /kónkáyv/ adj. having an outline or surface curved like the interior of a circle or sphere (cf. CONVEX). □□ **con·cave·ly** adv. **con·cav·i·ty** /–kávitee/ n. [L *concavus* (as COM-, *cavus* hollow), or through F *concave*]

con·ceal /kənseél/ v.tr. **1** (often foll. by *from*) keep secret (*concealed her motive from him*). **2** not allow to be seen; hide (*concealed the letter in her pocket*). □□ **con·ceal·er** n. **con·ceal·ment** n. [ME f. OF *conceler* f. L *concelare* (as COM-, *celare* hide)]

con·cede /kənseéd/ v.tr. **1 a** (often foll. by *that* + clause) admit (a defeat, etc.) to be true (*conceded that his work was inadequate*). **b** admit defeat in. **2** (often foll. by *to*) grant, yield, or surrender (a right, a privilege, points or a start in a game, etc.). **3** *Sports* allow an opponent to score (a run, goal, etc.) or to win (a match), etc. □□ **con·ced·er** n. [F *concéder* or L *concedere concess-* (as COM-, *cedere* yield)]

con·ceit /kənseét/ n. **1** personal vanity; pride. **2** *literary* **a** a farfetched comparison, esp. as a stylistic affectation; a convoluted or unlikely metaphor. **b** a fanciful notion. [ME f. CONCEIVE after *deceit, deceive*, etc.]

con·ceit·ed /kənseétid/ adj. vain; proud. □□ **con·ceit·ed·ly** adv. **con·ceit·ed·ness** n.

con·ceiv·a·ble /kənseévəbəl/ adj. capable of being grasped or imagined; understandable. □□ **con·ceiv·a·bil·i·ty** /–bílitee/ n. **con·ceiv·a·bly** adv.

con·ceive /kənseév/ v. **1** intr. become pregnant. **2** tr. become pregnant with (a child). **3** tr. (often foll. by *that* + clause) **a** imagine; fancy; think (*can't conceive that he could be guilty*). **b** (usu. in passive) formulate; express (a belief, a plan, etc.). □ **conceive of** form in the mind; imagine. [ME f. OF *conceiv-* stressed stem of *concevoir* f. L *concipere concept-* (as COM-, *capere* take)]

con·cel·e·brate /kónsélibrayt/ v.intr. *RC Ch.* **1** (of two or more priests) celebrate the mass together. **2** (esp. of a newly ordained priest) celebrate the mass with the ordaining bishop. □□ **con·cel·e·brant** /–brənt/ n. **con·cel·e·bra·tion** /–bráyshən/ n. [L *concelebrare* (as COM-, *celebrare* CELEBRATE)]

con·cen·ter /kənséntər/ v.tr. & intr. (*Brit.* **con·cen·tre**) bring or come to a common center. [F *concentrer*: see CONCENTRATE]

con·cen·trate /kónsəntrayt/ v. & n. • v. **1** intr. (often foll. by *on, upon*) focus all one's attention or mental ability. **2** tr. bring together (troops, power, attention, etc.) to one point; focus. **3** tr. increase the strength of (a liquid, etc.) by removing water or any other diluting agent. **4** tr. (as **concentrated** adj.) (of hate, etc.) intense; strong. • n. **1** a concentrated substance. **2** a concentrated form of esp. food. □□ **con·cen·trat·ed·ly** adv. **con·cen·tra·tive** /–tráytiv, –séntrə–/ adj. **con·cen·tra·tor** n. [after *concentre* f. F *concentrer* (as CON- + CENTER)]

con·cen·tra·tion /kónsəntráyshən/ n. **1 a** the act or power of concentrating (*needs to develop concentration*). **b** an instance of this (*interrupted my concentration*). **2** something concentrated (*a concentration of resources*). **3** something brought together; a gathering. **4** the weight of a substance in a given weight or volume of material.

con·cen·tra·tion camp n. a camp for the detention of political prisoners, internees, etc., esp. in Nazi Germany.

con·cen·tric /kənséntrik/ adj. (often foll. by *with*) (esp. of circles) having a common center (cf. ECCENTRIC). □□ **con·cen·tri·cal·ly** adv. **con·cen·tric·i·ty** /kónsentrísitee/ n. [ME f. OF *concentrique* or med.L *concentricus* (as COM-, *centricus* as CENTER)]

con·cept /kónsept/ n. **1** a general notion; an abstract idea (*the concept of evolution*). **2** *colloq.* an idea or invention to help sell or publicize a commodity (*a new concept in swimwear*). **3** *Philos.* an idea or mental pic-

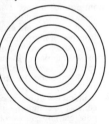
concentric circles

ture of a group or class of objects formed by combining all their aspects. [LL *conceptus* f. *concept-*: see CONCEIVE]

con·cep·tion /kənsépshən/ n. **1 a** the act or an instance of conceiving; the process of being conceived. **b** the faculty of conceiving in the mind; apprehension; imagination. **2** an idea or plan, esp. as being new or daring (*the whole conception showed originality*). □ **no conception of** an inability to imagine. □□ **con·cep·tion·al** *adj.* [ME f. OF f. L *conceptio –onis* (as CONCEPT)]

con·cep·tive /kənséptiv/ *adj.* **1** conceiving mentally. **2** of conception. [L *conceptivus* (as CONCEPTION)]

con·cep·tu·al /kənsépchoŏəl/ *adj.* of mental conceptions or concepts. □□ **con·cep·tu·al·ly** *adv.* [med.L *conceptualis* (*conceptus* as CONCEPT)]

con·cep·tu·al·ism /kənsépchoŏəlizəm/ n. *Philos.* the theory that universals exist, but only as concepts in the mind. □□ **con·cep·tu·al·ist** n.

con·cep·tu·al·ize /kənsépchoŏəlīz/ *v.tr.* form a concept or idea of. □□ **con·cep·tu·al·i·za·tion** n.

con·cern /kənsórn/ *v. & n.* ● *v.tr.* **1 a** be relevant or important to (*this concerns you*). **b** relate to; be about. **2** (usu. *refl.*; often foll. by *with, in, about,* or *to* + infin.) interest or involve oneself (*don't concern yourself with my problems*). **3** worry; cause anxiety to (*it concerns me that he is always late*). ● n. **1 a** anxiety; worry (*felt a deep concern*). **b** solicitous regard; care; consideration. **2 a** a matter of interest or importance to one (*no concern of mine*). **b** (usu. in *pl.*) affairs; private business (*meddling in my concerns*). **3** a business; a firm (*quite a prosperous concern*). **4** *colloq.* a complicated or awkward thing (*have lost the whole concern*). □ **have a concern in** have an interest or share in. **have no concern with** have nothing to do with. **to whom it may concern** to those who have a proper interest in the matter (as an address to the reader of a testimonial, reference, etc.). [F *concerner* or LL *concernere* (as COM-, *cernere* sift, discern)]

con·cerned /kənsórnd/ *adj.* **1** involved; interested (*the people concerned; concerned with proving their innocence*). **2** (often foll. by *that, about, at, for,* or *to* + infin.) troubled; anxious (*concerned about her; concerned to hear that*). □ **as** (or **so**) **far as I am concerned** as regards my interests. **be concerned** (often foll. by *in*) take part. **I am not concerned** it is not my business. □□ **con·cern·ed·ly** /-sórnidlee/ *adv.* **con·cern·ed·ness** /-sórnidnis/ n.

con·cern·ing /kənsórning/ *prep.* about; regarding.

con·cern·ment /kənsórnmənt/ n. *formal* **1** an affair or business. **2** importance. **3** (often foll. by *with*) a state of being concerned; anxiety.

con·cert n. *& v.* ● n. /kónsərt/ **1 a** a musical performance of usu. several separate compositions. **b** a comedy, etc., performance in a large hall. **2** agreement, accordance, harmony. **3** a combination of voices or sounds. ● *v.tr.* /kənsórt/ arrange (by mutual agreement or coordination). □ **in concert 1** (often foll. by *with*) acting jointly and accordingly. **2** (*predic.*) (of a musician) in a performance. [F *concert* (n.), *concerter* (v.) f. It. *concertare* harmonize]

con·cert·ed /kənsórtid/ *adj.* **1** combined together; jointly arranged or planned (*a concerted effort*). **2** *Mus.* arranged in parts for voices or instruments.

con·cert·go·er /kónsərtgōər/ n. a person who often goes to concerts. □□ **con·cert·go·ing** n.

con·cert grand n. the largest size of grand piano, used for concerts.

con·cer·ti·na /kónsərteénə/ n. *& v.* ● n. a musical instrument held in the hands and stretched and squeezed like bellows, having reeds and a set of buttons at each end to control the valves. ● *v.tr. & intr.* (**con·cer·ti·nas, con·cer·ti·naed** /-nəd/, **con·cer·ti·na·ing**) compress or collapse in folds like those of a concertina (*the car concertinaed into the bridge*). [CONCERT + -INA]

concertina

con·cer·ti·na wire n. coiled barbed wire placed on top of walls or fences for security.

con·cer·ti·no /kónchertéenō/ n. (*pl.* **-nos**) *Mus.* **1** a simple or short concerto. **2** a solo instrument or solo instruments playing in a concerto. [It., dimin. of CONCERTO]

con·cert·mas·ter /kónsərtmástər/ n. the leading first-violin player in some orchestras.

con·cer·to /kənchártō/ n. (*pl.* **con·cer·ti** /-tee/ or **·tos**) *Mus.* a composition for a solo instrument or instruments accompanied by an orchestra. [It.: *grosso* big]

con·cer·to gros·so /grósō/ n. (*pl.* **con·cer·ti gros·si** /-see/ or **con·cer·to gros·sos**) a composition for a group of solo instruments accompanied by an orchestra.

con·cert o·ver·ture n. *Mus.* a piece of music in the style of an overture but intended for independent performance.

con·cert per·for·mance n. *Mus.* a performance (of an opera, etc.) without scenery, costumes, or action.

con·cert pitch n. **1** *Mus.* the pitch internationally agreed in 1960 whereby the A above middle C = 440 Hz. **2** a state of unusual readiness, efficiency, and keenness (for action, etc.).

con·ces·sion /kənséshən/ n. **1 a** the act or an instance of conceding (*made the concession that we were right*). **b** a thing conceded. **2** a reduction in price for a certain category of person. **3 a** the right to use land or other property, granted esp. by a government or local authority, esp. for a specific use. **b** the right, given by a company, to sell goods, esp. in a particular territory. **c** the land or property used or given. □□ **con·ces·sion·ar·y** *adj.* (also **con·ces·sion·al**). [F *concession* f. L *concessio* (as CONCEDE)]

con·ces·sion·aire /kənséshənáir/ n. (also **con·ces·sion·er**) the holder of a concession or grant, esp. for the use of land or trading rights. [F *concessionnaire* (as CONCESSION)]

con·ces·sive /kənsésiv/ *adj.* **1** of or tending to concession. **2** *Gram.* **a** (of a preposition or conjunction) introducing a phrase or clause which might be expected to preclude the action of the main clause, but does not (e.g., *in spite of, although*). **b** (of a phrase or clause) introduced by a concessive preposition or conjunction. [LL *concessivus* (as CONCEDE)]

conch /kongk, konch/ n. (*pl.* **conchs** /kongks/ or **con·ches** /kónchiz/) **1 a** a thick, heavy spiral shell, occasionally bearing long projections, of various marine gastropod mollusks of the family Strombidae. **b** any of these gastropods. **2** *Archit.* the domed roof of a semicircular apse. **3** = CONCHA. [L *concha* shell f. Gk *kogkhē*]

conch

PRONUNCIATION TIP　**conch**

Strictly speaking, this word should be pronounced "KONK." This is how the inhabitants of Key West, Florida, pronounce it when they use the word *Conchs* to refer to the native inhabitants of their island. But because of the spelling, many speakers say "KONCH."

con·cha /kóngkə/ n. (*pl.* **con·chae** /-kee/) *Anat.* any part resembling a shell, esp. the depression in the external ear leading to its central cavity. [L: see CONCH]

con·chie /kónchee/ n. (also **con·chy**) (*pl.* **·chies**) *Brit. sl. derog.* a conscientious objector. [abbr.]

con·choi·dal /kongkóyd'l/ *adj. Mineral.* (of a solid fracture, etc.) resembling the surface of a bivalve shell.

con·chol·o·gy /kongkóləjee/ n. *Zool.* the scientific study of shells. □□ **con·cho·log·i·cal** /-kəlójikəl/ *adj.* **con·chol·o·gist** n. [Gk *kogkhē* shell + -LOGY]

con·chy var. of CONCHIE.

con·cierge /konseeáirzh, káwNsyáirzh/ n. **1** a hotel worker who arranges tours, transportation, etc., for guests. **2** (esp. in France) a doorkeeper or porter for an apartment building, etc. [F, prob. ult. f. L *conservus* fellow slave]

con·cil·i·ar /kənsíleeər/ *adj.* of or concerning a council, esp. an ecclesiastical council. [med.L *consiliarius* counselor]

con·cil·i·ate /kənsíleeayt/ *v.tr.* **1** make calm and amenable; pacify. **2** gain (esteem or goodwill). **3** *archaic* reconcile; make compatible. □□ **con·cil·i·a·tive** /-síleeǝtiv, -áytiv/ *adj.* **con·cil·i·a·tor** n. **con·cil·i·a·to·ry** /-síleeǝtáwree/ *adj.* **con·cil·i·a·to·ri·ness** n. [L *conciliare* combine, gain (*concilium* COUNCIL)]

con·cil·i·a·tion /kənsílee-áyshən/ n. the use of conciliating measures; reconcilement. [L *conciliatio* (as CONCILIATE)]

con·cin·ni·ty /kənsínitee/ n. elegance or neatness of literary style. □□ **con·cin·nous** *adj.* [L *concinnitas* f. *concinnus* well-adjusted]

con·cise /kǝnsís/ *adj.* (of speech, writing, style, or a person) brief but comprehensive in expression. □□ **con·cise·ly** *adv.* **con·cise·ness** n. [F *concis* or L *concisus* past part. of *concidere* (as COM-, *caedere* cut)]

con·ci·sion /kənsízhən/ n. (esp. of literary style) conciseness. [ME f. L *concisio* (as CONCISE)]

con·clave /kónklayv, kóng-/ n. **1** a private meeting. **2** *RC Ch.* **a** the assembly of cardinals for the election of a pope. **b** the meeting place for a conclave. [ME f. OF f. L *conclave* lockable room (as COM-, *clavis* key)]

con·clude /kənklôod/ *v.* **1** *tr. & intr.* bring or come to an end. **2** *tr.* (often foll. by *from,* or *that* + clause) infer (from given premises) (*what did you conclude?; concluded from the evidence that he had been mistaken*). **3** *tr.* settle; arrange (a treaty, etc.). **4** *intr.* decide. [ME f. L *concludere* (as COM-, *claudere* shut)]

con·clu·sion /kǝnklôozhǝn/ n. **1** a final result; a termination. **2** a judgment reached by reasoning. **3** the summing-up of an argument, article, book, etc. **4** a settling; an arrangement (*the conclusion of peace*). **5** *Logic* a proposition that is reached from given premises; the third and last part of a syllogism. □ **in conclusion** lastly; to conclude. **try conclusions with** engage in a trial of skill, etc., with. [ME f. OF *conclusion* or L *conclusio* (as CONCLUDE)]

con·clu·sive /kənklō̄osiv/ *adj.* decisive; convincing. □□ **con·clu·sive·ly** *adv.* **con·clu·sive·ness** *n.* [LL *conclusivus* (as CONCLUSION)]

con·coct /kənkókt/ *v.tr.* **1** make by mixing ingredients (*concocted a stew*). **2** invent (a story, a lie, etc.). □□ **con·coct·er** *n.* **con·coc·tion** /-kókshən/ *n.* **con·coct·or** *n.* [L *concoquere concoct-* (as COM-, *coquere* cook)]

con·com·i·tance /kənkómitns/ *n.* (also **con·com·i·tan·cy**) **1** coexistence. **2** *Theol.* the doctrine of the coexistence of the body and blood of Christ both in the bread and in the wine of the Eucharist. [med.L *concomitantia* (as CONCOMITANT)]

con·com·i·tant /kənkómitnt/ *adj. & v.* ● *adj.* going together; associated (*concomitant circumstances*). ● *n.* an accompanying thing. □□ **con·com·i·tant·ly** *adv.* [LL *concomitari* (as COM-, *comitari* f. L *comes –mitis* companion)]

con·cord /kónkawrd, kóng-/ *n.* **1** agreement or harmony between people or things. **2** a treaty. **3** *Mus.* a chord that is pleasing or satisfactory in itself. **4** *Gram.* agreement between words in gender, number, etc. [ME f. OF *concorde* f. L *concordia* f. *concors* of one mind (as COM-, *cors* f. *cor cordis* heart)]

con·cord·ance /kənkáwrdns/ *n.* **1** agreement. **2** a book containing an alphabetical list of the important words used in a book or by an author, usu. with citations of the passages concerned. [ME f. OF f. med.L *concordantia* (as CONCORDANT)]

con·cord·ant /kənkáwrdnt/ *adj.* **1** (often foll. by *with*) agreeing; harmonious. **2** *Mus.* in harmony. □□ **con·cord·ant·ly** *adv.* [ME f. OF f. L *concordare* f. *concors* (as CONCORD)]

con·cor·dat /kənkáwrdat/ *n.* an agreement, esp. between the Roman Catholic Church and a nation. [F *concordat* or L *concordatum* neut. past part. of *concordare* (as CONCORDANCE)]

con·course /kónkawrs/ *n.* **1** a crowd. **2** a coming together; a gathering (*a concourse of ideas*). **3** an open central area in a large public building, a railroad station, etc. [ME f. OF *concours* f. L *concursus* (as CONCUR)]

con·cres·cence /kənkrésəns/ *n.* *Biol.* coalescence; growing together. □□ **con·cres·cent** /-sənt/ *adj.* [CON-, after *excrescence*, etc.]

con·crete /kónkreet, kóng-, konkréet, kong-/ *adj., n., & v.* ● *adj.* **1 a** existing in a material form; real. **b** specific; definite (*concrete evidence; a concrete proposal*). **2** *Gram.* (of a noun) denoting a material object as opposed to an abstract quality, state, or action. ● *n.* (often *attrib.*) a composition of gravel, sand, cement, and water, used for building. ● *v.* **1** *tr.* **a** cover with concrete. **b** embed in concrete. **2** /kónkreet, kong-/ **a** *tr. & intr.* form into a mass; solidify. **b** *tr.* make concrete instead of abstract. □ **in the concrete** esp. *Brit.* in reality or in practice. □□ **con·crete·ly** *adv.* **con·crete·ness** *n.* [F *concret* or L *concretus* past part. of *concrescere* (as COM-, *crescere cret-* GROW)]

con·crete mix·er *n.* = CEMENT MIXER.

con·crete mu·sic *n.* = MUSIQUE CONCRÈTE.

con·crete po·e·try *n.* poetry using unusual typographical layout to enhance the effect on the page.

con·cre·tion /kənkréeshən/ *n.* **1 a** a hard, solid concreted mass. **b** the forming of this by coalescence. **2** *Med.* a stony mass formed within the body. **3** *Geol.* a small, round mass of rock particles embedded in limestone or clay. □□ **con·cre·tion·ar·y** *adj.* [F f. L *concretio* (as CONCRETE)]

con·cre·tize /kónkritiz/ *v.tr.* make concrete instead of abstract. □□ **con·cret·i·za·tion** *n.*

con·cu·bi·nage /konkyō̄obinij/ *n.* **1** the cohabitation of a man and woman not married to each other. **2** the state of being or having a concubine. [ME f. F (as CONCUBINE)]

con·cu·bine /kóngkyəbin/ *n.* **1** a woman who lives with a man as his wife. **2** (among polygamous peoples) a secondary wife. □□ **con·cu·bi·nar·y** /kənkyō̄obineree/ *adj.* [ME f. OF f. L *concubina* (as COM-, *cubina* f. *cubare* lie)]

con·cu·pis·cence /konkyō̄opisəns/ *n.* formal sexual desire. □□ **con·cu·pis·cent** /-sənt/ *adj.* [ME f. OF f. LL *concupiscentia* f. L *concupiscere* begin to desire (as COM-, inceptive f. *cupere* desire)]

con·cur /kənkár/ *v.intr.* (**con·curred, con·cur·ring**) **1** happen together; coincide. **2** (often foll. by *with*) **a** agree in opinion. **b** express agreement. **3** combine together for a cause; act in combination. [L *concurrere* (as COM-, *currere* run)]

con·cur·rent /kənkárənt, –kúr–/ *adj.* **1** (often foll. by *with*) **a** existing or in operation at the same time (*served two concurrent sentences*). **b** existing or acting together. **2** *Geom.* (of three or more lines) meeting at or tending toward one point. **3** agreeing; harmonious. □□ **con·cur·rence** /–rəns/ *n.* **con·cur·rent·ly** *adv.*

con·cuss /kənkús/ *v.tr.* **1** subject to concussion. **2** shake violently. **3** *archaic* intimidate. [L *concutere concuss-* (as COM-, *cutere = quatere* shake)]

con·cus·sion /kənkúshən/ *n.* **1** *Med.* temporary unconsciousness or incapacity due to injury to the head. **2** violent shaking; shock. [L *concussio* (as CONCUSS)]

con·demn /kəndém/ *v.tr.* **1** express utter disapproval of; censure (*was condemned for her irresponsible behavior*). **2 a** find guilty; convict. **b** (usu. foll. by *to*) sentence to (a punishment, esp. death). **c** bring about the conviction of (*his looks condemn him*). **3** pronounce (a building, etc.) unfit for use or habitation. **4** (usu. foll. by *to*) doom or assign (to something unwelcome or painful) (*condemned to spending hours at the kitchen sink*). **5 a** declare (smuggled goods, property, etc.) to be forfeited. **b** pronounce incurable. □□ **con·dem·na·ble** /–démnəbəl/ *adj.* **con·dem·na·tion** /kóndemnáyshən/ *n.* **con·dem·na·to·ry** /–démnətáwree/ *adj.* [ME f. OF *condem(p)ner* f. L *condemnare* (as COM-, *damnare* DAMN)]

con·den·sate /kəndénsayt, kóndən–/ *n.* a substance produced by condensation.

con·den·sa·tion /kóndensáyshən/ *n.* **1** the act of condensing. **2** any condensed material (esp. water on a cold surface). **3** an abridgment. **4** *Chem.* the combination of molecules with the elimination of water or other small molecules. [LL *condensatio* (as CONDENSE)]

con·den·sa·tion trail *n.* = VAPOR TRAIL.

con·dense /kəndéns/ *v.* **1** *tr.* make denser or more concentrated. **2** *tr.* express in fewer words; make concise. **3** *tr. & intr.* reduce or be reduced from a gas or vapor to a liquid or solid. □□ **con·den·sa·ble** *adj.* [F *condenser* or L *condensare* (as COM-, *densus* thick)]

con·densed milk *n.* milk thickened by evaporation and sweetened.

con·dens·er /kəndénsər/ *n.* **1** an apparatus or vessel for condensing vapor. **2** *Electr.* = CAPACITOR. **3** a lens or system of lenses for concentrating light. **4** a person or thing that condenses.

con·de·scend /kóndisénd/ *v.intr.* **1** (usu. foll. by *to* + infin.) be gracious enough (to do a thing) esp. while showing one's sense of dignity or superiority (*condescended to attend the meeting*). **2** (foll. by *to*) behave as if one is on equal terms with (an inferior), usu. while maintaining an attitude of superiority. **3** (as **condescending** *adj.*) patronizing; kind to inferiors. □□ **con·de·scend·ing·ly** *adv.* [ME f. OF *condescendre* f. eccl.L *condescendere* (as COM-, DESCEND)]

con·de·scen·sion /kóndisénshən/ *n.* **1** a patronizing manner. **2** affability toward inferiors. [obs. F f. eccl.L *condescensio* (as CONDESCEND)]

con·dign /kəndín/ *adj.* (of a punishment, etc.) severe and well-deserved. □□ **con·dign·ly** *adv.* [ME f. OF *condigne* f. L *condignus* (as COM-, *dignus* worthy)]

con·di·ment /kóndimənt/ *n.* a seasoning or relish for food. [ME f. L *condimentum* f. *condire* pickle]

con·di·tion /kəndíshən/ *n. & v.* ● *n.* **1** a stipulation; something upon the fulfillment of which something else depends. **2 a** the state of being or fitness of a person or thing (*arrived in bad condition; not in a condition to be used*). **b** an ailment or abnormality (*a heart condition*). **3** (in *pl.*) circumstances, esp. those affecting the functioning or existence of something (*working conditions are good*). **4** *archaic* social rank (*all sorts and conditions of men*). **5** *Gram.* a clause expressing a condition. **6** a requirement that a student must pass an examination, etc., within a stated time to receive credit for a course. **b** the grade indicating this. ● *v.tr.* **1 a** bring into a good or desired state or condition. **b** make fit (esp. dogs or horses). **2** teach or accustom to adopt certain habits, etc. (*conditioned by society*). **3** govern; determine (*his behavior was conditioned by his drunkenness*). **4 a** impose conditions on. **b** be essential to (*the two things condition each other*). **5** test the condition of (textiles, etc.). **6** subject (a student) to a condition. □ **in** (or **out of**) **condition** in good (or bad) condition. **in no condition** to certainly not fit to. **on condition that** with the stipulation that. [ME f. OF *condicion* (n.), *condicionner* (v.) or med.L *condicionare* f. L *condicio –onis* f. *condicere* (as COM-, *dicere* say)]

con·di·tion·al /kəndíshənəl/ *adj. & n.* ● *adj.* **1** (often foll. by *on*) dependent; not absolute; containing a condition or stipulation (*a conditional offer*). **2** *Gram.* (of a clause, mood, etc.) expressing a condition. ● *n.* *Gram.* **1** a conditional clause, etc. **2** the conditional mood. □□ **con·di·tion·al·i·ty** /–nálitee/ *n.* **con·di·tion·al·ly** *adv.* [ME f. OF *condicionel* or f. LL *conditionalis* (as CONDITION)]

con·di·tioned re·flex *n.* an automatic response to a nonnatural stimulus, established by training.

con·di·tion·er /kəndíshənər/ *n.* an agent that brings something into good condition, esp. a substance applied to the hair.

con·do /kóndō/ *n.* (pl. **-dos**) *colloq.* a condominium. [abbr.]

con·do·la·to·ry /kəndólətawree/ *adj.* expressing condolence. [CONDOLE, after *consolatory*, etc.]

con·dole /kəndól/ *v.intr.* (foll. by *with*) express sympathy with a person over a loss, grief, etc. [LL *condolēre* (as COM-, *dolēre* suffer)] ▶Often confused with *console*.

con·do·lence /kəndólləns/ *n.* (often in *pl.*) an expression of sympathy (*sent my condolences*).

con·dom /kóndom/ *n.* a rubber sheath worn on the penis during sexual intercourse as a contraceptive or to prevent infection. [18th c.: orig. unkn.]

con·do·min·i·um /kóndəmíneeəm/ *n.* **1** a building or complex containing apartments that are individually owned. **2** the joint control of a nation's affairs by other nations. [mod.L (as COM-, *dominium* DOMINION)]

con·done /kəndṓn/ *v.tr.* **1** forgive or overlook (an offense or wrong-doing). **2** approve or sanction, usu. reluctantly. **3** (of an action) atone for (an offense); make up for. □□ **con·do·na·tion** /kòndənáyshən/ *n.* **con·don·er** *n.* [L *condonare* (as COM-, *donare* give)]

con·dor /kóndawr/ *n.* **1** (in full **Andean condor**) a large vulture, *Vultur gryphus*, of S. America, having black plumage with a white neck ruff and a fleshy wattle on the forehead. **2** (in full **California condor**) a small vulture, *Gymnogyps californianus*, of California. [Sp. f. Quechua *cuntur*]

con·dot·tie·re /kòndətyáiree, –tyáiray/ *n.* (*pl.* **con·dot·tie·ri** /–tyáiree/) *hist.* a leader or a member of a troop of mercenaries in Italy, etc. [It. f. *condotto* troop under contract (*condotta*) (as CON-DUCT)]

con·duce /kəndóōs, –dyóōs/ *v.intr.* (foll. by *to*) (usu. of an event or attribute) lead or contribute to (a result). [L *conducere conduct-* (as COM-, *ducere duct-* lead)]

con·du·cive /kəndóōsiv, –dyóō–/ *adj.* (often foll. by *to*) contributing or helping (toward something) (*not a conducive atmosphere for negotiation; good health is conducive to happiness*).

con·duct *n. & v.* ● *n.* /kóndukt/ **1** behavior (esp. in its moral aspect). **2** the action or manner of directing or managing (business, war, etc.). **3** *Art* mode of treatment; execution. **4** leading; guidance. ● *v.* /kəndúkt/ **1** *tr.* lead or guide (a person or persons). **2** *tr.* direct or manage (business, etc.). **3** *tr.* (also *absol.*) be the conductor of (an orchestra, choir, etc.). **4** *tr.* transmit (heat, electricity, etc.) by conduction; serve as a channel for. **5** *refl.* behave (*conducted himself appropriately*). □□ **con·duct·i·ble** /kəndúktibəl/ *adj.* **con·duct·i·bil·i·ty** *n.* [ME f. L *conductus* (as COM-, *ducere duct-* lead): (v.) f. OF *conduire* past part. of *conduire*]

con·duct·ance /kəndúktəns/ *n. Physics* the power of a specified material to conduct electricity.

con·duct·ed tour *n.* a tour led by a guide on a fixed itinerary.

con·duc·tion /kəndúkshən/ *n.* **1 a** the transmission of heat through a substance from a region of higher temperature to a region of lower temperature. **b** the transmission of electricity through a substance by the application of an electric field. **2** the transmission of impulses along nerves. **3** the conducting of liquid through a pipe, etc. [F *conduction* or L *conductio* (as CONDUCT)]

con·duc·tive /kəndúktiv/ *adj.* having the property of conducting (esp. heat, electricity, etc.). □□ **con·duc·tive·ly** *adv.*

con·duc·tiv·i·ty /kónduktívitee/ *n.* the conducting power of a specified material.

con·duc·tor /kəndúktər/ *n.* **1** a person who directs the performance of an orchestra or choir, etc. **2** (*fem.* **con·duc·tress** /–tris/) **a** an official in charge of a train. **b** a person who collects fares in a bus, etc. **3** *Physics* **a** a thing that conducts or transmits heat or electricity, esp. regarded in terms of its capacity to do this (*a poor conductor*). **b** = LIGHTNING ROD. **4** a guide or leader. **5** a manager or director. □□ **con·duc·tor·ship** *n.* [ME f. F *conducteur* f. L *conductor* (as CONDUCT)]

con·duc·tus /kəndúktəs/ *n.* (*pl.* **con·duc·ti** /–tī/) a musical composition of the 12th–13th c., with Latin text. [med.L: see CONDUIT]

con·duit /kóndōit, –dyōōit, –dit/ *n.* **1** a channel or pipe for conveying liquids. **2 a** a tube or trough for protecting insulated electric wires. **b** a length or stretch of this. [ME f. OF *conduit* f. med.L *conductus* CONDUCT *n.*]

con·dyle /kóndil, –d'l/ *n. Anat.* a rounded process at the end of some bones, forming an articulation with another bone. □□ **con·dy·lar** *adj.* **con·dy·loid** *adj.* [F f. L *condylus* f. Gk *kondulos* knuckle]

cone /kōn/ *n. & v.* ● *n.* **1** a solid figure with a circular (or other curved) plane base, tapering to a point. **2** a thing of a similar shape, solid or hollow, e.g., as used to mark off areas of roads. **3** the dry fruit of a conifer. **4** a cone-shaped wafer for holding ice cream. **5** any of the minute cone-shaped structures in the retina. **6** a conical mountain esp. of volcanic origin. **7** (in full **cone shell**) any marine gastropod mollusk of the family Conidae. **8** *Pottery* a ceramic pyramid, melting at a known temperature, used to indicate the temperature of a kiln. ● *v.tr.* **1** shape like a cone. **2** (foll. by *off*) *Brit.* mark off (a road, etc.) with cones. [F *cône* f. L *conus* f. Gk *kōnos*]

Con·es·to·ga /konəstṓgə/ *n.* **1** a N. American people native to the northeastern US. **2** a member of this people.

co·ney /kṓnee/ *n.* (also **co·ny**) (*pl.* **·neys** or **·nies**) **1 a** a rabbit. **b** its fur. **2** *Bibl.* a hyrax. [ME *cunin(g)* f. AF *coning*, OF *conin*, f. L *cuniculus*]

con·fab /kónfab/ *n. & v. colloq.* ● *n.* = confabulation (see CONFABU-LATE). ● *v.intr.* (**con·fabbed, con·fab·bing**) = CONFABULATE. [abbr.]

con·fab·u·late /kənfábyəlayt/ *v.intr.* **1** converse; chat. **2** *Psychol.* fabricate imaginary experiences as compensation for the loss of memory. □□ **con·fab·u·la·tion** /–láyshən/ *n.* **con·fab·u·la·to·ry** /–lətáwree/ *adj.* [L *confabulari* (as COM-, *fabulari* f. *fabula* tale)]

con·fect /kənfékt/ *v.tr. literary* make by putting together ingredients. [L *conficere confect-* put together (as COM-, *facere* make)]

con·fec·tion /kənfékshən/ *n.* **1** a dish or delicacy made with sweet ingredients. **2** mixing; compounding. **3** a fashionable or elaborate

article of women's dress. □□ **con·fec·tion·ar·y** *adj.* (in sense 1). [ME f. OF f. L *confectio –onis* (as CONFECT)]

con·fec·tion·er /kənfékshənər/ *n.* a maker or retailer of confectionery.

con·fec·tion·ers' sug·ar *n.* very fine powdered sugar with cornstarch added, used for making icings and candy.

con·fec·tion·er·y /kənfékshəneree/ *n.* candy and other confections.

con·fed·er·a·cy /kənfédərəsee/ *n.* (*pl.* **·cies**) **1** a league or alliance, esp. of confederate nations. **2** a league for an unlawful or evil purpose; a conspiracy. **3** the condition or fact of being confederate; alliance; conspiracy. **4** (**the Confederacy**) = CONFEDERATE STATES OF AMERICA. [ME, AF, OF *confederacie* (as CONFEDERATE)]

con·fed·er·ate *adj., n., & v.* ● *adj.* /kənfédərət/ esp. *Polit.* allied; joined by an agreement or treaty. ● *n.* /kənfédərət/ **1** an ally, esp. (in a bad sense) an accomplice. **2** (**Confederate**) a supporter of the Confederate States of America. ● *v.* /kənfédərayt/ (often foll. by *with*) **1** *tr.* bring (a person, state, or oneself) into alliance. **2** *intr.* come into alliance. [LL *confoederatus* (as COM-, FEDERATE)]

Con·fed·er·ate States of A·mer·i·ca *n.* the eleven Southern states that seceded from the US in 1860–61.

con·fed·er·a·tion /kənfédəráyshən/ *n.* **1** a union or alliance of nations, etc. **2** the act or an instance of confederating; the state of being confederated. [F *confédération* (as CONFEDERATE)]

con·fer /kənfór/ *v.* (**con·ferred, con·fer·ring**) **1** *tr.* (often foll. by *on, upon*) grant or bestow (a title, degree, favor, etc.). **2** *intr.* (often foll. by *with*) converse; consult. □□ **con·fer·ra·ble** *adj.* [L *conferre* (as COM-, *ferre* bring)]

con·fer·ee /kónfəree/ *n.* **1** a person on whom something is conferred. **2** a participant in a conference.

con·fer·ence /kónfərəns, –frəns/ *n.* **1** consultation; discussion. **2** a meeting for discussion, esp. a regular one held by an association or organization. **3** an annual assembly of the Methodist Church. **4** an association in commerce, sports, etc. **5** the linking of several telephones, computer terminals, etc., so that each user may communicate with the others simultaneously. □ **in conference** engaged in discussion. □□ **con·fer·en·tial** /kónfərénshəl/ *adj.* [F *conférence* or med.L *conferentia* (as CONFER)]

con·fer·ence call *n.* a telephone call in which three or more people are connected.

con·fer·ment /kənfórmənt/ *n.* **1** the conferring of a degree, honor, etc. **2** an instance of this.

con·fer·ral /kənfórəl/ *n.* esp. *US* = CONFERMENT.

con·fess /kənfés/ *v.* **1 a** *tr.* (also *absol.*) acknowledge or admit (a fault, wrongdoing, etc.). **b** *intr.* (foll. by *to*) admit to (*confessed to having lied*). **2** *tr.* admit reluctantly (*confessed it would be difficult*). **3 a** *tr.* (also *absol.*) declare (one's sins) to a priest. **b** *tr.* (of a priest) hear the confession of. **c** *refl.* declare one's sins to a priest. [ME f. OF *confesser* f. Rmc f. L *confessus* past part. of *confitēri* (as COM-, *fatēri* declare, avow)]

con·fes·sant /kənfésənt/ *n.* a person who confesses to a priest.

con·fess·ed·ly /kənfésidlee/ *adv.* by one's own or general admission.

con·fes·sion /kənféshən/ *n.* **1 a** confessing or acknowledgment of a fault, wrongdoing, a sin to a priest, etc. **b** an instance of this. **c** a thing confessed. **2** (in full **confession of faith**) **a** a declaration of one's religious beliefs. **b** a statement of one's principles. □□ **con·fes·sion·ar·y** *adj.* [ME f. OF f. L *confessio –onis* (as CONFESS)]

con·fes·sion·al /kənféshənəl/ *n. & adj.* ● *n.* an enclosed stall in a church in which a priest hears confessions. ● *adj.* **1** of or relating to confession. **2** denominational. [F f. It. *confessionale* f. med.L, neut. of *confessionalis* (as CONFESSION)]

con·fes·sor /kənfésər/ *n.* **1** a person who makes a confession. **2** a priest who hears confessions and gives spiritual counsel. **3** a person who avows a religion in the face of its suppression, but does not suffer martyrdom. [ME f. AF *confessur*, OF *–our*, f. eccl.L *confessor* (as CONFESS)]

con·fet·ti /kənfétee/ *n.* small bits of colored paper thrown during celebrations, etc. [It., = sweetmeats f. L (as COMFIT)]

con·fi·dant /kónfidánt, –daánt/ *n.* (*fem.* **con·fi·dante** *pronunc.* same) a person trusted with knowledge of one's private affairs. [18th-c. for earlier CONFIDENT *n.*, prob. to represent the pronunc. of F *confidente* (as CONFIDE)]

con·fide /kənfíd/ *v.* **1** *tr.* (usu. foll. by *to*) tell (a secret, etc.) in confidence. **2** *tr.* (foll. by *to*) entrust (an object of care, a task, etc.) to. **3** *intr.* (foll. by *in*) **a** have trust or confidence in. **b** talk confidentially to. □□ **con·fid·ing·ly** *adv.* [L *confidere* (as COM-, *fidere* trust)]

con·fi·dence /kónfidəns/ *n.* **1** firm trust (*have confidence in his ability*). **2 a** a feeling of reliance or certainty. **b** a sense of self-reliance; boldness. **3 a** something told confidentially. **b** the telling of private matters with mutual trust. □ **in confidence** as a secret. **in a person's confidence** trusted with a person's secrets. **take into one's confidence** confide in. [ME f. L *confidentia* (as CONFIDE)]

con·fi·dence game *n.* (*Brit.* **con·fi·dence trick**) a swindle in which the victim is persuaded to trust the swindler in some way.

con·fi·dence man *n.* a man who robs by means of a confidence game.

con·fi·dent /kónfid'nt/ *adj. & n.* • *adj.* **1** feeling or showing confidence; self-assured; bold (*spoke with a confident air*). **2** (often foll. by *of*, or *that* + clause) assured; trusting (*confident of your support*; *confident that she will come*). • *n.* *archaic* = CONFIDANT. □□ **con·fi·dent·ly** *adv.* [F f. It. *confidente* (as CONFIDE)]

con·fi·den·tial /kónfidénshəl/ *adj.* **1** spoken or written in confidence. **2** entrusted with secrets (*a confidential secretary*). **3** confiding. □□ **con·fi·den·ti·al·i·ty** /‑sheeálitee/ *n.* **con·fi·den·tial·ly** *adv.*

con·fig·u·ra·tion /kənfigyəráyshən/ *n.* **1 a** an arrangement of parts or elements in a particular form or figure. **b** the form, shape, or figure resulting from such an arrangement. **2** *Astron. & Astrol.* the relative position of planets, etc. **3** *Psychol.* = GESTALT. **4** *Physics* the distribution of electrons among the energy levels of an atom, or of nucleons among the energy levels of a nucleus, as specified by quantum numbers. **5** *Chem.* the fixed three-dimensional relationship of the atoms in a molecule. **6** *Computing* **a** the interrelating or interconnecting of a computer system or elements of it so that it will accommodate a particular specification. **b** an instance of this. □□ **con·fig·u·ra·tion·al** *adj.* **con·fig·ure** *v.tr.* (in senses 1, 2, 6). [LL *configuratio* f. L *configurare* (as COM-, *figurare* fashion)]

con·fine *v. & n.* • *v.tr.* /kənfín/ (often foll. by *in*, *to*, *within*) **1** keep or restrict (within certain limits, etc.). **2** hold captive; imprison. • *n.* /kónfín/ (usu. in *pl.*) a limit or boundary (*within the confines of the town*). □ **be confined** be in childbirth. [(v.) f. F *confiner*, (n.) ME f. F *confins* (pl.), f. L *confinia* (as COM-, *finia* neut. pl. f. *finis* end, limit)]

con·fine·ment /kənfínmənt/ *n.* **1** the act or an instance of confining; the state of being confined. **2** the time of a woman's giving birth.

con·firm /kənfərm/ *v.tr.* **1** provide support for the truth or correctness of; make definitely valid (*confirmed my suspicions; confirmed his arrival time*). **2** ratify (a treaty, possession, title, etc.); make formally valid. **3** (foll. by *in*) encourage (a person) in (an opinion, etc.). **4** establish more firmly (power, possession, etc.). **5** administer the religious rite of confirmation to. □□ **con·firm·a·tive** *adj.* **con·firm·a·to·ry** *adj.* [ME f. OF *confermer* f. L *confirmare* (as COM-, FIRM¹)]

con·fir·mand /kónfərmand/ *n.* *Eccl.* a person who is to be or has just been confirmed.

con·fir·ma·tion /kónfərmáyshən/ *n.* **1 a** the act or an instance of confirming; the state of being confirmed. **b** an instance of this. **2 a** a religious rite confirming a baptized person, esp. at the age of discretion, as a member of the Christian Church. **b** a ceremony of confirming persons of about this age in the Jewish faith. [ME f. OF f. L *confirmatio –onis* (as CONFIRM)]

con·firmed /kənfərmd/ *adj.* firmly settled in some habit or condition (*confirmed in her ways; a confirmed bachelor*).

con·fis·cate /kónfiskayt/ *v.tr.* **1** take or seize by authority. **2** appropriate to the public treasury (by way of a penalty). □□ **con·fis·ca·ble** /kənfískəbəl/ *adj.* **con·fis·ca·tion** /‑káyshən/ *n.* **con·fis·ca·tor** *n.* **con·fis·ca·to·ry** /kənfiskətáwree/ *adj.* [L *confiscare* (as COM-, *fiscare* f. *fiscus* treasury)]

con·fla·gra·tion /kónfləgráyshən/ *n.* a great and destructive fire. [L *conflagratio* f. *conflagrare* (as COM-, *flagrare* blaze)]

con·flate /kənfláyt/ *v.tr.* blend or fuse together (esp. two variant texts into one). □□ **con·fla·tion** /‑fláyshən/ *n.* [L *conflare* (as COM-, *flare* blow)]

con·flict *n. & v.* • *n.* /kónflikt/ **1 a** a state of opposition or hostilities. **b** a fight or struggle. **2** (often foll. by *of*) **a** the clashing of opposed principles, etc. **b** an instance of this. **3** *Psychol.* **a** the opposition of incompatible wishes or needs in a person. **b** an instance of this. **c** the distress resulting from this. • *v.intr.* /kənflíkt/ **1** clash; be incompatible. **2** (often foll. by *with*) struggle or contend. **3** (as **conflicting** *adj.*) contradictory. □ **in conflict** conflicting. □□ **con·flic·tion** /‑flíkshən/ *n.* **con·flic·tu·al** /kənflíkchōōəl/ *adj.* [ME f. L *configere* *conflict-* (as COM-, *fligere* strike)]

con·flu·ence /kónflōōəns/ *n.* **1** a place where two rivers meet. **2 a** a coming together. **b** a crowd of people. [L *confluere* (as COM-, *fluere* flow)]

con·flu·ent /kónflōōənt/ *adj. & n.* • *adj.* flowing together; uniting. • *n.* a stream joining another.

con·flux /kónfluks/ *n.* = CONFLUENCE. [LL *confluxus* (as CONFLUENCE)]

con·form /kənfáwrm/ *v.* **1** *intr.* comply with rules or general custom. **2** (often foll. by *to*) be or make accordant or suitable. **3** *tr.* (often foll. by *to*) form according to a pattern; make similar. **4** *intr.* (foll. by *to*, *with*) comply with; be in accordance with. □□ **con·form·er** *n.* [ME f. OF *conformer* f. L *conformare* (as COM-, FORM)]

con·form·a·ble /kənfáwrməbəl/ *adj.* **1** (often foll. by *to*) similar. **2** (often foll. by *with*) consistent. **3** (often foll. by *to*) adapted. **4** tractable; submissive. **5** *Geol.* (of strata in contact) lying in the same direction. □□ **con·form·a·bil·i·ty** *n.* **con·form·a·bly** *adv.* [med.L *conformabilis* (as CONFORM)]

con·for·mal /kənfáwrməl/ *adj.* (of a map) showing any small area in its correct shape. □□ **con·for·mal·ly** *adv.* [LL *conformalis* (as CONFORM)]

con·form·ance /kənfáwrməns/ *n.* (often foll. by *to*, *with*) = CONFORMITY 1, 2.

con·for·ma·tion /kónfawrmáyshən/ *n.* **1** the way in which a thing is formed; shape; structure. **2** (often foll. by *to*) adjustment in form or character; adaptation. **3** *Chem.* any spatial arrangement of atoms in a molecule from the rotation of part of the molecule about a single bond. [L *conformatio* (as CONFORM)]

con·form·ist /kənfáwrmist/ *n. & adj.* • *n.* **1** a person who conforms to an established practice; a conventional person. **2** *Brit.* a person who conforms to the practices of the Church of England. • *adj.* (of a person) conforming to established practices; conventional. □□ **con·form·ism** *n.*

con·form·i·ty /kənfáwrmitee/ *n.* **1** (often foll. by *to*, *with*) action or behavior in accordance with established practice; compliance. **2** (often foll. by *to*, *with*) correspondence in form or manner; likeness; agreement. **3** *Brit.* compliance with the practices of the Church of England. [ME f. OF *conformité* or LL *conformitas* (as CONFORM)]

con·found /kənfównd/ *v. & int.* • *v.tr.* **1** throw into perplexity or confusion. **2** mix up; confuse (in one's mind). **3** *archaic* defeat; overthrow. • *int.* expressing annoyance (*confound you!*). [ME f. AF *conf(o)undre*, OF *confondre* f. L *confundere* mix up (as COM-, *fundere fus-* pour)]

con·found·ed /kənfówndid/ *adj.* *colloq.* damned (*a confounded nuisance!*). □□ **con·found·ed·ly** *adv.*

con·fra·ter·ni·ty /kónfrətérnitee/ *n.* (*pl.* **·ties**) a brotherhood, esp. religious or charitable. [ME f. OF *confraternité* f. med.L *confraternitas* (as COM-, FRATERNITY)]

con·frere /kónfrair/ *n.* (also **con·frère**) a fellow member of a profession, scientific body, etc. [ME f. OF f. med.L *confrater* (as COM-, *frater* brother)]

con·front /kənfrúnt/ *v.tr.* **1 a** face in hostility or defiance. **b** face up to and deal with (a problem, difficulty, etc.). **2** (of a difficulty, etc.) present itself to (*countless obstacles confronted us*). **3** (foll. by *with*) **a** bring (a person) face to face with (a circumstance, etc., esp. by way of accusation (*confronted them with the evidence*). **b** set (a thing) face to face with (another) for comparison. **4** meet or stand facing. □□ **con·fron·ta·tion** /kónfruntáyshən/ *n.* **con·fron·ta·tion·al** /kónfruntáyshənəl/ *adj.* [F *confronter* f. med.L *confrontare* (as COM-, *frontare* f. *frons frontis* face)]

Con·fu·cian /kənfyōōshən/ *adj. & n.* • *adj.* of or relating to Confucius, Chinese philosopher d. 479 BC, or his philosophy. • *n.* a follower of Confucius. □□ **Con·fu·cian·ism** *n.* **Con·fu·cian·ist** *n.* [*Confucius*, Latinization of *Kongfuze* Kong the master]

con·fus·a·ble /kənfyōōzəbəl/ *adj.* that is able or liable to be confused. □□ **con·fus·a·bil·i·ty** /‑bilitee/ *n.*

con·fuse /kənfyōōz/ *v.tr.* **1 a** disconcert; perplex; bewilder. **b** embarrass. **2** mix up in the mind; mistake (one for another). **3** make indistinct (*that point confuses the issue*). **4** (as **confused** *adj.*) mentally decrepit. **b** puzzled; perplexed. **5** (often as **confused** *adj.*) make muddled or disorganized; throw into disorder (*a confused jumble of clothes*). □□ **con·fus·ed·ly** /kənfyōōzidlee/ *adv.* **con·fus·ing** *adj.* **con·fus·ing·ly** *adv.* [19th-c. back-form. f. *confused* (14th c.) f. OF *confus* f. L *confusus*: see CONFOUND]

con·fu·sion /kənfyōōzhən/ *n.* **1 a** the act of confusing (*the confusion of fact and fiction*). **b** an instance of this; a misunderstanding (*confusions arise from a lack of communication*). **2 a** the result of confusing; a confused state; embarrassment; disorder (*thrown into confusion by his words; trampled in the confusion of battle*). **b** (foll. by *of*) a disorderly jumble (*a confusion of ideas*). **3 a** civil commotion (*confusion broke out at the announcement*). **b** an instance of this. [ME f. OF *confusion* or L *confusio* (as CONFUSE)]

con·fute /kənfyōōt/ *v.tr.* **1** prove (a person) to be in error. **2** prove (an argument) to be false. □□ **con·fu·ta·tion** /kónfyootáyshən/ *n.* [L *confutare* restrain]

Cong. *abbr.* **1** Congress. **2** Congressional. **3** Congregational.

con·ga /kónggə/ *n. & v.* **1** a Latin American dance of African origin, usu. with several persons in a single line, one behind the other. **2** (also **con·ga drum**) a tall, narrow, low-toned drum beaten with the hands. • *v.intr.* (**con·gas**, **con·gaed** /‑gəd/, **con·ga·ing** /‑gəing/) perform the conga. [Amer. Sp. f. Sp. *conga* (fem.) of the Congo]

con·gé /kónzhay, kawnzháy/ *n.* an unceremonious dismissal; leave-taking. [F: earlier *congee*, ME f. OF *congié* f. L *commeatus* leave of absence f. *commeare* go and come (as COM-, *meare* go): now usu. treated as mod. F]

con·geal /kənjéel/ *v.tr. & intr.* **1** make or become semisolid by cooling. **2** (of blood, etc.) coagulate. □□ **con·geal·a·ble** *adj.* **con·geal·ment** *n.* [ME f. OF *congeler* f. L *congelare* (as COM-, *gelare* f. *gelu* frost)]

con·ge·la·tion /kónjiláyshən/ *n.* **1** the process of congealing. **2** a congealed state. **3** a congealed substance. [ME f. OF *congelation* or L *congelatio* (as CONGEAL)]

con•ge•ner /kónjənər/ *n.* a thing or person of the same kind or category as another, esp. animals or plants of a specified genus (*the goldfinch is a congener of the canary*). [L (as CON-, GENUS)]

con•ge•ner•ic /kónjinérik/ *adj.* **1** of the same genus, kind, or race. **2** allied in nature or origin; akin. □□ **con•gen•er•ous** /kənjénərəs/ *adj.*

con•gen•ial /kənjéenyəl/ *adj.* **1** (often foll. by *with, to*) (of a person, character, etc.) pleasant because akin to oneself in temperament or interests. **2** (often foll. by *to*) suited or agreeable. □□ **con•ge•ni•al•i•ty** /–jéeneeálitee/ *n.* **con•gen•ial•ly** *adv.* [CON- + GENIAL[1]]

con•gen•i•tal /kənjénitəl/ *adj.* **1** (esp. of a disease, defect, etc.) existing from birth. **2** that is (or as if) such from birth (*a congenital liar*). □□ **con•gen•i•tal•ly** *adv.* [L *congenitus* (as COM-, *genitus* past part. of *gigno* beget)]

con•ger /kónggər/ *n.* (in full **conger eel**) any large marine eel of the family Congridae. [ME f. OF *congre* f. L *conger, congrus*, f. Gk *goggros*]

con•ge•ries /kənjéereez, kónjə–/ *n.* (*pl.* same) a disorderly collection; a mass or heap. [L, formed as CONGEST]

con•gest /kənjést/ *v.tr.* (esp. as **congested** *adj.*) affect with congestion; obstruct, block (*congested streets; congested lungs*). □□ **con•ges•tive** *adj.* [L *congerere congest-* (as COM-, *gerere* bring)]

con•ges•tion /kənjés-chən/ *n.* abnormal accumulation, crowding, or obstruction, esp. of traffic, etc. or of blood or mucus in a part of the body. [F f. L *congestio –onis* (as CONGEST)]

con•glom•er•ate *adj., n., & v.* •*adj.* /kənglómərət/ **1** gathered into a rounded mass. **2** *Geol.* (of rock) made up of small stones held together (cf. AGGLOMERATE). •*n.* /kənglómərət/ **1** a number of things or parts forming a heterogeneous mass. **2** a group or corporation formed by the merging of separate and diverse firms. **3** *Geol.* conglomerate rock. •*v.tr. & intr.* /kənglómərayt/ collect into a coherent mass. □□ **con•glom•er•a•tion** /–ráyshən/ *n.* [L *conglomeratus* past part. of *conglomerare* (as COM-, *glomerare* f. *glomus –eris* ball)]

Con•go•lese /kónggəléez/ *adj. & n.* •*adj.* of or relating to the Republic of the Congo in Central Africa, or the region surrounding the Congo River. •*n.* a native of either of these regions. [F *congolais*]

con•gou /kónggoo, –gó/ *n.* a variety of black China tea. [Chin. dial. *kung hu tē* tea labored for]

con•grats /kəngráts/ *n.pl. & int. colloq.* congratulations. [abbr.]

con•grat•u•late /kəngráchəlayt, –gráj–, kəng–/ *v.tr. & refl.* (often foll. by *on, upon*) **1** *tr.* express pleasure at the happiness or good fortune or excellence of (a person) (*congratulated them on their success*). **2** *refl.* think oneself fortunate or clever. □□ **con•grat•u•lant** *adj. & n.* **con•grat•u•la•tor** *n.* **con•grat•u•la•to•ry** /–lətáwree/ *adj.* [L *congratulari* (as COM-, *gratulari* show joy f. *gratus* pleasing)]

con•grat•u•la•tion /kəngráchəláyshən –gráj–, kəng–/ *n.* **1** congratulating. **2** (also as *int.*; usu. in *pl.*) an expression of this (*congratulations on winning!*). [L *congratulatio* (as CONGRATULATE)]

con•gre•gant /kónggrigənt/ *n.* a member of a congregation. [L *congregare* (as CONGREGATE)]

con•gre•gate /kónggrigayt/ *v.intr. & tr.* collect or gather into a crowd or mass. [ME f. L *congregare* (as COM-, *gregare* f. *grex gregis* flock)]

con•gre•ga•tion /kónggrigáyshən/ *n.* **1** the process of congregating; collection into a crowd or mass. **2** a crowd or mass gathered together. **3 a** a body assembled for religious worship. **b** a body of persons regularly attending a particular church, etc. **c** *RC Ch.* a body of persons obeying a common religious rule. **d** *RC Ch.* any of several permanent committees of the Roman Catholic College of Cardinals. **4** (**Congregation**) *Brit.* (in some universities) a general assembly of resident senior members. [ME f. OF *congregation* or L *congregatio* (as CONGREGATE)]

con•gre•ga•tion•al /kónggrigáyshənəl/ *adj.* **1** of a congregation. **2** (**Congregational**) of or adhering to Congregationalism.

Con•gre•ga•tion•al•ism /kónggrigáyshənəlizəm/ *n.* a system of ecclesiastical organization whereby individual churches are largely self-governing. □□ **Con•gre•ga•tion•al•ist** *n.* **Con•gre•ga•tion•al•ize** *v.tr.*

con•gress /kónggris/ *n.* **1** a formal meeting of delegates for discussion. **2** (**Congress**) a national legislative body, esp. that of the US. **3** a society or organization. **4** coming together; meeting. □□ **con•gres•sion•al** /kəngréshən'l/ *adj.* [L *congressus* f. *congredi* (as COM-, *gradi* walk)]

Con•gres•sion•al Med•al of Hon•or *n.* = *Medal of Honor.*

con•gress•man /kónggrismən/ *n.* (*pl.* •**men**; *fem.* **con•gress•wom•an**, *pl.* •**wom•en**) a member of the US Congress, esp. of the US House of Representatives.

con•gru•ence /kónggrōōəns, kəngrōō–/ *n.* (also **con•gru•en•cy** /–ənsee/) **1** agreement; consistency. **2** *Geom.* the state of being congruent. [ME f. L *congruentia* (as CONGRUENT)]

con•gru•ent /kónggrōōənt, kəngrōō–/ *adj.* **1** (often foll. by *with*) suitable; agreeing. **2** *Geom.* (of figures) coinciding exactly when superimposed. □□ **con•gru•ent•ly** *adv.* [ME f. L *congruere* agree]

con•gru•ous /kónggrōōəs/ *adj.* (often foll. by *with*) suitable; agree-

ing; fitting. □□ **con•gru•i•ty** /–grŏŏitee/ *n.* **con•gru•ous•ly** *adv.* [L *congruus* (as CONGRUENT)]

con•ic /kónik/ *adj. & n.* •*adj.* of a cone. •*n.* **1** a conic section. **2** (in *pl.*) the study of conic sections. [mod.L *conicus* f. Gk *kōnikos* (as CONE)]

con•i•cal /kónikəl/ *adj.* cone-shaped. □□ **con•i•cal•ly** *adv.*

con•ic sec•tion *n.* a figure formed by the intersection of a cone and a plane.

co•nid•i•um /kənídeeəm/ *n.* (*pl.* **co•nid•i•a** /–deeə/) a spore produced asexually by various fungi. [mod.L dimin. f. Gk *konis* dust]

co•ni•fer /kónifər, kó–/ *n.* any evergreen tree of a group usu. bearing cones, including pines, yews, cedars, and redwoods. □□ **con•if•er•ous** /kənífərəs/ *adj.* [L (as CONE, –FEROUS)]

co•ni•form /kónifawrm/ *adj.* cone-shaped. [L *conus* cone + –FORM]

co•ni•ine /kónee-een/ *n.* a poisonous alkaloid found in hemlock that paralyzes the nerves. [*conium* f. Gk *kōneion* hemlock]

conj. *abbr.* conjunction.

con•jec•tur•al /kənjékchərəl/ *adj.* based on, involving, or given to conjecture. □□ **con•jec•tur•al•ly** *adv.* [F f. L *conjecturalis* (as CONJECTURE)]

con•jec•ture /kənjékchər/ *n. & v.* •*n.* **1 a** the formation of an opinion on incomplete information; guessing. **b** an opinion or conclusion reached in this way. **2 a** (in textual criticism) the guessing of a reading not in the text. **b** a proposed reading. •*v.* **1** *tr. & intr.* guess. **2** *tr.* (in textual criticism) propose (a reading). □□ **con•jec•tur•a•ble** *adj.* [ME f. OF *conjecture* or L *conjectura* f. *conjicere* (as COM-, *jacere* throw)]

con•join /kənjóyn/ *v.tr. & intr.* join; combine. [ME f. OF *conjoign-* pres. stem of *conjoindre* f. L *conjungere* (as COM-, *jungere junct-* join)]

con•joint /kənjóynt/ *adj.* associated, conjoined. □□ **con•joint•ly** *adv.* [ME f. OF, past part. (as CONJOIN)]

con•ju•gal /kónjəgəl/ *adj.* of marriage or the relation between husband and wife. □□ **con•ju•gal•i•ty** /–gálitee/ *n.* **con•ju•gal•ly** *adv.* [L *conjugalis* f. *conjux* consort (as COM-, *–jux –jugis* f. root of *jungere* join)]

con•ju•gal rights *n.* those rights (esp. to sexual relations) regarded as exercisable in law by each partner in a marriage.

con•ju•gate *v., adj., & n.* •*v.* /kónjəgayt/ **1** *tr. Gram.* give the different forms of (a verb). **2** *intr.* **a** unite sexually. **b** (of gametes) become fused. **3** *intr. Chem.* (of protein) combine with nonprotein. •*adj.* /kónjəgət, –gayt/ **1** joined together, esp. as a pair. **2** *Gram.* derived from the same root. **3** *Biol.* fused. **4** *Chem.* (of an acid or base) related by loss or gain of an electron. **5** *Math.* joined in a reciprocal relation, esp. having the same real parts, and equal magnitudes but opposite signs of imaginary parts. •*n.* /kónjəgət, –gayt/ a conjugate word or thing. □□ **con•ju•gate•ly** *adv.* [L *conjugare* yoke together (as COM-, *jugare* f. *jugum* yoke)]

con•ju•ga•tion /kónjəgáyshən/ *n.* **1** *Gram.* a system of verbal inflection. **2 a** the act or an instance of conjugating. **b** an instance of this. **3** *Biol.* the fusion of two gametes in reproduction. □□ **con•ju•ga•tion•al** *adj.* [L *conjugatio* (as CONJUGATE)]

con•junct /kənjúngkt/ *adj.* joined together; combined; associated. [ME f. L *conjunctus* (as CONJOIN)]

con•junc•tion /kənjúngkshən/ *n.* **1 a** the action of joining; the condition of being joined. **b** an instance of this. **2** *Gram.* a word used to connect clauses or sentences or words in the same clause (e.g., *and, but, if*). **3 a** a combination (of events or circumstances). **b** a number of associated persons or things. **4** *Astron. & Astrol.* the alignment of two bodies in the solar system so that they have the same longitude as seen from the earth. ▪ **in conjunction with** together with. □□ **con•junc•tion•al** *adj.* [ME f. OF *conjonction* f. L *conjunctio –onis* (as CONJUNCT)]

GRAMMAR TIP conjunction

Conjunctions join together words or word groups. There are **coordinating, correlative**, and **subordinating** conjunctions.

Coordinating conjunctions are the simplest, linking two words or word groups that are grammatically the same ("she bought meat *and* potatoes."). Other coordinating conjunctions are *but* and *yet*. When two coordinating conjunctions are used together, they are called *correlative conjunctions* ("*Both* Henry *and* Bill are gone"). Other correlative conjunctions are *either . . . or, though . . . yet.*

Subordinating conjunctions connect a subordinate clause to the main clause of a sentence. In the following instance, the subordinating conjunction *because* introduces the subordinate clause ("Mary was happy *because* she found her mother at home."). Other subordinating conjunctions include *as, before, if, since*, and *unless.*

---

con•junc•ti•va /kónjungktívə, kənjúngktivə/ *n.* (*pl.* **con•junc•ti•vas** or **con•junc•ti•vae** /–vee/) *Anat.* the mucous membrane that covers the front of the eye and lines the inside of the eyelids. □□ **con·junc·ti·val** *adj.* [med.L (*membrana*) *conjunctiva* (as CONJUNCTIVE)]

con·junc·tive /kənjúngktiv/ *adj. & n.* • *adj.* **1** serving to join; connective. **2** *Gram.* of the nature of a conjunction. • *n. Gram.* a conjunctive word. □□ **con·junc·tive·ly** *adv.* [LL *conjunctivus* (as CONJOIN)]

con·junc·ti·vi·tis /kənjúngktivítis/ *n.* inflammation of the conjunctiva.

con·junc·ture /kənjúngkchər/ *n.* a combination of events; a state of affairs. [obs. F f. It. *congiuntura* (as CONJOIN)]

con·jur·a·tion /kónjəráyshən/ *n.* an incantation; a magic spell. [ME f. OF f. L *conjuratio* –*onis* (as CONJURE)]

con·jure /kónjər/ *v.* **1** *tr.* call upon (a spirit) to appear. **2** *tr.* (usu. foll. by *out of, away, to,* etc.) cause to appear or disappear as if by magic (*conjured a rabbit out of a hat; conjured them to a desert island; his pain was conjured away*). **3** *intr.* esp. *Brit.* perform tricks that are seemingly magical, esp. by rapid movements of the hands. **4** *intr.* perform marvels. **5** *tr.* /kənjóor/ (often foll. by *to* + infin.) appeal solemnly to (a person). □ **conjure up 1** bring into existence or cause to appear as if by magic. **2** cause to appear to the eye or mind; evoke. [ME f. OF *conjurer* plot, exorcise f. L *conjurare* band together by oath (as COM-, *jurare* swear)]

con·jur·er /kónjərər, kún–/ *n.* (also **con·jur·or**) **1** a person who conjures. **2** *Brit.* = MAGICIAN 2. [CONJURE + –ER[1] & AF *conjurour* (OF –*eor*) f. med.L *conjurator* (as CONJURE)]

conk[1] /kongk/ *v.intr.* (usu. foll. by *out*) *colloq.* **1** (of a machine, etc.) break down. **2** (of a person) become exhausted and give up; faint; die. [20th c.: orig. unkn.]

conk[2] /kongk/ *v. tr. sl.* hit on the head, etc. [19th c.: perh. = CONCH]

conk·er /kóngkər/ *n. Brit.* **1** the hard fruit of a horse chestnut. **2** (in *pl.*) *Brit.* a children's game played with conkers on strings, one hit against another to try to break it. [dial. *conker* snail shell (orig. used in the game), assoc. with CONQUER]

con man *n.* = CONFIDENCE MAN.

con mo·to /kón mótō, káwn/ *adv. Mus.* with movement. [It., = with movement]

Conn. *abbr.* Connecticut.

conn /kon/ *n. & v. Naut.* • *v.tr.* direct the steering of (a ship). • *n.* **1** the act of conning. **2** the responsibility or station of one who conns. [app. weakened form of obs. *cond, condie,* f. F *conduire* f. L *conducere* CONDUCT]

con·nate /kónayt/ *adj.* **1** existing in a person or thing from birth; innate. **2** formed at the same time. **3** allied; congenial. **4** *Bot.* (of organs) congenitally united so as to form one part. **5** *Geol.* (of water) trapped in sedimentary rock during its deposition. [LL *connatus* past part. of *connasci* (as COM-, *nasci* be born)]

con·nat·u·ral /kənáchərəl/ *adj.* **1** (often foll. by *to*) innate; belonging naturally. **2** of like nature. □□ **con·nat·u·ral·ly** *adv.* [LL *connaturalis* (as COM-, NATURAL)]

con·nect /kənékt/ *v.* **1 a** *tr.* (often foll. by *to, with*) join (one thing with another) (*connected the hose to the faucet*). **b** *tr.* join (two things) (*a track connected the two villages*). **c** *intr.* be joined or joinable (*the two parts do not connect*). **2** *tr.* (often foll. by *with*) associate mentally or practically (*did not connect the two ideas; never connected her with the theater*). **3** *intr.* (foll. by *with*) (of a train, etc.) be synchronized at its destination with another train, etc., so that passengers can transfer (*the train connects with the boat*). **4** *tr.* put into communication by telephone. **5 a** *tr.* (usu. in *passive*; foll. by *with*) unite or associate with others in relationships, etc. (*am connected with the royal family*). **b** *intr.* form a logical sequence; be meaningful. **6** *intr. colloq.* hit or strike effectively. □□ **con·nect·a·ble** *adj.* **con·nect·or** *n.* [L *connectere connex–* (as COM-, *nectere* bind)]

con·nect·ed /kənéktid/ *adj.* **1** joined in sequence. **2** (of ideas, etc.) coherent. **3** related or associated. □ **well-connected** associated, esp. by birth, with persons of good social position. □□ **con·nect·ed·ly** *adv.* **con·nect·ed·ness** *n.*

con·nect·ing rod *n.* the rod between the piston and the crankshaft, etc., in an internal combustion engine or between the wheels of a locomotive.

con·nec·tion /kənékshən/ *n.* (also *Brit.* **con·nex·ion**) **1 a** the act of connecting; the state of being connected. **b** an instance of this. **2** the point at which two things are connected (*broke at the connection*). **3 a** a thing or person that connects; a link; a relationship or association (*a radio formed the only connection with the outside world; cannot see the connection between the two ideas*). **b** a telephone link (*got a bad connection*). **4** arrangement or opportunity for catching a connecting train, etc.; the train, etc., itself (*missed the connection*). **5** *Electr.* **a** the linking up of an electric current by contact. **b** a device for effecting this. **6** (often in *pl.*) a relative or associate, esp. one with influence (*has connections in the State Department; heard it through a business connection*). **7** a relation of ideas; a context (*in this connection I have to disagree*). **8** *sl.* **a** a transaction involving illegal drugs. **b** a supplier of narcotics. **9** a religious body, esp. Methodist. □ **in connection with** with reference to. **in this** (or *that*) **connection** with reference to this (or that). □□ **con·nec·tion·al** *adj.* [L *connexio* (as CONNECT): spelling –*ct*- after CONNECT]

con·nec·tive /kənéktiv/ *adj. & n.* • *adj.* serving or tending to connect. • *n.* something that connects.

con·nec·tive tis·sue *n. Anat.* a fibrous tissue that supports, binds, or separates other tissues or organs.

conn·ing tow·er /kóning/ *n.* **1** the superstructure of a submarine from which steering, firing, etc., are directed on or near the surface, and which contains the periscope. **2** the armored pilothouse of a warship. [CON[4] + –ING[1]]

con·nip·tion /kənípshən/ *n.* a fit of anger, agonized distress, or hysteria. [orig. unknown]

con·niv·ance /kənívəns/ *n.* **1** (often foll. by *at, in*) conniving (*connivance in the crime*). **2** tacit permission (*done with his connivance*). [F *connivence* or L *conniventia* (as CONNIVE)]

con·nive /kəní͟v/ *v.intr.* **1** (foll. by *at*) disregard or tacitly consent to (a wrongdoing). **2** (usu. foll. by *with*) conspire. □□ **con·niv·er** *n.* [F *conniver* or L *connivēre* shut the eyes (to)]

con·nois·seur /kónəsŏr/ *n.* (often foll. by *of, in*) an expert judge in matters of taste (*a connoisseur of fine wine*). □□ **con·nois·seur·ship** *n.* [F, obs. spelling of *connaisseur* f. pres. stem of *connaître* know + –*eur*–OR[1]: cf. *reconnoiter*]

con·no·ta·tion /kónətáyshən/ *n.* **1** that which is implied by a word, etc., in addition to its literal or primary meaning (*a letter with sinister connotations*). **2** the act of connoting or implying.

con·note /kənṓt/ *v.tr.* **1** (of a word, etc.) imply in addition to the literal or primary meaning. **2** (of a fact) imply as a consequence or condition. **3** mean; signify. □□ **con·no·ta·tive** /kónətaytiv, kənṓtətiv/ *adj.* [med.L *connotare* mark in addition (as COM-, *notare* f. *nota* mark)]

▶**Connote** means 'suggest': *"Mother" connotes warmth, concern, and security.* **Denote** refers to the literal meaning: *"Mother" denotes a female who has given birth.*

con·nu·bi·al /kənŏŏbeeəl, kənyŏŏ–/ *adj.* of or relating to marriage or the relationship of husband and wife. □□ **con·nu·bi·al·i·ty** /–beeálitee/ *n.* **con·nu·bi·al·ly** *adv.* [L *connubialis* f. *connubium* (*nubium* f. *nubere* marry)]

co·noid /kónoyd/ *adj. & n.* • *adj.* (also **co·noi·dal** /–nóyd'l/) cone-shaped. • *n.* a cone-shaped object.

con·quer /kóngkər/ *v.tr.* **1 a** overcome and control (an enemy or territory) by military force. **b** *absol.* be victorious. **2** overcome (a habit, emotion, disability, etc.) by effort (*conquered his fear*). **3** climb (a mountain) successfully. □□ **con·quer·a·ble** *adj.* [ME f. OF *conquerre* f. Rmc f. L *conquirere* (as COM-, *quaerere* seek, get)]

con·quer·or /kóngkərər/ *n.* **1** a person who conquers. **2** *Brit.* = CONKER. [ME f. AF *conquerour* (OF –*eor*) f. *conquerre* (as CONQUER)]

con·quest /kóngkwest/ *n.* **1** the act or an instance of conquering; the state of being conquered. **2 a** a conquered territory. **b** something won. **3** a person whose affection or favor has been won. **4** (**the Conquest** *or* **Norman Conquest**) the conquest of England by William ("the Conqueror") of Normandy in 1066. □ **make a conquest of** win the affections of. [ME f. OF *conquest(e)* f. Rmc (as CONQUER)]

con·quis·ta·dor /konkwístədawr, kongkéestə–/ *n.* (*pl.* **con·quis·ta·dores** /–dáwrez/ *or* **con·quis·ta·dors**) a conqueror, esp. one of the Spanish conquerors of Mexico and Peru in the 16th c. [Sp.]

Cons. *abbr.* Conservative.

con·san·guin·e·ous /kónsanggwíneeəs/ *adj.* descended from the same ancestor; akin. □□ **con·san·guin·i·ty** *n.* [L *consanguineus* (as COM-, *sanguis* –*inis* blood)]

con·science /kónshəns/ *n.* **1** a moral sense of right and wrong esp. as felt by a person and affecting behavior (*my conscience won't allow me to do that*). **2** an inner feeling as to the goodness or otherwise of one's behavior (*my conscience is clear; has a guilty conscience*). □ **for conscience** (or **conscience's**) **sake** to satisfy one's conscience. **in all conscience** *colloq.* by any reasonable standard; by all that is fair. **on one's conscience** causing one feelings of guilt. □□ **con·science·less** *adj.* [ME f. OF f. L *conscientia* f. *conscire* be privy to (as COM-, *scire* know)]

▶See note at CONSCIOUS.

con·science clause *n.* a clause in a law that makes concessions to the consciences or religions of those affected by the law.

con·science mon·ey *n.* a sum paid to relieve one's conscience, esp. about a payment previously evaded.

con·science-strick·en *adj.* (also **con·science-struck**) made uneasy by a guilty conscience.

con·sci·en·tious /kónshee-énshəs/ *adj.* (of a person or conduct) governed by a sense of duty; diligent and scrupulous. □□ **con·sci·en·tious·ly** *adv.* **con·sci·en·tious·ness** *n.* [F *consciencieux* f. med.L *conscientiosus* (as CONSCIENCE)]

con·sci·en·tious ob·jec·tor *n.* a person who, on moral or religious grounds, objects to conforming to a requirement, esp. that of military service.

con·scious /kónshəs/ *adj. & n.* • *adj.* **1** awake and aware of one's surroundings and identity. **2** (usu. foll. by *of*, or *that* + clause) aware; knowing (*conscious of his inferiority*). **3** (of actions, emotions, etc.) realized or recognized by the doer; intentional (*made a conscious effort not to laugh*). **4** (in *comb.*) aware of; concerned with (*appearance-conscious*). • *n.* (prec. by *the*) the conscious mind. □□ **con·scious·ly**

adv. [L *conscius* knowing with others or in oneself f. *conscire* (as COM-, *scire* know)]

▶**Conscious** is an adjective meaning 'aware' (*I was conscious of her presence in the room*). **Conscience** is a noun meaning 'an inner sense of right and wrong' (*you'll have to let your conscience be your guide in this matter*).

con·scious·ness /kónshəsnis/ *n.* **1** the state of being conscious (*lost consciousness during the fight*). **2 a** awareness; perception (*had no consciousness of being ridiculed*). **b** (in *comb.*) awareness of (*class consciousness*). **3** the totality of a person's thoughts and feelings, or of a class of these (*moral consciousness*).

con·scious·ness-rais·ing *n.* the activity of increasing esp. social or political sensitivity or awareness.

con·scribe /kənskríb/ *v.tr.* = CONSCRIPT *v.* [L *conscribere* (as CONSCRIPTION)]

con·script *v. & n.* ● *v.tr.* /kənskrípt/ enlist by conscription. ● *n.* /kónskript/ a person enlisted by conscription. [(v.) back-form. f. CON-SCRIPTION: (n.) f. F *conscrit* f. L *conscriptus* (as CONSCRIPTION)]

con·scrip·tion /kənskrípshən/ *n.* compulsory enlistment for government service, esp. military service. [F f. LL *conscriptio* levying of troops f. L *conscribere conscript-* enroll (as COM-, *scribere* write)]

con·se·crate /kónsikrayt/ *v.tr.* **1** make or declare sacred; dedicate formally to a religious or divine purpose. **2** (in Christian belief) make (bread and wine) into the body and blood of Christ. **3** (foll. by *to*) devote (one's life, etc.) to (a purpose). **4** ordain (esp. a bishop) to a sacred office. □□ **con·se·cra·tion** /-kráyshən/ *n.* **con·se·cra·tor** *n.* **con·se·cra·to·ry** /-krətáwree/ *adj.* [ME f. L *consecrare* (as COM-, *secrare* = *sacrare* dedicate f. *sacer* sacred)]

con·se·cu·tion /kónsikyōoshən/ *n.* **1** logical sequence (in argument or reasoning). **2** sequence; succession (of events, etc.). [L *consecutio* f. *consequi consecut-* overtake (as COM-, *sequi* pursue)]

con·sec·u·tive /kənsékyətiv/ *adj.* **1 a** following continuously. **b** in unbroken or logical order. **2** *Gram.* expressing consequence. □□ **con·sec·u·tive·ly** *adv.* **con·sec·u·tive·ness** *n.* [F *consécutif –ive* f. med.L *consecutivus* (as CONSECUTION)]

con·sec·u·tive in·ter·vals *n. Mus.* intervals of the same kind (esp. fifths or octaves), occurring in succession between two voices or parts in harmony.

con·sen·su·al /kənséshōoəl/ *adj.* of or by consent or consensus. □□ **con·sen·su·al·ly** *adv.* [L *consensus* (see CONSENSUS) + −AL]

con·sen·sus /kənsénsəs/ *n.* (often foll. by *of*) **1 a** general agreement (of opinion, testimony, etc.). **b** an instance of this. **2** (*attrib.*) majority view; collective opinion (*consensus politics*). [L, = agreement (as CONSENT)]

con·sent /kənsént/ *v. & n.* ● *v.intr.* (often foll. by *to*) express willingness; give permission; agree. ● *n.* voluntary agreement; permission; compliance. [ME f. OF *consentir* f. L *consentire* (as COM-, *sentire* sens-feel)]

con·sen·tient /kənsénshənt/ *adj.* **1** agreeing; united in opinion. **2** concurrent. **3** (often foll. by *to*) consenting. [L *consentient-* (as CONSENT)]

con·sent·ing a·dult *n.* an adult who consents to something, esp. a sexual act.

con·se·quence /kónsikwens, –kwəns/ *n.* **1** the result or effect of an action or condition. **2 a** importance (*it is of no consequence*). **b** social distinction (*persons of consequence*). **3** (in *pl.*) a game in which a narrative is made up by the players, each ignorant of what has already been contributed. □ **in consequence** as a result. **take the consequences** accept the results of one's choice or action. [ME f. OF f. L *consequentia* (as CONSEQUENT)]

con·se·quent /kónsikwənt/ *adj. & n.* ● *adj.* **1** (often foll. by *on, upon*) following as a result or consequence. **2** logically consistent. ● *n.* **1** a thing that follows another. **2** *Logic* the second part of a conditional proposition, dependent on the antecedent. [ME f. OF f. L *consequi* (as CONSECUTION)]

con·se·quen·tial /kónsikwénshəl/ *adj.* **1** following as a result or consequence. **2** resulting indirectly (*consequential damage*). **3 a** significant. **b** (of a person) self-important. □□ **con·se·quen·ti·al·i·ty** /–sheeálitee/ *n.* **con·se·quen·tial·ly** *adv.* [L *consequentia*]

con·se·quent·ly /kónsikwentlee/ *adv. & conj.* as a result; therefore.

con·serv·an·cy /kənsórvənsee/ *n.* (*pl.* **·cies**) **1** a body concerned with the preservation of natural resources (*Nature Conservancy*). **2** conservation; official preservation (of forests, etc.). **3** *Brit.* a commission, etc., controlling a port, river, etc. (*Thames Conservancy*). [18th c. alt. of obs. *conservacy* f. AF *conservacie* f. AL *conservatia* f. L *conservatio* (as CONSERVE)]

con·ser·va·tion /kónsərváyshən/ *n.* preservation, esp. of the natural environment. □□ **con·ser·va·tion·al** *adj.* [ME f. OF *conservation* or L *conservatio* (as CONSERVE)]

con·ser·va·tion a·re·a *n.* an area containing a noteworthy environment and specially protected by law against undesirable changes.

con·ser·va·tion·ist /kónsərváyshənist/ *n.* a supporter or advocate of environmental conservation.

con·ser·va·tion of en·er·gy *n.* (or **mass** or **mo·men·tum**, etc.) *Physics* the principle that the total quantity of energy, etc., of any system not subject to external action remains constant.

con·serv·a·tive /kənsórvətiv/ *adj. & n.* ● *adj.* **1 a** averse to rapid change. **b** (of views, taste, etc.) moderate; avoiding extremes (*conservative in her dress*). **2** (of an estimate, etc.) purposely low; moderate; cautious. **3** (**Conservative**) of or characteristic of Conservatives or the Conservative party. **4** tending to conserve. ● *n.* **1** a conservative person. **2** (**Conservative**) a supporter or member of the Conservative party. □□ **con·serv·a·tism** *n.* **con·serv·a·tive·ly** *adv.* **con·serv·a·tive·ness** *n.* [ME f. LL *conservativus* (as CON-SERVE)]

Con·serv·a·tive Ju·da·ism *n.* Judaism allowing only minor changes in traditional ritual, etc.

Con·serv·a·tive par·ty *n.* **1** a British political party promoting free enterprise and private ownership. **2** a similar party elsewhere.

con·ser·va·toire /kənsórvətwaár/ *n.* a (usu. European) school of music or other arts. [F f. It. *conservatorio* (as CONSERVATORY)]

con·ser·va·tor /kənsórvətər, kónsərvaytər/ *n.* a person who preserves something; an official custodian (of a museum, etc.). [ME f. AF *conservatour*, OF *–ateur* f. L *conservator –oris* (as CONSERVE)]

con·serv·a·to·ri·um /kənsórvətáwreeəm/ *n. Austral.* = CONSERVA-TOIRE.

con·ser·va·to·ry /kənsórvətawree/ *n.* (*pl.* **·ries**) **1** a greenhouse for tender plants, esp. one attached to and communicating with a house. **2** = CONSERVATOIRE. [LL *conservatorium* (as CONSERVE): sense 2 through It. *conservatorio*]

con·serve /kənsórv/ *v. & n.* ● *v.tr.* **1** store up; keep from harm or damage, esp. for later use. **2** *Physics* maintain a quantity of (heat, etc.). **3** preserve (food, esp. fruit), usu. with sugar. ● *n.* /also kónsərv/ **1** fruit, etc., preserved in sugar. **2** fresh fruit jam. [ME f. OF *conserver* f. L *conservare* (as COM-, *servare* keep)]

con·sid·er /kənsídər/ *v.tr.* (often *absol.*) **1** contemplate mentally, esp. in order to reach a conclusion. **2** examine the merits of (a course of action, a candidate, claim, etc.). **3** give attention to. **4** reckon with; take into account. **5** (foll. by *that* + clause) have the opinion. **6** (foll. by compl.) believe; regard as (*consider it to be genuine; consider it settled*). **7** (as **considered** *adj.*) formed after careful thought (*a considered opinion*). □ **all things considered** taking everything into account. [ME f. OF *considerer* f. L *considerare* examine]

con·sid·er·a·ble /kənsídərəbəl/ *adj.* **1** enough in amount or extent to need consideration. **2** much; a lot of (*considerable pain*). **3** notable; important. □□ **con·sid·er·a·bly** *adv.*

con·sid·er·ate /kənsídərət/ *adj.* **1** thoughtful toward other people; careful not to cause hurt or inconvenience. **2** *archaic* careful. □□ **con·sid·er·ate·ly** *adv.*

con·sid·er·a·tion /kənsídəráyshən/ *n.* **1** the act of considering; careful thought. **2** thoughtfulness for others; being considerate. **3** a fact or a thing taken into account in deciding or judging something. **4** compensation; a payment or reward. **5** *Law* (in a contractual agreement) anything given or promised or forborne by one party in exchange for the promise or undertaking of another. **6** *archaic* importance or consequence. □ **in consideration of** in return for; on account of. **take into consideration** include as a factor, reason, etc.; make allowance for. **under consideration** being considered. [ME f. OF *consideration –onis* (as CONSIDER)]

con·sid·er·ing /kənsídəring/ *prep.* **1** in view of; taking into consideration (*considering their youth; considering that it was snowing*). **2** (without compl.) *colloq.* all in all; taking everything into account (*not so bad, considering*).

con·sign /kənsín/ *v.tr.* (often foll. by *to*) **1** hand over; deliver to a person's possession or trust. **2** assign; commit decisively or permanently (*consigned it to the trash can; consigned to years of misery*). **3** transmit or send (goods), usu. by a public carrier. □□ **con·sign·ee** /kónsínee/ *n.* **con·sign·or** *n.* [ME f. F *consigner* or L *consignare* mark with a seal (as COM-, SIGN)]

con·sign·ment /kənsínmənt/ *n.* **1** the act or an instance of consigning; the process of being consigned. **2** a batch of goods consigned. **3** an agreement to pay a supplier of goods after the goods are sold.

con·sist /kənsíst/ *v.intr.* **1** (foll. by *of*) be composed; have specified ingredients or elements. **2** (foll. by *in, of*) have its essential features as specified (*its beauty consists in the use of color*). **3** (usu. foll. by *with*) harmonize; be consistent. [L *consistere* exist (as COM-, *sistere* stop)]

con·sist·en·cy /kənsístənsee/ *n.* (also **con·sist·ence**) (*pl.* **·cies** or **·ces**) **1** the degree of density, firmness, or viscosity, esp. of thick liquids. **2** the state of being consistent; conformity with other or earlier attitudes, practice, etc. **3** the state or quality of holding or sticking together and retaining shape. [F *consistence* or LL *consistentia* (as CONSIST)]

con·sist·ent /kənsístənt/ *adj.* (usu. foll. by *with*) **1** compatible or in harmony; not contradictory. **2** (of a person) constant to the same principles of thought or action. □□ **con·sist·ent·ly** *adv.* [L *consistere* (as CONSIST)]

con·sis·to·ry /kənsístəree/ n. (pl. **·ries**) **1** RC Ch. the council of cardinals (with or without the pope). **2** (in full **consistory court**) (in the Church of England) a court presided over by a bishop, for the administration of ecclesiastical law in a diocese. **3** (in other churches) a local administrative body. □□ **con·sis·to·ri·al** /kónsistáwreeəl/ adj. [ME f. AF consistorie, OF –oire f. LL consistorium (as CONSIST)]

con·so·ci·a·tion /kənsôsheeáyshən, kənsôsee–/ n. **1** close association, esp. of churches or religious communities. **2** Ecol. a closely related subgroup of plants having one dominant species. [L consociatio, –onis f. consociare (as COM–, socius fellow)]

con·so·la·tion /kónsəláyshən/ n. **1** the act or an instance of consoling; the state of being consoled. **2** a consoling thing, person, or circumstance. □□ **con·sol·a·to·ry** /kənsôlətawree, –sól–/ adj. [ME f. OF, f. L consolatio –onis (as CONSOLE[1])]

con·so·la·tion prize n. a prize given to a competitor who loses or narrowly fails to win.

con·sole[1] /kənsôl/ v.tr. comfort, esp. in grief or disappointment. □□ **con·sol·a·ble** adj. **con·sol·er** n. **con·sol·ing·ly** adv. [F consoler f. L consolari]

▶Often confused with condole.

con·sole[2] /kónsōl/ n. **1** a panel or unit accommodating a set of switches, controls, etc. **2** a cabinet for television or radio equipment, etc. **3** Mus. a cabinet with the keyboards, stops, pedals, etc., of an organ. **4** an ornamented bracket supporting a shelf, etc. [F, perh. f. consolider (as CONSOLIDATE)]

con·sole ta·ble n. a table supported by a bracket against a wall.

con·sol·i·date /kənsólidayt/ v. **1** tr. & intr. make or become strong or solid. **2** tr. reinforce or strengthen (one's position, power, etc.). **3** tr. combine (territories, companies, debts, etc.) into one whole. □□ **con·sol·i·da·tion** /–dáyshən/ n. **con·sol·i·da·tor** n. **con·sol·i·da·to·ry** adj. [L consolidare (as COM–, solidare f. solidus solid)]

Con·sol·i·dat·ed Fund n. Brit. a Bank of England fund into which tax revenue is paid and from which payments not dependent on annual votes in Parliament are made.

con·sols /kónsolz/ n.pl. British government securities without redemption date and with fixed annual interest. [abbr. of consolidated annuities]

con·som·mé /kónsəmáy/ n. a clear soup made with meat stock. [F, past part. of consommer f. L consummare (as CONSUMMATE)]

con·so·nance /kónsənəns/ n. **1** agreement; harmony. **2** Prosody a recurrence of similar-sounding consonants. **3** Mus. a harmonious combination of notes; a harmonious interval. [ME f. OF consonance or L consonantia (as CONSONANT)]

con·so·nant /kónsənənt/ n. & adj. ● n. **1** a speech sound in which the breath is at least partly obstructed, and which to form a syllable must be combined with a vowel. **2** a letter or letters representing this. ● adj. (foll. by with, to) **1** consistent; in agreement or harmony. **2** similar in sound. **3** Mus. making a concord. □□ **con·so·nan·tal** /–nánt'l/ adj. **con·so·nant·ly** adv. [ME f. F f. L consonare (as COM–, sonare sound f. sonus)]

con sor·di·no /kón sawrdeénō, káwn/ adv. Mus. with the use of a mute. [It.]

con·sort[1] n. & v. ● n. /kónsawrt/ **1** a wife or husband, esp. of royalty (prince consort). **2** a companion or associate. **3** a ship sailing with another. ● v. /kənsórt/ **1** intr. (usu. foll. by with, together) **a** keep company; associate. **b** harmonize. **2** tr. class or bring together. [ME f. F f. L consors sharer, comrade (as COM–, sors sortis lot, destiny)]

con·sort[2] /kónsawrt/ n. Mus. a group of players or instruments, esp. playing early music (recorder consort). [earlier form of CONCERT]

con·sor·ti·um /kənsáwrsheeəm, –teeəm/ n. (pl. **con·sor·ti·a** /–sheeə, –teeə/ or **con·sor·ti·ums**) **1** an association, esp. of several business companies. **2** Law the right of association with a husband or wife (loss of consortium). [L = partnership (as CONSORT[1])]

con·spe·cif·ic /kónspisífik/ adj. Biol. of the same species.

con·spec·tus /kənspéktəs/ n. **1** a general or comprehensive survey. **2** a summary or synopsis. [L f. conspicere conspect- (as COM–, spicere look at)]

con·spic·u·ous /kənspíkyōōəs/ adj. **1** clearly visible; striking to the eye; attracting notice. **2** remarkable of its kind (conspicuous extravagance). □□ **con·spic·u·ous·ly** adv. **con·spic·u·ous·ness** n. [L conspicuus (as CONSPECTUS)]

con·spir·a·cy /kənspírəsee/ n. (pl. **·cies**) **1** a secret plan to commit a crime or do harm, often for political ends; a plot. **2** the act of conspiring. [ME f. AF conspiracie, alt. form of OF conspiration f. L conspiratio –onis (as CONSPIRE)]

con·spir·a·cy of si·lence n. an agreement to say nothing.

con·spir·a·tor /kənspírətər/ n. a person who takes part in a conspiracy. □□ **con·spir·a·to·ri·al** /–táwreeəl/ adj. **con·spir·a·to·ri·al·ly** adv. [ME f. AF conspiratour, OF –teur (as CONSPIRE)]

con·spire /kənspír/ v.intr. **1** combine secretly to plan and prepare an unlawful or harmful act. **2** (often foll. by against, or to + infin.) (of events or circumstances) seem to be working together, esp. disadvantageously. [ME f. OF conspirer f. L conspirare agree, plot (as COM–, spirare breathe)]

con·sta·ble /kónstəbəl, kún–/ n. **1** esp. Brit. **a** a policeman or policewoman. **b** (also **po·lice con·sta·ble**) a police officer of the lowest rank. **2** the governor of a royal castle. **3** hist. the principal officer in a royal household. [ME f. OF conestable f. LL comes stabuli count of the stable]

con·stab·u·lar·y /kənstábyəleree/ n. & adj. ● n. **1** (pl. **·ies**) an organized body of police; a police force. **2** armed police organized as a military unit. ● attrib.adj. of or concerning the police force. [med.L constabularius (as CONSTABLE)]

con·stan·cy /kónstənsee/ n. **1** the quality of being unchanging and dependable; faithfulness. **2** firmness; endurance. [L constantia (as CONSTANT)]

con·stant /kónstənt/ adj. & n. ● adj. **1** continuous (needs constant attention). **2** occurring frequently (receive constant complaints). **3** (often foll. by to) unchanging; faithful; dependable. ● n. **1** anything that does not vary. **2** Math. a component of a relationship between variables that does not change its value. **3** Physics **a** a number expressing a relation, property, etc., and remaining the same in all circumstances. **b** such a number that remains the same for a substance in the same conditions. □□ **con·stant·ly** adv. [ME f. OF f. L constare (as COM–, stare stand)]

con·stant·an /kónstəntan/ n. an alloy of copper and nickel used in electrical equipment. [CONSTANT + –AN]

con·stel·late /kónstəlayt/ v.tr. **1** form into (or as if into) a constellation. **2** adorn as with stars.

con·stel·la·tion /kónstəláyshən/ n. **1** a group of fixed stars whose outline is traditionally regarded as forming a particular figure. **2** a group of associated persons, ideas, etc. [ME f. OF f. LL constellatio –onis (as COM–, stella star)]

con·ster·nate /kónstərnayt/ v.tr. (usu. in passive) dismay; fill with anxiety. [L consternare (as COM–, sternere throw down)]

con·ster·na·tion /kónstərnáyshən/ n. anxiety or dismay causing mental confusion. [F consternation or L consternatio (as CONSTERNATE)]

con·sti·pate /kónstipayt/ v.tr. (esp. as **constipated** adj.) affect with constipation. [L constipare (as COM–, stipare press)]

con·sti·pa·tion /kónstipáyshən/ n. **1** a condition with hardened feces and difficulty in emptying the bowels. **2** a restricted state. [ME f. OF constipation or LL constipatio (as CONSTIPATE)]

con·stit·u·en·cy /kənstíchōōənsee/ n. (pl. **·cies**) **1** a body of voters in a specified area who elect a representative member to a legislative body. **2** the area represented in this way. **3** a body of customers, supporters, etc.

con·stit·u·ent /kənstíchōōənt/ adj. & n. ● adj. **1** composing or helping to make up a whole. **2** able to make or change a (political, etc.) constitution (constituent assembly). **3** appointing or electing. ● n. **1** a member of a constituency (esp. political). **2** a component part. **3** Law a person who appoints another as agent. [L constituent- partly through F –ant (as CONSTITUTE)]

con·sti·tute /kónstitōōt, tyōōt/ v.tr. **1** be the components or essence of; make up; form. **2 a** be equivalent or tantamount to (this constitutes an official warning). **b** formally establish (does not constitute a precedent). **3** give legal or constitutional form to; establish by law. □□ **con·sti·tu·tor** n. [L constituere (as COM–, statuere set up)]

con·sti·tu·tion /kónstitōōshən, –tyōō–/ n. **1** the act or method of constituting; the composition (of something). **2 a** the body of fundamental laws, principles, or established precedents according to which a nation, state, or other organization is acknowledged to be governed. **b** a (usu. written) record of this. **c** (**Constitution**) the US Constitution. **3** a person's physical state as regards vitality, health, strength, etc. **4** a person's mental or psychological makeup. **5** hist. a decree or ordinance. [ME f. OF constitution or L constitutio (as CONSTITUTE)]

con·sti·tu·tion·al /kónstitōōshənəl, –tyōō–/ adj. & n. ● adj. **1** of, consistent with, authorized by, or limited by a political constitution (constitutional duties of office). **2** inherent in, stemming from, or affecting the physical or mental constitution. ● n. a walk taken regularly to maintain or restore good health. □□ **con·sti·tu·tion·al·i·ty** /–nálitee/ n. **con·sti·tu·tion·al·ize** v.tr. **con·sti·tu·tion·al·ly** adv.

con·sti·tu·tion·al·ism /kónstitōōshənəlizəm, –tyōō–/ n. **1** a constitutional system of government. **2** the adherence to or advocacy of such a system. □□ **con·sti·tu·tion·al·ist** n.

con·sti·tu·tive /kónstitōōtiv, –tyōō–/ adj. **1** able to form or appoint. **2** component. **3** essential. □□ **con·sti·tu·tive·ly** adv. [LL constitutivus (as CONSTITUTE)]

con·strain /kənstráyn/ v.tr. **1** compel; urge irresistibly or by necessity. **2 a** confine forcibly; imprison. **b** restrict severely as regards action, behavior, etc. **3** bring about by compulsion. **4** (as **constrained** adj.) forced; embarrassed (a constrained voice; a constrained manner). □□ **con·strain·ed·ly** /–nidlee/ adv. [ME f. OF constraindre f. L constringere (as COM–, stringere strict- tie)]

con·straint /kənstráynt/ n. **1** the act or result of constraining or being constrained; restriction of liberty. **2** something that constrains; a limitation on motion or action. **3** the restraint of natural feelings or their expression; a constrained manner. [ME f. OF constreinte, fem. past part. (as CONSTRAIN)]

con•strict /kənstríkt/ v.tr. **1** make narrow or tight; compress. **2** Biol. cause (organic tissue) to contract. □□ **con•stric•tion** /-stríkshən/ n. **con•stric•tive** adj. [L (as CONSTRAIN)]

con•stric•tor /kənstríktər/ n. **1** any snake (esp. a boa) that kills by coiling around its prey and compressing it. **2** Anat. any muscle that compresses or contracts an organ or part of the body. [mod.L (as CONSTRICT)]

con•struct v. & n. • v.tr. /kənstrúkt/ **1** make by fitting parts together; build; form (something physical or abstract). **2** Geom. draw or delineate, esp. accurately to given conditions (construct a triangle). • n. /kónstrukt/ **1** a thing constructed, esp. by the mind. **2** Linguistics a group of words forming a phrase. □□ **con•struct•or** n. [L construere construct- (as COM-, struere pile, build)]

con•struc•tion /kənstrúkshən/ n. **1** the act or a mode of constructing. **2** a thing constructed. **3** an interpretation or explanation (they put a generous construction on his act). **4** Gram. an arrangement of words according to syntactical rules. □□ **con•struc•tion•al** adj. **con•struc•tion•al•ly** adv. [ME f. OF f. L constructio –onis (as CONSTRUCT)]

con•struc•tion•ism /kənstrúkshənizəm/ n. **1** Law interpretation of a law or constitution in a particular way (strict constructionism). **2** = CONSTRUCTIVISM. □□ **con•struc•tion•ist** n.

con•struc•tive /kənstrúktiv/ adj. **1 a** of construction; tending to construct. **b** tending to form a basis for ideas (constructive criticism). **2** helpful; positive (a constructive approach). **3** derived by inference; not expressed (constructive permission). **4** belonging to the structure of a building. □□ **con•struc•tive•ly** adv. **con•struc•tive•ness** n. [LL constructivus (as CONSTRUCT)]

con•struc•tiv•ism /kənstrúktivizəm/ n. Art a Russian movement in which assorted (usu. mechanical or industrial) objects are combined into nonrepresentational and mobile structural forms. □□ **con•struc•tiv•ist** n. [Russ. konstruktivizm (as CONSTRUCT)]

con•strue /kənstrṓ/ v.tr. (**con•strues, con•strued, con•stru•ing**) **1** interpret (words or actions) (their decision can be construed in many ways). **2** (often foll. by with) combine (words) grammatically ("rely" is construed with "on"). **3** analyze the syntax of (a sentence). **4** translate word for word. □□ **con•stru•a•ble** adj. **con•stru•al** n. [ME f. L construere CONSTRUCT]

con•sub•stan•tial /kónsəbstánshəl/ adj. Theol. of the same substance (esp. of the three persons of the Trinity). □□ **con•sub•stan•ti•al•i•ty** /-sheeálitee/ n. [ME f. eccl.L consubstantialis, transl. Gk homoousios (as COM-, SUBSTANTIAL)]

con•sub•stan•ti•a•tion /kónsəbstánsheeáyshən/ n. Theol. the doctrine of the real substantial presence of the body and blood of Christ in and with the bread and wine in the Eucharist. [mod.L consubstantiatio, after transubstantiatio TRANSUBSTANTIATION]

con•sue•tude /kónswitōod, –tyōod/ n. a custom, esp. one having legal force in Scotland. □□ **con•sue•tu•di•nar•y** /kónswitōod'neree, –tyōod–/ adj. [ME f. OF consuetude or L consuetudo –dinis f. consuetus accustomed]

con•sul /kónsəl/ n. **1** an official appointed by a government to live in a foreign city and protect the government's citizens and interests there. **2** hist. either of two annually elected chief magistrates in ancient Rome. **3** any of the three chief magistrates of the French republic (1799–1804). □□ **con•su•lar** adj. **con•sul•ship** n. [ME f. L, rel. to consulere CONSULT take counsel]

con•su•late /kónsələt/ n. **1** the building officially used by a consul. **2** the office, position, or period of office of a consul. **3** hist. government by consuls. **4** hist. the period of office of a consul. **5** hist. (**Consulate**) the government of France by three consuls (1799–1804). [ME f. L consulatus (as CONSUL)]

con•sult /kənsúlt/ v. & n. **1** tr. seek information or advice from (a person, book, watch, etc.). **2** intr. (often foll. by with) refer to a person for advice, an opinion, etc. **3** tr. seek permission or approval from (a person) for a proposed action. **4** tr. take into account; consider (feelings, interests, etc.). • n. /kónsult/ = CONSULTATION 1, 2. □□ **con•sul•ta•tive** /-súltətiv/ adj. [F consulter f. L consultare frequent. of consulere consult- take counsel]

con•sult•an•cy /kənsúlt'nsee/ n. (pl. •cies) the professional practice or position of a consultant.

con•sult•ant /kənsúlt'nt/ n. **1** a person providing professional advice, etc., esp. for a fee. **2** Brit. a senior specialist in a branch of medicine responsible for patients in a hospital. [prob. F (as CONSULT)]

con•sul•ta•tion /kónsəltáyshən/ n. **1** a meeting arranged to consult (esp. with a consultant). **2** the act or an instance of consulting. **3** a conference. [ME f. OF consultation or L consultatio (as CONSULTANT)]

con•sult•ing /kənsúlting/ attrib.adj. giving professional advice to others working in the same field or subject (consulting physician).

con•sum•a•ble /kənsōoməbəl/ adj. & n. • adj. that can be consumed; intended for consumption. • n. (usu. in pl.) a commodity that is eventually used up, worn out, or eaten.

con•sume /kənsōom/ v.tr. **1** eat or drink. **2** completely destroy; reduce to nothing or to tiny particles (fire consumed the building). **3** (often as **consumed** adj.) possess or entirely take up (foll. by with: consumed with rage). **4** use up (time, energy, etc.). □□ **con•sum•ing•**

203

constrict ~ contaminate

ly adv. [ME f. L consumere (as COM-, sumere sumpt- take up): partly through F consumer]

con•sum•er /kənsōomər/ n. **1** a person who consumes, esp. one who uses a product. **2** a purchaser of goods or services.

con•sum•er goods n. goods bought and used by consumers, rather than by manufacturers for producing other goods (opp. CAPITAL GOODS).

con•sum•er•ism /kənsōomərizəm/ n. the protection or promotion of consumers' interests in relation to the producer. □□ **con•sum•er•ist** adj. & n.

con•sum•er re•search n. investigation of purchasers' needs and opinions.

con•sum•er so•ci•e•ty n. a society in which the marketing of goods and services is an important social and economic activity.

con•sum•mate v. & adj. • v.tr. /kónsəmayt/ **1** complete; make perfect. **2** complete (a marriage) by sexual intercourse. • adj. /kənsúmit, kónsəmit/ complete; perfect; fully skilled (a consummate general). □□ **con•sum•mate•ly** adv. **con•sum•ma•tive** /kónsəmáy-/ adj. **con•sum•ma•tor** n. [L consummare (as COM-, summare complete f. summus utmost)]

PRONUNCIATION TIP **consummate**

As an adjective, this word may be pronounced either "kun-SUM-it" or "KAHN-suh-mit." As a verb, it is correctly pronounced "-KAHN-suh-MATE."

con•sum•ma•tion /kónsəmáyshən/ n. **1** completion, esp. of a marriage by sexual intercourse. **2** a desired end or goal; perfection. [ME f. OF consommation or L consummatio (as CONSUMMATE)]

con•sump•tion /kənsúmpshən/ n. **1** the act or an instance of consuming; the process of being consumed. **2** any disease causing wasting of tissues, esp. pulmonary tuberculosis. **3** an amount consumed. **4** the purchase and use of goods, etc. [ME f. OF consomption f. L consumptio (as CONSUME)]

con•sump•tive /kənsúmptiv/ adj. & n. • adj. **1** of or tending to consumption. **2** tending to or affected with pulmonary tuberculosis. • n. a consumptive patient. □□ **con•sump•tive•ly** adv. [med.L consumptivus (as CONSUMPTION)]

cont. abbr. **1** contents. **2** continued.

con•tact n. & v. • n. /kóntakt/ **1** the state or condition of touching, meeting, or communicating. **2** a person who is or may be communicated with for information, supplies, assistance, etc. **3** Electr. **a** a connection for the passage of a current. **b** a device for providing this. **4** a person likely to carry a contagious disease through being associated with an infected person. **5** (usu. in pl.) colloq. a contact lens. • v.tr. /kóntakt, kəntákt/ **1** get into communication with. **2** begin correspondence or personal dealings with. □□ **con•tact•a•ble** adj. [L contactus f. contingere (as COM-, tangere touch)]

con•tact lens n. a thin plastic lens placed directly on the surface of the eye to correct the vision.

con•tact print n. a photographic print made by placing a negative directly on sensitized paper, etc., and illuminating it.

con•tact sport n. a sport in which participants necessarily come into bodily contact with one another.

con•ta•gion /kəntáyjən/ n. **1 a** the communication of disease from one person to another by bodily contact. **b** a contagious disease. **2** a contagious or harmful influence. **3** moral corruption, esp. when tending to be widespread. [ME f. L contagio (as COM-, tangere touch)]

con•ta•gious /kəntáyjəs/ adj. **1 a** (of a person) likely to transmit disease by contact. **b** (of a disease) transmitted in this way. **2** (of emotions, reactions, etc.) likely to affect others (contagious enthusiasm). □□ **con•ta•gious•ly** adv. **con•ta•gious•ness** n. [ME f. LL contagiosus (as CONTAGION)]

con•ta•gious a•bor•tion n. brucellosis of cattle.

con•tain /kəntáyn/ v.tr. **1** hold or be capable of holding within itself; include; comprise. **2** (of measures) consist of or be equal to (a gallon contains eight pints). **3** prevent (an enemy, difficulty, etc.) from moving or extending. **4** control or restrain (oneself, one's feelings, etc.). **5** (of a number) be divisible by (a factor) without a remainder. □□ **con•tain•a•ble** adj. [ME f. OF contenir f. L continēre content- (as COM-, tenēre hold)]

con•tain•er /kəntáynər/ n. **1** a vessel, box, etc., for holding particular things. **2** a large boxlike receptacle of standard design for the transport of goods, esp. one readily transferable from one form of transport to another (also attrib.: container ship).

con•tain•er•ize /kəntáynəriz/ v.tr. **1** pack in or transport by container. **2** adapt to transport by container. □□ **con•tain•er•i•za•tion** n.

con•tain•ment /kəntáynmənt/ n. the action or policy of preventing the expansion of a hostile country or influence.

con•tam•i•nate /kəntámináyt/ v.tr. **1** pollute, esp. with radioactivity. **2** infect; corrupt. □□ **con•tam•i•nant** /-minənt/ n. **con•tam•i•na•tion**

See page xx for the **Key to Pronunciation**.

/–náyshən/ *n.* **con•tam•i•na•tor** *n.* [L *contaminare* (as COM-, *tamen-* rel. to *tangere* touch)]

con•tang•o /kəntánggō/ *n.* (*pl.* **-os**) *Brit. Stock Exch.* **1** the postponement of the transfer of stock from one account day to the next. **2** a percentage paid by the buyer for such a postponement. [19th c.: prob. an arbitrary formation]

con•te /kont/ *n.* **1** a short story (as a form of literary composition). **2** a medieval narrative tale. [F]

con•temn /kəntém/ *v.tr. literary* despise; treat with disregard. □□ **con• temn•er** /–témər, –témnər/ *n.* [ME f. OF *contemner* or L *contemnere* (as COM-, *temnere tempt-* despise)]

con•tem•plate /kóntəmplayt/ *v.* **1** *tr.* survey with the eyes or in the mind. **2** *tr.* regard (an event) as possible. **3** *tr.* intend; have as one's purpose (*we contemplate leaving tomorrow*). **4** *intr.* meditate. □□ **con• tem•pla•tion** /–pláyshən/ *n.* **con•tem•pla•tor** *n.* [L *contemplari* (as COM-, *templum* place for observations)]

con•tem•pla•tive /kəntémplətiv, kóntəmpláy–/ *adj. & n.* • *adj.* of or given to (esp. religious) contemplation; meditative. • *n.* a person whose life is devoted to religious contemplation. □□ **con•tem•pla• tive•ly** *adv.* [ME f. OF *contemplatif –ive*, or L *contemplativus* (as CONTEMPLATE)]

con•tem•po•ra•ne•ous /kəntémpəráyneeəs/ *adj.* (usu. foll. by *with*) **1** existing or occurring at the same time. **2** of the same period. □□ **con•tem•po•ra•ne•i•ty** /–pəranáyitee, –née–/ *n.* **con•tem•po•ra• ne•ous•ly** *adv.* **con•tem•po•ra•ne•ous•ness** *n.* [L *contemporaneus* (as COM-, *temporaneus* f. *tempus –oris* time)]

con•tem•po•rar•y /kəntémpəreree/ *adj. & n.* • *adj.* **1** living or occurring at the same time. **2** approximately equal in age. **3** following modern ideas or fashion in style or design. • *n.* (*pl.* **-ies**) **1** a person or thing living or existing at the same time as another. **2** a person of roughly the same age as another. □□ **con•tem•po•rar•i•ly** /–rérilee/ *adv.* **con•tem•po•rar•i•ness** *n.* **con•tem•po•ra•rize** /–tém–/ *v.tr.* [med.L *contemporarius* (as CONTEMPORANEOUS)]

con•tempt /kəntémpt/ *n.* **1** a feeling that a person or a thing is beneath consideration or worthless, or deserving scorn or extreme reproach. **2** the condition of being held in contempt. **3** (in full con•tempt of court) disobedience to or disrespect for a court of law and its officers. □ beneath contempt utterly despicable. hold in contempt despise. [ME f. L *contemptus* (as CONTEMN)]

con•tempt•i•ble /kəntémptibəl/ *adj.* deserving contempt; despicable. □□ **con•tempt•i•bil•i•ty** /–bilitee/ *n.* **con•tempt•i•bly** *adv.* [ME f. OF or LL *contemptibilis* (as CONTEMN)]

con•temp•tu•ous /kəntémpchŏŏəs/ *adj.* (often foll. by *of*) showing contempt; scornful; insolent. □□ **con•temp•tu•ous•ly** *adv.* [med.L *contemptuosus* f. L *contemptus* (as CONTEMPT)]

con•tend /kənténd/ *v.* **1** *intr.* (usu. foll. by *with*) strive; fight. **2** *intr.* compete (*fatigue contended with our desire to finish the project*). **3** *tr.* (usu. foll. by *that* + clause) assert; maintain. □□ **con•tend•er** *n.* [OF *contendre* or L *contendere* (as COM-, *tendere tent-* stretch, strive)]

con•tent¹ /kəntént/ *adj., v., & n.* • *predic.adj.* **1** satisfied; adequately happy; in agreement. **2** (foll. by *to* + infin.) willing. • *v.tr.* make content; satisfy. • *n.* a contented state; satisfaction. □ to one's heart's content to the full extent of one's desires. [ME f. OF f. L *contentus* satisfied, past part. of *continēre* (as CONTAIN)]

con•tent² /kóntent/ *n.* **1** (usu. in *pl.*) what is contained in something, esp. in a vessel, book, or house. **2** the amount of a constituent contained (*low sodium content*). **3** the substance or material dealt with (in a speech, work of art, etc.) as distinct from its form or style; significance. **4** the capacity or volume of a thing. [ME f. med.L *contentum* (as CONTAIN)]

con•tent•ed /kəntséntid/ *adj.* (often foll. by *with*, or *to* + infin.) **1** happy; satisfied. **2** (foll. by *with*) willing to be content (*was contented with the outcome*). □□ **con•tent•ed•ly** *adv.* **con•tent•ed•ness** *n.*

con•ten•tion /kənténshən/ *n.* **1** a dispute or argument; rivalry. **2** a point contended for in an argument (*it is my contention that you are wrong*). **3** a contention competing, esp. with a good chance of success. [ME f. OF *contention* or L *contentio* (as CONTEND)]

con•ten•tious /kənténshəs/ *adj.* **1** argumentative; quarrelsome. **2** likely to cause an argument; disputed; controversial. □□ **con•ten• tious•ly** *adv.* **con•ten•tious•ness** *n.* [ME f. OF *contentieux* f. L *contentiosus* (as CONTENTION)]

con•tent•ment /kənténtmənt/ *n.* a satisfied state; tranquil happiness.

con•ter•mi•nous /kəntórminəs/ *adj.* (often foll. by *with*) **1** having a common boundary. **2** coextensive; coterminous. □□ **con•ter•mi• nous•ly** *adv.* [L *conterminus* (as COM-, *terminus* boundary)]

con•tes•sa /kóntésə/ *n.* an Italian countess. [It. f. LL *comitissa*: see COUNTESS]

con•test *n. & v.* • *n.* /kóntest/ **1** a process of contending; a competition. **2** a dispute; a controversy. • *v.tr.* /kəntést, kóntest/ **1** challenge or dispute (a decision, etc.). **2** debate (a point, statement, etc.). **3** contend or compete for (a prize, parliamentary seat, etc.); compete in (an election). □□ **con•test•a•ble** /kəntéstəbəl/ *adj.* **con• test•er** /kəntéstər/ *n.* [L *contestari* (as COM-, *testis* witness)]

con•test•ant /kəntéstənt/ *n.* a person who takes part in a contest or competition.

con•tes•ta•tion /kóntestáyshən/ *n.* **1** a disputation. **2** an assertion contended for. [L *contestatio* partly through F (as CONTEST)]

con•text /kóntekst/ *n.* **1** the parts of something written or spoken that immediately precede and follow a word or passage and clarify its meaning. **2** the circumstances relevant to something under consideration (*must be seen in context*). □ out of context without the surrounding natural or spoken circumstances and so not fully understandable. □□ **con•tex•tu•al** /kóntéks-chŏŏəl/ *adj.* **con•tex•tu•al•ize** /kóntéks-chŏŏəlīz/ *v.tr.* **con•tex•tu•al•i•za•tion** *n.* **con•tex•tu•al•ly** *adv.* [ME f. L *contextus* (as COM-, *texere text-* weave)]

con•ti•gu•i•ty /kóntigyŏŏitee/ *n.* **1** being contiguous; proximity; contact. **2** *Psychol.* the proximity of ideas or impressions in place or time, as a principle of association.

con•tig•u•ous /kəntígyŏŏəs/ *adj.* (usu. foll. by *with, to*) touching, esp. along a line or border; in contact. □□ **con•tig•u•ous•ly** *adv.* [L *contiguus* (as COM-, *tangere* touch)]

con•ti•nent¹ /kóntinənt/ *n.* **1** any of the main continuous expanses of land (Europe, Asia, Africa, N. and S. America, Australia, Antarctica). **2** (the Continent) *Brit.* the mainland of Europe as distinct from the British Isles. **3** continuous land; a mainland. [L *terra continens* (see CONTAIN) continuous land]

con•ti•nent² /kóntinənt/ *adj.* **1** able to control movements of the bowels and bladder. **2** exercising self-restraint, esp. sexually. □□ **con•ti•nence** /–nəns/ *n.* **con•ti•nent•ly** *adv.* [ME f. L (as CONTAIN)]

con•ti•nen•tal /kóntinént'l/ *adj. & n.* • *adj.* **1** of or characteristic of a continent. **2** (Continental) *Brit.* of, relating to, or characteristic of mainland Europe. • *n.* an inhabitant of mainland Europe. □□ **con• ti•nen•tal•ly** *adv.*

con•ti•nen•tal break•fast *n.* a light breakfast of coffee, rolls, etc.

con•ti•nen•tal cli•mate *n.* a climate having wide variations of temperature.

Con•ti•nen•tal Di•vide *n.* (also called Great Divide) the high ridge of the Rocky mountains, watershed of the North American continent, separating the river systems flowing either W or E and S.

con•ti•nen•tal drift *n. Geol.* the hypothesis that the continents are moving slowly over the surface of the earth on a deep-lying plastic substratum.

con•ti•nen•tal quilt *n. Brit.* a duvet.

con•ti•nen•tal shelf *n.* an area of relatively shallow seabed between the shore of a continent and the deeper ocean.

con•tin•gen•cy /kəntínjənsee/ *n.* (*pl.* **-cies**) **1** a future event or circumstance regarded as likely to occur, or as influencing present action. **2** something dependent on another uncertain event or occurrence. **3** uncertainty of occurrence. **4 a** one thing incident to another. **b** an incidental or unanticipated expense, etc. [earlier *contingence* f. LL *contingentia* (as CONTINGENT)]

con•tin•gen•cy fund *n.* a fund to cover incidental or unforeseen expenses.

con•tin•gent /kəntínjənt/ *adj. & n.* • *adj.* **1** (usu. foll. by *on, upon*) conditional; dependent (on an uncertain event or circumstance). **2** associated. **3** (usu. foll. by *to*) incidental. **4 a** that may or may not occur. **b** fortuitous; occurring by chance. **5** true only under existing or specified conditions. • *n.* a body (esp. of troops, ships, etc.) forming part of a larger group. □□ **con•tin•gent•ly** *adv.* [L *contingere* (as COM-, *tangere* touch)]

con•tin•u•al /kəntínyŏŏəl/ *adj.* constantly or frequently recurring; always happening. □□ **con•tin•u•al•ly** *adv.* [ME f. OF *continuel* f. *continuer* (as CONTINUE)]

▶ In precise usage, **continual** means 'frequent, repeating at intervals' and **continuous** means 'going on without pause or interruption': *We suffered from the continual attacks of mosquitoe*; *The waterfall's continuous flow creates an endless roar*.

con•tin•u•ance /kəntínyŏŏəns/ *n.* **1** a state of continuing in existence or operation. **2** the duration of an event or action. **3** *Law* a postponement or adjournment. [ME f. OF (as CONTINUE)]

con•tin•u•ant /kəntínyŏŏənt/ *n. & adj. Phonet.* • *n.* a speech sound in which the vocal tract is only partly closed, allowing the breath to pass through and the sound to be prolonged (as with *f, r, s, v*). • *adj.* of or relating to such a sound. [F *continuant* and L *continuare* (as CONTINUE)]

con•tin•u•a•tion /kəntínyŏŏ-áyshən/ *n.* **1** the act or an instance of continuing; the process of being continued. **2** a part that continues something else. **3** *Brit. Stock Exch.* the carrying over of an account to the next settling day. [ME f. OF f. L *continuatio –onis* (as CONTINUE)]

con•tin•u•a•tive /kəntínyŏŏ-áytiv, –ətiv/ *adj.* tending to or serving to continue. [LL *continuativus* (as CONTINUATION)]

con•tin•ue /kəntínyŏŏ/ *v.* (con•tin•ues, con•tin•ued, con•tin•u•ing) **1** *tr.* (often foll. by verbal noun, or to + infin.) persist in, maintain, not stop (an action, etc.). **2 a** *tr.* (also *absol.*) resume or prolong (a narrative, journey, etc.). **b** *intr.* recommence after a pause (*the concert will continue shortly*). **3** *tr.* be a sequel to. **4** *intr.* **a** remain in existence or unchanged. **b** (with compl.) remain in a specified state (*the weather continued fine*). **5** *tr. Law* postpone or adjourn (proceedings). □□ **con·tin·u·a·ble** *adj.* **con·tin·u·er** *n.* [ME f. OF *continuer* f. L *continuare* make or be CONTINUOUS]

con·ti·nu·i·ty /kóntinōŏitee, –nyōŏ–/ *n.* (*pl.* **·ties**) **1 a** the state of being continuous. **b** an unbroken succession. **c** a logical sequence. **2** the detailed and self-consistent scenario of a film or broadcast. **3** the linking of broadcast items. [F *continuité* f. L *continuitas –tatis* (as CONTINUOUS)]

con·tin·u·o /kəntínyōŏ–ō/ *n.* (*pl.* **·os**) *Mus.* an accompaniment providing a bass line and harmonies which are indicated by figures, usu. played on a keyboard instrument. [*basso continuo* (It., = continuous bass)]

con·tin·u·ous /kəntínyōŏəs/ *adj.* **1** unbroken; uninterrupted; connected throughout in space or time. **2** *Gram.* = PROGRESSIVE. □□ **con·tin·u·ous·ly** *adv.* **con·tin·u·ous·ness** *n.* [L *continuus* uninterrupted f. *continēre* (as COM–, *tenēre* hold)]
▶See note at CONTINUAL.

con·tin·u·ous cre·a·tion *n.* the creation of the universe or the matter in it regarded as a continuous process.

con·tin·u·um /kəntínyōŏəm/ *n.* (*pl.* **con·tin·u·a** /–yōŏə/ or **con·tin·u·ums**) anything seen as having a continuous, not discrete, structure (*space-time continuum*). [L, neut. of *continuus*: see CONTINUOUS]

con·tort /kəntáwrt/ *v.tr.* twist or force out of normal shape. [L *contorquēre contort–* (as COM–, *torquēre* twist)]

con·tor·tion /kəntáwrshən/ *n.* **1** the act or process of twisting. **2** a twisted state, esp. of the face or body. [L *contortio* (as CONTORT)]

con·tor·tion·ist /kəntáwrshənist/ *n.* an entertainer who adopts contorted postures.

con·tour /kóntŏŏr/ *n. & v.* ● *n.* **1** an outline, esp. representing or bounding the shape or form of something. **2** the outline of a natural feature, e.g., a coast or mountain mass. **3** a line separating differently colored parts of a design. ● *v.tr.* **1** mark with contour lines. **2** carry (a road or railroad) around the side of a hill. [F f. It. *contorno* f. *contornare* draw in outline (as COM–, *tornare* turn)]

con·tour line *n.* a line on a map joining points of equal altitude.

con·tour map *n.* a map marked with contour lines.

con·tour plow·ing *n.* plowing along lines of constant altitude to minimize soil erosion.

con·tra /kóntrə/ *n.* (*pl.* **con·tras**) a member of a counterrevolutionary guerrilla force in Nicaragua. [abbr. of Sp. *contrarevolucionario* counterrevolutionary]

contra- /kóntrə/ *comb. form* **1** against; opposite (*contradict*). **2** *Mus.* (of instruments, organ stops, etc.) pitched an octave below (*contrabassoon*). [L *contra* against]

con·tra·band /kóntrəband/ *n. & adj.* ● *n.* **1** goods that have been smuggled, or imported or exported illegally. **2** prohibited trade; smuggling. **3** (in full **contraband of war**) goods forbidden to be supplied by neutrals to belligerents. ● *adj.* **1** forbidden to be imported or exported (at all or without payment of duty). **2** concerning traffic in contraband (*contraband trade*). □□ **con·tra·band·ist** *n.* [Sp. *contrabanda* f. It. (as CONTRA–, *bando* proclamation)]

con·tra·bass /kóntrəbays/ *n. Mus.* = double bass. [It. (*basso* BASS¹)]

con·tra·cep·tion /kóntrəsépshən/ *n.* the intentional prevention of pregnancy; the use of contraceptives. [CONTRA– + CONCEPTION]

con·tra·cep·tive /kóntrəséptiv/ *adj. & n.* ● *adj.* preventing pregnancy. ● *n.* a contraceptive device or drug.

con·tract *n. & v.* ● *n.* /kóntrakt/ **1** a written or spoken agreement between two or more parties, intended to be enforceable by law. **2** a document recording this. **3** marriage regarded as a binding commitment. **4** *Bridge*, etc., an undertaking to win the number of tricks bid. ● *v.* /kəntrákt, kóntrakt/ **1** *tr. & intr.* make or become smaller. **2 a** *intr.* (usu. foll. by *with*) make a contract. **b** *intr.* (usu. foll. by *for*, or *to* + infin.) enter formally into a business or legal arrangement. **c** *tr.* (often foll. by *out*) arrange (work) to be done by contract. **3** *tr.* catch or develop (a disease). **4** *tr.* form or develop (a friendship, habit, etc.). **5** *tr.* enter into (marriage). **6** *tr.* incur (a debt, etc.). **7** *tr.* shorten (a word) by combination or elision. **8** *tr.* draw (one's muscles, brow, etc.) together. □ **contract in** (or **out**) (also *refl.*) *Brit.* choose to be involved in (or withdraw or remain out of) a scheme or commitment. □□ **con·trac·tive** /kəntráktiv/ *adj.* [earlier as *adj.*, = contracted: OF, f. L *contractus* (as COM–, *trahere tract–* draw)]

con·tract·a·ble /kəntráktəbəl/ *adj.* (of a disease) that can be contracted.

con·tract bridge *n.* the most common form of bridge, in which only tricks bid and won count toward the game.

con·tract·i·ble /kəntráktibəl/ *adj.* able to be shrunk or capable of contracting.

con·trac·tile /kəntráktˌl, tīl/ *adj.* capable of or producing contraction. □□ **con·trac·til·i·ty** /kóntraktílitee/ *n.*

con·trac·tion /kəntrákshən/ *n.* **1** the act of contracting. **2** *Med.* (usu. in *pl.*) shortening of the uterine muscles during childbirth. **3** shrinking; diminution. **4 a** a shortening of a word by combination or elision. **b** a contracted word or group of words. [F f. L *contractio –onis* (as CONTRACT)]

con·trac·tor /kóntraktər, kəntrák–/ *n.* a person who undertakes a

contract, esp. to provide materials, conduct building operations, etc. [LL (as CONTRACT)]

con·trac·tu·al /kəntrákchōŏəl/ *adj.* of or in the nature of a contract. □□ **con·trac·tu·al·ly** *adv.*

con·tra·dict /kóntrədíkt/ *v.tr.* **1** deny or express the opposite of (a statement). **2** deny or express the opposite of a statement made by (a person). **3** be in opposition to or in conflict with (*new evidence contradicted our theory*). □□ **con·tra·dic·tion** *n.* **con·tra·dic·tor** *n.* [L *contradicere contradict–* (as CONTRA–, *dicere* say)]

con·tra·dic·tion /kóntrədíkshən/ *n.* **1 a** a statement of the opposite; denial. **b** an instance of this. **2** inconsistency. [ME f. OF f. L *contradictio –onis* (as CONTRADICT)]

con·tra·dic·tion in terms *n.* a statement or group of words associating objects or ideas that are incompatible (*true fiction*).

con·tra·dic·to·ry /kóntrədíktəree/ *adj.* **1** expressing a denial or opposite statement. **2** (of statements, etc.) mutually opposed or inconsistent. **3** (of a person) inclined to contradict. **4** *Logic* (of two propositions) so related that one and only one must be true. □□ **con·tra·dic·to·ri·ly** *adv.* **con·tra·dic·to·ri·ness** *n.* [ME f. LL *contradictorius* (as CONTRADICT)]

con·tra·dis·tinc·tion /kóntrədistíngkshən/ *n.* a distinction made by contrasting.

con·tra·dis·tin·guish /kóntrədistínggwish/ *v.tr.* (usu. foll. by *from*) distinguish two things by contrasting them.

con·tra·flow /kóntrəflō/ *n. Brit.* a flow (esp. of road traffic) alongside, and in a direction opposite to, an established or usual flow, esp. as a temporary or emergency arrangement.

con·trail /kóntrayl/ *n.* a condensation trail, esp. from an aircraft. [abbr.]

con·tra·in·di·cate /kóntrəíndikayt/ *v.tr. Med.* act as an indication against (the use of a particular substance or treatment). □□ **con·tra·in·di·ca·tion** /–káyshən/ *n.*

con·tral·to /kəntráltō/ *n.* (*pl.* **·tos**) **1 a** the lowest female singing voice. **b** a singer with this voice. **2** a part written for contralto. [It. (as CONTRA–, ALTO)]

con·tra·po·si·tion /kóntrəpəzíshən/ *n.* **1** opposition or contrast. **2** *Logic* conversion of a proposition from *all A is B* to *all not-B is not-A.* □□ **con·tra·pos·i·tive** /–pózitiv/ *adj. & n.* [LL *contrapositio* (as CONTRA–, *ponere posit–* place)]

con·trap·tion /kəntrápshən/ *n.* often *derog.* or *joc.* a machine or device, esp. a strange or cumbersome one. [19th c.: perh. f. CONTRIVE, INVENTION: assoc. with TRAP¹]

con·tra·pun·tal /kóntrəpúnt'l/ *adj. Mus.* of or in counterpoint. □□ **con·tra·pun·tal·ly** *adv.* **con·tra·pun·tist** *n.* [It. *contrappunto* counterpoint]

con·tra·ri·e·ty /kóntrərí–itee/ *n.* **1** opposition in nature, quality, or action. **2** disagreement; inconsistency. [ME f. OF *contrarieté* f. LL *contrarietas –tatis* (as CONTRARY)]

con·trar·i·wise /kəntráireewīz/ *adv.* **1** on the other hand. **2** in the opposite way. **3** perversely. [ME f. CONTRARY + –WISE]

con·trar·y /kóntreree/ *adj., n., & adv.* ● *adj.* **1** (usu. foll. by *to*) opposed in nature or tendency. **2** (also /kəntráiree/) *colloq.* perverse; self-willed. **3** (of a wind) unfavorable; impeding. **4** mutually opposed. **5** opposite in position or direction. ● *n.* (*pl.* **·ies**) (prec. by *the*) the opposite. ● *adv.* (foll. by *to*) in opposition or contrast (*contrary to expectations it rained*). □ **on the contrary** intensifying a denial of what has just been implied or stated. **to the contrary** to the opposite effect (*can find no indication to the contrary*). □□ **con·trar·i·ly** /–trérilee/ *adv.* **con·trar·i·ness** /–tréreenis/ *n.* [ME f. AF *contrarie*, OF *contraire*, f. L *contrarius* f. *contra* against]

PRONUNCIATION TIP contrary

It is customary to place the stress on the first syllable of this word (KON-tray-ree), whether it is used as an adjective or a noun. But if the adjective is used to mean 'perverse' or 'stubbornly opposed,' the stress is frequently placed on the second syllable, as in the old nursery rhyme: "Mary, Mary, quite contrary."

GRAMMAR TIP contraction

A **contraction** is the result of compressing (or contracting) two words into one by dropping a letter or letters and replacing them with an apostrophe. *He is* becomes *he's*, *they are* becomes *they're*, *I will* becomes *I'll*, and so on. Contractions are common in spoken English, and they can give writing the informality and naturalness of speech (as in dialogues). It is permissible to use contractions in all but the most formal writing, and even here they can be used sparingly if writing out the two words separately sounds stilted or artificial. On the other hand, avoiding the use of a contraction when one would be expected is useful to give emphasis (*I simply will not go along with you*).

con·trast n. & v. ● n. /kóntrast/ **1 a** a juxtaposition or comparison showing striking differences. **b** a difference so revealed. **2** (often foll. by *to*) a thing or person having qualities noticeably different from another. **3 a** the degree of difference between tones in a television picture or a photograph. **b** the change of apparent brightness or color of an object caused by the juxtaposition of other objects. ● v. /kəntrást, kóntrast/ (often foll. by *with*) **1** tr. distinguish or set together so as to reveal a contrast. **2** intr. have or show a contrast. □□ **con·trast·ing·ly** /-trást-/ adv. **con·tras·tive** /-trástiv/ adj. [F *contraste, contraster,* f. It. *contrasto* f. med.L *contrastare* (as CONTRA-, *stare* stand)]

▶Contrast means 'note the differences.' Compare, though, means 'note the similarities.'

con·trast·y /kontrástee, kón-/ adj. (of photographic negatives or prints or of a television picture) showing a high degree of contrast.

con·tra·sug·gest·i·ble /kóntrəsəgéstibəl, -sójés-/ adj. Psychol. tending to respond to a suggestion by believing or doing the contrary.

con·trate wheel /kóntrayt/ n. = CROWN WHEEL. [med.L & Rmc *contrata:* see COUNTRY]

con·tra·vene /kóntrəveén/ v.tr. **1** infringe (a law or code of conduct). **2** (of things) conflict with. □□ **con·tra·ven·er** n. [LL *contravenire* (as CONTRA-, *venire vent-* come)]

con·tra·ven·tion /kóntrəvénshən/ n. **1** infringement. **2** an instance of this. □ **in contravention** of infringing; violating (a law, etc.). [F f. med.L *contraventio* (as CONTRAVENE)]

con·tre·temps /kóntrətóN/ n. **1** an awkward or unfortunate occurrence. **2** an unexpected mishap. [F]

con·trib·ute /kəntríbyŏŏt/ v. (often foll. by *to*) **1** tr. give (money, an idea, help, etc.) toward a common purpose (*contributed $5 to the fund*). **2** intr. help to bring about a result, etc. (*contributed to their downfall*). **3** tr. (also *absol.*) supply (an article, etc.) for publication with others in a journal, etc. □□ **con·trib·u·tive** adj. [L *contribuere contribut-* (as COM-, *tribuere* bestow)]

con·tri·bu·tion /kóntribyŏŏshən/ n. **1** the act of contributing. **2** something contributed, esp. money. **3** an article, etc., contributed to a publication. [ME f. OF *contribution* or LL *contributio* (as CONTRIBUTE)]

con·trib·u·tor /kəntríbyətər/ n. a person who contributes (esp. an article or literary work).

con·trib·u·to·ry /kəntríbyətawree/ adj. **1** that contributes. **2** operated by means of contributions (*contributory pension plan*). [med.L *contributorius* (as CONTRIBUTE)]

con·trib·u·to·ry neg·li·gence n. Law negligence on the part of the injured party through failure to take precautions against an accident.

con·trite /kəntrít, kóntrit/ adj. **1** completely penitent. **2** feeling remorse or penitence; affected by guilt. **3** (of an action) showing a contrite spirit. □□ **con·trite·ly** adv. **con·trite·ness** n. [ME f. OF *contrit* f. L *contritus* bruised (as COM-, *terere trit-* rub)]

con·tri·tion /kəntríshən/ n. the state of being contrite; thorough penitence. [ME f. OF f. LL *contritio –onis* (as CONTRITE)]

con·triv·ance /kəntrívəns/ n. **1** something contrived, esp. a mechanical device or a plan. **2** an act of contriving, esp. deceitfully. **3** inventive capacity.

con·trive /kəntrív/ v.tr. **1** devise; plan or make resourcefully or with skill. **2** (often foll. by to + infin.) manage (*contrived to make matters worse*). □□ **con·triv·a·ble** adj. **con·triv·er** n. [ME f. OF *controver* find, imagine f. med.L *contropare* compare]

con·trived /kəntrívd/ adj. planned so carefully as to seem unnatural; artificial; forced (*the plot seemed contrived*).

con·trol /kəntról/ n. & v. ● n. **1** the power of directing; command (*under the control of*). **2** the power of restraining, esp. self-restraint. **3** a means of restraint; a check. **4** (usu. in *pl.*) a means of regulating prices, etc. **5** (usu. in *pl.*) switches and other devices by which a machine, esp. an aircraft or vehicle, is controlled (also *attrib.: control panel; control room*). **6 a** a place where something is controlled or verified. **b** a person or group that controls something. **7** (also *attrib.: control group*) a standard of comparison for checking the results of a survey or experiment. ● v.tr. (**con·trolled, con·trol·ing**) **1** have control or command of; dominate. **2** exert control over; regulate. **3** hold in check; restrain (*told him to control himself*). **4** serve as control to. **5** check; verify. □ **in control** (often foll. by *of*) directing an activity. **out of control** no longer subject to containment, restraint, or guidance. **under control** being controlled; in order. □□ **con·trol·la·ble** adj. **con·trol·la·bil·i·ty** n. **con·trol·la·bly** adv. [ME f. AF *contreroller* keep a copy of a roll of accounts, f. med.L *contrarotulare* (as CONTRA-, *rotulus* ROLL n.): (n.) perh. f. F *contrôle*]

con·trol·ler /kəntrólər/ n. **1** a person or thing that controls. **2** a person in charge of expenditure, esp. a steward or comptroller. □□ **con·trol·ler·ship** n. [ME *counterroller* f. AF *contrerollour* (as CONTROL)]

con·trol·ling in·ter·est n. a means of determining the policy of a business, etc., esp. by ownership of a majority of the stock.

con·trol rod n. a rod of neutron-absorbing material used to vary the output power of a nuclear reactor.

con·trol tow·er n. a tall building at an airport, etc., from which air traffic is controlled.

con·tro·ver·sial /kóntrəvórshəl/ adj. **1** causing or subject to controversy. **2** of controversy. **3** given to controversy. □□ **con·tro·ver·sial·ism** n. **con·tro·ver·sial·ist** n. **con·tro·ver·sial·ly** adv. [LL *controversialis* (as CONTROVERSY)]

con·tro·ver·sy /kóntrəvərsee/ n. (pl. **·sies**) a prolonged argument or dispute, esp. when conducted publicly. [ME f. L *controversia* (as CONTROVERT)]

con·tro·vert /kóntrəvórt/ v.tr. **1** dispute; deny. **2** argue about; discuss. □□ **con·tro·vert·i·ble** adj. [orig. past part.; f. F *controvers(e)* f. L *controversus* (as CONTRA-, *vertere vers-* turn)]

con·tu·ma·cious /kóntŏŏmáyshəs, -tyŏŏ-/ adj. insubordinate; stubbornly or willfully disobedient, esp. to a court order. □□ **con·tu·ma·cious·ly** adv. [L *contumax,* perh. rel. to *tumēre* swell]

con·tu·ma·cy /kóntŏŏməsee/ n. stubborn refusal to obey or comply. [L *contumacia* f. *contumax:* see CONTUMACIOUS]

con·tu·me·li·ous /kóntŏŏmeéleeəs, -tyŏŏ-/ adj. reproachful, insulting, or insolent. □□ **con·tu·me·li·ous·ly** adv. [ME f. OF *contumelieus* f. L *contumeliosus* (as CONTUMELY)]

con·tu·me·ly /kóntŏŏmələe, -tŏŏmlee, -tŏŏ, -tyŏŏ/ n. **1** insolent or reproachful language or treatment. **2** disgrace. [ME f. OF *contumelie* f. L *contumelia* (as COM-, *tumēre* swell)]

con·tuse /kəntŏŏz, -tyŏŏz/ v.tr. injure without breaking the skin; bruise. □□ **con·tu·sion** /-zhən/ n. [L *contundere contus-* (as COM-, *tundere* thump)]

co·nun·drum /kənúndrəm/ n. **1** a riddle, esp. one with a pun in its answer. **2** a hard or puzzling question. [16th c.: orig. unkn.]

con·ur·ba·tion /kónərbáyshən/ n. an extended urban area, esp. one consisting of several towns and merging suburbs. [CON- + L *urbs urbis* city + –ATION]

con·ure /kónyər/ n. any medium-sized parrot of the genus *Pyrrhura,* with mainly green plumage and a long gradated tail. [mod.L *conurus* f. Gk *kōnos* cone + *oura* tail]

con·va·lesce /kónvəlés/ v.intr. recover one's health after illness or medical treatment. [ME f. L *convalescere* (as COM-, *valēre* be well)]

con·va·les·cent /kónvəlésənt/ adj. & n. ● adj. **1** recovering from an illness. **2** of or for persons in convalescence. /-səns/ ● n. a convalescent person. □□ **con·va·les·cence** /-səns/ n.

con·vec·tion /kənvékshən/ n. **1** transference of heat in a gas or liquid by upward movement of the heated and less dense medium. **2** Meteorol. the transfer of heat by the upward flow of hot air or downward flow of cold air. □□ **con·vec·tion·al** adj. **con·vec·tive** adj. [LL *convectio* f. L *convehere convect-* (as COM-, *vehere vect-* carry)]

con·vec·tion cur·rent n. circulation that results from convection.

con·vec·tor /kənvéktər/ n. a heating appliance that circulates warm air by convection.

con·ve·nance /kónvənaáns/ n. (usu. in *pl.*) conventional propriety. [F f. *convenir* be fitting (as CONVENE)]

con·vene /kənveén/ v. **1** tr. summon or arrange (a meeting, etc.). **2** intr. assemble. **3** tr. summon (a person) before a tribunal. □□ **con·ven·a·ble** adj. **con·ven·er** n. **con·ve·nor** n. [ME f. L *convenire convent-* assemble, agree, fit (as COM-, *venire* come)]

con·ven·ience /kənveényəns/ n. & v. **1** the quality of being convenient; suitability. **2** freedom from difficulty or trouble; material advantage (*for convenience*). **3** an advantage (*a great convenience*). **4** a useful thing, esp. an installation or piece of equipment. **5** Brit. a bathroom or toilet, esp. a public one. ● v.tr. afford convenience to; suit; accommodate. □ **at one's convenience** at a time or place that suits one. **at one's earliest convenience** as soon as one can. **make a convenience of** take advantage of (a person) insensitively. [ME f. L *convenientia* (as CONVENE)]

con·ven·ience food n. food, esp. complete meals, that has been preprepared commercially and so requires little preparation by the consumer.

con·ven·ience store n. a store with extended opening hours and in a convenient location, stocking a limited range of basic household goods and groceries.

con·ven·ient /kənveényənt/ adj. **1** (often foll. by *for, to*) **a** serving one's comfort or interests; easily accessible. **b** suitable. **c** free of trouble or difficulty. **2** available or occurring at a suitable time or place (*will try to find a convenient moment*). **3** well situated for some purpose (*convenient for shopping*). □□ **con·ven·ient·ly** adv. [ME (as CONVENE)]

con·vent /kónvent, -vənt/ n. **1** a religious community, esp. of nuns, under vows. **2** the premises occupied by this. **3** (in full **convent school**) a school attached to and run by a convent. [ME f. AF *covent,* OF *convent* f. L *conventus* assembly (as CONVENE)]

con·ven·ti·cle /kənvéntikəl/ n. esp. hist. **1** a secret or unlawful religious meeting, esp. of dissenters. **2** a building used for this. [ME f. L *conventiculum* (place of) assembly, dimin. of *conventus* (as CONVENE)]

con·ven·tion /kənvénshən/ n. **1 a** general agreement, esp. agreement on social behavior, etc., by implicit consent of the majority. **b** a custom or customary practice, esp. an artificial or formal one. **2 a** a formal assembly or conference for a common purpose. **b** an assembly of the delegates of a political party to select candidates for office. **c** *Brit. hist.* a meeting of Parliament without a summons from the sovereign. **3 a** a formal agreement. **b** an agreement between nations, esp. one less formal than a treaty. **4** *Cards* an accepted method of play (in leading, bidding, etc.) used to convey information to a partner. **5** the act of convening. [ME f. OF f. L *conventio –onis* (as CONVENE)]

con•ven•tion•al /kənvénshənəl/ *adj.* **1** depending on or according to convention. **2** (of a person) attentive to social conventions. **3** usual; of agreed significance. **4** not spontaneous nor sincere nor original. **5** (of weapons or power) nonnuclear. **6** *Art* following tradition rather than nature. □□ **con•ven•tion•al•ism** *n.* **con•ven•tion•al•ist** *n.* **con•ven•tion•al•i•ty** /–shənálitee/ *n.* **con•ven•tion•al•ize** *v.tr.* **con•ven•tion•al•ly** *adv.* [F *conventionnel* or LL *conventionalis* (as CONVENTION)]

con•ven•tion•eer /kənvénshəneér/ *n.* a person attending a convention.

con•ven•tu•al /kənvénchōōəl/ *adj. & n.* ● *adj.* **1** of or belonging to a convent. **2** of the less strict branch of the Franciscans, living in large convents. ● *n.* **1** a member of a convent. **2** a conventual Franciscan. [ME f. med.L *conventualis* (as CONVENT)]

con•verge /kənvérj/ *v.intr.* **1** come together as if to meet or join. **2** (of lines) tend to meet at a point. **3** (foll. by *on, upon*) approach from different directions. **4** *Math.* (of a series) approximate in the sum of its terms toward a definite limit. [LL *convergere* (as COM-, *vergere* incline)]

con•ver•gent /kənvérjənt/ *adj.* **1** converging. **2** *Biol.* (of unrelated organisms) having the tendency to become similar while adapting to the same environment. **3** *Psychol.* (of thought) tending to reach only the most rational result. □□ **con•ver•gence** /–jəns/ *n.* **con•ver•gen•cy** *n.*

con•ver•sant /kənvérsənt, kónvərs–/ *adj.* (foll. by *with*) well experienced or acquainted with a subject, person, etc. □□ **con•ver•sance** /–vórsəns/ *n.* **con•ver•san•cy** *n.* [ME f. OF, pres. part. of *converser* CONVERSE[1]]

con•ver•sa•tion /kónvərsáyshən/ *n.* **1** the informal exchange of ideas by spoken words. **2** an instance of this. [ME f. OF f. L *conversatio –onis* (as CONVERSE[1])]

con•ver•sa•tion•al /kónvərsáyshənəl/ *adj.* **1** of or in conversation. **2** fond of or good at conversation. **3** colloquial. □□ **con•ver•sa•tion•al•ly** *adv.*

con•ver•sa•tion•al•ist /kónvərsáyshənəlist/ *n.* one who is good at or fond of conversing.

con•ver•sa•tion piece *n.* **1** a type of genre painting in which a group of figures are posed in a landscape or domestic setting, popular esp. in the 18th century. **2** an object that serves as a topic of conversation because of its unusual quality.

con•ver•sa•tion stop•per *n. colloq.* an unexpected remark, esp. one that cannot readily be answered.

con•ver•sa•zi•o•ne /kónvərsáatseeónee, káwnveraátsyáwne/ *n.* (*pl.* **con•ver•sa•zi•o•nes** or **con•ver•sa•zi•o•ni** /–tseeónee, tsyáwnee/) a social gathering held by a learned or art society. [It. f. L (as CONVERSATION)]

con•verse[1] *v. & n.* ● *v.intr.* /kənvérs/ (often foll. by *with*) engage in conversation (*conversed with him about various subjects*). ● *n.* /kónvərs/ *archaic* conversation. □□ **con•vers•er** /kənvórsər/ *n.* [ME f. OF *converser* f. L *conversari* keep company (with), frequent. of *convertere* (CONVERT)]

con•verse[2] *adj. & n.* ● *adj.* /kənvórs, kónvərs/ opposite; contrary; reversed. ● *n.* /kónvərs/ **1** something that is opposite or contrary. **2** a statement formed from another statement by the transposition of certain words, e.g., *some philosophers are men* from *some men are philosophers*. **3** *Math.* a theorem whose hypothesis and conclusion

are the conclusion and hypothesis of another. □□ **con•verse•ly** *adv.* [L *conversus*, past part. of *convertere* (CONVERT)]

con•ver•sion /kənvórzhən, –shən/ *n.* **1** the act or an instance of converting or the process of being converted, esp. in belief or religion. **2 a** an adaptation of a building for new purposes. **b** a converted building. **3** transposition; inversion. **4** *Theol.* the turning of sinners to God. **5** the transformation of fertile into fissile material in a nuclear reactor. **6** *Football* the scoring of an extra point or points after scoring a touchdown. **7** *Psychol.* the change of an unconscious conflict into a physical disorder or disease. [ME f. OF f. L *conversio –onis* (as CONVERT)]

con•vert *v. & n.* ● *v.* /kənvórt/ **1** *tr.* (usu. foll. by *into*) change in form, character, or function. **2** *tr.* cause (a person) to change beliefs, opinion, party, etc. **3** *tr.* change (money, stocks, units in which a quantity is expressed, etc.) into others of a different kind. **4** *tr.* make structural alterations in (a building) to serve a new purpose. **5** *tr.* (also *absol.*) *Football* score an extra point or points after a touchdown. **6** *intr.* be converted or convertible (*the sofa converts into a bed*). **7** *tr.* *Logic* interchange the terms of (a proposition). ● *n.* /kónvərt/ (often foll. by *to*) a person who has been converted to a different belief, opinion, etc. □ **convert to one's own use** wrongfully make use of (another's property). [ME f. OF *convertir* ult. f. L *convertere* *convers-* turn about (as COM-, *vertere* turn)]

con•vert•er /kənvórtər/ *n.* (also **con•ver•tor**) **1** a person or thing that converts. **2** *Electr.* **a** an electrical apparatus for the interconversion of alternating current and direct current. **b** *Electronics* an apparatus for converting a signal from one frequency to another. **3** a reaction vessel used in making steel.

con•vert•er re•ac•tor *n.* a nuclear reactor that converts fertile material into fissile material.

con•vert•i•ble /kənvórtibəl/ *adj. & n.* ● *adj.* **1** that may be converted. **2** (of currency, etc.) that may be converted into other forms, esp. into gold or US dollars. **3** (of a car) having a folding or detachable roof. **4** (of terms) synonymous. ● *n.* a car with a folding or detachable roof. □□ **con•vert•i•bil•i•ty** *n.* **con•vert•i•bly** *adv.* [OF f. L *convertibilis* (as CONVERT)]

con•vex /kónveks, kənvéks/ *adj.* having an outline or surface curved like the exterior of a circle or sphere (cf. CONCAVE). □□ **con•vex•i•ty** /–véksitee/ *n.* **con•vex•ly** *adv.* [L *convexus* vaulted, arched]

con•vey /kənváy/ *v.tr.* **1** transport or carry (goods, passengers, etc.). **2** communicate (an idea, meaning, etc.). **3** *Law* transfer the title to (property). **4** transmit (sound, smell, etc.). □□ **con•vey•a•ble** *adj.* [ME f. OF *conveier* f. med.L *conviare* (as COM-, L *via* way)]

con•vey•ance /kənváyəns/ *n.* **1 a** the act or process of carrying. **b** the communication (of ideas, etc.). **c** transmission. **2** a means of transport; a vehicle. **3** *Law* **a** the transfer of property from one owner to another. **b** a document effecting this. □□ **con•vey•anc•er** *n.* (in sense 3). **con•vey•anc•ing** *n.* (in sense 3).

convex and concave

con•vey•or /kənváyər/ *n.* (also **con•vey•er**) a person or thing that conveys.

con•vey•or belt *n.* an endless moving belt for conveying articles or materials, esp. in a factory or at a supermarket checkout.

con•vict *v. & n.* ● *v.tr.* /kənvíkt/ **1** (often foll. by *of*) prove to be guilty (of a crime, etc.). **2** declare guilty by the verdict of a jury or the decision of a judge. ● *n.* /kónvikt/ **1** a person found guilty of a criminal offense. **2** a person serving a prison sentence. [ME f. L *convincere* *convict-* (as COM-, *vincere* conquer): noun f. obs. *convict* convicted]

con•vic•tion /kənvíkshən/ *n.* **1 a** the act or process of proving or finding guilty. **b** an instance of this (*has two previous convictions*). **2 a** the action or resulting state of being convinced. **b** a firm belief or opinion. **c** an act of convincing. [L *convictio* (as CONVICT)]

con•vince /kənvíns/ *v.tr.* **1** (often foll. by *of*, or *that* + clause) persuade (a person) to believe or realize. **2** (as **convinced** *adj.*) firmly persuaded (*a convinced pacifist*). □□ **con•vinc•er** *n.* **con•vin•ci•ble** *adj.* [L (as CONVICT)]

con•vinc•ing /kənvínsing/ *adj.* **1** able to or such as to convince. **2** leaving no margin of doubt; substantial (*a convincing victory*). □□ **con•vinc•ing•ly** *adv.*

con•viv•i•al /kənvíveeəl/ *adj.* **1** fond of good company; sociable and lively. **2** festive (*a convivial atmosphere*). □□ **con•viv•i•al•i•ty** /–veeálitee/ *n.* **con•viv•i•al•ly** *adv.* [L *convivialis* f. *convivium* feast (as COM-, *vivere* live)]

con•vo•ca•tion /kónvəkáyshən/ *n.* **1** the act of calling together. **2** a large formal gathering of people, esp.: **a** *US* a formal ceremony at a university, as for giving awards. **b** *Brit.* a provincial synod of the

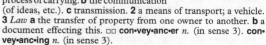

Anglican clergy of Canterbury or York. **c** *Brit.* a legislative or deliberative assembly of a university. □□ **con•vo•ca•tion•al** *adj.* [ME f. L *convocatio* (as CONVOKE)]

con•voke /kənvṓk/ *v.tr. formal* call (people) together to a meeting, etc.; summon to assemble. [L *convocare convocat-* (as COM-, *vocare* call)]

con•vo•lut•ed /kónvəlŏŏtid/ *adj.* **1** coiled; twisted. **2** complex; intricate. □□ **con•vo•lut•ed•ly** *adv.* [past part. of convolute f. L *convolutus* (as COM-, *volvere volut-* roll)]

con•vo•lu•tion /kónvəlŏŏshən/ *n.* **1** coiling; twisting. **2** a coil or twist. **3** complexity. **4** a sinuous fold in the surface of the brain. □□ **con•vo•lu•tion•al** *adj.* [med.L *convolutio* (as CONVOLUTED)]

con•volve /kənvólv/ *v.tr. & intr.* (esp. as **convolved** *adj.*) roll together; coil up. [L *convolvere* (as COM-, *vellere* pull)]

con•vol•vu•lus /kənvólvyələs/ *n.* any twining plant of the genus *Convolvulus*, with trumpet-shaped flowers, e.g., bindweed. [L]

con•voy /kónvoy/ *n. & v.* **1** a group of ships traveling together or under escort. **2** a supply of provisions, etc., under escort. **3** a group of vehicles traveling on land together or under escort. **4** the act of traveling or moving in a group or under escort. • *v.tr.* **1** (of a warship) escort (a merchant or passenger vessel). **2** escort, esp. with armed force. [OF *convoyer* var. of *conveier* CONVEY]

con•vul•sant /kənvúlsənt/ *adj. & n. Pharm.* • *adj.* producing convulsions. • *n.* a drug that may produce convulsions. [F f. *convulser* (as CONVULSE)]

con•vulse /kənvúls/ *v.tr.* **1** (usu. in *passive*) affect with convulsions. **2** cause to laugh uncontrollably. **3** shake violently; agitate; disturb. [L *convellere convuls-* (as COM-, *vellere* pull)]

con•vul•sion /kənvúlshən/ *n.* **1** (usu. in *pl.*) violent irregular motion of a limb or limbs or the body caused by involuntary contraction of muscles, esp. as a disorder of infants. **2** a violent natural disturbance, esp. an earthquake. **3** violent social or political agitation. **4** (in *pl.*) uncontrollable laughter. □□ **con•vul•sion•ar•y** *adj.* [F *convulsion* or L *convulsio* (as CONVULSE)]

con•vul•sive /kənvúlsiv/ *adj.* **1** characterized by or affected with convulsions. **2** producing convulsions. □□ **con•vul•sive•ly** *adv.*

co•ny var. of CONEY.

coo /kŏŏ/ *n., v., & int.* • *n.* a soft murmuring sound like that of a dove or pigeon. • *v.* (**coos, cooed**) **1** *intr.* make the sound of a coo. **2** *intr. & tr.* talk or say in a soft or amorous voice. • *int. Brit. sl.* expressing surprise or incredulity. □□ **coo•ing•ly** *adv.* [imit.]

coo•ee /kŏŏ-ee/ *n., int., & v. Brit. colloq.* • *n. & int.* a sound used to attract attention, esp. at a distance. • *v.intr.* (**coo•ees, coo•eed, coo•ee•ing**) make this sound. □ **within cooee** (or **a cooee**) **of** *Austral. & NZ colloq.* very near to. [imit. of a signal used by Australian Aboriginals and copied by settlers]

cook /kŏŏk/ *v. & n.* • *v.* **1** *tr.* prepare (food) by heating it. **2** *intr.* (of food) undergo cooking. **3** *tr. colloq.* falsify (accounts, etc.); alter to produce a desired result. **4** *tr. sl.* ruin; spoil. **5** *tr.* (esp. as **cooked** *adj.*) *Brit. sl.* fatigue; exhaust. **6** *tr. & intr. colloq.* do or proceed successfully. **7** *intr.* (as **be cooking**) *colloq.* be happening or about to happen (*went to find out what was cooking*). • *n.* a person who cooks, esp. professionally or in a specified way (*a good cook*). □ **cook a person's goose** ruin a person's chances. **cook up** *colloq.* invent or concoct (a story, excuse, etc.). □□ **cook•a•ble** *adj. & n.* [OE *cōc* f. pop.L *cocus* for L *coquus*]

cook•book /kŏŏkbŏŏk/ *n.* a book containing recipes and other information about cooking.

cook•er /kŏŏkər/ *n.* **1 a** a container or device for cooking food. **b** *Brit.* an appliance powered by gas, electricity, etc., for cooking food. **2** *Brit.* a fruit, etc., (esp. an apple) that is more suitable for cooking than for eating raw.

cook•er•y /kŏŏkəree/ *n.* (*pl.* **•ies**) the art or practice of cooking.

cook•house /kŏŏk-hows/ *n.* **1** a camp kitchen. **2** an outdoor kitchen in warm countries. **3** a ship's galley.

cook•ie /kŏŏkee/ *n.* (also **cook•y**) (*pl.* **cook•ies**) a small sweet cake. □ **that's the way the cookie crumbles** *colloq.* that is how things turn out; that is the unalterable state of affairs. [Du. *koekje* dimin. of *koek* cake]

cook•ie cut•ter *n.* a device with sharp edges for cutting cookie dough into a particular shape.

cook•ie-cut•ter *adj.* denoting something mass-produced or lacking any distinguishing characterstics; unvarying (*cookie-cutter apartment in a high-rise building*).

cook•ing /kŏŏking/ *n.* **1** the art or process by which food is cooked. **2** (*attrib.*) suitable for or used in cooking (*cooking apple; cooking utensils*).

cook•out /kŏŏkowt/ *n.* a gathering with an open-air cooked meal; a barbecue.

cook•shop /kŏŏkshop/ *n.* an establishment where prepared food is served or sold; a restaurant.

cook•ware /kŏŏkwair/ *n.* utensils for cooking, esp. dishes, pans, etc.

cool /kŏŏl/ *adj., n., & v.* • *adj.* **1** of or at a fairly low temperature, fairly cold (*a cool day; a cool bath*). **2** suggesting or achieving coolness

(*cool colors; cool clothes*). **3 a** (of a person) calm; unexcited. **b** (of an act) done without emotion. **4** lacking zeal or enthusiasm. **5** unfriendly; lacking cordiality (*got a cool reception*). **6** (of jazz playing) restrained; relaxed. **7** calmly audacious (*a cool customer*). **8** (prec. by *a*) *colloq.* at least; not less than (*cost me a cool thousand*). **9** *sl.* excellent; marvelous; suave; stylish. • *n.* **1** coolness. **2** cool air; a cool place. **3** *sl.* calmness; composure (*keep one's cool; lose one's cool*). • *v.* (often foll. by *down, off*) **1** *tr. & intr.* make or become cool. **2** *intr.* (of anger, emotions, etc.) lessen; become calmer. □ **cool one's heels** see HEEL[1]. **cool it** *sl.* relax, calm down. □□ **cool•ish** *adj.* **cool•ly** /kŏŏl-lee/ *adv.* **cool•ness** *n.* [OE *cōl, cōlian,* f. Gmc: cf. COLD]

coo•la•bah /kŏŏləbaa/ *n.* (also **coo•li•bah** /–libaa/) *Austral.* any of various gum trees, esp. *Eucalyptus microtheca.* [Aboriginal]

cool•ant /kŏŏlənt/ *n.* **1** a cooling agent, esp. fluid, to remove heat from an engine, nuclear reactor, etc. **2** a fluid used to lessen the friction of a cutting tool. [COOL + –ANT after *lubricant*]

cool•er /kŏŏlər/ *n.* **1** a vessel in which a thing is cooled. **2 a** a refrigerated room. **b** an insulated container for keeping foods, etc., cold. **3** a tall drink, esp. a spritzer; assist. **2** *sl.* prison or a prison cell.

cool•head•ed /kŏŏlhédid/ *adj.* not easily excited.

coo•li•bah var. of COOLABAH.

coo•lie /kŏŏlee/ *n. offens.* (also **coo•ly**) (*pl.* **•lies**) an unskilled native laborer in Asian countries. [perh. f. *Kulī,* an aboriginal tribe of Gujarat, India]

coo•lie hat *n.* a broad conical hat as worn by coolies.

cool•ing-off pe•ri•od *n.* **1** an interval to allow for a change of mind before commitment to action. **2** an interval after a sale contract is agreed to during which the purchaser can decide to cancel without loss.

cool•ing tow•er *n.* a tall, cylindrical concrete structure used for cooling water or condensing steam from an industrial process.

coomb /kŏŏm/ *n.* (also **combe**) *Brit.* **1** a valley or hollow on the side of a hill. **2** a short valley running up from the coast. [OE *cumb:* cf. CWM]

coon /kŏŏn/ *n.* **1** a raccoon. **2** *sl. offens.* a black person. [abbr.]

coon•can /kŏŏnkan/ *n.* a simple card game like rummy (orig. Mexican). [Sp. *con quién* with whom?]

coon•skin /kŏŏnskin/ *n.* **1** the skin of a raccoon. **2** a cap, etc., made of this.

coop /kŏŏp/ *n. & v.* • *n.* **1** a cage placed over sitting or fattening fowls. **2** building for keeping chickens, etc. **3** a small place of confinement, esp. a prison. **4** *Brit.* a basket used in catching fish. • *v.tr.* **1** put or keep (a fowl) in a coop. **2** (often foll. by *up, in*) confine (a person) in a small space. [ME *cupe* basket f. MDu., MLG *kūpe,* ult. f. L *cupa* cask]

co-op /kṓ-op/ *n. colloq.* **1** a cooperative business or enterprise. **2** = COOPERATIVE. [abbr.]

coop•er /kŏŏpər/ *n. & v.* • *n.* a maker or repairer of casks, barrels, etc. • *v.tr.* make or repair (a cask). [ME f. MDu., MLG *kūper* f. *kūpe* COOP]

coop•er•age /kŏŏpərij/ *n.* **1** the work or establishment of a cooper. **2** money payable for a cooper's work.

co•op•er•ate /kō-ópərayt/ *v.intr.* (also **co-op•er•ate**) **1** (often foll. by *with*) work or act together; assist. **2** (of things) concur in producing an effect. □□ **co•op•er•ant** /–rənt/ *adj.* **co•op•er•a•tor** *n.* [eccl.L *cooperari* (as CO-, *operari* f. *opus operis* work)]

co•op•er•a•tion /kō-ópəráyshən/ *n.* (also **co-op•er•a•tion**) **1** working together to the same end; assistance. **2** *Econ.* the formation and operation of cooperatives. [ME f. L *cooperatio* (as COOPERATE): partly through F *coopération*]

co•op•er•a•tive /kō-ópərətiv, –óprə–/ *adj. & n.* (also **co-op•er•a•tive**) • *adj.* **1** of or affording cooperation. **2** willing to cooperate. **3** *Econ.* (of a farm, shop, or other business) owned and run jointly by its members, with profits shared among them. **4** (of an apartment building) with individual units owned by their occupiers. • *n.* a cooperative farm or society or business. □□ **co•op•er•a•tive•ly** *adv.* **co•op•er•a•tive•ness** *n.* [LL *cooperativus* (as COOPERATE)]

co-opt /kō-ópt, kṓ-opt/ *v.tr.* appoint to membership of a body by invitation of the existing members. □□ **co-op•ta•tion** /–optáyshən/ *n.* **co-op•tion** /–ópshən/ *n.* **co-op•tive** *adj.* [L *cooptare* (as CO-, *optare* choose)]

co•or•di•nate *v., adj., & n.* (also **co-or•di•nate**) • *v.* /kō– áwrd'nayt/ **1** *tr.* bring (various parts, movements, etc.) into a proper or required relation to ensure harmony or effective operation, etc. **2** *intr.* work or act together effectively. **3** *tr.* make coordinate; organize; classify. • *adj.* /kō-áwrd'nət/ **1** equal in rank or importance. **2** in which the parts are coordinated; involving coordination. **3** *Gram.* (of parts of a compound sentence) equal in status (cf. SUBORDINATE). **4** *Chem.* denoting a type of covalent bond in which one atom provides both the shared electrons. • *n.* /kō-áwrd'nət/ **1** *Math.* each of a system of magnitudes used to fix the position of a point, line, or plane. **2** a person or thing equal in rank or importance. **3** (in *pl.*) matching items of clothing. □□ **co•or•di•nate•ly** *adv.* **co•or•di•na•tion** /–d'náyshən/ *n.* **co•or•di•na•tive** *adj.* **co•or•di•na•tor** *n.* [CO- + L *ordinare ordinat-* f. *ordo –inis* order]

coot /kŏŏt/ *n.* **1** any black aquatic bird of the genus *Fulica,* esp. F *atra* with the upper mandible extended backward to form a white plate on the forehead. **2** *colloq.* a stupid person. [ME, prob. f. LG]

coot·ie /kŏotee/ *n. sl.* a body louse. [perh. f. Malay *kutu* a biting parasite]

cop[1] /kop/ *n. & v. sl.* ● *n.* **1** a policeman. **2** *Brit.* a capture or arrest (*it's a fair cop*). ● *v.tr.* (**copped, cop·ping**) **1** catch or arrest (an offender). **2** *Brit.* receive; suffer. **3** take; seize. □ **cop it** *Brit.* **1** get into trouble; be punished. **2** be killed. **cop out 1** withdraw; give up an attempt. **2** go back on a promise. **3** escape. **2** an escape; a way of escape. **cop a plea** *sl.* = PLEA BARGAIN. **not much** (or **no**) **cop** *Brit.* of little or no value or use. [perh. f. obs. *cap* arrest f. OF *caper* seize f. L *capere*: (n.) cf. COPPER[2]]

cop[2] /kop/ *n.* (in spinning) a conical ball of thread wound on a spindle. [OE *cop* summit]

co·pa·cet·ic /kópəsétik/ *adj. sl.* excellent; in good order. [20th c.: orig. unkn.]

co·pai·ba /kəpíbə, -páy-/ *n.* an aromatic oil or resin from any plant of the genus *Copaifera*, used in medicine and perfumery. [Sp. & Port. f. Guarani *cupauba*]

co·pal /kópəl/ *n.* a resin from any of various tropical trees, used for varnish. [Sp. f. Aztec *copalli* incense]

co·part·ner /kópáartnər/ *n.* a partner or associate, esp. when sharing equally. □□ **co·part·ner·ship** *n.*

cope[1] /kōp/ *v.intr.* **1** (foll. by *with*) deal effectively or contend successfully with a person or task. **2** manage successfully; deal with a situation or problem (*found they could no longer cope*). [ME f. OF *coper, colper* f. *cop, colp* blow f. med.L *colpus* f. L *colaphus* f. Gk *kolaphos* blow with the fist]

cope[2] /kōp/ *n. & v.* ● *n.* **1** *Eccl.* a long, cloaklike vestment worn by a priest or bishop in ceremonies and processions. **2** esp. *poet.* a covering compared with a cope. ● *v.tr.* cover with a cope or coping. [ME ult. f. LL *cappa* CAP, CAPE[1]]

co·peck var. of KOPECK.

co·pe·pod /kópəpod/ *n.* any small aquatic crustacean of the class Copepoda, many of which form the minute components of plankton. [Gk *kōpē* oar-handle + *pous podos* foot]

Co·per·ni·can sys·tem /kəpərnikən/ *n.* (also **Co·per·ni·can the·o·ry**) *Astron.* the theory that the planets (including the earth) move around the sun (cf. PTOLEMAIC SYSTEM). [*Copernicus* latinized f. M. *Kopernik*, Polish astronomer d. 1543]

cope·stone /kópstōn/ *n.* **1** a stone used in a coping. **2** a finishing touch. [COPE[2] + STONE]

cop·i·a·ble /kópeeəbəl/ *adj.* that can or may be copied.

cop·i·er /kópeeər/ *n.* a machine or person that copies (esp. documents).

co·pi·lot /kópílət/ *n.* a second pilot in an aircraft.

cop·ing /kóping/ *n.* the top (usu. sloping) course of masonry in a wall or parapet.

cop·ing saw /kóping/ *n.* a D-shaped saw for cutting curves in wood. [*cope* cut wood f. OF *coper*: see COPE[1]]

cop·ing·stone /kópingstōn/ *n.* esp. *Brit.* = COPESTONE.

co·pi·ous /kópeeəs/ *adj.* **1** abundant; plentiful. **2** producing much. **3** providing much information. **4** profuse in speech. □□ **co·pi·ous·ly** *adv.* **co·pi·ous·ness** *n.* [ME f. OF *copieux* or f. L *copiosus* f. *copia* plenty]

co·pi·ta /kəpéetə/ *n.* **1** a tulip-shaped sherry glass. **2** a glass of sherry. [Sp., dimin. of *copa* cup]

co·pla·nar /kópláynər/ *adj. Geom.* in the same plane. □□ **co·pla·nar·i·ty** /-plənáiritee/ *n.*

co·pol·y·mer /kópólimər/ *n. Chem.* a polymer with units of more than one kind. □□ **co·po·lym·er·ize** *v.tr. & intr.*

cop-out *n.* **1** a cowardly or feeble evasion.

cop·per[1] /kópər/ *n., adj., & v.* ● *n.* **1** *Chem.* a malleable, red-brown metallic element of the transition series occurring naturally, esp. in cuprous oxide and malachite, and used esp. for electrical cables and apparatus. ¶ Symb.: **Cu**. **2** a bronze coin. **3** *Brit.* a large metal vessel for boiling, esp. laundry. ● *adj.* made of or colored like copper. ● *v.tr.* cover (a ship's bottom, a pan, etc.) with copper. [OE *copor, coper*, ult. f. L *cyprium aes* Cyprus metal]

cop·per[2] /kópər/ *n. sl.* a policeman. [COP[1] + -ER[1]]

cop·per·as /kópərəs/ *n.* green iron-sulfate crystals. [ME *coperose* f. OF *couperose* f. med.L *cup(e)rosa*: perh. orig. *aqua cuprosa* copper water]

cop·per beech *n.* a variety of beech with copper-colored leaves.

cop·per belt *n.* a copper-mining area of Central Africa.

cop·per·head /kópərhed/ *n.* **1** a venomous viper, *Agkistrodon contortrix*, native to N. America. **2** a venomous cobra, *Denisonia superba*, native to Australia.

cop·per·plate /kópərplayt/ *n. & adj.* ● *n.* **1 a** a polished copper plate for engraving or etching. **b** a print made from this. **2** an ornate style of handwriting resembling that orig. used in engravings. ● *adj.* of or in copperplate writing.

cop·per py·ri·tes *n.* a double sulfide of copper and iron. Also called **chalcopyrite**.

cop·per·smith /kópərsmith/ *n.* a person who works in copper.

cop·per sul·fate *n.* a blue crystalline solid used in electroplating, textile dyeing, and as a fungicide.

cop·per·y /kópəree/ *adj.* of or like copper, esp. in color.

cop·pice /kópis/ *n. & v.* ● *n.* an area of undergrowth and small trees, grown for periodic cutting. ● *v.tr.* cut back (young trees) periodically to stimulate growth of shoots. □□ **cop·piced** *adj.* [OF *copeïz* ult. f. med.L *colpus* blow: see COPE[1]]

cop·ra /kóprə/ *n.* the dried kernels of the coconut. [Port. f. Malayalam *koppara* coconut]

co·pre·cip·i·ta·tion /kóprisípitáyshən/ *n. Chem.* the simultaneous precipitation of more than one compound from a solution.

copro- /kóprō/ *comb. form* dung; feces. [Gk *kopros* dung]

co·pro·duc·tion /kóprədúkshən/ *n.* a production of a play, broadcast, etc., jointly by more than one company.

cop·ro·lite /kóprəlīt/ *n. Archaeol.* fossil dung or a piece of it.

cop·roph·a·gous /koprófəgəs/ *adj. Zool.* dung-eating. [COPRO-]

cop·ro·phil·i·a /kóprəfileeə/ *n.* an abnormal interest in feces and defecation.

co·pros·ma /kəprózmə/ *n.* any small evergreen plant of the genus *Coprosma*, native to Australasia. [mod.L f. Gk *kopros* dung + *osmē* smell]

copse /kops/ *n.* **1** = COPPICE. **2** (in general use) a small forest. □□ **copsy** *adj.* [shortened f. COPPICE]

copse·wood /kópswŏod/ *n.* undergrowth.

cop shop *n. slang* a police station.

Copt /kopt/ *n.* **1** a native Egyptian in the Hellenistic and Roman periods. **2** a native Christian of the independent Egyptian Church. [F *Copte* or mod.L *Coptus* f. Arab. *al-kibṭ, al- kubṭ* Copts f. Coptic *Gyptios* f. Gk *Aiguptios* Egyptian]

cop·ter /kóptər/ *n.* a helicopter. [shortening f. *helicopter*]

Cop·tic /kóptik/ *n. & adj.* ● *n.* the language of the Copts, now used only in the Coptic Church. ● *adj.* of or relating to the Copts.

cop·u·la /kópyələ/ *n.* (*pl.* **cop·u·las** or **cop·u·lae** /-lee/) *Logic & Gram.* a connecting word, esp. a part of the verb *be* connecting a subject and predicate. □□ **cop·u·lar** *adj.* [L (as CO-, *apere* fasten)]

cop·u·late /kópyəlayt/ *v.intr.* (often foll. by *with*) have sexual intercourse. □□ **cop·u·la·to·ry** /-látawree/ *adj.* [L *copulare* fasten together (as COPULA)]

cop·u·la·tion /kópyəláyshən/ *n.* **1** sexual union. **2** a grammatical or logical connection. [ME f. OF f. L *copulatio* (as COPULATE)]

cop·u·la·tive /kópyəlaytiv, -lətiv/ *adj.* **1** serving to connect. **2** *Gram.* **a** (of a word) that connects words or clauses linked in sense (cf. DISJUNCTIVE). **b** connecting a subject and predicate. **3** relating to sexual union. □□ **cop·u·la·tive·ly** *adv.* [ME f. OF *copulatif -ive* or LL *copulativus* (as COPULATE)]

cop·y /kópee/ *n. & v.* ● *n.* (*pl.* **-ies**) **1** a thing made to imitate or be identical to another. **2** a single specimen of a publication or issue (*ordered twenty copies*). **3 a** matter to be printed. **b** material for a newspaper or magazine article (*scandals make good copy*). **c** the text of an advertisement. **4 a** a model to be copied. **b** a page written after a model (of penmanship). ● *v.* (**-ies, -ied**) **1** *tr.* **a** make a copy of. **b** (often foll. by *out*) transcribe. **2** *intr.* make a copy, esp. clandestinely. **3** *tr.* (foll. by *to*) send a copy of (a letter) to a third party. **4** *tr.* do the same as; imitate. [ME f. OF *copie, copier*, ult. f. L *copia* abundance (in med.L = transcript)]

cop·y·book /kópeebŏok/ *n.* **1** a book containing models of handwriting for learners to imitate. **2** (*attrib.*) **a** tritely conventional. **b** accurate, exemplary.

cop·y·cat /kópeekat/ *n. colloq.* a person who copies another, esp. closely.

cop·y·desk /kópeedesk/ *n.* the desk at which copy is edited for printing.

cop·y·ed·it /kópee-édit/ *v.tr.* edit (copy) for printing.

cop·y ed·i·tor *n.* a person who edits text to be printed for consistency and accuracy.

cop·y·hold /kópeehōld/ *n. Brit. hist.* **1** tenure of land based on manorial records. **2** land held in this way. □□ **cop·y·hold·er** *n.*

cop·y·ist /kópee-ist/ *n.* **1** a person who makes (esp. written) copies. **2** an imitator. [earlier *copist* f. F *copiste* or med.L *copista* (as COPY)]

cop·y·read·er /kópeereedər/ *n.* a person who reads and edits copy for a newspaper or book. □□ **cop·y·read** *v.tr.*

cop·y·right /kópeerīt/ *n., adj., & v.* ● *n.* the exclusive legal right granted for a specified period to an author, designer, etc., or another appointed person, to print, publish, perform, film, or record original literary, artistic, or musical material. ● *adj.* (of such material) protected by copyright. ● *v.tr.* secure copyright for (material).

cop·y·right li·brar·y *n. Brit.* a library entitled to a free copy of each book published in the UK.

cop·y typist *n.* a person who makes typewritten transcripts of written or dictated material.

cop·y·writ·er /kópeerītər/ *n.* a person who writes or prepares copy (esp. of advertising material) for publication. □□ **cop·y·writ·ing** *n.*

coq au vin /kōk ō vÁN/ n. a casserole of chicken pieces cooked in wine. [F]

co•quet•ry /kókitree, kōkétree/ n. (pl. •ries) 1 coquettish behavior. 2 a coquettish act. 3 trifling with serious matters. [F coquetterie f. coqueter (as COQUETTE)]

co•quette /kōkét/ n. 1 a woman who flirts. 2 any crested hummingbird of the genus Lophornis. □□ **co•quet•tish** adj. **co•quet•tish•ly** adv. **co•quet•tish•ness** n. [F, fem. of coquet wanton, dimin. of coq cock]

co•qui•na /kōke̅enə/ n. a soft limestone of broken shells, used in roadmaking. [Sp., = cockle]

co•qui•to /kōke̅eto̅/ n. (pl. •tos) a palm tree, Jubaea chilensis, native to Chile, yielding honey from its sap, and fiber. [Sp., dimin. of coco coconut]

Cor. abbr. 1 Corinthians (New Testament). 2 coroner.

cor /kawr/ int. Brit. sl. expressing surprise, alarm, exasperation, etc. [corrupt. of God]

cor- /kər/ prefix assim. form of COM- before r.

cor•a•cle /káwrəkəl, kór–/ n. Brit. a small boat of wickerwork covered with watertight material, used on Welsh and Irish lakes and rivers. [Welsh corwgl (corwg = Ir. currach boat: cf. CURRACH)]

cor•a•coid /káwrəkoyd, kór–/ n. (in full **coracoid process**) a short projection from the shoulder blade in vertebrates. [mod.L coracoides f. Gk korakoeidēs ravenlike f. korax –akos raven]

cor•al /káwrəl, kór–/ n. & adj. • n. 1 a a hard red, pink, or white calcareous substance secreted by various marine polyps for support and habitation. b any of these usu. colonial organisms. 2 the unimpregnated roe of a lobster or scallop. • adj. 1 like coral, esp. in color. 2 made of coral. [ME f. OF f. L corallum f. Gk korallion, prob. of Semitic orig.]

cor•al•line /káwrəlin, –lin, kór–/ n. & adj. • n. 1 any seaweed of the genus Corallina having a calcareous jointed stem. 2 (in general use) the name of various plantlike compound organisms. • adj. 1 coral red. 2 of or like coral. [F corallin & It. corallina f. LL corallinus (as CORAL)]

cor•al•lite /káwrəlit, kór–/ n. 1 the coral skeleton of a marine polyp. 2 fossil coral. [L corallum CORAL]

cor•al•loid /káwrəloyd, kór–/ adj. & n. • adj. like or akin to coral. • n. a coralloid organism.

cor•al reef n. (also **cor•al is•land**) a reef formed by the growth of coral.

cor•al snake n. any of various brightly colored poisonous snakes, esp. Micrurus fulvius, native to the southeastern US.

co•ram po•pu•lo /káwrəm pópyəlō/ adv. in public. [L, = in the presence of the people]

cor an•glais /káwr ONgláy/ n. (pl. **cors an•glais** pronunc. same) esp. Brit. = ENGLISH HORN.

cor•bel /káwrbəl, –bel/ n. & v. Archit. • n. 1 a projection of stone, timber, etc., jutting out from a wall to support a weight. 2 a short timber laid longitudinally under a beam to help support it. • v.tr. & intr. (**cor•beled, cor•bel•ing**; esp. Brit. **cor•belled, cor•bel•ling**) (foll. by out, off) support or project on corbels. [ME f. OF, dimin. of corp: see CORBIE]

cor•bel steps n. = CORBIESTEPS.

cor•bel ta•ble n. a projecting course of bricks or stones resting on corbels.

cor•bie /káwrbee/ n. Sc. 1 a raven. 2 a carrion crow. [ME f. OF corb, corp f. L corvus crow]

cor•bie•steps /káwrbeesteps/ n. the steplike projections on the sloping sides of a gable.

cor bli•mey int. see BLIMEY.

cord /kawrd/ n. & v. • n. 1 a long, thin, flexible material made from several twisted strands. b a piece of this. 2 Anat. a structure in the body resembling a cord (spinal cord). 3 a ribbed fabric, esp. corduroy. b (in pl.) corduroy trousers. c a cordlike rib on fabric. 4 an electric flex. 5 a measure of cut wood (usu. 128 cu.ft., 3.6 cubic meters). 6 a moral or emotional tie (cords of affection; fourfold cord of evidence). • v.tr. 1 fasten or bind with cord. 2 (as **corded** adj.) a (of cloth) ribbed. b provided with cords. c (of muscles) standing out like taut cords. □□ **cord•like** adj. [ME f. OF corde f. L chorda f. Gk khordē gut, string of musical instrument]

cord•age /káwrdij/ n. cords or ropes, esp. in the rigging of a ship. [ME f. F (as CORD)]

cor•date /káwrdayt/ adj. heart-shaped. [mod.L cordatus f. L cor cordis heart]

cor•de•lier /káwrd'leer/ n. a Franciscan friar of the strict rule (wearing a knotted cord around the waist). [ME f. OF f. cordele dimin. of corde CORD]

cor•dial /káwrjəl/ adj. & n. • adj. 1 heartfelt; sincere. 2 warm; friendly. • n. 1 a a liqueur. b Brit. a fruit-flavored drink. □□ **cor•dial•i•ty** /–jeeálitee/ n. **cor•dial•ly** adv. [ME f. med.L cordialis f. L cor cordis heart]

cor•dil•le•ra /káwrd'lyáirə, kawrdílərə/ n. a system or group of usu. parallel mountain ranges together with intervening plateaus, etc.,

esp. of the Andes and in Central America and Mexico. [Sp. f. cordilla dimin. of cuerda CORD]

cord•ite /káwrdīt/ n. a smokeless explosive made from cellulose nitrate and nitroglycerine. [CORD (from its appearance) + –ITE[1]]

cord•less /káwrdlis/ adj. (of an electrical appliance, telephone, etc.) working from an internal source of energy, etc. (esp. a battery), and without a connection to an electrical supply or central unit.

cor•don /káwrd'n/ n. & v. • n. 1 a line or circle of police, soldiers, guards, etc., esp. preventing access to or from an area. 2 a an ornamental cord or braid. b the ribbon of a knightly order. 3 a fruit tree trained to grow as a single stem. 4 Archit. a stringcourse. • v.tr. (often foll. by off) enclose or separate with a cordon of police, etc. [It. cordone augmentative of corda CORD, & F cordon (as CORD)]

cor•don bleu /káwrdawN blŏ/ adj. & n. Cooking • adj. of the highest class. • n. a cook of this class. [F, = blue ribbon]

cor•don sa•ni•taire /kawrdáwN sáneetáir/ n. 1 a guarded line between infected and uninfected districts. 2 any measure designed to prevent communication or the spread of undesirable influences.

cor•do•van /káwrdəvən/ n. a kind of soft leather. [Sp. cordovan of Cordova (Córdoba) where it was orig. made]

cor•du•roy /káwrdəroy/ n. 1 a thick cotton fabric with velvety ribs. 2 (in pl.) corduroy trousers. [18th c.: prob. f. CORD ribbed fabric + obs. duroy coarse woolen fabric]

cor•du•roy road n. a road made of tree trunks laid across a swamp.

cord•wain•er /káwrdwaynər/ n. Brit. archaic a shoemaker (usu. in names of guilds, etc.). [obs. cordwain CORDOVAN]

cord•wood /káwrdwŏod/ n. wood that is or can easily be measured in cords.

CORE /kawr/ abbr. Congress of Racial Equality.

core /kawr/ n. & v. • n. 1 the horny central part of various fruits, containing the seeds. 2 a the central or most important part of anything (also attrib.: core curriculum). b the central part, of different character from the surroundings. 3 the central region of the earth. 4 the central part of a nuclear reactor, containing the fissile material. 5 a magnetic structural unit in a computer, storing one bit of data (see BIT[4]). 6 the inner strand of an electric cable, rope, etc. 7 a piece of soft iron forming the center of an electromagnet or an induction coil. 8 an internal mold filling a space to be left hollow in a casting. 9 the central part cut out (esp. of rock, etc., in boring). 10 Archaeol. a piece of flint from which flakes or blades have been removed. • v.tr. remove the core from. □□ **cor•er** n. [ME: orig. unkn.]

co•re•la•tion esp. Brit. var. of CORRELATION.

co•re•li•gion•ist /kórilíjənist/ n. an adherent of the same religion.

co•rel•la /kərélə/ n. Austral. either of two small white cockatoos, Cacatua tenuirostris or C. sanguinea. [app. Latinized f. Aboriginal ca-rall]

co•re•op•sis /káwreeópsis/ n. any composite plant of the genus Coreopsis, having rayed usu. yellow flowers. [mod.L f. Gk koris bug + opsis appearance, with ref. to the shape of the seed]

co•re•spond•ent /kó-rispóndənt/ n. a person cited in a divorce case as having committed adultery with the respondent.

corf /kawrf/ n. (pl. **corves** /kawrvz/) Brit. 1 a basket in which fish are kept alive in the water. 2 a small wagon, formerly a large basket, used in mining. [MDu., MLG korf, OHG chorp, korb f. L corbis basket]

cor•gi /káwrgee/ n. (pl. **cor•gis**) (in full **Welsh corgi**) 1 a dog of a short-legged breed with foxlike head. 2 this breed. [Welsh f. cor dwarf + ci dog]

co•ri•a•ceous /káwree-áyshəs/ adj. like leather; leathery. [LL coriaceus f. corium leather]

co•ri•an•der /káwreeándər/ n. 1 a plant, Coriandrum sativum, with leaves used for flavoring and small, round, aromatic fruits. 2 (also **co•ri•an•der seed**) the dried fruit used for flavoring curries, etc. [ME f. OF coriandre f. L coriandrum f. Gk koriannon]

Co•rin•thi•an /kəríntheeən/ adj. & n. • adj. 1 of ancient Corinth in southern Greece. 2 Archit. of an order characterized by ornate decoration and flared capitals with rows of acanthus leaves, used esp. by the Romans. 3 archaic profligate. • n. a native of Corinth. [L Corinthius f. Gk Korinthios + –AN]

Co•ri•o•lis ef•fect /káwreeólis/ n. a hypothetical force used to explain rotating systems, such that the movement of air or water over the surface of the rotating earth is directed clockwise in the northern hemisphere and counterclockwise in the southern hemisphere. [G. G. Coriolis, Fr. scientist d. 1843]

co•ri•um /káwreeəm/ n. Anat. the dermis. [L, = skin]

cork /kawrk/ n. & v. • n. 1 the buoyant light-brown bark of the cork oak. 2 a bottle stopper of cork or other material. 3 a float of cork used in fishing, etc. 4 Bot. a protective layer of dead cells immediately below the bark of woody plants. 5 (attrib.) made of cork. • v.tr. (often foll. by up) 1 stop or confine. 2 restrain (feelings, etc.). 3 blacken with burned cork. □□ **cork•like** adj. [ME f. Du. & LG kork f. Sp. alcorque cork sole, perh. f. Arab.]

cork•age /káwrkij/ n. a charge made by a restaurant or hotel for serving wine, etc., when brought in by customers.

corked /kawrkt/ adj. 1 stopped with a cork. 2 (of wine) spoiled by a decayed cork. 3 blackened with burned cork.

cork•er /káwrkər/ n. sl. an excellent or astonishing person or thing.

cork•ing /káwrking/ adj. sl. strikingly large or splendid.

cork oak n. a S. European oak, *Quercus suber*.

cork•screw /káwrkskrōō/ n. & v. • n. 1 a spirally twisted steel device for extracting corks from bottles. 2 (often *attrib.*) a thing with a spiral shape. • v.tr. & intr. move spirally; twist.

cork•wood /káwrkwŏŏd/ n. 1 any shrub of the genus *Duboisia*, yielding a light porous wood. 2 this wood.

cork•y /káwrkee/ adj. (cork•i•er, cork•i•est) 1 corklike. 2 (of wine) corked.

corm /kawrm/ n. Bot. an underground swollen stem base of some plants, e.g., crocus. [mod.L *cormus* f. Gk *kormos* trunk with boughs lopped off]

cor•mo•rant /káwrmərənt, –mərant/ n. any diving sea bird of the family Phalacrocoracidae, esp. *Phalacrocorax carbo* having lustrous black plumage. [ME f. OF *cormaran* f. med.L *corvus marinus* sea raven: for ending –*ant* cf. *peasant, tyrant*]

corn[1] /kawrn/ n. & v. • n. 1 a a tall-growing orig. N. American cereal plant, *Zea mays*, cultivated in many varieties, bearing kernels on a long ear (cob). b the cobs or kernels of this plant. 2 Brit. a any cereal before or after harvesting, esp. the chief crop of a region. b a grain or seed of a cereal plant. 3 colloq. something corny or trite. • v.tr. (as **corned** adj.) sprinkled or preserved with salt or brine (*corned beef*). [OE f. Gmc: rel. to L *granum* grain]

corn

corn[2] /kawrn/ n. a small area of horny usu. tender skin esp. on the toes, extending into subcutaneous tissue. [ME f. AF f. L *cornu* horn]

corn•ball /kórnbawl/ n. & adj. • n. an unsophisticated or mawkishly sentimental person. • adj. = CORNY adj. 1.

corn•brash /káwrnbrash/ n. Geol. Brit. an earthy limestone layer of the Jurassic period. [CORN[1] + BRASH[2]]

corn bread n. bread made with cornmeal.

corn•cob /káwrnkaab/ n. the cylindrical center of the corn ear to which rows of grains (kernels) are attached.

corn•cob pipe n. a tobacco pipe with a bowl made from a dried corncob.

corn cock•le n. see COCKLE[2].

corn crake /káwrnkrayk/ n. a rail, *Crex crex*, inhabiting grassland and nesting on the ground.

corn dog n. a hot dog covered in cornmeal batter, fried, and served on a stick.

corn dol•ly n. a symbolic or decorative figure made of plaited straw, corn husks, etc.

cor•ne•a /káwrneeə/ n. the transparent circular part of the front of the eyeball. □□ **cor•ne•al** adj. [med.L *cornea tela* horny tissue, f. L *corneus* horny f. *cornu* horn]

cor•nel /káwrnəl, –nel/ n. any plant of the genus *Cornus*, esp. a dwarf kind, *C. suecica*. [ME f. L *cornus*]

cor•nel•ian var. of CARNELIAN.

cor•ne•ous /káwrneeəs/ adj. hornlike; horny. [L *corneus* f. *cornu* horn]

cor•ner /káwrnər/ n. & v. • n. 1 a place where converging sides or edges meet. 2 a projecting angle, esp. where two streets meet. 3 the internal space or recess formed by the meeting of two sides, esp. of a room. 4 a difficult position, esp. one from which there is no escape (*driven into a corner*). 5 a secluded or remote place. 6 a region or quarter, esp. a remote one (*from the four corners of the earth*). 7 the action or result of buying or controlling the whole available stock of a commodity, thereby dominating the market. 8 Boxing & Wrestling a an angle of the ring, esp. one where a contestant rests between rounds. b a contestant's supporters offering assistance at the corner between rounds. 9 Soccer a free kick or hit from a corner of the field after the ball has been kicked over the goal line by a defending player. • v. 1 tr. force (a person or animal) into a difficult or inescapable position. 2 tr. a establish a corner in (a commodity). b dominate (dealers or the market) in this way. 3 intr. (esp. of or in a vehicle) go around a corner. □ **just around the corner** colloq. very near; imminent. [ME f. AF ult. f. L *cornu* horn]

cor•ner•stone /káwrnərstōn/ n. 1 a a stone in a projecting angle of a wall. b a foundation stone. 2 an indispensable part or basis of something.

cor•ner•wise /káwrnərwīz/ adv. diagonally.

cor•net[1] n. 1 /kawrnét/ Mus. a a brass instrument resembling a trumpet but shorter and wider. b its player. c an organ stop with the quality of a cornet. d a cornetto. 2 /káwrnit, kawrnét/ Brit. an ice-cream cone. □□ **cor•net•ist** or **cor•net•tist** n. [ME f. OF ult. f. L *cornu* horn]

cor•net[2] /káwrnit/ n. Brit. hist. the fifth commissioned officer in a cavalry troop, who carried the colors. □□ **cor•net•cy** n. (pl. •**cies**) [earlier sense 'pennon, standard' f. F *cornette* dimin. of *corne* ult. f. L *cornua* horns]

cor•nett /kawrnét/ n. Mus. = CORNETTO. [var. of CORNET[1]]

cor•net•to /kawrnétō/ n. (pl. **cor•net•ti** /–tee/) Mus. an old woodwind instrument like a flageolet. [It., dimin. of *corno* horn (as CORNET[1])]

corn•field /káwrnfeeld/ n. a field in which corn is being grown.

corn•flake /káwrnflayk/ n. 1 (in pl.) a breakfast cereal of toasted flakes made from cornmeal. 2 a flake of this cereal.

corn•flow•er /káwrnflowər/ n. any plant of the genus *Centaurea* growing among corn, esp. *C. cyanus*, with deep-blue flowers.

cor•nice /káwrnis/ n. 1 Archit. a an ornamental molding around the wall of a room just below the ceiling. b a horizontal molded projection crowning a building or structure, esp. the uppermost member of the entablature of an order, surmounting the frieze. 2 Mountaineering an overhanging mass of hardened snow at the edge of a precipice. □□ **cor•niced** adj. [F *corniche*, etc., f. It. *cornice*, perh. f. L *cornix –icis* crow]

cor•niche /káwrnish, kawrnéesh/ n. (in full **corniche road**) 1 a road cut into the edge of a cliff, etc. 2 a coastal road with wide views. [F: see CORNICE]

Cor•nish /káwrnish/ adj. & n. • adj. of or relating to Cornwall in SW England. • n. the ancient Celtic language of Cornwall.

corn mar•i•gold n. a daisylike, yellow-flowered plant, *Chrysanthemum segetum*.

corn•meal /káwrnmeel/ n. meal ground from corn.

corn•row /kórnrō/ n. & v. • n. any of usu. several narrow plaits of hair braided close to the scalp. • v.tr. plait (hair) in cornrows.

corn sal•ad n. a plant, *Valerianella locusta*, eaten in salads.

corn•starch /káwrnstaarch/ n. finely-ground corn flour, used as a thickener in cooking.

corn•stone /káwrnstōn/ n. Brit. Geol. a mottled red and green limestone usu. formed under arid conditions, esp. in the Devonian period.

cor•nu•co•pi•a /káwrnəkópeeə, –nyə–/ n. 1 a a symbol of plenty consisting of a goat's horn overflowing with flowers, fruit, etc. b an ornamental vessel shaped like this. 2 an abundant supply. □□ **cor•nu•co•pi•an** adj. [LL f. L *cornu copiae* horn of plenty]

corn whis•key n. whiskey distilled from corn.

corn•y /káwrnee/ adj. (corn•i•er, corn•i•est) 1 colloq. a trite. b feebly humorous. c sentimental. d old-fashioned; out of date. 2 of or abounding in corn. □□ **corn•i•ly** adv. **corn•i•ness** n. [CORN[1] + –Y[1]: sense 1 f. sense 'rustic']

co•rol•la /kərólə, –rō–/ n. Bot. a whorl or whorls of petals forming the inner envelope of a flower. [L, dimin. of *corona* crown]

cor•ol•lar•y /káwrəleree, kór–/ n. & adj. • n. (pl. •**ies**) 1 a a proposition that follows from (and is often appended to) one already proved. b an immediate deduction. 2 (often foll. by *of*) a natural consequence or result. • adj. 1 supplementary; associated. 2 (often foll. by *to*) forming a corollary. [ME f. L *corollarium* money paid for a garland; gratuity: neut. adj. f. COROLLA]

co•ro•na[1] /kərónə/ n. (pl. **co•ro•nas** or **co•ro•nae** /–nee/) 1 a a small circle of light around the sun or moon. b the rarefied gaseous envelope of the sun, seen as an irregularly shaped area of light around the moon's disk during a total solar eclipse. 2 a circular chandelier hung from a roof. 3 Anat. a crown or crownlike structure. 4 Bot. a crownlike outgrowth from the inner side of a corolla. 5 Archit. a broad vertical face of a cornice, usu. of considerable projection. 6 Electr. the glow around a conductor at high potential. [L, = crown]

co•ro•na[2] /kərónə/ n. a long cigar with straight sides. [Sp. *La Corona* the crown]

cor•o•nach /káwrənək, –nəkh/ n. Sc. & Ir. a funeral song or dirge. [Ir. *coranach*, Gael. *corranach* f. *comh–* together + *rànach* outcry]

co•ro•na•graph /kərónəgraf/ n. an instrument for observing the sun's corona, esp. other than during a solar eclipse.

cor•o•nal[1] /kərónəl, káwrən'l, kór–/ adj. 1 Astron. & Bot. of a corona. 2 Anat. of the crown of the head. [F *coronal* or L *coronalis* (as CORONA[1])]

cor•o•nal[2] /káwrən'l, kór–/ n. 1 a circlet (esp. of gold or gems) for the head. 2 a wreath or garland. [ME, app. f. AF f. *corone* CROWN]

cor•o•nal bone n. the frontal bone of the skull.

cor•o•nal plane n. an imaginary plane dividing the body into dorsal and ventral parts.

cor•o•nal su•ture n. Anat. the transverse suture of the skull separating the frontal bone from the parietal bones.

cor•o•nar•y /káwrəneree, kór–/ adj. & n. • adj. Anat. resembling or encircling like a crown. • n. (pl. •**ies**) 1 = CORONARY THROMBOSIS. 2 a heart attack. [L *coronarius* f. *corona* crown]

cor•o•nar•y ar•te•ry n. an artery supplying blood to the heart.

cor•o•nar•y care u•nit n. a hospital unit providing specialized care for patients with serious heart conditions.

cor•o•nar•y throm•bo•sis n. Med. a blockage of the blood flow caused by a blood clot in a coronary artery.

cor•o•na•tion /káwrənáyshən, kór–/ n. the ceremony of crowning a sovereign or a sovereign's consort. [ME f. OF f. med.L *coronatio –onis* f. *coronare* to crown f. CORONA[1]]

cor·o·ner /káwrənər, kór–/ *n.* an officer of a county, district, or municipality, holding inquests on deaths thought to be violent or accidental, and *Brit.* inquiries in cases of treasure trove. □□ **cor·o·ner·ship** *n.* [ME f. AF *cor(o)uner* f. *coro(u)ne* CROWN]

cor·o·net /káwrənit, –nét, kór–/ *n.* **1** a small crown (esp. as worn, or used as a heraldic device, by a peer or peeress). **2** a circlet of precious materials, esp. as a woman's headdress or part of one. **3** a garland for the head. **4** the lowest part of a horse's pastern. **5** a ring of bone at the base of a deer's antler. □□ **cor·o·net·ed** *adj.* [OF *coronet(t)e* dimin. of *corone* CROWN]

co·ro·zo /kərózó/ *n.* (*pl.* ·zos) *Bot.* any of various palm trees native to S. America. [Sp.]

co·ro·zo nut *n.* a seed of one species of palm, *Phytelephas macrocarpa*, which when hardened forms vegetable ivory. Also called **ivory nut.**

Corp. *abbr.* **1** corporal. **2** corporation.

cor·po·ra *pl.* of CORPUS.

cor·po·ral[1] /káwrpərəl, káwrprəl/ *n.* **1** a noncommissioned army, air force, or marine officer ranking next below sergeant. **2** (in full **ship's corporal**) *Brit.* an officer under the master-at-arms, attending to police matters. **3** a freshwater fallfish, *Semotilus corporalis.* [obs. F, var. of *caporal* f. It. *caporale* prob. f. L *corporalis* (as CORPORAL[2]), confused with It. *capo* head]

cor·po·ral[2] /káwrpərəl, káwrprəl/ *adj.* of or relating to the human body (cf. CORPOREAL). □□ **cor·po·ral·ly** *adv.* [ME f. OF f. L *corporalis* f. *corpus –oris* body]

cor·po·ral[3] /káwrpərəl, káwrprəl/ *n.* a cloth on which the vessels containing the consecrated elements are placed during the celebration of the Eucharist. [OE f. OF *corporal* or med.L *corporale pallium* body cloth (as CORPORAL[2])]

cor·po·ral pun·ish·ment *n.* punishment inflicted on the body, esp. by beating.

cor·po·rate /káwrpərət, káwrprit/ *adj.* **1** forming a corporation (*corporate body*; *body corporate*). **2** forming one body of many individuals. **3** of or belonging to a corporation or group (*corporate responsibility*). **4** corporative. □□ **cor·po·rate·ly** *adv.* **cor·po·rat·ism** *n.* [L *corporare corporat-* form into a body (*corpus –oris*)]

cor·po·rate raid·er *n.* a financier who makes a practice of making hostile takeover bids for companies, either to control their policies or to resell them for a profit.

cor·po·ra·tion /káwrpəráyshən/ *n.* **1** a group of people authorized to act as an individual and recognized in law as a single entity, esp. in business. **2** (in the UK) the municipal authorities of a borough, town, or city. **3** *joc.* a protruding stomach. [LL *corporatio* (as CORPORATE)]

cor·po·ra·tive /káwrpərətiv, –ráytiv/ *adj.* **1** of a corporation. **2** governed by or organized in corporations, esp. of employers and employed. □□ **corporativism** *n.*

cor·po·re·al /kawrpáwreeəl/ *adj.* **1** bodily, physical, material, esp. as distinct from spiritual (cf. CORPORAL[2]). **2** *Law* consisting of material objects. □□ **cor·po·re·al·i·ty** /–reeálitee/ *n.* **cor·po·re·al·ly** *adv.* [LL *corporealis* f. L *corporeus* f. *corpus –oris* body]

cor·po·re·ity /káwrpəréeitee, –ráy–/ *n.* **1** the quality of being or having a material body. **2** bodily substance. [F *corporéité* or med.L *corporeitas* f. L *corporeus* (as CORPOREAL)]

cor·po·sant /káwrpəzant/ *n.* = ST. ELMO'S FIRE. [OSp., Port., It. *corpo santo* holy body]

corps /kawr/ *n.* (*pl.* **corps** /kawrz/) **1** *Mil.* **a** a body of troops with special duties (*intelligence corps*; *Marine Corps*). **b** a main subdivision of an army in the field, consisting of two or more divisions. **2** a body of people engaged in a special activity (*diplomatic corps*; *press corps*). [F (as CORPSE)]

SPELLING TIP   **corps**

A *corps* is a body of live men. Don't kill it by adding an *e* (*corpse*).

---

corps de bal·let /káwr də baláy/ *n.* the company of ensemble dancers in a ballet. [F]

corps d'é·lite /káwrdayleét/ *n.* a select group. [F]

corps dip·lo·mat·ique /káwrdípləmateék/ *n.* a diplomatic corps. [F]

corpse /kawrps/ *n.* a dead (usu. human) body.

WORD HISTORY   **corpse**

Middle English (denoting the living body of a person or animal): alteration of archaic *corse* by association with Latin *corpus*, a change which also took place in French (Old French *cors* becoming *corps*). The *p* was originally silent, as in French; the final *e* was rare before the 19th century, but now distinguishes *corpse* from *corps*.

---

cor·pu·lent /káwrpyələnt/ *adj.* bulky in body; fat. □□ **cor·pu·lence** /–ləns/ *n.* **cor·pu·len·cy** *n.* [ME f. L *corpulentus* f. *corpus* body]

cor·pus /káwrpəs/ *n.* (*pl.* **cor·po·ra** /káwrpərə/ or **cor·pus·es**) **1** a

body or collection of writings, texts, spoken material, etc. **2** *Anat.* a structure of a special character in the animal body. [ME f. L, = body]

Cor·pus Chris·ti /káwrpəs krístee/ *n.* a feast commemorating the Eucharist, observed on the Thursday after Trinity Sunday. [ME f. L, = Body of Christ]

cor·pus·cle /káwrpusəl/ *n.* a minute body or cell in an organism, esp. (in *pl.*) the red or white cells in the blood of vertebrates. □□ **cor·pus·cu·lar** /kawrpúskyələr/ *adj.* [L *corpusculum* (as CORPUS)]

cor·pus de·lic·ti /káwrpəs dilíkti/ *n. Law* the facts and circumstances constituting a breach of a law. [L, = body of offense]

cor·pus lu·te·um /káwrpəs lóoteeəm/ *n.* (*pl.* **cor·po·ra lu·te·a** /lóoteeə/) *Anat.* a body developed in the ovary after discharge of the ovum, remaining in existence only if pregnancy has begun. [mod.L f. CORPUS + *luteus, –um* yellow]

corr. *abbr.* **1** correction. **2** correspondence.

cor·ral /kərál/ *n. & v.* ● *n.* **1** a pen for cattle, horses, etc. **2** an enclosure for capturing wild animals. **3** *hist.* a defensive circle of wagons in an encampment. ● *v.tr.* (**cor·ralled, cor·ral·ling**) **1** put or keep in a corral. **2** form (wagons) into a corral. **3** *colloq.* gather in; acquire. [Sp. & OPort. (as KRAAL)]

cor·ra·sion /kəráyzhən/ *n. Geol.* erosion of the earth's surface by rock material being carried over it by water, ice, etc. [L *corradere corras-* scrape together (as COM-, *radere* scrape)]

cor·rect /kərékt/ *adj. & v.* ● *adj.* **1** true; right; accurate. **2** (of conduct, manners, etc.) proper; right. **3** in accordance with good standards of taste, etc. ● *v.tr.* **1** set right; amend (an error, omission, etc., or the person responsible for it). **2** mark the errors in (written or printed work, etc.). **3** substitute the right thing for (the wrong one). **4 a** admonish or rebuke (a person). **b** punish (a person or fault). **5** counteract (a harmful quality). **6** adjust (an instrument, etc.) to function accurately or accord with a standard. □□ **cor·rect·ly** *adv.* **cor·rect·ness** *n.* [ME (adj. through F) f. L *corrigere correct-* (as COM-, *regere* guide)]

cor·rec·tion /kərékshən/ *n.* **1 a** the act or process of correcting. **b** an instance of this. **2** a thing substituted for what is wrong. **3** a program of incarceration, parole, probation, etc., for dealing with convicted offenders. **4** *archaic* punishment. □□ **cor·rec·tion·al** *adj.* [ME f. OF f. L *correctio –onis* (as CORRECT)]

cor·rec·ti·tude /kəréktitōod, –tyōod/ *n.* correctness, esp. conscious correctness of conduct. [19th c., f. CORRECT + RECTITUDE]

cor·rec·tive /kəréktiv/ *adj. & n.* ● *adj.* serving or tending to correct or counteract something undesired or harmful. ● *n.* a corrective measure or thing. □□ **cor·rec·tive·ly** *adv.* [F *correctif –ive* or LL *correctivus* (as CORRECT)]

cor·rec·tor /kəréktər/ *n.* a person who corrects or points out faults. [ME f. AF *correctour* f. L *corrector* (as CORRECT)]

cor·re·late /káwrəlayt, kór–/ *n. & v.* ● *v.* **1** *tr.* (foll. by *with, to*) have a mutual relation. **2** *tr.* (usu. foll. by *with*) bring into a mutual relation. ● *n.* each of two related or complementary things (esp. so related that one implies the other). [back-form. f. CORRELATION, CORRELATIVE]

cor·re·la·tion /káwrəláyshən, kór–/ *n.* (also esp. *Brit.* **co·re·la·tion** /kó-ree–/) **1** a mutual relation between two or more things. **2 a** interdependence of variable quantities. **b** a quantity measuring the extent of this. **3** the act of correlating. □□ **cor·re·la·tion·al** *adj.* [med.L *correlatio* (as CORRELATIVE)]

cor·rel·a·tive /kərélətiv/ *adj. & n.* ● *adj.* **1** (often foll. by *with, to*) having a mutual relation. **2** *Gram.* (of words) corresponding to each other and regularly used together (as *neither* and *nor*). ● *n.* a correlative word or thing. □□ **cor·rel·a·tive·ly** *adv.* **cor·rel·a·tiv·i·ty** /–tívitee/ *n.* [med.L *correlativus* (as COM-, RELATIVE)]

cor·re·spond /káwrispónd, kór–/ *v.intr.* **1 a** (usu. foll. by *to*) be analogous or similar. **b** (usu. foll. by *to*) agree in amount, position, etc. **c** (usu. foll. by *with, to*) be in harmony or agreement. **2** (usu. foll. by *with*) communicate by interchange of letters. □□ **cor·re·spond·ing·ly** *adv.* [F *correspondre* f. med.L *correspondere* (as COM-, RESPOND)]

cor·re·spond·ence /káwrispóndəns, kór–/ *n.* **1** (usu. foll. by *with, to, between*) agreement, similarity, or harmony. **2 a** communication by letters. **b** letters sent or received. [ME f. OF f. med.L *correspondentia* (as CORRESPOND)]

cor·re·spond·ence course *n.* a course of study in which student and teachers communicate by mail.

cor·re·spond·ence school *n.* (also **cor·re·spond·ence col·lege**) a college conducting correspondence courses.

cor·re·spond·ent /káwrispóndənt, –kór–/ *n. & adj.* ● *n.* **1** a person who writes letters to a person or a newspaper, esp. regularly. **2** a person employed to contribute material for publication in a periodical or for broadcasting (*our business correspondent*; *NBC's Moscow correspondent*). **3** a person or firm having regular business relations with another, esp. in another country. ● *adj.* (often foll. by *to, with*) *archaic* corresponding. □□ **cor·re·spond·ent·ly** *adv.* [ME f. OF *correspondant* or med.L (as CORRESPOND)]

cor·re·spond·ing mem·ber *n.* an honorary member of a learned society, etc., with no voice in the society's affairs.

cor·ri·da /kawreédə, –thaa/ *n.* **1** a bullfight. **2** bullfighting. [Sp. *corrida de toros* running of bulls]

cor·ri·dor /káwridər, –dor, kór–/ *n.* **1** a passage from which doors lead into rooms (orig. an outside passage connecting parts of a building, now usu. a main passage in a large building). **2** *Brit.* a passage in a railroad car from which doors lead into compartments. **3** a strip of the territory of one nation passing through that of another, esp. securing access to the sea. **4** a route to which aircraft are restricted, esp. over a foreign country. [F f. It. *corridore* corridor for *corridojo* running-place f. *correre* run, by confusion with *corridore* runner]

cor·ri·dors of pow·er *n.* places where covert influence is said to be exerted in government.

cor·rie /káwree, kór–/ *n. Sc.* a circular hollow on a mountainside; a cirque. [Gael. *coire* cauldron]

cor·ri·gen·dum /káwrijéndəm, kór–/ *n.* (*pl.* **cor·ri·gen·da** /–də/) a thing to be corrected, esp. an error in a printed book. [L, neut. gerundive of *corrigere*: see CORRECT]

cor·ri·gi·ble /káwrijibəl, kór–/ *adj.* **1** capable of being corrected. **2** (of a person) submissive; open to correction. □□ **cor·ri·gi·bly** *adv.* [ME f. F f. med.L *corrigibilis* (as CORRECT)]

cor·rob·o·rate /kəróbərayt/ *v.tr.* confirm or give support to (a statement or belief, or the person holding it), esp. in relation to witnesses in a court of law. □□ **cor·rob·o·ra·tion** /–ráyshən/ *n.* **cor·rob·o·ra·tive** /–rətiv, –ráytiv/ *adj.* **cor·rob·o·ra·tor** *n.* **cor·rob·o·ra·to·ry** /–rətawree/ *adj.* [L *corroborare* strengthen (as COM-, *roborare* f. *robur* –*oris* strength)]

cor·rob·o·ree /kəróbəree/ *n.* **1** a festive or warlike dance-drama with song of Australian Aboriginals. **2** a noisy party. [Aboriginal dial.]

cor·rode /kəród/ *v.* **1 a** *tr.* wear away, esp. by chemical action. **b** *intr.* be worn away; decay. **2** *tr.* destroy gradually (*optimism corroded by recent misfortunes*). □□ **cor·rod·i·ble** *adj.* [ME f. L *corrodere corros-* (as COM-, *rodere* gnaw)]

cor·ro·sion /kərózhən/ *n.* **1** the process of corroding, esp. of a rusting metal. **2 a** damage caused by corroding. **b** a corroded area.

cor·ro·sive /kərósiv/ *adj. & n.* • *adj.* tending to corrode or consume. • *n.* a corrosive substance. □□ **cor·ro·sive·ly** *adv.* **cor·ro·sive·ness** *n.* [ME f. OF *corosif –ive* (as CORRODE)]

cor·ro·sive sub·li·mate *n.* mercuric chloride, a strong acid poison, used as a fungicide, antiseptic, etc.

cor·ru·gate /káwrəgayt, kór–/ *v.* **1** *tr.* (esp. as **corrugated** *adj.*) form into alternate ridges and grooves, esp. to strengthen (*corrugated iron; corrugated cardboard*). **2** *tr. & intr.* contract into wrinkles or folds. □□ **cor·ru·ga·tion** /–gáyshən/ *n.* [L *corrugare* (as COM-, *rugare* f. *ruga* wrinkle)]

cor·ru·ga·tor /káwrəgaytər, kór–/ *n. Anat.* either of two muscles that contract the brow in frowning. [mod.L (as CORRUGATE)]

cor·rupt /kərúpt/ *adj. & v.* • *adj.* **1** morally depraved; wicked. **2** influenced by or using bribery or fraudulent activity. **3** (of a text, language, etc.) harmed (esp. made suspect or unreliable) by errors or alterations. **4** rotten. • *v.* **1** *tr. & intr.* make or become corrupt or depraved. **2** *tr.* affect or harm by errors or alterations. **3** *tr.* infect; taint. □□ **cor·rupt·er** *n.* **cor·rupt·i·ble** *adj.* **cor·rupt·i·bil·i·ty** *n.* **cor·rup·tive** *adj.* **cor·rupt·ly** *adv.* **cor·rupt·ness** *n.* [ME f. OF *corrupt* or L *corruptus* past part. of *corrumpere corrupt-* (as COM-, *rumpere* break)]

cor·rup·tion /kərúpshən/ *n.* **1** moral deterioration, esp. widespread. **2** use of corrupt practices, esp. bribery or fraud. **3 a** irregular alteration (of a text, language, etc.) from its original state. **b** an irregularly altered form of a word. **4** decomposition, esp. of a corpse or other organic matter. [ME f. OF *corruption* or L *corruptio* (as CORRUPT)]

cor·rupt prac·tic·es *n.* fraudulent activity, esp. at elections.

cor·sage /kawrsaázh/ *n.* **1** a small bouquet worn by a woman. **2** the bodice of a woman's dress. [ME f. OF f. *cors* body: see CORPSE]

cor·sair /káwrsair/ *n.* **1** a pirate ship. **2** a pirate. **3** *hist.* a privateer, esp. of the Barbary Coast. [F *corsaire* f. med.L *cursarius* f. *cursus* inroad f. *currere* run]

corse /kawrs/ *n. archaic* a corpse. [var. of CORPSE]

cor·se·let /káwrsəlét/ *n.* **1** (also **cor·se·lette**) a woman's foundation garment combining girdle and brassiere. **2** (also **cors·let** /káwrslit/) *hist.* a piece of armor covering the trunk. [OF *corselet,* dimin. formed as CORSET]

cor·se·lette var. of CORSELET. [Trademark]

cor·set /káwrsit/ *n. & v.* • *n.* **1** a closely fitting undergarment worn by women to support the abdomen. **2** a similar garment worn by men and women because of injury, weakness, or deformity. • *v.tr.* **1** provide with a corset. **2** control closely. □□ **cor·set·ed** *adj.* **cor·set·ry** *n.* [ME f. OF, dimin. of *cors* body: see CORPSE]

cor·se·tiere /káwrsityáir/ *n.* a woman who makes or fits corsets. [F, fem. of *corsetier* (as CORSET, –IER)]

Cor·si·can /káwrsikən/ *adj. & n.* • *adj.* of or relating to Corsica, an island in the Mediterranean under French rule. • *n.* **1** a native of Corsica. **2** the Italian dialect of Corsica.

cors·let var. of CORSELET.

cor·tege /kawrtéyzh/ *n.* (also **cor·tège**) **1** a procession, esp. for a funeral. **2** a train of attendants. [F]

Cor·tes /kawrtéz, –tés/ *n.* the legislative assembly of Spain and formerly of Portugal. [Sp. & Port., pl. of *corte* COURT]

cor·tex /káwrteks/ *n.* (*pl.* **cor·ti·ces** /–tiseez/ or **cor·tex·es**) **1** *Anat.* the outer part of an organ, esp. of the brain (**cerebral cortex**) or kidneys (**renal cortex**). **2** *Bot.* **a** an outer layer of tissue immediately below the epidermis. **b** bark. □□ **cor·ti·cal** /káwrtikəl/ *adj.* [L *cortex, –icis* bark]

cor·ti·cate /káwrtikayt/ *adj.* (also **cor·ti·cat·ed**) **1** having bark or rind. **2** barklike. [L *corticatus* (as CORTEX)]

cor·ti·co·troph·ic hor·mone /káwrtikōtrófik, –tróf–/ *adj.* (also **cor·ti·co·trop·ic**) = ADRENOCORTICOTROPHIC HORMONE.

cor·ti·co·troph·in /káwrtikōtrófin/ *n.* (also **cor·ti·co·tro·pin**) = ADRENOCORTICOTROPHIN.

cor·ti·sone /káwrtisōn, –zōn/ *n. Biochem.* a steroid hormone produced by the adrenal cortex or synthetically, used medicinally esp. against inflammation and allergy. [Chem. name 17-hydroxy-11-dehydro*cortic*osterone]

co·run·dum /kərúndəm/ *n. Mineral.* extremely hard crystallized alumina, used esp. as an abrasive, and varieties of which, e.g., ruby and sapphire, are used for gemstones. [Tamil *kurundam* f. Skr. *kuruvinda* ruby]

cor·us·cate /káwrəskayt, kór–/ *v.intr.* **1** give off flashing light; sparkle. **2** be showy or brilliant. □□ **cor·us·ca·tion** /–káyshən/ *n.* [L *coruscare* glitter]

cor·vée /kawrváy/ *n.* **1** *hist.* a day's work of unpaid labor due to a lord from a vassal. **2** labor exacted in lieu of paying taxes. **3** an onerous task. [ME f. OF ult. f. L *corrogare* ask for, collect (as COM-, *rogare* ask)]

corves *pl.* of CORF.

cor·vette /kawrvét/ *n. Naut.* **1** a small naval escort vessel. **2** *hist.* a flush-decked warship with one tier of guns. [F f. MDu. *korf* kind of ship + dimin. –ETTE]

cor·vine /káwrvīn, –vin/ *adj.* of or akin to the raven or crow. [L *corvinus* f. *corvus* raven]

cor·y·ban·tic /káwribántik, kór–/ *adj.* wild; frenzied. [*Corybantes* priests of Cybele performing wild dances (L f. Gk *Korubantes*)]

cor·ymb /káwrimb, –im, kór–/ *n. Bot.* a flat-topped cluster of flowers with the flower stalks proportionally longer lower down the stem. □□ **cor·ym·bose** *adj.* [F *corymbe* or L *corymbus* f. Gk *korumbos* cluster]

cor·y·phée /káwrifay, kór–/ *n.* a leading dancer in a corps de ballet. [F f. Gk *koruphaios* leader of a chorus f. *koruphē* head]

co·ry·za /kəríza/ *n.* **1** a catarrhal inflammation of the mucous membrane in the nose; a cold in the head. **2** any disease with this as a symptom. [L f. Gk *koruza* running at the nose]

cos[1] /kaws, kos/ *n.* a variety of lettuce with crisp narrow leaves forming a long, upright head. [L f. Gk *Kōs,* island in the Aegean, where it originated]

cos[2] /kos, koz/ *abbr.* cosine.

cos[3] /kawz, koz/ *conj. & adv.* (also **'cos**) *colloq.* because. [abbr.]

Co·sa Nos·tra /kósə nóstrə/ *n.* a US criminal organization resembling and related to the Mafia. [It., = our affair]

co·sec /kósek/ *abbr.* cosecant.

co·se·cant /kōseékant, –kənt/ *n. Math.* the ratio of the hypotenuse (in a right triangle) to the side opposite an acute angle; the reciprocal of sine. [mod.L *cosecans* and F *cosécant* (as CO-, SECANT)]

co·seis·mal /kōsízməl/ *adj.* & *n.* • *adj.* of or relating to points of simultaneous arrival of an earthquake wave. • *n.* a straight line or a curve connecting these points. [CO- + *seismal* (see SEISMIC)]

co·set /kóset/ *n. Math.* a set composed of all the products obtained by multiplying on the right or on the left each element of a subgroup in turn by one particular element of the group containing the subgroup. [CO- + SET[2]]

cosh[1] /kosh/ *n. & v. Brit. colloq.* • *n.* a heavy blunt weapon. • *v.tr.* hit with a cosh. [19th c.: orig. unkn.]

cosh[2] /kosh, kosáych/ *abbr. Math.* hyperbolic cosine.

co·sign /kós;amin/ *v.tr.* sign (a promissory note) jointly with another person. □□ **co·sign·er** *n.*

co·sig·na·to·ry /kōsígnətáwree/ *n. & adj.* • *n.* (*pl.* **·tor·ies**) a person or nation signing (a treaty, etc.) jointly with others. • *adj.* signing jointly.

co·sine /kósin/ *n. Math.* the ratio of the side adjacent to an acute angle (in a right triangle) to the hypotenuse. [mod.L *cosinus* (as CO-, SINE)]

cos·met·ic /kozmétik/ *adj. & n.* • *adj.* **1** intended to adorn or beautify the body, esp. the face. **2** intended to improve only appearances; superficially improving or beneficial (*the reform package was merely a cosmetic exercise*). **3** (of surgery or a prosthetic device) imitating, restoring, or enhancing the normal appearance. • *n.* (usu. **cosmetics**) a product applied to the body, esp. the face, to improve its appearance. □□ **cos·met·i·cal·ly** *adv.* [F *cosmétique* f. Gk *kosmētikos* f. *kosmeō* adorn f. *kosmos* order, adornment]

cos·me·tol·o·gy /kozmətóləjee/ n. the art and technique of treating the skin, nails, and hair with cosmetic preparations. □□ **cos·me·tol·o·gist** n. [f. F *cosmétologie*]

cos·mic /kózmik/ adj. 1 of the universe or cosmos, esp. as distinct from the earth. 2 of or for space travel. □□ **cos·mi·cal** adj. **cos·mi·cal·ly** adv.

cos·mic dust n. small particles of matter distributed throughout space.

cos·mic rays n. (also **cos·mic ra·di·a·tion**) radiations from space, etc., that reach the earth from all directions, usu. with high energy and penetrative power.

cos·mog·o·ny /kozmógənee/ n. (pl. ·nies) 1 the branch of science that deals with the origin of the universe, esp. the solar system. 2 a theory regarding this. □□ **cos·mo·gon·ic** /–məgónik/ adj. **cos·mo·gon·i·cal** adj. **cos·mog·o·nist** /–móg–/ n. [Gk *kosmogonia* f. *kosmos* world + –*gonia* –begetting]

cos·mog·ra·phy /kozmógrəfee/ n. (pl. ·phies) a description or mapping of general features of the universe. □□ **cos·mog·ra·pher** n. **cos·mo·graph·ic** /–məgráfik/ adj. **cos·mo·graph·i·cal** adj. [ME f. F *cosmographie* or f. LL f. Gk *kosmographia* (as COSMOS[1], –GRAPHY)]

cos·mol·o·gy /kozmóləjee/ n. the science of the origin and development of the universe. □□ **cos·mo·log·i·cal** /–məlójikəl/ adj. **cos·mol·o·gist** n. [F *cosmologie* or mod.L *cosmologia* (as COSMOS[1], –LOGY)]

cos·mo·naut /kózmənawt/ n. a Russian astronaut. [Russ. *kosmonavt*, as COSMOS[1], after *astronaut*]

cos·mop·o·lis /kozmópəlis/ n. a cosmopolitan city. [Gk *kosmos* world + *polis* city]

cos·mo·pol·i·tan /kózməpólit'n/ adj. & n. ● adj. 1 a of or from or knowing many parts of the world. b consisting of people from many or all parts. 2 free from national limitations or prejudices. 3 Ecol. (of a plant, animal, etc.) widely distributed. ● n. a cosmopolitan person. 2 Ecol. a widely distributed animal or plant. □□ **cos·mo·pol·i·tan·ism** n. **cos·mo·pol·i·tan·ize** v.tr. & intr. [COSMOPOLITE + –AN]

cos·mop·o·lite /kozmópəlīt/ n. & adj. ● n. 1 a cosmopolitan person. 2 Ecol. = COSMOPOLITAN n. 2. ● adj. free from national attachments or prejudices. [F f. Gk *kosmopolitēs* f. *kosmos* world + *politēs* citizen]

cos·mos[1] /kózmōs, –məs, –mos/ n. 1 the universe, esp. as a well-ordered whole. 2 a an ordered system of ideas, etc. b a sum total of experience. [Gk *kosmos*]

cos·mos[2] /kózməs, –mos, –mōs/ n. any composite plant of the genus *Cosmos*, bearing single dahlialike blossoms of various colors. [mod.L f. Gk *kosmos* in sense 'ornament']

Cos·sack /kósak/ n. & adj. ● n. 1 a member of a people of southern Imperial Russia, Ukraine, and Siberia, orig. famous for their horsemanship and military skill. 2 a member of a Cossack military unit. ● adj. of, relating to, or characteristic of the Cossacks. [F *cosaque* f. Russ. *kazak* f. Turki *quzzāq* nomad, adventurer]

cos·set /kósit/ v.tr. pamper. [dial. *cosset* = pet lamb, prob. f. AF *coscet*, *cozet* f. OE *cotsǣta* cottager (as COT[2], SIT)]

cos·sie /kózee/ n. (also **coz·zie**) chiefly Austral. sl. a swimming costume. [abbr.]

cost /kawst/ v. & n. ● v. (past and past part. **cost**) 1 tr. be obtainable for (a sum of money); have as a price (*what does it cost?*; *it cost me $50*). 2 tr. involve as a loss or sacrifice (*it cost them much effort*; *it cost him his life*). 3 tr. (past and past part. **cost·ed**) fix or estimate the cost or price of. 4 colloq. a tr. be costly to (*it'll cost you*). b intr. be costly. ● n. 1 what a thing costs; the price paid or to be paid. 2 a loss or sacrifice; an expenditure of time, effort, etc. 3 (in pl.) legal expenses, esp. those allowed in favor of the winning party or against the losing party in a suit. □ **at all costs** (or **at any cost**) no matter what the cost or risk may be. **at cost** at the initial cost; at cost price; without profit to the seller. **at the cost of** at the expense of losing or sacrificing. **cost a person dearly** (or **dear**) involve someone in a serious loss or heavy penalty. [ME f. OF *coster*, *couster*, *coust* ult. f. L *constare* stand firm, stand at a price (as COM-, *stare* stand)]

cost ac·count·ant n. an accountant who records costs and (esp. overhead) expenses in a business concern.

cos·tal /kóst'l, káwst'l/ adj. of the ribs. [F f. mod.L *costalis* f. L *costa* rib]

co·star /kóstaar/ n. & v. ● n. a movie or stage star appearing with another or others of equal importance. ● v. (·starred, ·starring) 1 intr. take part as a costar. 2 tr. (of a production) include as a costar.

cos·tard /kóstərd/ n. Brit. 1 a large ribbed variety of apple. 2 archaic joc. the head. [ME f. AF f. *coste* rib f. L *costa*]

cos·tate /kóstayt, káw–/ adj. ribbed; having ribs or ridges. [L *costatus* f. *costa* rib]

cost-ef·fec·tive adj. effective or productive in relation to its cost.

cos·ter /kóstər/ n. Brit. = COSTERMONGER. [abbr.]

cos·ter·mon·ger /kóstərmunggər, –monggər/ n. Brit. a person who sells fruit, vegetables, etc., in the street from a barrow. [COSTARD + MONGER]

cos·tive /kóstiv/ adj. 1 constipated. 2 slow or reluctant in speech or action. □□ **cos·tive·ly** adv. **cos·tive·ness** n. [ME f. OF *costivé* f. L *constipatus*: see CONSTIPATE]

cost·ly /kawstlee/ adj. (**cost·li·er**, **cost·li·est**) 1 costing much; expensive. 2 of great value. □□ **cost·li·ness** n.

cost·mar·y /káwstmairee/ n. (pl. ·ies) an aromatic composite plant, *Balsamita major*, formerly used in medicine and for flavoring beer, etc. [OE *cost* f. L *costum* f. Gk *kostos* f. Arab. *kust* an aromatic plant + (*St.*) *Mary* (with whom it was associated in medieval times)]

cost of liv·ing n. the level of prices esp. of the basic necessities of life.

cost-plus adj. calculated as the basic cost plus a profit factor.

cost-push n. Econ. factors other than demand that cause inflation.

cos·tume /kóstōōm, –tyōōm/ n. & v. ● n. 1 a style or fashion of dress, esp. that of a particular place, time, or class. 2 a set of clothes. 3 clothing for a particular activity (*dancing costume*). 4 an actor's clothes for a part. 5 a woman's matching jacket and skirt. ● v.tr. provide with a costume. [F f. It. f. L *consuetudo* CUSTOM]

cos·tume jew·el·ry n. jewelry made with inexpensive materials or imitation gems.

cos·tume play n. (also **cos·tume dra·ma**) a play or television drama in which the actors wear historical costume.

cos·tum·er /kóstōōmər, –tyōō–/ n. (also esp. Brit. **cos·tum·i·er** /kostōōmeeər, –tyōō–/) a person who makes or deals in costumes, esp. for theatrical use. [F *costumier* (as COSTUME)]

co·sy esp. Brit. var. of COZY.

cot[1] /kot/ n. 1 a small folding bed. 2 a hospital bed. 3 Brit. a small bed with high sides, esp. for a baby or very young child; crib. 4 Ind. a light bedstead. 5 Naut. a kind of swinging bed hung from deck beams, formerly used by officers. [Anglo-Ind., f. Hindi *khāt* bedstead, hammock]

cot[2] /kot/ n. & v. ● n. 1 a small shelter; a cote. 2 poet. a cottage. ● v.tr. (**cot·ted**, **cot·ting**) put (sheep) in a cot. [OE f. Gmc, rel. to COTE]

cot[3] /kot/ abbr. Math. cotangent.

co·tan·gent /kōtánjənt/ n. Math. the ratio of the side adjacent to an acute angle (in a right triangle) to the opposite side.

cote /kōt/ n. a shelter, esp. for animals or birds; a shed or stall (*sheepcote*). [OE f. Gmc, rel. to COT[2]]

co·te·rie /kótəree/ n. 1 an exclusive group of people sharing interests. 2 a select circle in society. [F, orig. = association of tenants, ult. f. MLG *kote* COTE]

co·ter·mi·nous /kōtɔ́rminəs/ adj. (often foll. by with) having the same boundaries or extent (in space, time, or meaning). [CO- + TERMINUS + –OUS]

coth /koth/ abbr. Math. hyperbolic cotangent.

co·tid·al line /kōtíd'l/ n. a line on a map connecting points at which tidal levels (as high tide or low tide) occur simultaneously.

co·til·lion /kətílyən/ n. 1 any of various French dances with elaborate steps, figures, and ceremonial. 2 a a ballroom dance resembling a quadrille. b a formal ball. [F *cotillon* petticoat, dimin. of *cotte* f. OF *cote* COAT]

co·to·ne·as·ter /kətóneeástər/ n. any rosaceous shrub of the genus *Cotoneaster*, bearing usu. bright red berries. [mod.L f. L *cotoneum* QUINCE + –ASTER]

cot·ta /kótə/ n. Eccl. a short surplice. [It., formed as COAT]

cot·tage /kótij/ n. 1 a small, simple house, esp. in the country. 2 a dwelling forming part of a farm establishment, used by a worker. □□ **cot·ta·gey** adj. [ME f. AF, formed as COT[2], COTE]

cot·tage cheese n. soft white cheese made from curds of skimmed milk without pressing.

cot·tage in·dus·try n. a business activity partly or wholly carried on at home.

cot·tage pie n. Brit. a dish of ground meat topped with browned mashed potato.

cot·tag·er /kótijər/ n. a person who lives in a cottage.

cot·tar /kótər/ n. (also **cot·ter**) Sc. & hist. a farm laborer or tenant occupying a cottage in return for labor as required. [COT[2] + –ER[1] (Sc. –ar)]

cot·ter /kótər/ n. 1 a bolt or wedge for securing parts of machinery, etc. 2 (in full **cotter pin**) a split pin that opens after passing through a hole. [17th c. (rel. to earlier *cotterel*): orig. unkn.]

cot·ton /kót'n/ n. & v. ● n. 1 a soft, white fibrous substance covering the seeds of certain plants. 2 a (in full **cotton plant**) such a plant, esp. any of the genus *Gossypium*. b cotton plants cultivated as a crop for the fiber or the seeds. 3 (*attrib.*) made of cotton. ● v.intr. (foll. by to) be attracted by (a person). □ **cotton to** (or **on to**) colloq. 1 begin to be fond of or agreeable to. 2 begin to understand. □□ **cot·ton·y** adj. [ME f. OF *coton* f. Arab. *kutn*]

cot·ton cake n. compressed cotton seed used as food for cattle.

cot·ton can·dy n. a fluffy mass of spun sugar, usu. served on a stick.

cot·ton gin n. a machine for separating cotton from its seeds.

cot·ton grass n. any grasslike plant of the genus *Eriophorum*, with long, white silky hairs.

cot·ton·mouth /kót'nmowth/ n. a venomous pit viper, *Agkistrodon piscivorus*, of swampy areas of the southeastern US, related to the coppermouth. Also called **water moccasin**. [f. the whitish lining of its mouth]

cot·ton-pick·ing *adj. sl.* unpleasant; wretched.

cot·ton·tail /kót'ntayl/ *n.* any rabbit of the genus *Sylvilagus*, native to America, having a mainly white fluffy tail.

cot·ton·wood /kót'nwŏŏd/ *n.* **1** any of several poplars, native to N. America, having seeds covered in white cottony hairs. **2** any of several trees native to Australia, esp. a downy-leaved tree, *Bedfordia arborescens*.

cotton wool *n.* **1** esp. *Brit.* fluffy wadding of a kind orig. made from raw cotton. **2** raw cotton.

cot·y·le·don /kót'leéd'n/ *n.* **1** an embryonic leaf in seed-bearing plants. **2** any succulent plant of the genus *Umbilicus*, e.g., pennywort. □□ **cot·y·le·don·ar·y** *adj.* **cot·y·le·don·ous** *adj.* [L, = pennywort, f. Gk *kotulēdōn* cup-shaped cavity f. *kotulē* cup]

cou·cal /kŏŏkəl/ *n.* any ground-nesting bird of the genus *Centropus*, related to the cuckoos. [F, perh. f. *coucou* cuckoo + *alouette* lark]

couch[1] /kowch/ *n. & v.* ● *n.* **1** an upholstered piece of furniture for several people; a sofa. **2** a long padded seat with a headrest at one end, esp. one on which a psychiatrist's or doctor's patient reclines during examination. ● *v.* **1** *tr.* (foll. by *in*) express in words of a specified kind (*couched in simple language*). **2** *tr.* lay on or as on a couch. **3** *intr.* a (of an animal) lie, esp. in its lair. **b** lie in ambush. **4** *tr.* lower (a spear, etc.) to the position for attack. **5** *tr. Med.* treat (a cataract) by displacing the lens of the eye. [ME f. OF *couche, coucher* f. L *collocare* (as COM-, *locare* place)]

couch[2] /kowch, kŏŏch/ *n.* (in full **couch grass**) any of several grasses of the genus *Agropyron*, esp. *A. repens*, having long, creeping roots. [var. of QUITCH]

couch·ant /kówchənt/ *adj.* (placed after noun) *Heraldry* (of an animal) lying with the body resting on the legs and the head raised. [F, pres. part. of *coucher*: see COUCH[1]]

cou·chette /kŏŏshét/ *n.* **1** a railroad car with seats convertible into sleeping berths. **2** a berth in this. [F, = little bed, dimin. of *couche* COUCH[1]]

couch po·ta·to *n. sl.* a person who likes lazing at home, esp. watching television.

cou·dé /kŏŏdáy/ *adj. & n.* ● *adj.* of or relating to a telescope in which rays are bent to a focus off the axis. ● *n.* such a telescope. [F, past part. of *couder* bend at right angles f. *coude* elbow formed as CUBIT]

Cou·é·ism /kŏŏáyizəm/ *n.* a system of usu. optimistic autosuggestion as psychotherapy. [E. *Coué*, Fr. psychologist d. 1926]

cou·gar /kŏŏgər/ *n.* a puma. [F, repr. Guarani *guaçu ara*]

cough /kawf, kof/ *v. & n.* ● *v.intr.* **1** expel air from the lungs with a sudden, sharp sound produced by abrupt opening of the glottis, to remove an obstruction or congestion. **2** (of an engine, gun, etc.) make a similar sound. ● *n.* **1** an act of coughing. **2** a condition of the respiratory organs causing coughing. **3** a tendency to cough. □ **cough out 1** eject by coughing. **2** say with a cough. **cough up 1** = *cough out*. **2** *sl.* bring out or give (money or information) reluctantly. **3** *sl.* confess. □□ **cough·er** *n.* [ME *coghe, cowhe*, rel. to MDu. *kuchen*, MHG *kūchen*, of imit. orig.]

cough drop *n.* a medicated lozenge to relieve a cough.

could *past* of CAN[1].
▶In spoken American English, the words *could have* are often pronounced so that they sound like *could of*. This mark of informalism should be avoided in writing. The same is true for *should have, would have, might have,* and *may have*.

could·n't /kŏŏd'nt/ *contr.* could not.

cou·lee /kŏŏlee/ *n. Geol.* **1** a solidified lava flow. **2** a deep ravine. [F, fem. past part. of *couler* flow, f. L *colare* strain, filter]

cou·lisse /kŏŏleés/ *n.* **1** (usu. in *pl.*) *Theatr.* a piece of side scenery or a space between two of these; the wings. **2** a place of informal discussion or negotiation. [F f. *coulis* sliding: see PORTCULLIS]

cou·loir /kŏŏlwaár/ *n.* a steep, narrow gully on a mountainside. [F f. *couler* glide: see COULEE]

cou·lomb /kŏŏlom/ *n. Electr.* the SI unit of electric charge, equal to the quantity of electricity conveyed in one second by a current of one ampere. ¶ Symb.: **C**. [C. A. de *Coulomb*, Fr. physicist d. 1806]

cou·lom·e·try /kŏŏlómitree/ *n. Chem.* a method of chemical analysis by measurement of the number of coulombs used in electrolysis. □□ **cou·lo·met·ric** /kŏŏləmétrik/ *adj.*

coul·ter *Brit.* var. of COLTER.

cou·ma·rin /kŏŏmərin/ *n.* an aromatic substance found in many plants and formerly used for flavoring food. [F *coumarine* f. Tupi *cumarú* tonka bean]

cou·ma·rone /kŏŏmərōn/ *n.* an organic liquid obtained from coal tar by synthesis and used in paints and varnishes. [COUMARIN + –ONE]

cou·ma·rone res·in *n.* a thermoplastic resin formed by polymerization of coumarone.

coun·cil /kównsəl/ *n.* **1** a an advisory, deliberative, or administrative body of people formally constituted and meeting regularly. **b** a meeting of such a body. **2** a the elected local legislative body of a town, city, or county. **3** a body of persons chosen as advisers. **4** an ecclesiastical assembly (*ecumenical council*). [ME f. AF *cuncile* f. L *concilium* convocation, assembly f. *calare* summon: cf. COUNSEL]

coun·ci·lor /kównsələr, –slər/ *n.* an elected member of a council, esp. a local one. □□ **coun·ci·lor·ship** *n.* [ME, alt. of COUNSELOR: assim. to COUNCIL]
▶See note at COUNSELOR.

coun·cil·man /kównsəlmən/ *n.* (*pl.* **·men**; *fem.* **coun·cil·wom·an**, *pl.* **·wom·en**) a member of a council.

coun·cil of war *n.* **1** an assembly of officers called in a special emergency. **2** any meeting held to plan a response to an emergency.

coun·sel /kównsəl/ *n. & v.* ● *n.* **1** advice, esp. formally given. **2** consultation, esp. to seek or give advice. **3** (*pl.* same) an attorney or other legal adviser; a body of these advising in a case. **4** a plan of action. ● *v.tr.* **1** (often foll. by *to* + infin.) advise (a person). **2 a** give advice to (a person) on social or personal problems, esp. professionally. **b** assist or guide (a person) in resolving personal difficulties. **3** (often foll. by *that*) recommend (a course of action). □ **keep one's own counsel** not confide in others. **take counsel** (usu. foll. by *with*) consult. [ME f. OF *c(o)unseil, conseiller* f. L *consilium* consultation, advice]

coun·sel·ing /kównsəling, –sling/ *n.* **1** the act or process of giving counsel. **2** the process of assisting and guiding clients, esp. by a trained person on a professional basis, to resolve esp. personal, social, or psychological problems and difficulties (cf. COUNSEL *v.* 2b).

coun·sel of de·spair *n.* action to be taken when all else fails.

coun·se·lor /kównsələr, –slər/ *n.* **1** a person who gives counsel; an adviser. **2** a person trained to give guidance on personal, social, or psychological problems (*marriage counselor; guidance counselor*). **3** a senior officer in the diplomatic service. **4** (also **coun·se·lor-at-law**) a lawyer, esp. one who gives advice in law. [ME f. OF *conseiller* (f. L *consiliarius*), *conseillour, –eur* (f. L *consiliator*): see COUNSEL]
▶A **counselor** is someone who gives advice or counsel, especially an attorney. A **councilor** is a member of a council, such as a town or city council. Confusion arises because many *counselors* sit on councils, and *councilors* are often called on to give counsel.

count[1] /kownt/ *v. & n.* ● *v.* **1** *tr.* determine the total number or amount of, esp. by assigning successive numbers (*count the stations*). **2** *intr.* repeat numbers in ascending order; conduct a reckoning. **3 a** *tr.* (often foll. by *in*) include in one's reckoning or plan (*you can count me in; fifteen people, counting the guide*). **b** *intr.* be included in a reckoning or plan. **4** *tr.* consider (a thing or a person) to be (lucky, etc.) (*count no man happy until he is dead*). **5** *intr.* (often foll. by *for*) have value; matter (*his opinion counts for a great deal*). ● *n.* **1 a** the act of counting; a reckoning (*after a count of fifty*). **b** the sum total of a reckoning (*blood count; pollen count*). **2** *Law* each charge in an indictment (*guilty on ten counts*). **3** a count of up to ten seconds by a referee when a boxer is knocked down. **4** *Polit.* the act of counting the votes after a general or local election. **5** one of several points under discussion. **6** the measure of the fineness of a yarn expressed as the weight of a given length or the length of a given weight. **7** *Physics* the number of ionizing particles detected by a counter. □ **count against** be reckoned to the disadvantage of. **count one's blessings** be grateful for what one has. **count one's chickens before they're hatched** be overoptimistic or hasty in anticipating good fortune. **count the cost** consider the risks before taking action; calculate the damage resulting from an action. **count the days** (or **hours**, etc.) be impatient. **count down** recite numbers backward to zero, esp. as part of a rocket-launching procedure. **count on** depend on; rely on; expect confidently. **count out 1** count while taking from a stock. **2** complete a count of ten seconds over (a fallen boxer, etc.), indicating defeat. **3** (in children's games) select (a player) for dismissal or a special role by use of a counting rhyme, etc. **4** *colloq.* exclude from a plan or reckoning (*I'm too tired, count me out*). **5** *Brit. Polit.* procure the adjournment of (the House of Commons) when fewer than 40 members are present. **count up** find the sum of. **down for the count 1** *Boxing* defeated by being unable to rise within ten seconds. **2 a** defeated or demoralized. **b** sound asleep. **keep count** take note of how many there have been, etc. **lose count** fail to take note of the number, etc. **not counting** excluding from the reckoning. **take the count** *Boxing* be defeated. [ME f. OF *co(u)nter, co(u)nte* f. LL *computus, computare* COMPUTE]

count[2] /kownt/ *n.* a noble of continental Europe corresponding in rank to a British earl. □□ **count·ship** *n.* [OF *conte* f. L *comes comitis* companion]

count·a·ble /kówntəbəl/ *adj.* **1** that can be counted. **2** *Gram.* (of a noun) that can form a plural or be used with the indefinite article (e.g., *book, kindness*).

count·down /kówntdown/ *n.* **1 a** the act of counting down, esp. at

SPELLING TIP council

For spelling, try this mnemonic: "A *council*, a group that meets to give advice, needs a *pencil* to record its meetings."

the launching of a rocket, etc. **b** the procedures carried out during this time. **2** the final moments before any significant event.

coun·te·nance /kówntinəns/ n. & v. •n. **1** a person's face or facial expression (*his inscrutable countenance gave little away*). **2** composure. **3** moral support. •v.tr. **1** give approval to (an act, etc.) (*cannot countenance this breach of the rules*). **2** (often foll. by *in*) encourage (a person or a practice). □ **change countenance** alter one's expression as an effect of emotion. **keep one's countenance** maintain composure, esp. by refraining from laughter. **keep a person in countenance** support or encourage a person. **lose countenance** become embarrassed. **out of countenance** disconcerted. [ME f. AF c(o)untenance, OF contenance bearing f. contenir: see CONTAIN]

coun·ter¹ /kówntər/ n. **1 a** a long, flat-topped fixture in a store, bank, etc., across which business is conducted with customers. **b** a similar structure used for serving food, etc., in a cafeteria or bar. **2 a** a small disk used for keeping the score, etc., esp. in board games. **b** a token representing a coin. **c** something used in bargaining; a pawn (*a counter in the struggle for power*). **3** an apparatus used for counting. **4** *Physics* an apparatus used for counting individual ionizing particles, etc. **5** a person or thing that counts. □ **under the counter** (esp. of the sale of scarce goods) surreptitiously, esp. illegally. [AF count(e)our, OF conteo(i)r, f. med.L computatorium (as COMPUTE)]

coun·ter² /kówntər/ v., adv., adj., & n. •v. **1** tr. **a** oppose; contradict (*countered our proposal with their own*). **b** meet by a countermove. **2** intr. **a** make a countermove. **b** make an opposing statement ("*I shall!*" *he countered*). **3** intr. *Boxing* give a return blow while parrying. •adv. **1** in the opposite direction (*ran counter to the fox*). **2** contrary (*her action was counter to my wishes*). •adj. **1** opposed; opposite. **2** duplicate; serving as a check. •n. **1** a parry; a countermove. **2** something opposite or opposed. □ **act** (or **go**) **counter to** disobey (instructions, etc.). **go** (or **run** or *Brit.* **hunt**) **counter** run or ride against the direction taken by a quarry. **run counter to** act contrary to. [ME f. OF countre f. L contra against: see COUNTER-]

coun·ter³ /kówntər/ n. **1** the part of a horse's breast between the shoulders and under the neck. **2** the curved part of the stern of a ship. **3** *Printing* a part of a printing type, etc., that is completely enclosed by an outline (e.g., the loop of P). [17th c.: orig. unkn.]

coun·ter⁴ /kówntər/ n. the back part of a shoe or a boot around the heel. [abbr. of counterfort buttress]

counter- /kówntər/ comb. form denoting: **1** retaliation, opposition, or rivalry (*counterthreat*; *countercheck*). **2** opposite direction (*countercurrent*). **3** correspondence, duplication, or substitution (*counterpart*; *countersign*). [from or after AF countre-, OF contre f. L contra against]

coun·ter·act /kówntərákt/ v.tr. **1** hinder or oppose by contrary action. **2** neutralize. □□ **coun·ter·ac·tion** /-ákshən/ n. **coun·ter·ac·tive** adj.

coun·ter·at·tack n. & v. •n. /kówntərətak/ an attack in reply to an attack by an enemy or opponent. •v.tr. & intr. /kówntərəták/ attack in reply.

coun·ter·at·trac·tion /kówntərətrákshən/ n. **1** a rival attraction. **2** the attraction of a contrary tendency.

coun·ter·bal·ance n. & v. •n. /kówntərbaləns/ **1** a weight balancing another. **2** an argument, force, etc., balancing another. •v.tr. /kówntərbáləns/act as a counterbalance to.

coun·ter·blast /kówntərblast/ n. (often foll. by *to*) an energetic or violent verbal or written reply to an argument, etc.

coun·ter·change /kówntərcháynj/ v. **1** tr. change (places or parts); interchange. **2** tr. literary checker, esp. with contrasting colors, etc. **3** intr. change places or parts. [F contrechanger (as COUNTER-, CHANGE)]

coun·ter·charge n. & v. •n. /kówntərchaarj/ a charge or accusation in return for one received. •v.tr. /kówntərcháarj/make a countercharge against.

coun·ter·check n. & v. •n. /kówntərchek/ **1 a** a restraint that opposes something. **b** a restraint that operates against another. **2** a second check, esp. for security or accuracy. **3** archaic a retort. •v.tr. /kówntərchék/ make a countercheck on.

coun·ter·claim n. & v. •n. /kówntərklaym/ **1** a claim made against another claim. **2** *Law* a claim made by a defendant in a suit against the plaintiff. •v.tr. & intr. /kówntərkláym/ make a counterclaim (for).

coun·ter·clock·wise /kówntərklókwiz/ adv. & adj. •adv. in a curve opposite in direction to the movement of the hands of a clock. •adj. moving counterclockwise.

coun·ter·cul·ture /kówntərkulchər/ n. a way of life, etc., opposed to that usually considered normal.

coun·ter·es·pi·o·nage /kówntəréspeeənaazh, –nij/ n. action taken to frustrate enemy spying.

coun·ter·feit /kówntərfit/ adj., n., & v. •adj. **1** (of a coin, writing, etc.) made in imitation; not genuine; forged. **2** (of a claimant, etc.) pretended. •n. a forgery; an imitation. •v.tr. **1 a** imitate fraudulently (a coin, handwriting, etc.); forge. **b** make an imitation of.

2 simulate (feelings, etc.) (*counterfeited interest*). **3** resemble closely. □□ **coun·ter·feit·er** n. [ME f. OF countrefet, –fait, past part. of contrefaire f. Rmc]

coun·ter·in·tel·li·gence /kówntərintéllijəns/ n. = COUNTERESPIONAGE.

coun·ter·ir·ri·tant /kówntərírit'nt/ n. **1** *Med.* something used to produce surface irritation of the skin, thereby counteracting more painful symptoms. **2** anything resembling a counterirritant in its effects. □□ **coun·ter·ir·ri·ta·tion** /–iritáyshən/ n.

coun·ter·mand v. & n. •v.tr. /kówntərmánd/ **1** *Mil.* **a** revoke (an order or command). **b** recall (forces, etc.) by a contrary order. **2** cancel an order for (goods, etc.). •n. /kówntərmand/ an order revoking a previous one. [ME f. OF contremander f. med.L contramandare (as CONTRA-, mandare order)]

coun·ter·march v. & n. •v.intr. & tr. /kówntərmaarch/ esp. Mil. march or cause to march in the opposite direction, e.g., with the front marchers turning and marching back through the ranks. •n. /kówntərmaarch/ an act of countermarching.

coun·ter·meas·ure /kówntərmezhər/ n. an action taken to counteract a danger, threat, etc.

coun·ter·mine n. & v. •n. /kówntərmin/ **1** *Mil.* **a** a mine dug to intercept another dug by an enemy. **b** a submarine mine sunk to explode an enemy's mines. **2** a counterplot. •v.tr. /kówntərmín/ make a countermine against.

coun·ter·move n. & v. •n. /kówntərmōōv/ a move or action in opposition to another. •v.intr. /kówntərmóōv/ make a countermove. □□ **coun·ter·move·ment** n.

coun·ter·of·fen·sive /kówntərəfénsiv/ n. **1** *Mil.* an attack made from a defensive position in order to effect an escape. **2** any attack made from a defensive position.

coun·ter·pane /kówntərpayn/ n. a bedspread. [alt. (with assim. to pane in obs. sense 'cloth') f. obs. counterpoint f. OF contrepointe alt. f. cou(l)tepointe f. med.L culcita puncta quilted mattress]

coun·ter·part /kówntərpaart/ n. **1 a** a person or thing extremely like another. **b** a person or thing forming a natural complement or equivalent to another. **2** *Law* one of two copies of a legal document.

coun·ter·plot n. & v. •n. /kówntərplot/ a plot intended to defeat another plot. •v. /kówntərplót/ (·plot·ted, ·plot·ting) **1** intr. make a counterplot. **2** tr. make a counterplot against.

coun·ter·point /kówntərpoynt/ n. & v. •n. **1** *Mus.* **a** the art or technique of setting, writing, or playing a melody or melodies in conjunction with another, according to fixed rules. **b** a melody played in conjunction with another. **2** a contrasting argument, plot, idea, or literary theme, etc., used to set off the main element. •v.tr. **1** *Mus.* add counterpoint to. **2** set (an argument, plot, etc.) in contrast to (a main element). [OF contrepoint f. med.L contrapunctum pricked or marked opposite, i.e., to the original melody (as CONTRA-, pungere punct- prick)]

coun·ter·poise n. & v. •n. /kówntərpoyz/ **1** a force, etc., equivalent to another on the opposite side. **2** a state of equilibrium. **3** a counterbalancing weight. •v.tr. /kówntərpóyz/ **1** counterbalance. **2** compensate. **3** bring into or keep in equilibrium. [ME f. OF contrepeis, –pois, contrepeser (as COUNTER-, peis, pois f. L pensum weight: cf. POISE¹)]

coun·ter·pro·duc·tive /kówntərprədúktiv/ adj. having the opposite of the desired effect.

coun·ter·ref·or·ma·tion /kówntəréfərmáyshən/ n. **1** (**Counter-Reformation**) hist. the reform of the Roman Catholic Church in the 16th and 17th centuries that took place in response to the Protestant Reformation. **2** a reformation running counter to another.

coun·ter·rev·o·lu·tion /kówntərévəlōōshən/ n. a revolution opposing a former one or reversing its results. □□ **coun·ter·rev·o·lu·tion·ar·y** adj. & n. (pl. ·ies).

coun·ter·scarp /kówntərskaarp/ n. *Mil.* the outer wall or slope of a ditch in a fortification. [F contrescarpe f. It. contrascarpa (as CONTRA-, SCARP)]

coun·ter·shaft /kówntərshaft/ n. an intermediate shaft driven by a main shaft and transmitting motion to a particular machine, etc.

coun·ter·sign /kówntərsin/ v. & n. •v.tr. **1** add a signature to (a document already signed by another). **2** ratify. •n. **1** a watchword or password spoken to a person on guard. **2** a mark used for identification, etc. □□ **coun·ter·sig·na·ture** /–sígnəchər/ n. [F contresigner (v.), contresigne (n.) f. It. contrasegno (as COUNTER-, SIGN)]

coun·ter·sink /kówntərsingk/ v.tr. (past and past part. ·sunk) **1** enlarge and bevel (the rim of a hole) so that a screw or bolt can be inserted flush with the surface. **2** sink (a screw, etc.) in such a hole.

coun·ter·stroke /kówntərstrōk/ n. a blow given in return for another.

coun·ter·ten·or /kówntərtenər/ n. *Mus.* **1 a** the highest adult male singing voice, above tenor. **b** a singer with this voice. **2** a part written for countertenor. [ME f. F contre-teneur f. obs. It. contratenore (as CONTRA-, TENOR)]

coun·ter·top /kówntərtop/ n. a horizontal, flat work surface, as in a kitchen.

coun·ter·vail /kówntərváyl/ v. **1** tr. counterbalance. **2** tr. & intr. (often foll. by *against*) oppose forcefully and usu. successfully. [ME f. AF *contrevaloir* f. L *contra valēre* be of worth against]

coun·ter·vail·ing du·ty *n.* a tax put on imports to offset a subsidy in the exporting country or a tax on similar goods not from abroad.

coun·ter·weight /kówntərwayt/ *n.* a counterbalancing weight.

count·ess /kówntis/ *n.* **1** the wife or widow of a count or an earl. **2** a woman holding the rank of count or earl. [ME f. OF *contesse, cuntesse,* f. LL *comitissa* fem. of *comes* COUNT²]

count·ing·house /kówntinghows/ *n.* where accounts are kept.

count·less /kówntlis/ *adj.* too many to be counted.

count noun *n.* a countable noun (see COUNTABLE 2).

count pal·a·tine *n. hist.* **1** a feudal lord having royal authority within a region of a kingdom. **2** a high official of the Holy Roman Empire with royal authority within his domain.

coun·tri·fied /kúntrifīd/ *adj.* (also **coun·try·fied**) often *derog.* rural or rustic, esp. of manners, appearance, etc. [past part. of *countrify* f. COUNTRY]

coun·try /kúntree/ *n.* (*pl.* **·tries**) **1 a** the territory of a nation with its own government; a nation. **b** a territory possessing its own language, people, culture, etc. **2** (often *attrib.*) rural districts as opposed to towns and cities or the capital (*a cottage in the country; a country town*). **3** the land of a person's birth or citizenship; a fatherland. **4 a** a territory, esp. an area of interest or knowledge. **b** a region associated with a particular person, esp. a writer (*Faulkner country*). **5** a national population, esp. as voters (*the country won't stand for it*). □ **across country** not keeping to roads. [ME f. OF *cuntree,* f. med.L *contrata* (*terra*) (land) lying opposite (CONTRA)]

coun·try and west·ern *n.* a form of popular music originating from folk music of the rural South and cowboy music of the West, usu. a mixture of ballads and dance tunes played on fiddle, banjo, guitar, and pedal steel guitar.

coun·try club *n.* a golfing and social club, often in a suburban setting.

coun·try cous·in *n.* often *derog.* a person with a countrified appearance or manners.

coun·try dance *n.* a traditional sort of dance, esp. English, with couples facing each other in long lines.

coun·try·fied var. of COUNTRIFIED.

coun·try gen·tle·man *n.* a wealthy man who owns and lives on an estate in a rural area.

coun·try·man /kúntreemən/ *n.* (*pl.* **·men**; *fem.* **coun·try·wom·an**, *pl.* **·wom·en**) **1** a person living in a rural area. **2 a** a person of one's own country or district. **b** (often in *comb.*) a person from a specified country or district (*north-countryman*).

coun·try mu·sic *n.* = COUNTRY AND WESTERN.

coun·try·side /kúntreesīd/ *n.* **1 a** a rural area. **b** rural areas in general. **2** the inhabitants of a rural area.

coun·try·wide /kúntreewíd/ *adj.* extending throughout a nation.

coun·ty /kówntee/ *n.* (*pl.* **·ties**) **1** *US* a political and administrative division of a state. **2** any of the territorial divisions of some countries, forming the chief unit of local administration. [ME f. AF *counté,* OF *conté, cunté,* f. L *comitatus* (as COUNT²)]

coun·ty court *n.* a judicial court for civil and criminal cases.

coun·ty seat *n.* the administrative capital of a county.

coup /koo/ *n.* (*pl.* **coups** /kooz/) **1** a notable or successful stroke or move. **2** = COUP D'ÉTAT. [F f. med.L *colpus* blow: see COPE¹]

coup de grâce /koo də graás/ *n.* a finishing stroke, esp. to kill a wounded animal or person. [F, lit. stroke of grace]

coup de main /koo də mán/ *n.* a sudden vigorous attack. [F, lit. stroke of the hand]

coup d'é·tat /koo daytaá/ *n.* a violent or illegal seizure of power. [F, lit. stroke of the state]

coupe¹ /koop/ *n.* **1** a shallow glass or dish used for serving fruit, ice-cream, etc. **2** fruit, ice-cream, etc., served in this. [F, = goblet]

coupe² /koop/ *n.* (also **cou·pé** /koopáy/) **1** a two-door car with a hard top. **2** *hist.* a four-wheeled enclosed carriage for two passengers and a driver. [F, past part. of *couper* cut (formed as COUP)]

cou·ple /kúpəl/ *n. & v.* ● *n.* **1** (usu. foll. by *of*; often as *sing.*) **a** two (*a couple of girls*). **b** about two (*a couple of hours*). **2** (often as *sing.*) **a** a married or engaged pair. **b** a pair of partners in a dance, a game, etc. **c** a pair of rafters. **3** (*pl.* **couple**) a pair of hunting dogs (*six couple of hounds*). **4** (in *pl.*) a pair of joined collars used for holding hounds together. **5** *Mech.* a pair of equal and parallel forces acting in opposite directions, and tending to cause rotation about an axis perpendicular to the plane containing them. ● *v.* **1** *tr.* fasten or link together; connect (esp. railroad car). **2** *tr.* (often foll. by *together, with*) associate in thought or speech (*papers coupled their names; couple our congratulations with our best wishes*). **3** *intr.* copulate. **4** *tr.* *Physics* connect (oscillators) with a coupling. [ME f. OF *cople, cuple, copler, cupler* f. L *copulare,* L COPULA]

cou·pler /kúplər/ *n.* **1** *Mus.* **a** a device in an organ for connecting two manuals, or a manual with pedals, so that they both sound when only one is played. **b** (also **oc·tave cou·pler**) a similar device for connecting notes with their octaves above or below. **2** anything that connects two things, esp. a transformer used for connecting electric circuits.

cou·plet /kúplit/ *n. Prosody* two successive lines of verse, usu. rhyming and of the same length. [F dimin. of *couple,* formed as COUPLE]

cou·pling /kúpling/ *n.* **1 a** a link connecting railroad car, etc. **b** a device for connecting parts of machinery. **2** *Physics* a connection between two systems, causing one to oscillate when the other does so. **3** *Mus.* **a** the arrangement of items on a phonograph record. **b** each such item. **4** (an act of) sexual intercourse.

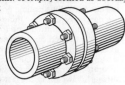

coupling 1

cou·pon /kóopon, kyóo–/ *n.* **1** a form, etc., in a newspaper, magazine, etc., that may be filled in and sent as an application for a purchase, information, etc., or that may be redeemed for a discount on a product or service. **2** *Brit.* an entry form for a soccer pool or other competition. **3** a voucher given with a retail purchase, a certain number of which entitle the holder to a discount, etc. **4 a** a detachable ticket entitling the holder to a ration of food, clothes, etc., esp. in wartime. **b** a similar ticket entitling the holder to payment, goods, a discount, services, etc. [F, = piece cut off f. *couper* cut: see COUPE²]

cour·age /kórij, kúr–/ *n.* the ability to disregard fear; bravery. □ **courage of one's convictions** the courage to act on one's beliefs. **lose courage** become less brave. **pluck up** (or **take**) **courage** muster one's courage. **take one's courage in both hands** nerve oneself to a venture. [ME f. OF *corage,* f. L *cor* heart]

SYNONYM TIP courage

FORTITUDE, GUTS, NERVE, PLUCK, RESOLUTION, TENACITY. **Courage** is what makes someone capable of facing extreme danger and difficulty without retreating (*the courage to confront the enemy head-on*). It implies not only bravery and a dauntless spirit but the ability to endure in times of adversity (*a mother's courage in the face of her loss*). Someone who has **guts**, a slang word indicating an admirable display of courage when it really counts (*having the guts to stand up to one's boss*), might also be described as having "intestinal fortitude," a cliché that is more formal and means the same thing. **Fortitude** is the most formal of any of these words; it suggests firmness or strength of mind rather than physical bravery (*the fortitude to stand up for his beliefs*). **Resolution** also implies firmness of mind rather than fearlessness, but the emphasis is on the determination to achieve a goal in spite of opposition or interference (*a woman of strong resolution, not easily held back by her male superiors*). **Tenacity** goes one step beyond *resolution,* adding stubborn persistence and unwillingness to acknowledge defeat (*the tenacity of a bulldog*). **Nerve** and **pluck** are informal words. *Pluck* connotes high spirits, conviction, and eagerness (*the pluck to volunteer her time even after she'd been laid off*), while *nerve* is the cool, unflappable daring with which someone takes a calculated risk (*the nerve to take over the controls and land the plane safely*). *Nerve* can also refer to brashness or even rudeness in social situations (*She had the nerve to go to his house without calling first*).

cou·ra·geous /kəráyjəs/ *adj.* brave; fearless. □□ **cou·ra·geous·ly** *adv.* **cou·ra·geous·ness** *n.* [ME f. AF *corageous,* OF *corageus* (as COURAGE)]

cou·rante /kooraánt/ *n.* **1** *hist.* a running or gliding dance. **2** *Mus.* the music used for this, esp. as a movement of a suite. [F, fem. pres. part. (as noun) of *courir* run f. L *currere*]

cour·gette /koorzhét/ *n. Brit.* = ZUCCHINI. [F, dimin. of *courge* gourd]

cour·i·er /kóoreeər, kór–, kúr–/ *n.* **1** a person employed, usu. by a travel company, to guide and assist a group of tourists. **2** a special messenger. [ME f. obs. F, f. It. *corriere,* & f. OF *coreor,* both f. L *currere* run]

course /kawrs/ *n. & v.* ● *n.* **1** a continuous onward movement or progression. **2 a** a line along which a person or thing moves; a direction taken (*has changed course; the course of the winding river*). **b** a correct or intended direction or line of movement. **c** the direction taken by a ship or aircraft. **3 a** the ground on which a race (or other sport involving extensive linear movement) takes place. **b** a series of fences, hurdles, or other obstacles to be crossed in a race, etc. **4 a** a series of lectures, lessons, etc., in a particular subject. **b** a book for such a course (*A Modern French Course*). **5** any of the successive parts of a meal. **6** *Med.* a sequence of medical treatment, etc. (*prescribed a course of antibiotics*). **7** a line of conduct (*disappointed by the course he took*). **8** *Archit.* a continuous horizontal layer of brick, stone, etc., in a building. **9** a channel in which water flows. **10** the pursuit of game (esp. hares) with hounds, esp. greyhounds, by sight rather than scent. **11** *Naut.* a sail on a square-rigged ship (*fore course; main course*). ● *v.* **1** *intr.* (esp. of liquid) run, esp. fast (*blood coursed through his veins*). **2** *tr.* (also *absol.*) **a** use (hounds) to hunt. **b** pursue (hares, etc.) in hunting. □ **the course of nature** ordinary events or procedure. **in the course of** during. **in the course of time** as time goes by; eventually. **a matter of course** the natural or expected thing. **of course** naturally; as is or was to be expected; admittedly. **on** (or **off**) **course** following (or deviating from) the desired direction or goal. **run** (or **take**) **its course** (esp. of an illness) complete its natural development. □□ **cours•er** *n.* (in sense 2 of *v.*). [ME f. OF *cours* f. L *cursus* f. *currere curs-* run]

cours•er[1] /káwrsər/ *n. poet.* a swift horse. [ME f. OF *corsier* f. Rmc]

cours•er[2] /káwrsər/ *n.* any fast-running ploverlike bird of the genus *Cursorius*, native to Africa and Asia, having long legs and a slender bill. [LL *cursorius* adapted for running]

court /kawrt/ *n. & v.* • *n.* **1** (in full **court of law**) **a** a judge or assembly of judges or other persons acting as a tribunal in civil and criminal cases. **b** = COURTROOM. **2 a** an enclosed quadrangular area for games, which may be open or covered (*tennis court; squash court*). **b** an area marked out for lawn tennis, etc. (*hit the ball out of court*). **3 a** a small enclosed street in a town, having a yard surrounded by houses, and adjoining a larger street. **b** *Brit.* = COURTYARD. **c** the name of a large house, block of apartments, street, etc. (*Grosvenor Court*). **d** (at Cambridge University) a college quadrangle. **e** a subdivision of a building, usu. a large hall extending to the ceiling with galleries and staircases. **4 a** the establishment, retinue, and courtiers of a sovereign. **b** a sovereign and his or her councilors, constituting a ruling power. **c** a sovereign's residence. **d** an assembly held by a sovereign; a state reception. **5** attention paid to a person whose favor, love, or interest is sought (*paid court to her*). **6 a** the qualified members of a company or a corporation. **c** a meeting of a court. • *v.tr.* **1 a** try to win the affection or favor of (a person). **b** pay amorous attention to (*courting couples*). **2** seek to win (applause, fame, etc.). **3** invite (misfortune) by one's actions (*you are courting disaster*). □ **go to court** take legal action. **in court** appearing as a party or an advocate in a court of law. **out of court 1** (of a plaintiff) not entitled to be heard. **2** (of a settlement) arranged before a hearing or judgment can take place. **3** not worthy of consideration (*that suggestion is out of court*). [ME f. AF *curt*, OF *cort*, ult. f. L *cohors, -hortis* yard, retinue: (v.) after OIt. *corteare*, OF *courtoyer*]

court bouil•lon /kōōr bōōlyón, -yáwn, káwr-; *Fr.* kōōrbōōyón/ *n.* (*pl.* **courts bouil•lons** /kōōr bōōlyónz, -yáwnz; *Fr.* kōōr bōōyón/) stock usu. made from wine, vegetables, etc., often used in fish dishes. [F f. *court* short + BOUILLON]

court dress *n.* formal dress worn at a royal court.

cour•te•ous /kártees/ *adj.* polite, kind, or considerate in manner; well-mannered. □□ **cour•te•ous•ly** *adv.* **cour•te•ous•ness** *n.* [ME f. OF *corteis, curteis* f. Rmc (as COURT): assim. to words in -OUS]

cour•te•san /káwrtizán/ *n. literary* **1** a prostitute, esp. one with wealthy or upper-class clients. **2** the mistress of a wealthy man. [F *courtisane* f. It. *cortigiana*, fem. of *cortigiano* courtier f. *corte* COURT]

cour•te•sy /kártisee/ *n.* (*pl.* **-sies**) **1** courteous behavior; good manners. **2** a courteous act. **3** *archaic* = CURTSY. □ **by courtesy** by favor, not by right. **by courtesy of** with the formal permission of (a person, etc.). [ME f. OF *curtesie, co(u)rtesie* f. *curteis*, etc., COURTEOUS]

cour•te•sy light *n.* a light in a car that is switched on by opening a door.

court•house /káwrthows/ *n.* **1** a building in which a judicial court is held. **2** a building containing the administrative offices of a county.

cour•ti•er /káwrteeər/ *n.* a person who attends or frequents a sovereign's court. [ME f. AF *courte(i)our*, f. OF f. *cortoyer* be present at court]

court•ly /káwrtlee/ *adj.* (**court•li•er, court•li•est**) **1** polished or refined in manners. **2** obsequious. **3** punctilious. □□ **court•li•ness** *n.* [COURT]

court•ly love *n.* the conventional medieval tradition of knightly love for a lady, and the etiquette used in its (esp. literary) expression.

court-mar•tial /káwrt maíarshəl/ *n. & v.* • *n.* (*pl.* **courts-mar•tial**) a judicial court for trying members of the armed services. • *v.tr.* try by a court-martial.

court of rec•ord *n.* a court whose proceedings are recorded and available as evidence of fact.

Court of St. James's *n.* the British sovereign's court.

court or•der *n.* a direction issued by a court or a judge, usu. requiring a person to do or not do something.

court re•port•er *n.* a stenographer who makes a verbatim record and transcription of the proceedings in a court of law.

court•room /káwrtrōōm, -rŏŏm/ *n.* the place or room in which a court of law meets.

court•ship /káwrtship/ *n.* **1 a** courting with a view to marriage. **b** the courting behavior of male animals, birds, etc. **c** a period of courting. **2** an attempt, often protracted, to gain advantage by flattery, attention, etc.

court ten•nis *n.* the original form of tennis played on an indoor court.

court•yard /káwrtyaard/ *n.* an area enclosed by walls or buildings, often opening off a street.

cous•cous /kōōskōōs/ *n.* **1** a type of N. African semolina in granules made from crushed durum wheat. **2** a spicy dish made by steaming or soaking such granules and adding meat, vegetables, or fruit. [F f. Arab. *kuskus* f. *kaskasa* to pound]

cous•in /kúzən/ *n.* **1** (also **first cous•in, cous•in-ger•man**) the child of one's uncle or aunt. **2** (usu. in *pl.*) applied to the people of kindred races or nations (*our British cousins*). **3** *hist.* a title formerly used by a sovereign in addressing another sovereign or a noble of his or her own country. □□ **cous•in•hood** *n.* **cous•in•ly** *adj.* **cous•in•ship** *n.* [ME f. OF *cosin, cusin,* f. L *consobrinus* mother's sister's child]

couth /kōōth/ *adj. joc.* cultured; well-mannered. [back-form. as antonym of UNCOUTH]

cou•ture /kōōtŌŌr, -tŢ;AAYr/ *n.* the design and manufacture of fashionable clothes; = HAUTE COUTURE. [F, = sewing, dressmaking]

cou•tu•ri•er /kōōtŌŌree-ay, -eeər/ *n.* (*fem.* **cou•tu•ri•ère** /-reeáir/) a fashion designer or dressmaker. [F]

cou•vade /kōōvaád/ *n.* a custom by which a father appears to undergo labor and childbirth when his child is being born. [F f. *couver* hatch f. L *cubare* lie down]

cou•vert /kōōváir/ *n.* = COVER *n.* 5. [F]

co•va•lence /kōváyləns/ *n.* (*Brit.* **co•va•len•cy** /-váylənsee/) *Chem.* **1** the linking of atoms by a covalent bond. **2** the number of pairs of electrons an atom can share with another.

co•va•lent /kōváylənt/ *adj. Chem.* of, relating to, or characterized by covalency. □□ **co•va•lence** *n.* **co•va•lent•ly** *adv.* [CO- + *valent,* after *trivalent,* etc.]

co•va•lent bond *n. Chem.* a bond formed by sharing of electrons usu. in pairs by two atoms in a molecule.

cove[1] /kōv/ *n. & v.* • *n.* **1** a small, esp. sheltered, bay or creek. **2** a sheltered recess. **3** *Archit.* a concave arch or arched molding, esp. one formed at the junction of a wall with a ceiling. • *v.tr. Archit.* **1** provide (a room, ceiling, etc.) with a cove. **2** slope (the sides of a fireplace) inward. [OE *cofa* chamber f. Gmc]

cove[2] /kōv/ *n. Brit. sl. archaic* a fellow; a chap. [16th c. cant: orig. unkn.]

cov•en /kúvən/ *n.* an assembly of witches. [var. of *covent;* see CONVENT]

cov•e•nant /kúvənənt/ *n. & v.* • *n.* **1** an agreement; a contract. **2** *Law* **a** a contract drawn up under a seal, esp. undertaking to make regular payments to a charity. **b** a clause of a covenant. **3** (**Covenant**) *Bibl.* the agreement between God and the Israelites (see ARK OF THE COVENANT). • *v.tr. & intr.* agree, esp. by legal covenant. □□ **cov•e•nan•tal** /-nánt'l/ *adj.* **cov•e•nan•tor** *n.* [ME f. OF, pres. part. of *co(n)venir,* formed as CONVENE]

cov•e•nant•ed /kúvənəntid/ *adj.* bound by a covenant.

cov•e•nant•er /kúvənəntər, -nántər/ *n.* **1** a person who covenants. **2** (**Covenanter**) *hist.* an adherent of the National Covenant or the Solemn League and Covenant in 17th-c. Scotland, in support of Presbyterianism.

cov•er /kúvər/ *v. & n.* • *v.tr.* **1 a** (often foll. by *with*) protect or conceal by means of a cloth, lid, etc. **b** prevent the perception or discovery of; conceal (*to cover my embarrassment*). **2 a** extend over; occupy the whole surface of (*covered in dirt; covered with writing*). **b** (often foll. by *with*) strew thickly or thoroughly (*covered the floor with straw*). **c** lie over; be a covering to (*the blanket scarcely covered him*). **3 a** protect; clothe. **b** (as **covered** *adj.*) wearing a hat; having a roof. **4** include; comprise; deal with (*the talk covered recent discoveries*). **5** travel (a specified distance) (*covered sixty miles*). **6** *Journalism* **a** report (events, a meeting, etc.). **b** investigate as a reporter. **7** be enough to defray (expenses, a bill, etc.) (*$20 should cover it*). **8 a** *refl.* take precautionary measures so as to protect oneself (*had covered myself by saying I might be late*). **b** (*absol.*; foll. by *for*) deputize or stand in for (a colleague, etc.) (*will you cover for me?*). **9** *Mil.* **a** aim a gun, etc., at. **b** (of a fortress, guns, etc.) command (a territory). **c** stand behind (a person in the front rank). **d** protect (an exposed person, etc.) by being able to return fire. **10** (also *absol.*) (in some card games) play a card higher than (one already played to the same trick). **11** (of a stallion, a bull, etc.) copulate with. • *n.* **1** something that covers or protects, esp.: **a** a lid. **b** the binding of a book. **c** either board of this. **d** an envelope or the wrapping of a mailed package (*under separate cover*). **e** the outer case of a pneumatic tire. **f** (in *pl.*) bedclothes. **2** a hiding place; a shelter. **3** woods or undergrowth sheltering game or covering the ground (see COVERT). **4 a** a pretense; a screen (*under cover of humility*). **b** a spy's pretended identity or activity, intended as concealment. **c** *Mil.* a supporting force protecting an advance party from attack. **5** a place setting at table, esp. in a restaurant. □ **break cover** (of an animal, esp. game, or a hunted person) leave a place of shelter, esp. vegetation. **cover one's tracks** conceal evidence of what one has done. **cover up 1** completely cover or conceal. **2** conceal (circumstances, etc., esp. illicitly) (also *absol.*: *refused to cover up for them*). **from cover to cover** from beginning to end of a book, etc. **take cover** use a natural or prepared shelter against an attack. □□ **cov•er•a•ble** *adj.* **cov•er•er** *n.* [ME f. OF *covrir, cuvrir* f. L *cooperire* (as CO-, *operire opert-* cover)]

cov•er•age /kúvərij/ n. **1** an area or an amount covered. **2** *Journalism* the amount of press, etc., publicity received by a particular story, person, etc. **3** a risk covered by an insurance policy. **4** an area reached by a particular broadcasting station or advertising medium.

cov•er•all /kúvərawl/ n. & adj. • n. **1** something that covers entirely. **2** (usu. in pl.) a full-length protective outer garment often zipped up the front. • attrib.adj. covering entirely (a coverall term).

cov•er charge n. an extra fee, in addition to the cost of food and drink, charged per person for admission to a restaurant, nightclub, etc.

cov•er crop n. a crop grown for the protection and enrichment of the soil.

covered wagon n. a wagon with an arched canvas cover, used esp. by American pioneers traveling westward across the prairies.

covered wagon

cov•er girl n. a female model whose picture appears on magazine covers, etc.

cov•er•ing /kúvəring/ n. something that covers, esp. a bedspread, blanket, etc., or clothing.

cov•er•let /kúvərlit/ n. a bedspread. [ME f. AF covrelet, –lit f. OF covrir cover + lit bed]

cov•er let•ter n. an explanatory letter sent with another document or parcel of goods.

cov•er sto•ry n. a news story in a magazine, that is illustrated or advertised on the front cover.

co•vert /kóvərt, kōvərt, kú–/ adj. & n. • adj. secret or disguised (a covert glance; covert operations). • n. **1** a shelter, esp. a thicket hiding game. **2** a feather covering the base of a bird's flight feather. □□ **co•vert•ly** adv. **co•vert•ness** n. [ME f. OF covert past part. of covrir COVER]

PRONUNCIATION TIP covert

The traditional pronunciation of this word, still widely used in British English, is "KUH-vert" (reflecting its relation to the word *cover*). But the newer pronunciation uses a "long o" sound, rhyming with *overt*, and is now regularly used in America.

---

co•ver•ture /kúvərchər/ n. **1** covering; shelter. **2** *Law hist.* the position of a married woman, considered to be under her husband's protection. [ME f. OF (as COVERT)]

cov•er-up n. an act of concealing circumstances, esp. illicitly.

cov•et /kúvit/ v. tr. desire greatly (esp. something belonging to another person) (coveted her friend's earrings). □□ **cov•et•a•ble** adj. [ME f. OF cu–, coveitier f. Rmc]

cov•et•ous /kúvitəs/ adj. (usu. foll. by of) **1** greatly desirous (esp. of another person's property). **2** grasping; avaricious. □□ **cov•et•ous•ly** adv. **cov•et•ous•ness** n. [ME f. OF coveitous f. Gallo-Roman]

cov•ey /kúvee/ n. (pl. ·eys) **1** a brood of partridges. **2** a small party or group of people or things. [ME f. OF covee f. Rmc f. L cubare lie]

cov•in /kúvin/ n. **1** *Law* a conspiracy to commit a crime, etc., against a third party. **2** *archaic* fraud; deception. [ME f. OF covin(e) f. med.L convenium –ia f. convenire: see CONVENE]

cow¹ /kow/ n. **1** a fully grown female of any bovine animal, esp. of the genus Bos, used as a source of milk and beef. **2** the female of other large animals, esp. the elephant, whale, and seal. **3** sl. derog. **a** a woman, esp. a coarse or unpleasant one. **b** *Austral.* & *NZ* an unpleasant person, thing, situation, etc. □ **till the cows come home** colloq. an indefinitely long time. [OE cū f. Gmc, rel. to L bos, Gk bous]

cow² /kow/ v. tr. (usu. in passive) intimidate or dispirit (cowed by ill-treatment). [prob. f. ON kúga oppress]

cow•ard /kówərd/ n. & adj. • n. a person who is easily frightened or intimidated by danger or pain. • adj. poet. easily frightened. [ME f. OF cuard, couard ult. f. L cauda tail]

cow•ard•ice /kówərdis/ n. a lack of bravery. [ME f. OF couardise (as COWARD)]

cow•ard•ly /kówərdlee/ adj. & adv. • adj. **1** of or like a coward; lacking courage. **2** (of an action) done against one who cannot retaliate. • adv. archaic like a coward. □□ **cow•ard•li•ness** n.

---

cow•bane /kówbayn/ n. = WATER HEMLOCK.

cow•bell /kówbel/ n. **1** a bell worn around a cow's neck for easy location of the animal. **2** a similar bell used as a percussion instrument.

cow•ber•ry /kówberee/ n. (pl. ·ries) **1** an evergreen shrub, Vaccinium vitis-idaea, bearing dark-red berries. **2** the berry of this plant.

cow•boy /kówboy/ n. **1** (fem. **cow•girl**) a person who herds and tends cattle, esp. in the western US. **2** this as a conventional figure in American folklore, esp. in films. **3** colloq. an unscrupulous or reckless person in business, esp. an unqualified one.

cow•catch•er /kówkachər/ n. a peaked metal frame at the front of a locomotive for pushing aside obstacles on the line.

cow•er /kowər/ v. intr. **1** crouch or shrink back, esp. in fear; cringe. **2** stand or squat in a bent position. [ME f. MLG kūren lie in wait, of unkn. orig.]

cow•fish /kówfish/ n. **1** any of several plant-eating marine mammals, e.g., the manatee. **2** a marine fish, Lactoria diaphana, covered in hard bony plates and having hornlike spines over the eyes and on other parts of the body.

cow•hage /kówij/ n. (also **cow•age**) a climbing plant, Mucuna pruritum, having hairy pods which cause stinging and itching. [Hindi kawānch]

cow•hand /kówhand/ n. = COWBOY n. 1.

cow•herd /kówhərd/ n. a person who tends cattle.

cow•hide /kówhīd/ n. **1 a** a cow's hide. **b** leather made from this. **2** a leather whip made from cowhide.

cow•house /kówhows/ n. esp. Brit. a shed or shelter for cows.

cowl /kowl/ n. **1 a** the hood of a monk's habit. **b** a loose hood. **c** a monk's hooded habit. **2** the hood-shaped covering of a chimney or ventilating shaft. **3** the removable cover of a vehicle or aircraft engine. □□ **cowled** adj. (in sense 1). [OE cugele, cūle f. eccl.L cuculla f. L cucullus hood of a cloak]

cow•lick /kówlik/ n. a projecting lock of hair.

cowl•ing /kówling/ n. = COWL 3.

cow•man /kówmən/ n. (pl. ·men) **1** = COWHERD. **2** a cattle owner.

co•work•er /kō-wórkər/ n. a person who works in collaboration with another.

cow•pat /kówpat/ n. a flat, round piece of cow dung.

cow•pea /kówpee/ n. **1** a plant of the pea family, Vigna unguiculata, grown esp. in the southern US for forage and green manure. **2** its edible seed. Also called **black-eyed pea**.

cow•poke /kówpōk/ n. = COWBOY 1.

cow•pox /kówpoks/ n. a disease of cows, of which the virus was formerly used in vaccination against smallpox.

cow•punch•er /kówpunchər/ n. = COWBOY 1.

cow•rie /kówree/ n. (also **cow•ry**) (pl. ·ries) **1** any gastropod mollusk of the family Cypraeidae, having a smooth, glossy, and usu. brightly colored shell. **2** its shell, esp. used as money in parts of Africa and S. Asia. [Urdu & Hindi kaurī]

cow•shed /kówshed/ n. **1** a shed for cattle that are not at pasture. **2** a milking shed.

cow•slip /kówslip/ n. **1** a primula, Primula veris, with fragrant yellow flowers and growing in pastures. **2** a marsh marigold. [OE cūslyppe f. cū COW¹ + slyppe slimy substance, i.e., cow dung]

cow tree n. a tree, Brosimum galactodendron, native to S. America, yielding a milklike juice which is used as a substitute for cow's milk.

cox /koks/ n. & v. • n. a coxswain, esp. of a racing boat. • v. **1** intr. act as a cox (coxed for Harvard). **2** tr. act as cox for (coxed the winning boat). [abbr.]

cox•a /kóksə/ n. (pl. **cox•ae** /–see/) **1** *Anat.* the hipbone or hip joint. **2** *Zool.* the first segment of an insect's leg. □□ **cox•al** adj. [L]

cox•comb /kókskōm/ n. an ostentatiously conceited man; a dandy. □□ **cox•comb•ry** /–kōmree, –kəmree/ n. (pl. ·ries). [= cock's comb (see COCK¹), orig. (a cap worn by) a jester]

cox•swain /kóksən, –swayn/ n. & v. • n. a person who steers and directs the crew, esp. in a rowing boat. • v. **1** intr. act as a coxswain. **2** tr. act as a coxswain of. □□ **cox•swain•ship** n. [ME f. cock (see COCKBOAT) + SWAIN: cf. BOATSWAIN]

coy /koy/ adj. (**coy•er**, **coy•est**) **1** archly or affectedly shy. **2** irritatingly reticent (always coy about her age). **3** (esp. of a girl) modest or shy. □□ **coy•ly** adv. **coy•ness** n. [ME f. OF coi, quei f. L quietus QUIET]

coy•o•te /kīyōtee, kíyōt/ n. (pl. same or **coy•o•tes**) a wolflike wild dog, Canis latrans, native to N. America. [Mex. Sp. f. Aztec coyotl]

coy•pu /kóypōo/ n. (pl. **coy•pus**) = NUTRIA 1. [Araucan]

coz /kuz/ n. archaic cousin. [abbr.]

coz•en /kúzən/ v. literary **1** tr. (often foll. by of, out of) cheat; defraud. **2** tr. (often foll. by into) beguile; persuade. **3** intr. act deceitfully. □□ **coz•en•age** n. [16th c. cant, perh. rel. to COUSIN]

co•zy /kốzee/ adj., n., & v. (esp. Brit. **co•sy**) • adj. (**coz•i•er**, **coz•i•est**) **1** comfortable and warm; snug. **2** derog. complacent; self-serving. **3** warm and friendly. • n. (pl. ·zies) **1** a cover to keep something hot, esp. a teapot or a boiled egg. **2** *Brit.* a canopied corner seat for two. • *v.tr.* (**·zies, ·zied**) (often foll. by *along*) *colloq.* reassure, esp. deceptively. □ **cozy up to** *colloq.* **1** ingratiate oneself with. **2** snuggle up to. □□ **co·zi·ly** *adv.* **co·si·ness** *n.* [18th c. f. Sc., of unkn. orig.]

coz·zie var. of COSSIE.

cp. *abbr.* compare.

c.p. *abbr.* candlepower.

CPA *abbr.* certified public accountant.

cpd. *abbr.* compound.

CPI *abbr.* consumer price index.

Cpl. *abbr.* corporal.

CPR *abbr.* cardiopulmonary resuscitation.

cps *abbr.* (also **c.p.s.**) **1** *Computing* characters per second. **2** cycles per second.

Cpt. *abbr.* captain.

CPU *abbr. Computing* central processing unit.

Cr *symb. Chem.* the element chromium.

crab[1] /krab/ *n.* **1 a** any of numerous ten-footed crustaceans having the first pair of legs modified as pincers. **b** the flesh of a crab, esp. *Cancer pagurus*, as food. **2** (**the Crab**) the zodiacal sign or constellation Cancer. **3** (in full **crab louse**) (often in *pl.*) a parasitic louse, *Phthirus pubis*, infesting hairy parts of the body and causing extreme irritation. **4** a machine for hoisting heavy weights. □ **catch a crab** *Rowing*

crab

effect a faulty stroke in which the oar is jammed under water or misses the water altogether. □□ **crab·like** *adj.* [OE *crabba*, rel. to ON *krafla* scratch]

crab[2] /krab/ *n.* **1** (in full **crab apple**) a small sour, applelike fruit. **2** (in full **crab tree** or **crab apple tree**) any of several trees bearing this fruit. **3** a sour person. [ME, perh. alt. (after CRAB[1] or CRABBED) of earlier *scrab*, prob. of Scand. orig.]

crab[3] /krab/ *v.* (**crabbed, crab·bing**) *colloq.* **1** *tr. & intr.* criticize adversely or captiously; grumble. **2** *tr.* act so as to spoil (*the mistake crabbed his chances*). [orig. of hawks fighting, f. MLG *krabben*]

crabbed /krábid/ *adj.* **1** irritable or morose. **2** (of handwriting) illformed and hard to decipher. **3** perverse or cross-grained. **4** difficult to understand. □□ **crab·bed·ly** *adv.* **crab·bed·ness** *n.* [ME f. CRAB[1], assoc. with CRAB[2]]

crab·by /krábee/ *adj.* (**crab·bi·er, crab·bi·est**) = CRABBED 1,3. □□ **crab·bi·ly** *adv.* **crab·bi·ness** *n.*

crab·grass /krábgras/ *n.* a creeping grass infesting lawns.

crab·wise /krábwīz/ *adv. & attrib.adj.* (of movement) sideways or backward like a crab.

crack /krak/ *n., v., & adj.* • *n.* **1 a** a sudden sharp or explosive noise (*the crack of a whip; a loud crack of thunder*). **b** (in a voice) a sudden harshness or change in pitch. **2** a sharp blow (*a crack on the head*). **3 a** a narrow opening between two surfaces, esp. ones that have broken or been moved apart (*the door opened a tiny crack*). **b** a partial fracture, with the parts still joined (*a hairline crack down the middle of the glass*). **4** *colloq.* a mischievous or malicious remark or aside (*a nasty crack about my age*). **5** *colloq.* an attempt (*I'll have a crack at it*). **6** the exact moment (*at the crack of noon; the crack of dawn*). **7** *sl.* a potent hard crystalline form of cocaine broken into small pieces and inhaled or smoked. • *v.* **1** *tr. & intr.* break without a complete separation of the parts (*cracked the window; the cup cracked on hitting the floor*). **2** *intr. & tr.* make or cause to make a sudden sharp or explosive sound. **3** *intr. & tr.* break or cause to break with a sudden, sharp sound. **4** *intr. & tr.* give way or cause to give way under torture, pressure, or strain; yield. **5** *intr.* (of the voice, esp. of an adolescent boy or a person under strain) become dissonant; break. **6** *tr. colloq.* find a solution to (a problem, code, etc.). **7** *tr.* say (a joke, etc.) in a jocular way. **8** *tr. colloq.* hit sharply or hard (*cracked her head on the ceiling*). **9** *tr. Chem.* decompose (heavy oils) by heat and pressure with or without a catalyst to produce lighter hydrocarbons (such as gasoline). **10** *tr.* break (wheat) into coarse pieces. • *attrib.adj. colloq.* excellent; first-rate (*a crack regiment; a crack shot*). □ **crack a bottle** open a bottle, esp. of wine, and drink it. **crack down on** *colloq.* take severe measures against. **crack up** *colloq.* **1** collapse under strain. **2** laugh. **3** repute (*not all it's cracked up to be*). **get cracking** *colloq.* begin promptly and vigorously. **have a crack at** *colloq.* attempt. [OE *cracian* resound]

crack·brain /krákbrayn/ *n.* a crackpot. □□ **crack·brained** *adj.*

crack·down /krákdown/ *n. colloq.* severe measures (esp. against lawbreakers, etc.).

cracked /krakt/ *adj.* **1** having cracks. **2** (*predic.*) *sl.* crazy.

cracked wheat *n.* grains of wheat that have been crushed into small pieces.

crack·er /krákər/ *n.* **1** a thin, dry biscuit often eaten with cheese. **2** a firework exploding with a sharp noise. **3** (usu. in *pl.*) an instrument

for cracking (*nutcrackers*). **4** a paper cylinder both ends of which are pulled at Christmas, etc., making a sharp noise and releasing a small toy, etc. **5** *Brit. sl.* a notable or attractive person. **6** *offens.* = *poor white.*

crack·er-bar·rel *n.* (of philosophy, etc.) homespun; unsophisticated.

crack·er·jack /krákərjak/ *adj. & n. sl.* • *adj.* exceptionally fine or expert. • *n.* an exceptionally fine thing or person.

crack·ers /krákərz/ *predic.adj. sl.* crazy.

crack·ing /kráking/ *adj. & adv. Brit. sl.* • *adj.* **1** outstanding; very good (*a cracking performance*). **2** (*attrib.*) fast and exciting (*a cracking speed*). • *adv.* outstandingly (*a cracking good time*).

crack·le /krákəl/ *v. & n.* • *v.intr.* make a repeated slight cracking sound (*radio crackled; fire was crackling*). • *n.* **1** such a sound. **2 a** paintwork, china, or glass decorated with a pattern of minute surface cracks. **b** the smooth surface of such paintwork, etc. □□ **crack·ly** *adj.* [CRACK + -LE[4]]

crack·ling /krákling/ *n.* **1** the crisp skin of roast pork. **2** *Brit. joc.* or *offens.* attractive women regarded collectively as objects of sexual desire.

crack·nel /kráknəl/ *n.* a light, crisp biscuit. [ME f. F *craquelin* f. MDu. *krākelinc* f. *krāken* CRACK]

crack·pot /krákpot/ *n. & adj. sl.* • *n.* an eccentric or impractical person. • *adj.* mad; unworkable (*a crackpot scheme*).

cracks·man /kráksmən/ *n.* (*pl.* **·men**) *sl.* a burglar, esp. a safecracker.

crack-up *n. colloq.* **1** a mental breakdown. **2** a car crash.

crack·y /krákee/ *adj.* covered with cracks. □□ **crack·i·ness** *n.*

-cracy /krəsee/ *comb. form* denoting a particular form of government, rule, or influence (*aristocracy; bureaucracy*). [from or after F *-cratie* f. med.L *-cratia* f. Gk *-kratia* f. *kratos* strength, power]

cra·dle /kráyd'l/ *n. & v.* • *n.* **1 a** a child's bed, esp. one mounted on rockers. **b** a place in which a thing begins, esp. a civilization, etc., or is nurtured in its infancy (*cradle of choral singing; cradle of democracy*). **2** a framework resembling a cradle, esp.: **a** that on which a ship, a boat, etc., rests during construction or repairs. **b** that on which a worker is suspended to work on a ceiling, a ship, the vertical side of a building, etc. **c** the part of a telephone on which the receiver rests when not in use. • *v.tr.* **1** contain or shelter as if in a cradle (*cradled his head in her arms*). **2** place in a cradle. □ **from the cradle** from infancy. **from the cradle to the grave** from infancy till death (esp. of government welfare). [OE *cradol*, perh. rel. to OHG *kratto* basket]

cra·dle-rob·ber *n.* (also **cra·dle-snatch·er**) *sl.* a person amorously attached to a much younger person.

cra·dle·song /kráyd'lsong/ *n.* a lullaby.

cra·dling /kráydling/ *n. Archit.* a wooden or iron framework, esp. one used as a structural support in a ceiling.

craft /kraft/ *n. & v.* • *n.* **1** skill, esp. in practical arts. **2 a** a trade or an art (*statecraft; handicraft; priestcraft; the craft of pottery*). **b** the members of such a craft. **3** (*pl.* **craft**) a boat or vessel. **b** an aircraft or spacecraft. **4** cunning or deceit. **5** (**the Craft**) the brotherhood of Freemasons. • *v.tr.* make in a skillful way (*crafted a poem; a well-crafted piece of work*). [OE *cræft*]

craft guild *n. hist.* a guild of workers of the same trade.

crafts·man /kráftsmən/ *n.* (*pl.* **·men;** *fem.* **crafts·wom·an,** *pl.* **·wom·en**) **1** a skilled worker; an artisan. **2** a person who practices a handicraft. □□ **crafts·man·ship** *n.* [ME, orig. *craft's man*]

craft·y /kráftee/ *adj.* (**craft·i·er, craft·i·est**) cunning; artful; wily. □□ **craft·i·ly** *adv.* **craft·i·ness** *n.* [OE *cræftig*]

crag[1] /krag/ *n.* a steep or rugged rock. [ME, of Celt. orig.]

crag[2] /krag/ *n. Geol.* rock consisting of a shelly sand. [18th c.: perh. f. CRAG[1]]

crag·gy /krágee/ *adj.* (**crag·gi·er, crag·gi·est**) **1** (esp. of a person's face) rugged; rough-textured. **2** (of a landscape) having crags. □□ **crag·gi·ly** *adv.* **crag·gi·ness** *n.*

crags·man /krágzmən/ *n.* (*pl.* **·men**) a skilled climber of crags.

crake /krayk/ *n.* **1** any rail (see RAIL[3]), esp. a corncrake. **2** the cry of a corncrake. [ME f. ON *kráka* (imit.): cf. CROAK]

cram /kram/ *v.* (**crammed, cram·ming**) **1** *tr.* **a** fill to bursting; stuff (*the room was crammed*). **b** (foll. by *in, into*) force (a thing) into (*cram the sandwiches into the bag*). **2** *tr. & intr.* prepare for an examination by intensive study. **3** *tr.* (often foll. by *with*) feed (poultry, etc.) to excess. **4** *tr. & intr. colloq.* eat greedily. □ **cram in** push in to bursting point (*crammed in another five minutes' work*). [OE *crammian* f. Gmc]

cram·bo /krámbō/ *n.* a game in which a player gives a word or line of verse to which each of the others must find a rhyme. [earlier *crambe*, app. allusive f. L *crambe repetita* cabbage served up again]

cram-full *adj.* as full as possible.

cramp /kramp/ *n. & v.* • *n.* **1 a** a painful involuntary contraction of a muscle or muscles from the cold, exertion, etc. **b** = WRITER'S CRAMP (see WRITER). **2** (also **cramp iron**) a metal bar with bent ends for holding masonry, etc., together. **3** a portable tool for holding two planks, etc., together; a clamp. **4** a restraint. • *v.tr.* **1** affect with cramp. **2** confine narrowly. **3** restrict (energies, etc.). **4** (as **cramped**

adj.) **a** (of handwriting) small and difficult to read. **b** (of a room, etc.) uncomfortably crowded; lacking space. **5** fasten with a cramp. □ **cramp a person's style** prevent a person from acting freely or naturally. **cramp up** confine narrowly. [ME f. OF *crampe* f. MDu., MLG *krampe*, OHG *krampfo* f. adj. meaning 'bent': cf. CRIMP]

cram·pon /krámpon/ *n.* (also **cram·poon** /–pōōn/) (usu. in *pl.*) **1** an iron plate with spikes fixed to a boot for walking on ice, climbing, etc. **2** a metal hook for lifting timber, rock, etc.; a grappling iron. [ME f. F (as CRAMP)]

cran·age /kráynij/ *n.* **1** the use of a crane or cranes. **2** the money paid for this.

cran·ber·ry /kránberee/ *n.* (*pl.* **·ries**) **1** any evergreen shrub of the genus *Vaccinium*, esp. *V. macrocarpon* of America and *V. oxycoccos* of Europe, yielding small, red, acid berries. **2** a berry from this used for a sauce and in cooking. [17th c.: named by Amer. colonists f. G *Kranbeere*, LG *kranebere* crane berry]

crane /krayn/ *n. & v.* • *n.* **1** a machine for moving heavy objects, usu. by suspending them from a projecting arm or beam. **2** any tall wading bird of the family Gruidae, with long legs, long neck, and straight bill. **3** a moving platform supporting a television camera or movie camera. • *v.tr.* **1** (also *absol.*) stretch out (one's neck) in order to see something. **2** *tr.* move (an object) by a crane. [OE *cran*, rel. to L *grus*, Gk *geranos*]

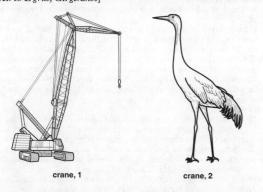

crane, 1   crane, 2

crane fly *n.* (*pl.* **flies**) any fly of the family Tipulidae, having two wings and long legs, resembling a large mosquito.

cranes·bill /kráynzbil/ *n.* any of various plants of the genus *Geranium*, having a long spur on the fruit.

cra·ni·al /kráyneeəl/ *adj.* of or relating to the skull. [CRANIUM + –AL]

cra·ni·al in·dex *n.* = CEPHALIC INDEX.

cra·ni·ate /kráyneeət, –ayt/ *adj. & n.* • *adj.* having a skull. • *n.* a craniate animal. [mod.L *craniatus* f. CRANIUM]

cranio- /kráyneeō/ *comb. form* cranium.

cra·ni·ol·o·gy /kráyneeóləjee/ *n.* the scientific study of the shape and size of the human skull. □□ **cra·ni·o·log·i·cal** /–neeəlójikəl/ *adj.* **cra·ni·ol·o·gist** *n.*

cra·ni·om·e·try /kráyneeómitree/ *n.* the scientific measurement of skulls. □□ **cra·ni·o·met·ric** /–neeəmétrik/ *adj.*

cra·ni·ot·o·my /kráyneeótəmee/ *n.* (*pl.* **·mies**) **1** surgical removal of a portion of the skull. **2** surgical perforation of the skull of a dead fetus to ease delivery.

cra·ni·um /kráyneeəm/ *n.* (*pl.* **cra·ni·ums** or **cra·ni·a** /–neeə/) **1** the skull. **2** the part of the skeleton that encloses the brain. [ME f. med.L f. Gk *kranion* skull]

crank¹ /krangk/ *n. & v.* • *n.* **1** part of an axle or shaft bent at right angles for interconverting reciprocal and circular motion. **2** an elbow-shaped connection in bell hanging. • *v.tr.* **1** cause to move by means of a crank. **2 a** bend into a crank shape. **b** furnish or fasten with a crank. □ **crank up 1** start (a car engine) by turning a crank. **2** *sl.* increase (speed, etc.) by intensive effort. [OE *cranc*, app. f. *crincan*, rel. to *cringan* fall in battle, orig. 'curl up']

crank² /krangk/ *n.* **1 a** an eccentric person, esp. one obsessed by a particular theory (*health-food crank*). **b** a bad-tempered person. **2** *literary* a fanciful turn of speech (*quips and cranks*). [back-form. f. CRANKY]

crank³ /krangk/ *adj.* *Naut.* liable to capsize. [perh. f. *crank* weak, shaky, or CRANK¹]

crank·case /krángk-kays/ *n.* a case enclosing a crankshaft.

crank·pin /krángkpin/ *n.* a pin by which a connecting rod is attached to a crank.

crank·shaft /krángkshaft/ *n.* a shaft driven by a crank (see CRANK¹ *n.* 1).

crank·y /krángkee/ *adj.* (**crank·i·er**, **crank·i·est**) **1** ill-tempered or crotchety. **2** working badly; shaky. **3** *colloq.* eccentric, esp. obsessed with a particular theory (*cranky ideas about women*). □□ **crank·i·ly** *adv.* **crank·i·ness** *n.* [perh. f. obs. *crank* rogue feigning sickness]

cran·nog /kránəg/ *n.* an ancient lake-dwelling in Scotland or Ireland. [Ir. f. *crann* tree, beam]

cran·ny /kránee/ *n.* (*pl.* **·nies**) a chink; a crevice; a crack. □□ **cran·nied** /–need/ *adj.* [ME f. OF *crané* past part. of *craner* f. *cran* f. pop.L *crena* notch]

crap¹ /krap/ *n. & v. coarse sl.* • *n.* **1** (often as *int.*) nonsense; rubbish (*he talks crap*). **2** feces. • *v.intr.* (**crapped, crap·ping**) defecate. □ **crap out 1** be unsuccessful. **2** withdraw from a game, etc. [earlier senses 'chaff, refuse from fat-boiling': ME f. Du. *krappe*]
▶This is usually considered a taboo word.

crap² /krap/ *n.* a losing throw of 2, 3, or 12 in craps. □ **crap game** a game of craps. [formed as CRAPS]

crape /krayp/ *n.* **1** crepe, usu. of black silk or imitation silk, formerly used for mourning clothes. **2** a band of this formerly worn around a person's hat, etc., as a sign of mourning. □□ **crap·y** *adj.* [earlier *crispe*, *crespe* f. F *crespe* CREPE]

crape fern *n.* a NZ fern, *Leptopteris superba*, with tall dark-green fronds.

crap·py /krápee/ *adj.* (**crap·pi·er**, **crap·pi·est**) *coarse sl.* **1** rubbishy; cheap. **2** disgusting.

craps /kraps/ *n.pl.* a gambling game played with dice. □ **shoot craps** play craps. [19th c.: perh. f. *crab* lowest throw at dice]

crap·shoot /krápshōōt/ *n. sl.* a venture marked by uncertainty and risk.

crap·u·lent /krápyələnt/ *adj.* **1** given to indulging in alcohol. **2** resulting from drunkenness. **3 a** drunk. **b** suffering from the effects of drunkenness. □□ **crap·u·lence** /–ləns/ *n.* **crap·u·lous** *adj.* [LL *crapulentus* very drunk f. L *crapula* inebriation f. Gk *kraipalē* drunken headache]

cra·que·lure /kráklōōr, kraklōōr/ *n.* a network of fine cracks in a painting or its varnish. [F]

crash¹ /krash/ *v., n., & adv.* • *v.* **1** *intr. & tr.* make or cause to make a loud smashing noise (*the cymbals crashed; crashed the plates together*). **2** *tr. & intr.* throw, drive, move, or fall with a loud smashing noise. **3** *intr. & tr.* **a** collide or cause (a vehicle) to collide violently with another vehicle, obstacle, etc.; overturn at high speed. **b** fall or cause (an aircraft) to fall violently on to the land or the sea (*crashed the plane; the pilot crashed into the sea*). **4** *intr.* (usu. foll. by *into*) collide violently (*crashed into the window*). **5** *intr.* undergo financial ruin. **6** *tr. colloq.* enter without permission (*crashed the cocktail party*). **7** *intr. colloq.* be heavily defeated (*crashed to a 4–0 defeat*). **8** *intr. Computing* (of a machine or system) fail suddenly. **9** *tr. Brit. colloq.* pass (a red traffic light, etc.). **10** *intr.* (often foll. by *out*) *sl.* sleep for a night, esp. in an improvised setting. • *n.* **1 a** a loud and sudden smashing noise (*a thunder crash; the crash of dishes*). **b** a breakage (esp. of china, pottery, glass, etc.). **2 a** a violent collision, esp. of one vehicle with another or with an object. **b** the violent fall of an aircraft on to the land or sea. **3** ruin, esp. financial. **4** *Computing* a sudden failure which puts a system out of action. **5** (*attrib.*) done rapidly or urgently (*a crash course in first aid*). • *adv.* with a crash (*the window went crash*). [ME: imit.]

crash² /krash/ *n.* a coarse plain linen, cotton, etc., fabric. [Russ. *krashenina* colored linen]

crash-dive *v.* **1** *intr.* **a** (of a submarine or its pilot) dive hastily and steeply in an emergency. **b** (of an aircraft or pilot) dive and crash. **2** *tr.* cause to crash-dive.

crash dive *n.* a steep, rapid dive made by a submarine or aircraft.

crash hel·met *n.* a helmet worn by a motorcyclist or race car driver to protect the head in a crash.

crash·ing /kráshing/ *adj. colloq.* overwhelming (*a crashing bore*).

crash-land *v.* **1** *intr.* (of an aircraft or airman) land hurriedly with a crash, usu. without lowering the undercarriage. **2** *tr.* cause (an aircraft) to crash-land. □□ **crash land·ing** *n.*

crash pad *n. sl.* a temporary place to sleep or live at no cost.

cra·sis /kráysis/ *n.* (*pl.* **cra·ses** /–seez/) the contraction of two adjacent vowels in ancient Greek into one long vowel or diphthong. [Gk *krasis* mixture]

crass /kras/ *adj.* **1** grossly stupid (*a crass idea*). **2** gross (*crass stupidity*). **3** *literary* thick or gross. □□ **cras·si·tude** *n.* **crass·ly** *adv.* **crass·ness** *n.* [L *crassus* solid, thick]

-crat /krat/ *comb. form* a member or supporter of a particular form of government or rule (*autocrat; democrat*). [from or after F *–crate*: see –CRACY]

crate /krayt/ *n. & v.* • *n.* **1** a large wickerwork basket or slatted wooden case, etc., for packing esp. fragile goods for transportation. **2** *sl.* an old airplane or other vehicle. • *v.tr.* pack in a crate. □□ **crate·ful** *n.* (*pl.* **·fuls**). [ME, perh. f. Du. *krat* basket, etc.]

cra·ter /kráytər/ *n. & v.* • *n.* **1** the mouth of a volcano. **2** a bowl-shaped cavity, esp. that made by the explosion of a shell or bomb. **3** *Astron.* a hollow with a raised rim on the surface of a planet or moon, caused by the impact of a meteorite. • *v.tr.* form a crater in. □□ **cra·ter·ous** *adj.* [L f. Gk *kratēr* mixing bowl: see CRASIS]

-cratic /krátik/ *comb. form* (also **–cratical**) denoting a particular kind of government or rule (*autocratic*; *democratic*). □□ **–cratically** *comb. form (adv.)* [from or after F *–cratique*: see **–CRACY**]

cra·vat /krəvát/ *n.* **1** a scarf worn by men inside an open-necked shirt. **2** *hist.* a necktie. □□ **cra·vat·ted** *adj.*

WORD HISTORY cravat

Mid-17th century: from French *cravate*, from *Cravate* 'Croat' (from German *Krabat*, from Croat *Hrvat*), because of the scarf worn by Croatian mercenaries in France.

---

crave /krayv/ *v.* **1** *tr.* **a** long for (*craved affection*). **b** beg for (*craves a blessing*). **2** *intr.* (foll. by *for*) long for; beg for (*craved for comfort*). □□ **crav·er** *n.* [OE *crafian*, rel. to ON *krefja*]

cra·ven /kráyvən/ *adj. & n.* **•** *adj.* (of a person, behavior, etc.) cowardly; abject. **•** *n.* a cowardly person. □□ **cra·ven·ly** *adv.* **cra·ven·ness** *n.* [ME *cravand*, etc., perh. f. OF *cravanté* defeated, past part. of *cravaner* ult. f. L *crepare* burst; assim. to **–EN**[3]]

crav·ing /kráyving/ *n.* (usu. foll. by *for*) a strong desire or longing.

craw /kraw/ *n.* *Zool.* the crop of a bird or insect. □ **stick in one's craw** be unacceptable. [ME, rel. to MDu. *crāghe*, MLG *krage*, MHG *krage* neck, throat]

craw·fish /kráwfish/ *n. & v.* **•** *n.* = **CRAYFISH**. **•** *v.intr.* retreat; back out. [var. of **CRAYFISH**]

crawl /krawl/ *v. & n.* **•** *v.intr.* **1** move slowly, esp. on hands and knees. **2** (of an insect, snake, etc.) move slowly with the body close to the ground, etc. **3** walk or move slowly (*the train crawled into the station*). **4** (often foll. by *to*) *colloq.* behave obsequiously or ingratiatingly in the hope of advantage. **5** (often foll. by *with*) be covered or filled with crawling or moving things, or with people, etc., compared to this. **6** (esp. of the skin) feel a creepy sensation. **7** swim with a crawl stroke. **•** *n.* **1** an act of crawling. **2** a slow rate of movement. **3** a high-speed swimming stroke with alternate overarm movements and rapid straight-legged kicks. **4** *Brit.* **a** (usu. in *comb.*) *colloq.* a leisurely journey between places of interest (*church crawl*). **b** = **PUB-CRAWL**. □□ **crawl·ing·ly** *adv.* **crawl·y** *adj.* (in senses 5, 6 of *v.*). [ME: orig. unkn.: cf. Sw. *kravla*, Da. *kravle*]

crawl·er /kráwlər/ *n.* **1** (usu. in *pl.*) a baby's overall for crawling in. **2** anything that crawls, esp. an insect. **3** *sl.* a person who behaves obsequiously in the hope of advantage.

cray /kray/ *n.* *Austral. & NZ* = **CRAYFISH**.

cray·fish /kráyfish/ *n.* (also **craw·dad** or **craw·fish**) (*pl.* same) **1** a small, lobsterlike freshwater crustacean. **2** a large marine spiny lobster. [ME f. OF *crevice*, *crevis*, ult. f. OHG *krebiz* **CRAB**[1]: assim. to **FISH**[1]]

cray·on /kráyon/ *n. & v.* **•** *n.* **1** a stick or pencil of colored chalk, wax, etc., used for drawing. **2** a drawing made with this. **•** *v.tr.* draw with crayons. [F f. *craie* f. L *creta* chalk]

craze /krayz/ *v. & n.* **•** *v.tr.* (usu. as **crazed** *adj.*) make insane (*crazed with grief*). **2 a** *tr.* produce fine surface cracks on (pottery glaze, etc.). **b** *intr.* develop such cracks. **•** *n.* **1 a** a usu. temporary enthusiasm (*a craze for hula hoops*). **b** the object of this. **2** an insane fancy or condition. [ME, orig. = break, shatter, perh. f. ON]

cra·zy /kráyzee/ *adj.* (**cra·zi·er**, **cra·zi·est**) **1** *colloq.* (of a person, an action, etc.) insane or mad; foolish. **2** *colloq.* (usu. foll. by *about*) extremely enthusiastic. **3** *sl.* exciting; unrestrained. **4** (*attrib.*) (of paving, a quilt, etc.) made of irregular pieces fitted together. **5** *archaic* (of a ship, building, etc.) unsound; shaky. □ **like crazy** *colloq.* = *like mad* (see **MAD**). □□ **cra·zi·ly** *adv.* **cra·zi·ness** *n.*

cra·zy bone *n.* the funny bone.

creak /kreek/ *n. & v.* **•** *n.* a harsh scraping or squeaking sound. **•** *v.intr.* **1** make a creak. **2 a** move with a creaking noise. **b** move stiffly and awkwardly. **c** show weakness or frailty under strain. □□ **creak·ing·ly** *adv.* [ME, imit.: cf. **CRAKE**, **CROAK**]

creak·y /kréekee/ *adj.* (**creak·i·er**, **creak·i·est**) **1** liable to creak. **2 a** stiff or frail (*creaky joints*). **b** (of a practice, institution, etc.) decrepit; dilapidated; outmoded. □□ **creak·i·ly** *adv.* **creak·i·ness** *n.*

cream /kreem/ *n., v., & adj.* **•** *n.* **1 a** the fatty content of milk which gathers at the top and can be made into butter by churning. **b** this eaten (often whipped) with a dessert, as a cake filling, etc. (*strawberries and cream*; *cream cake*). **2** the part of a liquid that gathers at the top. **3** (usu. prec. by *the*) the best or choicest part of something, esp.: **a** the point of an anecdote. **b** an elite group of people (*the cream of the crop*). **4** a creamlike preparation, esp. a cosmetic (*hand cream*). **5** a very pale yellow or off-white color. **6 a** a dish like or made with cream. **b** a soup or sauce containing milk or cream. **c** a full-bodied, mellow, sweet sherry. **d** a chocolate-covered usu. fruit-flavored fondant confection. **•** *v.* **1** *tr.* (usu. foll. by *off*) **a** take the

cream from (milk). **b** take the best or a specified part from (*creamed off the brightest pupils*). **2** *tr.* work (butter, etc.) to a creamy consistency. **3** *tr.* treat (the skin, etc.) with cosmetic cream. **4** *tr.* add cream to (coffee, etc.). **5** *intr.* (of milk or any other liquid) form a cream or scum. **6** *tr. colloq.* defeat soundly or by a wide margin (esp. in a sporting contest). **•** *adj.* pale yellow; off-white. [ME f. OF *cre(s)me* f. LL *cramum* (perh. f. Gaulish) & eccl.L *chrisma* **CHRISM**]

cream cheese *n.* a soft, rich cheese made from unskimmed milk and cream.

cream·er /kréemər/ *n.* **1** a cream or milk substitute for adding to coffee or tea. **2** a flat dish used for skimming the cream off milk. **3** a machine used for separating cream from milk. **4** a small pitcher for cream.

cream·er·y /kréeməree/ *n.* (*pl.* **-ies**) **1** a factory producing butter and cheese. **2** a store where milk, cream, etc., are sold; a dairy. [**CREAM**, after F *crémerie*]

cream of tar·tar *n.* purified and crystallized potassium hydrogen tartrate, used in medicine, baking powder, etc.

cream puff *n.* **1** a cake made of puff pastry filled with custard or whipped cream. **2** *colloq.* an ineffectual or effeminate person. **3** a second-hand car or other item maintained in excellent condition.

cream soda *n.* a carbonated vanilla-flavored soft drink.

cream·y /kréemee/ *adj.* (**cream·i·er**, **cream·i·est**) **1** like cream in consistency or color. **2** rich in cream. □□ **cream·i·ly** *adv.* **cream·i·ness** *n.*

crease[1] /krees/ *n. & v.* **•** *n.* **1 a** a line in paper, etc., caused by folding. **b** a fold or wrinkle. **2** an area near the goal in ice hockey or lacrosse into which the puck or the ball must precede the players. **3** *Cricket* a line marking the position of the bowler or batsman (see **BOWLING CREASE**). **•** *v.* **1** *tr.* make creases in (material). **2** *intr.* become creased (*linen creases badly*). **3** *tr. & intr. Brit. sl.* (often foll. by *up*) make or become incapable through laughter. [earlier *creast* = **CREST** ridge in material]

crease[2] var. of **KRIS**.

cre·ate /kree-áyt/ *v.* **1** *tr.* **a** (of natural or historical forces) bring into existence; cause (*poverty creates resentment*). **b** (of a person or persons) make or cause (*create a diversion*; *create a good impression*). **2** *tr.* originate (*an actor creates a part*). **3** *tr.* invest (a person) with a rank (*created him a lord*). **4** *intr. Brit. sl.* make a fuss; grumble. □□ **cre·at·a·ble** *adj.* [ME f. L *creare*]

cre·a·tine /kréeəteen, -tin/ *n.* a product of protein metabolism found in the muscles of vertebrates. [Gk *kreas* meat + **–INE**[4]]

cre·a·tion /kree-áyshən/ *n.* **1 a** the act of creating. **b** an instance of this. **2 a** (usu. **the Creation**) the creating of the universe regarded as an act of God. **b** (usu. **Creation**) everything so created; the universe. **3** a product of human intelligence, esp. of imaginative thought or artistic ability. **4 a** the act of investing with a title or rank. **b** an instance of this. [ME f. OF f. L *creatio –onis* (as **CREATE**)]

cre·a·tion·ism /kree-áyshənizəm/ *n.* *Theol.* a theory attributing all matter, biological species, etc., to separate acts of creation, rather than to evolution. □□ **cre·a·tion·ist** *n.*

cre·a·tive /kree-áytiv/ *adj.* **1** inventive and imaginative. **2** creating or able to create. □□ **cre·a·tive·ly** *adv.* **cre·a·tive·ness** *n.* **cre·a·tiv·i·ty** /–aytívitee, –ətív–/ *n.*

SYNONYM TIP creative

INVENTIVE, ORIGINAL, RESOURCEFUL, IMAGINATIVE, INGENIOUS. Everyone likes to think that he or she is *creative*, which is used to describe the active, exploratory minds possessed by artists, writers, and inventors (*a creative approach to problem-solving*). Today, however, *creative* has become an advertising buzzword (*creative cooking*, *creative hair-styling*) that simply means new or different. **Original** is more specific and limited in scope. Someone who is *original* comes up with things that no one else has thought of (*an original approach to constructing a doghouse*), or thinks in an independent and creative way (*a highly original filmmaker*). **Imaginative** implies having an active and creative imagination, which often means that the person visualizes things quite differently than the way they appear in the real world (*imaginative illustrations for a children's book*). The practical side of *imaginative* is **inventive**; the *inventive* person figures out how to make things work (*an inventive solution to the problem of getting a wheelchair into a van*). But where an *inventive* mind tends to comes up with solutions to problems it has posed for itself, a **resourceful** mind deals successfully with externally imposed problems or limitations (*A resourceful child can amuse herself with simple wooden blocks*). Someone who is **ingenious** is both *inventive* and *resourceful*, with a dose of cleverness thrown in (*the ingenious idea of using recycled plastic to create a warm, fleecelike fabric*).

---

cre·a·tor /kree-áytər/ *n.* **1** a person who creates. **2** (as **the Creator**) God. [ME f. OF *creat(o)ur* f. L *creator –oris* (as **CREATE**)]

crea·ture /kréechər/ *n.* **1 a** an animal, as distinct from a human being. **b** any living being (*we are all fellow creatures on this planet*). **c** a fictional or imaginary being (*a creature from outer space*). **2** a person of a specified kind (*poor creature*). **3** a person owing status to

crayfish

and obsequiously subservient to another. **4** anything created; a creation. □□ **crea·ture·ly** adj. [ME f. OF f. LL creatura (as CREATE)]

crea·ture com·forts n. material comforts such as good food, warmth, etc.

crea·ture of hab·it n. a person set in an unvarying routine.

crèche /kresh/ n. **1** a representation of a Nativity scene. **2** Brit. a day nursery for babies and young children. [OF creche f. Gmc: rel. to CRIB]

cred·al see CREED.

cre·dence /kreéd'ns/ n. **1** belief. **2** (in full **credence table**) a small table, shelf, or niche which holds the elements of the Eucharist before they are consecrated. □ **give credence to** believe. [ME f. OF f. med.L credentia f. credere believe]

cre·den·tial /kridénshəl/ n. (usu. in pl.) **1** evidence of a person's achievements or trustworthiness, usu. in the form of certificates, references, etc. **2** a letter or letters of introduction. [med.L credentialis (as CREDENCE)]

cre·den·za /kridénzə/ n. a sideboard or cupboard. [It. f. med.L (as CREDENCE)]

cred·i·bil·i·ty /krédibílitee/ n. **1** the condition of being credible or believable. **2** reputation; status.

cred·i·bil·i·ty gap n. an apparent difference between what is said and what is true.

cred·i·ble /krédibəl/ adj. **1** (of a person or statement) believable or worthy of belief. **2** (of a threat, etc.) convincing. □□ **cred·i·bly** adv. [ME f. L credibilis f. credere believe]

cred·it /krédit/ n. & v. • n. **1** (usu. of a person) a source of honor, pride, etc. (is a credit to the school). **2** the acknowledgment of merit (must give her credit for consistency). **3** a good reputation (his credit stands high). **4** a belief or trust (I place credit in that). **b** something believable or trustworthy (that statement has credit). **5 a** a person's financial standing; the sum of money at a person's disposal in a bank, etc. **b** the power to obtain goods, etc., before payment (based on the trust that payment will be made). **6** (usu. in pl.) an acknowledgment of a contributor's services to a film, television program, etc. **7** Brit. a grade above a pass in an examination. **8** a reputation for solvency and honesty in business. **9 a** (in bookkeeping) the acknowledgment of being paid by an entry on the credit side of an account. **b** the sum entered. **c** the credit side of an account. **10** a certification indicating that a student has completed a course. • v.tr. **1** believe (cannot credit it). **2** (usu. foll. by to, with) **a** enter on the credit side of an account (credited $20 to him; credited him with $20). **b** ascribe a good quality or achievement to (the goal was credited to Barnes; he was credited with the improved sales). □ **credit a person with** ascribe (a good quality) to a person. **do credit to** (or **do a person credit**) enhance the reputation of. **get credit for** be given credit for it. **give a person credit for 1** enter (a sum) to a person's credit. **2** ascribe (a good quality) to a person. **give credit to** believe. **on credit** with an arrangement to pay later. **to one's credit** in one's praise, commendation, or defense (to his credit, he refused the offer). [F crédit f. It. credito or L creditum f. credere credit- believe, trust]

cred·it·a·ble /kréditəbəl/ adj. (often foll. by to) bringing credit or honor. □□ **cred·it·a·bil·i·ty** n. **cred·it·a·bly** adv.

cred·it card n. a small plastic card issued by a bank, business, etc., allowing the holder to purchase goods or services on credit.

cred·i·tor /kréditər/ n. **1** a person to whom a debt is owing. **2** a person or company that gives credit for money or goods (cf. DEBTOR). [ME f. AF creditour (OF –eur) f. L creditor -oris (as CREDIT)]

cred·it rat·ing n. an estimate of the ability of a person or organization to fulfill their financial commitments, based on previous dealings.

cred·it ti·tle n. a person's name appearing at the beginning or end of a movie or broadcast, etc., as an acknowledgment.

cred·it trans·fer n. a transfer from one person's bank account to another's.

cred·it un·ion n. a cooperative association that makes low-interest loans to its members.

cred·it·wor·thy /kréditwərthee/ adj. considered suitable to receive commercial credit. □□ **cred·it·wor·thi·ness** n.

cre·do /kreéydō, kráy–/ n. (pl. **-dos**) **1** (**Credo**) a statement of belief; a creed, esp. the Apostles' or Nicene Creed beginning in Latin with credo. **2** a musical setting of the Nicene Creed. [ME f. L, = I believe]

cred·u·lous /kréjələs/ adj. **1** too ready to believe; gullible. **2** (of behavior) showing such gullibility. □□ **cre·du·li·ty** /kridoôlitee, –dyoô–/ n. **cred·u·lous·ly** adv. **cred·u·lous·ness** n. [L credulus f. credere believe]

▶ See note at INCREDIBLE.

Cree /kree/ n. & adj. • n. (pl. same or **Crees**) **1 a** a N. American people of E. and central Canada. **b** a member of this people. **2** the language of this people. • adj. of or relating to the Crees or their language. [Canadian F Cris (earlier Cristinaux) f. Algonquian]

creed /kreed/ n. **1** a set of principles or opinions, esp. as a philosophy of life (his creed is moderation in everything). **2 a** (often **the Creed**) = Apostles' Creed (see APOSTLE). **b** a brief formal summary of Christian doctrine (cf. NICENE CREED, ATHANASIAN CREED). **c** the

Creed as part of the Mass. □□ **creed·al** /kreéd'l/ adj. **cred·al** adj. [OE crēda f. L CREDO]

Creek /kreek/ n. **1 a** a confederacy of N. American peoples that formerly occupied much of Alabama and Georgia. **b** a member of these peoples. **2** the language used by these peoples.

creek /kreek, krik/ n. **1** US Regional a stream. **2** Brit. **a** a small bay or harbor on a seacoast. **b** a narrow inlet on a seacoast or in a riverbank. □ **up shit creek** coarse sl. = up the creek. **up the creek** sl. in difficulties or trouble. [ME crike f. ON kriki nook (or partly f. OF crique f. ON), & ME crēke f. MDu. krēke (or f. crike by lengthening): ult. orig. unkn.]

creel /kreel/ n. **1** a large wicker basket for fish. **2** an angler's fishing basket. [ME, orig. Sc.: ult. orig. unkn.]

creep /kreep/ v. & n. • v.intr. (past and past part. **crept** /krept/) **1** move with the body prone and close to the ground; crawl. **2** (often foll. by in, out, up, etc.) come, go, or move slowly and stealthily or timidly (crept out without being seen). **3** enter slowly (into a person's affections, life, awareness, etc.) (a feeling crept over her; crept into her heart). **4** colloq. act abjectly or obsequiously in the hope of advancement. **5** (of a plant) grow along the ground or up a wall by means of tendrils, etc. **6** (as **creeping** adj.) developing slowly and steadily (creeping inflation). **7** (of the flesh) feel as if insects, etc., were creeping over it, as a result of fear, horror, etc. **8** (of metals, etc.) undergo deformation. • n. **1 a** the act of creeping. **b** an instance of this. **2** (in pl.; prec. by the) colloq. a nervous feeling of revulsion or fear (gives me the creeps). **3** sl. an unpleasant person. **4** the gradual downward movement of disintegrated rock due to gravitational forces, etc. **5** (of metals, etc.) a gradual change of shape under stress. **6** a low arch under a railroad embankment, road, etc. □ **creep up on** approach (a person) stealthily or unnoticed. [OE crēopan f. Gmc]

creep·er /kreépər/ n. **1** Bot. any climbing or creeping plant. **2** any bird that climbs, esp. a tree creeper. **3** sl. a soft-soled shoe.

creep·ing Jen·ny n. (also **Creep·ing Jen·nie**) any of various creeping plants, esp. moneywort.

creep·ing Je·sus n. Brit. sl. an abject or hypocritical person.

creep·y /kreépee/ adj. (**creep·i·er, creep·i·est**) **1** colloq. having or producing a creeping of the flesh (I feel creepy; a creepy movie). **2** given to creeping. □□ **creep·i·ly** adv. **creep·i·ness** n. [CREEP]

creep·y-crawl·y /kreépeekráwlee/ n. & adj. colloq. • n. (pl. **·ies**) an insect, worm, etc. • adj. creeping and crawling.

creese var. of KRIS.

cre·mate /kreémayt, krimáyt/ v.tr. consume (a corpse, etc.) by fire. □□ **cre·ma·tion** /krimáyshən/ n. **cre·ma·tor** n. [L cremare burn]

cre·ma·to·ri·um /kreémətəwreeəm/ n. (pl. **cre·ma·to·ri·ums** or **cre·ma·to·ri·a** /–reeə/) a place for cremating corpses in a furnace. [mod.L (as CREMATE, –ORY)]

cre·ma·to·ry /kreémətəwree, krém–/ adj. & n. • adj. of or relating to cremation. • n. (pl. **·ries**) = CREMATORIUM.

crème /krem/ n. **1** = CREAM n. 6a. **2** a name for various creamy liqueurs (crème de cassis). [F, = cream]

crème brû·lée /broôlay/ n. a custard topped with caramelized sugar.

crème car·a·mel n. a custard coated with caramel.

crème de la crème /də laa krém/ n. the best part; the elite.

crème de menthe /də maáNt, ménth, mínt/ n. a peppermint-flavored liqueur.

cre·nate /kreénayt/ adj. Bot. & Zool. having a notched edge or rounded teeth. □□ **cre·nat·ed** adj. **cre·na·tion** /krináyshən/ n. **cren·a·ture** /krénətyoor, kreé–/ n. [mod.L crenatus f. pop.L crena notch]

cren·el /krénəl/ n. (also **cren·elle** /krinél/) an indentation or gap in the parapet of a tower, castle, etc., orig. for shooting through, etc. [ME f. OF crenel, ult. f. pop.L crena notch]

cren·el·late /krénəlayt/ v.tr. provide (a tower, etc.) with battlements or loopholes. □□ **cren·el·la·tion** /–láyshən/ n. [F créneler (as CRENEL)]

Cre·ole /kreé-ōl/ n. & adj. • n. **1 a** a descendant of European (esp. Spanish) settlers in the W. Indies or Central or S. America. **b** a white descendant of French settlers, esp. in Louisiana. **c** a person of mixed European and black descent. **2** a mother tongue formed from the contact of a European language (esp. English, French, or Portuguese) with another (esp. African) language. • adj. **1** of or relating to a Creole or Creoles. **2** (usu. **creole**) of Creole origin or production (creole cooking). [F créole, criole f. Sp. criollo, prob. f. Port. crioulo home-born slave f. criar breed f. L creare CREATE]

cre·o·lize /kreéəliz/ v.tr. form a Creole from (another language). □□ **cre·o·li·za·tion** n.

cre·o·sote /kreéəsōt/ n. & v. • n. **1** (in full **creosote oil**) a dark-brown oil distilled from coal tar, used as a wood preservative. **2** a colorless oily fluid distilled from wood tar, used as an antiseptic. • v.tr. treat with creosote. [G Kreosote f. Gk kreas flesh + sōtēr preserver, with ref. to its antiseptic properties]

crepe /krayp/ *n.* (also **crêpe**) **1** a fine, often gauzelike fabric with a wrinkled surface. **2** a thin pancake, usu. with a savory or sweet filling. **3** (also **crepe rub·ber**) a very hard-wearing wrinkled sheet rubber used for the soles of shoes, etc. □□ **crepe·y** or **crep·y** *adj.* [F f. OF *crespe* curled f. L *crispus*]

crepe de chine /dəsheén/ *n.* (also **crêpe de chine** or **Chine**) a fine silk crepe.

crêpe pa·per *n.* thin crinkled paper.

crêpe su·zette /sōōzét/ *n.* (also **crêpe Su·zette**) a small dessert pancake flamed in alcohol at the table.

crep·i·tate /krépitayt/ *v.intr.* **1** make a crackling sound. **2** *Zool.* (of a beetle) eject pungent fluid with a sharp report. □□ **crep·i·tant** *adj.* [L *crepitare* frequent. of *crepare* creak]

crep·i·ta·tion /krépitáyshən/ *n.* **1** *Med.* = CREPITUS. **2** the action or sound of crackling or rattling.

crep·i·tus /krépitəs/ *n. Med.* **1** a grating noise from the ends of a fractured bone rubbing together. **2** a similar sound heard from the chest in pneumonia, etc. [L f. *crepare* rattle]

crept *past* and *past part.* of CREEP.

cre·pus·cu·lar /kripúskyələr/ *adj.* **1 a** of twilight. **b** dim. **2** *Zool.* appearing or active in twilight. [L *crepusculum* twilight]

Cres. *abbr.* Crescent.

cresc. *abbr.* (also **cres.**) *Mus.* = CRESCENDO.

cre·scen·do /krishéndō/ *n., adv., adj.,* & *v. ● n.* (*pl. ·dos*) **1** *Mus.* a passage gradually increasing in loudness. **2 a** progress toward a climax (*a crescendo of emotions*). **b** *disp.* a climax (*reached a crescendo then died away*). ● *adv.* & *adj.* with a gradual increase in loudness. ● *v.intr.* (*·does, ·doed*) increase gradually in loudness or intensity. [It., part. of *crescere* grow (as CRESCENT)]

cres·cent /krésənt/ *n.* & *adj. ● n.* **1** the curved sickle shape of the waxing or waning moon. **2** anything of this shape, esp. *Brit.* a street forming an arc. **3** the crescent-shaped emblem of Islam or Turkey. **b** (**the Crescent**) the world or power of Islam. ● *adj.* **1** *poet.* increasing. **2** crescent-shaped. □□ **cres·cen·tic** /kriséntik/ *adj.* [ME f. AF *cressaunt*, OF *creissant*, f. L *crescere* grow]

cre·sol /kréesawl/ *n.* any of three isomeric phenols present in creosote and used as disinfectants. □□ **cre·syl** /kréesil/ *adj.* [CREOSOTE + -OL2]

cress /kres/ *n.* any of various cruciferous plants usu. with pungent edible leaves, e.g., watercress. [OE *cresse* f.WG]

cres·set /krésit/ *n. hist.* a metal container filled with fuel, lighted and usu. mounted on a pole for illumination. [ME f. OF *cresset, craisset*, f. *craisse* = *graisse* GREASE]

crest /krest/ *n.* & *v. ● n.* **1 a** a comb or tuft of feathers, fur, etc., on a bird's or animal's head. **b** something resembling this, esp. a plume of feathers on a helmet. **c** a helmet; the top of a helmet. **2** the top of something, esp. of a mountain, wave, roof, etc. **3** *Heraldry* **a** a device above the shield and helmet of a coat of arms. **b** such a device reproduced on writing paper or on a seal, signifying a family. **4 a** a line along the top of the neck of some animals. **b** the hair growing from this; a mane. **5** *Anat.* a ridge along the surface of a bone. ● *v.* **1** *tr.* reach the crest of (a hill, wave, etc.). **2** *tr.* provide with a crest. **b** serve as a crest to. **3** *intr.* (of a wave) form into a crest. □ **on the crest of a wave** at the most favorable moment in one's progress. □□ **crest·ed** *adj.* (also in *comb.*). **crest·less** *adj.* [ME f. OF *creste* f. L *crista* tuft]

crest·fal·len /kréstfawlən/ *adj.* **1** dejected; dispirited. **2** with a fallen or drooping crest.

cre·ta·ceous /kritáyshəs/ *adj.* & *n. ● adj.* **1** of the nature of chalk. **2** (**Cretaceous**) *Geol.* of or relating to the last period of the Mesozoic era, with evidence of the first flowering plants, the extinction of dinosaurs, and extensive deposits of chalk. ● *n. Geol.* this era or system. [L *cretaceus* f. *creta* chalk]

Cre·tan /kréeton/ *n.* & *adj. ● n.* a native of Crete, an island SE of the Greek mainland. ● *adj.* of or relating to Crete or the Cretans. [L *Cretanus f. Creta* f. Gk *Krētē* Crete]

cre·tic /kréetik/ *n. Prosody* a foot containing one short or unstressed syllable between two long or stressed ones. [L *Creticus* f. Gk *Krētikos* (as CRETAN)]

cre·tin /kréetin/ *n.* **1** a person who is deformed and mentally retarded as the result of a thyroid deficiency. **2** *colloq.* a stupid person. □□ **cre·tin·ism** *n.* **cre·tin·ize** *v.tr.* **cre·tin·ous** *adj.* [F *crétin* f. Swiss F. *cretin, crestin* f. L *Christianus* CHRISTIAN]

cre·tonne /krétən, kréeton/ *n.* (often *attrib.*) a heavy cotton fabric with a usu. floral pattern printed on one or both sides, used for upholstery. [F f. *Creton* in Normandy]

cre·vasse /krəvás/ *n.* **1** a deep open crack, esp. in a glacier. **2** a breach in a river levee. [F f. OF *crevace*: see CREVICE]

crev·ice /krévis/ *n.* a narrow opening or fissure, esp. in a rock or building, etc. [ME f. OF *crevace* f. *crever* burst f. L *crepare*]

crew1 /krōō/ *n.* & *v. ● n.* (often treated as *pl.*) **1 a** a body of people manning a ship, aircraft, train, etc. **b** such a body as distinguished from the captain or officers. **c** a body of people working together; a team. **2** *colloq.* a company of people; a gang (*a motley crew*). ● *v.*

1 *tr.* supply or act as a crew or member of a crew for. **2** *intr.* act as a crew or member of a crew. [ME f. OF *creüe* increase, fem. past part. of *croistre* grow f. L *crescere*]

crew2 esp. *Brit. past* of CROW2.

crew cut *n.* a very short haircut orig. for men and boys.

crew·el /krōōəl/ *n.* a thin worsted yarn used for tapestry and embroidery. [ME *crule*, etc., of unkn. orig.]

crew·el·work /krōōəlwərk/ *n.* a design worked in crewel on linen or other fabric.

crew·man /krōōmən/ *n.* (*pl. ·men*) a member of a crew.

crew neck *n.* a close-fitting round neckline, esp. on a sweater.

crib /krib/ *n.* & *v. ● n.* **1 a** a child's bed with barred or latticed sides. **2** a barred container or rack for animal fodder. **3** *colloq.* **a** a translation of a text for the (esp. surreptitious) use of students. **b** plagiarized work, etc. **4** a small house or cottage. **5** a framework lining the shaft of a mine. **6** *colloq.* **a** cribbage. **b** a set of cards given to the dealer at cribbage by all the players. **7** heavy crossed timbers used in foundations in loose soil, etc. **8** *sl.* a brothel. **9** *Austral.* & *NZ* a light meal; food. ● *v.tr.* (also *absol.*) (**cribbed, crib·bing**) **1** *colloq.* copy (another person's work) unfairly or without acknowledgment. **2** confine in a small space. **3** *colloq.* pilfer; steal. **4** *Brit. colloq.* grumble. □□ **crib·ber** *n.* [OE *crib(b)*]

crib·bage /kríbij/ *n.* a card game for two, three, or four players, in which the dealer may score from the cards in the crib (see CRIB *n.* 6b). [17th c.: orig. unkn.]

crib·bage board *n.* a board with pegs and holes used for scoring at cribbage.

crib bit·ing *n.* a horse's habit of biting the manger while noisily breathing in and swallowing.

crib death *n.* = SUDDEN INFANT DEATH SYNDROME.

cri·bo /kríbō, krībō/ *n.* (*pl. ·bos*) a large harmless snake, *Drymarchon corais,* of tropical America. Also called **gopher snake**. [19th c.: orig. unkn.]

crib·ri·form /kríbrifawrm/ *adj. Anat.* & *Bot.* having numerous small holes. [L *cribrum* sieve + -FORM]

crib·work /kríbwərk/ *n.* = CRIB *n.* 7.

crick /krik/ *n.* & *v. ● n.* a sudden painful stiffness in the neck or the back, etc. ● *v.tr.* produce a crick in (the neck, etc.). [ME: orig. unkn.]

crick·et1 /kríkit/ *n.* & *v. ● n.* a game played on a grass field with two teams of 11 players taking turns to bowl at a wicket defended by a batting player of the other team. ● *v.intr.* play cricket. □ **not cricket** *Brit. colloq.* underhand or unfair behavior. □□ **crick·et·er** *n.* [16th c.: orig. uncert.]

crick·et2 /kríkit/ *n.* any of various grasshopperlike insects of the order Orthoptera, the males of which produce a characteristic chirping sound. [ME f. OF *criquet* f. *criquer* creak, etc. (imit.)]

cri·coid /kríkoyd/ *adj.* & *n. ● adj.* ring-shaped. ● *n.* (in full **cricoid cartilage**) *Anat.* the ring-shaped cartilage of the larynx. [mod.L *cricoides* f. Gk *krikoeidēs* f. *krikos* ring]

cricket2

cri de coeur /kree də kör/ *n.* (*pl. cris de coeur pronunc.* same) a passionate appeal, complaint, or protest. [F, = cry from the heart]

cried *past* and *past part.* of CRY.

cri·er /kríər/ *n.* (also **cry·er**) **1** a person who cries. **2** an officer who makes public announcements in a court of justice. **3** = TOWN CRIER. [ME f. AF *criour*, OF *criere* f. *crier* CRY]

cri·key /kríkee/ *int. Brit. sl.* an expression of astonishment. [euphem. for CHRIST]

crim /krim/ *n.* & *adj. Austral. sl.* = CRIMINAL. [abbr.]

crime /krīm/ *n.* **1 a** an offense punishable by law. **b** illegal acts as a whole (*resorted to crime*). **2** an evil act (*a crime against humanity*). **3** *colloq.* a shameful act (*a crime to tease them*). [ME f. OF f. L *crimen -minis* judgment, offense]

crime of pas·sion *n.* a crime, esp. murder, committed in a fit of sexual jealousy.

crime wave *n.* a sudden increase in crime.

crim·i·nal /kríminəl/ *n.* & *adj. ● n.* a person who has committed a crime or crimes. ● *adj.* **1** of, involving, or concerning crime (*criminal records*). **2** having committed (and usu. been convicted of) a crime. **3** *Law* relating to or expert in criminal law rather than civil or political matters (*criminal code; criminal lawyer*). **4** *colloq.* scandalous; deplorable. □□ **crim·i·nal·i·ty** *n.* /-nálitee/ **crim·i·nal·ly** *adv.* [ME f. LL *criminalis* (as CRIME)]

crim·i·nal·ist /kríminəlist/ *n.* one who practices this science, esp. for a law enforcement agency.

crim·i·nal·is·tic /kríminəlístik/ *adj.* relating to criminals or their habits.

crim·i·nal·is·tics /kríminəlístiks/ *n.pl.* forensic science.

crim·i·nal law *n.* law concerned with punishment of offenders (opp. CIVIL LAW).

crim·i·nol·o·gy /kríminóləjee/ *n.* the scientific study of crime. □□ **crim·i·no·log·i·cal** /–nəlójikəl/ *adj.* **crim·i·nol·o·gist** *n.* [L *crimen –minis* CRIME + –OLOGY]

crimp /krimp/ *v. & n.* ● *v.tr.* **1** compress into small folds or ridges; frill. **2** make narrow wrinkles or flutings in; corrugate. **3** make waves in (the hair) with a hot iron. ● *n.* a crimped thing or form. □ **put a crimp in** *sl.* thwart; interfere with. □□ **crimp·er** *n.* **crimp·y** *adj.* **crimp·i·ly** *adv.* **crimp·i·ness** *n.* [ME, prob. ult. f. OHG *krimphan*]

crim·son /krímzən/ *adj., n., & v.* ● *adj.* of a rich, deep red inclining to purple. ● *n.* this color. ● *v.tr. & intr.* make or become crimson. [ME *cremesin, crimesin,* ult. f. Arab. *ḳirmizī* KERMES]

cringe /krinj/ *v. & n.* ● *v.intr.* **1** shrink back in fear or apprehension; cower. **2** (often foll. by *to*) behave obsequiously. ● *n.* the act or an instance of cringing. □□ **cring·er** *n.* [ME *crenge, crenche,* OE *cringan, crincan:* see CRANK[1]]

crin·gle /krínggəl/ *n. Naut.* an eye of rope containing a thimble for another rope to pass through. [LG *kringel* dimin. of *kring* ring f. root of CRANK[1]]

crin·kle /kríngkəl/ *n. & v.* ● *n.* a wrinkle or crease in paper, cloth, etc. ● *v.* **1** *intr.* form crinkles. **2** *tr.* form crinkles in. □□ **crin·kly** *adj.* [ME f. OE *crincan:* see CRANK[1]]

crin·kle-cut *adj.* (of vegetables) cut with wavy edges.

cri·noid /krínoyd/ *n. & adj.* ● *n.* any echinoderm of the class Crinoidea, usu. sedentary with feathery arms, e.g., sea lilies and feather stars. ● *adj.* lily-shaped. □□ **cri·noi·dal** /–nóyd'l/ *adj.* [Gk *krinoeidēs* f. *krinon* lily]

crin·o·line /krínəlin/ *n.* **1** a stiffened or hooped petticoat formerly worn to make a long skirt stand out. **2** a stiff fabric of horsehair, etc., used for linings, hats, etc. [F f. L *crinis* hair + *linum* thread]

cripes /krīps/ *int. sl.* expressing surprise, anger, etc. [early 20th c.: alteration of CHRIST]

crip·ple /krípəl/ *n. & v.* ● *n.* usu. *offens.* a person or animal who is permanently lame. ● *v.tr.* **1** cause someone to become unable to move or walk properly (*crippled by polio*). **2** disable; impair. **3** weaken or damage (an institution, enterprise, etc.) seriously (*crippled by the loss of funding*). □□ **crip·ple·dom** *n.* **crip·ple·hood** *n.* **crip·pler** *n.* [OE *crypel,* rel. to CREEP]

cris var. of KRIS.

cri·sis /krísis/ *n.* (*pl.* **cri·ses** /–seez/) **1 a** a time of intense difficulty or danger. **b** a time when a difficult or important decision must be made. **c** a severe problem or breakdown. **2** the turning point of a disease when an important change takes place, indicating recovery or death. [L f. Gk *krisis* decision f. *krinō* decide]

crisp /krisp/ *adj., n., & v.* ● *adj.* **1** hard but brittle. **2 a** (of air) bracing. **b** (of a style or manner) lively; brisk and decisive. **c** (of features, etc.) neat and clear-cut. **d** (of paper) stiff and crackling. **e** (of hair) closely curling. ● *n.* **1** (in full **potato crisp**) *Brit.* **2** a thing overdone in roasting, etc. (*burned to a crisp*). ● *v.tr. & intr.* **1** make or become crisp. **2** curl in short, stiff folds or waves. □□ **crisp·ly** *adv.* **crisp·ness** *n.* [OE f. L *crispus* curled]

cris·pate /kríspayt/ *adj.* **1** crisped. **2** *Bot. & Zool.* having a wavy margin. [L *crispare* curl]

crisp·bread /kríspbred/ *n.* **1** a thin, crisp cracker of crushed rye, etc. **2** these collectively (*a box of crispbread*).

crisp·er /kríspər/ *n.* a compartment in a refrigerator for storing fruit and vegetables.

crisp·y /kríspee/ *adj.* (**crisp·i·er, crisp·i·est**) **1** crisp; brittle. **2** curly. **3** brisk. □□ **crisp·i·ness** *n.*

criss·cross /krískraws, –krós/ *n., adj., adv., & v.* ● *n.* **1** a pattern of crossing lines. **2** the crossing of lines or currents, etc. ● *adj.* crossing; in cross lines (*crisscross marking*). ● *adv.* crosswise; at cross purposes. ● *v.* **1** *intr.* **a** intersect repeatedly. **b** move crosswise. **2** *tr.* mark or make with a crisscross pattern. [15th c., f. *Christ's cross:* later treated as redupl. of CROSS]

cris·ta /krístə/ *n.* (*pl.* **cris·tae** /–tee/) **1** *Anat. & Zool.* a ridge or crest. **2** *Anat.* an infold of the inner membrane of a mitochondrion. □□ **cris·tate** *adj.* [L]

cris·to·bal·ite /kristóbəlīt/ *n. Mineral.* a principal form of silica, occurring as opal. [G *Cristobalit* f. Cerro San *Cristóbal* in Mexico]

cri·te·ri·on /krīteéreeən/ *n.* (*pl.* **cri·te·ri·a** /–reeə/ or **cri·te·ri·ons**) a principle or standard that a thing is judged by. □□ **cri·te·ri·al** *adj.* [Gk *kritērion* means of judging (cf. CRITIC)]

SPELLING TIP **criterion**

Criterion is singular. It involves *one* point or item; remember the "on" in *one.* The plural is *criteria* in this word deriving from Greek.

---

crit·ic /krítik/ *n.* **1** a person who censures. **2** a person who reviews or judges the merits of literary, artistic, or musical works, etc., esp. regularly or professionally. **3** a person engaged in textual criticism. [L *criticus* f. Gk *kritikos* f. *kritēs* judge f. *krinō* judge, decide]

crit·i·cal /krítikəl/ *adj.* **1 a** making or involving adverse or censorious comments or judgments. **b** expressing or involving criticism. **2** skillful at or engaged in criticism. **3** providing textual criticism (*a critical edition of Frost*). **4 a** of or at a crisis; involving risk or suspense (*in a critical condition; a critical operation*). **b** decisive; crucial

(*of critical importance; at the critical moment*). **5 a** *Math. & Physics* marking transition from one state, etc., to another (*critical angle*). **b** *Physics* (of a nuclear reactor) maintaining a self-sustaining chain reaction. □□ **crit·i·cal·i·ty** /–kálitee/ *n.* (in sense 5). **crit·i·cal·ly** *adv.* **crit·i·cal·ness** *n.* [L *criticus:* see CRITIC]

crit·i·cal ap·pa·rat·us *n.* = APPARATUS 4.

crit·i·cal list *n.* a list of those critically ill, esp. in a hospital.

crit·i·cal mass *n. Physics* the amount of fissile material needed to maintain a nuclear chain reaction.

crit·i·cal path *n.* the sequence of stages determining the minimum time needed for an operation or task, esp. when analyzed on a computer for a large organization.

crit·i·cal tem·per·a·ture *n. Chem.* the temperature above which a gas cannot be liquefied.

crit·ic·as·ter /krítikástər/ *n.* a minor or inferior critic.

crit·i·cism /krítisizəm/ *n.* **1 a** finding fault; censure. **b** a statement or remark expressing this. **2 a** the work of a critic. **b** an article, essay, etc., expressing or containing an analytical evaluation of something. [CRITIC or L *criticus* + –ISM]

crit·i·cize /krítisīz/ *v.tr.* (also *absol.*) **1** find fault with; censure. **2** discuss critically. □□ **crit·i·ciz·a·ble** *adj.* **crit·i·ciz·er** *n.*

cri·tique /kriteék/ *n. & v.* ● *n.* a critical essay or analysis; an instance or the process of formal criticism. ● *v.tr.* (**cri·tiques, cri·tiqued, cri·ti·quing**) discuss critically. [F f. Gk *kritikē tekhnē* critical art]

crit·ter /krítər/ *n.* **1** *dial.* or *joc.* a creature. **2** *derog.* a person. [var. of CREATURE]

croak /krōk/ *n. & v.* ● *n.* **1** a deep, hoarse sound as of a frog or a raven. **2** a sound resembling this. ● *v.* **1 a** *intr.* utter a croak. **b** *tr.* utter with a croak or in a dismal manner. **2** *sl.* **a** *intr.* die. **b** *tr.* kill. [ME: imit.]

croak·er /krókər/ *n.* **1** an animal that croaks. **2** a prophet of evil.

croak·y /krókee/ *adj.* (**croak·i·er, croak·i·est**) (of a voice) croaking; hoarse. □□ **croak·i·ly** *adv.* **croak·i·ness** *n.*

Cro·at /krō-at/ *n. & adj.* ● *n.* **1 a** a native of Croatia in the former Yugoslavia. **b** a person of Croatian descent. **2** the Slavonic dialect of the Croats (cf. SERBO-CROAT). ● *adj.* of or relating to the Croats or their dialect. [mod.L *Croatae* f. Serbo-Croatian *Hrvat*]

Cro·a·tian /krō-áyshən/ *n. & adj.* = CROAT.

croc /krok/ *n. colloq.* a crocodile. [abbr.]

cro·ce·ate /króseeayt/ *adj.* saffron-colored. [L *croceus* f. CROCUS]

cro·chet /krōsháy/ *n. & v.* ● *n.* **1** a handicraft in which yarn is made up into a patterned fabric by means of a hooked needle. **2** work made in this way. ● *v.* (**cro·cheted** /–sháyd/; **cro·chet·ing** /–sháying/) **1** *tr.* make by crocheting. **2** *intr.* do crochet. □□ **cro·chet·er** *n.* [F, dimin. of *croc* hook]

cro·cid·o·lite /krōsídəlīt/ *n.* a fibrous blue or green silicate of iron and sodium; blue asbestos. [Gk *krokis –idos* nap of cloth]

crock[1] /krok/ *n.* **1** an earthenware pot or jar. **2** a broken piece of earthenware. [OE *croc(ca)*]

crock[2] /krok/ *n. colloq.* nonsense; exaggeration (*his explanation is just a crock*). [perhaps for *crock of shit*; CROCK[1]]

crock[3] /krok/ *n. & v. Brit. colloq.* **1** an inefficient, broken-down, or worn-out person. **2** a worn-out vehicle, ship, etc. ● *v.* **1** *intr.* (foll. by *up*) break down; collapse. **2** *tr.* (often foll. by *up*) disable; cause to collapse. [orig. Sc., perh. f. Flem.]

crock·er·y /krókəree/ *n.* earthenware or china dishes, plates, etc. [obs. *crocker* potter: see CROCK[2]]

crock·et /krókit/ *n. Archit.* a small carved ornament (usu. a bud or curled leaf) on the inclined side of a pinnacle, etc. [ME f. var. of OF *crochet:* see CROCHET]

croc·o·dile /krókədil/ *n.* **1 a** any large tropical amphibious reptile of the order Crocodilia, with thick scaly skin, long tail, and long jaws. **b** leather from its skin, used to make bags, shoes, etc. **2** *Brit. colloq.* a line of schoolchildren, etc., walking in pairs. □□ **croc·o·dil·i·an** /–díleeən/ *adj.* [ME f. OF *cocodrille* f. med.L *cocodrillus* f. L *crocodilus* f. Gk *krokodilos* f. *krokē* pebble + *drilos* worm]

crocodile

croc·o·dile tears *n.* insincere grief (from the belief that crocodiles wept while devouring or alluring their prey).

cro·cus /krókəs/ *n.* (*pl.* **cro·cus·es**) any dwarf plant of the genus *Crocus,* growing from a corm and having brilliant usu. yellow or purple flowers. [ME, = saffron, f. L f. Gk *krokos* crocus, of Semitic orig.]

Croe·sus /kreésəs/ *n.* a person of great wealth. [name of a king of Lydia (6th c. BC)]

croft /krawft, kroft/ *n. & v. Brit.* ● *n.* **1** an enclosed piece of (usu. arable) land. **2** a small rented farm in Scotland or N. of England. ● *v.intr.* farm a croft; live as a crofter. [OE: orig. unkn.]

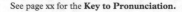

croft•er /kráwftər, króf–/ *n. Brit.* a person who rents a small piece of land, esp. a joint tenant of a divided farm in parts of Scotland.

crois•sant /krwaasáaN, krəsánt/ *n.* a crescent-shaped roll made of rich yeast pastry. [F, formed as CRESCENT]

Cro-Mag•non /krōmágnən, –mányən/ *adj. Anthropol.* of a tall, broad-faced European race of late Paleolithic times. [name of a hill in the Dordogne, France, where remains were found in 1868]

crom•lech /krómlekh, –lek/ *n.* **1** a dolmen; a megalithic tomb. **2** a circle of upright prehistoric stones. [Welsh f. *crom* fem. of *crwm* bent + *llech* flat stone]

crone /krōn/ *n.* **1** a withered old woman. **2** an old ewe. [ME, ult. f. ONF *carogne* CARRION]

cronk /krongk, krawngk/ *adj. Austral. colloq.* **1** unsound; liable to collapse. **2 a** fraudulent. **b** (of a horse) dishonestly run; unfit. [19th c.: cf. CRANK[3]]

cro•ny /krőnee/ *n.* (*pl.* **•nies**) a close friend or companion. [17th c. *chrony*, university sl. f. Gk *khronios* long-standing f. *khronos* time]

crook /krʊk/ *n., v., & adj.* •*n.* **1** the hooked staff of a shepherd or bishop. **2 a** a bend, curve, or hook. **b** anything hooked or curved. **3** *colloq.* **a** a rogue; a swindler. **b** a professional criminal. •*v.tr. & intr.* bend; curve. •*adj.* **1** *Brit.* crooked. **2** *Austral. & NZ colloq.* **a** unsatisfactory; out of order; (of a person) unwell or injured. **b** unpleasant. **c** dishonest; unscrupulous. **d** bad-tempered; irritable; angry. □ **go crook** (usu. foll. by *at, on*) *Austral. & NZ colloq.* lose one's temper; become angry. □□ **crook•er•y** *n.* [ME f. ON *krókr* hook]

crook•back /krʊ́kbak/ *n.* a hunchback. □□ **crook•backed** *adj.*

crook•ed /krʊ́kid/ *adj.* (**crook•ed•er, crook•ed•est**) **1 a** not straight or level; bent; curved; twisted. **b** deformed; bent with age. **2** *colloq.* not straightforward; dishonest. **3** /krʊkt/ *Austral. & NZ sl.* = CROOK *adj.* 2. **4** (foll. by *on*) *Austral. sl.* hostile to. □□ **crook•ed•ly** *adv.* **crook•ed•ness** *n.* [ME f. CROOK, prob. after ON *krókóttr*]

croon /krōōn/ *v. & n.* •*v.tr. & intr.* hum or sing in a low subdued voice, esp. in a sentimental manner. •*n.* such singing. □□ **croon•er** *n.* [ME (orig. Sc. & N.Engl.) f. MDu. & MLG *krōnen* groan, lament]

crop /krop/ *n. & v.* •*n.* **1 a** the produce of cultivated plants, esp. cereals. **b** the season's total yield of this (*a good crop*). **2** a group or an amount produced or appearing at one time (*this year's crop of students*). **3** (in full **hunting crop**) the stock or handle of a whip. **4 a** a style of hair cut very short. **b** the cropping of hair. **5** *Zool.* **a** the pouch in a bird's gullet where food is prepared for digestion. **b** a similar organ in other animals. **6** the entire tanned hide of an animal. **7** a piece cut off or out of something. •*v.* (**cropped, cropping**) **1** *tr.* **a** cut off. **b** (of animals) bite off (the tops of plants). **2** *tr.* cut (hair, cloth, edges of a book, etc.) short. **3** *tr.* gather or reap (produce). **4** *tr.* (foll. by *with*) sow or plant (land) with a crop. **5** *intr.* (of land) bear a crop. □ **crop out** *Geol.* appear at the surface. **crop up 1** (of a subject, circumstance, etc.) appear or come to one's notice unexpectedly. **2** *Geol.* appear at the surface. [OE *crop(p)*]

crop cir•cle *n.* an area of standing crops that has been flattened in the form of a circle without an apparent reason.

crop-dust•ing *n.* the sprinkling of powdered insecticide or fertilizer on crops, esp. from the air.

crop-eared *adj.* having the ears (esp. of animals) or hair cut short.

crop•per /krópər/ *n.* a crop-producing plant of specified quality (*a good cropper; a heavy cropper*). □ **come a cropper** *sl.* **1** fall heavily. **2** fail badly.

cro•quet /krōkáy/ *n. & v.* •*n.* **1** a game played on a lawn, with wooden balls which are driven through a series of hoops with mallets. **2** the act of croqueting a ball. •*v.tr.* (**cro•queted** /–káyd/; **cro•quet•ing** /–káying/) drive away (one's opponent's ball in croquet) by placing one's own against it and striking one's own. [perh. dial. form of F CROCHET hook]

cro•quette /krōkét/ *n.* a fried, breaded roll or ball of mashed potato or ground meat, etc. [F f. *croquer* crunch]

crore /krawr/ *n. Ind.* **1** ten million. **2** one hundred lakhs (of rupees, units of measurement, persons, etc.). [Hindi *k(a)rōr*, ult. f. Skr. *koṭi* apex]

cro•sier /krőzhər/ *n.* (also **cro•zier**) **1** a hooked staff carried by a bishop as a symbol of pastoral office. **2** a crook. [orig. = bearer of a crook, f. OF *crocier* & OF *croisier* f. *crois* CROSS]

cross /kraws, kros/ *n., v., & adj.* •*n.* **1** an upright post with a transverse bar, as used in antiquity for crucifixion. **2 a** (**the Cross**) in Christianity, the cross on which Christ was crucified. **b** a representation of this as an emblem of Christianity. **c** = SIGN OF THE CROSS. **3** a staff surmounted by a cross and borne before an archbishop or in a religious procession. **4** a thing or mark shaped like a cross, esp. a figure made by two short intersecting lines (+ or x). **b** a monument in the form of a cross, esp. one in the center of a town or on a tomb. **5** a cross-shaped decoration indicating rank in some orders of knighthood or awarded for personal valor. **6 a** an intermixture of animal breeds or plant varieties. **b** an animal or plant resulting from this. **7** (foll. by *between*) a mixture or compromise of two things. **8 a** a crosswise movement, e.g., of an actor on

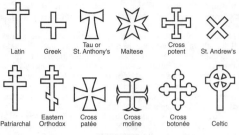

| Latin | Greek | Tau or St. Anthony's | Maltese | Cross potent | St. Andrew's |

| Patriarchal | Eastern Orthodox | Cross patée | Cross moline | Cross botonée | Celtic |

crosses

stage. **b** *Soccer*, etc., a pass of the ball across the direction of play. **c** *Boxing* a blow with a crosswise movement of the fist. **9** a trial or affliction; something to be endured (*bear one's crosses*). •*v.* **1** *tr.* (often foll. by *over*; also *absol.*) go across or to the other side of (a road, river, sea, etc.). **2 a** *intr.* intersect or be across one another (*the roads cross near the bridge*). **b** *tr.* cause to do this; place crosswise (*cross one's legs*). **3** *tr.* **a** draw a line or lines across. **b** *Brit.* mark (a check) with two parallel lines, and often an annotation, to indicate that it must be paid into a named bank account. **4** *tr.* (foll. by *off, out, through*) cancel or obliterate or remove from a list with lines drawn across. **5** *tr.* (often *refl.*) make the sign of the cross on or over. **6** *intr.* **a** pass in opposite or different directions. **b** (of letters between two correspondents) each be dispatched before receipt of the other. **c** (of telephone lines) become wrongly interconnected so that intrusive calls can be heard. **7** *tr.* **a** cause to interbreed. **b** cross-fertilize (plants). **8** *tr.* thwart or frustrate (*crossed in love*). **9** *tr. sl.* cheat. •*adj.* **1** (often foll. by *with*) peevish; angry. **2** (usu. *attrib.*) transverse; reaching from side to side. **3** (usu. *attrib.*) intersecting. **4** (usu. *attrib.*) contrary; opposed; reciprocal. □ **at cross purposes** misunderstanding or conflicting with one another. **cross one's fingers** (or **keep one's fingers crossed**) **1** put one finger across another as a sign of hoping for good luck. **2** trust in good luck. **cross the floor** *Brit.* join the opposing side in a debating assembly. **cross one's heart** make a solemn pledge, esp. by crossing one's front. **cross one's mind** (of a thought, etc.) occur to one, esp. transiently. **cross a person's palm** (usu. foll. by *with*) **1** pay a person for a favor. **2** bribe. **cross the path of 1** meet with (a person). **2** thwart. **cross swords** (often foll. by *with*) encounter in opposition; have an argument or dispute. **cross wires** (or **get one's wires crossed**) **1** become wrongly connected by telephone. **2** have a misunderstanding. **on the cross** *Brit.* **1** diagonally. **2** *sl.* fraudulently; dishonestly. □□ **cross•ly** *adv.* **cross•ness** *n.* [OE *cros* f. ON *kross* f. OIr. *cros* f. L *crux cruc*–]

cross- /kraws, kros/ *comb. form* **1** denoting movement or position across something (*cross-channel; cross-country*). **2** denoting interaction (*crossbreed; cross-cultural; cross-fertilize*). **3** passing from side to side; transverse (*crossbar; crosscurrent*). **b** having a transverse part (*crossbow*). **4** describing the form or figure of a cross (*crossroads*).

cross•bar /kráwsbaar, krós–/ *n.* a horizontal bar, esp. held on a pivot or between two upright bars, etc., e.g., of a bicycle or of a football goal.

cross-bed•ding /kráwsbeding, krós–/ *n. Geol.* lines of stratification crossing the main rock strata.

cross•bill /kráwsbil, krós–/ *n.* any stout finch of the genus *Loxia*, having a bill with crossed mandibles for opening pine cones.

cross•bones /kráwsbōnz, krós–/ *n.* a representation of two crossed leg or arm bones, usu. below a skull, as an emblem of piracy or death.

cross•bow /kráwsbō, krós–/ *n.* esp. *hist.* a bow fixed across a wooden stock, with a groove for an arrow and a mechanism for drawing and releasing the string. □□ **cross•bow•man** *n.* (*pl.* **•men**).

cross•breed *n. & v.* •*n.* /kráwsbreed, krós–/ **1** a breed of animals or plants produced by crossing. **2** an individual animal or plant of a crossbreed. •*v.tr.* /kráwsbreed, krós–/ (*past* and *past part.* **•bred**) produce by crossing.

cross-check *v. & n.* •*v.tr.* /kraws-chék, krós–/ check by a second or alternative method, or by several methods. •*n.* /kráws-chek, krós–/ an instance of cross-checking.

cross-coun•try /kráwskúntree, krós–/ *adj. & adv.* **1** across fields or open country. **2** not keeping to main or direct roads.

cross•cut *adj. & n.* •*adj.* /kráwskút, krós–/ cut across the main grain or axis. •*n.* /kráwskut, krós–/ a diagonal cut, path, etc.

crosscut saw *n.* a saw for cutting across the grain of wood.

cross-dat•ing /kráwsdáyting, krós–/ *n. Archaeol.* dating by correlation with another site or level.

cross-dress *v.intr.* to wear clothing typically worn by members of the opposite sex.

crosse /kraws, kros/ *n.* a stick with a triangular net at the end for conveying the ball in lacrosse. [F f. OF *croce, croc* hook]

cross-ex•am•ine /kráwsigzámin, krós–/ *v.tr.* examine (esp. a witness in a court of law) to check or extend testimony already given. □□ **cross-ex·am·i·na·tion** /–náyshən/ n. **cross-ex·am·in·er** n.

cross-eyed /kráwsíd, krós–/ adj. (as a disorder) having one or both eyes turned permanently inward toward the nose.

cross-fade /kráwsfáyd, krós–/ v.intr. Radio, etc., fade in one sound as another is faded out.

cross-fer·ti·lize /kráwsfért'líz, krós–/ v.tr. 1 fertilize (an animal or plant) from one of a different species. 2 help by the interchange of ideas, etc. □□ **cross-fer·ti·li·za·tion** n.

cross·fire /kráwsfír, krós–/ n. (also **cross fire**) 1 firing in two crossing directions simultaneously. 2 a attack or criticism from several sources at once. b a lively or combative exchange of views, etc.

cross-grain /kráwsgrayn, krós–/ n. a grain in lumber, running across the regular grain.

cross-grained /kráwsgráynd, krós–/ adj. 1 (of lumber) having a cross-grain. 2 perverse; intractable.

cross·hair /kráws-hair, krós–/ n. a fine wire at the focus of an optical instrument, gun, sight, etc.

cross·hatch /kráws-hách, krós–/ v.tr. (in drawing or graphics) shade an area with intersecting sets of parallel lines.

cross·head /kráws-hed, krós–/ n. 1 a bar between the piston rod and connecting rod in a steam engine. 2 = CROSSHEADING.

cross·head·ing /kráws-heding, krós–/ n. a heading to a paragraph printed across a column in the body of an article in a newspaper, etc.

cross·ing /kráwsing, krós–/ n. 1 a place where things (e.g. roads) cross. 2 a place at which one may cross a street, etc. (pedestrian crossing). 3 a journey across water (had a smooth crossing). 4 the intersection of a church nave and transepts. 5 Biol. mating.

cross·ing o·ver n. Biol. an exchange of genes between homologous chromosomes (cf. RECOMBINATION).

cross-leg·ged /kráwslégid, –légd, krós–/ adj. with one leg crossed over the other.

cross-link /kráwslingk, krós–/ n. (also **cross-link·age**) Chem. a bond between chains of atoms in a polymer, etc.

cross-match /kráwsmách, krós–/ v.tr. Med. test the compatibility of (a donor's and a recipient's blood). □□ **cross-match·ing** n. **cross-match** n.

cross·o·ver /kráwsóvər, krós–/ n. & adj. ● n. a point or place of crossing from one side to the other. ● adj. having a crossover.

cross·patch /kráwspach, krós–/ n. colloq. a bad-tempered person. [CROSS adj. 1 + obs. patch fool, clown]

cross·piece /kráwspees, krós–/ n. a beam or bar fixed or placed across something else.

cross-pol·li·nate /kráwspólinayt, krós–/ v.tr. pollinate (a plant) from another. □□ **cross-pol·li·na·tion** /–náyshən/ n.

cross-ques·tion /kráwskwés-chən, krós–/ v.tr. = CROSS-EXAMINE.

cross-re·fer /kráwsrifér, krós–/ v.intr. (·re·ferred, ·re·fer·ring) refer from one part of a book, article, etc., to another.

cross-ref·er·ence /kráwsréfərəns, krós–/ n. & v. ● n. a reference from one part of a book, article, etc., to another. ● v.tr. provide with cross-references.

cross·road /kráwsród, krós–/ n. 1 (usu. in pl.) an intersection of two or more roads. 2 a road that crosses a main road or joins two main roads. □ **at the crossroads** at a critical point in one's life.

cross·ruff /kráwsrúf, krós–/ n. & v. Bridge, etc. ● n. the alternate trumping of partners' leads. ● v.intr. play in this way.

cross sec·tion /kráws-sékshən, krós–/ n. 1 a a cutting of a solid at right angles to an axis. b a plane surface produced in this way. c a representation of this. 2 a representative sample, esp. of people. 3 Physics a quantity expressing the probability of interaction between particles. □□ **cross-sec·tion·al** adj.

cross-stitch /kráws-stich, krós–/ n. & v. ● n. 1 a stitch formed of two stitches crossing each other. 2 needlework done using this stitch. ● v.intr. & v.tr. work in cross-stitch.

cross·talk /kráws-tawk, krós–/ n. (also **cross talk**) 1 unwanted transfer of signals between communication channels. 2 Brit. witty talk; repartee.

cross·trees /kráws-treéz, krós–/ n.pl. Naut. a pair of horizontal timbers at the top of a lower mast, supporting the topmast.

cross-vot·ing /kráwsvóting, krós–/ n. voting for a party not one's own, or for more than one party.

cross·walk /kráwswawk, krós–/ n. a pedestrian crossing.

cross·ways /kráwsways, krós–/ adv. = CROSSWISE.

cross·wind /kráwswind, krós–/ n. a wind blowing across one's direction of travel.

cross·wise /kráwswíz, krós–/ adj. & adv. 1 in the form of a cross; intersecting. 2 transverse or transversely.

cross·word /kráwswərd, krós–/ n. (also **cross·word puz·zle**) a puzzle of a grid of squares and blanks into which words crossing ver-

WORD HISTORY crossword

Said to have been invented by the journalist Arthur Wynne, whose puzzle (called a 'word cross') appeared in a Sunday newspaper, the New York World, on December 21, 1913.

tically and horizontally have to be filled in according to provided clues.

crotch /kroch/ n. a place where something forks, esp. the legs of the human body or a garment (cf. CRUTCH). [perh. = ME & OF croc(he) hook, formed as CROOK]

crotch·et /króchit/ n. 1 a whimsical fancy. 2 a small hook. 3 Brit. = QUARTER NOTE. [ME f. OF crochet dimin. of croc hook (see CROTCH)]

crotch·et·y /króchitee/ adj. peevish; irritable. □□ **crotch·et·i·ness** n. [CROTCHET + –Y¹]

cro·ton /krót'n/ n. 1 any of various small tropical trees or shrubs of the genus Croton, producing a capsulelike fruit. 2 any small tree or shrub of the genus Codiaeum, esp. C. variegatum, with colored ornamental leaves. [mod.L f. Gk krotōn sheep tick, croton (from the shape of its seeds)]

cro·ton oil n. a powerful purgative obtained from the fruit of Croton tiglium.

crouch /krowch/ v. & n. ● v.intr. lower the body with the limbs close to the chest, esp. for concealment, or (of an animal) before pouncing; be in this position. ● n. an act of crouching; a crouching position. [ME, perh. f. OF crochir be bent f. croc hook: cf. CROOK]

croup¹ /kroōp/ n. an inflammation of the larynx and trachea in children, with a hard cough and difficulty in breathing. □□ **croup·y** adj. [croup to croak (imit.)]

croup² /kroōp/ n. the rump or hindquarters esp. of a horse. [ME f. OF croupe, rel. to CROP]

croup·i·er /kroōpeeər, –eeay/ n. 1 the person in charge of a gaming table, raking in and paying out money, etc. 2 the assistant chairperson at a public dinner, seated at the foot of the table. [F, orig. = rider on the crup: see CROUP²]

PRONUNCIATION TIP croupier

With the growing popularity of gambling casinos in the United States, this French word no longer seems foreign; a widely heard American pronunciation rhymes with snoopier. But the pronunciation "KROO-pee-ay," reflective of the French origin, is still widely used.

crou·ton /kroōton/ n. a small piece of fried or toasted bread served with soup or used as a garnish. [F f. croûte CRUST]

Crow /krō/ n. 1 a a N. American people native to eastern Montana. b a member of this people. 2 the language of this people.

crow¹ /krō/ n. 1 any large, black bird of the genus Corvus, having a powerful black beak. 2 any similar bird of the family Corvidae, e.g., the raven, rook, and jackdaw. 3 sl. derog. a woman, esp. an old or ugly one. □ **as the crow flies** in a straight line. **eat crow** submit to humiliation. [OE crāwe ult. f. WG]

crow² /krō/ v. & n. ● v.intr. 1 (past **crowed** or esp. Brit. **crew** /kroō/) (of a cock) utter its characteristic loud cry. 2 (of a baby) utter happy cries. 3 (usu. foll. by over) express unrestrained gleeful satisfaction. ● n. 1 the cry of a cock. 2 a happy cry of a baby. [OE crāwan, of imit. orig.]

crow

crow·bar /króbaar/ n. an iron bar with a flattened end, used as a lever.

crow·ber·ry /króberee/ n. (pl. ·ries) 1 a a heathlike evergreen shrub Empetrum nigrum, bearing black berries. b the flavorless edible berry of this plant. 2 a cranberry.

crowd /krowd/ n. & v. ● n. 1 a large number of people gathered together, usu. without orderly arrangement. 2 a mass of spectators; an audience. 3 colloq. a particular company or set of people (met the crowd from the sales department). 4 (prec. by the) the mass or multitude of people (go along with the crowd). 5 a large number (of things). 6 actors representing a crowd. ● v. 1 a intr. come together in a crowd. b tr. cause to do this. c intr. force one's way. 2 tr. a (foll. by into) force or compress into a confined space. b (often foll. by with; usu. in passive) fill or make abundant with (was crowded with tourists). 3 tr. a (of a number of people) come aggressively close to. b colloq. harass or pressure (a person). □ **crowd out** exclude by crowding. □□ **crowd·ed·ness** n. [OE crūdan press, drive]

crow·foot /krófoot/ n. (pl. **crow·foots** for 1 & 2, **crow·feet** for 3 & 4) 1 any of various plants of the genus Ranunculus, esp. buttercup, often characterized by divided leaves that resemble a crow's foot. 2 any of various other plants whose leaves, etc., bear a similar resemblance. 3 Mil. a caltrop. 4 a three-legged antislip support for a motion-picture camera's tripod.

crown /krown/ n. & v. ● n. 1 a monarch's ornamental and usu. jeweled headdress. 2 (**the Crown**) a the monarch, esp. as head of state.

See page xx for the **Key to Pronunciation**.

b the power or authority residing in the monarchy. **3 a** a wreath of leaves or flowers, etc., worn on the head, esp. as an emblem of victory. **b** an award or distinction gained by a victory or achievement, esp. in sport. **4** a crown-shaped thing, esp. a device or ornament. **5** the top part of a thing, esp. of the head or a hat. **6 a** the highest or central part of an arched or curved thing (*crown of the road*). **b** a thing that completes or forms the summit. **7** the part of a plant just above and below the ground. **8** the upper part of a cut gem above the girdle. **9 a** the part of a tooth projecting from the gum. **b** an artificial replacement or covering for this. **10 a** a former British coin equal to five shillings (25 pence). **b** any of several foreign coins with a name meaning 'crown,' esp. the krona or krone. **11** a former size of paper, 504 x 384 mm. • *v.tr.* **1** put a crown on (a person or a person's head). **2** invest (a person) with a royal crown or authority. **3** be a crown to; encircle or rest on the top of. **4 a** (often as **crowning** *adj.*) be or cause to be the consummation, reward, or finishing touch to (*the crowning glory*). **b** bring (efforts) to a happy issue. **5** fit a crown to (a tooth). **6** *sl.* hit on the head. [ME f. AF *corune*, OF *corone* f. L *corona*]

crown col•o•ny *n.* (also **Crown Col•o•ny**) a British colony controlled by the Crown.

crown court *n.* a court of criminal jurisdiction in England and Wales.

crown glass *n.* glass made without lead or iron and orig. in a circular sheet; used formerly in windows, now as optical glass of low refractive index.

crown im•pe•ri•al *n.* a tall fritillary, *Fritillaria imperialis*, with a flower cluster at the top of the stalk.

crown jew•els *n.* the regalia and other jewelry worn by the sovereign on certain state occasions.

crown of thorns *n.* any starfish of the genus *Acanthaster* feeding on coral.

crown prince *n.* a male heir to a sovereign throne.

crown prin•cess *n.* **1** the wife of a crown prince. **2** a female heir to a sovereign throne.

crown roast *n.* a roast of rib pieces of pork or lamb arranged like a crown.

crown wheel *n.* a wheel with teeth set at right angles to its plane, esp. in the gears of motor vehicles.

crow's-foot *n.* (*pl.* **-feet**) **1** (usu. in *pl.*) a wrinkle at the outer corner of a person's eye. **2** *Mil.* a caltrop.

crow's nest *n.* a barrel or platform fixed at the masthead of a sailing vessel as a shelter for a lookout.

crow•steps /krṓsteps/ *n.* = CORBIESTEPS.

cro•zier var. of CROSIER.

CRT *abbr.* cathode-ray tube.

cru /krōō/ *n.* **1 a** a French vineyard or wine-producing region. **2** the grade of wine produced from it. [F f. *crû* grown]

cru•ces *pl.* of CRUX.

cru•cial /krōōshəl/ *adj.* **1** decisive; critical. **2** *colloq. disp.* very important. **3** *sl.* excellent. □□ **cru•ci•al•i•ty** /–sheeálitee/ *n.* (*pl.* **-lities**). **cru•cial•ly** *adv.* [F f. L *crux crucis* cross]

▶**Crucial** is used in formal contexts to mean 'decisive, critical,' e.g., *The testimony of the only eyewitness was crucial to the case.* Its broader use to mean 'very important,' as in *It is crucial to get good light for your photographs,* should be restricted to informal contexts.

cru•cian /krōōshən/ *n.* a yellow cyprinoid fish, *Carassius carassius*, allied to the goldfish. [LG *karusse*, etc.]

cru•ci•ate /krōōsheeayt/ *adj. Zool.* cross-shaped. [mod.L *cruciatus* f. L (as CRUCIBLE)]

cru•ci•ble /krōōsibəl/ *n.* **1** a melting pot for metals, etc. **2** a severe test or trial. [ME f. med.L *crucibulum* night lamp, crucible, f. L *crux crucis* cross]

cru•ci•fer /krōōsifər/ *n.* **1** one who carries a cross in an ecclesiastical procession. **2** a cruciferous plant.

cru•cif•er•ous /krōōsífərəs/ *adj. Bot.* of the family Cruciferae, having flowers with four petals arranged in a cross. [LL *crucifer* (as CRUCIAL, –FEROUS)]

cru•ci•fix /krōōsifiks/ *n.* a model or image of a cross with a figure of Christ on it. [ME f. OF f. eccl.L *crucifixus* f. L *cruci fixus* fixed to a cross]

cru•ci•fix•ion /krōōsifíkshən/ *n.* **1 a** crucifying or being crucified. **b** an instance of this. **2** (**Crucifixion**) **a** the crucifixion of Christ. **b** a representation of this. [eccl.L *crucifixio* (as CRUCIFIX)]

cru•ci•form /krōōsifawrm/ *adj.* cross-shaped (esp. of a church with transepts). [L *crux crucis* cross + –FORM]

cru•ci•fy /krōōsifī/ *v.tr.* (**-fies**, **-fied**) **1** put to death by fastening to a cross. **2 a** cause extreme pain to. **b** persecute; torment. **c** *sl.* defeat thoroughly in an argument, match, etc. □□ **cru•ci•fi•er** *n.* [ME f. OF *crucifier* f. LL *crucifigere* (as CRUCIFIX)]

cruck /kruk/ *n. Brit. hist.* either of a pair of curved timbers extending to the ground in the framework of a type of medieval house roof. [var. of CROOK]

crud /krud/ *n. sl.* **1 a** a deposit of unwanted impurities, grease, etc. **b** something disgusting or undesirable **c** a corrosive deposit in a nuclear reactor. **2** an unpleasant person. **3** nonsense. □□ **crud•dy** *adj.* (**crud•di•er**, **crud•di•est**). [var. of CURD]

crude /krōōd/ *adj. & n.* • *adj.* **1 a** in the natural or raw state; not refined. **b** rough; unpolished; lacking finish. **2 a** (of an action or statement or manners) rude; blunt. **b** offensive; indecent (*a crude gesture*). **3 a** *Statistics* (of numerical totals) not adjusted or corrected. **b** rough (*a crude estimate*). • *n.* natural mineral oil. □□ **crude•ly** *adv.* **crude•ness** *n.* **cru•di•ty** *n.* [ME f. L *crudus* raw, rough]

cru•di•tés /krōōditáy/ *n.pl.* an hors-d'oeuvre of mixed raw vegetables, often served with a sauce into which they are dipped. [F]

cru•el /krōōəl/ *adj.* (**cru•el•er**, **cru•el•est**) **1** indifferent to or gratified by another's suffering. **2** causing pain or suffering, esp. deliberately. □□ **cru•el•ly** *adv.* **cru•el•ness** *n.* [ME f. OF f. L *crudelis*, rel. to *crudus* (as CRUDE)]

cru•el•ty /krōōəltee/ *n.* (*pl.* **-ties**) **1** a cruel act or attitude; indifference to another's suffering. **2** a succession of cruel acts; a continued cruel attitude (*suffered much cruelty*). **3** *Law* physical or mental harm inflicted (whether or not intentional), esp. as a ground for divorce. [OF *crualté* ult. f. L *crudelitas*]

cru•el•ty-free *adj.* (of cosmetics, etc.) produced without involving any cruelty to animals in the development or manufacturing process.

cru•et /krōōit/ *n.* **1** a small container for oil or vinegar for use at the table. **2** (in full **cruet-stand**) a stand holding cruets. **3** *Eccl.* a small container for the wine and water in the celebration of the Eucharist. [ME through AF f. OF *crue* pot f. OS *krūka*: rel. to CROCK[2]]

cruise /krōōz/ *v. & n.* • *v.* **1** *intr.* make a journey by sea calling at a series of ports usu. according to a predetermined plan, esp. for pleasure. **2** *intr.* sail about without a precise destination. **3** *intr.* **a** (of a motor vehicle or aircraft) travel at a moderate or economical speed. **b** (of a vehicle or its driver) travel at random, esp. slowly. **4** *intr.* achieve an objective, win a race, etc., with ease. **5** *intr. & tr. sl.* walk or drive about (the streets, etc.) in search of a sexual (esp. homosexual) partner. • *n.* a cruising voyage, esp. as a vacation. [prob. f. Du. *kruisen* f. *kruis* CROSS]

cruise con•trol *n.* a device on a motor vehicle that automatically maintains a constant speed and relieves the operator of the need to depress the accelerator.

cruise mis•sile *n.* a low-flying missile that is guided to its target by an on-board computer.

cruis•er /krōōzər/ *n.* **1** a warship of high speed and medium armament. **2** = CABIN CRUISER. **3** a police patrol car. [Du. *kruiser* (as CRUISE)]

cruis•er•weight /krōōzərwayt/ *n.* a weight class in professional boxing between light heavyweight and heavyweight.

cruis•ing speed *n.* a comfortable and economical speed for a motor vehicle, below its maximum speed.

crul•ler /krúlər/ *n.* a small cake made of a rich dough twisted or curled and fried in fat. [prob. f. Du. *krullen* curl]

crumb /krum/ *n. & v.* • *n.* **1 a** a small fragment, esp. of bread. **b** a small particle (*a crumb of comfort*). **2** the soft inner part of a loaf of bread. **3** *sl.* an objectionable person. • *v.tr.* **1** cover with breadcrumbs. **2** break into crumbs. [OE *cruma*]

crum•ble /krúmbəl/ *v. & n.* • *v.* **1** *tr. & intr.* break or fall into crumbs or fragments. **2** *intr.* (of power, a reputation, etc.) gradually disintegrate. • *n.* **1** a crumbly or crumbled substance. **2** *Brit.* a mixture of flour and fat, rubbed to the texture of breadcrumbs and cooked as a topping for fruit, etc. (*apple crumble; vegetable crumble*). [ME f. OE, formed as CRUMB]

crum•bly /krúmblee/ *adj.* (**crum•bli•er**, **crum•bli•est**) consisting of, or apt to fall into, crumbs or fragments. □□ **crum•bli•ness** *n.*

crumbs /krumz/ *int. Brit. sl.* expressing dismay or surprise. [euphem. for *Christ*]

crumb·y /krúmee/ *adj.* (**crumb·i·er**, **crumb·i·est**) **1** like or covered in crumbs. **2** = CRUMMY.

crum·horn var. of KRUMMHORN.

crum·my /krúmee/ *adj.* (**crum·mi·er**, **crum·mi·est**) *colloq.* dirty; squalid; inferior; worthless. □□ **crum·mi·ly** *adv.* **crum·mi·ness** *n.* [var. of CRUMBY]

crump /krump/ *n. & v. Mil. sl.* ● *n.* the sound of a bursting bomb or shell. ● *v.intr.* make this sound. [imit.]

crum·pet /krúmpit/ *n.* **1 a** a soft, flat cake of a yeast mixture cooked on a griddle and eaten toasted and buttered. **2** *Brit. joc.* or *offens.* **a** a sexually attractive person, esp. a woman. **b** women regarded collectively, esp. as objects of sexual desire. [17th c.: orig. uncert.]

crum·ple /krúmpəl/ *v. & n.* ● *v.* **1** *tr. & intr.* (often foll. by *up*) **a** crush or become crushed into creases. **b** ruffle; wrinkle. **2** *intr.* (often foll. by *up*) collapse; give way. ● *n.* a crease or wrinkle. □□ **crum·ply** *adj.* [obs. *crump* (v. & adj.) (make or become) curved]

crum·ple zone *n.* a part of a motor vehicle, esp. the extreme front and rear, designed to crumple easily in a crash and absorb impact.

crunch /krunch/ *v. & n.* ● *v.* **1** *tr.* **a** crush noisily with the teeth. **b** grind (gravel, dry snow, etc.) under foot, wheels, etc. **2** *intr.* (often foll. by *up, through*) make a crunching sound in walking, moving, etc. ● *n.* **1** crunching; a crunching sound. **2** *colloq.* a decisive event or moment. **3** a physical exercise designed to strengthen the abdominal muscles; a sit-up. [earlier *cra(u)nch*, assim. to *munch*]

crunch·y /krúnchee/ *adj.* (**crunch·i·er**, **crunch·i·est**) that can be or has been crunched or crushed into small pieces; hard and crispy. □□ **crunch·i·ly** *adv.* **crunch·i·ness** *n.*

crup·per /krúpər/ *n.* **1** a strap buckled to the back of a saddle and looped under the horse's tail to hold the harness back. **2** the hindquarters of a horse. [ME f. OF *cropiere* (cf. CROUP²)]

cru·ral /krŏorəl/ *adj. Anat.* of the leg. [F *crural* or L *cruralis* f. *crus cruris* leg]

cru·sade /krŏosáyd/ *n. & v.* ● *n.* **1 a** any of several medieval military expeditions made by Europeans to recover the Holy Land from the Muslims. **b** a war instigated by the Roman Catholic Church for alleged religious ends. **2** a vigorous campaign in favor of a cause. ● *v.intr.* engage in a crusade. □□ **cru·sad·er** *n.* [earlier *croisade* (F f. *croix* cross) or *crusado* (Sp. f. *cruz* cross)]

cruse /krŏoz/ *n. archaic* an earthenware pot or jar. [OE *crúse*, of unkn. orig.]

crush /krush/ *v. & n.* ● *v.tr.* **1** compress with force or violence, so as to break, bruise, etc. **2** reduce to powder by pressure. **3** crease or crumple by rough handling. **4** defeat or subdue completely (*crushed by my reply*). ● *n.* **1** an act of crushing. **2** a crowded mass of people. **3** a drink made from the juice of crushed fruit. **4** *colloq.* **a** (usu. foll. by *on*) a (usu. passing) infatuation. **b** the object of an infatuation (*who's the latest crush?*). □□ **crush·a·ble** *adj.* **crush·er** *n.* **crush·ing·ly** *adv.* [ME f. AF *crussir*, *corussier*, OF *croissir*, *cruissir*, gnash (teeth), crack, f. Rmc]

crust /krust/ *n. & v.* ● *n.* **1 a** the hard outer part of a loaf of bread. **b** a piece of this with some soft bread attached. **c** a hard, dry scrap of bread. **d** esp. *Austral. sl.* a livelihood (*what do you do for a crust?*). **2** the pastry covering of a pie. **3** a hard casing of a softer thing, e.g., a harder layer over soft snow. **4** *Geol.* the outer portion of the earth. **5 a** a coating or deposit on the surface of anything. **b** a hard, dry formation on the skin; a scab. **6** a deposit of tartar formed in bottles of old wine. **7 a** *sl.* impudence (*you have a lot of crust!*). **b** a superficial hardness of manner. ● *v.tr. & intr.* **1** cover or become covered with a crust. **2** form into a crust. □□ **crus·tal** *adj.* (in sense 4 of *n.*). [ME f. OF *crouste* f. L *crusta* rind, shell]

crus·ta·cean /krustáyshən/ *n. & adj.* ● *n.* any arthropod of the class Crustacea, having a hard shell and usu. aquatic, e.g., the crab, lobster, and shrimp. ● *adj.* of or relating to crustaceans. □□ **crus·ta·ce·ol·o·gy** /–sheeóləjee/ *n.* **crus·ta·ceous** /–shəs/ *adj.* [mod.L *crustaceus* f. *crusta*: see CRUST]

crust·ed /krústid/ *adj.* **1 a** having a crust. **b** (of wine) having deposited a crust. **2** antiquated; venerable (*crusted prejudice*).

crust·y /krústee/ *adj.* (**crust·i·er**, **crust·i·est**) **1** having a crisp crust (*a crusty loaf*). **2** irritable; curt. **3** hard; crustlike. □□ **crust·i·ly** *adv.* **crust·i·ness** *n.*

crutch /kruch/ *n.* **1** a support for a lame person, usu. with a crosspiece at the top fitting under the armpit (*pair of crutches*). **2** any support or prop. **3** the crotch of the human body or garment. [OE *cryc(c)* f. Gmc]

crux /kruks/ *n.* (*pl.* **crux·es** or **cru·ces** /krŏoseez/) **1** the decisive point at issue. **2** a difficult matter; a puzzle. [L, = cross]

cru·za·do /krŏozaádō/ *n.* (*pl.* **·dos**) the chief monetary unit of Brazil from 1986 to 1994. [Port. *cruzado*, *crusado*, = marked with the cross]

cru·zei·ro /krŏozáirō/ *n.* (*pl.* **·ros**) the monetary unit of Brazil before 1986 and (as *cruzeiro real*) since July 1994. [Port., = large cross]

cry /krī/ *v. & n.* ● *v.* (**cries**, **cried**) **1** *intr.* (often foll. by *out*) make a loud or shrill sound, esp. to express pain, grief, etc., or to appeal for help. **2 a** *intr.* shed tears; weep. **b** *tr.* shed (tears). **3** *tr.* (often foll. by *out*) say or exclaim loudly or excitedly. **4** *intr.* (of an animal, esp. a bird) make a loud call. **5** *tr.* (of a hawker, etc.) proclaim (wares, etc.) in the street. ● *n.* (*pl.* **cries**) **1** a loud inarticulate utterance of grief, pain, fear, joy, etc. **2** a loud excited utterance of words. **3** an urgent appeal or entreaty. **4** a spell of weeping. **5 a** a public demand; a strong movement of opinion. **b** a watchword or rallying call. **6** the natural utterance of an animal, esp. of hounds on the scent. **7** the street call of a hawker, etc. □ **cry down** disparage; belittle. **cry one's eyes** (or **heart**) **out** weep bitterly. **cry from the heart** a passionate appeal or protest. **cry out for** demand as a self-evident requirement or solution. **cry over spilled milk** see MILK. **cry wolf** see WOLF. **a far cry 1** a long way. **2** a very different thing. **for crying out loud** *colloq.* an exclamation of surprise or annoyance. **in full cry** (of hounds) in keen pursuit. [ME f. OF *crier*, *cri* f. L *quiritare* wail]

cry·ba·by /kríbaybee/ *n.* a person, esp. a child, who sheds tears frequently.

cry·er var. of CRIER.

cry·ing /krí-ing/ *attrib.adj.* (of an injustice or other evil) flagrant; demanding redress (*a crying need*; *a crying shame*).

cryo- /krīō/ *comb. form* (extreme) cold. [Gk *kruos* frost]

cry·o·bi·ol·o·gy /krīōbióləjee/ *n.* the biology of organisms below their normal temperatures. □□ **cry·o·bi·o·log·i·cal** /–bīəlójikəl/ *adj.* **cry·o·bi·ol·o·gist** *n.*

cry·o·gen /kríəjən/ *n.* a freezing mixture; a substance used to produce very low temperatures.

cry·o·gen·ics /krīəjéniks/ *n.* the branch of physics dealing with the production and effects of very low temperatures. □□ **cry·o·gen·ic** *adj.*

cry·o·lite /kríəlīt/ *n. Mineral.* a lustrous mineral of sodium aluminum fluoride, used in the manufacture of aluminum.

cry·o·pump /kríōpump/ *n.* a vacuum pump using liquefied gases.

cry·o·stat /kríəstat/ *n.* an apparatus for maintaining a very low temperature.

cry·o·sur·ger·y /krīōsə́rjəree/ *n.* surgery using the local application of intense cold for anesthesia or therapy.

crypt /kript/ *n.* an underground room or vault, esp. one beneath a church, used usu. as a burial place. [ME f. L *crypta* f. Gk *kruptē* f. *kruptos* hidden]

crypt·a·nal·y·sis /kríptənálisis/ *n.* the art or process of deciphering cryptograms by analysis. □□ **crypt·an·a·lyst** /–tánəlist/ *n.* **crypt·an·a·lyt·ic** /–tanəlítik/ *adj.* **crypt·an·a·lyt·i·cal** *adj.* [CRYPTO- + ANALYSIS]

cryp·tic /kríptik/ *adj.* **1 a** obscure in meaning. **b** (of a crossword clue, etc.) indirect; indicating the solution in a way that is not obvious. **c** secret; mysterious; enigmatic. **2** *Zool.* (of coloration, etc.) serving for concealment. □□ **cryp·ti·cal·ly** *adv.* [LL *crypticus* f. Gk *kruptikos* (as CRYPTO-)]

cryp·to /kríptō/ *n.* (*pl.* **·tos**) *colloq.* a person having a secret allegiance to a political creed, etc., esp. communism. [as CRYPTO-]

crypto- /kríptō/ *comb. form* concealed; secret (*crypto-communist*). [Gk *kruptos* hidden]

cryp·to·crys·tal·line /kríptōkrístəlin, –līn/ *adj.* having a crystalline structure visible only when magnified.

cryp·to·gam /kríptəgam/ *n.* a plant that has no true flowers or seeds, e.g., ferns, mosses, algae, and fungi. □□ **cryp·to·gam·ic** *adj.* **cryp·tog·a·mous** /–tógəməs/ *adj.* [F *cryptogame* f. mod.L *cryptogamae* (*plantae*) formed as CRYPTO- + Gk *gamos* marriage]

cryp·to·gram /kríptəgram/ *n.* a text written in code.

cryp·tog·ra·phy /kríptógrəfee/ *n.* the art of writing or solving codes and ciphers. □□ **cryp·tog·ra·pher** *n.* **cryp·to·graph·ic** /–təgráfik/ *adj.* **cryp·to·graph·i·cal·ly** *adv.*

cryp·to·me·ri·a /kríptəmeéreeə/ *n.* a tall evergreen tree, *Cryptomeria japonica*, native to China and Japan, with long, curved, spirally arranged leaves and short cones. Also called **Japanese cedar**. [CRYPTO- + Gk *meros* part (because the seeds are enclosed by scales)]

crys·tal /kríst'l/ *n. & adj.* ● *n.* **1 a** a clear transparent mineral, esp. rock crystal. **b** a piece of this. **2** (in full **crystal glass**) a highly transparent glass; flint glass. **b** articles made of this. **3** the glass over a watch face. **4** *Electronics* a crystalline piece of semiconductor. **5** *Chem.* **a** an aggregation of molecules with a definite internal structure and the external form of a solid enclosed by symmetrically arranged plane faces. **b** a solid whose constituent particles are symmetrically arranged. ● *adj.* (usu. *attrib.*) made of, like, or clear as crystal. □ **crystal clear** unclouded; transparent. [OE f. OF *cristal* f. L *crystallum* f. Gk *krustallos* ice, crystal]

crys·tal ball *n.* a solid globe of glass or rock crysal, used by fortune tellers and clairvoyants for crystal gazing.

crys·tal class *n. Crystallog.* any of 32 categories of crystals classified according to their symmetry.

crys·tal gaz·ing *n.* the process of concentrating one's gaze on a crystal ball supposedly in order to obtain a picture of future events, etc.

See page xx for the **Key to Pronunciation**.

crys·tal lat·tice *n. Crystallog.* the regular repeating pattern of atoms, ions, or molecules in a crystalline substance.

crys·tal·line /krís'lin, –lín/ *adj.* **1** of, like, or clear as crystal. **2** *Chem. & Mineral.* having the structure and form of a crystal. □□ **crys·tal·lin·i·ty** /–línitee/ *n.* [ME f. OF *cristallin* f. L *crystallinus* f. Gk *krustallinos* (as CRYSTAL)]

crys·tal·line lens *n.* a transparent lens enclosed in a membranous capsule behind the iris of the eye.

crys·tal·lite /kríst'lít/ *n.* **1** a small crystal. **2** an individual perfect crystal or grain in a metal, etc. **3** *Bot.* a region of cellulose, etc., with a crystallike structure.

crys·tal·lize /kríst'líz/ *v.* **1** *tr. & intr.* form or cause to form crystals. **2** (often foll. by *out*) **a** *intr.* (of ideas or plans) become definite. **b** *tr.* make definite. **3** *tr. & intr.* coat or impregnate or become coated or impregnated with sugar (*crystallized fruit*). □□ **crys·tal·liz·a·ble** *adj.* **crys·tal·li·za·tion** *n.*

crys·tal·log·ra·phy /kríst'lógrəfee/ *n.* the science of crystal form and structure. □□ **crys·tal·log·ra·pher** *n.* **crys·tal·lo·graph·ic** /–ləgráfik/ *adj.*

crys·tal·loid /kríst'loyd/ *adj. & n.* ● *adj.* **1** crystallike. **2** having a crystalline structure. ● *n.* a substance that in solution is able to pass through a semipermeable membrane (cf. COLLOID).

crys·tal set *n.* a simple early form of radio receiving apparatus with a crystal touching a metal wire as the rectifier.

crys·tal sys·tem *n. Crystallog.* any of seven possible unique combinations of unit cells, crystal lattices, and symmetry elements of a crystal class.

Cs *symb. Chem.* the element cesium.

c/s *abbr.* cycles per second.

csar·das var. of CZARDAS.

C-section *abbr.* of CESAREAN SECTION.

CSF *abbr.* cerebrospinal fluid.

CST *abbr.* central standard time.

CT *abbr.* Connecticut (in official postal use).

ct. *abbr.* **1** carat. **2** cent.

cte·noid /teénoyd, tén–/ *adj. Zool.* (of fish scales) characterized by tiny toothlike processes (cf. PLACOID). [Gk *kteis ktenos* comb]

cten·o·phore /teénəfawr, tén–/ *n.* any marine animal of the phylum Ctenophora, having a jellyfishlike body bearing rows of cilia, e.g., sea gooseberries. [mod.L *ctenophorus* (as CTENOID)]

ctn. *abbr.* **1** carton. **2** cotangent.

Cu *symb. Chem.* the element copper.

cu. *abbr.* cubic.

cub /kub/ *n. & v.* ● *n.* **1** the young of a fox, bear, lion, etc. **2** an ill-mannered young man. **3** (**Cub**) (in full **Cub Scout**) a member of the junior branch of the Boy Scouts. **4** (in full **cub reporter**) *colloq.* a young or inexperienced newspaper reporter. **5** an apprentice. ● *v.tr.* (**cubbed, cubbing**) (also *absol.*) give birth to (cubs). □□ **cub·hood** *n.* [16th c.: orig. unkn.]

Cu·ban /kyoobən/ *adj. & n.* ● *adj.* of or relating to Cuba, an island republic in the Caribbean, or its people. ● *n.* a native or national of Cuba.

Cu·ban heel *n.* a moderately high straight heel of a woman's shoe.

cub·by /kúbee/ *n.* (*pl.* **·bies**) (in full **cubbyhole**) **1** a very small room. **2** a snug or confined space. **3** a boxlike compartment for storage, etc. [dial. *cub* stall, pen, of LG orig.]

cube /kyoob/ *n. & v.* ● *n.* **1** a solid contained by six equal squares. **2** a cube-shaped block. **3** *Math.* the product of a number multiplied by its square. ● *v.tr.* **1** find the cube of (a number). **2** cut (food for cooking, etc.) into small cubes. **3** tenderize (meat) by scoring it in a crisscross pattern. □□ **cub·er** *n.* [F *cube* or L *cubus* f. Gk *kubos*]

cu·beb /kyoobeb/ *n.* **1** a climbing plant, *Piper cubeba*, bearing pungent berries. **2** this berry crushed for use in medicated cigarettes. [ME f. OF *cubebe, quibibe* ult. f. Arab. *kobāba, kubāba*]

cube root *n.* the number which produces a given number when cubed.

cube steak *n.* a thin slice of steak that has been cubed.

cu·bic /kyoobik/ *adj.* **1** cube-shaped. **2** of three dimensions. **3** involving the cube (and no higher power) of a number (*cubic equation*). **4** denoting a unit of measurement equal to the volume of a cube whose side is one of the linear unit specified (*cubic foot*). **5** *Crystallog.* having three equal axes at right angles. [F *cubique* or L *cubicus* f. Gk *kubikos* (as CUBE)]

cu·bi·cal /kyoobikəl/ *adj.* cube-shaped. □□ **cu·bi·cal·ly** *adv.*

cu·bic con·tent *n.* the volume of a solid expressed in cubic units.

cu·bi·cle /kyoobikəl/ *n.* **1** a small partitioned space, screened for privacy. **2** a small, separate sleeping compartment. [L *cubiculum* f. *cubare* lie down]

cu·bi·form /kyoobifawrm/ *adj.* cube-shaped.

cub·ism /kyoobizəm/ *n.* a style and movement in art, esp. painting, in which objects are represented as an assemblage of geometrical forms. □□ **cub·ist** *n. & adj.* [F *cubisme* (as CUBE)]

cu·bit /kyoobit/ *n.* an ancient measure of length, approximately equal to the length of a forearm. [ME f. L *cubitum* elbow, cubit]

cu·bi·tal /kyoobit'l/ *adj.* **1** *Anat.* of the forearm. **2** *Zool.* of the corresponding part in animals. [ME f. L *cubitalis* (as CUBIT)]

cu·boid /kyooboyd/ *adj. & n.* ● *adj.* cube-shaped; like a cube. ● *n.* **1** *Geom.* a rectangular parallelepiped. **2** (in full **cuboid bone**) *Anat.* the outer bone of the tarsus. □□ **cu·boi·dal** /–bóyd'l/ *adj.* [mod.L *cuboides* f. Gk *kuboeidēs* (as CUBE)]

cuck·ing stool /kúkingstool/ *n. hist.* a chair on which disorderly offenders were ducked in water, publicly mocked, etc., as a punishment. [ME f. obs. *cuck* defecate]

cuck·old /kúköld/ *n. & v.* ● *n.* the husband of an adulteress. ● *v.tr.* make a cuckold of. □□ **cuck·old·ry** *n.* [ME *cukeweld, cokewold,* f. OF *cucu* cuckoo]

cuck·oo /kookoo/ *n. & adj.* ● *n.* any bird of the family Cuculidae, esp. *Cuculus canorus*, having a characteristic cry, and depositing its eggs in the nests of small birds. ● *predic.adj. sl.* crazy; foolish. [ME f. OF *cucu*, imit.]

cuckoo clock *n.* a clock that strikes the hour with a sound like a cuckoo's call, usu. with the emergence on each note of a mechanical cuckoo.

cuck·oo·flow·er /kookooflówər/ *n.* **1** a meadow plant, *Cardamine pratensis*, with pale lilac flowers. **2** = RAGGED ROBIN.

cuck·oo·pint /kookoopint/ *n.* a wild arum, *Arum maculatum*, with arrow-shaped leaves and scarlet berries.

cuck·oo spit *n.* froth exuded by larvae of insects of the family Cercopidae on leaves, stems, etc.

cu·cum·ber /kyookumbər/ *n.* **1** a long, green, fleshy fruit, used in salads. **2** the climbing plant, *Cucumis sativus*, yielding this fruit. [ME f. OF *co(u)combre* f. L *cucumer*]

cu·cur·bit /kyookórbit/ *n.* = GOURD. □□ **cu·cur·bi·ta·ceous** /–táyshəs/ *adj.* [L *cucurbita*]

cud /kud/ *n.* half-digested food returned from the first stomach of ruminants to the mouth for further chewing. [OE *cwidu, cudu* what is chewed, corresp. to OHG *kuti, quiti* glue]

cud·dle /kúd'l/ *v. & n.* ● *v.* **1** *tr.* hug; embrace; fondle. **2** *intr.* nestle together; lie close and snug; kiss and fondle amorously. ● *n.* a prolonged and fond hug. □□ **cud·dle·some** *adj.* [16th c.: perh. f. dial. *couth* snug]

cud·dly /kúdlee/ *adj.* (**cud·dli·er, cud·dli·est**) tempting to cuddle; given to cuddling.

cud·dy /kúdee/ *n.* (*pl.* **·dies**) *Sc.* **1** a donkey. **2** a stupid person. [perh. a pet-form of the name *Cuthbert*]

cudg·el /kújəl/ *n. & v.* ● *n.* a short, thick stick used as a weapon. ● *v.tr.* beat with a cudgel. □ **cudgel one's brains** think hard about a problem. **take up the cudgels** (often foll. by *for*) make a vigorous defense. [OE *cycgel*, of unkn. orig.]

cud·weed /kúdweed/ *n.* any wild composite plant of the genus *Gnaphalium*, with scales and round flower heads, formerly given to cattle that had lost their cud.

cue[1] /kyoo/ *n. & v.* ● *n.* **1 a** the last words of an actor's speech serving as a signal to another actor to enter or speak. **b** a similar signal to a singer or player, etc. **2 a** a stimulus to perception, etc. **b** a signal for action. **c** a hint on how to behave in particular circumstances. **3** a facility for or an instance of cueing audio equipment (see sense 2 of *v.*). ● *v.tr.* (**cues, cued, cu·ing** or **cue·ing**) **1** give a cue to. **2** put (a piece of audio equipment, esp. a record player or tape recorder) in readiness to play a particular part of the recorded material. □ **cue in 1** insert a cue for. **2** give information to. **on cue** at the correct moment. **take one's cue from** follow the example or advice of. [16th c.: orig. unkn.]

cue[2] /kyoo/ *n. & v. Billiards,* etc. ● *n.* a long, straight, tapering rod for striking the ball. ● *v.* (**cues, cued, cu·ing** or **cue·ing**) **1** *tr.* strike (a ball) with a cue. **2** *intr.* use a cue. □□ **cue·ist** *n.* [var. of QUEUE]

cue ball *n.* the ball that is to be struck with the cue in billiards, etc.

cue bid *n. Bridge* an artificial bid to show a particular card, etc., in the bidder's hand.

cue card *n. colloq.* a card or board displaying a television script to a speaker as an aid to memory.

cues·ta /kwéstə/ *n. Geog.* a gentle slope, esp. one ending in a steep drop. [Sp., = slope, f. L *costa*: see COAST]

cuff[1] /kuf/ *n.* **1 a** the end part of a sleeve. **b** a separate band of linen worn around the wrist so as to appear under the sleeve. **c** the part of a glove covering the wrist. **2** a turned-up hem on pants. **3** (in *pl.*) *colloq.* handcuffs. □□ **cuffed** *adj.* (also in *comb.*). [ME: orig. unkn.]

cuff[2] /kuf/ *v. & n.* ● *v.tr.* strike with an open hand. ● *n.* such a blow. [16th c.: perh. imit.]

cuff link *n.* a device of two joined studs, etc., to fasten the sides of a shirt cuff together.

Cu·fic var. of KUFIC.

cui bo·no /kwee bónō/ who stands, or stood, to gain? (with the implication that this person is responsible). [L, = to whom (is it) a benefit?]

cui·rass /kwirás/ *n.* **1** *hist.* a piece of armor consisting of breastplate and backplate fastened together. **2** a device for artificial respiration. [ME f. OF *cuirace*, ult. f. LL *coriaceus* f. *corium* leather]

cui·ras·sier /kwírəseér/ *n. hist.* a cavalry soldier wearing a cuirass. [F (as CUIRASS)]

cuish var. of CUISSE.

cui·sine /kwizéen/ n. a style or method of cooking, esp. of a particular country or establishment. [F f. L *coquina* f. *coquere* to cook]

cuisse /kwis/ n. (also **cuish** /kwish/) (usu. in *pl.*) *hist.* thigh armor. [ME, f. OF *cuisseaux* pl. of *cuissel* f. LL *coxale* f. *coxa* hip]

cul-de-sac /kúldəsak, kŏŏl–/ n. (*pl.* **culs-de-sac** *pronunc.* same) **1 a** street or passage closed at one end. **2** a route or course leading nowhere; a position from which one cannot escape. **3** *Anat.* = DIVERTICULUM. [F, = sack bottom]

-cule /kyŏŏl/ *suffix* forming (orig. diminutive) nouns (*molecule*). [F –*cule* or L –*culus*]

cu·li·nar·y /kyŏŏləneree, kúl–/ adj. of or for cooking or the kitchen. □□ **cu·li·nar·i·ly** adv. [L *culinarius* f. *culina* kitchen]

cull /kul/ v. & n. ● v.tr. **1** select, choose, or gather from a large quantity or amount (*knowledge culled from books*). **2** pick or gather (flowers, fruit, etc.). **3** select (animals) according to quality, esp. poor surplus specimens for killing. ● n. **1** an act of culling. **2** an animal or animals culled. □□ **cull·er** n. [ME f. OF *coillier*, etc., ult. f. L *colligere* COLLECT¹]

cul·let /kúlit/ n. recycled waste or broken glass used in glassmaking. [var. of COLLET]

culm¹ /kulm/ n. **1** coal dust, esp. of anthracite. **2** *Geol.* strata under coal measures, esp. in SW England. [ME, prob. rel. to COAL]

culm² /kulm/ n. *Bot.* the stem of a plant, esp. of grasses. □□ **cul·mif·er·ous** /–mífərəs/ adj. [L *culmus* stalk]

cul·mi·nant /kúlminənt/ adj. **1** at or forming the top. **2** *Astron.* on the meridian. [as CULMINATE + –ANT]

cul·mi·nate /kúlminayt/ v. **1** intr. (usu. foll. by *in*) reach its highest or final point (*the antagonism culminated in war*). **2** tr. bring to its highest or final point. **3** intr. *Astron.* be on the meridian. □□ **cul·mi·na·tion** /–náyshən/ n. [LL *culminare culminat-* f. *culmen* summit]

cu·lottes /kŏŏlóts, kyŏŏ–/ n.pl. women's (usu. short) trousers cut to resemble a skirt. [F, = knee-breeches]

cul·pa·ble /kúlpəbəl/ adj. deserving blame. □□ **cul·pa·bil·i·ty** n. **cul·pa·bly** adv. [ME f. OF *coupable* f. L *culpabilis* f. *culpare* f. *culpa* blame]

cul·prit /kúlprit/ n. a person accused of or guilty of an offense. [17th c.: orig. in the formula *Culprit, how will you be tried?*, said by the clerk of the Crown to a prisoner pleading 'not guilty': perh. abbr. of AF *Culpable: prest d'averrer*, etc. (You are) guilty: (I am) ready to prove, etc.]

culottes

cult /kult/ n. **1** a system of religious worship esp. as expressed in ritual. **2 a** devotion or homage to a person or thing (*the cult of aestheticism*). **b** a popular fashion esp. followed by a specific section of society. **3** (*attrib.*) denoting a person or thing popularized in this way (*cult film; cult figure*). □□ **cul·tic** adj. **cult·ism** n. **cult·ist** n. [F *culte* or L *cultus* worship f. *colere cult-* inhabit, till, worship]

cul·ti·var /kúltivaar/ n. *Bot.* a plant variety produced by cultivation. [CULTIVATE + VARIETY]

cul·ti·vate /kúltivayt/ v.tr. **1 a** prepare and use (soil, etc.) for crops or gardening. **b** break up (the ground) with a cultivator. **2 a** raise or produce (crops). **b** culture (bacteria, etc.). **3 a** (often as **culti·vated** adj.) apply oneself to improving or developing (the mind, manners, etc.). **b** pay attention to or nurture (a person or a person's friendship); ingratiate oneself with (a person). □□ **cul·ti·va·ble** adj. **cul·ti·vat·a·ble** adj. **cul·ti·va·tion** n. [med.L *cultivare* f. *cultiva* (*terra*) arable (land) (as CULT)]

cul·ti·va·tor /kúltivaytər/ n. **1** a mechanical implement for breaking up the ground and uprooting weeds. **2** a person or thing that cultivates.

cul·tur·al /kúlchərəl/ adj. of or relating to the cultivation of the mind or manners, esp. through artistic or intellectual activity. □□ **cul·tur·al·ly** adv.

cul·ture /kúlchər/ n. & v. ● n. **1 a** the arts and other manifestations of human intellectual achievement regarded collectively (*a city*

lacking in culture. **b** a refined understanding of this; intellectual development (*a person of culture*). **2** the customs, civilization, and achievements of a particular time or people (*studied Chinese culture*). **3** improvement by mental or physical training. **4 a** the cultivation of plants; the rearing of bees, silkworms, etc. **b** the cultivation of the soil. **5** a quantity of microorganisms and the nutrient material supporting their growth. ● v.tr. maintain (bacteria, etc.) in conditions suitable for growth.

cul·tured /kúlchərd/ adj. having refined taste and manners and a good education.

cul·tured pearl n. a pearl formed by an oyster after the insertion of an irritant, such as a grain of sand, into its shell.

cul·ture shock n. the feeling of disorientation experienced by a person suddenly subjected to an unfamiliar culture or way of life.

cul·ture vul·ture n. *colloq.* a person who is excessively interested in the arts.

cul·tus /kúltəs/ n. a system of religious worship; a cult. [L: see CULT]

cul·ver·in /kúlvərin/ n. *hist.* **1** a long cannon. **2** a small firearm. [ME f. OF *couleuvrine* f. *couleuvre* snake ult. f. L *colubra*]

cul·vert /kúlvərt/ n. an underground channel carrying water across a road, etc. [18th c.: orig. unkn.]

cum /kum/ prep. (usu. in *comb.*) with; combined with; also used as (*a bedroom-cum-study*). [L]

cum. abbr. cumulative.

cum·ber /kúmbər/ v. & n. ● v.tr. *literary* hamper; hinder; inconvenience. ● n. a hindrance, obstruction, or burden. [ME, prob. f. ENCUMBER]

cum·ber·some /kúmbərsəm/ adj. inconvenient in size, weight, or shape; unwieldy. □□ **cum·ber·some·ly** adv. **cum·ber·some·ness** n. [ME f. CUMBER + –SOME¹]

Cum·bri·an /kúmbreeən/ adj. & n. ● adj. **1** of Cumberland. **2 a** of the ancient British kingdom of Cumbria. **b** of the modern county of Cumbria. ● n. a native of Cumberland or of ancient or modern Cumbria. [med.L *Cumbria* f. Welsh *Cymry* Welshmen + –AN]

cum·brous /kúmbrəs/ adj. = CUMBERSOME. □□ **cum·brous·ly** adv. **cum·brous·ness** n. [CUMBER + –OUS]

cum gra·no sal·is /kúm gráanō sáalis/ adv. with a grain of salt (see *take with a grain of salt* (see SALT)). [L]

cum·in /kúmin, kŏŏ–, kyŏŏ–/ n. **1** an umbelliferous plant, *Cuminum cyminum*, bearing aromatic seeds. **2** these seeds used as flavoring, esp. ground and used in curry powder. [ME f. OF *cumin, comin* f. L *cuminum* f. Gk *kuminon*, prob. of Semitic orig.]

cum·mer·bund /kúmərbund/ n. a waist sash.

cummerbund

cum·quat var. of KUMQUAT.

cu·mu·late v. & adj. ● v.tr. & intr. /kyŏŏmyəlayt/ accumulate; amass; combine. ● adj. /kyŏŏmyələt/ heaped up, massed. □□ **cu·mu·la·tion** /–láyshən/ n. [L *cumulare* f. *cumulus* heap]

cu·mu·la·tive /kyŏŏmyələtiv, –láytiv/ adj. **1 a** increasing or increased in amount, force, etc., by successive additions (*cumulative evidence*). **b** formed by successive additions (*learning is a cumulative process*). **2** *Stock Exch.* (of shares) entitling holders to arrears of interest before any other distribution is made. □□ **cu·mu·la·tive·ly** adv. **cu·mu·la·tive·ness** n.

cu·mu·la·tive vot·ing n. a system in which each voter has as many votes as there are candidates and may give all to one candidate.

cumulo- /kyŏŏmyəlō/ *comb. form* cumulus (cloud).

cu·mu·lus /kyŏŏmyələs/ n. (*pl.* **cu·mu·li** /–lī/) a cloud formation consisting of rounded masses heaped on each other above a horizontal base. □□ **cu·mu·lous** adj. [L, = heap]

cu·ne·ate /kyŏŏneeət, –ayt/ adj. wedge-shaped. [L *cuneus* wedge]

cu·ne·i·form /kyŏŏneeəfawrm, kyŏŏneeə–, kyŏŏni–/ adj. & n. ● adj. **1** wedge-shaped. **2** of, relating to, or using the wedge-shaped writing impressed usu. in clay in ancient Babylonian, etc., inscriptions. ● n. cuneiform writing. [F *cunéiforme* or mod.L *cuneiformis* f. L *cuneus* wedge]

cun·ni·lin·gus /kúnilínggəs/ n. (also **cun·ni·linc·tus** /–língktəs/) oral stimulation of the female genitals. [L f. *cunnus* vulva + *lingere* lick]

cun·ning /kúning/ adj. & n. ● adj. **1 a** skilled in ingenuity or deceit. **b** selfishly clever or crafty. **2** ingenious (*a cunning device*). **3** attractive; quaint. ● n. **1** craftiness; skill in deceit. **2** skill; ingenuity. □□ **cun·ning·ly** adv. **cun·ning·ness** n. [ME f. ON *kunnandi* knowing f. *kunna* know: cf. CAN¹]

cunt /kunt/ *n. coarse sl.* **1** the female genitals. **2** *offens.* an unpleasant or stupid person. [ME f. Gmc]

▶This is a highly taboo word.

cup /kup/ *n. & v.* • *n.* **1** a small bowl-shaped container, usu. with a handle for drinking from. **2 a** its contents (*a cup of tea*). **b** = CUP-FUL. **3** a cup-shaped thing, esp. the calyx of a flower or the socket of a bone. **4** flavored wine, cider, etc., usu. chilled. **5** an ornamental cup-shaped trophy as a prize for victory or prowess, esp. in a sports contest. **6** one's fate or fortune (*a bitter cup*). **7** either of the two cup-shaped parts of a brassiere. **8** the chalice used or the wine taken at the Eucharist. **9** *Golf* the hole on a putting green or the metal container in it. • *v.tr.* (**cupped, cup•ping**) **1** form (esp. one's hands) into the shape of a cup. **2** take or hold as in a cup. **3** *hist.* bleed (a person) by using a glass in which a partial vacuum is formed by heating. □ **one's cup of tea** *colloq.* what interests or suits one. **in one's cups** while drunk; drunk. [OE *cuppe* f. med.L *cuppa* cup, prob. differentiated from L *cupa* tub]

cup•bear•er /kúpbairər/ *n.* a person who serves wine, esp. an officer of a royal or noble household.

cup•board /kúbərd/ *n.* a recess or piece of furniture with a door and (usu.) shelves, in which things are stored. [ME f. CUP + BOARD]

cup•board love *n.* a display of affection meant to secure some gain.

cup•cake /kúpkayk/ *n.* a small cake baked in a cup-shaped metal, foil, or paper container and often iced.

cu•pel /kyóōpəl/ *n. & v.* • *n.* a small, flat, porous vessel used in assaying gold or silver in the presence of lead. • *v.tr.* assay or refine in a cupel. □□ **cu•pel•la•tion** /-pəláyshən/ *n.* [F *coupelle* f. LL *cupella* dimin. of *cupa*: see CUP]

cup•ful /kúpfŏŏl/ *n.* (*pl.* **•fuls**) **1** the amount held by a cup, esp. a half-pint (8-ounce) measure in cooking. **2** a cup full of a substance (*drank a cupful of water*).

▶A *cupful* is a measure, and so *three cupfuls* is a quantity regarded in terms of a cup; *three cups full* denotes the actual cups, as in *three cups full of water*. Sense 2 is an intermediate use.

Cu•pid /kyóōpid/ *n.* **1** (in Roman mythology) the Roman god of love represented as a naked winged boy with a bow and arrows. **2** (also **cu•pid**) a representation of Cupid. [ME f. L *Cupido* f. *cupere* desire]

cu•pid•i•ty /kyóōpíditee/ *n.* greed for gain; avarice. [ME f. OF *cupidité* or L *cupiditas* f. *cupidus* desirous]

Cu•pid's bow *n.* the upper lip, etc., shaped like the double-curved bow carried by Cupid.

cup li•chen *n.* a lichen, *Cladonia pyxidata*, with cup-shaped processes arising from the thallus.

cu•po•la /kyóōpələ/ *n.* **1 a** a rounded dome forming a roof or ceiling. **b** a small rounded dome adorning a roof. **2** a revolving dome protecting mounted guns on a warship or in a fort. **3** (in full **cupola furnace**) a furnace for melting metals. □□ **cu•po•laed** /-ləd/ *adj.* [It. f. LL *cupula* dimin. of *cupa* cask]

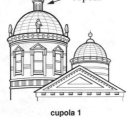
cupola

cupola 1

cup•pa /kúpə/ *n.* (also **cup•per** /kúpə/) *Brit. colloq.* **1** a cup of. **2** a cup of tea. [corruption]

cu•pram•mo•ni•um /kyóōprəmóneeəm/ *n.* a complex ion of divalent copper and ammonia, solutions of which dissolve cellulose. [LL *cuprum* + AMMONIUM]

cu•pre•ous /kóōpreeəs, kyóō-/ *adj.* of or like copper. [LL *cupreus* f. *cuprum* copper]

cu•pric /kóōprik, kyóō-/ *adj.* of copper, esp. divalent copper. □□ **cu•prif•er•ous** /-prífərəs/ *adj.* [LL *cuprum* copper]

cupro- /kóōprō, kyóō-/ *comb. form* copper (*cupronickel*).

cu•pro•nick•el /kóōprōníkəl, kyóō-/ *n.* an alloy of copper and nickel, esp. in the proportions 3:1 as used in 'silver' coins.

cu•prous /kóōprəs, kyóō-/ *adj.* of copper, esp. monovalent copper. [LL *cuprum* copper]

cu•pule /kyóōpyŏŏl/ *n. Bot. & Zool.* a cup-shaped organ, receptacle, etc. [LL *cupula* CUPOLA]

cur /kər/ *n.* **1** a worthless or snappy dog. **2** *colloq.* a contemptible person. [ME, prob. orig. in *cur-dog*, perh. f. ON *kurr* grumbling]

cur. *abbr.* **1** currency. **2** current.

cur•a•ble /kyóōrəbəl/ *adj.* that can be cured. □□ **cur•a•bil•i•ty** *n.* [CURE]

cu•ra•çao /kyóōrəsó, –sów/ *n.* (also **cu•ra•çoa** /–sóə/) (*pl.* **•aos** or **cu•ra•çoas**) a liqueur of spirits flavored with the peel of bitter oranges. [F *Curaçao*, name of the Caribbean island producing these oranges]

cu•ra•cy /kyóōrəsee/ *n.* (*pl.* **•cies**) a curate's office or the tenure of it.

cu•ra•re /kyŏŏráaree, kŏŏ–/ *n.* a resinous bitter substance prepared from S. American plants of the genera *Strychnos* and *Chondodendron*, paralyzing the motor nerves, used by native peoples to poison arrows and blowpipe darts, and formerly used as a muscle relaxant in surgery. [Carib]

cu•ras•sow /kyóōrəsō, kŏŏr–/ *n.* any game bird of the family Cracidae, found in Central and S. America. [Anglicized f. CURAÇAO]

cu•rate /kyóōrət/ *n.* **1** a member of the clergy engaged as assistant to a parish priest. **2** *archaic* an ecclesiastical pastor. [ME f. med.L *curatus* f. L *cura* CURE]

cu•rate's egg *n.* esp. *Brit.* a thing that is partly good and partly bad.

cur•a•tive /kyóōrətiv/ *adj. & n.* • *adj.* tending or able to cure (esp. disease). • *n.* a curative medicine or agent. [F *curatif –ive* f. med.L *curativus* f. L *curare* CURE]

cu•ra•tor /kyŏŏráytər, kyóōrə–/ *n.* a keeper or custodian of a museum or other collection. □□ **cu•ra•to•ri•al** /kyóōrətáwreeəl/ *adj.* **cu•ra•tor•ship** *n.* [ME f. AF *curatour* (OF *–eur*) or L *curator* (as CURATIVE)]

curb /kərb/ *n. & v.* • *n.* **1** a check or restraint. **2** a rim of concrete, stone, etc., along the side of a paved road. **3** a strap, etc., fastened to the bit and passing under a horse's lower jaw, used as a check. **4** an enclosing border or edging such as the frame around the top of a well or a fender around a hearth. • *v.tr.* **1** restrain. **2** put a curb on (a horse). [ME f. OF *courber* f. L *curvare* bend, CURVE]

curb roof *n.* the shallow upper slopes of a mansard roof.

curb•side /kərbsīd/ *n.* the side of a paved road or roadbed bordered by a curb.

curb•stone /kərbstōn/ *n.* each of a series of stones forming a curb, as along a street.

cur•cu•ma /kórkyəmə/ *n.* **1** the spice turmeric. **2** any tuberous plant of the genus *Curcuma*, yielding this and other commercial substances. [med.L f. mod.L f. Arab. *kurkum* saffron f. Skr. *kuṅkama^m*]

curd /kərd/ *n.* **1** (often in *pl.*) a coagulated substance formed by the action of acids on milk, which may be made into cheese or eaten as food. **2** a fatty substance found between flakes of boiled salmon flesh. **3** the edible head of a cauliflower. □□ **curd•y** *adj.* [ME: orig. unkn.]

cur•dle /kərd'l/ *v.tr. & intr.* make into or become curds, (of milk) turn sour; congeal. □ **make one's blood curdle** fill one with horror. □□ **cur•dler** *n.* [frequent. form of CURD (as verb)]

cure /kyŏŏr/ *n. & v.* • *v.* **1** *tr.* (often foll. by *of*) restore (a person or animal) to health (*was cured of pleurisy*). **2** *tr.* eliminate (a disease, evil, etc.). **3** *tr.* preserve (meat, fruit, tobacco, or skins) by salting, drying, etc. **4** *tr.* **a** vulcanize (rubber). **b** harden (concrete or plastic). **5** *intr.* effect a cure. **6** *intr.* undergo a process of curing. • *n.* **1** restoration to health. **2** a thing that effects a cure. **3** a course of medical or healing treatment. **4 a** the office or function of a curate. **b** a parish or other sphere of spiritual ministration. **5 a** the process of curing rubber or plastic. **b** (with qualifying adj.) the degree of this. □□ **cur•er** *n.* [ME f. OF *curer* f. L *curare* take care of f. *cura* care]

cu•ré /kyŏŏráy, kyóōray/ *n.* a parish priest in France, etc. [F f. med.L *curatus*: see CURATE]

cure-all *n.* a panacea; a universal remedy.

cu•ret•tage /kyŏŏritáazh/ *n.* the use of or an operation involving the use of a curette. [F (as CURETTE)]

cu•rette /kyŏŏrét/ *n. & v.* • *n.* a surgeon's small scraping instrument. • *v.tr. & intr.* clean or scrape with a curette. [F, f. *curer* cleanse (as CURE)]

cur•few /kərfyŏŏ/ *n.* **1 a** a regulation restricting or forbidding the public circulation of people, esp. requiring people to remain indoors between specified hours, usu. at night. **b** the hour designated as the beginning of such a restriction. **c** a daily signal indicating this. **2** *hist.* **a** a medieval regulation requiring people to extinguish fires at a fixed hour in the evening. **b** the hour for this. **c** the bell announcing it. **3** the ringing of a bell at a fixed evening hour. [ME f. AF *coeverfu*, OF *cuevrefeu* f. the stem of *couvrir* COVER + *feu* fire]

cu•ri•a /kyóōreeə/ *n.* (also **Cu•ri•a**) (*pl.* **cu•ri•ae**) the papal court; the government departments of the Vatican. □□ **Cu•ri•al** *adj.* [L: orig. a division of an ancient Roman tribe, the senate house at Rome, a feudal court of justice]

cu•rie /kyóōree/ *n.* **1** a unit of radioactivity, corresponding to 3.7 x 10¹⁰ disintegrations per second. ¶ Abbr.: **Ci. 2** a quantity of radioactive substance having this activity. [P. Curie, Fr. scientist d. 1906]

cu•ri•o /kyóōreeō/ *n.* (*pl.* **•os**) a rare or unusual object or person. [-19th-c. abbr. of CURIOSITY]

cu•ri•o•sa /kyóōreeósə/ *n.pl.* **1** curiosities. **2** erotic or pornographic books. [neut. pl. of L *curiosus*: see CURIOUS]

cu•ri•os•i•ty /kyóōreeósitee/ *n.* (*pl.* **•ties**) **1** an eager desire to know; inquisitiveness. **2** strangeness. **3** a strange, rare, or interesting object. [ME f. OF *curiouseté* f. L *curiositas –tatis* (as CURIOUS)]

cu•ri•ous /kyóōreeəs/ *adj.* **1** eager to learn; inquisitive. **2** strange; surprising; odd. **3** *euphem.* (of books, etc.) erotic; pornographic. □□ **cu•ri•ous•ly** *adv.* **cu•ri•ous•ness** *n.* [ME f. OF *curios* f. L *curiosus* careful f. *cura* care]

cu•ri•um /kyóōreeəm/ *n.* an artificially made transuranic radioactive metallic element, first produced by bombarding plutonium with helium ions. ¶ Symb.: **Cm.** [M. Curie d. 1934 and P. Curie d. 1906, Fr. scientists]

curl /kərl/ *v. & n.* • *v.* **1** *tr. & intr.* (often foll. by *up*) bend or coil into a spiral; form or cause to form curls. **2** *intr.* move in a spiral form (*smoke curling upward*). **3 a** *intr.* (of the upper lip) be raised slightly on one side as an expression of contempt or disapproval. **b** *tr.* cause (the lip) to do this. **4** *intr.* play curling. • *n.* **1** a lock of curled hair. **2** anything spiral or curved inward. **3 a** a curling movement or act. **b** the state of being curled. **4** a disease of plants in which the leaves are curled up. □ **curl up 1** lie or sit with the knees drawn up. **2** *colloq.* writhe with embarrassment, horror, or amusement. **make a person's hair curl** *colloq.* shock or horrify a person. [ME; earliest form *crolled*, *crulled* f. obs. adj. *crolle*, *crulle* curly f. MDu. *krul*]

curl·er /kɔ́rlər/ *n.* **1** a pin or roller, etc., for curling the hair. **2** a player in the game of curling.

cur·lew /kɔ́rlōō, -lyōō/ *n.* any wading bird of the genus *Numenius*, esp. *N. arquatus*, possessing a usu. long, slender, down-curved bill. [ME f. OF *courlieu*, *courlis* orig. imit., but assim. to *courliu* courier f. *courre* run + *lieu* place]

curl·i·cue /kɔ́rlikyōō/ *n.* a decorative curl or twist. [CURLY + CUE² (= pigtail) or Q¹]

curl·ing /kɔ́rling/ *n.* **1** in senses of CURL *v.* **2** a game played on ice, esp. in Canada and Scotland, in which large, round, flat stones are slid across the surface toward a mark. □ **curling iron** a heated device for shaping the hair into curls.

curl·y /kɔ́rlee/ *adj.* (**curl·i·er**, **curl·i·est**) **1** having or arranged in curls. **2** moving in curves. □□ **curl·i·ness** *n.*

cur·mudg·eon /kərmújən/ *n.* a bad-tempered person. □□ **cur·mudg·eon·ly** *adj.* [16th c.: orig. unkn.]

cur·rach /kúrəkh, kúrə/ *n.* (also **cur·ragh**) *Ir.* a coracle. [Ir.: cf. CORACLE]

cur·ra·jong var. of KURRAJONG.

cur·rant /kɔ́rənt, kúr-/ *n.* **1** a dried fruit of a small seedless variety of grape grown esp. in California and in the Levant and much used in cooking. **2 a** any of various shrubs of the genus *Ribes* producing red, white, or black berries. **b** a berry of these shrubs. [ME *raysons of coraunce* f. AF, = grapes of Corinth (the orig. source)]

cur·ra·wong /kúrəwawng, -wong/ *n. Austral.* any crowlike songbird of the genus *Strepera*, possessing a resonant call. [Aboriginal]

cur·ren·cy /kɔ́rənsee, kúr-/ *n.* (*pl.* **·cies**) **1 a** the money in general use in a country. **b** any other commodity used as a medium of exchange. **2** the condition of being current; prevalence (e.g., of words or ideas). **3** the time during which something is current.

cur·rent /kɔ́rənt, kúr-/ *adj. & n.* • *adj.* **1** belonging to the present time; happening now (*current events*; *the current week*). **2** (of money, opinion, a rumor, a word, etc.) in general circulation or use. • *n.* **1** a body of water, air, etc., moving in a definite direction, esp. through a stiller surrounding body. **2 a** an ordered movement of electrically charged particles. **b** a quantity representing the intensity of such movement. **3** (usu. foll. by *of*) a general tendency or course (of events, opinions, etc.). □ **pass current** *Brit.* be generally accepted as true or genuine. □□ **cur·rent·ness** *n.* [ME f. OF *corant* f. L *currere* run]

cur·rent·ly /kɔ́rəntlee, kúr-/ *adv.* at the present time; now.

cur·ri·cle /kúrikəl/ *n. hist.* a light, open two-wheeled carriage drawn by two horses abreast.

cur·ric·u·lum /kəríkyələm/ *n.* (*pl.* **cur·ric·u·la** /-lə/ or **cur·ric·u·lums**) **1** the subjects that are studied or prescribed for study in a school (*not part of the school curriculum*). **2** any program of activities. □□ **cur·ric·u·lar** *adj.* [L, = course, race-chariot, f. *currere* run]

cur·ric·u·lum vi·tae /kəríkyələm vítee, veétī/ *n.* (*pl.* **cur·ric·u·la vi·tae**) a brief account of one's education, qualifications, and previous occupations. [L, = course of life]

cur·ri·er /kɔ́reeər, kúr-/ *n.* a person who dresses and colors tanned leather. [ME f. OF *corier*, f. L *coriarius* f. *corium* leather]

cur·rish /kɔ́rish, kúr-/ *adj.* **1** like a cur; snappish. **2** ignoble. □□ **cur·rish·ly** *adv.* **cur·rish·ness** *n.*

cur·ry¹ /kɔ́ree, kúree/ *n. & v.* • *n.* (*pl.* **·ries**) a dish of meat, vegetables, etc., cooked in a sauce of hot-tasting spices, usu. served with rice. • *v.tr.* (**·ries**, **·ried**) prepare or flavor with a sauce of hot-tasting spices (*curried eggs*). [Tamil]

cur·ry² /kɔ́ree, kúree/ *v.tr.* (**·ries**, **·ried**) **1** groom (a horse) with a currycomb. **2** treat (tanned leather) to improve its properties. **3** thrash. □ **curry favor** ingratiate oneself. [ME f. OF *correier* ult. f. Gmc]

cur·ry·comb /kɔ́reekōm, kúree-/ *n. & v.* • *n.* a handheld metal serrated device for grooming horses. • *v.tr.* use a currycomb.

cur·ry pow·der *n.* a preparation of ground spices, such as turmeric, coriander, and ginger, for making curry.

curse /kɔrs/ *n. & v.* • *n.* **1** a solemn utterance intended to invoke a supernatural power to inflict destruction or punishment on a person or thing. **2** the evil supposedly resulting from a curse. **3** a violent exclamation of anger; a profane oath. **4** a thing that causes evil or harm. **5** (prec. by *the*) *colloq.* menstruation. **6** a sentence of excommunication. • *v.* **1** *tr.* **a** utter a curse against. **b** (in *imper.*) may God curse. **2** *tr.* (usu. in *passive*; foll. by *with*) afflict with (*cursed with blindness*). **3** *intr.* utter expletive curses; swear. **4** *tr.* excommunicate. □□ **curs·er** *n.* [OE *curs*, *cursian*, of unkn. orig.]

curs·ed /kɔ́rsid, kɔrst/ *adj.* damnable; abominable. □□ **curs·ed·ly** *adv.* **curs·ed·ness** *n.*

cur·sive /kɔ́rsiv/ *adj. & n.* • *adj.* (of writing) done with joined characters. • *n.* cursive writing (cf. PRINT *v.* 4, UNCIAL). □□ **cur·sive·ly** *adv.* [med.L (*scriptura*) *cursiva* f. L *currere curs-* run]

cur·sor /kɔ́rsər/ *n.* **1** *Computing* a movable indicator on a monitor screen identifying a particular position in the display, esp. the position that the program will operate on with the next keystroke. **2** *Math.*, etc., a transparent slide engraved with a hairline and forming part of a slide rule. [L, = runner (as CURSIVE)]

cur·so·ri·al /kɔrsáwreeəl/ *adj. Anat.* having limbs adapted for running. [as CURSOR + –IAL]

cur·so·ry /kɔ́rsəree/ *adj.* hasty, hurried (*a cursory glance*). □□ **cur·so·ri·ly** *adv.* **cur·so·ri·ness** *n.* [L *cursorius* of a runner (as CURSOR)]

curst *archaic* var. of CURSED.

curt /kɔrt/ *adj.* noticeably or rudely brief. □□ **curt·ly** *adv.* **curt·ness** *n.* [L *curtus* cut short, abridged]

cur·tail /kərtáyl/ *v.tr.* **1** cut short; reduce; terminate esp. prematurely (*curtailed his visit to Italy*). **2** (foll. by *of*) *archaic* deprive of. □□ **cur·tail·ment** *n.* [obs. *curtal* horse with docked tail. F *courtault* f. *court* short f. L *curtus*: assim. to *tail*]

cur·tain /kɔ́rtən/ *n. & v.* • *n.* **1** a piece of cloth, etc., hung up as a screen, usu. moveable sideways or upward, esp. at a window or between the stage and auditorium of a theater. **2** *Theatr.* **a** the rise or fall of the stage curtain at the beginning or end of an act or scene. **b** = CURTAIN CALL. **3** a partition or cover. **4** (in *pl.*) *sl.* the end. • *v.tr.* **1** furnish or cover with a curtain or curtains. **2** (foll. by *off*) shut off with a curtain or curtains. [ME f. OF *cortine* f. LL *cortina* transl. Gk *aulaia* f. *aulē* court]

cur·tain call *n. Theatr.* an audience's summons to actor(s) to take a bow after the fall of the curtain.

cur·tain lec·ture *n. dated* a wife's private reproof to her husband, orig. behind bed curtains.

cur·tain-rais·er *n.* **1** *Theatr.* a piece prefaced to the main performance. **2** a preliminary event.

cur·tain wall *n.* **1** *Fortification* the plain wall of a fortified place, connecting two towers, etc. **2** *Archit.* a piece of plain wall not supporting a roof.

cur·ta·na /kərtáynə, -táanə/ *n. Brit.* an unpointed sword borne before English sovereigns at their coronation, as an emblem of mercy. [ME f. AL *curtana* (*spatha* sword) f. AF *curtain*, OF *cortain* name of Roland's similar sword f. *cort* short (as CURT)]

cur·ti·lage /kɔ́rt'lij/ *n.* an area attached to a house and forming one enclosure with it. [ME f. AF *curtilage*, OF *co(u)rtillage* f. *co(u)rtil* small court f. *cort* COURT]

curt·sy /kɔ́rtsee/ *n. & v.* (also **curt·sey**) • *n.* (*pl.* **·sies** or **·seys**) a woman's or girl's formal greeting or salutation made by bending the knees and lowering the body. • *v.intr.* (**·sies**, **·sied** or **·seys**, **·seyed**) make a curtsy.

WORD HISTORY curtsy

Early 16th century: variant of COURTESY. Both forms were used to denote the expression of respect or courtesy by a gesture, especially in phrases such as *do courtesy*, *make courtesy*, and from this arose the current use (late 16th century).

cu·rule /kyōōrōōl/ *adj. Rom.Hist.* designating or relating to the authority exercised by the senior Roman magistrates, chiefly the consul and praetor, who were entitled to use the *sella curulis* ('curule seat' or seat of office). [L *curulis* f. *currus* chariot (in which the chief magistrate was conveyed to the seat of office)]

cur·va·ceous /kərváyshəs/ *adj. colloq.* (esp. of a woman) having a shapely curved figure.

cur·va·ture /kɔ́rvəchər/ *n.* **1** the act or state of curving. **2** a curved form. **3** *Geom.* **a** the deviation of a curve from a straight line, or of a curved surface from a plane. **b** the quantity expressing this. [OF f. L *curvatura* (as CURVE)]

curve /kɔrv/ *n. & v.* • *n.* **1** a line or surface having along its length a regular deviation from being straight or flat, as exemplified by the surface of a sphere or lens. **2** a curved form or thing. **3** a curved line on a graph. **4** *Baseball* a ball caused to deviate by the pitcher's spin. • *v.tr. & intr.* bend or shape so as to form a curve. □□ **curved** *adj.* (in *curve line*) f. L *curvus* bent: (v.) f. L *curvare*]

curve·ball /kɔ́rvbawl/ *n.* = CURVE *n.* 4.

cur·vet /kərvét/ *n. & v.* • *n.* a horse's leap with the forelegs raised together and the hind legs raised with a spring before the forelegs reach the ground. • *v.intr.* (**cur·vet·ted**, **cur·vet·ting** or **cur·vet·ed**, **cur·vet·ing**) (of a horse or rider) make a curvet. [It. *corvetta* dimin. of *corva* CURVE]

cur·vi- /kɔ́rvee/ *comb. form* curved. [L *curvus* curved]

cur·vi·fo·li·ate /kɔ́rvifōleeət, -ayt/ *adj. Bot.* with the leaves bent back.

cur·vi·form /kɔ́rvifawrm/ *adj.* having a curved shape.

cur·vi·lin·e·ar /kɔ́rvilíneeər/ *adj.* contained by or consisting of curved lines. □□ **cur·vi·lin·e·ar·ly** *adv.* [CURVI- after *rectilinear*]

cur·vi·ros·tral /kɔ́rvirɔ́strəl/ *adj.* with a curved beak.

curv·y /kɔ́rvee/ *adj.* (**curv·i·er, curv·i·est**) **1** having many curves. **2** (of a woman's figure) shapely. □□ **curv·i·ness** *n.*

cus·cus[1] /kúskəs/ *n.* the aromatic fibrous root of an E. Indian grass, *Vetiveria zizanoides*, used for making fans, etc. [Pers. *k̲a̲šk̲a̲š*]

cus·cus[2] /kúskəs/ *n.* any of several nocturnal, usu. arboreal, marsupial mammals of the genus *Phalanger*, native to New Guinea and N. Australia. [native name]

cu·sec /kyōŏsek/ *n.* a unit of flow (esp. of water) equal to one cubic foot per second. [abbr.]

cush /kōŏsh/ *n.* esp. *Billiards colloq.* a cushion. [abbr.]

cush-cush /kōŏshkōŏsh/ *n.* a yam, *Dioscorea trifida*, native to S. America. [native name]

cush·ion /kōŏshən/ *n. & v.* ● *n.* **1** a bag of cloth, etc., stuffed with a mass of soft material, used as a soft support for sitting or leaning on, etc. **2** a means of protection against shock. **3** the elastic lining of the sides of a billiard table, from which the ball rebounds. **4** a body of air supporting a hovercraft, etc. **5** the frog of a horse's hoof. ● *v.tr.* **1** provide or protect with a cushion or cushions. **2** provide with a defense; protect. **3** mitigate the adverse effects of (*cushioned the blow*). **4** quietly suppress. **5** place or bounce (the ball) against the cushion in billiards. □□ **cush·ion·y** *adj.* [ME f. OF *co(i)ssin*, *cu(i)ssin* f. Gallo-Roman f. L *culcita* mattress, cushion]

Cush·it·ic /kōŏshítik/ *n. & adj.* ● *n.* a group of E. African languages of the Hamitic type. ● *adj.* of this group. [*Cush* an ancient country in the Nile valley + –ITE[1] + –IC]

cush·y /kōŏshee/ *adj.* (**cush·i·er, cush·i·est**) *colloq.* **1** (of a job, etc.) easy and pleasant. **2** (of a seat, surroundings, etc.) soft; comfortable. □□ **cush·i·ness** *n.* [Anglo-Ind. f. Hind. *k̲hūsh* pleasant]

cusp /kusp/ *n.* **1** an apex or peak. **2** the horn of a crescent moon, etc. **3** *Astrol.* the initial point of a house. **4** *Archit.* a projecting point between small arcs in Gothic tracery. **5** *Geom.* the point at which two arcs meet from the same direction terminating with a common tangent. **6** *Bot.* a pointed end, esp. of a leaf. **7** a cone-shaped prominence on the surface of a tooth esp. a molar or premolar. **8** a pocket or fold in a valve of the heart. □□ **cusped** *adj.* **cus·pi·dal** /kúspid'l/ *adj.* [L *cuspis, –idis* point, apex]

cus·pi·dor /kúspidawr/ *n.* a spittoon. [Port., = spitter f. *cuspir* spit f. L *conspuere*]

cuss /kus/ *n. & v. colloq.* ● *n.* **1** a curse. **2** usu. *derog.* a person; a creature. ● *v.tr. & intr.* curse. [var. of CURSE]

cuss·ed /kúsid/ *adj. colloq.* awkward and stubborn. □□ **cuss·ed·ly** *adv.* **cuss·ed·ness** *n.* [var. of CURSED]

cuss·word /kúswərd/ *n.* a swearword.

cus·tard /kústərd/ *n.* **1** a dish made with milk and eggs, usu. sweetened. **2** a sweet sauce made with milk and flavored cornstarch. [ME, earlier *crusta(r)de* f. AF f. OF *crouste* CRUST]

cus·tard ap·ple *n.* a W. Indian fruit, *Annona reticulata*, with a custardlike pulp.

cus·tard-pie *adj.* denoting slapstick comedy, in which performers threw pies containing custard at each other.

cus·to·di·an /kustṓdeeən/ *n.* a guardian or keeper, esp. of a public building, etc. □□ **cus·to·di·an·ship** *n.* [CUSTODY + –AN, after *guardian*]

cus·to·dy /kústədee/ *n.* **1** guardianship; protective care. **2** imprisonment. □ **take into custody** arrest. □□ **cus·to·di·al** /kustṓdeeəl/ *adj.* [L *custodia* f. *custos –odis* guardian]

cus·tom /kústəm/ *n.* **1 a** the usual way of behaving or acting (*a slave to custom*). **b** a particular established way of behaving (*our customs seem strange to foreigners*). **2** *Law* established usage having the force of law. **3** esp. *Brit.* business patronage; regular dealings or customers (*lost a lot of custom*). **4** (in *pl.*; also treated as *sing.*) **a** a duty levied on certain imported and exported goods. **b** the official department that administers this. **c** the area at a port, frontier, etc., where customs officials deal with incoming goods, baggage, etc. [ME and OF *custume* ult. f. L *consuetudo –dinis*: see CONSUETUDE]

cus·tom·ar·y /kústəmeree/ *adj. & n.* ● *adj.* **1** usual; in accordance with custom. **2** *Law* in accordance with custom. ● *n.* (*pl.* **·ies**) *Law* a book, etc., listing the customs and established practices of a community. □□ **cus·tom·ar·i·ly** *adv.* **cus·tom·ar·i·ness** *n.* [med.L *custumarius* f. *custuma* f. AF *custume* (as CUSTOM)]

cus·tom-built *adj.* (also **cus·tom-made**, etc.) made to a customer's order.

cus·tom·er /kúst əmər/ *n.* **1** a person who buys goods or services from a store or business. **2** a person one has to deal with (*an awkward customer*). [ME f. AF *customer* (as CUSTOMARY), or f. CUSTOM + –ER[1]]

cus·tom·house /kústəmhows/ *n.* (also **cus·toms·house**) the office at a port or international border, etc., at which customs duties are levied.

cus·tom·ize /kústəmīz/ *v.tr.* make to order or modify according to individual requirements.

cus·toms u·nion *n.* a group of nations with an agreed common tariff, and usu. free trade with each other.

cut /kut/ *v. & n.* ● *v.* (**cut·ting**; *past* and *past part.* **cut**) **1** *tr.* (also *absol.*) penetrate or wound with a sharp-edged instrument (*cut his finger; the knife won't cut*). **2** *tr. & intr.* (often foll. by *into*) divide or be divided with a knife, etc. (*cut the bread; cut the cloth into yard lengths*). **3** *tr.* **a** trim or reduce the length of (hair, a hedge, etc.) by cutting. **b** detach all or the significant part of (flowers, grain, etc.) by cutting. **c** reduce the length of (a book, movie, etc.). **4** *tr.* (foll. by *loose, open*, etc.) make loose, open, etc. by cutting. **5** *tr.* (esp. as **cutting** *adj.*) cause sharp physical or mental pain to (*a cutting remark; a cutting wind; was cut to the quick*). **6** *tr.* (often foll. by *down*) **a** reduce (wages, prices, time, etc.). **b** reduce or cease (services, etc.). **7** *tr.* **a** shape or fashion (a coat, gem, key, record, etc.) by cutting. **b** make (a path, tunnel, etc.) by removing material. **8** *tr.* perform; execute; make (*cut a caper; cut a sorry figure; cut a deal*). **9** *tr.* (also *absol.*) cross; intersect (*the line cuts the circle at two points; the two lines cut*). **10** *intr.* (foll. by *across, through*, etc.) pass or traverse, esp. in a hurry or as a shorter way (*cut across the grass*). **11** *tr.* **a** ignore or refuse to recognize (a person). **b** renounce (a connection). **12** *tr.* deliberately fail to attend (a class, etc.). **13** *Cards* **a** *tr.* divide (a deck) into two parts. **b** *intr.* select a dealer, etc., by dividing the deck. **14** *Cinematog.* **a** *tr.* edit (a movie or tape). **b** *intr.* (often in *imper.*) stop filming or recording. **c** *intr.* (foll. by *to*) go quickly to (another shot). **15** *tr.* switch off (an engine, etc.). **16** *tr.* **a** hit (a ball) with a chopping motion. **b** *Golf* slice (the ball). **17** *tr.* dilute; adulterate. **18** *tr.* (as **cut** *adj.*) *Brit. sl.* drunk. **19** *intr. Cricket* (of the ball) turn sharply on pitching. **20** *intr. sl.* run. **21** *tr.* castrate. ● *n.* **1** an act of cutting. **2** a division or wound made by cutting. **3** a stroke with a knife, sword, whip, etc. **4** a reduction (in prices, wages, etc.). **5** an excision of part of a play, movie, book, etc. **6** a wounding remark or act. **7** the way or style in which a garment, the hair, etc., is cut. **8** a piece of meat, etc., cut from a carcass. **9** *colloq.* commission; a share of profits. **10** *Tennis*, etc., a stroke made by cutting. **11** ignoring of or refusal to recognize a person. **12 a** an engraved block for printing. **b** a woodcut or other print. **13** a railroad cutting. **14** a new channel made for a river. □ **a cut above** *colloq.* noticeably superior to. **be cut out** (foll. by *for*, or to + infin.) be suited (*was not cut out to be a teacher*). **cut across 1** transcend or take no account of (normal limitations, etc.). **2** (*their concern cuts across normal rivalries*). **2** see sense 10 of *v.* **cut and run** *sl.* run away. **cut and thrust 1** a lively interchange of argument, etc. **2** the use of both the edge and the point of a sword. **cut back 1** reduce (expenditure, etc.). **2** prune (a tree, etc.). **3** *Cinematog.* repeat part of a previous scene for dramatic effect. **cut both ways 1** serve both sides of an argument, etc. **2** (of an action) have both good and bad effects. **cut corners** do a task, etc., perfunctorily or incompletely, esp. to save time. **cut dead** *Brit.* completely refuse to recognize (a person). **cut down 1 a** bring or throw down by cutting. **b** kill by means of a sword or disease. **2** see sense 6 of *v.* **3** reduce the length of (*cut down the pants to make shorts*). **4** (often foll. by *on*) reduce one's consumption (*tried to cut down on chocolate*). **cut a person down to size** *colloq.* ruthlessly expose the limitations of a person's importance, ability, etc. **cut one's eyeteeth** (or **teeth**) attain worldly wisdom. **cut in 1** interrupt. **2** pull in too closely in front of another vehicle (esp. having overtaken it). **3** give a share of profits, etc., to (a person). **4** connect (a source of electricity). **5** join in a card game by taking the place of a player who cuts out. **6** interrupt a dancing couple to take over from one partner. **cut into 1** make a cut in (*they cut into the cake*). **2** interfere with and reduce (*traveling cuts into my free time*). **cut it fine** see FINE[1]. **cut it out** (usu. in *imper.*) *sl.* stop doing that (esp. quarreling). **cut loose 1** begin to act freely. **2** see sense 4 of *v.* **cut one's losses** abandon an unprofitable enterprise before losses become too great. **cut the mustard** *sl.* reach the required standard. **cut no ice** *sl.* **1** have no influence or importance. **2** achieve little or nothing. **cut off 1** remove (an appendage) by cutting. **2 a** (often in *passive*) bring to an abrupt end or (esp. early) death. **b** intercept; interrupt; prevent from continuing (*cut off supplies*). **c** disconnect (a person engaged in a telephone conversation) (*was suddenly cut off*). **3 a** prevent from traveling or venturing out (*was cut off by the snow*). **b** (as **cut off** *adj.*) isolated; remote (*felt cut off in the country*). **4 a** disinherit (*was cut off without a penny*). **b** sever a relationship (*was cut off from the children*). **cut out 1** remove from the inside by cutting. **2** make by cutting from a larger whole. **3** omit; leave out. **4** *colloq.* stop doing or using (something) (*managed to cut out chocolate; let's cut out the arguing*). **5** cease or cause to cease functioning (*the engine cut out*). **6** outdo or supplant (a rival). **7** detach (an animal) from the herd. **8** *Cards* be excluded from a card game as a result of cutting the deck. **9** *colloq.* prepare; plan (*has his work cut out*). **cut short 1** interrupt; terminate prematurely (*cut short his visit*). **2** make shorter or more concise. **cut one's teeth on** acquire initial practice or experience from (something). **cut a tooth** have it appear through the gum. **cut up 1** cut into pieces. **2** destroy utterly. **3** criticize severely. **4** behave in a comical or unruly manner. **have one's work cut out** see WORK. [ME *cutte, kitte, kette*, perh. f. OE *cyttan* (unrecorded)]

cut-and-dried *adj.* (also **cut-and-dry**) **1** completely decided; pre-arranged; inflexible. **2** (of opinions, etc.) ready-made; lacking freshness.

cu•ta•ne•ous /kyŏŏtáyneeəs/ *adj.* of the skin. [mod.L *cutaneus* f. L *cutis* skin]

cut•a•way /kútəway/ *adj.* **1** (of a diagram, etc.) with some parts left out to reveal the interior. **2** (of a coat) with the front below the waist cut away.

cut•back /kútbak/ *n.* an instance or the act of cutting back, esp. a reduction in expenditure.

cutch var. of COUCH².

cute /kyŏŏt/ *adj. colloq.* **1 a** attractive; quaint. **b** affectedly attractive. **2** clever; ingenious. □□ **cute•ly** *adv.* **cute•ness** *n.* [shortening of ACUTE]

cut glass *n.* glass that has been ornamented by having patterns cut into it by grinding and polishing.

cu•ti•cle /kyŏŏtikəl/ *n.* **1 a** the dead skin at the base of a fingernail or toenail. **b** the epidermis or other superficial skin. **2** *Bot.* a thin surface film on plants. □□ **cu•tic•u•lar** /–tíkyələr/ *adj.* [L *cuticula*, dimin. of *cutis* skin]

cut•ie /kyŏŏtee/ *n. sl.* an attractive or endearing person.

cut-in *n. Cinematog.* an insertion of another image, as a still photo, caption, etc., into motion picture footage.

cu•tis /kyŏŏtis/ *n. Anat.* the true skin or dermis, underlying the epidermis. [L, = skin]

cut•lass /kútləs/ *n.* a short sword with a slightly curved blade, esp. of the type formerly used by sailors. [F *coutelas* ult. f. L *cultellus*: see CUTLER]

cut•ler /kútlər/ *n.* a person who makes or deals in knives and similar utensils. [ME f. AF *cotillere*, OF *coutelier* f. *coutel* f. L *cultellus* dimin. of *culter* COLTER]

cut•ler•y /kútləree/ *n.* knives, forks, and spoons for use at table. [OF & F *coutel(l)erie* (as CUTLER)]

cut•let /kútlit/ *n.* **1** a small piece of veal, etc., for frying. **2** a flat cake of ground meat or nuts and breadcrumbs, etc. [F *côtelette*, OF *costelet* dimin. of *coste* rib f. L *costa*]

cutlass *(caption)*

cut•line /kútlīn/ *n.* **1** a caption to an illustration. **2** the line in squash above which a served ball must strike the wall.

cut•off /kútawf/ *n.* **1** the point at which something is cut off. **2** a device for stopping a flow. **3** a shortcut. **4** (in *pl.*) shorts made from jeans, etc., whose legs have been cut off.

cut•out /kútowt/ *n.* **1** a figure cut out of paper, etc. **2** a device for automatic disconnection, the release of exhaust gases, etc.

cut•out box *n.* = FUSE BOX.

cut•purse /kútpərs/ *n. archaic* a pickpocket; a thief.

cut-rate *adj.* **1** selling or sold at a reduced price (*cut-rate tickets*). **2** offering goods at reduced prices (*a cut-rate furniture store*).

cut•ter /kútər/ *n.* **1** a tailor, etc., who takes measurements and cuts cloth. **2** *Naut.* **a** a small, fast sailing ship. **b** a small boat carried by a large ship. **3** *Cricket* a ball turning sharply on pitching. **4** a light horse-drawn sleigh.

cut•throat /kútthrōt/ *n. & adj.* **•** *n.* **1** a murderer. **2** *Brit.* (in full **cut•throat razor**) a straight-edge razor. **3** a species of trout, *Salmo clarki*, with a red mark under the jaw. **•** *adj.* **1** (of competition) ruthless and intense. **2** (of a person) murderous. **3** (of a card game) three-handed.

cut•ting /kúting/ *n. & adj.* **•** *n.* **1** a piece cut from a plant for propagation. **2** an excavated channel through high ground for a railroad or road. **•** *adj.* see CUT *v.* 5. □□ **cut•ting•ly** *adv.*

cut•ting edge *n.* the forefront; the vanguard (*the cutting edge in compact disc reproduction*).

cut•tle /kútl/ *n.* **1** = CUTTLEFISH. **2** = CUTTLEBONE.

cut•tle•bone /kútlbōn/ *n.* the internal shell of the cuttlefish crushed and used for polishing teeth, etc., or as a supplement to the diet of a cage bird. [OE *cudele*, ME *codel*, rel. to *cod* bag, with ref. to its ink-bag]

cut•tle•fish /kútlfish/ *n.* any marine cephalopod mollusk of the genera *Sepia* and *Sepiola*, having ten arms and ejecting a black fluid when threatened or pursued.

cut•ty /kútee/ *adj. & n. Sc. & No. of Engl.* **•** *adj.* cut short; abnormally short. **•** *n.* (*pl.* **•ties**) a short tobacco pipe.

cut•ty stool *n. Scot. hist.* a stool on which an offender was publicly rebuked during a church service.

cut-up /kútup/ *n.* a person who clowns around; prankster.

cut•wa•ter /kútwawtər, –woter/ *n.* **1** the forward edge of a ship's prow. **2** a wedge-shaped projection from a pier or bridge.

cut•worm /kútwərm/ *n.* any of various caterpillars that eat through the stems of young plants level with the ground.

cu•vée /kyŏŏváy/ *n.* a blend or batch of wine. [F, = vatful f. *cuve* cask f. L *cupa*]

cu•vette /kŏŏvét, kyŏŏ–/ *n.* a shallow vessel for liquid. [F, dimin. of *cuve* cask f. L *cupa*]

c.v. *abbr.* curriculum vitae.

cwm /kŏŏm/ *n.* **1** (in Wales) = COOMB. **2** *Geog.* a cirque. [Welsh]

cwo *abbr.* **1** chief warrant officer. **2** cash with order.

cwt. *abbr.* hundredweight.

-cy /see/ *suffix* (see also –ACY, –ANCY, –CRACY, –ENCY, –MANCY). **1** denoting state or condition (*bankruptcy*; *idiocy*). **2** denoting rank or status (*captaincy*). [from or after L –*cia*, –*tia*, Gk –*k(e)ia*, –*t(e)ia*]

cy•an /sían/ *adj. & n.* **•** *adj.* of a greenish-blue. **•** *n.* a greenish-blue color. [Gk *kuan(e)os* dark blue]

cy•an•a•mide /sīánəmīd, mīd/ *n. Chem.* a colorless crystalline amide of cyanogen; any salt of this, esp. the calcium one which is used as a fertilizer. ¶ Chem. formula: CH_2N_2. [CYANOGEN + AMIDE]

cy•an•ic ac•id /siánik/ *n.* an unstable, colorless, pungent acid gas. ¶ Chem. formula: HCNO. [CYANOGEN]

cy•a•nide /síənīd/ *n.* any of the highly poisonous salts or esters of hydrocyanic acid, esp. the potassium salt used in the extraction of gold and silver. [CYANOGEN + –IDE]

cy•a•no•bac•te•ri•um /síənōbakteéreeəm, sīánō–/ *n.* any prokaryotic organism of the division Cyanobacteria, found in many environments and capable of photosynthesizing. Also called **blue-green alga**. [CYANOGEN + BACTERIUM]

cy•a•no•co•bal•a•min /síənōkōbálǝmin, sīánō–/ *n.* a vitamin of the B complex, found in foods of animal origin such as liver, fish, and eggs, a deficiency of which can cause pernicious anemia. Also called **vitamin B$_{12}$**. [CYANOGEN + *cobalamin* f. COBALT + VITAMIN]

cy•a•no•gen /síánəjən/ *n. Chem.* a colorless, highly poisonous gas intermediate in the preparation of many fertilizers. ¶ Chem. formula: C_2N_2. [F *cyanogène* f. Gk *kuanos* dark-blue mineral, as being a constituent of Prussian blue]

cy•a•no•sis /síənósis/ *n. Med.* a bluish discoloration of the skin due to the presence of oxygen-deficient blood. □□ **cy•a•not•ic** /–nótik/ *adj.* [mod.L f. Gk *kuanōsis* blueness (as CYANOGEN)]

cy•ber•na•tion /síbərnáyshən/ *n.* control by machines. □□ **cy•ber•nate** *v. tr.* [CYBERNETICS + –ATION]

cy•ber•net•ics /síbərnétiks/ *n.pl.* (usu. treated as *sing.*) the science of communications and automatic control systems in both machines and living things. □□ **cy•ber•net•ic** *adj.* **cy•ber•ne•ti•cian** /–nítishən/ *n.* **cy•ber•net•i•cist** /–tisist/ *n.* [Gk *kubernētēs* steersman]

cy•ber•space /síbərspays/ *n.* an environment in which information exchange by computer occurs.

cy•borg /síbawrg/ *n.* (in science fiction) a human being whose biological functions are bionically enhanced. [*cyb*ernetic *org*anism]

cy•cad /síkad/ *n. Bot.* any of the palmlike plants of the order Cycadales (including fossil forms) inhabiting tropical and subtropical regions and often growing to a great height. [mod.L *cycas*, *cycad*- f. supposed Gk *kukas*, scribal error for *koikas*, pl. of *koix* Egyptian palm]

Cy•clad•ic /síkládik, see–/ *adj.* of the Cyclades, a group of islands east of the Greek mainland, esp. of the Bronze Age civilization that flourished there. [*Cyclades*, L f. Gk *Kuklades* f. *kuklos* circle (of islands)]

cy•cla•mate /síkləmayt, sík–/ *n.* any of various salts or esters of sulfamic acid formerly used as artificial sweetening agents. [Chem. name *cyclohexylsulfamate*]

cy•cla•men /síkləmən, sík–/ *n.* **1** any plant of the genus *Cyclamen*, originating in Europe, having pink, red, or white flowers with reflexed petals, often grown in pots. **2** the shade of color of the red or pink cyclamen flower. [med.L f. Gk *kuklaminos*, perh. f. *kuklos* circle, with ref. to its bulbous roots]

cy•cle /síkəl/ *n. & v.* **•** *n.* **1 a** a recurrent round or period (of events, phenomena, etc.). **b** the time needed for one such round or period. **2 a** *Physics*, etc., a recurrent series of operations or states. **b** *Electr.* = HERTZ. **3** a series of songs, poems, etc., usu. on a single theme. **4** a bicycle, tricycle, or similar machine. **•** *v.intr.* **1** ride a bicycle, etc. **2** move in cycles. [ME f. OF, or f. LL *cyclus* f. Gk *kuklos* circle]

cy•clic /síklik, sík–/ *adj.* **1 a** recurring in cycles. **b** belonging to a chronological cycle. **2** *Chem.* with constituent atoms forming a ring. **3** of a cycle of songs, etc. **4** *Bot.* (of a flower) with its parts arranged in whorls. **5** *Math.* of a circle or cycle. [F *cyclique* or L *cyclicus* f. Gk *kuklikos* (as CYCLE)]

cy•cli•cal /síklikəl, sík–/ *adj.* = CYCLIC 1. □□ **cy•cli•cal•ly** *adv.*

cy•clist /síklist/ *n.* a rider of a bicycle.

cyclo- /síklō/ *comb. form* circle, cycle, or cyclic (*cyclometer*; *cyclorama*). [Gk *kuklos* circle]

cy•clo•al•kane /síklō-álkayn/ *n. Chem.* a saturated cyclic hydrocarbon.

cy•clo•graph /síkləgraf/ *n.* an instrument for tracing circular arcs.

cy•clo•hex•ane /síklōhéksayn/ *n. Chem.* a colorless liquid cycloalkane used as a solvent and paint remover. ¶ Chem. formula: C_6H_{12}.

cy•cloid /síkloyd/ *n. Math.* a curve traced by a point on a circle when the circle is rolled along a straight line. □□ **cy•cloi•dal** /–klóyd'l/ *adj.* [Gk *kukloeidēs* (as CYCLE, –OID)]

cy·clom·e·ter /síklómitər/ *n.* **1** an instrument for measuring circular arcs. **2** an instrument for measuring the distance traversed by a bicycle, etc.

cy·clone /síklōn/ *n.* **1** a system of winds rotating inward to an area of low barometric pressure; a depression. **2** a violent hurricane of limited diameter. □□ **cy·clon·ic** /–klónik/ *adj.* **cy·clon·i·cal·ly** *adv.* [prob. repr. Gk *kuklōma* wheel, coil of a snake]

cy·clo·par·af·fin /síklōpárəfin/ *n. Chem.* = CYCLOALKANE.

cy·clo·pe·an /síkləpeeən, –klópeeən/ *adj.* (also **Cy·clo·pe·an**) **1** (of ancient masonry) made with massive irregular blocks. **2** of or resembling a Cyclops.

cy·clo·pe·di·a /síkləpeedeeə/ *n.* (also esp. *Brit.* **cy·clo·pae·di·a**) an encyclopedia. □□ **cy·clo·pe·dic** *adj.* [shortening of ENCYCLOPEDIA]

cy·clo·pro·pane /síklōprópayn/ *n. Chem.* a colorless, gaseous cycloalkane used as a general anesthetic. ¶ *Chem.* formula: C_3H_6.

Cy·clops /síklops/ *n.* **1** (*pl.* **Cy·clopes** /síklópeez/) (in Greek mythology) a member of a race of one-eyed giants. **2** (**cyclops**) (*pl.* **cy·clops** or **cy·clopes**) *Zool.* a crustacean of the genus *Cyclops*, with a single central eye. [L f. Gk *Kuklōps* f. *kuklos* circle + *ōps* eye]

cy·clo·ram·a /síklərámə, -raámə/ *n.* a circular panorama, curved wall, or cloth at the rear of a stage, esp. one used to represent the sky. □□ **cy·clo·ram·ic** /–rámik/ *adj.*

cy·clo·stome /síkləstōm/ *n.* any fishlike, jawless vertebrate of the subclass Cyclostomata, having a large sucking mouth, e.g., a lamprey. □□ **cy·clos·to·mate** /–klóstəmayt, –mət/ *adj.* [CYCLO- + Gk *stoma* mouth]

cy·clo·style /síkləstīl/ *n. & v.* ● *n.* an apparatus for printing copies of writing from a stencil. ● *v.tr.* print or reproduce with this.

cy·clo·thy·mi·a /síkləthímeeə/ *n. Psychol.* a disorder characterized by the occurrence of marked swings of mood from cheerfulness to misery. □□ **cy·clo·thy·mic** *adj.* [CYCLO- + Gk *thumos* temper]

cy·clo·tron /síklətron/ *n. Physics* an apparatus in which charged atomic and subatomic particles are accelerated by an alternating electric field while following an outward spiral or circular path in a magnetic field.

cy·der *Brit.* var. of CIDER.

cyg·net /sígnit/ *n.* a young swan. [ME f. AF *cignet* dimin. of OF *cigne* swan f. med.L *cycnus* f. Gk *kuknos*]

cyl. *abbr.* cylinder.

cyl·in·der /sílindər/ *n.* **1 a** a uniform solid or hollow body with straight sides and a circular section. **b** a thing of this shape, e.g., a container for liquefied gas. **2** a cylinder-shaped part of various machines, esp. a piston chamber in an engine. **3** *Printing* a metal roller. □□ **cy·lin·dri·cal** /silíndrikəl/ *adj.* **cy·lin·dri·cal·ly** *adv.* [L *cylindrus* f. Gk *kulindros* f. *kulindō* roll]

cyl·in·der seal *n. Antiq.* a small barrel-shaped object of stone or baked clay bearing a cuneiform inscription, esp. for use as a seal.

cy·ma /símə/ *n.* **1** *Archit.* an ogee molding of a cornice. **2** = CYME. [mod.L f. Gk *kuma* wave, wavy molding]

cym·bal /símbəl/ *n.* a musical instrument consisting of a concave brass or bronze plate, struck with another or with a stick, etc., to make a ringing sound. □□ **cym·bal·ist** *n.* [ME f. L *cymbalum* f. Gk *kumbalon* f. *kumbē* cup]

cym·ba·lom /símbələm/ *n.* (also **cim·ba·lom**) a dulcimer. [Magyar f. It. *cembalo*]

cym·bid·i·um /simbídeeəm/ *n.* any tropical orchid of the genus *Cymbidium*, with a recess in the flower lip. [mod.L f. Gk *kumbē* cup]

cymbals

cym·bi·form /símbifawrm/ *adj. Anat. & Bot.* boat-shaped. [L *cymba* f. Gk *kumbē* boat + –FORM]

cyme /sīm/ *n. Bot.* an inflorescence in which the primary axis bears a single terminal flower that develops first, the system being continued by the axes of secondary and higher orders each with a flower (cf. RACEME). □□ **cy·mose** *adj.* [F, var. of *cime* summit, ult. f. Gk *kuma* wave]

Cym·ric /kímrik, sím–/ *adj.* Welsh. [Welsh *Cymru* Wales]

cyn·ic /sínik/ *n. & adj.* ● *n.* **1** a person who has little faith in human sincerity and goodness. **2** (**Cynic**) one of a school of ancient Greek philosophers founded by Antisthenes, marked by ostentatious contempt for ease and pleasure. ● *adj.* **1** (**Cynic**) of the Cynics. **2** = CYNICAL. □□ **cyn·i·cism** /–nisizəm/ *n.* [L *cynicus* f. Gk *kunikos* f. *kuōn kunos* dog, nickname for a Cynic]

cyn·i·cal /sínikəl/ *adj.* **1** of or characteristic of a cynic; incredulous of human goodness. **2** (of behavior, etc.) disregarding normal standards. **3** sneering; mocking. □□ **cyn·i·cal·ly** *adv.*

cyn·o·ceph·a·lus /sínōséfələs/ *n.* **1** a fabled dog-headed man. **2** any flying lemur of the genus *Cynocephalus*, native to SE Asia. [Gk *kunokephalos* f. *kuōn kunos* dog + *kephalē* head]

cy·no·sure /sínəshŏŏr, sin–/ *n.* **1** a center of attraction or admiration. **2** a guiding star. [F *cynosure* or L *cynosura* f. Gk *kunosoura* dog's tail, Ursa Minor f. *kuōn kunos* dog + *oura* tail]

cy·pher var. of CIPHER.

cy pres /seé práy/ *adv. & adj. Law* as near as possible to the testator's or donor's intentions when these cannot be precisely followed. [AF, = *si près* so near]

cy·press /síprəs/ *n.* **1** any coniferous tree of the genus *Cupressus* or *Chamaecyparis*, with hard wood and dark foliage. **2** this, or branches from it, as a symbol of mourning. [ME f. OF *cipres* f. LL *cypressus* f. Gk *kuparissos*]

Cyp·ri·an /sípreeən/ *n. & adj.* = CYPRIOT. [L *Cyprius* of Cyprus]

cyp·ri·noid /síprinoyd/ *adj. & n.* ● *adj.* of or like a carp. ● *n.* a carp or related fish. [L *cyprinus* f. Gk *kuprinos* carp]

Cyp·ri·ot /sípreeət/ *n. & adj.* (also **Cyp·ri·ote** /–ōt/) ● *n.* a native or national of Cyprus. ● *adj.* of Cyprus. [Gk *Kupriōtes* f. *Kupros* Cyprus in E. Mediterranean]

cyp·ri·pe·di·um /sípripeédeeəm/ *n.* any orchid of the genus *Cypripedium*, esp. the lady's slipper. [mod.L f. Gk *Kupris* Aphrodite + *pedilon* slipper]

cyp·se·la /sipsilə/ *n.* (*pl.* **cyp·se·lae** /–lee/) *Bot.* a dry single-seeded fruit formed from a double ovary of which only one develops into a seed, characteristic of the daisy family Compositae. [mod.L f. Gk *kupselē* hollow vessel]

Cy·ril·lic /sirílik/ *adj. & n.* ● *adj.* denoting the alphabet used by the Slavonic peoples of the Orthodox Church; now used esp. for Russian and Bulgarian. ● *n.* this alphabet. [St. *Cyril* d. 869, its reputed inventor]

cyst /sist/ *n.* **1** *Med.* a sac containing morbid matter, a parasitic larva, etc. **2** *Biol.* **a** a hollow organ, bladder, etc., in an animal or plant, containing a liquid secretion. **b** a cell or cavity enclosing reproductive bodies, an embryo, parasite, microorganism, etc. [LL *cystis* f. Gk *kustis* bladder]

cys·te·ine /sístee-een, –tee-in/ *n. Biochem.* a sulfur-containing amino acid, essential in the human diet and a constituent of many enzymes. [*cystine* (rel to CYST)+ –*eine* (var. of –INE[4])]

cys·tic /sístik/ *adj.* **1** of the urinary bladder. **2** of the gallbladder. **3** of the nature of a cyst. [F *cystique* or mod.L *cysticus* (as CYST)]

cys·tic fi·bro·sis *n. Med.* a hereditary disease affecting the exocrine glands and usu. resulting in respiratory infections.

cys·ti·tis /sistítis/ *n.* an inflammation of the urinary bladder, often caused by infection, and usu. accompanied by frequent painful urination.

cysto- /sístō/ *comb. form* the urinary bladder (*cystoscope; cystotomy*). [Gk *kustē, kustis* bladder]

cys·to·scope /sístəskōp/ *n.* an instrument inserted in the urethra for examining the urinary bladder. □□ **cys·to·scop·ic** /–skópik/ *adj.* **cys·tos·co·py** /sístóskəpee/ *n.*

cys·tot·o·my /sistótəmee/ *n.* (*pl.* **·mies**) a surgical incision into the urinary bladder.

-cyte /sīt/ *comb. form Biol.* a mature cell (*leukocyte*) (cf. –BLAST). [Gk *kutos* vessel]

cyt·i·dine /sítideen/ *n.* a nucleoside obtained from RNA by hydrolysis. [G *Cytidin* (as –CYTE)]

cyto- /sítō/ *comb. form Biol.* cells or a cell. [as –CYTE]

cy·to·chrome /sítəkrōm/ *n. Biochem.* a compound consisting of a protein linked to a heme, which is involved in electron transfer reactions.

cy·to·ge·net·ics /sítōjinétiks/ *n.* the study of inheritance in relation to the structure and function of cells. □□ **cy·to·ge·net·ic** *adj.* **cy·to·ge·net·i·cal** *adj.* **cy·to·ge·net·i·cal·ly** *adv.* **cy·to·ge·net·i·cist** /–néti-sist/ *n.*

cy·tol·o·gy /sītóləjee/ *n.* the study of cells. □□ **cy·to·log·i·cal** /sítəlójikəl/ *adj.* **cy·to·log·i·cal·ly** *adv.* **cy·tol·o·gist** *n.*

cy·to·plasm /sítəplazəm/ *n.* the protoplasmic content of a cell apart from its nucleus. □□ **cy·to·plas·mic** /–plázmik/ *adj.*

cy·to·sine /sítəseen/ *n.* one of the principal component bases of the nucleotides and the nucleic acids DNA and RNA, derived from pyrimidine.

cy·to·tox·ic /sítətóksik/ *adj.* toxic to cells.

czar /zaar/ *n.* (also **tsar**) **1** *hist.* the title of the former emperor of Russia. **2** a person with great authority. □□ **czar·dom** *n.* **czar·ism** *n.* **czar·ist** *n.* [Russ. *tsar'*, ult. f. L *Caesar*]

czar·das /chaárdaash/ *n.* (also **csar·das**) (*pl.* same) a Hungarian dance with a slow start and a quick, wild finish. [Magyar *csárdás* f. *csárda* inn]

czar·e·vich /zaárivich/ *n.* (also **tsar·e·vich**) *hist.* the eldest son of an emperor of Russia. [Russ. *tsarevich* son of a czar]

cza·ri·na /zaareénə/ *n.* (also **tsa·ri·na**) *hist.* the title of the former empress of Russia. [It. & Sp. *(c)zarina* f. G *Czarin, Zarin,* fem. of *Czar, Zar*]

Czech /chek/ *n. & adj.* ● *n.* **1** a native or national of the Czech Republic, Bohemia, or (*hist.*) Czechoslovakia. **2** the West Slavonic language of the Czech people. ● *adj.* of or relating to the Czechs or their language. [Pol. spelling of Bohemian *Čech*]

Czech·o·slo·vak /chékəslóvak, -vaak/ *n. & adj.* (also **Czech·o·slo·va·ki·an** /–sləvaákeeən/) ● *n.* a native or national of Czechoslovakia, a former nation in central Europe including Bohemia, Moravia, and Slovakia. ● *adj.* of or relating to Czechoslovaks or the former nation of Czechoslovakia. [CZECH + SLOVAK]

D

D¹ /dee/ *n.* (also **d**) (*pl.* **ds** or **D's**) **1** the fourth letter of the alphabet. **2** *Mus.* the second note of the diatonic scale of C major. **3** (as a Roman numeral) 500. **4** = DEE. **5** the fourth highest class or category (of academic marks, etc.).

D² *symb. Chem.* the element deuterium.

D³ *abbr.* (also **D.**) **1** Democrat. **2** dimension (*3-D*).

d. *abbr.* **1** died. **2** departs. **3** delete. **4** daughter. **5** *Brit.* (predecimal) penny. **6** depth. **7** deci–. [sense 5 f. L *denarius* silver coin]

'd *v. colloq.* (usu. after pronouns) had; would (*I'd; he'd*). [abbr.]

DA *abbr.* **1** district attorney. **2** *sl.* = DUCK'S ASS.

D/A *abbr. Computing* digital to analog.

da *abbr.* deca–.

dab¹ /dab/ *v. & n.* ● *v.* (**dabbed, dab·bing**) **1** *tr.* press (a surface) briefly with a cloth, sponge, etc., without rubbing, esp. in cleaning or to apply a substance. **2** *tr.* press (a sponge, etc.) lightly on a surface. **3** *tr.* (foll. by *on*) apply (a substance) by dabbing a surface. **4** *intr.* (usu. foll. by *at*) aim a feeble blow; tap. **5** *tr.* strike lightly; tap. ● *n.* **1** a brief application of a cloth, sponge, etc., to a surface without rubbing. **2** a small amount of something applied in this way (*a dab of paint*). **3** a light blow or tap. **4** (in *pl.*) *Brit. sl.* fingerprints. □□ **dab·ber** *n.* [ME, imit.]

dab² /dab/ *n.* any flatfish of the genus *Limanda*. [15th c.: orig. unkn.]

dab·ble /dábəl/ *v.* **1** *intr.* (usu. foll. by *in, at*) take a casual or superficial interest or part (in a subject or activity). **2** *intr.* move the feet, hands, etc., about in (usu. a small amount of) liquid. **3** *tr.* wet partly or intermittently; moisten; stain; splash. □□ **dab·bler** *n.* [16th c.: f. Du. *dabbelen* or DAB¹]

dab·chick /dábchik/ *n.* = *little grebe* (see GREBE). [16th c., in earlier forms *dap-, dop-*: perh. rel. to OE *dūfedoppa*, DEEP, DIP]

dab hand /dab/ *n.* esp. *Brit. colloq.* (usu. foll. by *at*) a person especially skilled (in) (*a dab hand at cooking*). [17th c.: orig. unkn.]

da ca·po /daa kaápō/ *adv. Mus.* repeat from the beginning. [It.]

dace /days/ *n.* (*pl.* same) any small freshwater fish, esp. of the genus *Leuciscus*, related to the carp. [OF *dars*: see DART]

da·cha /daáchə/ *n.* a country house or cottage in Russia. [Russ., = gift]

dachs·hund /daáks-hŏont, daák-sənt/ *n.* **1** a dog of a short-legged, long-bodied breed. **2** this breed. [G, = badger dog]

da·coit /dəkóyt/ *n.* (in India or Burma) a member of a band of armed robbers. [Hindi *ḍakait* f. *ḍākā* gang-robbery]

Da·cron /dáykron/ *n. Trademark* a synthetic polyester fiber used in textiles.

dachshund

dac·tyl /dáktil/ *n.* a metrical foot (‾ ˘ ˘) consisting of one long (or stressed) syllable followed by two short (or unstressed). [ME f. L *dactylus* f. Gk *daktulos* finger, the three bones corresponding to the three syllables]

dac·tyl·ic /daktílik/ *adj. & n.* ● *adj.* of or using dactyls. ● *n.* (usu. in *pl.*) dactylic verse. [L *dactylicus* f. Gk *daktulikos* (as DACTYL)]

dac·tyl·ic hex·am·e·ter *n.* a hexameter having five dactyls and a spondee or trochee, any of the first four feet, and sometimes the fifth, being replaceable by a spondee.

dad /dad/ *n. colloq.* father. [perh. imit. of a child's *da, da* (cf. DADDY)]

Da·da /daádaa/ *n.* an early 20th-c. international movement in art, literature, music, and film, repudiating and mocking artistic and social conventions. □□ **Da·da·ism** /daádəizəm/ *n.* **Da·da·ist** *n. & adj.* **Da·da·is·tic** *adj.* [F (the title of an early 20th-c. review) f. *dada* hobby-horse]

dad·dy /dádee/ *n.* (*pl.* **-dies**) *colloq.* **1** father. **2** (usu. foll. by *of*) the oldest or supreme example (*had a daddy of a headache*). [DAD + –Y³]

dad·dy long·legs *n.* an arachnid of the order Opiliones, with long, thin, bent legs. Also called **harvestman**.

da·do /dáydō/ *n.* (*pl.* **-dos**) **1** the lower part of the wall of a room when visually distinct from the upper part. **2** the plinth of a column. **3** the cube of a pedestal between the base and the cornice. [It., = DIE²]

dae·mon var. of DEMON¹ 5.

dae·mon·ic var. of DEMONIC.

daff /daf/ *n. colloq.* = DAFFODIL. [abbr.]

daf·fo·dil /dáfədil/ *n.* **1 a** a bulbous plant, *Narcissus pseudonarcissus,* with a yellow trumpet-shaped crown. **b** any of various other large-flowered plants of the genus *Narcissus.* **c** a flower of any of these plants. **2** a pale-yellow color. [earlier *affodill,* as ASPHODEL]

daf·fy /dáfee/ *adj.* (**daf·fi·er, daf·fi·est**) *sl.* = DAFT. □□ **daf·fi·ly** *adv.* **daf·fi·ness** *n.* [*daff* simpleton + –Y²]

daft /daft/ *adj. colloq.* **1** silly; foolish; crazy. **2** (foll. by *about*) fond of; infatuated with. □□ **daft·ly** *adv.* **daft·ness** *n.* [ME *daffte* = OE *gedæfte* mild, meek, f. Gmc]

dag¹ /dag/ *n. & v. Austral. & NZ* ● *n.* (usu. in *pl.*) a lock of wool clotted with dung on the hinder parts of a sheep. ● *v.tr.* (**dagged, dag·ging**) remove dags from (a sheep). □ **rattle one's dags** *sl.* hurry up. □□ **dag·ger** *n.* [orig. Engl. dial.]

daffodil 1

dag² /dag/ *n. Austral. & NZ sl.* an eccentric or noteworthy person; a character (*he's a bit of a dag*). [orig. Engl. dial., = a dare, challenge]

dag·ga /dágə/ *n. S.Afr.* **1** hemp used as a narcotic. **2** any plant of the genus *Leontis* used similarly. [Afrik. f. Hottentot *dachab*]

dag·ger /dágər/ *n.* **1** a short stabbing weapon with a pointed and edged blade. **2** *Printing* = OBELUS. □ **at daggers drawn** in bitter enmity. **look daggers at** glare angrily or venomously at. [ME, perh. f. obs. *dag* pierce, infl. by OF *dague* long dagger]

da·go /dáygō/ *n.* (*pl.* **-gos** or **-goes**) *sl. offens.* a person of Italian, Spanish, or Portuguese ancestry. [Sp. *Diego* = James]

da·guerre·o·type /dəgérətip/ *n.* **1** a photograph taken by an early photographic process employing an iodine-sensitized silvered plate and mercury vapor. **2** this process. [L. *Daguerre,* Fr. inventor d. 1851]

dagger 1

dah /daa/ *n. Telegraphy* (in the Morse system) = DASH (cf. DIT). [imit.]

dahl·ia /dályə, daál–, dáyl–/ *n.* any composite garden plant of the genus *Dahlia,* of Mexican origin, cultivated for its many-colored single or double flowers. [A. *Dahl,* Sw. botanist d. 1789]

Dáil /doyl/ *n.* (in full **Dáil Éireann** /áirən/) the lower House of Parliament in the Republic of Ireland. [Ir., = assembly (of Ireland)]

dai·ly /dáylee/ *adj., adv., & n.* ● *adj.* **1** done, produced, or occurring every day or every weekday. **2** constant; regular. **3** from day to day. **2** constantly. ● *n.* (*pl.* **-lies**) *colloq.* **1** a daily newspaper. **2** *Brit.* a cleaning woman or domestic help working daily. [ME f. DAY + –LY¹, –LY²]

dai·ly bread *n.* necessary food; a livelihood.

dai·ly doz·en *n. colloq.* regular exercises, esp. on rising.

dai·mon /dímōn/ *n.* = DEMON¹ 5. □□ **dai·mon·ic** /–mónik/ *adj.* [Gk, = deity]

dain·ty /dáyntee/ *adj. & n.* ● *adj.* (**dain·ti·er, dain·ti·est**) **1** delicately pretty. **2** delicate of build or in movement. **3** (of food) choice. **4** fastidious; having delicate taste and sensibility. ● *n.* (*pl.* **-ties**) a choice morsel; a delicacy. □□ **dain·ti·ly** *adv.* **dain·ti·ness** *n.* [AF *dainté,* OF *daintié, deintié* f. L *dignitas –tatis* f. *dignus* worthy]

dai·qui·ri /dákəree, dí–/ *n.* (*pl.* **dai·qui·ris**) a cocktail of rum, lime juice, etc. [*Daiquiri* in Cuba]

dair·y /dáiree/ *n.* (*pl.* **-ies**) **1** a building or room for the storage, processing, and distribution of milk and its products. **2** a store where milk and milk products are sold. **3** (*attrib.*) **a** of, containing, or concerning milk and its products (and sometimes eggs). **b** used for dairy products (*dairy cow*). [ME *deierie* f. *deie* maidservant f. OE *dǣge* kneader of dough]

dair·y·ing /dáireeing/ *n.* the business of producing, storing, and distributing milk and its products.

dair·y·maid /dáireemayd/ *n.* a woman employed in a dairy.

dair·y·man /dáireemən/ *n.* (*pl.* **-men**) **1** a person dealing in dairy products. **2** a person employed in a dairy.

da·is /dáyis, dí–, days/ *n.* a low platform, usu. at the upper end of a hall and used to support a table, lectern, etc. [ME f. OF *deis* f. L *discus* disk, dish, in med.L = table]

dai·sy /dáyzee/ *n. (pl.* **·sies) 1 a** a small composite plant, *Bellis perennis*, bearing flowers each with a yellow disk and white rays. **b** any other plant with daisylike flowers, esp. the larger oxeye daisy, the Michaelmas daisy, or the Shasta daisy. **2** *sl.* a first-rate specimen of anything. □ **pushing up daisies** *sl.* dead and buried. [OE *dæges ēage* day's eye, the flower opening in the morning]

dai·sy-chain *v.tr. Computing* connect (several devices) together in a linear series.

dai·sy chain *n.* **1** a string of daisies threaded together. **2** *sl.* a sexual activity in which participants serve as partners to different people simultaneously.

dai·sy wheel *n.* a disk of spokes extending radially from a central hub, each terminating in a printing character, used as a printer in word processors and typewriters.

Dak. *abbr.* Dakota.

Da·ko·ta /dəkṓtə/ *n.* **1 a** a N. American people native to the northern Mississippi valley. **b** a member of this people. **2** the language of this people. Also called **Lakota** or **Sioux.** □□ **Da·ko·tan** *adj.*

dal /daal/ *n.* (also **dhal) 1** a kind of split pulse, a common foodstuff in India. **2** a dish made with this. [Hindi]

Da·lai la·ma /dáalī láamə/ *n.* the spiritual head of Tibetan Buddhism, formerly also the chief ruler of Tibet (see LAMA). [Mongolian *dalai* ocean; see LAMA]

dale /dayl/ *n.* a valley, esp. a broad one. [OE *dæl* f. Gmc]

dales·man /dáylzmən/ *n. (pl.* **·men)** an inhabitant of the dales in Northern England.

dal·li·ance /dáleeəns, –yəns/ *n.* **1** a leisurely or frivolous passing of time. **2** the act or an instance of lighthearted flirting. [DALLY + –ANCE]

dal·ly /dálee/ *v.intr.* (**·lies, ·lied) 1** delay; waste time, esp. frivolously. **2** (often foll. by *with*) play about; flirt; treat frivolously (*dallied with her affections*). □ **dally away** waste or fritter (one's time, life, etc.). [ME f. OF *dalier* chat]

Dal·ma·tian /dalmáyshən/ *n.* **1** a dog of a large, white, short-haired breed with dark spots. **2** this breed. [*Dalmatia* in Croatia]

dal·mat·ic /dalmátik/ *n.* a wide-sleeved, long, loose vestment open at the sides, worn by deacons and bishops, and by a monarch at his or her coronation. [ME f. OF *dalmatique* or LL *dalmatica (vestis* robe) of Dalmatia]

Dalmatian

dal se·gno /daal sáynyō/ *adv. Mus.* repeat from the point marked by a sign. [It., = from the sign]

dal·ton·ism /dáwltənizəm/ *n.* color blindness, esp. a congenital inability to distinguish between red and green. [F *daltonisme* f. J. *Dalton*, Engl. chemist d. 1844, who suffered from it]

dam¹ /dam/ *n. & v.* ● *n.* **1** a barrier constructed to hold back water and raise its level, forming a reservoir or preventing flooding. **2** a barrier constructed in a stream by a beaver. **3** anything functioning as a dam does. **4** a causeway. ● *v.tr.* (**dammed, dam·ming) 1** furnish or confine with a dam. **2** (often foll. by *up*) block up; hold back; obstruct. [ME f. MLG, MDu.]

dam² /dam/ *n.* the female parent of an animal, esp. a four-footed one. [ME: var. of DAME]

dam·age /dámij/ *n. & v.* ● *n.* **1** harm or injury impairing the value or usefulness of something, or the health or normal function of a person. **2** (in *pl.*) *Law* a sum of money claimed or awarded in compensation for a loss or an injury. **3** the loss of what is desirable. **4** (prec. by *the*) *sl.* cost (*what's the damage?*). ● *v.tr.* **1** inflict damage on. **2** (esp. as **damaging** *adj.*) detract from the reputation of (*a most damaging admission*). □□ **dam·ag·ing·ly** *adv.* [ME f. OF *damage* (n.), *damagier* (v.), f. *dam(me)* loss f. L *damnum* loss, damage]

dam·a·scene /dáməseén/ *v., n., & adj.* ● *v.tr.* decorate (metal, esp. iron or steel) by etching or inlaying, esp. with gold or silver, or with a watered pattern produced in welding. ● *n.* a design or article produced in this way. ● *adj.* of, relating to, or produced by this process. [*Damascene* of Damascus, f. L *Damascenus* f. Gk *Damaskēnos*]

dam·ask /dáməsk/ *n., adj., & v.* ● *n.* **1 a** a figured woven fabric (esp. silk or linen) with a pattern visible on both sides. **b** twilled table linen with woven designs shown by the reflection of light. **2** a tablecloth made of this material. **3** *hist.* steel with a watered pattern produced in welding. ● *adj.* **1** made of or resembling damask. **2** colored like a damask rose, velvety pink or vivid red. ● *v.tr.* **1** weave with figured designs. **2** = DAMASCENE *v.* **3** ornament. [ME, ult. f. L *Damascus*]

dam·ask rose *n.* an old sweet-scented variety of rose, with very soft velvety petals, used to make attar.

dame /daym/ *n.* **1 (Dame) a** (in the UK) the title given to a woman with the rank of Knight Commander or holder of the Grand Cross in the Orders of Chivalry. **b** a woman holding this title. **2** *Brit.* a comic middle-aged woman in modern pantomime, usu. played by a man. **3** *archaic* a mature woman. **4** *sl.* a woman. [ME f. OF f. L *domina* mistress]

dame school *n. hist.* a small primary school run by an elderly woman, esp. in her own home.

dam·fool /dámfōol/ *n. & adj. colloq.* ● *n.* a foolish or stupid person. ● *adj.* (also **dam·fool·ish** /dámfōolish/) foolish; stupid. [DAMN + FOOL¹]

dam·mar /dámər/ *n.* **1** any E. Asian tree, esp. one of the genus *Agathis* or *Shorea*, yielding a resin used in making varnish. **2** this resin. [Malay *damar*]

dam·mit /dámit/ *int.* damn it.

damn /dam/ *v., n., adj., & adv.* ● *v.tr.* **1** (often *absol.* or as *int.* of anger or annoyance, = *may God damn*) curse (a person or thing). **2** doom to hell; cause the damnation of. **3** condemn; censure (*a reviewing damning the performance*). **4 a** (often as **damning** *adj.*) (of a circumstance, piece of evidence, etc.) show or prove to be guilty; bring condemnation upon (*evidence against them was damning*). **b** be the ruin of. ● *n.* **1** an uttered curse. **2** *sl.* a negligible amount (*not worth a damn*). ● *adj. & adv. colloq.* = DAMNED. □ **damn with faint praise** commend so unenthusiastically as to imply disapproval. **I'll be damned if** *colloq.* I certainly do not, will not, etc. **not give a damn** see GIVE. **well I'll be damned** *colloq.* exclamation of surprise, dismay, etc. □□ **damn·ing·ly** *adv.* [ME f. OF *damner* f. L *damnare* inflict loss on f. *damnum* loss]

dam·na·ble /dámnəbəl/ *adj.* hateful; annoying. □□ **dam·na·bly** *adv.* [ME f. OF *damnable* (as DAMN)]

dam·na·tion /damnáyshən/ *n. & int.* ● *n.* condemnation to eternal punishment, esp. in hell. ● *int.* expressing anger or annoyance. [ME f. OF *damnation* (as DAMN)]

dam·na·to·ry /dámnətawree/ *adj.* conveying or causing censure or damnation. [L *damnatorius* (as DAMN)]

damned /damd/ *adj. & adv. colloq.* ● *adj.* damnable; infernal; unwelcome. ● *adv.* extremely (*damned hot; damned lovely*). □ **damned well** (as an emphatic) simply (*you've damned well got to!*). **do one's damnedest** do one's utmost.

dam·ni·fy /dámnifī/ *v.tr.* (**·fies, ·fied)** *Law* cause injury to. □□ **dam·ni·fi·ca·tion** /–fikáyshən/ *n.* [OF *damnifier*, etc., f. LL *damnificare* injure (as DAMN)]

damp /damp/ *adj., n., & v.* ● *adj.* slightly wet; moist. ● *n.* **1** diffused moisture in the air, on a surface, or in a solid, esp. as a cause of inconvenience or danger. **2** dejection; discouragement. **3** = FIREDAMP. ● *v.tr.* **1** make damp; moisten. **2** (often foll. by *down*) **a** take the force or vigor out of (*damp one's enthusiasm*). **b** make flaccid or spiritless. **c** make (a fire) burn less strongly by reducing the flow of air to it. **3** reduce or stop the vibration of (esp. the strings of a musical instrument). **4** quiet. □ **damp off** (of a plant) die from a fungus attack in damp conditions. □□ **damp·ly** *adv.* **damp·ness** *n.* [ME f. MLG, = vapor, etc., OHG *dampf* steam f. WG]

damp·en /dámpən/ *v.* **1** *v.tr. & intr.* make or become damp. **2** *tr.* make less forceful or vigorous; stifle; choke. □□ **damp·en·er** *n.*

damp·er /dámpər/ *n.* **1** a person or thing that discourages, or tempers enthusiasm. **2** a device that reduces shock or noise. **3** a metal plate in a flue to control the draft, and so the rate of combustion. **4** *Mus.* a pad silencing a piano string except when removed by means of a pedal or by the note's being struck. **5** esp. *Austral. & NZ* unleavened bread or cake of flour and water baked in wood ashes. □ **put a damper on** take the enjoyment out of.

dam·sel /dámzəl/ *n. archaic* or *literary* a young unmarried woman. [ME f. OF *dam(e)isele* ult. f. L *domina* mistress]

dam·sel·fish /dámzəlfish/ *n.* a small, brightly colored fish, *Chromis chromis*, found in or near coral reefs.

dam·sel·fly /dámzəlflī/ *n. (pl.* **·flies)** any of various insects of the order Odonata, like a dragonfly but with its wings folded over the body when resting.

dam·son /dámzən, –sən/ *n. & adj.* ● *n.* **1** (in full **damson plum) a** a small, dark-purple, plumlike fruit. **b** the small deciduous tree, *Prunus institia*, bearing this. **2** a dark-purple color. ● *adj.* damson-colored. [ME *damacene, –scene, –sene* f. L *damascenum (prunum* plum) of *Damascus*: see DAMASCENE]

Dan. *abbr.* Daniel (Old Testament).

dan¹ /daan, dan/ *n.* **1** any of twelve degrees of advanced proficiency in judo. **2** a person who has achieved any of these. [Jap.]

dan² /dan/ *n.* (in full **dan buoy)** a small buoy used as a marker in deep-sea fishing, or to mark the limits of an area cleared by minesweepers. [17th c.: orig. unkn.]

dance /dans/ *v. & n.* ● *v.* **1** *intr.* move about rhythmically alone or with a partner or in a set, usu. in fixed steps or sequences to music, for pleasure or as entertainment. **2** *intr.* move in a lively way; skip or jump about. **3** *tr.* **a** perform (a specified dance or form of dancing). **b** perform (a specified role) in a ballet, etc. **4** *intr.* move up and down (on water, in the field of vision, etc.). **5** *tr.* move (esp. a child) up and down; dandle. ● *n.* **1 a** a piece of dancing; a sequence of steps in dancing. **b** a special form of this. **2** a single round or turn of a dance. **3** a social gathering for dancing; a ball. **4** a piece of music for dancing to or in a dance rhythm. **5** a dancing or lively motion. □ **dance attendance on** follow or wait on (a person) obsequiously. **dance to a person's tune** accede obsequiously to a person's demands and wishes. **lead a person a dance** (or **merry dance**) *Brit.* cause a person much trouble in following a course one has instigated. □□ **dance·a·ble** *adj.* [ME f. OF *dance, danse* (n.), *dancer, danser* (v.), f. Rmc, of unkn. orig.]

dance·hall /dáns-hawl/ *n.* a public hall for dancing.

dance of death *n.* (also **danse ma·ca·bre**) a medieval dance in which a personified Death is represented as leading all to the grave.

danc·er /dánsər/ *n.* **1** a person who performs a dance. **2** a person whose profession is dancing.

d. and c. *abbr.* dilatation and curettage.

dan·de·li·on /dánd'líən/ *n.* a composite plant, *Taraxacum officinale*, with jagged leaves and a large, bright-yellow flower on a hollow stalk, followed by a globular head of seeds with downy tufts. [F *dent-de-lion* transl. med.L *dens leonis* lion's tooth]

dan·der /dándər/ *n. colloq.* temper; anger; indignation. □ **get one's dander up** lose one's temper; become angry. [19th c.: orig. uncert.]

dan·di·fy /dándifí/ *v.tr.* (**·fies, ·fied**) cause to resemble a dandy.

dan·dle /dánd'l/ *v.tr.* **1** dance (a child) on one's knees or in one's arms. **2** pamper; pet. [16th c.: orig. unkn.]

dan·druff /dándruf/ *n.* **1** dead skin in small scales among the hair. **2** the condition of having this. [16th c.: *–ruff* perh. rel. to ME *rove* scurfiness f. ON *hrufa* or MLG, MDu. *rōve*]

dan·dy /dándee/ *n. & adj.* ● *n.* (*pl.* **·dies**) **1** a man unduly devoted to style, smartness, and fashion in dress and appearance. **2** *colloq.* an excellent thing. ● *adj.* (**dan·di·er, dan·di·est**) *colloq.* very good of its kind; splendid; first-rate. □□ **dan·dy·ish** *adj.* **dan·dy·ism** *n.* [18th c.: perh. orig. = *Andrew*, in *Jack-a-dandy*]

dan·dy brush *n.* a brush for grooming a horse.

dan·dy roll *n.* (also **dan·dy roll·er**) a device for solidifying, and impressing a watermark in, paper during manufacture.

Dane /dayn/ *n.* **1** a native or national of Denmark. **2** *hist.* a Viking invader of England in the 9th–11th c. □ **Great Dane 1** a dog of a very large, short-haired breed. **2** this breed. [ME f. ON *Danir* (pl.), LL *Dani*]

dane·geld /dáyngeld/ *n. hist.* (also **Danegeld**) **1** (in medieval England) an annual tax to raise funds for protection against Danish invaders. **2** appeasement by bribery. [OE (as DANE + ON *gjald* payment)]

Dane·law /dáynlaw/ *n. hist.* the part of N. & E. England occupied or administered by Danes in the 9th–11th c. [OE *Dena lagu* Danes' law]

dan·ger /dáynjər/ *n.* **1** liability or exposure to harm. **2** a thing that causes or is likely to cause harm. **3** the status of a railroad signal directing a halt or caution. □ **in danger of** likely to incur or to suffer from. [earlier sense 'jurisdiction, power': ME f. OF *dangier* ult. f. L *dominus* lord]

dan·ger list *n. Brit.* = CRITICAL LIST.

dan·ger·ous /dáynjərəs/ *adj.* involving or causing danger. □□ **dan·ger·ous·ly** *adv.* **dan·ger·ous·ness** *n.* [ME f. AF *dangerous, daunger-ous*, OF *dangereus* (as DANGER)]

dan·gle /dánggəl/ *v.* **1** *intr.* be loosely suspended, so as to be able to sway to and fro. **2** *tr.* hold or carry loosely suspended. **3** *tr.* hold out (a hope, temptation, etc.) enticingly. □□ **dan·gler** *n.* [16th c. (imit.): cf. Sw. *dangla*, Da. *dangle*]

Dan·ish /dáynish/ *adj. & n.* ● *adj.* of or relating to Denmark or the Danes. ● *n.* **1** the Danish language. **2** (prec. by *the*; treated as *pl.*) the Danish people. [ME f. AF *danes*, OF *daneis* f. med.L *Danensis* (as DANE)]

Dan·ish blue *n.* a soft, salty white cheese with blue veins.

Dan·ish pas·try *n.* a cake of sweetened yeast pastry topped with icing, fruit, nuts, etc.

dank /dangk/ *adj.* disagreeably damp and cold. □□ **dank·ly** *adv.* **dank·ness** *n.* [ME prob. f. Scand.: cf. Sw. *dank* marshy spot]

danse ma·ca·bre /dóns məkaábrə/ *n.* = DANCE OF DEATH. [F (as DANCE, MACABRE)]

dan·seur /donsőr/ *n.* (*fem.* **dan·seuse** /–sőz/) a ballet dancer. [F, = dancer]

Dan·te·an /dánteeən, dantéeən/ *adj. & n.* ● *adj.* **1** of Dante. **2** in the style of or reminiscent of Dante's writings. ● *n.* a student or imitator of Dante. □□ **Dan·tesque** /–tésk/ *adj.* [*Dante* Alighieri, It. poet d. 1321]

dap /dap/ *v.* (**dapped, dap·ping**) **1** *intr.* fish by letting the bait bob on the water. **2** *tr. & intr.* dip lightly. **3** *tr. & intr.* bounce on the ground. [cf. DAB¹]

daph·ne /dáfnee/ *n.* any flowering shrub of the genus *Daphne*, e.g., the spurge laurel or mezereon. [ME, = laurel, f. Gk *daphnē*]

daph·ni·a /dáfneeə/ *n.* any freshwater branchiopod crustacean of the genus *Daphnia*, enclosed in a transparent carapace and with long antennae and prominent eyes. Also called **freshwater flea**. [mod.L f. *Daphne* name of a nymph in Gk mythol., f. DAPHNE]

dap·per /dápər/ *adj.* **1** neat and precise, esp. in dress or movement.

2 sprightly. □□ **dap·per·ly** *adv.* **dap·per·ness** *n.* [ME f. MLG, MDu. *dapper* strong, stout]

dap·ple /dápəl/ *v. & n.* ● *v.* **1** *tr.* mark with spots or rounded patches of color or shade. **2** *intr.* become marked in this way. ● *n.* **1** a dappled effect. **2** a dappled animal, esp. a horse. [ME *dappled, dappeld*, (adj.), of unkn. orig.]

dap·ple gray *adj. & n.* ● *adj.* (of a horse) gray or white with darker spots. ● *n.* a horse of this color.

D.A.R. *abbr.* Daughters of the American Revolution.

dar·bies /daárbeez/ *n.pl. Brit. sl.* handcuffs. [allusive use of *Father Darby's bands*, some rigid form of agreement for debtors (16th c.)]

Dar·by and Joan /daárbee ənd jón/ *n. Brit.* a devoted old married couple. [18th c.: perh. f. a poem of 1735 in the *Gentleman's Magazine*]

dare /dair/ *v. & n.* ● *v.tr.* (*3rd sing. present* usu. **dare** before an expressed or implied infinitive without *to*) **1** (foll. by infin. with or without *to*) venture (to); have the courage or impudence (to) (*dare he do it?; if they dare to come; how dare you?; I dare not speak; I do not dare to jump*). **2** (usu. foll. by *to* + infin.) defy or challenge (a person) (*I dare you to own up*). **3** *literary* attempt; take the risk of (*dare all things; dared their anger*). ● *n.* **1** an act of daring. **2** a challenge, esp. to prove courage. □ **I daresay 1** (often foll. by *that* + clause) it is probable. **2** probably; I grant that much (*I daresay, but you are still wrong*). □□ **dar·er** *n.* [OE *durran* with Gmc cognates: cf. Skr. *dhṛsh*, Gk *tharseō* be bold]

dare·dev·il /dáirdevəl/ *n. & adj.* ● *n.* a recklessly daring person. ● *adj.* recklessly daring. □□ **dare·dev·il·ry** *n.* **dare·dev·il·try** *n.*

dar·ing /dáiring/ *n. & adj.* ● *n.* adventurous courage. ● *adj.* adventurous; bold; prepared to take risks. □□ **dar·ing·ly** *adv.*

Dar·jee·ling /daarjéeling/ *n.* a high-quality tea from Darjeeling in NE India.

dark /daark/ *adj. & n.* ● *adj.* **1** with little or no light. **2** of a deep or somber color. **3** (of a person) with deep brown or black hair, complexion, or skin. **4** gloomy; depressing; dismal (*dark thoughts*). **5** evil; sinister (*dark deeds*). **6** sullen; angry (*a dark mood*). **7** remote; secret; mysterious; little-known (*the dark and distant past; keep it dark*). **8** ignorant; unenlightened. ● *n.* **1** absence of light. **2** nightfall (*don't go out after dark*). **3** a dark area or color, esp. in painting (*the skilled use of lights and darks*). □ **in the dark** lacking information. □□ **dark·ish** *adj.* **dark·ly** *adv.* **dark·ness** *n.* **dark·some** *poet. adj.* [OE *deorc* prob. f. Gmc]

Dark Ag·es *n.* (also **Dark Age**) **1** the period of European history preceding the Middle Ages, esp. the 5th–10th c. **2** any period of supposed unenlightenment.

dark choc·o·late *n.* chocolate without added milk.

Dark Con·ti·nent *n.* a name for Africa, esp. when little known to Europeans.

dark·en /daárkən/ *v.* **1** *tr.* make dark or darker. **2** *intr.* become dark or darker. □ **never darken a person's door** keep away permanently. □□ **dark·en·er** *n.*

dark glass·es *n.* eyeglasses with dark-tinted lenses.

dark horse *n.* a little-known person or competitor who is unexpectedly successful or prominent.

dark·ie var. of DARKY.

dark·ling /daárkling/ *adj. & adv. poet.* in the dark; in the night.

dark·room /daárkroom, –room/ *n.* a room for photographic work, with normal light excluded.

dark star *n.* an invisible star known to exist from reception of physical data other than light.

dark·y /daárkee/ *n.* (also **dark·ie**) (*pl.* **·ies**) *sl. offens.* a black person.

dar·ling /daárling/ *n. & adj.* ● *n.* **1** a beloved or lovable person or thing. **2** a favorite. **3** *colloq.* a pretty or endearing person or thing. ● *adj.* **1** beloved; lovable. **2** favorite. **3** *colloq.* charming or pretty. [OE *dēorling* (as DEAR, –LING¹)]

darn¹ /daarn/ *v. & n.* ● *v.tr.* **1** mend (esp. knitted material, or a hole in it) by interweaving yarn across the hole with a needle. **2** embroider with a large running stitch. ● *n.* a darned area in material. [16th c.: perh. f. obs. *dern* hide]

darn² /daarn/ *v.tr., int., adj., & adv. colloq.* = DAMN (in imprecatory senses). [corrupt. of DAMN]

darned /daarnd/ *adj. & adv. colloq.* = DAMNED.

dar·nel /daárnəl/ *n.* any of several grasses of the genus *Lolium*, growing as weeds among cereal crops. [ME: cf. Walloon *darnelle*]

darn·er /daárnər/ *n.* a person or thing that darns, esp. a darning needle.

darn·ing /daárning/ *n.* **1** the action of a person who darns. **2** things to be darned.

darn·ing nee·dle *n.* **1** a long needle with a large eye, used in darning. **2** a dragonfly.

dart /daart/ *n. & v.* ● *n.* **1** a small pointed missile used as a weapon or in a game. **2** (in *pl.*; usu. treated as *sing.*) an indoor game in which light feathered darts are thrown at a circular target to score points. **3** a sudden rapid movement. **4** *Zool.* a dartlike structure, such as an insect's sting or the calcareous projections of a snail (used during copulation). **5** a tapering tuck stitched in a garment. ● *v.* **1** *intr.* (often foll. by *out, in, past,* etc.) move or go suddenly or rapidly (*darted into the store*). **2** *tr.* throw (a missile). **3** *tr.* direct suddenly (a glance, etc.). [ME f. OF *darz, dars,* f. Frank.]

dart·board /dáartbawrd/ *n.* a circular board marked with numbered segments, used as a target in darts.

dart·er /dáartər/ *n.* **1** any large waterbird of the genus *Anhinga,* having a narrow head and long, thin neck. **2** any of various small, quickmoving freshwater fish of the family Percidae, native to N. America.

Dart·moor· po·ny /dáartmŏŏr, –mawr/ *n.* **1** a small pony of a shaggy-coated breed. **2** this breed. [*Dartmoor* in SW England]

Dar·win·i·an /daarwíneeən/ *adj. & n.* ● *adj.* of or relating to Darwin's theory of the evolution of species by the action of natural selection. ● *n.* an adherent of this theory. □□ **Dar·win·ism** /dáarwinizəm/ *n.* **Dar·win·ist** *n.* [C. *Darwin,* Engl. naturalist d. 1882]

dash /dash/ *v. & n.* ● *v.* **1** *intr.* rush hastily or forcefully (*dashed up the stairs*). **2** *tr.* strike or fling with great force, esp. so as to shatter (*dashed it to the ground; the cup was dashed from my hand*). **3** *tr.* frustrate; daunt; dispirit (*dashed their hopes*). **4** *tr. colloq.* (esp. **dash it** or **dash it all**) = DAMN *v.* 1. ● *n.* **1** a rush or onset; a sudden advance (*made a dash for shelter*). **2** a horizontal stroke in writing or printing to mark a pause or break in sense or to represent omitted letters or words. **3** impetuous vigor or the capacity for this. **4** showy appearance or behavior. **5** a sprinting race. **6** the longer signal of the two used in Morse code (cf. DOT¹ *n.* 3). **7** a slight admixture, esp. of a liquid. **8** = DASHBOARD. □ **cut a dash** *Brit.* make a brilliant show. **dash down** (or **off**) write or finish hurriedly. [ME, prob. imit.]

dash·board /dáshbawrd/ *n.* **1** the surface below the windshield inside a motor vehicle or aircraft, containing instruments and controls. **2** *hist.* a board of wood or leather in front of a carriage, to keep out mud.

da·shi·ki /daasheékee/ *n.* a loose, brightly colored shirt worn orig. by men in Africa. [W. Afr.]

dash·ing /dáshing/ *adj.* **1** spirited; lively. **2** stylish. □□ **dash·ing·ly** *adv.* **dash·ing·ness** *n.*

dash·pot /dáshpot/ *n.* a device for damping shock or vibration.

das·sie /dásee, daás–/ *n. S.Afr.* **1** the Cape hyrax *Procavia capensis.* Also called **rock rabbit. 2** a small coastal fish *Diplodus sargus* with rows of black stripes. [Afrik. f. Du. *dasje* dimin. of *das* badger]

das·tard·ly /dástərdlee/ *adj.* cowardly; despicable. □□ **das·tard·li·ness** *n.* [*dastard* base coward, prob. f. *dazed* past part. + –ARD, or obs. *dasart* dullard, DOTARD]

das·y·ure /dáseeyŏŏr/ *n.* any small, carnivorous marsupial of the genus *Dasyurus.* [F f. mod.L *dasyurus* f. Gk *dasus* rough + *oura* tail]

DAT *abbr.* digital audiotape.

da·ta /dáytə, dátə, daá–/ *n.pl.* (also treated as *sing.,* as in *that is all the data we have,* although the singular form is strictly *datum*) **1** known facts or things used as a basis for inference or reckoning. **2** quantities or characters operated on by a computer, etc. [pl. of DATUM]

▶Data was originally the plural of the Latin word *datum,* 'something (e.g., a piece of information) given.' **Data** is now used as a singular where it means 'information': *This data was prepared for the conference.* It is used as a plural in technical contexts and when the collection of bits of information is stressed: *All recent data on hurricanes are being compared.*

da·ta bank *n.* **1** a store or source of data. **2** = DATABASE.

da·ta·base /dáytəbays, dátə–/ *n.* a structured set of data held in a computer, esp. one that is accessible or that can be arranged in various ways.

dat·a·ble /dáytəbəl/ *adj.* (often foll. by *to*) capable of being dated (to a particular time).

da·ta cap·ture *n.* the action or process of entering data into a computer.

da·ta proc·ess·ing *n.* a series of operations on data, esp. by a computer, to retrieve or classify, etc., information. □□ **da·ta proc·es·sor** *n.*

da·ta pro·tec·tion *n.* legal control over access to data stored in computers.

date¹ /dayt/ *n. & v.* ● *n.* **1** a day of the month, esp. specified by a number. **2** a particular day or year, esp. when a given event occurred. **3** a statement (usu. giving the day, month, and year) in a document or inscription, etc., of the time of composition or publication. **4** the period to which a work of art, etc., belongs. **5** the time when an event happens or is to happen. **6** *colloq.* **a** an engagement or appointment, esp. with a person of the opposite sex. **b** a person with whom one has a social engagement. ● *v.* **1** *tr.* mark with a date. **2** *tr.* **a** assign a date to (an object, event, etc.). **b** (foll. by *to*) assign to a particular time, period, etc. **3** *intr.* (often foll. by *from, back to,* etc.) have its origins at a particular time. **4** *intr.* be recog-

nizable as from a past or particular period; become evidently out of date (*a design that does not date*). **5** *tr.* indicate or expose as being out of date (*that hat really dates you*). **6** *colloq.* **a** *tr.* make an arrangement with (a person) to meet socially. **b** *intr.* meet socially by agreement (*they are now dating regularly*). □ **to date** until now.

Middle English: via Old French from medieval Latin *data,* feminine past participle of *dare* 'give'; from the Latin formula used in dating letters, *data (epistola)* '(letter) given or delivered,' to record a particular time or place.

date² /dayt/ *n.* **1** a dark, oval, single-stoned fruit. **2** (in full **date palm**) the tall tree *Phoenix dactylifera,* native to W. Asia and N. Africa, bearing this fruit. [ME f. OF f. L *dactylus* f. Gk *daktulos* finger, from the shape of its leaf]

dat·ed /dáytid/ *adj.* **1** showing or having a date (*a dated letter*). **2** old-fashioned; out-of-date.

date·less /dáytlis/ *adj.* **1** having no date. **2** of immemorial age. **3** not likely to become out of date.

date·line /dáytlin/ *n.* **1** (also **date line**; in full **international date line**) the line from north to south partly along the 180th meridian, to the east of which the date is a day earlier than it is to the west. **2** a line at the head of a dispatch or special article in a newspaper showing the date and place of writing.

date rape *n.* sexual assault involving two people who have met socially.

date stamp *n.* **1** a stamped mark indicating a date, typically used on food packaging or mailed envelopes. **2** an adjustable device used to make such a mark.

date-stamp *v.tr.* mark with a date stamp.

da·tive /dáytiv/ *n. & adj. Gram.* ● *n.* the case of nouns and pronouns (and words in grammatical agreement with them) indicating an indirect object or recipient. ● *adj.* of or in the dative. □□ **da·ti·val** /daytívəl/ *adj.* **da·tive·ly** *adv.* [ME f. L (*casus*) *dativus* f. *dare* dat-give]

da·tum /dáytəm, dátəm, daátəm/ *n.* (*pl.* **da·ta**: see DATA as main entry). **1** a piece of information. **2** a thing known or granted; an assumption or premise from which inferences may be drawn (see SENSE-DATUM). **3** a fixed starting point of a scale, etc. (*datum-line*). [L, = thing given, neut. past part. of *dare* give]

da·tu·ra /dətŏŏrə, –tyŏŏrə/ *n.* any poisonous plant of the genus *Datura,* e.g., the thorn apple. [mod.L f. Hindi *dhatura*]

daub /dawb/ *v. & n.* ● *v.tr.* **1** spread (paint, plaster, or some other thick substance) crudely or roughly on a surface. **2** coat or smear (a surface) with paint, etc. **3 a** (also *absol.*) paint crudely or unskillfully. **b** lay (colors) on crudely and clumsily. ● *n.* **1** paint or other substance daubed on a surface. **2** plaster, clay, etc., for coating a surface, esp. mixed with straw and applied to laths or wattles to form a wall. **3** a crude painting. [ME f. OF *dauber* f. L *dealbare* whitewash f. *albus* white]

daube /dōb/ *n.* a stew of braised meat (usu. beef) with wine, etc. [F]

daugh·ter /dáwtər/ *n.* **1** a girl or woman in relation to either or both of her parents. **2** a female descendant. **3** (foll. by *of*) a female member of a family, nation, etc. **4** (foll. by *of*) a woman who is regarded as the spiritual descendant of, or as spiritually attached to, a person or thing. **5** a product or attribute personified as a daughter in relation to its source (*Fortune and its daughter Confidence*). **6** *Physics* a nuclide formed by the radioactive decay of another. **7** *Biol.* a cell, etc., formed by the division, etc., of another. □□ **daugh·ter·hood** *n.* **daugh·ter·ly** *adj.* [OE *dohtor* f. Gmc]

daugh·ter-in-law *n.* (*pl.* **daughters-in-law**) the wife of one's son.

daunt /dawnt/ *v.tr.* discourage; intimidate. □□ **daunt·ing** *adj.* **daunt·ing·ly** *adv.* [ME f. AF *daunter,* OF *danter, donter* f. L *domitare* frequent. of *domare* tame]

daunt·less /dáwntlis/ *adj.* intrepid; persevering. □□ **daunt·less·ly** *adv.* **daunt·less·ness** *n.*

dau·phin /dáwfin, dōfáN/ *n. hist.* the eldest son of the king of France. [ME f. F, ult. f. L *delphinus* DOLPHIN, as a family name]

dav·en·port /dávənpawrt/ *n.* **1** a large, heavily upholstered sofa. **2** esp. *Brit.* an ornamental writing desk with drawers and a sloping surface for writing. [19th c.: from the name *Davenport*]

da·vit /dávit, dáyvit/ *n.* a small crane on board a ship, esp. one of a pair for suspending or lowering a lifeboat. [AF & OF *daviot* dimin. of *Davi* David]

Da·vy /dáyvee/ *n.* (*pl.* **·vies**) (in full **Davy lamp**) a miner's safety lamp with the flame enclosed by wire gauze to prevent an explosion of gas. [Sir H. *Davy,* Engl. chemist d. 1829, who invented it]

Da·vy Jones /jōnz/ *n. sl.* **1** (in full **Davy Jones's locker**) the bottom of the sea, esp. regarded as the grave of those drowned at sea. **2** the evil spirit of the sea. [18th c.: orig. unkn.]

daw /daw/ *n.* = JACKDAW. [ME: cf. OHG *tāha*]

daw·dle /dáwd'l/ *v. & n.* ● *v.* **1** *intr.* **a** walk slowly and idly. **b** delay; waste time. **2** *tr.* (foll. by *away*) waste (time). ● *n.* an act or instance of dawdling. □□ **daw·dler** *n.* [perh. rel. to dial. *daddle, doddle* idle, dally]

dawn /dawn/ *n. & v.* ● *n.* **1** the first light of day; daybreak. **2** the beginning or incipient appearance of something. ● *v.intr.* **1** (of a day) begin; grow light. **2** begin to appear or develop. **3** (often foll. by *on, upon*) begin to become evident or understood (by a person). [orig. as verb: back-form. f. *dawning*, ME f. earlier *dawing* after Scand. (as DAY)]

dawn cho•rus *n.* the singing of many birds at the break of day.

dawn•ing /dáwning/ *n.* **1** daybreak. **2** the first beginning of something.

day /day/ *n.* **1** the time between sunrise and sunset. **2 a** a period of 24 hours as a unit of time, esp. from midnight to midnight, corresponding to a complete revolution of the earth on its axis. **b** a corresponding period on other planets (*Martian day*). **3** daylight (*clear as day*). **4** the time in a day during which work is normally done (*an eight-hour day*). **5 a** (also *pl.*) a period of the past or present (*the modern day; the old days*). **b** (prec. by *the*) the present time (*the issues of the day*). **6** the lifetime of a person or thing, esp. regarded as useful or productive (*have had my day; in my day things were different*). **7** a point of time (*will do it one day*). **8 a** the date of a specific festival. **b** a day associated with a particular event or purpose (*graduation day; payday; Christmas Day*). **9** a particular date; a date agreed on. **10** a day's endeavor, or the period of an endeavor, esp. as bringing success (*win the day*). □ **all in a** (or the) **day's work** part of normal routine. **at the end of the day** in the final reckoning, when all is said and done. **call it a day** end a period of activity, esp. resting content that enough has been done. **day after day** without respite. **day and night** all the time. **day by day** gradually. **day in, day out** routinely; constantly. **day of rest** the Sabbath. **from day one** *colloq.* originally. **not one's day** a day of successive misfortunes for a person. **on one's day** at one's peak of capability. **one of these days** before very long. **one of those days** a day when things go badly. **that will be the day** *colloq.* that will never happen. **this day and age** the present time or period. □□ **day•less** *adj.* [OE *dæg* f. Gmc]

Day•ak /díak/ *n.* (also **Dy•ak**) an aboriginal of Borneo or Sarawak. [Malay *dayak* up-country]

day•book /dáybŏŏk/ *n.* an account book in which a day's transactions are entered, for later transfer to a ledger.

day•break /dáybrayk/ *n.* the first appearance of light in the morning.

day care *n.* the supervision and care of young children, the elderly, the disabled, etc., during the day.

day•dream /dáydreem/ *n. & v.* ● *n.* a pleasant fantasy or reverie. ● *v.intr.* indulge in this. □□ **day•dream•er** *n.*

Day-Glo /dáyglō/ *n. & adj.* ● *n. Trademark* a brand of fluorescent paint or other coloring. ● *adj.* colored with or like this. [DAY + GLOW]

day la•bor•er *n.* an unskilled laborer hired by the day.

day•light /dáylīt/ *n.* **1** the light of day. **2** dawn (*before daylight*). **3 a** openness; publicity. **b** open knowledge. **4** a visible gap or interval, e.g., between boats in a race. **5** (usu. in *pl.*) *sl.* one's life or consciousness (orig. the internal organs), esp. as representing vulnerability to fear, attack, etc. (*scared the daylights out of me; beat the living daylights out of them*). □ **see daylight** begin to understand what was previously obscure.

day•light rob•ber•y *n. Brit. colloq.* a blatantly excessive charge.

day•light sav•ing time *n.* (also **daylight savings time**) time as adjusted to achieve longer evening daylight, esp. in summer, by setting the clocks an hour ahead of the standard time.

day•lil•y /dáylilee/ *n.* any plant of the genus *Hemerocallis*, whose flowers last only a day.

day•long /dáylawng, –long/ *adj.* lasting for a day.

day nur•ser•y *n.* a nursery where children are looked after during the working day.

Day of A•tone•ment *n.* the most solemn religious fast of the Jewish year, eight days after the Jewish New Year.

Day of Judg•ment *n.* = JUDGMENT DAY.

day of reck•on•ing *n.* the time when something must be atoned for or avenged.

day•room /dáyrŏŏm/ *n.* a room, esp. a communal room for leisure in an institution, used during the day.

day school *n.* a school, esp. private, for students living at home.

day•side /dáysīd/ *n.* **1** staff, esp. of a newspaper, who work during the day. **2** *Astron.* the side of a planet that faces the sun.

days of grace *n.* = GRACE PERIOD.

day stu•dent *n.* a student who attends classes at a boarding school or college but who does not live at the school.

day•time /dáytīm/ *n.* the part of the day when there is natural light.

day-to-day *adj.* **1** happening regularly every day (*day-to-day management*). **2** ordinary; mundane; routine (*our day-to-day domestic life*).

day-trip *n.* a trip or excursion completed in one day. □□ **day-trip•per** *n.*

day•work /dáywərk/ *n.* work paid for according to the time taken.

daze /dayz/ *v. & n.* ● *v.tr.* stupefy; bewilder. ● *n.* a state of confusion or bewilderment (*in a daze*). □□ **daz•ed•ly** /–zidlee/ *adv.* [ME *dased* past part., f. ON *dasathr* weary]

daz•zle /dázəl/ *v. & n.* ● *v.* **1** *tr.* blind temporarily or confuse the sight

of by an excess of light. **2** *tr.* impress or overpower (a person) with knowledge, ability, or any brilliant display or prospect. **3** *intr. archaic* (of eyes) be dazzled. ● *n.* bright confusing light. □□ **daz•zle•ment** *n.* **daz•zler** *n.* **daz•zling** *adj.* **daz•zling•ly** *adv.* [ME, f. DAZE + –LE⁴]

dB *abbr.* decibel(s).

DBE *abbr.* (in the UK) Dame Commander of the Order of the British Empire.

DBMS *abbr. Computing* database management system.

DBS *abbr.* **1** direct broadcast satellite. **2** direct broadcasting by satellite.

DC *abbr.* **1** (also **d.c.**) direct current. **2** District of Columbia. **3** da capo.

DCL *abbr.* doctor of civil law.

DD *abbr.* doctor of divinity.

D day /déeday/ *n.* (also **D Day**) **1** the day (June 6, 1944) on which Allied forces invaded N. France. **2** the day on which an important operation is to begin or a change to take effect. [*D* for *day* + DAY]

D.D.S. *abbr.* **1** doctor of dental science. **2** doctor of dental surgery.

DDT *abbr.* dichlorodiphenyltrichloroethane, a colorless chlorinated hydrocarbon used as an insecticide.

DE *abbr.* Delaware (in official postal use).

de- /dee, di/ *prefix* **1** forming verbs and their derivatives: **a** down; away (*descend; deduct*). **b** completely (*declare; denude; deride*). **2** added to verbs and their derivatives to form verbs and nouns implying removal or reversal (*decentralize; de-ice; demoralization*). [from or after L *de* (adv. & prep.) = off, from: sense 2 through OF *des*– f. L *dis*–]

dea•con /déekən/ *n. & v.* ● *n.* **1** (in Catholic, Anglican, and Orthodox churches) a minister of the third order, below bishop and priest. **2** (in various, esp. Protestant, churches) a lay officer attending to a congregation's secular affairs. **3** (in the early Christian church) an appointed minister of charity. ● *v.tr.* appoint or ordain as a deacon. □□ **dea•con•ate** *n.* **dea•con•ship** *n.* [OE *diacon* f. eccl.L *diaconus* f. Gk *diakonos* servant]

dea•con•ess /déekənes, déekənis/ *n.* a woman in the early Christian church and in some modern churches with functions analogous to a deacon's. [DEACON, after LL *diaconissa*]

de•ac•ti•vate /deeáktivayt/ *v.tr.* make inactive or less reactive. □□ **de•ac•ti•va•tion** /–váyshən/ *n.* **de•ac•ti•va•tor** *n.*

dead /ded/ *adj., adv., & n.* ● *adj.* **1** no longer alive. **2** *colloq.* extremely tired or unwell. **3** benumbed; affected by loss of sensation (*my fingers are dead*). **4** (foll. by *to*) unappreciative or unconscious of; insensitive to. **5** no longer effective or in use; obsolete; extinct. **6** (of a match, of coal, etc.) no longer burning; extinguished. **7** inanimate. **8 a** lacking force or vigor; dull; lusterless; muffled. **b** (of sound) not resonant. **c** (of sparkling wine, etc.) no longer effervescent. **9 a** quiet; lacking activity (*the dead season*). **b** motionless; idle. **10 a** (of a microphone, telephone, etc.) not transmitting any sound, esp. because of a fault. **b** (of a circuit, conductor, etc.) carrying or transmitting no current; not connected to a source of electricity (*a dead battery*). **11** (of the ball in a game) out of play. **12** abrupt; complete; exact; unqualified; unrelieved (*come to a dead stop; a dead faint; a dead calm; in dead silence; a dead certainty*). **13** without spiritual life. ● *adv.* **1** absolutely; exactly; completely (*dead on target; dead level; dead tired*). **2** *colloq.* very; extremely (*dead good; dead easy*). ● *n.* (prec. by *the*) **1** (treated as *pl.*) those who have died. **2** a time of silence or inactivity (*the dead of night*). □ **dead as the dodo** see DODO. **dead as a doornail** see DOORNAIL. **dead beat** *colloq.* exhausted. **dead from the neck up** *colloq.* stupid. **dead in the water** unable to move or to function. **dead to the world** *colloq.* fast asleep; unconscious. **wouldn't be seen dead in** (or with, etc.) *colloq.* shall have nothing to do with; shall refuse to wear, etc. □□ **dead•ness** *n.* [OE *dēad* f. Gmc, rel. to DIE¹]

dead•beat /dédbeet/ *n. & adj.* ● *n.* **1** *colloq.* a penniless person. **2** *sl.* a person constantly in debt. ● *adj. Physics* (of an instrument) without recoil.

dead•bolt /dédbōlt/ *n.* a bolt engaged by turning a knob or key, rather than by spring action.

dead cen•ter *n.* **1** the exact center. **2** the position of a crank, etc., in line with the connecting rod and not exerting torque.

dead duck *n. sl.* **1** an unsuccessful or useless person or thing. **2** a person who is beyond help; one who is doomed.

dead•en /déd'n/ *v.* **1** *tr. & intr.* deprive of or lose vitality, force, brightness, sound, feeling, etc. **2** *tr.* (foll. by *to*) make insensitive. □□ **dead•en•er** *n.*

dead end *n.* a closed end of a road, passage, etc. from which no exit is possible.

dead-end *adj.* a situation offering no prospects of progress or advancement (*a dead-end job*).

dead•eye /dédī/ *n.* **1** *Naut.* a circular wooden block with a groove around the circumference to take a lanyard, used singly or in pairs to tighten a shroud. **2** *colloq.* an expert marksman.

dead·fall /dédfawl/ n. a trap in which a raised weight is made to fall on and kill esp. large game.

dead hand n. an oppressive persisting influence, esp. posthumous control; mortmain.

dead·head /dédhed/ n. & v. • n. 1 (**Deadhead**) a fan and follower of the rock group The Grateful Dead. 2 a boring or unenterprising person. 3 a passenger or member of an audience who has made use of a free ticket. 4 Brit. a faded flower head. • v. 1 intr. (of a commercial driver, etc.) complete a trip in an empty vehicle with no passengers or freight. 2 tr. remove faded flower heads from (a plant).

dead heat n. 1 a race in which two or more competitors finish in a tie. 2 the result of such a race.

dead lan·guage n. a language no longer commonly spoken, e.g., Latin.

dead let·ter n. 1 a law or practice no longer observed or recognized. 2 a letter that is undeliverable and unreturnable, esp. one with an incorrect address. □ **dead-letter office** n. the post office department that handles dead letters.

dead lift n. the exertion of one's utmost strength to lift something.

dead·light /dédlit/ n. Naut. 1 a shutter inside a porthole. 2 a skylight that cannot be opened.

dead·line /dédlin/ n. 1 a time limit for the completion of an activity, etc. 2 hist. a line beyond which prisoners were not allowed to go.

dead·lock /dédlok/ n. & v. • n. 1 a situation, esp. one involving opposing parties, in which no progress can be made. 2 a type of lock requiring a key to open or close it. • v.tr. & intr. bring or come to a standstill.

dead·ly /dédlee/ adj. & adv. • adj. (**dead·li·er, dead·li·est**) 1 a causing or able to cause fatal injury or serious damage. b poisonous (deadly snake). 2 intense; extreme (deadly dullness). 3 (of an aim, etc.) extremely accurate or effective. 4 deathlike (deadly pale; deadly faintness; deadly gloom). 5 colloq. dreary; dull. 6 implacable. • adv. 1 like death; as if dead (deadly faint). 2 extremely; intensely (deadly serious). □□ **dead·li·ness** n. [OE déadlic, déadlīce (as DEAD, -LY[1])]

dead·ly night·shade n. a poisonous plant, Atropa belladonna, with drooping purple flowers and black cherrylike fruit. Also called **belladonna**.

dead·ly sin n. a sin regarded as leading to damnation, esp. pride, covetousness, lust, gluttony, envy, anger, and sloth.

dead man's han·dle n. (also **dead man's pedal**, etc.) a control on an electric train, allowing power to be connected only as long as the operator presses on it.

dead march n. a funeral march.

dead men's shoes n. property or a position, etc., coveted by a prospective successor but available only on a person's death.

dead-net·tle n. any plant of the genus Lamium, having nettlelike leaves but without stinging hairs.

dead-on n. exactly right.

dead·pan /dédpán/ adj. & adv. with a face or manner totally lacking expression or emotion.

dead reck·on·ing n. Naut. calculation of a ship's position from the log, compass, etc., when observations are impossible.

dead ring·er n. a person or thing that strongly resembles someone or something else.

dead shot n. one who is extremely accurate.

dead sol·diers n. colloq. bottles (esp. of beer, liquor, etc.) after the contents have been drunk.

dead time n. Physics the period after the recording of a pulse, etc., when the detector is unable to record another.

dead·weight /dédwáyt/ n. (also **dead weight**) 1 a an inert mass. b a heavy weight or burden. 2 a debt not covered by assets. 3 the total weight carried on a ship.

dead·wood /dédwŏod/ n. 1 dead trees or branches. 2 colloq. one or more useless people or things. 3 Bowling knocked-down pins that remain on the alley.

de·aer·ate /dee-áirayt/ v.tr. remove air from. □□ **de·aer·a·tion** /-ráyshən/ n.

deaf /def/ adj. 1 wholly or partly without hearing (deaf in one ear). 2 (foll. by to) refusing to listen or comply. 3 insensitive to harmony, rhythm, etc. (tone-deaf). □ **deaf as a post** completely deaf. **fall on deaf ears** be ignored. **turn a deaf ear** (usu. foll. by to) be unresponsive. □□ **deafly** adv. **deaf·ness** n. [OE déaf f. Gmc]

deaf-and-dumb adj. offens. deaf-mute.

deaf·en /défən/ v.tr. (often as **deafening** adj.) overpower with sound. 2 deprive of hearing by noise, esp. temporarily. □□ **deaf·en·ing·ly** adv.

deaf-mute n. & adj. • n. a person who is both deaf and unable to speak. • adj. (of a person) both deaf and unable to speak.

deal[1] /deel/ v. & n. • v. (past and past part. **dealt** /delt/) 1 intr. a (foll. by with) take measures concerning (a problem, person, etc.), esp. in order to put something right. b (foll. by with) do business with; associate with. c (foll. by with) discuss or treat (a subject). d (of-

ten foll. by by) behave in a specified way toward a person (dealt honorably by them). 2 intr. (foll. by in) to sell or be concerned with commercially (deals in insurance). 3 tr. (often foll. by out) distribute or apportion to several people, etc. 4 tr. (also absol.) distribute (cards) to players for a game or round. 5 tr. cause to be received; administer (deal a heavy blow). 6 tr. assign as a share or deserts to a person (life dealt them much happiness). 7 tr. (foll. by in) colloq. include (a person) in an activity (you can deal me in). • n. 1 (usu. a **good** or **great deal**) colloq. a a large amount (a good deal of trouble). b to a considerable extent (is a great deal better). 2 colloq. a business arrangement; a transaction. 3 a specified form of treatment given or received (gave them a bad deal; got a fair deal). 4 a the distribution of cards by dealing. b a player's turn to do this (it's my deal). c the round of play following this. d a set of hands dealt to players. □ **it's a deal** colloq. expressing assent to an agreement. [OE dǽl, dǽlan, f. Gmc]

deal[2] /deel/ n. 1 fir or pine timber, esp. sawn into boards of a standard size. 2 a a board of this timber. b such boards collectively. [ME f. MLG, MDu. dele plank f. Gmc]

deal·er /déelər/ n. 1 a person or business dealing in (esp. retail) goods (contact your dealer; car dealer; a dealer in plumbing supplies). 2 the player dealing at cards. 3 a person who sells illegal drugs. □□ **deal·er·ship** n. (in sense 1).

deal·ings /déelingz/ n.pl. contacts or transactions, esp. in business. □ **have dealings with** associate with.

dealt past and past part. of DEAL[1].

dean[1] /deen/ n. 1 a a college or university official, esp. one with disciplinary and advisory functions. b the head of a university faculty or department or of a medical school. 2 a the head of the chapter of a cathedral or collegiate church. b (usu. **rural dean**) Brit. a member of the clergy exercising supervision over a group of parochial clergy within a division of an archdeaconry. 3 = DOYEN. [ME f. AF deen, OF deien, f. LL decanus f. decem ten; orig. = chief of a group of ten]

dean[2] Brit. var. of DENE[1].

dean·er·y /déenəree/ n. (pl. **-ies**) 1 a dean's house or office. 2 Brit. the group of parishes presided over by a rural dean.

dear /deer/ adj., n., adv., & int. • adj. 1 a beloved or much esteemed. b as a merely polite or ironic form (my dear man). 2 used as a formula of address, esp. at the beginning of letters (Dear Sir). 3 (often foll. by to) precious; much cherished. 4 (usu. in superl.) earnest; deeply felt (my dearest wish). 5 a high-priced relative to its value. b having high prices. c (of money) available as a loan only at a high rate of interest. • n. (esp. as a form of address) dear person. • adv. at a high price or great cost (buy cheap and sell dear; will pay dear). • int. expressing surprise, dismay, pity, etc. (dear me!; oh dear!; dear, dear!). □ **for dear life** see LIFE. □□ **dear·ly** adv. (esp. in sense 3 of adj.). **dear·ness** n. [OE déore f. Gmc]

dear·ie /déeree/ n. (esp. as a form of address) usu. joc. or iron. my dear. □ **dearie me!** int. expressing surprise, dismay, etc.

Dear John letter n. (also **Dear John**) colloq. a letter from a woman to a man, terminating a personal relationship.

dearth /dərth/ n. scarcity or lack, esp. of food. [ME, formed as DEAR]

dea·sil /désəl, deézəl/ adv. Sc. in the direction of the sun's apparent course (considered as lucky); clockwise. [Gael. deiseil]

death /deth/ n. 1 the final cessation of vital functions in an organism; the ending of life. 2 the event that terminates life. 3 a the fact or process of being killed or killing (stone to death; fight to the death). b the fact or state of being dead (eyes closed in death; their deaths caused rioting). 4 a the destruction or permanent cessation of something (was the death of our hopes). b colloq. something terrible or appalling. 5 (usu. **Death**) a personification of death, esp. as a destructive power, usu. represented by a skeleton. 6 a lack of religious faith or spiritual life. □ **as sure as death** quite certain. **at death's door** close to death. **be in at the death** 1 be present when an animal is killed, esp. in hunting. 2 witness the (esp. sudden) ending of an enterprise, etc. **be the death of** 1 cause the death of. 2 be very harmful to. **catch one's death** colloq. catch a serious chill, etc. **do to death** 1 kill. 2 overdo. **fate worse than death** colloq. a disastrous misfortune or experience. **like death warmed over** sl. very tired or ill. **put to death** kill or cause to be killed. **to death** to the utmost; extremely (bored to death; worked to death). □□ **death·less** adj. **death·less·ness** n. **death·like** adj. [OE déath f. Gmc: rel. to DIE[1]]

death ad·der n. any of various venomous snakes of the genus Acanthopis, esp. A. antarcticus of Australia.

death·bed /déthbed/ n. a bed as the place where a person is dying or has died.

death·blow /déthblō/ n. 1 a blow or other action that causes death. 2 an event or circumstance that abruptly ends an activity, enterprise, etc.

death cap n. (also **death cup**) a poisonous mushroom, Amanita phalloides.

death cer·tif·i·cate n. an official statement of the cause and date and place of a person's death.

death knell n. 1 the tolling of a bell to mark a person's death. 2 an event that heralds the end or destruction of something.

death·ly /déthlee/ *adj. & adv.* • *adj.* (**death·li·er, death·li·est**) suggestive of death (*deathly silence*). • *adv.* in a deathly way (*deathly pale*).

death mask *n.* a cast taken of a dead person's face.

death pen·al·ty *n.* punishment by being put to death.

death rate *n.* the number of deaths per thousand of population per year.

death rat·tle *n.* a gurgling sound sometimes heard in a dying person's throat.

death row *n.* a prison block or section for prisoners sentenced to death.

death's-head *n.* a human skull as an emblem of mortality.

death's-head moth *n.* (also **death's-head hawkmoth**) a large, dark hawkmoth, *Acherontia atropos*, with skull-like markings on the back of the thorax.

death squad *n.* an armed paramilitary group, esp. in Central America, formed to kill political enemies, etc.

death tax *n.* a tax on property payable on the owner's death.

death toll *n.* the number of people killed in an accident, battle, etc.

death trap *n. colloq.* a dangerous or unhealthy building, vehicle, etc.

death war·rant *n.* **1** an order for the execution of a condemned person. **2** anything that causes the end of an established practice, etc.

death·watch /déthwawch/ *n.* **1** (in full **death·watch bee·tle**) a small beetle, *Xestobium rufovillosum*, which makes a sound like a watch ticking, once supposed to portend death, and whose larva bores in old wood. **2** a vigil kept beside a dead or dying individual. **3** a guard set over a person due for execution.

death wish *n. Psychol.* a desire (usu. unconscious) for the death of oneself or another.

deb /deb/ *n. colloq.* a debutante. [abbr.]

de·ba·cle /daybaákəl, –bákel, də–/ *n.* (also **dé·bâ·cle**) **1 a** an utter defeat or failure. **b** a sudden collapse or downfall. **2** a confused rush or rout; a stampede. **3 a** a breakup of ice in a river, with resultant flooding. **b** a sudden rush of water carrying along blocks of stone and other debris. [F f. *débâcler* unbar]

PRONUNCIATION TIP   debacle

Although it is usually written without its original French accents, this word has managed to stay fairly close to its original French pronunciation ("dih-BAH-kul" or "day-BAH-kul"). In American English, the last two syllables are also commonly rhymed with *jackal* ("dih-BAK-ul" or "day-BAK-ul"). All of these pronunciations are heard, although placing the stress on the first syllable (DEB-uh-kul) has not yet gained wide acceptance.

---

de·bag /deebág/ *v.tr.* (**de·bagged, de·bag·ging**) *Brit. sl.* remove the pants of (a person), esp. as a joke.

de·bar /deebaár/ *v.tr.* (**de·barred, de·bar·ring**) (foll. by *from*) exclude from admission or from a right; prohibit from an action (*was debarred from entering*). □□ **de·bar·ment** *n.* [ME f. F *débarrer*, OF *desbarrer* (as DE-, BAR[1])]

de·bark[1] /dibaárk/ *v.tr. & intr.* land from a ship. □□ **de·bar·ka·tion** /–káyshən/ *n.* [F *débarquer* (as DE-, BARK[3])]

de·bark[2] /déebaárk/ *v.tr.* remove the bark from (a tree).

de·base /dibáys/ *v.tr.* **1** lower in quality, value, or character. **2** depreciate (coin) by alloying, etc. □□ **de·base·ment** *n.* **de·bas·er** *n.* [DE- + obs. *base* for ABASE]

de·bat·a·ble /dibáytəbəl/ *adj.* **1** questionable; subject to dispute. **2** capable of being debated. □□ **de·bat·a·bly** *adv.* [OF *debatable* or AL *debatabilis* (as DEBATE)]

de·bate /dibáyt/ *v. & n.* • *v.* **1** *tr.* (also *absol.*) discuss or dispute about (an issue, proposal, etc.) esp. formally in a legislative assembly, public meeting, etc. **2 a** *tr.* consider; ponder (a matter). **b** *intr.* consider different sides of a question. • *n.* **1** a formal discussion on a particular matter, esp. in a legislative assembly, etc. **2** debating; discussion (*open to debate*). □□ **de·bat·er** *n.* [ME f. OF *debatre, debat* f. Rmc (as DE-, BATTLE)]

de·bat·ing point *n.* an inessential piece of information used to gain advantage in a debate.

de·bauch /dibáwch/ *v. & n.* • *v.tr.* **1** corrupt morally. **2** make intemperate or sensually indulgent. **3** deprave or debase (taste or judgment). **4** (as **debauched** *adj.*) dissolute. **5** seduce (a woman). • *n.* **1** a bout of sensual indulgence. **2** debauchery. □□ **de·bauch·er** *n.* [F *débauche(r)*, OF *desbaucher* of unkn. orig.]

deb·au·chee /dibawchée, –shée, déb–/ *n.* a person addicted to excessive sensual indulgence. [F *débauché* past part.: see DEBAUCH]

de·bauch·er·y /dibáwchəree/ *n.* excessive sensual indulgence.

de·ben·ture /dibénchər/ *n.* **1** (in full **debenture bond**) a fixed-interest bond of a company or corporation, backed by general credit rather than specified assets. **2** *Brit.* an acknowledgment of indebtedness, esp. a bond of a company or corporation acknowledging a debt and providing for payment of interest at fixed intervals. [ME f. L *debentur* are owing f. *debēre* owe: assim. to –URE]

de·bil·i·tate /dibílitayt/ *v.tr.* enfeeble; enervate. □□ **de·bil·i·tat·ing·ly** *adv.* **de·bil·i·ta·tion** /–táyshən/ *n.* **de·bil·i·ta·tive** *adj.* [L *debilitare* (as DEBILITY)]

de·bil·i·ty /dibílitee/ *n.* feebleness, esp. of health. [ME f. OF *debilité* f. L *debilitas –tatis* f. *debilis* weak]

deb·it /débit/ *n. & v.* • *n.* **1** an entry in an account recording a sum owed. **2** the sum recorded. **3** the total of such sums. **4** the debit side of an account. • *v.tr.* (**deb·it·ed, deb·it·ing**) **1** (foll. by *against, to*) enter (an amount) on the debit side of an account (*debited $500 against me*). **2** (foll. by *with*) enter (a person) on the debit side of an account (*debited me with $500*). [F *débit* f. L *debitum* DEBT]

deb·it card *n.* a card issued by a bank allowing the holder to transfer deposited funds electronically, as to make a purchase.

deb·o·nair /débənáir/ *adj.* **1** carefree; cheerful; self-assured. **2** having pleasant manners. □□ **deb·o·nair·ly** *adv.* [ME f. OF *debonaire* = *de bon aire* of good disposition]

de·bouch /dibówch, –boosh/ *v.intr.* **1** (of troops or a stream) issue from a ravine, wood, etc., into open ground. **2** (often foll. by *into*) (of a river, road, etc.) merge into a larger body or area. □□ **de·bouch·ment** *n.* [F *déboucher* (as DE-, *bouche* mouth)]

de·brief /deebréef/ *v.tr. colloq.* interrogate (a person, e.g., a diplomat or pilot) about a completed mission or undertaking. □□ **de·brief·ing** *n.*

de·bris /dəbrée, day–, débree/ *n.* **1** scattered fragments, esp. of something wrecked or destroyed. **2** *Geol.* an accumulation of loose material, e.g., from rocks or plants. [F *débris* f. obs. *débriser* break down (as DE-, *briser* break)]

debt /det/ *n.* **1** something that is owed, esp. money. **2** a state of obligation to pay something owed (*in debt; out of debt; get into debt*). □ **in a person's debt** under an obligation to a person. [ME *det(te)* f. OF *dette* (later *debte*) ult. f. L *debitum* past part. of *debēre* owe]

debt col·lec·tor *n.* a person who is employed to collect debts for creditors.

debt of hon·or *n.* a debt not legally recoverable, esp. a sum lost in gambling.

debt·or /détər/ *n.* a person who owes a debt, esp. money. [ME f. OF *det(t)or, –our* f. L *debitor* (as DEBT)]

de·bug /deebúg/ *v.tr.* (**de·bugged, de·bug·ging**) **1** *colloq.* trace and remove concealed listening devices from (a room, etc.). **2** *colloq.* identify and remove defects from (a machine, computer program, etc.). **3** remove bugs from.

de·bunk /deebúngk/ *v.tr. colloq.* **1** show the good reputation or aspirations of (a person, institution, etc.) to be spurious. **2** expose the falseness of (a claim, etc.). □□ **de·bunk·er** *n.*

de·bus /deebús/ *v.tr. & intr.* (**de·bused, de·bus·ing** or **de·bussed, de·bus·sing**) esp. *Mil.* unload (personnel or stores) or alight from a motor vehicle.

de·but /daybyōo, dáybyoo/ *n. & v.* • *n.* (also **dé·but**) **1** the first public appearance of a performer on stage, etc., or the opening performance of a show, etc. **2** the first appearance of a debutante in society. • *v.* **1** *intr.* make a debut. **2** *tr.* introduce, esp. a performance, etc. [F f. *débuter* lead off]

▶**Debut** (pronounced "day-BYOO" or "DAY-byoo") is used widely as a verb in the context of entertainment and the performing arts (*her new album will debut in April*). It is less widely accepted, however, as a transitive verb (taking a direct object) (*she debuted her new column in the local paper; Ford will debut its new luxury sedan next year*).

deb·u·tante /débyətaant, dáybyoo–/ *n.* a (usu. wealthy) young woman making her social debut. [F, fem. part. of *débuter*: see DEBUT]

Dec. *abbr.* December.

dec. *abbr.* **1** deceased. **2** declared.

deca- /dékə/ *comb. form* (also **dec-** before a vowel) **1** having ten. **2** tenfold. **3** ten, esp. of a metric unit (*decagram; decaliter*). [Gk *deka* ten]

dec·ade /dékayd/ *n.* **1** a period of ten years. **2** a set, series, or group of ten. □□ **dec·a·dal** /dékəd'l/ *adj.* [ME f. F *décade* f. LL *decas –adis* f. Gk f. *deka* ten]

dec·a·dence /dékəd'ns/ *n.* **1** moral or cultural deterioration, esp. after a peak or culmination of achievement. **2** decadent behavior; a state of decadence. [F *décadence* f. med.L *decadentia* f. *decadere* DECAY]

dec·a·dent /dékədənt/ *adj. & n.* • *adj.* **1 a** in a state of moral or cultural deterioration; showing or characterized by decadence. **b** of a period of decadence. **2** self-indulgent. • *n.* a decadent person. □□ **dec·a·dent·ly** *adv.* [F *décadent* (as DECADENCE)]

de·caf·fein·ate /deekáfinayt/ *v.tr.* remove the caffeine from. **2** reduce the quantity of caffeine in (usu. coffee).

dec·a·gon /dékəgən/ *n.* a plane figure with ten sides and angles. □□ **dec·ag·o·nal** /dikágənəl/ *adj.* [med.L *decagonum* f. Gk *dekagōnon* (as DECA-, –GON)]

de·cag·y·nous /dikájinəs/ *adj. Bot.* having ten pistils. [mod.L *decagynus* (as DECA-, Gk *gūne* woman)]

dec·a·he·dron /dékəheédrən/ *n.* a solid figure with ten faces. □□ **dec·a·he·dral** *adj.* [DECA- + –HEDRON after POLYHEDRON]

de·cal /deékal/ n. = DECALCOMANIA 2. [abbr.]

de·cal·ci·fy /deekálsifī/ v.tr. (·fies, ·fied) remove lime or calcareous matter from (a bone, tooth, etc.). □□ **de·cal·ci·fi·ca·tion** /–fikáyshən/ n. **de·cal·ci·fi·er** n.

de·cal·co·ma·ni·a /deekálkəmáyneeə/ n. **1** a process of transferring designs from specially prepared paper to the surface of glass, porcelain, etc. **2** a picture or design made by this process. [F décalcomanie f. décalquer transfer]

dec·a·li·ter /dékəleetər/ n. a metric unit of capacity, equal to 10 liters.

Dec·a·logue /dékəlawg, –log/ n. the Ten Commandments. [ME f. F décalogue or eccl.L decalogus f. Gk dekalogos (after hoi deka logoi the Ten Commandments)]

dec·a·me·ter /dékəmeetər/ n. a metric unit of length, equal to 10 meters.

de·camp /dikámp/ v.intr. **1** break up or leave a camp. **2** depart suddenly; abscond. □□ **de·camp·ment** n. [F décamper (as DE-, CAMP[1])]

dec·a·nal /dékənəl, dikáy–/ adj. **1** of a dean or deanery. **2** of the south side of a choir, the side on which the dean sits (cf. CANTORIAL). [med.L decanalis f. LL decanus DEAN[1]]

de·can·drous /dikándrəs/ adj. Bot. having ten stamens. [DECA- + Gk andr- man (= male organ)]

de·ca·ni /dikáyní/ adj. Mus. to be sung by the decanal side in antiphonal singing (cf. CANTORIS). [L, genit. of decanus DEAN[1]]

de·cant /dikánt/ v.tr. **1** gradually pour off (liquid, esp. wine or a solution) from one container to another, esp. without disturbing the sediment. **2** empty out; move as if by pouring. [med.L decanthare (as DE-, L canthus f. Gk kanthos canthus, used of the lip of a beaker)]

de·cant·er /dikántər/ n. a stoppered glass container into which wine or brandy, etc., is decanted.

de·cap·i·tate /dikápitayt/ v.tr. **1** behead (esp. as a form of capital punishment). **2** cut the head or end from. □□ **de·cap·i·ta·tion** /–táyshən/ n. **de·cap·i·ta·tor** n. [LL decapitare (as DE-, caput –itis head)]

dec·a·pod /dékəpod/ n. **1** any crustacean of the chiefly marine order Decapoda, characterized by five pairs of walking legs, e.g., shrimps, crabs, and lobsters. **2** any of various mollusks of the class Cephalopoda, having ten tentacles, e.g., squids and cuttlefish. □□ **de·cap·o·dan** /dikápəd'n/ adj. [F décapode f. Gk deka ten + pous podos foot]

de·car·bon·ize /deekáarbəníz/ v.tr. remove carbon or carbonaceous deposits from (an internal combustion engine, etc.). □□ **de·car·bon·i·za·tion** n.

dec·a·style /dékəstīl/ n. & adj. Archit. • n. a ten-columned portico. • adj. having ten columns. [Gk dekastulos f. deka ten + stulos column]

dec·a·syl·la·ble /dékəsiləbəl/ n. a metrical line of ten syllables. □□ **dec·a·syl·lab·ic** /–silábik/ adj. & n.

de·cath·lon /dikáthlən, –lon/ n. an athletic contest in which each competitor takes part in ten events. □□ **de·cath·lete** /–leet/ n. [DECA- + Gk athlon contest]

de·cay /dikáy/ v. & n. **1 a** intr. rot; decompose. **b** tr. cause to rot or decompose. **2** intr. & tr. decline or cause to decline in quality, power, wealth, energy, beauty, etc. **3** intr. Physics **a** (usu. foll. by to) (of a substance, etc.,) undergo change by radioactivity. **b** undergo a gradual decrease in magnitude of a physical quantity. • n. **1** a rotten or ruinous state; a process of wasting away. **2** decline in health, quality, etc. **3** Physics **a** change into another substance, etc. by radioactivity. **b** a decrease in the magnitude of a physical quantity, esp. the intensity of radiation or amplitude of oscillation. **4** decayed tissue. □□ **de·cay·a·ble** adj. [ME f. OF decair f. Rmc (as DE-, L cadere fall)]

de·cease /disées/ n. & v. formal esp. Law • n. death. • v.intr. die. [ME f. OF deces f. L decessus f. decedere (as DE-, cedere cess- go)]

de·ceased /disées't/ adj. & n. formal • adj. dead. • n. (usu. prec. by the) a person who has died, esp. recently.

de·ce·dent /disée'd'nt/ n. Law a deceased person. [L decedere die: see DECEASE]

de·ceit /diséet/ n. **1** the act or process of deceiving or misleading, esp. by concealing the truth. **2** a dishonest trick or stratagem. **3** willingness to deceive. [ME f. OF f. past part. of deceveir f. L decipere deceive (as DE-, capere take)]

de·ceit·ful /diséetfool/ adj. **1** (of a person) using deceit, esp. habitually. **2** (of an act, practice, etc.) intended to deceive. □□ **de·ceit·ful·ly** adv. **de·ceit·ful·ness** n.

de·ceive /diséev/ v. **1** tr. make (a person) believe what is false; mislead purposely. **2** tr. be unfaithful to, esp. sexually. **3** intr. use deceit. **4** tr. archaic disappoint (esp. hopes). □ **be deceived** be mistak-

en or deluded. **deceive oneself** persist in a mistaken belief. □□ **de·ceiv·a·ble** adj. **de·ceiv·er** n. [ME f. OF deceivre or deceiv- stressed stem of deceveir (as DECEIT)]

de·cel·er·ate /deesélərayt/ v. **1** intr. & tr. begin or cause to begin to reduce speed. **2** tr. make slower (decelerated motion). □□ **de·cel·er·a·tion** /–ráyshən/ n. **de·cel·er·a·tor** n. **de·cel·er·om·e·ter** /–rómitər/ n. [DE-, after ACCELERATE]

De·cem·ber /disémbər/ n. the twelfth month of the year. [ME f. OF decembre f. L December f. decem ten: orig. the tenth month of the Roman year]

de·cen·cy /deésənsee/ n. (pl. ·cies) **1** correct and tasteful standards of behavior as generally accepted. **2** conformity with current standards of behavior or propriety. **3** avoidance of obscenity. **4** (in pl.) the requirements of correct behavior. [L decentia f. decēre be fitting]

de·cen·ni·al /diséneeəl/ adj. **1** lasting ten years. **2** recurring every ten years. □□ **de·cen·ni·al·ly** adv. [L decennis of ten years f. decem ten + annus year]

de·cent /deésənt/ adj. **1 a** conforming with current standards of behavior or propriety. **b** avoiding obscenity. **2** respectable. **3** acceptable; passable; good enough. **4** kind; obliging; generous (was decent enough to apologize). □□ **de·cent·ly** adv. [F décent or L decēre be fitting]

de·cen·tral·ize /deeséntrəlīz/ v.tr. **1** transfer (powers, etc.) from a central to a local authority. **2** reorganize (a centralized institution, organization, etc.) on the basis of greater local autonomy. □□ **de·cen·tral·ist** /–list/ n. & adj. **de·cen·tral·i·za·tion** n.

de·cep·tion /disépshən/ n. **1** the act or an instance of deceiving; the process of being deceived. **2** a thing that deceives; a trick or sham. [ME f. OF or LL deceptio f. decipere (as DECEIT)]

de·cep·tive /diséptiv/ adj. apt to deceive; easily mistaken for something else or as having a different quality. □□ **de·cep·tive·ly** adv. **de·cep·tive·ness** n. [OF deceptif –ive or LL deceptivus (as DECEPTION)]

de·cer·e·brate /deeséribrayt/ adj. having had the cerebrum removed.

deci- /désee/ comb. form one-tenth, esp. of a unit in the metric system (deciliter; decimeter). [L decimus tenth]

dec·i·bel /désibel/ n. a unit (one-tenth of a bel) used in the comparison of two power levels relating to electrical signals or sound intensities, one of the pair usually being taken as a standard. ¶ Abbr.: **dB**.

de·cide /disíd/ v. **1 a** intr. (often foll. by on, about) come to a resolution as a result of consideration. **b** tr. (usu. foll. by to + infin., or that + clause) have or reach as one's resolution about something (decided to stay; decided that we should leave). **2** tr. a Brit. cause (a person) to reach a resolution (was unsure about going but the weather decided me). **b** resolve or settle (a question, dispute, etc.). **3** intr. (usu. foll. by between, for, against, in favor of, or that + clause) give a judgment concerning a matter. □□ **de·cid·a·ble** adj. [ME f. F décider f. L decidere (as DE-, cædere cut)]

de·cid·ed /disídid/ adj. **1** (usu. attrib.) definite; unquestionable (a decided difference). **2** (of a person, esp. as a characteristic) having clear opinions, resolute, not vacillating. □□ **de·cid·ed·ness** n.

de·cid·ed·ly /disídidlee/ adv. undoubtedly; undeniably.

de·cid·er /disídər/ n. **1** a game, race, etc., to decide between competitors finishing equal in a previous contest. **2** any person or thing that decides.

de·cid·u·ous /disíjōoəs/ adj. **1** (of a tree) shedding its leaves annually. **2** (of leaves, horns, teeth, etc.) shed periodically. **3** (of an ant, etc.) shedding its wings after copulation. **4** fleeting; transitory. □□ **de·cid·u·ous·ness** n. [L deciduus f. decidere f. cadere fall]

dec·i·gram /désigram/ n. a metric unit of mass, equal to 0.1 gram.

dec·ile /désil, –il/ n. Statistics any of the nine values of a random variable which divide a frequency distribution into ten groups, each containing one-tenth of the total population. [F décile, ult. f. L decem ten]

dec·i·li·ter /désileetər/ n. a metric unit of capacity, equal to 0.1 liter.

dec·i·mal /désiməl/ adj. & n. • adj. **1** (of a system of numbers, weights, measures, etc.) based on the number ten, in which the smaller units are related to the principal units as powers of ten (units, tens, hundreds, thousands, etc.). **2** of tenths or ten; reckoning or proceeding by tens. • n. a decimal fraction. □□ **dec·i·mal·ly** adv. [mod.L decimalis f. L decimus tenth]

dec·i·mal frac·tion n. a fraction whose denominator is a power of ten, esp. when expressed positionally by units to the right of a decimal point.

dec·i·mal·ize /désiməlīz/ v.tr. **1** express as a decimal. **2** convert to a decimal system (esp. of coinage). □□ **dec·i·mal·i·za·tion** n.

dec·i·mal point n. a period or dot placed before a numerator in a decimal fraction.

dec·i·mal scale n. a scale with successive places denoting units, tens, hundreds, etc.

dec·i·mal sys·tem n. a numerical system based on units of ten.

dec·i·mate /désimayt/ v.tr. **1** disp. destroy a large proportion of. **2** orig. Mil. kill or remove one in every ten of. □□ **dec·i·ma·tion** /–máyshən/ n. **dec·i·ma·tor** n.

►The usual sense of **decimate** is now 'destroy a large proportion of': *the project would decimate the fragile wetland wilderness.* The original and literal sense is ' kill or remove one in ten of.' In any case, do not use **decimate** to mean 'defeat utterly.'

dec·i·me·ter /désimeetər/ *n.* a metric unit of length, equal to 0.1 meter.

de·ci·pher /disífər/ *v.tr.* **1** convert (a text written in cipher) into an intelligible script or language. **2** determine the meaning of (anything obscure or unclear). □□ **de·ci·pher·a·ble** *adj.* **de·ci·pher·ment** *n.*

de·ci·sion /disízhən/ *n.* **1** the act or process of deciding. **2** a conclusion or resolution reached, esp. as to future action, after consideration (*have made my decision*). **3** (often foll. by *of*) **a** the settlement of a question. **b** a formal judgment. **4** a tendency to decide firmly; resoluteness. [ME f. OF *decision* or L *decisio* (as DECIDE)]

de·ci·sive /disísiv/ *adj.* **1** that decides an issue; conclusive. **2** (of a person, esp. as a characteristic) able to decide quickly and effectively. □□ **de·ci·sive·ly** *adv.* **de·ci·sive·ness** *n.* [F *décisif –ive* f. med.L *decisivus* (as DECIDE)]

deck /dek/ *n. & v.* ●*n.* **1 a** a platform in a ship covering all or part of the hull's area at any level and serving as a floor. **b** the accommodation on a particular deck of a ship. **2** anything compared to a ship's deck, e.g., the floor or compartment of a bus. **3** a component, usu. a flat horizontal surface, that carries a particular recording medium (such as a disk or tape) in sound-reproduction equipment. **4 a** a pack of cards. **b** *sl.* a packet of narcotics. **5** *sl.* the ground. **6 a** any floor or platform, esp. the floor of a pier or a platform for sunbathing. **b** a platformlike structure, usu. made of lumber and unroofed, attached to a house, etc. **7** a level of a large, open building, esp. a sports stadium. ●*v.tr.* **1** (often foll. by *out*) decorate; adorn. **2** knock (someone) to the ground with a punch. **3** furnish with or cover as a deck. □ **below deck** (or **decks**) in or into the space below the main deck. **on deck 1** in the open air on a ship's main deck. **2** ready for action, work, etc. [ME, = covering f. MDu. *dec* roof, cloak]

deck chair *n.* a folding chair of wood and canvas, of a kind used on deck on passenger ships.

-decker /dékər/ *comb. form* having a specified number of decks or layers (*double-decker*).

deck·hand /dékhand/ *n.* a person employed in cleaning and odd jobs on a ship's deck.

deck·le /dékəl/ *n.* a device in a papermaking machine for limiting the size of the sheet. [G *Deckel* dimin. of *Decke* cover]

deck·le edge *n.* the rough uncut edge formed by a deckle.

deck·le-edged *adj.* having a deckle edge.

deck ten·nis *n.* a game in which a ring of rope or rubber is tossed back and forth over a net, played esp. on cruise ships.

de·claim /dikláym/ *v.* **1** *intr. & tr.* speak or utter rhetorically or affectedly. **2** *intr.* practice oratory or recitation. **3** *intr.* (foll. by *against*) protest forcefully. **4** *intr.* deliver an impassioned (rather than reasoned) speech. □□ **de·claim·er** *n.* [ME f. F *déclamer* or f. L *declamare* (as DE-, CLAIM)]

dec·la·ma·tion /dékləmáyshən/ *n.* **1** the act or art of declaiming. **2** a rhetorical exercise or set speech. **3** an impassioned speech; a harangue. □□ **de·clam·a·to·ry** /diklámətawree/ *adj.* [F *déclamation* or L *declamatio* (as DECLAIM)]

de·clar·ant /dikláirənt/ *n.* a person who makes a legal declaration. [F *déclarant* part. of *déclarer* (as DECLARE)]

dec·la·ra·tion /dékləráyshən/ *n.* **1** the act or process of declaring. **2 a** a formal, emphatic, or deliberate statement or announcement. **b** a statement asserting or protecting a legal right. **3** a written public announcement of intentions, terms of an agreement, etc. **4** *Cricket* an act of declaring an innings closed. **5** *Cards* **a** the naming of trump. **b** an announcement of a combination held. **6** *Law* **a** a plaintiff's statement of claim. **b** an affirmation made instead of taking an oath. [ME f. L *declaratio* (as DECLARE)]

Dec·la·ra·tion of In·dul·gence *n.* the proclamation of religious liberties, esp. under Charles II in 1672 and James II in 1687.

de·clare /dikláir/ *v.* **1** *tr.* announce openly or formally (*declare war; declare a dividend*). **2** *tr.* pronounce (a person or thing) to be something (*declared him to be an impostor; declared it invalid*). **3** *tr.* (usu. foll. by *that* + clause) assert emphatically; state explicitly. **4** *tr.* acknowledge possession of (dutiable goods, income, etc.). **5** *tr.* (as **declared** *adj.*) who admits to be such (*a declared atheist*). **6** *tr.* (also *absol.*) *Cricket* close (an innings) voluntarily before all the wickets have fallen. **7** *tr.* *Cards* **a** (also *absol.*) name (the trump suit). **b** announce that one holds (certain combinations of cards, etc.).

8 *tr.* (of things) make evident; prove (*your actions declare your honesty*). **9** *intr.* (foll. by *for, against*) take the side of one party or another. □ **declare oneself** reveal one's intentions or identity. **well, I declare** (or **I do declare**) an exclamation of incredulity, surprise, or vexation. □□ **de·clar·a·ble** *adj.* **de·clar·a·tive** /–klárətiv/ *adj.* **de·clar·a·tive·ly** *adv.* **de·clar·a·to·ry** /–klárətawree/ *adj.* **de·clar·ed·ly** /–ridlee/ *adv.* **de·clar·er** *n.* [ME f. L *declarare* (as DE-, *clarare* f. *clarus* clear)]

dé·clas·sé /dayklasáy/ *adj.* (*fem.* **dé·clas·sée**) that has fallen in social status. [F]

de·clas·si·fy /deeklásifí/ *v.tr.* (**·fies, ·fied**) declare (information, etc.) to be no longer secret. □□ **de·clas·si·fi·ca·tion** /–fikáyshən/ *n.*

de·clen·sion /diklénshən/ *n.* *Gram.* **a** a variation of the form of a noun, pronoun, or adjective, by which its grammatical case, number, and gender are identified. **b** the class in which a noun, etc., is put according to the exact form of this variation. **2** deterioration; declining. □□ **de·clen·sion·al** *adj.* [OF *declinaison* f. *decliner* DECLINE after L *declinatio*: assim. to ASCENSION, etc.]

dec·li·na·tion /déklináyshən/ *n.* **1** a downward bend or turn. **2** *Astron.* the angular distance of a star, etc., north or south of the celestial equator. **3** *Physics* the angular deviation of a compass needle from true north. **4** a formal refusal. □□ **dec·li·na·tion·al** *adj.* [ME f. L *declinatio* (as DECLINE)]

de·cline /diklín/ *v. & n.* ●*v.* **1** *intr.* deteriorate; lose strength or vigor; decrease. **2 a** *tr.* reply with formal courtesy that one will not accept (an invitation, honor, etc.). **b** *tr.* refuse, esp. formally and courteously (*declined to be made use of; declined doing anything*). **c** *tr.* turn away from (a challenge, battle, discussion, etc.). **d** *intr.* give or send a refusal. **3** *intr.* slope downward. **4** *intr.* bend down; droop. **5** *tr.* *Gram.* state the forms of (a noun, pronoun, or adjective) corresponding to cases, number, and gender. **6** *intr.* (of a day, life, etc.) draw to a close. **7** *intr.* decrease in price, etc. **8** *tr.* bend down. ●*n.* **1** gradual loss of vigor or excellence (*on the decline*). **2** decay; deterioration. **3** setting; the last part of the course (of the sun, of life, etc.). **4** a fall in price. **5** *archaic* tuberculosis or a similar wasting disease. □ **on the decline** in a declining state. □□ **de·clin·a·ble** *adj.* **de·clin·er** *n.* [ME f. OF *decliner* f. L *declinare* (as DE-, *clinare* bend)]

de·cliv·i·ty /diklívitee/ *n.* (*pl.* **·ties**) a downward slope, esp. a piece of sloping ground. □□ **de·cliv·i·tous** *adj.* [L *declivitas* f. *declivis* (as DE-, *clivus* slope)]

de·clutch /deeklúch/ *v.intr.* disengage the clutch of a motor vehicle.

dec·o /dékō/ *n.* (also **Deco**) (usu. *attrib.*) = *art deco.* [F *décoratif* DEC-ORATIVE]

de·coct /dikókt/ *v.tr.* extract the essence from by decoction. [ME f. L *decoquere* boil down]

de·coc·tion /dikókshən/ *n.* **1** the liquor resulting from concentrating the essence of a substance by heating or boiling, esp. a medicinal preparation made from a plant. **2** the action or process of extracting the essence of something. [ME f. OF *decoction* or LL *decoctio* (as DE-, L *coquere coct-* boil)]

de·code /deekṓd/ *v.tr.* convert (a coded message) into intelligible language. □□ **de·cod·a·ble** *adj.*

de·cod·er /deekṓdər/ *n.* **1** a person or thing that decodes. **2** an electronic device for analyzing signals and feeding separate amplifier channels.

de·col·late /dikólayt/ *v.tr.* *formal* **1** behead. **2** truncate. □□ **de·col·la·tion** /deekəláyshən/ *n.* [L *decollare decollat-* (as DE-, *collum* neck)]

dé·colle·tage /dáykawltáazh/ *n.* a low neckline of a woman's dress, etc. [F (as DE-, *collet* collar of a dress)]

dé·colle·té /daykawltáy/ *adj. & n.* ●*adj.* **1** (of a dress, etc.) having a low neckline. **2** (of a woman) wearing a dress with a low neckline. ●*n.* a low neckline. [F (as DÉCOLLETAGE)]

de·col·o·nize /deekólənīz/ *v.tr.* (of a nation) withdraw from (a colony), leaving it independent. □□ **de·col·o·ni·za·tion** *n.*

de·col·or·ize /deekúlərīz/ *v.* **1** *tr.* remove the color from. **2** *intr.* lose color. □□ **de·col·or·i·za·tion** *n.*

de·com·mis·sion /deekəmíshən/ *v.tr.* **1** close down (a nuclear reactor, etc.). **2** take (a ship) out of service.

de·com·pose /deekəmpṓz/ *v.* **1** *intr.* decay; rot. **2** *tr.* separate (a substance, light, etc.) into its elements or simpler constituents. **3** *intr.* disintegrate; break up. □□ **de·com·po·si·tion** /deekompəzíshən/ *n.* [F *décomposer* (as DE-, COMPOSE)]

de·com·press /deekəmprés/ *v.tr.* subject to decompression; relieve or reduce the compression on.

de·com·pres·sion /deekəmpréshən/ *n.* **1** release from compression. **2** a gradual reduction of air pressure on a person who has been subjected to high pressure (esp. underwater).

de·com·pres·sion cham·ber *n.* a small room in which the air pressure can be varied, used chiefly to allow deep-sea divers to adjust gradually to mornal air pressure.

de·com·pres·sion sick·ness *n.* = AEROEMBOLISM.

de·com·pres·sor /deékəmprésər/ n. a device for reducing pressure in the engine of a motor vehicle.

de·con·ges·tant /deékənjéstənt/ adj. & n. •adj. that relieves (esp. nasal) congestion. •n. a medicinal agent that relieves nasal congestion.

de·con·se·crate /deekónsikrayt/ v.tr. transfer (esp. a building) from sacred to secular use. □□ **de·con·se·cra·tion** /–kráyshən/ n.

de·con·struct /deékənstrúkt/ v.tr. subject to deconstruction. □□ **de·con·struc·tive** adj. [back-form. f. DECONSTRUCTION]

de·con·struc·tion /deékənstrúkshən/ n. a method of critical analysis of philosophical and literary language. □□ **de·con·struc·tion·ism** n. **de·con·struc·tion·ist** adj. & n. [F déconstruction (as DE-, CONSTRUCTION)]

de·con·tam·i·nate /deékəntáminayt/ v.tr. remove contamination from (an area, person, clothes, etc.). □□ **de·con·tam·i·na·tion** /–náyshən/ n.

de·con·trol /deékəntról/ v. & n. •v.tr. (**de·con·trolled, de·con·trol·ling**) release (a commodity, etc.) from controls or restrictions, esp. those imposed by the government. •n. the act of decontrolling.

de·cor /daykáwr, dáykawr/ n. (also **dé·cor**) 1 the furnishing and decoration of a room, etc. 2 the decoration and scenery of a stage. [F f. décorer (as DECORATE)]

dec·o·rate /dékərayt/ v.tr. 1 provide with adornments. 2 provide (a room or building) with new paint, wallpaper, etc. 3 serve as an adornment to. 4 confer an award or distinction on. [L decorare decorat- f. decus –oris beauty]

dec·o·rat·ed adj. (or **Decorated**) Archit. denoting a stage of English Gothic church architecture typical of the 14th century (between Early English and Perpendicular), with increasing use of decoration and geometrical, curvilinear, and reticulated tracery.

dec·o·ra·tion /dékəráyshən/ n. 1 the process or art of decorating. 2 a thing that decorates or serves as an ornament. 3 a medal, etc., conferred and worn as an honor. 4 (in pl.) flags, etc., put up on an occasion of public celebration. [F décoration or LL decoratio (as DECORATE)]

Dec·o·ra·tion Day n. = MEMORIAL DAY.

dec·o·ra·tive /dékərətiv, dékrə–, –əray–/ adj. serving to decorate. □□ **dec·o·ra·tive·ly** adv. **dec·o·ra·tive·ness** n. [F décoratif (as DECORATE)]

dec·o·ra·tor /dékəraytər/ n. a person who decorates, esp. one who paints or papers houses professionally.

dec·o·rous /dékərəs/ adj. 1 respecting good taste or propriety. 2 dignified and decent. □□ **dec·o·rous·ly** adv. **dec·o·rous·ness** n. [L decorus seemly]

de·cor·ti·cate /deekáwrtikayt/ v.tr. 1 remove the bark, rind, or husk from. 2 remove the outside layer from (the kidney, brain, etc.). [L decorticare decorticat- (as DE-, cortex –icis bark)]

de·cor·ti·ca·tion /deékawrtikáyshən/ n. 1 the removal of the outside layer from an organ (e.g., the kidney) or structure. 2 an operation removing the blood clot and scar tissue formed after bleeding in the chest cavity.

de·co·rum /dikáwrəm/ n. 1 a seemliness; propriety. b behavior required by politeness or decency. 2 a particular requirement of this kind. 3 etiquette. [L, neut. of decorus seemly]

de·cou·page /dáykōopáazh/ n. (also **dé·cou·page**) the decoration of surfaces with paper cutouts. [F, = the action of cutting out]

de·cou·ple /deekúpəl/ v.tr. 1 Electr. make the interaction between (oscillators, etc.) so weak that there is little transfer of energy between them. 2 separate; disengage; dissociate.

de·coy n. & v. •n. /deékoy, dikóy/ 1 a a person or thing used to lure an animal or person into a trap or danger. b a bait or enticement. 2 a pond with narrow, netted arms into which wild duck may be tempted in order to catch them. •v.tr. /dikóy/ (often foll. by into, out of) allure or entice, esp. by means of a decoy.

WORD HISTORY decoy

Mid-16th century (earlier as coy): from Dutch de kooi 'the decoy,' from Middle Dutch de kouw 'the cage,' from Latin cavea 'cage.' The meaning derives from the practice of using tamed ducks to lead wild ones along channels into captivity.

---

de·crease v. & n. •v.tr. & intr. /dikreés/ make or become smaller or fewer. •n. /deékrees/ 1 the act or an instance of decreasing. 2 the amount by which a thing decreases. □□ **de·creas·ing·ly** adv. [ME f. OF de(s)creiss-, pres. stem of de(s)creistre ult. f. L decrescere (as DE-, crescere cret- grow)]

de·cree /dikreé/ n. & v. •n. 1 an official order issued by a legal authority. 2 a judgment or decision of certain courts of law, esp. in matrimonial cases. •v.tr. (**de·crees, de·creed, de·cree·ing**) ordain by decree. [ME f. OF decré f. L decretum neut. past part. of decernere decide (as DE-, cernere sift)]

de·cree ab·so·lute n. a final order for divorce, enabling either party to remarry.

de·cree ni·si /nísī/ n. a provisional order for divorce, made absolute unless cause to the contrary is shown within a fixed period.

dec·re·ment /dékrimənt/ n. 1 Physics the ratio of the amplitudes in successive cycles of a damped oscillation. 2 the amount lost by diminution or waste. 3 the act of decreasing. [L decrementum (as DECREASE)]

de·crep·it /dikrépit/ adj. 1 weakened or worn out by age and infirmity. 2 worn out by long use; dilapidated. □□ **de·crep·i·tude** n. [ME f. L decrepitus (as DE-, crepitus past part. of crepare creak)]

de·crep·i·tate /dikrépitayt/ v. 1 tr. roast or calcine (a mineral or salt) until it stops crackling. 2 intr. crackle under heat. □□ **de·crep·i·ta·tion** /–táyshən/ n. [prob. mod.L decrepitare f. DE- + L crepitare crackle]

de·cre·scen·do /deékrishéndō, dáy–/ adv., adj., & n. (pl. **·dos**) = DIMINUENDO. [It., part. of decrescere DECREASE]

de·cres·cent /dikrésənt/ adj. (usu. of the moon) waning; decreasing. [L decrescere: see DECREASE]

de·cre·tal /dikreét'l/ n. 1 a papal decree. 2 (in pl.) a collection of these, forming part of canon law. [ME f. med.L decretale f. LL (epistola) decretalis (letter) of decree f. L decernere: see DECREE]

de·crim·i·nal·ize /deekríminəlīz/ v.tr. cease to treat (an action, etc.) as criminal. □□ **de·crim·i·nal·i·za·tion** n.

de·cry /dikrí/ v.tr. (**·cries, ·cried**) disparage; belittle. □□ **de·cri·er** n. [after F décrier: cf. cry down]

de·crypt /deekrípt/ v.tr. decipher (a cryptogram), with or without knowledge of its key. □□ **de·cryp·tion** /–krípshən/ n. [DE- + CRYPTOGRAM]

de·cum·bent /dikúmbənt/ adj. Bot. & Zool. (of a plant, shoot, or bristles) lying along the ground or a surface. [L decumbere decumbent- lie down]

de·curve /deekúrv/ v.tr. & intr. Zool. & Bot. (esp. as **decurved** adj.) curve or bend down (a decurved bill). □□ **de·cur·va·ture** n.

de·cus·sate /deekúsayt/ adj. & v. •adj. 1 X-shaped. 2 Bot. with pairs of opposite leaves, etc., each at right angles to the pair below. •v.tr. & intr. 1 arrange or be arranged in a decussate form. 2 intersect. □□ **de·cus·sa·tion** /–sáyshən/ n. [L decussatus past part. of decussare divide in a cross shape f. decussis the numeral ten or the shape X f. decem ten]

de·dans /dədón/ n. 1 (in court tennis) the open gallery at the end of the service side of a court. 2 the spectators watching a match. [F, = inside]

ded·i·cate /dédikayt/ v.tr. 1 (foll. by to) devote (esp. oneself) to a special task or purpose. 2 (foll. by to) dedicate (a book, piece of music, etc.) as a compliment to a friend, patron, etc. 3 (often foll. by to) devote (a building, etc.) to a deity or a sacred person or purpose. 4 (as **dedicated** adj.) a (of a person) devoted to an aim or vocation; having single-minded loyalty or integrity. b (of equipment, esp. a computer) designed for a specific purpose. □□ **ded·i·ca·tee** /–kaytee/ n. **ded·i·ca·tive** adj. **ded·i·ca·tor** n. **ded·i·ca·to·ry** /–kətáwree/ adj. [L dedicare (DE-, dicare declare, dedicate)]

ded·i·ca·tion /dédikáyshən/ n. 1 the act or an instance of dedicating; the quality or process of being dedicated. 2 the words with which a book, etc., is dedicated. 3 a dedicatory inscription. [ME f. OF dedicacion or L dedicatio (as DEDICATE)]

de·duce /didōōs, –dyōōs/ v.tr. 1 (often foll. by from) infer; draw as a logical conclusion. 2 archaic trace the course or derivation of. □□ **de·duc·i·ble** adj. [L deducere (as DE-, ducere duct- lead)]

de·duct /didúkt/ v.tr. (often foll. by from) subtract, take away, withhold (an amount, portion, etc.). [L (as DEDUCE)]

de·duct·i·ble /didúktibəl/ adj. & n. •adj. that may be deducted, esp. from tax to be paid or taxable income. •n. part of an insurance claim to be paid by the insured, esp. by prior agreement.

de·duc·tion /didúkshən/ n. 1 a the act of deducting. b an amount deducted. 2 a the inferring of particular instances from a general law (cf. INDUCTION). b a conclusion deduced. [ME f. OF deduction or L deductio (as DEDUCE)]

de·duc·tive /didúktiv/ adj. of or reasoning by deduction. □□ **de·duc·tive·ly** adv. [med.L deductivus (as DEDUCE)]

dee /dee/ n. 1 the letter D. 2 a a thing shaped like this. b Physics either of two hollow semicircular electrodes in a cyclotron. [the name of the letter]

deed /deed/ n. & v. •n. 1 a thing done intentionally or consciously. 2 a brave, skillful, or conspicuous act. 3 actual fact or performance (kind in word and deed; in deed and not in name). 4 Law a written or printed document often used for a legal transfer of ownership and bearing the disposer's signature. •v.tr. convey or transfer by legal deed. [OE dēd f. Gmc: cf. DO¹]

deed poll n. (pl. **deeds poll**) a deed made and executed by one party only, esp. to change one's name.

dee·jay /deéjáy/ n. sl. a disk jockey. [abbr. DJ]

deem /deem/ v.tr. formal regard; consider; judge (deem it my duty; was deemed sufficient). [OE dēman f. Gmc, rel. to DOOM]

de-em·pha·size /dee-émfəsīz/ v.tr. 1 remove emphasis from. 2 reduce emphasis on.

deem·ster /deémstər/ n. a judge of the Isle of Man. [DEEM + –STER]

deep /deep/ adj., n., & adv. •adj. 1 a extending far down from the top (*deep hole; deep water*). **b** extending far in from the surface or edge (*deep wound; deep plunge; deep shelf; deep border*). **2** (*predic.*) **a** extending to or lying at a specified depth (*water 6 feet deep; ankle-deep in mud*). **b** in a specified number of ranks one behind another (*soldiers drawn up six deep*). **3** situated far down or back or in (*hands deep in his pockets*). **4** coming or brought from far down or in (*deep breath; deep sigh*). **5** low-pitched; full-toned; not shrill (*deep voice; deep note; deep bell*). **6** intense; vivid; extreme (*deep disgrace; deep sleep; deep color; deep secret*). **7** heartfelt; absorbing (*deep affection; deep feelings; deep interest*). **8** (*predic.*) fully absorbed or overwhelmed (*deep in a book; deep in debt*). **9** profound; penetrating; not superficial; difficult to understand (*deep thinker; deep thought; deep insight; deep learning*). **10** *Cricket* distant from the batsman (*deep mid-off*). **11** *Football, Soccer, etc.* distant from the front line of one's team. **12** *sl.* cunning or secretive (*a deep one*). • *n.* **1** (prec. by *the*) *poet.* the sea. **2** a deep part of the sea. **3** an abyss, pit, or cavity. **4** (prec. by *the*) *Cricket* the position of a fielder distant from the batsman. **5** a deep state (*deep of the night*). **6** *poet.* a mysterious region of thought or feeling. • *adv.* deeply; far down or in (*dig deep; read deep into the night*). □ **deep kiss** a kiss with contact between tongues. **go off the deep end** *colloq.* give way to anger or emotion. **in deep water** (or **waters**) in trouble or difficulty. **jump** (or **be thrown**) **in at the deep end** face a difficult problem, undertaking, etc., with little experience of it. □□ **deep•ly** *adv.* **deep•ness** *n.* [OE *dēop* (adj.), *dīope, dēope* (adv.), f. Gmc: rel. to DIP]

deep-drawn *adj.* (of metal, etc.) shaped by forcing through a die when cold.

deep•en /deepən/ *v.tr. & intr.* make or become deep or deeper.

deep•en•ing /deepəning/ *n.* the act or process of making deeper, esp. the implementation of measures (such as economic and monetary union) to deepen and strengthen the ties among EC countries.

deep freeze *n.* **1** a refrigerator in which food can be quickly frozen and kept for long periods at a very low temperature. **2** a suspension of activity. □□ **deep-freeze** *v.tr.*

deep-fry *v.tr.* (**•fries, •fried**) fry (food) in an amount of fat or oil sufficient to cover it.

deep-laid *adj.* (of a scheme) secret and elaborate.

deep mourn•ing *n.* mourning expressed by wearing only black clothes.

deep-root•ed *adj.* (esp. of convictions) firmly established.

deep-sea *adj.* denoting the deeper parts of the ocean (*deep-sea diving*).

deep-seat•ed *adj.* (of emotion, disease, etc.) firmly established; profound.

Deep South *n.* the region of the SE US, usu. including South Carolina, Georgia, Alabama, Mississippi, and Louisiana.

deep space *n.* the regions of outer space beyond the solar system.

deer /deer/ *n.* (pl. same) any four-hoofed grazing animal of the family Cervidae, the males of which usu. have deciduous branching antlers. [OE *dēor* animal, deer]

deer•fly /deerfli/ *n.* any bloodsucking fly of the genus *Chrysops*.

deer•hound /deerhownd/ *n.* a large, rough-haired greyhound.

deer lick *n.* a spring or damp spot either artificially or naturally impregnated with salt, where deer come to lick.

deer•skin /deerskin/ *n. & adj.* • *n.* leather from a deer's skin. • *adj.* made from a deer's skin.

whitetail deer

deer•stalk•er /deerstawkər/ *n.* **1** a soft cloth cap with peaks in front and behind and earflaps often joined at the top. **2** a person who stalks deer.

de-es•ca•late /dee-éskəlayt/ *v.tr.* reduce the level or intensity of. □□ **de-es•ca•la•tion** /-láyshən/ *n.*

de•face /difáys/ *v.tr.* **1** spoil the appearance of; disfigure. **2** make illegible. □□ **de•face•a•ble** *adj.* **de•face•ment** *n.* **de•fac•er** *n.* [ME f. F *défacer* f. OF *desfacier* (as DE-, FACE)]

de fac•to /di fáktō, day/ *adv., adj., & n.* • *adv.* in fact, whether by right or not. • *adj.* that exists or is such in fact (*a de facto ruler*). • *n.* (in full **de facto wife** or **husband**) a person living with another as if married. [L]

de•fal•cate /deefálkayt, –fáwl–/ *v.intr. formal* misappropriate property in one's charge, esp. money. □□ **de•fal•ca•tor** *n.* [med.L *defalcare* lop (as DE-, L *falx –cis* sickle)]

de•fal•ca•tion /deefalkáyshən, –fawl–/ *n.* **1** *Law* **a** a misappropriation of money. **b** an amount misappropriated. **2** *formal* a shortcoming. **3** *formal* defection. [ME f. med.L *defalcatio* (as DEFALCATE)]

de•fame /difáym/ *v.tr.* attack the good reputation of; speak ill of. □□ **def•a•ma•tion** /défəmáyshən/ *n.* **de•fam•a•to•ry** /difámətawree/ *adj.* **de•fam•er** *n.* [ME f. OF *diffamer*, etc. f. L *diffamare* spread evil report (as DIS-, *fama* report)]

de•fat /deefát/ *v.tr.* (**de•fat•ted, de•fat•ting**) remove fat or fats from.

de•fault /difáwlt/ *n. & v.* • *n.* **1** failure to fulfill an obligation, esp. to appear, pay, or act in some way. **2** lack; absence. **3** a preselected option adopted by a computer program when no alternative is specified by the user or programmer. • *v.* **1** *intr.* fail to fulfill an obligation, esp. to pay money or to appear in a court of law. **2** *tr.* declare (a party) in default and give judgment against that party. □ **go by default 1** be ignored because of absence. **2** be absent. **in default of** because of the absence of. **judgment by default** judgment given for the plaintiff on the defendant's failure to plead. **win by default** win because an opponent fails to be present. [ME f. OF *defaut(e)* f. *defaillir* fail f. Rmc (as DE-, L *fallere* deceive): cf. FAIL]

de•fault•er /difáwltər/ *n.* a person who defaults, esp. *Brit.* a soldier guilty of a military offense.

de•fea•sance /difeezəns/ *n.* the act or process of rendering null and void. [ME f. OF *defesance* f. *de(s)faire* undo (as DE-, *faire* make f. L *facere*)]

de•fea•si•ble /difeezibəl/ *adj.* **1** capable of annulment. **2** liable to forfeiture. □□ **de•fea•si•bil•i•ty** *n.* **de•feas•i•bly** *adv.* [AF (as DEFEASANCE)]

de•feat /difeet/ *v. & n.* • *v.tr.* **1** overcome in a battle or other contest. **2** frustrate; baffle. **3** reject (a motion, etc.) by voting. **4** *Law* annul. • *n.* the act or process of defeating or being defeated. [ME f. OF *deffait, desfait* past part. of *desfaire* f. med.L *disfacere* (as DIS-, L *facere* do)]

de•feat•ism /difeetizəm/ *n.* **1** an excessive readiness to accept defeat. **2** conduct conducive to this. □□ **de•feat•ist** *n. & adj.* [F *défaitisme* f. *défaite* DEFEAT]

def•e•cate /défikayt/ *v.intr.* discharge feces from the body. □□ **def•e•ca•tion** /–káyshən/ *n.* [earlier as adj., = purified, f. L *defaecare* (as DE-, *faex faecis* dregs)]

de•fect *n. & v.* /deefekt, difékt/ **1** lack of something essential or required; imperfection. **2** a shortcoming or failing. **3** a blemish. **4** the amount by which a thing falls short. • *v.intr.* /difékt/ abandon one's country or cause in favor of another. □□ **de•fec•tor** *n.* [L *defectus* f. *deficere* desert, fail (as DE-, *facere* do)]

de•fec•tion /difékshən/ *n.* **1** the abandonment of one's country or cause. **2** ceasing in allegiance to a leader, party, religion, or duty. [L *defectio* (as DEFECT)]

de•fec•tive /diféktiv/ *adj. & n.* • *adj.* **1** having a defect or defects; incomplete; imperfect; faulty. **2** often *offens.* mentally subnormal. **3** (usu. foll. by *in*) lacking; deficient. **4** *Gram.* not having all the usual inflections. • *n. offens.* a mentally defective person. □□ **de•fec•tive•ly** *adv.* **de•fec•tive•ness** *n.* [ME f. OF *defectif –ive* or LL *defectivus* (as DEFECT)]

de•fence *Brit.* var. of DEFENSE.

de•fend /difénd/ *v.tr.* (also *absol.*) **1** (often foll. by *against, from*) resist an attack made on; protect (a person or thing) from harm or danger. **2** support or uphold by argument; speak or write in favor of. **3** conduct the case for (a defendant in a lawsuit). □□ **de•fend•a•ble** *adj.* **de•fend•er** *n.* [ME f. OF *defendre* f. L *defendere*: cf. OFFEND]

de•fend•ant /diféndənt, –ant/ *n.* a person, etc., sued or accused in a court of law. [ME f. OF, part. of *defendre*: see DEFEND]

de•fen•es•tra•tion /deefénistráyshən/ *n. formal* or *joc.* the action of throwing (esp. a person) out of a window. □□ **de•fen•es•trate** /deefénistrayt/ *v.tr.* [mod.L *defenestratio* (as DE-, L *fenestra* window)]

de•fense /diféns/ *n.* (*Brit.* **de•fence**) **1** the act of defending from or resisting attack. **2 a** a means of resisting attack. **b** a thing that protects. **c** the military resources of a country. **3** (in *pl.*) fortifications. **4 a** a justification; vindication. **b** a speech or piece of writing used to this end. **5 a** the defendant's case in a lawsuit. **b** the counsel for the defendant. **6** /deefens/ **a** the action or role of defending one's goal, etc., against attack. **b** the players on a team who perform this role. □□ **de•fense•less** *adj.* **de•fense•less•ly** *adv.* **de•fense•less•ness** *n.* [ME f. OF *defens(e)* f. LL *defensum, –a,* past part. of *defendere*: see DEFEND]

de•fense mech•an•ism *n.* **1** an automatic reaction of the body against disease-causing organisms. **2** a usu. unconscious mental process such as denial or rationalization, initiated to avoid conscious conflict or anxiety.

de•fen•si•ble /difénsibəl/ *adj.* **1** justifiable; supportable by argument. **2** that can be easily defended militarily. □□ **de•fen•si•bil•i•ty** *n.* **de•fen•si•bly** *adv.* [LL *defensibilis* (as DEFEND)]

de•fen•sive /difénsiv/ *adj.* **1** done or intended for defense or to defend. **2** (of a person or attitude) concerned to challenge criticism. □ **on the defensive 1** expecting criticism. **2** in an attitude or position of defense. □□ **de•fen•sive•ly** *adv.* **de•fen•sive•ness** *n.* [ME f. F *défensif –ive* f. med.L *defensivus* (as DEFEND)]

de•fer[1] /difér/ *v.tr.* (**de•ferred, de•fer•ring**) **1** put off to a later time; postpone. **2** postpone the conscription of (a person). □□ **de•fer•ment** *n.* **de•fer•ra•ble** *adj.* **de•fer•ral** *n.* [ME, orig. the same as DIFFER]

de·fer[2] /difór/ *v.intr.* (**de·ferred, de·fer·ring**) (foll. by *to*) yield or make concessions in opinion or action. □□ **de·fer·rer** *n.* [ME f. F *déférer* f. L *deferre* (as DE-, *ferre* bring)]

def·er·ence /défərəns, défrəns/ *n.* 1 courteous regard; respect. 2 compliance with the advice or wishes of another (*pay deference to*). □ **in deference to** out of respect for. [F *déférence* (as DEFER[2])]

def·er·en·tial /défərénshəl/ *adj.* showing deference; respectful. □□ **def·er·en·tial·ly** *adv.* [DEFERENCE, after PRUDENTIAL, etc.]

de·ferred pay·ment *n.* the temporary postponing of payment of an outstanding debt, usually involving repayment by installments.

de·fi·ance /difîəns/ *n.* 1 open disobedience; bold resistance. 2 a challenge to fight or maintain a cause, assertion, etc. □ **in defiance of** disregarding; in conflict with. [ME f. OF (as DEFY)]

de·fi·ant /difîənt/ *adj.* 1 showing defiance. 2 openly disobedient. □□ **de·fi·ant·ly** *adv.*

de·fib·ril·la·tion /déefibriláyshən/ *n. Med.* the stopping of the fibrillation of the heart. □□ **de·fib·ril·la·tor** /deefíbrilaytər/ *n.*

de·fi·cien·cy /difíshənsee/ *n.* (*pl.* **·cies**) 1 the state or condition of being deficient. 2 (usu. foll. by *of*) a lack or shortage. 3 a thing lacking. 4 the amount by which a thing, esp. revenue, falls short.

de·fi·cien·cy dis·ease *n.* a disease caused by the lack of some essential or important element in the diet.

de·fi·cient /difíshənt/ *adj.* 1 (usu. foll. by *in*) incomplete; not having enough of a specified quality or ingredient. 2 insufficient in quantity, force, etc. 3 (in full **mentally deficient**) incapable of adequate social or intellectual behavior through imperfect mental development. □□ **de·fi·cient·ly** *adv.* [L *deficiens* part. of *deficere* (as DEFECT)]

def·i·cit /défisit/ *n.* 1 the amount by which a thing (esp. a sum of money) is too small. 2 an excess of liabilities over assets in a given period, esp. a financial year (opp. SURPLUS). [F *déficit* f. L *deficit* 3rd sing. pres. of *deficere* (as DEFECT)]

def·i·cit fi·nanc·ing *n.* financing of (esp. government) spending by borrowing.

def·i·cit spend·ing *n.* spending, esp. by a government, financed by borrowing.

de·fi·er /difîər/ *n.* a person who defies.

de·fi·lade /défiláyd, -laád/ *v.* & *n.* • *v.tr.* secure (a fortification) against enfilading fire. • *n.* this precaution or arrangement. [DEFILE[2] + –ADE[1]]

de·file[1] /difíl/ *v.tr.* 1 make dirty; pollute; befoul. 2 corrupt. 3 desecrate; profane. 4 deprive (esp. a woman) of virginity. 5 make ceremonially unclean. □□ **de·file·ment** *n.* **de·fil·er** *n.* [ME *defoul* f. OF *defouler* trample down, outrage (as DE-, *fouler* tread, trample) altered after obs. *befile* f. OE *befylan* (BE-, *fūl* FOUL)]

de·file[2] /difíl/ *n.* & *v.* • *n.* also /deéfil/ 1 a narrow way through which troops can only march in file. 2 a gorge. • *v.intr.* march in file. [F *défiler* and *défilé* past part. (as DE-, FILE[2])]

de·fine /difín/ *v.tr.* 1 give the exact meaning of (a word, etc.). 2 describe or explain the scope of (*define one's position*). 3 make clear, esp. in outline (*well-defined image*). 4 mark out the boundary or limits of. 5 (of properties) make up the total character of. □□ **de·fin·a·ble** *adj.* **de·fin·er** *n.* [ME f. OF *definer* ult. f. L *definire* (as DE-, *finire* finish, f. *finis* end)]

def·i·nite /définit/ *adj.* 1 having exact and discernible limits. 2 clear and distinct; not vague. □□ **def·i·nite·ness** *n.* [L *definitus* past part. of *definire* (as DEFINE)]

▶See note at *definitive*.

def·i·nite ar·ti·cle *n. Gram.* the word (*the* in English) preceding a noun and implying a specific or known instance (as in *the book on the table*; *the art of government*; *the famous university at Oxford*).

def·i·nite in·te·gral *n.* see INTEGRAL.

def·i·nite·ly /définitlee/ *adv.* & *int.* • *adv.* 1 in a definite manner. 2 certainly; without doubt (*they were definitely there*). • *int. colloq.* yes, certainly.

def·i·ni·tion /définíshən/ *n.* 1 **a** the act or process of defining. **b** a statement of the meaning of a word or the nature of a thing. 2 **a** the degree of distinctness in outline of an object or image (esp. of an image produced by a lens or shown in a photograph or on a motion picture or television screen). **b** making or being distinct in outline. [ME f. OF f. L *definitio* (as DEFINE)]

de·fin·i·tive /difínitiv/ *adj.* 1 (of an answer, treaty, verdict, etc.) decisive; unconditional; final. 2 (of an edition of a book, etc.) most authoritative. 3 *Philately* (of a series of stamps) for permanent use, not commemorative, etc. □□ **de·fin·i·tive·ly** *adv.* [ME f. OF *definitif* –*ive* f. L *definitivus* (as DEFINE)]

▶**Definitive** in the sense 'decisive, unconditional, final' is sometimes confused with **definite**. However, **definite** does not have the connotations of authority: a *definite no* is simply a firm refusal, whereas a *definitive no* is an authoritative judgment or decision that something is not the case.

def·la·grate /défləgrayt/ *v.tr.* & *intr.* burn away with sudden flame. □□ **def·la·gra·tion** /-gráyshən/ *n.* **def·la·gra·tor** *n.* [L *deflagrare* (as DE-, *flagrare* blaze)]

de·flate /difláyt/ *v.* 1 **a** let air or gas out of (a tire, balloon, etc.). **b** *intr.* be emptied of air or gas. 2 **a** *tr.* cause to lose confidence or conceit. **b** *intr.* lose confidence. 3 *Econ.* **a** *tr.* subject (a currency or economy) to deflation. **b** *intr.* pursue a policy of deflation. 4 *tr.* reduce the importance of, depreciate. □□ **de·fla·tor** *n.* [DE- + INFLATE]

de·fla·tion /difláyshən/ *n.* 1 the act or process of deflating or being deflated. 2 *Econ.* reduction of the amount of money in circulation to increase its value as a measure against inflation. 3 *Geol.* the removal of particles of rock, etc., by the wind. □□ **de·fla·tion·ar·y** *adj.* **de·fla·tion·ist** *n.*

de·flect /diflékt/ *v.* 1 *tr.* & *intr.* bend or turn aside from a straight course or intended purpose. 2 (often foll. by *from*) **a** *tr.* cause to deviate. **b** *intr.* deviate. [L *deflectere* (as DE-, *flectere flex*- bend)]

de·flec·tion /diflékshən/ *n.* (also *Brit.* **de·flex·ion**) 1 the act or process of deflecting or being deflected. 2 a lateral bend or turn; a deviation. 3 *Physics* the displacement of a pointer on an instrument from its zero position. [LL *deflexio* (as DEFLECT)]

de·flec·tor /difléktər/ *n.* a thing that deflects, esp. a device for deflecting a flow of air, etc.

def·lo·ra·tion /déeflawráyshən/ *n.* deflowering. [ME f. OF or f. LL *defloratio* (as DEFLOWER)]

de·flow·er /diflówr/ *v.tr.* 1 deprive (esp. a woman) of virginity. 2 ravage; spoil. 3 strip of flowers. [ME f. OF *deflourer*, *des-*, ult. f. LL *deflorare* (as DE-, L *flos floris* flower)]

de·fo·cus /deefókəs/ *v.tr.* & *intr.* (**de·fo·cused, de·fo·cus·ing** or **de·fo·cussed, de·fo·cus·sing**) put or go out of focus.

de·fo·li·ate /deefóleeayt/ *v.tr.* remove leaves from, esp. as a military tactic. □□ **de·fo·li·ant** *n.* & *adj.* **de·fo·li·a·tion** /-áyshən/ *n.* **de·fo·li·a·tor** *n.* [LL *defoliare* f. *folium* leaf]

de·for·est /deefáwrist, -fór-/ *v.tr.* clear of forests or trees. □□ **de·for·est·a·tion** *n.*

de·form /difáwrm/ *v.* 1 *tr.* make ugly; deface. 2 *tr.* put out of shape; misshape. 3 *intr.* undergo deformation; be deformed. □□ **de·form·a·ble** *adj.* [ME f. OF *deformer*, etc., f. med.L *difformare* ult. f. L *deformare* (as DE-, *formare* f. *forma* shape)]

de·for·ma·tion /déefawrmáyshən/ *n.* 1 disfigurement. 2 *Physics* **a** (often foll. by *of*) change in shape. **b** a quantity representing the amount of this change. 3 a perverted form of a word (e.g., *dang* for *damn*). □□ **de·for·ma·tion·al** *adj.* [ME f. OF *deformation* or L *deformatio* (as DEFORM)]

de·formed /difáwrmd/ *adj.* (of a person or limb) misshapen.

de·form·i·ty /difáwrmitee/ *n.* (*pl.* **·ties**) 1 the state of being deformed; ugliness; disfigurement. 2 a malformation, esp. of body or limb. 3 a moral defect; depravity. [ME f. OF *deformité*, etc., f. L *deformitas* –*tatis* f. *deformis* (as DE-, *forma* shape)]

de·fraud /difráwd/ *v.tr.* (often foll. by *of*) cheat by fraud. □□ **de·fraud·er** *n.* [ME f. OF *defrauder* or L *defraudare* (as DE-, FRAUD)]

de·fray /difráy/ *v.tr.* provide money to pay (a cost or expense). □□ **de·fray·a·ble** *adj.* **de·fray·al** *n.* **de·fray·ment** *n.* [F *défrayer* (as DE-, obs. *frai(t)* cost, f. med.L *fredum*, –*us* fine for breach of the peace)]

de·frock /deefrók/ *v.tr.* deprive (a person, esp. a priest) of ecclesiastical status. [F *défroquer* (as DE-, FROCK)]

de·frost /difráwst, –fróst/ *v.* 1 *tr.* **a** free (the interior of a refrigerator) of excess frost, usu. by turning it off for a period. **b** remove frost or ice from (esp. the windshield of a motor vehicle). 2 *tr.* unfreeze (frozen food). 3 *intr.* become unfrozen. □□ **de·frost·er** *n.*

deft /deft/ *adj.* neatly skillful or dexterous; adroit. □□ **deft·ly** *adv.* **deft·ness** *n.* [ME, var. of DAFT in obs. sense 'meek']

de·funct /difúngkt/ *adj.* 1 no longer existing. 2 no longer used or in fashion. 3 dead or extinct. □□ **de·funct·ness** *n.* [L *defunctus* dead, past part. of *defungi* (as DE-, *fungi* perform)]

de·fuse /deefyóoz/ *v.tr.* 1 remove the fuse from (an explosive device). 2 reduce the tension or potential danger in (a crisis, difficulty, etc.).

de·fy /difî/ *v.tr.* (**·fies, ·fied**) 1 resist openly; refuse to obey. 2 (of a thing) present insuperable obstacles to (*defies solution*). 3 (foll. by *to* + infin.) challenge (a person) to do or prove something. 4 *archaic* challenge to combat. [ME f. OF *defier* f. Rmc (as DIS-, L *fidus* faithful)]

deg. *abbr.* degree.

dé·ga·gé /daygaazháy/ *adj.* (*fem.* **dé·ga·gée**) easy; unconstrained. [F, past part. of *dégager* set free]

de·gas /deegás/ *v.tr.* (**de·gassed, de·gas·sing**) remove unwanted gas from.

de·gauss /deegóws/ *v.tr.* neutralize the magnetism in (a thing) by encircling it with a current-carrying conductor. □□ **de·gauss·er** *n.* [DE- + GAUSS]

de·gen·er·ate *adj.*, *n.*, & *v.* • *adj.* /díjénərət/ 1 having lost the qualities that are normal and desirable or proper to its kind; fallen from former excellence. 2 *Biol.* having changed to a lower type. • *n.* /díjénərət/ a degenerate person or animal. • *v.intr.* /díjénərayt/ become degenerate. □□ **de·gen·er·a·cy** *n.* **de·gen·er·ate·ly** *adv.* [L *degeneratus* past part. of *degenerare* (as DE-, *genus* –*eris* race)]

de·gen·er·a·tion /díjénəráyshən/ *n.* 1 **a** the process of becoming degenerate. **b** the state of being degenerate. 2 *Med.* morbid deterioration of tissue or change in its structure. [ME f. F *dégéneration* or f. LL *degeneratio* (as DEGENERATE)]

de·gen·er·a·tive /dijénərətiv/ *adj.* **1** of or tending to degeneration. **2** (of disease) characterized by progressive often irreversible deterioration.

de·grade /digráyd/ *v.* **1** *tr.* reduce to a lower rank, esp. as a punishment. **2** *tr.* bring into dishonor or contempt. **3** *tr. Chem.* reduce to a simpler molecular structure. **4** *tr. Physics* reduce (energy) to a less convertible form. **5** *tr. Geol.* wear down (rocks, etc.) by disintegration. **6** *intr.* degenerate. **7** *intr. Chem.* disintegrate. □□ **de·grad·a·ble** *adj.* **deg·ra·da·tion** /dégrədáyshən/ *n.* **deg·ra·da·tive** /–dáytiv/ *adj.* **de·grad·er** *n.* [ME f. OF *degrader* f. eccl.L *degradare* (as DE-, L *gradus* step)]

de·grad·ing /digráyding/ *adj.* humiliating; causing a loss of self-respect. □□ **de·grad·ing·ly** *adv.*

de·grease /deegreés/ *v.tr.* remove unwanted grease or fat from.

de·gree /digreé/ *n.* **1** a stage in an ascending or descending scale, series, or process. **2** a stage in intensity or amount (*to a high degree; in some degree*). **3** relative condition (*each is good in its degree*). **4** *Math.* a unit of measurement of angles, one-ninetieth of a right angle or the angle subtended by one-three-hundred-and-sixtieth of the circumference of a circle. ¶ Symb.: ° (as in 45°). **5** *Physics* a unit in a scale of temperature, hardness, etc. ¶ Abbr.: **deg.** (or omitted in the Kelvin scale of temperature). **6** *Med.* an extent of burns on a scale characterized by the destruction of the skin. **7** an academic rank conferred by a college or university after examination or after completion of a course, or conferred as an honor on a distinguished person. **8** a grade of crime or criminality (*murder in the first degree*). **9** a step in direct genealogical descent. **10** social or official rank. **11** *Math.* the highest power of unknowns or variables in an equation, etc. (*equation of the third degree*). **12** a masonic rank. **13** a thing placed like a step in a series; a tier or row. **14** *Mus.* the classification of a note by its position in the scale. □ **by degrees** a little at a time; gradually. **to a degree** *colloq.* considerably. □□ **de·gree·less** *adj.* [ME f. OF *degré* f. Rmc (as DE-, L *gradus* step)]

de·gree-day *n.* a unit of measurement equal to one degree of variation between a standard temperature and the mean temperature on a given day.

de·gree of free·dom *n.* **1** *Physics* the independent direction in which motion can occur. **2** *Chem.* the number of independent factors required to specify a system at equilibrium. **3** *Statistics* the number of independent values or quantities that can be assigned to a statistical distribution.

de·grees of com·par·i·son *n.* see COMPARISON.

de·gres·sive /digrésiv/ *adj.* **1** (of taxation) at successively lower rates on low amounts. **2** reducing in amount. [L *degredi* (as DE-, *gradi* walk)]

de haut en bas /də ót awN baá/ *adv.* in a condescending or superior manner. [F, = from above to below]

de·hisce /dihís/ *v.intr.* gape or burst open (esp. of a pod or seed vessel or of a cut or wound). □□ **de·his·cence** *n.* **de·his·cent** *adj.* [L *dehiscere* (as DE-, *hiscere* incept. of *hiare* gape)]

de·horn /deéháwrn/ *v.tr.* remove the horns from (an animal).

de·hu·man·ize /deehyoómənīz/ *v.tr.* **1** deprive of human characteristics. **2** make impersonal or machinelike. □□ **de·hu·man·i·za·tion** *n.*

de·hu·mid·i·fy /deéhyoómídifī/ *v.tr.* (·**fies**, ·**fied**) reduce the degree of humidity of; remove moisture from (a gas, esp. air). □□ **de·hu·mid·i·fi·ca·tion** /–fikáyshən/ *n.* **de·hu·mid·i·fi·er** *n.*

de·hy·drate /deéhīdráyt/ *v.* **1** *tr.* **a** remove water from (esp. foods for preservation and storage in bulk). **b** make dry, esp. make (the body) deficient in water. **c** render lifeless or uninteresting. **2** *intr.* lose water. □□ **de·hy·dra·tion** /–dráyshən/ *n.* **de·hy·dra·tor** *n.*

de·hy·dro·gen·ate /deéhīdrójinayt/ *v.tr. Chem.* remove a hydrogen atom or atoms from (a compound). □□ **de·hy·dro·gen·a·tion** /–náyshən/ *n.*

de·ice /deeís/ *v.tr.* **1** remove ice from. **2** prevent the formation of ice on.

de·ic·er /deeísər/ *n.* a device or substance for deicing, esp. a windshield or an aircraft.

de·i·cide /deé-isīd, dáy-/ *n.* **1** the killer of a god. **2** the killing of a god. [eccl.L *deicida* f. L *deus* god + –CIDE]

deic·tic /díktik/ *adj. & n. Philol. & Gram.* • *adj.* pointing; demonstrative. • *n.* a deictic word. [Gk *deiktikos* f. *deiktos* capable of proof f. *deiknumi* show]

de·i·fy /deé-ifī, dáyee–/ *v.tr.* (·**fies**, ·**fied**) **1** make a god of. **2** regard or worship as a god. □□ **de·i·fi·ca·tion** /–fikáyshən/ *n.* [ME f. OF *deifier* f. eccl.L *deificare* f. *deus* god]

deign /dayn/ *v.* **1** *intr.* (foll. by *to* + infin.) think fit; condescend. **2** *tr.* (usu. with *neg.*) *archaic* condescend to give (an answer, etc.). [ME f. OF *degnier, deigner, daigner* f. L *dignare, –ari* deem worthy f. *dignus* worthy]

De·i gra·ti·a /dáyee gráateeə, deé-ī, graásheeə/ *adv.* by the grace of God. [L]

de·in·sti·tu·tion·al·ize /deé-institoóshənəliz, –tyoó–/ *v.tr.* (usu. as **de·institutionalized** *adj.*) remove from an institution or from the effects of institutional life. □□ **de·in·sti·tu·tion·al·i·za·tion** *n.*

de·i·on·ize /deeíənīz/ *v.tr.* remove the ions or ionic constituents from (water, air, etc.). □□ **de·i·on·i·za·tion** /–ízáyshən/ *n.* **de·i·on·iz·er** *n.*

deip·nos·o·phist /dipnósəfist/ *n.* a person skilled in dining and table talk. [Gk *deipnosophistēs* (in pl. as title of a work by Athenaeus (3rd c.) describing long discussions at a banquet) f. *deipnon* dinner + *sophistēs* wise man: see SOPHIST]

de·ism /deéizəm, dáy–/ *n.* belief in the existence of a supreme being arising from reason rather than revelation (cf. THEISM). □□ **de·ist** *n.* **de·is·tic** *adj.* **de·is·ti·cal** *adj.* [L *deus* god + –ISM]

de·i·ty /deéitee, dáy–/ *n.* (*pl.* ·**ties**) **1** a god or goddess. **2** divine status, quality, or nature. **3** (**the Deity**) the Creator, God. [ME f. OF *deité* f. eccl.L *deitas* –*tatis* transl. Gk *theotēs* f. *theos* god]

dé·jà vu /dáyzhaa voó/ *n.* **1** *Psychol.* an illusory feeling of having already experienced a present situation. **2** something tediously familiar. [F, = already seen]

de·ject /dijékt/ *v.tr.* (usu. as **dejected** *adj.*) make sad or dispirited; depress. □□ **de·ject·ed·ly** *adv.* [ME f. L *dejicere* (DE-, *jacĕre* throw)]

de·jec·tion /dijékshən/ *n.* a dejected state; low spirits. [ME f. L *dejectio* (as DEJECT)]

de ju·re /dee joóree, day joóray/ *adj. & adv.* • *adj.* rightful. • *adv.* rightfully; by right. [L]

dek·ko /dékō/ *n.* (*pl.* ·**kos**) *Brit. sl.* a look or glance (*took a quick dekko*). [Hindi *dekho*, imper. of *dekhnā* look]

Del. *abbr.* Delaware.

Del·a·ware /déləwair/ *n.* **1 a** a N. American people native to the northeastern US. **b** a member of this people. **2** the language of this people. Also called Lenape or Lenni Lenape.

de·late /diláyt/ *v.tr. archaic* **1** inform against; impeach (a person). **2** report (an offense). □□ **de·la·tion** /–láyshən/ *n.* **de·la·tor** *n.* [L *delat*- (as DE-, *lat*- past part. stem of *ferre* carry)]

de·lay /diláy/ *v. & n.* • *v.* **1** *tr.* postpone; defer. **2** *tr.* make late (*was delayed by the traffic lights*). **3** *intr.* loiter; be late (*don't delay!*). • *n.* **1** the act or an instance of delaying; the process of being delayed. **2** time lost by inaction or the inability to proceed. **3** a hindrance. □□ **de·lay·er** *n.* [ME f. OF *delayer* (v.), *delai* (n.), prob. f. *des*- DIS- + *laier* leave: see RELAY]

de·layed-ac·tion *adj.* (esp. of a bomb, camera, etc.) operating or effective after a predetermined length of time.

de·lay line *n. Electr.* a device producing a desired delay in the transmission of a signal.

de·le /deélee/ *v. & n. Printing* • *v.tr.* (**de·led, de·le·ing**) delete or mark for deletion (a letter, word, etc., struck out of a text). • *n.* a sign marking something to be deleted; a deletion. [L, imper. of *delēre*: see DELETE]

de·lec·ta·ble /diléktəbəl/ *adj.* esp. *literary* delightful; pleasant. □□ **de·lec·ta·bil·i·ty** /–bílitee/ *n.* **de·lec·ta·bly** *adv.* [ME f. OF f. L *delectabilis* f. *delectare* DELIGHT]

de·lec·ta·tion /deélektáyshən/ *n. literary* pleasure; enjoyment (*sang for his delectation*). [ME f. OF (as DELECTABLE)]

del·e·ga·cy /déligəsee/ *n.* (*pl.* ·**cies**) **1** a system of delegating. **2 a** an appointment as a delegate. **b** a body of delegates; a delegation.

del·e·gate *n. & v.* • *n.* /déligət/ **1** an elected representative sent to a conference. **2** a member of a committee. **3** a member of a deputation. • *v.tr.* /déligayt/ **1** (often foll. by *to*) **a** commit (authority, power, etc.) to an agent or deputy. **b** entrust (a task) to another person. **2** send or authorize (a person) as a representative; depute. □□ **del·e·ga·ble** /–gəbəl/ *adj.* [ME f. L *delegatus* (as DE-, *legare* depute)]

del·e·ga·tion /déligáyshən/ *n.* **1** a body of delegates; a deputation. **2** the act or process of delegating or being delegated. [L *delegatio* (as DELEGATE)]

de·lete /dileét/ *v.tr.* remove or obliterate (written or printed matter), esp. by striking out. □□ **de·le·tion** /–leéshən/ *n.* [L *delēre delet*- efface]

del·e·te·ri·ous /délitee̓reeəs/ *adj.* harmful (to the mind or body). □□ **del·e·te·ri·ous·ly** *adv.* [med.L *deleterius* f. Gk *dēlētērios* noxious]

delft /delft/ *n.* (also **delft·ware** /délftwair/) glazed, usu. blue and white, earthenware, made in Delft in Holland.

del·i /délee/ *n.* (*pl.* **del·is**) *colloq.* a delicatessen. [abbr.]

de·lib·er·ate *adj. & v.* • *adj.* /dilíbərət/ **1** intentional (*a deliberate foul*). **b** fully considered; not impulsive (*made a deliberate choice*). **2** slow in deciding; cautious (*a ponderous and deliberate mind*). **3** (of movement, etc.) leisurely and unhurried. • *v.* /dilíbərayt/ **1** *intr.* think carefully; take counsel (*the jury deliberated for an hour*). **2** *tr.* consider; discuss carefully (*deliberated the question*). □□ **de·lib·er·ate·ly** /dilíbərətlee/ *adv.* **de·lib·er·ate·ness** *n.* **de·lib·er·a·tor** *n.* [L *deliberatus* past part. of *deliberare* (as DE-, *librare* weigh f. *libra* balance)]

de·lib·er·a·tion /dilíbəráyshən/ *n.* **1** careful consideration. **2 a** the discussion of reasons for and against. **b** a debate or discussion. **3 a** caution and care. **b** (of action or behavior) purposefulness; deliberateness. **c** (of movement) slowness or ponderousness. [ME f. OF f. L *deliberatio* –*onis* (as DELIBERATE)]

de·lib·er·a·tive /dilíbərətiv, –ráytiv/ *adj.* of, or appointed for the purpose of, deliberation or debate (*a deliberative assembly*). □□ **de·lib·er·a·tive·ly** *adv.* **de·lib·er·a·tive·ness** *n.* [F *délibératif –ive* or L *deliberativus* (as DELIBERATE)]

del·i·ca·cy /délikəsee/ *n.* (*pl.* **·cies**) **1** (esp. in craftsmanship or artistic or natural beauty) fineness or intricacy of structure or texture; gracefulness. **2** susceptibility to injury or disease; weakness. **3** the quality of requiring discretion or sensitivity (*a situation of some delicacy*). **4** a choice or expensive food. **5 a** consideration for the feelings of others. **b** avoidance of immodesty or vulgarity. **6** (esp. in a person, a sense, or an instrument) accuracy of perception; sensitiveness. [ME f. DELICATE + –ACY]

del·i·cate /délikət/ *adj.* **1 a** fine in texture or structure; soft, slender, or slight. **b** of exquisite quality or workmanship. **c** (of color) subtle or subdued; not bright. **d** subtle; hard to appreciate. **2 a** (of a person) easily injured; susceptible to illness. **b** (of a thing) easily spoiled or damaged. **3 a** requiring careful handling; tricky (*a delicate situation*). **b** (of an instrument) highly sensitive. **4** deft (*a delicate touch*). **5** (of a person) avoiding the immodest or offensive. **6** (esp. of actions) considerate. **7** (of food) dainty; suitable for an invalid. □ **in a delicate condition** *archaic* pregnant. □□ **del·i·cate·ly** *adv.* **del·i·cate·ness** *n.* [ME f. OF *delicat* or L *delicatus*, of unkn. orig.]

del·i·ca·tes·sen /délikətésən/ *n.* **1** a store selling cooked meats, cheeses, and unusual or foreign prepared foods. **2** (often *attrib.*) such foods collectively (*a delicatessen counter*). [G *Delikatessen* or Du. *delicatessen* f. F *délicatesse* f. *délicat* (as DELICATE)]

De·li·cious /dilíshəs/ *n.* a red or yellow variety of apple cultivated orig. in the US.

de·li·cious /dilíshəs/ *adj.* **1** highly delightful and enjoyable to the taste or sense of smell. **2** (of a joke, etc.) very witty. □□ **de·li·cious·ly** *adv.* **de·li·cious·ness** *n.* [ME f. OF f. LL *deliciosus* f. L *deliciae* delight]

de·lict /dilíkt/ *n. archaic* a violation of the law; an offense. [L *delictum* neut. past part. of *delinquere* offend (as DE-, *linquere* leave)]

de·light /dilít/ *v. & n.* ●*v.* **1** *tr.* (often foll. by *with*, or *that* + clause, or *to* + infin.) please greatly (*the gift delighted them*; *was delighted with the result*; *was delighted that you won*; *would be delighted to help*). **2** *intr.* (often foll. by *in*, or *to* + infin.) take great pleasure; be highly pleased (*he delighted in her success*; *they delight to humor him*). ●*n.* **1** great pleasure. **2** something giving pleasure (*her singing is a delight*). □□ **de·light·ed** *adj.* **de·light·ed·ly** *adv.* [ME f. OF *delitier*, *delit*, f. L *delectare* frequent. of *delicere*: alt. after *light*, etc.]

de·light·ful /dilítfŏŏl/ *adj.* causing great delight; pleasant; charming. □□ **de·light·ful·ly** *adv.* **de·light·ful·ness** *n.*

De·li·lah /dilílə/ *n.* a seductive and wily temptress. [*Delilah*, betrayer of Samson (Judges 16)]

de·lim·it /dilímit/ *v.tr.* **1** determine the limits of. **2** fix the territorial boundary of. □□ **de·lim·i·ta·tion** /–táyshən/ *n.* [F *délimiter* f. L *delimitare* (as DE-, *limitare* f. *limes –itis* boundary)]

de·lin·e·ate /dilíneeayt/ *v.tr.* portray by drawing, etc., or in words (*delineated her character*). □□ **de·lin·e·a·tion** /–áyshən/ *n.* **de·lin·e·a·tor** *n.* [L *delineare delineat-* (as DE-, *lineare* f. *linea* line)]

del·in·quen·cy /dilíngkwənsee/ *n.* (*pl.* **·cies**) **1 a** a crime, usu. not of a serious kind; a misdeed. **b** minor crime in general, esp. that of young people (*juvenile delinquency*). **2** wickedness (*moral delinquency*; *an act of delinquency*). **3** neglect of one's duty. [eccl. L *delinquentia* f. *delinquens* part. of *delinquere* (as DELICT)]

de·lin·quent /dilíngkwənt/ *n. & adj.* ●*n.* an offender (*juvenile delinquent*). ●*adj.* **1** guilty of a minor crime or a misdeed. **2** failing in one's duty. **3** in arrears. □□ **de·lin·quent·ly** *adv.*

del·i·quesce /délikwés/ *v.intr.* **1** become liquid; melt. **2** *Chem.* dissolve in water absorbed from the air. □□ **del·i·ques·cence** *n.* **del·i·ques·cent** *adj.* [L *deliquescere* (as DE-, *liquescere* incept. of *liquēre* be liquid)]

de·lir·i·ous /dilíreeəs/ *adj.* **1** affected with delirium; temporarily or apparently mad; raving. **2** wildly excited; ecstatic. **3** (of behavior) betraying delirium or ecstasy. □□ **de·lir·i·ous·ly** *adv.*

de·lir·i·um /dilíreeəm/ *n.* **1** an acutely disordered state of mind involving incoherent speech, hallucinations, and frenzied excitement, occurring in metabolic disorders, intoxication, fever, etc. **2** great excitement; ecstasy. [L f. *delirare* be deranged (as DE-, *lira* ridge between furrows)]

de·lir·i·um tre·mens /treemənz, –menz/ *n.* a psychosis of chronic alcoholism involving tremors and hallucinations.

de·liv·er /dilívər/ *v.tr.* **1 a** distribute (letters, packages, ordered goods, etc.) to the addressee or the purchaser. **b** (often foll. by *to*) hand over (*delivered the boy safely to his teacher*). **2** (often foll. by *from*) save, rescue, or set free (*delivered him from his enemies*). **3 a** give birth to (*delivered a girl*). **b** (in *passive*; often foll. by *of*) give birth (*was delivered of a child*). **c** assist at the birth of (*delivered six babies that week*). **d** assist in giving birth (*delivered the patient successfully*). **4 a** (often *refl.*) utter or recite (an opinion, a speech, etc.) (*deliv-*

ered himself of the observation; *delivered the sermon well*). **b** (of a judge) pronounce (a judgment). **5** (often foll. by *up*, *over*) abandon; resign; hand over (*delivered his soul up to God*). **6** present or render (an account). **7** launch or aim (a blow, a ball, or an attack). **8** *Law* hand over formally (esp. a sealed deed to a grantee). **9** *colloq.* = *deliver the goods*. **10** cause (voters, etc.) to support a candidate. □ **deliver the goods** *colloq.* carry out one's part of an agreement. □□ **de·liv·er·a·ble** *adj.* **de·liv·er·er** *n.* [ME f. OF *delivrer* f. Gallo-Roman (as DE-, LIBERATE)]

de·liv·er·ance /dilívərəns/ *n.* **1 a** the act or an instance of rescuing; the process of being rescued. **b** a rescue. **2** a formally expressed opinion. [ME f. OF *delivrance* (as DELIVER)]

de·liv·er·y /dilívəree/ *n.* (*pl.* **·ies**) **1 a** the delivering of letters, etc. **b** a regular distribution of letters, etc. (*two deliveries a day*). **c** something delivered. **2 a** the process of childbirth. **b** an act of this. **3** deliverance. **4 a** an act of throwing, as of a baseball. **b** the style of such an act (*a good delivery*). **5** the act of giving or surrendering (*delivery of the town to the enemy*). **6 a** the uttering of a speech, etc. **b** the manner or style of such a delivery (*a measured delivery*). **7** *Law* **a** the formal handing over of property. **b** the transfer of a deed to a grantee or a third party. □ **take delivery of** receive (something purchased). [ME f. AF *delivree* fem. past part. of *delivrer* (as DELIVER)]

dell /del/ *n.* a small usu. wooded hollow or valley. [OE f. Gmc]

Del·la Crus·can /délə krúskən/ *adj. & n.* ●*adj.* **1** of or relating to the Academy della Crusca in Florence, concerned with the purity of Italian. **2** of or concerning a late 18th–c. school of English poets with an artificial style. ●*n.* a member of the Academy della Crusca or the late 18th–c. school of English poets. [It. (*Accademia*) *della Crusca* (Academy) of the bran (with ref. to sifting)]

de·lo·cal·ize /deelókəlīz/ *v.tr.* **1 a** detach or remove (a thing) from its place. **b** not limit to a particular location. **2** (as **delocalized** *adj.*) *Chem.* (of electrons) shared among more than two atoms in a molecule. □□ **de·lo·cal·i·za·tion** *n.*

de·louse /deelóws/ *v.tr.* rid (a person or animal) of lice.

Del·phic /délfik/ *adj.* (also **Del·phi·an** /–feeən/) **1** (of an utterance, prophecy, etc.) obscure, ambiguous, or enigmatic. **2** of or concerning the ancient Greek oracle at Delphi.

del·phin·i·um /delfineeəm/ *n.* any ranunculaceous garden plant of the genus *Delphinium*, with tall spikes of usu. blue flowers. [mod.L f. Gk *delphinion* larkspur f. *delphin* dolphin]

del·phi·noid /délfinoyd/ *adj. & n.* ●*adj.* **1** of the family that includes dolphins, porpoises, grampuses, etc. dolphinlike. ●*n.* **1** a member of the delphinoid family of aquatic mammals. **2** a dolphinlike animal. [Gk *delphinoeidēs* f. *delphin* dolphin]

del·ta /déltə/ *n.* **1** a triangular tract of deposited earth, alluvium, etc., at the mouth of a river, formed by its diverging outlets. **2 a** the fourth letter of the Greek alphabet (Δ, δ). **b** a fourth-class mark given for a piece of work or in an examination. **3** *Astron.* the fourth star in a constellation. **4** *Math.* an increment of a variable. □□ **del·ta·ic** /deltáyik/ *adj.* [ME f. Gk f. Phoen. *daleth*]

del·ta con·nec·tion *n.* *Electr.* a triangular arrangement of three-phase windings with circuit wire from each angle.

del·ta rays *n.* *Physics* rays of low penetrative power consisting of slow electrons ejected from an atom by the impact of ionizing radiation.

del·ta rhythm *n.* (also **delta wave**) low-frequency electrical activity of the brain during sleep.

del·ta wing *n.* each of the pair of wings of some supersonic and military aircraft that extend to the back of the plane, forming the shape of a triangle.

del·ti·ol·o·gy /délteeóləjee/ *n.* the collecting and study of postcards. □□ **del·ti·ol·o·gist** *n.* [Gk *deltion* dimin. of *deltos* writing-- tablet + –LOGY]

del·toid /déltoyd/ *adj. & n.* ●*adj.* triangular; like a river delta. ●*n.*

delta wing

(in full **deltoid muscle**) a thick triangular muscle covering the shoulder joint and used for raising the arm away from the body. [F *deltoïde* or mod.L *deltoides* f. Gk *deltoeidēs* (as DELTA, –OID)]

de·lude /dilóŏd/ *v.tr.* deceive or mislead (*deluded by false optimism*). □□ **de·lud·er** *n.* [ME f. L *deludere* mock (as DE-, *ludere lus-* play)]

del·uge /délyŏŏj, –yoozh/ *n. & v.* ●*n.* **1** a great flood. **2** (**the Deluge**) the biblical Flood (Gen. 6–8). **3** a great outpouring (of words, paper, etc.). **4** a heavy fall of rain. ●*v.tr.* **1** flood. **2** inundate with a great number or amount (*deluged with complaints*). [ME f. OF f. L *diluvium*, rel. to *lavare* wash]

de·lu·sion /dilóŏzhən/ *n.* **1** a false belief or impression. **2** *Psychol.* this as a symptom or form of mental disorder. □□ **de·lu·sion·al** *adj.* [ME f. LL *delusio* (as DELUDE)]

de·lu·sions of gran·deur *n.* a false idea of oneself as being important, noble, famous, etc.

de·lu·sive /dilóŏsiv/ *adj.* **1** deceptive or unreal. **2** disappointing. □□ **de·lu·sive·ly** *adv.* **de·lu·sive·ness** *n.*

de·lu·so·ry /dilŏŏsəree, –zə–/ *adj.* = DELUSIVE. [LL *delusorius* (as DE-LUSION)]

de·lust·er /deelústər/ *v.tr.* (*Brit.* **de·lust·re**) remove the luster from (a textile).

de·luxe /də lúks, lŏŏks/ *adj.* **1** luxurious or sumptuous. **2** of a superior kind. [F, = of luxury]

delve /delv/ *v.* **1** *intr.* (often foll. by *in, into*) **a** search energetically (*delved into his pocket*). **b** make a laborious search in documents, etc.; research (*delved into his family history*). **2** *tr. & intr. poet.* dig. □□ **delv·er** *n.* [OE *delfan* f. WG]

Dem. *abbr.* Democrat.

de·mag·net·ize /deemágnitīz/ *v.tr.* remove the magnetic properties of. □□ **de·mag·net·i·za·tion** /–tizáyshən/ *n.* **de·mag·net·iz·er** *n.*

dem·a·gogue /démagog, –gawg/ *n.* (also **–gog**) **1** a political agitator appealing to the basest instincts of a mob. **2** *hist.* a leader of the people, esp. in ancient times. □□ **dem·a·gog·ic** /–gójik, –gógik, –gṓ–/ *adj.* **dem·a·gogu·er·y** /–gógəree, –gáwg–/ *n.* **dem·a·go·gy** /–gójee, –gáw–/ *n.* [Gk *dēmagōgos* f. *dēmos* the people + *agōgos* leading]

de·mand /dimánd/ *n. & v.* ● *n.* **1** an insistent and peremptory request, made as of right. **2** *Econ.* the desire of purchasers or consumers for a commodity (*no demand for solid tires these days*). **3** an urgent claim (*care of her mother makes demands on her*). ● *v.tr.* **1** (often foll. by *of, from*, or *to* + infin., or *that* + clause) ask for (something) insistently and urgently, as of right (*demanded to know*; *demanded five dollars from him*; *demanded that his wife be present*). **2** require or need (*a task demanding skill*). **3** insist on being told (*demanded the truth*). **4** (as **demanding** *adj.*) making demands; requiring skill, effort, etc. (*a demanding but worthwhile job*). □ **in demand** sought after. **on demand** as soon as a demand is made (*a check payable on demand*). □□ **de·mand·a·ble** *adj.* **de·mand·er** *n.* **de·mand·ing·ly** *adv.* [ME f. OF *demande* (n.), *demander* (v.) f. L *demandare* entrust (as DE-, *mandare* order: see MANDATE)]

de·mand feed·ing *n.* the practice of feeding a baby when it cries for food rather than at set times.

de·mand note *n.* **1** a written request for payment. **2** a bill payable at sight.

de·mand pull *adj. Econ.* relating to inflation caused by an excess of demand over supply.

de·man·toid /dimántoyd/ *n.* a lustrous green garnet. [G]

de·mar·ca·tion /deemaarkáyshən/ *n.* **1** the act of marking a boundary or limits. **2** the trade-union practice of strictly assigning specific jobs to different unions. □□ **de·mar·cate** /dimaárkayt, deémaar–/ *v.tr.* **de·mar·ca·tor** *n.* [Sp. *demarcación* f. *demarcar* mark the bounds of (as DE-, MARK[1])]

dé·marche /daymaársh/ *n.* a political step or initiative. [F f. *démarcher* take steps (as DE-, MARCH[1])]

de·ma·te·ri·al·ize /deemətéereeəlīz/ *v.tr. & intr.* make or become nonmaterial or spiritual (esp. of psychic phenomena, etc.). □□ **de·ma·te·ri·al·i·za·tion** *n.*

deme /deem/ *n.* **1 a** a political division of Attica in ancient Greece. **b** an administrative division in modern Greece. **2** *Biol.* a local population of closely related plants or animals. [Gk *dēmos* the people]

de·mean[1] /dimeén/ *v.tr.* (usu. *refl.*) lower the dignity of (*would not demean myself to take it*). [DE- + MEAN[2], after *debase*]

de·mean[2] /dimeén/ *v.refl.* (with *adv.*) behave (*demeaned himself well*). [ME f. OF *demener* f. Rmc (as DE-, L *minare* drive animals f. *minari* threaten)]

de·mean·or /dimeénər/ *n.* (*Brit.* **de·mean·our**) outward behavior or bearing. [DEMEAN[2], prob. after obs. *havour* behavior]

de·ment /dimént/ *n. archaic* a demented person. [orig. adj.f. F *dément* or L *demens* (as DEMENTED)]

de·ment·ed /diméntid/ *adj.* mad; crazy. □□ **de·ment·ed·ly** *adv.* **de·ment·ed·ness** *n.* [past part. of *dement* verb f. OF *dementer* or f. LL *dementare* f. *demens* out of one's mind (as DE-, *mens mentis* mind)]

dé·men·ti /daymóntee/ *n.* an official denial of a rumor, etc. [F f. *démentir* accuse of lying]

de·men·tia /diménshə/ *n. Med.* a chronic or persistent disorder of the mental processes marked by memory disorders, personality changes, impaired reasoning, etc., due to brain disease or injury. [L f. *demens* (as DEMENTED)]

de·men·tia prae·cox /preékoks/ *n.* schizophrenia.

dem·e·ra·ra /déməráirə/ *n.* light-brown cane sugar coming orig. and chiefly from Demerara. [*Demerara* in Guyana]

de·mer·it /dimérit/ *n.* **1** a quality or action deserving blame; a fault. **2** a mark given to an offender. □□ **de·mer·i·to·ri·ous** /–táwreeəs/ *adj.* [ME f. OF *de(s)merite* or L *demeritum* neut. past part. of *demerēri* deserve]

de·mer·sal /dimérsəl/ *adj.* (of a fish, etc.) being or living near the sea bottom (cf. PELAGIC). [L *demersus* past part. of *demergere* (as DE-, *mergere* plunge)]

de·mesne /dimáyn, –meén/ *n.* **1 a** a sovereign's or nation's territory; a domain. **b** land attached to a mansion, etc. **c** landed property; an estate. **2** (usu. foll. by *of*) a region or sphere. **3** *Law hist.* possession (of real property) as one's own. □ **held in demesne** (of an es-

tate) occupied by the owner, not by tenants. [ME f. AF, OF *demeine* (later AF *demesne*) belonging to a lord f. L *dominicus* (as DOMINICAL)]

demi- /démee/ *prefix* **1** half; half-size. **2** partially or imperfectly such (*demigod*). [ME f. F f. med.L *dimedius* half, for L *dimidius*]

dem·i·god /démeegod/ *n.* (*fem.* **·god·dess** /–godis/) **1 a** a partly divine being. **b** the offspring of a god or goddess and a mortal. **2** *colloq.* a person of compelling beauty, powers, or personality.

dem·i·john /démeejon/ *n.* a bulbous, narrow-necked bottle holding from 3 to 10 gallons and usu. in a wicker cover. [prob. corrupt. of F *dame-jeanne* Lady Jane, assim. to DEMI- + the name *John*]

de·mil·i·ta·rize /deemílitərīz/ *v.tr.* remove a military organization or forces from (a frontier, a zone, etc.). □□ **de·mil·i·ta·ri·za·tion** *n.*

dem·i·mon·daine /démeemondayn/ *n.* a woman of a demimonde.

dem·i·monde /démeemond, –máwND/ *n.* **1 a** *hist.* a class of women in 19th-c. France considered to be of doubtful social standing and morality. **b** a similar class of women in any society. **2** any group considered to be on the fringes of respectable society. [F, = half-world]

de·min·er·al·ize /deemínərəlīz/ *v.tr.* remove salts from (sea water, etc.). □□ **de·min·er·al·i·za·tion** *n.*

de·mi-pen·sion /dəmeepáwNsyawN/ *n.* hotel accommodations with bed, breakfast, and one main meal per day. [F (as DEMI-, PENSION[2])]

dem·i·rep /démeerep/ *n. archaic* a woman of doubtful sexual reputation. [abbr. of *demi-reputable*]

de·mise /dimíz/ *n. & v.* ● *n.* **1** death (*left a will on her demise; the demise of the agreement*). **2** *Law* conveyance or transfer (of property, a title, etc.) by demising. ● *v.tr. Law* **1** convey or grant (an estate) by will or lease. **2** transmit (a title, etc.) by death. [AF use of past part. of OF *de(s)mettre* DISMISS, in refl. abdicate]

dem·i·sem·i·qua·ver /démeesémeekwayvər/ *n. Mus.* esp. *Brit.* = THIRTY-SECOND NOTE.

de·mist /deemíst/ *v.tr. Brit.* defrost (a windscreen, etc.). □□ **de·mist·er** *n.*

de·mit /dimít/ *v.tr.* (**de·mit·ted, de·mit·ting**) (often *absol.*) resign or abdicate (an office, etc.). □□ **de·mis·sion** /–míshən/ *n.* [F *démettre* f. L *demittere* (as DE-, *mittere miss-* send)]

dem·i·tasse /démeetas, –taas/ *n.* **1** a small coffee cup. **2** its contents. [F, = half-cup]

dem·i·urge /démeeərj/ *n.* **1** (in the philosophy of Plato) the creator of the universe. **2** (in Gnosticism, etc.) a heavenly being subordinate to the Supreme Being. □□ **dem·i·ur·gic** *adj.* [eccl.L f. Gk *dēmiourgos* craftsman f. *dēmios* public f. *dēmos* people + *–ergos* working]

dem·o /démō/ *n.* (*pl.* **·os**) *colloq.* = DEMONSTRATION 2, 3. [abbr.]

de·mob /deemób/ *v. & n. Brit. colloq.* ● *v.tr.* (**de·mobbed, de·mobbing**) demobilize. ● *n.* demobilization. [abbr.]

de·mo·bi·lize /deemóbilīz/ *v.tr.* disband (troops, ships, etc.). □□ **de·mo·bi·li·za·tion** *n.* (as DE-, MOBILIZE)]

de·moc·ra·cy /dimókrəsee/ *n.* (*pl.* **·cies**) **1 a** a system of government by the whole population, usu. through elected representatives. **b** a nation so governed. **c** any organization governed on democratic principles. **2** a classless and tolerant form of society. **3 a** the principles of the Democratic party. **b** its members. [F *démocratie* f. LL *democratia* f. Gk *dēmokratia* f. *dēmos* the people + *–CRACY*]

dem·o·crat /déməkrat/ *n.* **1** an advocate of democracy. **2** (**Democrat**) a member of the Democratic party. □□ **dem·o·crat·ism** /dimókrətizəm/ *n.* [F *démocrate* (as DEMOCRACY), after *aristocrate*]

dem·o·crat·ic /déməkrátik/ *adj.* **1** of, like, practicing, advocating, or constituting democracy or a democracy. **2** favoring social equality. □□ **dem·o·crat·i·cal·ly** *adv.* [F *démocratique* f. med.L *democraticus* f. Gk *dēmokratikos* f. *dēmokratia* DEMOCRACY]

dem·o·crat·ic cen·tral·ism *n.* the Leninist organizational system in which policy is decided centrally and is binding on all members.

Dem·o·crat·ic par·ty *n.* one of the two main US political parties, considered to support social reform and strong federal powers. (cf. *Republican party*).

de·moc·ra·tize /dimókrətīz/ *v.tr.* make (a nation, institution, etc.) democratic. □□ **de·moc·ra·ti·za·tion** *n.*

dé·mo·dé /dáymódáy/ *adj.* out of fashion. [F, past part. of *démoder* (as DE-, *mode* fashion)]

de·mod·u·late /deemójələyt/ *v.tr. Physics* extract (a modulating signal) from its carrier. □□ **de·mod·u·la·tion** /–láyshən/ *n.* **de·mod·u·la·tor** *n.*

de·mog·ra·phy /dimógrəfee/ *n.* the study of the statistics of births, deaths, disease, etc., as illustrating the conditions of life in communities. □□ **de·mog·ra·pher** *n.* **dem·o·graph·ic** /déməgráfik/ *adj.* **dem·o·graph·i·cal** *adj.* **dem·o·graph·i·cal·ly** *adv.* [Gk *dēmos* the people + –GRAPHY]

dem·oi·selle /démwazél/ *n.* **1** *Zool.* a small crane, *Anthropoides virgo*, native to Asia and N. Africa. **2 a** a damselfly. **b** a damselfish. **3** *archaic* a young woman. [F, = DAMSEL]

de·mol·ish /dimólish/ v.tr. **1 a** pull down (a building). **b** completely destroy or break. **2** overthrow (an institution). **3** refute (an argument, theory, etc.). **4** joc. eat up completely and quickly. □□ **de·mol·ish·er** n. **dem·o·li·tion** /démlíshn/ n. **dem·o·li·tion·ist** n. [F démolir f. L demoliri (as DE-, moliri molit- construct f. moles mass)]

de·mon[1] /déemn/ n. **1 a** an evil spirit or devil, esp. one thought to possess a person. **b** the personification of evil passion. **2** a malignant supernatural being; the Devil. **3** (often attrib.) a forceful, fierce, or skillful performer (a demon on the tennis court; a demon player). **4** a cruel or destructive person. **5** (also **dae·mon**) **a** an inner or attendant spirit; a genius (the demon of creativity). **b** a supernatural being in ancient Greece. □ **a demon for work** colloq. a person who works strenuously. [ME f. med.L demon f. L daemon f. Gk daimōn deity]

de·mon[2] /déemn/ n. Austral. sl. a police officer. [app. f. Van Diemen's Land, early name for Tasmania, after DEMON[1]]

de·mon·e·tize /deemónitíz, −mún−/ v.tr. withdraw (a coin, etc.) from use as money. □□ **de·mon·e·ti·za·tion** n. [F démonétiser (as DE-, L moneta MONEY)]

de·mo·ni·ac /dimóneeak/ adj. & n. ● adj. **1** fiercely energetic or frenzied. **2 a** supposedly possessed by an evil spirit. **b** of or concerning such possession. **3** of or like demons. ● n. a person possessed by an evil spirit. □□ **de·mo·ni·a·cal** /déemnéeakl/ adj. **de·mo·ni·a·cal·ly** adv. [ME f. OF demoniaque f. eccl.L daemoniacus f. daemonium f. Gk daimonion dimin. of daimōn: see DEMON[1]]

de·mon·ic /dimónik/ adj. (also **dae·monic**) **1** = DEMONIAC. **2** having or seeming to have supernatural genius or power. [LL daemonicus f. Gk daimonikos (as DEMON[1])]

de·mon·ism /déemnizm/ n. belief in the power of demons.

de·mon·ize /déemníz/ v.tr. **1** make into or like a demon. **2** represent as a demon.

de·mon·ol·a·try /déemnólatree/ n. the worship of demons.

de·mon·ol·o·gy /déemnóljee/ n. the study of demons, etc. □□ **de·mon·ol·o·gist** n.

de·mon·stra·ble /dimónstrbl/ adj. capable of being shown or logically proved. □□ **de·mon·stra·bil·i·ty** n. **de·mon·stra·bly** adv. [ME f. L demonstrabilis (as DEMONSTRATE)]

dem·on·strate /démnstrayt/ v. **1** tr. show evidence of (feelings, etc.). **2** tr. describe and explain (a scientific proposition, machine, etc.) by experiment, practical use, etc. **3** tr. **a** logically prove the truth of. **b** be proof of the existence of. **4** intr. take part in or organize a public demonstration. **5** intr. act as a demonstrator. [L demonstrare (as DE-, monstrare show)]

dem·on·stra·tion /démnstráyshn/ n. **1** (foll. by of) **a** the outward showing of feeling, etc. **b** an instance of this. **2** a public meeting, march, etc., for a political or moral purpose. **3 a** the exhibiting or explaining of specimens or experiments as a method of esp. scientific teaching. **b** an instance of this. **4** proof provided by logic, argument, etc. **5** Mil. a show of military force. □□ **dem·on·stra·tion·al** adj. [ME f. OF demonstration or L demonstratio (as DEMONSTRATE)]

de·mon·stra·tive /dimónstrtiv/ adj. & n. ● adj. **1** given to or marked by an open expression of feelings, esp. of affection (a very demonstrative person). **2** (usu. foll. by of) logically conclusive; giving proof (the work is demonstrative of their skill). **3 a** serving to point out or exhibit. **b** involving esp. scientific demonstration (demonstrative technique). **4** Gram. (of an adjective or pronoun) indicating the person or thing referred to (e.g., this, that, those). ● n. Gram. a demonstrative adjective or pronoun. □□ **de·mon·stra·tive·ly** adv. **de·mon·stra·tive·ness** n. [ME f. OF demonstratif −ive f. L demonstrativus (as DEMONSTRATION)]

GRAMMAR TIP demonstrative

Demonstrative Pronouns. Demonstrative pronouns specify or single out the person or thing to which they refer. There are only four of them: this, that, these, and those. Using there or here after a demonstrative pronoun (this here typewriter is broken) is best avoided.

dem·on·stra·tor /démnstraytr/ n. **1** a person who takes part in a political demonstration, etc. **2** a person who demonstrates, esp. machines, equipment, etc., to prospective customers. **3** a person who teaches by demonstration, esp. in a laboratory, etc. [L (as DEMONSTRATE)]

de·mor·al·ize /dimáwrlíz, −mór−/ v.tr. **1** destroy (a person's) morale; make hopeless. **2** archaic corrupt (a person's) morals. □□ **de·mor·al·i·za·tion** n. **de·mor·al·iz·ing** adj. **de·mor·al·iz·ing·ly** adv. [F démoraliser (as DE-, MORAL)]

de·mote /dimót/ v.tr. reduce to a lower rank or class. □□ **de·mo·tion** /−móshn/ n. [DE- + PROMOTE]

de·mot·ic /dimótik/ n. & adj. ● n. **1** the popular colloquial form of a language. **2** a popular simplified form of ancient Egyptian writing (cf. HIERATIC). ● adj. **1** (esp. of language) popular, colloquial, or vulgar. **2** of or concerning the ancient Egyptian or modern Greek demotic. [Gk dēmotikos f. dēmotēs one of the people (dēmos)]

de·mo·ti·vate /déemótivayt/ v.tr. (also absol.) cause to lose motivation; discourage. □□ **de·mo·ti·va·tion** /−váyshn/ n.

de·mount /déemównt/ v.tr. **1** take (apparatus, a gun, etc.) from its mounting. **2** dismantle for later reassembly. □□ **de·mount·a·ble** adj. & n. [F démonter: cf. DISMOUNT]

de·mul·cent /dimúlsnt/ adj. & n. ● adj. soothing. ● n. an agent that forms a protective film soothing irritation or inflammation in the mouth. [L demulcēre (as DE-, mulcēre soothe)]

de·mur /dimór/ v. & n. ● v.intr. (**de·murred**, **de·mur·ring**) **1** (often foll. by to, at) raise scruples or objections. **2** Law put in a demurrer. ● n. (also **de·mur·ral** /dimórl/) (usu. in neg.) **1** an objection (agreed without demur). **2** the act or process of objecting. □□ **de·mur·rant** /dimórnt/ n. (in sense 2 of v.). [ME f. OF demeure (n.), demeurer (v.) f. Rmc (as DE-, L morari delay)]

de·mure /dimyóor/ adj. (**de·mur·er**, **de·mur·est**) **1** composed, quiet, and reserved; modest. **2** affectedly shy and quiet; coy. **3** decorous (a demure high collar). □□ **de·mure·ly** adv. **de·mure·ness** n. [ME, perh. f. AF demuré f. OF demoré past part. of demorer remain, stay (as DEMUR): infl. by OF meür f. L maturus ripe]

de·mur·ra·ble /dimórbl/ adj. esp. Law open to objection.

de·mur·rage /dimórij, −múr−/ n. **1 a** a rate or amount payable to a shipowner by a charterer for failure to load or discharge a ship within the time agreed. **b** a similar charge on railroad trucks or goods. **2** such a detention or delay. [OF demo(u)rage f. demorer (as DEMUR)]

de·mur·rer /dimórr, −múr−/ n. Law an objection raised or exception taken. [AF (infin. as noun), = DEMUR]

de·my /dimí/ n. Printing a size of paper, 564 x 444 mm. [ME, var. of DEMI-]

de·mys·ti·fy /deemístifí/ v.tr. (**·fies**, **·fied**) **1** clarify (obscure beliefs or subjects, etc.). **2** reduce or remove the irrationality in (a person). □□ **de·mys·ti·fi·ca·tion** /−fikáyshn/ n.

de·my·thol·o·gize /déemithóljíz/ v.tr. **1** remove mythical elements from (a legend, famous person's life, etc.). **2** reinterpret what some consider to be the mythological elements in (the Bible).

den /den/ n. **1** a wild animal's lair. **2** a place of crime or vice (den of iniquity; opium den). **3** a small private room for pursuing a hobby, etc. [OE denn f. Gmc, rel. to DEAN[2]]

de·nar·i·us /dináreeəs/ n. (pl. **de·nar·i·i** /−ree-ī/) an ancient Roman silver coin. [L, = (coin) of ten asses (as DENARY: see AS[2])]

den·a·ry /dínaree, deé−/ adj. of ten; decimal. [L denarius containing ten (deni by tens)]

den·a·ry scale n. = DECIMAL SCALE.

de·na·tion·al·ize /deenáshnəlíz/ v.tr. **1** transfer (a nationalized industry or institution, etc.) from public to private ownership. **2 a** deprive (a nation) of its status or characteristics as a nation. **b** deprive (a person) of nationality or national characteristics. □□ **de·na·tion·al·i·za·tion** n. [F dénationaliser (as DE-, NATIONAL)]

de·nat·u·ral·ize /deenáchərəlíz/ v.tr. **1** change the nature or properties of; make unnatural. **2** deprive of the rights of citizenship. **3** = DENATURE v. 1. □□ **de·nat·u·ral·i·za·tion** n.

de·na·ture /deenáychər/ v.tr. **1** change the properties of (a protein, etc.) by heat, acidity, etc. **2** make (alcohol) unfit for drinking, esp. by the addition of another substance. □□ **de·na·tur·ant** n. **de·na·tur·a·tion** /deenáychəráyshn/ n. [F dénaturer (as DE-, NATURE)]

den·drite /déndrīt/ n. **1 a** a stone or mineral with natural treelike or mosslike markings. **b** such marks on stones or minerals. **2** Chem. a crystal with branching treelike growth. **3** Zool. & Anat. a branching process of a nerve cell conducting signals to a cell body. [F f. Gk dendritēs (adj.) f. dendron tree]

den·drit·ic /dendrítik/ adj. **1** of or like a dendrite. **2** treelike in shape or markings. □□ **den·drit·i·cal·ly** adv.

den·dro·chro·nol·o·gy /déndrōkrənóljee/ n. **1** a system of dating using the characteristic patterns of annual growth rings of trees to assign dates to timber. **2** the study of these growth rings. □□ **den·dro·chron·o·log·i·cal** /−krónəlójikəl/ adj. **den·dro·chro·nol·o·gist** n. [Gk dendron tree + CHRONOLOGY]

den·droid /déndroyd/ adj. tree-shaped. [Gk dendrōdēs treelike + -OID]

den·drol·o·gy /dendróljee/ n. the scientific study of trees. □□ **den·dro·log·i·cal** /−drəlójikəl/ adj. **den·drol·o·gist** n. [Gk dendron tree + -LOGY]

dene[1] /deen/ n. (also **dean**) Brit. **1** a narrow wooded valley. **2** a vale (esp. as the ending of place-names). [OE denu, rel. to DEN]

dene[2] /deen/ n. Brit. a bare sandy tract, or a low sand hill, by the sea. [orig. unkn.: cf. DUNE]

den·gue /dénggay, −gee/ n. an infectious viral disease of the tropics causing a fever and acute pains in the joints. [W. Ind. Sp., f. Swahili denga, dinga, with assim. to Sp. dengue fastidiousness, with ref. to the stiffness of the patient's neck and shoulders]

de·ni·a·ble /diníəbl/ adj. that may be denied. □□ **de·ni·a·bil·i·ty** n.

de·ni·al /diníəl/ n. **1** the act or an instance of denying. **2** a refusal of a request or wish. **3** a statement that a thing is not true; a rejection (denial of the accusation). **4** a disavowal of a person as one's leader, etc. **5** = SELF-DENIAL.

de·ni·er /dényr, dənyáy, dəneér/ n. a unit of weight by which the fineness of silk, rayon, or nylon yarn is measured. [orig. the name of a small coin: ME f. OF f. L denarius]

den•i•grate /dénigrayt/ v.tr. defame or disparage the reputation of (a person); blacken. □□ **den•i•gra•tion** /–gráyshən/ n. **den•i•gra•tor** n. **den•i•gra•to•ry** /–grətáwree/ adj. [L denigrare (as DE-, nigrare f. niger black)]

den•im /dénim/ n. 1 (often attrib.) a usu. blue, hard-wearing, cotton twill fabric used for jeans, overalls, etc., (a denim skirt). 2 (in pl.) colloq. jeans, overalls, etc., made of this. [for serge de Nim f. Nîmes in S. France]

de•ni•tri•fy /deenítrifī/ v.tr. (•fies, •fied) remove the nitrates or nitrites from (soil, etc.). □□ **de•ni•tri•fi•ca•tion** /–fikáyshən/ n.

den•i•zen /dénizən/ n. 1 a foreigner admitted to certain rights in his or her adopted country. 2 a naturalized foreign word, animal, or plant. 3 (usu. foll. by of) an inhabitant or occupant. □□ **den•i•zen•ship** n. [ME f. AF deinzein f. OF deinz within f. L de from + intus within + –ein f. L –aneus: see –ANEOUS]

de•nom•i•nate /dinóminayt/ v.tr. 1 give a name to. 2 call or describe (a person or thing) as. [L denominare (as DE-, NOMINATE)]

de•nom•i•na•tion /dinóminayshən/ n. 1 a church or religious sect. 2 a class of units within a range or sequence of numbers, weights, money, etc. (money of small denominations). 3 a a name or designation, esp. a characteristic or class name. b a class or kind having a specific name. 4 the rank of a playing card within a suit, or of a suit relative to others. □□ **de•nom•i•na•tion•al** adj. [ME f. OF dénomination or L denominatio (as DENOMINATE)]

de•nom•i•na•tive /dinóminaytiv, –nətiv/ adj. serving as or giving a name. [LL denominativus (as DENOMINATION)]

de•nom•i•na•tor /dinóminaytər/ n. Math. the number below the line in a vulgar fraction; a divisor. [F dénominateur or med.L denominator (as DE-, NOMINATE)]

de nos jours /də nō zhoŏr/ adj. (placed after noun) of the present time. [F, = of our days]

de•note /dinōt/ v.tr. 1 be a sign of; indicate (the arrow denotes direction). 2 (usu. foll. by that + clause) mean; convey. 3 stand as a name for; signify. □□ **de•no•ta•tion** /deenōtáyshən/ n. **de•no•ta•tive** /deenōtáytiv, dinōtátiv/ adj. [F dénoter or f. L denotare (as DE-, notare mark f. nota NOTE)]

▶See note at CONNOTE.

de•noue•ment /daynoōmóN/ n. (also **dé•noue•ment**) 1 the final unraveling of a plot or complicated situation. 2 the final scene in a play, novel, etc., in which the plot is resolved. [F dénouement f. dénouer unknot (as DE-, L nodare f. nodus knot)]

de•nounce /dinówns/ v.tr. 1 accuse publicly; condemn (denounced him as a traitor). 2 inform against (denounced her to the police). 3 give notice of the termination of (an armistice, treaty, etc.). □□ **de•nounce•ment** n. **de•nounc•er** n. [ME f. OF denoncier f. L denuntiare (as DE-, nuntiare make known f. nuntius messenger)]

de nou•veau /də noōvō/ adv. starting again; anew. [F]

de no•vo /dee nōvō, day/ adv. starting again; anew. [L]

dense /dens/ adj. 1 closely compacted in substance; thick (dense fog). 2 crowded together (the population is less dense on the outskirts). 3 colloq. stupid. □□ **dense•ly** adv. **dense•ness** n. [F dense or L densus]

den•si•tom•e•ter /dénsitómitər/ n. an instrument for measuring the photographic density of an image on a film or photographic print.

den•si•ty /dénsitee/ n. (pl. •ties) 1 the degree of compactness of a substance. 2 Physics degree of consistency measured by the quantity of mass per unit volume. 3 the opacity of a photographic image. 4 a crowded state. 5 stupidity. [F densité or L densitas (as DENSE)]

dent /dent/ n. & v. ●n. 1 a slight mark or hollow in a surface made by, or as if by, a blow with a hammer, etc. 2 a noticeable effect (lunch made a dent in our funds). ●v.tr. 1 mark with a dent. 2 have (esp. an adverse) effect on (the news dented our hopes). [ME, prob. f INDENT[1]]

dent. abbr. 1 dental. 2 dentist. 3 dentistry.

den•tal /dént'l/ adj. 1 of the teeth; or of relating to dentistry. 2 Phonet. (of a consonant) produced with the tip of the tongue against the upper front teeth (as th) or the ridge of the teeth (as n, s, t). □□ **den•tal•ize** v.tr. [LL dentalis f. L dens dentis tooth]

den•tal floss n. a thread of nylon, silk, etc., used to clean between the teeth.

den•tal hy•gien•ist n. a person who is trained and licensed to clean and examine teeth, and who usu. works with or for a dentist.

den•ta•li•um /dentáyleeəm/ n. (pl. **den•ta•li•a** /–leeə/) 1 any marine mollusk of the genus Dentalium, having a conical foot protruding from a tusklike shell. 2 this shell used as an ornament or as a form of currency. [mod.L f. LL dentalis: see DENTAL]

den•tal tech•ni•cian n. a person who makes and repairs artificial teeth.

den•tate /déntayt/ adj. Bot. & Zool. toothed; with toothlike notches; serrated. [L dentatus f. dens dentis tooth]

den•ti•cle /déntikəl/ n. Zool. a small tooth or toothlike projection, scale, etc. □□ **den•tic•u•late** /déntíkyoŏlət/ adj. [ME f. L denticulus dimin. of dens dentis tooth]

den•ti•frice /déntifris/ n. a paste or powder for cleaning the teeth. [F f. L dentifricium f. dens dentis tooth + fricare rub]

den•til /déntil/ n. Archit. each of a series of small rectangular blocks

as a decoration under the molding of a cornice in classical architecture. [obs. F dentille dimin. of dent tooth f. L dens dentis]

den•ti•lin•gual /déntilínggwəl/ adj. Phonet. formed by the teeth and the tongue.

den•tin /dént'n/ n. (also **den•tine** /–teen/) a hard, dense, bony tissue forming the bulk of a tooth. □□ **den•tin•al** /déntinəl, dentée–/ adj. [L dens dentis tooth + –INE[4]]

den•tist /déntist/ n. a person who is qualified to treat the diseases and conditions that affect the mouth, jaws, teeth, and their supporting tissues, esp. the repair and extraction of teeth and the insertion of artificial ones. □□ **den•tis•try** n. [F dentiste f. dent tooth]

den•ti•tion /dentíshən/ n. 1 the type, number, and arrangement of teeth in a species, etc. 2 the cutting of teeth; teething. [L dentitio f. dentire to teethe]

den•ture /dénchər/ n. a removable artificial replacement for one or more teeth carried on a removable plate or frame. [F f. dent tooth]

de•nu•cle•ar•ize /deenóōkleeəriz, –nyóō–/ v.tr. remove nuclear armaments from (a country, etc.). □□ **de•nu•cle•ar•i•za•tion** n.

de•nude /dinóōd, –nyóōd/ v.tr. 1 make naked or bare. 2 (foll. by of) a strip of clothing, a covering, etc. b deprive of a possession or attribute. 3 Geol. lay (rock or a formation, etc.) bare by removing what lies above. □□ **den•u•da•tion** /deenōōdáyshən, –nyoō–, dényoō–/ n. **de•nu•da•tive** /–dətiv/ adj. [L denudare (as DE-, nudus naked)]

de•nu•mer•able /dinóōmərəbəl, –nyoō–/ adj. Math. countable by correspondence with the infinite set of integers. □□ **de•nu•mer•a•bil•i•ty** n. **de•nu•mer•a•bly** adv. [LL denumerare (as DE-, numerare NUMBER)]

de•nun•ci•a•tion /dinúnsee-áyshən, –shee–/ n. 1 the act of denouncing (a person, policy, etc.); public condemnation. 2 an instance of this. □□ **de•nun•ci•ate** /–seeayt/ v.tr. **de•nun•ci•a•tive** /–seeaytiv/ adj. **de•nun•ci•a•tor** n. **de•nun•ci•a•to•ry** /–seeətawree/ adj. [F dénonciation or L denunciatio (as DENOUNCE)]

de•ny /diní/ v.tr. (•nies, •nied) 1 declare untrue or nonexistent (denied the charge; denied that it is so; denied having lied). 2 repudiate or disclaim (denied his faith; denied her signature). 3 (often foll. by to) refuse (a person or thing, or something to a person) (this was denied to me; denied him the satisfaction). 4 refuse access to (a person sought) (denied him his son). □ **deny oneself** be abstinent. □□ **de•ni•er** n. [ME f. OF denier f. L denegare (as DE-, negare say no)]

deoch an do•ris /dáwkh ən dáwris, dók ən dóris/ n. (also **doch-an-dor•ris**) Sc. & Ir. a drink taken at parting; a stirrup cup. [Gael. deoch an doruis drink at the door]

de•o•dar /deeədaar/ n. the Himalayan cedar Cedrus deodara, the tallest of the cedar family, with drooping branches bearing large, barrel-shaped cones. [Hindi dě' odār f. Skr. deva-dāru divine tree]

de•o•dor•ant /deeōdərənt/ n. (often attrib.) a substance sprayed or rubbed on to the body or sprayed into the air to remove or conceal unpleasant smells (a roll-on deodorant; has a deodorant effect). [as DEODORIZE + –ANT]

de•o•dor•ize /deeōdəriz/ v.tr. remove or destroy the (usu. unpleasant) smell of. □□ **de•o•dor•i•za•tion** n. **de•o•dor•iz•er** n. [DE- + L odor smell]

De•o gra•ti•as /dáyō graátee-aas, graásheeəs/ int. thanks be to God. [L, = (we give) thanks to God]

de•on•tic /deeóntik/ adj. Philos. of or relating to duty and obligation as ethical concepts. [Gk deont- part. stem of dei it is right]

de•on•tol•o•gy /deeóntóləjee/ n. Philos. the study of duty. □□ **de•on•to•log•i•cal** /–təlójikəl/ adj. **de•on•tol•o•gist** n.

De•o vo•len•te /dáyō vəléntay/ adv. God willing; if nothing prevents it. [L]

de•ox•y•gen•ate /deeóksijənayt/ v.tr. remove oxygen, esp. free oxygen, from. □□ **de•ox•y•gen•a•tion** n.

de•ox•y•ri•bo•nu•cle•ic ac•id /deeókseeríbonōōkleéik, –kláyik, –nyoō–/ n. see DNA. [DE- + OXYGEN + RIBONUCLEIC (ACID)]

dep. abbr. 1 departs. 2 deputy.

de•part /dipaárt/ v. 1 intr. a (usu. foll. by from) go away; leave (the train departs from this platform). b (usu. foll. by for) start; set out (flights depart for New York every hour). 2 intr. (usu. foll. by from) diverge; deviate (departs from standard practice). 3 a intr. leave by death; die. b tr. formal or literary leave by death (departed this life). [ME f. OF departir ult. f. L dispertire divide]

de•part•ed /dipaártid/ adj. & n. ●adj. bygone (departed greatness). ●n. (prec. by the) euphem. a particular dead person or dead people (we are here to mourn the departed).

de•part•ment /dipaártmənt/ n. 1 a separate part of a complex whole, esp.: a a branch of municipal or federal administration (State Department; Department of Agriculture). b a branch of study and its administration at a university, school, etc. (the physics department). c a specialized section of a large store (hardware department). 2 colloq. an area of special expertise. 3 an administrative district in France and other countries. [F département (as DEPART)]

de·part·men·tal /deepaartmént'l/ adj. of or belonging to a department. □□ **de·part·men·tal·ism** n. **de·part·men·tal·ize** v.tr. **de·part·men·tal·i·za·tion** n. **de·part·men·tal·ly** adv.

de·part·ment store n. a large retail establishment stocking many varieties of goods in different departments.

de·par·ture /dipáarchər/ n. 1 the act or an instance of departing. 2 (often foll. by from) a deviation (from the truth, a standard, etc.). 3 (often attrib.) the starting of a train, an aircraft, etc. (the departure was late; departure lounge). 4 a new course of action or thought (driving a car is rather a departure for him). 5 Naut. the amount of a ship's change of longitude. [OF departeüre (as DEPART)]

de·pas·ture /deepáschər/ v. 1 a tr. (of cattle) graze upon. b intr. graze. c tr. put (cattle) to graze. 2 tr. (of land) provide pasturage for (cattle). □□ **de·pas·tur·age** n.

de·pend /dipénd/ v.intr. 1 (often foll. by on, upon) be controlled or determined by (success depends on hard work; it depends on whether they agree; it depends how you tackle the problem). 2 (foll. by on, upon) a be unable to do without (depends on her mother). b rely on (- I'm depending on you to come). 3 (foll. by on, upon) be grammatically dependent on. 4 (often foll. by from) archaic poet. hang down. □ **depend upon it!** you may be sure! **it** (or **it all** or **that**) **depends** expressing uncertainty or qualification in answering a question (Will they come? It depends). [ME f. OF dependre ult. f. L dependēre (as DE-, pendēre hang)]

de·pend·a·ble /dipéndəbəl/ adj. reliable. □□ **de·pend·a·bil·i·ty** n. **de·pend·a·ble·ness** n. **de·pend·a·bly** adv.

SPELLING TIP dependable

Someone who is *able* is usually depend*able*.

de·pend·ant Brit. var. of DEPENDENT n..

de·pend·ence /dipéndəns/ n. 1 the state of being dependent, esp. on financial or other support. 2 reliance; trust; confidence (shows great dependence on his judgment). [F dépendance (as DEPEND)]

de·pend·en·cy /dipéndənsee/ n. (pl. ·cies) 1 a country or province controlled by another. 2 anything subordinate or dependent.

de·pend·ent /dipéndənt/ adj. & n. ● adj. 1 (usu. foll. by on) depending, conditional, or subordinate. 2 unable to do without (esp. a drug). 3 maintained at another's cost. 4 Math. (of a variable) having a value determined by that of another variable. 5 Gram. (of a clause, phrase, or word) subordinate to a sentence or word. ● n. 1 a person who relies on another, esp. for financial support. 2 a servant. □□ **de·pend·ent·ly** adv. [F dépendant pres. part. of dépendre (as DEPEND)]

de·per·son·a·li·za·tion /deepérsənəlizáyshən/ n. esp. Psychol. the loss of one's sense of identity.

de·per·son·al·ize /deepérsənəlīz/ v.tr. 1 make impersonal. 2 deprive of personality.

de·pict /dipíkt/ v.tr. 1 represent in a drawing or painting, etc. 2 portray in words; describe (the play depicts him as vain and petty). □□ **de·pict·er** n. **de·pic·tion** /–píkshən/ n. **de·pic·tive** adj. **de·pic·tor** n. [L depingere depict- (as DE-, pingere paint)]

dep·i·late /dépilayt/ v.tr. remove the hair from. □□ **dep·i·la·tion** /–láyshən/ n. [L depilare (as DE-, pilare f. pilus hair)]

de·pil·a·to·ry /dipílətawree/ adj. & n. ● adj. capable of removing unwanted hair. ● n. (pl. ·ries) a cream or lotion that removes unwanted hair from the body.

de·plane /deepláyn/ v. 1 intr. disembark from an airplane. 2 tr. remove from an airplane.

de·plete /dipleét/ v.tr. (esp. in passive) 1 reduce in numbers or quantity (depleted forces). 2 empty out; exhaust (their energies were depleted). □□ **de·ple·tion** /–pleéshən/ n. [L deplēre (as DE-, plēre plet- fill)]

de·plor·a·ble /dipláwrəbəl/ adj. 1 exceedingly bad (a deplorable meal). 2 that can be deplored. □□ **de·plor·a·bly** adv.

de·plore /dipláwr/ v.tr. 1 grieve over; regret. 2 be scandalized by; find exceedingly bad. □□ **de·plor·ing·ly** adv. [F déplorer or It. deplorare f. L deplorare (as DE-, plorare bewail)]

de·ploy /diplóy/ v. 1 Mil. a tr. cause (troops) to spread out from a column into a line. b intr. (of troops) spread out in this way. 2 tr. bring (arguments, forces, etc.) into effective action. □□ **de·ploy·ment** n. [F déployer f. L displicare (as DIS-, plicare fold) & LL deplicare explain]

de·plume /deeplóom/ v.tr. 1 strip of feathers; pluck. 2 deprive of honors, etc. [ME f. F déplumer or f. med.L deplumare (as DE-, L pluma feather)]

de·po·lar·ize /deepólərīz/ v.tr. Physics reduce or remove the polarization of. □□ **de·po·lar·i·za·tion** n.

de·po·lit·i·cize /deepəlítisiz/ v.tr. 1 make (a person, an organization, etc.) nonpolitical. 2 remove from political activity or influence. □□ **de·po·lit·i·ci·za·tion** n.

de·po·lym·er·ize /deepólimərīz/ v.tr. & intr. Chem. break down into monomers or other smaller units. □□ **de·po·lym·er·i·za·tion** n.

de·po·nent /dipónənt/ adj. & n. ● adj. Gram. (of a verb, esp. in Latin or Greek) passive or middle in form but active in meaning. ● n.

1 Gram. a deponent verb. 2 Law a a person making a deposition under oath. b a witness giving written testimony for use in court, etc. [L deponere (as DE-, ponere posit- place): adj. from the notion that the verb had laid aside the passive sense]

de·pop·u·late /deepópyəlayt/ v. 1 tr. reduce the population of. 2 intr. decline in population. □□ **de·pop·u·la·tion** /–láyshən/ n. [L depopulari (as DE-, populari lay waste f. populus people)]

de·port /dipáwrt/ v.tr. 1 a remove (an immigrant or foreigner) forcibly to another country; banish. b exile (a native) to another country. 2 refl. conduct (oneself) or behave (in a specified manner) (deported himself well). □□ **de·port·a·ble** adj. **de·por·ta·tion** /–táyshən/ n. [OF deporter and (sense 1) F déporter (as DE-, L portare carry)]

de·por·tee /deepawrteé/ n. a person who has been or is being deported.

de·port·ment /dipáwrtmənt/ n. bearing, demeanor, or manners, esp. of a cultivated kind. [F déportement (as DEPORT)]

de·pose /dipóz/ v. 1 tr. remove from office, esp. dethrone. 2 intr. Law (usu. foll. by to, or that + clause) bear witness, esp. on oath in court. [ME f. OF deposer after L deponere: see DEPONENT, POSE1]

de·pos·it /dipózit/ n. & v. ● n. 1 a a sum of money placed in an account in a bank. b anything stored or entrusted for safekeeping, usu. in a bank. 2 a a sum payable as a first installment on a time-payment purchase, or as a pledge for a contract. b a returnable sum payable on the short-term rental of a car, boat, etc. 3 a a natural layer of sand, rock, coal, etc. b a layer of precipitated matter on a surface, e.g., on the inside of a kettle. ● v.tr. (**de·pos·it·ed, de·pos·it·ing**) 1 a put or lay down in a (usu. specified) place (deposited the book on the floor). b (of water, wind, etc.) leave (matter, etc.) lying in a displaced position. 2 a store or entrust for keeping. b pay (a sum of money) into a bank account, esp. a deposit account. 3 pay (a sum) as a first installment or as a pledge for a contract. [L depositum (n.), med.L depositare f. L deponere deposit- (as DEPONENT)]

de·pos·i·tar·y /dipózitéree/ n. (pl. ·ies) a person to whom something is entrusted; a trustee. [LL depositarius (as DEPOSIT)]

dep·o·si·tion /dépəzíshən/ n. 1 the act or an instance of deposing, esp. a monarch; dethronement. 2 Law a the process of giving sworn evidence; allegation. b an instance of this. c evidence given under oath; a testimony. 3 the act or an instance of depositing. 4 (**the Deposition**) a the taking down of the body of Christ from the Cross. b a representation of this. [ME f. OF f. L depositio –onis f. deponere: see DEPOSIT]

de·pos·i·tor /dipózitər/ n. a person who deposits money, property, etc.

de·pos·i·to·ry /dipózitawree/ n. (pl. ·ries) 1 a a storehouse for furniture, etc. b a store (of wisdom, knowledge, etc.) (the book is a depository of wit). 2 = DEPOSITARY. [LL depositorium (as DEPOSIT)]

de·pot /deépō, dépō/ n. 1 a storehouse. 2 Mil. a a storehouse for equipment, etc. b Brit. the headquarters of a regiment. 3 a a building for the servicing, parking, etc., of esp. buses, trains, or goods vehicles. b a railroad or bus station. [F dépôt, OF depost f. L (as DEPOSIT)]

de·prave /dipráyv/ v.tr. pervert or corrupt, esp. morally. □□ **dep·ra·va·tion** /déprəvaŷshən/ n. [ME f. OF depraver or L depravare (as DE-, pravare f. pravus crooked)]

de·praved /dipráyvd/ adj. morally corrupt.

SYNONYM TIP depraved

CORRUPT, DEBASED, DEGENERATE, PERVERTED, VILE. There are many terms to describe the dark side of human nature. Someone who preys on young children would be considered **depraved**, a term that means totally immoral and implies a warped character or a twisted mind (a depraved man who stole money from his own mother and eventually murdered her). While depraved suggests an absolute condition, **degenerate** is a relative term that implies deterioration from a mental, moral, or physical standard (her degenerate habits eventually led to her arrest for possession of drugs). **Corrupt** also suggests a deterioration or loss of soundness, particularly through a destructive or contaminating influence. But unlike depraved, which usually applies to the lower end of the human spectrum, people in high positions are often referred to as corrupt (a corrupt politician from a prominent family). To say that someone or something is **debased** suggests a lowering in quality, value, dignity, or character (debased by having to spend time in prison). **Perverted** and **vile** are the strongest of these words describing lack of moral character. Perverted suggests a distortion of someone or something from what is right, natural, or true; in a moral sense, it means to use one's appetites or natural desires for other ends than those which are considered normal or natural (a perverted individual who never should have been left alone with young children). Most people find criminals who prey on either very old or very young victims to be **vile**, a more general term for whatever is loathsome, repulsive, or utterly despicable (a vile killer who deserved the maximum sentence).

de·prav·i·ty /diprávitee/ n. (pl. ·ties) 1 a moral corruption; wickedness. b an instance of this; a wicked act. 2 Theol. the innate corruptness of human nature. [DE- + obs. *pravity* f. L *pravitas* (as DE-PRAVE)]

dep·re·cate /déprikayt/ *v.tr.* **1** express disapproval of or a wish against; deplore (*deprecate hasty action*). **2** plead earnestly against. **3** *archaic* pray against. □□ **dep·re·cat·ing·ly** *adv.* **dep·re·ca·tion** /–káyshən/ *n.* **dep·re·ca·tive** /–kaytiv, –kətiv/ *adj.* **dep·re·ca·tor** *n.* **dep·re·ca·to·ry** /–kətawree/ *adj.* [L *deprecari* (as DE-, *precari* pray)]
▶ **Deprecate** means 'to express disapproval of, to deplore,' e.g., *The mainstream press began by deprecating the film's attitude towards terrorism*, while **depreciate** (apart from its financial senses) means 'to disparage or belittle,' e.g., *He is always depreciating his own skills out of a strong sense of humility.*

de·pre·ci·ate /dipréesheeayt/ *v.* **1** *tr. & intr.* diminish in value (*the car has depreciated*). **2** *tr.* disparage; belittle (*they are always depreciating his taste*). **3** *tr.* reduce the purchasing power of (money). □□ **de·pre·ci·at·ing·ly** *adv.* **de·pre·ci·a·to·ry** /–sheeətáwree/ *adj.* [LL *depretiare* (as DE-, *pretiare* f. *pretium* price)]
▶ See note at DEPRECATE.

de·pre·ci·a·tion /dipreesheeáyshən/ *n.* **1** the amount of wear and tear of a property, etc.) for which a reduction may be made in a valuation, an estimate, or a balance sheet. **2** *Econ.* a decrease in the value of a currency. **3** the act or an instance of depreciating; belittlement.

dep·re·da·tion /dépridáyshən/ *n.* (usu. in *pl.*) **1** despoiling, ravaging, or plundering. **2** an instance or instances of this. [F *déprédation* f. LL *depraedatio* (as DE-, *praedatio –onis* f. L *praedari* plunder)]

dep·re·da·tor /dépridaytər/ *n.* a despoiler or pillager. □□ **dep·re·da·to·ry** /dedpridáytoree, dipréddətawree/ *adj.* [LL *depraedator* (as DEPREDATION)]

de·press /diprés/ *v.tr.* **1** push or pull down; lower (*depressed the lever*). **2** make dispirited or dejected. **3** *Econ.* reduce the activity of (esp. trade). **4** (as **depressed** *adj.*) **a** dispirited or miserable. **b** *Psychol.* suffering from depression. □□ **de·pres·si·ble** *adj.* **de·press·ing** *adj.* **de·press·ing·ly** *adv.* [ME f. OF *depresser* f. LL *depressare* frequent. of *premere* press)]

de·pres·sant /diprésənt/ *adj. & n.* ● *adj.* **1** that depresses. **2** *Med.* sedative. ● *n.* **1** *Med.* an agent, esp. a drug, that sedates. **2** an influence that depresses.

de·pressed ar·e·a *n.* an area suffering from economic depression.

de·pres·sion /dipréshən/ *n.* **1 a** *Psychol.* a state of extreme dejection or morbidly excessive melancholy; a mood of hopelessness and feelings of inadequacy, often with physical symptoms. **b** a reduction in vitality, vigor, or spirits. **2 a** a long period of financial and industrial decline; a slump. **b** (**the Depression**) the depression of 1929–34. **3** *Meteorol.* a lowering of atmospheric pressure, esp. the center of a region of minimum pressure or the system of winds around it. **4** a sunken place or hollow on a surface. **5 a** a lowering or sinking (often foll. by *of*: *depression of freezing point*). **b** pressing down. **6** *Astron. & Geog.* the angular distance of an object below the horizon or a horizontal plane. [ME f. OF or L *depressio* (as DE-, *premere* press- press)]

de·pres·sive /diprésiv/ *adj. & n.* ● *adj.* **1** tending to depress. **2** *Psychol.* involving or characterized by depression. ● *n. Psychol.* a person suffering with a tendency to suffer from depression. [F *dépressif –ive* or med.L *depressivus* (as DEPRESSION)]

de·pres·sor /diprésər/ *n.* **1** *Anat.* **a** (in full **depressor muscle**) a muscle that causes the lowering of some part of the body. **b** a nerve that lowers blood pressure. **2** *Surgery* an instrument for pressing down an organ, etc. [L (as DEPRESSION)]

de·pres·sur·ize /deepréshəriz/ *v.tr.* cause an appreciable drop in the pressure of the gas inside (a container), esp. to the ambient level. □□ **de·pres·sur·i·za·tion** *n.*

dep·ri·va·tion /déprivávshən/ *n.* **1** (usu. foll. by *of*) the act or an instance of depriving; the state of being deprived (*deprivation of liberty; suffered many deprivations*). **2 a** deposition from esp. an ecclesiastical office. **b** an instance of this. [med.L *deprivatio* (as DEPRIVE)]

de·prive /diprív/ *v.tr.* **1** (usu. foll. by *of*) strip, dispossess; debar from enjoying (*illness deprived him of success*). **2** (as **deprived** *adj.*) **a** (of a child, etc.) suffering from the effects of a poor or loveless home. **b** (of an area) with inadequate housing, facilities, employment, etc. **3** *archaic* depose (esp. a clergyman) from office. □□ **de·priv·a·ble** *adj.* **de·priv·al** *n.* [ME f. OF *depriver* f. med.L *deprivare* (as DE-, L *privare* deprive)]

de pro·fun·dis /dáy prōfoŏndis/ *adv. & n.* ● *adv.* from the depths (of sorrow, etc.). ● *n.* a cry from the depths. [opening L words of Ps. 130]

Dept. *abbr.* Department.

depth /depth/ *n.* **1 a** a deepness (*the depth is not great at the edge*). **b** the measurement from the top down, from the surface inward, or from the front to the back (*depth of the drawer is 12 inches*). **2** difficulty; abstruseness. **3 a** sagacity; wisdom. **b** intensity of emotion, etc. (*the poem has little depth*). **4** an intensity of color, darkness, etc. **5** (in *pl.*) **a** deep water, a deep place; an abyss. **b** a low, depressed state. **c** the lowest or inmost part (*the depths of the country*). **6** the middle (*in the depth of winter*). □ **in depth** comprehensively, thoroughly, or pro-

foundly. **out of one's depth 1** in water over one's head. **2** engaged in a task or on a subject too difficult for one. [ME (as DEEP, –TH[2])]

depth charge *n.* (also **depth bomb**) a bomb capable of exploding under water, esp. for dropping on a submerged submarine, etc.

depth·less /dépthlis/ *adj.* **1** extremely deep; fathomless. **2** shallow; superficial.

depth psy·chol·o·gy *n.* psychoanalysis to reveal hidden motives, etc.

dep·u·rate /dépyərayt/ *v.tr. & intr.* make or become free from impurities. □□ **dep·u·ra·tion** /–ráyshən/ *n.* **dep·u·ra·tive** *adj. & n.* **dep·u·ra·tor** *n.* [med.L *depurare* (as DE-, *purus* pure)]

dep·u·ta·tion /dépyōōtáyshən/ *n.* a group of people appointed to represent others, usu. for a specific purpose; a delegation. [ME f. LL *deputatio* (as DEPUTE)]

de·pute *v. & n.* ● *v.tr.* /dipyóōt/ (often foll. by *to*) **1** appoint as a deputy. **2** delegate (a task, authority, etc.) (*deputed the leadership to her*). ● *n.* /dépyōōt/ *Sc.* a deputy. [ME f. OF *député* past part. of *deputer* f. L *deputare* regard as, allot (as DE-, *putare* think)]

dep·u·tize /dépyətiz/ *v.intr.* (usu. foll. by *for*) act as a deputy or understudy.

dep·u·ty /dépyətee/ *n.* (*pl.* **·ties**) **1** a person appointed or delegated to act for another or others (also *attrib.*: *deputy sheriff*). **2** *Polit.* a parliamentary representative in certain countries, e.g., France. □ **by deputy** by proxy. □□ **dep·u·ty·ship** *n.* [ME var. of DEPUTE *n.*]

de·rac·in·ate /di-rásinayt/ *v.tr. literary* **1** tear up by the roots. **2** obliterate; expunge. □□ **de·rac·i·na·tion** /–náyshən/ *n.* [F *déraciner* (as DE-, *racine* f. LL *radicina* dimin. of *radix* root)]

de·rail /diráyl/ *v.tr.* (usu. in *passive*) cause (a train, etc.) to leave the rails. □□ **de·rail·ment** *n.* [F *dérailler* (as DE-, RAIL[1])]

de·rail·leur /dəráylər/ *n.* a gear-shifting mechanism on a bicycle that moves the chain from one sprocket wheel to another. [F]

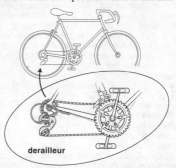

derailleur

de·range /diráynj/ *v.tr.* **1** throw into confusion; disorganize; cause to act irregularly. **2** (esp. as **deranged** *adj.*) make insane (*deranged by the tragic events*). **3** disturb; interrupt. □□ **de·range·ment** *n.* [F *déranger* (as DE-, *rang* RANK[1])]

de·ra·tion /dée-ráshən/ *v.tr.* free (food, etc.) from rationing.

der·by /dórbee/ *n.* (*pl.* **·bies**) **1** any of several horse races that are run annually, esp. for three-year olds (*Kentucky Derby*). **2** a sporting contest, etc., esp. one open to all comers. **3** a bowler hat. [the 12th Earl of *Derby* d. 1834, founder in 1780 of a horse race at Epsom Downs, England]

de·reg·u·late /dee-régyəlayt/ *v.tr.* remove regulations or restrictions from. □□ **de·reg·u·la·tion** /–láyshən/ *n.*

der·e·lict /dérilikt/ *adj. & n.* ● *adj.* **1** abandoned; ownerless (esp. of a ship at sea or an empty decrepit property). **2** (esp. of property) ruined; dilapidated. **3** negligent (of duty, etc.). ● *n.* **1** a social outcast; a person without a home, a job, or property. **2** abandoned property, esp. a ship. [L *derelictus* past part. of *derelinquere* (as DE-, *relinquere* leave)]

derby 3

der·e·lic·tion /dérilíkshən/ *n.* **1** (usu. foll. by *of*) **a** neglect; failure to carry out one's obligations (*dereliction of duty*). **b** an instance of this. **2** the act or an instance of abandoning; the process of being abandoned. **3 a** the retreat of the sea exposing new land. **b** the land so exposed. [L *derelictio* (as DERELICT)]

de·req·ui·si·tion /dee-rékwizíshən/ *v.tr.* return (requisitioned property) to its former owner.

de·re·strict /dée-ristríkt/ *v.tr.* **1** remove restrictions from. **2** remove speed restrictions from (a road, area, etc.). □□ **de•re•stric•tion** /–tríkshən/ *n.*

de•ride /diríd/ *v.tr.* laugh scornfully at; mock. □□ **de•rid•er** *n.* **de•rid•ing•ly** *adv.* [L *deridēre* (as DE-, *ridēre ris-* laugh)]

de ri•gueur /də rigő́r/ *predic.adj.* required by custom or etiquette (*evening dress is de rigueur*). [F, = of strictness]

de•ri•sion /dirízhən/ *n.* ridicule; mockery (*bring into derision*). □ **hold** (or **have**) **in derision** *archaic* mock at. □□ **de•ris•i•ble** /dirízibəl/ *adj.* [ME f. OF f. LL *derisio -onis* (as DERIDE)]

de•ri•sive /dirísiv/ *adj.* scoffing; ironical; scornful (*derisive cheers*). □□ **de•ri•sive•ly** *adv.* **de•ri•sive•ness** *n.*

de•ri•so•ry /dirísəree, zə-/ *adj.* **1** = DERISIVE. **2** so small or unimportant as to be ridiculous (*derisory offer; derisory costs*). [LL *derisorius* (as DERISION)]

der•i•va•tion /dérivávyshən/ *n.* **1** the act or an instance of deriving or obtaining from a source; the process of being derived. **2 a** the formation of a word from another word or from a root. **b** a derivative. **c** the tracing of the origin of a word. **d** a statement or account of this. **3** extraction; descent. **4** *Math.* a sequence of statements showing that a formula, theorem, etc., is a consequence of previously accepted statements. □□ **der•i•va•tion•al** *adj.* [F *dérivation* or L *derivatio* (as DERIVE)]

de•riv•a•tive /dirívətiv/ *adj. & n.* ● *adj.* derived from another source; not original (*his music is derivative and uninteresting*). ● *n.* **1** something derived from another source, esp.: **a** a word derived from another or from a root (e.g., *quickly* from *quick*). **b** *Chem.* a chemical compound that is derived from another. **2** *Math.* a quantity measuring the rate of change of another. □□ **de•riv•a•tive•ly** *adv.* [F *dérivatif -ive* f. L *derivativus* (as DERIVE)]

de•rive /dirív/ *v.* **1** *tr.* (usu. foll. by *from*) get, obtain, or form (*derived satisfaction from work*). **2** *intr.* (foll. by *from*) arise from, originate in, be descended or obtained from (*happiness derives from many things*). **3** *tr.* gather or deduce (*derived the information from the clues*). **4** *tr.* **a** trace the descent of (a person). **b** show the origin of (a thing). **5** *tr.* (usu. foll. by *from*) show or state the origin or formation of (a word, etc.) (*derived the word from Latin*). **6** *tr. Math.* obtain (a function) by differentiation. □□ **de•riv•a•ble** *adj.* [ME f. OF *deriver* or f. L *derivare* (as DE-, *rivus* stream)]

der•ma var. of DERMIS.

der•ma•ti•tis /dərmətítis/ *n.* inflammation of the skin. [Gk *derma -atos* skin + ;n-ITIS]

der•mat•o•glyph•ics /dərmətōglífiks/ *n.* the science or study of skin markings or patterns, esp. of the fingers, hands, and feet. □□ **der•mat•o•glyph•ic** *adj.* **der•mat•o•glyph•i•cal•ly** *adv.* [as DERMATITIS + Gk *gluphē* carving: see GLYPH]

der•ma•tol•o•gy /dərmətóləjee/ *n.* the study of the diagnosis and treatment of skin disorders. □□ **der•ma•to•log•i•cal** /–təlójikəl/ *adj.* **der•ma•tol•o•gist** *n.* [as DERMATITIS + ;n-LOGY]

der•mis /dərmis/ *n.* (also **der•ma** /dərmə/) **1** (in general use) the skin. **2** *Anat.* the true skin, the thick layer of living tissue below the epidermis. □□ **der•mal** *adj.* **der•mic** *adj.* [mod.L, after EPIDERMIS]

der•nier cri /dáirnyay kreé/ *n.* the very latest fashion. [F, = last cry]

der•o•gate /dérəgayt/ *v.intr.* (foll. by *from*) *formal* **1 a** take away a part from; detract from (a merit, a right, etc.). **b** disparage. **2** deviate from (correct behavior, etc.). □□ **de•rog•a•tive** /dirógətiv/ *adj.* [L *derogare* (as DE-, *rogare* ask)]

der•o•ga•tion /dérəgáyshən/ *n.* **1** (foll. by *of*) a lessening or impairment of (a law, authority, position, dignity, etc.). **2** deterioration; debasement. [ME f. OF *dérogation* or L *derogatio* (as DEROGATE)]

de•rog•a•to•ry /dirógətawree/ *adj.* (often foll. by *to*) involving disparagement or discredit; insulting; depreciatory (*made a derogatory remark; derogatory to my position*). □□ **de•rog•a•to•ri•ly** *adv.* [LL *derogatorius* (as DEROGATE)]

der•rick /dérik/ *n.* **1** a kind of crane for moving or lifting heavy weights, having a movable pivoted arm. **2** the framework over an oil well or similar excavation, holding the drilling machinery. [obs. senses *hangman, gallows*, f. the name of a London hangman *c.*1600]

der•ri•ere /déreeáir/ *n. colloq. euphem.* (also **der•ri•ère**) the buttocks. [F, = behind]

der•ring-do /déringdóo/ *n. literary joc.* heroic courage or action. [ME, = *daring to do*, misinterpreted by Spenser and by Scott]

der•rin•ger /dérinjər/ *n.* a small large-bore pistol. [H. *Deringer*, Amer. inventor d. 1868]

der•ris /déris/ *n.* **1** any woody, tropical climbing leguminous plant of the genus *Derris*, bearing leathery pods. **2** an insecticide made from the powdered root of some kinds of derris. [mod.L f. Gk, = leather covering (with ref. to its pod)]

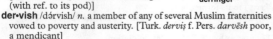

derringer

der•vish /dérvish/ *n.* a member of any of several Muslim fraternities vowed to poverty and austerity. [Turk. *derviş* f. Pers. *darvēsh* poor, a mendicant]

de•sal•i•nate /deesálinayt/ *v.tr.* remove salt from (esp. sea water). □□ **de•sal•i•na•tion** /–náyshən/ *n.*

de•salt /deesáwlt/ *v.tr.* = DESALINATE.

de•sa•pa•re•ci•do /désaapaarəseédō/ *n.* (esp. in South America) a person who has disappeared, presumed killed by members of the armed services or the police. [Sp., lit. 'disappeared']

de•scale /deeskáyl/ *v.tr.* remove the scale from.

des•cant *n. & v.* ● *n.* /déskant/ **1** *Mus.* an independent treble melody usu. sung or played above a basic melody, esp. of a hymn tune. **2** *poet.* a melody; a song. ● *v.intr.* /diskánt/ **1** (foll. by *on, upon*) talk lengthily and prosily, esp. in praise of. **2** *Mus.* sing or play a descant. [ME f. OF *deschant* f. med.L *discantus* (as DIS-, *cantus* song, CHANT)]

des•cant re•cord•er *n.* the most common size of recorder (musical instrument), with a range of two octaves.

de•scend /disénd/ *v.* **1** *tr. & intr.* go or come down (a hill, stairs, etc.). **2** *intr.* (of a thing) sink; fall (*rain descended heavily*). **3** *intr.* slope downward; lie along a descending slope (*fields descended to the beach*). **4** *intr.* (usu. foll. by *on*) **a** make a sudden attack. **b** make an unexpected and usu. unwelcome visit (*hope they don't descend on us during the weekend*). **5** *intr.* (usu. foll. by *from, to*) (of property, qualities, rights, etc.) be passed by inheritance (*the house descends from my grandmother; the property descended to me*). **6** *intr.* **a** sink in rank, quality, etc. **b** (foll. by *to*) degrade oneself morally to (an unworthy act) (*descend to violence*). **7** *intr. Mus.* (of sound) become lower in pitch. **8** *intr.* (usu. foll. by *to*) proceed (in discourse or writing): **a** in time (to a subsequent event, etc.). **b** from the general (to the particular) (*now let's descend to details*). **9** *tr.* go along (a river, etc.) to the sea, etc. **10** *intr. Printing* (of a letter) have its tail below the line. □ **be descended from** have as an ancestor. □□ **de•scend•ent** *adj.* [ME f. OF *descendre* f. L *descendere* (as DE-, *scandere* climb)]

de•scend•ant /diséndənt/ *n.* (often foll. by *of*) a person or thing descended from another (*a descendant of John Adams*). [F, part. of *descendre* (as DESCEND)]

SPELLING TIP descendant

Remember the *an* in *descendant* by using the mnemonic: "A *descendant* must have an *an*cestor."

---

de•scend•er /diséndər/ *n. Printing* a part of a letter that extends below the level of the base of a letter, as in *g* or *p*.

de•scend•i•ble /diséndibəl/ *adj.* **1** (of a slope, etc.) that may be descended. **2** *Law* capable of descending by inheritance. [OF *descendable* (as DESCEND)]

de•scent /disént/ *n.* **1 a** the act of descending. **b** an instance of this. **c** a downward movement. **2 a** a way or path, etc., by which one may descend. **b** a downward slope. **3 a** being descended; lineage; family origin (*traces his descent from Sitting Bull*). **b** the transmission of qualities, property, privileges, etc., by inheritance. **4 a** a decline; a fall. **b** a lowering (of pitch, temperature, etc.). **5** a sudden violent attack. [ME f. OF *descente* f. *descendre* DESCEND]

de•scram•ble /deeskrámbəl/ *v.tr.* **1** convert or restore (a signal) to intelligible form. **2** counteract the effects of (a scrambling device). **3** recover an original signal from (a scrambled signal). □□ **de•scram•bler** *n.*

de•scribe /diskríb/ *v.tr.* **1 a** state the characteristics, appearance, etc., of, in spoken or written form (*described the landscape*). **b** (foll. by *as*) assert to be; call (*described him as a habitual liar*). **2 a** mark out or draw (esp. a geometrical figure) (*described a triangle*). **b** move in (a specified way, esp. a curve) (*described a parabola through the air*). □□ **de•scrib•a•ble** *adj.* **de•scrib•er** *n.* [L *describere* (as DE-, *scribere script-* write)]

de•scrip•tion /diskrípshən/ *n.* **1 a** the act or an instance of describing; the process of being described. **b** a spoken or written representation (of a person, object, or event). **2** a sort, kind, or class (*no food of any description*). □ **answers** (or **fits**) **the description** has the qualities specified. [ME f. OF f. L *descriptio -onis* (as DESCRIBE)]

de•scrip•tive /diskríptiv/ *adj.* **1** serving or seeking to describe (*a descriptive writer*). **2** describing or classifying without expressing feelings or judging (*a purely descriptive account*). **3** *Linguistics* describing a language without comparing, endorsing, or condemning particular usage, vocabulary, etc. **4** *Gram.* (of an adjective) describing the noun, rather than its relation, position, etc., e.g., *blue* as distinct from *few*. □□ **de•scrip•tive•ly** *adv.* **de•scrip•tive•ness** *n.* [LL *descriptivus* (as DESCRIBE)]

de•scrip•tor /diskríptər/ *n. Linguistics* a word or expression, etc., used to describe or identify. [L, = describer (as DESCRIBE)]

de•scry /diskrí/ *v.tr.* (**-scries, -scried**) *literary* catch sight of; discern (*descried him in the crowd; descries no glimmer of light in her situation*). [ME (earlier senses 'proclaim, DECRY') f. OF *descrier*: prob. confused with var. of obs. *descrive* f. OF *describe* DESCRIBE]

des•e•crate /désikrayt/ *v.tr.* **1** violate (a sacred place or thing) with violence, profanity, etc. **2** deprive (a church, a sacred object, etc.) of sanctity; deconsecrate. □□ **des•e•cra•tion** /–kráyshən/ *n.* **des•e•cra•tor** *n.* [DE- + CONSECRATE]

de•seed /deeseéd/ v.tr. remove the seeds from (a plant, vegetable, etc.).

de•seg•re•gate /deeségrigayt/ v.tr. abolish racial segregation in (schools, etc.) or of (people, etc.). □□ **de•seg•re•ga•tion** /–gáyshən/ n.

de•se•lect /deésilékt/ v.tr. **1** dismiss (esp. a trainee); discharge; reject. **2** Polit. decline to select or retain as a constituency candidate in an election. □□ **de•se•lec•tion** /–lékshən/ n.

de•sen•si•tize /deesénsitiz/ v.tr. reduce or destroy the sensitiveness of (photographic materials, an allergic person, etc.). □□ **de•sen•si•ti•za•tion** n. **de•sen•si•tiz•er** n.

de•sert¹ /dizə́rt/ v. **1** tr. abandon; give up; leave (deserted the sinking ship). **2** tr. forsake or abandon (a cause or a person, people, etc., having claims on one) (deserted his wife and children). **3** tr. fail (his presence of mind deserted him). **4** intr. Mil. run away (esp. from military service). **5** tr. (as **deserted** adj.) empty; abandoned (a deserted house). □□ **de•sert•er** n. (in sense 4 of v.). **de•ser•tion** /–zə́rshən/ n. [F déserter f. LL desertare f. L desertus (as DESERT²)]

des•ert² /dézərt/ n. & adj. ● n. a dry, barren, often sand-covered area of land, characteristically desolate, waterless, and without vegetation; an uninteresting or barren subject, period, etc. (a cultural desert). ● adj. **1** uninhabited; desolate. **2** uncultivated; barren. [ME f. OF f. L desertus, eccl.L desertum (n.), past part. of deserere leave, forsake]

<table>
<tr><td>**SPELLING TIP** desert²</td></tr>
</table>

See note at DESSERT.

de•sert³ /dizə́rt/ n. **1** (in pl.) **a** acts or qualities deserving reward or punishment. **b** such reward or punishment (has gotten his just deserts). **2** the fact of being worthy of reward or punishment; deservingness. [ME f. OF f. deservir DESERVE]

Des•ert boot Trademark a suede, etc., boot reaching to or extending just above the ankle.

de•sert•i•fi•ca•tion /dizə́rtifikáyshən/ n. the process of making or becoming a desert.

des•ert is•land n. a remote (usu. tropical) island presumed to be uninhabited.

des•ert rat n. **1** any of various small rodents of arid regions. **2** desert dweller (esp. in US West), esp. a prospector. **3** a soldier (esp. Brit.) in the N. African desert campaign of 1941–42.

de•serve /dizə́rv/ v.tr. **1** (often foll. by to + infin.) show conduct or qualities worthy of (reward, punishment, etc.) (deserves to be imprisoned; deserves a prize). **2** (as **deserved** adj.) rightfully merited or earned (a deserved win). □ **deserve well** (or **ill**) **of** esp. Brit. be worthy of good (or bad) treatment at the hands of (deserves well of the electorate). □□ **de•serv•ed•ly** /–vidlee/ adv. **de•serv•ed•ness** n. **de•serv•er** n. [ME f. OF deservir f. L deservire (as DE-, servire serve)]

de•serv•ing /dizə́rving/ adj. meritorious. □ **deserving of** showing conduct or qualities worthy of (praise, blame, help, etc.). □□ **de•serv•ing•ly** adv. **de•serv•ing•ness** n.

de•sex /deeséks/ v.tr. **1** castrate or spay (an animal). **2** deprive of sexual qualities or attractions.

de•sex•u•al•ize /deesékshooəliz/ v.tr. deprive of sexual character or of the distinctive qualities of a sex.

des•ha•bille var. of DISHABILLE.

des•ic•cant /désikənt/ n. Chem. a hygroscopic substance used as a drying agent.

des•ic•cate /désikayt/ v.tr. remove the moisture from, dry (esp. food for preservation) (desiccated coconut). □□ **des•ic•ca•tion** /–káyshən/ n. **des•ic•ca•tive** adj. [L desiccare (as DE-, siccus dry)]

des•ic•ca•tor /désikaytər/ n. **1** an apparatus for desiccating. **2** Chem. an apparatus containing a drying agent to remove the moisture from specimens.

de•sid•er•ate /disídərayt/ v.tr. archaic feel to be missing; regret the absence of; wish to have. [L desiderare (as DE-, siderare as in CONSIDER)]

de•sid•er•a•tive /disídərətiv, –ráytiv/ adj. & n. ● adj. **1** Gram. (of a verb, conjugation, etc.) formed from another verb, etc., and denoting a desire to perform the action of that verb, etc. **2** desiring. ● n. Gram. a desiderative verb, conjugation, etc. [LL desiderativus (as DESIDERATE)]

de•sid•er•a•tum /disídəráytəm, –ráatəm/ n. (pl. **de•sid•er•a•ta** /–tə/) something lacking but needed or desired. [L neut. past part.: see DESIDERATE]

de•sign /dizín/ n. & v. ● n. **1 a** a preliminary plan or sketch for the making or production of a building, machine, garment, etc. **b** the art of producing these. **2** a scheme of lines or shapes forming a pattern or decoration. **3** a plan, purpose, or intention. **4** the general arrangement or layout of a product. **b** an established version of a product (one of our most popular designs). ● v. **1** tr. produce a design for (a building, machine, picture, garment, etc.). **2** tr. intend, plan, or purpose (the remark was designed to offend; a course designed for beginners; designed an attack). **3** absol. be a designer. □ **argument from design** Theol. the argument that God's existence is provable by the evidence of design in the universe. **by design** on purpose.

have designs on plan to harm or appropriate. [F désigner appoint or obs. F desseing ult. f. L designare DESIGNATE]

des•ig•nate v. & adj. ● v.tr. /dézignayt/ **1** (often foll. by as) appoint to an office or function (designated him as postmaster general; designated her own successor). **2** specify or particularize (receives guests at designated times). **3** (often foll. by as) describe as; entitle; style. **4** serve as the name or distinctive mark of (English uses French words to designate ballet steps). ● adj. /dézignət/ (placed after noun) appointed to an office but not yet installed (bishop designate). □□ **des•ig•na•tor** n. [L designare, past part. designatus (as DE-, signare f. signum mark)]

des•ig•nat•ed driv•er n. one member of a group who abstains from alcohol in order to drive the others safely.

des•ig•nat•ed hit•ter n. Baseball a batter in the lineup who hits for the pitcher. ¶ Abbr.: **DH**.

des•ig•na•tion /dézignáyshən/ n. **1** a name, description, or title. **2** the act or process of designating. [ME f. OF designation or L designatio (as DESIGNATE)]

de•sign•ed•ly /dizínidlee/ adv. by design; on purpose.

de•sign•er /dizínər/ n. **1** a person who makes artistic designs or plans for construction, e.g., for clothing, machines, theater sets; a draftsman. **2** (attrib.) (of clothing, etc.) bearing the name or label of a famous designer; prestigious.

de•sign•er drug n. **1** a synthetic analog of an illegal drug, esp. one devised to circumvent drug laws. **2** a fashionable artificial drug.

de•sign•ing /dizíning/ adj. crafty, artful, or scheming. □□ **de•sign•ing•ly** adv.

de•sir•a•ble /dizírəbəl/ adj. **1** worth having or wishing for (it is desirable that nobody should smoke). **2** arousing sexual desire; very attractive. □□ **de•sir•a•bil•i•ty** n. **de•sir•a•ble•ness** n. **de•sir•a•bly** adv. [ME f. OF (as DESIRE)]

de•sire /dizír/ n. & v. ● n. **1 a** an unsatisfied longing or craving. **b** an expression of this; a request (expressed a desire to rest). **2** lust. **3** something desired (achieved her heart's desire). ● v.tr. **1** (often foll. by to + infin., or that + clause) long for; crave. **2** request (desires a cup of coffee). **3** archaic pray, entreat, or command (desire him to wait). [ME f. OF desir f. desirer f. L desiderare DESIDERATE]

de•sir•ous /dizírəs/ predic.adj. **1** (usu. foll. by of) ambitious; desiring (desirous of stardom; desirous of doing well). **2** (usu. foll. by to + infin., or that + clause) wishful; hoping (desirous to do the right thing). [ME f. AF desirous, OF desireus f. Rmc (as DESIRE)]

de•sist /dizíst/ v.intr. (often foll. by from) literary abstain; cease (please desist from interrupting; when requested, he desisted). [OF desister f. L desistere (as DE-, sistere stop, redupl. f. stare stand)]

desk /desk/ n. **1** a piece of furniture or a portable box with a flat or sloped surface for writing on, and often drawers. **2** a counter in a hotel, bank, etc., which separates the customer from the assistant. **3** a section of a newspaper office, etc., dealing with a specified topic (the sports desk; the features desk). **4** Mus. a music stand in an orchestra regarded as a unit of two players. [ME f. med.L desca f. L DISCUS disk]

desk•bound /déskbownd/ adj. obliged to remain working at a desk.

desk•top /désktop/ n. **1 a** the working surface of a desk. **b** the working area for manipulating windows, icons, etc., in some computer software environments. **2** (attrib.) (esp. of a microcomputer) suitable for use at an ordinary desk.

desk•top pub•lish•ing n. the production of printed matter with a desktop computer and printer.

des•man /désmən/ n. (pl. **des•mans**) any aquatic carnivorous shrewlike mammal of two species, one originating in Russia (Desmana moschata) and one in the Pyrenees (Galemys pyrenaicus). [F & G f. Sw. desman-råtta muskrat]

des•o•late adj. & v. ● adj. /désələt/ **1** left alone; solitary. **2** (of a building or place) uninhabited; ruined; neglected; barren; dreary; empty (a desolate beach). **3** forlorn; wretched; miserable (was left desolate and weeping). ● v.tr. /désəlayt/ **1** depopulate or devastate; lay waste to. **2** (esp. as **desolated** adj.) make wretched or forlorn (desolated by grief; inconsolable and desolated). □□ **des•o•late•ly** /–lətlee/ adv. **des•o•late•ness** n. **des•o•la•tor** n. [ME f. L desolatus past part. of desolare (as DE-, solare f. solus alone)]

des•o•la•tion /désəláyshən/ n. **1 a** the act of desolating. **b** the process of being desolated. **2** loneliness, grief, or wretchedness, esp. caused by desertion. **3** a neglected, ruined, barren, or empty state. [ME f. LL desolatio (as DESOLATE)]

de•sorb /disáwrb, –záwrb/ v. **1** tr. cause the release of (an adsorbed substance) from a surface. **2** intr. (of an adsorbed substance) become released. □□ **de•sor•bent** adj. & n. **de•sorp•tion** n. [DE-, after ADSORB]

de•spair /dispáir/ n. & v. ● n. the complete loss or absence of hope. ● v.intr. **1** (often foll. by of) lose or be without hope (despaired of ever seeing her again). **2** (foll. by of) lose hope about (his life is despaired of). □ **be the despair of** be the cause of despair by badness or unapproachable excellence (*he's the despair of his parents*). □□ **de‧spair‧ing‧ly** *adv.* [ME f. OF *desespeir, desperer* f. L *desperare* (as DE-, *sperare* hope)]

des‧patch var. of DISPATCH.

des‧per‧a‧do /déspəraádō/ *n.* (*pl.* **·does** or **·dos**) a desperate or reckless person, esp. a criminal. [after DESPERATE (obs. n.) & words in −ADO]

des‧per‧ate /déspərət, –prit/ *adj.* **1** reckless from despair; violent and lawless. **2 a** extremely dangerous or serious (*a desperate situation*). **b** staking all on a small chance (*a desperate remedy*). **3** very bad (*a desperate night; desperate poverty*). **4** (usu. foll. by *for*) needing or desiring very much (*desperate for recognition*). □□ **des‧per‧ate‧ly** *adv.* **des‧per‧ate‧ness** *n.* **des‧per‧a‧tion** /–ráyshən/ *n.* [ME f. L *desperatus* past part. of *desperare* (as DE-, *sperare* hope)]

des‧pi‧ca‧ble /déspikəbəl, dispík–/ *adj.* vile; contemptible, esp. morally. □□ **des‧pi‧ca‧bly** *adv.* [LL *despicabilis* f. *despicari* (as DE-, *specere* look at)]

de‧spise /dispíz/ *v.tr.* look down on as inferior, worthless, or contemptible. □□ **de‧spis‧er** *n.* [ME f. *despis-* pres. stem of OF *despire* f. L *despicere* (as DE-, *specere* look at)]

SYNONYM TIP despise

ABHOR, CONTEMN, DETEST, DISDAIN, LOATHE, SCORN. It's one thing to dislike someone; it's quite another to **despise** or **detest** the person. Both are strong words, used to describe extreme dislike or hatred. *Detest* is probably the purest expression of hatred (*she detested the woman who had raised her, and longed to find her own mother*), while *despise* suggests looking down with great contempt and regarding the person as mean, petty, weak, or worthless (*he despised men whose only concern was their own safety*). **Disdain** carries even stronger connotations of superiority, often combined with self-righteousness (*to disdain anyone lacking a college education*). **Scorn** is a stronger word for *disdain*, and it implies an attitude of not only contempt but of haughty rejection or refusal (*to scorn the woman he'd once loved*). To **loathe** something is to feel utter disgust toward it (*he grew to loathe peanut butter and jelly sandwiches*) and to **abhor** it is to feel a profound, shuddering, repugnance (*she abhorred the very idea of asking her husband for the money*). **Contemn** is a more literary word meaning to treat with disdain, scorn, or contempt.

de‧spite /dispít/ *prep. & n.* • *prep.* in spite of. • *n.* archaic or literary **1** outrage; injury. **2** malice; hatred (*died of mere despite*). □ **despite** (or **in despite**) **of** archaic in spite of. □□ **de‧spite‧ful** *adj.* [ME f. OF *despit* f. L *despectus* noun f. *despicere* (as DESPISE)]

de‧spoil /dispóyl/ *v.tr.* literary (often foll. by *of*) plunder; rob; deprive. □□ **de‧spoil‧er** *n.* **de‧spoil‧ment** *n.* **de‧spo‧li‧a‧tion** /dispóleeáyshən/ *n.* [ME f. OF *despoill(i)er* f. L *despoliare* (as DE-, *spoliare* SPOIL)]

de‧spond /dispónd/ *v. & n.* • *v.intr.* lose heart or hope; be dejected. • *n.* archaic despondency. [L *despondēre* give up, abandon (as DE-, *spondēre* promise)]

de‧spond‧ent /dispóndənt/ *adj.* in low spirits; dejected. □□ **de‧spond‧ence** /–dəns/ *n.* **de‧spond‧en‧cy** *n.* **de‧spond‧ent‧ly** *adv.*

des‧pot /déspət/ *n.* **1** an absolute ruler. **2** a tyrant or oppressor. □□ **des‧pot‧ic** /–spótik/ *adj.* **des‧pot‧i‧cal‧ly** *adv.* [F *despote* f. med.L *despota* f. Gk *despotēs* master, lord]

des‧pot‧ism /déspətizəm/ *n.* **1 a** rule by a despot. **b** a country ruled by a despot. **2** absolute power or control; tyranny.

des‧qua‧mate /déskwəmayt/ *v.intr.* Med. (esp. of the skin) come off in scales (as in some diseases). □□ **des‧qua‧ma‧tion** /–máyshən/ *n.* **des‧qua‧ma‧tive** /diskwáamətiv/ *adj.* **des‧qua‧ma‧to‧ry** /diskwáamətawree/ *adj.* [L *desquamare* (as DE-, *squama* scale)]

des res /dez réz/ *n. Brit. sl.* a desirable residence. [abbr.]

des‧sert /dizórt/ *n.* **1** the sweet course of a meal, served at or near the end. **2** *Brit.* a course of fruit, nuts, etc., served after a meal. [F, past part. of *desservir* clear the table (as DIS-, *servir* SERVE)]

SPELLING TIP dessert

The Sahara has only one *s*—it's a *desert*. *Dessert* has two *s*'s because you always want seconds.

des‧sert‧spoon /dizórtspoon/ *n.* **1** a spoon used for dessert, smaller than a tablespoon and larger than a teaspoon. **2** the amount held by this. □□ **des‧sert‧spoon‧ful** *n.* (*pl.* **·fuls**)

des‧sert wine *n.* usu. sweet wine drunk with or following dessert.

de‧sta‧bi‧lize /deestáybilīz/ *v.tr.* **1** render unstable. **2** subvert (esp. a foreign government). □□ **de‧sta‧bi‧li‧za‧tion** *n.*

des‧ti‧na‧tion /déstináyshən/ *n.* a place to which a person or thing is going. [OF *destination* or L *destinatio* (as DESTINE)]

des‧tine /déstin/ *v.tr.* (often foll. by *to, for,* or *to* + infin.) set apart; appoint; preordain; intend (*destined him for the navy*). □ **be destined to** be fated or preordained to (*was destined to become a great surgeon*). [ME f. F *destiner* f. L *destinare* (as DE-, *stanare* (unrecorded) settle f. *stare* stand)]

des‧ti‧ny /déstinee/ *n.* (*pl.* **·nies**) **1 a** the predetermined course of events; fate. **b** this regarded as a power. **2** what is destined to happen to a particular person, etc. (*it was their destiny to be rejected*). [ME f. OF *destinée* f. Rmc, past part. of *destinare*: see DESTINE]

des‧ti‧tute /déstitoot, –tyoot/ *adj.* **1** without food, shelter, etc.; completely impoverished. **2** (usu. foll. by *of*) lacking (*destitute of friends*). □□ **des‧ti‧tu‧tion** /–tooshən, –tyoo–/ *n.* [ME f. L *destitutus* past part. of *destituere* forsake (as DE-, *statuere* place)]

des‧tri‧er /déstreeər/ *n. hist.* a war-horse. [ME f. AF *destrer*, OF *destrier* ult. f. L DEXTER[1] right (as the knight's horse was led by the squire with the right hand)]

de‧stroy /distróy/ *v.tr.* **1** pull or break down; demolish (*destroyed the bridge*). **2** end the existence of (*the accident destroyed her confidence*). **3** kill (esp. a sick or savage animal). **4** make useless; spoil utterly. **5** ruin financially, professionally, or in reputation. **6** defeat (*destroyed the enemy*). [ME f. OF *destruire* ult. f. L *destruere* (as DE-, *struere struct-* build)]

SYNONYM TIP destroy

ANNIHILATE, DEMOLISH, ERADICATE, EXTERMINATE, EXTIRPATE, RAZE. If you're interested in getting rid of something, you've got a number of options at your disposal. **Destroy** is a general term covering any force that wrecks, ruins, kills, etc. (*to destroy an ant hill by pouring boiling water on it*). If it's a building, you'll want to **demolish** or **raze** it, two words that are generally applied only to very large things. *Raze* is used almost exclusively with structures; it means to bring something down to the level of the ground (*they razed the apartment building to make way for the new hospital*). **Demolish** implies pulling or smashing something to pieces; when used with regard to buildings, it conjures up a vision of complete wreckage and often a heap of rubble (*their new house was demolished by the first hurricane of the season*). But unlike *raze*, *demolish* can also be applied to non-material things (*to demolish the theory with a few simple experiments*). If you **eradicate** something, you eliminate it completely, literally, pull it out by the roots (*to eradicate smallpox with a vaccine*) and prevent its reappearance. **Extirpate**, like *eradicate*, implies the utter destruction of something (*the species was extirpated from the park by the flooding*). If you're dealing with cockroaches, you'll probably want to **exterminate** them, which means to wipe out or kill in great numbers. Or better yet, you'll want to **annihilate** them, which is the most extreme word in this group and literally means to reduce to nothingness.

de‧stroy‧er /distróyər/ *n.* **1** a person or thing that destroys. **2** *Naut.* a fast warship with guns and torpedoes used to protect other ships.

de‧struct /distrúkt/ *v. & n.* esp. *Astronaut.* • *v.* **1** *tr.* destroy (one's own rocket, etc.) deliberately, esp. for safety reasons. **2** *intr.* be destroyed in this way. • *n.* an act of destructing. [L *destruere* (as DE-, STROY) or as back-form. f. DESTRUCTION]

de‧struct‧i‧ble /distrúktibəl/ *adj.* able to be destroyed. □□ **de‧struct‧i‧bil‧i‧ty** /–bílitee/ *n.* [F *destructible* or LL *destructibilis* (as DESTROY)]

de‧struc‧tion /distrúkshən/ *n.* **1** the act or an instance of destroying; the process of being destroyed. **2** a cause of ruin; something that destroys (*greed was their destruction*). [ME f. OF f. L *destructio –onis* (as DESTROY)]

de‧struc‧tive /distrúktiv/ *adj.* **1** (often foll. by *to, of*) destroying or tending to destroy (*destructive of her peace of mind; is destructive to organisms; a destructive child*). **2** negative in attitude or criticism; refuting without suggesting, helping, amending, etc. (opp. CONSTRUCTIVE) (*has only destructive criticism to offer*). □□ **de‧struc‧tive‧ly** *adv.* **de‧struc‧tive‧ness** *n.* [ME f. OF *destructif –ive* f. LL *destructivus* (as DESTROY)]

de‧struc‧tor /distrúktər/ *n. Brit.* a refuse-burning furnace.

des‧ue‧tude /déswitood, –tyood/ *n.* a state of disuse (*the custom fell into desuetude*). [F *désuétude* or L *desuetudo* (as DE-, *suescere suet-* be accustomed)]

des‧ul‧to‧ry /désəltáwree/ *adj.* **1** going constantly from one subject to another, esp. in a halfhearted way. **2** disconnected; unmethodical; superficial. □□ **des‧ul‧to‧ri‧ly** *adv.* **des‧ul‧to‧ri‧ness** *n.* [L *desultorius* superficial f. *desultor* vaulter f. *desult-* (as DE-, *salt-* past part. stem of *salire* leap)]

PRONUNCIATION TIP desultory

Although many Americans are tempted to pronounce this word with the stress on the second syllable, it is correctly pronounced with both the first and third syllables stressed, as "DESS-ul-TOR-ee."

de‧tach /ditách/ *v.tr.* **1** (often foll. by *from*) unfasten or disengage and remove (*detached the buttons; detached himself from the group*). **2** *Mil.* send (a ship, regiment, officer, messenger, etc.) on a separate mission. □□ **de‧tached** *adj.* **a** impartial; unemotional (*a detached viewpoint*). **b** (esp. of a house) not joined to another or others; separate. □□ **de‧tach‧a‧ble** *adj.* **de‧tach‧ed‧ly** /ditáchidlee/ *adv.* [F *détacher* (as DE-, ATTACH)]

de‧tach‧ment /ditáchmənt/ *n.* **1 a** a state of aloofness from or indifference to other people, one's surroundings, public opinion, etc. **b** disinterested independence of judgment. **2 a** the act or process of detaching or being detached. **b** an instance of this. **3** *Mil.* a separate group or unit of an army, etc., used for a specific purpose. [F *détachement* (as DETACH)]

de·tail /dítáyl, deétayl/ *n. & v.* • *n.* **1 a** a small or subordinate particular; an item. **b** such a particular, considered (ironically) to be unimportant (*the truth of the statement is just a detail*). **2 a** small items or particulars (esp. in an artistic work) regarded collectively (*has an eye for detail*). **b** the treatment of them (*the detail was insufficient and unconvincing*). **3** (often in *pl.*) a number of particulars; an aggregate of small items (*filled in the details on the form*). **4 a** a minor decoration on a building, in a picture, etc. **b** a small part of a picture, etc., shown alone. **5** *Mil.* **a** the distribution of orders for the day. **b** a small detachment of soldiers, etc., for special duty. • *v.tr.* **1** give particulars of (*detailed the plans*). **2** relate circumstantially (*detailed the anecdote*). **3** *Mil.* assign for special duty. **4** (as **detailed** *adj.*) **a** (of a picture, story, etc.) having many details. **b** itemized (*a detailed list*). □ **go into detail** give all the items or particulars. **in detail** item by item, minutely. [F *détail, détailler* as DE-, *tailler* cut, formed as TAIL[2]]

de·tain /ditáyn/ *v.tr.* **1** keep in confinement or under restraint. **2** keep waiting; delay. □□ **de·tain·ment** *n.* [ME f. OF *detenir* ult. f. L *detinēre detent-* (as DE-, *tenēre* hold)]

de·tain·ee /deétaynee/ *n.* a person detained in custody, esp. for political reasons.

de·tain·er /ditáynər/ *n. Law* **1** the wrongful detaining of goods taken from the owner for distraint, etc. **2** the detention of a person in prison, etc. [AF *detener* f. OF *detenir* (as DETAIN)]

de·tect /ditékt/ *v.tr.* **1 a** reveal the guilt of; discover (*detected him in his crime*). **b** discover (a crime). **2** discover or perceive the existence or presence of (*detected a smell of burning*; *do I detect a note of sarcasm?*). **3** *Physics* use an instrument to observe (a signal, radiation, etc.). □□ **de·tect·a·ble** *adj.* **de·tect·a·bly** *adv.* [L *detegere detect-* (as DE-, *tegere* cover)]

de·tec·tion /ditékshən/ *n.* **1 a** the act or an instance of detecting; the process of being detected. **b** an instance of this. **2** the work of a detective. **3** *Physics* the extraction of a desired signal; a demodulation. [LL *detectio* (as DETECT)]

de·tec·tive /ditéktiv/ *n. & adj.* • *n.* (often *attrib.*) a person, esp. a member of a police force, employed to investigate crime. • *adj.* serving to detect. [DETECT]

de·tec·tor /ditéktər/ *n.* **1** a person or thing that detects. **2** *Physics* a device for the detection or demodulation of signals.

de·tent /ditént/ *n.* **1** a catch by the removal of which machinery is allowed to move. **2** (in a clock, etc.) a catch that regulates striking. [F *détente* f. OF *destente* f. *destendre* slacken (as DE-, L *tendere*)]

dé·tente /daytóNt/ *n.* an easing of strained relations, esp. between nations. [F, = relaxation]

de·ten·tion /diténshən/ *n.* **1** detaining or being detained. **2 a** being kept in school after hours as a punishment. **b** an instance of this. **3** custody; confinement. [F *détention* or LL *detentio* (as DETAIN)]

de·ter /ditór/ *v.tr.* (**de·terred, de·ter·ring**) **1** (often foll. by *from*) discourage or prevent (a person) through fear or dislike of the consequences. **2** discourage, check, or prevent (a thing, process, etc.). □□ **de·ter·ment** *n.* [L *deterrēre* (as DE-, *terrēre* frighten)]

de·ter·gent /ditórjənt/ *n. & adj.* • *n.* a cleansing agent, esp. a synthetic substance (usu. other than soap) used with water as a means of removing dirt, etc. • *adj.* cleansing, esp. in the manner of a detergent. [L *detergēre* (as DE-, *tergēre ters-* wipe)]

de·te·ri·o·rate /ditéereeərayt/ *v.tr. & intr.* make or become bad or worse (*food deteriorates in hot weather*; *his condition deteriorated after the operation*). □□ **de·te·ri·o·ra·tion** /-ráyshən/ *n.* **de·te·ri·o·ra·tive** *adj.* [LL *deteriorare deteriorat-* f. L *deterior* worse]

de·ter·mi·nant /ditórminənt/ *adj. & n.* • *adj.* serving to determine or define. • *n.* **1** a determining factor, element, word, etc. **2** *Math.* a quantity obtained by the addition of products of the elements of a square matrix according to a given rule. [L *determinare* (as DETERMINE)]

de·ter·mi·nate /ditórminət/ *adj.* **1** limited in time, space, or character. **2** of definite scope or nature. □□ **de·ter·mi·na·cy** /-nəsee/ *n.* **de·ter·mi·nate·ly** *adv.* **de·ter·mi·nate·ness** *n.* [ME f. L *determina-tus* past part. (as DETERMINE)]

de·ter·mi·na·tion /ditórmináyshən/ *n.* **1** firmness of purpose; resoluteness. **2** the process of deciding, determining, or calculating. **3 a** the conclusion of a dispute by the decision of an arbitrator. **b** the decision reached. **4** *Law* the cessation of an estate or interest. **5** *Law* a judicial decision or sentence. **6** *archaic* a tendency to move in a fixed direction. [ME (in sense 4) f. OF f. L *determinatio –onis* (as DETERMINE)]

de·ter·mi·na·tive /ditórmənáytiv, –nətiv/ *adj. & n.* • *adj.* serving to define, qualify, or direct. • *n.* a determinative thing or circumstance. □□ **de·ter·mi·na·tive·ly** *adv.* [F *déterminatif –ive* (as DETERMINE)]

de·ter·mine /ditórmin/ *v.* **1** *tr.* find out or establish precisely (*have to determine the extent of the problem*). **2** *tr.* decide or settle (*determined who should go*). **3** *tr.* be a decisive factor in regard to (*demand*

determines supply). **4** *intr. & tr.* make or cause (a person) to make a decision (*we determined to go at once*; *what determined you to do it?*). **5** *tr. & intr.* esp. *Law* bring or come to an end. **6** *tr. Geom.* fix or define the position of. □ **be determined** be resolved (*was determined not to give up*). □□ **de·ter·mi·na·ble** *adj.* [ME f. OF *determiner* f. L *determinare* (as DE-, *terminus* end)]

de·ter·mined /ditórmind/ *adj.* **1** showing determination; resolute; unflinching. **2** fixed in scope or character; settled; determinate. □□ **de·ter·mined·ly** *adv.* **de·ter·mined·ness** *n.*

de·ter·min·er /ditórminər/ *n.* **1** a person or thing that determines. **2** *Gram.* any of a class of words (e.g., *a, the, every*) that determine the kind of reference a noun or noun substitute has.

de·ter·min·ism /ditórminizəm/ *n. Philos.* the doctrine that all events, including human action, are determined by causes regarded as external to the will. □□ **de·ter·min·ist** *n.* **de·ter·min·is·tic** / *adj.* **de·ter·min·is·ti·cal·ly** /–nístikəlee/ *adv.*

de·ter·rent /ditórənt, –túr–/ *adj. & n.* • *adj.* that deters. • *n.* a deterrent thing or factor, esp. a nuclear weapon regarded as deterring an enemy from attack. □□ **de·ter·rence** /–rəns/ *n.*

de·test /ditést/ *v.tr.* hate; loathe. □□ **de·test·er** *n.* [L *detestari* (as DE-, *testari* call to witness f. *testis* witness)]

de·test·a·ble /ditéstəbəl/ *adj.* intensely disliked; hateful. □□ **de·test·a·bly** *adv.*

de·tes·ta·tion /deétestáyshən/ *n.* **1** intense dislike; hatred. **2** a detested person or thing. [ME f. OF f. L *detestatio –onis* (as DETEST)]

de·throne /deethrón/ *v.tr.* **1** remove from the throne; depose. **2** remove from a position of authority or influence. □□ **de·throne·ment** *n.*

det·o·nate /dét'nayt/ *v.intr. & tr.* explode with a loud noise. □□ **det·o·na·tive** *adj.* [L *detonare detonat-* (as DE-, *tonare* thunder)]

det·o·na·tion /dét'náyshən/ *n.* **1 a** the act or process of detonating. **b** a loud explosion. **2** the premature combustion of fuel in an internal combustion engine, causing it to knock. [F *détonation* f. *détoner* (as DETONATE)]

det·o·na·tor /dét'naytər/ *n.* **1** a device for detonating an explosive. **2** a fog signal that detonates, e.g., as used on railroads.

de·tour /deétoor, ditór/ *n. & v.* • *n.* **1** a divergence from a direct or intended route; a roundabout course. **2** an alternative route, when a road is temporarily closed to traffic. • *v.intr. & tr.* make or cause to make a detour. [F *détour* change of direction f. *détourner* turn away (as DE-, TURN)]

de·tox·i·cate /deetóksikayt/ *v.tr.* = DETOXIFY. □□ **de·tox·i·ca·tion** /–káyshən/ *n.* [DE- + L *toxicum* poison, after *intoxicate*]

de·tox·i·fy /deetóksifī/ *v.tr.* remove the poison from. □□ **de·tox·i·fi·ca·tion** /–fikáyshən/ *n.* [DE- + L *toxicum* poison]

de·tract /ditrákt/ *v.tr.* (usu. foll. by *from*) take away (a part of something); reduce; diminish (*self-interest detracted nothing from their achievement*). □□ **de·trac·tion** /–trákshən/ *n.* **de·trac·tive** *adj.* **de·trac·tor** *n.* [L *detrahere detract-* (as DE-, *trahere* draw)]

de·train /deetráyn/ *v.intr. & tr.* alight or cause to alight from a train. □□ **de·train·ment** *n.*

de·trib·al·ize /deetríbəliz/ *v.tr.* **1** make (a person) no longer a member of a tribe. **2** destroy the tribal habits of. □□ **de·trib·al·i·za·tion** *n.*

det·ri·ment /détrimənt/ *n.* **1** harm; damage. **2** something causing this. [ME f. OF *detriment* or L *detrimentum* (as DE-, *terere trit-* rub, wear)]

det·ri·men·tal /détrimént'l/ *adj.* harmful; causing loss. □□ **det·ri·men·tal·ly** *adv.*

de·tri·tion /ditríshən/ *n.* wearing away by friction. [med.L *detritio* (as DETRIMENT)]

de·tri·tus /ditrítəs/ *n.* **1** matter produced by erosion, such as gravel, sand, silt, rock debris, etc. **2** debris of any kind; rubbish; waste. □□ **de·tri·tal** /ditrít'l/ *adj.* [after F *détritus* f. L *detritus* (n.) = wearing down (as DETRIMENT)]

de trop /də trố/ *predic.adj.* not wanted; unwelcome; in the way. [F, = excessive]

de·tu·mes·cence /deétoōmésəns, –tyoō–/ *n.* subsidence from a swollen state. [L *detumescere* (as DE-, *tumescere* swell)]

deuce[1] /doōs, dyoōs/ *n.* **1** the two on dice or playing cards. **2** (in tennis) the score of 40 all, at which two consecutive points are needed to win. [OF *deus* f. L *duo* (accus. *duos*) two]

deuce[2] /doōs, dyoōs/ *n.* misfortune; the Devil, used esp. *colloq.* as an exclamation of surprise or annoyance (*who the deuce are you?*). □ **a** (or **the**) **deuce of** a very bad or remarkable (*a deuce of a problem*; *a deuce of a fellow*). **the deuce to pay** trouble to be expected. [LG *duus*, formed as DEUCE[1], two aces at dice being the worst throw]

deuc·ed /doōsid, dyoō–, doōst, dyoōst/ *adj. & adv.* Brit. archaic damned; confounded (*a deuced liar*). □□ **deuc·ed·ly** /doōsidlee, dyoō–/ *adv.*

de·us ex ma·chi·na /dáyəs eks maákinə, mák–/ *n.* an unexpected power or event saving a seemingly hopeless situation, esp. in a play or novel. [mod.L transl. of Gk *theos ek mēkhanēs*, = god from the machinery (by which in the Greek theater the gods were suspended above the stage)]

Deut. *abbr.* Deuteronomy (Old Testament).

deu·ter·ag·o·nist /dōŏtərágənist, dyōō–/ *n.* the person second in importance to the protagonist in a drama. [Gk *deuteragōnistēs* (as DEUTERO-, *agōnistēs* actor)]

deu·ter·ate /dōŏtərayt, dyōō–/ *v.tr.* replace the usual isotope of hydrogen in (a substance) by deuterium. □□ **deu·ter·a·tion** /–ráyshən/ *n.*

deu·te·ri·um /dōōtēéreeəm, dyōō–/ *n. Chem.* a stable isotope of hydrogen with a mass about double that of the usual isotope. [mod.L, formed as DEUTERO- + –IUM]

deutero- /dōŏtərō, dyōō–/ *comb. form* second. [Gk *deuteros* second]

Deu·ter·o-I·sa·iah /dōŏtərō-īzáyə, –zíə, dyōō–/ *n.* the supposed later author of Isaiah 40–55.

deu·ter·on /dōŏtəron, dyōō–/ *n. Physics* the nucleus of a deuterium atom, consisting of a proton and a neutron. [DEUTERIUM + –ON]

deut·sche mark /dóychmaark/ *n.* (also **Deut·sche·mark** /dóychə maark/) the basic monetary unit of Germany. [G, = German mark (see MARK²)]

deut·zi·a /dōŏtseeə, dyōŏt–, dóyt–/ *n.* any ornamental shrub of the genus *Deutzia*, with usu. white flowers. [J. *Deutz* 18th-c. Du. patron of botany]

de·val·ue /deevályōō/ *v.tr.* (**de·val·ues, de·val·ued, de·val·u·ing**) **1** reduce the value of. **2** *Econ.* reduce the value of (a currency) in relation to other currencies or to gold (opp. REVALUE). □□ **de·val·u·a·tion** *n.*

De·va·na·ga·ri /dáyvənáagəree/ *n.* the alphabet used for Sanskrit, Hindi, and other languages of India. [Skr., = divine town script]

dev·as·tate /dévəstayt/ *v.tr.* **1** lay waste; cause great destruction to. **2** (often in *passive*) overwhelm with shock or grief; upset deeply. □□ **dev·as·ta·tion** /–táyshən/ *n.* **dev·as·ta·tor** *n.* [L *devastare devastat-* (as DE-, *vastare* lay waste)]

dev·as·tat·ing /dévəstayting/ *adj.* **1** crushingly effective; overwhelming. **2** *colloq.* **a** incisive; savage (*devastating accuracy, devastating wit*). **b** extremely impressive or attractive (*she wore a devastating black silk dress*). □□ **dev·as·tat·ing·ly** *adv.*

de·vel·op /divéləp/ *v.* (**de·vel·oped, de·vel·op·ing**) **1** *tr. & intr.* **a** make or become bigger or fuller or more elaborate or systematic (*the new town developed rapidly*). **b** bring or come to an active or visible state or to maturity (*developed a plan of action*). **2 a** *tr.* begin to exhibit or suffer from (*developed a rattle*). **b** *intr.* come into existence; originate; emerge (*a fault developed in the engine*). **3** *tr.* **a** construct new buildings on (land). **b** convert (land) to a new purpose so as to use its resources more fully. **4** *tr.* treat (photographic film, etc.) to make the latent image visible. **5** *tr. Mus.* elaborate (a theme) by modification of the melody, harmony, rhythm, etc. **6** *tr. Chess* bring (a piece) into position for effective use. □□ **de·vel·op·er** *n.* [F *développer* f. Rmc (as DIS-, orig. of second element unknown)]

de·vel·op·a·ble /divéləpəbəl/ *adj.* that can be developed. □ **developable surface** *Geom.* a surface that can be flattened into a plane without overlap or separation, e.g., a cylinder.

de·vel·op·ment /divéləpmənt/ *n.* **1** the act or an instance of developing; the process of being developed. **2 a** a stage of growth or advancement. **b** a thing that has developed, esp. an event or circumstance (*the latest developments*). **3** a full-grown state. **4** the process of developing a photograph. **5** a developed area of land. **6** *Mus.* the elaboration of a theme or themes, esp. in the middle section of a sonata movement. **7** *Chess* the developing of pieces from their original position.

de·vel·op·men·tal /divéləpmént'l/ *adj.* **1** incidental to growth (*developmental diseases*). **2** evolutionary. □□ **de·vel·op·men·tal·ly** *adv.*

de·vi·ant /déeveeənt/ *adj. & n.* ● *adj.* that deviates from the normal, esp. with reference to sexual practices. ● *n.* a deviant person or thing. □□ **de·vi·ance** /–veeəns/ *n.* **de·vi·an·cy** *n.* [ME (as DEVIATE)]

de·vi·ate *v. & n.* ● *v.intr.* /déeveeayt/ (often foll. by *from*) turn aside or diverge (from a course of action, rule, truth, etc.); digress. ● *n.* /déeveeət/ a deviant, esp. a sexual pervert. □□ **de·vi·a·tor** *n.* **de·vi·a·to·ry** /–veeətáwree/ *adj.* [LL *deviare deviat-* (as DE-, *via* way)]

de·vi·a·tion /déeveeáyshən/ *n.* **1 a** deviating; digressing. **b** an instance of this. **2** *Polit.* a departure from accepted (esp. Communist) party doctrine. **3** *Statistics* the amount by which a single measurement differs from the mean. **4** *Naut.* the deflection of a ship's compass needle caused by iron in the ship, etc. □□ **de·vi·a·tion·al** *adj.* **de·vi·a·tion·ism** *n.* **de·vi·a·tion·ist** *n.* [F *déviation* f. med.L *deviatio –onis* (as DEVIATE)]

de·vice /divís/ *n.* **1 a** a thing made or adapted for a particular purpose, esp. a mechanical contrivance. **b** an explosive contrivance; a

bomb. **2** a plan, scheme, or trick. **3 a** an emblematic or heraldic design. **b** a drawing or design. **4** *archaic* make, look (*things of rare device*). □ **leave a person to his** (or **her**) **own devices** leave a person to do as he or she wishes.

dev·il /dévəl/ *n. & v.* ● *n.* **1** (usu. **the Devil**) (in Christian and Jewish belief) the supreme spirit of evil; Satan. **2 a** an evil spirit; a demon; a superhuman malignant being. **b** a personified evil force or attribute. **3 a** a wicked or cruel person. **b** a mischievously energetic, clever, or self-willed person. **4** *colloq.* a person; a fellow (*lucky devil*). **5** fighting spirit; mischievousness (*the devil is in him tonight*). **6** *colloq.* something difficult or awkward (*this door is a devil to open*). **7** (**the devil** or **the Devil**) *colloq.* used as an exclamation of surprise or annoyance (*who the devil are you?*). **8** a literary hack exploited by an employer. **9** *Brit.* a junior legal counsel. **10** = TASMANIAN DEVIL. **11** applied to various instruments and machines, esp. when used for destructive work. ● *v.* (**dev·iled, dev·il·ing;** *esp. Brit.* **dev·illed, dev·il·ling**) **1** *tr.* cook (food) with hot seasoning. **2** *intr.* act as a devil for an author or barrister. **3** *tr.* harass; worry. □ **between the devil and the deep blue sea** in a dilemma. **a devil of** *colloq.* considerable, difficult, or remarkable (*a devil of a time*). **devil take the hindmost** a motto of selfish competition. **the devil to pay** trouble to be expected. **go to the devil 1** be damned. **2** (in *imper.*) depart at once. **like the devil** with great energy. **play the devil with** cause severe damage to. **speak** (or **talk**) **of the devil** said when a person appears just after being mentioned. **the very devil** (*predic.*) *colloq.* a great difficulty or nuisance.

dev·il·fish /dévəlfish/ *n.* (*pl.* same or **·fish·es**) **1** = *devil ray.* **2** any of various fish, esp. the stonefish. **3** *hist.* an octopus.

dev·il·ish /dévəlish/ *adj. & adv.* ● *adj.* **1** of or like a devil; wicked. **2** mischievous. ● *adv. colloq.* very; extremely. □□ **dev·il·ish·ly** *adv.* **dev·il·ish·ness** *n.*

dev·il-may-care *adj.* cheerful and reckless.

dev·il·ment /dévəlmənt/ *n.* mischief; wild spirits.

dev·il ray *n.* any cartilaginous fish of the family Mobulidae, esp. the manta.

dev·il·ry /dévilree/ *n.* (also **dev·il·try** /–tree/) (*pl.* **·ries**) **1 a** wickedness; reckless mischief. **b** an instance of this. **2 a** black magic. **b** the Devil and his works. [OF *diablerie: –try* wrongly after *harlotry,* etc.]

dev·il's ad·vo·cate *n.* a person who expresses a contentious opinion in order to provoke debate or test the strength of the opposing arguments.

dev·il's-bit *n.* any of various plants whose roots look bitten off, esp. a kind of scabious (*Succisa pratensis*).

dev·il's darn·ing nee·dle *n.* a dragonfly or damselfly.

dev·il's own *adj. colloq.* very difficult or unusual (*the devil's own job*).

de·vi·ous /déeveeəs/ *adj.* **1** (of a person, etc.) not straightforward; underhand. **2** winding; circuitous. **3** erring; straying. □□ **de·vi·ous·ly** *adv.* **de·vi·ous·ness** *n.* [L *devius* f. DE- + *via* way]

de·vise /divíz/ *v. & n.* ● *v.tr.* **1** plan or invent by careful thought. **2** *Law* leave (real estate) by the terms of a will (cf. BEQUEATH). ● *n.* **1** the act or an instance of devising. **2** *Law* a devising clause in a will. □□ **de·vis·a·ble** *adj.* **de·vi·see** /–zeé/ *n.* (in sense 2 of *v.*). **de·vis·er** *n.* **de·vi·sor** *n.* (in sense 2 of *v.*). [ME f. OF *deviser* ult. f. L *dividere divis-* DIVIDE: (n.) f. OF *devise* f. med.L *divisa* fem. past part. of *dividere*]

de·vi·tal·ize /deevít'līz/ *v.tr.* take away strength and vigor from. □□ **de·vi·tal·i·za·tion** *n.*

de·vit·ri·fy /deevítrifī/ *v.tr.* (**·fies, ·fied**) deprive of vitreous qualities; make (glass or vitreous rock) opaque and crystalline. □□ **de·vit·ri·fi·ca·tion** /–fikáyshən/ *n.*

de·void /divóyd/ *predic.adj.* (foll. by *of*) quite lacking or free from (*a book devoid of all interest*). [ME, past part. of obs. *devoid* f. OF *devoidier* (as DE-, VOID)]

de·voir /dəvwaár, dévwaar/ *n. archaic* **1** duty; one's best (*do one's devoir*). **2** (in *pl.*) courteous or formal attentions; respects (*pay one's devoirs to*). [ME f. AF *dever* = OF *deveir* f. L *debēre* owe]

de·vo·lute /déevəlōōt/ *v.tr.* transfer by devolution. [as DEVOLVE]

dev·o·lu·tion /déevəlóoshən/ *n.* **1** the delegation of power, esp. by central government to local or regional administration. **2 a** a descent or passing on through a series of stages. **b** descent by natural or due succession from one to another of property or qualities. **3** the lapse of an unexercised right to an ultimate owner. **4** *Biol.* degeneration. □□ **dev•o•lu•tion•ar•y** *adj.* **dev•o•lu•tion•ist** *n.* [LL *devolutio* (as DEVOLVE)]

de•volve /divólv/ *v.* **1** (foll. by *on, upon,* etc.) **a** *tr.* pass (work or duties) to (a deputy, etc.). **b** *intr.* (of work or duties) pass to (a deputy, etc.). **2** *intr.* (foll. by *on, to, upon*) *Law* (of property, etc.) descend or fall by succession to. □□ **de•volve•ment** *n.* [ME f. L *devolvere devolut-* (as DE-, *volvere* roll)]

De•vo•ni•an /divóneən/ *adj. & n.* ● *adj.* **1** of or relating to Devon in SW England. **2** *Geol.* of or relating to the fourth period of the Paleozoic era with evidence of the first amphibians and tree forests. ● *n.* **1** this period or system. **2** a native of Devon. [med.L *Devonia* Devonshire]

de•vote /divót/ *v.tr. & refl.* **1** (foll. by *to*) apply or give over (resources, etc., or oneself) to (a particular activity or purpose or person) (*devoted their time to reading; devoted himself to his guests*). **2** *archaic* doom to destruction. □□ **de•vote•ment** *n.* [L *devovēre devot-* (as DE-, *vovēre* vow)]

de•vot•ed /divótid/ *adj.* very loving or loyal (*a devoted husband*). □□ **de•vot•ed•ly** *adv.* **de•vot•ed•ness** *n.*

dev•o•tee /dévətee, –táy/ *n.* **1** (usu. foll. by *of*) a zealous enthusiast or supporter. **2** a zealously pious or fanatical person.

de•vo•tion /divóshən/ *n.* **1** (usu. foll. by *to*) enthusiastic attachment or loyalty (to a person or cause); great love. **2** a religious worship. **b** (in *pl.*) prayers. **c** devoutness; religious fervor. □□ **de•vo•tion•al** *adj.* [ME f. OF *devotion* or L *devotio* (as DEVOTE)]

de•vour /divówr/ *v.tr.* **1** eat hungrily or greedily. **2** (of fire, etc.) engulf; destroy. **3** take in greedily with the eyes or ears (*devoured book after book*). **4** absorb the attention of (*devoured by anxiety*). □□ **de•vour•er** *n.* **de•vour•ing•ly** *adv.* [ME f. OF *devorer* f. L *devorare* (as DE-, *vorare* swallow)]

de•vout /divówt/ *adj.* **1** earnestly religious. **2** earnestly sincere (*devout hope*). □□ **de•vout•ly** *adv.* **de•vout•ness** *n.* [ME f. OF *devot* f. L *devotus* past part. (as DEVOTE)]

DEW *abbr.* distant early warning.

dew /doo, dyoo/ *n. & v.* ● *n.* **1** atmospheric vapor condensing in small drops on cool surfaces at night. **2** beaded or glistening moisture resembling this, e.g., tears. **3** freshness; refreshing quality. ● *v.tr.* wet with or as with dew. □ **dew point** the temperature at which dew forms. [OE *dēaw* f. Gmc]

de•wan /diwáan/ *n.* the prime minister or finance minister of an E. Indian state. [Arab. & Pers. *diwān* fiscal register]

dew•ar /dóoər, dyóoər/ *n. Physics* (also **Dewar**) a double-walled flask with a vacuum between the walls to reduce the transfer of heat. [Sir James *Dewar*, Brit. physicist d. 1923]

dew•ber•ry /dóoberee, dyóo–/ *n.* (*pl.* **•ries**) **1** a bluish fruit like the blackberry. **2** the shrub, *Rubus caesius,* bearing this.

dew•claw /dóoklaw, dyóo–/ *n.* **1** a rudimentary inner toe found on some dogs. **2** a false hoof on a deer, etc.

dew•drop /dóodrop, dyóo–/ *n.* a drop of dew.

Dew•ey sys•tem /dóo-ee, dyóo-ee/ *n.* a decimal system of library classification. [M. *Dewey,* Amer. librarian d. 1931, its deviser]

dew•fall /dóofawl, dyóo–/ *n.* **1** the time when dew begins to form. **2** the formation of dew.

dew•lap /dóolap, dyóo–/ *n.* **1** a loose fold of skin hanging from the throat of cattle, dogs, etc. **2** similar loose skin around the throat of an elderly person. [ME f. DEW + LAP[1], perh. after ON (unrecorded) *döggleppr*]

dew•y /dóo-ee, dyóo-ee/ *adj.* (**dewier, dewiest**) **1 a** wet with dew. **b** moist as if with dew. **2** of or like dew. □□ **dew•i•ly** *adv.* **dew•i•ness** *n.* [OE *dēawig* (as DEW, –Y[1])]

dew•y-eyed *adj.* innocently trusting; naively sentimental.

dex•ter[1] /dékstər/ *adj.* esp. *Heraldry* on or of the right-hand side (the observer's left) of a shield, etc. [L, = on the right]

dewlap 1

dex•ter[2] /dékstər/ *n.* (also **Dex•ter**) **1** an animal of a small hardy breed of Irish cattle. **2** this breed. [19th c.: perh. f. the name of a breeder]

dex•ter•i•ty /dekstéritee/ *n.* **1** skill in handling. **2** manual or mental adroitness. **3** right-handedness; using the right hand. [F *dextérité* f. L *dexteritas* (as DEXTER[1])]

dex•ter•ous /dékstrəs, –stərəs/ *adj.* (also **dex•trous,** –strəs) having or showing dexterity. □□ **dex•ter•ous•ly** *adv.* **dex•ter•ous•ness** *n.* [L DEXTER[1] + –OUS]

dex•tral /dékstrəl/ *adj. & n.* ● *adj.* **1** (of a person) right-handed. **2** of or on the right. **3** *Zool.* (of a spiral shell) with whorls rising to the right and coiling in an anticlockwise direction. **4** *Zool.* (of a flatfish) with the right side uppermost. ● *n.* a right-handed person. □□ **dex•tral•i•ty** /–trálitee/ *n.* **dex•tral•ly** *adv.* [med.L *dextralis* f. L *dextra* right hand]

dex•tran /dékstran, –strən/ *n. Chem. & Pharm.* **1** an amorphous gum formed by the fermentation of sucrose, etc. **2** a degraded form of this used as a substitute for blood plasma. [G (as DEXTRO- + –*an* as in Chem. names)]

dex•trin /dékstrin/ *n. Chem.* a soluble gummy substance obtained from starch and used as an adhesive. [F *dextrine* f. L *dextra:* see DEXTRO-, –IN]

dextro- /dékstrō/ *comb. form* on or to the right (*dextrorotatory; dextrose*). [L *dexter, dextra* on or to the right]

dex•tro•ro•ta•to•ry /dékstrō-rótətawree/ *adj. Chem.* having the property of rotating the plane of a polarized light ray to the right (cf. LEVOROTATORY). □□ **dex•tro•ro•ta•tion** /–táyshən/ *n.*

dex•trorse /dékstrawrs/ *adj.* rising toward the right, esp. of a spiral stem. [L *dextrorsus* (as DEXTRO-)]

dex•trose /dékstrōs/ *n. Chem.* the dextrorotatory form of glucose. [formed as DEXTRO- + –OSE[2]]

dex•trous var. of DEXTEROUS.

DF *abbr.* **1** Defender of the Faith. **2** direction finder. [in sense 1 f. L *Defensor Fidei*]

DFC *abbr.* Distinguished Flying Cross.

DG *abbr.* **1** *Dei gratia* (by the grace of God). **2** *Deo gratias* (thanks be to God). **3** director general.

DH *abbr. Baseball* designated hitter.

dhal var. of DAL.

dhar•ma /daármə/ *n. Ind.* **1** social custom; the right behavior. **2** the Buddhist truth. **3** the Hindu social or moral law. [Skr., = decree, custom]

dho•ti /dótee/ *n.* (*pl.* **dho•tis**) the loincloth worn by male Hindus. [Hindi *dhotī*]

dhow /dow/ *n* a lateen-rigged ship used esp. on the Arabian Sea. [19th c.: orig. unkn.]

dhur•ra var. of DURRA.

DI *abbr. Mil* drill instructor.

di-[1] /dī/ *comb. form* **1** twice, two–, double. **2** *Chem.* containing two atoms, molecules, or groups of a specified kind (*dichromate; dioxide*). [Gk f. *dis* twice]

di-[2] /dī, dee/ *prefix* form of DIS- occurring before *l, m, n, r, s* (foll. by a consonant), *v,* usu. *g,* and sometimes *j.* [L var. of *dis*–]

di-[3] /dī/ *prefix* form of DIA- before a vowel.

dia. *abbr.* diameter.

dia- /díə/ *prefix* (also **di-** before a vowel) **1** through (*diaphanous*). **2** apart (*diacritical*). **3** across (*diameter*). [Gk f. *dia* through]

di•a•be•tes /díəbeetis, –teez/ *n.* **1** any disorder of the metabolism with excessive thirst and the production of large amounts of urine. **2** (in full **diabetes mellitus**) the commonest form of diabetes in which sugar and starch are not properly absorbed from the blood, with thirst, emaciation, and excessive excretion of urine with glucose. [orig. = siphon: L f. Gk f. *diabainō* go through]

di•a•be•tes in•sip•i•dus *n.* a rare metabolic disorder due to a pituitary deficiency, with excessive urination and thirst.

di•a•bet•ic /díəbétik/ *adj. & n.* ● *adj.* **1** of or relating to or having diabetes. **2** for use by diabetics. ● *n.* a person suffering from diabetes.

di•a•ble•rie /dee-aabləree, –áblə–/ *n.* **1** the devil's work; sorcery. **2** wild recklessness. **3** the realm of devils; demon lore. [F f. *diable* f. L *diabolus* DEVIL]

di•a•bol•ic /díəbólik/ *adj.* (also **di•a•bol•i•cal** /–bólikəl/) **1** of the Devil. **2** devilish; inhumanly cruel or wicked. **3** fiendishly clever or cunning or annoying. **4** *colloq.* disgracefully bad or defective; outrageous, atrocious. □□ **di•a•bol•i•cal•ly** *adv.* [ME f. OF *diabolique* or LL *diabolicus* f. L *diabolos* (as DEVIL)]

di•ab•o•lism /díábəlizəm/ *n.* **1 a** belief in or worship of the Devil. **b** sorcery. **2** devilish conduct or character. □□ **di•ab•o•list** *n.* [Gk *diabolos* DEVIL]

di•ab•o•lize /díábəliz/ *v.tr.* make into or represent as a devil.

di•ab•o•lo /deeábəlō/ *n.* (*pl.* **•los**) **1** a game in which a two-headed top is thrown up and caught with a string stretched between two sticks. **2** the top itself. [It., = DEVIL; formerly called *devil on two sticks.*]

di•a•chron•ic /díəkrónik/ *adj. Linguistics,* etc., concerned with the historical development of a subject (esp. a language) (opp. SYNCHRONIC). □□ **di•a•chron•i•cal•ly** *adv.* **di•a•chron•ism** /díákrənizəm/ *n.* **di•a•chron•ous** /díákrənəs/ *adj.* **di•ach•ro•ny** /díákrənee/ *n.* [F *diachronique* (as DIA-, CHRONIC)]

di•ac•o•nal /díákənəl/ *adj.* of a deacon. [eccl.L *diaconalis* f. *diaconus* DEACON]

di•ac•o•nate /díákənayt, –nət/ *n.* **1 a** the office of deacon. **b** a person's time as deacon. **2** a body of deacons. [eccl.L *diaconatus* (as DIACONAL)]

di•a•crit•ic /díəkritik/ *n. & adj.* ● *n.* a sign (e.g., an accent, diaeresis, cedilla) used to indicate different sounds or values of a letter. ● *adj.* = DIACRITICAL.

di•a•crit•i•cal /díəkritikəl/ *adj. & n.* ● *adj.* distinguishing; distinctive. ● *n.* (in full **diacritical mark** or **sign**) = DIACRITIC.

di•a•del•phous /díədélfəs/ *adj. Bot.* with the stamens united in two bundles (cf. MONADELPHOUS, POLYADELPHOUS). [DI-[1] + Gk *adelphos* brother]

di·a·dem /díədem/ n. & v. •n. 1 a crown or headband worn as a sign of sovereignty. 2 a wreath of leaves or flowers worn around the head. 3 sovereignty. 4 a crowning distinction or glory. •v.tr. (esp. as **diademed** adj.) adorn with or as with a diadem. [ME f. OF diademe f. L diadema f. Gk diadēma (as DIA-, deō bind)]

di·aer·e·sis /dī-érəsis/ n. (also **di·er·e·sis**) (pl. **·ses** /-seez/) 1 a mark (as in naïve) over a vowel to indicate that it is sounded separately. 2 Prosody a break where a foot ends at the end of a word. [L f. Gk, = separation]

diag. abbr. 1 diagonal. 2 diagram.

di·a·gen·e·sis /díəjénisis/ n. Geol. the transformation occurring during the conversion of sedimentation to sedimentary rock.

di·ag·nose /díəgnōs, -nōz/ v.tr. make a diagnosis of (a disease, a mechanical fault, etc.) from its symptoms. □□ **di·ag·nos·a·ble** adj.

di·ag·no·sis /díəgnósis/ n. (pl. **diagnoses** /-seez/) 1 a the identification of a disease by means of a patient's symptoms. b an instance or formal statement of this. 2 a the identification of the cause of a mechanical fault, etc. b an instance of this. 3 a the distinctive characterization in precise terms of a genus, species, etc. b an instance of this. [mod.L f. Gk (as DIA-, gignōskō recognize)]

di·ag·nos·tic /díəgnóstik/ adj. & n. • adj. of or assisting diagnosis. •n. a symptom. □□ **di·ag·nos·ti·cal·ly** adv. **di·ag·nos·ti·cian** /-nostíshən/ n. [Gk diagnōstikos (as DIAGNOSIS)]

di·ag·nos·tics /díəgnóstiks/ n. 1 (treated as pl.) Computing programs and other mechanisms used to detect and identify faults in hardware or software. 2 (treated as sing.) the science or study of diagnosing disease.

di·ag·o·nal /díágənəl/ adj. & n. • adj. 1 crossing a straight-sided figure from corner to corner. 2 slanting; oblique. •n. a straight line joining two nonadjacent corners. □□ **di·ag·o·nal·ly** adv. [L diagonalis f. Gk diagōnios (as DIA-, gōnia angle)]

di·a·gram /díəgram/ n. & v. •n. 1 a drawing showing the general scheme or outline of an object and its parts. 2 a graphic representation of the course or results of an action or process. 3 Geom. a figure made of lines used in proving a theorem, etc. •v.tr. (**diagramed, diagraming** or **diagrammed, diagramming**) represent by means of a diagram. □□ **di·a·gram·mat·ic** /-grəmátik/ adj. **di·a·gram·mat·i·cal·ly** adv. [L f. Gk diagramma f. Gk (as DIA-, -GRAM)]

di·a·grid /díəgrid/ n. Archit. a supporting structure of diagonally intersecting ribs of metal, etc. [DIAGONAL + GRID]

di·a·ki·ne·sis /díəkineésis, -kī-/ n. (pl. **diakineses** /-seez/) Biol. a stage during the prophase of meiosis when the separation of homologous chromosomes is complete and crossing over has occurred. [mod.L f. G Diakinese (as DIA-, Gk kinēsis motion)]

di·al /díəl/ n. & v. •n. 1 the face of a clock or watch, marked to show the hours, etc. 2 a similar flat plate marked with a scale for measuring weight, volume, pressure, consumption, etc., indicated by a pointer. 3 a movable disk on a telephone, with finger holes and numbers for making a connection. 4 a a plate or disk, etc., on a radio or television set for selecting wavelength or channel. b a similar selecting device on other equipment, e.g., a washing machine. 5 Brit. sl. a person's face. •v. 1 tr. (also absol.) select (a telephone number) by means of a dial or set of buttons (dialed 911). 2 tr. measure, indicate, or regulate by means of a dial. □□ **di·al·er** n. [ME, = sundial, f. med.L diale clock dial ult. f. L dies day]

di·a·lect /díəlekt/ n. 1 a form of speech peculiar to a particular region. 2 a subordinate variety of a language with nonstandard vocabulary, pronunciation, or grammar. □□ **di·a·lec·tal** /-lékt'l/ adj. **di·a·lec·tol·o·gy** /-tóləjee/ n. **di·a·lec·tol·o·gist** /-tólǝjist/ n. [F dialecte or L dialectus f. Gk dialektos discourse f. dialegomai converse]

di·a·lec·tic /díəléktik/ n. & adj. •n. 1 (often in pl.) a the art of investigating the truth of opinions; the testing of truth by discussion. b logical disputation. 2 Philos. a inquiry into metaphysical contradictions and their solutions, esp. in the thought of Kant and Hegel. b the existence or action of opposing social forces, etc. • adj. 1 of or relating to logical disputation. 2 fond of or skilled in logical disputation. [ME f. OF dialectique or L dialectica f. Gk dialektikē (tekhnē) (art) of debate (as DIALECT)]

di·a·lec·ti·cal /díəléktikəl/ adj. of dialectic or dialectics. □□ **di·a·lec·ti·cal·ly** adv.

di·a·lec·ti·cal ma·te·ri·al·ism n. the Marxist theory that political and historical events are due to a conflict of social forces caused by man's material needs.

di·a·lec·ti·cian /díəlektíshən/ n. a person skilled in dialectic. [F dialecticien f. L dialecticus]

di·a·lec·tics /díəléktiks/ n. (treated as sing. or pl.) = DIALECTIC n.

di·a·log·ic /díəlójik/ adj. of or in dialogue. [LL dialogicus f. Gk dialogikos (as DIALOGUE)]

di·a·lo·gist /díáləjist/ n. a speaker in or writer of dialogue. [LL dialogista f. Gk dialogistēs (as DIALOGUE)]

di·a·logue /díəlawg, -log/ n. (also **di·a·log**) 1 a conversation. b conversation in written form; this as a form of composition. 2 a a discussion, esp. one between representatives of two political groups. b a conversation; a talk (long dialogues between the two main characters). [ME f. OF dialoge f. L dialogus f. Gk dialogos f. dialegomai converse]

di·al tone n. a sound that a telephone produces indicating that a caller may start to dial.

di·a·lyse Brit. var. of DIALYZE.

di·al·y·sis /díálisis/ n. (pl. **di·al·y·ses** /-seez/) 1 Chem. the separation of particles in a liquid by differences in their ability to pass through a membrane and into another liquid. 2 Med. the clinical purification of blood by this technique. □□ **di·a·lyt·ic** /díəlítik/ adj. [L f. Gk dialusis (as DIA-, luō set free)]

di·a·lyze /díəlīz/ v.tr. separate by means of dialysis.

diam. abbr. diameter.

di·a·mag·net·ic /díəmagnétik/ adj. & n. • adj. tending to become magnetized in a direction at right angles to the applied magnetic field. • n. a diamagnetic body or substance. □□ **di·a·mag·net·i·cal·ly** adv. **di·a·mag·net·ism** /-mágnitizəm/ n.

di·a·man·té /deeəmoNtáy/ adj. & n. • adj. decorated with powdered crystal or another sparkling substance. • n. fabric or costume jewelry so decorated. [F, past part. of diamanter set with diamonds f. diamant DIAMOND]

di·a·man·tine /díəmántin, -teen/ adj. esp. Brit. of or like diamonds. [F diamantin f. diamant DIAMOND]

di·am·e·ter /díámitər/ n. 1 a a straight line passing from side to side through the center of a body or figure, esp. a circle or sphere. b the length of this line. 2 a transverse measurement; width; thickness. 3 a unit of linear measurement of magnifying power (a lens magnifying 2000 diameters). □□ **di·am·e·tral** adj. [ME f. OF diametre f. L diametrus f. Gk diametros (grammē) (line) measuring across f. metron measure]

di·a·met·ri·cal /díəmétrikəl/ adj. (also **di·a·met·ric**) 1 of or along a diameter. 2 (of opposition, difference, etc.) complete, like that between opposite ends of a diameter. □□ **di·a·met·ri·cal·ly** adv. [Gk diametrikos (as DIAMETER)]

di·a·mond /dímənd, díə-/ n., adj., & v. •n. 1 a precious stone of pure carbon crystallized in octahedrons, etc., the hardest naturally occurring substance. 2 a figure shaped like the cross section of a diamond; a rhombus. 3 a a playing card of a suit denoted by a red rhombus. b (in pl.) this suit. 4 a glittering particle or point (of frost, etc.). 5 a tool with a small diamond for cutting glass. 6 Baseball a the space delimited by the bases. b the entire field. • adj. 1 made of or set with diamonds or a diamond. 2 rhombus-shaped. •v.tr. adorn with or as with diamonds. □□ **dia·mond·if·er·ous** /-difərəs/ adj. [ME f. OF diamant f. med.L diamas diamant- var. of L adamas ADAMANT f. Gk]

dia·mond·back /díməndbak, díə-/ n. 1 an edible freshwater terrapin, Malaclemys terrapin, native to N. America, with diamond-shaped markings on its shell. 2 any rattlesnake of the genus Crotalus, native to N. America, with diamond-shaped markings.

di·a·mond·if·er·ous /dímandífərəs/ adj. Mining diamond-yielding. [F diamantifère f. diamant DIAMOND]

di·a·mond ju·bi·lee n. the 60th (or 75th) anniversary of an event, esp. a sovereign's accession.

SYNONYM TIP dialect

ARGOT, CANT, JARGON, LINGO, SLANG, VERNACULAR. When a New York City cab driver calls out the window, "Hey, wassa madda wichoo?" he is using the **vernacular**, which is the authentic, natural pattern of speech among those belonging to a certain community. In some areas of London, on the other hand, one might hear the Cockney **dialect**, which is a form or variety of a language that is confined to a specific group or locality; it has its own pronunciation, usage, and vocabulary, and may persist for generations or even centuries (he spoke in the dialect of the Appalachian backwoodsman). A teenager who tells his parents to "Chill out" is using **slang**, which is a very informal language that includes "substitute" vocabulary ("wheels" for car, "rug" for toupee), grammatical distortions, and other departures from formal or polite usage. **Argot** refers to the slang of a group that feels threatened by the hostility of society as a whole; it traditionally refers to the slang used by criminals and thieves, although it may refer to any peculiar language that a clique or other closely knit group uses to communicate with each other. At one time **cant** was a synonym for argot, but now it usually refers to pompous, inflated language or the hackneyed use of words and phrases by members of a particular class or profession (the cant of the fashion industry). In contrast to cant, which can at least be understood, **jargon** is nearly impossible for the average person to decipher. This term refers to the technical or highly specialized language used by members of an occupational or professional group (medical jargon; the jargon of the theater). If you are frustrated because you can't understand the language used by a particular class or group, you're apt to refer to their way of talking as **lingo**, which is a term for any language that is not readily understood (she tried to reason with the cab driver, but she couldn't understand his lingo).

di•an•drous /díándrəs/ *adj.* having two stamens. [DI-[1] + Gk *anēr andr-man*]

di•an•thus /díánthəs/ *n.* any flowering plant of the genus *Dianthus*, e.g., a carnation or pink. [Gk *Dios* of Zeus + *anthos* flower]

di•a•pa•son /díəpáyzən, –sən/ *n. Mus.* **1** the compass of a voice or musical instrument. **2** a fixed standard of musical pitch. **3** (in full **open** or **stopped diapason**) either of two main organ stops extending through the organ's whole compass. **4 a** a combination of notes or parts in a harmonious whole. **b** a melodious succession of notes, esp. a grand swelling burst of harmony. **5** an entire compass, range, or scope. [ME in sense 'octave' f. L *diapason* f. Gk *dia pasōn* (*khordōn*) through all (notes)]

di•a•pause /díəpawz/ *n.* a period of retarded or suspended development in some insects.

dia•per /dípər, díəpər/ *n. & v.* ● *n.* **1** a piece of toweling or other absorbent material wrapped around a baby to retain urine and feces. **2 a** a linen or cotton fabric with a small diamond pattern. **b** this pattern. **3** a similar ornamental design of diamonds, etc., for panels, walls, etc. ● *v.tr.* decorate with a diaper pattern.

> **WORD HISTORY** diaper
>
> Middle English: from Old French *diapre*, from medieval Latin *diasprum*, from medieval Greek *diaspros* (adjective), from *dia* 'across' + *aspros* 'white.' The term seems originally to have denoted a costly fabric, but after the 15th century it was used of a fabric woven with a repeating diamond pattern. This sort of fabric came to be used as a wrap for babies.

dia•per rash *n.* inflammation of a baby's skin, caused by prolonged contact with a damp diaper.

di•aph•a•nous /díáfənəs/ *adj.* (of fabric, etc.) light and delicate, and almost transparent. □□ **di•aph•a•nous•ly** *adv.* [med.L *diaphanus* f. Gk *diaphanes* (as DIA-, *phainō* show)]

di•a•pho•re•sis /díəfərēesis/ *n.* (*pl.* **diaphoreses**) *Med.* sweating, esp. artificially induced. [LL f. Gk f. *diaphoreō* carry through]

di•a•pho•ret•ic /díəfərétik/ *adj. & n.* ● *adj.* inducing perspiration. ● *n.* an agent inducing perspiration. [LL *diaphoreticus* f. Gk *diaphorētikos* (formed as DIAPHORESIS)]

di•a•phragm /díəfram/ *n.* **1** a muscular partition separating the thorax from the abdomen in mammals. **2** a partition in animal and plant tissues. **3** a disk pierced by one or more holes in optical and acoustic systems, etc. **4** a device for varying the effective aperture of the lens in a camera, etc. **5** a thin contraceptive cap fitting over the cervix. **6** a thin sheet of material used as a partition, etc. □□ **di•a•phrag•mat•ic** /–fragmátik/ *adj.* [ME f. LL *diaphragma* f. Gk (as DIA-, *phragma –atos* f. *phrassō* fence in)]

di•a•phragm pump *n.* a pump using a flexible diaphragm in place of a piston.

di•a•pos•i•tive /díəpózitiv/ *n.* a positive photographic slide or transparency.

di•ar•chy /díaarkee/ *n.* (also **dy•ar•chy**) (*pl.* **•chies**) **1** government by two independent authorities (esp. in India 1921–37). **2** an instance of this. □□ **di•ar•chal** /díaárkəl/ *adj.* **di•ar•chic** *adj.* [DI-[1] + Gk –*arkhia* rule, after *monarchy*]

di•a•rist /díərist/ *n.* a person who keeps a diary. □□ **di•a•ris•tic** *adj.*

di•a•rize /díəriz/ *v.* **1** *intr.* keep a diary. **2** *tr.* enter in a diary.

di•ar•rhe•a /díəréeə/ *n.* a condition of excessively frequent and loose bowel movements. □□ **di•ar•rhe•al** *adj.* **di•ar•rhe•ic** *adj.* [ME f. LL f. Gk *diarrhoia* (as DIA-, *rheō* flow)]

di•a•ry /díəree/ *n.* (*pl.* **•ries**) **1** a daily record of events or thoughts. **2** a book for this or for noting future engagements, usu. printed and with a calendar and other information. [L *diarium* f. *dies* day]

di•a•scope /díəskōp/ *n.* an optical projector giving images of transparent objects.

Di•as•po•ra /díáspərə/ *n.* **1** (prec. by *the*) **a** the dispersion of the Jews among the Gentiles mainly in the 8th–6th c. BC. **b** Jews dispersed in this way. **2** (also **diaspora**) **a** any group of people similarly dispersed. **b** their dispersion. [Gk f. *diaspeirō* (as DIA-, *speirō* scatter)]

di•a•stase /díəstayz, –stayz/ *n. Biochem.* = AMYLASE. □□ **di•a•sta•sic** /–stáysik, –zik/ *adj.* **di•a•stat•ic** /–státik/ *adj.* [F f. Gk *diastasis* separation (as DIA-, *stasis* placing)]

di•as•to•le /díástəlee/ *n. Physiol.* the period between two contractions of the heart when the heart muscle relaxes and allows the chambers to fill with blood (cf. SYSTOLE). □□ **di•as•tol•ic** /díəstólik/ *adj.* [LL f. Gk *diastellō* (as DIA-, *stellō* place)]

di•a•ther•man•cy /díəthérmənsee/ *n.* the quality of transmitting radiant heat. □□ **di•a•ther•mic** *adj.* **di•a•ther•mous** *adj.* [F *diathermansie* f. Gk *dia* through + *thermansis* heating: assim. to –ANCY]

di•a•ther•my /díəthərmee/ *n.* the application of high-frequency electric currents to produce heat in the deeper tissues of the body. [G *Diathermie* f. Gk *dia* through + *thermon* heat]

di•ath•e•sis /díáthisis/ *n. Med.* a constitutional predisposition to a certain state, esp. a diseased one. [mod.L f. Gk f. *diatithēmi* arrange]

di•a•tom /díətom/ *n.* a microscopic unicellular alga with a siliceous cell wall, found as plankton and forming fossil deposits. □□ **di•a•to-**

ma•ceous /–máyshəs/ *adj.* [mod.L *Diatoma* (genus-name) f. Gk *diatomos* (as DIA-, *temnō* cut)]

di•a•tom•ic /díətómik/ *adj.* consisting of two atoms. [DI-[1] + ATOM]

di•at•o•mite /díátəmīt/ *n.* a deposit composed of the siliceous skeletons of diatoms.

di•a•ton•ic /díətónik/ *adj. Mus.* **1** (of a scale, interval, etc.) involving only notes proper to the prevailing key without chromatic alteration. **2** (of a melody or harmony) constructed from such a scale. [F *diatonique* or LL *diatonicus* f. Gk *diatonikos* at intervals of a tone (as DIA-, TONIC)]

di•a•tribe /díətrīb/ *n.* a forceful verbal attack; a piece of bitter criticism. [F f. L *diatriba* f. Gk *diatribē* spending of time, discourse f. *diatribō* (as DIA-, *tribō* rub)]

di•az•e•pam /díázipam/ *n.* a tranquilizing muscle-relaxant drug with anticonvulsant properties used to relieve anxiety, tension, etc. [ben-zodiazepine + am]

di•az•o /díázō, –áyzō/ *n.* (in full **diazotype**) a copying or coloring process using a diazo compound decomposed by light. [DI-[1] + AZO-]

di•az•o com•pound *n. Chem.* a chemical compound containing two usu. multiply bonded nitrogen atoms, often highly colored and used as dyes.

dib /dib/ *v.intr.* (**dibbed, dibbing**) = DAP. [var. of DAB[1]]

di•ba•sic /díbáysik/ *adj. Chem.* having two replaceable protons. [DI-[1] + BASE[1] 6]

dib•ber /dibər/ *n.* = DIBBLE.

dib•ble /dibəl/ *n. & v.* ● *n.* a hand tool for making holes in the ground for seeds or young plants. ● *v.* **1** *tr.* sow or plant with a dibble. **2** *tr.* prepare (soil) with a dibble. **3** *intr.* use a dibble. [ME: perh. rel. to DIB]

dibs /dibz/ *n.pl. sl.* **1** money. **2** rights; claim (*I have dibs on the last slice of pizza*). [earlier sense 'pebbles for game,' also *dib-stones*, perh. f. DIB]

dice /dīs/ *n. & v.* ● *n.pl.* **1 a** small cubes with faces bearing 1–6 spots used in games of chance. **b** (treated as *sing.*) one of these cubes (see DIE[2]). **2** a game played with one or more such cubes. **3** food cut into small cubes for cooking. ● *v.* **1 a** *intr.* play dice. **b** *intr.* take risks; gamble (*dicing with death*). **c** *tr.* (foll. by *away*) gamble away. **2** *tr.* cut (food) into small cubes. **3** *tr. Austral.* reject; leave alone. **4** *tr.* mark with squares. ● **no dice** *sl.* no success or prospect of it. □□ **dic•er** *n.* (in sense 1 of *v.*). [pl. of DIE[2]]

dibble

dic•ey /dísee/ *adj.* (**dic•i•er, dic•i•est**) *sl.* risky; unreliable. [DICE + –Y[1]]

di•chot•o•my /dīkótəmee/ *n.* (*pl.* **•mies**) **1 a** a division into two, esp. a sharply defined one. **b** the result of such a division. **2** binary classification. **3** *Bot. & Zool.* repeated bifurcation. □□ **di•cho•to•mic** /–kətómik/ *adj.* **di•chot•o•mize** *v.* **di•chot•o•mous** *adj.* [mod.L *dichotomia* f. Gk *dikhotomia* f. *dikho-* apart + –TOMY]

di•chro•ic /díkróik/ *adj.* (esp. of doubly refracting crystals) showing two colors. □□ **di•chro•ism** *n.* [Gk *dikhroos* (as DI-[1], *khrōs* color)]

di•chro•mat•ic /díkrōmátik/ *adj.* **1** two-colored. **2** (of animal species) having individuals that show different colorations. **b** having vision sensitive to only two of the three primary colors. □□ **di•chro•ma•tism** /díkrōmətizəm/ *n.* [DI-[1] + Gk *khrōmatikos* f. *khrōma –atos* color]

dick[1] /dik/ *n.* **1** *coarse sl.* the penis. **2** *Brit. colloq.* (in certain set phrases) fellow; person (*clever dick*). [pet form of the name *Richard*] ▶In sense 1 usually considered a taboo word.

dick[2] /dik/ *n. sl.* a detective. [perh. abbr.]

dick[3] /dik/ *n. Brit.* □ **take one's dick** (often foll. by *that* + clause) *sl.* swear; affirm. [abbr. of *declaration*]

dick•ens /díkinz/ *n.* (usu. prec. by *how, what, why,* etc., *the*) *colloq.* (esp. in exclamations) deuce; the Devil (*what the dickens are you doing here?*). [16th c.: prob. a use of the surname *Dickens*]

Dick•en•si•an /dikénzeeən/ *adj. & n.* ● *adj.* **1** of or relating to Charles Dickens, Engl. novelist d. 1870, or his work. **2** resembling or reminiscent of the situations, poor social conditions, or comically repulsive characters described in Dickens's work. ● *n.* an admirer or student of Dickens or his work. □□ **Dick•en•si•an•ly** *adv.*

dick•er /díkər/ *v. & n.* ● *v.* **1 a** *intr.* bargain; haggle. **b** *tr.* barter; exchange. **2** *intr.* hesitate. ● *n.* a deal; a barter. □□ **dick•er•er** *n.* [perh. f. *dicker* set of ten (hides), as a unit of trade]

dick•ey[1] /díkee/ *n.* (also **dick•y**) (*pl.* **•eys** or **•ies**) *colloq.* **1** a false shirt-front. **2** (in full **dickeybird**) a child's word for a little bird. **3** *Brit.* a driver's seat in a carriage. **4** *Brit.* an extra folding seat at the back of a vehicle; rumble seat. [some senses f. *Dicky* (as DICK[1])]

dick•ey[2] /díkee/ *adj.* (**dick•i•er, dick•i•est**) *sl.* unsound; likely to collapse or fail. [19th c.: perh. f. 'as queer as Dick's hatband']

dick•head /dík-hed/ *n. coarse sl.* a stupid or obnoxious person.

di•cot /díkot/ *n.* = DICOTYLEDON. [abbr.]

di·cot·y·le·don /díkot'leéd'n/ *n.* any flowering plant having two cotyledons. □□ **di·cot·y·le·don·ous** *adj.* [mod.L *dicotyledones* (as DI-[1], COTYLEDON)]

di·crot·ic /díkrótik/ *adj.* (of the pulse) having a double beat. [Gk *dikrotos*]

dict. *abbr.* **1** dictionary. **2** dictation.

dic·ta *pl.* of DICTUM.

Dic·ta·phone /díktəfōn/ *n. Trademark* a machine for recording and playing back dictated words. [DICTATE + PHONE]

dic·tate *v. & n.* ● *v.* /díktayt, diktáyt/ **1** *tr.* say or read aloud (words to be written down or recorded). **2 a** *tr.* prescribe or lay down authoritatively (terms, things to be done). **b** *intr.* lay down the law; give orders. ● *n.* /díktayt/ (usu. in *pl.*) an authoritative instruction (*dictates of conscience*). [L *dictare dictat-* frequent. of *dicere dict-* say]

dic·ta·tion /diktáyshən/ *n.* **1 a** the saying of words to be written down or recorded. **b** an instance of this, esp. as a school exercise. **c** the material that is dictated. **2 a** authoritative prescription. **b** an instance of this. **c** a command.

dic·ta·tor /díktaytər, diktáy–/ *n.* **1** a ruler with (often usurped) unrestricted authority. **2** a person with supreme authority in any sphere. **3** a domineering person. **4** a person who dictates for transcription. **5** *Rom.Hist.* a chief magistrate with absolute power, appointed in an emergency. [ME f. L (as DICTATE)]

dic·ta·to·ri·al /díktətáwreeəl/ *adj.* **1** of or like a dictator. **2** imperious; overbearing. □□ **dic·ta·to·ri·al·ly** *adv.* [L *dictatorius* (as DICTATOR)]

dic·ta·tor·ship /diktáytərship/ *n.* **1** a nation ruled by a dictator. **2 a** the position, rule, or period of rule of a dictator. **b** rule by a dictator. **3** absolute authority in any sphere.

dic·tion /díkshən/ *n.* **1** the manner of enunciation in speaking or singing. **2** the choice of words or phrases in speech or writing. [F *diction* or L *dictio* f. *dicere dict-* say]

dic·tion·ar·y /díkshəneree/ *n.* (*pl.* **·ies**) **1** a book that lists (usu. in alphabetical order) and explains the words of a language or gives equivalent words in another language. **2** a reference book on any subject, the items of which are arranged in alphabetical order (*dictionary of architecture*). [med.L *dictionarium* (*manuale* manual) & *dictionarius* (*liber* book) f. L *dictio* (as DICTION)]

dic·tum /díktəm/ *n.* (*pl.* **dic·ta** /–tə/ or **dic·tums**) **1** a formal utterance or pronouncement. **2** a saying or maxim. **3** *Law* = OBITER DICTUM. [L, = neut. past part. of *dicere* say]

dic·ty /díktee/ *adj. sl.* **1** conceited; snobbish. **2** elegant; stylish. [20th c.: orig. unkn.]

did *past* of DO[1].

di·dac·tic /dīdáktik/ *adj.* **1** meant to instruct. **2** (of a person) tediously pedantic. □□ **di·dac·ti·cal·ly** *adv.* **di·dac·ti·cism** /–tisizəm/ *n.* [Gk *didaktikos* f. *didaskō* teach]

did·di·kai /dídikī/ *n. sl.* a gypsy; an itinerant tinker. [Romany]

did·dle /díd'l/ *v. colloq.* **1** *tr.* cheat; swindle. **2** *intr.* waste time. □□ **did·dler** *n.* [prob. back-form. f. Jeremy *Diddler* in Kenney's 'Raising the Wind' (1803)]

did·dly /dídlee/ *n.* (also **did·dly squat**) *sl.* the slightest amount (*he hasn't done diddly to help us out*).

did·dums /dídəmz/ *int. Brit.* expressing commiseration, esp. to a child. [= *did* 'em, i.e., did they (tease you, etc.)?]

did·ger·i·doo /díjəreedoō/ *n.* (also **did·jer·i·doo** or **did·jer·i·du**) an Australian Aboriginal musical wind instrument of long tubular shape. [imit.]

didn't /díd'nt/ *contr.* did not.

di·do /dídō/ *n.* (*pl.* **·does** or **·dos**) *colloq.* an antic; a caper; a prank. □ **cut** (or **cut up**) **didoes** play pranks. [19th c.: orig. unkn.]

didst /didst/ *archaic 2nd sing. past* of DO[1].

di·dym·i·um /dīdímeeəm/ *n.* a mixture of prasodymium and neodymium, orig. regarded as an element. [mod.L f. Gk *didumos* twin (from being closely associated with lanthanum)]

die[1] /dī/ *v.* (**dies, died, dy·ing** /dī-ing/) **1** *intr.* (often foll. by *of*) (of a person, animal, or plant) cease to live; expire, lose vital force (*died of hunger*). **2** *intr.* **a** come to an end; cease to exist; fade away (*the project died within six months*). **b** cease to function; break down (*the engine died*). **c** (of a flame) go out. **3** *intr.* (foll. by *on*) die or cease to function while in the presence or charge of (a person). **4** *intr.* (usu. foll. by *of, from, with*) be exhausted or tormented (*nearly died of boredom; was dying from the heat*). **5** *tr.* suffer (a specified death) (*died a natural death*). □ **be dying** (foll. by *for*, or *to* + infin.) wish for longingly or intently (*was dying for a drink; am dying to see you*). **die away** become weaker or fainter to the point of extinction. **die back** (of a plant) decay from the tip toward the root. **die down** become less loud or strong. **die hard** die reluctantly; not without a struggle (*old habits die hard*). **die off** die one after another until few or none are left. **die out** become extinct; cease to exist. **never say die** keep up courage, not give in. [ME, prob. f. ON *deyja* f. Gmc]

die[2] /dī/ *n.* **1** *sing.* of DICE. **1 a**. **2** (*pl.* **dies**) **a** an engraved device for stamping a design on coins, medals, etc. **b** a device for stamping, cutting, or molding material into a particular shape. **3** (*pl.* **dice**

/dīs/) *Archit.* the cubical part of a pedestal between the base and the cornice; a dado or plinth. □ **as straight** (or **true**) **as a die 1** quite straight. **2** entirely honest or loyal. **the die is cast** an irrevocable step has been taken. [ME f. OF *de* f. L *datum* neut. past part. of *dare* give, play]

▶*Dice* is now standard in general use for both the singular and the plural in sense 1.

die cast·ing *n.* the process or product of pouring molten metal into molds to shape into objects. □□ **die cast** *v.tr.*

die·hard /díhaard/ *n.* a person who strongly opposes change or who continues to support something in spite of opposition.

die-hard *adj.* stubborn; strongly devoted.

diel·drin /deéldrin/ *n.* a crystalline insecticide produced by the oxidation of aldrin. [O. *Diels*, Ger. chemist d. 1954 + ALDRIN]

di·e·lec·tric /dí-iléktrik/ *adj. & n. Electr.* ● *adj.* insulating. ● *n.* an insulating medium or substance. □□ **di·e·lec·tri·cal·ly** *adv.* [DI-[3] + ELECTRIC = through which electricity is transmitted (without conduction)]

di·e·lec·tric con·stant *n.* permittivity.

di·ene /dí-een, dī-eén/ *n. Chem.* any organic compound possessing two double bonds between carbon atoms. [DI-[1] + –ENE]

di·er·e·sis var. of DIAERESIS.

die·sel /deézəl/ *n.* **1** (in full **diesel engine**) an internal combustion engine in which the heat produced by the compression of air in the cylinder ignites the fuel. **2** a vehicle driven by a diesel engine. **3** fuel for a diesel engine. □□ **die·sel·ize** *v.tr.* [R. *Diesel*, Ger. engineer d. 1913]

die·sel-e·lec·tric *n. & adj.* ● *n.* a vehicle driven by the electric current produced by a diesel-engined generator. ● *adj.* of or powered by this means.

die·sel oil *n.* a heavy petroleum distillate used as fuel in diesel engines.

die·sink·er /dísingkər/ *n.* an engraver of dies.

Di·es I·rae /deé-ays eéray/ *n.* a Latin hymn sung in a mass for the dead. [L (its first words), = day of wrath]

di·es non /dí-eez nón, deé-ays nón/ *n. Law* **1** a day on which no legal business can be done. **2** a day that does not count for legal purposes. [L, short for *dies non juridicus* nonjudicial day]

di·et[1] /díət/ *n. & v.* ● *n.* **1** the kinds of food that a person or animal habitually eats. **2** a special course of food to which a person is restricted, esp. for medical reasons or to control weight. **3** a regular occupation or series of activities to which one is restricted or which form one's main concern, usu. for a purpose (*a diet of light reading and fresh air*). ● *v.* (**dieted, dieting**) **1** *intr.* restrict oneself to small amounts or special kinds of food, esp. to control one's weight. **2** *tr.* restrict (a person or animal) to a special diet. □□ **di·et·er** *n.* [ME f. OF *diete* (n.), *dieter* (v.) f. L *diaeta* f. Gk *diaita* a way of life]

di·et[2] /díət/ *n.* **1** a legislative assembly in certain countries. **2** *hist.* a national or international conference, esp. of a federal government or confederation. **3** *Sc. Law* a meeting or session of a court. [ME f. med.L *dieta* day's work, wages, etc.]

di·e·tar·y /díəteree/ *adj. & n.* ● *adj.* of or relating to a diet. ● *n.* (*pl.* **·ies**) a regulated or restricted diet. [ME f. med.L *dietarium* (as DIET[1])]

di·e·tet·ic /díətétik/ *adj.* of or relating to diet. □□ **di·e·tet·i·cal·ly** *adv.* [L *dieteticus* f. Gk *diaitētikos* (as DIET[1])]

di·e·tet·ics /díətétiks/ *n.pl.* (usu. treated as *sing.*) the scientific study of diet and nutrition.

di·eth·yl e·ther /dī-éthəl/ *n. Chem.* = ETHER 1.

di·e·ti·tian /díətishən/ *n.* (also **di·e·ti·cian**) an expert in dietetics.

dif- /dif/ *prefix* assim. form of DIS- before *f*. [L var. of DIS-]

dif·fer /dífər/ *v.intr.* **1** (often foll. by *from*) be unlike or distinguishable. **2** (often foll. by *with*) disagree; be at variance (with a person). [ME f. OF *differer* f. L *differre*, differ, DEFER[1], (as DIS-, *ferre* bear, tend)]

dif·fer·ence /dífrəns/ *n. & v.* ● *n.* **1** the state or condition of being different or unlike. **2** a point in which things differ; a distinction. **3** a degree of unlikeness. **4 a** the quantity by which amounts differ; a deficit (*will have to make up the difference*). **b** the remainder left after subtraction. **5 a** a disagreement, quarrel, or dispute. **b** the grounds of disagreement (*put aside their differences*). **6** a notable change (*the difference in his behavior is remarkable*). **7** *Heraldry* an alteration in a coat of arms distinguishing members of a family. ● *v.tr. Heraldry* alter (a coat of arms) to distinguish members of a family. □ **make a** (or **all the**, etc.) **difference** (often foll. by *to*) have a significant effect or influence (on a person, situation, etc.). **make no difference** (often foll. by *to*) have no effect (on a person, situation, etc.). **with a difference** having a new or unusual feature. [ME f. OF f. L *differentia* (as DIFFERENT)]

dif·fer·ent /dífrənt/ *adj.* **1** (often foll. by *from, to, than*) unlike; distinguishable in nature, form, or quality (from another). **2** distinct; separate; not the same one (as another). **3** *colloq.* unusual (*wanted to do something different*). **4** of various kinds; assorted; several; miscellaneous (*available in different colors*). □□ **dif·fer·ent·ly** *adv.* **dif·fer·ent·ness** *n.* [ME f. OF *different* f. L *different-* (as DIFFER)]

▶Many traditional critics regard **different than** as an improper substitute for **different from**: *My opinion is quite different from his*. But **different than** now appears widely in good writing, as well as in informal contexts.

dif•fer•en•ti•a /dífərénsheeə/ *n*. (*pl.* **dif•fer•en•ti•ae** /–shee-ee/) a distinguishing mark, esp. between species within a genus. [L: see DIFFERENCE]

dif•fer•en•tial /dífərénshəl/ *adj. & n.* ● *adj.* **1 a** of, exhibiting, or depending on a difference. **b** varying according to circumstances. **2** *Math.* relating to infinitesimal differences. **3** constituting a specific difference; distinctive; relating to specific differences (*differential diagnosis*). **4** *Physics & Mech.* concerning the difference of two or more motions, pressures, etc. ● *n.* **1** a difference between individuals or examples of the same kind. **2** *Brit.* a difference in wage or salary between industries or categories of employees in the same industry. **3** a difference between rates of interest, etc. **4** *Math.* **a** an infinitesimal difference between successive values of a variable. **b** a function expressing this as a rate of change with respect to another variable. **5** (in full **differential gear**) a gear allowing a vehicle's driven wheels to revolve at different speeds in cornering. □□ **dif•fer•en•tial•ly** *adv.* [med. & mod.L *differentialis* (as DIFFERENCE)]

dif•fer•en•tial cal•cu•lus *n. Math.* a method of calculating rates of change, maximum or minimum values, etc. (cf. INTEGRAL CALCULUS).

dif•fer•en•tial co•ef•fi•cient *n. Math.* = DERIVATIVE.

dif•fer•en•tial e•qua•tion *n. Math.* an equation involving differentials among its quantities.

dif•fer•en•ti•ate /dífərénsheeayt/ *v.* **1** *tr.* constitute a difference between or in. **2** *tr. & (often foll. by between) intr.* find differences (between); discriminate. **3** *tr. & intr.* make or become different in the process of growth or development (species, word forms, etc.). **4** *tr. Math.* transform (a function) into its derivative. □□ **dif•fer•en•ti•a•tion** /–sheeáyshən/ *n.* **dif•fer•en•ti•a•tor** *n.* [med.L *differentiare differentiat-* (as DIFFERENCE)]

dif•fi•cult /dífikult, –kəlt/ *adj.* **1 a** needing much effort or skill. **b** troublesome; perplexing. **2** (of a person): **a** not easy to please or satisfy. **b** uncooperative; troublesome. **3** characterized by hardships or problems (*a difficult period in his life*). □□ **dif•fi•cult•ly** *adv.* **dif•fi•cult•ness** *n.* [ME, back-form. f. DIFFICULTY]

dif•fi•cul•ty /dífikultee, –kəl–/ *n.* (*pl.* **-ties**) **1** the state or condition of being difficult. **2 a** a difficult thing; a problem or hindrance. **b** (often in *pl.*) a cause of distress or hardship (*in financial difficulties; there was someone in difficulties in the water*). □ **make difficulties** be intransigent or unaccommodating. **with difficulty** not easily. [ME f. L *difficultas* (as DIS–, *facultas* FACULTY)]

dif•fi•dent /dífidənt/ *adj.* **1** shy; lacking self-confidence. **2** excessively modest and reticent. □□ **dif•fi•dence** /–dəns/ *n.* **dif•fi•dent•ly** *adv.* [L *diffidere* (as DIS–, *fidere* trust)]

dif•fract /difrákt/ *v.tr. Physics* (of the edge of an opaque body, a narrow slit, etc.) break up (a beam of light) into a series of dark or light bands or colored spectra, or (a beam of radiation or particles) into a series of alternately high and low intensities. □□ **dif•frac•tion** /–frákshən/ *n.* **dif•frac•tive** *adj.* **dif•frac•tive•ly** *adv.* [L *diffringere diffract-* (as DIS–, *frangere* break)]

dif•frac•tom•e•ter /dífraktómitər/ *n.* an instrument for measuring diffraction, esp. in crystallographic work.

dif•fuse *adj. & v.* ● *adj.* /difyōōs/ **1** (of light, inflammation, etc.) spread out; diffused; not concentrated. **2** (of prose, speech, etc.) not concise; long-winded; verbose. ● *v.tr. & intr.* /difyōōz/ **1** disperse or be dispersed from a center. **2** spread or be spread widely; reach a large area. **3** *Physics* (esp. of fluids) intermingle by diffusion. □□ **dif•fuse•ly** /difyōōslee/ *adv.* **dif•fuse•ness** /difyōōsnis/ *n.* **dif•fus•i•ble** /difyōōzibəl/ *adj.* **dif•fu•sive** /difyōōsiv/ *adj.* [ME f. F *diffus* or L *diffusus* extensive (as DIS–, *fusus* past part. of *fundere* pour)]

dif•fus•er /difyōōzər/ *n.* (also **dif•fu•sor**) **1** a person or thing that diffuses, esp. a device for diffusing light. **2** *Engin.* a duct for broadening an airflow and reducing its speed.

dif•fu•sion /difyōōzhən/ *n.* **1** the act or an instance of diffusing; the process of being diffused. **2** *Physics & Chem.* the interpenetration of substances by the natural movement of their particles. **3** *Anthropol.* the spread of elements of culture, etc., to another region or people. □□ **dif•fu•sion•ist** *n.* [ME f. L *diffusio* (as DIFFUSE)]

dig /dig/ *v. & n.* ● *v.* (**dig•ging**; *past* and *past part.* **dug** /dug/) **1** *intr.* break up and remove or turn over soil, ground, etc., with a tool, one's hands, (of an animal) claws, etc. **2** *tr.* break up and displace (the ground, etc.) in this way. **b** (foll. by *up*) break up the soil of (fallow land). **3** *tr.* make (a hole, grave, tunnel, etc.) by digging. **4** *tr.* (often foll. by *out*) obtain or remove by digging. **b** find or discover after searching. **5** *tr.* (also *absol.*) excavate (an archaeological site). **6** *tr. sl.* like, appreciate, or understand. **7** *tr. & intr.* (foll. by *in, into*) thrust or poke into or down into. **8** *intr.* make one's way by digging (*dug through the mountainside*). **9** *intr.* (usu. foll. by *into*) investigate or study closely; probe. ● *n.* **1** a piece of digging. **2** a thrust or poke (*a dig in the ribs*). **3** *colloq.* (often foll. by *at*) a pointed or critical remark. **4** an archaeological excavation. **5** (in *pl.*) *colloq.* living quarters. □ **dig one's feet** (or **heels** or **toes**) **in** be obstinate. **dig in** *colloq.* begin eating. **dig oneself in 1** prepare a de-

fensive trench or pit. **2** establish one's position. [ME *digge*, of uncert. orig.: cf. OE *dīc* ditch]

di•gam•ma /dígámə/ *n.* the sixth letter (F, Ϝ) of the early Greek alphabet (prob. with a pronunciation similar to that of "w"), later disused. [L f. Gk (as DI–[1], GAMMA)]

di•gas•tric /dígástrik/ *adj. & n. Anat.* ● *adj.* (of a muscle) having two wide parts with a tendon between. ● *n.* the muscle that opens the jaw. [mod.L *digastricus* (as DI–[1], Gk *gastēr* belly)]

di•gest *v. & n.* ● *v.tr.* /díjést, dī–/ **1** assimilate (food) in the stomach and bowels. **2** understand and assimilate mentally. **3** *Chem.* treat (a substance) with heat, enzymes, or a solvent in order to decompose it, extract the essence, etc. **4 a** reduce to a systematic or convenient form; classify; summarize. **b** think over; arrange in the mind. **5** bear without resistance; tolerate; endure. ● *n.* /díjest/ **1 a** a methodical summary, esp. of a body of laws. **b** (**the Digest**) the compendium of Roman law compiled in the reign of Justinian (6th c. AD). **2 a** a compendium or summary of information; a résumé. **b** a regular or occasional synopsis of current literature or news. □□ **di•gest•er** *n.* **di•gest•i•ble** *adj.* **di•gest•i•bil•i•ty** *n.* [ME f. L *digerere digest-* distribute, dissolve, digest (as DI–[2], *gerere* carry)]

di•ges•tion /díjés-chən, dī–/ *n.* **1** the process of digesting. **2** the capacity to digest food (*has a weak digestion*). **3** digesting a substance by means of heat, enzymes, or a solvent. [ME f. OF f. L *digestio –onis* (as DIGEST)]

di•ges•tive /díjéstiv, dī–/ *adj. & n.* ● *adj.* **1** of or relating to digestion. **2** aiding or promoting digestion. ● *n.* **1** a substance that aids digestion. **2** (in full **digestive biscuit**) *Brit.* a usu. round semisweet wholewheat cookie. □□ **di•ges•tive•ly** *adv.* [ME f. OF *digestif –ive* or L *digestivus* (as DIGEST)]

dig•ger /dígər/ *n.* **1** a person or machine that digs, esp. a mechanical excavator. **2** a miner, esp. a gold digger. **3** *colloq.* an Australian or New Zealander, esp. a private soldier. **4** *Austral. & NZ colloq.* (as a form of address) mate; fellow.

dig•gings /dígingz/ *n.pl.* **1 a** a mine or goldfield. **b** material dug out of a mine, etc. **2** *Brit. colloq.* lodgings; accommodation.

dight /dīt/ *adj. archaic* clothed; arrayed. [past part. of *dight* (v.) f. OE *dihtan* f. L *dictare* DICTATE]

dig•it /díjit/ *n.* **1** any numeral from 0 to 9, esp. when forming part of a number. **2** *Anat. & Zool.* a finger, thumb, or toe. [ME f. L *digitus*]

dig•it•al /díjit'l/ *adj.* **1** of or using a digit or digits. **2** (of a clock, watch, etc.) that gives a reading by means of displayed digits instead of hands. **3** (of a computer) operating on data represented as a series of usu. binary digits or in similar discrete form. **4 a** (of a recording) with sound information represented in digits for more reliable transmission. **b** (of a recording medium) using this process. □□ **dig•it•al•ize** *v.tr.* **dig•it•al•ly** *adv.* [L *digitalis* (as DIGIT)]

dig•it•al au•di•o tape *n.* magnetic tape on which sound is recorded digitally.

dig•i•tal•in /díjitálin/ *n.* the pharmacologically active constituent(s) of the foxglove. [DIGITALIS + –IN]

dig•i•tal•is /díjitális/ *n.* a drug prepared from the dried leaves of foxgloves and containing substances that stimulate the heart muscle. [mod.L, genus name of foxglove after G *Fingerhut* thimble: see DIGITAL]

dig•i•tate /díjitayt/ *adj.* **1** *Zool.* having separate fingers or toes. **2** *Bot.* having deep radiating divisions. □□ **dig•i•tate•ly** *adv.* **dig•i•ta•tion** /–táyshən/ *n.* [L *digitatus* (as DIGIT)]

dig•i•ti•grade /díjitigrayd/ *adj. & n. Zool* ● *adj.* (of an animal) walking on its toes and not touching the ground with its heels, e.g., dogs, cats, and rodents. ● *n.* a digitigrade animal (cf. PLANTIGRADE). [F f. L *digitus* + *–gradus* –walking]

dig•i•tize /díjitīz/ *v.tr.* convert (data, etc.) into digital form, esp. for processing by a computer. □□ **dig•i•ti•za•tion** *n.*

dig•ni•fied /dígnifīd/ *adj.* having or expressing dignity; noble or stately in appearance or manner. □□ **dig•ni•fied•ly** *adv.*

dig•ni•fy /dígnifī/ *v.tr.* (**-fies, -fied**) **1** give dignity or distinction to. **2** ennoble; make worthy or illustrious. **3** give the form or appearance of dignity to (*dignified the house with the name of mansion*). [obs. F *dignifier* f. OF *dignefier* f. LL *dignificare* f. *dignus* worthy]

dig•ni•tar•y /dígniteree/ *n.* (*pl.* **-ies**) a person holding high rank or office. [DIGNITY + –ARY[1], after PROPRIETARY]

dig•ni•ty /dígnitee/ *n.* (*pl.* **-ties**) **1** a composed and serious manner or style. **2** the state of being worthy of honor or respect. **3** worthiness; excellence (*the dignity of work*). **4** a high or honorable rank or position. **5** high regard or estimation. **6** self-respect. □ **beneath one's dignity** not considered worthy enough for one to do. **stand on one's dignity** insist (esp. by one's manner) on being treated with due respect. [ME f. OF *digneté, dignité* f. L *dignitas –tatis* f. *dignus* worthy]

di•graph /dígraf/ *n.* a group of two letters representing one sound, as in *ph* and *ey*. □□ **di•graph•ic** /–gráfik/ *adj.*

di·gress /dīgrés/ *v.intr.* depart from the main subject temporarily in speech or writing. □□ **di·gress·er** *n.* **di·gres·sion** *n.* /–greshən/ **di·gres·sive** *adj.* **di·gres·sive·ly** *adv.* **di·gres·sive·ness** *n.* [L *digredi digress-* (as DI-², *gradi* walk)]

digs *colloq.* living quarters.

di·he·dral /dīheˈedrəl/ *adj. & n.* • *adj.* having or contained by two plane faces. • *n.* = DIHEDRAL ANGLE. [*dihedron* f. DI-¹ + –HEDRON]

di·he·dral an·gle *n.* an angle formed by two plane surfaces, esp. by an aircraft wing with the horizontal.

di·hy·dric /dīhídrik/ *adj. Chem.* containing two hydroxyl groups. [DI-¹ + *hydric* containing hydrogen]

dik-dik /díkdik/ *n.* any dwarf antelope of the genus *Madoqua*, native to Africa. [name in E. Africa and in Afrik.]

dike¹ /dīk/ *n. & v.* (also **dyke**) • *n.* **1** a long wall or embankment built to prevent flooding, esp. from the sea. **2 a** a ditch or artificial watercourse. **b** *Brit.* a natural watercourse. **3 a** a low wall, esp. of turf. **b** a causeway. **4** a barrier or obstacle; a defense. **5** *Geol.* an intrusion of igneous rock across sedimentary strata. **6** esp. *Austral. sl.* a toilet. • *v.tr.* provide or defend with a dike or dikes. [ME f. ON *dík* or MLG *dīk* dam, MDu. *dijc* ditch, dam: cf. DITCH]

dike² var. of DYKE².

dik·tat /diktát/ *n.* a categorical statement or decree, esp. terms imposed after a war by a victor. [G, = DICTATE]

di·lap·i·date /dilápidayt/ *v.intr. & tr.* fall or cause to fall into disrepair or ruin. [L *dilapidare* demolish, squander (as DI-², *lapis lapid-* stone)]

di·lap·i·dat·ed /dilápidaytid/ *adj.* in a state of disrepair or ruin, esp. as a result of age or neglect.

di·lap·i·da·tion /dilápidáyshən/ *n.* **1 a** the process of dilapidating. **b** a state of disrepair. **2** (in *pl.*) repairs required at the end of a tenancy or lease. **3** *Eccl.* a sum charged against an incumbent for wear and tear during a tenancy. [ME f. LL *dilapidatio* (as DILAPIDATE)]

dil·a·ta·tion /dilətáyshən, dī–/ *n.* **1** the widening or expansion of a hollow organ or cavity. **2** the process of dilating.

dil·a·ta·tion and cu·ret·tage *n.* an operation in which the cervix is expanded and the womb lining scraped off with a curette.

di·late /dīláyt, dīlayt/ *v.* **1** *tr. & intr.* make or become wider or larger (esp. of an opening in the body) (*dilated pupils*). **2** *intr.* (often foll. by *on, upon*) speak or write at length. □□ **di·lat·a·ble** *adj.* **di·la·tion** /–láyshən/ *n.* [ME f. OF *dilater* f. L *dilatare* spread out (as DI-², *latus* wide)]

dil·a·tor /dīláytər, dīlay–/ *n.* **1** *Anat.* a muscle that dilates an organ. **2** *Surgery* an instrument for dilating a tube or cavity in the body.

dil·a·to·ry /dílətawree/ *adj.* given to or causing delay. □□ **dil·a·to·ri·ly** *adv.* **dil·a·to·ri·ness** *n.* [LL *dilatorius* (as DI-², *dilat-* past part. stem of *differre* DEFER¹)]

dil·do /díldō/ *n.* (*pl.* **-dos** or **-does**) an object shaped like an erect penis and used, esp. by women, for sexual stimulation. [17th c.: orig. unkn.]

di·lem·ma /dilémə/ *n.* **1** a situation in which a choice has to be made between two equally undesirable alternatives. **2** a state of indecision between two alternatives. **3** *disp.* a difficult situation. **4** an argument forcing an opponent to choose either of two unfavorable alternatives. [L f. Gk as DI-¹, *lēmma* premise)]

▶Dilemma should be used with regard to situations in which a difficult choice has to be made between undesirable alternatives, as in *You see his dilemma? He would have to give up either his childhood home or his dreams of traveling.* It is imprecise to use **dilemma** to mean simply 'a difficult situation.'

dil·et·tante /dílitáànt/ *n. & adj.* • *n.* (*pl.* **dil·et·tantes** or **dil·et·tan·ti** /–tee/) **1** a person who studies a subject or area of knowledge superficially. **2** a person who enjoys the arts. • *adj.* trifling; not thorough; amateurish. □□ **dil·et·tant·ish** *adj.* **dil·et·tant·ism** *n.* [It. f. pres. part. of *dilettare* delight f. L *delectare*]

dil·i·gence¹ /dílijəns/ *n.* **1** careful and persistent application or effort. **2** (as a characteristic) industriousness. [ME f. OF f. L *diligentia* (as DILIGENT)]

dil·i·gence² /dílijəns, deèleezhóns/ *n. hist.* a public stagecoach, esp. in France. [F, for *carrosse de diligence* coach of speed]

dil·i·gent /dílijənt/ *adj.* **1** careful and steady in application to one's work or duties. **2** showing care and effort. □□ **dil·i·gent·ly** *adv.* [ME f. OF f. L *diligens* assiduous, part. of *diligere* love, take delight in (as DI-², *legere* choose)]

dill¹ /dil/ *n.* **1** an umbelliferous herb, *Anethum graveolens*, with yellow flowers and aromatic seeds. **2** the leaves or seeds of this plant used for flavoring and medicinal purposes. [OE *dile*]

dill² /dil/ *n. Austral. sl.* **1** a fool or simpleton. **2** the victim of a trickster. [app. back-form. f. DILLY²]

dill pick·le *n.* pickled cucumber, etc., flavored with dill.

dil·ly¹ /dílee/ *n.* (*pl.* **-lies**) *sl.* a remarkable or excellent person or thing. (adj.) f. DELIGHTFUL or DELICIOUS]

dil·ly² /dílee/ *adj. Austral. sl.* **1** odd or eccentric. **2** foolish; stupid; mad. [perh. f. DAFT, SILLY]

dil·ly-bag /díleebag/ *n. Austral.* a small bag or basket. [Aboriginal *dilly* + BAG]

dil·ly-dal·ly /díleedálee/ *v.intr.* (·lies, ·lied) *colloq.* **1** dawdle; loiter. **2** vacillate. [redupl. of DALLY]

dil·u·ent /dílyo͞oənt/ *adj. & n. Chem. & Biochem.* • *adj.* that serves to dilute. • *n.* a diluting agent. [L *diluere diluent-* DILUTE]

di·lute /dīlo͞ot, dī–/ *v. & adj.* • *v.tr.* **1** reduce the strength of (a fluid) by adding water or another solvent. **2** weaken or reduce the strength or forcefulness of, esp. by adding something. • *adj.* also /dí–/ **1** (esp. of a fluid) diluted; weakened. **2** (of a color) washed out; low in saturation. **3** *Chem.* **a** (of a solution) having relatively low concentration of solute. **b** (of a substance) in solution (*dilute sulfuric acid*). □□ **di·lut·er** *n.* **di·lu·tion** /–lo͞oshən/ *n.* [L *diluere dilut-* (as DI-², *luere* wash)]

di·lu·vi·al /dílo͞oveeəl/ *adj.* **1** of a flood, esp. of the Flood in Genesis. **2** *Geol.* of the Glacial Drift formation (see DRIFT *n.* 8). [LL *diluvialis* f. *diluvium* DELUGE]

di·lu·vi·um /dílo͞oveeəm/ *n.* (*pl.* **diluvia** /–veeə/ or **diluviums**) *Geol.* = DRIFT *n.* 8. [L: see DILUVIAL]

dim /dim/ *adj. & v.* • *adj.* (**dim·mer, dim·mest**) **1 a** only faintly luminous or visible; not bright. **b** obscure; ill-defined. **2** not clearly perceived or remembered. **3** *colloq.* stupid; slow to understand. **4** (of the eyes) not seeing clearly. • *v.* (**dimmed, dim·ming**) **1** *tr. & intr.* make or become dim or less bright. **2** *tr.* switch (headlights) to low beam. □ **take a dim view of** *colloq.* **1** disapprove of. **2** feel gloomy about. □□ **dim·ly** *adv.* **dim·mish** *adj.* **dim·ness** *n.* [OE *dim, dimm,* of unkn. orig.]

dim. *abbr.* diminuendo.

dime /dīm/ *n. US & Can.* **1** a ten-cent coin. **2** *colloq.* a small amount of money. □ **a dime a dozen** very cheap or commonplace. **turn on a dime** *colloq.* make a sharp turn in a vehicle. [ME (orig. = tithe) f. OF *disme* f. L *decima pars* tenth part]

dime nov·el *n.* a cheap popular novel, typically a melodramatic romance or adventure story, formerly selling for ten cents.

di·men·sion /diménshən, dī–/ *n. & v.* • *n.* **1** a measurable extent of any kind, as length, breadth, depth, area, and volume. **2** (in *pl.*) size; scope; extent. **3** an aspect or facet of a situation, problem, etc. **4** *Algebra* one of a number of unknown or variable quantities contained as factors in a product (x^3, x^2y, xyz, are all of three dimensions). **5** *Physics* the product of mass, length, time, etc., raised to the appropriate power, in a derived physical quantity. • *v.tr.* (usu. as **dimensioned** *adj.*) mark the dimensions on (a diagram, etc.). □□ **di·men·sion·al** *adj.* (also in *comb.*). **di·men·sion·less** *adj.* [ME f. OF f. L *dimensio –onis* (as DI-², *metiri mensus* measure)]

di·mer /dímər/ *n. Chem.* a compound consisting of two identical molecules linked together (cf. MONOMER). □□ **di·mer·ic** /–mérik/ *adj.* [DI-¹ + *–mer* after POLYMER]

dim·er·ous /dímərəs/ *adj.* (of a plant) having two parts in a whorl, etc. [mod.L *dimerus* f. Gk *dimerēs* bipartite]

dime store *n.* = FIVE-AND-DIME.

dim·e·ter /dímitər/ *n. Prosody* a line of verse consisting of two metrical feet. [LL *dimetrus* f. Gk *dimetros* (as DI-¹, METER)]

di·min·ish /dimínish/ *v.* **1** *tr. & intr.* make or become smaller or less. **2** *tr.* lessen the reputation or influence of (a person). □□ **di·min·ish·a·ble** *adj.* [ME, blending of earlier *minish* f. OF *menusier* (formed as MINCE) and *diminue* f. OF *diminuer* f. L *diminuere diminut-* break up small]

di·min·ished /dimínisht/ *adj.* **1** reduced; made smaller or less. **2** *Mus.* (of an interval, usu. a seventh or fifth) less by a semitone than the corresponding minor or perfect interval.

di·min·u·en·do /dimínyo͞o-éndō/ *adv. & n. Mus.* • *adv.* with a gradual decrease in loudness. • *n.* (*pl.* **·dos**) a passage to be played in this way. [It., part. of *diminuire* DIMINISH]

dim·i·nu·tion /dìminóoshən, –nyo͞o–/ *n.* **1 a** the act or an instance of diminishing. **b** the amount by which something diminishes. **2** *Mus.* the repetition of a passage in notes shorter than those originally used. [ME f. OF f. L *diminutio –onis* (as DIMINISH)]

di·min·u·tive /dimínyətiv/ *adj. & n.* • *adj.* **1** remarkably small; tiny. **2** *Gram.* (of a word or suffix) implying smallness, either actual or imputed in token of affection, scorn, etc. (e.g., *–let, –kins*). • *n. Gram.* a diminutive word or suffix. □□ **di·min·u·ti·val** /–tíval/ *adj.* **di·min·u·tive·ly** *adv.* **di·min·u·tive·ness** *n.* [ME f. OF *diminutif, –ive* f. LL *diminutivus* (as DIMINISH)]

dim·is·so·ry /dimísəree/ *adj.* **1** ordering or permitting to depart. **2** *Eccl.* granting permission for a candidate to be ordained outside the bishop's own see (*dimissory letters*). [ME f. LL *dimissorius* f. *dimittere dimiss-* send away (as DI-², *mittere* send)]

dim·i·ty /dímitee/ *n.* (*pl.* **·ties**) a cotton fabric woven with stripes or checks. [ME f. It. *dimito* f. med.L *dimitum* f. Gk *dimitos* (as DI-¹, *mitos* warp-thread)]

dim·mer /dímər/ *n.* **1** a device for varying the brightness of an electric light. **2 a** (in *pl.*) small parking lights on a motor vehicle. **b** headlights on low beam.

di·mor·phic /dīmáwrfik/ *adj.* (also **di·mor·phous** /dímáwrfəs/) *Biol., Chem.,* & *Mineral.* exhibiting, or occurring in, two distinct forms. □□ **di·mor·phism** *n.* [Gk *dimorphos* (as DI-¹, *morphē* form)]

dim•ple /dímpəl/ *n. & v.* ● *n.* a small hollow or dent in the flesh, esp. in the cheeks or chin. ● *v.* 1 *intr.* produce or show dimples. 2 *tr.* produce dimples in (a cheek, etc.). □□ **dim•ply** *adj.* [ME prob. f. OE *dympel* (unrecorded) f. a Gmc root *dump-*, perh. a nasalized form rel. to DEEP]

dim sum /dim súm/ *n.* (also **dim sim** /sim/) 1 a meal or course of savory Cantonese-style snacks. 2 (usu. **dim sim**) *Austral.* a dish of Cantonese origin, consisting of steamed or fried meat cooked in thin dough. [Cantonese *dim-săm*, lit. 'dot of the heart']

dim•wit /dímwit/ *n. colloq.* a stupid person.

dim-wit•ted *adj.. colloq.* stupid; unintelligent.

DIN /din/ *n.* any of a series of technical standards originating in Germany and used internationally, esp. to designate electrical connections, film speeds, and paper sizes. [G, f. *Deutsche Industrie-Norm*]

din /din/ *n. & v.* ● *n.* a prolonged loud and distracting noise. ● *v.* (**dinned, din•ning**) 1 *tr.* (foll. by *into*) instill (something to be learned) by constant repetition. 2 *intr.* make a din. [OE *dyne, dynn, dynian* f. Gmc]

di•nar /dinaár, deénaar/ *n.* 1 the chief monetary unit of Yugoslavia. 2 the chief monetary unit of certain countries of the Middle East and N. Africa. [Arab. & Pers. *dīnār* f. Gk *dēnarion* f. L *denarius*: see DENIER]

dine /dīn/ *v.* 1 *intr.* eat dinner. 2 *tr.* give dinner to. □ **dine out** 1 dine away from home. 2 (foll. by *on*) *Brit.* be invited to dinner, etc., on account of one's ability to relate an interesting event, story, etc. [ME f. OF *diner, disner*, ult. f. DIS- + LL *jejunare* f. *jejunus* fasting]

din•er /dínər/ *n.* 1 a person who dines, esp. in a restaurant. 2 a railroad dining car. 3 a small restaurant. 4 a small dining room.

di•nette /dīnét/ *n.* 1 a small room or part of a room used for eating meals. 2 (in full **dinette set**) table and chairs designed for such a room.

ding[1] /ding/ *v. & n.* ● *v.intr.* make a ringing sound. ● *n.* a ringing sound, as of a bell. [imit.: infl. by DIN]

ding[2] /ding/ *v. & n.* ● *v.tr.* cause surface damage; dent. ● *n.* nick; minor surface damage; dent. [ME *dingen*]

ding-a-ling /díngəling/ *n.* a foolish, flighty, or eccentric person.

ding an sich /díng an zíkh/ *n. Philos.* (in Kant's philosophy) a thing in itself, not mediated through perception by the senses or conceptualization, and therefore unknowable. [G]

ding•bat /díngbat/ *n. sl.* 1 a stupid or eccentric person. 2 *Printing* an ornamental design in typography. [19th c.: perh. f. *ding* to beat + BAT[1]]

ding•dong /díngdawng, –dong/ *n., adj., & adv.* ● *n.* 1 the sound of alternate chimes, as of two bells. 2 *colloq.* an intense argument or fight. 3 *colloq.* a riotous party. ● *adj.* (of a contest, etc.) evenly matched and intensely waged; thoroughgoing. ● *adv.* with vigor and energy (*hammer away at it dingdong*). [16th c.: imit.]

dinge /dinj/ *n.* the condition of dinginess.

din•ghy /díngee, dínggee/ *n.* (*pl.* **•ghies**) 1 a small boat carried by a ship. 2 a small pleasure boat. 3 a small inflatable rubber boat (esp. for emergency use). [orig. a row boat used in India f. Hindi *dĭṅgī, ḍēṅgī*]

din•gle /dínggəl/ *n.* a deep, wooded valley or dell. [ME: orig. unkn.]

din•go /dínggō/ *n.* (*pl.* **•goes**) 1 a wild or half-domesticated Australian dog, *Canis dingo.* 2 *Austral. sl.* a coward or scoundrel. [Aboriginal]

din•gy /dínjee/ *adj.* (**din•gi•er, din•gi•est**) dirty-looking; drab; dull-colored. □□ **din•gi•ly** *adv.* **din•gi•ness** *n.* [perh. ult. f. OE *dynge* DUNG]

din•ing car *n.* a railroad car equipped as a restaurant.

din•ing room *n.* a room in which meals are eaten.

din•kum /díngkəm/ *adj. & n. Austral. & NZ colloq.* ● *adj.* genuine, right. ● *n.* work, toil. □ **fair dinkum** genuine or true (*it's a fair dinkum Aussie wedding*). **dinkum oil** the honest truth. [19th c.: orig. unkn.]

dink•y /díngkee/ *adj.* (**dink•i•er, dink•i•est**) *colloq.* 1 trifling; insignificant. 2 *Brit.* (esp. of a thing) neat and attractive; small; dainty. [Sc. *dink* neat, trim, of unkn. orig.]

din•ner /dínər/ *n.* 1 the main meal of the day, taken either at midday or in the evening. 2 a formal evening meal, often in honor of a person or event. [ME f. OF *diner, disner*: see DINE]

din•ner dance *n.* a formal dinner followed by dancing.

din•ner jack•et *n.* a man's, usu. black, formal jacket for evening wear; a tuxedo.

din•ner serv•ice *n.* a set of usu. matching dishes, etc., for serving a meal.

din•ner•ware /dínərwair/ *n.* tableware, usu. including plates, glassware, and cutlery.

di•no•saur /dínəsawr/ *n.* 1 an extinct reptile of the Mesozoic era, often of enormous size. 2 a large, unwieldy system or organization, esp. one not adapting to new conditions. □□ **di•no•sau•ri•an** *adj. & n.* [mod.L *dinosaurus* f. Gk *deinos* terrible + *sauros* lizard]. See illustration on following page.

di•no•there /dínətheer/ *n.* any elephantlike animal of the extinct genus *Deinotherium*, having downward-curving tusks. [mod.L *dinotherium* f. Gk *deinos* terrible + *thērion* wild beast]

dint /dint/ *n. & v.* ● *n.* 1 a dent. 2 *archaic* a blow or stroke. ● *v.tr.* mark with dints. □ **by dint of** by force or means of. [ME f. OE *dynt*, and partly f. cogn. ON *dyntr*: ult. orig. unkn.]

di•oc•e•san /dīósisən/ *adj. & n.* ● *adj.* of or concerning a diocese. ● *n.* the bishop of a diocese. [ME f. F *diocésain* f. LL *diocesanus* (as DIOCESE)]

di•o•cese /dīəsis, –sees, –seez/ *n.* a district under the pastoral care of a bishop. [ME f. OF *diocise* f. LL *diocesis* f. L *dioecesis* f. Gk *dioikēsis* administration (as DI-[3], *oikeō* inhabit)]

di•ode /dīód/ *n. Electronics* 1 a semiconductor allowing the flow of current in one direction only and having two terminals. 2 a thermionic valve having two electrodes. [DI-[1] + ELECTRODE]

di•oe•cious /dī-eéshəs/ *adj.* 1 *Bot.* having male and female organs on separate plants. 2 *Zool.* having the two sexes in separate individuals (cf. MONOECIOUS). [DI-[1] + Gk *–oikos* –housed]

di•ol /díawl, –ol/ *n. Chem.* any alcohol containing two hydroxyl groups in each molecule. [DI-[1] + –OL[1]]

Di•o•nys•i•ac /dīəníseeak/ *adj.* (also **Di•o•ny•sian** /–níshən, –nízhən, –níseeən/) 1 wildly sensual; unrestrained 2 (in Greek mythology) of or relating to Dionysus, the Greek god of wine, or his worship. [LL *Dionysiacus* f. L *Dionysus* f. Gk *Dionusos*]

Di•o•phan•tine e•qua•tion /dīōfántin, –tīn/ *n. Math.* an equation with integral coefficients for which integral solutions are required. [*Diophantus* of Alexandria, mathematician of uncert. date]

di•op•ter /dīóptər/ *n.* (*Brit.* **di•op•tre**) *Optics* a unit of refractive power of a lens, equal to the reciprocal of its focal length in meters. [F *dioptre* f. L *dioptra* f. Gk *dioptra*: see DIOPTRIC]

di•op•tric /dīóptrik/ *adj. Optics* 1 serving as a medium for sight; assisting sight by refraction (*dioptric glass; dioptric lens*). 2 of refraction; refractive. [Gk *dioptrikos* f. *dioptra* a kind of theodolite]

di•op•trics /dīóptriks/ *n. Optics* the part of optics dealing with refraction.

di•o•ram•a /dīərámə, –raámə/ *n.* 1 a scenic painting in which changes in color and direction of illumination simulate a sunrise, etc. 2 a small representation of a scene with three-dimensional figures, viewed through a window, etc. 3 a small-scale model or movie set, etc. □□ **di•o•ram•ic** /–rámik/ *adj.* [DI-[3] + Gk *horama* –*atos* f. *horaō* see]

di•o•rite /dīərīt/ *n.* a coarse-grained, plutonic igneous rock containing quartz. □□ **di•o•rit•ic** /–rítik/ *adj.* [F f. Gk *diorizō* distinguish]

di•ox•ane /dīóksayn/ *n.* (also **di•ox•an** /–óksən/) *Chem.* a colorless toxic liquid used as a solvent. ¶ Chem. formula: $C_4H_8O_2$.

di•ox•ide /dīóksīd/ *n. Chem.* an oxide containing two atoms of oxygen which are not linked together (*carbon dioxide*).

DIP /dip/ *n. Computing* a form of integrated circuit consisting of a small plastic or ceramic slab with two parallel rows of pins. [abbr. of *dual in-line package*]

dip. *abbr.* diploma.

dip /dip/ *v. & n.* ● *v.* (**dipped, dip•ping**) 1 *tr.* put or let down briefly into liquid, etc.; immerse. 2 *intr.* a go below a surface or level (*the sun dipped below the horizon*). b (of a level of income, activity, etc.) decline slightly, esp. briefly (*profits dipped in May*). 3 *intr.* extend downward; take or have a downward slope (*the road dips after the curve*). 4 *intr.* go under water and emerge quickly. 5 *intr.* (foll. by *into*) a read briefly from (a book, etc.). b take a cursory interest in (a subject). 6 (foll. by *into*) a *intr.* put a hand, ladle, etc., into a container to take something out. b *tr.* put (a hand, etc.) into a container to do this. c *intr.* spend from or make use of one's resources (*dipped into our savings*). 7 *tr. & intr.* lower or be lowered, esp. in salute. 8 *tr. Brit.* lower the beam of (a vehicle's headlights). 9 *tr.* color (a fabric) by immersing it in dye. 10 *tr.* wash (esp. sheep) by immersion in a vermin-killing liquid. 11 *tr.* make (a candle) by immersing a wick briefly in hot tallow. 12 *tr.* baptize by immersion. 13 *tr.* (often foll. by *up, out of*) remove or scoop up (liquid, grain, etc., or something from liquid). ● *n.* 1 an act of dipping or being dipped. 2 a liquid into which something is dipped. 3 a brief swim in the ocean, lake, etc. 4 a brief downward slope, followed by an upward one, in a road, etc. 5 a sauce or dressing into which food is dipped before eating. 6 a depression in the skyline. 7 *Astron. & Surveying* the apparent depression of the horizon from the line of observation, due to the curvature of the earth. 8 *Physics* the angle made with the horizontal at any point by the earth's magnetic field. 9 *Geol.* the angle a stratum makes with the horizon. 10 *sl.* a pickpocket. 11 a quantity dipped up. 12 a candle made by dipping. [OE *dyppan* f. Gmc: rel. to DEEP]

di•pep•tide /dīpéptīd/ *n. Biochem.* a peptide formed by the combination of two amino acids.

diph•the•ri•a /diftheéreeə, dip–/ *n.* an acute infectious bacterial disease with inflammation of a mucous membrane esp. of the throat, resulting in the formation of a false membrane causing difficulty in breathing and swallowing. □□ **diph•the•ri•al** *adj.* **diph•ther•ic** /–thérik/ *adj.* **diph•the•rit•ic** /–thərítik/ *adj.* **diph•the•roid**

See inside front cover for the **Pronunciation Guide** & **Symbols Key**.

pterodactyl

Jurassic and Cretaceous,
213-65 millon years ago

velociraptor

Cretaceous, 144-65 million
years ago

stegosaurus

Jurassic, 213-144 million
years ago

tyrannosaurus

Cretaceous, 144-65 million
years ago

triceratops

Cretaceous, 144-65 million
years ago

apatosaurus

Jurassic, 213-144 million
years ago

dinosaurs

/dífthəroyd, díp–/ adj. [mod.L f. F diphthérie, earlier diphthérite f. Gk diphthera skin, hide]

PRONUNCIATION TIP diphtheria

The proper way to pronounce this word is with the -ph sounding like an f. The pronunciation beginning with "dip-," however, has become so widespread in American English, even among medical professionals, that it is now considered an acceptable variant.

diph·thong /dífthawng, –thong, díp–/ n. **1** a speech sound in one syllable in which the articulation begins as for one vowel and moves as for another (as in coin, loud, and side). **2 a** a digraph representing the sound of a diphthong or single vowel (as in feat). **b** a compound vowel character; a ligature (as æ). □□ **diph·thon·gal** /–tháwnggəl, –thóng–/ adj. [F diphtongue f. LL diphthongus f. Gk diphthoggos (as DI-[1], phthoggos voice)]

diph·thong·ize /dífthawngīz, –thong–, díp–/ v.tr. pronounce as a diphthong. □□ **diph·thong·i·za·tion** n.

diplo- /díplō/ comb. form double. [Gk diplous double]

di·lo·coc·cus /díplōkókəs/ n. (pl. **dip·lo·coc·ci** /–sī, –kī/) Biol. any coccus that occurs mainly in pairs.

di·plod·o·cus /diplódəkəs, dī–/ n. a giant plant-eating dinosaur of the order Sauropoda, with a long neck and tail. [DIPLO- + Gk dokos wooden beam]

dip·loid /díployd/ adj. & n. Biol. • adj. (of an organism or cell) having two complete sets of chromosomes per cell. • n. a diploid cell or organism. [G (as DIPLO-, –OID)]

dip·loid·y /díploydee/ n. Biol. the condition of being diploid.

di·plo·ma /diplómə/ n. (pl. **di·plo·mas**) **1** a certificate of qualification awarded by a college, etc. **2** a document conferring an honor or privilege. **3** (pl. also **di·plo·ma·ta** /–mətə/) a state paper; an official document; a charter. □□ **di·plo·maed** /–məd/ adj. [L f. Gk diplōma –atos folded paper f. diploō to fold f. diplous double]

di·plo·ma·cy /diplóməsee/ n. **1 a** the management of international relations. **b** expertise in this. **2** the art of dealing with people in a sensitive and effective way; tact. [F diplomatie f. diplomatique DIPLOMATIC after aristocratic]

dip·lo·mat /dípləmat/ n. **1** an official representing a country abroad; a member of a diplomatic service. **2** a tactful person. [F diplomate, back-form. f. diplomatique: see DIPLOMATIC]

dip·lo·mate /dípləmayt/ n. a person who holds a diploma, esp. in medicine.

dip·lo·mat·ic /dípləmátik/ adj. **1 a** of or involved in diplomacy. **b** skilled in diplomacy. **2** tactful; adroit in personal relations. **3** (of an edition, etc.) exactly reproducing the original. □□ **dip·lo·mat·i·cal·ly** adv. [mod.L diplomaticus and F diplomatique f. L DIPLOMA]

dip·lo·mat·ic corps n. the body of diplomats residing in a particular country.

dip·lo·mat·ic im·mu·ni·ty n. the privilege of exemption from certain laws and taxes granted to diplomats by the country in which they are working.

dip·lo·mat·ic pouch n. a container in which official mail, etc., is dispatched to or from an embassy, not usu. subject to customs inspection.

dip·lo·mat·ic serv·ice n. the branch of public service concerned with the representation of a country abroad.

di·plo·ma·tist /diplómətist/ n. esp. Brit. = DIPLOMAT.

dip·lont /díplont/ n. Biol. an animal or plant which has a diploid number of chromosomes in its somatic cells. [DIPLO- + Gk ont- stem of ōn being]

dip·lo·tene /díplōteen/ n. Biol. a stage during the prophase of meiosis where paired chromosomes begin to separate. [DIPLO- + Gk tainia band]

di·po·lar /dípōlər/ adj. having two poles, as in a magnet.

di·pole /dípōl/ n. **1** Physics two equal and oppositely charged or magnetized poles separated by a distance. **2** Chem. a molecule in which a concentration of positive charges is separated from a concentration of negative charges. **3** an aerial consisting of a horizontal metal rod with a connecting wire at its center.

dip·per /dípər/ n. **1** a diving bird, Cinclus cinclus. Also called **water ouzel**. **2** a ladle. **3** colloq. an Anabaptist or Baptist.

dip·py /dípee/ adj. (**dip·pi·er, dip·pi·est**) sl. crazy; silly. [20th c.: orig. uncert.]

dip·so /dípsō/ n. (pl. ·**sos**) colloq. a dipsomaniac. [abbr.]

dip·so·ma·ni·a /dípsōmáyneeə/ n. an abnormal craving for alcohol. □□ **dip·so·ma·ni·ac** /–máyneeak/ n. [Gk dipso- f. dipsa thirst + –MANIA]

dip·stick /dípstik/ n. a graduated rod for measuring the depth of a liquid, esp. in a vehicle's engine.

DIP switch n. an arrangement of switches on a printer for selecting a printing mode (acronym for dual in-line package).

dip·ter·al /díptərəl/ adj. Archit. having a double peristyle. [L dipteros f. Gk (as DI-[1], pteron wing)]

dip·ter·an /díptərən/ n. & adj. • n. a dipterous insect. • adj. = DIPTEROUS 1. [mod.L diptera f. Gk diptera neut. pl. of dipterous two-winged (as DI-[2], pteron wing)]

dip·ter·ous /díptərəs/ adj. **1** (of an insect) of the order Diptera, having two membranous wings, e.g., the fly, gnat, or mosquito. **2** Bot. having two winglike appendages. [mod.L dipterus f. Gk dipteros: see DIPTERAN]

dip·tych /díptik/ n. **1** a painting, esp. an altarpiece, on two hinged, usu. wooden panels which may be closed like a book. **2** an ancient writing tablet consisting of two hinged leaves with waxed inner sides. [LL diptycha f. Gk diptukha (as DI-[1], ptukhē fold)]

dire /dīr/ adj. **1 a** calamitous; dreadful (in dire straits). **b** ominous (dire warnings). **2** urgent (in dire need). □□ **dire·ly** adv. **dire·ness** n. [L dirus]

di·rect /dirékt, dī–/ adj., adv., & v. • adj. **1** extending or moving in a straight line or by the shortest route; not crooked or circuitous. **2 a** straightforward; going straight to the point. **b** frank; not ambiguous. **3** without intermediaries or the intervention of other factors (direct rule; the direct result; made a direct approach). **4** (of descent) lineal; not collateral. **5** exact; complete; greatest possible (esp. where contrast is implied) (the direct opposite). **6** Mus. (of an interval or chord) not inverted. **7** Astron. (of planetary, etc., motion) proceeding from East to West; not retrograde. • adv. **1** in a direct way or manner; without an intermediary or intervening factor (dealt with them direct). **2** frankly; without evasion. **3** by a direct route (send it direct to Chicago). • v.tr. **1** control; guide; govern the movements of. **2** (foll. by to + infin., or that + clause) give a formal order or command to. **3** (foll. by to) **a** address or give indications for the delivery of (a letter, etc.). **b** tell or show (a person) the way to a destination. **4** (foll. by at, to, toward) **a** point, aim, or cause (a blow or missile) to move in a certain direction. **b** point or address (one's attention, a remark, etc.). **5** guide as an adviser, as a principle, etc. (I do as duty directs me). **6 a** (also absol.) supervise the performing, staging, etc., of (a movie, play, etc.). **b** supervise the performance of (an actor, etc.). **7** (also absol.) guide the performance of (a group of musicians), esp. as a participant. □□ **di·rect·ness** n. [ME f. L directus past part. of dirigere direct- (as DI-[2], regere put straight)]

di·rect ac·cess n. the facility of retrieving data immediately from any part of a computer file.

di·rect ac·tion n. action such as a strike or sabotage directly affecting the community and meant to reinforce demands on a government, employer, etc.

di·rect ad·dress n. Computing an address which specifies the location of data to be used in an operation. (see ADDRESS n. 1c)

di·rect cur·rent n. (¶ Abbr.: DC, d.c.) an electric current flowing in one direction only.

di·rec·tion /dirékshən, dī–/ n. **1** the act or process of directing; supervision. **2** (usu. in pl.) an order or instruction, esp. each of a set guiding use of equipment, etc. **3 a** the course or line along which a person or thing moves or looks, or which must be taken to reach a destination (sailed in an easterly direction). **b** (in pl.) instructions on how to reach a destination or how to do something (give me directions to your house; directions for making puff pastry). **c** the point to or from which a person or thing moves or looks. **4** the tendency or scope of a theme, subject, or inquiry. □□ **di·rec·tion·less** adj. [ME f. F direction or L directio (as DIRECT)]

di·rec·tion·al /dirékshənəl, dī–/ adj. **1** of or indicating direction. **2** Electronics **a** concerned with the transmission of radio or sound waves in a particular direction. **b** (of equipment) designed to receive radio or sound waves most effectively from a particular direction or directions and not others. □□ **di·rec·tion·al·i·ty** /–álitee/ n. **di·rec·tion·al·ly** adv.

di·rec·tion find·er n. a system of antennas for determining the source of radio waves, esp. as an aid in navigation.

di·rec·tive /diréktiv, dī–/ n. & adj. • n. a general instruction from one in authority. • adj. serving to direct. [ME f. med.L directivus (as DIRECT)]

di·rect·ly /diréktlee, dī–/ adv. & conj. • adv. **1 a** at once; without delay. **b** presently; shortly. **2** exactly; immediately (directly opposite; directly after lunch). **3** in a direct manner. • conj. Brit. colloq. as soon as (will tell you directly they come).

di·rect meth·od n. a system of teaching a foreign language using only that language and without the study of formal grammar.

di·rect ob·ject n. Gram. a noun phrase denoting a person or thing that is the recipient of the action of a transitive verb, e.g., the dog in he fed the dog.

Di·rec·toire /díréktwaar/ adj. Needlework & Art in imitation of styles prevalent during the French Directory. [F (as DIRECTORY)]

di·rec·tor /diréktər, dī–/ n. **1** a person who directs or controls something. **2** a member of the managing board of a commercial company. **3** a person who directs a movie, play, etc., esp. professionally. **4** a person acting as spiritual adviser. **5** = CONDUCTOR 1. □□ **di·rec·to·ri·al** /–táwreeəl/ adj. **di·rec·tor·ship** n. (esp. in sense 2). [AF directour f. LL director governor (as DIRECT)]

di·rec·to·rate /diréktərət, di–/ *n.* **1** a board of directors. **2** the office of director.

di·rec·tor gen·er·al *n.* the chief executive of a large (esp. public) organization.

di·rec·to·ry /diréktəree, di–/ *n.* (*pl.* **·ries**) **1** a book listing alphabetically or thematically a particular group of individuals (e.g., telephone subscribers) or organizations with various details. **2 a** (**Directory**) *hist.* the revolutionary executive of five persons in power in France 1795–99. **b** a body of directors. **3** a book of rules, esp. for the order of private or public worship. [LL *directorium* (as DIRECT)]

di·rect pro·por·tion *n.* the relation between quantities whose ratio is constant (*sensors emit an electronic signal in direct proportion to the amount of light detected.*

di·rec·trix /diréktriks, di–/ *n.* (*pl.* **directrixes** or **directrices** /–triseéz/) *Geom.* a fixed line used in describing a curve or surface. [med.L f. LL *director*: see DIRECTOR, –TRIX]

di·rect speech *n.* the reporting of speech by repeating the actual words of a speaker, e.g., *"I'm going," she said.* (cf. REPORTED SPEECH).

di·rect tax *n.* a tax, such as income tax, that is levied on the income or profits of the person who pays it, rather than on goods or services.

dire·ful /dírfŏŏl/ *adj. literary* terrible; dreadful. □□ **dire·ful·ly** *adv.* [DIRE + –FUL]

dirge /dərj/ *n.* **1** a lament for the dead, esp. forming part of a funeral service. **2** any mournful song or lament. □□ **dirge·ful** *adj.* [ME f. L *dirige* (imper.) direct, the first word in the Latin antiphon (from Ps. 5:8) in the matins part of the Office for the Dead]

dir·ham /dirám, dírəm/ *n.* the principal monetary unit of Morocco and the United Arab Emirates. [Arab. f. L DRACHMA]

dir·i·gi·ble /dírijibəl, dirij–/ *adj. & n.* ● *adj.* capable of being guided. ● *n.* a dirigible balloon or airship. [L *dirigere* arrange, direct: see DIRECT]

dir·i·ment /dírəmənt/ *adj. Law* nullifying. [L *dirimere* f. *dir–* = DIS– + *emere* take]

dir·i·ment im·ped·i·ment *n.* a factor (e.g., the existence of a prior marriage) rendering a marriage null and void from the beginning.

dirk /dərk/ *n.* a long dagger, esp. as formerly worn by Scottish Highlanders. [17th-c. *durk*, of unkn. orig.]

dirn·dl /dórnd'l/ *n.* **1** a woman's dress styled in imitation of Alpine peasant costume, with close-fitting bodice, tight waistband, and full skirt. **2** a full skirt of this kind. [G dial., dimin. of *Dirne* girl]

dirt /dərt/ *n.* **1** unclean matter that soils. **2 a** earth; soil. **b** earth; cinders, etc., used to make a surface for a road, etc. (usu. *attrib.*: *dirt track*; *dirt road*). **3 a** foul or malicious words or talk. **b** scurrilous information; scandal; gossip; the lowdown. **4** excrement. **5** a dirty condition. **6** a person or thing considered worthless. □ **do a person dirt** *sl.* harm or injure a person's reputation maliciously. **eat dirt 1** suffer insults, etc., without retaliating. **2** make a humiliating confession. **treat like dirt** treat (a person) contemptuously; abuse. [ME f. ON *drit* excrement]

dirt bike *n.* a motorcycle designed for use on rough terrain, such as unpaved roads or tracks.

dirt cheap *n. colloq.* extremely cheap.

dirt poor *adj.* extremely poor; lacking basic necessities.

dirt·y /dórtee/ *adj., adv., & v.* ● *adj.* (**dirtier, dirtiest**) **1** soiled; unclean. **2** causing one to become dirty (*a dirty job*). **3** sordid; lewd; morally illicit or questionable (*dirty joke*). **4** unpleasant; nasty. **5** dishonest; dishonorable; unfair (*dirty play*). **6** (of weather) rough; stormy. **7** (of a color) not pure nor clear; dingy. **8** *colloq.* (of a nuclear weapon) producing considerable radioactive fallout. ● *adv. Brit. sl.* (with adjectives expressing magnitude) very (*a dirty great diamond*). ● *v.tr. & intr.* (**·ies, ·ied**) make or become dirty. □ **the dirty end of the stick** *colloq.* the difficult or unpleasant part of an undertaking, situation, etc. **do the dirty on** esp. *Brit. colloq.* play a mean trick on. □□ **dirt·i·ly** *adv.* **dirt·i·ness** *n.*

dirt·y lin·en *n.* (also **dirty laundry**) *colloq.* intimate secrets, esp. of a scandalous nature.

dirt·y look *n. colloq.* a look of disapproval, anger, or disgust.

dirt·y trick *n.* **1** a dishonorable and deceitful act. **2** (in *pl.*) underhand political activity, esp. to discredit an opponent.

dirt·y word *n.* **1** an offensive or taboo word. **2** a word for something which is disapproved of (*profit is a dirty word*).

dirt·y work *n.* **1** unpleasant tasks. **2** dishonorable or illegal activity, esp. done clandestinely.

dis /dis/ *v.tr.* (also **diss**) *sl.* (**dissed, dissing**) act or speak in a disrespectful way toward. [shortened f. DISRESPECT]

dis– /dis/ *prefix* forming nouns, adjectives, and verbs: **1** expressing negation (*dishonest*). **2** indicating reversal or absence of an action or state (*disengage*; *disbelieve*). **3** indicating removal of a thing or quality (*dismember*; *disable*). **4** indicating separation (*distinguish*; *dispose*). **5** indicating completeness or intensification of the action (*disembowel*; *disgruntled*). **6** indicating expulsion from (*disbar*). [L *dis–*, sometimes through OF *des–*]

dis·a·bil·i·ty /dísəbílitee/ *n.* (*pl.* **·ties**) **1** physical incapacity, either congenital or caused by injury, disease, etc. **2** a lack of some asset, quality, or attribute, that prevents one's doing something. **3** a legal disqualification.

dis·a·ble /disáybəl/ *v.tr.* **1** render unable to function; deprive of an ability. **2** (often as **disabled** *adj.*) deprive of or reduce the power to walk or do other normal activities, esp. by crippling. □□ **dis·a·ble·ment** *n.*

dis·a·buse /dísəbyŏŏz/ *v.tr.* **1** (foll. by *of*) free from a mistaken idea. **2** disillusion; undeceive.

dis·ac·cord /dísakáwrd/ *n. & v.* ● *n.* disagreement; disharmony. ● *v.intr.* (usu. foll. by *with*) disagree; be at odds. [ME f. F *désaccorder* (as ACCORD)]

dis·ad·van·tage /dísədvántij/ *n. & v.* ● *n.* **1** an unfavorable circumstance or condition. **2** damage to one's interest or reputation. ● *v.tr.* cause disadvantage to. □ **at a disadvantage** in an unfavorable position or aspect. [ME f. OF *desavantage*: see ADVANTAGE]

dis·ad·van·taged /dísədvántijd/ *adj.* placed in unfavorable circumstances (esp. of a person lacking the normal social opportunities).

dis·ad·van·ta·geous /disádvəntáyjəs, dísad–/ *adj.* **1** involving disadvantage or discredit. **2** derogatory. □□ **dis·ad·van·ta·geous·ly** *adv.*

dis·af·fect·ed /dísəféktid/ *adj.* **1** disloyal, esp. to one's superiors. **2** estranged; no longer friendly; discontented. □□ **dis·af·fect·ed·ly** *adv.* [past part. of *disaffect* (v.), orig. = dislike, disorder (as DIS–, AFFECT²)]

dis·af·fec·tion /dísəfékshən/ *n.* **1** disloyalty. **2** political discontent.

dis·af·fil·i·ate /dísəfileeayt/ *v.* **1** *tr.* end the affiliation of. **2** *intr.* end one's affiliation. **3** *tr. & intr.* detach. □□ **dis·af·fil·i·a·tion** /–leeáyshən/ *n.*

dis·af·firm /dísəfərm/ *v.tr. Law* **1** reverse (a previous decision). **2** repudiate (a settlement). □□ **dis·af·fir·ma·tion** /–máyshən/ *n.*

dis·af·for·est /dísəfáwrist, –fór–/ *v.tr. Brit.* **1** clear of forests or trees. **2** reduce from the legal status of forest to that of ordinary land. □□ **dis·af·for·est·a·tion** *n.* [ME f. AL *disafforestare* (as DIS–, AFFOREST)]

dis·a·gree /dísəgreé/ *v.intr.* (**·a·grees**, **·a·greed**, **·a·gree·ing**) (often foll. by *with*) **1** hold a different opinion. **2** quarrel. **3** (of factors or circumstances) not correspond. **4** have an adverse effect upon (a person's health, digestion, etc.). □□ **dis·a·gree·ment** *n.* [ME f. OF *desagreer* (as DIS–, AGREE)]

dis·a·gree·a·ble /dísəgreéəbəl/ *adj.* **1** unpleasant; not to one's liking. **2** quarrelsome; rude or bad-tempered. □□ **dis·a·gree·a·ble·ness** *n.* **dis·a·gree·a·bly** *adv.* [ME f. OF *desagreable* (as DIS–, AGREEABLE)]

dis·al·low /dísəlów/ *v.tr.* refuse to allow or accept as valid; prohibit. □□ **dis·al·low·ance** *n.* [ME f. OF *desalouer* (as DIS–, ALLOW)]

dis·am·big·u·ate /dísambígyŏŏ-ayt/ *v.tr.* remove ambiguity from. □□ **dis·am·big·u·a·tion** /–áyshən/ *n.*

dis·a·men·i·ty /dísəménitee/ *n.* (*pl.* **·ties**) an unpleasant feature (of a place, etc.); a disadvantage.

dis·ap·pear /dísəpeér/ *v.intr.* **1** cease to be visible; pass from sight. **2** cease to exist or be in circulation or use (*rotary telephones had all but disappeared*). □□ **dis·ap·pear·ance** *n.*

dis·ap·point /dísəpóynt/ *v.tr.* **1** (also *absol.*) fail to fulfill a desire or expectation of (a person). **2** frustrate (hopes, etc.); cause the failure of (a plan, etc.). □ **be disappointed** (foll. by *with, at, in,* or *to* + infin., or *that* + clause) fail to have one's expectation, etc., fulfilled in some regard (*was disappointed in you; disappointed at the result; am disappointed to be last*). □□ **dis·ap·point·ed** *adj.* **dis·ap·point·ed·ly** *adv.* **dis·ap·point·ing** *adj.* **dis·ap·point·ing·ly** *adv.* [ME f. F *désappointer* (as DIS–, APPOINT)]

dis·ap·point·ment /dísəpóyntmənt/ *n.* **1** an event, thing, or person that disappoints. **2** a feeling of distress, vexation, etc., resulting from this (*I cannot hide my disappointment*).

dis·ap·pro·ba·tion /dísáprəbáyshən/ *n.* strong (esp. moral) disapproval.

dis·ap·prove /dísəprŏŏv/ *v.* **1** *intr.* (usu. foll. by *of*) have or express an unfavorable opinion. **2** *tr.* be displeased with. □□ **dis·ap·prov·al** *n.* **dis·ap·prov·er** *n.* **dis·ap·prov·ing** *adj.* **dis·ap·prov·ing·ly** *adv.*

dis·arm /disaárm/ *v.* **1** *tr.* **a** take weapons away from (a person, nation, etc.) (often foll. by *of: were disarmed of their rifles*). **b** *Fencing*, etc., deprive of a weapon. **2** *tr.* deprive (a ship, etc.) of its means of defense. **3** *intr.* (of a nation, etc.) disband or reduce its armed forces. **4** *tr.* remove the fuse from (a bomb, etc.). **5** *tr.* deprive of the power to injure. **6** *tr.* pacify or allay the hostility or suspicions of; mollify; placate. □□ **dis·arm·er** *n.* **dis·arm·ing** *adj.* (esp. in sense 6). **dis·arm·ing·ly** *adv.* [ME f. OF *desarmer* (as DIS–, ARM²)]

dis·ar·ma·ment /disaárməmənt/ *n.* the reduction by a nation of its military forces and weapons.

dis·ar·range /dísəráynj/ *v.tr.* bring into disorder. □□ **dis·ar·range·ment** *n.*

dis·ar·ray /dísəráy/ *n. & v.* ● *n.* (often prec. by *in, into*) disorder; confusion (esp. among people). ● *v.tr.* throw into disorder.

dis·ar·tic·u·late /dísaartíkyəlayt/ *v.tr. & intr.* separate at the joints. □□ **dis·ar·tic·u·la·tion** /–láyshən/ *n.*

dis·as·sem·ble /dísəsémbəl/ *v.tr.* take (a machine, etc.) to pieces. □□ **dis·as·sem·bly** *n.*

dis•as•so•ci•ate /dísəsôsheeayt, –seeayt/ *v.tr. & intr.* = DISSOCIATE. □□ **dis•as•so•ci•a•tion** /–áyshən/ *n.*

dis•as•ter /dizástər/ *n.* **1** a great or sudden misfortune. **2 a** a complete failure. **b** a person or enterprise ending in failure. □□ **dis•as•trous** *adj.* **dis•as•trous•ly** *adv.* [orig. 'unfavorable aspect of a star,' f. F *désastre* or It. *disastro* (as DIS-, *astro* f. L *astrum* star)]

PRONUNCIATION TIP | **disastrous**

Avoid pronouncing this word with a fourth syllable ("dih-ZAS-ter-us").

dis•a•vow /dísəvów/ *v.tr.* disclaim knowledge of, responsibility for, or belief in. □□ **dis•a•vow•al** *n.* [ME f. OF *desavouer* (as DIS-, AVOW)]

dis•band /disbánd/ *v.* **1** *intr.* (of an organized group, etc.) cease to work or act together; disperse. **2** *tr.* cause (such a group) to disband. □□ **dis•band•ment** *n.* [obs. F *desbander* (as DIS-, BAND[1] *n.* 6)]

dis•bar /disbaár/ *v.tr.* (**dis•barred, dis•bar•ring**) deprive (an attorney) of the right to practice; expel from the bar. □□ **dis•bar•ment** *n.*

dis•be•lieve /dísbileév/ *v.* **1** *tr.* be unable or unwilling to believe (a person or statement). **2** *intr.* have no faith. □□ **dis•be•lief** /–leéf/ *n.* **dis•be•liev•er** *n.* **dis•be•liev•ing•ly** *adv.*

dis•bound /disbównd/ *adj.* (of a pamphlet, etc.) removed from a bound volume.

dis•bud /disbúd/ *v.tr.* (**dis•bud•ded, dis•bud•ding**) remove (esp. superfluous) buds from.

dis•bur•den /disbórd'n/ *v.tr.* **1** (often foll. by *of*) relieve (a person, one's mind, etc.) of a burden. **2** get rid of; discharge (a duty, anxiety, etc.).

dis•burse /disbórs/ *v.* **1** *tr.* expend (money). **2** *tr.* defray (a cost). **3** *intr.* pay money. □□ **dis•bur•sal** *n.* **dis•burse•ment** *n.* **dis•burs•er** *n.* [OF *desbourser* (as DIS-, BOURSE)]

disc var. of DISK.

dis•calced /diskálst/ *adj.* (of a friar or a nun) barefoot or wearing only sandals. [var. of *discalceated* (after F *déchaux*) f. L *discalceatus* (as DIS-, *calceatus* f. *calceus* shoe)]

dis•card *v. & n.* ● *v.tr.* /diskaárd/ **1** reject or get rid of as unwanted or superfluous. **2** (also *absol.*) *Cards* remove or put aside (a card) from one's hand. ● *n.* /dískaard/ (often in *pl.*) a discarded item, esp. a card in a card game. □□ **dis•card•a•ble** *adj.* [DIS- + CARD[1]]

dis•car•nate /diskaárnət, –nayt/ *adj.* having no physical body; separated from the flesh. [DIS-, L *caro carnis* flesh]

dis•cern /disórn/ *v.tr.* **1** perceive clearly with the mind or the senses. **2** make out by thought or by gazing, listening, etc. □□ **dis•cern•er** *n.* **dis•cern•i•ble** *adj.* **dis•cern•i•bly** *adv.* [ME f. OF *discerner* f. L (as DIS-, *cernere cret-* separate)]

dis•cern•ing /disórning/ *adj.* having or showing good judgment or insight. □□ **dis•cern•ing•ly** *adv.*

dis•cern•ment /disórnmənt/ *n.* good judgment or insight.

dis•cerp•ti•ble /disórptibəl/ *adj. literary* able to be plucked apart; divisible. □□ **dis•cerp•ti•bil•i•ty** *n.* [L *discerpere discerpt-* (as DIS-, *carpere* pluck)]

dis•cerp•tion /disórpshən/ *n. archaic* **1 a** pulling apart; severance. **b** an instance of this. **2** a severed piece. [LL *discerptio* (as DIS-CERPTIBLE)]

dis•charge *v. & n.* ● *v.* /dischaárj/ **1** *tr.* **a** let go or, release, esp. from a duty, commitment, or period of confinement. **b** relieve (a bankrupt) of residual liability. **2** *tr.* dismiss from office, employment, army commission, etc. **3** *tr.* **a** fire (a gun, etc.). **b** (of a gun, etc.) fire (a bullet, etc.). **4 a** *tr.* (also *absol.*) pour out or cause to pour out (pus, liquid, etc.) (*the wound was discharging*). **b** *tr.* throw; eject (*discharged a stone at the gopher*). **c** *tr.* utter (abuse, etc.). **d** *intr.* (foll. by *into*) (of a river, etc.) flow into (esp. the sea). **5** *tr.* **a** carry out; perform (a duty or obligation). **b** relieve oneself of (a financial commitment) (*discharged his debt*). **6** *tr.* *Law* cancel (an order of court). **7** *tr.* *Physics* release an electrical charge from. **8** *tr.* **a** relieve (a ship, etc.) of its cargo. **b** unload (a cargo) from a ship. ● *n.* /díschaarj, dischaárj/ **1** the act or an instance of discharging; the process of being discharged. **2** a dismissal, esp. from the armed services. **3 a** a release, exemption, acquittal, etc. **b** a written certificate of release, etc. **4** an act of firing a gun, etc. **5 a** an emission (of pus, liquid, etc.). **b** the liquid or matter so discharged. **6** (usu. foll. by *of*) **a** the payment (of a debt). **b** the performance (of a duty, etc.). **7** *Physics* **a** the release of a quantity of electric charge from an object. **b** a flow of electricity through the air or other gas, esp. when accompanied by the emission of light. **c** the conversion of chemical energy in a cell into electrical energy. **8** the unloading (of a ship or a cargo). □□ **dis•charge•a•ble** *adj.* **dis•charg•er** *n.* (in sense 7 of *v.*). [ME f. OF *descharger* (as DIS-, CHARGE)]

dis•ci•ple /disípəl/ *n.* **1** a follower or pupil of a leader, teacher, philosophy, etc. (*a disciple of Zen Buddhism*). **2** any early believer in Christ, esp. one of the twelve Apostles. □□ **dis•ci•ple•ship** *n.* **dis•cip•u•lar** /disípyo͞olər/ *adj.* [OE *discipul* f. L *discipulus* f. *discere* learn]

dis•ci•pli•nar•i•an /dísiplináireeən/ *n.* a person who upholds or practices firm discipline (*a strict disciplinarian*).

dis•ci•pli•nar•y /dísiplínéree/ *adj.* of, promoting, or enforcing discipline. [med.L *disciplinarius* (as DISCIPLINE)]

dis•ci•pline /dísiplin/ *n. & v.* ● *n.* **1 a** control or order exercised over people or animals, esp. children, prisoners, military personnel, church members, etc. **b** the system of rules used to maintain this control. **c** the behavior of groups subjected to such rules (*poor discipline in the ranks*). **2 a** mental, moral, or physical training. **b** adversity as used to bring about such training (*left the course because he couldn't take the discipline*). **3** a branch of instruction or learning (*philosophy is a hard discipline*). **4** punishment. **5** *Eccl.* mortification by physical self-punishment, esp. scourging. ● *v.tr.* **1** punish; chastise. **2** bring under control by training in obedience; drill. □□ **dis•ci•plin•a•ble** *adj.* **dis•ci•pli•nal** /dísiplín'l, díisiplín'l/ *adj.* [ME f. OF *discipliner* or LL & med.L *disciplinare, disciplina* f. *discipulus* DISCIPLE]

dis•claim /diskláym/ *v.tr.* **1** deny or disown (*disclaim all responsibility*). **2** (often *absol.*) *Law* renounce a legal claim to (property, etc.). [ME f. AF *desclaim-* stressed stem of *desclamer* (as DIS-, CLAIM)]

dis•claim•er /diskláymər/ *n.* a renunciation or disavowal, esp. of responsibility. [ME f. AF (= DISCLAIM as noun)]

dis•close /disklóz/ *v.tr.* **1** make known; reveal (*disclosed the truth*). **2** remove the cover from; expose to view. □□ **dis•clos•er** *n.* [ME f. OF *desclos-* stem of *desclore* f. Gallo-Roman f. L (as DIS-, CLOSE[2])]

dis•clo•sure /disklózhər/ *n.* **1** the act or an instance of disclosing; the process of being disclosed. **2** something disclosed; a revelation. [DISCLOSE + –URE after *closure*]

dis•co /dískō/ *n. & v. colloq.* ● *n.* (*pl.* **•cos**) = DISCOTHEQUE. ● *v.intr.* (**•coes, •coed**) **1** attend a discotheque. **2** dance to disco music (*discoed the night away*). [abbr.]

dis•cob•o•lus /diskóbələs/ *n.* (*pl.* **dis•cob•o•li** /–lī/) **1** a discus thrower in ancient Greece. **2** a statue of a discobolus. [L f. Gk *diskobolos* f. *diskos* DISCUS + –*bolos* –throwing f. *ballō* to throw]

dis•cog•ra•phy /diskógrəfee/ *n.* (*pl.* **•phies**) **1** a descriptive catalog of recordings, esp. of a particular performer or composer. **2** the study of recordings. □□ **dis•cog•ra•pher** *n.* [DISC + –GRAPHY after *biography*]

dis•coid /dískoyd/ *adj.* disk-shaped. [Gk *diskoeidēs* (as DISCUS, –OID)]

dis•col•or /diskúlər/ *v.tr. & intr.* (*Brit.* **dis•col•our**) spoil or cause to spoil the color of; stain; tarnish. □□ **dis•col•or•a•tion** *n.* [ME f. OF *descolorer* or med.L *discolorare* (as DIS-, COLOR)]

dis•com•bob•u•late /diskəmbóbyəlayt/ *v.tr. joc.* disturb; disconcert. [prob. based on *discompose* or *discomfit*]

dis•com•fit /diskúmfit/ *v.tr.* **1 a** disconcert or baffle. **b** thwart. **2** *archaic* defeat in battle. □□ **dis•com•fi•ture** *n.* [ME f. OF *disconfit* f. OF past part. of *desconfire* f. Rmc (as DIS-, L *conficere* put together: see CONFECTION)]

dis•com•fort /diskúmfərt/ *n. & v.* ● *n.* **1 a** a lack of ease; slight pain (*tight collar caused discomfort*). **b** mental uneasiness (*his presence caused her discomfort*). **2** a lack of comfort. ● *v.tr.* make uneasy. [ME f. OF *desconfort(er)* (as DIS-, COMFORT)]

dis•com•mode /diskəmód/ *v.tr.* inconvenience (a person, etc.). □□ **dis•com•mo•di•ous** *adj.* [obs. F *discommoder* var. of *incommoder* (as DIS-, INCOMMODE)]

dis•com•pose /dískəmpóz/ *v.tr.* disturb the composure of; agitate; disturb. □□ **dis•com•po•sure** /–pózhər/ *n.*

dis•co mu•sic *n.* pop music intended mainly for dancing to at discos, typically soul-influenced and melodic with a regular bass beat, popular particularly in the late 1970s.

dis•con•cert /dískənsórt/ *v.tr.* **1** (often as **disconcerted** *adj.*) disturb the composure of; agitate; fluster (*disconcerted by his expression*). **2** spoil or upset (plans, etc.). □□ **dis•con•cert•ed•ly** *adv.* **dis•con•cert•ing** *adj.* **dis•con•cert•ing•ly** *adv.* **dis•con•cer•tion** /–sórshən/ *n.* **dis•con•cert•ment** *n.* [obs. F *desconcerter* (as DIS-, CONCERT)]

dis•con•firm /dískənfórm/ *v.tr. formal* disprove or tend to disprove (a hypothesis, etc.). □□ **dis•con•fir•ma•tion** /–kónfərmáyshən/ *n.*

dis•con•form•i•ty /dískənfáwrmitee/ *n.* (*pl.* **•ties**) **1 a** a lack of conformity. **b** an instance of this. **2** *Geol.* a difference of plane between two parallel, approximately horizontal sets of strata.

dis•con•nect /dískənékt/ *v.tr.* **1** (often foll. by *from*) break the connection of (things, ideas, etc.). **2** put (an electrical device) out of action by disconnecting the parts, esp. by pulling out the plug.

dis•con•nect•ed /dískənéktid/ *adj.* **1** not connected; detached; separated. **2** (of speech, writing, argument, etc.) incoherent and illogical. □□ **dis•con•nect•ed•ly** *adv.* **dis•con•nect•ed•ness** *n.*

dis•con•nec•tion /dískənékshən/ *n.* the act or an instance of disconnecting; the state of being disconnected.

dis•con•so•late /diskónsələt/ *adj.* **1** forlorn or inconsolable. **2** unhappy or disappointed. □□ **dis•con•so•late•ly** *adv.* **dis•con•so•late•ness** *n.* **dis•con•so•la•tion** /–láyshən/ *n.* [ME f. med.L *disconsolatus* (as DIS-, *consolatus* past part. of L *consolari* console)]

dis•con•tent /dískəntént/ *n., adj., & v.* ● *n.* lack of contentment; restlessness, dissatisfaction. ● *adj.* dissatisfied (*was discontent with his lot*). ● *v.tr.* (esp. as **discontented** *adj.*) make dissatisfied. □□ **dis•con•tent•ed•ly** *adv.* **dis•con•tent•ed•ness** *n.* **dis•con•tent•ment** *n.*

dis·con·tin·ue /dískəntínyōō/ v. (·con·tin·ues, ·con·tin·ued, ·con·tin·u·ing) **1** intr. & tr. cease or cause to cease to exist or be made (a discontinued line). **2** tr. give up; cease from (discontinued his visits). **3** tr. cease taking or paying (a newspaper, a subscription, etc.). □□ **dis·con·tin·u·ance** n. **dis·con·tin·u·a·tion** n. [ME f. OF discontinuer f. med.L discontinuare (as DIS-, CONTINUE)]

dis·con·tin·u·ous /dískəntínyōōəs/ adj. lacking continuity in space or time; intermittent. □□ **dis·con·ti·nu·i·ty** /–kontinóō-itee, –nyóō–/ n. **dis·con·tin·u·ous·ly** adv. [med.L discontinuus (as DIS-, CONTINUOUS)]

dis·cord n. & v. ● n. /dískawrd/ **1** disagreement; strife. **2** harsh clashing noise; clangor. **3** Mus. **a** a lack of harmony between notes sounding together. **b** an unpleasing or unfinished chord needing to be completed by another. **c** any interval except unison, an octave, a perfect fifth and fourth, a major and minor third and sixth, and their octaves. **d** a single note dissonant with another. ● v.intr. /diskáwrd/ **1** (usu. foll. by with) **a** disagree or quarrel. **b** be different or inconsistent. **2** jar; clash; be dissonant. [ME f. OF descord, (n.), descorder (v.) f. L discordare f. discors discordant (as DIS-, cor cord- heart)]

dis·cord·ant /diskáwrd'nt/ adj. (usu. foll. by to, from, with) **1** disagreeing; at variance. **2** (of sounds) not in harmony; dissonant. □□ **dis·cord·ance** /–d'ns/ n. **dis·cor·dan·cy** n. **dis·cord·ant·ly** adv. [ME f. OF, part. of discorder: see DISCORD]

dis·co·theque /dískəték/ n. **1** a club, etc., for dancing to recorded popular music. **2 a** the professional lighting and sound equipment used at a discotheque. **b** a business that provides this. **3** a party with dancing to popular music, esp. using such equipment. [F, = record library]

dis·count n. & v. ● n. /dískownt/ **1** a deduction from a bill or amount due given esp. in consideration of prompt or advance payment or to a special class of buyers. **2** a deduction from the amount of a bill of exchange, etc., by a person who gives value for it before it is due. **3** the act or an instance of discounting. ● v.tr. /diskównt/ **1** disregard as being unreliable or unimportant (discounted his story). **2** reduce the effect of (an event, etc.) by previous action. **3** detract from; lessen; deduct (esp. an amount from a bill, etc.). **4** give or get the present worth of (a bill not yet due). □ **at a discount 1** below the nominal or usual price (cf. PREMIUM). **2** not in demand; depreciated. □□ **dis·count·a·ble** adj. **dis·count·er** n. [obs. F descompte, –conte, descompter or It. (di)scontare (as DIS-, COUNT¹)]

dis·coun·te·nance /diskówntinəns/ v.tr. **1** (esp. in passive) disconcert (was discountenanced by his abruptness). **2** refuse to countenance; show disapproval of.

dis·count house n. = DISCOUNT STORE.

dis·count rate n. the minimum interest rate set by the Federal Reserve for lending to other banks.

dis·count store n. a store, etc., that sells goods at less than the normal retail price.

dis·cour·age /diskórij, –kúr–/ v.tr. **1** deprive of courage, confidence, or energy. **2** (usu. foll. by from) dissuade (discouraged her from going). **3** inhibit or seek to prevent (an action, etc.) by showing disapproval; oppose (smoking is discouraged). □□ **dis·cour·age·ment** n. **dis·cour·ag·ing·ly** adv. [ME f. OF descouragier (as DIS-, COURAGE)]

dis·course n. & v. ● n. /dískawrs/ **1** literary **a** conversation; talk. **b** a dissertation or treatise on an academic subject. **c** a lecture or sermon. **2** Linguistics a connected series of utterances; a text. ● v. /diskórs/ **1** intr. talk; converse. **2** intr. (usu. foll. by of, on, upon) speak or write learnedly or at length (on a subject). **3** tr. archaic give forth (music, etc.). [ME f. L discursus (as DIS-, COURSE): (v.) partly after F discourir]

dis·cour·te·ous /diskórteeəs/ adj. impolite; rude. □□ **dis·cour·te·ous·ly** adv. **dis·cour·te·ous·ness** n.

dis·cour·te·sy /diskórtəsee/ n. (pl. ·sies) **1** bad manners; rudeness. **2** an impolite act or remark.

dis·cov·er /diskúvər/ v.tr. **1** (often foll. by that + clause) **a** find out or become aware of, whether by research or searching or by chance (discovered a new entrance; discovered that they had been overpaid). **b** be the first to find or find out (who discovered America?). **c** devise or pioneer (discover new techniques). **2** give (check) in a game of chess by removing one's own obstructing piece. **3** (in show business) find and promote as a new singer, actor, etc. **4** archaic **a** make known. **b** exhibit; manifest. **c** disclose; betray. **d** catch sight of; espy. □□ **dis·cov·er·a·ble** adj. **dis·cov·er·er** n. [ME f. OF descovrir f. LL discooperire (as DIS-, COVER)]

dis·cov·er·y /diskúvəree/ n. (pl. ·ies) **1 a** the act or process of discovering or being discovered. **b** an instance of this (the discovery of a new planet). **2** a person or thing discovered. **3** Law the compulsory disclosure, by a party to an action, of facts or documents on which the other party wishes to rely. [DISCOVER after recover, recovery]

dis·cred·it /diskrédit/ n. & v. ● n. **1** harm to reputation (brought discredit on the enterprise). **2** a person or thing causing this (he is a discredit to his family). **3** lack of credibility; doubt; disbelief (throws

discredit on her story). **4** the loss of commercial credit. ● v.tr. **1** harm the good reputation of. **2** cause to be disbelieved. **3** refuse to believe.

dis·cred·it·a·ble /diskréditəbəl/ adj. bringing discredit; shameful. □□ **dis·cred·it·a·bly** adv.

dis·creet /diskreét/ adj. **1 a** circumspect in speech or action, esp. to avoid social disgrace or embarrassment. **b** tactful; trustworthy. **2** unobtrusive (a discreet touch of rouge). □□ **dis·creet·ly** adv. **dis·creet·ness** n. [ME f. OF discret –ete f. L discretus separate (as DIS-, cretus past part. of cernere sift), with LL sense f. its derivative discretio discernment]

▶Discreet, meaning 'prudent; cautious,' and discrete, meaning 'separate' are different words: Be discreet and don't give away the surprise. I can see three discrete possibilities causing this problem.

dis·crep·an·cy /diskrépənsee/ n. (pl. ·cies) **1** difference; failure to correspond; inconsistency. **2** an instance of this. □□ **dis·crep·ant** adj. [L discrepare be discordant (as DIS-, crepare creak)]

dis·crete /diskreét/ adj. individually distinct; separate; discontinuous. □□ **dis·crete·ly** adv. **dis·crete·ness** n. [ME f. L discretus: see DISCREET]

▶See note at DISCREET.

dis·cre·tion /diskréshən/ n. **1** being discreet; discreet behavior (treats confidences with discretion). **2** prudence; self-preservation. **3** the freedom to act and think as one wishes, usu. within legal limits (it is within his discretion to leave). **4** Law a court's freedom to decide a sentence, etc. □ **at discretion** as one pleases. **at the discretion of** to be settled or disposed of according to the judgment or choice of. **discretion is the better part of valor** reckless courage is often self-defeating. **use one's discretion** act according to one's own judgment. **years** (or **age**) **of discretion** the esp. legal age at which a person is able to manage his or her own affairs. □□ **dis·cre·tion·ar·y** adj. [ME f. OF f. L discretio –onis (as DISCREET)]

dis·crim·i·nate /diskríminayt/ v. **1** intr. (often foll. by between) make or see a distinction; differentiate (cannot discriminate between right and wrong). **2** intr. make a distinction, esp. unjustly and on the basis of race, color, or sex. **3** intr. (usu. foll. by against) select for unfavorable treatment. **4** tr. (usu. foll. by from) make or see or constitute a difference in or between (many things discriminate one person from another). **5** intr. (esp. as **discriminating** adj.) observe distinctions carefully; have good judgment. **6** tr. mark as distinctive; be a distinguishing feature of. □□ **dis·crim·i·nate·ly** /–nətlee/ adv. **dis·crim·i·na·tive** /–nətiv/ adj. **dis·crim·i·na·tor** n. **dis·crim·i·na·to·ry** /–nətáwree/ adj. [L discriminare f. discrimen –minis distinction f. discernere DISCERN]

dis·crim·i·nat·ing /diskríminayting/ adj. **1** able to discern, esp. distinctions. **2** having good taste. □□ **dis·crim·i·nat·ing·ly** adv.

dis·crim·i·na·tion /diskrímináyshən/ n. **1** unfavorable treatment based on prejudice, esp. regarding race, color, age, or sex. **2** good taste or judgment in artistic matters, etc. **3** the power of discriminating or observing differences. **4** a distinction made with the mind or in action.

dis·cur·sive /diskórsiv/ adj. **1** rambling or digressive. **2** Philos. proceeding by argument or reasoning (opp. INTUITIVE). □□ **dis·cur·sive·ly** adv. **dis·cur·sive·ness** n. [med.L discursivus f. L discurrere discurs- (as DIS-, currere run)]

dis·cus /dískəs/ n. (pl. **dis·cus·es**) **1** a heavy, thick-centered disk thrown in ancient Greek games. **2** a similar disk thrown in modern field events. [L f. Gk diskos]

dis·cuss /diskús/ v.tr. **1** hold a conversation about (discussed their vacations). **2** talk or write about a topic in detail; examine different ideas (Chapter Two discusses problems). □□ **dis·cuss·a·ble** adj. **dis·cus·sant** n. **dis·cuss·er** n. **dis·cuss·i·ble** adj. [ME f. L discutere discuss- disperse (as DIS-, quatere shake)]

dis·cus·sion /diskúshən/ n. **1** a conversation, esp. on specific subjects; a debate (had a discussion about what they should do). **2** an examination by argument, written or spoken. [ME f. OF f. LL discussio –onis (as DISCUSS)]

discus thrower

dis·dain /disdáyn/ n. & v. ● n. scorn; contempt. ● v.tr. **1** regard with disdain. **2** think oneself superior to; reject (disdained his offer; dis-

dained to enter; disdained answering). [ME f. OF *desdeign(ier)* ult. f. L *dedignari* (as DE-, *dignari* f. *dignus* worthy)]

dis·dain·ful /disdáynfŏŏl/ *adj.* showing disdain or contempt. □□ **dis·dain·ful·ly** *adv.* **dis·dain·ful·ness** *n.*

dis·ease /dizéez/ *n.* **1** an unhealthy condition of the body (or a part of it) or the mind; illness; sickness. **2** a corresponding physical condition of plants. **3** a particular kind of disease with special symptoms or location. [ME f. OF *desaise*]

dis·eased /dizéezd/ *adj.* **1** affected with disease. **2** abnormal; disordered. [ME, past part. of *disease* (v.) f. OF *desaisier* (as DISEASE)]

dis·e·con·o·my /dísikónəmee/ *n.* *Econ.* the absence or reverse of economy, esp. the increase of costs in a large-scale operation.

dis·em·bark /dísimbaárk/ *v.tr. & intr.* put or go ashore or land from a ship or an aircraft. □□ **dis·em·bar·ka·tion** *n.* [F *désembarquer* (as DIS-, EMBARK)]

dis·em·bar·rass /dísimbárəs/ *v.tr.* **1** (usu. foll. by *of*) relieve (of a load, etc.). **2** free from embarrassment. □□ **dis·em·bar·rass·ment** *n.*

dis·em·bod·y /dísimbódee/ *v.tr.* (**·ies, ·ied**) **1** (esp. as **disembodied** *adj.*) separate or free (esp. the soul) from the body or a concrete form (*disembodied spirit*). **2** *archaic* disband (troops). □□ **dis·em·bod·i·ment** *n.*

dis·em·bogue /dísimbóg/ *v.tr. & intr.* (**dis·em·bogues, dis·em·bogued, dis·em·bogu·ing**) (of a river, etc.) pour forth (waters) at the mouth. [Sp. *desembocar* (as DIS-, *en* in, *boca* mouth)]

dis·em·bow·el /dísimbówəl/ *v.tr.* (**·em·bow·eled, ·em·bow·el·ing**; esp. *Brit.* **·em·bow·elled, ·em·bow·el·ling**) remove the bowels or entrails of. □□ **dis·em·bow·el·ment** *n.*

dis·em·broil /dísimbróyl/ *v.tr.* extricate from confusion or entanglement.

dis·en·chant /dísinchánt/ *v.tr.* free from enchantment; disillusion. □□ **dis·en·chant·ing·ly** *adv.* **dis·en·chant·ment** *n.* [F *désenchanter* (as DIS-, ENCHANT)]

dis·en·cum·ber /dísinkúmbər/ *v.tr.* free from encumbrance.

dis·en·dow /dísindów/ *v.tr.* strip (esp. a church) of endowments. □□ **dis·en·dow·ment** *n.*

dis·en·fran·chise var. of DISFRANCHISE.

dis·en·gage /dísingáyj/ *v.tr. & n.* ● *v.tr.* **1 a** *tr.* detach, free, loosen, or separate (parts, etc.) (*disengaged the clutch*). **b** *refl.* detach oneself; get loose (*disengaged ourselves from their company*). **2** *tr.* *Mil.* remove (troops) from a battle or a battle area. **3** *intr.* become detached. **4** *intr.* *Fencing* pass the point of one's sword to the other side of one's opponent's. **5** *intr.* (as **disengaged** *adj.*) **a** unoccupied; free; vacant. **b** uncommitted, esp. politically. ● *n.* *Fencing* a disengaging movement.

dis·en·gage·ment /dísingáyjmənt/ *n.* **1 a** the act of disengaging. **b** an instance of this. **2** freedom from ties; detachment. **3** the dissolution of an engagement to marry. **4** ease of manner or behavior. **5** *Fencing* = DISENGAGE.

dis·en·tail /dísintáyl/ *v.tr.* *Law* free (property) from entail; break the entail of.

dis·en·tan·gle /dísintánggəl/ *v.* **1** *tr.* **a** unravel; untwist. **b** free from complications; extricate (*disentangled her from the difficulty*). **2** *intr.* become disentangled. □□ **dis·en·tan·gle·ment** *n.*

dis·en·thrall /dísinthráwl/ *v.tr.* (also **dis·en·thral**) *literary* free from enthrallment. □□ **dis·en·thrall·ment** *n.*

dis·en·ti·tle /dísintít'l/ *v.tr.* (usu. foll. by *to*) deprive of any rightful claim.

dis·en·tomb /dísintŏŏm/ *v.tr.* *literary* **1** remove from a tomb; disinter. **2** unearth. □□ **dis·en·tomb·ment** /–tŏŏm-mənt/ *n.*

dis·e·qui·lib·ri·um /díseekwilíbreeəm/ *n.* a lack or loss of equilibrium; instability.

dis·es·tab·lish /dísistáblish/ *v.tr.* **1** deprive (a church) of government support. **2** depose from an official position. **3** terminate the establishment of. □□ **dis·es·tab·lish·ment** *n.*

dis·es·teem /dísistéem/ *v. & n.* ● *v.tr.* have a low opinion of; despise. ● *n.* low esteem or regard.

di·seuse /deezőz/ *n.* (*masc.* **di·seur** /deezőr/) a female entertainer who performs monologues. [F, = talker f. *dire* di- say]

dis·fa·vor /disfáyvər/ *n. & v.* (*Brit.* **dis·fa·vour**) ● *n.* **1** disapproval or dislike. **2** the state of being disliked (*fell into disfavor*). ● *v.tr.* regard or treat with disfavor.

dis·fig·ure /disfígyər/ *v.tr.* spoil the beauty of; deform; deface. □□ **dis·fig·ure·ment** *n.* [ME f. OF *desfigurer* f. Rmc (as DIS-, FIGURE)]

dis·for·est /disfáwrist, –fór–/ *v.tr.* *Brit.* = DISAFFOREST. □□ **dis·for·est·a·tion** *n.*

dis·fran·chise /disfránchīz/ *v.tr.* (also **dis·en·fran·chise** /disinfránchīz/) **1 a** deprive (a person) of the right to vote. **b** deprive (a place) of the right to send a representative to parliament. **2** deprive (a person) of rights as a citizen or of a franchise held. □□ **dis·fran·chise·ment** *n.*

dis·frock /disfrók/ *v.tr.* unfrock.

dis·gorge /disgáwrj/ *v.tr.* **1** eject from the throat or stomach. **2** pour forth; discharge (contents, ill-gotten gains, etc.). □□ **dis·gorge·ment** *n.* [ME f. OF *desgorger* (as DIS-, GORGE)]

dis·grace /disgráys/ *n. & v.* ● *n.* **1** the loss of reputation; shame; ig-

---

nominy (*brought disgrace on his family*). **2** a dishonorable, inefficient, or shameful person, thing, state of affairs, etc. (*the bus service is a disgrace*). ● *v.tr.* **1** bring shame or discredit on; be a disgrace to. **2** degrade from a position of honor; dismiss from favor. □ **in disgrace** having lost respect or reputation; out of favor. [F *disgrâce*, *disgracier* f. It. *disgrazia, disgraziare* (as DIS-, GRACE)]

dis·grace·ful /disgráysfŏŏl/ *adj.* shameful; dishonorable; degrading. □□ **dis·grace·ful·ly** *adv.*

dis·grun·tled /disgrúnt'ld/ *adj.* discontented; moody; sulky. □□ **dis·grun·tle·ment** *n.* [DIS- + *gruntle* obs. frequent. of GRUNT]

dis·guise /disgíz/ *v. & n.* ● *v.tr.* **1** (often foll. by *as*) alter the appearance, sound, smell, etc., of, so as to conceal the identity; make unrecognizable (*disguised herself as a police officer; disguised the taste by adding sugar*). **2** misrepresent or cover up (*disguised the truth; disguised their intentions*). ● *n.* **1 a** a costume, false beard, makeup, etc., used to alter the appearance so as to conceal or deceive. **b** any action, manner, etc., used for deception. **2 a** the act or practice of disguising; the concealment of reality. **b** an instance of this. □ **in disguise 1** wearing a concealing costume, etc. **2** appearing to be the opposite (*a blessing in disguise*). □□ **dis·guise·ment** *n.* [ME f. OF *desguis(i)er* (as DIS-, GUISE)]

dis·gust /disgúst/ *n. & v.* ● *n.* (usu. foll. by *at, for*) **1** strong aversion; repugnance; profound indignation. **2** strong distaste for (some item of) food, drink, medicine, etc.; nausea. ● *v.tr.* cause disgust in (*their behavior disgusts me; was disgusted to find a slug*). □ **in disgust** as a result of disgust (*left in disgust*). □□ **dis·gust·ed·ly** *adv.* [OF *degoust, desgouster*, or It. *disgusto, disgustare* (as DIS-, GUSTO)]

dis·gust·ful /disgústfŏŏl/ *adj.* **1** disgusting; repulsive. **2** (of curiosity, etc.) caused by disgust.

dis·gust·ing /disgústing/ *adj.* arousing aversion or indignation (*disgusting behavior*). □□ **dis·gust·ing·ly** *adv.* **dis·gust·ing·ness** *n.*

dish /dish/ *n. & v.* ● *n.* **1 a** a shallow, usu. flat-bottomed container for cooking or serving food, made of glass, ceramics, metal, etc. **b** the food served in a dish (*all the dishes were delicious*). **c** a particular kind of food (*a meat dish*). **2** (in *pl.*) dirty plates, utensils, cooking pots, etc. after a meal. **3 a** a dish-shaped receptacle, object, or cavity. **b** = SATELLITE DISH. **4** *sl.* a sexually attractive person. ● *v.tr.* **1** put (food) into a dish ready for serving. **2** *colloq.* **a** outmaneuver. **b** *Brit.* destroy (one's hopes, chances, etc.). **3** make concave or dish-shaped. □ **dish out** *sl.* distribute, esp. carelessly or indiscriminately. **dish up 1** serve or prepare to serve (food). **2** *colloq.* seek to present (facts, argument, etc.) attractively. □□ **dish·ful** *n.* (*pl.* **·fuls**). **dish·like** *adj.* [OE *disc* plate, bowl (with Gmc and ON cognates) f. L *discus* DISK]

dis·ha·bille /disəbéel, –bée/ *n.* (also **des·ha·bille** /dezəbéel, –bée/) a state of being only partly or carelessly clothed. [F, = undressed]

dis·har·mo·ny /dis-haármənee/ *n.* a lack of harmony; discord. □□ **dis·har·mo·ni·ous** /–móneeəs/ *adj.* **dis·har·mo·ni·ous·ly** *adv.* **dis·har·mo·nize** /–nīz/ *v.tr.*

dish·cloth /díshklawth, –kloth/ *n.* a usu. open-weave cloth for washing dishes. □ **dishcloth gourd** a loofah.

dis·heart·en /dis-haárt'n/ *v.tr.* cause to lose courage or confidence; make despondent. □□ **dis·heart·en·ing·ly** *adv.* **dis·heart·en·ment** *n.*

di·shev·eled /dishévəld/ *adj.* (esp. *Brit.* **di·shev·elled**) (of the hair, a person, etc.) untidy; ruffled; disordered. □□ **di·shev·el** *v.tr.* (**di·shev·eled, di·shev·el·ing**; esp. *Brit.* **di·shev·elled, di·shev·el·ling**). **di·shev·el·ment** *n.* [ME *dischevelee* f. OF *deschevelé* past part. (as DIS-, *chevel* hair f. L *capillus*)]

dis·hon·est /disónist/ *adj.* (of a person, act, or statement) fraudulent or insincere. □□ **dis·hon·est·ly** *adv.* [ME f. OF *deshoneste* (as DIS-, HONEST)]

dis·hon·es·ty /disónistee/ *n.* (*pl.* **·ties**) **1 a** a lack of honesty. **b** deceitfulness; fraud. **2** a dishonest or fraudulent act. [ME f. OF *deshon(n)esté* (as DISHONEST)]

dis·hon·or /disónər/ *n. & v.* (*Brit.* **dis·hon·our**) ● *n.* **1** a state of shame or disgrace; discredit. **2** something that causes dishonor (*a dishonor to her profession*). ● *v.tr.* **1** treat without honor or respect. **2** disgrace (*dishonored his name*). **3** refuse to accept or pay (a check or a bill of exchange). **4** *archaic* violate the chastity of; rape. [ME f. OF *deshonor, deshonorer* f. med.L *dishonorare* (as DIS-, HONOR)]

dis·hon·or·a·ble /disónərəbəl/ *adj.* (*Brit.* **dis·hon·our·a·ble**) **1** causing disgrace; ignominious. **2** unprincipled. □□ **dis·hon·or·a·ble·ness** *n.* **dis·hon·or·a·bly** *adv.*

dish·pan /díshpan/ *n.* a large, deep, usu. circular pan for washing dishes.

dish·rag /díshrag/ *n.* = DISHCLOTH.

dish·wash·er /díshwoshər, –wawshər/ *n.* **1** a machine for automatically washing dishes. **2** a person employed to wash dishes. □ **dull as dishwater** extremely dull; boring.

dish·wa·ter /díshwawtər, –woter/ *n.* water in which dishes are being or have been washed.

dish·y /díshee/ *adj.* (**dish·i·er, dish·i·est**) *Brit. colloq.* sexually attractive. [DISH *n.* 4 + -Y[1]]

dis·il·lu·sion /dísilóōzhən/ *n. & v.* ● *n.* freedom from illusions; disenchantment. ● *v.tr.* rid of illusions; disenchant. □□ **dis·il·lu·sion·ize** *v.tr.* **dis·il·lu·sion·ment** *n.*

dis·in·cen·tive /dísinséntiv/ *n. & adj.* ● *n.* **1** something that tends to discourage a particular action, etc. **2** *Econ.* a source of discouragement to productivity or progress. ● *adj.* tending to discourage.

dis·in·cli·na·tion /dísinklináyshən/ *n.* (usu. foll. by *for*, or *to* + infin.) the absence of willingness; a reluctance (*a disinclination for work*; *disinclination to go*).

dis·in·cline /dísinklín/ *v.tr.* (usu. foll. by *to* + infin. or *for*) **1** make unwilling or reluctant. **2** (as **disinclined** *adj.*) unwilling; averse.

dis·in·cor·po·rate /dísinkáwrpərayt/ *v.tr.* dissolve (a corporate body).

dis·in·fect /dísinfékt/ *v.tr.* cleanse (a wound, a room, clothes, etc.) of infection, esp. with a disinfectant. □□ **dis·in·fec·tion** /–fékshən/ *n.* [F *désinfecter* (as DIS-, INFECT)]

dis·in·fect·ant /dísinféktənt/ *n. & adj.* ● *n.* a usu. commercially produced chemical liquid that destroys germs, etc. ● *adj.* causing disinfection.

dis·in·fest /dísinfést/ *v.tr.* rid (a person, a building, etc.) of vermin, infesting insects, etc. □□ **dis·in·fes·ta·tion** /–stáyshən/ *n.*

dis·in·fla·tion /dísinfláyshən/ *n. Econ.* a policy designed to counteract inflation without causing deflation. □□ **dis·in·fla·tion·ar·y** *adj.*

dis·in·for·ma·tion /dísinfərmáyshən/ *n.* false information, intended to mislead.

dis·in·gen·u·ous /dísinjényōōəs/ *adj.* having secret motives; dishonest; insincere. □□ **dis·in·gen·u·ous·ly** *adv.* **dis·in·gen·u·ous·ness** *n.*

dis·in·her·it /dísinhérit/ *v.tr.* reject as one's heir; deprive of the right of inheritance. □□ **dis·in·her·i·tance** *n.* [ME f. DIS- + INHERIT in obs. sense 'make heir']

dis·in·te·grate /dísíntigrayt/ *v.* **1** *tr. & intr.* **a** separate into component parts or fragments. **b** lose or cause to lose cohesion. **2** *intr. colloq.* deteriorate mentally or physically; decay. **3** *intr. & tr. Physics* undergo or cause to undergo disintegration. □□ **dis·in·te·gra·tor** *n.*

dis·in·te·gra·tion /dísíntigráyshən/ *n.* **1** the act or an instance of disintegrating. **2** *Physics* any process in which a nucleus emits a particle or particles or divides into smaller nuclei.

dis·in·ter /dísintér/ *v.tr.* (**dis·in·terred, dis·in·ter·ring**) **1** remove (esp. a corpse) from the ground; unearth; exhume. **2** find after a protracted search (*disinterred the letter from the back of the drawer*). □□ **dis·in·ter·ment** *n.* [F *désenterrer* (as DIS-, INTER)]

dis·in·ter·est /dísíntrist, –íntərist/ *n.* **1** impartiality. **2** *disp.* lack of interest; unconcern.

dis·in·ter·est·ed /dísíntristid, –íntəri–/ *adj.* **1** not influenced by one's own advantage; impartial. **2** *disp.* uninterested. □□ **dis·in·ter·est·ed·ly** *adv.* **dis·in·ter·est·ed·ness** *n.* [past part. of *disinterest* (v.) divest of interest]

▶**Disinterested** means 'not having a personal interest, impartial': *A juror must be disinterested in the case being tried*. **Uninterested** means 'not interested; indifferent': *On the other hand, a juror must not be uninterested*.

dis·in·vest /dísinvést/ *v.intr.* (foll. by *from*, or *absol.*) reduce or dispose of one's investment (in a place, company, etc.). □□ **dis·in·vest·ment** *n.*

dis·jec·ta mem·bra /disjéktə mémbrə/ *n.pl.* scattered remains; fragments, esp. of written work. [L, alt. of *disjecti membra poetae* (Horace) limbs of a dismembered poet]

dis·join /disjóyn/ *v.tr.* separate or disunite; part. [ME f. OF *desjoindre* f. L *disjungere* (as DIS-, *jungere junct-* join)]

dis·joint /disjóynt/ *v. & adj.* ● *v.tr.* **1** take apart at the joints. **2** (as **disjointed** *adj.*) (esp. of conversation) incoherent; desultory. **3** disturb the working or connection of; dislocate. ● *adj.* (of two or more sets) having no elements in common. □□ **dis·joint·ed·ly** *adv.* **dis·joint·ed·ness** *n.* [ME f. obs. *disjoint* (adj.) f. past part. of OF *desjoindre* (as DISJOIN)]

dis·junc·tion /disjúngkshən/ *n.* **1** the process of disjoining; separation. **2** an instance of this. [ME f. OF *disjunction* or L *disjunctio* (as DISJOIN)]

dis·junc·tive /disjúngktiv/ *adj. & n.* ● *adj.* **1** involving separation; disjoining. **2** *Gram.* (esp. of a conjunction) expressing a choice between two words, etc., e.g., *or* in *asked if he were going or staying* (cf. COPULATIVE). **3** *Logic* (of a proposition) expressing alternatives. ● *n.* **1** *Gram.* a disjunctive conjunction or other word. **2** *Logic* a disjunctive proposition. □□ **dis·junc·tive·ly** *adv.* [ME f. L *disjunctivus* (as DISJOIN)]

disk /disk/ *n.* (also **disc**) **1 a** a flat thin circular object. **b** a round, flat or apparently flat surface (*the sun's disk*). **c** a mark of this shape. **2** a layer of cartilage between vertebrae. **3 a** a phonograph record. **b** = COMPACT DISC. **4 a** (in full **magnetic disk**) a computer storage device consisting of several flat, circular, magnetically coated plates formed into a rotatable disk. **b** (in full **optical disc** or **disk**) a smooth nonmagnetic disk with large storage capacity for data recorded and read by laser. **5** *Brit.* a device with a pointer or rotating disk indi-

cating time of arrival or latest permitted time of departure, for display in a parked motor vehicle. [F *disque* or L *discus*: see DISCUS]

disk brake *n.* (often **disc brake**) a brake employing the friction of pads against a disk.

disk drive *n. Computing* a mechanism for rotating a disk and reading or writing data from or to it.

disk har·row *n.* a harrow with cutting edges consisting of a row of concave disks set at an oblique angle.

disk jock·ey *n.* (also **disc jock·ey**) a person who introduces and plays recorded popular music, esp. on the radio or at a disco.

disk·ette /diskét/ *n. Computing* = *floppy disk*.

dis·like /dislík/ *v. & n.* ● *v.tr.* have an aversion or objection to; not like. ● *n.* **1** a feeling of repugnance or not liking. **2** an object of dislike. □□ **dis·lik·a·ble** *adj.* (also **dis·like·a·ble**)

dis·lo·cate /díslókayt, disló–/ *v.tr.* **1** disturb the normal connection of (esp. a joint in the body). **2** disrupt; put out of order. **3** displace. [prob. back-form. f. DISLOCATION]

dis·lo·ca·tion /díslōkáyshən/ *n.* **1** the act or result of dislocating. **2** *Crystallog.* the displacement of part of a crystal lattice structure. [ME f. OF *dislocation* or med.L *dislocatio* f. *dislocare* (as DIS-, *locare* place)]

dis·lodge /dislój/ *v.tr.* remove from an established or fixed position (*was dislodged from his directorship*). □□ **dis·lodge·ment** *n.* (also **dis·lodge·ment**). [ME f. OF *dislog(i)er* (as DIS-, LODGE)]

dis·loy·al /dislóyəl/ *adj.* (often foll. by *to*) **1** not loyal; unfaithful. **2** untrue to one's allegiance; treacherous to one's government, etc. □□ **dis·loy·al·ist** *n.* **dis·loy·al·ly** *adv.* **dis·loy·al·ty** *n.* [ME f. OF *desloial* (as DIS-, LOYAL)]

dis·mal /dízməl/ *adj.* **1** causing or showing gloom; miserable. **2** dreary or somber (*dismal brown walls*). **3** *colloq.* feeble or inept (*a dismal performance*). □□ **dis·mal·ly** *adv.* **dis·mal·ness** *n.*

WORD HISTORY dismal

Late ME: from earlier *dismal* (noun), denoting the two days in each month that in medieval times were believed to be unlucky, from Anglo-Norman French *dis mal*, from medieval Latin *dies mali* 'evil days.'

dis·mal sci·ence *n.* esp. *Brit. joc.* economics.

dis·man·tle /dismánt'l/ *v.tr.* **1** take to pieces; pull down. **2** deprive of defenses or equipment. **3** (often foll. by *of*) strip of covering or protection. □□ **dis·man·tle·ment** *n.* **dis·man·tler** *n.* [OF *desmanteler* (as DIS-, MANTLE)]

dis·mast /dismást/ *v.tr.* deprive (a ship) of masts; break down the mast or masts of.

dis·may /dismáy/ *v. & n.* ● *v.tr.* fill with consternation or anxiety; discourage or depress; reduce to despair. ● *n.* **1** consternation or anxiety. **2** depression or despair. [ME f. *desmaïer* (unrecorded) ult. f. a Gmc root = deprive of power (as DIS-, MAY)]

dis·mem·ber /dismémbər/ *v.tr.* **1** tear or cut the limbs from. **2** partition or divide up (an empire, country, etc.). □□ **dis·mem·ber·ment** *n.* [ME f. OF *desmembrer* f. Rmc (as DIS-, L *membrum* limb)]

dis·miss /dismís/ *v.* **1 a** *tr.* send away; cause to leave one's presence; disperse; disband (an assembly or army). **b** *intr.* (of an assembly, etc.) disperse; break ranks. **2** *tr.* discharge from employment, office, etc., esp. dishonorably. **3** *tr.* put out of one's thoughts; cease to feel or discuss (*dismissed him from memory*). **4** *tr.* treat (a subject) summarily (*dismissed his application*). **5** *tr. Law* refuse further hearing to (a case); send out of court. **6** *tr. Cricket* put (a batsman or a side) out (*was dismissed for 75 runs*). **7** *intr.* (in *imper.*) *Mil.* a word of command at the end of drilling. □□ **dis·mis·sal** *n.* **dis·miss·i·ble** *adj.* **dis·mis·sion** *n.* [ME, orig. as past part. after OF *desmis* f. med.L *dismissus* (as DIS-, L *mittere miss-* send)]

dis·mis·sive /dismísiv/ *adj.* tending to dismiss from consideration; disdainful. □□ **dis·mis·sive·ly** *adv.* **dis·mis·sive·ness** *n.*

dis·mount *v. & n.* ● *v.* (dismount) **1 a** *intr.* alight from a horse, bicycle, etc. **b** *tr.* (usu. in *passive*) throw from a horse; unseat. **2** *tr.* remove (a thing) from its mounting (esp. a gun from its carriage). ● *n.* /dismównt, dis–/ the act of dismounting.

dis·o·be·di·ent /dísəbeedeeənt/ *adj.* disobeying; rebellious; rule-breaking. □□ **dis·o·be·di·ence** /–deeəns/ *n.* **dis·o·be·di·ent·ly** *adv.* [ME f. OF *desobedient* (as DIS-, OBEDIENT)]

dis·o·bey /dísəbáy/ *v.tr.* (also *absol.*) fail or refuse to obey; disregard (orders); break (rules) (*disobeyed his mother*; *how dare you disobey!*). □□ **dis·o·bey·er** *n.* [ME f. OF *desobeir* f. Rmc (as DIS-, OBEY)]

dis·o·blige /dísəblíj/ *v.tr.* **1** refuse to consider the convenience or wishes of. **2** (as **disobliging** *adj.*) uncooperative. [F *désobliger* f. Rmc (as DIS-, OBLIGE)]

dis·or·der /disáwrdər/ *n. & v.* ● *n.* **1** a lack of order; confusion. **2** a riot; a commotion. **3** *Med.* a usu. minor ailment or disease. ● *v.tr.* **1** throw into confusion; disarrange. **2** *Med.* put out of good health; upset. [ME, alt. after ORDER v. of earlier *disordain* f. OF *desordener* (as DIS-, ORDAIN)]

dis·or·der·ly /disáwrdərlee/ *adj.* **1** untidy; confused. **2** irregular; unruly; riotous. **3** *Law* contrary to public order or morality. □□ **dis·or·der·li·ness** *n.*

dis•or•der•ly house n. Law dated a brothel.

dis•or•gan•ize /disáwrgənīz/ v.tr. **1** destroy the system or order of; throw into confusion. **2** (as **disorganized** adj.) lacking organization or system. □□ **dis•or•gan•i•za•tion** n. [F désorganiser (as DIS-, ORGANIZE)]

dis•o•ri•ent /disáwreeənt/ v.tr. **1** confuse (a person) as to his or her whereabouts or bearings. **2** (often as **disoriented** adj.) confuse (a person) (disoriented by his unexpected behavior). [F désorienter (as DIS-, ORIENT v.)]

dis•o•ri•en•tate /disáwriəntayt/ v.tr. = DISORIENT. □□ **dis•o•ri•en•ta•tion** /–táyshən/ n.

dis•own /disón/ v.tr. **1** refuse to recognize; repudiate; disclaim. **2** renounce one's connection with or allegiance to. □□ **dis•own•er** n.

dis•par•age /dispárij/ v.tr. **1** speak slightingly of; depreciate. **2** bring discredit on. □□ **dis•par•age•ment** n. **dis•par•ag•ing•ly** adv. [ME f. OF desparagier marry unequally (as DIS-, parage equality of rank ult. f. L par equal)]

dis•pa•rate /dispərət, dispár–/ adj. & n. • adj. essentially different in kind; without comparison or relation. • n. (in pl.) things so unlike that there is no basis for their comparison. □□ **dis•pa•rate•ly** adv. **dis•pa•rate•ness** n. [L disparatus separated (as DIS-, paratus past part. of parare prepare), infl. in sense by L dispar unequal]

dis•par•i•ty /dispáritee/ n. (pl. **–ties**) **1** inequality; difference; incongruity. **2** an instance of this. [F disparité f. LL disparitas –tatis (as DIS-, PARITY[1])]

dis•pas•sion•ate /dispáshənət/ adj. free from passion; calm; impartial. □□ **dis•pas•sion•ate•ly** adv. **dis•pas•sion•ate•ness** n.

dis•patch /dispách/ v. & n. (also **des•patch**) • v.tr. **1** send off to a destination or for a purpose (dispatched her with the message; dispatched the letter yesterday). **2** perform (business, a task, etc.) promptly; finish off. **3** kill; execute (dispatched him with the revolver). **4** colloq. eat (food, a meal, etc.) quickly. • n. **1** the act or an instance of sending (a messenger, letter, etc.). **2** the act or an instance of killing; execution. **3** (also /díspach/) **a** an official written message on state or esp. military affairs. **b** a report sent in by a newspaper's correspondent, usu. from a foreign country. **4** promptness; efficiency (done with dispatch). □□ **dis•patch•er** n. [It. dispacciare or Sp. despachar expedite (as DIS-, It. impacciare and Sp. empachar hinder, of uncert. orig.)]

dis•pel /dispél/ v.tr. (**dis•pelled, dis•pel•ling**) dissipate; disperse; scatter (the dawn dispelled their fears). □□ **dis•pel•ler** n. [L dispellere (as DIS-, pellere drive)]

dis•pen•sa•ble /dispénsəbəl/ adj. **1** able to be done without; unnecessary. **2** (of a law, etc.) able to be relaxed in special cases. □□ **dis•pen•sa•bil•i•ty** n. [med.L dispensabilis (as DISPENSE)]

dis•pen•sa•ry /dispénsəree/ n. (pl. **–ries**) **1** a place where medicines, etc., are dispensed. **2** a public or charitable institution for medical advice and the dispensing of medicines. [med.L dispensarius (as DISPENSE)]

dis•pen•sa•tion /díspənsáyshən/ n. **1 a** the act or an instance of dispensing or distributing. **b** (foll. by with) the state of doing without (a thing). **c** something distributed. **2** (usu. foll. by from) **a** exemption from a penalty or duty; an instance of this. **b** permission to be exempted from a religious observance; an instance of this. **3** a religious or political system obtaining in a nation, etc. (the Christian dispensation). **4 a** the ordering or management of the world by providence. **b** a specific example of such ordering (of a community, a person, etc.). □□ **dis•pen•sa•tion•al** adj. [ME f. OF dispensation or L dispensatio (as DISPENSE)]

dis•pense /dispéns/ v. **1** tr. distribute; deal out. **2** tr. administer (a sacrament, justice, etc.). **3** tr. make up and give out (medicine, etc.) according to a doctor's prescription. **4** tr. (usu. foll. by from) grant a dispensation to (a person) from an obligation, esp. a religious observance. **5** intr. (foll. by with) **a** do without; render needless. **b** give exemption from (a rule). [ME f. OF despenser f. L dispensare frequent. of dispendĕre weigh or pay out (as DIS-, pendĕre pens- weigh)]

dis•pens•er /dispénsər/ n. **1** a person or thing that dispenses something, e.g., medicine, good advice. **2** an automatic machine or container that is designed to release a specific amount of something (a paper towel dispenser).

dis•per•sant /dispérsənt/ n. Chem. an agent used to disperse small particles in a medium.

dis•perse /dispérs/ v. **1** intr. & tr. go, send, drive, or distribute in different directions or over a wide area. **2 a** intr. (of people at a meeting, etc.) leave and go their various ways. **b** tr. cause to do this. **3** tr. send to or station at separate points. **4** tr. put in circulation; disseminate. **5** tr. Chem. distribute (small particles) uniformly in a medium. **6** tr. Physics divide (white light) into its colored constituents. □□ **dis•pers•a•ble** adj. **dis•per•sal** n. **dis•pers•er** n. **dis•pers•i•ble** adj. **dis•per•sive** adj. [ME f. L dispergere dispers- (as DIS-, spargere scatter)]

dis•per•sion /dispérzhən, –shən/ n. **1** the act or an instance of dispersing; the process of being dispersed. **2** Chem. a mixture of one substance dispersed in another. **3** Physics the separation of white light into colors or of any radiation according to wavelength. **4** Statistics the extent to which values of a variable differ from the

mean. **5** (**the Dispersion**) the Jews dispersed among the Gentiles after the Captivity in Babylon. [ME f. LL dispersio (as DISPERSE), transl. Gk diaspora: see DIASPORA]

dis•pir•it /dispírit/ v.tr. **1** (esp. as **dispiriting** adj.) make despondent; discourage. **2** (as **dispirited** adj.) dejected; discouraged. □□ **dis•pir•it•ed•ly** adv. **dis•pir•it•ed•ness** n. **dis•pir•it•ing•ly** adv.

dis•place /displáys/ v.tr. **1** shift from its accustomed place. **2** remove from office. **3** take the place of; oust.

dis•placed per•son n. a person who is forced to leave his or her home country because of war, persecution, etc.; a refugee.

dis•place•ment /displáysmənt/ n. **1 a** the act or an instance of displacing; the process of being displaced. **b** an instance of this. **2** Physics the amount of a fluid displaced by a solid floating or immersed in it (a ship with a displacement of 11,000 tons). **3** Psychol. **a** the substitution of one idea or impulse for another. **b** the unconscious transfer of strong unacceptable emotions from one object to another. **4** the amount by which a thing is shifted from its place.

dis•play /displáy/ v. & n. • v.tr. **1** expose to view; exhibit; show. **2** show ostentatiously. **3** allow to appear; reveal; betray (displayed his ignorance). • n. **1** the act or an instance of displaying. **2** an exhibition or show. **3** ostentation; flashiness. **4** the distinct behavior of some birds and fish, esp. used to attract a mate. **5 a** the presentation of signals or data on a visual display unit, etc. **b** the information so presented. **6** Printing the arrangement and choice of type in order to attract attention. □□ **dis•play•er** n. [ME f. OF despleier f. L displicare (as DIS-, plicare fold): cf. DEPLOY]

dis•please /displeéz/ v.tr. make indignant or angry; offend; annoy. □ **be displeased** (often foll. by at, with) be indignant or dissatisfied; disapprove. □□ **dis•pleas•ing•ly** adv. [ME f. OF desplaisir (as DIS-, L placēre please)]

dis•pleas•ure /displézhər/ n. & v. • n. disapproval; anger; dissatisfaction. • v.tr. archaic cause displeasure to; annoy. [ME f. OF (as DISPLEASE): assim. to PLEASURE]

dis•port /dispáwrt/ v. & n. • v.intr. & refl. frolic; gambol; enjoy oneself (disported on the beach; disported themselves in the ocean). • n. archaic **1** relaxation. **2** a pastime. [ME f. AF & OF desporter (as DIS-, porter carry f. L portare)]

dis•pos•a•ble /dispózəbəl/ adj. & n. • adj. **1** intended to be used once and then thrown away (disposable diapers). **2** that can be got rid of, made over, or used. **3** (esp. of financial assets) at the owner's disposal. • n. a thing designed to be thrown away after one use. □□ **dis•pos•a•bil•i•ty** n.

dis•pos•a•ble in•come n. income after taxes, etc., available for spending.

dis•pos•al /dispózəl/ n. (usu. foll. by of) **1** the act or an instance of disposing of something. **2** the arrangement, disposition, or placing of something. **3** control or management (of a person, business, etc.). **4** (esp. as **garbage disposal**) an electrical device under a sink for grinding up food waste so it can be flushed away. □ **at one's disposal 1** available for one's use. **2** subject to one's orders or decisions.

dis•pose /dispóz/ v. **1** tr. (usu. foll. by to, or to + infin.) **a** make willing; incline (disposed him to the idea; was disposed to release them). **b** give a tendency to (the wheel was disposed to buckle). **2** tr. place suitably or in order (disposed the pictures in sequence). **3** tr. (as **disposed** adj.) have a specified mental inclination (usu. in comb.: ill-disposed). **4** intr. determine the course of events (man proposes, God disposes). □ **dispose of 1 a** deal with. **b** get rid of. **c** finish. **d** kill. **e** distribute; dispense; bestow. **2** sell. **3** prove (a claim, an argument, an opponent, etc.) to be incorrect. **4** consume (food). □□ **dis•pos•er** n. [ME f. OF disposer (as DIS-, POSE[1]) after L disponere disposit–]

dis•po•si•tion /díspəzíshən/ n. **1 a** (often foll. by to) a natural tendency; an inclination (a disposition to overeat). **b** a person's temperament or attitude, esp. as displayed in dealings with others (a happy disposition). **2 a** setting in order; arranging. **b** the relative position of parts; an arrangement. **3** (usu. in pl.) **a** Mil. the stationing of troops ready for attack or defense. **b** preparations; plans. **4 a** a bestowal by deed or will. **b** control; the power of disposing. **5** ordinance; dispensation. [ME f. OF f. L dispositio (as DIS-, ponere posit– place)]

dis•pos•sess /díspəzéss/ v.tr. **1** dislodge; oust (a person). **2** (usu. foll. by of) deprive. □□ **dis•pos•ses•sion** /–zéshən/ n. [OF despossesser (as DIS-, POSSESS)]

dis•praise /dispráyz/ v. & n. • v.tr. express disapproval or censure of. • n. disapproval; censure. [ME f. OF despreisier ult. f. LL depretiare DEPRECIATE]

dis•proof /disproóf/ n. **1** something that disproves. **2 a** refutation. **b** an instance of this.

dis•pro•por•tion /dísprəpáwrshən/ n. **1 a** lack of proportion. **2** an instance of this. □□ **dis•pro•por•tion•al** adj. **dis•pro•por•tion•al•ly** adv.

dis•pro•por•tion•ate /dísprəpáwrshənət/ adj. **1** lacking proportion.

2 relatively too large or small, long or short, etc. □□ **dis•pro•por•tion•ate•ly** adv. **dis•pro•por•tion•ate•ness** n.

dis•prove /disprōōv/ v.tr. prove false; refute. □□ **dis•prov•a•ble** adj. **dis•prov•al** n. [ME f. OF desprover (as DIS-, PROVE)]

dis•put•a•ble /dispyōōtəbəl/ adj. open to question; uncertain. □□ **dis•put•a•bly** adv. [F or f. L disputabilis (as DISPUTE)]

dis•pu•ta•tion /díspyətáyshən/ n. **1 a** disputing; debating. **b** an argument; a controversy. **2** a formal debate. [ME f. F disputation or L disputatio (as DISPUTE)]

dis•pu•ta•tious /díspyətáyshəs/ adj. fond of or inclined to argument. □□ **dis•pu•ta•tious•ly** adv. **dis•pu•ta•tious•ness** n.

dis•pute /dispyōōt/ v. & n. ● v. **1** intr. (usu. foll. by with, against) **a** debate; argue (was disputing with them about the meaning of life). **b** quarrel. **2** tr. discuss, esp. heatedly (disputed whether it was true). **3** tr. question the truth or correctness or validity of (a statement, alleged fact, etc.) (I dispute that number). **4** tr. contend for; strive to win (disputed the crown; disputed the title). **5** tr. resist (a landing, advance, etc.). ● n. **1** a controversy; a debate. **2** a quarrel. **3** a disagreement between management and employees, esp. one leading to industrial action. **4** archaic a fight or altercation; a struggle. □ **beyond** (or **past** or **without**) **dispute 1** certainly; indisputably. **2** certain; indisputable. **in dispute 1** being argued about. **2** (of a workforce) involved in industrial action. □□ **dis•pu•tant** /-spyōōt'nt/ n. **dis•put•er** n. [ME f. OF desputer f. L disputare estimate (as DIS-, putare reckon)]

dis•qual•i•fi•ca•tion /diskwólifikáyshən/ n. **1** the act or an instance of disqualifying; the state of being disqualified. **2** something that disqualifies.

dis•qual•i•fy /diskwólifī/ v.tr. (•fies, •fied) **1** (often foll. by from) debar from a competition or pronounce ineligible as a winner because of an infringement of the rules, etc. (disqualified from the race for taking drugs). **2** (often foll. by from) make or pronounce ineligible or unsuitable (his age disqualifies him for the job; a criminal record disqualified him from applying). **3** (often foll. by from) incapacitate legally; pronounce unqualified (disqualified from practicing as a doctor).

dis•qui•et /diskwíət/ v. & n. ● v.tr. deprive of peace; worry. ● n. anxiety; unrest. □□ **dis•qui•et•ing** adj. **dis•qui•et•ing•ly** adv.

dis•qui•e•tude /diskwíətōōd, -tyōōd/ n. a state of uneasiness; anxiety.

dis•qui•si•tion /dískwizíshən/ n. a long or elaborate treatise or discourse on a subject. □□ **dis•qui•si•tion•al** adj. [F f. L disquisitio (as DIS-, quaerere quaesit- seek)]

dis•rate /disráyt/ v.tr. Naut. reduce (a sailor) to a lower rating or rank.

dis•re•gard /dísrigaárd/ v. & n. ● v.tr. **1** pay no attention to; ignore. **2** treat as of no importance. **3** archaic neglect contemptuously; slight; snub. ● n. (often foll. by of, for) indifference; neglect. □□ **dis•re•gard•ful** adj. **dis•re•gard•ful•ly** adv.

dis•rel•ish /disrélish/ n. & v. ● n. dislike; distaste. ● v.tr. regard with dislike or distaste.

dis•re•mem•ber /dísrimémbər/ v.tr. & intr. dial. fail to remember; forget.

dis•re•pair /dísripáir/ n. poor condition due to neglect (in disrepair; in a state of disrepair).

dis•rep•u•ta•ble /disrépyətəbəl/ adj. **1** of bad reputation; discreditable. **2** not respectable in appearance; dirty; untidy. □□ **dis•rep•u•ta•ble•ness** n. **dis•rep•u•ta•bly** adv.

dis•re•pute /dísripyōōt/ n. a lack of good reputation or respectability; discredit (esp. fall into disrepute).

dis•re•spect /dísrispékt/ n. a lack of respect; discourtesy. □□ **dis•re•spect•ful** adj. **dis•re•spect•ful•ly** adv.

dis•robe /disrōb/ v.tr. & refl. (also absol.) **1** divest (oneself or another) of a robe or a garment; undress. **2** divest (oneself or another) of office, authority, etc.

dis•rupt /disrúpt/ v.tr. **1** interrupt the flow or continuity of (a meeting, speech, etc.); bring disorder to. **2** separate forcibly; shatter. □□ **dis•rupt•er** n. (also **dis•rup•tor**). **dis•rup•tion** /-rúpshən/ n. **dis•rup•tive** adj. **dis•rup•tive•ly** adv. **dis•rup•tive•ness** n. [L disrumpere disrupt- (as DIS-, rumpere break)]

diss /dis/ v.tr. var. of DIS

dis•sat•is•fy /disátisfī/ v.tr. (•fies, •fied) (often as **dissatisfied** adj.) make discontented; fail to satisfy (dissatisfied with the accommodation; dissatisfied to find him gone). □□ **dis•sat•is•fac•tion** /-fákshən/ n. **dis•sat•is•fac•to•ry** /-fáktəree/ adj. **dis•sat•is•fied•ly** adv.

dis•sect /disékt, dī-/ v.tr. **1** cut into pieces. **2** cut up (a plant or animal) to examine its parts, structure, etc., or (a corpse) for a post mortem. **3** analyze; criticize or examine in detail. □□ **dis•sec•**

PRONUNCIATION TIP dissect

The traditional pronunciation of this word is "di-SEKT." Many people still object to rhyming it with bisect, although this pronunciation has been widely used for several decades.

tion /-sékshən/ n. **dis•sec•tor** n. [L dissecare dissect- (as DIS-, secare cut)]

dis•sem•ble /disémbəl/ v. **1** intr. conceal one's motives; talk or act hypocritically. **2** tr. **a** disguise or conceal (a feeling, intention, act, etc.). **b** simulate (dissembled grief in public). □□ **dis•sem•blance** n. **dis•sem•bler** n. **dis•sem•bling•ly** adv. [ME, alt. after semblance of obs. dissimule f. OF dissimuler f. L dissimulare (as DIS-, SIMULATE)]

SPELLING TIP dissemble

Those who dissemble take on the semblance of someone or something else.

dis•sem•i•nate /diséminayt/ v.tr. scatter about; spread (esp. ideas) widely. □□ **dis•sem•i•na•tion** /-náyshən/ n. **dis•sem•i•na•tor** n. [L disseminare (as DIS-, semen -inis seed)]

dis•sen•sion /disénshən/ n. disagreement giving rise to discord. [ME f. OF f. L dissensio (as DIS-, sentire sens- feel)]

dis•sent /disént/ v. & n. ● v.intr. (often foll. by from) **1** think differently; disagree; express disagreement. **2** differ in religious opinion, esp. from the doctrine of an established or orthodox church. ● n. **1 a** a difference of opinion. **b** an expression of this. **2** the refusal to accept the doctrines of an established or orthodox church; nonconformity. □□ **dis•sent•ing** adj. **dis•sent•ing•ly** adv. [ME f. L dissentire (as DIS-, sentire feel)]

dis•sent•er /diséntər/ n. **1** a person who dissents. **2** (**Dissenter**) Brit. a member of a nonestablished church; a Nonconformist.

dis•sen•tient /disénshənt/ adj. & n. ● adj. disagreeing with a majority or official view. ● n. a person who dissents. [L dissentire (as DIS-, sentire feel)]

dis•ser•ta•tion /dísərtáyshən/ n. a detailed discourse on a subject, esp. one submitted in partial fulfillment of the requirements of a degree or diploma. □□ **dis•ser•ta•tion•al** adj. [L dissertatio f. dissertare discuss, frequent. of disserere dissert- examine (as DIS-, serere join)]

dis•serv•ice /dis-sórvis/ n. an ill turn; a harmful action. □□ **dis•serve** v.tr. archaic.

dis•sev•er /disévər/ v.tr. & intr. sever; divide into parts. □□ **dis•sev•er•ance** n. **dis•sev•er•ment** n. [ME f. AF dis(c)everer, OF dessevrer f. LL disseparare (as DIS-, SEPARATE)]

dis•si•dence /dísid'ns/ n. disagreement; dissent. [F dissidence or L dissidentia (as DISSIDENT)]

dis•si•dent /dísid'nt/ adj. & n. ● adj. disagreeing, esp. with an established government, system, etc. ● n. a dissident person. [F or f. L dissidēre disagree (as DIS-, sedēre sit)]

dis•sim•i•lar /dissímilər/ adj. (often foll. by to) unlike; not similar. □□ **dis•sim•i•lar•i•ty** /-láritee/ n. (pl. •ties). **dis•sim•i•lar•ly** adv.

dis•sim•i•late /dissímilayt/ v. (often foll. by to) Phonet. **1** tr. change (a sound or sounds in a word) to another when the word originally had the same sound repeated, as in cinnamon, orig. cinnamom. **2** intr. (of a sound) be changed in this way. □□ **dis•sim•i•la•tion** /-láyshən/ n. **dis•sim•i•la•to•ry** /-lətáwree/ adj. [L dissimilis (as DIS-, similis like), after assimilate]

dis•si•mil•i•tude /dísimílitōōd, tyōōd/ n. unlikeness; dissimilarity. [L dissimilitudo (as DISSIMILATE)]

dis•sim•u•late /dissímyəlayt/ v.tr. & intr. dissemble. □□ **dis•sim•u•la•tion** /-láyshən/ n. **dis•sim•u•la•tor** n. [L dissimulare (as DIS-, SIMULATE)]

dis•si•pate /dísipayt/ v. **1 a** intr. disperse or scatter (the cloud of smoke dissipated). **b** intr. (of a feeling or other intangible thing) disappear or be dispelled (her concern for him had wholly dissipated). **3** tr. cause (a feeling or other intangible thing) to disappear or disperse (he wanted to dissipate his anger). **3** tr. squander (money, energy, or resources). **4** intr. (as **dissipated** adj.) dissolute. □□ **dis•si•pat•er** n. **dis•si•pa•tive** adj. **dis•si•pa•tor** n. [L dissipare dissipat- (as DIS-, sipare (unrecorded) throw)]

dis•si•pa•tion /dísipáyshən/ n. **1** intemperate, dissolute, or debauched living. **2** (usu. foll. by of) wasteful expenditure (dissipation of resources). **3** scattering, dispersion, or disintegration. **4** a frivolous amusement. [F dissipation or L dissipatio (as DISSIPATE)]

dis•so•ci•ate /disósheeayt, -seeayt/ v. **1** tr. & intr. (usu. foll. by from) disconnect or become disconnected; separate (dissociated her from their guilt). **2** tr. Chem. decompose, esp. reversibly. **3** tr. Psychol. cause (a person's mind) to develop more than one center of consciousness. □ **dissociate oneself from 1** declare oneself unconnected with. **2** decline to support or agree with (a proposal, etc.). □□ **dis•so•ci•a•tive** /-sheeətiv, -seeətiv/ adj. [L dissociare (as DIS-, socius companion)]

dis•so•ci•at•ed per•son•al•i•ty n. Psychol. the pathological coexistence of two or more distinct personalities in the same person.

dis•so•ci•a•tion /disóseeáyshən, -shee-/ n. **1** the act or an instance of dissociating. **2** Psychol. the state of suffering from dissociated personality.

dis•sol•u•ble /disólyəbəl/ adj. able to be disintegrated, loosened, or disconnected; soluble □□ **dis•sol•u•bil•i•ty** n. **dis•sol•u•bly** adv. [F dissoluble or L dissolubilis (as DIS-, SOLUBLE)]

dis•so•lute /dísəlōōt/ adj. lax in morals; licentious. □□ **dis•so•lute•ly**

dis•so•lu•tion /dísəlóoshən/ *n.* **1** disintegration; decomposition. **2** (usu. foll. by *of*) the undoing or relaxing of a bond, esp.: **a** a marriage. **b** a partnership. **c** an alliance. **3** the dismissal or dispersal of an assembly, esp. of a parliament at the end of its term. **4** death. **5** bringing or coming to an end; fading away; disappearance. **6** dissipation; debauchery. [ME f. OF *dissolution* or L *dissolutio* (as DISSOLVE)]

dis•solve /dizólv/ *v. & n.* ● *v.* **1** *tr. & intr.* make or become liquid, esp. by immersion or dispersion in a liquid. **2** *intr. & tr.* disappear or cause to disappear gradually. **3 a** *tr.* dismiss or disperse (an assembly, esp. parliament). **b** *intr.* (of an assembly) be dissolved (cf. DISSOLUTION 3). **4** *tr.* annul or put an end to (a partnership, marriage, etc.). **5** *intr.* (of a person) become enfeebled or emotionally overcome (*completely dissolved when he saw her; dissolved into tears*). **6** *intr.* (often foll. by *into*) *Cinematog.* change gradually (from one picture into another). ● *n. Cinematog.* the act or process of dissolving a picture. □□ **dis•solv•a•ble** *adj.* [ME f. L *dissolvere dissolut-* (as DIS-, *solvere* loosen)]

dis•sol•vent /dizólvənt/ *adj. & n.* ● *adj.* tending to dissolve or dissipate. ● *n.* a dissolvent substance. [L *dissolvere* (as DISSOLVE)]

dis•so•nant /dísənənt/ *adj.* **1** *Mus.* harsh-toned; inharmonious. **2** incongruous; clashing. □□ **dis•so•nance** /-nəns/ *n.* **dis•so•nant•ly** *adv.* [ME f. OF *dissonant* or L *dissonare* (as DIS-, *sonare* sound)]

dis•suade /diswáyd/ *v.tr.* (often foll. by *from*) discourage (a person); persuade against (*dissuaded him from continuing; was dissuaded from his belief*). □□ **dis•suad•er** *n.* **dis•sua•sion** /-swáyzhən/ *n.* **dis•sua•sive** *adj.* [L *dissuadēre* (as DIS-, *suadēre suas-* persuade)]

dis•syl•la•ble var. of DISYLLABLE.

dis•sym•me•try /dis-símitree/ *n.* (*pl.* **•tries**) **1 a** lack of symmetry. **b** an instance of this. **2** symmetry as of mirror images or the left and right hands (esp. of crystals with two corresponding forms). □□ **dis•sym•met•ri•cal** /dis-simétrikəl/ *adj.*

dis•taff /dístaf/ *n.* **1 a** a cleft stick holding wool or flax wound for spinning by hand. **b** the corresponding part of a spinning wheel. **2** *archaic* women's work. [OE *distæf* (as STAFF[1]), the first element being app. rel. to LG *diesse*, MLG *dise(ne)* bunch of flax]

dis•taff side *n.* the female branch of a family.

dis•tal /díst'l/ *adj. Anat.* situated away from the center of the body or point of attachment; terminal. □□ **dis•tal•ly** *adv.* [DISTANT + -AL]

dis•tance /dístəns/ *n. & v.* ● *n.* **1** the condition of being far off; remoteness. **2 a** a space or interval between two things. **b** the length of this (*a distance of twenty miles*). **3** a distant point or place (*came from a distance*). **4** the avoidance of familiarity; aloofness; reserve (*there was a certain distance between them*). **5** a remoter field of vision (*saw him in the distance*). **6** an interval of time (*can't remember what happened at this distance*). **7 a** the full length of a race, etc. **b** *Brit. Racing* a length of 240 yards from the winning post on a racecourse. **c** *Boxing* the scheduled length of a fight. ● *v.tr.* (often *refl.*) **1** place far off (*distanced herself from them; distanced the painful memory*). **2** leave far behind in a race or competition. □ **at a distance** far off. **go the distance 1** *Boxing* complete a fight without being knocked out. **2** complete, esp. a hard task; endure an ordeal. **keep one's distance** maintain one's reserve. **within walking distance** near enough to reach by walking. [ME f. OF *distance, destance* f. L *distantia* f. *distare* stand apart (as DI-[2], *stare* stand)]

dis•tant /dístənt/ *adj.* **1 a** far away in space or time. **b** (usu. *predic.*; often foll. by *from*) at a specified distance (*three miles distant from them*). **2** remote or far apart in position, time, resemblance, etc. (*a distant prospect; a distant relation; a distant likeness*). **3** not intimate; reserved; cool (*a distant nod*). **4** remote; abstracted (*a distant stare*). **5** faint; vague (*he was a distant memory to her*). □□ **dis•tant•ly** *adv.* [ME f. OF *distant* or L *distant-* part. stem of *distare*: see DISTANCE]

dis•tant ear•ly warn•ing *n.* a radar system for the early detection of a missile attack.

dis•taste /dístáyst/ *n.* (usu. foll. by *for*) dislike; repugnance; aversion, esp. slight (*a distaste for prunes; a distaste for polite company*). □□ **dis•taste•ful** *adj.* **dis•taste•ful•ly** *adv.* **dis•taste•ful•ness** *n.*

dist. atty. *abbr.* district attorney.

dis•tem•per[1] /dístémpər/ *n. & v.* ● *n.* **1** a kind of paint using glue or size instead of an oil base, for use on walls or for scene painting. **2** a method of mural and poster painting using this. ● *v.tr.* paint (walls, etc.) with distemper. [earlier as verb, f. OF *destremper* or LL *distemperare* soak, macerate: see DISTEMPER[2]]

dis•tem•per[2] /dístémpər/ *n.* **1** a disease of some animals, esp. dogs, causing fever, coughing, and catarrh. **2** *archaic* political disorder. [earlier as verb, = upset, derange: ME f. LL *distemperare* (as DIS-, *temperare* mingle correctly)]

dis•tend /disténd/ *v.tr. & intr.* swell out by pressure from within (*distended stomach*). □□ **dis•ten•si•ble** /-sténsibəl/ *adj.* **dis•ten•si•bil•i•ty** /-sténsibílitee/ *n.* **dis•ten•sion** /-sténshən/ *n.* [ME f. L *distendere* (as DIS-, *tendere tens-* stretch)]

dis•tich /dístik/ *n. Prosody* a pair of verse lines; a couplet. [L *distichon* f. Gk *distikhon* (as DI-[1], *stikhos* line)]

dis•ti•chous /dístikəs/ *adj. Bot.* arranged in two opposite vertical rows. [L *distichus* (as DISTICH)]

dis•till /distíl/ *v.* (*Brit.* **dis•til**) (**dis•tilled, dis•til•ling**) **1** *tr. Chem.* purify (a liquid) by vaporizing it with heat, then condensing it with cold and collecting the result. **2** *tr.* **a** *Chem.* extract the essence of (a plant, etc.) usu. by heating it in a solvent. **b** extract the essential meaning or implications of (an idea, etc.). **3** *tr.* make (whiskey, essence, etc.) by distilling raw materials. **4** *tr.* (foll. by *off, out*) *Chem.* drive (the volatile constituent) off or out by heat. **5** *tr. & intr.* come as or give forth in drops; exude. **6** *intr.* undergo distillation. □□ **dis•til•la•to•ry** *adj.* [ME f. L *distillare* f. *destillare* (as DE-, *stilla* drop)]

dis•til•late /dístilit, - áyt/ *n.* a product of distillation.

dis•til•la•tion /dístiláyshən/ *n.* **1** the process of distilling or being distilled (in various senses). **2** something distilled.

dis•till•er /dístilər/ *n.* a person who distills, esp. a manufacturer of alcoholic liquor.

dis•till•er•y /dístiləree/ *n.* (*pl.* **•ies**) a place where alcoholic liquor is distilled.

dis•tinct /distíngkt/ *adj.* **1** (often foll. by *from*) **a** not identical; separate; individual. **b** different in kind or quality; unlike. **2 a** clearly perceptible; plain. **b** clearly understandable; definite. **3** unmistakable, decided (*had a distinct impression of being watched*). □□ **dis•tinct•ly** *adv.* **dis•tinct•ness** *n.* [ME f. L *distinctus* past part. of *distinguere* DISTINGUISH]

dis•tinc•tion /distíngkshən/ *n.* **1 a** the act or an instance of discriminating or distinguishing. **b** an instance of this. **c** the difference made by distinguishing. **2 a** something that differentiates, e.g., a mark, name, or title. **b** the fact of being different. **3** special consideration or honor. **4** distinguished character; excellence; eminence (*a film of distinction; shows distinction in his bearing*). **5** a grade in an examination denoting great excellence (*passed with distinction*). □ **distinction without a difference** a merely nominal or artificial distinction. [ME f. OF f. L *distinctio -onis* (as DISTINGUISH)]

dis•tinc•tive /distíngktiv/ *adj.* distinguishing; characteristic. □□ **dis•tinc•tive•ly** *adv.* **dis•tinc•tive•ness** *n.*

dis•tin•gué /dístanggáy, deestaNgáy/ *adj.* (*fem.* **dis•tin•guée** *pronunc.* same) having a distinguished air, features, manner, etc. [F, past part. of *distinguer*: see DISTINGUISH]

dis•tin•guish /distínggwish/ *v.* **1** *tr.* (often foll. by *from*) **a** see or point out the difference of; draw distinctions between (*cannot distinguish one from the other*). **b** constitute such a difference (*the mole distinguishes him from his twin*). **c** draw distinctions between; differentiate. **2** *tr.* be a mark or property of; characterize (*distinguished by her greed*). **3** *tr.* discover by listening, looking, etc. (*could distinguish two voices*). **4** *tr.* (usu. *refl.*; often foll. by *by*) make prominent or noteworthy (*distinguished himself by winning first prize*). **5** *tr.* (often foll. by *into*) divide; classify. **6** *intr.* (foll. by *between*) make or point out a difference between. □□ **dis•tin•guish•a•ble** *adj.* [F *distinguer* or L *distinguere* (as DIS-, *stinguere stinct-* extinguish): cf. EXTINGUISH]

SYNONYM TIP distinguish

DESCRY, DIFFERENTIATE, DISCERN, DISCRIMINATE. What we **discern** we see apart from all other objects (*to discern the lighthouse beaming on the far shore*). **Descry** puts even more emphasis on the distant or unclear nature of what we're seeing (*the lookout was barely able to descry a man approaching in the dusk*). To **discriminate** is to perceive the differences between or among things that are very similar; it may suggest that some aesthetic evaluation is involved (*to discriminate between two painters' styles*). **Distinguish** requires making even finer distinctions among things that resemble each other even more closely (*unable to distinguish the shadowy figures moving through the forest*). *Distinguish* can also mean recognizing by some special mark or outward sign (*the sheriff could be distinguished by his silver badge*). **Differentiate**, on the other hand, suggests the ability to perceive differences between things that are easily confused. In contrast to *distinguish*, *differentiate* suggests subtle differences that must be compared in some detail (*the color of her dress was difficult to differentiate from the color of the chair in which she was seated; it took a sharp eye to distinguish where her skirt ended and the upholstery began*) If you have trouble *differentiating* among these closely related verbs, you're not alone.

dis•tin•guished /distínggwisht/ *adj.* **1** (often foll. by *for, by*) of high standing; eminent; famous. **2** = DISTINGUÉ.

Dis•tin•guished Fly•ing Cross *n.* a US military decoration for heroism or extraordinary achievement in aerial flight.

Dis•tin•guished Serv•ice Cross *n.* a US Army decoration for extraordinary heroism in combat.

Dis•tin•guished Serv•ice Med•al *n.* a US military decoration for exceptionally meritorious service in a duty of great responsibility.

dis•tort /distáwrt/ *v.tr.* **1 a** put out of shape; make crooked or unshapely. **b** distort the appearance of, esp. by curved mirrors, etc.

2 misrepresent (motives, facts, statements, etc.). □□ **dis•tort•ed•ly** *adv.* **dis•tort•ed•ness** *n.* [L *distorquēre distort-* (as DIS-, *torquēre* twist)]

dis•tor•tion /distáwrshən/ *n.* **1** the act or an instance of distorting; the process of being distorted. **2** *Electronics* a change in the form of a signal during transmission, etc., usu. with some impairment of quality. □□ **dis•tor•tion•al** *adj.* **dis•tor•tion•less** *adj.* [L *distortio* (as DISTORT)]

distr. *abbr.* **1** distribution. **2** distributor. **3** district.

dis•tract /distrákt/ *v.tr.* **1** (often foll. by *from*) draw away the attention of (a person, the mind, etc.). **2** bewilder; perplex. **3** (as **distracted** *adj.*) troubled or distraught (*distracted by grief*; *distracted with worry*). **4** amuse, esp. in order to take the attention from pain or worry. □□ **dis•tract•ed•ly** *adv.* [ME f. L *distrahere distract-* (as DIS-, *trahere* draw)]

dis•trac•tion /distrákshən/ *n.* **1 a** the act of distracting, esp. the mind. **b** something that distracts; an interruption. **2** a relaxation from work; an amusement. **3** a lack of concentration. **4** confusion; perplexity. **5** frenzy; madness. □ **to distraction** almost to a state of madness. [ME f. OF *distraction* or L *distractio* (as DISTRACT)]

dis•train /distráyn/ *v.intr. Law* (usu. foll. by *upon*) impose distraint (on a person, goods, etc.). □□ **dis•train•ee** /–neé/ *n.* **dis•train•er** *n.* **dis•train•ment** *n.* [ME f. OF *destreindre* f. L *distringere* (as DIS-, *stringere strict-* draw tight)]

dis•traint /distráynt/ *n. Law* the seizure of chattels to make a person pay rent, etc., or meet an obligation, or to obtain satisfaction by their sale. [DISTRAIN, after *constraint*]

dis•trait /distráy/ *adj.* (*fem.* **dis•traite** /–stráyt/) not paying attention; absentminded; distraught. [ME f. OF *destrait* past part. of *destraire* (as DISTRACT)]

dis•traught /distráwt/ *adj.* distracted with worry, fear, etc.; extremely agitated. [ME, alt. of obs. *distract* (adj.) (as DISTRACT), after *straught* obs. past part. of STRETCH]

dis•tress /distrés/ *n. & v.* ● *n.* **1** severe pain, sorrow, anguish, etc. **2** the lack of money or comforts. **3** *Law* = DISTRAINT. **4** breathlessness; exhaustion. ● *v.tr.* **1** subject to distress; exhaust; afflict. **2** cause anxiety to; make unhappy; vex. □ **in distress 1** suffering or in danger. **2** (of a ship, aircraft, etc.) in danger or damaged. □□ **dis•tress•ful** *adj.* **dis•tress•ing•ly** *adv.* [ME f. OF *destresse*, etc., AF *destresser*, OF *–ecier* f. Gallo-Roman]

dis•tressed /distrést/ *adj.* **1** suffering from distress. **2** impoverished (*in distressed circumstances*). **3** (of furniture, leather, etc.) having simulated marks of age and wear.

dis•tressed ar•e•a *n.* a region needful of food, shelter, government aid, etc., due to the devastation of flood, earthquake, hurricane, etc.

dis•tress sig•nal *n.* a signal from a ship, aircraft, etc., in danger.

dis•trib•u•tar•y /distríbyəteree/ *n.* (*pl.* **·ies**) a branch of a river or glacier that does not return to the main stream after leaving it (as in a delta).

dis•trib•ute /distríbyōot/ *v.tr.* **1** give shares of; deal out. **2** spread about; scatter (*distributed the seeds evenly over the garden*). **3** divide into parts; arrange; classify. **4** *Printing* separate (type that has been set up) and return the characters to their separate boxes. **5** *Logic* use (a term) to include every individual of the class to which it refers. □□ **dis•trib•ut•a•ble** *adj.* [ME f. L *distribuere distribut-* (as DIS-, *tribuere* assign)]

dis•tri•bu•tion /distribyóoshən/ *n.* **1** the act or an instance of distributing; the process of being distributed. **2** *Econ.* **a** the dispersal of goods, etc., among consumers, brought about by commerce. **b** the extent to which different groups, classes, or individuals share in the total production or wealth of a community. **3** *Statistics* the way in which a characteristic is spread over members of a class. □□ **dis•tri•bu•tion•al** *adj.* [ME f. OF *distribution* or L *distributio* (as DISTRIBUTE)]

dis•trib•u•tive /distríbyətiv/ *adj. & n.* ● *adj.* **1** of, concerned with, or produced by distribution. **2** *Logic & Gram.* (of a pronoun, etc.) referring to each individual of a class, not to the class collectively (e.g., *each*, *either*). ● *n. Gram.* a distributive word. □□ **dis•trib•u•tive•ly** *adv.* [ME f. F *distributif –ive* or LL *distributivus* (as DISTRIBUTE)]

dis•trib•u•tor /distríbyətər/ *n.* **1** a person or thing that distributes. **2** an agent who supplies goods. **3** *Electr.* a device in an internal combustion engine for passing current to each spark plug in turn.

dis•trict /distrikt/ *n. & v.* ● *n.* **1 a** (often *attrib.*) a territory marked off for special administrative purposes. **b** *Brit.* an administrative division of a county or region. **2** an area which has common characteristics; a region (*the wine-growing district*). ● *v.tr.* divide into districts. [F f. med.L *districtus* (territory of) jurisdiction (as DISTRAIN)]

dis•trict at•tor•ney *n.* the prosecuting officer of a district.

dis•trict court *n.* **1** (in several US states) the court of general jurisdiction. **2** the federal trial court in each federal judicial district.

dis•trict heat•ing *n.* a supply of heat or hot water from one source to a district or a group of buildings.

dis•trust /distrúst/ *n. & v.* ● *n.* a lack of trust; doubt; suspicion. ● *v.tr.* have no trust or confidence in; doubt. □□ **dis•trust•er** *n.* **dis•trust•ful** *adj.* **dis•trust•ful•ly** *adv.*

dis•turb /distérb/ *v.tr.* **1** break the rest, calm, or quiet of; interrupt. **2 a** agitate; worry (*your story disturbs me*). **b** irritate. **3** move from a settled position; disarrange (*the papers had been disturbed*). **4** (as **disturbed** *adj.*) *Psychol.* emotionally or mentally unstable or abnormal. □□ **dis•turb•er** *n.* **dis•turb•ing** *adj.* **dis•turb•ing•ly** *adv.* [ME f. OF *desto(u)rber* f. L *disturbare* (as DIS-, *turbare* f. *turba* tumult)]

dis•turb•ance /distérbəns/ *n.* **1** the act or an instance of disturbing; the process of being disturbed **2** a tumult; an uproar. **3** agitation; worry. **4** an interruption. **5** *Law* interference with rights or property; molestation. [ME f. OF *desto(u)rbance* (as DISTURB)]

di•sul•fide /dísúlfíd/ *n.* (esp. *Brit.* **di•sul•phide**) *Chem.* a binary chemical containing two atoms of sulfur in each molecule.

dis•un•ion /disyóonyən/ *n.* a lack of union; separation; dissension. □□ **dis•u•nite** /dísyōonít/ *v.tr. & intr.* **dis•u•nity** *n.*

dis•use *n. & v.* ● *n.* /disyóos/ **1** lack of use or practice; discontinuance. **2** a disused state. ● *v.tr.* /disyóoz/ (esp. as **disused** *adj.*) cease to use. □ **fall into disuse** cease to be used. [ME f. OF *desuser* (as DIS-, USE)]

dis•u•til•i•ty /dísyōotílitee/ *n.* (*pl.* **·ties**) **1** harmfulness; injuriousness. **2** a factor tending to nullify the utility of something; a drawback.

di•syl•la•ble /dísíləbəl, di–/ *n.* (also **dis•syl•la•ble**) *Prosody* a word or metrical foot of two syllables. □□ **di•syl•lab•ic** /–lábik/ *adj.* [F *disyllabe* f. L *disyllabus* f. Gk *disullabos* (as DI-[1], SYLLABLE)]

dit /dit/ *n. Telegraphy* (in the Morse system) = DOT[1] 3 (cf. DAH). [imit.]

ditch /dich/ *n. & v.* ● *n.* **1** a long, narrow excavated channel esp. for drainage or to mark a boundary. **2** a watercourse, stream, etc. ● *v.* **1** *intr.* make or repair ditches. **2** *tr.* provide with ditches; drain. **3** *tr. sl.* leave in the lurch; abandon. **4** *tr. colloq.* **a** bring (an aircraft) down on water in an emergency. **b** drive (a vehicle) into a ditch. **5** *intr. colloq.* (of an aircraft) make a forced landing on water. **6** *tr. sl.* defeat; frustrate. **7** *tr.* derail (a train). □□ **ditch•er** *n.* [OE *dīc*, of unkn. orig.: cf. DIKE[1]]

ditch•wa•ter /díchwawtər/ *n.* stagnant water in a ditch. □ **dull as ditchwater** = *dull as dishwater* (see DISHWATER).

di•the•ism /dítheeizəm/ *n. Theol.* **1** a belief in two gods; dualism. **2** a belief in equal independent ruling principles of good and evil. □□ **di•the•ist** *n.*

dith•er /díthər/ *v. & n.* ● *v.intr.* **1** hesitate; be indecisive. **2** *dial.* tremble; quiver. ● *n. colloq.* **1** a state of agitation or apprehension. **2** a state of hesitation; indecisiveness. □ **in a dither** *colloq.* in a state of extreme agitation or vacillation. □□ **dith•er•er** *n.* **dith•er•y** *adj.* [var. of *didder*, DODDER[1]]

dith•y•ramb /díthiram, –ramb/ *n.* **1 a** a wild choral hymn in ancient Greece, esp. to Dionysus. **b** a bacchanalian song. **2** any passionate or inflated poem, speech, etc. □□ **dith•y•ram•bic** /–rámbik/ *adj.* [L *dithyrambus* f. Gk *dithurambos*, of unkn. orig.]

dit•sy /dítsee/ *adj.* (also **dit•zy**; **dit•si•er** or **dit•zi•er**, **dit•si•est** or **dit•zi•est**) *colloq.* silly; foolishly giddy; scatterbrained. [perh. f. DOTTY and DIZZY]

dit•ta•ny /dít'nee/ *n.* (*pl.* **·nies**) **1** a purple-flowered herb of the mint family, formerly used medicinally. **2** = FRAXINELLA [ME f. OF *dita(i)n* f. med.L *dictamus* f. L *dictamnus* f. Gk *diktamnon* perh. f. *Diktē*, a mountain in Crete]

dit•to /dítō/ *n. & v.* ● *n.* (*pl.* **·tos**) **1** (in accounts, inventories, lists, etc.) the aforesaid; the same. **2** *colloq.* (replacing a word or phrase to avoid repetition) the same (*came in late last night and ditto the night before*). **3** a similar thing; a duplicate. ● *v.tr.* (**·toes**, **·toed**) repeat (another's action or words). □ **say ditto to** esp. *Brit. colloq.* agree with; endorse. [It. dial. f. L *dictus* past part. of *dicere* say] ▶Often represented by " under the word or sum to be repeated.

dit•tog•ra•phy /ditógrəfee/ *n.* (*pl.* **·phies**) **1** a copyist's mistaken repetition of a letter, word, or phrase. **2** an example of this. □□ **dit•to•graph•ic** /dítəgráfik/ *adj.* [Gk *dittos* double + –GRAPHY]

dit•to marks *n.* quotation marks representing 'ditto.'

dit•ty /dítee/ *n.* (*pl.* **·ties**) a short simple song. [ME f. OF *dité* composition f. L *dictatum* neut. past part. of *dictare* DICTATE]

dit•ty bag /díteebag/ *n.* (also **dit•ty box** /–boks/) a sailor's or fisherman's receptacle for odds and ends. [19th c.: orig. unkn.]

ditz /dits/ *n. sl.* a ditsy person.

di•u•re•sis /díəreéesis/ *n. Med.* an increased excretion of urine. [mod.L f. Gk (as DI-[3], *ourēsis* urination)]

di•u•ret•ic /díərétik/ *adj. & n.* ● *adj.* causing increased output of urine. ● *n.* a diuretic drug. [ME f. OF *diuretique* or LL *diureticus* f. Gk *diourētikos* f. *dioureō* urinate]

di•ur•nal /dī–érnəl/ *adj.* **1** of or during the day; not nocturnal. **2** daily; of each day. **3** *Astron.* occupying one day. **4** *Zool.* (of animals) active in the daytime. **5** *Bot.* (of plants) open only during the day. □□ **di•ur•nal•ly** *adv.* [ME f. LL *diurnalis* f. L *diurnus* f. *dies* day]

div. *abbr.* division.

di•va /deévə/ *n.* (*pl.* **di•vas** or **di•ve** /–vay/) a great or famous woman singer; a prima donna. [It. f. L, = goddess]

di•va•gate /dívəgayt, dív–/ *v.intr. literary* stray; digress. □□ **di•va•ga•tion** /–gáyshən/ *n.* [L *divagari* (as DIS-, *vagari* wander)]

di•va•lent /díváylənt/ *adj. Chem.* **1** having a valence of two; bivalent. **2** having two valencies. □□ **di•va•lence** *n.* [DI-[1] + *valent-* part. stem (as VALENCE)]

di·van /diván, dī–/ *n.* **1 a** a long, low, padded seat set against a wall; a backless sofa. **b** a bed consisting of a base and mattress, usu. with no board at either end. **2 a** Middle Eastern state legislative body, council chamber, or court of justice. **3** *archaic* **a** a tobacco shop. **b** a smoking room attached to such a shop. [F *divan* or It. *divano* f. Turk. *dīvān* f. Arab. *dīwān* f. Pers. *dīvān* anthology, register, court, bench]

di·var·i·cate /divárikayt, dee–/ *v.intr.* diverge; branch; separate widely. □□ **di·var·i·cate** /–kət/ *adj.* **di·var·i·ca·tion** /–káyshən/ *n.* [L *divaricare* (as DI-², *varicus* straddling)]

dive /dīv/ *v. & n.* ●*v.* (**dived** or **dove** /dōv/) **1** *intr.* plunge head first into water, esp. as a sport. **2** *intr.* **a** *Aeron.* (of an aircraft) plunge steeply downward at speed. **b** *Naut.* (of a submarine) submerge. **c** (of a person) plunge downward. **3** *intr.* (foll. by *into*) *colloq.* **a** put one's hand into (a pocket, handbag, vessel, etc.) quickly and deeply. **b** occupy oneself suddenly and enthusiastically with (a subject, meal, etc.). **4** *tr.* (foll. by *into*) plunge (a hand, etc.) into. ●*n.* **1** an act of diving; a plunge. **2 a** the submerging of a submarine. **b** the steep descent of an aircraft. **3** a sudden darting movement. **4** *colloq.* a disreputable nightclub, drinking establishment, etc. **5** *Boxing sl.* a pretended knockout (*took a dive in the second round*). □ **dive in** *colloq.* help oneself (to food). [OE *dūfan* (v.intr.) dive, sink, and *dȳfan* (v.tr.) immerse, f. Gmc: rel. to DEEP, DIP]

dive-bomb *v.tr.* bomb (a target) while diving steeply downward in an aircraft. □□ **dive-bomb·er** *n.*

div·er /dívər/ *n.* **1** a person who dives. **2 a** a person who wears a diving suit to work under water for long periods. **b** a pearl diver, etc. **3** any of various diving birds, esp. large waterbirds of the family Gaviidae.

di·verge /dīvérj/ *v.* **1** *intr.* **a** proceed in a different direction or in different directions from a point (*diverging rays; the path diverges here*). **b** take a different course or different courses (*their interests diverged*). **2** *intr.* **a** (often foll. by *from*) depart from a set course (*diverged from the track; diverged from his parents' wishes*). **b** differ markedly (*they diverged as to the best course*). **3** *tr.* cause to diverge; deflect. **4** *intr. Math.* (of a series) increase indefinitely as more of its terms are added. [med.L *divergere* (as DI-², L *vergere* incline)]

di·ver·gent /dīvérjənt/ *adj.* **1** diverging. **2** *Psychol.* (of thought) tending to reach a variety of possible solutions when analyzing a problem. **3** *Math.* (of a series) increasing indefinitely as more of its terms are added; not convergent. □□ **di·ver·gence** /–jəns/ *n.* **di·ver·gen·cy** *n.* **di·ver·gent·ly** *adv.*

di·vers /dívərz/ *adj. archaic* or *literary* more than one; sundry; several. [ME f. OF f. L *diversus* DIVERSE (as DI-², *versus* past part. of *vertere* turn)]

di·verse /dīvérs, dī–/ *adj.* unlike in nature or qualities; varied. □□ **di·verse·ly** *adv.* [ME (as DIVERS)]

di·ver·si·fy /dīvérsifī, dī–/ *v.* (**·fies, ·fied**) **1** *tr.* make diverse; vary; modify. **2** *tr. Commerce* **a** spread (investment) over several enterprises or products, esp. to reduce the risk of loss. **b** introduce a spread of investment in (an enterprise, etc.). **3** *intr.* (often foll. by *into*) esp. *Commerce* (of a firm, etc.) expand the range of products handled. □□ **di·ver·si·fi·ca·tion** /–fikáyshən/ *n.* [ME f. OF *diversifier* f. med.L *diversificare* (as DIVERS)]

di·ver·sion /dīvérzhən, dī–/ *n.* **1 a** the act of diverting; deviation. **b** an instance of this. **2 a** the diverting of attention deliberately. **b** a stratagem for this purpose (*created a diversion to secure their escape*). **3** a recreation or pastime. **4** *Brit.* = DETOUR *n.* 2. □□ **di·ver·sion·al** *adj.* **di·ver·sion·ar·y** *adj.* [LL *diversio* (as DIVERT)]

di·ver·sion·ist /dīvérzhənist, dī–/ *n.* **1** a person who engages in disruptive or subversive activities. **2** *Polit.* (esp. used by Communists) a conspirator against the government; a saboteur.

di·ver·si·ty /dīvérsitee, dī–/ *n.* (*pl.* **·ties**) **1** being diverse; variety. **2** a different kind; a variety. [ME f. OF *diversité* f. L *diversitas –tatis* (as DIVERS)]

di·vert /dīvért, dī–/ *v.tr.* **1** (often foll. by *from, to*) a turn aside; deflect. **b** draw the attention of; distract. **2** (often as **diverting** *adj.*) entertain; amuse. □□ **di·vert·ing·ly** *adv.* [ME f. F *divertir* f. L *divertere* (as DI-², *vertere* turn)]

di·ver·tic·u·lar /dívərtíkyələr/ *adj. Med.* of or relating to a diverticulum.

di·ver·tic·u·li·tis /dívərtíkyəlítis/ *n. Med.* inflammation of a diverticulum.

di·ver·tic·u·lum /dívərtíkyələm/ *n.* (*pl.* **di·ver·tic·u·la** /–lə/) *Anat.* a blind tube forming at weak points in a cavity or passage esp. of the alimentary tract. □□ **di·ver·tic·u·lo·sis** /–lósis/ *n.* [med.L, var. of L *deverticulum* byway f. *devertere* (as DE-, *vertere* turn)]

di·ver·ti·men·to /dívərtiméntō, diváir–/ *n.* (*pl.* **divertimenti** /–tee/ or **·tos**) *Mus.* a light and entertaining composition, often in the form of a suite for chamber orchestra. [It., = diversion]

di·ver·tisse·ment /dívərtésmənt, deevaírteesmóN/ *n.* **1** a diversion; an entertainment. **2** a short ballet, etc., between acts or longer pieces. [F, f. *divertiss-* stem of *divertir* DIVERT]

Di·ves /díveez/ *n.* a rich man. [L, in Vulgate transl. of Luke 16]

di·vest /divést, dī–/ *v.tr.* **1** (usu. foll. by *of*; often *refl.*) unclothe; strip (*divested himself of his jacket*). **2** deprive; dispossess; free; rid (*can-*

not divest herself of the idea). □□ **di·vest·i·ture** *n.* **di·vest·ment** *n.* **di·ves·ture** *n.* [earlier *devest* f. OF *desvestir*, etc. (as DIS-, L *vestire* f. *vestis* garment)]

di·vide /divíd/ *v. & n.* ●*v.* **1** *tr. & intr.* (often foll. by *in, into*) separate or be separated into parts; break up; split (*the river divides into two; the road divides; divided them into three groups*). **2** *tr. & intr.* (often foll. by *out*) distribute; deal; share (*divided it out between them*). **3** *tr.* **a** cut off; separate; part (*divide the sheep from the goats*). **b** mark out into parts (*a ruler divided into inches*). **c** specify different kinds of, classify (*people can be divided into two types*). **4** *tr.* cause to disagree; set at variance (*religion divided them*). **5** *Math.* **a** *tr.* find how many times (a number) contains another (*divide 20 by 4*). **b** *intr.* (of a number) be contained in (a number) without a remainder (*4 divides into 20*). **c** *intr.* be susceptible of division (*10 divides by 2 and 5*). **d** *tr.* find how many times (a number) is contained in another (*divide 4 into 20*). **6** *intr. Math.* do division (*can divide well*). **7** *Parl.* **a** *intr.* (of a legislative assembly, etc.) part into two groups for voting (*the House divided*). **b** *tr.* so divide (a parliament, etc.) for voting. ●*n.* **1** a dividing or boundary line (*the divide between rich and poor*). **2** a watershed. □ **divided against itself** formed into factions. [ME f. L *dividere divis-* (as DI-², *vid-* separate)]

di·vid·ed high·way *n.* a highway with a median strip separating the two opposing flows of traffic.

div·i·dend /dívidend/ *n.* **1 a** a sum of money to be divided among a number of persons, esp. that paid by a company to shareholders. **b** a similar sum payable to winners in a betting pool, to members of a cooperative, or to creditors of an insolvent estate. **c** an individual's share of a dividend. **2** *Math.* a number to be divided by a divisor. □ a benefit from any action (*their long training paid dividends*). □ **dividend yield** a dividend expressed as a percentage of a current share price. [AF *dividende* f. L *dividendum* (as DIVIDE)]

di·vid·er /dívídər/ *n.* **1** a screen, piece of furniture, etc., dividing a room into two parts. **2** (in *pl.*) a measuring compass, esp. with a screw for making fine adjustments.

div·i·div·i /díveedivee/ *n.* (*pl.* **div·i·div·is**) **1** a small tree, *Caesalpinia coriaria*, native to tropical Africa, bearing curved pods. **2** this pod used as a source of tannin. [Carib]

div·i·na·tion /dívináyshən/ *n.* **1** supposed insight into the future or the unknown gained by supernatural means. **2 a** a skillful and accurate forecast. **b** a good guess. □□ **di·vin·a·to·ry** /–vínətáwree/ *adj.* [ME f OF *divination* or L *divinatio* (as DIVINE)]

di·vine /divín/ *adj., v., & n.* ●*adj.* (**di·vin·er, di·vin·est**) **1 a** of, from, or like God or a god. **b** devoted to God; sacred (*divine service*). **2 a** more than humanly excellent, gifted, or beautiful. **b** *colloq.* excellent; delightful. ●*v.* **1** *tr.* discover by guessing, intuition, inspiration, or magic. **2** *tr.* foresee; predict; conjecture. **3** *intr.* practice divination. **4** *intr.* dowse. ●*n.* **1** a cleric, usu. an expert in theology. **2** (**the Divine**) providence or God. □□ **di·vine·ly** *adv.* **di·vine·ness** *n.* **di·vin·er** *n.* **di·vin·ize** /dívinīz/ *v.tr.* [ME f. OF *devin –ine* f. L *divinus* f. *divus* godlike]

SYNONYM TIP divine

HOLY, SACRED, HALLOWED, CONSECRATED. **Holy** is the only one of these words associated with religion and worship that may be applied directly to the Supreme Being. Something that is *holy* is regarded with the highest reverence because of its connection with God or a god (*Christmas is a holy day in the Christian calendar*). Something that is **sacred**, on the other hand, is set apart as *holy* or is dedicated to some exalted purpose (*sacred music*) but may derive its holiness from a human source rather than from God (*a sacred oath between brothers*). In its strictest sense, **divine** means associated with or derived from God (*the divine right of kings*), but it has also been used to describe anything that is admirable or treasured (*her wedding dress was divine*). **Hallowed** and **consecrated** refer to what has been made sacred or holy, with *hallowed* connotating intrinsic holiness (*they walked on hallowed ground*) and *consecrated* meaning blessed by a formal rite or formally dedicated to some religious use (*the old building had been consecrated as a church*).

divine of·fice *n.* see OFFICE.

di·vine right of kings *n.* the doctrine that kings derive their sovereignty and authority from God, not from their subjects.

div·ing bell *n.* an open-bottomed box or bell, supplied with air, in which a person can descend into deep water.

div·ing board *n.* an elevated board projecting over a swimming pool or other body of water, from which people dive or jump in.

div·ing suit *n.* a watertight suit usu. with a helmet and an air supply, worn for working under water.

di·vin·ing rod *n.* = DOWSING ROD.

di·vin·i·ty /dívínitee/ *n.* (*pl.* **·ties**) **1** the state or quality of being divine. **2 a** a god; a divine being. **b** (as **the Divinity**) God. **3** the study of religion; theology. [ME f. OF *divinité* f. L *divinitas –tatis* (as DIVINE)]

di•vis•i•ble /divízibəl/ *adj.* **1** capable of being divided, physically or mentally. **2** (foll. by *by*) *Math.* containing (a number) a number of times without a remainder (*15 is divisible by 3 and 5*). □□ **di•vis•ibil•i•ty** /–bílitee/ *n.* [F *divisible* or LL *divisibilis* (as DIVIDE)]

di•vi•sion /divízhən/ *n.* **1** the act or an instance of dividing; the process of being divided. **2** *Math.* the process of dividing one number by another (see also *long division* (see LONG¹), *short division*). **3** disagreement or discord (*division of opinion*). **4** *Parl.* the separation of members of a legislative body into two sets for counting votes for and against. **5 a** one of two or more parts into which a thing is divided. **b** the point at which a thing is divided. **6** a major unit of administration or organization, esp.: **a** a group of army brigades or regiments. **b** *Sports* a grouping of teams within a league. **7 a** a district defined for administrative purposes. **b** *Brit.* a part of a county or borough returning a Member of Parliament. **8 a** *Bot.* a major taxonomic grouping. **b** *Zool.* a subsidiary category between major levels of classification. **9** *Logic* a classification of kinds, parts, or senses. □□ **di•vi•sion•al** *adj.* **di•vi•sion•al•ly** *adv.* **di•vi•sion•ar•y** *adj.* [ME f. OF *divisiun* f. L *divisio –onis* (as DIVIDE)]

di•vi•sion of la•bor *n.* the improvement of efficiency by giving different parts of a manufacturing process, etc., to different people.

di•vi•sion sign *n.* the symbol (÷) indicating that one quantity is to be divided by another.

di•vi•sive /divísiv/ *adj.* tending to divide, esp. in opinion; causing disagreement. □□ **di•vi•sive•ly** *adv.* **di•vi•sive•ness** *n.* [LL *divisivus* (as DIVIDE)]

di•vi•sor /divízər/ *n. Math.* **1** a number by which another is to be divided. **2** a number that divides another without a remainder. [ME f. F *diviseur* or L *divisor* (as DIVIDE)]

di•vorce /diváwrs/ *n. & v. • n.* **1 a** the legal dissolution of a marriage. **b** a legal decree of this. **2** a severance or separation (*a divorce between thought and feeling*). *• v.* **1 a** *tr.* (usu. as **divorced** *adj.*) (often foll. by *from*) legally dissolve the marriage of (*a divorced couple; he wants to get divorced from her*). **b** *intr.* separate by divorce (*they divorced last year*). **c** *tr.* end one's marriage with (*divorced him for neglect*). **2** *tr.* (often foll. by *from*) detach; separate (*divorced from reality*). **3** *tr. archaic* dissolve (a union). □□ **di•vorce•ment** *n.* [ME f. OF *divorce* (n.), *divorcer* (v.) f. LL *divortiare* f. L *divortium* f. *divortere* (as DI-², *vertere* turn)]

di•vor•cé /divawrsáy/ *n.* a divorced man.

di•vor•cée /divawrsáy/ *n.* a divorced woman.

div•ot /dívət/ *n.* **1** a piece of turf cut out by a golf club in making a stroke. **2** esp. *Sc.* a piece of turf; a sod. [16th c.: orig. unkn.]

di•vulge /divúlj, dī–/ *v.tr.* disclose; reveal (a secret, etc.). □□ **di•vulga•tion** /–vulgáyshən/ *n.* **di•vulge•ment** *n.* **di•vul•gence** *n.* [L *divulgare* (as DI-², *vulgare* publish f. *vulgus* common people)]

div•vy /dívee/ *n. & v. colloq. • n.* (*pl.* **-vies**) **1** a distribution. **2** *Brit.* a dividend; a share, esp. of profits earned by a cooperative. *• v.tr.* (**-vies, -vied**) (often foll. by *up*) share out; divide. [abbr. of DIVIDEND]

Di•wa•li /deewaálee/ *n.* a Hindu festival with illuminations, held between September and November. [Hind. *dīwalī* f. Skr. *dīpāvalī* row of lights f. *dīpa* lamp]

Dix•ie /díksee/ *n.* the southern states of the US. [19th c.: orig. uncert.]

dix•ie /díksee/ *n.* a large iron cooking pot used by campers, etc. [Hind. *degchī* cooking pot f. Pers. *degcha* dimin. of *deg* pot]

Dix•ie•land /díkseeland/ *n.* **1** = DIXIE. **2** a kind of jazz with a strong, two-beat rhythm and collective improvisation. [DIXIE]

diz•zy /dízee/ *adj. & v. • adj.* (**diz•zi•er, diz•zi•est**) **1 a** giddy; unsteady. **b** lacking mental stability; confused. **2** causing giddiness (*dizzy heights; dizzy speed*). *• v.tr.* **1** make dizzy. **2** bewilder. □□ **diz•zi•ly** *adv.* **diz•zi•ness** *n.* [OE *dysig* f. WG]

DJ *abbr.* **1** disk jockey. **2** district judge.

djel•la•ba /jəlaábə/ *n.* (also **djel•la•bah, jel•la•ba**) a loose, hooded, usu. woolen cloak worn or as worn by Arab men. [Arab. *jallaba, jallābīya*]

djib•ba (also **djib•bah**) var. of JIBBA.

DL *abbr. Sports* disabled list.

dl *abbr.* deciliter(s).

D-layer /déelayər/ *n.* the lowest layer of the ionosphere able to reflect low-frequency radio waves. [*D* (arbitrary)]

D.Litt. *abbr.* Doctor of Letters. [L *Doctor Litterarum*]

DM *abbr.* (also **D-mark**) deutsche mark.

dm *abbr.* decimeter(s).

D.M.D. *abbr.* doctor of dental medicine. [L *Dentariae Medicinae Doctor* or *Doctor Medicinae Dentalis*]

D.Mus. *abbr.* Doctor of Music.

DMZ *abbr.* demilitarized zone.

DNA *abbr.* deoxyribonucleic acid, the self-replicating material present in nearly all living organisms, esp. as a constituent of chromosomes, which is the carrier of genetic information.

DNA fin•ger•print•ing *n.* the identification of an individual by analysis of DNA structure from body tissue, hair, blood, etc., esp. as used for forensic purposes.

D-no•tice /déenōtis/ *n. Brit.* a government notice to news editors not to publish items on specified subjects, for reasons of security. [*defense* + NOTICE]

do¹ /dōō/ *v. & n. • v.* (*3rd sing. present* **does** /duz/; *past* **did** /did/; *past part.* **done** /dun/) **1** *tr.* perform; carry out; achieve; complete (work, etc.) (*did his homework; there's a lot to do; he can do anything*). **2** *tr.* **a** produce; make (*she was doing a painting; I did a translation; decided to do a casserole*). **b** provide (*do you do lunches?*). **3** *tr.* bestow; grant; have a specified effect on (*a walk would do you good; do me a favor*). **4** *intr.* act; behave; proceed (*do as I do; she would do well to accept the offer*). **5** *tr.* work at; study; be occupied with (*what does your father do?; we're doing Chaucer next term*). **6 a** *intr.* be suitable or acceptable; suffice (*this dress won't do for a wedding; a sandwich will do until we get home; that will never do*). **b** *tr.* satisfy; be suitable for (*that hotel will do me nicely*). **7** *tr.* deal with; put in order (*the garden needs doing; the barber will do you next; I must do my hair before we go*). **8** *intr.* **a** fare; get on (*the patients were doing excellently; he did badly in the test*). **b** perform; work (*could do better*). **9** *tr.* solve; work out (*we did the puzzle*). **b** (*prec. by can or be able to*) be competent at (*can you do cartwheels?; I never could do algebra*). **10** *tr.* **a** traverse (a certain distance) (*we did fifty miles today*). **b** travel at a specified speed (*he overtook us doing about eighty*). **11** *tr. colloq.* **a** act or behave like (*did a Houdini*). **b** esp. *Brit.* play the part of (*she was asked to do hostess*). **12** *intr.* **a** *colloq.* finish (*are you done annoying me?; I'm done in the bathroom*). **b** (as **done** *adj.*) be over (*the day is done*). **13** *tr.* produce or give a performance of (*the school does many plays and concerts; we've never done* Pygmalion). **14** *tr.* cook, esp. to the right degree (*do it in the oven; the potatoes aren't done yet*). **15** *intr.* be in progress (*what's doing?*). **16** *tr. colloq.* visit; see the sights of (*we did all the art galleries*). **17** *tr. colloq.* **a** (often as **done** *adj.*; often foll. by *in*) exhaust; tire out (*the climb has completely done me in*). **b** beat up; defeat; kill. **c** ruin (*now you've done it*). **18** *tr.* (foll. by *into*) translate or transform (*the book was done into French*). **19** *tr.* esp. *Brit. colloq.* (with qualifying adverb) provide food, etc., for in a specified way (*they do one very well here*). **20** *tr. sl.* **a** rob (*they did a liquor store downtown*). **b** swindle (*I was done at the market*). **21** *tr. Brit. sl.* prosecute; convict (*they were done for shoplifting*). **22** *tr. sl.* undergo (a specified term of imprisonment) (*he did two years for fraud*). **23** *tr. coarse sl.* have sexual intercourse with. **24** *tr. sl.* take (a drug). *• v.aux.* **1 a** (except with *be, can, may, ought, shall, will*) in questions and negative statements (*do you understand?; I don't smoke*). **b** (except with *can, may, ought, shall, will*) in negative commands (*do be silly; do not come tomorrow*). **2** ellipt. or in place of verb or verb and object (*you know her better than I do; I wanted to go and I did so; tell me, do!*). **3** forming emphatic present and past tenses (*I do want to; do tell me; they did go but she was out*). **4** in inversion for emphasis (*rarely does it happen; did she but know it*). *• n.* (*pl.* **dos** or **do's**) **1** *colloq.* an elaborate event, party, or operation. **2** *Brit. sl.* a swindle or hoax. □ **be done with** see DONE. **do about** see ABOUT *prep.* 1d. **do away with** *colloq.* **1** abolish. **2** kill. **do battle** enter into combat. **do one's best** see BEST. **do one's bit** see BIT¹. **do by** treat or deal with in a specified way (*do as you would be done by*). **do credit to** see CREDIT. **do for** **1** be satisfactory or sufficient for. **2** *colloq.* (esp. as **done for** *adj.*) destroy; ruin; kill (*he knew he was done for*). **3** esp. *Brit. colloq.* act as housekeeper for. **do one's head** (or **nut**) *Brit. sl.* be extremely angry or agitated. **do the honors** see HONOR. **do in 1** *sl.* **a** kill. **b** ruin; do injury to. **2** *colloq.* exhaust; tire out. **do justice to** see JUSTICE. **do nothing for** (or **to**) *colloq.* detract from the appearance or quality of (*such behavior does nothing for our reputation*). **do or die** persist regardless of danger. **do out** *Brit. colloq.* clean or redecorate (a room). **do a person out of** *colloq.* unjustly deprive a person of; swindle out of (*he was done out of his pension*). **do over** **1** *sl.* attack; beat up. **2** *colloq.* redecorate, refurbish. **3** *colloq.* do again. **do proud** see PROUD. **dos and don'ts** rules of behavior. **do something for** (or **to**) *colloq.* enhance the appearance or quality of (*that carpet does something for the room*). **do to** (*archaic* **unto**) = *do by.* **do to death** see DEATH. **do the trick** see TRICK. **do up 1** fasten; secure. **2** *colloq.* a refurbish; renovate. **b** adorn; dress up. **3** *Brit. sl.* **a** ruin; get the better of. **b** beat up. **do well for oneself** prosper. **do well out of** profit by. **do with** (*prec. by could*) would be glad to have; would profit by (*I could do with a rest; you could do with a wash*). **do without** manage without; forgo (also *absol.*: *we shall just have to do without*). **have nothing to do with 1** have no connection or dealings with (*our problem has nothing to do with the latest news; after the disagreement he had nothing to do with his father*). **2** be no business or concern of (*the decision has nothing to do with her*). **have to do** (or **something to do**) **with** be connected with (*his limp has to do with a car accident*). [OE *dōn* f. Gmc: rel. to Skr *dádhāmi* put, Gk *tithemi* place, L *facere* do]

do² /dō/ *n.* (also **doh**) *Mus.* **1** (in tonic sol-fa) the first and eighth notes of a major scale. **2** the note C in the fixed-do system. [18th c.: f. It. *do*]

do. *abbr.* ditto.

DOA *abbr.* dead on arrival (at a hospital, etc.).

do·a·ble /dóóəbəl/ adj. that can be done.

DOB abbr. date of birth.

dob·bin /dóbin/ n. a draft horse; a farm horse. [pet form of the name *Robert*]

Do·ber·man /dóbərmən/ n. (in full **Doberman pinscher** /pínshər/) **1** a large dog of a German breed with a smooth coat. **2** this breed. [L. *Dobermann*, 19th-c. Ger. dog breeder + G *Pinscher* terrier]

doc /dok/ n. colloq. doctor. [abbr.]

do·cent /dósənt/ n. **1** a teacher or lecturer in a college or university. **2** a person who serves as a well-informed guide, as in a museum. [f. G *Dozent*, f. L *docere* to teach]

doc·ile /dósəl/ adj. **1** submissive, easily managed. **2** archaic teachable. □□ **doc·ile·ly** adv. **do·cil·i·ty** /–sílitee/ n. [ME f. L *docilis* f. *docēre* teach]

dock[1] /dok/ n. & v. • n. **1** a structure extending out from the shore into a body of water, to which boats may be moored; a pier. **2** an artificially enclosed body of water for the loading, unloading, and repair of ships. **3** (in pl.) a range of docks with wharves and offices; a dockyard. **4** a ship's berth, a wharf. **5** = DRY DOCK. **6** Theatr. = SCENE DOCK. • v. **1** tr. & intr. bring or come into a dock. **2 a** tr. join (spacecraft) together in space. **b** intr. (of spacecraft) be joined. **3** tr. provide with a dock or docks. □ **in dock** Brit. colloq. in the hospital or (of a vehicle) awaiting repairs. [MDu. *docke*, of unkn. orig.]

dock[2] /dok/ n. the enclosure in a criminal court for the accused. □ **in the dock** on trial. [16th c.: prob. orig. cant = Flem. *dok* cage, of unkn. orig.]

dock[3] /dok/ n. any weed of the genus *Rumex*, with broad leaves. [OE *docce*]

dock[4] /dok/ v. & n. • v.tr. **1 a** cut short (an animal's tail). **b** cut short the tail of (an animal). **2 a** (often foll. by *from*) deduct (a part) from wages, supplies, etc. **b** reduce (wages, etc.) in this way. • n. **1** the solid, bony part of an animal's tail. **2** the crupper of a saddle or harness. □ **dock-tailed** having a docked tail. [ME, of uncert. orig.]

dock·age /dókij/ n. **1** the charge made for using docks. **2** dock accommodation. **3** the berthing of vessels in docks.

dock·er /dókər/ n. a person employed to load and unload ships.

dock·et /dókit/ n. & v. • n. **1** a list of causes for trial or persons having causes pending. **2** a list of things to be done. **3** Brit. **a** a document or label listing goods delivered or the contents of a package, or recording payment of customs dues, etc. **b** a voucher; an order form. • v.tr. label with a docket. [15th c.: orig. unkn.]

dock·hand /dókhand/ n. a person employed to load and unload ships; a longshoreman.

dock·land /dókland/ n. a district near docks. [DOCK[1]]

dock·side /dóksīd/ n. the area adjacent to a dock (*boats tethered at dockside*).

dock·yard /dókyaard/ n. an area with docks and equipment for building and repairing ships, esp. for naval use.

doc·tor /dóktər/ n. & v. • n. **1 a** a qualified practitioner of medicine; a physician. **b** a qualified dentist or veterinary surgeon. **2** a person who holds a doctorate (*Doctor of Civil Law*). **3** colloq. a person who carries out repairs. **4** archaic a teacher or learned man. **5** sl. a cook on board a ship or in a camp. **6** (in full **doctor-blade**) Printing esp. Brit. a blade for removing surplus ink, etc. **7** an artificial fishing fly. • v. colloq. **1 a** tr. treat medically. **b** intr. (esp. as **doctoring** n.) practice as a physician. **2** tr. Brit. castrate or spay. **3** tr. patch up (machinery, etc.); mend. **4** tr. adulterate. **5** tr. tamper with; falsify. **6** tr. confer a degree of doctor on. □ **go for the doctor** Austral. sl. **1** make an all-out effort. **2** bet all one has. **(just) what the doctor ordered** colloq. something beneficial or desirable. □□ **doc·tor·hood** n. **doc·to·ri·al** /–táwreeəl/ adj. **doc·tor·ly** adj. **doc·tor·ship** n. [ME f. OF *doctour* f. L *doctor* f. *docēre* doct- teach]

doc·tor·al /dóktərəl/ adj. of or for a degree of doctor.

doc·tor·ate /dóktərət/ n. the highest university degree in any faculty, often honorary.

Doc·tor of Phi·los·o·phy n. a doctorate in a discipline other than education, law, medicine, or sometimes theology.

Doc·tor of the Church n. any of several early ecclesiastics of noted learning.

doc·tri·naire /dóktrináir/ adj. & n. • adj. seeking to apply a theory or doctrine in all circumstances without regard to practical considerations; theoretical and impractical. • n. a doctrinaire person; a pedantic theorist. □□ **doc·tri·nair·ism** n. **doc·tri·nar·i·an** n. [F f. *doctrine* DOCTRINE + –*aire* –ARY[1]]

doc·tri·nal /dóktrinəl/ adj. of or inculcating a doctrine or doctrines. □□ **doc·tri·nal·ly** adv. [LL *doctrinalis* (as DOCTRINE)]

doc·trine /dóktrin/ n. **1** what is taught; a body of instruction. **2 a** a principle of religious or political, etc., belief. **b** a set of such principles; dogma. □□ **doc·trin·ism** n. **doc·trin·ist** n. [ME f. OF f. L *doctrina* teaching (as DOCTOR)]

doc·u·dra·ma /dókyōōdraamə, –dramə/ n. a dramatized television movie based on real events. [DOCUMENTARY + DRAMA]

doc·u·ment n. & v. • n. /dókyəmənt/ a piece of written or printed matter that provides a record or evidence of events, an agreement, ownership, identification, etc. • v.tr. /dókyəmənt/ **1** prove by or provide with documents or evidence. **2** record in a document. □□ **doc·**

u·men·tal /mént'l/ adj. [ME f. OF f. L *documentum* proof f. *docēre* teach]

doc·u·men·tal·ist /dókyəmént'list/ n. a person engaged in documentation.

doc·u·men·ta·ry /dókyəméntəree/ adj. & n. • adj. **1** consisting of documents (*documentary evidence*). **2** providing a factual record or report. • n. (pl. **-ries**) a documentary film, etc. □□ **doc·u·men·tar·i·ly** adv.

doc·u·men·ta·tion /dókyəmentáyshən/ n. **1** the accumulation, classification, and dissemination of information. **2** the material collected or disseminated. **3** the collection of documents relating to a process or event, esp. the written specification and instructions accompanying a computer program.

DOD abbr. Department of Defense.

dod·der[1] /dódər/ v.intr. tremble or totter, esp. from age. □□ **dod·der·er** n. **dod·der·ing** adj. [17th c.: var. of obs. dial. *dadder*]

dod·der[2] /dódər/ n. any climbing parasitic plant of the genus *Cuscuta*, with slender, leafless, threadlike stems. [ME f. Gmc]

dod·dered /dódərd/ adj. (of a tree, esp. an oak) having lost its top or branches. [prob. f. obs. *dod* poll, lop]

dod·der·y /dódəree/ adj. tending to tremble or totter, esp. from age. □□ **dod·der·i·ness** n. [DODDER[1] + –Y[1]]

dod·dle /dód'l/ n. Brit. colloq. an easy task. [perh. f. *doddle* = TODDLE]

dodeca- /dódekə/ comb. form twelve. [Gk *dōdeka* twelve]

do·dec·a·gon /dōdékəgon/ n. a plane figure with twelve sides.

do·dec·a·he·dron /dódekəheedrən/ n. a solid figure with twelve faces. □□ **do·dec·a·he·dral** adj.

do·dec·a·phon·ic /dódekəfónik/ adj. Mus. = TWELVE-TONE.

dodge /doj/ v. & n. • v. **1** intr. (often foll. by *about, behind, around*) move quickly to one side or quickly change position, to elude a pursuer, blow, etc. (*dodged behind the chair*). **2** tr. **a** evade by cunning or trickery (*dodged paying the fare*). **b** elude (a pursuer, opponent, blow, etc.) by a sideward movement, etc. **3** tr. Austral. sl. acquire dishonestly. **4** intr. (of a bell in change ringing) move one place contrary to the normal sequence. • n. **1** a quick movement to avoid or evade something. **2** a clever trick or expedient. **3** the dodging of a bell in change ringing. [16th c.: orig. unkn.]

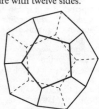

dodecahedron

dodg·em /dójəm/ n. (also **Dodgem**) = bumper cars.

dodg·er /dójər/ n. **1** a person who dodges, esp. an artful or elusive person. **2** a screen on a ship's bridge, etc., as protection from spray, etc. **3** a small handbill. **4** (in full **corn dodger**) e.g. southern US a small, hard cornmeal cake. **b** esp. S. Atlantic US a boiled cornmeal dumpling. **5** esp. Austral. sl. a sandwich; bread; food.

dodg·y /dójee/ adj. (**dodg·i·er**, **dodg·i·est**) **1** colloq. awkward; unreliable; tricky. **2** Brit. cunning; artful.

do·do /dódō/ n. (pl. **-does** or **-dos**) **1** any large flightless bird of the extinct family Raphidae, formerly native to Mauritius. **2** an old-fashioned, stupid, or inactive person. □ **as dead as the** (or a) **dodo 1** completely or unmistakably dead. **2** entirely obsolete. [Port. *doudo* simpleton]

DOE abbr. Department of Energy.

doe /dō/ n. a female fallow deer, reindeer, hare, or rabbit. [OE *dā*]

do·er /dóōər/ n. **1** a person who does something. **2** one who acts rather than merely talking or thinking. **3** (in full **hard doer**) Austral. an eccentric or amusing person.

does 3rd sing. present of DO[1].

doe·skin /dóskin/ n. **1 a** the skin of a doe fallow deer. **b** leather made from this. **2** a fine cloth resembling it.

does·n't /dúzənt/ contr. does not.

do·est /dóóist/ archaic 2nd sing. present of DO[1].

do·eth /dóóith/ archaic = DOTH.

doff /dawf, dof/ v.tr. literary take off (one's hat, clothing). [ME, = *do off*]

dog /dawg, dog/ n. & v. • n. **1** any four-legged, carnivorous animal of the genus *Canis*, of many breeds domesticated and wild, kept as pets or for work or sport. **2** the male of the dog, or of the fox (also **dog fox**) or wolf (also **dog wolf**). **3 a** colloq. a despicable person. **b** colloq. a person or fellow of a specified kind (*a lucky dog*). **c** Austral. sl. an informer; a traitor. **d** sl. a horse that is difficult to handle. **e** sl. derog. an unattractive or slovenly woman. **4** a mechanical device for gripping. **5** sl. something poor; a failure. **6** = FIREDOG. **7** (in pl.; prec. by the) Brit. colloq. greyhound racing. • v.tr. (**dogged, dog·ging**) **1** follow closely and persistently; pursue; track. **2** Mech. grip with a dog. □ **go to the dogs** sl. deteriorate, be ruined. **like a dog's dinner** Brit. colloq. smartly or flashily (dressed, arranged, etc.). **not a dog's chance** no chance at all. **put on the dog**

colloq. behave pretentiously. □□ **dog•like** *adj.* [OE *docga*, of unkn. orig]

dog•ber•ry /dáwgberee, dóg–/ *n.* (*pl.* **•ries**) the fruit of the dogwood.

dog bis•cuit *n.* a hard, thick biscuit for dogs, usu. containing ground meat and bones.

dog•cart /dáwgkaart, dóg–/ *n.* a two-wheeled driving cart with cross seats back to back.

dog•catch•er /dáwgkachər, dóg–/ *n.* an official who rounds up and impounds stray dogs in a community.

dog clutch *n. Mech.* a device for coupling two shafts in the transmission of power, one member having teeth which engage with slots in another.

dog col•lar *n.* **1** a collar for a dog. **2 a** *colloq.* a clerical collar. **b** a straight high collar.

dog days *n.* the hottest period of the year (reckoned in antiquity from the heliacal rising of the Dog Star).

doge /dōj/ *n. hist.* the chief magistrate of Venice or Genoa. [F f. It. f. Venetian *doze* f. L *dux ducis* leader]

dog-eared *adj.* (of a book, etc.) with the corners worn or battered with use.

dog-eat-dog *adj. colloq.* ruthlessly competitive.

dog•fight /dáwgfīt, dóg–/ *n.* **1** a close combat between fighter aircraft. **2** uproar; a fight like that between dogs.

dog•fish /dáwgfish, dóg–/ *n.* (*pl.* same or **dog•fish•es**) any of various small sharks, esp. of the families Scyliorhinidae or Squalidae.

dog•ged /dáwgid, dóg–/ *adj.* tenacious; grimly persistent. □□ **dog•ged•ly** *adv.* **dog•ged•ness** *n.* [ME f. DOG + –ED[1]]

dog•ger[1] /dáwgər, dóg–/ *n.* a two-masted, bluff-bowed Dutch fishing boat. [ME f. MDu., = fishing boat]

dog•ger[2] /dáwgər, dóg–/ *n. Geol.* a large spherical concretion occurring in sedimentary rock. [dial., = kind of ironstone, perh. f. DOG]

dog•ger•el /dáwgərəl, dóg–/ *n.* poor or trivial verse. [ME, app. f. DOG: cf. –REL]

dog•gie var. of DOGGY *n.*

dog•gish /dáwgish, dóg–/ *adj.* **1** of or like a dog. **2** currish; malicious; snappish. □□ **dog•gish•ly** *adv.* **dog•gish•ness** *n.*

dog•go /dáwgō, dógō/ *adv.* □ **lie doggo** *Brit. sl.* lie motionless or hidden, making no sign. [prob. f. DOG: cf. –o]

dog•gone /dáwg-gon, dóg–/ *adj., adv., & int. sl.* • *adj.* damned. • *int.* expressing annoyance. [prob. f. *dog on it* = *God damn it*]

dog•gy /dáwgee, dógee/ *adj. & n.* • *adj.* **1** of or like a dog. **2** devoted to dogs. • *n.* (also **dog•gie**) (*pl.* **•gies**) a little dog; a pet name for a dog. □□ **dog•gi•ness** *n.*

dog•gy bag *n.* (also **doggie bag**) a bag given to a customer in a restaurant or to a guest at a party, etc., for putting leftovers in to take home.

dog•house /dáwghows, dóg–/ *n.* a dog's shelter. □ **in the doghouse** *sl.* in disgrace or disfavor.

do•gie /dōgee/ *n.* a motherless or neglected calf. [19th c.: orig. unkn.]

dog in the man•ger *n.* a person who prevents others from using something, although that person has no use for it.

dog•leg /dáwgleg, dóg–/ *n., adj., & v.* • *n.* something with a sharp, abrupt bend, as a road. • *adj.* (also **dog-leg-ged**) bent like a dog's hind leg. • *v. intr.* proceed around a dogleg or on a dogleg course.

dog•leg hole *n. Golf* a hole at which a player cannot aim directly at the green from the tee.

dog•ma /dáwgmə, dóg–/ *n.* **1 a** a principle, tenet, or system of these, esp. as laid down by the authority of a church. **b** such principles collectively. **2** an arrogant declaration of opinion. [L f. Gk *dogma –matos* opinion f. *dokeō* seem]

dog•mat•ic /dawgmátik, dóg–/ *adj.* **1 a** (of a person) given to asserting or imposing personal opinions; arrogant. **b** intolerantly authoritative. **2 a** of or in the nature of dogma; doctrinal. **b** based on a priori principles, not on induction. □□ **dog•mat•i•cal•ly** *adv.* [LL *dogmaticus* f. Gk *dogmatikos* (as DOGMA)]

dog•mat•ics /dawgmátiks, dóg–/ *n.* **1** the study of religious dogmas; dogmatic theology. **2** a system of dogma. [DOGMATIC]

dog•ma•tism /dáwgmətizəm, dóg–/ *n.* a tendency to be dogmatic. □□ **dog•ma•tist** *n.* [F *dogmatisme* f. med.L *dogmatismus* (as DOGMA)]

dog•ma•tize /dáwgmətīz, dóg–/ *v.* **1** *intr.* make positive unsupported assertions; speak dogmatically. **2** *tr.* express (a principle, etc.) as a dogma. [F *dogmatiser* or f. LL *dogmatizare* f. Gk (as DOGMA)]

do-good•er /dōˊgŏŏdər/ *n.* a well-meaning but unrealistic philanthropist or reformer. □□ **do-good** /dōˊgŏŏd/ *adj. & n.* **do-good•er•y** *n.* **do-good•ism** *n.*

dog pad•dle *n.* an elementary swimming stroke in which the arms and legs alternately paddle underwater. □□ **dog-pad•dle** *v. intr.*

dog rose *n.* a wild rose, *Rosa canina.* Also called **brier rose.**

dogs•bod•y /dáwgzbodee, dógz–/ *n.* (*pl.* **•ies**) *Brit.* **1** *colloq.* a person who is given menial tasks to do; a drudge. **2** *Naut. sl.* a junior officer.

dog's break•fast *n.* (also **dog's dinner**) *Brit. & Can. colloq.* a mess.

dog's dis•ease *n. Austral. sl.* influenza.

dog•shore /dáwgshawr, dóg–/ *n.* a temporary wooden support for a ship just before launching.

dog's life *n.* a life of misery or harassment.

dogs of war *n. poet.* the havoc accompanying war.

Dog Star *n.* the chief star of the constellation Canis Major or Minor, esp. Sirius.

dog tag *n.* **1** a usu. metal plate attached to a dog's collar, giving owner's address, etc. **2** an identification tag, esp. as worn by a member of the military.

dog-tired *adj.* extremely tired; worn out.

dog•tooth /dáwgtōōth, dóg–/ *n.* **1** a small pointed ornament or molding esp. in Norman and Early English architecture. **2** *Brit.* a houndstooth check.

dog•tooth vi•o•let *n.* any liliaceous plant of the genus *Erythronium*, esp. *E. dens-canis* with speckled leaves, purple flowers, and a toothed perianth.

dog•trot /dáwgtrot, dóg–/ *n.* a gentle easy trot.

dog•watch /dáwgwoch, dóg–/ *n. Naut.* either of two short watches (4–6 or 6–8 p.m.).

dog•wood /dáwgwŏŏd, dóg–/ *n.* **1** any of various shrubs of the genus *Cornus*, esp. the wild cornel with dark red branches, greenish-white flowers, and purple berries, found in woods and hedgerows. **2** any of various similar trees. **3** the wood of the dogwood.

doh var. of DO[2].

DOI *abbr.* (in the US) Department of the Interior.

doi•ly /dóylee/ *n.* (also **doy•ley**) (*pl.* **•lies** or **•leys**) a small ornamental mat typically made of lace and placed under decorative objects. [orig. the name of a fabric: f. *Doiley*, the name of a draper]

do•ing /dóōing/ *n.* **1 a** (usu. in *pl.*) an action; the performance of a deed (*famous for his doings; it was my doing*). **b** activity; effort (*it takes a lot of doing*). **2** *colloq.* a scolding; a beating. **3** (in *pl.*) *sl.* things needed; adjuncts; things whose names are not known (*have we got all the doings?*).

doit /doyt/ *n. archaic* a very small amount of money. [MLG *doyt*, MDu. *duit*, of unkn. orig.]

do-it-your•self *adj. & n.* • *adj.* (of work, esp. building, painting, decorating, etc.) done or to be done by an amateur at home. • *n.* such work.

do•jo /dójō/ *n.* (*pl.* **•jos**) **1** a room or hall in which judo and other martial arts are practiced. **2** a mat on which judo, etc., is practiced. [Jap.]

dol. *abbr.* dollar(s).

Dol•by /dólbee/ *n. Trademark* an electronic noise-reduction system used esp. in tape recording to reduce hiss. [R. M. *Dolby*, US inventor]

dol•ce far nien•te /dólchay faár nyéntay/ *n.* pleasant idleness. [It., = sweet doing nothing]

dol•ce vi•ta /dólchay véetə/ *n.* a life of pleasure and luxury. [It., = sweet life]

dol•drums /dóldrəmz/ *n. pl.* (usu. prec. by *the*) **1** low spirits; a feeling of boredom or depression. **2** a period of inactivity or state of stagnation. **3** an equatorial ocean region of calms, sudden storms, and light unpredictable winds. [prob. after *dull* and *tantrum*]

dole[1] /dōl/ *n. & v.* • *n.* **1** (usu. prec. by *the*) *Brit. colloq.* benefit claimable by the unemployed from the government. **2 a** charitable distribution. **b** a charitable (esp. sparing, niggardly) gift of food, clothes, or money. **3** *archaic* one's lot or destiny. • *v. tr.* (usu. foll. by *out*) deal out sparingly. □ **on the dole** *colloq.* receiving welfare, etc., payments from the government. [OE *dāl* f. Gmc]

dole[2] /dōl/ *n. poet.* grief; woe; lamentation. [ME f. OF *do(e)l*, etc., f. pop. L *dolus* f. L *dolēre* grieve]

dole bludg•er *n. Austral. sl.* one who allegedly prefers the dole to work.

dole•ful /dólfŏŏl/ *adj.* **1** mournful; sad. **2** dreary; dismal. □□ **dole•ful•ly** *adv.* **dole•ful•ness** *n.* [ME f. DOLE[2] + –FUL]

dol•er•ite /dólərīt/ *n.* a coarse basaltic rock. [F *dolérite* f. Gk *doleros* deceptive (because it is difficult to distinguish from diorite)]

dol•i•cho•ce•phal•ic /dólikōsifálik/ *adj.* (also **dol•i•cho•ceph•a•lous** /–séfələs/) having a long or narrow head. [Gk *dolikhos* long + –CEPHALIC, –CEPHALOUS]

do•li•na /dəleénə/ *n.* (also **do•line** /dəleén/) *Geol.* an extensive depression or basin. [Russ. *dolina* valley]

doll /dol/ *n. & v.* • *n.* **1** a small model of a human figure, esp. a baby or a child, as a child's toy. **2 a** *colloq.* a pretty but silly young woman. **b** *sl.* a young woman, esp. an attractive one. **3** a ventriloquist's dummy. • *v. tr. & intr.* (foll. by *up*; often *refl.*) dress up smartly. [pet form of the name *Dorothy*]

dol•lar /dólər/ *n.* **1** the chief monetary unit in the US, Canada, and Australia. **2** the chief monetary unit of certain countries in the Pacific, West Indies, SE Asia, Africa, and S. America. □ **dollar diplomacy** diplomatic activity aimed at advancing a country's international influence by furthering its financial and commercial interests abroad.

dol•lar gap *n.* (also **dollar shortage**) the difference, in U.S. dollars, between the amount needed for a country's import trade over payments received through their export trade.

dol·lar sign *n.* the symbol $, placed before a number to indicate currency in dollars.

dol·lar·spot /dólərspot/ *n.* **1** a fungal disease of lawns, etc. **2** a discolored patch caused by this.

doll·house /dólhows/ *n.* **1** a miniature toy house for dolls. **2** a very small house.

dol·lop /dóləp/ *n. & v.* • *n.* a shapeless lump of food, etc. • *v.tr.* (usu. foll. by *out*) serve out in large, shapeless quantities. [perh. f. Scand.]

dol·ly /dólee/ *n. & v.* • *n.* (*pl.* **·lies**) **1** a child's name for a doll. **2** a platform or cart on wheels used for moving heavy objects, typically film or television cameras. **3** *Cricket colloq.* an easy catch or hit. **4** *hist.* a wooden pole for stirring clothes in a washtub. **5** = CORN DOLLY. • *v.intr.* (**·lies, ·lied**) move a film or television camera in or up to a subject, or out from it.

dol·ly bird *n. Brit. colloq.* an attractive and stylish young woman.

Dol·ly Var·den /dólee vaárd'n/ *n.* **1** a woman's large hat with one side drooping and with a floral trimming. **2** a brightly spotted char, *Salvelinus malma*, of western N. America. [a character in Dickens's *Barnaby Rudge*]

dol·ma /dólmə/ *n.* (*pl.* **dol·mas** or **dol·mades** /–maáthez/) a SE European delicacy of spiced rice or meat, etc., wrapped in vine or cabbage leaves. [Turk. f. *dolmak* fill, be filled: *dolmades* f. mod.Gk]

dol·man /dólmən/ *n.* **1** a long Turkish robe open in front. **2** a hussar's jacket worn with the sleeves hanging loose. **3** a woman's mantle with capelike or dolman sleeves. [ult. f. Turk. *dolama*]

dol·man sleeve *n.* a long loose sleeve tapered at the wrist, cut from one piece with the body of the coat, etc.

dol·men /dólmən/ *n.* a megalithic tomb with a large, flat stone laid on upright ones. [F, perh. f. Cornish *tolmēn* hole of stone]

do·lo·mite /dóləmīt, dól–/ *n.* a mineral or rock of calcium magnesium carbonate. □□ **dol·o·mit·ic** /–mítik/ *adj.* [F f. D. de *Dolomieu*, Fr. geologist d. 1801]

dolmen

do·lor /dólər/ *n.* (*Brit* **do·lour**) *literary* sorrow; distress. [ME f. OF f. L *dolor* –*oris* pain, grief]

do·lor·ous /dólərəs/ *adj. literary* or *joc.* **1** distressing; painful; doleful; dismal. **2** distressed; sad. □□ **dol·or·ous·ly** *adv.* [ME f. OF *doleros* f. LL *dolorosus* (as DOLOR)]

dol·phin /dólfin/ *n.* **1** any of various porpoiselike sea mammals of the family Delphinidae having a slender, beaklike snout. **2** (in general use) = DORADO 1. **3** a pile or buoy for mooring. **4** a structure for protecting the pier of a bridge. **5** a curved fish in heraldry, sculpture, etc. [ME, also *delphin* f. L *delphinus* f. Gk *delphis* –*inos*]

dol·phi·nar·i·um /dólfináreeəm/ *n.* (*pl.* **dol·phi·nar·i·ums**) an aquarium for dolphins, esp. one open to the public.

dolt /dōlt/ *n.* a stupid person. □□ **dolt·ish** *adj.* **dolt·ish·ly** *adv.* **dolt·ish·ness** *n.* [app. related to *dol, dold*, obs. var. of DULL]

Dom /dom/ *n.* **1** a title prefixed to the names of some Roman Catholic dignitaries, and Benedictine and Carthusian monks. **2** the Portuguese equivalent of Don (see DON¹). [L *dominus* master: sense 2 through Port.]

-dom /dəm/ *suffix* forming nouns denoting: **1** state or condition (*freedom*). **2** rank or status (*earldom*). **3** domain (*kingdom*). **4** a class of people (or the attitudes, etc., associated with them) regarded collectively (*officialdom*). [OE –*dōm*, orig. = DOOM]

do·main /dōmáyn/ *n.* **1** an area under one rule; a realm. **2** an estate or lands under one control. **3** a sphere of control or influence. **4** *Math.* the set of possible values of an independent variable. **5** *Physics* a discrete region of magnetism in ferromagnetic material. □□ **do·ma·ni·al** /–máyneeəl/ *adj.* [ME f. F *domaine*, OF *demeine* DEMESNE, assoc. with L *dominus* lord]

do·maine /dōmáyn/ *n.* a vineyard. [F: see DOMAIN]

dome /dōm/ *n. & v.* • *n.* **1 a** a rounded vault as a roof, with a circular, elliptical, or polygonal base; a large cupola. **b** the revolving, openable hemispherical roof of an observatory. **2 a** a natural vault or canopy (of the sky, trees, etc.). **b** the rounded summit of a hill, etc. **3** *Geol.* a dome-shaped structure. **4** *sl.* the head. **5** *poet.* a stately building. • *v.tr.* (usu. as **domed** *adj.*) cover with or shape as a dome. □□ **dome·like** *adj.* [F *dôme* f. It. *duomo* cathedral, dome f. L *domus* house]

Domes·day /dóomzday/ *n.* (also **Domes·day Book; Dooms·day**

From early Flemish or Low German *daler*, from German *Taler*, formerly spelled *Thaler*, short for *Joachimsthaler*, a coin from the silver mine of *Joachimsthal* ('Joachim's valley'), now *Jáchymov* in the Czech Republic. Originally denoting a German *thaler* coin, the term was later applied to a Spanish coin used in the Spanish American colonies. The Spanish coin was also widely used in the British North American colonies at the time of the Revolutionary War and its name was adopted as the name of the US monetary unit in the late 18th century.

Book) a record of the lands of England made in 1086 by order of William I. [ME var. of *doomsday*, as being a book of final authority]

do·mes·tic /dəmestik/ *adj. & n.* • *adj.* **1** of the home, household, or family affairs. **2 a** of one's own country, not foreign or international. **b** homegrown or homemade. **3** (of an animal) kept by or living with humans. **4** fond of home life. • *n.* a household servant. □□ **do·mes·ti·cal·ly** *adv.* [F *domestique* f. L *domesticus* f. *domus* home]

do·mes·ti·cate /dəmestikayt/ *v.tr.* **1** tame (an animal) to live with humans. **2** accustom to home life and management. **3** naturalize (a plant or animal) □□ **do·mes·ti·ca·ble** /–kəbəl/ *adj.* **do·mes·ti·ca·tion** /–káyshən/ *n.* [med.L *domesticare* (as DOMESTIC)]

do·mes·tic·i·ty /dómestísitee/ *n.* **1** the state of being domestic. **2** domestic or home life.

do·mes·tic sci·ence *n.* the study of household management.

dom·i·cile /dómisīl, –sil, dó–/ *n. & v.* (also **dom·i·cil** /–sil/) • *n.* **1** a dwelling place; one's home. **2** *Law* **a** a place of permanent residence. **b** the fact of residing. **3** the place at which a bill of exchange is made payable. • *v.tr.* **1** (usu. as **domiciled** *adj.*) (usu. foll. by *at, in*) establish or settle in a place. **2** (usu. foll. by *at*) make (a bill of exchange) payable at a certain place. [ME f. OF f. L *domicilium* f. *domus* home]

dom·i·cil·i·ar·y /dómisílee-eree/ *adj.* of a dwelling place (esp. of a doctor's, official's, etc., visit to a person's home). [F *domiciliaire* f. med.L *domiciliarius* (as DOMICILE)]

dom·i·nance /dóminəns/ *n.* **1** the state of being dominant. **2** control, authority.

dom·i·nant /dóminənt/ *adj. & n.* • *adj.* **1** dominating; prevailing; most influential. **2** (of a high place) prominent; overlooking others. **3 a** (of an allele) expressed even when inherited from only one parent. **b** (of an inherited characteristic) appearing in an individual even when its allelic counterpart is also inherited (cf. RECESSIVE). • *n. Mus.* the fifth note of the diatonic scale of any key. □□ **dom·i·nant·ly** *adv.* [F f. L *dominari* (as DOMINATE)]

dom·i·nate /dóminayt/ *v.* **1** *tr.* & (foll. by *over*) *intr.* have a commanding influence on; exercise control over (*fear dominated them for years*; *dominates over his friends*). **2** *intr.* (of a person, sound, feature of a scene, etc.) be the most influential or conspicuous. **3** *tr.* & (foll. by *over*) *intr.* (of a building, etc.) have a commanding position over; overlook. □□ **dom·i·na·tor** *n.* [L *dominari dominat-* f. *dominus* lord]

dom·i·na·tion /dómináyshən/ *n.* **1 a** command; control. **b** oppression; tyranny. **2** the act or an instance of dominating; the process of being dominated. **3** (in *pl.*) angelic beings of the fourth order of the celestial hierarchy. [ME f. OF f. L *dominatio* –*onis* (as DOMINATE)]

dom·i·neer /dóminéer/ *v.intr.* (often as **domineering** *adj.*) behave in an arrogant and overbearing way. □□ **dom·i·neer·ing·ly** *adv.* [Du. *dominieren* f. F *dominer*]

do·min·i·cal /dəminikəl/ *adj.* **1** of the Lord's day, of Sunday. **2** of the Lord (Jesus Christ). [F *dominical* or L *dominicalis* f. L *dominicus* f. *dominus* lord]

do·min·i·cal let·ter *n.* the one of the seven letters A–G indicating the dates of Sundays in a year.

Do·min·i·can /dəminikən/ *adj. & n.* • *adj.* **1** of or relating to St. Dominic or the order of preaching friars which he founded in 1215–16. **2** of or relating to either of the two orders of female religious founded on Dominican principles. • *n.* a Dominican friar, nun, or sister (see also *Black Friar*). [med.L *Dominicanus* f. *Dominicus* L name of *Domingo* de Guzmán (St. Dominic)]

dom·i·nie /dóminee/ *n. Sc.* a schoolmaster. [later spelling of *domine* sir, voc. of L *dominus* lord]

do·min·ion /dəminyən/ *n.* **1** sovereignty; control. **2** the territory of a sovereign or government; a domain. **3** *hist.* the title of each of the self-governing territories of the British Commonwealth. [ME f. OF f. med.L *dominio* –*onis* f. L *dominium* f. *dominus* lord]

dom·i·no /dóminō/ *n.* (*pl.* **·noes** or **·nos**) **1 a** any of 28 small oblong pieces marked with 0–6 dots in each half. **b** (in *pl.*, usu. treated as *sing.*) a game played with these. **2 a** a loose cloak with a mask for the upper part of the face, worn at masquerades. [F, prob. f. L *dominus* lord, but unexplained]

domino 1

dom·i·no the·o·ry *n.* the theory that a political event, etc., in one country will cause similar events in neighboring countries, like a row of falling dominoes.

don¹ /don/ *n.* **1** a university teacher, esp. a senior member of a college at Oxford or Cambridge. **2** (**Don**) **a** a Spanish title prefixed to a forename. **b** a Spanish gentleman; a Spaniard. [Sp. f. L *dominus* lord]

don[2] /don/ *v.tr.* (**donned, don•ning**) put on (clothing). [= *do on*]

do•na /dónə/ *n.* (also **do•nah**) *Brit. sl.* a woman; a sweetheart. [Sp. *doña* or Port. *dona* f. L (as DONNA)]

do•nate /dónayt, dōnáyt/ *v.tr.* give or contribute (money, etc.), esp. voluntarily to a fund or institution. □□ **do•na•tor** *n.* [back-form. f. DONATION]

do•na•tion /dōnáyshən/ *n.* **1** the act or an instance of donating. **2** something, esp. an amount of money, donated. [ME f. OF f. L *donatio* *–onis* f. *donare* give f. *donum* gift]

don•a•tive /dónətiv, dón–/ *n. & adj.* ● *n.* a gift or donation, esp. one given formally or officially as a largesse. ● *adj.* **1** given as a donation or bounty. **2** *hist.* (of a benefice) given directly, not presentative. [ME f. L *donativum* gift, largesse f. *donare*: see DONATION]

done /dun/ *past part.* of DO[1]. ● *adj.* **1** *colloq.* socially acceptable (*the done thing; it isn't done*). **2** (often with *in, up*) *colloq.* tired out. **3** (esp. as *int.* in reply to an offer, etc.) accepted. □ **be done with** be finished with. **done for** *colloq.* in serious trouble. **have done** have ceased or finished. **have done with** be rid of; have finished dealing with.

do•nee /dōneé/ *n.* the recipient of a gift. [DONOR + –EE]

dong[1] /dawng, dong/ *v. & n.* ● *v.* **1** *intr.* make the deep sound of a large bell. **2** *tr. Austral. & NZ colloq.* hit; punch. ● *n.* **1** the deep sound of a large bell. **2** *Austral. & NZ colloq.* a heavy blow. [imit.]

dong[2] /dawng, dong/ *n.* the chief monetary unit of Vietnam. [Vietnamese]

don•ga /dónggə, dáwng–/ *n. S.Afr. & Austral.* **1** a dry watercourse. **2** a ravine caused by erosion. [Zulu]

don•gle /dáwnggəl, dóng–/ *n. Computing sl.* a security attachment required by a computer to enable protected software to be used. [arbitrary form.]

don•jon /dónjən, dún–/ *n.* the great tower or innermost keep of a castle. [archaic spelling of DUNGEON]

Don Juan /don waán, hwaán, jōōən/ *n.* a seducer of women; a libertine. [name of a legendary Sp. nobleman celebrated in fiction, e.g., by Byron]

don•key /dóngkee, dúng–, dáwng–/ *n.* (*pl.* **•keys**) **1** a domestic ass. **2** *colloq.* a stupid or foolish person. [earlier with pronunc. as *monkey*: perh. f. DUN[1], or the Christian name *Duncan*]

don•key en•gine *n.* a small auxiliary engine.

don•key jack•et *n. Brit.* a heavy jacket with a patch of waterproof leather or plastic across the shoulders, worn typically by building workers.

don•key•work /dónkeewərk, dúng–, dáwng–/ *n.* the laborious part of a job; drudgery.

don•na /dónə/ *n.* **1** an Italian lady. **2** (**Donna**) the title of such a lady. [It. f. L *domina* mistress fem. of *dominus*: cf. DON[1]]

don•née /donáy, daw–/ *n.* **1** the subject or theme of a story, etc. **2** a basic fact or assumption. [F, fem. or masc. past part. of *donner* give]

don•nish /dónish/ *adj.* like or resembling a college don, esp. in supposed pedantry. □□ **don•nish•ly** *adv.* **don•nish•ness** *n.*

don•ny•brook /dóneebrŏŏk/ *n.* (also **Donnybrook**) an uproar; a wild fight. [*Donnybrook* near Dublin, Ireland, formerly site of annual fair]

do•nor /dónər/ *n.* **1** a person who gives or donates something (e.g., to a charity). **2** one who provides blood for a transfusion, semen for insemination, or an organ or tissue for transplantation. **3** *Chem.* an atom or molecule that provides a pair of electrons in forming a coordinate bond. **4** *Physics* an impurity atom in a semiconductor which contributes a conducting electron to the material. [ME f. AF *donour*, OF *doneur* f. L *donator* *–oris* f. *donare* give]

SPELLING TIP donor

Remember the *-nor* ending of this word by using the mnemonic: "You should never say *no* to a do*nor*."

do•nor card *n.* an official card authorizing use of organs for transplant, carried by the donor.

don't /dōnt/*contr. & n.* ● *contr.* do not. ● *n.* a prohibition (*dos and don'ts*).

▶ The use of **don't** as a singular is now generally regarded as uneducated, although it was once standard and is now often employed informally for effect, e.g., "It don't mean a thing to me."

do•nut var. of DOUGHNUT.

doo•dad /dóodad/ *n.* **1** a fancy article; a trivial ornament. **2** a gadget or thingamajig. [20th c.: orig. unkn.]

doo•dle /dóod'l/ *v. & n.* ● *v.intr.* scribble or draw, esp. absentmindedly. ● *n.* a scrawl or drawing made. □□ **doo•dler** *n.* [orig. = foolish person; cf. LG *dudeldopf*]

doo•dle•bug /dóod'lbug/ *n.* **1** any of various insects, esp. the larva of an ant lion. **2** an unscientific device for locating minerals. **3** *colloq.* a robot bomb.

doo•hick•ey /dóohikee/ *n.* (*pl.* **•eys** or **•ies**) *US colloq.* a small object, esp. mechanical. [DOODAD + HICKEY]

doom /dōōm/ *n. & v.* ● *n.* **1 a** a grim fate or destiny. **b** death or ruin. **2 a** a condemnation; a judgment or sentence. **b** the Last Judgment (*the crack of doom*). **3** *hist.* a statute, law, or decree. ● *v.tr.* **1** (usu. foll. by *to*) condemn or destine (*a city doomed to destruction*). **2** (esp. as **doomed** *adj.*) consign to misfortune or destruction. [OE *dōm* statute, judgment f. Gmc: rel. to DO[1]]

doom palm *n.* var. of DOUM palm.

dooms•day /dōōmzday/ *n.* the day of the Last Judgment. □ **till doomsday** forever (cf. DOMESDAY). [OE *dōmes dæg*: see DOOM]

doom•watch /dōōmwoch/ *n.* organized vigilance or observation to avert danger, esp. from environmental pollution. □□ **doom•watch•er** *n.*

door /dawr/ *n.* **1 a** a hinged, sliding, or revolving barrier for closing and opening an entrance to a building, room, cupboard, etc. **b** this as representing a house, etc. (*lives two doors away*). **2 a** an entrance or exit; a doorway. **b** a means of access or approach. □ **close the door to** exclude the opportunity for. **lay** (or **lie**) **at the door of** impute (or be imputable) to. **leave the door open** ensure that an option remains available. **open the door** create an opportunity for. **out of doors** in or into the open air. □□ **doored** *adj.* (also in *comb.*). [OE *duru, dor* f. Gmc]

door•bell /dáwrbel/ *n.* a bell in a house, etc., rung by visitors outside to signal their arrival.

door•case /dáwrkays/ *n.* the outermost part of a doorframe.

door•frame /dáwrfraym/ *n.* the framework of a doorway.

door•keep•er /dáwrkeepər/ *n.* = DOORMAN 1.

door•knob /dáwrnob/ *n.* a knob for turning to release the latch of a door.

door•man /dáwrman, –mən/ *n.* (*pl.* **•men**) **1** a person on duty at the door to a large building. **2** *Brit.* a janitor or porter.

door•mat /dáwrmat/ *n.* **1** a mat at an entrance for wiping mud, etc., from the shoes. **2** a feebly submissive person.

door•nail /dáwrnayl/ *n.* a nail with which doors were studded for strength or ornament. □ **dead as a doornail** completely or unmistakably dead.

door•plate /dáwrplayt/ *n.* a plate on the door of a house or room bearing the name of the occupant.

door•post /dáwrpōst/ *n.* each of the uprights of a doorframe, on one of which the door is hung.

door prize *n.* a prize awarded usu. by lottery at a dance, party, charity event, etc.

door•step /dáwrstep/ *n. & v.* ● *n.* **1** a step leading up to the outer door of a house, etc. **2** *Brit. sl.* a thick slice of bread. ● *v.intr.* (**• stepped, •step•ping**) go from door to door selling, canvassing, etc. □ **on one's** (or **the**) **doorstep** very close.

door•stop /dáwrstop/ *n.* a device for keeping a door open or to prevent it from striking a wall, etc., when opened.

door-to-door *adj.* (of selling, etc.) done at each house in turn.

door•way /dáwrway/ *n.* an opening filled by a door.

door•yard /dáwryaard/ *n.* a yard or garden near the door of a house.

doo•zy /dóozee/ *n.* (*pl.* **doo•zies**) (also **doo•zie**) *colloq.* one that is outstanding of its kind (*a mistake that was a doozy*). [orig. unknown]

do•pa /dópə/ *n. Pharm.* a crystalline amino acid derivative used in the treatment of Parkinson's disease. [G f. Dioxyphenylalanine, former name of the compound]

dop•ant /dópənt/ *n. Electronics* a substance used in doping a semiconductor.

dope /dōp/ *n. & v.* ● *n.* **1** a varnish applied to the cloth surface of airplane parts to strengthen them, keep them airtight, etc. **2** a thick liquid used as a lubricant, etc. **3** a substance added to gasoline, etc., to increase its effectiveness. **4 a** *sl.* a narcotic; a stupefying drug. **b** a drug, etc., given to a horse or greyhound, or taken by an athlete, to affect performance. **5** *sl.* a stupid person. **6** *sl.* **a** information about a subject, esp. if not generally known. **b** misleading information. ● *v.* **1** *tr.* administer dope to; drug. **2** *tr. Electronics* add an impurity to (a semiconductor) to produce a desired electrical characteristic. **3** *tr.* smear; daub; apply dope to. **4** *intr.* take addictive drugs. □ **dope out** *sl.* discover. □□ **dop•er** *n.* [Du. *doop* sauce f. *doopen* to dip]

dope•y /dópee/ *adj.* (also **dop•y**) (**dop•i•er, dop•i•est**) *colloq.* **1 a** half asleep. **b** stupefied by or as if by a drug. **2** stupid; silly. □□ **dop•i•ly** *adv.* **dop•i•ness** *n.*

dop•pel•gäng•er /dópəlgangər/ *n.* an apparition or double of a living person. [G, = double-goer]

Dop•pler ef•fect /dóplər/ *n.* (also **Dop•pler shift**) *Physics* an increase (or decrease) in the frequency of sound, light, or other waves as the source and observer move toward (or away) from each other. [C. J. *Doppler*, Austrian physicist d. 1853]

Dop•pler ra•dar /dóplər/ *n.* a radar system using the Doppler effect to determine velocity and location, as of storm clouds, etc.

dop•y var. of DOPEY.

do•ra•do /dəraádō/ *n.* (*pl.* **•dos**) **1** a blue and silver marine fish, *Coryphaena hippurus*, showing brilliant colors when dying out of water. **2** a brightly colored freshwater fish, *Salminus maxillosus*, native to S. America. [Sp. f. LL *deauratus* gilt f. *aurum* gold]

Do•ri•an /dáwreeən/ *n. & adj.* ● *n.* (in *pl.*) a Greek-speaking people thought to have entered Greece from the north *c.*1100 BC and settled in parts of Central and S. Greece. ● *adj.* of or relating to the

Dorians or to Doris in Central Greece. [L *Dorius* f. Gk *Dōrios* f. *Dōros*, the mythical ancestor]

Do·ri·an mode *n. Mus.* the mode represented by the natural diatonic scale D–D.

Dor·ic /dáwrik, dór–/ *adj. & n.* ● *adj.* **1** (of a dialect) broad; rustic. **2** *Archit.* of the oldest, sturdiest, and simplest of the Greek orders. ● *n.* **1** rustic English or esp. Scots. **2** *Archit.* the Doric order. **3** the dialect of the Dorians in ancient Greece. [L *Doricus* f. Gk *Dōrikos* (as DORIAN)]

dork /dawrk/ *n. sl.* a dull, slow-witted, or oafish person. □□ **dork·y** *adj.*

dorm /dawrm/ *n. colloq.* dormitory. [abbr.]

dor·mant /dáwrmənt/ *adj.* **1** lying inactive as in sleep; sleeping. **2 a** (of a volcano, etc.) temporarily inactive. **b** (of potential faculties, etc.) in abeyance. **3** (of plants) alive but not actively growing. **4** *Heraldry* (of a beast) lying with its head on its paws. □□ **dor·man·cy** *n.* [ME f. OF, pres. part. of *dormir* f. L *dormire* sleep]

dor·mer /dáwrmər/ *n.* (in full **dormer window**) a projecting upright window in a sloping roof. [OF *dormĕor* (as DORMANT)]

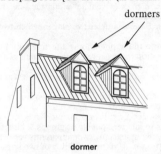

dormers

dormer

dor·mi·to·ry /dáwrmitáwree/ *n.* (*pl.* **·ries**) **1** a sleeping room with several beds, esp. in a school or institution. **2** (in full **dormitory town**, etc.) esp. *Brit.* a small town or suburb from which people travel to work in a city, etc. **3** a university or college hall of residence or hostel. [ME f. L *dormitorium* f. *dormire* dormit- sleep]

dor·mouse /dáwrmows/ *n.* (*pl.* **dor·mice**) any small, mouselike hibernating rodent of the family Gliridae, having a long, bushy tail. [ME: orig. unkn., but assoc. with F *dormir*, L *dormire*: see DORMANT]

do·ron·i·cum /dərónikəm/ *n.* = LEOPARD'S-BANE. [mod.L (Linnaeus) ult. f. Arab. *darānaj*]

dorp /dawrp/ *n. S.Afr.* a village or small township. [Du. (as THORP)]

dor·sal /dáwrsəl/ *adj. Anat., Zool., & Bot.* **1** of, on, or near the back (cf. VENTRAL). **2** ridge-shaped. □□ **dor·sal·ly** *adv.* [F *dorsal* or LL *dorsalis* f. L *dorsum* back]

do·ry¹ /dáwree/ *n.* (*pl.* **·ries**) any of various marine fish having a compressed body and flat head, esp. the John Dory, used as food. [ME f. F *dorée* fem. past part. of *dorer* gild (as DORADO)]

do·ry² /dáwree/ *n.* (*pl.* **·ries**) a flat-bottomed fishing boat with high bow and flaring sides. [Miskito *dóri* dugout]

DOS /dos, daws/ *n. Computing* a software operating system for personal computers. [abbr. of *disk* operating *system*]

dos-à-dos /dózaadó/ *adj. & n.* ● *adj.* (of two books) bound together with a shared central board and facing in opposite directions. ● *n.* (*pl.* same) a seat, carriage, etc., in which the occupants sit back to back (cf. DO-SI-DO). [F, = back to back]

dos·age /dósij/ *n.* **1** the giving of medicine in doses. **2** the size of a dose.

dose /dōs/ *n. & v.* ● *n.* **1** an amount of a medicine or drug for taking or taken at one time. **2** a quantity of something administered or allocated (e.g., work, praise, punishment, etc.). **3** the amount of ionizing radiation received by a person or thing. **4** *sl.* a venereal infection. ● *v.tr.* **1** treat (a person or animal) with doses of medicine. **2** give a dose or doses to. **3** adulterate or blend (esp. wine with spirit). □ **like a dose of salts** *Brit. colloq.* very fast and efficiently. [F f. LL *dosis* f. Gk *dosis* gift f. *didōmi* give]

do-si-do /dóseedó/ *n.* (*pl.* **·dos**) a figure in which two dancers pass around each other back to back and return to their original positions. [corrupt. of DOS-À-DOS]

do·sim·e·ter /dōsímitər/ *n.* a device used to measure an absorbed dose of ionizing radiation. □□ **do·si·met·ric** /–métrik/ *adj.* **do·sim·e·try** *n.*

doss /dos/ *v. & n. Brit. sl.* ● *v.intr.* (often foll. by *down*) sleep, esp. roughly or in a cheap rooming house, motel, etc. ● *n.* a bed, esp. in a cheap rooming house, motel, etc. □ **doss-house** a cheap rooming house, motel, etc., esp. for vagrants. [prob. = *doss* ornamental covering for a seat back, etc., f. OF *dos* ult. f. L *dorsum* back]

dos·sal /dósəl/ *n.* a hanging cloth behind an altar or around a chancel. [med.L *dossale* f. LL *dorsalis* DORSAL]

dos·ser /dósər/ *n. Brit. sl.* **1** a person who dosses. **2** = *doss-house.*

dos·si·er /dósee-ay, dáw–/ *n.* a set of documents, esp. a collection

of information about a person, event, or subject. [F, so called from the label on the back, f. *dos* back f. L *dorsum*]

dost /dust/ *archaic 2nd sing. present* of DO¹.

DOT *abbr.* Department of Transportation.

dot¹ /dot/ *n. & v.* ● *n.* **1 a** a small spot, speck, or mark. **b** such a mark written or printed as part of an *i* or *j*, as a diacritical mark, as one of a series of marks to signify omission, or as a full stop. **c** a decimal point. **2** *Mus.* a dot used to denote the lengthening of a note or rest, or to indicate staccato. **3** the shorter signal of the two used in Morse code (cf. DASH n. 6). **4** a tiny or apparently tiny object (*a dot on the horizon*). ● *v.tr.* (**dot·ted, dot·ting**) **1** mark with a dot or dots. **b** place a dot over (a letter). **2** *Mus.* mark (a note or rest) to show that the time value is increased by half. **3** (often foll. by *about*) scatter like dots. **4** partly cover as with dots (*an ocean dotted with ships*). **5** *Brit. sl.* hit (*dotted him one in the eye*). □ **dot the i's and cross the t's** *colloq.* **1** be minutely accurate; emphasize details. **2** add the final touches to a task, exercise, etc. **on the dot** exactly on time. □□ **dot·ter** *n.* [OE *dott* head of a boil, perh. infl. by Du. *dot* knot]

dot² /dot/ *n.* a woman's dowry. [F f. L *dos dotis*]

dot·age /dótij/ *n.* feeble-minded senility (*in his dotage*).

do·tard /dótərd/ *n.* a person who is feeble-minded, esp. from senility. [ME f. DOTE + –ARD]

dote /dōt/ *v.intr.* **1** (foll. by *on, upon*) be foolishly or excessively fond of. **2** be silly or feeble-minded, esp. from old age. □□ **dot·er** *n.* **dot·ing·ly** *adv.* [ME, corresp. to MDu. *doten* be silly]

doth /duth/ *archaic 3rd sing. present* of DO¹.

dot ma·trix print·er *n. Computing* a printer with that forms images of letters, numbers, etc., from a number of tiny dots.

dot·ted line *n.* a line on a document or contract made up of dots or dashes, esp. to show a space left for a signature.

dot·ter·el /dótərəl/ *n.* a small migrant plover, *Eudromias morinellus.* [ME f. DOTE + –REL, named from the ease with which it is caught, taken to indicate stupidity]

dot·tle /dót'l/ *n.* a remnant of unburned tobacco in a pipe. [DOT¹ + –LE¹]

dot·ty /dótee/ *adj.* (**dot·ti·er, dot·ti·est**) *colloq.* **1** feeble-minded, silly. **2** eccentric. **3** absurd. **4** (foll. by *about, on*) infatuated with; obsessed by. □□ **dot·ti·ly** *adv.* **dot·ti·ness** *n.* [earlier = unsteady: f. DOT¹ + –Y¹]

douane /doo-aán/ *n.* a foreign customhouse. [F f. It. *do(g)ana* f.Turk. *duwan*, Arab. *dīwān*: cf. DIVAN]

Dou·ay Bi·ble /dóo-ay, doo-áy/ *n.* (also **Dou·ay Ver·sion**) an English translation of the Bible formerly used in the Roman Catholic Church, completed at Douai in France early in the seventeenth century.

dou·ble /dúbəl/ *adj., adv., n., & v.* ● *adj.* **1 a** consisting of two usu. equal parts or things; twofold. **b** consisting of two identical parts. **2** twice as much or many (*double the amount; double the number; double thickness*). **3** having twice the usual size, quantity, strength, etc. (*double whiskey*). **4** designed for two people (*double bed*). **5 a** having some part double. **b** (of a flower) having more than one circle of petals. **c** (of a domino) having the same number of pips on each half. **6** having two different roles or interpretations, esp. implying confusion or deceit (*double meaning; leads a double life*). **7** *Mus.* lower in pitch by an octave (*double bassoon*). ● *adv.* **1** at or to twice the amount, etc. (*counts double*). **2** two together (*sleep double*). ● *n.* **1 a** a double quantity or thing; twice as much or many. **b** *colloq.* a double measure of liquor. **2 a** a counterpart of a person or thing; a person who looks exactly like another. **b** an understudy. **c** a wraith. **3** (in *pl.*) *Sports* (esp. tennis) a game between two pairs of players. **4** *Sports* a pair of victories over the same team, a pair of championships at the same game, etc. **5** a system of betting in which the winnings and stake from the first bet are transferred to a second. **6** *Bridge* the doubling of an opponent's bid. **7** *Darts* a hit on the narrow ring enclosed by the two outer circles of a dartboard, scoring double. **8** a sharp turn, esp. of the tracks of a hunted animal, or the course of a river. ● *v.* **1** *tr. & intr.* make or become twice as much or many; increase twofold; multiply by two. **2** *tr.* amount to twice as much as. **3 a** *tr.* fold or bend (paper, cloth, etc.) over on itself. **b** *intr.* become folded. **4 a** *tr.* (of an actor) play (two parts) in the same piece. **b** *intr.* (often foll. by *for*) be understudy, etc. **5** *intr.* (usu. foll. by *as*) play a twofold role. **6** *intr.* turn sharply in flight or pursuit; take a tortuous course. **7** *tr. Naut.* sail around (a headland). **8** *tr. Bridge* make a call increasing the value of the points to be won or lost on (an opponent's bid). **9** *Mus.* **a** *intr.* (often foll. by *on*) play two or more musical instruments (*the clarinettist doubles on tenor sax*). **b** *tr.* add the same note in a higher or lower octave to (a note). **10** *tr.* clench (a fist). **11** *intr.* move at twice the usual speed; run. **12** *Billiards* **a** *intr.* rebound. **b** *tr.* cause to rebound. □ **double back** take a new direction opposite to the previous one. **double cross** *n.* an act of double-crossing. **double or nothing** (or esp. *Brit.* **quits**) a gamble to decide whether a player's loss or debt be doubled or canceled. **double up 1 a** bend or curl up. **b** cause to do this, esp. by a blow. **2** be overcome with pain or laughter. **3** share or assign to a room, quarters, etc., with another or others. **4** fold or become folded. **5** use winnings from a bet as stake for another. **on** (or *Brit.* **at**) **the double** running; hurrying. □□ **dou•bler** *n.* **dou•bly** *adv.* [ME f. OF *doble, duble* (n.), *dobler, dubler* (v.) f. L *duplus* DUPLE]

dou•ble a•cros•tic *n.* an acrostic in which the first and last letters of each line form a hidden word or words. see ACROSTIC.

dou•ble a•gent *n.* an agent who spies simultaneously for two rival countries, etc.

dou•ble axe *n.* an axe with two blades.

dou•ble-bar•reled *adj.* **1** (of a gun) having two barrels. **2** twofold; having a dual purpose.

dou•ble bass *n.* **1** the largest and lowest-pitched instrument of the violin family. **2** (also **dou•ble bass•ist**) its player.

dou•ble bill *n.* a program of entertainment with two principal items or personalities.

dou•ble-bill *v.tr.* charge (different accounts) for the same expenses (*her two restaurants were double-billed for the one refrigerator*).

dou•ble bind *n.* a dilemma.

dou•ble-blind *adj. & n.* ● *adj.* (of a test or experiment) in which neither the tester nor the subject has knowledge of identities, etc., that might lead to bias. ● *n.* such a test or experiment.

dou•ble boil•er *n.* a saucepan with a detachable upper compartment heated by boiling water in the lower one.

dou•ble bond *n. Chem.* a pair of bonds between two atoms in a molecule.

dou•ble-book *v.tr.* accept two reservations simultaneously for (the same seat, room, etc.).

dou•ble-breast•ed *adj.* (of a jacket or coat) having a substantial overlap of material at the front and showing two rows of buttons when fastened.

dou•ble-check *v.tr.* verify (something) a second time to ensure that it is accurate or safe.

dou•ble chin *n.* a chin with a fold of loose flesh below it. □□ **dou•ble-chinned** *adj.*

dou•ble co•co•nut *n.* = COCO-DE-MER.

dou•ble con•cer•to *n.* a concerto for two solo instruments.

dou•ble cream *n.* **1** a soft French cheese. **2** *Brit.* thick cream with a high fat content.

dou•ble-cross *v. & n.* ● *v.tr.* deceive or betray (a person one is supposedly helping). ● *n.* a betrayal of someone with whom one is supoosedly cooperating. □□ **dou•ble-cross•er** *n.*

dou•ble dag•ger *n. Printing* a symbol (‡) used to introduce a reference.

dou•ble-deal•ing *n. & adj.* ● *n.* deceit, esp. in business. ● *adj.* deceitful; practicing deceit. □□ **dou•ble-deal•er** *n.*

dou•ble-deck•er *n.* **1** esp. *Brit.* a bus having an upper and lower deck. **2** *colloq.* anything consisting of two layers.

dou•ble de•com•po•si•tion *n. Chem.* a chemical reaction involving exchange of radicals between two reactants. Also called **metathesis.**

dou•ble den•si•ty *adj. Computing* designating a storage device, esp. a disk, having twice the basic capacity.

dou•ble dum•my *n. Bridge* play with two hands exposed, allowing every card to be located.

dou•ble Dutch *n.* **1** a synchronized jump-rope game using two outstretched ropes swung in opposite directions. **2** *Brit. colloq* incomprehensible talk.

dou•ble ea•gle *n.* **1** a figure of a two-headed eagle. **2** *Golf* a score of three strokes under par at any hole. **3** *hist.* a U.S. coin worth twenty dollars.

dou•ble-edged *adj.* **1** having two functions or (often contradictory) applications. **2** (of a knife, etc.) having two cutting edges.

dou•ble en•ten•dre /dúbəl aantaándrə, dóoblaan taándrə/ *n.* **1** a word or phrase open to two interpretations, one usu. risqué. **2** humor using such words or phrases. [obs. F, = double understanding]

dou•ble en•try *n.* a system of bookkeeping in which each transaction is entered as a debit in one account and a credit in another.

dou•ble ex•po•sure *n. Photog.* the accidental or deliberate repeated exposure of a plate, film, etc.

dou•ble-faced *adj.* **1** insincere. **2** (of a fabric or material) finished on both sides so that either may be used as the right side.

dou•ble fault *n.* (in tennis) two consecutive faults in serving.

dou•ble fea•ture *n.* a movie program with two full-length films.

dou•ble first *n. Brit.* **1** first-class honors in two subjects or examinations at a university. **2** a person achieving this.

dou•ble-gang•er /dúblgangər/ *n.* = DOPPELGÄNGER.

dou•ble glaz•ing *n.* **1** a window consisting of two layers of glass with a space between them, designed to reduce loss of heat and exclude noise. **2** the provision of this.

dou•ble•head•er /dúbəlhedər/ *n.* **1** a train pulled by two locomo-

tives coupled together. **2 a** two games (esp. baseball), etc., in succession between the same opponents. **b** two games (esp. basketball), etc., in succession between different opponents. **3** *Austral. colloq.* a coin with a head on both sides.

dou•ble he•lix *n.* a pair of parallel helices with a common axis, esp. in the structure of the DNA molecule.

dou•ble in•dem•ni•ty *n.* a clause in a life-insurance policy providing double payment to the beneficiary if the insured person dies accidentally.

dou•ble-joint•ed *adj.* having joints that allow unusual bending of the fingers, limbs, etc.

dou•ble-knit *adj.* (of fabric) knit of two joined layers for extra thickness.

dou•ble-lock *v.tr.* lock (a door) with two complete turns of the key so as to engage a second bolt.

dou•ble na•po•le•on *n. hist.* a forty-franc piece.

dou•ble neg•a•tive *n. Gram.* a negative statement containing two negative elements (e.g., *didn't say nothing*).
▶Considered ungrammatical in standard English.

dou•ble-park *v.tr.* park (a vehicle) alongside one that is already parked at the roadside.

dou•ble play *n. Baseball* a defensive play in which two runners are put out.

dou•ble pneu•mo•nia *n.* pneumonia affecting both lungs.

dou•ble re•frac•tion *n. Optics* refraction forming two separate rays from a single incident ray.

dou•ble rhyme *n.* a rhyme including two syllables, as in *station, nation.*

dou•ble salt *n. Chem.* a salt composed of two simple salts and having different crystal properties from either.

dou•ble stand•ard *n.* **1** a rule or principle that is unfairly applied in different ways to different people or groups. **2** bimetallism.

dou•ble star *n.* two stars actually or apparently very close together.

dou•ble-stop•ping *n. Mus.* the sounding of two strings at once on a violin, etc.

dou•blet /dúblit/ *n.* **1** either of a pair of similar things, esp. either of two words of the same derivation but different sense (e.g., *fashion* and *faction, cloak* and *clock*). **2** *hist.* a man's short, close-fitting jacket, with or without sleeves. **3** a historical or biblical account occurring twice in differing contexts, usu. traceable to different sources. **4** (in *pl.*) the same number on two dice thrown at once. **5** a pair of associated lines close together in a spectrum. **6** a combination of two simple lenses. [ME f. OF f. *double*: see DOUBLE]

dou•ble take *n.* a delayed reaction to a situation, etc., immediately after one's first reaction.

dou•ble-talk *n.* verbal expression that is (usu. deliberately) ambiguous or misleading.

dou•ble•think /dúbəlthingk/ *n.* the mental capacity to accept contrary opinions or beliefs at the same time, esp. as a result of political indoctrination.

dou•ble time *n.* **1** payment of an employee at twice the normal rate, sometimes paid for working on holidays or for overtime. **2** *Mil.* a marching pace of 180 three-foot steps per minute. **3** *Mus.* a rhythm that is twice as fast as an earlier one.

dou•ble-tongu•ing *n.* rapid articulation in playing a wind instrument.

dou•bloon /dublóon/ *n.* **1** *hist.* a Spanish gold coin. **2** (in *pl.*) *sl.* money. [F *doublon* or Sp. *doblón* (as DOUBLE)]

dou•blure /dəblóor, dōō-/ *n.* an ornamental lining, usu. leather, inside a book cover. [F, = lining (*doubler* to line)]

doubt /dowt/ *n. & v.* ● *n.* **1** a feeling of uncertainty; an undecided state of mind (*be in no doubt about; have no doubt that*). **2** (often foll. by *of, about*) an inclination to disbelieve (*have one's doubts about*). **3** an uncertain state of things. **4** a lack of full proof or clear indication (*benefit of the doubt*). ● *v.* **1** *tr.* (often foll. by *whether, if, that* + clause; also foll. (after *neg.* or *interrog.*) by *but, but that*) feel uncertain or undecided about (*I doubt that you are right*). **2** *tr.* hesitate to believe or trust. **3** *intr.* (often foll. by *of*) feel uncertain or undecided; have doubts (*never doubted of success*). □ **beyond doubt** certainly. **in doubt** uncertain; open to question. **no doubt** certainly; probably; admittedly. **without doubt** (or **a doubt**) certainly. □□ **doubt•a•ble** *adj.* **doubt•ing•ly** *adv.* [ME *doute* f. OF *doute* (n.), *douter* (v.) f. L *dubitare* hesitate; mod. spelling after L]

doubt•ful /dówtfŏol/ *adj.* **1** feeling doubt or misgivings; unsure or guarded in one's opinion. **2** causing doubt; ambiguous; uncertain in meaning, etc. **3** unreliable (*a doubtful ally*). □□ **doubt•ful•ly** *adv.* **doubt•ful•ness** *n.*

doubt•ing Thom•as *n.* an incredulous or skeptical person (after John 20: 24–29).

doubt•less /dówtlis/ *adv.* (often qualifying a sentence) **1** certainly; no doubt. **2** probably. □□ **doubt•less•ly** *adv.*

douce /dōōs/ *adj. Sc.* sober; gentle; sedate. [ME f. OF *dous douce* f. L *dulcis* sweet]

douche /dōōsh/ *n. & v.* ● *n.* **1** a jet of liquid applied to a body part or cavity for cleansing or medicinal purposes. **2** a device for producing such a jet. ● *v.* **1** *tr.* treat with a douche. **2** *intr.* use a douche.

[F f. It. *doccia* pipe f. *docciare* pour by drops ult. f. L *ductus*: see DUCT]

dough /dō/ n. **1** a thick mixture of flour, etc., and liquid (usu. water), for baking into bread, pastry, etc. **2** *sl.* money. [OE *dāg* f. Gmc]

dough·boy /dóboy/ n. **1** *colloq.* a United States infantryman, esp. in World War I. **2** a boiled dumpling.

dough·nut /dónut/ n. (also **do·nut**) **1** a small fried cake of sweetened dough, usu. in the shape of a ball or ring. **2** a ring-shaped object, esp. *Physics* a vacuum chamber for acceleration of particles in a betatron or synchrotron.

dough·ty /dówtee/ adj. (**dough·ti·er, dough·ti·est**) *archaic or joc.* valiant; stouthearted. □□ **dough·ti·ly** adv. **dough·ti·ness** n. [OE *dohtig* var. of *dyhtig* f. Gmc]

dough·y /dóee/ adj. (**dough·i·er, dough·i·est**) **1** having the form or consistency of dough. **2** pale and sickly in color. □□ **dough·i·ness** n.

Doug·las fir /dúgləs/ n. (also **Doug·las pine** or **spruce**) any large conifer of the genus *Pseudotsuga*, of Western N. America. [D. *Douglas*, Sc. botanist d. 1834]

doum /dōom, dowm/ n. (in full **doum palm**; also **doom palm**) a palm tree, *Hyphaene thebaica*, with edible fruit. [Arab. *dawm, dūm*]

dour /door, dowr/ adj. severe, stern, or sullenly obstinate in manner or appearance. □□ **dour·ly** adv. **dour·ness** n. [ME (orig. Sc.), prob. f. Gael. *dúr* dull, obstinate, perh. f. L *durus* hard]

PRONUNCIATION TIP   **dour**

The traditional pronunciation of this word rhymes with *tour*, but the pronunciation that rhymes with *sour* is considered an acceptable variant.

---

dou·rou·cou·li /dŏŏrəkŏŏlee/ n. (pl. **dou·rou·cou·lis**) any nocturnal monkey of the genus *Aotus*, native to S. America, having large staring eyes. [Indian name]

douse /dows/ v.tr. (also **dowse**) **1 a** throw water over. **b** plunge into water. **2** extinguish (a light). **3** *Naut.* **a** lower (a sail). **b** close (a porthole). [16th c.: perh. rel. to MDu., LG *dossen* strike]

dove[1] /duv/ n. **1** any bird of the family Columbidae, with short legs, small head, and large breast. **2** a gentle or innocent person. **3** *Polit.* an advocate of peace or peaceful policies (cf. HAWK[1]). **4** (**Dove**) *Relig.* a representation of the Holy Spirit (John 1:32). **5** a soft gray color. □□ **dove·like** adj. [ME f. ON *dúfa* f. Gmc]

dove[2] past and past part. of DIVE.

dove·cote /dúvkōt, –kot/ n. (also **dove·cot**) a shelter with nesting holes for domesticated pigeons.

dove·tail /dúvtayl/ n. & v. • n. **1** a joint formed by a mortise with a tenon shaped like a dove's spread tail or a reversed wedge. **2** such a tenon. • v. **1** tr. join together by means of a dove-

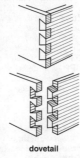

dovetail

SYNONYM TIP   **doubtful**

AMBIGUOUS, DUBIOUS, ENIGMATIC, EQUIVOCAL, PROBLEMATIC, QUESTIONABLE. If you are **doubtful** about the outcome of a situation, you might be understandably **dubious** about getting involved in it. While all of these adjectives express suspicion, indecision, or a lack of clarity, *doubtful* carries such strong connotations of uncertainty that the thing being described is as good as worthless, unsound, invalid, unlikely, or doomed to fail (*it was doubtful that the plane could land safely*). *Dubious* is not quite as strong, suggesting suspicion, mistrust, or hesitation (*a dubious reputation*). It can also mean inclined to doubt or full of hesitation. If you're *doubtful* about the outcome of a particular situation, it means that you are fairly certain it will not turn out well. If you're *dubious*, on the other hand, it means that you're wavering or hesitating in your opinion. **Questionable** may merely imply the existence of doubt (*a questionable excuse*), but like *dubious*, it also has connotations of dishonesty and immorality (*a place where questionable activities were going on*). **Problematic**, in contrast to both *dubious* and *questionable*, is free from any suggestion of moral judgment or suspicion. It is applied to things that are genuinely uncertain, and to outcomes that are as likely to be positive as negative (*getting everyone in the family to agree could be problematic*). **Ambiguous** and **equivocal** refer to lack of clarity. But while *ambiguous* can refer to either an intentional or unintentional lack of clarity (*her ambiguous replies to our questions*), *equivocal* suggests an intentional wish to remain unclear (*his equivocal responses indicated that he wasn't keen to cooperate*). It can also mean capable of different interpretations (*an equivocal statement that could be taken to mean opposite things*). Something that is **enigmatic** is likely to be intentionally unclear as well (*an enigmatic statement designed to provoke controversy*), although *enigmatic* can also mean perplexing or mysterious.

---

tail. **2** tr. & intr. (often foll. by *into, with*) fit readily together; combine neatly or compactly.

dow·a·ger /dówəjər/ n. **1** a widow with a title or property derived from her late husband (*Queen dowager; dowager duchess*). **2** *colloq.* a dignified elderly woman. [OF *douag(i)er* f. *douage* (as DOWER)]

dow·dy /dówdee/ adj. & n. • adj. (**dow·di·er, dow·di·est**) **1** (of clothes) unattractively dull; unfashionable. **2** (of a person, esp. a woman) dressed in dowdy clothes. • n. (pl. **·dies**) a dowdy woman. □□ **dow·di·ly** adv. **dow·di·ness** n. [ME *dowd* slut, of unkn. orig.]

dow·el /dówəl/ n. & v. • n. a headless peg of wood, metal, or plastic for holding together components of a structure. • v.tr. (**dow·eled, dow·el·ing**; esp. *Brit.* **dow·elled, dow·el·ling**) fasten with a dowel or dowels. [ME f. MLG *dovel*: cf. THOLE[1]]

dow·el·ing /dówəling/ n. round rods for cutting into dowels.

dow·er /dowər/ n. & v. • n. **1** a widow's share for life of her husband's estate. **2** *archaic* a dowry. **3** a natural gift or talent. • v.tr. **1** *archaic* give a dowry to. **2** (foll. by *with*) endow with talent, etc. □□ **dow·er·less** adj. [ME f. OF *douaire* f. med.L *dotarium* f. L *dos dotis*]

dowel

dow·er house n. *Brit.* a smaller house near a big one, forming part of a widow's dower.

Dow–Jones av·er·age /dówjōnz/ n. (also **Dow–Jones in·dex**) a figure based on the average price of selected stocks, indicating the relative price of shares on the New York Stock Exchange. [C. H. *Dow* d. 1902 & E. D. *Jones* d. 1920, Amer. economists]

down[1] /down/ adv., prep., adj., v., & n. • adv. (superl. **down·most**) **1** into or toward a lower place, esp. to the ground (*fall down; knelt down*). **2** in a lower place or position (*blinds were down*). **3** to or in a place regarded as lower, esp.: **a** southward. **b** *Brit.* away from a major city or a university. **4 a** in or into a low or weaker position, mood, or condition (*hit a man when he's down; many down with colds*). **b** in a position of lagging or loss (*our team was three goals down; $5 down on the transaction*). **c** (of a computer system) out of action or unavailable for use (esp. temporarily). **5** from an earlier to a later time (*customs handed down; down to 1600*). **6** to a finer or thinner consistency or a smaller amount or size (*grind down; water down; boil down*). **7** cheaper; lower in price or value (*bread is down; stocks are down*). **8** into a more settled state (*calm down*). **9** in writing; in or into recorded or listed form (*copy it down; I got it down on tape; you are down to speak next*). **10** (of part of a larger whole) paid; dealt with (*$5 down, $20 to pay; three down, six to go*). **11** *Naut.* **a** with the current or wind. **b** (of a ship's helm) with the rudder to windward. **12** inclusively of the lower limit in a series (*read down to the third paragraph*). **13** (as *int.*) lie down, put (something) down, etc. **14** (of a crossword clue or answer) read vertically (*cannot do five down*). **15** downstairs, esp. after rising (*is not down yet*). **16** swallowed (*could not get the pill down*). **17** *Football* (of the ball) no longer in play. • prep. **1** downward along, through, or into. **2** from top to bottom of. **3** along (*walk down the road; cut down the middle*). **4** at or in a lower part of (*situated down the river*). • adj. (superl. **down·most**) **1** directed downward. **2** *Brit.* of travel away from a capital or center (*the down train; the down platform*). **3** *colloq.* unhappy; depressed. • v.tr. *colloq.* **1** knock or bring down. **2** swallow (a drink). • n. **1** an act of putting down (as an opponent in wrestling). **2** a reverse of fortune (*ups and downs*). **3** *colloq.* a period of depression. **4** *Football* **a** one of a series of plays (up to four) in which the offensive team must advance the ball 10 yards in order to keep the ball. **b** the declaring of the ball as no longer in play. □ **be down on** *colloq.* disapprove of; show animosity toward. **be down to 1** be attributable to. **2** be the responsibility of. **3** have used up everything except (*down to their last can of rations*). **down on one's luck** *colloq.* **1** temporarily unfortunate. **2** dispirited by misfortune. **down to the ground** *colloq.* completely. **down tools** *Brit. colloq.* cease work, esp. to go on strike. **down with** int. expressing strong disapproval or rejection of a specified person or thing. [OE *dūn(e)* f. *adūne* off the hill]

down[2] /down/ n. **1 a** the first covering of young birds. **b** a bird's under-plumage, used in cushions, etc. **c** a layer of fine, soft feathers. **2** fine, soft hair esp. on the face. **3** short, soft hairs on some leaves, fruit, seeds, etc. **4** a fluffy substance, e.g., thistledown. [ME f. ON *dúnn*]

down[3] /down/ n. **1** an area of open rolling land. **2** (in pl.; usu. prec. by *the*) **a** undulating chalk and limestone uplands esp. in S. England, with few trees and used mainly for pasture. **b** (**Downs**) a part of the sea (opposite the North Downs) off E. Kent, England. □□ **down·y** adj. [OE *dūn* perh. f. OCelt.]

down-and-out adj. & n. • adj. **1** penniless; destitute. **2** *Boxing* unable to resume the fight. • n. a destitute person.

down•at•the•heels *adj.* (also **down-at-heel, down-at-the-heel**) shabby; slovenly.

down•beat /dównbeet/ *n. & adj.* ● *n. Mus.* an accented beat, usu. the first of the bar. ● *adj.* **1** pessimistic; gloomy. **2** relaxed.

down•cast /dównkast/ *adj. & n.* ● *adj.* **1** (of eyes) looking downward. **2** (of a person) dejected. ● *n.* a shaft dug in a mine for extra ventilation.

down•com•er /dównkumər/ *n.* a pipe for downward transport of water or gas.

down•draft /dówndraft/ *n.* a downward draft, esp. one down a chimney into a room.

down•er /dównər/ *n. sl.* **1** a depressant or tranquilizing drug, esp. a barbiturate. **2** a depressing person or experience; a failure. **3** = DOWNTURN.

down•fall /dównfawl/ *n.* **1 a** a fall from prosperity or power. **b** the cause of this. **2** a sudden heavy fall of rain, etc.

down•fold /dównfōld/ *n. Geol.* a syncline.

down•grade *v. & n.* ● *v.tr.* /dówngráyd/ **1** make lower in rank or status. **2** speak disparagingly of. ● *n.* /dówngrayd/ **1** a descending slope of a road or railroad. **2** a deterioration. □ **on the downgrade** in decline.

down•heart•ed /dównhaártid/ *adj.* dejected; in low spirits. □□ **down•heart•ed•ly** *adv.* **down•heart•ed•ness** *n.*

down•hill *adv., adj., & n.* ● *adv.* /dównhíl/ in a descending direction, esp. toward the bottom of an incline. ● *adj.* /dównhil/ **1** sloping down; descending. **2** declining; deteriorating. ● *n.* /dównhil/ **1** *Skiing* a downhill race. **2** a downward slope. **3** a decline. □ **go downhill** *colloq.* decline; deteriorate (in health, state of repair, moral state, etc.).

down•land /dównlənd/ *n.* = DOWN[3].

down•load /dównlōd/ *v.tr. Computing* transfer (data) from one storage device or system to another (esp. smaller remote one).

down-mar•ket *adj. & adv. colloq.* toward or relating to the cheaper or less affluent sector of the market.

down•most /dównmōst/ *adj. & adv.* the furthest down.

down pay•ment *n.* a partial payment made at the time of purchase.

down•pipe /dównpīp/ *n. Brit.* = DOWNSPOUT.

down•play /dównpláy/ *v.tr.* play down; minimize the importance of.

down•pour /dównpawr/ *n.* a heavy fall of rain.

down•right /dównrīt/ *adj. & adv.* ● *adj.* **1** plain; definite; straightforward; blunt. **2** utter; complete (*a downright lie; downright nonsense*). ● *adv.* thoroughly; completely; positively (*downright rude*). □□ **down•right•ness** *n.*

down•scale /dównskáyl/ *v. & adj.* ● *v.tr.* reduce or restrict in size, scale, or extent. ● *adj.* at the lower end of a scale, esp. a social scale; inferior.

down•shift /dównshift/ *v.intr. & tr.* shift (an automotive vehicle) into a lower gear.

down•side /dównsīd/ *n.* a downward movement of share prices, etc.

down•size /dównsīz/ *v.tr.* (**down•sized, down•siz•ing**) **1** reduce in size; make smaller. **2** cut back on the number of employees in (a company).

down•spout /dównspowt/ *n.* a pipe to carry rainwater from a roof to a drain or to ground level.

Down's syn•drome /downz/ *n. Med.* (also **Down syn•drome**) a congenital disorder due to a chromosome defect, characterized by mental retardation and physical abnormalities (cf. MONGOLISM). [J. L. H. *Down*, Engl. physician d. 1896]

down•stage /dównstayj/ *n., adj., & adv. Theatr.* ● *n.* the frontmost portion of the stage. ● *adj. & adv.* at or to the front of the stage.

down•stairs *adv., adj., & n.* ● *adv.* /dównstáirz/ **1** down a flight of stairs. **2** to or on a lower floor. ● *adj.* /dównstairz/ (also **down•stair**) situated downstairs. ● *n.* /dównstáirz/ the lower floor.

down•state /dównsáyt/ *adj., n., & adv.* ● *adj.* of or in a southern part of a state. ● *n.* a downstate area. ● *adv.* in a downstate area.

down•stream /dównstreém/ *adv. & adj.* ● *adv.* in the direction of the flow of a stream, etc. ● *adj.* moving downstream.

down•stroke /dównstrōk/ *n.* a stroke made or written downward.

down•throw /dównthrō/ *n. Geol.* a downward dislocation of strata.

down•time /dówntīm/ *n.* time during which a machine, esp. a computer, is out of action or unavailable for use.

down-to-earth *adj.* practical; realistic.

down•town /dówntówn/ *adj., n., & adv.* ● *adj.* of or in the lower or more central part, or the business part, of a town or city. ● *n.* a downtown area. ● *adv.* in or into a downtown area.

down•trod•den /dówntród’n/ *adj.* oppressed; badly treated; kept under.

down•turn /dówntərn/ *n.* a decline, esp. in economic or business activity.

down un•der *adv. & n. colloq.* (also **Down Un•der**) ● *adv.* in or to Australia or New Zealand. ● *n.* Australia and New Zealand.

down•ward /dównwərd/ *adv. & adj.* ● *adv.* (also **down•wards**) toward what is lower, inferior, less important, or later. ● *adj.* moving, extending, pointing, or leading downward. □□ **down•ward•ly** *adv.*

down•warp /dównwawrp/ *n. Geol.* a broad surface depression; a syncline.

down•wind /dównwínd/ *adj. & adv.* in the direction in which the wind is blowing.

down•y /dównee/ *adj.* (**down•i•er, down•i•est**) **1 a** of, like, or covered with down. **b** soft and fluffy. **2** *Brit. sl.* aware; knowing. □□ **down•i•ly** *adv.* **down•i•ness** *n.*

dow•ry /dówree/ *n.* (*pl.* **•ries**) **1** property or money brought by a bride to her husband. **2** a talent; a natural gift. [ME f. AF *dowarie*, OF *douaire* DOWER]

dowse[1] /dowz/ *v.intr.* search for underground water or minerals by holding a Y-shaped stick or rod which supposedly dips abruptly when over the right spot. □□ **dows•er** *n.* [17th c.: orig. unkn.]

dowse[2] var. of DOUSE.

dows•ing rod *n.* (also **di•vin•ing rod**) a stick or rod that supposedly dips abruptly when held over ground under which water or minerals can be found.

dox•ol•o•gy /doksóləjee/ *n.* (*pl.* **•gies**) a liturgical formula of praise to God. □□ **dox•o•log•i•cal** /–səlójikəl/ *adj.* [med.L *doxologia* f. Gk *doxologia* f. *doxa* glory + –LOGY]

dox•y /dóksee/ *n.* (also **dox•ie**) (*pl.* **•ies**) *literary* **1** a lover or mistress. **2** a prostitute. [16th-c. cant: orig. unkn.]

doy•en /doyén, dóyən, dwaáyaN/ *n.* (*fem.* **doy•enne** /doyén, dwaayén/) the senior member of a body of colleagues, esp. the senior ambassador at a court. [F (as DEAN[1])]

doy•ley var. of DOILY.

doz. *abbr.* dozen.

doze /dōz/ *v. & n.* ● *v.intr.* sleep lightly; be half asleep. ● *n.* a short, light sleep. □ **doze off** fall lightly asleep. □□ **doz•er** *n.* [17th c.: cf. Da. *døse* make drowsy]

doz•en /dúzən/ *n.* **1** (prec. by *a* or a number) (*pl.* **doz•en**) twelve, regarded collectively (*a dozen eggs; two dozen packages; ordered three dozen*). **2** a set or group of twelve (*packed in dozens*). **3** *colloq.* about twelve, a fairly large indefinite number. **4** (in *pl.*; usu. foll. by *of*) *colloq.* very many (*made dozens of mistakes*). **5** (**the dozens**) a game or ritualized exchange of verbal insults. □ **by the dozen** in large quantities. **talk nineteen to the dozen** *Brit.* talk incessantly. □□ **doz•enth** *adj. & n.* [ME f. OF *dozeine*, ult. f. L *duodecim* twelve]

doz•er /dózər/ *n. colloq.* = BULLDOZER. [abbr.]

doz•y /dózee/ *adj.* (**doz•i•er, doz•i•est**) **1** drowsy; tending to doze. **2** *Brit. colloq.* stupid or lazy. □□ **doz•i•ly** *adv.* **doz•i•ness** *n.*

DP *abbr.* **1** data processing. **2** displaced person.

D.Ph. *abbr.* Doctor of Philosophy.

DPP *abbr.* deferred payment plan.

DPT *abbr.* (vaccination against) diphtheria, pertussis, and tetanus.

Dr. *abbr.* **1** Doctor. **2** Drive. **3** debtor.

dr. *abbr.* **1** dram(s). **2** drachma(s).

drab[1] /drab/ *adj. & n.* ● *adj.* (**drab•ber, drab•best**) **1** dull; uninteresting. **2** of a dull brownish color. ● *n.* **1** drab color. **2** monotony. □□ **drab•ly** *adv.* **drab•ness** *n.* [prob. f. obs. *drap* cloth f. OF f. LL *drappus*, perh. of Celt. orig.]

drab[2] /drab/ see DRIBS AND DRABS.

drab[3] /drab/ *n.* **1** a slut; a slattern. **2** a prostitute. [perh. rel. to LG *drabbe* mire, Du. *drab* dregs]

drab•ble /drábəl/ *v.intr. & tr.* become or make dirty and wet with water or mud. [ME f. LG *drabbelen* paddle in water or mire: cf. DRAB[3]]

drachm /dram/ *n. Brit.* var. of DRAM 2. [ME *dragme* f. OF *dragme* or LL *dragma* f. L *drachma* f. Gk *drakhmē* Attic weight and coin]

drach•ma /drákmə/ *n.* (*pl.* **drach•mas** or **drach•mai** /–mi/ or **drach•mae** /–mee/) **1** the chief monetary unit of Greece. **2** a silver coin of ancient Greece. [L f. Gk *drakhmē*]

drack /drak/ *adj. Austral. sl.* **1** (esp. of a woman) unattractive. **2** dismal; dull. [20th c.: orig. unkn.]

dra•cone /drákōn/ *n.* a large flexible container for liquids, towed on the surface of the sea. [L *draco –onis* (as DRAGON)]

dra•co•ni•an /drəkóneeən, dray–/ *adj.* (also **dra•con•ic** /–kónik/) very harsh or severe (esp. of laws and their application). [*Drakōn*, 7th-c. BC Athenian legislator]

draff /draf/ *n.* **1** dregs; lees. **2** refuse. [ME, perh. repr. OE *dræf* (unrecorded)]

draft /draft/ *n. & v.* ● *n.* **1 a** a preliminary written version of a speech, document, etc. **b** a rough preliminary outline of a scheme. **c** a sketch of work to be carried out. **2 a** a written order for payment of money by a bank. **b** the drawing of money by means of this. **3** (foll. by *on*) a demand made on a person's confidence, friendship, etc. **4 a** a party detached from a larger group for a special duty or purpose. **b** the selection of this. **5** compulsory military service. **6** a reinforcement. **7** a current of air in a confined space (e.g., a room or chimney). **8** pulling; traction. **9** *Naut.* the depth of water needed to float a ship. **10** the drawing of liquor from a cask, etc. **11 a** a single act of drinking. **b** the amount drunk in this. **c** a dose of liquid medicine. **12 a** the drawing in of a fishing net. **b** the fish taken at one drawing. □ **feel the draft** *Brit. colloq.* suffer from adverse (usu. financial) conditions. ● *v.tr.* **1** prepare a draft of (a document, scheme, etc.). **2** select for a special duty or purpose. **3** con-

draft beer *n*. beer drawn from a cask, not bottled.

draft board *n*. a board of civilians that selects and classifies persons for compulsory US military service.

draft horse *n*. a horse used for pulling heavy loads, esp. a cart or plow.

drafts•man /dráftsmən/ *n*. (*pl*. **•men**) **1** a person who makes drawings, plans, or sketches. **2** a person who drafts documents. □□ **drafts•man•ship** *n*.

draft•y /dráftee/ *adj*. (*Brit*. **draughty**) (**•i•er**, **•i•est**) (of a room, etc.) letting in sharp currents of air. □□ **draft•i•ly** *adv*. **draft•i•ness** *n*.

drag /drag/ *v. & n*. • *v*. (**dragged**, **drag•ging**) **1** *tr*. pull along with effort or difficulty. **2 a** *tr*. allow (one's feet, tail, etc.) to trail along the ground. **b** *intr*. trail along the ground. **c** *intr*. (of time, etc.) go or pass heavily or slowly or tediously. **3 a** *intr*. (usu. foll. by *for*) use a grapnel or drag (to find a drowned person or lost object). **b** *tr*. search the bottom of (a river, etc.) with grapnels, nets, or drags. **4** *tr*. (often foll. by *to*) *colloq*. take (a person to a place, etc., esp. against his or her will). **5** *intr*. (foll. by *on, at*) draw on (a cigarette, etc.). **6** *intr*. (often foll. by *on*) continue at tedious length. • *n*. **1 a** an obstruction to progress. **b** *Aeron*. the longitudinal retarding force exerted by air. **c** slow motion; impeded progress. **d** an iron shoe for retarding a horse-drawn vehicle downhill. **2** *colloq*. **a** a boring or dreary person, duty, performance, etc. **3 a** a strong-smelling lure drawn before hounds as a substitute for a fox. **b** a hunt using this. **4** an apparatus for dredging or recovering drowned persons, etc. from under water. **5** = DRAGNET. **6** *sl*. a draw on a cigarette, etc. **7** *sl*. **a** women's clothes worn by men. **b** a party at which these are worn. **c** clothes in general. **8** an act of dragging. **9** *sl*. (in full **drag race**) an acceleration race between cars, usu. for a short distance. **10** *sl*. influence; pull. **11** *sl*. a street or road (*the main drag*). **12** *hist*. a private vehicle like a stagecoach, drawn by four horses. □ **drag anchor** (of a ship) move from a moored position when the anchor fails to hold. **drag-anchor** *n*. = SEA ANCHOR. **drag one's feet** (or **heels**) be deliberately slow or reluctant to act. **drag in** introduce (a subject) irrelevantly. **drag out** protract. **drag through the mud** see MUD. **drag up** *colloq*. **1** deliberately mention (an unwelcome subject). **2** esp. *Brit*. rear (a child) roughly and without proper training. [ME f. OE *dragan* or ON *draga* DRAW]

dra•gée /drazháy/ *n*. **1** a sugar-coated almond, etc. **2** a small silver ball for decorating a cake. **3** a chocolate-coated candy. [F: see DREDGE²]

drag•gle /drágəl/ *v*. **1** *tr*. make dirty or wet or limp by trailing. **2** *intr*. hang trailing. **3** *intr*. lag; straggle in the rear. [DRAG + -LE⁴]

drag•gle-tailed *adj*. (of a woman) with untidily trailing skirts.

drag•gy /drágee/ *adj*. (**drag•gi•er**, **drag•gi•est**) *colloq*. **1** tedious. **2** unpleasant.

drag•hound /drághownd/ *n*. a hound used to hunt with a drag.

drag•line /drághn/ *n*. an excavator with a bucket pulled in by a wire rope.

drag•net /drágnet/ *n* **1** a net drawn through a river or across ground to trap fish or game. **2** a systematic hunt for criminals, etc.

drag•o•man /drágəmən/ *n*. (*pl*. **drag•o•mans** or **drag•o•men**) an interpreter or guide, esp. in countries speaking Arabic, Turkish, or Persian. [F f. It. *dragomano* f. med.Gk *dragomanos* f. Arab. *tarjumān* f. *tarjama* interpret, f. Aram. *targēm* f. Assyr. *targumānu* interpreter]

drag•on /drágən/ *n*. **1** a mythical monster like a reptile, usu. with wings and claws and able to breathe out fire. **2** a fierce person, esp. a woman. **3** (in full **flying dragon**) a lizard, *Draco volans*, with a long tail and membranous winglike structures. Also called **flying lizard**. [ME f. OF f. L *draco -onis* f. Gk *drakōn* serpent]

drag•on•et /drágənit/ *n*. any marine spiny fish of the family Callionymidae, the males of which are brightly colored. [ME f. F, dimin. of DRAGON]

drag•on•fish /drágənfish/ *n*. (*pl*. same or **•fish•es**) any marine deepwater fish of the family Stomiatidae, having a long, slender body and a barbel on the chin with luminous tissue, serving to attract prey.

drag•on•fly /drágənfh/ *n*. (*pl*. **•flies**) any of various insects of the order Odonata, having a long, slender body and two pairs of large transparent wings usu. spread when resting.

drag•on•nade /drágənáyd/ *n. & v*. • *n*. a persecution by use of troops, esp. (in *pl*.) of French Protestants under Louis XIV by quartering dragoons on them. • *v.tr*. subject to a dragonnade. [F f. *dragon*: see DRAGOON]

dra•gon's blood *n*. a red gum that exudes from the fruit of some palms and the dragon tree.

dra•gon's teeth *n. Mil. colloq*. obstacles resembling teeth pointed upward, used esp. against tanks.

dra•gon tree *n*. a tree, *Dracaena draco*, native to the Canary Islands.

dra•goon /drəgoon/ *n. & v*. • *n*. **1** a cavalryman (orig. a mounted infantryman armed with a carbine). **2** a rough, fierce fellow. **3** a variety of pigeon. • *v.tr*. **1** (foll. by *into*) coerce into doing something, esp. by use of strong force. **2** persecute, esp. with

troops. [orig. = carbine (thought of as breathing fire) f. F *dragon* DRAGON]

drag queen *n. sl*. a male transvestite.

drag race *n*. a race between two or more vehicles to determine which accelerates the fastest.

drag•ster /drágstər/ *n*. a car built or modified to take part in drag races.

drag strip *n*. a straight stretch of road on which drag races are held.

drail /drayl/ *n*. a fishhook and line weighted with lead for dragging below the surface of the water. [app. var. of TRAIL]

drain /drayn/ *v. & n*. • *v*. **1** *tr*. draw off liquid from, esp.: **a** make (land, etc.) dry by providing an outflow for moisture. **b** (of a river) carry off the superfluous water of (a district). **c** remove purulent matter from (an abscess). **2** *tr*. (foll. by *off, away*) draw off (liquid) esp. by a pipe. **3** *intr*. (foll. by *away, off, through*) flow or trickle away. **4** *intr*. (of a wet cloth, a vessel, etc.) become dry as liquid flows away (*put it there to drain*). **5** *tr*. (often foll. by *of*) exhaust or deprive (a person or thing) of strength, resources, property, etc. **6** *tr*. **a** drink (liquid) to the dregs. **b** empty (a vessel) by drinking the contents. • *n*. **1 a** a channel, conduit, or pipe carrying off liquid, esp. an artificial conduit for water or sewage. **b** a tube for drawing off the discharge from an abscess, etc. **2** a constant outflow, withdrawal, or expenditure (*a great drain on my resources*). □ **down the drain** *colloq*. lost; wasted. **laugh like a drain** *Brit*. laugh copiously; guffaw. [OE *drē(a)hnian* f. Gmc]

drain•age /dráynij/ *n*. **1** the process or means of draining (*the land has poor drainage*). **2** a system of drains, artificial or natural. **3** what is drained off, esp. sewage.

drain•board /dráynbawrd/ *n*. a sloping usu. grooved surface beside a sink, on which washed dishes, etc., are left to drain.

drain•er /dráynər/ *n*. **1** a device for draining; anything on which things are put to drain, e.g., a drainboard. **2** a person who drains.

drain•pipe /dráynpīp/ *n*. **1** a pipe for carrying off water, sewage, etc., from a building. **2** (*attrib*.) *Brit*. (of pants, etc.) very narrow. **3** (in *pl*.) *Brit*. (also **drainpipe trousers**) very narrow pants.

drake /drayk/ *n*. a male duck. [ME prob. f. Gmc]

dram /dram/ *n*. **1** a small drink of liquor. **2** a weight or measure formerly used by apothecaries, equivalent to 60 grains or one eighth of an ounce, or (in full **fluid dram**) 60 minims, one eighth of a fluid ounce. [ME f. OF *drame* or med.L *drama, dragma*: cf. DRAM]

dra•ma /drámə, draámə/ *n*. **1** a play for acting on stage or for broadcasting. **2** (often prec. by *the*) the art of writing and presenting plays. **3** an exciting or emotional event, set of circumstances, etc. **4** dramatic quality (*the drama of the situation*). [LL f. Gk *drama –atos* f. *draō* do]

dra•mat•ic /drəmátik/ *adj*. **1** of drama or the study of drama. **2** (of an event, circumstance, etc.) sudden and exciting or unexpected. **3** vividly striking. **4** (of a gesture, etc.) theatrical; overdone; absurd. □□ **dra•mat•i•cal•ly** *adv*. [LL *dramaticus* f. Gk *dramatikos* (as DRAMA)]

dra•mat•ic i•ro•ny *n*. = TRAGIC IRONY.

dra•mat•ics /drəmátiks/ *n.pl*. (often treated as *sing*.) **1** the production and performance of plays. **2** exaggerated or showy behavior.

dram•a•tis per•so•nae /drámətis pərsónee, draámətis pərsóni/ *n.pl*. (often treated as *sing*.) **1** the characters in a play. **2** a list of these. [L, = persons of the drama]

dram•a•tist /drámətist, draámə–/ *n*. a writer of dramas.

dram•a•tize /drámətīz, draámə–/ *v*. **1** *tr*. adapt (a novel, etc.) to form a stage play. **b** *intr*. admit of such adaptation. **2** *tr*. make a drama or dramatic scene of. **3** *tr*. (also *absol*.) express or react to in a dramatic way. □□ **dram•a•ti•za•tion** *n*.

dram•a•turge /drámətərj, draámə–/ *n*. (also **dram•a•turg**) **1** a specialist in theatrical production. **2** a dramatist. [F f. Gk *dramatourgos* (as DRAMA, *–ergos* worker)]

dram•a•tur•gy /drámətərjee, draámə–/ *n*. **1** the art of theatrical production; the theory of dramatics. **2** the application of this. □□ **dram•a•tur•gic** *adj*. **dram•a•tur•gi•cal** *adj*.

Dram•bu•ie /drambóoee/ *n*. Trademark a Scotch whiskey liqueur. [Gael. *dram buidheach* satisfying drink]

drank *past* of DRINK.

drape /drayp/ *v. & n*. • *v.tr*. **1** hang, cover loosely, or adorn with cloth, etc. **2** arrange (clothes or hangings) carefully in folds. • *n*. **1** (often in *pl*.) a curtain or drapery. **2** a piece of drapery. **3** the way in which a garment or fabric hangs. [ME f. OF *draper* f. *drap* f. LL *drappus* cloth]

drap•er /dráypər/ *n. Brit*. a retailer of textile fabrics. [ME f. AF, OF *drapier* (as DRAPE)]

dra•per•y /dráypəree/ *n* (*pl*. **•ies**) **1** clothing or hangings arranged in folds. **2** (often in *pl*.) a curtain or hanging. **3** *Brit*. cloth; textile fabrics. **4** *Brit*. the trade of a draper. **5** the arrangement of clothing in sculpture or painting. [ME f. OF *draperie* f. *drap* cloth]

dras•tic /drástik/ *adj*. having a strong or far-reaching effect; severe. □□ **dras•ti•cal•ly** *adv*. [Gk *drastikos* f. *draō* do]

drat /drat/ *v. & int. colloq.* •*v.tr.* (**drat·ted, drat·ting** usu. as an exclam.) curse; confound (*drat the thing!*). •*int.* expressing anger or annoyance. □□ **drat·ted** *adj.* [for '*od* (= God) *rot*]

draught /dráft/ *n., v. & adj.* •*n.* (in *pl.*; usu. treated as *sing.*) *Brit.* = *checkers* (see CHECKER²). •*v.tr. & adj. Brit.* = DRAFT. [ME *draht*, perh. f. ON *drahtr*, *dráttr* f. Gmc, rel. to DRAW]

draught·board /dráftbawrd/ *n. Brit.* a checkerboard, as used in checkers (*Brit.* draughts).

draughts·man /dráftsmən/ *n.* (*pl.* •**men**) **1** *Brit.* = DRAFTSMAN. **2** /dráftsmən/ *Brit.* a piece in the game of draughts.

draught·y *Brit.* var. of DRAFTY.

Dra·vid·i·an /drəvídeeən/ *n. & adj.* •*n.* **1** a member of a dark-skinned aboriginal people of S. India and Sri Lanka (including the Tamils and Kanarese). **2** any of the group of languages spoken by this people. •*adj.* of or relating to this people or group of languages. [Skr. *Dravida*, a province of S. India]

draw /draw/ *v. & n.* •*v.* (*past* **drew** /droo/; *past part.* **drawn** /drawn/) **1** *tr.* pull or cause to move toward or after one. **2** *tr.* pull (a thing) up, over, or across. **3** *tr.* pull (curtains, etc.) open or shut. **4** *tr.* take (a person) aside, esp. to talk to. **5** *tr.* attract; bring to oneself or to something; take in (*drew a deep breath; I felt drawn to her; drew my attention to the matter; draw him into conversation; the match drew large crowds*). **6** *intr.* (foll. by *at, on*) suck smoke from (a cigarette, pipe, etc.). **7** *tr.* **a** (also *absol.*) take out; remove (e.g., a tooth, a gun from a holster, etc.). **b** select by taking out (e.g., a card from a pack). **8** *tr.* obtain or take from a source (*draw a salary; draw inspiration*). **9** *tr.* trace (a line, mark, furrow, or figure). **10 a** *tr.* produce (a picture) by tracing lines and marks. **b** *tr.* represent (a thing) by this means. **c** *absol.* make a drawing. **11** *tr.* (also *absol.*) finish (a contest or game) with neither side winning. **12** *intr.* make one's or its way; proceed; move; come (*drew near the bridge; draw to a close; the second horse drew even; drew ahead of the field; the time draws near*). **13** *tr.* infer; deduce (a conclusion). **14** *tr.* **a** elicit; evoke. **b** bring about; entail (*draw criticism*). **c** induce (a person) to reveal facts, feelings, or talent (*refused to be drawn*). **d** (foll. by *to* + infin.) induce (a person) to do something. **e** *Cards* cause to be played (*drew all the trump*). **15** *tr.* haul up (water) from a well. **16** *tr.* bring out (liquid from a vessel or blood from a wound). **17** *tr.* extract a liquid essence from. **18** *intr.* (of a chimney or pipe) promote or allow a draft. **19** *intr.* (of tea) infuse. **20 a** *tr.* obtain by lot (*drew the winner*). **b** *absol.* draw lots. **21** *intr.* (foll. by *on*) make a demand on a person, a person's skill, memory, imagination, etc. **22** *tr.* write out (a bill, check, or draft) (*drew a check on the bank*). **23** *tr.* frame (a document) in due form; compose. **24** *tr.* formulate or perceive (a comparison or distinction). **25** *tr.* (of a ship) require (a specified depth of water) to float in. **26** *tr.* disembowel (*hang, and quarter; draw the fowl before cooking it*). **27** *tr. Hunting* search (cover) for game. **28** *tr.* drag (a badger or fox) from a hole. **29** *tr.* **a** protract; stretch; elongate (*long-drawn agony*). **b** make (wire) by pulling a piece of metal through successively smaller holes. **30** *tr.* **a** *Golf* drive (the ball) to the left (or, of a left-handed player, the right) esp. purposely. **b** *Bowls* cause (a bowl) to travel in a curve to the desired point. **31** *intr.* (of a sail) swell tightly in the wind. •*n.* **1** an act of drawing. **2 a** a person or thing that draws custom, attention, etc. **b** the power to attract attention. **3** the drawing of lots, esp. a raffle. **4** a drawn game. **5** a suck on a cigarette, etc. **6** the act of removing a gun from its holster in order to shoot (*quick on the draw*). **7** strain; pull. **8** the movable part of a drawbridge. □ **draw back** withdraw from an undertaking. **draw a bead on** see BEAD. **draw bit** = *draw rein*. **draw a blank** see BLANK. **draw bridle** = *draw rein*. **draw a person's fire** attract hostility, criticism, etc., away from a more important target. **draw in 1 a** (of successive days) become shorter because of the changing seasons. **b** (of a day) approach its end. **c** (of successive evenings or nights) start earlier because of the changing seasons. **2** persuade to join; entice. **3** (of a train, etc.) arrive at a station. **draw in one's horns** become less assertive or ambitious; draw back. **draw the line at** set a limit (of tolerance, etc.) at. **draw lots** see LOT. **draw off 1** withdraw (troops). **2** drain off (a liquid), esp. without disturbing sediment. **draw on 1** approach; come near. **2** lead to; bring about. **3** allure. **4** put (gloves, boots, etc.) on. **draw out 1** prolong. **2** elicit. **3** induce to talk. **4** (of successive days) become longer because of the changing seasons. **5** (of a train, etc.) leave a station, etc. **6** write out in proper form. **7** lead out, detach, or array (troops). **draw rein** see REIN. **draw one's sword against** attack. **draw up 1** compose or draft (a document, etc.). **2** bring or come into regular order. **3** come to a halt. **4** make (oneself) stiffly erect. **5** (foll. by *with, to*) gain on or overtake. **quick on the draw** quick to act or react. [OE *dragan* f. Gmc]

draw·back /dráwbak/ *n.* **1** a thing that impairs satisfaction; a disadvantage. **2** (foll. by *from*) a deduction. **3** an amount of excise or import duty paid back or remitted on goods exported.

draw·back lock *n.* a lock with a spring bolt that can be drawn back by an inside knob.

draw·bridge /dráwbrij/ *n.* a bridge, esp. over water, hinged at one end so that it may be raised to prevent passage or to allow ships, etc., to pass.

drawbridge

draw·ee /drawee/ *n.* the person on whom a draft or bill is drawn.

draw·er *n.* **1** /dráwər/ a person or thing that draws, esp. a person who draws a check, etc. **2** /drawr/ a boxlike storage compartment without a lid, sliding in and out of a frame, table, etc. (*chest of drawers*). **3** (in *pl.*) /drawrz/ an undergarment worn next to the body below the waist. □□ **draw·er·ful** *n.* (*pl.* •**fuls**)

draw·ing /dráwing/ *n.* **1 a** the art of representing by line. **b** delineation without color or with a single color. **c** the art of representing with pencils, pens, crayons, etc., rather than paint. **2** a picture produced in this way. □ **out of drawing** incorrectly depicted.

draw·ing board *n.* a board for spreading drawing paper on. □ **back to the drawing board** *colloq.* back to begin afresh (after earlier failure).

draw·ing pin *n. Brit.* a thumbtack.

draw·ing room /dráwingroom, –room/ *n.* **1** a room for comfortable sitting or entertaining in a private house. **2** (*attrib.*) restrained; observing social proprieties (*drawing room conversation*). **3** a private compartment in a train. **4** *Brit. hist.* a levee, a formal reception esp. at court. [earlier *withdrawing room*, because orig. used for women to withdraw to after dinner]

drawl /drawl/ *v. & n.* •*v.* **1** *intr.* speak with drawn-out vowel sounds. **2** *tr.* utter in this way. •*n.* a drawling utterance or way of speaking. □□ **drawl·er** *n.* [16th c.: prob. orig. cant, f. LG, Du. *dralen* delay, linger]

drawn /drawn/ *past part.* of DRAW. •*adj.* **1** looking strained from fear, anxiety, or pain. **2** (of butter) melted. **3** (of a position in chess, etc.) that will result in a draw if both players make the best moves available.

drawn·work /dráwnwərk/ *n.* ornamental work on linen, etc., done by drawing out threads, usu. with additional needlework.

draw·sheet /dráwsheet/ *n.* a sheet that can be taken from under a patient without remaking the bed.

draw·string /dráwstring/ *n.* a string that can be pulled to tighten the mouth of a bag, the waist of a garment, etc.

draw-well *n. Brit.* a deep well with a rope and a bucket.

dray¹ /dray/ *n.* **1** a low cart without sides for heavy loads, esp. beer barrels. **2** *Austral. & NZ* a two-wheeled cart. □ **dray horse** a large, powerful horse. [ME f. OE *dræge* dragnet, *dragan* DRAW]

dray² var. of DREY.

dray·man /dráymən/ *n.* (*pl.* •**men**) a brewer's driver.

dread /dred/ *v., n., & adj.* •*v.tr.* **1** (foll. by *that*, or *to* + infin.) fear greatly. **2** shrink from; look forward to with great apprehension. **3** be in great fear of. •*n.* **1** great fear; apprehension; awe. **2** an object of fear or awe. •*adj.* **1** dreaded. **2** *archaic* awe-inspiring; revered. [OE *ādrǽdan, ondrǽdan*]

dread·ful /drédfool/ *adj. & adv.* **1** terrible; inspiring fear or awe. **2** *colloq.* troublesome; disagreeable; very bad •*adv. colloq.* dreadfully; very. □□ **dread·ful·ly** *adv.* **dread·ful·ness** *n.*

dread·locks /drédloks/ *n.pl.* **1** a Rastafarian hairstyle in which the hair is twisted into tight braids or ringlets hanging down on all sides. **2** hair dressed in this way.

dread·nought /drédnawt/ *n.* **1** (usu. **Dreadnought**) *Brit. hist.* a type of battleship greatly superior in armament to all its predecessors (from the name of the first, launched in 1906). **2** *archaic* a fearless person. **3** *archaic* **a** a thick coat for stormy weather. **b** the cloth used for such coats.

dream /dreem/ *n. & v.* •*n.* **1 a** a series of pictures or events in the mind of a sleeping person. **b** the act or time of seeing this. **c** (in full **waking dream**) a similar experience of one awake. **2** a daydream or fantasy. **3** an ideal, aspiration, or ambition, esp. of a nation. **4** a beautiful or ideal person or thing. **5** a state of mind without proper perception of reality (*goes about in a dream*). •*v.* (*past* and *past part.* **dreamed** or **dreamt** /dremt/) **1** *intr.* experience a dream. **2** *tr.* imagine in or as if in a dream. **3** (usu. with *neg.*) **a** *intr.* (foll. by *of*) contemplate the possibility of; have any conception or intention of (*would not dream of upsetting them*). **b** *tr.* (often foll. by *that* + clause) think of as a possibility (*never dreamed that he would come*). **4** *tr.* (foll. by *away*) spend (time) unprofitably. **5** *intr.* be inactive or unpractical. **6** *intr.* fall into a reverie. □ **dream up** imagine; invent. **like a dream** *colloq.* easily; effortlessly. □□ **dream·ful** *adj.* **dream·less** *adj.* **dream·like** *adj.* [ME f. OE *drēam* joy, music]

dream·boat /dréembōt/ *n. colloq.* **1** a very attractive or ideal person, esp. of the opposite sex. **2** a very desirable or ideal thing.

dream·er /dreemər/ *n.* **1** a person who dreams. **2** a romantic or unpractical person.

dream·land /dréemland/ *n.* an ideal or imaginary land.

dream·time /dréemtīm/ *n. Austral.* the alcheringa.

dream·y /dréemee/ adj. (**dream·i·er, dream·i·est**) **1** given to daydreaming; fanciful; unpractical. **2** dreamlike; vague; misty. **3** colloq. delightful; marvelous. **4** poet. full of dreams. □□ **dream·i·ly** adv. **dream·i·ness** n.

drear /dreer/ adj. poet. = DREARY. [abbr.]

drear·y /dréeree/ adj. (**drear·i·er, drear·i·est**) dismal; dull; gloomy. □□ **drear·i·ly** adv. **drear·i·ness** n. [OE drēorig f. drēor gore: rel. to drēosan to drop f. Gmc]

dreck /drek/ n. sl. (also **drek**) rubbish, trash. [Yiddish drek f. G Dreck filth, dregs]

dredge[1] /drej/ v. & n. • v. **1** tr. **a** (often foll. by up) bring up (lost or hidden material) as if with a dredge (don't dredge all that up again). **b** (often foll. by away, up, out) bring up or clear (mud, etc.) from a river, harbor, etc. with a dredge. **2** tr. clean (a harbor, river, etc.) with a dredge. **3** intr. use a dredge. • n. an apparatus used to scoop up oysters, specimens, etc., or to clear mud, etc., from a riverbed or seabed. [15th-c. Sc. dreg, perh. rel. to MDu. dregghe]

dredge[2] /drej/ v.tr. **1** sprinkle with flour, sugar, etc. **2** (often foll. by over) sprinkle (flour, etc.) on. [obs. dredge sweetmeat f. OF dragie, dragee, perh. f. L tragemata f. Gk trăgēmata spices]

dredg·er[1] /dréjər/ n. **1** a machine used for dredging rivers, etc.; a dredge. **2** a boat containing this.

dredg·er[2] /dréjər/ n. a container with a perforated lid used for sprinkling flour, sugar, etc.

dree /dree/ v.tr. (**drees, dreed, dree·ing**) Sc. or archaic endure (something burdensome or painful). □ **dree one's weird** submit to one's destiny. [OE drēogan f. Gmc]

dreg /dreg/ n. **1** (usu. in pl.) **a** a sediment; grounds, lees, etc. **b** a worthless part; refuse (the dregs of humanity). **2** a small remnant (not a dreg). □ **drain** (or **drink**) **to the dregs** consume leaving nothing (drained life to the dregs). □□ **dreg·gy** adj. colloq. [ME prob. f. ON dreggjar]

drench /drench/ v. & n. • v.tr. **1 a** wet thoroughly (was drenched by the rain). **b** saturate; soak (in liquid). **2** force (an animal) to take medicine. **3** archaic cause to drink. • n. **1** a soaking; a downpour. **2** medicine administered to an animal. **3** archaic a medicinal or poisonous draft. [OE drencan, drenc f. Gmc: rel. to DRINK]

Dres·den chi·na /drézdən/ n. (also **Dres·den por·ce·lain**) **1** delicate and elaborate chinaware orig. made at Dresden in Germany, now made at nearby Meissen. **2** (attrib.) delicately pretty.

dress /dres/ v. & n. • v. **1 a** tr. clothe; array (dressed in rags; dressed her quickly). **b** intr. wear clothes of a specified kind or in a specified way (dresses well). **2** intr. **a** put on clothes. **b** put on formal or evening clothes, esp. for dinner. **3** tr. esp. Brit. decorate or adorn. **4** tr. Med. **a** treat (a wound) with ointment, etc. **b** apply a dressing to (a wound). **5** tr. trim, comb, brush, or smooth (the hair). **6** tr. **a** clean and prepare (poultry, a crab, etc.) for cooking or eating. **b** add a dressing to (a salad, etc.). **7** tr. apply manure, etc., to a field, garden, etc. **8** tr. finish the surface of (fabric, building stone, etc.). **9** tr. groom (a horse). **10** tr. curry (leather, etc.). **11** Mil. **a** tr. correct the alignment of (troops, etc.). **b** intr. (of troops) come into alignment. **12** tr. make (an artificial fly) for use in fishing. • n. **1** a one-piece woman's garment consisting of a bodice and skirt. **2** clothing, esp. a whole outfit, etc. (fussy about his dress; wore the dress of a Cherokee). **3** formal or ceremonial costume (evening dress; morning dress). **4** an external covering; the outward form (birds in their winter dress). □ **dress down** colloq. **1** reprimand or scold. **2** dress casually, esp. for an informal affair. **dress out** attire conspicuously. **dress shield** a piece of waterproof material fastened in the armpit of a dress to protect it from perspiration. **dress up 1** dress (oneself or another) elaborately for a special occasion. **2** dress in fancy dress. **3** disguise (unwelcome facts) by embellishment. [ME f. OF dresser ult. f. L directus DIRECT]

dres·sage /drisáazh, dre–/ n. the training of a horse in obedience and deportment, esp. for competition. [F f. dresser to train]

dress cir·cle n. the first gallery in a theater, in which evening dress was formerly required.

dress coat n. a man's swallow-tailed evening coat; a tailcoat.

dress code n. a set of rules, usu. written, describing acceptable dress, as at a school, restaurant, etc.

dres·ser[1] /drésər/ n. **1** a kitchen sideboard with shelves above for displaying plates, etc. **2** a dressing table or chest of drawers. [ME f. OF dresseur f. dresser prepare: cf. med.L directorium]

dres·ser[2] /drésər/ n. **1** a person who assists actors to dress, takes care of their costumes, etc. **2** Med. a surgeon's assistant in operations. **3** a person who dresses elegantly or in a specified way (a snappy dresser).

dress·ing /drésing/ n. **1** in senses of DRESS v. **2 a** an accompaniment to salads, usu. a mixture of oil with other ingredients; a sauce or seasoning (French dressing). **b** stuffing, esp. for poultry. **3 a** a bandage for a wound. **b** ointment, etc., used to dress a wound. **4** size or stiffening used to finish fabrics. **5** compost, etc., spread over land (a top dressing of peat).

dress·ing case n. dated a case for carrying toiletries, etc.

dress·ing-down n. colloq. a scolding; a severe reprimand.

dress·ing gown n. esp. Brit. = ROBE n. 2.

dress·ing room n. **1** a room for changing clothes, etc., in a theater, sports facility, etc. **2** a small room attached to a bedroom, containing clothes.

dress·ing sta·tion n. esp. Mil. a place for giving emergency treatment to the wounded, esp. in battle.

dress·ing ta·ble n. a table with mirror and drawers, used to sit at while applying makeup, etc.

dress·mak·er /drésmaykər/ n. a person who makes clothes professionally. □□ **dress·mak·ing** n.

dress pa·rade n. **1** Mil. a military parade in full dress uniform. **2** a display of clothes worn by models.

dress re·hears·al n. the final rehearsal of a live performance, in which everything is done as it would be in a real performance.

dress shirt n. **1** a man's usu. starched white shirt worn with evening dress. **2** a man's long-sleeved shirt, buttoned down the front, suitable for wearing with a tie.

dress·y /drésee/ adj. (**dress·i·er, dress·i·est**) **1 a** fond of smart clothes. **b** overdressed. **c** (of clothes) stylish or elaborate. **2** overelaborate (the design is rather dressy). □□ **dress·i·ness** n.

drew past of DRAW.

drey /dray/ n. Brit. (also **dray**) a squirrel's nest. [17th c.: orig. unkn.]

drib·ble /dríbəl/ v. & n. • v. **1** intr. allow saliva to flow from the mouth. **2** intr. & tr. flow or allow to flow in drops or a trickling stream. **3** tr. (also absol.) **a** Basketball bounce (the ball) repeatedly, esp. to retain control of it. **b** esp. Soccer & Hockey move (the ball, puck, etc.) forward with slight touches of the feet, the stick, etc. • n. **1** the act or an instance of dribbling. **2** a small trickling stream. □□ **drib·bler** n. **drib·bly** adj. [frequent. of obs. drib, var. of DRIP]

drib·let /dríblit/ n. **1 a** a small quantity. **b** a petty sum. **2** a thin stream; a dribble. [drib (see DRIBBLE) + –LET]

dribs and drabs /dríbz ənd drábz/ n.pl. colloq. small scattered amounts (did the work in dribs and drabs). [as DRIBBLE + drab redupl.]

dried past and past part. of DRY.

dri·er[1] compar. of DRY.

dri·er[2] /dríər/ n. **1** var. of DRYER 1. **2** a substance mixed with oil paint or ink to promote drying.

dri·est superl. of DRY.

drift /drift/ n. & v. • n. **1 a** a slow movement or variation. **b** such movement caused by a slow current. **2** the intention, meaning, scope, etc. of what is said, etc. (didn't understand his drift). **3** a large mass of snow, sand, etc., accumulated by the wind. **4** esp. derog. a state of inaction. **5 a** Naut. a ship's deviation from its course, due to currents. **b** Aeron. an aircraft's deviation due to side winds. **c** a projectile's deviation due to its rotation. **d** a controlled slide of a racing car, etc. **6** Mining a horizontal passage following a mineral vein. **7** a large mass of esp. flowering plants (a drift of bluebells). **8** Geol. **a** material deposited by the wind, a current of water, etc. **b** (**Drift**) Pleistocene ice detritus, e.g., boulder clay. **9** the movement of cattle, esp. a gathering on an appointed day to determine ownership, etc. **10** a tool for enlarging or shaping a hole in metal. • v. **1** intr. be carried by or as if by a current of air or water. **2** intr. move or progress passively, casually, or aimlessly (drifted into teaching). **3** tr. & intr. pile or be piled by the wind into drifts. **b** tr. cover (a field, a road, etc.) with drifts. **4** tr. form or enlarge (a hole) with a drift. **5** tr. (of a current) carry. □□ **drift·age** n. [ME f. ON & MDu., MHG trift movement of cattle: rel. to DRIVE]

drift·er /dríftər/ n. **1** an aimless or rootless person. **2** a boat used for drift-net fishing.

drift ice n. ice driven or deposited by water.

drift net n. a large net for catching herring and similar fish, kept upright by weights at the bottom and floats at the top and allowed to drift with the tide.

drift·wood /dríftwŏŏd/ n. wood, etc., driven or deposited by water.

drill[1] /dril/ n. & v. • n. **1** a pointed, esp. revolving, steel tool or machine used for boring cylindrical holes, sinking wells, etc. **2 a** esp. Mil. instruction or training in military exercises. **b** rigorous discipline or methodical instruction, esp. when learning or performing tasks. **c** routine procedure to be followed in an emergency (fire drill). **d** a routine or exercise (drills in irregular verb patterns). **3** colloq. a recognized procedure (I expect you know the drill). **4** any of various mollusks, esp. Urosalpinx cinera, that bore into the shells of young oysters. • v. **1** tr. (also absol.) **a** (of a person or a tool) make a hole with a drill through or into (wood, metal, etc.). **b** make (a hole) with a drill. **2** tr. & intr.

drill[1] 1

esp. *Mil.* subject to or undergo discipline by drill. **3** *tr.* impart (knowledge, etc.) by a strict method. **4** *tr. sl.* shoot with a gun (*drilled him full of holes*). □□ **drill•er** *n.* [earlier as verb, f. MDu. *drillen* bore, of unkn. orig.]

drill² /dril/ *n. & v.* ● *n.* **1** a machine used for making furrows, sowing, and covering seed. **2** a small furrow for sowing seed in. **3** a ridge with such furrows on top. **4** a row of plants so sown. ● *v.tr.* **1** sow (seed) with a drill. **2** plant (the ground) in drills. [perh. f. obs. *drill* rill (17th c., of unkn. orig.)]

drill³ /dril/ *n.* a W. African baboon, *Papio leucophaeus*, related to the mandrill. [prob. a native name: cf. MANDRILL]

drill⁴ /dril/ *n.* a coarse twilled cotton or linen fabric. [earlier *drilling* f. G *Drillich* f. L *trilix* –*licis* f. *tri*- three + *licium* thread]

drill•mas•ter /drílmàstər/ *n.* **1** *Mil.* one who instructs or leads others (often recruits) in military drill. **2** a rigorous, exacting, or severe instructor.

drill press *n.* a drilling machine with a vertical bit that is lowered into the item being drilled.

drill rig *n.* a structure with equipment for drilling an oil well.

drill ser•geant *n.* **1** *Mil.* a noncommissioned officer who trains soldiers, esp. new recruits. **2** a strict disciplinarian.

dri•ly var. of DRYLY.

drink /dringk/ *v. & n.* ● *v.* (*past* **drank** /drangk/; *past part.* **drunk** /drungk/) **1 a** *tr.* swallow (a liquid). **b** *tr.* swallow the liquid contents of (a vessel). **c** *intr.* swallow liquid; take drafts (*drank from the stream*). **2** *intr.* take alcohol, esp. to excess (*I have heard that she drinks*). **3** *tr.* (of a plant, porous material, etc.) absorb (moisture). **4** *refl.* bring (oneself, etc.) to a specified condition by drinking (*drank himself into a stupor*). **5** *tr.* (usu. foll. by *away*) spend (wages, etc.) on drink (*drank away the money*). **6** *tr.* wish (a person's good health, luck, etc.) by drinking (*drank his health*). ● *n.* **1 a** a liquid for drinking (*milk is a high-cholesterol drink*). **b** a draft or specified amount of this (*had a drink of milk*). **2 a** alcoholic liquor (*got the drink for Christmas*). **b** a portion, glass, etc., of this (*have a drink*). **c** excessive indulgence in alcohol (*drink is his vice*). **3** (as **the drink**) *colloq.* the sea. □ **drink deep** take a large draft or drafts. **drink in** listen to closely or eagerly (*drank in his every word*). **drink off** *Brit.* drink the whole (contents) of at once. **drink to** toast; wish success to. **drink a person under the table** remain sober longer than one's drinking companion. **drink up** drink the whole of; empty. **in drink** drunk. □□ **drink•a•ble** *adj.* **drink•er** *n.* [OE *drincan* (v.), *drinc(a)* (n.) f. Gmc]

drink•ing song *n.* a song sung while drinking, usu. concerning drink.

drip /drip/ *v. & n.* ● *v.* (**dripped**, **drip•ping**) **1** *intr. & tr.* fall or let fall in drops. **2** *intr.* (often foll. by *with*) be so wet as to shed drops (*dripped with sweat*). ● *n.* **1 a** the act or an instance of dripping (*the steady drip of rain*). **b** a drop of liquid (*a drip of paint*). **c** a sound of dripping. **2** *colloq.* a stupid, dull, or ineffective person. **3** (*Med.* **drip-feed**) the drip-by-drip intravenous administration of a solution of salt, sugar, etc. **4** *Archit.* a projection, esp. from a windowsill, keeping the rain off the walls. □ **dripping wet** very wet. [MDa. *drippe* f. Gmc (cf. DROP)]

drip-dry *v. & adj.* ● *v.* (·**dries**, ·**dried**) **1** *intr.* (of fabric, etc.) dry crease-free when hung up to drip. **2** *tr.* leave (a garment, etc.) hanging up to dry. ● *adj.* able to be drip-dried.

drip-mat *n. Brit.* a small mat under a glass; a coaster.

drip•ping /dríping/ *n.* (usu. *pl.*) **1** fat melted from roasted meat and used for cooking or as a spread. **2** water, grease, etc., dripping from anything.

drip•py /drípee/ *adj.* (**drip•pi•er**, **drip•pi•est**) **1** tending to drip. **2** *sl.* (of a person) ineffectual; sloppily sentimental. □□ **drip•pi•ly** *adv.* **drip•pi•ness** *n.*

drip•stone /drípstōn/ *n.* **1** *Archit.* a stone, etc., projection that deflects rain, etc., from walls. **2** calcium carbonate in the form of stalagmites and stalactites.

drive /drīv/ *v. & n.* ● *v.* (*past* **drove** /drōv/; *past part.* **driv•en** /drívən/) **1** *tr.* (usu. foll. by *away, back, in, out, to*, etc.) urge in some direction, esp. forcibly (*drove back the wolves*). **2** *tr.* **a** (usu. foll. by *to* + infin., or *to* + verbal noun) compel or constrain forcibly (*was driven to complain; drove her to stealing*). **b** (often foll. by *to*) force into a specified state (*drove him mad; drove to despair*). **c** (often *refl.*) urge to overwork (*drives himself too hard*). **3 a** *tr.* (also *absol.*) operate and direct the course of (a vehicle, a locomotive, etc.) (*drove a sports car; drives well*). **b** *tr. & intr.* convey or be conveyed in a vehicle (*drove them to the station; drove to the station in a bus*) (cf. RIDE). **c** *tr.* (also *absol.*) be licensed or competent to drive (a vehicle) (*does he drive?*). **d** *tr.* (also *absol.*) urge and direct the course of (an animal drawing a vehicle or plow). **4** *tr.* (of wind, water, etc.) carry along, propel, send, or cause to go in some direction (*pure as the driven snow*). **5** *tr.* **a** (often foll. by *into*) force (a stake, nail, etc.) into place by blows (*drove the nail home*). **b** *Mining* bore (a tunnel, horizontal cavity, etc.). **6** *tr.* effect or conclude forcibly (*drove a hard bargain; drove her point home*). **7** *tr.* (of steam or other power) set or keep (machinery) going. **8** *intr.* (usu. foll. by *at*) work hard; dash;

rush, or hasten. **9** *tr.* *Baseball & Tennis* hit (the ball) hard from a freely swung bat or racket. **10** *tr.* (often *absol.*) *Golf* strike (a ball) with a driver from the tee. **11** *tr.* chase or frighten (game, wild beasts, an enemy in warfare, etc.) from a large area to a smaller, to kill or capture; corner. **12** *tr. Brit.* hold a drift in (a forest, etc.) (see DRIFT *n.* 9). ● *n.* **1** an act of driving in a motor vehicle; a journey or excursion in such a vehicle (*went for a pleasant drive; lives an hour's drive from us*). **2 a** the capacity for achievement; motivation and energy (*lacks the drive needed to succeed*). **b** *Psychol.* an inner urge to attain a goal or satisfy a need (*unconscious emotional drives*). **3 a** a usu. landscaped street or road. **b** *Brit.* a usu. private road through a garden or park to a house; a driveway. **4** *Golf, Cricket, & Tennis* a driving stroke of the club, etc. **5** *Golf* a shot from the tee, usu. with a driver. **6** an organized effort to achieve a usu. charitable purpose (*a famine-relief drive*). **7 a** the transmission of power to machinery, the wheels of a motor vehicle, etc. (*belt drive; front-wheel drive*). **b** the position of a steering wheel in a motor vehicle (*left-hand drive*). **c** *Computing* = DISK DRIVE. **8** *Brit.* an organized competition, for many players, of whist, bingo, etc. **9** an act of driving game or an enemy. **10** *Austral. & NZ* a line of partly cut trees on a hillside felled when the top one topples on the others. □ **drive at** seek, intend, or mean (*what is he driving at?*). **drive out** take the place of; oust; exorcize; cast out. **let drive** aim a blow or missile. □□ **driv•a•ble** *adj.* [OE *drífan* f. Gmc]

drive-by *adj.* (of a crime, etc.) carried out from a moving vehicle (-*drive-by shooting*).

drive-in *attrib.adj. & n.* ● *attrib.adj.* (of a bank, movie theater, etc.) able to be used while sitting in one's car. ● *n.* such a bank, movie theater, etc.

driv•el /drívəl/ *n. & v.* ● *n.* silly nonsense; twaddle. ● *v.* (**driv•eled**, **driv•el•ing**; esp. *Brit.* **driv•elled**, **driv•el•ling**) **1** *intr.* run at the mouth or nose; dribble. **2** *intr.* talk childishly or idiotically. **3** *tr.* (foll. by *away*) fritter; squander away. □□ **driv•el•er** *n.* (esp. *Brit.* **driv•el•ler**). [OE *dreflian* (v.)]

driv•en *past part.* of DRIVE.

drive-on *adj.* denoting a ferry or train onto which motor vehicles may be driven.

driv•er /drívər/ *n.* **1** (often in *comb.*) a person who drives a vehicle (*bus driver*). **2** *Golf* a club with a flat face and wooden head, used for driving from the tee. **3** *Electr.* a device or part of a circuit providing power for output. **4** *Mech.* a wheel, etc., receiving power directly and transmitting motion to other parts. □ **in the driver's seat** in charge. □□ **driv•er•less** *adj.*

driv•er's li•cense *n.* a license permitting a person to drive a motor vehicle.

drive•shaft /drívshaft/ *n.* a rotating shaft that transmits power to machinery.

drive•train /drívtrayn/ *n.* the components in an automotive vehicle that connect the transmission with the driving wheels.

drive•way /drívway/ *n.* a usu. private road from a public street, etc., to a house, garage, etc.

driv•ing *adj.* **1** (of rain or snow) falling and being blown by the wind with great force (*driving rain*). **2** having a strong and controlling influence (*she was the driving force behind the plan*).

driv•ing range *n. Golf* an area for practicing long-distance shots, usu. equipped with distance markers and with balls and clubs for rent.

driv•ing test *n.* an official test of a motorist's competence that must be passed to obtain a driver's license.

driv•ing wheel *n.* **1** any of the large wheels of a locomotive, to which power is applied either directly or via coupling rods. **2** a wheel transmitting motive power in machinery.

driz•zle /drízəl/ *n. & v.* ● *n.* very fine rain. ● *v.intr.* (esp. of rain) fall in very fine drops (*it's drizzling again*). □□ **driz•zly** *adj.* [prob. f. ME *drēse*, OE *drēosan* fall]

drogue /drōg/ *n.* **1** *Naut.* **a** a buoy at the end of a harpoon line. **b** a sea anchor. **2** *Aeron.* a truncated cone of fabric used as a brake, a target for gunnery, a wind sock, etc. [18th c.: orig. unkn.]

droit /droyt/ *n. Law* a right or due. [ME f. OF f. L *directum* (n.) f. *directus* DIRECT]

droit de sei•gneur /drwaá də senyór/ *n. hist.* the alleged right of a feudal lord to have sexual intercourse with a vassal's bride on her wedding night. [F, = lord's right]

droll /drōl/ *adj. & n.* ● *adj.* **1** quaintly amusing. **2** strange; odd; surprising. ● *n. archaic* **1** a jester; an entertainer. **2** a quaintly amusing person. □□ **droll•er•y** *n.* (*pl.* ·**ies**). **drol•ly** *adv.* **droll•ness** *n.* [F *drôle*, perh. f. MDu. *drolle* little man]

-drome /drōm/ *comb. form* forming nouns denoting: **1** a place for running, racing, or other forms of movement (*aerodrome; hippodrome*). **2** a thing that runs or proceeds in a certain way (*palindrome; syndrome*). [Gk *dromos* course, running]

drom•e•dar•y /drómidèree, drúm-/ *n.* (*pl.* ·**ies**) a one-humped camel, *Camelus dromedarius*, bred for riding and racing. Also called **Arabian camel**. [ME f. OF *dromedaire* or LL *dromedarius* ult. f. Gk *dromas* –*ados* runner]

drom•ond /drómənd, drúm-/ *n. hist.* a large medieval ship used for war or commerce. [ME f. OF *dromon(t)* f. LL *dromo –onis* f. late Gk *dromōn* light vessel]

drone /drōn/ *n. & v.* ● *n.* **1** a nonworking male of certain bees, as the honeybee, whose sole function is to mate with fertile females. **2** an idler. **3** a deep humming sound. **4** a monotonous speech or speaker. **5 a** a pipe, esp. of a bagpipe, sounding a continuous note of fixed low pitch. **b** the note emitted by this. **6** a remote-controlled pilotless aircraft or missile. ● *v.* **1** *intr.* make a deep humming sound. **2** *intr. & tr.* speak or utter monotonously. **3 a** *intr.* be idle. **b** *tr.* (often foll. by *away*) idle away (one's time, etc.). [OE *drān*, *drēn* prob. f. WG]

dron·go /dróngō/ *n.* (*pl.* **·gos**) **1** any black bird of the family Dicruridae, native to India, Africa, and Australia, having a long, forked tail. **2** *Austral. & NZ sl. derog.* a simpleton. [Malagasy]

droob /drōōb/ *n. Austral. sl.* a hopeless-looking ineffectual person. [perh. f. DROOP]

drool /drōōl/ *v. & n.* ● *v.intr.* **1** drivel; slobber. **2** (often foll. by *over*) show much pleasure or infatuation. ● *n.* slobbering; driveling. [contr. of *drivel*]

droop /drōōp/ *v. & n.* ● *v.* **1** *intr. & tr.* hang or allow to hang down; languish, decline, or sag, esp. from weariness. **2** *intr.* **a** (of the eyes) look downward. **b** *poet.* (of the sun) sink. **3** *intr.* lose heart; be dejected; flag. ● *n.* **1** a drooping attitude. **2** a loss of spirit or enthusiasm. [ME f. ON *drúpa* hang the head f. Gmc: cf. DROP]

droop-snoot *adj. & n. Brit. colloq.* ● *adj.* (of an aircraft) having an adjustable nose or leading-edge flap. ● *n.* such an aircraft.

droop·y /drōōpee/ *adj.* (**droop·i·er**, **droop·i·est**) **1** drooping. **2** dejected; gloomy. □□ **droop·i·ly** *adv.* **droop·i·ness** *n.*

drop /drop/ *n. & v.* ● *n.* **1 a** a small, round or pear-shaped portion of liquid that hangs or falls or adheres to a surface (*drops of dew*; *tears fell in large drops*). **b** a very small amount of usu. drinkable liquid (*just a drop left in the glass*). **c** a glass, etc., of alcoholic liquor (*take a drop with us*). **2 a** an abrupt fall or slope. **b** the amount of this (*a drop of fifteen feet*). **c** an act of falling or dropping (*had a nasty drop*). **d** a reduction in prices, temperature, etc. **e** a deterioration or worsening (*a drop in status*). **3** something resembling a drop, esp.: **a** a pendant or earring. **b** a crystal ornament on a chandelier, etc. **c** (often in *comb.*) a candy or lozenge (*lemon drop*; *cough drop*). **4** something that drops or is dropped, esp.: **a** *Theatr.* a painted curtain or scenery let down on to the stage. **b** a platform or trapdoor on a gallows, the opening of which causes the victim to fall. **5** *Med.* **a** the smallest separable quantity of a liquid. **b** (in *pl.*) liquid medicine to be measured in drops (*eye drops*). **6** a minute quantity (*not a drop of pity*). **7** *sl.* **a** a hiding place for stolen or illicit goods. **b** a secret place where documents, etc., may be left or passed on in espionage. **8** *sl.* a bribe. **9** a box for letters, etc. ● *v.* (**dropped**, **drop·ping**) **1** *intr. & tr.* fall or let fall in drops (*tears dropped on to the book*; *dropped the soup down her shirt*). **2** *intr. & tr.* fall or allow to fall; relinquish; let go (*dropped the box*; *the egg dropped from my hand*). **3 a** *intr. & tr.* sink or cause to sink or fall to the ground from exhaustion, a blow, a wound, etc. **b** *intr.* die. **4 a** *intr. & tr.* cease or cause to cease; lapse or let lapse; abandon (*the connection dropped*; *dropped the friendship*; *drop everything and come at once*). **b** *tr. colloq.* cease to associate with. **5** *tr.* set down (a passenger, etc.) (*drop me at the station*). **6** *tr. & intr.* utter or be uttered casually (*dropped a hint*; *the remark dropped into the conversation*). **7** *tr.* send casually (*drop me a postcard*). **8 a** *intr. & tr.* fall or allow to fall in direction, amount, condition, degree, pitch, etc. (*his voice dropped*; *the wind dropped*; *we dropped the price by $20*; *the road dropped southward*). **b** *intr.* (of a person) jump down lightly; let oneself fall. **c** *tr.* remove (clothes, esp. trousers) rapidly, allowing them to fall to the ground. **9** *tr. colloq.* lose (money, esp. in gambling). **10** *tr.* **a** omit (*drop this article*). **b** omit (a letter, esp. 'h,' a syllable, etc.) in speech. **11** *tr.* (as **dropped** *adj.*) in a lower position than usual (*dropped handlebars*; *dropped waist*). **12** *tr.* give birth to (esp. a lamb, a kitten, etc.). **13 a** *intr.* (of a card) be played in the same trick as a higher card. **b** *tr.* play or cause (a card) to be played in this way. **14** *tr. Sports* lose (a game, a point, a contest, a match, etc.). **15** *tr. Aeron.* deliver (supplies, etc.) by parachute. **16** *tr. Football* **a** send (a ball) by a dropkick. **b** score points by a dropkick. **17** *tr. colloq.* dismiss or exclude (*was dropped from the team*). □ **at the drop of a hat** given the slightest excuse. **drop anchor** anchor ship. **drop asleep** fall gently asleep. **drop away** decrease or depart gradually. **drop back** (or **behind** or **to the rear**) fall back; get left behind. **drop back into** esp. *Brit.* return to (a habit, etc.). **drop a brick** *Brit. colloq.* make an indiscreet or embarrassing remark. **drop a curtsy** *Brit.* make a curtsy. **drop dead!** *sl.* an exclamation of intense scorn. **drop down** descend a hill, etc. **drop in** (or **by**) *colloq.* call casually as a visitor. **a drop in the ocean** (or **a bucket**) a very small amount, esp. compared with what is needed or expected. **drop into** *colloq.* **1** call casually at (a place). **2** esp. *Brit.* fall into (a habit, etc.). **drop it!** *sl.* stop that! **drop off 1** decline gradually. **2** *colloq.* fall asleep. **3** = sense 5 of *v.* **drop on** reprimand or punish. **drop out** *colloq.* cease to participate, esp. in a race, a course of study, or in conventional society. **drop a stitch** let a stitch fall off the end of a knitting needle. **have had a drop too much** *colloq.* be

slightly drunk. **ready to drop** extremely tired. □□ **drop·let** *n.* [OE *dropa*, *drop(p)ian* ult. f. Gmc: cf. DRIP, DROOP]

drop cur·tain *n. Theatr.* a curtain or painted cloth lowered vertically onto a theater stage.

drop-forg·ing *n.* a method of forcing white-hot metal through an open-ended die by a heavy weight.

drop ham·mer *n.* a heavy weight raised mechanically and allowed to drop, as used in drop-forging and pile-driving.

drop·head /dróphed/ *n. Brit.* **1** a convertible automobile. **2** the adjustable roof of such an automobile.

drop·kick /drópkik/ *n. Football* a kick made by dropping the ball and kicking it on the bounce.

drop-leaf *adj.* (of a table) having a hinged leaf attached to the side or end that can be raised to make the table surface larger or folded down when not in use.

drop·out /drópowt/ *n. colloq.* a person who has dropped out, esp. from school.

drop·per /drópər/ *n.* **1** a device for administering liquid, esp. medicine, in drops. **2** *Austral., NZ, & S.Afr.* a light vertical stave in a fence.

drop·pings /drópingz/ *n.pl.* **1** the dung of animals or birds. **2** something that falls or has fallen in drops, e.g., wax from candles.

drop shot *n.* (in tennis) a shot dropping abruptly over the net.

drop·sy /drópsee/ *n.* (*pl.* **·sies**) **1** = EDEMA. **2** *sl.* a tip or bribe. □□ **drop·si·cal** /-sikəl/ *adj.* (in sense 1). [ME f. *idrop(e)sie* f. OF *idropesie* ult. f. L *hydropisis* f. Gk *hudrōps* dropsy (*as* HYDRO-)]

drop·wort /drópwərt, –wawrt/ *n.* a plant, *Filipendula vulgaris*, with tuberous root fibers.

drosh·ky /dróshkee/ *n.* (*pl.* **·kies**) a Russian low, four-wheeled open carriage. [Russ. *drozhki* dimin. of *drogi* wagon f *droga* shaft]

dro·soph·i·la /drəsófilə/ *n.* any fruit fly of the genus *Drosophila*, used extensively in genetic research. [mod.L f. Gk *drosos* dew, moisture + *philos* loving]

dross /draws, dros/ *n.* **1** rubbish; refuse. **2 a** the scum separated from metals in melting. **b** foreign matter mixed with anything; impurities. □□ **dross·y** *adj.* [OE *drōs*: cf. MLG *drōsem*, OHG *truosana*]

drought /drowt/ *n.* **1** the continuous absence of rain; dry weather. **2** the prolonged lack of something. **3** *archaic* a lack of moisture; thirst; dryness. □□ **drought·y** *adj.* [OE *drūgath* f. *drȳge* DRY]

drouth /drowth/ *n. poet.* var. of DROUGHT.

drove[1] *past* of DRIVE.

drove[2] /drōv/ *n.* **1 a** a large number (of people, etc.) moving together; a crowd; a multitude; a shoal. **b** (in *pl.*) *colloq.* a great number (*people arrived in droves*). **2** a herd or flock being driven or moving together. [OE *drāf* f. *drīfan* DRIVE]

dro·ver /drōvər/ *n.* a person who drives herds to market; a cattle dealer. □□ **drove** *v.tr.* **drov·ing** *n.*

drove road *n.* an ancient cattle track.

drown /drown/ *v.* **1** *tr. & intr.* kill or be killed by submersion in liquid. **2** *tr.* submerge; flood; drench (*drowned the fields in six feet of water*). **3** *tr.* (often foll. by *in*) deaden (grief, etc.) with drink (*drowned his sorrows in drink*). **4** *tr.* (often foll. by *out*) make (a sound) inaudible by means of a louder sound. □ **drown out** drive out by flood. **like a drowned rat** *colloq.* extremely wet and bedraggled. [ME (orig. north.) *drun(e)*, *droun(e)*, perh. f. OE *drūnian* (unrecorded), rel. to DRINK]

PRONUNCIATION TIP   **drowned**

This is a one-syllable word ("DROWND"). Don't pronounce it as if it had an extra -*ed* at the end.

drowned val·ley *n.* a valley partly or wholly submerged by a rise in sea level.

drowse /drowz/ *v. & n.* ● *v.* **1** *intr.* be dull and sleepy or half asleep. **2** *tr.* **a** (often foll. by *away*) pass (the time) in drowsing. **b** make drowsy. **3** *intr. archaic* be sluggish. ● *n.* a condition of sleepiness. [-back-form. f. DROWSY]

drow·sy /drówzee/ *adj.* (**drow·si·er**, **drow·si·est**) **1** half asleep; dozing. **2** soporific; lulling. **3** sluggish. □□ **drow·si·ly** *adv.* **drow·si·ness** *n.* [prob. rel. to OE *drūsian* be languid or slow, *drēosan* fall: cf. DREARY]

drub /drub/ *v.tr.* (**drubbed**, **drub·bing**) **1** thump; belabor. **2** beat in a fight. **3** (usu. foll. by *into*, *out of*) beat (an idea, attitude, etc.) into or out of a person. □□ **drub·bing** *n.* [ult. f. Arab. *ḍaraba* beat]

drudge /druj/ *n. & v.* ● *n.* a servile worker, esp. at menial tasks; a hack. ● *v.intr.* (often foll. by *at*) work slavishly (at menial, hard, or dull work). □□ **drudg·er·y** /drújəree/ *n.* [15th c.: perh. rel. to DRAG]

drug /drug/ *n. & v.* ● *n.* **1** a medicinal substance. **2** a narcotic, hallucinogen, or stimulant, esp. one causing addiction. ● *v.* (**drugged**, **drug·ging**) **1** *tr.* add a drug to (food or drink). **2** *tr.* **a** administer a drug to. **b** stupefy with a drug. **3** *intr.* take drugs as an addict. [ME *drogges*, *drouges* f. OF *drogue*, of unkn. orig.]

drug ad•dict *n.* a person who is addicted to a narcotic drug.

drug•get /drúgit/ *n.* **1** a coarse woven fabric used as a floor or table covering. **2** such a covering. [F *droguet*, of unkn. orig.]

drug•gie /drúgee/ *n. & adj. colloq.* ● *n.* (also **drug•gy**) (*pl.* **•gies**) a drug addict. ● *adj.* of or associated with narcotic drugs.

drug•gist /drúgist/ *n.* a pharmacist. [F *droguiste* (as DRUG)]

drug•push•er /drúgpŏŏshər/ *n.* a person who sells esp. addictive drugs illegally.

drug•store /drúgstawr/ *n.* a pharmacy also selling miscellaneous drugs, cosmetics, and often light refreshments.

Dru•id /drŏŏid/ *n.* (*fem.* **Dru•id•ess**) **1** an ancient Celtic priest, magician, or soothsayer of Gaul, Britain, or Ireland. **2** a member of a Welsh, etc., Druidic order, esp. the Gorsedd. □□ **Dru•id•ism** *n.* **Dru•id•ic** /–ídik/ *adj.* **Dru•id•i•cal** /–ídikəl/ *adj.* [F *druide* or L pl. *druidae*, *–des*, Gk *druidai* f. Gaulish *druides*]

drum[1] /drum/ *n. & v.* ● *n.* **1 a** a percussion instrument or toy made of a hollow cylinder or hemisphere covered at one or both ends with stretched skin or parchment and sounded by striking (*bass drum; kettledrum*). **b** (often in *pl.*) a drummer or a percussion section (*the drums are playing too loud*). **c** a sound made by or resembling that of a drum. **2** something resembling a drum in shape, esp.: **a** a cylindrical container or receptacle for oil, dried fruit, etc. **b** a cylinder or barrel in machinery on which something is wound, etc. **c** *Archit.* the solid part of a Corinthian or composite capital. **d** *Archit.* a stone block forming a section of a shaft. **3** *Zool. & Anat.* the membrane of the middle ear; the eardrum. **4** *Brit. sl.* **a** a house. **b** a nightclub. **c** a brothel. **5** (in full **drumfish**) any marine fish of the family Sciaenidae, having a swim bladder that produces a drumming sound. **6** *hist.* an evening or afternoon tea party. **7** *Austral. sl.* a piece of reliable information, esp. a racing tip. ● *v.* (**drummed, drum•ming**) **1** *intr. & tr.* play on a drum. **2** *tr. & intr.* beat, tap, or thump (knuckles, feet, etc.) continuously (on something) (*drummed on the table; drummed his feet; drumming at the window*). **3** *intr.* (of a bird or an insect) make a loud, hollow noise with quivering wings. **4** *tr. Austral. sl.* provide with reliable information. □ **drum into** drive (a lesson) into (a person) by persistence. **drum out** *Mil.* cashier (a soldier) by the beat of a drum; dismiss with ignominy. **drum up** summon, gather, or call up (*needs to drum up more support*). [obs. *drombslade, drombyllsclad,* f. LG *trommelslag* drumbeat f. *trommel* drum + *slag* beat]

drum[2] /drum/ *n.* (also **drum•lin** /drúmlin/) *Geol.* a long, oval mound of boulder clay molded by glacial action. □□ **drumlinoid** *n.* [Gael. & Ir. *druim* ridge: *–lin* perh. for −LING[1]]

drum•beat /drúmbeet/ *n.* the sound of a drum or drums being beaten.

drum brake *n.* a brake in which shoes on a vehicle press against the drum on a wheel.

drum•fire /drúmfīr/ *n.* **1** *Mil.* heavy continuous rapid artillery fire, usu. heralding an infantry attack. **2** a barrage of criticism, etc.

drum•fish /drúmfish/ *n.* see DRUM[1] n. 5.

drum•head /drúmhed/ *n.* **1** the skin or membrane of a drum. **2** an eardrum. **3** the circular top of a capstan. **4** (*attrib.*) improvised (*drumhead court-martial*).

drum•lin var. of DRUM[2].

drum ma•chine *n.* a programmable electronic device that imitates the sound of percussion instruments.

drum ma•jor *n.* **1** the leader of a marching band. **2** *archaic* an NCO commanding the drummers of a regiment.

drum ma•jor•ette *n.* a female member of a baton-twirling parading group.

drum•mer /drúmər/ *n.* **1** a person who plays a drum or drums. **2** *colloq.* a commercial traveler. **3** *Brit. sl.* a thief.

drum•stick /drúmstik/ *n.* **1** a stick used for beating a drum. **2** the lower joint of the leg of a cooked chicken, turkey, etc.

drunk /drungk/ *adj. & n.* ● *adj.* **1** rendered incapable by alcohol (*blind drunk; dead drunk; drunk as a skunk*). **2** (often foll. by *with*) overcome or elated with joy, success, power, etc. ● *n.* **1** a habitually drunk person. **2** *sl.* a drinking bout; a period of drunkenness. [past part. of DRINK]

drunk•ard /drúngkərd/ *n.* a person who is drunk, esp. habitually.

drunk driv•ing *n.* the act of driving a vehicle with an excess of alcohol in the blood. □□ **drunk driv•er**

drunk•en /drúngkən/ *adj.* (usu. *attrib.*) **1** = DRUNK. **2** caused by or exhibiting drunkenness (*a drunken brawl*). **3** fond of drinking; often drunk. □□ **drunk•en•ly** *adv.* **drunk•en•ness** *n.*

drupe /drŏŏp/ *n.* any fleshy or pulpy fruit enclosing a stone containing one or a few seeds, e.g., an olive, plum, or peach. □□ **dru•pa•ceous** /–páyshəs/ *adj.* [L *drupa* f. Gk *druppa* olive]

drupe•let /drŏŏplit/ *n.* a small drupe usu. in an aggregate fruit, e.g., a blackberry or raspberry.

druse /drŏŏz/ *n.* **1** a crust of crystals lining a rock cavity. **2** a cavity lined with this. [F f. G, = weathered ore]

druth•ers /drúthərz/ *n.pl. colloq.* preference; choice (*if I had my druthers, I'd stay at home*). [alt. of *would rather*]

Druze /drŏŏz/ *n.* (often *attrib.*) (also **Druse**) a member of a political or religious sect linked with Islam and living near Mt. Lebanon (*Druze militia*). [F f. Arab. *durūz* (pl.), prob. f. their founder *al-Darazī* (11th c.)]

dry /drī/ *adj., v., & n.* ● *adj.* (**dri•er** /drīər/; **dri•est** /drī-ist/) **1** free from moisture, not wet, esp.: **a** with any moisture having evaporated, drained, or been wiped away (*the clothes are not dry yet*). **b** (of the eyes) free from tears. **c** (of a climate, etc.) with insufficient rainfall; not rainy (*a dry spell*); (of land, etc.) receiving little rain. **d** (of a river, well, etc.) dried up; not yielding water. **e** (of a liquid) having disappeared by evaporation, etc. **f** not connected with or for use without moisture (*dry shampoo*). **g** (of a shave) with an electric razor. **2** (of wine, etc.) not sweet (*dry sherry*). **3 a** meager, plain, or bare (*dry facts*). **b** uninteresting; dull (*dry as dust*). **4** (of a sense of humor, a joke, etc.) subtle, ironic, and quietly expressed; not obvious. **5** (of a country, of legislation, etc.) prohibiting the sale of alcoholic drink. **6** (of toast, bread, etc.) without butter, margarine, etc. **7** (of provisions, groceries, etc.) solid; not liquid (*dry goods*). **8** impassive; unsympathetic; hard; cold. **9** (of a cow, etc.) not yielding milk. **10** *colloq.* thirsty or thirst-making (*feel dry; this is dry work*). **11** *Polit. Brit. colloq.* of or being a political 'dry'. ● *v.* (**dries, dried**) **1** *tr. & intr.* make or become dry by wiping, evaporation, draining, etc. **2** *tr.* (usu. as **dried** *adj.*) preserve (food, etc.) by removing the moisture (*dried egg; dried fruit; dried flowers*). **3** *intr.* (often foll. by *up*) *Theatr. colloq.* forget one's lines. **4** *tr. & intr.* (often foll. by *off*) cease or cause (a cow, etc.) to cease yielding milk. ● *n.* (*pl.* **dries**) **1** the process or an instance of drying. **2** *Brit. sl.* a politician, esp. a Conservative, who advocates individual responsibility, free trade, and economic stringency, and opposes high government spending. **3 a** (prec. by *the*) esp. *Austral. colloq.* the dry season. **b** *Austral.* a desert area; waterless country. **4** a prohibitionist. **5** esp. *Brit.* **a** a dry ginger ale. **b** dry wine, sherry, etc. □ **dry out 1** become fully dry. **2** (of a drug addict, alcoholic, etc.) undergo treatment to cure addiction. **dry up 1** make utterly dry. **2** (of moisture) disappear ut-

ARID, DEHYDRATED, DESSICATED, PARCHED, SERE. Almost anything lacking in moisture (in relative terms)—whether it's a piece of bread, the basement of a house, or the state of Arizona—may be described as **dry**, a word that also connotes a lack of life or spirit (*a dry lecture on cell division*). **Arid**, on the other hand, applies to places or things that have been deprived of moisture and are therefore extremely or abnormally *dry* (*one side of the island was arid*); it is most commonly used to describe a desertlike region or climate that is lifeless or barren. **Desiccated** is used as a technical term for something from which moisture has been removed, and in general use it suggests lifelessness, although it is applied very often to people who have lost their vitality (*a desiccated old woman who never left her house*) or to animal and vegetable products that have been completely deprived of their vital juices (*desiccated oranges hanging limply from the tree*). **Dehydrated** is very close in meaning to desiccated and is often the preferred adjective when describing foods from which the moisture has been extracted (*they lived on dehydrated fruit*). *Dehydrated* may also refer to an unwanted loss of moisture (*the virus had left him seriously dehydrated*), as may the less formal term **parched**, which refers to an undesirable or uncomfortable lack of water in either a human being or a place (*parched with thirst; the parched landscape*). **Sere** is associated primarily with places and means *dry* or *arid* (*a harsh, sere land where few inhabitants could survive*).

BLOTTO, DRUNKEN, INEBRIATED, INTOXICATED, TIGHT, TIPSY. Anyone who is obviously or legally under the influence of alcohol is said to be **drunk**. **Drunken** means the same thing, but only *drunk* should be used predicatively, that is, after a linking verb (*she was drunk*) while *drunken* is more often used to modify a noun (*a drunken sailor*) and, in some cases, to imply habitual drinking to excess. *Drunken* is also used to modify nouns that do not refer to a person (*a drunken celebration*). To say **intoxicated** or **inebriated** is a more formal and less offensive way of calling someone *drunk*, with *intoxicated* implying that the individual is only slightly drunk, and *inebriated* implying drunkenness to the point of excitement or exhilaration (*the streets were filled with inebriated revelers*). **Tight** and **tipsy** are two of the more common slang expressions (there are literally hundreds more) meaning *drunk*. Like *intoxicated*, *tipsy* implies that someone is only slightly drunk, while *tight* implies obvious drunkenness but without any loss of muscular coordination. An elderly woman who has had one sherry too many might be described as *tipsy*, but someone who has been drinking all evening and is still able to stand up and give a speech might be described as *tight*. Either condition is preferable to being **blotto**, a word that means drunk to the point of incomprehensibility or unconsciousness.

terly. **3** (of a well, etc.) cease to yield water. **4** *colloq.* (esp. in *imper.*) cease talking. **go dry** enact legislation for the prohibition of alcohol. □□ **dry•ish** *adj.* **dry•ness** *n.* [OE *drȳge*, *drygan*, rel. to MLG *dröge*, MDu. *drȫghe*, f. Gmc]

dry•ad /dríad, dríad/ *n. Mythol.* a nymph inhabiting a tree; a wood nymph. [ME f. OF *dryade* f. L f. Gk *druas –ados* f. *drus* tree]

dry bat•ter•y *n. Electr.* an electric battery consisting of dry cells.

dry cell *n. Electr.* a cell in which the electrolyte is absorbed in a solid and cannot be spilled.

dry-clean *adj.* clean (clothes, etc.) with organic solvents without using water. □□ **dry clean•er** *n.*

dry-cure *v.tr.* = DRY-SALT.

dry dock *n.* an enclosed dock that can be drained of water to allow the inspection and repair of a ship.

dry•er /dríər/ *n.* **1** a machine for drying the hair, laundry, etc. **2** var. of DRIER² 2.

dry-fly *adj. & v.* ● *adj.* (of fishing) with an artificial fly floating on the surface. ● *v.intr.* (**•flies, •flied**) fish by such a method.

dry goods *n.* fabric, thread, clothing, and related merchandise, esp. as distinct from hardware and groceries.

dry ice *n.* solid carbon dioxide.

dry•lands *n.* an arid area; a region with low rainfall.

dry•ly /dríle/ *adv.* (also **dri•ly**) **1** (said) in a dry manner; humorously. **2** in a dry way or condition.

dry meas•ure *n.* a measure of volume for loose dry commodities such as grain, tea, and sugar.

dry milk *n.* dehydrated milk that has been reduced to a powder.

dry nurse *n.* a nurse for young children, not required to breastfeed.

dry plate *n. Photog.* a glass plate coated with a light-sensitive, gelatin-based emulsion.

dry•point /drípoynt/ *n.* **1** a needle for engraving on a bare copper plate without acid. **2** an engraving produced with this.

dry rot *n.* **1** a decayed state of wood when not ventilated, caused by certain fungi. **2** these fungi.

dry run *n. colloq.* a rehearsal of a performance or procedure before the real one.

dry-salt *v.tr.* cure (meat or fish) with salt instead of liquid.

dry•salt•er /drísawltər/ *n. Brit.* a dealer in dyes, gums, drugs, oils, pickles, canned meats, etc.

dry-shod *adj.* without wetting the shoes.

dry•stone /dríston/ *adj.* esp. *Brit.* (of a wall, etc.) built without mortar.

dry•wall /dríwawl/ *n.* = PLASTERBOARD.

DS *abbr.* **1** dal segno. **2** disseminated sclerosis.

DSC *abbr.* Distinguished Service Cross.

D.Sc. *abbr.* Doctor of Science.

DSM *abbr.* Distinguished Service Medal.

DST *abbr.* daylight saving(s) time.

DT *abbr.* (also **DT's** /deéteéz/) delirium tremens.

DTP *abbr.* desktop publishing.

du•al /dóoəl, dyóoəl/ *adj., n., & v.* ● *adj.* **1** of two; twofold. **2** divided in two; double (*dual ownership*). **3** *Gram.* (in some languages) denoting two persons or things (additional to singular and plural). ● *n.* (also **du•al num•ber**) *Gram.* a dual form of a noun, verb, etc. ● *v.tr. Brit.* convert (a road) into a divided highway. □□ **du•al•i•ty** /-álitee/ *n.* **du•al•ize** *v.tr.* **du•al•ly** *adv.* [L *dualis* f. *duo* two]

du•al car•riage•way *n. Brit.* a divided highway.

du•al con•trol *n.* (of a vehicle or an aircraft) having two sets of controls, one of which is used by the instructor.

du•al in-line pack•age *n. Computing* see DIP.

du•al•ism /dóoəlizəm, dyóo–/ *n.* **1** being twofold; duality. **2** *Philos.* the theory that in any domain of reality there are two independent underlying principles, e.g., mind and matter, form and content (cf. IDEALISM, MATERIALISM). **3** *Theol.* **a** the theory that the forces of good and evil are equally balanced in the universe. **b** the theory of the dual (human and divine) personality of Christ. □□ **du•al•ist** *n.* **du•al•is•tic** *adj.* **du•al•is•ti•cal•ly** *adv.*

du•al-pur•pose *adj.* serving two purposes or functions.

dub¹ /dub/ *v.tr.* (**dubbed, dub•bing**) **1** make (a person) a knight by touching his shoulders with a sword. **2** give (a person) a name, nickname, or title (*dubbed him a crank*). **3** *Brit.* dress (an artificial fishing fly). **4** smear (leather) with grease. [OE f. AF *duber*, *aduber*, OF *adober* equip with armor, repair, of unkn. orig.]

dub² /dub/ *v.tr.* (**dubbed, dub•bing**) **1** provide (a movie, etc.) with an alternative soundtrack, esp. in a different language. **2** add (sound effects or music) to a movie or a broadcast. **3** combine (soundtracks) into one. **4** transfer or make a copy of (a soundtrack). [abbr. of DOUBLE]

dub³ /dub/ *n. sl.* an inexperienced or unskillful person. [perh. f. DUB¹ in sense 'beat flat']

dub⁴ /dub/ *v.intr.* (**dubbed, dub•bing**) *Brit. sl.* (foll. by *in, up*) pay up; contribute money. [19th c.: orig. uncert.]

dub•bin /dúbin/ *n. & v.* ● *n.* (also **dub•bing** /dúbing/) prepared grease for softening and waterproofing leather. ● *v.tr.* (**dub•bined, dub•bin•ing**) apply dubbin to (boots, etc.). [see DUB¹ 4]

dub•bing /dúbing/ *n.* an alternative soundtrack to a movie, etc.

du•bi•e•ty /doobíətee, dyoo–/ *n.* (*pl.* **•ties**) *literary* **1** a feeling of doubt. **2** a doubtful matter. [LL *dubietas* f. *dubium* doubt]

du•bi•ous /dóobeeəs, dyoo–/ *adj.* **1** hesitating or doubting (*dubious about going*). **2** of questionable value or truth (*a dubious claim*). **3** unreliable; suspicious (*dubious company*). **4** of doubtful result (*a dubious undertaking*). □□ **du•bi•ous•ly** *adv.* **du•bi•ous•ness** *n.* [L *dubiosus* f. *dubium* doubt]

du•bi•ta•tion /doobitáyshən, dyoo–/ *n. literary* doubt; hesitation. [ME f. OF *dubitation* or L *dubitatio* f. *dubitare* DOUBT]

du•bi•ta•tive /dóobitaytiv, dyoo–/ *adj. literary* of, expressing, or inclined to doubt or hesitation. □□ **du•bi•ta•tive•ly** *adv.* [F *dubitatif –ive* or LL *dubitativus* (as DUBITATION)]

Du•bon•net /doobonáy, dyoo–/ *n. Trademark* **1** a sweet French aperitif. **2** a glass of this. [name of a family of French wine merchants]

du•cal /dóokəl, dyoo–/ *adj.* of, like, or bearing the title of a duke. [F f. *duc* DUKE]

duc•at /dúkət/ *n.* **1** *hist.* a gold coin, formerly current in most European countries. **2 a** a coin. **b** (in *pl.*) money. **3** a ticket to a performance. [ME f. It. *ducato* or med.L *ducatus* DUCHY]

Du•ce /dóochay/ *n.* a leader, esp. (**Il Duce**) the title assumed by Mussolini (d. 1945). [It., = leader]

duch•ess /dúchis/ *n.* (as a title usu. **Duchess**) **1** a duke's wife or widow. **2** a woman holding the rank of duke in her own right. [ME f. OF *duchesse* f. med.L *ducissa* (as DUKE)]

duch•esse /dooshés, dúchis/ *n.* **1** a soft heavy kind of satin. **2** a dressing table with a pivoting mirror. [F, = DUCHESS]

duch•esse lace *n.* a kind of Brussels pillow lace with bold floral patterns worked with a fine thread.

duch•esse po•ta•toes *n.* mashed potatoes mixed with egg and butter, formed into shapes and baked.

duch•esse set *n.* a set of fabric or lace mats for a dressing table.

duch•y /dúchee/ *n.* (*pl.* **•ies**) **1** the territory of a duke or duchess; a dukedom. **2** (often as **the Duchy**) the royal dukedom of Cornwall or Lancaster, each with certain estates, revenues, and jurisdiction of its own. [ME f. OF *duché(e)* f. med.L *ducatus* f. L *dux ducis* leader]

duck¹ /duk/ *n.* (*pl.* same or **ducks**) **1 a** any of various swimming birds of the family Anatidae, esp. the domesticated form of the mallard or wild duck. **b** the female of this (opp. DRAKE). **c** the flesh of a duck as food. **2** *Cricket* (in full **duck-egg**) a batsman's score of zero. **3** (also **ducks**) *Brit. colloq.* (esp. as a form of address) dear; darling. □ **like a duck to water** adapting very readily. **like water off a duck's back** *colloq.* (of remonstrances, etc.) producing no effect. **play ducks and drakes with** *colloq.* squander. [OE *duce, dūce:* rel. to DUCK²]

duck² /duk/ *v. & n.* ● *v.* **1** *intr. & tr.* plunge, dive, or dip under water and emerge (*ducked him in the pond*). **2** *intr. & tr.* bend (the head or the body) quickly to avoid a blow or being seen, or as a bow or curtsy; bob (*ducked out of sight*). **3** *tr. & intr. colloq.* avoid or dodge; withdraw (from) (*ducked out of the engagement; ducked the meeting*). **4** *intr. Bridge* lose a trick deliberately by playing a low card. ● *n.* **1** a quick dip or swim. **2** a quick lowering of the head, etc. □□ **duck•er** *n.* [OE *dūcan* (unrecorded) f. Gmc]

duck³ /duk/ *n.* **1** a strong, untwilled linen or cotton fabric used for small sails and the outer clothing of sailors. **2** (in *pl.*) pants made of this (*white ducks*). [MDu. *doek*, of unkn. orig.]

duck⁴ /duk/ *n. colloq.* an amphibious landing craft. [*DUKW*, its official designation]

duck•bill /dúkbil/ *n.* (also **duck-billed plat•y•pus**) = PLATYPUS.

duck•board /dúkbawrd/ *n.* (usu. in *pl.*) a path of wooden slats placed over muddy ground or in a trench.

duck hawk *n. dated* the peregrine falcon.

duck•ing stool *n. hist.* a chair fastened to the end of a pole, which could be plunged into a pond, used formerly for punishing public offenders, etc.

duck•ling /dúkling/ *n.* **1** a young duck. **2** its flesh as food

ducks and drakes *n.* a game of making a flat stone skim along the surface of water.

duck's ass *n. coarse sl.* a haircut with the hair on the back of the head shaped like a duck's tail (usu. abbr. as **DA**).

duck soup *n. sl.* an easy task.

duck•weed /dúkweed/ *n.* any of various aquatic plants, esp. of the genus *Lemna*, growing on the surface of still water.

duck•y /dúkee/ *n. & adj.* esp. *Brit. colloq.* ● *n.* (*pl.* **•ies**) darling; dear. ● *adj.* sweet; pretty; splendid.

duct /dukt/ *n. & v.* ● *n.* **1** a channel or tube for conveying fluid, cable, etc. **2 a** a tube in the body conveying secretions such as tears, etc. **b** *Bot.* a tube formed by cells that have lost their intervening end walls, holding air, water, etc. ● *v.tr.* convey through a duct. [L *ductus* leading, aqueduct f. *ducere duct-* lead]

duc•tile /dúktəl, –tíl/ *adj.* **1** (of a metal) capable of being drawn into wire; pliable, not brittle **2** (of a substance) easily molded. **3** (of a person) docile, gullible. □□ **duc•til•i•ty** /-tílitee/ *n.* [ME f. OF *ductile* or L *ductilis* f. *ducere duct-* lead]

duct•ing /dúkting/ *n.* **1** a system of ducts. **2** material in the form of a duct or ducts.

duct•less /dúktlis/ *adj.* lacking or not using a duct or ducts. □ **ductless gland** a gland secreting directly into the bloodstream. Also called **endocrine gland.**

duct•work /dúktwərk/ *n.* a series of interlinked ducts, as for a ventilation system.

dud /dud/ *n. & adj. sl.* • *n.* **1** a futile or ineffectual person or thing (*a dud at the job*). **2** a counterfeit article. **3** a shell, etc., that fails to explode. **4** (in *pl.*) clothes. • *adj.* **1** useless, worthless; unsatisfactory or futile. **2** counterfeit. [ME: orig. unkn.]

dude /dood, dyood/ *n. sl.* **1** a fastidious aesthetic person, usu. male; a dandy. **2** a vacationer on a ranch in the western US, esp. when unused to ranch life. **3** a fellow; a guy. □ **dude up** *colloq.* dress up; dress in one's best or showiest clothing. □□ **dud•ish** *adj.* [19th c.: prob. f. G dial. *dude* fool]

dude ranch *n.* a cattle ranch converted to a vacation resort for tourists, etc.

dudg•eon /dújən/ *n.* a feeling of offense; resentment. □ **in high dudgeon** very angry or angrily. [16th c.: orig. unkn.]

due /doo, dyoo/ *adj., n., & adv.* • *adj.* **1** (*predic.*) owing or payable as a debt or an obligation (*our thanks are due to him; $500 was due on the 15th*). **2** (often foll. by *to*) merited; appropriate; fitting (*her due reward; received the applause due to a hero*). **3** rightful; proper; adequate (*after due consideration*). **4** (*predic.*; foll. by *to*) to be ascribed to (a cause, an agent, etc.) (*the discovery was due to Edison*). **5** (*predic.*) intended to arrive at a certain time (*a train is due at 7:30*). **6** (foll. by *to* + infin.) under an obligation or agreement to do something (*due to speak tonight*). • *n.* **1** a person's right; what is owed to a person (*a fair hearing is my due*). **2** (in *pl.*) **a** what one owes (*pays his dues*). **b** a legally demandable toll or fee (*harbor dues; university dues*). • *adv.* (of a point of the compass) exactly, directly (*went due east; a due north wind*). □ **due to** *disp.* because of; owing to (*was late due to an accident*) (cf. sense 4 of *adj.*). **fall** (or **become**) **due** (of a bill, etc.) be immediately payable. **in due course 1** at about the appropriate time. **2** in the natural order. [ME f. OF *deü* ult. f. L *debitus* past part. of *debēre* owe]

▶ The use of **due to** meaning 'because of', as in *we were late due to circumstances beyond our control,* is widely used and generally accepted, although some traditionalists hold that **due** is properly a predicate adjective and restrict its use to follow forms of the verb *to be,* e.g., *The collapse was due to flooding.*

du•el /dóoəl, dyóoəl/ *n. & v.* • *n.* **1** *hist.* a contest with deadly weapons between two people, in the presence of two seconds, to settle a point of honor. **2** any contest between two people, parties, causes, animals, etc. (*a duel of wits*). • *v.intr.* fight a duel or duels. □□ **du•el•er** *n.* **du•el•ist** *n..*

WORD HISTORY duel

Late 15th century: from Latin *duellum,* archaic and literary form of *bellum* 'war,' used in medieval Latin with the meaning 'combat between two persons,' partly influenced by *dualis* 'of two.' The original sense was 'single combat used to decide a judicial dispute'; the sense 'contest to decide a point of honor' dates from the early 17th century.

duen•de /doo-énday/ *n.* **1** an evil spirit. **2** inspiration. [Sp.]

du•en•na /doo-énə, dyoo-/ *n.* an older woman acting as a governess and companion in charge of girls, esp. in a Spanish family; a chaperon. [Sp. *dueña* f. L *domina* mistress]

due proc•ess *n.* a course of legal proceedings in accordance with a state's or nation's legal system, such that individual rights are protected.

du•et /doo-ét, dyoo-/ *n.* **1** *Mus.* **a** a performance by two voices, instrumentalists, etc. **b** a composition for two performers. **2** a dialogue. □□ **du•et•tist** *n.* [G *Duett* or It. *duetto* dimin. of *duo* duet f. L *duo* two]

duff¹ /duf/ *n.* a boiled pudding. [North of Engl. form of DOUGH]

duff² /duf/ *adj. Brit. sl.* **1** worthless; counterfeit. **2** useless; broken. [perh. = DUFF¹]

duff³ /duf/ *v.tr. sl.* **1** *Brit. Golf* mishit (a shot, a ball); bungle. **2** *Austral.* steal and alter brands on (cattle). □ **duff up** *Brit. sl.* beat; thrash. [perh. back-form. f. DUFFER]

duf•fel /dúfəl/ *n.* (also **duf•fle**) **1** a coarse woolen cloth with a thick nap. **2** a sportsman's or camper's equipment. [*Duffel* in Belgium]

duf•fel bag *n.* a cylindrical canvas, etc., bag closed by a drawstring and carried over the shoulder.

duf•fer /dúfər/ *n. sl.* **1** an inefficient, useless, or stupid person. **2** *Austral.* a person who duffs cattle. **3** *Austral.* an unproductive mine. [perh. f. Sc. *doofart* stupid person f. *douf* spiritless]

duf•fle coat *n.* (or **duffel coat**) a hooded overcoat of heavy esp. woolen fabric, usu. fastened with toggles.

dug¹ *past* and *past part.* of DIG.

dug² /dug/ *n.* **1** the udder, breast, teat, or nipple of a female animal. **2** *derog.* the breast of a woman. [16th c.: orig. unkn.]

du•gong /dóogawng, –gong/ *n.* (*pl.* same or **dugongs**) a marine mammal, *Dugong dugon,* of Asian seas and coasts. Also called **sea cow.** [ult. f. Malay *dūyong*]

dug•out /dúgowt/ *n.* **1 a** a roofed shelter esp. for troops in trenches. **b** an underground air-raid or nuclear shelter. **c** *Baseball* a roofed seating area for players, facing the field. **2** a canoe made from a hollowed tree trunk. **3** *Brit. sl.* a retired officer, etc., recalled to service.

dui•ker /díkər/ *n.* **1** any African antelope of the genus *Cephalophus,* usu. having a crest of long hair between its horns. **2** *S.Afr.* the long-tailed cormorant, *Phalacrocorax africanus.* [Du. *duiker* diver: in sense 1, from plunging through bushes when pursued]

duke /dook, dyook/ *n.* (as a title usu. **Duke**) **1 a** a person holding the highest hereditary title of the nobility. **b** a sovereign prince ruling a duchy or small state. **2** (usu. in *pl.*) *sl.* the hand; the fist (*put up your dukes!*). **3** *Bot.* a kind of cherry, neither very sweet nor very sour. [ME f. OF *duc* f. L *dux ducis* leader]

duke•dom /dóokdəm, dyóok–/ *n.* **1** a territory ruled by a duke. **2** the rank of duke.

dul•cet /dúlsit/ *adj.* (esp. of sound) sweet and soothing. [ME, earlier *doucet* f. OF dimin. of *doux* f. L *dulcis* sweet]

dul•ci•fy /dúlsifī/ *v.tr.* (**•fies, •fied**) *literary* **1** make gentle. **2** sweeten. □□ **dul•ci•fi•ca•tion** /–fikáyshən/ *n.* [L *dulcificare* f. *dulcis* sweet]

dul•ci•mer /dúlsimər/ *n.* a musical instrument with strings of graduated length stretched over a sounding board or box, played by being struck with hammers. [OF *doulcemer,* said to repr. L *dulce* sweet, *melos* song]

dul•ci•tone /dúlsitōn/ *n. Mus.* a keyboard instrument with steel tuning forks which are struck by hammers. [L *dulcis* sweet + TONE]

du•li•a /doolíə, dyoo–/ *n. RC Ch.* the reverence accorded to saints and angels. [med.L f. Gk *douleia* servitude f. *doulos* slave]

dull /dul/ *adj. & v.* • *adj.* **1** slow to understand; stupid. **2** tedious; boring. **3** (of the weather) overcast; gloomy. **4 a** (esp. of a knife edge, etc.) blunt. **b** (of color, light, sound, or taste) not bright, shining, vivid, or keen. **5** (of a pain, etc.) not acute; prolonged and indistinct; not acute (*a dull ache*). **6 a** (of a person, an animal, trade, etc.) sluggish, slow-moving, or stagnant. **b** (of a person) listless; depressed (*he's a dull fellow since the accident*). **7** (of the ears, eyes, etc.) without keen perception. • *v.tr. & intr.* make or become dull. □ **dull the edge of** make less sensitive, interesting, effective, amusing, etc.; blunt. □□ **dull•ish** *adj.* **dull•ness** *n.* (also **dul•ness**). **dul•ly** *adv.* [ME f. MLG, MDu. *dul,* corresp. to OE *dol* stupid]

dull•ard /dúlərd/ *n.* a stupid person.

dull-wit•ted *adj.* = DULL *adj.* 1.

dulse /duls/ *n.* an edible seaweed, *Rhodymenia palmata,* with red wedge-shaped fronds. [Ir. & Gael. *duileasg*]

du•ly /dóolee, dyóo–/ *adv.* **1** in due time or manner. **2** rightly; properly; fitly.

du•ma /dóomə/ *n. hist.* a Russian council of state, esp. the elected body existing between 1905 and 1917. [Russ.: orig. an elective municipal council]

dumb /dum/ *adj.* **1 a** (of a person) unable to speak, usu. because of a congenital defect or deafness. **b** (of an animal) naturally unable to speak (*our dumb friends*). **2** silenced by surprise, shyness, etc. (*struck dumb by this revelation*). **3** taciturn or reticent, esp. insultingly (*dumb insolence*). **4** (of an action, etc.) performed without speech. **5** (often in *comb.*) giving no sound; without voice or some other property normally belonging to things of the name (*a dumb piano*). **6** *colloq.* stupid; ignorant. **7** (usu. of a class, population, etc.) having no voice in government; inarticulate (*the dumb masses*). **8** (of a computer terminal, etc.) able only to transmit data to or receive data from a computer; not programmable (opp. INTELLIGENT). □□ **dumb•ly** /dúmlee/ *adv.* **dumb•ness** /dúmnis/ *n.* [OE: orig. unkn.: sense 6 f. G *dumm*]

dumb•bell /dúmbel/ *n.* **1** a short bar with a weight at each end, used for exercise, muscle-building, etc. **2** *sl.* a stupid person.

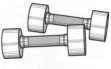
dumbbells 1

dumb cluck *n. sl.* a stupid person.

dumb•found /dúmfównd/ *v.tr.* (also **dum•found;** esp. as **dumbfounded** *adj.*) strike dumb; confound; nonplus. [DUMB, CONFOUND]

dumb•head /dúmhed/ *n. sl.* a stupid person.

dum•bo /dúmbō/ *n.* (*pl.* **•bos**) *sl.* a stupid person; a fool. [DUMB + –O]

dumb show *n.* **1** significant gestures or mime, used when words are inappropriate. **2** a part of a play in early drama, acted in mime.

dumb•struck /dúmstruk/ *adj.* greatly shocked or surprised and so lost for words.

dumb•wait•er /dúmwaytər/ *n.* **1** a small elevator for carrying food, plates, etc., between floors. **2** a movable table, esp. with revolving shelves, used in a dining room.

dum•dum /dúmdum/ *n.* (in full **dumdum bullet**) a kind of soft-nosed bullet that expands on impact and inflicts a severe wound. [*Dum-Dum* in India, where it was first produced]

dum•my /dúmee/ *n., adj., & v. • n. (pl. •mies)* **1** a model of a human being, esp.: **a** a ventriloquist's doll. **b** a figure used to model clothes in a store window, etc. **c** a target used for firearms practice. **2** (often *attrib.*) **a** a counterfeit object used to replace or resemble a real or normal one. **b** a prototype, esp. in publishing. **3** *colloq.* a stupid person. **4** a person taking no significant part; a figurehead. **5** *Brit.* a baby's pacifier. **6** an imaginary fourth player at whist, whose hand is turned up and played by a partner. **7** *Bridge* **a** the partner of the declarer, whose cards are exposed after the first lead. **b** this player's hand. **8** *Mil.* a blank round of ammunition. **9** *colloq.* a dumb person. • *adj.* sham; counterfeit. □ **dummy up** *sl.* keep quiet; give no information. [DUMB + −Y²]

dum•my run *n.* **1** a practice attack, etc.; a trial run. **2** a rehearsal.

dump /dump/ *n. & v. • n.* **1 a** a place for depositing trash, garbage, etc. **b** a heap of trash, garbage, etc. **2** *colloq.* an unpleasant or dreary place. **3** *Mil.* a temporary store of ammunition, provisions, etc. **4** an accumulated pile of ore, earth, etc. **5** *Computing* **a** a printout of stored data. **b** the process or result of dumping data. • *v.tr.* **1** put down firmly or clumsily (*dumped the shopping on the table*). **2** deposit or dispose of (rubbish, etc.). **3** *colloq.* abandon; desert. **4** *Mil.* leave (ammunition, etc.) in a dump. **5** *Econ.* send (goods unsalable at a high price in the home market) to a foreign market for sale at a low price, to keep up the price at home, and to capture a new market. **6** *Computing* **a** copy (stored data) to a different location. **b** reproduce the contents of (a store) externally. □ **dump on** *sl.* criticize or abuse; get the better of. □□ **dump•ing** *n.* [ME perh. f. Norse; cf. Da. *dumpe*, Norw. *dumpa* fall suddenly]

dump•er /dúmpər/ *n.* **1** a person or thing that dumps. **2** *Austral. & NZ* a large wave that breaks and hurls the swimmer or surfer on to the beach.

dump•ling /dúmpling/ *n.* **1 a** a small ball of usu. shortening, flour, and water, boiled in stew or water, and eaten. **b** a dessert consisting of apple or other fruit enclosed in dough and baked. **2** a small fat person. [app. dimin., of *dump* small round object, but recorded much earlier]

dumps /dumps/ *n.pl. colloq.* depression; melancholy (*in the dumps*). [prob. f. LG or Du., fig. use of MDu. *domp* exhalation, haze, mist: rel. to DAMP]

Dump•ster /dúmpstər/ *n. Trademark* a large trash receptacle designed to be hoisted and emptied into a truck.

dump truck *n.* a truck with a body that tilts or opens at the back for unloading.

dump•y /dúmpee/ *adj* (**dump•i•er, dump•i•est**) short and stout. □□ **dump•i•ly** *adv.* **dump•i•ness** *n.* [*dump* (cf. DUMPLING) + −Y¹]

dun¹ /dun/ *adj. & n. • adj.* **1** dull grayish brown. **2** *poet.* dark; dusky. • *n.* **1** a dun color. **2** a dun horse. **3** (in full **dun fly**) a dark fishing fly. [OE *dun, dunn*]

dun² /dun/ *v. & n. • v.tr.* (**dunned, dunning**) make persistent demands on someone, esp. for payment of a debt. • *n.* **1** a debt collector or an insistent creditor. **2** a demand for payment. [abbr. of obs. *dunkirk* privateer, f. *Dunkirk* in France]

dunce /duns/ *n.* a person slow at learning; a dullard. [John *Duns* Scotus, scholastic theologian d. 1308, whose followers were ridiculed by 16th-c. humanists and reformers as enemies of learning]

dunce cap *n.* (also **dunce's cap**) a paper cone formerly put on the head of a dunce at school as a mark of disgrace.

dun•der•head /dúndərhed/ *n.* a stupid person. □□ **dun•der•head•ed** *adj.* [17th c.: perh. rel. to dial. *dunner* resounding noise]

dune /doon, dyoon/ *n.* a mound or ridge of loose sand, etc., formed by the wind, esp. beside the sea or in a desert. □ **dune buggy** a low, wide-wheeled motor vehicle for driving on sand. [F f MDu. *dûne*: cf. DOWN³]

dung /dung/ *n. & v. • n.* the excrement of animals; manure. • *v.tr.* apply dung to; manure (land). [OE, rel. to OHG *tunga*, Icel. *dyngja*, of unkn. orig.]

dun•ga•ree /dúnggəreé/ *n.* **1** (in *pl.*) **a** overalls, etc., usu. made of blue denim, worn esp. by workers. **b** blue jeans. **2** a coarse E. Indian calico. [Hindi *dungrī*]

dung bee•tle *n.* any of a family of beetles whose larvae develop in dung.

dun•geon /dúnjən/ *n. & v. • n.* **1** a strong underground cell for prisoners. **2** *archaic* a donjon. • *v.tr. archaic* (usu. foll. by *up*) imprison in a dungeon. [orig. = *donjon*: ME f. OF *donjon* ult. f. L *dominus* lord]

dung fly *n.* any of various flies feeding on dung.

dung•hill /dúnghil/ *n.* a heap of dung or refuse, esp. in a farmyard.

dunk /dungk/ *v.tr.* **1** dip (a doughnut, etc.) into milk, coffee, etc. before eating. **2** immerse; dip (*was dunked in the river*). □ **dunk shot** *Basketball* a shot made by a player jumping up and thrusting the ball down through the basket. [Pennsylvanian G *dunke* to dip f. G *tunken*]

dun•lin /dúnlin/ *n.* a long-billed sandpiper, *Calidris alpina.* [prob. f. DUN¹ + −LING¹]

dun•nage /dúnij/ *n.* **1** *Naut.* mats, brushwood, etc., stowed under or among cargo to prevent wetting or chafing. **2** *colloq.* miscellaneous baggage. **3** cushioning packing material for shipping. [AL *dennagium*, of unkn. orig.]

dun•no /dənố/ *colloq.* (I) do not know. [corrupt.]

dun•nock /dúnək/ *n. Brit.* the hedge sparrow. [app. f. DUN¹ + −OCK, from its brown and gray plumage]

dun•ny /dúnee/ *n. (pl. •nies)* **1** *Sc.* an underground passage or cellar, esp. in an apartment building. **2** esp. *Austral. & NZ sl.* an outhouse; privy. [20th c.: orig. uncert.]

du•o /doó-ō, dyoó-ō/ *n. (pl. •os)* **1** a pair of actors, entertainers, singers, etc. (*a comedy duo*). **2** *Mus.* a duet. [It. f. L, = two]

du•o•dec•i•mal /doó-ōdésiməl, dyoó–/ *adj. & n. • adj.* relating to or using a system of numerical notation that has 12 as a base. • *n.* **1** the duodecimal system. **2** duodecimal notation. □□ **du•o•dec•i•mal•ly** *adv.* [L *duodecimus* twelfth f. *duodecim* twelve]

du•o•dec•i•mo /doó-ōdésimō, dyoó–/ *n. (pl. •mos) Printing* **1** a book size in which each leaf is one-twelfth of the size of the printing sheet. **2** a book of this size. [L (*in*) *duodecimo* in a twelfth (as DUODECIMAL)]

du•o•den•a•ry /doóədénəree, –deénə–, dyoó–/ *adj.* proceeding by twelves or in sets of twelve. [L *duodenarius* f. *duodeni* distrib. of *duodecim* twelve]

du•o•de•num /doóədeénəm, dyoó–, doō-ód'nəm, dyoó–/ *n. Anat.* the first part of the small intestine immediately below the stomach. □□ **du•o•de•nal** *adj.* **du•o•de•ni•tis** /–nítis/ *n.* [ME f. med.L f. *duodeni* (see DUODENARY) from its length of about 12 fingers' breadth]

du•o•logue /doóəlawg, –log, dyoó–/ *n.* **1** a conversation between two people. **2** a play or part of a play for two actors. [irreg. f. L *duo* or Gk *duo* two, after *monologue*]

duo•mo /dwômō/ *n. (pl. •mos)* an Italian cathedral. [It., = DOME]

du•op•o•ly /doó-ópəlee, dyoó–/ *n. (pl. •lies) Econ.* the possession of trade in a commodity, etc., by only two sellers. [Gk *duo* two + *pōleō* sell, after *monopoly*]

du•o•tone /doóətōn, dyoó–/ *n. & adj. Printing • n.* **1** a halftone illustration in two colors from the same original with different screen angles. **2** the process of making a duotone. • *adj.* in two colors. [L *duo* two + TONE]

dupe /doop, dyoop/ *n. & v. • n.* a victim of deception. • *v.tr.* make a fool of; cheat; gull. □□ **dup•a•ble** *adj.* **dup•er** *n.* **dup•er•y** *n.* [F f. dial. F *dupe* hoopoe, from the bird's supposedly stupid appearance]

du•pi•on /doópeeən, dyoó–/ *n.* **1** a rough silk fabric woven from the threads of double cocoons. **2** an imitation of this with other fibers. [F *doupion* f. It. *doppione* f. *doppio* double]

du•ple /doópəl, dyoó–/ *adj.* of two parts. [L *duplus* f. *duo* two]

du•ple ra•ti•o *n. Math.* a ratio of 2 to 1.

du•ple time *n. Mus.* based on two beats to the bar.

du•plex /doópleks, dyoó–/ *n. & adj. • n.* **1** an apartment on two levels. **2** a house subdivided for two families. • *adj.* **1** having two elements; twofold. **2 a** (of an apartment) two-story. **b** (of a house) for two families. **3** *Computing* (of a circuit) allowing the transmission of signals in both directions simultaneously (opp. SIMPLEX). [L *duplex duplicis* f. *duo* two + *plic-* fold]

du•pli•cate *adj., n., & v. • adj.* /doóplikət, dyoó–/ **1** exactly like something already existing; copied (esp. in large numbers). **2 a** having two corresponding parts. **b** existing in two examples; paired. **c** twice as large or many; doubled. • *n.* /doóplikət, dyoó–/ **1 a** one of two or more identical things, esp. a copy of an original. **b** one of two or more specimens of a thing exactly or almost identical. **2** *Law* a second copy of a letter or document. **3** (in full **duplicate bridge** or whist) a form of bridge or whist in which the same hands are played successively by different players. **4** *archaic* a pawnbroker's ticket. • *v.tr.* /doóplikayt, dyoó–/ **1** multiply by two; double. **2 a** make or be an exact copy of. **b** make or supply copies of (*duplicated the leaflet for distribution*). **3** repeat (an action, etc.), esp. unnecessarily. □ **in duplicate** consisting of two exact copies. □□ **du•pli•ca•ble** /doóplikəbəl, dyoó–/ *adj.* **du•pli•ca•tion** /–káyshən/ *n.* [L *duplicatus* past part. of *duplicare* (as DUPLEX)]

du•pli•ca•tor /doóplikaytər, dyoó–/ *n.* **1** a machine for making copies of a document, leaflet, etc. **2** a person or thing that duplicates.

du•plic•i•ty /doóplísitee, dyoó–/ *n.* **1** double-dealing; deceitfulness. **2** *archaic* doubleness. □□ **du•plic•i•tous** *adj.* [ME f. OF *duplicité* or LL *duplicitas* (as DUPLEX)]

du•ra•ble /doórəbəl, dyoó–/ *adj. & n. • adj.* **1** capable of lasting; hard-wearing. **2** (of goods) not for immediate consumption; able to be kept. • *n.* (in *pl.*) durable goods. □□ **du•ra•bil•i•ty** *n.* **du•ra•ble•ness** *n.* **du•ra•bly** *adv.* [ME f. OF f. L *durabilis* f. *durare* endure f. *durus* hard]

du•ral•u•min /doorályəmin, dyoor–/ *n.* a light, hard alloy of aluminum with copper, etc. [perh. f. *Düren* in the Rhineland or L *durus* hard + ALUMINUM]

du•ra ma•ter /doórə máytər, maá–, dyoórə/ *n. Anat.* the tough outermost membrane enveloping the brain and spinal cord (see MENINX). [med.L = hard mother, transl. Arab. *al-'umm al-jāfiya* ('mother' in Arab. indicating the relationship of things)]

du·ra·men /dooráymen, dyoor–/ *n.* = HEARTWOOD. [L f. *durare* harden]

dur·ance /doorəns, dyoor–/ *n.* *archaic* imprisonment (*in durance vile*). [ME f. F f. *durer* last f. L *durare*: see DURABLE]

du·ra·tion /dooráyshən, dyoor–/ *n.* **1** the length of time for which something continues. **2** a specified length of time (*after the duration of a minute*). □ **for the duration 1** until the end of something obstructing normal activities, as a war. **2** for a very long time. □□ **du·ra·tion·al** *adj.* [ME f. OF f. med.L *duratio –onis* (as DURANCE)]

dur·a·tive /doorətiv, dyoor–/ *adj.* *Gram.* denoting continuing action.

dur·bar /dərbaar/ *n.* *hist.* **1** the court of an E. Indian ruler. **2** a public levee of an E. Indian prince or an Anglo-Indian governor or viceroy. [Urdu f. Pers. *darbār* court]

du·ress /doorés, dyoo–/ *n.* **1** compulsion, esp. imprisonment, threats, or violence, illegally used to force a person to act against his or her will (*under duress*). **2** forcible restraint or imprisonment. [ME f. OF *duresse* f. L *duritia* f. *durus* hard]

du·ri·an /dooreeən/ *n.* **1** a large tree, *Durio zibethinus*, native to SE Asia, bearing oval spiny fruits containing a creamy pulp with a fetid smell and an agreeable taste. **2** this fruit. [Malay *durian* f *dūrī* thorn]

dur·ing /dooring, dyoor–/ *prep.* **1** throughout the course or duration of (*read during the meal*). **2** at some point in the duration of (*came in during the evening*). [ME f. OF *durant* ult. f. L *durare* last, continue]

dur·mast /dərmast, –maast/ *n.* an oak tree, *Quercus petraea*, having sessile flowers. [*dur–* (perh. erron. for DUN¹) + MAST²]

durn *dial.* var. of DARN².

durned *dial.* var. of DARNED.

dur·ra /doorə/ *n.* (also **dhur·ra**) a kind of sorghum, *Sorghum vulgare*, native to Asia, Africa, and the US. [Arab. *dura, durra*]

durst /dərst/ *archaic past* of DARE.

du·rum /doorəm, dyoo–/ *n.* a kind of wheat, *Triticum turgidum*, having hard seeds and yielding a flour used in the manufacture of spaghetti, etc. [L, neut of *durus* hard]

dusk /dusk/ *n., adj., & v.* ● *n.* **1** the darker stage of twilight. **2** shade; gloom. ● *adj. poet.* shadowy; dim; dark-colored. ● *v.tr. & intr. poet.* make or become shadowy or dim. [ME *dosk, dusk* f. OE *dox* dark, swarthy, *doxian* darken in color]

dusk·y /dúskee/ *adj.* (**dusk·i·er, dusk·i·est**) **1** shadowy; dim. **2** dark-colored, darkish. □□ **dusk·i·ly** *adv.* **dusk·i·ness** *n.*

dust /dust/ *n. & v.* ● *n.* **1 a** finely powdered earth, dirt, etc., lying on the ground or on surfaces, and blown about by the wind. **b** fine powder of any material (*pollen dust; gold dust*). **c** a cloud of dust. **2 a** dead person's remains (*honored dust*). **3** confusion or turmoil (*raised quite a dust*). **4** *archaic* or *poet.* the mortal human body (*we are all dust*). **5** the ground; the earth (*kissed the dust*). ● *v.* **1** *tr.* (also *absol.*) clear (furniture, etc.) of dust, etc., by wiping, brushing, etc. **2** *tr.* **a** sprinkle (esp. a cake) with powder, dust, sugar, etc. **b** sprinkle or strew (sugar, powder, etc.). **3** *tr.* make dusty. **4** *intr. archaic* (of a bird) take a dust-bath. □ **dust down** *Brit.* **1** dust the clothes of (a person). **2** *colloq.* reprimand. **3** = *dust off.* **dust off 1** remove the dust from (an object on which it has long been allowed to settle). **2** take up and enjoy again after a long period of neglect. **in the dust 1** humiliated. **2** dead. **when the dust settles** when things quiet down. □□ **dust·less** *adj.* [OE *dūst*: cf. LG *dunst* vapor]

dust·bin /dústbin/ *n.* *Brit.* a garbage can, esp. one kept outside.

dust bowl *n.* **1** an area denuded of vegetation by drought or erosion and reduced to desert. **2** (**Dust Bowl**) areas of Oklahoma and other prairie states affected by severe soil erosion in the early 1930s.

dust·cart /dústkaart/ *n.* *Brit.* a garbage truck.

dust·cov·er /dústkuvər/ *n.* **1** a cloth put over furniture to protect it from dust. **2** = DUST JACKET.

dust dev·il *n.* a whirlwind visible as a column of dust.

dust·er /dústər/ *n.* **1 a** a cloth for dusting furniture, etc. **b** a person or contrivance that dusts. **2** a woman's light, loose, full-length coat.

dust·ing pow·der *n.* **1** talcum powder. **2** any dusting or drying powder.

dust jack·et *n.* a usu. decorated paper cover used to protect a book from dirt, etc.

dust·man /dústmən/ *n.* (*pl.* **·men**) *Brit.* **1** a person employed to clear household refuse; garbage collector. **2** the sandman.

dust·pan /dústpan/ *n.* a small pan into which dust, etc., is brushed from the floor.

dust shot *n.* the smallest size of shot for a shotgun.

dust storm *n.* a strong, turbulent wind that carries clouds of dust, soil, and sand over a large area.

dust·up /dústup/ *n.* *colloq.* a fight.

dust·y /dústee/ *adj.* (**dust·i·er, dust·i·est**) **1** full of, covered with, or resembling dust. **2** dry as dust; uninteresting. **3** (of a color) dull or muted. □ **dusty answer** *Brit.* a curt rejection of a request. **dusty**

mill·er 1 any of various plants, esp. *Artemisia stelleriana*, having white down on the leaves and flowers. **2** an artificial fishing fly. **not so dusty** *Brit. sl.* fairly good. □□ **dust·i·ly** *adv.* **dust·i·ness** *n.* [OE *dūstig* (as DUST)]

Dutch /duch/ *adj. & n.* ● *adj.* **1** of, relating to, or associated with the Netherlands. **2** *sl.* German. **3** *S.Afr.* of Dutch descent. **4** *archaic* Germany including the Netherlands. ● *n.* **1 a** the language of the Netherlands. **b** *S.Afr.* usu. *derog.* Afrikaans. **2** (prec. by *the*; treated as *pl.*) **a** the people of the Netherlands. **b** *S.Afr.* Afrikaans speakers. **3** *archaic* the language of Germany including the Netherlands. □ **beat the Dutch** *colloq.* do something remarkable. **go Dutch** share expenses equally. [MDu. *dutsch*, etc., Hollandish, Netherlandish, German, OHG *diutisc* national]

dutch /duch/ *n.* *Brit. sl.* a wife (esp. old dutch). [abbr. of *duchess* (also in this sense)]

Dutch auc·tion *n.* a sale, usu. public, of goods in which the price is reduced by the auctioneer until a buyer is found.

Dutch barn *n.* *Brit.* a barn roof over hay, etc., set on poles and having no walls.

Dutch cap *n.* **1** a contraceptive diaphragm. **2** a woman's lace cap with triangular flaps on each side.

Dutch cour·age *n.* false courage gained from alcohol.

Dutch doll *n.* a jointed wooden doll.

Dutch door *n.* a door divided into two parts horizontally allowing one part to be shut and the other open.

Dutch elm dis·ease *n.* a disease affecting elms caused by the fungus *Ceratocystis ulmi*, first found in the Netherlands.

Dutch hoe *n.* a hoe used with a pushing action just under the surface of the soil so as to kill weeds at this level.

Dutch in·te·ri·or a painting of Dutch domestic life in a style characteristic of the work of 17th-century genre painters.

Dutch·man /dúchmən/ *n.* (*pl.* **·men**; *fem.* **Dutch·wom·an**, *pl.* **·wom·en**) **1 a** a native or national of the Netherlands. **b** a person of Dutch descent. **2** a Dutch ship. **3** *sl.* a German. □ **I'm a Dutchman** *Brit.* expression of disbelief or refusal.

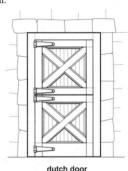

dutch door

Dutch·man's-breech·es *n.* a plant, *Dicentra cucullaria*, with white flowers and finely divided leaves.

Dutch met·al *n.* a copper-zinc alloy imitating gold leaf.

Dutch ov·en *n.* **1** a metal box the open side of which is turned toward a fire. **2** a covered cooking pot for braising, etc.

Dutch treat *n.* a party, outing, meal, etc. at which each person pays for their share of the expenses.

Dutch un·cle *n.* a person giving advice with benevolent firmness.

Dutch wife *n.* a framework of cane, etc., or a bolster, used for resting the legs in bed.

du·te·ous /dooteeəs, dyoo–/ *adj.* *literary* (of a person or conduct) dutiful; obedient. □□ **du·te·ous·ly** *adv.* **du·te·ous·ness** *n.* [DUTY + –OUS: cf. *beauteous*]

du·ti·a·ble /dooteeəbəl, dyoo–/ *adj.* liable to customs or other duties.

du·ti·ful /dootifool, dyoo–/ *adj.* doing or observant of one's duty; obedient. □□ **du·ti·ful·ly** *adv.* **du·ti·ful·ness** *n.*

du·ty /dootee, dyoo–/ *n.* (*pl.* **·ties**) **1 a** a moral or legal obligation; a responsibility (*her duty to report it*). **b** the binding force of what is right (*strong sense of duty*). **c** what is required of one (*do one's duty*). **2** payment to the public revenue, esp.: **a** that levied on the import, export, manufacture, or sale of goods (*customs duty*). **b** that levied on the transfer of property, licenses, the legal recognition of documents, etc. (*death duty; probate duty*). **3** a job or function (*his duties as caretaker*). **4** the behavior due to a superior; deference, respect. **5** the measure of an engine's effectiveness in units of work done per unit of fuel. **6** *Eccl.* the performance of church services. □ **do duty for** serve as or pass for (something else). **on** (or **off**) **duty** engaged (or not engaged) in one's work. [AF *deweté, dueté* (as DUE)]

du·ty-free *adj. & adv.* **1** exempt from payment of duty. **2** selling goods that are exempt from duty (*duty-free shop*).

du·ty of·fi·cer *n.* the officer currently on duty.

du·um·vir /doo-úmvər, dyoo–/ *n.* *Rom.Hist.* one of two coequal magistrates or officials. □□ **du·um·vi·rate** /–virət/ *n.* [L f. *duum virum* of the two men]

du·vet /doováy/ *n.* a thick, soft quilt with a detachable cover, used instead of an upper sheet and blankets. [F]

dux /duks/ *n.* *Sc., Austral., NZ, & S.Afr.* the top pupil in a class or in a school. [L, = leader]

DV *abbr.* Deo volente.

DVD *abbr.* digital videodisc, a CD-ROM technology designed for high quality video display. D.V.M.

D.V.M. *abbr.* doctor of veterinary medicine.

dwarf /dwawrf/ *n. & v.* ● *n.* (*pl.* **dwarfs** or **dwarves** /dwawrvz/)
1 a *Offens.* a person of abnormally small stature, esp. one with a
normal-sized head and body but short limbs. b an animal or plant
much below the ordinary size for the species. 2 a small mythological being with supernatural powers. 3 (in full **dwarf star**) a small
usu. dense star. 4 (*attrib.*) a of a kind very small in size (*dwarf bean*).
b puny; stunted. ● *v.tr.* 1 stunt in growth. 2 cause (something similar or comparable) to seem small or insignificant (*efforts dwarfed
by their rivals' achievements*). □□ **dwarf•ish** *adj.* [OE *dweorg* f. Gmc]
dwarf•ism /dwáwrfizəm/ *n.* the condition of being a dwarf.
dweeb /dweeb/ *n. sl.* a studious or tedious person. [orig. unkn.]
dwell /dwel/ *v. & n.* ● *v.intr.* (*past* and *past part.* **dwelled** or **dwelt**)
1 *literary* (usu. foll. by *in, at, near, on*, etc.) live; reside (*dwelt in the
forest*). 2 (of a horse) be slow in raising its feet; pause before taking a fence. ● *n.* a slight, regular pause in the motion of a machine.
□ **dwell on** (or **upon**) 1 spend time on; linger over; write, brood, or
speak at length on (a specified subject) (*always dwells on his grievances*). 2 prolong (a note, a syllable, etc.). □□ **dwell•er** *n.* [OE *dwellan*
lead astray, later 'continue in a place,' f. Gmc]
dwell•ing /dwéling/ *n.* (also **dwell•ing place**) *formal* a house; a residence; an abode.
dwell•ing house *n.* a house used as a residence and not for business purposes.
DWI *abbr.* 1 driving while intoxicated. 2 Dutch West Indies.
dwin•dle /dwind'l/ *v.intr.* 1 become gradually smaller; shrink; waste
away. 2 lose importance; decline; degenerate. [*dwine* fade away f.
OE *dwīnan*, ON *dvina*]
dwt. *abbr. hist.* pennyweight.
d.w.t. *abbr.* deadweight ton(s); deadweight tonnage.
Dy *symb. Chem.* the element dysprosium.
dy•ad /díad/ *n. Math.* an operator which is a combination of two vectors. □□ **dy•ad•ic** /–ádik/ *adj.* [LL *dyas dyad-* f. Gk *duas duados* f.
duo two]
Dy•ak /díak/ *n.* var. of DAYAK.
dy•ar•chy var. of DIARCHY.
dyb•buk /díbook, deebóok/ *n.* (*pl.* **dybbukim** /dibóokim, dée-
bóokeem/ or **dybbuks**) a malevolent spirit in Jewish folklore. [Heb.
dibbūk f. *dābak* cling]
dye /dī/ *n. & v.* ● *n.* 1 a a substance used to change the color of hair,
fabric, wood, etc. b a color produced by this. 2 (in full **dyestuff**) a
substance yielding a dye, esp. for coloring materials in solution.
● *v.tr.* (**dye•ing**) 1 impregnate with dye. 2 make (a thing) a specified color with dye (*dyed it yellow*). □□ **dye•a•ble** *adj.* [OE *deag, dea-
gian*]
dyed-in-the-wool *adj.* 1 out and out; unchangeable; inveterate (-
dyed-in-the-wool conservative). 2 (of a fabric) made of yarn dyed in
its raw state.
dye•line /dílin/ *n.* a print made by the diazo process.
dy•er /díər/ *n.* a person who dyes cloth, etc.
dy•er's broom *n.* (also **dyer's greenweed, woadwaxen** a bushy,
yellow-flowered Eurasian plant, *Genista tinctoria*, formerly used to
make a yellow or green dye.
dy•ing /dí-ing/ *adj.* about to die, mortally ill; connected with, or at
the time of, death (*his dying words*). □ **to one's dying day** for the
rest of one's life. [pres. part. of DIE¹]
dyke¹ var. of DIKE¹.
dyke² /dīk/ *n.* (also **dike**) *sl.* (*often offensive*) a lesbian. [20th c.: orig.
unkn.]
dyn *abbr.* dyne(s).
dy•na•mic /dīnámik/ *adj. & n.* ● *adj.* (also **dy•nam•i•cal**) 1 energetic;
active; potent. 2 *Physics* a concerning motive force (opp. STATIC).
b concerning force in actual operation. 3 of or concerning dynamics. 4 *Mus.* relating to the volume of sound. 5 *Philos.* relating to dynamism. 6 (as **dynamical**) *Theol.* (of inspiration) endowing with
divine power, not impelling mechanically. ● *n.* 1 an energizing or
motive force. 2 *Mus.* = DYNAMICS 3. □□ **dy•nam•i•cal•ly** *adv.* [F
dynamique f. Gk *dunamikos* f. *dunamis* power]
dy•nam•ics /dīnámiks/ *n.pl.* 1 (usu. treated as *sing.*) a *Mech.* the
branch of mechanics concerned with the motion of bodies under
the action of forces (cf. STATICS). b the branch of any science in
which forces or changes are considered (*aerodynamics; population
dynamics*). 2 the motive forces, physical or moral, affecting behavior and change in any sphere. 3 *Mus.* the varying degree of volume of sound in musical performance. □□ **dynamicist** /–məsist/ *n.*
(in sense 1).

dy•nam•ic vis•cos•i•ty *n.* a quantity measuring the force needed to
overcome internal friction in a fluid.
dy•na•mism /dínəmizəm/ *n.* 1 energizing or dynamic action or power. 2 *Philos.* the theory that phenomena of matter or mind are due
to the action of forces (rather than to motion or matter). □□ **dy•na•
mist** *n.* [Gk *dunamis* power + –ISM]
dy•na•mite /dínəmīt/ *n. & v.* ● *n.* 1 a high explosive consisting of nitroglycerine mixed with an absorbent. 2 a potentially dangerous
person, thing, or situation. 3 *sl.* a narcotic, esp. heroin. ● *v.tr.* charge
or shatter with dynamite. □□ **dy•na•mit•er** *n.* [formed as DYNAMISM
+ –ITE¹]
dy•na•mo /dínəmō/ *n.* (*pl.* **•mos**) 1 a machine converting mechanical into electrical energy, esp. by rotating coils of copper wire in a
magnetic field. 2 *colloq.* an energetic person. [abbr. of *dynamoelec-
tric machine* f. Gk *dunamis* power, force]
dy•na•mom•e•ter /dínəmómitər/ *n.* an instrument measuring energy
expended. [F *dynamomètre* f. Gk *dunamis* power, force]
dy•nast /dínast, –nəst/ *n.* 1 a ruler. 2 a member of a dynasty. [L f.
Gk *dunastēs* f. *dunamai* be able]
dy•nas•ty /dínəstee/ *n.* (*pl.* **•ties**) 1 a line of hereditary rulers. 2 a succession of leaders in any field. □□ **dy•nas•tic** /–nástik/ *adj.* **dy•nas•
ti•cal•ly** *adv.* [F *dynastie* or LL *dynastia* f. Gk *dunasteia* lordship (as
DYNAST)]
dy•na•tron /dínətron/ *n. Electronics* a thermionic valve, used to generate continuous oscillations. [Gk *dunamis* power + –TRON]
dyne /dīn/ *n. Physics* a unit of force that, acting on a mass of one
gram, increases its velocity by one centimeter per second every second along the direction that it acts. ¶ Abbr.: **dyn.** [F f. Gk *dunamis*
force, power]
dys- /dis/ *comb. form* esp. *Med.* bad; difficult. [Gk *dus-* bad]
dys•en•ter•y /dísənteree/ *n.* a disease with inflammation of the
intestines, causing severe diarrhea with blood and mucus. □□ **dys•
en•ter•ic** *adj.* [OF *dissenterie* or L *dysenteria* f. Gk *dusenteria* (as DYS-,
enteria f. *entera* bowels)]
dys•func•tion /dísfúngkshən/ *n.* an abnormality or impairment of
function. □□ **dys•func•tion•al** *adj.*
dys•graph•i•a /disgráfeeə/ *n.* an inability to write coherently. □□ **dys•
graph•ic** *adj.* [DYS- + Gk *graphia* writing]
dys•lex•i•a /dislékseeə/ *n.* an abnormal difficulty in reading and
spelling, caused by a condition of the brain. □□ **dys•lex•ic** *adj. &
n.* **dys•lec•tic** /–léktik/ *adj. & n.* [G *Dyslexie* (as DYS-, Gk *lexis*
speech)]
dys•men•or•rhe•a /dísmenəréeə/ *n.* painful or difficult menstruation.
dys•pep•sia /dispépseeə/ *n.* indigestion. [L *dyspepsia* f. Gk *duspep-
sia* (as DYS-, *peptos* cooked, digested)]
dys•pep•tic /dispéptik/ *adj. & n.* ● *adj.* of or relating to dyspepsia or
the resulting depression. ● *n.* a person suffering from dyspepsia.
dys•pha•sia /disfáyzhə, –zheeə/ *n. Med.* lack of coordination in
speech, owing to brain damage. □□ **dys•pha•sic** /–zik, –sik/ *adj.* [Gk
dusphatos hard to utter (as DYS-, PHATIC)]
dys•pho•ri•a /disfáwreeə/ *n.* a state of unease or mental discomfort.
□□ **dys•phor•ic** /–fáwrik/ *adj.* [Gk *dusphoria* f. *dusphoros* hard to bear
(as DYS-, *pherō* bear)]
dys•pla•sia /displáyzhə, –zheeə/ *n. Med.* abnormal growth of tissues,
etc. □□ **dys•plas•tic** /–plástik/ *adj.* [mod.L, formed as DYS- + Gk *plasis* formation]
dysp•ne•a /dispneéə/ *n.* (*Brit.* **dysp•noe•a**) *Med.* difficult or labored
breathing. □□ **dysp•ne•ic** *adj.* [L f. Gk *duspnoia* (as DYS-, *pneō*
breathe)]
dys•pro•si•um /disprózeeəm/ *n. Chem.* a naturally occurring soft
metallic element of the lanthanide series, used as a component in
certain magnetic alloys. ¶ Symb.: **Dy.** [mod.L f. Gk *dusprositos* hard
to get at + –IUM]
dys•to•cia /distóshə/ *n. Med.* difficult or prolonged childbirth. [DYS-
+ Gk *tokos* childbirth]
dys•tro•phy /dístrəfee/ *n.* defective nutrition. □□ **dys•troph•ic** /dis-
trófik, –tró–/ *adj.* [mod.L *dystrophia* formed as DYS- + Gk –*trophia*
nourishment]
dys•u•ri•a /disyóoreeə/ *n.* painful or difficult urination. [LL f. Gk
dusouria (as DYS-, *ouron* urine)]
dz. *abbr.* dozen.
dzho /zō, dzō, zhō/ *n.* (also **dzo, zho**) (*pl.* same or **zhos**) a hybrid of
a cow and a yak. [Tibetan *ṃdso*]

E

E¹ /ee/ *n.* (also **e**) (*pl.* **Es** or **E's**) **1** the fifth letter of the alphabet. **2** *Mus.* the third note of the diatonic scale of C major.

E² *abbr.* (also **E.**) **1** east; eastern. **2** English. **3** energy. **4** see E-NUMBER.

e *symb.* **1** *Math.* the base of natural logarithms, equal to approx. 2.71828. **2** used on packaging (in conjunction with specification of weight, size, etc.) to indicate compliance with EEC regulations.

e- /ee, e/ *prefix* form of EX-¹ 1 before some consonants.

ea. *abbr.* each.

each /eech/ *adj. & pron.* ● *adj.* every one of two or more persons or things, regarded separately (*each person; five in each class*). ● *pron.* each person or thing (*each of us; have two books each; cost a penny each*). □ **each and every** every single. [OE *ælc* f.WG (as AYE², ALIKE)]
▶See note at BOTH.

each oth·er one another (used as a compound reciprocal pron.: *they hate each other; they wore each other's hats*).

ea·ger /eégər/ *adj.* **1 a** full of keen desire; enthusiastic. **b** (of passions, etc.) keen; impatient. **2** keen; impatient; strongly desirous (*eager to learn; eager for news*). □□ **ea·ger·ly** *adv.* **ea·ger·ness** *n.* [ME f. AF *egre*, OF *aigre* keen, ult. f. L *acer acris*]
▶See note at ANXIOUS.

ea·ger bea·ver *n. colloq.* a very or excessively diligent person; an over-zealous person.

ea·gle /eégəl/ *n.* **1 a** any of various large birds of prey of the family Accipitridae, with keen vision and powerful flight. **b** a figure of an eagle, esp. as a symbol of the US, or formerly as a Roman or French ensign. **2** *Golf* a score of two strokes under par at any hole. **3** *US* a gold coin worth ten dollars. [ME f. AF *egle*, OF *aigle* f. L *aquila*]

ea·gle eye *n.* keen sight, watchfulness. □□ **ea·gle-eyed** *adj.*

ea·gle owl *n.* any large owl of the genus *Bubo*, with long ear tufts.

Ea·gle Scout *n.* the highest rank a Boy Scout can attain.

ea·glet /eéglit/ *n.* a young eagle. [OE *ēare* f. Gmc: rel. to L *auris*, Gk *ous*]

ea·gre /eégər, áygər/ *n.* esp. *Brit.* = BORE³. [17th c.: orig. unkn.]

-ean /eéən/ *suffix* var. of –AN.

ear¹ /eer/ *n.* **1 a** the organ of hearing and balance in humans and other vertebrates, esp. the external part of this. **b** an organ sensitive to sound in other animals. **2** the faculty for discriminating sounds (*an ear for music*). **3** an ear-shaped thing, esp. the handle of a jug. **4** listening; attention. □ **all ears** listening attentively. **bring about one's ears** bring down upon oneself. **give ear to** listen to. **have a person's ear** receive a favorable hearing. **have** (or **keep**) **an ear to the ground** be alert to rumors or the trend of opinion. **in one ear and out the other** heard but disregarded or quickly forgotten. **out on one's ear** dismissed ignominiously. **up to one's ears** (often foll. by *in*) *colloq.* deeply involved or occupied. □□ **eared** *adj.* (also in *comb.*). **ear·less** *adj.* [OE *ēare* f. Gmc: rel. to L *auris*, Gk *ous*]

ear² /eer/ *n.* the seed-bearing head of a cereal plant. [OE *ēar* f. Gmc]

ear·ache /eérayk/ *n.* a (usu. prolonged) pain in the ear.

ear·bash /eérbash/ *v.tr.* esp. *Austral. sl.* talk inordinately to; harangue. □□ **ear·bash·er** *n.*

ear·drop /eérdrop/ *n.* a hanging earring.

ear drops *n.* medicinal drops for the ears.

ear·drum /eérdrum/ *n.* the membrane of the middle ear (= TYMPANIC MEMBRANE).

ear·ful /eérfŏŏl/ *n.* (*pl.* **-fuls**) *colloq.* **1** a copious or prolonged amount of talking. **2** a strong reprimand.

earl /ərl/ *n.* a British nobleman ranking between a marquess and a viscount (cf. COUNT²). □□ **earl·dom** *n.* [OE *eorl*, of unkn. orig.]

earl·lobe /eérlōb/ *n.* the lower soft pendulous external part of the ear.

earl pal·a·tine *n. hist.* an earl having royal authority within his country or domain.

ear·ly /ə́rlee/ *adj., adv., & n.* ● *adj. & adv.* (**ear·li·er**, **ear·li·est**) **1** before the due, usual, or expected time (*was early for my appointment; the train arrived early*). **2 a** not far on in the day or night, or in time (*early evening; at the earliest opportunity*). **b** prompt (*early payment appreciated; at your earliest convenience*). **3 a** not far on in a period, development, or process of evolution; being the first stage (*Early English architecture; the early Christians; early spring*). **b** of the distant past (*early man*). **c** not far on in a sequence or serial order (*the early chapters; appears early on the list*). **4 a** of childhood, esp. the preschool years (*early learning*). **b** (of a piece of writing, music, etc.) immature; youthful (*an early work*). **5** forward in flowering, ripening, etc. (*early peaches*). ● *n.* (*pl.* **-lies**) (usu. in *pl.*) an early fruit or vegetable, esp. potatoes. □ **at the earliest** (often placed after a specified time) not before (*will arrive on Monday at the earliest*). **early** (or **earlier**) **on** at an early (or earlier) stage. □□ **ear·li·ness** *n.* [orig. as adv., f. OE *ǣrlīce, ārlīce* (*ǣr* ERE)]

ear·ly bird *n. colloq.* one who arrives, gets up, etc., early.

ear·ly grave *n.* an untimely or premature death.

ear·ly warn·ing *n.* an advance indication of a dangerous or threatening situation.

ear·mark /eérmaark/ *n. & v.* ● *n.* **1** an identifying mark. **2** an owner's mark on the ear of an animal. ● *v.tr.* **1** set aside (money, etc.) for a special purpose. **2** mark (sheep, etc.) with such a mark.

ear·muff /eérmuf/ *n.* a wrap or cover for the ears, protecting them from cold, noise, etc.

earn /ərn/ *v.tr.* **1** (also *absol.*) **a** (of a person) obtain (income) in the form of money in return for labor or services (*earn a weekly wage; happy to be earning at last*). **b** (of capital invested) bring in as interest or profit. **2 a** deserve; be entitled to; obtain as the reward for hard work or merit (*have earned a vacation; earned our admiration; earn one's keep*). **b** incur (a reproach, reputation, etc.). [OE *earnian* f.WG, rel. to Gmc roots assoc. with reaping]

earned in·come *n.* income derived from wages, etc. (opp. UNEARNED INCOME).

earn·er /ə́rnər/ *n.* **1** a person or thing that earns (often in *comb.*: *wage earner*). **2** *Brit. sl.* a lucrative job or enterprise.

ear·nest¹ /ə́rnist/ *adj. & n.* ● *adj.* ardently or intensely serious; zealous; not trifling or joking. ● *n.* seriousness. □ **in** (or **in real**) **earnest** serious(ly), not joking(ly); with determination. □□ **ear·nest·ly** *adv.* **ear·nest·ness** *n.* [OE *eornust, eornost* (with Gmc cognates): cf. ON *ern* vigorous]

ear·nest² /ə́rnist/ *n.* **1** money paid as an installment, esp. to confirm a contract, etc. **2** a token or foretaste (*in earnest of what is to come*). [ME *ernes*, prob. var. of *erles, arles* prob. f. med.L *arrhula* (unrecorded) f. *arr(h)a* pledge]

earn·ings /ə́rningz/ *n.pl.* money earned.

earn·ings-re·lat·ed *adj.* (of benefit, a pension, etc.) calculated on the basis of past or present income.

ear·phone /eérfōn/ *n.* a device applied to the ear to aid hearing or receive radio or telephone communications.

ear·piece /eérpees/ *n.* the part of a telephone, etc., applied to the ear during use.

ear-pierc·ing *adj.* loud and shrill (*an ear-piercing scream*).

ear·plug /eérplug/ *n.* a piece of wax, etc., placed in the ear to protect against cold air, water, or noise.

ear·ring /eéring/ *n.* a piece of jewelry worn in or on (esp. the lobe of) the ear.

ear·shot /eérshot/ *n.* the distance over which something can be heard (esp. within or out of earshot).

ear-split·ting /eérspliting/ *adj.* excessively loud.

earth /ərth/ *n. & v.* ● *n.* **1 a** (also **Earth**) one of the planets of the solar system orbiting about the sun between Venus and Mars; the planet on which we live. **b** land and sea, as distinct from sky. **2 a** dry land; the ground (*fell to earth*). **b** soil; clay; mold. **c** bodily matter (*earth to earth*). **3** *Relig.* the present abode of mankind, as distinct from heaven or hell; the world. **4** *Brit. Electr.* = GROUND¹ *n.* 11. **5** the hole of a badger, fox, etc. **6** (prec. by *the*) *colloq.* a huge amount; everything (*cost the earth*; *want the earth*). • *v.* **1** *tr.* (foll. by *up*) cover (the roots and lower stems of plants) with heaped-up earth. **2** *a tr.* drive (a fox) to its earth. **b** *intr.* (of a fox, etc.) run to its earth. **3** *tr. Brit. Electr.* = GROUND[1] *v.* 5. □ **come back** (or **down**) **to earth** return to reality. **gone to earth** in hiding. **on earth** *colloq.* **1** existing anywhere (*the happiest man on earth*; *looked like nothing on earth*. **2** as an intensifier (*what on earth?*). □□ **earth·ward** *adj. & adv.* **earth·wards** *adv.* [OE *eorthe* f. Gmc]

earth·bound /ə́rthbownd/ *adj.* **1** attached to the earth or earthly things. **2** moving toward the earth.

earth·en /ə́rthən/ *adj.* **1** made of earth. **2** made of baked clay.

earth·en·ware /ə́rthənwair/ *n. & adj.* • *n.* pottery, vessels, etc., made of clay fired to a porous state, which can be made impervious to liquids by the use of a glaze (cf. PORCELAIN). • *adj.* made of fired clay. [EARTHEN + WARE[1]]

earth·ling /ə́rthling/ *n.* an inhabitant of the earth, esp. as regarded in fiction by outsiders.

earth·ly /ə́rthlee/ *adj.* **1 a** of the earth; terrestrial. **b** of human life on earth; worldly; material; carnal. **2** (usu. with *neg.*) *colloq.* remotely possible or conceivable (*is no earthly use*; *there wasn't an earthly reason*). □ **not stand** (or **have**) **an earthly chance** *Brit. colloq.* have no chance at all. □□ **earth·li·ness** *n.*

earth moth·er *n.* **1** *Mythol.* a spirit or deity symbolizing the earth. **2** a sensual and maternal woman.

earth·mov·er /ə́rthmoovər/ *n.* a tractorlike vehicle, as a bulldozer, for pushing and hauling large amounts of earth at excavation sites.

earth·nut /ə́rthnut/ *n.* any of various plants, or its edible roundish tuber, esp.: **1** an umbelliferous woodland plant, *Conopodium majus.* **2** the peanut.

earth·quake /ə́rthkwayk/ *n.* **1** a convulsion of the superficial parts of the earth due to the release of accumulated stress as a result of faults in strata or volcanic action. **2** a social, etc., disturbance.

earth sci·enc·es *n.* the sciences concerned with the earth or part of it, or its atmosphere (e.g., geology, oceanography, meteorology).

earth·shat·ter·ing *n. colloq.* having a traumatic or devastating effect. □□ **earth·shat·ter·ing·ly** *adv.*

earth·shine /ə́rthshīn/ *n. Astron.* **1** the unilluminated portion of a crescent moon shining faintly because of sunlight reflected from the earth to the moon. **2** illumination on the moon's surface caused by this.

earth·star /ə́rthstaar/ *n.* any woodland fungus of the genus *Geastrum*, esp. *G. triplex*, with a spherical spore-containing fruit body surrounded by a fleshy star-shaped structure.

earth·work /ə́rthwərk/ *n.* **1** an artificial bank of earth in fortification or road building, etc. **2** the process of excavating soil in civil engineering work.

earth·worm /ə́rthwərm/ *n.* any of various annelid worms, esp. of the genus *Lumbricus* or *Allolobophora*, living and burrowing in the ground.

earth·y /ə́rthee/ *adj.* (**earth·i·er**, **earth·i·est**) **1** of or like earth or soil. **2** somewhat coarse or crude; unrefined (*earthy humor*). □□ **earth·i·ly** *adv.* **earth·i·ness** *n.*

ear trum·pet *n.* a trumpet-shaped device formerly used as a hearing aid.

ear·wax /ə́erwaks/ *n.* a yellow waxy secretion produced by the ear, = CERUMEN.

ear·wig /ə́erwig/ *n. & v.* • *n.* **1** any small elongate insect of the order Dermaptera, with a pair of terminal appendages in the shape of forceps. **2** a small centipede. • *v.tr.* (**ear·wigged**, **ear·wig·ging**) *archaic* influence (a person) by secret communication. [OE *ēarwicga* f. *ēare* EAR[1] + *wicga* earwig, prob. rel. to *wiggle*: once thought to enter the head through the ear]

ease /eez/ *n. & v.* • *n.* **1** absence of difficulty; facility; effortlessness (*did it with ease*). **2 a** freedom or relief from pain, anxiety, or trouble. **b** freedom from embarrassment or awkwardness. **c** freedom or relief from constraint or formality. **d** freedom from poverty. • *v.* **1** *tr.* **a** relieve from pain or anxiety, etc. (often foll. by *of*: *eased my mind*; *eased me of the burden*). **b** make easy or easier; help; facilitate. **2** *intr.* (often foll. by *off*, *up*) **a** become less painful or burdensome. **b** relax; begin to take it easy. **c** slow down; moderate one's behavior, habits, etc. **3** *tr. joc.* rob or extract money, etc., from (*let me ease you of your loose change*). **4** *intr. Meteorol.* become less severe (*the wind will ease tonight*). **5 a** *tr.* relax; slacken; make a less tight fit. **b** *tr. & intr.* (foll. by *through*, *into*, etc.) move or be moved carefully into place (*eased it into the hole*). **6** *intr.* (often foll. by *off*) *Stock Exch.* (of shares, etc.) descend in price or value. □ **at ease 1** free from anxiety or constraint. **2** *Mil.* **a** in a relaxed attitude, with the feet apart. **b** the order to stand in this way. **at one's ease** free from embarrassment, awkwardness, or undue formality. **ease away** (or **down** or **off**) *Naut.*

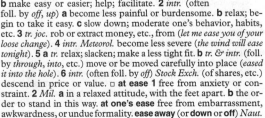

earwig 1

slacken (a rope, sail, etc.). □□ **eas·er** *n.* [ME f. AF *ese*, OF *eise*, ult. f. L *adjacens* ADJACENT]

ea·sel /ee´zəl/ *n.* **1** a standing frame, usu. of wood, for supporting an artist's work, a blackboard, etc. **2** an artist's work collectively. [Du. *ezel* = G *Esel* ASS[1]]

ease·ment /ee´zmənt/ *n. Law* a right of way or a similar right over another's land. [ME f. OF *aisement*]

eas·i·ly /ee´zilee/ *adv.* **1** without difficulty. **2** by far (*easily the best*). **3** very probably (*it could easily snow*).

east /eest/ *n., adj., & adv.* • *n.* **1 a** the point of the horizon where the sun rises at the equinoxes (cardinal point 90° to the right of north). **b** the compass point corresponding to this. **c** the direction in which this lies. **2** (usu. **the East**) **a** the regions or countries lying to the east of Europe. **b** the formerly Communist nations of eastern Europe. **3** the eastern part of a country, town, etc. **4** (**East**) *Bridge* a player occupying the position designated "east." • *adj.* **1** toward, at, near, or facing east. **2** coming from the east (*east wind*). • *adv.* **1** toward, at, or near the east. **2** (foll. by *of*) further east than. □ **to the east** (often foll. by *of*) in an easterly direction. [OE *ēast-* f. Gmc]

easel

east·bound /ee´stbownd/ *adj.* traveling or leading eastward.

East End *n.* the part of London east of the city as far as the River Lea.

Eas·ter /ee´stər/ *n.* **1** (also **Eas·ter Sun·day** or **Day**) the festival (held on a variable Sunday in March or April) commemorating Christ's resurrection. **2** the season in which this occurs, esp. the weekend from Good Friday to Easter Monday. [OE *ēastre* app. f. *Ēostre*, a goddess associated with spring, f. Gmc]

Eas·ter egg *n.* **1** an egg that is dyed and often decorated as part of the Easter celebration. **2** an artificial usu. chocolate egg given at Easter, esp. to children.

east·er·ly /ee´stərlee/ *adj., adv., & n.* • *adj. & adv.* **1** in an eastern position or direction. **2** (of a wind) blowing from the east. • *n.* (*pl.* **·lies**) a wind blowing from the east.

east·ern /ee´stərn/ *adj.* **1** of or in the east; inhabiting the east. **2** lying or directed toward the east. **3** (**Eastern**) of or in the Far, Middle, or Near East. □□ **east·ern·most** *adj.* [OE *ēasterne* (as EAST, –ERN)]

East·ern Church *n.* **1** another name for the Orthodox Church. **2** any of the Christian churches originating in eastern Europe and the Middle East.

East·ern·er /ee´stərnər/ *n.* a native or inhabitant of the east; esp. in the US.

east·ern hem·i·sphere *n.* (also **East·ern Hem·i·sphere**) the half of the earth containing Europe, Asia, and Africa.

East·ern time *n.* standard time used in the eastern US and eastern Canada or in eastern Australia.

Eas·ter·tide /ee´stərtīd/ *n.* the period following Easter.

East Ger·man·ic *n.* an extinct group of Germanic languages, including Gothic.

East In·di·a·man *n. hist.* a large ship engaged in trade with the East Indies.

East In·dies *n.* the islands, etc., east of India, esp. the Malay archipelago.

east·ing /ee´sting/ *n. Naut.*, etc., the distance traveled or the angle of longitude measured eastward from either a defined north–south grid line or a meridian.

east-north-east *n.* (also **east-south-east**) the direction or compass point midway between east and northeast (or southeast).

east·ward /ee´stwərd/ *adj., adv., & n.* • *adj. & adv.* (also **east·wards**) toward the east. • *n.* an eastward direction or region. □□ **east·ward·ly** *adj. & adv.*

eas·y /ee´zee/ *adj., adv., & int.* (**eas·i·er**, **eas·i·est**) • *adj.* **1** not difficult; achieved without great effort. **2 a** free from pain, discomfort, anxiety, etc. **b** comfortably off; affluent (*easy circumstances*). **3** free from embarrassment, awkwardness, constraint, or pressure; relaxed and pleasant (*an easy manner*). **4 a** not strict; tolerant. **b** compliant; obliging; easily persuaded (*an easy touch*). **5** *Stock Exch.* (of goods, money on loan, etc.) not much in demand. • *adv.* with ease; in an effortless or relaxed manner. • *int.* go carefully; move gently. □ **easy as pie** see PIE[1]. **easy come easy go** *colloq.* what is easily obtained is soon lost or spent. **easy does it** *colloq.* go carefully. **easy of access** easily entered or approached. **easy on the eye** (or **ear**, etc.) *colloq.* pleasant to look at (or listen to, etc.). **go easy** (foll. by *with*, *on*) be sparing or cautious. **I'm easy** *colloq.* I have no preference. **of easy virtue** (of a woman) sexually promiscuous. **stand easy!** *Brit. Mil.* permission to a squad standing at ease to relax their attitude further. **take it easy 1** proceed gently or carefully. **2** relax; avoid overwork. □□ **eas·i·ness** *n.* [ME f. AF *aisé*, OF *aisié* past part. of *aisier* EASE]

easy chair *n.* a large, comfortable, upholstered chair, usu. an armchair.

eas•y•go•ing /éezeegóing/ *adj.* **1** placid and tolerant; relaxed in manner; accepting things as they are. **2** (of a horse) having an easy gait.

eas•y mon•ey *n.* money obtained without effort (esp. of dubious legality).

eas•y street *n. colloq.* a situation of ease or affluence.

eas•y touch *n. sl.* a person who readily parts with money.

eat /eet/ *v.* (*past* **ate** /ayt/, esp. *Brit.* /et/; *past part.* **eat•en** /éet'n/) **1 a** *tr.* take into the mouth, chew, and swallow (food). **b** *intr.* consume food; take a meal. **c** *tr.* devour (*eaten by a lion*). **2** *intr.* (foll. by *away*, *into*, or *up*) **a** destroy gradually, esp. by corrosion, erosion, disease, etc. **b** begin to consume or diminish (resources, etc.). **3** *tr. colloq.* trouble; vex (*what's eating you?*). □ **eat dirt** see DIRT. **eat one's hat** *colloq.* admit one's surprise in being wrong (only as a proposition unlikely to be fulfilled: *said he would eat his hat*). **eat one's heart out** suffer from excessive longing or envy. **eat humble pie** see HUMBLE. **eat out** have a meal away from home, esp. in a restaurant. **eat out of a person's hand** be entirely submissive to a person. **eat salt with** see SALT. **eat up 1** (also *absol.*) eat or consume completely. **2** use or deal with rapidly or wastefully (*eats up time; eats up the miles*). **3** encroach upon or annex (*eating up the neighboring countries*). **4** absorb; preoccupy (*eaten up with pride*). **eat one's words** admit that one was wrong. [OE *etan* f. Gmc]

eat•a•ble /éetəbəl/ *adj.* & *n.* • *adj.* that is in a condition to be eaten (cf. EDIBLE). • *n.* (usu. in *pl.*) food.

eat•er /éetər/ *n.* **1** a person who eats (*a big eater*). **2** *Brit.* an eating apple, etc.

eat•er•y /éetəree/ *n.* (*pl.* **•ies**) *colloq.* a restaurant, esp. a diner, luncheonette, etc.

eat•ing /éeting/ *adj.* **1** suitable for eating (*eating apple*). **2** used for eating (*eating room*).

eat•ing dis•or•der *n.* a neurotic condition, such as anorexia nervosa or bulimia, in which a person does not eat normally.

eats /eets/ *n.pl. colloq.* food.

eau de co•logne /ódəkəlón/ *n.* an alcohol-based perfume of a kind made orig. at Cologne. [F, lit. 'water of Cologne']

eau-de-vie /ódəvée/ *n.* spirits, esp. brandy. [F, lit. 'water of life']

eaves /eevz/ *n.pl.* the underside of a projecting roof. [orig. sing., f. OE *efes*: prob. rel. to OVER]

eaves•drop /éevzdrop/ *v.intr.* (**•dropped, •drop•ping**) listen secretly to a private conversation. □□ **eaves•drop•per** *n.*

WORD HISTORY eavesdrop

Early 17th century: back-formation from *eavesdropper* (late Middle English) 'a person who listens from under the eaves,' from the obsolete noun *eavesdrop* 'the ground on to which water drips from the eaves,' probably from Old Norse *upsardropi*, from *ups* 'eaves' + *dropi* 'a drop.'

ebb /eb/ *n.* & *v.* • *n.* **1** the movement of the tide out to sea (also *attrib.*: *ebb tide*). **2** the process of draining away of floodwater, etc. **3** the process of declining or diminishing; the state of being in decline. • *v.intr.* (often foll. by *away*) **1** (of tidewater) flow out to sea; recede; drain away. **2** decline; run low (*his life was ebbing away*). □ **at a low ebb** in a poor condition or state of decline. **on the ebb** in decline. [OE *ebba*, *ebbian*]

ebb and flow *n.* a continuing process of decline and upturn in circumstances.

E•bon•ics /eebóniks/ *n.pl.* the English used by Black Americans, regarded as a language in its own right.

eb•on•ite /ébənīt/ *n.* = VULCANITE. [EBONY + -ITE[1]]

eb•on•y /ébənee/ *n.* & *adj.* • *n.* (*pl.* **•ies**) **1** a heavy, hard, dark wood used for furniture. **2** any of various trees of the genus *Diospyros* producing this. • *adj.* **1** made of ebony. **2** black like ebony. [earlier *hebeny* f. (*h*)*eben*(*e*) = *ebon*, perh. after *ivory*]

e•bul•lient /ibúlyənt, ibŏŏl-/ *adj.* **1** exuberant; high-spirited. **2** *Chem.* boiling. □□ **e•bul•lience** /-yəns/ *n.* **e•bul•lien•cy** *n.* **e•bul•lient•ly** *adv.* [L *ebullire ebullient-* bubble out (as E-, *bullire* boil)]

EC *abbr.* **1** European Community. **2** executive committee.

ecad /éekad/ *n. Ecol.* an organism modified by its environment. [Gk *oikos* house + -AD[1]]

é•car•té /aykaartáy/ *n.* **1** a card game for two persons in which cards from a player's hand may be exchanged for others from the pack. **2** a position in classical ballet with one arm and leg extended. [F, past part. of *écarter* discard]

ecce homo /ékay hómō, éksee/ *n. Art* one of the subjects of the Passion cycle: in Renaissance painting typically a depiction of Christ wearing the crown of thorns. [L, = 'behold the man,' the words of Pilate to the Jews after the crowning with thorns (John 19:5)]

ec•cen•tric /ikséntrik, ek-/ *adj.* & *n.* • *adj.* **1** odd or capricious in behavior or appearance; whimsical. **2 a** not placed or not having its axis, etc., placed centrally. **b** (often foll. by *to*) (of a circle) not concentric (to another). **c** (of an orbit) not circular. • *n.* **1** an eccentric person. **2** *Mech.* an eccentric contrivance for changing rotatory into backward-and-forward motion, e.g., the cam used in an internal combustion engine. □□ **ec•cen•tri•cal•ly** *adv.* **ec•cen•tric•i•ty** /éksentrísitee/ *n.* (*pl.* **•ties**). [LL *eccentricus* f. Gk *ekkentros* f. *ek* out of + *kentros* CENTER]

eccl. *abbr.* **1** ecclesiastic. **2** ecclesiastical.

Eccles. *abbr.* Ecclesiastes (Old Testament).

ec•cle•si•al /ikléezeeəl/ *adj.* of or relating to a church. [Gk *ekklesia* assembly, church f. *ekklētos* summoned out f. *ek* out + *kaleō* call]

ec•cle•si•as•tic /ikléezeeástik/ *n.* & *adj.* • *n.* a priest or clergyman. • *adj.* = ECCLESIASTICAL. □□ **ec•cle•si•as•ti•cism** /-tisizəm/ *n.* [F *ecclésiastique* or LL *ecclesiasticus* f. Gk *ekklēsiastikos* f. *ekklēsia* assembly, church: see ECCLESIAL]

ec•cle•si•as•ti•cal /ikléezeeástikəl/ *adj.* of the church or the clergy. □□ **ec•cle•si•as•ti•cal•ly** *adv.*

ec•cle•si•ol•o•gy /ikléezeeóləjee/ *n.* **1** the study of churches, esp. church building and decoration. **2** theology as applied to the nature and structure of the Christian Church. □□ **ec•cle•si•o•log•i•cal** /-zeeəlójikəl/ *adj.* **ec•cle•si•ol•o•gist** *n.* [Gk *ekklēsia* assembly, church (see ECCLESIAL) + -LOGY]

Ecclus. *abbr.* Ecclesiasticus (Apocrypha).

ec•crine /ékrin, -rīn, -reen/ *adj.* (of a gland, e.g., a sweat gland) secreting without loss of cell material. [Gk *ek* out of + *krinō* sift]

ec•dy•sis /ékdisis/ *n.* the action of casting off skin or shedding an exoskeleton, etc. [mod.L f. Gk *ekdusis* f. *ekduō* put off]

ECG *abbr.* electrocardiogram.

ech•e•lon /éshəlon/ *n.* & *v.* • *n.* **1** a level or rank in an organization, in society, etc.; those occupying it (often in *pl.*: *the upper echelons*). **2** *Mil.* a formation of troops, ships, aircraft, etc., in parallel rows with the end of each row projecting further than the one in front (*in echelon*). • *v.tr.* arrange in an echelon. [F *échelon* f. *échelle* ladder f. L *scala*]

ech•e•ve•ri•a /échəvərée̱ə/ *n.* any succulent plant of the genus *Echeveria*, native to Central and S. America. [M. *Echeveri*, 19th-c. Mex. botanical illustrator]

e•chid•na /ikídnə/ *n.* any of several egg-laying, pouch-bearing mammals native to Australia and New Guinea, with a covering of spines, and having a long snout and long claws. Also called **spiny anteater**. [mod.L f. Gk *ekhidna* viper]

e•chi•no•derm /ikínədərm/ *n.* any marine invertebrate of the phylum Echinodermata, usu. having a spiny skin, e.g., starfish and sea urchins. [ECHINUS + Gk *derma -atos* skin]

e•chi•noid /ikínoyd/ *n.* a sea urchin.

e•chi•nus /ikínəs/ *n.* **1** any sea urchin of the genus *Echinus*, including the common European edible urchin, *E. esculentus*. **2** *Archit.* a rounded molding below an abacus on a Doric or Ionic capital. [ME f. L f. Gk *ekhinos* hedgehog, sea urchin]

ech•o /ékō/ *n.* & *v.* • *n.* (*pl.* **•oes** or **•os**) **1 a** the repetition of a sound by the reflection of sound waves. **b** the secondary sound produced. **2** a reflected radio or radar beam. **3** a close imitation or repetition of something already done. **4** a person who slavishly repeats the words or opinions of another. **5** (often in *pl.*) circumstances or events reminiscent of or remotely connected with earlier ones. **6** *Bridge*, etc., a conventional mode of play to show the number of cards held in the suit led, etc. • *v.* (**•oes, •oed**) **1** *intr.* **a** (of a place) resound with an echo. **b** (of a sound) be repeated; resound. **2** *tr.* repeat (a sound) by an echo. **3** *tr.* **a** repeat (another's words). **b** imitate the words, opinions, or actions of (a person). □□ **ech•o•er** *n.* **ech•o•less** *adj.* [ME f. OF or L f. Gk *ēkhō*, rel. to *ēkhē* a sound]

ech•o•car•di•o•gram /ékōkaárdeeəgram/ *n. Med.* a record produced by echocardiography.

ech•o•car•di•og•ra•phy /ékōkaárdeeógrəfee/ *n. Med.* the use of ultrasound waves to investigate the action of the heart. □□ **ech•o•car•di•o•graph** /-deeəgraf/ *n.* **ech•o•car•di•og•ra•pher** *n.*

ech•o cham•ber *n.* an enclosure with sound-reflecting walls, used esp. for recording purposes.

ech•o•en•ceph•a•lo•gram /ékōenséfələgram/ *n. Med.* a record produced by echoencephalography.

ech•o•en•ceph•a•log•ra•phy /ékōenséfəlógrəfee/ *n. Med.* the use of ultrasound waves to investigate intracranial structures.

ech•o•gram /ékōgram/ *n.* a record made by an echo sounder.

ech•o•graph /ékōgraf/ *n.* a device for automatically recording echograms.

e•cho•ic /ekóik/ *adj. Phonet.* (of a word) imitating the sound it represents; onomatopoeic. □□ **e•cho•i•cal•ly** *adv.*

ech•o•ism /ékōizəm/ *n.* = ONOMATOPOEIA.

ech•o•la•li•a /ékōláyleeə/ *n.* **1** the meaningless repetition of another person's spoken words. **2** the repetition of speech by a child learning to talk. [mod.L f. Gk *ēkhō* echo + *lalia* talk]

ech•o•lo•ca•tion /ékōlōkáyshən/ *n.* the location of objects by reflected sound.

ech•o sound•er *n.* sounding apparatus for determining the depth of the sea beneath a ship by measuring the time taken for an echo to be received. □□ **ech•o-sound•ing** *n.*

ech·o verse *n.* a verse form in which a line repeats the last syllables of the previous line.

ech·o·vi·rus /ékōvīrəs/ *n.* (also **ECHO vi·rus**) any of a group of enteroviruses sometimes causing mild meningitis, encephalitis, etc. [f. *enteric cytopathogenic human orphan* (because not originally assignable to any known disease) + VIRUS]

echt /ekht/ *adj.* authentic; genuine; typical. [G]

é·clair /aykláir/ *n.* a small, elongated light pastry filled with whipped cream or custard and iced with chocolate or coffee icing. [F, lit. lightning, flash]

é·clair·cisse·ment /aykláirseesmón/ *n. archaic* an enlightening explanation of something hitherto inexplicable (e.g., conduct, etc.). [F f. *éclaircir* clear up]

ec·lamp·si·a /iklámpseeə/ *n.* a condition involving convulsions leading to coma, occurring esp. in pregnant women. □□ **ec·lamp·tic** *adj.* [mod.L f. F *eclampsie* f. Gk *eklampsis* sudden development f. *eklampō* shine forth]

é·clat /aykláá/ *n.* **1** brilliant display; dazzling effect. **2** social distinction; conspicuous success; universal approbation (*with great éclat*). [F f. *éclater* burst out]

ec·lec·tic /ikléktik/ *adj. & n.* ● *adj.* **1** deriving ideas, tastes, style, etc., from various sources. **2** *Philos. & Art* selecting one's beliefs, etc., from various sources; attached to no particular school of philosophy. ● *n.* **1** an eclectic person. **2** a person who subscribes to an eclectic school of thought. □□ **ec·lec·ti·cal·ly** *adv.* **ec·lec·ti·cism** /–tisizəm/ *n.* [Gk *eklektikos* f. *eklegō* pick out]

e·clipse /iklíps/ *n. & v.* ● *n.* **1** the obscuring of the reflected light from one celestial body by the passage of another between it and the eye or between it and its source of illumination. **2 a** a deprivation of light or the period of this. **b** obscuration or concealment; a period of this. **3** a rapid or sudden loss of importance or prominence, esp. in relation to another or a newly arrived person or thing. ● *v.tr.* **1** (of a celestial body) obscure the light from or to (another). **2** intercept (light, esp. of a lighthouse). **3** deprive of prominence or importance; outshine; surpass. □ **in eclipse 1** surpassed; in decline. **2** (of a bird) having lost its courting plumage. □□ **e·clips·er** *n.* [ME f. OF f. L f. Gk *ekleipsis* f. *ekleipō* fail to appear, be eclipsed f. *leipō* leave]

e·clip·tic /iklíptik/ *n. & adj.* ● *n.* the sun's apparent path among the stars during the year. ● *adj.* of an eclipse or the ecliptic. [ME f. L f. Gk *ekleiptikos* (as ECLIPSE)]

ec·logue /éklawg, –log/ *n.* a short poem, esp. a pastoral dialogue. [L *ecloga* f. Gk *eklogē* selection f. *eklegō* pick out]

e·clo·sion /iklṓzhən/ *n.* the emergence of an insect from a pupa case or of a larva from an egg. [F *éclosion* f. *éclore* hatch (as EX-[1], L *claudere* to close)]

eco- /ékō, éekō/ *comb. form* ecology, ecological.

e·co·cli·mate /ékōklīmit, éekō–/ *n.* climate considered as an ecological factor.

ecol. *abbr.* **1** ecological. **2** ecologist. **3** ecology.

E. co·li /éekṓlī/ *n.* a species of anaerobic bacteria in the large intestine of human and other animals; it is toxic in large quantities. ¶ Abbr. for **Esch·e·rich·i·a co·li.**

e·col·o·gy /ikóləjee/ *n.* **1** the branch of biology dealing with the relations of organisms to one another and to their physical surroundings. **2** (in full **human ecology**) the study of the interaction of people with their environment. □□ **ec·o·log·i·cal** /ékəlójikəl, éekə–/ *adj.* **ec·o·log·i·cal·ly** *adv.* **ec·ol·o·gist** *n.* [G *Ökologie* f. Gk *oikos* house]

econ. *abbr.* **1** economics. **2** economy.

e·con·o·met·rics /ikónəmétriks/ *n.pl.* (usu. treated as *sing.*) a branch of economics concerned with the application of mathematical economics to economic data by the use of statistics. □□ **e·con·o·met·ric** *adj.* **e·con·o·met·ri·cal** *adj.* **e·con·o·me·tri·cian** /–mətríshən/ *n.* **e·con·o·met·rist** *n.* [ECONOMY + METRIC]

ec·o·nom·ic /ékənómik, éekə–/ *adj.* **1** of or relating to economics. **2** maintained for profit; on a business footing. **3** adequate to repay or recoup expenditure with some profit (*not economic to run buses on Sunday; an economic rent*). **4** practical; considered or studied with regard to human needs (*economic geography*). [ME f. OF *economique* or L *oeconomicus* f. Gk *oikonomikos* (as ECONOMY)]

▶**Economic** means 'concerning economics': *He's rebuilding a solid economic base for the country's future.* **Economical** is commonly used to mean 'thrifty; avoiding waste': *Small cars should be inexpensive to buy and economical to run.*

ec·o·nom·i·cal /ékənómikəl, éekə–/ *adj.* sparing in the use of resources; avoiding waste. □□ **ec·o·nom·i·cal·ly** *adv.*

▶See note at ECONOMIC.

ec·o·nom·ics /ékənómiks, éekə–/ *n.pl.* (often treated as *sing.*) **1 a** the science of the production and distribution of wealth. **b** the application of this to a particular subject (*the economics of publishing*). **2** the condition of a country, etc., as regards material prosperity.

economies of scale *n.* proportionate savings gained by using larger quantities.

e·con·o·mist /ikónəmist/ *n.* **1** an expert in or student of economics.

2 a person who manages financial or economic matters. [Gk *oikonomos* (as ECONOMY) + –IST]

e·con·o·mize /ikónəmīz/ *v.intr.* **1** be economical; make economies; reduce expenditure. **2** (foll. by *on*) use sparingly; spend less on. □□ **e·con·o·mi·za·tion** *n.* **e·con·o·miz·er** *n.*

e·con·o·my /ikónəmee/ *n.* (*pl.* **·mies**) **1 a** the wealth and resources of a community, esp. in terms of the production and consumption of goods and services. **b** a particular kind of this (*a capitalist economy*). **c** the administration or condition of an economy. **2 a** the careful management of (esp. financial) resources; frugality. **b** (often in *pl.*) an instance of this (*made many economies*). **3** sparing or careful use (*economy of language*). **4** (also **e·con·o·my class**) the cheapest class of air travel. **5** (*attrib.*) (also **e·con·o·my-size**) (of goods) consisting of a large quantity for a proportionally lower cost. [F *économie* or L *oeconomia* f. Gk *oikonomia* household management f. *oikos* house + *nemō* manage]

ec·o·sphere /ékōsfeer, éekə–/ *n.* the region of space including planets where conditions are such that living things can exist.

ec·o·sys·tem /ékōsistəm, éekō–/ *n.* a biological community of interacting organisms and their physical environment.

ec·ru /ékrōō, áykrōō/ *n.* the color of unbleached linen; light fawn. [F *écru* unbleached]

ec·sta·size /ékstəsīz/ *v.tr. & intr.* throw or go into ecstasies.

ec·sta·sy /ékstəsee/ *n.* (*pl.* **·sies**) **1** an overwhelming feeling of joy or rapture. **2** *Psychol.* an emotional or religious frenzy or trancelike state. **3** *sl.* methylene dioxymethamphetamine, a powerful stimulant and hallucinatory drug (see MDA). [ME f. OF *extasie* f. LL *extasis* f. Gk *ekstasis* standing outside oneself f. *ek* out + *histēmi* to place]

ec·stat·ic /ikstátik, ek–/ *adj. & n.* ● *adj.* **1** in a state of ecstasy. **2** very enthusiastic or excited (*was ecstatic about her new job*). **3** producing ecstasy; sublime (*an ecstatic embrace*). ● *n.* a person subject to (usu. religious) ecstasy. □□ **ec·stat·i·cal·ly** *adv.* [F *extatique* f. Gk *ekstatikos* (as ECSTASY)]

ECT *abbr.* electroconvulsive therapy.

ecto- /éktō/ *comb. form* outside. [Gk *ekto-* stem of *ektos* outside]

ec·to·blast /éktōblast/ *n.* = ECTODERM. □□ **ec·to·blas·tic** *adj.*

ec·to·derm /éktōdərm/ *n. Biol.* the outermost layer of an animal embryo in early development. □□ **ec·to·der·mal** *adj.*

ec·to·gen·e·sis /éktōjénisis/ *n. Biol.* the production of structures outside the organism. □□ **ec·to·ge·net·ic** /–jinétik/ *adj.* **ec·to·gen·ic** /–jénik/ *adj.* **ec·tog·e·nous** /ektójinəs/ *adj.* [mod.L (as ECTO-, GENESIS)]

ec·to·morph /éktəmawrf/ *n.* a person with a lean body build. (cf. ENDOMORPH, MESOMORPH). □□ **ec·to·mor·phic** *adj.* **ec·to·morph·y** *n.* [ECTO- + Gk *morphē* form]

-ectomy /éktəmee/ *comb. form* denoting a surgical operation in which a part of the body is removed (*appendectomy*). [Gk *ektomē* excision f. *ek* out + *temnō* cut]

ec·top·ic /ektópik/ *adj. Med.* in an abnormal place or position. [mod.L *ectopia* f. Gk *ektopos* out of place]

ec·top·ic preg·nan·cy *n.* a pregnancy occurring outside the uterus.

ec·to·plasm /éktəplazəm/ *n.* **1** the dense outer layer of the cytoplasm (cf. ENDOPLASM). **2** the supposed viscous substance exuding from the body of a spiritualistic medium during a trance. □□ **ec·to·plas·mic** *adj.*

ec·to·zo·on /éktzṓ-on/ *n. Biol.* a parasite that lives on the outside of its host.

ECU *abbr.* (also **e·cu** /ékyōō/) European currency unit.

ec·u·men·i·cal /ékyōōménikəl/ *adj.* **1** of or representing the whole

---

SYNONYM TIP *economical*

FRUGAL, MISERLY, PARSIMONIOUS, PROVIDENT, PRUDENT, SPARING, THRIFTY. If you don't like to spend money unnecessarily, you may simply be **economical**, which means that you manage your finances wisely and avoid any unnecessary expenses. If you're **thrifty**, you're both industrious and clever in managing your resources (*a thrifty shopper who never leaves home without her coupons*). **Frugal**, on the other hand, means that you tend to be sparing with money— sometimes getting a little carried away in your efforts—by avoiding any form of luxury or lavishness (*too frugal to take a taxi, even at night*). If you're **sparing**, you exercise such restraint in your spending that you sometimes deprive yourself (*sparing to the point where she allowed herself only one new item of clothing a season*). If you're **provident**, however, you're focused on providing for the future (*never one to be provident, she spent her allowance the day she received it*). **Miserly** and **parsimonious** are both used to describe frugality in its most extreme form. But while being *frugal* might be considered a virtue, being *parsimonious* is usually considered to be a fault or even a vice (*they could have been generous with their wealth, but they chose to lead a parsimonious life*). And no one wants to be called *miserly*, which implies being stingy out of greed rather than need (*so miserly that he reveled in his riches while those around him were starving*).

Christian world. **2** seeking or promoting worldwide Christian unity. □□ **ec•u•men•i•cal•ly** *adv.* [LL *oecumenicus* f. Gk *oikoumenikos* of the inhabited earth (*oikoumenē*)]

ec•u•men•i•cal•ism /ékyōōménikəlizəm/ *n.* (also **ec•u•me•nism** /ékyəminizəm, ikyōōmənizəm/) the principle or aim of the unity of Christians worldwide.

ec•ze•ma /éksimə, égzi–, igzeé–/ *n.* inflammation of the skin, with itching and discharge from blisters. □□ **ec•zem•a•tous** /igzémətəs, egzém–, –zeé–/ *adj.* [mod.L f. Gk *ekzema –atos* f. *ek* out + *zeō* boil]

ed. *abbr.* **1** edited by. **2** edition. **3** editor. **4** educated; education.

-ed[1] /əd, id/ *suffix* forming adjectives: **1** from nouns, meaning 'having, wearing, affected by, etc.' (*talented; trousered; diseased*). **2** from phrases of adjective and noun (*good-humored; three-cornered*). [OE *-ede*]

-ed[2] /əd, id/ *suffix* forming: **1** the past tense and past participle of weak verbs (*needed; risked*). **2** participial adjectives (*escaped prisoner; a pained look*). [OE *-ed, –ad, –od*]

e•da•cious /idáyshəs/ *adj. literary* or *joc.* **1** greedy. **2** of eating. □□ **e•dac•i•ty** *n.* /idásitee/ [L *edax –acis* f. *edere* eat]

E•dam /eédəm, eédam/ *n.* a round Dutch cheese, usu. pale yellow with a red rind. [*Edam* in Holland]

e•daph•ic /idáfik/ *adj.* **1** *Bot.* of the soil. **2** *Ecol.* produced or influenced by the soil. [G *edaphisch* f. Gk *edaphos* floor]

Ed•da /édə/ *n.* **1** (also **Eld•er Ed•da, Po•et•ic Ed•da**) a collection of medieval Icelandic poems on Norse legends. **2** (also **Young•er Ed•da, Prose Ed•da**) a 13th-c. miscellaneous handbook to Icelandic poetry. [perh. a name in a Norse poem or f. ON *óthr* poetry]

ed•do /édō/ *n.* (*pl.* **•does**) = TARO. [Afr. word]

ed•dy /édee/ *n. & v.* ● *n.* (*pl.* **•dies**) **1** a circular movement of water causing a small whirlpool. **2** a movement of wind, fog, or smoke resembling this. ● *v.tr. & intr.* (**•dies, •died**) whirl around in eddies. [prob. OE *ed-* again, back, perh. of Scand. orig.]

ed•dy cur•rent *n. Electr.* a localized current induced in a conductor by a varying magnetic field.

e•del•weiss /áyd'lvīs/ *n.* an Alpine plant, *Leontopodium alpinum*, with woolly white bracts around the flower heads, growing in rocky places. [G f. *edel* noble + *weiss* white]

e•de•ma /ideémə/ *n.* a condition characterized by an excess of watery fluid collecting in the cavities or tissues of the body. Also called **dropsy.** □□ **e•dem•a•tose** /idémətōs, idee–/ *adj.* **e•dem•a•tous** *adj.* [LL f. GK *oidēma –atos* f. *oideō* swell]

E•den /eédən/ *n.* (also **Gar•den of E•den**) a place or state of great happiness; paradise (with reference to the abode of Adam and Eve in the biblical account of the Creation). [ME f. LL f. Gk *Ēdēn* f. Heb. *'ēden*, orig. = delight]

e•den•tate /idéntayt/ *adj. & n.* ● *adj.* having no or few teeth. ● *n.* any mammal, esp. of the order Edentata, having no or few teeth, e.g., an anteater or sloth. [L *edentatus* (as E–, *dens dentis* tooth)]

edge /ej/ *n. & v.* ● *n.* **1** a boundary line or margin of an area or surface. **2** a narrow surface of a thin object. **3** the meeting line of two surfaces of a solid. **4 a** the sharpened side of the blade of a cutting instrument or weapon. **b** the sharpness of this (*the knife has lost its edge*). **5** the area close to a steep drop (*along the edge of the cliff*). **6** anything compared to an edge, esp. the crest of a ridge. **7 a** effectiveness, force; incisiveness. **b** keenness; excitement (esp. as an element in an otherwise routine situation). **8** an advantage; superiority. ● *v.* **1** *tr. & intr.* (often foll. by *in, into, out*, etc.) move gradually or furtively toward an objective (*edged it into the corner; they all edged toward the door*). **2** *tr.* **a** provide with an edge or border. **b** form a border to. **c** trim the edge of. **3** *tr.* sharpen (a knife, tool, etc.). □ **have the edge on** (or **over**) have a slight advantage over. **on edge 1** tense and restless or irritable. **2** eager; excited. **on the edge of** almost involved in or affected by. **set a person's teeth on edge** (of a taste or sound) cause an unpleasant nervous sensation. **take the edge off** dull; weaken; make less effective or intense. □□ **edge•less** *adj.* **edg•er** *n.*

edge•wise /éjwiz/ *adv.* (/–wayz/) **1** with the edge uppermost or toward the viewer. **2** edge to edge. □ **get a word in edgewise** contribute to a conversation when the dominant speaker pauses briefly.

edg•ing /éjing/ *n.* **1** something forming an edge or border, e.g., a fringe or lace. **2** the process of making an edge.

edg•y /éjee/ *adj.* (**edg•i•er, edg•i•est**) **1** irritable; nervously anxious. **2** disjointed (*edgy rhythms*). □□ **edg•i•ly** *adv.* **edg•i•ness** *n.*

edh /eth/ *n.* (also **eth** /eth/) the name of an Old English and Icelandic letter, = th. [Icel.]

ed•i•ble /édibəl/ *adj. & n.* ● *adj.* fit or suitable to be eaten (cf. EATABLE). ● *n.* (in *pl.*) food. □□ **ed•i•bil•i•ty** *n.* [LL *edibilis* f. *edere* eat]

e•dict /eédikt/ *n.* an order proclaimed by authority. □□ **e•dic•tal** /eédíkt'l/ *adj.* [ME f. L *edictum* f. *edicere* proclaim]

---

ed•i•fice /édifis/ *n.* **1** a building, esp. a large imposing one. **2** a complex organizational or conceptual structure. [ME f. OF f. L *aedificium* f. *aedis* dwelling + *–ficium* f. *facere* make]

ed•i•fy /édifī/ *v.tr.* (**•fies, •fied**) (of a circumstance, experience, etc.) instruct and improve morally or intellectually. □□ **ed•i•fi•ca•tion** /–fikáyshən/ *n.* **ed•i•fy•ing** *adj.* **ed•i•fy•ing•ly** *adv.*

ed•it /édit/ *v. & n.* ● *v.tr.* **1 a** assemble, prepare, modify, or condense (written material, esp. the work of another or others) for publication. **b** prepare an edition of (an author's work). **2** be in overall charge of the content and arrangement of (a newspaper, journal, etc.). **3** take extracts from and collate (movies, tape recordings, etc.) to form a unified sequence. **4 a** prepare (data) for processing by a computer. **b** alter (a text entered in a word processor, etc.). **5 a** reword to correct, or to alter the emphasis. **b** (foll. by *out*) remove (part) from a text, etc. ● *n.* **a** a piece of editing. **b** an edited item. **c** a change or correction made as a result of editing. [F *éditer* (as EDITION): partly a back-form. f. EDITOR]

e•di•tion /idíshən/ *n.* **1 a** one of the particular forms in which a literary work, etc., is published (*paperback edition; pocket edition*). **b** a copy of a book in a particular form (*a first edition*). **2** a whole number of copies of a book, newspaper, etc., issued at one time. **3** a particular version or instance of a broadcast, esp. of a regular program or feature. **4** a person or thing similar to or resembling another (*a miniature edition of her mother*). [F *édition* f. L *editio –onis* f. *edere* edit- put out (as E–, *dare* give)]

e•di•ti•o prin•ceps /idísheeō prínseps, edíteeō príngkeps/ *n.* (*pl.* **e•di•ti•o•nes prin•ci•pes** /idísheeōneez prínsipeez/) the first printed edition of a book, text, etc. [L]

ed•i•tor /éditər/ *n.* **1** a person who edits material for publication or broadcasting. **2** a person who directs the preparation of a newspaper or periodical, or a particular section of one (*sports editor*). **3** a person who selects or commissions material for publication. **4** a person who edits film, sound track, etc. **5** a computer program for modifying data. □□ **ed•i•tor•ship** *n.* [LL, = producer (of games), publisher (as EDIT)]

ed•i•to•ri•al /éditáwreeəl/ *adj. & n.* ● *adj.* **1** of or connected with editing or editors. **2** written or approved by an editor. ● *n.* a newspaper article written by or on behalf of an editor, esp. one giving an opinion on a topical issue. □□ **ed•i•to•ri•al•ist** *n.* **ed•i•to•ri•al•ize** *v.intr.* **ed•i•to•ri•al•ly** *adv.*

-edly /idlee/ *suffix* forming adverbs from verbs, meaning 'in a manner characterized by performance of or undergoing of the verbal action' (*allegedly; disgustedly; hurriedly*).

EDP *abbr.* electronic data processing.

EDT *abbr.* eastern daylight time.

ed•u•cate /éjəkayt/ *v.tr.* (also *absol.*) **1** give intellectual, moral, and social instruction to (a pupil, esp. a child), esp. as a formal and prolonged process. **2** provide education for. **3** (often foll. by *in,* or *to* + infin.) train or instruct for a particular purpose. **4** advise; give information to. □□ **ed•u•ca•ble** /–kəbəl/ *adj.* **ed•u•ca•bil•i•ty** /–kəbílitee/ *n.* **ed•u•cat•a•ble** *adj.* **ed•u•ca•tive** *adj.* **ed•u•ca•tor** *n.* [L *educare educat-*, rel. to *educere* EDUCE]

ed•u•cat•ed /éjəkaytid/ *adj.* **1** having had an education, esp. to a higher level than average. **2** resulting from a (good) education (*an educated accent*). **3** based on experience or study (*an educated guess*).

ed•u•ca•tion /éjəkáyshən/ *n.* **1 a** the act or process of educating or being educated; systematic instruction. **b** the knowledge gained from this. **2** a particular kind of or stage in education (*further education; a classical education*). **3 a** development of character or mental powers. **b** a stage in or aspect of this (*travel will be an education for you*). □□ **ed•u•ca•tion•al** *adj.* **ed•u•ca•tion•al•ist** *n.* **ed•u•ca•tion•al•ly** *adv.* **ed•u•ca•tion•ist** *n.* [F *éducation* or L *educatio* (as EDUCATE)]

e•duce /idōōs, idyōōs/ *v.tr.* **1** bring out or develop from latent or potential existence; elicit. **2** infer; assume (a principle, number, etc., from data. □□ **e•duc•i•ble** *adj.* **e•duc•tion** /idúkshen/ *n.* **e•duc•tive** /idúktiv/ *adj.* [ME f. L *educere educt-* lead out (as E–, *ducere* lead)]

Ed•ward•i•an /edwáwrdeeən, –waár–/ *adj. & n.* ● *adj.* of, characteristic of, or associated with the reign of King Edward VII of England (1901–10). ● *n.* a person belonging to this period.

-ee /ee/ *suffix* forming nouns denoting: **1** the person affected by the verbal action (*addressee; employee; lessee*). **2** a person concerned with or described as (*absentee; refugee*). **3** an object of smaller size (*bootee*). [from or after AF past part. in *–é* f. L *-atus*]

EEC *abbr.* European Economic Community.

EEG *abbr.* electroencephalogram.

eel /eel/ *n.* **1** any of various snakelike fish, with slender body and poorly developed fins. **2** a slippery or evasive person or thing. □□ **eel·like** *adj.* **eel·y** *adj.* [OE *ǣl* f. Gmc]

eel

eel·grass /éelgras/ *n.* **1** any marine plant of the genus *Zostera*, with long ribbonlike leaves. **2** any submerged freshwater plant of the genus *Vallisneria*.

eel·pout /éelpowt/ *n.* **1** any fish of the family Zoarcidae, with slender body and dorsal and anal fins meeting to fuse with the tail. Also called **pout.** **2** = BURBOT. [OE *ǣleputa* (as EEL, POUT²)]

eel·worm /éelwərm/ *n.* any of various small nematode worms infesting plant roots.

e'en¹ /een/ *archaic* or *poet.* var. of EVEN¹.

e'en² /een/ *Sc.* var. of EVEN².

-een /een/ *suffix Ir.* forming diminutive nouns (*colleen*). [Ir. *-ín* dimin. suffix]

EEOC *abbr.* Equal Employment Opportunity Commission.

e'er /air/ *poet.* var. of EVER.

-eer /eer/ *suffix* forming: **1** nouns meaning 'person concerned with or engaged in' (*auctioneer, mountaineer, profiteer*). **2** verbs meaning 'be concerned with' (*electioneer*). [from or after F *-ier* f. L *-arius*: cf. –IER, –ARY¹]

ee·rie /éeree/ *adj.* (**ee·ri·er, ee·ri·est**) gloomy and strange; weird, frightening (*an eerie silence*). □□ **ee·ri·ly** *adv.* **ee·ri·ness** *n.* [orig. No. of Engl. and Sc. *eri*, of obscure orig.: cf. OE *earg* cowardly]

ef- /if, ef/ *prefix* assim. form of EX-¹ 1 before *f*.

ef·face /ifáys/ *v.* **1** *tr.* rub or wipe out (a mark, etc.). **2** *tr.* (in abstract senses) obliterate; wipe out (*effaced it from his memory*). **3** *tr.* utterly surpass; eclipse (*success has effaced all previous attempts*). **4** *refl.* treat or regard oneself as unimportant (*self-effacing*). □□ **ef·face·ment** *n.* [F *effacer* (as EX-¹, FACE)]

ef·fect /ifékt/ *n. & v.* ● *n.* **1** the result or consequence of an action, etc.; the significance or implication of this. **2** efficacy (*had little effect*). **3** an impression produced on a spectator, hearer, etc. (*lights had a pretty effect; my words had no effect*). **4** (in *pl.*) property; luggage. **5** (in *pl.*) the lighting, sound, etc., used to accompany a play, movie, broadcast, etc. **6** *Physics* a physical phenomenon, usually named after its discoverer (*Doppler effect*). **7** the state of being operative. ● *v.tr.* **1** bring about; accomplish. **2** cause to exist or occur. □ **bring** (or **carry**) **into effect** accomplish. **for effect** to create an impression. **give effect to** make operative. **in effect** for practical purposes; in reality. **take effect** become operative. **to the effect that** the general substance or gist being. **to that effect** having that result or implication. [ME f. OF *effect* or L *effectus* (as EX-¹, *facere* make)] ▶See note at AFFECT.

ef·fec·tive /iféktiv/ *adj. & n.* ● *adj.* **1** having a definite or desired effect. **2** powerful in effect; impressive. **3** actual; existing in fact rather than officially or theoretically (*took effective control in their absence*). **b** actually usable; realizable; equivalent in its effect (*effective money; effective demand*). **4** coming into operation (*effective as of May 1*). **5** (of manpower) fit for work or service. ● *n.* a soldier available for service. □□ **ef·fec·tive·ly** *adv.* **ef·fec·tive·ness** *n.* [ME f. L *effectivus* (as EFFECT)]

SYNONYM TIP effective

EFFECTUAL, EFFICACIOUS, EFFICIENT. All of these adjectives mean producing or capable of producing a result, but they are not interchangeable. Use **effective** when you want to describe something that produces a definite effect or result (*an effective speaker who was able to rally the crowd's support*) and **efficacious** when it produces the desired effect or result (*an efficacious remedy that cured her almost immediately*). If something produces the desired effect or result in a decisive manner, use **effectual** (*an effectual recommendation that got him the job*), an adjective that is often employed when looking back after an event is over (*an effectual strategy that finally turned the tide in their favor*). Reserve the use of **efficient** for when you want to imply skill and economy of energy in producing the desired result (*so efficient in her management of the company that layoffs were not necessary*). When applied to people, **efficient** means capable or competent (*an efficient homemaker*) and places less emphasis on the achievement of results and more on the skills involved.

ef·fec·tor /iféktər/ *adj. & n. Biol.* ● *adj.* acting in response to a stimulus. ● *n.* an effector organ.

ef·fec·tu·al /ifékchōōəl/ *adj.* **1** capable of producing the required result or effect; answering its purpose. **2** valid. □□ **ef·fec·tu·al·i·ty** /-chōōálitee/ *n.* **ef·fec·tu·al·ly** *adv.* **ef·fec·tu·al·ness** *n.* [ME f. med.L *effectualis* (as EFFECT)]

ef·fec·tu·ate /ifékchōō-ayt/ *v.tr.* cause to happen; accomplish. □□ **ef·fec·tu·a·tion** *n.* [med.L *effectuare* (as EFFECT)]

ef·fem·i·nate /iféminət/ *adj.* (of a man) feminine in appearance or manner; unmasculine. □□ **ef·fem·i·na·cy** *n.* **ef·fem·i·nate·ly** *adv.* [ME f. L *effeminatus* past part. of *effeminare* (as EX-¹, *femina* woman)]

ef·fen·di /eféndee/ *n.* (*pl.* **ef·fen·dis**) **1** a man of education or standing in eastern Mediterranean or Arab countries. **2** a former title of respect or courtesy in Turkey. [f. Turk. *efendi* f. mod. Gk *aféntēs* f. Gk *authentēs* lord, master: see AUTHENTIC]

ef·fer·ent /éfərənt/ *adj. Physiol.* conducting outward (*efferent nerves; efferent vessels*) (opp. AFFERENT). □□ **ef·fer·ence** /-rəns/ *n.* [L *efferre* (as EX-¹, *ferre* carry)]

ef·fer·vesce /éfərvés/ *v.intr.* **1** give off bubbles of gas; bubble. **2** (of a person) be lively or energetic. □□ **ef·fer·ves·cence** *n.* **ef·fer·ves·cen·cy** *n.* **ef·fer·ves·cent** *adj.* [L *effervescere* (as EX-¹, *fervēre* be hot)]

ef·fete /iféet/ *adj.* **1 a** feeble and incapable. **b** effeminate. **2** worn out; exhausted of its essential quality or vitality. □□ **ef·fete·ness** *n.* [L *effetus* worn out by bearing young (as EX-¹, FETUS)]

ef·fi·ca·cious /éfikáyshəs/ *adj.* (of a thing) producing or sure to produce the desired effect. □□ **ef·fi·ca·cious·ly** *adv.* **ef·fi·ca·cious·ness** *n.* **ef·fi·ca·cy** /éfikəsee/ *n.* [L *efficax* (as EFFICIENT)]

ef·fi·cien·cy /ifishənsee/ *n.* (*pl.* **·cies**) **1** the state or quality of being efficient. **2** *Mech. & Physics* the ratio of useful work performed to the total energy expended or heat taken in. [L *efficientia* (as EFFICIENT)]

ef·fi·cient /ifishənt/ *adj.* **1** productive with minimum waste or effort. **2** (of a person) capable; acting effectively. □□ **ef·fi·cient·ly** *adv.* [ME f. L *efficere* (as EX-¹, *facere* make, accomplish)]

ef·fi·cient cause *n. Philos.* an agent that brings a thing into being or initiates a change.

ef·fi·gy /éfijee/ *n.* (*pl.* **·gies**) a sculpture or model of a person. □ **in effigy** in the form of a (usu. crude) representation of a person. [L *effigies* f. *effingere* to fashion]

ef·fleu·rage /éflöráazh/ *n. & v.* ● *n.* a form of massage involving a circular inward stroking movement made with the palm of the hand, used esp. during childbirth. ● *v.intr.* massage with a circular stroking movement. [F f. *effleurer* to skim]

ef·flo·resce /éflərés/ *v.intr.* **1** burst out into flower. **2** *Chem.* **a** (of a substance) turn to a fine powder on exposure to air. **b** (of salts) come to the surface and crystallize on it. **c** (of a surface) become covered with salt particles. □□ **ef·flo·res·cence** *n.* **ef·flo·res·cent** *adj.* [L *efflorescere* (as EX-¹, *flōrēre* to bloom f. *flos floris* flower)]

ef·flu·ence /éflŏŏəns/ *n.* **1** a flowing out (of light, electricity, etc.). **2** that which flows out. [F *effluence* or med.L *effluentia* f. L *effluere* *efflux-* flow out (as EX-¹, *fluere* flow)]

ef·flu·ent /éflŏŏənt/ *adj. & n.* ● *adj.* flowing forth or out. ● *n.* **1** sewage or industrial waste discharged into a river, the sea, etc. **2** a stream or lake flowing from a larger body of water.

ef·flu·vi·um /iflŏŏveeəm/ *n.* (*pl.* **ef·flu·vi·a** /-veeə/) an unpleasant or noxious odor or exhaled substance affecting the lungs or the sense of smell, etc. [L (as EFFLUENT)]

ef·flux /éfluks/ *n.* = EFFLUENCE. □□ **ef·flux·ion** /eflúkshən/ *n.* [med.L *effluxus* (as EFFLUENT)]

ef·fort /éfərt/ *n.* **1** strenuous physical or mental exertion. **2** a vigorous or determined attempt. **3** *Mech.* a force exerted. **4** *colloq.* the result of an attempt; something accomplished (*not bad for a first effort*). □□ **ef·fort·ful** *adj.* [F f. OF *esforcier* ult. f. L *fortis* strong]

ef·fort·less /éfərtlis/ *adj.* **1** seemingly without effort; natural; easy. **2** requiring no effort (*effortless contemplation*). □□ **ef·fort·less·ly** *adv.* **ef·fort·less·ness** *n.*

ef·fron·ter·y /ifrúntəree/ *n.* (*pl.* **·ies**) **1** shameless insolence; impudent audacity (esp. have the effrontery to). **2** an instance of this. [F *effronterie* f. *effronté* ult. f. LL *effrons* *-ontis* shameless (as EX-¹, *frons* forehead)]

ef·ful·gent /ifúljənt/ *adj. literary* radiant; shining brilliantly. □□ **ef·ful·gence** /-jəns/ *n.* **ef·ful·gent·ly** *adv.* [L *effulgēre* shine forth (as EX-¹, *fulgēre* shine)]

ef·fuse *adj. & v.* ● *adj.* /ifyŏŏs/ *Bot.* (of an inflorescence, etc.) spreading loosely. ● *v.tr.* /ifyŏŏz/ **1** pour forth (liquid, light, etc.). **2** give out (ideas, etc.). [ME f. L *effusus* past part. of *effundere* *effus-* pour out (as EX-¹, *fundere* pour)]

ef·fu·sion /ifyŏŏzhən/ *n.* **1** a copious outpouring. **2** usu. *derog.* an unrestrained flow of speech or writing. [ME f. OF *effusion* or L *effusio* (as EFFUSE)]

ef·fu·sive /ifyŏŏsiv/ *adj.* **1** gushing; demonstrative; exuberant (*effusive praise*). **2** *Geol.* (of igneous rock) poured out when molten and later solidified; volcanic. □□ **ef·fu·sive·ly** *adv.* **ef·fu·sive·ness** *n.*

EFL *abbr.* English as a foreign language.

eft /eft/ *n.* a newt. [OE *efeta*, of unkn. orig.]

EFTA /éftə/ *n.* European Free Trade Association. [abbr.]

EFTPOS /éftpoz/ *abbr.* electronic funds transfer at point of sale.

e.g. *abbr.* for example. [L *exempli gratia*]

e·gad /eegád, igád/ *int. archaic* or *joc.* by God. [prob. orig. *a* ah + GOD]

e·gal·i·tar·i·an /igálitáireeən/ *adj. & n.* ● *adj.* **1** of or relating to the principle of equal rights and opportunities for all (*an egalitarian society*). **2** advocating this principle. ● *n.* a person who advocates or supports egalitarian principles. □□ e•gal•i•tar•i•an•ism *n.* [F *égali-taire* f. *égal* EQUAL]

egg[1] /eg/ *n.* **1 a** the spheroidal reproductive body produced by females of animals such as birds, reptiles, fish, etc., enclosed in a protective layer and capable of developing into a new individual. **b** the egg of the domestic hen, used for food. **2** *Biol.* the female reproductive cell in animals and plants. **3** *colloq.* a person or thing qualified in some way (*a tough egg*). **4** anything resembling or imitating an egg, esp. in shape or appearance. □ **as sure as eggs is** (or **are**) **eggs** *Brit. colloq.* without any doubt. **have** (or **put**) **all one's eggs in one basket** *colloq.* risk everything on a single venture. **with egg on one's face** *colloq.* made to look foolish. □□ **egg•less** *adj.* **egg•y** *adj.* (**egg•i•er**, **egg•i•est**). [ME f. ON, rel. to OE *ǣg*]

egg[2] /eg/ *v.tr.* (foll. by *on*) urge (*egged us on to it*; *egged them on to do it*). [ME f. ON *eggja* = EDGE]

egg•beat•er /égbeetər/ *n.* **1** a device for beating eggs. **2** *sl.* a helicopter.

egg•cup /égkup/ *n.* a cup for holding a boiled egg.

egg•er /égər/ *n.* (also **eg•gar**) any of various large moths of the family Lasiocampidae, esp. *Lasiocampa quercus*, with an egg-shaped cocoon; tent caterpillar. [prob. f. EGG[1] + –ER[1]]

egg-flip *n. Brit.* = EGGNOG.

egg•head /éghed/ *n. colloq.* an intellectual; an expert.

egg•nog /égnog/ *n.* a drink made from a mixture of eggs, cream, and flavorings, often with alcohol.

egg•plant /égplant/ *n.* **1** a tropical plant, *Solanum melongena*, having erect or spreading branches bearing purple or white egg-shaped fruit. **2** this fruit eaten as a vegetable. **3** the dark purple color of this fruit.

egg roll *n.* a Chinese-style snack similar to a spring roll, consisting of diced meat or shrimp and shredded vegetables encased in a dough made with egg and deep fried.

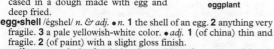

eggplant

egg•shell /égshel/ *n. & adj.* • *n.* **1** the shell of an egg. **2** anything very fragile. **3** a pale yellowish-white color. • *adj.* **1** (of china) thin and fragile. **2** (of paint) with a slight gloss finish.

egg tim•er *n.* a device for timing the cooking of an egg, traditionally in the form of a miniature hourglass.

egg tooth *n.* a projection of an embryo bird or reptile used for breaking out of the shell.

egg white *n.* the clear, viscous substance around the yolk of an egg that turns white when cooked or beaten. Also called albumen.

eg•lan•tine /égləntīn, –teen/ *n.* sweetbrier. [ME f. F *églantine* f. OF *aiglent* ult. f. L *acus* needle]

e•go /éegō/ *n.* (*pl.* **•gos**) **1** *Metaphysics* a conscious thinking subject. **2** *Psychol.* the part of the mind that reacts to reality and has a sense of individuality. **3** self-esteem. [L, = I]

e•go•cen•tric /éegōséntrik, égō–/ *adj.* **1** centered in the ego. **2** self-centered; egoistic. □□ **e•go•cen•tri•cal•ly** *adv.* **e•go•cen•tric•i•ty** /–trísitee/ *n.* [EGO + –CENTRIC after *geocentric*, etc.]

e•go i•de•al *n.* **1** *Psychol.* the part of the mind developed from the ego by an awareness of social standards. **2** (in general use) idealization of oneself.

e•go•ism /éegōizəm, égō–/ *n.* **1** an ethical theory that treats self-interest as the foundation of morality. **2** systematic selfishness. **3** self-opinionatedness. **4** = EGOTISM. □□ **e•go•ist** *n.* **e•go•is•tic** *adj.* **e•go•is•ti•cal** *adj.* [F *égoïsme* ult. f. mod.L *egoismus* (as EGO)]

e•go•ma•ni•a /éegōmáyneeə, égō–/ *n.* morbid egotism. □□ **e•go•ma•ni•ac** *n.* **e•go•ma•ni•a•cal** /–mənīəkəl/ *adj.*

e•go•tism /éegətizəm, égə–/ *n.* **1** excessive use of 'I' and 'me.' **2** the practice of talking about oneself. **3** an exaggerated opinion of oneself. **4** selfishness. □□ **e•go•tist** *n.* **e•go•tis•tic** *adj.* **e•go•tis•ti•cal** *adj.* **e•go•tis•ti•cal•ly** *adv.* **e•go•tize** *v.intr.* [EGO + –ISM with intrusive –*t*–] ▶See note at EGOIST.

e•go trip *n. colloq.* activity, etc., devoted entirely to one's own interests or feelings.

e•gre•gious /igréejəs/ *adj.* **1** outstandingly bad; shocking (*egregious folly*; *an egregious ass*). **2** *archaic* or *joc.* remarkable. □□ **e•gre•gious•ly** *adv.* **e•gre•gious•ness** *n.* [L *egregius* illustrious, lit. 'standing out from the flock' f. *grex gregis* flock]

e•gress /éegres/ *n.* **1 a** going out. **b** the right of going out. **2** an exit; a way out. **3** *Astron.* the end of an eclipse or transit. □□ **e•gres•sion** /–gréshən/ *n.* (in senses 1, 2). [L *egressus* f. *egredi egress-* (as E–, *gradi* to step)]

e•gret /éegrit/ *n.* any of various herons of the genus *Egretta* or *Bulbulcus*, usu. having long white feathers in the breeding season. [ME, var. of AIGRETTE]

E•gyp•tian /ijípshən/ *adj. & n.* • *adj.* **1** of or relating to Egypt in NE Africa. **2** of or for Egyptian antiquities (e.g., in a museum) (*Egyptian room*). • *n.* **1** a native of ancient or modern Egypt; a national of the Arab Republic of Egypt. **2** the Hamitic language used in ancient Egypt until the 3rd c. AD. □□ **E•gyp•tian•ize** *v.tr.* **E•gyp•tian•i•za•tion** *n.*

E•gyp•tol•o•gy /éejiptólajee/ *n.* the study of the language, history, and culture of ancient Egypt. □□ **E•gyp•tol•o•gist** *n.*

eh /ay/ *int. colloq.* **1** expressing inquiry or surprise. **2** inviting assent. **3** asking for something to be repeated or explained. [ME *ey*, instinctive exclam.]

-eian /eeən/ *suffix* corresp. to –*ey* (or –*y*) + –*an* (*Bodleian*; *Rugbeian*).

ei•der /ídər/ *n.* **1** (in full **eider duck**) any of various large northern ducks, esp. of the genus *Somateria*. **2** = EIDERDOWN 1. [Icel. *aethr*]

ei•der•down /ídərdown/ *n.* **1** small, soft feathers from the breast of the eider duck. **2** a quilt stuffed with down (orig. from the eider) or some other soft material, esp. as the upper layer of bedclothes.

ei•det•ic /ídétik/ *adj. & n.* • *adj. Psychol.* (of a mental image) having unusual vividness and detail, as if actually visible. • *n.* a person able to see eidetic images. □□ **ei•det•i•cal•ly** *adv.* [G *eidetisch* f. Gk *eidētikos* f. *eidos* form]

ei•do•lon /īdṓlən/ *n.* (*pl.* **ei•do•lons** or **ei•do•la** /–lə/) **1** a specter; a phantom. **2** an idealized figure. [Gk *eidōlon*: see IDOL]

eigen- /ígən/ *comb. form Math. & Physics* proper; characteristic. [G *eigen* OWN]

ei•gen•fre•quen•cy /ígənfreekwənsee/ *n.* (*pl.* **•cies**) *Math. & Physics* one of the natural resonant frequencies of a system.

ei•gen•func•tion /ígənfungkshən/ *n. Math. & Physics* that function which under a given operation generates some multiple of itself.

ei•gen•val•ue /ígənvalyōō/ *n. Math. & Physics* that value by which an eigenfunction of an operation is multiplied after the eigenfunction has been subjected to that operation.

eight /ayt/ *n. & adj.* • *n.* **1** one more than seven, or two less than ten; the product of two units and four units. **2** a symbol for this (8, viii, VIII). **3** a figure resembling the form of 8. **4** a size, etc., denoted by eight. **5** an eight-oared rowing boat or its crew. **6** the time of eight o'clock (*is it eight yet?*). **7** a card with eight pips. • *adj.* that amount to eight. □ **have one over the eight** *Brit. sl.* get slightly drunk. [OE *ehta, eahta*]

eight•ball /áytbawl/ *n.* **1** *Billiards* the black ball, numbered eight. **2** *sl.* a portion of an illegal drug weighing an eighth of an ounce. □ **behind the eight ball** *sl.* at a disadvantage.

eight-ball *n.* a game of pool in which one side must pocket all of the striped or solid balls and finally the eight ball to win.

eight•een /áyteén/ *n. & adj.* • *n.* **1** one more than seventeen, or eight more than ten; the product of two units and nine units. **2** a symbol for this (18, xviii, XVIII). **3** a size, etc., denoted by eighteen. **4** a set or team of eighteen individuals. • *adj.* that amount to eighteen. □□ **eight•eenth** *adj. & n.* [OE *ehtatēne, eaht–*]

eight•een•mo /áyteénmō/ *n.* = OCTODECIMO.

eight•een-wheel•er *n.* a large tractor-trailer with eighteen wheels.

eight•fold /áytfóld/ *adj. & adv.* • *adj.* **1** eight times as much or as many. **2** having eight parts or elements. • *adv.* by eight times; to eight times the number or amount.

eighth /ayt-th, ayth/ *n. & adj.* • *n.* **1** the position in a sequence corresponding to the number 8 in the sequence 1–8. **2** something occupying this position. **3** one of eight equal parts of a thing. • *adj.* that is the eighth. □□ **eighth•ly** *adv.*

eighth note *n. Mus.* a note having the time value of an eighth of a whole note and represented by a large dot with a hooked stem. Also called *Brit.* **quaver.**

eight•some /áytsəm/ *n.* **1** (in full **eightsome reel**) a lively Scottish reel for eight dancers. **2** the music for this.

eight•y /áytee/ *n. & adj.* • *n.* (*pl.* **•ies**) **1** the product of eight and ten.

2 a symbol for this (80, lxxx, LXXX). **3** (in *pl.*) the numbers from 80 to 89, esp. the years of a century or of a person's life. ● *adj.* that amount to eighty. □□ **eight•i•eth** *adj. & n.* **eight•y•fold** *adj. & adv.* [OE *–eahtatig* (as EIGHT, –TY²)]

eight•y-first *n.* (**eighty-second**, etc.) the ordinal numbers between eightieth and ninetieth.

eight•y-one *n.* (**eighty-two**, etc.) the cardinal numbers between eighty and ninety.

ein•korn /ínkawrn/ *n.* a kind of wheat (*Triticum monococcum*). [G f. *ein* one + *Korn* seed]

ein•stein•i•um /ínstíneeəm/ *n. Chem.* a transuranic radioactive metallic element produced artificially from plutonium. ¶ Symb.: **Es**. [A. *Einstein*, Ger.-Amer. physicist d. 1955]

ei•ren•ic var. of IRENIC.

eis•tedd•fod /ístéthvod, aystéth-/ *n.* (*pl.* **eis•tedd•fods** or **eisteddfod•au** /–dí/) a congress of Welsh bards; a national or local festival for musical competitions, etc. □□ **eis•tedd•fod•ic** /–vódik/ *adj.* [Welsh, lit. = session, f. *eistedd* sit]

ei•ther /éethər, íthər/ *adj., pron., adv., & conj.* ● *adj. & pron.* **1** one or the other of two (*either of you can go; you may have either book*). **2** each of two (*houses on either side of the road; either will do*). ● *adv. & conj.* **1** as one possibility (*is either black or white*). **2** as one choice or alternative; which way you will (*either come in or go out*). **3** (with *neg.* or *interrog.*) **a** any more than the other (*I didn't like it either; if you do not go, I shall not either*). **b** moreover (*there is no time to lose, either*). □ **either-or** *n.* an unavoidable choice between alternatives. ● *adj.* involving such a choice. **either way** in either case or event. [OE *ǣgther* f. Gmc]

e•jac•u•late *v. & n.* ● *v.tr.* /ijákyəlayt/ (also *absol.*) **1** utter suddenly (words esp. of prayer or other emotion). **2** eject (fluid, etc., esp. semen) from the body. ● *n.* /ijákyələt/ semen that has been ejaculated from the body. □□ **e•jac•u•la•tion** /–láyshən/ *n.* **e•jac•u•la•tor** *n.* **e•jac•u•la•to•ry** /ijákyələtáwree/ *adj.* [L *ejaculari* to dart (as E-, *jaculum* javelin)]

e•ject /ijékt/ *v.tr.* **1 a** send or drive out precipitately or by force, esp. from a building or other property; compel to leave. **b** dismiss from employment or office. **2 a** cause (the pilot, etc.) to be propelled from an aircraft or spacecraft in an emergency. **b** (*absol.*) (of the pilot, etc.) be ejected in this way (*they both ejected at 1,000 feet*). **3** cause to be removed or drop out (e.g., a spent cartridge from a gun). **4** dispossess (a tenant, etc.) by legal process. **5** dart forth; emit. □□ **e•jec•tive** *adj.* **e•ject•ment** *n.* [L *ejicere eject-* (as E-, *jacere* throw)]

e•jec•tion /ijékshən/ *n.* the act or an instance of ejecting; the process of being ejected.

e•jec•tion seat *n.* a device for the automatic ejection of the pilot, etc., of an aircraft or spacecraft in an emergency.

e•jec•tor /ijéktər/ *n.* a device for ejecting.

e•jec•tor seat *n.* = EJECTION SEAT.

eke /eek/ *v.tr.* □ **eke out 1** (foll. by *with*, *by*) supplement; make the best use of (defective means, etc.). **2** contrive to make (a livelihood) or support (an existence). [OE *ēacan*, rel. to L *augēre* increase]

EKG *abbr.* electrocardiogram. [L, ult. f. Gk *elektron* + *kardio* + *gram*]

-el var. of –LE².

e•lab•o•rate *adj. & v.* ● *adj.* /ilábərət/ **1** carefully or minutely worked out. **2** highly developed or complicated. ● *v.* /ilábərayt/ **1 a** *tr.* work out or explain in detail. **b** *tr.* make more intricate or ornate. **c** *intr.* (often foll. by *on*) go into details (*I need not elaborate*). **2** *tr.* produce by labor. **3** *tr.* (of a natural agency) produce (a substance, etc.) from its elements or sources. □□ **e•lab•o•rate•ly** *adv.* **e•lab•o•rate•ness** *n.* **e•lab•o•ra•tion** /–ráyshən/ *n.* **e•lab•o•ra•tive** *adj.* **e•lab•o•ra•tor** *n.* [L *elaboratus* past part. of *elaborare* (as E-, *labor* work)]

é•lan /aylón, aylón/ *n.* vivacity; dash. [F f. *élancer* launch]

e•land /éelənd/ *n.* any antelope of the genus *Taurotragus*, native to Africa, having spirally twisted horns, esp. the largest of living antelopes *T. derbianus*. [Du.,= elk]

e•lapse /iláps/ *v.intr.* (of time) pass by. [L *elabor elaps-* slip away]

e•las•mo•branch /ilázməbrangk/ *n. Zool.* any cartilaginous fish of the subclass Chondrichthyes, e.g., sharks, skates, rays. [mod.L *elasmobranchii* f. Gk *elasmos* beaten metal + *bragkhia* gills]

e•las•mo•sau•rus /ilázməsáwrəs/ *n.* a large extinct marine reptile with paddlelike limbs and tough crocodilelike skin. [mod.L f. Gk *elasmos* beaten metal + *sauros* lizard]

e•las•tic /ilástik/ *adj. & n.* ● *adj.* **1** able to resume its normal bulk or shape spontaneously after contraction, dilatation, or distortion. **2** springy. **3** (of a person or feelings) buoyant. **4** flexible; adaptable (*elastic conscience*). **5** *Econ.* (of demand) variable according to price. **6** *Physics* (of a collision) involving no decrease of kinetic energy. ● *n.* **1** elastic cord or fabric, usu. woven with strips of rubber. **2** (in full **elastic band**) = RUBBER BAND. □□ **e•las•ti•cal•ly** *adv.* **e•las•tic•i•ty** /ílástisitee, eelas–/ *n.* **e•las•ti•cize** /ilástisiz/ *v.tr.* [mod.L *elasticus* f. Gk *elastikos* propulsive f. *elaunō* drive]

e•las•ti•cat•ed /ilástikaytid/ *adj.* (of a fabric) made elastic by weaving with rubber thread.

e•las•to•mer /ilástəmər/ *n.* a natural or synthetic rubber or rubberlike plastic. □□ **e•las•to•mer•ic** /–mérik/ *adj.* [ELASTIC, after *isomer*]

e•late /iláyt/ *v. & adj.* ● *v.tr.* **1** (esp. as **elated** *adj.*) inspirit; stimulate. **2** make proud. ● *adj. archaic* in high spirits; exultant; proud. □□ **e•lat•ed•ly** *adv.* **e•lat•ed•ness** *n.* **e•la•tion** /–láyshən/ *n.* [ME f. L *efferre elat-* raise]

el•a•ter /élətər/ *n.* CLICK BEETLE. [mod.L f. Gk *elatēr* driver f. *elaunō* drive]

E lay•er /éelayər/ *n.* a layer of the ionosphere able to reflect medium-frequency radio waves. [*E* (arbitrary) + LAYER]

el•bow /élbō/ *n. & v.* ● *n.* **1 a** the joint between the forearm and the upper arm. **b** the part of the sleeve of a garment covering the elbow. **2** an elbow-shaped bend or corner; a short piece of piping bent through a right angle. ● *v.tr.* (foll. by *in*, *out*, *aside*, etc.) **1** thrust or jostle (a person or oneself). **2** make (one's way) by thrusting or jostling. **3** nudge or poke with the elbow. □ **at one's elbow** close at hand. **give a person the elbow** *colloq.* send a person away; dismiss or reject a person. **out at the elbows 1** (of a coat) worn out. **2** (of a person) ragged; poor. [OE *elboga, elnboga*, f. Gmc (as ELL¹, BOW¹)]

el•bow grease *n. colloq.* hard physical work, esp. vigorous polishing or cleaning (*you should be able to get the rust off with a wire brush and elbow grease*).

el•bow•room /élbōrōōm/ *n.* plenty of room to move or work in.

eld /eld/ *n. archaic* or *poet.* **1** old age. **2** olden time. [OE *(i)eldu* f. Gmc: cf. OLD]

eld•er¹ /éldər/ *adj. & n.* ● *attrib.adj.* (of two indicated persons, esp. when related) senior; of a greater age (*my elder brother*). ● *n.* (often prec. by *the*) **1** the older or more senior of two indicated (esp. related) persons (*which is the elder?; is my elder by ten years*). **2** (in *pl.*) **a** persons of greater age or seniority (*respect your elders*). **b** persons venerable because of age. **3** a person advanced in life. **4** *hist.* a member of a senate or governing body. **5** an official in the early Christian, Presbyterian, or Mormon churches. □□ **eld•er•ship** *n.* [OE *eldra*, rel. to OLD]

eld•er² /éldər/ *n.* any shrub or tree of the genus *Sambucus*, with white flowers and usu. blue-black or red berries. [OE *ellærn*]

eld•er•ber•ry /éldərberee/ *n.* (*pl.* **•ries**) the berry of the elder, esp. common elder (*Sambucus nigra*) used for making jelly, wine, etc.

eld•er hand *n. Cards* the first player.

eld•er•ly /éldərlee/ *adj. & n.* ● *adj.* **1** somewhat old. **2** (of a person) past middle age. ● *n.* (*collect.*) (prec. by *the*) elderly people. □□ **eld•er•li•ness** *n.*

eld•er states•man *n.* an influential experienced person, esp. a politician, of advanced age.

eld•est /éldist/ *adj. & n.* ● *adj.* first-born or oldest surviving (member of a family, son, daughter, etc.). ● *n.* (often prec. by *the*) the eldest of three or more indicated (*who is the eldest?*). [OE (as ELDER¹)]

eld•est hand *n. Cards* the first player.

El Do•ra•do /éldəraadó/ *n.* (*pl.* **•dos**) **1** any imaginary country or city abounding in gold. **2** a place of great abundance. [Sp. *el dorado* the gilded]

el·dritch /éldrich/ *adj. Sc.* **1** weird. **2** hideous. [16th c.: perh. f. OE *elfrīce* (unrecorded) 'fairy realm']

elec. *abbr.* **1** electric. **2** electrical. **3** electricity.

el·e·cam·pane /élikampáyn/ *n.* **1** a sunflowerlike plant, *Inula helenium*, with bitter aromatic leaves and roots, used in herbal medicine and cooking. **2** an esp. candied confection flavored with this. [corrupt. of med.L *enula* (for L *inula* f. Gk *helenion*) *campana* (prob. = of the fields)]

e·lect /ilékt/ *v. & adj.* ● *v.tr.* **1** (usu. foll. by *to* + infin.) choose (*the principles they elected to follow*). **2** choose (a person) by vote (*elected a new chairman*). **3** *Theol.* (of God) choose (persons) in preference to others for salvation. ● *adj.* **1** chosen. **2** select; choice. **3** *Theol.* chosen by God. **4** (after a noun designating office) chosen but not yet in office (*president elect*). [ME f. L *electus* past part. of *eligere elect-* (as E-, *legere* pick)]

e·lec·tion /ilékshən/ *n.* **1** the process of electing or being elected, esp. of members of a political body. **2** the act or an instance of electing. [ME f. OF f. L *electio –onis* (as ELECT)]

e·lec·tion·eer /ilékshəneér/ *v. & n.* ● *v.intr.* take part in an election campaign. ● *n.* a person who electioneers.

e·lec·tive /iléktiv/ *adj. & n.* ● *adj.* **1 a** (of an office or its holder) filled or appointed by election. **b** (of authority) derived from election. **2** (of a body) having the power to elect. **3** having a tendency to act on or be concerned with some things rather than others (*elective affinity*). **4** (of a course of study) chosen by the student; optional. **5** (of a surgical operation, etc.) optional; not urgently necessary. ● *n.* an elective course of study. □□ **e·lec·tive·ly** *adv.* [F *électif –ive* f. LL *electivus* (as ELECT)]

e·lec·tor /iléktər/ *n.* **1** a person who has the right of voting. **2** (also **E·lec·tor**) *hist.* a German prince entitled to take part in the election of the emperor. **3** a member of the electoral college. □□ **e·lec·tor·ship** *n.* [ME f. F *électeur* f. L *elector* (as ELECT)]

e·lec·tor·al /iléktərəl/ *adj.* relating to or ranking as electors. □□ **e·lec·tor·al·ly** *adv.*

e·lec·tor·al col·lege *n.* **1** a body of persons representing each of the states of the US, who cast votes for the election of the president and vice president. **2** a body of electors.

e·lec·tor·ate /iléktərət/ *n.* **1** a body of electors. **2** *Austral. & NZ* an area represented by one member of parliament. **3** *hist.* the office or territories of a German elector.

E·lec·tra com·plex /iléktrə/ *n. Psychol.* a daughter's subconscious sexual attraction to her father and hostility toward her mother, corresponding to the Oedipus complex in a son. [*Electra* in Gk tragedy, who caused her mother to be murdered for having murdered Electra's father]

e·lec·tret /iléktrit/ *n. Physics* a permanently polarized piece of dielectric material, analogous to a permanent magnet. [ELECTRICITY + MAGNET]

e·lec·tric /iléktrik/ *adj. & n.* ● *adj.* **1** of, worked by, or charged with electricity; producing or capable of generating electricity. **2** causing or charged with sudden and dramatic excitement (*the news had an electric effect; the atmosphere was electric*). ● *n.* **1** an electric light, vehicle, etc. **2** (in *pl.*) electrical equipment. □□ **e·lec·tri·cal·ly** *adv.* [mod.L *electricus* f. L *electrum* f. Gk *ēlektron* amber, the rubbing of which causes electrostatic phenomena]

e·lec·tri·cal /iléktrikəl/ *adj.* **1** of or concerned with or of the nature of electricity. **2** operating by electricity. **3** suddenly or dramatically exciting (*the effect was electrical*).

e·lec·tri·cal tape *n.* an adhesive tape used to cover exposed electrical wires, etc.

e·lec·tric blan·ket *n.* a blanket that can be heated electrically by an internal element.

e·lec·tric chair *n.* a chair in which criminals sentenced to death are executed by electrocution.

e·lec·tric eel *n.* an eellike freshwater fish, *Electrophorus electricus*, native to S. America, that kills its prey by electric shock.

e·lec·tric eye *n. colloq.* a photoelectric cell operating a relay when the beam of light illuminating it is obscured.

e·lec·tric fence *n.* a fence through which an electric current can be passed, giving an electric shock to any person or animal touching it.

e·lec·tric field *n.* a region around a charged particle or object within which a force would be exerted on other charged particles or objects.

e·lec·tric fire *n. Brit.* a usu. portable electric heater.

e·lec·tric gui·tar *n.* a guitar with a built-in sound pickup that converts sound vibrations into electrical signals for amplification.

e·lec·tri·cian /iléktríshən, eélek–/ *n.* a person who installs or maintains electrical equipment, esp. professionally.

e·lec·tric·i·ty /iléktrísitee, eélek–/ *n.* **1** a form of energy resulting from the existence of charged particles (electrons, protons, etc.), either statically as an accumulation of charge or dynamically as a current. **2** the branch of physics dealing with electricity. **3** a supply of electric current for heating, lighting, etc. **4** a state of heightened emotion; excitement; tension.

e·lec·tric or·gan *n.* **1** *Biol.* an organ in some fishes that is used to

produce an electrical discharge for stunning prey, for sensing surroundings, or as a defense. **2** *Mus.* an electrically operated organ.

e·lec·tric ray *n.* any of several marine rays of the family Torpedinidae that can produce an electric shock for the capture of prey and for defense.

e·lec·tric ra·zor *n.* (also **electric shaver**) an electrical device for shaving, with oscillating blades behind a metal guard.

e·lec·tric shock *n.* the effect of a sudden discharge of electricity on a person or animal, usually with stimulation of the nerves and contraction of the muscles.

e·lec·tric storm *n.* a thunderstorm or other violent disturbance of the electrical condition of the atmosphere.

e·lec·tri·fy /iléktrifī/ *v.tr.* (·**fies**, ·**fied**) **1** charge (a body) with electricity. **2** convert (machinery or the place or system employing it) to the use of electric power. **3** cause dramatic or sudden excitement in. □□ **e·lec·tri·fi·ca·tion** /–fikáyshən/ *n.* **e·lec·tri·fi·er** *n.*

e·lec·tro /iléktrō/ *n. & v.* ● *n.* (*pl.* ·**tros**) **1** = ELECTROTYPE *n.* **2** = ELECTROPLATE *n.* ● *v.tr.* (·**troes**, ·**troed**) *colloq.* **1** = ELECTROTYPE *v.* **2** = ELECTROPLATE *v.* [abbr.]

electro- /iléktrō/ *comb. form Electr.* of, relating to, or caused by electricity (*electrocute; electromagnet*). [Gk *ēlektron* amber: see ELECTRIC]

e·lec·tro·bi·ol·o·gy /iléktrōbīóləjee/ *n.* the study of the electrical phenomena of living things.

e·lec·tro·car·di·o·gram /iléktrōkaárdeeəgram/ *n.* a record of the heartbeat traced by an electrocardiograph. [G *Elektrokardiogramm* (as ELECTRO-, CARDIO-, –GRAM)]

e·lec·tro·car·di·o·graph /iléktrōkaárdeeəgraf/ *n.* an instrument recording the electric currents generated by a person's heartbeat. □□ **e·lec·tro·car·di·o·graph·ic** *adj.* **e·lec·tro·car·di·og·ra·phy** /–deeógrəfee/ *n.*

e·lec·tro·chem·i·cal /iléktrōkémikəl/ *adj.* involving electricity as applied to or occurring in chemistry. □□ **e·lec·tro·chem·ist** *n.* **e·lec·tro·chem·is·try** *n.*

e·lec·tro·con·vul·sive /iléktrōkənvúlsiv/ *adj.* (of a therapy) employing the use of the convulsive response to the application of electric shocks.

e·lec·tro·cute /iléktrəkyōōt/ *v.tr.* **1** injure or kill someone by electric shock. **2** execute (a convicted criminal) by means of the electric chair. □□ **e·lec·tro·cu·tion** /–kyōóshən/ *n.* [ELECTRO-, after EXECUTE]

e·lec·trode /iléktrōd/ *n.* a conductor through which electricity enters or leaves an electrolyte, gas, vacuum, etc. [ELECTRIC + Gk *hodos* way]

e·lec·tro·di·al·y·sis /iléktrōdiálisis/ *n.* dialysis in which electrodes are placed on either side of a semipermeable membrane, as used in obtaining pure water from salt water.

e·lec·tro·dy·nam·ics /iléktrōdīnámiks/ *n.pl.* (usu. treated as *sing.*) the branch of mechanics concerned with electric current applied to motive forces. □□ **e·lec·tro·dy·nam·ic** *adj.*

e·lec·tro·en·ceph·a·lo·gram /iléktrōïnséfələgram/ *n.* a record of the brain's activity traced by an electroencephalograph. [G *Elektrenkephalogramm* (as ELECTRO-, ENCEPHALO-, –GRAM)]

e·lec·tro·en·ceph·a·lo·graph /iléktrōïnséfələgraf/ *n.* an instrument recording the electrical activity of the brain. □□ **e·lec·tro·en·ceph·a·log·ra·phy** /–lógrəfee/ *n.*

e·lec·tro·lu·mi·nes·cence /iléktrōlóóminésəns/ *n. Chem.* luminescence produced electrically, esp. by the application of a voltage. □□ **e·lec·tro·lu·mi·nes·cent** /–sənt/ *adj.*

e·lec·trol·y·sis /iléktrólisis, eélek–/ *n.* **1** *Chem.* the decomposition of a substance by the application of an electric current. **2** *Med.* this process applied to the destruction of tumors, hair roots, etc. □□ **e·lec·tro·lyt·ic** /iléktrōlítik/ *adj.* **e·lec·tro·lyt·i·cal** *adj.* **e·lec·tro·lyt·i·cal·ly** *adv.* [ELECTRO- + –LYSIS]

e·lec·tro·lyte /iléktrəlit/ *n.* **1** a substance that conducts electricity when molten or in solution, esp. in an electric cell or battery. **2** a solution of this. [ELECTRO- + Gk *lutos* released f. *luō* loosen]

e·lec·tro·lyze /iléktrəliz/ *v.tr.* subject to or treat by electrolysis. □□ **e·lec·tro·lyz·er** *n.* [ELECTROLYSIS after *analyze*]

e·lec·tro·mag·net /iléktrōmágnit/ *n.* a soft metal core made into a magnet by the passage of electric current through a coil surrounding it.

e·lec·tro·mag·net·ic /iléktrōmagnétik/ *adj.* having both an electrical and a magnetic character or properties. □□ **e·lec·tro·mag·net·i·cal·ly** *adv.*

e·lec·tro·mag·net·ic ra·di·a·tion *n.* a kind of radiation including visible light, radio waves, gamma rays, X rays, etc., in which electric and magnetic fields vary simultaneously.

e·lec·tro·mag·net·ic spec·trum *n.* the range of wavelengths over which electromagnetic radiation extends.

e·lec·tro·mag·net·ic u·nits *n.pl.* a system of electrical units derived primarily from the magnetic properties of electric currents.

e·lec·tro·mag·net·ism /iléktrōmágnitizəm/ *n.* **1** the magnetic forces produced by electricity. **2** the study of this.

e·lec·tro·me·chan·i·cal /iléktrōmikánikəl/ adj. relating to the application of electricity to mechanical processes, devices, etc.

e·lec·trom·e·ter /ilektrómitər, eélek–/ n. an instrument for measuring electrical potential without drawing any current from the circuit. □□ **e·lec·tro·met·ric** /–métrik/ adj. **e·lec·trom·e·try** n.

e·lec·tro·mo·tive /iléktrōmótiv/ adj. producing or tending to produce an electric current.

e·lec·tro·mo·tive force n. a force set up in an electric circuit by a difference in potential.

e·lec·tron /iléktron/ n. a stable elementary particle with a charge of negative electricity, found in all atoms and acting as the primary carrier of electricity in solids. [ELECTRIC + –ON]

e·lec·tron beam n. a stream of electrons in a gas or vacuum.

e·lec·tron dif·frac·tion n. the diffraction of a beam of electrons by atoms or molecules, used for determining crystal structures, etc.

e·lec·tro·neg·a·tive /iléktrōnégətiv/ adj. **1** electrically negative. **2** Chem. (of an element) tending to acquire electrons.

e·lec·tron gun n. a device that produces a narrow stream of electrons from a heated cathode.

e·lec·tron·ic /ilektrónik, eélek–/ adj. **1 a** produced by or involving the flow of electrons. **b** of or relating to electrons or electronics. **2** (of a device) using electronic components. **3 a** (of music) produced by electronic means, and usu. recorded on tape. **b** (of a musical instrument) producing sounds by electronic means. □□ **e·lec·tron·i·cal·ly** adv.

e·lec·tron·ic flash n. a device that produces a flash of light from a gas-discharge tube, used in high-speed photography.

e·lec·tron·ic mail n. messages distributed by electronic means, esp. from one computer system to one or more recipients. Also called E-mail.

e·lec·tron·ic pub·lish·ing n. the issuing of books and other material in machine-readable form rather than on paper.

e·lec·tron·ics /ilektróniks, eélek–/ n.pl. (usu. treated as sing.) **1** a branch of physics and technology concerned with the behavior and movement of electrons in a vacuum, gas, semiconductor, etc. **2** the circuits used in this.

e·lec·tron lens n. a device for focusing a stream of electrons by means of electric or magnetic fields.

e·lec·tron mi·cro·scope n. a microscope with high magnification and resolution, employing electron beams in place of light and using electron lenses.

e·lec·tron pair n. an electron and a positron.

e·lec·tron spin res·o·nance n. a spectroscopic method of locating electrons within the molecules of a paramagnetic substance. ¶ Abbr.: ESR.

e·lec·tron·volt /iléktronvōlt/ n. a unit of energy equal to the work done on an electron in accelerating it through a potential difference of one volt. ¶ Abbr.: eV.

e·lec·tro·phil·ic /iléktrōfilik/ adj. Chem. having an affinity for electrons. □□ **e·lec·tro·phile** /iléktrōfil/ n.

e·lec·tro·pho·re·sis /iléktrōfəreésis/ n. Physics & Chem. the movement of colloidal particles in a fluid under the influence of an electric field. □□ **e·lec·tro·pho·ret·ic** /–fərétik/ adj. [ELECTRO- + Gk phorēsis being carried]

e·lec·troph·o·rus /iléktrófərəs, eélek–/ n. a device for repeatedly generating static electricity by induction. [mod.L f. ELECTRO- + Gk –phoros bearing]

e·lec·tro·plate /iléktrəplayt/ v. & n. •v.tr. coat (a utensil, etc.) by electrolytic deposition with chromium, silver, etc. •n. electroplated articles. □□ **e·lec·tro·plat·er** n.

e·lec·tro·pos·i·tive /iléktrōpózitiv/ adj. **1** electrically positive. **2** Chem. (of an element) tending to lose electrons.

e·lec·tro·scope /iléktrəskōp/ n. an instrument for detecting and measuring electricity, esp. as an indication of the ionization of air by radioactivity. □□ **e·lec·tro·scop·ic** /–skópik/ adj.

e·lec·tro·shock /iléktrōshok/ attrib.adj. (of medical treatment) by means of electric shocks.

e·lec·tro·stat·ic /iléktrōstátik/ adj. of electricity at rest. [ELECTRO- + STATIC after hydrostatic]

e·lec·tro·stat·ics /iléktrōstátiks/ n.pl. (treated as sing.) the study of electricity at rest.

e·lec·tro·stat·ic u·nits n. a system of units based primarily on the forces between electric charges.

e·lec·tro·tech·nol·o·gy /iléktrōteknólajee/ n. the science of the application of electricity in technology. □□ **e·lec·tro·tech·nic** /–téknik/ adj. **e·lec·tro·tech·ni·cal** adj. **e·lec·tro·tech·nics** n.

e·lec·tro·ther·a·py /iléktrōthérəpee/ n. the treatment of diseases by the use of electricity. □□ **e·lec·tro·ther·a·peu·tic** /–pyóŏtik/ adj. **e·lec·tro·ther·a·peu·ti·cal** adj. **e·lec·tro·ther·a·pist** n.

e·lec·tro·ther·mal /iléktrōthérmal/ adj. relating to heat electrically derived.

e·lec·tro·type /iléktrōtīp/ v. & n. •v.tr. copy by the electrolytic deposition of copper on a mold, esp. for printing. •n. a copy so formed. □□ **e·lec·tro·typ·er** n.

e·lec·tro·va·lent /iléktrōváylənt/ adj. Chem. linking ions by a bond resulting from electrostatic attraction. □□ **e·lec·tro·va·lence** /–ləns/ n. **e·lec·tro·va·len·cy** n. [ELECTRO- + –valent after trivalent, etc.]

e·lec·trum /iléktrəm/ n. **1** an alloy of silver and gold used in ancient times. **2** native argentiferous gold ore. [ME f. L f. Gk ēlektron amber, electrum]

e·lec·tu·ar·y /iliékchōoeree/ n. (pl. ·ies) medicinal powder, etc., mixed with honey or other sweet substance. [ME f. LL electuarium, prob. f. Gk ekleikton f. ekleikhō lick up]

el·ee·mos·y·nar·y /élǝmósineree, –móz–, éleeǝ–/ adj. **1** of or dependent on alms. **2** charitable. **3** gratuitous. [med.L eleemosynarius f. LL eleemosyna: see ALMS]

el·e·gant /éligənt/ adj. **1** graceful in appearance or manner. **2** tasteful; refined. **3** (of a mode of life, etc.) of refined luxury. **4** ingeniously simple and pleasing. **5** excellent. □□ **el·e·gance** /–gəns/ n. **el·e·gant·ly** adv. [F élégant or L elegant-, rel. to eligere: see ELECT]

el·e·gi·ac /élijíak, ileéjeeak/ adj. & n. •adj. **1** (of a meter) used for elegies. **2** mournful. •n. (in pl.) verses in an elegiac meter. □□ **el·e·gi·a·cal·ly** adv. [F élégiaque or f. LL elegiacus f. Gk elegeiakos: see ELEGY]

el·e·gi·ac coup·let n. a pair of lines consisting of a dactylic hexameter and a pentameter, esp. in Greek and Latin verse.

el·e·gize /élijiz/ v. **1** intr. (often foll. by upon) write an elegy. **2** intr. write in a mournful strain. **3** tr. write an elegy upon. □□ **el·e·gist** n.

el·e·gy /élijee/ n. (pl. ·gies) **1** a song of lament, esp. for the dead (sometimes vaguely used of other poems). **2** a poem in elegiac meter. [F élégie or L elegia f. Gk elegeia f. elegos mournful poem]

elem. abbr. elementary.

el·e·ment /élimənt/ n. **1** a component part or group; a contributing factor or thing. **2** Chem. & Physics any of the hundred or so substances that cannot be resolved by chemical means into simpler substances. **3 a** any of the four substances (earth, water, air, and fire) in ancient and medieval philosophy. **b** any of these as a being's natural abode or environment. **c** a person's appropriate or preferred sphere of operation. **4** Electr. a resistance wire that heats up in an electric heater, cooker, etc.; an electrode. **5** (in pl.) atmospheric agencies, esp. wind and storm. **6** (in pl.) the rudiments of learning or of a branch of knowledge. **7** (in pl.) the bread and wine of the Eucharist. **8** Math. & Logic an entity that is a single member of a set. □ **in** (or **out of**) **one's element** in (or out of) one's accustomed or preferred surroundings. **reduced to its elements** analyzed. [ME f. OF f. L elementum]

el·e·men·tal /élimént'l/ adj. & n. •adj. **1** of the four elements. **2** of the powers of nature (elemental worship). **3** comparable to a force of nature (elemental grandeur; elemental tumult). **4** uncompounded (elemental oxygen). **5** essential. •n. an entity or force thought to be physically manifested by occult means. □□ **el·e·men·tal·ism** n. (in senses 1, 2). [med.L elementalis (as ELEMENT)]

el·e·men·ta·ry /éliméntəree, –tree/ adj. **1 a** dealing with or arising from the simplest facts of a subject; rudimentary; introductory. **b** simple. **2** Chem. not decomposable. □□ **el·e·men·tar·i·ly** /–tərəlee/ adv. **el·e·men·tar·i·ness** n. [ME f. L elementarius (as ELEMENT)]

el·e·men·ta·ry par·ti·cle n. Physics any of several subatomic particles supposedly not decomposable into simpler ones.

el·e·men·ta·ry school n. a primary school for the first five, six, or eight grades.

el·en·chus /iléngkǝs/ n. (pl. **e·len·chi** /–kī/) Logic logical refutation. □□ **e·lenc·tic** adj. [L f. Gk elegkhos]

el·e·phant /élifənt/ n. (pl. same or **el·e·phants**) **1** the largest living land animal, of which two species survive, the larger African (Loxodonta africana) and the smaller Indian (Elephas maximus), both with a trunk and long curved ivory tusks. **2** Brit. a size of paper (23 x 28 in). □□ **el·e·phan·toid** /–fantóyd/ adj. [ME olifaunt, etc., f. OF oli-, elefant ult. f. L elephantus, elephans f. Gk elephas –antos ivory, elephant]

African elephant   Indian elephant

el·e·phant grass n. any of various tall African grasses, esp. Pennisetum purpureum.

el·e·phan·ti·a·sis /élifəntíəsis/ n. gross enlargement of the body, esp. the limbs, caused by lymphatic obstruction, esp. by a nematode parasite. [L f. Gk (as ELEPHANT)]

el·e·phan·tine /élifánteen, –tīn, éləfən–/ adj. **1** of elephants. **2 a** huge. **b** clumsy; unwieldy (elephantine movements; elephantine humor). [L elephantinus f. Gk elephantinos (as ELEPHANT)]

el·e·phant seal n. a large seal of the genus Mirounga of Antarctica and the west coast of North America, the male of which has an inflatable proboscis. Also called **sea elephant**.

el·e·phant shrew *n.* any small insect-eating mammal of the family Macroscelididae, native to Africa, having a long snout and long hind limbs.

El·eu·sin·i·an /élyōōsíneeən/ *adj.* of or relating to Eleusis near Athens. [L *Eleusinius* f. Gk *Eleusinios*]

El·eu·sin·i·an mys·ter·ies *n. Gk Hist.* the annual celebrations held at ancient Eleusis in honor of Demeter.

elev. *abbr.* elevation.

el·e·vate /élivayt/ *v.tr.* **1** bring to a higher position. **2** *Eccl.* hold up (the Host or the chalice) for adoration. **3** raise; lift (one's eyes, etc.). **4** raise the axis of (a gun). **5** raise (a railroad, etc.) above ground level. **6** exalt in rank, etc. **7** (usu. as **elevated** *adj.*) **a** raise the spirits of; elate. **b** raise morally or intellectually (*elevated style*). **8** (as **elevated** *adj.*) *colloq.* slightly drunk. □□ **el·e·va·to·ry** *adj.* [L *elevare* raise (as E-, *levis* light)]

el·e·va·tion /élivávshən/ *n.* **1 a** the process of elevating or being elevated. **b** the angle with the horizontal, esp. of a gun or of the direction of a heavenly body. **c** the height above a given level, esp. sea level. **d** a raised area; a swelling on the skin. **2** loftiness; grandeur; dignity. **3 a** a drawing or diagram made by projection on a vertical plane (cf. PLAN). **b** a flat drawing of the front, side, or back of a house, etc. **4** *Ballet* **a** the capacity of a dancer to attain height in springing movements. **b** the action of tightening the muscles and uplifting the body. □□ **el·e·va·tion·al** *adj.* (in sense 2). [ME f. OF *elevation* or L *elevatio*: see ELEVATE]

el·e·va·tor /élivaytər/ *n.* **1** a hoisting machine. **2** *Aeron.* the movable part of a tailplane for changing the pitch of an aircraft. **3 a** a platform or compartment housed in a shaft for raising and lowering persons or things to different floors of a building or different levels of a mine, etc. **b** a place for lifting and storing quantities of grain. **4** that which elevates, esp. a muscle that raises a limb. [mod.L (as ELEVATE)]

e·lev·en /ilévən/ *n. & adj.* ● *n.* **1** one more than ten; the sum of six units and five units. **2** a symbol for this (11, xi, XI). **3** a size, etc., denoted by eleven. **4** a set or team of eleven individuals. **5** the time of eleven o'clock (*is it eleven yet?*). ● *adj.* that amount to eleven. [OE *endleofon* f. Gmc]

e·lev·en·fold /ilévənfōld/ *adj. & adv.* **1** eleven times as much or as many. **2** consisting of eleven parts.

e·lev·ens·es /ilévənziz/ *n.* (usu. in *pl.*) *Brit. colloq.* light refreshment, usu. with tea or coffee, taken about 11 a.m.

e·lev·enth /ilévənth/ *n. & adj.* ● *n.* **1** the position in a sequence corresponding to the number 11 in the sequence 1– 11. **2** something occupying this position. **3** one of eleven equal parts of a thing. **4** *Mus.* **a** an interval or chord spanning an octave and a third in the diatonic scale. **b** a note separated from another by this interval. ● *adj.* that is the eleventh.

e·lev·enth hour *n.* the last possible moment.

el·e·von /élivon/ *n. Aeron.* the movable part of the trailing edge of a delta wing. [ELEVATOR + AILERON]

elf /elf/ *n.* (*pl.* **elves** /elvz/) **1** a mythological being, esp. one that is small and mischievous. **2** a sprite or little creature. □□ **elf·ish** *adj.* **elv·ish** *adj.* [OE f. Gmc]

elf·in /élfin/ *adj. & ● n.* ● *adj.* of elves; elflike; tiny; dainty. ● *n. archaic* a dwarf; a child. [ELF, perh. infl. by ME *elvene* genit. pl. of *elf*, and by *Elphin* in Arthurian romance]

elf·lock /élflok/ *n.* (usu. in *pl.*) a tangled mass of hair.

e·lic·it /ilísit/ *v.tr.* **1** draw out; evoke (an admission, response, etc.). **2** draw forth (what is latent). □□ **e·lic·i·ta·tion** *n.* **e·lic·i·tor** *n.* [L *elicere elicit-* (as E-, *lacere* entice)]

▶To elicit is to call forth (*it was difficult to elicit any information from her when she was so upset*). **Illicit** is an adjective meaning "unlawful" (*he was engaged in an illicit activity*).

e·lide /ilíd/ *v.tr.* omit (a vowel or syllable) by elision. [L *elidere elis-* crush out (as E-, *laedere* knock)]

el·i·gi·ble /élijibəl/ *adj.* **1** (often foll. by *for*) fit or entitled to be chosen (*eligible for a rebate*). **2** desirable or suitable, esp. as a partner in marriage. □□ **el·i·gi·bil·i·ty** *n.* **el·i·gi·bly** *adv.* [F *éligible* f. LL *eligibilis* (as ELECT)]

e·lim·i·nate /iliminayt/ *v.tr.* **1 a** remove; get rid of. **b** kill; murder. **2** exclude from consideration; ignore as irrelevant. **3** exclude from further participation in a competition, etc., on defeat. **4** *Physiol.* discharge (waste matter). **5** *Chem.* remove (a simpler substance) from a compound. **6** *Algebra* remove (a quantity) by combining equations. □□ **e·lim·i·na·tion** /–náyshən/ *n.* **e·lim·i·na·tor** *n.* **e·lim·i·na·to·ry** /–nətáwree/ *n.* [L *eliminare* (as E-, *limen liminis* threshold)]

e·li·sion /ilízhən/ *n.* **1** the omission of a vowel or syllable in pronouncing (as in *I'm, let's, e'en*). **2** the omission of a passage in a book, etc. [LL *elisio* (as ELIDE)]

e·lite /ayleét, əleét/ *adj. & n.* ● *n.* **1** (prec. by *the*) the best or choice part of a larger body or group. **2** a select group or class. **3** a size of letter in typewriting (12 per inch). ● *adj.* of or belonging to an elite; exclusive. [F f. past part. of *élire* f. Rmc: rel. to ELECT]

e·lit·ism /ayleétizəm, əleet–/ *n.* **1** advocacy of or reliance on leadership or dominance by a select group. **2** a sense of belonging to an elite. □□ **e·lit·ist** *n. & adj.*

e·lix·ir /ilíksər/ *n.* **1** *Alchemy* **a** a preparation supposedly able to change metals into gold. **b** (in full **elixir of life**) a preparation supposedly able to prolong life indefinitely. **c** a supposed remedy for all ills. **2** *Pharm.* an aromatic solution used as a medicine or flavoring. **3** the quintessence or kernel of a thing. [ME f. med.L f. Arab. *al-iksīr* f. *al* the + *iksīr* prob. f. Gk *xērion* powder for drying wounds f. *xēros* dry]

E·liz·a·be·than /ilízəbeéthən/ *adj. & n.* ● *adj.* of the time of England's Queen Elizabeth I (1558–1603) or of Queen Elizabeth II (1952–). ● *n.* a person, esp. a writer, of the time of Queen Elizabeth I or II.

elk /elk/ *n.* (*pl.* same or **elks**) **1** a large deer, *Cervus canadensis*, native to North America. Also called **wapiti**. **2** a large deer, *Alces alces*, of N. Europe and Asia; a moose. [ME, prob. repr. OE *elh, eolh*]

elk·hound /élkhownd/ *n.* (in full **Norwegian elkhound**) a large Scandinavian hunting dog with a shaggy coat.

ell¹ /el/ *n. hist.* a former measure of length, about 45 inches. [OE *eln*, rel. to L *ulna*: see ULNA]

ell² *n.* something that is L-shaped or that creates an L shape, in particular: **1** an extension of a building or room that is at right angles to the main part. **2** a bend or joint for connecting two pipes at right angles.

el·lipse /ilíps/ *n.* a regular oval, traced by a point moving in a plane so that the sum of its distances from two other points is constant, or resulting when a cone is cut by a plane that does not intersect the base and makes a smaller angle with the base than the side of the cone makes (cf. HYPERBOLA). [F f. L *ellipsus* f. Gk *elleipsis* f. *elleipō* come short f. *en* in + *leipō* leave]

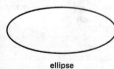
ellipse

el·lip·sis /ilípsis/ *n.* (*pl.* **el·lip·ses** /–seez/) **1** the omission from a sentence of words needed to complete the construction or sense. **2** the omission of a sentence at the end of a paragraph. **3** a set of three dots, etc., indicating an omission.

el·lip·soid /ilípsoyd/ *n.* a solid of which all the plane sections normal to one axis are circles and all the other plane sections are ellipses. □□ **el·lip·soi·dal** /–sóyd'l/ *adj.*

el·lip·tic /ilíptik/ *adj.* (also **el·lip·ti·cal**) of, relating to, or having the form of an ellipse or ellipsis. □□ **el·lip·ti·cal·ly** *adv.* **el·lip·tic·i·ty** /élip-tísitee/ *n.* [Gk *elleiptikos* defective f. *elleipō* (as ELLIPSE)]

elm /elm/ *n.* **1** any tree of the genus *Ulmus*, esp. *U. procera* with rough serrated leaves. **2** (in full **elmwood**) the wood of the elm. □□ **elm·y** *adj.* [OE, rel. to L *ulmus*]

el·o·cu·tion /éləkyōōshən/ *n.* **1** the art of clear and expressive speech, esp. of distinct pronunciation and articulation. **2** a particular style of speaking. □□ **el·o·cu·tion·ar·y** *adj.* **el·o·cu·tion·ist** *n.* [L *elocutio* f. *eloqui elocut-* speak out (as E-, *loqui* speak)]

e·lon·gate /iláwnggayt, –long–/ *v. & adj.* ● *v.* **1** *tr.* lengthen; prolong. **2** *intr. Bot.* be of slender or tapering form. ● *adj. Bot. & Zool.* long in proportion to width. [LL *elongare* (as E-, L *longus* long)]

e·lon·ga·tion /ilawnggáyshən, ilong–, eélawng–, eélong–/ *n.* **1** the act or an instance of lengthening; the process of being lengthened. **2** a part of a line, etc., formed by lengthening. **3** *Mech.* the amount of extension under stress. **4** *Astron.* the angular separation of a planet from the sun or of a satellite from a planet. [ME f. LL *elongatio* (as ELONGATE)]

e·lope /ilóp/ *v.intr.* **1** run away to marry secretly, esp. without parental consent. **2** run away with a lover. □□ **e·lope·ment** *n.* **e·lop·er** *n.* [AF *aloper* perh. f. a ME form *alope*, rel. to LEAP]

el·o·quence /éləkwəns/ *n.* **1** fluent and effective use of language. **2** rhetoric. [ME f. OF f. L *eloquentia* f. *eloqui* speak out (as E-, *loqui* speak)]

el·o·quent /éləkwənt/ *adj.* **1** possessing or showing eloquence. **2** (often foll. by *of*) clearly expressive or indicative. □□ **el·o·quent·ly** *adv.* [ME f. OF f. L *eloqui* (as ELOQUENCE)]

else /els/ *adv.* **1** (prec. by indef. or interrog. pron.) besides; in addition (*someone else; nowhere else; who else*). **2** instead; other; different (*what else could I say?; he did not love her, but someone else*). **3** otherwise; if not (*run, (or) else you will be late*). [OE *elles*, rel. to L *alius*, Gk *allos*]

else·where /éls-hwair, –wáir/ *adv.* in or to some other place. [OE *elles hwǣr* (as ELSE, WHERE)]

el·u·ant /élyōōənt/ *n.* (also **el·u·ent**) *Chem.* a fluid used for elution. [L *eluere* wash out (as E-, *luere* lut–wash)]

el·u·ate /élyōō–it, –ayt/ *n. Chem.* a solution or gas stream obtained by elution. [formed as ELUENT]

e·lu·ci·date /ilōōsidáyt/ *v.tr.* throw light on; explain. □□ **e·lu·ci·da·**

tion /–dáyshən/ *n.* **e•lu•ci•da•tive** *adj.* **e•lu•ci•da•tor** *n.* **e•lu•ci•da•to•ry** *adj.* [LL *elucidare* (as E-, LUCID)]

e•lude /ilóod / *v. tr.* **1** escape adroitly from (a danger, difficulty, pursuer, etc.); dodge. **2** avoid compliance with (a law, request, etc.) or fulfillment of (an obligation). **3** (of a fact, solution, etc.) escape from or baffle (a person's memory or understanding). □□ **e•lu•sion** /ilóozhən/ *n.* **e•lu•so•ry** /–lóosəree/ *adj.* [L *eludere elus-* (as E-, *ludere* play)]

el•u•ent var. of ELUANT.

e•lu•sive /ilóosiv/ *adj.* **1** difficult to find or catch; tending to elude. **2** difficult to remember or recall. **3** (of an answer, etc.) avoiding the point raised; seeking to elude. □□ **e•lu•sive•ly** *adv.* **e•lu•sive•ness** *n.*

e•lute /ilóot/ *v. tr.* Chem. remove (an adsorbed substance) by washing. □□ **e•lu•tion** /–lóoshən/ *n.* [G *eluieren* (as ELUENT)]

e•lu•tri•ate /ilóotreeayt/ *v. tr.* Chem. separate (lighter and heavier particles in a mixture) by suspension in an upward flow of liquid or gas. □□ **e•lu•tri•a•tion** /–áyshən/ *n.* [L *elutriare elutriat-* (as E-, *lutriare* wash)]

el•ver /élvər/ *n.* a young eel. [var. of *eel-fare* (see FARE) = a brood of young eels]

elves *pl.* of ELF.

elv•ish see ELF.

E•ly•si•um /ilízeeəm, ilízh–/ *n.* **1** (also **E•ly•sian fields**) (in Greek mythology) the abode of the blessed after death. **2** a place or state of ideal happiness. □□ **e•ly•sian** or **E•ly•sian** *adj.* [L f. Gk *Elusion* (*pedion* plain)]

el•y•tron /élitron/ *n.* (*pl.* **el•y•tra** /–trə/) the outer hard, usu. brightly colored wing case of a coleopterous insect. [Gk *elutron* sheath]

em /em/ *n.* Printing **1** a unit for measuring the amount of printed matter in a line, usually equal to the nominal width of capital M. **2** a unit of measurement equal to 12 points. [name of the letter *M*]

em- /im, em/ *prefix* assim. form of EN-¹, EN-² before *b*, *p*.

'em /əm/ *pron.* colloq. them (*let 'em all come*). [orig. a form of ME *hem*, dative and accus. 3rd pers. pl. pron.: now regarded as an abbr. of THEM]

e•ma•ci•ate /imáysheeayt/ *v. tr.* (esp. as **emaciated** *adj.*) make abnormally thin or feeble. □□ **e•ma•ci•a•tion** /–áyshən/ *n.* [L *emaciare emaciat-* (as E-, *macies* leanness)]

e-mail /eémayl/ *n.* (also **E-mail**) = ELECTRONIC MAIL.

GRAMMAR TIP e-mail

E-mail Acronyms and Emoticons. Because **e-mail** is characterized by speed and informality, users have developed a number of ways to get their ideas across while saving keystrokes. **Acronyms** (very often used in lower case) that stand for commonly used expressions include:

bbl	=	be back later
bfn	=	bye for now
btw	=	by the way
fwiw	=	for what it's worth
hsik	=	how should I know?
imo	=	in my opinion
lol	=	laughing out loud
otl	=	out to lunch
otoh	=	on the other hand
tic	=	tongue in cheek
ttfn	=	ta ta for now
ttyl	=	talk to you later

E-mail users also rely on **emoticons** or "smileys" to summarize emotions via keystrokes (to be viewed sideways):

:-)	=	happy
:-(	=	sad
:-	=	upset
:-D	=	laughing
:-|	=	bored
8-O	=	extremely shocked
:-\	=	undecided
;-)	=	winking

em•a•nate /émənayt/ *v.* **1** *intr.* (usu. foll. by *from*) (of an idea, rumor, etc.) issue; originate (from a source). **2** *intr.* (usu. foll. by *from*) (of gas, light, etc.) proceed; issue. **3** *tr.* emit; send forth. [L *emanare* flow out]

em•a•na•tion /émənáyshən/ *n.* **1** the act or process of emanating. **2** something that emanates from a source (esp. of virtues, qualities, etc.). **3** Chem. a radioactive gas formed by radioactive decay. □□ **em•a•na•tive** *adj.* [LL *emanatio* (as EMANATE)]

e•man•ci•pate /imánsipayt/ *v. tr.* **1** free from restraint, esp. legal, social, or political. **2** (usu. as **emancipated** *adj.*) cause to be less inhibited by moral or social convention. **3** free from slavery. □□ **e•man•ci•pa•tion** /–páyshən/ *n.* **e•man•ci•pa•tor** *n.* **e•man•ci•pa•to•ry**

adj. [L *emancipare* transfer property (as E-, *manus* hand + *capere* take)]

e•mas•cu•late *v. & adj.* ● *v. tr.* /imáskyəlayt/ **1** deprive of force or vigor; make feeble or ineffective. **2** castrate. ● *adj.* /imáskyələt/ **1** deprived of force or vigor. **2** castrated. **3** effeminate. □□ **e•mas•cu•la•tion** /–láyshən/ *n.* **e•mas•cu•la•tor** *n.* **e•mas•cu•la•to•ry** /–lətáwree/ *adj.* [L *emasculatus* past part. of *emasculare* (as E-, *masculus* dimin. of *mas* male)]

em•balm /embaám, im–/ *v. tr.* **1** preserve (a corpse) from decay orig. with spices, now by means of arterial injection. **2** preserve from oblivion. **3** endue with balmy fragrance. □□ **em•balm•er** *n.* **em•balm•ment** *n.* [ME f. OF *embaumer* (as EN-¹, BALM)]

em•bank /embángk, im–/ *v. tr.* shut in or confine (a river, etc.) with an artificial bank.

em•bank•ment /embángkmənt, im–/ *n.* an earth or stone bank for keeping back water, or for carrying a road or railroad.

em•bar•go /embaárgō/ *n. & v.* ● *n.* (*pl.* **-goes**) **1** an order of a government forbidding foreign ships to enter, or any ships to leave, its ports. **2** an official suspension of commerce or other activity (*be under an embargo*). **3** an impediment. ● *v. tr.* (**-goes, -goed**) **1** place (ships, trade, etc.) under embargo. **2** seize (a ship, goods) for government service. [Sp. f. *embargar* arrest f. Rmc (as IN-², BAR¹)]

em•bark /embaárk, im–/ *v.* **1** *tr. & intr.* (often foll. by *for*) put or go on board a ship or aircraft (to a destination). **2** *intr.* (foll. by *on, upon*) engage in an activity or undertaking. □□ **em•bar•ka•tion** *n.* (in sense 1). [F *embarquer* (as IN-², BARK³)]

em•bar•ras de choix /óNbaraá də shwaá/ *n.* (also **em•bar•ras de ri•chesses** /reeshés/) more options or resources than one knows what to do with. [F, = embarrassment of choice, riches]

em•bar•rass /embárəs, im–/ *v. tr.* **1 a** cause (a person) to feel awkward or self-conscious or ashamed. **b** (as **embarrassed** *adj.*) having or expressing a feeling of awkwardness or self-consciousness. **2** (as **embarrassed** *adj.*) encumbered with debts. **3** encumber; impede. **4** complicate (a question, etc.). **5** perplex. □□ **em•bar•rassed•ly** *adv.* **em•bar•rass•ing•ly** *adv.* **em•bar•rass•ing•ly** *adv.* **em•bar•rass•ment** *n.* [F *embarrasser* (orig. = hamper) f. Sp. *embarazar* f. It. *imbarrare* bar in (as IN-², BAR¹)]

em•bas•sy /émbəsee/ *n.* (*pl.* **-sies**) **1 a** the residence or offices of an ambassador. **b** the ambassador and staff attached to an embassy. **2** a deputation or mission to a foreign country. [earlier *ambassy* f. OF *ambassée*, etc., f. med.L *ambasciata* f. Rmc (as AMBASSADOR)]

em•bat•tle /embát'l, im–/ *v. tr.* **1 a** set (an army, etc.) in battle array. **b** fortify against attack. **2** provide (a building or wall) with battlements. **3** (as **embattled** *adj.*) **a** prepared or arrayed for battle. **b** involved in a conflict or difficult undertaking. **c** Heraldry like battlements in form. [ME f. OF *embataillier* (as EN-¹, BATTLE): see BATTLEMENT]

em•bay /embáy, im–/ *v. tr.* **1** enclose in or as in a bay; shut in. **2** form (a coast) into bays. □□ **em•bay•ment** *n.*

em•bed /embéd, im–/ *v. tr.* (also **im•bed**) (**-bed•ded, -bed•ding**) **1** (esp. as **embedded** *adj.*) fix firmly in a surrounding mass (*embedded in concrete*). **2** (of a mass) surround so as to fix firmly. **3** place in or as in a bed. □□ **em•bed•ment** *n.*

em•bel•lish /embélish, im–/ *v. tr.* **1** beautify; adorn. **2** add interest to (a narrative) with fictitious additions. □□ **em•bel•lish•er** *n.* **em•bel•lish•ment** *n.* [ME f. OF *embellir* (as EN-¹, *bel* handsome f. L *bellus*)]

em•ber¹ /émbər/ *n.* **1** (usu. in *pl.*) a small piece of glowing coal or wood in a dying fire. **2** an almost extinct residue of a past activity, feeling, etc. [OE *ǣmyrge* f. Gmc]

em•ber² /émbər/ *n.* (in full **ember-goose**) = GREAT NORTHERN DIVER. [Norw. *emmer*]

em•ber day /émbər/ *n. pl.* any of the days in the quarterly three-day periods traditionally reserved for fasting and prayer in the Christian Church, now associated with ordinations. [OE *ymbren* (n.), perh. f. *ymbryne* period f. *ymb* about + *ryne* course]

em•bez•zle /embézəl, im–/ *v. tr.* (also *absol.*) divert (money, etc.) fraudulently to one's own use. □□ **em•bez•zle•ment** *n.* **em•bez•zler** *n.* [AF *embesiler* (as EN-¹, OF *besillier* maltreat, ravage, of unkn. orig.)]

em•bit•ter /embítər, im–/ *v. tr.* **1** arouse bitter feelings in (a person). **2** make more bitter or painful. **3** render (a person or feelings) hostile. □□ **em•bit•ter•ment** *n.*

em•bla•zon /embláyzən, im–/ *v. tr.* **1 a** portray conspicuously, as on a heraldic shield. **b** adorn (a shield) with heraldic devices. **2** adorn brightly and conspicuously. **3** celebrate, extol. □□ **em•bla•zon•ment** *n.*

em•blem /émbləm/ *n.* **1** a symbol or representation typifying or identifying an institution, quality, etc. **2** (foll. by *of*) (of a person) the type (*the very emblem of courage*). **3** a heraldic device or symbolic object as a distinctive badge. □□ **em•blem•at•ic** /–mátik/ *adj.* **em•blem•at•i•cal** *adj.* **em•blem•at•i•cal•ly** *adv.* [ME f. L *emblema* f. Gk *emblēma –matos* insertion f. *emballō* throw in (as EN-¹, *ballō* throw)]

em•blem•a•tize /imblémətiz/ *v. tr.* **1** serve as an emblem of. **2** represent by an emblem.

em•ble•ments /émbləmənts/ *n. pl.* Law crops normally harvested annually, regarded as personal property. [ME f. OF *emblaement* f. *emblaier* (as EN-¹, *blé* grain)]

em·bod·y /embódee, im–/ *v.tr.* (·**ies**, ·**ied**) **1** give a concrete or discernible form to (an idea, concept, etc.). **2** (of a thing or person) be an expression of (an idea, etc.). **3** express tangibly (*courage embodied in heroic actions*). **4** form into a body. **5** include; comprise. **6** provide (a spirit) with bodily form. □□ **em·bod·i·ment** *n.*

em·bold·en /embóldən, im–/ *v.tr.* (often foll. by *to* + infin.) make bold; encourage.

em·bo·lism /émbəlizəm/ *n.* an obstruction of any artery by a clot of blood, air bubble, etc. [ME, = 'intercalation' f. LL *embolismus* f. Gk *embolismos* f. *emballō* (as EMBLEM)]

em·bo·lus /émbələs/ *n.* (*pl.* **em·bo·li** /–lī/) an object causing an embolism. [L, = piston, f. Gk *embolos* peg, stopper]

em·bon·point /óⁿbawⁿpwáⁿ/ *n.* plumpness (of a person). [F *en bon point* in good condition]

em·bos·om /embóozəm, im–/ *v.tr. literary* **1** embrace. **2** enclose; surround.

em·boss /embós, im–/ *v.tr.* **1** carve or mold in relief. **2** form figures, etc., so that they stand out on (a surface). **3** make protuberant. □□ **em·boss·er** *n.* **em·boss·ment** *n.* [ME, f. OF (as EN-¹, BOSS²)]

em·bou·chure /ómbooshŏŏr/ *n.* **1** *Mus.* **a** the mode of applying the mouth to the mouthpiece of a brass or wind instrument. **b** the mouthpiece of some instruments. **2** the mouth of a river. **3** the opening of a valley. [F f. *s'emboucher* discharge itself by the mouth (as EN-¹, *bouche* mouth)]

em·bow·el /embówəl, im–/ *v.tr.* (**em·bow·eled, em·bow·el·ing;** esp. *Brit.* **em·bow·elled, em·bow·el·ling**) *archaic* = DISEMBOWEL. [OF *emboweler* f. *esboueler* (as EX-¹, BOWEL)]

em·bow·er /embówr, im–/ *v.tr. literary* enclose as in a bower.

em·brace /embráys, im–/ *v. & v.* ● *v.tr.* **1 a** hold (a person) closely in the arms, esp. as a sign of affection. **b** (*absol.*, of two people) hold each other closely. **2** clasp; enclose. **3** accept eagerly (an offer, opportunity, etc.). **4** adopt (a course of action, doctrine, cause, etc.). **5** include; comprise. **6** take in with the eye or mind. ● *n.* an act of embracing; holding in the arms. □□ **em·brace·a·ble** *adj.* **em·brace·ment** *n.* **em·brac·er** *n.* [ME f. OF *embracer*, ult. f. L *in*- IN-¹ + *bracchium* arm]

em·branch·ment /embránchmənt, im–/ *n.* a branching out (of the arm of a river, etc.). [F *embranchement* BRANCH (as EN-¹, BRANCH)]

em·bra·sure /embráyzhər, im–/ *n.* **1** the beveling of a wall at the sides of a door or window; splaying. **2** a small opening in a parapet of a fortified building, splayed on the inside. □□ **em·bra·sured** *adj.* [F f. *embraser* splay, of unkn. orig.]

em·brit·tle /embrít'l, im–/ *v.tr.* make brittle. □□ **em·brit·tle·ment** *n.*

em·bro·ca·tion /émbrōkáyshən/ *n.* a liquid used for rubbing on the body to relieve muscular pain, etc. [F *embrocation* or med.L *embrocatio* ult. f. Gk *embrokhē* lotion]

em·broi·der /embróydər, im–/ *v.tr.* **1** (also *absol.*) **a** decorate (cloth, etc.) with needlework. **b** create (a design) in this way. **2** add interest to (a narrative) with fictitious additions. □□ **em·broi·der·er** *n.* [ME f. AF *enbrouder* (as EN-¹, OF *brouder, broisder* f. Gmc)]

em·broi·der·y /embróydəree, im–/ *n.* (*pl.* ·**ies**) **1** the art of embroidering. **2** embroidered work; a piece of this. **3** unnecessary or extravagant ornament. [ME f. AF *enbrouderie* (as EMBROIDER)]

em·broil /embróyl, im–/ *v.tr.* **1** (often foll. by *with*) involve (a per-

---

SYNONYM TIP emblem

ATTRIBUTE, IMAGE, SIGN, SYMBOL, TOKEN, TYPE. When it comes to representing or embodying the invisible or intangible, you can't beat a **symbol**. It applies to anything that serves as an outward sign of something immaterial or spiritual (*the cross as a symbol of salvation; the crown as a symbol of monarchy*), although the association between the symbol and what it represents does not have to be based on tradition or convention and may, in fact, be quite arbitrary (*the annual gathering at the cemetery became a symbol of the family's long and tragic history*). An **emblem** is a visual symbol or pictorial device that represents the character or history of a family, a nation, or an office (*the eagle is an emblem of the United States*). It is very close in meaning to **attribute**, which is an object that is conventionally associated with either an individual, a group, or an abstraction (*the spiked wheel as an attribute of St. Catherine; the scales as an attribute of Justice*). An **image** is also a visual representation or embodiment, but in a much broader sense (*veins popping, he was the image of the angry father*). **Sign** is often used in place of *symbol* to refer to a simple representation of an agreed-upon meaning (*the upraised fist as a sign of victory; the white flag as a sign of surrender*), but a *symbol* usually embodies a wider range of meanings, while a *sign* can be any object, event, or gesture from which information can be deduced (*her faltering voice was a sign of her nervousness*). A **token**, on the other hand, is something offered as a symbol or reminder (*he gave her his class ring as a token of his devotion*) and a **type**, particularly in a religious context, is a symbol or representation of something not present (*Jerusalem as the type of heaven; the paschal lamb as the type of Christ*).

---

son) in conflict or difficulties. **2** bring (affairs) into a state of confusion. □□ **em·broil·ment** *n.* [F *embrouiller* (as EN-¹, BROIL²)]

em·bry·o /émbreeō/ *n.* (*pl.* ·**os**) **1 a** an unborn or unhatched offspring. **b** a human offspring in the first eight weeks from conception. **2** a rudimentary plant contained in a seed. **3** a thing in a rudimentary stage. **4** (*attrib.*) undeveloped; immature. □ **in embryo** undeveloped. □□ **em·bry·oid** /–breeoyd/ *adj.* **em·bry·o·nal** /émbreeənəl, émbreeónəl/ *adj.* **em·bry·on·ic** /émbreeónik/ *adj.* **em·bry·on·i·cal·ly** *adv.* [LL *embryo* –*onis* f. Gk *embruon* fetus (as EN-², *bruō* swell, grow)]

embryo- /émbreeō/ *comb. form* embryo.

em·bry·o·gen·e·sis /émbreeōjénisis/ *n.* the formation of an embryo.

em·bry·ol·o·gy /émbreeóləjee/ *n.* the study of embryos. □□ **em·bry·o·log·ic** /–breeəlójik/ *adj.* **em·bry·o·log·i·cal** *adj.* **em·bry·o·log·i·cal·ly** *adv.* **em·bry·ol·o·gist** *n.*

em·bus /embús, im–/ *v.* (**em·bused, em·bus·ing** or **em·bussed, em·bus·sing**) *Mil.* **1** *tr.* put (men or equipment) into a motor vehicle. **2** *intr.* board a motor vehicle.

em·cee /émseé/ *n. & v. colloq.* ● *n.* a master of ceremonies. ● *v.tr. & intr.* (**em·cees, em·ceed**) act as a master of ceremonies. [the letters *MC*]

em dash *n.* a long dash used in punctuation.

-eme /eem/ *suffix Linguistics* forming nouns denoting units of structure, etc. (*grapheme; morpheme*). [F *–ème* unit f. Gk *–ēma*]

e·mend /iménd/ *v.tr.* edit (a text, etc.) to remove errors and corruptions. □□ **e·men·da·tion** /éemendáyshən/ *n.* **e·men·da·tor** *n.* **e·men·da·to·ry** *adj.* [ME f. L *emendare* (as E-, *menda* fault)]

em·er·ald /émərəld, émrəld/ *n.* **1** a bright-green precious stone, a variety of beryl. **2** (also **em·er·ald green**) the color of this. □□ **em·er·ald·ine** /–dīn, –din/ *adj.* [ME f. OF *emeraude, esm-*, ult. f. Gk *smaragdos*]

Em·er·ald Isle *n. literary* Ireland.

e·merge /imórj/ *v.intr.* (often foll. by *from*) **1** come up or out into view, esp. when formerly concealed. **2** come up out of a liquid. **3** (of facts, circumstances, etc.) come to light; become known, esp. as a result of inquiry, etc. **4** become recognized or prominent (*emerged as a leading contender*). **5** (of a question, difficulty, etc.) become apparent. **6** survive (an ordeal, etc.) with a specified result (*emerged unscathed*). □□ **e·mer·gence** *n.* [L *emergere emers-* (as E-, *mergere* dip)]

e·mer·gen·cy /imórjənsee/ *n.* (*pl.* ·**cies**) **1** a sudden state of danger, conflict, etc., requiring immediate action. **2 a** a medical condition requiring immediate treatment. **b** a patient with such a condition. **3** (*attrib.*) characterized by or for use in an emergency. [med.L *emergentia* (as EMERGE)]

e·mer·gen·cy med·i·cal tech·ni·cian *n.* a person trained and licensed to provide basic medical assistance in emergencies. ¶ Abbr.: **EMT.**

e·mer·gen·cy room *n.* the part of a hospital that treats those requiring immediate medical attention. □□

e·mer·gent /imórjənt/ *adj.* **1** becoming apparent; emerging. **2** (of a nation) newly formed or made independent.

e·mer·i·tus /iméritəs/ *adj.* **1** retired and retaining one's title as an honor (*emeritus professor; professor emeritus*). **2** honorably discharged from service. [L, past part. of *emerēri* (as E-, *merēri* earn)]

e·mer·sion /imórzhən, –shən/ *n.* **1** the act or an instance of emerging. **2** *Astron.* the reappearance of a celestial body after its eclipse or occultation. [LL *emersio* (as EMERGE)]

em·er·y /éməree/ *n.* **1** a coarse rock of corundum and magnetite or hematite used for polishing metal or other hard materials. **2** (*attrib.*) covered with emery. [F *émeri(l)* f. It. *smeriglio* ult. f. Gk *smuris, smēris* polishing powder]

em·er·y board *n.* a strip of thin wood or board coated with emery or another abrasive, used as a nail file.

em·er·y cloth *n.* cloth or paper covered with emery, used for polishing or cleaning metals, etc.

e·met·ic /imétik/ *adj. & n.* ● *adj.* that causes vomiting. ● *n.* an emetic medicine. [Gk *emetikos* f. *emeō* vomit]

EMF *abbr.* electromotive force.

-emia /éemeeə/ *comb. form* (also **–hemia** /héemeeə/, esp. *Brit.* **–aemia**, **–haemia** /héemeeə/) forming nouns denoting that a substance is (esp. excessively) present in the blood (*bacteremia; pyemia*). [mod.L f. GK *–aimia* f. *haima* blood]

em·i·grant /émigrənt/ *n. & adj.* ● *n.* a person who emigrates. ● *adj.* emigrating.

em·i·grate /émigrayt/ *v.* **1** *intr.* leave one's own country to settle in another. **2** *tr.* assist (a person) to emigrate. □□ **em·i·gra·tion** /–gráyshən/ *n.* **em·i·gra·to·ry** /–grətáwree/ *adj.* [L *emigrare emigrat-* (as E-, *migrare* depart)]

▶ To **emigrate** is to leave a country, especially one's own, intending to remain away. To **immigrate** is to enter a country, intending to remain there. From the point of view of the receiving country, one might say: *My aunt emigrated from Poland and immigrated into Canada.*

é·mi·gré /émigray/ *n.* (also **e·mi·gré**) an emigrant, esp. a political exile. [F, past part. of *émigrer* EMIGRATE]

em·i·nence /éminəns/ *n.* **1** distinction; recognized superiority. **2** a piece of rising ground. **3** (**Eminence**) a title used in addressing or referring to a cardinal (*Your Eminence*; *His Eminence*). **4** an important person. [L *eminentia* (as EMINENT)]

é·mi·nence grise /áymeenóns greéz/ *n.* (*pl.* **é·mi·nences grises** *pronunc.* same) **1** a person who exercises power or influence without holding office. **2** a confidential agent. [F, = gray cardinal (see EMINENCE): orig. applied to Cardinal Richelieu's private secretary, Père Joseph d. 1638]

em·i·nent /éminənt/ *adj.* **1** distinguished; notable. **2** (of qualities) remarkable in degree. □□ **em·i·nent·ly** *adv.* [ME f. L *eminēre* eminent-jut]

▶**Eminent** means 'outstanding; famous': *The book was written by an eminent authority on folk art.* **Imminent** means 'about to happen': *People brushed aside the possibility that war was imminent.* **Immanent**, often used in religious or philosophical contexts, means 'inherent': *He believed in the immanent unity of nature taught by the Hindus.*

em·i·nent do·main *n.* sovereign control over all property in a government jurisdiction, with the right of expropriation.

e·mir /əmeér/ *n.* **1** a title of various Muslim rulers. **2** *archaic* a male descendant of Muhammad. [F *émir* f. Arab. ʿamīr: cf. AMIR]

e·mir·ate /imeérit, –ayt, aymeér–, émərit/ *n.* the rank, domain, or reign of an emir.

em·is·sar·y /émiseree/ *n.* (*pl.* ·**ies**) a person sent on a special mission (usu. diplomatic, formerly usu. odious or underhand). [L *emissarius* scout, spy (as EMIT)]

e·mis·sion /imíshən/ *n.* **1** (often foll. by *of*) the process or an act of emitting. **2** a thing emitted. [L *emissio* (as EMIT)]

e·mis·sive /imísiv/ *adj.* having the power to radiate light, heat, etc. □□ **em·is·siv·i·ty** /éemisívitee/ *n.*

e·mit /imít/ *v.tr.* (**e·mit·ted, e·mit·ting**) **1 a** send out (heat, light, vapor, etc.). **b** discharge from the body. **2** utter (a cry, etc.). [L *emittere emiss-* (as E-, *mittere* send)]

e·mit·ter /imítər/ *n.* that which emits, esp. a region in a transistor producing carriers of current.

Em·men·ta·ler /émantaalər/ *n.* (also **Em·men·tha·ler** or **Em·men·tal** or **Em·men·thal**) a kind of hard Swiss cheese with many holes in it, similar to Gruyère. [G *Emmentaler* f. *Emmental* in Switzerland]

em·mer /émər/ *n.* a kind of wheat, *Triticum dicoccum*, grown mainly for fodder. [G dial.]

em·met /émit/ *n. archaic* or *dial.* an ant. [OE *ǣmete*: see ANT]

Em·my /émee/ *n.* (*pl.* ·**mies**) one of the statuettes awarded annually to outstanding television programs and performers. [perh. f. *Immy* = image orthicon tube]

e·mol·li·ent /imólyənt/ *adj. & n.* ● *adj.* that softens or soothes the skin. ● *n.* an emollient agent. □□ **e·mol·lience** /–yəns/ *n.* [L *emollire* (as E-, *mollis* soft)]

e·mol·u·ment /imólyəmənt/ *n.* a salary, fee, or profit from employment or office. [ME f. OF *emolument* or L *emolumentum*, orig. prob. 'payment for grain-grinding,' f. *emolere* (as E-, *molere* grind)]

e·mote /imót/ *v.intr. colloq.* show excessive emotion. □□ **e·mot·er** *n.* [back-form. f. EMOTION]

e·mo·tion /imóshən/ *n.* a strong mental or instinctive feeling such as love or fear. [earlier = agitation, disturbance of the mind, f. F *émotion* f. *émouvoir* excite]

SYNONYM TIP emotion

AFFECT, FEELING, PASSION, SENTIMENT. A **feeling** can be almost any subjective reaction or state—pleasant or unpleasant, strong or mild, positive or negative—that is characterized by an emotional response (*a feeling of insecurity; a feeling of pleasure*). An **emotion** is a very intense feeling, which often involves a physical as well as a mental response and implies outward expression or agitation (*to be overcome with emotion*). **Passion** suggests a powerful or overwhelming emotion, with connotations of sexual love (*their passion remained undiminished after 30 years of marriage*) or intense anger (*a passion for revenge*). There is more intellect and less feeling in **sentiment**, which is often applied to an emotion inspired by an idea (*political sentiments; antiwar sentiments*). *Sentiment* also suggests a refined or slightly artificial feeling (*a speech marked by sentiment rather than passion*). **Affect** is a formal psychological term that refers to an observed emotional state (*heavily sedated, he spoke without affect*).

---

e·mo·tion·al /imóshən əl/ *adj.* **1** of or relating to the emotions. **2** (of a person) liable to excessive emotion. **3** expressing or based on emotion (*an emotional appeal*). **4** likely to excite emotion (*an emotional issue*). □□ **e·mo·tion·al·ism** *n.* **e·mo·tion·al·ist** *n.* **e·mo·tion·al·i·ty** /– álitee/ *n.* **e·mo·tion·al·ize** *v.tr.* **e·mo·tion·al·ly** *adv.*

e·mo·tive /imótiv/ *adj.* **1** of or characterized by emotion. **2** tending

---

to excite emotion. **3** arousing feeling; not purely descriptive. □□ **e·mo·tive·ly** *adv.* **e·mo·tive·ness** *n.* **e·mo·tiv·i·ty** /éemōtívitee/ *n.* [L *emovēre emot-* (as E-, *movēre* move)]

em·pan·el /empánəl, im–/ esp. *Brit.* var. of IMPANEL.

em·pa·thize /émpəthīz/ *v. Psychol.* **1** *intr.* (usu. foll. by *with*) exercise empathy. **2** *tr.* treat with empathy.

em·pa·thy /émpəthee/ *n. Psychol.* the power of identifying oneself mentally with (and so fully comprehending) a person or object of contemplation. □□ **em·pa·thet·ic** /–thétik/ *adj.* **em·pa·thet·i·cal·ly** *adv.* **em·path·ic** /empáthik/ *adj.* **em·path·i·cal·ly** *adv.* **em·path·ist** *n.* [transl. G *Einfühlung* f. *ein* in + *Fühlung* feeling, after Gk *empatheia*: see SYMPATHY]

em·pen·nage /empénij/ *n. Aeron.* an arrangement of stabilizing surfaces at the tail of an aircraft. [F f. *empenner* to feather (an arrow)]

em·per·or /émpərər/ *n.* **1** the sovereign of an empire. **2** a sovereign of higher rank than a king. □□ **em·per·or·ship** *n.* [ME f. OF *emperere*, *empereor* f. L *imperator –oris* f. *imperare* command]

em·per·or moth *n.* a large moth, *Saturnia pavonia*, of the silk-moth family, with eyespots on all four wings.

em·per·or pen·guin *n.* the largest known penguin, *Aptenodytes forsteri*, of the Antarctic.

em·pha·sis /émfəsis/ *n.* (*pl.* **em·pha·ses** /–seez/) **1** special importance or prominence attached to a thing, fact, idea, etc. (*emphasis on economy*). **2** stress laid on a word or words to indicate special meaning or importance. **3** vigor or intensity of expression, feeling, action, etc. **4** prominence, sharpness of contour. [L f. Gk f. *emphainō* exhibit (as EN-[2], *phainō* show)]

em·pha·size /émfəsīz/ *v.tr.* **1** bring (a thing, fact, etc.) into special prominence. **2** lay stress on (a word in speaking).

em·phat·ic /emfátik/ *adj.* **1** (of language, tone, or gesture) forcibly expressive. **2** of words: **a** bearing the stress. **b** used to give emphasis. **3** expressing oneself with emphasis. **4** (of an action or process) forcible; significant. □□ **em·phat·i·cal·ly** *adv.* [LL *emphaticus* f. Gk *emphatikos* (as EMPHASIS)]

em·phy·se·ma /émfiseémə, –zeémə/ *n.* **1** enlargement of the air sacs of the lungs causing breathlessness. **2** a swelling caused by the presence of air in the connective tissues of the body. [LL f. Gk *emphusēma* f. *emphusaō* puff up]

em·pire /émpīr/ *n.* **1** an extensive group of lands or countries under a single supreme authority, esp. an emperor. **2 a** supreme dominion. **b** (often foll. by *over*) *archaic* absolute control. **3** a large commercial organization, etc., owned or directed by one person or group. **4** (**the Empire**) *hist.* **a** the British Empire. **b** the Holy Roman Empire. **5** a type or period of government in which the sovereign is called emperor. **6** (**Empire**) (*attrib.*) **a** denoting a style of furniture or dress fashionable during the first (1804–14) or second (1852–70) French Empire. **b** *Brit.* denoting produce from the Commonwealth. [ME f. OF f. L *imperium* rel. to *imperare*: see EMPEROR]

Em·pire Day *n. hist.* former name of COMMONWEALTH DAY

em·pir·ic /empírik, im–/ *adj. & n.* ● *adj.* = EMPIRICAL. ● *n. archaic* **1** a person relying solely on experiment. **2** a quack doctor. □□ **em·pir·i·cism** /–sizəm/ *n.* **em·pir·i·cist** *n.* [L *empiricus* f. Gk *empeirikos* f. *empeiria* experience f. *empeiros* skilled]

em·pir·i·cal /empírikəl, im–/ *adj.* **1** based or acting on observation or experiment, not on theory. **2** *Philos.* regarding sense-data as valid information. **3** deriving knowledge from experience alone. □□ **em·pir·i·cal·ly** *adv.*

em·pir·i·cal for·mu·la *n. Chem.* a formula giving the proportions of the elements present in a compound but not the actual numbers or arrangement of atoms.

em·place·ment /empláysmənt, im–/ *n.* **1** the act or an instance of putting in position. **2** a platform or defended position where a gun is placed for firing. **3** situation; position. [F (as EN-[1], PLACE)]

em·plane var. of ENPLANE.

em·ploy /emploý/ *v. & n.* ● *v.tr.* **1** use the services of (a person) in return for payment; keep (a person) in one's service. **2** (often foll. by *for, in, on*) use (a thing, time, energy, etc.) esp. to good effect. **3** (often foll. by *in*) keep (a person) occupied. ● *n.* the state of being employed, esp. for wages. □ **in the employ of** employed by. □□ **em·ploy·a·ble** *adj.* **em·ploy·a·bil·i·ty** *n.* **em·ploy·er** *n.* [ME f. OF *employer* ult. f. L *implicari* be involved f. *implicare* enfold: see IMPLICATE]

em·ploy·ee /émployée, –ployeé/ *n.* (also **em·ploy·e**) a person employed for wages or salary, esp. at a nonexecutive level.

em·ploy·ment /emploýmənt, im–/ *n.* **1** the act of employing or the state of being employed. **2** a person's regular trade or profession.

em·ploy·ment a·gen·cy *n.* a business that finds employers or employees for those seeking them.

em·po·ri·um /empáwreeəm/ *n.* (*pl.* ·**ums** or **emporia** /–reeə/) **1** a large retail store selling a wide variety of goods. **2** a center of commerce; a market. [L f. Gk *emporion* f. *emporos* merchant]

em·pow·er /empówər, im–/ *v.tr.* (foll. by *to* + infin.) **1** authorize, license. **2** give power to; make able. □□ **em·pow·er·ment** *n.*

em·press /émpris/ *n.* **1** the wife or widow of an emperor. **2** a woman emperor. [ME f. OF *emperesse* fem. of *emperere* EMPEROR]

emp·ty /émptee/ *adj., v., & n.* ● *adj.* (**emp·ti·er, emp·ti·est**) **1** containing nothing. **2** (of a space, place, house, etc.) unoccupied; uninhabited; deserted; unfurnished. **3** (of a transport vehicle, etc.) without a load, passengers, etc. **4 a** meaningless; hollow; insincere (*empty threats; an empty gesture*). **b** without substance or purpose (*an empty existence*). **c** (of a person) lacking sense or knowledge; vacant; foolish. **5** *colloq.* hungry. **6** (foll. by *of*) devoid; lacking. ● *v.* (**·ties, ·tied**) **1** *tr.* **a** make empty; remove the contents of. **b** (foll. by *of*) deprive of certain contents (*emptied the room of its chairs*). **c** remove (contents) from a container, etc. **2** *tr.* (often foll. by *into*) transfer (the contents of a container). **3** *intr.* become empty. **4** *intr.* (usu. foll. by *into*) (of a river) discharge itself (into the sea, etc.). ● *n.* (*pl.* **·ties**) *colloq.* a container (esp. a bottle) left empty of its contents. □ **on an empty stomach** see STOMACH. □□ **emp·ti·ly** *adv.* **emp·ti·ness** *n.* [OE *ǣmtig, ǣmetig* f. *ǣmetta* leisure]

emp·ty-hand·ed *adj.* **1** bringing or taking nothing. **2** having achieved or obtained nothing.

emp·ty-head·ed *adj.* foolish; lacking common sense.

emp·ty nest·er *n.* either of a couple whose children have grown up and left home.

em·pur·ple /empúrpəl, im–/ *v.tr.* **1** make purple or red. **2** make angry.

em·py·e·ma /émpī-éemə/ *n.* a collection of pus in a cavity, esp. in the pleura. [LL f. Gk *empuēma* f. *empueō* suppurate (as EN-², *puon* pus)]

em·py·re·an /émpəréeən, empíreeən/ *n. & adj.* ● *n.* **1** the highest heaven, as the sphere of fire in ancient cosmology or as the abode of God in early Christianity. **2** the visible heavens. ● *adj.* of the empyrean. □□ **em·pyr·e·al** /empíreeəl, émpíréeəl/ *adj.* [med.L *empyreus* f. Gk *empurios* (as EN-², *pur* fire)]

EMS *abbr.* European Monetary System.

EMT *abbr.* emergency medical technician.

e·mu /éemyoō/ *n.* a large flightless bird, *Dromaius novaehollandiae*, native to Australia, and capable of running at high speed. [earlier *emia, eme* f. Port. *ema*]

e.m.u. *abbr.* electromagnetic unit(s).

em·u·late /émyəlayt/ *v.tr.* **1** try to equal or excel. **2** imitate zealously. **3** rival. □□ **em·u·la·tion** /–láyshən/ *n.* **em·u·la·tive** *adj.* **em·u·la·tor** *n.* [L *aemulari* (as EMULOUS)]

em·u·lous /émyələs/ *adj.* **1** (usu. foll. by *of*) seeking to emulate. **2** actuated by a spirit of rivalry. □□ **em·u·lous·ly** *adv.* [ME f. L *aemulus* rival]

e·mul·si·fi·er /imúlsifīər/ *n.* **1** any substance that stabilizes an emulsion, esp. a food additive used to stabilize processed foods. **2** an apparatus used for producing an emulsion.

e·mul·si·fy /imúlsifī/ *v.tr.* (**·fies, ·fied**) convert into an emulsion. □□ **e·mul·si·fi·a·ble** *adj.* **e·mul·si·fi·ca·tion** /–fikáyshən/ *n.*

e·mul·sion /imúlshən/ *n.* **1** a fine dispersion of one liquid in another, esp. as paint, medicine, etc. **2** a mixture of a silver compound suspended in gelatin, etc., for coating plates or films. □□ **e·mul·sion·ize** /–siv/ *adj.* **e·mul·sive** /–siv/ *adj.* [F *émulsion* or mod.L *emulsio* f. *emulgēre* (as E–, *mulgēre* muls– to milk)]

e·mul·sion paint *n.* a water-thinned paint containing a nonvolatile substance, e.g., synthetic resin, as its binding medium.

en /en/ *n. Printing* a unit of measurement equal to half an em. [name of the letter *N*]

en-¹ /en, in/ *prefix* (also **em-** before *b, p*) forming verbs, = IN-¹: **1** from nouns, meaning 'put into or on' (*engulf; entrust; embed*). **2** from nouns or adjectives, meaning 'bring into the condition of' (*enslave*); often with the suffix *–en* (*enlighten*). **3** from verbs: **a** in the sense 'in, into, on' (*enfold*). **b** as an intensive (*entangle*). [from or after F *en-* f. L *in-*]

en-² /en, in/ *prefix* (also **em-** before *b, p*) in, inside (*energy; enthusiasm*). [Gk]

-en¹ /ən/ *suffix* forming verbs: **1** from adjectives, usu. meaning 'make or become so or more so' (*deepen; fasten; moisten*). **2** from nouns (*happen; strengthen*). [OE *–nian* f. Gmc]

-en² /ən/ *suffix* (also *–n*) forming adjectives from nouns, meaning: **1** made or consisting of (often with extended and figurative senses) (*wooden*). **2** resembling or of the nature of (*golden; silvern*). [OE f. Gmc]

-en³ /ən/ *suffix* (also *–n*) forming past participles of strong verbs: **1** as a regular inflection (*spoken; sworn*). **2** with restricted sense (*drunken*). [OE f. Gmc]

-en⁴ /ən/ *suffix* forming the plural of a few nouns (*children; brethren; oxen*). [ME reduction of OE *–an*]

-en⁵ /ən/ *suffix* forming diminutives of nouns (*chicken; maiden*). [OE f. Gmc]

-en⁶ /ən/ *suffix* **1** forming feminine nouns (*vixen*). **2** forming abstract nouns (*burden*). [OE f. Gmc]

en·a·ble /enáybəl/ *v.tr.* **1** (foll. by *to* + infin.) give (a person, etc.) the means or authority to do something. **2** make possible. **3** esp. *Computing* make (a device) operational; switch on. □□ **en·a·bler** *n.*

en·a·bling act *n.* **1** a statute empowering a person or body to take certain action. **2** a statute legalizing something otherwise unlawful.

en·act /enákt, in–/ *v.tr.* **1 a** (often foll. by *that* + clause) ordain; decree. **b** make (a bill, etc.) law. **2** play (a part or scene on stage or in life). □□ **en·act·a·ble** *adj.* **en·ac·tion** /–akshən/ *n.* **en·ac·tive** *adj.* **en·ac·tor** *n.* **en·ac·to·ry** *adj.*

en·act·ment /enáktmənt, in–/ *n.* **1** a law enacted. **2** the process of enacting.

e·nam·el /ináməl/ *n. & v.* ● *n.* **1** a glasslike opaque or semitransparent coating on metallic or other hard surfaces for ornament or as a preservative lining. **2 a** a smooth, hard coating. **b** a cosmetic simulating this. **3** the hard, glossy natural coating over the crown of a tooth. **4** painting done in enamel. **5** *poet.* a smooth, bright surface coloring, verdure, etc. ● *v.tr.* (**e·nam·eled, e·nam·el·ing;** esp. *Brit.* **e·nam·elled, e·nam·el·ling**) **1** inlay or encrust (a metal, etc.) with enamel. **2** portray (figures, etc.) with enamel. **3** *archaic* adorn with varied colors. □□ **e·nam·el·er** *n.* **e·nam·el·work** *n.* [ME f. AF *enamel-er, enamailler* (as EN-¹, OF *esmail* f. Gmc)]

e·nam·el·ware /ináməlwair/ *n.* enameled kitchenware.

en·am·or /inámər/ *v.tr.* (usu. in *passive*; foll. by *of*) **1** inspire with love or liking. **2** charm; delight. [ME f. OF *enamourer* f. *amourer* (as EN-¹, AMOUR)]

en·an·the·ma /énantheémə/ *n. Med.* an eruption occurring on a mucus-secreting surface such as the inside of the mouth. [mod.L f. Gk *enanthēma* eruption (as EN-¹, EXANTHEMA)]

en·an·ti·o·mer /enánteeəmər/ *n. Chem.* a molecule with a mirror image. □□ **en·an·ti·o·mer·ic** /–mérik/ *adj.* [Gk *enantios* opposite + –MER]

en·an·ti·o·morph /enánteeəmawrf/ *n.* a mirror image; a form (esp. of a crystal structure, etc.) related to another as an object is to its mirror image. □□ **en·an·ti·o·mor·phic** *adj.* **en·an·ti·o·mor·phism** *n.* **en·an·ti·o·mor·phous** *adj.* [G f. Gk *enantios* opposite + *morphē* form]

en·ar·thro·sis /énaarthrósis/ *n.* (*pl.* **en·ar·thro·ses** /–seez/) *Anat.* a ball-and-socket joint. [Gk f. *enarthros* jointed (as EN-¹, *arthron* joint)]

en bloc /on bláwk/ *adv.* in a block; all at the same time; wholesale. [F]

en brosse /on bráws/ *adj.* (of hair) cut short and bristly. [F]

en·cae·nia /enseéneeə/ *n.* **1** (at Oxford University, England) an annual celebration in memory of founders and benefactors. **2** a dedication festival. [L f. Gk *egkainia* (as EN-², *kainos* new)]

en·cage /enkáyj/ *v.tr.* confine in or as in a cage.

en·camp /enkámp/ *v.tr. & intr.* **1** settle in a military camp. **2** lodge in the open in tents.

en·camp·ment /enkámpmənt, in–/ *n.* **1** a place with temporary accommodations for troops or nomads. **2** the process of setting up a camp.

en·cap·su·late /enkápsəlayt, –syoō–, in–/ *v.tr.* **1** enclose in or as in a capsule. **2** summarize; express the essential features of. **3** isolate. □□ **en·cap·su·la·tion** /–láyshən/ *n.* [EN-¹ + L *capsula* CAPSULE]

en·case /enkáys, in–/ *v.tr.* (also **in·case**) **1** put into a case. **2** surround as with a case. □□ **en·case·ment** *n.*

en·cash /enkásh, in–/ *v.tr. Brit.* **1** convert (bills, etc.) into cash. **2** receive in the form of cash; realize. □□ **en·cash·a·ble** *adj.* **en·cash·ment** *n.*

en·caus·tic /enkáwstik, in–/ *adj. & n.* ● *adj.* **1** (in painting, ceramics, etc.) using pigments mixed with hot wax, which are burned in as an inlay. **2** (of bricks and tiles) inlaid with differently colored clays burned in. ● *n.* **1** the art of encaustic painting. **2** a painting done with this technique. [L *encausticus* f. Gk *egkaustikos* (as EN-², CAUSTIC)]

-ence /əns/ *suffix* forming nouns expressing: **1** a quality or state or an instance of one (*patience; an impertinence*). **2** an action (*reference; reminiscence*). [from or after F *–ence* f. L *–entia, –antia* (cf. –ANCE) f. pres. part. stem *–ent-, –ant–*]

en·ceinte /ensáynt, aansánt, ONSÁNT/ *n. & adj.* ● *n.* an enclosure, esp. in fortification. ● *adj. archaic* pregnant. [F, ult. f. L *cingere cinct-gird*: see CINCTURE]

en·ce·phal·ic /énsifálik/ *adj.* of or relating to the brain. [Gk *egkephalos* brain (as EN-², *kephalē* head)]

en·ceph·a·li·tis /enséfəlítis/ *n.* inflammation of the brain. □ **encephalitis lethargica** /lithaárjikə/ an infectious encephalitis caused by a virus, with headache and drowsiness leading to coma; sleepy sickness. □□ **en·ceph·a·lit·ic** /–lítik/ *adj.*

encephalo- /enséfəlō/ *comb. form* brain. [Gk *egkephalos* brain]

en·ceph·a·lo·gram /enséfəlogram/ *n.* an X-ray photograph of the brain.

en·ceph·a·lo·graph /enséfələgraf/ *n.* an instrument for recording the electrical activity of the brain.

en·ceph·a·lon /enséfəlon/ *n. Anat.* the brain.

en·ceph·a·lop·a·thy /enséfəlópəthee/ *n.* disease of the brain.

en·chain /encháyn, in–/ *v.tr.* **1** chain up; fetter. **2** hold fast (the attention, emotions, etc.). □□ **en·chain·ment** *n.* [ME f. F *enchaîner* ult. f. L *catena* chain]

en·chant /enchánt, in–/ *v.tr.* **1** charm; delight. **2** bewitch. □□ **en·**

chant·ed·ly adv. **en·chant·ing** adj. **en·chant·ing·ly** adv. **en·chant·ment** n. [ME f. F *enchanter* f. L *incantare* (as IN-[2], *canere cant-* sing)]

en·chant·er /enchántər, in–/ n. (*fem.* **en·chant·ress**) a person who enchants, esp. by supposed use of magic.

en·chant·er's night·shade n. a woodland plant, *Circaea lutetiana*, with white flowers, native to Eurasia and the eastern US.

en·chase /encháys, in–/ v.tr. **1** (foll. by *in*) place (a jewel) in a setting. **2** (foll. by *with*) set (gold, etc.) with gems. **3** inlay with gold, etc. **4** adorn with figures in relief. **5** engrave. [ME f. F *enchâsser* (as EN-[1], CHASE[2])]

en·chi·la·da /énchiláadə/ n. a tortilla with chili sauce and usu. a filling, esp. meat. [Amer. Sp., fem. past part. of *enchilar* season with chili]

en·chi·rid·i·on /énkīrídeeən/ n. (*pl.* **en·chi·rid·i·a** /–deeə/ or **en·chi·rid·i·ons**) *formal* a handbook. [LL f. Gk *egkheiridion* (as EN-[2], *kheir* hand, *–idion* dimin. suffix)]

en·ci·pher /ensífər, in–/ v.tr. **1** write (a message, etc.) in cipher. **2** convert into coded form using a cipher. □□ **en·ci·pher·ment** n.

en·cir·cle /ensúrkəl, in–/ v.tr. **1** (usu. foll. by *with*) surround; encompass. **2** form a circle around. □□ **en·cir·cle·ment** n.

encl. abbr. **1** enclosed. **2** enclosure.

en clair /ON kláir/ adj. & adv. (of a telegram, official message, etc.) in ordinary language (not in code or cipher). [F, lit. 'in clear']

en·clasp /enklásp, in–/ v.tr. hold in a clasp or embrace.

en·clave /énklayv, ón–/ n. **1** a portion of territory of one country surrounded by territory of another or others, as viewed by the surrounding territory (cf. EXCLAVE). **2** a group of people who are culturally, intellectually, or socially distinct from those surrounding them. [F *enclave* ult. f. L *clavis* key]

en·clit·ic /enklítik/ adj. & n. *Gram.* • adj. (of a word) pronounced with so little emphasis that it forms part of the preceding word. • n. such a word, e.g., *not* in *cannot*. □□ **en·clit·i·cal·ly** adv. [LL *encliticus* f. Gk *egklitikos* (as EN-[2], *klinō* lean)]

en·close /enklóz, in–/ v.tr. (also **in·close**) **1** (often foll. by *with, in*) **a** surround with a wall, fence, etc. **b** shut in on all sides. **2** fence in (common land) so as to make it private property. **3** put in a receptacle (esp. in an envelope together with a letter). **4** (usu. as **enclosed** adj.) seclude (a religious community) from the outside world. **5** esp. Math. bound on all sides; contain. **6** hem in on all sides. [ME f. OF *enclos* past part. of *enclore* ult. f. L *includere* (as INCLUDE)]

en·clo·sure /enklózhər, in–/ n. (also **in·clo·sure**) **1** the act of enclosing, esp. of common land. **2** *Brit.* an enclosed space or area, esp. for a special class of persons at a sporting event. **3** a thing enclosed with a letter. **4** an enclosing fence, etc. [AF & OF (as ENCLOSE)]

en·code /enkód, in–/ v.tr. put (a message, etc.) into code or cipher. □□ **en·cod·er** n.

en·co·mi·ast /enkómeeast/ n. **1** the composer of an encomium. **2** a flatterer. □□ **en·co·mi·as·tic** /–ástik/ adj. [Gk *egkōmiastēs* (as ENCOMIUM)]

en·co·mi·um /enkómeeəm/ n. (*pl.* **en·co·mi·ums** or **en·co·mi·a** /–meeə/) a formal or high-flown expression of praise. [L f. Gk *egkōmion* (as EN-[2], *kōmos* revelry)]

en·com·pass /enkúmpəs, in–/ v.tr. **1** surround or form a circle about, esp. to protect or attack. **2** contain. □□ **en·com·pass·ment** n.

en·core /óngkawr/ n., v., & int. • n. **1** a call by an audience or spectators for the repetition of an item, or for a further item. **2** such an item. • v.tr. **1** call for the repetition of (an item). **2** call back (a performer) for this. • int. also /–kór/ again; once more. [F, = again]

en·coun·ter /enkówntər, in–/ v. & n. • v.tr. **1** meet by chance or unexpectedly. **2** meet as an adversary. **3** meet with; experience (problems, opposition, etc.). • n. **1** a meeting by chance. **2** a meeting in conflict. **3** participation in an encounter group. [ME f. OF *encontrer, encontre* ult. f. L *contra* against]

en·coun·ter group n. a group of persons seeking psychological benefit by freely expressing their emotions with one another.

en·cour·age /enkúrij, –kúr–, in–/ v.tr. **1** give courage, confidence, or hope to. **2** (foll. by *to* + infin.) urge; advise. **3** stimulate by help, reward, etc. **4** promote or assist (an enterprise, opinion, etc.). □□ **en·cour·age·ment** n. **en·cour·ag·er** n. **en·cour·ag·ing·ly** adv. [ME f. F *encourager* (as EN-[1], COURAGE)]

en·croach /enkróch, in–/ v.intr. **1** (foll. by *on, upon*) intrude, esp. on another's territory or rights. **2** advance gradually beyond due limits. □□ **en·croach·er** n. **en·croach·ment** n. [ME f. OF *encrochier* (as EN-[1], *crochier* f. *croc* hook: see CROOK)]

en·crust /enkrúst, in–/ v. (also **in·crust**) **1** tr. cover with a crust. **2** tr. overlay with an ornamental crust of precious material. **3** intr. form a crust. □□ **en·crust·ment** n. [F *incruster* f. L *incrustare* (as IN-[2], *crustare* f. *crusta* CRUST)]

en·crus·ta·tion var. of INCRUSTATION.

en·crypt /enkrípt, in–/ v.tr. **1** convert (data) into code, esp. to prevent unauthorized access. **2** conceal by this means. □□ **en·cryp·tion** /–krípshən/ n. [EN-[1] + Gk *kruptos* hidden]

en·cum·ber /enkúmbər, in–/ v.tr. **1** be a burden to. **2** hamper; impede. **3** burden (a person or estate) with debts, esp. mortgages. **4** fill or block (a place), esp. with lumber. □□ **en·cum·ber·ment** n. [ME f. OF *encombrer* block up f. Rmc]

en·cum·brance /enkúmbrəns, in–/ n. **1** a burden. **2** an impediment. **3** a mortgage or other charge on property. **4** an annoyance. [ME f. OF *encombrance* (as ENCUMBER)]

ency. abbr. (also **encyc.**) encyclopedia.

-ency /ənsee/ suffix forming nouns denoting a quality (*efficiency; fluency*) or state (*presidency*) but not action (cf. –ENCE). [L –*entia* (cf. –ANCY)]

en·cyc·li·cal /ensíklikəl/ n. & adj. • n. a papal letter sent to all bishops of the Roman Catholic Church. • adj. (of a letter) for wide circulation. [LL *encyclicus* f. Gk *egkuklios* (as EN-[2], *kuklos* circle)]

en·cy·clo·pe·di·a /ensíkləpeédeeə/ n. (also **en·cy·clo·pae·di·a**) a book, often in several volumes, giving information on many subjects, or on many aspects of one subject, usu. arranged alphabetically. [mod.L f. spurious Gk *egkuklopaideia* for *egkuklios paideia* all-around education: cf. ENCYCLICAL]

en·cy·clo·pe·dic /ensíkləpeédik/ adj. (also **en·cy·clo·pae·dic**) (of knowledge or information) comprehensive.

en·cy·clo·pe·dism /ensíkləpeédizəm/ n. (also **en·cy·clo·pae·dism**) encyclopedic learning.

en·cy·clo·pe·dist /ensíkləpeédist/ n. (also **en·cy·clo·pae·dist**) a person who writes, edits, or contributes to an encyclopedia.

en·cyst /ensíst, in–/ v.tr. & intr. *Biol.* enclose or become enclosed in a cyst. □□ **en·cys·ta·tion** /–táyshən/ n. **en·cyst·ment** n.

end /end/ n. & v. • n. **1 a** the extreme limit; the point beyond which a thing does not continue. **b** an extremity of a line, or of the greatest dimension of an object. **c** the furthest point (*to the ends of the earth*). **2** the surface bounding a thing at either extremity; an extreme part (*a piece of wood with a nail in one end*). **3 a** a conclusion; finish (*no end to his misery*). **b** the latter or final part. **c** death; destruction; downfall (*met an untimely end*). **d** result; outcome. **e** an ultimate state or condition. **4 a** a thing one seeks to attain; a purpose (*will do anything to achieve her ends; to what end?*). **b** the object for which a thing exists. **5** a remnant; a piece left over (*a board end*). **6** (prec. by *the*) *colloq.* the limit of endurability. **7** the half of a sports field or court occupied by one team or player. **8** the part or share with which a person is concerned (*no problem at my end*). **9** *Football* a player at the extremity of the offensive or defensive line. • v. **1** tr. & intr. bring or come to an end. **2** tr. put an end to; destroy. **3** intr. (foll. by *in*) have as its result (*will end in tears*). **4** intr. (foll. by *by*) do or achieve eventually (*ended by marrying an heiress*). □ **at an end** exhausted or completed. **at the end of one's rope** having no patience or energy left to cope with something. **come to a bad end** meet with ruin or disgrace. **come to an end 1** be completed or finished. **2** become exhausted. **end it all** (or **end it**) *colloq.* commit suicide. **end of the road** the point at which a hope or endeavor has to be abandoned. **end of the world** the cessation of mortal life. **end on** with the end facing one, or with the end adjoining the end of the next object. **end to end** with the end of each of a series adjoining the end of the next. **end up** reach a specified state, action, or place eventually (*ended up a drunk; ended up making a fortune*). **in the end** finally; after all. **keep one's end up** do one's part despite difficulties. **make an end of** put a stop to. **make ends meet** live within one's income. **no end** *colloq.* to a great extent; very much. **no end of** *colloq.* much or many of. **on end 1** upright (*hair stood on end*). **2** continuously (*for three weeks on end*). **put an end to 1** stop (an activity, etc.). **2** abolish; destroy. □□ **end·er** n. [OE *ende, endian,* f. Gmc]

-end /end, ənd/ suffix forming nouns in the sense 'person or thing to be treated in a specified way' (*dividend; reverend*). [L gerundive ending –*endus*]

en·dan·ger /endáynjər, in–/ v.tr. place in danger. □ **endangered species** a species in danger of extinction. □□ **en·dan·ger·ment** n.

end a·round *n. & adj.* ● *n. Football* an offensive play in which an end carries the ball around the opposite end. ● *adj. Computing* involving the transfer of a digit from one end of a register to the other.

en dash *n.* a short dash used in punctuation.

en·dear /endéer, in–/ *v.tr.* (usu. foll. by *to*) make dear to or beloved by.

en·dear·ing /endéering, in–/ *adj.* inspiring affection. □□ **en·dear·ing·ly** *adv.*

en·dear·ment /endéermənt, in–/ *n.* **1** an expression of affection. **2** liking; affection.

en·deav·or /endévər, in–/ *v. & n.* (*Brit.* **en·deav·our**) ● *v.* **1** *tr.* (foll. by *to* + infin.) try earnestly. **2** *intr.* (foll. by *after*) *archaic* strive. ● *n.* (often foll. by *at*, or *to* + infin.) effort directed toward a goal; an earnest attempt. [ME f. *put oneself* in DEVOIR]

en·dem·ic /endémik/ *adj. & n.* ● *adj.* regularly or only found among a particular people or in a certain region. ● *n.* an endemic disease or plant. □□ **en·dem·i·cal·ly** *adv.* **en·de·mic·i·ty** /éndimísitee/ *n.* **en·de·mism** *n.* [F *endémique* or mod.L *endemicus* f. Gk *endēmos* native (as EN-², *dēmos* the people)]

▶See note at EPIDEMIC.

en·der·mic /endérmik/ *adj.* acting on or through the skin. □□ **en·der·mi·cal·ly** *adv.* [EN-² + Gk *derma* skin]

end·game /éndgaym/ the final stage of a game (esp. chess), when few pieces remain.

end·ing /énding/ *n.* **1** an end or final part, esp. of a story. **2** an inflected final part of a word. [OE (as END, –ING¹)]

en·dive /éndiv, óndeev/ *n.* **1** a curly-leaved plant, *Cichorium endivia*, used in salads. **2** a chicory crown. [ME f. OF f. LL *endivia* ult. f. Gk *entubon*]

end·less /éndlis/ *adj.* **1** infinite; without end; eternal. **2** continual; incessant (*tired of their endless complaints*). **3** *colloq.* innumerable. **4** (of a belt, chain, etc.) having the ends joined for continuous action over wheels, etc. □□ **end·less·ly** *adv.* **end·less·ness** *n.* [OE *endelēas* (as END, –LESS)]

end·most /éndmōst/ *adj.* nearest the end.

end·note /éndnōt/ *n.* a note printed at the end of a book or section of a book.

endo- /éndō/ *comb. form* internal. [Gk *endon* within]

en·do·car·di·tis /éndōkaardítis/ *n.* inflammation of the endocardium. □□ **en·do·car·dit·ic** /–dítik/ *adj.*

en·do·car·di·um /éndōkaárdeeəm/ *n.* the lining membrane of the heart. [ENDO- + Gk *kardia* heart]

en·do·carp /éndōkaarp/ *n.* the innermost layer of the pericarp. □□ **en·do·carp·ic** *adj.* [ENDO- + PERICARP]

en·do·crine /éndōkrin, –kreen, –krīn/ *adj.* (of a gland) secreting directly into the blood; ductless. [ENDO- + Gk *krinō* sift]

en·do·cri·nol·o·gy /éndōkrinólǝjee/ *n.* the study of the structure and physiology of endocrine glands. □□ **en·do·crin·o·log·i·cal** /–nəlójikəl/ *adj.* **en·do·cri·nol·o·gist** *n.*

en·do·derm /éndōdərm/ *n. Biol.* the innermost layer of an animal embryo in early development. □□ **en·do·der·mal** *adj.* **en·do·der·mic** *adj.* [ENDO- + Gk *derma* skin]

en·dog·a·my /endógəmee/ *n.* **1** *Anthropol.* marrying within the same tribe. **2** *Bot.* pollination from the same plant. □□ **en·dog·a·mous** *adj.* [ENDO- + Gk *gamos* marriage]

en·dog·e·nous /endójinəs/ *adj.* growing or originating from within. □□ **en·do·gen·e·sis** /éndəjénisis/ *n.* **en·dog·e·ny** /endójinee/ *n.*

en·do·lymph /éndōlimf/ *n.* the fluid in the membranous labyrinth of the ear.

en·do·me·tri·o·sis /éndōméetreeōsis/ *n. Medicine* a condition marked by the appearance of endometrial tissue outside the uterus and pelvic cavity.

en·do·me·tri·um /éndōméetreeəm/ *n. Anat.* the mucous membrane lining the uterus, which thickens during the menstrual cycle in preparation for possible implantation of an embryo. □□ **en·do·me·tri·tis** /éndōmītrítis/ *n.* [ENDO- + Gk *mētra* womb]

en·do·morph /éndōmawrf/ *n.* **1** a person with a soft, round body build and a high proportion of fat tissue (cf. ECTOMORPH, MESOMORPH). **2** *Mineral.* a mineral enclosed within another. □□ **en·do·mor·phic** *adj.* **en·do·mor·phy** *n.* [ENDO- + Gk *morphē* form]

en·do·par·a·site /éndōpárəsīt/ *n.* a parasite that lives on the inside of its host.

en·do·plasm /éndōplazəm/ *n.* the inner fluid layer of the cytoplasm.

en·do·plas·mic re·tic·u·lum /éndōplázmik/ *n. Biol.* a system of membranes within the cytoplasm of a eukaryotic cell forming a link between the cell and nuclear membranes and usu. having ribosomes attached to its surface.

en·dor·phin /endáwrfin/ *n. Biochem.* any of a group of peptide neurotransmitters occurring naturally in the brain and having pain-relieving properties. [F *endorphine* f. *endogène* endogenous + MORPHINE]

en·dorse /endáwrs, in–/ *v.tr.* (also **in·dorse**) **1 a** confirm (a statement or opinion). **b** declare one's approval of. **2** sign or write on the back of (a document), esp. the back of (a bill, check, etc.) as the payee or to specify another as payee. **3** write (an explanation or comment) on the back of a document. □□ **en·dors·a·ble** *adj.* **en-**

317   **end around ~ enemy**

dor·see /éndorsée/ *n.* **en·dors·er** *n.* [med.L *indorsare* (as IN-², L *dorsum* back)]

en·dorse·ment /endáwrsmənt, in–/ *n.* (also **in·dorse·ment**) **1** the act or an instance of endorsing. **2** something with which a document, etc., is endorsed, esp. a signature.

en·do·scope /éndōskōp/ *n. Surgery* an instrument for viewing the internal parts of the body. □□ **en·do·scop·ic** /–skópik/ *adj.* **en·do·scop·i·cal·ly** *adv.* **en·dos·co·pist** /endóskəpist/ *n.* **en·dos·co·py** /endóskəpee/ *n.*

en·do·skel·e·ton /éndōskélitən/ *n.* an internal skeleton, as found in vertebrates.

en·do·sperm /éndəspərm/ *n.* albumen enclosed with the germ in seeds.

en·do·spore /éndəspawr/ *n.* **1** a spore formed by certain bacteria. **2** the inner coat of a spore.

en·do·the·li·um /éndōthéeleeəm/ *n. Anat.* a layer of cells lining the blood vessels, heart, and lymphatic vessels. [ENDO- + Gk *thēlē* teat]

en·do·ther·mic /éndōthérmik/ *adj.* occurring or formed with the absorption of heat.

en·dow /endów, in–/ *v.tr.* **1** bequeath or give a permanent income to (a person, institution, etc.). **2** (esp. as **endowed** *adj.*) (usu. foll. by *with*) provide (a person) with talent, ability, etc. □□ **en·dow·er** *n.* [ME f. AF *endouer* (as EN-¹, OF *douer* f. L *dotare* f. *dos dotis* DOWER)]

en·dow·ment /endówmənt, in–/ *n.* **1** the act or an instance of endowing. **2** assets, esp. property or income, with which a person or body is endowed. **3** (usu. in *pl.*) skill, talent, etc., with which a person is endowed. **4** (*attrib.*) denoting forms of life insurance involving payment by the insurer of a fixed sum on a specified date, or on the death of the insured person if earlier.

end·pa·per /éndpaypər/ *n.* a usu. blank leaf of paper at the beginning and end of a book, fixed to the inside of the cover.

end·play /éndplay/ *n. Bridge* a method of play in the last few tricks to force an opponent to make a disadvantageous lead.

end·point /éndpoynt/ *n.* (also **end point**) *Math.* a point or value that marks the end of a ray or one of the ends of a line segment or interval.

end point *n.* **1** the final stage of a process, esp. the point at which an effect is observed in titration, dilution, etc. **2** var. of ENDPOINT.

end prod·uct *n.* that which is produced as the final result of an activity or process, esp. the finished article in a manufacturing process.

end run *n.* **1** *Football* an attempt by the ballcarrier to run around the offensive end. **2** an evasive tactic, esp. in war or politics.

end-stopped *adj.* (of verse) having a pause at the end of each line.

en·due /endōo, –dyōo, in–/ *v.tr.* (also **in·due**) (foll. by *with*) invest or provide (a person) with qualities, powers, etc. [earlier = induct, put on clothes: ME f. OF *enduire* f. L *inducere* lead in, assoc. in sense with L *induere* put on (clothes)]

en·dur·ance /endōorəns, –dyōor–, in–/ *n.* **1** the power or habit of enduring (*beyond endurance*). **2** the ability to withstand prolonged strain (*endurance test*). **3** the act of enduring. **4** ability to last; enduring quality. [OF f. *endurer:* see ENDURE]

en·dure /endōor, –dyōor, in–/ *v.* **1** *tr.* undergo (a difficulty, hardship, etc.). **2** *tr.* **a** tolerate (a person) (*cannot endure him*). **b** (esp. with *neg.*; foll. by *to* + infin.) bear. **3** *intr.* (often as **enduring** *adj.*) remain in existence; last. **4** *tr.* submit to. □□ **en·dur·a·ble** *adj.* **en·dur·a·bil·i·ty** *n.* **en·dur·ing·ly** *adv.* [ME f. OF *endurer* f. L *indurare* harden (as IN-², *durus* hard)]

en·dur·o /endōorō, –dyōorō, in–/ *n.* (*pl.* **-os**) a long-distance race for motor vehicles, designed to test endurance.

end us·er *n.* the person, customer, etc., who is the ultimate user of a product.

end·ways /éndwayz/ *adv.* **1** with its end uppermost or foremost or turned toward the viewer. **2** end to end.

end·wise /éndwiz/ *adv.* = ENDWAYS.

end zone *n. Football* the area at each end of a football field where points are scored.

ENE *abbr.* east-northeast.

-ene /een/ *suffix* **1** forming names of inhabitants of places (*Nazarene*). **2** *Chem.* forming names of unsaturated hydrocarbons containing a double bond (*benzene*; *ethylene*). [from or after Gk –*ēnos*]

en·e·ma /énimə/ *n.* (*pl.* **en·e·mas** or **en·e·ma·ta** /inémətə/) **1** the injection of liquid or gas into the rectum, esp. to expel its contents. **2** a fluid or syringe used for this. [LL f. Gk *enema* f. *eniēmi* inject (as EN-², *hiēmi* send)]

en·e·my /énəmee/ *n.* (*pl.* **-mies**) **1** a person or group actively opposing or hostile to another, or to a cause, etc. **2 a** a hostile nation or army, esp. in war. **b** a member of this. **c** a hostile ship or aircraft. **3** (usu. foll. by *of, to*) an adversary or opponent. **4** a thing that harms or injures. **5** (*attrib.*) of or belonging to an enemy (*destroyed by enemy action*). [ME f. OF *enemi* f. L *inimicus* (as IN-¹, *amicus* friend)]

See page xx for the **Key to Pronunciation.**

en·er·get·ic /énərjétik/ *adj.* **1** strenuously active. **2** forcible; vigorous. **3** powerfully operative. □□ **en·er·get·i·cal·ly** *adv.* [Gk *energētikos* f. *energeō* (as EN-², *ergon* work)]

en·er·get·ics /énərjétiks/ *n.pl.* the science of energy.

en·er·gize /énərjīz/ *v.tr.* **1** infuse energy into (a person or work). **2** provide energy for the operation of (a device). □□ **en·er·giz·er** *n.*

en·er·gy /énərjee/ *n.* (*pl.* **·gies**) **1** force; vigor; capacity for activity. **2** (in *pl.*) individual powers in use (*devote your energies to this*). **3** *Physics* the capacity of matter or radiation to do work. **4** the means of doing work by utilizing matter or radiation. [F *énergie* or LL *energia* f. Gk *energeia* f. *ergon* work]

en·er·vate *v. & adj.* ● *v.tr.* /énərvayt/ deprive of vigor or vitality. ● *adj.* /inərvət/ enervated. □□ **en·er·va·tion** /-váyshən/ *n.* [L *enervatus* past part. of *enervare* (as E-, *nervus* sinew)]

en fa·mille /óN faméey/ *adv.* **1** in or with one's family. **2** at home. [F, = in family]

en·fant ter·ri·ble /aaNfaaN tereéblə/ *n.* a person who causes embarrassment by indiscreet or unruly behavior. [F, = terrible child]

en·fee·ble /enfeébəl, in-/ *v.tr.* make feeble. □□ **en·fee·ble·ment** *n.* [ME f. OF *enfeblir* (as EN-¹, FEEBLE)]

en fête /oN fét/ *adv. & predic.adj.* holding or ready for a holiday or celebration. [F, = in festival]

en·fet·ter /enfétər, in-/ *v.tr. literary* **1** bind in or as in fetters. **2** (foll. by *to*) enslave.

en·fi·lade /énfiláyd, -laád/ *n. & v.* ● *n.* gunfire directed along a line from end to end. ● *v.tr.* direct an enfilade at (troops, a road, etc.). [F f. *enfiler* (as EN-¹, *fil* thread)]

en·fold /enfóld, in-/ *v.tr.* (also **in·fold**) **1** (usu. foll. by *in, with*) wrap up; envelop. **2** clasp; embrace.

en·force /enfáwrs, in-/ *v.tr.* **1** compel observance of (a law, etc.). **2** (foll. by *on, upon*) impose (an action, conduct, one's will). **3** persist in (a demand or argument). □□ **en·force·a·ble** *adj.* **en·force·a·bil·i·ty** *n.* **en·force·ed·ly** /-sidlee/ *adv.* **en·forc·er** *n.* [ME f. OF *enforcir, -ier* ult. f. L *fortis* strong]

en·force·ment /enfáwrsmənt, in-/ *n.* the act or an instance of enforcing. [ME f. OF, as ENFORCE + -MENT]

en·fran·chise /enfránchīz, in-/ *v.tr.* **1** give (a person) the right to vote. **2** give (a town, city, etc.) municipal or parliamentary rights. **3** *hist.* free (a slave, villein, etc.). □□ **en·fran·chise·ment** *n.* [OF *enfranchir* (as EN-¹, *franc franche* FRANK)]

ENG *abbr.* electronic news gathering.

en·gage /en-gáyj, in-/ *v.* **1** *tr.* employ or hire (a person). **2** *tr.* **a** (usu. in *passive*) employ busily; occupy (*he was engaged as a trainee copywriter*). **b** hold fast (a person's attention). **3** *tr.* (usu. in *passive*) bind by a promise, esp. of marriage. **4** *tr.* (usu. foll. by *to* + infin.) bind by a contract. **5** *tr.* arrange beforehand to occupy (a room, seat, etc.). **6** (usu. foll. by *with*) *Mech.* **a** *tr.* interlock (parts of a gear, etc.); cause (a part) to interlock. **b** *intr.* (of a part, gear, etc.) interlock. **7 a** *intr.* (usu. foll. by *with*) (of troops, etc.) come into battle. **b** *tr.* bring (troops) into battle. **c** *tr.* come into battle with (an enemy, etc.). **8** *intr.* take part (*engage in politics*). **9** *intr.* (foll. by *that* + clause or *to* + infin.) pledge oneself. **10** *tr.* (usu. as **engaged** *adj.*) *Archit.* attach (a column) to a wall. **11** *tr.* (of fencers, etc.) interlock (weapons). □□ **en·gag·er** *n.* [F *engager*, rel. to GAGE¹]

en·ga·gé /oN-gazháy/ *adj.* (of a writer, artist, etc.) morally committed to a particular aim or cause. [F, past part. of *engager*: see ENGAGE]

en·gaged /en-gáyjd, in-/ *adj.* **1** under a promise to marry. **2 a** occupied; busy. **b** reserved; booked. **3** *Brit.* (of a telephone line) unavailable because already in use.

en·gage·ment /en-gáyjmənt, in-/ *n.* **1** the act or state of engaging or being engaged. **2** an appointment with another person. **3** a betrothal. **4** an encounter between hostile forces. **5** a moral commitment. **6** a period of paid employment; a job. [F f. *engager*: see ENGAGE]

en·gage·ment ring *n.* a ring given by a man to a woman when they promise to marry.

en·gag·ing /en-gáyjing, in-/ *adj.* attractive; charming. □□ **en·gag·ing·ly** *adv.* **en·gag·ing·ness** *n.*

en·gen·der /enjéndər, in-/ *v.tr.* **1** give rise to; bring about (a feeling, etc.). **2** *archaic* beget. [ME f. OF *engendrer* f. L *ingenerare* (as IN-², *generare* GENERATE)]

en·gine /énjin/ *n.* **1** a mechanical contrivance consisting of several parts working together, esp. as a source of power. **2 a** a railroad locomotive. **b** = FIRE ENGINE. **c** = STEAM ENGINE. **3** *archaic* a machine or instrument; a contrivance used in warfare. □□ **en·gined** *adj.* (also in *comb.*). **en·gine·less** *adj.* [OF *engin* f. L *ingenium* talent, device: cf. INGENIOUS]

▶An **engine** is a machine that (via combustion) converts fuel into energy, to drive something: *an automobile engine, a steam engine*. **Motor** is also used of a car's engine, but is also used of a wide range of machines that move something, like *electric motors*.

en·gi·neer /énjineér/ *n. & v.* ● *n.* **1** a person qualified in a branch of engineering, esp. as a professional. **2** = CIVIL ENGINEER. **3** a person who makes or is in charge of engines. **4** the operator or supervisor of an engine, esp. a railroad locomotive. **5** a person who designs and constructs military works; a soldier trained for this purpose. **6** (foll. by *of*) a skillful or artful contriver. ● *v.* **1** *tr.* arrange, contrive, or bring about, esp. artfully. **2** *intr.* act as an engineer. **3** *tr.* construct or manage as an engineer. □□ **en·gi·neer·ship** *n.* [ME f. OF *engineor* f. med.L *ingeniator –oris* f. *ingeniare* (as ENGINE)]

en·gi·neer·ing /énjineéring/ *n.* the application of science to the design, building, and use of machines, constructions, etc. □ **engineering science** engineering as a field of study.

en·gine room *n.* a room containing engines (esp. in a ship).

en·gine·ry /énjinree/ *n.* engines and machinery generally.

en·gird /en-gúrd, in-/ *v.tr.* surround with or as with a girdle.

en·gir·dle /en-gúrdəl, in-/ *v.tr.* engird.

Eng·lish /íngglish/ *adj. & n.* ● *adj.* of or relating to England or its people or language. ● *n.* **1** the language of England, now used in many varieties in the British Isles, the United States, and most Commonwealth or ex-Commonwealth countries, and often internationally. **2** (prec. by *the*; treated as *pl.*) the people of England. **3** *Billiards* a spinning motion given to the cue ball by striking it off center. □□ **Eng·lish·ness** *n.* [OE *englisc, ænglisc* (as ANGLE, -ISH¹)]

Eng·lish bond *n. Building* a bond of brickwork arranged in alternate courses of stretchers and headers.

Eng·lish horn *n. Mus.* **1** an alto woodwind instrument of the oboe family. **2** its player. **3** an organ stop with the quality of an English horn.

Eng·lish·man /íngglishmən/ *n.* (*pl.* **·men**) a person who is English by birth or descent.

Eng·lish muf·fin *n.* a flat, round, bread roll made from yeast dough, served sliced, toasted, and buttered.

Eng·lish·wom·an /íngglishwoomən/ *n.* (*pl.* **·wom·en**) a woman who is English by birth or descent.

en·gorge /en-gáwrj, in-/ *v.tr.* **1** (in *passive*) **a** be crammed. **b** *Med.* be congested with blood. **2** devour greedily. □□ **en·gorge·ment** *n.* [F *engorger* (as EN-¹, GORGE)]

English Horn

engr. *abbr.* **1** engineer. **2** engraved. **3** engraver. **4** engraving.

en·graft /en-gráft, in-/ *v.tr.* (also **in·graft**) **1** *Bot.* (usu. foll. by *into, upon*) insert (a scion of one tree into another). **2** (usu. foll. by *in*) implant (principles, etc.) in a person's mind. **3** (usu. foll. by *into*) incorporate permanently. □□ **en·graft·ment** *n.*

en·grail /en-gráyl, in-/ *v.tr.* (usu. as **engrailed** *adj.*) esp. Heraldry indent the edge of; give a serrated appearance to. [ME f. OF *engresler* (as EN-¹, *gresle* hail)]

en·grain /en-gráyn, in-/ *v.tr.* **1** implant (a habit, belief, or attitude) ineradicably in a person (see also INGRAINED). **2** cause (dye, etc.) to sink deeply into a thing. [ME f. OF *engrainer* dye in grain (*en graine*): see GRAIN]

en·grained /en-gráynd, in-/ *adj.* inveterate (see also INGRAINED).

en·gram /éngram/ *n.* a memory trace, a supposed permanent change in the brain accounting for the existence of memory. □□ **en·gram·mat·ic** /-grəmátik/ *adj.* [G *Engramm* f. Gk *en* in + *gramma* letter of the alphabet]

en·grave /en-gráyv, in-/ *v.tr.* **1** (often foll. by *on*) inscribe, cut, or carve (a text or design) on a hard surface. **2** (often foll. by *with*) inscribe or ornament (a surface) in this way. **3** cut (a design) as lines on a metal plate, block, etc., for printing. **4** (often foll. by *on*) impress deeply on a person's memory, etc. □□ **en·grav·er** *n.* [EN-¹ + GRAVE³]

en·grav·ing /en-gráyving, in-/ *n.* a print made from an engraved plate, block, or other surface.

en·gross /en-gróss, in-/ *v.tr.* **1** absorb the attention of; occupy fully (*engrossed in studying*). **2** make a fair copy of a legal document. **3** reproduce (a document, etc.) in larger letters or larger format. **4** *archaic* monopolize (a conversation, etc.). □□ **en·gross·ing** *adj.* (in sense 1). **en·gross·ment** *n.* [ME f. AF *engrosser*: senses 2 and 3 f. *en* in + *grosse* large writing: senses 1 and 4 f. *en gros* wholesale]

en·gulf /en-gúlf, in-/ *v.tr.* (also **in·gulf**) **1** flow over and swamp; overwhelm. **2** swallow or plunge into a gulf. □□ **en·gulf·ment** *n.*

en·hance /enháns, in-/ *v.tr.* heighten or intensify (qualities, powers, value, etc.); improve (something already of good quality). □□ **en·hance·ment** *n.* **en·hanc·er** *n.* [ME f. AF *enhauncer*, prob. alt. f. OF *enhaucier* ult. f. L *altus* high]

en·har·mon·ic /énhaarmónik/ *adj. Mus.* of or having intervals smaller than a semitone (esp. such intervals as that between G sharp and A flat, these notes being made the same in a scale of equal temperament). □□ **en·har·mon·i·cal·ly** *adv.* [LL *enharmonicus* f. Gk *enarmonikos* (as EN-², *harmonia* HARMONY)]

e·nig·ma /inígmə/ *n.* **1** a puzzling thing or person. **2** a riddle or paradox. □□ **en·ig·mat·ic** /énigmátik/ *adj.* **en·ig·mat·i·cal** *adj.* **en·ig·mat·**

i•cal•ly adv. e•nig•mat•ize /inígmətīz/ v.tr. [L aenigma f. Gk ainigma –matos f. ainissomai speak allusively f. ainos fable]

en•jamb•ment /enjámənt/ n. (also **en•jambe•ment**) Prosody the continuation of a sentence without a pause beyond the end of a line, couplet, or stanza. [F enjambement f. enjamber (as EN-¹, jambe leg)]

en•join /enjóyn/ in–/ v.tr. **1 a** (foll. by to + infin.) command or order (a person). **b** (foll. by that + clause) issue instructions. **2** (often foll. by on) impose or prescribe (an action or conduct). **3** (usu. foll. by from) Law prohibit (a person) by order. □□ **en•join•ment** n. [ME f. OF enjoindre f. L injungere (as IN-², jungere join)]

en•joy /enjóy/ in–/ v.tr. **1** take delight or pleasure in. **2** have the use or benefit of. **3** experience (enjoy poor health). □ **enjoy oneself** experience pleasure. □□ **en•joy•er** n. **en•joy•ment** n. [ME f. OF enjoier give joy to or enjoïr enjoy, ult. f. L gaudēre rejoice]

en•joy•a•ble /enjóyəbəl, in–/ adj. pleasant; giving enjoyment. □□ **en•joy•a•bil•i•ty** n. **en•joy•a•ble•ness** n. **en•joy•a•bly** adv.

en•keph•al•in /enkéfəlin/ n. Biochem. either of two morphinelike peptides occurring naturally in the brain and thought to control levels of pain. [Gk egkephalos brain]

en•kin•dle /enkíndəl, in–/ v.tr. literary **1 a** cause (flames) to flare up. **b** stimulate (feeling, passion, etc.). **2** inflame with passion.

en•lace /enláys, in–/ v.tr. **1** encircle tightly. **2** entwine. **3** enfold. □□ **en•lace•ment** n. [ME f. OF enlacier ult. f. L laqueus noose]

en•large /enláarj, in–/ v. **1** tr. & intr. make or become larger or wider. **2 a** tr. describe in greater detail. **b** intr. (usu. foll. by upon) expatiate. **3** tr. Photog. produce an enlargement of (a negative). [ME f. OF enlarger (as EN-¹, LARGE)]

en•large•ment /enláarjmənt, in–/ n. **1** the act or an instance of enlarging; the state of being enlarged. **2** Photog. a print that is larger than the negative from which it is produced.

en•larg•er /enláarjər, in–/ n. Photog. an apparatus for enlarging or reducing negatives or positives.

en•light•en /enlít'n, in–/ v.tr. **1 a** (often foll. by on) instruct or inform (a person) about a subject. **b** (as **enlightened** adj.) well-informed; knowledgeable. **2** (esp. as **enlightened** adj.) free from prejudice or superstition. **3** rhet. or poet. **a** shed light on (an object). **b** give spiritual insight to (a person). □□ **en•light•en•er** n.

en•light•en•ment /enlít'nmənt, in–/ n. **1** the act or an instance of enlightening; the state of being enlightened. **2** (**the Enlightenment**) the 18th-c. philosophy emphasizing reason and individualism rather than tradition.

en•list /enlíst, in–/ v. **1** intr. & tr. enroll in the armed services. **2** tr. secure as a means of help or support. □□ **en•list•er** n. **en•list•ment** n.

en•list•ed man n. a soldier or sailor below the rank of officer.

en•liv•en /enlívən, in–/ v.tr. **1** give life or spirit to. **2** make cheerful; brighten (a picture or scene). □□ **en•liv•en•er** n. **en•liv•en•ment** n.

en masse /on más/ adv. **1** all together. **2** in a mass. [F]

en•mesh /enmésh, in–/ v.tr. entangle in or as in a net. □□ **en•mesh•ment** n.

en•mi•ty /énmitee/ n. (pl. **•ties**) **1** the state of being an enemy. **2** a feeling of hostility. [ME f. OF enemitié f. Rmc (as ENEMY)]

en•ne•ad /éneead/ n. a group of nine. [Gk enneas enneados f. ennea nine]

en•no•ble /enóbəl, in–/ v.tr. **1** make (a person) a noble. **2** make noble; elevate. □□ **en•no•ble•ment** n. [F ennoblir (as EN-¹, NOBLE)]

en•nui /onwée/ n. mental weariness from lack of occupation or interest; boredom. [F f. L in odio: cf. ODIUM]

e•nol•o•gy /eenóləjee/ n. (Brit. **oe•nol•o•gy**) the study of wines. □□ **e•no•log•i•cal** /éenəlójikəl/ adj. **e•nol•o•gist** n. [GK oinos wine]

e•nor•mi•ty /ináwrmitee/ n. (pl. **•ties**) **1** extreme wickedness. **2** an act of extreme wickedness. **3** a serious error. **4** disp. great size; enormousness.

▶This word is imprecisely used to mean 'great size,' e.g., it's difficult to recognize the enormity of the continent, but the original and preferred meaning is 'extreme wickedness,' as in the enormity of the crime.

WORD HISTORY enormity

Late Middle English: via Old French from Latin enormitas, from enormis, from e- (variant of ex-) 'out of' + norma 'pattern, standard.' The word originally meant 'deviation from legal or moral rectitude' and 'transgression.' Current senses have been influenced by enormous.

e•nor•mous /ináwrməs/ adj. very large; huge (enormous animals; an enormous difference). □□ **e•nor•mous•ly** adv. **e•nor•mous•ness** n. [L enormis (as E-, norma pattern, standard)]

e•no•sis /inósis, énōsees/ n. the political union of Cyprus and Greece, as an ideal or proposal. [mod. Gk enōsis f. ena one]

e•nough /inúf/ adj., n., adv., & int. • adj. as much or as many as required (we have enough apples; we do not have enough sugar; earned enough money to buy a house). • n. an amount or quantity that is enough (we have enough of everything now; enough is as good as a feast). • adv. **1** to the required degree; adequately (are you warm enough?). **2** fairly (she sings well enough). **3** very; quite (you know well

319

enjambment ~ entablature

enough what I mean; oddly enough). • int. that is enough (in various senses, esp. to put an end to an action, thing said, etc.). □ **have had enough of** want no more of; be satiated with or tired of. [OE genog f. Gmc]

en pas•sant /ón pasón/ adv. **1** by the way. **2** Chess used with reference to the permitted capture of an opponent's pawn that has just advanced two squares in its first move with a pawn that could have taken it if it had advanced only one square. [F, = in passing]

en•plane /enpláyn, in–/ v.intr. & tr. (also **em•plane** /em–, im–/) go or put on board an airplane.

en•quire var. of INQUIRE.

en•quir•y var. of INQUIRY.

en•rage /enráyj, in–/ v.tr. (often foll. by at, by, with) make furious. □□ **en•rage•ment** n. [F enrager (as EN-¹, RAGE)]

en rap•port /ón rapáwr/ adv. (usu. foll. by with) in harmony or rapport. [F: see RAPPORT]

en•rap•ture /enrápchər, in–/ v.tr. give intense delight to.

en•rich /enrích, in–/ v.tr. **1** make rich or richer. **2** make richer in quality, flavor, nutritive value, etc. **3** add to the contents of (a collection, museum, or book). **4** increase the content of an isotope in (material), esp. enrich uranium with isotope U-235. □□ **en•rich•ment** n. [ME f. OF enrichir (as EN-¹, RICH)]

en•robe /enrób, in–/ v.intr. put on a robe, vestment, etc.

en•roll /enról, in–/ v. (also **en•rol**) (**en•rolled, en•rol•ling**) **1** intr. enter one's name on a list, esp. as a commitment to membership. **2** tr. **a** write the name of (a person) on a list. **b** (usu. foll. by in) incorporate (a person) as a member of a society, etc. **3** tr. hist. enter (a deed, etc.) among the rolls of a court of justice. **4** tr. record. □□ **en•roll•ee** /–leé/ n. **en•roll•er** n. [ME f. OF enroller (as EN-¹, rolle ROLL)]

en•roll•ment /enrólmənt, in–/ n. (also **en•rol•ment**) **1** the act or an instance of enrolling; the state of being enrolled. **2** the number of persons enrolled, esp. at a school or college.

en route /on róōt/ adv. (usu. foll. by to, for) on the way. [F]

Ens. abbr. ensign.

en•sconce /enskóns, in–/ v.tr. (usu. refl. or in passive) establish or settle comfortably, safely, or secretly.

en•sem•ble /onsómbəl/ n. **1 a** a thing viewed as the sum of its parts. **b** the general effect of this. **2** a set of clothes worn together; an outfit. **3** a group of actors, dancers, musicians, etc., performing together, esp. subsidiary dancers in ballet, etc. **4** Mus. **a** a concerted passage for an ensemble. **b** the manner in which this is performed (good ensemble). **5** Physics a group of systems with the same constitution but possibly in different states. [F, ult. f. L insimul (as IN-², simul at the same time)]

en•shrine /enshrín, in–/ v.tr. **1** enclose in or as in a shrine. **2** serve as a shrine for. **3** preserve or cherish. □□ **en•shrine•ment** n.

en•shroud /enshrówd, in–/ v.tr. literary **1** cover with or as with a shroud. **2** cover completely; hide from view.

en•sign /énsin, –sín/ n. **1 a** a banner or flag, esp. the military or naval flag of a nation. **b** Brit. a flag with the union in the corner. **2** a standard-bearer. **3 a** hist. the lowest commissioned infantry officer. **b** the lowest commissioned officer in the US Navy or US Coast Guard. □□ **en•sign•cy** n. [ME f. OF enseigne f. L insignia: see INSIGNIA]

en•si•lage /énsilij/ n. & v. • n. = SILAGE. • v.tr. treat (fodder) by ensilage. [F (as ENSILE)]

en•sile /ensíl, in–/ v.tr. **1** put (fodder) into a silo. **2** preserve (fodder) in a silo. [F ensiler f. Sp. ensilar (as EN-¹, SILO)]

en•slave /ensláyv, in–/ v.tr. make (a person) a slave. □□ **en•slave•ment** n. **en•slav•er** n.

en•snare /ensnáir, in–/ v.tr. catch in or as in a snare; entrap. □□ **en•snare•ment** n.

en•sue /ensóō, in–/ v.intr. **1** happen afterward. **2** (often foll. by from, on) occur as a result. [ME f. OF ensuivre ult. f. L sequi follow]

en suite /on sweét/ adv. forming a single unit (bedroom with bathroom en suite). [F, = in sequence]

en•sure /enshóōr, in–/ v.tr. **1** (often foll. by that + clause) make certain. **2** (usu. foll. by to, for) secure (a thing for a person, etc.). **3** (usu. foll. by against) make safe. □□ **en•sur•er** n. [ME f. AF enseürer f. OF aseürer ASSURE]

▶See note at INSURE.

en•swathe /enswáyth, in–/ v.tr. bind or wrap in or as in a bandage. □□ **en•swathe•ment** n.

ENT abbr. ear, nose, and throat.

-ent /ənt, ent/ suffix **1** forming adjectives denoting attribution of an action (consequent) or state (existent). **2** forming nouns denoting an agent (coefficient; president). [from or after F –ent or L –ent– pres. part. stem of verbs (cf. –ANT)]

en•tab•la•ture /entábləchər, in–/ n. Archit. the upper part of a classical building supported by columns or a colonnade, comprising architrave, frieze, and cornice. [It. intavolatura f. intavolare board up (as IN-², tavola table)]

en·ta·ble·ment /entáybəlmənt, in–/ *n.* a platform supporting a statue, above the dado and base. [F, f. *entabler* (as EN-¹, TABLE)]

en·tail /entáyl, in–/ *v. & n.* • *v.tr.* **1 a** necessitate or involve unavoidably (*the work entails much effort*). **b** give rise to; involve. **2** *Law* bequeath (property, etc.) so that it remains within a family. **3** (usu. foll. by *on*) bestow (a thing) inalienably. • *n. Law* **1** an entailed estate. **2** the succession to such an estate. □□ **en·tail·ment** *n.* [ME, f. EN-¹ + AF *taile* TAIL²]

en·tan·gle /entánggəl, in–/ *v.tr.* **1** cause to get caught in a snare or among obstacles. **2** cause to become tangled. **3** involve in difficulties or illicit activities. **4** make (a thing) tangled or intricate; complicate.

en·tan·gle·ment /entánggəlmənt, in–/ *n.* **1** the act or condition of entangling or being entangled. **2 a** a thing that entangles. **b** *Mil.* an extensive barrier erected to obstruct an enemy's movements (esp. one made of stakes and interlaced barbed wire). **3** a compromising (esp. amorous) relationship.

en·ta·sis /éntəsis/ *n. Archit.* a slight convex curve in a column shaft to correct the visual illusion that straight sides give of curving inward. [mod.L f. Gk f. *enteinō* to stretch]

en·tel·lus /entéləs, in–/ *n.* = HANUMAN. [name of a Trojan in Virgil's *Aeneid*]

en·tente /aantaánt/ *n.* **1** = ENTENTE CORDIALE. **2** a group of nations in such a relation. [F, = understanding (as INTENT)]

en·tente cor·diale /oNtóNt kawrdyaál/ *n.* a friendly understanding between nations, esp. (often **Entente Cordiale**) that reached in 1904 between Britain and France. [F, = cordial understanding: see EN-TENTE]

en·ter /éntər/ *v.* **1 a** *intr.* (often foll. by *into*) go or come in. **b** *tr.* go or come into. **c** *intr.* come on stage (as a direction: *enter Macbeth*). **2** *tr.* penetrate; go through; spread through (*a bullet entered his chest; a smell of toast entered the room*). **3** *tr.* (often foll. by *up*) write (a name, details, etc.) in a list, book, etc. **4 a** *intr.* register or announce oneself as a competitor (*entered the long jump*). **b** *tr.* become a competitor in (an event). **c** *tr.* record the name of (a person, etc.) as a competitor (*entered two horses for the Kentucky Derby*). **5** *tr.* **a** become a member of (a society, etc.). **b** enroll as a member or prospective member of a society, school, etc.; admit or obtain admission for. **7** *tr.* make known; present for consideration (*entered a protest*). **8** *intr.* (foll. by *into*) **a** engage in (conversation, relations, an undertaking, etc.). **b** subscribe to; bind oneself by (an agreement, etc.). **c** form part of (one's calculations, plans, etc.). **d** sympathize with (feelings, etc.). **9** *intr.* (foll. by *on*, *upon*) **a** begin; undertake; begin to deal with (a subject). **b** assume the functions of (an office). **c** assume possession of (property). **10** *intr.* (foll. by *up*) complete a series of entries in (account books, etc.). □□ **en·ter·er** *n.* [ME f. OF *entrer* f. L *intrare*]

en·ter·ic /entérik/ *adj. & n.* • *adj.* of the intestines. • *n.* (in full **enteric fever**) typhoid. □□ **en·ter·i·tis** /éntərítis/ *n.* [Gk *enterikos* (as ENTERO-)]

entero- /éntərō/ *comb. form* intestine. [Gk *enteron* intestine]

en·ter·os·to·my /éntəróstəmee/ *n.* (*pl.* **·mies**) *Surgery* a surgical operation in which the small intestine is brought through the abdominal wall and opened, in order to bypass the stomach or the colon.

en·ter·ot·o·my /éntərótəmee/ *n.* (*pl.* **·mies**) *Surgery* the surgical cutting open of the intestine.

en·ter·o·vi·rus /éntərōvírəs/ *n.* a virus infecting the intestines and sometimes spreading to other parts of the body, esp. the central nervous system.

en·ter·prise /éntərprīz/ *n.* **1** an undertaking, esp. a bold or difficult one. **2** (as a personal attribute) readiness to engage in such undertakings (*has no enterprise*). **3** a business firm. □□ **en·ter·pris·er** *n.* [ME f. OF *entreprise* fem. past part. of *entreprendre* var. of *emprendre* ult. f. L *prendere, prehendere* take]

en·ter·prise zone *n.* a depressed (usu. urban) area where government incentives such as tax concessions are available to encourage investment.

en·ter·pris·ing /éntərprīzing/ *adj.* **1** ready to engage in enterprises. **2** resourceful; imaginative; energetic. □□ **en·ter·pris·ing·ly** *adv.*

en·ter·tain /éntərtáyn/ *v.tr.* **1** amuse; occupy agreeably. **2 a** receive or treat as a guest. **b** (*absol.*) receive guests (*they entertain a great deal*). **3** give attention or consideration to (an idea, feeling, or proposal). [ME f. F *entretenir* ult. f. L *tenēre* hold]

en·ter·tain·er /éntərtáynər/ *n.* a person who entertains, esp. professionally on stage, etc.

en·ter·tain·ing /éntərtáyning/ *adj.* amusing; diverting.

en·ter·tain·ment /éntərtáynmənt/ *n.* **1** the act or an instance of entertaining; the process of being entertained. **2** a public performance or show. **3** diversions or amusements for guests, etc. **4** amusement (*much to my entertainment*). **5** hospitality.

en·ter·tain·ment cen·ter *n.* a piece of furniture, usu. with several shelves to accommodate a television, video cassette recorder, stereo system, etc.

en·thal·py /énthəlpee, enthálpee/ *n. Physics* the total thermodynamic heat content of a system. [Gk *enthalpō* warm in (as EN-¹, *thalpō* to heat)]

en·thrall /enthráwl, in–/ *v.tr.* (also **en·thral, in·thral, in·thrall**) (·**thralled, ·thrall·ing**) **1** (often as **enthralling** *adj.*) captivate; please greatly. **2** enslave. □□ **en·thrall·ment** *n.* [EN-¹ + THRALL]

en·throne /enthrón, in–/ *v.tr.* **1** install (a king, bishop, etc.) on a throne, esp. ceremonially. **2** exalt. □□ **en·throne·ment** *n.*

en·thuse /enthōōz, in–/ *v.intr. & tr. colloq.* be or make enthusiastic. [back-form. f. ENTHUSIASM]

▶ The verb **enthuse**, meaning 'show enthusiasm,' is a 19th-century American invention, a back-formation from the noun **enthusiasm**. It is now widely accepted in both Britain and the United States, although many continue to disapprove of it. The same goes for the adjective **enthused**. Many careful speakers and writers prefer **enthusiastic** (*he was very enthusiastic about the performance*).

en·thu·si·asm /enthōōzeeazəm, in–/ *n.* **1** (often foll. by *for, about*) **a** strong interest or admiration. **b** great eagerness. **2** an object of enthusiasm. **3** *archaic* extravagant religious emotion. [F *enthousiasme* or LL *enthusiasmus* f. Gk *entheos* possessed by a god, inspired (as EN-², *theos* god)]

en·thu·si·ast /enthōōzeeast, in–/ *n.* **1** (often foll. by *for*) a person who is full of enthusiasm. **2** a visionary; a self-deluded person. [F *enthousiaste* or eccl.L *enthusiastes* f. Gk (as ENTHUSIASM)]

en·thu·si·as·tic /enthōōzeeástik, in–/ *adj.* having or showing enthusiasm. □□ **en·thu·si·as·ti·cal·ly** *adv.* [Gk *enthousiastikos* (as ENTHU-SIASM)]

en·thy·meme /énthimeem/ *n. Logic* a syllogism in which one premise is not explicitly stated. [L *enthymema* f. Gk *enthumēma* f. *enthumeomai* consider (as EN-², *thumos* mind)]

en·tice /entís, in–/ *v.tr.* (often foll. by *from, into,* or *to* + infin.) persuade by the offer of pleasure or reward. □□ **en·tice·ment** *n.* **en·tic·er** *n.* **en·tic·ing·ly** *adv.* [ME f. OF *enticier* prob. f. Rmc]

en·tire /entír, in–/ *adj. & n.* • *adj.* **1** whole; complete. **2** not broken or decayed. **3** unqualified; absolute (*an entire success*). **4** in one piece; continuous. **5** not castrated. **6** *Bot.* without indentation. **7** pure; unmixed. • *n.* an uncastrated animal. [ME f. AF *enter*, OF *entier* f. L *integer* (as IN-², *tangere* touch)]

en·tire·ly /entírlee, in–/ *adv.* **1** wholly; completely (*the stock is entirely exhausted*). **2** solely; exclusively (*did it entirely for my benefit*).

en·tire·ty /entírtee, in–/ *n.* (*pl.* **·ties**) **1** completeness. **2** (usu. foll. by *of*) the sum total. □ **in its entirety** in its complete form; completely. [ME f. OF *entiereté* f. L *integritas –tatis* f. *integer*: see EN-TIRE]

en·ti·tle /entítəl, in–/ *v.tr.* **1 a** (usu. foll. by *to*) give (a person, etc.) a just claim. **b** (foll. by *to* + infin.) give (a person, etc.) a right. **2 a** give (a book, etc.) the title of. **b** *archaic* give (a person) the title of (*entitled him sultan*). □□ **en·ti·tle·ment** *n.* [ME f. AF *entitler*, OF *entitel-er* f. LL *intitulare* (as IN-², TITLE)]

en·ti·ty /éntitee/ *n.* (*pl.* **·ties**) **1** a thing with distinct existence, as opposed to a quality or relation. **2** a thing's existence regarded distinctly; a thing's essential nature. □□ **en·ti·ta·tive** /–titáytiv/ *adj.* [F *entité* or med.L *entitas* f. LL *ens* being]

ento- /éntō/ *comb. form* within. [Gk *entos* within]

en·tomb /entōōm, in–/ *v.tr.* **1** place in or as in a tomb. **2** serve as a tomb for. □□ **en·tomb·ment** *n.* [OF *entomber* (as EN-¹, TOMB)]

entomo- /éntəmō/ *comb. form* insect. [Gk *entomos* cut up (in neut. = INSECT) f. EN-² + *temnō* cut]

en·to·mol·o·gy /éntəmóləjee/ *n.* the study of the forms and behavior of insects. □□ **en·to·mo·log·i·cal** /–məlójikəl/ *adj.* **en·to·mol·o·gist** *n.* [F *entomologie* or mod.L *entomologia* (as ENTOMO-, –LOGY)]

en·to·moph·a·gous /éntəmófəgəs/ *adj. Zool.* insect-eating.

en·to·moph·i·lous /éntəmófiləs/ *adj. Biol.* pollinated by insects.

en·to·phyte /éntōfit/ *n. Bot.* a plant growing inside a plant or animal.

en·tou·rage /óntooraázh/ *n.* **1** people attending an important person. **2** surroundings. [F f. *entourer* surround]

en·tr'acte /aantrákt, áan–/ *n.* **1** an interval between two acts of a play. **2** a piece of music or a dance performed during this. [F f. *entre* between + *acte* act]

en·trails /éntraylz, -trəlz/ *n.pl.* **1** the bowels and intestines of a person or animal. **2** the innermost parts (*entrails of the earth*). [ME f. OF *entrailles* f. med.L *intralia* alt. f. L *interaneus* internal f. *inter* among]

en·train¹ /entráyn, in–/ *v.intr. & tr.* go or put on board a train. □□ **en·train·ment** *n.*

en·train² /entráyn, in–/ *v.tr.* **1** (of a fluid) carry (particles, etc.) along in its flow. **2** drag along. □□ **en·train·ment** *n.* [F *entraîner* (as EN-¹, *traîner* drag, formed as TRAIN)]

en·trance¹ /éntrəns, in–/ *n.* **1** the act or an instance of going or coming in. **2** a door, passage, etc., by which one enters. **3** right of admission. **4** the coming of an actor on stage. **5** *Mus.* = ENTRY 8. **6** (foll. by *into, upon*) entering into office, etc. **7** (in full **entrance fee**) a fee paid for admission to a society, club, exhibition, etc. [OF (as EN-TER, –ANCE)]

en·trance² /entráns, in–/ *v.tr.* **1** enchant; delight. **2** put into a trance.

3 (often foll. by *with*) overwhelm with strong feeling. □□ **en·trance·ment** *n.* **en·tranc·ing** *adj.* **en·tranc·ing·ly** *adv.*

en·trant /éntrənt/ *n.* a person who enters (esp. an examination, profession, etc.). [F, part. of *entrer*: see ENTER]

en·trap /entráp, in–/ *v.tr.* (**en·trapped, en·trap·ping**) **1** catch in or as in a trap. **2** (often foll. by *into* + verbal noun) beguile or trick (a person). □□ **en·trap·per** *n.* [OF *entraper* (as EN-[1], TRAP[1])]

en·trap·ment /entrápmənt, in–/ *n.* **1** the act or an instance of entrapping; the process of being entrapped. **2** *Law* inducement to commit a crime, esp. by the authorities to secure a prosecution.

en·treat /entreét, in–/ *v.tr.* **1 a** (foll. by *to* + infin. or *that* + clause) ask (a person) earnestly. **b** ask earnestly for (a thing). **2** *archaic* treat; act toward (a person). □□ **en·treat·ing·ly** *adv.* [ME f. OF *entraiter* (as EN-[1], *traiter* TREAT)]

en·treat·y /entreétee, in–/ *n.* (*pl.* **·ies**) an earnest request; a supplication. [ENTREAT, after TREATY]

en·tre·chat /óntrəshaá/ *n.* a leap in ballet, with one or more crossings of the legs while in the air. [F f. It. (*capriola*) *intrecciata* complicated (caper)]

en·tre·côte /óntrəkōt/ *n.* a boned steak cut off the sirloin. [F f. *entre* between + *côte* rib]

en·trée /óntray/ *n.* (also **en·tree**) **1** *Cooking* **a** esp. *US* the main dish of a meal. **b** *Brit.* a dish served between the fish and meat courses. **2** the right or privilege of admission. [F, = ENTRY]

en·tre·mets /óntrəmáy/ *n.* **1** a sweet dish. **2** any light dish served between two courses. [F f. *entre* between + *mets* dish]

en·trench /entrénch, in–/ *v.* (also **in·trench**) **1** *tr.* establish firmly (in a defensible position, in office, etc.). **2** *tr.* surround (a post, army, town, etc.) with a trench as a fortification. **3** *tr.* apply extra safeguards to (rights, etc., guaranteed by legislation). **4** *intr.* entrench oneself. **5** *intr.* (foll. by *upon*) encroach; trespass. □ **entrench oneself** adopt a well-defended position. □□ **en·trench·ment** *n.*

en·tre nous /óntrə nōō/ *adv.* **1** between you and me. **2** in private. [F, = between ourselves]

en·tre·pôt /óntrəpō/ *n.* **1** a warehouse for temporary storage of goods in transit. **2** a commercial center for import and export, and for collection and distribution. [F f. *entreposer* store f. *entre-* INTER- + *poser* place]

en·tre·pre·neur /óntrəprənóōr/ *n.* **1** a person who undertakes an enterprise or business, with the chance of profit or loss. **2** a contractor acting as an intermediary. **3** the person in effective control of a commercial undertaking. **4** a person who organizes entertainments, esp. musical performances. □□ **en·tre·pre·neur·i·al** *adj.* **en·tre·pre·neur·i·al·ism** *n.* (also **en·tre·pre·neur·ism**). **en·tre·pre·neur·i·al·ly** *adv.* **en·tre·pre·neur·ship** *n.* [F f. *entreprendre* undertake: see ENTERPRISE]

en·tre·sol /óntrəsol/ *n.* a low story between the first and the ground floor; a mezzanine floor. [F f. *entre* between + *sol* ground]

en·trism var. of ENTRYISM.

en·tro·py /éntrəpee/ *n.* **1** *Physics* a measure of the unavailability of a system's thermal energy for conversion into mechanical work. **2** *Physics* a measure of the disorganization or degradation of the universe. **3** a measure of the rate of transfer of information in a message, etc. □□ **en·tro·pic** /–trópik/ *adj.* **en·tro·pi·cal·ly** *adv.* [G *Entropie* (as EN-[2], Gk *tropē* transformation)]

en·trust /entrúst, in–/ *v.tr.* (also **in·trust**) **1** (foll. by *to*) give responsibility for (a person or a thing) to a person in whom one has confidence. **2** (foll. by *with*) assign responsibility for a thing to (a person). □□ **en·trust·ment** *n.*

en·try /éntree/ *n.* (*pl.* **·tries**) **1 a** the act or an instance of going or coming in. **b** the coming of an actor on stage. **c** ceremonial entrance. **2** liberty to go or come in. **3 a** a place of entrance; a door, gate, etc. **b** a lobby. **4** *Brit.* a passage between buildings. **5** the mouth of a river. **6 a** an item entered (in a diary, list, account book, etc.). **b** the recording of this. **7 a** a person or thing competing in a race, contest, etc. **b** a list of competitors. **8** the start or resumption of music for a particular instrument in an ensemble. **9** *Law* the act of taking possession. **10** *Bridge* **a** the transfer of the lead to one's partner's hand. **b** a card providing this. [ME f. OF *entree* ult. f. L *intrare* ENTER]

en·try form *n.* an application form for a competition.

en·try·ism /éntreeizəm/ *n.* (also **entrism**) infiltration into a political organization to change or subvert its policies or objectives. □□ **en·trist** *n.* **en·try·ist** *n.*

en·twine /entwín, in–/ *v.* (also **in·twine** /in–/) **1** *tr. & intr.* (foll. by *with, about, around*) twine together (a thing with or around another). **2** *tr.* (as **entwined** *adj.*) entangled. **3** *tr.* interweave. □□ **en·twine·ment** *n.*

e·nu·cle·ate /inóōkleeayt, inyóō–/ *v.tr. Surgery* extract (a tumor, etc.). □□ **e·nu·cle·a·tion** /–áyshən/ *n.* [L *enucleare* (as E-, NUCLEUS)]

E-num·ber /éenumbər/ *n.* the letter E followed by a code number, designating food additives according to EC directives.

e·nu·mer·ate /inóōmərayt, inyóō–/ *v.tr.* **1** specify (items); mention one by one. **2** count; establish the number of. □□ **e·nu·mer·a·ble** *adj.* **e·nu·mer·a·tion** /–ráyshən/ *n.* **e·nu·mer·a·tive** /–raytiv, –rətiv/ *adj.* [L *enumerare* (as E-, NUMBER)]

e·nu·mer·a·tor /inóōmərayter, inyóō–/ *n.* **1** a person who enumerates. **2** a person employed in census taking.

e·nun·ci·ate /inúnseeayt/ *v.tr.* **1** pronounce (words) clearly. **2** express (a proposition or theory) in definite terms. **3** proclaim. □□ **e·nun·ci·a·tion** /–áyshən/ *n.* **e·nun·ci·a·tive** /–seeətiv/ *adj.* **e·nun·ci·a·tor** *n.* [L *enuntiare* (as E-, *nuntiare* announce f. *nuntius* messenger)]

en·ure /inyóōr/ *v.intr. Law* take effect. [var. of INURE]

en·u·re·sis /ényōōreésis/ *n. Med.* involuntary urination, esp. while sleeping. □□ **en·u·ret·ic** /–rétik/ *adj. & n.* [mod.L f. Gk *enoureō* urinate in (as EN-[2], *ouron* urine)]

en·vel·op /envéləp, in–/ *v.tr.* (**en·vel·oped, en·vel·op·ing**) **1** (often foll. by *in*) **a** wrap up or cover completely. **b** make obscure; conceal (*was enveloped in mystery*). **2** *Mil.* completely surround (an enemy). □□ **en·vel·op·ment** *n.* [ME f. OF *envoluper* (as EN-[1]: cf. DEVELOP)]

en·vel·ope /énvəlōp, ón–/ *n.* **1** a folded paper container, usu. with a sealable flap, for a letter, etc. **2** a wrapper or covering. **3** the structure within a balloon or airship containing the gas. **4** the outer metal or glass housing of a vacuum tube, electric light, etc. **5** *Electr.* a curve joining the successive peaks of a modulated wave. **6** *Bot.* any enveloping structure, esp. the calyx or corolla (or both). **7** *Math.* a line or curve tangent to each line or curve of a given family. [F *enveloppe* (as ENVELOP)]

> **PRONUNCIATION TIP envelope**
>
> Some people consider the pronunciation "ON-ve-lope" to be pseudo-French. Although the Anglicized pronunciation "EN-ve-lope" is more widely used, the French variant is considered acceptable.

en·ven·om /envénəm, in–/ *v.tr.* **1** put poison on or into; make poisonous. **2** infuse venom or bitterness into (feelings, words, or actions). [ME f. OF *envenimer* (as EN-[1], *venim* VENOM)]

en·vi·a·ble /énveeəbəl/ *adj.* (of a person or thing) exciting or likely to excite envy. □□ **en·vi·a·bly** *adv.*

en·vi·ous /énveeəs/ *adj.* (often foll. by *of*) feeling or showing envy. □□ **en·vi·ous·ly** *adv.* [ME f. AF *envious*, OF *envieus* f. *envie* ENVY]

en·vi·ron /envírən, víərn, in–/ *v.tr.* encircle; surround (esp. hostilely or protectively). [ME f. OF *environer* f. *environ* surroundings f. *en* in + *viron* circuit f. *virer* turn, VEER[1]]

en·vi·ron·ment /envírənmənt, –víərn–, in–/ *n.* **1** physical surroundings and conditions, esp. as affecting people's lives. **2** conditions or circumstances of living. **3** *Ecol.* external conditions affecting the growth of plants and animals. **4** a structure designed to be experienced from inside as a work of art. **5** *Computing* the overall structure within which a user, computer, or program operates. □□ **en·vi·ron·men·tal** /–ment'l/ *adj.* **en·vi·ron·men·tal·ist** *n.* **en·vi·ron·men·tal·ly** *adv.*

en·vi·ron·men·tal·ist /envírənméntəlist, –víərn–, in–/ *n.* **1** a person who is concerned with or advocates the protection of the environment. **2** a person who considers that environment has the primary influence on the development of a person or group. □□ **en·vi·ron·men·tal·ism** *n.*

en·vi·ron·ment-friend·ly *n.* not harmful to the environment.

en·vi·rons /envírənz, –víərnz, in–/ *n.pl.* a surrounding district, esp. around an urban area.

en·vis·age /envízij, in–/ *v.tr.* **1** have a mental picture of (a thing or conditions not yet existing). **2** contemplate or conceive, esp. as a possibility or desirable future event. **3** *archaic* **a** face (danger, facts, etc.). **b** look in the face of. □□ **en·vis·age·ment** *n.* [F *envisager* (as EN-[1], VISAGE)]

en·vi·sion /envízhən, in–/ *v.tr.* envisage; visualize.

en·voy[1] /énvoy, ón–/ *n.* **1** a messenger or representative, esp. on a diplomatic mission. **2** (in full **envoy extraordinary**) a minister plenipotentiary, ranking below ambassador and above chargé d'affaires. □□ **en·voy·ship** *n.* [F *envoyé*, past part. of *envoyer* send f. *en voie* on the way f. L *via*]

en·voy[2] /énvoy, ón–/ *n.* (also **en·voi**) **1** a short stanza concluding a ballade, etc. **2** *archaic* an author's concluding words. [ME f. OF *envoi* f. *envoyer* (as ENVOY[1])]

en·vy /énvee/ *n. & v.* • *n.* (*pl.* **·vies**) **1** a feeling of discontent or resentful longing aroused by another's better fortune, etc. **2** the object or ground of this feeling (*their house is the envy of the neighborhood*). • *v.tr.* (**·vies, ·vied**) feel envy of (a person, circumstances, etc.) (*I envy you your position*). □□ **en·vi·er** *n.* [ME f. OF *envie* f. L *invidia* f. *invidēre* envy (as IN-[1], *vidēre* see)]

en·weave var. of INWEAVE.

en·wrap /enráp, in–/ *v.tr.* (also **in·wrap**) (**·wrapped, ·wrap·ping**) (often foll. by *in*) *literary* wrap or enfold.

en·wreathe /enreéth, in–/ *v.tr.* (also **in·wreathe**) *literary* surround with or as with a wreath.

En·zed /énzéd/ *n. Austral. & NZ colloq.* a popular written form of:

1 New Zealand. **2** a New Zealander. □□ **En·zed·der** *n.* [pronunc. of *NZ*]

en·zo·ot·ic /énzō-ótik/ *adj. & n.* ● *adj.* regularly affecting animals in a particular district or at a particular season (cf. ENDEMIC, EPIZOOTIC). ● *n.* an enzootic disease. [Gk *en* in + *zōion* animal]

en·zyme /énzīm/ *n. Biochem.* a protein acting as a catalyst in a specific biochemical reaction. □□ **en·zy·mat·ic** /–zīmátik/ *adj.* **en·zy·mic** *adj.* **en·zy·mol·o·gy** /–zīmóləjee/ *n.* [G *Enzym* f. med. Gk *enzumos* leavened f. Gk *en* in + *zumē* leaven]

E·o·cene /ée∂seen/ *adj. & n. Geol.* ● *adj.* of or relating to the second epoch of the Tertiary period with evidence of an abundance of mammals including horses, bats, and whales. ● *n.* this epoch or system. [Gk *ēōs* dawn + *kainos* new]

e·o·li·an /ee-ólee-∂n/ *adj.* (*Brit.* **ae·o·li·an**) wind-borne. [as AEOLIAN]

e·o·lith /ée∂lith/ *n. Archaeol.* any of various flint objects found in Tertiary strata and thought to be early artifacts. [Gk *ēōs* dawn + *lithos* stone]

e·o·lith·ic /ée∂líthik/ *adj. Archaeol.* of the period preceding the Paleolithic age, thought to include the earliest use of flint tools. [F *éolithique* (as EOLITH)]

e.o.m. *abbr.* (also **E.O.M.**) end of month.

e·on /ée∂n/ *n.* (also **ae·on**) **1** a very long or indefinite period. **2** an age of the universe. **3** a billion years. **4** an eternity. **5** *Philos.* (in Neoplatonism, Platonism, and Gnosticism) a power existing from eternity, an emanation or phase of the supreme deity. [eccl.L f. GK *aiōn* age]

e·o·sin /ée∂sin/ *n.* a red fluorescent dyestuff used esp. as a stain in optical microscopy. [Gk *ēōs* dawn + –IN]

e·o·sin·o·phil /ée∂sinǒfil/ *n.* a white blood cell readily stained by eosin.

-eous /ee∂s/ *suffix* forming adjectives meaning 'of the nature of' (*erroneous; gaseous*).

EP *abbr.* **1** European plan. **2** extended play.

Ep. *abbr.* Epistle.

ep- /ep, ip, eep/ *prefix* form of EPI- before a vowel or *h.*

EPA *abbr.* Environmental Protection Agency.

e·pact /éepakt/ *n.* the number of days by which the solar year exceeds the lunar year. [F *épacte* f. LL *epactae* f. Gk *epaktai* (*hēmerai*) intercalated (days) f. *epagō* intercalate (as EPI-, *agō* bring)]

ep·arch /éepaark/ *n.* the chief bishop of an eparchy. [Gk *eparkhos* (as EPI-, *arkhos* ruler)]

ep·ar·chy /éepaarkee/ *n.* (*pl.* **·chies**) a province of the Orthodox Church. [Gk *eparkhia* (as EPARCH)]

ep·au·let /éep∂lét/ *n.* (also **ep·au·lette**) an ornamental shoulder piece on a coat, dress, etc., esp. on a uniform. [F *épaulette* dimin. of *épaule* shoulder f. L *spatula*: see SPATULA]

epaulet

epaulet

é·pée /aypáy, épay/ *n.* a sharp-pointed dueling sword, used (with the end blunted) in fencing. □□ **é·pée·ist** *n.* [F, = sword, f. OF *espee*: see SPAY]

ep·ei·rog·e·ny /épírójənee/ *n.* (also **ep·ei·ro·gen·e·sis** /epírō jénisis, ipí–/) *Geol.* the regional uplift of extensive areas of the earth's crust. □□ **e·pei·ro·gen·ic** /–jénik/ *adj.* [Gk *ēpeiros* mainland + –*genesis*, –*geny*]

ep·en·the·sis /épénthisis/ *n.* (*pl.* **ep·en·the·ses** /–seez/) the insertion of a letter or sound within a word, e.g., in the pronunciation of *elm* as "el∂m." □□ **ep·en·thet·ic** /épenthétik/ *adj.* [LL f. Gk f. *epentithēmi* insert (as EPI- + EN-[2] + *tithēmi* place)]

e·pergne /ipárn, aypérn/ *n.* an ornament (esp. in branched form) for the center of a dinner-table, holding flowers or fruit. [18th c.: perh. a corrupt. of F *épargne* saving, economy]

ep·ex·e·ge·sis /épéksijéesis/ *n.* (*pl.* **ep·ex·e·ge·ses** /–seez/) **1** the addition of words to clarify meaning (e.g., *to do* in *difficult to do*). **2** the words added. □□ **ep·ex·e·get·ic** /–jétik/ *adj.* **ep·ex·e·get·i·cal** *adj.* **ep·ex·e·get·i·cal·ly** *adv.* [Gk *epexēgēsis* (as EPI-, EXEGESIS)]

Eph. *abbr.* Ephesians (New Testament).

e·phebe /éfeeb, iféeb/ *n. Gk Hist.* a young man of 18–20 undergoing military training. □□ **e·phe·bic** /iféebik/ *adj.* [L *ephebus* f. Gk *ephēbos* (as EPI-, *hēbē* early manhood)]

e·phed·ra /iféedr∂/ *n.* any evergreen shrub of the genus *Ephedra*, with trailing stems and scalelike leaves. [mod.L f. Gk *ephedra* sitting upon]

e·phed·rine /iféedrin, éf∂dreen/ *n.* an alkaloid drug found in some ephedras, causing constriction of the blood vessels and widening of the bronchial passages, used to relieve asthma, etc. [EPHEDRA + –INE[4]]

e·phem·er·a[1] /ifém∂r∂/ *n.* (*pl.* **e·phem·er·a** or **e·phem·er·ae** /–ree/ or

e·phem·er·as) **1 a** an insect living only a day or a few days. **b** any insect of the order Ephemeroptera, e.g., the mayfly. **2** = EPHEMERON. [mod.L f. Gk *ephēmeros* lasting only a day (as EPI-, *hēmera* day)]

e·phem·er·a[2] *pl.* of EPHEMERON 1.

e·phem·er·al /ifém∂r∂l/ *adj.* **1** lasting or of use for only a short time; transitory. **2** lasting only a day. **3** (of an insect, flower, etc.) lasting a day or a few days. □□ **e·phem·er·al·i·ty** /–rálitee/ *n.* **e·phem·er·al·ly** *adv.* **e·phem·er·al·ness** *n.* [Gk *ephēmeros*: see EPHEMERA]

e·phem·er·is /iféméris/ *n.* (*pl.* **e·phe·mer·i·des** /éfimérideez/) *Astron.* an astronomical almanac or table of the predicted positions of celestial bodies. [L f. Gk *ephēmeris* diary (as EPHEMERAL)]

e·phem·er·ist /ifém∂rist/ *n.* a collector of ephemera.

e·phem·er·on /ifém∂r∂n/ *n.* **1** (*pl.* **e·phem·er·a** /–r∂/) (usu. in *pl.*) **a** a thing (esp. a printed item) of short-lived interest or usefulness. **b** a short-lived thing. **2** (*pl.* **e·phem·er·ons**) = EPHEMERA[1] 1. [as EPHEMERA[1]]

eph·od /éfod, eéfod/ *n.* a Jewish priestly vestment. [ME f. Heb. *'ēpōd*]

eph·or /éfawr/ *n. Gk Hist.* any of five senior magistrates in ancient Sparta. □□ **eph·or·ate** *n.* [Gk *ephoros* overseer (as EPI-, *horaō* see)]

epi- /épi–/ *prefix* (usu. **ep-** before a vowel or *h*) **1** upon (*epicycle*). **2** above (*epicotyl*). **3** in addition (*epiphenomenon*). [Gk *epi* (prep.)]

ep·i·blast /épiblast/ *n. Biol.* the outermost layer of a gastrula, etc.; the ectoderm. [EPI- + –BLAST]

ep·ic /épik/ *n. & adj.* ● *n.* **1** a long poem narrating the adventures or deeds of one or more heroic or legendary figures, e.g., the *Iliad*, *Paradise Lost*. **2** an imaginative work of any form, embodying a nation's conception of its history. **3** a book or motion picture based on an epic narrative or heroic in type or scale. **4** a subject fit for recital in an epic. ● *adj.* **1** of or like an epic. **2** grand; heroic. □□ **ep·i·cal** *adj.* **ep·i·cal·ly** *adv.* [L *epicus* f. Gk *epikos* f. *epos* word, song]

ep·i·carp /épikaarp/ *n. Bot.* the outermost layer of the pericarp. [EPI- + Gk *karpos* fruit]

ep·i·ce·di·um /épiseédeeəm/ *n.* (*pl.* **ep·i·ce·di·a** /–deeə/) a funeral ode. □□ **ep·i·ce·di·an** *adj.* [L f. Gk *epikēdeion* (as EPI-, *kēdos* care)]

ep·i·cene /épiseen/ *adj. & n.* ● *adj.* **1** *Gram.* denoting either sex without change of gender. **2** of, for, or used by both sexes. **3** having characteristics of both sexes. **4** having no characteristics of either sex. **5** effete; effeminate. ● *n.* an epicene person. [ME f. LL *epicoenus* f. Gk *epikoinos* (as EPI-, *koinos* common)]

ep·i·cen·ter /épisentər/ *n.* **1** *Geol.* the point at which an earthquake reaches the earth's surface. **2** the central point of a difficulty. □□ **ep·i·cen·tral** /–séntrəl/ *adj.* [Gk *epikentros* (adj.) (as EPI-, CENTER)]

ep·i·con·ti·nen·tal /épikóntinént'l/ *adj.* (of the sea) over the continental shelf.

ep·i·cot·yl /épikót'l/ *n. Bot.* the region of an embryo or seedling stem above the cotyledon(s).

ep·i·cure /épikyŏŏr/ *n.* a person with refined tastes, esp. in food and drink. □□ **ep·i·cur·ism** *n.* [med.L *epicurus* one preferring sensual enjoyment: see EPICUREAN]

Ep·i·cu·re·an /épikyŏŏréeən, –kyŏŏree–/ *n. & adj.* ● *n.* **1** a disciple or student of the Greek philosopher Epicurus (d. 270 BC), who taught that the highest good is personal happiness. **2** (**epicurean**) a person devoted to (esp. sensual) enjoyment. ● *adj.* **1** of or concerning Epicurus or his ideas. **2** (**epicurean**) characteristic of an epicurean. □□ **Ep·i·cu·re·an·ism** *n.* [F *épicurien* or L *epicureus* f. Gk *epikoureios* f. *Epikouros* Epicurus]

ep·i·cy·cle /épisikəl/ *n. Geom.* a small circle moving around the circumference of a larger one. □□ **ep·i·cy·clic** /–síklik, –síklik/ *adj.* [ME f. OF or LL *epicyclus* f. Gk *epikuklos* (as EPI-, *kuklos* circle)]

ep·i·cy·cloid /épisíkloyd/ *n. Math.* a curve traced by a point on the circumference of a circle rolling on the exterior of another circle. □□ **ep·i·cy·cloi·dal** *adj.*

ep·i·deic·tic /épidíktik/ *adj.* meant for effect or display, esp. in speaking. [Gk *epideiktikos* (as EPI-, *deiknumi* show)]

ep·i·dem·ic /épidémik/ *n. & adj.* ● *n.* **1** a widespread occurrence of a disease in a community at a particular time. **2** such a disease. **3** (foll. by *of*) a wide prevalence of something usu. undesirable. ● *adj.* in the nature of an epidemic (cf. ENDEMIC). □□ **ep·i·dem·i·cal·ly** *adv.* [F *épidémique* f. *épidémie* f. LL *epidemia* f. Gk *epidēmia* prevalence of disease f. *epidēmios* (adj.) (as EPI-, *dēmos* the people)]

▶A disease that quickly affects a large number of people and then subsides is an **epidemic**: *Throughout the Middle Ages, successive epidemics of the plague killed millions.* Epidemic is also used as an adjective: *She studied the causes of epidemic cholera.* A disease that is continually present in a one area is **endemic**: *Malaria is endemic in hot, moist climates.*

ep·i·de·mi·ol·o·gy /épideemeeóləjee/ *n.* the study of the incidence and distribution of diseases, and of their control and prevention. □□ **ep·i·de·mi·o·log·i·cal** /–meeəlójikəl/ *adj.* **ep·i·de·mi·o·log·ist** *n.*

ep·i·der·mis /épidərmis/ *n.* **1** the outer cellular layer of the skin. **2** *Bot.* the outer layer of cells of leaves, stems, roots, etc. □□ **ep·i·der·mal** *adj.* **ep·i·der·mic** *adj.* **ep·i·der·moid** *adj.* [LL f. Gk (as EPI-, DERMIS)]

ep·i·di·a·scope /épidíəskōp/ *n.* an optical projector capable of giving images of both opaque and transparent objects. [EPI- + DIA- + –SCOPE]

ep•i•did•y•mis /épidídimis/ n. (pl. **ep•i•di•dym•i•des** /–didímideez/) Anat. a convoluted duct behind the testis, along which sperm passes to the vas deferens. [Gk epididumis (as EPI-, didumoi testicles)]

ep•i•du•ral /épidốôrəl, –dyốôr–/ adj. & n. • adj. **1** Anat. on or around the dura mater. **2** (of an anesthetic) introduced into the space around the dura mater of the spinal cord. • n. an epidural anesthetic, used esp. in childbirth to produce loss of sensation below the waist. [EPI- + DURA (MATER)]

ep•i•fau•na /épifawnə/ n. animals living on the seabed, either attached to animals, plants, etc., or free-living. [Da. (as EPI-, FAUNA)]

ep•i•gas•tri•um /épigástreeəm/ n. (pl. **ep•i•gas•tri•a** /–reeə/) Anat. the part of the abdomen immediately over the stomach. □□ **ep•i•gas•tric** adj. [LL f. Gk epigastrion (neut. adj.) (as EPI-, gastēr belly)]

ep•i•ge•al /épijeéəl/ adj. Bot. **1** having one or more cotyledons above the ground. **2** growing above the ground. [Gk epigeios (as EPI-, gē earth)]

ep•i•gene /épijeen/ adj. Geol. produced on the surface of the earth. [F épigène f. Gk epigenēs (as EPI-, genēs born)]

ep•i•glot•tis /épiglótis/ n. Anat. a flap of cartilage at the root of the tongue, which is depressed during swallowing to cover the windpipe. □□ **ep•i•glot•tal** adj. **ep•i•glot•tic** adj. [Gk epiglōttis (as EPI-, glōtta tongue)]

ep•i•gone /épigòn/ n. (pl. **ep•i•gones** or **ep•ig•o•ni** /ipígənī/) one of a later (and less distinguished) generation. [pl. f. F épigones f. L epigoni f. Gk epigonoi those born afterward (as EPI-, root of gignomai be born)]

ep•i•gram /épigram/ n. **1** a short poem with a witty ending. **2** a saying or maxim, esp a proverbial one. **3 a** a pointed remark or expression, esp. a witty one. **b** the use of concise witty remarks. □□ **ep•i•gram•mat•ic** /–grəmátik/ adj. **ep•i•gram•mat•i•cal•ly** adv. **ep•i•gram•ma•tist** /–grámətist/ n. **ep•i•gram•ma•tize** /–grámətīz/ v.tr. & intr. [F épigramme or L epigramma f. Gk epigramma –atos (as EPI-, –GRAM)]

ep•i•graph /épigraf/ n. an inscription on a statue or coin, at the head of a chapter, etc. [Gk epigraphē f. epigraphō (as EPI-, graphō write)]

e•pig•ra•phy /ipígrəfee/ n. the study of (esp. ancient) inscriptions. □□ **ep•i•graph•ic** /épigráfik/ adj. **ep•i•graph•i•cal** adj. **ep•i•graph•i•cal•ly** adv. **e•pig•ra•phist** /–pígrəfist/ n.

ep•i•late /épilayt/ v.tr. remove hair from. □□ **ep•i•la•tion** /–láyshən/ n. [F épiler (cf. DEPILATE)]

ep•i•lep•sy /épilepsee/ n. a nervous disorder with convulsions and often loss of consciousness. [F épilepsie or LL epilepsia f. Gk epilēpsia f. epilambanō attack (as EPI-, lambanō take)]

ep•i•lep•tic /épiléptik/ adj. & n. • adj. of or relating to epilepsy. • n. a person with epilepsy. [F épileptique f. LL epilepticus f. Gk epilēptikos (as EPILEPSY)]

ep•i•lim•ni•on /épilímneeən/ n. (pl. **ep•i•lim•ni•a** /–neeə/) the upper layer of water in a stratified lake. [EPI- + Gk limnion dimin. of limnē lake]

e•pil•o•gist /ipíləjist/ n. the writer or speaker of an epilogue.

ep•i•logue /épilawg, –og/ n. (also **ep•i•log**) **1 a** the concluding part of a literary work. **b** an appendix. **2 a** a speech or short poem addressed to the audience by an actor at the end of a play. **3** Brit. a short piece at the end of a day's broadcasting (cf. PROLOGUE). [ME f. F épilogue f. L epilogus f. Gk epilogos (as EPI-, logos speech)]

ep•i•mer /épimər/ n. Chem. either of two isomers with different configurations of atoms about one of several asymmetric carbon atoms present. □□ **ep•i•mer•ic** /–mérik/ adj. **ep•i•mer•ism** n. [G (as EPI-, –MER)]

ep•i•mer•ize /épimərīz/ v.tr. Chem. convert (one epimer) into the other.

ep•i•nas•ty /épinastee/ n. Bot. a tendency in plant organs to grow more rapidly on the upper side. [EPI- + Gk nastos pressed]

ep•i•neph•rine /épinéfrin/ n. (also **ep•i•neph•rin**) **1** Biochem. a hormone secreted by the adrenal glands, affecting circulation and muscular action, and causing excitement and stimulation. **2** Pharm. the same substance obtained from animals or by synthesis, used as a stimulant. Also called **adrenaline**. [EPI- + nephros kidney]

e•piph•a•ny /ipífənee/ n. (pl. **•nies**) **1** (Epiphany) **a** the manifestation of Christ to the Magi according to the biblical account. **b** the festival commemorating this on January 6. **2** any manifestation of a god or demigod. □□ **ep•i•phan•ic** /épifánik/ adj. [ME f. Gk epiphaneia manifestation f. epiphainō reveal (as EPI-, phainō show): sense 1 through OF epiphanie and eccl.L epiphania]

ep•i•phe•nom•e•non /épifinóminən/ n. (pl. **ep•i•phe•nom•e•na** /–nə/) **1** a secondary symptom, which may occur simultaneously with a disease, etc., but is not regarded as its cause or result. **2** Psychol. consciousness regarded as a by-product of brain activity. □□ **ep•i•phe•nom•e•nal** adj.

e•piph•y•sis /ipífisis/ n. (pl. **e•piph•y•ses** /–seez/) Anat. **1** the end part of a long bone, initially growing separately from the shaft. **2** = PINEAL GLAND. [mod.L f. Gk epiphusis (as EPI-, phusis growth)]

ep•i•phyte /épifīt/ n. a plant growing but not parasitic on another, e.g., a moss. □□ **ep•i•phyt•al** /–fīt'l/ adj. **ep•i•phyt•ic** /–fítik/ adj. [EPI- + Gk phuton plant]

e•pis•co•pa•cy /ipískəpəsee/ n. (pl. **•cies**) **1** government of a church by bishops. **2** (prec. by the) the bishops.

e•pis•co•pal /ipískəpəl/ adj. **1** of a bishop or bishops. **2** (of a Church) constituted on the principle of government by bishops. □□ **e•pis•co•pal•ism** n. **e•pis•co•pal•ly** adv. [ME f. F épiscopal or eccl.L episcopalis f. episcopus BISHOP]

E•pis•co•pal Church n. a Protestant Church in the US and Scotland, with elected bishops, and doctrine, forms of worship, etc., inherited from the Church of England.

e•pis•co•pa•lian /ipískəpáyleeən/ adj. & n. • adj. **1** of or advocating government of a church by bishops. **2** of or belonging to an episcopal church or (**Episcopalian**) the Episcopal Church. • n. **1** an adherent of episcopacy. **2** (**Episcopalian**) a member of the Episcopal Church. □□ **e•pis•co•pa•lian•ism** n.

e•pis•co•pate /ipískəpət/ n. **1** the office or tenure of a bishop. **2** (prec. by the) the bishops collectively. [eccl.L episcopatus f. episcopus BISHOP]

ep•i•scope /épiskōp/ n. an optical projector giving images of opaque objects.

ep•i•se•mat•ic /épisimátik/ adj. Zool. (of coloration, markings, etc.) serving to help recognition by animals of the same species. [EPI- + Gk sēma sēmatos sign]

e•pi•si•ot•o•my /ipeézeeótəmee/ n. (pl. **•mies**) a surgical cut made at the opening of the vagina during childbirth, to aid delivery. [Gk epision pubic region]

ep•i•sode /épisōd/ n. **1** one event or a group of events as part of a sequence. **2** each of the parts of a serial story or broadcast. **3** an incident or set of incidents in a narrative. **4** an incident that is distinct but contributes to a whole (a romantic episode in her life). **5** Mus. a passage containing distinct material or introducing a new subject. **6** the part between two choric songs in Greek tragedy. [Gk epeisodion (as EPI- + eisodos entry f. eis into + hodos way)]

ep•i•sod•ic /épisódik/ adj. (also **ep•i•sod•i•cal** /–sódikəl/) **1** in the nature of an episode. **2** sporadic; occurring at irregular intervals. □□ **ep•i•sod•i•cal•ly** adv.

ep•i•stax•is /épistáksis/ n. Med. a nosebleed. [mod.L f. Gk (as EPI-, stazō drip)]

ep•i•ste•mic /épisteémik, –stémik/ adj. Philos. relating to knowledge or to the degree of its validation. □□ **ep•i•ste•mi•cal•ly** adv. [Gk epistēmē knowledge]

e•pis•te•mol•o•gy /ipístimóləjee/ n. the theory of knowledge, esp. with regard to its methods and validation. □□ **e•pis•te•mo•log•i•cal** /–məlójikəl/ adj. **e•pis•te•mo•log•i•cal•ly** adv. **e•pis•te•mol•o•gist** n.

e•pis•tle /ipísəl/ n. **1** formal or joc. a letter, esp. a long one on a serious subject. **2** (**Epistle**) **a** any of the letters of the apostles in the New Testament. **b** an extract from an Epistle read in a church service. **3** a poem or other literary work in the form of a letter or series of letters. [ME f. OF f. L epistola f. Gk epistolē f. epistellō send news (as EPI-, stellō send)]

e•pis•to•lar•y /ipístəleree/ adj. **1** in the style or form of a letter or letters. **2** of, carried by, or suited to letters. [F épistolaire or L epistolaris (as EPISTLE)]

e•pis•tro•phe /ipístrəfee/ n. the repetition of a word at the end of successive clauses. [Gk (as EPI-, strophē turning)]

ep•i•style /épistīl/ n. Archit. = ARCHITRAVE. [F épistyle or L epistylium f. Gk epistulion (as EPI-, stulos pillar)]

ep•i•taph /épitaf/ n. words written in memory of a person who has died, esp. as a tomb inscription. [ME f. OF epitaphe f. L epitaphium f. Gk epitaphion funeral oration (as EPI-, taphos tomb)]

ep•i•tax•y /épitaksee/ n. Crystallog. the growth of a thin layer on a single-crystal substrate that determines the lattice structure of the layer. □□ **ep•i•tax•i•al** /–tákseeəl/ adj. [F épitaxie (as EPI-, Gk taxis arrangement)]

ep•i•tha•la•mi•um /épithəláymeeəm/ n. (pl. **ep•i•tha•la•mi•ums** or **ep•i•tha•la•mi•a** /–meeə/) a song or poem celebrating a marriage. □□ **ep•i•tha•la•mic** adj. **ep•i•tha•lam•ic** /–lámik/ adj. [L f. Gk epithalamion (as EPI-, thalamos bridal chamber)]

ep•i•the•li•um /épitheéleeəm/ n. (pl. **ep•i•the•li•a** /–leeə/ or **ep•i•the•li•ums**) the tissue forming the outer layer of the body surface and lining many hollow structures. □□ **ep•i•the•li•al** adj. [mod.L f. EPI- + Gk thēlē teat]

ep•i•thet /épithet/ n. **1** an adjective or other descriptive word expressing a quality or attribute, esp. used with or as a name. **2** such a word as a term of abuse. □□ **ep•i•thet•ic** /–thétik/ adj. **ep•i•thet•i•cal** adj. **ep•i•thet•i•cal•ly** adv. [F épithète or L epitheton f. Gk epitheton f. epitithēmi add (as EPI-, tithēmi place)]

ep•i•to•me /ipítəmee/ n. **1** a person or thing embodying a quality, class, etc. **2** a thing representing another in miniature. **3** a summary of a written work; an abstract. □□ **e•pit•o•mist** n. [L f. Gk epitomē f. epitemnō abridge (as EPI-, temnō cut)]

e•pit•o•mize /ipítəmīz/ v.tr. **1** be a perfect example of (a quality, etc.); typify. **2** make an epitome of (a work). □□ **e•pit•o•mi•za•tion** n.

ep•i•zo•on /épizó-on/ n. (pl. **ep•i•zo•a** /-zóə/) an animal living on another animal. [mod.L (as EPI-, Gk zōion animal)]

ep•i•zo•ot•ic /épizō-ótik/ adj. & n. • adj. (of a disease) temporarily prevalent among animals (cf. ENZOOTIC). • n. an outbreak of such a disease. [F épizootique f. épizootie (as EPIZOON)]

ep•och /épək, eepok/ n. 1 a period of history or of a person's life marked by notable events. 2 the beginning of an era. 3 Geol. a division of a period, corresponding to a set of strata. □□ **ep•och•al** adj. [mod.L epocha f. Gk epokhē stoppage]

> **PRONUNCIATION TIP**   epoch
>
> The preferred British English pronunciation of this word is "EE-pok." In American English, "EP-ik" is more common.

ep•och-mak•ing adj. remarkable; historic; of major importance.

ep•ode /épōd/ n. 1 a form of lyric poem written in couplets each of a long line followed by a shorter one. 2 the third section of an ancient Greek choral ode or of one division of it. [F épode or L epodos f. Gk epōidos (as EPI-, ODE)]

ep•o•nym /épənim/ n. 1 a person (real or imaginary) after whom a discovery, invention, place, institution, etc., is named or thought to be named. 2 the name given. □□ **ep•on•y•mous** /ipónimǝs/ adj. [Gk epōnumos (as EPI-, –ōnumos f. onoma name)]

ep•ox•ide /ipóksid/ n. Chem. a compound containing an oxygen atom bonded in a triangular arrangement to two carbon atoms. [EPI- + OXIDE]

ep•ox•y /ipóksee/ adj. Chem. relating to or derived from an epoxide. [EPI- + OXY-²]

ep•ox•y res•in n. a synthetic thermosetting resin containing epoxy groups.

ep•si•lon /épsilon/ n. the fifth letter of the Greek alphabet (E, ∈). [ME f. Gk, = bare E f. psilos bare]

Ep•som salts /épsəm/ n. a preparation of magnesium sulfate used as a purgative, etc. [Epsom in Surrey, England, where it was first found occurring naturally]

e•pyl•lion /epíleeən/ n. (pl. **e•pyl•li•a** /-leeə/) a miniature epic poem. [Gk epullion dimin. of epos word, song]

eq•ua•ble /ékwəbəl/ adj. 1 even; not varying. 2 uniform and moderate (an equable climate). 3 (of a person) not easily disturbed or angered. □□ **eq•ua•bil•i•ty** /-bílitee/ n. **eq•ua•bly** adv. [L aequabilis (as EQUATE)]

e•qual /éekwəl/ adj., n., & v. • adj. 1 (often foll. by to, with) the same in quantity, quality, size, degree, rank, level, etc. 2 evenly balanced (an equal contest). 3 having the same rights or status (human beings are essentially equal). 4 uniform in application or effect. • n. a person or thing equal to another, esp. in rank, status, or characteristic quality (their treatment of the subject has no equal; is the equal of any man). • v.tr. (**e•qualed, e•qual•ing;** esp. Brit. **e•qualled, e•qual•ling**) 1 be equal to in number, quality, etc. 2 achieve something that is equal to (an achievement) or to the achievement of (a person). □ **be equal to** have the ability or resources for. **equal** (or **equals**) **sign** the symbol =. [ME f. L aequalis f. aequus even]

e•qual•i•tar•i•an /ikwólitáireeən/ n. = EGALITARIAN. □□ **e•qual•i•tar•i•an•ism** n. [EQUALITY, after humanitarian, etc.]

e•qual•i•ty /ikwólitee/ n. the state of being equal. [ME f. OF equalité f. L aequalitas –tatis (as EQUAL)]

e•qual•ize /éekwəliz/ v. 1 tr. & intr. make or become equal. 2 intr. reach one's opponent's score in a game, after being behind. □□ **e•qual•i•za•tion** n.

e•qual•iz•er /éekwəlizər/ n. 1 an equalizing score or goal, etc., in a game. 2 sl. a weapon, esp. a gun. 3 Electr. a connection in a system that compensates for any undesirable frequency or phase response with the system.

e•qual•ly /éekwəlee/ adv. 1 in an equal manner (treated them all equally). 2 to an equal degree (is equally important).

▶In sense 2 construction with as (equally as important) is often found, but is considered incorrect by many.

e•qual op•por•tu•ni•ty n. (often in pl.) the opportunity or right to be employed, paid, etc., without discrimination on grounds of sex, race, etc.

e•qua•nim•i•ty /éekwənímitee, ékwə–/ n. mental composure; evenness of temper, esp. in misfortune. □□ **e•quan•i•mous** /ikwánimǝs/ adj. [L aequanimitas f. aequanimis f. aequus even + animus mind]

e•quate /ikwáyt/ v. 1 tr. (usu. foll. by to, with) regard as equal or equivalent. 2 intr. (foll. by with) a be equal or equivalent to. b agree or correspond. □□ **e•quat•a•ble** adj. [ME f. L aequare aequat- f. aequus equal]

e•qua•tion /ikwáyzhən/ n. 1 the process of equating or making equal; the state of being equal. 2 Math. a statement that two mathematical expressions are equal (indicated by the sign =). 3 Chem. a formula indicating a chemical reaction by means of symbols for the elements taking part. □□ **e•qua•tion•al** adj. [ME f. OF equation or L aequatio (as EQUATE)]

e•qua•tor /ikwáytər/ n. 1 an imaginary line around the earth or other body, equidistant from the poles. 2 Astron. = CELESTIAL EQUATOR. [ME f. OF equateur or med.L aequator (as EQUATION)]

e•qua•to•ri•al /ékwətáwreeəl, eekwə–/ adj. of or near the equator. □□ **e•qua•to•ri•al•ly** adv.

e•qua•to•ri•al tel•e•scope n. a telescope attached to an axis perpendicular to the plane of the equator.

eq•uer•ry /ékwəree/ n. (pl. **-ries**) 1 an officer of the British royal household attending members of the royal family. 2 hist. an officer of a prince's or noble's household in charge of the horses. [earlier esquiry f. OF esquierie company of squires, prince's stables, f. OF esquier ESQUIRE: perh. assoc. with L equus horse]

e•ques•tri•an /ikwéstreeən/ adj. & n. • adj. 1 of or relating to horses and horseback riding. 2 on horseback. • n. (fem. **e•ques•tri•enne** /–tree-én/) a rider or performer on horseback. □□ **e•ques•tri•an•ism** n. [L equestris f. eques horseman, knight, f. equus horse]

equi- /éekwee, ékwi/ comb. form equal. [L aequi- f. aequus equal]

e•qui•an•gu•lar /éekweeángyələr, ékwee–/ adj. having equal angles.

e•qui•dis•tant /éekwidístənt, ékwi–/ adj. at equal distances. □□ **e•qui•dis•tant•ly** adv.

e•qui•lat•er•al /éekwilátərəl, ékwi–/ adj. having all its sides equal in length.

e•quil•i•brate /ikwílibrayt, eékwilíbrayt/ v. 1 tr. cause (two things) to balance. 2 intr. be in equilibrium; balance. □□ **e•quil•i•bra•tion** n. **e•quil•i•bra•tor** n. [LL aequilibrare aequilibrat- (as EQUI-, libra balance)]

e•quil•i•brist /ikwílibrist/ n. an acrobat, esp. on a high rope.

e•qui•lib•ri•um /éekwilíbreeəm, ékwi–/ n. (pl. **e•qui•lib•ri•ums** or **e•qui•lib•ri•a** /–reeə/) 1 a state of physical balance. 2 a state of mental or emotional equanimity. 3 a state in which the energy in a system is evenly distributed and forces, influences, etc., balance each other. [L (as EQUI-, libra balance)]

e•quine /éekwin, ékwin/ adj. of or like a horse. [L equinus f. equus horse]

e•qui•noc•tial /éekwinókshəl, ékwi–/ adj. & n. • adj. 1 happening at or near the time of an equinox (equinoctial gales). 2 of or relating to equal day and night. 3 at or near the (terrestrial) equator. • n. (in full **equinoctial line**) = CELESTIAL EQUATOR. [ME f. OF equinoctial or L aequinoctialis (as EQUINOX)]

e•qui•noc•tial point n. the point at which the ecliptic cuts the celestial equator (twice each year at an equinox).

e•qui•noc•tial year n. see YEAR.

e•qui•nox /éekwinoks, ékwi–/ n. 1 the time or date (about March 20 (vernal equinox) and September 22 (autumnal equinox) each year) at which the sun crosses the celestial equator, when day and night are of equal length. 2 = EQUINOCTIAL POINT. [ME f. OF equinoxe or med.L aequinoxium f. L aequinoctium (as EQUI-, nox noctis night)]

e•quip /ikwíp/ v.tr. (**e•quipped, e•quip•ping**) supply with what is needed. □□ **e•quip•per** n. [F équiper, prob. f. ON skipa to man (a ship) f. skip SHIP]

eq•ui•page /ékwipij/ n. 1 a requisites for an undertaking. b an outfit for a special purpose. 2 a carriage and horses with attendants. [F équipage (as EQUIP)]

e•quip•ment /ikwípmənt/ n. 1 the necessary articles, clothing, etc., for a purpose. 2 the process of equipping or being equipped. [F équipement (as EQUIP)]

e•qui•poise /éekwipoyz, ékwi–/ n. 1 equilibrium; a balanced state. 2 a counterbalancing thing. • v.tr. counterbalance.

e•qui•pol•lent /éekwipólənt, ékwi–/ adj. & n. • adj. 1 equal in power, force, etc. 2 practically equivalent. • n. an equipollent thing. □□ **e•qui•pol•lence** n. **e•qui•pol•len•cy** n. [ME f. OF equipolent f. L aequipollens –entis of equal value (as EQUI-, pollēre be strong)]

e•qui•po•ten•tial /éekwipəténshəl, ékwi–/ adj. & n. Physics • adj. (of a surface or line) having the potential of a force the same or constant at all its points. • n. an equipotential line or surface.

e•qui•prob•a•ble /éekwipróbəbəl, ékwi–/ adj. Logic equally probable. □□ **e•qui•prob•a•bil•i•ty** n.

eq•ui•ta•ble /ékwitəbəl/ adj. 1 fair; just. 2 Law valid in equity as distinct from law. □□ **eq•ui•ta•ble•ness** n. **eq•ui•ta•bly** adv. [F équitable (as EQUITY)]

eq•ui•ta•tion /ékwitáyshən/ n. the art and practice of horsemanship and horseback riding. [F équitation or L equitatio f. equitare ride a horse f. eques equitis horseman f. equus horse]

eq•ui•ty /ékwitee/ n. (pl. **-ties**) 1 fairness. 2 the application of the principles of justice to correct or supplement the law. 3 a the value of the shares issued by a company. b (in pl.) stocks and shares not bearing fixed interest. 4 the net value of a mortgaged property after the deduction of charges. 5 (**Equity**) = ACTORS' EQUITY ASSOCIATION. [ME f. OF equité f. L aequitas –tatis f. aequus fair]

e•quiv•a•lent /ikwívələnt/ adj. & n. • adj. 1 (often foll. by to) equal in value, amount, importance, etc. 2 corresponding. 3 (of words) having the same meaning. 4 having the same result. 5 /éekwəváylənt/ Chem. (of a substance) equal in combining or displacing capacity. • n. 1 an equivalent thing, amount, word, etc. 2 (in full **equivalent weight**) Chem. the weight of a substance that can combine with or displace one gram of hydrogen or eight grams of oxygen. □□ **e•quiv•a•lence** /–ləns/ n. **e•quiv•a•len•cy** n. **e•quiv•a•lent•ly** adv. [ME f. OF f. LL aequivalēre (as EQUI-, valēre be worth)]

e·quiv·o·cal /ikwívəkəl/ *adj.* **1** of double or doubtful meaning; ambiguous. **2** of uncertain nature. **3** (of a person, character, etc.) questionable; suspect. □□ **e·quiv·o·cal·i·ty** /–kálitee/ *n.* **e·quiv·o·cal·ly** *adv.* **e·quiv·o·cal·ness** *n.* [LL *aequivocus* (as EQUI-, *vocare* call)]

e·quiv·o·cate /ikwívəkayt/ *v.intr.* use ambiguity to conceal the truth. □□ **e·quiv·o·ca·cy** *n.* **e·quiv·o·ca·tion** /–káyshən/ *n.* **e·quiv·o·ca·tor** *n.* **e·quiv·o·ca·to·ry** *adj.* [ME f. LL *aequivocare* (as EQUIVOCAL)]

eq·ui·voque /ékwivōk, éékwi–/ *n.* (also **eq·ui·voke**) a pun or ambiguity. [ME in the sense 'equivocal' f. OF *equivoque* or LL *aequivocus* EQUIVOCAL]

ER *abbr.* **1** emergency room. **2** Queen Elizabeth. [L *Elizabetha Regina*.]

Er *symb. Chem.* the element erbium.

er /ər/ *int.* expressing hesitation or a pause in speech. [imit.]

-er[1] /ər/ *suffix* forming nouns from nouns, adjectives, and many verbs, denoting: **1** a person, animal, or thing that performs a specified action or activity (*cobbler; lover; executioner; poker; computer; eye-opener*). **2** a person or thing that has a specified attribute or form (*foreigner; four-wheeler; second-rater*). **3** a person concerned with a specified thing or subject (*hatter; geographer*). **4** a person belonging to a specified place or group (*villager; New Zealander; sixth-grader*). [orig. 'one who has to do with': OE *–ere* f. Gmc]

-er[2] /ər/ *suffix* forming the comparative of adjectives (*wider; hotter*) and adverbs (*faster*). [OE *–ra* (adj.), *–or* (adv.) f. Gmc]

-er[3] /ər/ *suffix* used in slang formations usu. distorting the root word (*rugger; soccer*). [prob. an extension of –ER[1]]

-er[4] /ər/ *suffix* forming iterative and frequentative verbs (*blunder; glimmer; twitter*). [OE *–erian, –rian* f. Gmc]

-er[5] /ər/ *suffix* **1** forming nouns and adjectives through OF or AF, corresponding to: **a** L *–aris* (*sampler*) (cf. –AR[1]). **b** L *–arius, –arium* (*butler; carpenter; danger*). **c** (through OF *–eûre*) L *–atura* or (through OF *–eōr*) L *–atorium* (see COUNTER[1], FRITTER[2]). **2** = –OR.

-er[6] /ər/ *suffix esp. Law* forming nouns denoting verbal action or a document effecting this (*disclaimer; misnomer*). [AF infin. ending of verbs]

▶The same ending occurs in *dinner* and *supper*.

ERA *abbr.* **1** *Baseball* earned run average. **2** Equal Rights Amendment.

e·ra /éerə, érə/ *n.* **1** a system of chronology reckoning from a noteworthy event (*the Christian era*). **2** a large distinct period of time, esp. regarded historically (*the pre-Roman era*). **3** a date at which an era begins. **4** *Geol.* a major division of time. [LL *aera* number expressed in figures (pl. of *aes aeris* money, treated as fem. sing.)]

e·rad·i·cate /irádikayt/ *v.tr.* root out; destroy completely; get rid of. □□ **e·rad·i·ca·ble** *adj.* **e·rad·i·ca·tion** /–káyshən/ *n.* **e·rad·i·ca·tor** *n.* [ME f. L *eradicare* tear up by the roots (as E-, *radix –icis* root)]

e·rase /iráys/ *v.tr.* **1** rub out; obliterate. **2** remove all traces of (*erased it from my memory*). **3** remove recorded material from (a magnetic tape or medium). □□ **e·ras·a·ble** *adj.* **e·ra·sure** *n.* [L *eradere eras-* (as E-, *radere* scrape)]

e·ras·er /iráysər/ *n.* a thing that erases, esp. a piece of rubber or plastic used for removing pencil and ink marks.

er·bi·um /ə́rbeeəm/ *n. Chem.* a soft, silvery, metallic element of the lanthanide series, occurring naturally in apatite and xenotine. ¶ Symb.: **Er**. [mod.L f. *Ytterby* in Sweden]

ere /air/ *prep. & conj. poet.* or *archaic* before (of time) (*ere noon; ere they come*). [OE *ǣr* f. Gmc]

e·rect /irékt/ *adj. & v.* ● *adj.* **1** upright; vertical. **2** (of the penis, clitoris, or nipples) enlarged and rigid, esp. in sexual excitement. **3** (of hair) bristling, standing up from the skin. ● *v.tr.* **1** raise; set upright. **2** build. **3** establish (*erect a theory*). □□ **e·rect·a·ble** *adj.* **e·rect·ly** *adv.* **e·rect·ness** *n.* **e·rec·tor** *n.* [ME f. L *erigere erect-* set up (as E-, *regere* direct)]

e·rec·tile /irékt'l, –tīl/ *adj.* that can be erected or become erect. □ **erectile** *Physiol.* animal tissue that is capable of becoming rigid, esp. with sexual excitement. [F *érectile* (as ERECT)]

e·rec·tion /irékshən/ *n.* **1** the act or an instance of erecting; the state of being erected. **2** a building or structure. **3** *Physiol.* an enlarged and erect state of erectile tissue, esp. of the penis. [F *érection* or L *erectio* (as ERECTILE)]

E re·gion the part of the ionosphere that contains the E layer.

er·e·mite /érəmīt/ *n.* a hermit or recluse (esp. Christian). □□ **er·e·mit·ic** /–mítik/ *adj.* **er·e·mit·i·cal** *adj.* **er·e·mit·ism** *n.* [ME f. OF, var. of *hermite, ermite* HERMIT]

er·e·thism /érithizəm/ *n.* **1** an excessive sensitivity to stimulation of any part of the body, esp. the sexual organs. **2** a state of abnormal mental excitement or irritation. [F *éréthisme* f. Gk *erethismos* f. *erethizō* irritate]

erg[1] /ərg/ *n. Physics* a unit of work or energy, equal to the work done by a force of one dyne when its point of application moves one centimeter in the direction of action of the force. [Gk *ergon* work]

erg[2] /erg/ *n.* (pl. **ergs** or **areg** /áareg/) an area of shifting sand dunes in the Sahara. [F f. Arab. *'irj*]

er·go /ə́rgō, ér–/ *adv.* therefore. [L]

er·go·cal·cif·er·ol /ə́rgōkalsífə–rōl, –rol/ *n.* = CALCIFEROL. [ERGOT + CALCIFEROL]

er·go·nom·ics /ə́rgənómiks/ *n.* the study of the efficiency of persons in their working environment. □□ **er·go·nom·ic** *adj.* **er·gon·o·mist** /ergónəmist/ *n.* [Gk *ergon* work: cf. ECONOMICS]

er·gos·ter·ol /ərgóstərawl, –rōl/ *n. Biochem.* a plant sterol that is converted to vitamin D_2 when irradiated with ultraviolet light. [ERGOT, after CHOLESTEROL]

er·got /ə́rgət, –got/ *n.* **1** a disease of rye and other cereals caused by the fungus *Claviceps purpurea*. **2 a** this fungus. **b** the dried spore-containing structures of this, used as a medicine to aid childbirth. [F f. OF *argot* cock's spur, from the appearance produced]

er·got·ism /ə́rgətizəm/ *n.* poisoning produced by eating food affected by ergot.

er·i·ca /érikə/ *n.* any shrub or heath of the genus *Erica*, with small leathery leaves and bell-like flowers. □□ **er·i·ca·ceous** /–káyshəs/ *adj.* [L f. Gk *ereikē* heath]

e·rig·er·on /irígəron/ *n.* any hardy composite herb of the genus *Erigeron*, with daisylike flowers. [Gk *ērigerōn* f. *ēri* early + *gerōn* old man, because some species bear gray down]

Er·in /érin/ *n. archaic* or *poet.* Ireland. [Ir.]

E·rin·ys /erínis/ *n.* (pl. **E·rin·y·es** /–nee-eez/) *Mythol.* a Fury. [Gk]

er·is·tic /erístik/ *adj. & n.* ● *adj.* **1** of or characterized by disputation. **2** (of an argument or arguer) aiming at winning rather than at reaching the truth. ● *n.* **1** the practice of disputation. **2** an exponent of disputation. □□ **er·is·ti·cal·ly** *adv.* [Gk *eristikos* f. *erizō* wrangle f. *eris* strife]

erk /ərk/ *n. Brit. sl.* **1** a naval rating. **2** an aircraftman. **3** a disliked person. [20th c.: orig. unkn.]

erl·king /ə́rl-king/ *n.* (in Germanic mythology) a bearded giant or goblin who lures little children to the land of death. [G *Erlkönig* alder-king, a mistransl. of Da. *ellerkonge* king of the elves]

er·mine /ə́rmin/ *n.* (pl. same or **er·mines**) **1** the stoat, esp. when in its white winter fur. **2** its white fur, used as trimming for the robes of judges, peers, etc. **3** *Heraldry* a white fur marked with black spots. □□ **er·mined** *adj.* [ME f. OF (*h)ermine* prob. f. med.L (*mus*) *Armenius* Armenian (mouse)]

ern var. of ERNE.

-ern /ərn/ *suffix* forming adjectives (*northern*). [OE *–erne* f. Gmc]

erne /ern/ *n.* (also **ern**) *poet.* a sea eagle. [OE *earn* f. Gmc]

e·rode /irṓd/ *v.* **1** *tr. & intr.* wear away; destroy or be destroyed gradually. **2** *tr. Med.* (of ulcers, etc.) destroy (tissue) little by little. □□ **e·rod·i·ble** *adj.* [F *éroder* or L *erodere eros-* (as E-, *rodere ros-* gnaw)]

e·rog·e·nous /irójinəs/ *adj.* **1** (esp. of a part of the body) sensitive to sexual stimulation. **2** giving rise to sexual desire or excitement. [as EROTIC + –GENOUS]

e·ro·sion /irṓzhən/ *n.* **1** *Geol.* the wearing away of the earth's surface by the action of water, wind, etc. **2** the act or an instance of eroding; the process of being eroded. □□ **e·ro·sion·al** *adj.* **e·ro·sive** *adj.* [F *érosion* f. L *erosio* (as ERODE)]

e·rot·ic /irótik/ *adj.* of or causing sexual love, esp. tending to arouse sexual desire or excitement. □□ **e·rot·i·cal·ly** *adv.* [F *érotique* f. Gk *erōtikos* f. *erōs erōtos* sexual love]

e·rot·i·ca /irótikə/ *n.pl.* erotic literature or art.

e·rot·i·cism /irótisizəm/ *n.* **1** erotic nature or character. **2** the use of or reponse to erotic images or stimulation.

er·o·tism /érətizəm/ *n.* sexual desire or excitement; eroticism.

eroto- /irótō, iró–/ *comb. form* erotic; eroticism. [Gk *erōs erōtos* sexual love]

er·o·to·gen·ic /irótəjénik, iró–/ *adj.* = EROGENOUS.

er·o·tol·o·gy /érətóləjee/ *n.* the study of sexual love.

e·ro·to·ma·ni·a /irótəmáyneeə, iró–/ *n.* **1** excessive or morbid erotic desire. **2** a preoccupation with sexual passion. □□ **e·ro·to·ma·ni·ac** /–neeak/ *n.*

err /ər, er/ *v.intr.* **1** be mistaken or incorrect. **2** do wrong; sin. □ **err on the right side** act so that the least harmful of possible errors is the most likely to occur. **err on the side of** act with a specified bias (*errs on the side of generosity*). [ME f. OF *errer* f. L *errare* stray; rel. to Goth. *airzei* error, *airzjan* lead astray]

PRONUNCIATION TIP **err**

How this word is pronounced varies widely, but the usual American English pronunciation rhymes with *pair*. The older, more traditional pronunciation rhymes with *fur*. Both are acceptable, though purists insist on the latter pronunciation.

---

er·rand /érənd/ *n.* **1** a short journey, esp. on another's behalf, to take a message, collect goods, etc. **2** the object of such a journey. [OE *ǣrende*]

er·rant /érənt/ *adj.* **1** erring; deviating from an accepted standard. **2** *literary* or *archaic* traveling in search of adventure (*knight errant*). □□ **er·ran·cy** /–ənsee/ *n.* (in sense 1). **er·rant·ry** *n.* (in sense 2). [ME: sense 1 formed as ERR: sense 2 f. OF *errer* ult. f. LL *itinerare* f. *iter* journey]

er•rat•ic /irátik/ *adj.* **1** inconsistently variable in conduct, opinions, etc.; unpredictable; eccentric. **2** uncertain in movement. □□ **er•rat•i•cal•ly** *adv.* [ME f. OF *erratique* f. L *erraticus* (as ERR)]

er•rat•ic block *n. Geol.* a large rock carried from a distance by glacial action.

er•ra•tum /iráatəm, irát–/ *n.* (*pl.* **er•ra•ta** /–tə/) an error in printing or writing, esp. (in *pl.*) a list of corrected errors attached to a book, etc. [L, neut. past part. (as ERR)]

er•ro•ne•ous /iróneeəs/ *adj.* incorrect; arising from error. □□ **er•ro•ne•ous•ly** *adv.* **er•ro•ne•ous•ness** *n.* [ME f. OF *erroneus* or L *erroneus* f. *erro –onis* vagabond (as ERR)]

er•ror /érər/ *n.* **1** a mistake. **2** the condition of being wrong in conduct or judgment (*led into error*). **3** a wrong opinion or judgment. **4** the amount by which something is incorrect or inaccurate in a calculation or measurement. □□ **er•ror•less** *adj.* [ME f. OF *errour* f. L *error –oris* (as ERR)]

er•satz /érzaats, –saats, erzáats, –sáats/ *adj. & n.* • *adj.* substitute; imitation (esp. of inferior quality). • *n.* an ersatz thing. [G, = replacement]

Erse /ərs/ *adj. & n.* • *adj.* Irish or Highland Gaelic. • *n.* the Gaelic language. [early Sc. form of IRISH]

erst /ərst/ *adv.* archaic formerly; of old. [OE *ǣrest* superl. of *ǣr*: see ERE]

erst•while /ə́rst-hwīl, –wīl/ *adj. & adv.* • *adj.* former; previous. • *adv.* archaic = ERST.

e•ru•bes•cent /éroōbésənt/ *adj.* reddening; blushing. [L *erubescere* (as E-, *rubescere* f. *rubēre* be red)]

e•ruc•ta•tion /iruktáyshən, éeruk–/ *n.* the act or an instance of belching. [L *eructatio* f. *eructare* (as E-, *ructare* belch)]

er•u•dite /éryədīt, érə–/ *adj.* **1** (of a person) learned. **2** (of writing, etc.) showing great learning. □□ **er•u•dite•ly** *adv.* **er•u•di•tion** /–díshən/ *n.* [ME f. L *eruditus* past part. of *erudire* instruct, train (as E-, *rudis* untrained)]

e•rupt /irúpt/ *v.intr.* **1** break out suddenly or dramatically. **2** (of a volcano) become active and eject lava, etc. **3 a** (of a rash, boil, etc.) appear on the skin. **b** (of the skin) produce a rash, etc. **4** (of the teeth) break through the gums in normal development. □□ **e•rup•tion** /–rúpshən/ *n.* **e•rup•tive** *adj.* [L *erumpere erupt-* (as E-, *rumpere* break)]

-ery /əree/ *suffix* forming nouns denoting: **1** a class or kind (*greenery; machinery*). **2** employment; state or condition (*archery; dentistry; slavery; bravery*). **3** a place of work or cultivation or breeding (*brewery; rookery*). **4** behavior (*mockery*). **5** often *derog.* all that has to do with (*knavery; popery; tomfoolery*). [ME, from or after F *–erie*, *–ere* ult. f. L *–ario-, –ator*]

er•y•sip•e•las /érisípiləs/ *n. Med.* a streptococcal infection producing inflammation and a deep red color on the skin, esp. of the face and scalp. [ME f. L f. Gk *erusipelas*, perh. rel. to *eruthros* red + a root *pel-* skin]

er•y•the•ma /érithéemə/ *n.* a superficial reddening of the skin, usu. in patches. □□ **er•y•the•mal** *adj.* **er•y•the•mat•ic** /–thimátik/ *adj.* [mod.L f. Gk *eruthēma* f. *eruthainō* be red f. *eruthros* red]

erythro- /iríthrō/ *comb. form* red. [Gk *eruthros* red]

e•ryth•ro•blast /iríthrəblast/ *n.* an immature erythrocyte. [G]

e•ryth•ro•cyte /iríthrəsīt/ *n.* a red blood cell, which contains the pigment hemoglobin and transports oxygen and carbon dioxide to and from the tissues. □□ **e•ryth•ro•cyt•ic** /–sítik/ *adj.*

e•ryth•roid /érithroyd/ *adj.* of or relating to erythrocytes.

Es *symb. Chem.* the element einsteinium.

-es¹ /iz/ *suffix* forming plurals of nouns ending in sibilant sounds (such words in *–e* dropping the *e*) (*kisses; cases; boxes; churches*). [var. of –S¹]

-es² /iz, z/ *suffix* forming the 3rd person sing. present of verbs ending in sibilant sounds (such words in *–e* dropping the *e*) and ending in *–o* (but not *–oo*) (*goes; places; pushes*). [var. of –S²]

ESA *abbr.* European Space Agency.

es•ca•drille /éskədril/ *n.* a French squadron of airplanes. [F]

es•ca•lade /éskəláyd, –láad/ *n.* the scaling of fortified walls with ladders, as a military attack. [F f. Sp. *escalada*, *–ado* f. med.L *scalare* f. *scala* ladder]

es•ca•late /éskəlayt/ *v.* **1** *intr. & tr.* increase or develop (usu. rapidly) by stages. **2** *tr.* cause (an action, activity, or process) to become more intense. □□ **es•ca•la•tion** /–láyshən/ *n.* [back-form. f. ESCALATOR]

es•ca•la•tor /éskəlaytər/ *n.* a moving staircase consisting of a circulating belt forming steps. [f. the stem of *escalade* 'climb a wall by ladder' + –ATOR]

es•cal•lo•ni•a /éskəlóneeə/ *n.* any evergreen shrub of the genus *Escallonia*, bearing rose-red flowers. [*Escallon*, 18th-c. Sp. traveler]

es•cal•lop /iskáləp/ *n.* **1** = SCALLOP 1, 2. **2** = ESCALOPE. **3** (in *pl.*) = SCALLOP 3. **4** *Heraldry* a scallop shell as a device. [formed as ESCALOPE]

es•ca•lope /éskəlóp/ *n.* a thin slice of meat without any bone, esp. from a leg of veal. [F (in OF = shell): see SCALLOP]

es•ca•pade /éskəpáyd/ *n.* an act or incident involving excitement, daring, or adventure. [F f. Prov. or Sp. *escapada* (as ESCAPE)]

es•cape /iskáyp/ *v. & n.* • *v.* **1** *intr.* (often foll. by *from*) get free of the restriction or control of a place, person, etc. **2** *intr.* (of a gas, liquid, etc.) leak from a container or pipe, etc. **3** *intr.* succeed in avoiding danger, punishment, etc.; get off safely. **4** *tr.* get completely free of (a person, grasp, etc.). **5** *tr.* avoid or elude (a commitment, danger, etc.). **6** *tr.* elude the notice or memory of (*nothing escapes you; the name escaped me*). **7** *tr.* (of words, etc.) issue unawares from (a person, a person's lips). • *n.* **1** the act or an instance of escaping; avoidance of danger, injury, etc. **2** the state of having escaped (*was a narrow escape*). **3** a means of escaping (often *attrib.*: *escape hatch*). **4** a leakage of gas, etc. **5** a temporary relief from reality or worry. **6** a garden plant running wild. □□ **es•cap•a•ble** *adj.* **es•cap•er** *n.* [ME f. AF, ONF *escaper* ult. f. med.L (as EX-¹, *cappa* cloak)]

es•cape clause *n. Law* a clause specifying the conditions under which a contracting party is free from an obligation.

es•cap•ee /iskaypée/ *n.* a person, esp. a prisoner, who has escaped.

es•cape•ment /iskáypmənt/ *n.* **1** the part of a clock or watch that connects and regulates the motive power. **2** the part of the mechanism in a piano that enables the hammer to fall back immediately after striking the string. **3** *archaic* a means of escape. [F *échappement* f. *échapper* ESCAPE]

es•cape ve•loc•i•ty *n.* the minimum velocity needed to escape from the gravitational field of a body.

es•cape wheel *n.* a toothed wheel in the escapement of a watch or clock.

es•cap•ism /iskáypizəm/ *n.* the tendency to seek distraction and relief from reality, esp. in the arts or through fantasy. □□ **es•cap•ist** *n. & adj.*

es•cap•ol•o•gy /éskəpóləjee/ *n.* the methods and techniques of escaping from confinement, esp. as a form of entertainment. □□ **es•cap•ol•o•gist** *n.*

es•car•got /eskaargố/ *n.* an edible snail. [F]

es•carp•ment /iskáarpmənt/ *n.* (also **es•carp**) *Geol.* a long, steep slope at the edge of a plateau, etc. [F *escarpement* f. *escarpe* SCARP]

-esce /es/ *suffix* forming verbs, usu. initiating action (*effervesce; fluoresce*). [from or after L *–escere*]

-escent /ésənt/ *suffix* forming adjectives denoting the beginning of a state or action (*effervescent; fluorescent*). □□ **–escence** *suffix* forming nouns. [from or after F *–escent* or L *–escent-*, pres. part. stem of verbs in *–escere*]

es•cha•tol•o•gy /éskətóləjee/ *n.* the part of theology concerned with death and final destiny. □□ **es•cha•to•log•i•cal** /–təlójikəl/ *adj.* **es•cha•tol•o•gist** *n.* [Gk *eskhatos* last + –LOGY]

es•cheat /ischéet/ *n. & v. hist.* • *n.* **1** the reversion of property to the state, or (in feudal law) to a lord, on the owner's dying without legal heirs. **2** property affected by this. • *v.* **1** *tr.* hand over (property) as an escheat. **2** *tr.* confiscate. **3** *intr.* revert by escheat. [ME f. OF *eschete*, ult. f. L *excidere* (as EX-¹, *cadere* fall)]

es•chew /eschōo/ *v.tr. literary* avoid; abstain from. □□ **es•chew•al** *n.* [ME f. OF *eschiver*, ult. f. Gmc: rel. to SHY¹]

esch•scholt•zi•a /eshốltseeə/ *n.* any yellow-flowering plant of the genus *Eschscholtzia*, esp. the Californian poppy (see POPPY). [J. F. von *Eschscholtz*, Ger. botanist d. 1831]

es•cort *n. & v.* • *n.* /éskawrt/ **1** one or more persons, vehicles, ships, etc., accompanying a person, vehicle, etc., esp. for protection or security or as a mark of rank or status. **2** a person accompanying a person of the opposite sex socially. **3** a person or group acting as a guide or leader, esp. on a journey. • *v.tr.* /iskáwrt/ act as an escort to. [F *escorte, escorter* f. It. *scorta* fem. past part. of *scorgere* conduct]

es•cri•toire /éskritwáar/ *n.* a writing desk with drawers, etc. [F f. L *scriptorium* writing room: see SCRIPTORIUM]

es•crow /éskrō/ *n. & v. Law* • *n.* **1** money, property, or a written bond, kept in the custody of a third party until a specified condition has been fulfilled. **2** the status of this (*in escrow*). • *v.tr.* place in escrow. [AF *escrowe*, OF *escroe* scrap, scroll, f. med.L *scroda* f. Gmc]

es•cu•do /eskốōdō/ *n.* (*pl.* **•dos**) the principal monetary unit of Portugal and Chile. [Sp. & Port. f. L *scutum* shield]

es•cu•lent /éskyələnt/ *adj. & n.* • *adj.* fit to eat; edible. • *n.* an edible substance. [L *esculentus* f. *esca* food]

es•cutch•eon /iskúchən/ *n.* **1** a shield or emblem bearing a coat of arms. **2** the middle part of a ship's stern where the name is placed. **3** the protective plate around a keyhole or door handle. □□ **es•cutch•eoned** *adj.* [AF & ONF *escuchon* ult. f. L *scutum* shield]

Esd. *abbr.* Esdras (Apocrypha).

ESE *abbr.* east-southeast.

-ese /eez/ *suffix* forming adjectives and nouns denoting: **1** an inhabitant or language of a country or city (*Japanese; Milanese; Viennese*). **2** often *derog.* character or style, esp. of language (*officialese*). [OF *–eis* ult. f. L *–ensis*]

▶Plural forms are the same.

es•ker /éskər/ *n. Geol.* a long ridge of postglacial gravel in river valleys. [Ir. *eiscir*]

Es·ki·mo /éskimō/ n. & adj. • n. (pl. same or **·mos**) **1** a member of a people inhabiting N. Canada, Alaska, Greenland, and E. Siberia. **2** the language of this people. • adj. of or relating to the Eskimos or their language. [Da. f. F *Esquimaux* (pl.) f. Algonquian] ▶The term *Inuit* is preferred by the people themselves.

ESL abbr. English as a second language.

e·soph·a·gus /isófəgəs, ee–/ n. (Brit. **oe·soph·a·gus**) (pl. **e·soph·a·gi** /–gī, –jī/) the part of the alimentary canal from the mouth to the stomach; the gullet. □□ **e·soph·a·ge·al** /isófəjeéəl, eesəfájeeəl/ adj. [ME f. GK *oisophagos*]

es·o·ter·ic /ésətérik/ adj. **1** intelligible only to those with special knowledge. **2** (of a belief, etc.) intended only for the initiated. □□ **es·o·ter·i·cal** adj. **es·o·ter·i·cal·ly** adv. **es·o·ter·i·cism** /–rəsizəm/ n. **es·o·ter·i·cist** n. [Gk *esōterikos* f. *esōterō* compar. of *esō* within]

ESP abbr. extrasensory perception.

es·pa·drille /éspədríl/ n. a light canvas shoe with a plaited fiber sole. [F f. Prov. *espardillo* f. *espart* ESPARTO]

es·pal·ier /ispályər, –yay/ n. **1** a latticework along which the branches of a tree or shrub are trained to grow flat against a wall, etc. **2** a tree or shrub trained in this way. [F f. It. *spalliera* f. *spalla* shoulder]

es·par·to /espaártō/ n. (pl. **·tos**) (in full **esparto grass**) a coarse grass, *Stipa tenacissima*, native to Spain and N. Africa, with tough, narrow leaves, used to make ropes, wickerwork, and good-quality paper. [Sp. f. L *spartum* f. Gk *sparton* rope]

es·pe·cial /ispéshəl/ adj. **1** notable; exceptional. **2** attributed or belonging chiefly to one person or thing (*your especial charm*). [ME f. OF f. L *specialis* special]

es·pe·cial·ly /ispéshəlee, espésh–/ adv. chiefly; much more than in other cases.

Es·pe·ran·to /éspərántō, –ráan–/ n. an artificial universal language devised in 1887, based on roots common to the chief European languages. □□ **Es·pe·ran·tist** n. [the pen name (f. L *sperare* hope) of its inventor, L. L. Zamenhof, Polish physician d. 1917]

es·pi·al /ispíəl/ n. **1** the act or an instance of catching sight of or of being seen. **2** archaic spying. [ME f. OF *espiaille* f. *espier*: see ESPY]

es·pi·o·nage /éspeeənaazh/ n. the practice of spying or of using spies, esp. by governments. [F *espionnage* f. *espionner* f. *espion* SPY]

es·pla·nade /ésplənaád, –náyd/ n. **1** a long, open level area for walking on, esp. beside the ocean. **2** a level space separating a fortress from a town. [F f. Sp. *esplanada* f. *esplanar* make level f. L *explanare* (as EX–, *planus* level)]

es·pous·al /ispówzəl, –səl/ n. **1** (foll. by *of*) the espousing of a cause, etc. **2** archaic a marriage or betrothal. [ME f. OF *espousailles* f. L *sponsalia* neut. pl. of *sponsalis* (as ESPOUSE)]

es·pouse /ispówz/ v.tr. **1** adopt or support (a cause, doctrine, etc.). **2** archaic **a** (usu. of a man) marry. **b** (usu. foll. by *to*) give (a woman) in marriage. □□ **es·pous·er** n. [ME f. OF *espouser* f. L *sponsare* f. *sponsus* past part. of *spondēre* betroth]

es·pres·so /esprésō/ n. (also **ex·pres·so** /eksprésō/) (pl. **·sos**) **1** strong, concentrated black coffee made under steam pressure. **2** a machine for making this. [It., = pressed out]

PRONUNCIATION TIP espresso

This Italian word is short for *caffè espresso*, that is, "pressed-out coffee." The variant *expresso*, which probably came about because it sounded like the word *express*, is an invented word that has gained widespread use but is best avoided.

es·prit /espreé/ n. sprightliness; wit. [F f. L *spiritus* SPIRIT (+ *corps* body, *escalier* stairs)]

es·prit de corps /espreé də káwr/ n. a feeling of devotion to and pride in the group one belongs to.

es·prit de l'es·ca·lier /espreé də leskalyáy/ n. an apt retort or clever remark that comes to mind after the chance to make it is gone.

es·py /ispí/ v.tr. (**·pies**, **·pied**) literary catch sight of; perceive. [ME f. OF *espier*: see SPY]

Esq. abbr. esquire.

-esque /esk/ suffix forming adjectives meaning 'in the style of' or 'resembling' (*romanesque*; *Schumannesque*; *statuesque*). [F f. It. *-esco* f. med.L *-iscus*]

Es·qui·mau /éskimō/ n. (pl. **·maux** /–mōz/) = ESKIMO. [F]

es·quire /éskwir, iskwír/ n. **1** (usu. as abbr. **Esq.**) **a** a title appended to a man's surname when no other form of address is used, esp. as a form of address for letters. **b** a title placed after the name of an attorney (male or female), esp. in correspondence. **2** archaic = SQUIRE. [ME f. OF *esquier* f. L *scutarius* shield-bearer f. *scutum* shield]

ESR abbr. Physics electron spin resonance.

-ess¹ /is/ suffix forming nouns denoting females (*actress*; *lioness*; *mayoress*). [from or after F *-esse* f. LL *-issa* f. Gk *-issa*]

-ess² /es/ suffix forming abstract nouns from adjectives (*duress*). [ME f. F *-esse* f. L *-itia*; cf. –ICE]

es·say n. & v. • n. /ésay/ **1** a composition, usu. short and in prose, on any subject. **2** (often foll. by *at, in*) formal an attempt. • v.tr. /esáy/ formal attempt, try. [ME f. ASSAY, assim. to F *essayer* ult. f. LL *exagium* weighing f. *exigere* weigh: see EXACT]

es·say·ist n. a person who writes essays, esp. as a literary genre.

es·sence /ésəns/ n. **1** the indispensable quality or element identifying a thing or determining its character; fundamental nature or inherent characteristics. **2 a** an extract obtained by distillation, etc., esp. a volatile oil. **b** a perfume or scent, esp. made from a plant or animal substance. **3** the constituent of a plant that determines its chemical properties. **4** an abstract entity; the reality underlying a phenomenon or all phenomena. □ **in essence** fundamentally. **of the essence** indispensable; vital. [ME f. OF f. L *essentia* f. *esse* be]

Es·sene /éseen, eseén/ n. a member of an ancient Jewish ascetic sect living communally. [L pl. *Esseni* f. Gk pl. *Essēnoi*]

es·sen·tial /isénshəl/ adj. & n. • adj. **1** absolutely necessary; indispensable. **2** fundamental; basic. **3** of or constituting the essence of a person or thing. **4** (of a disease) with no known external stimulus or cause; idiopathic. • n. (esp. in pl.) a basic or indispensable element or thing. □□ **es·sen·ti·al·i·ty** /–sheeálitee/ n. **es·sen·tial·ly** adv. **es·sen·tial·ness** n. [ME f. LL *essentialis* (as ESSENCE)]

es·sen·tial oil n. a natural oil typically obtained by distillation and having the characteristic fragrance of the plant or other souce from which it is extracted.

EST abbr. **1** eastern standard time. **2** electroshock treatment.

est. abbr. **1** established. **2** estimate. **3** estimated.

-est¹ /ist/ suffix forming the superlative of adjectives (*widest*; *nicest*; *happiest*) and adverbs (*soonest*). [OE *-ost-*, *-ust-*, *-ast-*]

-est² /ist/ suffix (also **-st**) archaic forming the 2nd person sing. of verbs (*canst*; *findest*; *gavest*). [OE *-est*, *-ast*, *-st*]

es·tab·lish /istáblish/ v.tr. **1** set up or consolidate (a business, system, etc.) on a permanent basis. **2** (foll. by *in*) settle (a person or oneself) in some capacity. **3** (esp. as **established** adj.) achieve permanent acceptance for (a custom, belief, practice, institution, etc.). **4** validate; place beyond dispute (a fact, etc.). □□ **es·tab·lish·er** n. [ME f. OF *establir* (stem *establiss-*) f. L *stabilire* f. *stabilis* STABLE¹]

es·tab·lished church n. a church recognized by the government as the national church.

es·tab·lish·ment /istáblishmənt/ n. **1** the act or an instance of establishing; the process of being established. **2 a** a business organization or public institution. **b** a place of business. **c** a residence. **3 a** the staff or equipment of an organization. **b** a household. **4** any organized body permanently maintained for a purpose. **5** a church system organized by law. **6** (**the Establishment**) **a** the group in a society exercising authority or influence, and seen as resisting change. **b** any influential or controlling group (*the literary Establishment*).

es·tab·lish·men·tar·i·an /istáblishməntáireeən/ adj. & n. • adj. adhering to or advocating the principle of an established church. • n. a person adhering to or advocating this. □□ **es·tab·lish·men·tar·i·an·ism** n.

es·ta·mi·net /estaameenáy/ n. a small French café, etc., selling alcoholic drinks. [F f. Walloon *staminé* byre f. *stamo* a pole for tethering a cow, prob. f. G *Stamm* stem]

es·tate /istáyt/ n. **1** a property consisting of an extensive area of land usu. with a large house. **2** Brit. a housing development. **3** all of a person's assets and liabilities, esp. at death. **4** a property where rubber, tea, grapes, etc., are cultivated. **5** (in full **estate of the realm**) a group or social class having specific political powers, esp. (in Britain) one of the three groups constituting Parliament, now the Lords Spiritual (the heads of the Church), the Lords Temporal (the peerage), and the Commons. **6** archaic or literary a state or position in life (*the estate of holy matrimony*; *poor man's estate*). [ME f. OF *estat* (as STATUS)]

es·tate agent n. Brit. **1** a real-estate agent. **2** the steward of an estate.

es·tate car n. Brit. a station wagon.

es·tate tax n. a tax levied on the net value of property of a deceased person.

es·teem /isteém/ v. & n. • v.tr. **1** (usu. in passive) have a high

SYNONYM TIP esteem

ADMIRE, APPRECIATE, PRIZE, REGARD, RESPECT. If you're a classical music aficionado, you might **appreciate** a good symphony orchestra, **admire** someone who plays the oboe, and **esteem** the works of Beethoven above all other classical composers. All three of these verbs are concerned with recognizing the worth of something, but in order to *appreciate* it you have to understand it well enough to judge it critically. If you *admire* something, you appreciate its superiority (*to admire a pianist's performance*), while *esteem* goes one step further, implying that your admiration is of the highest degree (*a musician esteemed throughout the music world*). You **prize** what you value highly or cherish, especially if it is a possession (*she prized her Stradivarius violin*), while **regard** is a more neutral term meaning to look at or to have a certain mental view of something, either favorable or unfavorable (*to regard him as a great musician*; *to regard her as a ruthless competitor*). To **respect** is to have a deferential regard for someone or something because of its worth or value (*to respect the conductor's interpretation of the music*).

regard for; greatly respect; think favorably of. **2** *formal* consider; deem (*esteemed it an honor*). ● *n.* high regard; respect; favor (*held them in esteem*). [ME f. OF *estimer* f. L *aestimare* fix the price of]

es·ter /éstər/ *n. Chem.* any of a class of organic compounds produced by replacing the hydrogen of an acid by an alkyl, aryl, etc., radical, many of which occur naturally as oils and fats. □□ **es·ter·i·fy** /estérifī/ *v.tr.* (**·fies**, **·fied**). [G, prob. f. *Essig* vinegar + *Äther* ether]

Esth. *abbr.* Esther (Old Testament & Apocrypha).

es·thete var. of AESTHETE.

es·thet·ic var. of AESTHETIC.

es·ti·ma·ble /éstiməbəl/ *adj.* worthy of esteem. □□ **es·ti·ma·bly** *adv.* [F f. L *aestimabilis* (as ESTEEM)]

es·ti·mate *n. & v.* ● *n.* /éstimət/ **1** an approximate judgment, esp. of cost, value, size, etc. **2** a price specified as that likely to be charged for work to be undertaken. **3** opinion; judgment; estimation. ● *v.tr.* (also *absol.*) /éstimayt/ **1** form an estimate or opinion of. **2** (foll. by *that* + clause) make a rough calculation. **3** (often foll. by *at*) form an estimate; adjudge. **4** fix (a price, etc.) by estimate. □□ **es·ti·ma·tive** *adj.* **es·ti·ma·tor** *n.* [L *aestimare aestimat-* fix the price of]

es·ti·ma·tion /éstimáyshən/ *n.* **1** the process or result of estimating. **2** judgment or opinion of worth (*in my estimation*). **3** *archaic* esteem (*hold in estimation*). [ME f. OF *estimation* or L *aestimatio* (as ESTIMATE)]

es·ti·val /éstəvəl, estívəl/ *adj.* (also **aes·ti·val**) *formal* belonging to or appearing in summer. [ME f. OF *estival* f. L *aestivalis* f. *aestivus* f. *aestus* heat]

es·ti·vate /éstəvayt/ *v.intr.* (also **aes·ti·vate**) **1** *Zool.* spend the summer or dry season in a state of torpor. **2** *formal* pass the summer. [L *aestivare aestivat–*]

es·ti·va·tion /éstiváyshən/ *n.* (also **aes·ti·va·tion**) **1** *Bot.* the arrangement of petals in a flower bud before it opens (cf. VERNATION) **2** *Zool.* spending the summer or dry season in a state of torpor.

Es·to·ni·an /estóneeən/ *n. & adj* ● *n.* **1 a** a native of Estonia, a Baltic republic. **b** a person of Estonian descent. **2** the Finno-Ugric language of Estonia. ● *adj.* of or relating to Estonia or its people or language.

es·top /estóp/ *v.tr.* (**es·topped**, **es·top·ping**) (foll. by *from*) *Law* bar or preclude, esp. by estoppel. □□ **es·top·page** *n.* [ME f. AF, OF *estoper* f. LL *stuppare* stop up f. L *stuppa* tow: cf. STOP, STUFF]

es·top·pel /estópəl/ *n. Law* the principle which precludes a person from asserting something contrary to what is implied by a previous action or statement of that person or by a previous pertinent judicial determination. [OF *estouppail* bung f. *estoper* (as ESTOP)]

es·to·vers /estóvərz/ *n.pl. hist.* necessaries allowed by law to a tenant (esp. fuel, or wood for repairs). [AF *estovers*, OF *estoveir* be necessary, f. L *est opus*]

es·trange /istráynj/ *v.tr.* (usu. in *passive*; often foll. by *from*) cause (a person or group) to turn away in feeling or affection; alienate. □□ **es·trange·ment** *n.* [ME f. AF *estraunger*, OF *estranger* f. L *extraneare* treat as a stranger f. *extraneus* stranger]

es·treat /estreét/ *n. & v. Brit. Law* ● *n.* **1** a copy of a court record of a fine, etc., for use in prosecution. **2** the enforcement of a fine or forfeiture of a recognizance. ● *v.tr.* enforce the forfeit of (a fine, etc., esp. surety for bail). [ME f. AF *estrete* f. OF *estraite* f. *estraire* f. L *extrahere* EXTRACT]

es·tro·gen /éstrəjən/ *n.* (*Brit.* **oes·tro·gen** /eés-/) **1** any of various steroid hormones developing and maintaining female characteristics of the body. **2** this hormone produced artificially for use in oral contraceptives, etc. □□ **es·tro·gen·ic** /–jénik/ *adj.* **es·tro·gen·i·cal·ly** /–jénikəlee/ *adv.* [ESTRUS + –GEN]

es·trus /éstrəs/ *n.* (also **es·trum**, *Brit.* **oes·trus**, **oes·trum** /eés–/) a recurring period of sexual receptivity in many female mammals; heat. □□ **estrous** *adj.* [GK *oistros* gadfly, frenzy]

es·tu·ar·y /és–chōoeree/ *n.* (*pl.* **·ies**) a wide tidal mouth of a river. □□ **es·tu·a·rine** /–əriin, –əreen/ *adj.* [L *aestuarium* tidal channel f. *aestus* tide]

e.s.u. *abbr.* electrostatic unit(s).

e·su·ri·ent /isŏoreeənt/ *adj. archaic* or *joc.* **1** hungry. **2** impecunious and greedy. □□ **e·su·ri·ent·ly** *adv.* [L *esurire* (v.) hunger f. *edere* eat]

ET *abbr.* extraterrestrial.

-et[1] /it/ *suffix* forming nouns (orig. diminutives) (*baronet; bullet; sonnet*). [OF *–et –ete*]

-et[2] /it/ *suffix* (also **–ete** /eet/) forming nouns usu. denoting persons (*comet; poet; athlete*). [Gk *–ētēs*]

ETA *abbr.* estimated time of arrival.

e·ta /áytə, eétə/ *n.* the seventh letter of the Greek alphabet (H, η). [Gk]

et al. /et ál/ *abbr.* and others. [L *et alii, et alia,* etc.]

▶Use **et al.** for an unnamed list of people (*Johnson et al. were the authors of the work*). Use **etc.** for an unnamed list of things (*they looked at houses, apartments, etc.*).

e·ta·lon /áyt'lon/ *n. Physics* a device consisting of two reflecting plates, for producing interfering light beams. [F *étalon* standard]

etc. *abbr.* = ET CETERA.
▶See note at ET AL.

et cet·er·a /et sétərə, sétrə/ *adv. & n.* (also **et·cet·er·a**) ● *adv.* **1 a** and the rest; and similar things or people. **b** or similar things or people. **2** and so on. ● *n.* (in *pl.*) the usual sundries or extras. [ME f. L]

etch /ech/ *v. & n.* ● *v.* **1 a** *tr.* reproduce (a picture, etc.) by engraving a design on a metal plate with acid (esp. to print copies). **b** *tr.* engrave (a plate) in this way. **2** *intr.* practice this craft. **3** *tr.* (foll. by *on, upon*) impress deeply (esp. on the mind). ● *n.* the action or process of etching. □□ **etch·er** *n.* [Du. *etsen* f. G *ätzen* etch f. OHG *azzen* cause to eat or to be eaten f. Gmc]

etch·ant /échənt/ *n.* a corrosive used in etching.

etch·ing /éching/ *n.* **1** a print made from an etched plate. **2** the art of producing these plates.

ETD *abbr.* estimated time of departure.

-ete *suffix* var. of –ET[2].

e·ter·nal /itúrnəl/ *adj.* **1** existing always; without an end or (usu.) beginning in time. **2** essentially unchanging (*eternal truths*). **3** *colloq.* constant; seeming not to cease (*your eternal nagging*). □ **the Eternal God.** □□ **e·ter·nal·i·ty** /–nálitee/ *n.* **e·ter·nal·ize** *v.tr.* **e·ter·nal·ly** *adv.* **e·ter·nal·ness** *n.* **e·ter·nize** *v.tr.* [ME f. OF f. LL *aeternalis* f. L *aeternus* f. *aevum* age]

E·ter·nal Cit·y *n.* Rome.

e·ter·nal tri·an·gle *n.* a relationship of three people involving sexual rivalry.

e·ter·ni·ty /itúrnitee/ *n.* (*pl.* **·ties**) **1** infinite or unending (esp. future) time. **2** *Theol.* endless life after death. **3** the state of being eternal. **4** *colloq.* (often prec. by *an*) a very long time. **5** (in *pl.*) eternal truths. [ME f. OF *eternité* f. L *aeternitas –tatis* f. *aeternus*: see ETERNAL]

e·te·sian /iteézhən/ *adj.* annually-occurring. [L *etesius* f. Gk *etēsios* annual f. *etos* year]

E·te·sian winds *n.* NW winds blowing each summer in the E. Mediterranean.

eth var. of EDH.

-eth[1] var. of –TH[1].

-eth[2] /ith/ *suffix* (also **–th**) *archaic* forming the 3rd person sing. present of verbs (*doeth; saith*). [OE *–eth, –ath, –th*]

eth·a·nal /éthənal/ *n.* = ACETALDEHYDE. [ETHANE + ALDEHYDE]

eth·ane /éthayn/ *n. Chem.* a gaseous hydrocarbon of the alkane series, occurring in natural gas. ¶ *Chem.* formula: C_2H_6. [ETHER + –ANE[2]]

eth·a·nol /éthənawl, –nol/ *n. Chem.* = ALCOHOL 1. [ETHANE + ALCOHOL]

eth·ene /étheen/ *n. Chem.* = ETHYLENE. [ETHER + –ENE]

e·ther /eéthər/ *n.* **1** *Chem.* **a** a colorless volatile organic liquid used as an anesthetic or solvent. Also called **diethyl ether.** ¶ *Chem.* formula: $C_2H_5OC_2H_5$. **b** any of a class of organic compounds with a similar structure to this, having an oxygen joined to two alkyl, etc., groups. **2** a clear sky; the upper regions of air beyond the clouds. **3** *hist.* **a** a medium formerly assumed to permeate space and fill the interstices between particles of matter. **b** a medium through which electromagnetic waves were formerly thought to be transmitted. □□ **e·ther·ic** /eethérik/ *adj.* [ME f. OF *ether* or L *aether* f. Gk *aithēr* f. root of *aithō* burn, shine]

e·the·re·al /itheéreeəl/ *adj.* **1** light; airy. **2** highly delicate, esp. in appearance. **3** heavenly; celestial. **4** *Chem.* of or relating to ether. □□ **e·the·re·al·i·ty** /–reeálitee/ *n.* **e·the·re·al·ly** *adv.* [L *aethereus, –ius* f. Gk *aitherios* (as ETHER)]

e·ther·ize /éethərīz/ v.tr. hist. treat or anesthetize with ether. □□ **e·ther·i·za·tion** n.

eth·ic /éthik/ n. & adj. ● n. a set of moral principles (the Quaker ethic). ● adj. = ETHICAL. [ME f. OF éthique or L ethicus f. Gk ēthikos (as ETHOS)]

eth·i·cal /éthikəl/ adj. 1 relating to morals, esp. as concerning human conduct. 2 morally correct; honorable. 3 (of a medicine or drug) not advertised to the general public, and usu. available only on a doctor's prescription. □□ **eth·i·cal·i·ty** /-kálitee/ n. **eth·i·cal·ly** adv.

eth·i·cal in·vest·ment n. investment in companies that meet ethical and moral criteria specified by the investor.

eth·ics /éthiks/ n.pl. (also treated as sing.) 1 the science of morals in human conduct. 2 a moral principles; rules of conduct. b a set of these (medical ethics). □□ **eth·i·cist** /éthisist/ n.

E·thi·o·pi·an /éetheeópeeən/ n. & adj. ● n. 1 a a native or national of Ethiopia in NE Africa. b a person of Ethiopian descent. 2 archaic a black person. ● adj. of or relating to Ethiopia. [Ethiopia f. L Aethiops f. Gk Aithiops f. aithō burn + ōps face]

E·thi·op·ic /éetheeópik, -ṓpik/ n. & adj. ● n. the Christian liturgical language of Ethiopia. ● adj. of or in this language. [L aethiopicus f. Gk aithiopikos: see ETHIOPIAN]

eth·moid /éthmoyd/ adj. sievelike. □□ **eth·moi·dal** /-móyd'l/ adj. [Gk ēthmoeidēs f. ēthmos sieve]

eth·moid bone n. a square bone at the root of the nose, with many perforations through which the olfactory nerves pass to the nose.

eth·nic /éthnik/ adj. & n. ● adj. 1 a (of a social group) having a common national or cultural tradition. b (of clothes, etc.) resembling those of a non-European exotic people. 2 denoting origin by birth or descent rather than nationality (ethnic Turks). 3 relating to race or culture (ethnic group; ethnic origins). 4 archaic pagan; heathen. ● n. 1 a member of an (esp. minority) ethnic group. 2 (in pl., usu. treated as sing.) = ETHNOLOGY. □□ **eth·ni·cal·ly** adv. **eth·nic·i·ty** /-nísitee/ n. [ME f. eccl.L ethnicus f. Gk ethnikos heathen f. ethnos nation]

eth·ni·cal /éthnikəl/ adj. relating to ethnology.

eth·nic cleans·ing n. euphem. the practice of mass expulsion or killing of people from opposing ethnic or religious groups within a certain area.

eth·nic mi·nor·i·ty n. a (usu. identifiable) group differentiated from the main population of a community by racial origin or cultural background.

ethno- /éthnō/ comb. form ethnic; ethnological. [Gk ethnos nation]

eth·no·ar·chae·ol·o·gy /éthnō-aárkeeóləjee/ n. the study of a society's institutions based on examination of its material attributes. □□ **eth·no·ar·chae·o·log·i·cal** /-keeəlójikəl/ adj. **eth·no·ar·chae·ol·o·gist** n.

eth·no·cen·tric /éthnōséntrik/ adj. evaluating other races and cultures by criteria specific to one's own. □□ **eth·no·cen·tri·cal·ly** adv. **eth·no·cen·tric·i·ty** /-trísitee/ n. **eth·no·cen·trism** n.

eth·nog·ra·phy /ethnógrəfee/ n. the scientific description of races and cultures of mankind. □□ **eth·nog·ra·pher** n. **eth·no·graph·ic** /-nəgráfik/ adj. **eth·no·graph·i·cal** adj.

eth·nol·o·gy /ethnóləjee/ n. the comparative scientific study of human peoples. □□ **eth·no·log·ic** /-nəlójik/ adj. **eth·no·log·i·cal** adj. **eth·nol·o·gist** n.

eth·no·mu·si·col·o·gy /éthnōmyōōzikóləjee/ n. the study of the music of one or more (esp. non-European) cultures. □□ **eth·no·mu·si·col·o·gist** n.

e·tho·gram /éethəgram/ n. Zool. a list of the kinds of behavior or activity observed in an animal. [Gk ētho- (see ETHOS) + -GRAM]

e·thol·o·gy /eethóləjee/ n. 1 the science of animal behavior. 2 the science of character formation in human behavior. □□ **e·tho·log·i·cal** /éethəlójikəl/ adj. **e·thol·o·gist** n. [L ethologia f. Gk ēthologia (as ETHOS)]

e·thos /éethos/ n. the characteristic spirit or attitudes of a community, people, or system, or of a literary work, etc. [mod.L f. Gk ēthos nature, disposition]

eth·yl /éthil/ n. (attrib.) Chem. the univalent radical derived from ethane by removal of a hydrogen atom (ethyl alcohol). [G (as ETHER, -YL)]

eth·yl·ene /éthileen/ n. Chem. a gaseous hydrocarbon of the alkene series, occurring in natural gas and used in the manufacture of polyethylene. Also called ethene. ¶ Chem. formula: C_2H_4. □□ **eth·yl·e·nic** /-léenik, -lénik/ adj.

eth·yl·ene gly·col n. Chem. a colorless viscous hygroscopic liquid used as an antifreeze and in the manufacture of polyesters. ¶ Chem. formula: $C_2H_6O_2$.

-etic /étik/ suffix forming adjectives and nouns (ascetic; emetic; genetic; synthetic). [Gk -ētikos or -ētikos: cf. -IC]

e·ti·o·late /éeteeəláyt/ v.tr. 1 make (a plant) pale by excluding light. 2 give a sickly hue to (a person). □□ **e·ti·o·la·tion** /-láyshən/ n. [F étioler f. Norman F étieuler make into haulm f. éteule ult. f. L stipula straw]

e·ti·ol·o·gy /éeteeóləjee/ n. (esp. Brit. **ae·ti·ol·o·gy**) 1 the assignment of a cause or reason. 2 the philosophy of causation. 3 Med. the science of the causes of disease. □□ **e·ti·o·log·ic** /-teeəlójik/ adj. **e·ti·o·log·i·cal** /-teeəlójikəl/ adj. **e·ti·o·log·i·cal·ly** /-teeəlójikəlee/ adv. [LL aetiologia f. GK aitiologia f. aitia cause]

et·i·quette /étiket, -kit/ n. 1 the conventional rules of social behavior. 2 a the customary behavior of members of a profession toward each other. b the unwritten code governing this (medical etiquette). [F étiquette label, etiquette]

E·ton col·lar /éet'n/ n. a broad stiff collar worn outside the coat collar, esp. of an Eton jacket.

E·to·ni·an /eetóneeən/ n. a past or present member of Eton College in S. England.

E·ton jack·et /éet'n/ n. a short jacket reaching only to the waist, as formerly worn by pupils of Eton College.

étri·er /aytree-áy/ n. Mountaineering a short rope ladder with a few rungs of wood or metal. [F, = stirrup]

E·trus·can /itrúskən/ adj. & n. ● adj. of ancient Etruria in Italy, esp. its pre-Roman civilization and physical remains. ● n. 1 a native of Etruria. 2 the language of Etruria. □□ **E·trus·col·o·gy** /-kóləjee/ n. [L Etruscus]

et seq. abbr. (also **et seqq.**) and the following (pages, etc.). [L et sequentia]

-ette /et/ suffix forming nouns meaning: 1 small (kitchenette; cigarette). 2 imitation or substitute (leatherette; flannelette). 3 often offens. female (usherette; suffragette). [from or after OF -ette, fem. of -ET[1]]

é·tude /áytōōd, -tyōōd/ n. a short musical composition or exercise, usu. for one instrument, designed to improve the technique of the player. [F, = study]

e·tui /etwee/ n. a small case for needles, etc. [F étui f. OF estui prison]

-etum /éetəm/ suffix forming nouns denoting a collection of trees or other plants (arboretum; pinetum). [L]

etym. abbr. 1 etymological. 2 etymology.

et·y·mol·o·gize /étimóləjiz/ v. 1 tr. give or trace the etymology of. 2 intr. study etymology. [med.L etymologizare f. L etymologia (as ETYMOLOGY)]

et·y·mol·o·gy /étimóləjee/ n. (pl. ·gies) 1 a the historically verifiable sources of the formation of a word and the development of its meaning. b an account of these. 2 the branch of linguistic science concerned with etymologies. □□ **et·y·mo·log·i·cal** /-məlójikəl/ adj. **et·y·mo·log·i·cal·ly** adv. **et·y·mol·o·gist** n. [OF ethimologie f. L etymologia f. Gk etumologia (as ETYMON, -LOGY)]

et·y·mon /étimən/ n. (pl. **et·y·ma** /-mə/ or **et·y·mons**) the word that gives rise to a derivative or a borrowed or later form. [L f. Gk etumon (neut. of etumos true), the literal sense or original form of a word]

EU abbr. European Union.

Eu symb. Chem. the element europium.

eu- /yōō/ comb. form well; easily. [Gk]

eu·ca·lyp·tus /yōōkəlíptəs/ n. (also **eu·ca·lypt** (pl. **eu·ca·lyp·ti** /-tī/ or **eu·ca·lyp·tus·es** or **eu·ca·lypts**) 1 any tree of the genus Eucalyptus, native to Australasia, cultivated for its wood and for the oil from its leaves. 2 (in full **eucalyptus oil**) this oil used as an antiseptic, etc. [mod.L f. EU- + Gk kaluptos covered f. kaluptō to cover, the unopened flower being protected by a cap]

eu·car·y·ote var. of EUKARYOTE.

eu·cha·ris /yōōkəris/ n. any bulbous plant of the genus Eucharis, native to S. America, with white umbellate flowers. [Gk eukharis pleasing (as EU-, kharis grace)]

Eu·cha·rist /yōōkərist/ n. 1 the Christian sacrament commemorating the Last Supper, in which bread and wine are consecrated and consumed. 2 the consecrated elements, esp. the bread (receive the Eucharist). □□ **Eu·cha·ris·tic** adj. **Eu·cha·ris·ti·cal** adj. [ME f. OF eucariste, ult. f. eccl.Gk eukharistia thanksgiving f. Gk eukharistos grateful (as EU-, kharizomai offer willingly)]

eu·chre /yōōkər/ n. & v. ● n. a card game for two, three, or four players. ● v.tr. 1 (in euchre) gain the advantage over (another player) when that player fails to take three tricks. 2 deceive; outwit. 3 Austral. exhaust; ruin. [19th c.: orig. unkn.]

eu·clid·e·an /yōōklídeeən/ adj. (also **Eu·clid·e·an**) of or relating to Euclid, 3rd-c. BC Alexandrian geometrician, esp. the system of geometry based on his principles. [L Euclideus f. Gk Eukleideios]

eu·clid·e·an space n. space for which euclidean geometry is valid.

eu·de·mon·ic /yōōdimónik/ adj. (also **eu·dae·mon·ic**) conducive to happiness. [Gk eudaimonikos (as EUDEMONISM)]

eu·de·mon·ism /yōōdéemənizəm/ n. (also **eu·dae·mon·ism**) a system of ethics that bases moral obligation on the likelihood of actions producing happiness. □□ **eu·de·mon·ist** n. **eu·de·mon·is·tic** adj. [Gk eudaimonismos system of happiness f. eudaimōn happy (as EU-, daimōn guardian spirit)]

eu·di·om·e·ter /yōōdeeómitər/ n. Chem. a graduated glass tube in which gases may be chemically combined by an electric spark, used to measure changes in volume of gases during chemical reactions.

□□ **eu•di•o•met•ric** /–deeəmétrik/ *adj.* **eu•di•o•met•ri•cal** *adj.* **eu•di•om•e•try** *n.* [Gk *eudios* clear (weather): orig. used to measure the amount of oxygen, thought to be greater in clear air]

eu•gen•ics /yo͞ojéniks/ *n.pl.* (also treated as *sing.*) the science of improving the (esp. human) population by controlled breeding for desirable inherited characteristics. □□ **eu•gen•ic** *adj.* **eu•gen•i•cal•ly** *adv.* **eu•gen•i•cist** /yo͞ojénisist/ *n.* **eu•ge•nist** /yo͞ójinist/ *n.*

eu•kar•y•ote /yo͞okáreeōt/ *n.* (also **eu•car•y•ote**) *Biol.* an organism consisting of a cell or cells in which the genetic material is contained within a distinct nucleus (cf. PROKARYOTE). □□ **eu•kar•y•ot•ic** /–reeótik/ *adj.* [EU- + KARYO- + –*ote* as in ZYGOTE]

eu•lo•gi•um /yo͞olójeeəm/ *n.* (*pl.* **eu•lo•gi•a** /–jeeə/ or •**ums**) = EULOGY. [med.L: see EULOGY]

eu•lo•gize /yo͞oləjīz/ *v.tr.* praise in speech or writing. □□ **eu•lo•gist** /–jist/ *n.* **eu•lo•gis•tic** *adj.* **eu•lo•gis•ti•cal•ly** *adv.*

eu•lo•gy /yo͞oləjee/ *n.* (*pl.* •**gies**) **1 a** speech or writing in praise of a person. **b** an expression of praise. **2** a funeral oration in praise of a person.

WORD HISTORY	eulogy

Late Middle English (in the sense 'high praise'): from medieval Latin *eulogium, eulogia* (from Greek *eulogia* 'praise'), apparently influenced by Latin *elogium* 'inscription on a tomb' (from Greek *elegia* 'elegy'). The current sense dates from the late 16th century.

---

eu•nuch /yo͞onək/ *n.* **1** a castrated man, esp. one formerly employed at an Oriental harem or court. **2** a person lacking effectiveness (*political eunuch*). [ME f. L *eunuchus* f. Gk *eunoukhos* lit. bedchamber attendant f. *eunē* bed + second element rel. to *ekhō* hold]

eu•on•y•mus /yo͞o-óniməs/ *n.* any tree of the genus *Euonymus*, e.g., the spindle tree. [L f. Gk *euōnumos* of lucky name (as EU-, *onoma* name)]

eu•pep•tic /yo͞opéptik/ *adj.* of or having good digestion. [Gk *eupeptos* (as EU-, *peptō* digest)]

eu•phe•mism /yo͞ofimizəm/ *n.* **1** a mild or vague expression substituted for one thought to be too harsh or direct (e.g., *pass over for die*). **2** the use of such expressions. □□ **eu•phe•mist** *n.* **eu•phe•mis•tic** *adj.* **eu•phe•mis•ti•cal•ly** *adv.* **eu•phe•mize** *v.tr. & intr.* [Gk *euphēmismos* f. *euphēmos* (as EU-, *phēmē* speaking]

eu•pho•ni•ous /yo͞ofóneeəs/ *adj.* **1** sounding pleasant; harmonious. **2** concerning euphony. □□ **eu•pho•ni•ous•ly** *adv.*

eu•pho•ni•um /yo͞ofóneeəm/ *n.* a brass wind instrument of the tuba family. [mod.L f. Gk *euphōnos* (as EUPHONY)]

eu•pho•ny /yo͞ofónee/ *n.* (*pl.* •**nies**) **1 a** pleasantness of sound, esp. of a word or phrase; harmony. **b** a pleasant sound. **2** the tendency to make a phonetic change for ease of pronunciation. □□ **eu•phon•ic** /–fónik/ *adj.* **eu•pho•nize** *v.tr.* [F *euphonie* f. LL *euphonia* f. Gk *euphōnos* (as EU-, *phōnē* sound)]

eu•phor•bi•a /yo͞ofáwrbeeə/ *n.* any plant of the genus *Euphorbia*, including spurges. [ME f. L *euphorbea* f. *Euphorbus*, 1st-c. Gk physician]

eu•pho•ri•a /yo͞ofáwreeə/ *n.* a feeling of well-being, esp. one based on overconfidence or overoptimism. □□ **eu•phor•ic** /–fáwrik, fór–/ *adj.* **eu•phor•i•cal•ly** *adv.* [Gk f. *euphoros* well-bearing (as EU-, *pherō* bear)]

eu•pho•ri•ant /yo͞ofáwreeənt/ *adj. & n.* •*adj.* inducing euphoria. •*n.* a euphoriant drug.

eu•phu•ism /yo͞ofo͞oizəm/ *n.* an affected or high-flown style of writing or speaking. □□ **eu•phu•ist** *n.* **eu•phu•is•tic** *adj.* **eu•phu•is•ti•cal•ly** *adv.* [Gk *euphuēs* well endowed by nature: orig. of writing imitating Lyly's *Euphues* (1578–80)]

Eur•a•sian /yo͞oráyzhən/ *adj. & n.* •*adj.* **1** of mixed European and Asian parentage. **2** of Europe and Asia. •*n.* a Eurasian person.

Eur•at•om /yo͞orátəm/ *n.* European Atomic Energy Community. [abbr.]

eu•re•ka /yo͞oréekə/ *int. & n.* •*int.* I have found it! (announcing a discovery, etc.). •*n.* the exultant cry of 'eureka'. [Gk *heurēka* 1st pers. sing. perfect of *heuriskō* find: attributed to Archimedes]

eu•rhyth•mic var. of EURYTHMIC.

eu•rhyth•mics var. of EURYTHMICS.

eu•ro /yo͞orō/ *n.* (*pl.* •**ros**) *Austral.* a large reddish kangaroo. [Aboriginal]

Euro- /yo͞orō/ *comb. form* Europe; European. [abbr.]

Eu•ro•com•mu•nism /yo͞orōkómyənizəm/ *n.* a form of communism in Western European countries independent of the former Soviet Communist party. □□ **Eu•ro•com•mu•nist** *adj. & n.*

Eu•ro•crat /yo͞orōkrat/ *n.* usu. *derog.* a bureaucrat in the administration of the European Community.

Eu•ro•dol•lar /yo͞orōdolər/ *n.* a dollar held in Europe or elsewhere outside the US.

Eu•ro•pe•an /yo͞orəpeeən/ *adj. & n.* •*adj.* **1** of or in Europe. **2 a** descended from natives of Europe. **b** originating in or characteristic of Europe. **3 a** happening in or extending over Europe. **b** concerning Europe as a whole rather than its individual countries. **4** of

or relating to the European Economic Community. •*n.* **1 a** a native or inhabitant of Europe. **b** a person descended from natives of Europe. **c** a white person. **2** a person concerned with European matters. □□ **Eu•ro•pe•an•ism** *n.* **Eu•ro•pe•an•ize** *v.tr. & intr.* **Eu•ro•pe•an•i•za•tion** *n.* [F *européen* f. L *europaeus* f. L *Europa* f. Gk *Eurōpē* Europe]

Eu•ro•pe•an Com•mu•ni•ty *n.* (also **European Economic Community**) an economic and political association of certain European countries as a unit with internal free trade and common external tariffs.

Eu•ro•pe•an plan *n.* a system of charging for a hotel room only without meals.

Eu•ro•pe•an U•nion *n.* name used by the European Community since November 1993.

eu•ro•pi•um /yo͞orópeeəm/ *n. Chem.* a soft, silvery metallic element of the lanthanide series, occurring naturally in small quantities. ¶ Symb.: **Eu.** [mod.L f. *Europe*]

Eu•ro•vi•sion /yo͞orōvizhən/ *n.* a network of European television production administered by the European Broadcasting Union.

eu•ryth•mic /yo͞oríthmik/ *adj.* (also **eu•rhyth•mic**) of or in harmonious proportion (esp. of architecture). [*eurhythmy* harmony of proportions f. L *eur(h)ythmia* f. Gk *eurhuthmia* (as EU-, *rhuthmos* proportion, rhythm)]

eu•ryth•mics /yo͞oríthmiks/ *n.pl.* (also treated as *sing.*) (also **eu•rhyth•mics**) harmony of bodily movement, esp. as developed with music and dance into a system of education.

Eu•sta•chian tube /yo͞ostáyshən, –keeən/ *n. Anat.* a tube leading from the pharynx to the cavity of the middle ear and equalizing the pressure on each side of the eardrum. [L *Eustachius* = B. *Eustachio*, It. anatomist d. 1574]

eu•sta•sy /yo͞ostəsee/ *n.* a change in sea level throughout the world caused by tectonic movements, melting of glaciers, etc. □□ **eu•stat•ic** /–státik/ *adj.* [back-form. f. G *eustatisch* (adj.) (as EU-, STATIC)]

eu•tec•tic /yo͞otéktik/ *adj. & n. Chem.* •*adj.* (of a mixture, alloy, etc.) having the lowest freezing point of any possible proportions of its constituents. •*n.* a eutectic mixture. [Gk *eutēktos* (as EU-, *tēkō* melt)]

eu•tec•tic point *n.* (also **eutectic temperature**) the minimum freezing point for a eutectic mixture.

eu•tha•na•sia /yo͞othənáyzhə/ *n.* **1** the bringing about of a gentle and easy death in the case of incurable and painful disease. **2** such a death. [Gk (as EU-, *thanatos* death)]

eu•troph•ic /yo͞otrófik, –trōfik/ *adj.* (of a lake, etc.) rich in nutrients and therefore supporting a dense plant population, which kills animal life by depriving it of oxygen. □□ **eu•troph•i•cate** *v.tr.* **eu•troph•i•ca•tion** *n.* **eu•tro•phy** /yo͞otrəfee/ *n.* [*eutrophy* f. Gk *eutrophia* (as EU-, *trephō* nourish)]

eV *abbr.* electronvolt.

EVA *abbr. Astronaut.* extravehicular activity.

e•vac•u•ate /iváykyo͞o-ayt/ *v.tr.* **1 a** remove (people) from a place of danger to stay elsewhere for the duration of the danger. **b** empty or leave (a place) in this way. **2** make empty (a vessel of air, etc.). **3** (of troops) withdraw from (a place). **4 a** empty (the bowels or other bodily organ). **b** discharge (feces, etc.). □□ **e•vac•u•ant** *n. & adj.* **e•vac•u•a•tion** /–áyshən/ *n.* **e•vac•u•a•tive** *adj. & n.* **e•vac•u•a•tor** *n.* [L *evacuare* (as E-, *vacuus* empty)]

e•vac•u•ee /iváykyo͞o-eé/ *n.* a person evacuated from a place of danger.

e•vade /iváyd/ *v.tr.* **1 a** escape from, avoid, esp. by guile or trickery. **b** avoid doing (one's duty, etc.). **c** avoid answering (a question) or yielding to (an argument). **2 a** fail to pay (tax due). **b** defeat the intention of (a law, etc.), esp. while complying with its letter. **3** (of a thing) elude or baffle (a person). □□ **e•vad•a•ble** *adj.* **e•vad•er** *n.* [F *évader* f. L *evadere* (as E-, *vadere* vas- go)]

e•vag•i•nate /ivájinayt/ *v.tr. Med. & Physiol.* turn (a tubular organ) inside out. □□ **e•vag•i•na•tion** /–náyshən/ *n.* [L *evaginare* (as E-, *vaginare* as VAGINA)]

e•val•u•ate /ivályo͞o-ayt/ *v.tr.* **1** assess; appraise. **2 a** find or state the number or amount of. **b** find a numerical expression for. □□ **e•val•u•a•tion** /–áyshən/ *n.* **e•val•u•a•tive** *adj.* **e•val•u•a•tor** *n.* [back-form. f. *evaluation* f. F *évaluation* f. *évaluer* (as E-, VALUE)]

ev•a•nesce /évənés/ *v.intr.* **1** fade from sight; disappear. **2** become effaced. [L *evanescere* (as E-, *vanus* empty)]

ev•a•nes•cent /évənésənt/ *adj.* (of an impression or appearance, etc.) quickly fading. □□ **ev•a•nes•cence** /–səns/ *n.* **ev•a•nes•cent•ly** *adv.*

e•van•gel /ivánjəl/ *n.* **1** *archaic* **a** the gospel. **b** any of the four Gospels. **2** a basic doctrine or set of principles. **3** = EVANGELIST. [ME f. OF *evangile* f. eccl.L *evangelium* f. Gk *euaggelion* good news (as EU-, ANGEL)]

e•van•gel•ic /éevanjélik, évən–/ *adj.* = EVANGELICAL.

e•van•gel•i•cal /éevanjélikəl, évən–/ *adj. & n.* •*adj.* **1** of or according to the teaching of the gospel or the Christian religion. **2** of the Protestant school maintaining that the doctrine of salvation by faith in the Atonement is the essence of the gospel. •*n.* a member of the evangelical school. □□ **e•van•gel•i•cal•ism** *n.* **e•van•gel•i•cal•ly** *adv.* [eccl.L *evangelicus* f. eccl.Gk *euaggelikos* (as EVANGEL)]

e•van•ge•lism /ivánjəlizəm/ *n.* **1** the preaching or promulgation of the gospel. **2** evangelicalism.

e•van•ge•list /ivánjəlist/ *n.* **1** any of the writers of the four Gospels (Matthew, Mark, Luke, John). **2** a preacher of the gospel. **3** a lay person doing missionary work.

e•van•ge•lis•tic /ivánjəlístik/ *adj.* **1** = EVANGELICAL. **2** of preachers of the gospel. **3** of the four evangelists.

e•van•ge•lize /ivánjəlīz/ *v.tr.* **1** (also *absol.*) preach the gospel to. **2** convert (a person) to Christianity. □□ **e•van•ge•li•za•tion** *n.* **e•van•ge•liz•er** *n.* [ME f. eccl.L *evangelizare* f. Gk *euaggelizomai* (as EVANGEL)]

e•vap•o•rate /ivápərayt/ *v.* **1** *intr.* turn from solid or liquid into vapor. **2** *intr. & tr.* lose or cause to lose moisture as vapor. **3** *intr. & tr.* disappear or cause to disappear (*our courage evaporated*). □□ **e•vap•o•ra•ble** *adj.* **e•vap•o•ra•tion** /–ráyshən/ *n.* **e•vap•o•ra•tive** /–vápərətiv, –raytiv/ *adj.* **e•vap•o•ra•tor** *n.* [L *evaporare* (as E–, *vapor* rare as VAPOR)]

e•vap•o•rat•ed milk *n.* milk concentrated by partial evaporation.

e•va•sion /iváyzhən/ *n.* **1** the act or a means of evading. **2** a subterfuge or a prevaricating excuse. **b** an evasive answer. [ME f. OF f. L *evasio –onis* (as EVADE)]

e•va•sive /iváysiv/ *adj.* **1** seeking to evade something. **2** not direct in one's answers, etc. **3** enabling or effecting evasion (*evasive action*). **4** (of a person) tending to evasion; habitually practicing evasion. □□ **e•va•sive•ly** *adv.* **e•va•sive•ness** *n.*

eve /eev/ *n.* **1** the evening or day before a church festival or any date or event (*Christmas Eve; the eve of the funeral*). **2** the time just before anything (*the eve of the election*). **3** *archaic* evening. [ME, = EVEN[2]]

e•vec•tion /ivékshən/ *n.* *Astron.* a perturbation of the moon's motion caused by the sun's attraction. [L *evectio* (as E–, *vehere vect*- carry)]

e•ven[1] /éevən/ *adj., adv., & v.* ● *adj.* (**e•ven•er, e•ven•est**) **1** level; flat and smooth. **2 a** uniform in quality; constant. **b** equal in number or amount or value, etc. **c** equally balanced. **3** (usu. foll. by *with*) in the same plane or line. **4** (of a person's temper, etc.) equable; calm. **5 a** (of a number such as 4, 6) divisible by two without a remainder. **b** bearing such a number (*no parking on even days*). **c** not involving fractions; exact (*in even dozens*). ● *adv.* **1** used to invite comparison of the stated assertion, negation, etc., with an implied one that is less strong or remarkable (*never even opened* [let alone read] *the letter; does he even suspect* [not to say realize] *the danger?; ran even faster* [not just as fast as before]; *even if my watch is right we shall be late* [later if it is slow]). **2** used to introduce an extreme case (*even you must realize it; it might even cost $100*). **3** (sometimes foll. by *with* or *though*) in spite of; notwithstanding (*even with the delays, we arrived on time*). ● *v.* **1** *tr. & intr.* (often foll. by *up* or *out*) make or become even. **2** *tr.* (often foll. by *to*) *archaic* treat as equal or comparable. □ **even as** at the very moment that. **even now 1** now as well as before. **2** at this very moment. **even so 1** notwithstanding that; nevertheless. **2** quite so. **3** in that case as well as in others. **get** (or **be**) **even with** have one's revenge on. **of even date** *Law & Commerce* of the same date. **on an even keel 1** (of a ship or aircraft) not listing. **2** (of a plan or person) untroubled. □□ **e•ven•ly** *adv.* **e•ven•ness** *n.* [OE *efen, efne*]

e•ven[2] /éevən/ *n.* *poet.* evening. [OE *æfen*]

e•ven break *n.* *colloq.* an equal chance.

e•ven•hand•ed /éevənhándid/ *adj.* impartial; fair. □□ **e•ven•hand•ed•ly** *adv.* **e•ven•hand•ed•ness** *n.*

eve•ning /éevning/ *n. & int.* ● *n.* **1** the end part of the day, esp. from about 6 p.m. to bedtime (*this evening; during the evening; evening meal*). **2** this time spent in a particular way (*had a lively evening*). **3** a time compared with this, esp. the last part of a person's life. ● *int.* = good evening (see GOOD *adj.* 14). [OE *æfnung*, rel. to EVEN[2]]

eve•ning dress *n.* formal dress for evening wear.

eve•ning prim•rose *n.* any plant of the genus *Oenothera* with pale yellow flowers that open in the evening.

eve•ning star *n.* a planet, esp. Venus, conspicuous in the west after sunset.

e•ven mon•ey *n.* **1** betting odds offering the gambler the chance of winning the amount he or she staked. **2** equally likely to happen or not (*it's even money he'll fail to arrive*).

e•ven•song /éevənsawng, –song/ *n.* a service of evening prayer esp. in the Anglican Church. [EVEN[2] + SONG]

e•ven-ste•ven *adj.* (or **even-Steven**) *colloq.* even; equal; level.

e•vent /ivént/ *n.* **1** a thing that happens or takes place, esp. one of importance. **2 a** the fact of a thing's occurring. **b** a result or outcome. **3** an item in a sports program, or the program as a whole. **4** *Physics* a single occurrence of a process, e.g., the ionization of one atom. **5** something on the result of which money is staked. □ **in any event** (or **at all events**) whatever happens. **in the event** as it turns (or turned) out. **in the event of** if (a specified thing) happens. **in the event that** *disp.* if it happens that. [L *eventus* f. *evenire event*- happen (as E–, *venire* come)]

e•vent•ful /ivéntfʊl/ *adj.* marked by noteworthy events. □□ **e•vent•ful•ly** *adv.* **e•vent•ful•ness** *n.*

e•vent hor•i•zon *n.* *Astron.* the gravitational boundary enclosing a black hole, from which no light escapes.

e•ven•tide /éevəntīd/ *n.* *archaic* or *poet.* = EVENING. [OE *æfentīd* (as EVEN[2], TIDE)]

e•vent•ing /ivénting/ *n.* *Brit.* participation in equestrian competitions, esp. dressage and show jumping. [EVENT 3 as in *three-day event*]

e•vent•less /ivéntlis/ *adj.* without noteworthy or remarkable events. □□ **e•vent•less•ly** *adv.*

e•ven•tu•al /ivénchōōəl/ *adj.* occurring or existing in due course or at last; ultimate. □□ **e•ven•tu•al•ly** *adv.* [as EVENT, after *actual*]

e•ven•tu•al•i•ty /ivénchōō-álitee/ *n.* (*pl.* **-ties**) a possible event or outcome.

e•ven•tu•ate /ivénchōō-ayt/ *v.intr.* *formal* **1** turn out in a specified way as the result. **2** (often foll. by *in*) result. □□ **e•ven•tu•a•tion** /–áyshən/ *n.* [as EVENT, after *actuate*]

ev•er /évər/ *adv.* **1** at all times; always (*ever hopeful; ever after*). **2** at any time (*have you ever been to Paris? nothing ever happens; as good as ever*). **3** as an emphatic word: **a** in any way; at all (*how ever did you do it?; when will they ever learn?*). **b** (prec. by *as*) in any manner possible (*be as quick as ever you can*). **4** (in *comb.*) constantly (*ever-present; ever-recurring*). **5** (foll. by *so, such*) esp. *Brit. colloq.* very; very much (*is ever so easy; was ever such a nice man; thanks ever so*). **6** (foll. by *compar.*) constantly; increasingly (*grew ever larger*). □ **did you ever?** *colloq.* did you ever hear or see the like? **ever since** throughout the period since. [OE *æfre*]

ev•er•green /évərgreen/ *adj. & n.* ● *adj.* **1** always green or fresh. **2** (of a plant) retaining green leaves throughout the year. ● *n.* an evergreen plant (cf. DECIDUOUS).

ev•er•last•ing /évərlásting/ *adj. & n.* ● *adj.* **1** lasting forever. **2** lasting for a long time, esp. so as to become unwelcome. **3** (of flowers) keeping their shape and color when dried. ● *n.* **1** eternity. **2** = IMMORTELLE. □□ **ev•er•last•ing•ly** *adv.* **ev•er•last•ing•ness** *n.*

ev•er•more /évərmáwr/ *adv.* forever; always.

e•vert /ivért/ *v.tr.* turn outward or inside out. □□ **e•ver•sion** /–vórzhən/ *n.* [L *evertere* (as E–, *vertere vers*- turn)]

eve•ry /évree/ *adj.* **1** each single (*heard every word; watched her every move*). **2** each at a specified interval in a series (*take every third one; comes every four days*). **3** all possible; the utmost degree of (*there is every prospect of success*). □ **every bit as** *colloq.* (in comparisons) quite as (*every bit as good*). **every now and again** (or **now and then**) from time to time. **every one** each one (see also EVERYONE). **every other** each second in a series (*every other day*). **every so often** at intervals; occasionally. **every time** *colloq.* **1** without exception. **2** without hesitation. **every which way** *colloq.* **1** in all directions. **2** in a disorderly manner. [OE *æfre ælc* ever each]

eve•ry•bod•y /évreebodee, –budee/ *pron.* every person.

▶**Everybody,** along with **everyone,**, traditionally used a singular pronoun of reference: *Everybody must sign his* (not *their*) *own name.* Because the use of *his* in this context is now perceived as sexist by some, a second option became popular: *Everybody must sign his or her own name.* But *his or her* is often awkward, and many feel that the plural simply makes more sense: *Everybody must sign their own name.* Although this violates logic, it is standard in British English and informal US usage. In some sentences, only *they* makes grammatical sense: *Everybody agreed to convict the defendant, and they so voted unanimously.*

eve•ry•day /évreedáy/ *adj.* **1** occurring every day. **2** suitable for or used on ordinary days. **3** commonplace; usual. **4** mundane; mediocre; inferior.

eve•ry•man /évreeman/ *n.* (also **Eve•ry•man**) the ordinary or typical human being; the "man in the street." [the principal character in a 15th-c. morality play]

eve•ry•one /évreewun/ *pron.* every person; everybody.

▶See note at EVERYBODY.

eve•ry•thing /évreething/ *pron.* **1** all things; all the things of a group or class. **2** *colloq.* a great deal (*gave me everything*). **3** an essential consideration (*speed is everything*). □ **have everything** *colloq.* possess all the desired attributes, etc.

eve•ry•where /évreehwair, évreewair/ *adv.* **1** in every place. **2** *colloq.* in many places.

▶See note at ANYWAY.

e•vict /ivíkt/ *v.tr.* expel (a tenant) from a property by legal process. □□ **e•vic•tion** /–víkshən/ *n.* **e•vic•tor** *n.* [L *evincere evict*- (as E–, *vincere* conquer)]

ev•i•dence /évidəns/ *n. & v.* ● *n.* **1** (often foll. by *for, of*) the available facts, circumstances, etc., supporting or otherwise a belief, proposition, etc., or indicating whether or not a thing is true or valid. **2** *Law* **a** information given personally or drawn from a document, etc., and tending to prove a fact or proposition. **b** statements or proofs admissible as testimony in a court of law. **3** clearness; obviousness. ● *v.tr.* be evidence of; attest. □ **call in evidence** *Law* summon (a person) as a witness. **in evidence** noticeable; conspicuous. [ME f. OF f. L *evidentia* (as EVIDENT)]

ev·i·dent /évidənt/ *adj.* **1** plain or obvious (visually or intellectually); manifest. **2** seeming; apparent (*his evident anxiety*). [ME f. OF *evident* or L *evidēre evident-* (as E-, *vidēre* see)]

ev·i·den·tial /évidénshəl/ *adj.* of or providing evidence. □□ **ev·i·den·tial·ly** *adv.*

ev·i·den·tia·ry /évidénshəree, –shee-eree/ *adj.* = EVIDENTIAL.

ev·i·dent·ly /évidəntlee, –déntlee/ *adv.* **1** as shown by evidence. **2** seemingly; as it appears (*was evidently unwilling to go*).

e·vil /ēevəl/ *adj. & n. • adj.* **1** morally bad; wicked. **2** harmful or tending to harm, esp. intentionally or characteristically. **3** disagreeable or unpleasant (*has an evil temper*). **4** unlucky; causing misfortune (*evil days*). *• n.* **1** an evil thing; an instance of something evil. **2** evil quality; wickedness; harm. □ **speak evil of** slander. □□ **e·vil·ly** *adv.* **e·vil·ness** *n.* [OE *yfel* f. Gmc]

e·vil·do·er /ēevəldōoər/ *n.* a person who does evil. □□ **e·vil·do·ing** *n.*

e·vil eye *n.* a gaze or stare superstitiously believed to be able to cause material harm.

e·vil-mind·ed *adj.* having evil intentions.

e·vince /ivíns/ *v.tr.* **1** indicate or make evident. **2** show that one has (a quality). □□ **e·vin·ci·ble** *adj.* **e·vin·cive** *adj.* [L *evincere*: see EVICT]

e·vis·cer·ate /ivísərayt/ *v.tr. formal* **1** disembowel. **2** empty or deprive of essential contents. □□ **e·vis·cer·a·tion** /–ráyshən/ *n.* [L *eviscerare* *eviscerat-* (as E-, VISCERA)]

e·voc·a·tive /ivókətiv/ *adj.* tending to evoke (esp. feelings or memories). □□ **e·voc·a·tive·ly** *adv.* **e·voc·a·tive·ness** *n.*

e·voke /ivók/ *v.tr.* **1** inspire or draw forth (memories, feelings, a response, etc.). **2** summon (a supposed spirit from the dead). □□ **ev·o·ca·tion** /évəkáyshən, eevō–/ *n.* **e·vok·er** *n.* [L *evocare* as E-, *vocare* call)]

ev·o·lute /évəlōot/ *n.* (in full **evolute curve**) *Math.* a curve which is the locus of the centers of curvature of another curve that is its involute. [L *evolutus* past part. (as EVOLVE)]

ev·o·lu·tion /évəlōoshən/ *n.* **1** gradual development, esp. from a simple to a more complex form. **2** a process by which species develop from earlier forms, as an explanation of their origins. **3** the appearance or presentation of events, etc., in due succession (*the evolution of the plot*). **4** a change in the disposition of troops or ships. **5** the giving off or evolving of gas, heat, etc. **6** an opening out. **7** the unfolding of a curve. **8** *Math.* the extraction of a root from any given power (cf. INVOLUTION). □□ **ev·o·lu·tion·al** *adj.* **ev·o·lu·tion·al·ly** *adv.* **ev·o·lu·tion·ar·y** *adj.* **ev·o·lu·tion·ar·i·ly** *adv.* [L *evolutio* unrolling (as EVOLVE)]

ev·o·lu·tion·ist /évəlōoshənist/ *n.* a person who believes in evolution as explaining the origin of species. □□ **ev·o·lu·tion·ism** *n.* **ev·o·lu·tion·is·tic** /–nístik/ *adj.*

e·volve /ivólv/ *v.* **1** *intr. & tr.* develop gradually by a natural process. **2** *tr.* work out or devise (a theory, plan, etc.). **3** *intr. & tr.* unfold; open out. **4** *tr.* give off (gas, heat, etc.). □□ **e·volv·a·ble** *adj.* **e·volve·ment** *n.* [L *evolvere* *evolut-* (as E-, *volvere* roll)]

ev·zone /évzōn/ *n.* a member of a select Greek infantry regiment. [mod. Gk *euzōnos* f. Gk, = dressed for exercise (as EU-, *zōnē* belt)]

ewe /yōo/ *n.* a female sheep. [OE *ēowu* f. Gmc]

ewe-necked *adj.* (of a horse) having a thin concave neck.

ew·er /yōoər/ *n.* a large pitcher or water jug with a wide mouth. [ME f. ONF *eviere*, OF *aiguiere*, ult. f. L *aquarius* of water f. *aqua* water]

ex¹ /eks/ *prep.* **1** (of goods) sold from (*ex factory*). **2** (of stocks or shares) without; excluding. [L, = out of]

ex² /eks/ *n. colloq.* a former husband or wife. [absol. use of EX-¹ 2]

ex-¹ /eks/ *prefix* (also **e-** before some consonants, **ef-** before *f*) **1** forming verbs meaning: **a** out; forth (*exclude*; *exit*). **b** upward (*extol*). **c** thoroughly (*excruciate*). **d** bring into a state (*exasperate*). **e** remove or free from (*expatriate*; *exonerate*). **2** forming nouns from titles of office, status, etc., meaning 'formerly' (*ex-convict*; *ex-president*; *ex-wife*). [L f. *ex* out of]

▶Use **ex** when you're talking about the person who immediately precedes the current holder of a position (*the company's ex-president*; *her ex-husband*). Use **former** when talking about everyone who held the position earlier than the **ex** (*my ex-wife is very friendly with my two former wives*).

ex-² /eks/ *prefix* out (*exodus*). [Gk f. *ex* out of]

exa- /éksə/ *comb. form* denoting a factor of 10^{18}. [perh. f. HEXA-]

ex·ac·er·bate /igzásərbayt/ *v.tr.* **1** make (pain, anger, etc.) worse. **2** irritate (a person). □□ **ex·ac·er·ba·tion** /–báyshən/ *n.* [L *exacerbare* (as EX-¹, *acerbus* bitter)]

ex·act /igzákt/ *adj. & v. • adj.* **1** accurate; correct in all details (*an exact description*). **2 a** precise. **b** (of a person) tending to precision. *• v.tr.* (often foll. by *from, of*) **1** demand and enforce payment of (money, fees, etc.) from a person. **2 a** demand; insist on. **b** (of circumstances) require urgently. □□ **ex·act·a·ble** *adj.* **ex·ac·ti·tude** *n.* **ex·act·ness** *n.* **ex·ac·tor** *n.* [L *exigere exact-* (as EX-¹, *agere* drive)]

ex·act·ing /igzákting/ *adj.* **1** making great demands. **2** calling for much effort. □□ **ex·act·ing·ly** *adv.* **ex·act·ing·ness** *n.*

ex·ac·tion /igzákshən/ *n.* **1** the act or an instance of exacting; the process of being exacted. **2 a** an illegal or exorbitant demand; an extortion. **b** a sum or thing exacted. [ME f. L *exactio* (as EXACT)]

ex·act·ly /igzáktlee/ *adv.* **1** accurately; precisely; in an exact manner (*worked it out exactly*). **2** in exact terms (*exactly when did it happen?*). **3** (said in reply) quite so; I quite agree. **4** just; in all respects. □ **not exactly** *colloq.* **1** by no means. **2** not precisely.

ex·act sci·ence *n.* a science admitting of absolute or quantitative precision.

ex·ag·ger·ate /igzájərayt/ *v.tr.* **1** (also *absol.*) give an impression of (a thing), esp. in speech or writing, that makes it seem larger or greater, etc., than it really is. **2** enlarge or alter beyond normal or due proportions (*spoke with exaggerated politeness*). □□ **ex·ag·ger·at·ed·ly** *adv.* **ex·ag·ger·at·ing·ly** *adv.* **ex·ag·ger·a·tion** /–ráyshən/ *n.* **ex·ag·ger·a·tive** *adj.* **ex·ag·ger·a·tor** *n.*

WORD HISTORY   exaggerate

Mid-16th century: from Latin *exaggerat-* 'heaped up,' from the verb *exaggerare*, from *ex-* 'thoroughly' + *aggerare* 'heap up' (from *agger* 'heap'). The word originally meant 'pile up, accumulate,' later 'intensify praise or blame,' 'dwell on a virtue or fault,' giving rise to current senses.

---

ex·alt /igzáwlt/ *v.tr.* **1** raise in rank or power, etc. **2** praise highly. **3** (usu. as **exalted** *adj.*) **a** make lofty or noble (*exalted aims*; *an exalted style*). **b** make rapturously excited. **4** (as **exalted** *adj.*) elevated in rank or character; eminent; celebrated. **5** stimulate (a faculty, etc.) to greater activity; intensify; heighten. □□ **ex·alt·ed·ly** *adv.* **ex·alt·ed·ness** *n.* **ex·alt·er** *n.* [ME f. L *exaltare* (as EX-¹, *altus* high)]

ex·al·ta·tion /égzawltáyshən/ *n.* **1** the act or an instance of exalting; the state of being exalted. **2** elation; rapturous emotion. [ME f. OF *exaltation* or LL *exaltatio* (as EXALT)]

ex·am /igzám/ *n.* = EXAMINATION 3.

ex·am·i·na·tion /igzámináyshən/ *n.* **1** the act or an instance of examining; the state of being examined. **2** a detailed inspection. **3** the testing of the proficiency or knowledge of students or other candidates for a qualification by oral or written questions. **4** an instance of examining or being examined medically. **5** *Law* the formal questioning of the accused or of a witness in court. □□ **ex·am·i·na·tion·al** *adj.* [ME f. OF f. L *examinatio –onis* (as EXAMINE)]

ex·am·ine /igzámin/ *v.* **1** *tr.* inquire into the nature or condition, etc., of. **2** *tr.* look closely or analytically at. **3** *tr.* test the proficiency of, esp. by examination (see EXAMINATION 3). **4** *tr.* check the health of (a patient) by inspection or experiment. **5** *tr.* *Law* formally question (the accused or a witness) in court. **6** *intr.* (foll. by *into*) inquire. □□ **ex·am·in·a·ble** *adj.* **ex·am·in·ee** /–née/ *n.* **ex·am·in·er** *n.* [ME f. OF *examiner* f. L *examinare* weigh, test f. *examen* tongue of a balance, ult. f. *exigere* examine, weigh: see EXACT]

ex·am·ple /igzámpəl/ *n. & v. • n.* **1** a thing characteristic of its kind or illustrating a general rule. **2** a person, thing, or piece of conduct, regarded in terms of its fitness to be imitated (*must set him an example*; *you are a bad example*). **3** a circumstance or treatment seen as a warning to others; a person so treated (*shall make an example of you*). **4** a problem or exercise designed to illustrate a rule. *• v.tr.* (usu. in *passive*) serve as an example of. □ **for example** by way of illustration. [ME f. OF f. L *exemplum* (as EXEMPT)]

ex·an·i·mate /igzánimət/ *adj.* **1** dead; lifeless (esp. in appearance); inanimate. **2** lacking animation or courage. [L *exanimatus* past part. of *exanimare* deprive of life, f. EX-¹ + *anima* breath of life]

ex·an·the·ma /éksanthéemə, égzan–/ *n. Med.* a skin rash accompanying any eruptive disease or fever. [LL f. Gk *exanthēma* eruption f. *exantheō* (as EX-², *anthos* blossom)]

ex·arch /éksaark/ *n.* in the Orthodox Church, a bishop lower in rank than a patriarch and having jurisdiction wider than the metropolitan of a diocese. □□ **ex·ar·chate** *n.* [eccl.L f. Gk *exarkhos* (as EX-², *arkhos* ruler)]

ex·as·per·ate /igzáaspərayt/ *v.tr.* **1** (often as **exasperated** *adj.* or **exasperating** *adj.*) irritate intensely; infuriate; enrage. **2** make (a pain, ill feeling, etc.) worse. □□ **ex·as·per·at·ed·ly** *adv.* **ex·as·per·at·ing·ly** *adv.* **ex·as·per·a·tion** /–ráyshən/ *n.* [L *exasperare exasperat-* (as EX-¹, *asper* rough)]

ex ca·the·dra /éks kəthéedrə/ *adj. & adv.* with full authority (esp. of a papal pronouncement, implying infallibility as doctrinally defined). [L, = from the (teacher's) chair]

ex·ca·vate /ékskəvayt/ *v.tr.* **1 a** make (a hole or channel) by digging. **b** dig out material from (the ground). **2** reveal or extract by digging. **3** (also *absol.*) *Archaeol.* dig systematically into the ground to explore (a site). □□ **ex·ca·va·tion** /–váyshən/ *n.* **ex·ca·va·tor** *n.* [L *excavare* (as EX-¹, *cavus* hollow)]

ex·ceed /ikseéd/ *v.tr.* **1** (often foll. by *by* an amount) be more or greater than (in number, extent, etc.). **2** go beyond or do more than is warranted by (a set limit, esp. of one's instructions or rights). **3** surpass; excel (a person or achievement). [ME f. OF *exceder* f. L *excedere* (as EX-¹, *cedere cess-* go)]

ex·ceed·ing /ikseéding/ *adj. & adv. • adj.* **1** surpassing in amount or degree. **2** preeminent. *• adv. archaic* = EXCEEDINGLY 2.

ex·ceed·ing·ly /ikseéding-lee/ adv. **1** very; to a great extent. **2** surpassingly; preeminently.

ex·cel /iksél/ v. (**ex·celled, ex·cel·ling**) (often foll. by in, at) **1** tr. be superior to. **2** intr. be preeminent or the most outstanding (excels at games). □ **excel oneself** Brit. surpass one's previous performance. [ME f. L excellere (as EX-¹, celsus lofty)]

ex·cel·lence /éksələns/ n. **1** the state of excelling; surpassing merit or quality. **2** the activity, etc., in which a person excels. [ME f. OF excellence or L excellentia (as EXCEL)]

Ex·cel·len·cy /éksələnsee/ n. (pl. **·cies**) (usu. prec. by Your, His, Her, Their) a title used in addressing or referring to certain high officials, e.g., ambassadors and governors, and (in some countries) senior church dignitaries. [ME f. L excellentia (as EXCEL)]

ex·cel·lent /éksələnt/ adj. extremely good; preeminent. □□ **ex·cel·lent·ly** adv. [ME f. OF (as EXCEL)]

ex·cel·si·or /iksélseeэr/ int. & n. • int. higher; outstanding (esp. as a motto or trademark). • n. soft wood shavings used for stuffing, packing, etc. [L, compar. of excelsus lofty]

ex·cept /iksépt/ v., prep., & conj. • v.tr. (often as **excepted** adj. placed after object) exclude from a general statement, condition, etc. (excepted him from the amnesty; present company excepted). • prep. (often foll. by for or that) not including; other than (all failed except her; all here except for John; is all right except that it is too long). • conj. archaic unless (except he be born again). [ME f. L excipere except- (as EX-¹, capere take)]

▶See note at ACCEPT.

ex·cept·ing /iksépting/ prep. & conj. • prep. = EXCEPT prep. • conj. archaic = EXCEPT conj.

ex·cep·tion /iksépshən/ n. **1** the act or an instance of excepting; the state of being excepted (made an exception in my case). **2** a thing that has been or will be excepted. **3** an instance that does not follow a rule. □ **take exception** (often foll. by to) object; be resentful (about). **with the exception of** except; not including. [ME f. OF f. L exceptio –onis (as EXCEPT)]

ex·cep·tion·a·ble /iksépshənəbəl/ adj. open to objection. □□ **ex·cep·tion·a·bly** adv.

▶Exceptionable means 'open to objection,' e.g., There was nothing exceptionable in the evidence, and is usually found in negative contexts. It is sometimes confused with the much more common exceptional, meaning 'unusual, outstanding.'

ex·cep·tion·al /iksépshənəl/ adj. **1** forming an exception. **2** unusual; not typical (exceptional circumstances). **3** unusually good; outstanding. □□ **ex·cep·tion·al·i·ty** /–nálitee/ n. **ex·cep·tion·al·ly** adv.

▶See note at EXCEPTIONABLE.

ex·cerpt n. & v. • n. /éksərpt/ a short extract from a book, motion picture, piece of music, etc. • v.tr. /iksérpt/ (also absol.) **1** take an excerpt or excerpts from (a book, etc.). **2** take (an extract) from a book, etc. □□ **ex·cerpt·i·ble** adj. **ex·cerp·tion** /–sórpshən/ n. [L excerpere excerpt- (as EX-¹, carpere pluck)]

ex·cess /iksés, ékses/ n. & adj. • n. **1** the state or an instance of exceeding. **2** the amount by which one quantity or number exceeds another. **3** exceeding of a proper or permitted limit. **4 a** the overstepping of the accepted limits of moderation, esp. intemperance in eating or drinking. **b** (in pl.) outrageous or immoderate behavior. **5** an extreme or improper degree or extent (an excess of cruelty). **6** part of an insurance claim to be paid by the insured, esp. by prior agreement. • attrib.adj. usu. /ékses/ **1** that exceeds a limited or prescribed amount (excess weight). **2** required as extra payment (excess postage). □ **in** (or **to**) **excess** exceeding the proper amount or degree. **in excess of** more than; exceeding. [ME f. OF exces f. L excessus (as EXCEED)]

ex·cess bag·gage n. **1** exceeding a weight allowance and liable to an extra charge. **2** something unnecessary and burdensome.

ex·ces·sive /iksésiv/ adj. **1** too much or too great. **2** more than what is normal or necessary. □□ **ex·ces·sive·ly** adv. **ex·ces·sive·ness** n.

ex·change /ikscháynj/ n. & v. • n. **1** the act or an instance of giving one thing and receiving another in its place. **2 a** the giving of money for its equivalent in the money of the same or another country. **b** the fee or percentage charged for this. **3** the central telephone office of a district, where connections are effected. **4** a place where merchants, bankers, etc., gather to transact business. **5 a** an office where certain information is given or a service provided, usu. involving two parties. **b** an employment office. **6** a system of settling debts between persons (esp. in different countries) without the use of money, by bills of exchange (see BILL¹). **7 a** a short conversation, esp. a disagreement or quarrel. **b** a sequence of letters between correspondents. **8** Chess the capture of an important piece (esp. a rook) by one player at the loss of a minor piece to the opposing player. **9** (attrib.) forming part of an exchange, e.g., of personnel between institutions (an exchange student). • v. **1** tr. (often foll. by for) give or receive (one thing) in place of another. **2** tr. give and receive as equivalents (e.g., things or people, blows, information, etc.); give one and receive another of. **3** intr. (often foll. by with) make an exchange. □ **in exchange** (often foll. by for) as a thing exchanged (for). □□ **ex·change·a·ble** adj. **ex·change·a·bil·i·ty** n. **ex·chang·er** n. [ME f. OF eschangier f. Rmc (as EX-¹, CHANGE)]

ex·change rate n. the value of one currency in terms of another.

ex·cheq·uer /ikschékər/ n. **1** Brit. the former government department in charge of national revenue. **2** a royal or national treasury. **3** the money of a private individual or group. [ME f. AF escheker, OF eschequier f. med.L scaccarium chessboard (its orig. sense, with ref. to keeping accounts on a checkered cloth)]

▶The functions of the government department in the United Kingdom (sense 1) now belong to the Treasury, although the name formally survives, esp. in the title Chancellor of the Exchequer.

ex·cise¹ /éksīz/ n. & v. • n. **1** a duty or tax levied on goods and commodities produced or sold within the country of origin. **2** a tax levied on certain licenses. • v.tr. **1** charge excise on (goods). **2** force (a person) to pay excise. [MDu. excijs, accijs, perh. f. Rmc: rel. to CENSUS]

ex·cise² /iksíz/ v.tr. **1** remove (a passage of a book, etc.). **2** cut out (an organ, etc.) by surgery. □□ **ex·ci·sion** /iksízhən/ n. [L excidere excis- (as EX-¹, caedere cut)]

ex·cise·man /éksīzmən/ n. (pl. **·men**) Brit. hist. an officer responsible for collecting excise duty.

ex·cit·a·ble /iksítəbəl/ adj. **1** (esp. of a person) easily excited. **2** (of an organism, tissue, etc.) responding to a stimulus, or susceptible to stimulation. □□ **ex·cit·a·bil·i·ty** n. **ex·cit·a·bly** adv.

ex·ci·ta·tion /éksitáyshən/ n. **1 a** the act or an instance of exciting. **b** the state of being excited; excitement. **2** the action of an organism, tissue, etc., resulting from stimulation. **3** Electr. **a** the process of applying current to the winding of an electromagnet to produce a magnetic field. **b** the process of applying a signal voltage to the control electrode of an electron tube or the base of a transistor. **4** Physics the process in which an atom, etc., acquires a higher energy state.

ex·cite /iksít/ v.tr. **1 a** rouse the feelings or emotions of (a person). **b** bring into play; rouse up (feelings, faculties, etc.). **c** arouse sexually. **2** provoke; bring about (an action or active condition). **3** promote the activity of (an organism, tissue, etc.) by stimulus. **4** Electr. **a** cause (a current) to flow in the winding of an electromagnet. **b** supply a signal. **5** Physics **a** cause the emission of (a spectrum). **b** cause (a substance) to emit radiation. **c** put (an atom, etc.) into a state of higher energy. □□ **ex·cit·ant** /éksit'nt, iksít'nt/ adj. & n. **ex·ci·ta·tive** /–tətiv/ adj. **ex·ci·ta·to·ry** /–tətawree/ adj. **ex·cit·ed·ly** adv. **ex·cit·ed·ness** n. **ex·cite·ment** n. **ex·cit·er** n. (esp. in senses 4, 5). [ME f. OF exciter or L excitare frequent. of exciēre (as EX-¹, ciēre set in motion)]

ex·cit·ing /iksíting/ adj. arousing great interest or enthusiasm; stirring. □□ **ex·cit·ing·ly** adv. **ex·cit·ing·ness** n.

ex·ci·ton /eksíton, éksiton/ n. Physics a combination of an electron with a hole in a crystalline solid. [EXCITATION + –ON]

ex·claim /ikskláym/ v. **1** intr. cry out suddenly, esp. in anger, surprise, pain, etc. **2** tr. (foll. by that) utter by exclaiming. [F exclamer or L exclamare (as EX-¹: cf. CLAIM)]

ex·cla·ma·tion /ékskləmáyshən/ n. **1** the act or an instance of exclaiming. **2** words exclaimed; a strong sudden cry. [ME f. OF exclamation or L exclamatio (as EXCLAIM)]

ex·cla·ma·tion point n. (also esp. Brit. **exclamation mark**) a punctuation mark (| ! |) indicating an exclamation.

ex·clam·a·to·ry /iksklámətawree/ adj. of or serving as an exclamation.

ex·clave /éksklayv/ n. a portion of territory of one country completely surrounded by territory of another or others, as viewed by the home territory (cf. ENCLAVE). [EX-¹ + ENCLAVE]

ex·clo·sure /iksklózhər/ n. Forestry, etc., an area from which unwanted animals are excluded. [EX-¹ + ENCLOSURE]

ex·clude /iksklōōd/ v.tr. **1** shut or keep out (a person or thing) from a place, group, privilege, etc. **2** expel and shut out. **3** remove from consideration (no theory can be excluded). **4** prevent the occurrence of; make impossible (excluded all doubt). □□ **ex·clud·a·ble** adj. **ex·clud·er** n. [ME f. L excludere exclus- (as EX-¹, claudere shut)]

ex·clud·ed mid·dle n. Logic the principle that of two contradictory propositions one must be true.

ex·clu·sion /iksklōōzhən/ n. the act or an instance of excluding; the state of being excluded. □ **to the exclusion of** so as to exclude. □□ **ex·clu·sion·ar·y** adj. [L exclusio (as EXCLUDE)]

ex·clu·sion·ist /iksklōōzhənist/ adj. & n. • adj. favoring exclusion, esp. from rights or privileges. • n. a person favoring exclusion.

ex·clu·sion prin·ci·ple n. Physics see PAULI EXCLUSION PRINCIPLE.

ex·clu·sive /iksklōōsiv/ adj. & n. • adj. **1** excluding other things. **2** (predic.; foll. by of) not including; except for. **3** tending to exclude others, esp. socially; select. **4** catering for few or select customers; high-class. **5 a** (of a commodity) not obtainable elsewhere. **b** (of a newspaper article) not published elsewhere. **6** (predic.; foll. by to) restricted or limited to; existing or available only in. **7** (of terms, etc.) excluding all but what is specified. **8** employed or followed or held to the exclusion of all else (my exclusive occupation; exclusive *rights*). ● *n.* an article or story published by only one newspaper or periodical. □□ **ex•clu•sive•ly** *adv.* **ex•clu•sive•ness** *n.* **ex•clu•siv•i•ty** /ékskloosívitee/ *n.* [med.L *exclusivus* (as EXCLUDE)]

ex•cog•i•tate /ekskójitayt/ *v.tr.* think out; contrive. □□ **ex•cog•i•ta•tion** /–táyshən/ *n.* [L *excogitare excogitat-* (as EX-¹, *cogitare* COGITATE)]

ex•com•mu•ni•cate *v., adj., & n. Eccl.* ● *v.tr.* /ékskəmyóōnikayt/ officially exclude (a person) from participation in the sacraments, or from formal communion with the church. ● *adj.* /ékskəmyóōnikət/ excommunicated. ● *n.* /ékskəmyóōnikət/ an excommunicated person. □□ **ex•com•mu•ni•ca•tion** /–káyshən/ *n.* **ex•com•mu•ni•ca•tive** /–kətiv, –kaytiv/ *adj.* **ex•com•mu•ni•ca•tor** *n.* **ex•com•mu•ni•ca•to•ry** /–kətáwree/ *adj.* [L *excommunicare –atus* (as EX-¹, *communis* COMMON)]

ex-con /ékskón/ *n. colloq.* an ex-convict; a former inmate of a prison. [abbr.]

ex•co•ri•ate /ekskáwreeayt/ *v.tr.* **1 a** remove part of the skin of (a person, etc.) by abrasion. **b** strip or peel off (skin). **2** censure severely. □□ **ex•co•ri•a•tion** /–áyshən/ *n.* [L *excoriare excoriat-* (as EX-¹, *corium* hide)]

ex•cre•ment /ékskrimənt/ *n.* (in *sing.* or *pl.*) feces. □□ **ex•cre•men•tal** /–mént'l/ *adj.* [F *excrément* or L *excrementum* (as EXCRETE)]

ex•cres•cence /ikskrésəns/ *n.* **1** an abnormal or morbid outgrowth on the body or a plant. **2** an ugly addition. □□ **ex•cres•cent** /–sənt/ *adj.* **ex•cres•cen•tial** /ékskrisénshəl/ *adj.* [L *excrescentia* (as EX-¹, *crescere* grow)]

ex•cre•ta /ikskréetə/ *n.pl.* waste discharged from the body, esp. feces and urine. [L neut. pl.: see EXCRETE]

ex•crete /ikskréet/ *v.tr.* (also *absol.*) (of an animal or plant) separate and expel (waste matter) as a result of metabolism. □□ **ex•cret•er** *n.* **ex•cre•tion** /–kréeshən/ *n.* **ex•cre•tive** *adj.* **ex•cre•to•ry** /ékskrətáwree/ *adj.* [L *excernere excret-* (as EX-¹, *cernere* sift)]

ex•cru•ci•ate /ikskróōsheeayt/ *v.tr.* (esp. as **excruciating** *adj.*) torment acutely (a person's senses); torture mentally. □□ **ex•cru•ci•at•ing•ly** *adv.* **ex•cru•ci•a•tion** /–sheeáyshən/ *n.* [L *excruciare excruciat-* (as EX-¹, *cruciare* torment f. *crux crucis* cross)]

ex•cul•pate /ékskulpayt, ikskúl–/ *v.tr. formal* **1** free from blame. **2** (foll. by *from*) clear (a person) of a charge. □□ **ex•cul•pa•tion** /–páyshən/ *n.* **ex•cul•pa•to•ry** /–kúlpətáwree/ *adj.* [med.L *exculpare exculpat-* (as EX-¹, *culpa* blame)]

ex•cur•sion /ikskə́rzhən/ *n.* **1** a short journey or ramble for pleasure, with return to the starting point. **2** a digression. **3** *Astron.* a deviation from a regular path. **4** *archaic* a sortie (see ALARUM). □□ **ex•cur•sion•al** *adj.* **ex•cur•sion•ar•y** *adj.* **ex•cur•sion•ist** *n.* [L *excursio* f. *excurrere excurs-* (as EX-¹, *currere* run)]

ex•cur•sive /ikskə́rsiv/ *adj.* digressive; diverse. □□ **ex•cur•sive•ly** *adv.* **ex•cur•sive•ness** *n.*

ex•cur•sus /ikskə́rsəs/ *n.* **1** a detailed discussion of a special point in a book, usu. in an appendix. **2** a digression in a narrative. [L, verbal noun formed as EXCURSION]

ex•cuse *v. & n.* ● *v.tr.* /ikskyóōz/ **1** attempt to lessen the blame attaching to (a person, act, or fault). **2** (of a fact or circumstance) serve in mitigation of (a person or act). **3** obtain exemption for (a person or oneself). **4** (foll. by *from*) release (a person) from a duty, etc. (*excused from kitchen duties*). **5** overlook or forgive (a fault or offense). **6** (foll. by *for*) forgive (a person) for a fault. **7** not insist upon (what is due). **8** *refl.* apologize for leaving. ● *n.* /ikskyóōs/ **1** a reason put forward to mitigate or justify an offense, fault, etc. **2** an apology (*made my excuses*). **3** (foll. by *for*) a poor or inadequate example of. **4** the action of excusing; indulgence; pardon. □ **be excused** be allowed to leave a room, etc., e.g., to go to the bathroom. **excuse me** a polite apology for lack of ceremony, for an interruption, etc., or for disagreeing. □□ **ex•cus•a•ble** /–kyóōzəbəl/ *adj.* **ex•cus•a•bly** *adv.* **ex•cus•a•to•ry** /–kyóōzətáwree/ *adj.* [ME f. OF *escuser* f. L *excusare* (as EX-¹, *causa* CAUSE, accusation)]

ex-di•rec•to•ry /éksdiréktəree, –dī–/ *adj. Brit.* not listed in a telephone directory, at the wish of the subscriber.

ex div. *abbr.* ex dividend.

ex div•i•dend /eks dívidend/ *adj. & adv.* (of stocks or shares) exclusive of dividend; not including the previously announced dividend.

ex•e•at /ékseeat/ *n.* **1** *Brit.* permission granted to a student by a college for temporary absence. **2** permission granted to a priest by a bishop to move to another diocese. [L, 3rd sing. pres. subjunctive of *exire* go out (as EX-¹, *ire* go)]

ex•ec /igzék/ *n.* an executive. [abbr.]

ex•e•cra•ble /éksikrəbəl/ *adj.* abominable; detestable. □□ **ex•e•cra•bly** *adv.* [ME f. OF f. L *execrabilis* (as EXECRATE)]

ex•e•crate /éksikrayt/ *v.* **1** *tr.* express or feel abhorrence for. **2** *tr.* curse (a person or thing). **3** *intr.* utter curses. □□ **ex•e•cra•tion** /–kráyshən/ *n.* **ex•e•cra•tive** *adj.* **ex•e•cra•to•ry** /–krətáwree/ *adj.* [L *exsecrare* (as EX-¹), *sacrare* devote f. *sacer* sacred, accursed)]

ex•ec•u•tant /igzékyətənt/ *n. formal* **1** a performer, esp. of music. **2** one who carries something into effect. [F *exécutant* pres. part. (as EXECUTE)]

ex•e•cute /éksikyōot/ *v.tr.* **1 a** carry out a sentence of death on (a condemned person). **b** kill as a political act. **2** carry into effect; perform (a plan, duty, command, operation, etc.). **3 a** carry out a design for (a product of art or skill). **b** perform (a musical composition, dance, etc.). **4** make (a legal instrument) valid by signing, sealing, etc. **5** put into effect (a judicial sentence, the terms of a will, etc.). □□ **ex•e•cut•a•ble** *adj.* [ME f. OF *executer* f. med.L *executare* f. L *exsequi exsecut-* (as EX-¹, *sequi* follow)]

ex•e•cu•tion /éksikyóōshən/ *n.* **1** the carrying out of a sentence of death. **2** the act or an instance of carrying out or performing something. **3** technique or style of performance in the arts, esp. music. **4 a** seizure of the property or person of a debtor in default of payment. **b** a judicial writ enforcing a judgment. □□ **ex•e•cu•tion•ar•y** *adj.* [ME f. OF f. L *executio –onis* (as EXECUTE)]

ex•e•cu•tion•er /éksikyóōshənər/ *n.* an official who carries out a sentence of death.

ex•ec•u•tive /igzékyətiv/ *n. & adj.* ● *n.* **1** a person or body with managerial or administrative responsibility in a business organization, etc.; a senior businessman. **2** a branch of a government or organization concerned with executing laws, agreements, etc., or with other administration or management. ● *adj.* **1** concerned with executing laws, agreements, etc., or with other administration or management. **2** relating to or having the function of executing. □□ **ex•ec•u•tive•ly** *adv.* [med.L *executivus* (as EXECUTE)]

ex•ec•u•tive coun•cil *n.* **1** a council with executive authority. **2** a council that advises the head of government.

ex•ec•u•tive of•fi•cer *n.* **1** *Mil.* an officer second in command. **2** (in a corporation, organization, etc.) one with executive duties.

ex•ec•u•tive ses•sion *n.* a usu. private meeting of a legislative body for executive business.

ex•ec•u•tor /igzékyətər/ *n.* (*fem.* **ex•ec•u•trix** /–triks/, *pl.* •**trices** /–tríseez/ or •**trixes**) a person appointed by a testator to carry out the terms of his or her will. □□ **ex•ec•u•to•ri•al** /–táwreeəl/ *adj.* **ex•ec•u•tor•ship** *n.* **ex•ec•u•to•ry** *adj.* [ME f. AF *executor, –our* f. L *executor –oris* (as EXECUTE)]

ex•e•ge•sis /éksijéesis/ *n.* (*pl.* **ex•e•ge•ses** /–seez/) critical explanation of a text, esp. of Scripture. □□ **ex•e•gete** /éksijeet/ *n.* **ex•e•get•ic** /–jétik/ *adj.* **ex•e•get•i•cal** *adj.* **ex•e•get•ist** /–jétist/ *n.* [Gk *exēgēsis* f. *exēgeomai* interpret (as EX-², *hēgeomai* lead)]

ex•em•plar /igzémplər, –plaar/ *n.* **1** a model or pattern. **2** a typical instance of a class of things. **3** a parallel instance. [ME f. OF *exemplaire* f. LL *exemplarium* (as EXAMPLE)]

ex•em•pla•ry /igzémploree/ *adj.* **1** fit to be imitated; outstandingly good. **2 a** serving as a warning. **b** *Law* (of damages) exceeding the amount needed for simple compensation. **3** illustrative; representative. □□ **ex•em•pla•ri•ly** *adv.* **ex•em•pla•ri•ness** *n.* [LL *exemplaris* (as EXAMPLE)]

ex•em•pli•fy /igzémplifī/ *v.tr.* (•**fies**, •**fied**) **1** illustrate by example. **2** be an example of. **3** *Law* make an attested copy of (a document) under an official seal. □□ **ex•em•pli•fi•ca•tion** /–fikáyshən/ *n.* [ME f. med.L *exemplificare* (as EXAMPLE)]

ex•em•plum /igzémpləm/ *n.* (*pl.* **ex•em•pla** /–plə/) an example or model, esp. a moralizing or illustrative story. [L: see EXAMPLE]

ex•empt /igzémpt/ *adj., n., & v.* ● *adj.* **1** free from an obligation or liability, etc., imposed on others. **2** (foll. by *from*) not liable to. ● *n.* a person who is exempt, esp. from payment of tax. ● *v.tr.* (usu. foll. by *from*) free from an obligation, esp. one imposed on others. □□ **ex•emp•tion** /–zémpshən/ *n.* [ME f. L *exemptus* past part. of *eximere exempt-* (as EX-¹, *emere* take)]

ex•e•quies /éksikweez/ *n.pl. formal* funeral rites. [ME f. OF f. L *exsequiae* (as EX-¹, *sequi* follow)]

ex•er•cise /éksərsīz/ *n. & v.* ● *n.* **1** activity requiring physical effort, done esp. as training or to sustain or improve health. **2** mental or spiritual activity, esp. as practice to develop a skill. **3** (often in *pl.*) a particular task or set of tasks devised as exercise, practice in a technique, etc. **4 a** the use or application of a mental faculty, right, etc. **b** practice of an ability, quality, etc. **5** (often in *pl.*) military drill or maneuvers. **6** (foll. by *in*) a process directed at or concerned with something specified (*was an exercise in public relations*). ● *v.* **1** *tr.* use or apply (a faculty, right, influence, restraint, etc.). **2** *tr.* perform (a function). **3 a** *intr.* take (esp. physical) exercise; do exercises. **b** *tr.* provide (an animal) with exercise. **c** *tr.* train (a person). **4** *tr.* a tax the powers of. **b** perplexy; worry. □□ **ex•er•cis•a•ble** *adj.* **ex•er•cis•er** *n.* [ME f. OF *exercice* f. L *exercitium* f. *exercere exercit-* keep at work (as EX-¹, *arcēre* restrain)]

ex•ergue /eksórg/ *n.* **1** a small space usu. on the reverse of a coin or medal, below the principal device. **2** an inscription on this space. [F f. med.L *exergum* f. Gk *ex-* (as EX-²) + *ergon* work]

ex•ert /igzórt/ *v.tr.* **1** exercise; bring to bear (a quality, force, influence, etc.). **2** *refl.* (often foll. by *to* + infin.) use one's efforts or endeavors; strive. □□ **ex•er•tion** /–zórshən/ *n.* [L *exserere exsert-* put forth (as EX-¹, *serere* bind)]

ex•e•unt /ékseeənt, –ōont/ *v.intr.* used as a stage direction in a printed play to indicate that a group of characters leave the stage (*exeunt Hamlet and Polonius*). □ **exeunt omnes** all leave the stage. [L, = they go out: 3rd pl. pres. of *exire* go out: see EXIT]

ex•fil•trate /éksfiltrayt/ *v.tr.* (also *absol.*) withdraw (troops, spies, etc.) surreptitiously, esp. from danger. □□ **ex•fil•tra•tion** /-tráyshən/ *n.*

ex•fo•li•ate /eksfóleeayt/ *v.intr.* **1** (of bone, the skin, a mineral, etc.) come off in scales or layers. **2** (of a tree) throw off layers of bark. □□ **ex•fo•li•a•tion** /-áyshən/ *n.* **ex•fo•li•a•tive** *adj.* [LL *exfoliare exfoliat-* (as EX-¹, *folium* leaf)]

ex gra•ti•a /eks gráysheeə/ *adv. & adj.* ● *adv.* as a favor rather than from an (esp. legal) obligation. ● *adj.* granted on this basis. [L, = from favor]

ex•ha•la•tion /éks-həláyshən/ *n.* **1 a** an expiration of air. **b** a puff of breath. **2** a mist; vapor. **3** an emanation or effluvium. [ME f. L *exhalatio* (as EXHALE)]

ex•hale /eks-háyl/ *v.* **1** *tr.* (also *absol.*) breathe out (esp. air or smoke) from the lungs. **2** *tr. & intr.* give off or be given off in vapor. □□ **ex•hal•a•ble** *adj.* [ME f. OF *exhaler* f. L *exhalare* (as EX-¹, *halare* breathe)]

ex•haust /igzáwst/ *v. & n.* ● *v.tr.* **1** consume or use up the whole of. **2** (often as **exhausted** *adj.* or **exhausting** *adj.*) use up the strength or resources of (a person); tire out. **3** study or expound on (a subject) completely. **4** (often foll. by *of*) empty (a vessel, etc.) of its contents. **5** (often as **exhausted** *adj.*) drain of strength or resources; (of land) make barren. ● *n.* **1 a** waste gases, etc., expelled from an engine after combustion. **b** (also **exhaust pipe**) the pipe or system by which these are expelled. **c** the process of expulsion of these gases. **2 a** the production of an outward current of air by the creation of a partial vacuum. **b** an apparatus for this. □□ **ex•haust•er** *n.* **ex•haust•i•ble** *adj.* **ex•haust•i•bil•i•ty** *n.* **ex•haust•i•bly** *adv.* [L *exhaurire exhaust-* (as EX-¹, *haurire* draw (water), drain)]

ex•haus•tion /igzáwschən/ *n.* **1** the action or process of draining or emptying something; the state of being depleted or emptied. **2** a total loss of strength or vitality. **3** the process of establishing a conclusion by eliminating alternatives. [LL *exhaustio* (as EX-HAUST)]

ex•haus•tive /igzáwstiv/ *adj.* **1** thorough; comprehensive. **2** tending to exhaust a subject. □□ **ex•haus•tive•ly** *adv.* **ex•haus•tive•ness** *n.*

ex•hib•it /igzíbit/ *v. & n.* ● *v.tr.* **1** show or reveal publicly (for amusement, in competition, etc.). **2 a** show; display. **b** manifest (a quality). **3** submit for consideration. ● *n.* **1** a thing or collection of things forming part or all of an exhibition. **2** a document or other item or object produced in a court of law as evidence. □□ **ex•hib•i•to•ry** *adj.* [L *exhibēre exhibit-* (as EX-¹, *habēre* hold)]

ex•hi•bi•tion /éksibíshən/ *n.* **1** a display (esp. public) of works of art, industrial products, etc. **2** the act or an instance of exhibiting; the state of being exhibited. **3** *Brit.* a scholarship, esp. from the funds of a school, college, etc. □ **make an exhibition of oneself** behave so as to appear ridiculous or foolish. [ME f. OF f. LL *exhibitio –onis* (as EXHIBIT)]

ex•hi•bi•tion•er /éksibíshənər/ *n. Brit.* a student who has been awarded an exhibition.

ex•hi•bi•tion•ism /éksibíshənizəm/ *n.* **1** a tendency toward display or extravagant behavior. **2** *Psychol.* a mental condition characterized by the compulsion to display one's genitals indecently in public. □□ **ex•hi•bi•tion•ist** *n.* **ex•hi•bi•tion•is•tic** *adj.* **ex•hi•bi•tion•is•ti•cal•ly** *adv.*

ex•hib•i•tor /igzíbitər/ *n.* a person who provides an item or items for an exhibition.

ex•hil•a•rate /igzílərayt/ *v.tr.* (often as **exhilarating** *adj.* or **exhilarated** *adj.*) affect with great liveliness or joy; raise the spirits of. □□ **ex•hil•a•rant** *adj. & n.* **ex•hil•a•rat•ing•ly** *adv.* **ex•hil•a•ra•tion** /-ráyshən/ *n.* **ex•hil•a•ra•tive** *adj.* [L *exhilarare* (as EX-¹, *hilaris* cheerful)]

ex•hort /igzáwrt/ *v.tr.* (often foll. by *to* + infin.) urge or advise strongly or earnestly. □□ **ex•hor•ta•tive** /-tətiv/ *adj.* **ex•hor•ta•to•ry** /-tətáwree/ *adj.* **ex•hort•er** *n.* [ME f. OF *exhorter* or L *exhortari* (as EX-¹, *hortari* exhort)]

ex•hor•ta•tion /égzawrtáyshən/ *n.* **1** the act or an instance of exhorting; the state of being exhorted. **2** a formal or liturgical address. [ME f. OF *exhortation* or L *exhortatio* (as EXHORT)]

ex•hume /igzóóm, –zyóóm, eks-hyóóm/ *v.tr.* dig out; unearth (esp. a buried corpse). □□ **ex•hu•ma•tion** *n.* [F *exhumer* f. med.L *exhumare* (as EX-¹, *humus* ground)]

ex hy•poth•e•si /éks hīpóthəsee/ *adv.* according to the hypothesis proposed. [mod.L]

ex•i•gen•cy /éksijənsee, igzíj–/ *n.* (*pl.* •cies) (also **ex•i•gence** /éksijəns/) **1** an urgent need or demand. **2** an emergency. [F *exigence* & LL *exigentia* (as EXIGENT)]

ex•i•gent /éksijənt/ *adj.* **1** requiring much; exacting. **2** urgent; pressing. [ME f. L *exigere* EXACT]

ex•ig•u•ous /igzígyőőəs, iksig–/ *adj.* scanty; small. □□ **ex•i•gu•i•ty** /éksigyőőitee/ *n.* **ex•ig•u•ous•ly** *adv.* **ex•ig•u•ous•ness** *n.* [L *exiguus* scanty f. *exigere* weigh exactly: see EXACT]

ex•ile /éksīl, égzīl/ *n. & v.* ● *n.* **1** expulsion, or the state of being expelled, from one's native land or (**internal exile**) native town, etc. **2** long absence abroad, esp. enforced. **3** a person expelled or long absent from his or her native country. **4** (**the Exile**) the captivity of the Jews in Babylon in the 6th c. BC. ● *v.tr.* (foll. by *from*) officially expel (a person) from his or her native country or town, etc. □□ **ex•**

il•ic /–sílik, –zílik/ *adj.* (esp. in sense 4 of *n.*). [ME f. OF *exil, exiler* f. L *exilium* banishment]

ex•ist /igzíst/ *v.intr.* **1** have a place as part of objective reality. **2 a** have being under specified conditions. **b** (foll. by *as*) exist in the form of. **3** (of circumstances, etc.) occur; be found. **4** live with no pleasure under adverse conditions (*felt he was merely existing*). **5** continue in being; maintain life (*can hardly exist on this salary*). **6** be alive; live. [prob. back-form. f. EXISTENCE; cf. LL *existere*]

ex•ist•ence /igzístəns/ *n.* **1** the fact or condition of being or existing. **2** continued being; the manner of one's existing or living, esp. under adverse conditions (*a wretched existence*). **3** an existing thing. **4** all that exists. [ME f. OF *existence* or LL *existentia* f. L *exsistere* (as EX-¹, *stare* stand)]

ex•ist•ent /igzístənt/ *adj.* existing; actual; current.

ex•is•ten•tial /égzisténshəl/ *adj.* **1** of or relating to existence. **2** *Logic* (of a proposition, etc.) affirming or implying the existence of a thing. **3** *Philos.* concerned with existence, esp. with human existence as viewed by existentialism. □□ **ex•is•ten•tial•ly** *adv.* [LL *existentialis* (as EXISTENCE)]

ex•is•ten•tial•ism /égzisténshəlizəm/ *n.* a philosophical theory emphasizing the existence of the individual person as a free and responsible agent determining his or her own development. □□ **ex•is•ten•tial•ist** *n.* [G *Existentialismus* (as EXISTENTIAL)]

ex•it /égzit, éksit/ *n. & v.* ● *n.* **1** a passage or door by which to leave a room, building, etc. **2 a** the act of going out. **b** the right to go out. **3** a place where vehicles can leave a highway or major road. **4** the departure of an actor from the stage. **5** death. ● *v.intr.* **1** go out of a room, building, etc. **2** (as a stage direction) (an actor) leaves the stage (*exit Macbeth*). **3** die. [L, 3rd sing. pres. of *exire* go out (as EX-¹, *ire* go): cf. L *exitus* going out]

ex•it per•mit *n.* (also **exit visa**) authorization to leave a particular country.

ex•it poll *n.* a survey usu. of voters leaving voting booths, used to predict an election's outcome, analyze voting patterns, etc.

ex li•bris /eksleébris/ *n.* (*pl.* same) a usu. decorated bookplate or label bearing the owner's name, pasted into the front of a book. [L *ex libris* among the books of]

ex ni•hi•lo /eks níhilō, neé–/ *adv.* out of nothing (*creation ex nihilo*). [L]

exo- /éksō/ *comb. form* external. [Gk *exō* outside]

ex•o•bi•ol•o•gy /éksōbiólōjee/ *n.* the study of life outside the earth. □□ **ex•o•bi•ol•o•gist** *n.*

Ex•o•cet /éksōset/ *n. Trademark* a short-range guided missile used esp. in sea warfare. [F *exocet* flying fish]

ex•o•crine /éksəkrin, –kreen, –krīn/ *adj.* (of a gland) secreting through a duct (cf. ENDOCRINE). [EXO- + Gk *krīnō* sift]

Exod. *abbr.* Exodus (Old Testament).

ex•o•dus /éksədəs/ *n.* **1** a mass departure of people (esp. emigrants). **2** (**Exodus**) *Bibl.* **a** the departure of the Israelites from Egypt. **b** the book of the Old Testament relating this. [eccl.L f. Gk *exodos* (as EX-², *hodos* way)]

ex of•fi•ci•o /éksəfisheeō/ *adv. & adj.* by virtue of one's office or status. [L]

ex•og•a•my /eksógəmee/ *n.* **1** *Anthropol.* marriage of a man outside his own tribe. **2** *Biol.* the fusion of reproductive cells from distantly related or unrelated individuals. □□ **ex•og•a•mous** *adj.*

ex•og•e•nous /eksójinəs/ *adj. Biol.* growing or originating from outside. □□ **ex•og•e•nous•ly** *adv.*

ex•on /ékson/ *n. Brit.* each of the four officers acting as commanders of the Yeomen of the Guard. [repr. F pronunc. of EXEMPT]

ex•on•er•ate /igzónərayt/ *v.tr.* (often foll. by *from*) **1** free or declare free from blame, etc. **2** release from a duty, etc. □□ **ex•on•er•a•tion** /-ráyshən/ *n.* **ex•on•er•a•tive** *adj.* [L *exonerare exonerat-* (as EX-¹, *onus, oneris* burden)]

ex•oph•thal•mos /éksofthálməs/ *n.* (also **ex•oph•thal•mus, ex•oph•thal•mi•a** /-meeə/) *Med.* abnormal protrusion of the eyeball. □□ **ex•oph•thal•mic** *adj.* [mod.L f. Gk *exophthalmos* having prominent eyes (as EX-², *ophthalmos* eye)]

exor. *abbr.* executor.

ex•or•bi•tant /igzáwrbit'nt/ *adj.* (of a price, demand, etc.) grossly excessive. □□ **ex•or•bi•tance** /-təns/ *n.* **ex•or•bi•tant•ly** *adv.* [LL *exorbitare* (as EX-¹, *orbita* ORBIT)]

ex•or•cize /éksawrsīz, –sər–/ *v.tr.* **1** expel (a supposed evil spirit) by invocation or by use of a holy name. **2** (often foll. by *of*) free (a person or place) of a supposed evil spirit. □□ **ex•or•cism** /-sizəm/ *n.* **ex•or•cist** *n.* **ex•or•ci•za•tion** /-sizáyshən/ *n.* [F *exorciser* or eccl.L *exorcizare* f. Gk *exorkizō* (as EX-², *horkos* oath)]

ex•or•di•um /eksáwrdeeəm/ *n.* (*pl.* **ex•or•di•ums** or **ex•or•di•a** /-deeə/) the beginning or introductory part, esp. of a discourse or treatise. □□ **ex•or•di•al** *adj.* **ex•or•di•al•ly** *adv.* [L f. *exordiri* (as EX-¹, *ordiri* begin)]

ex•o•skel•e•ton /éksōskélit'n/ *n.* a rigid external covering for the body in certain animals, esp. arthropods, providing support and protection. □□ **ex•o•skel•e•tal** *adj.*

ex•o•sphere /éksōsfeer/ *n.* the layer of atmosphere furthest from the earth.

ex•o•ther•mic /éksōthórmik/ *adj.* (also **ex•o•ther•mal** /–məl/) esp. Chem. occurring or formed with the evolution of heat. □□ **ex•o•ther•mal•ly** *adv.* **ex•o•ther•mi•cal•ly** *adv.*

ex•ot•ic /igzótik/ *adj. & n.* • *adj.* **1** introduced from or originating in a foreign (esp. tropical) country (*exotic fruits*). **2** attractively or remarkably strange or unusual; bizarre. **3** (of a fuel, metal, etc.) of a kind newly brought into use. • *n.* an exotic person or thing. □□ **ex•ot•i•cal•ly** *adv.* **ex•ot•i•cism** /–tisizəm/ *n.* [L *exoticus* f. Gk *exōtikos* f. *exō* outside]

ex•ot•i•ca /igzótikə/ *n.pl.* remarkably strange or rare objects. [L, neut. pl. of *exoticus*: see EXOTIC]

ex•ot•ic danc•er *n.* a striptease dancer.

ex•pand /ikspánd/ *v.* **1** *tr. & intr.* increase in size or bulk or importance. **2** *intr.* (often foll. by *on*) give a fuller description or account. **3** *intr.* become more genial or effusive; discard one's reserve. **4** *tr.* set or write out in full (something condensed or abbreviated). **5** *tr. & intr.* spread out flat. □□ **ex•pand•a•ble** *adj.* **ex•pand•er** *n.* **ex•pan•si•ble** /ikspánsibəl/ *adj.* **ex•pan•si•bil•i•ty** /–bílitee/ *n.* [ME f. L *expandere expans-* spread out (as EX-¹, *pandere* spread)]

ex•pand•ed met•al *n.* sheet metal slit and stretched into a mesh, used to reinforce concrete and other brittle materials.

ex•panse /ikspáns/ *n.* **1** a wide continuous area or extent of land, space, etc. **2** an amount of expansion. [mod.L *expansum* neut. past part. (as EXPAND)]

ex•pan•sile /ikspánsəl, –sīl/ *adj.* **1** of expansion. **2** capable of expansion.

ex•pan•sion /ikspánshən/ *n.* **1** the act or an instance of expanding; the state of being expanded. **2** enlargement of the scale or scope of (esp. commercial) operations. **3** increase in the amount of a country's territory or area of control. **4** an increase in the volume of fuel, etc., on combustion in the cylinder of an engine. **5** the action of making or becoming greater in area, bulk, capacity, etc.; dilatation; the degree of this (*alternate expansion and contraction of the muscle*). □□ **ex•pan•sion•ar•y** *adj.* **ex•pan•sion•ism** *n.* **ex•pan•sion•ist** *n.* **ex•pan•sion•is•tic** *adj.* (all in senses 2, 3). [LL *expansio* (as EXPAND)]

ex•pan•sive /ikspánsiv/ *adj.* **1** able or tending to expand. **2** extensive, wide-ranging. **3** (of a person, feelings, or speech) effusive; open. □□ **ex•pan•sive•ly** *adv.* **ex•pan•sive•ness** *n.* **ex•pan•siv•i•ty** /–sívitee/ *n.*

ex par•te /eks paártee/ *adj. & adv. Law* in the interests of one side only or of an interested outside party. [L]

ex•pat /ékspát/ *n. & adj. Brit. colloq.* = EXPATRIATE. [abbr.]

ex•pa•ti•ate /ikspáysheeayt/ *v.intr.* (usu. foll. by *on, upon*) speak or write at length or in detail. □□ **ex•pa•ti•a•tion** /–áyshən/ *n.* **ex•pa•ti•a•to•ry** /–sheeətáwree/ *adj.* [L *exspatiari* digress (as EX-¹, *spatium* SPACE)]

ex•pa•tri•ate *adj., n., & v.* • *adj.* /ékspáytreeət/ **1** living abroad, esp. for a long period. **2** expelled from one's country; exiled. • *n.* /ekspáytreeət/ an expatriate person. • *v.tr.* /ekspáytreeayt/ **1** expel or remove (a person) from his or her native country. **2** *refl.* withdraw (oneself) from one's citizenship or allegiance. □□ **ex•pa•tri•a•tion** /–áyshən/ *n.* [med.L *expatriare* (as EX-¹, *patria* native country)]

ex•pect /ikspékt/ *v.tr.* **1** (often foll. by *to* + infin., or *that* + clause) **a** regard as likely; assume as a future event or occurrence. **b** (often foll. by *of*) look for as appropriate or one's due (from a person) (*I expect cooperation*; *expect you to be here*; *expected better of you*). **2** *colloq.* (often foll. by *that* + clause) think; suppose (*I expect we'll be on time*). **3** be shortly to have (a baby) (*is expecting twins*). □ **be expecting** *colloq.* be pregnant. □□ **ex•pect•a•ble** *adj.* [L *exspectare* (as EX-¹, *spectare* look, frequent. of *specere* see)]

ex•pect•an•cy /ikspéktənsee/ *n.* (*pl.* **-cies**) **1** a state of expectation. **2** a prospect, esp. of future possession. **3** (foll. by *of*) a prospective chance. [L *expectantia*, f. (as EXPECT)]

ex•pect•ant /ikspéktənt/ *adj. & n.* • *adj.* **1** (often foll. by *of*) expecting. **2** having the expectation of possession, status, etc. **3** (*attrib.*) expecting a baby (said of the mother or father). • *n.* **1** one who expects. **2** a candidate for office, etc. □□ **ex•pect•ant•ly** *adv.*

ex•pec•ta•tion /ékspektáyshən/ *n.* **1** the act or an instance of expecting or looking forward. **2** something expected or hoped for. **3** (foll. by *of*) the probability of an event. **4** (in *pl.*) one's prospects of inheritance. [L *expectatio* (as EXPECT)]

ex•pec•to•rant /ikspéktərənt/ *adj. & n.* • *adj.* causing the coughing out of phlegm, etc. • *n.* an expectorant medicine.

ex•pec•to•rate /ikspéktərayt/ *v.tr.* (also *absol.*) cough or spit out (phlegm, etc.) from the chest or lungs. □□ **ex•pec•to•ra•tion** /–ráyshən/ *n.* **ex•pec•to•ra•tor** *n.* [L *expectorare expectorat-* (as EX-¹, *pectus -oris* breast)]

ex•pe•di•ent /ikspéedeeənt/ *adj. & n.* • *adj.* **1** advantageous; advisable on practical rather than moral grounds. **2** suitable; appropri-

ate. • *n.* a means of attaining an end; a resource. □□ **ex•pe•di•ence** /–əns/ *n.* **ex•pe•di•en•cy** *n.* **ex•pe•di•ent•ly** *adv.* [ME f. L *expedire*: see EXPEDITE]

ex•pe•dite /ékspidīt/ *v.tr.* **1** assist the progress of; hasten (an action, process, etc.). **2** accomplish (business) quickly. □□ **ex•pe•dit•er** *n.* [L *expedire expedit-* extricate, put in order (as EX-¹, *pes pedis* foot)]

ex•pe•di•tion /ékspidíshən/ *n.* **1** a journey or voyage for a particular purpose, esp. exploration, scientific research, or war. **2** the personnel or ships, etc., undertaking this. **3** promptness; speed. □□ **ex•pe•di•tion•ist** *n.* [ME f. OF f. L *expeditio –onis* (as EXPEDITE)]

ex•pe•di•tion•ar•y /ékspidíshəneree/ *adj.* of or used in an expedition, esp. military.

ex•pe•di•tious /ékspidíshəs/ *adj.* **1** acting or done with speed and efficiency. **2** suited for speedy performance. □□ **ex•pe•di•tious•ly** *adv.* **ex•pe•di•tious•ness** *n.* [EXPEDITION + –OUS]

ex•pel /ikspél/ *v.tr.* (**ex•pelled, ex•pel•ling**) (often foll. by *from*) **1** deprive (a person) of the membership of or involvement in (a school, society, etc.). **2** force out or eject (a thing from its container, etc.). **3** order or force to leave a building, etc. □□ **ex•pel•la•ble** *adj.* **ex•pel•lee** /–leé/ *n.* **ex•pel•lent** *adj.* **ex•pel•ler** *n.* [ME f. L *expellere expuls-* (as EX-¹, *pellere* drive)]

ex•pend /ikspénd/ *v.tr.* spend or use up (money, time, etc.). [ME f. L *expendere expens-* (as EX-¹, *pendere* weigh)]

ex•pend•a•ble /ikspéndəbəl/ *adj.* **1** that may be sacrificed or dispensed with, esp. to achieve a purpose. **2 a** not regarded as worth preserving or saving. **b** unimportant; insignificant. **3** not normally reused. □□ **ex•pend•a•bil•i•ty** *n.* **ex•pend•a•bly** *adv.*

ex•pen•di•ture /ikspéndichər/ *n.* **1** the process or an instance of spending or using up. **2** a thing (esp. a sum of money) expended. [EXPEND, after obs. *expenditor* officer in charge of expenditure, f. med.L f. *expenditus* irreg. past part. of L *expendere*]

ex•pense /ikspéns/ *n.* **1** cost incurred; payment of money. **2** (usu. in *pl.*) **a** costs incurred in doing a particular job, etc. (*will pay your expenses*). **b** an amount paid to reimburse this (*offered me $40 per day expenses*). **3** a thing that is a cause of much expense (*the house is a real expense to run*). □ **at the expense of** so as to cause loss or damage or discredit to. [ME f. AF, alt. of OF *espense* f. LL *expensa* (money) spent, past part. of L *expendere* EXPEND]

ex•pense ac•count *n.* a list of an employee's expenses payable by the employer.

ex•pen•sive /ikspénsiv/ *adj.* **1** costing much. **2** making a high charge. **3** causing much expense (*has expensive tastes*). □□ **ex•pen•sive•ly** *adv.* **ex•pen•sive•ness** *n.*

ex•pe•ri•ence /ikspeéreeəns/ *n. & v.* • *n.* **1** actual observation of or practical acquaintance with facts or events. **2** knowledge or skill resulting from this. **3 a** an event regarded as affecting one (*an unpleasant experience*). **b** the fact or process of being so affected (*learned by experience*). • *v.tr.* **1** have experience of; undergo. **2** feel or be affected by (an emotion, etc.). □□ **ex•pe•ri•ence•a•ble** *adj.* [ME f. OF f. L *experientia* f. *experiri expert-* try]

ex•pe•ri•enced /ikspeéreeənst/ *adj.* **1** having had much experience. **2** skilled from experience (*an experienced driver*).

ex•pe•ri•en•tial /ikspeéree-énshəl/ *adj.* involving or based on experience. □□ **ex•pe•ri•en•tial•ism** *n.* **ex•pe•ri•en•tial•ist** *n.* **ex•pe•ri•en•tial•ly** *adv.*

ex•pe•ri•en•tial phi•los•o•phy *n.* a philosophy that treats all knowledge as based on experience.

ex•per•i•ment /ikspérimənt/ *n. & v.* • *n.* **1** a procedure adopted on the chance of its succeeding, for testing a hypothesis, etc., or to demonstrate a known fact. **2** (foll. by *of*) a test or trial of. • *v.intr.* (often foll. by *on, with*) make an experiment. □□ **ex•per•i•men•ta•tion** *n.* **ex•per•i•ment•er** *n.* [ME f. OF *experiment* or L *experimentum* (as EXPERIENCE)]

ex•per•i•men•tal /ikspérimént'l/ *adj.* **1** based on or making use of experiment (*experimental psychology*). **2 a** used in experiments. **b** serving or resulting from (esp. incomplete) experiment; tentative, provisional. **3** based on experience, not on authority or conjecture. □□ **ex•per•i•men•tal•ism** *n.* **ex•per•i•men•tal•ist** *n.* **ex•per•i•men•tal•ize** *v.intr.* **ex•per•i•men•tal•ly** *adv.* [ME f. med.L *experimentalis* (as EXPERIMENT)]

ex•pert /ékspərt/ *adj. & n.* • *adj.* **1** (often foll. by *at, in*) having special knowledge or skill in a subject. **2** involving or resulting from this (*expert evidence; an expert piece of work*). • *n.* (often foll. by *at, in*) a person having special knowledge or skill. □□ **ex•pert•ly** *adv.* **ex•pert•ness** *n.* [ME f. OF f. L *expertus* past part. of *experiri*: see EXPERIENCE]

ex•per•tise /ékspərteéz/ *n.* expert skill, knowledge, or judgment. [F (as EXPERT)]

ex•pert•ize /ékspərtīz/ *v.* **1** *intr.* give an expert opinion. **2** *tr.* give an expert opinion concerning.

ex•pi•ate /ékspeeayt/ *v.tr.* **1** pay the penalty for (wrongdoing). **2** make amends for. □□ **ex•pi•a•ble** /–peeəbəl/ *adj.* **ex•pi•a•to•ry** /–peeətawree/ *adj.* **ex•pi•a•tion** /–áyshən/ *n.* **ex•pi•a•tor** *n.* [L *expiare expiat-* (as EX-¹, *pius* devout)]

ex•pi•ra•tion /ékspəráyshən/ *n.* **1** breathing out. **2** the end of the validity or duration of something. [L *expiratio* (as EXPIRE)]

ex•pire /ikspír/ *v.* **1** *intr.* (of a period of time, validity, etc.) come to an end. **2** *intr.* (of a document, authorization, etc.) cease to be valid; become void. **3** *intr.* (of a person) die. **4** *tr.* (usu. foll. by *from*; also *absol.*) exhale (air, etc.) from the lungs. □□ **ex·pir·a·to·ry** *adj.* (in sense 4). [ME f. OF *expirer* f. L *exspirare* (as EX-¹, *spirare* breathe)]

ex·pi·ry /ikspíree/ *n.* **1** expiration. **2** death.

ex·plain /ikspláyn/ *v.tr.* **1** make clear or intelligible with detailed information, etc. (also *absol.*: *let me explain*). **2** (foll. by *that* + clause) say by way of explanation. **3** account for (one's conduct, etc.). □ **explain away** minimize the significance of (a difficulty or mistake) by explanation. **explain oneself 1** make one's meaning clear. **2** give an account of one's motives or conduct. □□ **ex·plain·a·ble** *adj.* **ex·plain·er** *n.* [L *explanare* (as EX-¹, *planus* flat, assim. to PLAIN¹)]

ex·pla·na·tion /éksplənáyshən/ *n.* **1** the act or an instance of explaining. **2** a statement or circumstance that explains something. **3** a declaration made with a view to mutual understanding or reconciliation. [ME f. L *explanatio* (as EXPLAIN)]

ex·plan·a·to·ry /iksplánətawree/ *adj.* serving or intended to serve to explain. □□ **ex·plan·a·to·ri·ly** *adv.* [LL *explanatorius* (as EXPLAIN)]

ex·plant /eksplánt/ *v. & n. Biol.* ● *v.tr.* transfer (living cells, tissues, or organs) from animals or plants to a nutrient medium. ● *n.* a piece of explanted tissue, etc. □□ **ex·plan·ta·tion** *n.* [mod.L *explantare* (as EX-¹, *plantare* PLANT)]

ex·ple·tive /éksplətiv/ *n. & adj.* ● *n.* **1** an oath, swearword, or other expression, used in an exclamation. **2** a word used to fill out a sentence, etc., esp. in verse. ● *adj.* serving to fill out (esp. a sentence, line of verse, etc.).

WORD HISTORY   expletive

Late Middle English (as an adjective): from late Latin *expletivus*, from *explere* 'fill out,' from *ex-* 'out' + *plere* 'fill.' The general noun sense 'word used merely to fill out a sentence' (early 17th century) was applied specifically to an oath or swear word in the early 19th century.

---

ex·pli·ca·ble /éksplikəbəl, iksplík–/ *adj.* that can be explained.

ex·pli·cate /éksplikayt/ *v.tr.* **1** develop the meaning or implication of (an idea, principle, etc.). **2** make clear; explain (esp. a literary text). □□ **ex·pli·ca·tion** *n.* /éksplikaytiv, iksplíkətiv/ *adj.* **ex·pli·ca·tor** *n.* **ex·pli·ca·to·ry** /éksplikətáwree, iksplík–/ *adj.* [L *explicare explicat-* unfold (as EX-¹, *plicare plicat-* or *plicit-* fold)]

ex·plic·it /iksplísit/ *adj.* **1** expressly stated, leaving nothing merely implied; stated in detail. **2** (of knowledge, a notion, etc.) definite; clear. **3** (of a person, book, etc.) expressing views unreservedly; outspoken. □□ **ex·plic·it·ly** *adv.* **ex·plic·it·ness** *n.* [F *explicite* or L *explicitus* (as EXPLICATE)]

▶See note at IMPLICIT.

ex·plode /iksplód/ *v.* **1 a** *intr.* (of gas, gunpowder, a bomb, a boiler, etc.) expand suddenly with a loud noise owing to a release of internal energy. **b** *tr.* cause (a bomb, etc.) to explode. **2** *intr.* give vent suddenly to emotion, esp. anger. **3** *intr.* (of a population, etc.) increase suddenly or rapidly. **4** *tr.* show (a theory, etc.) to be false or baseless. **5** *tr.* (as **exploded** *adj.*) (of a drawing, etc.) showing the components of a mechanism as if separated by an explosion but in the normal relative positions. □□ **ex·plod·er** *n.* [earliest in sense 4: L *explodere* hiss off the stage (as EX-¹, *plodere plos-* = *plaudere* clap)]

ex·ploit *n. & v.* ● *n.* /éksployt/ a bold or daring feat. ● *v.tr.* /iksplóyt/ **1** make use of (a resource, etc.); derive benefit from. **2** usu. *derog.* utilize or take advantage of (esp. a person) for one's own ends. □□ **ex·ploit·a·ble** *adj.* **ex·ploi·ta·tion** *n.* **ex·ploi·ta·tive** /iksplóytətiv/ *adj.* **ex·ploit·er** *n.* **ex·ploi·tive** *adj.* [ME f. OF *esploit*, *exploiter* ult. f. L *explicare*: see EXPLICATE]

ex·plo·ra·tion /ékspləráyshən/ *n.* **1** an act or instance of exploring. **2** the process of exploring. □□ **ex·plo·ra·tion·al** *adj.*

ex·plor·a·to·ry /ikspláwrətawree/ *adj.* **1** (of discussion, etc.) preliminary; serving to establish procedure, etc. **2** of or concerning exploration or investigation (*exploratory surgery*).

ex·plore /ikspláwr/ *v.tr.* **1** travel extensively through (a country, etc.) in order to learn or discover about it. **2** inquire into; investigate thoroughly. **3** *Surgery* examine (a part of the body) in detail. □□ **ex·plor·a·tive** /–rətiv/ *adj.* [F *explorer* f. L *explorare*]

ex·plor·er /ikspláwrər/ *n.* a traveler into undiscovered or uninvestigated territory, esp. to get scientific information.

ex·plo·sion /iksplóuzhən/ *n.* **1** the act or an instance of exploding. **2** a loud noise caused by something exploding. **3 a** a sudden outburst of noise. **b** a sudden outbreak of feeling, esp. anger. **4** a rapid or sudden increase, esp. of population. [L *explosio* scornful rejection (as EXPLODE)]

ex·plo·sive /iksplósiv/ *adj. & n.* ● *adj.* **1** able or tending or likely to explode. **2** likely to cause a violent outburst, etc.; (of a situation, etc.) dangerously tense. ● *n.* an explosive substance. □□ **ex·plo·sive·ly** *adv.* **ex·plo·sive·ness** *n.*

ex·po /ékspō/ *n.* (also **Ex·po**) (*pl.* **·pos**) a large international exhibition. [abbr. of EXPOSITION 4]

ex·po·nent /ikspónənt/ *n. & adj.* ● *n.* **1** a person who favors or promotes an idea, etc. **2** a representative or practitioner of an activity,

profession, etc. **3** a person who explains or interprets something. **4** an executant (of music, etc.). **5** a type or representative. **6** *Math.* a raised symbol or expression beside a numeral indicating how many times it is to be multiplied by itself (e.g., 2^3 = 2 x 2 x 2). ● *adj.* that sets forth or interprets. [L *exponere* (as EX-¹, *ponere pos-it-* put)]

ex·po·nen·tial /ékspənénshəl/ *adj.* **1** *Math.* of or indicated by a mathematical exponent. **2** (of an increase, etc.) more and more rapid. □□ **ex·po·nen·tial·ly** *adv.* [F *exponentiel* (as EXPONENT)]

ex·po·nen·tial func·tion *n. Math.* a function that increases as a quantity raised to a power determined by the variable on which the function depends.

ex·po·nen·tial growth *n. Biol.* a form of population growth in which the rate of growth is related to the number of individuals present.

ex·port *v. & n.* ● *v.tr.* /ekspáwrt, éks–/ send out (goods or services) esp. for sale in another country. ● *n.* /ékspawrt/ **1** the process of exporting. **2 a** an exported article or service. **b** (in *pl.*) an amount exported (*exports exceeded $50 billion*). **3** (*attrib.*) suitable for export, esp. of better quality. □□ **ex·port·a·ble** *adj.* **ex·port·a·bil·i·ty** *n.* **ex·por·ta·tion** *n.* **ex·port·er** *n.* [L *exportare* (as EX-¹, *portare* carry)]

ex·pose /ikspóz/ *v.tr.* **1** leave uncovered or unprotected, esp. from the weather. **2** (foll. by *to*) **a** cause to be liable to or in danger of (*was exposed to great danger*). **b** lay open to the action or influence of; introduce to (*exposed to bad influences, exposed to Hemingway at a young age*). **3** (as **exposed** *adj.*) **a** (foll. by *to*) open to; unprotected from (*exposed to the east*). **b** vulnerable; risky. **4** *Photog.* subject (film) to light, esp. by operation of a camera. **5** reveal the identity or fact of (esp. a person or thing disapproved of or guilty of crime, etc.). **6** disclose; make public. **7** exhibit; display. **8** put up for sale. □ **expose oneself** display one's body, esp. the genitals, publicly and indecently. □□ **ex·pos·er** *n.* [ME f. OF *exposer* after L *exponere*: see EXPONENT, POSE¹]

ex·po·sé /ékspōzáy/ *n.* (also **ex·pose**) **1** an orderly statement of facts. **2** the act or an instance of revealing something discreditable. [F, past part. of *exposer* (as EXPOSE)]

ex·po·si·tion /ékspəzíshən/ *n.* **1** an explanatory statement or account. **2** an explanation or commentary; an interpretative article or treatise. **3** *Mus.* the part of a movement, esp. in sonata form, in which the principal themes are first presented. **4** a large public exhibition. **5** *archaic* exposure. □□ **ex·po·si·tion·al** *adj.* **ex·pos·i·tive** /–pózitiv/ *adj.* [ME f. OF *exposition*, or L *expositio* (as EXPONENT)]

ex·pos·i·tor /ikspózitər/ *n.* an expounder or interpreter. □□ **ex·pos·i·to·ry** *adj.*

ex post fac·to /éks pōst fáktō/ *adj. & adv.* with retrospective action or force. [L *ex postfacto* in the light of subsequent events]

ex·pos·tu·late /ikspóschəlayt/ *v.intr.* (often foll. by *with* a person) make a protest; remonstrate earnestly. □□ **ex·pos·tu·la·tion** /–láyshən/ *n.* **ex·pos·tu·la·to·ry** /–lətáwree/ *adj.* [L *expostulare expostulat-* (as EX-¹, *postulare* demand)]

ex·po·sure /ikspózhər/ *n.* **1** (foll. by *to*) the act or condition of exposing or being exposed (to air, cold, danger, etc.). **2** the condition of being exposed to the elements, esp. in severe conditions (*died from exposure*). **3** the revelation of an identity or fact, esp. when concealed or likely to find disapproval. **4** *Photog.* **a** the action of exposing film, etc., to the light. **b** the duration of this action. **c** the area of film, etc., affected by it. **5** an aspect or outlook (*has a fine southern exposure*). **6** experience, esp. of a specified kind of work. [EXPOSE after *enclosure*, etc.]

ex·po·sure me·ter *n. Photog.* a device for measuring the strength of the light to determine the correct duration of exposure.

ex·pound /ikspównd/ *v.tr.* **1** set out in detail (a doctrine, etc.). **2** explain or interpret (a literary or doctrinal work). □□ **ex·pound·er** *n.* [ME f. OF *espondre* (as EXPONENT)]

ex·press¹ /iksprés/ *v.tr.* **1** represent or make known (thought, feelings, etc.) in words or by gestures, conduct, etc. **2** *refl.* say what one thinks or means. **3** esp. *Math.* represent by symbols. **4** squeeze out (liquid or air). □□ **ex·press·er** *n.* **ex·press·i·ble** *adj.* [ME f. OF *expresser* f. Rmc (as EX-¹, PRESS¹)]

ex·press² /iksprés/ *adj., adv., n., & v.* ● *adj.* **1** operating at high speed. **2** also /ékspres/ **a** definitely stated, not merely implied. **b** *archaic* (of a likeness) exact. **3 a** done, made, or sent for a special purpose. **b** (of messages or goods) delivered by a special messenger or service. ● *adv.* **1** at high speed. **2** by express messenger or train. ● *n.* **1 a** an express train or messenger. **b** an express rifle. **2** a company undertaking the transport of packages, etc. ● *v.tr.* send by express messenger or delivery. □□ **ex·press·ly** *adv.* (in senses 2 and 3a of *adj.*). [ME f. OF *expres* f. L *expressus* distinctly shown, past part. of *exprimere* (as EX-¹, *premere* press)]

ex·pres·sion /ikspréshən/ *n.* **1** the act or an instance of expressing. **2 a** a word or phrase expressed. **b** manner or means of expressing in language; wording; diction. **3** *Math.* a collection of symbols expressing a quantity. **4** a person's facial appearance or intonation of voice, esp. as indicating feeling. **5** depiction of feeling, movement, etc., in art. **6** conveying of feeling in the performance of a piece of music. □□ **ex•pres•sion•al** *adj.* **ex•pres•sion•less** *adj.* **ex•pres•sion•less•ly** *adv.* **ex•pres•sion•less•ness** *n.* [ME f. OF *expression* or L *expressio* f. *exprimere*: see EXPRESS[1]]

ex•pres•sion•ism /ikspréshənizəm/ *n.* a style of painting, music, drama, etc., in which an artist or writer seeks to express emotional experience rather than impressions of the external world. □□ **ex•pres•sion•ist** *n. & adj.* **ex•pres•sion•is•tic** *adj.* **ex•pres•sion•is•ti•cal•ly** *adv.*

ex•pres•sive /iksprésiv/ *adj.* **1** full of expression (*an expressive look*). **2** (foll. by *of*) serving to express (*words expressive of contempt*). □□ **ex•pres•sive•ly** *adv.* **ex•pres•sive•ness** *n.* **ex•pres•siv•i•ty** /–sívitee/ *n.* [ME f. F *expressif –ive* or med.L *expressivus* (as EXPRESSION)]

ex•pres•so var. of ESPRESSO.

ex•press train *n.* a fast train, stopping at few intermediate stations.

ex•press•way /iksprésway/ *n.* a divided highway for high-speed traffic.

ex•pro•pri•ate /ekspróspreeayt/ *v.tr.* **1** (esp. of the government) take away (property) from its owner. **2** (foll. by *from*) dispossess. □□ **ex•pro•pri•a•tion** /–áyshən/ *n.* **ex•pro•pri•a•tor** *n.* [med.L *expropriare expropriat-* (as EX-[1], *proprium* property: see PROPER)]

ex•pul•sion /ikspúlshən/ *n.* the act or an instance of expelling; the process of being expelled. □□ **ex•pul•sive** /–púlsiv/ *adj.* [ME f. L *expulsio* (as EXPEL)]

ex•punge /ikspúnj/ *v.tr.* (foll. by *from*) erase; remove (esp. a passage from a book or a name from a list). □□ **ex•punc•tion** /ikspúngkshən/ *n.* **ex•pung•er** *n.* [L *expungere expunct-* (as EX-[1], *pungere* prick)]

ex•pur•gate /ékspərgayt/ *v.tr.* **1** remove matter thought to be objectionable from (a book, etc.). **2** remove (such matter). □□ **ex•pur•ga•tion** /–gáyshən/ *n.* **ex•pur•ga•tor** *n.* **ex•pur•ga•to•ri•al** /ikspórgatáwreeəl/ *adj.* **ex•pur•ga•to•ry** *adj.* [L *expurgare expurgat-* (as EX-[1], *purgare* cleanse)]

ex•quis•ite /ékskwizit, ikskwízit/ *adj. & n. • adj.* **1** extremely beautiful or delicate. **2** acute; keenly felt (*exquisite pleasure*). **3 a** keen; highly sensitive or discriminating (*exquisite taste*). **b** elaborately devised or accomplished; consummate; perfect. • *n.* a person of refined (esp. affected) tastes. □□ **ex•quis•ite•ly** *adv.* **ex•quis•ite•ness** *n.* [ME f. L *exquirere exquisit-* (as EX-[1], *quaerere* seek)]

ex•san•gui•nate /iksánggwinayt/ *Med. v.tr.* drain of blood. □□ **ex•san•gui•na•tion** /–náyshən/ *n.* [L *exsanguinatus* as EX-[1], *sanguis –inis* blood)]

ex•sert /iksórt/ *v.tr. Biol.* put forth. [L *exserere*: see EXERT]

ex•serv•ice /éks-sórvis/ *adj. Brit.* **1** having formerly been a member of the armed forces. **2** relating to former servicemen and –women.

ex•serv•ice•man /éks-sórvismən/ *n.* (*pl.* **•men**) a former member of the armed forces.

ex•serv•ice•wom•an /éks-sórviswŏŏmən/ *n.* (*pl.* **•wom•en**) a former woman member of the armed forces.

ext. *abbr.* **1** exterior. **2** external.

ex•tant /ékstənt, ekstánt/ *adj.* (esp. of a document, etc.) still existing; surviving. [L *exstare exstant-* (as EX-[1], *stare* stand)]

ex•tem•po•ra•ne•ous /ikstémpəráyneeəs/ *adj.* spoken or done without preparation. □□ **ex•tem•po•ra•ne•ous•ly** *adv.* **ex•tem•po•ra•ne•ous•ness** *n.*

ex•tem•po•rar•y /ikstémp əreree/ *adj.* = EXTEMPORANEOUS. □□ **ex•tem•po•rar•i•ly** /–ráiralee/ *adv.* **ex•tem•po•rar•i•ness** *n.*

ex•tem•po•re /ikstémpəree/ *adj. & adv.* **1** without preparation. **2** offhand. [L *ex tempore* on the spur of the moment, lit. out of the time f. *tempus* time]

ex•tem•po•rize /ikstémpəriz/ *v.tr.* (also *absol.*) compose or produce (music, a speech, etc.) without preparation; improvise. □□ **ex•tem•po•ri•za•tion** *n.*

ex•tend /iksténd/ *v.* **1** *tr. & intr.* lengthen or make larger in space or time. **2 a** *tr.* stretch or lay out at full length. **b** *tr. & intr.* (often foll. by *over*) (cause to) stretch or span over a period of time. **3** *intr. & tr.* (foll. by *to, over*) reach or be or make continuous over a certain area. **4** *intr.* (foll. by *to*) have a certain scope (*the permit does not extend to camping*). **5** *tr.* offer or accord (an invitation, hospitality, kindness, etc.). **6** *tr.* (usu. *refl.* or in *passive*) tax the powers of (an athlete, horse, etc.) to the utmost. □□ **ex•tend•a•ble** *adj.* **ex•tend•a•bil•i•ty** *n.* **ex•tend•i•ble** *adj.* **ex•tend•i•bil•i•ty** *n.* **ex•ten•si•ble** /–sténsibəl/ *adj.* **ex•ten•si•bil•i•ty** *n.* [ME f. L *extendere extens-* or *extent-* stretch out (as EX-[1], *tendere* stretch)]

ex•tend•ed fam•i•ly *n.* **1** a family group that includes relatives living in one household. **2** all the members of a family, including cousins, in-laws, etc.

ex•tend•ed-play *adj.* (of a phonograph record) playing for longer than most singles, usu. at 45 r.p.m.; (of a videocassette recording) playing at the slowest recordable speed.

ex•tend•er /iksténdər/ *n.* **1** a person or thing that extends. **2** a substance added to paint, ink, glue, etc., to dilute its color or increase its bulk.

ex•ten•sile /iksténsəl, –sīl/ *adj.* capable of being stretched out or protruded.

ex•ten•sion /iksténshən/ *n.* **1** the act or an instance of extending; the process of being extended. **2** prolongation; enlargement. **3** a part enlarging or added on to a main structure or building. **4** an additional part of anything. **5 a** a subsidiary telephone on the same line as the main one. **b** its number. **6 a** an additional period of time, esp. extending allowance for a project, etc. **b** permission for the sale of alcoholic drinks until later than usual, granted to licensed premises on special occasions. **7** extramural instruction by a university or college (*extension course*). **8** extent; range. **9** *Logic* a group of things denoted by a term. □□ **ex•ten•sion•al** *adj.* [ME f. LL *extensio* (as EXTEND)]

ex•ten•sive /iksténsiv/ *adj.* **1** covering a large area in space or time. **2** having a wide scope; far-reaching; comprehensive (*an extensive knowledge of music*). **3** *Agriculture* involving cultivation from a large area, with a minimum of special resources (cf. INTENSIVE). □□ **ex•ten•sive•ly** *adv.* **ex•ten•sive•ness** *n.* [F *extensif –ive* or LL *extensivus* (as EXTENSION)]

ex•ten•som•e•ter /ékstensómitər/ *n.* **1** an instrument for measuring deformation of metal under stress. **2** an instrument using such deformation to record elastic strains in other materials. [L *extensus* (as EXTEND) + –METER]

ex•ten•sor /iksténsər/ *n.* (in full **extensor muscle**) *Anat.* a muscle that extends or straightens out part of the body (cf. FLEXOR). [mod.L (as EXTEND)]

ex•tent /ikstént/ *n.* **1** the space over which a thing extends. **2** the width or limits of application; scope (*to a great extent; to the full extent of their power*). [ME f. AF *extente* f. med.L *extenta* past part. of L *extendere*: see EXTEND]

ex•ten•u•ate /ikstényoo-ayt/ *v.tr.* (often as **extenuating** *adj.*) lessen the seeming seriousness of (guilt or an offense) by reference to some mitigating factor. □□ **ex•ten•u•at•ing•ly** *adv.* **ex•ten•u•a•tion** /–áyshən/ *n.* **ex•ten•u•a•to•ry** /–yŏŏətáwree/ *adj.* [L *extenuare extenuat-* (as EX-[1], *tenuis* thin)]

ex•te•ri•or /iksteéreeər/ *adj. & n. • adj.* **1 a** of or on the outer side (opp. INTERIOR). **b** (foll. by *to*) situated on the outside of (a building, etc.). **c** coming from outside. **2** *Cinematog.* outdoor. • *n.* **1** the outward aspect or surface of a building, etc. **2** the outward or apparent behavior or demeanor of a person. **3** *Cinematog.* an outdoor scene. □□ **ex•te•ri•or•i•ty** /–ree-áwritee, –ree-ór–/ *n.* **ex•te•ri•or•ize** *v.tr.* **ex•te•ri•or•ly** *adv.* [L, compar. of *exterus* outside]

ex•te•ri•or an•gle *n.* the angle between the side of a rectilinear figure and the adjacent side extended outward.

ex•ter•mi•nate /ikstórminayt/ *v.tr.* **1** destroy utterly (esp. something living). **2** get rid of; eliminate (a pest, disease, etc.). □□ **ex•ter•mi•na•tion** /–náyshən/ *n.* **ex•ter•mi•na•tor** *n.* **ex•ter•mi•na•to•ry** /–nətáwree/ *adj.* [L *exterminare exterminat-* (as EX-[1], *terminus* boundary)]

ex•ter•nal /ikstórnəl/ *adj. & n. • adj.* **1 a** of or situated on the outside or visible part (opp. INTERNAL). **b** coming or derived from the outside or an outside source. **2** relating to a country's foreign affairs. **3** outside the conscious subject (*the external world*). **4** (of medicine, etc.) for use on the outside of the body. **5** for or concerning students taking the examinations of a university without attending it. • *n.* (in *pl.*) **1** the outward features or aspect. **2** external circumstances. **3** inessentials. □□ **ex•ter•nal•i•ty** /–nálitee/ *n.* (*pl.* **•ties**). **ex•ter•nal•ly** *adv.* [med.L f. L *externus* f. *exterus* outside]

SYNONYM TIP extemporaneous

IMPROMPTU, IMPROVISED, IMPULSIVE, OFFHAND, SPONTANEOUS, UNPREMEDITATED. If you're the kind of person who acts first and thinks about it later, your friends are likely to describe you as **spontaneous**, which means that you behave in a very natural way, without prompting or premeditation (*a spontaneous embrace; a spontaneous burst of applause*). Or they may call you **impulsive**, which has somewhat less positive connotations, suggesting someone who is governed by his or her own moods and whims without regard for others. Although *impulsive* behavior may be admirable (*his impulsive generosity prompted him to empty his pockets*), it is just as likely to be ugly or disruptive (*impulsive buying; an impulsive temper*). **Offhand** also has negative overtones, implying behavior that is spontaneous to the point of being cavalier or brusque (*her offhand remarks offended them*). **Unpremeditated** is a more formal term, often used in a legal context to describe an impulsive crime committed without forethought (*unpremeditated murder*). In the world of public speaking, an **extemporaneous** speech is one that is delivered without referring to a written text, although the speaker may have been aware that he or she would be called upon to speak, while an **impromptu** speech is one that the speaker was not expecting to give. **Improvised** is often used in the context of a musical or theatrical performance, suggesting a basic structure within which the performers are free to play in a spontaneous manner (*by its very nature, jazz is improvised*). But it has broader applications as well; in fact, anything that is devised on the spur of the moment may be described as *improvised*.

ex·ter·nal ev·i·dence *n.* evidence derived from a source independent of the thing discussed.

ex·ter·nal·ize /ikstɔ́rnəlīz/ *v.tr.* **1** give or attribute external existence or form to (*elements of the internal construction were externalized onto the façade*). **2** express (a thought or feeling) in words or actions. **3** *Psychol.* project (a mental image or process) onto a figure outside oneself (*one is generally externalizing when he attributes his own feelings to forces outside himself*). □□ **ex·ter·nal·i·za·tion** *n.*

ex·ter·o·cep·tive /ékstərōséptiv/ *adj.* *Biol.* relating to stimuli produced outside an organism. [irreg. f. L *externus* exterior + RECEPTIVE]

ex·ter·ri·to·ri·al /éksteritáwreeəl/ *adj.* = EXTRATERRITORIAL. □□ **ex·ter·ri·to·ri·al·i·ty** /–reeálitee/ *n.*

ex·tinct /ikstíngkt/ *adj.* **1** (of a family, class, or species) that has died out. **2 a** (of fire, etc.) no longer burning. **b** (of a volcano) that no longer erupts. **3** (of life, hope, etc.) terminated; quenched. **4** (of an office, etc.) obsolete. **5** (of a title of nobility) having no qualified claimant. [ME f. L *exstinguere exstinct-* (as EX-¹, *stinguere* quench)]

ex·tinc·tion /ikstíngkshən/ *n.* **1** the act of making extinct; the state of being or process of becoming extinct. **2** the act of extinguishing; the state of being extinguished. **3** total destruction or annihilation. **4** the wiping out of a debt. **5** *Physics* a reduction in the intensity of radiation by absorption, scattering, etc. □□ **ex·tinc·tive** *adj.* [L *extinctio* (as EXTINCT)]

ex·tin·guish /ikstínggwish/ *v.tr.* **1** cause (a flame, light, etc.) to die out; put out. **2** make extinct; annihilate; destroy (*a program to extinguish disease*). **3** put an end to; terminate; obscure utterly (a feeling, quality, etc.). **4 a** abolish; wipe out (a debt). **b** *Law* render void. **5** *colloq.* reduce to silence (*the argument extinguished the opposition*). **6** *archaic* surpass by superior brilliance. □□ **ex·tin·guish·a·ble** *adj.* **ex·tin·guish·ment** *n.* [irreg. f. L *extinguere* (as EXTINCT): cf. *distinguish*]

ex·tin·guish·er /ikstínggwishər/ *n.* a person or thing that extinguishes, esp. = FIRE EXTINGUISHER.

ex·tir·pate /ékstərpayt/ *v.tr.* root out; destroy completely. □□ **ex·tir·pa·tion** /–páyshən/ *n.* **ex·tir·pa·tor** *n.* [L *exstirpare exstirpat-* (as EX-¹, *stirps* stem)]

ex·tol /ikstṓl/ *v.tr.* (**ex·tolled, ex·tol·ling**) praise enthusiastically. □□ **ex·tol·ler** *n.* **ex·tol·ment** *n.* [L *extollere* (as EX-¹, *tollere* raise)]

ex·tort /ikstáwrt/ *v.tr.* obtain by force, threats, persistent demands, etc. □□ **ex·tort·er** *n.* **ex·tor·tive** *adj.* [L *extorquēre extort-* (as EX-¹, *torquēre* twist)]

ex·tor·tion /ikstáwrshən/ *n.* **1** the act or an instance of extorting, esp. money. **2** illegal exaction. □□ **ex·tor·tion·er** *n.* **ex·tor·tion·ist** *n.* [ME f. LL *extortio* (as EXTORT)]

ex·tor·tion·ate /ikstáwrshənət/ *adj.* **1** (of a price, etc.) exorbitant. **2** using or given to extortion (*extortionate methods*). □□ **ex·tor·tion·ate·ly** *adv.*

ex·tra /ékstrə/ *adj., adv., & n.* ● *adj.* additional; more than is usual or necessary or expected. ● *adv.* **1** more than usually. **2** additionally (*was charged extra*). ● *n.* **1** an extra thing. **2** a thing for which an extra charge is made; such a charge. **3** a person engaged temporarily to fill out a scene in a motion picture or play, esp. as one of a crowd. **4** a special issue of a newspaper, etc. [prob. a shortening of EXTRAORDINARY]

extra- /ékstrə/ *comb. form* **1** outside; beyond (*extragalactic*). **2** beyond the scope of (*extracurricular*). [med.L f. L *extra* outside]

ex·tra·cel·lu·lar /ékstrəsélyələr/ *adj.* situated or taking place outside a cell or cells.

ex·tract *v. & n.* ● *v.tr.* /ikstrákt/ **1** remove or take out, esp. by effort or force (anything firmly rooted). **2** obtain (money, an admission, etc.) with difficulty or against a person's will. **3** obtain (a natural resource) from the earth. **4** select or reproduce for quotation or performance (a passage of writing, music, etc.). **5** obtain (juice, etc.) by suction, pressure, distillation, etc. **6** derive (pleasure, etc.). **7** *Math.* find (the root of a number). **8** *archaic* deduce (a principle, etc.). ● *n.* /ékstrakt/ **1** a short passage taken from a book, piece of music, etc.; an excerpt. **2** a preparation containing the active principle of a substance in concentrated form (*malt extract*). □□ **ex·tract·a·ble** *adj.* **ex·tract·a·bil·i·ty** *n.* [L *extrahere extract-* (as EX-¹, *trahere* draw)]

ex·trac·tion /ikstrákshən/ *n.* **1** the act or an instance of extracting; the process of being extracted. **2** the removal of a tooth. **3** origin; lineage; descent (*of German extraction*). **4** something extracted; an extract. [ME f. F f. LL *extractio –onis* (as EXTRACT)]

ex·trac·tive /ikstráktiv/ *adj.* of or involving extraction, esp. extensive extracting of natural resources without provision for their renewal.

ex·trac·tor /ikstráktər/ *n.* **1** a person or machine that extracts. **2** (*attrib.*) (of a device) that extracts bad air, etc., or ventilates a room (*extractor fan; extractor hood*).

ex·tra·cur·ric·u·lar /ékstrəkəríkyələr/ *adj.* (of a subject of study) not included in the normal curriculum.

ex·tra·dit·a·ble /ékstrədītəbəl/ *adj.* **1** liable to extradition. **2** (of a crime) warranting extradition.

ex·tra·dite /ékstrədīt/ *v.tr.* hand over (a person accused or convicted of a crime) to the country, state, etc., in which the crime was committed.

ex·tra·di·tion /ékstrədíshən/ *n.* **1** the extraditing of a person accused or convicted of a crime. **2** *Psychol.* the localizing of a sensation at a distance from the center of sensation.

ex·tra·dos /ékstrədos, –dōs, ekstráydos/ *n.* *Archit.* the upper or outer curve of an arch (opp. INTRADOS). [EXTRA- + *dos* back f. L *dorsum*]

ex·tra·ga·lac·tic /ékstrəgəláktik/ *adj.* occurring or existing outside the galaxy.

ex·tra·ju·di·cial /ékstrəjōōdíshəl/ *adj.* **1** not legally authorized. **2** (of a confession) not made in court. □□ **ex·tra·ju·di·cial·ly** *adv.*

ex·tra·mar·i·tal /ékstrəmárit'l/ *adj.* (esp. of sexual relations) occurring outside marriage. □□ **ex·tra·mar·i·tal·ly** *adv.*

ex·tra·mun·dane /ékstrəmundáyn/ *adj.* outside or beyond the physical world.

ex·tra·mu·ral /ékstrəmyо́orəl/ *adj. & n.* ● *adj.* **1** taught or conducted off the premises of a university, college, or school. **2** additional to normal teaching or studies, esp. for nonresident students. **3** outside the walls or boundaries of a town or city. ● *n.* an extramural lesson, course, etc. □□ **ex·tra·mu·ral·ly** *adv.* [L *extra muros* outside the walls]

ex·tra·ne·ous /ikstráyneeəs/ *adj.* **1** of external origin. **2** (often foll. by *to*) **a** separate from the object to which it is attached, etc. **b** external to; irrelevant or unrelated to. **c** inessential; superfluous. □□ **ex·tra·ne·ous·ly** *adv.* **ex·tra·ne·ous·ness** *n.* [L *extraneus*]

ex·traor·di·nar·y /ikstráwrd'neree, ékstrəáwr–/ *adj.* **1** unusual or remarkable; out of the usual course. **2** unusually great (*an extraordinary talent*). **3** so exceptional as to provoke astonishment or admiration. **4 a** (of an official, etc.) additional; specially employed (*envoy extraordinary*). **b** (of a meeting) specially convened. □□ **ex·traor·di·nar·i·ly** *adv.* **ex·traor·di·nar·i·ness** *n.* [L *extraordinarius* f. *extra ordinem* outside the usual order]

SPELLING TIP **extraordinary**

Someone who is extraordinary is *extra ordinary.*

ex·trap·o·late /ikstrápəlayt/ *v.tr.* (also *absol.*) **1** *Math. & Philos.* **a** calculate approximately from known values, data, etc. (others which lie outside the range of those known). **b** calculate on the basis of (known facts) to estimate unknown facts, esp. extend (a curve) on a graph. **2** infer more widely from a limited range of known facts. □□ **ex·trap·o·la·tion** /–láyshən/ *n.* **ex·trap·o·la·tive** *adj.* **ex·trap·o·la·tor** *n.* [EXTRA- + INTERPOLATE]

ex·tra·sen·so·ry /ékstrəsénsəree/ *adj.* regarded as derived by means other than the known senses, e.g., by telepathy, clairvoyance, etc.

ex·tra·sen·so·ry per·cep·tion *n.* a person's supposed faculty of perceiving things by means other than the known senses, e.g., by telepathy or clairvoyance. ¶ Abbr.: ESP.

ex·tra·ter·res·tri·al /ékstrətərréstreeəl/ *adj. & n.* ● *adj.* **1** outside the earth or its atmosphere. **2** (in science fiction) from outer space. ● *n.* (in science fiction) a being from outer space.

ex·tra·ter·ri·to·ri·al /ékstrətéritáwreeəl/ *adj.* **1** situated or (of laws, etc.) valid outside a country's territory. **2** (of an ambassador, etc.) free from the jurisdiction of the territory of residence. □□ **ex·tra·ter·ri·to·ri·al·i·ty** /–reeálitee/ *n.* [L *extra territorium* outside the territory]

ex·tra time *n.* *Sports Brit.* = OVERTIME 3.

ex·trav·a·gance /ikstrávəgəns/ *n.* **1** excessive spending or use of resources; being extravagant. **2** an instance or item of this. **3** unrestrained or absurd behavior, speech, thought, or writing. □□ **ex·trav·a·gan·cy** *n.* (*pl.* **·cies**) [F (as EXTRAVAGANT)]

ex·trav·a·gant /ikstrávəgənt/ *adj.* **1** spending (esp. money) excessively; immoderate or wasteful in use of resources. **2** exorbitant; costing much. **3** exceeding normal restraint or sense; unreasonable; absurd (*extravagant claims*). □□ **ex·trav·a·gant·ly** *adv.* [ME f. med.L *extravagari* (as EXTRA-, *vagari* wander)]

ex·trav·a·gan·za /ikstrávəgánzə/ *n.* **1** a fanciful literary, musical, or dramatic composition. **2** a spectacular theatrical or television production, esp. of light entertainment. [It. *estravaganza* extravagance]

ex·trav·a·sate /ikstrávəsayt/ *v.* **1** *tr.* force out (a fluid, esp. blood) from its proper vessel. **2** *intr.* (of blood, lava, etc.) flow out. □□ **ex·trav·a·sa·tion** /–sáyshən/ *n.* [L *extra* outside + *vas* vessel]

ex·tra·ve·hic·u·lar /ékstrəvihíkyələr/ *adj.* outside a vehicle, esp. a spacecraft.

ex·tre·ma *pl.* of EXTREMUM.

ex·treme /ikstréem/ *adj. & n.* ● *adj.* **1** reaching a high or the highest degree; exceedingly great or intense; exceptional (*extreme old age; in extreme danger*). **2 a** severe; stringent; lacking restraint or moderation (*take extreme measures; an extreme reaction*). **b** (of a person, opinion, etc.) going to great lengths; advocating immoderate measures. **3** outermost; furthest from the center; situated at either end (*the extreme edge*). **4** *Polit.* on the far left or right of a party. **5** utmost; last. ● *n.* **1** (often in *pl.*) one or other of two things as remote or as different as possible. **2** a thing at either end of anything. **3** the highest degree of anything. **4** *Math.* the first or the last term of a ratio or series. **5** *Logic* the subject or predicate in a proposition; the major or the minor term in a syllogism. □ **go to extremes** take an extreme course of action. **go to the other extreme** take a diametrically opposite course of action. **in the extreme** to an extreme degree. □□ **ex·treme·ly** *adv.* **ex·treme·ness** *n.* [ME f. OF f. L *extremus* superl. of *exterus* outward]

ex·treme unc·tion *n.* the last rites in the Roman Catholic and Orthodox churches.

ex·trem·ist /ikstreémist/ *n.* (also *attrib.*) a person who holds extreme or fanatical political or religious views and esp. resorts to or advocates extreme action. □□ **ex·trem·ism** *n.*

ex·trem·i·ty /ikstrémitee/ *n.* (*pl.* **·ties**) **1** the extreme point; the very end. **2** (in *pl.*) the hands and feet. **3** a condition of extreme adversity or difficulty. **4** excessiveness; extremeness. [ME f. OF *extremité* or L *extremitas* (as EXTREME)]

ex·tre·mum /ikstreéməm/ *n.* (*pl.* **ex·tre·ma** /-mə/) *Math.* the maximum or minimum value of a function. □□ **ex·tre·mal** *adj.* [L, neut. of *extremus* EXTREME]

ex·tri·cate /ékstrikayt/ *v.tr.* (often foll. by *from*) free or disentangle from a constraint or difficulty. □□ **ex·tri·ca·ble** *adj.* **ex·tri·ca·tion** /-káyshən/ *n.* [L *extricare extricat-* (as EX-¹, *tricae* perplexities)]

ex·trin·sic /ekstrínsik, -zik/ *adj.* **1** not inherent or intrinsic; not essential (opp. INTRINSIC). **2** (often foll. by *to*) extraneous; lying outside; not belonging (to). **3** originating or operating from without. □□ **ex·trin·si·cal·ly** *adv.* [LL *extrinsicus* outward f. L *extrinsecus* (adv.) f. *exter* outside + *secus* beside]

ex·tro·vert /ékstrəvərt/ *n. & adj.* ● *n.* **1** *Psychol.* a person predominantly concerned with external things or objective considerations. **2** an outgoing or sociable person. ● *adj.* typical or characteristic of an extrovert. □□ **ex·tro·ver·sion** /-vórzhən/ *n.* **ex·tro·vert·ed** *adj.* [*extro-* = EXTRA- (after *intro-*) + L *vertere* turn]

ex·trude /ikstroód/ *v.tr.* **1** (foll. by *from*) thrust or force out. **2** shape metal, plastics, etc., by forcing them through a die. □□ **ex·tru·sion** /-troózhən/ *n.* **ex·tru·sile** /-troósəl, -sīl/ *adj.* **ex·tru·sive** /-troósiv/ *adj.* [L *extrudere extrus-* (as EX-¹, *trudere* thrust)]

ex·u·ber·ant /igzoóbərənt/ *adj.* **1** lively, high-spirited. **2** (of a plant, etc.) prolific; growing copiously. **3** (of feelings, etc.) abounding; lavish; effusive. □□ **ex·u·ber·ance** /-rəns/ *n.* **ex·u·ber·ant·ly** *adv.* [F *exubérant* f. L *exuberare* (as EX-¹, *uberare* be fruitful f. *uber* fertile)]

ex·u·ber·ate /igzoóbərayt/ *v.intr.* be exuberant.

ex·ude /igzoód, iksoód/ *v.* **1** *tr. & intr.* (of a liquid, moisture, etc.) escape or cause to escape gradually; ooze out; give off. **2** *tr.* emit (a smell). **3** *tr.* display (an emotion, etc.) freely or abundantly (*exuded displeasure*). □□ **ex·u·date** /éksyoódayt, éksə-/ *n.* **ex·u·da·tion** *n.* **ex·u·da·tive** *adj.* [L *exsudare* (as EX-¹, *sudare* sweat)]

ex·ult /igzúlt/ *v.intr.* (often foll. by *at, in, over,* or *to* + infin.) **1** be greatly joyful. **2** (often foll. by *over*) have a feeling of triumph (over a person). □□ **ex·ul·tan·cy** /-tənsee/ *n.* **ex·ul·ta·tion** /égzultáyshən, éksul-/ *n.* **ex·ul·tant** *adj.* **ex·ul·tant·ly** *adv.* **ex·ul·ting·ly** *adv.* [L *exsultare* (as EX-¹, *saltare* frequent. of *salire salt-* leap)]

ex·urb /éksərb, égzərb/ *n.* a district outside a city or town, esp. a prosperous area beyond the suburbs. □□ **ex·ur·ban** *adj.* **ex·ur·ban·ite** /eksórbənīt, égzór-/ *n.* [L *ex* out of + *urbs* city, or back-form. f. *exurban* (as EX-¹ + URBAN, after *suburban*)]

ex·ur·bi·a /eksórbeeə, egzór-/ *n.* the exurbs collectively; the region beyond the suburbs. [EX-¹, after *suburbia*]

ex·u·vi·ae /igzoóvee-ee/ *n.pl.* (also treated as *sing.*) an animal's cast skin or covering. □□ **ex·u·vi·al** *adj.* [L, = animal's skins, spoils of the enemy, f. *exuere* divest oneself of]

ex·u·vi·ate /igzoóveeayt/ *v.tr.* shed (a skin, etc.). □□ **ex·u·vi·a·tion** /-áyshən/ *n.*

ex vo·to /eks vótō/ *n.* (*pl.* **·tos**) an offering made in pursuance of a vow. [L, = out of a vow]

-ey /ee/ *suffix* var. of -Y².

ey·as /íəs/ *n.* a young hawk, esp. one taken from the nest for training in falconry. [orig. *nyas* f. F *niais* ult. f. L *nidus* nest: for loss of *n-* cf. ADDER]

eye /ī/ *n. & v.* ● *n.* **1 a** the organ of sight in humans and other animals. **b** the light-detecting organ in some invertebrates. **2** the eye characterized by the color of the iris (*has blue eyes*). **3** the region around the eye (*eyes red from crying*). **4** a glass or plastic ball serving as an artificial eye. **5** (in *sing.* or *pl.*) sight; the faculty of sight (*demonstrate to the eye; need perfect eyes to be a pilot*). **6** a particular visual faculty or talent; visual appreciation; perspicacity (*a straight eye; cast an expert eye over*). **7 a** (in *sing.* or *pl.*) a look, gaze, or glance, esp. as indicating the disposition of the viewer (*a friendly eye*). **b** (**the eye**) a flirtatious or sexually provocative glance. **8** mental awareness; consciousness. **9** a person or animal, etc., that sees on behalf of another. **10 a** = ELECTRIC EYE. **b** = PRIVATE EYE. **11** a thing like an eye, esp.: **a** a spot on a peacock's tail. **b** the leaf bud of a potato.

12 the center of something circular, e.g., a flower or target. **13** the relatively calm region at the center of a storm or hurricane. **14** an aperture in an implement, esp. a needle, for the insertion of something, e.g., thread. **15** a ring or loop for a bolt or hook, etc., to pass through. ● *v.tr.* (**eyes, eyed, eye·ing** or **ey·ing**) watch or observe closely, esp. admiringly or with curiosity or suspicion. □ **all eyes 1** watching intently. **2** general attention (*all eyes were on us*). **before one's** (or **one's very**) **eyes** right in front of one. **an eye for an eye** retaliation in kind (Exodus 21:24). **have one's eye on** wish or plan to procure. **have an eye for 1** be quick to notice. **2** be partial to. **have an eye to** have as one's objective; prudently consider. **have eyes for** be interested in; wish to acquire. **have an eye to** have as one's objective; prudently consider. **hit a person in the eye** (or **between the eyes**) *colloq.* be very obvious or impressive. **keep an eye on 1** pay attention to. **2** look after; take care of. **keep an eye open** (or **out**) (often foll. by *for*) watch carefully. **keep one's eyes open** (or **peeled**) watch out; be on the alert. **lower one's eyes** look modestly or sheepishly down or away. **make eyes at** look amorously or flirtatiously at. **my eye** *sl.* nonsense. **open a person's eyes** be enlightening or revealing to a person. **raise one's eyes** look upward. **see eye to eye** (often foll. by *with*) be in full agreement. **set eyes on** catch sight of. **take one's eyes off** (usu. in *neg.*) stop watching; stop paying attention to. **under the eye of** under the supervision or observation of. **up to one's eyes in 1** deeply engaged or involved in; inundated with (*up to my eyes in work*). **2** to the utmost limit (*mortgaged up to the eyes*). **with one's eyes open** deliberately; with full awareness. **with one's eyes shut** (or **closed**) **1** easily; with little effort. **2** without awareness; unobservant (*goes around with his eyes shut*). **with an eye to** with a view to; prudently considering. **with a friendly** (or **jealous,** etc.) **eye** with a feeling of friendship, jealousy, etc. **with one eye on** directing one's attention partly to. **with one eye shut** *colloq.* easily; with little effort (*could do this with one eye shut*). □□ **eyed** *adj.* (also in *comb.*). **eye·less** *adj.* [OE *ēage* f. Gmc]

eye·ball /íbawl/ *n. & v.* ● *n.* the ball of the eye within the lids and socket. ● *v. sl.* **1** *tr.* look or stare at. **2** *intr.* look or stare. □ **eyeball to eyeball** *colloq.* confronting closely. **to** (or **up to**) **the eyeballs** *colloq.* completely (permeated, soaked, etc.).

eye bath *n.* = EYECUP.

eye·black /íblak/ *n. Brit.* = MASCARA.

eye·bolt /íbōlt/ *n.* a bolt or bar with an eye at the end for a hook, etc.

eye·bright /íbrīt/ *n.* any plant of the genus *Euphrasia,* formerly used as a remedy for weak eyes.

eye·brow /íbrow/ *n.* the line of hair growing on the ridge above the eye socket. □ **raise one's eyebrows** show surprise, disbelief, or mild disapproval.

eye-catch·ing *adj. colloq.* striking; attractive.

eye con·tact *n.* looking directly into another person's eyes.

eye·cup /íkup/ *n.* a small glass or vessel for applying eyewash to the eye.

eye·drop·per /ídropər/ *n.* DROPPER *n.* 1.

eye·ful /ífool/ *n.* (*pl.* **·fuls**) *colloq.* **1** a long, steady look. **2** a visually striking person or thing. **3** anything thrown or blown into the eye.

eye·glass /íglas/ *n.* **1 a** a lens for correcting or assisting defective sight. **b** (in *pl.*) a pair of these, usu. set into a frame that rests on the nose and has side pieces that curve over the ears. **2** an eyecup.

eye·hole /íhōl/ *n.* a hole to look through.

eye·lash /ílash/ *n.* each of the hairs growing on the edges of the eyelids. □ **by an eyelash** by a very small margin.

eye·let /ílit/ *n. & v.* ● *n.* **1** a small hole in paper, leather, cloth, etc., for string or rope, etc., to pass through. **2** a metal ring reinforcement for this. **3** a small eye, esp. the ocellus on a butterfly's wing. **4** a form of decoration in embroidery. **5** a small hole for observation, shooting through, etc. ● *v.tr.* (**eye·let·ed, eye·let·ing; eye·let·ted, eye·let·ting**) provide with eyelets. [ME f. OF *oillet* dimin. of *oil* eye f. L *oculus*]

eye lev·el *n.* the level seen by the eyes looking horizontally (*put it at eye level*).

eye·lid /ílid/ *n.* the upper or lower fold of skin closing to cover the eye.

eye·lin·er /ílīnər/ *n.* a cosmetic applied as a line around the eye.

eye mask *n.* **1** a covering of soft material saturated with a lotion for refreshing the eyes. **2** a covering for the eyes.

eye-o·pen·er *n. colloq.* **1** an enlightening experience; an unexpected revelation. **2** an alcoholic drink taken on waking up.

eye·piece /ípees/ *n.* the lens or lenses at the end of a microscope, telescope, etc., to which the eye is applied.

eye rhyme *n.* a correspondence of words in spelling but not in pronunciation (e.g., *love* and *move*).

eyes front *n.* (also **eyes left** or **eyes right**) *Mil.* a command to turn the head in the direction stated.

eye·shade /íshayd/ *n.* a device, esp. a visor, to protect the eyes, esp. from strong light.

eye shad·ow *n.* a colored cosmetic applied to the eyelids.

eye·shot /íshot/ *n.* seeing distance (*out of eyeshot*).

eye·sight /ísīt/ *n.* the faculty or power of seeing.

eye·sore /ísawr/ *n.* a visually offensive or ugly thing, esp. a building.

eye·spot /íspot/ *n.* **1 a** a light-sensitive area on the bodies of some invertebrate animals, e.g., flatworms, starfish, etc.; an ocellus. **b** *Bot.* an area of light-sensitive pigment found in some algae, etc. **2** any of several fungus diseases of plants characterized by yellowish oval spots on the leaves and stems.

eye·stalk /ístawk/ *n. Zool.* a movable stalk carrying the eye, esp. in crabs, shrimps, etc.

eye·strain /ístrayn/ *n.* fatigue of the (internal or external) muscles of the eye.

eye·tooth /ítooth/ *n.* a canine tooth just under or next to the eye, esp. in the upper jaw.

eye·wash /íwosh, íwawsh/ *n.* **1** lotion for the eye. **2** *sl.* nonsense; bunkum; pretentious or insincere talk.

eye·wear /íwair/ *n.* spectacles, goggles, or lenses for improving eyesight or protecting the eyes.

eye·wit·ness /íwítnis/ *n.* a person who has personally seen a thing done or happen and can give evidence of it.

eye worm *n.* a nematode worm, *Loa loa*, parasitic on humans and other primates in Central and West Africa.

ey·ot *Brit.* var. of AIT.

ey·ra /áirə/ *n. Zool.* a red form of jaguarundi. [Tupi (*e*)*irara*]

ey·rie var. of AERIE.

Ezek. *abbr.* Ezekiel (Old Testament).

F

F¹ /ef/ *n.* (also **f**) (*pl.* **Fs** or **F's**) **1** the sixth letter of the alphabet. **2** *Mus.* the fourth note of the diatonic scale of C major. **3** a grade indicating failure.

F² *abbr.* (also **F.**) **1** Fahrenheit. **2** farad(s). **3** female. **4** US fighter aircraft designation **5** *Brit.* fine (pencil lead). **6** formula motor racing (*an F1 driver*).

F³ *symb. Chem.* the element fluorine.

f *abbr.* (also **f.**) **1** female. **2** feminine. **3** following page, etc. **4** *Mus.* forte. **5** folio. **6** focal length (cf. F-NUMBER). **7** = FEMTO-. **8** filly. **9** foreign. **10** frequency.

fa /faa/ *n.* (also **fah**) *Mus.* **1** (in tonic sol-fa) the fourth note of a major scale. **2** the note F in the fixed-do system. [ME *fa* f. L *famuli*: see GAMUT]

FAA *abbr.* Federal Aviation Administration.

fab /fab/ *adj. colloq.* fabulous; marvelous. [abbr.]

Fa•bi•an /fáybeeən/ *n. & adj.* ● *n.* a member or supporter of the Fabian Society, an organization of socialists aiming at a gradual rather than revolutionary achievement of socialism; founded in England (1884). ● *adj.* **1** relating to or characteristic of the Fabians. **2** employing a cautiously persistent and dilatory strategy to wear out an enemy (*Fabian tactics*). □□ **Fa•bi•an•ism** *n.* **Fa•bi•an•ist** *n.* [L *Fabianus* f. the name of Q. *Fabius* Maximus Cunctator (= delayer), Roman general of the 3rd c. BC, noted for cautious strategies]

fa•ble /fáybəl/ *n. & v.* ● *n.* **1** a a supernatural one, not based on fact. **b** a tale, esp. with animals as characters, conveying a moral. **2** (*collect.*) myths and legendary tales (*in fable*). **3 a** a false statement; a lie. **b** a thing only supposed to exist. ● *v.* **1** *intr.* tell fictitious tales. **2** *tr.* describe fictitiously. **3** *tr.* (as **fabled** *adj.*) celebrated in fable; famous; legendary. □□ **fa•bler** /fáyblər/ *n.* [ME f. OF *fabler* f. L *fabulari* f. *fabula* discourse f. *fari* speak]

fab•li•au /fáybleeō/ *n.* (*pl.* **fab•li•aux** /-ōz/) a metrical tale in early French poetry, often coarsely humorous. [F f. OF dialect *fabliaux*, *-ax* pl. of *fablel* dimin. (as FABLE)]

fab•ric /fábrik/ *n.* **1 a** a woven material; a textile. **b** other material resembling woven cloth. **2** a structure or framework, esp. the walls, floor, and roof of a building. **3** (in abstract senses) the essential structure or essence of a thing (*the fabric of society*). [ME f. F *fabrique* f. L *fabrica* f. *faber* metal worker, etc.]

fab•ri•cate /fábrikayt/ *v.tr.* **1** construct or manufacture, esp. from prepared components. **2** invent or concoct (a story, evidence, etc.). **3** forge (a document). □□ **fab•ri•ca•tor** *n.* [L *fabricare fabricat-* (as FABRIC)]

fab•ri•ca•tion /fábrikáyshən/ *n.* **1** the action or process of manufacturing or constructing something. **2** the invention of a lie, forging of a document, etc. **3** an invention or falsehood; a forgery. [L *fabricatio* (as FABRICATE)]

fab•u•list /fábyəlist/ *n.* **1** a composer of fables. **2** a liar. [F *fabuliste* f. L *fabula:* tale]

fab•u•lous /fábyələs/ *adj.* **1** incredible; exaggerated; absurd (*fabulous wealth*). **2** *colloq.* marvelous (*looking fabulous*). **3 a** celebrated in fable. **b** legendary; mythical. □□ **fabulosity** /-lósitee/ *n.* **fab•u•lous•ly** *adv.* **fab•u•lous•ness** *n.* [F *fabuleux* or L *fabulosus* (as FABLE)]

fa•çade /fəsaád/ *n.* **1** the face of a building, esp. its principal front. **2** an outward appearance or front, esp. a deceptive one. [F (as FACE)]

face /fays/ *n. & v.* ● *n.* **1** the front of the head from the forehead to the chin. **2 a** the expression of the facial features (*had a happy face*). **b** an expression of disgust; a grimace (*make a face*). **3** composure; coolness; effrontery. **4** the surface of a thing, esp. as regarded or approached, esp.: **a** the visible part of a celestial body. **b** a side of a mountain, etc. (*the north face*). **c** the (usu. vertical) surface of a coal seam, excavation, etc. **d** *Geom.* each surface of a solid. **e** the façade of a building. **f** the plate of a clock or watch bearing the digits, hands, etc. **5 a** the functional or working side of a tool, etc. **b** the distinctive side of a playing card. **c** the obverse of a coin. **6** = TYPEFACE. **7 a** the outward appearance or aspect (*the unacceptable face of capitalism*). **b** outward show; disguise; pretense (*put on a brave face*). **8** a person, esp. conveying some quality or association (*a face from the past; some young faces for a change*). **9** credibility or respect; good reputation; dignity (*lose face*). ● *v.* **1** *tr.* **a** look or be positioned toward or in a certain direction (*face toward the window; facing the window; the room faces north*). **2** *tr.* be opposite (*facing page 20*). **3** *tr.* **a** meet resolutely or defiantly; confront (*face one's critics*). **b** not shrink from (*face the facts*). **4** *tr.* present itself to; confront (*the problem that faces us; faces us with a problem*). **5** *tr.* **a** cover the surface of (a thing) with a coating, extra layer, etc.

b put a facing on (a garment). **6** *intr. & tr.* turn or cause to turn in a certain direction. □ **face down** (or **downward**) with the face or surface turned toward the ground, floor, etc. **face a person down** overcome a person by a show of determination or by browbeating. **face facts** (or **the facts**) recognize the truth. **face the music** *colloq.* put up with or stand up to unpleasant consequences, esp. criticism. **face to face** (often foll. by *with*) facing; confronting each other. **face up** (or **upward**) with the face or surface turned up to view. **face up to** accept bravely; confront; stand up to. **have the face** be shameless enough. **in one's** (or **the**) **face 1** straight against one; as one approaches. **2** confronting. **in the face of 1** despite. **2** confronted by. **let's face it** *colloq.* we must be honest or realistic about it. **on the face of it** as it would appear. **put a bold** (or **brave**) **face on it** accept difficulty, etc., cheerfully or with courage. **put one's face on** *colloq.* apply makeup to one's face. **put a good face on** make (a matter) look good. **put a new face on** alter the aspect of. **save face** preserve esteem; avoid humiliation. **save a person's face** enable a person to save face; forbear from humiliating a person. **show one's face** see SHOW. **set one's face against** oppose or resist with determination. **to a person's face** openly in a person's presence. □□ **faced** *adj.* (also in *comb.*). **fac•ing** *adj.* (also in *comb.*). [ME f. OF ult. f. L *facies*]

face card *n.* *Cards* a king, queen, or jack.

face cloth *n.* **1** a cloth for washing one's face; a washcloth. **2** *Brit.* a smooth-surfaced woolen cloth.

face flan•nel *n. Brit.* = FACE CLOTH 1.

face•less /fáyslis/ *adj.* **1** without identity; purposely not identifiable. **2** lacking character. **3** without a face. □□ **face•less•ly** *adv.* **face•less•ness** *n.*

face-lift *n.* **1** (also **face-lifting**) cosmetic surgery to remove wrinkles, etc., by tightening the skin of the face. **2** a procedure to improve the appearance of something (*the station has undergone a multimillion dollar face-lift*).

face pow•der *n.* a cosmetic for reducing the shine on the face.

fac•er /fáysər/ *n. colloq.* **1** *Brit.* a sudden difficulty or obstacle. **2** a blow in the face. **3** one that faces.

face-sav•ing *adj.* preserving one's reputation, credibility, or dignity.

fac•et /fásit/ *n.* **1** a particular aspect of a thing. **2** one side of a many-sided body, esp. a flat surface of a cut gem, a bone, etc. **3** one segment of a compound eye. □□ **fac•et•ed** *adj.* (also in *comb.*). [F *facette* dimin. (as FACE, -ETTE)]

fa•ce•ti•ae /fəseéeshee-ee/ *n.pl.* pleasantries; witticisms. [L, pl. of *facetia* jest f. *facetus* witty]

fa•ce•tious /fəseéeshəs/ *adj.* **1** characterized by flippant or inappropriate humor. **2** (of a person) intending to be amusing, esp. inappropriately. □□ **fa•ce•tious•ly** *adv.* **fa•ce•tious•ness** *n.* [F *facétieux* f. *facétie* f. L *facetia* jest]

face val•ue *n.* **1** the nominal value as printed or stamped on money. **2** the superficial appearance or implication of a thing.

fa•cia var. of FASCIA.

fa•cial /fáyshəl/ *adj. & n.* ● *adj.* of or for the face. ● *n.* a beauty treatment for the face. □□ **fa•cial•ly** *adv.* [med.L *facialis* (as FACE)]

-facient /fáyshənt/ *comb. form* forming adjectives and nouns indicating an action or state produced (*abortifacient*). [from or after L *-faciens -entis* part. of *facere* make]

fa•ci•es /fáyshee-eez, -sheez/ *n.* (*pl.* same) **1** *Med.* the appearance or facial expression of an individual. **2** *Geol.* the character of rock, etc., expressed by its composition, fossil content, etc. [L, = FACE]

fac•ile /fásil/ *adj.* usu. *derog.* **1** easily achieved but of little value. **2** (of speech, writing, etc.) fluent; ready; glib. □□ **fac•ile•ly** *adv.* **fac•ile•ness** *n.* [F *facile* or L *facilis* f. *facere* do]

fa•cil•i•tate /fəsílitayt/ *v.tr.* make easy or less difficult or more easily achieved. □□ **fa•cil•i•ta•tion** /-táyshən/ *n.* **fa•cil•i•ta•tive** *adj.* **fa•cil•i•ta•tor** *n.* [F *faciliter* f. It. *facilitare* f. *facile* easy f. L *facilis*]

fa•cil•i•ty /fəsílitee/ *n.* (*pl.* **-ties**) **1** ease; absence of difficulty. **2** fluency; dexterity; aptitude (*facility of expression*). **3** (esp. in *pl.*) an opportunity, the equipment, or the resources for doing something. **4** a plant, installation, or establishment. **5** *euphem.* (in *pl.*) a (public) toilet. [F *facilité* or L *facilitas* (as FACILE)]

fac•ing /fáysing/ *n.* **1 a** a layer of material covering part of a garment, etc., for contrast or strength. **b** (in *pl.*) the cuffs, collar, etc., of a military jacket. **2** an outer layer covering the surface of a wall, etc.

fac•sim•i•le /faksímilee/ *n. & v.* ● *n.* **1** an exact copy, esp. of writing, printing, a picture, etc. (often *attrib.*: *facsimile edition*). **2 a** production of an exact copy of a document, etc., by electronic scanning and transmission of the resulting data (see also FAX). **b** a copy produced in this way. • *v. tr.* (**fac·sim·i·led, fac·sim·i·le·ing**) make a facsimile of. □ **in facsimile** as an exact copy. [mod.L f. L *fac* imper. of *facere* make + *simile* neut. of *similis* like]

fact /fakt/ *n.* **1** a thing that is known to have occurred, to exist, or to be true. **2** a datum of experience (often foll. by an explanatory clause or phrase: *the fact that fire burns*; *the fact of my having seen them*). **3** (usu. in *pl.*) an item of verified information; a piece of evidence. **4** truth; reality. **5** a thing assumed as the basis for argument or inference. □ **before** (or **after**) **the fact** before (or after) the committing of a crime. **a fact of life** something that must be accepted. **facts and figures** precise details. **in** (or **in point of**) **fact 1** in reality; as a matter of fact. **2** (in summarizing) in short. [L *factum* f. *facere* do]

fac·tion[1] /fákshən/ *n.* **1** a small organized dissenting group within a larger one, esp. in politics. **2** a state of dissension within an organization. [F f. L *factio* -*onis* f. *facere* fact- do, make]

fac·tion[2] /fákshən/ *n.* a book, movie, etc., using real events as a basis for a fictional narrative or dramatization. [blend of FACT and FICTION]

-faction /fákshən/ *comb. form* forming nouns of action from verbs ending in -*fy* (*petrifaction*; *satisfaction*). [from or after L -*factio* -*factionis* f. -*facere* do, make]

fac·tion·al /fákshənəl/ *adj.* **1** of or characterized by faction. **2** belonging to a faction. □□ **fac·tion·al·ism** *n.* **fac·tion·al·ize** *v. tr. & intr.* **fac·tion·al·ly** *adv.* [FACTION[1]]

fac·tious /fákshəs/ *adj.* of, characterized by, or inclined to faction. □□ **fac·tious·ly** *adv.* **fac·tious·ness** *n.*

fac·ti·tious /faktíshəs/ *adj.* **1** contrived; not genuine (*factitious value*). **2** artificial; not natural (*factitious joy*). □□ **fac·ti·tious·ly** *adv.* **fac·ti·tious·ness** *n.* [L *facticius* f. *facere* fact- do, make]

fac·ti·tive /fáktitiv/ *adj. Gram.* (of a verb) having a sense of regarding or designating, and taking a complement as well as an object (e.g., *appointed me captain*). [mod.L *factitivus*, irreg. f. L *factitare* frequent. of *facere* do, make]

fac·toid /fáktoyd/ *n. & adj.* • *n.* **1** an assumption or speculation that is reported and repeated so often that it becomes accepted as fact; a simulated or imagined fact. **2** a trivial fact or news item. • *adj.* being or having the character of a factoid; containing factoids.

fac·tor /fáktər/ *n. & v.* • *n.* **1** a circumstance, fact, or influence contributing to a result. **2** *Math.* a whole number, etc., that when multiplied with another produces a given number or expression. **3** *Biol.* a gene, etc., determining hereditary character. **4** (foll. by identifying number) *Med.* any of several substances in the blood contributing to coagulation (*factor eight*). **5 a** a business agent; a merchant buying and selling on commission. **b** *Sc.* a land agent or steward. **c** an agent or a deputy. **6** an agent or company that buys a manufacturer's invoices and takes responsibility for collecting the payments due on them; a backer. • *v. tr.* **1** *Math.* resolve into factors or components. **2** *tr.* sell (one's receivable debts) to a factor. □□ **fac·tor·a·ble** *adj.* [F *facteur* or L *factor* f. *facere* fact- do, make]

fac·tor·age /fáktərij/ *n.* **1** commission or charges payable to a factor. **2** the business of a factor.

fac·tor a·nal·y·sis *n. Statistics* a process by which the relative importance of variables in the study of a sample is assessed by mathematical techniques.

fac·to·ri·al /faktáwreeəl/ *n. & adj. Math.* • *n.* **1** the product of a number and all the whole numbers below it (*four factorial = 4 x 3 x 2 x 1*). ¶ Symb.: ! (as in 4!). **2** the product of a series of factors in an arithmetical progression. • *adj.* of a factor or factorial. □□ **fac·to·ri·al·ly** *adv.*

fac·tor·ize /fáktərīz/ *v. Math.* **1** *tr.* resolve into factors. **2** *intr.* be capable of resolution into factors. □□ **fac·tor·i·za·tion** *n.*

fac·to·ry /fáktəree/ *n.* (*pl.* -**ries**) **1** a building or buildings containing equipment for manufacturing machinery or goods. **2** (usu. *derog.*) a place producing mass quantities or a low quality of goods, etc. (*a degree factory*). **3** *hist.* a merchant company's foreign trading station. [Port. *feitoria* and LL *factorium*]

fac·to·ry farm·ing *n.* a system of rearing livestock using industrial or intensive methods, by which poultry, pigs, or cattle are confined indoors under strictly controlled conditions. □□ **fac·to·ry farm** *n.*

fac·to·ry ship *n.* a fishing ship with facilities for immediate processing of the catch.

fac·to·tum /faktótəm/ *n.* (*pl.* **fac·to·tums**) an employee who does all kinds of work. [med.L f. L *fac* imper. of *facere* do, make + *totum* neut. of *totus* whole]

facts of life *n.* information about sexual functions and practices, esp. as given to children.

fac·tu·al /fákchoõəl/ *adj.* **1** based on or concerned with fact or facts. **2** actual; true. □□ **fac·tu·al·i·ty** /—chooálitee/ *n.* **fac·tu·al·ly** *adv.* **fac·tu·al·ness** *n.* [FACT, after *actual*]

fac·tum /fáktəm/ *n.* (*pl.* **fac·tums** or **fac·ta** /—tə/) *Law* **1** an act or deed. **2** a statement of the facts. [F f. L: see FACT]

fac·ture /fákchər/ *n.* the quality or manner of execution of an artwork, etc. [ME f. OF f. L *factura* f. *facere* fact- do, make]

fac·u·la /fákyələ/ *n.* (*pl.* **fac·u·lae** /—lee/) *Astron.* a bright spot or streak on the sun. □□ **fac·u·lar** *adj.* **fac·u·lous** *adj.* [L, dimin. of *fax facis* torch]

fac·ul·ta·tive /fákəltaytiv/ *adj.* **1** *Law* enabling an act to take place. **2** that may occur. **3** *Biol.* not restricted to a particular function, mode of life, etc. **4** of a faculty. □□ **fac·ul·ta·tive·ly** *adv.* [F *facultatif* -*ive* (as FACULTY)]

fac·ul·ty /fákəltee/ *n.* (*pl.* -**ties**) **1** an aptitude or ability for a particular activity. **2** an inherent mental or physical power. **3 a** the teaching staff of a university, college, or secondary school. **b** a department of a university, etc., teaching a specific branch of learning (*faculty of modern languages*). **c** *Brit.* a branch of art or science; those qualified to teach it. **4** the members of a particular profession, esp. medicine. **5** authorization; power conferred by an authority. [ME f. OF *faculté* f. L *facultas* -*tatis* f. *facilis* easy]

FAD *abbr.* flavin adenine dinucleotide.

fad /fad/ *n.* **1** a craze. **2** a peculiar notion or idiosyncrasy. □□ **fad·dish** *adj.* **fad·dish·ly** *adv.* **fad·dish·ness** *n.* **fad·dism** *n.* **fad·dist** *n.* [19th c. (orig. dial.): prob. f. *fidfad* f. FIDDLE-FADDLE]

fad·dy /fádee/ *adj.* (**fad·di·er, fad·di·est**) *Brit.* having arbitrary likes and dislikes, esp. about food. □□ **fad·di·ly** *adv.* **fad·di·ness** *n.*

fade /fayd/ *v. & n.* • *v.* **1** *intr.* lose or cause to lose color. **2** *intr.* lose freshness or strength; (of flowers, etc.) droop; wither. **3** *intr.* **a** (of color, light, etc.) disappear gradually; grow pale or dim. **b** (of sound) grow faint. **4** *intr.* (of a feeling, etc.) diminish. **5** *intr.* (foll. by *away*, *out*) (of a person, etc.) disappear or depart gradually. **6** *tr.* (foll. by *in*, *out*) *Cinematog. & Broadcasting* **a** cause (a picture) to come gradually in or out of view on a screen, or to merge into another shot. **b** make (the sound) more or less audible. **7** *intr.* (of a radio signal) vary irregularly in intensity. **8** *intr.* (of a brake) temporarily lose effectiveness. **9** *Golf* **a** *intr.* (of a ball) deviate from a straight course, esp. in a deliberate slice. **b** *tr.* cause (a ball) to fade. • *n.* the action or an instance of fading. □ **fade away** *colloq.* languish; grow thin. □□ **fade·less** *adj.* **fad·er** *n.* (in sense 6 of *v.*). [ME f. OF *fader* f. *fade* dull, insipid prob. ult. f. L *fatuus* silly + *vapidus* VAPID]

fade-in *n. Cinematog. & Broadcasting* the action or an instance of fading in a picture or sound.

fade-out *n.* **1** *colloq.* disappearance; death. **2** *Cinematog. & Broadcasting* the action or an instance of fading out a picture or sound.

fadge /faj/ *n. Austral. & NZ* **1** a limp package of wool. **2** a loosely packed wool bale. [16th-c. Engl. dial.: orig. uncert.]

fae·ces *Brit.* var. of FECES.

fa·er·ie /fáiree/ *n.* (also **fa·er·y**) *archaic* **1** fairyland; the fairies, esp. as represented by Spenser (*the Faerie Queene*). **2** (*attrib.*) visionary; imagined. [var. of FAIRY]

Faer·o·ese /fáirō-eéz/ *adj. & n.* (also **Far·o·ese**) • *adj.* of or relating to the Faeroes, an island group in the N. Atlantic between Norway and Iceland. • *n.* (*pl.* same) **1** a native of the Faeroes; a person of Faeroese descent. **2** the Norse language of this people.

faff /faf/ *v. & n. Brit. colloq.* • *v. intr.* (often foll. by *about*, *around*) fuss; dither. • *n.* a fuss. [imit.]

fag[1] /fag/ *n. & v.* • *n.* **1** esp. *Brit. colloq.* a piece of drudgery; a wearisome or unwelcome task. **2** *sl.* a cigarette. **3** *Brit.* (at public schools) a junior pupil who runs errands for a senior. • *v.* (**fagged, fag·ging**) **1** *colloq.* **a** *tr.* (often foll. by *out*) tire out; exhaust. **b** *intr. Brit.* toil. **2** *intr. Brit.* (in public schools) act as a fag. **3** *tr. Naut.* (often foll. by *out*) fray (the end of a rope, etc.). [orig. unkn.: cf. FLAG[1]]

fag[2] /fag/ *n. sl.* often *offens.* a male homosexual. [abbr. of FAGGOT]

fag end *n. sl.* **1** an inferior or useless remnant (*the fag ends of rope*). **2** *Brit.* a cigarette butt.

fag·got /fágət/ *n.* **1** *sl. derog.* **a** often *offens.* a male homosexual. **b** *Brit.* an unpleasant woman. **2** *Brit.* (usu. in *pl.*) a ball or roll of seasoned chopped liver, etc., baked or fried. □□ **fag·got·y** *adj.* [ME f. OF *fagot*, of uncert. orig.]

fag·ot /fágət/ *n. & v.* • *n.* (also **fag·got**) **1** a bundle of sticks or twigs bound together as fuel. **2** a bundle of iron rods for heat treatment. **3** a bunch of herbs. • *v. tr.* (**fag·ot·ed, fag·ot·ing**) **1** bind in or make into fagots. **2** join by fagoting (see FAGOTING).

fag·ot·ing /fágəting/ *n.* (also **fag·got·ing**) **1** embroidery in which threads are fastened together like a fagot. **2** the joining of materials in a similar manner.

fah var. of FA.

Fahr. *abbr.* Fahrenheit.

Fahr·en·heit /fárənhīt/ *adj.* of or measured on a scale of temperature on which water freezes at 32° and boils at 212° under standard conditions. [G. *Fahrenheit*, Ger. physicist d. 1736]

fa·ience /fī-óNs, fay-/ *n.* decorated and glazed earthenware and porcelain, e.g., delft or majolica. [F *faïence* f. *Faenza* in Italy]

fail /fayl/ *v. & n.* • *v.* **1** *intr.* not succeed (*failed in persuading*; *failed to qualify*; *tried but failed*). **2 a** *tr. & intr.* be unsuccessful in (an examination, test, interview, etc.; be rejected as a candidate. **b** *tr.* (of a commodity, etc.) not pass (a test of quality). **c** *tr.* reject (a candidate, etc.); adjudge or grade as unsuccessful. **3** *intr.* be unable to; neglect to; choose not to (*I fail to see the reason; he failed to appear*). **4** *tr.* disappoint; let down; not serve when needed. **5** *intr.* (of supplies, crops, etc.) be or become lacking or insufficient. **6** *intr.* become weaker; cease functioning; break down (*her health is failing; the engine has failed*). **7** *intr.* **a** (of an enterprise) collapse; come to nothing. **b** become bankrupt. • *n.* a failure in an examination or test. □ **without fail** for certain; whatever happens. [ME f. OF *faillir* (v.), *fail(l)e* (n.) ult. f. L *fallere* deceive]

failed /fayld/ *adj.* **1** unsuccessful; not good enough (*a failed actor*). **2** weak; deficient; broken down (*a failed crop; a failed battery*).

fail·ing /fáyling/ *n. & prep.* • *n.* a fault or shortcoming; a weakness, esp. in character. • *prep.* in default of; if not.

fail-safe *adj.* **1** causing a piece of machinery to revert to a safe condition in the event of a breakdown or malfunction (*a forklift truck with a fail-safe device*). **2** unlikely or unable to fail (*that computer is supposed to be fail-safe*).

fail·ure /fáylyər/ *n.* **1** lack of success; failing. **2** an unsuccessful person, thing, or attempt. **3** nonperformance; nonoccurrence. **4** breaking down or ceasing to function (*heart failure; engine failure*). **5** running short of supply, etc. **6** bankruptcy; collapse. [earlier *failer* f. AF, = OF *faillir* FAIL]

fain /fayn/ *adj. & adv. archaic* • *predic.adj.* (foll. by *to* + infin.) **1** willing under the circumstances to. **2** left with no alternative but to. • *adv.* gladly (esp. would fain). [OE *fægen* f. Gmc]

fai·né·ant /fáyneeənt, faynayóN/ *n. & adj.* • *n.* an idle or ineffective person. • *adj.* idle; inactive. □□ **fai·né·an·cy** /–ənsee/ *n.* [F f. *fait* does + *néant* nothing]

faint /faynt/ *adj., v., & n.* • *adj.* **1** indistinct; pale; dim; quiet; not clearly perceived. **2** (of a person) weak or dizzy; inclined to faint. **3** slight; remote; inadequate (*a faint chance*). **4** feeble; halfhearted (*faint praise*). **5** timid (*a faint heart*). • *v.intr.* **1** lose consciousness. **2** become faint. • *n.* a sudden loss of consciousness; fainting. □ **not have the faintest** *colloq.* have no idea. □□ **faint·ness** *n.* [ME f. OF, past part. of *faindre* FEIGN]

faint-heart·ed *adj.* cowardly; timid. □□ **faint-heart·ed·ly** *adv.* **faint·heart·ed·ness** *n.*

faint·ly /fáyntlee/ *adv.* **1** very slightly (*faintly amused*). **2** indistinctly; feebly.

fair[1] /fair/ *adj., adv., n., & v.* • *adj.* **1** just; unbiased; equitable; in accordance with the rules. **2** blond; light or pale in color or complexion. **3 a** (of only) moderate quality or amount; average. **b** considerable; satisfactory (*a fair chance of success*). **4** (of weather) fine and dry; (of the wind) favorable. **5** clean; clear; unblemished (*fair copy*). **6** beautiful; attractive. **7** *archaic* kind; gentle. **8 a** false, despite being initially attractive or pleasing; specious. **b** complimentary (*fair words*). **9** *Austral. & NZ* complete; unquestionable. **10** unobstructed; open. • *adv.* **1** in a fair manner (*play fair*). **2** *Brit.* exactly; completely (*was hit fair on the jaw*). • *n.* **1** a fair thing. **2** *archaic* a beautiful woman. • *v.* **1** *tr.* make (the surface of a ship, aircraft, etc.) smooth and streamlined. **2** *intr. dial.* (often foll. by *off, up*) (of the weather) become fair. □ **fair and square** *adv. & adj.* **1** exactly. **2** straightforward; honest; aboveboard. **fair enough** *colloq.* that is reasonable or acceptable. **the fair** (or **fairer**) **sex** women. **fair's fair** *colloq.* all involved should act fairly. **in a fair way to do something** *dated* having nearly done something, and likely to achieve it. □□ **fair·ish** *adj.* **fair·ness** *n.* [OE *fæger* f. Gmc]

fair[2] /fair/ *n.* **1** a gathering of stalls, amusements, etc., for public (usu. outdoor) entertainment. **2** a periodical gathering for the sale of goods, often with entertainments. **3** an exhibition of farm products, usu. held annually, with competitions, entertainments, etc. **4** an exhibition, esp. to promote particular products. [ME f. OF *feire* f. LL *feria* sing. f. L *feriae* holiday]

Fair Deal *n.* a Democratic Party social program during the administration of Pres. Harry Truman.

fair deal *n.* equitable treatment.

fair game *n.* a thing or person one may legitimately pursue, exploit, etc.

fair·ground /fáirgrownd/ *n.* an outdoor area where a fair is held.

fair·ing[1] /fáiring/ *n.* **1** an external structure added to increase streamlining and reduce drag, esp. on a high-performance car, motorcycle, boat, or aircraft. **2** the process of streamlining. [FAIR[1] *v.* 1 + –ING[1]]

fair·ing[2] /fáiring/ *n. Brit. archaic* a present bought at a fair.

Fair Isle /fáir íl/ *n.* (also *attrib.*) a piece of clothing knitted in a characteristic multicolored design. [*Fair Isle* in the Shetlands, where the design was first devised]

fair·lead /fáirleed/ *n. Naut.* a device to guide rope, etc., e.g., to prevent cutting or chafing.

fair·ly /fáirlee/ *adv.* **1** in a fair manner; justly. **2** moderately; acceptably (*fairly good*). **3** to a noticeable degree (*fairly narrow*). **4** utterly; completely (*fairly beside himself*). **5** actually (*fairly jumped for joy*).

fair-mind·ed *adj.* just; impartial. □□ **fair-mind·ed·ly** *adj.* **fair-mind·ed·ness** *n.*

fair play *n.* respect for the rules or equal treatment of all concerned.

fair-spo·ken *adj.* courteous.

fair·wa·ter /fáirwawtər, –wotər/ *n.* a structure that improves the streamlining of a ship to assist its smooth passage through water.

fair·way /fáirway/ *n.* **1** a navigable channel; a regular course or track of a ship. **2** the part of a golf course between a tee and its green, kept free of rough grass.

fair-weath·er friend *n.* a friend or ally who is unreliable in times of difficulty.

fair·y /fáiree/ *n. & adj.* • *n.* (*pl.* **-ies**) **1** a small imaginary being with magical powers. **2** *sl. derog.* a male homosexual. • *adj.* of fairies; fairylike; delicate; small. □□ **fair·y·like** *adj.* [ME f. OF *faerie* f. *fae* FAY]

fair·y cake *n. Brit.* a small individual frosted sponge cake.

fair·y cy·cle *n. Brit.* a small bicycle for a child.

fair·y god·moth·er *n.* a benefactress.

fair·y·land /fáireeland/ *n.* **1** the imaginary home of fairies. **2** an enchanted region.

fair·y ring *n.* a ring of mushrooms or darker grass caused by fungi.

fair·y tale *n.* (also **fair·y sto·ry**) **1** a tale about fairies or other fantastic creatures. **2** an incredible story; a fabrication.

fait ac·com·pli /fet aakawNplee, –komplee/ *n.* a thing that has been done and is past arguing about or altering. [F]

faith /fayth/ *n.* **1** complete trust or confidence. **2** firm belief, esp. without logical proof. **3 a** a system of religious belief (*the Christian faith*). **b** belief in religious doctrines. **c** spiritual apprehension of divine truth apart from proof. **d** things believed or to be believed. **4** duty or commitment to fulfill a trust, promise, etc.; obligation; allegiance (*keep faith*). **5** (*attrib.*) concerned with a supposed ability to cure by faith rather than treatment (*faith healing*). [ME f. AF *fed* f. OF *feid* f. L *fides*]

faith·ful /fáythfool/ *adj.* **1** showing faith. **2** (often foll. by *to*) loyal; trustworthy; constant. **3** accurate; true to fact (*a faithful account*). **4** thorough in performing one's duty; conscientious. **5** (**the Faithful**) the believers in a religion, esp. Christianity or Islam. □□ **faith·ful·ness** *n.*

faith·ful·ly /fáythfoolee/ *adv.* in a faithful manner. □ **yours faithfully** a formula for ending a business or formal letter.

faith heal·er *n.* one who uses religious faith and prayer to heal.

faith·less /fáythlis/ *adj.* **1** false; unreliable; disloyal. **2** without religious faith. □□ **faith·less·ly** *adv.* **faith·less·ness** *n.*

fa·ji·tas /faaheeətəs, fə–/ *n.pl. Mexican Cooking* thin strips of fried or broiled meat, usu. seasoned with salsa. [Amer. Sp., pl. of *fajita* little sash, f. Sp. *faja* belt, sash, strip]

fake[1] /fayk/ *n., adj., & v.* • *n.* **1** a thing or person that is not genuine. **2** a trick. **3** *Sport* a feint. • *adj.* counterfeit; not genuine. • *v.tr.* **1** make (a false thing) appear genuine; forge; counterfeit. **2** make a pretense of having (a feeling, illness, etc.). **3** *Sport* feint. **4** improvise (*I'm not exactly sure, but I can fake it*). □□ **fak·er** *n.* **fak·er·y** *n.* [obs. *feak*, *feague* thrash f. G *fegen* sweep, thrash]

fake[2] /fayk/ *n. & v. Naut.* • *n.* one loop of a coil of rope. • *v.tr.* coil (rope). [ME: cf. Scottish *faik* fold]

fa·kir /fəkeer, fáykeer/ *n.* (also **fa·quir**) a Muslim or Hindu religious mendicant or ascetic. [Arab. *fakīr* needy man]

fa·la·fel /fəláafəl/ *n.* (also **fe·la·fel**) (in Near Eastern countries) a spicy dish of fried patties made from mashed chick peas or beans. [Arab. *falāfil*]

Fa·lange /falánj/ *n.* the Fascist movement in Spain, founded in 1933. □□ **Fa·lan·gism** *n.* **Fa·lan·gist** *n.* [Sp., = PHALANX]

fal·cate /fálkayt/ *adj. Anat.* curved like a sickle. [L *falcatus* f. *falx falcis* sickle]

fal·chion /fáwlchən/ *n. hist.* a broad curved sword with a convex edge. [ME *fauchoun* f. OF *fauchon* ult. f. L *falx falcis* sickle]

fal·ci·form /fálsifawrm/ *adj. Anat.* curved like a sickle. [L *falx falcis* sickle]

fal·con /fálkən, fáwl–/ *n.* **1** any diurnal bird of prey of the family Falconidae, having long pointed wings, and sometimes trained to hunt small game for sport. **2** (in falconry) a female falcon (cf. TERCEL). [ME f. OF *faucon* f. LL *falco –onis*, perh. f. L *falx* scythe or f. Gmc]

fal·con·er /fálkənər, fáwl–/ *n.* **1** a keeper and trainer of hawks. **2** a person who hunts with hawks. [ME f. AF *fauconer*, OF *fauconier* (as FALCON)]

fal·co·net /fálkənit, fáwl–/ *n.* **1** *hist.* a light cannon. **2** *Zool.* a small falcon. [sense 1 f. It. *falconetto* dimin. of *falcone* FALCON: sense 2 f. FALCON + –ET[1]]

fal·con·ry /fálkənree, fáwl–/ *n.* the breeding and training of hawks; the sport of hawking. [F *fauconnerie* (as FALCON)]

fal·de·ral /fáldəral/ *n.* (also **fol·de·rol** /fóldərol/) **1** a gewgaw or trifle. **2 a** a nonsensical refrain in a song. **b** nonsense. [perh. f. *falbala* trimming on a dress]

fald·stool /fáwldstool/ *n.* **1** a bishop's backless folding chair. **2** a small movable desk for kneeling at prayer. [OE *fældestōl* f. med.L *faldistolium* f. WG (as FOLD[1], STOOL)]

fall /fawl/ v. & n. ● v.intr. (past **fell** /fel/; past part. **fallen** /fáwlən/) **1 a** go or come down freely; descend rapidly from a higher to a lower level (*fell from the top floor; rain was falling*). **b** drop or be dropped (*supplies fell by parachute; the curtain fell*). **2 a** (often foll. by *over* or *down*) cease to stand; come suddenly to the ground from loss of balance, etc. **b** collapse forward or downward, esp. of one's own volition (*fell into my arms*). **3** become detached and descend or disappear. **4** take a downward direction: **a** (of hair, clothing, etc.) hang down. **b** (of ground, etc.) slope. **c** (foll. by *into*) (of a river, etc.) discharge into. **5 a** find a lower level; sink lower. **b** subside; abate. **6** (of a barometer, thermometer, etc.) show a lower reading. **7** occur; become apparent or present (*darkness fell*). **8** decline; diminish (*demand is falling; standards have fallen*). **9 a** (of the face) show dismay or disappointment. **b** (of the eyes or a glance) look downward. **10 a** lose power or status (*the government will fall*). **b** lose esteem, moral integrity, etc. **11** commit sin; yield to temptation. **12** take or have a particular direction or place (*his eye fell on me; the accent falls on the first syllable*). **13 a** find a place; be naturally divisible (*the subject falls into three parts*). **b** (foll. by *under, within*) be classed among. **14** occur at a specified time (*Easter falls early this year*). **15** come by chance or duty (*it fell to me to answer*). **16 a** pass into a specified condition (*fall into decay; fell ill*). **b** become (*fall asleep*). **17 a** (of a position, etc.) be overthrown or captured; succumb to attack. **b** be defeated; fail. **18** die (*fall in battle*). **19** (foll. by *on, upon*) **a** attack. **b** meet with. **c** embrace or embark on avidly. **20** (foll. by *to* + verbal noun) begin (*fell to wondering*). **21** (foll. by *to*) lapse; revert (*revenues fall to the state*). ● n. **1** the act or an instance of falling; a sudden rapid descent. **2** that which falls or has fallen, e.g., snow, rocks, etc. **3** the recorded amount of rainfall, etc. **4** a decline or diminution; depreciation in price, value, demand, etc. **5** overthrow; downfall (*the fall of Rome*). **6 a** succumbing to temptation. **b** (the **Fall**) the biblical sin of Adam and its consequences, as described in Genesis. **7** (of material, land, light, etc.) a downward direction; a slope. **8** (also **Fall**) autumn. **9** (esp. in *pl.*) a waterfall, cataract, or cascade. **10** *Mus.* a cadence. **11 a** a wrestling bout; a throw in wrestling that keeps the opponent on the ground for a specified time. **b** a controlled act of falling, esp. as a stunt or in judo, etc. **12 a** the birth of young of certain animals. **b** the number of young born. **13** a rope of a hoisting tackle. □ **fall about** *Brit. colloq.* be helpless, esp. with laughter. **fall apart** (or **to pieces**) **1** break into pieces. **2** (of a situation, etc.) disintegrate; be reduced to chaos. **3** lose one's capacity to cope. **fall away 1** (of a surface) incline abruptly. **2** become few or thin; gradually vanish. **3** desert; revolt; abandon one's principles. **fall back** retreat. **fall back on** have recourse to in difficulty. **fall behind 1** be outstripped by one's competitors, etc.; lag. **2** be in arrears. **fall down** (often foll. by *on*) *colloq.* fail; perform poorly; fail to deliver (payment, etc.). **fall flat** fail to achieve expected success or evoke a desired response. **fall for** *colloq.* **1** be captivated or deceived by. **2** yield to the charms or merits of. **fall foul of** come into conflict with; quarrel with. **fall in 1 a** take one's place in military formation. **b** (as *int.*) the order to do this. **2** collapse inward. **fall in love** see LOVE. **fall into line 1** take one's place in the ranks. **2** conform or collaborate with others. **fall into place** begin to make sense or cohere. **fall in with 1** meet or become involved with by chance. **2** agree with; accede to; humor. **3** coincide with. **fall off 1** (of demand, etc.) decrease; deteriorate. **2** withdraw. **fall out 1** quarrel. **2** (of the hair, teeth, etc.) become detached. **3** *Mil.* come out of formation. **4** result; come to pass; occur. **fall out of** gradually discontinue (a habit, etc.). **fall over oneself** *colloq.* **1** be eager or competitive. **2** be awkward; stumble through haste, confusion, etc. **fall short 1** be or become deficient or inadequate. **2** (of a missile, etc.) not reach its target. **fall short of** fail to reach or obtain. **fall through** fail; come to nothing; miscarry. **fall to** begin an activity, e.g., eating or working. [OE *fallan, feallan* f. Gmc]

fal·la·cy /fáləsee/ n. (pl. **·cies**) **1** a mistaken belief, esp. based on unsound argument. **2** faulty reasoning; misleading or unsound argument. **3** *Logic* a flaw that vitiates an argument. □□ **fal·la·cious** /fəláyshəs/ adj. **fal·la·cious·ly** adv. **fal·la·cious·ness** n. [L *fallacia* f. *fallax –acis* deceiving f. *fallere* deceive]

fall·back /fáwlbak/ n. **1** (also *attrib.*) an alternative resource or plan that may be used in an emergency. **2** a reduction or retreat (*the offering will hit the market after a fallback from record highs*).

fall·en past part. of FALL v. ● adj. **1** (*attrib.*) having lost one's honor or reputation. **2** killed in war. □□ **fall·en·ness** n.

fall·fish /fáwlfish/ n. a N. American freshwater fish, *Semotilus corporalis.*

fall guy n. *sl.* **1** an easy victim. **2** a scapegoat.

fal·li·ble /fálibəl/ adj. **1** capable of making mistakes. **2** liable to be erroneous. □□ **fal·li·bil·i·ty** n. **fal·li·bly** adv. [med.L *fallibilis* f. L *fallere* deceive]

fall·ing star n. a meteor.

fall·off /fáwlawf/ n. a decrease, deterioration, withdrawal, etc.

Fal·lo·pi·an tube /fəlópeeən/ n. *Anat.* either of two tubes in female mammals along which ova travel from the ovaries to the uterus. [*Fallopius*, Latinized name of G. *Fallopio*, It. anatomist d. 1562]

fall·out /fáwlowt/ n. **1** radioactive debris caused by a nuclear explosion or accident. **2** the adverse side effects of a situation, etc.

fal·low[1] /fálō/ adj., n., & v. ● adj. **1 a** (of land) plowed and harrowed but left unsown for a year. **b** uncultivated. **2** (of an idea, etc.) potentially useful but not yet in use. **3** inactive. **4** (of a sow) not pregnant. ● n. fallow or uncultivated land. ● v.tr. break up (land) for sowing or to destroy weeds. □□ **fal·low·ness** n. [ME f. OE *fealh* (n.), *fealgian* (v.)]

fal·low[2] /fálō/ adj. of a pale brownish or reddish yellow. [OE *falu, fealu* f. Gmc]

fal·low deer n. any small deer of the genus *Dama*, having a white-spotted reddish brown coat in the summer.

false /fawls/ adj. & adv. ● adj. **1** not according with fact; wrong; incorrect (*a false idea*). **2 a** spurious; sham; artificial (*false teeth; false modesty*). **b** acting as such; appearing to be such, esp. deceptively (*a false lining*). **3** illusory; not actually so (*a false economy*). **4** improperly so called (*false acacia*). **5** deceptive. **6** (foll. by *to*) deceitful, treacherous, or unfaithful. **7** illegal (*false imprisonment*). ● adv. in a false manner (esp. play false). □□ **false·ly** adv. **false·ness** n. **fal·si·ty** n. (pl. **·ties**). [OE *fals* and OF *fals, faus* f. L *falsus* past part. of *fallere* deceive]

false a·ca·cia n. see ACACIA.

false a·larm n. an alarm given needlessly.

false dawn n. a transient light in the east before dawn.

false·hood /fáwls-hood/ n. **1** the state of being false, esp. untrue. **2** a false or untrue thing. **3 a** the act of lying. **b** a lie or lies.

false move n. an unwise or careless action that could have dangerous consequences (*one false move could lead to nuclear war*).

false pre·tens·es n. misrepresentations made with intent to deceive (esp. under false pretenses).

false rib = FLOATING RIB.

false scent n. **1** a scent trail laid to deceive. **2** false clues, etc., intended to deflect pursuers.

false start n. **1** an invalid or disallowed start in a race. **2** an unsuccessful attempt to begin something.

false step n. a slip; a mistake.

false to·paz n. = CITRINE.

fal·set·to /fawlsétō/ n. (pl. **·tos**) **1** a method of voice production used by male singers, esp. tenors, to sing notes higher than their normal range. **2** a singer using this method. [It., dimin. of *falso* FALSE]

false·work /fáwlswərk/ n. a temporary framework or support used during building to form arches, etc.

fals·ies /fáwlseez/ n.pl. *colloq.* padded material to increase the apparent size of the breasts.

fal·si·fy /fáwlsifi/ v.tr. (**·fies, ·fied**) **1** fraudulently alter or make false (a document, evidence, etc.). **2** misrepresent. **3** make wrong; pervert. **4** show to be false. **5** disappoint (a hope, fear, etc.). □□ **fal·si·fi·a·ble** adj. **fal·si·fi·a·bil·i·ty** n. **fal·si·fi·ca·tion** n. [ME f. F *falsifier* or med.L *falsificare* f. L *falsificus* making false f. *falsus* false]

fal·ter /fáwltər/ v. **1** intr. stumble; stagger; go unsteadily. **2** intr. waver; lose courage. **3** tr. & intr. stammer; speak hesitatingly. □□ **fal·ter·er** n. **fal·ter·ing·ly** adv. [ME: orig. uncert.]

fame /faym/ n. **1** renown; the state of being famous. **2** reputation. **3** *archaic* public report; rumor. [ME f. OF f. L *fama*]

famed /faymd/ adj. **1** (foll. by *for*) famous; much spoken of (*famed for its good food*). **2** *archaic* currently reported.

fa·mil·ial /fəmílyəl, –leeəl/ adj. of, occurring in, or characteristic of a family or its members. [F f. L *familia* FAMILY]

fa·mil·iar /fəmílyər/ adj. & n. ● adj. **1 a** (often foll. by *to*) well known; no longer novel. **b** common; usual; often encountered or experienced. **2** (foll. by *with*) knowing a thing well or in detail (*am familiar with all the problems*). **3** (often foll. by *with*) **a** well acquainted (with a person); in close friendship; intimate. **b** sexually intimate. **4** excessively informal; impertinent. **5** unceremonious; informal. **6** (of animals) tame. ● n. **1** a close friend or associate. **2** a person rendering certain services in a high-ranking household. **3** (in full **familiar spirit**) a demon, esp. in animal form, supposedly attending and obeying a witch, etc. □□ **fa·mil·iar·ly** adv. [ME f. OF *familier* f. L *familiaris* (as FAMILY)]

fa·mil·i·ar·i·ty /fəmileeáritee, –yár–/ n. (pl. **·ties**) **1** the state of being well known (*the familiarity of the scene*). **2** (foll. by *with*) close acquaintance. **3** a close relationship. **4 a** sexual intimacy. **b** (in *pl.*) acts of physical intimacy. **5** familiar or informal behavior, esp. excessively so. [ME f. OF *familiarité* f. L *familiaritas –tatis* (as FAMILIAR)]

fa·mil·iar·ize /fəmílyərīz/ v.tr. **1** (foll. by *with*) make (a person) conversant or well acquainted. **2** make (a thing) well known. □□ **fa·mil·iar·i·za·tion** n. [F *familiariser* f. *familiaire* (as FAMILIAR)]

fa·mille /famée/ n. a Chinese enameled porcelain with a predominant color: (**famille jaune** /zhōn/) yellow, (**famille noire** /nwaar/) black, (**famille rose** /rōz/) red, (**famille verte** /vairt/) green. [F, = family]

fam·i·ly /fámilee/ n. (pl. **·lies**) **1** a set of parents and children, or of relations, living together or not. **2 a** the members of a household, esp. parents and their children. **b** a person's children. **c** (*attrib.*) serving the needs of families (*family butcher*). **3 a** all the descendants of a common ancestor; a house; a lineage. **b** a race or group of peoples from a common stock. **4** all the languages ultimately derived from a particular early language, regarded as a group. **5 a** brotherhood of persons or nations united by political or religious ties. **6** a group of objects distinguished by common features. **7** *Math.* a group of curves, etc., obtained by varying one quantity. **8** *Biol.* a group of related genera of organisms within an order in taxonomic classification. □ **in the** (or **a**) **family way** *colloq.* pregnant. [ME f. L *familia* household f. *famulus* servant]

fam·i·ly man *n.* a man having a wife and children, esp. one fond of family life.

fam·i·ly name *n.* a surname.

fam·i·ly plan·ning *n.* the practice of controlling the number of children in a family by using contraception.

fam·i·ly prac·tice *n.* a medical specialty in which a physician provides general care for individuals and families.

fam·i·ly tree *n.* a chart showing relationships and lines of descent.

fam·ine /fámin/ *n.* **1 a** extreme scarcity of food. **b** a shortage of something specified (*water famine*). **2** *archaic* hunger; starvation. [ME f. OF f. *faim* f. L *fames* hunger]

fam·ish /fámish/ *v.tr. & intr.* (usu. in *passive*) **1** reduce or be reduced to extreme hunger. **2** *colloq.* (esp. as **famished** *adj.*) feel very hungry. [ME f. obs. *fame* f. OF *afamer* ult. f. L *fames* hunger]

fa·mous /fáyməs/ *adj.* **1** (often foll. by *for*) celebrated; well known. **2** *colloq.* excellent. □□ **fa·mous·ness** *n.* [ME f. AF, OF *fameus* f. L *famosus* f. *fama* fame]

fa·mous·ly /fáyməslee/ *adv.* **1** *colloq.* excellently (*got on famously*). **2** notably.

fam·u·lus /fámyələs/ *n.* (*pl.* **fam·u·li** /-lī/) *hist.* an attendant to a magician or scholar. [L, = servant]

fan[1] /fan/ *n. & v.* ● *n.* **1** an apparatus, usu. with rotating blades, giving a current of air for ventilation, etc. **2** a device, usu. folding and forming a semicircle when spread out, for agitating the air to cool oneself. **3** anything spread out like a fan, e.g., a bird's tail or kind of ornamental vaulting (*fan tracery*). **4** a device for winnowing grain. **5** a fan-shaped deposit of alluvium, esp. where a stream begins to descend a gentler slope. **6** a small sail for keeping the head of a windmill toward the wind. ● *v.* (**fanned, fan·ning**) **1** *tr.* **a** blow a current of air on, with or as with a fan. **b** agitate (the air) with a fan. **2** *tr.* (of a breeze) blow gently on; cool. **3** *tr.* **a** winnow (grain). **b** winnow away (chaff). **4** *tr.* sweep away by or as by the wind from a fan. **5** *intr. & tr.* (usu. foll. by *out*) spread out in the shape of a fan. **6 a** *tr.* strike (a batter) out. **b** *intr.* strike out. □□ **fan·like** *adj.* **fan·ner** *n.* [OE *fann* (in sense 4 of *n.*) f. L *vannus* winnowing fan]

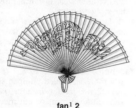

fan[1] 2

fan[2] /fan/ *n.* a devotee of a particular activity, performer, etc. (*theater fan; football fan*). □□ **fan·dom** *n.* [abbr. of FANATIC]

fa·nat·ic /fənátik/ *n. & adj.* ● *n.* a person filled with excessive and often misguided enthusiasm for something. ● *adj.* excessively enthusiastic. □□ **fa·nat·i·cal** *adj.* **fa·nat·i·cal·ly** *adv.* **fa·nat·i·cism** /-tisizəm/ *n.* **fa·nat·i·cize** /-tisiz/ *v.intr. & tr.* [F *fanatique* or L *fanaticus* f. *fanum* temple (orig. in religious sense)]

fan belt *n.* a belt that drives a fan to cool the radiator in a motor vehicle.

fan·ci·er /fánseeər/ *n.* a connoisseur or follower of some activity or thing (*cat fancier*).

fan·ci·ful /fánsifŏŏl/ *adj.* **1** existing only in the imagination or fancy. **2** indulging in fancies; whimsical; capricious. **3** fantastically designed, ornamented, etc.; odd looking. □□ **fan·ci·ful·ly** *adv.* **fan·ci·ful·ness** *n.*

fan club *n.* an organized group of devotees of a famous person.

fan·cy /fánsee/ *n., adj., & v.* ● *n.* (*pl.* **·cies**) **1** an individual taste or inclination (*take a fancy to*). **2** a caprice or whim. **3** a thing favored, e.g., a horse to win a race. **4** an arbitrary supposition. **5 a** the faculty of using imagination or of inventing imagery. **b** a mental image. **6** delusion; unfounded belief. **7** (prec. by *the*) those who have a certain hobby; fanciers, esp. patrons of boxing. ● *adj.* (usu. *attrib.*) (**fan·ci·er, fan·ci·est**) **1** ornamental; not plain. **2** capricious; whimsical; extravagant (*at a fancy price*). **3** based on imagination, not fact. **4 a** (of foods, etc.) above average quality. **b** of superior skill. **5** (of flowers, etc.) particolored. **6** (of an animal) bred for particular points of beauty, etc. ● *v.tr.* (**·cies, ·cied**) **1** (foll. by *that* + clause) be inclined to suppose. **2** *colloq.* feel a desire for (*do you fancy a drink?*). **3** *colloq.* find sexually attractive. **4** *Brit. colloq.* have an unduly high opinion of (oneself, one's ability, etc.). **5** (in *imper.*) an exclamation of surprise (*fancy their doing that!*). **6 a** picture to oneself; conceive; imagine. **b** (as **fancied** *adj.*) having no basis in fact; imaginary. □ **catch** (or **take**) **the fancy of** please; appeal to.

□□ **fan·ci·a·ble** *adj.* (in sense 3 of *v.*). **fan·ci·ly** *adv.* **fan·ci·ness** *n.* [contr. of FANTASY]

fan·cy dress *n.* fanciful costume, esp. for masquerading as a different person or as an animal, etc., at a party.

fan·cy-free *adj.* without (esp. emotional) commitments.

fan·cy goods *n.pl. dated* items or novelties for sale that are purely ornamental.

fan·cy man *n. sl. derog.* **1** a woman's lover. **2** a pimp.

fan·cy wom·an *n. sl. derog.* a mistress.

fan·cy·work /fánseewərk/ *n.* ornamental sewing, etc.

fan dance *n.* a dance in which the dancer is (apparently) nude and partly concealed by fans.

fan·dan·go /fandánggō/ *n.* (*pl.* **·goes** or **·gos**) **1 a** a lively Spanish dance for two. **b** the music for this. **2** nonsense; tomfoolery. [Sp.: orig. unkn.]

fane /fayn/ *n. poet.* = TEMPLE[1]. [ME f. L *fanum*]

fan·fare /fánfair/ *n.* **1** a short showy or ceremonious sounding of trumpets, bugles, etc. **2** an elaborate display; a burst of publicity. [F, imit.]

fan·fa·ron·ade /fánfarənáyd, –naád/ *n.* **1** arrogant talk; bravado. **2** a fanfare. [F *fanfaronnade* f. *fanfaron* braggart (as FANFARE)]

fang /fang/ *n.* **1** a canine tooth, esp. of a dog or wolf. **2** the tooth of a venomous snake, by which poison is injected. **3** the root of a tooth or its prong. **4** *colloq.* a person's tooth. □□ **fanged** *adj.* (also in *comb.*). **fang·less** *adj.* [OE f. ON *fang* f. a Gmc root = to catch]

fan heat·er *n.* an electric heater in which a fan drives air over an element.

fan-jet *n.* = TURBOFAN.

fan·light /fánlit/ *n.* a small, orig. semicircular window over a door or another window.

fan mail *n.* letters from fans.

fan·ny /fánee/ *n.* (*pl.* **·nies**) **1** *sl.* the buttocks. **2** *Brit. coarse sl.* the female genitals. [20th c.: orig. unkn.]

fangs of a common viper

▶Usually considered a taboo word in British use.

Fan·ny Ad·ams /fáneeádəmz/ *n. Brit. sl.* **1** (also **sweet Fan·ny Ad·ams**) nothing at all. **2** *Naut.* **a** canned meat. **b** stew. [name of a murder victim *c.*1870]

▶Sometimes understood as a euphemism for *fuck all*.

fan·ny pack *n.* a pouch for personal items, worn on a belt around the waist or hips.

fan palm *n.* a palm tree with fan-shaped leaves.

fan·tail /fántayl/ *n.* **1** a pigeon with a broad, fan-shaped tail. **2** any flycatcher of the genus *Rhipidura*, with a fan-shaped tail. **3** a fan-shaped tail or end. **4** the fan of a windmill. **5** the projecting part of a boat's stern. □□ **fan·tailed** *adj.*

fan-tan /fántan/ *n.* **1** a Chinese gambling game in which players try to guess the remainder after the banker has divided a number of hidden objects into four groups. **2** a card game in which players build on sequences of sevens. [Chin. = repeated divisions]

fan·ta·sia /fantáyzhə, –zheeə, fántəzeeə/ *n.* a musical or other composition free in form and often in improvisatory style, or that is based on several familiar tunes. [It. = FANTASY]

fan·ta·size /fántəsiz/ *v.* **1** *intr.* have a fantasy or fanciful vision. **2** *tr.* imagine; create a fantasy about. □□ **fan·ta·sist** *n.*

fan·tast /fántast/ *n.* a visionary; a dreamer. [med.L f. Gk *phantastēs* boaster f. *phantazomai* make a show f. *phainō* show]

fan·tas·tic /fantástik/ *adj.* (also **fan·tas·ti·cal**) **1** *colloq.* excellent; extraordinary. **2** extravagantly fanciful; capricious; eccentric. **3** grotesque or bizarre in design, etc. □□ **fan·tas·ti·cal·i·ty** /-kálitee/ *n.* **fan·tas·ti·cal·ly** *adv.* [ME f. OF *fantastique* f. med.L *fantasticus* f. LL *phantasticus* f. Gk (as FANTAST)]

fan·tas·ti·cate /fantástikayt/ *v.tr.* make fantastic. □□ **fan·tas·ti·ca·tion** /-káyshən/ *n.*

fan·ta·sy /fántəsee, –zee/ *n. & v.* ● *n.* (*pl.* **·sies**) **1** the faculty of inventing images, esp. extravagant or visionary ones. **2** a fanciful mental image; a daydream. **3** a whimsical speculation. **4** a fantastic invention or composition; a fantasia. **5** fabrication; pretense; make-believe (*his account was pure fantasy*). **6** a fiction genre that features supernatural, magical, or otherworldly elements. ● *v.tr.* (**·sies, ·sied**) imagine in a visionary manner. [ME f. OF *fantasie* f. L *phantasia* appearance f. Gk (as FANTAST)]

Fan·ti /fántee, faán-/ *n.* (also **Fan·te** (*pl.* same or **Fan·tis**)) **1** a member of a people native to Ghana. **2** the language of this people. [native name]

FAO *abbr.* Food and Agriculture Organization (of the United Nations).

far /faar/ *adv. & adj.* (**far·ther, far·thest** or **fur·ther, fur·thest**) ● *adv.* **1** at or to or by a great distance (*far away; far off; far out*). **2** a long way (off) in space or time (*are you traveling far?; we talked far into* *the night*). **3** to a great extent or degree; by much (*far better*; *far too early*). • *adj.* **1** situated at or extending over a great distance in space or time; remote (*a far cry*; *a far country*). **2** more distant (*the far end of the hall*). **3** extreme (*far right militants*). □ **as far as 1** to the distance of (a place). **2** to the extent that (*travel as far as you like*). **by far 1** by a great amount. **2** (as an intensifier) without doubt. **far and away** by a very large amount. **far and near** everywhere. **far and wide** over a large area. **far be it from me** (foll. by *to* + infin.) I am reluctant to (esp. express criticism, etc.). **far from** very different from; tending to the opposite of (*the problem is far from being solved*). **go far 1** achieve much. **2** contribute greatly. **3** be adequate. **go too far** go beyond the limits of what is reasonable, polite, etc. **how far** to what extent. **so far 1** to such an extent or distance; to this point. **2** until now. **so** (or **in so**) **far as** (or **that**) to the extent that. **so far so good** progress has been satisfactory up to now. □□ **far•ness** *n.* [OE *feorr*]

far•ad /fárəd, –ad/ *n. Electr.* a unit of capacitance, such that one coulomb of charge causes a potential difference of one volt. ¶ Abbr.: **F.** [shortening of FARADAY]

far•a•day /fárəday/ *n.* (also **Far•a•day's con•stant**) *Electr.* the quantity of electric charge carried by one mole of electrons. ¶ Abbr.: **f.** [M. *Faraday*, Engl. physicist d. 1867]

Far•a•day cage *n. Electr.* a grounded metal screen used for shielding electrostatic influences.

Far•a•day ef•fect *n. Physics* the rotation of the plane of polarization of electromagnetic waves in certain substances in a magnetic field.

fa•rad•ic /fərádik/ *adj.* (also **fa•rad•aic** /fárədáyik/) *Electr.* inductive; induced. [see FARADAY]

far•an•dole /fárəndōl/ *n.* **1** a lively Provençal dance. **2** the music for this. [F f. mod. Prov. *farandoulo*]

far•a•way /fáarəwày/ *adj.* **1** remote; long past. **2** (of a look) dreamy. **3** (of a voice) sounding as if from a distance.

farce /faars/ *n.* **1 a** a broadly comic dramatic work based on ludicrously improbable events. **b** this branch of drama. **2** absurdly futile proceedings; pretense; mockery. [F, orig. = stuffing, f. OF *farsir* f. L *farcire* to stuff, used metaph. of interludes, etc.]

far•ceur /faarsőr/ *n.* **1** a joker or wag. **2** an actor or writer of farces. [F f. *farcer* act farces]

far•ci•cal /fáarsikəl/ *adj.* **1** extremely ludicrous or futile. **2** of or like farce. □□ **far•ci•cal•i•ty** /–kálitee/ *n.* **far•ci•cal•ly** *adv.*

far cry *n.* a long way.

far•cy /fáarsee/ *n.* a form of glanders in horses or cattle, with inflammation of the lymph vessels. [ME f. earlier & OF *farcin* f. LL *farciminum* f. *farcire* to stuff]

far•cy bud *n.* (also **far•cy but•ton**) a small lymphatic tumor as a result of farcy.

fard•ed /fáardid/ *adj. archaic* (of a face, etc.) painted with cosmetics. [past part. of obs. *fard* f. OF *farder*]

fare /fair/ *n. & v.* • *n.* **1 a** the price a passenger has to pay to be conveyed by bus, train, etc. **b** a passenger paying to travel in a public vehicle. **2** a range of food provided by a restaurant, etc. • *v.intr.* **1** progress; get on (*how did you fare?*). **2** happen; turn out. **3** journey; go; travel. [OE *fær, faru* journeying, *faran* (v.), f. Gmc]

Far East *n.* China, Japan, and other countries of E. Asia. □□ **Far East•ern** *adj.*

fare•well /fáirwél/ *int. & n.* • *exclam.* good-bye; adieu. • *n.* **1** leave-taking; departure (also *attrib.*: *a farewell kiss*). **2** parting good wishes. [ME f. imper. of FARE + WELL[1]]

far-fetched *adj.* (of an explanation, etc.) strained; unconvincing.

far-flung *adj.* **1** extending far; widely distributed. **2** remote; distant.

far gone *adj.* **1** in a bad or worsening state, esp. so as to be beyond recovery. **2** advanced in time.

fa•ri•na /fəréenə/ *n.* **1** the flour or meal of cereal, nuts, or starchy roots. **2** a powdery substance. **3** *Brit.* starch. □□ **far•i•na•ceous** /fárináyshəs/ *adj.* [L f. *far* corn]

farl /faarl/ *n. Sc.* a thin cake, orig. triangular, of oatmeal or flour. [obs. *fardel* quarter (as FOURTH, DEAL[1])]

farm /faarm/ *n. & v.* • *n.* **1** an area of land and its buildings used under one management for growing crops, rearing animals, etc. **2** a place or establishment for breeding a particular type of animal, growing fruit, etc. (*trout farm*; *mink farm*). **3** = FARMHOUSE. **4** a place with many tanks for the storage of oil or oil products. • *v.* **1 a** *tr.* use (land) for growing crops, rearing animals, etc. **b** *intr.* be a farmer; work on a farm. **2** *tr.* breed (fish, etc.) commercially. **3** *tr.* (often foll. by *out*) **a** delegate or subcontract (work) to others. **b** contract (the collection of taxes) to another for a fee. **c** arrange for (a person) to be looked after by another, with payment. **4** *tr.* lease the labor or services of (a person) for hire. **5** *tr.* contract to maintain and care for (a person, esp. a child) for a fixed sum. □□ **farm•a•ble** *adj.* **farm•ing** *n.* [ME f. OF *ferme* f. med.L *firma* fixed payment f. L *firmus* FIRM[1]: orig. applied only to leased land]

farm•er /fáarmər/ *n.* **1** a person who cultivates a farm. **2** a person to whom the collection of taxes is contracted for a fee. **3** a person who looks after children or performs other services for payment.

[ME f. AF *fermer*, OF *fermier* f. med.L *firmarius*, *firmator* f. *firma* FIRM[2]]

farm hand *n.* a worker on a farm.

farm•house /fáarmhows/ *n.* a dwelling place (esp. the main one) attached to a farm.

farm•land /fáarmland/ *n.* land used or suitable for farming.

farm•stead /fáarmsted/ *n.* a farm and its buildings regarded as a unit.

farm•yard /fáarmyaard/ *n.* a yard or enclosure attached to a farmhouse or other farm buildings.

far•o /fáirō/ *n.* a gambling card game in which bets are placed on the order of appearance of the cards. [F *pharaon* PHARAOH (said to have been the name of the king of hearts)]

Far•o•ese var. of FAEROESE.

fa•rouche /fəróosh/ *adj.* **1** sullen; shy. **2** wild; fierce. [F f. OF *faroche*, *forache* f. med.L *forasticus* f. L *foras* out of doors]

far out *adj.* **1** unconventional or avant-garde. **2** *sl.* (often as exclam.) excellent.

far•ra•go /fəráagō, –ráy–/ *n.* (*pl.* •**goes** or *Brit.* •**gos**) a medley or hodgepodge. □□ **far•rag•i•nous** /–ráajinəs/ *adj.* [L *farrago farraginis* mixed fodder f. *far* corn]

far-reach•ing *adj.* having important and widely applicable effects or implications (*a case of far-reaching political reforms*).

far•ri•er /fáreeər/ *n.* **1** a smith who shoes horses. **2** *Brit.* a horse doctor. □□ **far•ri•er•y** *n.* [OF *ferrier* f. L *ferrarius* f. *ferrum* iron, horseshoe]

far•row /fárō/ *n. & v.* • *n.* **1** a litter of pigs. **2** the birth of a litter. • *v.tr.* (also *absol.*) (of a sow) produce (pigs). [OE *fearh, færh* pig f. WG]

far•ru•ca /fəróokə/ *n.* a type of flamenco dance. [Sp.]

far•see•ing /fáarseeíng/ *adj.* shrewd in judgment; prescient.

Far•si /fáarsee/ *n.* the modern Persian language. [Pers.: cf. PARSEE]

far•sight•ed /fáarsítid/ *adj.* **1** having foresight; prudent. **2** able to see clearly only what is comparatively distant. □□ **far•sight•ed•ly** *adv.* **far•sight•ed•ness** *n.*

fart /faart/ *v. & n. coarse sl.* • *v.intr.* **1** emit intestinal gas from the anus. **2** (foll. by *around*) behave foolishly; waste time. • *n.* **1** an emission of intestinal gas from the anus. **2** an unpleasant person. [OE (recorded in *feorting* verbal noun) f. Gmc]
▶Usually considered a taboo word.

far•ther /fáarthər/ *adv. & adj.* (also **fur•ther** /főrthər/) • *adv.* **1** to or at a more advanced point in space or time (*unsafe to proceed farther*). **2** at a greater distance (*nothing was farther from his thoughts*). • *adj.* more distant or advanced (*on the farther side*). □□ **far•ther•most** *adj.*
▶Traditionally, **farther**, **farthest** were used in referring to physical distance: *The falls were still two or three miles farther up the path.* **Further**, **furthest** were held to be restricted to figurative or abstract senses: *We decided to consider the matter further.* Although **farther**, **farthest** are still properly restricted to measurable distances, **further** is now common in both senses: *Put those plants the furthest from the window.*

far•thest /fáarthist/ *adj. & adv.* (also **fur•thest** /fúrthist/) • *adj.* most distant. • *adv.* to or at the greatest distance. □ **at the farthest** (or **at farthest**) at the greatest distance; at the latest; at most. [ME, superl. f. FARTHER]

far•thing /fáarthing/ *n.* **1** (in the UK) a former coin and monetary unit worth a quarter of an old penny. **2** the least possible amount (*it doesn't matter a farthing*). [OE *fēorthing* f. *fēortha* fourth]

far•thin•gale /fáarthinggayl/ *n. hist.* a hooped petticoat or a stiff curved roll to extend a woman's skirt. [earlier *vardingale*, *verd-* f. F *verdugale* f. Sp. *verdugado* f. *verdugo* rod]

fas•ces /fáseez/ *n.pl.* **1** *Rom.Hist.* a bundle of rods with a projecting ax blade, carried by a lictor as a symbol of a magistrate's power. **2** *hist.* (in Fascist Italy) emblems of authority. [L, pl. of *fascis* bundle]

fasces 1

fas•ci•a /fáysheeə/ *n.* **1** a stripe or band. **2** *Archit.* **a** a long flat surface between moldings on the architrave in classical architecture. **b** a flat surface, usu. of wood, covering the ends of rafters. **3** /fásheeə/ *Anat.* a thin sheath of fibrous connective tissue. **4** /fáysh/ *Brit.* (also **fa•cia**) **a** the instrument panel of a motor vehicle. **b** any similar panel for operating machinery. **5** *Brit.* the upper part of a storefront with the store's name, etc. □□ **fas•ci•al** *adj.* [L, = band, door frame, etc.]

fas•ci•ate /fásheeayt/ *adj.* (also **fas•ci•at•ed**) **1** *Bot.* (of contiguous parts) compressed or growing into one. **2** striped or banded. □□ **fas•ci•a•tion** /–áyshən/ *n.* [L *fasciatus* past part. of *fasciare* swathe (as FASCIA)]

fas•ci•cle /fásikəl/ *n.* **1** (also **fas•ci•cule** /–kyōōl/) a separately published installment of a book, usu. not complete in itself. **2** a bunch or bundle. **3** (also **fas•cic•u•lus** /fasíkyələs/) *Anat.* a bundle of fibers. □□ **fas•ci•cled** *adj.* **fas•cic•u•lar** /fasíkyələr/ *adj.* **fas•cic•u•late** /–síkyōōlayt/ *adj.* **fas•cic•u•la•tion** /–síkyōōláyshən/ *n.* [L *fasciculus* bundle, dimin. of *fascis*: see FASCES]

fas•ci•nate /fásinayt/ *v.tr.* **1** capture the interest of; attract irresistibly. **2** (esp. of a snake) paralyze (a victim) with fear. □□ **fas•ci•nat•**

fas·cine /faseén/ *n.* a long fagot used for engineering purposes and (esp. in war) for lining trenches, filling ditches, etc. [F f. L *fascina* f. *fascis* bundle: see FASCES]

Fas·cism /fáshizəm/ *n.* **1** the totalitarian principles and organization of the extreme right-wing nationalist movement in Italy (1922–43). **2** (also **fascism**) **a** any similar nationalist and authoritarian movement. **b** *disp.* any system of extreme right-wing or authoritarian views. □□ **Fas·cist** *n. & adj.* (also **fas·cist**). **Fas·cis·tic** *adj.* (also **fas·cis·tic**). [It. *fascismo* f. *fascio* political group f. L *fascis* bundle: see FASCES]

fash·ion /fáshən/ *n. & v.* ● *n.* **1** the current popular custom or style, esp. in dress or social conduct. **2** a manner or style of doing something (*in a peculiar fashion*). **3** (in *comb.*) in a specified manner (*in a peaceable fashion*). **4** fashionable society (*a woman of fashion*). ● *v.tr.* (often foll. by *into*) make into a particular or the required form. □ **after** (or **in**) **a fashion** as well as is practicable, though not satisfactorily. **in** (or **out of**) **fashion** fashionable (or not fashionable) at the time in question. □□ **fash·ion·er** *n.* [ME f. AF *fasun*, OF *façon*, f. L *factio* –*onis* f. *facere fact*- do, make]

fash·ion·a·ble /fáshənəbəl/ *adj.* **1** following, suited to, or influenced by the current fashion. **2** characteristic of or favored by those who are leaders of social fashion. □□ **fash·ion·a·ble·ness** *n.* **fash·ion·a·bly** *adv.*

fast¹ /fast/ *adj. & adv.* ● *adj.* **1** rapid; quick-moving. **2** capable of high speed (*a fast car*). **3** enabling or causing or intended for high speed (*a fast road*; *fast lane*). **4** (of a clock, etc.) showing a time ahead of the correct time. **5** (of a field, etc., in a sport) likely to make the ball bounce or run quickly. **6 a** (of a photographic film) needing only a short exposure. **b** (of a lens) having a large aperture. **7 a** firmly fixed or attached. **b** secure; firmly established (*a fast friendship*). **8** (of a color) not fading in light or when washed. **9** (of a person) immoral; dissipated. ● *adv.* **1** quickly; in quick succession. **2** firmly; tightly; securely (*stand fast*; *eyes fast shut*). **3** soundly; completely (*fast asleep*). **4** close; immediately (*fast on their heels*). **5** in a dissipated manner; extravagantly; immorally. □ **pull a fast one** (often foll. by *on*) *colloq.* try to deceive or gain an unfair advantage. [OE *fæst* f. Gmc]

fast² /fast/ *v. & n.* ● *v.intr.* abstain from all or some kinds of food or drink, esp. as a religious observance. ● *n.* an act or period of fasting. □□ **fast·er** *n.* [ON *fasta* f. Gmc (as FAST¹)]

fast·back /fástbak/ *n.* **1** an automobile with the rear sloping continuously down to the bumper. **2** such a back.

fast breed·er *n.* (also **fast breed·er re·ac·tor**) a reactor using fast neutrons to produce the same fissile material as it uses.

fast buck *n. sl.* easily and quickly earned money.

fast·en /fásən/ *v.* **1** *tr.* make or become fixed or secure. **2** *tr.* (foll. by *in, up*) lock securely; shut in. **3** *tr.* **a** (foll. by *on, upon*) direct (a look, thoughts, etc.) fixedly or intently. **b** focus or direct the attention fixedly upon (*fastened him with her eyes*). **4** *tr.* (foll. by *on, upon*) fix (a designation or imputation, etc.). **5** *intr.* (foll. by *on, upon*) **a** take hold of. **b** single out. □□ **fast·en·er** *n.* [OE *fæstnian* f. Gmc]

fast·en·ing /fásəning/ *n.* a device that fastens something; a fastener.

fast food *n.* food that can be prepared and served quickly and easily, sold esp. in a snack bars or restaurants as a quick meal or to be taken out.

fas·tid·i·ous /fastídeeəs/ *adj.* **1** very careful in matters of choice or taste; fussy. **2** easily disgusted; squeamish. □□ **fas·tid·i·ous·ly** *adv.* **fas·tid·i·ous·ness** *n.* [ME f. L *fastidiosus* f. *fastidium* loathing]

fas·tig·i·ate /fastíjeeət/ *adj. Bot.* **1** having a conical or tapering outline. **2** having parallel upright branches. [L *fastigium* gable top]

fast·ness /fástnis/ *n.* **1** a stronghold or fortress. **2** the state of being secure. [OE *fæstnes* (as FAST¹)]

fast neu·tron *n.* a neutron with high kinetic energy, esp. one released by nuclear fission and not slowed by any moderator.

fast re·ac·tor *n.* a nuclear reactor using mainly fast neutrons.

fast-talk *n. colloq.* persuade by rapid or deceitful talk.

fast track *n.* a course or situation leading to rapid advancement or promotion, as in a career.

fast work·er *n. colloq.* a person who achieves quick results, esp. in love affairs.

fat /fat/ *n., adj., & v.* ● *n.* **1** a natural oily or greasy substance occurring esp. in animal bodies. **2** the part of anything containing this. **3** excessive presence of fat in a person or animal; corpulence. **4** *Chem.* any of a group of natural esters of glycerol and various fatty acids existing as solids at room temperature. **5** overabundance or excess. ● *adj.* (**fat·ter, fat·test**) **1** (of a person or animal) having excessive fat; corpulent. **2** (of an animal) made plump for slaughter; fatted. **3** containing much fat. **4** greasy; oily; unctuous. **5** (of land or resources) fertile; rich; yielding abundantly. **6 a** thick; substantial in content (*a fat book*). **b** substantial as an asset or opportunity (*a fat check*; *was given a fat part in the play*). **7 a** (of coal) bituminous. **b** (of clay, etc.) sticky. **8** *colloq. iron.* very little; not much (*a fat chance*). **9** *Baseball* (of a pitch) easy to hit. ● *v.tr. & intr.* (**fat·**

ted, fat·ting) make or become fat. □ **the fat is in the fire** trouble is imminent. **kill the fatted calf** celebrate, esp. at a prodigal's return (Luke 15). **live off** (or **on**) **the fat of the land** have the best of everything. □□ **fat·less** *adj.* **fat·ly** *adv.* **fat·ness** *n.* **fat·tish** *adj.* [OE *fæt* (adj.), *fættian* (v.) f. Gmc]

fa·tal /fáytəl/ *adj.* **1** causing or ending in death (*a fatal accident*). **2** (often foll. by *to*) destructive; ruinous; ending in disaster (*was fatal to their chances*; *made a fatal mistake*). **3** fateful; decisive. □□ **fa·tal·ly** *adv.* **fa·tal·ness** *n.* [ME f. OF *fatal* or L *fatalis* (as FATE)]

fa·tal·ism /fáytˈlizəm/ *n.* **1** the belief that all events are predetermined and therefore inevitable. **2** a submissive attitude to events as being inevitable. □□ **fa·tal·ist** *n.* **fa·tal·is·tic** *adj.* **fa·tal·is·ti·cal·ly** /-lístiklee/ *adv.*

fa·tal·i·ty /fətálətee, fay-/ *n.* (*pl.* **-ties**) **1 a** an occurrence of death by accident or in war, etc. **b** a person killed in this way. **2** a fatal influence. **3** a predestined liability to disaster. **4** subjection to or the supremacy of fate. **5** a disastrous event; a calamity. [F *fatalité* or LL *fatalitas* f. L *fatalis* FATAL]

fat cat *n. sl.* **1** a wealthy person, esp. as a benefactor. **2** a highly paid executive or official.

fat cit·y *n. sl.* a situation or condition of ease, prosperity, comfort, etc. (*since winning the lottery, she's living in fat city*).

fate /fayt/ *n. & v.* ● *n.* **1** a power regarded as predetermining events unalterably. **2 a** the future regarded as determined by such a power. **b** an individual's appointed lot. **c** the ultimate condition or end of a person or thing (*that sealed our fate*). **3** death; destruction. **4** (usu. **Fate**) a goddess of destiny, esp. one of three Greek or Scandinavian goddesses. ● *v.tr.* **1** (usu. in *passive*) preordain (*was fated to win*). **2** (as **fated** *adj.*) a doomed to destruction. **b** preordained; fateful. □ **fate worse than death** see DEATH. [ME f. It. *fato* & L *fatum* that which is spoken, f. *fari* speak]

fate·ful /fáytfŏol/ *adj.* **1** important; decisive; having far-reaching consequences. **2** controlled as if by fate. **3** causing or likely to cause disaster. **4** prophetic. □□ **fate·ful·ly** *adv.* **fate·ful·ness** *n.*

fat·head /fat-hed/ *n. colloq.* a stupid person. □□ **fat·head·ed** *adj.* **fat·head·ed·ness** *n.*

fa·ther /fáathər/ *n. & v.* ● *n.* **1 a** a man in relation to a child or children born from his fertilization of an ovum. **b** a man who has continuous care of his offspring, esp. by adoption. **2** any male animal in relation to its offspring. **3** (usu. in *pl.*) a progenitor or forefather. **4** an originator, designer, or early leader. **5** a person who deserves special respect (*the father of his country*). **6** (**Fathers** or Fathers of the Church) early Christian theologians whose writings were regarded as especially authoritative. **7** (also **Father**) **a** (often as a title or form of address) a priest, esp. of a religious order. **b** a religious leader. **8** (**the Father**) (in Christian belief) the first person of the Trinity. **9** (**Father**) a venerable person, esp. as a title in personifications (*Father Time*). **10** the oldest member or doyen. **11** (usu. in *pl.*) the leading men or elders in a city, etc. (*city fathers*). ● *v.tr.* **1** beget; be the father of. **2** behave as a father toward. **3** originate (a scheme, etc.). **4** appear as or admit that one is the father or originator of. **5** (foll. by *on*) assign the paternity of (a child, book, etc.) to a person. □□ **fa·ther·hood** *n.* **fa·ther·less** *adj.* **fa·ther·less·ness** *n.* **fa·ther·like** *adj. & adv.* **fa·ther·ship** *n.* [OE *fæder* with many Gmc cognates: rel. to L *pater*, Gk *patēr*]

fa·ther fig·ure *n.* an older man who is respected like a father; a trusted leader.

fa·ther-in-law *n.* (*pl.* **fa·thers-in-law**) the father of one's husband or wife.

fa·ther·land /fáathərland/ *n.* one's native country.

fa·ther·ly /fáathərlee/ *adj.* **1** like or characteristic of a father in affection, care, etc. (*fatherly concern*). **2** of or proper to a father. □□ **fa·ther·li·ness** *n.*

Fa·ther's Day *n.* a day (usu. the third Sunday in June) established for a special tribute to fathers.

Fa·ther Time *n.* the personification of time, esp. as an old man with a scythe and hourglass.

fath·om /fáthəm/ *n. & v.* ● *n.* (*pl.* often **fathom** when prec. by a number) **1** a measure of six feet, esp. used in taking depth soundings. **2** *Brit.* a quantity of wood six feet square in cross section. ● *v.tr.* **1** grasp or comprehend (a problem or difficulty). **2** measure the depth of (water) with a sounding line. □□ **fath·om·a·ble** *adj.* **fath·om·less** *adj.* [OE *fæthm* outstretched arms f. Gmc]

Fa·thom·e·ter /fəthómitər/ *n. Trademark* a type of echo sounder.

fa·tigue /fəteég/ *n. & v.* ● *n.* **1** extreme tiredness after exertion. **2** weakness in materials, esp. metal, caused by repeated variations of stress. **3** a reduction in the efficiency of a muscle, organ, etc., after prolonged activity. **4** an activity that causes fatigue. **5 a** a nonmilitary duty in the army, often as a punishment. **b** (in full **fatigue party**) a group of soldiers ordered to do fatigues. **c** (in *pl.*) work clothing worn by soldiers on fatigue duty. ● *v.tr.* (**fa·tigues, fa·tigued, fa·ti·guing**) **1** cause fatigue in; tire; exhaust. **2** (as **fatigued**

adj.) weary; listless. □□ **fat·i·ga·ble** /–gəbəl/ *adj.* **fat·i·ga·bil·i·ty** *n.* **fa·tigue·less** *adj.* [F *fatigue, fatiguer* f. L *fatigare* tire out]

Fat·i·mid /fátimid/ *n.* (also **Fat·i·mite** /–mīt/) **1** a descendant of Fatima, the daughter of Muhammad. **2** a member of a dynasty ruling in N. Africa in the 10th–12th c.

fat·ling /fátling/ *n.* a young fatted animal.

fat·so /fátsō/ *n.* (*pl.* **·soes**) *sl. joc.* or *offens.* a fat person. [prob. f. FAT or the designation *Fats*]

fat·stock /fátstok/ *n. Brit.* livestock fattened for slaughter.

fat·ten /fát'n/ *v.* **1** *tr. & intr.* (esp. with ref. to meat-producing animals) make or become fat. **2** *tr.* enrich (soil).

fat·ty /fátee/ *adj. & n.* ● *adj.* (**fat·ti·er, fat·ti·est**) **1** like fat; oily; greasy. **2** consisting of or containing fat; adipose. **3** marked by abnormal deposition of fat, esp. in fatty degeneration. ● *n.* (*pl.* **·ties**) *colloq.* usu. *offens.* a fat person (esp. as a nickname). □□ **fat·ti·ly** *adv.* **fat·ti·ness** *n.*

fat·ty ac·id *n. Chem.* any of a class of organic compounds consisting of a hydrocarbon chain and a terminal carboxyl group, esp. those occurring as constituents of lipids.

fat·ty oil *n.* = FIXED OIL.

fat·u·ous /fáchōoəs/ *adj.* vacantly silly; purposeless; idiotic. □□ **fa·tu·i·ty** /fətōoitee, –tyōo–/ *n.* (*pl.* **·ties**). **fat·u·ous·ly** *adv.* **fat·u·ous·ness** *n.* [L *fatuus* foolish]

fat·wa /fátwaa/ *n.* (in Islamic countries) an authoritative ruling on a religious matter. [Arab. *fatwa*]

fau·bourg /fóbōorg/ *n.* a suburb, esp. of a French city or New Orleans. [F: cf. med.L *falsus burgus* not the city proper]

fau·ces /fáwseez/ *n.pl. Anat.* a cavity at the back of the mouth. □□ **fau·cial** /fáwshəl/ *adj.* [L, = throat]

fau·cet /fáwsit/ *n.* a device by which a flow of liquid from a pipe or vessel can be controlled. [ME f. OF *fausset* vent peg f. Prov. *falset* f. *falsar* to bore]

fault /fawlt/ *n. & v.* ● *n.* **1** a defect or imperfection of character or of structure, appearance, etc. **2** a break or other defect in an electric circuit. **3** a transgression, offense, or thing wrongly done. **4** a *Tennis,* etc., a service of the ball not in accordance with the rules. **b** (in show jumping) a penalty for an error. **5** responsibility for wrongdoing, error, etc. (*it will be your own fault*). **6** a defect regarded as the cause of something wrong (*the fault lies in the teaching methods*). **7** *Geol.* an extended break in the continuity of strata or a vein. ● *v.* **1** *tr.* find fault with; blame. **2** *tr.* declare to be faulty. **3** *tr. Geol.* break the continuity of (strata or a vein). **4** *intr.* commit a fault. **5** *intr. Geol.* show a fault. □ **at fault** guilty; to blame. **find fault** (often foll. by *with*) make an adverse criticism; complain. **to a fault** (usu. of a commendable quality, etc.) excessively (*generous to a fault*). [ME *faut(e)* f. OF ult. f. L *fallere* FAIL]

SYNONYM TIP *fault*

BLEMISH, DEFECT, FAILING, FLAW, FOIBLE, SHORTCOMING. No one is perfect. But when it comes to cataloging your own imperfections, it's best to start with your **foibles**—the slight weaknesses or eccentricities for which you will be most quickly forgiven. You also have a good chance of being forgiven for your **shortcomings**, which are not necessarily damaging to others (*his ardent devotion to his dog was a shortcoming that was readily overlooked*). **Failing** suggests a more severe shortcoming, usually with more serious consequences (*chronic tardiness was one of her failings*), but a *failing* can also be a weakness of character that you're not responsible for and perhaps not even aware of (*pride is a common failing among those who have met with great success early in life*). **Fault** also implies failure—but not necessarily a serious failure or even moral perfection (*his major fault was his outspokenness*). While *fault* usually indicates something inherent in your nature rather than external to it, a **flaw** can be either superficial (*a flaw in his otherwise immaculate appearance*) or profound (*a personality flaw that made her impossible to work with*), and it can refer to things as well as people (*a flaw in the table's finish*). A **blemish** is usually a physical flaw (*a facial blemish*), although it can be anything that disfigures or mars the perfection of someone or something (*a blemish on her otherwise spotless academic record*). You can get rid of a blemish and even overcome your shortcomings, but a **defect** is a flaw so serious that you may never be able to get rid of it (*a defect in his hearing*).

---

fault·find·er /fáwltfīndər/ *n.* a person given to continually finding fault.

fault·find·ing /fáwltfīnding/ *n. & adj.* ● *n.* continual criticism. ● *adj.* given to finding fault; carping.

fault·less /fáwltlis/ *adj.* without fault; free from defect or error. □□ **fault·less·ly** *adv.* **fault·less·ness** *n.*

fault·y /fáwltee/ *adj.* (**fault·i·er, fault·i·est**) *adj.* having faults; imperfect; defective. □□ **fault·i·ly** *adv.* **fault·i·ness** *n.*

faun /fawn/ *n.* a Roman rural deity with a human face and torso and a goat's horns, legs, and tail. [ME f. OF *faune* or L *Faunus,* a Roman god identified with Gk Pan]

fau·na /fáwnə/ *n.* (*pl.* **fau·nas** or **fau·nae** /–nee/) **1** the animal life of a region or geological period (cf. FLORA). **2** a treatise on or list of this. □□ **fau·nal** *adj.* **fau·nist** *n.* **fau·nis·tic** /–nístik/ *adj.* [mod.L f. the name of a rural goddess, sister of Faunus: see FAUN]

faute de mieux /fṓt də myṓ/ *adv.* for want of a better alternative. [F]

fau·teuil /fṓtil, fōtṓ–ĭ/ *n.* an armchair with open sides and upholstered arms. [F f. OF *faudestuel, faldestoel* FALDSTOOL]

fauve /fōv/ *n.* a person who practices or favors fauvism.

fauv·ism /fōvizəm/ *n.* a style of painting with vivid use of color. □□ **fauv·ist** *n.* [F *fauve* wild beast, applied to painters of the school of Matisse]

faux /fō/ *adj.* imitation; counterfeit (*faux emeralds*). [F, false]

faux pas /fō paa/ *n.* (*pl.* same, *pronunc.* /paaz/) **1** a tactless mistake; a blunder. **2** a social indiscretion. [F, = false step]

fave /fayv/ *n. & adj. sl.* = FAVORITE. [abbr.]

fa·ve·la /fəvélə/ *n.* a Brazilian shack, slum, or shanty town. [Port.]

fa·vor /fáyvər/ *n. & v.* ● *n.* **1** an act of kindness beyond what is due or usual (*did it as a favor*). **2** esteem; liking; approval; goodwill; friendly regard (*gained their favor, look with favor on*). **3** partiality; too lenient or generous treatment. **4** aid; support (*under favor of night*). **5** a thing given or worn as a mark of favor or support, e.g., a badge or a knot of ribbons. **6** a small present or token given out, as at a party. **7** *archaic* leave; pardon (*by your favor*). **8** *Commerce archaic* a letter (*your favor of yesterday*). **9** *archaic* appearance; features. ● *v.tr.* **1** regard or treat with favor or partiality. **2** give support or approval to; promote; prefer. **3 a** be to the advantage of (a person). **b** facilitate (a process, etc.). **4** tend to confirm (an idea or theory). **5** (foll. by *with*) oblige (*favor me with a reply*). **6** (as **favored** *adj.*) **a** having special advantages. **b** preferred; favorite. **7** *colloq.* resemble in features. **8** treat gingerly or gently. (*favored her injured wrist*). □ **in favor 1** meeting with approval. **2** (foll. by *of*) **a** in support of. **b** to the advantage of. **out of favor** lacking approval. □□ **fa·vor·er** *n.* [ME f. OF f. L *favor –oris* f. *favēre* show kindness to]

fa·vor·a·ble /fáyvərəbəl/ *adj.* **1** a well-disposed; propitious. **b** commendatory; approving. **2** giving consent (*a favorable answer*). **3** promising; auspicious; satisfactory (*a favorable aspect*). **4** (often foll. by *to*) helpful; suitable. □□ **fa·vor·a·ble·ness** *n.* **fa·vor·a·bly** *adv.* [ME f. OF *favorable* f. L *favorabilis* (as FAVOR)]

fa·vor·ite /fáyvorit, fáyvrit/ *adj. & n.* ● *adj.* preferred to all others (*my favorite book*). ● *n.* **1** a particularly favored person. **2** *Sports* a competitor thought most likely to win. [obs. F *favorit* f. It. *favorito* past part. of *favorire* favor]

fa·vor·ite son *n.* **1** a person preferred as the presidential candidate by delegates from the candidate's home state. **2** a celebrity particularly popular in his hometown.

fa·vor·it·ism /fáyvoritizəm, fáyvri–/ *n.* the unfair favoring of one person or group at the expense of another.

fawn¹ /fawn/ *n., adj., & v.* ● *n.* **1** a young deer in its first year. **2** a light yellowish brown. ● *adj.* fawn colored. ● *v.tr.* (also *absol.*) (of a deer) bring forth (young). □ **in fawn** (of a deer) pregnant. [ME f. OF *faon,* etc., ult. f. L *fetus* offspring: cf. FETUS]

fawn² /fawn/ *v.intr.* **1** (often foll. by *on*) (of a person) behave servilely; cringe. **2** (of an animal, esp. a dog) show extreme affection. □□ **fawn·er** *n.* **fawn·ing** *adj.* **fawn·ing·ly** *adv.* [OE *fagnian, fægnian* (as FAIN)]

fax /faks/ *n. & v.* ● *n.* **1** facsimile transmission (see FACSIMILE *n.* 2). **2 a** a copy produced by this. **b** a machine for transmitting and receiving these. ● *v.tr.* transmit (a document) in this way. [abbr. of FACSIMILE]

fay /fay/ *n. literary* a fairy. [ME f. OF *fae, faie* f. L *fata* (pl.) the Fates]

faze /fayz/ *v.tr.* (often as **fazed** *adj.*) *colloq.* disconcert; perturb; disorient. [var. of *feeze* drive off, f. OE *fēsian,* of unkn. orig.]

FBA *abbr.* Fellow of the British Academy.

FBI *abbr.* Federal Bureau of Investigation.

FCC *abbr.* Federal Communications Commission.

fcp. *abbr.* foolscap.

FD *abbr.* **1** fire department. **2** Defender of the Faith. [L *Fidei Defensor*]

FDA *abbr.* Food and Drug Administration.

FDIC *abbr.* Federal Deposit Insurance Corporation.

Fe *symb. Chem.* the element iron.

fe·al·ty /féeəltee/ *n.* (*pl.* **·ties**) **1** *hist.* **a** a feudal tenant's or vassal's fidelity to a lord. **b** an acknowledgment of this. **2** allegiance. [ME f. OF *feaulté* f. L *fidelitas –tatis* f. *fidelis* faithful f. *fides* faith]

fear /feer/ *n. & v.* ● *n.* **1 a** an unpleasant emotion caused by exposure to danger, expectation of pain, etc. **b** a state of alarm (*be in fear*). **2** a cause of fear (*all fears removed*). **3** (often foll. by *of*) dread or fearful respect (for) (*had a fear of heights*). **4** anxiety for the safety of (*in fear of their lives*). **5** danger; likelihood (of something unwelcome) (*there is little fear of failure*). ● *v.* **1 a** *tr.* feel fear about or toward (a person or thing). **b** *intr.* (foll. by *for*) feel anxiety or apprehension about (*feared for my life*). **2** *intr.* (foll. by *for*) feel anxiety or apprehension about (*feared for my life*). **3** *tr.* apprehend; have uneasy expectation of (*fear the worst*). **4** *tr.* (foll. by *that* + clause) apprehend with fear or regret (*I fear that you are wrong*). **5** *tr.* **a** (foll. by *to* + infin.) hesitate. **b** (foll. by verbal noun) shrink from; be apprehensive about (*he feared meeting his ex-wife*). **6** *tr.*

show reverence toward. □ **for fear of** (or **that**) to avoid the risk of (or that). **never fear** there is no danger of that. [OE f. Gmc]

fear·ful /féerfŏŏl/ *adj.* **1** (usu. foll. by *of*, or *that* + clause) afraid. **2** terrible; awful. **3** *colloq.* extremely unwelcome or unpleasant (*a fearful row*). □□ **fear·ful·ly** *adv.* **fear·ful·ness** *n.*

fear·less /féerlis/ *adj.* **1** courageous; brave. **2** (foll. by *of*) without fear. □□ **fear·less·ly** *adv.* **fear·less·ness** *n.*

fear·some /féersəm/ *adj.* **1** appalling or frightening, esp. in appearance. **2** timid; fearful. □□ **fear·some·ly** *adv.* **fear·some·ness** *n.*

fea·si·bil·i·ty /féezibílitee/ *n.* the state or degree of being feasible.

fea·si·ble /féezibəl/ *adj.* **1** practicable; possible; easily or conveniently done. **2** *disp.* likely; probable (*it is feasible that they will get the job*). □□ **fea·si·bly** *adv.* [ME f. OF *faisable*, *–ible* f. *fais-* stem of *faire* f. L *facere* do, make]
▶The correct meaning of **feasible** is 'practicable' or 'possible,' e.g., *walking at night was not feasible without the aid of a flashlight*. It should not be used to mean 'likely' or 'probable.'

feast /feest/ *n. & v.* ●*n.* **1** a large or sumptuous meal, esp. with entertainment. **2** a gratification to the senses or mind. **3 a** an annual religious celebration. **b** a day dedicated to a particular saint. ●*v.* **1** *intr.* partake of a feast; eat and drink sumptuously. **2** *tr.* **a** regale. **b** pass (time) in feasting. □ **feast one's eyes on** take pleasure in beholding. □□ **feast·er** *n.* [ME f. OF *feste*, *fester* f. L *festus* joyous]

feast day *n.* a day on which a feast, esp. an annual religious holiday or saint's day, is held.

Feast of Tab·er·na·cles *n.* = SUCCOTH.

feat /feet/ *n.* a noteworthy act or achievement. [ME f. OF *fait*, *fet* (as FACT)]

feath·er /féthər/ *n. & v.* ●*n.* **1** any of the appendages growing from a bird's skin, with a horny hollow stem and fine strands. **2** one or more of these as decoration, fletching on an arrow, etc. **3** (*collect.*) **a** plumage. **b** game birds. ●*v.* **1** *tr.* cover or line with feathers. **2** *tr. Rowing* turn (an oar) so that it passes through the air edgewise. **3** *tr. Aeron. & Naut.* **a** cause (the propeller blades) to rotate in such a way as to lessen the air or water resistance. **b** vary the angle of incidence of (helicopter blades). **4** *intr.* float, move, or wave like feathers. □ **a feather in one's cap** an achievement to one's credit. **feather one's nest** enrich oneself. **in fine** (or **high**) **feather** *colloq.* in good spirits. □□ **feath·ered** *adj.* (also in *comb.*). **feath·er·less** *adj.* **feath·er·y** *adj.* **feath·er·i·ness** *n.* [OE *fether*, *gefithrian*, f. Gmc]

feath·er·bed /féthərbed/ *v.tr.* (**·bed·ded**, **·bed·ding**) provide with (esp. financial) advantages.

feath·er bed *n.* a bed with a mattress stuffed with feathers.

feath·er·bed·ding /féthərbeding/ *n.* the employment of excess staff, esp. due to union rules.

feath·er·brain /féthərbrayn/ *n.* (also **feath·er·head**) a silly or absent-minded person. □□ **feath·er·brained** *adj.*

feath·er·edge /féthərej/ *n.* a fine edge produced by tapering a board, plank, or other object.

feath·er·ing /féthəring/ *n.* **1** bird's plumage. **2** the feathers of an arrow. **3** a featherlike structure in an animal's coat. **4** *Archit.* cusps in tracery.

feath·er·stitch /féthərstich/ *n.* ornamental zigzag sewing.

feath·er·weight /féthərwayt/ *n.* **1 a** any of various weight classes in certain sports intermediate between bantamweight and lightweight. **b** a boxer, weightlifter, etc., of this weight. **2** a very light person or thing. **3** (usu. *attrib.*) a trifling or unimportant thing.

fea·ture /féechər/ *n. & v.* ●*n.* **1** a distinctive or characteristic part of a thing. **2** (usu. in *pl.*) (a distinctive part of) the face, esp. with regard to shape and visual effect. **3 a** a distinctive or regular article in a newspaper or magazine. **b** a special attraction at an event, etc. **4 a** (in full **feature film**) a full-length movie intended as the main at a showing. **b** (in full **feature program**) a broadcast devoted to a particular topic. ●*v.* **1** *tr.* make a special display or attraction of; give special prominence to. **2** *tr. & intr.* have as or be an important actor, participant, or topic in a movie, broadcast, etc. **3** *intr.* be a feature. □□ **fea·tured** *adj.* (also in *comb.*). **fea·ture·less** *adj.* [ME f. OF *feture*, *faiture* form f. L *factura* formation: see FACTURE]

Feb. *abbr.* February.

feb·ri·fuge /fébrifyŏŏj/ *n.* a medicine or treatment that reduces fever; a cooling drink. □□ **fe·brif·u·gal** /fibrífyəgəl, fébrifyŏŏgəl/ *adj.* [F *fébrifuge* f. L *febris* fever + –FUGE]

fe·brile /fébrəl, fée–/ *adj.* of or relating to fever; feverish. □□ **fe·bril·i·ty** /fibrílitee/ *n.* [F *fébrile* or med.L *febrilis* f. L *febris* fever]

Feb·ru·ar·y /fébrŏŏeree, fébyŏŏ–/ *n.* (*pl.* **·ies**) the second month of the year. [ME f. OF *fevrier* ult. f. L *februarius* f. *februa* a purification feast held in this month]

fe·ces /féeseez/ *n.pl.* (*Brit.* **fae·ces**) waste matter discharged from the bowels. □□ **fe·cal** /féekəl/ *adj.* [L, pl. of *faex* dregs]

feck·less /féklis/ *adj.* **1** feeble; ineffective. **2** unthinking; irresponsible (*feckless gaiety*). □□ **feck·less·ly** *adv.* **feck·less·ness** *n.* [Sc. *feck* f. *effeck* var. of EFFECT]

fec·u·lent /fékyələnt/ *adj.* **1** murky; filthy. **2** containing sediments or dregs. □□ **fec·u·lence** *n.* [F *féculent* or L *faeculentus* (as FECES)]

fe·cund /féekənd, fék–/ *adj.* **1** prolific; fertile. **2** fertilizing. □□ **fe·cun·di·ty** /fikúnditee/ *n.* [ME f. F *fécond* or L *fecundus*]

fe·cun·date /féekəndayt, fék–/ *v.tr.* **1** make fruitful. **2** = FERTILIZE 2. □□ **fe·cun·da·tion** /–dáyshən/ *n.* [L *fecundare* f. *fecundus* fruitful]

Fed /fed/ *n. sl.* **1** a federal agent or official, esp. a member of the FBI. **2 a** the Federal Reserve System. **b** the Federal Reserve Board. [abbr. of FEDERAL]

fed *past and past part.* of FEED. □ **fed up** (often foll. by *with*) discontented or bored, esp. from a surfeit of something (*am fed up with the rain*).

fe·da·yeen /fédaayéen/ *n.pl.* Arab guerrillas operating esp. against Israel. [colloq. Arab. *fidā'iyīn* pl. f. Arab. *fidā'ī* adventurer]

fed·er·al /fédərəl/ *adj.* **1** of a system of government in which several states or provinces, etc., form a union but remain independent in internal affairs. **2** relating to or affecting such a federation (*federal laws*). **3** relating to or favoring centralized government. **4** (**Federal**) of or loyal to the Union army and federal government in the US Civil War. **5** comprising an association of largely independent units. □□ **fed·er·al·ism** *n.* **fed·er·al·ist** *n.* **fed·er·al·ize** *v.tr.* **fed·er·al·i·za·tion** *n.* **fed·er·al·ly** *adv.* [L *foedus –eris* league, covenant]

Fed·er·al Re·serve Board *n.* the governing body of the Federal Reserve System.

Fed·er·al Re·serve Sys·tem *n.* a national system of reserve cash available to banks.

fed·er·ate *v. & adj.* ●*v.tr. & intr.* /fédərayt/ organize or be organized on a federal basis. ●*adj.* /fédərət/ having a federal organization. □□ **fed·er·a·tive** /fédəraytiv, –rətiv/ *adj.* [LL *foederare foederat-* (as FEDERAL)]

fed·er·a·tion /fédəráyshən/ *n.* **1** a federal group of states. **2** a federated society or group. **3** the act or an instance of federating. □□ **fed·er·a·tion·ist** *n.* [F *fédération* f. LL *foederatio* (as FEDERAL)]

fe·do·ra /fidáwrə/ *n.* a soft felt hat with a low crown creased lengthways. [*Fédora*, drama by V. Sardou (1882)]

fee /fee/ *n. & v.* ●*n.* **1 a** a payment made to a professional person or to a professional or public body in exchange for advice or services. **2** money paid as part of a special transaction, for a privilege, admission to a society, etc. (*enrollment fee*). **3** (in *pl.*) money regularly paid (esp. to a school) for continuing services. **4** *Law* an inherited estate, unlimited (**fee simple**) or limited (**fee tail**) as to the category of heir. **5** *hist.* a fief; a feudal benefice. ●*v.tr.* (**fee'd** or **feed**) **1** pay a fee to. **2** engage for a fee. [ME f. AF, = OF *feu*, *fieu*, etc. f. med.L *feodum*, *feudum*, perh. f. Frank.: cf. FEUD², FIEF]

fedora

fee·ble /féebəl/ *adj.* **1** weak; infirm. **2** lacking energy, force, or effectiveness. **3** dim; indistinct. **4** deficient in character or intelligence. □□ **fee·ble·ness** *n.* **fee·blish** *adj.* **fee·bly** *adv.* [ME f. AF & OF *feble*, *fieble*, *flexible* f. L *flēbilis* lamentable f. *flēre* weep]

fee·ble·mind·ed /féebəlmíndid/ *adj.* **1** unintelligent. **2** mentally deficient. □□ **fee·ble·mind·ed·ly** *adv.* **fee·ble·mind·ed·ness** *n.*

feed /feed/ *v. & n.* ●*v.* (*past and past part.* **fed** /fed/) **1** *tr.* **a** supply with food. **b** put food into the mouth of. **2** *tr.* **a** give as food, esp. to animals. **b** graze (cattle). **3** *tr.* serve as food for. **4** *intr.* (usu. foll. by *on*) (esp. of animals, or *colloq.* of people) take food; eat. **5** *tr.* nourish; make grow. **6 a** *tr.* maintain supply of raw material, fuel, etc., to (a fire, machine, etc.). **b** (foll. by *into*) supply (material) to a machine, etc. **c** *tr.* supply or send (an electronic signal) for broadcast, etc. **d** *intr.* (often foll. by *into*) (of a river, etc.) flow into another body of water. **e** *tr.* insert further coins into (a meter) to continue its function, validity, etc. **7** *intr.* (foll. by *on*) **a** be nourished by. **b** derive benefit from. **8** *tr.* use (land) as pasture. **9** *tr. Theatr. sl.* supply (an actor, etc.) with cues. **10** *tr. Sports* send passes to (a player) in a basketball game, soccer or hockey match, etc. **11** *tr.* gratify (vanity, etc.). **12** *tr.* provide (advice, information, etc.) to. ●*n.* **1** an amount of food, esp. for animals or (*Brit.*) infants. **2** the act or an instance of feeding; the giving of food. **3** *colloq.* a meal. **4** pasturage; green crops. **5 a** a supply of raw material to a machine, etc. **b** the provision of this or a device for it. **c** an electronic signal fed to a television or radio station. **6** the charge of a gun. **7** *Theatr.*

sl. an actor who supplies another with cues. □ **feed back** produce feedback. **feed the fishes 1** meet one's death by drowning. **2** be seasick. **feed up 1** fatten. **2** satiate (cf. *fed up* (see FED)). □□ **feed•a•ble** *adj.* [OE *fēdan* f. Gmc]

feed•back /féedbak/ *n.* **1** information about the result of an experiment, etc.; response. **2** *Electronics* **a** the return of a fraction of the output signal from one stage of a circuit, amplifier, etc., to the input of the same or a preceding stage. **b** a signal so returned. **3** *Biol.*, etc., the modification or control of a process or system by its results or effects, esp. by the difference between the desired and the actual result.

feed bag *n.* a bag containing fodder, hung on a horse's head.

feed•er /féedər/ *n.* **1** a person or thing that feeds. **2** a person who eats in a specified manner. **3** *Brit.* a baby's bottle. **4** *Brit.* a bib for an infant. **5** a tributary stream. **6** a branch road, railroad line, etc., linking outlying districts with a main communication system. **7** *Electr.* a main conductor carrying electricity to a distribution point. **8** a hopper or feeding apparatus in a machine.

feel /feel/ *v. & n.* ● *v.* (*past* and *past part.* **felt** /felt/) **1** *tr.* **a** examine or search by touch. **b** (*absol.*) have the sensation of touch (*was unable to feel*). **2** *tr.* perceive or ascertain by touch; have a sensation of (*could feel the warmth; felt that it was cold*). **3** *tr.* **a** undergo; experience (*shall feel my anger*). **b** exhibit or be conscious of (an emotion, sensation, conviction, etc.). **4 a** *intr.* have a specified feeling or reaction (*felt strongly about it*). **b** *tr.* be emotionally affected by (*felt the rebuke deeply*). **5** *tr.* (usu. foll. by *that* + clause) have a vague or unreasoned impression (*I feel that I am right*). **6** *tr.* consider; think (*I feel it is useful to go*). **7** *intr.* seem; give an impression of being; be perceived as (*the air feels chilly*). **8** *intr.* be consciously; consider oneself (*I feel happy; do not feel well*). **9** *intr.* **a** (foll. by *with*) have sympathy with. **b** (foll. by *for*) have pity or compassion for. **10** *tr.* (often foll. by *up*) *sl.* fondle the breasts or genitals of. ● *n.* **1** the act or an instance of feeling; testing by touch. **2** the sensation characterizing a material, situation, etc. **3** the sense of touch. □ **feel free** (often foll. by *to* + infin.) not be reluctant or hesitant (*do feel free to criticize*). **feel like** have a wish for; be inclined toward. **feel one's oats** see OAT. **feel oneself** be fit or confident, etc. **feel out** investigate cautiously. **feel strange** see STRANGE. **feel up to** be ready to face or deal with. **feel one's way** proceed carefully; act cautiously. **get the feel of** become accustomed to using. **make one's influence** (or **presence, etc.**) **felt** assert one's influence; make others aware of one's presence, etc. [OE *fēlan* f. WG]

feel•er /féelər/ *n.* **1** an organ in certain animals for testing things by touch or for searching for food. **2** a tentative proposal or suggestion, esp. to elicit a response (*put out feelers*). **3** a person or thing that feels.

feel•er gauge *n.* a gauge equipped with blades for measuring narrow gaps, etc.

feel•ing /féeling/ *n. & adj.* ● *n.* **1 a** the capacity to feel; a sense of touch (*lost all feeling in his arm*). **b** a physical sensation. **2 a** (often foll. by *of*) a particular emotional reaction; an atmosphere (*a feeling of despair*). **b** (in *pl.*) emotional susceptibilities or sympathies (*hurt my feelings; had strong feelings about it*). **c** intense emotion (*said it with such feeling*). **3** a particular sensitivity (*had a feeling for literature*). **4 a** an opinion or notion, esp. a vague or irrational one (*my feelings on the subject; had a feeling she would be there*). **b** vague awareness (*had a feeling of safety*). **c** sentiment (*the general feeling was against it*). **5** readiness to feel sympathy or compassion. **6 a** the general emotional response produced by a work of art, piece of music, etc. **b** emotional commitment or sensibility in artistic execution (*played with feeling*). ● *adj.* **1** sensitive; sympathetic. **2** showing emotion or sensitivity. □□ **feel•ing•less** *adj.* **feel•ing•ly** *adv.*

feet *pl.* of FOOT.

feign /fayn/ *v.* **1** *tr.* simulate; pretend to be affected by (*feign illness*). **2** *tr. archaic* invent (an excuse, etc.). **3** *intr.* indulge in pretense. [ME f. *feign-* stem of OF *feindre* f. L *fingere* mold, contrive]

fei•jo•a /fayóə/ *n.* **1** any evergreen shrub or tree of the genus *Feijoa*, bearing edible guavalike fruit. **2** this fruit. [mod.L f. J. da Silva *Feijo*, 19th-c. Brazilian naturalist]

feint /faynt/ *n. & v.* ● *n.* **1** a sham attack or blow, etc., used to divert attention or fool an opponent or enemy. **2** pretense. ● *v.intr.* make a feint. [F *feinte*, fem. past part. of *feindre* FEIGN]

feist•y /fístee/ *adj.* (**feist•i•er, feist•i•est**) *sl.* **1** aggressive; exuberant. **2** touchy. □□ **feist•i•ness** *n.* [*feist* (= fist) small dog]

fe•la•fel var. of FALAFEL.

feld•spar /féldspaar/ *n.* (also esp. *Brit.* **fel•spar** /félspaar/) *Mineral.* any of a group of aluminum silicates of potassium, sodium, or calcium, which are the most abundant minerals in the earth's crust. □□ **feld•spath•ic** /–spáthik/ *adj.* **feld•spath•oid** /féldspəthoyd, félspə–/ *n.* [G *Feldspat, –spath* f. *Feld* FIELD + *Spat, Spath* SPAR³: *felspar* by false assoc. with G *Fels* rock]

fe•lic•i•tate /fəlísitayt/ *v.tr.* congratulate. □□ **fe•lic•i•ta•tion** /–táyshən/ *n.* (usu. in *pl.*). [LL *felicitare* make happy f. L *felix –icis* happy]

fe•lic•i•tous /fəlísitəs/ *adj.* (of an expression, quotation, civilities, or

a person making them) strikingly apt; pleasantly ingenious. □□ **fe•lic•i•tous•ly** *adv.* **fe•lic•i•tous•ness** *n.*

fe•lic•i•ty /fəlísitee/ *n.* (*pl.* **•ties**) **1** intense happiness; being happy. **2** a cause of happiness. **3 a** a capacity for apt expression; appropriateness. **b** an appropriate or well-chosen phrase. **4** a fortunate trait. [ME f. OF *felicité* f. L *felicitas –tatis* f. *felix –icis* happy]

fe•line /féelīn/ *adj. & n.* ● *adj.* **1** of or relating to the cat family. **2** catlike, esp. in beauty or slyness. ● *n.* an animal of the cat family Felidae. □□ **fe•lin•i•ty** /filínitee/ *n.* [L *felinus* f. *feles* cat]

fell¹ *past* of FALL *v.*

fell² /fel/ *v. & n.* ● *v.tr.* **1** cut down (esp. a tree). **2** strike or knock down (a person or animal). **3** stitch down (the edge of a seam) to lie flat. ● *n.* an amount of timber cut. □□ **fell•er** *n.* [OE *fellan* f. Gmc, rel. to FALL]

fell³ /fel/ *n. No. of Engl.* **1** a hill. **2** a stretch of hills or moorland. [ME f. ON *fjall, fell* hill]

fell⁴ /fel/ *adj. poet.* or *rhet.* **1** fierce; ruthless. **2** terrible; destructive. □ **at** (or **in**) **one fell swoop** in a single (orig. deadly) action. [ME f. OF *fel* f. Rmc FELON¹]

fell⁵ /fel/ *n.* an animal's hide or skin with its hair. [OE *fel, fell* f. Gmc]

fel•lah /félə/ *n.* (*pl.* **fel•la•hin** /–ləheén/) an Egyptian peasant. [Arab. *fallāḥ* husbandman f. *falaḥa* till the soil]

fel•la•ti•o /fláysheeō, feláateeō/ *n.* oral stimulation of the penis. □□ **fel•late** /filáyt/ *v.tr.* **fel•la•tor** /filáytər/ *n.* [mod.L f. L *fellare* suck]

fell•er /félər/ *n.* = FELLOW 1, 2. [repr. an affected or sl. pronunc.]

fel•loe /félō/ *n.* (also **fel•ly** /félee/) (*pl.* **•loes** or **•lies**) the outer circle (or a section of it) of a wheel, to which the spokes are fixed. [OE *felg*, of unkn. orig.]

fel•low /félō/ *n.* **1** *colloq.* a man or boy (*poor fellow!; my dear fellow*). **2** *derog.* a person regarded with contempt. **3** (usu. in *pl.*) a person associated with another; a comrade (*were separated from their fellows*). **4** a counterpart or match; the other of a pair. **5** an equal; one of the same class. **6** a contemporary. **7 a** *Brit.* an incorporated senior member of a college. **b** a selected graduate receiving a stipend for a period of research. **c** a member of the governing body in some universities. **8** a member of a learned society. **9** (*attrib.*) belonging to the same class or activity (*fellow soldier; fellow citizen*). [OE *fēolaga* f. ON *félagi* f. *fé* cattle, property, money: see LAY¹]

fel•low feel•ing *n.* sympathy from common experience.

fel•low•ship /félōship/ *n.* **1** companionship; friendliness. **2** participation; sharing; community of interest. **3** a body of associates; a company. **4** a brotherhood or fraternity. **5** a guild or corporation. **6** a financial grant to a scholar. **7** *Brit.* the status or emoluments of a fellow of a college or society.

fel•low trav•el•er *n.* **1** a person who travels with another. **2** a sympathizer with, or a secret member of, the Communist Party.

fel•ly var. of FELLOE.

fel•on¹ /félən/ *n. & adj.* ● *n.* a person who has committed a felony. ● *adj. archaic* cruel; wicked. □□ **fel•on•ry** *n.* [ME f. OF f. med.L *felo –onis*, of unkn. orig.]

fel•on² /félən/ *n.* an inflamed sore on the finger near the nail. [ME, perh. as FELON¹: cf. med.L *felo, fello* in the same sense]

fe•lo•ni•ous /filóneeəs/ *adj.* **1** criminal. **2** *Law* **a** of or involving felony. **b** who has committed felony. □□ **fe•lo•ni•ous•ly** *adv.*

fel•o•ny /félənee/ *n.* (*pl.* **•nies**) a crime regarded by the law as grave, and usu. involving violence. [ME f. OF *felonie* (as FELON¹)]

fel•spar var. of FELDSPAR.

felt¹ /felt/ *n. & v.* ● *n.* **1** a kind of cloth made by rolling and pressing wool, etc., or by weaving and shrinking it. **2** a similar material made from other fibers. ● *v.* **1** *tr.* make into felt; mat together. **2** *tr.* cover with felt. **3** *intr.* become matted. □□ **felt•y** *adj.* [OE f. WG]

felt² *past* and *past part.* of FEEL.

felt-tipped pen *n.* (or **felt-tip pen**) a pen with a writing point made of felt or fiber.

fe•luc•ca /filúkə, –loōkə/ *n.* a small Mediterranean coasting vessel with oars or lateen sails or both. [It. *felucca* f. obs. Sp. *faluca* f. Arab. *fulk*, perh. f. Gk *epholkion* sloop]

FEMA /féemə/ *abbr.* Federal Emergency Management Agency.

fe•male /féemayl/ *adj. & n.* ● *adj.* **1** of the sex that can bear offspring or produce eggs. **2** (of plants or their parts) fruit-bearing; having a pistil and no stamens. **3** of or consisting of women or female animals or female plants. **4** (of a screw, socket, etc.) manufactured hollow to receive a corresponding inserted part. ● *n.* a female person, animal, or plant. □□ **fe•male•ness** *n.* [ME f. OF *femelle* (n.) f. L *femella* dimin. of *femina* a woman, assim. to *male*]

fe•male im•per•son•a•tor *n.* a male performer impersonating a woman.

feme /fem/ *n. Law* a woman or wife. □ **feme covert** a married woman. **feme sole** a woman without a husband (esp. if divorced). [ME f. AF & OF f. L *femina* woman]

fem•i•nine /féminin/ *adj. & n.* ● *adj.* **1** of or characteristic of women. **2** having qualities associated with women. **3** womanly; effeminate. **4** *Gram.* of or denoting the gender proper to women's names. ● *n. Gram.* a feminine gender or word. □□ **fem•i•nine•ly** *adv.* **fem•i•nine•ness** *n.* **fem•i•nin•i•ty** /–nínitee/ *n.* [ME f. OF *feminin –ine* or L *femininus* f. *femina* woman]

fem·i·nism /féminizəm/ *n.* **1** the advocacy of women's rights on the ground of the equality of the sexes. **2** *Med.* the development of female characteristics in a male person. □□ **fem·i·nist** *n.* (in sense 1). [L *femina* woman (in sense 1 after F *féminisme*)]

fe·min·i·ty /féminitee/ *n.* = *femininity* (see FEMININE). [ME f. OF *féminité* f. med.L *feminitas –tatis* f. L *femina* woman]

fem·i·nize /féminīz/ *v.tr. & intr.* make or become feminine or female. □□ **fem·i·ni·za·tion** *n.*

femme fa·tale /fém fətál, –taál, fay–/ *n.* (*pl.* **femmes fa·tales** *pronunc.* same) a seductively attractive woman. [F]

femto- /fémtō/ *comb. form* denoting a factor of 10⁻¹⁵ (*femtometer*). [Da. or Norw. *femten* fifteen]

fe·mur /féemər/ *n.* (*pl.* **fe·murs** or **fem·o·ra** /fémərə/) **1** *Anat.* the thigh bone, the thick bone between the hip and the knee. **2** the corresponding part of an insect. □□ **fem·o·ral** /fémərəl/ *adj.* [L *femur femoris* thigh]

fen /fen/ *n.* a low marshy or flooded area of land. □□ **fen·ny** *adj.* [OE *fenn* f. Gmc]

fence /fens/ *n. & v.* • *n.* **1** a barrier or railing or other upright structure enclosing an area of ground, esp. to prevent or control access. **2** a large upright obstacle in steeplechasing or show jumping. **3** *sl.* a receiver of stolen goods. **4** a guard or guide in machinery. • *v.* **1** *tr.* surround with or as with a fence. **2** *tr.* **a** (foll. by *in, off*) enclose or separate with or as with a fence. **b** (foll. by *up*) seal with or as with a fence. **3** *tr.* (foll. by *from, against*) screen; shield; protect. **4** *tr.* (foll. by *out*) exclude with or as with a fence; keep out. **5** *tr.* (also *absol.*) *sl.* deal in (stolen goods). **6** *intr.* practice the sport of fencing; use a sword. **7** *intr.* (foll. by *with*) evade answering (a person or question). **8** *intr.* (of a horse, etc.) leap fences. □ **sit on the fence** remain neutral or undecided in a dispute, etc. □□ **fence·less** *adj.* **fenc·er** *n.* [ME f. DEFENSE]

fenc·ing /fénsing/ *n.* **1** a set or extent of fences. **2** material for making fences. **3** the art or sport of swordplay.

fend /fend/ *v.* **1** *intr.* (foll. by *for*) look after (esp. oneself). **2** *tr.* (usu. foll. by *off*) keep away; ward off (an attack, etc.). [ME f. DEFEND]

fend·er /féndər/ *n.* **1** a low frame bordering a fireplace to keep in falling coals, etc. **2** *Naut.* a piece of old timber, matting, etc., hung over a vessel's side to protect it against impact. **3 a** a thing used to keep something off, prevent a collision, etc. **b** a device or enclosure over or around the wheel of a motor vehicle, bicycle, etc.

fe·nes·tra /finéstrə/ *n.* (*pl.* **fe·nes·trae** /–tree/) **1** *Anat.* a small hole or opening in a bone, etc., esp. one of two (**fenestra ovalis** /ōváylis/, **fenestra rotunda**) in the inner ear. **2** a perforation in a surgical instrument. **3** a hole made by surgical fenestration. [L, = window]

fe·nes·trate /fénistrayt, finés–/ *adj. Bot. & Zool.* having small windowlike perforations or transparent areas. [L *fenestratus* past part. of *fenestrare* f. *fenestra* window]

fe·nes·trat·ed /fénistraytid, finés–/ *adj.* **1** *Archit.* having windows. **2** perforated. **3** = FENESTRATE. **4** *Surgery* having fenestrae.

fen·es·tra·tion /fénistráyshən/ *n.* **1** *Archit.* the arrangement of windows in a building. **2** *Bot. & Zool.* being fenestrate. **3** a surgical operation in which a new opening is formed, esp. in the bony labyrinth of the inner ear, as a form of treatment in some cases of deafness.

Fe·ni·an /féeneeən/ *n. & adj.* • *n. hist.* a member of a 19th-c. league among the Irish in the US & Ireland for promoting revolution and overthrowing British government in Ireland. • *adj.* of or relating to the Fenians. □□ **Fe·ni·an·ism** *n.* [OIr. *féne* name of an ancient Irish people, confused with *fiann* guard of legendary kings]

fen·nec /fénik/ *n.* a small fox, *Vulpes zerda*, native to N. Africa, having large pointed ears. [Arab. *fanak*]

fen·nel /fénəl/ *n.* **1** a yellow-flowered fragrant umbelliferous plant, *Foeniculum vulgare*, with leaves or leaf stalks used in salads, soups, etc. **2** the seeds of this used as flavoring. [OE *finugl*, etc. & OF *fenoil* f. L *feniculum* f. *fenum* hay]

fen·u·greek /fényəgreek, fénə–/ *n.* **1** a leguminous plant, *Trigonella foenum-graecum*, having aromatic seeds. **2** these seeds used as flavoring, esp. ground and used in curry powder. [OE *fenogrecum*, superseded in ME f. OF *fenugrec* f. L *faenugraecum* (*fenum graecum* Greek hay), used by the Romans as fodder]

feoff·ment /féfmənt, feéf–/ *n. hist.* a mode of conveying a freehold estate by a formal transfer of possession. □□ **feoff·ee** /fefée, feefée/ *n.* **feoff·or** *n.* [ME f. AF *feoffement*, rel. to FEE]

fe·ral /féerəl, férəl/ *adj.* **1** (of an animal or plant) wild; untamed; uncultivated. **2 a** (of an animal) in a wild state after escape from captivity. **b** born in the wild of such an animal. **3** brutal. [L *ferus* wild]

fer de lance /fáir də láns/ *n.* a large highly venomous snake, *Bothrops atrox*, native to Central and S. America. [F, = iron (head) of a lance]

fe·ri·al /féereeəl, féreeəl/ *adj. Eccl.* **1** (of a day) ordinary; not appointed for a festival or fast. **2** (of a service, etc.) for use on a ferial day. [ME f. OF *ferial* or med.L *ferialis* f. L *feriae*: see FAIR²]

fer·ma·ta /fermaátə/ *n.* (*pl.* **fer·ma·tas**) *Mus.* **1** an unspecified prolongation of a note or rest. **2** a sign ⌢ indicating a prolonged note or rest. [It.]

fer·ment *n. & v.* • *n.* /fərment/ **1** agitation; excitement; tumult.

2 a fermenting; fermentation. **b** a fermenting agent or leaven. • *v.* /fərment/ **1** *intr. & tr.* undergo or subject to fermentation. **2** *intr. & tr.* effervesce or cause to effervesce. **3** *tr.* excite; stir up; foment. □□ **fer·ment·a·ble** *adj.* **fer·ment·er** /–méntər/ *n.* [ME f. OF *ferment* or L *fermentum* f. L *fervēre* boil]

fer·men·ta·tion /fərmentáyshən/ *n.* **1** the breakdown of a substance by microorganisms, such as yeasts and bacteria, usu. in the absence of oxygen, esp. of sugar to ethyl alcohol in making beers, wines, and spirits. **2** agitation; excitement. □□ **fer·ment·a·tive** /–méntətiv/ *adj.* [ME f. LL *fermentatio* (as FERMENT)]

fer·mi /férmee, fér–/ *n.* (*pl.* **fer·mis**) a unit of length equal to 10⁻¹⁵ meter, formerly used in nuclear physics. [E. *Fermi*, Ital.-Amer. physicist d. 1954]

fer·mi·on /férmeeon, fér–/ *n. Physics* any of several elementary particles with half-integral spin, e.g., nucleons (cf. BOSON). [as FERMI + –ON]

fer·mi·um /férmeeəm, fér–/ *n. Chem.* a transuranic radioactive metallic element produced artificially. ¶ Symb.: **Fm**. [as FERMI + –IUM]

fern /fərn/ *n.* (*pl.* same or **ferns**) any flowerless plant of the order Filicales, reproducing by spores and usu. having feathery fronds. □□ **fern·less** *adj.* **fern·y** *adj.* [OE *fearn* f. WG]

fe·ro·cious /fəróshəs/ *adj.* fierce; savage; wildly cruel. □□ **fe·ro·cious·ly** *adv.* **fe·ro·cious·ness** *n.* [L *ferox –ocis*]

fe·roc·i·ty /fərósitee/ *n.* (*pl.* **·ties**) a ferocious nature or act. [F *férocité* or L *ferocitas* (as FEROCIOUS)]

-ferous /fərəs/ *comb. form* (usu. **–iferous**) forming adjectives with the sense 'bearing,' 'having' (*auriferous; odoriferous*). □□ **–ferous·ly** *suffix* forming adverbs. **–ferous·ness** *suffix* forming nouns. [from or after F *–fère* or L *–fer* producing f. *ferre* bear]

fer·rate /férayt/ *n. Chem.* a salt of (the hypothetical) ferric acid. [L *ferrum* iron]

fer·ret /férit/ *n. & v.* • *n.* **1** a small semidomesticated polecat, *Mustela putorius furo*, used in catching rabbits, rats, etc. **2** a person who searches assiduously. • *v.* **1** *intr.* hunt with ferrets. **2** *intr.* rummage; search out. **3** *tr.* (often foll. by *about, away, out,* etc.) a clear out (holes or an area of ground) with ferrets. **b** take or drive away (rabbits, etc.) with ferrets. **4** *tr.* (foll. by *out*) search out (secrets, criminals, etc.). □□ **fer·ret·er** *n.* **fer·ret·y** *adj.* [ME f. OF *fu(i)ret* alt. f. *fu(i)ron* f. LL *furo –onis* f. L *fur* thief]

ferret 1

ferri- /féree/ *comb. form Chem.* containing iron, esp. in ferric compounds. [L *ferrum* iron]

fer·ri·age /féreeij/ *n.* **1** conveyance by ferry. **2** a charge for using a ferry.

fer·ric /férik/ *adj.* **1** of iron. **2** *Chem.* containing iron in a trivalent form (cf. FERROUS).

fer·ri·mag·net·ism /férimágnitizəm/ *n. Physics* a form of ferromagnetism with nonparallel alignment of neighboring atoms or ions. □□ **fer·ri·mag·net·ic** /–magnétik/ *adj.* [F *ferrimagnétisme* (as FERRI-, MAGNETISM)]

Fer·ris wheel /féris/ *n.* a carnival ride consisting of a tall revolving vertical wheel with passenger cars suspended on its outer edge. [G. W. G. *Ferris*, Amer. engineer d. 1896]

fer·rite /férīt/ *n. Chem.* **1** a magnetic substance, a compound of ferric oxide and another metallic oxide. **2** an allotrope of pure iron occurring in low-carbon steel. □□ **fer·ri·tic** /férítik/ *adj.* [L *ferrum* iron]

ferro- /férō/ *comb. form Chem.* **1** iron, esp. in ferrous compounds (*ferrocyanide*). **2** (of alloys) containing iron (*ferromanganese*). [L *ferrum* iron]

fer·ro·con·crete /férōkónkreet/ *n. & adj.* • *n.* concrete reinforced with steel. • *adj.* made of reinforced concrete.

Ferris wheel

fer·ro·e·lec·tric /féroiléktrik/ *adj. & n. Physics* • *adj.* exhibiting permanent electric polarization that varies in strength with the applied electric field. • *n.* a ferroelectric substance. □□ **fer·ro·e·lec·tric·i·ty** /–trísitee/ *n.* [ELECTRIC after *ferromagnetic*]

fer·ro·mag·net·ism /férōmágnitizəm/ *n. Physics* a phenomenon in which there is a high susceptibility to magnetization, the strength of which varies with the applied magnetizing field, and which may persist after removal of the applied field. □□ fer·ro·mag·net·ic /–magnétik/ adj.

fer·rous /férəs/ adj. **1** containing iron (ferrous and nonferrous metals). **2** Chem. containing iron in a divalent form (cf. FERRIC). [L ferrum iron]

fer·ru·gi·nous /fərōōjinəs/ adj. **1** of or containing iron rust, or iron as a chemical constituent. **2** rust colored; reddish brown. [L ferrugo –ginis rust f. ferrum iron]

fer·rule /férōōl/ n. **1** a ring or cap strengthening the end of a stick or tube. **2** a band strengthening or forming a joint. [earlier verrel, etc., f. OF virelle, virol(e), f. L viriola dimin. of viriae bracelet: assim. to L ferrum iron]

fer·ry /féree/ n. & v. ● n. (pl. ·ries) **1** a boat or aircraft, etc., for conveying passengers and goods, esp. across water and as a regular service. **2** the service itself or the place where it operates. ● v. (·ries, ·ried) **1** tr. & intr. convey or go in a boat, etc., across water. **2** intr. (of a boat, etc.) pass back and forth across water. **3** tr. transport from one place to another, esp. as a regular service. □□ fer·ry·man /–mən/ n. (pl. ·men). [ME f. ON ferja f. Gmc]

fer·tile /fórt'l/ adj. **1** (of soil) producing abundant vegetation or crops. **b** fruitful. **2 a** (of a seed, egg, etc.) capable of becoming a new individual. **b** (of animals and plants) able to conceive young or produce fruit. **3** (of the mind) inventive. **4** (of nuclear material) able to become fissile by the capture of neutrons. □□ fer·til·i·ty /–tílitee/ n. [ME f. F f. L fertilis]

PRONUNCIATION TIP | fertile

In British English, this word is pronounced "FUR-tile." In American English, the standard pronunciation is "FUR-tul."

SYNONYM TIP | fertile

FECUND, FRUITFUL, PROLIFIC. A **fertile** woman is one who has the power to produce offspring, just as fertile soil produces crops and a fertile imagination produces ideas. This adjective pertains to anything in which seeds (or thoughts) can take root and grow. A woman with ten children might be described as **fecund**, which means that she is not only capable of producing many offspring but has actually done it. A woman can be fertile, in other words, without necessarily being fecund. **Fruitful**, whose meaning is very close to that of fecund when used to describe plants and may replace fertile in reference to soil or land, pertains specifically to something that promotes fertility or fecundity (a fruitful downpour). It can also apply in a broader sense to anything that bears or promotes results (a fruitful idea; a fruitful discussion). While it's one thing to call a woman with a large family fecund, **prolific** is more usually applied to animals or plants in the literal sense of fertility, and suggests reproducing in great quantity or with rapidity. Figuratively, prolific is often used of highly productive creative efforts (a prolific author with 40 titles published).

Fer·tile Cres·cent n. the fertile region extending in a crescent shape from the E. Mediterranean to the Persian Gulf.

fer·til·i·za·tion /fórt'lizáyshən/ n. **1** Biol. the fusion of male and female gametes during sexual reproduction to form a zygote. **2 a** the act or an instance of fertilizing. **b** the process of being fertilized.

fer·ti·lize /fórt'līz/ v.tr. **1** make (soil, etc.) fertile or productive. **2** cause (an egg, female animal, or plant) to develop a new individual by introducing male reproductive material. □□ fer·ti·liz·a·ble adj.

fer·ti·liz·er /fórt'līzər/ n. a chemical or natural substance added to soil to make it more fertile.

fer·u·la /féroolə, féryə–/ n. **1** any plant of the genus Ferula, esp. the giant fennel (F. communis), having a tall sticklike stem and thick roots. **2** = FERULE. [ME f. L, = giant fennel, rod]

fer·ule /férəl, –rool/ n. & v. ● n. a flat ruler with a widened end formerly used for beating children. ● v.tr. beat with a ferule. [ME as FERULA]

fer·vent /fórvənt/ adj. **1** ardent; impassioned; intense (fervent admirer; fervent hatred). **2** hot; glowing. □□ fer·ven·cy n. fer·vent·ly adv. [ME f. OF f. L fervēre boil]

fer·vid /fórvid/ adj. **1** ardent; intense. **2** hot; glowing. □□ fer·vid·ly adv. [L fervidus (as FERVENT)]

fer·vor /fórvər/ n. (Brit. fer·vour) **1** vehemence; passion; zeal. **2** a glowing condition; intense heat. [ME f. OF f. L fervor –oris (as FERVENT)]

fes·cue /féskyōō/ n. any grass of the genus Festuca, valuable for pasture and fodder. [ME festu(e) f. OF festu ult. f. L festuca stalk, straw]

fess /fes/ n. (also fesse) Heraldry a horizontal stripe across the middle of a shield. □ in fess arranged horizontally. [ME f. OF f. L fascia band]

fess point n. a point at the center of a shield.

fes·tal /fést'l/ adj. **1** joyous; merry. **2** engaging in holiday activities. **3** of a feast. □□ fes·tal·ly adv. [OF f. LL festalis (as FEAST)]

fes·ter /féstər/ v. & n. ● v. **1** tr. & intr. make or become septic. **2** intr. cause continuing annoyance. **3** intr. rot; stagnate. ● n. a pus-filled sore. [ME f. OF festrir, f. OF festre f. L fistula: see FISTULA]

fes·ti·val /féstivəl/ n. & adj. ● n. **1** a day or period of celebration, religious or secular. **2** a concentrated series of concerts, plays, etc., held regularly in a town, etc. ● attrib.adj. of or concerning a festival. [earlier as adj.: ME f. OF f. med.L festivalis (as FESTIVE)]

fes·ti·val of lights n. **1** = HANUKKAH. **2** = DIWALI.

fes·tive /féstiv/ adj. **1** of or characteristic of a festival. **2** joyous. **3** fond of feasting; jovial. □□ fes·tive·ly adv. fes·tive·ness n. [L festivus f. festum (as FEAST)]

fes·tiv·i·ty /festívitee/ n. (pl. ·ties) **1** gaiety; rejoicing. **2 a** a festive celebration. **b** (in pl.) festive proceedings. [ME f. OF festivité or L festivitas (as FESTIVE)]

fes·toon /festōōn/ n. & v. ● n. **1** a chain of flowers, leaves, ribbons, etc., hung in a curve as a decoration. **2** a carved or molded ornament representing this. ● v.tr. (often foll. by with) adorn with or form into festoons; decorate elaborately. □□ fes·toon·er·y n. [F feston f. It. festone f. festa FEAST]

Fest·schrift /féstshrift/ n. (also fest·schrift) (pl. ·schrift·en or ·schrifts) a collection of writings published in honor of a scholar. [G f. Fest celebration + Schrift writing]

fet·a /fétə/ n. a crumbly white ewe's milk or goat's milk cheese cured in brine, made esp. in Greece. [mod.Gk pheta]

fetch¹ /fech/ v. & n. ● v.tr. **1** go for and bring back (a person or thing) (fetch a doctor). **2** be sold for; realize (a price) (fetched $50). **3** cause (blood, tears, etc.) to flow. **4** draw (breath); heave (a sigh). **5** colloq. give (a blow, slap, etc.) (usu. with recipient stated: fetched him a slap on the face). **6** excite the emotions of; delight or irritate. **7** Naut. to arrive at; to reach, esp. by sailing. ● n. **1** an act of fetching. **2** a dodge or trick. **3** Naut. **a** the distance traveled by wind or waves across open water. **b** the distance a vessel must sail to reach open water. □ fetch and carry run backward and forward with things; be a servant. fetch up colloq. **1** arrive; come to rest. **2** Brit. vomit. □□ fetch·er n. [OE fecc(e)an var. of fetian, prob. rel. to a Gmc root = grasp]

fetch² /fech/ n. a person's wraith or double, doppelgänger. [18th c.: orig. unkn.]

fetch·ing /féching/ adj. attractive. □□ fetch·ing·ly adv.

fête /fayt, fet/ n. & v. ● n. **1** a great entertainment; a festival. **2** Brit. an outdoor function with the sale of goods, amusements, etc., esp. to raise funds for charity. **3** a saint's day. ● v.tr. honor or entertain lavishly. [F fête (as FEAST)]

fête cham·pê·tre /fáyt shonpáytrə/ n. an outdoor entertainment; a rural festival. [F (as FÊTE, champêtre rural)]

fet·id /fétid, féetid/ adj. (also foe·tid) stinking. □□ fet·id·ly adv. fet·id·ness n. [L fetidus f. fetēre stink]

fet·ish /fétish/ n. **1** Psychol. a thing abnormally stimulating or attracting sexual desire. **2 a** an inanimate object worshiped for its supposed inherent magical powers or as being inhabited by a spirit. **b** a thing evoking irrational devotion or respect. □□ fet·ish·ism n. fet·ish·ist n. fet·ish·is·tic /–shístik/ adj.

WORD HISTORY | fetish

Early 17th century (originally denoting an object used by the peoples of West Africa as an amulet or charm): from French fétiche, from Portuguese feitiço 'charm, sorcery' (originally an adjective meaning 'made by art'), from Latin factitius (source of factitious).

---

fet·lock /fétlok/ n. part of the back of a horse's leg above the hoof where a tuft of hair grows. [ME fetlak, etc., rel. to G Fessel fetlock f. Gmc]

fe·tor /féetər/ n. a stench. [L (as FETID)]

fet·ter /fétər/ n. & v. ● n. **1 a** a shackle for holding a prisoner by the ankles. **b** any shackle or bond. **2** (in pl.) captivity. **3** a restraint or check. ● v.tr. **1** put into fetters. **2** restrict; restrain; impede. [OE feter f. Gmc]

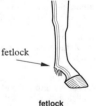
fetlock

fetlock

fet·tle /fét'l/ n. & v. ● n. condition or trim (in fine fettle). ● v.tr. **1** trim or clean (the rough edge of a metal casting, pottery before firing, etc.). **2** line a hearth, furnace, etc., with loose sand or gravel. [earlier as verb, f. dial. fettle (n.) = girdle, f. OE fetel f. Gmc]

fet·tuc·ci·ne /fetəcheenee/ n. (also fet·tuc·ci·ni) pasta in the form of long flat ribbons. [It, f. fetta ribbon, slice]

fe·tus /féetəs/ n. (Brit. foe·tus) an unborn or unhatched offspring of a mammal, esp. a human one more than eight weeks after w4conception. □□ fe·tal adj. fe·ti·cide /–tisīd/ n. [ME f. L fetus offspring]

feud¹ /fyōōd/ n. & v. ● n. **1** prolonged mutual hostility, esp. between two families, tribes, etc., with murderous assaults in revenge for a previous injury (a family feud; be at feud with). **2** a prolonged or bitter quarrel or dispute. ● v.intr. conduct a feud. [ME fede f. OF feide, fede f. MDu., MLG vēde f. Gmc, rel. to FOE]

feud[2] /fyōōd/ n. a piece of land held under the feudal system or in fee; a fief. [med.L *feudum*: see FEE]

feu·dal /fyōōd'l/ adj. **1** of, according to, or resembling the feudal system. **2** of a feud or fief. **3** outdated (*had a feudal attitude*). □□ **feu·dal·ism** n. **feu·dal·ist** n. **feu·dal·is·tic** adj. **feu·dal·ize** v.tr. **feu·dal·i·za·tion** n. **feu·dal·ly** adv. [med.L *feudalis, feodalis* f. *feudum, feodum* FEE, perh. f. Gmc]

feu·dal·i·ty /fyōōdálitee/ n. (pl. **·ties**) **1** the feudal system or its principles. **2** a feudal holding; a fief. [F *féodalité* f. *féodal* (as FEUDAL)]

feu·dal sys·tem n. the social system in medieval Europe whereby a vassal held land from a superior in exchange for allegiance and service.

feu·da·to·ry /fyōōdətáwree/ adj. & n. • adj. (often foll. by *to*) feudally subject; under overlordship. • n. (pl. **·ries**) a feudal vassal. [med.L *feudatorius* f. *feudare* enfeoff (as FEUD[2])]

feud·ist /fyōōdist/ n. a person who is conducting a feud.

feuil·le·ton /fő-yotáwN/ n. **1** a part of a European newspaper, etc., devoted to fiction, criticism, light literature, etc. **2** an item printed in this. [F, = leaflet]

fe·ver /féevər/ n. & v. • n. **1 a** an abnormally high body temperature, often with delirium, etc. **b** a disease characterized by this (*scarlet fever; typhoid fever*). **2** nervous excitement; agitation. • v.tr. (esp. as **fevered** adj.) affect with nervous excitement. [OE *fēfor* & AF *fevre*, OF *fievre* f. L *febris*]

fe·ver·few /féevərfyōō/ n. an aromatic bushy European plant, *Chrysanthemum parthenium*, with feathery leaves and white daisylike flowers, formerly used to reduce fever. [OE *feferfuge* f. L *febrifuga* (as FEBRIFUGE)]

fe·ver·ish /féevərish/ adj. **1** having the symptoms of a fever. **2** excited; fitful; restless. **3** (of a place) infested by fever; feverous. □□ **fe·ver·ish·ly** adv. **fe·ver·ish·ness** n.

fe·ver pitch n. a state of extreme excitement (*the football crowd was at fever pitch*).

few /fyōō/ adj. & n. • adj. not many (*few doctors smoke; visitors are few*). • n. (as pl.) **1** (prec. by *a*) some but not many (*a few words should be added; a few of his friends were there*). **2** a small number; not many (*many are called but few are chosen*). **3** (prec. by *the*) **a** the minority. **b** the elect. **4** (**the Few**) Brit. colloq. the RAF pilots who took part in the Battle of Britain. □ **every few** once in every small group of (*every few days*). **few and far between** scarce. **a good few** Brit. colloq. a fairly large number. **have a few** colloq. have several alcoholic drinks. **no fewer than** as many as (a specified number). **not a few** a considerable number. **some few** some but not at all many. □□ **few·ness** n. [OE *fēawe, fēawa* f. Gmc]

▶**Fewer**, the comparative of *few*, properly refers to a countable quantity: *This has one-third fewer calories than regular sour cream.* Formally, **less** refers to uncountable, mass quantities: *less sand; less water in this glass than that; less time to work with.* Today informal speakers rarely use **fewer** for **less**, but often use **less** where **fewer** has been preferred: *There are less people in the room than there were before lunch.*

fey /fay/ adj. **1 a** strange; otherworldly; elfin; whimsical. **b** clairvoyant. **2** Sc. **a** fated to die soon. **b** overexcited or elated, as formerly associated with the state of mind of a person about to die. □□ **fey·ly** adv. **fey·ness** n. [OE *fǣge* f. Gmc]

fez /fez/ n. (pl. **fez·zes**) a flat-topped conical red cap with a tassel, worn by men in some Muslim countries. □□ **fezzed** adj. [Turk., perh. f. *Fez* (now *Fès*) in Morocco]

ff abbr. Mus. fortissimo.

ff. abbr. **1** following pages, etc. **2** folios.

FHA abbr. Federal Housing Administration.

fi·a·cre /fiáakər/ n. a small four-wheeled carriage. [the Hôtel de St. Fiacre, Paris]

fi·an·cé /féeonsáy, fónsay/ n. (fem. **fi·an·cée** pronunc. same) a person to whom another is engaged to be married. [F, past part. of *fiancer* betroth f. OF *fiance* a promise, ult. f. L *fidere* to trust]

fi·an·chet·to /féeənchétō/ n. & v. Chess • n. (pl. **·toes**) the development of a bishop to a long diagonal of the board. • v.tr. (**·toes**, **·toed**) develop (a bishop) in this way. [It., dimin. of *fianco* FLANK]

fez

fi·as·co /feeáskō/ n. (pl. **·cos**) a ludicrous or humiliating failure or breakdown (orig. in a dramatic or musical performance); an ignominious result. [It., = bottle (with unexplained allusion): see FLASK]

fi·at /féeot, -at, -aat, fíat, fíot/ n. **1** an authorization. **2** a decree or order. [L, = let it be done]

fi·at money n. inconvertible paper money made legal tender by a government decree.

fib /fib/ n. & v. • n. a trivial or venial lie. • v.intr. (**fibbed, fib·bing**) tell a fib. □□ **fib·ber** n. **fib·ster** n. [perh. f. obs. *fible-fable* nonsense, redupl. of FABLE]

fi·ber /fíbər/ n. (Brit. **fi·bre**) **1** Biol. any of the threads or filaments forming animal or vegetable tissue and textile substances. **2** a piece of glass in the form of a thread. **3 a** a substance formed of fibers. **b** a substance that can be spun, woven, or felted. **4** the structure, grain, or character of something (*lacks moral fiber*). **5** dietary material that is resistant to the action of digestive enzymes; roughage. □□ **fi·bered** adj. (also in comb.). **fi·ber·less** adj. **fi·bri·form** /fíbrifawrm/ adj. [ME f. F f. L *fibra*]

fi·ber·board /fíbərbawrd/ n. a building material made of wood or other plant fibers compressed into boards.

fi·ber·glass /fíbərglas/ n. & v. • n. **1** a textile fabric made from woven glass fibers. **2** a plastic reinforced by glass fibers. • v.tr. repair or reinforce with fiberglass.

fi·ber op·tics n. optics employing thin glass fibers, usu. for the transmission of light, esp. modulated to carry signals.

Fi·bo·nac·ci se·ries /feebənáachee/ n. Math. a series of numbers in which each number (**Fibonacci number**) is the sum of the two preceding numbers, esp. 1, 1, 2, 3, 5, 8, etc. [L. *Fibonacci*, It. mathematician *fl.* 1200]

fi·bre Brit. var. of FIBER.

fi·bril /fíbril, fíb–/ n. **1** a small fiber. **2** a subdivision of a fiber. □□ **fi·bril·lar** adj. **fi·bril·lar·y** adj. [mod.L *fibrilla* dimin. of L *fibra* fiber]

fi·bril·late /fíbrilayt, fī–/ v. **1** intr. **a** (of a fiber) split up into fibrils. **b** (of a muscle, esp. in the heart) undergo a quivering movement in fibrils. **2** tr. break (a fiber) into fibrils. □□ **fi·bril·la·tion** /–láyshən/ n.

fi·brin /fíbrin/ n. an insoluble protein formed during blood clotting from fibrinogen. □□ **fi·bri·noid** adj. [FIBER + –IN]

fi·brin·o·gen /fíbrínəjən/ n. a soluble blood plasma protein that produces fibrin when acted upon by the enzyme thrombin.

fibro- /fíbrō/ comb. form fiber.

fi·broid /fíbroyd/ adj. & n. • adj. **1** of or characterized by fibrous tissue. **2** resembling or containing fibers. • n. a benign tumor of muscular and fibrous tissues, one or more of which may develop in the wall of the uterus.

fi·bro·in /fíbrōin/ n. a protein that is the chief constituent of silk. [FIBRO– + –IN]

fi·bro·ma /fíbrómə/ n. (pl. **fi·bro·mas** or **fi·bro·ma·ta** /–mətə/) a fibrous tumor. [mod.L f. L *fibra* fiber + –OMA]

fi·bro·sis /fíbrósis/ n. Med. a thickening and scarring of connective tissue, usu. as a result of injury or disease. □□ **fi·brot·ic** /–brótik/ adj. [mod.L f. L *fibra* fiber + –OSIS]

fi·bro·si·tis /fíbrəsítis/ n. an inflammation of fibrous connective tissue, usu. rheumatic and painful. □□ **fi·bro·si·tic** /–sítik/ adj. [mod.L f. L *fibrosus* fibrous + –ITIS]

fi·brous /fíbrəs/ adj. consisting of or like fibers. □□ **fi·brous·ly** adv. **fi·brous·ness** n.

fib·u·la /fíbyələ/ n. (pl. **fib·u·lae** /–lee/ or **fib·u·las**) **1** Anat. the smaller and outer of the two bones between the knee and the ankle in terrestrial vertebrates. **2** Antiq. a brooch or clasp. □□ **fib·u·lar** adj. [L, perh. rel. to *figere* fix]

-fic /fik/ suffix (usu. as –ific) forming adjectives meaning 'producing,' 'making' (*prolific; pacific*). □□ **–fically** suffix forming adverbs. [from or after F –*fique* or L –*ficus* f. *facere* do, make]

FICA /fíkə/ abbr. Federal Insurance Contributions Act.

-fication /fikáyshən/ suffix (usu. as –ification /ifikáyshən/) forming nouns of action from verbs in –*fy* (*acidification; purification; simplification*). [from or after F –*fication* or L –*ficatio* –*onis* f. –*ficare*: see –FY]

fiche /feesh/ n. (pl. same or **fich·es**) a microfiche. [F, = slip of paper]

fich·u /físhoo, feeshoo/ n. a woman's small triangular shawl of lace, etc., for the shoulders and neck. [F]

fick·le /fíkəl/ adj. inconstant or changeable, esp. in loyalty. □□ **fick·le·ness** n. **fick·ly** adv. [OE *ficol*: cf. *befician* deceive, *fǣcne* deceitful]

fic·tile /fíktəl, –tíl/ adj. **1** made of earth or clay by a potter. **2** of pottery. [L *fictilis* f. *fingere* fict- fashion]

fic·tion /fíkshən/ n. **1** an invented idea or statement or narrative; an imaginary thing. **2** literature, esp. novels, describing imaginary events and people. **3** a conventionally accepted falsehood (*legal fiction; polite fiction*). **4** the act or process of inventing imaginary things. □□ **fic·tion·al** adj. **fic·tion·al·i·ty** /–nálitee/ n. **fic·tion·al·ize** v.tr. **fic·tion·al·i·za·tion** n. **fic·tion·al·ly** adv. **fic·tion·ist** n. [ME f. OF f. L *fictio –onis* (as FICTILE)]

SYNONYM TIP fiction

DECEPTION, FABLE, FABRICATION, FALSEHOOD, FIGMENT. If a young child tells you there is a dinosaur under his bed, you might assume that his story is a **fiction**, but it is probably a **figment**. A *fiction* is a story that is invented either to entertain or to deceive (*her excuse was ingenious, but it was pure fiction*), while *figment* suggests the operation of fancy or imagination (*a figment of his imagina-*

tion). If a child hides his sandwich under the sofa cushions and tells you that a dinosaur ate it, this would be a **fabrication**, which is a story that is intended to deceive. Unlike a *figment*, which is mostly imagined, a *fabrication* is a false but thoughtfully constructed story in which some truth is often interwoven (*the city's safety record was a fabrication designed to lure tourists downtown*). A **falsehood** is basically a lie—a statement or story that one knows to be false but tells with intent to deceive (*a deliberate falsehood about where the money had come from*). A **deception**, on the other hand, is an act that deceives but not always intentionally (*a foolish deception designed to prevent her parents from worrying*). A **fable** is a fictitious story that deals with events or situations that are clearly fantastic, impossible, or incredible. It often gives animals or inanimate objects the power to speak and conveys a lesson of practical wisdom, as in *Aesop's Fables*.

fic·ti·tious /fiktíshəs/ *adj.* **1** imaginary; unreal. **2** counterfeit; not genuine. **3** (of a name or character) assumed. **4** of or in novels. □□ **fic·ti·tious·ly** *adv.* **fic·ti·tious·ness** *n.* [L *ficticius* (as FICTILE)]

fic·tive /fíktiv/ *adj.* **1** creating or created by imagination. **2** not genuine. □□ **fic·tive·ly** *adv.* **fic·tive·ness** *n.* [F *fictif –ive* or med.L *fictivus* (as FICTILE)]

fid /fid/ *n.* **1** *Brit.* a small thick piece or wedge or heap of anything. **2** *Naut.* **a** a square wooden or iron bar to support the topmast. **b** a conical wooden pin used in splicing. [17th c.: orig. unkn.]

fid·dle /fíd'l/ *n. & v.* ● *n.* **1** a stringed instrument played with a bow, esp. a violin. **2** *Brit. colloq.* an instance of cheating or fraud. **3** *Naut.* a contrivance for stopping things from rolling or sliding off a table in bad weather. ● *v.* **1** *intr.* **a** (often foll. by *with*) play restlessly. **b** (often foll. by *about*) move aimlessly. **c** act idly or frivolously. **d** (usu. foll. by *with*) make minor adjustments; tinker (esp. in an attempt to make improvements). **2** *tr. Brit. sl.* **a** cheat; swindle. **b** falsify. **c** get by cheating. **3 a** *intr.* play the fiddle. **b** *tr.* play (a tune, etc.) on the fiddle. □ **as fit as a fiddle** in very good health. **face as long as a fiddle** a dismal face. **play second** (or **first**) **fiddle** take a subordinate (or leading) role. [OE *fithele* f. Gmc f. a Rmc root rel. to VIOL]

fid·dle·back *n. & adj.* ● *n.* a thing shaped like the back of a violin, with the sides deeply curved inward, such as the back of a chair. ● *adj.* denoting something shaped like a fiddle.

fid·dle-de-dee /fíd'ldeedeé/ *int. & n.* nonsense.

fid·dle-fad·dle /fíd'lfad'l/ *n., v., int., & adj.* ● *n.* trivial matters. ● *v.intr.* fuss; trifle. ● *int.* nonsense! ● *adj.* (of a person or thing) petty; fussy. [redupl. of FIDDLE]

fid·dle·head /fíd'lhed/ *n.* **1** a scroll-like carving at a ship's bow. **2** the coiled frond of some ferns eaten as a vegetable.

fid·dle pat·tern *n.* a style of spoons and forks, with handles shaped like the body of a violin.

fid·dler /fídlər/ *n.* **1** a fiddle player. **2** any small N. American crab of the genus *Uca*, the male having one of its claws enlarged and held in a position like a violinist's arm. **3** *Brit. sl.* a swindler; a cheat. ┐[OE *fithelere* (as FIDDLE)]

fid·dle·stick /fíd'lstik/ *n.* **1** (in *pl.*; as *int.*) nonsense! **2** *colloq.* a bow for a fiddle.

fid·dling /fídling/ *adj.* **1 a** petty; trivial. **b** contemptible; futile. **2** that fiddles.

fi·de·ism /féedayizəm, fídee–/ *n.* the doctrine that all or some knowledge depends on faith or revelation. □□ **fi·de·ist** *n.* **fi·de·is·tic** *adj.* [L *fides* faith + –ISM]

fi·del·i·ty /fidélitee/ *n.* **1** (often foll. by *to*) faithfulness; loyalty. **2** strict conformity to truth or fact. **3** exact correspondence to the original. **4** precision in reproduction of sound or video (*high fidelity*). [F *fidélité* or L *fidelitas* (as FEALTY)]

fidg·et /fíjit/ *v. & n.* ● *v.* (**fidg·et·ed**, **fidg·et·ing**) **1** *intr.* move or act restlessly or nervously, usu. while maintaining basically the same posture. **2** *intr.* be uneasy; worry. **3** *tr.* make (a person) uneasy or uncomfortable. ● *n.* **1** a person who fidgets. **2** (usu. in *pl.*) **a** bodily uneasiness seeking relief in spasmodic movements; such movements. **b** a restless mood. □□ **fidg·et·y** *adj.* **fidg·et·i·ness** *n.* [obs. or dial. *fidge* to twitch]

fi·du·cial /fidoŏshəl, –dyoŏ–/ *adj.* *Surveying, Astron.*, etc., (of a line, point, etc.) assumed as a fixed basis of comparison; a standard reference. [LL *fiducialis* f. *fiducia* trust f. *fidere* to trust]

fi·du·ci·ar·y /fidoŏshee-eree, –shəree, –dyoŏ–, fi–/ *adj. & n.* ● *adj.* **1 a** of a trust, trustee, or trusteeship. **b** held or given in trust. **2** (of a paper currency) depending for its value on public confidence or securities. ● *n.* (*pl.* **-ies**) a trustee. [L *fiduciarius* (as FIDUCIAL)]

fie /fí/ *int.* expressing disgust, shame, or a pretense of outraged propriety. [ME f. OF f. L *fi* exclam. of disgust at a stench]

fief /feef/ *n.* **1** a piece of land held under the feudal system or in fee. **2** a person's sphere of operation or control. [F (as FEE)]

fief·dom /féefdəm/ *n.* a fief.

field /feeld/ *n. & v.* ● *n.* **1** an area of open land, esp. one used for pasture or crops, often bounded by hedges, fences, etc. **2** an area rich

in some natural product (*gas field*; *diamond field*). **3** a piece of land for a specified purpose, esp. **a** an area marked out for a game or sport (*football field*), or **b** an airfield. **4 a** the participants in a contest or sport. **b** all the competitors in a race or all except those specified. **5** *Baseball* the defensive positions collectively (*he's fast enough in the field and on the bases*). **6** an expanse of ice, snow, sea, sky, etc. **7 a** the ground on which a battle is fought; a battlefield (*left his rival in possession of the field*). **b** the scene of a campaign. **c** (*attrib.*) (of artillery, etc.) light and mobile for use on campaign. **d** a battle. **8** an area of operation or activity; a subject of study (*each supreme in his own field*). **9 a** the region in which a force is effective (*gravitational field*; *magnetic field*). **b** the force exerted in such an area. **10** a range of perception (*field of view*; *wide field of vision*; *filled the field of the telescope*). **11** *Math.* a system subject to two operations analogous to those for the multiplication and addition of real numbers. **12** (*attrib.*) **a** (of an animal or plant) found in the countryside; wild (*field mouse*). **b** carried out or working in the natural environment, not in a laboratory, etc. (*field test*). **13 a** the background of a picture, coin, flag, etc. **b** *Heraldry* the surface of an escutcheon or of one of its divisions. **14** *Computing* a part of a database record, representing an item of data. ● *v.* **1** *Baseball, Cricket,* etc. **a** *intr.* act as a fielder. **b** *tr.* catch (and return) (the ball). **2** *tr.* select (a team or individual) to play in a game. **3** *tr.* deal with (a succession of questions, etc.). □ **hold the field** not be defeated; remain in battle. **in the field 1** campaigning. **2** working, etc., away from one's laboratory, headquarters, etc. **keep the field** continue a campaign. **play the field** *colloq.* avoid exclusive attachment to one person or activity, etc. **take the field 1** begin a battle. **2** (of a sports team) go on to a field to begin a game. [OE *feld* f. WG]

field day *n.* **1** wide scope for action or success; a time occupied with exciting events (*when crowds form, pickpockets have a field day*). **2** *Mil.* an exercise, esp. in maneuvering; a review. **3** a day spent in exploration, scientific investigation, etc., in the natural environment. **4** an all-day sports or athletics meet, esp. at a school.

field·er /féeldər/ *n.* *Baseball* a member of the team that is fielding.

field e·vents *n.* contests at a track meet other than races (e.g., shot-putting, jumping, discus throwing).

field·fare /féeldfair/ *n.* a European thrush, *Turdus pilaris*, having gray plumage with a speckled breast. [ME *feldefare*, perh. as FIELD + FARE]

field glass·es *n.* binoculars for outdoor use.

field goal 1 *Football* a score of three points by a kick from the field. **2** *Basketball* a goal scored when the ball is in normal play.

field grade *n.* any rank in the air force, army, or marines above captain and below general.

field hock·ey *n.* a team game played between two teams of eleven players each, using hooked sticks with which the players try to drive a small hard ball toward goals at opposite ends of a field.

field hos·pi·tal *n.* a temporary hospital near a battlefield.

field mar·shal *n. Brit.* an army officer of the highest rank.

field mouse *n.* **1** a small mouse, *Apodemus sylvaticus*, with prominent ears and a long tail. **2** various similar rodents inhabiting fields.

field mush·room *n.* the edible fungus *Agaricus campestris*.

field of·fi·cer *n.* an army officer of field grade or (*Brit.*) rank.

field of hon·or *n.* the place where a duel or battle is fought.

field of vi·sion *n.* all that comes into view when the eyes are turned in some direction.

fields·man /féeldzmən/ *n.* (*pl.* **-men**) *Cricket* = FIELDER.

field·stone /féeldstōn/ *n.* stone used in its natural form.

field·work /féeldwərk/ *n.* **1** the practical work of a surveyor, collector of scientific data, sociologist, etc., conducted in the natural environment rather than a laboratory, office, etc. **2** a temporary fortification. □□ **field·work·er** *n.*

fiend /feend/ *n.* **1 a** an evil spirit; a demon. **b** (prec. by *the*) the Devil. **2 a** a very wicked or cruel person. **b** a person causing mischief or annoyance. **3** (with a qualifying word) *sl.* a devotee or addict (*a fitness fiend*). **4** something difficult or unpleasant. □□ **fiend·ish** *adj.* **fiend·ish·ly** *adv.* **fiend·ish·ness** *n.* **fiend·like** *adj.* [OE *fēond* f. Gmc]

fierce /feers/ *adj.* (**fierc·er**, **fierc·est**) **1** vehemently aggressive or frightening in temper or action; violent. **2** eager; intense; ardent. **3** unpleasantly strong or intense; uncontrolled (*fierce heat*). **4** (of a mechanism) not smooth or easy in action. □□ **fierce·ly** *adv.* **fierce·ness** *n.* [ME f. AF *fers*, OF *fiers fier* proud f. L *ferus* savage]

fi·e·ri fa·ci·as /fíóri fáysheeəs, –shəs, fíeri/ *n. Law* a writ to a sheriff for executing a judgment. [L, = cause to be made or done]

fi·er·y /fíree/ *adj.* (**fi·er·i·er**, **fi·er·i·est**) **1 a** consisting of or flaming with fire. **b** (of an arrow, etc.) fire-bearing. **2** like fire in appearance; bright red. **3 a** hot as fire. **b** acting like fire; producing a burning sensation. **4** flashing; ardent (*fiery eyes*). **b** eager; pugnacious; spirited; irritable (*fiery temper*). **c** (of a horse) mettlesome. **5** (of gas, a mine, etc.) flammable; liable to explode. □□ **fi·er·i·ly** *adv.* **fi·er·i·ness** *n.*

PRONUNCIATION TIP **fiery**

This word has three syllables. Pronounce all three (FIE-er-ee) and you'll be less likely to misspell it.

fier•y cross *n.* a wooden cross charred or set on fire as a symbol.

fi•es•ta /fee-éstə/ *n.* **1** a holiday or festivity. **2** a religious festival in Spanish-speaking countries. [Sp., = feast]

FIFA /féefə/ *abbr.* International Football Federation. [F *Fédération Internationale de Football Association*]

fi. fa. *abbr.* fieri facias.

fife /fíf/ *n. & v.* ● *n.* **1** a kind of small shrill flute used with the drum in military music. **2** its player. ● *v.* **1** *intr.* play the fife. **2** *tr.* play (an air, etc.) on the fife. □□ **fif•er** *n.* [G *Pfeife* PIPE, or F *fifre* f. Swiss G *Pfifre* piper]

fife rail /fíf rayl/ *n. Naut.* a rail around the mainmast with belaying pins. [18th c.: orig. unkn.]

fif•teen /fíftéen/ *n. & adj.* ● *n.* **1** one more than fourteen, or five more than ten; the product of three units and five units. **2** a symbol for this (15, xv, XV). **3** a size, etc., denoted by fifteen. **4** a team of fifteen players, esp. in rugby. **5** (**the Fifteen**) *hist.* the Jacobite rebellion of 1715. ● *adj.* that amount to fifteen. □□ **fif•teenth** *adj. & n.* [OE *fíftēne* (as FIVE, –TEEN)]

fifth /fífth/ *n. & adj.* ● *n.* **1** the position in a sequence corresponding to that of the number 5 in the sequence 1–5. **2** something occupying this position. **3** the fifth person, etc., in a race or competition. **4** any of five equal parts of a thing. **5** *Mus.* **a** an interval or chord spanning five consecutive notes in the diatonic scale (e.g., C to G). **b** a note separated from another by this interval. **6 a** a fifth of a gallon of liquor. **b** a bottle containing this. **7** (**the Fifth**) the Fifth Amendment to the US Constitution. ● *adj.* that is the fifth. □ **take the Fifth** exercise the right guaranteed by the Fifth Amendment to the Constitution of refusing to answer questions in order to avoid incriminating oneself. □□ **fifth•ly** *adv.* [earlier and dial. *fift* f. OE *fífta* f. Gmc, assim. to FOURTH]

fifth col•umn *n.* a group within a country at war who are sympathetic to or working for its enemies (from the Spanish Civil War, when General Mola, leading four columns of troops toward Madrid, declared that he had a fifth column inside the city). □□ **fifth col•um•nist** *n.*

fifth gen•er•a•tion *n. Computing* a stage in computer design involving machines that make use of artificial intelligence.

fifth wheel *n.* **1** an extra wheel of a carriage. **2** a superfluous person or thing. **3** a horizontal turntable over the front axle of a carriage as an extra support to prevent its tipping. **4** a round coupling device to connect a tractor and trailer.

fif•ty /fíftee/ *n. & adj.* ● *n.* (*pl.* **-ties**) **1** the product of five and ten. **2** a symbol for this (50, l (letter), L). **3** (in *pl.*) the numbers from 50 to 59, esp. the years of a century or of a person's life. **4** a set of fifty persons or things. **5** a large indefinite number (*have fifty things to tell you*). **6** a fifty-dollar bill. ● *adj.* that amount to fifty. □□ **fif•ti•eth** *adj. & n.* **fif•ty•fold** *adj. & adv.* [OE *fíftig* (as FIVE, –TY²)]

fif•ty-fif•ty *adj. & adv.* ● *adj.* equal; with equal shares, chances, or proportions (*fifty-fifty partners; a fifty-fifty chance of surviving*). ● *adv.* equally; half and half (*split the money fifty-fifty*).

fif•ty-first *adj.* (**fifty-second**, etc.) the ordinal numbers between fiftieth and sixtieth.

fif•ty-one *n.* (**fifty-two**, etc.) the cardinal numbers between fifty and sixty.

fig¹ /fíg/ *n.* **1 a** a soft pear-shaped fruit with many seeds, eaten fresh or dried. **b** (in full **fig tree**) any deciduous tree of the genus *Ficus*, esp. *F. carica*, having broad leaves and bearing figs. **2** a valueless thing (*don't care a fig for*). [ME f. OF *figue* f. Prov. *fig(u)a* ult. f. L *ficus*]

fig² /fíg/ *n. & v.* ● *n.* **1** dress or equipment (*in full fig*). **2** condition or form (*in good fig*). ● *v.tr.* (**figged, fig•ging**) **1** (foll. by *out*) dress up (a person). **2** (foll. by *out, up*) make (a horse) lively. [var. of obs. *feague* (v.) f. G *fegen*: see FAKE¹]

fig. *abbr.* figure.

fight /fít/ *v. & n.* ● *v.* (*past* and *past part.* **fought** /fawt/) **1** *intr.* **a** (often foll. by *against, with*) contend or struggle in war, battle, single combat, etc. **b** (often foll. by *with*) argue; quarrel. **2** *tr.* contend with (an opponent) in this way. **3** *tr.* take part or engage in (a battle, war, duel, boxing match, etc.). **4** *tr.* contend about (an issue, an election); maintain (a lawsuit, cause, etc.) against an opponent. **5** *intr.* campaign or strive determinedly to achieve something. **6** *tr.* strive to overcome (disease, fire, fear, etc.). **7** *tr.* make (one's way) by fighting. **8** *tr.* cause (cocks or dogs) to fight. **9** *tr.* handle (troops, a ship, etc.) in battle. ● *n.* **1 a** a combat, esp. unpremeditated, between two or more persons, animals, or parties. **b** a boxing match. **c** a battle. **d** an argument. **2** a conflict or struggle; a vigorous effort in the face of difficulty. **3** power or inclination to fight (*has no fight left; showed fight*). □ **fight back 1** counterattack. **2** suppress (one's feelings, tears, etc.). **fight down** suppress (one's feelings, tears, etc.). **fight for 1** fight on behalf of. **2** fight to secure (a thing). **fight off** repel with effort. **fight out** (usu. **fight it out**) settle (a dispute, etc.) by fighting. **fight shy of** avoid; be unwilling to approach (a person, task, etc.). **put up a fight** offer resistance. [OE *feohtan, feoht(e),* f. WG]

fight•er /fítər/ *n.* **1** a person or animal that fights. **2** a fast military aircraft designed for attacking other aircraft.

fight•er-bomb•er *n.* an aircraft serving as both fighter and bomber.

fight•ing chair *n.* a chair secured to the deck of a boat for use when catching large fish.

fight•ing chance *n.* an opportunity to succeed by great effort.

fight•ing fish *n.* (in full **Siamese fighting fish**) a freshwater fish, *Betta splendens*, native to Thailand, the males of which sometimes kill each other during fights for territory.

fig leaf *n.* **1** a leaf of a fig tree. **2** a device for concealing something, esp. the genitals (Gen. 3:7).

fig•ment /fígmənt/ *n.* a thing invented or existing only in the imagination. [ME f. L *figmentum*, rel. to *fingere* fashion]

fig•ur•al /fígyərəl/ *adj.* **1** figurative. **2** relating to figures or shapes. **3** *Mus.* florid in style. [OF *figural* or LL *figuralis* f. *figura* FIGURE]

fig•u•ra•tion /fígyəráyshən/ *n.* **1 a** the act of formation. **b** a mode of formation; a form. **c** a shape or outline. **2 a** ornamentation by designs. **b** *Mus.* ornamental patterns of scales, arpeggios, etc., often derived from an earlier motif. **3** allegorical representation. [ME f. F or f. L *figuratio* (as FIGURE)]

fig•ur•a•tive /fígyərətiv/ *adj.* **1** metaphorical, not literal. **b** metaphorically so called. **2** characterized by or addicted to figures of speech. **3** of pictorial or sculptural representation. **4** emblematic; serving as a type. □□ **fig•ur•a•tive•ly** *adv.* **fig•ur•a•tive•ness** *n.* [ME f. LL *figurativus* (as FIGURE)]

fig•ure /fígyər/ *n. & v.* ● *n.* **1 a** the external form or shape of a thing. **b** bodily shape (*has a model's figure*). **2 a** a person as seen in outline but not identified (*saw a figure leaning against the door*). **b** a person as contemplated mentally (*a public figure*). **3** appearance as giving a certain impression (*cut a poor figure*). **4 a** a representation of the human form in drawing, sculpture, etc. **b** an image or likeness. **c** an emblem or type. **5** *Geom.* a two-dimensional space enclosed by a line or lines, or a three-dimensional space enclosed by a surface or surfaces; any of the classes of these, e.g., the triangle, the sphere. **6 a** a numerical symbol, esp. any of the ten in Arabic notation. **b** a number so expressed. **c** an amount of money; a value (*cannot put a figure on it*). **d** (in *pl.*) arithmetical calculations. **7** a diagram or illustrative drawing. **8** a decorative pattern as in a textile. **9 a** a division of a set dance. **b** (in skating) a prescribed pattern of movements from a stationary position. **10** *Mus.* a short succession of notes producing a single impression, a brief melodic or rhythmic formula out of which longer passages are developed. **11** (in full **figure of speech**) a recognized form of rhetorical expression giving variety, force, etc., esp. metaphor or hyperbole. **12** *Gram.* a permitted deviation from the usual rules of construction, e.g., ellipsis. **13** *Logic* the form of a syllogism, classified according to the position of the middle term. ● *v.* **1** *intr.* appear or be mentioned, esp. prominently. **2** *tr.* represent in a diagram or picture. **3** *tr.* imagine; picture to oneself. **4 a** *tr.* embellish with a pattern (*figured satin*). **b** *tr. Mus.* embellish with figures. **c** *intr.* perform a figure in skating or dancing. **5** *tr.* mark with numbers (*figured bass*) or prices. **6 a** *tr.* calculate. **b** *intr.* do arithmetic. **7** *tr.* be a symbol of; represent typically. **8 a** *intr.* understand; ascertain; consider. **b** *intr. colloq.* be likely or understandable (*that figures*). □ **figure on** count on; expect. **figure out 1** work out by arithmetic or logic. **2** estimate. **3** understand. □□ **fig•ure•less** *adj.* [ME f. OF *figure* (n.), *figurer* (v.) f. L *figura, figurare,* rel. to *fingere* fashion]

fig•ured bass *n. Mus.* = CONTINUO.

fig•ure•head /fígyərhed/ *n.* **1** a nominal leader or head without real power. **2** a carving, usu. a bust or a full-length figure, at a ship's prow.

fig•ure skat•ing *n.* the sport of performing jumps and spins, etc., in a dance-like performance while ice skating, and also including skating in prescribed patterns from a stationary position. □□ **fig•ure skat•er** *n.*

fig•ur•ine /fígyəréen/ *n.* a statuette. [F f. It. *figurina* dimin. of *figura* FIGURE]

fig•wort /fígwərt, –wawrt/ *n.* any aromatic green-flowered plant of the genus *Scrophularia*, once believed to be useful against scrofula.

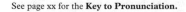

figurehead 2

fil•a•gree var. of FILIGREE.

fil•a•ment /fíləmənt/ *n.* **1** a slender threadlike body or fiber (esp. in animal or vegetable structures). **2** a conducting wire or thread with a high melting point in an electric bulb or vacuum tube, heated or made incandescent by an electric current. **3** *Bot.* the part of the stamen that supports the anther. **4** *archaic* (of air, light, etc.) a notional train of particles following each other. □□ **fil•a•men•ta•ry** /–méntəree/ *adj.* **fil•a•ment•ed** *adj.* **fil•a•men•tous** /–méntəs/ *adj.* [F *filament* or mod.L *filamentum* f. LL *filare* spin f. L *filum* thread]

fi•lar•ia /filáireeə/ *n.* (*pl.* **fi•lar•i•ae** /–ree-ee/) any threadlike parasitic nematode worm of the family Filariidae introduced into the blood by certain biting flies and mosquitoes. □□ **fi•lar•i•al** *adj.* [mod.L f. L *filum* thread]

fil•a•ri•a•sis /filərı́əsis/ *n.* a disease common in the tropics, caused by the presence of filarial worms in the lymph vessels.

fil•a•ture /filəchər/ *n.* an establishment for or the action of reeling silk from cocoons. [F f. It. *filatura* f. *filare* spin]

fil•bert /filbərt/ *n.* **1** the cultivated hazel, *Corylus maxima*, bearing edible ovoid nuts. **2** this nut. [ME *philliberd*, etc., f. AF *philbert*, dial. F *noix de filbert*, a nut ripe about St. Philibert's day (Aug. 20)]

filch /filch/ *v.tr.* pilfer; steal. □□ **filch•er** *n.* [16th-c. thieves' sl.: orig. unkn.]

file[1] /fil/ *n. & v.* •*n.* **1** a folder, box, etc., for holding loose papers, esp. arranged for reference. **2** a set of papers kept in this. **3** *Computing* a collection of (usu. related) data stored under one name. **4** a series of issues of a newspaper, etc., in order. **5** a stiff pointed wire on which documents, etc., are impaled for keeping. •*v.tr.* **1** place (papers) in a file or among (esp. public) records; classify or arrange (papers, etc.). **2** submit (a petition for divorce, an application for a patent, etc.) to the appropriate authority. **3** (of a reporter) send (a story, information, etc.) to a newspaper. □□ **fil•er** *n.* [F *fil* f. L *filum* thread]

file[2] /fil/ *n. & v.* •*n.* **1** a line of persons or things one behind another. **2** *Chess* a line of squares from player to player (cf. RANK[1]). •*v.intr.* walk in a file. [F *file* f. LL *filare* spin or L *filum* thread]

file[3] /fil/ *n. & v.* •*n.* a tool with a roughened surface or surfaces, usu. of steel, for smoothing or shaping wood, fingernails, etc. •*v.tr.* smooth or shape with a file. □ **file away** (or **off**) remove (roughness, etc.) with a file. □□ **fil•er** *n.* [OE *fil* f. WG]

file•fish /filfish/ *n.* any fish of the family Ostracionidae, with sharp dorsal fins and usu. bright coloration.

fi•let /filáy, filit/ *n.* **1** a kind of net or lace with a square mesh. **2** a fillet of meat. [F, = thread]

fi•let mi•gnon /filáy minyón/ *n.* a small tender piece of beef from the end of the tenderloin.

fil•i•al /fileeəl/ *adj.* **1** of or due from a son or daughter. **2** *Biol.* bearing the relation of offspring (cf. F[2] 5). □□ **fil•i•al•ly** *adv.* [ME f. OF *filial* or LL *filialis* f. *filius* son, *filia* daughter]

fil•i•a•tion /fileeáyshən/ *n.* **1** being the child of one or two specified parents. **2** (often foll. by *from*) descent or transmission. **3** the formation of offshoots. **4** a branch of a society or language. **5** a genealogical relation or arrangement. [F f. LL *filiatio –onis* f. L *filius* son]

fil•i•bus•ter /filibustər/ *n. & v.* •*n.* **1** a the obstruction of progress in a legislative assembly, esp. by prolonged speaking. **b** a person who engages in a filibuster. **2** esp. *hist.* a person engaging in unauthorized warfare against a foreign nation. •*v.* **1** *intr.* act as a filibuster. **2** *tr.* act in this way against (a motion, etc.). □□ **fil•i•bus•ter•er** *n.*

WORD HISTORY   **filibuster**

Late 18th century: from French *flibustier*, first applied to pirates who pillaged the Spanish Colonies in the West Indies. In the mid-19th century (via Spanish *filibustero*), the term denoted American adventurers who incited revolution in several Latin American states. The verb was soon extended to describe tactics intended to sabotage legislative proceedings, whence sense 1.

---

fil•i•gree /filigree/ *n.* (also **fil•a•gree** /filə–/) **1** ornamental work of gold or silver or copper as fine wire formed into delicate tracery; fine metal openwork. **2** anything delicate resembling this. □□ **fil•i•greed** *adj.* [earlier *filigreen*, *filigrane* f. F *filigrane* f. It. *filigrana* f. L *filum* thread + *granum* seed]

fil•ing /filing/ *n.* (usu. in *pl.*) a particle rubbed off by a file.

fil•ing cab•i•net *n.* a case with drawers for storing documents.

Fil•i•pi•no /filipeénō/ *n. & adj.* •*n.* (*pl.* •nos; *fem.* **Filipina** /–nə/) a native or inhabitant of the Philippines, a group of islands in the SW Pacific. •*adj.* of or relating to the Philippines or the Filipinos. [Sp., = Philippine]

fill /fil/ *v. & n.* •*v.* **1** *tr. & intr.* (often foll. by *with*) make or become full. **2** *tr.* occupy completely; spread over or through; pervade. **3** *tr.* block up (a cavity or hole in a tooth) with cement, amalgam, gold, etc.; drill and put a filling into (a decayed tooth). **4** *tr.* make level or raise the level of (low-lying land). **5** *tr.* appoint a person to hold (a vacant post). **6** *tr.* hold (a position); discharge the duties of (an office). **7** *tr.* carry out or supply (an order, commission, etc.). **8** *tr.* occupy (vacant time). **9** *intr.* (of a sail) be distended by wind. **10** *tr.* (usu. as **filling** *adj.*) (esp. of food) satisfy; satiate. **11** *tr.* satisfy; fulfill (a need or requirement). **12** *tr. Poker*, etc., complete (a straight or flush, etc.) by drawing the necessary cards. **13** *tr.* stock abundantly. •*n.* **1** (prec. by possessive) as much as one wants or can bear (*eat your fill*). **2** enough to fill something (*a fill of tobacco*). **3** earth, etc., used to fill a cavity. □ **fill the bill** be suitable or adequate. **fill in 1** add information to complete (*Brit.* a form, document, blank check, etc.). **2 a** complete (a drawing, etc.) within an outline. **b** fill (an outline) in this way. **3** fill (a hole, etc.) completely. **4** (often foll. by *for*) act as a substitute. **5** occupy oneself during

(time between other activities). **6** *colloq.* inform (a person) more fully. **7** *Brit. sl.* thrash, beat. **fill out 1** enlarge to the required size. **2** become enlarged or plump. **3** add information to complete (a document, etc.). **fill up 1** make or become completely full. **2** *Brit.* fill in (a document, etc.). **3** fill the fuel tank of (a car, etc.). **4** provide what is needed to occupy vacant parts or places or deal with deficiencies in. **5** do away with (a pond, etc.) by filling. [OE *fyllan* f. Gmc, rel. to FULL[1]]

filled gold *n.* gold in the form of a thin coating applied to a baser metal by rolling.

fill•er /filər/ *n.* **1** material or an object used to fill a cavity or increase bulk. **2** an item filling space in a newspaper, etc. **3** paper for filling a binder or notebook. **4** a person or thing that fills.

fil•let /filit/ *n. & v.* •*n.* **1** (usu. /filáy/) **a** a fleshy boneless piece of meat from near the loins or the ribs. **b** (in full **fillet steak**) the tenderloin. **c** a boned longitudinal section of a fish. **2 a** a headband, ribbon, string, or narrow band, for binding the hair or worn around the head. **b** a band or bandage. **3 a** a thin narrow strip of anything. **b** a raised rim or ridge on any surface. **4** *Archit.* **a** a narrow flat band separating two moldings. **b** a small band between the flutes of a column. **5** *Carpentry* an added triangular piece of wood to round off an interior angle. **6 a** a plain line impressed on the cover of a book. **b** a roller used to impress this. **7** *Heraldry* a horizontal division of a shield, a quarter of the depth of a chief. •*v.tr.* (**fil•let•ed, fil•let•ing**) **1** (also /filáy, filay/) **a** remove bones from (fish or meat). **b** divide (fish or meat) into fillets. **2** bind or provide with a fillet or fillets. **3** encircle with an ornamental band. □□ **fil•let•er** *n.* [ME f. OF *filet* f. Rmc dimin. of L *filum* thread]

fill•ing /filing/ *n.* **1** any material that fills or is used to fill, esp.: **a** a piece of material used to fill a cavity in a tooth. **b** the edible substance between the bread in a sandwich or between the pastry crusts in a pie. **2** weft.

fill•ing sta•tion *n.* a service station.

fil•lip /filip/ *n. & v.* •*n.* **1** a stimulus or incentive. **2 a** a sudden release of a finger or thumb when it has been bent and checked by a thumb or finger. **b** a slight sharp stroke given in this way. •*v.* (**fil•liped, fil•lip•ing**) **1** *tr.* stimulate (*fillip one's memory*). **2** *tr.* strike slightly and sharply. **3** *tr.* propel (a coin, marble, etc.) with a fillip. **4** *intr.* make a fillip. [imit.]

fill-up *n.* **1** a thing that fills something up. **2** an act of filling something up.

fil•ly /filee/ *n.* (*pl.* •lies) **1** a young female horse, usu. before it is four years old. **2** *colloq.* a girl or young woman. [ME, prob. f. ON *fylja* f. Gmc (as FOAL)]

film /film/ *n. & v.* •*n.* **1** a thin coating or covering layer. **2** *Photog.* a strip or sheet of plastic or other flexible base coated with light-sensitive emulsion for exposure in a camera, either as individual visual representations or as a sequence, forming the illusion of movement when shown in rapid succession. **3 a** a representation of a story, episode, etc., on a film, with the illusion of movement; a movie. **b** a story represented in this way; a movie. **c** (in *pl.*) the movie industry. **4** a slight veil or haze, etc. **5** a dimness or morbid growth affecting the eyes. **6** a fine thread or filament. •*v.* **1 a** *tr.* make a photographic film of (a scene, person, etc.). **b** *tr.* (also *absol.*) make a movie or television film of (a book, etc.). **c** *intr.* be (well or ill) suited for reproduction on film. **2** *tr. & intr.* cover or become covered with or as with a film. [OE *filmen* membrane f. WG, rel. to FELL[5]]

film•go•er /filmgōər/ *n.* a person who frequents movie theaters.

film•ic /filmik/ *adj.* of or relating to movies or cinematography.

film•mak•er /filmaykər/ *n.* a person who makes motion pictures.

film•og•ra•phy /filmógrəfee/ *n.* (*pl.* •phies) a list of movies by one director, etc., or on one subject. [FILM + –GRAPHY after *bibliography*]

film•set /filmset/ *v.tr.* (•set•ting; *past* and *past part.* •set) *Printing* set (material for printing) by filmsetting. □□ **film•set•ter** *n.*

film•set•ting /filmseting/ *n.* = PHOTOCOMPOSITION.

film star *n.* a celebrated actor or actress in films.

film•strip /filmstrip/ *n.* a series of transparencies in a strip for projection as still pictures.

film•y /filmee/ *adj.* (**film•i•er, film•i•est**) **1** thin and translucent. **2** covered with or as with a film. □□ **film•i•ly** *adv.* **film•i•ness** *n.*

fi•lo /féelō/ *n.* (also **phyl•lo**) dough that can be stretched into very thin layers; pastry made from this dough. [mod.Gk *phullo* leaf]

fils /fees/ *n.* (added to a surname to distinguish a son from a father) the son; junior (cf. PÈRE). [F, = son]

fil•ter /filtər/ *n. & v.* •*n.* **1** a porous device for removing impurities or solid particles from a liquid or gas passed through it. **2** = FILTER TIP. **3** a screen or attachment for absorbing or modifying light, X rays, etc. **4** a device for suppressing electrical or sound waves of frequencies not required. **5** *Brit.* **a** an arrangement for filtering traffic. **b** a traffic light signaling this. •*v.* **1** *tr. & intr.* pass or cause to pass through a filter. **2** *tr.* (foll. by *out*) remove (impurities, etc.) by means of a filter. **3** *intr.* (foll. by *through, into*, etc.) make way gradually. **4** *intr.* (foll. by *out*) leak or cause to leak. **5** *tr. & intr. Brit.* allow (traffic) or (of traffic) be allowed to pass to the left or right at a junction while traffic going straight ahead is halted (esp. at traffic lights). [F *filtre* f. med.L *filtrum* felt used as a filter, f. WG]

fil•ter•a•ble /fíltərəbəl/ *adj.* (also **fil•tra•ble** /fíltrəbəl/) **1** *Med.* (of a virus) able to pass through a filter that retains bacteria. **2** that can be filtered.

fil•ter bed *n.* a tank or pond containing a layer of sand, etc., for filtering large quantities of liquid.

fil•ter pa•per *n.* porous paper for filtering.

fil•ter tip *n.* **1** a filter attached to a cigarette for removing impurities from the inhaled smoke. **2** a cigarette with this.

filth /filth/ *n.* **1** repugnant or extreme dirt; excrement; refuse. **2** vileness; corruption; obscenity. **3** foul or obscene language. [OE *fȳlth* (as FOUL, –TH[2])]

filth•y /filthee/ *adj. & adv.* • *adj.* (**filth•i•er, filth•i•est**) **1** extremely or disgustingly dirty. **2** obscene. **3** *Brit. colloq.* (of weather) very unpleasant. **4** vile; disgraceful. • *adv.* **1** filthily (*filthy dirty*). **2** *colloq.* extremely (*filthy rich*). ▫▫ **filth•i•ly** *adv.* **filth•i•ness** *n.*

filth•y lu•cre *n.* money, esp. when gained in a dishonest or dishonorable way.

fil•tra•ble var. of FILTERABLE.

fil•trate /filtrayt/ *v. & n.* • *v.tr.* filter. • *n.* filtered liquid. ▫▫ **fil•tra•tion** /–tráyshən/ *n.* [mod.L *filtrare* (as FILTER)]

fim•bri•at•ed /fímbreeaytid/ *adj.* (also **fim•bri•ate**) **1** *Bot. & Zool.* fringed or bordered with hairs, etc. **2** *Heraldry* having a narrow border. [L *fimbriatus* f. *fimbriae* fringe]

fin[1] /fin/ *n. & v.* • *n.* **1** an organ on various parts of the body of many aquatic vertebrates and some invertebrates, including fish and cetaceans, for propelling, steering, and balancing (*dorsal fin; anal fin*). **2** a small projecting surface or attachment on an aircraft, rocket, or automobile for ensuring aerodynamic stability. **3** an underwater swimmer's flipper. **4** a sharp lateral projection on the share or colter of a plow. **5** a finlike projection on any device, for improving heat transfer, etc. • *v.* (**finned, fin•ning**) **1** *tr.* provide with fins. **2** *intr.* swim under water. ▫▫ **fin•less** *adj.* **finned** *adj.* (also in *comb.*). [OE *fin(n)*]

fin[2] /fin/ *n. sl.* a five-dollar bill. [f. Yiddish *finf* five]

fin•a•ble see FINE[2].

fi•na•gle /fináygəl/ *v.intr. & tr. colloq.* act or obtain dishonestly or deviously. ▫▫ **fi•na•gler** *n.* [dial. *fainaigue* cheat]

fi•nal /fínəl/ *adj. & n.* • *adj.* **1** situated at the end; coming last. **2** conclusive; decisive; unalterable; putting an end to doubt. **3** concerned with the purpose or end aimed at. • *n.* **1** (also in *pl.*) the last or deciding heat or game in sports or in a competition. **2** the edition of a newspaper published latest in the day. **3** an examination at the end of an academic course. **4** *Mus.* the principal or tonic note in any mode. ▫▫ **fi•nal•ly** *adv.* [ME f. OF or f. L *finalis* f. *finis* end]

fi•nal cause *n. Philos.* the end toward which a thing naturally develops or at which an action aims.

fi•nal clause *n. Gram.* a clause expressing purpose, introduced by *in order that, lest,* etc.

fi•na•le /finaálee, –nálee/ *n.* **1 a** the last movement of an instrumental composition. **b** a piece of music closing an act in an opera. **2** the close of a drama, etc. **3** a conclusion. [It. (as FINAL)]

fi•nal•ism /fínəlizəm/ *n.* the doctrine that natural processes (e.g., evolution) are directed toward some goal. ▫▫ **fi•nal•is•tic** *adj.*

fi•nal•ist /fínəlist/ *n.* a competitor in the final of a competition, etc.

fi•nal•i•ty /fínálitee, fə–/ *n.* (*pl.* **•ties**) **1** the quality or fact of being final. **2** the belief that something is final. **3** a final act, state, or utterance. **4** the principle of final cause viewed as operative in the universe. [F *finalité* f. LL *finalitas –tatis* (as FINAL)]

fi•nal•ize /fínəlīz/ *v.tr.* **1** put into final form. **2** complete; bring to an end. **3** approve the final form or details of. ▫▫ **fi•nal•i•za•tion** *n.*

fi•nal so•lu•tion *n.* the Nazi policy (1941–45) of exterminating European Jews.

fi•nance /fináns, fī–, fínans/ *n. & v.* • *n.* **1** the management of (esp. public) money. **2** monetary support for an enterprise. **3** (in *pl.*) the money resources of a government, company, or person. • *v.tr.* provide capital for (a person or enterprise). [ME f. OF f. *finer* settle a debt f. *fin* end: see FINE[2]]

fi•nance com•pa•ny *n.* a company concerned mainly with providing money, e.g., for short-term loans.

fi•nan•cial /finánshəl, fī–/ *adj.* **1** of finance. **2** *Austral. & NZ sl.* possessing money. ▫▫ **fi•nan•cial•ly** *adv.*

fi•nan•cial year *n. Brit.* = FISCAL YEAR.

fin•an•cier /finənseér, fənan–, fínən–/ *n. & v.* • *n.* a person engaged in large-scale finance. • *v.intr.* usu. *derog.* conduct financial operations. [F (as FINANCE)]

fin•back /finbak/ *n.* (or **fin whale**) a rorqual, *Balaenoptera physalus.*

finch /finch/ *n.* any small seed-eating passerine bird of the family Fringillidae (esp. one of the genus *Fringilla*), including crossbills, canaries, and chaffinches. [OE *finc* f. WG]

find /find/ *v. & n.* • *v.tr.* (*past* and *past part.* **found** /fownd/) **1 a** discover by chance or effort (*found a key*). **b** become aware of. **2 a** get possession of by chance (*found a treasure*). **b** obtain; receive (*idea found acceptance*). **c** succeed in obtaining (*cannot find the money; can't find time to read*). **d** summon up (*found courage to protest*). **e** *Brit. sl.* steal. **3 a** seek out and provide (*will find you a book*). **b** supply; furnish (*each finds his own equipment*). **4** ascertain by study or calculation or inquiry (*could not find the answer*). **5 a** perceive or experience (*find no sense in it; find difficulty in breathing*). **b** (often in *passive*) recognize or discover to be present (*the word is not found in Shakespeare*). **c** regard or discover from experience (*finds Canada too cold; you'll find it pays*). **6** *Law* (of a jury, judge, etc.) decide and declare (*found him guilty; found it murder*). **7** reach by a natural or normal process (*water finds its own level*). **8 a** (of a letter) reach (a person). **b** (of an address) be adequate to enable a letter, etc., to reach (a person). **9** *archaic* reach the conscience of. • *n.* **1** a discovery of treasure, minerals, etc. **2** a thing or person discovered, esp. when of value. ▫ **all found** *Brit.* (of an employee's wages) with board and lodging provided free. **find against** *Law* decide against (a person); judge to be guilty. **find fault** see FAULT. **find favor** prove acceptable. **find one's feet 1** become able to walk. **2** develop one's independent ability. **find for** *Law* decide in favor of (a person); judge to be innocent. **find it in one's heart** (esp. with *neg.*; foll. by *to* + infin.) prevail upon oneself; be willing. **find oneself 1** discover that one is (*woke to find myself in the hospital; found herself agreeing*). **2** discover one's own talents, strengths, etc. **find out 1** discover or detect (a wrongdoer, etc.). **2** (often foll. by *about*) get information (*find out about vacationing abroad*). **3** discover (*find out where we are*). **4** (often foll. by *about*) discover the truth, a fact, etc. (*he never found out*). **5** devise. **6** solve. **find one's way 1** (often foll. by *to*) manage to reach a place. **2** (often foll. by *into*) be brought or get. ▫▫ **find•a•ble** *adj.* [OE *findan* f. Gmc]

▶See note at LOCATE.

find•er /fíndər/ *n.* **1** a person who finds. **2** a small telescope attached to a large one to locate an object for observation. **3** the viewfinder of a camera.

fin de siè•cle /fáN də syéklə/ *adj.* **1** characteristic of the end of the nineteenth century. **2** decadent. [F, = end of century]

find•ing /fínding/ *n.* **1** (often in *pl.*) a conclusion reached by an inquiry. **2** (in *pl.*) small parts or tools used by artisans.

fine[1] /fīn/ *adj., n., adv., & v.* • *adj.* **1** of high quality (*they sell fine fabrics*). **2 a** excellent; of notable merit (*a fine painting*). **b** good; satisfactory (*that will be fine*). **c** fortunate (*has been a fine thing for him*). **d** well conceived or expressed (*a fine saying*). **3 a** pure; refined. **b** (of gold or silver) containing a specified proportion of pure metal. **4** of handsome appearance or size; imposing; dignified (*fine buildings*). **5** in good health (*I'm fine, thank you*). **6** (of weather, etc.) bright and clear with sunshine; free from rain. **7 a** thin; sharp. **b** in small particles. **c** worked in slender thread. **d** (esp. of print) small. **e** (of a pen) narrow-pointed. **8** *Cricket* behind the wicket and near the line of flight of the ball. **9** tritely complimentary; euphemistic (*say fine things about a person; call things by fine names*). **10** ornate; showy; smart. **11** fastidious; dainty; pretending refinement; (of speech or writing) affectedly ornate. **12 a** capable of delicate perception or discrimination. **b** perceptible only with difficulty (*a fine distinction*). **13 a** delicate; subtle; exquisitely fashioned. **b** (of feelings) refined; elevated. **14** (of wine or other goods) of a high standard; conforming to a specified grade. • *n.* **1** (in *pl.*) very small particles in mining, milling, etc. **2** *Brit.* fine weather (*in rain or fine*). • *adv.* **1** finely. **2** *colloq.* very well (*suits me fine*). • *v.* **1** (often foll. by *down*) **a** *tr.* make (beer or wine) clear. **b** *intr.* (of liquid) become clear. **2** *tr. & intr.* (often foll. by *away, down, off*) make or become finer, thinner, or less coarse; dwindle or taper, or cause to do so. ▫ **cut it fine** allow very little margin of time, etc. **fine up** *Austral. colloq.* (of the weather) become fine. **not to put too fine a point on it** (as a parenthetic remark) to speak bluntly. ▫▫ **fine•ly** *adv.* **fine•ness** *n.* [ME f. OF *fin* ult. f. L *finire* finish]

fine[2] /fīn/ *n. & v.* • *n.* **1** a sum of money exacted as a penalty. **2** *hist.* a sum of money paid by an incoming tenant in return for the rent's being small. • *v.tr.* punish by a fine (*fined him $5*). ▫ **in fine** to sum up; in short. ▫▫ **fin•a•ble** /fínəbəl/ *adj.* [ME f. OF *fin* f. med.L *finis* sum paid on settling a lawsuit f. L *finis* end]

SYNONYM TIP financial

MONETARY, PECUNIARY, FISCAL. What's the difference between a **financial** crisis and a **fiscal** one? It all depends on who's having trouble with money and the scale of the difficulties. *Financial* usually applies to money matters involving large sums or transactions of considerable importance (*the auction was a financial success*). *Fiscal* refers specifically to the financial affairs of a government, organization, or corporation (*the end of the company's fiscal year*), while **pecuniary** refers to money matters of a more personal or practical nature and is preferred to *financial* when money is being discussed on a smaller scale (*pecuniary motives; pecuniary assistance; pecuniary difficulties*). Of all these words, **monetary** refers most directly to money as such and is often used when discussing the coinage, distribution, and circulation of money (*the European monetary system; the monetary unit of a country*).

fine arts *n.* those appealing to the mind or to the sense of beauty, as poetry, music, and esp. painting, sculpture, and architecture.

fine-draw *v.tr.* sew together (two pieces of cloth, edges of a tear, parts of a garment) so that the join is imperceptible.

fine-drawn *adj.* 1 extremely thin. 2 subtle.

fine print *n.* detailed printed information, esp. in legal documents, instructions, etc.

fin·er·y[1] /fínəree/ *n.* showy dress or decoration. [FINE[1] + -ERY, after BRAVERY]

fin·er·y[2] /fínəree/ *n.* (*pl.* **-ies**) *hist.* a hearth where pig iron was converted into wrought iron. [F *finerie* f. *finer* refine, FINE[1]]

fines herbes /feen áirb, feenz/ *n.pl.* mixed herbs used in cooking. [F, = fine herbs]

fine-spun *adj.* 1 delicate. 2 (of a theory, etc.) too subtle; unpractical.

fi·nesse /finés/ *n. & v.* ● *n.* 1 refinement. 2 subtle or delicate manipulation. 3 artfulness, esp. in handling a difficulty tactfully. 4 *Cards* an attempt to win a trick with a card that is not the highest held. ● *v.* 1 *intr. & tr.* use or achieve by finesse. 2 *Cards* **a** *intr.* make a finesse. **b** *tr.* play (a card) by way of finesse. 3 *tr.* evade or trick by finesse. [F, rel. to FINE[1]]

fine-tooth comb *n.* (also **fine-toothed comb**) a comb with narrow close-set teeth. □ **go over with a fine-tooth comb** (also **-toothed comb**) check or search thoroughly.

fine-tune *v.tr.* make small adjustments to (a mechanism, etc.) in order to obtain the best possible results.

fin·ger /fínggər/ *n. & v.* ● *n.* 1 any of the terminal projections of the hand (including or excluding the thumb). 2 the part of a glove, etc., intended to cover a finger. 3 **a** a fingerlike object (*chicken finger*). **b** a long narrow structure. 4 *colloq.* a measure of liquor in a glass, based on the breadth of a finger. 5 *sl.* **a** an informer. **b** *Brit.* a pickpocket. **c** *Brit.* a policeman. ● *v.tr.* 1 touch, feel, or handle with the fingers. 2 *Mus.* **a** play (a passage) with fingers used in a particular way. **b** mark (music) with signs showing which fingers are to be used. **c** play upon (an instrument) with the fingers. 3 *sl.* indicate (a victim, or a criminal to the police). □ **all fingers and thumbs** *Brit.* clumsy. **get** (or **pull**) **one's finger out** *Brit. sl.* cease prevaricating and start to act. **have a finger in** (or **in the pie**) be (esp. officiously) concerned in (the matter). **lay a finger on** touch however slightly. **point the finger at** *colloq.* accuse; blame. **put one's finger on** locate or identify exactly. **put the finger on** *sl.* 1 inform against. 2 identify (an intended victim). **slip through one's fingers** escape. **twist** (or **wind** or **wrap**) **around one's finger** (or **little finger**) persuade (a person) without difficulty; dominate (a person) completely. **work one's fingers to the bone** see BONE. □□ **fin·gered** *adj.* (also in *comb.*). **fin·ger·less** *adj.* [OE f. Gmc]

fin·ger·board /fínggərbawrd/ *n.* a flat strip at the top end of a stringed instrument, against which the strings are pressed to determine tones.

finger bowl *n.* a small bowl for rinsing the fingers at the table.

fin·ger·ing[1] /fínggəring/ *n.* 1 a manner or technique of using the fingers, esp. to play an instrument. 2 an indication of this in a musical score.

fin·ger·ing[2] /fínggəring/ *n.* fine wool for knitting. [earlier *fingram*, perh. f. F *fin grain*, as GROGRAM f. *gros grain*]

fin·ger·ling /fínggərling/ *n.* a young fish, esp. a small salmon or trout.

fin·ger mark *n.* a mark left on a surface by a finger.

fin·ger·nail /fínggərnayl/ *n.* the nail at the tip of each finger.

fin·ger paint *n. & v.* ● *n.* paint that can be applied with the fingers. ● *v.tr.* apply paint with the fingers.

fin·ger plate *n.* a plate fixed to a door above the handle to prevent finger marks.

fin·ger·post *n.* a post at a road junction from which signs project in the direction of the place or route indicated.

fin·ger·print /fínggərprint/ *n. & v.* ● *n.* 1 an impression made on a surface by the fine ridges on the fingertips, esp. as used for identifying individuals. 2 a distinctive characteristic, spectrum, etc. ● *v.tr.* record the fingerprints of (a person).

fin·ger·spell·ing /fínggər-spéling/ *n.* a form of sign language in which individual letters are formed by the fingers to spell out words.

fin·ger·tip /fínggərtip/ *n.* the tip of a finger. □ **have at one's fingertips** be thoroughly familiar with (a subject, etc.).

fin·i·al /fíneeəl/ *n. Archit.* 1 an ornament finishing off the apex of a roof, pediment, gable, tower corner, canopy, etc. 2 the topmost part of a pinnacle. [ME f. OF *fin* f. L *finis* end]

fin·i·cal /fínikəl/ *adj.* = FINICKY. □□ **fin·i·cal·i·ty** /-kálitee/ *n.* **fin·i·cal·ly** *adv.* **fin·i·cal·ness** *n.* [16th c.: prob. orig. university sl. f. FINE[1] + -ICAL]

fin·ick·ing /fíniking/ *adj.* = FINICKY. [FINICAL + -ING[2]]

fin·ick·y /fínikee/ *adj.* 1 overly particular; fastid-

finial 1

ious. 2 needing much care or attention to detail. □□ **fin·ick·i·ness** *n.*

fin·is /fínis, feenée, fínis/ *n.* 1 (at the end of a book) the end. 2 the end of anything, esp. of life. [L]

fin·ish /fínish/ *v. & n.* ● *v.* 1 *tr.* **a** (often foll. by *off*) bring to an end; come to the end of; complete. **b** (usu. foll. by *off*) *colloq.* kill; overcome completely. **c** (often foll. by *off, up*) consume or get through the whole or the remainder of (food or drink) (*finish your dinner*). 2 *intr.* **a** come to an end; cease. **b** reach the end, esp. of a race. **c** = *finish up*. 3 *tr.* **a** complete the manufacture of (cloth, woodwork, etc.) by surface treatment. **b** put the final touches to; make perfect or highly accomplished (*finished manners*). **c** prepare (a girl) for entry into fashionable society. ● *n.* 1 **a** the end; the last stage. **b** the point at which a race, etc., ends. **c** the death of a fox in a hunt (*be in at the finish*). 2 a method, material, or texture used for surface treatment of wood, cloth, etc. (*mahogany finish*). 3 what serves to give completeness. 4 an accomplished or completed state. □ **fight to the finish** fight until one party is completely beaten. **finish off** provide with an ending. **finish up** (often foll. by *in, by*) end in something, end by doing something (*he finished up last in the race; the plan finished up in the waste-basket; finished up by apologizing*). **finish with** have no more to do with; complete one's use of or association with. [ME f. OF *fenir* f. L *finire* f. *finis* end]

fin·ish·er /fínishər/ *n.* 1 a person who finishes something. 2 a worker or machine doing the last operation in a manufacturing process. 3 *colloq.* a discomfiting thing, a crushing blow, etc.

fin·ish·ing school *n.* a private school where girls are prepared for entry into fashionable society.

fin·ish·ing stroke *n.* a coup de grâce; a final and fatal stroke.

fin·ish·ing touch *n.* (also **touch·es**) the final details completing and enhancing a piece of work, etc. finite

fi·nite /fínit/ *adj.* 1 limited; bounded; not infinite. 2 *Gram.* (of a part of a verb) having a specific number and person. 3 not infinitely small. □□ **fi·nite·ly** *adv.* **fi·nite·ness** *n.* **fin·i·tude** /fínitōōd, -tyōōd/ *n.* [L *finitus* past part. of *finire* FINISH]

fi·nit·ism /fínitizəm/ *n.* belief in the finiteness of the world, God, etc. □□ **fi·nit·ist** /-tist/ *n.*

fink /fingk/ *n. & v. sl.* ● *n.* 1 an unpleasant person. 2 an informer. 3 a strikebreaker. ● *v.intr.* (foll. by *on*) inform on. [20th c.: orig. unkn.]

Finn /fin/ *n.* a native or inhabitant of Finland; a person of Finnish descent. [OE *Finnas* pl.]

fin·nan /fínən/ *n.* (in full **finnan haddie** or **haddock**) a haddock cured with the smoke of green wood, turf, or peat. [*Findhorn* or *Findon* in Scotland]

Finn·ic /fínik/ *adj.* 1 of the group of peoples related to the Finns. 2 of the group of languages related to Finnish.

Finn·ish /fínish/ *adj. & n.* ● *adj.* of the Finns or their language. ● *n.* the language of the Finns.

Finn·no-U·gric /fínō-ōōgrik, -yōōgrik/ *adj. & n.* (also **Fin·no-u·gri·an** /-ōōgreeən, -yōōgreeən/) ● *adj.* belonging to the group of Uralic languages including Finnish, Estonian, Lapp, and Magyar. ● *n.* this group.

fin·ny /fínee/ *adj.* 1 having fins; like a fin. 2 *poet.* of or teeming with fish.

fi·no /feenō/ *n.* (*pl.* **-nos**) a light-colored dry sherry. [Sp., = fine]

fiord var. of FJORD.

fio·ri·tu·ra /fee-áwritōōrə/ *n.* (*pl.* **fio·ri·tu·re** /-tōōray/) *Mus.* the usu. improvised decoration of a melody. [It., = flowering f. *fiorire* to flower]

fip·ple /fípəl/ *n.* a plug at the mouth end of a wind instrument. [17th c.: orig. unkn.]

fip·ple flute *n.* a flute played by blowing endwise, e.g., a recorder.

fir /fər/ *n.* 1 (in full **fir tree**) any evergreen coniferous tree, esp. of the genus *Abies*, with needles borne singly on the stems (cf. PINE[1]). 2 the wood of the fir. □ **fir cone** *Brit.* the fruit of the fir. □□ **fir·ry** *adj.* [ME, prob. f. ON *fyri-* f. Gmc]

fire /fīr/ *n. & v.* ● *n.* 1 **a** the state or process of combustion, in which substances combine chemically with oxygen from the air and usu. give out bright light and heat. **b** the active principle operative in this. **c** flame or incandescence. 2 a conflagration; a destructive burning (*forest fire*). 3 burning fuel in a fireplace, furnace, etc. 4 firing of guns (*open fire*). 5 **a** fervor; spirit; vivacity. **b** poetic inspiration; lively imagination. **c** vehement emotion. 6 burning heat; fever. 7 luminosity; glow (*St. Elmo's fire*). ● *v.* 1 **a** *tr.* discharge (a gun, etc.). **b** *tr.* propel (a missile) from a gun, etc. **c** *tr.* propel (a ball) with force or high speed. **d** *intr.* (often foll. by *at, into, on*) fire a gun or missile. **e** *tr.* produce (a broadside, salute, etc.) by discharge of guns. **f** *intr.* (of a gun, etc.) be discharged. 2 *tr.* cause (explosive) to explode. 3 *tr.* deliver or utter in rapid succession (*fired insults at us*). 4 *tr. sl.* dismiss (an employee) from a job. 5 *tr.* **a** set fire to with the intention of destroying. **b** kindle (explosives). 6 *intr.* catch fire. 7 *intr.* (of an internal combustion engine, or a cylinder in one) undergo ignition of its fuel. 8 *tr.* supply (a furnace, engine, boiler, or power station) with fuel. 9 *tr.* **a** stimulate (the imagination or emotion). **b** fill (a person) with enthusiasm. 10 *tr.* **a** bake or dry (pottery, bricks, etc.). **b** cure (tea or tobacco) by artificial heat. 11 *intr.*

become heated or excited. **12** *tr.* cause to glow or redden. □ **catch fire** begin to burn. **fire away** *colloq.* begin; go ahead. **fire up 1** start up, as an engine. **2** show sudden anger. **go through fire and water** face all perils. **on fire 1** burning. **2** excited. **set fire to** (or **set on fire**) ignite; kindle; cause to burn. **set the world on fire** do something remarkable or sensational. **take fire** catch fire. **under fire 1** being shot at. **2** being rigorously criticized or questioned. □□ **fire·less** *adj.* **fir·er** *n.* [OE *fȳr*, *fȳrian*, f. WG]

fire a·larm *n.* a device making a loud noise that gives warning of fire.

fire and brim·stone *n.* the supposed torments of hell.

fire·arm /fīraarm/ *n.* (usu. in *pl.*) a gun, esp. a pistol or rifle.

fire·back /fīrbak/ *n.* **1 a** the back wall of a fireplace. **b** an iron sheet for this. **2** a SE Asian pheasant of the genus *Lophura*.

fire·ball /fīrbawl/ *n.* **1** a large meteor. **2** a ball of flame, esp. from a nuclear explosion. **3** an energetic person. **4** ball lightning. **5** *Mil. hist.* a ball filled with combustibles.

fire bal·loon *n.* a balloon made buoyant by the heat of a fire burning at its mouth.

fire blight *n.* a disease of plants, esp. hops and fruit trees, causing a scorched appearance.

fire·bomb /fīrbom/ *n.* an incendiary bomb.

fire·box /fīrboks/ *n.* **1** the fuel chamber of a steam engine or boiler. **2** an alarm box used to alert a fire department.

fire·brand /fīrbrand/ *n.* **1** a piece of burning wood. **2** a cause of trouble, esp. a person causing unrest.

fire·break /fīrbrayk/ *n.* an obstacle to the spread of fire in a forest, etc., esp. an open space.

fire·brick /fīrbrik/ *n.* a fireproof brick used in a grate.

fire bri·gade *n.* esp. *Brit.* = FIRE DEPARTMENT.

fire·bug /fīrbug/ *n. colloq.* a pyromaniac.

fire·clay /fīrklay/ *n.* clay capable of withstanding high temperatures, often used to make firebricks.

fire com·pa·ny *n.* **1** = FIRE DEPARTMENT. **2** a fire-insurance company.

fire·crack·er /fīrkrakər/ *n.* an explosive firework.

fire·crest /fīrkrest/ *n.* a European warbler, *Regulus ignicapillus*, with red and orange crown feathers, which may be erected.

fire·damp /fīrdamp/ *n.* a miners' name for methane, which is explosive when mixed in certain proportions with air.

fire de·part·ment *n.* an organized body of firefighters trained and employed to extinguish fires.

fire·dog /fīrdawg, –dog/ *n.* a metal support for burning wood or for a grate or fire irons.

fire door *n.* a fire-resistant door to prevent the spread of fire.

fire·drake /fīrdrayk/ *n.* (in Germanic mythology) a fiery dragon.

fire drill *n.* **1** a rehearsal of the procedures to be used in case of fire. **2** a primitive device for kindling fire with a stick and wood.

fire-eat·er *n.* **1** a performer who appears to swallow fire. **2** a person fond of quarreling or fighting.

fire en·gine *n.* a vehicle carrying equipment for fighting large fires.

fire es·cape *n.* an emergency staircase or apparatus for escape from a building on fire.

fire ex·tin·guish·er *n.* an apparatus with a jet for discharging liquid chemicals, water, or foam to extinguish a fire.

fire·fight·er /fīrfītər/ *n.* a person whose task is to extinguish fires.

fire·fly /fīrflī/ *n.* (*pl.* **·flies**) any soft-bodied beetle of the family Lampyridae, emitting phosphorescent light, including glowworms.

fire·guard /fīrgaard/ *n.* **1** a fire screen. **2** a fire-watcher. **3** a firebreak.

fire hose *n.* a hose used in extinguishing fires.

fire·house /fīrhows/ *n.* a fire station.

fire i·rons *n.* tongs, poker, and shovel, for tending a domestic fire.

fire·light /fīrlīt/ *n.* light from a fire in a fireplace. [OE *fȳr-leoht* (as FIRE, LIGHT[1])]

fire·lock /fīrlok/ *n. hist.* a musket in which the priming was ignited by sparks.

fire·man /fīrmən/ *n.* (*pl.* **·men**) **1** a member of a fire department; a person employed to extinguish fires. **2** a person who tends a furnace or the fire of a steam engine or steamship.

fire o·pal *n.* girasol.

fire·place /fīrplays/ *n. Archit.* **1** a place for a domestic fire, esp. a grate or hearth at the base of a chimney. **2** a structure surrounding this. **3** the area in front of this.

fire·plug /fīrplug/ *n.* a hydrant for a fire hose.

fire·pow·er /fīrpowər/ *n.* **1** the destructive capacity of guns, missiles, or a military force, used with reference to the number and size of guns available. **2** financial, intellectual, or emotional strength (*well-funded legal firepower*).

fire·proof /fīrproof/ *adj. & v.* ● *adj.* able to resist fire or great heat. ● *v.tr.* make fireproof.

fire screen *n.* **1** a screen to keep off the direct heat of a fire. **2** a protective screen or grid placed in front of a fireplace. **3** an ornamental screen for a fireplace.

fire ship *n. hist.* a ship loaded with combustibles and set adrift to ignite an enemy's ships, etc.

fire·side /fīrsīd/ *n.* **1** the area around a fireplace. **2** a person's home or home life.

fire·side chat *n.* an informal talk.

fire sta·tion *n.* the headquarters of a fire department.

fire·stone /fīrstōn/ *n.* stone that resists fire, used for furnaces, etc.

fire storm *n.* **1** a high wind or storm following a very intense fire. **2** a sudden outburst, esp. of criticism, etc.

fire·trap /fīrtrap/ *n.* a building without proper provision for escape in case of fire.

firewall /fīrwawl/ *n.* **1** a wall, usu. constructed of fireproof material, intended to prevent the spread of fire. **2** *Computing* a part of a computer system or network designed to block unauthorized access while permitting outward communication.

fire war·den *n.* a person employed to prevent or extinguish fires, esp. in a town, camp, or forest.

fire·wa·ter /fīrwawtər/ *n. colloq.* strong alcoholic liquor.

fire·weed /fīrweed/ *n.* any of several plants that spring up on burned land, esp. willow herb.

fire·wood /fīrwŏŏd/ *n.* wood for use as fuel.

fire·work /fīrwərk/ *n.* **1** a device containing combustible chemicals that cause explosions or spectacular effects. **2** (in *pl.*) **a** an outburst of passion, esp. anger. **b** a display of wit or brilliance.

fir·ing /fīring/ *n.* **1** the discharging of guns. **2** material for a fire; fuel. **3** the heating process that hardens clay into pottery, etc.

fir·ing line *n.* **1** the front line in a battle. **2** the leading part in an activity, etc.

fir·ing squad *n.* a group detailed to shoot a condemned person.

fir·kin /fərkin/ *n.* **1** a small cask for liquids, butter, fish, etc. **2** *Brit.* (as a measure) half a kilderkin (1/4 barrel or 8 or 9 imperial gallons). [ME *ferdekyn*, prob. f. MDu. *vierdekijn* (unrecorded) dimin. of *vierde* fourth]

firm[1] /fərm/ *adj., adv., & v.* ● *adj.* **1 a** of solid or compact structure. **b** fixed; stable. **c** steady; not shaking. **2 a** resolute; determined. **b** not easily shaken (*firm belief*). **c** steadfast; constant (*a firm friend*). **3 a** (of an offer, etc.) not liable to cancellation after acceptance. **b** (of a decree, law, etc.) established; immutable. **4** *Commerce* (of prices or goods) maintaining their level or value. ● *adv.* firmly (*stand firm*; *hold firm to*). ● *v.* **1** *tr. & intr.* make or become firm, secure, compact, or solid. **2** *tr.* fix (plants) firmly in the soil. □□ **firm·ly** *adv.* **firm·ness** *n.* [ME f. OF *ferme* f. L *firmus*]

firm[2] /fərm/ *n.* **1 a** a business concern. **b** the partners in such a concern. **2** *Brit.* a group of persons working together, esp. of hospital doctors and assistants. [earlier = signature, style: Sp. & It. *firma* f. med.L, f. L *firmare* confirm f. *firmus* FIRM[1]]

fir·ma·ment /fərməmənt/ *n. literary* the sky regarded as a vault or arch. □□ **fir·ma·men·tal** /–mént'l/ *adj.* [ME f. OF f. L *firmamentum* f. *firmare* (as FIRM[2])]

firm·ware /fərmwair/ *n. Computing* a permanent kind of software programmed into a read-only memory.

fir·ry see FIR.

first /fərst/ *adj., n., & adv.* ● *adj.* **1 a** earliest in time or order. **b** coming next after a specified or implied time (*shall take the first train*; *the first cuckoo*). **2** foremost in position, rank, or importance (*first mate*). **3** *Mus.* performing the highest or chief of two or more parts for the same instrument or voice. **4** most willing or likely (*should be the first to admit the problem*). **5** basic or evident (*first principles*). ● *n.* **1** (prec. by *the*) the person or thing first mentioned or occurring. **2** the first occurrence of something notable. **3** *Brit.* **a** a place in the first class in an examination. **b** a person having this. **4** the first day of a month. **5** first gear. **6 a** first place in a race. **b** the winner of this. **7** (in *pl.*) goods of the best quality. **8** first base. ● *adv.* **1** before any other person or thing (*first of all*; *first and foremost*; *first come first served*). **2** before someone or something else (*must get this done first*). **3** for the first time (*when did you first see her?*). **4** in preference; sooner (*will see him damned first*). □ **at first** at the beginning. **first and last** taking one thing with another; on the whole. **first off** *colloq.* at first; first of all. **first or last** sooner or later. **first up** *Austral.* first of all; at the first attempt. **from the first** from the beginning. **from first to last** throughout. **get to first base** achieve the first step toward an objective. **in the first place** as the first consideration. **of the first water** see WATER. [OE *fyrst* f. Gmc]

▶**First, second, third**, etc., are adverbs as well as adjectives: *first, dice three potatoes; second, add the bouillon*. **Firstly, secondly**, etc., are not wrong, but make sure not to mix the two groups: *first, second, third*; not *first, secondly, thirdly*. See also note at FORMER.

first aid *n.* help given to an injured person until proper medical treatment is available.

first base *n. Baseball* **1** the base touched first by a base runner. **2 a** the fielder stationed nearest first base. **b** the position nearest first base.

first blood *n.* **1** the first shedding of blood, esp. in boxing. **2** the first point gained in a contest, etc.

first-born *adj. & n.* ● *adj.* eldest. ● *n.* the eldest child of a person.

first cause *n.* the creator or source of the universe.

first class *n.* **1** a set of persons or things grouped together as the best. **2** the best accommodations in a plane, train, or ship (*a seat in first class*). **3** the class of mail given priority in handling. **4** *Brit.* **a** the highest division in an examination list. **b** a place in this.

first-class *adj. & adv.* ● *adj.* **1** belonging to or traveling by the first class (*first-class accommodations*). **2** of the best quality; very good (*a first-class performance*). ● *adv.* (usu. **first class**)by first class (*travels first class; sent the package first class*).

first cous•in *n.* see COUSIN.

first-day cov•er *n.* an envelope bearing a stamp or set of stamps postmarked on their first day of issue.

first-de•gree *adj. Med.* denoting burns that affect only the surface of the skin, causing reddening.

first fin•ger *n.* the finger next to the thumb.

first fruit *n.* (usu. in *pl.*) **1** the first agricultural produce of a season, esp. as an offering. **2** the first results of work, etc. **3** *hist.* a payment to a superior by the new holder of an office.

first gear *n.* (also *Brit.* **bottom gear**) the lowest gear in a series.

first•hand /fə́rst-hánd/ *attrib. adj. & adv.* from the original source; direct.

first in•ten•tions *n.pl.* **1** *Med.* the healing of a wound by natural contact of the parts. **2** *Logic* one's primary conception of things, formed by the direct application of the mind to the thing itself, as distinct from abstract conceptions (second intentions) formed by consideration of these.

first la•dy *n.* the wife of the US president.

first lieu•ten•ant *n.* an army or air force officer ranking below captain.

first light *n.* the time when light first appears in the morning.

first•ling /fə́rstling/ *n.* (usu. in *pl.*) **1** the first result of anything; first fruits. **2** the first offspring; the first born in a season.

first•ly /fə́rstlee/ *adv.* (in enumerating topics, arguments, etc.) in the first place; first (cf. FIRST *adv.*).
▶See note at FIRST.

first mate *n.* (on a merchant ship) the officer second in command to the master.

first name *n.* a personal name other than a surname.

first night *n.* the first public performance of a play, etc.

first-night•er *n.* a habitual attender of first nights.

first of•fend•er *n.* a criminal against whom no previous conviction is recorded.

first of•fi•cer *n.* the first mate on a merchant ship.

first per•son see PERSON.

first-rate *adj. & adv.* ● *adj.* of the highest class; excellent. ● *adv. colloq.* **1** very well (*feeling first-rate*). **2** excellently.

first read•ing *n.* the occasion when a bill is presented to a legislature to permit its introduction.

first re•fus•al *n.* the privilege of deciding whether to accept or reject something before it is offered to others..

First Reich *n.* the Holy Roman Empire, 962–1806.

first ser•geant *n.* (in the US army) the highest ranking noncommissioned officer in a company.

first-strike *n.* denoting a first aggressive attack with nuclear weapons.

first thing *adv. & n.* ● *adv. colloq.* before anything else; very early in the morning (*shall do it first thing*). ● *n.* even the most elementary fact or principle (*does not know the first thing about it*). □ **first things first** the most important things before any others (*we must do first things first*).

firth /fə́rth/ *n.* (also **frith** /frith/) **1** a narrow inlet of the sea. **2** an estuary. [ME (orig. Sc.) f. ON *fjǫrthr* FIORD]

fisc /fisk/ *n. Rom.Hist.* the public treasury; the emperor's privy purse. [F *fisc* or L *fiscus* rush basket, purse, treasury]

fis•cal /fískəl/ *adj. & n.* ● *adj.* of public revenue; of financial matters. ● *n.* a legal official in some countries. □□ **fis•cal•ly** *adv.* [F *fiscal* or L *fiscalis* (as FISC)]

fis•cal•i•ty /fiskálitee/ *n.* (*pl.* **-ties**) **1** (in *pl.*) fiscal matters. **2** excessive regard for these.

fis•cal year *n.* a 12-month period as reckoned for taxing or accounting purposes.

fish¹ /fish/ *n. & v.* ● *n.* (*pl.* same or **fish•es**) **1** a vertebrate cold-blooded animal with gills and fins living wholly in water. **2** any animal living wholly in water, e.g., cuttlefish, shellfish, jellyfish. **3** the flesh of fish as food. **4** *colloq.* a person remarkable in some way (usu. unfavorable) (*an odd fish*). **5** (**the Fish** or **Fishes**) the zodiacal sign or constellation Pisces. **6** *Naut. sl.* a torpedo; a submarine. ● *v.* **1** *intr.* try to catch fish, esp. with a line or net. **2** *tr.* fish for (a certain kind of fish) or in (a certain stretch of water). **3** *intr.* (foll. by *for*) **a** search for in water or a concealed place. **b** seek by indirect means (*fishing for compliments*). **4** *tr.* (foll. by *up, out*, etc.) retrieve with careful or awkward searching. □ **drink like a fish** drink excessively. **fish out of water** a person in an unsuitable or unwelcome environment or situation. **other fish to fry** other matters to attend to. □□ **fish•like** *adj.* [OE *fisc, fiscian* f. Gmc]

fish² /fish/ *n. & v.* ● *n.* **1** a flat plate of iron, wood, etc., to strength-

en a beam or joint. **2** *Naut.* a piece of wood used to strengthen a mast, etc. ● *v.tr.* **1** mend or strengthen (a spar, etc.) with a fish. **2** join (rails) with a fishplate. [orig. as verb: f. F *ficher* fix ult. f. L *figere*]

fish-bolt *n.* a bolt used to fasten fishplates and rails together.

fish cake *n.* a cake of shredded fish and mashed potato, usu. eaten pan fried.

fish duck *n.* a merganser.

fish ea•gle *n.* **1** any large eagle of the genus *Haliaeetus*, with long broad wings, strong legs, and a strong tail. **2** any of several other eagles catching and feeding on fish.

fish•er /físhər/ *n.* **1** any animal that catches fish, esp. the marten, *Martes pennanti*, valued for its fur. **2** *archaic* a fisherman. [OE *fiscere* f. Gmc (as FISH¹)]

fish•er•man /físhərmən/ *n.* (*pl.* **-men**) **1** a person who catches fish as a livelihood or for recreation. **2** a fishing boat.

fish•er•y /físhəree/ *n.* (*pl.* **-ies**) **1** a place where fish or other aquatic animals are caught or reared. **2** the occupation or industry of catching or rearing fish or other aquatic animals.

fish-eye lens *n.* a wide-angle lens with a field of vision covering up to 180°, the scale being reduced toward the edges.

fish farm *n.* a place where fish are bred for food.

fish hawk *n.* an osprey, *Pandion haliaeetus*.

fish•hook /fish-hŏŏk/ *n.* a barbed hook for catching fish.

fish•ing /físhing/ *n.* the activity of catching fish, esp. for food or as recreation.

fish•ing line *n.* a long thread of nylon filament, silk, etc., with a baited hook, sinker, float, etc., used for catching fish.

fish•ing rod *n.* a long tapering usu. jointed rod to which a fishing line is attached.

fish knife *n.* a blunt knife with a broad blade for eating or serving fish.

fish lad•der *n.* (also **fish leap**) a series of steps or other arrangement incorporated in a dam to allow fish to pass upstream.

fish meal *n.* ground dried fish used as fertilizer or animal feed.

fish•mon•ger /físhmunggər, –mong–/ *n.* esp. *Brit.* a dealer in fish.

fish•net /fishnet/ *n.* (often *attrib.*) an open-meshed fabric (*fishnet stockings*).

fish•plate /físhplayt/ *n.* **a** a flat piece of iron, etc., connecting railroad rails. **b** a flat piece of metal with ends like a fish's tail, used to position masonry.

fish•pond /fishpond/ *n.* a pond or pool in which fish are kept.

fish stick *n.* (also *Brit.* **fish finger**) a small oblong piece of fish dipped in batter or breadcrumbs and fried.

fish sto•ry *n. colloq.* an exaggerated account.

fish•tail /fishtayl/ *n. & v.* ● *n.* a device, etc., shaped like a fish's tail. ● *v.intr.* move the tail of a vehicle from side to side. □ **fishtail burner** a kind of burner producing a broadening jet of flame.

fish•wife /fishwīf/ *n.* (*pl.* **-wives**) **1** an ill-mannered or noisy woman. **2** a woman who sells fish.

fish•y /físhee/ *adj.* (**fish•i•er, fish•i•est**) **1 a** smelling or tasting like fish. **b** like that of a fish. **c** (of an eye) dull; vacant-looking. **d** consisting of fish (*a fishy repast*). **e** *joc.* or *poet.* abounding in fish. **2** *sl.* of dubious character; questionable; suspect. □□ **fish•i•ly** *adv.* **fish•i•ness** *n.*

fisk /fisk/ *n. Sc.* the national treasury; the exchequer. [var. of FISC]

fis•sile /físəl, –īl/ *adj.* **1** capable of undergoing nuclear fission. **2** cleavable; tending to split. □□ **fis•sil•i•ty** /–sílitee/ *n.* [L *fissilis* (as FISSURE)]

fis•sion /físhən/ *n. & v.* ● *n.* **1** *Physics* the spontaneous or impact-induced splitting of a heavy atomic nucleus, accompanied by a release of energy. **2** *Biol.* the division of a cell, etc., into new cells, etc., as a mode of reproduction. ● *v.intr. & tr.* undergo or cause to undergo fission. □ **fission bomb** an atomic bomb. □□ **fis•sion•a•ble** *adj.* [L *fissio* (as FISSURE)]

fis•sip•a•rous /fisípərəs/ *adj.* **1** *Biol.* reproducing by fission. **2** tending to split. □□ **fis•sip•a•ri•ty** /fisipáritee/ *n.* **fis•sip•a•rous•ly** *adv.* **fis•sip•a•rous•ness** *n.* [L *fissus* past part. (as FISSURE) after *viviparous*]

fis•sure /físhər/ *n. & v.* ● *n.* **1** an opening, usu. long and narrow, made esp. by cracking, splitting, or separation of parts. **2** *Bot. & Anat.* a narrow opening in an organ, etc., esp. a depression between convolutions of the brain. **3** a cleavage. ● *v.tr. & intr.* split or crack. [ME f. OF *fissure* or L *fissura* f. *findere fiss-* cleave]

fist /fist/ *n. & v.* ● *n.* **1** a tightly closed hand. **2** *sl.* handwriting (*writes a good fist; I know his fist*). **3** *sl.* a hand (*give us your fist*). **4** = INDEX *n.* 9. ● *v.tr.* **1** close into a fist. **2** *Naut.* handle (a sail, an oar, etc.). □ **make a good** (or **poor**, etc.) **fist** (foll. by *at, of*) *colloq.* make a good (or poor, etc.) attempt at. □□ **fist•ed** *adj.* (also in *comb.*). **fist•ful** *n.* (*pl.* **-fuls**) [OE *fȳst* f. WG]

fist•fight /fistfīt/ *n.* a fight with bare fists.

fist•ic /fístik/ *adj.* (also **fist•i•cal**) *joc.* pugilistic.

fist•i•cuffs /fístikufs/ *n.pl.* fighting with fists. [prob. obs. *fisty* adj. = FISTIC, + CUFF²]

fis•tu•la /físchələ/ *n.* (*pl.* **fis•tu•las** or **fis•tu•lae** /–lee/) **1** an abnormal or surgically made passage between a hollow organ and the body surface or between two hollow organs. **2** a natural pipe or spout in whales, insects, etc. □□ **fis•tu•lar** *adj.* **fis•tu•lous** *adj.* [L, = pipe, flute]

fit[1] /fit/ *adj., v., n., & adv.* • *adj.* (**fit·ter, fit·test**) **1 a** (usu. foll. by *for*, or *to* + infin.) well adapted or suited. **b** (foll. by *to* + infin.) qualified; competent; worthy. **c** (foll. by *for*, or *to* + infin.) in a suitable condition; ready. **d** (foll. by *for*) good enough (*a dinner fit for a king*). **e** (foll. by *to* + infin.) sufficiently exhausted, troubled, or angry (*fit to drop*). **2** in good health or athletic condition. **3** proper; becoming; right (*it is fit that*). • *v.* (**fit·ted, fit·ting**) **1 a** *tr.* (also *absol.*) be of the right shape and size for (*the dress fits her; the key doesn't fit the lock; these shoes don't fit*). **b** *tr.* make, fix, or insert (a thing) so that it is of the right size or shape (*fitted shelves in the alcoves*). **c** *intr.* (often foll. by *in, into*) (of a component) be correctly positioned (*that piece fits here*). **d** *tr.* find room for (*can't fit another person on the bench*). **2** *tr.* (foll. by *for*, or *to* + infin.) **a** make suitable; adapt. **b** make competent (*fitted him to be a priest*). **3** *tr.* (usu. foll. by *with*) supply; furnish (*fitted the boat with a new rudder*). **4** *tr.* fix in place (*fit a lock on the door*). **5** *tr.* try on (a garment). **6** *tr.* be in harmony with; befit; become (*it fits the occasion; the punishment fits the crime*). • *n.* the way in which a garment, component, etc., fits (*a bad fit; a tight fit*). • *adv.* (foll. by *to* + infin.) *colloq.* in a suitable manner; appropriately (*was laughing fit to bust*). □ **fit the bill** = *fill the bill*. **fit in 1** (often foll. by *with*) be (esp. socially) compatible or accommodating (*doesn't fit in with the rest of the group; tried to fit in with their plans*). **2** find space or time for (an object, engagement, etc.) (*the dentist fitted me in at the last minute*). **fit on** *Brit.* try on (a garment). **fit out** (or **up**) (often foll. by *with*) equip. **see** (or **think**) **fit** (often foll. by *to* + infin.) decide or choose (a specified course of action). □□ **fit·ly** *adv.* **fit·ness** *n.* [ME: orig. unkn.]

fit[2] /fit/ *n.* **1** a sudden seizure of epilepsy, hysteria, apoplexy, fainting, or paralysis, with unconsciousness or convulsions. **2** a sudden brief attack of an illness or of symptoms (*fit of coughing*). **3** a sudden short bout or burst (*fit of energy; fit of giggles*). **4** *colloq.* an attack of strong feeling (*fit of rage*). **5** a capricious impulse; a mood (*when the fit was on him*). □ **by** (or **in**) **fits and starts** spasmodically. **give a person a fit** *colloq.* surprise or outrage him or her. **have a fit** *colloq.* be greatly surprised or outraged. **in fits** laughing uncontrollably. [ME, = position of danger, perh. = OE *fitt* conflict (?)]

fit[3] /fit/ *n.* (also **fytte**) *archaic* a section of a poem. [OE *fitt*]

fitch /fich/ *n.* **1** a polecat. **2 a** the hair or fur of a polecat. **b** a brush made from this or similar hair. [MDu. *fisse*, etc.: cf. FITCHEW]

fitch·ew /fichoō/ *n.* a polecat. [14th c. f. OF *ficheau, fissel* dimin. of MDu. *fisse*]

fit·ful /fitfool/ *adj.* active or occurring spasmodically or intermittently. □□ **fit·ful·ly** *adv.* **fit·ful·ness** *n.*

fit·ment /fitmənt/ *n.* (usu. in *pl.*) esp. *Brit.* a fixed item of furniture.

fit·ted /fitid/ *adj.* **1** made or shaped to fill a space or cover something closely or exactly (*a fitted sheet*). **2** esp. *Brit.* provided with appropriate equipment, fittings, etc. (*a fitted kitchen*). **3** esp. *Brit.* built-in; filling an alcove, etc. (*fitted cupboards*).

fit·ter /fitər/ *n.* **1** a person who supervises the cutting, fitting, altering, etc., of garments. **2** a mechanic who fits together and adjusts machinery.

fit·ting /fiting/ *n. & adj.* • *n.* **1** the process or an instance of having a garment, etc., fitted (*needed several fittings*). **2 a** (in *pl.*) the fixtures and furnishings of a building. **b** a piece of apparatus or a detachable part of a machine, fixture, etc. • *adj.* proper; becoming; right. □□ **fit·ting·ly** *adv.* **fit·ting·ness** *n.*

fit-up *n. Brit. Theatr. sl.* **1** a temporary stage, etc. **2** a traveling company.

Fitz·Ger·ald con·trac·tion /fitsjérəld/ *n.* (also **Fitz·Ger·ald ef·fect**) (in full **FitzGerald-Lorentz**) *Physics* the shortening of a moving body in the direction of its motion, esp. at speeds close to that of light. [G. F. *FitzGerald*, Ir. physicist d. 1901 and H. A. *Lorentz*, Du. physicist d. 1928]

five /fīv/ *n. & adj.* • *n.* **1** one more than four or one half of ten; the sum of three units and two units. **2** a symbol for this (5, v, V). **3** a size, etc., denoted by five. **4** a set or team of five individuals. **5** the time of five o'clock (*is it five yet?*). **6** a card with five pips. **7** a five-dollar bill. • *adj.* that amount to five. [OE *fīf* f. Gmc]

five-and-dime *n.* (also **five-and-ten**) a store with a variety of inexpensive household sundries, toiletries, etc., originally sold for five or ten cents.

five-fin·ger ex·er·cise *n.* **1** an exercise on the piano involving all the fingers. **2** an easy task.

five·fold /fīvfōld/ *adj. & adv.* **1** five times as much or as many. **2** consisting of five parts. **3** amounting to five.

five o'clock shad·ow *n.* beard growth visible on a man's face in the latter part of the day.

fiv·er /fīvər/ *n. colloq.* **1** a five-dollar bill. **2** *Brit.* a five-pound note.

fives /fīvz/ *n.* esp. *Brit.* a game in which a ball is hit with a gloved hand or a bat against the walls of a court with three walls (**Eton fives**) or four walls (**Rugby fives**). [*pl.* of FIVE used as *sing.*: significance unkn.]

five-star *adj.* **1** (esp. of accommodations or service) of the highest class or quality (*a luxury five-star hotel*). **2** having or denoting the highest military rank, distinguished in the US armed forces by five stars on the uniform (*a five-star general*).

five·stones /fīvstōnz/ *n. Brit.* jacks played with five pieces of metal, etc., and usu. without a ball.

five-year plan *n.* **1** (esp. in China and the former USSR) a government plan for economic development over five years. **2** a similar plan in another country.

fix /fiks/ *v. & n.* • *v.* **1** *tr.* make firm or stable; fasten; secure (*fixed a picture to the wall*). **2** *tr.* decide; settle; specify (a price, date, etc.). **3** *tr.* mend; repair. **4** *tr.* implant (an idea or memory) in the mind (*couldn't get the rules fixed in his head*). **5** *tr.* **a** (foll. by *on, upon*) direct steadily; set (one's eyes, gaze, attention, or affection). **b** attract and hold (a person's attention, eyes, etc.). **c** (foll. by *with*) single out with one's eyes, etc. **6** *tr.* place definitely or permanently; establish; station. **7** *tr.* determine the exact nature, position, etc., of; refer (a thing or person) to a definite place or time; identify, locate. **8 a** *tr.* make (eyes, features, etc.) rigid. **b** *intr.* (of eyes, features, etc.) become rigid. **9** *tr. colloq.* prepare (food or drink) (*fixed me a drink*). **10 a** *tr.* deprive of fluidity or volatility; congeal. **b** *intr.* lose fluidity or volatility; become congealed. **11** *tr. colloq.* punish; kill; silence; deal with; take revenge on (a person). **12** *tr. colloq.* **a** secure the support of (a person) fraudulently, esp. by bribery. **b** arrange the result of (a race, match, etc.) fraudulently (*the competition was fixed*). **13** *sl.* **a** *tr.* inject (a person, esp. oneself) with a narcotic. **b** *intr.* take an injection of a narcotic. **14** *tr.* make (a color, photographic image, or microscope specimen) fast or permanent. **15** *tr.* (of a plant or microorganism) assimilate (nitrogen or carbon dioxide) by forming a nongaseous compound. **16** *tr.* castrate or spay (an animal). **17** *tr.* arrest changes or development in (a language or literature). **18** *tr.* determine the incidence of (liability, etc.). **19** *intr. archaic* take up one's position. **20** (as **fixed** *adj.*) **a** permanently placed; stationary. **b** without moving; rigid; (of a gaze, etc.) steady or intent. **c** definite. **d** *sl.* dishonest; fraudulent. • *n.* **1** *colloq.* a position hard to escape from; a dilemma or predicament. **2 a** the act of finding one's position by bearings or astronomical observations (*get a fix on that star*). **b** a position found in this way. **3** *sl.* a dose of a narcotic drug to which one is addicted. **4** *sl.* bribery. □ **be fixed** (usu. foll. by *for*) be disposed or affected (regarding) (*how is he fixed for money?; how are you fixed for Friday?*). **fix on** (or **upon**) choose; decide on. **fix up 1** arrange; organize; prepare. **2** accommodate. **3** (often foll. by *with*) provide (a person) with (*fixed me up with a job*). **4** restore; refurbish (*fixed up the old house*). □□ **fix·a·ble** *adj.* /fiksidlee/ *adv.* **fix·ed·ness** /fiksidnis/ *n.* [ME, partly f. obs. *fix* fixed f. OF *fix* or L *fixus* past part. of *figere* fix, fasten, partly f. med.L *fixare* f. *fixus*]

fix·ate /fiksáyt/ *v.tr.* **1** direct one's gaze on. **2** *Psychol.* **a** (usu. in *passive*; often foll. by *on, upon*) cause (a person) to acquire an abnormal attachment to persons or things (*was fixated on his son*). **b** arrest (part of the libido) at an immature stage, causing such attachment. [L *fixus* (see FIX) + -ATE[3]]

fix·a·tion /fiksáyshən/ *n.* **1** the act or an instance of being fixated. **2** an obsession; concentration on a single idea. **3** fixing or being fixed. **4** the process of rendering solid; coagulation. **5** the process of assimilating a gas to form a solid compound. [ME f. med.L *fixatio* f. *fixare*: see FIX]

fix·a·tive /fiksətiv/ *adj. & n.* • *adj.* tending to fix or secure. • *n.* a substance used to fix colors, hair, microscope specimens, etc.

fixed cap·i·tal *n.* machinery, etc., that remains in the owner's use.

fixed-do /fikst dō/ *n. Mus.* applied to a system of sight-singing in which C is called 'do,' D is called 're,' etc., irrespective of the key in which they occur (cf. MOVABLE-DO).

fixed fo·cus *n.* a camera focus at a distance from a lens that is not adjustable.

fixed i·de·a *n.* = IDÉE FIXE.

fixed in·come *n.* income deriving from a pension, investment at fixed interest, etc.

fixed odds *n.* odds in betting that are predetermined, as opposed to a pool system or a starting price.

fixed oil *n.* a nonvolatile oil of animal or plant origin used in varnishes, lubricants, illuminants, soaps, etc. Also called **fatty oil**.

fixed star *n. Astron.* a star so far from the earth as to appear motionless.

fix·er /fiksər/ *n.* **1** a person or thing that fixes. **2** *Photog.* a substance used for fixing a photographic image, etc. **3** *colloq.* a person who makes arrangements, esp. of an illicit kind.

fix·ings /fiksingz/ *n.pl.* **1** apparatus or equipment. **2** the trimmings for a dish. **3** the trimmings of a dress, etc.

fix·i·ty /fiksitee/ *n.* **1** a fixed state. **2** stability; permanence. [obs. *fix* fixed: see FIX]

fix·ture /fikschər/ *n.* **1 a** something fixed or fastened in position. **b** an attached appliance, apparatus, etc. (*an electrical fixture*). **c** (usu. *predic.*) *colloq.* a person or thing confined to or established in one place (*he seems to be a fixture*). **2** *Brit.* **a** a sporting event, esp. a match, race, etc. **b** the date agreed for this. **3** (in *pl.*) *Law* articles attached to a house or land and regarded as legally part of it. [alt. of obs. *fixure* f. LL *fixura* f. L *figere fix-* fix]

fizz /fiz/ *v. & n.* ● *v.intr.* **1** make a hissing or spluttering sound. **2** (of a drink) make bubbles; effervesce. ● *n.* **1** effervescence. **2** esp. *Brit. colloq.* a carbonated drink, esp. champagne. [imit.]

fizz•er /fizər/ *n.* **1** *Brit.* an excellent or first-rate thing. **2** *Cricket colloq.* a very fast ball, or one that deviates with unexpected speed. **3** *Austral. sl.* a disappointing failure or fiasco.

fiz•zle /fizəl/ *v. & n.* ● *v.intr.* make a feeble hissing or spluttering sound. ● *n.* such a sound. □ **fizzle out** end feebly (*the party fizzled out at 10 o'clock*). [formed as FIZZ + –LE⁴]

fizz•y /fizee/ *adj.* (**fizz•i•er, fizz•i•est**) effervescent; carbonated. □□ **fizz•i•ly** *adv.* **fizz•i•ness** *n.*

fjord /fyawrd/ *n.* (also **fiord**) a long narrow inlet of sea between high cliffs, as in Norway. [Norw. f. ON *fjörthr* f. Gmc: cf. FIRTH, FORD]

FL *abbr.* Florida (in official postal use).

fl. *abbr.* **1** floor. **2** floruit. **3** fluid.

Fla. *abbr.* Florida.

flab /flab/ *n. colloq.* fat; flabbiness. [imit., or back-form. f. FLABBY]

flab•ber•gast /flabərgast/ *v.tr.* (esp. as **flabbergasted** *adj.*) *colloq.* overwhelm with astonishment; dumbfound. [18th c.: perh. f. FLAB-BY + AGHAST]

flab•by /flabee/ *adj.* (**flab•bi•er, flab•bi•est**) **1** (of flesh, etc.) hanging down; limp; flaccid. **2** (of language or character) feeble. □□ **flab•bi•ly** *adv.* **flab•bi•ness** *n.* [alt. of earlier *flappy* f. FLAP]

flac•cid /flásid, fláksid/ *adj.* **1 a** (of flesh, etc.) hanging loose or wrinkled; limp; flabby. **b** (of plant tissue) soft; less rigid. **2** relaxed; drooping. **3** lacking vigor; feeble. □□ **flac•cid•i•ty** /–síditee/ *n.* **flac•cid•ly** *adv.* [F *flaccide* or L *flaccidus* f. *flaccus* flabby]

flack¹ /flak/ *n. & v. sl.* ● *n.* a publicity agent. ● *v.intr.* act as a publicity agent. [20th c.: orig. unkn.]

flack² var. of FLAK.

flag¹ /flag/ *n. & v.* ● *n.* **1 a** a piece of cloth, usu. oblong or square, attachable by one edge to a pole or rope and used as a country's emblem or as a standard, signal, etc. **b** a small toy, device, etc., resembling a flag. **2** *Brit.* an oblong strip of metal, etc., that can be raised or lowered to indicate whether a taxi is available or occupied. **3** *Naut.* a flag carried by a flagship as an emblem of an admiral's rank afloat. ● *v.* (**flagged, flag•ging**) **1** *intr.* **a** grow tired; lose vigor; lag (*his energy flagged after the first lap*). **b** hang down; droop; become limp. **2** *tr.* **a** place a flag on or over. **b** mark out with or as if with a flag or flags. **3** *tr.* (often foll. by *that*) **a** inform (a person) by flag signals. **b** communicate (information) by flagging. □ **flag down** signal to (a vehicle or driver) to stop. **keep the flag flying** continue the fight. **put the flag out** celebrate victory, success, etc. **show the flag 1** make an official visit to a foreign port, etc. **2** ensure that notice is taken of one's country, oneself, etc.; make a patriotic display. □□ **flag•ger** *n.* [16th c.: perh. f. obs. *flag* drooping]

flag² /flag/ *n. & v.* ● *n.* (also **flag•stone**) **1** a flat usu. rectangular stone slab used for paving. **2** (in *pl.*) a pavement made of these. ● *v.tr.* (**flagged, flag•ging**) pave with flags. [ME, = sod: cf. Icel. *flag* spot from which a sod has been cut out, ON *flaga* slab of stone, and FLAKE¹]

flag³ /flag/ *n.* **1** any plant with a bladed leaf (esp. several of the genus *Iris*) growing on moist ground. **2** the long slender leaf of such a plant. [ME: cf. MDu. *flag*, Da. *flæg*]

flag⁴ /flag/ *n.* (in full **flag feather**) a quill feather of a bird's wing. [perh. rel. to obs. *fag* loose flap: cf. FLAG¹ *v.*]

flag day *n. Brit.* a day on which money is raised for a charity by the sale of small paper flags, etc., in the street.

Flag Day *n.* June 14, the anniversary of the adoption of the Stars and Stripes as the official US flag in 1777.

flag•el•lant /flájələnt, fləjélənt/ *n. & adj.* ● *n.* **1** a person who scourges himself or herself or others as a religious discipline. **2** a person who engages in flogging as a sexual stimulus. ● *adj.* of or concerning flagellation. [L *flagellare* to whip f. FLAGELLUM]

flag³

flag•el•late¹ /flájəlayt/ *v.tr.* scourge; flog (cf. FLAGELLANT). □□ **flag•el•la•tion** /–láyshən/ *n.* **flag•el•la•tor** *n.* **flag•el•la•to•ry** /–lətawree/ *adj.*

flag•el•late² /flájilit, –layt/ *adj. & n.* ● *adj.* having flagella (see FLAGELLUM). ● *n.* a protozoan having one or more flagella.

fla•gel•lum /fləjéləm/ *n.* (*pl.* **fla•gel•la** /–lə/) **1** *Biol.* a long lashlike appendage found principally on microscopic organisms. **2** *Bot.* a runner; a creeping shoot. □□ **fla•gel•lar** /–lər/ *adj.* **fla•gel•li•form** /–láwrm/ *adj.* [L, = whip, dimin. of *flagrum* scourge]

flag•eo•let¹ /flájəlét, –láy/ *n.* **1** a small flute blown at the end, like a recorder but with two thumb holes. **2** an organ stop having a similar sound. [F, dimin. of OF *flag(e)ol* f. Prov. *flajol*, of unkn. orig.]

flag•eo•let² /flájəláy, –lét/ *n.* a kind of French kidney bean. [F]

flag•i•tious /fləjíshəs/ *adj.* deeply criminal; utterly villainous. □□ **fla•**

gi•tious•ly *adv.* **fla•gi•tious•ness** *n.* [ME f. L *flagitiosus* f. *flagitium* shameful crime]

flag•man /flágmən/ *n.* (*pl.* **•men**) a person who signals with or as with a flag, e.g., in highway construction.

flag of con•ven•ience *n.* a foreign flag under which a ship is registered, usu. to avoid financial charges, etc.

flag of truce *n.* a white flag indicating a desire for a truce.

flag•on /flágən/ *n.* **1** a large bottle in which wine, cider, etc., are sold, usu. holding 1.13 liters. **2 a** a large vessel usu. with a handle, spout, and lid, to hold wine, etc. **b** *Eccl.* a similar vessel used for the Eucharist. [ME *flakon* f. OF *flacon* ult. f. LL *flasco –onis* FLASK]

flag•pole /flágpōl/ *n.* a pole on which a flag may be hoisted.

fla•grant /fláygrənt/ *adj.* (of an offense or an offender) glaring; notorious; scandalous. □□ **fla•gran•cy** /–grənsee/ *n.* **fla•grant•ly** *adv.* [F *flagrant* or L *flagrant-* part. stem of *flagrare* blaze]

flag•ship /flágship/ *n.* **1** a ship having an admiral on board. **2** something that is held to be the best or most important of its kind; a leader.

flag•staff /flágstaf/ *n.* = FLAGPOLE.

flag sta•tion *n.* (also **flag stop**) a station at which trains stop only if signaled.

flag•stone /flágstōn/ *n.* = FLAG².

flag-wav•ing *n.* populist agitation; patriotic chauvinism. □□ **flag-wav•er** *n.*

flail /flayl/ *n. & v.* ● *n.* a threshing tool consisting of a wooden staff with a short heavy stick swinging from it. ● *v.* **1** *tr.* beat or strike with or as if with a flail. **2** *intr.* wave or swing wildly or erratically (*went into the fight with arms flailing*). [OE prob. f. L *FLAGELLUM*]

flair /flair/ *n.* **1** an instinct for selecting or performing what is excellent, useful, etc.; a talent (*has a flair for knowing what the public wants; has a flair for languages*). **2** talent or ability, esp. artistic or stylistic. [F *flairer* to smell f. L *fragrare* see FRAGRANT]

flak /flak/ *n.* (also **flack**) **1** antiaircraft fire. **2** adverse criticism; abuse. [abbr. of G *Fliegerabwehrkanone*, lit. aviator-defense-gun]

flake¹ /flayk/ *n. & v.* ● *n.* **1 a** a small thin light piece of snow. **b** a similar piece of another material. **2** a thin broad piece of material peeled or split off. **3** *Archaeol.* a piece of hard stone chipped off and used as a tool. **4** a natural division of the flesh of some fish. **5** the dogfish or other shark as food. **6** *sl.* a crazy or eccentric person. ● *v.tr. & intr.* (often foll. by *away, off*) **1** take off or come away in flakes. **2** sprinkle with or fall in snowlike flakes. □ **flake out** *colloq.* **1** fall asleep or drop from exhaustion; faint. **2** act strangely. [ME: orig. unkn.: cf. ON *flakna* flake off]

flake² /flayk/ *n.* a stage for drying fish, storing produce, etc. [ME, perh. f. ON *flaki, fleki* wicker shield]

flak jack•et *n.* a protective jacket reinforced with bulletproof material, worn by soldiers, etc.

flak•y /fláykee/ *adj.* (**flak•i•er, flak•i•est**) **1** of or like flakes; separating easily into flakes. **2** *sl.* crazy; eccentric. □ **flaky pastry** pastry consisting of thin light layers. □□ **flak•i•ly** *adv.* **flak•i•ness** *n.*

flambé /flaambáy/ *adj.* (of food) covered with alcohol and set alight briefly. [F, past part. of *flamber* singe (as FLAMBEAU)]

flam•beau /flámbō/ *n.* (*pl.* **flam•beaus** or **flam•beaux** /–bōz/) **1** a flaming torch, esp. composed of several thick waxed wicks. **2** a branched candlestick. [F f. *flambe* f. L *flammula* dimin. of *flamma* flame]

flam•boy•ant /flambóyənt/ *adj.* **1** ostentatious; showy. **2** floridly decorated. **3** gorgeously colored. **4** *Archit.* (of decoration) marked by wavy flamelike lines. □□ **flam•boy•ance** /–əns/ *n.* **flam•boy•an•cy** *n.* **flam•boy•ant•ly** *adv.* [F (in Archit. sense), pres. part. of *flamboyer* f. *flambe*: see FLAMBEAU]

flame /flaym/ *n. & v.* ● *n.* **1 a** ignited gas (*the fire burned with a steady flame*). **b** one portion of this (*the fire flickered and died*). **c** (usu. in *pl.*) visible combustion (*burst into flames*). **2 a** a bright light; brilliant coloring. **b** a brilliant orange-red color. **3 a** a strong passion, esp. love (*fan the flame*). **b** *colloq.* a boyfriend or girlfriend. ● *v.* **1** *intr. & tr.* (often foll. by *away, forth, out, up*) emit or cause to emit flames. **2** *intr.* (often foll. by *out, up*) **a** (of passion) break out. **b** (of a person) become angry. **3** *intr.* shine or glow like flame (*leaves flamed in the autumn sun*). **4** *intr. poet.* move like flame. **5** *tr.* send (a signal) by means of flame. **6** *tr.* subject to the action of flame. □ **flame out** (of a jet engine) lose power through imperfect combustion in the combustion chamber. **go up in flames** be consumed by fire. □□ **flame•less** *adj.* **flame•like** *adj.* **flam•y** *adj.* [ME f. OF *flame, flam(m)er* f. L *flamma*]

flame gun *n.* a device for producing a jet of flame, esp. for destroying weeds.

fla•men /fláymən/ *n. Rom.Hist.* a priest serving a particular deity. [ME f. L]

fla•men•co /fləméngkō/ *n.* (*pl.* **•cos**) **1** a style of music played (esp. on the guitar) and sung by Spanish gypsies. **2** a dance performed to this music. [Sp., = Flemish]

flame•proof /fláymprōof/ *adj.* (esp. of a fabric) treated so as to be nonflammable.

flame•throw•er /fláymthrōər/ *n.* a weapon for throwing a spray of flame.

flame tree *n.* any of various trees with brilliant red flowers, esp. *Brachychiton acerifolius*, native to Australia.

flam•ing /fláyming/ *adj.* 1 emitting flames. 2 very hot (*flaming day*). 3 *colloq.* a passionate; intense (*a flaming argument*). b expressing annoyance, or as an intensifier (*that flaming idiot*). 4 bright colored (*flaming red hair*).

fla•min•go /fləmínggō/ *n.* (*pl.* •gos or •goes) any tall long-necked web-footed wading bird of the family Phoenicopteridae, with crooked bill and pink, scarlet, and black plumage. [Port. *flamengo* f. Prov. *flamenc* f. *flama* flame + *−enc = −*ING³]

flam•ma•ble /flámməbəl/ *adj.* easily set on fire; inflammable. □□ flam•ma•bil•i•ty *n.* [L *flammare* f. *flamma* flame]
▶See note at INFLAMMABLE.

flan /flan/ *n.* 1 a an open pastry case with a savory or sweet filling. b a custard topped with caramel glaze. 2 a disk of metal from which a coin, etc., is made. [F (orig. = round cake) f. OF *flaon* f. med.L *flado −onis* f. Frank.]

flange /flanj/ *n. & v. Engin.* •*n.* a projecting flat rim, collar, or rib, used for strengthening or attachment. •*v.tr.* provide with a flange. □□ flange•less *n.* [17th c.: perh. f. *flange* widen out f. OF *flangir*, rel. to FLANK]

flamingo

flange

flank /flangk/ *n. & v.* •*n.* 1 a the side of the body between the ribs and the hip. b the side of an animal carved as meat (*flank of beef*). 2 the side of a mountain, building, etc. 3 the right or left side of an army or other body of persons. •*v.tr.* 1 (often in *passive*) be situated at both sides of (*a road flanked by mountains*). 2 *Mil.* a guard or strengthen on the flank. b menace the flank of. [ME f. OF *flanc* f. Frank.]

flank•er /flángkər/ *n.* 1 *Mil.* a fortification guarding or menacing the flank. 2 anything that flanks another thing. 3 a *Football* an offensive back positioned outside the tackle and behind the line of scrimmage. b *Rugby* a flank forward. 4 *Brit. sl.* a trick; a swindle (*pulled a flanker*).

flan•nel /flánəl/ *n. & v.* •*n.* 1 a a kind of woven wool fabric, usu. with a slight nap. b (in *pl.*) flannel garments, esp. underwear or trousers. 2 *Brit.* = WASHCLOTH. 3 *Brit. sl.* nonsense; flattery. •*v.* (flan•neled, flan•nel•ing; *Brit.* flan•nelled, flan•nel•ling) *Brit.* 1 *sl.* a *tr.* flatter. b *intr.* use flattery. 2 *tr.* wash or clean with a flannel. □□ flan•nel•ly *adj.* [perh. f. Welsh *gwlanen* f. *gwlân* wool]

flan•nel•board /flánəlbawrd/ *n.* a piece of flannel as a base for paper or cloth cutouts, used as a toy or a teaching aid.

flan•nel•ette /flánəlét/ *n.* a napped cotton fabric similar to flannel. [FLANNEL]

flan•nel•mouth /flánəlmowth/ *n. sl.* a flatterer; a braggart.

flap /flap/ *v. & n.* •*v.* (flapped, flap•ping) 1 a *tr.* move (wings, the arms, etc.) up and down when flying, or as if flying. b *intr.* (of wings, the arms, etc.) move up and down; beat. 2 *intr. colloq.* be agitated or panicky. 3 *intr.* (esp. of curtains, loose cloth, etc.) swing or sway about; flutter. 4 *tr.* (usu. foll. by *away, off*) strike (flies, etc.) with something broad; drive. 5 *intr. colloq.* (of ears) listen intently. •*n.* 1 a piece of cloth, wood, paper, etc., hinged or attached by one side only and often used to cover a gap, e.g., a pocket cover, the folded part of an envelope, a table leaf. 2 one up-and-down motion of a wing, an arm, etc. 3 *colloq.* a state of agitation; panic (*don't get into a flap*). 4 a hinged or sliding section of a wing used to control lift and drag. 5 a light blow with something broad. 6 an open mushroom top. □□ flap•py *adj.* [ME, prob. imit.]

flap•doo•dle /flápdōōd'l/ *n. colloq.* nonsense. [19th c.: orig. unkn.]

flap•jack /flápjak/ *n.* a pancake. [FLAP + JACK¹]

flap•per /flápər/ *n.* 1 a person or thing that flaps. 2 an instrument that is flapped to kill flies, scare birds, etc. 3 a person who panics easily or is easily agitated. 4 *sl.* (in the 1920s) a young unconventional or lively woman. 5 *Brit.* a young mallard or partridge.

flare /flair/ *v. & n.* •*v.* 1 *intr. & tr.* widen or cause to widen, esp. toward the bottom (*flared trousers*). 2 *intr. & tr.* burn or cause to burn suddenly with a bright unsteady flame. 3 *intr.* burst into anger; burst forth. •*n.* 1 a a dazzling irregular flame or light, esp. in the open air. b a sudden outburst of flame. 2 a a signal light used at sea. b a bright light used as a signal. c a flame dropped from an aircraft to illuminate a target, etc. 3 *Astron.* a sudden burst of radiation from a star. 4 a a gradual widening, esp. of a skirt or trousers. b (in *pl.*) wide-bottomed trousers. 5 an outward bulge in a ship's sides. 6 *Photog.* unnecessary illumination on a lens caused by internal reflection, etc. □ flare up 1 burst into a sudden blaze. 2 become suddenly angry or active. [16th c.: orig. unkn.]

flare-up *n.* an outburst of flame, anger, activity, etc.

flash /flash/ *v., n., & adj.* •*v.* 1 *intr. & tr.* emit or reflect or cause to emit or reflect light briefly, suddenly, or intermittently; gleam or cause to gleam. 2 *intr.* break suddenly into flame; give out flame or sparks. 3 *tr.* send or reflect like a sudden flame or blaze (*his eyes flashed fire*). 4 *intr.* a burst suddenly into view or perception (*the explanation flashed upon me*). b move swiftly (*the train flashed through the station*). 5 *tr.* a send (news, etc.) by radio, telegraph, etc. (*flashed a message to her*). b signal to (a person) by shining lights or headlights briefly. 6 *tr. colloq.* show ostentatiously (*flashed her engagement ring*). 7 *intr.* (of water) rush along; rise and flow. 8 *intr. sl.* indecently expose oneself. •*n.* 1 a sudden bright light or flame, e.g., of lightning. 2 a very brief time; an instant (*all over in a flash*). 3 a a brief, sudden burst of feeling (*a flash of hope*). b a sudden display (of wit, understanding, etc.). 4 = NEWS FLASH. 5 *Photog.* = FLASHLIGHT 2. 6 a a rush of water, esp. down a weir to take a boat over shallows. b a contrivance for producing this. 7 *Brit. Mil.* a colored patch of cloth on a uniform, etc., as a distinguishing emblem. 8 vulgar display; ostentation. 9 a bright patch of color. 10 *Cinematog.* the momentary exposure of a scene. 11 excess plastic or metal oozing from a mold during molding. •*adj. Brit. colloq.* 1 gaudy; showy; vulgar (*a flash car*). 2 sudden; happening quickly. 3 counterfeit (*flash notes*). 4 connected with thieves, the underworld, etc. □ flash in the pan a promising start followed by failure (from the priming of old guns). flash over *Electr.* make an electric circuit by sparking across a gap. [ME orig. with ref. to the rushing of water: cf. SPLASH]

flash•back /fláshbak/ *n.* a scene in a movie, novel, etc., set in a time earlier than the main action.

flash•board /fláshbawrd/ *n.* a board used for increasing the depth of water behind a dam.

flash•bulb *n.* a bulb that flashes to illuminate a photographic subject.

flash burn *n.* a burn caused by sudden intense radiation, esp. from a nuclear explosion.

flash card *n.* a card containing a small amount of information, held up for students to see, as an aid to learning.

flash•cube /fláshkyōōb/ *n. Photog.* a set of four flashbulbs arranged as a cube and operated in turn.

flash•er /fláshər/ *n.* 1 *sl.* a person, esp. a man, who indecently exposes himself. 2 a an automatic device for switching lights rapidly on and off. b a sign or signal using this. 3 a person or thing that flashes.

flash flood *n.* a sudden local flood due to heavy rain, etc.

flash•gun /fláshgun/ *n. Photog.* a device used to operate a photographic flashlight.

flash•ing /fláshing/ *n.* a strip of metal used to stop water from penetrating the junction of a roof with another surface, such as a wall or chimney. [dial. *flash* seal with lead sheets or obs. *flash* flashing]

flash•ing point *n.* = FLASH POINT.

flash lamp *n.* a portable flashing electric lamp used in photography.

flash•light /fláshlīt/ *n.* 1 a battery-operated portable light. 2 a a light giving an intense flash, used for photographing by night, indoors, etc. b a picture so taken. 3 a flashing light used for signals and in lighthouses.

flash•o•ver /fláshōvər/ *n.* an instance of flashing over.

flash point *n.* 1 the temperature at which vapor from oil, etc., will ignite in air. 2 the point at which anger, indignation, etc., becomes uncontrollable.

flash•y /fláshee/ *adj.* (flash•i•er, flash•i•est) showy; gaudy; cheaply attractive. □□ flash•i•ly *adv.* flash•i•ness *n.*

flask /flask/ *n.* 1 a narrow-necked bulbous bottle for wine, etc., or as used in chemistry. 2 = HIP FLASK. 3 *Brit.* = THERMOS. 4 *hist.* = POWDER FLASK.

WORD HISTORY flask

Middle English (in the sense 'cask'): from medieval Latin *flasca*. From the mid-16th century the word denoted a case of horn, leather, or metal for carrying gunpowder. The sense 'glass container' (late 17th century) was influenced by Italian *fiasco*, from medieval Latin *flasco*.

flat[1] /flat/ *adj., adv., n., & v.* • *adj.* (**flat·ter, flat·test**) **1 a** horizontally level (*a flat roof*). **b** even; smooth; unbroken; without projection or indentation (*a flat stomach*). **c** with a level surface and little depth; shallow (*a flat cap; a flat heel*). **2** unqualified; plain; downright (*a flat refusal; a flat denial*). **3 a** dull; lifeless; monotonous (*spoke in a flat tone*). **b** without energy; dejected. **4** (of a carbonated drink) having lost its effervescence; stale. **5** *Brit.* (of a battery, etc.) having exhausted its charge. **6** *Mus.* **a** below true or normal pitch (*the violins are flat*). **b** (of a key) having a flat or flats in the signature. **c** (as B, E, etc., **flat**) a half step lower than B, E, etc. **7** *Photog.* lacking contrast. **8 a** (of paint, etc.) not glossy; matte. **b** (of a tint) uniform. **9** (of a tire) punctured; deflated. **10** (of a market, prices, etc.) inactive; sluggish. **11** of or relating to flat racing. • *adv.* **1** lying at full length; spread out, esp. on another surface (*lay flat on the floor; the ladder was flat against the wall*). **2** *colloq.* **a** completely; absolutely (*turned it down flat; flat broke*). **b** exactly (*in five minutes flat*). **3** *Mus.* below the true or normal pitch (*always sings flat*). • *n.* **1** the flat part of anything; something flat (*the flat of the hand*). **2** level ground, esp. a plain or swamp. **3** *Mus.* **a** a note lowered a half step below natural pitch. **b** the sign (♭) indicating this. **4** (as **the flat**) *Brit.* **a** flat racing. **b** the flat racing season. **5** *Theatr.* a flat section of scenery mounted on a frame. **6** *colloq.* a flat tire. **7** a shallow planter box for starting seedlings. • *v.tr.* (**flat·ted, flat·ting**) **1** make flat; flatten (esp. in technical use). **2** *Mus.* make (a note) flat. □ **fall flat** fail to live up to expectations; not win applause. **flat out 1** at top speed. **2** without hesitation or delay. **3** using all one's strength, energy, or resources. □□ **flat·ly** *adv.* **flat·ness** *n.* **flat·tish** *adj.* [ME f. ON *flatr* f. Gmc]

flat[2] /flat/ *n. & v.* • *n.* esp. *Brit.* = APARTMENT 1. • *v.intr.* (**flat·ted, flat·ting**) (often foll. by *with*) *Austral.* share a flat (apartment) with. □□ **flat·let** *n.* [alt. f. obs. *flet* floor, dwelling f. Gmc (as FLAT[1])]

flat arch *n. Archit.* an arch with a flat lower or inner curve.

flat·boat /flátbōt/ *n.* (or **flat-bot·tomed boat**) a boat with a flat bottom for transport in shallow water.

flat·car /flátkaar/ *n.* a railroad car without raised sides or ends.

flat·fish /flátfish/ *n.* any marine fish of various families having an asymmetric appearance with both eyes on one side of a flattened body, including sole, turbot, plaice, etc.

flat·foot /flátfŏŏt/ *n. sl., dated* a police officer.

flat foot *n.* a foot with a less than normal arch.

flat-foot·ed /flátfŏŏtid/ *adj.* **1** having flat feet. **2** *colloq.* downright; positive. **3** *colloq.* unprepared; off guard (*was caught flat-footed*). □□ **flat-foot·ed·ly** *adv.* **flat-foot·ed·ness** *n.*

flat·head /fláthed/ *n.* any marine fish of the family Platycephalidae, having a flattened body with both eyes on the top side.

flat·i·ron /fláti̇ərn/ *n.* an iron heated externally and used for pressing clothes, etc.

flat·mate /flátmayt/ *n. Brit.* a person in relation to one or more others living in the same flat.

flat race *n.* a horse race over level ground, as opposed to a steeplechase or hurdles. □□ **flat rac·ing**

flat rate *n.* a charge that is the same in all cases, not varying in proportion with something (*a system of charging a flat rate per household*).

flat spin *n.* **1** *Aeron.* a nearly horizontal spin. **2** *Brit. colloq.* a state of agitation or panic.

flat·ten /flát'n/ *v.* **1** *tr. & intr.* make or become flat. **2** *tr. colloq.* **a** humiliate. **b** knock down. □ **flatten out** bring an aircraft parallel to the ground. □□ **flat·ten·er** *n.*

flat·ter /flátər/ *v.tr.* **1** compliment unduly; overpraise, esp. for gain or advantage. **2** (usu. *refl.*; usu. foll. by *that* + clause) please, congratulate, or delude (oneself, etc.) (*I flatter myself that I can sing*). **3 a** (of a color, a style, etc.) make (a person) appear to the best advantage (*that blouse flatters you*). **b** (esp. of a portrait, a painter, etc.) represent too favorably. **4** gratify the vanity of; make (a person) feel honored. **5** inspire (a person) with hope, esp. unduly (*was flattered into thinking himself invulnerable*). **6** please or gratify (the ear, the eye, etc.). □□ **flat·ter·er** *n.* **flat·ter·ing** *adj.* **flat·ter·ing·ly** *adv.* [ME, perh. rel. to OF *flater* to smooth]

flat·ter·ing unc·tion *n.* a salve that one administers to one's own conscience or self-esteem (Shakesp. esp. *Hamlet* III. iv. 136).

flat·ter·y /flátəree/ *n.* (*pl.* **·ies**) **1** exaggerated or insincere praise. **2** the act or an instance of flattering.

flat·top /flát-top/ *n.* **1** *Aeron. sl.* an aircraft carrier. **2** *sl.* a man's hairstyle in which the hair is cropped short so that it bristles up into a flat surface.

flat·u·lent /fláchələnt/ *adj.* **1 a** causing formation of gas in the alimentary canal. **b** caused by or suffering from this. **2** (of speech, etc.) inflated; pretentious. □□ **flat·u·lence** *n.* **flat·u·len·cy** *n.* **flat·u·lent·ly** *adv.* [F f. mod.L *flatulentus* (as FLATUS)]

fla·tus /fláytəs/ *n.* gas in or from the stomach or intestines, produced by bacterial fermentation. [L, = blowing f. *flare* blow]

flat·ware /flátwair/ *n.* **1** forks, knives, spoons, etc.; cutlery. **2** plates, saucers, etc. (opp. HOLLOWARE).

flat·worm /flátwərm/ *n.* any worm of the phylum Platyhelminthes, having a flattened body and no body cavity or blood vessels, including turbellaria, flukes, etc.

flaunt /flawnt/ *v. & n.* • *v.tr. & intr.* **1** (often *refl.*) display ostentatiously (oneself or one's belongings); show off; parade (*liked to flaunt his gold cuff links; flaunted themselves before the crowd*). **2** wave or cause to wave proudly (*flaunted the banner*). • *n.* an act or instance of flaunting. □□ **flaunt·er** *n.* **flaunt·y** *adj.* [16th c.: orig. unkn.]

▶**Flaunt** and **flout** are often confused because both suggest arrogance or showing off. However, **flaunt** means 'display ostentatiously,' e.g., *he liked to flaunt his wealth,*' while **flout** means 'express contempt for or disobey (laws, convention, etc.),' e.g., *the fine is too low for those who flout the law so egregiously.*

flau·tist /fláwtist, flów–/ *n.* a flute player. [It. *flautista* f. *flauto* FLUTE]

fla·ves·cent /fləvésənt/ *adj.* turning yellow; yellowish. [L *flavescere* f. *flavus* yellow]

fla·vin /fláyvin/ *n.* (also **fla·vine** /–veen/) **1** the chemical compound forming the nucleus of various natural yellow pigments. **2** a yellow dye obtained from dyer's oak. [L *flavus* yellow + –IN]

fla·vin ad·e·nine di·nu·cle·o·tide // *n.* a coenzyme derived from riboflavin, important in various biochemical reactions. ¶ Abbr.: **FAD**.

fla·vine /fláyveen/ *n. Pharm.* an antiseptic derived from acridine. [as FLAVIN + –INE[4]]

fla·vone /fláyvōn/ *n. Biochem.* any of a group of naturally occurring white or yellow pigments found in plants. [as FLAVINE + –ONE]

fla·vo·pro·tein /fláyvōprōteen/ *n. Biochem.* any of a group of conjugated proteins containing flavin that are involved in oxidation reactions in cells. [FLAVINE + PROTEIN]

fla·vor /fláyvər/ *n. & v.* • *n.* **1** a distinctive mingled sensation of smell and taste (*has a cheesy flavor*). **2** an indefinable characteristic quality (*music with a romantic flavor*). **3** (usu. foll. by *of*) a slight admixture of a usu. undesirable quality (*the flavor of failure hangs over the enterprise*). **4** = FLAVORING. • *v.tr.* give flavor to; season. □ **flavor of the month** (or **week**) a temporary trend or fashion. □□ **fla·vor·ful** *adj.* **fla·vor·less** *adj.* **fla·vor·some** *adj.* [ME f. OF *flaor* perh. f. L *flatus* blowing & *foetor* stench: assim. to *savor*]

fla·vor·ing /fláyvəring/ *n.* a substance used to flavor food or drink.

fla·vor·ous /fláyvərəs/ *adj.* having a pleasant or pungent flavor.

flaw[1] /flaw/ *n. & v.* • *n.* **1** an imperfection; a blemish (*has a character without a flaw*). **2** a crack or similar fault (*the cup has a flaw*). **3** *Law* an invalidating defect in a legal matter. • *v.tr. & intr.* crack; damage; spoil. □□ **flawed** *adj.* **flaw·less** *adj.* **flaw·less·ly** *adv.* **flaw·less·ness** *n.* [ME perh. f. ON *flaga* slab f. Gmc: cf. FLAKE[1], FLAG[2]]

flaw[2] /flaw/ *n.* a squall of wind; a short storm. [prob. f. MDu. *vlāghe*, MLG *vlāge*, perh. = stroke]

flax /flaks/ *n.* **1 a** a blue-flowered plant, *Linum usitatissimum*, cultivated for its textile fiber and its seeds (see LINSEED). **b** a plant resembling this. **2 a** dressed or undressed flax fibers. **b** *archaic* linen; cloth of flax. [OE *flæx* f. WG]

flax·en /fláksən/ *adj.* **1** of flax. **2** (of hair) colored like dressed flax; pale yellow.

flax lil·y *n.* (*pl.* **·ies**) *NZ* any plant of the genus *Phormium*, yielding valuable fiber.

flax·seed /flákseed/ *n.* linseed.

flay /flay/ *v.tr.* **1** strip the skin or hide off, esp. by beating. **2** criticize severely (*the play was flayed by the critics*). **3** peel off (skin, bark, peel, etc.). **4** strip (a person) of wealth by extortion or exaction. □□ **flay·er** *n.* [OE *flēan* f. Gmc]

F lay·er /éf layər/ *n.* the highest and most strongly ionized region of the ionosphere. [F (arbitrary) + LAYER]

flea /flee/ *n.* **1** a small wingless jumping insect of the order Siphonaptera, feeding on human and other blood. **2 a** (in full **flea beetle**) a small jumping beetle infesting hops, cabbages, etc. **b** (in full **water flea**) daphnia. □ **a flea in one's ear** a sharp reproof. [OE *flēa, flēah* f. Gmc]

flea·bag /fleebag/ *n. sl.* a shabby or unattractive place or thing.

flea·bane /fleebayn/ *n.* any of various composite plants of the genus *Inula* or *Pulicaria*, supposed to drive away fleas.

flea·bite /fleebīt/ *n.* **1** the bite of a flea. **2** a trivial injury or inconvenience.

flea-bit·ten *adj.* **1** bitten by or infested with fleas. **2** shabby.

flea col·lar *n.* an insecticidal collar for dogs and cats.

flea mar·ket *n.* a market selling secondhand goods, etc.

flea-pit *n. Brit.* a dingy dirty place, esp. a run-down movie theater.

flea·wort /fleewawrt/ *n.* any of several plants supposed to drive away fleas.

flèche /flesh, flaysh/ *n.* a slender spire, often perforated with windows, esp. at the intersection of the nave and the transept of a church. [F, orig. = arrow]

fleck /flek/ *n. & v.* • *n.* **1** a small patch of color or light (*eyes with green flecks*). **2** a small particle or speck, esp. of dust. **3** a spot on the skin; a freckle. • *v.tr.* mark with flecks; dapple; variegate. [perh. f. ON *flekkr* (n.), *flekka* (v.), or MLG, MDu. *vlecke*, OHG *flec, flecho*]

flec·tion var. of FLEXION.

fled *past* and *past part.* of FLEE.

fledge /flej/ *v.* **1** *intr.* (of a bird) grow feathers. **2** *tr.* provide (an arrow) with feathers. **3** *tr.* bring up (a young bird) until it can fly. **4** *tr.* (as **fledged** *adj.*) **a** able to fly. **b** independent; mature. **5** *tr.* deck or provide with feathers or down. [obs. *fledge* (adj.) 'fit to fly,' f. OE *flycge* (recorded in *unfligge*) f. a Gmc root rel. to FLY¹]

fledg·ling /fléjling/ *n.* (also *Brit.* **fledge·ling**) **1** a young bird. **2** an inexperienced person. [FLEDGE + ‑LING¹]

flee /flee/ *v.* (*past* and *past part.* **fled** /fled/) **1** *intr.* (often foll. by *from*, *before*) **a** run away. **b** seek safety by fleeing. **2** *tr.* run away from; leave abruptly; shun (*fled the room; fled his attentions*). **3** *intr.* vanish; cease; pass away. □□ **flee·er** /fléeər/ *n.* [OE *flēon* f. Gmc]

fleece /flees/ *n. & v.* • *n.* **1 a** the woolly covering of a sheep or a similar animal. **b** the amount of wool sheared from a sheep at one time. **2** something resembling a fleece, esp.: **a** a woolly or rough head of hair. **b** a soft warm fabric with a pile, used for lining coats, etc. **c** a white cloud, a blanket of snow, etc. **3** *Heraldry* a representation of a fleece suspended from a ring. • *v.tr.* **1** (often foll. by *of*) strip (a person) of money, valuables, etc.; swindle. **2** remove the fleece from (a sheep, etc.); shear. **3** cover as if with a fleece (*a sky fleeced with clouds*). □□ **fleece·a·ble** *adj.* **fleeced** *adj.* (also in *comb.*). [OE *flēos*, *flēs* f. WG]

fleec·y /fléesee/ *adj.* (**fleec·i·er**, **fleec·i·est**) **1** of or like a fleece. **2** covered with a fleece. □□ **fleec·i·ly** *adv.* **fleec·i·ness** *n.*

fle·er /fleer/ *v. & n.* • *v.intr.* laugh impudently or mockingly; sneer; jeer. • *n.* a mocking look or speech. [ME, prob. f. Scand.: cf. Norw. & Sw. dial. *flira* to grin]

fleet¹ /fleet/ *n.* **1 a** a number of warships under one commander. **b** (prec. by *the*) all the warships and merchant ships of a nation. **2** a number of ships, aircraft, buses, trucks, taxis, etc., operating together or owned by one proprietor. [OE *flēot* ship, shipping f. *flēotan* float, FLEET⁵]

fleet² /fleet/ *adj.* swift; nimble. □□ **fleet·ly** *adv.* **fleet·ness** *n.* [prob. f. ON *fljótr* f. Gmc: cf. FLEET⁵]

fleet³ /fleet/ *n. Brit. dial.* a creek; an inlet. [OE *flēot* f. Gmc: cf. FLEET⁵]

fleet⁴ /fleet/ *adj. & adv. Brit. dial.* • *adj.* (of water) shallow. • *adv.* at or to a small depth (*plow fleet*). [orig. uncert.: perh. f. OE *flēat* (unrecorded), rel. to FLEET⁵]

fleet⁵ /fleet/ *v.intr. archaic* **1** glide away; vanish; be transitory. **2** (usu. foll. by *away*) (of time) pass rapidly; slip away. **3** move swiftly; fly. [OE *flēotan* float, swim f. Gmc]

Fleet Ad·mi·ral *n.* an admiral of the highest rank in the US navy.

fleet·ing /fléeting/ *adj.* transitory; brief. □□ **fleet·ing·ly** *adv.* [FLEET⁵ + ‑ING²]

Fleet Street *n.* a street in central London in which the offices of national newspapers were located until the mid 1980s (often used to refer to the British press).

Flem·ing /fléming/ *n.* **1** a native of medieval Flanders in the Low Countries. **2** a member of a Flemish-speaking people inhabiting N. and W. Belgium (see also WALLOON). [OE f. ON *flæmingi* & MDu. *Vlāming* f. root of *Vlaanderen* Flanders]

Flem·ish /flémish/ *adj. & n.* • *adj.* of or relating to Flanders. • *n.* the language of the Flemings. [MDu. *Vlāmisch* (as FLEMING)]

Flemish bond *n. Building* a bond in which each course of bricks consists of alternate headers and stretchers.

flense /flens/ *v.tr.* (also **flench** /flench/, **flinch** /flinch/) **1** cut up (a whale or seal). **2** flay (a seal). [Da. *flense*: cf. Norw. *flinsa*, *flunsa* flay]

flesh /flesh/ *n. & v.* • *n.* **1 a** the soft substance consisting of muscle and fat found between the skin and bones of an animal or a human. **b** plumpness; fat (*has put on flesh*). **c** *archaic* meat, esp. excluding poultry, game, and offal. **2** the body as opposed to the mind or the soul, esp. considered as sinful. **3** the pulpy substance of a fruit or a plant. **4 a** the visible surface of the human body with ref. to its color or appearance. **b** (also **flesh col·or**) a yellowish pink color. **5** animal or human life. • *v.tr.* **1** embody in flesh. **2** incite (a hound, etc.) by the taste of blood. **3** initiate, esp. by aggressive or violent means, esp.: **a** use (a sword, etc.) for the first time on flesh. **b** use (wit, the pen, etc.) for the first time. **c** inflame (a person) by the foretaste of success. □ **all flesh** all human and animal life. **flesh out** make or become substantial. **flesh tints** flesh colors as rendered by a painter. **in the flesh** in bodily form; in person. **lose** (or **put on**) **flesh** grow thinner or fatter. **make a person's flesh creep** (or **crawl**) frighten or horrify a person, esp. with tales of the supernatural, etc. **sins of the flesh** unchastity. **the way of all flesh** experience common to all humankind. □□ **flesh·less** *adj.* [OE *flǣsc* f. Gmc]

flesh and blood *n. & adj.* • *n.* **1** the body or its substance. **2** humankind. **3** human nature, esp. as being fallible. • *adj.* actually living, not imaginary or supernatural. □ **one's own flesh and blood** near relatives; descendants.

flesh·er /fléshər/ *n. Sc.* a butcher.

flesh fly *n.* (*pl.* **flies**) any fly of the family Sarcophagidae that deposits eggs or larvae in dead flesh.

flesh·ings /fléshingz/ *n.pl.* an actor's flesh-colored tights.

flesh·ly /fléshlee/ *adj.* (**flesh·li·er**, **flesh·li·est**) **1** (of desire, etc.) bod-ily; lascivious; sensual. **2** mortal; not divine. **3** worldly. □□ **flesh·li·ness** *n.* [OE *flǣsclic* (as FLESH)]

flesh·pots /fléshpots/ *n.pl.* places providing luxurious or hedonistic living (from the biblical allusion to the *fleshpots of Egypt* Exod. 16:3).

flesh side *n.* the side of a hide that adjoined the flesh.

flesh wound *n.* a wound not reaching a bone or a vital organ.

flesh·y /fléshee/ *adj.* (**flesh·i·er**, **flesh·i·est**) **1** plump; fat. **2** of flesh; without bone. **3** (of plant or fruit tissue) pulpy. **4** like flesh. □□ **flesh·i·ness** *n.*

fletch·er /fléchər/ *n.* a maker or seller of arrows. [ME f. OF *flech(i)er* f. *fleche* arrow]

fleur-de-lis /flŏrdəlée/ *n.* (also **fleur-de-lys**) (*pl.* **fleurs-** *pronunc.* same) **1** the iris flower. **2** *Heraldry* **a** a lily composed of three petals bound together near their bases. **b** the former royal arms of France. [ME f. OF *flour de lys* flower of lily]

fleu·ret /flŏrét/ *n.* an ornament like a small flower. [F *fleurette* f. *fleur* flower]

fleu·ron /flŏron, flŏr‑/ *n.* a flower-shaped ornament on a building, a coin, a book, etc. [ME f. OF *floron* f. *flour* FLOWER]

fleu·ry /flŏree, flŏoree/ *adj.* (also **flo·ry** /flóree/) *Heraldry* decorated with fleurs-de-lis. [ME f. OF *flo(u)ré* (as FLEURON)]

fleur-de-lis 2

flew *past* of FLY¹.

flews /flooz/ *n.pl.* the hanging lips of a bloodhound, etc. [16th c.: orig. unkn.]

flex¹ /fleks/ *v.* **1** *tr. & intr.* bend (a joint, limb, etc.) or be bent. **2** *tr. & intr.* move (a muscle) or (of a muscle) be moved to bend a joint. **3** *tr. Geol.* bend (strata). **4** *tr. Archaeol.* place (a corpse) with the legs drawn up under the chin. [L *flectere flex‑* bend]

flex² /fleks/ *n. Brit.* a flexible insulated cable used for carrying electric current to an appliance. [abbr. of FLEXIBLE]

flex·i·ble /fléksibəl/ *adj.* **1** able to bend without breaking; pliable; pliant. **2** easily led; manageable; docile. **3** adaptable; versatile; variable (*works flexible hours*). □□ **flex·i·bil·i·ty** *n.* **flex·i·bly** *adv.* [ME f. OF *flexible* or L *flexibilis* (as FLEX¹)]

SYNONYM TIP flexible

ELASTIC, LIMBER, PLIABLE, PLIANT, RESILIENT, SUPPLE. If you can bend over and touch your toes, you are **flexible**. But a dancer or gymnast is **limber**, an adjective that specifically applies to a body that has been brought into condition through training (*to stay limber, she did yoga every day*). *Flexible* applies to whatever can be bent without breaking, whether or not it returns to its original shape (*a flexible plastic hose; a flexible electrical conduit*); it does not necessarily refer, as *limber* does, to the human body. Unlike *flexible*, **resilient** implies the ability to spring back into shape after being bent or compressed, or to recover one's health or spirits quickly (*so young and resilient that she was back at work in a week*). **Elastic** is usually applied to substances or materials that are easy to stretch or expand and that quickly recover their shape or size (*pants with an elastic waist*), while **supple** is applied to whatever is easily bent, twisted, or folded without breaking or cracking (*a soft, supple leather*). When applied to the human body, *supple* suggests the ability to move effortlessly. **Pliant** and **pliable** may be used to describe either people or things that are easily bent or manipulated. *Pliant* suggests a tendency to bend without force or pressure from the outside, while *pliable* suggests the use of force or submission to another's will. A *pliant* person is merely adaptable, but a *pliable* person is easy to influence and eager to please.

---

flex·ile /fléksəl, ‑sīl/ *adj. archaic* **1** supple; mobile. **2** tractable; manageable. **3** versatile. □□ **flex·il·i·ty** /‑sílitee/ *n.* [L *flexilis* (as FLEX¹)]

flex·ion /flékshən/ *n.* (also **flec·tion**) **1 a** the act of bending or the condition of being bent, esp. of a limb or joint. **b** a bent part; a curve. **2** *Gram.* inflection. **3** *Math.* = FLEXURE. □□ **flex·ion·al** *adj.* (in sense 2). **flex·ion·less** *adj.* (in sense 2). [L *flexio* (as FLEX¹)]

flex·i·time /fléksitim/ *n.* var. of FLEXTIME.

flex·og·ra·phy /fleksógrəfee/ *n. Printing* a rotary letterpress technique using rubber or plastic plates and synthetic inks or dyes for printing on fabrics, plastics, etc., as well as on paper. □□ **flex·o·graph·ic** /‑səgráfik/ *adj.* [L *flexus* a bending f. *flectere* bend + ‑GRA-PHY]

flex·or /fléksər/ *n.* (in full **flexor muscle**) a muscle that bends part of the body (cf. EXTENSOR). [mod.L (as FLEX¹)]

flex·time /flékstim/ *n.* **1** a system of working a set number of hours with the starting and finishing times chosen within agreed limits by the employee. **2** the hours worked in this way. [FLEXIBLE + TIME]

flex·u·ous /flékshōos/ *adj.* full of bends; winding. □□ **flex·u·os·i·ty**

/–yōō-ósitee/ *n.* **flex•u•ous•ly** *adv.* [L *flexuosus* f. *flexus* bending formed as FLEX[1]]

flex•ure /flékshər/ *n.* **1 a** the act of bending or the condition of being bent. **b** a bend, curve, or turn. **2** *Math.* the curving of a line, surface, or solid, esp. from a straight line, plane, etc. **3** *Geol.* the bending of strata under pressure. ▫▫ **flex•ur•al** *adj.* [L *flexura* (as FLEX[1])]

flib•ber•ti•gib•bet /flíbərteejíbit/ *n.* a gossiping, frivolous, or restless person. [imit. of chatter]

flick /flik/ *n.* & *v.* • *n.* **1 a** a light, sharp, quickly retracted blow with a whip, etc. **b** the sudden release of a bent finger or thumb, esp. to propel a small object. **2** a sudden movement or jerk. **3** a quick turn of the wrist in playing games, esp. in throwing or striking a ball. **4** a slight, sharp sound. **5** *colloq.* **a** a movie. **b** (in *pl.*; prec. by *the*) the movies. • *v.* **1** *tr.* (often foll. by *away, off*) strike or move with a flick (*flicked the ash off his cigar; flicked away the dust*). **2** *tr.* give a flick with (a whip, towel, etc.). **3** *intr.* make a flicking movement or sound. ▫ **flick through** = *flip through.* [ME, imit.]

flick•er[1] /flíkər/ *v.* & *n.* • *v.intr.* **1** (of light) shine unsteadily or fitfully. **2** (of a flame) burn unsteadily, alternately flaring and dying down. **3 a** (of a flag, a reptile's tongue, an eyelid, etc.) move or wave to and fro; quiver; vibrate. **b** (of the wind) blow lightly and unsteadily. **4** (of hope, etc.) increase and decrease unsteadily and intermittently. • *n.* a flickering movement, light, thought, etc. ▫ **flicker out** die away after a final flicker. [OE *flicorian, flycerian*]

flick•er[2] /flíkər/ *n.* any woodpecker of the genus *Colaptes*, a ground-feeder native to N. America. [imit. of its note]

flick-knife *n. Brit.* a switchblade knife.

fli•er /flíər/ *n.* (also **fly•er**) *colloq.* **1** an airman or airwoman. **2** a thing that flies in a specified way (*a poor flier*). **3** a fast-moving animal or vehicle. **4** an ambitious or outstanding person. **5** (usu. **fly•er**) a small handbill or circular. **6** a speculative investment. **7** a flying jump.

flight[1] /flīt/ *n.* & *v.* • *n.* **1 a** the act or manner of flying through the air (*studied swallows' flight*). **b** the swift movement or passage of a projectile, etc., through the air (*the flight of an arrow*). **2 a** a journey made through the air or in space. **b** a timetabled journey made by an airline. **c** a military air unit of two or more aircraft. **3 a** a flock or large body of birds, insects, etc., esp. when migrating. **b** a migration. **4** (usu. foll. by *of*) a series, esp. of stairs between floors, or of hurdles across a race track (*lives up six flights*). **5** an extravagant soaring; a mental or verbal excursion or sally (of wit, etc.) (*a flight of fancy; a flight of ambition*). **6** the trajectory and pace of a ball in games. **7** the distance that a bird, aircraft, or missile can fly. **8** (usu. foll. by *of*) a volley (*a flight of arrows*). **9** the tail of a dart. **10** the pursuit of game by a hawk. **11** swift passage (of time). • *v.tr.* **1** provide (an arrow) with feathers. **2** shoot (wildfowl, etc.) in flight. **3** *Brit.* vary the trajectory and pace of (a cricket ball, etc.). ▫ **in the first** (or **top**) **flight** taking a leading place. **take** (or **wing**) **one's flight** fly. [OE *flyht* f. WG: rel to FLY[1]]

flight[2] /flīt/ *n.* **1 a** the act or manner of fleeing. **b** a hasty retreat. **2** *Econ.* the selling of currency, investments, etc., in anticipation of a fall in value (*flight from the dollar*). ▫ **put to flight** cause to flee. **take** (or **take to**) **flight** flee. [OE f. Gmc: rel. to FLEE]

flight at•tend•ant *n.* an airline employee who attends to passengers' safety and comfort during flights.

flight bag *n.* a small, zippered, shoulder bag carried by air travelers.

flight con•trol *n.* an internal or external system directing the movement of aircraft.

flight deck *n.* **1** the deck of an aircraft carrier used for takeoff and landing. **2** the forward compartment occupied by the pilot, navigator, etc., in an aircraft.

flight feath•er *n.* any of the large primary or secondary feathers in a bird's wing or tail, supporting it in flight.

flight•less /flítlis/ *adj.* (of a bird, etc.) naturally unable to fly.

flight path *n.* the planned course of an aircraft or spacecraft.

flight re•cord•er *n.* a device in an aircraft to record technical details during a flight, which may be used in the event of an accident to discover its cause.

flight-test *v.tr.* test (an aircraft, rocket, etc.) during flight.

flight•y /flítee/ *adj.* (**flight•i•er, flight•i•est**) **1** frivolous; fickle; changeable. **2** slightly crazy. ▫▫ **flight•i•ly** *adv.* **flight•i•ness** *n.* [FLIGHT[1] + –Y[1]]

flim•flam /flímflam/ *n.* & *v.* • *n.* **1** a trifle; nonsense; idle talk. **2** humbug; deception. • *v.tr.* (**flim•flammed, flim•flam•ming**) cheat; deceive. ▫▫ **flim•flam•mer** *n.* **flim•flam•mer•y** /–məree/ *n.* (*pl.* **•ies**). [imit. redupl.]

flim•sy /flímzee/ *adj.* & *n.* • *adj.* (**flim•si•er, flim•si•est**) **1** lightly or carelessly assembled; insubstantial; easily damaged (*a flimsy structure*). **2** (of an excuse, etc.) unconvincing (*a flimsy pretext*). **3** paltry; trivial; superficial (*a flimsy play*). **4** (of clothing) thin (*a flimsy blouse*). • *n. Brit.* (*pl.* **•sies**) **1 a** a very thin paper. **b** a document, esp. a copy, made on this. **2** a flimsy thing, esp. women's underwear. ▫▫ **flim•si•ly** *adv.* **flim•si•ness** *n.* [17th c.: prob. f. FLIMFLAM: cf. TIPSY]

flinch[1] /flinch/ *v.* & *n.* • *v.intr.* **1** draw back in pain or expectation of a blow, etc.; wince. **2** (often foll. by *from*) give way; shrink; turn aside (*flinched from his duty*). • *n.* an act or instance of flinching. ▫▫ **flinch•er** *n.* **flinch•ing•ly** *adv.* [OF *flenchir, flainchir* f. WG]

flinch[2] var. of FLENSE.

flin•ders /flíndərz/ *n.pl.* fragments; splinters. [ME, prob. f. Scand.]

fling /fling/ *v.* & *n.* • *v.* (*past* and *past part.* **flung** /flung/) **1** *tr.* throw or hurl (an object) forcefully. **2** *refl.* **a** (usu. foll. by *into*) rush headlong (into a person's arms, a train, etc.). **b** (usu. foll. by *into*) embark wholeheartedly (on an enterprise). **c** (usu. foll. by *on*) throw (oneself) on a person's mercy, etc. **3** *tr.* utter (words) forcefully. **4** *tr.* (usu. foll. by *out*) suddenly spread (the arms). **5** *tr.* (foll. by *on, off*) put on or take off (clothes) carelessly or rapidly. **6** *intr.* go angrily or violently; rush (*flung out of the room*). **7** *tr.* put or send suddenly or violently (*was flung into jail*). **8** *tr.* (foll. by *away*) discard or put aside thoughtlessly or rashly (*flung away their reputation*). **9** *intr.* (usu. foll. by *out*) (of a horse, etc.) kick and plunge. **10** *tr. archaic* send; emit (sound, light, smell). • *n.* **1** an act or instance of flinging; a throw; a plunge. **2 a** a spell of indulgence or wild behavior (*he's had his fling*). **b** *colloq.* an attempt (*give it a fling*). **3** a brief or casual romance. **4** an impetuous, whirling Scottish dance, esp. the Highland fling. ▫ **have a fling at 1** make an attempt at. **2** jeer at. ▫▫ **fling•er** *n.* [ME, perh. f. ON]

flint /flint/ *n.* **1 a** a hard gray stone of nearly pure silica occurring naturally as nodules or bands in chalk. **b** a piece of this, esp. as flaked or shaped to form a primitive tool or weapon. **2** a piece of hard alloy of rare earth metals used to give an igniting spark in a cigarette lighter, etc. **3** a piece of flint used with steel to produce fire, esp. in a flintlock gun. **4** anything hard and unyielding. ▫▫ **flint•y** *adj.* (**flint•i•er, flint•i•est**). **flint•i•ly** *adv.* **flint•i•ness** *n.* [OE]

flint corn *n.* a variety of corn having hard translucent kernels.

flint glass *n.* a pure lustrous kind of glass orig. made with flint.

flint•lock /flíntlok/ *n. hist.* **1** an old type of gun fired by a spark from a flint. **2** the lock producing such a spark.

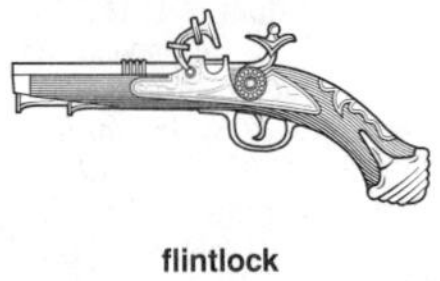

flintlock

flip[1] /flip/ *v., n.,* & *adj.* • *v.* (**flipped, flip•ping**) **1** *tr.* **a** flick or toss (a coin, ball, etc.) with a quick movement so that it spins in the air. **b** remove (a small object) from a surface with a flick of the fingers. **2** *tr.* **a** strike or flick (a person's ear, cheek, etc.) lightly or smartly. **b** move (a fan, whip, etc.) with a sudden jerk. **3** *tr.* turn or turn over. **4** *intr.* **a** make a fillip or flicking noise with the fingers. **b** (foll. by *at*) strike smartly at. **5** *intr.* move about with sudden jerks. **6** *intr. sl.* (often foll. by *out*) become suddenly angry, excited, or enthusiastic. • *n.* **1** a smart light blow; a flick. **2** a somersault, esp. while in the air. **3** an act of flipping over (*gave the stone a flip*). **4** *colloq.* **a** a short pleasure flight in an aircraft. **b** a quick tour, etc. • *adj. colloq.* glib; flippant. ▫ **flip one's lid** *sl.* **1** lose self-control. **2** go crazy. **flip through 1** turn over (cards, pages, etc.). **2 a** turn over the pages, etc., of, by a rapid movement of the fingers. **b** look cursorily through (a book, etc.). [prob. f. FILLIP]

flip[2] /flip/ *n.* **1** a drink of heated beer and liquor. **2** = EGG-FLIP. [perh. f. FLIP[1] in the sense *whip up*]

flip chart *n.* a large pad erected on a stand and bound so that one page can be turned over at the top to reveal the next.

flip-flop /flípflop/ *n.* & *v.* • *n.* **1** a usu. rubber sandal with a thong between the big and second toe. **2** a backward somersault. **3** an electronic switching circuit changed from one stable state to another, or through an unstable state back to its stable state, by a triggering pulse. **4** an esp. sudden change of direction, attitude, policy, etc. • *v.intr.* (**•flopped, •flop•ping**) **1** move with a sound or motion suggested by "flip-flop." **2** to change direction, attitude, policy, etc., esp. suddenly. [imit.]

flip•pant /flípənt/ *adj.* lacking in seriousness; treating serious things lightly; disrespectful. ▫▫ **flip•pan•cy** /–pənsee/ *n.* **flip•pant•ly** *adv.* [FLIP[1] + –ANT]

flip•per /flípər/ *n.* **1** a broadened limb of a tortoise, penguin, etc., used in swimming. **2** a flat rubber, etc., attachment worn on the foot for underwater swimming. **3** *sl.* a hand.

flip•ping /flíping/ *adj.* & *adv. Brit. sl.* expressing annoyance, or as an intensifier (*where's the flipping towel?; he flipping beat me*). [FLIP[1] + –ING[2]]

flip side *n. colloq.* the less important side of something (orig. of a phonograph record).

flirt /flərt/ *v.* & *n.* • *v.* **1** *intr.* (usu. foll. by *with*) behave in a frivolously amorous or sexually enticing manner. **2** *intr.* (usu. foll. by *with*) **a** superficially interest oneself (with an idea, etc.). **b** trifle (with danger, etc.) (*flirted with disgrace*). **3** *tr.* wave or move (a fan, a bird's tail, etc.) briskly. **4** *intr.* & *tr.* move or cause to move with a jerk. • *n.* **1** a person who indulges in flirting. **2** a quick movement; a sudden jerk. ▫▫ **flir•ta•tion** *n.* **flir•ta•tious** *adj.* **flir•ta•tious•ly** *adv.* **flir•ta•tious•ness** *n.* **flirt•y** *adj.* (**flirt•i•er, flirt•i•est**). [imit.]

flit /flit/ *v.* & *n.* • *v.intr.* (**flit•ted, flit•ting**) **1** move lightly, softly, or rapidly (*flitted from one room to another*). **2** fly lightly; make short flights (*flitted from branch to branch*). **3** *Brit. colloq.* leave one's house, etc., secretly to escape creditors or obligations. **4** esp. *Sc. & No. of Engl.* change one's home; move. ●*n.* **1** an act of flitting. **2** (also **moon-light flit**) a secret change of abode in order to escape creditors, etc. □□ **flit·ter** *n.* [ME f. ON *flytja*: rel. to FLEET⁵]

flitch /flich/ *n.* **1** a side of bacon. **2** a slab of timber from a tree trunk, usu. from the outside. **3** (in full **flitch plate**) a strengthening plate in a beam, etc. [OE *flicce* f. Gmc]

flitch beam *n.* a compound beam, esp. of an iron plate between two slabs of wood.

flit·ter /flítər/ *v.intr.* flit about; flutter. [FLIT + −ER⁴]

fliv·ver /flívər/ *n. Old-fash. sl.* a cheap, old car. [20th c.: orig. uncert.]

float /flōt/ *v. & n.* ●*v.* **1** *intr. & tr.* **a** rest or move or cause (a buoyant object) to rest or move on the surface of a liquid without sinking. **b** get afloat or set (a stranded ship) afloat. **2** *intr.* move with a liquid or current of air; drift (*the clouds floated high up*). **3** *intr. colloq.* **a** move in a leisurely or casual way (*floated about humming quietly*). **b** (often foll. by *before*) hover before the eye or mind (*the prospect of lunch floated before them*). **4** *intr.* (often foll. by *in*) move or be suspended freely in a liquid or a gas. **5** *tr.* **a** bring (a company, scheme, etc.) into being; launch. **b** offer (stock, shares, etc.) on the stock market. **6** *Commerce* **a** *intr.* (of currency) be allowed to have a fluctuating exchange rate. **b** *tr.* cause (currency) to float. **c** *intr.* (of an acceptance) be in circulation. **7** *tr.* (of water, etc.) support; bear along (a buoyant object). **8** *intr. & tr.* circulate or cause (a rumor or idea) to circulate. **9** *tr.* put forward as a proposal. **10** waft (a buoyant object) through the air. **11** *tr. archaic* cover with liquid; inundate. ●*n.* **1** a thing that floats, esp.: **a** a raft. **b** a cork or other buoyant object on a fishing line as an indicator of a fish biting. **c** a cork supporting the edge of a fishing net. **d** the hollow or inflated part or organ supporting a fish, etc., in the water; an air bladder. **e** a hollow structure fixed underneath an aircraft enabling it to float on water. **f** a floating device on the surface of water, fuel, etc., controlling the flow. **2** *Brit.* a small vehicle or cart, esp. one powered by electricity (*milk float*). **3** a platform mounted on a truck or trailer and carrying a display in a parade, etc. **4 a** an amount of money outstanding but not yet collected by a bank, etc., such as checks written but not yet collected. **b** the time between the writing of a check, etc., and the actual collection of funds. **5** *Brit.* **a** a sum of money used at the beginning of a period of selling in a shop, etc., to provide change. **b** a small sum of money for minor expenditure; petty cash. **6** *Theatr. Brit.* (in *sing.* or *pl.*) footlights. **7** a tool used for smoothing plaster or concrete. □□ **float·a·ble** *adj.* **float·a·bil·i·ty** /−təbílitee/ *n.* [OE *flot, flotian* float, OE *flota* ship, ON *flota, floti* rel. to FLEET⁵: in ME infl. by OF *floter*]

float·age var. of FLOTAGE.

float·a·tion var. of FLOTATION.

float·er /flótər/ *n.* **1** a person or thing that floats. **2 a** a floating voter. **b** one who votes fraudulently, esp. repeatedly. **3** *Brit. sl.* a mistake; a gaffe. **4** a person who frequently changes occupations or duties. **5** *Stock Exch.* a government stock certificate, etc., recognized as a security. **6** an insurance policy for movable valuables, such as jewelry, etc.

float glass *n.* a kind of glass made by drawing the molten glass continuously onto a surface of molten metal for hardening.

float·ing /flóting/ *adj.* not settled in a definite place; fluctuating; variable (*the floating population*). □□ **float·ing·ly** *adv.*

float·ing an·chor *n.* a sea anchor.

float·ing bridge *n.* a bridge supported by pontoons or other floating vessels.

float·ing debt *n.* a usu. short-term debt repayable on demand, or at a stated time.

float·ing dock *n.* a floating structure that can be submerged to allow the entry of a boat, and then raised to lift the boat from the water.

float·ing kidney *n.* **1** an abnormal condition in which the kidneys are unusually movable. **2** such a kidney.

float·ing point *n. Computing* a decimal, etc., point that does not occupy a fixed position in the numbers processed.

float·ing rib *n.* any of the lower ribs, which are not attached to the breastbone.

float·ing voter *n.* a voter without allegiance to any political party.

float·y /flótee/ *adj.* (esp. of a woman's garment or a fabric) light and airy. [FLOAT]

floc /flok/ *n.* a flocculent mass of fine particles. [abbr. of FLOCCULUS]

floc·cu·late /flókyəlayt/ *v.tr. & intr.* form into flocculent masses. □□ **floc·cu·la·tion** /−láyshən/ *n.*

floc·cule /flókyōōl/ *n.* a small portion of matter resembling a tuft of wool.

floc·cu·lent /flókyələnt/ *adj.* **1** like tufts of wool. **2** consisting of or showing tufts; downy. **3** *Chem.* (of precipitates) loosely massed. □□ **floc·cu·lence** /−lens/ *n.* [L *floccus* FLOCK²]

floc·cu·lus /flókyələs/ *n.* (*pl.* **floc·cu·li** /−lī/) **1** a floccule. **2** *Anat.* a small ovoid lobe on the underside of the cerebellum. **3** *Astron.* a small cloudy wisp on the sun's surface. [mod.L, dimin. of FLOCCUS]

floc·cus /flókəs/ *n.* (*pl.* **floc·ci** /flóksī/) a tuft of woolly hairs or filaments. [L, = FLOCK²]

flock¹ /flok/ *n. & v.* ●*n.* **1 a** a number of animals of one kind, esp. birds, feeding or traveling together. **b** a number of domestic animals, esp. sheep, goats, or geese, kept together. **2** a large crowd of people. **3 a** a Christian congregation or body of believers, esp. in relation to one minister. **b** a family of children, a number of pupils, etc. ●*v.intr.* **1** congregate; mass. **2** (usu. foll. by *to, in, out, together*) go together in a crowd; troop (*thousands flocked to the polls*). [OE *flocc*]

flock² /flok/ *n.* **1** a lock or tuft of wool, cotton, etc. **2 a** (also in *pl.*; often *attrib.*) material for quilting and stuffing made of wool refuse or torn-up cloth (*a flock pillow*). **b** powdered wool or cloth. □□ **flock·y** *adj.* [ME f. OF *floc* f. L *floccus*]

flock pa·per *n.* (also **flock wallpaper**) wallpaper sized and sprinkled with powdered wool to make a raised pattern.

floe /flō/ *n.* a sheet of floating ice. [prob. f. Norw. *flo* f. ON *fló* layer]

flog /flawg, flog/ *v.* (**flogged, flog·ging**) **1** *tr.* **a** beat with a whip, stick, etc. (as a punishment or to urge on). **b** make work through violent effort (*flogged the engine*). **2** *sl.* sell or promote aggressively. **3** *tr.* (usu. foll. by *into, out of*) drive (a quality, knowledge, etc.) into or out of a person, esp. by physical punishment. **4** *intr. & refl. Brit. sl.* proceed with violent or painful effort. □ **flog** (also **beat**) **a dead horse** waste energy on something unalterable. **flog to death** *colloq.* talk about or promote at tedious length. □□ **flog·ger** *n.* [17th-c. cant: prob. imit. or f. L *flagellare* to whip]

flood /flud/ *n. & v.* ●*n.* **1 a** an overflowing or influx of water beyond its normal confines, esp. over land; an inundation. **b** the water that overflows. **2 a** an outpouring of water; a torrent (*a flood of rain*). **b** something resembling a torrent (*a flood of tears, a flood of relief*). **c** an abundance or excess. **3** the inflow of the tide (also in *comb.*: *flood tide*). **4** *colloq.* a floodlight. **5** (**the Flood**) the flood described in Genesis. **6** *poet.* a river; a stream; a sea. ●*v.* **1** *tr.* **a** cover with or overflow in a flood (*rain flooded the cellar*). **b** overflow as if with a flood (*the market was flooded with foreign goods*). **2** *tr.* irrigate (*flooded the rice paddies*). **3** *tr.* deluge (a burning house, a mine, etc.) with water. **4** *intr.* (often foll. by *in, through*) arrive in great quantities (*complaints flooded in; fear flooded through them*). **5** *intr.* become inundated (*the bathroom flooded*). **6** *tr.* overfill (a carburetor) with fuel. **7** *intr.* experience a uterine hemorrhage. **8** *tr.* (of rain, etc.) fill (a river) to overflowing. □ **flood out** drive out (of one's home, etc.) with a flood. [OE *flōd* f. Gmc]

flood·gate /flúdgayt/ *n.* **1** a gate opened or closed to admit or exclude water, esp. the lower gate of a lock. **2** (usu. in *pl.*) a last restraint holding back tears, rain, anger, etc.

flood·light /flúdlīt/ *n. & v.* ●*n.* **1** a large powerful light (usu. one of several) to illuminate a building, stadium, stage, etc. **2** the illumination so provided. ●*v.tr.* illuminate with floodlights.

flood·plain /flúdplayn/ *n.* flat terrain alongside a river that is subject to inundation when the river floods.

flood tide *n.* the incoming or rising tide.

flood·wa·ter /flúdwawtər, −wo−/ *n.* the water overflowing as the result of a flood.

floor /flawr/ *n. & v.* ●*n.* **1 a** the lower surface of a room. **b** the boards, etc., of which it is made. **2 a** the bottom of the sea, a cave, a cavity, etc. **b** any level area. **3** all the rooms, etc., on the same level of a building; a story (*lives on the first floor; walked up to the fourth floor*). **4 a** (in a legislative assembly) the part of the house in which members sit and from which they speak. **b** the right to speak next in debate (*gave him the floor*). **5** *Stock Exch.* the large central hall where trading takes place. **6** the minimum of prices, wages, etc. **7** *colloq.* the ground. ●*v.tr.* **1** furnish with a floor; pave. **2** bring to the ground; knock (a person) down. **3** *colloq.* confound; baffle (*was floored by the puzzle*). **4** *colloq.* get the better of; overcome. **5** serve as the floor of (*leopard skins floored the hall*). **6** cause a vehicle to accelerate rapidly. □ **from the floor** (of a speech, etc.) given by a member of the audience, not by those on the platform, etc. **take the floor 1** begin to dance on a dance floor, etc. **2** speak in a debate. □□ **floor·less** *adj.* [OE *flōr* f. Gmc]

floor·board /flawrbawrd/ *n.* a long wooden board used for flooring.

floor·cloth /fláwrklawth, −kloth/ *n.* a thin canvas rug or similar light floor covering.

floor ex·er·cise *n.* a routine of gymnastic exercises performed without the use of apparatus.

floor·ing /fláwring/ *n.* the boards, etc., of which a floor is made.

floor lamp *n.* a lamp with a base that rests on the floor.

floor lead·er *n.* the organizational or strategical leader of a party in a legislative assembly.

floor man·a·ger *n.* **1** the stage manager of a television production. **2** a person who directs activities, etc., from the floor, as at a political convention. **2** an employee in a large store who supervises other salespeople.

floor plan *n.* a diagram of the rooms, etc., on one floor of a building.

floor price *n.* = RESERVE PRICE.

floor show *n.* an entertainment presented at a nightclub, restaurant, or similar venue.

floor·walk·er /fláwrwawkər/ *n.* a person employed in a retail store who assists customers and supervises other workers.

floo·zy /flŏ̄ozee/ *n.* (also **floo·zie**) (*pl.* **·zies**) *colloq.* a girl or a woman, esp. a disreputable one. [20th c.: cf. FLOSSY and dial. *floosy* fluffy]

flop /flop/ *v., n., & adv.* ● *v.intr.* (**flopped, flop·ping**) **1** sway about heavily or loosely (*hair flopped over his face*). **2** move in an ungainly way (*flopped along the beach in flippers*). **3** (often foll. by *down, on, into*) sit, kneel, lie, or fall awkwardly or suddenly (*flopped down on to the bench*). **4** *sl.* (esp. of a play, movie, book, etc.) fail; collapse (*flopped on Broadway*). **5** *sl.* sleep. **6** make a dull sound as of a soft body landing, or of a flat thing slapping water. ● *n.* **1 a** a flopping movement. **b** the sound made by it. **2** *sl.* a failure. **3** *sl.* a place to sleep, esp. cheaply. **4** a piece of cow dung. ● *adv.* with a flop. [var. of FLAP]

flop·house /flop-hows/ *n.* a cheap hotel or rooming house.

flop·py /flópee/ *adj. & n.* ● *adj.* (**flop·pi·er, flop·pi·est**) tending to flop; not firm or rigid. ● *n.* (*pl.* **·pies**) (in full **floppy disk**) *Computing* a flexible removable magnetic disk for the storage of data. □□ **flop·pi·ly** *adv.* **flop·pi·ness** *n.*

flor. *abbr.* floruit.

flo·ra /fláwrə/ *n.* (*pl.* **flo·ras** or **flo·rae** /–ree/) **1** the plants of a particular region, geological period, or environment. **2** a treatise on or list of these. [mod.L f. the name of the goddess of flowers f. L *flos floris* flower]

flo·ral /fláwrəl/ *adj.* **1** of flowers. **2** decorated with or depicting flowers. **3** of flora or floras. □□ **flo·ral·ly** *adv.* [L *floralis* or *flos floris* flower]

flo·re·at /fláwreeat/ *v.intr.* may (he, she, or it) flourish. [L, 3rd sing. pres. subj. of *florēre* flourish]

Flor·en·tine /fláwrənteen, –tīn, flór–/ *adj. & n.* ● *adj.* **1** of or relating to Florence in Italy. **2** (**florentine** /–teen/) (of a dish) served on a bed of spinach. ● *n.* a native or citizen of Florence. [F *Florentin –ine* or L *Florentinus* f. *Florentia* Florence]

flo·res·cence /fláwrésəns/ *n.* the process, state, or time of flowering. □□ **flo·res·cent** *adj.* [mod.L *florescentia* f. L *florescere* f. *florēre* bloom]

flo·ret /fláwrit/ *n. Bot.* **1** each of the small flowers making up a composite flower head. **2** each of the flowering stems making up a head of cauliflower, broccoli, etc. **3** a small flower. [L *flos floris* flower]

flo·ri·ate /fláwriayt/ *v.tr.* decorate with flower designs, etc.

flo·ri·bun·da /fláwribúndə/ *n.* a plant, esp. a rose, bearing dense clusters of flowers. [mod.L f. *floribundus* freely flowering f. L *flos floris* flower, infl. by L *abundus* copious]

flo·ri·cul·ture /fláwrikulchər/ *n.* the cultivation of flowers. □□ **flo·ri·cul·tur·al** *adj.* **flo·ri·cul·tur·ist** *n.* [L *flos floris* flower + CULTURE, after *horticulture*]

flor·id /fláwrid, flór–/ *adj.* **1** ruddy; flushed (*a florid complexion*). **2** (of a book, a picture, music, architecture, etc.) elaborately ornate; ostentatious; showy. **3** adorned with or as with flowers; flowery. □□ **flo·rid·i·ty** *n.* **flor·id·ly** *adv.* **flor·id·ness** *n.* [F *floride* or L *floridus* f. *flos floris* flower]

flo·rif·er·ous /fláwrífərəs/ *adj.* (of a seed or plant) producing many flowers. [L *flos floris* flower]

flo·ri·le·gi·um /fláwrileéjeeəm/ *n.* (*pl.* **flo·ri·le·gi·a** /–jeeə/ or **flo·ri·le·gi·ums**) an anthology. [mod.L f. L *flos floris* flower + *legere* gather, transl. of Gk *anthologion* ANTHOLOGY]

flor·in /fláwrin, flór–/ *n. hist.* **1 a** a British silver or alloy two-shilling coin of the 19th–20th c. **b** an English gold coin of the 14th c. **2** a foreign coin of gold or silver, esp. a Dutch guilder. [ME f. OF f. It. *fiorino* dimin. of *fiore* flower f. L *flos floris*, the orig. coin having a figure of a lily on it]

flo·rist /fláwrist, flór–/ *n.* a person who deals in or grows flowers. □□ **flo·rist·ry** *n.* [L *flos floris* flower + –IST]

flo·ris·tic /fláwrístik/ *adj.* relating to the study of the distribution of plants. □□ **flo·ris·ti·cal·ly** *adv.* **flo·ris·tics** *n.*

flo·ru·it /fláwrŏ̄oit, flór–/ *v. & n.* ● *v.intr.* (he or she) was alive and working; flourished (used of a person, esp. a painter, a writer, etc., whose exact dates are unknown). ● *n.* the period or date at which a person lived or worked. [L, = he or she flourished]

flo·ry var. of FLEURY.

flos·cu·lar /flóskyələr/ *adj.* (also **flos·cu·lous** /–kyŏ̄oləs/) having florets or composite flowers. [L *flosculus* dimin. of *flos* flower]

floss /flaws, flos/ *n. & v.* ● *n.* **1** the rough silk enveloping a silkworm's

cocoon. **2** untwisted silk thread used in embroidery. **3** = DENTAL FLOSS. ● *v.tr.* (also *absol.*) clean (the teeth) with dental floss. [F (*soie*) *floche* floss(-silk) f. OF *flosche* floss, nap of velvet]

floss·y /fláwsee, flósee/ *adj.* (**floss·i·er, floss·i·est**) **1** of or like floss. **2** *colloq.* fancy; showy.

flo·tage /flótij/ *n.* **1** the act or state of floating. **2 a** a floating objects or masses; flotsam. **b** *Brit.* the right of appropriating flotsam. **3 a** ships, etc., afloat on a river. **b** the part of a ship above the water line. **4** buoyancy; floating power.

flo·ta·tion /flótáyshən/ *n.* (also **floa·ta·tion**) **1** the process of launching or financing a commercial enterprise. **2** the separation of the components of crushed ore, etc., by their different capacities to float. **3** the capacity to float. [alt. of *floatation* f. FLOAT, after *rotation*, etc.]

flo·til·la /flótílə/ *n.* **1** a small fleet. **2** a fleet of boats or small ships. [Sp., dimin. of *flota* fleet, OF *flote* multitude]

flot·sam /flótsəm/ *n.* wreckage found floating. [AF *floteson* f. *floter* FLOAT]

flot·sam and jet·sam *n.* **1** odds and ends; rubbish. **2** vagrants, etc.

flounce[1] /flowns/ *v. & n.* ● *v.intr.* (often foll. by *away, off, out*) go or move with an agitated, violent, or impatient motion (*flounced out in a huff*). ● *n.* a flouncing movement. [16th c.: orig. unkn.: perh. imit., as *bounce, pounce*]

flounce[2] /flowns/ *n. & v.* ● *n.* a wide ornamental strip of material gathered and sewn to a skirt, dress, etc.; a frill. ● *v.tr.* trim with a flounce or flounces. [alt. of earlier *frounce* fold, pleat, f. OF *fronce* f. *froncir* wrinkle]

floun·der[1] /flówndər/ *v. & v.* ● *v.intr.* **1** struggle in mud, or as if in mud, or when wading. **2** perform a task badly or without knowledge; be out of one's depth. ● *n.* an act of floundering. □□ **floun·der·er** *n.* [imit.: perh. assoc. with *founder, blunder*]

floun·der[2] /flówndər/ *n.* **1** an edible flatfish, *Pleuronectes flesus*, native to European shores. **2** any of various flatfish native to N. American shores. [ME f. AF *floundre*, OF *flondre*, prob. of Scand. orig.]

flour /flowər/ *n. & v.* ● *n.* **1** a meal or powder obtained by grinding and usu. sifting grain, esp. wheat. **2** any fine powder. ● *v.tr.* **1** sprinkle with flour. **2** grind into flour. □□ **flour·y** *adj.* (**flour·i·er, flour·i·est**). **flour·i·ness** *n.* [ME, different. spelling of FLOWER in the sense 'finest part']

flour·ish /flórish, flúr–/ *v. & n.* ● *v.* **1** *intr.* **a** grow vigorously; thrive. **b** prosper; be successful. **c** be in one's prime. **d** be in good health. **e** (as **flourishing** *adj.*) successful; prosperous. **2** *intr.* (usu. foll. by *in, at, about*) spend one's life; be active (at a specified time) (*flourished in the Middle Ages*) (cf. FLORUIT). **3** *tr.* show ostentatiously (*flourished her checkbook*). **4** *tr.* wave (a weapon, one's limbs, etc.) vigorously. ● *n.* **1** an ostentatious gesture with a weapon, a hand, etc. (*removed his hat with a flourish*). **2** an ornamental curving decoration of handwriting. **3** a florid verbal expression; a rhetorical embellishment. **4** *Mus.* **a** a fanfare played by brass instruments. **b** an ornate musical passage. **c** an extemporized addition played esp. at the beginning or end of a composition. **5** *archaic* an instance of prosperity; a flourishing. □□ **flour·ish·er** *n.* **flour·ish·y** *adj.*

flout /flowt/ *v. & n.* ● *v.* **1** *tr.* express contempt for (the law, rules, etc.) by word or action; mock; insult (*flouted convention by shaving her head*). **2** *intr.* (often foll. by *at*) mock or scoff. ● *n.* a flouting speech or act. [perh. f. Du. *fluiten* whistle, hiss: cf. FLUTE]
▶See note at FLAUNT.

flow /flō/ *v. & n.* ● *v.intr.* **1** glide along as a stream (*the Thames flows through London*). **2 a** (of a liquid, esp. water) gush out; spring. **b** (of blood, liquid, etc.) be spilled. **3** (of blood, money, electric current, etc.) circulate. **4** (of people or things) come or go in large numbers or smoothly (*traffic flowed along the highway*). **5** (of talk, literary style, etc.) proceed easily and smoothly. **6** (of a garment, hair, etc.) hang easily or gracefully; undulate. **7** (often foll. by *from*) result from; be caused by (*his failure flows from his diffidence*). **8** (esp. of the tide) be in flood; run full. **9** (of wine) be poured out copiously. **10** (of a rock or metal) undergo a permanent change of shape under stress. **11** menstruate. **12** (foll. by *with*) *archaic* be plentifully supplied with (*land flowing with milk and honey*). ● *n.* **1 a** a flowing movement in a stream. **b** the manner in which a thing flows (*a sluggish flow*). **c** a flowing liquid (*couldn't stop the flow*). **d** a copious outpouring; a stream (*a continuous flow of complaints*). **e** a hardened mass that formerly flowed (*walked out onto the lava flow*). **2** the rise of a tide or a river (*ebb and flow*). **3** the gradual deformation of a rock or metal under stress. **4** menstruation. **5** *Sc.* a bog or morass. [OE *flōwan* f. Gmc, rel. to blood]

flow chart *n.* (also **flow di·a·gram** or **flow sheet**) **1** a diagram of the movement or action of things or persons engaged in a complex activity. **2** a graphical representation of a computer program in relation to its sequence of functions (as distinct from the data it processes).

flow·er /flowər/ *n. & v.* ● *n.* **1** the part of a plant from which the fruit or seed is developed. **2** the reproductive organ in a plant containing one or more pistils or stamens or both, and usu. a corolla and calyx. **3** a blossom, esp. on a stem and used in bunches for decoration. **4** a plant cultivated or noted for its flowers. **5** (in *pl.*) ornamental phrases (*flowers of speech*). **6** the finest time, group, example, etc.; the peak.

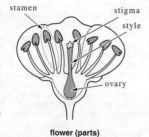

stamen
stigma
style
ovary

flower (parts)

● *v.* **1** *intr.* (of a plant) produce flowers; bloom or blossom. **2** *intr.* reach a peak. **3** *tr.* cause or allow (a plant) to flower. **4** *tr.* decorate with worked flowers or a floral design. □ **the flower of** the best or best part of. **in flower** with the flowers out. □□ **flow·ered** *adj.* (also in *comb.*). **flow·er·less** *adj.* **flow·er·like** *adj.* [ME f. AF *flur*, OF *flour*, *flor*, f. L *flos floris*]

flow·er·er /flówərər/ *n.* a plant that flowers at a specified time (*a late flowerer*).

flow·er·et /flówərit/ *n.* a small flower.

flow·er girl *n.* **1** a girl who carries flowers at a wedding as an attendant to the bride. **2** *Brit.* a woman who sells flowers, esp. in the street.

flow·er head *n.* a compact mass of flowers at the top of a stem, esp. a capitulum.

flow·er·ing /flówəring/ *adj.* (of a plant) capable of producing flowers.

flow·er·ing cur·rant *n.* an ornamental species of currant native to N. America.

flow·er peo·ple *n.* (esp. in the 1960s) hippies carrying or wearing flowers as symbols of peace and love.

flow·er·pot /flówərpot/ *n.* a pot in which a plant may be grown.

flow·er pow·er *n.* (esp. in the 1960s) the ideas of the flower people regarded as an instrument in changing the world.

flow·ers of sul·fur *n.pl. Chem.* a fine powder produced when sulfur evaporates and condenses.

flow·ers of zinc *n.pl.* = ZINC OXIDE.

flow·er·y /flówəree/ *adj.* **1** decorated with flowers or floral designs. **2** (of literary style, manner of speech, etc.) highly embellished; ornate. **3** full of flowers (*a flowery meadow*). □□ **flow·er·i·ness** *n.*

flow·ing /flóing/ *adj.* **1** (of literary style, etc.) fluent; easy. **2** (of a line, a curve, or a contour) smoothly continuous; not abrupt. **3** (of hair, a garment, a sail, etc.) unconfined. □□ **flow·ing·ly** *adv.*

flown *past part.* of FLY[1].

flow·stone /flóstōn/ *n.* rock deposited in a thin sheet by a flow of water.

fl. oz. *abbr.* fluid ounce(s).

FLQ *abbr.* Front de Libération du Québec.

flu /floo/ *n. colloq.* influenza. [abbr.]

flub /flub/ *v. & n. colloq.* ● *v.tr. & intr.* (**flubbed, flub·bing**) botch; bungle. ● *n.* something badly or clumsily done. [20th c.: orig. unkn.]

fluc·tu·ate /flúkchoo-ayt/ *v.intr.* vary irregularly; be unstable; vacillate; rise and fall. □□ **fluc·tu·a·tion** /–áyshən/ *n.* [L *fluctuare* f. *fluctus* flow, wave f. *fluere fluct-* flow]

flue /floo/ *n.* **1** a smoke duct in a chimney. **2** a channel for conveying heat, esp. a hot-air passage in a wall; a tube for heating water in some kinds of boiler. [16th c.: orig. unkn.]

flue-cure *v.tr.* cure (tobacco) by artificial heat from flues.

flu·ence /flóoəns/ *n. Brit. colloq.* influence. ● **put the fluence on** apply hypnotic, etc., suggestion to (a person). [shortening of INFLUENCE]

flu·en·cy /flóoənsee/ *n.* **1** a smooth, easy flow, esp. in speech or writing. **2** a ready command of words or of a specified foreign language.

flu·ent /flóoənt/ *adj.* **1 a** (of speech or literary style) flowing naturally and readily. **b** having command of a foreign language (*is fluent in German*). **c** able to speak quickly and easily. **2** flowing easily or gracefully (*the fluent line of her arabesque*). **3** *archaic* liable to change; unsettled. □□ **flu·ent·ly** *adv.* [L *fluere* flow]

flue pipe *n.* an organ pipe into which the air enters directly, not striking a reed.

fluff /fluf/ *n. & v.* ● *n.* **1** soft, light, feathery material coming off blankets, etc. **2** soft fur or feathers. **3** *sl.* **a** a mistake in delivering theatrical lines, in playing music, etc. **b** a mistake in playing a game. ● *v.* **1** *tr. & intr.* (often foll. by *up*) shake into or become a soft mass. **2** *tr. & intr. colloq.* make a mistake in (a theatrical part, a game, playing music, a speech, etc.); blunder (*fluffed his opening line*). **3** *tr.* make into fluff. **4** *tr.* put a soft surface on (the flesh side of leather). □ **bit of fluff** esp. *Brit. sl. offens.* a woman regarded as an object of sexual desire. [prob. dial. alt. of *flue* fluff]

fluff·y /flúfee/ *adj.* (**fluff·i·er, fluff·i·est**) **1** of or like fluff. **2** covered in fluff; downy. **3** nonintellectual; frivolous; superficial. □□ **fluff·i·ly** *adv.* **fluff·i·ness** *n.*

flu·gel·horn /flóogəlhawrn/ *n.* a valved brass wind instrument like a cornet but with a broader tone. [G *flügelhorn* f. *flügel* wing + *Horn* horn]

flu·id /flóoid/ *n. & adj.* ● *n.* **1** a substance, esp. a gas or liquid, lacking definite shape and capable of flowing and yielding to the slightest pressure. **2** a fluid part or secretion. ● *adj.* **1** able to flow and alter shape freely. **2** constantly changing or fluctuating (*the situation is fluid*). **3** (of a clutch, coupling, etc.) in which liquid is used to transmit power. □□ **flu·id·i·fy** /–ídifī/ *v.tr.* (**·fies, ·fied**). **flu·id·i·ty** /–íditee/ *n.* **flu·id·ly** *adv.* **flu·id·ness** *n.* [F *fluide* or L *fluidus* f. *fluere* flow]

flu·id dram *n.* a weight or measure formerly used by apothecaries, equivalent to one eighth of a fluid ounce.

flu·id·ics /flóoidiks/ *n.pl.* (usu. treated as *sing.*) the study and technique of using small interacting flows and fluid jets for functions usu. performed by electronic devices. □□ **flu·id·ic** *adj.*

flu·id·ize /flóoidiz/ *v.tr.* cause (a finely divided solid) to acquire the characteristics of a fluid by the upward passage of a gas, etc. □□ **flu·id·i·za·tion** /–dizáyshən/ *n.*

flu·id ounce *n.* **1** a unit of capacity equal to one-sixteenth of a pint (approx. 0.034 liter). **2** *Brit.* a unit of capacity equal to one-twentieth of a pint (approx. 0.028 liter).

flu·i·dram /flóoidram/ *n.* a fluid dram.

fluke[1] /flook/ *n. & v.* ● *n.* **1 a** a lucky accident (*won by a fluke*). **2** a chance breeze. ● *v.tr.* achieve by a fluke (*fluked that shot*). [19th c.: perh. f. dial. *fluke* guess]

fluke[2] /flook/ *n.* **1** any parasitic flatworm of the class Digenea or Monogenea, including liver flukes and blood flukes. **2** a flatfish, esp. a flounder. [OE *flōc*]

fluke[3] /flook/ *n.* **1** *Naut.* a broad triangular plate on the arm of an anchor. **2** the barbed head of a lance, harpoon, etc. **3** *Zool.* either of the lobes of a whale's tail. [16th c.: perh. f. FLUKE[2]]

fluk·y /flóokee/ *adj.* (**fluk·i·er, fluk·i·est**) of the nature of a fluke; obtained or occurring more by chance than skill. □□ **fluk·i·ly** *adv.* **fluk·i·ness** *n.*

flume /floom/ *n. & v.* ● *n.* **1 a** an artificial channel conveying water, etc., for industrial use. **b** a water slide into a swimming pool, etc. **2** a ravine with a stream. ● *v.* **1** *intr.* build flumes. **2** *tr.* convey down a flume. [ME f. OF *flum, flun* f. L *flumen* river f. *fluere* flow]

flum·mer·y /flúməree/ *n.* (*pl.* **·ies**) **1** empty compliments; trifles; nonsense. **2** any of various sweet dishes made with beaten eggs, sugar, etc. [Welsh *llymru*, of unkn. orig.]

flum·mox /flúməks/ *v.tr. colloq.* bewilder; confound; disconcert. [19th c.: prob. dial., imit.]

flump /flump/ *v. & n.* ● *v.* (often foll. by *down*) **1** *intr.* fall or move heavily. **2** *tr.* set or throw down with a heavy thud. ● *n.* the action or sound of flumping. [imit.]

flung *past* and *past part.* of FLING.

flunk /flungk/ *v. & n. colloq.* ● *v.tr.* **1 a** fail (an examination, etc.). **b** fail (an examination candidate). **2** *intr.* (often foll. by *out*) fail utterly; give up. ● *n.* an instance of flunking. □ **flunk out** be dismissed from school, etc., after failing an examination, course, etc. [cf. FUNK[1] and obs. *flink* be a coward]

flun·ky /flúngkee/ *n.* (also **flun·key**) (*pl.* **·kies** or **·keys**) usu. *derog.* **1** a liveried servant. **2** a toady. **3** a person who does menial work. [18th c. (orig. Sc.): perh. f. FLANK with the sense 'sidesman, flanker']

fluo·resce /flooréss, flaw–/ *v.intr.* be or become fluorescent.

fluo·res·cence /floorésəns, flaw–/ *n.* **1** the visible or invisible radiation produced from certain substances as a result of incident radiation of a shorter wavelength such as X rays, ultraviolet light, etc. **2** the property of absorbing light of short (invisible) wavelength and emitting light of longer (visible) wavelength. [FLUORSPAR (which fluoresces) after *opalescence*]

fluo·res·cent /floorésənt, flaw–/ *adj.* (of a substance) having or showing fluorescence. □ **fluorescent screen** a screen coated with fluorescent material to show images from X rays, etc.

SPELLING TIP **fluorescent**

See note at FLORESCENT.

fluo·res·cent lamp *n.* (also **fluorescent bulb**) a lamp or bulb radiating largely by fluorescence, esp. a tubular lamp in which phosphor on the inside surface of the tube is made to fluoresce by ultraviolet radiation from mercury vapor.

fluor·i·date /flóoridayt, fláw–/ *v.tr.* add traces of fluoride to (drinking water, etc.).

fluor·i·da·tion /flóoridáyshən, fláw–/ *n.* (also **fluor·i·di·za·tion**) the addition of traces of fluoride to drinking water in order to prevent or reduce tooth decay.

fluor·ide /flóorīd, fláw–/ *n.* any binary compound of fluorine.

fluor·i·nate /flóorinayt, fláw–/ *v.tr.* **1** = FLUORIDATE. **2** introduce fluorine into (a compound) (*fluorinated hydrocarbons*). ▫▫ **fluor·i·na·tion** /–náyshən/ *n.*

fluor·ine /flŏoreen, fláw–/ *n.* a poisonous pale yellow gaseous element of the halogen group occurring naturally in fluorite and cryolite, and the most reactive of all elements. ¶ Symb.: **f.** [F (as FLUORSPAR)]

fluo·rite /flŏorīt, fláw–/ *n.* a mineral form of calcium fluoride. [It. (as FLUORSPAR)]

fluoro- /flŏorō, fláw–/ *comb. form* **1** fluorine (*fluorocarbon*). **2** fluorescence (*fluoroscope*). [FLUORINE, FLUORESCENCE]

fluor·o·car·bon /flŏorōkaárbən, fláw–/ *n.* a compound formed by replacing one or more of the hydrogen atoms in a hydrocarbon with fluorine atoms.

fluor·o·scope /flŏorəskōp, fláw–/ *n.* an instrument with a fluorescent screen on which X-ray images may be viewed without taking and developing X-ray photographs.

fluo·ro·sis /flŏorṓsis, fláw–/ *n.* poisoning by fluorine or its compounds. [F *fluorose* (as FLUORO- 1)]

flu·or·spar /flŏorspaar, flŏr–/ *n.* = FLUORITE. [*fluor* a flow, any of the minerals used as fluxes, fluorspar, f. L *fluor* f. *fluere* flow + SPAR³]

flur·ry /flŏree, flúree/ *n. & v.* • *n.* (*pl.* **·ries**) **1** a gust or squall (esp. of snow). **2** a sudden burst of activity. **3** a commotion; excitement; nervous agitation (*a flurry of speculation; the flurry of the city*). • *v.tr.* (**·ries**, **·ried**) confuse by haste or noise; agitate. [imit.: cf. obs. *flurr* ruffle, *hurry*]

flush¹ /flush/ *v. & n.* • *v.* **1** *intr.* **a** blush; redden (*he flushed with embarrassment*). **b** glow with a warm color (*sky flushed pink*). **2** *tr.* (usu. as **flushed** *adj.*) cause to glow, blush, or be elated (often foll. by *with: flushed with pride*). **3** *tr.* **a** cleanse (a drain, toilet, etc.) by a rushing flow of water. **b** (often foll. by *away, down*) dispose of (an object) in this way (*flushed away the cigarette*). **4** *intr.* rush out; spurt. **5** *tr.* flood (*the river flushed the meadow*). **6** *intr.* (of a plant) throw out fresh shoots. • *n.* **1 a** a blush. **b** a glow of light or color. **2 a** a rush of water. **b** the cleansing of a drain, toilet, etc., by flushing. **3 a** a rush of emotion. **b** the elation produced by a victory, etc. (*the flush of triumph*). **4** sudden abundance. **5** freshness; vigor (*in the first flush of womanhood*). **6 a** (also **hot flush**) = HOT FLASH. **b** a feverish temperature. **c** facial redness, esp. caused by fever, alcohol, etc. **7** a fresh growth of grass, etc. ▫▫ **flush·er** *n.* [ME, perh. = FLUSH⁴ infl. by *flash* and *blush*]

flush² /flush/ *adj. & v.* • *adj.* **1** (often foll. by *with*) in the same plane; level; even (*the sink is flush with the counter; typed the numbers flush with the margin*). **2** (usu. *predic.*) *colloq.* **a** having plenty of money. **b** (of money) abundant; plentiful. **3** full to overflowing; in flood. • *v.tr.* **1** make (surfaces) level. **2** fill in (a joint) level with a surface. ▫▫ **flush·ness** *n.* [prob. f. FLUSH¹]

flush³ /flush/ *n.* a hand of cards all of one suit, esp. in poker. ▫ **royal flush** a straight flush in poker headed by an ace. **straight flush** a flush that is in numerical sequence. [OF *flus, flux* f. L *fluxus* FLUX]

flush⁴ /flush/ *v.* **1** *tr.* cause (esp. a game bird) to fly up. **2** *intr.* (of a bird) fly up and away. ▫ **flush out 1** reveal. **2** drive out. [ME, imit.: cf. *fly, rush*]

flus·ter /flústər/ *v. & n.* • *v.* **1** *tr. & intr.* make or become nervous or confused; flurry (*was flustered by the noise; he flusters easily*). **2** *tr.* confuse with drink; half-intoxicate. **3** *intr.* bustle. • *n.* a confused or agitated state. [ME: orig. unkn.: cf. Icel. *flaustr(a)* hurry, bustle]

flute /flŏot/ *n. & v.* • *n.* **1 a** a high-pitched woodwind instrument of metal or wood, having holes along it stopped by the fingers or keys, and held horizontally. **b** an organ stop having a similar sound. **c** any of various wind instruments resembling a flute. **d** a flute player. **2 a** *Archit.* an ornamental vertical groove in a column. **b** a trumpet-shaped frill on a dress, etc. **c** any similar cylindrical groove. **3** a tall narrow wineglass. • *v.* **1** *intr.* play the flute. **2** *intr.* speak, sing, or whistle in a fluting way. **3** *tr.* make flutes or grooves in. **4** *tr.* play (a tune, etc.) on a flute. ▫▫ **flute·like** *adj.* **flut·ing** *n.* **flut·ist** *n.* **flut·y** *adj.* (in sense 1a of *n.*). [ME f. OF *flëute, fläute, flahute*, prob. f. Prov. *fläut*]

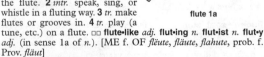

flute 1a

flut·ter /flútər/ *v. & n.* • *v.* **1 a** *intr.* flap the wings in flying or trying to fly (*butterflies fluttered in the sunshine*). **b** *tr.* flap (the wings). **2** *intr.*

fall with a quivering motion (*leaves fluttered to the ground*). **3** *intr. & tr.* move or cause to move irregularly or tremblingly (*the wind fluttered the flag*). **4** *intr.* go about restlessly; flit; hover. **5** *tr.* agitate; confuse. **6** *intr.* (of a pulse or heartbeat) beat feebly or irregularly. **7** *intr.* tremble with excitement or agitation. • *n.* **1 a** the act of fluttering. **b** an instance of this. **2** a tremulous state of excitement; a sensation (*was in a flutter; caused a flutter with his behavior*). **3** *Brit. sl.* a small bet, esp. on a horse. **4** an abnormally rapid but regular heartbeat. **5** *Aeron.* an undesired oscillation in a part of an aircraft, etc., under stress. **6** *Mus.* a rapid movement of the tongue (as when rolling one's *r*s) in playing a wind instrument. **7** *Electronics* a rapid variation of pitch, esp. of recorded sound (cf. WOW²). **8** a vibration. ▫ **flutter the dovecotes** esp. *Brit.* cause alarm among normally imperturbable people. ▫▫ **flut·ter·er** *n.* **flut·ter·y** *adj.* [OE *floterian, flotorian*, frequent. form rel. to FLEET⁵]

flu·vi·al /flŏoveeəl/ *adj.* of, found in, or produced by a river or rivers. [ME f. L *fluvialis* f. *fluvius* river f. *fluere* flow]

flu·vi·a·tile /flŏoveeətīl/ *adj.* of, found, or produced by rivers. [F f. L *fluviatilis* f. *fluviatus* moistened f. *fluvius*]

fluvio- /flŏoveeō/ *comb. form* river (*fluviometer*). [L *fluvius* river f. *fluere* flow]

flu·vi·o·gla·cial /flŏoveeōgláyshəl/ *adj.* of or caused by streams from glacial ice, or the combined action of rivers and glaciers.

flu·vi·om·e·ter /flŏoveeómitər/ *n.* an instrument for measuring the rise and fall of rivers.

flux /fluks/ *n. & v.* • *n.* **1** a process of flowing or flowing out. **2** an issue or discharge. **3** continuous change (*in a state of flux*). **4** *Metallurgy* a substance mixed with a metal, etc., to promote fusion. **5** *Physics* **a** the rate of flow of any fluid across a given area. **b** the amount of fluid crossing an area in a given time. **6** *Physics* the amount of radiation or particles incident on an area in a given time. **7** *Electr.* the total electric or magnetic field passing through a surface. **8** *Med.* an abnormal discharge of blood or excrement from the body. • *v.* **1** *tr. & intr.* make or become fluid. **2** *tr.* a fuse. **b** treat with a fusing flux. [ME f. OF *flux* or L *fluxus* f. *fluere* flux- flow]

flux·ion /flúkshən/ *n.* **1** an act or instance of flux or flowing. **2** *Math.* the rate at which a variable quantity changes; a derivative. [F *fluxion* or L *fluxio* (as FLUX)]

fly¹ /flī/ *v. & n.* • *v.* (**flies**; *past* **flew** /flŏo/; *past part.* **flown** /flōn/) **1** *intr.* move through the air under control, esp. with wings. **2** (of an aircraft or its occupants) **a** *intr.* travel through the air or through space. **b** *tr.* traverse (a region or distance) (*flew the English Channel*). **3** *tr.* **a** control the flight of (esp. an aircraft). **b** transport in an aircraft. **4** a *tr.* cause to fly or remain aloft. **b** *intr.* (of a flag, hair, etc.) wave or flutter. **5** *intr.* pass or rise quickly through the air or over an obstacle. **6** *intr.* go or move quickly; pass swiftly (*time flies*). **7** *intr.* **a** flee. **b** *colloq.* depart hastily. **8** *intr.* be driven or scattered; be forced off suddenly (*sent me flying; the door flew open*). **9** *intr.* (foll. by *at, upon*) **a** hasten or spring violently. **b** attack or criticize fiercely. **10** *tr.* flee from; escape in haste. **11** *intr.* *Baseball* hit a fly ball. • *n.* (*pl.* **·ies**) **1** an opening at the front of a pair of pants, closed with a zipper or buttons and covered with a flap. **2 a** a fabric cover pitched over a tent for extra protection from rain, etc. **b** a flap at the entrance of a tent. **3** (in *pl.*) the space over the proscenium in a theater. **4** the act or an instance of flying. **5** *Baseball* a fly ball. **6** (*pl.* usu. **flys**) *Brit. hist.* a one-horse hackney carriage. **7** a speed-regulating device in clockwork and machinery. ▫ **fly high 1** pursue a high ambition. **2** excel; prosper. **fly in the face of** openly disregard or disobey; conflict roundly with (probability, the evidence, etc.). **fly into a rage** (or **temper**, etc.) become suddenly or violently angry. **fly off the handle** *colloq.* lose one's temper suddenly and unexpectedly. ▫▫ **fly·a·ble** *adj.* [OE *flēogan* f. Gmc]

fly² /flī/ *n.* (*pl.* **flies**) **1** any insect of the order Diptera with two usu. transparent wings. **2** any other winged insect, e.g., a firefly or mayfly. **3** a disease of plants or animals caused by flies. **4** a natural or artificial fly used as bait in fishing. ▫ **fly in the ointment** a minor irritation that spoils enjoyment. **fly on the wall** an unnoticed observer. **like flies** in large numbers (usu. of people dying in an epidemic, etc.). **no flies on** *colloq.* nothing to diminish (a person's) astuteness. [OE *flȳge, flēoge* f. WG]

fly³ /flī/ *adj. Brit. sl.* knowing; clever; alert. ▫▫ **fly·ness** *n.* [19th c.: orig. unkn.]

fly ag·a·ric *n.* a poisonous fungus *Amanita Muscaria*, forming bright-red mushrooms with white flecks.

fly·a·way /flīəway/ *adj.* (of hair, etc.) tending to fly out or up; streaming.

fly ball *n. Baseball* a batted ball hit high in the air.

fly·blow /flíblō/ *n.* flies' eggs contaminating food, esp. meat.

fly·blown /flíblōn/ *adj.* tainted, esp. by flies.

fly-by *n.* (*pl.* **·bys**) **1** a flight past a position, esp. the approach of a spacecraft to a planet for observation. **2** = FLYOVER.

fly-by-night *adj. & n.* • *adj.* **1** unreliable. **2** short-lived. • *n.* an unreliable person.

fly·catch·er /flíkachər/ *n.* any bird of the families Tyrannidae and Muscicapidae, catching insects, esp. in short flights from a perch.

fly·er var. of FLIER.

fly-fishing *v.intr.* the sport of fishing using a rod and an artificial fly as bait. □□ **fly-fish** *v.intr.*

fly·ing /flí-ing/ *adj. & n.* ● *adj.* **1** fluttering or waving in the air; hanging loose. **2** hasty; brief (*a flying visit*). **3** designed for rapid movement. **4** (of an animal) able to make very long leaps by using winglike membranes, etc. ● *n.* flight, esp. in an aircraft. □ **with flying colors** with distinction.

fly·ing boat *n.* a seaplane with a boatlike fuselage.

fly·ing bomb *n.* = ROBOT BOMB.

fly·ing but·tress *n.* a buttress slanting from a separate column, usu. forming an arch with the wall it supports.

fly·ing doc·tor *n.* esp. *Austral.* a doctor (esp. in a large sparsely populated area) who visits distant patients by aircraft.

Fly·ing Dutch·man *n.* **1** a legendary Dutch ghost ship supposedly seen in the region of the Cape of Good Hope and presaging disaster. **2** the captain of this ship.

fly·ing fish *n.* any tropical fish of the family Exocoetidae, with winglike pectoral fins for gliding through the air.

fly·ing fox *n.* any of various fruit-eating bats esp. of the genus *Pteropus*, with a foxlike head.

fly·ing le·mur *n.* either of two mammals of the genus *Cynocephalus* of S. Asia, with a lemurlike appearance and having a membrane between the fore and hind limbs for gliding from tree to tree.

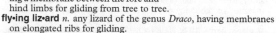
flying fish

fly·ing liz·ard *n.* any lizard of the genus *Draco*, having membranes on elongated ribs for gliding.

fly·ing pha·lan·ger *n.* any of various phalangers having a membrane between the fore and hind limbs for gliding.

fly·ing sau·cer *n.* any unidentified, esp. circular, flying object, popularly supposed to have come from space.

fly·ing squir·rel *n.* any of various squirrels, esp. of the genera *Glaucomys Pteromys*, with skin joining the fore and hind limbs for gliding from tree to tree.

fly·ing start *n.* **1** a start (of a race, etc.) in which the starting point is passed at full speed. **2** a vigorous start giving an initial advantage.

fly·ing wing *n.* an aircraft with little or no fuselage and no tail assembly.

fly·leaf /flíleef/ *n.* (*pl.* **·leaves**) a blank leaf at the beginning or end of a book.

fly·o·ver /flíōvər/ *n.* **1** a ceremonial flight of aircraft past a person or a place. **2** *Brit.* a bridge carrying one road or railroad over another.

fly·pa·per /flípaypər/ *n.* sticky treated paper for catching flies.

fly-past *n. Brit.* = FLYOVER.

fly-post *v.tr. Brit.* display (posters, etc.) rapidly in unauthorized places.

fly·sheet /flísheet/ *n.* **1** a tract or circular of two or four pages. **2** *Brit.* = FLY *n.* 2a.

fly swat·ter *n.* an implement for killing flies and other insects, usu. consisting of a flat mesh square attached to a handle.

fly-tip *v.intr. Brit.* illegally dump (waste). □□ **fly-tip·per** *n.*

fly·trap /flítrap/ *n.* any of various plants that catch flies, esp. the Venus flytrap.

fly·weight /flíwayt/ *n.* **1** a weight in certain sports intermediate between light flyweight and bantamweight. **2** a boxer, wrestler, etc., of this weight.

fly·wheel /flíhweel, –weel/ *n.* a heavy wheel on a revolving shaft used to regulate machinery or accumulate power.

FM *abbr.* **1** frequency modulation. **2** Field Marshal.

Fm *symb. Chem.* the element fermium.

fm. *abbr.* (also **fm**) fathom(s).

FNMA /fáneemáy/ *n.* Federal National Mortgage Association.

f-num·ber /éf numbər/ *n.* (also **f-stop**) *Photog.* the ratio of the focal length to the effective diameter of a lens (e.g., *f*/5, indicating that the focal length is five times the diameter). [*f* (denoting focal length) + NUMBER]

FO *abbr.* **1** financial officer. **2** *hist.* (in the UK) Foreign Office.

foal /fōl/ *n. & v.* ● *n.* the young of a horse or related animal. ● *v.tr.* (of a mare, etc.) give birth to (a foal). □ **in** (or **with**) **foal** (of a mare, etc.) pregnant. [OE *fola* f. Gmc: cf. FILLY]

foam /fōm/ *n. & v.* ● *n.* **1** a mass of small bubbles formed on or in liquid by agitation, fermentation, etc. **2** a froth of saliva or sweat. **3** a substance resembling these, e.g., rubber or plastic in a cellular mass. **4** the sea. ● *v.intr.* **1** emit foam; froth. **2** run with foam. **3** (of a vessel) be filled and overflow with foam. □ **foam at the mouth** be very angry. □□ **foam·less** *adj.* **foam·y** *adj.* (**foam·i·er, foam·i·est**). [OE *fām* f. WG]

foam rub·ber *n.* a light, spongy foam used for mattresses, pillows, cushions, etc.

fob[1] /fob/ *n. & v.* ● *n.* **1** (in full **fob chain**) a chain attached to a watch for carrying in a waistcoat or pocket. **2** a small pocket for carrying

a watch. **3** a tab on a key ring. ● *v.tr.* (**fobbed, fob·bing**) put in one's fob; pocket. [orig. cant, prob. f. G]

fob[2] /fob/ *v.tr.* (**fobbed, fob·bing**) cheat; deceive. □ **fob off 1** (often foll. by *with* a thing) deceive into accepting something inferior. **2** (often foll. by *on to* a person) palm or pass off (an inferior thing). [16th c.: cf. obs. *fop* to dupe, G *foppen* to banter]

f.o.b. *abbr.* free on board.

fo·cal /fókəl/ *adj.* of, at, or in terms of a focus. [mod.L *focalis* (as FOCUS)]

fo·cal·ize /fókəliz/ *v.tr.* = FOCUS *v.* □□ **fo·cal·i·za·tion** /–lizáyshən/ *n.*

fo·cal length *n.* the distance between the center of a mirror or lens and its focus.

fo·cal plane *n.* the plane through the focus perpendicular to the axis of a mirror or lens.

fo·cal point *n.* = FOCUS *n.* 1.

fo·c's·le var. of FORECASTLE.

fo·cus /fókəs/ *n. & v.* ● *n.* (*pl.* **fo·cus·es** or **fo·ci** /fósī/) **1** *Physics* **a** the point at which rays or waves meet after reflection or refraction. **b** the point from which diverging rays or waves appear to proceed. Also called **focal point. 2 a** *Optics* the point at which an object must be situated for an image of it given by a lens or mirror to be well defined (*bring into focus*). **b** the adjustment of the eye or a lens necessary to produce a clear image (*the binoculars were not in focus*). **c** a state of clear definition (*the photograph was out of focus*). **3** the center of interest or activity (*focus of attention*). **4** *Geom.* one of the points from which the distances to any point of a given curve are connected by a linear relation. **5** *Med.* the principal site of an infection or other disease. **6** *Geol.* the place of origin of an earthquake. ● *v.* (**fo·cused, fo·cus·ing** or **fo·cussed, fo·cus·sing**) **1** *tr.* bring into focus. **2** *tr.* adjust the focus of (a lens, the eye, etc.). **3** *tr. & intr.* (often foll. by *on*) concentrate or be concentrated on. **4** *intr. & tr.* converge or make converge to a focus. □□ **fo·cus·er** *n.* [L, = hearth]

fo·cus group *n.* a group that meets to discuss a particular problem, issue, etc.

fod·der /fódər/ *n. & v.* ● *n.* dried hay or straw, etc., for cattle, horses, etc. ● *v.tr.* give fodder to. [OE *fōdor* f. Gmc, rel. to FOOD]

foe /fō/ *n.* an enemy or opponent. [OE *fāh* hostile, rel. to FEUD[1]]

foehn /fön/ *n.* (also **föhn**) **1** a hot southerly wind on the northern slopes of the Alps. **2** a warm dry wind on the lee side of mountains. [G, ult. f. L *Favonius* mild west wind]

foet·id var. of FETID.

foe·tus *Brit.* var. of FETUS.

fog[1] /fawg, fog/ *n. & v.* ● *n.* **1 a** a thick cloud of water droplets or smoke suspended in the atmosphere at or near the earth's surface restricting or obscuring visibility. **b** obscurity in the atmosphere caused by this. **2** *Photog.* cloudiness on a developed negative, etc., obscuring the image. **3** an uncertain or confused position or state. ● *v.* (**fogged, fog·ging**) **1** *tr.* **a** (often foll. by *up*) cover with fog or condensed vapor. **b** bewilder or confuse as if with a fog. **2** *intr.* (often foll. by *up*) become covered with fog or condensed vapor. **3** *tr. Photog.* make (a negative, etc.) obscure or cloudy. □ **in a fog** puzzled; at a loss. [perh. back-form. f. FOGGY]

fog[2] /fawg, fog/ *n.* **1** *v.* esp. *Brit.* **1** a second growth of grass after cutting; aftermath. **2** long grass left standing in winter. ● *v.tr.* (**fogged, fog·ging**) **1** leave (land) under fog. **2** feed (cattle) on fog. [ME: orig. unkn.]

fog bank *n.* a mass of fog at sea or in the distance.

fog·bound /fáwgbownd, fóg–/ *adj.* unable to proceed because of fog.

fog·bow /fáwgbō, fóg–/ *n.* a manifestation like a rainbow, produced by light on fog.

fo·gey var. of FOGY.

fog·gy /fáwgee, fógee/ *adj.* (**fog·gi·er, fog·gi·est**) **1** (of the atmosphere) thick or obscure with fog. **2** of or like fog. **3** vague; confused; unclear. □ **not have the foggiest** *colloq.* have no idea at all. □□ **fog·gi·ly** *adv.* **fog·gi·ness** *n.*

fog·horn /fáwghawrn, fóg–/ *n.* **1** a deep-sounding instrument for warning ships in fog. **2** *colloq.* a loud penetrating voice.

fo·gy /fógee/ *n.* (also **fo·gey**) (*pl.* **·gies** or **·geys**) a dull old-fashioned person (esp. old fogy). □□ **fo·gy·dom** *n.* **fo·gy·ish** *adj.* [18th c.: rel. to sl. *fogram*, of unkn. orig.]

föhn var. of FOEHN.

foi·ble /fóybəl/ *n.* **1** a minor weakness or idiosyncrasy. **2** *Fencing* the part of a sword blade from the middle to the point (cf. FORTE[1] 2). [F, obs. form of *faible* (as FEEBLE)]

foie gras /fwaa graá/ *n. colloq.* = PÂTÉ DE FOIE GRAS.

foil[1] /foyl/ *v. & n.* ● *v.tr.* **1** frustrate; baffle; defeat. **2** *Hunting* **a** a run over or cross (ground or a scent) to confuse the hounds. **b** (*absol.*) (of an animal) spoil the scent in this way. ● *n.* **1** *Hunting* the track of a hunted animal. **2** *archaic* a repulse or defeat. [ME, = trample down, perh. f. OF *fouler* to full cloth, trample, ult. f. L *fullo* FULLER[1]]

foil² /foyl/ n. **1 a** metal hammered or rolled into a thin sheet (*tin foil*). **b** a sheet of this or another material attached to mirror glass as a reflector. **c** a leaf of foil placed under a precious stone, etc., to brighten or color it. **2** a person or thing that enhances the qualities of another by contrast. **3** *Archit.* a leaf-shaped curve formed by the cusping of an arch or circle. [ME f. OF f. L *folium* leaf, and f. OF *foille* f. L *folia* (pl.)]

foil³ /foyl/ n. a light blunt-edged sword with a button on its point used in fencing. [16th c.: orig. unkn.]

foil⁴ /foyl/ n. = HYDROFOIL. [abbr.]

foist /foyst/ v.tr. **1** (foll. by *on, upon*) impose (an unwelcome person or thing). **2** (foll. by *on, upon*) falsely fix the authorship of (a composition). **3** (foll. by *in, into*) introduce surreptitiously or unwarrantably. [orig. of palming a false die, f. Du. dial. *vuisten* take in the hand f. *vuist* FIST]

fol. abbr. folio.

fol·a·cin /fóləsin/ n. = FOLIC ACID. [*folic* acid + –IN]

fold¹ /fōld/ v. & n. • v. **1** tr. **a** bend or close (a flexible thing) over upon itself. **b** (foll. by *back, over, down*) bend a part of (a flexible thing) in the manner specified (*fold down the flap*). **2** intr. become or be able to be folded. **3** tr. (foll. by *away, up*) make compact by folding. **4** intr. colloq. **a** collapse; disintegrate. **b** (of an enterprise) fail; go bankrupt. **5** tr. poet. embrace (esp. fold in the arms or to the breast). **6** tr. (foll. by *about, around*) clasp (the arms); wrap; envelop. **7** tr. (foll. by *in*) mix (an ingredient with others) using a gentle cutting and turning motion. • n. **1** the act or an instance of folding. **2** a line made by or for folding. **3** a folded part. **4** esp. Brit. a hollow among hills. **5** Geol. a curvature of strata. □ **fold one's arms** place one's arms across the chest, side by side or entwined. **fold one's hands** clasp them. □□ **fold·a·ble** adj. [OE *falden, fealden* f. Gmc]

fold² /fōld/ n. & v. • n. **1** = SHEEPFOLD. **2** a body of believers or members of a church. • v.tr. enclose (sheep) in a fold. [OE *fald*]

-fold /fōld/ suffix forming adjectives and adverbs from cardinal numbers, meaning: **1** in an amount multiplied by (*repaid tenfold*). **2** consisting of so many parts (*threefold blessing*). [OE –*fald, –feald*, rel. to FOLD¹: orig. sense 'folded in so many layers']

fold·a·way /fōldəway/ adj. adapted or designed to be folded away.

fold·er /fōldər/ n. **1** a folding cover or holder for loose papers. **2** a folded leaflet.

fol·de·rol var. of FALDERAL.

fold·ing door n. a door with jointed sections, folding on itself when opened.

fold·ing mon·ey n. colloq. paper money.

fold·out /fōldowt/ n. an oversize page in a book, etc., to be unfolded by the reader.

fo·li·a·ceous /fólee–áyshəs/ adj. **1** of or like leaves. **2** having organs like leaves. **3** laminated. [L *foliaceus* leafy f. *folium* leaf]

fo·li·age /fóleeij/ n. **1** leaves; leafage. **2** a design in art resembling leaves. [ME f. F *feuillage* f. *feuille* leaf f. OF *foille*: see FOIL²]

fo·li·age leaf n. a leaf excluding petals and other modified leaves.

fo·li·ar /fóleeər/ adj. of or relating to leaves. [mod.L *foliaris* f. L *folium* leaf]

fo·li·ar feed n. feed supplied to leaves of plants.

fo·li·ate adj. & v. • adj. /fóleeət/ **1** leaflike. **2** having leaves. **3** (in comb.) having a specified number of leaflets (*trifoliate*). • v. /fóleeayt/ **1** intr. split into laminae. **2** tr. decorate with foils. **3** tr. number leaves (not pages) of (a volume) consecutively. □□ **fo·li·a·tion** /–áyshən/ n. [L *foliatus* leaved f. *folium* leaf]

fol·ic ac·id /fólik, fól–/ n. a vitamin of the B complex, found in leafy green vegetables, liver, and kidney, a deficiency of which causes pernicious anemia. Also called **folacin** or **pteroylglutamic acid**. [L *folium* leaf (because found esp. in green leaves) + –IC]

fo·li·o /fóleeō/ n. & adj. • n. (pl. **·os**) **1** a leaf of paper, etc., esp. one numbered only on the front. **2 a** a leaf number of a book. **b** a page number of a book. **3** a sheet of paper folded once making two leaves of a book. **4** a book made of such sheets. • adj. (of a book) made of folios, of the largest size. □ **in folio** made of folios. [L, ablat. of *folium* leaf, = *on leaf* (as specified)]

fo·li·ole /fóleeōl/ n. a division of a compound leaf; a leaflet. [F f. LL *foliolum* dimin. of *folium* leaf]

folk /fōk/ n. (pl. **folk** or **folks**) **1** (treated as pl.) people in general or of a specified class (*few folks about; townsfolk*). **2** (in pl.) (usu. **folks**) one's parents or relatives. **3** (treated as sing.) a people. **4** (treated as sing.) colloq. traditional music, esp. a style featuring acoustic guitar. **5** (attrib.) of popular origin; traditional (*folk art*). [OE *folc* f. Gmc]

folk dance n. **1** a dance of traditional origin. **2** the music for such a dance.

folk et·y·mol·o·gy n. a popular modifying of the form of a word or phrase to make it seem to be derived from a more familiar word (e.g., *woodchuck* from Algonquian *otchek*).

folk·ish /fókish/ adj. of the common people; traditional; unsophisticated.

folk·lore /fóklawr/ n. the traditional beliefs and stories of a people; the study of these. □□ **folk·lor·ic** adj. **folk·lor·ist** n. **folk·lor·is·tic** adj.

folk mem·o·ry n. recollection of the past persisting among a people.

folk mu·sic n. music that originates in traditional popular culture, typically of unknown authorship and transmitted orally from generation to generation.

folk sing·er n. a singer of folk songs.

folk song n. a song of popular or traditional origin or style.

folk·sy /fóksee/ adj. (**folk·si·er, folk·si·est**) **1** friendly; sociable; informal. **2 a** having the characteristics of folk art, culture, etc. **b** ostensibly or artificially folkish. □□ **folk·si·ness** n.

folk tale n. a popular or traditional story.

folk·ways /fókwayz/ n.pl. the traditional behavior of a people.

folk·y /fókee/ adj. (**folk·i·er, folk·i·est**) **1** = FOLKSY **2**. **2** = FOLKISH. □□ **folk·i·ness** n.

fol·li·cle /fólikəl/ n. **1** a small sac or vesicle. **2** a small sac-shaped secretory gland or cavity. **3** Bot. a single-carpelled dry fruit opening on one side only to release its seeds. □□ **fol·lic·u·lar** /folíkyələr/ adj. **fol·lic·u·late** /folíkyələt, –layt/ adj. **fol·lic·u·lat·ed** /–laytid/ adj. [L *folliculus* dimin. of *follis* bellows]

fol·low /fólō/ v. **1** tr. or (foll. by *after*) intr. go or come after (a person or thing proceeding ahead). **2** tr. go along (a route, path, etc.). **3** tr. & intr. come after in order or time (*Clinton followed Bush; dessert followed; my reasons are as follows*). **4** tr. take as a guide or leader. **5** tr. conform to (*follow your example*). **6** tr. practice (a trade or profession). **7** tr. undertake (a course of study, etc.). **8** tr. understand the meaning or tendency of (a speaker or argument). **9** tr. maintain awareness of the current state or progress of (events, etc., in a particular sphere). **10** tr. (foll. by *with*) provide with a sequel or successor. **11** intr. happen after something else; ensue. **12** intr. **a** be necessarily true as a result of something else. **b** (foll. by *from*) be a result of. **13** tr. strive after; aim at; pursue (*followed fame and fortune*). □ **follow one's nose** trust to instinct. **follow on 1** continue. **2** (of a cricket team) have to bat again immediately after the first innings. **follow out** carry out; adhere precisely to (instructions, etc.). **follow suit 1** Cards play a card of the suit led. **2** conform to another person's actions. **follow through 1** continue (an action, etc.) to its conclusion. **2** Sports continue the movement of a stroke after the ball has been struck. **follow up 1** (foll. by *with*) pursue; develop; supplement. **2** make further investigation of. [OE *folgian* f. Gmc]

fol·low·er /fólōər/ n. **1** an adherent or devotee. **2** a person or thing that follows.

fol·low·ing /fólōing/ prep., n., & adj. • prep. coming after in time; as a sequel to. • n. a body of adherents or devotees. • adj. that follows or comes after.

fol·low-on n. the action of occurring as a consequence or result of something (*follow-on treatment*).

fol·low the lead·er n. a children's game in which players copy the actions and words of a person who has been chosen as leader.

follow-through n. the continuing of an action or task to its conclusion.

follow-up n. a subsequent or continued action, measure, experience, etc.

fol·ly /fólee/ n. (pl. **·lies**) **1** foolishness; lack of good sense. **2** a foolish act, behavior, idea, etc. **3** an ornamental building, usu. a tower or mock Gothic ruin. **4** (in pl.) Theatr. **a** a revue with glamorous female performers, esp. scantily clad. **b** the performers. [ME f. OF *folie* f. *fol* mad, FOOL¹]

fo·ment /fōmént/ v.tr. **1** instigate or stir up (trouble, sedition, etc.). **2 a** bathe with warm or medicated liquid. **b** apply warmth to. □□ **fo·ment·er** n. [ME f. F *fomenter* f. LL *fomentare* f. L *fomentum* poultice, lotion f. *fovēre* heat, cherish]

fo·men·ta·tion /fómentáyshən/ n. **1** the act or an instance of fomenting. **2** materials prepared for application to a wound, etc. [ME f. OF or LL *fomentatio* (as FOMENT)]

fond /fond/ adj. **1** (foll. by *of*) having affection for or a liking for. **2** affectionate; loving; doting. **3** (of beliefs, etc.) foolishly optimistic or credulous; naive. □□ **fond·ly** adv. **fond·ness** n. [ME f. obs. *fon* fool, be foolish]

fon·dant /fóndənt/ n. a soft creamy candy of flavored sugar. [F, pres. part. of *fondre* melt f. L *fundere* pour]

fon·dle /fónd'l/ v.tr. touch or stroke lovingly; caress. □□ **fon·dler** n. [back-form. f. *fondling* fondled person (as FOND, –LING¹)]

fon·due /fondóo, –dyóo/ n. **1** a dish of flavored melted cheese. **2** a dish of small pieces of food cooked at the table by dipping in hot melted chocolate, cheese, etc. [F, fem. past part. of *fondre* melt f. L *fundere* pour]

font¹ /font/ n. **1** a receptacle in a church for baptismal water. **2** the reservoir for oil in a lamp. □□ **font·al** adj. (in sense 1). [OE *font, fant* f. OIr. *fant, font* f. L *fons fontis* fountain, baptismal water]

font² /font/ Printing a set of type of one face or size. [F *fonte* f. *fondre* FOUND³]

fon·ta·nel /fóntənél/ n. (esp. Brit. **fon·ta·nelle**) a membranous space in an infant's skull at the angles of the parietal bones. [F *fontanelle* f. mod.L *fontanella* f. OF *fontenelle* dimin. of *fontaine* fountain]

fonts (typefaces)

SERIF

Bookman
abcdefghijklmnopqrstuvwxyz 1234567890
ABCDEFGHIJKLMNOPQRSTUVWXYZ

Times
abcdefghijklmnopqrstuvwxyz 1234567890
ABCDEFGHIJKLMNOPQRSTUVWXYZ

SANS SERIF

Helvetica
abcdefghijklmnopqrstuvwxyz 1234567890
ABCDEFGHIJKLMNOPQRSTUVWXYZ

Avant Garde
abcdefghijklmnopqrstuvwxyz 1234567890
ABCDEFGHIJKLMNOPQRSTUVWXYZ

SQUARE SERIF

Courier
abcdefghijklmnopqrstuvwxyz 1234567890
ABCDEFGHIJKLMNOPQRSTUVWXYZ

SCRIPT

Boulevard
abcdefghijklmnopqrstuvwxyz 1234567890
ABCDEFGHIJKLMNOPQRSTU-
VWXYZ

DISPLAY

ITC Kabel Ultra
abcdefghijklmnopqrstuvwxyz 1234567890
ABCDEFGHIJKLMNOPQRSTUVWXYZ

food /fŏŏd/ *n.* **1** a nutritious substance, esp. solid in form, that can be taken into an animal or a plant to maintain life and growth. **2** ideas as a resource for or stimulus to mental work (*food for thought*). [OE *fōda* f. Gmc: cf. FEED]

food ad•di•tive *n.* a substance added to food to enhance its color, flavor, or presentation, or for any other nonnutritional purpose.

food chain *n. Ecol.* a series of organisms each dependent on the next for food.

food•ie /fŏŏdee/ *n.* (also **food•y**) (*pl.* **•ies**) *colloq.* a person who is particular about food; a gourmet.

food poi•son•ing *n.* illness caused by bacteria or other toxins in food, usu. with vomiting and diarrhea.

food pro•ces•sor *n.* an electric kitchen appliance used for chopping, mixing, or puréeing foods.

food pyr•a•mid *n.* **1** an ecological model of the food chain, with green plants at the base and predators at the apex. **2** a dietary model of recommended foods, with carbohydrates at the base and fats and sugars at the apex.

food•stuff /fŏŏdstuf/ *n.* any substance suitable as food.

fool[1] /fŏŏl/ *n., v., & adj.* ● *n.* **1** a person who acts unwisely or imprudently; a stupid person. **2** *hist.* a jester; a clown. **3** a dupe. **4** (often foll. by *for*) a devotee or fan (*a fool for the ballet*). ● *v.* **1** *tr.* deceive so as to cause to appear foolish. **2** *tr.* (foll. by *into* + verbal noun, or *out of*) trick; cause to do something foolish. **3** *tr.* play tricks on; dupe. **4** *intr.* act in a joking, frivolous, or teasing way. **5** *intr.* (foll. by *around*) behave in a playful or silly way. ● *adj. colloq.* foolish; silly. □ **act** (or **play**) **the fool** behave in a silly way. **make a fool of** make (a person or oneself) look foolish; trick or deceive. **no** (or **nobody's**) **fool** a shrewd or prudent person. [ME f. OF *fol* f. L *follis* bellows, empty-headed person]

fool[2] /fŏŏl/ *n.* esp. *Brit.* a dessert of usu. stewed fruit crushed and mixed with cream, custard, etc. [16th c.: perh. f. FOOL[1]]

fool•er•y /fŏŏləree/ *n.* (*pl.* **•ies**) **1** foolish behavior. **2** a foolish act.

fool•har•dy /fŏŏlhaardee/ *adj.* (**fool•har•di•er**, **fool•har•di•est**) rashly or foolishly bold; reckless. □□ **fool•har•di•ly** *adv.* **fool•har•di•ness** *n.* [ME f. OF *folhardi* f. *fol* foolish + *hardi* bold]

fool•ish /fŏŏlish/ *adj.* (of a person, action, etc.) lacking good sense or judgment; unwise. □□ **fool•ish•ly** *adv.* **fool•ish•ness** *n.*

fool•proof /fŏŏlproof/ *adj.* (of a procedure, mechanism, etc.) so straightforward or simple as to be incapable of misuse or mistake.

fools•cap /fŏŏlskap/ *n. Brit.* a size of paper, about 330 x 200 (or 400) mm. [named from the former watermark representing a fool's cap]

fool's er•rand *n.* a fruitless venture.

fool's gold *n.* iron pyrites, having a brassy yellow color than can be mistaken for gold.

fool's par•a•dise *n.* happiness founded on an illusion.

fool's pars•ley *n.* a species of hemlock resembling parsley.

foot /fŏŏt/ *n. & v.* ● *n.* (*pl.* **feet** /feet/) **1 a** the lower extremity of the leg below the ankle. **b** the part of a sock, etc., covering the foot. **2 a** the lower or lowest part of anything, e.g., a mountain, a page, stairs, etc. **b** the lower end of a table. **c** the end of a bed where the user's feet normally rest. **3** the base, often projecting, of anything extending vertically. **4** a step, pace, or tread; a manner of walking (*fleet of foot*). **5** (*pl.* **foot** or **feet**) a unit of linear measure equal to 12 inches (30.48 cm). **6** *Prosody* **a** a group of syllables (one usu. stressed) constituting a metrical unit. **b** a similar unit of speech, etc. **7** *Brit. hist.* infantry (*a regiment of foot*). **8** *Zool.* the locomotive or adhesive organ of invertebrates. **9** *Bot.* the part by which a petal is attached. **10** a device on a sewing machine for holding the material steady as it is sewn. **11** (*pl.* **foots**) dregs; oil refuse. **12** (usu. in *pl.*) footlights. ● *v. tr.* **1** (as **foot it**) a traverse (esp. a long distance) by foot. **b** dance. **2** pay (a bill, esp. one considered large). □ **at a person's feet** as a person's disciple or subject. **feet of clay** a fundamental weakness in a person otherwise revered. **get one's feet wet** begin to participate. **have one's** (or **both**) **feet on the ground** be practical. **have a foot in the door** have a prospect of success. **have one foot in the grave** be near death or very old. **my foot!** *int.* expressing strong contradiction. **off one's feet** so as to be unable to stand, or in a state compared with this (*was rushed off my feet*). **on one's feet** standing or walking. **on foot** walking; not riding, etc. **put one's best foot forward** make every effort; proceed with determination. **put one's feet up** *colloq.* take a rest. **put one's foot down** *colloq.* **1** be firmly insistent or repressive. **2** accelerate a motor vehicle. **put one's foot in it** *colloq.* commit a blunder or indiscretion. **set foot in** (or **on**) enter; go into. □□ **foot•ed** *adj.* (also in *comb.*). **foot•less** *adj.* [OE *fōt* f. Gmc]

foot•age /fŏŏtij/ *n.* **1** length or distance in feet. **2** an amount of film made for showing, broadcasting, etc.

foot-and-mouth dis•ease *n.* a contagious viral disease of cattle and other hoofed animals, causing ulceration of the hoofs and around the mouth.

foot•ball /fŏŏtbawl/ *n. & v.* ● *n.* **1** any of several outdoor games between two teams played with a ball on a field with goals at each end. **2** a large inflated ball of a kind used in these. **3** a topical issue or problem that is the subject of continued argument or controversy. ● *v. intr.* play football. □□ **foot•ball•er** *n.*

▶In N. America, **football** generally refers to American football, but elsewhere the word is used to refer to soccer or rugby.

foot•ball pool *n.* a form of gambling on the results of football games, the winners receiving sums accumulated from entry money.

foot•board /fŏŏtbawrd/ *n.* **1** a board to support the feet or a foot. **2** an upright board at the foot of a bed.

foot•brake /fŏŏtbrayk/ *n.* a brake operated by the foot in a motor vehicle.

foot•bridge /fŏŏtbrij/ *n.* a bridge for use by pedestrians.

foot•er[1] /fŏŏtər/ *n.* (in *comb.*) a person or thing of so many feet in length or height (*six-footer*).

foot•er[2] /fŏŏtər/ *n. Brit. colloq.* = FOOTBALL 1.

foot•fall /fŏŏtfawl/ *n.* the sound of a footstep.

foot fault *n.* (in tennis) incorrect placement of the feet while serving.

foot•hill /fŏŏt-hil/ *n.* (often in *pl.*) any of the low hills around the base of a mountain.

foot•hold /fŏŏt-hōld/ *n.* **1** a place, esp. in climbing, where a foot can be supported securely. **2** a secure initial position or advantage.

foot•ing /fŏŏting/ *n.* **1** a foothold; a secure position (*lost his footing*). **2** the basis on which an enterprise is established or operates; the position or status of a person in relation to others (*on an equal footing*). **3** the foundation of a wall, usu. with a course of brickwork wider than the base of the wall.

foot•le /fŏŏt'l/ *v. intr.* (usu. foll. by *around, about*) *colloq.* behave foolishly or trivially. [19th c.: perh. f. dial. *footer* idle]

foot•lights /fŏŏtlits/ *n. pl.* a row of lights along the front of a stage at the level of the actors' feet.

foot•ling /fŏŏtling/ *adj. colloq.* trivial; silly.

foot•lock•er /fŏŏtlokər/ *n.* a small trunk usu. kept at the foot of a soldier's or camper's bunk to hold items of clothing or equipment.

foot•loose /fŏŏtloos/ *adj.* free to go where or act as one pleases.

foot•man /fŏŏtmən/ *n.* (*pl.* **•men**) **1** a liveried servant attending at the door, at table, or on a carriage. **2** *hist.* an infantryman.

foot•mark /fŏŏtmaark/ *n.* a footprint.

foot•note /fŏŏtnōt/ *n. & v.* ● *n.* **1** an additional piece of information printed at the bottom of a page. **2** a thing that is additional or less important (*a mere footnote in history*). ● *v. tr.* add a footnote or footnotes to (a piece of writing).

foot•pad /fŏŏtpad/ *n. hist.* an unmounted highwayman.

foot•path /fŏŏtpath/ *n.* **1** a trail or path for pedestrians (in the woods, etc.). **2** *Brit.* a path for pedestrians; a pavement.

foot•plate /fŏŏtplayt/ *n.* esp. *Brit.* the platform in the cab of a locomotive for the crew.

foot-pound *n.* the amount of energy required to raise 1 lb. a distance of 1 foot.

foot-pound-second system *n.* a system of measurement with the foot, pound, and second as basic units.

foot•print /fŏŏtprint/ *n.* **1** the impression left by a foot or shoe. **2** *Computing* the area of desk space, etc., occupied by a computer or other piece of hardware. **3** the ground area covered by a communications satellite or affected by noise, etc., from aircraft.

foot•race /fŏŏtrays/ *n.* a race run by people on foot.

foot•rest /fŏŏtrest/ *n.* a support for the feet or a foot.

foot rot *n.* a bacterial disease of the feet in sheep and cattle.

foot•sie /fŏŏtsee/ *n. colloq.* amorous play with the feet. [joc. dimin. of FOOT]

foot•slog /fŏŏtslog/ *v. & n. Brit.* ● *v. intr.* (**•slogged**, **•slog•ging**) walk or march, esp. laboriously for a long distance. ● *n.* a laborious walk or march. □□ **foot•slog•ger** *n.*

foot sol•dier *n.* a soldier who fights on foot.

foot•sore /fŏŏtsawr/ *adj.* having sore feet, esp. from walking.

foot•stalk /fŏŏtstawk/ *n.* **1** *Bot.* a stalk of a leaf or peduncle of a flower. **2** *Zool.* an attachment of a barnacle, etc.

foot•step /fŏŏtstep/ *n.* **1** a step taken in walking. **2** the sound of this. □ **follow** (or **tread**) **in a person's footsteps** do as another person did before.

foot•stool /fŏŏtstool/ *n.* a stool for resting the feet on when sitting.

foot•way /fŏŏtway/ *n. Brit.* a path or way for pedestrians.

foot•wear /fŏŏtwair/ *n.* shoes, socks, etc.

foot•work /fŏŏtwərk/ *n.* the use of the feet, esp. skillfully, in sports, dancing, etc.

fop /fop/ *n.* an affectedly elegant or fashionable man; a dandy. □□ **fop•per•y** *n.* **fop•pish** *adj.* **fop•pish•ly** *adv.* **fop•pish•ness** *n.* [17th c.: perh. f. earlier *fop* fool]

for /fawr, fər/ *prep. & conj.* ● *prep.* **1** in the interest or to the benefit of; intended to go to (*these flowers are for you; wish to see it for myself; did it all for my country; silly for you to go*). **2** in defense, support, or favor of (*fight for one's rights*). **3** suitable or appropriate to (*a dance for beginners; not for me to say*). **4** in respect of or with reference to; regarding; so far as concerns (*usual for ties to be worn; don't care for him at all; ready for bed*). **5** representing or in place of (*here for my uncle*). **6** in exchange against (*swapped it for a bigger one*). **7 a** as the price of (*give me $5 for it*). **b** at the price of (*bought it for*

$5). **c** to the amount of (*a bill for $100*). **8** as the penalty of (*fined them heavily for it*). **9** in requital of (*that's for upsetting my sister*). **10** as a reward for (*here's $5 for your trouble*). **11 a** with a view to; in the hope or quest of; in order to get (*go for a walk; run for a doctor; did it for the money*). **b** on account of (*could not speak for laughing*). **12** corresponding to (*word for word*). **13** to reach; in the direction of; toward (*left for Rome; ran for the end of the road*). **14** conducive or conducively to; in order to achieve (*take the pills for a sound night's sleep*). **15** starting at (a specified time) (*we set the meeting for eight*). **16** through or over (a distance or period); during (*walked for miles; sang for two hours*). **17** in the character of; as being (*for the last time; know it for a lie; I for one refuse*). **18** because of; on account of (*could not see for tears*). **19** in spite of; notwithstanding (*for all we know; for all your fine words*). **20** considering or making due allowance in respect of (*good for a beginner*). **21** in order to be (*gone for a soldier*). • *conj.* because; since; seeing that. □ **oh for** I wish I had (*oh for a strong black coffee*). [OE, prob. a reduction of Gmc *fora* (unrecorded) BEFORE (of place and time)]

f.o.r. *abbr.* free on rail.

for- /fawr, fər/ *prefix* forming verbs and their derivatives meaning: **1** away; off; apart (*forget; forgive*). **2** prohibition (*forbid*). **3** abstention or neglect (*forgo; forsake*). **4** excess or intensity (*forlorn*). [OE *for-, fær-*]

for•age /fáwrij, fór-/ *n. & v.* • *n.* **1** food for horses and cattle. **2** the act or an instance of searching for food. • *v.* **1** *intr.* go searching; rummage (esp. for food). **2** *tr.* obtain food from; plunder. **3** *tr.* **a** get by foraging. **b** supply with food. □□ **for•ag•er** *n.* [ME f. OF *fourrage, fourrager*, rel. to FODDER]

for•age cap *n.* a billed cap forming part of a soldier's uniform.

fo•ra•men /fəráymen/ *n.* (*pl.* **fo•ram•i•na** /-rámina/) *Anat.* an opening, hole, or passage, esp. in a bone. □□ **fo•ram•i•nate** /-ráminət/ *adj.* [L *foramen –minis* f. *forare* bore a hole]

fo•ra•min•i•fer /fáwrəminifər, fór-/ *n.* (also **fo•ram•i•nif•er•an** /-fərən/) any protozoan of the order Foraminifera, having a perforated shell through which pseudopodia emerge. □□ **fo•ram•i•nif•er•ous** /-nifərəs/ *adj.*

fo•ram•i•nif•er•an var. of FORAMINIFER.

for•as•much as /fáwrəzmúch/ *conj. archaic* because; since. [= for as much]

for•ay /fáwray, fór-/ *n. & v.* • *n.* **1** a sudden attack; a raid or incursion. **2** an attempt or venture, esp. into a field not one's own. • *v.intr.* make or go on a foray. [ME, prob. earlier as verb: back-form. f. *forayer* f. OF *forrier* forager, rel. to FODDER]

for•bade (also **for•bad**) *past* of FORBID.

for•bear[1] /fáwrbáir/ *v.intr. & tr.* (*past* **for•bore** /-báwr/; *past part.* **for•borne** /-báwrn/) (often foll. by *from*, or *to* + infin.) *literary* abstain or desist (from) (*could not forbear (from) speaking out; forbore to mention it*). [OE *forberan* (as FOR-, BEAR[1])]

for•bear[2] var. of FOREBEAR.

for•bear•ance /fawrbáirəns/ *n.* patient self-control; tolerance.

for•bear•ing /fawrbáiring/ *adj.* patient; long-suffering. □□ **for•bear•ing•ly** *adv.*

for•bid /fərbíd, fawr-/ *v.tr.* (**for•bid•ding**; *past* **for•bade** /-bád, -báyd/ or **for•bad** /-bád/; *past part.* **for•bid•den** /-bíd'n/) **1** (foll. by *to* + infin.) order not (*I forbid you to go*). **2** refuse to allow (a thing, or a person to have a thing) (*I forbid it; was forbidden any wine*). **3** refuse a person entry to (*the gardens were forbidden to children*). □ **God forbid!** may it not happen! □□ **for•bid•dance** /-dəns/ *n.* [OE *forbēodan* (as FOR-, BID)]

for•bid•den de•grees *n.pl.* (also **pro•hib•it•ed de•grees**) a number of degrees of descent too few to allow marriage between two related persons.

for•bid•den fruit *n.* something desired or enjoyed all the more because not allowed.

for•bid•ding /fərbíding, fawr-/ *adj.* uninviting; repellent; stern. □□ **for•bid•ding•ly** *adv.*

for•bore *past* of FORBEAR[1].

for•borne *past part.* of FORBEAR[1].

for•bye /fawrbí/ *prep. & adv. archaic* or *Sc.* • *prep.* besides. • *adv.* in addition.

force[1] /fawrs/ *n. & v.* • *n.* **1** power; exerted strength or impetus; intense effort. **2** coercion or compulsion, esp. with the use or threat of violence. **3 a** military strength. **b** (in *pl.*) troops; fighting resources. **c** an organized body of people, esp. soldiers, police, or workers. **4** binding power; validity. **5** effect; precise significance (*the force of their words*). **6 a** mental or moral strength; influence; efficacy (*force of habit*). **b** vividness of effect (*described with much force*). **7** *Physics* **a** an influence tending to cause the motion of a body. **b** the intensity of this equal to the mass of the body and its accelera-

tion. **8** a person or thing regarded as exerting influence (*is a force for good*). • *v.* **1** *tr.* constrain (a person) by force or against his or her will. **2** *tr.* make a way through or into by force; break open by force. **3** *tr.* (usu. with prep. or adv.) drive or propel violently or against resistance (*forced it into the hole; the wind forced them back*). **4** *tr.* (foll. by *on, upon*) impose or press (on a person) (*forced their views on us*). **5** *tr.* **a** cause or produce by effort (*forced a smile*). **b** attain by strength or effort (*forced an entry; must force a decision*). **6** *tr.* strain or increase to the utmost; overstrain. **7** *tr.* artificially hasten the development or maturity of (a plant). **8** *tr.* seek or demand quick results from; accelerate the process of (*force the pace*). **9** *intr. Cards* make a play that compels another particular play. □ **by force of** by means of. **force the bidding** (at an auction) make bids to raise the price rapidly. **force a person's hand** make a person act prematurely or unwillingly. **force the issue** render an immediate decision necessary. **in force 1** valid; effective. **2** in great strength or numbers. **join forces** combine efforts. □□ **force•a•ble** *adj.* **forc•er** *n.* [ME f. OF *force, forcer* ult. f. L *fortis* strong]

force[2] /fawrs/ *n. No. of Engl.* a waterfall. [ON *fors*]

forced /fawrst/ *adj.* **1** obtained or imposed by force (*forced entry*). **2** (of a gesture, etc.) produced or maintained with effort; affected; unnatural (*a forced smile*).

forced land•ing *n.* the unavoidable landing of an aircraft in an emergency.

forced march *n.* a long and vigorous march, esp. by troops.

force-feed *v.tr.* **1** force (esp. a prisoner) to take food. **2** impose or force information or ideology upon (*(no group has the right to force-feed its beliefs on us*).

force field *n.* (in science fiction) an invisible barrier of force.

force•ful /fáwrsfŏŏl/ *adj.* **1** vigorous; powerful. **2** (of speech) compelling; impressive. □□ **force•ful•ly** *adv.* **force•ful•ness** *n.*

force ma•jeure /fáwrs mazhŏr/ *n.* **1** irresistible compulsion or coercion. **2** an unforeseeable course of events excusing a person from the fulfillment of a contract. [F, = superior strength]

force•meat /fáwrsmeet/ *n.* meat, etc., chopped and seasoned for use as a stuffing or a garnish. [obs. *force, farce* stuff f. OF *farsir*: see FARCE]

for•ceps /fáwrseps/ *n.* (*pl.* same) **1** surgical pincers, used for grasping and holding. **2** *Bot. & Zool.* an organ or structure resembling forceps. □□ **for•ci•pate** /-sipət/ *adj.* [L *forceps forcipis*]

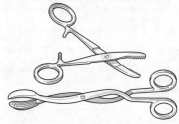

forceps 1

force pump *n.* a pump that forces water under pressure.

for•ci•ble /fáwrsibəl/ *adj.* done by or involving force; forceful. □□ **for•ci•ble•ness** *n.* **for•ci•bly** *adv.* [ME f. AF & OF (as FORCE[1])]

ford /fawrd/ *n. & v.* • *n.* a shallow place where a river or stream may be crossed by wading or in a vehicle. • *v.tr.* cross (water) at a ford. □□ **ford•a•ble** *adj.* **ford•less** *adj.* [OE f. WG]

fore /fawr/ *adj., n., int., & prep.* • *adj.* situated in front. • *n.* the front part, esp. of a ship; the bow. • *int. Golf* a warning to a person in the path of a ball. • *prep. archaic* (in oaths) in the presence of (*fore God*). □ **come to the fore** take a leading part. **to the fore** in front; conspicuous. [OE f. Gmc.: (adj. & n.) ME f. compounds with FORE-]

fore- /fawr/ *prefix* forming: **1** verbs meaning: **a** in front (*foreshorten*). **b** beforehand; in advance (*foreordain; forewarn*). **2** nouns meaning: **a** situated in front of (*forecourt*). **b** the front part of (*forehead*). **c** of or near the bow of a ship (*forecastle*). **d** preceding (*forerunner*).

fore and aft *n.* at bow and stern; all over the ship.

fore-and-aft *adj.* (of a sail or rigging) set lengthwise, not on the yards.

fore•arm[1] /fáwraarm/ *n.* **1** the part of the arm from the elbow to the wrist or the fingertips. **2** the corresponding part in a foreleg or wing.

fore•arm[2] /fawraárm/ *v.tr.* prepare or arm beforehand.

fore•bear /fáwrbair/ *n.* (also **for•bear**) (usu. in *pl.*) an ancestor. [FORE + obs. *bear, beer* (as BE, -ER[1])]

fore•bode /fawrbŏd/ *v.tr.* **1** betoken; be an advance warning of (an evil or unwelcome event). **2** have a presentiment of (usu. evil).

fore•bod•ing /fawrbṓding/ n. an expectation of trouble or evil; a presage or omen. □□ **fore•bod•ing•ly** adv.

fore•cast /fáwrkast/ v. & n. •v.tr. (past and past part. •cast or •cast•ed) predict; estimate or calculate beforehand. •n. a calculation or estimate of something future, esp. coming weather. □□ **fore•cast•er** n.

fore•cas•tle /fṓksəl/ n. (also fo'c's'le) Naut. **1** the forward part of a ship where the crew has quarters. **2** hist. a short raised deck at the bow.

> **PRONUNCIATION TIP**   forecastle
>
> See note at GUNWALE.

fore•close /fawrklṓz/ v.tr. **1** (also absol.; foll. by on) stop (a mortgage) from being redeemable or (a mortgager) from redeeming, esp. as a result of defaults in payment. **2** exclude; prevent. **3** shut out; bar. □□ **fore•clo•sure** /–klṓzhər/ n. [ME f. OF forclos past part. of forclore f. for- out f. L foras + CLOSE[2]]

fore•court /fáwrkawrt/ n. **1** an enclosed space in front of a building. **2** Tennis the part of the court between the service line and the net. **3** Brit. the part of a filling station where gasoline is supplied.

fore•deck /fṓrdek, fáwr–/ n. the forward section of a ship's main deck.

fore•doom /fawrdṓm/ v.tr. (often foll. by to) doom or condemn beforehand.

fore•fa•ther /fáwrfaathər/ n. (usu. in pl.) **1** an ancestor. **2** a member of a past generation of a family or people.

fore•fin•ger /fáwrfinggər/ n. the finger next to the thumb.

fore•foot /fáwrfŏŏt/ n. (pl. •feet) **1** either of the front feet of a four-footed animal. **2** Naut. the foremost section of a ship's keel.

fore•front /fáwrfrunt/ n. **1** the foremost part. **2** the leading position.

fore•gath•er var. of FORGATHER.

fore•go[1] /fáwrgṓ/ v.tr. & intr. (•goes; past •went /–wént/; past part. •gone /–gón/) precede in place or time. □□ **fore•go•er** n. [OE foregān]

fore•go[2] var. of FORGO.

fore•go•ing /fáwrgṓing/ adj. preceding; previously mentioned.

fore•gone /fáwrgawn, –gón/ past part. of FOREGO[1].• attrib.adj. previous; preceding; completed.

fore•gone con•clu•sion n. an easily foreseen or predictable result.

fore•ground /fáwrgrownd/ n. **1** the part of a view, esp. in a picture, that is nearest the observer. **2** the most conspicuous position. [Du. voorgrond (as FORE-, GROUND[1])]

fore•hand /fáwrhand/ n. **1** Tennis, etc. **a** a stroke played with the palm of the hand facing the opponent. **b** (attrib.) (also **fore•hand•ed**) of or made with a forehand. **2** the part of a horse in front of the seated rider.

fore•head /fáwrid, –hed, fór–/ n. the part of the face above the eyebrows. [OE forhēafod (as FORE-, HEAD)]

> **PRONUNCIATION TIP**   forehead
>
> Traditionally, forehead was pronounced with the stress on the first syllable and with the h silent, so that it almost rhymed with horrid. But today many pronounce it sounding the h and giving the element head secondary stress.

for•eign /fáwrin, fór–/ adj. **1** of or from or situated in or characteristic of a country or a language other than one's own. **2** dealing with other countries (foreign service). **3** of another district, society, etc. **4** (often foll. by to) unfamiliar; strange; uncharacteristic (his behavior is foreign to me). **5** coming from outside (a foreign body lodged in my eye). □□ **for•eign•ness** n. [ME f. OF forein, forain ult. f. L foras, –is outside: for –g– cf. sovereign]

for•eign aid n. money, food, etc., given or lent by one country to another.

for•eign•er /fáwrinər, fór–/ n. **1** a person born in or coming from a foreign country or place. **2** dial. a person not native to a place. **3 a** a foreign ship. **b** an imported animal or article.

for•eign ex•change n. **1** the currency of other countries. **2** dealings in these.

for•eign le•gion n. a body of foreign volunteers in an army (esp. the French army).

for•eign min•is•ter n. (also **foreign secretary**) (in some governments) a government minister in charge of his or her country's relations with other countries.

for•eign of•fice n. (in some governments) a government department dealing with other countries.

for•eign trade n. international trade.

fore•judge /fáwrjúj/ v.tr. judge or determine before knowing the evidence.

fore•know /fawrnṓ/ v.tr. (past •knew /–nṓŏ, –nyṓŏ/; past part. •known /–nṓn/) know beforehand; have prescience of. □□ **fore•knowl•edge** /fórnólij/ n.

fore•la•dy /fáwrlaydee/ n. (pl. •dies) dated = FOREWOMAN.

fore•land /fáwrland/ n. **1** a cape or promontory. **2** a piece of land in front of something.

fore•leg /fáwrleg/ n. each of the front legs of a quadruped.

fore•limb /fáwrlim/ n. any of the front limbs of an animal.

fore•lock /fáwrlok/ n. a lock of hair growing just above the forehead. □ **take time by the forelock** seize an opportunity.

fore•man /fáwrmən/ n. (pl. •men) **1** a worker with supervisory responsibilities. **2** the member of a jury who presides over its deliberations and speaks on its behalf.

fore•mast /fáwrmast, –məst/ n. the forward (lower) mast of a ship.

fore•most /fáwrmōst/ adj. & adv. • adj. **1** the chief or most notable. **2** the most advanced in position; the front. • adv. before anything else in position; in the first place (first and foremost). [earlier formost, formest, superl. of OE forma first, assim. to FORE, MOST]

fore•name /fáwrnaym/ n. a first name.

fore•noon /fáwrnōōn/ n. the part of the day before noon.

fo•ren•sic /fərénsik, –zik/ adj. **1** of or used in connection with courts of law (forensic science). **2** disp. of or involving forensic science (sent for forensic examination). □□ **fo•ren•si•cal•ly** adv. [L forensis f. FORUM]

fo•ren•sic med•i•cine n. the application of medical knowledge to legal problems.

fore•or•dain /fáwrawrdáyn/ v.tr. predestinate; ordain beforehand. □□ **fore•or•di•na•tion** /–d'náyshən/ n.

fore•paw /fáwrpaw/ n. either of the front paws of a quadruped.

fore•peak /fáwrpeek/ n. Naut. the end of the forehold in the angle of the bows.

fore•play /fáwrplay/ n. stimulation preceding sexual intercourse.

fore•run /fáwr-rún/ v.tr. (•run•ning; past •ran /–rán/; past part. •run) **1** go before. **2** indicate the coming of; foreshadow.

fore•run•ner /fáwr-runər/ n. **1** a predecessor. **2** an advance messenger.

fore•sail /fáwrsayl, –səl/ n. Naut. the principal sail on a foremast (the lowest square sail, or the fore-and-aft bent on the mast, or the triangular before the mast).

fore•see /fáwrseé/ v.tr. (past •saw /–sáw/; past part. •seen /–seén/) (often foll. by that + clause) see or be aware of beforehand. □□ **fore•see•a•ble** adj. **fore•see•a•bil•i•ty** n. **fore•se•er** /–seéər/ n. [OE foresēon (as FORE- + SEE[1])]

fore•shad•ow /fáwrshádō/ v.tr. be a warning or indication of (a future event).

fore•sheets /fáwrsheets/ n.pl. Naut. the inner part of the bows of a boat with gratings for the bowman to stand on.

fore•shore /fáwrshawr/ n. the part of the shore between high- and low-water marks, or between the water and cultivated or developed land.

fore•short•en /fáwrsháwrt'n/ v.tr. show or portray (an object) with the apparent shortening due to visual perspective.

fore•show /fáwrshṓ/ v.tr. (past part. •shown /–shṓn/) **1** foretell. **2** foreshadow; portend; prefigure.

fore•sight /fáwrsīt/ n. **1** regard or provision for the future. **2** the process of foreseeing. **3** the front sight of a gun. **4** Surveying a sight taken forward. □□ **fore•sight•ed** /–sítid/ adj. **fore•sight•ed•ly** adv. **fore•sight•ed•ness** n. [ME, prob. after ON forsjá, forsjó (as FORE-, SIGHT)]

fore•skin /fáwrskin/ n. the fold of skin covering the end of the penis. Also called **prepuce**.

for•est /fáwrist, fór–/ n. & v. • n. **1 a** (often attrib.) a large area covered chiefly with trees and undergrowth. **b** the trees growing in it. **c** a large number or dense mass of vertical objects (a forest of masts). **2** a district formerly a forest but now cultivated. **3** hist. (in the UK) an area usu. owned by the sovereign and kept for hunting. • v.tr. **1** plant with trees. **2** convert into a forest. [ME f. OF f. LL forestis silva wood outside the walls of a park f. L foris outside]

fore•stall /fáwrstáwl/ v.tr. **1** act in advance of in order to prevent. **2** anticipate (the action of another, or an event). **3** anticipate the action of. **4** deal with beforehand. **5** hist. buy up (goods) in order to profit by an enhanced price. □□ **fore•stall•er** n. **fore•stall•ment** n. [ME in sense 5: cf. AL forestallare f. OE foresteall an ambush (as FORE-, STALL)]

fore•stay /fáwrstay/ n. Naut. a stay from the head of the foremast to the ship's deck to support the foremast.

for•est•er /fáwristər, fór–/ n. **1** a person in charge of a forest or skilled in forestry. **2** a person or animal living in a forest. [ME f. OF forestier (as FOREST)]

for•est rang•er n. a government official who protects and preserves forests.

for•est•ry /fáwristree, fór–/ n. **1** the science or management of forests. **2** wooded country; forests.

fore•taste n. & v. • n. /fáwrtayst/ partial enjoyment or suffering in advance; anticipation. • v.tr. /fáwrtáyst/ taste beforehand; anticipate the experience of.

fore•tell /fáwrtél/ v.tr. (past and past part. •told /–tṓld/) **1** tell of (an event, etc.) before it takes place; predict; prophesy. **2** presage; be a precursor of. □□ **fore•tell•er** n.

fore•thought /fáwrthawt/ n. **1** care or provision for the future. **2** previous thinking or devising. **3** deliberate intention.

fore•to•ken n. & v. • n. /fáwrtōkən/ a sign of something to come.

● *v.tr.* /fáwrtókən/ portend; indicate beforehand. [OE *foretācn* (as FORE-, TOKEN)]

fore•told *past* and *past part.* of FORETELL.

fore•top /fáwrtop/ *n. Naut.* a platform at the top of a foremast (see TOP[1] *n.* 9).

fore•top-gal•lant mast /fôrtop gálənt; fór–; –tə gál–/ *n.* the mast above the fore-topmast.

fore•top-gal•lant-sail *n.* the sail above the fore-topsail.

fore•top•mast /fawrtópmast, –məst/ *n. Naut.* the mast above the foremast.

fore•top•sail /fawrtópsayl, –səl/ *n. Naut.* the sail above the foresail.

for•ev•er /fərévər, fawr–/ *adv.* **1** for all future time; for always (*he would love her forever*). **2** a very long time (used hyperbolically) (*it took forever to get a passport*). **3** continually; persistently (*is forever complaining*).

for•ev•er•more /fərévərmáwr, fawr–/ *adv.* an emphatic form of FOREVER.

fore•warn /fáwrwáwrn/ *v.tr.* warn beforehand. □□ **fore•warn•er** *n.*

fore•went *past* of FOREGO[1], FOREGO[2].

fore•wom•an /fáwrwŏomən/ *n.* (*pl.* **•wom•en**) **1** a female worker with supervisory responsibilities. **2** a woman who presides over a jury's deliberations and speaks on its behalf.

fore•word /fáwrwərd/ *n.* introductory remarks at the beginning of a book, often by a person other than the author. [FORE- + WORD after G *Vorwort*]

fore•yard /fáwryaard/ *n. Naut.* the lowest yard on a foremast.

for•feit /fáwrfit/ *n., adj., & v.* ● *n.* **1** a penalty for a breach of contract or neglect; a fine. **2 a** a trivial fine for a breach of rules in clubs, etc., or in a game. **b** (in *pl.*) a game in which forfeits are exacted. **3** something surrendered as a penalty. **4** the process of forfeiting. **5** *Law* property or a right or privilege lost as a legal penalty. ● *adj.* lost or surrendered as a penalty. ● *v.tr.* (**for•feit•ed, for•feit•ing**) lose the right to, be deprived of, or have to pay as a penalty. □□ **for•feit•a•ble** *adj.* **for•feit•er** *n.* **for•fei•ture** /–fichər/ *n.* [ME (= crime) f. OF *forfet, forfait* past part. of *forfaire* transgress (f. L *foris* outside) + *faire* f. L *facere* do]

for•fend /fawrfénd/ *v.tr.* **1** protect by precautions. **2** *archaic* avert; keep off.

for•gath•er /fáwrgáthər/ *v.intr.* (also **fore•gath•er**) assemble; meet together; associate. [16th-c. Sc. f. Du. *vergaderen*, assim. to FOR-, GATHER]

for•gave *past* of FORGIVE.

forge[1] /fawrj/ *v. & n.* ● *v.tr.* **1 a** write (a document or signature) in order to pass it off as written by another. **b** make (money, etc.) in fraudulent imitation. **2** fabricate; invent. **3** shape (esp. metal) by heating in a fire and hammering. ● *n.* **1** a blacksmith's workshop; a smithy. **2 a** a furnace or hearth for melting or refining metal. **b** a workshop containing this. □□ **forge•a•ble** *adj.* **forg•er** *n.* [ME f. OF *forge* (n.), *forger* (v.) f. L *fabricare* FABRICATE]

forge[2] /fawrj/ *v.intr.* move forward gradually or steadily. □ **forge ahead 1** take the lead in a race. **2** move forward or make progress rapidly. [18th c.: perh. an aberrant pronunc. of FORCE[1]]

for•ger•y /fáwrjəree/ *n.* (*pl.* **•ies**) **1** the act or an instance of forging, counterfeiting, or falsifying a document, etc. **2** a forged or spurious thing, esp. a document or signature.

for•get /fərgét/ *v.* (**for•get•ting;** *past* **for•got** /–gót/; *past part.* **for•got•ten** /–gót'n/ or esp. *US* **for•got**) **1** *tr. & (often foll. by about) intr.* lose the remembrance of; not remember (a person or thing). **2** *tr.* (foll. by clause or *to* + infin.) not remember; neglect (*forgot to come; forgot how to do it*). **3** *tr.* inadvertently omit to bring or mention or attend to. **4** *tr.* (also *absol.*) put out of mind; cease to think of (*forgive and forget*). □ **forget oneself 1** neglect one's own interests. **2** act unbecomingly or unworthily. □□ **for•get•ta•ble** *adj.* **for•get•ter** *n.* [OE *forgietan* f. WG (as FOR-, GET)]

for•get•ful /fərgétfŏol/ *adj.* **1** apt to forget; absent-minded. **2** (often foll. by *of*) forgetting; neglectful. □□ **for•get•ful•ly** *adv.* **for•get•ful•ness** *n.*

for•get-me-not *n.* any plant of the genus *Myosotis*, esp. *M. alpestris* with small yellow-eyed bright blue flowers.

for•give /fərgív/ *v.tr.* (also *absol.* or with double object) (*past* **for•gave;** *past part.* **for•giv•en**) **1** cease to feel angry or resentful toward; pardon (an offender or offense) (*forgive us our mistakes*). **2** remit or let off (a debt or debtor). □□ **for•giv•a•ble** *adj.* **for•giv•a•bly** *adv.* **for•giv•er** *n.* [OE *forgiefan* (as FOR-, GIVE)]

for•give•ness /fərgívnis/ *n.* **1** the act of forgiving; the state of being forgiven. **2** readiness to forgive. [OE *forgiefenes* (as FORGIVE)]

for•giv•ing /fərgíving/ *adj.* inclined readily to forgive. □□ **for•giv•ing•ly** *adv.*

for•go /fawrgó/ *v.tr.* (also **fore•go**) (**•goes;** *past* **•went** /–wént/; *past part.* **•gone** /–gáwn, –gón/) **1** abstain from; go without; relinquish. **2** omit or decline to take or use (a pleasure, advantage, etc.). [OE *forgān* (as FOR-, GO[1])]

for•got *past* of FORGET.

for•got•ten *past part.* of FORGET.

for•int /fáwrint/ *n.* the chief monetary unit of Hungary. [Magyar f. It. *fiorino:* see FLORIN]

fork /fawrk/ *n. & v.* ● *n.* **1** an instrument with two or more prongs used in eating or cooking. **2** a similar much larger instrument used for digging, lifting, etc. **3** any pronged device or component (*tuning fork*). **4** a forked support for a bicycle wheel. **5 a** a divergence of anything, e.g., a stick, road, or a river, into two parts. **b** the place where this occurs. **c** either of the two parts (*take the left fork*). **6** a flash of forked lightning. **7** *Chess* a simultaneous attack on two pieces by one. ● *v.* **1** *intr.* form a fork or branch by separating into two parts. **2** *intr.* take one or other road, etc., at a fork (*fork left for Danbury*). **3** *tr.* dig or lift, etc., with a fork. **4** *tr. Chess* attack (two pieces) simultaneously with one. □ **fork out** (or **over** or **up**) *sl.* hand over or pay, usu. reluctantly. [OE *forca, force* f. L *furca*]

forked /fawrkt/ *adj.* **1** having a fork or forklike end or branches. **2** divergent; cleft. **3** (in *comb.*) having so many prongs (*three-forked*).

forked light•ning *n.* a lightning flash in the form of a zigzag or branching line.

fork•lift /fáwrklift/ *n.* (also **forklift truck**) a vehicle with a pronged device in front for lifting and carrying heavy loads.

forklift

for•lorn /fawrláwrn/ *adj.* **1** sad and abandoned or lonely. **2** in a pitiful state; of wretched appearance. □□ **for•lorn•ly** *adv.* **for•lorn•ness** *n.* [past part. of obs. *forlese* f. OE *forlēosan* (as FOR-, LOSE): *forlorn hope* f. Du. *verloren hoop* lost troop, orig. of a storming party, etc.]

for•lorn hope *n.* **1** a faint remaining hope or chance. **2** a desperate enterprise.

form /fawrm/ *n. & v.* ● *n.* **1 a** a shape; an arrangement of parts. **b** the outward aspect (esp. apart from color) or shape of a body. **2** a person or animal as visible or tangible (*the familiar form of the teacher*). **3** the mode in which a thing exists or manifests itself (*took the form of a book*). **4** a species, kind, or variety. **5 a** a printed document with blank spaces for information to be inserted. **b** a regularly drawn document. **6** a class or grade, as in some private schools or a British school. **7** a customary method; what is usually done (*common form*). **8** a set order of words; a formula. **9** behavior according to a rule or custom. **10** (prec. by *the*) correct procedure (*knows the form*). **11 a** (of an athlete, horse, etc.) condition of health and training (*is in top form*). **b** *Racing* details of previous performances. **12** general state or disposition (*was in great form*). **13** *Brit. sl.* a criminal record. **14** formality or mere ceremony. **15** *Gram.* **a** one of the ways in which a word may be spelled or pronounced or inflected. **b** the external characteristics of words apart from meaning. **16** arrangement and style in literary or musical composition. **17** *Philos.* the essential nature of a species or thing. **18** *Brit.* a long bench without a back. **19** *Printing* **a** a body of type secured in a chase for printing at one impression. **b** a quantity of film arranged for making a plate, etc. **20** a hare's lair. **21** = FORMWORK. ● *v.* **1** *tr.* make or fashion into a certain shape or form. **2** *intr.* take a certain shape; be formed. **3** *tr.* be the material of; make up or constitute (*together form a unit; forms part of the structure*). **4** *tr.* train or instruct. **5** *tr.* develop or establish as a concept, institution, or practice (*form an idea; formed an alliance; form a habit*). **6** *tr.* (foll. by *into*) embody; organize. **7** *tr.* articulate (a word). **8** *tr. & intr.* (often foll. by *up*) esp. *Mil.* bring or be brought into a certain arrangement or formation. **9** *tr.* construct (a new word) by derivation, inflection, etc. □ **in form** fit for racing, etc. **off form** esp. *Brit.* not playing or performing well. **on form** esp. *Brit.* playing or performing well. **out of form** not fit for racing, etc. [ME f. OF *forme* f. L *forma* mold, form]

-form /fawrm/ *comb. form* (usu. as **–iform**) forming adjectives meaning: **1** having the form of (*cruciform; cuneiform*). **2** having such a number of (*uniform; multiform*). [from or after F *-forme* f. L *-formis* f. *forma* FORM]

for•mal /fáwrməl/ *adj. & n.* ● *adj.* **1** used or done or held in accordance with rules, convention, or ceremony (*formal dress; a formal occasion*). **2** ceremonial; required by convention (*a formal offer*). **3** precise or symmetrical (*a formal garden*). **4** prim or stiff in manner. **5** perfunctory; having the form without the spirit. **6** valid or correctly so called because of its form; explicit and definite (*a formal agreement*). **7** in accordance with recognized forms or rules. **8** of or concerned with (outward) form or appearance, esp. as distinct from content or matter. **9** *Logic* concerned with the form and not the matter of reasoning. **10** *Philos.* of the essence of a thing; essential; not material. ● *n.* **1** evening dress. **2** an occasion on which evening dress is worn. □□ **for•mal•ly** *adv.* **for•mal•ness** *n.* [ME f. L *formalis* (as FORM)]

SYNONYM TIP **formal**

CEREMONIAL, CEREMONIOUS, POMPOUS, PROPER, PUNCTILIOUS. **Formal** suggests a suit-and-tie approach to certain situations—reserved, conventional, obeying all the rules (*an engraved invitation to a formal dinner requiring black tie or evening gown*). **Proper**, in this regard, implies scrupulously correct behavior that observes rules of etiquette (*the proper way to serve a guest; the proper spoon for dessert*). **Punctilious** behavior observes all the proper formalities (a "*punctilio*" is a detail or fine point), but may verge on the annoying (*her punctilious attention to the correct placement of silverware made setting the table an ordeal*). Someone (usually a man) who likes to show off just how *formal* and *proper* he can be runs the risk of becoming the most dreaded dinner guest of all: the **pompous** ass. *Pompous* individuals may derive more than the normal amount of pleasure from participating in **ceremonial** acts or events, which are those performed according to set rules, but **ceremonious** suggests a less negative and more ritualized approach to formality (*the Japanese woman could not have been more ceremonious than when she was carrying out the ceremonial serving of tea*).

form·al·de·hyde /fawrmáldihīd/ *n.* a colorless pungent gas used as a disinfectant and preservative and in the manufacture of synthetic resins. ¶ Chem. formula: CH_2O. Also called **methanal**. [FORMIC (ACID) + ALDEHYDE]

for·ma·lin /fáwrməlin/ *n.* a colorless solution of formaldehyde in water used as a preservative for biological specimens, etc.

for·mal·ism /fáwrməlizəm/ *n.* **1 a** excessive adherence to prescribed forms. **b** the use of forms without regard to inner significance. **2** *derog.* an artist's concentration on form at the expense of content. **3** the treatment of mathematics as a manipulation of meaningless symbols. **4** *Theatr.* a symbolic and stylized manner of production. **5** *Physics & Math.* the mathematical description of a physical situation, etc. □□ **for·mal·ist** *n.* **for·mal·is·tic** *adj.*

for·mal·i·ty /fawrmálitee/ *n.* (*pl.* **·ties**) **1 a** a formal or ceremonial act, requirement of etiquette, regulation, or custom (often with an implied lack of real significance). **b** a thing done simply to comply with a rule. **2** the rigid observance of rules or convention. **3** ceremony; elaborate procedure. **4** being formal; precision of manners. **5** stiffness of design. [F *formalité* or med.L *formalitas* (as FORMAL)]

for·mal·ize /fáwrməlīz/ *v.tr.* **1** give definite shape or legal formality to. **2** make ceremonious, precise, or rigid; imbue with formalism. □□ **for·mal·i·za·tion** /-lizáyshən/ *n.*

for·mant /fáwrmənt/ *n. Phonetics* **1** the characteristic pitch constituent of a vowel. **2** a morpheme occurring only in combination in a word or word stem. [G f. L *formare formant-* to form]

for·mat /fáwrmat/ *n. & v.* • *n.* **1** the shape and size of a book, periodical, etc. **2** the style or manner of an arrangement or procedure. **3** *Computing* a defined structure for holding data, etc., in a record for processing or storage. • *v.tr.* (**for·mat·ted**, **for·mat·ting**) **1** arrange or put into a format. **2** *Computing* prepare (a storage medium) to receive data. [F f. G f. L *formatus* (*liber*) shaped (book), past part. of *formare* FORM]

for·mate see FORMIC ACID.

for·ma·tion /fawrmáyshən/ *n.* **1** the act or an instance of forming; the process of being formed. **2** a thing formed. **3** a structure or arrangement of parts. **4** a particular arrangement, e.g., of troops, aircraft in flight, etc. **5** *Geol.* an assemblage of rocks or series of strata having some common characteristic. □□ **for·ma·tion·al** *adj.* [ME f. OF *formation* or L *formatio* (as FORM]

for·ma·tive /fáwrmətiv/ *adj. & n.* • *adj.* **1** serving to form or fashion; of formation. **2** *Gram.* (of a flexional or derivative suffix or prefix) used in forming words. • *n. Gram.* a formative element. □□ **for·ma·tive·ly** *adv.* [ME f. OF *formatif -ive* or med.L *formativus* (as FORM)]

form class *n. Linguistics* a class of linguistic forms with grammatical or syntactical features in common.

form crit·i·cism *n.* textual analysis of the Bible, etc., by tracing the history of its content by forms (e.g., proverbs, myths).

forme /fawrm/ *n. Brit.* = FORM *n.* 19.

for·mer[1] /fáwrmər/ *attrib.adj.* **1** of or occurring in the past or an earlier period (*in former times*). **2** having been previously (*her former husband*). **3** (prec. by *the*; often *absol.*) the first or first mentioned of two (opp. LATTER). [ME f. *forme* first, after FOREMOST]

▶When two previously mentioned items are referred to, the one named first is the **former**, the second the **latter**: *the menu offered coconut-crusted shrimp and barbecued ribs—the former decidedly sweet, the latter absolutely mild.* If there are three or more, **first**, **second**, (etc.) and **last** should be used, even if all are not mentioned: *of winter, spring, and summer, I find the last most enjoyable.*

form·er[2] /fáwrmər/ *n.* **1** a person or thing that forms. **2** *Electr.* a frame or core for winding a coil on. **3** *Aeron.* a transverse strengthening member in a wing or fuselage. **4** esp. *Brit.* (in *comb.*) a pupil of a specified form in a school (*fourth-former*).

for·mer·ly /fáwrmərlee/ *adv.* in the past; in former times.

For·mi·ca /fawrmíkə/ *n. Trademark* a hard durable plastic laminate used for working surfaces, cupboard doors, etc. [20th c.: orig. uncert.]

for·mic ac·id /fáwrmik/ *n.* a colorless irritant volatile acid (HCOOH) contained in the fluid emitted by some ants. □□ **for·mate** /-mayt/ *n.* [L *formica* ant]

for·mi·ca·tion /fáwrmikáyshən/ *n.* a sensation as of ants crawling over the skin. [L *formicatio* f. *formica* ant]

for·mi·da·ble /fáwrmidəbəl, *disp.* formídəbəl/ *adj.* **1** inspiring fear or dread. **2** inspiring respect or awe. **3** likely to be hard to overcome, resist, or deal with. □□ **for·mi·da·ble·ness** *n.* **for·mi·da·bly** *adv.* [F *formidable* or L *formidabilis* f. *formidare* fear]

form·less /fáwrmlis/ *adj.* shapeless; without determinate or regular form. □□ **form·less·ly** *adv.* **form·less·ness** *n.*

form let·ter *n.* a standardized letter to deal with frequently occurring matters.

for·mu·la /fáwrmyələ/ *n.* (*pl.* **for·mu·las** or (esp. in senses 1, 2) **for·mu·lae** /-lee/) **1** *Chem.* a set of chemical symbols showing the constituents of a substance and their relative proportions. **2** *Math.* a mathematical rule expressed in symbols. **3 a** a fixed form of words, esp. one used on social or ceremonial occasions. **b** a rule unintelligently or slavishly followed; an established or conventional usage. **c** a form of words embodying or enabling agreement, resolution of a dispute, etc. **4 a** a list of ingredients; a recipe. **b** an infant's liquid food preparation given as a substitute for mother's milk. **5 a** classification of racing car, esp. by the engine capacity. □□ **for·mu·la·ic** /-láyik/ *adj.* **for·mu·lar·ize** /-lərīz/ *v.tr.* **for·mu·lize** *v.tr.* [L, dimin. of *forma* FORM]

for·mu·lar·y /fáwrmyəleree/ *n. & adj.* • *n.* (*pl.* **·ies**) **1** a collection of formulas or set forms, esp. for religious use. **2** *Pharm.* a compendium of formulae used in the preparation of medicinal drugs. • *adj.* **1** using formulae. **2** in or of formulae. [(n.) F *formulaire* or f. med.L *formularius* (*liber* book) f. L (as FORMULA): (adj.) f. FORMULA]

for·mu·late /fáwrmyəlayt/ *v.tr.* **1** express in a formula. **2** express clearly and precisely. **3** create or devise (a plan, etc.). **4** develop or prepare following a formula. □□ **for·mu·la·tion** /-láyshən/ *n.*

for·mu·la weight *n.* = MOLECULAR WEIGHT.

for·mu·lism /fáwrmyəlizəm/ *n.* adherence to or dependence on conventional formulas. □□ **for·mu·list** *n.* **for·mu·lis·tic** *adj.*

form·work /fáwrmwərk/ *n.* a temporary structure, usu. of wood, used to hold concrete during setting.

for·ni·cate /fáwrnikayt/ *v.intr.* (of people not married or not married to each other) have sexual intercourse voluntarily. □□ **for·ni·ca·tion** /-káyshən/ *n.* **for·ni·ca·tor** *n.* [eccl.L *fornicari* f. L *fornix –icis* brothel]

for·rad·er /fáwrədər/ *Brit. colloq. compar.* of FORWARD.

for·sake /fərsáyk, fawr–/ *v.tr.* (*past* **for·sook** /-sŏŏk/; *past part.* **for·sak·en** /-sáykən/) **1** give up; break off from; renounce. **2** withdraw one's help, friendship, or companionship from; desert; abandon. □□ **for·sak·en·ness** *n.* **for·sak·er** *n.* [OE *forsacan* deny, renounce, refuse, f. WG; cf. OE *sacan* quarrel]

for·sooth /fərsŏŏth, fawr–/ *adv. archaic* or *joc.* truly; in truth; no doubt. [OE *forsōth* (as FOR, SOOTH)]

for·swear /fáwrswáir/ *v.tr.* (*past* **for·swore** /-swáwr/; *past part.* **for·sworn** /-swáwrn/) **1** abjure; renounce on oath. **2** (in *refl.* or *passive*) swear falsely; commit perjury. [OE *forswerian* (as FOR-, SWEAR)]

for·syth·i·a /fawrsítheeə/ *n.* any ornamental shrub of the genus *Forsythia* bearing bright yellow flowers in early spring. [mod.L f. W. Forsyth, Engl. botanist d. 1804]

fort /fawrt/ *n.* **1** a fortified building or position. **2** *hist.* a trading post, orig. fortified. [F *fort* or It. *forte* f. L *fortis* strong]

forte[1] /fawrt, fáwrtay/ *n.* **1** a person's strong point; a thing in which a person excels. **2** *Fencing* the part of a sword blade from the hilt to the middle (cf. FOIBLE 2). [F *fort* strong f. L *fortis*]

for·te[2] /fórtay/ *adj., adv., & n. Mus.* • *adj.* performed loudly. • *adv.* loudly. • *n.* a passage to be performed loudly. [It., = strong, loud]

for·te·pia·no /fórtaypiánō, –aánō/ *n.* (*pl.* **·nos**) *Mus.* = PIANOFORTE esp. with ref. to an instrument of the 18th to early 19th c. [FORTE² + PIANO²]

for·te-pia·no *adj. & adv.* loud and then immediately soft.

forth /fawrth/ *adv. archaic* except in set phrases and after certain verbs, esp. *bring, come, go,* and *set.* **1** forward; into view. **2** onward in time (*from this time forth; henceforth*). **3** forward. **4** out from a starting point (*set forth*). □ **and so forth** and so on; and the like. [OE f. Gmc]

forth·com·ing /fáwrthkúming/ *attrib. adj.* **1 a** about or likely to appear or become available. **b** approaching. **2** produced when wanted (*no reply was forthcoming*). **3** (of a person) informative; responsive. □□ **forth·com·ing·ness** *n.*

forth·right /fáwrthrít/ *adj. & adv.* ● *adj.* **1** direct and outspoken; straightforward. **2** decisive; unhesitating. ● *adv.* in a direct manner; bluntly. □□ **forth·right·ly** *adv.* **forth·right·ness** *n.* [OE *forthriht* (as FORTH, RIGHT)]

forth·with /fáwrthwíth, –wíth/ *adv.* immediately; without delay. [earlier *forthwithal* (as FORTH, WITH, ALL)]

for·ti·fi·ca·tion /fáwrtifikáyshən/ *n.* **1** the act or an instance of fortifying; the process of being fortified. **2** *Mil.* **a** the art or science of fortifying. **b** (usu. in *pl.*) defensive works fortifying a position. [ME f. F f. LL *fortificatio –onis* act of strengthening (as FORTIFY)]

for·ti·fy /fáwrtifī/ *v.tr.* (**·fies, ·fied**) **1** provide or equip with defensive works so as to strengthen against attack. **2** strengthen or invigorate physically, mentally, or morally. **3** strengthen the structure of. **4** strengthen (wine) with alcohol. **5** increase the nutritive value of (food, esp. with vitamins). □□ **for·ti·fi·a·ble** *adj.* **for·ti·fi·er** *n.* [ME f. OF *fortifier* f. LL *fortificare* f. L *fortis* strong]

for·tis·si·mo /fawrtísimō/ *adj., adv., & n. Mus.* ● *adj.* performed very loudly. ● *adv.* very loudly. ● *n.* (*pl.* **·mos** or **for·tis·si·mi** /–mee/) a passage to be performed very loudly. [It., superl. of FORTE²]

for·ti·tude /fáwrtitōd, –tyōd/ *n.* courage in pain or adversity. [ME f. F f. L *fortitudo –dinis* f. *fortis* strong]

fort·night /fáwrtnīt/ *n.* **1** a period of two weeks. **2** *Brit.* (prec. by a specified day) two weeks after (that day) (*Tuesday fortnight*). [OE *fēowertíene niht* fourteen nights]

fort·night·ly /fáwrtnītlee/ *adj., adv., & n.* esp. *Brit.* ● *adj.* done, produced, or occurring once a fortnight. ● *adv.* every fortnight. ● *n.* (*pl.* **·lies**) a magazine, etc., issued every fortnight.

For·tran /fáwrtran/ *n.* (also **FORTRAN**) *Computing* a high-level programming language used esp. for scientific calculations. [*formula translation*]

for·tress /fáwrtris/ *n.* a military stronghold, esp. a strongly fortified town fit for a large garrison. [ME f. OF *forteresse*, ult. f. L *fortis* strong]

for·tu·i·tous /fawrtōoitəs, –tyōo–/ *adj.* due to or characterized by chance; accidental; casual. □□ **for·tu·i·tous·ly** *adv.* **for·tu·i·tous·ness** *n.* [L *fortuitus* f. *forte* by chance]

for·tu·i·ty /fawrtōoitee, –tyōo–/ *n.* (*pl.* **·ties**) **1** a chance occurrence. **2** accident or chance; fortuitousness.

for·tu·nate /fáwrchənət/ *adj.* **1** favored by fortune; lucky; prosperous. **2** auspicious; favorable. [ME f. L *fortunatus* (as FORTUNE)]

for·tu·nate·ly /fáwrchənətlee/ *adv.* **1** luckily; successfully. **2** (qualifying a whole sentence) it is fortunate that.

for·tune /fáwrchən/ *n.* **1 a** chance or luck as a force in human affairs. **b** a person's destiny. **2** (**Fortune**) this force personified, often as a deity. **3** (in *sing.* or *pl.*) the good or bad luck that befalls a person or an enterprise. **4** good luck. **5** prosperity; a prosperous condition. **6** (also *colloq.* small fortune) great wealth; a huge sum of money. □ **make a** (or **one's**) **fortune** acquire wealth or prosperity. **tell a person's fortune** make predictions about a person's future. [ME f. OF f. L *fortuna* luck, chance]

for·tune hunt·er *n. colloq.* a person seeking wealth by marriage.

for·tune-tell·er *n.* a person who claims to predict future events in a person's life. □□ **for·tune-tell·ing** *n.*

for·ty /fáwrtee/ *n. & adj.* ● *n.* (*pl.* **·ties**) **1** the product of four and ten. **2** a symbol for this (40, xl, XL). **3** (in *pl.*) the numbers from 40 to 49, esp. the years of a century or of a person's life. **4** (**the Forties**) *Brit.* the sea area between the NE coast of Scotland and the SW coast of Norway (so called from its depth of forty fathoms or more). ● *adj.* that amount to forty. □□ **for·ti·eth** *adj. & n.* **for·ty·fold** *adj. & adv.* [OE *fēowertig* (as FOUR, –TY²)]

for·ty-first *adj.* (**forty-second**, etc.) the ordinal numbers between fortieth and fiftieth.

for·ty-five *n.* **1** a phonograph record played at 45 r.p.m. **2** a .45 caliber handgun.

For·ty-five *n.* the Jacobite rebellion of 1745.

for·ty-nin·er *n.* a seeker for gold, etc., esp. in the California gold rush of 1849.

for·ty-one *n.* (**forty-two**, etc.) the cardinal numbers between forty and fifty.

for·ty winks *n. colloq.* a short sleep.

fo·rum /fáwrəm/ *n.* **1** a place of or meeting for public discussion. **2** a periodical, etc., giving an opportunity for discussion. **3** a court or tribunal. **4** *hist.* a public square or marketplace in an ancient Roman city used for judicial and other business. [L, in sense 4]

for·ward /fáwrwərd/ *adj., n., adv., & v.* ● *adj.* **1** lying in one's line of motion. **2 a** onward or toward the front. **b** *Naut.* belonging to the fore part of a ship. **3** precocious; bold in manner; presumptuous. **4** *Commerce* relating to future produce, delivery, etc. (*forward contract*). **5 a** advanced; progressing toward or approaching maturity or completion. **b** (of a plant, etc.) well advanced or early. ● *n.* an attacking player positioned near the front of a team in football, hockey, etc. ● *adv.* **1** to the front; into prominence (*come forward; move forward*). **2** in advance; ahead (*sent them forward*). **3** onward so as to make progress (*not getting any farther forward*). **4** toward the future; continuously onward (*from this time forward*). **5** (also **for·wards**) **a** toward the front in the direction one is facing. **b** in the normal direction of motion or of traversal. **c** with continuous forward motion (*backward and forward; rushing forward*). **6** *Naut. & Aeron.* in, near, or toward the bow or nose. ● *v.tr.* **1 a** send (a letter, etc.) on to a further destination. **b** esp. *Brit.* dispatch (goods, etc.) (*forwarding agent*). **2** help to advance; promote. □□ **for·ward·er** *n.* **for·ward·ly** *adv.* **for·ward·ness** *n.* (esp. in sense 3 of *adj.*). [OE *forweard*, var. of *forthweard* (as FORTH, –WARD)]

for·ward-look·ing *adj.* progressive; favoring change.

for·wards var. of FORWARD *adv.* 5.

for·went *past* of FORGO.

fos·sa /fósə/ *n.* (*pl.* **fos·sae** /–see/) *Anat.* a shallow depression or cavity. [L, = ditch, fem. past part. of *fodere* dig]

fosse /fos/ *n.* **1** a long narrow trench or excavation, esp. in a fortification. **2** *Anat.* = FOSSA. [ME f. OF f. L *fossa*: see FOSSA]

fos·sick /fósik/ *v.intr. Austral. & NZ colloq.* **1** (foll. by *about, around*) rummage; search. **2** search for gold, etc., in abandoned workings. □□ **fos·sick·er** *n.* [19th c.: cf. dial. *fossick* bustle about]

fos·sil /fósəl/ *n. & adj.* ● *n.* **1** the remains or impression of a (usu. prehistoric) plant or animal hardened in rock (often *attrib.: fossil bones; fossil shells*). **2** *colloq.* an antiquated or unchanging person or thing. **3** a word that has become obsolete except in set phrases or forms, e.g., *hue* in *hue and cry*. ● *adj.* **1** of or like a fossil. **2** antiquated; out of date. □□ **fos·sil·if·er·ous** /fósilífərəs/ *adj.* **fos·sil·ize** *v.tr. & intr.* **fos·sil·i·za·tion** *n.* [F *fossile* f. L *fossilis* f. *fodere* foss- dig]

fos·sil fuel *n.* a natural fuel such as coal or gas formed in the geological past from the remains of living organisms.

fos·sil i·vo·ry *n.* ivory from the tusks of a mammoth.

fos·so·ri·al /fosáwreeəl/ *adj.* **1** (of animals) burrowing. **2** (of limbs, etc.) used in burrowing. [med.L *fossorius* f. *fossor* digger (as FOSSIL)]

fos·ter /fáwstər, fós–/ *v. & adj.* ● *v.tr.* **1 a** promote the growth or development of. **b** encourage or harbor (a feeling). **2** (of circumstances) be favorable to. **3 a** bring up (a child that is not one's own by birth). **b** *Brit.* (of a local authority, etc.) place (a child) to be fostered. **4** cherish; have affectionate regard for (an idea, scheme, etc.). ● *adj.* **1** having a family connection by fostering and not by birth (*foster brother; foster child; foster parent*). **2** involving or concerned with fostering a child (*foster care; foster home*). □□ **fos·ter·age** *n.* (esp. in sense 3 of *v.*). **fos·ter·er** *n.* [OE *fōstrian, fōster*, rel. to FOOD]

fos·ter·ling /fáwstərling, fós–/ *n.* a foster child; a nursling. [OE *fōsterling* (as FOSTER)]

fouet·té /fwetáy/ *n. Ballet* a quick whipping movement of the raised leg. [F, past part. of *fouetter* whip]

fought *past* and *past part.* of FIGHT.

foul /fowl/ *adj., n., adv., & v.* ● *adj.* **1** offensive to the senses; loathsome; stinking. **2** dirty; soiled; filthy. **3** *colloq.* revolting; disgusting. **4 a** containing or charged with noxious matter (*foul air*). **b** clogged; choked. **5** morally polluted; disgustingly abusive or offensive (*foul language; foul deeds*). **6** unfair; against the rules of a game, etc. (*by fair means or foul*). **7** (of the weather) wet; rough; stormy. **8** (of a rope, etc.) entangled. **9** (of a ship's bottom) overgrown with weeds, barnacles, etc. ● *n.* **1** *Sports* an unfair or invalid stroke or action. **2** *Baseball* a batted ball not hit into fair territory. **3** a collision or entanglement, esp. in riding, rowing, or running. **4** a foul thing. ● *adv.* unfairly; contrary to the rules. ● *v.* **1** *tr. & intr.* make or become foul or dirty. **2** *tr.* (of an animal) make dirty with excrement. **3 a** *tr. Sports* commit a foul against (a player). **b** *intr.* commit a foul. **4** *tr. & intr. Sports* hit a ball foul. **5 a** *tr.* (often foll. by *up*) cause (an anchor, cable, etc.) to become entangled or muddled. **b** *intr.* become entangled. **6** *tr.* jam or block (a crossing, railway line, or traffic). **7** *tr.* (usu. foll. by *up*) *colloq.* spoil or bungle. **8** *tr.* run foul of; collide with. **9** *tr.* pollute with guilt; dishonor. □□ **foul·ly** *adv.* **foul·ness** *n.* [OE *fūl* f. Gmc]

fou·lard /fōoláard/ *n.* **1** a thin soft material of silk or silk and cotton. **2** an article made of this. [F]

foul ball *n.* = sense 2 of *n.*

foul brood *n.* a fatal bacterial disease of larval honeybees.

foul mouth *n.* a tendency to use offensive or obscene language.

foul play *n.* **1** unfair play in games. **2** treacherous or violent activity, esp. murder.

foul shot *n.* = FREE THROW.

foul-up *n.* a muddled or bungled situation.

found[1] *past* and *past part.* of FIND.

found[2] /fownd/ *v.* **1** *tr.* **a** establish (esp. with an endowment). **b** originate or initiate (an institution). **2** *tr.* be the original builder or begin the building of (a town, etc.). **3** *tr.* lay the base of (a building, etc.). **4** (foll. by *on, upon*) **a** *tr.* construct or base (a story, theory, rule, etc.) according to a specified principle or ground. **b** *intr.* have a basis in. [ME f. OF *fonder* f. L *fundare* f. *fundus* bottom]

found[3] /fownd/ *v.tr.* **1 a** melt and mold (metal). **b** fuse (materials for glass). **2** make by founding. □□ **found·er** *n.* [ME f. OF *fondre* f. L *fundere fus-* pour]

foun·da·tion /fowndáyshən/ *n.* **1 a** the solid ground or base, natural or artificial, on which a building rests. **b** (usu. in *pl.*) the lowest load-bearing part of a building, usu. below ground level. **2** a body or ground on which other parts are overlaid. **3** a basis or underlying principle; groundwork (*the report has no foundation*). **4 a** the act or an instance of establishing or constituting (esp. an endowed institution) on a permanent basis. **b** such an institution, e.g., a college or hospital. **5** a cream used as a base to even out facial skin tone before applying other cosmetics. **6** (in full **foundation garment**) a woman's supporting undergarment, e.g., a corset. □□ **foun·da·tion·al** *adj.* [ME f. OF *fondation* f. L *fundatio –onis* (as FOUND[2])]

foun·da·tion stone *n.* **1** a stone laid with ceremony to celebrate the founding of a building. **2** the main ground or basis of something.

found·er[1] /fówndər/ *n.* a person who founds an institution. □□ **found·er·ship** *n.*

found·er[2] /fówndər/ *v. & n.* • *v.* **1 a** *intr.* (of a ship) fill with water and sink. **b** *tr.* cause (a ship) to founder. **2** *intr.* (of a plan, etc.) fail. **3** *intr.* (of earth, a building, etc.) fall down or in; give way. **4 a** *intr.* (of a horse or its rider) fall to the ground, fall from lameness, stick fast in mud, etc. **b** *tr.* cause (a horse) to break down, esp. with founder. • *n.* **1** inflammation of a horse's foot from overwork. **2** rheumatism of the chest muscles in horses. [ME f. OF *fondrer, esfondrer* submerge, collapse, ult. f. L *fundus* bottom]

found·ing fa·ther *n.* a person associated with a founding, esp. (usu. *cap.*) an American statesman at the time of the Revolution.

found·ling /fówndling/ *n.* an abandoned infant of unknown parentage. [ME, perh. f. obs. *funding* (as FIND, –ING[3]), assim. to –LING[1]]

found·ry /fówndree/ *n.* (*pl.* **-ries**) a workshop for or a business of casting metal.

fount[1] /fownt/ *n. poet.* a spring or fountain; a source. [back-form. f. FOUNTAIN after MOUNT[2]]

fount[2] /fownt, font/ *n. Brit.* = FONT[2].

foun·tain /fówntin/ *n.* **1 a** a jet or jets of water made to spout for ornamental purposes or for drinking. **b** a structure provided for this. **2** a structure for the constant public supply of drinking water. **3** a natural spring of water. **4** a source (in physical or abstract senses). **5** = SODA FOUNTAIN. **6** a reservoir for oil, ink, etc. □□ **foun·tained** *adj.* (also in *comb.*). [ME f. OF *fontaine* f. LL *fontana* fem. of L *fontanus* (adj.) f. *fons fontis* a spring]

foun·tain·head /fównt'nhed/ *n.* an original source.

foun·tain pen *n.* a pen with a reservoir or cartridge holding ink.

fountain pen

four /fawr/ *n. & adj.* • *n.* **1** one more than three, or six less than ten; the product of two units and two units. **2** a symbol for this (4, iv, IV; *rarely* iiii, IIII). **3** a size, etc., denoted by four. **4** a four-oared rowing boat or its crew. **5** the time of four o'clock (*is it four yet?*). **6** a card with four pips. • *adj.* that amount to four. □ **four hundred** the social élite of a community. **on all fours** on hands and knees. [OE *fēower* f. Gmc]

four·chette /foorshét/ *n. Anat.* a thin fold of skin at the back of the vulva. [F, dimin. of *fourche* (as FORK)]

four-eyes *n. sl.* a person wearing glasses.

four flush *n. Cards* a poker hand of little value, having four cards of the same suit and one of another.

four-flush·er *n.* a bluffer, one who makes false claims.

four·fold /fáwrfold/ *adj. & adv.* **1** four times as much or as many. **2** consisting of four parts. **3** amounting to four.

four free·doms *n.* freedom of speech and religion, and freedom from fear and want (from a speech to Congress by F.D. Roosevelt in 1941).

Fou·ri·er a·nal·y·sis /fóoreeay/ *n. Math.* the resolution of periodic data into harmonic functions using a Fourier series. [J. B. J. *Fourier*, Fr. mathematician d. 1830]

Fou·ri·er se·ries /fóoreeay/ *n. Math.* an expansion of a periodic function as a series of trigonometric functions.

four-in-hand *n.* **1** a vehicle with four horses driven by one person. **2** a necktie worn with a knot and two hanging ends superposed.

four-leaf clo·ver *n.* a clover leaf with four leaflets, rather than the typical three, thought to bring good luck.

four-let·ter word *n.* any of several short words referring to sexual or excretory functions, regarded as coarse or offensive.

four-part *adj. Mus.* arranged for four voices to sing or instruments to play.

four·pence /fáwrpəns/ *n. Brit.* the sum of four pence.

four·pen·ny /fáwrpənee/ *adj. Brit.* costing four pence. □ **fourpenny one** *Brit. colloq.* a hit or blow.

four-post·er *n.* a bed with a post at each corner sometimes supporting a canopy.

four·score /fáwrskáwr/ *n. archaic* eighty.

four·some /fáwrsəm/ *n.* **1** a group of four persons. **2 a** a golf match between two pairs with partners playing the same ball. **b** a golf match with four players.

four·square /fáwrskwáir/ *adj. & adv.* • *adj.* **1** solidly based. **2** steady; resolute; forthright. **3** square shaped. • *adv.* steadily; resolutely.

four-stroke *adj.* (also **four-cycle**) (of an internal combustion engine) having a cycle of four strokes (intake, compression, combustion, and exhaust).

four·teen /fáwrteen/ *n. & adj.* • *n.* **1** one more than thirteen, or four more than ten; the product of two units and seven units. **2** a symbol for this (14, xiv, XIV). **3** a size, etc., denoted by fourteen. • *adj.* that amount to fourteen. □□ **four·teenth** *adj. & n.* [OE *fēowertīene* (as FOUR, –TEEN)]

fourth /fawrth/ *n. & adj.* • *n.* **1** the position in a sequence corresponding to that of the number 4 in the sequence 1–4. **2** something occupying this position. **3** the fourth person, etc., in a race or competition. **4** each of four equal parts of a thing; a quarter. **5** the fourth in a sequence of gears. **6** *Mus.* **a** an interval or chord spanning four consecutive notes in the diatonic scale (e.g., C to F). **b** a note separated from another by this interval. **7** (**Fourth**) the Fourth of July. • *adj.* that is the fourth. □□ **fourth·ly** *adv.* [OE *fēortha, fēowertha* f. Gmc]

fourth di·men·sion *n.* **1** a postulated dimension additional to those determining area and volume. **2** time regarded as equivalent to linear dimensions.

fourth es·tate *n.* the press; journalism.

four-wheel drive *n.* **1** a transmission system that provides power directly to all four wheels of a vehicle. **2** a vehicle with such a system, typically designed for off-road driving.

fo·ve·a /fóveeə/ *n.* (*pl.* **fo·ve·ae** /–vee-ee/) *Anat.* a small depression or pit, esp. the pit in the retina of the eye for focusing images. □□ **fo·ve·al** *adj.* **fo·ve·ate** /–veeayt/ *adj.* [L]

fowl /fowl/ *n. & v.* (*pl.* same or **fowls**) • *n.* **1** any domestic cock or hen of various gallinaceous birds, kept for eggs and flesh. **2** the flesh of birds, esp. a domestic cock or hen, as food. **3** *archaic* (except in *comb.* or *collect.*) a bird (*guineafowl; wildfowl*). • *v.intr.* catch or hunt wildfowl. □□ **fowl·er** *n.* **fowl·ing** *n.* [OE *fugol* f. Gmc]

fowl pest *n.* an infectious virus disease of fowls.

fowl-run *n. Brit.* **1** a place where fowls may run. **2** a breeding establishment for fowls.

Fox /foks/ *n.* **1 a** a N. American people native to the northeastern US. **b** a member of this people. **2** the language of this people.

fox /foks/ *n. & v.* • *n.* **1 a** any of various wild carnivorous mammals of the dog family, esp. of the genus *Vulpes*, with a sharp snout, bushy tail, and red or gray fur. **b** the fur of a fox. **2** a cunning or sly person. **3** *sl.* an attractive young woman or man. • *v.* **1 a** *intr.* act craftily. **b** *tr.* deceive; baffle; trick. **2** *tr.* (usu. as **foxed** *adj.*) discolor (the leaves of a book, engraving, etc.) with brownish marks. □□ **fox·ing** *n.* (in sense 2 of *v.*). **fox·like** *adj.* [OE f. WG]

red fox

fox·glove /fóksgluv/ *n.* any tall plant of the genus *Digitalis*, with erect spikes of purple or white flowers like glove fingers.

fox·hole /fóks-hōl/ *n.* **1** *Mil.* a hole in the ground used as a shelter against enemy fire or as a firing point. **2** a place of refuge or concealment.

fox·hound /fóks-hownd/ *n.* a kind of hound bred and trained to hunt foxes.

fox hunt /fóks-hunt/ *n. & v.* • *n.* **1** the hunting of foxes with hounds. **2** a particular group of people engaged in this. • *v.intr.* engage in a foxhunt. □□ **fox·hunt·er** *n.* **fox·hunt·ing** *n. & adj.*

fox·tail /fókstayl/ *n.* any of several grasses of the genus *Alopecurus*, with brushlike spikes.

fox ter·ri·er *n.* **1** a terrier of a short-haired breed originally used for digging out foxes. **2** this breed.

fox·trot /fókstrot/ *n. & v.* ● *n.* **1** a ballroom dance with slow and quick steps. **2** the music for this. ● *v.intr.* (**fox·trot·ted, fox·trot·ting**) perform this dance.

fox·y /fóksee/ *adj.* (**fox·i·er, fox·i·est**) **1** of or like a fox. **2** sly or cunning. **3** reddish brown. **4** (of paper) damaged, esp. by mildew. **5** *sl.* sexually attractive. □□ **fox·i·ly** *adv.* **fox·i·ness** *n.*

foy·er /fóyər, fóyay, fwáayay/ *n.* the entrance hall or other large area in a hotel, theater, etc. [F, = hearth, home, ult. f. L *focus* fire]

FP *abbr.* freezing point.

fp *abbr.* forte piano.

FPO *abbr.* **1** field post office. **2** fleet post office.

fps *abbr.* (also **f.p.s.**) **1** feet per second. **2** foot-pound-second.

Fr *symb. Chem.* the element francium.

Fr. *abbr.* (also **Fr**) **1** Father. **2** French.

fr. *abbr.* franc(s).

Fra /fraa/ *n.* a prefixed title given to an Italian monk or friar. [It., abbr. of *frate* brother]

frab·jous /fráebjəs/ *adj.* delightful; joyous. □□ **frab·jous·ly** *adv.* [devised by Lewis Carroll, app. to suggest *fair* and *joyous*]

fra·cas /fráykəs/ *n.* (*pl.* same, *pronunc.* /-kaaz/) a noisy disturbance or quarrel. [F f. *fracasser* f. It. *fracassare* make an uproar]

frac·tion /frákshən/ *n.* **1** a numerical quantity that is not a whole number (e.g., 0.5, ½). **2** a small, esp. very small, part, piece, or amount. **3** a portion of a mixture separated by distillation, etc. **4** *Polit.* any organized dissenting group, esp. a group of communists in a noncommunist organization. **5** *Eccl.* the division of the Eucharistic bread. □□ **frac·tion·ar·y** *adj.* **frac·tion·ize** *v.tr.* [ME f. OF f. LL *fractio* –*onis* f. L *frangere fract-* break]

frac·tion·al /frákshənəl/ *adj.* **1** of or relating to or being a fraction. **2** very slight; incomplete. **3** *Chem.* relating to the separation of parts of a mixture by making use of their different physical properties (*fractional crystallization; fractional distillation*). □□ **frac·tion·al·ize** *v.tr.* **frac·tion·al·ly** *adv.* (esp. in sense 2).

frac·tion·ate /frákshənayt/ *v.tr.* **1** break up into parts. **2** separate (a mixture) by fractional distillation, etc. □□ **frac·tion·a·tion** /-náyshən/ *n.*

frac·tious /frákshəs/ *adj.* **1** irritable; peevish. **2** unruly. □□ **frac·tious·ly** *adv.* **frac·tious·ness** *n.* [FRACTION in obs. sense 'brawling,' prob. after *factious*, etc.]

fracto- /fráktō/ *comb. form Meteorol.* (of a cloud form) broken or fragmentary (*fractocumulus; fractonimbus*). [L *fractus* broken: see FRACTION]

frac·ture /frákchər/ *n. & v.* ● *n.* **1 a** a breakage or breaking, esp. of a bone or cartilage. **b** the result of breaking; a crack or split. **2** the surface appearance of a freshly broken rock or mineral. **3** *Linguistics* **a** the substitution of a diphthong for a simple vowel owing to an influence esp. of a following consonant. **b** a diphthong substituted in this way. ● *v.intr. & tr.* **1** *Med.* undergo or cause to undergo a fracture. **2** break or cause to break. [ME f. F *fracture* or f. L *fractura* (as FRACTION)]

frae·nu·lum *Brit.* var. of FRENULUM.

frae·num *Brit.* var. of FRENUM.

frag·ile /frájil, –jīl/ *adj.* **1** easily broken; weak. **2** of delicate frame or constitution; not strong. □□ **frag·ile·ly** *adv.* **fra·gil·i·ty** /frəjílitee/ *n.* [F *fragile* or L *fragilis* f. *frangere* break]

PRONUNCIATION TIP **fragile**

Like many other adjectives that end in -*ile* (*docile, facile, fertile, futile*, etc.), the standard British English pronunciation is with a "long i" (rhyming with *pile*).

---

frag·ment *n. & v.* ● *n.* /frágmənt/ **1** a part broken off; a detached piece. **2** an isolated or incomplete part. **3** the remains of an otherwise lost or destroyed whole, esp. the extant remains or unfinished portion of a book or work of art. ● *v.tr. & intr.* /fragmént/ break or separate into fragments. □□ **frag·men·tal** /-mént'l/ *adj.* **frag·ment·ize** *v.tr.* [ME f. F *fragment* or L *fragmentum* (as FRAGILE)]

GRAMMAR TIP **fragment**

Sentence Fragments. A fragment is a partial sentence, usually missing either the subject or the main verb. Although **sentence fragments** are best avoided in formal, written English, they are quite common in the spoken language and recorded speech, and in written dialogue that mimics informal speech ("*Where to?" she asked. "Home," I said*).

---

frag·men·tar·y /frágmənteree/ *adj.* **1** consisting of fragments. **2** disconnected. **3** *Geol.* composed of fragments of previously existing rocks. □□ **frag·men·tar·i·ly** *adv.*

frag·men·ta·tion /frágməntáyshən/ *n.* the process or an instance of breaking into fragments.

frag·men·ta·tion bomb *n.* a bomb designed to break up into small rapidly-moving fragments when exploded.

fra·grance /fráygrəns/ *n.* **1** sweetness of smell. **2** a sweet scent. [F *fragrance* or L *fragrantia* (as FRAGRANT)]

fra·gran·cy /fráygrənsee/ *n.* (*pl.* **·cies**) = FRAGRANCE.

fra·grant /fráygrənt/ *adj.* sweet-smelling. □□ **fra·grant·ly** *adv.* [ME f. F *fragrant* or L *fragrare* smell sweet]

frail /frayl/ *adj. & n.* ● *adj.* **1** fragile; delicate. **2** in weak health. **3** morally weak; unable to resist temptation. **4** transient; insubstantial. ● *n. Old-fash.* (usu. *derog.*) *sl.* a woman. □□ **frail·ly** *adv.* **frail·ness** *n.* [ME f. OF *fraile, frele* f. L *fragilis* FRAGILE]

frail·ty /fráyltee/ *n.* (*pl.* **·ties**) **1** the condition of being frail. **2** liability to err or yield to temptation. **3** a fault, weakness, or foible. [ME f. OF *frailete* f. L *fragilitas* –*tatis* (as FRAGILE)]

Frak·tur /fráktoʊr/ *n.* a German style of black letter type. [G]

fram·be·sia /frambéezhə/ *n. Med.* = YAWS. [mod.L f. F *framboise* raspberry f. L *fraga ambrosia* ambrosial strawberry]

frame /fraym/ *n. & v.* ● *n.* **1** a case or border enclosing a picture, window, door, etc. **2** the basic rigid supporting structure of anything, e.g., of a building, motor vehicle, or aircraft. **3** (in *pl.*) the structure of spectacles holding the lenses. **4** a human or animal body, esp. with reference to its size or structure (*his frame shook with laughter*). **5** a framed work or structure (*the frame of heaven*). **6 a** an established order, plan, or system (*the frame of society*). **b** construction; constitution; build. **7** a temporary state (esp. in **frame of mind**). **8** a single complete image or picture on a movie or video film or transmitted in a series of lines by television. **9 a** a triangular structure for positioning the balls in pool, etc. **b** the balls positioned in this way. **c** a round of play in bowling, etc. **10** *Hort.* a boxlike structure of glass, etc., for protecting plants. **11** a removable box of slats for the building of a honeycomb in a beehive. **12** *sl.* = FRAME-UP. ● *v.tr.* **1 a** set in or provide with a frame. **b** serve as a frame for. **2** construct by a combination of parts or in accordance with a design or plan. **3** formulate or devise the essentials of (a complex thing, idea, theory, etc.). **4** (foll. by *to, into*) adapt or fit. **5** *colloq.* concoct a false charge or evidence against; devise a plot with regard to. **6** articulate (words). □□ **fram·a·ble** *adj.* (also **frame·a·ble**) **frame·less** *adj.* **fram·er** *n.* [OE *framian* be of service f. *fram* forward: see FROM]

frame house *n.* a house constructed of a wooden skeleton covered with boards, etc.

frame of ref·er·ence *n.* **1** a set of criteria or stated values in relation to which measurements of judgments can be made (*the observer interprets what he sees in terms of his own cultural frame of reference*). **2** *Geom.* a system of geometrical axes in relation to which measurements of size, position, or motion can be made.

frame-up *n. colloq.* a conspiracy, esp. to make an innocent person appear guilty.

frame·work /fráymwərk/ *n.* **1** an essential supporting structure. **2** a basic system.

fram·ing /fráyming/ *n.* a framework; a system of frames.

franc /frangk/ *n.* the chief monetary unit of France, Belgium, Switzerland, Luxembourg, and several other countries. [ME f. OF f. *Francorum Rex* king of the Franks, the legend on the earliest gold coins so called (14th c.): see FRANK]

fran·chise /fránchīz/ *n. & v.* ● *n.* **1 a** a right to vote in governmental elections. **b** the principle of qualification for this. **2** full membership of a corporation or nation; citizenship. **3** authorization granted to an individual or group by a company to sell its goods or services in a particular way. **4** *hist.* legal immunity or exemption from a burden or jurisdiction. **5** a right or privilege granted to a person or corporation. **6** a professional sports team, esp. as part of a league. ● *v.tr.* grant a franchise to. □□ **fran·chi·see** /-zée/ *n.* **fran·chis·er** *n.* (also **fran·chi·sor**). [ME f. OF f. *franc, franche* free: see FRANK]

Fran·cis·can /fransískən/ *n. & adj.* ● *n.* a friar, sister, or lay member of an order founded in 1209 by St. Francis of Assisi (see also GREY FRIAR). ● *adj.* of St. Francis or his order. [F *franciscain* f. mod.L *Franciscanus* f. *Franciscus* Francis]

fran·ci·um /fránseeəm/ *n. Chem.* a radioactive metallic element oc-

---

SYNONYM TIP **fragment**

FRACTION, PART, PIECE, PORTION, SECTION, SEGMENT. The whole is equal to the sum of its **parts**—*part* being a general term for any of the components of a whole. But how did the whole come apart? **Fragment** suggests that breakage has occurred (*fragments of pottery*) and often refers to a brittle substance such as glass or pottery. **Segment** suggests that the whole has been separated along natural or preexisting lines of division (*a segment of an orange*), and **section** suggests a substantial and clearly separate *part* that fits closely with other parts to form the whole (*a section of a bookcase*). **Fraction** usually suggests a less substantial but still clearly delineated *part* (*a fraction of her income*), and a **portion** is a *part* that has been allotted or assigned to someone (*her portion of the program*). Finally, the very frequently used **piece** is any *part* that is separate from the whole.

---

curring naturally in uranium and thorium ores. ¶ Symb.: **Fr**. [mod.L f. *France* (the discoverer's country)]

Franco- /fráŋkō/ *comb. form* **1** French; French and (*Franco-german*). **2** regarding France or the French (*Francophile*). [med.L *Francus* FRANK]

fran•co•lin /fráŋkōlin/ *n*. any medium-sized partridge of the genus *Francolinus*. [F f. It. *francolino*]

Fran•co•phile /fráŋkəfil/ *n*. a person who is fond of France or the French.

fran•co•phone /fráŋkəfōn/ *n. & adj*. • *n*. a French-speaking person. • *adj*. French-speaking. [FRANCO- + Gk *phōnē* voice]

fran•gi•ble /fránjibəl/ *adj*. breakable; fragile. [OF *frangible* or med.L *frangibilis* f. L *frangere* to break]

fran•gi•pane /fránjipayn/ *n*. **1 a** an almond-flavored cream or paste. **b** a flan filled with this. **2** = FRANGIPANI. [F prob. f. Marquis *Frangipani*, 16th-c. It. inventor of the perfume]

fran•gi•pan•i /fránjipánee, –páanee/ *n*. (*pl*. **fran•gi•pan•is**) **1** any tree or shrub of the genus *Plumeria*, native to tropical America, esp. *P. rubra* with clusters of fragrant white, pink, or yellow flowers. **2** the perfume from this plant. [var. of FRANGIPANE]

fran•glais /fróŋglay/ *n*. a version of French using many words and idioms borrowed from English. [F f. *français* French + *anglais* English]

Frank /fraŋk/ *n*. **1** a member of the Germanic nation or coalition that conquered Gaul in the 6th c. **2** (in the Levant) a person of Western nationality. □□ **Frank•ish** *adj*. [OE *Franca*, OHG *Franko*, perh. f. the name of a weapon: cf. OE *franca* javelin]

frank /fraŋk/ *adj., v., & n*. • *adj*. **1** candid; outspoken (*a frank opinion*). **2** undisguised; avowed (*frank admiration*). **3** ingenuous; open (*a frank face*). **4** *Med*. unmistakable. • *v.tr*. **1** stamp (a letter) with an official mark (esp. other than a normal postage stamp) to record the payment of postage. **2** *hist*. superscribe (a letter, etc.) with a signature ensuring conveyance without charge; send without charge. **3** *archaic* facilitate the coming and going of (a person). • *n*. **1** a franking signature or mark. **2** a franked cover. □□ **frank•a•ble** *adj*. **frank•er** *n*. **frank•ness** *n*. [ME f. OF *franc* f. med.L *francus* free, f. FRANK (since only Franks had full freedom in Frankish Gaul)]

Frank•en•stein /fráŋkənstīn/ *n*. (in full **Frankenstein's monster**) a thing that becomes terrifying to its maker; a monster. [Baron *Frankenstein*, a character in and the title of a novel (1818) by Mary Shelley]

frank•furt•er /fráŋkfərtər/ *n*. a seasoned sausage made of beef or beef and other meat, such as pork. [G *Frankfurter Wurst* Frankfurt sausage]

frank•in•cense /fráŋkinsens/ *n*. an aromatic gum resin obtained from trees of the genus *Boswellia*, used for burning as incense. [ME f. OF *franc encens* pure incense]

frank•lin /fráŋklin/ *n. hist*. a landowner of free but not noble birth in the 14th and 15th c. in England. [ME *francoleyn*, etc., f. AL *francalanus* f. *francalis* held without dues f. *francus* free: see FRANK]

Frank•lin stove /fráŋklin/ *n*. a cast-iron stove having the general shape of an open fireplace but often placed so as to be freestanding. [for its designer, US statesman Benjamin *Franklin* d. 1790]

Franklin stove

frank•ly /fráŋklee/ *adv*. **1** in a frank manner. **2** (qualifying a whole sentence) to be frank.

fran•tic /frántik/ *adj*. **1** wildly excited; frenzied. **2** characterized by great hurry or anxiety; desperate; violent. **3** *colloq*. extreme; very great. □□ **fran•ti•cal•ly** *adv*. **fran•tic•ly** *adv*. **fran•tic•ness** *n*. [ME *frentik, frantik* f. OF *frenetique* f. L *phreneticus*: see PHRENETIC]

frap /frap/ *v.tr*. (**frapped, frap•ping**) *Naut*. bind tightly. [F *frapper* bind, strike]

frap•pé /frapáy/ *adj. & n*. • *adj*. (esp. of wine) iced, cooled. • *n*. **1** an iced drink. **2** a soft semi-frozen drink or dessert. [F, past part. of *frapper* strike, ice (drink)]

frass /fras/ *n*. **1** a fine powdery refuse left by insects boring. **2** the excrement of insect larvae. [G f. *fressen* devour (as FRET[1])]

frat /frat/ *n. colloq*. a student fraternity.

fra•ter•nal /frətárnəl/ *adj*. **1** of a brother or brothers. **2** suitable to a brother; brotherly. **3** (of twins) developed from separate ova and not necessarily closely similar. **4** of or concerning a fraternity (see FRATERNITY 3). □□ **fra•ter•nal•ism** *n*. **fra•ter•nal•ly** *adv*. [med.L *fraternalis* f. L *fraternus* f. *frater* brother]

fra•ter•ni•ty /frətárnitee/ *n*. (*pl*. **-ties**) **1** a male students' society in a university or college. **2** a group or company with common interests, or of the same professional class. **3** a religious brotherhood. **4** being fraternal; brotherliness. [ME f. OF *fraternité* f. L *fraternitas –tatis* (as FRATERNAL)]

frat•er•nize /frátərnīz/ *v.intr*. (often foll. by *with*) **1** associate; make friends; behave as intimates. **2** (of troops) enter into friendly relations with enemy troops or the inhabitants of an occupied country. □□ **frat•er•ni•za•tion** *n*. [F *fraterniser* & med.L *fraternizare* f. L *fraternus*: see FRATERNAL]

frat•ri•cide /frátrisīd/ *n*. **1** the killing of one's brother or sister. **2** a person who does this. □□ **frat•ri•cid•al** /–síd'l/ *adj*. [F *fratricide* or LL *fratricidium*, L *fratricida*, f. *frater fratris* brother]

Frau /frow/ *n*. (*pl*. **Frau•en** /frówən/) (often as a title) a married or widowed German woman. [G]

fraud /frawd/ *n*. **1** criminal deception; the use of false representations to gain an unjust advantage. **2** a dishonest artifice or trick. **3** a person or thing not fulfilling what is claimed or expected of it. [ME f. OF *fraude* f. L *fraus fraudis*]

fraud•u•lent /fráwjələnt/ *adj*. **1** characterized or achieved by fraud. **2** guilty of fraud; intending to deceive. □□ **fraud•u•lence** /–ləns/ *n*. **fraud•u•lent•ly** *adv*. [ME f. OF *fraudulent* or L *fraudulentus* (as FRAUD)]

fraught /frawt/ *adj*. **1** (foll. by *with*) filled or attended with (*fraught with danger*). **2** *colloq*. causing or affected by great anxiety or distress. [ME, past part. of obs. *fraught* (v.) load with cargo f. MDu. *vrachten* f. *vracht* FREIGHT]

Fräu•lein /fróylīn, fröw–/ *n*. (often as a title or form of address) an unmarried (esp. young) German woman. [G, dimin. of FRAU]

Fraun•ho•fer lines /frównhōfər/ *n.pl*. the dark lines visible in solar and stellar spectra. [J. von *Fraunhofer*, Bavarian physicist d. 1826]

frax•i•nel•la /fráksinélə/ *n*. an aromatic plant *Dictamnus albus*, having foliage that emits an ethereal flammable oil. Also called **ditta-ny, gas plant**, or **burning bush**. [mod.L, dimin. of L *fraxinus* ash tree]

fray[1] /fray/ *v*. **1** *tr. & intr*. wear through or become worn, esp. (of woven material) unweave at the edges. **2** *intr*. (of nerves, temper, etc.) become strained; deteriorate. [F *frayer* f. L *fricare* rub]

fray[2] /fray/ *n*. **1** conflict; fighting (*eager for the fray*). **2** a noisy quarrel or brawl. [ME f. *fray* to quarrel f. *affray* (v.) (as AFFRAY)]

fra•zil /fráyzil/ *n*. ice crystals that form in a stream or on its bed. [Can.F *frasil* snow floating in the water; cf. F *fraisil* cinders]

fraz•zle /frázəl/ *n. & v. colloq*. • *n*. a worn or exhausted state (*burned to a frazzle*). • *v.tr*. (usu. as **frazzled** *adj*.) wear out; exhaust. [orig. uncert.]

freak /freek/ *n. & v*. • *n*. **1** (also **freak of na•ture**) a monstrosity; an abnormally developed individual or thing. **2** (often *attrib*.) an abnormal, irregular, or bizarre occurrence (*a freak storm*). **3** *colloq*. **a** an unconventional person. **b** a person with a specified enthusiasm or interest (*health freak*). **c** a person who undergoes hallucinations; a drug addict (see sense 2 of *v*.). **4 a** a caprice or vagary. **b** capriciousness. • *v*. (often foll. by *out*) *colloq*. **1** *intr. & tr*. become or make very angry. **2** *intr. & tr*. undergo or cause to undergo hallucinations or a strong emotional experience, esp. from use of narcotics. **3** *intr*. adopt a wildly unconventional lifestyle. [16th c.: prob. f. dial.]

freak•ish /freekish/ *adj*. **1** of or like a freak. **2** bizarre, unconventional. □□ **freak•ish•ly** *adv*. **freak•ish•ness** *n*.

freak-out *n. sl*. an act of freaking out; a hallucinatory or strong emotional experience.

freak•y /freekee/ *adj*. (**freak•i•er, freak•i•est**) = FREAKISH. □□ **freak•i•ly** *adv*. **freak•i•ness** *n*.

freck•le /frékəl/ *n. & v*. • *n*. (often in *pl*.) a light brown spot on the skin, usu. caused by exposure to the sun. • *v*. **1** *tr*. (usu. as **freckled** *adj*.) spot with freckles. **2** *intr*. be spotted with freckles. □□ **freck•ly** /fréklee/ *adj*. [ME *fracel*, etc., f. dial. *freken* f. ON *freknur* (pl.)]

free /free/ *adj., adv., & v*. • *adj*. (**fre•er** /freeər/; **fre•est** /freeist/) **1** not in bondage to or under the control of another; having personal rights and social and political liberty. **2** (of a nation, or its citizens or institutions) subject neither to foreign domination nor to despotic government; having national and civil liberty (*a free press; a free society*). **3 a** unrestricted; unimpeded; not restrained or fixed. **b** at liberty; not confined or imprisoned. **c** released from ties or duties; unimpeded. **d** unrestrained as to action; independent (*set free*). **4** (foll. by *of, from*) **a** not subject to; exempt from (*free of tax*). **b** not containing or subject to a specified (usu. undesirable) thing (*free of preservatives; free from disease*). **5** (foll. by *to* + infin.) able or permitted to take a specified action (*you are free to choose*). **6** unconstrained (*free gestures*). **7 a** available without charge; costing nothing. **b** not subject to tax, duty, trade restraint, or fees. **8 a** clear of engagements or obligations (*are you free tomorrow?*). **b** not occupied or in use (*the bathroom is free now*). **c** clear of obstructions. **9** spontaneous; unforced (*free compliments*). **10** open to all comers. **11** lavish; profuse; using or used without restraint (*very free with their money*). **12** frank; unreserved. **13** (of a literary, sporting, etc., style) not observing the strict laws of form. **14** (of a translation) conveying the broad sense; not literal. **15** forward; familiar; impudent. **16** (of talk, stories, etc.) slightly indecent. **17** *Physics* **a** not modified by an external force. **b** not bound in an atom or molecule. **18** *Chem*. not combined (*free oxygen*). **19** (of power or energy) disengaged or available. • *adv*. **1** in a free manner. **2** without

cost or payment. **3** *Naut.* not close-hauled. •*v.tr.* **1** make free; set at liberty. **2** (foll. by *of*, *from*) relieve from (something undesirable). **3** disengage; disentangle. □ **free and easy** informal; unceremonious. **free hand** freedom to act at one's own discretion (see also FREEHAND). □□ **free•ly** *adv.* **free•ness** *n.* [OE *frēo, frēon* f. Gmc]
▶<Free means 'without charge,' and a *gift* is 'something given without charge.' The expression "free gift" is therefore tautological.

-free /free/ *comb. form* free of or from (*duty-free; trouble-free*).

free a•gent *n.* a person with freedom of action, esp. a professional athlete to sign a contract with any team.

free as•so•ci•a•tion *n. Psychol.* a method of investigating a person's unconscious by eliciting from him or her spontaneous associations with ideas proposed by the examiner.

free•base /freebays/ *n. & v. sl.* •*n.* cocaine that has been purified by heating with ether, and is taken by inhaling the fumes or smoking the residue. •*v.tr.* purify (cocaine) for smoking or inhaling.

free•bie /freebee/ *n. colloq.* a thing provided free of charge. [arbitrary f. FREE]

free•board /freebawrd/ *n.* the part of a ship's side between the waterline and the deck.

free•boot•er /freebootǝr/ *n.* a pirate or buccaneer. □□ **free•boot** *v.intr.* [Du. *vrijbuiter* (as FREE, BOOTY): cf. FILIBUSTER]

free•born /freeborn/ *adj.* inheriting a citizen's rights and liberty.

free church *n.* a church dissenting or seceding from an established or state-controlled church.

freed•man /freedman/ *n.* (*pl.* •**men**) an emancipated slave.

free•dom /freedǝm/ *n.* **1** the condition of being free or unrestricted. **2** personal or civic liberty; absence of slave status. **3** the power of self-determination; the quality of not being controlled by fate or necessity. **4** the state of being free to act (often foll. by *to* + infin.: *we have the freedom to leave*). **5** frankness; outspokenness; undue familiarity. **6** (foll. by *from*) the condition of being exempt from or not subject to (a defect, burden, etc.). **7** (foll. by *of*) **a** full or honorary participation in (membership, privileges, etc.). **b** unrestricted use of (facilities, etc.). **8** a privilege possessed by a city or corporation. **9** facility or ease in action. **10** boldness of conception. [OE *frēodōm* (as FREE, -DOM)]

free•dom fight•er *n.* a person who takes part in violent resistance to an established political system, etc.

free•dom of con•science *n.* the right to follow one's own beliefs in matters of religion and morality.

free en•ter•prise *n.* a system in which private business operates in competition and largely free of government control.

free fall *n.* movement under the force of gravity only, esp.: **1** the part of a parachute descent before the parachute opens. **2** the movement of a spacecraft in space without thrust from the engines.

free-for-all *n.* a disorganized or unrestricted situation or event in which everyone may take part, esp. a fight, discussion, or trading market.

free-form *adj.* not conforming to a regular or formal structure or shape (*a free-form jazz improvisation*).

free•hand /freehand/ *adj. & adv.* •*adj.* (of a drawing or plan, etc.) done by hand without special instruments or guides. •*adv.* in a freehand manner.

free-hand•ed *n.* generous. □□ **free-hand•ed•ly** *adj.* **free-hand•ed•ness** *n.*

free•hold /freehōld/ *n. & adj.* •*n.* **1** tenure of land or property in fee simple or fee tail or for life. **2** *esp. Brit.* land or property or an office held by such tenure. •*adj.* held by or having the status of freehold. □□ **free•hold•er** *n.*

free house *n. Brit.* an inn or public house not controlled by a brewery and therefore not restricted to selling particular brands of beer or liquor.

free kick *n. Soccer*, etc., a set kick allowed to be taken by one side without interference from the other.

free la•bor *n. Brit.* the labor of workers not in a labor union.

free•lance /freelans/ *adj., adv., n., & v.* •*adj.* working for different companies at different times rather than being permanently employed by one company (*a freelance journalist*). •*adv.* earning one's living in such a way (*she went freelance last year*). •*n.***1** a person who earns their living in such a way. **2** *hist.* (often **free lance**) a medieval mercenary. •*v.intr.* earn one's living as a freelance (*she is freelancing now*). [19th c.: orig. in sense 2 of *n.*]

free•lanc•er *n.* a person who works freelance.

free-liv•ing *n.* **1** indulgence in pleasures, esp. that of eating. **2** *Biol.* living freely and independently; not attached to a substrate; not parasitic or symbiotic.

free•load•er /freelōdǝr/ *n. sl.* a person who eats, drinks, or lives at others' expense; a sponger. □□ **free•load** /-lōd/ *v.intr.*

free love *n.* sexual relations according to choice and unrestricted by marriage.

free•man /freemǝn/ *n.* (*pl.* •**men**) **1** a person who has the freedom of a city, company, etc. **2** a person who is not a slave or serf.

free mar•ket *n.* a market in which prices are determined by unrestricted competition.

free•mar•tin /freemaartin/ *n.* a hermaphrodite or imperfect female calf of oppositely sexed twins. [17th c.: orig. unkn.]

Free•ma•son /freemaysǝn/ *n.* a member of an international fraternity for mutual help and fellowship (the *Free and Accepted Masons*), with elaborate secret rituals.

Free•ma•son•ry /freemaysǝnree/ *n.* **1** the system and institutions of the Freemasons. **2** (**freemasonry**) instinctive sympathy or understanding.

free on board *adv. & adj.* (also **free on rail**) without charge for delivery to a ship or railroad freight car. ¶ Abbr.: **FOB**.

free port *n.* **1** a port area where goods in transit are exempt from customs duty. **2** a port open to all traders.

free•post /freepōst/ *n. Brit.* business reply mail.

fre•er *compar.* of FREE.

free rad•i•cal *n. Chem.* an unchanged atom or group of atoms with one or more unpaired electrons.

free-range *adj.* (of livestock, esp. poultry) kept in natural conditions, with freedom of movement.

free rein *n.* freedom of action or expression..

free school *n.* **1** a school for which no fees are charged. **2** a school run on the basis of freedom from restriction for the students.

free•si•a /freezhǝ, -zeeǝ/ *n.* any bulbous plant of the genus *Freesia*, native to Africa, having fragrant colored flowers. [mod.L f. F. H. T. *Freese*, Ger. physician d. 1876]

free speech *n.* the right to express opinions freely.

free-spo•ken *adj.* speaking candidly; not concealing one's opinions.

fre•est *superl.* of FREE.

free-stand•ing *adj.* not supported by another structure.

Free State *n.* a US state in which slavery was prohibited before the Civil War.

free•stone /freestōn/ *n.* **1** any fine-grained stone which can be cut easily, esp. sandstone or limestone. **2** a stone fruit, esp. a peach, in which the stone is loose when the fruit is ripe (cf. CLINGSTONE).

free•style /freestil/ *adj. & n.* •*adj.* (of a race or contest) in which all styles are allowed, esp.: **1** *Swimming* in which any stroke may be used. **2** *Wrestling* with few restrictions on the holds permitted. •*n.* = CRAWL³.

free•think•er /freethingkǝr/ *n.* a person who rejects dogma or authority, esp. in religious belief. □□ **free•think•ing** *n. & adj.*

free throw *n. Basketball* an unhindered shot at the basket made by a player after a foul has been called against the opposing team.

free trade *n.* international trade left to its natural course without restriction on imports or exports.

free verse *n.* verse without a fixed metrical pattern.

free vote *n.* (in a parliamentary system) a vote not subject to party discipline.

free•ware /freewair / *n. Computing* software that is distributed free and without technical support to users. [FREE + SOFTWARE]

free•way /freeway/ *n.* **1** an express highway, esp. with controlled access. **2** a toll-free highway.

free•wheel /freeweel/ *v.intr.* **1** move freely with gears disengaged, esp. downhill. **2** move or act without constraint or effort.

free wheel *n.* **1** a device in a motor vehicle transmission allowing the drive shaft to spin faster than the engine. **2** the driving wheel of a bicycle, able to revolve with the pedals at rest.

free will *n.* **1** the power of acting without the constraint of necessity or fate. **2** the ability to act at one's own discretion (*I did it of my own free will*).

free world *n.* the noncommunist countries, esp. during the Cold War.

freeze /freez/ *v. & n.* •*v.* (*past* **froze** /frōz/; *past part.* **fro•zen** /frōzǝn/) **1** *tr. & intr.* **a** turn or be turned into ice or another solid by cold. **b** (often foll. by *over*, *up*) make or become rigid or solid as a result of the cold. **2** *intr.* be or feel very cold. **3** *tr. & intr.* cover or become covered with ice. **4** *intr.* (foll. by *to*, *together*) adhere or be fastened by frost (*the curtains froze to the window*). **5** *tr.* preserve (food) by refrigeration below the freezing point. **6** *tr. & intr.* **a** make or become motionless or powerless through fear, surprise, etc. (*he froze in front of the audience*). **b** react or cause to react with sudden aloofness or detachment *she froze under cross-examination*. **7** *tr.* stiffen, harden, injure or kill by chilling (*frozen to death*). **8** *tr.* make (credits, assets, etc.) temporarily or permanently unrealizable. **9** *tr.* fix or stabilize (prices, wages, etc.) at a certain level. **10** *tr.* arrest (an action) at a certain stage of development. **11** *tr.* arrest (a movement in a movie, video, etc.) by repeating a frame or stopping the film at a frame. •*n.* **1** a state of frost; a period or the coming of

WORD HISTORY freeze

Old English *frēosan* (in the phrase *hit frēoseth* 'it is freezing, it is so cold that water turns to ice'), of Germanic origin; related to Dutch *vriezen* and German *frieren*, from an Indo-European root shared by Latin *pruina* 'hoar frost' and *frost*.

frost or very cold weather. **2** the fixing or stabilization of prices, wages, etc. **3** a film shot in which movement is arrested by the repetition of a frame. □ **freeze onto** *colloq.* take or keep tight hold of. **freeze out** *colloq.* exclude from business, society, etc., by competition or boycott, etc. **freeze up** obstruct or be obstructed by the formation of ice. □□ **freez•a•ble** *adj.* **fro•zen•ly** *adv.*

freeze-dry *v.tr.* (·**dries**, ·**dried**) freeze and dry by the sublimation of ice in a high vacuum.

freeze-frame *n.* = sense 3 of *n.*

freez•er /fréezər/ *n.* a refrigerated compartment, cabinet, or room for preserving food at very low temperatures; = DEEP FREEZE 1.

freeze-up *n.* a period or conditions of extreme cold.

freez•ing point *n.* the temperature at which a liquid, esp. water, freezes.

freez•ing works *n. Austral. & NZ* a place where animals are slaughtered and carcasses frozen for export.

freight /frayt/ *n. & v.* ● *n.* **1** the transport of goods in containers or by air or land or, esp. *Brit.*, water. **2** goods transported; cargo. **3** a charge for transportation of goods. **4** the lease of a ship or aircraft for transporting goods. **5** a load or burden. ● *v.tr.* **1** transport (goods) as freight. **2** load with freight. **3** lease out (a ship) for the transport of goods and passengers. [MDu., MLG *vrecht* var. of *vracht*: cf. FRAUGHT]

freight•age /fráytij/ *n.* **1 a** the transportation of freight. **b** the cost of this. **2** freight transported.

freight car *n.* a railroad car used for transporting freight.

freight•er /fráytər/ *n.* **1** a ship or aircraft designed to carry freight. **2** a person who loads or charters and loads a ship. **3** a person who consigns goods for transport inland. **4** a person whose business is to receive and forward freight.

freight•lin•er /fráytlinər/ *n. Brit.* a train carrying goods in containers.

freight ton *n.* see TON[1].

French /french/ *adj. & n.* ● *adj.* **1** of or relating to France or its people or language. **2** having the characteristics attributed to the French people. ● *n.* **1** the language of France, also used in Belgium, Switzerland, Canada, and elsewhere. **2** (prec. by *the*; treated as *pl.*) the people of France. **3** *colloq.* bad language (*excuse my French*). **4** *colloq.* dry vermouth (*gin and French*). □□ **French•ness** *n.* [OE *frencisc* f. Gmc]

French bean *n. Brit.* **1** a beanplant, *Phaseolus vulgaris*, having many varieties cultivated for their pods and seeds. **2 a** the pod used as food. **b** the seed used as food: also called HARICOT or KIDNEY BEAN.

French bread *n.* white bread in a long crisp loaf.

French Ca•na•di•an *n. & adj.* ● *n.* a Canadian whose principal language is French. ● *adj.* of or relating to French-speaking Canadians.

French chalk *n.* a kind of steatite used for marking cloth and removing grease and as a dry lubricant.

French cuff *n.* a double cuff formed by turning back a long cuff and fastening it.

French curve *n.* a template used for drawing curved lines.

French door *n.* **1** a door with glass panes throughout its length. **2** = FRENCH WINDOW.

French dress•ing *n.* **1 a** sweet, creamy, orange salad dressing prepared from oil, tomato purée, and spices. **2** a salad dressing of vinegar and oil, and seasonings.

French fries *n.pl.* (also **French fried potatoes**) potatoes cut into strips and deep-fried.

French doors

French horn *n.* a coiled brass wind instrument with a wide bell.

French•i•fy /frénchifí/ *v.tr.* (·**fies**, ·**fied**) (usu. as **Frenchified** *adj.*) make French in form, character, or manners.

French kiss *n.* a kiss with one partner's tongue inserted in the other's mouth.

French leave *n.* absence without permission.

French let•ter *n. Brit. colloq.* a condom.

French•man /frénchmən/ *n.* (*pl.* ·**men**) a man who is French by birth or descent.

French mus•tard *n. Brit.* a mild mustard mixed with vinegar.

French horn

French pol•ish *n.* shellac polish that produces a high gloss on wood.

French-pol•ish *v.tr.* treat wood with French polish.

French roof *n.* a mansard roof.

French seam *n.* a seam with the raw edges enclosed.

French toast *n.* **1** bread dipped in egg and milk and sautéed.

French win•dow *n.* a pair of casement windows extending to the floor in an outside wall, serving as a window and door.

French•wom•an /frénchwooman/ *n.* (*pl.* ·**wom•en**) a woman who is French by birth or descent.

fre•net•ic /frənétik/ *adj.* **1** frantic; frenzied. **2** fanatic. □□ **fre•net•i•cal•**

ly *adv.* [ME f. OF *frenetique* f. L *phreneticus* f. Gk *phrenitikos* f. *phrenitis* delirium f. *phrēn phrenos* mind]

fren•u•lum /frényələm/ *n.* (also *Brit.* **fraen•u•lum**) (*pl.* ·**la** /–lə/) *Anat.* a small frenum. [mod.L, dimin. of FRENUM]

fre•num /fréenəm/ *n.* (also *Brit.* **frae•num**) (*pl.* ·**na** /–nə/) *Anat.* a fold of mucous membrane or skin, esp. under the tongue, checking the motion of an organ. [L, = bridle]

fren•zy /frénzee/ *n. & v.* ● *n.* (*pl.* ·**zies**) **1** mental derangement; wild excitement or agitation. **2** delirious fury. ● *v.tr.* (·**zies**, ·**zied**) (usu. as **frenzied** *adj.*) drive to frenzy; infuriate. □□ **fren•zied•ly** *adv.* [ME f. OF *frenesie* f. med.L *phrenesia* f. L *phrenesis* f. Gk *phrēn* mind]

Fre•on /fréeon/ *n. Trademark* any of a group of halogenated hydrocarbons containing fluorine, chlorine, and sometimes bromine, used in aerosols, refrigerants, etc. (see also CFC).

fre•quen•cy /fréekwənsee/ *n.* (*pl.* ·**cies**) **1** commonness of occurrence. **2 a** the state of being frequent; frequent occurrence. **b** the process of being repeated at short intervals. **3** *Physics* the rate of recurrence of a vibration, oscillation, cycle, etc.; the number of repetitions in a given time, esp. per second. ¶ Abbr.: *f.* **4** *Statistics* the ratio of the number of actual to possible occurrences of an event. [L *frequentia* (as FREQUENT)]

fre•quen•cy band *n. Electronics* = BAND[1] *n.* 3a.

fre•quen•cy dis•tri•bu•tion *n. Statistics* a measurement of the frequency of occurrence of the values of a variable.

fre•quen•cy mod•u•la•tion *n. Electronics* a modulation in which the frequency of the carrier wave is varied. ¶ Abbr.: **FM**.

fre•quen•cy re•sponse *n. Electronics* the dependence on signal frequency of the output–input ratio of an amplifier, etc.

fre•quent *adj. & v.* /fréekwənt/ *adj.* **1** occurring often or in close succession. **2** habitual; constant (*a frequent caller*). **3** found near together; numerous; abundant. **4** (of the pulse) rapid. ● *v.tr.* /also frikwént/ attend or go to habitually. □□ **fre•quen•ta•tion** *n.* **fre•quent•er** /frikwéntər/ *n.* **fre•quent•ly** /fréekwəntlee/ *adv.* [F *fréquent* or L *frequens –entis* crowded]

fre•quen•ta•tive /frikwéntətiv/ *adj. & n. Gram.* ● *adj.* expressing frequent repetition or intensity of action. ● *n.* a verb or verbal form or conjugation expressing this (e.g., *chatter*, *twinkle*). [F *fréquentatif –ive* or L *frequentativus* (as FREQUENT)]

fres•co /fréskō/ *n.* (*pl.* ·**cos** or ·**coes**) **1** a painting done in watercolor on a wall or ceiling while the plaster is still wet. **2** this method of painting (esp. in fresco). □□ **fres•coed** *adj.* [It., = cool, fresh]

fres•co sec•co *n.* = SECCO.

fresh /fresh/ *adj., adv., & n.* ● *adj.* **1** newly made or obtained (*fresh sandwiches*). **2 a** other; different; not previously known or used (*start a fresh page; we need fresh ideas*). **b** additional (*fresh supplies*). **3** (foll. by *from*) lately arrived from (a specified place or situation). **4** not stale or musty or faded (*fresh flowers; fresh memories*). **5** (of food) not preserved by salting, canning, freezing, etc. **6** not salty (*fresh water*). **7 a** pure; untainted; refreshing; invigorating (*fresh air*). **b** bright and pure in color (*a fresh complexion*). **8** (of the wind) brisk; of fair strength. **9** alert; vigorous; fit (*never felt fresher*). **10** *colloq.* **a** cheeky; presumptuous. **b** amorously impudent. **11** young and inexperienced. ● *adv.* newly; recently (esp. in *comb.*: *fresh-baked; fresh-cut*). ● *n.* the fresh part of the day, year, etc. (*in the fresh of the morning*). □□ **fresh•ly** *adv.* **fresh•ness** *n.* [ME f. OF *freis fresche* ult. f. Gmc]

fresh•en /fréshən/ *v.* **1** *tr. & intr.* make or become fresh or fresher. **2** *intr. & tr.* (foll. by *up*) **a** wash, change one's clothes, etc. **b** revive; refresh; renew.

fresh•er /fréshər/ *n. Brit. colloq.* = FRESHMAN.

fresh•et /fréshit/ *n.* **1** a rush of fresh water flowing into the sea. **2** the flood of a river from heavy rain or melted snow. [prob. f. OF *freschete* f. *frais* FRESH]

fresh•man /fréshmən/ *n.* (*pl.* ·**men**) a first-year student at a high school, college, or university.

fresh•wa•ter /fréshwawtər, –wotər/ *adj.* **1** of or found in fresh water; not of the sea. **2** (esp. of a school or college) rustic or provincial.

fresh•wa•ter flea *n.* = DAPHNIA.

fret[1] /fret/ *v. & n.* ● *v.* (**fret•ted**, **fret•ting**) **1** *intr.* **a** be greatly and visibly worried or distressed. **b** be irritated or resentful. **2** *tr.* **a** cause anxiety or distress to. **b** irritate; annoy. **3** *tr.* wear or consume by gnawing or rubbing. **4** *tr.* form (a channel or passage) by wearing away. **5** *intr.* (of running water) flow or rise in little waves. ● *n. Brit.* irritation; vexation; querulousness (esp. in a fret). [OE *fretan* f. Gmc, rel. to EAT]

fret[2] /fret/ *n. & v.* ● *n.* **1** an ornamental pattern made of continuous combinations of straight lines joined usu. at right angles. **2** *Heraldry* a device of narrow bands and a diamond interlaced. ● *v.tr.* (**fret•ted**, **fret•ting**) **1** embellish or decorate with a fret. **2** adorn (esp. a ceiling) with carved or embossed work. [ME f. OF *frete* trelliswork and *freter* (v.)]

fret[3] /fret/ *n.* each of a sequence of bars or ridges on the fingerboard of some

frets

fret[3]

stringed musical instruments (esp. the guitar) fixing the positions of the fingers to produce the desired notes. □□ **fret•less** adj. [15th c.: orig. unkn.]

fret•ful /frétfŏŏl/ adj. visibly anxious, distressed, or irritated. □□ **fret•ful•ly** adv. **fret•ful•ness** n.

fret•saw /frétsaw/ n. a saw consisting of a narrow blade stretched on a frame, for cutting thin wood in patterns.

fret•work /frétwərk/ n. ornamental work in wood, done with a fretsaw.

Freud•i•an /fróydeeən/ adj. & n. Psychol. • adj. of or relating to the Austrian psychologist Sigmund Freud (d. 1939) or his methods of psychoanalysis, esp. with reference to the importance of sexuality in human behavior. • n. a follower of Freud or his methods. □□ **Freud•i•an•ism** n.

Freud•i•an slip n. an unintentional error regarded as revealing subconscious feelings.

F.R.G. abbr. Federal Republic of Germany.

Fri. abbr. Friday.

fri•a•ble /fríəbəl/ adj. easily crumbled. □□ **fri•a•bil•i•ty** n. **fri•a•ble•ness** n. [F friable or L friabilis f. friare crumble]

fri•ar /fríər/ n. a member of any of certain religious orders of men, esp. the four mendicant orders (Augustinians, Carmelites, Dominicans, and Franciscans). □□ **fri•ar•ly** adj. [ME & OF frere f. L frater fratris brother]

fri•ar's bal•sam n. (or **friars' bal•sam**) a solution containing benzoin in alcohol, used esp. as an inhalant.

fri•ar•y /fríəree/ n. (pl. **-ies**) a convent of friars.

fric•an•deau /fríkəndō/ n. & v. • n. (pl. **fric•an•deaux** /–dōz/) 1 a cushion-shaped piece of meat, esp. veal, cut from the leg. 2 a dish made from this, usu. braised or roasted and served with a sauce. • v.tr. (**fric•an•deaus, fric•an•deaued, fric•an•deau•ing**) make into fricandeaux. [F]

fric•as•see /fríkəsee/ n. & v. • n. a dish of stewed or fried pieces of meat served in a thick white sauce. • v.tr. (**fric•as•sees, fric•as•seed**) make a fricassee of. [F, fem. past part. of fricasser (v.)]

fric•a•tive /fríkətiv/ adj. & n. Phonet. • adj. made by the friction of breath in a narrow opening. • n. a consonant made in this way, e.g., f and th. [mod.L fricativus f. L fricare rub]

fric•tion /fríkshən/ n. 1 the action of one object rubbing against another. 2 the resistance an object encounters in moving over another. 3 a clash of wills, temperaments, or opinions; mutual animosity arising from disagreement. 4 (in comb.) of devices that transmit motion by frictional contact (friction clutch; friction disk). □□ **fric•tion•al** adj. **fric•tion•less** adj. [F f. L frictio -onis f. fricare frict-]

Fri•day /fríday, –dee/ n. & adv. • n. the sixth day of the week, following Thursday. • adv. colloq. 1 on Friday. 2 (**Fridays**) on Fridays; each Friday. [OE frīgedæg f. Gmc (named after Frigg the wife of Odin)]

fridge /frij/ n. colloq. = REFRIGERATOR. [abbr.]

friend /frend/ n. & v. • n. 1 a person with whom one enjoys mutual affection and regard (usu. exclusive of sexual or family bonds). 2 a sympathizer, helper, or patron (no friend to virtue; a friend of order). 3 a person who is not an enemy or who is on the same side (friend or foe?). 4 a a person already mentioned or under discussion (my friend at the next table then left the room). b a person known by sight. c used as a polite or ironic form of address. 5 (usu. in pl.) a regular contributor of money or other assistance to an institution. 6 (**Friend**) a member of the Society of Friends; a Quaker. 7 a helpful thing or quality. • v.tr. befriend; help. □ **be** (or Brit. **keep**) **friends with** be friendly with. **my honourable friend** Brit. used in the House of Commons to refer to another member of one's own party. **my learned friend** Brit. used by a lawyer in court to refer to another lawyer. **my noble friend** Brit. used in the House of Lords to refer to another member of one's own party. □□ **friend•ed** adj. **friend•less** adj. [OE frēond f. Gmc]

friend at court n. a friend whose influence may be made use of.

friend•ly /fréndlee/ adj. & adv. • adj. (**friend•li•er, friend•li•est**) 1 acting as or like a friend; well-disposed; kindly. 2 a (often foll. by with) on amicable terms. b not hostile. 3 characteristic of friends; showing or prompted by kindness. 4 favorably disposed; ready to approve or help. 5 a (of a thing) serviceable; convenient; opportune. b = USER-FRIENDLY. • adv. in a friendly manner. □□ **friend•li•ly** adv. **friend•li•ness** n.

friend•ly fire n. Mil. fire coming from one's own side in a conflict, esp. as the cause of accidental injury or damage to one's forces.

friend•ship /fréndship/ n. 1 being friends; the relationship between friends. 2 a friendly disposition felt or shown. [OE frēondscipe (as FRIEND, –SHIP)]

fri•er var. of FRYER.

Frie•sian /fréezhən/ n. & adj. Brit. = HOLSTEIN.

frieze[1] /freez/ n. 1 Archit. the part of an entablature between the architrave and the cornice. 2 Archit. a horizontal band of sculpture filling this. 3 a band of decoration elsewhere, esp. along a wall near the ceiling. [F frise f. med.L frisium, frigium f. L Phrygium (opus) (work) of Phrygia]

frieze[2] /freez/ n. coarse woolen cloth with a nap, usu. on one side only. [ME f. F frise, prob. rel. to FRISIAN]

frig[1] /frig/ v. & n. coarse sl. • v. (**frigged, frig•ging**) 1 a tr. & intr. have sexual intercourse (with). b masturbate. 2 tr. (usu. as an exclamation) = FUCK v. 3. 3 intr. (foll. by around, about) mess around; fool around. 4 intr. (foll. by off) go away. • n. an act of frigging. [perh. imit.: orig. senses 'move about, rub']

frig[2] /frij/ n. colloq. = REFRIGERATOR. [abbr.]

frig•ate /frígit/ n. 1 a a naval vessel between a destroyer and a cruiser in size. b Brit. a similar ship between a corvette and a destroyer in size. 2 hist. a warship next in size to ships of the line. [F frégate f. It. fregata, of unkn. orig.]

frig•ate bird n. any marine bird of the family Fregatidae, found in tropical seas, with a wide wingspan and deeply forked tail. Also called **hurricane bird**.

fright /frīt/ n. & v. • n. 1 a a sudden or extreme fear. b an instance of this (gave me a fright). 2 a person or thing looking grotesque or ridiculous. • v.tr. frighten. □ **take fright** become frightened. [OE fryhto, metathetic form of fyrhto, f. Gmc]

fright•en /frītən/ v. 1 tr. fill with fright; terrify (was frightened at the bang; is frightened of dogs). 2 tr. (foll. by away, off, out of, into) drive or force by fright (frightened it out of the room; frightened them into submission; frightened me into agreeing). 3 intr. become frightened (I frighten easily). □□ **fright•en•ing** adj. **fright•en•ing•ly** adv.

fright•en•er /frítnər/ n. a person or thing that frightens. □ **put the frighteners on** Brit. sl. intimidate.

fright•ful /frítfŏŏl/ adj. 1 a dreadful; shocking; revolting. b ugly; hideous. 2 colloq. extremely bad (a frightful idea). 3 colloq. very great; extreme. □□ **fright•ful•ly** adv.

fright•ful•ness /frítfŏŏlnis/ n. 1 being frightful. 2 (transl. G Schrecklichkeit) the terrorizing of a civilian population as a military resource.

frig•id /fríjid/ adj. 1 very cold in temperature. 2 lacking friendliness or enthusiasm; apathetic; formal; forced. 3 (of a woman) sexually unresponsive. □□ **fri•gid•i•ty** /–jíditee/ n. **fri•gid•ly** adv. **fri•gid•ness** n. [L frigidus f. frigēre be cold f. frigus (n.) cold]

frig•id zones n.pl. the parts of the earth north of the Arctic Circle and south of the Antarctic Circle.

fri•jo•les /freehólays/ n.pl. beans. [Sp., pl. of frijol bean ult. f. L phaseolus]

frill /fril/ n. & v. • n. 1 a a strip of material with one side gathered or pleated and the other left loose with a fluted appearance, used as an ornamental edging. b a similar paper ornament on a lamb chop, etc. c a natural fringe of feathers, hair, etc., on an animal (esp. a bird) or a plant. 2 (in pl.) a unnecessary embellishments or accomplishments. b airs; affectation (put on frills). • v.tr. 1 decorate with a frill. 2 form into a frill. □□ **frilled** adj. **frill•er•y** /–ləree/ n. [16th c.: orig. unkn.]

frilled liz•ard n. (also **frill-necked lizard**) a large N. Australian lizard, Chlamydosaurus kingii, with an erectile membrane round the neck.

frill•y /frílee/ adj. & n. • adj. (**frill•i•er, frill•i•est**) 1 having a frill or frills. 2 resembling a frill. • n. (pl. **•ies**) (in pl.) Brit. colloq. frilled underwear. □□ **frill•i•ness** n.

fringe /frinj/ n. & v. • n. 1 a an ornamental bordering of threads left loose or formed into tassels or twists. b such a bordering made separately. c any border or edging. 2 a Brit. a portion of the front hair hanging over the forehead; bangs. b a natural border of hair, etc., in an animal or plant. 3 an outer edge or margin; the outer limit of an area, population, etc. (often attrib.: fringe theater). 4 a thing, part, or area of secondary or minor importance. 5 a a band of contrasting brightness or darkness produced by diffraction or interference of light. b a strip of false color in an optical image. 6 a fringe benefit. • v.tr. 1 adorn or encircle with a fringe. 2 serve as a fringe to. □□ **fringe•less** adj. **fring•y** adj. [ME & OF frenge ult. f. LL fimbria (earlier only in pl.) fibers, fringe]

fringe ben•e•fit n. an extra benefit supplementing an employee's salary, such as a company car, health insurance, etc.

fring•ing /frínjing/ n. material for a fringe or fringes.

fring•ing reef n. a coral reef that fringes the shore.

frip•per•y /frípəree/ n. & adj. • n. (pl. **•ies**) 1 showy, tawdry, or unnecessary finery or ornament, esp. in dress. 2 empty display in speech, literary style, etc. 3 a knickknacks; trifles. b a knickknack or trifle. • adj. 1 frivolous. 2 contemptible. [F friperie f. OF freperie f. frepe rag]

frip•pet /frípit/ n. Brit. sl. a frivolous or showy young woman. [20th c.: orig. unkn.]

Fris•bee /frízbee/ n. Trademark a molded plastic disk for skimming through the air as an outdoor game. [perh. f. Frisbie bakery (Bridgeport, Conn.), whose pie tins could be used similarly]

Fri•sian /frízhən, free–/ adj. & n. • adj. of Friesland (an area comprising the NW Netherlands and adjacent islands). • n. 1 a native or inhabitant of Friesland. **2** the language of Friesland. [L *Frisii* pl. f. OFris. *Frīsa, Frēsa*]

frisk /frisk/ *v. & n.* ● *v.* **1** *intr.* leap or skip playfully. **2** *tr. sl.* feel over or search (a person) for a weapon, etc. (usu. rapidly). ● *n.* **1** a playful leap or skip. **2** *sl.* the frisking of a person. □□ **frisk·er** *n.* [obs. *frisk* (adj.) f. OF *frisque* lively, of unkn. orig.]

fris·ket /frískit/ *n.* *Printing* a thin iron frame keeping the sheet in position during printing on a hand press. [F *frisquette* f. Prov. *frisqueto* f. Sp. *frasqueta*]

frisk·y /frískee/ *adj.* (**frisk·i·er, frisk·i·est**) lively; playful. □□ **frisk·i·ly** *adv.* **frisk·i·ness** *n.*

fris·son /freesóN/ *n.* an emotional thrill. [F, = shiver]

frit /frit/ *n. & v.* ● *n.* **1** a calcined mixture of sand and fluxes as material for glass-making. **2** a vitreous composition from which soft porcelain, enamel, etc., are made. ● *v.tr.* (**frit·ted, frit·ting**) make into frit; partially fuse; calcine. [It. *fritta* fem. past part. of *friggere* FRY[1]]

frit·fly /frítflī/ *n.* (pl. **-flies**) a small fly, *Oscinella frit*, of which the larvae are destructive to grains. [19th c.: orig. unkn.]

frith var. of FIRTH.

frit·il·lar·y /frít'leree/ *n.* (pl. **-ies**) **1** any liliaceous plant of the genus *Fritillaria*, esp. snake's head, having pendent bell-like flowers. **2** any of various butterflies, esp. of the genus *Argynnis*, having reddish-brown wings checkered with black. [mod.L *fritillaria* f. L *fritillus* dice cup]

frit·ter[1] /frítər/ *v.tr.* **1** (usu. foll. by *away*) waste (money, time, energy, etc.) triflingly, indiscriminately, or on divided aims. **2** *archaic* subdivide. [obs. *n. fritter(s)* fragments = obs. *fitters* (n.pl.), perh. rel. to MHG *vetze* rag]

frit·ter[2] /frítər/ *n.* a piece of fruit, meat, etc., coated in batter and deep-fried (*apple fritter*). [ME f. OF *friture* ult. f. L *frigere* frict- FRY[1]]

frit·to mi·sto /fréetō méèstō/ *n.* a mixed grill. [It., = mixed fry]

fritz /frits/ *n.* □ **on the fritz** *sl.* out of order; unsatisfactory. [20th c.: orig. unkn.]

friv·ol /frívəl/ *v.* (**friv·oled, friv·ol·ing**; also **friv·olled, friv·ol·ling**) **1** *intr.* be a trifler; trifle. **2** *tr.* (foll. by *away*) spend (money or time) foolishly. [back-form. f. FRIVOLOUS]

friv·o·lous /frívələs/ *adj.* **1** not having any serious purpose or value (*rules to stop frivolous lawsuits*). **2** (of a person) lacking seriousness; given to trifling; silly. □□ **friv·ol·i·ty** /–vólitee/ *n.* (pl. **-ties**). **friv·o·lous·ly** *adv.* **friv·o·lous·ness** *n.* [L *frivolus* silly, trifling]

frizz /friz/ *v. & n.* ● *v.tr.* form (hair, etc.) into a mass of small curls. ● *n.* **1 a** a frizzed hair. **b** a row of curls. **2** a frizzed state. [F *friser*, perh. f. the stem of *frire* FRY[1]]

friz·zle[1] /frízəl/ *v.intr. & tr.* **1** fry, toast, or grill, with a sputtering noise. **2** (often foll. by *up*) burn or shrivel. [*frizz* (in the same sense) f. FRY[1], with imit. ending + –LE[4]]

friz·zle[2] /frízəl/ *v. & n.* ● *v.* **1** *tr.* form (hair) into tight curls. **2** *intr.* (often foll. by *up*) (of hair, etc.) curl tightly. ● *n.* frizzled hair. [16th c.: orig. unkn. (earlier from FRIZZ)]

friz·zly /frízlee/ *adj.* in tight curls.

friz·zy /frízee/ *adj.* (**friz·zi·er, friz·zi·est**) in a mass of small curls. □□ **friz·zi·ness** *n.*

Frl. *abbr.* Fräulein.

fro /frō/ *adv.* back (now only in *to and fro*: see TO). [ME f. ON *frá* FROM]

frock /frok/ *n. & v.* ● *n.* **1** esp. *Brit.* a woman's or girl's dress. **2 a** a monk's or priest's long gown with loose sleeves. **b** priestly office. **3** a smock. **4 a** a frock coat. **b** a military coat of similar shape. **5** a sailor's woolen jersey. ● *v.tr.* invest with priestly office (cf. UNFROCK). [ME f. OF *froc* f. Frank.]

frock coat *n.* a man's knee-length coat not cut away in front.

froe /frō/ *n.* (also **frow**) a cleaving tool with a handle at right angles to the blade. [abbr. of *frower* f. FROWARD 'turned away']

Froe·bel sys·tem /frŏbəl, frōbəl/ *n.* a system of education of children by means of kindergartens. □□ **Froe·bel·i·an** /–beéleeən/ *adj.* **Froe·bel·ism** *n.* [F. W. A. *Fröbel*, Ger. teacher d. 1852]

frog[1] /frawg, frog/ *n.* **1** any of various small amphibians of the order Anura, having a tailless smooth-skinned body with legs developed for jumping. **2** (**Frog**) *sl. offens.* a French person. **3** a hollow in the top face of a brick for holding the mortar. **4** the nut of a violin bow, etc. □ **frog in the** (or **one's**) **throat** *colloq.* hoarseness. [OE *frogga* f. Gmc]

frog¹ 1

frog[2] /frawg, frog/ *n.* an elastic horny substance in the sole of a horse's foot. [17th c.: orig. uncert. (perh. a use of FROG[1])]

frog[3] /frawg, frog/ *n.* **1** an ornamental coat fastening of a spindle-shaped button and loop. **2** an attachment to a belt to support a sword, bayonet, etc. □□ **frogged** *adj.* **frog·ging** *n.* [18th c.: orig. unkn.]

frog[4] /frawg, frog/ *n.* a grooved piece of iron at a place in a railroad line where tracks cross. [19th c.: orig. unkn.]

frog·fish /fráwgfish, fróg–/ *n.* = ANGLERFISH.

frog·gy /fráwgee, frógee/ *adj. & n.* ● *adj.* **1** of or like a frog or frogs. **2 a** cold as a frog. **b** abounding in frogs. **3** *sl. offens.* French. ● *n.* (**Froggy**) (pl. **-gies**) *sl. derog.* a French person.

frog·hop·per /fráwghopər, fróg–/ *n.* any jumping insect of the family Cercopidae, sucking sap and as larvae producing a protective mass of froth (see CUCKOO SPIT).

frog·man /fráwgman, fróg–, –mən/ *n.* (pl. **-men**) a person equipped with a rubber suit, flippers, and an oxygen supply for underwater swimming.

frog·march /fráwgmaarch, fróg–/ *v. & n.* ● *v.tr.* **1** hustle (a person) forward, holding and pinning the arms from behind. **2** carry (a person) in a frogmarch. ● *n.* the carrying of a person face downward by four others each holding a limb.

frog·mouth /fráwgmowth, fróg–/ *n.* any of various birds of Australia and SE Asia, esp. of the family Podargidae, having large wide mouths.

frol·ic /frólik/ *v., n., & adj.* ● *v.intr.* (**frol·icked, frol·ick·ing**) play about cheerfully; gambol. ● *n.* **1** cheerful play. **2** a prank. **3** a merry party. **4** an outburst of gaiety. **5** merriment. ● *adj. archaic* **1** full of pranks; sportive. **2** joyous; mirthful. □□ **frol·ick·er** *n.* [Du. *vrolijk* (adj.) f. *vro* glad + –*lijk* –LY[1]]

frol·ic·some /fróliksəm/ *adj.* merry; playful. □□ **frol·ic·some·ly** *adv.* **frol·ic·some·ness** *n.*

from /frum, from, frəm/ *prep.* expressing separation or origin, followed by: **1** a person, place, time, etc., that is the starting point of motion or action, or of extent in place or time (*rain comes from the clouds; repeated from mouth to mouth; dinner is served from 8; from start to finish*). **2** a place, object, etc., whose distance or remoteness is reckoned or stated (*ten miles from Los Angeles; I am far from admitting it; absent from home; apart from its moral aspect*). **3 a** a source (*dig gravel from a pit; a man from Idaho; draw a conclusion from premises; quotations from Whitman*). **b** a giver or sender (*presents from their parents; have not heard from her*). **4 a** a thing or person avoided, escaped, lost, etc. (*released him from prison; cannot refrain from laughing; dissuaded from folly*). **b** a person or thing deprived (*took his gun from him*). **5** a reason, cause, or motive (*died from fatigue; suffering from mumps; did it from jealousy; from her looks you might not believe it*). **6** a thing distinguished or unlike (*know black from white*). **7** a lower limit (*saw from 10 to 20 boats; tickets from $5*). **8** a state changed for another (*from being the victim he became the attacker; raised the penalty from a fine to imprisonment*). **9** an adverb or preposition of time or place (*from long ago; from elsewhere; from under the bed*). **10** the position of a person who observes or considers (*saw it from the roof; from his point of view*). **11** a model (*painted it from nature*). □ **from day to day** (or **hour to hour**, etc.) daily (or hourly, etc.); as the days (or hours, etc.) pass. **from home** out; away. **from now on** henceforward. **from time to time** occasionally. **from year to year** each year; as the years pass. [OE *fram, from* f. Gmc]

frond /frond/ *n.* **1** *Bot.* **a** a large usu. divided foliage leaf in various flowerless plants, esp. ferns and palms. **b** the leaflike thallus of some algae. **2** *Zool.* a leaflike expansion. □□ **fron·dage** *n.* **fron·dose** *adj.* [L *frons frondis* leaf]

fron·deur /frondőr/ *n.* a political rebel. [F, = slinger, applied to a party (the Fronde) rebelling during the minority of Louis XIV of France]

front /frunt/ *n., adj., & v.* ● *n.* **1** the side or part normally nearer or toward the spectator or the direction of motion (*the front of the car; the front of the chair; the front of the mouth*). **2** any face of a building, esp. that of the main entrance. **3** *Mil.* **a** the foremost line or part of an army, etc. **b** line of battle. **c** the part of the ground toward a real or imaginary enemy. **d** a scene of actual fighting (*go to the front*). **e** the direction in which a formed line faces. **4 a** a sector of activity regarded as resembling a military front. **b** an organized political group. **5 a** demeanor; bearing (*show a bold front*). **b** outward appearance. **6** a forward or conspicuous position (*come to the front*). **7 a** a bluff. **b** a pretext. **8** a person, etc., serving to cover subversive or illegal activities. **9** esp. *Brit.* (prec. by *the*) the promenade of a seaside resort. **10** *Meteorol.* the forward edge of an advancing mass of cold or warm air. **11** (prec. by *the*) the audience or auditorium of a theater. **12 a** a face. **b** *poet.* or *rhet.* a forehead. **13 a** the breast of a man's shirt. **b** a false shirtfront. **14** impudence. ● *attrib.adj.* **1** of the front. **2** situated in front. **3** *Phonet.* formed at the front of the mouth. ● *v.* **1** *intr.* (foll. by *on, to, toward, upon*) have the front facing or directed. **2** *intr.* (foll. by *for*) *sl.* act as a front or cover for. **3** *tr.* furnish with a front (*fronted with stone*). **4** *tr.* lead (a band). **5** *tr.* **a** stand opposite to; front toward. **b** have its front on the side of (a street, etc.). **6** *tr. archaic* confront; meet; oppose. □ **in front 1** in an advanced position. **2** facing the spectator. **in front of 1** ahead of; in advance of. **2** in the presence of; confronting. **on the front burner** see BURNER. □□ **front·less** *adj.* **front·ward** *adj. & adv.* **front·wards** *adv.* [ME f. OF *front* (n.), *fronter* (v.) f. L *frons frontis*]

front·age /frúntij/ *n.* **1** the front of a building. **2 a** land abutting on a street or on water. **b** the land between the front of a building and the road. **3** extent of front (*a store with little frontage*). **4 a** the way a thing faces. **b** outlook. □□ **front·ag·er** *n.*

front·age road *n.* a subsidiary road running parallel to a main road and giving access to houses, stores, and businesses. Also called **service road**).

fron·tal[1] /frúnt'l/ *adj.* **1 a** of, at, or on the front (*a frontal attack*). **b** of the front as seen by an onlooker (*a frontal view*). **2** of the forehead or front part of the skull (*frontal bone*). □□ **front·al·ly** *adv.* [mod.L *frontalis* (as FRONT)]

fron·tal[2] /frúnt'l/ *n.* **1** a covering for the front of an altar. **2** the façade of a building. [ME f. OF *frontel* f. L *frontale* (as FRONT)]

front bench *n. Brit.* the foremost seats in Parliament, occupied by leading members of the government and opposition. □□ **front·bench·er** *n.*

front door *n.* **1** the chief entrance of a house. **2** a chief means of approach or access to a place, situation, etc.

fron·tier /frúnteer/ *n.* **1 a** the border between two countries. **b** the district on each side of this. **2** the limits of attainment or knowledge in a subject. **3** the borders between settled and unsettled country. □□ **fron·tier·less** *adj.* [ME f. AF *frounter*, OF *frontiere* ult. f. L *frons frontis* FRONT]

fron·tiers·man /frúnteerzmən/ *n.* (*pl.* **·men**) a person living in the region of a frontier, esp. between settled and unsettled country.

fron·tis·piece /frúntispees/ *n.* **1** an illustration facing the title page of a book or of one of its divisions. **2** *Archit.* **a** the principal face of a building. **b** a decorated entrance. **c** a pediment over a door, etc. [F *frontispice* or LL *frontispicium* façade f. L *frons frontis* FRONT + *-spicium* f. *specere* look: assim. to PIECE]

front·let /frúntlit/ *n.* **1** a piece of cloth hanging over the upper part of an altar frontal. **2** a band worn on the forehead. **3** a phylactery. **4** an animal's forehead. [OF *frontelet* (as FRONTAL[2])]

front·line /frúntlīn/ *adj.* **1** *Mil.* relating to or located at a front line. **2** relating to the forefront of any activity.

front line *n. Mil.* = sense 3 of *n.*

front·man *n.* **1** a person who leads or represents a group or organization, esp. the lead singer of a pop group. **2** a person who represents an illegal or disreputable organization to give it an air of legitimacy.

front mat·ter *n. Printing* the title page, preface, etc., preceding the text proper.

front of·fice *n.* **1** the executives or executive branch of an organization. **2 a** a main office. **b** *Brit.* police headquarters.

fron·ton /frónton, -tón/ *n.* **1** a jai alai court. **2** a pediment. [F f. It. *frontone* f. *fronte* forehead]

front page *n.* the first page of a newspaper, esp. as containing important or remarkable news.

front run·ner *n.* **1** the contestant most likely to succeed. **2** an athlete or horse running best when in the lead.

front-wheel drive *n.* an automobile drive system in which power is transmitted from the engine to the front wheels.

frore /frawr/ *adj. poet.* frozen; frosty. [archaic past part. of FREEZE]

frost /frawst, frost/ *n. & v.* ● *n.* **1 a** a white frozen dew coating esp. the ground at night (*windows covered with frost*). **b** a consistent temperature below freezing point causing frost to form. **2** a chilling or dispiriting atmosphere. **3** *Brit. sl.* a failure. ● *v.* **1** *intr.* (usu. foll. by *over, up*) become covered with frost. **2** *tr.* **a** cover with or as if with frost, powder, etc. **b** injure (a plant, etc.) with frost. **3** *tr.* give a roughened or finely granulated surface to (glass, metal) (*frosted glass*). **4** *tr.* cover or decorate (a cake, etc.) with icing. □□ **frost·less** *adj.* [OE f. Gmc]

frost·bite /fráwstbīt, fróst-/ *n.* injury to body tissues, esp. the nose, fingers, or toes, due to freezing and often resulting in gangrene.

frost heave *n. Geol.* an upthrust of soil or pavement caused by the freezing of moist soil underneath.

frost·ing /fráwsting, fróst-/ *n.* **1** icing. **2** a rough surface on glass, etc.

frost·work /fráwstwərk, fróst-/ *n.* tracery made by frost on glass, etc.

frost·y /fráwstee, fróstee/ *adj.* (**frost·i·er**, **frost·i·est**) **1** cold with frost. **2** covered with or as with hoarfrost. **3** unfriendly in manner; lacking in warmth of feeling. □□ **frost·i·ly** *adv.* **frost·i·ness** *n.*

froth /frawth, froth/ *n. & v.* ● *n.* **1 a** a collection of small bubbles in liquid caused by shaking, fermenting, etc.; foam. **b** impure matter on liquid; scum. **2 a** idle talk or ideas. **b** anything unsubstantial or of little worth. ● *v.* **1** *intr.* emit or gather froth (*frothing at the mouth*). **2** *tr.* cause (beer, etc.) to foam. □□ **froth·i·ly** *adv.* **froth·i·ness** *n.* **froth·y** *adj.* (**froth·i·er**, **froth·i·est**). [ME f. ON *frotha*, *frauth* f. Gmc]

froth-blow·er *n. Brit. joc.* a beer drinker (esp. as a designation of a member of a charitable organization).

frot·tage /frawtaázh/ *n.* **1** *Psychol.* the practice of touching or rubbing against the clothed body of another person as a means of sexual gratification. **2** *Art* the technique or process of taking a rubbing from an uneven surface to form the basis of a work of art. [F, = rubbing f. *frotter* rub f. OF *froter*]

frou·frou /frōrfrōo/ *n.* **1** a rustling, esp. of a dress. **2** a frilly ornamentation. [F, imit.]

frow[1] /frow/ *n. Brit.* **1** a Dutchwoman. **2** a housewife. [ME f. Du. *vrouw* woman]

frow[2] var. of FROE.

fro·ward /fróərd/ *adj. archaic* perverse; difficult to deal with. □□ **fro·ward·ly** *adv.* **fro·ward·ness** *n.* [ME f. FRO + −WARD]

frown /frown/ *v. & n.* ● *v.* **1** *intr.* wrinkle one's brows, esp. in displeasure or deep thought. **2** *intr.* (foll. by *at, on, upon*) express disapproval. **3** *intr.* (of a thing) present a gloomy appearance. **4** *tr.* compel with a frown (*frowned them into silence*). **5** *tr.* express (defiance, etc.) with a frown. ● *n.* **1** an action of frowning; a vertically furrowed or wrinkled state of the brow. **2** a look expressing severity, disapproval, or deep thought. □□ **frown·er** *n.* **frown·ing·ly** *adv.* [ME f. OF *frongnier, froignier* f. *froigne* surly look f. Celt.]

frowst /frowst/ *n. & v. Brit. colloq.* ● *n.* fusty warmth in a room. ● *v. intr.* stay in or enjoy frowst. □□ **frowst·er** *n.* [back-form. f. FROWSTY]

frowst·y /frówstee/ *adj. Brit.* (**frowst·i·er**, **frowst·i·est**) fusty; stuffy. □□ **frowst·i·ness** *n.* [var. of FROWZY]

frowz·y /frówzee/ *adj.* (also **frows·y**) (**·ier**, **·iest**) **1** fusty; musty; malodorous; close. **2** slatternly; unkempt; dingy. □□ **frowz·i·ness** *n.* [17th c.: orig. unkn.: cf. earlier *frowy*]

froze *past* of FREEZE.

fro·zen *past part.* of FREEZE.

FRS *abbr.* **1** Federal Reserve System. **2** (in the UK) Fellow of the Royal Society.

fruc·tif·er·ous /fruktífərəs, frook-/ *adj.* bearing fruit. [L *fructifer* f. *fructus* FRUIT]

fruc·ti·fi·ca·tion /frúktifikáyshən, frook-/ *n. Bot.* **1** the process of fructifying. **2** any spore-bearing structure, esp. in ferns, fungi, and mosses. [LL *fructificatio* (as FRUCTIFY)]

fruc·ti·fy /frúktifī, frook-/ *v.* (**·fies, ·fied**) **1** *intr.* bear fruit. **2** *tr.* make fruitful; impregnate. [ME f. OF *fructifier* f. L *fructificare* f. *fructus* FRUIT]

fruc·tose /frúktōs, frook-/ *n. Chem.* a simple sugar found in honey and fruits. Also called **levulose** or **fruit sugar**. [L *fructus* FRUIT + −OSE[2]]

fruc·tu·ous /frúkchooəs, frook-/ *adj.* full of or producing fruit. [ME f. OF *fructuous* or L *fructuosus* (as FRUIT)]

fru·gal /fróogəl/ *adj.* **1** (often foll. by *of*) sparing or economical, esp. as regards food. **2** sparingly used or supplied; meager; costing little. □□ **fru·gal·i·ty** /−gálitee/ *n.* **fru·gal·ly** *adv.* **fru·gal·ness** *n.* [L *frugalis* f. *frugi* economical]

fru·giv·o·rous /froojívərəs/ *adj.* feeding on fruit. [L *frux frugis* fruit + −VOROUS]

fruit /froot/ *n. & v.* ● *n.* **1 a** the usu. sweet and fleshy edible product of a plant or tree, containing seed. **b** (in *sing.*) these in quantity (*eats fruit*). **2** the seed of a plant or tree with its covering, e.g., an acorn, pea pod, cherry, etc. **3** (usu. in *pl.*) vegetables, grains, etc., used for food (*fruits of the earth*). **4** (usu. in *pl.*) the result of action, etc., esp. as financial reward (*fruits of his labors*). **5** *derog. sl.* a male homosexual. **6** *Bibl.* an offspring (*the fruit of the womb; the fruit of his loins*). ● *v. intr. & tr.* bear or cause to bear fruit. □□ **fruit·age** *n.* **fruit·ed** *adj.* (also in *comb.*). [ME f. OF f. L *fructus* fruit, enjoyment f. *frui* enjoy]

fruit·ar·i·an /frootáireeən/ *n.* a person who eats only fruit. [FRUIT, after *vegetarian*]

fruit bat *n.* any large bat of the suborder Megachiroptera, feeding on fruit.

fruit·cake /frootkayk/ *n.* **1** a cake containing dried fruit. **2** *sl.* an eccentric or mad person.

fruit cock·tail *n.* a chopped usu. canned fruit salad.

fruit·er /frootər/ *n.* **1** a tree producing fruit, esp. with reference to its quality (*a poor fruiter*). **2** a fruit grower. **3** a ship carrying fruit. [ME f. OF *fruitier* (as FRUIT, −ER[5]): later f. FRUIT + −ER[1]]

fruit·er·er /frootərər/ *n. esp. Brit.* a dealer in fruit.

fruit fly *n.* (*pl.* **flies**) any of various flies, esp. of the genus *Drosophila*, having larvae that feed on fruit.

fruit·ful /frootfool/ *adj.* **1** producing much fruit; fertile; causing fertility. **2** producing good results; successful; beneficial; remunerative. **3** producing offspring, esp. prolifically. □□ **fruit·ful·ly** *adv.* **fruit·ful·ness** *n.*

fruit·ing bod·y *n.* (also **fruit bod·y**) (*pl.* **·ies**) the spore-bearing part of a fungus.

fru·i·tion /froo-íshən/ *n.* **1 a** the bearing of fruit. **b** the production of results. **2** the realization of aims or hopes. **3** enjoyment. [ME f. OF f. LL *fruitio -onis* f. *frui* enjoy, erron. assoc. with FRUIT]

fruit·less /frootlis/ *adj.* **1** not bearing fruit. **2** useless; unsuccessful; unprofitable. □□ **fruit·less·ly** *adv.* **fruit·less·ness** *n.*

fruit·let /frootlit/ *n.* = DRUPELET.

fruit ma·chine *n. Brit.* = SLOT MACHINE.

fruit sal·ad *n.* **1** various fruits cut up and served in syrup or juice. **2** *Mil. sl.* a display of medals.

fruit sug·ar *n.* fructose.

fruit·wood /frootwood/ *n.* the wood of a fruit tree, esp. when used in furniture.

fruit·y /frootee/ *adj.* (**fruit·i·er**, **fruit·i·est**) **1 a** of fruit. **b** tasting or smelling like fruit, esp. (of wine) tasting of the grape. **2** (of a voice, etc.) of full rich quality. **3** *sl.* crazy; silly. **4** *offens. sl.* homosexual. **5** *Brit. colloq.* full of rough humor or (usu. scandalous) interest; suggestive. □□ **fruit·i·ly** *adv.* **fruit·i·ness** *n.*

fru·men·ty /frōmantee/ *n.* (also **fur·me·ty** /fórmitee/) hulled wheat boiled in milk and seasoned with cinnamon, sugar, etc. [ME f. OF *frumentee* f. *frument* f. L *frumentum* grain]

frump /frump/ *n.* a dowdy, unattractive, old-fashioned woman. □□ **frump·ish** *adj.* **frump·ish·ly** *adv.* [16th c.: perh. f. dial. *frumple* (v.) wrinkle f. MDu. *verrompelen* (as FOR-, RUMPLE)]

frump·y /frúmpee/ *adj.* (**frump·i·er, frump·i·est**) dowdy, unattractive, and old-fashioned. □□ **frump·i·ly** *adv.* **frump·i·ness** *n.*

frus·trate /frústrayt/ *v. & adj.* ● *v.tr.* **1** make (efforts) ineffective. **2** prevent (a person) from achieving a purpose. **3** (as **frustrated** *adj.*) **a** discontented because unable to achieve one's desire. **b** sexually unfulfilled. **4** disappoint (a hope). ● *adj. archaic* frustrated. □□ **frus·trat·ed·ly** /-stráytidlee/ *adv.* **frus·trat·er** *n.* **frus·trat·ing** *adj.* **frus·trat·ing·ly** *adv.* **frus·tra·tion** /-stráyshən/ *n.* [ME f. L *frustrari frustrat-* f. *frustra* in vain]

frus·tule /frúschōōl/ *n. Bot.* the siliceous cell wall of a diatom. [F f. L *frustulum* (as FRUSTUM)]

frus·tum /frústəm/ *n.* (pl. **frus·ta** /-tə/ or **frus·tums**) *Geom.* **1** the remainder of a cone or pyramid whose upper part has been cut off by a plane parallel to its base. **2** the part of a cone or pyramid intercepted between two planes. [L, = piece cut off]

fru·tes·cent /frōōtésənt/ *adj. Bot.* of the nature of a shrub. [irreg. f. L *frutex* bush]

fru·tex /frōōteks/ *n.* (pl. **fru·ti·ces** /-tiseez/) *Bot.* a woody-stemmed plant smaller than a tree; a shrub. [L *frutex fruticis*]

fru·ti·cose /frōōtikōs/ *adj. Bot.* resembling a shrub. [L *fruticosus* f. FRUTEX)]

fry[1] /frī/ *v. & n.* ● *v.* (**fries, fried**) **1** *tr. & intr.* cook or be cooked in hot fat. **2** *tr. & intr. sl.* electrocute or be electrocuted. **3** *tr.* (as **fried** *adj.*) *sl.* drunk. **4** *intr. colloq.* be very hot. ● *n.* (pl. **fries**) **1** a French fry. **2** a social gathering serving fried food. **3** a dish of fried food, esp. meat. **4** various internal parts of animals usu. eaten fried (*lamb's fry*). □ **fry up** cook in a frying pan. **out of the frying pan into the fire** from a bad situation to a worse one. [ME f. OF *frire* f. L *frigere*]

fry[2] /frī/ *n.pl.* **1** young or newly hatched fishes. **2** the young of other creatures produced in large numbers, e.g., bees or frogs. □ **small fry** people of little importance; children. [ME f. ON *frjó*]

fry·er /fríər/ *n.* (also **fri·er**) **1** a person who fries. **2** a vessel for frying, esp. deep frying. **3** a young chicken suitable for frying.

fry·ing pan *n.* (also **fry pan**) a shallow pan used in frying.

fry-up *n. Brit. colloq.* a dish of miscellaneous fried food.

FSLIC *abbr.* Federal Savings and Loan Insurance Corporation.

f-stop /éf stop/ var. of F-NUMBER.

Ft. *abbr.* Fort.

ft. *abbr.* foot, feet.

FTC *abbr.* Federal Trade Commission.

fub·sy /fúbzee/ *adj.* (**fub·si·er, fub·si·est**) *Brit.* fat or squat. [obs. *fubs* small fat person + -Y[1]]

fuch·sia /fyōōshə/ *n.* any shrub of the genus *Fuchsia*, with drooping red or purple or white flowers. [mod.L f. L. *Fuchs*, Ger. botanist d. 1566]

fuch·sin /fōōksin/ *n.* (also **fuch·sine** /-seen/) a deep red aniline dye used in the pharmaceutical and textile-processing industries; rosaniline. [FUCHSIA (from its resemblance to the color of the flower)]

fuck /fuk/ *v., int., & n. coarse sl.* ● *v.* **1** *tr. & intr.* have sexual intercourse (with). **2** *intr.* (foll. by *around, about*) mess around; fool around. **3** *tr.* (usu. as an exclam.) curse; confound (*fuck the schedule!*). **4** *intr.* (as **fucking** *adj., adv.*) used as an intensive to express annoyance, etc. ● *int.* expressing anger or annoyance. ● *n.* **1 a** an act of sexual intercourse. **b** a partner in sexual intercourse. **2** the slightest amount (*don't give a fuck*). □ **fuck off** go away. **fuck up** make a mess of. □□ **fuck·er** *n.* (often as a term of abuse). [16th c.: orig. unkn.]

fuck-up *n.* a mess or muddle.

▶A highly taboo word.

fu·cus /fyōōkəs/ *n.* (pl. **fu·ci** /fyōōsī/) any seaweed of the genus *Fucus*, with flat leathery fronds. □□ **fu·coid** *adj.* [L, = rock lichen, f. Gk *phukos*, of Semitic orig.]

fud·dle /fúd'l/ *v. & n.* ● *v.* **1** *tr.* confuse or stupefy, esp. with alcoholic liquor. **2** *intr.* tipple; booze. ● *n.* **1** confusion. **2** intoxication. **3** *Brit.* a spell of drinking (*on the fuddle*). [16th c.: orig. unkn.]

fud·dy-dud·dy /fúdeedúdee/ *adj. & n. sl.* ● *adj.* old-fashioned or quaintly fussy. ● *n.* (pl. **·dies**) a fuddy-duddy person. [20th c.: orig. unkn.]

fudge /fuj/ *n., v., & int.* ● *n.* **1** a soft candy made with milk, sugar, butter, etc. **2** nonsense. **3** a piece of dishonesty or faking. **4** a piece of late news inserted in a newspaper page. ● *v.* **1** *tr.* put together in a makeshift or dishonest way; fake. **2** *tr.* deal with incompetently. **3** *intr.* practice such methods. ● *int.* expressing disbelief or annoyance. [perh. f. obs. *fadge* (v.) fit]

---

fueh·rer var. of FÜHRER.

fuel /fyōōəl/ *n. & v.* ● *n.* **1** material, esp. coal, wood, oil, etc., burned or used as a source of heat or power. **2** food as a source of energy. **3** material used as a source of nuclear energy. **4** anything that sustains or inflames emotion or passion. ● *v.* (**fueled, fuel·ing;** *Brit.* **fuelled, fuel·ling**) **1** *tr.* supply with fuel. **2** *tr.* sustain or inflame (an argument, feeling, etc.) (*liquor fueled his anger*). **3** *intr.* take in or get fuel. [ME f. AF *fuaille, fewaile*, OF *fouaille*, ult. f. L *focus* hearth]

fuel cell *n.* a cell producing an electric current direct from a chemical reaction.

fuel el·e·ment *n.* an element of nuclear fuel, etc., for use in a reactor.

fuel in·jec·tion *n.* the direct introduction of fuel under pressure into the combustion units of an internal combustion engine. □□ **fuel-injected** *adj.*

fuel oil *n.* oil used as fuel in an engine or furnace.

fug /fug/ *n. & v. Brit. colloq.* ● *n.* stuffiness or fustiness of the air in a room. ● *v.intr.* (**fugged, fug·ging**) stay in or enjoy a fug. □□ **fug·gy** *adj.* [19th c.: orig. unkn.]

fu·ga·cious /fyōōgáyshəs/ *adj.* fleeting; evanescent; hard to capture or keep. □□ **fu·ga·cious·ly** *adv.* **fu·ga·cious·ness** *n.* **fu·gac·i·ty** /-gásitee/ *n.* [L *fugax fugacis* f. *fugere* flee]

fu·gal /fyōōgəl/ *adj.* of the nature of a fugue. □□ **fu·gal·ly** *adv.*

-fuge /fyooj/ *comb. form* forming adjectives and nouns denoting expelling or dispelling (*febrifuge; vermifuge*). [from or after mod.L *-fugus* f. L *fugare* put to flight]

fu·gi·tive /fyōōjitiv/ *adj. & n.* ● *adj.* **1** fleeing; that runs or has run away. **2** transient; fleeting; of short duration. **3** (of literature) of passing interest; ephemeral. **4** flitting; shifting. ● *n.* **1** (often foll. by *from*) a person who flees, esp. from justice, an enemy, danger, or a master. **2** an exile or refugee. □□ **fu·gi·tive·ly** *adv.* [ME f. OF *fugitif -ive* f. L *fugitivus* f. *fugere fugit-* flee]

fu·gle /fyōōgəl/ *v.intr.* act as a fugleman. [back-form. f. FUGLEMAN]

fu·gle·man /fyōōgəlmən/ *n.* (pl. **-men**) **1** *hist.* a soldier placed in front of a regiment, etc., while drilling to show the motions and time. **2** a leader, organizer, or spokesman. [G *flügelmann* f. *flügel* wing + *Mann* man]

fugue /fyōōg/ *n. & v.* ● *n.* **1** *Mus.* a contrapuntal composition in which a short melody or phrase (the subject) is introduced by one part and successively taken up by others and developed by interweaving the parts. **2** *Psychol.* loss of awareness of one's identity, often coupled with flight from one's usual environment. ● *v.intr.* (**fugues, fugued, fugu·ing**) *Mus.* compose or perform a fugue. □□ **fu·guist** *n.* [F or It. f. L *fuga* flight]

fugued /fyōōgd/ *adj.* in the form of a fugue.

füh·rer /fyōōrər/ *n.* (also **fueh·rer**) a leader, esp. a tyrannical one. [G, = leader: part of the title assumed in 1934 by Hitler (see HITLER)]

-ful /fool/ *comb. form* forming: **1** adjectives from nouns, meaning: **a** full of (*beautiful*). **b** having the qualities of (*masterful*). **2** adjectives from adjectives or Latin stems with little change of sense (*direful; grateful*). **3** adjectives from verbs, meaning 'apt to,' 'able to,' 'accustomed to' (*forgetful; mournful; useful*). **4** nouns (pl. **·fuls**) meaning 'the amount needed to fill' (*handful; spoonful*).

▶The combining form **-ful** is used to form nouns meaning 'the amount needed to fill,' e.g., *cupful, spoonful.* The plural form of such words is -s, (*cupfuls, spoonfuls,* etc.). *Three cups full* would denote the individual cups rather than a quantity measured in cups: *on the sill were three cups full of milk.*

ful·crum /fŏōlkrəm, fŭl-/ *n.* (pl. **ful·cra** /-rə/ or **ful·crums**) **1** the point against which a lever is placed to get a purchase or on which it turns or is supported. **2** the means by which influence, etc., is brought to bear. [L, = post of a couch, f. *fulcire* to prop]

ful·fill /fŏōlfil/ *v.tr.* (**ful·filled, ful·fill·ing**) **1** bring to consummation; carry out (a prophecy or promise). **2** satisfy (a desire or prayer). **3 a** execute; obey (a command or law). **b** perform; carry out (a task). **4** comply with (conditions). **5** answer (a purpose). **6** bring to an end; finish; complete (a period or piece of work). □ **fulfill oneself** develop one's gifts and character to the full. □□ **ful·fill·a·ble** *adj.* **ful·fill·er** *n.* **ful·fill·ment** *n.* [OE *fullfyllan* (as FULL[1], FILL)]

ful·gent /fúljənt/ *adj. poet.* or *rhet.* shining; brilliant. [ME f. L *fulgēre* shine]

ful·gu·ra·tion /fúlgyəráyshən/ *n. Surgery* the destruction of tissue by means of high-voltage electricity. [L *fulguratio* sheet lightning f. *fulgur* lightning]

ful·gu·rite /fúlgyərīt/ *n. Geol.* a rocky substance of sand fused or vitrified by lightning. [L *fulgur* lightning]

fu·lig·i·nous /fyōōlíjinəs/ *adj.* sooty; dusky. [LL *fuliginosus* f. *fuligo -ginis* soot]

full[1] /fool/ *adj., adv., n., & v.* ● *adj.* **1** (often foll. by *of*) holding all its limits will allow (*the bucket is full; full of water*). **2** having eaten to one's limits or satisfaction. **3** abundant; copious; satisfying; sufficient (*a full program of events; led a full life; turned it to full account; give full details; the book is very full on this point*). **4** (foll. by *of*) having or holding an abundance of; showing marked signs of (*full of vitality; full of interest; full of mistakes*). **5** (foll. by *of*) **a** engrossed in thinking about (*full of himself; full of his work*). **b** unable to refrain from talking about (*full of the news*). **6 a** complete; perfect; reaching the specified or usual or utmost limit (*full membership*; *full daylight*; *waited a full hour*; *it was full summer*, *in full bloom*). **b** *Bookbinding* used for the entire cover (*full leather*). **7 a** (of tone or color) deep and clear; mellow. **b** (of light) intense. **c** (of motion, etc.) vigorous (*a full pulse*; *at full gallop*). **8** plump; rounded; protuberant (*a full figure*). **9** (of clothes) made of much material arranged in folds or gathers. **10** (of the heart, etc.) overcharged with emotion. **11** *Brit. sl.* drunk. **12** (foll. by *of*) *archaic* having had plenty of (*full of years and honors*). ● *adv.* **1** very (*you know full well*). **2** quite; fully (*full six miles*). **3** exactly (*hit him full on the nose*). **4** more than sufficiently (*full early*). ● *n.* **1** height; acme (*season is past the full*). **2** the state or time of full moon. **3** the whole; the complete amount (*cannot tell you the full of it*; *paid in full*). ● *v.intr. & tr.* be or become or make (esp. clothes) full. □ **at full length 1** lying stretched out. **2** without abridgment. **come full circle** see CIRCLE. **full blood** pure descent. **full speed** (or **steam**) **ahead!** an order to proceed at maximum speed or to pursue a course of action energetically. **full up** *colloq.* completely full. **in full 1** without abridgment. **2** to or for the full amount (*paid in full*). **in full swing** at the height of activity. **in full view** entirely visible. **on a full stomach** see STOMACH. **to the full** to the utmost extent. [OE f. Gmc]

full² /fŏol/ *v.tr.* cleanse and thicken (cloth). [ME, back-form. f. FULLER¹: cf. OF *fouler* (FOIL¹)]

full age *n. Brit.* adult status (esp. with ref. to legal rights and duties).

full•back /fŏolbak/ *n.* **1** an offensive player in the backfield in football. **2** a defensive player, or a position near the goal, in soccer, field hockey, etc.

full-blood•ed *adj.* **1** vigorous; hearty; sensual. **2** not hybrid. □□ **full-blood•ed•ly** *adv.* **full-blood•ed•ness** *n.*

full-blown *adj.* **1** fully developed (*a full-blown revolution*). **2** (of flowers) in full bloom.

full board *n. Brit.* provision of accommodation and all meals at a hotel, etc.

full-bod•ied *adj.* rich in quality, tone, etc. (*a full-bodied wine*; *a full-bodied voice*).

full-court press *n. Basketball* **1** an aggressive tactic in which members of a team cover their opponents throughout the court and not just in the region near their own basket. **2** an instance of aggressive pressure.

full dress *n.* formal clothes worn on great occasions.

full-dress *adj.* (of a debate, etc.) of major importance.

full em•ploy•ment *n.* **1** the condition in which there is no idle capital or labor of any kind that is in demand. **2** the condition in which virtually all who are able and willing to work are employed.

full•er¹ /fŏolər/ *n.* a person who fulls cloth. [OE *fullere* f. L *fullo*]

full•er² /fŏolər/ *n. & v.* ● *n.* **1** a grooved or rounded tool on which iron is shaped. **2** a groove made by this, esp. in a horseshoe. ● *v.tr.* stamp with a fuller. [19th c.: orig. unkn.]

full•er's earth *n.* a type of clay used in fulling cloth and as an adsorbent.

full face *adv.* with all the face visible; facing directly at someone or something.

full-face *adj.* **1** showing all of the face (*a full-face mugshot*). **2** covering all of the face (*a full-face motorcycle helmet*).

full-fash•ioned *adj. dated* (of women's clothing) shaped to fit the body.

full-fledged *adj.* mature.

full-fron•tal *adj.* **1** (of nudity or a nude figure) with full exposure at the front. **2** unrestrained; explicit; with nothing concealed.

full-grown *adj.* having reached maturity.

full house *n.* **1** a maximum or large attendance at a theater, etc. **2** *Poker* a hand with three of a kind and a pair.

full-length *adj.* **1** not shortened or abbreviated. **2** (of a mirror, portrait, etc.) showing the whole height of the human figure.

full marks *n.pl. Brit.* the maximum award in an examination or assessment; full credit.

full moon *n.* **1** the moon with its whole disk illuminated. **2** the time when this occurs.

full-mouthed *adj.* **1** (of cattle or sheep) having a full set of teeth. **2** (of a dog) baying loudly. **3** (of oratory, etc.) sonorous; vigorous.

full•ness /fŏolnis/ *n.* (also **ful•ness**) **1** being full. **2** (of sound, color, etc.) richness; volume; body. **3** all that is contained (in the world, etc.). □ **the fullness of the heart** emotion; genuine feelings. **the fullness of time** the appropriate or destined time.

full out *adj.* **1** *Printing* flush with the margin. **2** at full power. **3** complete.

full point *n.* = FULL STOP 1.

full pro•fes•sor *n.* a professor of the highest rank in a university, etc.

full-scale *adj.* **1** of the same size as the thing represented (*a full-scale model of a pirate ship*). **2** unrestricted in size, extent, or intensity; complete (*a full-scale invasion*).

full score *n. Mus.* a score giving the parts for all performers on separate staves.

full-ser•vice *adj.* (of a bank, service station, etc.) providing a wide range of services.

full stop *n.* **1** esp. *Brit.* = PERIOD n. 8. **2** a complete cessation.

full term *n.* the completion of a normal pregnancy.

full tilt *adv.* with maximum energy or force; at top speed.

full-time *adj. & adv.* ● *adj.* occupying or using the whole of someone's available working time, usu. 40 hours in a week (*a full-time job*). ● *adv.* on a full-time basis (*both parents were employed full-time*). □□ **full-tim•er** *n.*

ful•ly /fŏolee/ *adv.* **1** completely; entirely (*am fully aware*). **2** no less or fewer than (*fully 60*). [OE *fullīce* (as FULL¹, −LY²)]

-fully /fŏolee/ *comb. form* forming adverbs corresp. to adjectives in −*ful*.

ful•mar /fŏolmər/ *n.* any medium-sized sea bird of the genus *Fulmarus*, with stout body, robust bill, and rounded tail. [orig. Hebridean dial.: perh. f. ON *fúll* FOUL (with ref. to its smell) + *már* gull (cf. MEW²)]

ful•mi•nant /fŭlminənt, fŏol−/ *adj.* **1** fulminating. **2** *Med.* (of a disease or symptom) developing suddenly. [F *fulminant* or L *fulminant-* (as FULMINATE)]

ful•mi•nate /fŭlminayt, fŏol−/ *v. & n.* ● *v.intr.* **1** (often foll. by *against*) express censure loudly and forcefully. **2** explode violently; flash like lightning (*fulminating mercury*). **3** *Med.* (of a disease or symptom) develop suddenly. ● *n. Chem.* a salt or ester of fulminic acid. □□ **ful•mi•na•tion** /−náyshən/ *n.* **ful•mi•na•to•ry** /−nətáwree/ *adj.* [L *fulminare fulminat-* f. *fulmen −minis* lightning]

ful•min•ic ac•id /fŭlmínik, fŏol−/ *n. Chem.* an isomer of cyanic acid that is stable only in solution. ¶ Chem. formula: HONC. [L *fulmen*: see FULMINATE]

ful•ness var. of FULLNESS.

ful•some /fŏolsəm/ *adj.* **1** disgusting by excess of flattery, servility, or expressions of affection; excessive; cloying. **2** *disp.* copious. □□ **ful•some•ly** *adv.* **ful•some•ness** *n.* [ME f. FULL¹ + −SOME¹]
▶The earliest recorded use of **fulsome**, in the 13th century, had the meaning 'abundant,' but in modern use this is held by many to be incorrect. The correct current meaning is 'disgusting because overdone; excessive.' The word is still often used to mean 'abundant; copious,' but this use can give rise to ambiguity in such expressions as *fulsome praise*.

ful•vous /fŭlvəs/ *adj.* reddish yellow; tawny. □□ **ful•ves•cent** /−vésənt/ *adj.* [L *fulvus*]

fu•ma•role /fyŏomərōl/ *n.* an opening in or near a volcano, through which hot vapors emerge. □□ **fu•ma•rol•ic** /−rólik/ *adj.* [F *fumarolle*]

fum•ble /fŭmbəl/ *v. & n.* ● *v.* **1** *intr.* (often foll. by *at, with, for, after*) use the hands awkwardly or clumsily while doing or handling something (*he fumbled for his keys*). **2** *tr.* express oneself or deal with something with clumsily or nervously (*we fumbled through the interview*). **3 a** *Sports* fail to stop or catch (a ball, pass, shot, etc.) cleanly. **b** *Football* an act of dropping or losing control of the ball, typically causing a turnover. ● *n.* an act of fumbling. □□ **fum•bler** *n.* **fum•bling•ly** *adv.* [LG *fummeln, fommeln*, Du. *fommelen*]

fume /fyŏom/ *n. & v.* ● *n.* **1** (usu. in *pl.*) exuded gas or smoke or vapor, esp. when harmful or unpleasant. **2** a fit of anger (*in a fume*). ● *v.* **1 a** *intr.* emit fumes. **b** *tr.* give off as fumes. **2** *intr.* (often foll. by *at*) be affected by (esp. suppressed) anger (*was fuming at their inefficiency*). **3** *tr.* **a** fumigate. **b** subject to fumes, esp. those of ammonia (to darken tints in oak, photographic film, etc.). **4** *tr.* perfume with incense. □□ **fume•less** *adj.* **fum•ing•ly** *adv.* **fum•y** *adj.* (in sense 1 of *n.*). [ME f. OF *fum* f. L *fumus* smoke & OF *fume* f. *fumer* f. L *fumare* to smoke]

fume hood *n.* (also *Brit.* **fume cupboard**, or **fume chamber**, etc.) a ventilated structure in a laboratory, for storing or experimenting with noxious chemicals.

fu•mi•gate /fyŏomigayt/ *v.tr.* **1** disinfect or purify with fumes. **2** apply fumes to. □□ **fu•mi•gant** /−gənt/ *n.* **fu•mi•ga•tion** /−gáyshən/ *n.* **fu•mi•ga•tor** *n.* [L *fumigare fumigat-* f. *fumus* smoke]

fu•mi•to•ry /fyŏomitawree/ *n.* any plant of the genus *Fumaria*, esp. *F. officinalis*, formerly used against scurvy. [ME f. OF *fumeterre* f. med.L *fumus terrae* earth smoke]

fun /fun/ *n. & adj.* ● *n.* **1** amusement, esp. lively or playful. **2** a source of this. **3** (in full **fun and games**) exciting or amusing goings-on. ● *adj. disp. colloq.* amusing; entertaining; enjoyable (*a fun thing to do*). □ **be great** (or **good**) **fun** esp. *Brit.* be very amusing. **for fun** (or **for the fun of it**) not for a serious purpose. **have fun** enjoy oneself. **in fun** as a joke; not seriously. **like fun** an ironic exclamation of contradiction or disbelief in response to a statement. **make fun of** tease; ridicule. **what fun!** how amusing! [obs. *fun* (v.) var. of *fon* befool: cf. FOND]

fu•nam•bu•list /fyŏonámbyəlist/ *n.* a tightrope walker. [F *funambule* or L *funambulus* f. *funis* rope + *ambulare* walk]

func•tion /fúngkshən/ *n. & v.* ● *n.* **1 a** an activity proper to a person or institution. **b** a mode of action or activity by which a thing fulfills its purpose. **c** an official or professional duty; an employment, profession, or calling. **2 a** a public ceremony or occasion. **b** a social gathering, esp. a large, formal, or important one. **3** *Math.* a variable quantity regarded in relation to another or others in terms of which it may be expressed or on which its value depends (*x is a function of y and z*). **4** a part of a program that corresponds to a single value. ● *v.intr.* fulfill a function; operate; be in working order. □□ **func·tion·less** *adj.* [F *fonction* f. L *functio –onis* f. *fungi funct-* perform]

func·tion·al /fúngkshənəl/ *adj.* **1** of or serving a function. **2** (esp. of buildings) designed or intended to be practical rather than attractive; utilitarian. **3** *Physiol.* **a** (esp. of disease) of or affecting only the functions of an organ, etc., not structural or organic. **b** (of mental disorder) having no discernible organic cause. **c** (of an organ) having a function, not functionless or rudimentary. **4** *Math.* of a function. □□ **func·tion·al·i·ty** /–nálitee/ *n.* **func·tion·ai·ly** *adv.*

func·tion·al group *n. Chem.* a group of atoms that determine the reactions of a compound containing the group.

func·tion·al·ism /fúngkshənəlizəm/ *n.* belief in or stress on the practical application of a thing. □□ **func·tion·al·ist** *n.*

func·tion·ar·y /fúngkshəneree/ *n.* (pl. **·ies**) a person who has to perform official functions or duties; an official.

fund /fund/ *n. & v.* ● *n.* **1** a permanent stock of something ready to be drawn upon (*a fund of knowledge; a fund of tenderness*). **2** a stock of money, esp. one set apart for a purpose. **3** (in *pl.*) money resources. **4** (in *pl.*; prec. by *the*) *Brit.* the stock of the National Debt (as a mode of investment). ● *v.tr.* **1** provide with money. **2** convert (a floating debt) into a more or less permanent debt at fixed interest. **3** put into a fund. □ **in funds** *Brit. colloq.* having money to spend. [L *fundus* bottom, piece of land]

fun·da·ment /fúndəmənt/ *n. joc.* the buttocks or anus. [ME f. OF *fondement* f. L *fundamentum* (as FOUND²)]

fun·da·men·tal /fúndəmént'l/ *adj. & n.* ● *adj.* of, affecting, or serving as a base or foundation; essential; primary; original (*a fundamental change; the fundamental rules; the fundamental form*). ● *n.* **1** (usu. in *pl.*) a fundamental rule, principle, or article. **2** *Mus.* a fundamental note or tone. □□ **fun·da·men·tal·i·ty** /–tálitee/ *n.* **fun·da·men·tal·ly** *adv.* [ME f. F *fondamental* or LL *fundamentalis* (as FUNDAMENT)]

fun·da·men·tal·ism /fúndəméntəlizəm/ *n.* **1** (also **Fun·da·men·tal·ism**) strict maintenance of traditional Protestant beliefs such as the inerrancy of Scripture and literal acceptance of the creeds as fundamentals of Christianity. **2** strict maintenance of ancient or fundamental doctrines of any religion, esp. Islam. □□ **fun·da·men·tal·ist** *n.*

fun·da·men·tal note *n. Mus.* the lowest note of a chord in its original (uninverted) form.

fun·da·men·tal par·ti·cle *n. Physics* an elementary particle.

fun·da·men·tal tone *n. Mus.* the tone produced by vibration of the whole of a sonorous body (opp. HARMONIC).

fund-rais·er *n.* **1** a person whose job is to seek financial support for a charity, institution, or other enterprise. **2** an event held to generate financial support for such an enterprise. □□ **fund-rais·ing** *n.*

fun·dus /fúndəs/ *n.* (pl. **fun·di** /–dī/) *Anat.* the base of a hollow organ; the part furthest from the opening. [L, = bottom]

fu·ner·al /fyoonərəl/ *n. & adj.* ● *n.* **1 a** the ceremonies involved with burial or cremation of a dead person. **b** a burial or cremation procession. **2** *sl.* one's (usu. unpleasant) concern (*that's your funeral*). ● *attrib.adj.* of or used, etc., at a funeral (*funeral oration*). [ME f. OF *funeraille* f. med.L *funeralia* neut. pl. of LL *funeralis* f. L *funus –eris* funeral: (adj.) OF f. L *funeralis*]

fu·ner·al di·rec·tor *n.* an undertaker.

fu·ner·al par·lor *n.* (also **funeral home**) an establishment where the dead are prepared for burial or cremation.

fu·ner·al urn *n.* an urn holding the ashes of a cremated body.

fu·ner·ar·y /fyoonəreree/ *adj.* of or used at a funeral or funerals. [LL *funerarius* (as FUNERAL)]

fu·ne·re·al /fyoonéereeəl/ *adj.* **1** of or appropriate to a funeral. **2** gloomy; dismal; dark. □□ **fu·ne·re·al·ly** *adv.* [L *funereus* (as FUNERAL)]

fun·fair /fúnfair/ *n. Brit.* = AMUSEMENT PARK.

fun·gi *pl.* of FUNGUS.

fun·gi·ble /fúnjibəl/ *adj. Law* (of goods, etc., contracted for, when an individual specimen is not meant) that can serve for, or be replaced by, another answering to the same definition. □□ **fun·gi·bil·i·ty** *n.* [med.L *fungibilis* f. *fungi* (*vice*) serve (in place of)]

fun·gi·cide /fúnjisīd, fúnggi–/ *n.* a fungus-destroying substance. □□ **fun·gi·cid·al** /–síd'l/ *adj.*

fun·gi·stat·ic /fúnjistátik, fúnggi–/ *adj.* inhibiting the growth of fungi. □□ **fun·gi·stat·i·cal·ly** *adv.*

fun·goid /fúnggoyd/ *adj. & n.* ● *adj.* **1** resembling a fungus in texture or in rapid growth. **2** *Brit.* of a fungus or fungi. ● *n.* a fungoid plant.

fun·gous /fúnggəs/ *adj.* **1** having the nature of a fungus. **2** springing up like a mushroom; transitory. [ME f. L *fungosus* (as FUNGUS)]

fun·gus /fúnggəs/ *n.* (pl. **fun·gi** /–gī, –jī/ or **fun·gus·es**) **1** any of a group of unicellular, multicellular, or multinucleate nonphoto-

synthetic organisms feeding on organic matter, which include molds, yeast, mushrooms, and toadstools. **2** anything similar usu. growing suddenly and rapidly. **3** *Med.* a spongy morbid growth. □□ **fun·gal** /fúnggəl/ *adj.* **fun·gi·form** /fúnjifawrm, fúnggi–/ *adj.* **fun·giv·or·ous** /funjívərəs, funggív–/ *adj.* [L, perh. f. Gk *sp(h)oggos* SPONGE]

fu·nic·u·lar /fyooníkyələr, fə–/ *adj. & n.* ● *adj.* **1** (of a railway, esp. on a mountainside) operating by cable with ascending and descending cars counterbalanced. **2** of a rope or its tension. ● *n.* a funicular railway. [L *funiculus* f. *funis* rope]

funk¹ /fungk/ *n. & v. sl.* ● *n.* **1** fear; panic. **2** *Brit.* a coward. ● *v. Brit.* **1** *intr.* flinch; shrink; show cowardice. **2** *tr.* try to evade (an undertaking); shirk. **3** *tr.* be afraid of. □ **in a funk** dejected. [18th-c. Oxford sl.: perh. f. sl. FUNK² = tobacco smoke]

funk² /fungk/ *n. sl.* **1** funky music. **2** a strong smell. [*funk* blow smoke on, perh. f. F dial. *funkier* f. L (as FUMIGATE)]

fun·ki·a /fúngkeeə/ *n.* = HOSTA. [mod.L f. H. C. *Funck*, Prussian botanist d. 1839]

funk·y¹ /fúngkee/ *adj.* (**funk·i·er, funk·i·est**) *sl.* **1** (esp. of jazz or rock music) earthy, bluesy, with a heavy rhythmical beat. **2** fashionable. **3** odd; unconventional. **4** having a strong smell. □□ **funk·i·ly** *adv.* **funk·i·ness** *n.*

funk·y² /fúngkee/ *adj.* (**funk·i·er, funk·i·est**) *Brit. sl.* **1** terrified. **2** cowardly.

fun·nel /fúnəl/ *n. & v.* ● *n.* **1** a narrow tube or pipe widening at the top, for pouring liquid, powder, etc., into a small opening. **2** a metal chimney on a steam engine or ship. **3** something resembling a funnel in shape or use. ● *v.tr.* (**fun·neled, fun·nel·ing; fun·nelled, fun·nel·ling**) guide or move through or as through a funnel. □□ **fun·nel·like** *adj.* [ME f. Prov. *fonilh* f. LL *fundibulum* f. L *infundibulum* f. *infundere* (as IN–², *fundere* pour)]

fun·nies *n.* = FUNNY PAPERS

fun·ny /fúnee/ *adj. & n.* ● *adj.* (**fun·ni·er, fun·ni·est**) **1** amusing; comical. **2** strange; perplexing; hard to account for. **3** *colloq.* slightly unwell, eccentric, etc. ● *n.* (pl. **·ies**) (usu. in *pl.*) **1** a comic strip in a newspaper. **2** a joke. □ □ **fun·ni·ly** *adv.* **fun·ni·ness** *n.* [FUN + –Y¹]

fun·ny bone *n.* the part of the elbow over which the ulnar nerve passes, which when knocked or struck may cause numbness or tingling along the forearm and hand.

fun·ny busi·ness *n.* **1** *sl.* misbehavior or deception. **2** comic behavior, comedy.

fun·ny farm *n. sl.* a mental hospital.

fun·ny man *n.* a clown or comedian, esp. a professional.

fun·ny mon·ey *n. colloq.* **1** counterfeit money. **2** foreign currency. **3** inflated currency.

fun·ny pa·pers *n.pl.* a section of a newspaper containing comics and other humorous matter.

fun run *n. colloq.* an uncompetitive run, esp. for sponsored runners in support of a charity.

fur /fər/ *n. & v.* ● *n.* **1 a** the fine, soft hair of certain animals. **b** the skin of such an animal with the fur on it; a pelt. **2 a** the coat of certain animals as material for making, trimming, or lining clothes. **b** a trimming or lining made of the dressed coat of such animals, or of material imitating this. **c** a garment made of or trimmed or lined with fur. **3** *Brit.* (collect.) furred animals. **4 a** a coating formed on the tongue in sickness. **b** *Brit.* a coating formed on the inside surface of a pipe, kettle, etc., by hard water. **c** a crust adhering to a surface, e.g., a deposit from wine. **5** *Heraldry* a representation of tufts on a plain ground. ● *v.* (**furred, furring**) **1** *tr.* (esp. as **furred** *adj.*) **a** line or trim (a garment) with fur. **b** clothe (a person) with fur. **c** coat (a tongue, the inside of a kettle) with fur. **2** *intr.* (often foll. by *up*) (of a kettle, etc.) become coated with fur. **3** *tr.* level (floorboards) by inserting strips of wood. □ **make the fur fly** *colloq.* cause a disturbance; stir up trouble. □□ **fur·less** *adj.* [ME (earlier as v.) f. *forrer* f. *forre, fuerre* sheath f. Gmc]

fur. *abbr.* furlong(s).

fur·be·low /fŕbilō/ *n. & v.* ● *n.* **1** a gathered strip or pleated border of a skirt or petticoat. **2** (in *pl.*) *derog.* showy ornaments. ● *v.tr.* adorn with a furbelow or furbelows. [18th-c. var. of *falbala* flounce, trimming]

fur·bish /fŕbish/ *v.tr.* (often foll. by *up*) **1** remove rust from; polish; burnish. **2** give a new look to; renovate; revive (something antiquated). □□ **fur·bish·er** *n.* [ME f. OF *forbir* f. Gmc]

fur·cate /fŕkayt/ *adj. & v.* ● *adj.* also /fŕkət/ forked; branched. ● *v.intr.* form a fork; divide. □□ **fur·ca·tion** /–káyshən/ *n.* [L *furca* fork: (adj.) f. LL *furcatus*]

fur·fu·ra·ceous /fŕfəráyshəs/ *adj.* **1** *Med.* (of skin) resembling bran or dandruff; scaly. **2** *Bot.* covered with branlike scales. [*furfur* scurf f. L *furfur* bran]

fu·ri·ous /fyooreeəs/ *adj.* **1** extremely angry. **2** full of fury. **3** raging; violent; intense. □ **fast and furious** *adv.* **1** rapidly. **2** eagerly; uproariously. ● *adj.* (of mirth, etc.) eager; uproarious. □□ **fu·ri·ous·ly** *adv.* **fu·ri·ous·ness** *n.* [ME f. OF *furieus* f. L *furiosus* (as FURY)]

furl /fərl/ *v.* **1** *tr.* roll up and secure (a sail, umbrella, flag, etc.). **2** *intr.* become furled. **3** *tr.* **a** close (a fan). **b** fold up (wings). **c** draw away (a curtain). **d** relinquish (hopes). □□ **fur•a•ble** *adj.* [F *ferler* f. OF *fer(m)* FIRM[1] + *lier* bind f. L *ligare*]

fur•long /fórlawng, –long/ *n.* an eighth of a mile, 220 yards. [OE *furlang* f. *furh* FURROW + *lang* LONG[1]: orig. = length of a furrow in a common field]

fur•lough /fórlō/ *n. & v.* ● *n.* leave of absence, esp. granted to a member of the armed services or to a missionary. ● *v.* **1** *tr.* grant furlough to. **2** *intr.* spend furlough. **3** lay off. [Du. *verlof* after G *Verlaub* (as FOR-, LEAVE[2])]

fur•me•ty (also **fur•mi•ty**) vars. of FRUMENTY.

furn. *abbr.* **1** furnished. **2** furniture.

fur•nace /fórnis/ *n.* **1** an enclosed structure for intense heating by fire, esp. of metals or water. **2** a very hot place. [ME f. OF *fornais* f. L *fornax –acis* f. *fornus* oven]

fur•nish /fórnish/ *v.tr.* **1** provide (a house, room, etc.) with all necessary contents, esp. movable furniture. **2** (foll. by *with*) cause to have possession or use of. **3** provide; afford; yield. [OF *furnir* ult. f. WG]

fur•nished /fórnisht/ *adj.* (of a house, apartment, etc.) rented with furniture.

fur•nish•er /fórnishər/ *n.* **1** a person who sells furniture. **2** a person who furnishes.

fur•nish•ings /fórnishingz/ *n.pl.* the furniture and utensils, etc., in a house, room, etc.

fur•ni•ture /fórnichər/ *n.* **1** the movable equipment of a house, room, etc., e.g., tables, chairs, and beds. **2** *Naut.* a ship's equipment, esp. tackle, etc. **3** accessories, e.g., the handles and lock of a door. **4** *Printing* pieces of wood or metal placed round or between type to make blank spaces and fasten the matter in the chase. □ **part of the furniture** *colloq.* a person or thing taken for granted. [F *fourniture* f. *fournir* (as FURNISH)]

fur•ni•ture bee•tle *n.* a beetle, *Anobium punctatum*, the larvae of which bore into wood (see WOODWORM).

fu•ror /fyoorawr, –ər/ *n.* (*Brit.* **fu•rore** /fyooráwree, fyoorawr/) **1** an uproar; an outbreak of fury. **2** a wave of enthusiastic admiration; a craze. [It. f. L *furor –oris* f. *furere* be mad]

fur•phy /fórfee/ *n.* (*pl.* **•phies**) *Austral. sl.* **1** a false report or rumor. **2** an absurd story. [water and sanitary *Furphy carts* of World War I, made at a foundry set up by the Furphy family]

fur•ri•er /fóreeər/ *n.* a dealer in or dresser of furs. [ME *furrour* f. OF *forreor* f. *forrer* trim with fur, assim. to –IER]

fur•ri•er•y /fóree–əree/ *n.* the work of a furrier.

fur•row /fórō, fúr–/ *n. & v.* ● *n.* **1** a narrow trench made in the ground by a plow. **2** a rut, groove, or deep wrinkle. **3** a ship's track. ● *v.tr.* **1** plow. **2 a** make furrows, grooves, etc., in. **b** mark with wrinkles. □□ **fur•row•less** *adj.* **fur•row•y** *adj.* [OE *furh* f. Gmc]

fur•ry /fóree, fúree/ *adj.* (**fur•ri•er, fur•ri•est**) **1** of or like fur. **2** covered with or wearing fur. □□ **fur•ri•ness** *n.*

fur seal *n.* a sea lion with a valuable undercoat.

fur•ther /fórthər/ *adv., adj., & v.* ● *adv.* **1** = FARTHER. **2** to a greater extent; more (*will inquire further*). **3** in addition; furthermore (*I may add further*). ● *adj.* **1** = FARTHER. **2** more; additional; going beyond what exists or has been dealt with (*threats of further punishment*). ● *v.tr.* promote; favor; help; forward (a scheme, undertaking, movement, or cause). □ **until further notice** to continue until explicitly changed. □□ **fur•ther•er** *n.* **fur•ther•most** *adj.* [OE *furthor* (adv.), *furthra* (adj.), *fyrthrian* (v.), formed as FORTH, –ER[3]]

▶See note at FARTHER.

fur•ther•ance /fórthərəns/ *n.* furthering or being furthered; the advancement of a scheme, etc.

fur•ther ed•u•ca•tion *n. Brit.* education for persons above school age but usu. below degree level.

fur•ther•more /fórthərmáwr/ *adv.* in addition; besides (esp. introducing a fresh consideration in an argument).

fur•thest var. of FARTHEST.

fur•tive /fórtiv/ *adj.* **1** done by stealth; clandestine; meant to escape notice. **2** sly; stealthy. **3** stolen; taken secretly. **4** thievish; pilfering. □□ **fur•tive•ly** *adv.* **fur•tive•ness** *n.* [F *furtif –ive* or L *furtivus* f. *furtum* theft]

fu•run•cle /fyoorungkəl/ *n. Med.* = BOIL[2]. □□ **fu•run•cu•lar** /–rúngkyələr/ *adj.* **fu•run•cu•lous** /–rúngkyələs/ *adj.* [L *furunculus* f. *fur* thief]

fu•run•cu•lo•sis /fyoorúngkyəlósis/ *n.* **1** a diseased condition in which boils appear. **2** a bacterial disease of salmon and trout. [mod.L (as FURUNCLE)]

fu•ry /fyooree/ *n.* (*pl.* **•ies**) **1 a** wild and passionate anger; rage. **b** a fit of rage (*in a blind fury*). **c** impetuosity in battle, etc. **2** violence of a storm, disease, etc. **3** (**Fury**) (usu. in *pl.*) (in Greek mythology) each of three goddesses sent from Tartarus to avenge crime, esp. against kinship. **4** an avenging spirit. **5** an angry or spiteful woman; a virago. □ **like fury** *colloq.* with great force or effect. [ME f. OF *furie* f. L *furia* f. *furere* be mad]

furze /fərz/ *n. Brit.* = GORSE. □□ **furz•y** /fúrzee/ *adj.* [OE *fyrs*, of unkn. orig.]

fus•cous /fúskəs/ *adj.* somber; dark-colored. [L *fuscus* dusky]

fuse[1] /fyooz/ *v. & n.* ● *v.* **1** *tr. & intr.* melt with intense heat; liquefy.

2 *tr. & intr.* blend or amalgamate into one whole by or as by melting. **3** *tr.* provide (a circuit, plug, etc.) with a fuse. **4** *Brit.* **a** *intr.* (of an appliance) cease to function when a fuse blows. **b** *tr.* cause (an appliance) to do this. ● *n.* a device or component for protecting an electric circuit, containing a strip of wire of easily melted metal and placed in the circuit so as to break it by melting when an excessive current passes through. [L *fundere fus-* pour, melt]

fuse[2] /fyooz/ *n. & v.* (also **fuze**) ● *n.* **1** a device for igniting a bomb or explosive charge, consisting of a tube or cord, etc., filled or saturated with combustible matter. **2** a component in a shell, mine, etc., designed to detonate an explosive charge on impact, after an interval, or when subjected to a magnetic or vibratory stimulation. ● *v.tr.* fit a fuse to. □□ **fuse•less** *adj.* [It. *fuso* f. L *fusus* spindle]

fuse box *n.* a box housing the fuses for circuits in a building.

fu•see /fyoozée/ *n.* (also **fu•zee**) **1** a conical pulley or wheel, esp. in a watch or clock. **2** a large-headed match for lighting a cigar or pipe in a wind. **3** a railroad signal flare. [F *fusée* spindle ult. f. L *fusus*]

fu•se•lage /fyoosəlaazh, –lij, –zə–/ *n.* the body of an airplane. [F f. *fuseler* cut into a spindle f. *fuseau* spindle f. OF *fusel* ult. f. L *fusus*]

fu•sel oil /fyoozəl/ *n.* a mixture of several alcohols, chiefly amyl alcohol, produced usu. in small amounts during alcoholic fermentation. [G *Fusel* bad brandy, schnaps: cf. *fuseln* to bungle]

fu•si•ble /fyoozibəl/ *adj.* that can be easily fused or melted. □□ **fu•si•bil•i•ty** *n.*

fu•si•form /fyoozifawrm/ *adj. Bot. & Zool.* shaped like a spindle or cigar, tapering at both ends. [L *fusus* spindle + –FORM]

fu•sil /fyoozil/ *n. hist.* a light musket. [F ult. f. L *focus* hearth, fire]

fu•sil•ier /fyoozileér/ *n.* (also **fu•sil•eer**) **1** a member of any of several British regiments formerly armed with fusils. **2** *hist.* a soldier armed with a fusil. [F (as FUSIL)]

fu•sil•lade /fyoosiláyd, –laàd, –zi–/ *n. & v.* ● *n.* **1 a** a continuous discharge of firearms. **b** a wholesale execution by this means. **2** a sustained outburst of criticism, etc. ● *v.tr.* **1** assault (a place) by a fusillade. **2** shoot down (persons) with a fusillade. [F f. *fusiller* shoot]

fu•sion /fyoozhən/ *n.* **1** the act or an instance of fusing or melting. **2** a fused mass. **3** the blending of different things into one. **4** a coalition. **5** *Physics* = NUCLEAR FUSION. □□ **fu•sion•al** *adj.* [F *fusion* or L *fusio* (as FUSE[1])]

fu•sion bomb *n.* a bomb involving nuclear fusion, esp. a hydrogen bomb.

fuss /fus/ *n. & v.* ● *n.* **1** excited commotion; bustle; ostentatious or nervous activity. **2 a** excessive concern about a trivial thing. **b** abundance of petty detail. **3** a sustained protest or dispute. **4** a person who fusses. ● *v.* **1** *intr.* **a** make a fuss. **b** busy oneself restlessly with trivial things. **c** move fussily. **2** *tr. Brit.* agitate; worry. □ **make a fuss** complain vigorously. **make a fuss over** (or *Brit.* **of**) treat (a person or animal) with great or excessive attention. □□ **fuss•er** *n.* [18th c.: perh. Anglo-Ir.]

fuss•budg•et /fúsbəjət/ *n.* a person who habitually frets over minor matters.

fuss•pot /fúspot/ *n. colloq.* a person given to fussing.

fuss•y /fúsee/ *adj.* (**fus•si•er, fus•si•est**) **1** inclined to fuss. **2** full of unnecessary detail or decoration. **3** fastidious. □□ **fuss•i•ly** *adv.* **fuss•i•ness** *n.*

fus•ta•nel•la /fústənélə/ *n.* a man's stiff white kilt worn in Albania and Greece. [It. dimin. of mod. Gk *phoustani* prob. f. It. *fustagno* FUSTIAN]

fus•tian /fúschən/ *n. & adj.* ● *n.* **1** thick twilled cotton cloth with a short nap, usu. dyed in dark colors. **2** turgid speech or writing; bombast. ● *adj.* **1** made of fustian. **2** bombastic. **3** worthless. [ME f. OF *fustaigne* f. med.L *fustaneus* (adj.) relating to cloth from *Fostat* a suburb of Cairo]

fus•tic /fústik/ *n.* a yellow dye obtained from either of two kinds of wood, esp. old fustic. [F f. Sp. *fustoc* f. Arab. *fustuk* f. Gk *pistakē* pistachio]

fus•ty /fústee/ *adj.* (**fus•ti•er, fus•ti•est**) **1** stale-smelling; musty; moldy. **2** stuffy, close. **3** antiquated; old-fashioned. □□ **fus•ti•ly** *adv.* **fus•ti•ness** *n.* [ME f. OF *fusté* smelling of the cask f. *fust* cask, tree trunk, f. L *fustis* cudgel]

fu•thark /foothaark/ *n.* (also **fu•thore, fu•thork**) the Scandinavian runic alphabet. [its first six letters *f, u, th, a* (or *ō*), *r, k*]

fu•tile /fyoot'l, –tīl/ *adj.* **1** useless; ineffectual, vain. **2** frivolous; trifling. □□ **fu•tile•ly** *adv.* **fu•til•i•ty** /–tilitee/ *n.* [L *futilis* leaky, futile, rel. to *fundere* pour]

fu•ton /footon/ *n.* **1** a Japanese quilted mattress rolled out on the floor for use as a bed. **2** a type of low-slung wooden bed using this kind of mattress. [Jap.]

fut•tock /fútək/ *n.* each of the middle timbers of a ship's frame, between the floor and the top timbers. [ME *votekes*, etc., pl. f. MLG f. *fōt* FOOT + –*ken* –KIN]

fu•ture /fyoochər/ *adj. & n.* ● *adj.* **1 a** going or expected to happen or be or become (*his future career*). **b** that will be something specified (*my future wife*). **c** that will be after death (*a future life*). **2 a** of time to come (*future years*). **b** *Gram.* (of a tense or participle) describing an event yet to happen. • *n.* **1** time to come (*past, present, and future*). **2** what will happen in the future (*the future is uncertain*). **3** the future condition of a person, country, etc. **4** a prospect of success, etc. (*there's no future in it*). **5** *Gram.* the future tense. **6** (in *pl.*) *Stock Exch.* **a** goods and stocks sold for future delivery. **b** contracts for these. □ **for the future** from now onward. **in future** = *for the future*. □□ **fu•ture•less** *adj.* [ME f. OF *futur –ure* f. L *futurus* future part. of *esse* be f. stem *fu-* be]

fu•ture per•fect *n. Gram.* a tense of verbs expressing expected completion in the future, in English exemplified by *will have done*.

fu•ture shock *n.* inability to cope with rapid progress.

fu•tur•ism /fyōōchərizəm/ *n.* a movement in art, literature, music, etc., with violent departure from traditional forms so as to express movement and growth. [FUTURE + –ISM, after It. *futurismo*, F *futurisme*]

fu•tur•ist /fyōōchərist/ *n.* (often *attrib.*) **1** an adherent of futurism. **2** a believer in human progress. **3** a student of the future. **4** *Theol.* one who believes that biblical prophecies, esp. those of the Apocalypse, have yet to be fulfilled.

fu•tur•is•tic /fyōōchəristik/ *adj.* **1** suitable for the future; ultramodern. **2** of futurism. **3** relating to the future. □□ **fu•tur•is•ti•cal•ly** *adv.*

fu•tu•ri•ty /fyōōtōōritee, –tyōōr–, chōōr–/ *n.* (*pl.* **•ties**) **1** future time. **2** (in *sing.* or *pl.*) future events. **3** future condition; existence after death.

fu•tu•ri•ty rac•es *n.* (also **fu•tu•ri•ty stakes**) a horse race for young horses for which entries are made long in advance, sometimes before the horses are born.

fu•tur•ol•o•gy /fyōōchəróləjee/ *n.* systematic forecasting of the future, esp. from present trends in society. □□ **fu•tur•ol•o•gist** *n.*

fuze var. of FUSE[2].

fu•zee var. of FUSEE.

fuzz /fuz/ *n.* **1** fluff. **2** fluffy or frizzled hair. **3** *sl.* **a** the police. **b** a policeman. [17th c.: prob. f. LG or Du.: sense 3 perh. a different word]

fuzz•ball /fúzbawl/ *n.* a puffball fungus.

fuzz•y /fúzee/ *adj.* (**fuzz•i•er, fuzz•i•est**) **1 a** like fuzz. **b** frayed; fluffy. **c** frizzy. **2** blurred; indistinct. □□ **fuzz•i•ly** *adv.* **fuzz•i•ness** *n.*

fwd *abbr.* forward.

f.w.d. *abbr.* **1** four-wheel drive. **2** front-wheel drive.

FY *abbr.* fiscal year.

-fy /fī/ *suffix* forming: **1** verbs from nouns, meaning: **a** make; produce (*pacify; satisfy*). **b** make into (*deify; petrify*). **2** verbs from adjectives, meaning 'bring or come into such a state' (*Frenchify; solidify*). **3** verbs in causative sense (*horrify; stupefy*). [from or after F *–fier* f. L *–ficare, –facere* f. *facere* do, make]

fyl•fot /fílfət/ *n.* a swastika. [perh. f. *fill-foot*, pattern to fill the foot of a painted window]

fyrd /fərd/ *n. hist.* **1** the Anglo-Saxon militia before 1066. **2** the duty to serve in this. [OE f. Gmc (as FARE)]

fytte var. of FIT[3].

G

G¹ /jee/ n. (also **g**) (pl. **Gs** or **G's**) **1** the seventh letter of the alphabet. **2** Mus. the fifth note in the diatonic scale of C major.

G² abbr. (also **G.**) **1** gauss. **2** giga–. **3** gravitational constant. **4** sl. = GRAND n. 2.

g abbr. (also **g.**) **1** gelding. **2** gram(s). **3 a** gravity. **b** acceleration due to gravity.

GA abbr. Georgia (in official postal use).

Ga symb. Chem. the element gallium.

Ga. abbr. Georgia (US).

gab /gab/ n. & v. colloq. ● n. talk; chatter. ● v.intr. talk incessantly, trivially, or indiscreetly; chatter. □ **gift of gab** the facility of speaking eloquently or profusely. □□ **gab•ber** n. [17th-c. var. of GOB¹]

gab•ar•dine /gábərdeen/ n. (also **gab•er•dine**) **1** a smooth durable twilled cloth esp. of worsted or cotton. **2** Brit. a garment made of this, esp. a raincoat.

WORD HISTORY gabardine

Early 16th century: from Old French *gauvardine*, earlier *galle-vardine*, perhaps from Middle High German *wallevart* 'pilgrimage' and originally 'a garment worn by a pilgrim.' The textile sense is first recorded in the early 20th century.

---

gab•ble /gábəl/ v. & n. ● v. **1** intr. **a** talk volubly or inarticulately. **b** read aloud too fast. **2** tr. utter too fast, esp. in reading aloud. ● n. fast unintelligible talk. □□ **gab•bler** n. [MDu. *gabbelen* (imit.)]

gab•bro /gábrō/ n. (pl. **•bros**) a dark granular plutonic rock of crystalline texture. □□ **gab•bro•ic** /–bróik/ adj. **gab•broid** adv. [It. f. *Gabbro* in Tuscany]

gab•by /gábee/ adj. (**gab•bi•er**, **gab•bi•est**) colloq. talkative. [GAB + –Y¹]

gab•er•dine /gábərdeen/ n. **1** var. of GABARDINE. **2** hist. a loose long upper garment worn esp. by medieval Jews. [OF *gauvardine* perh. f. MHG *wallevart* pilgrimage]

ga•bi•on /gáybeeən/ n. a cylindrical wicker or metal basket for filling with earth or stones, used in engineering or (formerly) in fortification. □□ **ga•bi•on•age** n. [F f. It. *gabbione* f. *gabbia* CAGE]

ga•ble /gáybəl/ n. **1 a** the triangular upper part of a wall at the end of a ridged roof. **b** (in full **gable end**) a gable-topped wall. **2** a gable-shaped canopy over a window or door. □□ **ga•bled** adj. (also in comb.). [ME *gable* f. ON *gafl*]

gable

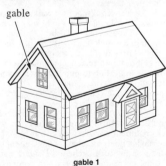

gable 1

gad¹ /gad/ v. & n. ● v.intr. (**gad•ded**, **gad•ding**) (foll. by *about*) go about idly or in search of pleasure. ● n. idle wandering or adventure. [back-form. f. obs. *gadling* companion f. OE *gædeling* f. *gæd* fellowship]

gad² /gad/ int. (also **by gad**) an expression of surprise or emphatic assertion. [= *God*]

gad•a•bout /gádəbowt/ n. a person who gads about; an idle pleasure seeker.

Gad•a•rene /gádəreen/ adj. involving or engaged in headlong or suicidal rush or flight. [LL *Gadarenus* f. Gk *Gadarēnos* of Gadara in anc. Palestine, with ref. to Matthew 8:28–32]

gad•fly /gádflī/ n. (pl. **•flies**) **1** a cattle-biting fly, esp. a warble fly, horsefly, or botfly. **2** an irritating or harassing person. [obs. *gad* goad, spike f. ON *gaddr*, rel. to YARD¹]

gadg•et /gájit/ n. any small and usu. ingenious mechanical or electronic device or tool. □□ **gadg•e•teer** /–téer/ n. **gadg•et•ry** n. **gadg•et•y** adj. [19th-c. Naut.: orig. unkn.]

ga•doid /gáydoyd, gád–/ n. & adj. ● n. any marine fish of the cod family Gadidae, including haddock and whiting. ● adj. belonging to or resembling the Gadidae. [mod.L *gadus* f. Gk *gados* cod + –OID]

gad•o•lin•ite /gád'linīt/ n. a dark crystalline mineral consisting of ferrous silicate of beryllium. [J. *Gadolin*, Finnish mineralogist d. 1852]

gad•o•lin•i•um /gád'líneeəm/ n. Chem. a soft silvery metallic element of the lanthanide series, occurring naturally in gadolinite. ¶ Symb.: **Gd**. [mod.L f. GADOLINITE]

ga•droon /gədroon/ n. a decoration on silverware, etc., consisting of convex curves in a series forming an ornamental edge like inverted fluting. [F *godron*: cf. *goder* pucker]

gad•wall /gádwawl/ n. a brownish gray freshwater duck, *Anas strepera*. [17th c.: orig. unkn.]

gad•zooks /gadzo͞oks/ int. archaic an expression of surprise, etc. [GAD² + *zooks* of unkn. orig.]

Gael /gayl/ n. **1** a Scottish Celt. **2** a Gaelic-speaking Celt. □□ **Gael•dom** n. [Gael. *Gaidheal*]

Gael•ic /gáylik, gálik/ n. & adj. ● n. any of the Celtic languages spoken in Ireland, Scotland, and the Isle of Man. ● adj. of or relating to the Celts or the Celtic languages.

Gael•tacht /gáyltəkht/ n. any of the regions in Ireland where the vernacular language is Irish. [Ir.]

gaff¹ /gaf/ n. & v. ● n. **1 a** a stick with an iron hook for landing large fish. **b** a barbed fishing spear. **2** a spar to which the head of a fore-and-aft sail is bent. ● v.tr. seize (a fish) with a gaff. [ME f. Prov. *gaf* hook]

gaff² /gaf/ n. Brit. sl. □ **blow the gaff** let out a plot or secret. [19th c., = nonsense: orig. unkn.]

gaffe /gaf/ n. a blunder; an indiscreet act or remark. [F]

gaf•fer /gáfər/ n. **1** an old fellow; an elderly rustic. **2** Brit. colloq. a foreman or boss. **3** colloq. the chief electrician in a movie or television production unit. [prob. contr. of GODFATHER]

gag /gag/ n. & v. ● n. **1** a piece of cloth, etc., thrust into or held over the mouth to prevent speaking or crying out, or to hold it open in surgery. **2** a joke or comic scene in a play, movie, etc., or as part of a comedian's act. **3** an actor's interpolation in a dramatic dialogue. **4** a thing or circumstance restricting free speech. **5 a** a joke or hoax. **b** a humorous action or situation. **6** an imposture or deception. **7** Brit. Parl. a closure or guillotine. ● v. (**gagged**, **gag•ging**) **1** tr. apply a gag to. **2** tr. silence; deprive of free speech. **3** tr. apply a gag bit to (a horse). **4 a** intr. choke or retch. **b** tr. cause to do this. **5** intr. Theatr. make gags. [ME, orig. as verb: orig. uncert.]

ga•ga /gáagaa/ adj. sl. **1** senile. **2** infatuated; overly fond. **3** fatuous; slightly crazy. [F, = senile]

gag bit n. a specially powerful bit for horse breaking.

gage¹ /gayj/ n. & v. ● n. **1** a pledge; a thing deposited as security. **2 a** a challenge to fight. **b** a symbol of this, esp. a glove thrown down. ● v.tr. archaic stake; pledge; offer as a guarantee. [ME f. OF *gage* (n.), F *gager* (v.) ult. f. Gmc, rel. to WED]

gage² var. of GAUGE.

gage³ /gayj/ n. = GREENGAGE. [abbr.]

gag•gle /gágəl/ n. & v. ● n. **1** a flock of geese. **2** colloq. a disorderly group of people. ● v.intr. (of geese) cackle. [ME, imit.: cf. *gabble*, *cackle*]

gag•man /gágman/ n. a deviser, writer, or performer of theatrical gags.

gag•ster /gágstər/ n. = GAGMAN.

gai•e•ty /gáyətee/ n. (also **gay•e•ty**) **1** the state of being lighthearted or merry; mirth. **2** merrymaking; amusement. **3** a bright appearance, esp. of dress. [F *gaieté* (as GAY)]

gail•lar•di•a /gaylaárdeeə/ n. any composite plant of the genus *Gaillardia*, with showy flowers. [mod.L f. *Gaillard* de Marentoneau, 18th-c. Fr. botanist]

gai•ly /gáylee/ adv. **1** in a gay or lighthearted manner. **2** with a bright or colorful appearance.

gain /gayn/ v. & n. ● v. **1** tr. obtain or secure (usu. something desired or favorable) (*gain an advantage*; *gain recognition*). **2** tr. acquire (a sum) as profits or as a result of changed conditions; earn. **3** tr. obtain as an increment or addition (*gain momentum*; *gain weight*). **4** tr. **a** win (a victory). **b** reclaim (land from the sea). **5** intr. (foll. by *in*) make a specified advance or improvement (*gained in stature*). **6** intr. & tr. (of a clock, etc.) become fast, or be fast by (a specified amount of time). **7** intr. (often foll. by *on*, *upon*) come closer to a person or thing pursued. **8** tr. **a** bring over to one's interest or views. **b** (foll.

by *over*) win by persuasion, etc. **9** *tr.* reach or arrive at (a desired place). ● *n.* **1** something gained, achieved, etc. **2** an increase of possessions, etc.; a profit, advance, or improvement. **3** the acquisition of wealth. **4** (in *pl.*) sums of money acquired by trade, etc.; emoluments; winnings. **5** an increase in amount. **6** *Electronics* **a** the factor by which power, etc., is increased. **b** the logarithm of this. □ **gain ground** see GROUND¹. □□ **gain·a·ble** *adj.* **gain·er** *n.* **gain·ings** *n.pl.* [OF *gaigner, gaaignier* to till, acquire, ult. f. Gmc]

gain·ful /gáynfŏŏl/ *adj.* **1** (of employment) paid. **2** lucrative; remunerative. □□ **gain·ful·ly** *adv.* **gain·ful·ness** *n.*

gain·say /gáynsáy/ *v.tr.* (*past* and *past part.* **gain·said** /-séd/) deny; contradict. □□ **gain·say·er** *n.* [ME f. obs. *gain-* against f. ON *gegn* straight f. Gmc + SAY]

'gainst /genst/ *prep. poet.* = AGAINST. [abbr.]

gait /gayt/ *n.* **1** a manner of walking; one's bearing or carriage as one walks. **2** the manner of forward motion of a runner, horse, vehicle, etc. [var. of GATE²]

gait·er /gáytər/ *n.* a garment of cloth or leather, covering the lower leg and part of the foot, used to protect against snow, mud, etc. □□ **gait·ered** *adj.* [F *guêtre*, prob. rel. to WRIST]

gal¹ /gal/ *n. sl.* a girl. [repr. var. pronunc.]

gal² /gal/ *n. Physics* a unit of acceleration for a gravitational field, equal to one centimeter per second per second. [*Galileo*: see GALILEAN¹]

Gal. *abbr.* Galatians (New Testament).

gal. *abbr.* gallon(s).

ga·la /gáylə, gaálə, gálə/ *n.* **1** (often *attrib.*) a festive or special occasion (*a gala performance*). **2** *Brit.* a festive gathering for sports, esp. swimming. [F or It. f. Sp. f. OF *gale* rejoicing f. Gmc]

ga·lac·ta·gogue /gəláktəgawg, –gog/ *adj. & n.* ● *adj.* inducing a flow of milk. ● *n.* a galactagogue substance. [Gk *gala galaktos* milk, + *agōgos* leading]

ga·lac·tic /gəláktik/ *adj.* of or relating to a galaxy or galaxies, esp. the Milky Way galaxy. [Gk *galaktias*, var. of *galaxias*: see GALAXY]

ga·la·go /gəláygō, –laá–/ *n.* (*pl.* **·gos**) any small tree-climbing primate of the genus *Galago*, found in southern Africa, with large eyes and ears and a long tail. Also called **bush baby**. [mod.L]

ga·lah /gəlaá/ *n. Austral.* **1** a small rosy-breasted gray-backed cockatoo, *Cacatua roseicapilla*. **2** *sl.* a fool. [Aboriginal]

Gal·a·had /gáləhad/ *n.* a person characterized by nobility, integrity, courtesy, etc. [name of a knight of the Round Table in Arthurian legend]

gal·an·tine /gálənteen/ *n.* white meat or fish boned, cooked, pressed, and served cold in aspic, etc. [ME f. OF, alt. f. *galatine* jellied meat f. med.L *galatina*]

gal·a·vant var. of GALLIVANT.

gal·ax·y /gáləksee/ *n.* (*pl.* **·ies**) **1** any of many independent systems of stars, gas, dust, etc., held together by gravitational attraction. **2** (often **the Galaxy**) the galaxy of which the solar system is a part. **3** (often **the Galaxy**) the irregular luminous band of stars indistinguishable to the naked eye encircling the heavens; the Milky Way. **4** (foll. by *of*) a brilliant company or gathering.

WORD HISTORY galaxy

Late Middle English (originally referring to the Milky Way): via Old French from medieval Latin *galaxia*, from Greek *galaxias (kuklos)* 'milky (vault),' from *gala, galakt-* 'milk.'

---

gal·ba·num /gálbənəm/ *n.* a bitter aromatic gum resin produced from kinds of ferula. [ME f. L f. Gk *khalbanē*, prob. of Semitic orig.]

gale¹ /gayl/ *n.* **1** a very strong wind, esp. (on the Beaufort scale) one of 32–63 m.p.h. **2** *Naut.* a storm. **3** an outburst, esp. of laughter. [16th c.: orig. unkn.]

gale² /gayl/ *n.* (in full **sweet gale**) bog myrtle. [OE *gagel(le)*, MDu. *gaghel*]

ga·le·a /gáyleeə/ *n.* (*pl.* **ga·le·ae** /–lee-ee/ or **·as**) *Bot. & Zool.* a structure like a helmet in shape, form, or function. □□ **ga·le·ate** /–lee-ayt/ *adj.* **ga·le·at·ed** *adj.* [L, = helmet]

ga·le·na /gəléenə/ *n.* a bluish, gray, or black mineral ore of lead sulfide. ¶ Chem. formula: PbS. [L, = lead ore (in a partly purified state)]

ga·len·ic var. of GALENICAL.

ga·len·i·cal /gəlénikəl/ *adj. & n.* (also **ga·len·ic** /–lénik/) ● *adj.* **1** of or relating to Galen, a Greek physician of the 2nd c. AD, or his methods. **2** made of natural as opposed to synthetic components. ● *n.* a drug or medicament produced directly from vegetable tissues.

gal Fri·day *n.* (also **girl Friday**) a female helper, esp. a junior office worker or a personal assistant to a business executive (1940s, after *man Friday* in Defoe's *Robinson Crusoe*).

Gal·i·le·an¹ /gálilávən, –léeən/ *adj.* of or relating to Galileo, Italian astronomer d. 1642, or his methods.

Gal·i·le·an² /gálileéən/ *adj. & n.* ● *adj.* **1** of Galilee in Palestine. **2** Christian. ● *n.* **1** a native of Galilee. **2** a Christian. **3** (prec. by *the*) *derog.* Christ.

---

gal·in·gale /gálinggayl/ *n.* **1** an aromatic rhizome of an E. Asian plant of the genus *Alpinia*, formerly used in cooking and medicine. **2** (in full **English galingale**) a sedge (*Cyperus longus*) having a root with similar properties. [OE *gallengar* OF *galingal* f. Arab. *kalanjān* f. Chin. *ge-liang-jiang* mild ginger from Ge in Canton]

gal·i·ot var. of GALLIOT.

gal·i·pot /gálipot/ *n.* a hardened deposit of resin formed on the stem of the cluster pine. [F: orig. unkn.]

gall¹ /gawl/ *n.* **1** *sl.* impudence. **2** asperity; rancor. **3** bitterness; anything bitter (*gall and wormwood*). **4** the bile of animals. **5** the gall-bladder and its contents. [ON, corresp. to OE *gealla*, f. Gmc]

gall² /gawl/ *n. & v.* ● *n.* **1** a sore on the skin made by chafing. **2 a** mental soreness or vexation. **b** a cause of this. **3** a place rubbed bare. ● *v.tr.* **1** rub sore; injure by rubbing. **2** vex; annoy; irritate. □□ **gall·ing·ly** *adv.* [ME f. LG or Du. *galle*, corresp. to OE *gealla* sore on a horse]

gall³ /gawl/ *n.* **1** a growth produced by insects or fungus, etc., on plants and trees, esp. on oak. **2** (*attrib.*) of insects producing galls. [ME f. OF *galle* f. L *galla*]

gal·lant *adj., n., & v.* ● *adj.* /gálənt/ **1** brave; chivalrous. **2 a** (of a ship, horse, etc.) grand; fine; stately. **b** *archaic* finely dressed. **3** /gálənt, gəlánt, –laánt/ **a** markedly attentive to women. **b** concerned with sexual love; amatory. ● *n.* /gálənt, gəlánt, –laánt/ **1** a ladies' man; a lover or paramour. **2** *archaic* a man of fashion; a fine gentleman. ● *v.* /gəlánt/ **1** *tr.* flirt with. **2** *tr.* escort; act as a cavalier to (a lady). **3** *intr.* **a** play the gallant. **b** (foll. by *with*) flirt. □□ **gal·lant·ly** /gáləntlee/ *adv.* [ME f. OF *galant* part. of *galer* make merry]

gal·lant·ry /gáləntree/ *n.* (*pl.* **·ries**) **1** courageous behavior, esp. in battle. **2** courtliness; respect given by men to women. **3** a polite act or speech. [F *galanterie* (as GALLANT)]

gall·blad·der /gáwlbladər/ *n.* the vessel storing bile after its secretion by the liver and before release into the intestine.

gal·le·on /gáleeən/ *n. hist.* **1** a ship of war (usu. Spanish). **2** a large Spanish merchant ship. **3** a vessel shorter and higher than a galley. [MDu. *galjoen* f. F *galion* f. *galie* galley, or f. Sp. *galeón*]

galleon

gal·le·ri·a /gálereéə/ *n.* a collection of small shops under a single roof; an arcade. [It.]

gal·ler·y /gáləree/ *n.* (*pl.* **·ies**) **1** a room or building for showing works of art. **2** a balcony, esp. a platform projecting from the inner wall of a church, hall, etc., providing extra room for spectators, etc., or reserved for musicians, etc. (*minstrels' gallery*). **3 a** the highest balcony in a theater. **b** its occupants. **4 a** a covered space for walking in, partly open at the side; a portico or colonnade. **b** a long narrow passage in the thickness of a wall or supported on corbels, open toward the interior of the building. **5** a long narrow room, passage, or corridor. **6** *Mil. & Mining* a horizontal underground passage. **7** a group of spectators at a golf or tennis match, etc. □ **play to the gallery** seek to win approval by appealing to popular taste. □□ **gal·ler·ied** *adj.* [F *galerie* f. It. *galleria* f. med.L *galeria*]

gal·ler·y·ite /gáləree-īt/ *n.* a person occupying a seat in a gallery; a spectator at a play, tennis match, etc.

gal·ley /gálee/ *n.* (*pl.* **·leys**) **1** *hist.* **a** a low flat single-decked vessel using sails and oars, and usu. rowed by slaves or criminals. **b** an ancient Greek or Roman warship with one or more banks of oars. **c** a large open rowing boat, e.g., that used by the captain of a man-of-war. **2** a ship's or aircraft's kitchen. **3** *Printing* **a** an oblong tray for set type. **b** the corresponding part of a composing machine. **c** (in full **galley proof**) a proof in the form of long single-column strips from type in a galley, not in sheets or pages. [ME f. OF *galie* f. med.L *galea*, med.Gk *galaia*]

gal·ley slave *n.* **1** *hist.* a person condemned to row in a galley. **2** a drudge.

gal·liard /gályaard/ *n. hist.* **1** a lively dance usu. in triple time for two persons. **2** the music for this. [ME f. OF *gaillard* valiant]

Gal·lic /gálik/ *adj.* **1** French or typically French. **2** of the Gauls; Gaulish. □□ **Gal·li·cize** /–lisīz/ *v.tr. & intr.* [L *Gallicus* f. *Gallus* a Gaul]

gal·lic ac·id /gálik/ *n. Chem.* an acid extracted from gallnuts, etc., formerly used in making ink. [F *gallique* f. *galle* GALL³]

Gal·li·cism /gálisizəm/ *n.* a French idiom, esp. one adopted in another language. [F *gallicisme* (as GALLIC)]

gal·li·gas·kins /gáligáskinz/ *n.pl. Brit. hist.* or *joc.* breeches; trousers; leggings. [orig. wide hose of the 16th–17th c., f. obs. F *garguesque* for *greguesque* f. It. *grechesca* fem. of *grechesco* Greek]

gal·li·mau·fry /gálimáwfree/ *n.* (*pl.* **·fries**) a heterogeneous mixture; a jumble or medley. [F *galimafrée*, of unkn. orig.]

gal·li·na·ceous /gálináyshəs/ *adj.* of or relating to the order Galliformes, which includes domestic poultry, pheasants, partridges, etc. [L *gallinaceus* f. *gallina* hen f. *gallus* cock]

gal·li·nule /gálinōol, –nyōol/ *n.* **1** a small aquatic bird, *Gallinula chloropus*, with long legs and a short reddish-yellow bill. **2** any of various similar birds of the genus *Porphyrula* or *Porphyrio*. [mod.L *gallinula*, dimin. of L *gallina* hen f. *gallus* cock]

gal·li·ot /gáleeət/ *n.* (also **gal·li·ot**) **1** a Dutch cargo boat or fishing vessel. **2** a small (usu. Mediterranean) galley. [ME f. OF *galiote* f. It. *galeotta* f. med.L *galea* galley]

gal·li·pot /gálipot/ *n.* a small pot of earthenware, metal, etc., used for ointments, etc. [prob. GALLEY + POT¹, because brought in galleys from the Mediterranean]

gal·li·um /gáleeəm/ *n. Chem.* a soft bluish white metallic element occurring naturally in coal, bauxite, and kaolin. ¶ Symb.: **Ga**. [mod.L f. L *Gallia* France (so named patriotically by its discoverer Lecoq de Boisbaudran d. 1912)]

gal·li·vant /gálivant/ *v.intr. colloq.* **1** gad about. **2** flirt. [orig. uncert.]

gal·li·wasp /gáliwosp/ *n.* a W. Indian lizard, *Diploglossus monotropis*. [18th c.: orig. unkn.]

gall·nut /gáwlnut/ *n.* = GALL³.

Gallo- /gálō/ *comb. form* **1** French; relating to France. **2** Gaul (*Gallo-Roman*). [L *Gallus* a Gaul]

gal·lon /gálən/ *n.* **1 a** a measure of capacity equivalent to four quarts (3785 cc), used for liquids. **b** (in full **imperial gallon**) *Brit.* a measure of capacity equal to eight pints and equivalent to four quarts (4546 cc), used for liquids and grain, etc. **2** (usu. in *pl.*) *colloq.* a large amount. □□ **gal·lon·age** *n.* [ME f. ONF *galon*, OF *jalon*, f. base of med.L *galleta*, *galletum*, perh. of Celtic orig.]

gal·loon /gəlōon/ *n.* a narrow braid of gold, silver, silk, cotton, nylon, etc., for trimming dresses, etc. [F *galon* f. *galonner* trim with braid, of unkn. orig.]

gal·lop /gáləp/ *n. & v.* ● *n.* **1** the fastest pace of a horse or other quadruped, with all the feet off the ground together in each stride. **2** a ride at this pace. **3** *Brit.* a track or ground for this. ● *v.* (**gal·loped**, **gal·lop·ing**) **1 a** *intr.* (of a horse, etc., or its rider) go at the pace of a gallop. **b** *tr.* make (a horse, etc.) gallop. **2** *intr.* (foll. by *through*, *over*) read, recite, or talk at great speed. **3** *intr.* move or progress rapidly (*galloping inflation*). □ **at a gallop** at the pace of a gallop. □□ **gal·lop·er** *n.* [OF *galop*, *galoper*: see WALLOP]

gal·lo·way /gáləway/ *n.* **1** an animal of a breed of hornless black beef cattle from Galloway in SW Scotland. **2** this breed.

gal·lows /gálōz/ *n.pl.* (usu. treated as *sing.*) **1** a structure, usu. of two uprights and a crosspiece, for the hanging of criminals. **2** (prec. by *the*) execution by hanging. [ME f. ON *gálgi*]

gal·lows hu·mor *n.* grim and ironic humor.

gall·stone /gáwlstōn/ *n.* a small hard mass forming in the gallbladder.

Gal·lup poll /gáləp/ = OPINION POLL. [G. H. *Gallup*, US statistician d. 1984]

gal·lus·es /gáləsiz/ *n.pl. dial. & old-fashioned* suspenders. [pl. of *gallus* var. of GALLOWS]

ga·loot /gəlōot/ *n. colloq.* a person, esp. a strange or clumsy one. [-19th-c. Naut. sl.: orig. unkn.]

gal·op /gáləp/ *n. & v.* **1** a lively dance in duple time. **2** the music for this. ● *v.intr.* (**gal·oped**, **gal·op·ing**) perform this dance. [F: see GALLOP]

ga·lore /gəláwr/ *adv.* in abundance (placed after noun: *flowers galore*). [Ir. *go leór* to sufficiency]

ga·losh /gəlósh/ *n.* (usu. **galoshes**) a high, waterproof overshoe, usu. of rubber. [ME f. OF *galoche* f. LL *gallicula* small Gallic shoe]

ga·lumph /gəlúmf/ *v.intr. colloq.* **1** move noisily or clumsily. **2** go prancing in triumph. [coined by Lewis Carroll (in sense 2), perh. f. GALLOP + TRIUMPH]

gal·van·ic /galvánik/ *adj.* **1 a** sudden and remarkable (*had a galvanic effect*). **b** stimulating; full of energy. **2** of or producing an electric current by chemical action. □□ **gal·van·i·cal·ly** *adv.*

gal·va·nism /gálvənizəm/ *n.* **1** electricity produced by chemical action. **2** the use of electricity for medical purposes. □□ **gal·va·nist** *n.* [F *galvanisme* f. L. *Galvani*, It. physiologist d. 1798]

gal·va·nize /gálvənīz/ *v.tr.* **1** (often foll. by *into*) rouse forcefully, esp. by shock or excitement (*was galvanized into action*). **2** stimulate by or as if by electricity. **3** coat (iron) with zinc (usu. without the use of electricity) as a protection against rust. □□ **gal·va·ni·za·tion** *n.* **gal·va·niz·er** *n.* [F *galvaniser*: see GALVANISM]

gal·va·nom·e·ter /gálvənómitər/ *n.* an instrument for detecting and measuring small electric currents. □□ **gal·va·no·met·ric** /–nəmétrik/ *adj.*

gam·bade /gambáad/ *n.* (also **gam·ba·do** /–báadō/) (*pl.* **gam·bades**; **·dos** or **·does**) **1** a horse's leap or bound. **2** a capering movement. **3** an escapade. [F *gambade* & Sp. *gambado* f. It. & Sp. *gamba* leg]

gam·bier /gámbeeər/ *n.* an astringent extract of an Eastern plant used in tanning, etc. [Malay *gambir* name of the plant]

gam·bit /gámbit/ *n.* **1** a chess opening in which a player sacrifices a piece or pawn to secure an advantage. **2** an opening move in a dis-

cussion, etc. **3** a trick or device. [earlier *gambett* f. It. *gambetto* tripping up f. *gamba* leg]

gam·ble /gámbəl/ *v. & n.* ● *v.* **1** *intr.* play games of chance for money, esp. for high stakes. **2** *tr.* a bet (a sum of money) in gambling. **b** (often foll. by *away*) lose (assets) by gambling. **3** *intr.* take great risks in the hope of substantial gain. **4** *intr.* (foll. by *on*) act in the hope or expectation of (*gambled on fine weather*). ● *n.* **1** a risky undertaking or attempt. **2** a spell or an act of gambling. □□ **gam·bler** *n.* [obs. *gamel* to sport, *gamene* GAME¹]

gam·boge /gambój, –bōozh/ *n.* a gum resin produced by various E. Asian trees and used as a yellow pigment and as a purgative. [mod.L *gambaugium* f. *Cambodia* in SE Asia]

gam·bol /gámbəl/ *v. & n.* ● *v.intr.* (**gam·boled**, **gam·bol·ing**; also **gam·bolled**, **gam·bol·ling**) skip or frolic playfully. ● *n.* a playful frolic. [GAMBADE]

gam·brel /gámbrəl/ *n.* (in full **gambrel roof**) **1** *US* a roof with gables and with each face having two slopes, the lower one steeper. **2** *Brit.* a roof like a hipped roof but with gablelike ends. [ONF *gamberel* f. *gambier* forked stick f. *gambe* leg (from the resemblance to the shape of a horse's hind leg)]

game¹ /gaym/ *n., adj., & v.* ● *n.* **1 a** a form or spell of play or sport, esp. a competitive one played according to rules and decided by skill, strength, or luck. **b** a specific instance of playing such a game; a match. **2** a single portion of play forming a scoring unit in some contests, e.g., bridge or tennis. **3** (in *pl.*) **a** *Brit.* athletics or sports as organized in a school, etc. **b** a meeting for athletic, etc., contests (*Olympic Games*). **4** a winning score in a game; the state of the score in a game (*the game is two all*). **5** the equipment for a game. **6** one's level of achievement in a game, as specified (*played a good game*). **7 a** a piece of fun; a jest (*was only playing a game with you*). **b** (in *pl.*) jokes; tricks (*none of your games!*). **8** a scheme or undertaking, etc., regarded as a game (*so that's your game*). **9 a** a policy or line of action. **b** an occupation or profession (*the fighting game*). **10** (*collect.*) **a** wild animals or birds hunted for sport or food. **b** the flesh of these. **11** a hunted animal; a quarry or object of pursuit or attack. **12** a kept flock of swans. ● *adj.* **1** spirited; eager and willing. **2** (foll. by *for*, or *to* + infin.) having the spirit or energy; eagerly prepared. ● *v.intr.* esp. *Brit.* play at games of chance for money; gamble. □ **the game is up** the scheme is revealed or foiled. **make game** (or **a game**) of mock; taunt. **off** (or **on**) one's game playing badly (or well). **on the game** *Brit. sl.* involved in prostitution or thieving. **play the game** behave fairly or according to the rules. □□ **game·ly** *adv.* **game·ness** *n.* **game·ster** *n.* [OE *gamen*]

game² /gaym/ *adj.* (of a leg, arm, etc.) lame; crippled. [18th-c. dial.: orig. unkn.]

game·cock /gáymkok/ *n.* (also **game·fowl** /–fowl/) a cock bred and trained for cockfighting.

game·keep·er /gáymkeepər/ *n.* a person employed to care for and protect game.

gam·e·lan /gáməlan/ *n.* **1** a type of orchestra found in SE Asia (esp. Indonesia), with string and woodwind instruments, and a wide range of percussion instruments. **2** a kind of xylophone used in this. [Jav.]

game of chance *n.* a game decided by luck, not skill.

game plan *n.* a strategy worked out in advance, esp. in sports, politics, or business.

game point *n. Tennis*, etc., a point which, if won, would win the game.

games·man /gáymzmən/ *n.* (*pl.* **·men**) an exponent of gamesmanship.

games·man·ship /gáymzmənship/ *n.* the art or practice of winning games or other contests by gaining a psychological advantage over an opponent.

game·some /gáymsəm/ *adj.* merry; sportive. □□ **game·some·ly** *adv.* **game·some·ness** *n.*

gam·e·tan·gi·um /gámitánjeeəm/ *n.* (*pl.* **gam·e·tan·gi·a** /–jeeə/) *Bot.* an organ in which gametes are formed. [as GAMETE + *aggeion* vessel]

gam·ete /gámeet, gəmeét/ *n. Biol.* a mature germ cell able to unite with another in sexual reproduction. □□ **ga·met·ic** /gəmétik/ *adj.* [mod.L *gameta* f. Gk *gametē* wife f. *gamos* marriage]

game the·o·ry *n.* (also **games the·o·ry**) the mathematical analysis of conflict in war, economics, games of skill, etc.

gameto- /gəmeétō/ *comb. form Biol.* gamete.

ga·me·to·cyte /gəmeétəsīt/ *n. Biol.* any cell that is in the process of developing into one or more gametes.

gam·e·to·gen·e·sis /gámeetəjénisis/ *n. Biol.* the process by which cells undergo meiosis to form gametes.

ga·me·to·phyte /gəmeétəfīt/ *n.* the gamete-producing form of a plant that has alternation of generations between this and the asexual form. □□ **ga·me·to·phyt·ic** /–fitik/ *adj.*

game war·den *n.* an official locally supervising game and hunting.

gam·in /gámin/ n. **1** a street urchin. **2** an impudent child. [F]

gam·ine /gámeen/ n. **1** a female street urchin. **2** a girl with mischievous or boyish charm. [F]

gam·ing house n. a place frequented for gambling; a casino.

gam·ing ta·ble n. a table used for gambling games.

gam·ma /gámə/ n. **1** the third letter of the Greek alphabet (Γ, γ). **2** Brit. a third-class mark given for a piece of work or in an examination. **3** Astron. the third brightest star in a constellation. **4** the third member of a series. [ME f. Gk]

gam·ma ra·di·a·tion n. (also **gam·ma rays**) electromagnetic radiation of very short wavelength emitted by some radioactive substances.

gam·mer /gámər/ n. Brit. archaic an old woman, esp. as a rustic name. [prob. contr. of GODMOTHER: cf. GAFFER]

gam·mon[1] /gámən/ n. & v. ● n. **1** the bottom piece of a side of bacon including a hind leg. **2** esp. Brit. the ham of a pig cured like bacon. ● v.tr. cure (bacon). [ONF gambon f. gambe leg: cf. JAMB]

gam·mon[2] /gámən/ n. & v. ● n. a victory in backgammon in which the opponent removes no pieces from the board. ● v.tr. defeat in this way. [app. = ME gamen GAME[1]]

gam·mon[3] /gámən/ n. & v. Brit. colloq. ● n. humbug; deception. ● v. **1** intr. a talk speciously. b pretend. **2** tr. hoax; deceive. [18th c.: orig. uncert.]

gam·my /gámee/ adj. (**gam·mi·er, gam·mi·est**) Brit. sl. (esp. of a leg) lame; permanently injured. [dial. form of GAME[2]]

gamp /gamp/ n. Brit. colloq. an umbrella, esp. a large unwieldy one. [Mrs. Gamp in Dickens's Martin Chuzzlewit]

gam·ut /gámət/ n. **1** the whole series or range or scope of anything (the whole gamut of crime). **2** Mus. **a** the whole series of notes used in medieval or modern music. **b** a major diatonic scale. **c** a people's or a period's recognized scale. **d** a voice's or instrument's compass. **3** Mus. the lowest note in the medieval sequence of hexachords, = modern G on the lowest line of the bass staff.

WORD HISTORY   **gamut**

Late Middle English (denoting the musical scale of seven hexachords): from medieval Latin gamma ut, from gamma (taken as the name for a note one tone lower than A of the classical scale) and ut, the first of six arbitrary names of the notes forming the hexachord, from the initial syllables of words in a Latin hymn: Ut queant laxis resonare fibris Mira gestorum famuli tuorum, Solve polluti labii reatum, Sancte Iohannes (a further note, si, was added later, from the initial letters of the last two words).

---

gam·y /gáymee/ adj. (**gam·i·er, gam·i·est**) **1** having the strong flavor or smell of game, esp. when it is slightly tainted. **2** scandalous; sensational; racy. **3** = GAME[1] adj. □□ **gam·i·ly** adv. **gam·i·ness** n.

gan·der /gándər/ n. & v. ● n. **1** a male goose. **2** sl. a look; a glance (take a gander). ● v.intr. look or glance. [OE gandra, rel. to GANNET]

gang[1] /gang/ n. & v. ● n. **1 a** a band of persons acting or going about together, esp. for criminal purposes. **b** colloq. such a band pursuing antisocial purposes. **2** a set of workers, slaves, or prisoners. **3** a set of tools arranged to work simultaneously. ● v.tr. arrange (tools, etc.) to work in coordination. □ **gang up** colloq. **1** (often foll. by with) act in concert. **2** (foll. by on) combine against. [orig. = going, journey, f. ON gangr, ganga GOING, corresp. to OE gang]

gang[2] /gang/ v.intr. Sc. go. □ **gang agley** (of a plan, etc.) go wrong. [OE gangan: cf. GANG[1]]

gang bang n. sl. an occasion on which several men successively have sexual intercourse, often forcibly, with one partner.

gang·board /gángbawrd/ n. = GANGPLANK.

gang·er /gángər/ n. Brit. the foreman of a gang of workers.

gang·land /gángland, –lənd/ n. the world of organized crime.

gan·gle /gánggəl/ v.intr. move ungracefully. [back-form. f. GANGLING]

gan·gling /gánggling/ adj. (of a person) loosely built; lanky. [frequent. of GANG[2]]

gan·gli·on /gánggleeən/ n. (pl. **gan·gli·a** /–leeə/ or **gan·gli·ons**) **1 a** an enlargement or knot on a nerve, etc., containing an assemblage of nerve cells. **b** a mass of gray matter in the central nervous system forming a nerve nucleus. **2** Med. a cyst, esp. on a tendon sheath. **3** a center of activity or interest. □□ **gan·gli·ar** /–gleeər/ adj. **gan·gli·form** /–glifawrm/ adj. **gan·gli·on·at·ed** adj. **gan·gli·on·ic** /–leeónik/ adj. [Gk gagglion]

gan·gly /gánglee/ adj. (**gan·gli·er, gan·gli·est**) = GANGLING.

gang·plank /gángplangk/ n. a movable plank usu. with cleats nailed on it for boarding or disembarking from a ship, etc.

gan·grene /gánggreen/ n. & v. ● n. **1** Med. death and decomposition of a part of the body tissue, usu. resulting from obstructed circulation. **2** moral corruption. ● v.tr. & intr. affect or become affected with gangrene. □□ **gan·gre·nous** /gánggrinəs/ adj. [F gangrène f. L gangraena f. Gk gaggraina]

gang·ster /gángstər/ n. a member of a gang of violent criminals. □□ **gang·ster·ism** n.

gangue /gang/ n. valueless earth, rock, etc., in which ore is found. [F f. G Gang lode = GANG[1]]

gang·way /gángway/ n. & int. ● n. **1 a** an opening in the bulwarks for a gangplank by which a ship is entered or left. **b** a bridge laid from ship to shore. **c** a passage on a ship, esp. a platform connecting the quarterdeck and forecastle. **2** a temporary bridge on a building site, etc. **3** Brit. a passage, esp. between rows of seats; an aisle. ● int. make way!

gan·is·ter /gánistər/ n. a close-grained, hard, siliceous stone found in the coal measures of northern England, and used for furnace linings. [19th c.: orig. unkn.]

gan·ja /gaánjə/ n. marijuana. [Hindi gānjhā]

gan·net /gánit/ n. **1** any sea bird of the genus Morus, esp. Morus bassanus, catching fish by plunge-diving. **2** Brit. sl. a greedy person. □□ **gan·net·ry** n. (pl. **·ries**) [OE ganot f. Gmc, rel. to GANDER]

gan·oid /gánoyd/ adj. & n. ● adj. **1** (of fish scales) enameled; smooth and bright. **2** having ganoid scales. ● n. a fish having ganoid scales. [F ganoïde f. Gk ganos brightness]

gant·let var. of GAUNTLET[2].

gan·try /gántree/ n. (pl. **·tries**) **1** an overhead structure with a platform supporting a traveling crane, or railroad or road signals. **2** a structure supporting a space rocket prior to launching. **3** (also **gaun·try** /gáwntree/) a wooden stand for barrels. [prob. f. gawn, dial. form of GALLON + TREE]

GAO abbr. General Accounting Office.

gaol Brit. var. of JAIL.

gaol·er Brit. var. of JAILER.

gap /gap/ n. **1** an unfilled space or interval; a blank; a break in continuity. **2** a breach in a hedge, fence, or wall. **3** a wide (usu. undesirable) divergence in views, sympathies, development, etc. (generation gap). **4** a gorge or pass. □ **fill** (or **close**, etc.) **a gap** make up a deficiency. □□ **gapped** adj. **gap·py** adj. [ME f. ON, = chasm, rel. to GAPE]

gape /gayp/ v. & n. ● v.intr. **1 a** open one's mouth wide, esp. in amazement or wonder. **b** be or become wide open. **2** (foll. by at) gaze curiously or wondrously. **3** split; part asunder. **4** yawn. ● n. **1** an open-mouthed stare. **2** a yawn. **3** (in pl.; prec. by the) **a** a disease of birds with gaping as a symptom, caused by infestation with gapeworm. **b** joc. a fit of yawning. **4 a** an expanse of open mouth or beak. **b** the part of a beak that opens. **5** a rent or opening. □□ **gap·ing·ly** adv. [ME f. ON gapa]

gap·er /gáypər/ n. **1** any bivalve mollusk of the genus Mya, with the shell open at one or both ends. **2** the comber fish, which gapes when dead. **3** a person who gapes.

gape·worm /gáypwərm/ n. a nematode worm, Syngamus tracheae, that infests the trachea and bronchi of birds and causes the gapes.

gap-toothed adj. having spaces between the teeth.

gar /gaar/ n. **1** any mainly marine fish of the family Belonidae, esp. Belone belone, having long beaklike jaws with sharp teeth. Also called **needlefish**. **2** any similar freshwater fish of the genus Lepisosteus, with ganoid scales. Also called **garfish** or **garpike**. **3** NZ & Austral. either of two marine fish of the genus Hemiramphus. Also called **halfbeak**. [app. f. OE gār spear + fisc FISH[1]]

ga·rage /gəraázh, –raáj/ n. & v. ● n. **1** a building or shed for the storage of a motor vehicle or vehicles. **2** an establishment selling gasoline, etc., or repairing and selling motor vehicles. ● v.tr. put or keep (a motor vehicle) in a garage. [F f. garer shelter]

ga·rage sale n. a sale of miscellaneous household goods held in the garage or yard of a private house. Also called **tag sale, yard sale**.

garb /gaarb/ n. & v. ● n. **1** clothing, esp. of a distinctive kind. **2** the way a person is dressed. ● v.tr. **1** (usu. in passive or refl.) put (esp. distinctive) clothes on (a person). **2** attire. [obs. F garbe f. It. garbo f. Gmc, rel. to GEAR]

gar·bage /gaárbij/ n. **1 a** refuse; filth. **b** domestic waste, esp. food wastes. **2** foul or inferior literature, etc. **3** nonsense. **4** incomprehensible or meaningless data, esp. in computing. [AF: orig. unkn.]

gar·bage can n. a plastic or metal container for household refuse.

gar·ble /gaárbəl/ v.tr. **1** unintentionally distort or confuse (facts, messages, etc.). **2 a** mutilate in order to misrepresent. **b** make (usu. unfair or malicious) selections from (facts, statements, etc.). □□ **gar·bler** n. [It. garbellare f. Arab. garbala sift, perh. f. LL cribellare to sieve f. L cribrum sieve]

gar·board /gaárbərd/ n. (in full **garboard strake**) the first range of planks or plates laid on a ship's bottom next to the keel. [Du. gaarboord, perh. f. garen GATHER + boord BOARD]

gar·çon /gaarsáwn/ n. a waiter in a French restaurant, hotel, etc. [F, lit. 'boy']

gar·den /gaárd'n/ n. & v. ● n. **1 a** a piece of ground used for growing esp. flowers or vegetables. **b** a piece of ground, usu. partly grassed and adjoining a private house, used for growing flowers, fruit, or vegetables, and as a place of recreation. **2** (esp. in pl.) ornamental grounds laid out for public enjoyment (botanical gardens). **3** a similar place with the service of refreshments (tea garden). **4** (attrib.) **a** (of plants) cultivated, not wild. **b** for use in a garden (garden seat). **5** (usu. in pl. prec. by a name) Brit. a street, square, etc. (Onslow Gardens). **6** an especially fertile region. **7** a large public hall. ●*v.intr.* cultivate or work in a garden. □□ **gar•den•esque** /–ésk/ *adj.* **gar•den•ing** *n.* [ME f. ONF *gardin* (OF *jardin*) ult. f. Gmc: cf. YARD²]

gar•den cen•ter *n.* an establishment where plants, garden equipment, etc., are sold.

gar•den cit•y *n.* an industrial or other town laid out systematically with spacious surroundings, parks, etc.

gar•den cress *n.* a cruciferous plant, *Lepidium sativum*, used in salads.

gar•den•er /gaárdnər/ *n.* a person who gardens or is employed to tend a garden. [ME ult. f. *jardinier* (as GARDEN)]

gar•den•er bird *n.* a bowerbird making a "garden" of moss, etc., in front of a bower.

gar•de•nia /gaardéenyə/ *n.* any tree or shrub of the genus *Gardenia*, with large white or yellow flowers and usu. a fragrant scent. [mod.L f. Dr. A. *Garden*, Sc. naturalist d. 1791]

gar•den par•ty *n.* a social event held on a lawn or in a garden.

gar•den war•bler *n.* a European woodland songbird, *Sylvia borin*.

gar•fish /gaárfish/ *n.* (*pl.* same) = GAR.

gar•gan•tu•an /gaargánchōŏən/ *adj.* enormous; gigantic. [the name of a giant in Rabelais' book *Gargantua* (1534)]

gar•get /gaárgit/ *n.* **1** inflammation of a cow's or ewe's udder. **2** pokeweed. [perh. f. obs. *garget* throat f. OF *gargate, –guete*]

gar•gle /gaárgəl/ *v.* & *n.* ●*v.* **1** *tr.* (also *absol.*) wash (one's mouth and throat), esp. for medicinal purposes, with a liquid kept in motion by breathing through it. **2** *Brit. intr.* make a sound as when doing this. ●*n.* **1** a liquid used for gargling. **2** *sl.* an alcoholic drink. [F *gargouiller* f. *gargouille*: see GARGOYLE]

gar•goyle /gaárgoyl/ *n.* a grotesque carved human or animal face or figure projecting from the gutter of a building, typically acting as a spout to carry water clear of a wall. □□ **gar•goyled** *adj.* [OF *gargouille* throat, gargoyle]

gar•goyl•ism /gaárgoylizəm/ *n. Med.* = HURLER'S SYNDROME.

gar•i•bal•di /gáribáwldee/ *n.* (*pl.* **gar•i•bal•dis**) **1** a kind of woman's or child's loose blouse, orig. of bright red material imitating the shirts worn by Garibaldi and his followers. **2** *Brit.* a cookie containing a layer of currants. **3** a small red Californian fish, *Hypsypops rubicundus*. [G. *Garibaldi*, It. patriot d. 1882]

gargoyle

gar•ish /gáirish/ *adj.* **1** obtrusively bright; showy. **2** gaudy; overdecorated. □□ **gar•ish•ly** *adv.* **gar•ish•ness** *n.* [16th-c. *gaurish* app. f. obs. *gaure* stare]

gar•land /gaárlənd/ *n.* & *v.* ●*n.* **1** a wreath of flowers, leaves, etc., worn on the head or hung as a decoration. **2** a prize or distinction. **3** a literary anthology or miscellany. ●*v.tr.* **1** adorn with garlands. **2** crown with a garland. [ME f. OF *garlande*, of unkn. orig.]

gar•lic /gaárlik/ *n.* **1** any of various alliaceous plants, esp. *Allium sativum*. **2** the strong-smelling pungent bulb of this plant, used as a flavoring in cooking. □□ **gar•lick•y** *adj.* [OE *gārleac* f. *gār* spear + *lēac* LEEK]

gar•lic press *n.* a hand-held device for crushing gloves of garlic.

gar•ment /gaármənt/ *n.* & *v.* ●*n.* **1 a** an article of dress. **b** (in *pl.*) clothes. **2** the outward and visible covering of anything. ●*v.tr.* (usu. in *passive*) *rhet.* attire. [ME f. OF *garnement* (as GARNISH)]

gar•ner /gaárnər/ *v.* & *n.* ●*v.tr.* **1** collect. **2** store; deposit. ●*n. literary* a storehouse or granary. [ME (orig. as noun) f. OF *gernier* f. L *granarium* GRANARY]

garlic press

gar•net /gaárnit/ *n.* a vitreous silicate mineral, esp. a transparent deep red kind used as a gem. [ME f. OF *grenat* f. med.L *granatum* POMEGRANATE, from its resemblance to the pulp of the fruit]

gar•nish /gaárnish/ *v.* & *n.* ●*v.tr.* **1** decorate or embellish (esp. food). **2** *Law* serve notice on (a person) for the purpose of legally seizing money belonging to a debtor or defendant. **b** summon (a person) as a party to litigation started between others. ●*n.* (also **gar•nish•ing**) a decoration or embellishment, esp. to food. □□ **gar•nish•ment** *n.* (in sense 2). [ME f. OF *garnir* f. Gmc]

gar•nish•ee /gaárnishée/ *n.* & *v. Law* ●*n.* a third party who is served notice by a court to surrender money in settlement of a debt or claim. ●*v.tr.* (**gar•nishees, gar•nish•eed**) = GARNISH 2.

gar•ni•ture /gaárnichər/ *n.* **1** decoration or trimmings, esp. of food. **2** accessories; appurtenances. [F (as GARNISH)]

ga•rotte var. of GARROTE.

gar•pike /gaárpik/ *n.* = GAR.

gar•ret /gárit/ *n.* **1** a top floor or attic room, esp. a dismal or unfurnished one. **2** an attic. [ME f. OF *garite* watchtower f. Gmc]

gar•ri•son /gárisən/ *n.* & *v.* ●*n.* **1** the troops stationed in a fortress, town, etc., to defend it. **2** the building occupied by them. ●*v.tr.*

1 provide (a place) with or occupy as a garrison. **2** place on garrison duty. [ME f. OF *garison* f. *garir* defend, furnish f. Gmc]

gar•rote /gərót/ *v.* & *n.* ●*v.tr.* **1** execute or kill by strangulation, esp. with an iron or wire collar, etc. **2** throttle in order to rob. ●*n.* **1 a** a Spanish method of execution by garroting. **b** the apparatus used for this. **2** highway robbery in which the victim is throttled. [F *garrotter* or Sp. *garrotear* f. *garrote* a cudgel, of unkn. orig.]

SPELLING TIP garrote

The standard American spelling of this word has two *r*'s and one *t*. Other acceptable spellings are *garrotte, garotte,* and *garote.*

gar•ru•lous /gárələs, gáryə–/ *adj.* **1** talkative, esp. on trivial matters. **2** loquacious; wordy. □□ **gar•ru•li•ty** /gərooólitee/ *n.* **gar•ru•lous•ly** *adv.* **gar•ru•lous•ness** *n.* [L *garrulus* f. *garrire* chatter]

gar•ter /gaártər/ *n.* & *v.* ●*n.* **1** a band worn to keep a sock or stocking or shirt sleeve up. **2** a strap hanging from a girdle, etc., for holding up a stocking. **3** (**the Garter**) *Brit.* **a** the highest order of English knighthood. **b** the badge of this. **c** membership of this. ●*v.tr.* fasten (a stocking) or encircle (a leg) with a garter. [ME f. OF *gartier* f. *garet* bend of the knee]

gar•ter belt *n.* a belt with hanging straps with fasteners attached to hold up stockings.

gar•ter snake a common, harmless snake of the genus *Thamnophis*, native to N. America, having well-defined longitudinal stripes.

gar•ter stitch a plain knitting stitch or pattern, forming ridges in alternate rows.

garth /gaarth/ *n. Brit.* **1** an open space within cloisters. **2** *archaic* **a** a yard or garden. **b** a paddock. [ME f. ON *garthr* = OE *geard* YARD²]

gas /gas/ *n.* & *v.* ●*n.* (*pl.* **gas•es**) **1** any airlike substance which moves freely to fill any space available, irrespective of its quantity. **2 a** such a substance (esp. found naturally or extracted from coal) used as a domestic or industrial fuel (also *attrib.: gas stove*). **b** an explosive mixture of firedamp with air. **3** nitrous oxide or another gas used as an anesthetic (esp. in dentistry). **4** a gas or vapor used as a poisonous agent to disable an enemy in warfare. **5** *colloq.* a gasoline. **b** motor vehicle's accelerator. **6** *sl.* pointless idle talk; boasting. **7** *sl.* an enjoyable, attractive, or amusing thing or person. ●*v.* (**gas•es, gassed, gas•sing**) **1** *tr.* expose to gas, esp. to kill or make unconscious. **2** *intr.* give off gas. **3** *tr.* (usu. foll. by *up*) *colloq.* fill (the tank of a motor vehicle) with gasoline. **4** *intr. colloq.* talk idly or boastfully. [invented by J. B. van Helmont, Belgian chemist d. 1644, after Gk *khaos* chaos]

gas•bag /gásbag/ *n.* **1** a container of gas, esp. for holding the gas for a balloon or airship. **2** *sl.* an idle talker.

gas cham•ber *n.* an airtight chamber that can be filled with poisonous gas to kill people or animals.

gas chro•ma•tog•ra•phy *n.* chromatography employing gas as the moving carrier medium.

Gas•con /gáskən/ *n.* **1** a native of Gascony, a region of France. **2** (**gascon**) a braggart. [F f. L *Vasco –onis*]

gas-cooled *adj.* (of a nuclear reactor, etc.) cooled by a current of gas.

gas•e•ous /gáseeəs, gáshəs/ *adj.* of or like gas. □□ **gas•e•ous•ness** *n.*

gas fire *n. Brit.* a domestic fire using gas as its fuel.

gas-fired *adj.* using gas as the fuel.

gas gan•grene *n.* a rapidly spreading gangrene of injured tissue infected by a soil bacterium and accompanied by the evolution of gas in the infected tissue.

gas-guz•zler *n.* colloq. a motor vehicle that gets relatively poor gas mileage.

gash¹ /gash/ *n.* & *v.* ●*n.* **1** a long and deep slash, cut, or wound. **2 a** a cleft such as might be made by a slashing cut. **b** the act of making such a cut. ●*v.tr.* make a gash in; cut. [var. of ME *garse* f. OF *garcer* scarify, perh. ult. f. Gk *kharassō*]

gash² /gash/ *adj. Brit. sl.* spare; extra. [20th-c. Naut. sl.: orig. unkn.]

gas•i•fy /gásifī/ *v.tr.* & *intr.* (**·fies, ·fied**) convert or be converted into gas. □□ **gas•i•fi•ca•tion** /–fikáyshən/ *n.*

gas•ket /gáskit/ *n.* **1** a sheet or ring of rubber, etc., shaped to seal the junction of metal surfaces. **2** a small cord securing a furled sail to a yard. □ **blow a gasket** *sl.* lose one's temper. [perh. f. F *garcette* thin rope (orig. little girl)]

gas•kin /gáskin/ *n.* the muscular part of the hind leg of a horse between the stifle and the hock. [perh. erron. f. GALLI-GASKINS]

gasket 1

gas•light /gáslīt/ *n.* **1** a jet of burning gas, usu. heating a mantle, to provide light. **2** light emanating from this.

gas mask *n.* a respirator used as a defense against poison gas.

gas me•ter *n.* an apparatus recording the amount of gas consumed.

gas oil *n.* a type of fuel oil distilled from petroleum and heavier than kerosene.

gas·o·lene var. of GASOLINE.

gas·o·line /gásəléen/ *n.* (also **gas·o·lene**) a volatile flammable liquid blended from petroleum and natural gas and used as a fuel. [GAS + -OL² + -INE⁴, -ENE]

gas·om·e·ter /gasómítər/ *n. Brit.* a large tank in which gas is stored for distribution by pipes to users. [F *gazomètre* f. *gaz* gas + -*mètre* -METER]

gasp /gasp/ *v. & n. ● v.* **1** *intr.* catch one's breath with an open mouth as in exhaustion or astonishment. **2** *intr.* (foll. by *for*) strain to obtain by gasping (*gasped for air*). **3** *tr.* (often foll. by *out*) utter with gasps. *● n.* a convulsive catching of breath. □ **at one's last gasp 1** at the point of death. **2** exhausted. [ME f. ON *geispa*: cf. *geip* idle talk]

gas·per /gáspər/ *n. Brit. sl.* a cigarette.

gas-per·me·a·ble *adj.* (esp. of a contact lens) allowing the diffusion of gases.

gas plant *n. Bot.* = FRAXINELLA.

gas ring *n.* a hollow ring perforated with gas jets, used esp. for cooking.

gas·ser /gásər/ *n.* **1** *colloq.* an idle talker. **2** *sl.* a very attractive or impressive person or thing.

gas sta·tion *n.* a service station.

gas·sy /gásee/ *adj.* (**gas·si·er, gas·si·est**) **1 a** of or like gas. **b** full of gas. **2** *colloq.* (of talk, etc.) pointless; verbose. □□ **gas·si·ness** *n.*

gast·haus /gaást-hows/ *n.* a small inn or hotel in German-speaking countries. [G f. *Gast* GUEST + *Haus* HOUSE]

gas·trec·to·my /gastréktəmee/ *n.* (*pl.* -**mies**) a surgical operation in which the whole or part of the stomach is removed. [GASTRO- + -ECTOMY]

gas·tric /gástrik/ *adj.* of the stomach. [mod.L *gastricus* f. Gk *gastēr gast(e)ros* stomach]

gas·tric juice *n.* a thin clear virtually colorless acid fluid secreted by the stomach glands and active in promoting digestion.

gas·tri·tis /gastrítis/ *n.* inflammation of the lining of the stomach.

gastro- /gástrō/ *comb. form* (also **gastr-** before a vowel) stomach. [Gk *gastēr gast(e)ros* stomach]

gas·tro·en·ter·ic /gástrōéntérik/ *adj.* of or relating to the stomach and intestines.

gas·tro·en·ter·i·tis /gástrō-éntərítis/ *n. Med.* inflammation of the stomach and intestines.

gas·tro·nome /gástrənōm/ *n.* a gourmet. [F f. *gastronomie* GASTRONOMY]

gas·tron·o·my /gastrónəmee/ *n.* the practice, study, or art of eating and drinking well. □□ **gas·tro·nom·ic** /gástrənómik/ *adj.* **gas·tro·nom·i·cal** *adj.* **gas·tro·nom·i·cal·ly** *adv.* [F *gastronomie* f. Gk *gastronomia* (as GASTRO-, *-nomia* f. *nomos* law)]

gas·tro·pod /gástrəpod/ *n.* any mollusk of the class Gastropoda that moves along by means of a large muscular foot, e.g., a snail, slug, etc. □□ **gas·trop·o·dous** /gastrópədəs/ *adj.* [F *gastéropode* f. mod.L *gasteropoda* (as GASTRO-, Gk *pous podos* foot)]

gas·tro·scope /gástrəskōp/ *n.* an optical instrument used for inspecting the interior of the stomach.

gas·tru·la /gástrələ/ *n.* (*pl.* **gas·tru·lae** /-lee/) *Zool.* an embryonic stage developing from the blastula. [mod.L f. Gk *gastēr gast(e)ros* belly]

gas tur·bine *n.* a turbine driven by a flow of gas or by gas from combustion.

gas·works /gáswərks/ *n.* a place where gas is manufactured and processed.

gat¹ /gat/ *n. sl.* a revolver or other firearm. [abbr. of GATLING]

gat² /gat/ *archaic past* of GET *v.*

gate¹ /gayt/ *n. & v. ● n.* **1 a** barrier, usu. hinged, made to close an opening used for entrance and exit through a wall, fence, tollbooth, etc. **2** such an opening, esp. in the wall of a city, enclosure, or large building. **3** a means of entrance or exit. **4** a numbered place of access to aircraft at an airport. **5** a mountain pass. **6** an arrangement of slots into which the gear lever of a motor vehicle moves to engage the required gear. **7** a device for holding the frame of a photographic film momentarily in position behind the lens of a camera or projector. **8 a** an electrical signal that causes or controls the passage of other signals. **b** an electrical circuit with an output which depends on the combination of several inputs. **9 a** device regulating the passage of water in a lock, etc. **10 a** the number of people entering by payment at the gates of a sports stadium, etc. **b** (in full **gate money**) the proceeds taken for admission. **11** *Brit. sl.* the mouth. **12** *sl.* dismissal. **13** = STARTING GATE. *● v.tr.* **1** *Brit.* confine to college or school entirely or after certain hours. **2** (as **gated** *adj.*) (of a road) having a gate or gates to control the movement of traffic or animals. [OE *gæt, geat,* pl. *gatu,* f. Gmc]

gate² /gayt/ *n.* (prec. or prefixed by a name) *Brit.* a street (*Westgate*). [ME f. ON *gata,* f. Gmc]

-gate /gayt/ *suffix* forming nouns denoting an actual or alleged scandal comparable in some way to the Watergate scandal of 1972 (*Irangate*). [f. (WATER)GATE]

ga·teau /gatố, gaa-/ *n.* (*pl.* **ga·teaus** or **ga·teaux** /-tốz/) any of various rich cakes, usu. containing cream or fruit. [F *gâteau* cake]

gate·crash·er /gáytkrashər/ *n.* an uninvited guest at a party, etc. □□ **gate·crash** *v.tr. & intr.*

gate·fold /gáytfōld/ *n.* a page in a book or magazine, etc., that folds out to be larger than the page format.

gate·house /gáyt-hows/ *n.* **1** a house standing by a gateway, esp. to a large house or park. **2** *hist.* a room over a city gate, often used as a prison. **3** a building in which the controls of a lock, dam, drawbridge, etc., are situated.

gate·keep·er /gáytkeepər/ *n.* **1** an attendant at a gate, controlling entrance and exit. **2** any of several large brown species of butterfly, esp. *Maniola tithonus*, frequenting hedgerows and woodland.

gate·leg /gáytleg/ *n.* (in full **gateleg table**) a table with hinged legs that swing out from the frame to support folding leaves that make the surface of table larger. □□ **gate·legged** *adj.*

gate·man /gáytmən/ *n.* (*pl.* -**men**) = GATEKEEPER 1.

gate·post /gáytpōst/ *n.* a post on which a gate is hung or against which it shuts. □ **between you and me and the gatepost** in strict confidence.

gate·way /gáytway/ *n.* **1** an entrance with or opening for a gate. **2** a frame or structure built over a gate. **3** an entrance or exit.

gath·er /gáthər/ *v. & n. ● v.* **1** *tr. & intr.* bring or come together; assemble; accumulate. **2** *tr.* (usu. foll. by *up*) **a** bring together from scattered places or sources. **b** take up together from the ground, a surface, etc. **c** draw into a smaller compass. **3** *tr.* acquire by gradually collecting; amass. **4** *tr.* **a** pick a quantity of (flowers, etc.). **b** collect (grain, etc.) as a harvest. **5** *tr.* (often foll. by *that* + clause) infer or understand. **6** *tr.* be subjected to or affected by the accumulation or increase of (*unread books gathering dust; gather speed; gather strength*). **7** *tr.* (often foll. by *up*) summon up (one's thoughts, energy, etc.) for a purpose. **8** *tr.* gain or recover (one's breath). **9** *tr.* **a** draw (material, or one's brow) together in folds or wrinkles. **b** pucker or draw together (part of a dress) by running a thread through. **10** *intr.* come to a head; develop a purulent swelling. *● n.* (in *pl.*) a part of a garment that is gathered or drawn in. □ **gather way** (of a ship) begin to move. □□ **gath·er·er** *n.* [OE *gaderian* f.WG]

ASSEMBLE, COLLECT, CONGREGATE, CONVENE, MARSHAL, MUSTER. **Gather** is the most general of these terms meaning to come or bring together. It implies bringing widely scattered things or people to one place but with no particular arrangement (*to gather shells at the beach; to gather the family in the living room*). **Collect**, on the other hand, implies both selectivity (*to collect evidence for the trial*) and organization (*to collect butterflies as a hobby*). To *gather* one's thoughts means to bring them together because they have been previously scattered; to *collect* one's thoughts is to organize them. **Assemble** pertains to objects or people who are brought together for a purpose (*to assemble data for a report; to assemble Congress so that legislation will be passed*), while *congregate* may be more spontaneous, done as a free choice (*people congregated in front of the palace, hoping to catch a glimpse of the queen*). **Convene** is a formal word meaning to assemble or meet in a body (*to convene an international conference on the subject of global warming*) **Marshal** and **muster** are usually thought of as military terms. *Muster* implies bringing together the parts or units of a force (*troops mustered for inspection*), and *marshal* suggests a very orderly and purposeful arrangement (*to marshal the allied forces along the battle front*).

gath·er·ing /gáthəring/ *n.* **1** an assembly or meeting. **2** a purulent swelling. **3** a group of leaves taken together in bookbinding.

Gat·ling /gátling/ *n.* (in full **Gatling gun**) a machine gun with clustered barrels. [R. J. *Gatling,* Amer. inventor d. 1903]

ga·tor /gáytər/ *n.* (also **ga·ter**) *colloq.* an alligator.

GATT /gat/ *abbr.* (also **Gatt**) General Agreement on Tariffs and Trade.

gauche /gōsh/ *adj.* **1** lacking ease or grace; socially awkward. **2** tactless. □□ **gauche·ly** *adv.* **gauche·ness** *n.* [F, = left-handed, awkward]

gau·che·rie /gốshəree/ *n.* **1** gauche manners. **2** a gauche action. [F]

gau·cho /gówchō/ *n.* (*pl.* -**chos**) a cowboy from the S. American pampas. [Sp. f. Quechua]

gaud /gawd/ *n.* a gaudy thing; a showy ornament. [perh. through AF f. OF *gaudir* rejoice f. L *gaudēre*]

gaud·y¹ /gáwdee/ *adj.* (**gaud·i·er, gaud·i·est**) tastelessly or extravagantly bright or showy. □□ **gaud·i·ly** *adv.* **gaud·i·ness** *n.* [prob. f. GAUD + -Y¹]

gaud·y² /gáwdee/ *n.* (*pl.* -**ies**) *Brit.* an annual feast or entertainment, esp. a college dinner for graduates, etc. [L *gaudium* joy or *gaude* imper. of *gaudēre* rejoice]

gauge /gayj/ *n. & v.* (also **gage**) *● n.* **1** a standard measure to which certain things must conform, esp.: **a** the measure of the capacity or contents of a barrel. **b** the fineness of a textile. **c** the diameter of a bullet. **d** the thickness of sheet metal. **2** any of various instruments for measuring or determining this, or for measuring length, thickness, or other dimensions or properties. **3** the distance between a pair of rails or the width of wheels on one axle. **4** the capacity, extent, or scope of something. **5** a means of estimating; a criterion or test. **6** a graduated instrument measuring the force or quantity of rainfall, stream, tide, wind, etc. **7** *Naut.* a relative position with respect to the wind. • *v.tr.* **1** measure exactly (esp. objects of standard size). **2** determine the capacity or content of. **3** estimate or form a judgment of (a person, temperament, situation, etc.). **4** make uniform; bring to a standard size or shape. □ **take the gauge** of estimate. □□ **gauge·a·ble** *adj.* **gaug·er** *n.* [ME f. ONF *gauge, gauger,* of unkn. orig.]

gauge pres·sure *n.* the amount by which the pressure measured in a fluid exceeds that of the atmosphere.

Gaul /gawl/ *n.* a native or inhabitant of ancient Gaul. [*Gaul* the country f. F *Gaule* f. Gmc]

gau·lei·ter /gówlītər/ *n.* **1** an official governing a district under Nazi rule. **2** a local or petty tyrant. [G f. *Gau* administrative district + *Leiter* leader]

Gaul·ish /gáwlish/ *adj. & n.* • *adj.* of or relating to the ancient Gauls. • *n.* their language.

Gaull·ism /gôlizəm, gáw–/ *n.* **1** the principles and policies of Charles de Gaulle, French military and political leader (d. 1970), characterized by their conservatism, nationalism, and advocacy of centralized government. **2** adherence to these. □□ **Gaull·ist** *n.* [F *Gaullisme*]

gault /gawlt/ *n. Geol. Brit.* **1** a series of Cretaceous clays and marls forming strata in southern England. **2** clay obtained from these beds. [16th c.: orig. unkn.]

gaunt /gawnt/ *adj.* **1** lean; haggard. **2** grim or desolate in appearance. □□ **gaunt·ly** *adv.* **gaunt·ness** *n.* [ME: orig. unkn.]

gaunt·let¹ /gáwntlit/ *n.* **1** a stout glove with a long loose wrist. **2** *hist.* an armored glove. **3** the part of a glove covering the wrist. **4** a challenge (esp. in **throw down the gauntlet**). [ME f. OF *gantelet* dimin. of *gant* glove f. Gmc]

gaunt·let² /gáwntlit/ *n.* (also **gant·let** /gánt–/) □ **run the gauntlet 1** be subjected to harsh criticism. **2** pass between two rows of people and receive blows from them, as a punishment or ordeal. [earlier *gantlope* f. Sw. *gatlopp* f. *gata* lane, *lopp* course, assim. to GAUNTLET¹]

gaun·try var. of GANTRY 3.

gaur /gowr/ *n.* a wild species of E. Indian cattle, *Bos gaurus.* [Hind.]

gauss /gows/ *n.* (pl. same or **gauss·es**) a unit of magnetic induction, equal to one ten-thousandth of a tesla. ¶ Abbr.: **G.** [K. *Gauss,* Ger. mathematician d. 1855]

Gauss·i·an dis·tri·bu·tion /gówseeən/ *n. Statistics* = NORMAL DISTRIBUTION. [as GAUSS]

gauze /gawz/ *n.* **1** a thin transparent fabric of silk, cotton, etc. **2** a fine mesh of wire, etc. **3** a slight haze. [F *gaze* f. *Gaza* in Palestine]

gauz·y /gáwzee/ *adj.* (**gauz·i·er, gauz·i·est**) **1** like gauze; thin and translucent. **2** flimsy; delicate. □□ **gauz·i·ly** *adv.* **gauz·i·ness** *n.*

gave past of GIVE.

gav·el /gávəl/ *n. & v.* • *n.* a small hammer used by an auctioneer, or for calling a meeting, courtroom, etc., to order. • *v.* (**gav·eled, gav·el·ing;** also **gav·elled, gav·el·ling**) **1** *intr.* use a gavel. **2** *tr.* (often foll. by *down*) end (a meeting) or dismiss (a speaker) by use of a gavel. [19th c.: orig. unkn.]

ga·vi·al /gáyveeəl/ *n.* (also **gha·ri·al** /gúreeəl/) a large crocodile of India, *Gavialis gangeticus,* having a long narrow snout widening at the nostrils. [Hind.]

ga·votte /gəvót/ *n.* **1** an old French dance in moderately quick 4/4 time beginning on the third beat of the bar. **2** the music for this, or a piece of music in the rhythm of this as a movement in a suite. [F f. Prov. *gavoto* f. *Gavot* native of a region in the Alps]

gawk /gawk/ *v. & n.* • *v.intr. colloq.* stare stupidly. • *n.* an awkward or bashful person. □□ **gawk·ish** *adj.* [rel. to obs. *gaw* gaze f. ON *gá* heed]

gawk·y /gáwkee/ *adj.* (**gawk·i·er, gawk·i·est**) awkward or ungainly. □□ **gawk·i·ly** *adv.* **gawk·i·ness** *n.*

gawp /gawp/ *v.intr. Brit. colloq.* stare stupidly or obtrusively. □□ **gawp·er** *n.* [earlier *gaup, galp* f. ME *galpen* yawn, rel. to YELP]

gay /gay/ *adj. & n.* • *adj.* **1** lighthearted and carefree; mirthful. **2** characterized by cheerfulness or pleasure (*a gay life*). **3 a** homosexual. **b** intended for or used by homosexuals (*a gay bar*). **4** brightly colored; showy; brilliant (*a gay scarf*). **5** *colloq.* dissolute; immoral. • *n.* a homosexual, esp. male. □□ **gay·ness** *n.* [ME f. OF *gai,* of unkn. orig.]

▶ *Gay* as a term referring to homosexuals is generally informal in use, but often favored by homosexuals with reference to themselves.

ga·yal /gəyál/ *n.* a wild species of E. Indian cattle, *Bos frontalis.* [Hindi]

gay·e·ty var. of GAIETY.

ga·za·ni·a /gəzáyneeə/ *n.* any herbaceous plant of the genus *Gazania,* with showy yellow or orange daisy-shaped flowers. [18th c.: f. Theodore of *Gaza,* Greek scholar d. 1478]

gaze /gayz/ *v. & n.* • *v.intr.* (foll. by *at, into, on, upon,* etc.) look fix-

edly. • *n.* a fixed or intent look. □□ **gaz·er** *n.* [ME: orig. unkn.; cf. obs. *gaw* GAWK]

ga·ze·bo /gəzeébō/ *n.* (*pl.* **·bos** or **·boes**) a small building or structure such as a summerhouse or turret, designed to give a wide view. [perh. joc. f. GAZE, in imitation of L futures in *–ēbo:* cf. LAVABO]

gazebo

ga·zelle /gəzél/ *n.* any of various small graceful soft-eyed antelopes of Asia or Africa, esp. of the genus *Gazella.* [F prob. f. Sp. *gacela* f. Arab. *ġazāl*]

ga·zette /gəzét/ *n. & v.* • *n.* **1** a newspaper, esp. the official one of an organization or institution (*University Gazette*). **2** *hist.* a news sheet; a periodical publication giving current events. **3** *Brit.* an official journal with a list of government appointments, bankruptcies, and other public notices. • *v.tr. Brit.* announce or publish in an official gazette.

WORD HISTORY gazette

Early 17th century: via French from Italian *gazzetta,* originally Venetian *gazeta de la novità* 'a halfpennyworth of news' (because the newssheet sold for a *gazeta,* a Venetian coin of small value).

gaz·et·teer /gázite͝er/ *n.* a geographical index or dictionary. [earlier = journalist, for whom such an index was provided: f. F *gazettier* f. It. *gazzettiere* (as GAZETTE)]

gaz·pa·cho /gəspaáchō/ *n.* (*pl.* **·chos**) a Spanish soup made with tomatoes, oil, garlic, onions, etc., and served cold. [Sp.]

ga·zump /gəzúmp/ *v.tr.* (also *absol.*) *Brit. colloq.* **1** (of a seller) raise the price of a property after having accepted an offer by (an intending buyer). **2** swindle. □□ **ga·zump·er** *n.* [20th c.: orig. uncert.]

ga·zund·er /gəzúndər/ *v.tr.* (also *absol.*) *Brit. colloq.* (of a buyer) lower the amount of an offer made to (the seller) for a property, esp. just before exchange of contracts. [GAZUMP + UNDER]

GB *abbr.* Great Britain.

Gd *symb. Chem.* the element gadolinium.

GDP *abbr.* gross domestic product.

GDR *abbr. hist.* German Democratic Republic.

Ge *symb. Chem.* the element germanium.

gear /geer/ *n. & v.* • *n.* **1** (often in *pl.*) **a** a set of toothed wheels that work together to transmit and control motion from an engine, esp. to the road wheels of a vehicle. **b** a mechanism for doing this. **2** a particular function or state of adjustment of engaged gears (*low gear; second gear*). **3** a mechanism of wheels, levers, etc., usu. for a special purpose (*winding gear*). **4** a particular apparatus or mechanism, as specified (*landing gear*). **5** equipment or tackle for a special purpose. **6** *colloq.* **a** clothing, esp. when modern or fashionable. **b** possessions in general. **7** goods; household utensils. **8** rigging. **9** a harness for a draft animal. • *v.* **1** *tr.* (foll. by *to*) adjust or adapt to suit a special purpose or need. **2** *tr.* (often foll. by *up*) equip with gears. **3** *tr.* (foll. by *up*) make ready or prepared. **4** *tr.* put (machinery) in gear. **5** *intr.* **a** *Brit.* be in gear. **b** (foll. by *with*) work smoothly with. □ **be geared (or all geared) up** (often foll. by *for,* or *to* + infin.) *colloq.* be ready or enthusiastic. **gear down** (or *up*) provide with or shift into a low (or high) gear. **in gear** with a gear engaged. **out of gear 1** with no gear engaged. **2** out of order. [ME f. ON *gervi* f. Gmc]

gear·box /geérboks/ *n.* **1** the casing that encloses a set of gears. **2** a set of gears with its casing, esp. in a motor vehicle; a transmission.

gear·ing /geéring/ *n.* **1** a set or arrangement of gears in a machine. **2** *Brit. Commerce* = LEVERAGE 5.

gear·shift /geérshift/ *n.* a lever used to engage or change gear, esp. in a motor vehicle.

gear·wheel /geérwheel, –weel/ *n.* **1** a toothed wheel in a set of gears. **2** (in a bicycle) the cogwheel driven directly by the chain.

geck·o /gékō/ *n.* (*pl.* **·os** or **·oes**) any of various house lizards found in warm climates, with adhesive feet for climbing vertical surfaces. [Malay *chichak,* etc., imit. of its cry]

gee¹ /jee/ *int.* (also **gee whiz** /wiz/) *colloq.* a mild expression of surprise, discovery, etc. [perh. abbr. of JESUS]

gee² /jee/ *int.* (often foll. by *up*) a command to a horse, etc., esp. to turn to the right or to go faster. [17th c.: orig. unkn.]

gee³ /jee/ *n. sl.* (usu. in *pl.*) a thousand dollars. [the letter *G,* as initial of GRAND]

gee-gee /jeéjee/ *n. Brit. colloq.* a horse. [orig. a child's word, f. GEE²]

geek¹ /geek/ *n. sl.* **1** a person who is socially inept or tediously conventional; a dupe. **2** a carnival performer who bites the heads off live chickens in performance. [var. of dial. *geck* fool, dupe]

geek[2] /geek/ *n. Austral. sl.* a look. [E dial.]

geese *pl.* of GOOSE.

gee-string var. of G-STRING 2.

gee·zer /ˈgeezər/ *n. sl.* a person, esp. an old man. [dial. pronunc. of *guiser* mummer]

Ge·hen·na /giˈhenə/ *n.* **1** (in the New Testament) hell. **2** a place of burning, torment, or misery. [eccl.L f. Gk f. Heb. *gê hinnōm* hell, orig. the valley of Hinnom near Jerusalem, where children were sacrificed]

Gei·ger count·er /ˈgīgər/ *n.* a device for measuring radioactivity by detecting and counting ionizing particles. [H. *Geiger*, Ger. physicist d. 1945]

gei·sha /ˈgāshə, ˈgē–/ *n. (pl.* same or **gei·shas**) a Japanese hostess trained in entertaining men with dance and song. [Jap.]

Geiss·ler tube /ˈgīslər/ *n.* a sealed tube of glass or quartz with a central constriction, filled with vapor for the production of a luminous electrical discharge. [H. *Geissler*, Ger. mechanic d. 1879]

gel /jel/ *n. & v.* • *n.* **1** a semisolid colloidal suspension or jelly, of a solid dispersed in a liquid. **2** a gelatinous hair-styling preparation. **3** *Theatr.* a thin sheet of colored gelatin used to color stage lights. • *v.intr.* **(gelled, gel·ling)** form a gel. □□ **ge·la·tion** /jeˈlāshən/ *n.* [abbr. of GELATIN]

gel·a·tin /ˈjelətin/ *n.* (also **gel·a·tine** /–teen/) **1** a virtually colorless, tasteless, transparent, water-soluble protein derived from collagen and used in food preparation, photography, etc. **2** a similar substance derived from vegetable matter. □□ **ge·lat·i·nize** /jiˈlatˌnīz/ *v.tr. & intr.* **ge·lat·i·ni·za·tion** /jiˌlatˌnizˈāshən/ *n.* [F *gélatine* f. It. *gelatina* f. *gelata* JELLY]

ge·lat·i·nous /jiˈlatˈnəs/ *adj.* **1** of or like gelatin. **2** of a jellylike consistency. □□ **ge·lat·i·nous·ly** *adv.*

ge·la·tion /jiˈlāshən/ *n.* solidification by freezing. [L *gelatio* f. *gelare* freeze]

ge·la·to /jəˈlaato/ *n.* a kind of Italian ice cream. [It.]

geld /geld/ *v.tr.* **1** deprive (usu. a male animal) of the ability to reproduce. **2** castrate or spay; excise the testicles or ovaries of. [ME f. ON *gelda* f. *geldr* barren f. Gmc]

geld·ing /ˈgelding/ *n.* a gelded animal, esp. a male horse. [ME f. ON *geldingr*: see GELD]

gel·id /ˈjelid/ *adj.* **1** icy; ice cold. **2** chilly; cool. [L *gelidus* f. *gelu* frost]

gel·ig·nite /ˈjelignīt/ *n.* an explosive made from nitroglycerine, cellulose nitrate, sodium or potassium nitrate, and wood pulp. [GELATIN + L *ignis* fire + –ITE[1]]

gel·ly /ˈjelee/ *n. Brit. sl.* gelignite. [abbr.]

gem /jem/ *n. & v.* • *n.* **1** a precious stone, esp. when cut and polished or engraved. **2** an object or person of great beauty or worth. • *v.tr.* **(gemmed, gem·ming)** adorn with or as with gems. □□ **gem·like** *adj.* **gem·my** *adj.* [ME f. OF *gemme* f. L *gemma* bud, jewel]

Ge·ma·ra /giˈmaarə, –ˈmawrə, –ˈmaaraa/ *n.* a rabbinical commentary on the Mishnah, forming the second part of the Talmud. [Aram. *gᵊmārâ* completion]

gem·i·nal /ˈjeminəl/ *adj. Chem.* (of molecules) having two functional groups attached to the same atom. □□ **gem·i·nal·ly** *adv.* [as GEMINATE + –AL]

gem·i·nate *adj. & v.* • *adj.* /ˈjemininət/ combined in pairs. • *v.tr.* /ˈjeminayt/ **1** double; repeat. **2** arrange in pairs. □□ **gem·i·na·tion** *n.* [L *geminatus* past part. of *geminare* f. *geminus* twin]

Gem·i·ni /ˈjeminī, –nee/ *n.* **1** a constellation, traditionally regarded as contained in the figures of twins. **2 a** the third sign of the zodiac (the Twins). **b** a person born when the sun is in this sign. □□ **Gem·i·ne·an** /ˌjeminˈeeən, –ˈnī–/ *n. & adj.* [ME f. L = twins]

gem·ma /ˈjemə/ *n. (pl.* **gem·mae** /–mee/) a small cellular body in cryptogams that separates from the mother plant and starts a new one; an asexual spore. [L: see GEM]

gem·ma·tion /jeˈmāshən/ *n.* reproduction by gemmae. [F f. *gemmer* to bud, *gemme* bud]

gem·mif·er·ous /jeˈmifərəs/ *adj.* **1** producing precious stones. **2** bearing buds. [L *gemmifer* (as GEMMA, –FEROUS)]

gem·mip·a·rous /jeˈmipərəs/ *adj.* of or propagating by gemmation. [mod.L *gemmiparus* f. L *gemma* bud + *parere* bring forth]

gem·mule /ˈjemyool/ *n.* an encysted embryonic cell cluster in sponges. [F *gemmule* or L *gemmula* little bud (as GEM)]

gem·ol·o·gy /jeˈmäləjee/ *n.* (also **gem·mol·o·gy**) the study of gems. □□ **gem·ol·o·gist** or **gem·mol·o·gist** *n.* [L *gemma* gem + –LOGY]

gem·stone /ˈjemstōn/ *n.* a precious stone used as a gem.

ge·müt·lich /gəˈmootlikh/ *adj.* **1** pleasant and comfortable. **2** genial; agreeable. [G]

Gen. *abbr.* **1** General. **2** Genesis (Old Testament).

gen /jen/ *n. & v. Brit. sl.* • *n.* information. • *v.tr. & intr.* **(genned, gen·ning)** (foll. by *up*) provide with or obtain information. [perh. f. first syll. of *general information*]

-gen /jən/ *comb. form* **1** Chem. that which produces (*hydrogen; antigen*). **2** *Bot.* growth (*endogen; exogen; acrogen*). [F *–gène* f. Gk *–genēs* –born, of a specified kind f. *gen–* root of *gignomai* be born, become]

gen·darme /ˈzhondaarm/ *n.* **1** a police officer, esp. in France. **2** a sol-

dier, mounted or on foot, employed in police duties, esp. in France. **3** a rock tower on a mountain, occupying and blocking an arête. [F f. *gens d'armes* men of arms]

gen·dar·me·rie /zhondaarˈməree/ *n.* **1** a force of gendarmes. **2** the headquarters of such a force.

gen·der /ˈjendər/ *n.* **1 a** the grammatical classification of nouns and related words, roughly corresponding to the two sexes and sexlessness. **b** each of the classes of nouns (see MASCULINE, FEMININE, NEUTER, COMMON *adj.* 6). **2** (of nouns and related words) the property of belonging to such a class. **3** *colloq.* a person's sex. [ME f. OF *gendre* ult. f. L GENUS]

▶**Gender-Neutral Language.** Until the 1960s and 1970s, the noun *man* and the pronouns *he*, *his*, *him*, and *himself* were generally used to refer to all human beings, whether they were men or women. Nowadays, careful writers and speakers try to avoid language that ignores or minimizes the existence of one **gender**. Sexist language can often be avoided by rephrasing, by including both feminine and masculine pronouns (*everyone should check his or her luggage at the hotel*), or simply by using plural nouns and pronouns instead of singular ones (*conferees should check their luggage at the hotel*). A plural verb is sometimes used with a singular antecedent (*everyone should check their luggage at the hotel*), although language purists object to this use. Using *he/she* or *s/he* is acceptable under some circumstances, particularly in written instructions and guidelines, but neither usage has enjoyed widespread acceptance.

gene /jeen/ *n.* a unit of heredity composed of DNA or RNA and forming part of a chromosome, etc., that determines a particular characteristic of an individual. [G *Gen*: see –GEN]

ge·ne·a·log·i·cal /ˌjeeneeəˈläjikəl/ *adj.* **1** of or concerning genealogy. **2** tracing family descent. □□ **ge·ne·a·log·i·cal·ly** *adv.* [F *généalogique* f. Gk *genealogikos* (as GENEALOGY)]

ge·ne·a·log·i·cal tree *n.* a chart like an inverted branching tree showing the descent of a family or of an animal species.

ge·ne·al·o·gy /ˌjeeneeˈaaləjee, –ˈäl–/jee/ *n. (pl.* **·gies**) **1 a** a line of descent traced continuously from an ancestor. **b** an account or exposition of this. **2** the study and investigation of lines of descent. **3** a plant's or animal's line of development from earlier forms. □□ **ge·ne·al·o·gist** *n.* **ge·ne·al·o·gize** *v.tr. & intr.* [ME f. OF *genealogie* f. LL *genealogia* f. Gk *genealogia* f. *genea* race]

PRONUNCIATION TIP   genealogy

There are so many words ending in *-ology*, such as *psychology, sociology,* and *pathology,* that this word is almost always pronounced as if it ended with *-ology* rather than *-alogy*. Both pronunciations, however, are considered acceptable.

gen·er·a *pl.* of GENUS.

gen·er·al /ˈjenərəl/ *adj. & n.* • *adj.* **1 a** completely or almost universal. **b** including or affecting all or nearly all parts or cases of things. **2** prevalent; widespread; usual. **3** not partial, particular, local, or sectional. **4** not limited in application; relating to whole classes or all cases. **5** including points common to the individuals of a class and neglecting the differences (*a general term*). **6** not restricted or specialized (*general knowledge*). **7 a** roughly corresponding or adequate. **b** sufficient for practical purposes. **8** not detailed (*a general resemblance; a general idea*). **9** vague; indefinite (*spoke only in general terms*). **10** chief or principal; having overall authority (*general manager; Secretary General*). • *n.* **1 a** an army officer ranking next above lieutenant general. **b** = BRIGADIER GENERAL, LIEUTENANT GENERAL, MAJOR GENERAL. **2** a commander of an army. **3** a tactician or strategist of specified merit (*a great general*). **4** the head of a religious order, e.g., of the Jesuits or Dominicans or the Salvation Army. **5** (prec. by *the*) *archaic* the public. □ **as a general rule** in most cases. **in general 1** as a normal rule; usually. **2** for the most part. □□ **gen·er·al·ness** *n.*

WORD HISTORY   general

Middle English: via Old French from Latin *generalis*, from *genus*, *gener-* 'class, race, kind.' The noun primarily denotes a person having overall authority: the sense 'army commander' is an abbreviation of *captain general*, from French *capitaine général* 'commander-in-chief.'

Gen·er·al A·mer·i·can *n.* a form of US speech not markedly dialectal or regional.

gen·er·al an·es·thet·ic *n.* an anesthetic that affects the whole body, usu. with loss of consciousness.

gen·er·al de·liv·er·y *n.* mail delivery to a post office where it is held for pickup by the addressee.

gen·er·al e·lec·tion *n.* the election of representatives to a legislature from constituencies throughout the country, esp. a final election between winners of earlier primary elections.

gen·er·al head·quar·ters *n.* the headquarters of a military commander.

gen·er·al·is·si·mo /ˌjenərəˈlisimō/ *n. (pl.* **·mos**) the commander of a combined military force in some countries consisting of army, navy, and air force units. [It., superl. of *generale* GENERAL]

gen·er·al·ist /jénərəlist/ n. a person competent in several different fields or activities (opp. SPECIALIST).

gen·er·al·i·ty /jénərálitee/ n. (pl. **·ties**) 1 a statement or principle, etc.; having general validity or force. 2 applicability to a whole class of instances. 3 vagueness; lack of detail. 4 the state of being general. 5 (foll. by *of*) the main body or majority. [F *généralité* f. LL *generalitas –tatis* (as GENERAL)]

gen·er·al·i·za·tion /jénərəlizáyshən/ n. 1 a general notion or proposition obtained by inference from (esp. limited or inadequate) particular cases. 2 the act or an instance of generalizing. [F *généralisation* (as GENERALIZE)]

gen·er·al·ize /jénərəliz/ v. 1 intr. **a** speak in general or indefinite terms. **b** form general principles or notions. 2 tr. reduce to a general statement, principle, or notion. 3 tr. **a** give a general character to. **b** call by a general name. 4 tr. infer (a law or conclusion) by induction. 5 tr. Math. & Philos. express in a general form; extend the application of. 6 tr. (in painting) render only the typical characteristics of. 7 tr. bring into general use. □□ **gen·er·al·iz·a·ble** /–rəbəl/ adj. **gen·er·al·iz·a·bil·i·ty** n. **gen·er·al·iz·er** n. [F *généraliser* (as GENERAL)]

gen·er·al·ly /jénərəlee/ adv. 1 usually; in most cases. 2 in a general sense; without regard to particulars or exceptions (*generally speaking*). 3 for the most part; extensively (*not generally known*). 4 in most respects (*they were generally well-behaved*).

general of the ar·my n. (also **gen·er·al of the air force**) the officer of the highest rank in the army or air force.

gen·er·al prac·ti·tion·er n. a doctor working in the community and treating cases of all kinds and patients of all ages, as distinct from a consultant or specialist. ¶ Abbr.: **GP**.

gen·er·al quar·ters n. a condition of full readiness for combat on a warship.

gen·er·al·ship /jénərəlship/ n. 1 the art or practice of exercising military command. 2 military skill; strategy. 3 skillful management; tact; diplomacy.

gen·er·al staff n. the staff assisting a military commander in planning and administration.

gen·er·al store n. a store, usu. located in a rural area, that carries a wide variety of items, as food, clothing, housewares, etc., without being divided into departments.

gen·er·al strike n. a strike of workers in all or most trades.

Gen·er·al Syn·od n. the highest governing body in the Church of England.

gen·er·ate /jénərayt/ v.tr. 1 bring into existence; produce; evolve. 2 produce (electricity). 3 Math. (of a point or line or surface conceived as moving) make (a line or surface or solid). 4 Math. & Linguistics produce (a set or sequence of items) by the formulation and application of precise criteria. □□ **gen·er·a·ble** /–rəbəl/ adj. [L *generare* beget (as GENUS)]

gen·er·a·tion /jénəráyshən/ n. 1 all the people born at a particular time, regarded collectively (*my generation; the next generation*). 2 a single step in descent or pedigree (*have known them for three generations*). 3 a stage in (esp. technological) development (*fourth-generation computers*). 4 the average time in which children are ready to take the place of their parents (usu. figured at about 30 years). 5 production by natural or artificial process, esp. the production of electricity or heat. 6 **a** procreation; the propagation of species. **b** the act of begetting or being begotten. □□ **gen·er·a·tion·al** adj. [ME f. OF f. L *generatio –onis* (as GENERATE)]

gen·er·a·tion gap n. differences of outlook or opinion between those of different generations.

Gen·er·a·tion X n. term used for the generation born after that of the baby boomers, roughly from the early 1960s to the mid 1970s. (fr. a novel by Douglas Coupland).

gen·er·a·tive /jénərətiv, –raytiv/ adj. 1 of or concerning procreation. 2 able to produce; productive. [ME f. OF *generatif* or LL *generativus* (as GENERATE)]

gen·er·a·tive gram·mar n. Linguistics a set of rules whereby permissible sentences may be generated from the elements of a language.

gen·er·a·tor /jénəraytər/ n. 1 a machine for converting mechanical into electrical energy. 2 an apparatus for producing gas, steam, etc. 3 a person who generates an idea, etc.; an originator.

ge·ner·ic /jinérik/ adj. 1 characteristic of or relating to a class; general, not specific or special. 2 Biol. characteristic of or belonging to a genus. 3 (of goods, esp. a drug) having no brand name; not protected by a registered trade mark. □□ **ge·ner·i·cal·ly** adv. [F *générique* f. L GENUS]

gen·er·ous /jénərəs/ adj. 1 giving or given freely. 2 magnanimous; noble-minded; unprejudiced. 3 **a** ample; abundant; copious (*a generous portion*). **b** (of wine) rich and full. □□ **gen·er·os·i·ty** /–rósitee/ n. **gen·er·ous·ly** adv. **gen·er·ous·ness** n. [OF *genereus* f. L *generosus* noble, magnanimous (as GENUS)]

gen·e·sis /jénisis/ n. 1 the origin, or mode of formation or generation, of a thing. 2 (**Genesis**) the first book of the Old Testament, with an account of the creation of the world. [L f. Gk f. *gen-* be produced, root of *gignomai* become]

403 generalist ~ genl.

gen·et /jénit/ n. (also **gen·ette** /jinét/) 1 any catlike mammal of the genus *Genetta*, native to Africa and S. Europe, with spotted fur and a long ringed bushy tail. 2 the fur of the genet. [ME f. OF *genete* f. Arab. *jarnait*]

gene ther·a·py n. Med. the introduction of normal genes into cells in place of defective or missing ones in order to correct genetic disorders.

ge·net·ic /jinétik/ adj. 1 of genetics or genes; inherited. 2 of, in, or concerning origin; causal. □□ **ge·net·i·cal·ly** adv. [GENESIS after *antithetic*]

ge·net·ic code n. Biochem. the means by which genetic information is stored as sequences of nucleotide bases in the chromosomal DNA.

ge·net·ic en·gi·neer·ing n. the deliberate modification of the characteristics of an organism by the manipulation of DNA and the transformation of certain genes.

ge·net·ic fin·ger·print·ing n. (also **ge·net·ic pro·fil·ing**) the analysis of characteristic patterns in DNA as a means of identifying individuals.

ge·net·ics /jinétiks/ n.pl. (usu. treated as *sing.*) the study of heredity and the variation of inherited characteristics. □□ **ge·net·i·cist** /–tisist/ n.

gen·ette var. of GENET.

ge·ne·va /jinéevə/ n. Dutch gin. [Du. *genever* f. OF *genevre* f. L *juniperus*, with assim. to the place name *Geneva*]

Ge·ne·va bands /jinéevə/ n.pl. two white cloth strips attached to the collar of some Protestants' clerical dress. [*Geneva* in Switzerland, where orig. worn by Calvinists]

Ge·ne·va Con·ven·tion /jinéevə/ n. an international agreement first made at Geneva in 1864 and later revised, governing the status and treatment of prisoners and the sick, wounded, and dead in battle.

gen·ial[1] /jéeneeəl/ adj. 1 jovial; sociable; kindly; cheerful. 2 (of the climate) mild and warm; conducive to growth. 3 cheering; enlivening. □□ **ge·ni·al·i·ty** /–neeálitee/ n. **gen·ial·ly** adv. [L *genialis* (as GENIUS)]

ge·ni·al[2] /jiníəl/ adj. Anat. of or relating to the chin. [Gk *geneion* chin f. *genus* jaw]

gen·ic /jéenik/ adj. of or relating to genes.

-genic /jénik/ comb. form forming adjectives meaning: 1 producing (*carcinogenic; pathogenic*). 2 well suited to (*photogenic; radiogenic*). 3 produced by (*iatrogenic*). □□ **-genically** suffix forming adverbs. [-GEN + –IC]

ge·nie /jéenee/ n. (pl. usu. **ge·nii** /jéenee-ī/) a jinnee, goblin, or familiar spirit of Arabian folklore. [F *génie* f. L GENIUS: cf. JINN]

ge·ni·i pl. of GENIE, GENIUS.

ge·nis·ta /jinístə/ n. any almost leafless shrub of the genus *Genista*, with a profusion of yellow pea-shaped flowers, e.g., dyer's broom. [L]

gen·i·tal /jénit'l/ adj. & n. ● adj. of or relating to animal reproduction. ● n. (in pl.) the external reproductive organs. [OF *génital* or L *genitalis* f. *gignere genit-* beget]

gen·i·ta·li·a /jénitáyleeə/ n.pl. the genitals. [L, neut. pl. of *genitalis*: see GENITAL]

gen·i·tive /jénitiv/ n. & adj. Gram. ● n. the case of nouns and pronouns (and words in grammatical agreement with them) corresponding to *of, from,* and other prepositions and indicating possession or close association. ● adj. of or in the genitive. □□ **gen·i·ti·val** /–tívəl/ adj. **gen·i·ti·val·ly** adv. [ME f. OF *genetif, –ive* or L *genitivus* f. *gignere genit-* beget]

genito- /jénitō/ comb. form genital.

gen·i·to·u·ri·nar·y /jénitōyŏ͝orineree/ adj. of the genital and urinary organs.

ge·nius /jéenyəs/ n. (pl. **ge·nius·es** or **gen·ii** /–nee-ī/) 1 (pl. **gen·ius·es**) **a** an exceptional intellectual or creative power or other natural ability or tendency. **b** a person having this. 2 the tutelary spirit of a person, place, institution, etc. 3 a person or spirit regarded as powerfully influencing a person for good or evil. 4 the prevalent feeling or associations, etc., of a nation, age, etc.

Late Middle English: from Latin, 'attendant spirit present from one's birth, innate ability or inclination,' from the root of *gignere* 'beget.' The original sense 'guardian spirit attendant on a person' gave rise to a sense 'a person's characteristic disposition' (late 16th century), which led to a sense 'a person's natural ability,' and finally 'exceptional natural ability' (mid-17th century).

ge·ni·zah /gənéezə, –neezaá/ n. a room attached to a synagogue and housing damaged, discarded, or heretical books, etc., and sacred relics. [Heb. *gĕnīzāh*, lit. hiding place f. *gānaz* hide, set aside]

genl. abbr. general.

gen·o·a jib n. (also **gen·o·a jen·ny**) a large jib or foresail used esp. on racing yachts.

gen·o·cide /jénəsīd/ n. the deliberate extermination of a people or nation. □□ **gen·o·cid·al** /-sídʹl/ adj. [Gk genos race + –CIDE]

ge·nome /jēenōm/ n. 1 the haploid set of chromosomes of an organism. 2 the genetic material of an organism. [GENE + CHROMOSOME]

gen·o·type /jēenətīp/ n. Biol. the genetic constitution of an individual. □□ **gen·o·typ·ic** /-típik/ adj. [G Genotypus (as GENE, TYPE)]

-genous /jénəs/ comb. form forming adjectives meaning 'produced' (endogenous).

gen·re /zhónrə/ n. 1 a kind or style, esp. of art or literature (e.g., novel, drama, satire). 2 (in full **genre painting**) the painting of scenes from ordinary life. [F, = a kind (as GENDER)]

gens /jenz/ n. (pl. **gen·tes** /jénteez/) 1 Rom.Hist. a group of families sharing a name and claiming a common origin. 2 Anthropol. a number of people sharing descent through the male line. [L, f. the root of gignere beget]

gent /jent/ n. colloq. (often joc.) 1 a gentleman. 2 (in pl.) Brit. (in shop titles) men (gents' outfitters). 3 (**the Gents**) Brit. colloq. a men's public toilet. [abbr. of GENTLEMAN]

gen·teel /jenteél/ adj. 1 polite, refined, respectable. 2 often iron. of or appropriate to the upper classes; polite or refined in an affected way. □□ **gen·teel·ly** adv. **gen·teel·ness** n. [earlier gentile, readoption of F gentil GENTLE]

gen·teel·ism /jenteélizəm/ n. a word used because it is thought to be less vulgar than the more common word (e.g., perspire for sweat).

gen·tes pl. of GENS.

gen·tian /jénshən/ n. 1 any plant of the genus Gentiana or Gentianella, found esp. in mountainous regions, and having usu. vivid blue flowers. 2 (in full **gentian bitter**) a liquor extracted from the root of the gentian. [OE f. L gentiana f. Gentius king of Illyria]

gen·tian vi·o·let n. a violet dye used as an antiseptic, esp. in the treatment of burns.

gen·tile /jéntīl/ adj. & n. • adj. 1 (**Gentile**) not Jewish; heathen. 2 of or relating to a nation or tribe. 3 Gram. (of a word) indicating nationality. 4 (**Gentile**) (in the Mormon Church) not Mormon. • n. 1 (**Gentile**) a person who is not Jewish. 2 Gram. a word indicating nationality. 3 (**Gentile**) (in the Mormon Church) a person who is not Mormon. [ME f. L gentilis f. gens gentis family: see GENS]

gen·til·i·ty /jentílitee/ n. 1 social superiority. 2 good manners; habits associated with the upper class. 3 people of high-class birth. [ME f. OF gentilité (as GENTLE)]

gen·tle /jéntʹl/ adj., v., & n. • adj. (**gen·tler, gen·tlest**) 1 not rough; mild or kind, esp. in temperament. 2 moderate; not severe or drastic (a gentle rebuke; a gentle breeze). 3 (of birth, pursuits, etc.) honorable; of or fit for people of good social position. 4 quiet; requiring patience (gentle art). 5 archaic generous; courteous. • v.tr. 1 make gentle or docile. 2 handle (a horse, etc.) firmly but gently. • n. archaic a person of high social status. □□ **gen·tle·ness** n. **gent·ly** adv. [ME f. OF gentil f. L gentilis: see GENTLE]

gen·tle·folk /jéntʹlfōk/ n.pl. literary people of good family.

gen·tle·man /jéntʹlmən/ n. (pl. **-men**) 1 a man (in polite or formal use). 2 a chivalrous or well-bred man. 3 a man of good social position or of wealth and leisure (country gentleman). 4 esp. Brit. a man of gentle birth attached to a royal household (gentleman in waiting). 5 (in pl. as a form of address) a male audience or the male part of an audience. [GENTLE + MAN after OF gentilz hom]

gen·tle·man-at-arms n. (in the UK) one of a sovereign's bodyguard.

gen·tle·man farm·er n. a country gentleman who farms.

gen·tle·man·ly /jéntʹlmənlee/ adj. like a gentleman in looks or behavior; befitting a gentleman. □□ **gen·tle·man·li·ness** n.

gen·tle·man's a·gree·ment n. (also **gen·tle·men's a·gree·ment**) one that is binding in honor but not legally enforceable.

gen·tle·wom·an /jéntʹlwŏŏmən/ n. (pl. **·wom·en**) archaic a woman of good birth or breeding.

gen·too /jéntŏŏ/ n. a penguin, Pygoscelis papua of the Antarctic region, esp. abundant in the Falkland Islands. [perh. f. Anglo-Ind. Gentoo = Hindu, f. Port. gentio GENTILE]

gen·tri·fi·ca·tion /jéntrifikáyshən/ n. the social advancement of an inner urban area by the refurbishing of buildings and arrival of affluent middle-class residents, usu. displacing poorer inhabitants. □□ **gen·tri·fy** /-fī/ v.tr. (**·fies, ·fied**).

gen·try /jéntree/ n. 1 people of good social position, specifically (in the UK) the class of people next below the nobility in position and birth. 2 people, esp. a specific group of people (one of the company gentry). [prob. f. obs. gentrice f. OF genterise var. of gentelise nobility f. gentil GENTLE]

gen·u·flect /jényəflekt/ v.intr. bend the knee, esp. in worship or as a sign of respect. □□ **gen·u·flec·tion** /-flékshən/ n. (also Brit. **gen·u·flex·ion**). **gen·u·flec·tor** n. [eccl.L genuflectere genuflex- f. L genu knee + flectere bend]

gen·u·ine /jényŏŏ-in/ adj. 1 actually coming from its stated, advertised, or reputed source; authentic. 2 properly so called; not a sham. 3 purebred. 4 (of a person) free from affectation or hypocrisy; honest. □□ **gen·u·ine·ly** adv. **gen·u·ine·ness** n. [L genuinus f. genu knee, with ref. to a father's acknowledging a newborn child by placing it on his knee: later associated with GENUS]

ge·nus /jēenəs/ n. (pl. **gen·e·ra** /jénərə/) 1 Biol. a taxonomic grouping of organisms having common characteristics distinct from those of other genera, usu. containing several or many species and being one of a series constituting a taxonomic family. 2 a kind or class having common characteristics. 3 Logic kinds of things including subordinate kinds or species. [L genus –eris birth, race, stock]

-geny /jənee/ comb. form forming nouns meaning 'mode of production or development of' (anthropogeny; ontogeny; pathogeny). [F –génie (as –GEN, –Y³)]

Geo. abbr. George.

geo- /jēe-ō/ comb. form earth. [Gk geō- f. gē earth]

ge·o·bot·a·ny /jēeōbótʹnee/ n. the study of the geographical distribution of plants. □□ **ge·o·bot·a·nist** n.

ge·o·cen·tric /jēeōséntrik/ adj. 1 considered as viewed from the center of the earth. 2 having or representing the earth as the center; not heliocentric. □□ **ge·o·cen·tri·cal·ly** adv.

ge·o·cen·tric lat·i·tude n. the latitude at which a planet would appear if viewed from the center of the earth.

ge·o·chem·is·try /jēeōkémistree/ n. the chemistry of the earth and its rocks, minerals, etc. □□ **ge·o·chem·i·cal** /-mikəl/ adj. **ge·o·chem·ist** /-mist/ n.

ge·o·chro·nol·o·gy /jēeōkrənóləjee/ n. 1 the study and measurement of geological time by means of geological events. 2 the ordering of geological events. □□ **ge·o·chron·o·log·i·cal** /-krónələjikəl/ adj. **ge·o·chro·nol·o·gist** n.

ge·ode /jēe-ōd/ n. 1 a small cavity lined with crystals or other mineral matter. 2 a rock containing such a cavity. □□ **ge·od·ic** /jee-ódik/ adj. [L geodes f. Gk geōdēs earthy f. gē earth]

ge·o·des·ic /jēeədeézik, –désik/ adj. (also **ge·o·det·ic** /-détik/) 1 of or relating to geodesy. 2 of, involving, or consisting of a geodesic line.

ge·o·des·ic dome n. a dome constructed of short struts along geodesic lines.

ge·o·des·ic line n. the shortest possible line between two points on a curved surface.

geodesic dome

ge·od·e·sy /jee-ódisee/ n. the branch of mathematics dealing with the shape and area of the earth or large portions of it. □□ **ge·od·e·sist** n. [mod.L f. Gk geōdaisia (as GEO-, daiō divide)]

ge·o·det·ic var. of GEODESIC.

geog. abbr. 1 geographer. 2 geographic. 3 geographical. 4 geography.

ge·o·graph·ic /jēeəgráfik/ adj. (also **ge·o·graph·i·cal** /-gráfikəl/) of or relating to geography. □□ **ge·o·graph·i·cal·ly** adv. [geographic f. F géographique or LL geographicus f. Gk geōgraphikos (as GEO-, –GRAPHIC)]

ge·o·graph·i·cal var. of GEOGRAPHIC.

ge·o·graph·i·cal lat·i·tude n. the angle made with the plane of the equator by a perpendicular to the earth's surface at any point.

ge·o·graph·i·cal mile n. a distance equal to one minute of longitude or latitude at the equator (about 1850 meters; a nautical mile).

ge·o·graph·ic in·for·ma·tion sys·tem(s) n. a computerized system for storing and manipulating geographical information for mapping, navigation, etc. ¶ Abbr.: **GIS.**

ge·og·ra·phy /jee-ógrəfee/ n. 1 the study of the earth's physical features, resources, and climate, and the physical aspects of its population. 2 the main physical features of an area. 3 the layout or arrangement of any set of constituent elements. □□ **ge·og·ra·pher** n. [F géographie or L geographia f. Gk geōgraphia (as GEO-, –GRAPHY)]

ge·oid /jēe-oyd/ n. 1 the shape of the earth. 2 a shape formed by the mean sea level and its imagined extension under land areas. **3** an oblate spheroid. [Gk *geōeidēs* (as GEO-, -OID)]

geol. *abbr.* **1** geologic. **2** geological. **3** geologist. **4** geology.

ge·ol·o·gy /jeeólэjee/ *n.* **1** the science of the earth, including the composition, structure, and origin of its rocks. **2** this science applied to any other planet or celestial body. **3** the geological features of a district. □□ **ge·o·log·ic** /jeeэlójik/ *adj.* **ge·o·log·i·cal** *adj.* **ge·o·log·i·cal·ly** *adv.* **ge·ol·o·gist** /-ólэjist/ *n.* **ge·ol·o·gize** *v.tr. & intr.* [mod.L *geologia* (as GEO-, -LOGY)]

geom. *abbr.* **1** geometric. **2** geometrical. **3** geometry.

ge·o·mag·net·ism /jeeōmágnitizэm/ *n.* the study of the magnetic properties of the earth. □□ **ge·o·mag·net·ic** /-magnétik/ *adj.* **ge·o·mag·net·i·cal·ly** *adv.*

ge·o·man·cy /jeeōmánsee/ *n.* divination from the configuration of a handful of earth or random dots, lines, or figures. □□ **ge·o·man·tic** /-mántik/ *adj.*

ge·om·e·ter /jeeómitэr/ *n.* **1** a person skilled in geometry. **2** (also **ge·om·e·trid**) any moth, esp. of the family Geometridae, having twiglike larvae that move in a looping fashion, seeming to measure the ground. [ME f. LL *geometra* f. L *geometres* f. Gk *geōmetrēs* (as GEO-, *metrēs* measurer)]

ge·o·met·ric /jeeэmétrik/ *adj.* (also **ge·o·met·ri·cal**) **1** of, according to, or like geometry. **2** (of a design, architectural feature, etc.) characterized by or decorated with regular lines and shapes. □□ **ge·o·met·ri·cal·ly** *adv.* [F *géométrique* f. L *geometricus* f. Gk *geōmetrikos* (as GEOMETER)]

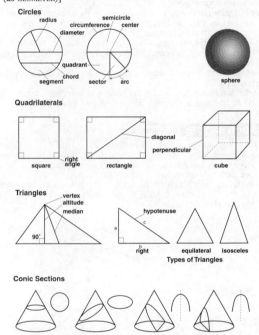

Circles

radius
circumference
semicircle
center
diameter
quadrant
chord
segment
sector
arc

sphere

Quadrilaterals

diagonal
perpendicular

square
right angle
rectangle
cube

Triangles

vertex
altitude
median
hypotenuse
90°
right
equilateral
isosceles

Types of Triangles

Conic Sections

circle
ellipse
parabola
hyperbola

Geometric Shapes and Forms

ge·o·met·ric mean *n.* the central number in a geometric progression, also calculable as the nth root of a product of n numbers (as 9 from 3 and 27).

ge·o·met·ric pro·gres·sion *n.* a progression of numbers with a constant ratio between each number and the one before (as 1, 3, 9, 27, 81).

ge·om·e·trid /jeeómitrid/ *n.* = GEOMETER 2.

ge·om·e·try /jeeómitree/ *n.* **1** the branch of mathematics concerned with the properties and relations of points, lines, surfaces, and solids. **2** the relative arrangement of objects or parts. □□ **ge·om·e·tri·cian** /jeeэmitríshэn/ *n.* [ME f. OF *geometrie* f. L *geometria* f. Gk (as GEO-, -METRY)]

ge·o·mor·phol·o·gy /jeeōmawrfólэjee/ *n.* the study of the physical features of the surface of the earth and their relation to its geological structures. □□ **ge·o·mor·pho·log·i·cal** /-fэlójikэl/ *adj.* **ge·o·mor·phol·o·gist** *n.*

ge·oph·a·gy /jeeófэjee/ *n.* the practice in some cultures of eating earth, esp. clay, to supplement diet. [GEO- + Gk *phagō* eat]

ge·o·phys·ics /jee-ōfíziks/ *n.* the physics of the earth. □□ **ge·o·phys·i·cal** *adj.* **ge·o·phys·i·cist** /-zisist/ *n.*

ge·o·pol·i·tics /jee-ōpólitiks/ *n.* **1** the politics of a country as determined by its geographical features. **2** the study of this. □□ **ge·o·po·lit·i·cal** /-pэlítikэl/ *adj.* **ge·o·po·lit·i·cal·ly** *adv.* **ge·o·pol·i·ti·cian** /-tíshэn/ *n.*

George /jawrj/ *n. Brit. sl.* the automatic pilot of an aircraft. [the name *George*]

George Cross /jawrj/ *n.* (also **George Med·al**) (in the UK) a decoration for bravery awarded esp. to civilians, instituted in 1940 by King George VI.

geor·gette /jawrjét/ *n.* a thin silk or crêpe dress material. [*Georgette* de la Plante, Fr. dressmaker]

Geor·gian[1] /jáwrjэn/ *adj. & n.* ● *adj.* of or relating to the state of Georgia. ● *n.* a native of Georgia.

Geor·gian[2] /jáwrjэn/ *adj.* **1** of or characteristic of the time of Kings George I–IV (1714–1830). **2** of or characteristic of the time of Kings George V and VI (1910–52), esp. of the literature of 1910–20.

Geor·gian[3] /jáwrjэn/ *adj. & n.* ● *adj.* of or relating to Georgia in the Caucasus. ● *n.* **1** a native of Georgia; a person of Georgian descent. **2** the language of Georgia.

ge·o·sphere /jeeэsfeer/ *n.* **1** the solid surface of the earth. **2** any of the almost spherical concentric regions of the earth and its atmosphere.

ge·o·stroph·ic /jee-ōstrófik/ *adj. Meteorol.* depending upon the rotation of the earth. [GEO- + Gk *strophē* a turning f. *strephō* to turn]

ge·o·syn·chro·nous /jee-ōsíngkrэnэs/ *adj.* (of an artificial satellite of the earth) moving in an orbit equal to the earth's period of rotation. Also called **geostationary**.

ge·o·ther·mal /jee-ōthórmэl/ *adj.* relating to, originating from, or produced by the internal heat of the earth.

ge·ot·ro·pism /jeeótrэpizэm/ *n.* plant growth in relation to gravity. □□ **ge·o·trop·ic** /jeeótrópik, -otrópik/ *adj.* [GEO- + Gk *tropikos* f. *tropē* a turning f. *trepō* to turn]

Ger. *abbr.* German.

ge·ra·ni·um /jэráyneeэm/ *n.* **1** any herb or shrub of the genus *Geranium* bearing fruit shaped like the bill of a crane, e.g., cranesbill. **2** (in general use) a cultivated pelargonium. **3** the color of the scarlet geranium. [L f. Gk *geranion* f. *geranos* crane]

ger·ber·a /jórbэrэ/ *n.* any composite plant of the genus *Gerbera* of Africa or Asia, esp. the Transvaal daisy. [T. *Gerber*, Ger. naturalist d. 1743]

ger·bil /jórbil/ *n.* (also **jer·bil**) a mouselike desert rodent of the subfamily Gerbillinae, with long hind legs. [F *gerbille* f. mod.L *gerbillus* dimin. of *gerbo* JERBOA]

ger·e·nuk /gérэnook/ *n.* an antelope, *Litocranius walleri*, native to E. Africa, with a very long neck and small head. [Somali]

ger·fal·con var. of GYRFALCON.

ger·i /jéree/ *n. Austral. colloq.* a geriatric person. [abbr.]

ger·i·at·ric /jéreeátrik/ *adj. & n.* ● *adj.* **1** of or relating to old people. **2** *colloq.* old; outdated. ● *n.* **1** an old person, esp. one receiving special care. **2** *colloq.* a person or thing considered as relatively old or outdated. [Gk *gēras* old age + *iatros* doctor]

ger·i·at·rics /jéreeátriks/ *n.pl.* (usu. treated as *sing.*) a branch of medicine or social science dealing with the health and care of old people. □□ **ger·i·a·tri·cian** /-эtríshэn/ *n.*

germ /jórm/ *n.* **1** a microorganism, esp. one that causes disease. **2 a** a portion of an organism capable of developing into a new one; the rudiment of an animal or plant. **b** an embryo of a seed (*wheat germ*). **3** an original idea, etc., from which something may develop; an elementary principle. □ **in germ** not yet developed. □□ **germ·y** *adj.* [F *germe* f. L *germen germinis* sprout]

Ger·man /jórmэn/ *n. & adj.* ● *n.* **1** a native or inhabitant of Germany; a person of German descent. **2** the language of Germany, also used in Austria and Switzerland. ● *adj.* of or relating to Germany or its people or language. [L *Germanus* with ref. to related peoples of Central and N. Europe, a name perh. given by Celts to their neighbors: cf. OIr. *gair* neighbor]

ger·man /jórmэn/ *adj.* (placed after *brother, sister,* or *cousin*) **1** having the same parents (*brother-german*). **2** having the same grandparents on one side (*cousin-german*). **3** *archaic* germane. [ME f. OF *germain* f. L *germanus* genuine, of the same parents]

ger·man·der /jэrmándэr/ *n.* any plant of the genus *Teucrium*. [ME f. med.L *germandra* ult. f. Gk *khamaidrus* f. *khamai* on the ground + *drus* oak]

ger·man·der speed·well *n.* a creeping plant, *Veronica chamaedrys*, with germanderlike leaves and blue flowers.

ger·mane /jэrmáyn/ *adj.* (usu. foll. by *to*) relevant (to a subject under consideration). □□ **ger·mane·ly** *adv.* **ger·mane·ness** *n.* [var. of GERMAN]

Ger·man·ic /jэrmánik/ *adj. & n.* ● *adj.* **1** having German characteristics. **2** *hist.* of the Germans. **3** of the Scandinavians, Anglo-Saxons, or Germans. **4** of the languages or language group called Germanic. ● *n.* **1** the branch of Indo-European languages including English, German, Dutch, and the Scandinavian languages. **2** the (unrecorded) early language from which other Germanic languages developed. [L *Germanicus* (as GERMAN)]

ger·man·ic /jərmánik/ *adj. Chem.* of or containing germanium, esp. in its tetravalent state.

Ger·man·ist /jŕrmənist/ *n.* an expert in or student of the language, literature, and civilization of Germany, or Germanic languages.

ger·ma·ni·um /jərmáyneeəm/ *n. Chem.* a lustrous brittle semi-metallic element occurring naturally in sulfide ores and used in semiconductors. ¶ Symb.: **ge.** [mod.L f. *Germanus* GERMAN]

Ger·man·ize /jŕrməniz/ *v. tr. & intr.* make or become German; adopt or cause to adopt German customs, etc. □□ **Ger·man·i·za·tion** *n.* **Ger·man·i·zer** *n.*

Ger·man mea·sles *n.* a contagious disease, rubella, with symptoms like mild measles.

Germano- /jŕrmánō/ *comb. form* German; German and.

ger·man·ous /jərmáynəs/ *adj. Chem.* containing germanium in the bivalent state.

Ger·man shep·herd *n.* **1** a large breed of dog used esp. in police work and as guide dogs for the blind. **2** a dog of this breed.

Ger·man sil·ver *n.* a white alloy of nickel, zinc, and copper.

germ cell *n.* **1** a cell containing half the number of chromosomes of a somatic cell and able to unite with one from the opposite sex to form a new individual; a gamete. **2** any embryonic cell with the potential of developing into a gamete.

ger·mi·cide /jŕrmisid/ *n.* a substance destroying germs, esp. those causing disease. □□ **ger·mi·cid·al** /síd'l/ *adj.*

ger·mi·nal /jŕrminəl/ *adj.* **1** relating to or of the nature of a germ or germs (see GERM 1). **2** in the earliest stage of development. **3** productive of new ideas. □□ **ger·mi·nal·ly** *adv.* [L *germen germin-* sprout: see GERM]

ger·mi·nate /jŕrminayt/ *v.* **1** *intr.* sprout, bud, or put forth shoots. **b** *tr.* cause to sprout or shoot. **2 a** *tr.* cause (ideas, etc.) to originate or develop. **b** *intr.* come into existence. □□ **ger·mi·na·tion** /-náyshən/ *n.* **ger·mi·na·tive** *adj.* **ger·mi·na·tor** *n.* [L *germinare germinat-* (as GERM)]

germ war·fare *n.* the systematic spreading of microorganisms to cause disease in an enemy population.

ger·on·tol·o·gy /jərontóləjee/ *n.* the scientific study of old age, the process of aging, and the special problems of old people. □□ **ge·ron·to·log·i·cal** /-təlójikəl/ *adj.* **ger·on·tol·o·gist** *n.* [Gk *gerōn -ontos* old man + -LOGY]

-gerous /jərəs/ *comb. form* forming adjectives meaning 'bearing' (*lanigerous*).

ger·ry·man·der /jérimándər/ *v. & n.* • *v. tr.* **1** manipulate the boundaries of (a constituency, etc.) so as to give undue influence to some party or class. **2** manipulate (a situation, etc.) to gain advantage. • *n.* this practice. □□ **ger·ry·man·der·er** *n.*

ger·und /jérənd/ *n. Gram.* a form of a verb functioning as a noun, orig. in Latin ending in *-ndum* (declinable), in English ending in *-ing* (e.g., *do you mind my asking you?*). [LL *gerundium* f. *gerundum* var. of *gerendum*, the gerund of L *gerere* do]

GRAMMAR TIP gerund

Gerunds and Possessive Pronouns. A **gerund** is a verb form ending in *-ing* that functions as a noun. It may be the subject of a sentence (*singing was her passion*), the object of a preposition (*he devoted most of his free time to volunteering at the soup kitchen*), or the object of a verb (*I adore cross-country skiing*). Some people insist that when a gerund is preceded by a noun or pronoun, the noun or pronoun must be possessive (*I can understand her wanting to go, but I can also understand their preventing her*), but personal pronouns before gerunds are also widely used (*she could imagine them missing their flight*).

---

ger·un·dive /jərúndiv/ *n. Gram.* a form of a Latin verb, ending in *-ndus* (declinable) and functioning as an adjective meaning 'that should or must be done,' etc. [LL *gerundivus* (*modus* mood) f. *gerundium*: see GERUND]

ges·so /jésō/ *n.* (*pl.* •**soes**) plaster of Paris or gypsum as used in painting or sculpture. [It. f. L *gypsum*: see GYPSUM]

ge·stalt /gəshtáalt, -stáalt, -shtáwlt, -stáwlt/ *n. Psychol.* an organized whole that is perceived as more than the sum of its parts. □□ **ge·stalt·ism** *n.* **ge·stalt·ist** *n.* [G, = form, shape]

ge·stalt psy·chol·o·gy *n.* a movement in psychology founded in Germany in 1912 seeking to explain perceptions in terms of gestalts rather than by analyzing their constituents.

Ge·sta·po /gestáapō, -shtáa-/ *n.* **1** the German secret police under Nazi rule. **2** *derog.* an organization compared to this. [G, f. *geheime Staatspolizei*]

ges·tate /jéstayt/ *v. tr.* **1** carry (a fetus) in gestation. **2** develop (an idea, etc.).

ges·ta·tion /jestáyshən/ *n.* **1 a** the process of carrying or being carried in the womb between conception and birth. **b** this period.

WORD HISTORY gerrymander

Early 19th century: from the name of Governor Elbridge Gerry of Massachusetts + *salamander*, from the supposed similarity between a salamander and the shape of a new voting district on a map drawn when he was in office (1812), the creation of which was felt to favor his party: the map (with claws, wings, and fangs added), was published in the Boston *Weekly Messenger*, with the title *The Gerry-Mander*.

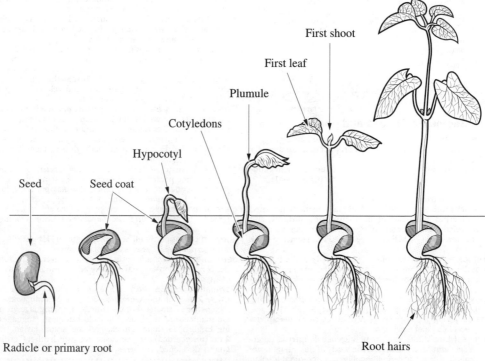

First shoot

First leaf

Plumule

Cotyledons

Hypocotyl

Seed

Seed coat

Radicle or primary root

Root hairs

germination of a bean

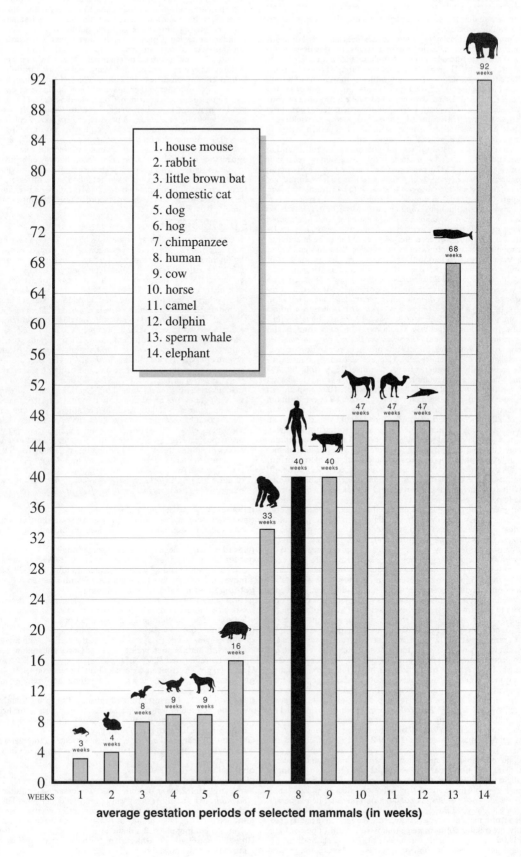

1. house mouse
2. rabbit
3. little brown bat
4. domestic cat
5. dog
6. hog
7. chimpanzee
8. human
9. cow
10. horse
11. camel
12. dolphin
13. sperm whale
14. elephant

average gestation periods of selected mammals (in weeks)

2 the private development of a plan, idea, etc. [L *gestatio* f. *gestare* frequent. of *gerere* carry]

ges•tic•u•late /jestíkyəlayt/ *v.* **1** *intr.* use gestures instead of or in addition to speech. **2** *tr.* express with gestures. □□ **ges•tic•u•la•tion** /–láyshən/ *n.* **ges•tic•u•la•tive** *adj.* **ges•tic•u•la•tor** *n.* **ges•tic•u•la•to•ry** /–lətáwree/ *adj.* [L *gesticulari* f. *gesticulus* dimin. of *gestus* GESTURE]

ges•ture /jés-chər/ *n.* & *v.* • *n.* **1** a significant movement of a limb or the body. **2** the use of such movements, esp. to convey feeling or as a rhetorical device. **3** an action to evoke a response or convey intention, usu. friendly. • *v.tr.* & *intr.* gesticulate. □□ **ges•tur•al** *adj.* **ges•tur•er** *n.* [ME f. med.L *gestura* f. L *gerere gest-* wield]

ge•sund•heit /gəzóont-hīt/ *int.* expressing a wish of good health, esp. to a person who has sneezed. [G, = health]

get /get/ *v.* & *n.* • *v.* (**get•ting**; *past* **got** /got/; *past part.* **got** or (and in *comb.*) **got•ten** /gót'n/) **1** *tr.* come into the possession of; receive or earn (*get a job; got $200 a week; got first prize*). **2** *tr.* **a** fetch; obtain; procure; purchase (*get my book for me; got a new car*). **b** capture; get hold of (a person). **3** *tr.* go to reach or catch (a bus, train, etc.). **4** *tr.* prepare (a meal, etc.). **5** *intr.* & *tr.* reach or cause to reach a certain state or condition; become or cause to become (*get rich; get one's feet wet; get to be famous; got them ready; got him into trouble; cannot get the key into the lock*). **6** *tr.* obtain as a result of calculation. **7** *tr.* contract (a disease, etc.). **8** *tr.* establish or be in communication with via telephone or radio; receive (a radio signal). **9** *tr.* experience or suffer; have inflicted on one; receive as one's lot or penalty (*got four years in prison*). **10 a** *tr.* succeed in bringing, placing, etc. (*get it around the corner; get it onto the agenda; flattery will get you nowhere*). **b** *intr.* & *tr.* succeed or cause to succeed in coming or going (*will get you there somehow; got absolutely nowhere*). **11** *tr.* (prec. by *have*) **a** possess (*haven't got a penny*). **b** (foll. by *to* + infin.) be bound or obliged (*have got to see you*). **12** *tr.* (foll. by *to* + infin.) induce; prevail upon (*got them to help me*). **13** *tr. colloq.* understand (a person or an argument) (*have you got that?; I get your point; do you get me?*). **14** *tr. colloq.* inflict punishment or retribution on, esp. in retaliation (*I'll get you for that*). **15** *tr. colloq.* **a** annoy. **b** move; affect emotionally. **c** attract; obsess. **d** amuse. **16** *tr.* (foll. by *to* + infin.) develop an inclination as specified (*am getting to like it*). **17** *intr.* (foll. by verbal noun) begin (*get going*). **18** *tr.* (esp. in *past* or *perfect*) catch in an argument; corner; puzzle. **19** *tr.* establish (an idea, etc.) in one's mind. **20** *intr. sl.* be off; go away. **21** *tr. archaic* beget. **22** *tr. archaic* learn; acquire (knowledge) by study. • *n.* **1** an act of begetting (of animals). **2** *dated* an offspring (of animals). **3** *Tennis* an exceptional return. □ **get across 1** manage to communicate (an idea, etc.). **2** (of an idea, etc.) be communicated successfully. **get ahead** be or become successful. **get along** (or **on**) **1** (foll. by *together, with*) live harmoniously; accord. **2** *Brit.* be off! nonsense! **3** leave; depart (*I must be getting along*). **4** manage to survive; have sufficient means. **get around 1** successfully coax or cajole (a person) esp. to secure a favor. **2** evade (a law, etc.). **3** circulate; go from place to place. **4** managed to walk, move about, etc., esp. after illness. **5** (of news) be circulated, esp. orally. **get around to** deal with (a task, etc.) in due course. **get at 1** reach; get hold of. **2** *colloq.* imply (*what are you getting at?*). **3** *colloq.* annoy; try to upset or irritate. **get away 1** escape. **2** leave, esp. on vacation. **3** (as *imper.*) *colloq.* expressing disbelief or skepticism. **4** (foll. by *with*) escape blame or punishment for. **get back at** *colloq.* retaliate against. **get by** *colloq.* **1** just manage, even with difficulty. **2** be acceptable. **get down 1** alight; descend (from a vehicle, ladder, etc.). **2** record in writing. **get a person down** depress or deject him or her. **get down to** begin working on or discussing. **get even** (often foll. by *with*) **1** achieve revenge; act in retaliation. **2** equalize the score. **get his** (or **hers**, etc.) *sl.* **1** be killed. **2** be avenged. **get hold** (or **ahold**) **of 1** grasp (physically). **2** grasp (intellectually); understand. **3** make contact with (a person). **4** acquire. **get in 1** enter. **2** be elected. **get into** become interested or involved in. **get it** *sl.* **1** understand. **2** be punished or in trouble. **get it into one's head** (foll. by *that* & clause) firmly believe or maintain; realize. **get off 1** *colloq.* be acquitted; escape with little or no punishment. **2** leave. **3** alight; alight from (a bus, etc.). **4** go, or cause to go, to sleep. **5** *sl.* to experience orgasm. **6** (foll. by *with, together*) *Brit. colloq.* form an amorous or sexual relationship, esp. abruptly or quickly. **get a person off** *colloq.* cause a person to be acquitted. **get off on** *sl.* be excited or aroused by; enjoy. **get on 1** make progress; manage. **2** enter (a bus, etc.). **3** esp. *Brit.* = *get along* 1. **4** *colloq.* become more advanced in time, age, etc. **get on to** *colloq.* **1** make contact with. **2** understand; become aware of. **get out 1** leave or escape. **2** manage to go outdoors. **3** alight from a vehicle. **4** transpire; become known. **5** succeed in uttering, publishing, etc. **6** *Brit.* solve or finish (a puzzle, etc.). **7** *Baseball, Cricket* be dismissed. **get a person out 1** help a person to leave or escape. **2** *Baseball, Cricket* dismiss (a batter or batsman). **get out of 1** avoid or escape (a duty, etc.). **2** abandon (a habit) gradually. **get a thing out of** manage to obtain it from (a person) esp. with difficulty. **get outside** (or **outside of**) *Brit. sl.* eat or drink. **get over 1** recover from (an illness, upset, etc.). **2** overcome (a difficulty). **3** manage to communicate (an idea, etc.). **get a thing over** (or **over with**) complete (a tedious task) promptly. **get one's own back** *colloq.* have one's revenge. **get rid of** see RID. **get somewhere** make progress; be initially successful. **get there** *colloq.* **1** succeed. **2** understand what is meant. **get through 1** pass or assist in passing (an examination, an ordeal, etc.). **2** finish or use up (esp. resources). **3** make contact by telephone. **4** (foll. by *to*) succeed in making (a person) listen or understand. **get a thing through** cause it to overcome obstacles, difficulties, etc. **get to 1** reach. **2** = *get down to*. **get together** gather; assemble. **get up 1** rise or cause to rise from sitting, etc., or from bed after sleeping or an illness. **2** ascend or mount, e.g., on horseback. **3** (of fire, wind, or the sea) begin to be strong or agitated. **4** prepare or organize. **5** enhance or refine one's knowledge of (a subject). **6** work up (a feeling, e.g., anger). **7** produce or stimulate (*get up steam; get up speed*). **8** (often *refl.*) dress or arrange elaborately; make presentable; arrange the appearance of. **9** (foll. by *to*) esp. *Brit. colloq.* indulge or be involved in (*always getting up to mischief*). **get the wind up** see WIND[1]. **get with child** *archaic* make pregnant. **have got it bad** *sl.* be obsessed or affected emotionally. □□ **get•ta•ble** *adj.* [ME f. ON *geta* obtain, beget, guess, corresp. to OE *gietan* (recorded only in compounds), f. Gmc]

SYNONYM TIP get

ACQUIRE, ATTAIN, GAIN, OBTAIN, PROCURE, SECURE. **Get** is a very broad term meaning to come into possession of. You can *get* something by fetching it (*get some groceries*), by receiving it (*get a birthday gift*), by earning it (*get interest on a bank loan*), or by any of a dozen other familiar means. It is such a common, over-used word that many writers try to substitute **obtain** for it whenever possible, perhaps because it sounds less colloquial. But it can also sound pretentious (*all employees were required to obtain an annual physical exam*) and should be reserved for contexts where the emphasis is on seeking something out (*to obtain blood samples*). **Acquire** often suggests a continued, sustained, or cumulative acquisition (*to acquire poise as one matures*), but it can also hint at deviousness (*to acquire the keys to the safe*). Use **procure** if you want to emphasize the effort involved in bringing something to pass (*procure a mediated divorce settlement*) or if you want to imply maneuvering to possess something (*procure a reserved parking space*). But beware: *Procure* is so often used to describe the act of obtaining partners to gratify the lust of others (*to procure a prostitute*) that it has acquired somewhat unsavory overtones. **Gain** also implies effort, usually in *getting* something advantageous or profitable (*gain entry, gain victory*). In a similar vein, **secure** underscores the difficulty involved in bringing something to pass and the desire to place it beyond danger (*secure a permanent peace; secure a lifeline*). **Attain** should be reserved for achieving a high goal or desirable result (*If she attains the summit of Mt. Everest, she will secure for herself a place in mountaineering history*).

get•at•a•ble /getátəbəl/ *adj. colloq.* accessible.

get•a•way /gétəway/ *n.* **1** an escape, esp. after committing a crime. **2 a** a vacation, esp. a brief one. **b** a place at which one spends such a vacation.

get-out *n. Brit.* a means of avoiding something.

get•ter /gétər/ *n.* & *v.* • *n.* **1** in senses of GET *v.* **2** *Physics* a substance used to remove residual gas from a vacuum tube. • *v.tr. Physics* remove (gas) or evacuate (a vacuum tube) with a getter.

get-to•geth•er *n. colloq.* a social gathering.

get•up (also **get-up**) *n. colloq.* **1** a style or arrangement of dress, etc., esp. an elaborate or unusual one (*he looks ridiculous in that getup!*). **2** a style of production or finish, esp. of a book.

get-up-and-go *n. colloq.* energy; vim; enthusiasm.

ge•um /jéeəm/ *n.* any rosaceous plant of the genus *Geum* including avens and herb bennet, with rosettes of leaves and yellow, red, or white flowers. [mod.L, var. of L *gaeum*]

GeV *abbr.* gigaelectronvolt (equivalent to 10^9 electronvolts).

gew•gaw /gyóogaw, góo–/ *n.* a gaudy plaything or ornament; a bauble. [ME: orig. unkn.]

gey•ser /gízər/ *n.* **1** an intermittently gushing hot spring that throws up a tall column of water. **2** /géezər/ *Brit.* an apparatus for heating water rapidly for domestic use. [Icel. *Geysir*, the name of a particular spring in Iceland, rel. to *geysa* to gush]

Gha•na•ian /gaáneeən/ *adj.* & *n.* • *adj.* of or relating to Ghana in W. Africa. • *n.* a native or inhabitant of Ghana; a person of Ghanaian descent.

gha•ri•al var. of GAVIAL.

ghast•ly /gástlee/ *adj.* & *adv.* • *adj.* (**ghast•li•er, ghast•li•est**) **1** horrible; frightful. **2** *colloq.* objectionable; unpleasant. **3** deathlike; pallid. • *adv.* in a ghastly or sickly way (*ghastly pale*). □□ **ghast•li•ly** *adv.* **ghast•li•ness** *n.* [ME *gastlich* f. obs. *gast* terrify: *gh* after *ghost*]

ghat /gaat, gat/ *n.* (also **ghaut**) in India: **1** steps leading down to a river. **2** a landing place. **3** a defile or mountain pass. [Hindi *ghāṭ*]

Gha•zi /gaázee/ *n.* (*pl.* **Gha•zis**) a Muslim fighter against non-muslims. [Arab. *al-ġāzī* part. of *ġazā* raid]

ghee /gee/ n. (also **ghi**) clarified butter esp. from the milk of a buffalo or cow. [Hindi *ghī* f. Skr. *ghritá-* sprinkled]

ghe•rao /gerów/ n. (pl. **•raos**) (in India and Pakistan) coercion of employers, by which their workers prevent them from leaving the premises until certain demands are met. [Hind. *gherna* besiege]

gher•kin /gérkin/ n. **1** a small variety of cucumber, or a young green cucumber, used for pickling. **2 a** a trailing plant, *Cucumis anguria*, with cucumberlike fruits used for pickling. **b** this fruit. [Du. *gurkkijn* (unrecorded), dimin. of *gurk*, f. Slavonic, ult. f. med. Gk *aggourion*]

ghet•to /gétō/ n. & v. •n. (pl. **•tos**) **1** a part of a city, esp. a slum area, occupied by a minority group or groups. **2** hist. the Jewish quarter in a city. **3** a segregated group or area. •v.tr. (**•toes**, **•toed**) put or keep (people) in a ghetto. [perh. f. It. *getto* foundry (applied to the site of the first ghetto in Venice in 1516)]

ghet•to blast•er n. sl. a large, powerful, portable radio, often with cassette or CD player; a boom box.

ghi var. of GHEE.

ghil•lie var. of GILLIE.

ghost /gōst/ n. & v. •n. **1** the supposed apparition of a dead person or animal; a disembodied spirit. **2** a shadow or mere semblance (*not a ghost of a chance*). **3** an emaciated or pale person. **4** a secondary or duplicated image produced by defective television reception or by a telescope. **5** archaic a spirit or soul. •v. **1** intr. (often foll. by *for*) act as ghostwriter. **2** tr. act as ghostwriter of (a work). □□ **ghost•like** adj. [OE *gāst* f. WG: *gh-* occurs first in Caxton, prob. infl. by Flem. *gheest*]

ghost•ing /gṓsting/ n. the appearance of a "ghost" (see GHOST n. 4) or secondary image in a television picture.

ghost•ly /gṓstlee/ adj. (**ghost•li•er**, **ghost•li•est**) like a ghost; spectral. □□ **ghost•li•ness** n. [OE *gāstlic* (as GHOST)]

ghost town n. a deserted town with few or no remaining inhabitants.

ghost•write /gṓstrīt/ v.tr. & intr. act as ghostwriter (of).

ghost•writ•er n. a person who writes on behalf of the credited author of a work.

ghoul /gool/ n. **1** a person morbidly interested in death, etc. **2** an evil spirit or phantom. **3** a spirit in Muslim folklore preying on corpses. □□ **ghoul•ish** adj. **ghoul•ish•ly** adv. **ghoul•ish•ness** n. [Arab. *gūl* protean desert demon]

GHQ abbr. General Headquarters.

ghyll Brit. var. of GILL[3].

GI /jée-í/ n. & adj. •n. an enlisted soldier in the US armed forces, esp. the army. •adj. of, for, or characteristic of US soldiers. [abbr. of *galvanized iron*, later taken as abbr. of *government* (or *general*) *issue*]

gi•ant /jíənt/ n. & adj. •n. **1** an imaginary or mythical being of human form but superhuman size. **2** (in Greek mythology) one of such beings who fought against the gods. **3** an abnormally tall or large person, animal, or plant. **4** a person of exceptional ability, integrity, courage, etc. **5** a large star. •attrib.adj. **1** of extraordinary size or force; gigantic; monstrous. **2** extra large (*giant package*). **3** (of a plant or animal) of a very large kind. □□ **gi•ant•ism** n. **gi•ant•like** adj. [ME *geant* (later infl. by L) f. OF, ult. f. L *gigas gigant-* f. Gk]

giaour /jówər/ n. derog. or literary a non-Muslim, esp. a Christian (orig. a Turkish name). [Pers. *gaur, gōr*]

Gib. /jib/ abbr. Gibraltar.

gib /gib/ n. a wood or metal bolt, wedge, or pin for holding a machine part, etc., in place. [18th c.: orig. unkn.]

gib•ber[1] /jíbər/ v. & n. •v.intr. speak fast and inarticulately; chatter incoherently. •n. such speech or sound. [imit.]

gib•ber[2] /gíbər/ n. Austral. a boulder or large stone. [Aboriginal]

gib•ber•el•lin /jíbərélin/ n. one of a group of plant hormones that stimulate the growth of leaves and shoots. [*Gibberella* a genus of fungi, dimin. of genus name *Gibbera* f. L *gibber* hump]

gib•ber•ish /jíbərish/ n. unintelligible or meaningless speech; nonsense. [perh. f. GIBBER[1] (but attested earlier) + -ISH[1] as used in *Spanish, Swedish*, etc.]

gib•bet /jíbit/ n. & v. •n. hist. **1 a** a gallows. **b** an upright post with an arm on which the bodies of executed criminals were hung up. **2** (prec. by *the*) death by hanging. •v.tr. (**gib•bet•ed, gib•bet•ing**) **1** put to death by hanging. **2** expose on a gibbet. **b** hang up as on a gibbet. **3** hold up to contempt. [ME f. OF *gibet* gallows dimin. of *gibe* club, prob. f. Gmc]

gib•bon /gíbən/ n. any small ape of the genus *Hylobates*, native to SE Asia, having a slender body and long arms. [F f. a native name]

gib•bous /gíbəs/ adj. **1** convex or protuberant. **2** (of a moon or planet) having the bright part greater than a semicircle and less than a circle. **3** humped or humpbacked. □□ **gib•bos•i•ty** /-bósitee/ n. **gib•bous•ly** adv. **gib•bous•ness** n. [ME f. LL *gibbosus* f. *gibbus* hump]

gibe /jīb/ v. & n. (also **jibe**) •v.intr. (often foll. by *at*) jeer; mock. •n. an instance of gibing; a taunt. □□ **gib•er** n. [perh. f. OF *giber* handle roughly]

▶See note at JIBE.

gib•lets /jíblits/ n.pl. the liver, gizzard, neck, etc., of a bird, usu. re-

moved and kept separate when the bird is prepared for cooking. [OF *gibelet* game stew, perh. f. *gibier* game]

gid•dy /gídee/ adj. & v. •adj. (**gid•di•er, gid•di•est**) **1** having a sensation of whirling and a tendency to fall, stagger, or spin around. **2 a** overexcited as a result of success, pleasurable emotion, etc.; mentally intoxicated. **b** excitable; frivolous. **3** tending to make one giddy. •v.tr. & intr. (**•dies, •died**) make or become giddy. □□ **gid•di•ly** adv. **gid•di•ness** n. [OE *gidig* insane, lit. 'possessed by a god']

gift /gift/ n. & v. •n. **1** a thing given; a present. **2** a natural ability or talent. **3** the power to give (*in his gift*). **4** the act or an instance of giving. **5** colloq. an easy task. •v.tr. **1** endow with gifts. **2 a** (foll. by *with*) give to as a gift. **b** bestow as a gift. □ **look a gift horse in the mouth** (usu. neg.) find fault with what has been given. [ME f. ON *gipt* f. Gmc, rel. to GIVE]

gift cer•tif•i•cate n. a voucher given as a gift that is exchangeable for a specified cash value of goods or services from a specific place of business.

gift•ed /giftid/ adj. exceptionally talented or intelligent. □□ **gift•ed•ly** adv. **gift•ed•ness** n.

gift of tongues n. see TONGUE.

gift-wrap v.tr. wrap (something) in decorative paper to present as a gift.

gig[1] /gig/ n. **1** a light two-wheeled one-horse carriage. **2** a light ship's boat for rowing or sailing. **3** a rowing boat esp. for racing. [ME in var. senses: prob. imit.]

gig[2] /gig/ n. & v. colloq. •n. an engagement of an entertainer, esp. a musician, usu. for a single appearance. •v.intr. (**gigged, gig•ging**) perform a gig. [20th c.: orig. unkn.]

gig[3] /gig/ n. a kind of fishing spear. [short for *fizgig, fishgig*: cf. Sp. *fisga* harpoon]

giga- /gígə, jígə/ comb. form denoting a factor of 10^9. [Gk *gigas* giant]

gig•a•bit /gígəbit, jígə-/ n. Computing a unit of information equal to one billion (10^9) bits.

gig•a•byte /gígəbīt, jígə-/ n. Computing a unit of information equal to one billion (10^9) bytes.

gig•a•me•ter /gigəmeetər, jígə-/ n. a metric unit equal to 10^9 meters.

gi•gan•tic /jīgántik/ adj. **1** very large; enormous. **2** like or suited to a giant. □□ **gi•gan•tesque** /-tésk/ adj. **gi•gan•ti•cal•ly** adv. [L *gigas gigantis* GIANT]

gi•gan•tism /jīgántizəm/ n. abnormal largeness, esp. Med. excessive growth due to hormonal imbalance, or to polyploidy in plants.

gig•gle /gígəl/ v. & n. •v.intr. laugh in half-suppressed spasms, esp. in an affected or silly manner. •n. **1** such a laugh. **2** esp. Brit. colloq. an amusing person or thing; a joke. □□ **gig•gler** n. **gig•gly** adj. (**gig•gli•er, gig•gli•est**). **gig•gli•ness** n. [imit.: cf. Du. *gichelen*, G *gickeln*]

GIGO /gígō/ n. Computing abbr. for garbage in, garbage out, an informal rule stating that the quality of the data input determines the quality of the results.

gig•o•lo /jígəlō, zhíg-/ n. (pl. **•los**) **1** a young man paid by an older woman to be her escort or lover. **2** a professional male dancing partner or escort. [F, formed as masc. of *gigole* dancehall woman]

gig•ot /jígət, zheegṓ/ n. a leg of mutton or lamb. [F, dimin. of dial. *gigue* leg]

gig•ot sleeve n. a leg-of-mutton sleeve.

gigue /zheeg/ n. **1** = JIG 1. **2** Mus. a lively dance usu. in a compound triple rhythm with two sections each repeated. [F: see JIG[1]]

Gi•la mon•ster /heelə/ n. a large venomous lizard, *Heloderma suspectum*, of the southwestern US, having orange, yellow, and black scales like beads. [*Gila* River, Arizona]

gild[1] /gild/ v.tr. (past part. **gild•ed** or as adj. in sense 1 **gilt**) **1** cover thinly with gold. **2** tinge with a golden color or light. **3** give a specious or false brilliance to. □ **gild the lily** try to improve what is already beautiful or excellent. □□ **gild•er** n. [OE *gyldan* f. Gmc]

gild[2] var. of GUILD.

gild•ed cage n. luxurious but restrictive surroundings.

gild•ed youth n. young people of wealth, fashion, and flair.

gild•ing /gílding/ n. **1** the act or art of applying gilt. **2** material used in applying gilt.

gil•gai /gílgī/ n. Austral. a hollow where rainwater collects; a waterhole. [Aboriginal]

gill[1] /gil/ n. & v. •n. (usu. in pl.) **1** the respiratory organ in fishes and other aquatic animals. **2** the vertical radial plates on the underside of mushrooms and other fungi. **3** the flesh below a person's jaws and ears (*green about the gills*). **4** the wattles or dewlap of fowls. •v.tr. **1** gut (a fish). **2** cut off the gills of (a mushroom). **3** catch in a gill net. □□ **gilled** adj. (also in comb.). [ME f. ON *gil* (unrecorded) f. Gmc]

gill[2] /jil/ n. **1** a unit of liquid measure, equal to a quarter of a pint. **2** Brit. dial. half a pint. [ME f. OF *gille*, med.L *gillo* f. LL *gello, gillo* water pot]

gill[3] /gil/ n. (also **ghyll**) Brit. **1** a deep usu. wooded ravine. **2** a narrow mountain torrent. [ME f. ON gil glen]

gill cov·er n. a bony case protecting a fish's gills; an operculum.

gil·lie /gílee/ n. (also **ghil·lie**) Sc. **1** a man or boy attending a person hunting or fishing. **2** hist. a Highland chief's attendant. [Gael. gille lad, servant]

gil·lion /jílyən/ n. Brit. **1** a thousand million. **2** a large number. [GIGA- + MILLION]

▶This term is mainly used to avoid the ambiguity of billion.

gill net n. a net for entangling fishes by the gills.

gil·ly·flow·er /jíleeflowr, gílee–/ n. **1** (in full **clove gillyflower**) a clove-scented pink (see CLOVE[1] 2). **2** any of various similarly scented flowers such as the wallflower, carnation, or white stock. [ME gilofre, gerofle f. OF gilofre, girofle, f. med.L f. Gk karuophullon clove tree f. karuon nut + phullon leaf, assim. to FLOWER]

gilt[1] /gilt/ adj. & n. ● adj. **1** covered thinly with gold. **2** gold-colored. ● n. **1** gold or a goldlike substance applied in a thin layer to a surface. **2** (often in pl.) Brit. a gilt-edged security. [past part. of GILD[1]]

gilt[2] /gilt/ n. a young unbred sow. [ME f. ON gyltr]

gilt-edged adj. **1** (of securities, stocks, etc.) having a high degree of reliability as an investment. **2** having a gilded edge.

gim·bals /gímbəlz, jím–/ n.pl. a contrivance, usu. of rings and pivots, for keeping a stove or instruments such as a compass and chronometer horizontal at sea, in the air, etc. [var. of earlier gimmal f. OF gemel double finger ring f. L gemellus dimin. of geminus twin]

gim·crack /jímkrak/ adj. & n. ● adj. showy but flimsy and worthless. ● n. a cheap showy ornament; a knickknack. □□ **gim·crack·er·y** n. **gim·crack·y** adj. [ME gibecrake a kind of ornament, of unkn. orig.]

gim·let /gímlit/ n. **1** a small tool with a screw tip for boring holes. **2** a cocktail usu. of gin and lime juice. [ME f. OF guimbelet, dimin. of guimble]

gim·let eye n. an eye that seems to give a piercing glance.

gim·mick /gímik/ n. colloq. a trick or device, esp. to attract attention, publicity, or trade. □□ **gim·mick·ry** n. **gim·mick·y** adj. [20th-c. US: orig. unkn.]

gimp[1] /gimp/ n. (also **guimp, gymp**) **1** a twist of silk, etc., with cord or wire running through it, used esp. as trimming. **2** fishing line of silk, etc., bound with wire. **3** a coarser thread outlining the design of lace. [Du.: orig. unkn.]

gimlet 1

gimp[2] /gimp/ n. & v. sl. ● n. a lame person, gait, or leg. ● v.intr. walk with a lame gait. □□ **gimp·y** adj.

gin[1] /jin/ n. an alcoholic spirit distilled from grain or malt and flavored with juniper berries. [abbr. of GENEVA]

gin[2] /jin/ n. & v. ● n. **1** a machine for separating cotton from its seeds. **2** a snare or trap. **3** a kind of crane and windlass. ● v.tr. (**ginned, gin·ning**) **1** treat (cotton) in a gin. **2** trap. □□ **gin·ner** n. [ME f. OF engin ENGINE]

gin·ger /jínjər/ n., adj., & v. ● n. **1 a** a hot spicy root usu. powdered for use in cooking, or preserved in syrup, or candied. **b** the plant, Zingiber officinale, of SE Asia, having this root. **2** a light reddish yellow color. **3** spirit; mettle. **4** stimulation. ● adj. of a ginger color. ● v.tr. **1** flavor with ginger. **2** (foll. by up) rouse or enliven. **3** Austral. colloq. steal from (a person). □□ **gin·ger·y** adj. [ME f. OE gingiber & OF gingi(m)bre, both f. med.L gingiber ult. f. Skr. śṛṅgaveram f. śṛṅgam horn + –vera body, with ref. to the antler shape of the root]

gin·ger ale n. a carbonated nonalcoholic clear drink flavored with ginger extract.

gin·ger beer n. a carbonated sometimes mildly alcoholic cloudy drink, made by fermenting a mixture of ginger and syrup.

gin·ger·bread /jínjərbred/ n. **1** a cake made with molasses or syrup and flavored with ginger. **2** (often attrib.) a gaudy, lavish, or superfluous decoration or ornament (a house with gingerbread trim).

gin·ger group n. Brit. a group within a party or movement that presses for stronger or more radical policy or action.

gin·ger·ly /jínjərlee/ adv. & adj. ● adv. in a careful or cautious manner. ● adj. showing great care or caution. □□ **gin·ger·li·ness** n. [perh. f. OF gensor delicate, compar. of gent graceful f. L genitus (well-)born]

gin·ger·snap /jínjərsnap/ n. a thin brittle cookie flavored with ginger.

ging·ham /gíng-əm/ n. a plain-woven cotton cloth, esp. striped or checked. [Du. gingang f. Malay ginggang (orig. adj. = striped)]

gin·gi·va /jínjívə, jínjivə/ n. (pl. **gin·gi·vae** /–vee/) the gums. □□ **gin·gi·val** /–jívəl, –jívəl/ adj. [L]

gin·gi·vi·tis /jínjivítis/ n. inflammation of the gums.

ging·ko var. of GINKGO.

ging·ly·mus /gíngglíməs, gíng–/ n. (pl. **gin·gly·mi** /–mī/) Anat. a hingelike joint in the body with motion in one plane only, e.g., the elbow or knee. [mod.L f. Gk gigglumos hinge]

gink[1] /gingk/ n. sl. often derog. a fellow; a man. [20th-c. US: orig. unkn.]

gink[2] /gingk/ n. Austral. a scrutinizing look. [prob. alt. of GEEK[1]]

gink·go /gíngkgō/ n. (also **ging·ko**) (pl. **·gos** or **·goes**) an orig. Chinese and Japanese tree, Ginkgo biloba, with fan-shaped leaves and yellow flowers. Also called **maidenhair tree**. [Jap. ginkyo f. Chin. yinxing silver apricot]

gin·or·mous /jīnáwrməs/ adj. Brit. sl. very large; enormous. [GIANT + ENORMOUS]

gin rum·my n. a form of the card game rummy in which a player holding unmatched cards totaling ten or less may terminate play.

gin·seng /jínseng/ n. **1** any of several medicinal plants of the genus Panax, found in E. Asia and N. America. **2** the root of this. [Chin. renshen perh. = man image, with allusion to its forked root]

gip·py tum·my /jípee/ n. (also **gyp·py tum·my**) Brit. colloq. diarrhea affecting visitors to hot countries. [abbr. of EGYPTIAN]

gip·sy var. of Gypsy.

gi·raffe /jiráf/ n. (pl. same or **gi·raffes**) a ruminant mammal, Giraffa camelopardalis of Africa, the tallest living animal, with a long neck and forelegs and a skin of dark patches separated by lighter lines.

Late 16th century: from French girafe, Italian giraffa, or Spanish and Portuguese girafa, based on Arabic zarāfa. The animal was known in Europe in the medieval period, and isolated instances of names for it based on the Arabic are recorded in Middle English, when it was commonly called the camelopard.

giraffe

gir·an·dole /jírəndōl/ n. **1** a revolving cluster of fireworks. **2** a branched candle bracket or candlestick. **3** an earring or pendant with a large central stone surrounded by small ones. [F f. It. girandola f. girare GYRATE]

gir·a·sol /jírəsawl, –sol/ n. (also **gir·a·sole** /–sōl/) **1** a kind of opal reflecting a reddish glow; a fire opal. **2** (usu. **gir·a·sole**) = JERUSALEM ARTICHOKE. [orig. = sunflower, f. F girasol or It. girasole f. girare (as GIRANDOLE) + sole sun]

gird[1] /gərd/ v.tr. (past and past part. **gird·ed** or **girt**) **1** encircle, attach, or secure with a belt or band. **2** secure (clothes) on the body with a girdle or belt. **3** enclose or encircle. **4 a** (foll. by with) equip with a sword in a belt. **b** fasten (a sword) with a belt. **5** (foll. by around) place (cord, etc.) around. □ **gird** (or **gird up**) **one's loins** prepare for action. [OE gyrdan f. Gmc (as GIRTH)]

gird[2] /gərd/ v. ● v.intr. (foll. by at) jeer or gibe. ● n. a gibe or taunt. [ME, = strike, etc.: orig. unkn.]

gird·er /gɔ́rdər/ n. a large iron or steel beam or compound structure for bearing loads, esp. in a bridge or building. [GIRD[1] + –ER[1]]

gir·dle[1] /gɔ́rd'l/ n. & v. ● n. **1** a belt or cord worn around the waist. **2** a woman's corset extending from waist to thigh. **3** a thing that surrounds like a girdle. **4** the bony support for a limb (pelvic girdle). **5** the part of a cut gem dividing the crown from the base and embraced by the setting. **6** a ring around a tree made by the removal of bark. ● v.tr. **1** surround with a girdle. **2** remove a ring of bark from (a tree), esp. to make it more fruitful. [OE gyrdel: see GIRD[1]]

gir·dle[2] /gɔ́rd'l/ n. Sc. & No. of Engl. = GRIDDLE n. 1.

girl /gɔ́rl/ n. **1** a female child or youth. **2** colloq. a young (esp. unmarried) woman. **3** colloq. a girlfriend or sweetheart. **4** derog. a female servant. □□ **girl·hood** n. [ME gurle, girle, gerle, perh. rel. to LG gör child]

girl·friend /gɔ́rlfrend/ n. **1** a regular female companion or lover. **2** a female friend.

girl·ie /gɔ́rlee/ adj. colloq. (of a magazine, etc.) depicting nude or partially nude young women in erotic poses.

girl·ish /gɔ́rlish/ adj. of or like a girl. □□ **girl·ish·ly** adv. **girl·ish·ness** n.

Girl Scout n. a member of an organization of girls, esp. the Girl Scouts of America, that promotes character, outdoor activities, community service, etc.

gi·ro /jírō/ n. & v. ● n. (pl. **·ros**) **1** a system of credit transfer between banks, post offices, etc., in Europe. **2** a check or payment by giro. ● v.tr. (**·roes, ·roed**) pay by giro. [G f. It., = circulation (of money)]

girt[1] past part. of GIRD[1].

girt[2] var. of GIRTH.

girth /gɔ́rth/ n. & v. (also **girt** /gərt/) ● n. **1** the distance around a thing. **2** a band around the body of a horse to secure the saddle, etc. ● v. **1** tr. **a** secure (a saddle, etc.) with a girth. **b** put a girth on (a horse). **2** tr. surround; encircle. **3** intr. measure (an amount) in girth. [ME f. ON gjörth, Goth. gairda f. Gmc]

GIS abbr. GEOGRAPHIC INFORMATION SYSTEM(S).

gist /jist/ n. **1** the substance or essence of a matter. **2** *Law* the real ground of an action, etc. [OF, 3rd sing. pres. of *gesir* lie f. L *jacēre*]

git /git/ n. *Brit. sl.* a silly or contemptible person. [var. of GET n.]

git•tern /gítərn/ n. a medieval stringed instrument, a forerunner of the guitar. [ME f. OF *guiterne*: cf. CITTERN, GUITAR]

give /giv/ v. & n. • v. (past **gave** /gayv/; past part. **giv•en** /gívən/) **1** tr. (also *absol.*; often foll. by *to*) transfer the possession of freely; hand over as a present (*gave them her old curtains; gives to cancer research*). **2** tr. **a** transfer the ownership of with or without actual delivery; bequeath (*gave him $200 in her will*). **b** transfer, esp. temporarily or for safe keeping; hand over; provide with (*gave him the dog to hold; gave them a drink*). **c** administer (medicine). **d** deliver (a message) (*give her my best wishes*). **3** tr. (usu. foll. by *for*) **a** pay (*gave him $30 for the bicycle*). **b** sell (*gave him the bicycle for $30*) **4** tr. **a** confer; grant (a benefit, an honor, etc.). **b** accord; bestow (one's affections, confidence, etc.). **c** award; administer (one's approval, blame, etc.); tell; offer (esp. something unpleasant) (*gave him a talking-to; gave him my blessing*). **d** pledge; assign as a guarantee (*gave his word*). **5** tr. **a** effect or perform (an action, etc.) (*gave him a kiss; gave a jump*). **b** utter (*gave a shriek*). **6** tr. allot; assign; grant (*give him the contract*). **7** tr. (in *passive*; foll. by *to*) be inclined to or fond of (*is given to speculation*). **8** tr. yield as a product or result (*the lamp gives a bad light; the field gives fodder for twenty cows*). **9** intr. **a** yield to pressure; become relaxed; lose firmness (*this elastic doesn't give properly*). **b** collapse (*the roof gave under the pressure*). **10** intr. (usu. foll. by *of*) grant; bestow (*gave freely of his time*). **11** tr. **a** commit, consign, or entrust (*gave him into custody; give her into your care*). **b** sanction the marriage of (a daughter, etc.). **12** tr. devote; dedicate (*gave his life to his job; shall give it my attention*). **13** tr. (usu. *absol.*) *colloq.* tell what one knows (*What happened? Come on, give!*). **14** tr. present; offer; show; hold out (*gives no sign of life; gave her his arm; give him your ear*). **15** tr. *Theatr.* read, recite, perform, act, etc. (*gave them Hamlet's soliloquy*). **16** tr. impart; be a source of (*gave him my sore throat; gave its name to the battle; gave them to understand; gives him a right to complain*). **17** tr. allow (esp. a fixed amount of time) (*can give you five minutes*). **18** tr. (usu. foll. by *for*) value (something) (*gives nothing for their opinions*). **19** tr. concede; yield (*I give you the victory*). **20** tr. deliver (a judgment, etc.) authoritatively (*gave his verdict*). **21** tr. toast (a person, cause, etc.) (*I give you our President*). **22** tr. provide (a party, meal, etc.) as host (*gave a banquet*). • n. **1** capacity to yield or bend under pressure; elasticity (*there is no give in a stone floor*). **2** ability to adapt or comply (*no give in his attitudes*). □ **give and take** v.tr. exchange (words, blows, or concessions). • n. an exchange of words, etc.; a compromise. **give as good as one gets** retort adequately in words or blows. **give away 1** transfer as a gift. **2** hand over (a bride) ceremonially to a bridegroom. **3** betray or expose to ridicule or detection. **give back** return (something) to its previous owner or in exchange. **give birth (to)** see BIRTH. **give chase** pursue a person, animal, etc.; hunt. **give forth** emit; publish; report. **give the game** (or **show**) **away** reveal a secret or intention. **give a hand** = *lend a hand* (see HAND). **give a person** (or **the devil**) **his or her due** acknowledge, esp. grudgingly, a person's rights, abilities, etc. **give in** cease fighting or arguing; yield; surrender. **give in marriage** sanction the marriage of (one's daughter, etc.). **give it to a person** *colloq.* scold or punish. **give me** I prefer or admire (*give me the Greek islands*). **give off** emit (vapor, etc.). **give oneself airs** act pretentiously or snobbishly. **give oneself up to 1** abandon oneself to an emotion, esp. despair. **2** addict oneself to. **give onto** (or **into**) (of a window, corridor, etc.) overlook or lead into. **give or take** *colloq.* add or subtract (a specified amount or number) in estimating. **give out 1** announce; emit; distribute. **2** cease or break down from exhaustion, etc. **3** run short. **give rise to** cause; induce; suggest. **give a person to understand** inform authoritatively. **give up 1** resign; surrender. **2** part with. **3** deliver (a

---

---

wanted person, etc.). **4** pronounce incurable or insoluble; renounce hope of. **5** renounce or cease (an activity). **give up the ghost** *archaic* or *colloq.* die. **give way** see WAY. **give a person what for** *colloq.* punish or scold severely. **give one's word** promise solemnly. **not give a damn** *colloq.* not care at all. **what gives?** *colloq.* what is the news?; what's happening? **would give the world** (or one's ears, eyes, etc.) for covet or wish for desperately. □□ **giv•a•ble**, **give•a•ble** adj. **giv•er** n. [OE *g(i)efan* f. Gmc]

give•a•way /gívəway/ n. & adj. • n. *colloq.* **1** an inadvertent betrayal or revelation (*the shape of the package was a dead giveaway*). **2** a thing that is given free, esp. for promotional purposes. • adj. **1a** free of charge (*giveaway goodies*). **b** (of prices) very low. **2** revealing (*small giveaway mannerisms*).

giv•en /gívən/ adj. & n. • adj. **1** as previously stated or assumed; granted; specified (*given that he is a liar, we cannot trust him; a given number of people*). **2** *Law* (of a document) signed and dated (*given this day the 30th of June*). • n. a known fact or situation. [past part. of GIVE]

giv•en name n. a name given as afirst name.

giz•mo /gízmō/ n. (also **gis•mo**) (pl. **-mos**) *sl.* a gadget. [20th c.: orig. unkn.]

giz•zard /gízərd/ n. **1** the second part of a bird's stomach, for grinding food usu. with grit. **2** a muscular stomach of some fish, insects, mollusks, and other invertebrates. □ **stick in one's gizzard** (or **craw**) *colloq.* be distasteful. [ME *giser* f. OF *giser, gesier*, etc., ult. f. L *gigeria* cooked entrails of fowl]

gla•bel•la /gləbélə/ n. (pl. **gla•bel•lae** /-lee/) the smooth part of the forehead above and between the eyebrows. □□ **gla•bel•lar** adj. [mod.L f. L *glabellus* (adj.) dimin. of *glaber* smooth]

gla•brous /gláybrəs/ adj. free from hair or down; smooth-skinned. [L *glaber glabri* hairless]

gla•cé /glasáy/ adj. **1** (of fruit, esp. cherries) preserved in sugar, usu. resulting in a glossy surface. **2** (of cloth, leather, etc.) smooth; polished. [F, past part. of *glacer* to ice, gloss f. *glace* ice: see GLACIER]

gla•cé ic•ing n. icing made with confectioner's sugar and water.

gla•cial /gláyshəl/ adj. **1** of ice; icy. **2** *Geol.* characterized or produced by the presence or agency of ice. **3** *colloq.* exceptionally slow. **4** *Chem.* forming icelike crystals upon freezing (*glacial acetic acid*). □□ **gla•cial•ly** adv. [F *glacial* or L *glacialis* icy f. *glacies* ice]

gla•cial ep•och n. (also **gla•cial pe•ri•od**) a period in the earth's history when polar and mountain ice sheets were exceptionally extensive across the earth's surface.

gla•ci•at•ed /gláyshee-aytid, -see–/ adj. **1** marked or polished by the action of ice. **2** covered or having been covered by glaciers or ice sheets. □□ **gla•ci•a•tion** /–áyshən/ n. [past part. of *glaciate* f. L *glaciare* freeze f. *glacies* ice]

gla•cier /gláyshər/ n. a mass of land ice formed by the accumulation of snow on high ground. [F f. *glace* ice ult. f. L *glacies*]

gla•ci•ol•o•gy /gláysheeólajee, –see–/ n. the science of the internal dynamics and effects of glaciers. □□ **gla•ci•o•log•i•cal** /–əlójikəl/ adj. **gla•ci•ol•o•gist** n. [L *glacies* ice + –LOGY]

gla•cis /gláysis, glás–/ n. (pl. same /–siz, –seez/) a bank sloping down from a fort, on which attackers are exposed to the defenders' missiles, etc. [F f. OF *glacier* to slip f. *glace* ice: see GLACIER]

glad¹ /glad/ adj. & v. • adj. (**glad•der**, **glad•dest**) **1** (*predic.*; usu. foll. by *to* & infin. or *Brit. of*) pleased; willing (*shall be glad to come*). **2 a** marked by, filled with, or expressing, joy (*a glad expression*). **b** (of news, events, etc.) giving joy (*glad tidings*). **3** (of objects) bright; beautiful. • v.tr. (**glad•ded**, **glad•ding**) *archaic* make glad. □□ **glad•ly** adv. **glad•ness** n. **glad•some** adj. *poet.* [OE *glæd* f. Gmc]

glad² /glad/ n. (also *Austral.* **glad•die** /gládee/) *colloq.* a gladiolus. [abbr.]

glad•den /glád'n/ v.tr. & intr. make or become glad. □□ **glad•den•er** n.

glade /glayd/ n. an open space in a wood or forest. [16th c.: orig. unkn.]

glad eye n. *colloq.* an amorous glance.

glad hand n. a warm and hearty, but often insincere, greeting or welcome.

glad-hand v.tr. (esp. of a politician) greet or welcome warmly or with the appearance of warmth (*glad-hand the loyal supporters*).

glad•i•a•tor /gládee-aytər/ n. **1** *hist.* a man trained to fight with a sword or other weapons at ancient Roman shows. **2** a person defending or opposing a cause. □□ **glad•i•a•to•ri•al** /–deeətáwreeəl/ adj. [L f. *gladius* sword]

glad•i•o•lus /gládeeóləs/ n. (pl. **glad•i•o•li** /–lī/ or **glad•i•o•lus•es**) any iridaceous plant of the genus *Gladiolus* with sword-shaped leaves and usu. brightly colored flower spikes. [L, dimin. of *gladius* sword]

glad rags n.pl. *colloq.* clothes for a special occasion; one's best clothes.

Glad•stone bag /gládstōn, –stən/ n. a suitcase that opens flat into two equal compartments. [W. E. *Gladstone*, Engl. statesman d. 1898]

Glag•o•lit•ic /glágəlítik/ *adj.* of or relating to the alphabet ascribed to St. Cyril and formerly used in writing some Slavonic languages. [mod.L *glagoliticus* f. Serbo-Croatian *glagolica* Glagolitic alphabet f. OSlav. *glagol* word]

glair /glair/ *n.* (also **glaire**) 1 white of egg. 2 an adhesive preparation made from this, used in bookbinding, etc. □□ **glair•e•ous** *adj.* **glair•y** *adj.* [ME f. OF *glaire*, ult. f. L *clara* fem. of *clarus* clear]

glaire var. of GLAIR.

glaive /glayv/ *n. archaic poet.* 1 a broadsword. 2 any sword. [ME f. OF, app. f. L *gladius* sword]

glam•or•ize /glámərīz/ *v.tr.* (also **glam•our•ize**) make glamorous or attractive. □□ **glam•or•i•za•tion** *n.*

glam•our /glámər/ *n. & v.* (also **glam•or**) •*n.* 1 physical attractiveness, esp. when achieved by makeup, etc. 2 alluring or exciting beauty or charm (*the glamour of New York*). •*v.tr.* 1 *poet.* affect with glamour; bewitch; enchant. 2 *colloq.* make glamorous. □ **cast a glamour over** enchant. □□ **glam•or•ous** *adj.* **glam•or•ous•ly** *adv.* [18th c.: var. of GRAMMAR, with ref. to the occult practices associated with learning in the Middle Ages]

glam•our girl *n.* (also **glam•our boy**) an attractive young woman (or man), esp. a model, etc.

glance[1] /glans/ *v. & n.* •*v.* 1 *intr.* (often foll. by *down, up,* etc.) cast a momentary look (*glanced up at the sky*). 2 *intr.* (often foll. by *off*) (esp. of a weapon) glide or bounce (off an object). 3 *intr.* (usu. foll. by *over, off, from*) (of talk or a talker) pass quickly over a subject or subjects (*glanced over the question of payment*). 4 *intr.* (of a bright object or light) flash, dart, or gleam; reflect (*the sun glanced off the knife*). 5 *tr.* (esp. of a weapon) strike (an object) obliquely. •*n.* 1 (usu. foll. by *at, into, over,* etc.) a brief look (*took a glance at the paper; threw a glance over her shoulder*). 2 a a flash or gleam (*a glance of sunlight*). b a sudden movement producing this. 3 a swift oblique movement or impact. □ **at a glance** immediately upon looking. **glance at** 1 give a brief look at. 2 make a passing and usu. sarcastic allusion to. **glance one's eye** (foll. by *at, over,* etc.) look at briefly (esp. a document). **glance over** (or **through**) read cursorily. □□ **glanc•ing•ly** *adv.* [ME *glence*, etc., prob. a nasalized form of obs. *glace* in the same sense, f. OF *glacier* to slip: see GLACIS]

glance[2] /glans/ *n.* any lustrous sulfide ore (*copper glance; lead glance*). [G *Glanz* luster]

gland[1] /gland/ *n.* 1 a an organ in an animal body secreting substances for use in the body or for ejection. b a structure resembling this, such as a lymph gland. 2 *Bot.* a secreting cell or group of cells on the surface of a plant structure. [F *glande* f. OF *glandre* f. L *glandulae* throat glands]

gland[2] /gland/ *n.* a sleeve used to produce a seal around a moving shaft. [19th c.: perh. var. of *glam, glan* a vice, rel. to CLAMP[1]]

glan•ders /glándərz/ *n.pl.* (also treated as *sing.*) 1 a contagious disease of horses, caused by a bacterium and characterized by swellings below the jaw and mucous discharge from the nostrils. 2 this disease in humans or other animals. □□ **glan•dered** *adj.* **glan•der•ous** *adj.* [OF *glandre*: see GLAND[1]]

glan•du•lar /glánjələr/ *adj.* of or relating to a gland or glands. □ **glandular fever** = INFECTIOUS MONONUCLEOSIS. [F *glandulaire* (as GLAND[1])]

glans /glanz/ *n.* (*pl.* **glan•des** /glándeez/) the rounded part forming the end of the penis or clitoris. [L, = acorn]

glare[1] /glair/ *v. & n.* •*v.* 1 *intr.* (usu. foll. by *at, upon*) look fiercely or fixedly. 2 *intr.* shine dazzlingly or disagreeably. 3 *tr.* express (hate, defiance, etc.) by a look. 4 *intr.* be overly conspicuous or obtrusive. •*n.* 1 a strong fierce light, esp. sunshine. b oppressive public attention (*the glare of fame*). 2 a fierce or fixed look (*a glare of defiance*). 3 tawdry brilliance. □□ **glar•y** *adj.* [ME, prob. ult. rel. to GLASS: cf. MDu. and MLG *glaren* gleam, glare]

glare[2] /glair/ *adj.* (esp. of ice) smooth and glassy. [perh. f. *glare* frost (16th c., of uncert. orig.)]

glar•ing /gláiring/ *adj.* 1 obvious; conspicuous (*a glaring error*). 2 shining oppressively. 3 staring fiercely. □□ **glar•ing•ly** *adv.* **glar•ing•ness** *n.*

glas•nost /gláasnəst, –nawst/ *n.* (in the former Soviet Union) the policy or practice of more open consultative government and wider dissemination of information. [Russ. *glasnost'*, lit. = publicity, openness]

glass /glas/ *n., v., & adj.* •*n.* 1 a (often *attrib.*) a hard, brittle, usu. transparent, translucent, or shiny substance, made by fusing sand with soda and lime and sometimes other ingredients (*a glass pitcher*) (cf. CROWN GLASS, FLINT GLASS, PLATE GLASS). b a substance of similar properties or composition. 2 (often *collect.*) an object or objects made from, or partly from, or originally from, glass, esp.: a a drinking vessel. b esp. *Brit.* a mirror; a looking glass. c an hourglass or sandglass. d a window. e a greenhouse (*rows of lettuce under glass*). f glass ornaments. g a barometer. h *Brit.* a glass disk covering a watch face. i a magnifying lens. j a monocle. 3 (in *pl.*) a eyeglasses. b field glasses; opera glasses. 4 the amount of liquid contained

in a glass; a drink (*he likes a glass of wine*). 5 fiberglass. •*v.tr.* 1 (usu. as **glassed** *adj.*) fit with glass; glaze. 2 *poet.* reflect as in a mirror. 3 *Mil.* look at or for with field glasses, etc. •*adj.* of or made from glass. □ **has had a glass too much** is rather drunk. □□ **glass•ful** *n.* (*pl.* •**fuls**). **glass•less** *adj.* **glass•like** *adj.* [OE *glæs* f. Gmc: cf. GLAZE]

glass•blow•er /glásblō̄ər/ *n.* a person who blows semimolten glass through a long tube to make glassware.

glass•blow•ing /glásblō̄ing/ *n.* the craft of blowing semimolten glass through a long tube to make glassware.

glass ceil•ing *n.* a barrier to advancement in a profession, esp. affecting women and minorities, that is not officially acknowledged.

glass cut•ter *n.* 1 a worker who cuts glass. 2 a tool used for cutting glass.

glass eye *n.* an artificial eye made from glass.

glass fi•ber *n. Brit.* 1 a filament or filaments of glass made into fabric; fiberglass. 2 such filaments embedded in plastic as reinforcement.

glass gall *n.* = SANDIVER.

glass•house /glás-hows/ *n.* 1 a building where glass is made. 2 *Brit.* a greenhouse. 3 *Brit. sl.* a military prison.

glass•ie var. of GLASSY *n.*

glass•ine /glaseén/ *n.* a glossy transparent paper. [GLASS]

glass•mak•ing /glásmayking/ *n.* the manufacture of glass.

glass snake *n.* any snakelike lizard of the genus *Ophisaurus*, with a very brittle tail.

glass•ware /gláswair/ *n.* articles made from glass, esp. drinking glasses, tableware, etc.

glass wool *n.* glass in the form of fine fibers used for packing and insulation.

glass•wort /gláswərt/ *n.* any plant of the genus *Salicornia* or *Salsola* formerly burned for use in glassmaking.

glass•y /glásee/ *adj. & n.* •*adj.* (**glass•i•er, glass•i•est**) 1 of or resembling glass, esp. in smoothness. 2 (of the eye, the expression, etc.) abstracted; dull; fixed (*fixed her with a glassy stare*). •*n.* (also **glass•ie**) a glass marble. □ **the** (or **just the**) **glassy** *Austral.* the most excellent person or thing. □□ **glass•i•ly** *adv.* **glass•i•ness** *n.*

Glas•we•gian /glazweéjən, glaas–/ *adj. & n.* •*adj.* of or relating to Glasgow in Scotland. •*n.* a native of Glasgow. [*Glasgow* after *Norwegian*, etc.]

Glau•ber's salt /glówbərz/ *n.* (also **Glau•ber's salts**) a crystalline hydrated form of sodium sulfate used esp. as a laxative. [J. R. *Glauber*, Ger. chemist d. 1668]

glau•co•ma /glawkṓmə, glou–/ *n.* an eye condition with increased pressure within the eyeball, causing gradual loss of sight. □□ **glau•co•ma•tous** *adj.* [L f. Gk *glaukōma –atos*, ult. f. *glaukos*: see GLAUCOUS]

glau•cous /gláwkəs/ *adj.* 1 of a dull grayish green or blue. 2 covered with a powdery bloom as of grapes. [L *glaucus* f. Gk *glaukos*]

glaze /glayz/ *v. & n.* •*v.* 1 *tr.* a fit (a window, picture, etc.) with glass. b provide (a building) with glass windows. 2 *tr.* a cover (pottery, etc.) with a glaze. b fix (paint) on pottery with a glaze. 3 *tr.* cover (pastry, meat, etc.) with a glaze. 4 *intr.* (often foll. by *over*) (of the eyes) become fixed or glassy (*his eyes glazed over*). 5 *tr.* cover (cloth, paper, leather, a painted surface, etc.) with a glaze or other similar finish. 6 *tr.* give a glassy surface to, e.g., by rubbing. •*n.* 1 a vitreous substance, usu. a special glass, used to glaze pottery. 2 a smooth shiny coating of milk, sugar, gelatin, etc., on food. 3 a thin topcoat of transparent paint used to modify the tone of the underlying color. 4 a smooth surface formed by glazing. 5 a thin coating of ice. □ **glaze in** enclose (a building, a window frame, etc.) with glass. □□ **glaz•er** *n.* **glaz•y** *adj.* [ME f. an oblique form of GLASS]

gla•zier /gláyzhər/ *n.* a person whose trade is glazing windows, etc. □□ **gla•zier•y** *n.*

OLD-FASHIONED   PORT   BRANDY   LIQUEUR

RED WINE   CHAMPAGNE   MARTINI   WHITE WINE

glasses: shapes

glaz•ing /gláyzing/ *n.* **1** the act or an instance of glazing. **2** windows (see also DOUBLE GLAZING). **3** material used to produce a glaze.

gleam /gleem/ *n. & v.* • *n.* **1** a faint or brief light (*a gleam of sunlight*). **2** a faint, sudden, intermittent, or temporary shine (*not a gleam of hope*). • *v.intr.* **1** emit gleams. **2** shine with a faint or intermittent brightness. **3** a brief instance of a quality or emotion, esp. a desirable one (*amusement gleamed in his eyes*). □□ **gleam•ing•ly** *adv.* **gleam•y** *adj.* [OE *glǣm*: cf. GLIMMER]

glean /gleen/ *v.* **1** *tr.* collect or scrape together (news, facts, gossip, etc.) in small quantities. **2 a** *tr.* (also *absol.*) gather (ears of grain, etc.) after the harvest. **b** *tr.* strip (a field, etc.) after a harvest. □□ **glean•er** *n.* [ME f. OF *glener* f. LL *glennare*, prob. of Celt. orig.]

glean•ings /gléeningz/ *n.pl.* things gleaned, esp. facts.

glebe /gleeb/ *n.* **1** a piece of land serving as part of a clergyman's benefice and providing income. **2** *poet.* earth; land; a field. [ME f. L *gl(a)eba* clod, soil]

glee /glee/ *n.* **1** mirth; delight (*watched the enemy's defeat with glee*). **2** a song for three or more, esp. adult male, voices, singing different parts simultaneously, usu. unaccompanied. □□ **glee•some** *adj.* [OE *glīo, glēo* minstrelsy, jest f. Gmc]

glee club *n.* a group organized for singing short choral pieces.

glee•ful /gléefŏol/ *adj.* joyful. □□ **glee•ful•ly** *adv.* **glee•ful•ness** *n.*

Gleich•schal•tung /glíkh-shaltŏong/ *n.* the standardization of political, economic, and social institutions in authoritarian countries. [G]

glen /glen/ *n.* a narrow valley. [Gael. & Ir. *gleann*]

glen•gar•ry /glengáree/ *n.* (*pl.* **-ries**) a brimless Scottish cap with a cleft down the center and usu. two ribbons hanging at the back. [*Glengarry* in Scotland]

gle•noid cav•i•ty /gléenoyd/ *n.* a shallow depression on a bone, esp. the scapula and temporal bone, into which another bone fits to form a joint. [F *glénoïde* f. Gk *glēnoeidēs* f. *glēnē* socket]

gley /glay/ *n.* a sticky waterlogged soil, gray to blue in color. [Ukrainian, = sticky blue clay, rel. to CLAY]

gli•a /glía/ *n.* = NEUROGLIA. □□ **gli•al** *adj.* [Gk, = glue]

glib /glib/ *adj.* (**glib•ber, glib•best**) **1** (of a speaker, speech, etc.) fluent and voluble but insincere and shallow. **2** *archaic* smooth; unimpeded. □□ **glib•ly** *adv.* **glib•ness** *n.* [rel. to obs. *glibbery* slippery f. Gmc: perh. imit.]

glide /glīd/ *v. & n.* • *v.* **1** *intr.* (of a stream, bird, snake, ship, train, skater, etc.) move with a smooth continuous motion. **2** *intr.* (of an aircraft, esp. a glider) fly without engine power. **3** *intr.* of time, etc.: **a** pass gently and imperceptibly. **b** (often foll. by *into*) pass and change gradually and imperceptibly (*night glided into day*). **4** *intr.* move quietly or stealthily. **5** *tr.* cause to glide (*breezes glided the boat on its course*). **6** *intr.* traverse or fly in a glider. • *n.* **1 a** the act of gliding. **b** an instance of this. **2** *Phonet.* a gradually changing sound made in passing from one position of the speech organs to another. **3** a gliding dance or dance step. **4** a flight in a glider. □□ **glid•ing•ly** *adv.* [OE *glīdan* f. WG]

glide path *n.* (also **glide slope**) an aircraft's line of descent to land, esp. as indicated by ground radar.

glid•er /glīdər/ *n.* **1 a** an aircraft that flies without an engine. **b** a glider pilot. **2** a type of porch swing with a gliding motion. **3** a person or thing that glides.

glim /glim/ *n.* **1** a faint light. **2** *archaic sl.* a candle; a lantern. [17th c.: perh. abbr. of GLIMMER or GLIMPSE]

glim•mer /glímər/ *v. & n.* • *v.intr.* shine faintly or intermittently. • *n.* **1** a feeble or wavering light. **2** (usu. foll. by *of*) a faint gleam (of hope, understanding, etc.). **3** a glimpse. □□ **glim•mer•ing•ly** *adv.* [ME prob. f. Scand. f. WG: see GLEAM]

glim•mer•ing /glíməring/ *n.* **1** = GLIMMER *n.* **2** an act of glimmering.

glimpse /glimps/ *n. & v.* • *n.* (often foll. by *of*) **1** a momentary or partial view (*caught a glimpse of her*). **2** a faint and transient appearance (*glimpses of the truth*). • *v.* **1** *tr.* see faintly or partly (*glimpsed his face in the crowd*). **2** *intr.* (often foll. by *at*) cast a passing glance. **3** *intr.* **a** shine faintly or intermittently. **b** *poet.* appear faintly; dawn. [ME *glimse* corresp. to MHG *glimsen* f. WG (as GLIMMER)]

glint /glint/ *v. & n.* • *v.intr. & tr.* flash or cause to flash; glitter; sparkle; reflect (*eyes glinted with amusement; the sword glinted fire*). • *n.* a brief flash of light; a sparkle. [alt. of ME *glent*, prob. of Scand. orig.]

glis•sade /glisáad, -sáyd/ *n. & v.* • *n.* **1** an act of sliding down a steep slope of snow or ice, usu. on the feet with the support of an ice ax, etc. **2** a gliding step in ballet. • *v.intr.* perform a glissade. [F f. *glisser* slip, slide]

glis•san•do /glisáandō/ *n.* (*pl.* **glis•san•di** /-dee/ or **-dos**) *Mus.* a continuous slide of adjacent notes upward or downward. [It. f. F *glissant* sliding (as GLISSADE)]

glis•ten /glísən/ *v. & n.* • *v.intr.* shine, esp. like a wet object, snow, etc.; glitter. • *n.* a glitter; a sparkle. [OE *glisnian* f. *glisian* shine]

glis•ter /glístər/ *v. & n. archaic* • *v.intr.* sparkle; glitter. • *n.* a sparkle; a gleam. [ME f. MLG *glistern*, MDu *glisteren*, rel. to GLISTEN]

glitch /glich/ *n. colloq.* a sudden jump or malfunction (of equipment, etc.). [20th c.: orig. unkn.]

glit•ter /glítər/ *v. & n.* • *v.intr.* **1** shine, esp. with a bright reflected light; sparkle. **2** (usu. foll. by *with*) **a** be a showy or splendid (*glittered*

with diamonds). **b** be ostentatious or flashily brilliant (*glittering rhetoric*). • *n.* **1** a gleam; a sparkle. **2** showiness; splendor. **3** tiny pieces of sparkling material used for decoration. □□ **glit•ter•ing•ly** *adv.* **glit•ter•y** *adj.* [ME f. ON *glitra* f. Gmc]

glit•te•ra•ti /glítəraátee/ *n.pl. sl.* the fashionable set of literary or show business people. [GLITTER + LITERATI]

glitz /glits/ *n. sl.* extravagant but superficial display; show business glamour. [back-form. f. GLITZY]

glitz•y /glítsee/ *adj.* (**glitz•i•er, glitz•i•est**) *sl.* extravagant; ostentatious; tawdry; gaudy. □□ **glitz•i•ly** *adv.* **glitz•i•ness** *n.* [GLITTER, after RITZY: cf. G *glitzerig* glittering]

gloam•ing /glōming/ *n. poet.* twilight; dusk. [OE *glōmung* f. *glōm* twilight, rel. to GLOW]

gloat /glōt/ *v. & n.* • *v.intr.* (often foll. by *on, upon, over*) consider or contemplate with lust, greed, malice, triumph, etc. (*gloated over his collection*). • *n.* **1** the act of gloating. **2** a look or expression of triumphant satisfaction. □□ **gloat•er** *n.* **gloat•ing•ly** *adv.* [16th c.: orig. unkn., but perh. rel. to ON *glotta* grin, MHG *glotzen* stare]

glob /glob/ *n.* a mass or lump of semiliquid substance, e.g., mud. [20th c.: perh. f. BLOB and GOB[1]]

glob•al /glōbəl/ *adj.* **1** worldwide (*global conflict*). **2** relating to or embracing a group of items, etc.; total. □□ **glob•al•ly** *adv.* [F (as GLOBE)]

glob•al warm•ing *n.* the increase in temperature of the earth's atmosphere caused by the greenhouse effect.

globe /glōb/ *n. & v.* • *n.* **1 a** (prec. by *the*) the planet earth. **b** a planet, star, or sun. **c** any spherical body; a ball. **2** a spherical representation of the earth or of the constellations with a map on the surface. **3** a golden sphere as an emblem of sovereignty; an orb. **4** any spherical glass vessel, esp. a fish bowl, a lamp, etc. **5** the eyeball. • *v.tr. & intr.* make (usu. in *passive*) or become globular. □□ **globe•like** *adj.* **glo•boid** *adj. & n.* **glo•bose** /-bōs/ *adj.* [F *globe* or L *globus*]

globe ar•ti•choke *n.* the partly edible head of the artichoke plant.

globe•fish /glōbfish/ *n.* = PUFFER **2**.

globe•flow•er /glōbflowər/ *n.* any ranunculaceous plant of the genus *Trollius* with globular usu. yellow flowers.

globe light•ning *n.* = ball lightning.

globe-trot•ter *n.* a person who travels widely. □□ **globe-trot•ting** *n.*

glo•big•er•i•na /glōbíjəríɴə, -réenə/ *n.* any planktonic protozoan of the genus *Globigerina*, living near the surface of the sea. [mod.L f. L *globus* globe + *-ger* carrying + -INA]

glob•u•lar /glóbyələr/ *adj.* **1** globe-shaped; spherical. **2** composed of globules. □□ **glob•u•lar•i•ty** /-láritee/ *n.* **glob•u•lar•ly** *adv.*

glob•ule /glóbyŏol/ *n.* a small globe or round particle; a drop. □□ **glob•u•lous** *adj.* [F *globule* or L *globulus* (as GLOBE)]

glob•u•lin /glóbyəlin/ *n.* any of a group of proteins found in plant and animal tissues and esp. responsible for the transport of molecules, etc.

glock•en•spiel /glókənspeel, -shpeel/ *n.* a musical instrument consisting of a series of bells or metal bars or tubes suspended or mounted in a frame and struck by hammers. [G, = bell-play]

glom /glom/ *v. sl.* (**glommed, glom•ming**) **1** *tr.* steal; grab. **2** *intr.* (usu. foll. by *on to*) steal; grab. [var. of Sc. *glaum* (18th c., of unkn. orig.)]

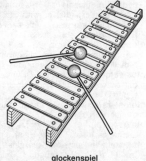
glockenspiel

glom•er•ate /glómərət/ *adj. Bot. & Anat.* compactly clustered. [L *glomeratus* past part. of *glomerare* f. *glomus -eris* ball]

glom•er•ule /glómərōol/ *n.* a clustered flower head.

glo•mer•u•lus /glōméryələs/ *n.* (*pl.* **glo•mer•u•li** /-lī/) a cluster of small organisms, tissues, or blood vessels, esp. of the capillaries of the kidney. □□ **glo•mer•u•lar** *adj.* [mod.L, dimin. of L *glomus -eris* ball]

gloom /glōom/ *n. & v.* • *n.* **1** darkness; obscurity. **2** melancholy; despondency. **3** *poet.* a dark place. • *v.* **1** *intr.* be gloomy or melancholy; frown. **2** *intr.* (of the sky, etc.) be dull or threatening; lower. **3** *intr.* appear darkly or obscurely. **4** *tr.* cover with gloom; make dark or dismal. [ME *gloum(b)e*, of unkn. orig.: cf. GLUM]

gloom•y /glōomee/ *adj.* (**gloom•i•er, gloom•i•est**) **1** dark; unlighted. **2** depressed; sullen. **3** dismal; depressing. □□ **gloom•i•ly** *adv.* **gloom•i•ness** *n.*

glop /glop/ *n. sl.* a liquid or sticky mess, esp. unappealing or inedible food. [imit.: cf. obs. *glop* swallow greedily]

Glo•ri•a /gláwreeə/ *n.* **1** any of various doxologies beginning with *Gloria*, esp. the hymn beginning with *Gloria in excelsis Deo* (Glory be to God in the highest). **2** an aureole. [L, = glory]

glo·ri·fy /gláwrifī/ v.tr. (·fies, ·fied) 1 exalt to heavenly glory; make glorious. 2 transform into something more splendid. 3 extol; praise. 4 (as **glorified** adj.) seeming or pretending to be better than in reality (just a glorified office boy). □□ **glo·ri·fi·ca·tion** n. **glo·ri·fi·er** n. [ME f. OF glorifier f. eccl.L glorificare f. LL glorificus f. L gloria glory]

glo·ri·ole /gláwreeōl/ n. an aureole; a halo. [F f. L gloriola dimin. of gloria glory]

glo·ri·ous /gláwreeəs/ adj. 1 possessing glory; illustrious. 2 conferring glory; honorable. 3 colloq. splendid; magnificent; delightful (a glorious day). 4 esp. Brit. iron. intense; unmitigated (a glorious muddle). 5 Brit. colloq. happily intoxicated. □□ **glo·ri·ous·ly** adv. **glo·ri·ous·ness** n. [ME f. AF glorious, OF glorios, –eus f. L gloriosus (as GLORY)]

glo·ry /gláwree/ n. & v. • n. (pl. ·ries) 1 high renown or fame; honor. 2 adoring praise and thanksgiving (Glory to the Lord). 3 resplendent majesty or magnificence; great beauty (the glory of Versailles; the glory of the rose). 4 a thing that brings renown or praise; a distinction. 5 the bliss and splendor of heaven. 6 colloq. a state of exaltation, prosperity, happiness, etc. (is in his glory playing with his trains). 7 an aureole; a halo. 8 an anthelion. • v.intr. (often foll. by in, or to + infin.) pride oneself; exult (glory in their skill). □ **glory be!** 1 a devout ejaculation. 2 colloq. an exclamation of surprise or delight. **go to glory** sl. die; be destroyed. [ME f. AF & OF glorie f. L gloria]

glo·ry hole n. 1 a small furnace used to keep glass malleable for handworking. 2 Brit. colloq. an untidy room, drawer, or receptacle. 3 an open quarry.

glory-of-the-snow n. = CHIONODOXA.

gloss¹ /glaws, glos/ n. & v. • n. 1 a surface shine or luster. b an instance of this; a smooth finish. 2 a deceptively attractive appearance. b an instance of this. 3 (in full **gloss paint**) paint formulated to give a hard glossy finish (cf. MATTE¹). • v.tr. make glossy. □ **gloss over** 1 seek to conceal beneath a false appearance. 2 conceal or evade by mentioning briefly or misleadingly. □□ **gloss·er** n. [16th c.: orig. unkn.]

gloss² /glaws, glos/ n. & v. • n. 1 a an explanatory word or phrase inserted between the lines or in the margin of a text. b a comment, explanation, interpretation, or paraphrase. 2 a misrepresentation of another's words. 3 a a glossary. b an interlinear translation or annotation. • v. 1 tr. a add a gloss or glosses to (a text, word, etc.). b read a different sense into; explain away. 2 intr. (often foll. by on) make (esp. unfavorable) comments. 3 intr. write or introduce glosses. □□ **gloss·er** n. [alt. of GLOZE after med.L glossa]

glos·sal /gláwsəl, glós–/ adj. Anat. of the tongue; lingual. [Gk glōssa tongue]

glos·sa·ry /gláwsəree, glós–/ n. (pl. ·ries) 1 (also **gloss**) an alphabetical list of terms or words found in or relating to a specific subject or text, esp. dialect, with explanations; a brief dictionary. 2 a collection of glosses. □□ **glos·sar·i·al** /–sáireeəl/ adj. **glos·sa·rist** n. [L glossarium f. glossa GLOSS²]

glos·sa·tor /glawsáytər, glo–/ n. 1 a writer of glosses or glossaries. 2 hist. a commentator on, or interpreter of, medieval law texts. [ME f. med.L glossator f. glossa GLOSS²]

glos·seme /gláwseem, glós–/ n. any meaningful feature of a language that cannot be analyzed into smaller meaningful units. [Gk glōssēma f. glōssa GLOSS²]

glos·si·tis /glawsítis, glo–/ n. inflammation of the tongue. [Gk glōssa tongue + –ITIS]

glos·sog·ra·pher /glawsógrəfər, glo–/ n. a writer of glosses or commentaries. [GLOSS² + –GRAPHER]

glos·so·la·li·a /gláwsəláyleeə, glós–/ n. = gift of tongues (see TONGUE). [mod.L f. Gk glōssa tongue + –lalia speaking]

glos·so·la·ryn·ge·al /gláwsōlərínjeeəl, glós–/ adj. of the tongue and larynx. [Gk glōssa tongue + LARYNGEAL]

gloss·y /gláwsee, glós–/ adj. & n. • adj. (**gloss·i·er, gloss·i·est**) 1 having a shine; smooth. 2 (of paper, etc.) smooth and shiny. 3 (of a magazine, etc.) printed on such paper; expensively produced and attractively presented, but sometimes lacking in content or depth. • n. (pl. ·ies) colloq. 1 a glossy magazine. 2 a photograph with a glossy surface. □□ **gloss·i·ly** adv. **gloss·i·ness** n.

glot·tal /glót'l/ adj. of or produced by the glottis.

glottal stop n. a sound produced by the sudden opening or shutting of the glottis.

glot·tis /glótis/ n. the space at the upper end of the windpipe and between the vocal cords, affecting voice modulation through expansion or contraction. □□ **glot·tic** /–tik/ adj. [mod.L f. Gk glōttis f. glōtta var. of glōssa tongue]

glove /gluv/ n. & v. • n. 1 a covering for the hand, of wool, leather, cotton, etc., worn esp. for protection against cold or dirt, and usu. having separate fingers. 2 a padded protective glove, esp.: a a boxing glove. b Baseball a fielder's glove. • v.tr. cover or provide with a glove or gloves. □ **fit like a glove** fit exactly. **throw down** (or **take up**) **the glove** issue (or accept) a challenge. **with the gloves off** mer-

cilessly; unfairly; with no compunction. □□ **glove·less** adj. **glov·er** n. [OE glōf, corresp. to ON glófi, perh. f. Gmc]

glove box n. 1 a sealed chamber with openings with attached gloves, allowing someone to reach in and handle sterile, radioactive, or other hazardous material without contamination. 3 = GLOVE COMPARTMENT.

glove com·part·ment n. a recess or cabinet for small articles in the dashboard of a motor vehicle.

glove pup·pet n. a small cloth puppet fitted on the hand and worked by the fingers.

glow /glō/ v. & n. • v.intr. 1 a throw out light and heat without flame; be incandescent. b shine like something heated in this way. 2 (of the cheeks) redden, esp. from cold or exercise. 3 (often foll. by with) a (of the body) be heated, esp. from exertion; sweat. b express or experience strong emotion (glowed with pride; glowing with indignation). 4 show a warm color (the painting glows with warmth). 5 (as **glowing** adj.) expressing pride or satisfaction (a glowing report). • n. 1 a glowing state. 2 a bright warm color, esp. the red of cheeks. 3 ardor; passion. 4 a feeling induced by good health, exercise, etc.; well-being. □ **in a glow** Brit. colloq. hot or flushed; sweating. □□ **glow·ing·ly** adv. [OE glōwan f. Gmc]

glow dis·charge n. a luminous sparkless electrical discharge from a pointed conductor in a gas at low pressure.

glow·er /glowr/ v. & n. • v.intr. (often foll. by at) stare or scowl, esp. angrily. • n. a glowering look. □□ **glow·er·ing·ly** adv. [orig. uncert.: perh. Sc. var. of ME glore f. LG or Scand., or f. obs. (ME) glow stare + –ER⁴]

glow plug n. a device in a diesel engine that heats air and fuel entering a cyclinder in order to facilitate combustion in a cold engine.

glow·worm /glówwərm/ n. any beetle of the genus Lampyris whose wingless female emits light from the end of the abdomen.

glox·in·i·a /gloksíneeə/ n. any tropical plant of the genus Gloxinia, native to S. America, with large bell flowers of various colors. [mod.L f. B. P. Gloxin, 18th-c. Ger. botanist]

gloze /glōz/ v. 1 tr. GLOSS², 1. 2 = gloss over (see GLOSS¹). 3 intr. archaic a (usu. foll. by on, upon) comment. b talk speciously; fawn. [ME f. OF gloser f. glose f. med.L glosa, gloza f. L glossa tongue, GLOSS²]

glu·ca·gon /glóokəgon/ n. a polypeptide hormone formed in the pancreas, which aids the breakdown of glycogen. [Gk glukus sweet + agōn leading]

glu·cose /glóokōs/ n. 1 a simple sugar containing six carbon atoms, found mainly in the form of dextrose. Glucose is an important energy source in living organisms and obtainable from some carbohydrates by hydrolysis. ¶ Chem. formula: $C_6H_{12}O_6$. 2 a syrup containing glucose sugars from the incomplete hydrolysis of starch. [F f. Gk gleukos sweet wine, rel. to glukus sweet]

glu·co·side /glóokəsīd/ n. a compound giving glucose and other products upon hydrolysis. □□ **glu·co·sid·ic** /–sídik/ adj.

glue /glōo/ n. & v. • n. an adhesive substance used for sticking objects or materials together. • v.tr. (**glues, glued, gluing** or **glueing**) 1 fasten or join with glue. 2 be paying very close attention to (something) (he was glued to the televsion during the Olympics). □□ **glue·like** adj. **glu·er** n. **glu·ey** /glóo-ee/ adj. (**glu·i·er, glu·i·est**) **glu·ey·ness** n. [ME f. OF glu (n.), gluer (v.), f. LL glus glutis f. L gluten]

glue·pot /glóopot/ n. 1 a pot with an outer vessel holding water to heat glue. 2 colloq. an area of sticky mud, etc.

glue sniff·ing n. the practice of inhaling the fumes from the solvents in adhesives for the intoxicating effects.

glug /glug/ n. & v. • n. a hollow, usu. repetitive gurgling sound. • v.intr. make a gurgling sound as of water from a bottle. [imit.]

glum /glum/ adj. (**glum·mer, glum·mest**) looking or feeling dejected; sullen; displeased. □□ **glum·ly** adv. **glum·ness** n. [rel. to dial. glum (v.) frown, var. of gloume GLOOM v.]

glume /glōom/ n. 1 a membranous bract surrounding the spikelet of grasses or the florets of sedges. 2 the husk of grain. □□ **glu·ma·ceous** /–máyshəs/ adj. **glu·mose** adj. [L gluma husk]

glu·on /glóo-on/ n. Physics any of a group of elementary particles that are thought to bind quarks together. [GLUE + –ON]

glut /glut/ *v. & n.* • *v.tr.* (**glut·ted, glut·ting**) **1** feed (a person, one's stomach, etc.) or indulge (an appetite, a desire, etc.) to the full; satiate; cloy. **2** fill to excess; choke up. **3** *Econ.* overstock (a market) with goods. • *n.* **1** *Econ.* supply exceeding demand; a surfeit (*a glut in the market*). **2** full indulgence; one's fill. [ME prob. f. OF *gloutir* swallow f. L *gluttire*: cf. GLUTTON]

glu·ta·mate /glo͞otəmayt/ *n.* any salt or ester of glutamic acid, esp. a sodium salt used to enhance the flavor of food.

glu·tam·ic ac·id /glo͞otámik/ *n.* a naturally occurring amino acid, a constituent of many proteins. [GLUTEN + AMINE + -IC]

glu·ten /glo͞otən/ *n.* **1** a mixture of proteins present in cereal grains. **2** *archaic* a sticky substance. [F f. L *gluten glutinis* glue]

glu·te·us /glo͞otee͡əs/ *n.* (*pl.* **glu·te·i** /-tee͡ī/) any of the three muscles in each buttock. □□ **glu·te·al** *adj.* [mod.L f. Gk *gloutos* buttock]

glu·ti·nous /glo͞ot'nəs/ *adj.* sticky; like glue. □□ **glu·ti·nous·ly** *adv.* **glu·ti·nous·ness** *n.* [F *glutineux* or L *glutinosus* (as GLUTEN)]

glut·ton[1] /glút'n/ *n.* **1** an excessively greedy eater. **2** (often foll. by *for*) *colloq.* a person insatiably eager (*a glutton for work*). **3** a voracious animal *Gulo gulo*, of the weasel family. Also called **wolverine**. □ **a glutton for punishment** a person eager to take on hard or unpleasant tasks. □□ **glut·ton·ize** *v.intr.* **glut·ton·ous** *adj.* **glut·ton·ous·ly** *adv.* [ME f. OF *gluton, gloton* f. L *glutto -onis* f. *gluttire* swallow, *gluttus* greedy]

glut·ton[2] *n.* a European wolverine, *Gulo gulo*.

glut·ton·y /glút'nee/ *n.* habitual greed or excess in eating. [OF *glutonie* (as GLUTTON)]

glyc·er·ide /glísərīd/ *n.* any fatty acid ester of glycerol.

glyc·er·in /glísərin/ *n.* (also **glyc·er·ine**) = GLYCEROL. [F *glycerin* f. Gk *glukeros* sweet]

glyc·er·ol /glísərawl, -rol/ *n.* a colorless sweet viscous liquid formed as a byproduct in the manufacture of soap, used as an emollient and laxative, in explosives, etc. ¶ *Chem.* formula: $C_3H_8O_3$. Also called **glycerin**. [GLYCERIN + -OL[1]]

gly·cine /glíseen/ *n.* the simplest naturally occurring amino acid, a general constituent of proteins. [G *Glycin* f. Gk *glukus* sweet]

glyco- /glíkō/ *comb. form* sugar. [Gk *glukus* sweet]

gly·co·gen /glíkəjən/ *n.* a polysaccharide serving as a store of carbohydrates, esp. in animal tissues, and yielding glucose on hydrolysis. □□ **gly·co·gen·ic** /-jénik/ *adj.*

gly·co·gen·e·sis /glíkəjénisis/ *n. Biochem.* the formation of glycogen from sugar.

gly·col /glíkawl, -kol/ *n.* an alcohol, esp. ethylene glycol. □□ **gly·col·ic** /-kólik/ *adj.* **gly·col·lic** *adj.* [GLYCERIN + -OL[1], orig. as being intermediate between glycerine and alcohol]

gly·col·y·sis /glikólisis/ *n. Biochem.* the breakdown of glucose by enzymes in most living organisms to release energy and pyruvic or lactic acid.

gly·co·pro·tein /glíkōpróteen/ *n.* any of a group of compounds consisting of a protein combined with a carbohydrate.

gly·co·side /glíkəsīd/ *n.* any compound giving sugar and other products on hydrolysis. □□ **gly·co·sid·ic** /-sídik/ *adj.* [GLYCO-, after GLUCOSIDE]

gly·cos·u·ri·a /glíkəsyo͞oree͡ə, -sho͞or-/ *n.* a condition characterized by an excess of sugar in the urine, associated with diabetes, kidney disease, etc. □□ **gly·cos·u·ric** *adj.* [F *glycose* glucose + -URIA]

glyph /glif/ *n.* **1** a sculptured character or symbol. **2** a vertical groove, esp. that on a Greek frieze. □□ **glyph·ic** *adj.* [F *glyphe* f. Gk *gluphē* carving f. *gluphō* carve]

glyp·tic /glíptik/ *adj.* of or concerning carving, esp. on precious stones. [F *glyptique* or Gk *gluptikos* f. *gluptēs* carver f. *gluphō* carve]

glyp·to·dont /glíptədont/ *n.* any extinct armadillolike edentate animal of the genus *Glyptodon* native to S. America, having fluted teeth and a body covered in a hard thick bony shell. [mod.L f. Gk *gluptos* carved + *odous odontos* tooth]

glyp·tog·ra·phy /gliptógrəfee/ *n.* the art or scientific study of engraving gems. [Gk *gluptos* carved + -GRAPHY]

GM *abbr.* **1** General Motors. **2** general manager. **3** (in the UK) George Medal.

gm *abbr.* gram(s).

G-man /jee͡man/ *n.* (*pl.* **G-men**) **1** *US colloq.* a federal officer, esp. an FBI agent. **2** *Ir.* a political detective. [Government + MAN]

GMT *abbr.* Greenwich Mean Time.

gnam·ma /námə/ *n.* (also **nam·ma**) *Austral.* a natural hole in a rock, containing water; a waterhole. [Aboriginal]

gnarled /naarld/ *adj.* (also **gnarl·y** /náarlee/) (of a tree, hands, etc.) knobbly; twisted; rugged. [var. of *knarled*, rel. to KNURL]

gnash /nash/ *v. & n.* • *v.* **1** *tr.* grind (the teeth). **2** *intr.* (of the teeth) strike together; grind. • *n.* an act of grinding the teeth. [var. of obs. *gnacche* or *gnast*, rel. to ON *gnastan* a gnashing (imit.)]

gnat /nat/ *n.* **1** any small two-winged biting fly of the genus *Culex*, esp. *C. pipiens*. **2** an insignificant annoyance. **3** a tiny thing. [OE *gnætt*]

gnath·ic /náthik/ *adj.* of or relating to the jaws. [Gk *gnathos* jaw]

gnaw /naw/ *v.* (*past part.* **gnawed** or **gnawn**) **1 a** *tr.* (usu. foll. by *away, off, in two*, etc.) bite persistently; wear away by biting. **b** *intr.* (often foll. by *at, into*) bite; nibble. **2 a** *intr.* (often foll. by *at, into*) (of a destructive agent, pain, fear, etc.) corrode; waste away; consume; torture. **b** *tr.* corrode, consume, torture, etc., with pain, fear, etc. (*was gnawed by doubt*). **3** *tr.* (as **gnawing** *adj.*) persistent; worrying. □□ **gnaw·ing·ly** *adv.* [OE *gnagan*, ult. imit.]

gneiss /nīs/ *n.* a usu. coarse-grained metamorphic rock foliated by mineral layers, principally of feldspar, quartz, and ferromagnesian minerals. □□ **gneiss·ic** *adj.* **gneiss·oid** *adj.* **gneiss·ose** *adj.* [G]

GNMA /jínee may/ *n.* Government National Mortgage Association.

gnoc·chi /nyáwkee/ *n.pl.* (in Italian cooking) small dumplings made from potato, semolina flour, etc., or from spinach and cheese, usu. served with a sauce. [It., pl. of *gnocco* f. *nocchio* knot in wood]

gnome[1] /nōm/ *n.* **1 a** a dwarfish legendary creature supposed to guard the earth's treasures underground; a goblin. **b** a figure of a gnome, esp. as a garden ornament. **2** (esp. in *pl.*) *colloq.* a person with sinister influence, esp. financial (*gnomes of Zurich*). □□ **gnom·ish** *adj.* [F f. mod.L *gnomus* (word invented by Paracelsus)]

gnome[2] /nōm, nōmee/ *n.* a maxim; an aphorism. [Gk *gnōmē* opinion f. *gignōskō* know]

gno·mic /nómik/ *adj.* **1** of, consisting of, or using gnomes or aphorisms; sententious (see GNOME[2]). **2** *Gram.* (of a tense) used without the implication of time to express a general truth, e.g., *men were deceivers ever*. □□ **gno·mi·cal·ly** *adv.* [Gk *gnōmikos* (as GNOME[2])]

gno·mon /nómon, -mən/ *n.* **1** the rod or pin, etc., on a sundial that shows the time by the position of its shadow. **2** *Geom.* the part of a parallelogram left when a similar parallelogram has been taken from its corner. **3** *Astron.* a column, etc., used in observing the sun's meridian altitude. □□ **gno·mon·ic** /-mónik/ *adj.* [F or L *gnomon* f. Gk *gnōmōn* indicator, etc., f. *gignōskō* know]

gno·sis /nósis/ *n.* knowledge of spiritual mysteries. [Gk *gnōsis* knowledge (as GNOMON)]

gnos·tic /nóstik/ *adj. & n.* • *adj.* **1** relating to knowledge, esp. esoteric mystical knowledge. **2** (**Gnostic**) concerning the Gnostics; occult; mystic. • *n.* (**Gnostic**) (usu. in *pl.*) a Christian heretic of the 1st–3rd c. claiming gnosis. □□ **Gnos·ti·cism** /-tisizəm/ *n.* **gnos·ti·cize** *v.tr. & intr.* [eccl.L *gnosticus* f. Gk *gnōstikos* (as GNOSIS)]

GNP *abbr.* gross national product.

gnu /no͞o, nyo͞o/ *n.* any antelope of the genus *Connochaetes*, native to S. Africa, with a large erect head and brown stripes on the neck and shoulders. Also called **wildebeest**. [Bushman *nqu*, prob. through Du. *gnoe*]

go[1] /gō/ *v., n., & adj.* • *v.* (*3rd sing. present* **goes** /gōz/; *past* **went** /went/; *past part.* **gone** /gon/) **1** *intr.* **a** start moving or be moving from one place or point in time to another; travel; proceed. **b** (foll. by *to* + infin., or *and* + verb) proceed in order to (*went to find him; go and buy some bread*). **c** (foll. by *and* + verb) *colloq.* expressing annoyance (*you went and told him; they've gone and broken it; she went and won*). **2** *intr.* (foll. by verbal noun) make a special trip for; participate in; proceed to do (*went skiing; then went shopping; often goes running*). **3** *intr.* lie or extend in a certain direction; lead to (*the road goes to the shore; where does that door go?*). **4** *intr.* **a** leave; depart (*they had to go*). **b** *colloq.* disappear; vanish (*my bag has gone*). **5** *intr.* move, act, work, etc. (*the clock doesn't go; his brain is going all the time*). **6** *intr.* **a** make a specified movement (*go like this with your foot*). **b** make a sound (often of a specified kind) (*the gun went bang; the door bell went*). **c** *colloq.* say (*so he goes to me "Why didn't you like it?"*). **d** (of an animal) make (its characteristic cry) (*the cow went "moo"*). **7** *intr.* be in a specified state (*go hungry; went in fear of his life*). **8** *intr.* **a** pass into a specified condition (*gone bad; went mad; went to sleep*). **b** *colloq.* die. **c** proceed or escape in a specified condition (*the poet went unrecognized; the crime went unnoticed*). **9** *intr.* **a** (of time or distance) pass; elapse; be traversed (*ten days to go before Easter; the last mile went quickly*). **b** be finished (*the movie went quickly*). **10** *intr.* **a** (of a document, verse, song, etc.) have a specified content or wording; run (*the tune goes like this*). **b** be current or accepted (*so the story goes*). **c** be suitable; fit; match (*the shoes don't go with the hat*). **d** be regularly kept or put (*the forks go here*). **e** find room; fit (*this won't go into the cupboard*). **11** *intr.* **a** turn out; proceed; take a course or view (*things went well; Massachusetts went Democratic*). **b** be successful (*make the party go*). **c** progress (*we've still got a long way to go*). **12** *intr.* **a** be sold (*went for $1; went cheap*). **b** (of money) be spent (*$200 went on a new jacket*). **13** *intr.* **a** be relinquished, dismissed, or abolished (*the car will have to go*). **b** fail; decline; give way; collapse (*his sight is going; the bulb has gone*). **14** *intr.* be acceptable or permitted; be accepted without question (*anything goes; what I say goes*). **15** *intr.* (often foll. by *by, with, on, upon*) be guided by; judge or act on or in harmony with (*have nothing to go on; a good rule to go by*). **16** *intr.* attend or visit or travel to regularly (*goes to church; goes to school; this train goes to Paris*). **17** *intr.* (foll. by *pres. part.*) *colloq.* proceed (often foolishly) to do (*went running to the police; don't go making him angry*). **18** *intr.* act or proceed to a certain point (*will go so far and no further; went as high as $100*). **19** *intr.* (of a number) be capable of being contained in another (6 *into 12 goes twice; 6 into 5 won't go*). **20** *tr. Cards* bid; declare (*has gone two spades*). **21** *intr.* (usu. foll. by *to*) be allotted or awarded; pass (*first prize went to the girl; the job went to his rival*). **22** *intr.* (foll. by *to, toward*) amount to; contribute to (*12 inches go to make a foot; this will go toward your vacation*). **23** *intr.* (in *imper.*) begin motion (a starter's order in a race) (*ready, set, go!*). **24** *intr.* (usu. foll. by *to*) refer or appeal (*go to him for help*). **25** *intr.* (often foll. by *on*) take up a specified profession (*went on the stage; gone soldiering; went to sea*). **26** *intr.* (usu. foll. by *by, under*) be known or called (*goes by the name of Max*). **27** *tr. colloq.* proceed to (*go jump in the lake*). **28** *intr.* (foll. by *for*) apply to; have relevance for (*that goes for me too*). **29** *intr. colloq.* urinate or defecate. • *n.* (*pl.* **goes**) **1** the act or an instance of going. **2** mettle; spirit; dash; animation (*she has a lot of go in her*). **3** vigorous activity (*it's all go*). **4** *colloq.* a success (*made a go of it*). **5** *colloq.* a turn; an attempt (*I'll have a go; it's my go; all in one go*). **6** permission; approval; go-ahead (*gave us a go on the new project*). **7** esp. *Brit. colloq.* a state of affairs (*a helluva go*). **8** esp. *Brit. colloq.* an attack of illness (*a bad go of flu*). **9** esp. *Brit. colloq.* a quantity of liquor, food, etc., served at one time. • *adj. colloq.* **1** functioning properly (*all systems are go*). **2** fashionable; progressive. □ **as** (or **so**) **far as it goes** an expression of caution against taking a statement too positively (*the work is good as far as it goes*). **as (a person or thing) goes** as the average is (*a good actor as actors go*). **from the word go** *colloq.* from the very beginning. **give it a go** *colloq.* make an effort to succeed. **go about 1** busy oneself with; set to work at. **2** be socially active. **3** (foll. by *pres. part.*) make a habit of doing (*goes about telling lies*). **4** *Naut.* change to an opposite tack. **go ahead** proceed without hesitation. **go all the way 1** win a contest, one's ultimate goal, etc. **2** engage in sexual intercourse. **go along with** agree to; take the same view as. **go around 1** spin, revolve. **2** be long enough to encompass. **3** (of food, etc.) suffice for everybody. **4** (usu. foll. by *to*) visit informally. **5** (foll. by *with*) be regularly in the company of. **6** = *go about* 3. **go at** take in hand energetically; attack. **go away** depart, esp. from home for a vacation, etc. **go back 1** return; revert. **2** extend backward (in time or space). **3** (foll. by *to*) have a history extending back to. **go back on** fail to keep (one's word, promise, etc.). **go bail** see BAIL¹. **go begging** see BEG. **go by 1** pass. **2** be dependent on; be guided by. **go by default** see DEFAULT. **go down 1 a** (of an amount) become less (*the coffee has gone down a lot*). **b** subside (*the flood went down*). **c** decrease in price; lose value. **2 a** (of a ship) sink. **b** (of the sun) set. **3** (usu. foll. by *to*) be continued to a specified point. **4** deteriorate; fail; (of a computer network, etc.) cease to function. **5** be recorded in writing. **6** be swallowed. **7** (often foll. by *with*) be received (in a specified way). **8** *Brit. colloq.* be sent to prison (*went down for ten years*). **9** (often foll. by *before*) fall (before a conqueror). **go Dutch** see DUTCH. **go far** be very successful. **go fly a kite** stop annoying, irritating, etc., (someone), as with unwanted suggestions. **go for 1** go to fetch. **2** be accounted as or achieve (*went for nothing*). **3** prefer; choose (*that's the one I go for*). **4** *colloq.* strive to attain (*go for it!*). **5** *colloq.* attack (*the dog went for him*). **go for broke** exert all one's strength or risk all one's resources. **go great guns** see GUN. **go halves** (often foll. by *with*) share equally. **go in 1** enter a room, house, etc. **2** (usu. foll. by *for*) enter as a competitor. **3** (of the sun, etc.) become obscured by cloud. **go in for** take as one's object, style, pursuit, principle, etc. **going, going, gone!** an auctioneer's announcement that bidding is closing or closed. **go into 1** enter (a profession, etc.). **2** take part in; be a part of. **3** investigate. **4** allow oneself to pass into (hysterics, etc.). **5** dress oneself in (mourning, etc.). **6** frequent (society); go in with join as a partner; share expenses for. **go it alone** see ALONE. **go a long way 1** (often foll. by *toward*) have a great effect. **2** (of food, money, etc.) last a long time; buy much. **3** = *go far*. **go off 1** explode. **2 a** leave the stage. **b** leave; depart. **3** gradually cease to be felt. **4** (esp. of foodstuffs) deteriorate; decompose. **5** go to sleep; become unconscious. **6** be extinguished. **7** die. **8** be got rid of by sale, etc. **9** sound, as an alarm, siren, etc. **go off at** *Austral. & NZ sl.* reprimand; scold. **go off well** (or **badly**, etc.) (of an enterprise, etc.) be received or accomplished well (or badly, etc.). **go on 1** (often foll. by *pres. part.*) continue; persevere (*decided to go on with it; went on trying; unable to go on*). **2** *colloq.* **a** talk at great length. **b** (foll. by *at*) admonish (*went on and on at him*). **3** (foll. by *to* + infin.) proceed (*went on to become a star*). **4** happen. **5** conduct oneself (*shameful, the way they went on*). **6** *Theatr.* appear on stage. **7** (of a garment) be large enough for its wearer. **8** take one's turn to do something. **9** *colloq.* use as evidence (*police don't have anything to go on*). **10** *colloq.* (esp. in *neg.*) **a** concern oneself about. **b** care for (*don't go much on red hair*). **11** become chargeable to (an expense account, etc.). **go on!** *colloq.* an expression of encouragement or disbelief. **go out 1** leave a room, house, etc. **2** be broadcast. **3** be extinguished. **4** (often foll. by *with*) be courting. **5** (of a government or elected official) leave office. **6** cease to be fashionable. **7** (usu. foll. by *to*) depart, esp. to a colony, etc. **8** *colloq.* lose consciousness. **9** (of workers) strike. **10** (usu. foll. by *to*) (of the heart, etc.) ex-

pand with sympathy, etc., toward (*my heart goes out to them*). **11** *Golf* play the first nine holes in a round. **12** *Cards* be the first to dispose of one's hand. **13** (of a tide) turn to low tide. **14** mix socially; attend (social) events. **go over 1** inspect the details of; rehearse; retouch. **2** (often foll. by *to*) change one's allegiance or religion. **3** (of a play, etc.) be received in a specified way (*went over well in Dallas*). **go public 1** offer (a corporation's) shares for sale to the general public. **2** disclose or admit publicly. **go through 1** be dealt with or completed. **2** discuss in detail; scrutinize in sequence. **3** perform (a ceremony, a recitation, etc.). **4** undergo. **5** *colloq.* use up; spend (money, etc.). **6** make holes in. **7** (of a book) be successively published (in so many editions). **go through with** not leave unfinished; complete. **go to blazes** (or **hell** or **Jericho**, etc.) *sl.* an exclamation of dismissal, contempt, etc. **go to the country** see COUNTRY. **go together 1** match; fit. **2** be courting. **go to it!** *colloq.* begin work! **go to show** (or **prove**) serve to demonstrate (or prove). **go to town 1** expend great effort; attack (a project) vigorously. **2** spend time, effort, money, etc. lavishly or indulgently. (*the committee really went to town on the decorations*). **go under** sink; fail; succumb. **go up 1** increase in price. **2** be consumed (in flames, etc.); explode. **go up in the world** attain a higher social position. **go with 1** be harmonious with; match. **2** agree to; take the same view as. **3 a** be a pair with. **b** be dating. **4** follow the drift of. **go without** manage without; forgo (also *absol.*: *we shall just have to go without*). **go with the tide** (or **times**) do as others do; follow the drift. **have a go at 1** esp. *Brit.* attack; criticize. **2** attempt; try. **no go 1** useless; unavailing. **2** canceled; not approved to proceed. **on the go** *colloq.* **1** in constant motion. **2** constantly working. **to go** (of food, etc.) to be eaten or drunk off the premises where sold (*burgers to go*). **who goes there?** a sentry's challenge. [OE *gān* f. Gmc]

go² /gō/ *n.* a Japanese board game of territorial possession and capture. [Jap.]

goad /gōd/ *n. & v.* • *n.* **1** a spiked stick used for urging cattle forward. **2** anything that torments, incites, or stimulates. • *v.tr.* **1** urge on with a goad. **2** (usu. foll. by *on, into*) irritate; stimulate (*goaded him into retaliating; goaded me on to win*). [OE *gād*, rel. to Lombard *gaida* arrowhead f. Gmc]

go-a·head *n. & adj.* • *n.* permission to proceed (*the government had given the go-ahead for the power station*). • *adj.* enterprising; enthusiastic (*a young and go-ahead managing director*)

goal /gōl/ *n.* **1** the object of a person's ambition or effort; a destination; an aim (*fame is his goal; Washington was our goal*). **2 a** *Football* a pair of posts with a crossbar between which the ball has to be sent to score. **b** *Soccer, Ice Hockey,* etc., a cage or basket used similarly. **c** a point or points won (*scored 3 goals*). **3** a point marking the end of a race. □ **in goal** in the position of goalkeeper. □□ **goal·less** *adj.* [16th c.: orig. unkn.: perh. identical with ME *gol* boundary]

goal·ball /gólbawl/ *n.* a team ball game for blind and visually handicapped players.

goal·ie /gólee/ *n. colloq.* = GOALKEEPER.

goal·keep·er /gólkeepər/ *n.* a player stationed to protect the goal in various sports.

goal kick *n. Soccer* a free kick taken by the defending side from within their goal area after attackers send the ball over the byline.

goal line *n. Sports* a line between each pair of goalposts on a football or hockey field, extended to form the end boundary of a field of play (cf. TOUCHLINE).

goal·mouth /gólmowth/ *n. Soccer, Ice Hockey* the space between or near the goalposts.

goal·post /gólpōst/ *n.* either of the two upright posts of a goal. □ **move the goalposts** alter the basis or scope of a procedure during its course, so as to fit adverse circumstances encountered.

goal·tend·er /góltendər/ *n.* a hockey goalkeeper.

go·an·na /gō-ánə/ *n. Austral.* a monitor lizard. [corrupt. of IGUANA]

goat /gōt/ *n.* **1 a** a hardy, lively, frisky shorthaired domesticated mammal, *Capra aegagrus,* having horns and (in the male) a beard, and kept for its milk and meat. **b** either of two similar mammals, the mountain goat and the Spanish goat. **2** any other mammal of the genus *Capra,* including the ibex. **3** a lecherous man. **4** *Brit. colloq.* a foolish person. **5** (**the Goat**) the zodiacal sign or constellation Capricorn. **6** a scapegoat. □ **get a person's goat** *colloq.* irritate a person.

mountain goat

□□ **goat·ish** *adj.* **goat·y** *adj.* [OE *gāt* she-goat f. Gmc]

goat an·te·lope *n.* any antelopelike member of the goat family, including the chamois and goral.

goat·ee /gōtée/ *n.* a small beard trimmed to a point on the chin (from its resemblance to a goat's beard).

goat god *n.* Pan.

goat·herd /gót-hərd/ *n.* a person who tends goats.

goat moth *n.* any of various large moths of the family Cossidae.

goats·beard /gōtsbeerd/ *n.* **1** a meadow plant, *Tragopogon pratensis*. **2** a herbaceous plant, *Aruncus dioicus*, with long spikes of white flowers.

goat·skin /gōtskin/ *n.* **1** the skin of a goat. **2** a garment or bottle made out of goatskin.

goat·suck·er /gōtsukər/ *n.* = NIGHTJAR.

gob[1] /gob/ *n. esp. Brit. sl.* the mouth. [perh. f. Gael. & Ir., = beak, mouth]

gob[2] /gob/ *n. & v. sl.* ● *n.* **1** a lump or clot of slimy matter. **2** (in *pl.*) large amounts (*gobs of cash*) ● *v.intr.* (**gobbed, gob·bing**) spit. [ME f. OF *go(u)be* mouthful]

gob[3] /gob/ *n. sl.* a sailor. [20th c.: cf. GOBBY]

gob·bet /gobit/ *n.* **1** a piece or lump of raw meat, flesh, food, etc. **2** an extract from a text, esp. one set for translation or comment in an examination. [ME f. OF *gobet* (as GOB[2])]

gob·ble[1] /gobəl/ *v.tr. & intr.* eat hurriedly and noisily. □□ **gob·bler** *n.* [prob. dial. f. GOB[2]]

gob·ble[2] /gobəl/ *v.intr.* **1** (of a male turkey) make a characteristic swallowing sound in the throat. **2** make such a sound when speaking, esp. when excited, angry, etc. [imit.: perh. based on GOBBLE[1]]

gob·ble·dy·gook /gobəldeegook/ *n.* (also **gob·ble·de·gook**) *colloq.* pompous or unintelligible jargon. [prob. imit. of a turkey]

gob·bler /goblər/ *n. colloq.* a male turkey.

gob·by /gobee/ *n.* (*pl.* **·bies**) *Brit. sl.* **1** a coastguard. **2** an American sailor. [perh. f. GOB[2] + -Y[1]]

Gob·e·lin /gobəlin, gōbəlin, gawblăn/ *n.* (in full **Gobelin tapestry**) **1** a tapestry made at the Gobelins factory. **2** a tapestry imitating this. [name of a factory in Paris, called *Gobelins* after its orig. owners]

gobe·mouche /gōbmoosh/ *n.* (*pl.* **gobe·mouches** *pronunc.* same) a gullible listener. [F *gobe-mouches*, = flycatcher f. *gober* swallow + *mouches* flies]

go-be·tween *n.* an intermediary; a negotiator.

gob·let /goblit/ *n.* **1** a drinking vessel with a foot and a stem, usu. of glass. **2** *archaic* a metal or glass bowl-shaped drinking cup without handles, sometimes with a foot and a cover. **3** *poet.* a drinking cup. [ME f. OF *gobelet* dimin. of *gobel* cup, of unkn. orig.]

gob·lin /goblin/ *n.* a mischievous, ugly, dwarflike creature of folklore. [ME prob. f. AF *gobelin*, med.L *gobelinus*, prob. f. name dimin. of *Gobel*, rel. to G *Kobold*: see COBALT]

gob·smacked /gobsmakt/ *adj. sl. Brit.* flabbergasted; struck dumb with awe or amazement. [GOB[1] + SMACK[1]]

gob·stop·per *n. Brit.* a very large piece of hard candy.

go·by /gōbee/ *n.* (*pl.* **·bies**) any small marine fish of the family Gobiidae, having ventral fins joined to form a sucker or disk. [L *gobius*, *cobius* f. Gk *kōbios* GUDGEON[1]]

go-by *n. colloq.* a snub; a slight (*gave it the go-by*).

go-cart *n.* **1** a handcart; a stroller. **2** = GO-KART. **3** *archaic* a baby walker.

god /god/ *n. & int.* ● *n.* **1 a** (in many religions) a superhuman being or spirit worshiped as having power over nature, human fortunes, etc.; a deity. **b** an image, idol, animal, or other object worshiped as divine or symbolizing a god. **2** (**God**) (in Christian and other monotheistic religions) the creator and ruler of the universe; the supreme being. **3 a** an adored, admired, or influential person. **b** something worshiped like a god (*makes a god of success*). **4** *Theatr.* (in *pl.*) **a** the gallery. **b** the people sitting in it. ● *int.* (**God!**) an exclamation of surprise, anger, etc. □ **by God!** an exclamation of surprise, etc. **for God's sake!** see SAKE[1]. **God bless** an expression of good wishes on parting. **God bless me** (or **my soul**) see BLESS. **God damn (you, him**, etc.) may (you, etc.) be damned. **God the Father, Son, and Holy Spirit** (or **Ghost**) (in the Christian tradition) the Persons of the Trinity. **God forbid** (foll. by *that* + clause, or *absol.*) may it not happen! **God grant** (foll. by *that* + clause) may it happen. **God help (you, him,** etc.) an expression of concern for or sympathy with a person. **God knows 1** it is beyond all knowledge (*God knows what will become of him*). **2** I call God to witness that (*God knows we tried hard enough*). **God willing** if fate allows. **good God!** an exclamation of surprise, anger, etc. **in God's name** an appeal for help. **in the name of God** an expression of surprise or annoyance. **my** (or **oh**) **God!** an exclamation of surprise, anger, etc. **play God** assume importance or superiority. **thank God!** an exclamation of pleasure or relief. **with God** dead and in heaven. □□ **god·hood** *n.* **god·ship** *n.* **god·ward** *adj. & adv.* **god·wards** *adv.* [OE f. Gmc]

god-aw·ful *adj. sl.* extremely unpleasant, nasty, etc.

god·child /godchild/ *n.* a person in relation to a godparent.

god·damn /godăm/ *adj.* (or **god·dam** or **god·damned** /-dămd/) *sl.* accursed; damnable.

god·daugh·ter /goddawtər/ *n.* a female godchild.

god·dess /godis/ *n.* **1** a female deity. **2** a woman who is adored, esp. for her beauty.

go·det /gōdét, gōdáy/ *n.* a triangular piece of material inserted in a dress, glove, etc. [F]

go-dev·il *n.* **1** a jointed apparatus used to clean the inside of pipes.

---

2 a crude sled with heavy runners for dragging heavy objects, used in farming, logging, etc. **3** a railroad handcar.

god·fa·ther /godfaathər/ *n.* **1** a male godparent. **2** a person directing an illegal organization, esp. the Mafia.

God-fear·ing *adj.* **1** earnestly religious. **2** devout; pious.

god·for·sak·en /godfərsaykən/ *adj.* (also **God·for·sak·en**) devoid of all merit; dismal; dreary.

god·head /godhed/ *n.* (also **God·head**) **1 a** the state of being God or a god. **b** divine nature. **2** a deity. **3** (**the Godhead**) God.

god·less /godlis/ *adj.* **1** not recognizing or obeying a god or gods; atheistic. **2** profane; wicked. □□ **god·less·ness** *n.*

god·like /godlīk/ *adj.* **1** resembling God or a god in some quality, esp. in physical beauty. **2** befitting or appropriate to a god.

god·ly /godlee/ *adj.* religious; pious; devout. □□ **god·li·ness** *n.*

god·moth·er /godmuthər/ *n.* a female godparent.

go·down /gōdown/ *n.* a warehouse in parts of E. Asia. [Port. *gudão* f. Malay *godong* perh. f. Telugu *gidangi* place where goods lie f. *kidu* lie]

god·par·ent /godpairənt/ *n.* a person who presents a child at baptism, promising to take responsibility for the child's religious education.

God's a·cre *n.* a churchyard.

god·send /godsend/ *n.* an unexpected but welcome event or acquisition.

god·son /godsun/ *n.* a male godchild.

God·speed /godspeed/ *int.* an expression of good wishes to a person starting a journey.

God squad *n. sl.* **1** a religious organization, esp. an evangelical Christian group. **2** its members.

God's truth *n.* the absolute truth.

god·wit /godwit/ *n.* any wading bird of the genus *Limosa*, with long legs and a long straight or slightly upcurved bill. [16th c.: of unkn. orig.]

God·wot·te·ry /godwótəree/ *n. Brit. joc.* affected, archaic, or excessively elaborate speech or writing, esp. regarding gardens. [*God wot* (in a poem on gardens, by T. E. Brown 1876)]

go·er /gōər/ *n.* **1** a person or thing that goes (*a slow goer*). **2** (often in *comb.*) a person who attends, esp. regularly (*a churchgoer*). **3** *Brit. colloq.* **a** a lively or persevering person. **b** a sexually promiscuous person. **4** *Austral. colloq.* a project likely to be accepted or to succeed.

goes *3rd sing. present of* GO[1].

go·est /gōist/ *archaic 2nd sing. present of* GO[1].

go·eth /gōith/ *archaic 3rd sing. present of* GO[1].

Goe·the·an /gōteeən/ *adj. & n.* (also **Goe·thi·an**) ● *adj.* of, relating to, or characteristic of the German writer J. W. von Goethe (d. 1832). ● *n.* an admirer or follower of Goethe.

go·fer /gōfər/ *n. sl.* a person who runs errands, esp. on a movie set or in an office. [*go for* (see GO[1])]

gof·fer /gōfər/ *v. & n.* ● *v.tr.* **1** make wavy, flute, or crimp (a lace edge, a trimming, etc.) with heated irons. **2** (as **goffered** *adj.*) (of the edges of a book) embossed. ● *n.* **1** an iron used for goffering. **2** ornamental braiding used for frills, etc. [F *gaufrer* stamp with a patterned tool f. *gaufre* honeycomb, rel. to WAFER, WAFFLE[2]]

go-get·ter *n. colloq.* an aggressively enterprising person.

gog·gle /gogəl/ *v., adj., & n.* ● *v.* **1** *intr.* **a** (often foll. by *at*) look with wide-open eyes. **b** (of the eyes) be rolled about; protrude. **2** *tr.* turn (the eyes) sideways or from side to side. ● *adj.* (usu. *attrib.*) (of the eyes) protuberant or rolling. ● *n.* **1** (in *pl.*) **a** eyeglasses for protecting the eyes from glare, dust, water, etc. **b** *colloq.* eyeglasses. **2** (in *pl.*) a sheep disease; the staggers. **3** a goggling expression. [ME, prob. from a base *gog* (unrecorded) expressive of oscillating movement]

gog·gle-box *n. Brit. colloq.* a television set.

gog·gle-eyed *adj.* having staring or protuberant eyes, esp. through astonishment or disbelief.

gog·let /goglit/ *n. Ind.* a long-necked usu. porous earthenware vessel used for keeping water cool. [Port. *gorgoleta*]

go-go *adj. colloq.* **1** relating to an unrestrained and erotic style of dancing to popular music (*a go-go bar; go-go dancers*). **2** assertively dynamic (*the go-go bravado of the 1980s*).

Goi·del /goyd'l/ *n.* a Celt who speaks Irish Gaelic, Scottish Gaelic, or Manx. □□ **Goi·del·ic** /-délik/ *n.* [OIr. *Góidel*]

go·ing /gōing/ *n. & adj.* ● *n.* **1 a** the act or process of going. **b** an instance of this; a departure. **2 a** the condition of the ground for walking, riding, etc. **b** progress affected by this (*found the going hard*). ● *adj.* **1** in or into action (*set the clock going*). **2** esp. *Brit.* existing; available; to be had (*there's hot soup going; one of the best writers going*). **3** current; prevalent (*the going rate*). □ **get going** start steadily talking, working, etc. (*can't stop him when he gets going*). **going away** a departure. **going for one** *colloq.* acting in one's favor (*he's got a lot going for him*). **going on fifteen**, etc., approaching one's fifteenth, etc., birthday. **going on for** *Brit.* approaching (a time, an age, etc.) (*must be going on for 6 years*). **going to** intending or intended to; about to; likely to (*it's going to sink!*). **heavy going** slow or difficult to progress with (*found Faulkner heavy going*). **to be going on with** to start with; for the time being. **while the going is good** while conditions are favorable. [GO¹: in some senses f. earlier *a--going*: see A²]

go•ing con•cern *n.* a thriving business.

go•ing-o•ver *n.* **1** *colloq.* a thorough treatment, esp. in cleaning or inspection (*give the place a going-over with the vacuum cleaner*). **2** *sl.* a beating. **3** *colloq.* a scolding.

go•ings-on /gōingzón, –áwn/ *n.pl.* events or behavior, esp. of an unusual or suspect nature.

goi•ter /góytər/ *n.* *Med.* a swelling of the neck resulting from enlargement of the thyroid gland. □□ **goi•trous** /–trus/ *adj.* [F, back-form. f. *goitreux* or f. Prov. *goitron*, ult. f. L *guttur* throat]

go-kart *n.* a small racing car with a lightweight body.

Gol•con•da /golkóndə/ *n.* a mine or source of wealth, advantages, etc. [city near Hyderabad, India, famous for its diamonds]

gold /gōld/ *n. & adj.* ● *n.* **1** a yellow, malleable, ductile, high density metallic element resistant to chemical reaction, occurring naturally in quartz veins and gravel, and precious as a monetary medium, in jewelry, etc. ¶ Symb.: **Au. 2** the color of gold. **3 a** coins or articles made of gold. **b** money in large sums; wealth. **4** something precious, beautiful, or brilliant (*all that glitters is not gold*). **5** = GOLD MEDAL. **6** gold used for coating a surface or as a pigment; gilding. **7** the bull's-eye of an archery target (usu. gilt). ● *adj.* **1** made wholly or chiefly of gold. **2** colored like gold. [OE f. Gmc]

gold a•mal•gam *n.* an easily molded combination of gold with mercury.

gold•beat•er's skin *n.* an animal membrane used to separate leaves of gold during beating.

gold•beat•ing /góldbeetər/ *n.* the act of beating gold into gold leaf.

gold bloc *n.* a bloc of countries having a gold standard.

gold brick *n.* *sl.* **1** a thing with only a surface appearance of value, but in fact worthless.

gold-brick *n. & v.* ● *n.* (also **gold•brick•er**) **1** a person who invents excuses to avoid a task; a shirker. **2** a confidence trickster. ● *v.intr.* **1** invent excuses to avoid a task. **2** swindle (someone).

gold card *n.* a credit card issued to people with a high credit rating, giving privileges and benefits not available to holders of the standard card.

gold•crest /góldkrest/ *n.* a small bird, *Regulus regulus*, with a golden crest.

gold dig•ger *n.* **1** *sl.* a person who associates with others purely to extract money from them, in particular a woman who strives to marry a wealthy man. **2** a person who digs for gold.

gold dust *n.* **1** gold in fine particles as often found naturally. **2** a plant, *Alyssum saxatile*, with many small yellow flowers.

gold•en /góldən/ *adj.* **1 a** made of or consisting of gold (*golden coin*). **b** yielding gold. **2** colored or shining like gold (*golden hair*). **3** precious; valuable; excellent; important (*a golden memory; a golden opportunity*). □□ **gold•en•ly** *adv.* **gold•en•ness** *n.*

gold•en age *n.* **1** a supposed past age when people were happy and innocent. **2** the period of a nation's greatest prosperity, literary merit, etc.

gold•en-ag•er *n.* an old person.

gold•en boy *n.* (also **gold•en girl**) *colloq.* a popular or successful person.

gold•en calf *n.* wealth as an object of worship, from a biblical reference in Exod. 32.

gold•en chain *n.* the laburnum.

Gold•en De•li•cious *n.* a variety of apple.

gold•en ea•gle *n.* a large eagle, *Aquila chrysaetos*, with yellow-tipped head feathers.

gold•en•eye /góldəní/ *n.* any marine duck of the genus *Bucephala*.

Gold•en Fleece *n.* (in Greek mythology) a fleece of gold sought and won by Jason.

gold•en goose *n.* a continuing source of wealth or profit that may be exhausted if misused (from a reference to one of Aesop's fables).

gold•en ham•ster *n.* a usu. tawny hamster, *Mesocricetus auratus*, kept as a pet or laboratory animal.

gold•en hand•shake *n.* *colloq.* a payment given to someone who is laid off from work or retires early.

Gold•en Horde *n.* the Tartar horde that overran E. Europe in the 13th c. (from the richness of the leader's tent).

Gold•en Horn *n.* the harbor of Istanbul.

gold•en ju•bi•lee *n.* **1** the fiftieth anniversary of a sovereign's accession. **2** any other fiftieth anniversary.

gold•en mean *n.* **1** the principle of moderation, as opposed to excess. **2** = GOLDEN SECTION.

gold•en old•ie *n.* *colloq.* an old hit record or movie, etc., that is still well known and popular.

gold•en o•ri•ole *n.* a European oriole, *Oriolus oriolus*, of which the

male has yellow and black plumage and the female has mainly green plumage.

gold•en par•a•chute *n.* an executive's contract that provides substantial severance pay, etc., in the event of job loss following the company's being sold or merged with another.

gold•en perch *n.* *Austral.* = CALLOP.

gold•en re•triev•er *n.* a retriever with a thick, golden-colored coat.

gold•en•rod /góldənrod/ *n.* any plant of the genus *Solidago* with a rodlike stem and small bright yellow flowerheads.

gold•en rule *n.* a basic principle of action, esp. "do unto others as you would have them do unto you."

gold•en sec•tion *n.* the division of a line so that the whole is to the greater part as that part is to the smaller part.

gold•en share *n.* the controlling interest in a company, esp. as retained by government after a nationalized industry is privatized.

gold•en State *n.* California.

gold•en syr•up *n.* *Brit.* a pale treacle.

gold•en wed•ding *n.* the fiftieth anniversary of a wedding.

gold field *n.* a district in which gold is found as a mineral.

gold•finch /góldfinch/ *n.* any of various brightly colored songbirds of the genus *Carduelis*, esp. the Eurasian *C. carduelis* and the N. American *c. tristis*. [OE *goldfinc* (as GOLD, FINCH)]

gold•fish /góldfish/ *n.* a small reddish golden Chinese carp kept for ornament, *Carassius auratus*.

gold•fish bowl *n.* **1** a globular glass container for goldfish. **2** a situation lacking privacy.

gold foil *n.* gold beaten into a thin sheet.

gold•i•locks /góldeeloks/ *n.* **1** a person with golden hair. **2 a** a kind of buttercup, *Ranunculus auricomus*. **b** a composite plant, *Aster linosyris*, like the goldenrod. [*goldy* f. GOLD + LOCK²]

gold leaf *n.* gold beaten into a very thin sheet, used in gilding.

gold med•al *n.* a medal of gold, usu. awarded as first prize.

gold mine *n.* **1** a place where gold is mined. **2** *colloq.* a source of wealth, valuable information, or resources (*this book is a gold mine of information*).

gold of pleas•ure *n.* an annual European yellow-flowered plant, *Camelina sativa*.

gold plate *n.* **1** a thin layer of gold, electroplated or otherwise applied as a coating to another metal. **2** objects coated with gold, esp. plates, dishes, etc.

gold-plate *v.tr.* cover (something) with a thin layer of gold.

gold re•serve *n.* a reserve of gold coins or bullion held by a central bank, government, etc., to support the issue of currency.

gold rush *n.* a rush of people to a newly discovered gold field, such as to California in 1848-49.

gold•smith /góldsmith/ *n.* a worker in gold; a manufacturer of gold articles. [OE (as GOLD, SMITH)]

gold stand•ard *n.* a system by which the value of a currency is defined in terms of gold, for which the currency may be exchanged.

Gold Stick *n.* **1** (in the UK) a gilt rod carried on state occasions by the colonel of the Life Guards or the captain of the gentlemen-at-arms. **2** the officer carrying this rod.

gold thread *n.* **1** a thread of silk, etc., with gold wire wound around it. **2** a bitter plant, *Coptis tinfolia*.

go•lem /gōləm/ *n.* **1** a clay figure supposedly brought to life in Jewish legend. **2** an automaton; a robot. [Yiddish *goylem* f. Heb. *gōlem* shapeless mass]

golf /golf, gawlf/ *n. & v.* ● *n.* a game played on a course set in open country, in which a small hard ball is driven with clubs into a series of 18 or 9 holes with the fewest possible strokes. ● *v.intr.* play golf. [15th-c. Sc.: orig. unkn.]

golf bag *n.* a bag used for carrying gold clubs and balls.

golf ball *n.* **1** a small hard ball used in golf. **2** *colloq.* a small ball used in some electric typewriters to carry the type.

golf cart *n.* **1** a cart used for carrying golf clubs. **2** a motorized cart for one or two golfers and their equipment.

golf club *n.* **1** a club used to hit the ball in golf, with a heavy wooden or metal head on a slender shaft. **2** an association of members for playing golf. **3** the premises used by a such an association.

golf course *n.* (also **golf links**) a large expanse of land on which golf is played.

golf•er /gólfər/ *n.* **1** a golf player. **2** *Brit.* a cardigan.

Gol•gi bod•y /gáwljee/ *n.* (also **Gol•gi ap•pa•ra•tus**) *Biol.* an organelle of vesicles and folded membranes within the cytoplasm of most eukaryotic cells, involved esp. in the secretion of substances. [C. Golgi, It. cytologist d. 1926]

Go•li•ath bee•tle /gəlíəth/ *n.* any large beetle of the genus *Goliathus*, esp. *G. giganteus* native to Africa. [LL f. Heb. *golya* giant slain by David (1 Sam. 17)]

gol•li•wog /góleewog/ *n.* (also **gol•li•wogg**) **1** a black-faced brightly dressed soft doll with fuzzy hair. **2** a grotesque person. [19th c.: perh. f. GOLLY¹ + POLLIWOG]

gol•lop /góləp/ *v. & n.* *colloq.* ● *v.tr.* (**gol•loped, gol•lop•ing**) swallow hastily or greedily. ● *n.* a hasty gulp. [perh. f. GULP, infl. by GOBBLE¹]

gol•ly¹ /gólee/ *int.* expressing surprise. [euphem. for GOD]

gol•ly² /gólee/ *n.* (*pl.* **•lies**) *colloq.* = GOLLIWOG. [abbr.]

gom·been /gombeˊen/ n. Ir. usury. [Ir. *gaimbín* perh. f. the same OCelt. source as med.L *cambire* CHANGE]

gom·been-man n. a moneylender.

-gon /gon; gən/ comb. form forming nouns denoting plane figures with a specified number of angles (*hexagon*; *polygon*). [Gk *-gōnos* -angled]

go·nad /gónad/ n. an animal organ producing gametes, e.g., the testis or ovary. □□ **go·nad·al** /-náďl/ adj. [mod.L *gonas gonad-* f. Gk *gonē*, *gonos* generation, seed]

go·nad·o·troph·ic hor·mone /gōnádətrófik, -trófik/ n. (also **go·nad·o·trop·ic hor·mone** /-trópik, -trópik/) Biochem. any of various hormones stimulating the activity of the gonads.

go·nad·o·tro·phin /gōnádətrófin, -trófin/ n. (also **go·nad·o·tro·pin**) = GONADOTROPHIC HORMONE.

gon·do·la /góndələ, gondóˊlə/ n. 1 a light flat-bottomed boat used on Venetian canals, with a central cabin and a high point at each end, worked by one oar at the stern. 2 a car suspended from an airship or balloon. 3 an island of shelves used to display goods in a supermarket. 4 (also **gon·do·la car**) a flat-bottomed open railroad freight car. 5 a car attached to a ski lift. [Venetian It., of obscure orig.]

gondola 1

gon·do·lier /góndəleeˊr/ n. the oarsman on a gondola. [F f. It. *gondoliere* (as GONDOLA)]

gone /gawn, gon/ adj. 1 a lost; hopeless. b dead. 2 colloq. pregnant for a specified time (*already three months gone*). 3 sl. completely enthralled or entranced, esp. by rhythmic music, drugs, etc. 4 Brit. (of time) past (*not until gone nine*). □ **all gone** consumed; finished; used up. **be gone** depart; leave temporarily (cf. BEGONE). **gone goose** (or **gosling**) colloq. a person or thing beyond hope. **gone on** sl. infatuated with. [past part. of GO¹]

gon·er /gáwnər, gón-/ n. sl. a person or thing that is doomed, ended, irrevocably lost, etc.; a dead person.

gon·fa·lon /gónfələn/ n. 1 a banner, often with streamers, hung from a crossbar. 2 hist. such a banner as the standard of some Italian republics. □□ **gon·fa·lon·ier** /gónfələneeˊr/ n. [It. *gonfalone* f. Gmc (cf. VANE)]

gong /gawng, gong/ n. & v. ● n. 1 a metal disk with a turned rim, giving a resonant note when struck. 2 a saucer-shaped bell. 3 Brit. sl. a medal; a decoration. ● v.tr. 1 summon with a gong. 2 (of traffic police in the UK) sound a gong, etc., to direct (a motorist) to stop. [Malay *gong*, *gung* of imit. orig.]

go·ni·om·e·ter /gōneeómitər/ n. an instrument for measuring angles. □□ **go·ni·om·e·try** n. **go·ni·o·met·ric** /-neeəmétrik/ adj. **go·ni·o·met·ri·cal** adj. [F *goniomètre* f. Gk *gōnia* angle]

gon·o·coc·cus /gónəkókəs/ n. (pl. **gon·o·coc·ci** /-kókī, -kóksī/) a bacterium causing gonorrhea. □□ **gon·o·coc·cal** adj. [Gk *gonos* generation, semen + COCCUS]

gon·or·rhe·a /gónəreeˊə/ n. (Brit. **gon·or·rhoe·a**) a venereal disease with inflammatory discharge from the urethra or vagina. □□ **gon·or·rhe·al** adj. [LL f. Gk *gonorrhoia* f. *gonos* semen + *rhoia* flux]

goo /goo/ n. 1 a sticky or viscous substance. 2 sickly sentiment. [20th c.: perh. f. *burgoo* (Naut. sl.) = porridge]

good /good/ adj., n., & adv. ● adj. (**bet·ter**, **best**) 1 having the right or desired qualities; satisfactory; adequate. 2 a (of a person) efficient; competent (*good at math*; *a good driver*). b (of a thing) reliable; efficient (*good brakes*). c (of health, etc.) strong (*good eyesight*). 3 a kind; benevolent (*good of you to come*). b morally excellent; virtuous (*a good deed*). c charitable (*good works*). d well-behaved (*a good child*). 4 enjoyable, agreeable (*a good party*). 5 thorough; considerable (*gave it a good wash*). 6 a not less than (*waited a good hour*). b considerable in number, quality, etc. (*a good many people*). 7 healthy; beneficial (*milk is good for you*). 8 a valid; sound (*a good reason*). b financially sound (*his credit is good*). 9 in exclamations of surprise (*good heavens!*). 10 right; proper; expedient (*thought it good to have a try*). 11 fresh; eatable; untainted (*is the meat still good?*). 12 (sometimes patronizing) commendable; worthy (*good old George*; *good men and true*; *my good man*). 13 well shaped; attractive (*has good legs*; *good looks*). 14 in courteous greetings and farewells (*good afternoon*). 15 promising or favorable (*a good omen*; *good news*). 16 expressing approval; complimentary (*a good review*). ● n. 1 (only in *sing.*) that which is good; what is beneficial or morally right (*only good can come of it*; *did it for your own good*; *what good will it do?*). 2 (only in *sing.*) a desirable end or object; a thing worth attaining (*sacrificing the present for a future good*). 3 (in *pl.*) a movable property or merchandise. b Brit. things to be transported, as distinct from passengers; freight. c (prec. by *the*) colloq. what one has

---

419   **gombeen ~ goodness**

undertaken to supply (esp. deliver the goods). **d** (prec. by *the*) sl. the real thing; the genuine article. **4** proof, esp. of guilt. **5** (as *pl.*; prec. by *the*) virtuous people. ● adv. colloq. well (*doing pretty good*). □ **as good as** practically (*he as good as told me*). **be so good as** (or **be good enough) to** (often in a request) be kind and do (a favor) (*be so good as to open the window*). **be (a certain amount) to the good** have as net profit or advantage. **do good** show kindness; act philanthropically. **do a person good** be beneficial to. **for good (and all)** finally; permanently. **good and** colloq. used as an intensifier before an adj. or adv. (*raining good and hard*; *was good and angry*). **good for 1** beneficial to; having a good effect on. **2** able to perform; inclined for (*good for a ten-mile walk*). **3** able to be trusted to pay (*is good for $100*). **good for you!** (or **him!**, **her!**, etc.) exclamation of approval toward a person. **good on you!** (or **him!**, etc.) *Austral., NZ, & Brit.* = *good for you!* **have a good mind** see MIND. **have the goods on a person** sl. have advantageous information about a person. **have a good time** enjoy oneself. **in a person's good books** see BOOK. **in good faith** with honest or sincere intentions. **in good time 1** with no risk of being late. **2** (also **all in good time**) in due course but without haste. **make good 1** make up for; compensate for; pay (an expense). **2** fulfill (a promise); effect (a purpose or an intended action). **3** demonstrate the truth of (a statement); substantiate (a charge). **4** gain and hold (a position). **5** replace or restore (a thing lost or damaged). **6** (*absol.*) accomplish what one intended. **no good 1** mischief (*is up to no good*). **2** useless; to no advantage (*it is no good arguing*). **take in good part** not be offended by. **to the good** having as profit or benefit. □□ **good·ish** adj. [OE *gōd* f. Gmc]

▶The adverb corresponding to the adjective **good** is **well**: *she is a good swimmer who performs well in meets*. Confusion sometimes arises because **well** is also an adjective meaning 'healthy' or 'fine,' and **good** is widely accepted as an informal substitute: *I feel well* (vs. informal "I feel good"). See note at BAD.

Good Book n. the Bible.

good-bye /goodbíˊ/ int. & n. (also **good·bye**, **good-by** or **goodby**) ● int. expressing good wishes on parting, ending a telephone conversation, etc., or said with reference to a thing gotten rid of or irrevocably lost. ● n. (pl. **good-byes**) the saying of "good-bye"; a parting; a farewell. [contr. of *God be with you!* with *good* substituted after *good night*, etc.]

good faith n. honesty or sincerity of intention.

good form n. 1 what complies with current social conventions (*it wasn't good form to show too much enthusiasm*). 2 in a state of good health or training.

good-for-noth·ing adj. & n. ● adj. worthless; useless. ● n. a worthless person.

Good Fri·day n. (in the Christian calender) the Friday before Easter commemorating the crucifixion of Christ.

good-heart·ed n. kindly; well-meaning.

good hu·mor n. a genial mood.

good-hu·mored /goodhyooˊmərd/ adj. genial; cheerful; amiable. □□ **good-hu·mored·ly** adv.

good-look·er n. a handsome or attractive person.

good-look·ing adj. handsome; attractive.

good luck n. 1 good fortune; happy chance. 2 an exclamation of well-wishing.

good·ly /goodlee/ adj. (**good·li·er**, **good·li·est**) 1 comely; handsome. 2 of imposing size, etc. □□ **good·li·ness** n. [OE *gōdlic* (as GOOD, -LY¹)]

good·man /goodmən/ n. (pl. **-men**) archaic the head of a household.

good mon·ey n. 1 genuine money; money that might usefully have been spent elsewhere. 2 colloq. high wages.

good na·ture n. a friendly disposition.

good-na·tured /goodnáychərd/ adj. kind; patient; easygoing. □□ **good-na·tured·ly** adv.

good·ness /goodnis/ n. & int. ● n. 1 virtue; excellence, esp. moral. 2 kindness; generosity (*had the goodness to wait*). 3 what is good or beneficial in a thing (*vegetables with all the goodness boiled out*). ● int. (as a substitution for "God") expressing surprise, anger, etc. (*goodness me!*; *goodness knows*; *for goodness' sake!*). [OE *gōdnes* (as GOOD, -NESS)]

SYNONYM TIP goodness

MORALITY, PROBITY, RECTITUDE, VIRTUE. Of all these words denoting moral excellence, **goodness** is the broadest in meaning. It describes an excellence so well established that it is thought of as inherent or innate and is associated with kindness, generosity, helpfulness, and sincerity (*she has more goodness in her little finger than most people have in their whole body*). **Morality**, on the other hand, is moral excellence based on a code of ethical conduct or religious teaching (*his behavior was kept in line by fear of punishment rather than morality*). Although it is often used as a synonym for

See page xx for the **Key to Pronunciation**.

goodness, **virtue** suggests moral excellence that is acquired rather than innate and that is consciously or steadfastly maintained, often in spite of temptations or evil influences (*her virtue was as unassailable as her noble character*). **Rectitude** is used to describe strict adherence to the rules of just or right behavior and carries strong connotations of sternness and self-discipline (*he had a reputation for rectitude and insisted on absolute truthfulness*). **Probity** describes an honesty or integrity that has been tried and proved (*as mayor, she displayed a probity that was rare in a politician*).

goods and chat·tels *n.pl. Law* all kinds of personal possessions..

Good Shep·herd *n.* Jesus Christ, according to John 10:11-14.

good-tem·pered /go͝odtémpərd/ *adj.* having a good temper; not easily annoyed. □□ **good-tem·pered·ly** *adv.*

good times *n.pl.* a period of prosperity, happiness, or success.

good·wife /go͝odwīf/ *n.* (*pl.* **-wives**) *archaic* the mistress of a household.

good·will /go͝odwíl/ *n.* **1** kindly feeling. **2** the established reputation of a business, etc., as enhancing its value. **3** cheerful consent or acquiescence; readiness; zeal.

goodwill *n.* friendly, helpful, or cooperative feelings or attitude (*the plan is dependent on goodwill between the two sides*).

good word *n.* (often in phr. **put in a good word for**) words in recommendation or defense of a person.

good·y[1] /go͝odee/ *n. & int.* ● *n.* (also **good·ie**) (*pl.* **-ies**) **1** (usu. in *pl.*) something good or attractive, esp. to eat. **2** *colloq.* a good or favored person, esp. a hero in a story, movie, etc. **3** = GOODY-GOODY *N.* ● *int.* expressing childish delight.

good·y[2] /go͝odee/ *n.* (*pl.* **good·ies**) *archaic* (often as a title prefixed to a surname) an elderly woman of humble station (*Goody Blake*). [for GOODWIFE: cf. HUSSY]

good·y-good·y *n. & adj.* ● *n.* a smug or obtrusively virtuous person. ● *adj.* obtrusively or smugly virtuous.

goo·ey /go͝o-ee/ *adj.* (**goo·i·er, goo·i·est**) *sl.* **1** viscous; sticky. **2** sickly; sentimental. □□ **goo·ey·ness** *n.* (also **goo·i·ness**). [GOO + -Y[2]]

goof /go͝of/ *n. & v. sl.* ● *n.* **1** a foolish or stupid person. **2** a mistake. ● *v.* **1** *tr.* bungle; mess up. **2** *intr.* blunder; make a mistake. **3** *intr.* (often foll. by *off*) idle. **4** *tr.* (as **goofed** *adj.*) stupefied with drugs. [var. of dial. *goff* f. F *goffe* f. It. *goffo* f. med.L *gufus* coarse]

goof·ball /go͝ofbawl/ *n. sl.* **1** a pill containing a barbiturate or a tranquilizer. **2** a silly, ridiculous, or inept person.

goof·y /go͝ofee/ *adj.* (**goof·i·er, goof·i·est**) *sl.* **1** stupid; silly. **2** *Brit.* having protruding or crooked front teeth. □□ **goof·i·ly** *adv.* **goof·i·ness** *n.*

goog /go͝og/ *n. Austral. sl.* an egg. □ **full as a goog** very drunk. [20th c.: orig. unkn.]

goo·gly /go͝oglee/ *n.* (*pl.* **-glies**) *Cricket* an off-break ball bowled with apparent leg-break action. [20th c.: orig. unkn.]

goo·gol /go͝ogawl/ *n.* ten raised to the hundredth power (10^{100}). [arbitrary formation]

▶This word is not used in formal contexts.

gook /go͝ok, go͝ok/ *n. sl. offens.* a foreigner, esp. a person from E. Asia. [20th c.: orig. unkn.]

gool·ie /go͝olee/ *n.* (also **gool·y**) (*pl.* **-ies**) **1** (usu. in *pl.*) *Brit. sl.* a testicle. **2** *Austral. sl.* a stone or pebble. [app. of Ind. orig.; cf. Hind. *golī* bullet, ball, pill]

goon /go͝on/ *n. sl.* **1** a stupid or playful person. **2** a person hired by racketeers, etc., to terrorize political or industrial opponents. [perh. f. dial. *gooney* booby: infl. by the subhuman cartoon character "Alice the *Goon*"]

goop[1] /go͝op/ *n. sl.* a stupid or fatuous person. [20th c.: cf. GOOF]

goop[2] /go͝op/ *n. colloq.* a viscous substance. [prob. f. GOO]

goop·y[1] /go͝opee/ *adj. Brit. sl.* (**goop·i·er, goop·i·est**) stupid; fatuous. □□ **goop·i·ness** *n.*

goop·y[2] /go͝opee/ *adj. colloq.* thick; viscous.

goos·an·der /go͝osándər/ *n.* a large diving duck, *Mergus merganser*, with a narrow serrated bill; a common merganser. [prob. f. GOOSE + *-ander* in *bergander* sheldrake]

goose /go͝os/ *n. & v.* ● *n.* (*pl.* **geese** /gees/) **1 a** any of various large water birds of the family Anatidae, with short legs, webbed feet, and a broad bill. **b** the female of this (opp. GANDER). **c** the flesh of a goose as food. **2** *colloq.* a simpleton. **3** (*pl.* **goos·es**) a tailor's smoothing iron, having a handle like a goose's neck. ● *v.tr. sl.* poke (a person) between the buttocks. [OE *gōs* f. Gmc]

goose-ber·ry /go͝osberee, –bəree, go͝oz–/ *n.* (*pl.* **-ries**) **1** a round edible yellowish green berry with a thin usu. translucent skin enclosing seeds in a juicy flesh. **2** the thorny shrub, *Ribes grossularia*, bearing this fruit. □ **play gooseberry** *Brit. colloq.* be an unwanted extra (usu. third) person. [perh. f. GOOSE + BERRY]

goose bumps *n.* (also **goose flesh** or **goose pim·ples** or **goose skin**) a bristling state of the skin produced by cold or fright.

goose egg *n.* a zero score in a game.

goose·foot /go͝osfo͝ot/ *n.* (*pl.* **-foots**) any plant of the genus *Chenopodium*, having leaves shaped like the foot of a goose.

goose·gog /go͝ozgog/ *n. Brit. colloq.* a gooseberry. [joc. corrupt.]

goose·grass /go͝osgras/ *n.* cleavers.

goose step *n.* a military marching step in which the legs are not bent, and knees are kept stiff.

GOP *abbr.* Grand Old Party (the Republican Party).

go·pher[1] /gófər/ *n.* **1** (in full **pocket gopher**) any burrowing rodent of the family Geomyidae, native to N. America, having external cheek pouches and sharp front teeth. **2** a N. American ground squirrel. **3** a tortoise, *Gopherus polyphemus*, native to the southern US, that excavates tunnels as shelter from the sun. [18th c.: orig. uncert.]

go·pher[2] /gófər/ *n.* **1** *Bibl.* a tree from the wood of which Noah's ark was made. **2** (in full **gopher wood**) a tree, *Cladrastis lutea*, yielding yellowish timber. [Heb. *gōper*]

go·pher snake *n.* a cribo.

go·ral /gáwrəl/ *n.* a goat antelope, *Nemorhaedus goral*, native to mountainous regions of N. India, having short horns curving to the rear. [native name]

gor·bli·mey /gáwrblīmee/ *int. & n. Brit. sl.* ● *int.* an expression of surprise, indignation, etc. ● *n.* (*pl.* **-meys**) a soft service cap. [corrupt. of *God blind me*]

Gor·di·an knot /gáwrdeeən/ *n.* **1** an intricate knot. **2** a difficult problem or task. □ **cut the Gordian knot** solve a problem by force or by evasion. [*Gordius*, king of Phrygia, who tied an intricate knot that remained tied until cut by Alexander the Great]

gor·do /gáwrdō/ *n. Austral.* a popular variety of grape. [Sp. *gordo blanco* fat white]

Gor·don set·ter /gáwrd'n/ *n.* **1** a setter of a black and tan breed, used as a gun dog. **2** this breed. [4th Duke of *Gordon*, d. 1827, promoter of the breed]

gore[1] /gawr/ *n.* **1** blood shed and clotted. **2** slaughter; carnage. [OE *gor* dung, dirt]

gore[2] /gawr/ *v.tr.* pierce with a horn, tusk, etc. [ME: orig. unkn.]

gore[3] /gawr/ *n. & v.* ● *n.* **1** a wedge-shaped piece in a garment. **2** a triangular or tapering piece in an umbrella, etc. **3** a small often wedge-shaped plot of land, as between larger tracts. ● *v.tr.* shape with a gore. [OE *gāra* triangular piece of land, rel. to OE *gār* spear, a spearhead being triangular]

gorge /gawrj/ *n. & v.* ● *n.* **1** a narrow opening between hills or a rocky ravine, often with a stream running through it. **2** an act of gorging; a feast. **3** the contents of the stomach; what has been swallowed. **4** the neck of a bastion or other outwork; the rear entrance to a work. **5** a mass of ice, etc., blocking a narrow passage. ● *v.* **1** *intr.* feed greedily. **2** *tr.* **a** (often *refl.*) satiate; glut. **b** swallow; devour greedily. □ **one's gorge rises at** one is sickened by. □□ **gorg·er** *n.* [ME f. OF *gorge* throat ult. f. L *gurges* whirlpool]

gore[3] 1

gor·geous /gáwrjəs/ *adj.* **1** richly colored; sumptuous; magnificent. **2** *colloq.* very pleasant; splendid (*gorgeous weather*). **3** *colloq.* strikingly beautiful. □□ **gor·geous·ly** *adv.* **gor·geous·ness** *n.* [earlier *gorgayse, -yas* f. OF *gorgias* fine, elegant, of unkn. orig.]

gor·get /górjit/ *n.* **1** *hist.* **a** a piece of armor for the throat. **b** a woman's wimple. **2** a patch of color on the throat of a bird, insect, etc. [OF *gorgete* (as GORGE)]

gor·gon /gáwrgən/ *n.* **1** (in Greek mythology) each of three snake-haired sisters (esp. Medusa) with the power to turn anyone who looked at them to stone. **2** a frightening or repulsive person, esp. a woman. □□ **gor·go·ni·an** /gawrgóneeən/ *adj.* [L *Gorgo -onis* f. Gk *Gorgō* f. *gorgos* terrible]

gor·go·ni·an /gawrgóneeən/ *n. & adj.* ● *n.* a usu. brightly colored horny coral of the order Gorgonacea, having a treelike skeleton bearing polyps, e.g., a sea fan. ● *adj.* of or relating to the Gorgonacea. [mod.L (as GORGON), with ref. to its petrifaction]

gor·gon·ize /gáwrgənīz/ *v.tr.* **1** stare at like a gorgon. **2** paralyze with terror, fascination.

Gor·gon·zo·la /gáwrgənzólə/ *n.* a type of rich cheese with bluish green veins. [*Gorgonzola* in Italy]

go·ril·la /gərílə/ *n.* the largest anthropoid ape, *Gorilla gorilla*, native to Central Africa, having a large head, short neck, and prominent mouth.

From an alleged African word for a wild or hairy person, found in the Greek account of the voyage of the Carthaginian explorer Hanno in the 5th or 6th century BC; adopted in 1847 as the specific name of the ape.

mountain gorilla

gor·mand·ize /gáwrməndīz/ *v. & n.* ● *v.* **1** *intr. & tr.* eat or devour voraciously.

2 *intr.* indulge in good eating. ● *n.* = GOURMANDISE. □□ **gor·mand·iz·er** *n.* [as GOURMANDISE]

gorm·less /gáwrmlis/ *adj.* esp. *Brit. colloq.* foolish; lacking sense. □□ **gorm·less·ly** *adv.* **gorm·less·ness** *n.* [orig. *gaumless* f. dial. *gaum* understanding]

gorse /gawrs/ *n.* any spiny yellow-flowered shrub of the genus *Ulex*, esp. growing on European wastelands. Also called **furze.** □□ **gors·y** *adj.* [OE *gors(t)* rel. to OHG *gersta*, L *hordeum*, barley]

Gor·sedd /gáwrseth/ *n.* a meeting of Welsh, etc., bards and druids (esp. as a daily preliminary to the eisteddfod). [Welsh, lit. 'throne']

gor·y /gáwree/ *adj.* (**gor·i·er, gor·i·est**) **1** involving bloodshed; bloodthirsty (*a gory film*). **2** covered in gore. □□ **gor·i·ly** *adv.* **gor·i·ness** *n.*

gosh /gosh/ *int.* expressing surprise. [euphem. for GOD]

gos·hawk /gós-hawk/ *n.* a large short-winged hawk, *Accipiter gentilis*. [OE *gōs-hafoc* (as GOOSE, HAWK[1])]

gos·ling /gózling/ *n.* a young goose. [ME, orig. *gesling* f. ON *gǽslin-gr*]

gos·pel /góspəl/ *n.* **1** the teaching or revelation of Christ. **2** (**Gospel**) **a** the record of Christ's life and teaching in the first four books of the New Testament. **b** each of these books. **c** a portion from one of them read at a service. **d** a similar book in the Apocrypha. **3** a thing regarded as absolutely true (*take my word as gospel*). **4** a principle one acts on or advocates. **5** (in full **gospel music**) African-American evangelical religious singing. [OE *gōdspel* (as GOOD, *spel* news, SPELL[1]), rendering eccl.L *bona annuntiatio, bonus nuntius* = *evangelium* EVANGEL: assoc. with GOD]

gos·pel·er /góspələr/ *n.* (also **gos·pel·ler**) the reader of the Gospel in the Mass.

Gos·pel side *n.* the north side of the altar in a church, at which the Gospel is read.

gos·pel truth *n.* something considered to be unquestionably true.

gos·sa·mer /gósəmər/ *n. & adj.* ● *n.* **1** a filmy substance of small spiders' webs. **2** delicate filmy material. **3** a thread of gossamer. ● *adj.* light and flimsy as gossamer. □□ **gos·sa·mered** *adj.* **gos·sa·mer·y** *adj.* [ME *gos(e)somer(e)*, app. f. GOOSE + SUMMER[1] (*goose summer* = St Martin's summer, i.e. early November when geese were eaten, gossamer being common then)]

gos·sip /gósip/ *n. & v.* ● *n.* **1 a** easy or unconstrained talk or writing esp. about persons or social incidents. **b** idle talk; groundless rumor. **2** an informal chat, esp. about persons or social incidents. **3** a person who indulges in gossip. ● *v.intr.* (**gos·siped, gos·sip·ing**) talk or write gossip. □□ **gos·sip·er** *n.* **gos·sip·y** *adj.* [earlier sense 'godparent': f. OE *godsibb* person related to one in GOD: see SIB]

gos·sip col·umn *n.* a section of a newspaper devoted to gossip about well-known people. □□ **gos·sip col·um·nist** *n.*

gos·sip·mon·ger /gósipmongər/ *n.* a perpetrator of gossip.

gos·soon /gosóōn/ *n. Ir.* a lad. [earlier *garsoon* f. F *garçon* boy]

got *past and past part.* of GET.

Goth /goth/ *n.* **1** a member of a Germanic tribe that invaded the Roman Empire in the 3rd–5th c. **2** an uncivilized or ignorant person. [LL *Gothi* (pl.) f. Gk *Go(t)thoi* f. Goth.]

goth /goth/ *n. Brit.* **1** a style of rock music with an intense or droning blend of guitars, bass, and drums, often with apocalyptic or mystical lyrics. **2** a performer or devotee of this music, often dressing in black clothing and wearing black make-up.

Goth·ic /góthik/ *adj. & n.* ● *adj.* **1** of the Goths or their language. **2** in the style of architecture prevalent in W. Europe in the 12th–16th c., characterized by pointed arches. **3** (of a novel, etc.) in a style popular in the 18th–19th c., with supernatural or horrifying events. **4** barbarous; uncouth. **5** *Printing* (of type) old-fashioned German, black letter, or sans serif. ● *n.* **1** the Gothic language. **2** Gothic architecture. **3** *Printing* Gothic type. □□ **Goth·i·cal·ly** *adv.* **Goth·i·cism** /–thisizəm/ *n.* **Goth·i·cize** /–thisīz/ *v.tr. & intr.* [F *gothique* or LL *gothicus* f. *Gothi*: see GOTH]

go-to-meet·ing *adj.* (also **Sun·day-go-to-meet·ing**) (of a hat, clothes, etc.) suitable for going to church in.

got·ta /gótə/ *colloq.* have got to (*we gotta go*). [corrupt.]

got·ten *past part.* of GET.

Göt·ter·däm·mer·ung /gótərdámərung, gótərdémərōong/ *n.* **1** the twilight (i.e., downfall) of the gods. **2** the complete downfall of a regime, etc. [G, esp. as the title of an opera by Wagner]

gouache /gwaash, gōō-aásh/ *n.* **1** a method of painting in opaque pigments ground in water and thickened with a gluelike substance. **2** these pigments. **3** a picture painted in this way. [F f. It. *guazzo*]

Gou·da /gōōdə, gów–/ *n.* a flat round usu. Dutch cheese with a yellow rind. [*Gouda* in Holland, where orig. made]

gouge /gowj/ *n. & v.* ● *n.* **1 a** a chisel with a concave blade, used in woodworking, sculpture, and surgery. **b** an indentation or groove made with or as with this. **2** *colloq.* a swindle. ● *v.* **1** *tr.* cut with or as with a gouge. **2** *tr.* **a** (foll. by *out*)

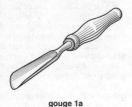

gouge 1a

---

force out (esp. an eye with the thumb) with or as with a gouge. **b** force out the eye of (a person). **3** *tr. colloq.* swindle; extort money from. **4** *intr. Austral.* dig for opal. □□ **goug·er** *n.* [F f. LL *gubia*, perh. of Celt. orig.]

gou·lash /gōōlaash, –lash/ *n.* **1** a highly seasoned Hungarian dish of meat and vegetables, usu. flavored with paprika. **2** (in contract bridge) a re-deal, several cards at a time, of the four hands (unshuffled, but with each hand arranged in suits and order of value) when no player has bid. [Magyar *gulyás-hús* f. *gulyás* herdsman + *hús* meat]

gou·ra·mi /gōōraámee, gōōrəmee/ *n.* **1 a** a large freshwater fish, *Osphronemus goramy*, native to SE Asia, used as food. **b** any small fish of the family Osphronemidae, usu. kept in aquariums. **2** any small brightly colored freshwater fish of the family Belontiidae, usu. kept in aquariums. Also called **labyrinth fish.** [Malay *gurámi*]

gourd /gōrd/ *n.* **1 a** any of various fleshy usu. large fruits with a hard skin, often used as containers, ornaments, etc. **b** any of various climbing or trailing plants of the family Cucurbitaceae bearing this fruit. Also called **cucurbit. 2** the hollow hard skin of the gourd fruit, dried and used as a drinking vessel, water container, etc. □□ **gourd·ful** *n.* (*pl.* **·fuls**). [ME f. AF *gurde*, OF *gourde* ult. f. L *cucurbita*]

gour·mand /gōōrmaánd/ *n. & adj.* ● *n.* **1** a glutton. **2** *disp.* a gourmet. ● *adj.* gluttonous; fond of eating, esp. to excess. □□ **gour·mand·ism** *n.* [ME f. OF, of unkn. orig.]

gour·man·dise /gōōrmoNdéez/ *n.* the habits of a gourmand; gluttony. [F (as GOURMAND)]

gour·met /gōōrmáy/ *n.* a connoisseur of good or delicate food. [F, = wine taster: sense infl. by GOURMAND]

gout /gowt/ *n.* **1** a disease with inflammation of the smaller joints, esp. the toe, as a result of excess uric acid salts in the blood. **2** *archaic* **a** a drop, esp. of blood. **b** a splash or spot. □□ **gout·y** *adj.* **gout·i·ly** *adv.* **gout·i·ness** *n.* [ME f. OF *goute* f. L *gutta* drop, with ref. to the medieval theory of the flowing down of humors]

Gov. *abbr.* **1** Government. **2** Governor.

gov. *abbr.* governor.

gov·ern /gúvərn/ *v.* **1 a** *tr.* rule or control (a nation, subject, etc.) with authority; conduct the policy and affairs of (an organization, etc.). **b** *intr.* be in government. **2 a** *tr.* influence or determine (a person or a course of action). **b** *intr.* be the predominating influence. **3** *tr.* be a standard or principle for; constitute a law for; serve to decide (a case). **4** *tr.* check or control (esp. passions and machinery). **5** *tr. Gram.* (esp. of a verb or preposition) have (a noun or pronoun or its case) depending on it. **6** *tr.* be in military command of (a fort, town). □□ **gov·ern·a·ble** *adj.* **gov·ern·a·bil·i·ty** *n.* **gov·ern·a·ble·ness** *n.* [ME f. OF *governer* f. L *gubernare* steer, rule f. Gk *kubernaō*]

gov·ern·ance /gúvərnəns/ *n.* **1** the act or manner of governing. **2** the office or function of governing. **3** sway; control. [ME f. OF (as GOVERN)]

gov·ern·ess /gúvərnis/ *n.* a woman employed to teach children in a private household. [earlier *governeress* f. OF *governeresse* (as GOVERNOR)]

gov·er·ness·y /gúvərnisee/ *adj.* characteristic of a governess; prim.

gov·ern·ing bod·y *n.* the managers of an institution.

gov·ern·ment /gúvə rnmənt/ *n.* **1** the act or manner of governing. **2** the system by which a nation or community is governed. **3 a** a body of persons governing a nation. **b** (usu. **Government**) a particular party or group of people in office. **4** the nation as an agent. **5** *Gram.* the relation between a governed and a governing word. □□ **gov·ern·men·tal** /–mént'l/ *adj.* **gov·ern·men·tal·ly** *adv.* [ME f. OF *governement* (as GOVERN)]

PRONUNCIATION TIP government

In informal English, there is a tendency not to pronounce the first *n* in this word, and some speakers skip the middle of the word altogether ("GUV-mint" or "GUM-mint"). But in careful speech it is best to say "GUV-urn-mint."

Gov·ern·ment House *n.* (in certain countries) the official residence of a governor.

gov·ern·ment is·sue *n.* (of equipment) provided by the government.

gov·ern·ment sur·plus *n.* unused equipment sold by the government.

gov·er·nor /gúvərnər/ *n.* **1** a person who governs; a ruler. **2** the executive head of each state of the US. **3 a** *hist.* an official governing a province, town, etc. **b** *Brit.* a representative of the British crown in a colony. **4** an officer commanding a fortress or garrison. **5** the head or a member of a governing body of an institution. **6** *Brit.* the official in charge of a prison. **7** *Brit.* **a** *sl.* one's employer. **b** *sl.* one's father. **c** *colloq.* (as a form of address) sir. **8** *Mech.* an automatic regulator controlling the speed of an engine, etc. □□ **gov•er•nor•ate** /-rət, -rayt/ *n.* **gov•er•nor•ship** *n.* [ME f. AF *gouvernour*, OF *gov-erneo(u)r* f. L *gubernator –oris* (as GOVERN)]

Gov•er•nor Gen•er•al *n.* **1** a high-ranking governor of a territory who presides over deputy governors. **2** the representative of the British crown in a Commonwealth country that regards the sovereign as head of state.

Govt. *abbr.* Government.

gow•an /gówən/ *n. Sc.* **1** a daisy. **2** any white or yellow field flower. [prob. var. of dial. *gollan* ranunculus, etc., and rel. to *gold* in *marigold*]

gowk /gowk/ *n. Brit. dial.* **1** a cuckoo. **2** an awkward or halfwitted person; a fool. [ME f. ON *gaukr* f. Gmc]

gown /gown/ *n. & v.* ● *n.* **1** a loose flowing garment, esp. a long dress worn by a woman. **2** the official robe of an alderman, judge, cleric, member of a university, etc. **3** a surgeon's robe, worn during surgery. **4** the members of a university as distinct from the permanent residents of the university town (cf. TOWN). ● *v.tr.* (usu. as **gowned** *adj.*) attire in a gown. [ME f. OF *goune, gon(n)e* f. LL *gunna* fur garment: cf. med. Gk *gouna* fur]

goy /goy/ *n.* (*pl.* **goy•im** /góyim/ or **goys**) *sl.* sometimes *derog.* a Jewish name for a non-Jew. □□ **goy•ish** *adj.* (also **goy•isch**). [Heb. *gōy* people, nation]

GP *abbr.* **1** general practitioner. **2** Grand Prix.

GPA *abbr.* grade point average.

GPO *abbr.* **1** General Post Office. **2** Government Printing Office.

gr *abbr.* (also **gr.**) **1** gram(s). **2** grain(s). **3** gross. **4** gray.

Graaf•i•an fol•li•cle /gráafeeən, gráf-/ *n.* a follicle in the mammalian ovary in which an ovum develops prior to ovulation. [R. de *Graaf*, Du. anatomist d. 1673]

grab /grab/ *v. & n.* ● *v.* (**grabbed, grab•bing**) **1** *tr.* **a** seize suddenly. **b** capture; arrest. **2** *tr.* take greedily or unfairly. **3** *tr. sl.* attract the attention of; impress. **4** *intr.* (foll. by *at*) make a sudden snatch at. **5** *intr.* (of the brakes of a motor vehicle) act harshly or jerkily. ● *n.* **1** a sudden clutch or attempt to seize. **2** a mechanical device for clutching. **3** the practice of grabbing; rapacious proceedings, esp. in politics and commerce. **4** a children's card game in which certain cards may be snatched from the table. □ **up for grabs** *sl.* easily obtainable; inviting capture. □□ **grab•ber** *n.* [MLG, MDu. *grabben*: cf. GRIP, GRIPE, GROPE]

grab bag *n.* **1** a container from which one removes a mystery gift, as at a party. **2** a miscellaneous group of items.

grab bar *n.* (also **grab han•dle, grab rail,** etc.) a bar, handle or rail, etc., for aid in balance, as in a moving vehicle or a bathtub, etc.

grab•ble /grábəl/ *v.intr.* **1** grope about; feel for something. **2** (often foll. by *for*) sprawl on all fours; scramble (for something). [Du. & LG *grabbeln* scramble for a thing (as GRAB)]

grab•by /grábee/ *adj. colloq.* tending to grab; greedy; grasping.

gra•ben /gráabən/ *n.* (*pl.* same or **gra•bens**) *Geol.* a depression of the earth's surface between faults. [G, orig. = ditch]

grace /grays/ *n. & v.* ● *n.* **1** attractiveness, esp. in elegance of proportion or manner or movement; gracefulness. **2** courteous good will (*had the grace to apologize*). **3** an attractive feature; an accomplishment (*social graces*). **4 a** (in Christian belief) the unmerited favor of God; a divine saving and strengthening influence. **b** the state of receiving this. **c** a divinely given talent. **5** goodwill; favor (*fall from grace*). **6** delay granted as a favor (*a year's grace*). **7** a short thanksgiving before or after a meal. **8** (**Grace**) (in Greek mythology) each of three beautiful sister goddesses, bestowers of beauty and charm. **9** (**Grace**) (prec. by *His, Her, Your*) forms of description or address for a duke, duchess, or archbishop. ● *v.tr.* **1** lend or add grace to; enhance or embellish. **2** (often foll. by *with*) confer honor or dignity on (*graced us with his presence*). □ **in a person's good** (or **bad**) **graces** regarded by a person with favor (or disfavor). **with good** (or **bad**) **grace** as if willingly (or reluctantly). [ME f. OF f. L *gratia* f. *gratus* pleasing: cf. GRATEFUL]

grace-and-fa•vor *adj. Brit.* denoting a house or other accommodations owned by a sovereign or government and occupied by a person by permission of that government.

grace•ful /gráysfool/ *adj.* having or showing grace or elegance. □□ **grace•ful•ly** *adv.* **grace•ful•ness** *n.*

grace•less /gráyslis/ *adj.* lacking grace or elegance or charm. □□ **grace•less•ly** *adv.* **grace•less•ness** *n.*

grace note *n. Mus.* an extra note as an embellishment not essential to the harmony or melody.

grace pe•ri•od *n.* the time allowed by law for payment of a debt beyond the due date of the debt.

grac•ile /grásil, -sil/ *adj.* slender; gracefully slender. [L *gracilis* slender]

gra•cil•i•ty /grəsílitee/ *n.* **1** slenderness. **2** (of literary style) unornamented simplicity.

gra•cious /gráyshəs/ *adj. & int.* ● *adj.* **1** kind; indulgent and beneficent to others. **2** (of God) merciful; benign. **3** kindly; courteous.

4 *Brit.* a polite epithet used of royal persons or their acts (*the gracious speech from the throne*). ● *int.* expressing surprise. □□ **gra•ci•os•i•ty** /–sheeósitee/ *n.* **gra•cious•ly** *adv.* **gra•cious•ness** *n.* [ME f. OF f. L *gratiosus* (as GRACE)]

grack•le /grákəl/ *n.* **1** any of various orioles, esp. of the genus *Quiscalus*, native to America, the males of which are shiny black with a blue-green sheen. Also called **blackbird**. **2** any of various mynahs, esp. of the genus *Gracula*, native to Asia. [mod.L *Gracula* f. L *graculus* jackdaw]

grad /grad/ *n. colloq.* = GRADUATE *n.* 1. [abbr.]

gra•date /gráydayt/ *v.* **1** *v.intr. & tr.* pass or cause to pass by gradations from one shade to another. **2** *tr.* arrange in steps or grades of size, etc. [back-form. f. GRADATION]

gra•da•tion /gráydáyshən/ *n.* (usu. in *pl.*) **1** a stage of transition or advance. **2 a** a certain degree in rank, intensity, merit, divergence, etc. **b** such a degree; an arrangement in such degrees. **3** (of paint, etc.) the gradual passing from one shade, tone, etc., to another. **4** *Philol.* ablaut. □□ **gra•da•tion•al** *adj.* **gra•da•tion•al•ly** *adv.* [L *gradatio* f. *gradus* step]

grade /grayd/ *n. & v.* ● *n.* **1 a** a certain degree in rank, merit, proficiency, quality, etc. **b** a class of persons or things of the same grade. **2** a mark indicating the quality of a student's work. **3** a class in school, concerned with a particular year's work and usu. numbered from the first upwards. **4** a gradient or slope. **5 a** the rate of ascent or descent. **5 a** a variety of cattle produced by crossing native stock with a superior breed. **b** a group of animals at a similar level of development. **6** *Philol.* a relative position in a series of forms involving ablaut. ● *v.* **1** *tr.* arrange in or allocate to grades; class; sort. **2** *intr.* (foll. by *up, down, off, into,* etc.) pass gradually between grades, or into a grade. **3** *tr.* give a grade to (a student). **4** *tr.* blend so as to affect the grade of color with tints passing into each other. **5** *tr.* reduce (a road, etc.) to easy gradients. **6** *tr.* (often foll. by *up*) cross (livestock) with a better breed. □ **at grade** on the same level. **make the grade** *colloq.* succeed; reach the desired standard. [F *grade* or L *gradus* step]

grade cross•ing *n.* a crossing of a roadway, etc., with a railroad track at the same level.

grade point *n.* the numerical equivalent of a scholastic letter grade. □ **grade point average** a scholastic average that is obtained by dividing the number of earned grade points by the number of credits taken.

grad•er /gráydər/ *n.* **1** a person or thing that grades. **2** a wheeled machine for leveling the ground, esp. in road-making. **3** (in *comb.*) a pupil of a specified grade in a school (*third grader*).

grade school *n.* elementary school.

gra•di•ent /gráydeeənt/ *n.* **1 a** a stretch of road, railroad, etc., that slopes from the horizontal. **b** the amount of such a slope. **2** the rate of rise or fall of temperature, pressure, etc., in passing from one region to another. [prob. formed on GRADE after *salient*]

gra•din /gráydin/ *n.* (also **gra•dine** /–deen/) **1** each of a series of low steps or a tier of seats. **2** a ledge at the back of an altar. [It. *gradino* dimin. of *grado* GRADE]

grad•u•al /grájʊəl/ *adj. & n.* ● *adj.* **1** taking place or progressing slowly or by degrees. **2** not rapid or steep or abrupt. ● *n. Eccl.* **1** a response sung or recited between the Epistle and Gospel in the Mass. **2** a book of music for the sung Mass. □□ **grad•u•al•ly** *adv.* **grad•u•al•ness** *n.* [med.L *gradualis, –ale* f. L *gradus* step, the noun referring to the altar steps on which the response is sung]

grad•u•al•ism /grájʊəlizəm/ *n.* a policy of gradual reform rather than sudden change or revolution. □□ **grad•u•al•ist** *n.* **grad•u•al•is•tic** *adj.*

grad•u•and /grájʊand/ *n. Brit.* a person about to receive an academic degree. [med.L *graduandus* gerundive of *graduare* GRADUATE]

grad•u•ate *n. & v.* ● *n.* /grájʊət/ **1** a person who has been awarded an academic degree (also *attrib.*: *graduate student*). **2** a person who has completed a course of study. ● *v.* /grájōō-áyt/ **1 a** *intr.* take an academic degree. **b** *tr.* admit to an academic degree or a certificate of completion of school studies. **2** *intr.* **a** (foll. by *from*) be a graduate of a specified university. **b** (foll. by *in*) be a graduate in a specified subject. **3** *tr.* send out as a graduate from a university, etc. **4** *intr.* **a** (foll. by *to*) move up to (a higher grade of activity, etc.). **b** (foll. by *as, in*) gain specified qualifications. **5** *tr.* mark out in degrees or parts. **6** *tr.* arrange in gradations; apportion (e.g., tax) according to a scale. **7** *intr.* (foll. by *into, away*) pass by degrees. □□ **grad•u•a•tor** *n.* [med.L *graduari* take a degree f. L *gradus* step] ▶ The traditional use of the verb *graduate* in sense 1 is "to be graduated from": *she will be graduated from medical school in June.* It is now more common to say "graduate from": *he will graduate from high school next year.* Avoid using *graduate* as a transitive verb, as in *he graduated high school last week.*

grad•u•at•ed pen•sion *n.* (in the UK) a system of pension contributions by employees in proportion to their wages or salary.

grad•u•ate school *n.* a division of a university for advanced work by graduates.

grad•u•a•tion /grájʊáyshən/ *n.* **1** the act or an instance of graduating or being graduated. **2** a ceremony at which degrees are conferred. **3** each or all of the marks on a vessel or instrument indicating degrees of quantity, etc.

Grae•cism var. of GRECISM.
Grae•cize var. of GRECIZE.
Graeco- var. of GRECO-.
Grae•co-Ro•man var. of GRECO-ROMAN.

graf•fi•to /grəféétō/ *n.* (*pl.* **graf•fi•ti** /-tee/) **1** (usu. in *pl.*) a piece of writing or drawing scribbled, scratched, or sprayed on a surface. **2** *Art* a form of decoration made by scratches on wet plaster, showing a different colored underside. [It. f. *graffio* a scratch]
▶The plural form *graffiti* is sometimes used with a singular verb, even though it is not a mass noun in this sense. Language purists would insist on a plural onstruction (*graffiti are an art form*).

graft[1] /graft/ *n. & v.* ● *n.* **1** *Bot.* **a** a shoot or scion inserted into a slit of stock, from which it receives sap. **b** the place where a graft is inserted. **2** *Surgery* a piece of living tissue, organ, etc., transplanted surgically. **3** *Brit. sl.* hard work. ● *v.* **1** *tr.* **a** (often foll. by *into, on, together,* etc.) insert (a scion) as a graft. **b** insert a graft on (a stock). **2** *intr.* insert a graft. **3** *tr. Surgery* transplant (living tissue). **4** *tr.* (foll. by *in, on*) insert or fix (a thing) permanently to another. **5** *intr. Brit. sl.* work hard. □□ **graft•er** *n.* [ME (earlier *graff*) f. OF *grafe, grefe* f. L *graphium* f. Gk *graphion* stylus f. *graphō* write]

graft[2] /graft/ *n. & v. colloq.* ● *n.* **1** practices, esp. bribery, used to secure illicit gains in politics or business. **2** such gains. ● *v.intr.* seek or make such gains. □□ **graft•er** *n.* [19th c.: orig. unkn.]

gra•ham crack•er /gram, gráyəm/ *n.* a crisp, slightly sweet cracker made from whole wheat flour. [after Sylvester *Graham* d. 1851, US dietary reformer]

Grail /grayl/ *n.* (in full **Holy Grail**) **1** (in medieval legend) the cup or platter used by Christ at the Last Supper, and in which Joseph of Arimathea received Christ's blood at the Cross, esp. as the object of quests by medieval knights. **2** any object of a quest. [ME f. OF *graal,* etc., f. med.L *gradalis* dish, of unkn. orig.]

grain /grayn/ *n. & v.* ● *n.* **1** **a** a fruit or seed of a cereal. **2 a** (*collect.*) wheat or any related grass used as food. **b** (*collect.*) their fruit. **c** any particular species of a cereal crop. **3 a** a small hard particle of salt, sand, etc. **b** a discrete particle or crystal, usu. small, in a rock or metal. **c** a piece of solid propellant for use in a rocket engine. **4** the smallest unit of weight in the troy system (equivalent to $1/480$ of an ounce), and in the avoirdupois system (equivalent to $1/437.5$ of an ounce). **5** the smallest possible quantity (*not a grain of truth in it*). **6 a** roughness of surface. **b** *Photog.* a granular appearance on a photograph or negative. **7** the texture of skin, wood, stone, textile, etc.; the arrangement and size of constituent particles. **8 a** a pattern of lines of fiber in wood or paper. **b** lamination or planes of cleavage in stone, coal, etc. **9** nature; temper; tendency. **10 a** *hist.* kermes or cochineal, or dye made from either of these. **b** *poet.* dye; color. ● *v.* **1** *tr.* paint in imitation of the grain of wood or marble. **2** *tr.* give a granular surface to. **3** *tr.* dye in grain. **4** *tr. & intr.* form into grains. **5** *tr.* remove hair from (hides). □ **against the grain** (often in phr. **go against the grain**) contrary to one's natural inclination or feeling. **in grain** thorough; genuine; by nature; downright; indelible. □□ **grained** *adj.* (also in *comb.*). **grain•er** *n.* **grain•less** *adj.* [ME f. OF f. L *granum*]

grain el•e•va•tor *n.* a building in which grain is stored, usu. with mechanical devices for lifting and lowering the grain.

grain leath•er *n.* leather dressed with the grain side out.

grain side *n.* the side of a hide on which the hair was.

grains of Par•a•dise *n.* capsules of a W. African plant (*Aframomum melegueta*), used as a spice and a drug.

grain•y /gráynee/ *adj.* (**grain•i•er, grain•i•est**) **1** granular. **2** resembling the grain of wood. **3** *Photog.* having a granular appearance. □□ **grain•i•ness** *n.*

gral•la•to•ri•al /grálətáwreeəl/ *adj. Zool.* of or relating to long-legged wading birds, e.g., storks, flamingos, etc. [mod.L *grallatorius* f. L *grallator* stilt-walker f. *grallae* stilts]

gram[1] /gram/ *n.* (also *Brit.* **gramme**) a metric unit of mass equal to one-thousandth of a kilogram. [F *gramme* f. Gk *gramma* small weight]

gram[2] /gram/ *n.* any of various beans used as food. [Port. *grão* f. L *granum* grain]

-gram /gram/ *comb. form* forming nouns denoting a thing written or recorded (often in a certain way) (*anagram; epigram; monogram; telegram*). □□ **–grammatic** /grəmátik/ *comb. form* forming adjectives. [from or after Gk *gramma –atos* thing written, letter of the alphabet, f. *graphō* write]

gram at•om *n. Chem.* the quantity of a chemical element equal to its relative atomic mass in grams (see MOLE[4]).

gram e•quiv•a•lent *n. Chem.* the quantity of a substance equal to its equivalent weight in grams.

gram•i•na•ceous /grámináyshəs/ *adj.* = GRAMINEOUS. [L *gramen –inis* grass]

gra•min•e•ous /grəmíneeəs/ *adj.* of or like grass; grassy. [L *gramineus* f. *gramen –inis* grass]

gram•i•niv•o•rous /grámínívərəs/ *adj.* feeding on grass, cereals, etc. [L *gramen –inis* grass + –VOROUS]

gram•ma•logue /grámələwg, –log/ *n.* **1** a word represented by a single shorthand sign. **2** a logogram. [irreg. f. Gk *gramma* letter of the alphabet + *logos* word]

gram•mar /grámər/ *n.* **1 a** the study or rules of a language's inflections or other means of showing the relation between words, including its phonetic system. **b** a body of form and usages in a specified language (*Latin grammar*). **2** a person's manner or quality of observance or application of the rules of grammar (*bad grammar*). **3** a book on grammar. **4** the elements or rudiments of an art or science. **5** *Brit. colloq.* = GRAMMAR SCHOOL. □□ **gram•mar•less** *adj.* [ME f. AF *gramere,* OF *gramaire* f. L *grammata* f. Gk *grammatikē* (*tekhnē*) (art) of letters f. *gramma –atos* letter of the alphabet]

> **SPELLING TIP** grammar
>
> Remember the *-ar* ending of this word with the mnemonic: "Don't *mar* your writing with poor gram*mar*."

gram•mar•i•an /grəmáireeən/ *n.* an expert in grammar or linguistics; a philologist. [ME f. OF *gramarien*]

gram•mar school *n.* **1** *US* an elementary school. **2** *Brit. esp. hist.* a selective state-supported secondary school with a mainly academic curriculum. **3** *Brit. hist.* a school founded in or before the 16th c. for teaching Latin, later becoming a secondary school teaching academic subjects.

gram•mat•i•cal /grəmátikəl/ *adj.* **1 a** of or relating to grammar. **b** determined by grammar, esp. by form or inflection (*grammatical gender*). **2** conforming to the rules of grammar, or to the formal principles of an art, science, etc. □□ **gram•mat•i•cal•ly** *adv.* **gram•mat•i•cal•ness** *n.* [F *grammatical* or LL *grammaticalis* f. L *grammaticus* f. Gk *grammatikos* (as GRAMMAR)]

gramme var. of GRAM[1].

gram mol•e•cule *n. Chem.* the quantity of a substance equal to its relative molecular mass in grams.

Gram-neg•a•tive *adj.* (of bacteria) that do not retain the dye when stained by Gram's stain.

gram•o•phone /gráməfōn/ *n.* = PHONOGRAPH. □□ **gram•o•phon•ic** /–fónik/ *adj.* [formed by inversion of PHONOGRAM]

Gram-pos•i•tive *adj.* (of bacteria) that do retain the dye when stained by Gram's stain.

gram•pus /grámpəs/ *n.* (*pl.* **gram•pus•es**) **1** a dolphin, *Grampus griseus,* with a blunt snout and long pointed black flippers. **2** a person breathing heavily and loudly. [earlier *graundepose, grapeys* f. OF *grapois,* etc., f. med.L *craspiscis* f. L *crassus piscis* fat fish]

Gram's stain /gramz/ *n.* (also **Gram stain, Gram's meth•od**) *Biol.* a method of differentiating bacteria by staining with a violet dye, then attempting to remove the dye with a solvent, for purposes of identification. [H. C. J. *Gram,* Da. physician d. 1938]

gran /gran/ *n. colloq.* grandmother (cf. GRANNY). [abbr.]

gran•a•dil•la /gránədílə, –déeyə/ *n.* (also **gren•a•dil•la** /grén–/) a passionfruit. [Sp., dimin. of *granada* pomegranate]

gra•na•ry /gránəree, gráy–/ *n.* (*pl.* **•ries**) **1** a storehouse for threshed grain. **2** a region producing, and esp. exporting, much grain. [L *granarium* f. *granum* grain]

grand /grand/ *adj. & n.* ● *adj.* **1 a** splendid; magnificent; imposing; dignified. **b** solemn or lofty in conception, execution, or expression; noble. **2** main; of chief importance (*grand staircase; grand entrance*). **3** (**Grand**) of the highest rank, esp. in official titles (*Grand Cross; Grand Inquisitor*). **4** *colloq.* excellent; enjoyable (*had a grand time*). **5** belonging to high society; wealthy (*the grand folk at the manor*). **6** (in *comb.*) in names of family relationships, denoting the second degree of ascent or descent (*granddaughter*). **7** (**Grand**) (in French phrases or imitations) great (*Grand Monarch; Grand Hotel*). **8** *Law* serious; important (*grand larceny*) (cf. COMMON, PETTY). ● *n.* **1** = GRAND PIANO. **2** (*pl.* same) *sl.* a thousand dollars or pounds sterling. □□ **grand•ly** *adv.* **grand•ness** *n.* [ME f. AF *graunt,* OF *grant* f. L *grandis* full-grown]

gran•dad /grándad/ *n.* (also **grand•dad**) *colloq.* **1** grandfather. **2** an elderly man.

gran•dam /grándam/ *n.* **1** (also **gran•dame**) *archaic* grandmother. **2** an old woman. **3** an ancestress. [ME f. AF *graund dame* (as GRAND, DAME)]

grand aunt *n.* a great-aunt (see GREAT *adj.* 11).

grand•child /gránchīld, gránd–/ *n.* (*pl.* **•chil•dren**) a child of one's son or daughter.

grand•dad•dy /grándadee/ *n.* (also **gran•dad•dy**) (*pl.* **•dies**) **1** *colloq.* a grandfather. **2** the original and usu. most venerated of its kind (*the granddaddy of symphony orchestras*).

grand•daugh•ter /grándawtər/ *n.* a female grandchild.

grand duch•y *n.* a nation ruled by a grand duke or duchess.

grand duke *n.* (or **grand duch•ess**) **1** a prince (or princess) or noble person ruling over a territory. **2** (**Grand Duke**) *hist.* the son or grandson of a Russian czar.

grande dame /groɴd daám/ *n.* a dignified woman of high rank. [F]

gran·dee /grandeé/ *n.* **1** a Spanish or Portuguese nobleman of the highest rank. **2** a person of high rank or eminence. [Sp. & Port. *grande*, assim. to –EE]

gran·deur /gránjər, –jōor/ *n.* **1** majesty; splendor; dignity of appearance or bearing. **2** high rank; eminence. **3** nobility of character. [F f. *grand* great, GRAND]

grand·fa·ther /gránfaathər, gránd–/ *n.* a male grandparent. □□ **grand·fa·ther·ly** *adj.*

grand·fa·ther clock *n.* a floor-standing pendulum clock in a tall wooden case.

Grand Gui·gnol /gróɴ geenyáwl/ *n.* a dramatic entertainment of a sensational or horrific nature. [the name (= Great Punch) of a theater in Paris]

gran·di·flo·ra /grándifláwrə/ *adj.* bearing large flowers. [mod.L (often used in specific names of large-flowered plants) f. L *grandis* great + FLORA]

gran·dil·o·quent /grandíləkwənt/ *adj.* **1** pompous or inflated in language. **2** given to boastful talk. □□ **gran·dil·o·quence** /–kwəns/ *n.* **gran·dil·o·quent·ly** *adv.* [L *grandiloquus* (as GRAND, *–loquus* –speaking f. *loqui* speak), after *eloquent*, etc.]

Grand In·quis·i·tor *n.* the director of the court of Inquisition in some countries.

gran·di·ose /grándeeōs/ *adj.* **1** producing or meant to produce an imposing effect. **2** planned on an ambitious or magnificent scale. □□ **gran·di·ose·ly** *adv.* **gran·di·os·i·ty** /–deeósitee/ *n.* [F f. It. *grandioso* (as GRAND, –OSE[1])]

grand ju·ry *n. Law* a jury selected to examine the validity of an accusation prior to trial.

grand lar·ce·ny *n. Law* larceny in which the value of the stolen property exceeds a certain legally established limit.

grand·ma /gránmaa, gránd–/ *n. colloq.* grandmother.

grand mal /groɴ maál, gránd mál/ *n.* a serious form of epilepsy with loss of consciousness (cf. PETIT MAL). [F, = great sickness]

grand·ma·ma /gránməmaa, –maamə, gránd–/ *n. archaic colloq.* = GRANDMA.

grand mas·ter *n.* **1** a chess player of the highest class. **2** the head of a military order of knighthood, of Freemasons, etc.

grand·moth·er /gránmuthər, gránd–/ *n.* a female grandparent. □ **teach one's grandmother to suck eggs** presume to advise a more experienced person. □□ **grand·moth·er·ly** *adj.*

grand·moth·er clock *n.* a clock like a grandfather clock but in a shorter case.

Grand Na·tion·al *n.* an annual horse race established in 1839, held at Aintree, Liverpool, England.

grand neph·ew *n.* (also **grand niece**) a great-nephew or great-niece (see GREAT *adj.* 11).

grand op·er·a *n.* opera on a serious theme, or in which the entire libretto (including dialogue) is sung.

grand·pa /gránpaa, gránd–/ *n. colloq.* grandfather.

grand·pa·pa /gránpəpaá, –paapə, gránd–/ *n. archaic colloq.* = GRANDPA.

grand·par·ent /gránpairənt, gránd–/ *n.* a parent of one's father or mother.

grand pi·an·o *n.* a large full-toned piano standing on three legs, with the body, strings, and soundboard arranged horizontally and in line with the keys.

Grand Prix /groɴ preé/ *n.* any of several important international automobile or motorcycle racing events. [F, = great or chief prize]

grand sei·gneur /groɴ/ *n.* a person of high rank or noble presence.

grand siè·cle /groɴ syéklə/ *n.* the classical or golden age, esp. the 17th c. in France. [F, = great century or age]

grand·sire /gránsīr, gránd–/ *n. archaic* **1** grandfather; old man; ancestor. **2** *Bell-ringing* a method of change-ringing.

grand slam *n.* **1** *Sports* the winning of all of a group of major championships. **2** *Bridge* the winning of all 13 tricks. **3** *Baseball* a home run hit with three runners on base.

grand·son /gránsun, gránd–/ *n.* a male grandchild.

grand·stand /gránstand, gránd–/ *n. & v.* • *n.* the main seating area, usu. roofed, for spectators at a racetrack or sports stadium. • *v.intr.* seek to attract applause or favorable attention from spectators or the media (*a politician who will grandstand to get votes*).

grand·stand fin·ish *n.* a close and exciting finish to a race, etc.

grand to·tal *n.* the final amount after everything is added up; the sum of other totals.

grand tour *n. hist.* a cultural tour of Europe, esp. in the 18th c. for educational purposes.

grange /graynj/ *n.* **1** esp. *Brit.* a country house with farm buildings. **2** (**Grange**) a farmer's social organization. **3** *archaic* a barn. [ME f. AF *graunge*, OF *grange* f. med.L *granica* (*villa*) ult. f. L *granum* GRAIN]

gra·nif·er·ous /grənífərəs/ *adj.* producing grain or a grainlike seed. □□ **gran·i·form** /gránifawrm/ *adj.* [L *granum* GRAIN]

gran·ite /gránit/ *n.* **1** a granular crystalline igneous rock of quartz,

mica, feldspar, etc., used for building. **2** a determined or resolute quality, attitude, etc. □□ **gra·nit·ic** /grənítik/ *adj.* **gran·it·oid** *adj. &* *n.* [It. *granito*, lit. grained f. *grano* f. L *granum* GRAIN]

gran·ite·ware /gránitwair/ *n.* **1** a speckled form of earthenware imitating the appearance of granite. **2** a kind of enameled ironware.

gra·niv·o·rous /grənívərəs/ *adj.* feeding on grain. □□ **gran·i·vore** /gránivawr/ *n.* [L *granum* GRAIN]

gran·ny /gránee/ *n.* (also **gran·nie**) (*pl.* **·nies**) *colloq.* grandmother. [obs. *grannam* for GRANDAM + –Y[2]]

gran·ny glass·es *n.* wire-frame eyeglasses with small lenses, often round or oval.

gran·ny knot *n.* a square knot crossed the wrong way and therefore insecure.

Gran·ny Smith /gránee smíth/ *n.* a crisp, green apple originating in Australia. [Maria Ann ("Granny") Smith d. 1870]

gra·no·la /grənōlə/ *n.* a breakfast or snack food consisting typically of a mixture of rolled oats, nuts, dried fruits, and brown sugar. [orig. f. *Granola*, a trademark]

grant /grant/ *v. & n.* • *v.tr.* **1 a** consent to fulfill (a request, wish, etc.) (*granted all he asked*). **b** allow (a person) to have (a thing) (*granted me my freedom*). **c** (as **granted**) *colloq.* apology accepted; pardon given. **2** give (rights, property, etc.) formally; transfer legally. **3** (often foll. by *that* + clause) admit as true; concede, esp. as a basis for argument. • *n.* **1** the process of granting or a thing granted. **2** a sum of money given by the government for any of various purposes, esp. to finance education. **3** *Law* **a** a legal conveyance by written instrument. **b** formal conferment. □ **take for granted 1** assume something to be true or valid. **2** cease to appreciate through familiarity. □□ **grant·a·ble** *adj.* **gran·tee** /–teé/ *n.* (esp. in sense 2 of *v.*). **grant·er** *n.* **gran·tor** /–tór/ *n.* (esp. in sense 2 of *v.*). [ME f. OF *gr(e)anter* var. of *creanter* ult. f. part. of L *credere* entrust]

Granth /grunt/ *n.* (also **Grunth**) the sacred scriptures of the Sikhs. [Hindi, = book, code f. Skr. *grantha* tying, literary composition]

grant-in-aid *n.* (*pl.* **grants-in-aid**) a grant by central government to local government or an institution.

gran·u·lar /grányələr/ *adj.* **1** of or like grains or granules. **2** having a granulated surface or structure. □□ **gran·u·lar·i·ty** /–láritee/ *n.* **gran·u·lar·ly** *adv.* [LL *granulum* GRANULE]

gran·u·late /grányəlayt/ *v.* **1** *tr. & intr.* form into grains (*granulated sugar*). **2** *tr.* roughen the surface of. **3** *intr.* (of a wound, etc.) form small prominences as the beginning of healing; heal; join. □□ **gran·u·la·tion** /–láyshən/ *n.* **gran·u·la·tor** *n.*

gran·ule /grányōol/ *n.* a small grain. [LL *granulum*, dimin. of L *granum* grain]

gran·u·lo·cyte /grányələsīt/ *n. Physiol.* any of various white blood cells having granules in their cytoplasm. □□ **gran·u·lo·cyt·ic** /–sítik/ *adj.*

gran·u·lo·met·ric /grányəlōmétrik/ *adj.* relating to the distribution of grain sizes in sand, etc. [F *granulométrique* (as GRANULE, METRIC)]

grape /grayp/ *n.* **1** a berry (usu. green, purple, or black) growing in clusters on a vine, used as fruit and in making wine. **2** (prec. by *the*) *colloq.* wine. **3** = GRAPESHOT. **4** (in *pl.*) a diseased growth like a bunch of grapes on the pastern of a horse, etc., or on a pleura in cattle. □□ **grap·y** *adj.* (also **grap·ey**). [ME f. OF *grape* bunch of grapes prob. f. *graper* gather (grapes) f. *grap(p)e* hook, ult. f. Gmc]

grape·fruit /gráypfrōot/ *n.* (*pl.* same) **1** a large round yellow citrus fruit with an acid juicy pulp. **2** the tree, *Citrus paradisi*, bearing this fruit.

grape hy·a·cinth *n.* any liliaceous plant of the genus *Muscari*, with clusters of usu. blue flowers.

grape·shot /gráypshot/ *n. hist.* small balls used as charge in a cannon and scattering when fired.

grape sug·ar *n.* dextrose.

grape·vine /gráypvīn/ *n.* **1** any of various vines of the genus *Vitis*, esp. *Vitis vinifera*. **2** *colloq.* the means of transmission of unofficial information or rumor (*heard it through the grapevine*).

graph[1] /graf/ *n. & v.* • *n.* **1** a diagram showing the relation between variable quantities, usu. of two variables, each measured along one of a pair of axes at right angles. **2** *Math.* a collection of points whose coordinates satisfy a given relation. • *v.tr.* plot or trace on a graph. [abbr. of *graphic formula*]

graph[2] /graf/ *n. Linguistics* a visual symbol, esp. a letter or letters, representing a unit of sound or other feature of speech. [Gk *graphē* writing]

-graph /graf/ *comb. form* forming nouns and verbs meaning: **1** a thing written or drawn, etc., in a specified way (*autograph*; *photograph*). **2** an instrument that records (*heliograph*; *seismograph*; *telegraph*).

graph·eme /gráfeem/ *n. Linguistics* **1** a class of letters, etc., representing a unit of sound. **2** a feature of a written expression that cannot be analyzed into smaller meaningful units. □□ **gra·phe·mic** /gráfeémik/ *adj.* **gra·phe·mi·cal·ly** *adv.* **gra·phe·mics** /gráfeémiks/ *n.* [GRAPH[2] + –EME]

-grapher /grəfər/ *comb. form* forming nouns denoting a person concerned with a specified subject (*geographer*; *radiographer*). [from or after Gk *–graphos* writer + –ER[1]]

graph·ic /gráfik/ *adj. & n.* • *adj.* **1** of or relating to the visual or descriptive arts, esp. writing and drawing. **2** vividly descriptive; conveying all (esp. unwelcome or unpleasant) details; unequivocal. **3** (of minerals) showing marks like writing on the surface or in a fracture. **4** = GRAPHICAL. • *n.* a product of the graphic arts (cf. GRAPHICS). □□ **graph·i·cal·ly** *adv.* **graph·ic·ness** *n.* [L *graphicus* f. Gk *graphikos* f. *graphē* writing]

-graphic /gráfik/ *comb. form* (also **–graphical** /gráfikəl/) forming adjectives corresponding to nouns in *–graphy* (see –GRAPHY). □□ **–graphically** /gráfikIee/ *comb. form* forming adverbs. [from or after Gk *–graphikos* (as GRAPHIC)]

graph·i·ca·cy /gráfikəsee/ *n.* the ability to read a map, graph, etc., or to present information by means of diagrams. [GRAPHIC, after *literacy, numeracy*]

graph·i·cal /gráfikəl/ *adj.* **1** of or in the form of graphs (see GRAPH[1]). **2** graphic. □□ **graph·i·cal·ly** *adv.*

graph·ic arts *n.* the visual and technical arts involving design, drawing, printing, the use of color, etc.

graph·ic e·qual·iz·er *n.* a device for the separate control of the strength and quality of selected audio frequency bands.

graph·ics /gráfiks/ *n.pl.* (usu. treated as *sing.*) **1** the products of the graphic arts, esp. commercial design or illustration. **2** the use of diagrams in calculation and design. **3** (in full **computer graphics**) *Computing* a mode of processing and output in which a significant part of the information is in pictorial form.

graph·ite /gráfīt/ *n.* a crystalline allotropic form of carbon used as a solid lubricant, in pencils, and as a moderator in nuclear reactors, etc. Also called **plumbago** or **black lead**. □□ **gra·phit·ic** /–fítik/ *adj.* **graph·i·tize** /–fītīz/ *v.tr. & intr.* [G *Graphit* f. Gk *graphō* write]

graph·ol·o·gy /grəfóləjee/ *n.* **1** the study of handwriting esp. as a supposed guide to character. **2** a system of graphic formulae; notation for graphs (see GRAPH[1]). **3** *Linguistics* the study of systems of writing. □□ **graph·o·log·i·cal** /gráfəlójikəl/ *adj.* **graph·ol·o·gist** *n.* [Gk *graphē* write]

graph pa·per *n.* paper printed with a network of lines as a basis for drawing graphs.

-graphy /grəfee/ *comb. form* forming nouns denoting: **1** a descriptive science (*bibliography; geography*). **2** a technique of producing images (*photography; radiography*). **3** a style or method of writing, drawing, etc. (*calligraphy*). [from or after F or G *–graphie* f. L *–graphia* f. Gk *–graphia* writing]

grap·nel /grápnəl/ *n.* **1** a device with iron claws, attached to a rope and used for dragging or grasping. **2** a small anchor with several flukes. [ME f. AF f. OF *grapon* f. Gmc: cf. GRAPE]

grap·pa /graápə/ *n.* a brandy distilled from the fermented residue of grapes after they have been pressed in wine-making. [It.]

grap·ple /grápəl/ *v. & n.* • *v.* **1** *intr.* (often foll. by *with*) fight at close quarters or in close combat. **2** *intr.* (foll. by *with*) try to manage or overcome a difficult problem, etc. **3** *tr.* a grip with the hands; come to close quarters with. **b** seize with or as with a grapnel; grasp. • *n.* **1 a** a hold or grip or in as in wrestling. **b** a contest at close quarters. **2** a clutching instrument; a grapnel. □□ **grap·pler** *n.* [OF *grapil* (n.) f. Prov., dimin. of *grapa* hook (as GRAPNEL)]

grapnel 2

grap·pling i·ron *n.* (also **grap·pling hook**) = GRAPNEL.

grap·to·lite /gráptəlīt/ *n.* an extinct marine invertebrate animal found as a fossil in lower Palaeozoic rocks. [Gk *graptos* marked with letters + -LITE]

grasp /grasp/ *v. & n.* • *v.* **1** *tr.* **a** clutch at; seize greedily. **b** hold firmly; grip. **2** *intr.* (foll. by *at*) try to seize; accept avidly. **3** *tr.* understand or realize (a fact or meaning). • *n.* **1** a firm hold; a grip. **2** (foll. by *of*) **a** mastery or control (*a grasp of the situation*). **b** a mental hold or understanding (*a grasp of the facts*). **3** mental agility (*a quick grasp*). □ **grasp at a straw** see STRAW. **within one's grasp** capable of

being grasped or comprehended by one. □□ **grasp·a·ble** *adj.* **grasp·er** *n.* [ME *graspe, grapse* perh. f. OE *grǣpsan* (unrecorded) f. Gmc, rel. to GROPE: cf. LG *grapsen*]

grasp·ing /grásping/ *adj.* avaricious; greedy. □□ **grasp·ing·ly** *adv.* **grasp·ing·ness** *n.*

grass /gras/ *n. & v.* • *n.* **1 a** vegetation belonging to a group of small plants with green blades that are eaten by cattle, horses, sheep, etc. **b** any species of this. **c** any plant of the family Gramineae, which includes cereals, reeds, and bamboos. **2** pasture land. **3** grass-covered ground; a lawn (*keep off the grass*). **4** grazing (*be at grass*). **5** *sl.* marijuana. **6** *Brit. sl.* an informer, esp. a police informer. **7** *sl.* asparagus; cress. • *v.* **1** *tr.* cover with turf. **2** *tr.* provide with pasture. **3** *Brit. sl.* **a** *tr.* betray, esp. to the police. **b** *intr.* inform the police. **4** *Brit. tr.* knock down; fell (an opponent). **5** *tr.* **a** bring (a fish) to the bank. **b** bring down (a bird) by a shot. □ **at grass** *Brit.* out of work, on vacation, retired, etc. **not let the grass grow under one's feet** be quick to act or to seize an opportunity. **out to grass 1** to pasture. **2** laid off; in retirement; on vacation. □□ **grass·less** *adj.* **grass·like** *adj.* [OE *græs* f. Gmc, rel. to GREEN, GROW]

grass bird *n. Austral.* any of various warblers, esp. of the genus *Megalurus*, living among reeds.

grass catch·er *n.* (or *Brit.* **grass box**) a receptacle for cut grass on a lawnmower.

grass cloth *n.* a linenlike cloth woven from ramie, etc.

grass court *n.* a grass-covered tennis court.

grass·hop·per /grás-hoppər/ *n.* a jumping and chirping plant-eating insect of the order Saltatoria.

grass·land /grásland/ *n.* a large open area covered with grass, esp. one used for grazing.

grass of Par·nas·sus *n.* a herbaceous plant, *Parnassia palustris*.

grass par·a·keet *n. Austral.* a parakeet, esp. of the genus *Neophema*, frequenting grassland.

grass roots *n.* **1** a fundamental or basic level of an activity or organization (*he appealed for unity at the grass roots*). **2** ordinary people, esp. as voters; the rank and file of an organization, esp. a political party.

grass-roots *adj.* denoting the basic level of an activity or organization (*improving the game at grass-roots level*). **2** denoting ordinary people (*the movement never gained any grass-roots support*).

grass skirt *n. Polynesia* a skirt made of long grass and leaves fastened to a waistband.

grass snake *n.* **1** the common greensnake, *Opheodrys vernalis*. **2** *Brit.* the common ringed snake, *Natrix natrix*.

grass tree *n.* = BLACKBOY.

grass wid·ow *n.* **1** a person whose husband is away for a prolonged period. **2** a divorced or separated woman. [early 16th c., from *grass* and *widow*, perhaps from the idea of the couple having lain on the grass instead of in bed]

grass·y /grásee/ *adj.* (**grass·i·er, grass·i·est**) **1** covered with or abounding in grass. **2** resembling grass. **3** of grass. □□ **grass·i·ness** *n.*

grate[1] /grayt/ *v.* **1** *tr.* reduce to small particles by rubbing on a serrated surface. **2** *intr.* (often foll. by *against, on*) rub with a harsh scraping sound. **3** *tr.* utter in a harsh tone. **4** *intr.* (often foll. by *on*) **a** sound harshly or discordantly. **b** have an irritating effect. **5** *tr.* grind (one's teeth). **6** *intr.* (of a hinge, etc.) creak. [ME f. OF *grater* ult. f. WG]

grate[2] /grayt/ *n.* **1** the recess of a fireplace or furnace. **2** a metal frame confining fuel in a grate. [ME, = grating f. OF ult. f. L *cratis* hurdle]

grate·ful /gráytfool/ *adj.* **1** thankful; feeling or showing gratitude (*am grateful to you for helping*). **2** pleasant; acceptable. □□ **grate·ful·ly** *adv.* **grate·ful·ness** *n.* [obs. *grate* (adj.) f. L *gratus* + –FUL]

grat·er /gráytər/ *n.* a device for reducing cheese or other food to small particles.

grat·i·cule /grátikyool/ *n.* **1** fine lines or fibers incorporated in a telescope or other optical instrument as a measuring scale or as an aid in locating objects. **2** *Surveying* a network of lines on paper representing meridians and parallels. [F f. med.L *graticula* for *craticula* gridiron f. L *cratis* hurdle]

grat·i·fy /grátifī/ *v.tr.* (**·fies, ·fied**) **1 a** please; delight. **b** please by compliance; assent to the wish of. **2** indulge in or yield to (a feeling or desire). □□ **grat·i·fi·ca·tion** *n.* **grat·i·fi·er** *n.* **gra·ti·fy·ing** *adj.* **gra·ti·fy·ing·ly** *adv.* [F *gratifier* or L *gratificari* do a favor to, make a present of, f. *gratus* pleasing]

grat·ing[1] /gráyting/ *adj.* **1** sounding harsh or discordant (*a grating laugh*). **2** having an irritating effect. □□ **grat·ing·ly** *adv.*

grat·ing[2] /gráyting/ *n.* **1** a framework of parallel or crossed metal bars. **2** *Optics* a set of parallel wires, lines ruled on glass, etc., for producing spectra by diffraction.

grat·is /grátis, graá–/ *adv. & adj.* free; without charge. [L, contracted ablat. pl. of *gratia* favor]

grat·i·tude /grátitōōd, –tyōōd/ *n.* being thankful; readiness to show appreciation for and to return kindness. [F *gratitude* or med.L *gratitudo* f. *gratus* thankful]

gra·tu·i·tous /grətōōitəs, tyōō–/ *adj.* **1** given or done free of charge. **2** uncalled-for; unwarranted; lacking good reason (*a gratuitous insult*). □□ **gra·tu·i·tous·ly** *adv.* **gra·tu·i·tous·ness** *n.* [L *gratuitus* spontaneous: cf. *fortuitous*]

gra·tu·i·ty /grətōōitee, –tyōō–/ *n.* (*pl.* **·ties**) money given in recognition of services; a tip. [OF *gratuité* or med.L *gratuitas* gift f. L *gratus* grateful]

grat·u·la·to·ry /gráchələtáwree/ *adj.* expressing congratulation. [LL *gratulatorius* f. L *gratus* grateful]

gra·va·men /grəváymen/ *n.* (*pl.* **gra·va·mens** or **gra·vam·i·na** /–váminə/) **1** the essence or most serious part of an argument. **2** a grievance. [LL, = inconvenience, f. L *gravare* to load f. *gravis* heavy]

grave[1] /grayv/ *n.* **1 a** a trench dug in the ground to receive a coffin for burial. **b** a mound or memorial stone placed over this. **2** (prec. by *the*) death, esp. as indicating mortal finality. **3** something compared to or regarded as a grave. □ **turn in one's grave** (of a dead person) be thought of in certain circumstances as likely to have been shocked or angry if still alive. □□ **grave·less** *adj.* **grave·ward** *adv.* & *adj.* [OE *græf* f. WG]

grave[2] /grayv/ *adj.* & *n.* ● *adj.* **1 a** serious; weighty; important (*a grave matter*). **b** dignified; solemn; somber (*a grave look*). **2** extremely serious or threatening (*grave danger*). ● *n.* /graav/ = GRAVE ACCENT. □□ **grave·ly** *adv.* **grave·ness** *n.* [F *grave* or L *gravis* heavy, serious]

grave[3] /grayv/ *v.tr.* (*past part.* **grav·en** or **graved**) **1** (foll. by *in, on*) fix indelibly (on one's memory). **2** engrave; carve. □ **graven image** an idol. [OE *grafan* dig, engrave f. Gmc: cf. GROOVE]

grave[4] /grayv/ *v.tr.* clean a ship's bottom) by burning off accretions and by tarring. [perh. F dial. *grave* = OF *greve* shore]

grave[5] /gráavay/ *adv., adj.* & *n.* ● *adv.* & *adj. Music* in slow time. ● *n.* a piece of music played in this manner.

grave ac·cent /graav, grayv/ *n.* a mark (`) placed over a vowel in some languages to denote pronunciation, length, etc., orig. indicating low or falling pitch.

grave·dig·ger /gráyvdigər/ *n.* **1** a person who digs graves. **2** (in full **gravedigger beetle**) a sexton beetle.

grav·el /grávəl/ *n.* & *v.* ● *n.* **1 a** a mixture of coarse sand and small waterworn or pounded stones, used for paths and roads and as an aggregate. **b** *Geol.* a stratum of this. **2** *Med.* aggregations of crystals forming in the urinary tract. ● *v.tr.* (**grav·eled, grav·el·ing**; also **grav·elled, grav·el·ling**) **1** lay or strew with gravel. **2** perplex; puzzle; nonplus (from an obs. sense 'run (a ship) aground'). [ME f. OF *gravel(e)* dimin. of *grave* (as GRAVE[4])]

grave·lax var. of GRAVLAX.

grav·el-blind *adj. literary* almost completely blind ("more than sand-blind," in Shakesp. *Merchant of Venice* II. ii. 33).

grav·el·ly /grávəlee/ *adj.* **1** of or like gravel. **2** having or containing gravel. **3** (of a voice) deep and rough sounding.

grav·en *past part.* of GRAVE[3].

grav·er /gráyvər/ *n.* **1** an engraving tool; a burin. **2** an engraver; a carver.

Graves /graav/ *n.* a light usu. white wine from the Graves district in France.

Graves' dis·ease /grayvz/ *n.* exophthalmic goiter with characteristic swelling of the neck and protrusion of the eyes, resulting from an overactive thyroid gland. [R. J. *Graves*, Ir. physician d. 1853]

grave·stone /gráyvstōn/ *n.* a stone (usu. inscribed) marking a grave.

grave·yard /gráyvyaard/ *n.* a burial ground, esp. by a church. □ **graveyard shift** a work shift that usu. starts about midnight and ends about eight o'clock in the morning.

grav·id /grávid/ *adj. literary* or *Zool.* pregnant. [L *gravidus* f. *gravis* heavy]

gra·vim·e·ter /grəvímitər/ *n.* an instrument for measuring the difference in the force of gravity from one place to another. [F *gravimètre* f. L *gravis* heavy]

grav·i·met·ric /grávimétrik/ *adj.* **1** of or relating to the measurement of weight. **2** denoting chemical analysis based on weight.

gra·vim·e·try /grəvímitree/ *n.* the measurement of weight.

grav·ing dock *n.* = DRY DOCK.

grav·i·tas /grávitaas/ *n.* solemn demeanor; seriousness. [L f. *gravis* serious]

grav·i·tate /grávitayt/ *v.* **1** *intr.* (foll. by *to, toward*) move or be attracted to some source of influence. **2** *tr.* & *intr.* **a** move or tend by force of gravity toward. **b** sink by or as if by gravity. [mod.L *gravitare* GRAVITAS]

grav·i·ta·tion /grávitáyshən/ *n. Physics* **1** a force of attraction between any particle of matter in the universe and any other. **2** the effect of this, esp. the falling of bodies to the earth. [mod.L *gravitatio* (as GRAVITY)]

grav·i·ta·tion·al /grávitáyshənəl/ *adj.* of or relating to gravitation. □□ **grav·i·ta·tion·al·ly** *adv.*

grav·i·ta·tion·al con·stant *n.* the constant in Newton's law of gravitation relating gravity to the masses and separation of particles. ¶ Symb.: G.

grav·i·ta·tion·al field *n.* the region of space surrounding a body in which another body experiences a force of attraction.

grav·i·ty /grávitee/ *n.* **1 a** the force that attracts a body to the center of the earth or other celestial body. **b** the degree of intensity of this measured by acceleration. **c** gravitational force. **2** the property of having weight. **3 a** importance; seriousness; the quality of being grave. **b** solemnity; sobriety; serious demeanor. [F *gravité* or L *gravitas* f. *gravis* heavy]

grav·i·ty feed *n.* the supply of material by its fall under gravity.

grav·lax /graávlaaks/ *n.* (also **grave·lax**) filleted salmon cured by marination in salt, sugar, and dill. [Sw.]

gra·vure /grəvyōōr/ *n.* = PHOTOGRAVURE. [abbr.]

gra·vy /gráyvee/ *n.* (*pl.* **·vies**) **1 a** the juices exuding from meat during and after cooking. **b** a sauce for food, made by thickening these, or from other materials. **2** *sl.* unearned or unexpected gains, esp. money. [ME, perh. from a misreading as *gravé* of OF *grané*, prob. f. *grain* spice: see GRAIN]

gra·vy boat *n.* a boat-shaped dish for serving gravy.

gra·vy train *n. sl.* a source of easy financial benefit.

gray[1] /gray/ *adj., n.,* & *v.* (also **grey**) ● *adj.* **1** of a color intermediate between black and white, as of ashes or lead. **2 a** (of the weather, etc.) dull; dismal; heavily overcast. **b** bleak; depressing; (of a person) depressed. **3 a** (of hair) turning white with age, etc. **b** (of a person) having gray hair. **4** anonymous; nondescript; unidentifiable. ● *n.* **1 a** a gray color or pigment. **b** gray clothes or material (*dressed in gray*). **2** a cold sunless light. **3** a gray or white horse. ● *v.tr.* & *intr.* make or become gray. □□ **gray·ish** *adj.* **gray·ly** *adv.* **gray·ness** *n.* [OE *græg* f. Gmc]

gray[2] /gray/ *n. Physics* the SI unit of the absorbed dose of ionizing radiation, corresponding to one joule per kilogram. ¶ Abbr.: **Gy**. [L. H. *Gray*, Engl. radiobiologist d. 1965]

gray ar·e·a *n.* **1** a situation or topic sharing features of more than one category and not clearly attributable to any one category; an ill-defined situation (*gray areas in the legislation have yet to be clarified*).

gray·beard /gráybeerd/ *n. archaic* **1** an old man. **2** a large stoneware jug for alcohol. **3** *Brit.* clematis in seed.

gray em·i·nence *n.* = ÉMINENCE GRISE.

gray goose *n.* = GREYLAG.

gray·ling /gráyling/ *n.* **1** any silver-gray freshwater fish of the genus *Thymallus*, with a long high dorsal fin. **2** a butterfly, *Hipparchia semele*, having wings with gray undersides and bright eye-spots on the upper side. [GRAY[1] + –LING[2]]

gray mat·ter *n.* **1** the darker tissues of the brain and spinal cord consisting of nerve cell bodies and branching dendrites. **2** *colloq.* intelligence.

gray squir·rel *n.* an American squirrel, *Sciurus carolinensis*, introduced to England in the 19th c.

gray·wacke /gráywakə, –wak/ *n.* (*Brit.* **grey·wacke**) *Geol.* a dark and coarse-grained sandstone, usu. with an admixture of clay. [Anglicized f. G *Grauwacke* f. *grau* gray: see WACKE]

graze[1] /grayz/ *v.* **1** *intr.* (of cattle, sheep, etc.) eat growing grass. **2** *tr.* **a** feed (cattle, etc.) on growing grass. **b** feed on (grass). **3** *intr.* pasture cattle. □□ **graz·er** *n.* [OE *grasian* f. *græs* GRASS]

graze[2] /grayz/ *v.* & *n.* ● *v.* **1** *tr.* rub or scrape (a part of the body, esp. the skin) so as to break the surface without causing bleeding or with only minor bleeding. **2 a** *tr.* touch lightly in passing. **b** *intr.* (foll. by *against, along,* etc.) move with a light passing contact. ● *n.* an act or instance of grazing. [perh. a specific use of GRAZE[1], as if 'take off the grass close to the ground' (of a shot, etc.)]

gra·zier /gráyzhər/ *n.* **1** a person who feeds cattle for market. **2** *Austral.* a large-scale sheep farmer or cattle farmer. □□ **gra·zier·y** *n.* [GRASS + –IER]

graz·ing /gráyzing/ *n.* grassland suitable for pasturage.

grease /grees/ *n.* & *v.* ● *n.* **1** oily or fatty matter esp. as a lubricant. **2** the melted fat of a dead animal. **3** oily matter in unprocessed wool. ● *v.tr.* also /greez/ smear or lubricate with grease. □ **grease the palm of** *colloq.* bribe. **like greased lightning** *colloq.* very fast. □□ **grease·less** *adj.* [ME f. AF *grece, gresse,* OF *graisse* ult. f. L *crassus* (adj.) fat]

grease gun *n.* a device for pumping grease under pressure to a particular point.

grease mon·key *n. sl.* a mechanic, esp. one who works on motor vehicles.

grease·paint /gréespaynt/ *n.* a waxy composition used as makeup for actors.

grease·proof /gréesprōof/ *adj.* impervious to the penetration of grease.

greas·er /gréesər/ *n.* **1** a person or thing that greases. **2** *sl.* a member of a gang of young street toughs. **3** *sl. offens.* a Mexican or Spanish-American. **4** a gentle landing of an aircraft.

greas·y /gréesee, gréezee/ *adj.* (**greas·i·er, greas·i·est**) **1 a** of or like grease. **b** smeared or covered with grease. **c** containing or having too much grease. **2 a** slippery. **b** (of a person or manner) unpleasantly unctuous; smooth. **c** objectionable. □□ **greas•i•ly** *adv.* **greas•i•ness** *n.*

greas•y spoon *n. sl.* an inexpensive small restaurant that serves fried food and that is often unsanitary.

great /grayt/ *adj. & n.* ● *adj.* **1 a** of a size, amount, extent, or intensity considerably above the normal or average; big (*made a great hole; take great care; lived to a great age*). **b** also with implied surprise, admiration, contempt, etc., esp. in exclamations (*great stuff!*). **c** reinforcing other words denoting size, quantity, etc. (*a great big hole; a great many*). **2** important; preeminent; worthy or most worthy of consideration. **3** grand; imposing (*a great occasion; the great hall*). **4 a** (esp. of a public or historic figure) distinguished; prominent. **b** (**the Great**) as a title denoting the most important of the name (*Alexander the Great*). **5 a** (of a person) remarkable in ability, character, achievement, etc. (*great men; a great thinker*). **b** (of a thing) outstanding of its kind (*the Great Depression*). **6** (foll. by *at*) competent; skilled; well-informed. **7** fully deserving the name of; doing a thing habitually or extensively (*a great reader; a great believer in tolerance; not a great one for traveling*). **8** (also **great•er**) the larger of the name, species, etc. (*great auk; greater celandine*). **9** (**Greater**) (of a city, etc.) including adjacent urban areas (*Greater Boston*). **10** *colloq.* **a** very enjoyable or satisfactory; attractive; fine (*had a great time; it would be great if we won*). **b** (as an exclam.) fine; very good. **11** (in *comb.*) (in names of family relationships) denoting one degree further removed upwards or downwards (*great-uncle; great-great-grandmother*). ● *n.* **1** a great or outstanding person or thing. **2** (in *pl.*) (**Greats**) *colloq.* (at Oxford University) an honors course or final examinations in classics and philosophy. □ **great and small** all classes or types. **great deal** see DEAL[1]. **the great majority** by far the most. **to a great extent** largely. □□ **great•ness** *n.* [OE *grēat* f. WG]

great auk *n.* an extinct flightless auk, *Alca impennis.*

Great Bear *n. Brit.* = *Big Dipper.*

Great Brit•ain *n.* England, Wales, and Scotland.

▶Great Britain is the name for the island that comprises England, Scotland, and Wales. The *United Kingdom* includes these and Northern Ireland. The *British Isles* include the United Kingdom and surrounding, smaller islands. The all-encompassing adjective *British* is unlikely to offend anyone from any of these places. *Welsh, Scottish,* and *English* should be used only if you are sure of a person's specific origin.

Great Char•ter *n.* = MAGNA CARTA.

great cir•cle *n.* (or **small circle**) a circle on the surface of a sphere whose plane passes (or does not pass) through the sphere's center.

great•coat /gráytkōt/ *n.* a long heavy overcoat.

Great Dane *n.* a dog of a very large, powerful, short-haired breed.

Great Di•vide *n.* **1** another name for CONTINENTAL DIVIDE. **2** the boundary between life and death.

great•heart•ed /gráyt-haártid/ *adj.* magnanimous; having a noble or generous mind. □□ **great•heart•ed•ness** *n.*

Great Lakes *n.* the Lakes Superior, Huron, Michigan, Erie, and Ontario, along the boundary of the US and Canada.

great•ly /gráytlee/ *adv.* by a considerable amount; much (*greatly admired; greatly superior*).

great north•ern div•er *n.* a diving sea bird, *Gavia immer,* of the northern hemisphere.

great or•gan *n.* the chief keyboard in a large organ, with its related pipes and mechanism.

Great Rus•sian *n. & adj.* ● *n.* a member or the language of the principal East Slavonic ethnic group, inhabiting mainly the Russian Republic; (a) Russian. ● *adj.* of or relating to this people or language.

great tit *n.* a Eurasian songbird, *Parus major,* with black and white head markings.

great toe *n.* the big toe.

Great War *n.* World War I (1914–18).

greave /greev/ *n.* (usu. in *pl.*) armor for the shin. [ME f. OF *greve* shin, greave, of unkn. orig.]

grebe /greeb/ *n.* any diving bird of the family Podicipedidae, with a long neck, lobed toes, and almost no tail. □ **little grebe** a small water bird of the grebe family, *Tachybaptus ruficollis.* [F *grèbe,* of unkn. orig.]

Gre•cian /greeshən/ *adj.* (of architecture or facial outline) following Greek models or ideals. [OF *grecien* or med.L *graecianus* (unrecorded) f. L *Graecia* Greece]

Gre•cian nose *n.* a straight nose that continues the line of the forehead without a dip.

Gre•cism /greesizəm/ *n.* (also **Grae•cism**) **1** a Greek idiom, esp. as imitated in another language. **2 a** the Greek spirit, style, mode of expression, etc. **b** the imitation of these. [F *grécisme* or med.L *Graecismus* f. *Graecus* GREEK]

Gre•cize /greesīz/ *v.tr.* (also **Grae•cize**) give a Greek character or form to. [L *Graecizare* (as GRECISM)]

Greco- /grékō/ *comb. form* (also **Graeco-**) Greek; Greek and. [L *Graecus* GREEK]

Gre•co-Ro•man /grékō-rṓmən, grékō–/ *adj.* **1** of or relating to the Greeks and Romans. **2** *Wrestling* denoting a style attacking only the upper part of the body.

greed /greed/ *n.* an excessive desire, esp. for food or wealth. [back-form. f. GREEDY]

greed•y /greedee/ *adj.* (**greed•i•er, greed•i•est**) **1** having or showing an excessive appetite for food or drink. **2** wanting wealth or pleasure to excess. **3** (foll. by *for,* or *to* + infin.) very keen or eager; needing intensely (*greedy for affection; greedy to learn*). □□ **greed•i•ly** *adv.* **greed•i•ness** *n.* [OE *grǣdig* f. Gmc]

SYNONYM TIP greedy

ACQUISITIVE, AVARICIOUS, COVETOUS, GLUTTONOUS, RAPACIOUS. The desire for money and the things it can buy is often associated with Americans. But not all Americans are **greedy**, which implies an insatiable desire to possess or acquire something, beyond what one needs or deserves (*greedy for profits*). Someone who is *greedy* for food might be called **gluttonous**, which emphasizes consumption as well as desire (*a gluttonous appetite for sweets*), but *greedy* is a derogatory term only when the object of longing is itself evil or when it cannot be possessed without harm to oneself or others (*a reporter greedy for information*). A *greedy* child may grow up to be an **avaricious** adult, which implies a fanatical greediness for money or other valuables. **Rapacious** is an even stronger term, with an emphasis on taking things by force (*so rapacious in his desire for land that he forced dozens of families from their homes*). **Acquisitive,** on the other hand, is a more neutral word suggesting a willingness to exert effort in acquiring things (*an acquisitive woman who filled her house with antiques and artwork*), and not necessarily material things (*a probing, acquisitive mind*). **Covetous,** in contrast to *acquisitive,* implies an intense desire for something as opposed to the act of acquiring or possessing it. It is often associated with the Ten Commandments (*Thou shalt not covet thy neighbor's wife*) and suggests a longing for something that rightfully belongs to another.

greed•y-guts *n. colloq.* a glutton.

Greek /greek/ *n. & adj.* ● *n.* **1 a** a native or inhabitant of modern Greece; a person of Greek descent. **b** a native or citizen of any of the ancient nation-states of Greece; a member of the Greek people. **2** the Indo-European language of Greece. ● *adj.* of Greece or its people or language; Hellenic. □ **Greek** (or **greek**) **to me** *colloq.* incomprehensible to me. □□ **Greek•ness** *n.* [OE *Grēcas* (pl.) f. Gmc f. L *Graecus* Greek f. Gk *Graikoi,* the prehistoric name of the Hellenes (in Aristotle)]

Greek Church *n.* (also **Greek Or•tho•dox Church**) the national church of Greece (see also ORTHODOX CHURCH).

Greek cross *n.* a cross with four equal arms.

Greek fire *n. hist.* a combustible composition for igniting enemy ships, etc.

green /green/ *adj., n., & v.* ● *adj.* **1** of the color between blue and yellow in the spectrum; colored like grass, emeralds, etc. **2 a** covered with leaves or grass; mild and without snow (*a green Christmas*). **3** (of fruit, etc., or wood) unripe or unseasoned. **4** not dried, smoked, or tanned. **5** inexperienced; naive; gullible. **6 a** (of the complexion) pale; sickly-hued. **b** jealous; envious. **7** young; flourishing. **8** not withered or worn out (*a green old age*). **9** vegetable (*green food; green salad*). **10** (also **Green**) concerned with or supporting protection of the environment as a political principle. **11** *archaic* fresh; not healed (*a green wound*). ● *n.* **1** a green color or pigment. **2** green clothes or material (*dressed in green*). **3 a** a piece of public or common grassy land (*village green*). **b** a grassy area used for a special purpose (*putting green; bowling green*). **c** *Golf* a putting green. **4** (in *pl.*) green vegetables. **5** vigor; youth; virility (*in the green*). **6** a green light. **7** a green ball, piece, etc., in a game or sport. **8** (also **Green**) a member or supporter of an environmentalist group or party. **9** (in *pl.*) *Brit. sl.* sexual intercourse. **10** *sl.* low-grade marijuana. **11** *sl.* money. **12** green foliage or growing plants. ● *v.* **1** *tr. & intr.* make or become green. **2** *tr. sl.* hoax; take in. □ **green in a person's eye** *Brit.* a sign of gullibility (*do you see any green in my eye?*). □□ **green•ish** *adj.* **green•ly** *adv.* **green•ness** *n.* [OE *grēne* (adj. & n.), *grēnian* (v.), f. Gmc, rel. to GROW]

green•back /greenbak/ *n.* **1** a US legal tender note; paper money. **2** any of various green-backed animals.

green bean *n.* (also **string bean**) the green pods of a young kidney bean, eaten as a vegetable.

green belt *n.* an area of open land around a city, designated for preservation.

Green Be•ret *n. Mil.* a member of the U.S. Army Special Forces.

green•bot•tle /greenbot'l/ *n.* any fly of the genus *Lucilia,* esp. *L. sericata* which lays eggs in the flesh of sheep.

green card *n.* **1** (in the US) a permit allowing a foreign national to live and work permanently in the US. **2** *Brit.* an international insurance document for motorists.

green cheese *n.* **1** *Brit.* cheese colored green with sage. **2** whey cheese. **3** unripened cheese.

green earth *n.* a hydrous silicate of potassium, iron, and other metals.

green•er•y /gréenəree/ *n.* green foliage or growing plants.

green-eyed *adj.* jealous.

green-eyed mon•ster *n.* jealousy personified.

green fat *n.* the green, gelatinous part of a turtle, highly regarded by gourmets.

green•feed /gréenfeed/ *n.* *Austral.* & *NZ* forage grown to be fed fresh to livestock.

green•field /gréenfeeld/ *n.* (*attrib.*) (of a site, in terms of its potential development) having no previous building development on it.

green•finch /gréenfinch/ *n.* a finch, *Carduelis chloris*, with green and yellow plumage.

green•fly /gréenflī/ *n.* (*pl.* **•flies**) **1** a green aphid. **2** these collectively.

green•gage /gréengayj/ *n.* a roundish green fine-flavored variety of plum. [Sir W. *Gage* d. 1727]

green goose *n.* a goose killed under four months old and eaten without stuffing.

green•gro•cer /gréengrósər/ *n.* a retailer of fruit and vegetables.

green•gro•cer•y /gréengrósəree/ *n.* (*pl.* **•ies**) *Brit.* **1** the business of a greengrocer. **2** goods sold by a greengrocer.

green•head /gréenhed/ *n.* **1** any biting fly of the genus *Chrysops* or other genera. **2** an Australian ant, *Chalcoponera metallica*, with a painful sting.

green•heart /gréenhaart/ *n.* **1** any of several tropical American trees, esp. *Ocotea rodiaei*. **2** the hard greenish wood of one of these.

green•hide /gréehīd/ *n.* *Austral.* the untanned hide of an animal.

green•horn /gréenhawrn/ *n.* **1** an inexperienced or foolish person; a new recruit. **2** a newcomer; an immigrant.

green•house /gréenhows/ *n.* a light structure with the sides and roof mainly of glass, for rearing delicate plants or hastening the growth of plants.

green•house ef•fect *n.* the trapping of the sun's warmth in the lower atmosphere of the earth caused by an increase in carbon dioxide, which is more transparent to solar radiation than to the reflected radiation from the earth.

green•house gas *n.* any of various gases, esp. carbon dioxide, that contribute to the greenhouse effect.

green•ing /gréening/ *n.* a variety of apple that is green when ripe. [prob. f. MDu. *groeninc* (as GREEN)]

green•keep•er *n.* var. of GREENSKEEPER.

green leek *n.* any of several green-faced Australian parakeets.

green•let /gréenlit/ *n.* = VIREO.

green light *n.* **1** a signal to proceed on a road, railroad, etc. **2** *colloq.* permission to go ahead with a project.

green lin•net *n.* = GREENFINCH.

green ma•nure *n.* growing plants plowed into the soil as fertilizer.

green pep•per *n.* the unripe bell or sweet pepper, *Capsicum annuum grossum*, eaten green as a vegetable.

green plov•er *n.* a lapwing.

green pound *n.* *Brit.* the exchange rate for the pound for payments for agricultural produce in the European Community.

green rev•o•lu•tion *n.* greatly increased crop production in underdeveloped countries.

green•room /gréenroom/ *n.* a room in a theater for actors and actresses who are off stage.

green•sand /gréensand/ *n.* **1** a greenish kind of sandstone, often imperfectly cemented. **2** a stratum largely formed of this sandstone.

greens fee *n.* (also **green fee**) *Golf* a charge for playing one round or session on a golf course.

green•shank /gréenshangk/ *n.* a large sandpiper, *Tringa nebularia*.

green•sick /gréensik/ *adj.* affected with chlorosis. □□ **green•sick•ness** *n.*

greens•keep•er /gréenzkéepər/ *n.* the keeper of a golf course.

green•stick frac•ture /gréenstik/ *n.* a bone fracture, esp. in children, in which one side of the bone is broken and one only bent.

green•stone /gréenstōn/ *n.* **1** a greenish igneous rock containing feldspar and hornblende. **2** a variety of jade found in New Zealand, used for tools, ornaments, etc.

green•stuff /gréenstuf/ *n.* vegetation; green vegetables.

green•sward /gréenswawrd/ *n.* *archaic* or *literary* **1** grassy turf. **2** an expanse of this.

green tea *n.* tea made from dried, not fermented, leaves.

green thumb *n.* skill in growing plants.

green tur•tle *n.* a green-shelled sea turtle, *Chelonia mydas*, highly regarded as food.

green vit•ri•ol *n.* ferrous sulfate crystals.

green•weed /gréenweed/ *n.* (in full **dyer's greenweed**) a bushy plant, *Genista tinctoria*, with deep yellow flowers.

Green•wich Mean Time /grénich, grínij/ *n.* (also **Green•wich Time**) the local time on the meridian of Greenwich, England, used as an international basis for reckoning time. [*Greenwich* in London, former site of the Royal Observatory]

green•wood /gréenwŏod/ *n.* a wood in summer, esp. as the scene of outlaw life.

green•y /gréenee/ *adj.* greenish (*greeny-yellow*).

green•yard /gréenyaard/ *n.* *Brit.* an enclosure for stray animals; a pound.

greet¹ /greet/ *v.tr.* **1** address politely or welcomingly on meeting or arrival. **2** receive or acknowledge in a specified way (*was greeted with derision*). **3** (of a sight, sound, etc.) become apparent to or noticed by. □□ **greet•er** *n.* [OE *grētan* handle, salute f. WG]

greet² /greet/ *v.intr.* *Sc.* weep. [OE *grētan*, *grēotan*, of uncert. orig.]

greet•ing /gréeting/ *n.* **1** the act or an instance of welcoming or addressing politely. **2** words, gestures, etc., used to greet a person. **3** (often in *pl.*) an expression of goodwill.

greet•ing card *n.* a decorative card sent to convey good wishes on some occasion.

gre•gar•i•ous /grigáireeəs/ *adj.* **1** fond of company. **2** living in flocks or communities. **3** growing in clusters. □□ **gre•gar•i•ous•ly** *adv.* **gre•gar•i•ous•ness** *n.* [L *gregarius* f. *grex gregis* flock]

Gre•go•ri•an cal•en•dar /grigáwreeən/ *n.* the calendar introduced in 1582 by Pope Gregory XIII, as a correction of the Julian calendar. [med.L *Gregorianus* f. LL *Gregorius* f. Gk *Grēgorios* Gregory]

Gre•go•ri•an chant /grigáwreeən/ *n.* plainsong ritual music, named after Pope Gregory I.

Gre•go•ri•an tel•e•scope /grigáwreeən/ *n.* a reflecting telescope in which light reflected from a secondary mirror passes through a hole in a primary mirror. [J. *Gregory*, Sc. mathematician d. 1675, who devised it]

grem•lin /grémlin/ *n.* *colloq.* **1** an imaginary mischievous sprite regarded as responsible for mechanical faults, esp. in aircraft. **2** any similar cause of trouble. [20th c.: orig. unkn., but prob. after *goblin*]

gre•nade /grináyd/ *n.* **1** a small bomb thrown by hand (**hand grenade**) or shot from a rifle. **2** a glass receptacle containing chemicals which disperse on impact, for testing drains, extinguishing fires, etc.

WORD HISTORY   grenade

Mid-16th century (in the sense 'pomegranate'): from French, alteration of Old French *(pome) grenate*, on the pattern of Spanish *granada*. The bomb was so named because of its original shape, supposedly resembling a pomegranate.

---

gren•a•dier /grénədeér/ *n.* **1 a** *Brit.* (**Grenadiers** or **Grenadier Guards**) the first regiment of the royal household infantry. **b** *hist.* a soldier armed with grenades. **2** any deep-sea fish of the family Macrouridae, with a long tapering body and pointed tail, and secreting luminous bacteria when disturbed. [F (as GRENADE)]

gren•a•dil•la var. of GRANADILLA.

gren•a•dine¹ /grénədeén/ *n.* a French syrup of pomegranates, etc., used in mixed drinks. [F f. *grenade*: see GRENADE]

gren•a•dine² /grénədeén/ *n.* a dress fabric of loosely woven silk or silk and wool. [F, earlier *grenade* grained silk f. *grenu* grained]

Gresh•am's law /gréshəmz/ *n.* the tendency for money of lower intrinsic value to circulate more freely than money of higher intrinsic and equal nominal value. [Sir T. *Gresham*, Engl. financier d. 1579]

gres•so•ri•al /gresáwreeəl/ *adj.* *Zool.* **1** walking. **2** adapted for walking. [mod.L *gressorius* f. L *gradi gress-* walk]

grew past of GROW.

grey var. of GRAY¹.

Grey Fri•ar *n.* a Franciscan friar.

grey•hound /gráyhownd/ *n.* **1** a dog of a tall slender breed having excellent sight and capable of high speed, used in racing and coursing. **2** this breed. [OE *grīghund* f. *grīeg* bitch (unrecorded: cf. ON *grey*) + *hund* dog, rel. to HOUND]

grey•lag /gráylag/ *n.* (in full **greylag goose**) a wild goose, *Anser anser*, native to Europe. [GREY + LAG¹ (because of its late migration)]

grey•wacke *Brit.* var. of GRAYWACKE.

greyhound

grid /grid/ *n.* **1** a framework of spaced parallel bars; a grating. **2** a system of numbered squares printed on a map and forming the basis of map references. **3** a network of lines, electrical power connections, gas supply lines, etc. **4** a pattern of lines marking the starting places on a motor-racing track. **5** the wire network between the filament and the anode of a vacuum tube, etc. **6** an arrangement of city streets in a rectangular pattern. □□ **grid•ded** *adj.* [back-form. f. GRIDIRON]

grid bi•as *n. Electr.* a fixed voltage applied between the cathode and the control grid of a vacuum tube which determines its operating conditions.

grid•dle /gríd'l/ *n. & v.* • *n.* **1** a circular iron plate placed over a fire or otherwise heated for baking, toasting, etc. **2** a miner's wire-bottomed sieve. • *v.tr.* **1** cook with a griddle; grill. **2** sieve with a griddle. [ME f. OF *gredil, gridil* gridiron ult. f. L *craticula* dimin. of *cratis* hurdle; cf. GRATE², GRILL¹]

grid•i•ron /grídíərn/ *n.* **1** a cooking utensil of metal bars for broiling or grilling. **2** a frame of parallel beams for supporting a ship in dock. **3** a football field (with parallel lines marking out the area of play). **4** *Theatr.* a plank structure over a stage supporting the mechanism for drop scenery, etc. **5** = GRID 6. [ME *gredire*, var. of *gredil* GRIDDLE, later assoc. with IRON]

grid•lock /grídlok/ *n.* **1** a traffic jam affecting a network of streets, caused by continuous lines of intersecting traffic. **2** a complete standstill in action or progress. □□ **gridlocked** *adj.*

grief /greef/ *n.* **1** deep or intense sorrow or mourning. **2** the cause of this. □ **come to grief** meet with disaster; fail. **good grief!** an exclamation of surprise, alarm, etc. [ME f. AF *gref*, OF *grief* f. *grever* GRIEVE¹]

griev•ance /gréevəns/ *n.* **1** a real or fancied cause for complaint. **2** a formal complaint. [ME, = injury, f. OF *grevance* (as GRIEF)]

grieve¹ /greev/ *v.* **1** *tr.* cause grief or great distress to. **2** *intr.* suffer grief, esp. at another's death. □□ **griev•er** *n.* [ME f. OF *grever* ult. f. L *gravare* f. *gravis* heavy]

grieve² /greev/ *n. Sc.* a farm bailiff; an overseer. [late 15th c.: cf. REEVE¹]

griev•ous /gréevəs/ *adj.* **1** (of pain, etc.) severe. **2** causing grief or suffering. **3** injurious. **4** flagrant; heinous. □□ **griev•ous•ly** *adv.* **griev•ous•ness** *n.* [ME f. OF *grevos* (as GRIEVE¹)]

PRONUNCIATION TIP grievous

Avoid pronouncing this word with three syllables, as if there were an *i* before the *-ous*.

---

griev•ous bod•i•ly harm *n. Law* serious injury inflicted intentionally on a person.

grif•fin /grifin/ *n.* (also **gryph•on, grif•fon**) a mythical creature with an eagle's head and wings and a lion's body. [ME f. OF *grifoun* ult. f. LL *gryphus* f. L *gryps* f. Gk *grups*]

grif•fon /grifən/ *n.* **1 a** a dog of a small terrierlike breed with coarse or smooth hair. **b** this breed. **2** (in full **griffon vulture**) a large S. European vulture, *Gyps fulvus*. **3** = GRIFFIN. [F (in sense 1) or var. of GRIFFIN]

griffin

grig /grig/ *n.* **1** a small eel. **2** a grasshopper or cricket. □ **merry** (or **lively**) **as a grig** full of fun; extravagantly lively. [ME, orig. = dwarf: orig. unkn.]

grill¹ /gril/ *n. & v.* • *n.* **1** = GRIDIRON 1. **2** a dish of food cooked on a grill. **3** (in full **grill room**) a restaurant serving grilled food. • *v.* **1** *tr. & intr.* cook or be cooked under a boiler or on a gridiron. **2** *tr. & intr.* subject or be subjected to extreme heat, esp. from the sun. **3** *tr.* subject to severe questioning or interrogation. □□ **grill•er** *n.* **grill•ing** *n.* (in sense 3 of *v.*). [F *gril* (n.), *griller* (v.), f. OF forms of GRILLE]

grill² var. of GRILLE.

gril•lage /grílij/ *n.* a heavy framework of cross-timbering or metal beams forming a foundation for building on difficult ground. [F (as GRILLE)]

grille /gril/ *n.* (also **grill**) **1** a grating or latticed screen, used as a partition or to allow discreet vision. **2** a metal grid protecting the radiator of a motor vehicle. [F f. OF *graille* f. med.L *graticula, craticula*: see GRIDDLE]

grill•work /grílwərk/ *n.* metal fashioned to form a grille (*a balcony of ornate grillwork*).

grilse /grils/ *n.* a young salmon that has returned to fresh water from the sea for the first time. [ME: orig. unkn.]

grim /grim/ *adj.* (**grim•mer, grim•mest**) **1** of a stern or forbidding appearance. **2 a** harsh; merciless; severe. **b** resolute; uncompromising (*grim determination*). **3** ghastly; joyless; sinister (*has a grim truth in it*). **4** unpleasant; unattractive. □ **like grim death** with great determination. □□ **grim•ly** *adv.* **grim•ness** *n.* [OE f. Gmc]

grim•ace /grímos, grimáys/ *n. & v.* • *n.* a distortion of the face made in disgust, etc., or to amuse. • *v.intr.* make a grimace. □□ **grim•ac•er** *n.* [F f. Sp. *grimazo* f. *grima* fright]

gri•mal•kin /grimálkin, –máwlkin/ *n. archaic* (esp. in fiction) **1** an old she-cat. **2** a spiteful old woman. [GRAY + *Malkin* dimin. of the name *Matilda*]

grime /grim/ *n. & v.* • *n.* soot or dirt ingrained in a surface, esp. of buildings or the skin. • *v.tr.* blacken with grime; befoul. [orig. as verb: f. MLG & MDu.]

grim•y /grímee/ *adj.* (**grim•i•er, grim•i•est**) covered with grime; dirty. □□ **grim•i•ly** *adv.* **grim•i•ness** *n.*

grin /grin/ *v. & n.* • *v.* (**grinned, grin•ning**) **1** *intr.* **a** smile broadly, showing the teeth. **b** make a forced, unrestrained, or stupid smile. **2** *tr.* express by grinning (*grinned his satisfaction*). • *n.* the act or action of grinning. □ **grin and bear it** take pain or misfortune stoically. □□ **grin•ner** *n.* **grin•ning•ly** *adv.* [OE *grennian* f. Gmc]

grind /grind/ *v. & n.* • *v.* (*past* and *past part.* **ground** /grownd/) **1 a** *tr.* reduce to small particles or powder by crushing esp. by passing through a mill. **b** *intr.* (of a mill, machine, etc.) move with a crushing action. **2 a** *tr.* reduce, sharpen, or smooth by friction. **b** *tr. & intr.* rub or rub together gratingly (*grind one's teeth*). **3** *tr.* (often foll. by *down*) oppress; harass with exactions (*grinding poverty*). **4** *intr.* **a** (often foll. by *away*) work or study hard. **b** (foll. by *out*) produce with effort (*grinding out verses*). **c** (foll. by *on*) (of a sound) continue gratingly or monotonously. **5** *tr.* turn the handle of e.g., a coffee mill, barrel organ, etc. **6** *intr. sl.* (of a dancer) rotate the hips. **7** *intr. Brit. coarse sl.* have sexual intercourse. • *n.* **1** the act or an instance of grinding. **2** *colloq.* hard dull work; a laborious task (*the daily grind*). **3** the size of ground particles. **4** *sl.* a dancer's rotary movement of the hips. **5** *Brit. coarse sl.* an act of sexual intercourse. □ **grind to a halt** stop laboriously. □□ **grind•ing•ly** *adv.* [OE *grindan*, of unkn. orig.]

grind•er /gríndər/ *n.* **1** a person or thing that grinds, esp. a machine (often in *comb.*: *coffee grinder, organ grinder*). **2** a molar tooth. **3** *US dial.* a submarine sandwich.

grind•stone /gríndstōn/ *n.* **1** a thick revolving disk used for grinding, sharpening, and polishing. **2** a kind of stone used for this. □ **keep one's nose to the grindstone** work hard and continuously.

grin•go /gríngō/ *n.* (*pl.* **-gos**) *colloq.* a foreigner, esp. a non-hispanic N. American, in a Spanish-speaking country. [Sp., = gibberish]

grip /grip/ *v. & n.* • *v.* (**gripped, grip•ping**) **1 a** *tr.* grasp tightly; take a firm hold of. **b** *intr.* take a firm hold, esp. by friction. **2** *tr.* (of a feeling or emotion) deeply affect (a person) (*was gripped by fear*). **3** *tr.* compel the attention or interest of (*a gripping story*). • *n.* **1 a** a firm hold; a tight grasp or clasp. **b** a manner of grasping or holding. **2** the power of holding attention. **3 a** mental or intellectual understanding or mastery. **b** effective control of a situation or one's behavior, etc. (*lose one's grip*). **4 a** a part of a machine that grips or holds something. **b** a part or attachment by which a tool, implement, weapon, etc., is held in the hand. **5** *Brit.* = HAIRGRIP. **6** a traveling bag. **7** an assistant in a theater, movie studio, etc. **8** *Austral. sl.* a job or occupation. □ **come** (or **get**) **to grips with** approach purposefully; begin to deal with. **get a grip (on oneself)** keep or recover one's self-control. **in the grip of** dominated or affected by (esp. an adverse circumstance or unpleasant sensation). **lose one's grip** lose control. □□ **grip•per** *n.* **grip•ping•ly** *adv.* [OE *gripe, gripa* handful (as GRIPE)]

gripe /grip/ *v. & n.* • *v.* **1** *intr. colloq.* complain, esp. peevishly. **2** *tr.* affect with gastric or intestinal pain. **3** *tr. archaic* clutch; grip. **4** *Naut.* **a** *tr.* secure with gripes. **b** *intr.* turn to face the wind in spite of the helm. • *n.* **1** (usu. in *pl.*) gastric or intestinal pain; colic. **2** *colloq.* **a** a complaint. **b** the act of griping. **3** a grip or clutch. **4** (in *pl.*) *Naut.* lashings securing a boat in its place. □□ **grip•er** *n.* **grip•ing•ly** *adv.* [OE *grīpan* f. Gmc: cf. GROPE]

grippe /grip/ *n. archaic* or *colloq.* influenza. [F f. *gripper* seize]

gri•saille /grizí, –záyl/ *n.* **1** a method of painting in gray monochrome, often to imitate sculpture. **2** a painting or stained glass window of this kind. [F f. *gris* gray]

gris•e•o•ful•vin /grízeeəfoolvin/ *n.* an antibiotic used against fungal infections of the hair and skin. [mod.L *griseofulvum* f. med.L *griseus* gray + L *fulvus* reddish yellow]

gri•sette /grizét/ *n.* a young working-class Frenchwoman. [F, orig. a gray dress material, f. *gris* gray]

gris•ly /grízlee/ *adj.* (**gris•li•er, gris•li•est**) causing horror, disgust, or fear. □□ **gris•li•ness** *n.* [OE *grislic* terrifying]

gri•son /gríson, grízən/ *n.* any weasellike mammal of the genus *Galictis*, with dark fur and a white stripe across the forehead. [F, app. f. *grison* gray]

grist /grist/ *n.* **1** grain to grind. **2** malt crushed for brewing. □ **grist to the** (or **a person's**) **mill** a source of profit or advantage. [OE f. Gmc, rel. to GRIND]

gris•tle /grísəl/ *n.* tough flexible tissue in vertebrates; cartilage. □□ **gris•tly** /gríslee/ *adj.* [OE *gristle*]

grit /grit/ *n. & v.* • *n.* **1** particles of stone or sand, esp. as causing discomfort, clogging machinery, etc. **2** coarse sandstone. **3** *colloq.* pluck; endurance; strength of character. • *v.* (**grit•ted, grit•ting**) **1** *tr.* spread grit on (icy roads, etc.). **2** *tr.* clench (the teeth). **3** *intr.* make or move with a grating sound. □□ **grit•ter** *n.* **grit•ty** *adj.* (**grit•ti•er, grit•ti•est**). **grit•ti•ly** *adv.* **grit•ti•ness** *n.* [OE *grēot* f. Gmc: cf. GRITS, GROATS]

grits /grits/ *n.pl.* **1** coarsely ground hulled grain, esp. hominy prepared by boiling, then sometimes frying. **2** *Brit.* oats that have been husked but not ground. [OE *grytt(e)*: cf. GRIT, GROATS]

griz·zle /grízǝl/ v.intr. Brit. colloq. **1** (esp. of a child) cry fretfully. **2** complain whiningly. □□ **griz·zler** n. **griz·zly** adj. [19th c.: orig. unkn.]

griz·zled /grízǝld/ adj. having, or streaked with, gray hair. [grizzle gray f. OF grisel f. gris gray]

griz·zly /grízlee/ adj. & n. ● adj. (griz·zli·er, griz·zli·est) gray, grayish, gray-haired. ● n. (pl. ·zlies) (in full **grizzly bear**) a large variety of brown bear found in N. America.

groan /grōn/ v. & n. ● v. **1** a intr. make a deep sound expressing pain, grief, or disapproval. **b** tr. utter with groans. **2** intr. complain inarticulately. **3** intr. (usu. foll. by under, beneath, with) be loaded or oppressed. ● n. the sound made in groaning. □ **groan inwardly** be distressed. □□ **groan·er** n. **groan·ing·ly** adv. [OE grānian f. Gmc, rel. to GRIN]

groat /grōt/ n. hist. **1** a silver coin worth four old English pence. **2** archaic a small sum (don't care a groat). [ME f. MDu. groot, orig. = great, i.e., thick (penny): cf. GROSCHEN]

groats /grōts/ n.pl. hulled or crushed grain, esp. oats. [OE grotan (pl.): cf. grot fragment, grēot GRIT, grytt bran]

gro·cer /grṓsǝr/ n. a dealer in food and household provisions. [ME & AF grosser, orig. one who sells in the gross, f. OF grossier f. med.L grossarius (as GROSS)]

gro·cer·y /grṓsǝree/ n. (pl. ·ies) **1** a grocer's trade or store. **2** (in pl.) provisions, esp. food, sold by a grocer.

grog /grog/ n. **1** a drink of liquor (orig. rum) and water. **2** Austral. & NZ colloq. alcoholic liquor, esp. beer. [said to be from "Old Grog," the reputed nickname (f. his GROGRAM cloak) of Admiral Vernon, who in 1740 first had diluted instead of neat rum served out to sailors]

grog·gy /grógee/ adj. (grog·gi·er, grog·gi·est) incapable or unsteady from being dazed or semiconscious. □□ **grog·gi·ly** adv. **grog·gi·ness** n.

grog·ram /grógrǝm, grṓ–/ n. a coarse fabric of silk, mohair and wool, or a mixture of these. [F gros grain coarse grain (as GROSS, GRAIN)]

groin[1] /groyn/ n. & v. ● n. **1** the depression between the belly and the thigh. **2** Archit. **a** an edge formed by intersecting vaults. **b** an arch supporting a vault. ● v.tr. Archit. build with groins. [ME grynde, perh. f. OE grynde depression]

groin[2] /groyn/ n. (also **groyn**) a wooden framework or low broad wall built out from a shore to check erosion of a beach. [dial. groin snout f. OF groign f. LL grunium pig's snout]

grom·met /grómit/ n. (also **grum·met** /grúmit/) **1** a metal, plastic, or rubber eyelet placed in a hole to protect or insulate a rope or cable, etc., passed through it. **2** a tube passed through the eardrum in surgery to make a connection with the middle ear. [obs. F grommette f. gourmer to curb, of unkn. orig.]

grom·well /grómwǝl/ n. any of various plants of the genus Lithospermum, with hard seeds formerly used in medicine. [ME f. OF gromil, prob. f. med.L gruinum milium (unrecorded) crane's millet]

groom /grōōm/ n. & v. ● n. **1** = BRIDEGROOM. **2** a person employed to take care of horses. **3** Brit. Mil. any of certain officers of the Royal Household. ● v.tr. **1** a curry or tend (a horse). **b** give a neat appearance to (a person, etc.). **2** (of an ape or monkey, etc.) clean and comb the fur of (its fellow) with the fingers. **3** prepare or train (a person) for a particular purpose or activity (was groomed for the top job). [ME, orig. = boy: orig. unkn.]

groove /grōōv/ n. & v. ● n. **1** a a channel or hollow, esp. one made to guide motion or receive a corresponding ridge. **b** a spiral track cut in a phonograph record. **2** an established routine or habit, esp. a monotonous one. ● v. **1** tr. make a groove or grooves in. **2** intr. sl. **a** enjoy oneself. **b** (often foll. by with) make progress; get on well. □ **in the groove** sl. **1** doing or performing well. **2** fashionable. [ME, = mine shaft, f. obs. Du. Du. groeve furrow f. Gmc]

▶The use of groove in sense 2 of the verb often occurs with reference to popular music or jazz; the use is becoming obsolete in general contexts.

groov·y /grṓvee/ adj. (groov·i·er, groov·i·est) **1** sl. or joc. fashionable and exciting; enjoyable; excellent. **2** of or like a groove. □□ **groov·i·ly** adv. **groov·i·ness** n.

grope /grōp/ v. & n. ● v. **1** intr. (usu. foll. by for) feel about or search blindly or uncertainly with the hands. **2** intr. (foll. by for, after) search mentally (was groping for the answer). **3** tr. feel (one's way) toward something. **4** tr. sl. fondle clumsily for sexual pleasure. ● n. the process or an instance of groping. □□ **grop·er** n. **grop·ing·ly** adv. [OE grāpian f. Gmc]

grop·er /grṓpǝr/ n. esp. Austral. & NZ = GROUPER. [var. of GROUPER]

gros·beak /grṓsbeek/ n. any of various finches of the families Cardinalidae and Fringillidae, having stout conical bills and usu. brightly colored plumage. [F grosbec (as GROSS)]

gro·schen /grṓshǝn/ n. **1** an Austrian coin and monetary unit, one hundredth of a schilling. **2** a German 10-pfennig piece. **3** hist. a small German silver coin. [G f. MHG gros, grosse f. med.L (denarius) grossus thick (penny): cf. GROAT]

gros·grain /grṓgrayn/ n. a corded fabric of silk, rayon, etc. [F, = coarse grain (as GROSS, GRAIN)]

gros point /grō póynt, pwáN/ n. cross-stitch embroidery on large-holed canvas. [F (as GROSS, POINT)]

gross /grōs/ adj., v., & n. ● adj. **1** overfed; bloated; repulsively fat. **2** (of a person, manners, or morals) noticeably coarse, unrefined, or indecent. **3** flagrant; conspicuously wrong (gross negligence). **4** total; without deductions; not net (gross tonnage; gross income). **5 a** luxuriant; rank. **b** thick; solid; dense. **6** (of the senses, etc.) dull; lacking sensitivity. **7** sl. repulsive; disgusting. ● v.tr. produce or earn as gross profit or income. ● n. (pl. same) an amount equal to twelve dozen, or 144, things. □ **by the gross** in large quantities; wholesale. **gross out** sl. disgust, esp. by repulsive or obscene behavior. **gross up** increase (a net amount) to its value before deductions. □□ **gross·ly** adv. **gross·ness** n. [ME f. OF gros grosse large f. LL grossus: (n.) f. F grosse douzaine large dozen]

gross do·mes·tic prod·uct n. the total value of goods produced and services provided in a country in one year. ¶ abbr.: **GDP**.

gross na·tion·al prod·uct n. the total value of goods produced and services provided by a country during one year, equal to the gross domestic product plus the net income from foreign investments. ¶ Abbr.: **GNP**.

grot /grot/ n. & adj. Brit. sl. ● n. rubbish; junk. ● adj. dirty. [backform. f. GROTTY]

gro·tesque /grōtésk/ adj. & n. ● adj. **1** comically or repulsively distorted; monstrous; unnatural. **2** incongruous; ludicrous; absurd. ● n. **1** a decorative form interweaving human and animal features. **2** a comically distorted figure or design. **3** Printing a family of sans serif typefaces. □□ **gro·tesque·ly** adv. **gro·tesque·ness** n. **gro·tes·quer·ie** /–téskǝree/ n.

WORD HISTORY　grotesque

Mid-16th century (as noun): from French crotesque (the earliest form in English), from Italian grottesca, from opera or pittura grottesca 'work or painting in a grotto'; 'grotto' here probably denoted the rooms of ancient buildings in Rome that had been revealed by excavations, and that contained murals in a distorted style.

grot·to /grótō/ n. (pl. ·toes or ·tos) **1** a small esp. picturesque cave. **2** an artificial ornamental cave, e.g., in a park or large garden. □□ **grot·toed** adj. [It. grotta ult. f. L crypta f. Gk kruptē CRYPT]

grot·ty /grótee/ adj. (grot·ti·er, grot·ti·est) Brit. sl. unpleasant; dirty; shabby; unattractive. □□ **grot·ti·ness** n. [shortening of GROTESQUE + –Y[1]]

grouch /growch/ v. & n. colloq. ● v.intr. grumble. ● n. **1** a discontented person. **2** a fit of grumbling or the sulks. **3** a cause of discontent. [var. of grutch: see GRUDGE]

grouch·y /grówchee/ adj. (grouch·i·er, grouch·i·est) colloq. discontented; grumpy. □□ **grouch·i·ly** adv. **grouch·i·ness** n.

ground[1] /grownd/ n. & v. ● n. **1 a** the surface of the earth, esp. as contrasted with the air around it. **b** a part of this specified in some way (low ground). **2** the substance of the earth's surface; soil; earth (stony ground; dug deep into the ground). **3 a** a position, area, or distance on the earth's surface. **b** the extent of activity, etc., achieved or of a subject dealt with (the book covers a lot of ground). **4** (often in pl.) a foundation, motive, or reason (there is ground for concern; there are grounds for believing; excused on the grounds of poor health). **5** an area of a special kind or designated for special use (often in comb.: fishing-grounds). **6** (in pl.) an area of sometimes enclosed land attached to a house, etc. **7** an area or basis for consideration, agreement, etc. (common ground; on firm ground). **8 a** (in painting) the prepared surface giving the predominant color or tone. **b** (in embroidery, ceramics, etc.) the undecorated surface. **9** (in full **ground bass**) Mus. a short theme in the bass constantly repeated with the upper parts of the music varied. **10** (in pl.) solid particles, esp. of coffee, forming a residue. **11** Electr. the connection to the ground that completes an electrical circuit. **12** the bottom of the sea (the ship touched ground). **13** Brit. the floor of a room, etc. **14** a piece of wood fixed to a wall as a base for boards, plaster, or joinery. **15** (attrib.) **a** (of animals) living on or in the ground; (of fish) living at the bottom of water; (of plants) dwarfish or trailing. **b** relating to or concerned with the ground (ground staff). ● v. **1** tr.**a** refuse authority for (a pilot or an aircraft) to fly. **b** restrict (esp. a child) from certain activities, places, etc., esp. as a form of punishment. **2 a** tr. run (a ship) aground; strand. **b** intr. (of a ship) run aground. **3** tr. (foll. by in) instruct thoroughly (in a subject). **4** tr. (often as **grounded** adj.) (foll. by on) base (a principle, conclusion, etc.) on. **5** tr. Electr. connect to the ground. **6** intr. alight on the ground. **7** tr. place or lay (esp. weapons) on the ground. □ **break new** (or **fresh**) **ground** treat a subject previously not dealt with. **cut the ground from under a person's feet** anticipate and preempt a person's arguments, plans, etc. **down to the ground** Brit. colloq. thoroughly; in every respect. **fall to the ground** (of a plan, etc.) fail. **from the ground up** gradually and thoroughly; from top to bottom. **gain** (or **make**) **ground 1** advance steadily; make progress. **2** (foll. by on) catch (a person) up. **get in on the ground floor** become part of an enterprise in its early stages. **get off the ground** *colloq.* make a successful start. **give** (or **lose**) **ground 1** retreat; decline. **2** lose the advantage or one's position in an argument, contest, etc. **go to ground 1** (of a fox, etc.) enter its burrow, etc. **2** (of a person) become inaccessible for a prolonged period. **hold one's ground** not retreat or give way. **into the ground** beyond what is reasonable, necessary, or productive. **on the ground** at the point of production or operation; in practical conditions. **on one's own ground** on one's own territory or subject; on one's own terms. **thin on the ground** not numerous. **work** (or **run**, etc.) **oneself into the ground** *colloq.* work, etc., to the point of exhaustion. □□ **ground•er** *n.* [OE *grund* f. Gmc]

ground² *past* and *past part.* of GRIND.

ground•age /gró͟wndij/ *n. Brit.* duty levied on a ship entering a port or lying on a shore.

ground bait *n.* bait thrown to the bottom of a fishing ground.

ground ball *n.* (also **ground•er**) *Baseball* a ball batted such that it bounces on the ground.

ground•break•ing /gró͟wndbrayking/ *adj.* innovative in character; pioneering (*groundbreaking techniques in electronic communication*).

ground con•trol *n.* the personnel and equipment that monitor and direct the flight and landing of aircraft or spacecraft.

ground cov•er *n.* plants covering the surface of the soil, esp. low-growing spreading plants that inhibit the growth of weeds.

ground crew *n.* mechanics who maintain and service aircraft.

ground•er /gró͟wndər/ *n. Baseball* = GROUND BALL.

ground•fish /gró͟wndfish/ *n.* a fish, as cod, flounder, etc., that lives at the bottom of oceans, lakes, rivers, etc.

ground floor *n.* the floor of a building at ground level.

ground frost *n.* frost on the surface of the ground or in the top layer of soil.

ground glass *n.* **1** glass with a smooth ground surface that renders it nontransparent while retaining its translucency. **2** glass ground into an abrasive powder.

ground•hog /gró͟wndhawg, –hog/ *n.* **1** a woodchuck; a marmot. **2** *Brit.* = AARDVARK.

ground•ing /gró͟wnding/ *n.* basic training or instruction in a subject.

ground•less /gró͟wndlis/ *adj.* without motive or foundation. □□ **ground•less•ly** *adv.* **ground•less•ness** *n.* [OE *grundlēas* (as GROUND¹, –LESS)]

ground lev•el *n.* **1** the level of the ground; the ground floor. **2** *Physics* = GROUND STATE.

ground•ling /gró͟wndling/ *n.* **1 a** a creeping or dwarf plant. **b** an animal that lives near the ground, at the bottom of a lake, etc., esp. a groundfish. **2** a person on the ground as opposed to one in an aircraft. **3** a spectator or reader of inferior taste (with ref. to Shakesp. *Hamlet* III. ii. 11).

ground•nut /gró͟wndnut/ *n.* **1 a** a N. American wild bean. **b** its edible tuber. **2** = PEANUT.

ground plan *n.* **1** the plan of a floor of a building. **2** the general outline of a scheme.

ground rules *n.pl.* basic principles or rules in a situation (*the journalists were given strict ground rules before the interview*).

ground•sel /gró͟wndsəl/ *n.* any composite plant of the genus *Senecio*, esp. *S. vulgaris*, used as a food for cage birds. [OE *grundeswylige*, *gundæswelgiæ* (perh. = pus absorber f. *gund* pus, with ref. to use for poultices)]

ground•sheet /gró͟wndsheet/ *n.* a waterproof sheet for spreading on the ground, esp. in or under a tent.

grounds•keep•er /gró͟wndzkeepər, gró͟wnz–/ *n.* a person who maintains the grounds of a sizable property, as a golf course or park.

grounds•man /gró͟wndzmən/ *n. Brit.* (*pl.* **•men**) a person who maintains a sports field; a groundskeeper.

ground speed *n.* an aircraft's speed relative to the ground.

ground squir•rel *n.* **1** a squirrellike rodent, e.g., a chipmunk, gopher, etc. **2** any squirrel of the genus *Spermophilus* living in burrows.

ground state *n. Physics* the lowest energy state of an atom, etc.

ground stroke *n. Tennis* a stroke played near the ground after the ball has bounced.

ground•swell /gró͟wndswel/ *n.* an increasingly forceful presence (esp. of public opinion).

ground swell *n.* **1** a heavy sea caused by a distant or past storm or an earthquake. **2** = GROUNDSWELL.

ground•wa•ter /gró͟wndwáwtər, –wotər/ *n.* water found in soil or in pores, crevices, etc., in rock.

ground•work /gró͟wndwərk/ *n.* **1** preliminary or basic work. **2** a foundation or basis.

ground ze•ro *n.* the point on the ground under an exploding (usu. nuclear) bomb.

group /gro͞op/ *n. & v.* ● *n.* **1** a number of persons or things located close together, or considered or classed together. **2** (*attrib.*) concerning or done by a group (*a group photograph*; *group therapy*). **3** a number of people working together or sharing beliefs, e.g., part of a political party. **4** a number of commercial companies under common ownership. **5** an ensemble playing popular music. **6** a division

of an air force or air fleet. **7** *Math.* a set of elements, together with an associative binary operation, which contains an inverse for each element and an identity element. **8** *Chem.* **a** a set of ions or radicals giving a characteristic qualitative reaction. **b** a set of elements having similar properties. **c** a combination of atoms having a recognizable identity in a number of compounds. ● *v.* **1** *tr. & intr.* form or be formed into a group. **2** *tr.* (often foll. by *with*) place in a group or groups. **3** *tr.* form (colors, figures, etc.) into a well-arranged and harmonious whole. **4** *tr.* classify. □□ **group•age** *n.* [F *groupe* f. It. *gruppo* f. Gmc, rel. to CROP]

group dy•nam•ics *n. Psychol.* the field of social psychology concerned with the nature, development, and interactions of human groups.

group•er /gro͞opər/ *n.* any marine fish of the family Serranidae, with heavy body, big head, and wide mouth. [Port. *garupa*, prob. f. native name in S. America]

group•ie /gro͞opee/ *n. sl.* an ardent follower of touring pop groups, esp. a young woman seeking sexual relations with them.

group•ing /gro͞oping/ *n.* **1** a process or system of allocation to groups. **2** the formation or arrangement so produced.

group prac•tice *n.* a medical practice in which several doctors are associated.

group ther•a•py *n.* therapy in which patients with a similar condition are brought together to assist one another psychologically.

group ve•loc•i•ty *n.* the speed of travel of the energy of a wave or wave group.

grouse¹ /grows/ *n.* (*pl.* same) **1** any of various game birds of the family Tetraonidae, with a plump body and feathered legs. **2** the flesh of a grouse used as food. [16th c.: orig. uncert.]

grouse² /grows/ *v. & n. colloq.* ● *v.intr.* grumble or complain pettily. ● *n.* a complaint. □□ **grous•er** *n.* [19th c.: orig. unkn.]

grouse³ /grows/ *adj. Austral. sl.* very good or excellent (*extra grouse*). [20th c.: orig. unkn.]

grout¹ /growt/ *n. & v.* ● *n.* a thin fluid mortar for filling gaps in tiling, etc. ● *v.tr.* provide or fill with grout. □□ **grout•er** *n.* [perh. f. GROUT², but cf. F dial. *grouter* grout a wall]

grout² /growt/ *n. Brit.* sediment; dregs. [OE *grūt*, rel. to GRITS, GROATS]

grout•er /gró͟wtər/ *n. Austral. sl.* an unfair advantage. [20th c.: orig. uncert.]

grove /grōv/ *n.* a small wood or group of trees. [OE *grāf*, rel. to *grǣfa* brushwood]

grov•el /gró͟vəl/ *v.intr.* (**grov•eled, grov•el•ing;** also **grov•elled, grov•el•ling**) **1** behave obsequiously in seeking favor or forgiveness. **2** lie prone in abject humility. □□ **grov•el•er** *n.* **grov•el•ing** *adj.* **grov•el•ing•ly** *adv.* [back-form. f. obs. *grovelling* (adv.) f. *gruf* face down f. *on grufe* f. ON *á grúfu*, later taken as pres. part.]

grow /grō/ *v.* (*past* **grew** /gro͞o/; *past part.* **grown** /grōn/) **1** *intr.* increase in size, height, quantity, degree, or in any way regarded as measurable (e.g., authority or reputation) (often foll. by *in*: *grew in stature*). **2** *intr.* **a** develop or exist as a living plant or natural product. **b** develop in a specific way or direction (*began to grow sideways*). **c** germinate; sprout; spring up. **3** *intr.* be produced; come naturally into existence; arise. **4** *intr.* (as **grown** *adj.*) fully matured; adult. **5** *intr.* **a** become gradually (*grow rich*; *grow less*). **b** (foll. by to + infin.) come by degrees (*grew to like it*). **6** *intr.* (foll. by *into*) **a** become or having grown or developed (*the acorn has grown into a tall oak*; *will grow into a fine athlete*). **b** become large enough for or suited to (*will grow into the coat*; *grew into her new job*). **7** *intr.* (foll. by *on*) become gradually more favored by. **8** *tr.* **a** produce (plants, fruit, wood, etc.) by cultivation. **b** bring forth. **c** cause (a beard, etc.) to develop. **9** *tr.* (in *passive*; foll. by *over*, *up*) be covered with a growth. □ **grow out of 1** become too large to wear (a garment). **2** become too mature to retain (a childish habit, etc.). **3** be the result or development of. **grow together** coalesce. **grow up 1 a** advance to maturity. **b** (esp. in *imper.*) begin to behave sensibly. **2** (of a custom) arise; become common. □□ **grow•a•ble** *adj.* [OE *grōwan* f. Gmc, rel. to GRASS, GREEN]

grow•er /gró͟ər/ *n.* **1** (often in *comb.*) a person growing produce (-*fruit-grower*). **2** a plant that grows in a specified way (*a fast grower*).

grow•ing pains *n.* **1** early difficulties in the development of an enterprise, etc. **2** neuralgic pain in children's legs due to fatigue, etc.

growl /growl/ *v. & n.* ● *v.* **1** *intr.* **a** (often foll. by *at*) (esp. of a dog) make a low guttural sound, usu. of anger. **b** murmur angrily. **2** *intr.* rumble. **3** *tr.* (often foll. by *out*) utter with a growl. ● *n.* **1** a growling sound, esp. made by a dog. **2** an angry murmur; complaint. **3** a rumble. □□ **growl•ing•ly** *adv.* [prob. imit.]

growl•er /gró͟lər/ *n.* **1** a person or thing that growls, esp. *sl.* a dog. **2** a small iceberg.

grown *past part.* of GROW.

grown-up *adj. & n.* ● *adj.* adult. ● *n.* an adult person.

growth /grōth/ *n.* **1** the act or process of growing. **2** an increase in size or value. **3** something that has grown or is growing. **4** *Med.* a morbid formation. **5** the cultivation of produce. **6** a crop or yield of grapes.

growth hor·mone *n. Biol.* a substance which stimulates the growth of a plant or animal.

growth in·dus·try *n.* an industry that is developing rapidly.

growth stock *n.* stock, etc., that tends to increase in capital value rather than yield high income.

groyne var. of GROIN².

grub /grub/ *n. & v.* ●*n.* **1** the larva of an insect, esp. of a beetle. **2** *colloq.* food. **3** a menial; a drudge. ●*v.* (**grubbed, grub·bing**) **1** *tr. & intr.* dig superficially. **2** *tr.* **a** clear (the ground) of roots and stumps. **b** clear away (roots, etc.). **3** *tr.* (foll. by *up, out*) **a** fetch by digging (*grubbing up weeds*). **b** extract (information, etc.) by searching in books, etc. **4** *intr.* search; rummage. **5** *intr.* (foll. by *on, along, away*) toil; plod. □□ **grub·ber** *n.* (also in *comb.*). [ME, (v.) perh. corresp. to OE *grybban* (unrecorded) f. Gmc]

grub·by /grúbee/ *adj.* (**grub·bi·er, grub·bi·est**) **1** dirty; grimy; slovenly. **2** of or infested with grubs. □□ **grub·bi·ly** *adv.* **grub·bi·ness** *n.*

grub·stake /grúbstayk/ *n. & v.* ●*n.* material or provisions supplied to an enterprise in return for a share in the resulting profits (orig. in prospecting for ore). ●*v.tr.* provide with a grubstake. □□ **grub·stak·er** *n.*

Grub Street /grúb/ *n.* (often *attrib.*) the world or class of literary hacks and impoverished authors. [name of a street (later Milton St.) in Moorgate, London, inhabited by these in the 17th c.]

grudge /gruj/ *n. & v.* ●*n.* a persistent feeling of ill will or resentment, esp. one due to an insult or injury (*bears a grudge against me*). ●*v.tr.* **1** be resentfully unwilling to give, grant, or allow (a thing). **2** (foll. by verbal noun or *to* + infin.) be reluctant to do (a thing) (*grudged paying so much*). □□ **grudg·er** *n.* [ME *grutch* f. OF *grouchier* murmur, of unkn. orig.]

grudg·ing /grújing/ *adj.* reluctant; not willing. □□ **grudg·ing·ly** *adv.* **grudg·ing·ness** *n.*

gru·el /gróoəl/ *n.* a liquid food of oatmeal, etc., boiled in milk or water chiefly for invalids. [ME f. OF, ult. f. Gmc, rel. to GROUT¹]

gru·el·ing /gróoəling/ *adj. & n.* (also **gruel·ling**) ●*adj.* extremely demanding, severe, or tiring. ●*n.* a harsh or exhausting experience; punishment. □□ **gru·el·ing·ly** *adv.* [GRUEL as verb, = exhaust, punish]

grue·some /gróosəm/ *adj.* horrible; grisly; disgusting. □□ **grue·some·ly** *adv.* **grue·some·ness** *n.* [Sc. *grue* to shudder f. Scand. + –SOME¹]

gruff /gruf/ *adj.* **1 a** (of a voice) low and harsh. **b** (of a person) having a gruff voice. **2** surly; laconic; rough-mannered. □□ **gruff·ly** *adv.* **gruff·ness** *n.* [Du., MLG *grof* coarse f. WG (rel. to ROUGH)]

grum·ble /grúmbəl/ *v. & n.* ●*v.* **1** *intr.* **a** (often foll. by *at, about, over*) complain peevishly. **b** be discontented. **2** *intr.* **a** utter a dull inarticulate sound; murmur; growl faintly. **b** rumble. **3** *tr.* (often foll. by *out*) utter complainingly. **4** *intr.* (as **grumbling** *adj.*) *colloq.* giving intermittent discomfort without causing illness (*a grumbling appendix*). ●*n.* **1** a complaint. **2 a** a dull inarticulate sound; a murmur. **b** a rumble. □□ **grum·bler** *n.* **grum·bling** *adj.* **grum·bling·ly** *adv.* **grum·bly** *adj.* [obs. *grumme*: cf. MDu. *grommen*, MLG *grommelen*, f. Gmc]

grum·met var. of GROMMET.

grump /grump/ *n. colloq.* **1** a grumpy person. **2** (in *pl.*) a fit of sulks. □□ **grump·ish** *adj.* **grump·ish·ly** *adv.* [imit.]

grump·y /grúmpee/ *adj.* (**grump·i·er, grump·i·est**) morosely irritable; surly. □□ **grump·i·ly** *adv.* **grump·i·ness** *n.*

Grun·dy /grúndee/ *n.* (*pl.* **·dies**) (in full **Mrs. Grundy**) a person embodying conventional propriety and prudery. □□ **Grun·dy·ism** *n.* [a person repeatedly mentioned in T. Morton's comedy *Speed the Plough* (1798)]

grunge /grunj/ *n. sl.* **1** grime; dirt. **2** an aggressive style of rock music characterized by a raucous guitar sound. **3** a style of youthful clothing and appearance marked by studied dishevelment. □□ **grun·gy** *adj.* [app. after GRUBBY, DINGY, etc.]

grun·ion /grúnyən/ *n.* a slender Californian marine fish, *Leuresthes tenuis*, that comes ashore to spawn. [prob. f. Sp. *gruñón* grunter]

grunt /grunt/ *n. & v.* ●*n.* **1** a low guttural sound made by a pig. **2** a sound resembling this. **3** any fish of the genus *Haemulon* that grunts when caught. ●*v.* **1** *intr.* (of a pig) make a grunt or grunts. **2** *intr.* (of a person) make a low inarticulate sound resembling this, esp. to express discontent, dissent, fatigue, etc. **3** *tr.* utter with a grunt. [OE *grunnettan*, prob. orig. imit.]

grunt·er /grúntər/ *n.* **1** a person or animal that grunts, esp. a pig. **2** a grunting fish, esp. = GRUNT *n.* 3.

Grunth var. of GRANTH.

Gru·yère /groo-yáir, gree-/ *n.* a firm pale cheese made from cow's milk. [*Gruyère*, a district in Switzerland where it was first made]

gr. wt. *abbr.* gross weight.

gryph·on var. of GRIFFIN.

grys·bok /grísbok/ *n.* any small antelope of the genus *Raphicerus*, native to S. Africa. [S.Afr. Du. f. Du. *grijs* gray + *bok* BUCK¹]

GSA *abbr.* **1** General Services Administration. **2** Girl Scouts of America.

G-string /jée-string/ *n.* **1** *Mus.* a string sounding the note G. **2** (also **gee-string**) a narrow strip of cloth, etc., covering only the genitals and attached to a string around the waist, as worn esp. by striptease artists.

G suit /jée-soot/ *n.* a garment with inflatable pressurized pouches, worn by pilots and astronauts to enable them to withstand high acceleration. [*g* = gravity + SUIT]

GT *n.* a high-performance two-door automobile. [abbr. f. It. *gran turismo* great touring]

Gt. *abbr.* Great.

Gt. Brit. *abbr.* Great Britain.

gua·ca·mo·le /gwaákəmólee/ *n.* a dish of mashed avocado mixed with chopped onion, tomatoes, chili peppers, and seasoning. [Amer. Sp. f. Nahuatl *ahuacamolli* f. *ahuacatl* avocado + *molli* sauce]

gua·cha·ro /gwaáchərō/ *n.* (*pl.* **·ros**) a nocturnal bird, *Steatornis caripensis*, native to S. America and feeding on fruit. Also called **oil·bird.** [S.Amer. Sp.]

guai·ac var. of GUAIACUM 2.

guai·a·cum /gwíəkəm/ *n.* **1** any tree of the genus *Guaiacum*, native to tropical America. **2** (also **guai·ac** /gwíak/) **a** the hard dense oily timber of some of these, esp. *G. officinale*. Also called **lignum vitae. b** the resin from this used medicinally. [mod.L f. Sp. *guayaco* of Haitian orig.]

guan /gwaan/ *n.* any of various game birds of the family Cracidae, of tropical America. [prob. f. a native name]

gua·na·co /gwənaákō/ *n.* (*pl.* **·cos**) a llamalike camelid, *Lama guanicoe*, with a coat of soft pale brown hair used for wool. [Quechua *huanaco*]

gua·nine /gwaáneen/ *n. Biochem.* a purine derivative found in all living organisms as a component base of DNA and RNA. [GUANO + –INE⁴]

gua·no /gwaánō/ *n. & v.* (*pl.* **·nos**) ●*n.* **1** the excrement of sea birds, used as manure. **2** an artificial manure, esp. that made from fish. ●*v.tr.* (**·noes, ·noed**) fertilize with guano. [Sp. f. Quechua *huanu* dung]

Gua·ra·ni /gwaáronee/ *n.* **1 a** a member of a S. American Indian people. **b** the language of this people. **2** (**guarani**) the monetary unit of Paraguay. [Sp.]

guar·an·tee /gárənt ée/ *n. & v.* ●*n.* **1 a** a formal promise or assurance, esp. that an obligation will be fulfilled or that something is of a specified quality and durability. **b** a document giving such an undertaking. **2** = GUARANTY. **3** a person making a guaranty or giving a security. ●*v.tr.* (**guar·an·tees, guar·an·teed**) **1 a** give or serve as a guarantee for; answer for the due fulfillment of (a contract, etc.) or the genuineness of (an article). **b** assure the permanence, etc., of. **c** provide with a guarantee. **2** (foll. by *that* + clause, or *to* + infin.) give a promise or assurance. **3 a** (foll. by *to*) secure the possession of (a thing) for a person. **b** make (a person) secure against a risk or in possession of a thing. [earlier *garante*, perh. f. Sp. *garante* = F *garant* WARRANT: later infl. by F *garantie* guaranty]

guar·an·tor /gárəntáwr, –tər/ *n.* a person who gives a guarantee or guaranty.

guar·an·ty /gárə ntee/ *n.* (*pl.* **·ties**) **1** a written or other undertaking to answer for the payment of a debt or for the performance of an obligation by another person liable in the first instance. **2** a thing serving as security for a guaranty. [AF *guarantie*, var. of *warantie* WARRANTY]

guard /gaard/ *v. & n.* ●*v.* **1** *tr.* (often foll. by *from, against*) watch over and defend or protect from harm. **2** *tr.* keep watch by (a door, etc.) so as to control entry or exit. **3** *tr.* supervise (prisoners, etc.) and prevent from escaping. **4** *tr.* provide (machinery) with a protective device. **5** *tr.* keep (thoughts or speech) in check. **6** *tr.* provide with safeguards. **7** *intr.* (foll. by *against*) take precautions. **8** *tr.* (in various games) protect (a piece, card, etc.) with set moves. ●*n.* **1** a state of vigilance or watchfulness. **2** a person who protects or keeps watch. **3** a body of soldiers, etc. serving to protect a place or person; an escort. **4** a person who keeps watch over prisoners. **5** a part of an army detached for some purpose (*advance guard*). **6** (in *pl.*) (usu. **Guards**) any of various bodies of troops nominally employed to guard a ruler. **7** a thing that protects or defends. **8** (often in *comb.*) a device fitted to a machine, vehicle, weapon, etc., to prevent injury or accident to the user (*fire guard*). **9** *Brit.* an official who rides with and is in general charge of a train. **10** in some sports: **a** a protective or defensive player. **b** a defensive posture or motion. □ **be on** (or **keep** or **stand**) **guard** (of a sentry, etc.) keep watch. **lower one's guard** reduce vigilance against attack. **off** (or **off one's**) **guard** unprepared for some surprise or difficulty. **on** (or **on one's**) **guard** prepared for all contingencies; vigilant. **raise one's guard** become vigilant against attack. □□ **guard·er** *n.* **guard·less** *adj.* [ME f. OF *garde, garder* ult. f. WG, rel. to WARD *n.*]

guard·ant /gaárd'nt/ *adj. Heraldry* depicted with the body sideways and the face toward the viewer.

guard cell *n. Bot.* either of a pair of cells surrounding the stomata in plants.

guard·ed /gáardid/ *adj.* (of a remark, etc.) cautious; avoiding commitment. □□ **guard·ed·ly** *adv.* **guard·ed·ness** *n.*

guard·house /gáardhows/ *n.* a building used to accommodate a military guard or to temporarily detain military prisoners.

guard·i·an /gáardeeən/ *n.* **1** a defender, protector, or keeper. **2** a person having legal custody of another person and his or her property when that person is incapable of managing his or her own affairs. **3** the superior of a Franciscan convent. □□ **guard·i·an·ship** *n.* [ME f. AF *gardein*, OF *garden* f. Frank., rel. to WARD, WARDEN]

guard·i·an an·gel *n.* a spirit conceived as watching over a person or place.

guard·rail /gáardrayl/ *n.* a rail, e.g., a handrail, fitted as a support or to prevent an accident.

guard·room /gáardrŏm, -rŏŏm/ *n.* a room with the same purpose as a guardhouse.

guards·man /gáardzmən/ *n.* (*pl.* **·men**) **1** a soldier belonging to a body of guards. **2** (in the UK) a soldier of a regiment of Guards.

gua·va /gwáavə/ *n.* **1** a small tropical American tree, *Psidium guajava*, bearing an edible pale yellow fruit with pink juicy flesh. **2** this fruit. [Sp. *guayaba* prob. f. a S. Amer. name]

gua·yu·le /gwiyŏŏlee/ *n.* **1** a silver-leaved shrub, *Parthenium argentatum*, native to Mexico. **2** a rubber substitute made from the sap of this plant. [Amer. Sp. f. Nahuatl *cuauhuli*]

gub·bins /gúbinz/ *n. Brit.* **1** a set of equipment or paraphernalia. **2** a gadget. **3** something of little value. **4** *colloq.* a foolish person (often with ref. to oneself). [orig. = fragments, f. obs. *gobbon*: perh. rel. to GOBBET]

gu·ber·na·to·ri·al /gŏŏbərnətáwreeəl, gyŏŏ-/ *adj.* of or relating to a governor. [L *gubernator* governor]

gudg·eon¹ /gújən/ *n.* **1** a small European freshwater fish, *Gobio gobio*, often used as bait. **2** a credulous or easily fooled person. [ME f. OF *goujon* f. L *gobio -onis* GOBY]

gudg·eon² /gújən/ *n.* **1** any of various kinds of pivot working a wheel, bell, etc. **2** the tubular part of a hinge into which the pin fits to effect the joint. **3** a socket at the stern of a boat, into which a rudder is fitted. **4** a pin holding two blocks of stone, etc., together. [ME f. OF *goujon* dimin. of *gouge* GOUGE]

guel·der rose /géldər/ *n.* a deciduous shrub, *Viburnum opulus*, with round bunches of creamy white flowers. Also called **snowball bush**. [Du. *geldersch* f. *Gelderland* a province in the Netherlands]

gue·non /gənón/ *n.* any African monkey of the genus *Cercopithecus*, having a characteristic long tail, e.g., the vervet. [F: orig. unkn.]

guer·don /gárdən/ *n. & v. poet.* ●*n.* a reward or recompense. ●*v.tr.* give a reward to. [ME f. OF *guerdon* f. med.L *widerdonum* f. WG *widarlōn* (as WITH, LOAN¹), assim. to L *donum* gift]

Guern·sey /gárnzee/ *n.* (*pl.* **·seys**) **1 a** an animal of a breed of dairy cattle from Guernsey in the Channel Islands. **b** this breed. **2** (**guernsey**) **a** a thick (usu. blue) woolen sweater of a distinctive pattern. **b** *Austral.* a soccer or football shirt. □ **get a guernsey** *Austral. colloq.* **1** be selected for a soccer or football team. **2** gain recognition.

guern·sey lil·y *n.* a kind of nerine orig. from S. Africa, with large pink lilylike flowers.

guer·ril·la /gəríla/ *n.* (also **gue·ril·la**) a member of a small independently acting (usu. political) group taking part in irregular fighting, esp. against larger regular forces. [Sp. *guerrilla*, dimin. of *guerra* war]

guer·ril·la war *n.* (also **guer·ril·la war·fare**) fighting by or with guerrillas.

guess /ges/ *v. & n.* ●*v.* **1** *tr.* (often *absol.*) estimate without calculation or measurement, or on the basis of inadequate data. **2** *tr.* (often foll. by *that*, etc. + clause, or *to* + infin.) form a hypothesis or opinion about; conjecture; think likely (*cannot guess how you did it*). **3** *tr.* conjecture or estimate correctly by guessing (*you have to guess the weight*). **4** *intr.* (foll. by *at*) make a conjecture about. ●*n.* an estimate or conjecture reached by guessing. □ **anybody's** (or **anyone's**) **guess** something very vague or difficult to determine. **I guess** *colloq.* I think it likely; I suppose. **keep a person guessing** *colloq.* withhold information. □□ **guess·a·ble** *adj.* **guess·er** *n.* [ME *gesse*, of uncert. orig.: cf. OSw. *gissa*, MLG, MDu. *gissen*: f. the root of GET *v.*]

guess-rope var. of GUEST-ROPE.

guess·ti·mate /géstimət/ *n.* (also **gues·ti·mate**) *colloq.* an estimate based on a mixture of guesswork and calculation. [GUESS + ESTIMATE]

guess·work /géswərk/ *n.* the process of or results got by guessing.

guest /gest/ *n. & v.* ●*n.* **1** a person invited to visit another's house or have a meal, etc., at the expense of the inviter. **2** a person lodging at a hotel, boarding house, etc. **3 a** an outside performer invited to take part with a regular body of performers. **b** a person who takes part by invitation in a radio or television program (often *attrib.*: *guest artist*). **4** (*attrib.*) **a** a serving or set aside for guests (*guest room*). **b** acting as a guest (*guest speaker*). **5** an organism living in close association with another. ●*v.intr.* be a guest on a radio or television show or in a theatrical performance, etc. □ **be my guest** *colloq.* make what use you wish of the available facilities. □□ **guest·ship** *n.* [ME f. ON *gestr* f. Gmc]

guest·house /gésthows/ *n.* a private house offering paid accommodation.

guest of hon·or *n.* the most important guest at an occasion.

guest-rope /géstrōp, gésrōp/ *n.* (also **guess-rope**) **1** a second rope fastened to a boat in tow to steady it. **2** a rope slung outside a ship to give a hold for boats coming alongside. [17th c.: orig. uncert.]

guff /guf/ *n. sl.* empty talk; nonsense. [19th c., orig. = 'puff': imit.]

guf·faw /gufáw/ *n. & v.* ●*n.* a loud or boisterous laugh. ●*v.* **1** *intr.* utter a guffaw. **2** *tr.* say with a guffaw. [orig. Sc.: imit.]

guid·ance /gíd'ns/ *n.* **1 a** advice or information aimed at resolving a problem, difficulty, etc. **b** leadership or direction. **2** the process of guiding or being guided.

guide /gīd/ *n. & v.* ●*n.* **1** a person who leads or shows the way, or directs the movements of a person or group. **2** a person who conducts travelers on tours, etc. **3** a professional mountain climber in charge of a group. **4** an adviser. **5** a directing principle or standard (*one's feelings are a bad guide*). **6** a book with essential information on a subject, esp. = GUIDEBOOK. **7** a thing marking a position or guiding the eye. **8** a soldier, vehicle, or ship whose position determines the movements of others. **9** *Mech.* **a** a bar, rod, etc., directing the motion of something. **b** a gauge, etc., controlling a tool. **10** (**Guide**) *Brit.* a member of an organization similar to the Girl Scouts. ●*v.tr.* **1 a** act as guide to; lead or direct. **b** arrange the course of (events). **2** be the principle, motive, or ground of (an action, judgment, etc.). **3** direct the affairs of (a government, etc.). □□ **guid·a·ble** *adj.* **guid·er** *n.* [ME f. OF *guide* (n.), *guider* (v.), earlier *guier* ult. f. Gmc, rel. to WIT²]

guide·book /gídbŏŏk/ *n.* a book of information about a place for visitors, tourists, etc.

guid·ed mis·sile *n.* a missile directed to its target by remote control or by equipment within itself.

guide dog *n.* a dog trained to guide a blind person.

guide·line /gídlīn/ *n.* a principle or criterion guiding or directing action.

guide·post /gídpōst/ *n.* = SIGNPOST.

guide rope *n.* a rope used to guide the movement of the load of a crane.

guide·way /gídway/ *n.* a groove or track that guides movement.

gui·don /gíd'n/ *n.* **1** a pennant narrowing to a point or fork at the free end, esp. one used as the standard of a military unit. **2** the soldier who carries it. [F f. It. *guidone* f. *guida* GUIDE]

guild /gild/ *n.* (also **gild**) **1** an association of people for mutual aid or the pursuit of a common goal. **2** a medieval association of craftsmen or merchants. [ME prob. f. MLG, MDu. *gilde* f. Gmc: rel. to OE *gild* payment, sacrifice]

guild·er /gíldər/ *n.* **1** the chief monetary unit of the Netherlands. **2** *hist.* a gold coin of the Netherlands and Germany. [ME, alt. of Du. *gulden*: see GULDEN]

guild·hall /gíldháwl/ *n.* **1** the meeting place of a guild or corporation; (*Brit.*) a town hall. **2** (**the Guildhall**) the hall of the Corporation of the City of London, used for ceremonial occasions.

guilds·man /gíldzmən/ *n.* (*pl.* **·men**; *fem.* **guilds·wom·an**, *pl.* **·wom·en**) a member of a guild.

guile /gīl/ *n.* treachery; deceit; cunning or sly behavior. □□ **guile·ful** *adj.* **guile·ful·ly** *adv.* **guile·ful·ness** *n.* **guile·less** *adj.* **guile·less·ly** *adv.* **guile·less·ness** *n.* [ME f. OF, prob. f. Gmc]

guil·le·mot /gíləmot/ *n.* any fast-flying sea bird of the genus *Uria* or *Cepphus*, nesting on cliffs or islands. [F f. *Guillaume* William]

guil·loche /gilósh, geeyósh/ *n.* an architectural or metalwork ornament imitating braided ribbons. [F *guillochis* (or *guilloche* the tool used)]

guil·lo·tine /gíləteen, gée-ə-/ *n. & v.* ●*n.* **1** a machine with a heavy knife blade dropping vertically in grooves, used for beheading. **2** a device for cutting paper, metal, etc. **3** a surgical instrument for excising the uvula, etc. **4** *Brit. Parl.* a method of preventing delay in the discussion of a legislative bill by fixing times at which various parts of it must be voted on. ●*v.tr.* **1** use a guillotine on. **2** *Brit. Parl.* end discussion of (a bill) by applying a guillotine. □□ **guil·lo·tin·er** *n.* [F f. J.-i. *Guillotin*, Fr. physician d. 1814, who recommended its use for executions in 1789]

guilt /gilt/ *n.* **1** the fact of having committed a specified or implied offense. **2 a** culpability. **b** the feeling of this. [OE *gylt*, of unkn. orig.]

guilt com·plex *n. Psychol.* a mental obsession with the idea of having done wrong.

guilt·less /gíltlis/ *adj.* **1** (often foll. by *of*) innocent. **2** (foll. by *of*) not having knowledge or possession of. □□ **guilt·less·ly** *adv.* **guilt·less·ness** *n.* [OE *gyltlēas* (as GUILT, –LESS)]

guilt·y /gíltee/ *adj.* (**guilt·i·er**, **guilt·i·est**) **1** culpable of or responsible for a wrong. **2** conscious of or affected by guilt (*a guilty conscience*; *a guilty look*). **3** concerning guilt (*a guilty secret*). **4 a** (often foll. by *of*) having committed a (specified) offense. **b** *Law* adjudged to have committed a specified offense, esp. by a verdict in a trial. □□ **guilt•i•ly** *adv.* **guilt•i•ness** *n.* [OE *gyltig* (as GUILT, –Y¹)]

guimp var. of GIMP¹.

guin•ea /gínee/ *n.* **1** *Brit. hist.* the sum of 21 old shillings, used esp. in determining professional fees. **2** *hist.* a former British gold coin worth 21 shillings, first coined for the African trade. [*Guinea* in W. Africa]

guin•ea fowl *n.* any African fowl of the family Numididae, esp. *Numida meleagris*, with slate-colored white-spotted plumage.

guin•ea pig *n.* **1** a domesticated S. American cavy, *Cavia porcellus*, kept as a pet or for research in biology, etc. **2** a person or thing used as a subject for experiment.

gui•pure /gipyŏor/ *n.* a heavy lace of linen pieces joined by embroidery. [F f. *guiper* cover with silk, etc., f. Gmc]

guise /giz/ *n.* **1** an assumed appearance; a pretense (*in the guise of*; *under the guise of*). **2** external appearance. **3** *archaic* style of attire; garb. [ME f. OF ult. f. Gmc]

gui•tar /gitaár/ *n.* a usu. six-stringed musical instrument with a fretted fingerboard, played by plucking with the fingers or a plectrum. □□ **gui•tar•ist** *n.* [Sp. *guitarra* (partly through F *guitare*) f. Gk *kithara*: see CITTERN, GITTERN]

gui•ver /gívər/ *n.* (also **gy•ver**) *Austral.* & *NZ sl.* **1** plausible talk. **2** affectation of speech or manner. [19th c.: orig. unkn.]

Gu•ja•ra•ti /gŏojəraátee/ *n.* & *adj.* ● *n.* (*pl.* **Gu•ja•ra•tis**) **1** the language of Gujarat in W. India. **2** a native of Gujarat. ● *adj.* of or relating to Gujarat or its language. [Hind.: see –I²]

guitar

gulch /gulch/ *n.* a ravine, esp. one in which a torrent flows. [perh. dial. *gulch* to swallow]

gul•den /gŏoldən, gŏol–/ *n.* = GUILDER. [Du. & G, = GOLDEN]

gules /gyŏolz/ *n.* & *adj.* (usu. placed after noun) *Heraldry* red. [ME f. OF *goules* red-dyed fur neck ornaments f. *gole* throat]

gulf /gulf/ *n.* & *v.* ● *n.* **1** a stretch of sea consisting of a deep inlet with a narrow mouth. **2** (**the Gulf**) **a** the Gulf of Mexico. **b** the Persian Gulf. **3** a deep hollow; a chasm or abyss. **4** a wide difference of feelings, opinion, etc. ● *v.tr.* engulf; swallow up. [ME f. OF *golfe* f. It. *golfo* ult. f. Gk *kolpos* bosom, gulf]

Gulf Stream *n.* an oceanic warm current flowing from the Gulf of Mexico to Newfoundland where it is deflected into the Atlantic Ocean.

gulf•weed /gúlfweed/ *n.* = SARGASSO.

gull¹ /gul/ *n.* any of various long-winged web-footed sea birds of the family Laridae, usu. having white plumage with a mantle varying from pearly gray to black, and a bright bill. □□ **gull•er•y** *n.* (*pl.* **-ies**). [ME ult. f. OCelt.]

gull² /gul/ *v.tr.* (usu. in *passive*; foll. by *into*) dupe; fool. [perh. f. obs. *gull* yellow f. ON *gulr*]

Gul•lah /gúlə/ *n.* **1** a member of a group of African-Americans living on the coast of S. Carolina or the nearby sea islands. **2** the Creole language spoken by them. [perh. a shortening of *Angola*, or f. a tribal name *Golas*]

gul•let /gúlit/ *n.* **1** the food passage extending from the mouth to the stomach; the esophagus. **2** the throat. [ME f. OF dimin. of *go(u)le* throat f. L *gula*]

gul•li•ble /gúlibəl/ *adj.* easily persuaded or deceived; credulous. □□ **gul•li•bil•i•ty** *n.* **gul•li•bly** *adv.* [GULL² + –IBLE]

gul•ly /gúlee/ *n.* & *v.* ● *n.* (*pl.* **-lies**) **1** a waterworn ravine. **2** a deep

artificial channel; a gutter or drain. **3** *Austral.* & *NZ* a river valley. **4** *Cricket* **a** the fielding position between point and slips. **b** a fielder in this position. ● *v.tr.* (**·lies, ·lied**) **1** form (channels) by water action. **2** make gullies in. [F *goulet* bottleneck (as GULLET)]

gulp /gulp/ *v.* & *n.* ● *v.* **1** *tr.* (often foll. by *down*) swallow hastily, greedily, or with effort. **2** *intr.* swallow gaspingly or with difficulty; choke. **3** *tr.* (foll. by *down, back*) stifle; suppress (esp. tears). ● *n.* **1** an act of gulping (*drained it at one gulp*). **2** an effort to swallow. **3** a large mouthful of a drink. □□ **gulp•er** *n.* **gulp•ing•ly** *adv.* **gulp•y** *adj.* [ME prob. f. MDu. *gulpen* (imit.)]

gum¹ /gum/ *n.* & *v.* ● *n.* **1 a** a viscous secretion of some trees and shrubs that hardens on drying but is soluble in water (cf. RESIN). **b** an adhesive substance made from this. **2** chewing gum. **3** = GUMDROP. **4** = GUM ARABIC. **5** = GUM TREE. **6** a secretion collecting in the corner of the eye. **7** = GUMBOOT. ● *v.* (**gummed, gum•ming**) **1** *tr.* smear or cover with gum. **2** *tr.* (usu. foll. by *down, together*, etc.) fasten with gum. **3** *intr.* exude gum. **4** *tr.* & *intr.* to clog or become clogged with or as if with gum. □ **gum up** (of a mechanism, etc.) become clogged or obstructed with stickiness. **2** *colloq.* interfere with the smooth running of (*gum up the works*). **up a gum tree** *Brit. colloq.* in great difficulties. [ME f. OF *gomme* ult. f. L *gummi, cummi* f. Gk *kommi* f. Egypt. *kemai*]

gum² /gum/ *n.* (usu. in *pl.*) the firm flesh around the roots of the teeth. [OE *gōma* rel. to OHG *guomo*, ON *gómr* roof or floor of the mouth]

gum³ /gum/ *n. colloq.* (in oaths) God (*by gum!*). [corrupt. of *God*]

gum ar•a•bic *n.* a gum exuded by some kinds of acacia and used as an emulsifier, in glue, and as the binder for watercolor paints.

gum ben•ja•min *n.* benzoin.

gum•bo /gúmbō/ *n.* (*pl.* **-bos**) **1** okra. **2** a soup thickened with okra pods. **3** (**Gumbo**) a patois of African-Americans and Creoles spoken esp. in Louisiana. [of Afr. orig.]

gum•boil /gúmboyl/ *n.* a small abscess on the gums.

gum•boot /gúmbōot/ *n.* a rubber boot.

gum•drop /gúmdrop/ *n.* a soft, colored candy made with gelatin or gum arabic.

gum•ma /gúmə/ *n.* (*pl.* **gum•mas** or **gum•ma•ta** /–mətə/) *Med.* a small soft swelling occurring in the connective tissue of the liver, brain, testes, and heart, and characteristic of the late stages of syphilis. □□ **gum•ma•tous** *adj.* [mod.L f. L *gummi* GUM¹]

gum•my¹ /gúmee/ *adj.* (**gum•mi•er, gum•mi•est**) **1** viscous; sticky. **2** abounding in or exuding gum. □□ **gum•mi•ness** *n.* [ME f. GUM¹ + –Y¹]

gum•my² /gúmee/ *adj.* & *n.* ● *adj.* (**gum•mi•er, gum•mi•est**) toothless. ● *n.* (*pl.* **-mies**) **1** *Austral.* a small shark, *Mustelus antarcticus*, having rounded teeth with which it crushes hard-shelled prey. **2** *Austral.* & *NZ* a toothless sheep. □□ **gum•mi•ly** *adv.* [GUM² + –Y¹]

gump•tion /gúmpshən/ *n. colloq.* **1** resourcefulness; initiative; enterprising spirit. **2** common sense. [18th-c. Sc.: orig. unkn.]

gum res•in *n.* a plant secretion of resin mixed with gum.

gum shield *n.* a pad protecting a boxer's teeth and gums.

gum•shoe /gúmshōo/ *n.* **1** *sl.* a detective. **2** a galosh.

gum tree *n.* a tree exuding gum, esp. a eucalyptus.

gun /gun/ *n.* & *v.* ● *n.* **1** any kind of weapon consisting of a metal tube and often held in the hand with a grip at one end, from which bullets or other missiles are propelled with great force, esp. by a contained explosion. **2** any device imitative of this, e.g., a starting pistol. **3** a device for discharging insecticide, grease, electrons, etc., in the required direction (often in *comb.*: *grease gun*). **4** *Brit.* a member of a shooting party. **5** a gunman. **6** the firing of a gun. **7** (in *pl.*) *Naut. sl.* a gunnery officer. ● *v.* (**gunned, gun•ning**) **1** *tr.* **a** (usu. foll. by *down*) shoot (a person) with a gun. **b** shoot at with a gun. **2** *tr. colloq.* accelerate (an engine or vehicle). **3** *intr.* go shooting. **4** *intr.* (foll. by *for*) seek out determinedly to attack or rebuke. □ **go great guns** *colloq.* proceed vigorously or successfully. **gun-shy 1** (esp. of a sporting dog) alarmed at the report of a gun. **2** nervous; distrustful; wary. **jump the gun** *colloq.* start before a signal is given, or before an agreed time. **stick to one's guns** *colloq.* maintain one's position under attack. □□ **gun•less** *adj.* **gunned** *adj.* [ME *gunne, gonne*, perh. f. the Scand. name *Gunnhildr*]

gun•boat /gúnbōt/ *n.* a small vessel of shallow draft and with relatively heavy guns.

gun•boat di•plo•ma•cy *n.* political negotiation supported by the use or threat of military force.

gun car•riage *n.* a wheeled support for a gun.

gun•cot•ton /gúnkotən/ *n.* an explosive used for blasting, made by steeping cotton in nitric and sulfuric acids.

gun crew *n.* a team of soldiers or sailors manning a heavy gun.

gun dog *n.* a dog trained to retrieve game for a hunter who is using a gun.

gun•dy /gúndee/ *n. Austral. colloq.* □ **no good to gundy** no good at all. [20th c.: orig. unkn.]

gun•fight /gúnfīt/ *n.* a fight with firearms. □□ **gun•fight•er** *n.*

gun•fire /gúnfīr/ *n.* **1** the firing of a gun or guns, esp. repeatedly. **2** the noise from this.

gunge /gunj/ *n.* & *v. Brit. colloq.* ● *n.* sticky or viscous matter, esp.

when messy or indeterminate. ● *v. tr.* (usu. foll. by *up*) clog or obstruct with gunge. □□ **gun·gy** *adj.* [20th c.: orig. uncert.: cf. GOO, GUNK]

gung-ho /gúnghó/ *adj.* enthusiastic; eager. [Chin. *gonghe* work together, slogan adopted by US Marines in 1942]

gunk /gungk/ *n. sl.* viscous or liquid material. [20th c.: orig. the name of a detergent (trademark)]

gun·lock /gúnlok/ *n.* a mechanism by which the charge of a gun is exploded.

gun·man /gúnmən/ *n.* (*pl.* **·men**) a man armed with a gun, esp. in committing a crime.

gun·met·al /gúnmetəl/ *n.* **1** a dull bluish gray color. **2** an alloy of copper and tin or zinc (formerly used for guns).

gun·nel[1] /gúnəl/ *n.* any small eel-shaped marine fish of the family Pholidae, esp. *Pholis gunnellus.* Also called **butterfish**. [17th c.: orig. unkn.]

gun·nel[2] var. of GUNWALE.

gun·ner /gúnər/ *n.* **1** an artillery soldier (esp. *Brit.* as an official term for a private). **2** *Naut.* a warrant officer in charge of a battery, magazine, etc. **3** a member of an aircraft crew who operates a gun. **4** a person who hunts game with a gun.

gun·ner·a /gúnərə/ *n.* any plant of the genus *Gunnera* from S. America and New Zealand, having huge leaves and often grown for ornament. [J. E. *Gunnerus*, Norw. botanist d. 1773]

gun·ner·y /gúnəree/ *n.* **1** the construction and management of large guns. **2** the firing of guns.

gun·ny /gúnee/ *n.* (*pl.* **·nies**) **1** coarse sacking, usu. of jute fiber. **2** a sack made of this. [Hindi & Marathi *gōnī* f. Skr. *gōṇi* sack]

gun·play /gúnplay/ *n.* the use of guns.

gun·point /gúnpoynt/ *n.* the point of a gun. □ **at gunpoint** threatened with a gun or an ultimatum, etc.

gun·pow·der /gúnpowdər/ *n.* **1** an explosive made of saltpeter, sulfur, and charcoal. **2** a fine green tea of granular appearance.

gun·pow·er /gúnpowər/ *n.* the strength or quantity of available guns.

gun·room /gúnroom, -room/ *n.* **1** a room in a house for storing sporting guns. **2** *Brit.* quarters for junior officers (orig. for gunners) in a warship.

gun·run·ner /gúnrunər/ *n.* a person engaged in the illegal sale or importing of firearms. □□ **gun·run·ning** *n.*

gun·sel /gúnsəl/ *n. sl.* a criminal, esp. a gunman. [Yiddish *gendzel* = G *Gänslein* gosling; infl. by GUN]

gun·ship /gúnship/ *n.* a heavily armed helicopter or other aircraft.

gun·shot /gúnshot/ *n.* **1** a shot fired from a gun. **2** the range of a gun (*within gunshot*).

gun·sling·er /gúnslingər/ *n. sl.* a gunman. □□ **gun·sling·ing** *n.*

gun·smith /gúnsmith/ *n.* a person who makes, sells, and repairs small firearms.

gun·stock /gúnstok/ *n.* the wooden mounting of the barrel of a gun.

Gun·ter's chain /gúntərz/ *n. Surveying* **1** a measuring chain of 66 ft. **2** this length as a unit. [E. *Gunter*, Engl. mathematician d. 1626]

gun·wale /gúnəl/ *n.* (also **gun·nel**) the upper edge of the side of a boat or ship. [GUN + WALE (because formerly used to support guns)]

PRONUNCIATION TIP gunwale

Like many nautical terms, *gunwale* is pronounced quite differently from the way it is spelled. Say "GUN-el"; avoid the pronunciation suggested by the spelling. Other nautical words with pronunciations that differ from their spellings include *forecastle* (say "FOKE-sel"), *boatswain* ("BO-sun"), *topmast* ("TOP-mist"), and *topsail* ("TOP-sel").

---

gun·yah /gúnyaa/ *n. Austral.* an Aboriginal bush hut. [Aboriginal]

gup·py /gúpee/ *n.* (*pl.* **·pies**) a freshwater fish, *Poecilia reticulata*, of the W. Indies and S. America, frequently kept in aquariums, and giving birth to live young. [R. J. L. *Guppy*, 19th-c. Trinidad clergyman who sent the first specimen to the British Museum]

gur·dwa·ra /gərdwáarə/ *n.* a Sikh temple. [Punjabi *gurduārā* f. Skr. *guru* teacher + *dvāra* door]

gur·gle /gɔ́rgəl/ *v. & n.* ● *v.* **1** *intr.* make a bubbling sound as of water from a bottle. **2** *tr.* utter with such a sound. ● *n.* a gurgling sound. □□ **gur·gler** *n.* [imit., or f. Du. *gorgelen*, G *gurgeln*, or med.L *gurgulare* f. L *gurgulio* gullet]

Gur·kha /gɔ́rkə/ *n.* **1** a member of the dominant Hindu people in Nepal. **2** a Nepalese soldier serving in the British army. [native name, f. Skr. *gāus* cow + *raksh* protect]

gur·nard /gɔ́rnərd/ *n.* (also **gur·net** /gɔ́rnit/) any marine fish of the family Triglidae, having a large spiny head with mailed sides, and three fingerlike pectoral rays used for walking on the sea bed, etc. [ME f. OF *gornart* f. *grondir* to grunt f. L *grunnire*]

gu·ru /goʻoroo/ *n.* **1** a Hindu spiritual teacher or head of a religious sect. **2 a** an influential teacher. **b** a revered mentor. [Hindi *gurū* teacher f. Skr. *gurús* grave, dignified]

gush /gush/ *v. & n.* ● *v.* **1** *tr. & intr.* emit or flow in a sudden and copious stream. **2** *intr.* speak or behave with effusiveness or sentimental affectation. ● *n.* **1** a sudden or copious stream. **2** an effusive or

sentimental manner. □□ **gush·ing** *adj.* **gush·ing·ly** *adv.* [ME *gosshe*, *gusche*, prob. imit.]

gush·er /gúshər/ *n.* **1** an oil well from which oil flows without being pumped. **2** an effusive person.

gush·y /gúshee/ *adj.* (**gush·i·er**, **gush·i·est**) excessively effusive or sentimental. □□ **gush·i·ly** *adv.* **gush·i·ness** *n.*

gus·set /gúsit/ *n.* **1** a piece inserted into a garment, etc., to strengthen or enlarge a part. **2** a bracket strengthening an angle of a structure. □□ **gus·set·ed** *adj.* [ME f. OF *gousset* flexible piece filling up a joint in armor f. *gousse* pod, shell]

gust /gust/ *n. & v.* ● *n.* **1** a sudden strong rush of wind. **2** a burst of rain, fire, smoke, or sound. **3** a passionate or emotional outburst. ● *v. intr.* blow in gusts. [ON *gustr*, rel. to *gjósa* to gush]

gus·ta·tion /gustáyshən/ *n.* the act or capacity of tasting. □□ **gus·ta·tive** /gústətiv/, **gus·ta·to·ry** /gústətáwree/ *adj.* [F *gustation* or L *gustatio* f. *gustare* f. *gustus* taste]

gus·to /gústō/ *n.* (*pl.* **·toes**) **1** zest; enjoyment or vigor in doing something. **2** (foll. by *for*) relish or liking. **3** *archaic* a style of artistic execution. [It. f. L *gustus* taste]

gust·y /gústee/ *adj.* (**gust·i·er**, **gust·i·est**) **1** characterized by or blowing in strong winds. **2** characterized by gusto. □□ **gust·i·ly** *adv.* **gust·i·ness** *n.*

gut /gut/ *n. & v.* ● *n.* **1** the lower alimentary canal or a part of this; the intestine. **2** (in *pl.*) the bowel or entrails, esp. of animals. **3** (in *pl.*) *colloq.* personal courage and determination; vigorous application and perseverance. **4** *colloq.* **a** (in *pl.*) the belly as the source of appetite. **b** the belly or abdomen. **5** (in *pl.*) **a** the contents of anything, esp. representing substantiality. **b** the essence of a thing, e.g., of an issue or problem. **6 a** material for violin or racket strings or surgical use made from the intestines of animals. **b** material for fishing lines made from the silk glands of silkworms. **7 a** a narrow water passage; a sound; straits. **b** a defile or narrow passage. **8** (*attrib.*) **a** instinctive (*a gut reaction*). **b** fundamental (*a gut issue*). ● *v. tr.* (**gut·ted**, **gut·ting**) **1** remove or destroy (esp. by fire) the internal fittings of (a house, etc.). **2** take out the guts of (a fish). **3** extract the essence of (a book, etc.). □ **hate a person's guts** *colloq.* dislike a person intensely. **sweat** (or **work**) **one's guts out** *colloq.* work extremely hard. [OE *guttas* (pl.), prob. rel. to *gēotan* pour]

gut·less /gútlis/ *adj. colloq.* lacking courage or determination; feeble. □□ **gut·less·ly** *adv.* **gut·less·ness** *n.*

guts·y /gútsee/ *adj.* (**guts·i·er**, **guts·i·est**) *colloq.* **1** courageous. **2** greedy. □□ **guts·i·ly** *adv.* **guts·i·ness** *n.*

gut·ta-per·cha /gútəpɔ́rchə/ *n.* a tough plastic substance obtained from the latex of various Malaysian trees. [Malay *getah* gum + *percha* name of a tree]

gut·tate /gútayt/ *adj. Biol.* having droplike markings. [L *guttatus* speckled f. *gutta* drop]

gut·ted /gútid/ *adj. sl.* utterly exhausted; devastated.

gut·ter /gútər/ *n. & v.* ● *n.* **1** a shallow trough along the eaves of a house, or a channel at the side of a street, to carry off rainwater. **2** (prec. by *the*) a poor or degraded background or environment. **3** an open conduit along which liquid flows out. **4** a groove. **5** a track made by the flow of water. **6** *Printing* the white space at the inside margin of two adjoining pages. ● *v.* **1** *intr.* flow in streams. **2** *tr.* furrow; channel. **3** *intr.* (of a candle) melt away as the wax forms channels down the side. □ **gutter press** esp. *Brit.* sensational journalism concerned esp. with the private lives of public figures. [ME f. AF *gotere*, OF *gotiere* ult. f. L *gutta* drop]

gut·ter·ing /gútəring/ *n.* **1 a** the gutters of a building, etc. **b** a section or length of a gutter. **2** material for gutters.

gut·ter·snipe /gútərsnip/ *n.* a street urchin.

gut·tur·al /gútərəl/ *adj. & n.* ● *adj.* **1** throaty, harsh sounding. **2 a** *Phonet.* (of a consonant) produced in the throat or by the back of the tongue and palate. **b** (of a sound) coming from the throat. **c** of the throat. ● *n. Phonet.* a guttural consonant (e.g., *k*, *g*). □□ **gut·tur·al·ly** *adv.* [F *guttural* or med.L *gutturalis* f. L *guttur* throat]

guv /guv/ *n. Brit. sl.* = GOVERNOR 7. [abbr.]

guy[1] /gi/ *n. & v.* ● *n.* **1** *colloq.* a man; a fellow. **2** (usu. in *pl.*) a person of either sex. **3** *Brit.* an effigy of Guy Fawkes in ragged clothing, burned on a bonfire on Nov. 5. **4** *Brit.* a grotesquely dressed person. ● *v. tr.* **1** ridicule. **2** *Brit.* exhibit in effigy. [*Guy* Fawkes, conspirator in the Gunpowder Plot to blow up Parliament in 1605]

guy[2] /gi/ *n. & v.* ● *n.* a rope or chain to secure a tent or steady a crane load, etc. ● *v. tr.* secure with a guy or guys. [prob. of LG orig.: cf. LG & Du. *gei* brail, etc.]

guz·zle /gúzəl/ *v. tr. & intr.* eat, drink, or consume excessively or greedily. □□ **guz·zler** *n.* [perh. f. OF *gosiller* chatter, vomit f. *gosier* throat]

gybe /jib/ *v. & n.* var. of JIBE[2].

gym /jim/ *n. colloq.* **1** a gymnasium. **2** gymnastics. [abbr.]

gym·kha·na /jimkáanə/ *n.* **1** a meeting for competition or display in a sport, esp. horse riding or automobile racing. **2** *Brit.* a public place with facilities for athletics. [Hind. *gendkhāna* ball house, racket court, assim. to GYMNASIUM]

gym•na•si•um /jimnáyzeeəm/ n. (*pl.* **gym•na•si•ums** or **gym•na•si•a** /–zeeə/) **1** a room or building equipped for indoor sports, often including gymnastics. **2** a school in Germany or Scandinavia that prepares pupils for university entrance. □□ **gym•na•si•al** /–zeeəl/ *adj.* [L f. Gk *gumnasion* f. *gumnazō* exercise f. *gumnos* naked]

gym•nast /jímnast, –nəst/ n. an expert in gymnastics. [F *gymnaste* or Gk *gumnastēs* athlete trainer f. *gumnazō*: see GYMNASIUM]

gym•nas•tic /jimnástik/ *adj.* of or involving gymnastics. □□ **gym•nas•ti•cal•ly** *adv.* [L *gymnasticus* f. Gk *gumnastikos* (as GYMNASIUM)]

gym•nas•tics /jimnástiks/ *n.pl.* (also treated as *sing.*) **1** exercises developing or displaying physical agility and coordination, usu. in competition. **2** other forms of physical or mental agility.

gymno- /jímnō/ *comb. form Biol.* bare; naked. [Gk *gumnos* naked]

gym•nos•o•phist /jimnósəfist/ n. a member of an ancient Hindu sect wearing little clothing and devoted to contemplation. □□ **gym•nos•o•phy** n. [ME f. F *gymnosophiste* f. L *gymnosophistae* (pl.) f. Gk *gumnosophistai*: see GYMNO-, SOPHIST]

gym•no•sperm /jímnəspərm/ n. any of various plants having seeds unprotected by an ovary, including conifers, cycads, and ginkgos (opp. ANGIOSPERM). □□ **gym•no•sper•mous** *adj.*

gymp var. of GIMP[1].

gyn. *abbr.* (also **gynecol.**) **1** gynecological. **2** gynecologist. **3** gynecology.

gyn•ae•ce•um var. of GYNOECIUM.

gy•nan•dro•morph /jinándrəmawrf, gī–/ n. *Biol.* an individual, esp. an insect, having male and female characteristics. □□ **gy•nan•dro•mor•phic** *adj.* **gy•nan•dro•morph•ism** n. [formed as GYNANDROUS + Gk *morphē* form]

gy•nan•drous /jinándrəs, gī–/ *adj. Bot.* with stamens and pistil united in one column as in orchids. [Gk *gunandros* of doubtful sex, f. *gunē* woman + *anēr andros* man]

gyneco- /gínikō, jínə–/ *comb. form* (*Brit.* **gynaeco-**) woman; women; female. [Gk *gunē gunaikos* woman]

gy•ne•col•o•gy /gínikóləjee, jínə–/ n. (*Brit.* **gy•nae•col•o•gy**) the science of the physiological functions and diseases of women and girls, esp. those affecting the reproductive system. □□ **gyn•e•co•log•ic** /–kəlójik/ *adj.* **gyn•e•co•log•i•cal** *adj.* **gyn•e•co•log•i•cal•ly** *adv.* **gy•ne•col•o•gist** /–kóləjist/ n.

gyn•e•co•mas•ti•a /gínikōmásteeə, jínə–/ n. (*Brit.* **gyn•ae•co•mas•ti•a**) *Med.* enlargement of a man's breasts, usu. due to hormone imbalance or hormone therapy.

gy•noe•ci•um /jineéseeəm, –shee–, gī–/ n. (also **gy•nae•ci•um**) (*pl.* **ci•a** /–seeə, –sheeə/) *Bot.* the carpels of a flower taken collectively. [mod.L f. Gk *gunaikeion* women's apartments (as GYNECO-, Gk *oikos* house)]

-gynous /jinəs, ginəs/ *comb. form Bot.* forming adjectives meaning 'having specified female organs or pistils' (*monogynous*). [Gk –*gunos* f. *gunē* woman]

gyp[1] /jip/ *v. & n. sl.* ● *v.tr.* (**gypped, gyp•ping**) cheat; swindle. ● n. an act of cheating; a swindle. [19th c.: perh. f. GYP[2]]

gyp[2] /jip/ n. *Brit. colloq.* **1** pain or severe discomfort. **2** a scolding (*gave them gyp*). [19th c.: perh. f. *gee-up* (see GEE[2])]

gyp[3] /jip/ n. *Brit.* a college servant at Cambridge and Durham. [perh. f. obs. *gippo* scullion, orig. a man's short tunic, f. obs. F *jupeau*]

gyp•py tum•my var. of GIPPY TUMMY.

gyp•soph•i•la /jipsófilə/ n. any plant of the genus *Gypsophila*, with a profusion of small usu. white composite flowers, as baby's breath. [mod.L f. Gk *gupsos* chalk + *philos* loving]

gyp•sum /jípsəm/ n. a hydrated form of calcium sulfate occurring naturally and used to make plaster of Paris and in the building industry. □□ **gyp•se•ous** *adj.* **gyp•sif•er•ous** /–sífərəs/ *adj.* [L f. Gk *gupsos*]

Gyp•sy /jípsee/ n. (also **Gip•sy**) (*pl.* **•sies**) **1** a member of a nomadic people of Europe and N. America, of Hindu origin with dark skin and hair, and speaking a language related to Hindi. **2** (**gypsy**) a person resembling or living like a Gypsy. □□ **Gyp•sy•dom** n. **Gyp•sy•fied** *adj.* **Gyp•sy•hood** n. **Gyp•sy•ish** *adj.* [earlier *gipcyan, gipsen* f. EGYPTIAN, from the supposed origin of Gypsies when they appeared in England in the early 16th c.]

gyp•sy moth n. a kind of tussock moth, *Lymantria dispar*, of which the larvae are very destructive to foliage.

gy•rate /jírayt/ v. & *adj.* ● *v.intr.* (also /jiráyt/) go in a circle or spiral; revolve; whirl. ● *adj. Bot.* arranged in rings or convolutions. □□ **gy•ra•tion** /–ráyshən/ n. **gy•ra•tor** n. **gy•ra•to•ry** /–rətáwree/ *adj.* [L *gyrare gyrat-* revolve f. *gyrus* ring f. Gk *guros*]

gyre /jir/ v. & n. esp. *poet.* ● *v.intr.* whirl or gyrate. ● n. a gyration. [L *gyrus* ring f. Gk *guros*]

gyr•fal•con /jórfalkən, –fawlkən/ n. (also **ger•fal•con**) a large falcon, *Falco rusticolus*, of the northern hemisphere. [ME f. OF *gerfaucon* f. Frank. *gērfalco* f. ON *geirfálki*: see FALCON]

gy•ro /jírō/ n. (*pl.* **•ros**) *colloq.* **1** = GYROSCOPE. **2** = GYROCOMPASS. [abbr.]

gyro- /jírō/ *comb. form* rotation. [Gk *guros* ring]

gy•ro•com•pass /jírōkumpəs, –kom–/ n. a nonmagnetic compass giving true north and bearings from it by means of a gyroscope.

gy•ro•graph /jírəgraf/ n. an instrument for recording revolutions.

gy•ro•mag•net•ic /jírōmagnétik/ *adj.* **1** *Physics* of the magnetic and mechanical properties of a rotating charged particle. **2** (of a compass) combining a gyroscope and a normal magnetic compass.

gy•ro•pi•lot /jírōpílət/ n. a gyrocompass used for automatic steering.

gy•ro•plane /jírəplayn/ n. a form of aircraft deriving its lift mainly from freely rotating overhead vanes.

gy•ro•scope /jírəskōp/ n. a rotating wheel whose axis is free to turn but maintains a fixed direction unless perturbed, esp. used for stabilization or with the compass in an aircraft, ship, etc. □□ **gy•ro•scop•ic** /–skópik/ *adj.* **gy•ro•scop•i•cal•ly** *adv.* [F (as GYRO-, SCOPE[2])]

gyroscope

gy•ro•sta•bi•liz•er /jírōstáybilizər/ n. a gyroscopic device for maintaining the equilibrium of a ship, aircraft, platform, etc.

gy•rus /jírəs/ n. (*pl.* **gy•ri** /–rī/) a fold or convolution, esp. of the brain. [L f. Gk *guros* ring]

gyt•tja /yíchə/ n. *Geol.* a lake deposit of a usu. black organic sediment. [Sw., = mud, ooze]

gy•ver var. of GUIVER.

H

H¹ /aych/ *n.* (also **h**) (*pl.* **Hs** or **H's**) **1** the eighth letter of the alphabet (see AITCH). **2** anything having the form of an H (esp. in *comb.*: *H-girder*).

H² *abbr.* (also **H.**) **1** hardness. **2** (of a pencil lead) hard. **3** henry; henrys. **4** (water) hydrant. **5** *sl.* heroin.

H³ *symb. Chem.* the element hydrogen.

h. *abbr.* **1** hecto-. **2** height. **3** horse. **4** hot. **5** hour(s). **6** husband. **7** Planck's constant. **8** *Baseball* hit; hits.

Ha *symb. Chem.* the element hahnium.

ha¹ /haa/ *int.* (also **hah**) expressing surprise, suspicion, triumph, etc. (cf. HA HA). [ME]

ha² *abbr.* hectare(s).

haar /haar/ *n.* a cold sea fog on the east coast of England or Scotland. [perh. f. ON *hárr* hoar, hoary]

Hab. *abbr.* Habakkuk (Old Testament).

ha·ba·ne·ra /haàbɔnáirɔ/ *n.* **1** a Cuban dance in slow duple time. **2** the music for this. [Sp., fem. of *habanero* of Havana in Cuba]

ha·be·as cor·pus /háybeeɔs káwrpɔs/ *n.* a writ requiring a person to be brought before a judge or into court, esp. to investigate the lawfulness of his or her detention. [L, = you must have the body]

hab·er·dash·er /hábɔrdashɔr/ *n.* **1** a dealer in men's clothing. **2** *Brit.* a dealer in dress accessories and sewing goods. □□ **hab·er·dash·er·y** *n.* (*pl.* **-ies**). [ME prob. ult. f. AF *hapertas* perh. the name of a fabric]

hab·er·geon /hábɔrjɔn/ *n. hist.* a sleeveless coat of mail. [ME f. OF *haubergeon* (as HAUBERK)]

ha·bil·i·ment /hɔbílimɔnt/ *n.* (usu. in *pl.*) **1** clothes suited to a particular purpose. **2** *joc.* ordinary clothes. [ME f. OF *habillement* f. *habiller* fit out f. *habile* ABLE]

ha·bil·i·tate /hɔbílitayt/ *v.intr.* qualify for office (esp. as a teacher in a German university). □□ **ha·bil·i·ta·tion** /-táyshɔn/ *n.* [med.L *habilitare* (as ABILITY)]

hab·it /hábit/ *n. & v.* ● *n.* **1** a settled or regular tendency or practice (often foll. by *of* + verbal noun: *has a habit of ignoring me*). **2** a practice that is hard to give up. **3** a mental constitution or attitude. **4** *Psychol.* an automatic reaction to a specific situation. **5** *colloq.* an addictive practice, esp. of taking drugs. **6 a** the dress of a particular class, esp. of a religious order. **b** (in full **riding habit**) a woman's riding dress. **c** *archaic* dress; attire. **7** a bodily constitution. **8** *Biol. & Crystallog.* a mode of growth. ● *v.tr.* (usu. as **habited** *adj.*) clothe. [ME f. OF *abit* f. L *habitus* f. *habēre* habit- have, be constituted]

hab·it·a·ble /hábitɔbɔl/ *adj.* that can be inhabited. □□ **hab·it·a·bil·i·ty** *n.* **hab·it·a·ble·ness** *n.* **hab·it·a·bly** *adv.* [ME f. OF f. L *habitabilis* (as HABIT)]

hab·i·tant *n.* **1** /hábit'nt/ an inhabitant. **2** /ábeetóN/ **a** an early French settler in Canada or Louisiana. **b** a descendant of these settlers. [F f. OF *habiter* f. L *habitare* inhabit (as HABIT)]

hab·i·tat /hábitat/ *n.* **1** the natural home of an organism. **2** a habitation. [L, = it dwells: see HABITANT]

hab·i·ta·tion /hábitáyshɔn/ *n.* **1** the process of inhabiting (*fit for human habitation*). **2** a house or home. [ME f. OF f. L *habitatio -onis* (as HABITANT)]

hab·it-form·ing *adj.* causing addiction.

ha·bit·u·al /hɔbíchooɔl/ *adj.* **1** done constantly or as a habit. **2** regular; usual. **3** given to a (specified) habit (*a habitual smoker*). □□ **ha·bit·u·al·ly** *adv.* **ha·bit·u·al·ness** *n.* [med.L *habitualis* (as HABIT)]

ha·bit·u·ate /hɔbíchoo-ayt/ *v.tr.* (often foll. by *to*) accustom; make used to something. □□ **ha·bit·u·a·tion** /-áyshɔn/ *n.* [LL *habituare* (as HABIT)]

hab·i·tude /hábitood, -tyood/ *n.* **1** a mental or bodily disposition. **2** a custom or tendency. [ME f. OF f. L *habitudo -dinis* f. *habēre* habit- have]

ha·bit·u·é /hɔbíchoo-áy/ *n.* a habitual visitor or resident. [F, past part. of *habituer* (as HABITUATE)]

ha·ček /háachek/ *n.* (also **há·ček**) a diacritical mark (ˇ) placed over letters to modify the sound in some Slavic and Baltic languages. [Czech, dimin. of *hák* hook]

ha·chures /hashyóòr/ *n.pl.* parallel lines used in shading hills on maps, their closeness indicating the steepness of gradient. [F f. *hacher* HATCH³]

ha·ci·en·da /haàsee-éndɔ/ *n.* in Spanish-speaking countries: **1** an estate or plantation with a dwelling house. **2** a factory. [Sp. f. L *facienda* things to be done]

hack¹ /hak/ *v. & n.* ● *v.* **1** *tr.* cut or chop roughly; mangle. **2** *Sports*

strike illegally at an opponent's arms, legs, etc., during a game. **3** *intr.* (often foll. by *at*) deliver cutting blows. **4** *tr.* cut (one's way) through thick foliage, etc. **5** *tr. colloq.* gain unauthorized access to (data in a computer). **6** *tr. sl.* **a** manage; cope with. **b** tolerate. **c** (often foll. by *off* or as **hacked off** *adj.*) annoy; disconcert. ● *n.* **1** a kick with the toe of a boot. **2** a gash or wound, esp. from a kick. **3 a** a mattock. **b** a miner's pick. [OE *haccian* cut in pieces f. WG]

hack² /hak/ *n., adj., & v.* ● *n.* **1 a** a horse for ordinary riding. **b** a horse let out for hire. **c** = JADE² 1. **2** a writer of mediocre literary work or journalism; *colloq.* usu. *derog.* a journalist. **3** a person hired to do dull routine work. **4** a taxi. ● *attrib.adj.* **1** used as a hack. **2** typical of a hack; commonplace (*hack work*). ● *v.* **1 a** *intr.* ride on horseback on a road at an ordinary pace. **b** *tr.* ride (a horse) in this way. **2** *tr.* make common or trite. **3** drive a taxi. [abbr. of HACKNEY]

hack³ /hak/ *n.* **1** *Falconry* a board on which a hawk's meat is laid. **2** a rack holding fodder for cattle. □ **at hack** *Falconry* (of a young hawk) not yet allowed to prey for itself. [var. of HATCH¹]

hack·ber·ry /hákberee/ *n.* (*pl.* **·ries**) **1** any tree of the genus *Celtis*, native to N. America, bearing purple edible berries. **2** the berry of this tree. [var. of *hagberry*, of Norse orig.]

hack·er /hákɔr/ *n.* **1** a person or thing that hacks or cuts roughly. **2** *colloq.* **a** a person who is very adept at programming and working with computers. **b** a person who uses computers to gain unauthorized access to data. **3** a golfer who plays poorly.

hack·le /hákɔl/ *n. & v.* ● *n.* **1** a long feather or series of feathers on the neck or saddle of a domestic fowl and other birds. **2** *Fishing* an artificial fly dressed with a hackle. **3** *Sc.* a feather in a Highland soldier's bonnet. **4** (in *pl.*) the erectile hairs along the back of a dog, which rise when it is angry or alarmed. **5** a steel comb for dressing flax. ● *v.tr.* dress or comb with a hackle. □ **raise a person's hackles** cause a person to be angry or indignant. [ME *hechele*, *hakele*, prob. f. OE f. WG]

hack·ney /háknee/ *n.* (*pl.* **·neys**) **1** a horse of average size and quality for ordinary riding. **2** (*attrib.*) designating any of various vehicles kept for hire. [ME, perh. f. *Hackney* (formerly *Hakenei*) in London, where horses were pastured]

hack·neyed /háknee'd/ *adj.* (of a phrase, etc.) made commonplace or trite by overuse.

hack·saw /háksaw/ *n.* a saw with a narrow blade set in a frame, for cutting metal.

had *past* and *past part.* of HAVE.

had·dock /hádɔk/ *n.* (*pl.* same) a marine fish, *Melanogrammus aeglefinus*, of the N. Atlantic, allied to cod, but smaller. [ME, prob. f. AF *hadoc*, OF (*h*)*adot*, of unkn. orig.]

hade /hayd/ *n. & v. Geol.* ● *n.* an incline from the vertical. ● *v.intr.* incline from the vertical. [17th c., perh. dial. form of *head*]

Ha·des /háydeez/ *n.* (in Greek mythology) the underworld; the abode of the spirits of the dead. □□ **Ha·de·an** /-deeɔn/ *adj.* [Gk *haidēs*, orig. a name of Pluto]

Ha·dith /hádith/ *n. Relig.* a body of traditions relating to Muhammad. [Arab. *ḥadīṯ* tradition]

hadj var. of HAJJ.

hadj·i var. of HAJJI.

had·n't /hád'nt/ *contr.* had not.

had·ron /hádron/ *n. Physics* any strongly interacting elementary particle. □□ **ha·dron·ic** /-drónik/ *adj.* [Gk *hadros* bulky]

hadst /hadst/ *archaic 2nd sing. past* of HAVE.

hae·re mai /híra mí/ *int.* NZ welcome. [Maori, lit. 'come hither']

ha·fiz /háafiz/ *n.* a Muslim who knows the Koran by heart. [Pers. f. Arab. *ḥāfiz* guardian]

haf·ni·um /háfneeɔm/ *n. Chem.* a silvery lustrous metallic element occurring naturally with zirconium, used in tungsten alloys for filaments and electrodes. ¶ Symb.: **Hf**. [mod.L f. *Hafnia* Copenhagen]

haft /haft/ *n. & v.* ● *n.* the handle of a dagger, knife, etc. ● *v.tr.* provide with a haft. [OE *hæft* f. Gmc]

Hag. *abbr.* Haggai (Old Testament).

hag¹ /hag/ *n.* **1** an ugly old woman. **2** a witch. **3** = HAGFISH. □□ **hag·gish** *adj.* [ME *hegge*, *hagge*, perh. f. OE *hægtesse*, OHG *hagazissa*, of unkn. orig.]

hag² /hag/ *n. Sc. & No. of Engl.* **1** a soft place on a moor. **2** a firm place in a bog. [ON *högg* gap, orig. 'cutting blow,' rel. to HEW]

hag·fish /hágfish/ *n.* any jawless fish of the family Myxinidae, with a rasplike tongue used for feeding on dead or dying fish. [HAG¹]

Hag·ga·dah /hɔgáádɔ, –gáwdɔ, haagaadáá/ *n.* **1** a legend, etc., used to illustrate a point of the Law in the Talmud; the legendary element of the Talmud. **2** a book recited at the Passover Seder service. □□ **Hag·gad·ic** /həgádik, –gaá–, –gáw–/ *adj.* [Heb., = tale, f. *higgíḍ* tell]

hag·gard /hágərd/ *adj. & n.* ● *adj.* **1** looking exhausted and distraught, esp. from fatigue, worry, privation, etc. **2** (of a hawk) caught and trained as an adult. ● *n.* a haggard hawk. □□ **hag·gard·ly** *adv.* **hag·gard·ness** *n.* [F *hagard*, of uncert. orig.: later infl. by HAG[1]]

hag·gis /hágis/ *n.* a Scottish dish consisting of a sheep's or calf's offal mixed with suet, oatmeal, etc., and boiled in a bag made from the animal's stomach or in an artificial bag. [ME: orig. unkn.]

hag·gle /hágəl/ *v. & n.* ● *v.intr.* (often foll. by *about, over*) dispute or bargain persistently. ● *n.* a dispute or wrangle. □□ **hag·gler** *n.* [earlier sense 'hack' f. ON *höggva* HEW]

hagio- /hágeeō, háyjeeō/ *comb. form* of saints or holiness. [Gk *hagios* holy]

Hag·i·og·ra·pha /hágeeógrəfə, háyjee–/ *n.pl.* the twelve books comprising the last of the three major divisions of the Hebrew Scriptures, along with the Law and the Prophets.

hag·i·og·ra·pher /hágeeógrəfər, háyjee–/ *n.* **1** a writer of the lives of saints. **2** a writer of any of the Hagiographa.

hag·i·og·ra·phy /hágeeógrəfee, háyjee–/ *n.* the writing of the lives of saints. □□ **hag·i·o·graph·ic** /–geeəgráfik/ *adj.* **hag·i·o·graph·i·cal** *adj.*

hag·i·ol·a·try /hágeeólətree, háyjee–/ *n.* the worship of saints.

hag·i·ol·o·gy /hágióləjee/ *n.* literature dealing with the lives and legends of saints. □□ **hag·i·o·log·i·cal** /–geeəlójikəl/ *adj.* **hag·i·ol·o·gist** *n.*

hag·rid·den /hágrid'n/ *adj.* afflicted by nightmares or anxieties.

hah var. of HA[1].

ha ha /haáhaá/ *int.* repr. laughter. [OE: cf. HA[1]]

ha-ha /haáhaá/ *n.* a ditch with a wall on its inner side below ground level, forming a boundary to a park or garden without interrupting the view. [F, perh. from the cry of surprise on encountering it]

hahn·i·um /haániəm/ *n. Chem.* an artificially produced radioactive element. ¶ Symb.: **Ha**. [O. *Hahn,* Ger. chemist d. 1968 + –IUM]

haik /hīk, hayk/ *n.* (also **haick**) an outer covering for head and body worn by Arabs. [Moroccan Arab. *ḥā'ik*]

hai·ku /híkoo/ *n.* (*pl.* same) **1** a Japanese three-line poem of usu. 17 syllables. **2** an English imitation of this. [Jap.]

hail[1] /hayl/ *n. & v.* ● *n.* **1** pellets of frozen rain falling in showers from cumulonimbus clouds. **2** (foll. by *of*) a barrage or onslaught (of missiles, curses, questions, etc.). ● *v.* **1** *intr.* (prec. by *it* as subject) hail falls (*it is hailing; if it hails*). **2 a** *tr.* pour down (blows, words, etc.). **b** *intr.* come down forcefully. [OE *hagol, hægl, hagalian* f. Gmc]

hail[2] /hayl/ *v., int., & n.* ● *v.* **1** *tr.* greet enthusiastically. **2** *tr.* signal to or attract the attention of (*hailed a taxi*). **3** *tr.* acclaim (*hailed him king; was hailed as a prodigy*). **4** *intr.* (foll. by *from*) have one's home or origins in (a place) (*hails from Mexico*). ● *int. archaic* or *rhet.* expressing greeting. ● *n.* **1** a greeting or act of hailing. **2** distance as affecting the possibility of hailing (*was within hail*). □□ **hail·er** *n.* [ellipt. use of obs. *hail* (adj.) f. ON *heill* sound, WHOLE]

hail-fellow-well-met *adj.* showing excessive familiarity (*a hail-fellow-well-met salesman*).

Hail Mary *n.* a prayer to the Virgin Mary, used chiefly by Roman Catholics.

hail·stone /háylstōn/ *n.* a pellet of hail.

hail·storm /háylstorm/ *n.* a period of heavy hail.

hair /hair/ *n.* **1 a** any of the fine threadlike strands growing from the skin of mammals, esp. from the human head. **b** these collectively (*his hair is falling out*). **c** a hairstyle or way of wearing the hair (*I like your hair today*). **2 a** an artificially produced hairlike strand, e.g., in a brush. **b** a mass of such hairs. **3** anything resembling a hair. **4** an elongated cell growing from the epidermis of a plant. **5** a very small quantity or extent (also *attrib.: a hair crack*). □ **get in a person's hair** *colloq.* encumber or annoy a person. **keep one's hair on** *Brit. colloq.* remain calm; not get angry. **let one's hair down** *colloq.* abandon restraint; behave freely or wildly. **make a person's hair stand on end** alarm or horrify a person. **not turn a hair** remain apparently unmoved or unaffected. □□ **haired** *adj.* (also in *comb.*). **hair·less** *adj.* **hair·like** *adj.* [OE *hēr* f. Gmc]

hair·ball /háirbawl/ *n.* (also **hair ball**) a compact ball of hair that accumulates in the stomach of a cat or other animal that grooms itself by licking its fur.

hair·breadth /háirbredth/ *n.* = HAIR'S BREADTH; (esp. *attrib.: a hairbreadth escape*).

hair·brush /háirbrush/ *n.* a brush for arranging or smoothing the hair.

hair·cloth /háirklawth, -kloth/ *n.* stiff cloth woven from hair, used, e.g., in upholstery.

hair·cut /háirkut/ *n.* **1** a cutting of the hair. **2** the style in which the hair is cut.

hair·do /háirdoo/ *n.* (*pl.* **-dos**) *colloq.* the style or an act of styling a woman's hair.

hair·dress·er /háirdresər/ *n.* **1** a person who cuts and styles hair,

esp. professionally. **2** the business or establishment of a hairdresser. □□ **hair·dress·ing** *n.*

hair dry·er *n.* (or **hair drier**) an electrical device for drying the hair by blowing warm air over it.

hair grass *n.* any of various grasses, esp. of the genus *Deschampsia, Corynephous, Aira,* etc., with slender stems.

hair·grip /háirgrip/ *n. Brit.* a flat hairpin with the ends close together; a bobby pin.

hair·line /háirlīn/ *n.* **1** the edge of a person's hair, esp. on the forehead. **2** a very thin line or crack, etc.

hair·net /háirnet/ *n.* a piece of fine mesh fabric for confining the hair.

hair of the dog *n.* an alcoholic drink taken to cure a hangover.

hair·piece /háirpees/ *n.* a quantity or switch of detached hair used to augment a person's natural hair.

hair·pin /háirpin/ *n.* a U-shaped pin for fastening the hair. □ **hairpin turn** (or **bend**) a sharp U-shaped bend in a road.

hair-rais·ing *adj.* extremely alarming; terrifying.

hair's breadth *n.* a very small amount or margin.

hair shirt *n.* a shirt of haircloth, worn formerly by penitents and ascetics.

hair·split·ting /háirspliting/ *adj. & n.* making overfine distinctions; quibbling. □□ **hair·split·ter** *n.*

hair spray *n.* a solution sprayed onto a person's hair to keep it in place.

hair·spring /háirspring/ *n.* a fine spring regulating the balance wheel in a watch.

hair·streak /háirstreek/ *n.* a butterfly of the genus *Strymonidia,* etc., with fine streaks or rows of spots on its wings.

hair·style /háirstīl/ *n.* a particular way of arranging or dressing the hair. □□ **hair·styl·ing** *n.* **hair·styl·ist** *n.*

hair trig·ger *n.* a trigger of a firearm set for release at the slightest pressure.

hair-trig·ger *adj.* reacting to the slightest pressure, stimulus, or provocation (*a hair-trigger temper*).

hair·y /háiree/ *adj.* (**hair·i·er, hair·i·est**) **1** made of or covered with hair. **2** having the feel of hair. **3** *sl.* **a** alarmingly unpleasant or difficult. **b** crude; clumsy. □□ **hair·i·ly** *adv.* **hair·i·ness** *n.*

hajj /haj/ *n.* (also **hadj**) the Islamic pilgrimage to Mecca. [Arab. *ḥajj* pilgrimage]

haj·ji /hájee/ *n.* (also **hadj·i**) (*pl.* **·jis**) a Muslim who has been to Mecca as a pilgrim: also (**Hajji**) used as a title. [Pers. *ḥājī* (partly through Turk. *hacı*) f. Arab. *ḥajj*: see HAJJ]

hake /hayk/ *n.* any marine fish of the genus *Merluccius,* esp. *M. merluccius* with an elongate body and large head. [ME perh. ult. f. dial. *hake* hook + FISH[1]]

hakenkreuz /haákənkroyts/ *n.* a swastika, esp. as a Nazi symbol. [G f. *Haken* hook + *Kreuz* CROSS]

ha·kim[1] /haakeém/ *n.* (in India and Islamic countries) **1** a wise man. **2** a physician. [Arab. *ḥakīm* wise man, physician]

ha·kim[2] /haákeem/ *n.* (in India and Muslim countries) a judge, ruler, or governor. [Arab. *ḥākim* governor]

Ha·la·kah /haalaakháá, həláakhə, –láw–/ *n.* (also **Ha·la·chah**) Jewish law and jurisprudence, based on the Talmud. □□ **Ha·la·chic** /–laákhik/ *adj.* [Aram. *həlākāh* law]

ha·lal /haalaál/ *v. & n.* (also **hal·lal**) ● *v.tr.* (**ha·lalled, ha·lal·ling**) kill (an animal) as prescribed by Muslim law. ● *n.* (often *attrib.*) meat prepared in this way; lawful food. [Arab. *ḥalāl* lawful]

ha·la·tion /haláyshən/ *n. Photog.* the spreading of light beyond its proper extent in a developed image, caused by internal reflection in the support of the emulsion. [irreg. f. HALO + –ATION]

hal·berd /hálbərd/ *n.* (also **hal·bert** /–bərt/) *hist.* a combined spear and battleax. [ME f. F *hallebarde* f. It *alabarda* f. MHG *helmbarde* f. *helm* handle + *barde* hatchet]

hal·berd·ier /hálbərdeér/ *n. hist.* a man armed with a halberd. [F *hallebardier* (as HALBERD)]

hal·cy·on /hálseeən/ *adj. & n.* ● *adj.* **1** calm; peaceful (*halcyon days*). **2** (of a period) happy, prosperous. ● *n.* **1** any kingfisher of the genus *Halcyon,* native to Europe, Africa, and Australasia, with brightly colored plumage. **2** *Mythol.* a bird thought in antiquity to breed in a nest floating at sea at the winter solstice, charming the wind and waves into calm. [ME f. L (*h*)*alcyon* f. Gk (*h*)*alkuōn* kingfisher]

hale[1] /hayl/ *adj.* (esp. of an old person) strong and healthy (esp. in **hale and hearty**). □□ **hale·ness** *n.* [OE *hāl* WHOLE]

hale[2] /hayl/ *v.tr.* drag or draw forcibly. [ME f. OF *haler* f. ON *hala*]

half /haf/ *n., adj., & adv.* ● *n.* (*pl.* **halves** /havz/) **1** either of two equal or corresponding parts or groups into which a thing is or might be divided. **2** *colloq.* = HALFBACK. **3** *Brit. colloq.* half a pint, esp. of beer, etc. **4** either of two equal periods of

halberd

play in sports. **5** *colloq.* a half-price fare or ticket, esp. for a child. **6** *Golf* a score that is the same as one's opponent's. ● *adj.* **1** of an amount or quantity equal to a half, or loosely to a part thought of as roughly a half (*take half the men; spent half the time reading; half a pint; a half pint; half-price*). **2** forming a half (*a half share*). ● *adv.* **1** (often in *comb.*) to the extent of half; partly (*only half cooked; half-frozen; half-laughing*). **2** to a certain extent; somewhat (esp. in idiomatic phrases: *half dead; am half inclined to agree*). **3** (in reckoning time) by the amount of half (an hour, etc.) (*half past two*). □ **at half cock** see COCK¹. **by half** (prec. by *too* + adj.) excessively (*too clever by half*). **by halves** imperfectly or incompletely (*never does things by halves*). **half the battle** see BATTLE. **half a chance** *colloq.* the slightest opportunity (esp. *given half a chance*). **half an eye** the slightest degree of perceptiveness. **half a mind** see MIND. **the half of it** *colloq.* the rest or more important part of something (usu. after *neg.*: *you don't know the half of it*). **half the time** see TIME. **not half 1** not nearly (*not half long enough*). **2** *colloq.* not at all (*not half bad*). **3** *Brit. sl.* to an extreme degree (*he didn't half get angry*). [OE *half, healf* f. Gmc, orig. = 'side']

half-and-half *n.* being half one thing and half another, esp. a liquid of half cream and half milk.

half•back /háfbak/ *n.* (in some sports) a player between the linemen and fullbacks, or behind the forward line.

half-baked *adj.* **1** incompletely considered or planned (*a half-baked scheme*). **2** (of enthusiasm, etc.) only partly committed. **3** foolish.

half•beak /háfbeek/ *n.* any fish of the family Hemirhamphidae with the lower jaw projecting beyond the upper.

half bind•ing *n.* a type of bookbinding in which the spine and corners are bound in one material (usu. leather) and the sides in another.

half-blood *n.* **1** a person having one parent in common with another. **2** this relationship. **3** = HALF BREED. □□ **half-blood•ed** *adj.*

half boot *n.* a boot reaching up to the calf.

half breed *n.* often *offens.* a person of mixed race.

half broth•er *n.* a brother with only one parent in common.

half caste *n. & adj.* often *offens.* ● *n.* a person whose parents are of different races, esp. the offspring of a European father and an E. Indian mother. ● *adj.* of or relating to such a person.

half crown *n.* (or **half a crown**) a former British coin and monetary unit worth two shillings and sixpence (12½ pence).

half-doz•en *n.* (or **half a dozen**) a set or group of six (*a half-dozen eggs*).

half du•plex *n. Computing* (of a circuit) allowing the transmission of signals in both directions but not simultaneously.

half-har•dy *adj.* (of a plant) able to grow in the open air at all times except in severe frost.

half•heart•ed /háfhaártid/ *adj.* lacking enthusiasm; feeble. □□ **half•heart•ed•ly** *adv.* **half•heart•ed•ness** *n.*

half hitch *n.* a noose or knot formed by passing the end of a rope around its standing part and then through the loop.

half-hol•i•day *n.* a day of which half (usu. the afternoon) is taken as a holiday.

half hour *n.* **1** (also **half an hour**) a period of 30 minutes. **2** a point of time 30 minutes after any full hour of the clock. □□ **half-hour•ly** *adv.*

half-inch *n. & v.* ● *n.* a unit of length half as large as an inch. ● *v.tr. Brit. rhyming sl.* steal (= *pinch*).

half-land•ing *n. Brit.* a landing part of the way up a flight of stairs, whose length is twice the width of the flight plus the width of the well.

half-lap *n.* the joining of rails, shafts, etc., by halving the thickness of each at one end and fitting them together.

half-length *n.* a portrait of a person's upper half.

half-life *n. Physics & Biochem.*, etc., the time taken for the radioactivity or some other property of a substance to fall to half its original value.

half-light *n.* a dim imperfect light.

half-mast *n.* the position of a flag halfway down the mast, as a mark of respect for a person who has died.

half moon *n.* **1** the moon when only half its illuminated surface is visible from earth. **2** the time when this occurs. **3** a semicircular object.

half nel•son *n. Wrestling* see NELSON.

half note *n. Mus.* a note whose duration is one half of a whole note; minim.

half pay *n.* half of a person's normal or previous salary or wages, esp. as paid to military officers on retirement.

half•pen•ny /háypnee/ *n.* (also **ha'pen•ny**) (*pl.* **•pen•nies** or **•pence** /háypəns/) (in the UK) a former bronze coin worth half a penny.

half•pen•ny•worth /háypəth/ *n. Brit.* (also **ha'p'orth**) **1** as much as could be bought for a halfpenny. **2** *colloq.* a negligible amount (esp. after *neg.*: *doesn't make a halfpennyworth of difference*).

▶The halfpenny was withdrawn from circulation in 1984.

half-seas-over *adj. Brit. sl.* partly drunk.

half sis•ter *n.* a sister with only one parent in common.

half sole *n.* the sole of a boot or shoe from the shank to the toe.

half sov•er•eign *n.* a former British gold coin and monetary unit worth ten shillings (50 pence).

half step *n. Mus.* a semitone.

half-term *n. Brit.* a period about halfway through a school term, when a short vacation is usually taken.

half-tim•bered *adj. Archit.* having walls with a timber frame and a brick or plaster filling.

half•time *n. & adj.* ● *n.* **1** the time at which half of a game or contest is completed. **2** a short intermission occurring at this time. ● *adj.* occurring during halftime (*a halftime Super Bowl show*).

half ti•tle *n.* **1** the title or short title of a book, printed on the recto of the leaf preceding the title page. **2** the title of a section of a book printed on the recto of the leaf preceding it.

half•tone /háftōn/ *n.* **1** a reproduction printed from a block (produced by photographic means) in which the various tones of gray are produced from small and large black dots. **2** *Mus.* (**half tone**) a semitone.

half-track *n.* **1** a propulsion system for land vehicles with wheels at the front and a continuous track at the back. **2** a vehicle equipped with this.

half-truth *n.* a statement that (esp. deliberately) conveys only part of the truth.

half vol•ley *n.* (*pl.* **•leys**) (in ball games) the playing of a ball as soon as it bounces off the ground.

half•way /háfwáy/ *adv. & adj.* ● *adv.* **1** at a point equidistant between two others (*we were halfway to Chicago*). **2** to some extent; more or less (*is halfway decent*). ● *adj.* situated halfway (*reached a halfway point*). □ **halfway line** a line midway between the ends of a sports field, esp. in soccer.

half•way house *n.* **1** a center for helping former drug addicts, prisoners, psychiatric patients, or others to adjust to life in general society. **2** the halfway point in a progression. **3** *hist.* an inn midway between two towns.

half•wit /háfwit/ *n.* **1** *colloq.* an extremely foolish or stupid person. **2** a person who is mentally deficient. □□ **half•wit•ted** /witid/ *adj.* **half•wit•ted•ly** *adv.* **half•wit•ted•ness** *n.*

half-year•ly *adj. & adv.* esp. *Brit.* at intervals of six months.

hal•i•but /hálibət/ *n.* /hól–/) (*pl.* same) a large marine flatfish, *Hippoglossus vulgaris*, used as food. [ME f. *haly* HOLY + BUTT³ flatfish, perh. because eaten on holy days]

hal•ide /hálid, háyl–/ *n. Chem.* **1** a binary compound of a halogen with another group or element. **2** any organic compound containing a halogen.

hal•i•eu•tic /hálee-ốotik/ *adj. formal* of or concerning fishing. [L *halieuticus* f. Gk *halieutikos* f. *halieutēs* fisherman]

hal•i•o•tis /háleeốtis/ *n.* any edible gastropod mollusk of the genus *Haliotis* with an ear-shaped shell lined with mother-of-pearl. [Gk *hals hali-* sea + *ous ōt-* ear]

hal•ite /hálit, háy–/ *n.* rock salt. [mod.L *halites* f. Gk *hals* salt]

hal•i•to•sis /hálitósis/ *n.* = BAD BREATH. [mod.L f. L *halitus* breath]

hall /hawl/ *n.* **1 a** a space or passage into which the front entrance of a house, etc., opens. **b** a corridor or passage in a building. **2 a** a large room or building for meetings, meals, concerts, etc. **b** *Brit.* (in *pl.*) music halls. **3** *Brit.* a large country house, esp. with a landed estate. **4** a university residence for students. **5 a** (in an English college, a residence hall, etc.) a common dining room. **b** *Brit.* dinner in this. **6** the building of a guild (*Fishmongers' Hall*). **7 a** a large public room in a palace, etc. **b** the principal living room of a medieval house. [OE = *hall* f. Gmc, rel. to HELL]

hal•lal var. of HALAL.

hal•le•lu•jah var. of ALLELUIA.

hal•liard var. of HALYARD.

hall•mark /háwlmaark/ *n. & v.* ● *n.* **1** a mark used at Goldsmiths' Hall in London (and by the UK assay offices) for marking the standard of gold, silver, and platinum. **2** any distinctive feature, esp. of excellence. ● *v.tr.* **1** stamp with a hallmark. **2** designate as excellent.

hal•lo esp. *Brit.* var. of HELLO.

Hall of Fame *n.* a building with memorials to individuals who excelled in a sport, etc.

hal•loo /hələ́o/ *int., v., & v.* ● *int.* **1** inciting dogs to the chase. **2** calling attention. **3** expressing surprise. ● *n.* the cry "halloo." ● *v.* (**halloos, hal•looed**) **1** *intr.* cry "halloo," esp. to dogs. **2** *intr.* shout to attract attention. **3** *tr.* urge on (dogs, etc.) with shouts. [perh. f. *hallow* pursue with shouts f. OF *halloer* (imit.)]

hal•low /hálō/ *v. & n.* ● *v.tr.* **1** make holy; consecrate. **2** honor as holy. ● *n. archaic* a saint or holy person. [OE *hālgian, hālga* f. Gmc]

Hal•low•een /hálōweén/ *n.* (also **Hal•low•e'en**) the eve of All Saints' Day, Oct. 31, esp. as celebrated by children dressing in costumes and collecting treats door-to-door. [HALLOW + EVEN²]

hall por•ter *n. Brit.* a porter who carries baggage, etc., in a hotel.

Hall•statt /háalshtaat/ *adj.* of or relating to the early Iron Age in Europe as attested by archaeological finds at Hallstatt in Upper Austria.

hal·lu·ces *pl.* of HALLUX.

hal·lu·ci·nate /həloõsinayt/ *v.* **1** *tr.* produce illusions in the mind of (a person). **2** *intr.* experience hallucinations. □□ **hal·lu·ci·nant** /–nənt/ *adj. & n.* **hal·lu·ci·na·tor** *n.* [L (*h*)*allucinari* wander in mind f. Gk *alussō* be uneasy]

hal·lu·ci·na·tion /həloõsináyshən/ *n.* the apparent or alleged perception of an object not actually present. □□ **hal·lu·ci·na·to·ry** /–sinətáwree/ *adj.* [L *hallucinatio* (as HALLUCINATE)]

hal·lu·ci·no·gen /həloõsinəjən/ *n.* a drug causing hallucinations. □□ **hal·lu·ci·no·gen·ic** /–jénik/ *adj.*

hal·lux /háluks/ *n.* (*pl.* **hal·lu·ces** /hályəseez/) **1** the big toe. **2** the innermost digit of the hind foot of vertebrates. [mod.L f. L *allex*]

hall·way /háwlway/ *n.* an entrance hall or corridor.

halm var. of HAULM.

hal·ma /hálmə/ *n.* a game played by two or four persons on a board of 256 squares, with men advancing from one corner to the opposite corner by being moved over other men into vacant squares. [Gk, = leap]

ha·lo /háylō/ *n. & v.* ● *n.* (*pl.* **·loes**) **1** a disk or circle of light shown in art surrounding the head of a sacred person. **2** the glory associated with an idealized person, etc. **3** a circle of white or colored light around a luminous body, esp. the sun or moon. **4** a circle or ring. ● *v.tr.* (**·loes, ·loed**) surround with a halo. [med.L f. L f. Gk *halōs* threshing floor, disk of the sun or moon]

hal·o·gen /hálǝjən/ *n. Chem.* any of the group of nonmetallic elements: fluorine, chlorine, bromine, iodine, and astatine, which form halides (e.g., sodium chloride) by simple union with a metal. □□ **hal·o·gen·ic** /–jénik/ *adj.* [Gk *hals halos* salt]

hal·o·gen·a·tion /hálǝjináyshǝn/ *n.* the introduction of a halogen atom into a molecule.

hal·on /háylon/ *n. Chem.* any of various gaseous compounds of carbon, bromine, and other halogens, used to extinguish fires. [as HALOGEN + –ON]

halt[1] /hawlt/ *n. & v.* ● *n.* **1** a stop (usu. temporary); an interruption of progress (*come to a halt*). **2** a temporary stoppage on a march or journey. **3** *Brit.* a minor stopping place on a local railroad line, usu. without permanent buildings. ● *v.intr. & tr.* stop; come or bring to a halt. □ **call a halt** (**to**) decide to stop. [orig. in phr. *make halt* f. G *Halt machen* f. *halten* hold, stop]

halt[2] /hawlt/ *v. & adj.* ● *v.intr.* **1** (esp. as **halting** *adj.*) lack smooth progress. **2** hesitate (*halt between two opinions*). **3** walk hesitatingly. **4** *archaic* be lame. ● *adj. archaic* lame or crippled. □□ **halt·ing·ly** *adv.* [OE *halt, healt, healtian* f. Gmc]

halt·er /háwltər/ *n. & v.* ● *n.* **1** a rope or strap with a noose or head-stall for horses or cattle. **2 a** a strap around the back of a woman's neck holding her dress top or blouse and leaving her shoulders and back bare. **b** a dress top or blouse held by this. **3 a** a rope with a noose for hanging a person. **b** death by hanging. ● *v.tr.* **1** put a halter on (a horse, etc.). **2** hang (a person) with a halter. [OE *hælftre*: cf. HELVE]

halt·er·break /háwltərbrayk/ *v.tr.* accustom (a horse) to a halter.

hal·te·res /hálteéreez/ *n.pl.* the balancing organs of dipterous insects. [Gk, = weights used to aid leaping f. *hallomai* to leap]

hal·vah /haálvaá/ *n.* (also **hal·va**) a Middle Eastern confection made of sesame flour and honey. [Yiddish f. Turk. *helva* f. Arab. *ḥalwa*]

halve /hav/ *v.tr.* **1** divide into two halves or parts. **2** reduce by half. **3** share equally (with another person, etc.). **4** *Golf* use the same number of strokes as one's opponent in (a hole or match). **5** fit (two pieces of wood) together by cutting out half the thickness of each. [ME *halfen* f. HALF]

halves *pl.* of HALF.

hal·yard /hályərd/ *n.* (also **hal·liard, haul·yard** /háwlyərd/) *Naut.* a rope or tackle for raising or lowering a sail or yard, etc. [ME *halier* f. HALE[2] + –IER, assoc. with YARD[1]]

ham /ham/ *n. & v.* ● *n.* **1 a** the upper part of a pig's leg salted and dried or smoked for food. **b** the meat from this. **2** the back of the thigh; the thigh and buttock. **3** *sl.* (often *attrib.*) an inexpert or unsubtle actor or piece of acting. **4** (in full **radio ham**) *colloq.* the operator of an amateur radio station or holder of an amateur radio license. ● *v.intr. & (*often foll. by *up*) *tr.* (**hammed, ham·ming**) *sl.* overact; act or treat emotionally or sentimentally.

> **WORD HISTORY** ham
>
> Old English *ham, hom* (originally denoting the back of the knee), from a Germanic base meaning 'be crooked.' In the late 15th century the term came to denote the back of the thigh, hence that part of the animal used as food.

ham·a·dry·ad /hámədríad/ *n.* **1** (in Greek and Roman mythology) a nymph who lives in a tree and dies when it dies. **2** the king cobra, *Naja bungarus*. [ME f. L *hamadryas* f. Gk *hamadruas* f. *hama* with + *drus* tree]

ham·a·dry·as /hámədríəs/ *n.* a large Arabian baboon, *Papio hamadryas*, with a silvery gray cape of hair over the shoulders, held sacred in ancient Egypt.

ham·a·mel·is /hámǝmeélis/ *n.* any shrub of the genus *Hamamelis*, e.g., witch hazel. [mod.L f. Gk *hamamēlis* medlar]

ham·ba /hámbə/ *int. S.Afr.* be off; go away. [Nguni *–hambe* go]

ham·bone /hámbōn/ *n. Austral. colloq.* a male striptease show. [20th c.: orig. uncert.]

ham·burg·er /hámbərgər/ *n.* **1** a round patty of ground beef, fried or grilled and typically served on a bun or roll and garnished with various condiments. **2** ground beef. [G, = of Hamburg in Germany]

hames /haymz/ *n.pl.* two curved pieces of iron or wood forming the collar or part of the collar of a draft horse, to which the traces are attached. [ME f. MDu. *hame*]

ham-fist·ed /hámfistid/ *adj. colloq.* clumsy; heavy-handed; bungling. □□ **ham-fist·ed·ly** *adv.* **ham-fist·ed·ness** *n.*

ham-hand·ed /hámhándid/ *adj. colloq.* = HAM-FISTED. □□ **ham-hand·ed·ly** *adv.* **ham-hand·ed·ness** *n.*

Ham·it·ic /həmítik/ *n. & adj.* ● *n.* a group of African languages including ancient Egyptian and Berber. ● *adj.* **1** of or relating to this group of languages. **2** of or relating to the Hamites, a group of peoples in Egypt and N. Africa, by tradition descended from Noah's son Ham (Gen. 10:6 ff.).

ham·let /hámlit/ *n.* a small village. [ME f. AF *hamelet(t)e*, OF *hamelet* dimin. of *hamel* dimin. of *ham* f. MLG *hamm*]

ham·mer /hámər/ *n. & v.* ● *n.* **1 a** a tool with a heavy metal head at right angles to the handle, used for breaking, driving nails, etc. **b** a machine with a metal block serving the same purpose. **c** a similar contrivance, as for exploding the charge in a gun, striking the strings of a piano, etc. **2** an auctioneer's mallet, indicating by a rap that an article is sold. **3 a** a metal ball of about 7 kg, attached to a wire for throwing in an athletic contest. **b** the sport of throwing the hammer. **4** a bone of the middle ear; the malleus. ● *v.* **1 a** *tr. & intr.* hit or beat with or as with a hammer. **b** *intr.* strike loudly; knock violently (esp. on a door). **2** *tr.* **a** drive in (nails) with a hammer. **b** fasten or secure by hammering (*hammered the lid down*). **3** *tr.* (often foll. by *in*) inculcate (ideas, knowledge, etc.) forcefully or repeatedly. **4** *tr. colloq.* utterly defeat; inflict heavy damage on. **5** *intr.* (foll. by *at, away at*) work hard or persistently at. **6** *tr. Brit. Stock Exch.* declare (a person or a business) a defaulter. □ **come under the hammer** be sold at an auction. **hammer out 1** make flat or smooth by hammering. **2** work out the details of (a plan, agreement, etc.) laboriously. **3** play (a tune, esp. on the piano) loudly or clumsily. □□ **ham·mer·ing** *n.* (esp. in sense 4 of *v.*). **ham·mer·less** *adj.* [OE *hamor, hamer*]

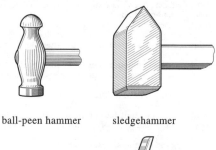

ball-peen hammer　　　sledgehammer

claw hammer　　　tack hammer

hammer 1

ham·mer and sick·le *n.* the symbols of the industrial worker and the peasant used as the emblem of the former USSR and of international communism.

ham·mer·beam /hámərbeem/ *n.* a wooden beam (often carved) projecting from a wall to support the principal rafter or the end of an arch.

ham·mer·head /hámərhed/ *n.* **1** the striking head of a hammer. **2** any shark

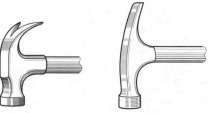

hammer and sickle

of the family Sphyrinidae, with a flattened head and eyes in lateral extensions of it. **3** a long-legged African marsh bird, *Scopus umbretta*, with a thick bill and an occipital crest.

ham•mer•lock /hámərlok/ *n. Wrestling* a hold in which the arm is twisted and bent behind the back.

ham•mer•toe /hámərtō/ *n.* a deformity in which the toe is bent permanently downwards.

ham•mock /hámək/ *n.* a bed of canvas or rope network, suspended by cords at the ends. [earlier *hamaca* f. Sp., of Carib orig.]

ham•my /hámee/ *adj.* (**ham•mi•er**, **ham•mi•est**) **1** of or like ham. **2** *colloq.* (of acting or an actor) exaggerated or over-theatrical. **3** (of a hand or thigh) thick and solid. □□ **ham•mi•ly** *adv.* **ham•mi•ness** *n.*

ham•per[1] /hámpər/ *n.* **1** a large basket, usu. with a hinged lid and containing laundry or (esp. *Brit.*) food (*clothes hamper; picnic hamper*). **2** *Brit.* a selection of food, drink, etc., for an occasion. [ME f. obs. *hanaper*, AF f. OF *hanapier* case for a goblet f. *hanap* goblet]

ham•per[2] /hámpər/ *v. & n.* ● *v.tr.* **1** prevent the free movement or activity of. **2** impede; hinder. ● *n. Naut.* necessary but cumbersome equipment on a ship. [ME: orig. unkn.]

ham•sin var. of KHAMSIN.

ham•ster /hámstər/ *n.* any of various rodents of the subfamily Cricetinae, esp. *Cricetus cricetus*, having a short tail and large cheek pouches for storing food, kept as a pet or laboratory animal. [G f. OHG *hamustro* weevil]

ham•string /hámstring/ *n. & v. Anat.* ● *n.* **1** each of five tendons at the back of the knee in humans. **2** the great tendon at the back of the hock in quadrupeds. ● *v.tr.* (*past* and *past part.* **ham•strung** or **ham•stringed**) **1** cripple by cutting the hamstrings of (a person or animal). **2** prevent the activity or efficiency of (a person or enterprise).

ham•u•lus /hámyələs/ *n.* (*pl.* **ham•u•li** /-lī/) *Anat., Zool., & Bot.* a hooklike process. [L, dimin. of *hamus* hook]

hand /hand/ *n. & v.* ● *n.* **1 a** the end part of the human arm beyond the wrist, including the fingers and thumb. **b** in other primates, the end part of a forelimb, also used as a foot. **2 a** (often in *pl.*) control; management; custody; disposal (*is in good hands*). **b** agency or influence (*suffered at their hands*). **c** a share in an action; active support. **3** a thing compared with a hand or its functions, esp. the pointer of a clock or watch. **4** the right or left side or direction relative to a person or thing. **5 a** a skill, esp. in something practical (*a hand for making pastry*). **b** a person skillful in some respect. **6** a person who does or makes something, esp. distinctively (*a picture by the same hand*). **7** an individual's writing or the style of this; a signature (*a legible hand; in one's own hand; witness the hand of . . .*). **8** a person, etc., as the source of information, etc. (*at first hand*). **9** a pledge of marriage. **10** a person as a source of manual labor, esp. in a factory, on a farm, or on board ship. **11 a** the playing cards dealt to a player. **b** the player holding these. **c** a round of play. **12** *colloq.* applause (*got a big hand*). **13** the unit of measure of a horse's height, equal to 4 inches (10.16 cm). **14** a forehock of pork. **15** a bunch of bananas. **16** (*attrib.*) **a** operated or held in the hand (*hand drill; hand luggage*). **b** done by hand and not by machine (*hand-knitted*). ● *v.tr.* **1** (foll. by *in, to, over*, etc.) deliver; transfer by hand or otherwise. **2** convey verbally (*handed me a lot of abuse*). **3** *colloq.* give away too readily (*handed them the advantage*). □ **all hands 1** the entire crew of a ship. **2** the entire workforce. **at hand 1** close by. **2** about to happen. **by hand 1** by a person and not a machine. **2** delivered privately and not by the public mail. **from hand to mouth** satisfying only one's immediate needs (also *attrib.: a hand-to-mouth existence*). **get** (or **have** or **keep**) **one's hand in** become (or be or remain) practiced in something. **hand around** distribute. **hand down 1** pass the ownership or use of to another. **2 a** transmit (a decision) from a higher court, etc. **b** express (an opinion or verdict). **hand in glove** in collusion or association. **hand in hand** in close association. **hand it to** *colloq.* acknowledge the merit of (a person). **hand off 1** *Football* hand (a football) to a teammate in the course of play. **2** pass along (responsibility, etc.) **3** *Rugby* push off (a tackling opponent) with the hand. **hand on** pass (a thing) to the next in a series or succession. **hand out 1** serve; distribute. **2** award; allocate (*the judges handed out stiff sentences*). **hand over** deliver; surrender possession of. **hands down** (esp. of winning) with no difficulty. **hands off 1** a warning not to touch or interfere with something. **2** *Computing*, etc., not requiring manual use of controls. **hands on 1** *Computing* of or requiring personal operation at a keyboard. **2** direct; practical; involving or offering active participation rather than theory. **hands up!** an instruction to raise one's hands in surrender or to signify assent or participation. **have** (or **take**) **a hand** (often foll. by *in*) share or take part. **have one's hands full** be fully occupied. **have one's hands tied** *colloq.* be unable to act. **hold one's hand** = *stay one's hand* (see HAND). **in hand 1** receiving attention. **2** in reserve; at one's disposal. **3** under one's control. **lay** (or **put**) **one's hands on** see LAY[1]. **lend** (or **give**) **a hand** assist in an action or enterprise. **off one's hands** no longer one's responsibility. **on every hand** (or **all hands**) to or from all directions. **on hand** available. **on one's hands** resting on one as a responsibility. **on the**

one (or **the other**) **hand** from one (or another) point of view. **out of hand 1** out of control. **2** peremptorily (*refused out of hand*). **put** (or **set**) **one's hand to** start work on; engage in. **stay one's hand** *archaic* or *literary* refrain from action. **to hand 1** within easy reach. **2** (of a letter) received. **turn one's hand to** undertake (as a new activity). □□ **hand•ed** *adj.* **hand•less** *adj.* [OE *hand, hond*]

hand and foot *adv.* completely; satisfying all demands (*waited on them hand and foot*).

hand•bag /hándbag/ *n. & v.* ● *n.* a small bag usu. with a handle or shoulder strap carried esp. by a woman and used to hold a wallet, cosmetics, etc. ● *v.tr. Brit.* (of a woman politician) treat (a person, idea, etc.) ruthlessly or insensitively.

hand•ball *n.* **1** /hándbawl/ one of several games with a ball thrown by hand among players or struck with an open hand against a wall. **2** /hándbáwl/ *Soccer* intentional touching of the ball with the hand or arm by a player other than the goalkeeper in the goal area, constituting a foul.

hand•bell /hándbel/ *n.* a small bell, usu. tuned to a particular note and rung by hand, esp. one of a set giving a range of notes.

hand•bill /hándbil/ *n.* a printed notice distributed by hand.

hand•book /hándbook/ *n.* a short manual or guidebook.

hand•brake /hándbrayk/ *n.* a brake operated by hand.

hand•cart /hándkaart/ *n.* a small cart pushed or drawn by hand.

hand•clap /hándklap/ *n.* a clapping of the hands.

hand•craft /hándkraft/ *n. & v.* ● *n.* = HANDICRAFT. ● *v.tr.* make by handicraft.

hand cream *n.* a lotion for softening the hands.

hand•cuff /hándkuf/ *n. & v.* ● *n.* (in *pl.*) a pair of lockable linked metal rings for securing a person's wrists. ● *v.tr.* put handcuffs on.

-handed /hándid/ *adj.* (in *comb.*) **1** for or involving a specified number of hands (in various senses) (*two-handed*). **2** using chiefly the hand specified (*left-handed*). □□ **-hand•ed•ly** *adv.* **-hand•ed•ness** *n.* (both in sense 2).

hand•ful /hándfool/ *n.* (*pl.* **-fuls**) **1** a quantity that fills the hand. **2** a small number or amount. **3** *colloq.* a troublesome person or task.

hand•glass /hándglas/ *n.* **1** a magnifying glass held in the hand. **2** a small mirror with a handle.

hand gre•nade *n.* a hand-thrown grenade..

hand•grip /hándgrip/ *n.* **1** a grasp with the hand. **2** a handle designed for easy holding.

hand•gun /hándgun/ *n.* a small firearm held in and fired with one hand.

hand•hold /hándhōld/ *n.* something for the hands to grip on (in climbing, sailing, etc.).

hand•i•cap /hándeekap/ *n. & v.* ● *n.* **1 a** a disadvantage imposed on a superior competitor in order to make the chances more equal. **b** a race or contest in which this is imposed. **2** the number of strokes by which a golfer normally exceeds par for the course. **3** a thing that makes progress or success difficult. **4** a physical or mental disability. ● *v.tr.* (**hand•i•capped**, **hand•i•cap•ping**) **1** impose a handicap on. **2** place (a person) at a disadvantage. □□ **hand•i•cap•per** *n.* [prob. from the phrase *hand i'* (= in) *cap* describing a kind of sporting lottery]

hand•i•capped /hándeekapt/ *adj.* having a physical or mental disability.

hand•i•craft /hándeekraft/ *n.* work that requires both manual and artistic skill. [ME, alt. of earlier HANDCRAFT after HANDIWORK]

hand•i•work /hándeewərk/ *n.* work done or a thing made by hand, or by a particular person. [OE *handgeweorc*]

hand•ker•chief /h ángkərchif, -cheef/ *n.* (*pl.* **hand•ker•chiefs** or **hand•ker•chieves** /-cheevz/) a square of cotton, linen, silk, etc., usu. carried in the pocket for wiping one's nose, etc.

SPELLING TIP handkerchief

Remember the *d* in spelling this word with this mnemonic: "If someone is crying, you should always *hand* him your *kerchief*."

han•dle /hánd'l/ *n. & v.* ● *n.* **1** the part by which a thing is held, carried, or controlled. **2** a fact that may be taken advantage of (*gave a handle to his critics*). **3** *colloq.* a personal title or nickname. **4** the feel of goods, esp. textiles, when handled. ● *v.tr.* **1** touch, feel, operate, or move with the hands. **2** manage or deal with; treat in a particular or correct way (*knows how to handle people; unable to handle the situation*). **3** deal in (goods). **4** discuss or write about (a subject). □ **get a handle on** *colloq.* understand the basis of or reason for a situation, circumstance, etc. □□ **han•dle•a•ble** *adj.* **han•dle•a•bil•i•ty** *n.* **han•dled** *adj.* (also in *comb.*). [OE *handle, handlian* (as HAND)]

han•dle•bar /hánd'lbaar/ *n.* (often in *pl.*) the steering bar of a bicycle, etc., with a handgrip at each end.

han•dle•bar mus•tache *n.* a thick mustache with curved ends resembling a handlebar.

han·dler /hándlər/ n. **1** a person who handles or deals in certain commodities. **2** a person who trains and looks after an animal (esp. a working or show dog).

hand·list /hándlist/ n. a short list of essential reading, reference books, etc.

hand·made /hándmáyd/ adj. made by hand and not by machine, esp. as designating superior quality.

hand·maid /hándmayd/ n. (also **hand·maid·en** /–máyd'n/) archaic a female servant or helper.

hand-me-down n. an article of clothing, etc., passed on from another person.

hand·out /hándowt/ n. **1** something given free to a needy person. **2** a statement given to the press, printed information given to a lecture audience, etc.

hand·over n. the act or an instance of handing over.

hand-over-fist adv. colloq. with rapid progress.

hand·pick /hándpik/ v.tr. choose carefully or personally. □□ **hand·picked** adj.

hand·rail /hándrayl/ n. a narrow rail for holding as a support on stairs, etc.

hand·saw /hándsaw/ n. a saw worked by one hand.

hand·sel /hánsəl/ n. & v. (also **han·sel**) • n. **1** a gift at the beginning of the new year, or on coming into new circumstances. **2** = EARNEST[2] 1. **3** a foretaste. • v.tr. (**hand·seled, hand·sel·ing**; or **hand·selled, hand·sel·ling**) **1** give a handsel to. **2** inaugurate. **3** be the first to try. [ME, corresp. to OE handselen giving into a person's hands, ON handsal giving of the hand (esp. in promise), formed as HAND + OE sellan SELL]

hand·set /hándset/ n. a telephone mouthpiece and earpiece forming one unit.

hand·shake /hándshayk/ n. the shaking of a person's hand by another's hand as a greeting, etc.

hand·some /hánsəm/ adj. (**hand·som·er, hand·som·est**) **1** (of a person) good-looking. **2** (of a building, etc.) imposing; attractive. **3 a** generous; liberal (a handsome present; handsome treatment). **b** (of a price, fortune, etc., as assets gained) considerable. □□ **hand·some·ness** n. [ME, = easily handled, f. HAND + –SOME[1]]

hand·some·ly /hánsəmlee/ adv. **1** generously; liberally. **2** finely; beautifully. **3** Naut. carefully.

hand·spike /hándspīk/ n. a wooden rod shod with iron, used on board ship and by artillery soldiers.

hand·spring /hándspring/ n. an acrobatic flip in which one lands first on the hands and then on the feet.

hand·stand /hándstand/ n. balancing on one's hands with the feet in the air or against a wall.

hand-to-hand adj. (of fighting) at close quarters.

hand·work /hándwərk/ n. work done with the hands, esp. as opposed to machinery. □□ **hand·worked** adj.

hand·writ·ing /hándrīting/ n. **1** writing with a pen, pencil, etc. **2** a person's particular style of writing. □□ **hand·writ·ten** /–rítən/ adj.

hand·y /hándee/ adj. (**hand·i·er, hand·i·est**) **1** convenient to handle or use; useful. **2** ready to hand; placed or occurring conveniently. **3** clever with the hands. □□ **hand·i·ly** adv. **hand·i·ness** n.

hand·y·man /hándeeman/ n. (pl. **·men**) a person able or employed to do occasional domestic repairs and minor renovations.

hang /hang/ v. & n. • v. (past and past part. **hung** /hung/ except in sense 7) **1** tr. **a** secure or cause to be supported from above, esp. with the lower part free. **b** (foll. by up, on, onto, etc.) attach loosely by suspending from the top. **2** tr. set up (a door, gate, etc.) on its hinges so that it moves freely. **3** tr. place (a picture) on a wall or in an exhibition. **4** tr. attach (wallpaper) in vertical strips to a wall. **5** tr. (foll. by on) colloq. attach the blame for (a thing) to (a person) (you can't hang that on me). **6** tr. (foll. by with) decorate by hanging pictures or decorations, etc. (a hall hung with tapestries). **7** tr. & intr. (past and past part. **hanged**) **a** suspend or be suspended by the neck, usu. with a noosed rope, until dead, esp. as a form of capital punishment. **b** as a mild oath (hang the expense; let everything go hang). **8** tr. let droop (hang one's head). **9** tr. suspend (meat or game) from a hook and leave it until dry or tender or high. **10** intr. be or remain hung (in various senses). **11** intr. remain static in the air. **12** intr. (often foll. by over) be present or imminent, esp. oppressively or threateningly (a hush hung over the room). **13** intr. (foll. by on) **a** be contingent or dependent on (everything hangs on the discussions). **b** listen closely to (hangs on their every word). **14** tr. colloq. make (a turn) (hang a right at the corner). • n. **1** the way a thing hangs or falls. **2** a downward droop or bend. □ **get the hang of** colloq. understand the technique or meaning of. **hang around** (or Brit. **about**) **1** loiter or dally; not move away. **2** (foll. by with) associate with (a person, etc.). **hang back 1** show reluctance to act or move. **2** remain behind. **hang fire** be slow in taking action or in progressing. **hang heavily** (or **heavy**) (of time) pass slowly. **hang in** colloq. **1** persist; persevere. **2** linger. **hang loose** colloq. relax; stay calm. **hang on** colloq. **1** continue or persevere, esp. with difficulty. **2** (often foll. by to) cling; retain one's grip. **3** (foll. by to) retain; fail to

give back. **4 a** wait for a short time. **b** (in telephoning) continue to listen during a pause in the conversation. **hang out 1** hang from a window, clothesline, etc. **2** protrude or cause to protrude downward. **3** (foll. by of) lean out of (a window, etc.). **4** sl. reside or be often present. **5** (foll. by with) sl. accompany; be friends with. **6** loiter; dally. **hang together 1** make sense. **2** remain associated. **hang up 1** hang from a hook, peg, etc. **2** (often foll. by on) end a telephone conversation, esp. abruptly (then he hung up on me). **3** cause delay or difficulty to. **4** (usu. in passive, foll. by on) sl. be a psychological or emotional obsession or problem to (is really hung up on her teacher). **let it all hang out** sl. be uninhibited or relaxed. **not care** (or **give**) **a hang** colloq. not care at all. [ON hanga (tr.) = OE hōn, & f. OE hangian (intr.), f. Gmc]

▶ A person suspended by the neck until dead is hanged, although hung is common in informal usage. Pictures, draperies, decorations, Christmas stockings, and the like are hung.

hang·ar /hángər/ n. a building with extensive floor area, for housing aircraft, etc. □□ **hang·a·rage** n. [F, of unkn. orig.]

hang·dog /hángdawg, –dog/ adj. having a dejected or guilty appearance; shamefaced.

hang·er[1] /hángər/ n. **1** a person or thing that hangs. **2** (in full **coat hanger**) a shaped piece of wood or plastic, etc., from which clothes may be hung.

hang·er[2] /hángər/ n. Brit. a wood on the side of a steep hill. [OE hangra f. hangian HANG]

hang·er-on n. (pl. **hang·ers-on**) a follower or dependent, esp. an unwelcome one.

hang glid·er n. a frame with a fabric airfoil stretched over it, from which the operator is suspended and controls flight by body movement. □□ **hang glid·ing** n.

hang glider

hang·ing /hánging/ n. & adj. • n. **1 a** the practice or an act of executing by hanging a person. **b** (attrib.) meriting or causing this (a hanging offense). **2** (usu. in pl.) draperies hung on a wall, etc. • adj. that hangs or is hung; suspended.

Hang·ing Gar·dens of Bab·y·lon n. legendary terraced gardens at Babylon, one of the Seven Wonders of the World.

hang·ing val·ley n. a valley that is cut across by a deeper valley or a cliff.

hang·man /hángmən/ n. (pl. **·men**) **1** an executioner who hangs condemned persons. **2** a word game for two players, in which the tally of failed guesses is kept by drawing a representation of a figure hanging from a gallows.

hang·nail /hángnayl/ n. **1** a piece of torn skin at the root of a fingernail. **2** the soreness resulting from this. [alt. of AGNAIL, infl. by HANG and taking nail as = NAIL n. 2a]

hang·out /hángowt/ n. sl. a place one lives in or frequently visits.

hang·o·ver /hángōvər/ n. **1** a severe headache or other aftereffects caused by drinking an excess of liquor. **2** a survival from the past.

hang-up n. sl. an emotional problem or inhibition.

hank /hangk/ n. **1** a coil or skein of wool or thread, etc. **2** any of several measures of length of cloth or yarn, e.g., 840 yds. for cotton yarn and 560 yds. for worsted. **3** Naut. a ring of rope, iron, etc., for securing the staysails to the stays. [ME f. ON hönk: cf. Sw. hank string, Da. hank handle]

hank·er /hángkər/ v.intr. (foll. by to + infin., for, or after) long for; crave. □□ **hank·er·er** n. **hank·er·ing** n. [obs. hank, prob. rel. to HANG]

han·ky /hángkee/ n. (also **han·kie**) (pl. **·kies**) colloq. a handkerchief. [abbr.]

han·ky-pan·ky /hángkeepángkee/ n. sl. **1** naughtiness, esp. sexual misbehavior. **2** dishonest dealing; trickery. [19th c.: perh. based on hocus-pocus]

Han·o·ve·ri·an /hánəveéreeən/ adj. of or relating to the British sovereigns from George I to Victoria (1714–1901). [Hanover in Germany, whose Elector became George I in 1714]

Han·sa /hánsə/ n. (also **Hanse**) **1 a** a medieval guild of merchants. **b** the entrance fee to a guild. **2** (also **Han·se·at·ic** /–seeátik/ **League**) a medieval political and commercial league of Germanic towns. □□ **Han·se·at·ic** adj. [MHG hanse, OHG, Goth. hansa company]

Han·sard /hánsaard/ n. the official verbatim record of debates in the British Parliament. [T. C. Hansard, Engl. printer d. 1833, who first printed it]

han·sel var. of HANDSEL.

Han·sen's disease /hánsənz/ *n.* leprosy. [G. H. A. *Hansen,* Norw. physician d. 1912]

han·som /hánsəm/ *n.* (in full **hansom cab**) *hist.* a two-wheeled horse-drawn carriage accommodating two inside, with the driver seated behind. [J. A. *Hansom,* Engl. architect d. 1882, who designed it]

Hants /hants/ *abbr.* Hampshire. [OE *Hantescire*]

Ha·nuk·kah /kha͝aánəkə, haá–/ *n.* (also **Cha·nuk·kah**) the Jewish festival of lights, commemorating the purification of the Temple in 165 BC. [Heb. *ḥānukkāh* consecration]

han·u·man /hún͝ooma͝aán/ *n.* **1** an Indian langur venerated by Hindus. **2** (**Hanuman**) (in Hindu mythology) the monkey god, a loyal helper of Rama. [Hindi]

hap /hap/ *n. & v. archaic* ● *n.* **1** chance; luck. **2** a chance occurrence. ● *v.intr.* (**happed, hap·ping**) **1** come about by chance. **2** (foll. by *to* + infin.) happen to. [ME f. ON *happ*]

hap·ax le·go·me·non /hápaks ligómɪnon, háypaks/ *n.* (*pl.* **hap·ax le·go·me·na** /–mínə/) a word of which only one instance of use is recorded in a document, a body of literature, etc. [Gk, = a thing said once]

ha'·pen·ny var. of HALFPENNY.

hap·haz·ard /hápházərd/ *adj. & adv.* ● *adj.* done, etc., by chance; random. ● *adv.* at random. □□ **hap·haz·ard·ly** *adv.* **hap·haz·ard·ness** *n.* [HAP & HAZARD]

hap·less /háplɪs/ *adj.* unlucky. □□ **hap·less·ly** *adv.* **hap·less·ness** *n.* [HAP + –LESS]

hap·log·ra·phy /haplógrəfee/ *n.* the accidental omission of letters when these are repeated in a word (e.g., *philogy* for *philology*). [Gk *haplous* single + –GRAPHY]

hap·loid /háployd/ *adj. & n. Biol.* ● *adj.* (of an organism or cell) with a single set of chromosomes. ● *n.* a haploid organism or cell. [G f. Gk *haplous* single + *eidos* form]

hap·lol·o·gy /haplóləjee/ *n.* the omission of a sound when this is repeated within a word (e.g., *February* pronounced /fébree/). [Gk *haplous* + –LOGY]

ha'p'orth *Brit.* var. of HALFPENNYWORTH.

hap·pen /hápən/ *v. & adv.* ● *v.intr.* **1** occur (by chance or otherwise). **2** (foll. by *to* + infin.) have the (good or bad) fortune to (*I happened to meet her*). **3** (foll. by *to*) be the (esp. unwelcome) fate or experience of (*what happened to you?*; *I hope nothing happens to them*). **4** (foll. by *on*) encounter or discover by chance. ● *adv. dial.* perhaps; maybe (*happen it'll rain*). □ **as it happens** in fact; in reality (*as it happens, it turned out well*). [ME f. HAP + –EN¹]

SYNONYM TIP happen

BEFALL, OCCUR, TRANSPIRE. When things **happen**, they come to pass either for a reason or by chance (*it happened the day after school started; she happened upon the scene of the accident*), but the verb is more frequently associated with chance (*it happened to be raining when we got there*). **Occur** can also refer either to something that comes to pass either accidentally or as planned, but it should only be used interchangeably with *happen* when the subject is a definite or actual event (*the tragedy occurred last winter*). Unlike *happen, occur* also carries the implication of something that presents itself to sight or mind (*it never occurred to me that he was lying*). **Transpire** is a more formal (and some would say undesirable) word meaning to *happen* or *occur,* and it conveys the sense that something has leaked out or become known (*he told her exactly what had transpired while she was away*). While things that *happen, occur,* or *transpire* can be either positive or negative, when something **befalls,** it is usually unpleasant (*he had no inkling of the disaster that would befall him when he got home*).

hap·pen·ing /hápəning/ *n. & adj.* ● **1** an event or occurrence. **2** an improvised or spontaneous theatrical, etc., performance. ● *adj. sl.* exciting, fashionable, trendy.

hap·pen·stance /hápənstans/ *n.* a thing that happens by chance. [HAPPEN + CIRCUMSTANCE]

hap·pi /hápee/ *n.* (*pl.* **hap·pis**) (also **hap·pi coat**) a loose informal Japanese jacket, sometimes sashed. [Jap.]

hap·py /hápee/ *adj.* (**hap·pi·er, hap·pi·est**) **1** feeling or showing pleasure or contentment. **2 a** fortunate; characterized by happiness. **b** (of words, behavior, etc.) apt; pleasing. **3** *colloq.* slightly drunk. **4** (in *comb.*) *colloq.* inclined to use excessively or at random (*trigger-happy*). □□ **hap·pi·ly** *adv.* **hap·pi·ness** *n.* [ME f. HAP + –Y¹]

hap·py fam·i·lies *n.pl. Brit.* a card game the object of which is to acquire four members of the same "family."

hap·py-go-luck·y *adj.* cheerfully casual.

hap·py hour *n.* a period of the day when drinks are sold at reduced prices in bars, hotels, etc.

hap·py hunt·ing ground *n.* **1** the conception of paradise for certain Native American tribes. **2** a place where success or enjoyment is obtained.

hap·py me·di·um *n.* a compromise; the avoidance of extremes.

hap·tic /háptik/ *adj.* relating to the sense of touch. [Gk *haptikos* able to touch f. *haptō* fasten]

ha·ra-ki·ri /hárəke͝eree, ha͝aáree–/ *n.* (also **ha·ri-ka·ri**) ritual suicide by

disembowelment with a sword, formerly practiced by samurai when disgraced or sentenced to death. [colloq. Jap. f. *hara* belly + *kiri* cutting]

ha·rangue /həráng/ *n. & v.* ● *n.* a lengthy and earnest speech. ● *v.tr.* lecture or make a harangue to. □□ **ha·rangu·er** *n.* [ME f. F f. OF *arenge* f. med.L *harenga,* perh. f. Gmc]

ha·rass /hərás, hárəs/ *v.tr.* **1** trouble and annoy continually or repeatedly. **2** make repeated attacks on (an enemy or opponent). □□ **ha·rass·er** *n.* **ha·rass·ing·ly** *adv.* **ha·rass·ment** *n.* [F *harasser* f. OF *harer* set a dog on]

PRONUNCIATION TIP harass

"HAR-ass," with the stress on the first syllable, is the older, more traditional pronunciation of this word and is still preferred by those for whom British pronunciation is a guide. "Ha-RASS" first occurred in American English and has gained wide acceptance over the last 50 years. The spelling, with its double-*s* ending and the similarity to words such as *morass,* has helped establish the second-syllable stress.

har·bin·ger /ha͝aárbinjər/ *n. & v.* ● *n.* **1** a person or thing that announces or signals the approach of another. **2** a forerunner. ● *v.tr.* announce the approach of. [earlier = 'one who provides lodging': ME *herbergere* f. OF f. *herberge* lodging f. Gmc]

har·bor /ha͝aárbər/ *n. & v.* ● *n.* **1** a place of shelter for ships. **2** a shelter; a place of refuge or protection. ● *v.* **1** *tr.* give shelter to (esp. a criminal or wanted person). **2** *tr.* keep in one's mind, esp. resentfully (*harbor a grudge*). **3** *intr.* come to anchor in a harbor. □□ **har·bor·less** *adj.* [OE *herebeorg* perh. f. ON, rel. to HARBINGER]

har·bor·age /ha͝aárbərij/ *n.* a shelter or place of shelter, esp. for ships.

har·bor mas·ter *n.* an official in charge of a harbor.

hard /haard/ *adj., adv., & n.* ● *adj.* **1** (of a substance, material, etc.) firm and solid; unyielding to pressure; not easily cut. **2 a** difficult to understand or explain (*a hard problem*). **b** difficult to accomplish (*a hard decision*). **c** (foll. by *to* + infin.) not easy (*hard to believe; hard to please*). **3** difficult to bear; entailing suffering (*a hard life*). **4** (of a person) unfeeling; severely critical. **5** (of a season or the weather) severe; harsh (*a hard winter; a hard frost*). **6** harsh or unpleasant to the senses (*a hard voice; hard colors*). **7 a** strenuous; enthusiastic; intense (*a hard worker; a hard fight*). **b** severe; uncompromising (*a hard blow; a hard bargain; hard words*). **c** *Polit.* extreme; most radical (*the hard right*). **8 a** (of liquor) strongly alcoholic. **b** (of drugs) potent and addictive. **c** (of radiation) highly penetrating. **d** (of pornography) highly suggestive and explicit. **9** (of water) containing mineral salts that make lathering difficult. **10** established; not disputable; reliable (*hard facts; hard data*). **11** *Stock Exch.* (of currency, prices, etc.) high; not likely to fall in value. **12** *Phonet.* (of a consonant) guttural (as *c* in *cat, g* in *go*). **13** (of a shape, boundary, etc.) clearly defined; unambiguous. ● *adv.* **1** strenuously; intensely; copiously; with one's full effort (*try hard; look hard at; is raining hard; hardworking*). **2** with difficulty or effort (*hard-earned*). **3** so as to be hard or firm (*hard-baked; the jelly set hard*). **4** *Naut.* fully; to the extreme (*hard to starboard*). ● *n. Brit.* **1** a sloping roadway across a foreshore. **2** *sl.* = HARD LABOR (*got two years hard*). □ **be hard on 1** be difficult for. **2** be severe in one's treatment or criticism of. **3** be unpleasant to (the senses). **be hard put** (usu. foll. by *to* + infin.) find it difficult. **go hard with** turn out to (a person's) disadvantage. **hard at it** *colloq.* busily working or occupied. **hard by** near; close by. **a hard case 1** *colloq.* **a** an intractable person. **b** *Austral. & NZ* an amusing or eccentric person. **2** a case of hardship. **hard hit** badly affected. **hard on** (or **upon**) close

SYNONYM TIP hard

ARDUOUS, DIFFICULT, LABORIOUS, TRYING For the student who does not read well, homework is **hard** work, which means that it demands great physical or mental effort. An English assignment to write an essay might be particularly **difficult,** meaning that it not only requires effort but skill. Where *hard* suggests toil, *difficult* emphasizes complexity (*a difficult math problem*). Memorizing long lists of vocabulary words would be **laborious,** which is even more restrictive than *hard* and suggests prolonged, wearisome toil with no suggestion of the skill required and no reference to the complexity of the task. Reading *War and Peace,* however, would be an **arduous** task, because it would require a persistent effort over a long period of time. A school assignment may be *difficult,* but is usually not *arduous;* that is, it may require skill rather than perseverance. It may also be *arduous* without being particularly *difficult,* as when a student is asked to write "I will not throw spitballs" five hundred times. A student who is new to a school may find it especially **trying,** which implies that it taxes the individual's patience, skill, or capabilities.

to in pursuit, etc. **put the hard word on** *Austral. & NZ sl.* ask a favor (esp. sexual or financial) of. □□ **hard•ish** *adj.* **hard•ness** *n.* [OE *hard, heard* f. Gmc]

hard and fast *adj.* (of a rule or a distinction made) definite; unalterable; strict.

hard•back /haárdbak/ *adj. & n.* ● *adj.* (of a book) bound in stiff covers. ● *n.* a hardback book.

hard•ball /haárdbawl/ *n. & v.* ● *n.* **1** = BASEBALL. **2** *sl.* uncompromising methods or dealings, esp. in politics or business (*play hardball*). ● *v.tr. sl.* pressure or coerce politically.

hard•bit•ten /haárdbítən/ *adj. colloq.* tough and cynical.

hard•board /haárdbawrd/ *n.* stiff board made of compressed and treated wood pulp.

hard-boiled *adj.* **1** (of an egg) boiled until the white and the yolk are solid. **2** (of a person) tough; shrewd.

hard cash *n.* negotiable coins and paper money.

hard coal *n.* anthracite.

hard copy *n.* printed material produced by computer, usu. on paper, suitable for ordinary reading.

hard core *n.* **1** an irreducible nucleus. **2** *colloq.* **a** the most active or committed members of a group or movement. **b** a conservative or reactionary minority. **3** *Brit.* solid material, esp. rubble, forming the foundation of a road, etc.

hard-core *adj.* blatant; uncompromising, esp.: **1** (of pornography) explicit; obscene. **2** (of drug addiction) relating to hard drugs, esp. heroin.

hard•cov•er /hárdkəvər/ *adj. & n.* ● *adj.* bound between rigid boards covered in cloth, paper, leather, or film (*a hardcover edition of the novel*). ● *n.* a hardcover book.

hard disk *n.* (also **hard drive**) *Computing* a rigid nonremovable magnetic disk with a large data storage capacity.

hard drive *n.* = HARD DISK.

hard•en /haárdən/ *v.* **1** *tr. & intr.* make or become hard or harder. **2** *intr. & tr.* become, or make (one's attitude, etc.), uncompromising or less sympathetic. **3** *intr.* (of prices, etc.) cease to fall or fluctuate. □ **harden off** inure (a plant) to cold by gradually increasing its exposure. □□ **hard•en•er** *n.*

hard•en•ing /haárdəning/ *n.* **1** the process or an instance of becoming hard. **2** (in full **hardening of the arteries**) *Med.* = ARTERIOSCLEROSIS.

hard er•ror *n. Computing* an error or hardware fault causing failure of a program or operating system, esp. one that gives no option of recovery.

hard feel•ings *n.pl.* feelings of resentment.

hard hat *n.* **1** a protective helmet worn on building sites, etc. **2** *colloq.* a reactionary person.

hard•head•ed /haárdhédid/ *adj.* practical; realistic; not sentimental. □□ **hard•head•ed•ly** *adv.* **hard•head•ed•ness** *n.*

hard•heart•ed /haárdhaártid/ *adj.* unfeeling; unsympathetic. □□ **hard•heart•ed•ly** *adv.* **hard•heart•ed•ness** *n.*

hard-hit•ting *adj.* aggressively critical.

har•di•hood /haárdeehood/ *n.* boldness; daring.

hard la•bor *n.* heavy manual work as a punishment, esp. in a prison.

hard land•ing *n.* **1** a clumsy or rough landing of an aircraft. **2** an uncontrolled landing in which a spacecraft crashes onto the surface of a planet and is destroyed.

hard line *n.* an unyielding adherence to a firm policy. □□ **hard•lin•er** *n.*

hard luck *n.* worse fortune than one deserves.

hard•ly /haárdlee/ *adv.* **1** scarcely; only just (*we hardly knew them*). **2** only with difficulty (*could hardly speak*). **3** harshly.

GRAMMAR TIP   **hardly**

See note at SCARCELY.

hard-nosed *adj. colloq.* realistic; uncompromising.

hard nut *n. sl.* a tough, aggressive person. □ **a hard nut to crack** *colloq.* **1** a difficult problem. **2** a person or thing not easily understood or influenced.

hard-on *n. coarse sl.* an erection of the penis.

hard pad *n.* hardening of the pads of the feet, a symptom of distemper in dogs and other animals.

hard pal•ate *n.* the front part of the palate.

hard•pan /haárdpan/ *n. Geol.* a hardened layer of clay occurring in or below the soil profile.

hard paste *adj.* denoting a Chinese or "true" porcelain made of fusible and infusible materials (usu. clay and stone) and fired at a high temperature.

hard-pressed *adj.* **1** closely pursued. **2** burdened with urgent business. **3** (also **hard pressed**) in difficulties.

hard rock *n. colloq.* highly amplified rock music with a heavy beat.

hard roe *n.* see ROE[1].

hard sauce *n.* a sauce of butter and sugar, often with brandy, etc., added.

hard sell *n.* aggressive salesmanship or advertising.

hard•shell /haárdshel/ *adj.* **1** having a hard shell. **2** rigid; orthodox; uncompromising.

hard•ship /haárdship/ *n.* **1** severe suffering or privation. **2** the circumstance causing this.

hard shoul•der *n. Brit.* a hardened strip alongside a motorway for stopping on in an emergency.

hard stuff *n. sl.* strong liquor, esp. whiskey.

hard•tack /haárdtak/ *n.* a hard biscuit, as that formerly given to sailors and soldiers as rations.

hard•top /haárdtop/ *n.* **1** an automobile without roof supports between the front and back windows. **2** an automobile with a rigid (usu. detachable) roof.

hard up *adj.* **1** short of money. **2** (foll. by *for*) at a loss for; lacking.

hard•ware /haárdwair/ *n.* **1** tools and household articles of metal, etc. **2** heavy machinery or armaments. **3** the mechanical and electronic components of a computer, etc. (cf. SOFTWARE).

hard-wear•ing /haárdwáiring/ *adj.* able to stand much wear.

hard wheat *n.* wheat with a hard grain rich in gluten.

hard-wired *adj.* involving or achieved by permanently connected circuits designed to perform a specific function.

hard•wood /haárdwood/ *n.* the wood from a deciduous broad-leaved tree as distinguished from that of conifers.

hard-work•ing /haárdwərking/ *adj.* diligent.

har•dy /haárdee/ *adj.* (**har•di•er, har•di•est**) **1** robust; capable of enduring difficult conditions. **2** (of a plant) able to grow in the open air all year round. □□ **har•di•ly** *adv.* **har•di•ness** *n.* [ME f. OF *hardi* past part. of *hardir* become bold, f. Gmc, rel. to HARD]

har•dy an•nu•al *n.* **1** an annual plant that may be sown outdoors. **2** *Brit. joc.* a subject that comes up at regular intervals.

hare /hair/ *n. & v.* ● *n.* **1** any of various mammals of the family Leporidae, esp. *Lepus europaeus*, like a large rabbit, with tawny fur, long ears, short tail, and hind legs longer than forelegs, inhabiting fields, hills, etc. **2** (in full **electric hare**) a dummy hare propelled by electricity, used in greyhound racing. ● *v.intr.* run with great speed. □ **run with the hare and hunt with the hounds** *Brit.* try to remain on good terms with both sides. **start a hare** *Brit.* raise a topic of conversation. [OE *hara* f. Gmc]

hare and hounds *n.* a game, esp. a paperchase, in which a group of people chase another person or group across the countryside.

hare•bell /háirbel/ *n.* **1** a plant, *Campanula rotundifolia*, with slender stems and pale blue bell-shaped flowers. **2** = BLUEBELL 2.

hare-brained /háirbraynd/ *adj.* rash; foolish; wild.

Hare Krish•na /haáree kríshnə/ *n.* **1** a sect devoted to the worship of the Hindu deity Krishna (an incarnation of Vishnu). **2** (*pl.* **Hare Krish•nas**) a member of this sect. [the title of a mantra based on the name *Krishna*, f. Skr. *O Hari!* an epithet of Krishna]

hare•lip /háirlip/ *n.* a congenital fissure of the upper lip. □□ **hare•lipped** *adj.*

har•em /háirəm, hár–/ *n.* **1 a** the women of a Muslim household, living in a separate part of the house. **b** their quarters. **2** a group of female animals sharing a mate. [Arab. *ḥarām, ḥarīm,* orig. = prohibited, prohibited place, f. *ḥarama* prohibit]

hare's-foot *n.* (in full **hare's-foot clover**) a clover, *Trifolium arvense*, with soft hair around the flowers.

hare•wood /háirwood/ *n.* stained sycamore wood used for making furniture. [G dial. *Ehre* f. L *acer* maple + WOOD]

har•i•cot /árikò/ *n.* **1** (in full **haricot vert** /ver/) a variety of French bean with small white seeds. **2** the dried seed of this used as a vegetable. [F]

Har•i•jan /hárijən/ *n.* a member of the class formerly called untouchables in India. [Skr., = a person dedicated to Vishnu, f. *Hari* Vishnu, *jana* person]

hark /haark/ *v.intr.* (usu. in *imper.*) *archaic* listen attentively. □ **hark back** revert to a topic discussed earlier. [ME *herkien* f. OE *heorcian* (unrecorded): cf. HEARKEN: *hark back* was orig. a hunting call to retrace steps]

hark•en var. of HEARKEN.

harl /haarl/ *n.* (also **harle, herl** /herl/) fiber of flax or hemp. [MLG *herle, harle* fiber of flax or hemp]

har•le•quin /haárlikwin/ *n. & adj.* ● *n.* **1** (**Harlequin**) **a** a mute character in pantomime, usu. masked and dressed in a diamond-patterned costume. **b** *hist.* a stock comic character in Italian *commedia dell'arte.* **2** (in full **harlequin duck**) an Icelandic duck, *Histrionicus histrionicus*, with variegated plumage. ● *adj.* in varied colors; variegated. [F f. earlier *Herlequin* leader of a legendary troup of demon horsemen]

har•le•quin•ade /haárlikwináyd/ *n.* **1** the part of a pantomime featuring Harlequin. **2** a piece of buffoonery. [F *arlequinade*, (as HARLEQUIN)]

har•lot /haárlət/ *n. archaic* a prostitute. □□ **har•lot•ry** *n.* [ME f. OF *harlot, herlot* lad, knave, vagabond]

harm /haarm/ *n. & v.* ● *n.* hurt; damage. ● *v.tr.* cause harm to. □ **out of harm's way** in safety. [OE *hearm, hearmian* f. Gmc]

har•mat•tan /haármətán/ *n.* a parching dusty wind of the W. African coast occurring from December to February. [Fanti or Twi *haramata*]

harm·ful /haarmfŏŏl/ *adj.* causing or likely to cause harm. □□ **harm·ful·ly** *adv.* **harm·ful·ness** *n.*

harm·less /haarmlis/ *adj.* **1** not able or likely to cause harm. **2** inoffensive. □□ **harm·less·ly** *adv.* **harm·less·ness** *n.*

har·mon·ic /haarmónik/ *adj. & n.* ● *adj.* **1** of or characterized by harmony; harmonious. **2** *Mus.* **a** of or relating to harmony. **b** (of a tone) produced by vibration of a string, etc., in an exact fraction of its length. **3** *Math.* of or relating to quantities whose reciprocals are in arithmetical progression (*harmonic progression*). ● *n.* **1** *Mus.* an overtone accompanying at a fixed interval (and forming a note with) a fundamental. **2** *Physics* a component frequency of wave motion. □□ **har·mon·i·cal·ly** *adv.* [L *harmonicus* f. Gk *harmonikos* (as HARMONY)]

har·mon·i·ca /haarmónikə/ *n.* a small rectangular wind instrument with a row of metal reeds along its length, held against the lips and moved from side to side to produce different notes by blowing or sucking. [L, fem. sing. or neut. pl. of *harmonicus*: see HARMONIC]

har·mon·ic mo·tion *n.* (in full **simple harmonic motion**) *Physics* oscillatory motion under a retarding force proportional to the amount of displacement from an equilibrium position.

har·mon·ic pro·gres·sion *n.* (also **harmonic series**) *Math.* a series of quantities whose reciprocals are in arithmetical progression.

har·mo·ni·ous /haarmóneeəs/ *adj.* **1** pleasant sounding; tuneful. **2** forming a pleasing or consistent whole; concordant. **3** free from disagreement or dissent. □□ **har·mo·ni·ous·ly** *adv.* **har·mo·ni·ous·ness** *n.*

har·mo·nist /haarmənist/ *n.* a person skilled in musical harmony; a harmonizer. □□ **har·mo·nis·tic** *adj.*

har·mo·ni·um /haarmóneeəm/ *n.* a keyboard instrument in which the notes are produced by air driven through metal reeds by bellows operated by the feet. [F f. L (as HARMONY)]

har·mo·nize /haarmənīz/ *v.* **1** *tr.* add notes to (a melody) to produce harmony. **2** *tr. & intr.* (often foll. by *with*) bring into or be in harmony. **3** *intr.* make or form a pleasing or consistent whole. □□ **har·mo·ni·za·tion** *n.* [f. F *harmoniser* (as HARMONY)]

har·mo·ny /haarmənee/ *n.* (*pl.* **·nies**) **1 a** a combination of simultaneously sounded musical notes to produce chords and chord progressions, esp. as having a pleasing effect. **b** the study of this. **2 a** an apt or aesthetic arrangement of parts. **b** the pleasing effect of this. **3** agreement; concord. **4** a collation of parallel narratives, esp. of the Gospels. □ **in harmony 1** (of singing, etc.) producing chords; not discordant. **2** (often foll. by *with*) in agreement. [ME f. OF *harmonie* f. L *harmonia* f. Gk *harmonia* joining, concord, f. *harmos* joint]

har·mo·ny of the spheres *n.* the natural harmonic tones supposedly produced by the movement of the celestial spheres or the bodies fixed in them.

har·ness /haarnis/ *n. & v.* ● *n.* **1** the equipment of straps and fittings by which a horse is fastened to a cart, etc., and controlled. **2** a similar arrangement for fastening a thing to a person's body, for restraining a young child, etc. ● *v.tr.* **1 a** put a harness on (esp. a horse). **b** (foll. by *to*) attach by a harness. **2** make use of (natural resources) esp. to produce energy. □ **in harness** in the routine of daily work. □□ **har·ness·er** *n.* [ME f. OF *harneis* military equipment f. ON *hernest* (unrecorded) f. *herr* army + *nest* provisions]

harp /haarp/ *n. & v.* ● *n.* a large upright roughly triangular musical instrument consisting of a frame housing a graduated series of vertical strings, played by plucking with the fingers. ● *v.intr.* **1** (foll. by *on*) talk repeatedly and tediously about. **2** play on a harp. □□ **harp·er** *n.* **harp·ist** *n.* [OE *hearpe* f. Gmc]

har·poon /haarpŏŏn/ *n. & v.* ● *n.* a barbed spearlike missile with a rope attached, for killing whales, etc. ● *v.tr.* spear with a harpoon. □□ **har·poon·er** *n.* [F *harpon* f. *harpe* clamp f. L *harpa* f. Gk *harpē* sickle]

har·poon gun *n.* a gun for firing a harpoon.

harp seal *n.* a Greenland seal, *Phoca groenlandica*, with a harp-shaped dark mark on its back.

harp·si·chord /haarpsikawrd/ *n.* a keyboard instrument with horizontal strings whose each plucked mechanically. □□ **harp·si·chord·ist** *n.* [obs. F *harpechorde* f. LL *harpa* harp, + *chorda* string, the *-s-* being unexplained]

har·py /haarpee/ *n.* (*pl.* **·pies**) **1** (in Greek and Roman mythology) a monster with a woman's head and

harp

body and bird's wings and claws. **2** a grasping unscrupulous person. [F *harpie* or L *harpyia* f. Gk *harpuiai* snatchers (cf. *harpazō* snatch)]

har·py ea·gle *n.* a S. American crested bird of prey, *Harpia harpyja*, one of the largest of eagles.

har·que·bus /haarkwibəs/ *n.* (also **ar·que·bus** /aar–/) *hist.* an early type of portable gun supported on a tripod or on a forked rest. [F (*h*)*arquebuse* ult. f. MLG *hakebusse* or MHG *hakenbühse*, f. *haken* hook + *busse* gun]

har·ri·dan /hárid'n/ *n.* a bad-tempered woman. [17th-c. cant, perhaps f. F *haridelle* old horse]

har·ri·er[1] /háreeər/ *n.* a person who harries or lays waste.

har·ri·er[2] /háreeər/ *n.* **1 a** a hound used for hunting hares. **b** (in *pl.*) a pack of these with huntsmen. **2** a runner or group of cross-country runners. [HARE + –IER, assim. to HARRIER[1]]

har·ri·er[3] /háreeər/ *n.* any bird of prey of the genus *Circus*, with long wings for swooping over the ground. [*harrower* f. *harrow* harry, rob, assim. to HARRIER[1]]

Har·ris tweed /háris/ *n.* a kind of tweed woven by hand in Harris in the Outer Hebrides of Scotland.

har·row /hárō/ *n. & v.* ● *n.* a heavy frame with iron teeth dragged over plowed land to break up clods, remove weeds, cover seed, etc. ● *v.tr.* **1** draw a harrow over (land). **2** (usu. as **harrowing** *adj.*) distress greatly. □□ **har·row·er** *n.* **har·row·ing·ly** *adv.* [ME f. ON *hervi*]

har·rumph /hərúmf/ *v.intr.* clear the throat or make a similar sound, esp. ostentatiously or to signal disapproval. [imit.]

har·ry /háree/ *v.tr.* (**·ries**, **·ried**) **1** ravage or despoil. **2** harass; worry. [OE *herian, hergian* f. Gmc, rel. to OE *here* army]

harsh /haarsh/ *adj.* **1** unpleasantly rough or sharp, esp. to the senses. **2** severe; cruel. □□ **harsh·en** *v.tr. & intr.* **harsh·ly** *adv.* **harsh·ness** *n.* [MLG *harsch* rough, lit. 'hairy,' f. *haer* HAIR]

hars·let var. of HASLET.

hart /haart/ *n.* esp. *Brit.* the male of the deer (esp. the red deer) usu. over five years old. [OE *heor(o)t* f. Gmc]

har·tal /haart'l/ *n.* the closing of shops and offices in India as a mark of protest or sorrow. [Hind. *hartāl, hattāl* f. Skr. *hatta* shop + *tālaka* lock]

har·te·beest /haartəbeest, haartbeest/ *n.* any large African antelope of the genus *Alcelaphus*, with ringed horns bent back at the tips. [Afrik. f. Du. *hert* HART + *beest* BEAST]

harts·horn /haarts-hawrn/ *n. archaic* **1** an ammonious substance obtained from the horns of a hart. **2** (in full **spirit of hartshorn**) an aqueous solution of ammonia. [OE (as HART, HORN)]

hart's tongue *n.* a fern, *Phyllitis scolopendrium*, with narrow undivided fronds.

har·um-scar·um /háirəmskáirəm/ *adj. & n. colloq.* ● *adj.* wild and reckless. ● *n.* such a person. [rhyming form. on HARE, SCARE]

ha·rus·pex /hərúspeks, hárəspeks/ *n.* (*pl.* **ha·rus·pi·ces** /–spiseez/) a Roman religious official who interpreted omens from the inspection of animals' entrails. □□ **ha·rus·pi·cy** /–spisee/ *n.* [L]

har·vest /haarvist/ *n. & v.* ● *n.* **1 a** the process of gathering in crops, etc. **b** the season when this takes place. **2** the season's yield or crop. **3** the product or result of any action. ● *v.tr.* **1 a** gather as a harvest; reap. **b** earn; obtain as a result of harvesting. **2** experience (consequences). □□ **har·vest·a·ble** *adj.* [OE *hærfest* f. Gmc]

har·vest·er /haarvistər/ *n.* **1** a reaper. **2** a reaping machine, esp. with sheaf-binding.

har·vest·man /haarvistmən/ *n.* (*pl.* **·men**) any of various arachnids of the family Opilionidae, with very long thin legs, found in humus and on tree trunks; a daddy-longlegs.

har·vest mite *n.* any arachnid larvae of the genus *Trombicula*, whose parasitic larvae live on or under the skin of warm-blooded animals, where they cause irritation and dermatitis.

har·vest moon *n.* the full moon nearest to the autumnal equinox (Sept. 22 or 23).

har·vest mouse *n.* a small rodent, *Micromys minutus*, that nests in the stalks of growing grain.

has *3rd sing. present* of HAVE.

has-been /házbin/ *n. colloq.* a person or thing that has lost a former importance or usefulness.

hash[1] /hash/ *n. & v.* ● *n.* **1** a dish of cooked meat and potatoes cut into small pieces and recooked. **2 a** a mixture; a jumble. **b** a mess. **3** reused or recycled material. ● *v.tr.* (often foll. by *up*) **1** make (meat, etc.) into a hash. **2** recycle (old material). □ **hash something out** come to agreement on something after lengthy and vigorous discussion. **make a hash of** *colloq.* make a mess of; bungle. **settle someone's hash** *colloq.* deal with and subdue a person. [F *hacher* f. *hache* HATCHET]

hash[2] /hash/ *n. colloq.* hashish. [abbr.]

hash·ish /hásheesh, hasheesh/ *n.* a resinous product of the top leaves and tender parts of hemp, smoked or chewed for its narcotic effects. [f. Arab. *ḥašīš* dry herb; powdered hemp leaves]

Ha·sid /khaásid, kháw–, haá–/ (*pl.* **Ha·sid·im** /–sídim, –seé–/) a member of any of several mystical Jewish sects, esp. one founded in the 18th c. □□ **Ha·sid·ic** /–sídik/ *adj.* [Heb. *ḥasíd* pious]

has·let /háslit, háyz–/ *n.* (also **hars·let** /háar–/) pieces of (esp. pig's) offal cooked together and usu. compressed into a meat loaf. [ME f. OF *hastelet* dimin. of *haste* roast meat, spit, f. OLG, OHG *harst* roast]

has·n't /házənt/ *contr.* has not.

hasp /hasp/ *n. & v.* ● *n.* a hinged metal clasp that fits over a staple and can be secured by a padlock. ● *v.tr.* fasten with a hasp. [OE *hæpse, hæsp*]

hasp

hasp

has·si·um /háseeəm/ *n.* a radioactive element. ¶ Symb.: **Hs**.

has·sle /hásəl/ *n. & v. colloq.* ● *n.* **1** a prolonged trouble or inconvenience. **2** an argument or involved struggle. ● *v.* **1** *tr.* harass; annoy; cause trouble to. **2** *intr.* argue; quarrel. [20th c.: orig. dial.]

has·sock /hásək/ *n.* **1 a** a thick firm cushion for kneeling on, esp. in church. **b** a similar cushion used as a footrest, etc. **2** a tuft of matted grass, etc. [OE *hassuc*]

hast /hast/ *archaic 2nd sing. present* of HAVE.

has·tate /hástayt/ *adj. Bot.* triangular; shaped like the head of a spear. [L *hastatus* f. *hasta* spear]

haste /hayst/ *n. & v.* ● *n.* **1** urgency of movement or action. **2** excessive hurry. ● *v.intr. archaic* = HASTEN. □ **in haste** quickly; hurriedly. **make haste** hurry; be quick. [ME f. OF *haste, haster* f.WG]

has·ten /háysən/ *v.* **1** *intr.* (often foll. by *to* + infin.) make haste; hurry. **2** *tr.* cause to occur or be ready or be done sooner.

hast·y /háystee/ *adj.* (**hast·i·er, hast·i·est**) **1** hurried; acting quickly or hurriedly. **2** said, made, or done too quickly or too soon; rash; unconsidered. **3** quick-tempered. □□ **hast·i·ly** *adv.* **hast·i·ness** *n.* [ME f. OF *hasti, hastif* (as HASTE, –IVE)]

hat /hat/ *n. & v.* ● *n.* **1** a covering for the head, often with a brim and worn out of doors. **2** *colloq.* a person's occupation or capacity, esp. one of several (*wearing his managerial hat*). ● *v.tr.* (**hat·ted, hat·ting**) cover or provide with a hat. □ **keep it under one's hat** *colloq.* keep it secret. **out of a hat** by random selection. **pass the hat** collect contributions of money. **take off one's hat to** (or **hats off to**) *colloq.* acknowledge admiration for. **throw one's hat in the ring** take up a challenge. □□ **hat·ful** *n.* (*pl.* **·fuls**) **hat·less** *adj.* [OE *hætt* f. Gmc]

hat·band /hátband/ *n.* a band of ribbon, etc., around a hat above the brim.

hat·box /hátboks/ *n.* a box to hold a hat, esp. for traveling.

hatch[1] /hach/ *n.* **1** an opening in the wall between two rooms, e.g., between a kitchen and a dining room for serving food. **2** an opening or door in an aircraft, spacecraft, etc. **3** *Naut.* **a** = HATCHWAY. **b** a trapdoor or cover for this (often in *pl.: batten the hatches*). **4** a floodgate. □ **down the hatch** *sl.* (as drinking a toast) drink up; cheers! [OE *hæcc* f. Gmc]

hatch[2] /hach/ *v. & n.* ● *v.* **1** *intr.* **a** (often foll. by *out*) (of a young bird or fish, etc.) emerge from the egg. **b** (of an egg) produce a young animal. **2** *tr.* incubate (an egg). **3** *tr.* (also foll. by *up*) devise (a plot, etc.). ● *n.* **1** the act or an instance of hatching. **2** a brood hatched. [ME *hacche*, of unkn. orig.]

hatch[3] /hach/ *v.tr.* mark (a surface, e.g., a map or drawing) with close parallel lines. [ME f. F *hacher* f. *hache* HATCHET]

hatch·back /háchbak/ *n.* a car with a sloping back hinged at the top to form a door.

hatch·er·y /háchəree/ *n.* (*pl.* **·ies**) a place for hatching eggs, esp. of fish or poultry.

hatch·et /háchit/ *n.* **1** a light short-handled ax for use with one hand. **2** TOMAHAWK. [ME f. OF *hachette* dimin. of *hache* ax f. med.L *hapia* f. Gmc]

hatch·et-faced *adj. colloq.* sharp-featured or grim looking.

hatch·et job *n. colloq.* a fierce destructive critique of a person, esp. in print.

hatch·et man *n. colloq.* **1** a hired killer. **2** a person employed to carry out a hatchet job.

hatch·ing /háching/ *n. Art & Archit.* close parallel lines forming shading, esp. on a map or an architectural drawing.

hatch·ling /háchling/ *n.* a bird or fish that has just hatched.

hatch·ment /háchmənt/ *n. Heraldry* a large usu. diamond-shaped tablet with a deceased person's coat of arms, affixed to that person's house, tomb, etc. [contr. of ACHIEVEMENT]

hatch·way /háchway/ *n.* an opening in a ship's deck for lowering cargo into the hold.

hate /hayt/ *v. & n.* ● *v.tr.* **1** dislike intensely; feel hatred toward. **2** *colloq.* **a** dislike. **b** (foll. by verbal noun or *to* + infin.) be reluctant (to do something) (*I hate to disturb you*). ● *n.* **1** hatred. **2** *colloq.* a hated person or thing. □□ **hat·a·ble** *adj.* (also **hate·a·ble**). **hat·er** *n.* [OE *hatian* f. Gmc]

hate·ful /háytfŏŏl/ *adj.* arousing hatred. □□ **hate·ful·ly** *adv.* **hate·ful·ness** *n.*

hath /hath/ *archaic 3rd sing. present* of HAVE.

hath·a yo·ga /háthə/ *n.* a system of physical exercises and breathing control used in yoga. [Skr. *haṭha* force: see YOGA]

hat·pin /hátpin/ *n.* a long pin, often decorative, for securing a hat to the head.

ha·tred /háytrid/ *n.* intense dislike or ill will. [ME f. HATE + –*red* f. OE *rǣden* condition]

hat·stand /hátstand/ *n.* a stand with hooks on which to hang hats.

hat·ter /hátər/ *n.* **1** a maker or seller of hats. **2** *Austral. & NZ* a person (esp. a miner or bushman) who lives alone. □ **as mad as a hatter** wildly eccentric.

hat trick *n. Sports* the scoring of three goals, etc., in a single game, match, etc.

hau·berk /háwbərk/ *n. hist.* a coat of mail. [ME f. OF *hau(s)berc* f. Frank., = neck protection, f. *hals* neck + *berg-* f. *beorg* protection]

haugh·ty /háwtee/ *adj.* (**haugh·ti·er, haugh·ti·est**) arrogantly self-admiring and disdainful. □□ **haugh·ti·ly** *adv.* **haugh·ti·ness** *n.* [extension of *haught* (adj.), earlier *haut* f. OF *haut* f. L *altus* high]

haul /hawl/ *v. & n.* ● *v.* **1** *tr.* pull or drag forcibly. **2** *tr.* transport by truck, cart, etc. **3** *intr.* turn a ship's course. **4** *tr. colloq.* (usu. foll. by *up*) bring for reprimand or trial. ● *n.* **1** the act or an instance of hauling. **2** an amount gained or acquired. **3** a distance to be traversed (*a short haul*). □ **haul over the coals** see COAL. [var. of HALE[2]]

haul·age /háwlij/ *n.* **1** the commercial transport of goods. **2** a charge for this.

haul·er /háwlər/ *n.* **1** a person or thing that hauls. **2** a miner who takes coal from the workface to the bottom of the shaft. **3** a person or business engaged in the transport of goods.

haul·ier /háwləər/ *n. Brit.* = HAULER.

haulm /hawm/ *n.* (also **halm**) **1** a stalk or stem. **2** the stalks or stems collectively of peas, beans, potatoes, etc., without the pods, etc. [OE *h(e)alm* f. Gmc]

haul·yard var. of HALYARD.

haunch /hawnch/ *n.* **1** the fleshy part of the buttock with the thigh, esp. in animals. **2** the leg and loin of a deer, etc., as food. **3** the side of an arch between the crown and the pier. [ME f. OF *hanche*, of Gmc orig.: cf. LG *hanke* hind leg of a horse]

haunt /hawnt/ *v. & n.* ● *v.* **1** *tr.* (of a ghost) visit (a place) regularly, usu. reputedly giving signs of its presence. **2** *tr.* (of a person or animal) frequent or be persistently in (a place). **3** *tr.* (of a memory, etc.) be persistently in the mind of. **4** *intr.* (foll. by *with, in*) stay habitually. **5** trouble; distress (*their shady financial dealings came back to haunt them*). ● *n.* **1** (often in *pl.*) a place frequented by a person. **2** a place frequented by animals, esp. for food and drink. □□ **haunt·er** *n.* [ME f. OF *hanter* f. Gmc]

haunt·ing /háwnting/ *adj.* (of a memory, melody, etc.) poignant; wistful; evocative. □□ **haunt·ing·ly** *adv.*

Hau·sa /hówzə/ *n. & adj.* ● *n.* (*pl.* same or **Hau·sas**) **1 a** a people of W. Africa and the Sudan. **b** a member of this people. **2** the Hamitic language of this people, widely used in W. Africa. ● *adj.* of or relating to this people or language. [native name]

haus·frau /hówsfrow/ *n.* a German housewife. [G f. *Haus* house + *Frau* woman]

haut·boy *archaic* var. of OBOE.

haute cou·ture /ót kōōtóor/ *n.* high fashion; the leading fashion houses or their products. [F, lit. = high dressmaking]

haute cui·sine /ót kwizeén/ *n.* cooking of a high standard, esp. of the French traditional school. [F, lit. = high cooking]

haute é·cole /ót aykól/ *n.* the art or practice of advanced classical dressage. [F, = high school]

hau·teur /hōtór/ *n.* haughtiness of manner. [F f. *haut* high]

haut monde /ō mawnd/ *n.* fashionable society. [F, lit. = high world]

Ha·van·a /həvánə/ *n.* a cigar made in Havana or elsewhere in Cuba.

have /hav/ *v. & n.* ● *v.* (*3rd sing. present* **has** /haz/; *past* and *past part.* **had** /had/) ● *v.tr.* **1** hold in possession as one's property or at one's disposal; be provided with (*has a car; had no time to read; has nothing to wear*). **2** hold in a certain relationship (*has a sister; had no equals*). **3** contain as a part or quality (*house has two floors; has green eyes*). **4 a** undergo; experience; enjoy; suffer (*had a good time; has a headache*). **b** be subjected to a specified state (*had my car stolen; the book has a page missing*). **c** cause, instruct, or invite (a person or thing) to be in a particular state or take a particular action (*had him dismissed; had us worried; had my hair cut; had a copy made; had them stay*). **5 a** engage in (an activity) (*had an argument*). **b** hold (a meeting, party, etc.). **6** eat or drink (*had a beer*). **7** (usu. in *neg.*) accept or tolerate; permit to (*I won't have it; will not have you say such things*). **8 a** let (a feeling, etc.) be present (*have no doubt; has a lot of sympathy for me; have nothing against them*). **b** show or feel (mercy, pity, etc.) toward another person (*have pity on him; have mercy!*). **c** (foll. by *to* + infin.) show by action that one is influenced by (a feeling, quality, etc.) (*have the goodness to leave now*). **9 a** give

birth to or beget (offspring). **b** conceive mentally (an idea, etc.).
10 receive; obtain (*had a letter from him; not a ticket to be had*). **11** be
burdened with or committed to (*has a job to do; have my garden to
attend to*). **12 a** have obtained (a qualification) (*has several degrees*).
b know (a language) (*has no Latin*). **13** *sl.* **a** get the better of (*I had
him there*). **b** (usu. in *passive*) cheat; deceive (*you were had*). **14** *coarse
sl.* have sexual intercourse with. • *v.aux.* (with *past part.* or *ellipt.*,
to form the perfect, pluperfect, and future perfect tenses, and the
conditional mood) (*have worked; had seen; will have been; had I
known, I would have gone; have you met her? yes, I have*). • *n.* **1** (usu.
in *pl.*) *colloq.* a person who has wealth or resources. **2** *Brit. sl.* a
swindle. □ **had best** see BEST. **had better** would find it prudent to.
had rather see RATHER. **have a care** see CARE. **have done, have done
with** see DONE. **have an eye for, have eyes for, have an eye to** see
EYE. **have a good mind to** see MIND. **have got to** *colloq.* = *have to*.
have had it *colloq.* **1** have missed one's chance. **2** (of a person) have
passed one's prime; (of a thing) be worn out or broken. **3** have been
killed, defeated, etc. **4** have suffered or endured enough. **have it
1** (foll. by *that* + clause) express the view that. **2** win a decision in
a vote, etc. **3** *colloq.* have found the answer, etc. **have it away** (or
off) *Brit. coarse sl.* have sexual intercourse. **have it both ways** see
BOTH. **have it in for** *colloq.* be hostile or ill-disposed toward. **have it
out** (often foll. by *with*) *colloq.* attempt to settle a dispute by discussion or argument. **have it one's own way** see WAY. **have nothing
to do with** see DO¹. **have on 1** be wearing (clothes). **2** be committed to (an engagement); have plans for. **3** *Brit. colloq.* tease; play a
trick on. **have out** get (a tooth, etc.) extracted (*had her tonsils out*).
have sex (often foll. by *with*) *colloq.* have sexual intercourse. **have
something** (or **nothing**) **on a person 1** know something (or nothing) discreditable or incriminating about a person. **2** have an (or
no) advantage or superiority over a person. **have to** be obliged to;
must. **have to do with** see DO¹. **have up** *Brit. colloq.* bring (a person) before a court of justice, interviewer, etc. [OE *habban* f. Gmc,
prob. rel. to HEAVE]

ha•ven /háyvən/ *n.* **1** a harbor or port. **2** a place of refuge. [OE *hæfen*
f. ON *höfn*]

have-not *n.* (usu. in *pl.*) *colloq.* a person lacking wealth or resources.

have•n't /hávənt/ *contr.* have not.

ha•ver /háyvər/ *v. & n.* • *v.intr. Brit.* **1** talk foolishly; babble. **2** vacillate; hesitate. • *n.* (usu. in *pl.*) *Sc.* foolish talk; nonsense. [18th c.:
orig. unkn.]

hav•er•sack /hávərsak/ *n.* a stout bag for provisions, etc., carried on
the back or over the shoulder. [F *havresac* f. G *Habersack* f. *Haber*
oats + *Sack* SACK¹]

hav•er•sine /hávərsin/ *n.* (also **hav•er•sin**) *Math.* half of a versed
sine. [contr.]

hav•oc /hávək/ *n. & v.* • *n.* widespread destruction; great confusion
or disorder. • *v.tr.* (**hav•ocked, hav•ock•ing**) devastate. □ **play havoc with** *colloq.* cause great confusion or difficulty to. [ME f. AF
havok f. OF *havo(t)*, of unkn. orig.]

haw¹ /haw/ *n.* the hawthorn or its fruit. [OE *haga* f. Gmc, rel. to
HEDGE]

haw² /haw/ *n.* the nictitating membrane of a horse, dog, etc., esp.
when inflamed. [16th c.: orig. unkn.]

haw³ /haw/ *int. & v.* • *int.* expressing hesitation. • *v.intr.* (in **hem and
haw**: see HEM²) [imit.: cf. HA¹]

haw⁴ /haw/ *int.* a command to a horse, etc., to turn to the left.

Ha•wai•ian /həwíən/ *n. & adj.* • *n.* **1 a** a native or inhabitant of
Hawaii, an island or island group (comprising a US state) in the
N. Pacific. **b** a person of Hawaiian descent. **2** the Malayo-
Polynesian language of Hawaii. • *adj.* of or relating to Hawaii or its
people or language.

haw•finch /háwfinch/ *n.* any large stout finch of the genus
Coccothraustes, with a thick beak for cracking seeds. [HAW¹ + FINCH]

hawk¹ /hawk/ *n. & v.* • *n.* **1** any of
various diurnal birds of prey of
the family Accipitridae, having
a characteristic curved beak,
rounded short wings, and a long
tail. **2** *Polit.* a person who advocates an aggressive or warlike policy, esp. in foreign affairs. **3** a rapacious person. • *v.* **1** *intr.* hunt
game with a hawk. **2** *intr.* (often
foll. by *at*) & *tr.* attack, as a hawk
does. **3** *intr.* (of a bird) hunt on the
wing for food. □□ **hawk•ish** *adj.* **hawk•ish•ness** *n.* **hawk•like** *adj.*
[OE *h(e)afoc, hæbuc* f. Gmc]

hawk¹ (Swainson's hawk)

hawk² /hawk/ *v.tr.* **1** carry about or offer around (goods) for sale.
2 (often foll. by *about*) relate (news, gossip, etc.) freely. [back-form.
f. HAWKER¹]

hawk³ /hawk/ *v.* **1** *intr.* clear the throat noisily. **2** *tr.* (foll. by *up*) bring
(phlegm, etc.) up from the throat. [prob. imit.]

hawk⁴ /hawk/ *n.* a plasterer's square board with a handle underneath
for carrying plaster or mortar. [17th c.: orig. unkn.]

hawk•er¹ /háwkər/ *n.* a person who travels about selling goods. [16th
c.: prob. f. LG or Du.; cf. HUCKSTER]

hawk•er² /háwkər/ *n.* a falconer. [OE *hafocere*]

hawk-eyed *adj.* keen-sighted.

hawk moth *n.* any darting and hovering moth of the family
Sphingidae, having narrow forewings and a stout body.

hawks•bill /háwksbil/ *n.* (in full **hawksbill turtle**) a small turtle,
Eretmochelys imbricata, yielding tortoiseshell.

hawk•weed /háwkweed/ *n.* any composite plant of the genus
Hieracium, with yellow flowers.

hawse /hawz/ *n.* **1** the part of a ship's bows in which hawseholes or
hawsepipes are placed. **2** the space between the head of an
anchored vessel and the anchors. **3** the arrangement of cables when
a ship is moored with port and starboard forward anchors. [ME
halse, prob. f. ON *háls* neck, ship's bow]

hawse•hole /háwzhōl/ *n.* a hole in the side of a ship through which
a cable or anchor rope passes.

hawse•pipe /háwzpip/ *n.* a metal pipe lining a hawsehole.

haw•ser /háwzər/ *n. Naut.* a thick rope or cable for mooring or towing a ship. [ME f. AF *haucer, hauceour* f. OF *haucier* hoist ult. f. L
altus high]

haw•thorn /háwthawrn/ *n.* any thorny shrub or tree of the genus
Crataegus, esp. *C. monogyna*, with white, red, or pink blossoms and
small dark red fruit or haws. [OE *hagathorn* (as HAW¹, THORN)]

hay¹ /hay/ *n. & v.* • *n.* grass mown and dried for fodder. • *v.* **1** *intr.*
make hay. **2** *tr.* put (land) under grass for hay. **3** *tr.* make into hay.
□ **make hay of** throw into confusion. **make hay (while the sun
shines)** seize opportunities for profit or enjoyment. [OE *hēg, hīeg,
hīg* f. Gmc]

hay² /hay/ *n.* (also **hey**) **1** a country dance with interweaving steps.
2 a figure in this. [obs. F *haie*]

hay•cock /háykok/ *n.* a conical heap of hay in a field.

hay fever *n.* a common allergy with respiratory symptoms, caused
by pollen or dust.

hay•field /háyfeeld/ *n.* a field where hay is being or is to be made.

hay•mak•er /háymaykər/ *n.* **1** a person who tosses and spreads hay
to dry after mowing. **2** an apparatus for shaking and drying hay.
3 *sl.* a forceful blow or punch. □□ **hay•mak•ing** *n.*

hay•mow /háymow/ *n.* hay stored in a stack or barn.

hay•rick /háyrik/ *n.* = HAYSTACK.

hay•seed /háyseed/ *n.* **1** grass seed obtained from hay. **2** *colloq.* a rustic or yokel.

hay•stack /háystak/ *n.* a packed pile of hay with a pointed or ridged
top.

hay•wire /háywir/ *adj. colloq.* **1** badly disorganized; out of control.
2 (of a person) badly disturbed; erratic. [HAY¹ + WIRE, from the use
of hay-baling wire in makeshift repairs]

haz•ard /házərd/ *n. & v.* • *n.* **1** a danger or risk. **2** a source of this.
3 chance. **4** a dice game with a complicated arrangement of
chances. **5** *Golf* an obstruction in playing a shot, e.g., a bunker, water, etc. • *v.tr.* **1** venture on (*hazard a guess*). **2** run the risk of. **3** expose to hazard. [ME f. OF *hasard* f. Sp. *azar* f. Arab. *az-zahr* chance,
luck]

haz•ard•ous /házərdəs/ *adj.* **1** risky; dangerous. **2** dependent on
chance. □□ **haz•ard•ous•ly** *adv.* **haz•ard•ous•ness** *n.* [F *hasardeux*
(as HAZARD)]

haze¹ /hayz/ *n.* **1** obscuration of the atmosphere near the earth by
fine particles of water, smoke, or dust. **2** mental obscurity or confusion. [prob. back-form. f. HAZY]

haze² /hayz/ *v.tr.* **1** *Naut.* harass with overwork. **2** seek to disconcert;
ridicule. **3** subject (fraternity initiates, etc.) to tricks, humiliation,
etc. [orig. uncert.: cf. obs. F *haser* tease, insult]

ha•zel /háyzəl/ *n.* **1** any shrub or small tree of the genus *Corylus*, esp.
C. avellana bearing round brown edible nuts. **2 a** wood from the
hazel. **b** a stick made of this. **3** a reddish brown or greenish brown
color (esp. of the eyes). [OE *hæsel* f. Gmc]

ha•zel grouse *n.* a European woodland grouse, *Tetrastes bonasia*.

ha•zel•nut /háyzəlnut/ *n.* the fruit of the hazel.

ha•zy /háyzee/ *adj.* (**ha•zi•er, ha•zi•est**) **1** misty. **2** vague; indistinct.
3 confused; uncertain. □□ **ha•zi•ly** *adv.* **ha•zi•ness** *n.* [17th c. in
Naut. use: orig. unkn.]

Hb *symb.* hemoglobin.

HBM *abbr.* Her or His Britannic Majesty (or Majesty's).

H-bomb /áychbom/ *n.* = HYDROGEN BOMB. [H³ + BOMB]

HC *abbr.* **1** Holy Communion. **2** (in the UK) House of Commons.

h.c. *abbr. honoris causa.*

HCF *abbr.* highest common factor.

hdbk. *abbr.* handbook.

HDTV *abbr.* high-definition television.

HE *abbr.* **1** high explosive. **2** His Eminence. **3** His or Her Excellency.

He *symb. Chem.* the element helium.

he /hee/ *pron. & n.* •*pron.* (*obj.* **him** /him/; *poss.* **his** /hiz/; *pl.* **they** /thay/) **1** the man or boy or male animal previously named or in question. **2** a person, etc., of unspecified sex, esp. referring to one already named or identified (*if anyone comes he will have to wait*). •*n.* **1** a male; a man. **2** (in *comb.*) male (*he-goat*). **3** *Brit.* a children's chasing game, with the chaser designated "he." [OE f. Gmc] ▶See note at EVERYBODY.

head /hed/ *n., adj., & v.* •*n.* **1** the upper part of the human body, or the foremost or upper part of an animal's body, containing the brain, mouth, and sense organs. **2 a** the head regarded as the seat of intellect or repository of comprehended information. **b** intelligence; imagination (*use your head*). **c** mental aptitude or tolerance (usu. foll. by *for*: *a good head for business; no head for heights*). **3** *colloq.* a headache, esp. resulting from a blow or from intoxication. **4** a thing like a head in form or position, esp.: **a** the operative part of a tool. **b** the flattened top of a nail. **c** the ornamented top of a pillar. **d** a mass of leaves or flowers at the top of a stem. **e** the flat end of a drum. **f** the foam on top of a glass of beer, etc. **g** the upper horizontal part of a window frame, door frame, etc. **5** life when regarded as vulnerable (*it cost him his head*). **6 a** a person in charge; a director or leader (esp. usu. *Brit.*) the principal teacher at a school or college). **b** a position of leadership or command. **7** the front or forward part of something, e.g., a line. **8** the upper end of something, e.g., a table or bed. **9** the top or highest part of something, e.g., a page, stairs, etc. **10** a person or individual regarded as a numerical unit (*$10 per head*). **11** (*pl.* same) **a** an individual animal as a unit. **b** (as *pl.*) a number of cattle or game as specified (*20 head*). **12 a** the side of a coin bearing the image of a head. **b** (usu. in *pl.*) this side as a choice when tossing a coin. **13 a** the source of a river or stream, etc. **b** the end of a lake at which a river enters it. **14** the height or length of a head as a measure. **15** the component of a machine that is in contact with or very close to what is being processed or worked on, esp.: **a** the component on a tape recorder that touches the moving tape in play and converts the signals. **b** the part of a record player that holds the playing cartridge and stylus. **c** = PRINTHEAD. **16 a** a confined body of water behind a dam, or steam in an engine, etc. **b** the pressure exerted by this. **17** a promontory (esp. in place-names) (*Nags Head*). **18** *Naut.* **a** the bows of a ship. **b** a ship's latrine. **19** a main topic or category for consideration or discussion. **20** *Journalism* = HEADLINE *n.* **21** a culmination, climax, or crisis. **22** the fully developed top of a boil, etc. **23** *sl.* a habitual taker of drugs; a drug addict. •*attrib.adj.* chief or principal (*head gardener; head office*). •*v.* **1** *tr.* be at the head or front of. **2** *tr.* be in charge of (*headed a small team*). **3** *tr.* **a** provide with a head or heading. **b** (of an inscription, title, etc.) be at the top of; serve as a heading for. **4 a** *intr.* face or move in a specified direction or toward a specified result (often foll. by *for*: *is heading for trouble*). **b** *tr.* direct in a specified direction. **5** *tr.* *Soccer* strike (the ball) with the head. **6 a** *tr.* (often foll. by *down*) cut the head off (a plant, etc.). **b** *intr.* (of a plant, etc.) form a head. □ **above** (or **over**) **one's head** beyond one's ability to understand. **come to a head** reach a crisis. **enter** (or **come into**) **one's head** *colloq.* occur to one. **from head to toe** (or **foot**) all over a person's body. **get one's head down** *Brit. sl.* **1** go to bed. **2** concentrate on the task in hand. **give a person his** or **her head** allow a person to act freely. **go out of one's head** go mad. **go to one's head 1** (of liquor) make one dizzy or slightly drunk. **2** (of success) make one conceited. **head and shoulders** *colloq.* by a considerable amount. **head back 1** get ahead of so as to intercept and turn back. **2** return home, etc. **head in the sand** refusal to acknowledge an obvious danger or difficulty. **head off 1** get ahead of so as to intercept and turn aside. **2** forestall. **head over heels 1** turning over completely in forward motion as in a somersault, etc. **2** topsy-turvy. **3** utterly; completely (*head over heels in love*). **heads up** (as an interjection) watch out; be alert. **heads will roll** *colloq.* people will be disgraced or dismissed. **head up** take charge of (a group of people). **hold up one's head** be confident or unashamed. **in one's head 1** in one's thoughts or imagination. **2** by mental process without use of physical aids. **keep one's head** remain calm. **keep one's head above water** *colloq.* **1** keep out of debt. **2** avoid succumbing to difficulties. **keep one's head down** *colloq.* remain inconspicuous in difficult or dangerous times. **lose one's head** lose self-control; panic. **make head or tail of** (usu. with *neg.* or *interrog.*) understand at all. **off one's head** *sl.* crazy. **off the top of one's head** *colloq.* impromptu; without careful thought or investigation. **on one's** (or **one's own**) **head** as one's sole responsibility. **out of one's head 1** *sl.* crazy. **2** from one's imagination or memory. **over one's head 1** beyond one's ability to understand. **2** without one's knowledge or involvement, esp. when one has a right to this. **3** with disregard for one's own (stronger) claim (*was promoted over their heads*). **put heads together** consult together. **put into a person's head** suggest to a person. **take** (or **get**) **it into one's head** (foll. by *that* + clause or *to* + infin.) form a definite idea or plan. **turn a person's head 1** make a person conceited. **2** cause a person to be distracted, confused, etc. **with one's head in the clouds** see

CLOUD. □□ **head•ed** *adj.* (also in *comb.*). **head•less** *adj.* **head•ward** *adj. & adv.* [OE *hēafod* f. Gmc]

-head /hed/ *suffix* = -HOOD (*godhead; maidenhead*). [ME *-hed, -hede* = -HOOD]

head•ache /hédayk/ *n.* **1** a continuous pain in the head. **2** *colloq.* **a** a worrying problem. **b** a troublesome person. □□ **head•ach•y** *adj.*

head•band /hédband/ *n.* a band worn around the head as decoration or to keep the hair off the face.

head•bang•er *n. sl.* **1** a young person dancing violently to heavy metal music. **2** a crazy or eccentric person.

head•board /hédbawrd/ *n.* an upright panel forming the head of a bed.

head•butt *n. & v.* •*n.* a forceful thrust with the top or front of the head into the chin, head, or body of another person. •*v.tr.* attack (another person) with a head-butt.

head count /hédkownt/ *n.* **1** a counting of individual people. **2** a total number of people, esp. the number of people employed in a particular organization.

head•dress /héd-dres/ *n.* an ornamental covering or band for the head.

head•er /hédər/ *n.* **1** *Soccer* a shot or pass made with the head. **2** *colloq.* a headlong fall or dive. **3** a brick or stone laid at right angles to the face of a wall. **4** (in full **header tank**) a tank of water, etc., maintaining pressure in a plumbing system. **5** *Computing* line or lines of information printed at the top of the page throughout a document.

head first *adj. & adv.* **1** with the head foremost (*dive head first into the water*). **2** without sufficient forethought.

head•gear /hédgeer/ *n.* a hat, headdress, or head covering.

head•hunt•ing /hédhunting/ *n.* **1** the practice among some peoples of collecting the heads of dead enemies as trophies. **2** the practice of filling a (usu. senior) business position by approaching a suitable person employed elsewhere. □□ **head•hunt** *v.tr.* (also *absol.*). **head•hunt•er** *n.*

head•ing /héding/ *n.* **1 a** a title at the head of a page or section of a book, etc. **b** a division or section of a subject of discourse, etc. **2 a** a horizontal passage made in preparation for building a tunnel. **b** *Mining* = DRIFT *n.* 6. **3** the extension of the top of a curtain above the tape that carries the hooks or the pocket for a rod. **4** the course of an aircraft, ship, etc.

head•lamp /hédlamp/ *n.* = HEADLIGHT.

head•land *n.* **1** /hédlənd/ a promontory. **2** /hédland/ a strip left unplowed at the end of a field, to allow machinery to pass through.

head•light /hédlīt/ *n.* **1** a strong light at the front of a motor vehicle or train engine. **2** the beam from this.

head•line /hédlīn/ *n. & v.* •*n.* **1** a heading at the top of an article or page, esp. in a newspaper. **2** (in *pl.*) the most important items of news in a newspaper or broadcast news bulletin. •*v.tr.* give a headline to. □ **hit** (or **make**) **the headlines** *colloq.* be given prominent attention as news.

head•lin•er /hédlīnər/ *n.* a star performer.

head•lock /hédlok/ *n.* *Wrestling* a hold with an arm around the opponent's head.

head•long /hédlawng, –lóng/ *adv. & adj.* **1** with head foremost. **2** in a rush. [ME *headling* (as HEAD, –LING²), assim. to –LONG]

head•man /hédmən/ *n.* (*pl.* **-men**) the chief man of a tribe, etc.

head•mas•ter /hédmástər/ *n.* (*fem.* **head•mis•tress** /–místris/) (esp. in the UK or in private schools in the US) the person in charge of a school.

head•most /hédmōst/ *adj.* (esp. of a ship) foremost.

head•on *adj.* **1** with the front foremost (*a head-on crash*). **2** in direct confrontation.

head•phone /hédfōn/ *n.* (usu. in *pl.*) a pair of earphones joined by a band placed over the head, for listening to audio equipment, etc.

head•piece /hédpees/ *n.* **1** an ornamental engraving at the head of a chapter, etc. **2 a** a helmet. **b** a ceremonial headdress. **3** intellect.

head•quar•ters /hédkwáwrtərz/ *n.* (as *sing.* or *pl.*) **1** the administrative center of an organization. **2** the premises occupied by a military commander and the commander's staff.

head•rest /hédrest/ *n.* a support for the head, esp. on a seat or chair.

head•room /hédrŏŏm, –rŏŏm/ *n.* **1** the space or clearance between the top of a vehicle and the underside of a bridge, etc., which it passes under. **2** the space above a driver's or passenger's head in a vehicle.

head•scarf /hédskaarf/ *n.* a scarf worn around the head and tied under the chin, instead of a hat.

head•set /hédset/ *n.* a set of headphones, often with a microphone attached, used esp. in telephone and radio communications.

head•ship /hédship/ *n.* the position of chief or leader, esp. of a headmaster or headmistress.

headset

head·shrink·er n. **1** hist. a headhunter who preserved and shrank the heads of his dead enemies. **2** sl. a psychiatrist.

heads·man /hédzmən/ n. (pl. ·men) **1** hist. an executioner who beheads. **2** a person in command of a whaling boat.

head·spring /hédspring/ n. **1** the main source of a stream. **2** a principal source of ideas, etc.

head·square /hédskwair/ n. a rectangular scarf for wearing on the head.

head·stall /hédstawl/ n. the part of a halter or bridle that fits around a horse's head.

head start n. an advantage granted or gained at an early stage.

head·stock /hédstok/ n. a set of bearings in a machine, supporting a revolving part.

head·stone /hédstōn/ n. a (usu. inscribed) stone set up at the head of a grave.

head·strong /hédstrawng, –strong/ adj. self-willed and obstinate. □□ **head·strong·ly** adv. **head·strong·ness** n.

head teach·er n. the teacher in charge of a department or school.

head-up adj. (of instrument readings in an aircraft, vehicle, etc.) shown so as to be visible without lowering the eyes.

head voice n. the high register of the voice in speaking or singing.

head·wa·ter /hédwawtər, –wotər/ n. (in sing. or pl.) streams flowing at the sources of a river.

head·way /hédway/ n. **1** progress. **2** the rate of progress of a ship. **3** = HEADROOM 1. □ **make headway** see MAKE.

headwind n. a wind blowing from directly in front, opposing forward motion.

head·word /hédwərd/ n. a word forming a heading, e.g., of an entry in a dictionary or encyclopedia.

head·work /hédwərk/ n. mental work or effort.

head·y /hédee/ adj. (head·i·er, head·i·est) **1** (of alcohol) potent; intoxicating. **2** (of success, etc.) likely to cause conceit. **3** (of a person, thing, or action) impetuous; violent. □□ **head·i·ly** adv. **head·i·ness** n.

heal /heel/ v. **1** intr. (often foll. by up) (of a wound or injury) become sound or healthy again. **2** tr. cause (a wound, disease, or person) to heal or be healed. **3** tr. put right (differences, etc.). **4** tr. alleviate (sorrow, etc.). □□ **heal·a·ble** adj. **heal·er** n. [OE hǣlan f. Gmc, rel. to WHOLE]

heal-all n. **1** a universal remedy; a panacea. **2** a popular name of various medicinal plants.

heald /heeld/ n. = HEDDLE. [app. f. OE hefel, hefeld, f. Gmc]

health /helth/ n. **1** the state of being well in body or mind. **2** a person's mental or physical condition (in poor health). **3** soundness, esp. financial or moral (the health of the nation). **4** a toast drunk in someone's honor. [OE hǣlth f. Gmc]

health farm n. a residential establishment where people seek improved health by a regimen of dieting, exercise, etc.

health food n. food thought to have health-giving or -sustaining qualities.

health·ful /hélthfŏol/ adj. conducive to good health; beneficial. □□ **health·ful·ly** adv. **health·ful·ness** n.

health main·te·nance or·gan·i·za·tion n. an organization that provides medical care to subscribers who have paid in advance, usu. through a health insurance plan. ¶ Abbr.: **HMO**

health ser·vice n. Brit. a public service providing medical care.

health spa n. **1** a resort, club, gym, etc., providing facilities for exercise and conditioning. **2** = HEALTH FARM.

health vis·i·tor n. Brit. a trained nurse who visits those in need of medical attention in their homes.

health·y /hélthee/ adj. (health·i·er, health·i·est) **1** having, showing, or promoting good health. **2** beneficial; helpful (a healthy respect for experience). □□ **health·i·ly** adv. **health·i·ness** n.

heap /heep/ n. & v. ● n. **1** a collection of things lying haphazardly one on another. **2** (esp. Brit. in pl.) colloq. a large number or amount (there's heaps of time; is heaps better; a heap of chores to finish). **3** sl. an old or dilapidated thing, esp. a motor vehicle or building. ● v. **1** tr. & intr. (foll. by up, together, etc.) collect or be collected in a heap. **2** tr. (foll. by with) load copiously or to excess. **3** tr. (foll. by on, upon) accord or offer copiously to (heaped insults on them). **4** tr. (as **heaping**, **heaped** adj.) (of a spoonful, etc.) with the contents piled above the brim. □ **heap coals of fire on a person's head** Brit. cause a person remorse by returning good for evil. [OE hēap, hēapian f. Gmc]

hear /heer/ v. (past and past part. **heard** /herd/) **1** tr. (also absol.) perceive (sound, etc.) with the ear. **2** tr. listen to (heard them on the radio). **3** tr. listen judicially to and judge (a case, plaintiff, etc.). **4** intr. (foll. by about, of, or that + clause) be told or informed. **5** intr. (foll. by from) be contacted by, esp. by letter or telephone. **6** tr. be ready to obey (an order). **7** tr. grant (a prayer). □ **have heard of** be aware of; know of the existence of. **hear! hear!** int. expressing agreement (esp. with something said in a speech). **hear a person out** listen to all that a person says. **hear say** (or **tell**) (usu. foll. by of, or that + clause) be informed. **will not hear of** will not allow or agree to. □□ **hear·a·ble** adj. **hear·er** n. [OE hīeran f. Gmc]

hear·ing /hééring/ n. **1** the faculty of perceiving sounds. **2** the range

within which sounds may be heard; earshot (within hearing; in my hearing). **3** an opportunity to state one's case (give them a fair hearing). **4** the listening to evidence and pleadings in a court of law.

hear·ing aid n. a small device to amplify sound, worn by a partially deaf person.

heark·en /haárkən/ v.intr. (also **hark·en**) archaic or literary (often foll. by to) listen. [OE heorcnian (as HARK)]

hear·say /héersay/ n. rumor; gossip.

hear·say ev·i·dence n. Law evidence given by a witness based on information received from others rather than personal knowledge.

hearse /hərs/ n. a vehicle for conveying the coffin at a funeral. [ME f. OF herse harrow f. med.L herpica ult. f. L hirpex –icis large rake]

heart /haart/ n. **1** a hollow muscular organ maintaining the circulation of blood by rhythmic contraction and dilation. **2** the region of the heart; the breast. **3 a** the heart regarded as the center of thought, feeling, and emotion (esp. love). **b** a person's capacity for feeling emotion (has no heart). **4 a** courage or enthusiasm (take heart; lose heart). **b** one's mood or feeling (change of heart). **5 a** the central or innermost part of something. **b** the vital part or essence (the heart of the matter). **6** the close compact center of a head of cabbage, lettuce, etc. **7 a** a heart-shaped thing. **b** a conventional representation of a heart with two equal curves meeting at a point at the bottom and a cusp at the top. **8 a** a playing card of a suit denoted by a red figure of a heart. **b** (in pl.) this suit. **c** (in pl.) a card game in which players avoid taking tricks containing a card of this suit. **9** condition of land as regards fertility (in good heart). □ **after one's own heart** such as one likes or desires. **at heart 1** in one's inmost feelings. **2** basically; essentially. **break a person's heart** overwhelm a person with sorrow. **by heart** in or from memory. **close to** (or **near**) **one's heart 1** dear to one. **2** affecting one deeply. **from the heart** (or **the bottom of one's heart**) sincerely; profoundly. **give** (or **lose**) **one's heart** (often foll. by to) fall in love (with). **have a heart** be merciful. **have the heart** (usu. with neg.; foll. by to + infin.) be insensitive or hard-hearted enough (didn't have the heart to ask him). **have** (or **put**) **one's heart in** be keenly involved in or committed to (an enterprise, etc.). **have one's heart in one's mouth** be greatly alarmed or apprehensive. **have one's heart in the right place** be sincere or well-intentioned. **heart to heart** candidly; intimately. **in one's heart of hearts** in one's inmost feelings. **take to heart** be much affected or distressed by. **to one's heart's content** see CONTENT¹. **wear one's heart on one's sleeve** make one's feelings apparent. **with all one's heart** sincerely; with all goodwill. **with one's whole heart** with enthusiasm; without doubts or reservations. □□ **heart·ed** adj. [OE heorte f. Gmc]

heart·ache /haártayk/ n. mental anguish or grief.

heart at·tack n. a sudden and sometimes fatal occurrence of coronary thrombosis, usu. resulting in the death of part of a heart muscle.

heart·beat /haártbeet/ n. a pulsation of the heart.

heart·break /haártbrayk/ n. overwhelming distress. □□ **heart·break·er** n. **heart·break·ing** adj. **heart·bro·ken** adj.

heart·burn /haártbərn/ n. a burning sensation in the chest resulting from indigestion; pyrosis.

heart·en /haárt'n/ v.tr. & intr. make or become more cheerful. □□ **heart·en·ing·ly** adv.

heart fail·ure n. a gradual failure of the heart to function properly, resulting in breathlessness, edema, etc.

heart·felt /haártfelt/ adj. sincere; deeply felt.

hearth /haarth/ n. **1 a** the floor of a fireplace. **b** the area in front of a fireplace. **2** this symbolizing the home. **3** the bottom of a blast furnace where molten metal collects. [OE heorth f. WG]

hearth·rug /haárthrug/ n. a rug laid before a fireplace.

hearth·stone /haárthstōn/ n. **1** a flat stone forming a hearth. **2** a soft stone used to whiten hearths, doorsteps, etc.

heart·i·ly /haártilee/ adv. **1** in a hearty manner; with goodwill, appetite, or courage. **2** very; to a great degree (esp. with ref. to personal feelings) (am heartily sick of it; disliked him heartily).

heart·land /haártland/ n. the central or most important part of an area.

heart·less /haártlis/ adj. unfeeling; pitiless. □□ **heart·less·ly** adv. **heart·less·ness** n.

heart-lung ma·chine n. a machine that temporarily takes over the functions of the heart and lungs, esp. in surgery.

heart of gold n. a generous nature.

heart of stone n. a stern or cruel nature.

heart-rend·ing adj. very distressing. □□ **heart-rend·ing·ly** adv.

heart-search·ing n. the thorough examination of one's own feelings and motives.

hearts·ease /haártseez/ n. (also **heart's-ease**) any plant of the genus Viola, esp. a pansy.

heart·sick /haártsik/ adj. very despondent. □□ **heart·sick·ness** n.

heart·sore /haártsawr/ adj. archaic or literary grieving; heartsick.

heart·strings /háartstringz/ *n.pl.* one's deepest feelings or emotions.

heart·throb /háart-throb/ *n.* **1** beating of the heart. **2** *colloq.* a person for whom one has (esp. immature) romantic feelings.

heart-to-heart *adj. & n.* •*adj.* (of a conversation, etc.) candid; intimate. •*n.* a candid or personal conversation.

heart·warm·ing /háartwawrming/ *adj.* emotionally rewarding or uplifting.

heart·wood /háartwŏŏd/ *n.* the dense inner part of a tree trunk, yielding the hardest timber.

heart·y /háartee/ *adj. & n.* •*adj.* (**heart·i·er, heart·i·est**) **1** strong; vigorous. **2** spirited. **3** (of a meal or appetite) large. **4** warm; friendly. **5** genuine; sincere. •*n.* **1** *Brit.* a hearty person, esp. one ostentatiously so. **2** (usu. in *pl.*) (as a form of address) fellows, esp. fellow sailors. □□ **heart·i·ness** *n.*

heat /heet/ *n. & v.* •*n.* **1 a** the condition of being hot. **b** the sensation or perception of this. **c** high temperature of the body. **2** *Physics* **a** a form of energy arising from the random motion of the molecules of bodies, which may be transferred by conduction, convection, or radiation. **b** the amount of this needed to cause a specific process, or evolved in a process (*heat of formation; heat of solution*). **3** hot weather (*succumbed to the heat*). **4 a** warmth of feeling. **b** anger or excitement (*the heat of the argument*). **5** (foll. by *of*) the most intense part or period of an activity (*in the heat of the battle*). **6 a** (usu. preliminary or trial) round in a race or contest. **7** the receptive period of the sexual cycle, esp. in female mammals. **8** redness of the skin with a sensation of heat (*prickly heat*). **9** pungency of flavor. **10** *sl.* intensive pursuit, e.g., by the police. **11** *sl.* criticism. •*v.* **1** *tr. & intr.* make or become hot or warm. **2** *tr.* inflame; excite or intensify. □ **in heat** (of mammals, esp. females) sexually receptive. **in the heat of the moment** during or resulting from intense activity, without pause for thought. **turn the heat on** *colloq.* concentrate an attack or criticism on (a person). [OE *hætu* f. Gmc]

heat bar·ri·er *n.* the limitation of the speed of an aircraft, etc., by heat resulting from air friction.

heat death *n. Physics* a state of uniform distribution of energy to which the universe is thought to be tending.

heat·ed /héetid/ *adj.* **1** (of a person, discussions, etc.) angry; inflamed with passion or excitement. **2** made hot. □□ **heat·ed·ly** *adv.*

heat en·gine *n.* a device for producing motive power from heat.

heat·er /héetər/ *n.* **1** a device for supplying heat to its environment. **2** a container with an element, etc., for heating the contents (*water heater*). **3** *sl.* a gun.

heat ex·chang·er *n.* a device for the transfer of heat from one medium to another.

heat ex·haus·tion *n.* (also **heat prostration**) a condition caused by prolonged exposure to or vigorous exercise in heat and characterized by faintness, nausea, and profuse sweating.

heath /heeth/ *n.* **1** an area of flattish uncultivated land with low shrubs. **2** a plant growing on a heath, esp. of the genus *Erica* or *Calluna* (e.g., heather). □□ **heath·less** *adj.* **heath·like** *adj.* **heath·y** *adj.* [OE *hæth* f. Gmc]

heath·en /héethən/ *n. & adj.* •*n.* **1** a person who does not belong to a widely held religion (esp. who is not Christian, Jewish, or Muslim) as regarded by those that do. **2** an unenlightened person; a person regarded as lacking culture or moral principles. **3** (**the heathen**) heathen people collectively. **4** *Bibl.* a Gentile. •*adj.* **1** of or relating to heathens. **2** having no religion. □□ **heath·en·dom** *n.* **heath·en·ism** *n.* [OE *hæthen* f. Gmc]

heath·er /héthər/ *n.* **1** an evergreen shrub, *Calluna vulgaris*, with purple bell-shaped flowers. **2** any of various shrubs of the genus *Erica* or *Daboecia*, growing esp. on moors and heaths or in acid soil. **3 a** a fabric of mixed hues supposed to resemble heather. **b** the color of this. □□ **heath·er·y** *adj.* [ME, Sc., & No. of Engl. *hathir*, etc., of unkn. orig.: assim. to *heath*]

Heath Rob·in·son /heeth róbinsən/ *adj. Brit.* absurdly ingenious and impracticable in design or construction. [W. *Heath Robinson*, Engl. cartoonist d. 1944 who drew such contrivances]

heat·ing /héeting/ *n.* **1** the imparting or generation of heat. **2** equipment or devices used to provide heat, esp. to a building.

heat lightning *n.* distant lightning seen as vivid flashes near the horizon, usu. without the sound of thunder and usu. occurring during late evening in summer.

heat pump *n.* a device for the transfer of heat from a colder area to a hotter area by using mechanical energy.

heat-seek·ing *adj.* (of a missile, etc.) able to detect infrared radiation to guide it to its target.

heat shield *n.* a device for protection from excessive heat, esp. fitted to a spacecraft.

heat sink *n.* a device or substance for absorbing excessive or unwanted heat.

heat·stroke /héetstrōk/ *n.* a severe feverish condition caused by excessive exposure to high temperature.

heat-treat *v.tr.* subject to heat treatment.

heat treat·ment *n.* **1** the use of heat for therapeutic purposes in med-

icine. **2** the use of heat to modify the properties of a material, esp. in metallurgy.

heat wave *n.* a prolonged period of abnormally hot weather.

heave /heev/ *v. & n.* •*v.* (*past* and *past part.* **heaved** or esp. *Naut.* **hove** /hōv/) **1** *tr.* lift or haul (a heavy thing) with great effort. **2** *tr.* utter with effort or resignation (*heaved a sigh*). **3** *tr. colloq.* throw. **4** *intr.* rise and fall rhythmically or spasmodically. **5** *tr. Naut.* haul by rope. **6** *intr.* retch. •*n.* **1** an instance of heaving. **2** *Geol.* a sideways displacement in a fault. **3** (in *pl.*) a disease of horses, with labored breathing. □ **heave in sight** *Naut.* or *colloq.* come into view. **heave to** esp. *Naut.* bring or be brought to a standstill. □□ **heav·er** *n.* [OE *hebban* f. Gmc, rel. to L *capere* take]

heave-ho *n.* **1** a sailors' cry, esp. on raising the anchor. **2** *sl.* (usu. prec. by *the*) a dismissal or rejection (*gave her husband the heave-ho*).

heav·en /hévən/ *n.* **1** a place regarded in some religions as the abode of God and the angels, and of the good after death, often characterized as above the sky. **2** a place or state of supreme bliss. **3** *colloq.* something delightful. **4** (usu. **Heaven**) **a** God; Providence. **b** (in *sing.* or *pl.*) an exclamation or mild oath (*by Heaven!*). **5** (**the heavens**) esp. *poet.* the sky as the abode of the sun, moon, and stars and regarded from earth. □ **in heaven's name** *colloq.* used as an exclamation of surprise or annoyance. **in seventh heaven** in a state of ecstasy. **move heaven and earth** (foll. by *to* + infin.) make extraordinary efforts. □□ **heav·en·ward** *adj. & adv.* **heav·en·wards** *adv.* [OE *heofon*]

heav·en·ly /hévənlee/ *adj.* **1** of heaven; divine. **2** of the heavens or sky. **3** *colloq.* very pleasing; wonderful. □□ **heav·en·li·ness** *n.* [OE *heofonlic* (as HEAVEN)]

heav·en·ly bod·ies *n.pl.* the sun, stars, planets, etc.

heav·en-sent *adj.* providential; wonderfully opportune.

heav·i·er-than-air *adj.* (of an aircraft) weighing more than the air it displaces.

Heav·i·side lay·er /héveesid/ *n.* (in full **Heaviside–Kennelly layer** /hévisídkénəlee/) = E LAYER. [O. *Heaviside*, Engl. physicist d. 1925, and A. E. *Kennelly*, US physicist d. 1939]

heav·y /hévee/ *adj., n., adv., & v.* •*adj.* (**heav·i·er, heav·i·est**) **1 a** of great or exceptionally high weight; difficult to lift. **b** (of a person) fat; overweight. **2 a** of great density. **b** *Physics* having a greater than the usual mass (esp. of isotopes and compounds containing them). **3** abundant; considerable (*a heavy crop*). **4** severe; intense; extensive; excessive (*heavy fighting; a heavy sleep*). **5** doing something to excess (*a heavy drinker*). **6 a** striking or falling with force (*heavy blows; heavy rain*). **b** (of the sea) having large powerful waves. **7** (of machinery, artillery, etc.) very large of its kind; large in caliber, etc. **8** causing a strong impact (*a heavy fall*). **9** needing much physical effort (*heavy work*). **10** (foll. by *with*) laden. **11** carrying heavy weapons (*the heavy brigade*). **12 a** (of a person, writing, music, etc.) serious or somber in tone or attitude; dull; tedious. **b** (of an issue, etc.) grave; important; weighty. **13 a** (of food) hard to digest. **b** (of a literary work, etc.) hard to read or understand. **14** (of temperament) dignified; stern. **15** (of bread, etc.) too dense from not having risen. **16** (of ground) difficult to traverse or work. **17 a** oppressive; hard to endure (*a heavy fate; heavy demands*). **b** (of the atmosphere, weather, etc.) overcast; oppressive; sultry. **18 a** coarse; ungraceful (*heavy features*). **b** unwieldy. •*n.* (*pl.* **-ies**) **1** *colloq.* a large violent person; a thug. **2** a villainous or tragic role or actor in a play, etc. **3** *Brit. colloq.* a serious newspaper. **4** *colloq.* an important or influential person. **5** anything large or heavy of its kind, e.g., a vehicle. •*adv.* heavily (esp. in *comb.*: *heavy-laden*). •*v.tr. colloq.* harass or pressurize (a person). □ **heavy-handed 1** clumsy. **2** overbearing; oppressive. **make heavy weather of** see WEATHER. □□ **heav·i·ly** *adv.*

SYNONYM TIP   heavy

BURDENSOME, CUMBERSOME, MASSIVE, PONDEROUS, WEIGHTY. Trying to move a refrigerator out of a third-floor apartment is difficult because it is **cumbersome**, which means that it is so heavy and bulky that it becomes unwieldy or awkward to handle. Cartons filled with books, on the other hand, are merely **heavy**, which implies greater density and compactness than the average load. A huge oak dining table might be described as **massive**, which stresses largeness and solidity rather than weight, while something that is **ponderous** is too large or too *massive* to move, or to be moved quickly (*a ponderous printing press*). Most of these terms can be used figuratively as well. *Heavy*, for example, connotes a pressing down on the mind, spirits, or senses (*heavy with fatigue; a heavy heart*) and *ponderous* implies a dull and labored quality (*a novel too ponderous to read*). **Burdensome**, which refers to something that is not only *heavy* but must be carried or supported, is even more likely to be used in an abstract way to describe something that is difficult but can, with effort, be managed (*a burdensome task*). Both a package and a problem may be described as **weighty**, meaning actually (as opposed to relatively) heavy; but it is more commonly used to mean 'very important or momentous' (*weighty matters to discuss*).

heav•i•ness *n.* **heav•y-hand•ed•ly** *adv.* **heav•y-hand•ed•ness** *n.* **heav•y•ish** *adj.* [OE *hefig* f. Gmc, rel. to HEAVE]

heav•y chem•i•cals *n.pl.* bulk chemicals used in industry and agriculture.

heav•y-du•ty *adj.* **1** intended to withstand hard use. **2** serious; grave.

heav•y-foot•ed *adj.* slow and laborious in movement.

heav•y go•ing *n.* a person or situation that is difficult or boring.

heav•y-heart•ed *adj.* sad; doleful.

heav•y hy•dro•gen *n.* = DEUTERIUM.

heav•y in•dus•try *n.* industry producing metal, machinery, heavy articles in bulk, etc.

heav•y met•al *n.* **1** a type of highly-amplified rock music with a strong beat. **2** metal of relatively high density, or of high relative atomic weight.

heav•y pet•ting *n.* erotic fondling between two people, stopping short of intercourse.

heav•y•set /héveesét/ *adj.* stocky; thickset.

heav•y wa•ter *n.* water in which the hydrogen in the molecules is partly or wholly replaced by the isotope deuterium, used esp. as a moderator in nuclear reactors.

heav•y•weight /héveewayt/ *n.* **1 a** a weight in certain sports, differing for professional and amateur boxers, wrestlers, and weightlifters. **b** a sports participant of this weight. **2** a person, animal, or thing of above average weight. **3** *colloq.* a person of influence or importance.

Heb. *abbr.* **1** Hebrew. **2** Hebrews (New Testament).

heb•dom•a•dal /hebdómad'l/ *adj.* weekly, esp. meeting weekly. [LL *hebdomadalis* f. Gk *hebdomas, –ados* f. *hepta* seven]

he•be /héebee/ *n.* any flowering shrub of the genus *Hebe*, with usu. overlapping scalelike leaves. [mod.L after the Gk goddess *Hēbē*]

heb•e•tude /hébitŏōd, –tyŏōd/ *n.* *literary* dullness. [LL *hebetudo* f. *hebes, –etis* blunt]

He•bra•ic /hibráyik/ *adj.* of Hebrew or the Hebrews. □□ **He•bra•i•cal•ly** *adv.* [LL f. Gk *Hebraikos* (as HEBREW)]

He•bra•ism /héebrayizəm/ *n.* **1** a Hebrew idiom or expression, esp. in the Greek of the Bible. **2** an attribute of the Hebrews. **3** the Hebrew system of thought or religion. □□ **He•bra•is•tic** *adj.* **He•bra•ize** *v.tr. & intr.* [F *hébraïsme* or mod.L *Hebraismus* f. late Gk *Hebraïsmos* (as HEBREW)]

He•bra•ist /héebrayist/ *n.* an expert in Hebrew.

He•brew /héebrŏō/ *n. & adj.* ●*n.* **1** a member of a Semitic people orig. centered in ancient Palestine. **2 a** the language of this people. **b** a modern form of this used esp. in Israel. ●*adj.* **1** of or in Hebrew. **2** of the Hebrews or the Jews. [ME f. OF *Ebreu* f. med.L *Ebreus* f. L *hebraeus* f. Gk *Hebraios* f. Aram. *'ibray* f. Heb. *'ibrī* one from the other side (of the river)]

Heb•ri•de•an /hébrideeən/ *adj. & n.* ●*adj.* of or relating to the Hebrides, an island group off the W. coast of Scotland. ●*n.* a native of the Hebrides.

hec•a•tomb /hékətōōm/ *n.* **1** (in ancient Greece or Rome) a great public sacrifice, orig. of 100 oxen. **2** any extensive sacrifice. [L *hecatombe* f. Gk *hekatombē* f. *hekaton* hundred + *bous* ox]

heck /hek/ *int. colloq.* a mild exclamation of surprise or dismay. [alt. f. HELL]

heck•le /hékəl/ *v.tr.* **1** interrupt and harass (a public speaker). **2** dress (flax or hemp). □□ **heck•ler** *n.* [ME, northern and eastern form of HACKLE]

hec•tare /héktair/ *n.* a metric unit of square measure, equal to 100 ares (2.471 acres or 10,000 square meters). □□ **hec•tar•age** /-tərij/ *n.* [F (as HECTO-, ARE²)]

hec•tic /héktik/ *adj. & n.* ●*adj.* **1** busy and confused; excited. **2** having a hectic fever; morbidly flushed. ●*n.* **1** a hectic fever or flush. **2** a patient suffering from this. □□ **hec•ti•cal•ly** *adv.* [ME *etik* f. OF *etique* f. LL *hecticus* f. Gk *hektikos* habitual f. *hexis* habit, assim. to F *hectique* or LL]

hec•tic fe•ver *n.* (also **flush**) *hist.* a fever which accompanies consumption and similar diseases, with flushed cheeks and hot dry skin.

hecto- /héktə/ *comb. form* a hundred, esp. of a unit in the metric system. ¶ Abbr.: **ha**. [F, irreg. f. Gk *hekaton* hundred]

hec•to•gram /héktəgram/ *n.* (also *Brit.* **hec•to•gramme**) a metric unit of mass, equal to one hundred grams.

hec•to•graph /héktəgraf/ *n.* an apparatus for copying documents by the use of a gelatin plate that receives an impression of the master copy.

hec•to•li•ter /héktəleetər/ *n.* a metric unit of capacity, equal to one hundred liters.

hec•to•me•ter /héktəmeetər, hektómitər/ *n.* a metric unit of length, equal to one hundred meters.

hec•tor /héktər/ *v. & n.* ●*v.tr.* bully; intimidate. ●*n.* a bully. □□ **hec•tor•ing•ly** *adv.* [*Hector*, L f. Gk *Hektōr*, Trojan hero and son of Priam in Homer's *Iliad*, f. its earlier use to mean 'swaggering fellow']

he'd /heed/ *contr.* **1** he had. **2** he would.

hed•dle /héd'l/ *n.* one of the sets of small cords or wires between which the warp is passed in a loom before going through the reed. [app. f. OE *hefeld*]

hedge /hej/ *n. & v.* ●*n.* **1** a fence or boundary formed by closely growing bushes or shrubs. **2** a protection against possible loss or diminution. ●*v.* **1** *tr.* surround or bound with a hedge. **2** *tr.* (foll. by *in*) enclose. **3 a** *tr.* reduce one's risk of loss on (a bet or speculation) by compensating transactions on the other side. **b** *intr.* avoid a definite decision or commitment. **4** *intr.* make or trim hedges. □□ **hedg•er** *n.* [OE *hegg* f. Gmc]

hedge•hog /héjhawg, -hog/ *n.* **1** any small nocturnal insect-eating mammal of the genus *Erinaceus*, esp. *E. europaeus*, having a piglike snout and a coat of spines, and rolling itself up into a ball for defense. **2** a porcupine or other animal similarly covered with spines. □□ **hedge•hog•gy** *adj.* [ME f. HEDGE (from its habitat) + HOG (from its snout)]

hedgehog 1

hedge•hop /héjhop/ *v.intr.* fly at a very low altitude.

hedge•row /héjrō/ *n.* a row of bushes, etc., forming a hedge.

hedge spar•row *n.* a common gray and brown bird, *Prunella modularis*; the dunnock.

he•don•ic /heedónik/ *adj.* **1** of or characterized by pleasure. **2** *Psychol.* of pleasant or unpleasant sensations. [Gk *hēdonikos* f. *hēdonē* pleasure]

he•don•ism /héed'nizəm/ *n.* **1** belief in pleasure as the highest good and the proper aim of humans. **2** behavior based on this. □□ **he•don•ist** *n.* **he•don•is•tic** *adj.* [Gk *hēdonē* pleasure]

-hedron /héedrən, hédrən/ *comb. form* (pl. **•hedra**) forming nouns denoting geometrical solids with various numbers or shapes of faces (*dodecahedron; rhombohedron*). □□ **–hedral** *comb. form* forming adjectives. [Gk *hedra* seat]

hee•bie-jee•bies /héebeejéebeez/ *n.pl.* (prec. by *the*) *sl.* a state of nervous depression or anxiety. [20th c.: orig. unkn.]

heed /heed/ *v. & n.* ●*v.tr.* attend to; take notice of. ●*n.* careful attention. □□ **heed•ful** *adj.* **heed•ful•ly** *adv.* **heed•ful•ness** *n.* **heed•less** *adj.* **heed•less•ly** *adv.* **heed•less•ness** *n.* [OE *hēdan* f. WG]

hee-haw /héehaw/ *n. & v.* ●*n.* the bray of a donkey. ●*v.intr.* (of or like a donkey) emit a braying sound, esp. a braying laugh. [imit.]

heel¹ /heel/ *n. & v.* ●*n.* **1** the back part of the foot below the ankle. **2** the corresponding part in vertebrate animals. **3 a** the part of a sock, etc., covering the heel. **b** the part of a shoe or boot supporting the heel. **4** a thing like a heel in form or position, e.g., the part of the palm next to the wrist, the end of a violin bow at which it is held, or the part of a golf club near where the head joins the shaft. **5** the crust end of a loaf of bread. **6** *colloq.* a person regarded with contempt or disapproval. **7** (as *int.*) a command to a dog to walk close to its owner's heel. ●*v.* **1** *tr.* fit or renew a heel on (a shoe or boot). **2** *intr.* touch the ground with the heel, as in dancing. **3** *intr.* (foll. by *out*) *Rugby* pass the ball with the heel. **4** *tr. Golf* strike (the ball) with the heel of the club. **5** *intr.* (of dog) follow at one's heels. □ **at** (or **to**) **heel 1** (of a dog) close behind its owner. **2** (of a person, etc.) under control. **at** (or **on**) **the heels of** following closely after (a person or event). **cool** (or *Brit.* **kick**) **one's heels** be kept waiting. **down at** (the) **heel(s)** see DOWN¹. **take to one's heels** run away. **to heel 1** (of a dog) close behind. **2** (of a person, etc.) under control. **turn on one's heel** turn sharply around. □□ **heel•less** *adj.* [OE *hēla, hǣla* f. Gmc]

heel² /heel/ *v. & n.* ●*v.* **1** *intr.* (of a ship, etc.) lean over owing to the pressure of wind or an uneven load (cf. LIST²). **2** *tr.* cause (a ship, etc.) to do this. ●*n.* the act or amount of heeling. [prob. f. obs. *heeld, hield* incline, f. OE *hieldan*, OS *–heldian* f. Gmc]

heel³ /heel/ *v.tr.* (also **hele**) (foll. by *in*) set (a plant) temporarily in the ground at an angle and cover its roots. [OE *helian* f. Gmc]

heel•ball /héelbawl/ *n.* **1** a mixture of hard wax and lampblack used by shoemakers for polishing. **2** this or a similar mixture used in brass-rubbing.

heel•tap /héeltap/ *n.* **1** a layer of leather, metal, etc., in a shoe heel. **2** liquor left at the bottom of a glass after drinking.

heft /heft/ *v. & n.* ●*v.tr.* lift (something heavy), esp. to judge its weight. ●*n.* weight; heaviness. [prob. f. HEAVE after *cleft, weft*]

heft•y /héftee/ *adj.* (**heft•i•er, heft•i•est**) **1** (of a person) big and strong. **2** (of a thing) large; heavy; powerful; sizable; considerable. □□ **heft•i•ly** *adv.* **heft•i•ness** *n.*

He•ge•li•an /haygáyleeən, hijée-/ *adj. & n.* ●*adj.* of or relating to the German philosopher G. W. F. Hegel (d. 1831) or his philosophy of objective idealism. ●*n.* an adherent of Hegel or his philosophy. □□ **He•ge•li•an•ism** *n.*

heg•e•mon•ic /héjimónik/ *adj.* ruling; supreme. [Gk *hēgemonikos* (as HEGEMONY)]

he•gem•o•ny /hijémənee, héjəmōnee/ *n.* leadership, esp. by one nation over others of a confederacy. [Gk *hēgemonia* f. *hēgemōn* leader f. *hēgeomai* lead]

he·gi·ra /hijírə, héjirə/ *n.* (also **he·ji·ra, hij·ra** /híjrə/) **1** (**Hegira**) **a** Muhammad's departure from Mecca to Medina in AD 622. **b** the Muslim era reckoned from this date. **2** a general exodus or departure. [med.L *hegira* f. Arab. *hijra* departure from one's country f. *hajara* separate]

heif·er /héfər/ *n.* **1 a** a young cow, esp. one that has not had more than one calf. **b** a female calf. **2** *Brit. sl. derog.* a woman. [OE *heahfore*]

heigh /hay, hī/ *int.* expressing encouragement or inquiry. □ **heigh-ho** /hí hṓ, háy–/ expressing boredom, resignation, etc. [imit.]

height /hīt/ *n.* **1** the measurement from base to top or (of a standing person) from head to foot. **2** the elevation above ground or a recognized level (usu. sea level). **3** any considerable elevation (*situated at a height*). **4 a** a high place or area. **b** rising ground. **5** the top of something. **6** *Printing* the distance from the foot to the face of type. **7 a** the most intense part or period of anything (*the battle was at its height*). **b** an extreme instance or example (*the height of fashion*) . [OE *hēhthu* f. Gmc]

PRONUNCIATION TIP height

Avoid pronouncing this word with a final *-th* sound. This mispronunciation has come about by analogy to the (correct) final *-th* in the related words *length* and *width*.

height·en /hítən/ *v.tr. & intr.* make or become higher or more intense.

Heim·lich ma·neu·ver /hímlik/ *n.* an emergency procedure for assisting a choking victim in which one applies sudden upward pressure with the fist against the victim's upper abdomen in order to dislodge the object causing the choking. [for US physician Henry J. *Heimlich* (b. 1920)]

hei·nous /háynəs/ *adj.* (of a crime or criminal) utterly odious or wicked. □□ **hei·nous·ly** *adv.* **hei·nous·ness** *n.* [ME f. OF *ha ïneus* ult. f. *haïr* to hate f. Frank.]

PRONUNCIATION TIP heinous

Avoid pronouncing this word as if the first syllable rhymed with *keen*.

heir /air/ *n.* **1** a person entitled to property or rank as the legal successor of its former owner (often foll. by *to: heir to the throne*). **2** a person deriving or morally entitled to some thing, quality, etc., from a predecessor. □□ **heir·dom** *n.* **heir·less** *adj.* **heir·ship** *n.* [ME f. OF *air* f. LL *herem* f. L *heres –edis*]

heir ap·par·ent *n.* an heir whose claim cannot be set aside by the birth of another heir.

heir-at-law *n.* (*pl.* **heirs-at-law**) an heir by right of blood, esp. to the real property of an intestate.

heir·ess /áiris/ *n.* a female heir, esp. to great wealth or high title.

heir·loom /áirlōom/ *n.* **1** a piece of personal property that has been in a family for several generations. **2** a piece of property received as part of an inheritance. [HEIR + LOOM[1] in the sense 'tool']

heir pre·sump·tive *n.* an heir whose claim may be set aside by the birth of another heir.

Hei·sen·berg un·cer·tain·ty prin·ci·ple /hízənbərg/ see UNCERTAINTY PRINCIPLE.

heist /hīst/ *n. & v. sl.* ● *n.* a robbery. ● *v.tr.* rob. [repr. a local pronunc. of HOIST]

he·ji·ra var. of HEGIRA.

He·La /hélə/ *adj.* of a strain of human epithelial cells maintained in tissue culture. [*Henrietta Lacks*, whose cervical carcinoma provided the original cells]

held *past* and *past part.* of HOLD[1].

hel·den·ten·or /héld'ntenər/ *n.* **1** a powerful tenor voice suitable for heroic roles in opera. **2** a singer with this voice. [G f. *Held* a hero]

hele var. of HEEL[3].

he·len·i·um /helé·eneeəm/ *n.* any composite plant of the genus *Helenium*, with daisylike flowers having prominent central disks. [mod.L f. Gk *helenion*, possibly commemorating Helen of Troy]

heli- /hélee/ *comb. form* helicopter (*heliport*).

he·li·a·cal /hilíəkəl/ *adj. Astron.* relating to or near the sun. [LL *heliacus* f. Gk *hēliakos* f. *hēlios* sun]

he·li·a·cal ris·ing *n.* (also **heliacal setting**) the first rising (or setting) of a star after (or before) a period of invisibility due to conjunction with the sun.

he·li·an·the·mum /héeleeánthəməm/ *n.* any evergreen shrub of the genus *Helianthemum*, with saucer-shaped flowers. Also called **rock rose**. [mod.L f. Gk *hēlios* sun + *anthemon* flower]

he·li·an·thus /héeleeánthəs/ *n.* any plant of the genus *Helianthus*, including the sunflower and Jerusalem artichoke. [mod.L f. Gk *hēlios* sun + *anthos* flower]

hel·i·cal /hélikəl, héeli–/ *adj.* having the form of a helix. □□ **hel·i·cal·ly** *adv.* **hel·i·coid** *adj. & n.*

hel·i·ces *pl.* of HELIX.

hel·i·chry·sum /hélikrízəm, héeli–/ *n.* any composite plant of the genus *Helichrysum*, with flowers retaining their appearance when dried. [L f. Gk *helikhrusos* f. *helix* spiral + *khrusos* gold]

hel·i·con /hélikən/ *n.* a large spiral bass tuba played encircling the player's head and resting on the shoulder. [L f. Gk *Helikōn* mountain sacred to the Muses: later assoc. with HELIX]

hel·i·cop·ter /hélikoptər/ *n. & v.* ● *n.* a type of aircraft without fixed wings, obtaining lift and propulsion from horizontally revolving overhead blades or rotors, and capable of moving vertically and horizontally. ● *v.tr. & intr.* transport or fly by helicopter. [F *hélicoptère* f. Gk *helix* (see HELIX) + *pteron* wing]

helicopter

helio- /héeleeō/ *comb. form* the sun. [Gk *hēlios* sun]

he·li·o·cen·tric /héeleeōséntrik/ *adj.* **1** regarding the sun as center. **2** considered as viewed from the sun's center. □□ **he·li·o·cen·tri·cal·ly** *adv.*

he·li·o·gram /héeleeəgram/ *n.* a message sent by heliograph.

he·li·o·graph /héeleeəgraf/ *n. & v.* ● *n.* **1 a** a signaling apparatus reflecting sunlight in flashes from a movable mirror. **b** a message sent by means of this; a heliogram. **2** an apparatus for photographing the sun. **3** an engraving obtained chemically by exposure to light. ● *v.tr.* send (a message) by heliograph. □□ **he·li·og·ra·phy** /–leeógrəfee/ *n.*

he·li·o·gra·vure /héeleeōgrəvyóor/ *n.* = PHOTOGRAVURE.

he·li·o·lith·ic /héeleeōlíthik/ *adj.* (of a civilization) characterized by sun worship and megaliths.

he·li·om·e·ter /héeleeómitər/ *n.* an instrument used for finding the angular distance between two stars (orig. used for measuring the diameter of the sun).

he·li·o·stat /héeleeəstat/ *n.* an apparatus with a mirror driven by clockwork to reflect sunlight in a fixed direction. □□ **he·li·o·stat·ic** *adj.*

he·li·o·ther·a·py /héeleeōthérəpee/ *n.* the use of sunlight in treating disease.

he·li·o·trope /héeleeətrōp/ *n.* **1 a** any plant of the genus *Heliotropium*, with fragrant purple flowers. **b** the scent of these. **2** a light purple color. **3** bloodstone. [L *heliotropium* f. Gk *hēliotropion* plant turning its flowers to the sun, f. *hēlios* sun + *–tropos* f. *trepō* turn]

he·li·ot·ro·pism /héeleeótrəpizəm/ *n.* the directional growth of a plant in response to sunlight (cf. PHOTOTROPISM). □□ **he·li·o·trop·ic** /–leeətrópik, –trópik/ *adj.*

he·li·o·type /héeleeōtīp/ *n.* a picture obtained from a sensitized gelatin film exposed to light.

hel·i·port /hélipawrt/ *n.* a place where helicopters take off and land. [HELI-, after *airport*]

he·li·um /héeleeəm/ *n. Chem.* a colorless, light, inert, gaseous element occurring in deposits of natural gas, used in airships and balloons and as a refrigerant. ¶ Symb.: **He**. [Gk *hēlios* sun (having been first identified in the sun's atmosphere)]

he·lix /héeliks/ *n.* (*pl.* **hel·i·ces** /–seez, hél–/) **1** a spiral curve (like a corkscrew) or a coiled curve (like a watch spring). **2** *Geom.* a curve that cuts a line on a solid cone or cylinder, at a constant angle with the axis. **3** *Archit.* a spiral ornament. **4** *Anat.* the rim of the external ear. [L *helix –icis* f. Gk *helix –ikos*]

hell /hel/ *n.* **1** a place regarded in some religions as the abode of the dead, or of condemned sinners and devils. **2** a place or state of misery or wickedness. **3** *colloq.* used as an exclamation of surprise or annoyance (*who the hell are you?; a hell of a mess*). **4** *colloq.* fun; high spirits. □ **beat** (*or* **knock, etc.**) **the hell out of** *colloq.* beat, etc., without restraint. **come hell or high water** no matter what the difficulties. **for the hell of it** *colloq.* for fun; on impulse. **get** (*or* **catch**) **hell** *colloq.* be severely scolded or punished. **give a person hell** *colloq.* scold or punish or make things difficult for a person. **hell of a** *colloq.* very much of a; extremely (*hell of a hot day*). **hell for leather** at full speed. **like hell** *colloq.* **1** not at all. **2** recklessly; exceedingly. **not a hope in hell** *colloq.* no chance at all. **play hell** (*or Brit.* **merry hell**) **with** *colloq.* be upsetting or disruptive to. **to hell with** *colloq.* (one is) finished with, disgusted with, or without a use for (something or someone). **what the hell** *colloq.* it is of no importance. □□ **hell-like** *adj.* **hell·ward** *adv. & adj.* [OE *hel, hell* f. Gmc]

he'll /heel/ *contr.* he will; he shall.

hel·la·cious /heláyshəs/ *adj. sl.* **1** impressive; terrific; tremendous; remarkable. **2** overwhelmingly powerful, severe, or difficult. [HELL + –ACIOUS]

Hel·lad·ic /heládik/ *adj.* of or belonging to the Bronze Age culture of mainland Greece. [Gk *Helladikos* f. *Hellas –ados* Greece]

hell-bent *adj.* (foll. by *on*) recklessly determined.

hell-cat /hélkat/ *n.* a spiteful violent woman.

hel·le·bore /hélibawr/ *n.* **1** any evergreen plant of the genus

Helleborus, having large white, green, or purplish flowers, e.g., the Christmas rose. **2** a liliaceous plant, *Veratrum album*. **3** *hist.* any of various plants supposed to cure madness. [ME f. OF *ellebre*, *elebore* or med.L *eleborus* f. L *elleborus* f. Gk (*h*)*eleboros*]

hel•leb•o•rine /hélibəreen/ *n.* any orchid of the genus *Epipactis* or *Cephalanthera*. [F or L *helleborine* or L f. Gk *helleborinē* plant like hellebore (as HELLEBORE)]

Hel•lene /héleen/ *n.* **1** a native of modern Greece. **2** an ancient Greek. □□ **Hel•len•ic** /helénik/ *adj.* [Gk *Hellēn* a Greek]

Hel•len•ism /hélinizəm/ *n.* **1** Greek character or culture (esp. of ancient Greece). **2** the study or imitation of Greek culture. □□ **Hel•len•ize** *v.tr. & intr.* **Hel•len•i•za•tion** *n.* [Gk *hellēnismos* f. *hellēnizō* speak Greek, make Greek (as HELLENE)]

Hel•len•ist /hélinist/ *n.* an expert on or admirer of Greek language or culture. [Gk *Hellēnistēs* (as HELLENISM)]

Hel•len•is•tic /hélinístik/ *adj.* of or relating to Greek history, language, and culture from the death of Alexander the Great to the time of Augustus (4th–1st c. BC).

hell•fire /hélfīr/ *n.* the fire or fires regarded as existing in hell.

hell•gram•mite /hélgrəmīt/ *n.* an aquatic larva of an American fly, *Corydalus cornutus*, often used as fishing bait. [19th c.: orig. unkn.]

hell•hole /hélhōl/ *n. colloq.* an oppressive or unbearable place.

hell•hound /hélhownd/ *n.* a fiend.

hel•lion /hélyən/ *n. colloq.* a mischievous or troublesome person, esp. a child. [perh. f. dial. *hallion* a worthless fellow, assim. to HELL]

hell•ish /hélish/ *adj. & adv.* ● *adj.* **1** of or like hell. **2** *colloq.* extremely difficult or unpleasant. ● *adv. Brit. colloq.* (as an intensifier) extremely (*hellish expensive*). □□ **hell•ish•ly** *adv.* **hell•ish•ness** *n.*

hel•lo /helō, hə–/ *int., n., & v.* (also esp. *Brit.* (**hul•lo** /hə–/, **hal•lo** /hə–/) ● *int.* **1 a** an expression of informal greeting, or esp. *Brit.* of surprise. **b** used to begin a telephone conversation. **2** a cry used to call attention. ● *n.* (*pl.* **•los**) a cry of "hello." ● *v.intr.* (**•loes**, **•loed**) cry "hello." [var. of earlier HOLLO]

hell-rais•er *n.* a person who causes trouble or creates chaos.

Hell's An•gel *n.* a member of a gang of motorcyclists notorious for outrageous or violent behavior.

helm[1] /helm/ *n. & v.* ● *n.* **1** a tiller or wheel by which a ship's rudder is controlled. **2** the amount by which this is turned (*more helm needed*). ● *v.tr.* steer or guide as if with a helm. □ **at the helm** in control; at the head of (an organization, etc.). [OE *helma*, prob. related to HELVE]

helm[2] /helm/ *n. archaic* helmet. □□ **helmed** *adj.* [OE f. Gmc]

hel•met /hélmit/ *n.* **1** any of various protective head coverings worn by soldiers, police officers, firefighters, divers, cyclists, etc. **2** *Bot.* the arched upper part of the corolla in some flowers. **3** the shell of a gastropod mollusk of the genus *Cassis*, used in jewelry. □□ **hel•met•ed** *adj.* [ME f. OF, dimin. of *helme* f. WG (as HELM[2])]

hel•minth /hélminth/ *n.* any of various parasitic worms including flukes, tapeworms, and nematodes. □□ **hel•min•thic** /–mínthik/ *adj.* **hel•min•thoid** *adj.* **hel•min•thol•o•gy** *n.* [Gk *helmins –inthos* intestinal worm]

hel•min•thi•a•sis /hélminthíəsis/ *n.* a disease characterized by the presence of any of several parasitic worms in the body.

helms•man /hélmzmən/ *n.* (*pl.* **•men**) a person who steers a vessel.

hel•ot /hélət/ *n.* a serf (esp. Helot), of a class in ancient Sparta. □□ **hel•ot•ism** *n.* **hel•ot•ry** *n.* [Gk *helotes* pl. f. Gk *heilōtes*, *–ōtai*, erron. taken as = inhabitants of *Helos*, a Laconian town]

help /help/ *v. & n.* ● *v.tr.* **1** provide (a person, etc.) with the means toward what is needed or sought (*helped me with my work*; *helped me (to) pay my debts*). **2** (foll. by *up*, *down*, etc.) assist or give support to (a person) in moving, etc., as specified (*helped her into the chair*; *helped him on with his coat*). **3** (often *absol.*) be of use or service to (a person) (*does that help?*). **4** contribute to alleviating (a pain or difficulty). **5** prevent or remedy (*it can't be helped*). **6** (usu. with *neg.*) **a** *tr.* refrain from (*can't help it*; *could not help laughing*). **b** *refl.* refrain from acting (*couldn't help himself*). **7** *tr.* (often foll. by *to*) serve (a person with food) (*shall I help you to more rice?*). ● *n.* **1** the act of helping or being helped (*we need your help*; *came to our help*). **2** a person or thing that helps. **3** a domestic servant or employee, or several collectively. **4** a remedy or escape (*there is no help for it*). □ **help oneself** (often foll. by *to*) **1** serve oneself (with food). **2** take without seeking help; take without permission; steal. **help a person off with** give a person help, esp. in difficulty. **so help me** (or **help me God**) (as an invocation or oath) I am speaking the truth. □□ **help•er** *n.* [OE *helpan* f. Gmc]

help•ful /hélpfŏol/ *adj.* (of a person or thing) giving help; useful. □□ **help•ful•ly** *adv.* **help•ful•ness** *n.*

help•ing /hélping/ *n.* a portion of food esp. at a meal.

help•ing hand *n.* assistance.

help•less /hélplis/ *adj.* **1** lacking help or protection; defenseless. **2** unable to act without help. □□ **help•less•ly** *adv.* **help•less•ness** *n.*

help•line /hélplīn/ *n.* a telephone service providing help with problems.

help•mate /hélpmayt/ *n.* a helpful companion or partner (usu. a husband or wife).

hel•ter-skel•ter /héltərskéltər/ *adv., adj., & n.* ● *adv.* in disorderly haste; confusedly. ● *adj.* characterized by disorderly haste or confusion. ● *n. Brit.* a tall spiral slide around a tower, at a fairground or carnival. [imit., orig. in a rhyming jingle, perh. f. ME *skelte* hasten]

helve /helv/ *n.* the handle of a weapon or a tool. [OE *helfe* f. WG]

Hel•ve•tian /helvéeshən/ *adj. & n.* ● *adj.* Swiss. ● *n.* a native of Switzerland. [L *Helvetia* Switzerland]

hem[1] /hem/ *n. & v.* ● *n.* the border of a piece of cloth, esp. a cut edge turned under and sewn down. ● *v.tr.* (**hemmed, hem•ming**) turn down and sew in the edge of (a piece of cloth, etc.). □ **hem in** confine; restrict the movement of. [OE, perh. rel. to dial. *ham* enclosure]

hem[2] /hem, həm/ *int., n., & v.* ● *int.* (also **a•hem**) calling attention or expressing hesitation by a slight cough or clearing of the throat. ● *n.* an utterance of this. ● *v.intr.* (**hemmed, hem•ming**) say *hem*; hesitate in speech. □ **hem and haw** hesitate, esp. in speaking. [imit.]

he•mal /héemal/ *adj.* (*Brit.* **hae•mal**) *Anat.* **1** of or concerning the blood. **2 a** situated on the same side of the body as the heart and major blood vessels. **b** ventral. [Gk *haima* blood]

he-man *n.* (*pl.* **-men**) a masterful or virile man.

he•mat•ic /himátik/ *adj.* (*Brit.* **hae•mat•ic**) *Med.* of or containing blood. [Gk *haimatikos* (as HEMATIN)]

he•ma•tin /héemətin, hém–/ *n.* (*Brit.* **hae•ma•tin**) *Anat.* a bluish black derivative of hemoglobin, formed by removal of the protein part and oxidation of the iron atom. [Gk *haima –matos* blood]

he•ma•tite /héemətīt, hém–/ *n.* (*Brit.* **hae•ma•tite**) a ferric oxide ore. [L *haematites* f. Gk *haimatitēs* (*lithos*) bloodlike (stone) (as HEMATIN)]

hemato- /héemətō, hém–/ *comb. form* (*Brit.* **haemato-**) blood. [Gk *haima haimat-* blood]

he•mat•o•cele /himátəseel, héemətəseel, hém–/ *n.* (*Brit.* **hae•mat•o•cele**) *Med.* a swelling caused by blood collecting in a body cavity.

he•mat•o•crit /himátəkrit/ *n.* (*Brit.* **hae•mat•o•crit**) *Physiol.* **1** the ratio of the volume of red blood cells to the total volume of blood. **2** an instrument for measuring this. [HEMATO- + Gk *kritēs* judge]

he•ma•tol•o•gy /héemətóləjee, hém–/ *n.* (*Brit.* **hae•ma•tol•o•gy**) the study of the physiology of the blood. □□ **he•ma•to•log•ic** /–təlójik/ *adj.* **he•ma•to•log•i•cal** *adj.* **he•ma•tol•o•gist** *n.*

he•ma•to•ma /héemətómə, hém–/ *n.* (*Brit.* **hae•ma•to•ma**) *Med.* a solid swelling of clotted blood within the tissues.

he•ma•tu•ri•a /héemətyŏóreeə, –tyŏór–, hém–/ *n.* (*Brit.* **hae•ma•tu•ri•a**) heem/ *n.* (also **haem**) a nonprotein compound containing iron, and responsible for the red color of hemoglobin. [Gk *haima* blood or f. HEMOGLOBIN]

hem•er•o•cal•lis /hémərōkális/ *n.* = DAYLILY. [L *hemerocallis* f. Gk *hēmerokalles* a kind of lily f. *hēmera* day + *kallos* beauty]

hemi- /héemee/ *comb. form* half. [Gk *hēmi-* = L *semi-*: see SEMI-]

-hemia *comb. form* var. of –EMIA.

hem•i•a•nop•si•a /hémeeənópseeə/ *n.* (also **hem•i•a•no•pi•a** /–nópeeə/) blindness over half the field of vision.

hem•i•cel•lu•lose /hémisélyəlōs/ *n.* any of various polysaccharides forming the matrix of plant cell walls in which cellulose is embedded. [G (as HEMI-, CELLULOSE)]

hem•i•cy•cle /hémisīkəl/ *n.* a semicircular figure.

hem•i•dem•i•sem•i•qua•ver /hémeedémeesémeekwayvər/ *n. Mus.* esp. *Brit.* = SIXTY-FOURTH NOTE.

hem•i•he•dral /hémihéedrəl/ *adj. Crystallog.* having half the number of planes required for symmetry of the holohedral form.

hem•i•ple•gi•a /hémipléejə, –jeeə/ *n. Med.* paralysis of one side of the body. □□ **hem•i•ple•gic** *n. & adj.* [mod.L f. Gk *hēmiplēgia* paralysis (as HEMI-, *plēgē* stroke)]

he•mip•ter•ous /hemíptərəs/ *adj.* of the insect order Hemiptera, including aphids, bugs, and cicadas, with piercing or sucking mouthparts. [HEMI- + Gk *pteron* wing]

hem•i•sphere /hémisfeer/ *n.* **1** half of a sphere. **2** a half of the earth, esp. as divided by the equator (into *northern* and *southern hemisphere*) or by a line passing through the poles (into *eastern* and *western hemisphere*). **3** either lateral half of the brain. □□ **hem•i•spher•ic** /–sféerik, –sférik/ *adj.* **hem•i•spher•i•cal** *adj.* [OF *emisphere* & L *hemisphaerium* f. Gk *hēmisphaira* (as HEMI-, SPHERE)]

hem•i•stich /hémistik/ *n.* half of a line of verse. [LL *hemistichium* f. Gk *hēmistikhion* (as HEMI-, *stikhion* f. *stikhos* line)]

hem•line /hémlīn/ *n.* the line or level of the lower edge of a skirt, dress, or coat.

hem•lock /hémlok/ *n.* **1 a** a poisonous umbelliferous plant, *Conium maculatum*, with fernlike leaves and small white flowers. **b** a poisonous potion obtained from this. **2** (in full **hemlock fir** or **spruce**) **a** any coniferous tree of the genus *Tsuga*, having foliage that smells like hemlock when crushed. **b** the lumber or pitch of these trees. [OE *hymlic(e)*]

hemo- /héemō, hémmō/ *comb. form* (*Brit.* **haemo-**) = HEMATO-. [abbr.]

he·mo·cy·a·nin /heˈeməsíənin, hém–/ n. (Brit. **hae·mo·cy·a·nin**) an oxygen-carrying substance containing copper, present in the blood plasma of arthropods and mollusks. [HEMO- + cyanin blue pigment (as CYAN)]

he·mo·di·al·y·sis /heˈemōdíálisis/ n. = DIALYSIS 2.

he·mo·glo·bin /heˈeməglóbin, hém–/ n. (Brit. **hae·mo·glo·bin**) a red oxygen-carrying substance containing iron, present in the red blood cells of vertebrates. [shortened f. hematoglobin, compound of HEMATIN + GLOBULIN]

he·mol·y·sis /heemólisis, hem–/ n. (Brit. **hae·mol·y·sis**) the loss of hemoglobin from red blood cells. □□ **he·mo·lyt·ic** /–məlítik/ adj.

he·mo·phil·i·a /heˈeməfíleeə, hém–/ n. (Brit. **hae·mo·phil·i·a**) Med. a usu. hereditary disorder with a tendency to bleed severely from even a slight injury, through the failure of the blood to clot normally. □□ **he·mo·phil·ic** adj. [mod.L (as HEMO-, –PHILIA)]

he·mo·phil·i·ac /heˈeməfíleeak, –féelee–, hém–/ n. (Brit. **hae·mo·phil·i·ac**) a person suffering from hemophilia.

hem·or·rhage /hémərij, hémrij/ n. & v. (Brit. **haem·or·rhage**) •n. 1 an escape of blood from a ruptured blood vessel, esp. when profuse. 2 an extensive damaging loss suffered by a government, organization, etc., esp. of people or assets. •v.intr. undergo a hemorrhage. □□ **hem·or·rhag·ic** /hémərájik/ adj. [earlier hemorrhagy f. F hémorr(h)agie f. L haemorrhagia f. Gk haimorrhagia f. haima blood + stem of rhēgnumi burst]

hem·or·rhoid /héməroyd/ n. (Brit. **haem·or·rhoid**) (usu. in pl.) swollen veins at or near the anus; piles. □□ **hem·or·rhoi·dal** adj. [ME emeroudis (Bibl. emerods) f. OF emeroyde f. L f. Gk haimorrhoides (phlebes) bleeding (veins) f. haima blood, –rhoos –flowing]

he·mos·ta·sis /himóstəsis, heˈeməstáysis, hém–/ n. (Brit. **hae·mos·ta·sis**) the stopping of the flow of blood. □□ **he·mo·stat·ic** /heˈeməstátik/ adj.

hemp /hemp/ n. 1 (in full Indian hemp) a herbaceous plant, Cannabis sativa, native to Asia. 2 its fiber extracted from the stem and used to make rope and strong fabrics. 3 any of several narcotic drugs made from the hemp plant (cf. CANNABIS, MARIJUANA). 4 any of several other plants yielding fiber, including Manila hemp and sunn hemp. [OE henep, hænep f. Gmc, rel. to Gk kannabis]

hemp ag·ri·mo·ny n. a composite plant, Eupatorium cannabinum, with pale purple flowers and hairy leaves.

hemp·en /hémpən/ adj. made from hemp.

hemp net·tle n. any of various nettlelike plants of the genus Galeopsis.

hem·stitch /hémstich/ n. & v. •n. a decorative stitch used in sewing hems. •v.tr. hem with this stitch.

hen /hen/ n. 1 a a female bird, esp. of a domestic fowl. b (in pl.) domestic fowls of either sex. 2 a female lobster or crab or salmon. [OE henn f. WG]

hen and chick·ens n. any of several succulent plants, esp. the houseleek.

hen·bane /hénbayn/ n. 1 a poisonous herbaceous plant, Hyoscyamus niger, with sticky hairy leaves and an unpleasant smell. 2 a narcotic drug obtained from this.

hence /hens/ adv. 1 from this time (two years hence). 2 for this reason; as a result of inference (hence we seem to be wrong). 3 archaic from here; from this place. [ME hens, hennes, henne f. OE heonan f. the root of HE]

hence·forth /hénsfáwrth/ adv. (also **hence·for·ward** /–fáwrwərd/) from this time onward.

hench·man /hénchmən/ n. (pl. **·men**) 1 a a trusted supporter or attendant. b often derog. a political supporter; a partisan. 2 hist. a squire; a page of honor. 3 Sc. the principal attendant of a Highland chief. [ME henxman, hengestman f. OE hengst male horse]

hen·coop /hénkoop/ n. a coop for keeping fowls in.

hendeca- /hendékə/ comb. form eleven. [Gk hendeka eleven]

hen·dec·a·gon /hendékəgon/ n. a plane figure with eleven sides and angles.

hen·di·a·dys /hendíədis/ n. the expression of an idea by two words connected with "and," instead of one modifying the other, e.g., nice and warm for nicely warm. [med.L f. Gk hen dia duoin one thing by two]

hen·e·quen /héniken/ n. 1 a Mexican agave, Agave fourcroydes. 2 the sisaline fiber obtained from this. [Sp. jeniquen]

henge /henj/ n. a prehistoric monument consisting of a circle of massive stone or wood uprights. [back-form. f. Stonehenge, such a monument in S. England]

hen·house /hénhows/ n. a small shed for fowls to roost in.

hen·na /hénə/ n. 1 a tropical shrub, Lawsonia inermis, having small pink, red, or white flowers. 2 the reddish dye from its shoots and leaves esp. used to color hair. [Arab. ḥinnā']

hen·naed /hénəd/ adj. treated with henna.

hen·o·the·ism /hénətheeízəm/ n. belief in or adoption of a particular god in a polytheistic system as the god of a tribe, class, etc. [Gk heis henos one + theos god]

hen par·ty n. colloq. often derog. a social gathering of women.

hen·peck /hénpek/ v.tr. (of a woman) constantly harass (a man, esp. her husband).

hen·ry /hénree/ n. (pl. **·ries** or **hen·rys**) Electr. the SI unit of inductance that gives an electromotive force of one volt in a closed circuit with a uniform rate of change of current of one ampere per second. ¶ Abbr.: **H**. [J. Henry, Amer. physicist d. 1878]

he·or·tol·o·gy /heˈeawrtóləjee/ n. the study of ecclesiastical festivals. [G Heortologie, F héortologie f. Gk heortē feast]

hep[1] var. of HIP[3].

hep[2] var. of HIP[2].

hep·a·rin /hépərin/ n. Biochem. a substance produced in liver cells, etc., which inhibits blood coagulation, and is used as an anticoagulant in the treatment of thrombosis. □□ **hep·a·rin·ize** v.tr. [L f. Gk hēpar liver]

he·pat·ic /hipátik/ adj. 1 of or relating to the liver. 2 dark brownish red; liver colored. [ME f. L hepaticus f. Gk hēpatikos f. hēpar –atos liver]

he·pat·i·ca /hipátikə/ n. any plant of the genus Hepatica, with reddish brown lobed leaves resembling the liver. [med.L fem. of hepaticus: see HEPATIC]

hep·a·ti·tis /hépətítis/ n. inflammation of the liver. [mod.L: see HEPATIC]

hep·cat /hépkat/ n. a hip person of the 1930s or 40s; a devotee of jazz or swing.

Hep·ple·white /hépəlwīt/ n. a light and graceful style of furniture. [G. Hepplewhite, Engl. cabinetmaker d. 1786]

hepta- /héptə/ comb. form seven. [Gk hepta seven]

hep·tad /héptad/ n. a group of seven. [Gk heptas –ados set of seven (hepta)]

hep·ta·gon /héptəgən/ n. a plane figure with seven sides and angles. □□ **hep·tag·o·nal** /–tágənəl/ adj. [F heptagone or med.L heptagonum f. Gk (as HEPTA-, –GON)]

hep·ta·he·dron /héptəheˈedrən/ n. a solid figure with seven faces. □□ **hep·ta·he·dral** adj. [HEPTA- + –HEDRON after POLYHEDRON]

hep·tam·e·ter /heptámitər/ n. a line or verse of seven metrical feet. [L heptametrum f. Gk (as HEPTA-, –METER)]

hep·tane /héptayn/ n. Chem. a liquid hydrocarbon of the alkane series, obtained from petroleum. ¶ Chem. formula: C_7H_{16}. [HEPTA- + –ANE[2]]

hep·tar·chy /héptaarkee/ n. (pl. **·chies**) 1 a a government by seven rulers. b an instance of this. 2 hist. the supposed seven kingdoms of the Angles and the Saxons in Britain in the 7th–8th c. □□ **hep·tar·chic** /–taárkik/ adj. **hep·tar·chi·cal** adj. [HEPTA- after tetrarchy]

Hep·ta·teuch /héptətook, –tyook/ n. the first seven books of the Old Testament. [L f. Gk f. hepta seven + teukhos book, volume]

hep·tath·lon /heptáthlon, –lən/ n. Sports a seven-event track and field competition esp. for women.

hep·ta·va·lent /héptəváylənt/ adj. Chem. having a valence of seven; septivalent.

her /hər/ pron. & poss.pron. •pron. 1 objective case of SHE (I like her). 2 colloq. she (it's her all right; am older than her). 3 archaic herself (she fell and hurt her). •poss.pron. (attrib.) 1 of or belonging to her or herself (her house; her own business). 2 Brit. (**Her**) (in titles) that she is (Her Majesty). [OE hi(e)re dative & genit. of hio, hēo fem. of HE]

her·ald /hérəld/ n. & v. •n. 1 an official messenger bringing news. 2 a forerunner (spring is the herald of summer). 3 a Brit. hist. an officer responsible for official ceremonies and etiquette. b Brit. an official of the Heralds' College. •v.tr. proclaim the approach of; usher in (the storm heralded trouble). [ME f. OF herau(l)t, herauder f. Gmc]

he·ral·dic /heráldik/ adj. of or concerning heraldry. □□ **he·ral·di·cal·ly** adv. [HERALD]

her·ald·ist /hérəldist/ n. an expert in heraldry. [HERALD]

her·ald·ry /hérəldree/ n. 1 the science or art of a herald, esp. in dealing with armorial bearings. 2 heraldic pomp. 3 armorial bearings.

Her·alds' Col·lege n. Brit. colloq. = COLLEGE OF ARMS.

herb /ərb, hərb/ n. 1 any nonwoody seed-bearing plant that dies down to the ground after flowering. 2 any plant with leaves, seeds, or flowers used for flavoring, food, medicine, scent, etc. 3 sl. marijuana. □ **give it the herbs** Austral. colloq. accelerate. □□ **her·bif·er·ous** /–bífərəs/ adj. **herb·like** adj. [ME f. OF erbe f. L herba grass, green crops, herb; herb bennet prob. f. med.L herba benedicta blessed herb (thought of as expelling the Devil)]

PRONUNCIATION TIP **herb**

In British English, this word is pronounced exactly as it is spelled, with an h—as are herbal, herbaceous, herbicide, and herbivore. In American English, herb and herbal are often pronounced without the initial h, although the h is pronounced in the derivatives herbaceous, herbicide, and herbivore.

---

her·ba·ceous /hərbáyshəs, ər–/ adj. of or like herbs (see HERB 1). [L herbaceus grassy (as HERB)]

her·ba·ceous pe·ren·ni·al n. a plant whose growth dies down annually but whose roots, etc., survive.

herb•age /ə́rbij, hə́r–/ *n.* **1** herbs collectively. **2** the succulent part of herbs, esp. as pasture. **3** *Law* the right of pasture on another person's land. [ME f. OF *erbage* f. med.L *herbaticum, herbagium* right of pasture, f. L *herba* herb]

herb•al /ə́rbəl, hə́r–/ *adj. & n.* ● *adj.* of herbs in medicinal and culinary use. ● *n.* a book with descriptions and accounts of the properties of these. [med.L *herbalis* (as HERB)]

herb•al•ist /ə́rbəlist, hə́r–/ *n.* **1** a dealer in medicinal herbs. **2** a person skilled in herbs, esp. an early botanical writer.

her•bar•i•um /hərbáireeəm, ər–/ *n.* (*pl.* **her•bar•i•a** /–reeə/) **1** a systematically arranged collection of dried plants. **2** a book, room, or building for these. [LL (as HERB)]

herb ben•net *n.* a common yellow-flowered European plant, *Geum urbanum.*

herb Chris•to•pher *n.* a white-flowered baneberry, *Actaea spicata.*

herb Ge•rard *n.* a white-flowered plant, *Aegopodium podagraria.*

herb•i•cide /hə́rbisīd, ə́r–/ *n.* a substance toxic to plants and used to destroy unwanted vegetation.

herb•biv•ore /hə́rbivawr, ə́r–/ *n.* an animal that feeds on plants. □□ **her•biv•o•rous** /–bívərəs/ *adj.* [L *herba* herb + *-vore* (see –VOROUS)]

herb Par•is *n.* a plant, *Paris quadrifolia,* with a single flower and four leaves in a cross shape on an unbranched stem.

herb Ro•bert *n.* a common cranesbill, *Geranium robertianum,* with red-stemmed leaves and pink flowers.

herb tea *n.* an infusion of herbs as a refreshing or medicinal drink.

herb to•bac•co *n.* a mixture of herbs smoked as a substitute for tobacco.

herb•y /ə́rbee, hə́r–/ *adj.* (**herb•i•er, herb•i•est**) **1** abounding in herbs. **2** of the nature of a culinary or medicinal herb.

Her•cu•le•an /hə́rkyəleeən, –kyóoleeən/ *adj.* having or requiring great strength or effort. [L *Herculeus* (as HERCULES)]

Her•cu•les /hə́rkyəleez/ *n.* a man of exceptional strength or size. [ME f. L f. Gk *Hēraklēs* a hero noted for his great strength]

Her•cu•les bee•tle *n. Zool.* a large S. American beetle, *Dynastes hercules,* with two horns extending from the head.

Her•cy•ni•an /hərsíneeən/ *adj. Geol.* of a mountain-forming time in the E. hemisphere in the late Paleozoic era. [L *Hercynia silva* forested mountains of central Germany]

herd /hərd/ *n. & v.* ● *n.* **1** a large number of animals, esp. cattle, feeding or traveling or kept together. **2** (often prec. by *the*) *derog.* a large number of people; a crowd; a mob (*prefers not to follow the herd*). **3** (esp. in *comb.*) a keeper of herds; a herdsman (*cowherd*). ● *v.* **1** *intr. & tr.* go or cause to go in a herd (*herded together for warmth; herded the cattle into the field*). **2** *tr.* tend (sheep, cattle, etc.) (*he herds the goats*). □ **ride herd on** keep watch on. □□ **herd•er** *n.* [OE *heord,* (in sense 3) *hirdi,* f. Gmc]

herd in•stinct *n.* the tendency to associate or conform with one's own kind for support, etc.

herds•man /hə́rdzmən/ *n.* (*pl.* **•men**) the owner or keeper of herds (of domesticated animals).

Herd•wick /hə́rdwik/ *n.* **1** a hardy mountain breed of sheep from the north of England. **2** this breed. [obs. *herdwick* pasture ground (as HERD, WICK²), perh. because this breed originated in Furness Abbey pastures]

here /heer/ *adv., n., & int.* ● *adv.* **1** in or at or to this place or position (*put it here; has lived here for many years; comes here every day*). **2** indicating a person's presence or a thing offered (*here is your coat; my son here will show you*). **3** at this point in the argument, situation, etc. (*here I have a question*). ● *n.* this place (*get out of here; lives near here; fill it up to here*). ● *int.* **1** calling attention: short for *come here, look here,* etc. (*here, where are you going with that?*). **2** indicating one's presence in a roll call: short for *I am here.* □ **here goes!** *colloq.* an expression indicating the start of a bold act. **here's to** I drink to the health of. **here we are** *colloq.* said on arrival at one's destination. **here we go again** *colloq.* the same, usu. undesirable, events are recurring. **here you are** said on handing something to somebody. **neither here nor there** of no importance or relevance. [OE *hēr* f. Gmc: cf. HE]

here•a•bouts /hee'rəbówts/ *adv.* (also **here•a•bout**) near this place.

here•af•ter /hee'ráftər/ *adv. & n.* ● *adv.* **1** from now on; in the future. **2** in the world to come (after death). ● *n.* **1** the future. **2** life after death.

here and now *n.* at this very moment; immediately.

here•at /hee'rát/ *adv. archaic* as a result of this.

here•by /hee'rbí/ *adv.* by this means; as a result of this.

he•red•i•ta•ble /hirédɪtəbəl/ *adj.* that can be inherited. [obs. F *héréditable* or med.L *hereditabilis* f. eccl.L *hereditare* f. L *heres –edis* heir]

her•e•dit•a•ment /héridɪtəmənt/ *n. Law* **1** any property that can be inherited. **2** inheritance. [med.L *hereditamentum* (as HEREDITABLE)]

he•red•i•tar•y /hirédɪtairee/ *adj.* **1** (of disease, instinct, etc.) able to be passed down from one generation to another. **2 a** descending by inheritance. **b** holding a position by inheritance. **3** the same as or resembling what one's parents had (*a hereditary hatred*). **4** of or relating to inheritance. □□ **he•red•i•tar•i•ly** *adv.* **he•red•i•tar•i•ness** *n.* [L *hereditarius* (as HEREDITY)]

he•red•i•ty /hirédɪtee/ *n.* **1 a** the passing on of physical or mental

characteristics genetically from one generation to another. **b** these characteristics. **2** the genetic constitution of an individual. [F *hérédité* or L *hereditas* heirship (as HEIR)]

Her•e•ford /hə́rfərd, hérifərd/ *n.* **1** an animal of a breed of red and white beef cattle. **2** this breed. [*Hereford* in England, where it originated]

here•in /hee'rín/ *adv. formal* in this matter, book, etc.

here•in•af•ter /hee'rináftər/ *adv. formal,* esp. *Law* in a later part of this document, etc.

here•in•be•fore /hee'rinbifáwr/ *adv. formal,* esp. *Law* in a preceding part of this document, etc.

here•of /hee'rúv, –óv/ *adv. formal* of this.

he•re•si•arch /hereezeeaark, hérisee–/ *n.* the leader or founder of a heresy. [eccl.L *haeresiarcha* f. Gk *hairesiarkhēs* (as HERESY + *arkhēs* ruler)]

her•e•sy /hérəsee/ *n.* (*pl.* **•sies**) **1 a** belief or practice contrary to the orthodox doctrine of esp. the Christian church. **b** an instance of this. **2 a** opinion contrary to what is normally accepted or maintained (*it's heresy to suggest that instant coffee is as good as the real thing*). **b** an instance of this. □□ **he•re•si•ol•o•gy** /hərəézeeóləjee, –seeóləjee/ *n.* [ME f. OF (*h*)*eresie,* f. eccl.L *haeresis,* in L = school of thought, f. Gk *hairesis* choice, sect f. *haireomai* choose]

her•e•tic /hérətik/ *n.* **1** the holder of an unorthodox opinion. **2** a person believing in or practicing religious heresy. □□ **he•ret•i•cal** /hirétikəl/ *adj.* **he•ret•i•cal•ly** *adv.* [ME f. OF *heretique* f. eccl.L *haereticus* f. Gk *hairetikos* able to choose (as HERESY)]

here•to /hee'rtóo/ *adv. formal* to this matter.

here•to•fore /hee'rtəfáwr/ *adv. formal* before this time.

here•un•der /hee'rúndər/ *adv. formal* below (in a book, legal document, etc.).

here•un•to /hee'rúntóo/ *adv. archaic* to this.

here•up•on /hee'rəpón, –páwn/ *adv.* after this; in consequence of this.

here•with /hee'rwith, –with/ *adv.* with this (esp. of an enclosure in a letter, etc.).

her•i•ot /hérēot/ *n. Brit. hist.* a tribute paid to a lord on the death of a tenant, consisting of a live animal, a chattel, or, orig., the return of borrowed equipment. [OE *heregeatwa* f. *here* army + *geatwa* trappings]

her•it•a•ble /hérɪtəbəl/ *adj.* **1** *Law* **a** (of property) capable of being inherited by heirs-at-law (cf. MOVABLE). **b** capable of inheriting. **2** *Biol.* (of a characteristic) transmissible from parent to offspring. □□ **her•it•a•bil•i•ty** *n.* **her•it•a•bly** *adv.* [ME f. OF f. *heriter* f. eccl.L *hereditare:* see HEREDITABLE]

her•it•age /hérɪtij/ *n.* **1** anything that is or may be inherited. **2** inherited circumstances, benefits, etc. (*a heritage of confusion*). **3** a nation's, state's, etc., historic buildings, monuments, countryside, etc., esp. when regarded as worthy of preservation. **4** *Bibl.* **a** the ancient Israelites. **b** the church. [ME f. OF (as HERITABLE)]

her•i•tor /hérɪtər/ *n.* (esp. in Scottish Law) a person who inherits. [ME f. AF *heriter,* OF *heritier* (as HEREDITARY), assim. to words in –OR¹]

herk•y-jerk•y /hə́rkeejórkee/ *adj.* marked by fitful, spastic, or unpredictable movement or manner. [redupl. of JERKY]

herl var. of HARL.

herm /hərm/ *n. GkAntiq.* a squared stone pillar with a head (esp. of Hermes) on top, used as a boundary marker, etc. (cf. TERMINUS 6). [L *Herma* f. Gk *Hermēs* messenger of the gods]

her•maph•ro•dite /hərmáfrədīt/ *n. & adj.* ● *n.* **1 a** *Zool.* an animal having both male and female sexual organs. **b** *Bot.* a plant having stamens and pistils in the same flower. **2** a human being in which both male and female sex organs are present, or in which the sex organs contain both ovarian and testicular tissue. **3** a person or thing combining opposite qualities or characteristics. ● *adj.* **1** combining both sexes. **2** combining opposite qualities or characteristics. □□ **her•maph•ro•dit•ic** /–dítik/ *adj.* **her•maph•ro•dit•i•cal** *adj.* **her•maph•ro•dit•ism** *n.* [L *hermaphroditus* f. Gk *hermaphroditos,* orig. the name of a son of Hermes and Aphrodite in Greek mythology, who became joined in one body with the nymph Salmacis]

her•maph•ro•dite brig *n. hist.* a two-masted sailing ship rigged on the foremast as a brig and on the mainmast as a schooner.

her•me•neu•tic /hərmɪnóotik, –nyóo–/ *adj.* concerning interpretation, esp. of Scripture or literary texts. □□ **her•me•neu•ti•cal** *adj.* **her•me•neu•ti•cal•ly** *adv.* [Gk *hermēneutikos* f. *herm ēneuō* interpret]

her•me•neu•tics /hərminóotiks, –nyóo–/ *n.pl.* (also treated as *sing.*) *Bibl.* interpretation, esp. of Scripture or literary texts.

her•met•ic /hərmétik/ *adj.* (also **her•met•i•cal**) **1** with an airtight closure. **2** protected from outside agencies. **3 a** of alchemy or other occult sciences (*hermetic art*). **b** esoteric. □□ **her•met•i•cal•ly** *adv.* [mod.L *hermeticus* irreg. f. *Hermes Trismegistus* thrice greatest Hermes (as the founder of alchemy)]

her•met•ic seal *n.* an airtight seal (orig. as used by alchemists).

her•mit /hə́rmit/ *n.* **1** an early Christian recluse. **2** any person living in solitude. □□ **her•mit•ic** /–mítik/ *adj.* [ME f. OF (*h*)*ermite* or f. LL *eremita* f. Gk *erēmitēs* f. *erēmia* desert f. *erēmos* solitary]

her•mit•age /hŕmitij/ *n.* **1** a hermit's dwelling. **2** a monastery. **3** a solitary dwelling. [ME f. OF (*h*)*ermitage* (as HERMIT)]

her•mit crab *n.* any crab of the family Paguridae that lives in a cast-off mollusk shell for protection.

her•mit thrush *n.* a migratory N. American thrush, *Catharus guttatus.*

her•ni•a /hŕneeə/ *n.* (*pl.* **her•ni•as** or **her•ni•ae** /–nee-ee/) the displacement and protrusion of part of an organ through the wall of the cavity containing it, esp. of the abdomen. □□ **her•ni•al** *adj.* **her•ni•ar•y** *adj.* **her•ni•at•ed** *adj.* [L]

he•ro /heerō/ *n.* (*pl.* **•roes**) **1 a** a person noted or admired for nobility, courage, outstanding achievements, etc. (*Newton, a hero of science*). **b** a great warrior. **2** the chief male character in a poem, play, story, etc. **3** *Gk Antiq.* a man of superhuman qualities, favored by the gods; a demigod. **4** *dial.* = SUBMARINE SANDWICH. [ME f. L *heros* f. Gk *hērōs*]

he•ro•ic /hirōik/ *adj. & n.* ● *adj.* **1 a** (of an act or a quality) of or fit for a hero. **b** (of a person) like a hero. **2 a** (of language) grand; high-flown; dramatic. **b** (of a work of art) heroic in scale or subject; unusually large or impressive. **3** of the heroes of Greek antiquity; (of poetry) dealing with the ancient heroes. ● *n.* (in *pl.*) **1 a** high-flown language or sentiments. **b** unduly bold behavior. **2** = HEROIC VERSE. □□ **he•ro•i•cal•ly** *adv.* [F *héroïque* or L *heroicus* f. Gk *hērōikos* (as HERO)]

he•ro•ic age *n.* the period in Greek history before the return from Troy.

he•ro•ic coup•let *n.* two lines of rhyming iambic pentameters.

he•ro•i•com•ic /hirōikómik/ *adj.* (also **he•ro•i•com•i•cal**) combining the heroic with the comic. [F *héroïcomique* (as HERO, COMIC)]

he•ro•ic verse *n.* a type of verse used for heroic poetry, esp. the hexameter, the iambic pentameter, or the alexandrine.

her•o•in /hérōin/ *n.* a highly addictive white crystalline analgesic drug derived from morphine, often used as a narcotic. [G (as HERO, supposedly from its effects on the user's self-esteem)]

her•o•ine /hérōin/ *n.* **1** a woman noted or admired for nobility, courage, outstanding achievements, etc. **2** the chief female character in a poem, play, story, etc. **3** *Gk Antiq.* a demigoddess. [F *héroïne* or L *heroina* f. Gk *hērōinē*, fem. of *hērōs* HERO]

her•o•ism /hérōizəm/ *n.* heroic conduct or qualities. [F *héroïsme* f. *héros* HERO]

her•o•ize /heerō-īz/ *v.* **1** *tr.* **a** make a hero of. **b** make heroic. **2** *intr.* play the hero.

her•on /hérən/ *n.* any of various large wading birds of the family Ardeidae, esp. *Ardea cinerea*, with long legs and a long S-shaped neck. □□ **her•on•ry** *n.* (*pl.* **•ries**). [ME f. OF *hairon* f. Gmc]

he•ro's wel•come *n.* a rapturous welcome, like that given to a successful warrior.

he•ro-wor•ship *n. & v.* ● *n.* **1** excessive admiration for someone. **2** *Gk Antiq.* the worship of superhuman heroes. ● *v.tr.* (**he•ro-wor•shiped**, **he•ro-wor•ship•ing** or **he•ro-wor•shipped**, **he•ro-wor•ship•ping**) admire (someone) excessively; idolize. □□ **he•ro-wor•ship•er** (or **–wor•ship•per**) *n.*

her•pes /hŕpeez/ *n.* a virus disease with outbreaks of blisters on the skin, etc. □□ **her•pet•ic** /–pétik/ *adj.* [ME f. L f. Gk *herpēs –ētos* shingles f. *herpō* creep: *zoster* f. Gk *zōstēr* belt, girdle]

her•pes sim•plex *n.* a viral infection which may produce blisters or conjunctivitis.

her•pes zos•ter /zóstər/ *n.* = SHINGLES.

her•pe•tol•o•gy /hŕpitóləjee/ *n.* the study of reptiles. □□ **her•pe•to•log•i•cal** /–tələjikəl/ *adj.* **her•pe•tol•o•gist** *n.* [Gk *herpeton* reptile f. *herpō* creep]

Herr /hair/ *n.* (*pl.* **Her•ren** /hérən/) **1** the title of a German man; Mr. **2** a German man. [G f. OHG *hērro* compar. of *hēr* exalted]

Her•ren•volk /hérənfawlk/ *n.* **1** the German nation characterized by the Nazis as born to mastery. **2** a group regarding itself as naturally superior. [G, = master race (as HERR, FOLK)]

her•ring /héring/ *n.* a N. Atlantic fish, *Clupea harengus*, coming near the coast in large shoals to spawn. [OE *hēring, hæring* f. WG]

her•ring•bone /héringbōn/ *n. & v.* ● *n.* **1** a stitch with a zigzag pattern, resembling the pattern of a herring's bones. **2** this pattern, or cloth woven in it. **3** any zigzag pattern, e.g., in building. **4** *Skiing* a method of ascending a slope with the skis pointing outwards. ● *v.* **1** *tr.* a work with a herringbone stitch. **b** mark with a herringbone pattern. **2** *intr. Skiing* ascend a slope using the herringbone technique.

her•ring gull *n.* a large gull, *Larus argentatus*, with dark wing tips.

hers /hŕz/ *poss.pron.* the one or ones belonging to or associated with her (*it is hers; hers are over there*). □ **of hers** of or belonging to her (*a friend of hers*).

her•self /hŕsélf/ *pron.* **1 a** *emphat. form* of SHE or HER (*she herself will do it*). **b** *refl. form* of HER (*she has hurt herself*). **2** in her normal state of body or mind (*does not feel quite herself today*). □ **be herself** act in her normal unconstrained manner. **by herself** see *by oneself*. [OE *hire self* (as HER, SELF)]

hertz /herts/ *n.* (*pl.* same) a unit of frequency, equal to one cycle per second. ¶ Abbr.: **Hz.** [H. R. *Hertz*, Ger. physicist d. 1894]

Hertz•ian wave /hŕtseeən/ *n.* an electromagnetic wave of a length suitable for use in radio.

he's /heez/ *contr.* **1** he is. **2** he has.

hes•i•tant /hézit'nt/ *adj.* **1** hesitating; irresolute. **2** (of speech) stammering; faltering. □□ **hes•i•tance** /–təns/ *n.* **hes•i•tan•cy** *n.* **hes•i•tant•ly** *adv.*

hes•i•tate /hézitayt/ *v.intr.* **1** (often foll. by *about, over*) show or feel indecision or uncertainty; pause in doubt (*hesitated over her choice*). **2** (often foll. by *to* + infin.) be deterred by scruples; be reluctant (*I hesitate to inform against him*). **3** stammer or falter in speech. □□ **hes•i•tat•er** *n.* **hes•i•tat•ing•ly** *adv.* **hes•i•ta•tion** /–táyshən/ *n.* **hes•i•ta•tive** *adj.* [L *haesitare* frequent. of *haerēre haes-* stick fast]

Hes•pe•ri•an /hespéereeən/ *adj. poet.* **1** western. **2** (in Greek mythology) of or concerning the Hesperides (nymphs who guarded the garden of golden apples at the western extremity of the earth). [L *Hesperius* f. Gk *Hesperios* (as HESPERUS)]

hes•per•id•i•um /héspərídeeəm/ *n.* (*pl.* **hes•per•id•i•a** /–deeə/) a fruit with sectioned pulp inside a separable rind, e.g., an orange or grapefruit. [Gk *Hesperides* daughters of Hesperus, nymphs in Greek mythology who guarded a tree of golden apples]

Hes•per•us /héspərəs/ *n.* the evening star, Venus. [ME f. L f. Gk *hesperos* (adj. & n.) western, evening (star)]

hes•sian /héshən/ *n. & adj.* ● *n.* **1** esp. *Brit.* a strong coarse sacking made of hemp or jute. **2** (**Hessian**) a native of Hesse in Germany. **3** (**Hes•sian**) a soldier from Hesse fighting for Britain during the Revolutionary War. ● *adj.* (**Hessian**) of or concerning Hesse. [*Hesse* in Germany]

Hes•sian boot *n.* a tasseled high boot first worn by Hessian troops.

Hes•sian fly *n.* a midge, *Mayetiola destructor*, whose larva destroys growing wheat (thought to have been brought to America by Hessian troops).

hest /hest/ *n. archaic* behest. [OE *hæs* (see HIGHT), assim. to ME nouns in –*t*]

he•tae•ra /hiteerə/ *n.* (also **he•tai•ra** /–tírə/) (*pl.* **•ras, he•tae•rae** /–teeree/, or **he•tai•rai** /–tírī/) a courtesan or mistress, esp. in ancient Greece. [Gk *hetaira*, fem. of *hetairos* companion]

he•tae•rism /hiteerizəm/ *n.* (also **he•tai•rism** /–tírizəm/) **1** a recognized system of concubinage. **2** communal marriage in a tribe. [Gk *hetairismos* prostitution (as HETAERA)]

het•er•o /hétərō/ *n.* (*pl.* **•os**) *colloq.* a heterosexual. [abbr.]

hetero- /hétərō/ *comb. form* other; different (often opp. HOMO-). [Gk *heteros* other]

het•er•o•chro•mat•ic /hétərōkrōmátik/ *adj.* of several colors.

het•er•o•clite /hétərōklīt/ *adj. & n.* ● *adj.* **1** abnormal. **2** *Gram.* (esp. of a noun) irregularly declined. ● *n.* **1** an abnormal thing or person. **2** *Gram.* an irregularly declined word, esp. a noun. [LL *heteroclitus* f. Gk *heteroklitos* f. *klitos* f. *klinō* bend, inflect)]

het•er•o•cy•clic /hétərōsíklik, –síklik/ *adj. Chem.* (of a compound) with a bonded ring of atoms of more than one kind.

het•er•o•dox /hétərədoks/ *adj.* (of a person, opinion, etc.) not orthodox. □□ **het•er•o•dox•y** *n.* [LL *heterodoxus* f. Gk (as HETERO-, *doxos* f. *doxa* opinion)]

het•er•o•dyne /hétərədīn/ *adj. & v. Radio* ● *adj.* relating to the production of a lower frequency from the combination of two almost equal high frequencies. ● *v.intr.* produce a lower frequency in this way.

het•er•og•a•mous /hétərógəməs/ *adj.* **1** *Bot.* irregular as regards stamens and pistils. **2** *Biol.* characterized by heterogamy or heterogony.

het•er•og•a•my /hétərógəmee/ *n.* **1** the alternation of generations, esp. of a sexual and parthenogenic generation. **2** sexual reproduction by fusion of unlike gametes. **3** *Bot.* a state in which the flowers of a plant are of two types.

het•er•o•ge•ne•ous /hétərōjéeneeəs, –nyəs/ *adj.* **1** diverse in character. **2** varied in content. **3** *Math.* incommensurable through being of different kinds or degrees. □□ **het•er•o•ge•ne•i•ty** /–jineeitee/ *n.* **het•er•o•ge•ne•ous•ly** *adv.* **het•er•o•ge•ne•ous•ness** *n.* [med.L *heterogeneus* f. Gk *heterogenēs* (as HETERO-, *genos* kind)]

het•er•o•gen•e•sis /hétərōjénisis/ *n.* **1** the birth of a living otherwise than from parents of the same kind. **2** spontaneous generation from inorganic matter. □□ **het•er•o•ge•net•ic** /–jinétik/ *adj.*

het•er•og•o•ny /hétərógənee/ *n.* the alternation of generations, esp. of a sexual and hermaphroditic generation. □□ **het•er•og•o•nous** *adj.*

het•er•o•graft /hétərōgraft/ *n.* living tissue grafted from one individual to another of a different species.

great blue heron

het·er·ol·o·gous /hétəróləgəs/ *adj.* not homologous. □□ **het·er·ol·o·gy** *n.*

het·er·om·er·ous /hétərómərəs/ *adj.* not isomerous.

het·er·o·mor·phic /hétərōmáwrfik/ *adj. Biol.* **1** of dissimilar forms. **2** (of insects) existing in different forms at different stages in their life cycle.

het·er·o·mor·phism /hétərōmáwrfizəm/ *n.* existing in various forms.

het·er·on·o·mous /hétərónəməs/ *adj.* **1** subject to an external law (cf. AUTONOMOUS). **2** *Biol.* subject to different laws (of growth, etc.).

het·er·on·o·my /hétərónəmee/ *n.* **1** the presence of a different law. **2** subjection to an external law.

het·er·o·path·ic /hétərōpáthik/ *adj.* **1** allopathic. **2** differing in effect.

het·er·o·phyl·lous /hétərófiləs/ *adj.* bearing leaves of different forms on the same plant. □□ **het·er·o·phyl·ly** *n.* [HETERO- + Gk *phullon* leaf]

het·er·o·po·lar /hétərōpṓlər/ *adj.* having dissimilar poles, esp. *Electr.* with an armature passing north and south magnetic poles alternately.

het·er·op·ter·an /hétəróptərən/ *n.* any insect of the suborder Heteroptera, including bugs, with nonuniform forewings having a thickened base and membranous tip (cf. HOMOPTERAN). □□ **het·er·op·ter·ous** *adj.* [HETERO- + Gk *pteron* wing]

het·er·o·sex·u·al /hétərōsékshooəl/ *adj. & n.* ● *adj.* **1** feeling or involving sexual attraction to persons of the opposite sex. **2** concerning heterosexual relations or people. **3** relating to the opposite sex. ● *n.* a heterosexual person. □□ **het·er·o·sex·u·al·i·ty** /-shooálitee/ *n.* **het·er·o·sex·u·al·ly** *adv.*

het·er·o·sis /hétərósis/ *n.* the tendency of a crossbred individual to show qualities superior to those of both parents. [Gk f. *heteros* different]

het·er·o·tax·y /hétərōtaksee/ *n.* the abnormal disposition of organs or parts. [HETERO- + Gk *taxis* arrangement]

het·er·o·trans·plant /hétərōtránsplaant/ *n.* = HETEROGRAFT.

het·er·o·tro·phic /hétərōtrófik, –trófik/ *adj. Biol.* deriving its nourishment and carbon requirements from organic substances; not autotrophic. [HETERO- + Gk *trophos* feeder]

het·er·o·zy·gote /hétərōzígōt/ *n. Biol.* **1** a zygote resulting from the fusion of unlike gametes. **2** an individual with dominant and recessive alleles determining a particular characteristic. □□ **het·er·o·zy·gous** *adj.*

het·man /hétmən/ *n.* (*pl.* **·men**) a Polish or Cossack military commander. [Pol., prob. f. G *Hauptmann* captain]

het up /hét úp/ *adj. colloq.* excited; overwrought. [*het* dial. past part. of HEAT]

heu·cher·a /hyóōkərə/ *n.* any N. American herbaceous plant of the genus *Heuchera*, with dark green round or heart-shaped leaves and tiny flowers. [mod.L f. J. H. von *Heucher*, Ger. botanist d. 1747]

heu·ris·tic /hyoōrístik/ *adj. & n.* ● *adj.* **1** allowing or assisting to discover on one's own. **2** *Computing* proceeding to a solution by trial and error. ● *n.* **1** the science of heuristic procedure. **2** a heuristic process or method. **3** (in *pl.*, usu. treated as *sing.*) *Computing* the study and use of heuristic techniques in data processing. □□ **heu·ris·ti·cal·ly** *adv.* [irreg. f. Gk *heuriskō* find]

heu·ris·tic meth·od *n.* a system of education under which students are trained to find out things for themselves.

he·ve·a /héeveeə/ *n.* any S. American tree of the genus *Hevea*, yielding a milky sap used for making rubber. [mod.L f. native name *hevé*]

HEW *abbr. US hist.* Department of Health, Education, and Welfare (1953-79).

hew /hyōō/ *v.* (*past part.* **hewn** /hyōōn/ or **hewed**) **1** *tr.* **a** (often foll. by *down, away, off*) chop or cut (a thing) with an ax, a sword, etc. **b** cut (a block of wood, etc.) into shape. **2** *intr.* (often foll. by *at, among*, etc.) strike cutting blows. **3** *intr.* (usu. foll. by *to*) conform. □ **hew one's way** make a way for oneself by hewing. [OE *hēawan* f. Gmc]

hew·er /hyóōər/ *n.* **1** a person who hews. **2** a person who cuts coal from a seam. □ **hewers of wood and drawers of water** menial drudges; laborers (Josh. 9:21).

hex /heks/ *v. & n.* ● *v.* **1** *intr.* practice witchcraft. **2** *tr.* cast a spell on; bewitch. ● *n.* **1** a magic spell; a curse. **2** a witch. [Pennsylvanian G *hexe* (v.), *Hex* (n.), f. G *hexen*, *Hexe*]

hexa- /héksə/ *comb. form* six. [Gk *hex* six]

hex·a·chord /héksəkawrd/ *n.* a diatonic series of six notes with a semitone between the third and fourth, used at three different pitches in medieval music. [HEXA- + CHORD[1]]

hex·ad /héksad/ *n.* a group of six. [Gk *hexas –ados* f. *hex* six]

hex·a·dec·i·mal /héksədésiməl/ *adj. & n.* (also **hex**) esp. *Computing* ● *adj.* relating to or using a system of numerical notation that has 16 rather than 10 as a base. ● *n.* the hexadecimal system; hexadecimal notation. □□ **hex·a·dec·i·mal·ly** *adv.*

hex·a·gon /héksəgon/ /–gən/ *n.* a plane figure with six sides and angles. □□ **hex·a·gon·al** /–ságənəl/ *adj.* [LL *hexagonum* f. Gk (as HEXA-, –GON)]

hex·a·gram /héksəgram/ *n.* **1** a figure formed by two intersecting equilateral triangles. **2** a figure of six lines. [HEXA- + Gk *gramma* line]

hex·a·he·dron /héksəheédrən/ *n.* a solid figure with six faces. □□ **hex·a·he·dral** *adj.* [Gk (as HEXA-, –HEDRON)]

hex·am·e·ter /heksámitər/ *n.* a line or verse of six metrical feet. □□ **hex·a·met·ric** /–sɔmétrik/ *adj.* **hex·a·met·rist** *n.* [ME f. L f. Gk *hexametros* (as HEXA-, *metron* measure)]

hex·ane /héksayn/ *n. Chem.* a liquid hydrocarbon of the alkane series. ¶ *Chem.* formula: C_6H_{14}. [HEXA- + –ANE[2]]

hex·a·pla /héksəplə/ *n.* a sixfold text, esp. of the Old Testament, in parallel columns. [Gk neut. pl. of *hexaploos* (as HEXA-, *ploos* –fold), orig. of Origen's OT text]

hex·a·pod /héksəpod/ *n. & adj.* ● *n.* any arthropod with six legs; an insect. ● *adj.* having six legs. [Gk *hexapous, hexapod-* (as HEXA-, *pous pod-* foot)]

hex·a·style /héksəstil/ *n. & adj.* ● *n.* a six-columned portico. ● *adj.* having six columns. [Gk *hexastulos* (as HEXA-, *stulos* column)]

Hex·a·teuch /héksətōōk, –tyōōk/ *n.* the first six books of the Old Testament. [Gk *hex* six + *teukhos* book]

hex·a·va·lent /héksəváylənt/ *adj.* having a valence of six; sexivalent.

hex·ose /héksōs/ *n. Biochem.* a monosaccharide with six carbon atoms in each molecule, e.g., glucose or fructose. [HEXA- + –OSE[2]]

hey[1] /hay/ *int.* calling attention or expressing joy, surprise, inquiry, enthusiasm, etc. [ME: cf. OF *hay*, Du., G *hei*]

hey[2] var. of HAY[2].

hey·day /háyday/ *n.* the flush or full bloom of youth, vigor, prosperity, etc. [archaic *heyday* expression of joy, surprise, etc.: cf. LG *heidi, heida*, excl. denoting gaiety]

HF *abbr.* high frequency.

Hf *symb. Chem.* the element hafnium.

hf. *abbr.* half.

HG *abbr.* Her or His Grace.

Hg *symb. Chem.* the element mercury. [mod.L *hydrargyrum*]

hg *abbr.* hectogram(s).

hgt. *abbr.* height.

hgwy. *abbr.* highway.

HH *abbr.* **1** His Holiness. **2** double hard (pencil lead). **3** *Brit.* Her or His Highness.

hh. *abbr.* hands (see HAND *n.* 13).

hhd. *abbr.* hogshead(s).

H-hour /áychowr/ *n.* the hour at which a military operation is scheduled to begin. [*H* for *hour* + HOUR]

HHS *abbr.* (Department of) Health and Human Services.

HI *abbr.* **1** Hawaii (also in official postal use). **2** the Hawaiian Islands.

hi /hī/ *int.* expression of greeting or (*Brit.*) to call attention. [parallel form to HEY[1]]

hi·a·tus /hiáytəs/ *n.* (*pl.* **hi·a·tus·es**) **1** a break or gap, esp. in a series, account, or chain of proof. **2** *Prosody & Gram.* a break between two vowels coming together but not in the same syllable, as in *though oft the ear*. □□ **hi·a·tal** *adj.* [L, = gaping f. *hiare* gape]

hi·ba·chi /həbáachee/ *n.* a small charcoal-burning brazier for grilling food. [Jap.]

hi·ber·nate /híbərnayt/ *v.intr.* **1** (of some animals) spend the winter in a dormant state. **2** remain inactive. □□ **hi·ber·na·tion** /–náyshən/ *n.* **hi·ber·na·tor** *n.* [L *hibernare* f. *hibernus* wintry]

Hi·ber·ni·an /hibə́rneeən/ *adj. & n. archaic poet.* ● *adj.* of or concerning Ireland. ● *n.* a native of Ireland. [L *Hibernia, Iverna* f. Gk *Iernē* f. OCelt.]

Hi·ber·ni·cism /hibə́rnisizəm/ *n.* an Irish idiom or expression; = BULL[3] 1. [as HIBERNIAN after *Anglicism*, etc.]

Hiberno- /hibə́rnō/ *comb. form* Irish (*Hiberno-British*). [med.L *hibernus* Irish (as HIBERNIAN)]

hi·bis·cus /hibískəs/ *n.* any tree or shrub of the genus *Hibiscus*, cultivated for its large bright-colored flowers. Also called **rose mallow**. [L f. Gk *hibiskos* marsh mallow]

hic /hik/ *int.* expressing the sound of a hiccup, esp. a drunken hiccup. [imit.]

hic·cup /híkup/ *n. & v.* (also **hic·cough**) ● *n.* **1 a** an involuntary spasm of the diaphragm and respiratory organs, with sudden closure of the glottis and characteristic coughlike sound. **b** (in *pl.*) an attack of such spasms. **2** a temporary or minor stoppage or difficulty. ● *v.* **1** *intr.* make a hiccup or series of hiccups. **2** *tr.* utter with a hiccup. □□ **hic·cup·y** *adj.* [imit.]

hic ja·cet /hik jáyset, heek yaáket/ *n.* an epitaph. [L, = here lies]

hick /hik/ *n. colloq.* a country dweller; a provincial. [nickname for the name *Richard*: cf. DICK[1]]

hick·ey /híkee/ *n.* (*pl.* **·eys**) *colloq.* **1** a gadget (cf. DOOHICKEY). **2** a reddish mark on the skin, esp. one produced by a sucking kiss. [20th c.: orig. unkn.]

hick·o·ry /híkəree/ *n.* (*pl.* **·ries**) **1** any N. American tree of the genus *Carya*, yielding tough heavy wood and bearing nutlike edible fruits (see PECAN). **2 a** the wood of these trees. **b** a stick made of this. [native Virginian *pohickery*]

hid *past of* HIDE[1].

hi·dal·go /hidálgō, eethaál–/ *n.* (*pl.* **·gos**) a Spanish gentleman. [Sp. f. *hijo dalgo* son of something]

hid·den *past part.* of HIDE[1] *adj.* kept out of sight; concealed. □□ **hid·den·ness** *n.*

hid·den a·gen·da *n.* a secret motivation behind a policy, statement, etc.; an ulterior motive.

hid·den re·serves *n.pl.* extra profits, resources, etc., kept concealed in reserve.

hide[1] /hīd/ *v. & n.* ● *v.* (*past* hid /hid/; *past part.* **hid·den** /hídən/ or *archaic* hid) **1** *tr.* put or keep out of sight (*hid it under the cushion*; *hid her in the closet*). **2** *intr.* conceal oneself. **3** *tr.* (usu. foll. by *from*) keep (a fact) secret (*hid his real motive from her*). **4** *tr.* conceal (a thing) from sight intentionally or not (*trees hid the house*). ● *n. Brit.* = BLIND 6. □ **hide one's head** keep out of sight, esp. from shame. **hide one's light under a bushel** conceal one's merits (Matthew 5:15). **hide out** remain in concealment. □□ **hid·den** *adj.* **hid·er** *n.* [OE *hȳdan* f. WG]

hide[2] /hīd/ *n. & v.* ● *n.* **1** the skin of an animal, esp. when tanned or dressed. **2** *colloq.* the human skin (*saved his own hide*; *I'll tan your hide*). **3** *Austral. & NZ colloq.* impudence; effrontery; nerve. ● *v.tr. colloq.* flog. □□ **hid·ed** *adj.* (also in *comb.*). [OE *hȳd* f. Gmc]

hide[3] /hīd/ *n.* a former English measure of land large enough to support a family and its dependents, usu. between 60 and 120 acres. [OE *hī(gi)d* f. *hīw-, hīg-* household]

hide-and-seek *n.* **1** a children's game in which one or more players seek a child or children hiding. **2** a process of attempting to find an evasive person or thing.

hide·a·way /hídəway/ *n.* a hiding place or place of retreat.

hide·bound /hídbownd/ *adj.* **1 a** narrow-minded; bigoted. **b** (of the law, rules, etc.) constricted by tradition. **2** (of cattle) with the skin clinging close as a result of bad feeding.

WORD HISTORY   hidebound

Mid-16th century (as a noun denoting a condition of cattle): from HIDE[2] + BOUND[4]. The earliest sense of the adjective (referring to cattle) was extended to emaciated human beings, and then applied figuratively in the sense 'narrow, cramped, or bigoted in outlook.'

---

hid·e·os·i·ty /hídeeósitee/ *n.* (*pl.* **·ties**) **1** a hideous object. **2** hideousness.

hid·e·ous /hídeeəs/ *adj.* **1** frightful, repulsive, or revolting, to the senses or the mind (*a hideous monster*; *a hideous pattern*). **2** *colloq.* unpleasant. □□ **hid·e·ous·ly** *adv.* **hid·e·ous·ness** *n.* [ME *hidous* f. AF *hidous*, OF *hidos, –eus*, f. OF *hide, hisde* fear, of unkn. orig.]

hide-out *n. colloq.* a hiding place, esp. one used by someone who has broken the law.

hid·ey-hole /hídeehōl/ *n. colloq.* a hiding place.

hid·ing[1] /hídiŋ/ *n. colloq.* a thrashing. □ **on a hiding to nothing** *Brit.* in a position from which there can be no successful outcome. [HIDE[2] + –ING[1]]

hid·ing[2] /hídiŋ/ *n.* **1** the act or an instance of hiding. **2** the state of remaining hidden (*go into hiding*). [ME, f. HIDE[1] + –ING[1]]

hi·dro·sis /hīdrósis/ *n. Med.* perspiration. □□ **hi·drot·ic** /–drótik/ *adj.* [mod.L f. Gk f. *hidrōs* sweat]

hie /hī/ *v.intr. & refl.* (**hies, hied, hie·ing** or **hy·ing**) esp. *archaic or poet.* go quickly (*hie to your chamber*; *hied him to the chase*). [OE *hīgian* strive, pant, of unkn. orig.]

hi·er·arch /híəraárk/ *n.* **1** a chief priest. **2** an archbishop. □□ **hi·er·ar·chal** *adj.* [med.L f. Gk *hierarkhēs* f. *hieros* sacred + *–arkhēs* ruler]

hi·er·ar·chy /híəraarkee/ *n.* (*pl.* **·chies**) **1 a** a system in which grades or classes of status or authority are ranked one above the other (*ranks third in the hierarchy*). **b** the hierarchical system (of government, management, etc.). **2 a** priestly government. **b** a priesthood organized in grades. **3 a** each of the three divisions of angels. **b** the angels. □□ **hi·er·ar·chic** *adj.* /–raárkik/ **hi·er·ar·chi·cal** *adj.* **hi·er·ar·chism** *n.* **hi·er·ar·chize** *v.tr.* [ME f. OF *ierarchie* f. med.L (h)*ierarchia* f. Gk *hierarkhia* (as HIERARCH)]

hi·er·at·ic /híərátik/ *adj.* **1** of or concerning priests; priestly. **2** of the ancient Egyptian writing of abridged hieroglyphics as used by priests (opp. DEMOTIC). **3** of or concerning Egyptian or Greek traditional styles of art. □□ **hi·er·at·i·cal·ly** *adv.* [L f. Gk *hieratikos* f. *hieraomai* be a priest f. *hiereus* priest]

hiero- /híró/ *comb. form* sacred; holy. [Gk *hieros* sacred + –o-]

hi·er·oc·ra·cy /hírókrəsee/ *n.* (*pl.* **·cies**) **1** priestly rule. **2** a body of ruling priests. [HIERO- + –CRACY]

hi·er·o·glyph /híərəglif/ *n.* **1 a** a picture of an object representing a word, syllable, or sound, as used in ancient Egyptian and other writing. **b** a writing consisting of characters of this kind. **2** a secret or enigmatic symbol. **3** (in *pl.*) = HIEROGLYPHIC *n.* 2. [back-form. f. HIEROGLYPHIC]

hi·er·o·glyph·ic /híərəglífik/ *adj. & n.* ● *adj.* **1** of or written in hieroglyphs. **2** symbolic. ● *n.* (in *pl.*) **1** hieroglyphs; hieroglyphic writing. **2** *joc.* writing difficult to read. □□ **hi·er·o·glyph·i·cal** *adj.* **hi·er·o·glyph·i·cal·ly** *adv.* [F *hiéroglyphique* or LL *hieroglyphicus* f. Gk *hieroglyphikos* (as HIERO-, *gluphikos* f. *gluphē* carving)]

hi·er·o·gram /híərəgram/ *n.* a sacred inscription or symbol.

hi·er·o·graph /híərəgraf/ *n.* = HIEROGRAM.

hi·er·ol·a·try /híərólətree/ *n.* the worship of saints or sacred things.

hi·er·ol·o·gy /híəróləjee/ *n.* sacred literature or lore.

hi·er·o·phant /híərəfant/ *n.* **1** *Gk Antiq.* an initiating or presiding priest; an official interpreter of sacred mysteries. **2** an interpreter of sacred mysteries or any esoteric principle. □□ **hi·er·o·phan·tic** /–fántik/ *adj.* [LL *hierophantes* f. Gk *hierophantēs* (as HIERO-, *phantēs* f. *phainō* show)]

hi-fi /hífí/ *adj. & n. colloq.* ● *adj.* of high fidelity. ● *n.* (*pl.* **hi-fis**) a set of equipment for high fidelity sound reproduction. [abbr.]

hig·gle /hígəl/ *v.intr.* dispute about terms; haggle. [var. of HAGGLE]

hig·gle·dy-pig·gle·dy /hígəldeepígəldee/ *adv., adj., & n. adj. & adv.* in confusion or disorder. ● *n.* a state of disordered confusion. [rhyming jingle, prob. with ref. to the irregular herding together of pigs]

high /hī/ *adj., n., & adv.* ● *adj.* **1 a** of great vertical extent (*a high building*). **b** (*predic.*; often in *comb.*) of a specified height (*one inch high*; *water was waist-high*). **2 a** far above ground or sea level, etc. (*a high altitude*). **b** inland, esp. when raised (*High Plains*). **3** extending above the normal or average level (*high boots*; *sweater with a high neck*). **4** of exalted, esp. spiritual, quality (*high minds*; *high principles*; *high art*). **5 a** of exalted rank (*in high society*; *is high in the government*). **b** important; serious; grave. **6 a** great; intense; extreme; powerful (*high praise*; *high temperature*). **b** greater than normal (*high prices*). **c** extreme in religious or political opinion (*high Tory*). **7** (of physical action, esp. athletics) performed at, to, or from a considerable height (*high diving*; *high flying*). **8 a** elated; merry. **b** *colloq.* (often foll. by *on*) intoxicated by alcohol or esp. drugs. **9** (of a sound or note) of high frequency; shrill; at the top end of the scale. **10** (of a period, an age, a time, etc.) at its peak (*high noon*; *high summer*; *High Renaissance*). **11 a** (of meat) beginning to go bad; off. **b** (of game) well-hung and slightly decomposed. **12** *Geog.* (of latitude) near the North or South Pole. **13** *Phonet.* (of a vowel) close (see CLOSE[1] *adj.* 14). ● *n.* **1** a high, or the highest, level or figure. **2** an area of high barometric pressure; an anticyclone. **3** *sl.* a euphoric drug-induced state. **4** top gear in a motor vehicle. **5** *colloq.* high school. **6** (**the High**) *Brit. colloq.* a High Street, esp. that in Oxford. ● *adv.* **1** far up; aloft (*flew the flag high*). **2** in or to a high degree. **3** at a high price. **4** (of a sound) at or to a high pitch (*sang high*). □ **ace** (or **king** or **queen**, etc.) **high** (in card games) having the ace, etc., as the highest-ranking card. **from on high** from heaven or a high place. **high old** *colloq.* most enjoyable (*had a high old time*). **high opinion of** a favorable opinion of. **high, wide, and handsome** *colloq.* in a carefree or stylish manner. **in high feather** see FEATHER. **the Most High** God. **on high** in or to heaven or a high place. **on one's high horse** *colloq.* behaving superciliously or arrogantly. **play high** *Brit.* **1** play for high stakes. **2** play a card of high value. **run high 1** (of the sea) have a strong current with high tide. **2** (of feelings) be strong. [OE *hēah* f. Gmc]

high and dry *adj. & adv.* **1** in a difficult position, esp. without resources; stranded. **2** (of a ship) out of the water.

high and mighty *adj.* **1** *colloq.* arrogant. **2** *archaic* of exalted rank.

high·ball /hībawl/ *n.* **1** a drink of liquor (esp. whiskey) and soda, etc., served with ice in a tall glass. **2** a railroad signal to proceed.

high beam *n.* the brightest setting of a vehicle's headlights.

high·bind·er /híbindər/ *n.* a ruffian; a swindler; an assassin.

high·born /hībáwrn/ *adj.* of noble birth.

high·boy /híboy/ *n.* a tall chest of drawers on legs.

high·brow /híbrow/ *adj. & n. colloq.* ● *adj.* intellectual; cultural. ● *n.* an intellectual or cultured person.

high card *n.* a card that outranks others, esp. the ace or a face card.

high chair *n.* an infant's chair with long legs and a tray, for use at meals.

High Church *n. & adj.* ● *n.* (in the Anglican communion) emphasizing Catholic tradition, as to ritual, church authority, and sacraments. ● *adj.* of or relating to this.

High Church·man *n.* (*pl.* **·men**) an advocate of High Church principles.

high-class *adj.* **1** of high quality. **2** characteristic of the upper class.

high color *n.* a flushed complexion.

high com·mand *n.* an army commander-in-chief and associated staff.

High Com·mis·sion *n.* an embassy from one British Commonwealth country to another.

High Court *n.* **1** the US Supreme Court. **2** (in England also **High Court of Justice**) a supreme court of justice for civil cases.

high en·e·ma *n.* an enema delivered into the colon.

high·er court *n. Law* a court that can overrule the decision of another.

high·er crit·i·cism *n.* criticism dealing with the origin and character, etc., of texts, esp. of biblical writings.

high·er ed·u·ca·tion *n.* education beyond high school, esp. to degree level.

high·er math·e·mat·ics *n.* advanced mathematics as taught at the college level.

high·er-up *n. colloq.* a person of higher rank.

high·est com·mon fac·tor *n. Math.* the highest number that can be divided exactly into each of two or more numbers.

high ex·plo·sive *n.* a chemical explosive that is rapid and destructive, used in shells and bombs.

high·fa·lu·tin /hífəlóot'n/ *adj. & n.* (also **high·fa·lu·ting** /–ing/) *colloq.* • *adj.* absurdly pompous or pretentious. • *n.* highfalutin speech or writing. [HIGH + –*falutin*, of unkn. orig.]

high fash·ion *n.* = HAUTE COUTURE.

high fi·del·i·ty *n.* the reproduction of sound with little distortion, giving a result very similar to the original. Also called **hi-fi**.

high fi·nance *n.* financial transactions involving large sums.

high five *n.* a gesture of celebration or greeting in which two people slap each other's raised palm.

high-flown *adj.* (of language, etc.) extravagant; bombastic.

high-fly·er *n.* (or **high-fli·er**) **1** an ambitious person. **2** a person or thing with great potential for achievement. □□ **high-fly·ing** *adj.*

high fre·quen·cy *n.* a frequency, esp. in radio, of 3 to 30 megahertz.

high gear *n.* (also **low gear**) a gear such that the driven end of a transmission revolves faster (or slower) than the driving end.

High Ger·man *n.* a literary and cultured form of German.

high-grade *adj.* of high quality.

high-hand·ed /híhándid/ *adj.* disregarding others' feelings; overbearing. □□ **high-hand·ed·ly** *adv.* **high-hand·ed·ness** *n.*

high hat *n.* **1** a tall hat; a top hat. **2** foot-operated cymbals. **3** a snobbish or overbearing person.

high-hat *adj. & v.* • *adj.* supercilious; snobbish. • *v.* (**·hat·ted**, **·hat·ting**) **1** *tr.* treat superciliously. **2** *intr.* assume a superior attitude.

High Hol·i·day *n.* (also **High Ho·ly Day**) the Jewish New Year or the Day of Atonement.

high jinks *n.* boisterous joking or merrymaking.

high jump *n.* **1** an athletic event consisting of jumping as high as possible over a bar of adjustable height. **2** *Brit. colloq.* a drastic punishment (*he's for the high jump*).

high-key *adj. Photog.* having a predominance of light tones.

high-keyed *adj.* emotionally taught; high-strung.

high·land /hílənd/ *n. & adj.* • *n.* (usu. in *pl.*) **1** an area of high land. **2** (the Highlands) the mountainous part of Scotland. • *adj.* of or in a highland or the Highlands. □□ **high·land·er** *n.* (also **High·land·er**). **High·land·man** *n.* (*pl.* **·men**). [OE *hēahlond* promontory (as HIGH, LAND)]

High·land cat·tle *n.* **1** a shaggy-haired breed of cattle with long, curved, widely spaced horns. **2** this breed.

High·land dress *n.* clothing in the traditional style of the Scottish Highlands, such as the kilt.

High·land fling *n.* a vigorous Scottish dance consisting of a series of complex steps performed solo, originally to celebrate victory.

high lat·i·tudes *n.* the regions near the poles.

high-lev·el *adj.* **1** (of negotiations, etc.) conducted by high-ranking people. **2** *Computing* (of a programming language) that is not machine-dependent and is usu. at a level of abstraction close to natural language.

high life *n.* (also **high living**) a luxurious existence ascribed to the upper classes.

high·light /hílīt/ *n. & v.* • *n.* **1** (in a painting, etc.) a light area, or one seeming to reflect light. **2** a moment or detail of vivid interest; an outstanding feature. **3** (usu. in *pl.*) a bright tint in the hair produced by bleaching. • *v.tr.* **1 a** bring into prominence; draw attention to. **b** mark with a highlighter. **2** create highlights in (the hair).

high·light·er /hílītər/ *n.* a marker pen that overlays color on a printed word, etc., leaving it legible and emphasized.

high-lows *n.pl. archaic* boots reaching over the ankles.

high·ly /hílee/ *adv.* **1** in a high degree (*highly amusing*; *highly probable*; *commend it highly*). **2** honorably; favorably (*think highly of him*). **3** in a high position or rank (*highly placed*). [OE *hēalīce* (as HIGH)]

High Mass *n.* a Catholic mass with full ceremonial, including music and incense and typically sung by the celebrant.

high-mind·ed /hímíndid/ *adj.* **1** having high moral principles. **2** proud; pretentious. □□ **high-mind·ed·ly** *adv.* **high-mind·ed·ness** *n.*

high-muck-a-muck /hímukəmuk/ *n.* (also **high-muck·e·ty-muck**) a person of great self-importance. [perh. f. Chinook *hiu* plenty + *muckamuck* food]

high·ness /hínis/ *n.* **1** the state of being high (cf. HEIGHT). **2** (**Highness**) a title used in addressing and referring to a prince or princess (*Her Highness*; *Your Royal Highness*). [OE *hēanes* (as HIGH)]

high-oc·cu·pan·cy ve·hi·cle *n.* a commuter vehicle carrying several (or many) passengers. ¶ Abbr.: **HOV.**

high-oc·tane *n.* denoting gasoline having a high octane number and thus good antiknock properties.

high-pitched *adj.* **1** (of a sound). high. **2** (of a roof) steep. **3** (of style, etc.) lofty. **4** at a high level of energy; intense.

high point *n.* the most enjoyable or significant part of an experience or period of time.

high pol·y·mer *n.* a polymer having a high molecular weight.

high-pow·ered *adj.* **1** having great power or energy. **2** important or influential.

high pres·sure *n.* **1** a high degree of activity or exertion. **2** a condition of the atmosphere with the pressure above average.

high priest *n.* **1** a chief priest, esp. in early Judaism. **2** the head of any cult.

high pro·file *n.* a position of attracting much attention or publicity (*he has a high profile in the community*).

high-pro·file *adj.* attracting much attention or publicity (*a high-profile military presence*).

high-rank·ing *adj.* of high rank; senior.

high re·lief *n.* a method of molding or carving or stamping in which the design or figures stand clearly out from the surface.

high-rise *adj. & n.* • *adj.* (of a building) having many stories. • *n.* a building with many stories.

high-risk *adj.* involving or exposed to danger (*high-risk sports*).

high road *n.* **1** (usu. foll. by *to*) a direct route (*on the high road to success*). **2** *Brit.* a main road.

high roll·er *n. sl.* a person who gambles large sums or spends freely.

high school *n.* **1** a school that typically comprises grades 9 through 12, attended after middle school.

high sea *n.* (also **high seas**) open seas not within any country's jurisdiction.

high sea·son *n.* the period of the greatest number of visitors at a vacation destination, etc.

High Sheriff see SHERIFF.

high sign *n. colloq.* a surreptitious gesture indicating that all is well or that the coast is clear.

high·sound·ing *adj.* pretentious; bombastic.

high-speed *adj.* **1** operating at great speed. **2** (of steel) suitable for cutting tools even when red-hot.

high-spir·it·ed *adj.* vivacious; energetic; cheerful. □□ **high-spir·it·ed·ness** *n.*

high spir·its *n.* vivacity; energy; cheerfulness.

high-step·per *n.* **1** a horse that lifts its feet high when walking or trotting. **2** a stately person.

High Stew·ard *n.* see STEWARD *n.* 6.

high-strung *adj.* very sensitive or nervous.

hight /hīt/ *adj. archaic poet.*, or *joc.* called; named. [past part. (from 14th c.) of OE *hātan* command, call]

high·tail /hítayl/ *v.intr. colloq.* move at high speed, esp. in retreat.

high tea *n. Brit.* a main evening meal usu. consisting of a cooked dish, bread and butter, tea, etc.

high tech *n. & adj.* • *n.* = HIGH TECHNOLOGY. • *adj.* **1** (of interior design, etc.) imitating styles more usual in industry, etc., esp. using steel, glass, or plastic in a functional way. **2** employing, requiring, or involved in high technology.

high tech·nol·o·gy *n.* advanced technological development, esp. in electronics.

high ten·sion *adj.* = HIGH-VOLTAGE 1.

high tide *n.* the state of the tide when at its highest level.

high time *n.* a time that is late or overdue (*it is high time they arrived*).

high-toned *adj.* stylish; dignified; superior.

high tops *n.pl.* shoes, esp. sports shoes or sneakers, that cover the ankle.

high trea·son *n.* see TREASON.

high-up *n. colloq.* a person of high rank.

high-volt·age *n.* **1** electrical potential causing some danger of injury or damage. **2** energetic; dynamic (*a high-voltage presentation*).

high wa·ter *n.* **1** the tide at its fullest. **2** the time of this.

high-wa·ter mark *n.* **1** the level reached at high water. **2** the maximum recorded value or highest point of excellence.

high·way /híway/ *n.* **1 a** a public road. **b** a main route (by land or water). **2** a direct course of action (*on the highway to success*).

high·way·man /híwaymən/ *n.* (*pl.* **·men**) *hist.* a robber of passengers, travelers, etc., usu. mounted. [HIGHWAY]

high·way pa·trol *n.* an organization of state police officers who patrol state highways.

high wire *n.* a high tightrope.

HIH *abbr. Brit.* Her or His Imperial Highness.

hi·jack /híjak/ *v. & n.* • *v.tr.* **1** seize control of (a loaded truck, an aircraft in flight, etc.), esp. to force it to a different destination. **2** seize (goods) in transit. **3** take over (an organization, etc.) by force or subterfuge in order to redirect it. • *n.* an instance of hijacking. □□ **hi·jack·er** *n.* [20th c.: orig. unkn.]

hij·ra var. of HEGIRA.

hike /hīk/ *n. & v.* ● *n.* **1** a long walk, esp. in the country or wilderness with backpacks, etc. **2** an increase (of prices, etc.). ● *v.* **1** *intr.* walk, esp. across country, for a long distance, esp. with boots, backpack, etc. **2** (usu. foll. by *up*) **a** *tr.* hitch up (clothing, etc.); hoist; shove. **b** *intr.* work upwards out of place; become hitched up. **3** *tr.* increase (prices, etc.). **4** *Football* put the ball in play by passing it back to an offensive player in the backfield. □□ **hik·er** *n.* [19th-c. dial.: orig. unkn.]

hi·la *pl.* of HILUM.

hi·lar·i·ous /hiláireeəs/ *adj.* **1** exceedingly funny. **2** boisterously merry. □□ **hi·lar·i·ous·ly** *adv.* **hi·lar·i·ous·ness** *n.* **hi·lar·i·ty** /-láritee/ *n.* [L *hilaris* f. Gk *hilaros* cheerful]

Hil·a·ry term /hílaree/ *n. Brit.* the university term beginning in January, esp. at Oxford. [*Hilarius* bishop of Poitiers d. 367, with a festival on Jan. 13.]

hill /hil/ *n. & v.* ● *n.* **1 a** a naturally raised area of land, not as high as a mountain. **b** (as **the hills**) *Anglo-Ind.* = HILL STATION. **2** (often in *comb.*) a heap; a mound (*anthill; dunghill*). **3** a sloping piece of road. ● *v.tr.* **1** form into a hill. **2** (usu. foll. by *up*) bank up (plants) with soil. □ **old as the hills** very ancient. **over the hill** *colloq.* **1** past the prime of life; declining. **2** past the crisis. **up hill and down dale** see UP. [OE *hyll*]

hill·bil·ly /hílbilee/ *n.* (*pl.* **·lies**) **1** *colloq.*, often *derog.* a person from a remote or mountainous area, esp. in the Appalachian mountains of the eastern US (cf. HICK). **2** country music of or like that originating in the Appalachian region.

hill climb *n.* a race for vehicles up a steep hill.

hill·ock /hílək/ *n.* a small hill or mound. □□ **hill·ock·y** *adj.*

hill·side /hílsīd/ *n.* the sloping side of a hill.

hill sta·tion *n.* a town in the low mountains of the Indian subcontinent, popular as a holiday resort during the hot season.

hill·top /híltop/ *n.* the summit of a hill.

hill·walk·ing /hílwawking/ *n.* the pastime of walking in hilly country. □□ **hill·walk·er** *n.*

hill·y /hílee/ *adj.* (**hill·i·er**, **hill·i·est**) having many hills. □□ **hill·i·ness** *n.*

hilt /hilt/ *n. & v.* ● *n.* **1** the handle of a sword, dagger, etc. **2** the handle of a tool. ● *v.tr.* provide with a hilt. □ **up to the hilt** completely. [OE *hilt(e)* f. Gmc]

hi·lum /híləm/ *n.* (*pl.* **hi·la** /-lə/) **1** *Bot.* the point of attachment of a seed to its vessel. **2** *Anat.* a notch or indentation where a vessel enters an organ. [L, = little thing, trifle]

HIM *abbr. Brit.* Her or His Imperial Majesty.

him /him/ *pron.* **1** *objective case* of HE (*I saw him*). **2** *colloq.* he (*it's him again; is taller than him*). **3** *archaic* himself (*fell and hurt him*). [OE, masc. and neut. dative sing. of HE, IT[1]]

Him·a·la·yan /híməláyən/ *adj.* of or relating to the Himalaya mountains in Nepal. [*Himalaya* Skr. f. *hima* snow + *ālaya* abode]

hi·mat·i·on /himáteeon/ *n. hist.* the outer garment worn by the ancient Greeks over the left shoulder and under the right. [Gk]

him·self /himsélf/ *pron.* **1 a** *emphat. form* of HE or HIM (*he himself will do it*). **b** *refl. form* of HIM (*he has hurt himself*). **2** in his normal state of body or mind (*does not feel quite himself today*). **3** esp. *Ir.* a third party of some importance; the master of the house. □ **be himself** act in his normal unconstrained manner. **by himself** see *by oneself*. [OE (as HIM, SELF)]

Hi·na·ya·na /heénəyaánə/ *n.* = THERAVADA. [Skr. f. *hīna* lesser + *yāna* vehicle]

hind[1] /hīnd/ *adj.* (esp. of parts of the body) situated at the back; posterior (*hind leg*) (opp. FORE). □ **on one's hind legs** see LEG. [ME, perh. shortened f. OE *bihindan* BEHIND]

hind[2] /hīnd/ *n.* a female deer (usu. a red deer or sika), esp. in and after the third year. [OE f. Gmc]

hind[3] /hīnd/ *n. hist.* **1** esp. *Sc.* a skilled farm worker, usu. married and with a tied cottage, and formerly having charge of two horses. **2** *Brit.* a steward on a farm. **3** a rustic; a boor. [ME *hine* f. OE *hīne* (pl.) app. f. *hī(g)na* genit. pl. of *hīgan*, *hīwan* 'members of a family' (cf. HIDE[3]): for *-d* cf. SOUND[1]]

hind·er[1] /híndər/ *v.tr.* (also *absol.*) impede; delay; prevent (*you will hinder him; hindered me from working*). [OE *hindrian* f. Gmc]

hind·er[2] /híndər/ *adj.* rear; hind (*the hinder part*). [ME, perh. f. OE *hinderweard* backward: cf. HIND[1]]

Hin·di /híndee/ *n. & adj.* ● *n.* **1** a group of spoken dialects of N. India. **2** a literary form of Hindustani with a Sanskrit-based vocabulary and the Devanagari script, an official language of India. ● *adj.* of or concerning Hindi. [Urdu *hindī* f. *Hind* India]

hind·most /híndmōst/ *adj.* farthest behind; most remote.

Hin·doo *archaic* var. of HINDU.

hind·quar·ters /híndkwáwrtərz/ *n.pl.* the hind legs and adjoining parts of a quadruped.

hin·drance /híndrəns/ *n.* **1** the act or an instance of hindering; the state of being hindered. **2** a thing that hinders; an obstacle.

hind·sight /híndsīt/ *n.* **1** wisdom after the event (*realized with hind-*

sight that they were wrong) (opp. FORESIGHT). **2** the backsight of a gun.

Hin·du /híndoō/ *n. & adj.* ● *n.* **1** a follower of Hinduism. **2** *archaic* a person of India. ● *adj.* **1** of or concerning Hindus or Hinduism. **2** *archaic* of India. [Urdu f. Pers. f. *Hind* India]

Hin·du·ism /híndooizəm/ *n.* the main religious and social system of India, including belief in reincarnation and the worship of several gods. □□ **Hin·du·ize** *v.tr.*

Hin·du·sta·ni /híndoōstaánee, –stánee/ *n. & adj.* ● *n.* **1** a language based on Western Hindi, with elements of Arabic, Persian, etc., used as a lingua franca in much of India. **2** *archaic* Urdu. ● *adj.* of or relating to Hindustan or its people, or Hindustani. [Urdu f. Pers. *hindūstānī* (as HINDU, *stān* country)]

hinge /hinj/ *n. & v.* ● *n.* **1 a** a movable, usu. metal, joint or mechanism such as that by which a door is hung on a side post. **b** *Biol.* a natural joint performing a similar function, e.g., that of a bivalve shell. **2** a central point or principle on which everything depends. ● *v.* **1** *intr.* (foll. by *on*) **a** depend (on a principle, an event, etc.) (*all hinges on his acceptance*). **b** (of a door, etc.) hang and turn (on a post, etc.). **2** *tr.* attach with or as if with a hinge. □□ **hinged** *adj.* **hinge·less** *adj.* **hinge·wise** *adv.* [ME *heng*, etc., rel. to HANG]

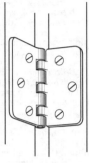

hinge 1a

hin·ny[1] /hínee/ *n.* (*pl.* **·nies**) the offspring of a female donkey and a male horse. [L *hinnus* f. Gk *hinnos*]

hin·ny[2] /hínee/ *n.* (also **hin·nie**) (*pl.* **·nies**) *Sc. & No. of Engl.* (esp. as a form of address) darling; sweetheart. [var. of HONEY]

hint /hint/ *n. & v.* ● *n.* **1** a slight or indirect indication or suggestion (*took the hint and left*). **2** a small piece of practical information (*handy hints on cooking*). **3** a very small trace; a suggestion (*a hint of perfume*). ● *v.tr.* (often foll. by *that* + clause) suggest slightly (*hinted that they were wrong*). □ **hint at** give a hint of; refer indirectly to. [app. f. obs. *hent* grasp, lay hold of, f. OE *hentan*, f. Gmc, rel. to HUNT]

hin·ter·land /híntərland/ *n.* **1** the often deserted or uncharted areas beyond a coastal district or a river's banks. **2** an area remote from but served by a port or other center. **3** a remote or fringe area. [G f. *hinter* behind + *Land* LAND]

hip[1] /hip/ *n.* **1** a projection of the pelvis and upper thigh bone on each side of the body in human beings and quadrupeds. **2** (often in *pl.*) the circumference of the body at the buttocks. **3** *Archit.* the sharp edge of a roof from ridge to eaves where two sides meet. □ **on the hip** *archaic* at a disadvantage. □□ **hip·less** *adj.* **hipped** *adj.* (also in *comb.*). [OE *hype* f. Gmc, rel. to HOP[1]]

hip[2] /hip/ *n.* (also **hep** /hep/) the fruit of a rose, esp. a wild kind. [OE *hēope*, *hīope* f. WG]

hip[3] /hip/ *adj.* (also **hep** /hep/) (**hip·per**, **hip·pest** or **hep·per**, **hep·pest**) *sl.* **1** following the latest fashion in music, clothes, etc.; stylish. **2** (often foll. by *to*) understanding; aware. □□ **hip·ness** *n.* [20th c.: orig. unkn.]

hip[4] /hip/ *int.* introducing a united cheer (*hip, hip, hooray*). [19th c.: orig. unkn.]

hip·bone /hípbōn/ *n.* a bone forming the hip, esp. the ilium.

hip flask *n.* a flask for liquor, etc., carried in a hip pocket.

SYNONYM TIP **hinder**

ENCUMBER, HAMPER, IMPEDE, OBSTRUCT, PREVENT. If you're about to set off on a cross-country trip by car and wake up to find that a foot of snow has fallen overnight, it would be correct to say that the weather has **hindered** you. But if you're trying to drive through a snowstorm and are forced to creep along at a snail's pace behind a snowplow, it would be correct to say you were **impeded**. To *hinder* is to delay or hold something back, especially something that is under way or is about to start (*she entered college but was hindered by poor study habits*); it connotes a thwarting of progress, either deliberate or accidental. *Impede*, on the other hand, means to slow the progress of someone or something and implies that the obstacles are more serious. *Impede* suggests that movement or progress is so slow that it is painful or frustrating (*the shoes were so tight they impeded his circulation*). Both **hamper** and **encumber** involve hindering by outside forces. To *hamper* is to impede by placing restraints on someone or something so as to make action difficult (*hampered by family responsibilities*), while **encumber** means to hinder by the placing of a burden (*encumbered with several heavy suitcases*). To **obstruct** is to place obstacles in the way, often bringing progress or movement to a complete halt (*obstruct traffic; obstruct justice*). **Prevent** suggests precautionary or restraining measures (*the police prevented him from entering the burning building*) and is also used to describe a nonhuman agency or cause that hinders something (*the snow prevented us from leaving that day*).

hip-hop *n.* a style of popular music of US black and Hispanic origin, and the subculture associated with it, including rap music, graffiti art, and breakdancing.

hip-hug·gers *n.pl.* pants hanging from the hips rather than from the waist.

hip joint *n.* the articulation of the head of the thigh bone with the ilium.

hip·pe·a·strum /hípeeástrəm/ *n.* any S. American bulbous plant of the genus *Hippeastrum* with showy white or red flowers. [mod.L f. Gk *hippeus* horseman (the leaves appearing to ride on one another) + *astron* star (from the flower-shape)]

hipped /hipt/ *adj.* (usu. foll. by *on*) *sl.* obsessed; infatuated. [past part. of *hip* (v.) = make hip (HIP³)]

hip·per /hípər/ *n. Austral.* a soft pad used to protect the hip when sleeping on hard ground.

hip·pie /hípee/ *n.* (also **hip·py**) (*pl.* **·pies**) *colloq.* **1** (esp. in the 1960s) a person of unconventional appearance, typically with long hair, jeans, beads, etc., often associated with hallucinogenic drugs and a rejection of conventional values. **2** = HIPSTER². [HIP³]

hip·po /hípō/ *n.* (*pl.* **·pos**) *colloq.* a hippopotamus. [abbr.]

hip·po·cam·pus /hípōkámpəs/ *n.* (*pl.* **hip·po·cam·pi** /–pī/) **1** any marine fish of the genus *Hippocampus*, swimming vertically and with a head suggestive of a horse; a sea horse. **2** *Anat.* the elongated ridges on the floor of each lateral ventricle of the brain, thought to be the center of emotion and the autonomic nervous system. [L f. Gk *hippokampos* f. *hippos* horse + *kampos* sea monster]

hip·po·cras /hípəkras/ *n. hist.* wine flavored with spices. [ME f. OF *ipocras* Hippocrates (see HIPPOCRATIC OATH), prob. because strained through a filter called "Hippocrates' sleeve"]

Hip·po·crat·ic oath /hípəkrátik/ *n.* an oath taken by doctors affirming their obligations and proper conduct. [med.L *Hippocraticus* f. *Hippocrates*, Gk physician of the 5th c. BC]

Hip·po·crene /hípəkreen/ *n. poet.* poetic or literary inspiration. [name of a fountain on Mount Helicon sacred to the Muses: L f. Gk f. *hippos* horse + *krēnē* fountain, as having been produced by a stroke of Pegasus' hoof]

hip·po·drome /hípədrōm/ *n.* **1** an arena used for equestrian or other sporting events. **2** (in classical antiquity) a course for chariot races, etc. [F *hippodrome* or L *hippodromus* f. Gk *hippodromos* f. *hippos* horse + *dromos* race, course]

hip·po·griff /hípəgrif/ *n.* (also **hip·po·gryph**) a mythical griffinlike creature with the body of a horse. [F *hippogriffe* f. It. *ippogrifo* f. Gk *hippos* horse + It. *grifo* GRIFFIN]

hip·po·pot·a·mus /hípəpótəməs/ *n.* (*pl.* **hip·po·pot·a·mus·es** or **hip·po·pot·a·mi** /–mī/) **1** a large thick-skinned four-legged mammal, *Hippopotamus amphibius*, native to Africa, inhabiting rivers, lakes, etc. **2** (in full **pygmy hippopotamus**) a smaller related mammal, *Choeropsis liberiensis*, native to Africa, inhabiting forests and swamps. [ME f. L f. Gk *hippopotamos* f. *hippos* horse + *potamos* river]

hippopotamus

hip·py¹ var. of HIPPIE.

hip·py² /hípee/ *adj.* having large hips.

hip roof *n.* (also **hipped roof**) a roof with the sides and the ends inclined.

hip·ster¹ /hípstər/ *adj. & n. Brit.* • *adj.* (of a garment) having the waistline at the hips rather than at the waist. • *n.* (in pl.) = HIP-HUGGERS.

hip·ster² /hípstər/ *n. sl.* a person who is stylish or hip. □□ **hip·ster·ism** *n.*

hi·ra·ga·na /héerəgáanə/ *n.* the cursive form of Japanese syllabic writing or kana (cf. KATAKANA). [Jap., = plain kana]

hir·cine /hársin, –sin/ *adj.* goatlike. [L *hircinus* f. *hircus* goat]

hire /hīr/ *v. & n.* • *v.tr.* **1** employ (a person) for wages or a fee. **2** (often foll. by *from*) procure the temporary use of (a thing) for an agreed payment; rent or lease. **3** *archaic* borrow (money). • *n.* **1** hiring or being hired. **2** *esp. Brit.* payment for this. **3** a person who is hired. □ **for** (or **on**) **hire** ready to be hired. **hire out** grant the temporary use of (a thing) for an agreed payment. □□ **hir·a·ble** *adj.* (also **hire·a·ble**). **hir·er** *n.* [OE *hȳrian*, *hȳr* f. WG]

hire·ling /hírling/ *n.* usu. *derog.* a person who works for hire. [OE *hȳrling* (as HIRE, –LING¹)]

hir·sute /hársyŏŏt/ *adj.* **1** hairy; shaggy. **2** untrimmed. □□ **hir·sute·ness** *n.* [L *hirsutus*]

hir·sut·ism /hársyŏŏtizəm/ *n.* the excessive growth of hair on the face and body.

his /hiz/ *poss.pron.* **1** (*attrib.*) of or belonging to him or himself (*his house; his own business*). **2** (**His**) (*attrib.*) (in titles) that he is (*His Majesty*). **3** the one or ones belonging to or associated with him (*it is his; his are over there*). □ **his and hers** *joc.* (of matching items) for husband and wife, or men and women. **of his** of or belonging to him (*a friend of his*). [OE, genit. of HE, IT¹]

His·pan·ic /hispánik/ *adj. & n.* • *adj.* **1** of or being a person of Latin-

American or Spanish or Portuguese descent in the US. **2** of or relating to Spain or to Spain and Portugal. **3** of Spain and other Spanish-speaking countries. • *n.* a Spanish-speaking person, esp. one of Latin-American descent, living in the US. □□ **His·pan·i·cize** /–nisiz/ *v.tr.* [L *Hispanicus* f. *Hispania* Spain]

His·pan·ist /híspənist/ *n.* (also **His·pan·i·cist** /hispánisist/) an expert in or student of the language, literature, and civilization of Spain.

Hispano- /hispánō/ *comb. form* Spanish. [L *Hispanus* Spanish]

his·pid /híspid/ *adj. Bot. & Zool.* **1** rough with bristles; bristly. **2** shaggy. [L *hispidus*]

hiss /his/ *v. & n.* • *v.* **1** *intr.* (of a person, snake, goose, etc.) make a sharp sibilant sound, esp. as a sign of disapproval or derision (*audience booed and hissed; the water hissed on the hot plate*). **2** *tr.* express disapproval of (a person, etc.) by hisses. **3** *tr.* whisper (a threat, etc.) urgently or angrily (*"Where's the door?" he hissed*). • *n.* **1** a sharp sibilant sound as of the letter *s*, esp. as an expression of disapproval or derision. **2** *Electronics* unwanted interference at audio frequencies. □ **hiss away** (or **down**) drive off, etc., by hisses. **hiss off** hiss (actors, etc.) so that they leave the stage. [ME: imit.]

hist /hist/ *int. archaic* used to call attention, enjoin silence, incite a dog, etc. [16th c.: natural excl.]

hist. *abbr.* **1** historian. **2** historical. **3** history.

his·ta·mine /hístəmin, –meen/ *n. Biochem.* an organic compound occurring in injured body tissues, etc., and also associated with allergic reactions. □□ **his·ta·min·ic** /–mínik/ *adj.* [HISTO- + AMINE]

his·ti·dine /hístideen/ *n. Biochem.* an amino acid from which histamine is derived. [Gk *histos* web, tissue]

histo- /hístō/ *comb. form* (before a vowel also **hist-**) *Biol.* tissue. [Gk *histos* web]

his·to·chem·is·try /hístōkémistree/ *n.* the study of the identification and distribution of the chemical constituents of tissues by means of stains, indicators, and microscopy. □□ **his·to·chem·i·cal** *adj.*

his·to·gen·e·sis /hístōjénisis/ *n.* the formation of tissues. □□ **his·to·ge·net·ic** /–jinétik/ *adj.*

his·tog·e·ny /histójinee/ *n.* = HISTOGENESIS. □□ **his·to·gen·ic** /hístəjénik/ *adj.*

his·to·gram /hístəgram/ *n. Statistics* a chart consisting of rectangles (usu. drawn vertically from a base line) whose areas and positions are proportional to the value or range of a number of variables. [Gk *histos* mast + –GRAM]

his·tol·o·gy /históləjee/ *n.* the study of the structure of tissues. □□ **his·to·log·i·cal** /hístəlójikəl/ *adj.* **his·tol·o·gist** /históləjist/ *n.*

his·tol·y·sis /histólisis/ *n.* the breaking down of tissues. □□ **his·to·lyt·ic** /–təlítik/ *adj.*

his·tone /hístōn/ *n. Biochem.* any of a group of proteins found in chromatin. [G *Histon* perh. f. Gk *histamai* arrest, or as HISTO-]

his·to·pa·thol·o·gy /hístōpəthóləjee/ *n.* **1** changes in tissues caused by disease. **2** the study of these.

his·to·ri·an /histáwreeən/ *n.* **1** a writer of history, esp. a critical analyst, rather than a compiler. **2** a person learned in or studying history (*English historian; ancient historian*). [F *historien* f. L (as HISTORY)]

his·to·ri·at·ed /histáwreeaytid/ *adj.* = STORIATED. [med.L *historiare* (as HISTORY)]

his·tor·ic /histáwrik, –stór–/ *adj.* **1** famous or important in history or potentially so (*a historic moment*). **2** *Gram.* (of a tense) normally used in the narration of past events (esp. Latin & Greek imperfect and pluperfect; (cf. PRIMARY)). **3** = HISTORICAL. [L *historicus* f. Gk *historikos* (as HISTORY)]

▶Historic and *historical* denote different things. The former means 'important; notable': *historic leaders, historic battles.* The latter means 'relating to history': *historical writings.* An event can be either historical or historic, depending on whether it is viewed as part of history or as extremely important. Note also that both of these words, traditionally preceded by *a*, are now often used with *an*: *a historic moment, an historic moment.*

his·tor·i·cal /histáwrikəl, –stór–/ *adj.* **1** of or concerning history (*historical evidence*). **2** belonging to history, not to prehistory or legend. **3** (of the study of a subject) based on an analysis of its development over a period. **4** belonging to the past, not the present. **5** (of a novel, a movie, etc.) dealing or professing to deal with historical events. **6** in connection with history; from the historian's point of view (*of purely historical interest*). □□ **his·tor·i·cal·ly** *adv.*

his·tor·ic in·fin·i·tive *n.* the infinitive when used instead of the indicative.

his·tor·i·cism /histáwrisizəm, –stór–/ *n.* **1 a** the theory that social and cultural phenomena are determined by history. **b** the belief that historical events are governed by laws. **2** the tendency to regard historical development as the most basic aspect of human existence. **3** an excessive regard for past styles, etc. □□ **his·tor·i·cist** *n.* [HISTORIC after G *Historismus*]

his·to·ric·i·ty /hístərísitee/ *n.* the historical genuineness of an event, etc.

his·tor·ic pres·ent *n.* the present tense used instead of the past in vivid narration.

his·to·ri·og·ra·pher /histáwreeógrəfər/ *n.* **1** an expert in or student of historiography. **2** a writer of history, esp. an official historian. [ME f. F *historiographe* or f. LL *historiographus* f. Gk *historiographos* (as HISTORY, –GRAPHER)]

his·to·ri·og·ra·phy /histáwreeógrəfee/ *n.* **1** the writing of history. **2** the study of historical writing. □□ **his·to·ri·o·graph·ic** /–reeəgráfik/ *adj.* **his·to·ri·o·graph·i·cal** *adj.* [med.L *historiographia* f. Gk *historiographia* (as HISTORY, –GRAPHY)]

his·to·ry /hístəree/ *n.* (*pl.* **-ries**) **1** a continuous, usu. chronological, record of important or public events. **2 a** the study of past events, esp. human affairs. **b** the total accumulation of past events, esp. relating to human affairs or to the accumulation of developments connected with a particular nation, person, thing, etc. (*our nation's history; the history of astronomy*). **c** the past in general; antiquity. **3** an eventful past (*this house has a history*). **4 a** a systematic or critical account of or research into a past event or events, etc. **b** a similar record or account of natural phenomena. **5** a historical play. □ **make history 1** influence the course of history. **2** do something memorable.

> **WORD HISTORY** | history
>
> Late Middle English (also as a verb): via Latin from Greek *historia* 'finding out, narrative, history,' from *histōr* 'learned, wise man,' from an Indo-European root shared by WIT[2].

his·tri·on·ic /hístreeónik/ *adj. & n.* • *adj.* **1** of or concerning actors or acting. **2** (of behavior) theatrical; dramatic. • *n.* **1** (in *pl.*) **a** insincere and dramatic behavior designed to impress. **b** theatricals; theatrical art. **2** *archaic* an actor. □□ **his·tri·on·i·cal·ly** *adv.* [LL *histrionicus* f. L *histrio –onis* actor]

hit /hit/ *v. & n.* • *v.* (**hit·ting**; *past* and *past part.* **hit**) **1** *tr.* **a** strike with a blow or a missile. **b** (of a moving body) strike (*the plane hit the ground*). **c** reach (a target, a person, etc.) with a directed missile (*hit the window with the ball*). **2** *tr.* cause to suffer or affect adversely; wound (*the loss hit him hard*). **3** *intr.* (often foll. by *at, against, upon*) direct a blow. **4** *tr.* (often foll. by *against, on*) knock (a part of the body) (*hit his head on the door frame*). **5** *tr.* light upon; get at (a thing aimed at) (*he's hit the truth at last; tried to hit the right tone in her apology*) (see *hit on*). **6** *tr. colloq.* **a** encounter (*hit a snag*). **b** arrive at (*hit an all-time low; hit the town*). **c** indulge in, esp. liquor, etc. (*hit the bottle*). **7** *tr. sl.* rob or kill. **8** *tr.* occur forcefully to (*the seriousness of the situation only hit him later*). **9** *tr. Sports* **a** propel (a ball, etc.) with a bat, etc. **b** score (runs, etc.) in this way. **c** (usu. foll. by *for*) strike (a ball or a pitcher, etc.) for a specific hit, result, etc. **10** *tr.* represent exactly. **11** *tr. sl.* (often foll. by *up*) ask (a person) for; beg. • *n.* **1 a** a blow; a stroke. **b** a collision. **2 a** shot, etc., that hits its target. **3** *colloq.* a popular success in entertainment. **4** a stroke of sarcasm, wit, etc. **5** a stroke of good luck. **6** *sl.* **a** a murder or other violent crime. **b** a drug injection, etc. **7** a successful attempt. **8** *Baseball* = BASE HIT. □ **hit and run 1** cause (accidental or willful) damage and escape or leave the scene before being discovered. **2** *Baseball* play in which a base runner begins running to the next base as the pitcher delivers the ball and the batter then tries to hit the thrown ball. **hit back** retaliate. **hit below the belt 1** esp. *Boxing* give a foul blow. **2** treat or behave unfairly. **hit for six** *Brit.* defeat in an argument. **hit the hay** (or **sack**) *colloq.* go to bed. **hit the headlines** see HEADLINE. **hit home** make a salutary impression. **hit it off** (often foll. by *with, together*) agree or be congenial. **hit the nail on the head** state the truth exactly. **hit on** (or **upon**) find (what is sought); esp. by chance. **hit out** deal vigorous physical or verbal blows (*hit out at her enemies*). **hit the road** (or **trail**) *sl.* depart. **hit the roof** see ROOF. **hit the spot** *colloq.* find out or do exactly what was needed. **hit up 1** sense 11 of *v.* **2** *Cricket* score (runs) energetically. **hit wicket** *Cricket* be out by striking the wicket with the bat, etc. **make a hit** (usu. foll. by *with*) be successful or popular. □□ **hit·ter** *n.* [ME f. OE *hittan* f. ON *hitta* meet with, of unkn. orig.]

hit-and-run *attrib.adj.* relating to or (of a person) committing an act or play of this kind.

hitch /hich/ *v. & n.* • *v.* **1 a** *tr.* fasten with a loop, hook, etc.; tether (*hitched the horse to the cart*). **b** *intr.* (often foll. by *in, onto*, etc.) become fastened in this way (*the rod hitched in to the bracket*). **2** *tr.* move (a thing) with a jerk; shift slightly (*hitched the pillow to a comfortable position*). **3** *colloq.* **a** *intr.* = HITCHHIKE. **b** *tr.* obtain (a ride) by hitchhiking. **4** *colloq.* (as **hitched** *adj.*) married. • *n.* **1** an impediment; a temporary obstacle. **2** an abrupt pull or push; a jerk. **3 a** a noose or knot of various kinds. **b** the connector assembly between a vehicle and something being towed. **4** *colloq.* a free ride in a vehicle. **5** *sl.* a period of service. □ **get hitched** *colloq.* marry. **hitch up** lift (esp. clothing) with a jerk. **hitch one's wagon to a star** make

use of powers higher than one's own. □□ **hitch·er** *n.* [ME: orig. uncert.]

hitch·hike /hích-hīk/ *v. & n.* • *v.intr.* travel by seeking free rides in passing vehicles. • *n.* a journey made by hitchhiking. □□ **hitch·hik·er** *n.*

hi-tech /híték/ *n.* = HIGH TECH. [abbr.]

hith·er /híthər/ *adv. & adj.* usu. *formal* or *literary* • *adv.* to or toward this place. • *adj.* situated on this side; the nearer (of two). [OE *hider*: cf. THITHER]

hith·er and thith·er *adv.* (also **hither and yon**) in various directions; esp. in a disorganized way.

hith·er·to /híthərtóō/ *adv.* until this time; up to now.

hith·er·ward /híthərwərd/ *adv. archaic* in this direction.

Hit·ler /hítlər/ *n.* a person who embodies the authoritarian characteristics of Adolf Hitler, Ger. dictator d. 1945. □□ **Hit·ler·ite** /–rīt/ *n. & adj.*

Hit·ler·ism /hítlərizəm/ *n.* the political principles or policy of the Nazi Party in Germany. [HITLER]

hit list *n. sl.* a list of prospective victims.

hit man *n.* (*pl.* **hit men**) *sl.* a hired assassin.

hit-or-miss *adj.* careless, haphazard.

hit pa·rade *n. colloq.* a list of the current best-selling records of popular music.

Hit·tite /hítīt/ *n. & adj.* • *n.* **1** a member of an ancient people of Asia Minor and Syria. **2** the extinct language of the Hittites. • *adj.* of or relating to the Hittites or their language. [Heb. *Hittīm*]

HIV *abbr.* human immunodeficiency virus, either of two retroviruses causing AIDS.

hive /hīv/ *n. & v.* • *n.* **1 a** a beehive. **b** the bees in a hive. **2** a busy swarming place. **3** a swarming multitude. **4** a thing shaped like a hive in being domed. • *v.* **1** *tr.* **a** place (bees) in a hive. **b** house (people, etc.) snugly. **2** *intr.* **a** enter a hive. **b** live together like bees. □ **hive off** esp. *Brit.* **1** separate from a larger group. **2 a** form into or assign (work) to a subsidiary department or company. **b** denationalize or privatize (an industry, etc.). **hive up** hoard. [OE *hȳf* f. Gmc]

hives /hīvz/ *n.pl.* a skin eruption, esp. nettle rash. [16th c. (orig. Sc.): orig. unkn.]

hiya /híyə/ *int. colloq.* a word used in greeting. [corrupt. of *how are you?*]

HK *abbr.* Hong Kong.

HL *abbr.* (in the UK) House of Lords.

hl *abbr.* hectoliter(s).

HM *abbr. Brit.* **1** headmaster or headmistress. **2** heavy metal (music). **3** Her (or His) Majesty('s)

hm *abbr.* hectometer(s).

h'm /hm/ *int. & n.* (also **hmm**) = HEM[2], HUM[2].

HMO *abbr.* health maintenance organization.

HMS *abbr.* Her or His Majesty's Ship.

Ho *symb. Chem.* the element holmium.

ho /hō/ *int.* **1 a** an expression of surprise, admiration, triumph, or (often repeated as **ho! ho!**, etc.) derision. **b** (in *comb.*) (*heigh-ho; what ho*). **2 a** call for attention. **b** (in *comb.*) *Naut.* an addition to the name of a destination, etc. (*westward ho*). [ME, imit.: cf. ON *hó*]

ho. *abbr.* house.

hoa·gie /hōgee/ *n.* (also **hoa·gy**) (*pl.* **-gies**) = SUBMARINE SANDWICH. [orig. unknown]

hoar /hawr/ *adj. & n. literary* • *adj.* **1** gray-haired with age. **2** grayish white. **3** (of a thing) gray with age. • *n.* **1** = HOARFROST. **2** hoariness. [OE *hār* f. Gmc]

hoard /hawrd/ *n. & v.* • *n.* **1** a stock or store (esp. of money) laid by. **2** an amassed store of facts, etc. **3** *Archaeol.* an ancient store of treasure, etc. • *v.* **1** *tr.* (often *absol.*; often foll. by *up*) amass (money, etc.) and put away; store. **2** *intr.* accumulate more than one's current requirements of food, etc., in a time of scarcity. **3** *tr.* store in the mind. □□ **hoard·er** *n.* [OE *hord* f. Gmc]

hoard·ing /háwrding/ *n.* **1** a board fence erected around a building site, etc., often used for displaying posters, etc. **2** *Brit.* a large, usu. wooden, structure used to carry advertisements, etc.; a billboard. [obs. *hoard* f. AF *h(o)urdis* f. OF *hourd, hort*, rel. to HURDLE]

hoar·frost /háwrfrawst/ *n.* frozen water vapor deposited in clear still weather on vegetation, etc.

hoar·hound var. of HOREHOUND.

hoarse /hawrs/ *adj.* **1** (of the voice) rough and deep; husky; croaking. **2** having such a voice. □□ **hoarse·ly** *adv.* **hoars·en** *v.tr. & intr.* **hoarse·ness** *n.* [ME f. ON *hārs* (unrecorded) f. Gmc]

hoar·stone /háwrstōn/ *n. Brit.* an ancient boundary stone.

hoar·y /háwree/ *adj.* (**hoar·i·er, hoar·i·est**) **1 a** (of hair) gray or white with age. **b** having such hair; aged. **2** old and trite (*a hoary joke*). **3** *Bot. & Zool.* covered with short white hairs. □□ **hoar·i·ly** *adv.* **hoar·i·ness** *n.*

ho·at·zin /hwaatseén/ *n.* a tropical American bird, *Opisthocomus hoatzin*, whose young climb by means of hooked claws on their wings. [native name, imit.]

hoax /hōks/ *n. & v.* • *n.* a humorous or malicious deception; a practical joke. ● *v. tr.* deceive (a person) with a hoax. □□ **hoax·er** *n.* [18th c.: prob. contr. f. HOCUS]

hob[1] /hob/ *n.* **1 a** a flat metal shelf at the side of a fireplace, having its surface level with the top of the grate, used esp. for keeping things warm. **b** *Brit.* a flat heating surface for a pan on a stove. **2** a tool used for cutting gear teeth, etc. **3** a peg or pin used as a mark in quoits, etc. **4** = HOBNAIL. [perh. var. of HUB, orig. = lump]

hob[2] /hob/ *n.* **1** a male ferret. **2** a hobgoblin. □ **play** (or **raise**) **hob** cause mischief. [ME, familiar form of *Rob*, short for *Robin* or *Robert*]

hob·bit /hóbit/ *n.* a member of an imaginary race of half-sized people in stories by Tolkien. □□ **hob·bi·try** *n.* [invented by J. R. R. Tolkien, Engl. writer d. 1973, and said by him to mean 'hole dweller']

hob·ble /hóbəl/ *v. & n.* ● *v.* **1** *intr.* **a** walk lamely; limp. **b** proceed haltingly in action or speech (*hobbled lamely to his conclusion*). **2** *tr.* **a** tie together the legs of (a horse, etc.) to prevent it from straying. **b** tie (a horse's, etc., legs). **3** *tr.* cause (a person, etc.) to limp. ● *n.* **1** an uneven or infirm gait. **2** a rope, etc., used for hobbling a horse, etc. □□ **hob·bler** *n.* [ME, prob. f. LG: cf. HOPPLE and Du. *hobbelen* rock from side to side]

hob·ble·de·hoy /hóbəldeehoy/ *n. colloq.* **1** a clumsy or awkward youth. **2** a hooligan. [16th c.: orig. unkn.]

hob·ble skirt *n.* a skirt so narrow at the hem as to impede walking, popular between 1910 and 1915.

hob·by[1] /hóbee/ *n.* (*pl.* **·bies**) **1** a favorite leisure time activity or occupation. **2** *archaic* a small horse. □□ **hob·by·ist** *n.* [ME *hobyn, hoby,* f. nicknames for *Robin:* cf. DOBBIN]

hob·by[2] /hóbee/ *n.* (*pl.* **·bies**) any of several small long-winged falcons, esp. *Falco subbuteo,* catching prey on the wing. [ME f. OF *hobé, hobet* dimin. of *hobe* small bird of prey]

hob·by·horse /hóbeehawrs/ *n.* **1** a child's toy consisting of a stick with a horse's head. **2** a preoccupation; a favorite topic of conversation. **3** a model of a horse, esp. of wicker, used in morris dancing, etc. **4** a rocking horse. **5** a horse on a merry-go-round.

hob·gob·lin /hóbgoblin/ *n.* a mischievous imp; a bogy; a bugbear. [HOB[2] + GOBLIN]

hob·nail /hóbnayl/ *n.* a heavy-headed nail used for boot soles. □□ **hob·nailed** *adj.* [HOB[1] + NAIL]

hob·nail liv·er *n.* (or **hob·nailed liv·er**) a liver having many small knobbly projections due to cirrhosis.

hob·nob /hóbnob/ *v.intr.* **1** (usu. foll. by *with*) mix socially or informally. **2** drink together. [*hob or nob* = give or take, of alternate drinking; earlier *hab nab,* = have or not have]

ho·bo /hóbō/ *n.* (*pl.* **·boes** or **·bos**) a wandering worker; a tramp. [19th c.: orig. unkn.]

Hob·son's choice /hóbsənz/ *n.* a choice of taking the thing offered or nothing. [T. *Hobson,* Cambridge liveryman d. 1631, who let out horses on the basis that customers must take the one nearest the door]

hock[1] /hok/ *n.* **1** the joint of a quadruped's hind leg between the knee and the fetlock. **2** a knuckle of pork; the lower joint of a ham. [obs. *hockshin* f. OE *hōhsinu:* see HOUGH]

hock[2] /hok/ *n. Brit.* a German white wine from the Rhineland (properly that of Hochheim on the river Main). [abbr. of obs. *hockamore* f. G *Hochheimer*]

hock[3] /hok/ *v. & n. colloq.* ● *v.tr.* pawn; pledge. ● *n.* a pawnbroker's pledge. □ **in hock 1** in pawn. **2** in debt. **3** in prison. [Du. *hok* hutch, prison, debt]

hock·ey /hókee/ *n.* **1** = ICE HOCKEY. **2** = FIELD HOCKEY. [16th c.: orig. unkn.]

Hock·tide /hóktīd/ *n. Brit. hist.* a festival formerly kept on the second Monday and Tuesday after Easter, orig. for raising money. [ME: orig. unkn.]

ho·cus /hókəs/ *v. tr.* (**ho·cussed, ho·cus·sing;** also **ho·cused, ho·cus·ing**) **1** take in; hoax. **2** stupefy (a person, animal, etc.) with drugs. **3** drug (liquor). [obs. noun *hocus* = HOCUS-POCUS]

ho·cus-po·cus /hókəspókəs/ *n. & v.* ● *n.* **1** deception; trickery. **2 a** a typical verbal formula used in conjuring. **b** language intended to mystify; mumbo-jumbo. **3** conjuring; sleight of hand. ● *v.* (**·po·cussed, ·po·cus·sing;** also **·po·cused, ·po·cus·ing**) **1** *intr.* (often foll. by *with*) play tricks. **2** *tr.* play tricks on; deceive.

WORD HISTORY hocus-pocus

Early 17th century: from *hax pax max Deus adimax,* a pseudo-Latin phrase used as a formula by magicians.

hod /hod/ *n.* **1** a V-shaped open trough on a pole used for carrying bricks, mortar, etc. **2** a portable receptacle for coal. [prob. = dial. *hot* f. OF *hotte* pannier, f. Gmc]

hod·die /hódee/ *n. Austral.* a bricklayer's laborer; a hodman. [HOD + ·IE]

Hodge /hoj/ *n. Brit.* a typical English agricultural laborer. [nickname for the name *Roger*]

hodge·podge /hójpoj/ *n.* a confused mixture, a jumble. [ME, assim. to HODGE]

Hodg·kin's dis·ease /hójkinz/ *n.* a malignant disease of lymphatic tissues usu. characterized by enlargement of the lymph nodes. [T. *Hodgkin,* Engl. physician d. 1866]

hod·man /hódmən/ *n. Brit.* (*pl.* **·men**) **1** a laborer who carries a hod. **2** a literary hack. **3** a person who works mechanically.

hod·o·graph /hódəgraf/ *n.* a curve in which the radius vector represents the velocity of a moving particle. [Gk *hodos* way + ·GRAPH]

hoe /hō/ *n. & v.* ● *n.* a long-handled tool with a thin metal blade, used for weeding, etc. ● *v.* (**hoes, hoed, hoe·ing**) **1** *tr.* weed (crops); loosen (earth); dig up or cut down with a hoe. **2** *intr.* use a hoe. □ **hoe** in *Austral. & NZ sl.* eat eagerly. **hoe into** *Austral. & NZ sl.* attack (food, a person, a task). □□ **ho·er** *n.* [ME *howe* f. OF *houe* f. Gmc]

hoe·cake /hókayk/ *n.* a coarse cake of cornmeal orig. baked on the blade of a hoe.

hoe·down /hódown/ *n.* a lively dance or dance party, esp. one with square dancing.

hog /hawg, hog/ *n. & v.* ● *n.* **1 a** a domesticated pig, esp. one over 120 pounds (54 kg.) and reared for slaughter. **b** any of several other pigs of the family Suidae, e.g., a warthog. **2** *colloq.* a greedy person. **3** (also **hogg**) *Brit. dial.* a young sheep before the first shearing. ● *v.* (**hogged, hog·ging**) **1** *tr. colloq.* take greedily; hoard selfishly. **2** *tr. & intr.* raise (the back), or rise in an arch in the center. □ **go the whole hog** *colloq.* do something completely or thoroughly. □□ **hog·ger** *n.* **hog·gish** *adj.* **hog·gish·ly** *adv.* **hog·gish·ness** *n.* **hog·like** *adj.* [OE *hogg, hocg,* perh. of Celt. orig.]

ho·gan /hógaan, -gən/ *n.* a Navajo dwelling of logs, etc. [Navajo]

hogan

hog·back /háwgbak, hóg–/ *n.* (also **hog's back**) a steep-sided ridge of a hill.

hogg var. of HOG *n.* 3.

hog·get /hógit/ *n. Brit.* a yearling sheep. [HOG]

hog·gin /hógin/ *n.* **1** a mixture of sand and gravel. **2** sifted gravel. [19th c.: orig. unkn.]

Hog·ma·nay /hógmənáy/ *n. Sc.* **1** New Year's Eve. **2** a celebration on this day. **3** a gift of cake, etc., demanded by children at Hogmanay. [17th c.: perh. f. Norman F *hoguinané* f. OF *aguillanneuf* (also = new year's gift)]

hog's back var. of HOGBACK.

hogs·head /háwgz-hed, hógz–/ *n.* **1** a large cask. **2** a liquid or dry measure, usu. about 63 gallons. [ME f. HOG, HEAD: reason for the name unkn.]

hog-tie *v.* (also **hogtie**) **1** secure by fastening the hands and feet or all four feet together. **2** impede or hinder greatly.

hog·wash /háwgwosh, –wawsh, hóg–/ *n.* **1** *colloq.* nonsense; rubbish. **2** kitchen swill, etc., for pigs.

hog·weed /háwgweed, hóg–/ *n.* any of various coarse weeds of the genus *Heracleum,* esp. *H. sphondylium.*

ho-ho /hóhó/ *int.* expressing surprise, triumph, or derision. [redupl. of HO]

ho-hum /hóhúm/ *int.* expressing boredom. [imit. of yawn]

hoick[1] /hoyk/ *v. & n. Brit. colloq.* ● *v.tr.* (often foll. by *out*) lift or pull, esp. with a jerk. ● *n.* a jerky pull; a jerk. [perh. var. of HIKE]

hoick[2] /hoyk/ *v.intr. Brit. sl.* spit. [perh. var. of HAWK[3]]

hoicks var. of YOICKS.

hoi pol·loi /hóy pólóy/ *n.* (often prec. by *the:* see note below) **1** the masses; the common people. **2** the majority. [Gk, = the many]

▶The phrase **hoi polloi** is often preceded by *the: the hoi polloi grew restless as candidate after candidate spoke.* Strictly speaking, the *the* is unnecessary because *hoi* means 'the' (in Greek). Perhaps because of confusion with *hoity-toity,* **hoi polloi** is sometimes wrongly taken to mean its opposite, 'the few, the elite.'

hoist /hoyst/ *v. & n.* ● *v.tr.* **1** raise or haul up. **2** raise by means of ropes and pulleys, etc. ● *n.* **1** an act of hoisting; a lift. **2** an apparatus for hoisting. **3 a** the part of a flag nearest the staff. **b** a group of flags raised as a signal. □ **hoist the flag** stake one's claim to discovered territory by displaying a flag. **hoist one's flag** signify that one takes command. **hoist with** (or **by**) **one's own petard** see PETARD. □□ **hoist·er** *n.* [16th c.: alt. of *hoise* f. (15th-c.) *hysse,* prob. f. LG orig.: cf. LG *hissen*]

hoi·ty-toi·ty /hóyteetóytee/ *adj., int., & n.* ● *adj.* **1** haughty; petulant; snobbish. **2** *archaic* frolicsome. ● *int.* expressing surprised protest at presumption, etc. • *n. archaic* riotous or giddy conduct. [obs. *hoit* indulge in riotous mirth, of unkn. orig.]

hok·ey /hṓkee/ *adj.* (also **hok·y**) (**hok·i·er, hok·i·est**) *sl.* sentimental; melodramatic; artificial. □□ **hok·ey·ness** *n.* (also **hok·i·ness**). **hok·i·ly** *adv.* [HOKUM + -Y²]

ho·key-co·key /hṓkeekṓkee/ *n. Brit.* a dance similar to the hokey-pokey.

ho·key-po·key /hṓkeepṓkee/ *n. colloq.* **1** = HOCUS-POCUS 1. **2** ice cream formerly sold esp. by Italian street vendors. **3** a communal dance performed in a circle with synchronized shaking of the limbs in turn. [perh. f. HOCUS-POCUS]

hok·ku /hṓkoo, hŏk-/ *n.* (*pl.* same) = HAIKU. [Jap.]

ho·kum /hṓkəm/ *n. sl.* **1** sentimental, popular, sensational, or unreal situations, dialogue, etc., in a movie or play, etc. **2** bunkum; rubbish. [20th c.: orig. unkn.]

hok·y var. of HOKEY.

Hol·arc·tic /hōlaárktik, -laártik/ *adj.* of or relating to the geographical distribution of animals in the whole northern or Arctic region. [HOLO- + ARCTIC]

hold¹ /hōld/ *v. & n.* • *v.* (*past* and *past part.* **held** /held/) **1** *tr.* **a** keep fast; grasp (esp. in the hands or arms). **b** (also *refl.*) keep or sustain (a thing, oneself, one's head, etc.) in a particular position (*hold it to the light; held himself erect*). **c** grasp so as to control (*hold the reins*). **2** *tr.* (of a vessel, etc.) contain or be capable of containing (*the pitcher holds two pints; the hall holds 900*). **3** *tr.* possess, gain, or have, esp.: **a** be the owner or tenant of (land, property, stocks, etc.) (*holds the farm from the trust*). **b** gain or have gained (a degree, record, etc.) (*holds the long-jump record*). **c** have the position of (a job or office). **d** have (a specified card) in one's hand. **e** keep possession of (a place, a person's thoughts, etc.) esp. against attack (*held the fort against the enemy; held his place in her estimation*). **4** *intr.* remain unbroken; not give way (*the roof held under the storm*). **5** *tr.* observe; celebrate; conduct (a meeting, festival, conversation, etc.). **6** *tr.* **a** keep (a person, etc.) in a specified condition, place, etc. (*held her prisoner; held him at arm's length*). **b** detain, esp. in custody (*hold him until I arrive*). **7** *tr.* **a** engross (a person or a person's attention) (*the book held him for hours*). **b** dominate (*held the stage*). **8** *tr.* (foll. by *to*) make (a person, etc.) adhere to (terms, a promise, etc.). **9** *intr.* (of weather) continue fine. **10** *tr.* (often foll. by *to* + infin., or *that* + clause) think; believe (*held it to be self-evident; held that the earth was flat*). **11** *tr.* regard with a specified feeling (*held him in contempt*). **12** *tr.* **a** cease; restrain (*hold your fire*). **b** *colloq.* withhold; not use (*a burger please, and hold the onions!*). **13** *tr.* keep or reserve (*will you hold our seats please?*). **14** *tr.* be able to drink (liquor) without effect (*can hold his liquor*). **15** *tr.* (usu. foll. by *that* + clause) (of a judge, a court, etc.) lay down; decide. **16** *intr.* keep going (*held on his way*). **17** *tr. Mus.* sustain (a note). **18** *intr. archaic* restrain oneself. • *n.* **1** a grasp (*catch hold of him; keep a hold on her*). **2** (often in *comb.*) a thing to hold by (*seized the handhold*). **3** (foll. by *on, over*) influence over (*has a strange hold over them*). **4** a manner of holding in wrestling, etc. **5** *archaic* a fortress. □ **hold (a thing) against (a person)** resent or regard it as discreditable to (a person). **hold aloof** avoid communication with people, etc. **hold back 1** impede the progress of; restrain. **2** keep (a thing) to or for oneself. **3** (often foll. by *from*) hesitate; refrain. **hold one's breath** see BREATH. **hold by** (or **to**) adhere to (a choice, purpose, etc.). **hold cheap** *Brit.* not value highly; despise. **hold the clock on** time (a sporting event, etc.). **hold court** preside over one's admirers, etc.; be the center of attention. **hold dear** regard with affection. **hold down 1** repress. **2** *colloq.* be competent enough to keep (one's job, etc.). **hold everything!** (or **it!**) cease action or movement. **hold for ransom 1** keep (a person) prisoner until a ransom is paid. **2** demand concessions from by threats of esp. damaging action. **hold the fort 1** act as a temporary substitute. **2** cope in an emergency. **hold forth 1** offer (an inducement, etc.). **2** usu. *derog.* speak at length or tediously. **hold good** (or **true**) be valid; apply. **hold one's ground** see GROUND¹. **hold one's hand** see HAND. **hold a person's hand** give a person guidance or moral support. **hold hands** grasp one another by the hand as a sign of affection or for support or guidance. **hold hard!** *Brit.* stop!; wait! **hold harmless** *Law* indemnify. **hold one's head high** behave proudly and confidently. **hold one's horses** *colloq.* stop; slow down. **hold in** keep in check; confine. **hold it good** *Brit.* think it advisable. **hold the line 1** not yield. **2** maintain a telephone connection. **hold one's nose** compress the nostrils to avoid a bad smell. **hold off 1** delay; not begin. **2** keep one's distance. **3** keep at a distance; fend off. **hold on 1** keep one's grasp on something. **2** wait a moment. **3** (when telephoning) not hang up. **hold out 1** stretch forth (a hand, etc.). **2** offer (an inducement, etc.). **3** maintain resistance. **4** persist or last. **hold out for** continue to demand. **hold out on** *colloq.* refuse something to (a person). **hold over 1** postpone. **2** retain. **hold something over** threaten (a person) constantly with something. **hold one's own** see OWN. **hold sway** rule or dominate. **hold to bail** *Law* bind by bail. **hold to a draw** manage to achieve a draw against (an opponent thought likely to win). **hold together**

1 cohere. **2** cause to cohere. **hold one's tongue** *colloq.* be silent. **hold up 1 a** support; sustain. **b** maintain (the head, etc.) erect. **c** last; endure. **2** exhibit; display. **3** arrest the progress of; obstruct. **4** stop and rob by violence or threats. **hold water** (of reasoning) be sound; bear examination. **hold with** (usu. with *neg.*) *colloq.* approve of (*don't hold with motorcycles*). **left holding the bag** (*Brit.* **baby**) left with unwelcome responsibility. **on hold 1** in abeyance; temporarily deferred. **2** (of a telephone call or caller) holding on (see *hold on* 3 above). **take hold** (of a custom or habit) become established. **there is no holding him** (or **her**, etc.) he (or she, etc.) is restive, high-spirited, determined, etc. **with no holds barred** with no restrictions; all methods being permitted. □□ **hold·a·ble** *adj.* [OE *h(e)aldan, heald*]

hold² /hōld/ *n.* a cavity in the lower part of a ship or aircraft in which the cargo is stowed. [obs. *holl* f. OE *hol* (orig. adj. = hollow), rel. to HOLE, assim. to HOLD¹]

hold·all /hṓldawl/ *n. esp. Brit.* a portable case for miscellaneous articles.

hold·back /hṓldbak/ *n.* a hindrance or thing held back.

hold·er /hṓldər/ *n.* **1** (often in *comb.*) a device or implement for holding something (*cigarette holder*). **2 a** the possessor of a title, etc. **b** the occupant of an office, etc. **3** = SMALLHOLDER.

hold·fast /hṓldfast/ *n.* **1** a firm grasp. **2** a staple or clamp securing an object to a wall, etc. **3** the attachment organ of an alga, etc.

hold·ing /hṓlding/ *n.* **1 a** land held by lease (cf. SMALLHOLDING). **b** the tenure of land. **2** stocks, property, etc., held.

hold·ing com·pa·ny *n.* a company created to hold the shares of other companies, which it then controls.

hold·o·ver /hṓldōvər/ *n.* a relic.

hold·up /hṓldəp/ *n.* **1** a stoppage or delay by traffic, fog, etc. **2** a robbery, esp. by the use of threats or violence.

hole /hōl/ *n. & v.* • *n.* **1 a** an empty space in a solid body. **b** an aperture in or through something. **c** flaw; weakness; gap. **2** an animal's burrow. **3** a cavity or receptacle for a ball in various sports or games. **4 a** *colloq.* a small, mean, or dingy abode. **b** a dungeon; a prison cell. **5** *colloq.* an awkward situation. **6** *Golf* **a** a point scored by a player who gets the ball from tee to hole with the fewest strokes. **b** the terrain or distance from tee to hole. **7** a position from which an electron is absent, esp. acting as a mobile positive particle in a semiconductor. • *v.tr.* **1** make a hole or holes in. **2** pierce the side of (a ship). **3** put into a hole. **4** (also *absol.*; often foll. by *out*) send (a golf ball) into a hole. □ **hole up** *colloq.* hide oneself. **in holes** worn so much that holes have formed. **make a hole in** use a large amount of. **a round** (or **square**) **peg in a square** (or **round**) **hole** see PEG. □□ **hol·ey** *adj.* [OE *hol, holian* (as HOLD²)]

hole-and-cor·ner *adj.* attempting to avoid public notice; secret.

hole in one *n. Golf* a shot that enters the hole from the tee.

hole in the heart *n.* a congenital defect in the heart septum.

hole in the wall *n.* a small dingy place (esp. of a business).

-holic var. of -AHOLIC.

hol·i·day /hóliday/ *n. & v.* • *n.* **1** a day of festivity or recreation when no work is done, esp. a religious festival, etc. **2** esp. *Brit.* (often in *pl.*) = VACATION. **3** (*attrib.*) (of clothes, etc.) festive. • *v.intr.* esp. *Brit.* spend a holiday in a specified place. □ **on holiday** (or **one's holidays**) *Brit.* in the course of one's vacation. **take a** (or *archaic* **make**) **holiday** have a break from work. [OE *hāligdæg* (HOLY, DAY)]

hol·i·day camp *n. Brit.* a vacation resort with accommodations, entertainment, and leisure facilities. on site.

hol·i·day-mak·er *n. esp. Brit.* a person on vacation away from home.

ho·li·er-than-thou *adj. colloq.* self-righteous.

ho·li·ly /hṓlilee/ *adv.* in a holy manner. [OE *hāliglīce* (as HOLY)]

ho·li·ness /hṓleenis/ *n.* **1** sanctity; the state of being holy. **2** (**Holiness**) a title used when referring to or addressing the Pope. [OE *hālignes* (as HOLY)]

ho·lism /hṓlizəm/ *n.* (also **who·lism**) **1** *Philos.* the theory that certain wholes are to be regarded as greater than the sum of their parts (cf. REDUCTIONISM). **2** *Med.* the treating of the whole person including mental and social factors rather than just the symptoms of a disease. □□ **ho·lis·tic** *adj.* **ho·lis·ti·cal·ly** *adv.* [as HOLO- + -ISM]

hol·la /hólə/ *int., n., & v.* • *int., n.* a cry of "holla." • *v.* (**hol·las, hol·laed** or **hol·la'd, hol·la·ing**) **1** *intr.* shout. **2** *tr.* call to (hounds). [F *holà* (as HO, *là* there)]

hol·land /hólənd/ *n.* a smooth, hard-wearing, linen fabric. [*Holland* = Netherlands: Du., earlier *Holtlant* f. *holt* wood + -*lant* land, describing the Dordrecht district]

hol·lan·daise sauce /hóləndáyz/ *n.* a creamy sauce of melted butter, egg yolks, and lemon juice or vinegar, etc., served esp. with fish, vegetables, etc. [F, fem. of *hollandais* Dutch f. *Hollande* Holland]

Hol·land·er /hóləndər/ *n.* **1** a native of Holland (the Netherlands). **2** a Dutch ship.

Hol·lands /hóləndz/ *n.* gin made in Holland. [Du. *hollandsch genever* Dutch gin]

hol·ler /hólər/ *v. & n. colloq.* • *v.* **1** *intr.* make a loud cry or noise. **2** *tr.* express with a loud cry or shout. • *n.* a loud cry, noise, or shout. [var. of HOLLO]

hol·lo /hólō/ *int., n., & v.* • *int.* = HOLLA. • *n.* (*pl.* **·los**) = HOLLA. • *v.* (· loes, ·loed) (also **hol·low** *pronunc.* same) = HOLLA. [rel. to HOLLA]

hol·low /hólō/ *adj., n., v., & adv.* • *adj.* **1 a** having a hole or cavity inside; not solid throughout. **b** having a depression; sunken (*hollow cheeks*). **2** (of a sound) echoing, as though made in or on a hollow container. **3** empty; hungry. **4** without significance; meaningless (*a hollow triumph*). **5** insincere; cynical; false (*a hollow laugh*; *hollow promises*). • *n.* **1** a hollow place; a hole. **2** a valley; a basin. • *v.tr.* (often foll. by *out*) make hollow; excavate. • *adv. colloq.* completely (*beaten hollow*). □ **in the hollow** (also **palm**) **of one's hand** entirely subservient to one. □□ **hol·low·ly** *adv.* **hol·low·ness** *n.* [ME *holg, holu, hol(e)we* f. OE *holh* cave, rel. to HOLE]

hol·low-eyed *adj.* having sunken eyes.

hol·low-heart·ed *adj.* insincere.

hol·low square *n. Mil. hist.* a body of infantry drawn up in a square with a space in the middle.

hol·low·ware /hólōwair/ *n.* hollow articles of metal, china, etc., such as pots, kettles, pitchers, etc. (opp. FLATWARE).

hol·ly /hólee/ *n.* (*pl.* **·lies**) **1** any evergreen shrub of the genus *Ilex*, often with prickly usu. dark green leaves, small white flowers, and red berries. **2** its branches and foliage used as decorations at Christmas. [OE *hole(g)n*]

hol·ly·hock /hóleehok/ *n.* a tall plant, *Alcea rosea*, with large showy flowers of various colors. [ME (orig. = marsh mallow) f. HOLY + obs. *hock* mallow, OE *hoc*, of unkn. orig.]

hol·ly oak *n.* a holm oak.

Hol·ly·wood /hóleewŏŏd/ *n.* the American movie industry or its products, with its principal center at Hollywood, California.

holm[1] /hōm/ *n.* (also **holme**) *Brit.* **1** an islet, esp. in a river or near a mainland. **2** a piece of flat ground by a river, which is submerged in time of flood. [ON *holmr*]

holm[2] /hōm/ *n.* (in full **holm oak**) an evergreen oak, *Quercus ilex*, with hollylike young leaves. [ME alt. of obs. *holin* (as HOLLY)]

hol·mi·um /hólmeeəm/ *n. Chem.* a soft silvery metallic element of the lanthanide series occurring naturally in apatite. ¶ Symb.: **Ho**. [mod.L f. *Holmia* Stockholm]

holo- /hólō/ *comb. form* whole (*Holocene*; *holocaust*). [Gk *holos* whole]

hol·o·caust /hóləkawst/ *n.* **1** a case of large-scale destruction or slaughter, esp. by fire or nuclear war. **2** (**the Holocaust**) the mass murder of the Jews by the Nazis in World War II. **3** a sacrifice wholly consumed by fire. [ME f. OF *holocauste* f. LL *holocaustum* f. Gk *holokauston* (as HOLO-, *kaustos* burned f. *kaiō* burn)]

Hol·o·cene /hóləseen/ *adj. & n. Geol.* • *adj.* of or relating to the most recent epoch of the Quaternary period with evidence of human development and intervention, and the extinction of large mammals. • *n.* this period or system. Also called **Recent**. [HOLO- + Gk *kainos* new]

hol·o·en·zyme /hólō-énzīm/ *n. Biochem.* a complex enzyme consisting of several components.

hol·o·gram /hóləgram/ *n. Physics* **1** a three-dimensional image formed by the interference of light beams from a coherent light source. **2** a photograph of the interference pattern, which when suitably illuminated produces a three-dimensional image.

hol·o·graph /hóləgraf/ *adj. & n.* • *adj.* wholly written by hand by the person named as the author. • *n.* a holograph document. [F *holographe* or LL *holographus* f. Gk *holographos* (as HOLO-, -GRAPH)]

hol·og·ra·phy /həlógrəfee/ *n. Physics* the study or production of holograms. □□ **hol·o·graph·ic** /hóləgráfik/ *adj.* **hol·o·graph·i·cal·ly** *adv.*

hol·o·he·dral /hóləheédrəl/ *adj. Crystallog.* having the full number of planes required by the symmetry of a crystal system.

hol·o·phyte /hóləfīt/ *n.* an organism that synthesizes complex organic compounds by photosynthesis. □□ **hol·o·phyt·ic** /-fítik/ *adj.*

hol·o·thu·ri·an /hóləthŏŏreeən/, –thyŏŏr–/ *n. & adj.* • *n.* any echinoderm of the class Holothurioidea, with a wormlike body, e.g., a sea cucumber. • *adj.* of or relating to this class. [mod.L *Holothuria* (n.pl.) f. Gk *holothourion*, a zoophyte]

hol·o·type /hólətīp/ *n.* the specimen used for naming and describing a species.

hols /holz/ *n.pl. Brit. colloq.* holidays. [abbr.]

Hol·stein /hólstīn, -steen/ *n. & adj.* • *n.* **1** a large animal of a usu. black and white breed of dairy cattle orig. from Friesland. **2** this breed. • *adj.* of or concerning Holsteins. [*Holstein* in NW Germany]

hol·ster /hólstər/ *n.* a leather case for a pistol or revolver, worn on a belt or under an arm or fixed to a saddle. [17th c., synonymous with Du. *holster*: orig. unkn.]

holt[1] /hōlt/ *n. Brit.* **1** an animal's (esp. an otter's) lair. **2** *colloq.* or *dial.* grip; hold. [var. of HOLD[1]]

holt[2] /hōlt/ *n. archaic* or *dial.* **1** a wood or copse. **2** a wooded hill. [OE f. Gmc]

holster

ho·lus-bo·lus /hóləsbólas/ *adv.* all in a lump; altogether. [app. sham L]

ho·ly /hólee/ *adj.* (**ho·li·er, ho·li·est**) **1** morally and spiritually excellent or perfect, and to be revered. **2** belonging to, devoted to, or empowered by, God. **3** consecrated; sacred. **4** used as an intensive and in trivial exclamations (*holy cow!*; *holy mackerel!*; *holy Moses!*; *holy smoke!*). [OE *hālig* f. Gmc, rel. to WHOLE]

Ho·ly Cit·y *n.* **1** a city held sacred by the adherents of a religion, esp. Jerusalem. **2** Heaven.

Ho·ly Com·mun·ion *n.* see COMMUNION.

ho·ly day *n.* a religious festival.

Ho·ly Fam·i·ly *n.* the young Jesus with his mother and St. Joseph (often with St. John the Baptist, St. Anne, etc.) as grouped in pictures, etc.

Ho·ly Fa·ther *n.* the Pope.

Ho·ly Ghost *n.* = HOLY SPIRIT.

Ho·ly Grail *n.* see GRAIL.

ho·ly Joe *n. orig. Naut. sl.* **1** a clergyman. **2** a pious person.

Ho·ly Land *n.* **1** W. Palestine, esp. Judaea. **2** a region similarly revered in non-Christian religions.

Ho·ly Of·fice *n.* an office of the Roman Catholic Church succeeding the Inquisition and charged with the protection of faith and morals.

ho·ly of ho·lies *n.* **1** the inner chamber of the sanctuary in the Jewish temple, separated by a veil from the outer chamber. **2** an innermost shrine. **3** a thing regarded as most sacred.

ho·ly or·ders *n.* the status of a member of the clergy, esp. the grades of bishop, priest, and deacon.

ho·ly place *n.* **1** (in *pl.*) places to which religious pilgrimage is made. **2** the outer chamber of the sanctuary in the Jewish temple.

Ho·ly Roll·er *n. sl.* a member of an evangelical Christian group that expresses religious fervor by frenzied excitement or trances.

Ho·ly Ro·man Em·pire *n.* the empire in western Europe following the coronation of Charlemagne as emperor in the year 800, created by the medieval papacy in an attempt to unite Christendom under one rule.

Ho·ly Rood Day *n.* the festival of the Invention (finding) of the Cross, May 3.

Ho·ly Sac·ra·ment *n.* see SACRAMENT.

Ho·ly Sat·ur·day *n.* the Saturday preceding Easter Sunday.

Ho·ly Scrip·ture *n.* the Bible.

Ho·ly See *n.* the papacy or the papal court.

Ho·ly Sep·ul·chre *n.* the tomb in which the body of Christ was laid.

Ho·ly Spir·it *n.* the third person of the Christian Trinity.

ho·ly·stone /hóleestōn/ *n. & v. Naut.* • *n.* a piece of soft sandstone used for scouring decks. • *v.tr.* scour with this. [19th c.: prob. f. HOLY + STONE: the stones were called *bibles*, etc., perh. because used while kneeling]

ho·ly ter·ror *n.* a troublesome person or thing.

Ho·ly Thurs·day *n.* **1** Maundy Thursday. **2** Ascension Day.

Ho·ly Trin·i·ty *n.* see TRINITY.

ho·ly war *n.* a war waged in support of a religious cause.

ho·ly wa·ter *n.* water dedicated to holy uses, or blessed by a priest.

Ho·ly Week *n.* the week before Easter.

Ho·ly Writ *n.* holy writings collectively, esp. the Bible.

Ho·ly Year *n. RC Ch.* a period of remission from the penal consequences of sin, granted under certain conditions for a year usu. at intervals of 25 years.

hom /hōm/ *n.* (also **ho·ma** /hómə/) **1** the soma plant. **2** the juice of this plant as a sacred drink of the Parsees. [Pers. *hōm, hūm*, Avestan *haoma*]

hom·age /hómij/ *n.* **1** acknowledgment of superiority; respect; dutiful reverence (*pay homage to*; *do homage to*). **2** *hist.* formal public acknowledgment of feudal allegiance. [ME f. OF (*h*)*omage* f. med.L *hominaticum* f. L *homo* –*minis* man]

hom·bre /ómbray/ *n.* a man. [Sp.]

Hom·burg /hómbərg/ *n.* a man's felt hat with a narrow curled brim and a lengthwise dent in the crown. [*Homburg* in Germany, where first worn]

home /hōm/ *n., adj., adv., & v.* • *n.* **1 a** the place where one lives; the fixed residence of a family or household. **b** a dwelling house. **2** the members of a family collectively; one's family background (*comes from a good home*). **3** the native land of a person or of a person's ancestors. **4** an institution for persons needing care, rest, or refuge (*nursing home*). **5** the place where a thing originates or is native or most common. **6 a** the finishing point in a race. **b** (in games) the place where one is free from attack; the goal. **c** *Baseball* home plate. **d** *Lacrosse* a player in an attacking position near the opponents' goal. **7** *Sports* a home game or win. • *attrib.adj.* **1 a** of or connected with one's home. **b** carried on, done, or made at home. **c** proceeding from home. **2 a** carried on or produced in one's own country (*home industries*; *the home market*). **b** dealing with the domestic affairs of a country. **3** *Sports* played on one's own field, etc. (*home game*; *home win*). **4** in the neighborhood of home. ● *adv.* **1 a** to one's home or country (*go home*). **b** arrived at home (*is he home yet?*). **c** at home (*stay home*). **2 a** to the point aimed at (*the thrust went home*). **b** as far as possible (*drove the nail home*; *pressed his advantage home*). ● *v.* **1** *intr.* (esp. of a trained pigeon) return home (cf. HOMING 1). **2** *intr.* (often foll. by *on*, *in on*) (of a vessel, missile, etc.) be guided toward a destination or target by a landmark, radio beam, etc. **3** *tr.* send or guide homewards. **4** *tr.* provide with a home. □ **at home 1** in one's own house or native land. **2** at ease as if in one's own home (*make yourself at home*). **3** (usu. foll. by *in*, *on*, *with*) familiar or well informed. **4** available to callers. ● *n.* a social reception in a person's home. **come home to** become fully realized by. **come home to roost** see ROOST. **close** (or **near**) **to home** (of a remark or topic of discussion) relevant or accurate to the point that one feels uncomfortable or embarrassed. **home and dry** *Brit.* having achieved one's purpose. **home away from home** a place other than one's home where one feels at home; a place providing homelike amenities. **home from home** = *home away from home.* **home, James!** *joc.* drive home quickly! □□ **home·like** *adj.* [OE *hām* f. Gmc]

home·bod·y /hómbodee/ *n.* (*pl.* **-ies**) a person who likes to stay at home.

home·boy /hómboy/ *n. colloq.* a person from one's own town or neighborhood.

home brew *n.* beer or other alcoholic drink brewed at home. □□ **home-brewed** *adj.*

home·com·ing /hómkəming/ *n.* **1** arrival at home. **2** a high school, college, or university game, dance, or other event to which alumni are invited to visit.

home ec·o·nom·ics *n.pl.* the study of household management.

home·grown /hómgrōn/ *adj.* grown or produced at home.

home guard *n. hist.* a volunteer group that provides local military defense when the regular army is elsewhere.

home·land /hómland/ *n.* **1** one's native land. **2** *hist.* an area in S. Africa formerly reserved for a particular African people (the official name for a Bantustan).

home·less /hómlis/ *adj. & n.* ● *adj.* lacking a home. ● *n.* (prec. by *the*) homeless people. □□ **home·less·ness** *n.*

home·ly /hómlee/ *adj.* (**home·li·er**, **home·li·est**) **1** (of people or their features) not attractive in appearance; ugly. **2 a** simple; plain. **b** unpretentious. **c** primitive. **3** comfortable in the manner of a home; cozy. **4** skilled at housekeeping. □□ **home·li·ness** *n.*

home·made /hómayd/ *adj.* made at home.

home·mak·er /hómaykər/ *n.* a person who manages a household, esp. as a fulltime occupation.

home mov·ie *n.* a film made at home or without professional equipment, esp. a movie of one's own activities.

Home Of·fice *n.* **1** the British government department dealing with law and order, immigration, etc., in England and Wales. **2** the building used for this.

ho·me·o·path /hómeeəpath/ *n.* a person who practices homeopathy. [G *Homöopath* (as HOMEOPATHY)]

ho·me·op·a·thy /hómeeópəthee/ *n.* (*Brit.* **ho·moe·op·a·thy**) the treatment of disease by minute doses of drugs that in a healthy person would produce symptoms of the disease (cf. ALLOPATHY). □□ **ho·me·o·path·ic** /–meeəpáthik/ *adj.* **ho·me·op·a·thist** *n.* [G *Homöopathie* f. Gk *homoios* like + *patheia* –PATHY]

ho·me·o·sta·sis /hómeeōstáysis/ *n.* (*Brit.* **ho·moe·o·sta·sis**) (*pl.* **·sta·ses** /–seez/) the tendency toward a relatively stable equilibrium between interdependent elements, esp. as maintained by physiological processes. □□ **ho·me·o·stat·ic** /–státik/ *adj.* [mod.L f. Gk *homoios* like + –STASIS]

ho·me·o·therm /hómeeəthérm/ *n.* (also **ho·moe·o·therm** or **ho·moi·o·therm**) an organism that maintains its body temperature at a constant level, usu. above that of the environment, by its metabolic activity; a warm-blooded organism (cf. POIKILOTHERM). □□ **ho·me·o·ther·mal** *adj.* **ho·me·o·ther·mic** *adj.* **ho·me·o·ther·my** *n.* [mod.L f. Gk *homoios* like + *thermē* heat]

home·own·er /hómōnər/ *n.* a person who owns his or her own home.

home plate *n. Baseball* a plate beside which the batter stands and which the runner must cross to score a run.

home port *n.* the port from which a ship originates.

ho·mer /hómər/ *n.* **1** *Baseball* a home run. **2** a homing pigeon.

Ho·mer·ic /hōmérik/ *adj.* **1** of, or in the style of, Homer or the epic poems ascribed to him. **2** of Bronze Age Greece as described in these poems. **3** epic; large-scale; titanic (*Homeric conflict*). [L *Homericus* f. Gk *Homērikos* f. *Homēros* Homer, traditional author of the *Iliad* and the *Odyssey*]

home rule *n.* the government of a country or region by its own citizens.

home run *n.* **1** *Baseball* a hit that allows the batter to make a complete circuit of the bases. **2** any singular success.

Home Sec·re·tar·y *n.* (in the UK) the Secretary of State in charge of the Home Office.

home·sick /hómsik/ *adj.* depressed by longing for one's home during absence from it. □□ **home·sick·ness** *n.*

home sig·nal *n.* a signal indicating whether a train may proceed into a station or to the next section of the line.

home·spun /hómspun/ *adj. & n.* ● *adj.* **1 a** (of cloth) made of yarn spun at home. **b** (of yarn) spun at home. **2** plain; simple; unsophisticated; homely. ● *n.* **1** homespun cloth. **2** anything plain or homely.

home·stead /hómsted/ *n.* **1** a house, esp. a farmhouse, and outbuildings. **2** *Austral. & NZ* the owner's residence on a sheep or cattle station. **3** an area of land (usu. 160 acres) granted to an early American settler as a home. □□ **home·stead·er** *n.* [OE *hāmstede* (as HOME, STEAD)]

homestretch *n.* (also **home stretch**) **1** the concluding straight part of a racetrack. **2** the last part of an activity or campaign.

home·style /hómstil/ *adj.* (esp. of food) of a kind made or done at home; homey.

home town *n.* the town of one's birth or early life or present fixed residence.

home trade *n.* trade carried on within a country.

home truth *n.* basic but unwelcome information concerning oneself.

home unit *n. Austral.* a private residence, usu. occupied by the owner, as one of several in a building.

home·ward /hómwərd/ *adv. & adj.* ● *adv.* (also **home·wards** /–wərdz/) toward home. ● *adj.* going or leading toward home. [OE *hāmweard(es)* (as HOME, –WARD)]

home·ward-bound *adj.* on the way home (*homeward-bound commuters*).

home·work /hómwərk/ *n.* **1** work to be done at home, esp. by a school pupil. **2** preparatory work or study.

hom·ey /hómee/ *adj.* (also **hom·y**) (**hom·i·er**, **hom·i·est**) suggesting home; cozy. □□ **hom·ey·ness** *n.* (also **hom·i·ness**).

hom·i·cide /hómisīd, hó–/ *n.* **1** the killing of a human being by another. **2** a person who kills a human being. □□ **hom·i·cid·al** /–síd'l/ *adj.* [ME f. OF f. L *homicidium* (sense 1), *homicida* (sense 2) (HOMO man)]

hom·i·let·ic /hómilétik/ *adj. & n.* ● *adj.* of homilies. ● *n.* (usu. in *pl.*) the art of preaching. [LL *homileticus* f. Gk *homilētikos* f. *homileō* hold converse, consort (as HOMILY)]

ho·mil·i·ar·y /homílee-eree/ *n.* (*pl.* **-ies**) a book of homilies. [med.L *homiliarius* (as HOMILY)]

hom·i·ly /hómilee/ *n.* (*pl.* **·lies**) **1** a sermon. **2** a tedious moralizing discourse. □□ **hom·i·list** *n.* [ME f. OF *omelie* f. eccl.L *homilia* f. Gk *homilia* f. *homilos* crowd]

hom·ing /hóming/ *attrib.adj.* **1** (of a pigeon) trained to fly home; bred for long-distance racing. **2** (of a device) for guiding to a target, etc. **3** that goes home.

hom·ing in·stinct *n.* the instinct of certain animals to return to the territory from which they have been moved.

hom·i·nid /hóminid/ *n. & adj.* ● *n.* any member of the primate family Hominidae, including humans and their fossil ancestors. ● *adj.* of or relating to this family. [mod.L *Hominidae* f. L *homo hominis* man]

hom·i·noid /hóminoyd/ *adj. & n.* ● *adj.* **1** like a human. **2** hominid or pongid. ● *n.* an animal resembling a human.

hom·i·ny /hóminee/ *n.* coarsely ground corn kernels soaked in lye then washed to remove the hulls. [Algonquian]

ho·mo¹ /hómō/ *n.* any primate of the genus *Homo*, including modern humans and various extinct species. [L = man]

ho·mo² /hómō/ *n.* (*pl.* **·mos**) *offens. colloq.* a homosexual. [abbr.]

homo- /hómō/ *comb.form* same (often opp. HETERO-). [Gk *homos* same]

ho·mo·cen·tric /hómōséntrik/ *adj.* having the same center.

ho·mo·e·rot·ic /hómōərótik/ *adj.* homosexual.

ho·mo·ga·met·ic /hómōgəméetik, –gəmét–/ *adj. Biol.* (of a sex or individuals of a sex) producing gametes that carry the same sex chromosome.

ho·mog·a·my /həmógəmee/ *n. Bot.* **1** a state in which the flowers of a plant are hermaphrodite or of the same sex. **2** the simultaneous ripening of the stamens and pistils of a flower. □□ **ho·mog·a·mous** *adj.* [Gk *homogamos* (as HOMO-, *gamos* marriage)]

ho·mog·e·nate /həmójinayt/ *n.* a suspension produced by homogenizing.

ho·mo·ge·ne·ous /hóməjeeneeəs, –yəs/ *adj.* **1** of the same kind. **2** consisting of parts all of the same kind; uniform. **3** *Math.* containing terms all of the same degree. □□ **ho·mo·ge·ne·i·ty** /–jinee-itee/ *n.* **ho·mo·ge·ne·ous·ness** *n.* [med.L *homogeneus* f. Gk *homogenēs* (as HOMO-, *genēs* f. *genos* kind)]

ho·mo·ge·net·ic /hómōjinétik/ *adj. Biol.* having a common descent or origin.

ho·mog·e·nize /həmójinīz/ *v.* **1** *tr. & intr.* make or become homogeneous. **2** *tr.* treat (milk) so that the fat droplets are emulsified and the cream does not separate. □□ **ho·mog·e·ni·za·tion** *n.* **ho·mog·e·niz·er** *n.*

ho·mog·e·ny /həmójinee/ *n. Biol.* similarity due to common descent. □□ **ho·mog·e·nous** *adj.*

ho·mo·graft /hómǝgraft, hóm–/ n. a graft of living tissue from one to another of the same species but different genotype.

ho·mo·graph /hómǝgraf, hó–/ n. a word spelled like another but of different meaning or origin (e.g., *quail* ['a bird'] and *quail* ['recoil in dread']).

ho·moi·o·therm var. of HOMEOTHERM.

ho·moi·ou·si·an /hómoy-ōōseeǝn,–zee–,–ów–/ n. *hist.* a person who held that God the Father and God the Son are of like but not identical substance (cf. HOMOOUSIAN). [eccl.L f. Gk *homoiousios* f. *homoios* like + *ousia* essence]

ho·mo·log var. of HOMOLOGUE.

ho·mol·o·gate /hǝmólǝgayt/ v.tr. 1 acknowledge; admit. 2 confirm; accept. 3 approve (a car, boat, engine, etc.) for use in a particular class of racing. □□ **ho·mol·o·ga·tion** /–gáyshǝn/ n. [med.L *homologare* agree f. Gk *homologeō* (as HOMO-, *logos* word)]

ho·mol·o·gize /hǝmólǝjīz/ v. 1 intr. be homologous; correspond. 2 tr. make homologous.

ho·mol·o·gous /hǝmólǝgǝs/ adj. 1 a having the same relation, relative position, etc. b corresponding. 2 *Biol.* (of organs, etc.) similar in position and structure but not necessarily in function. 3 *Biol.* (of chromosomes) pairing at meiosis and having the same structural features and pattern of genes. 4 *Chem.* (of a series of chemical compounds) having the same functional group but differing in composition by a fixed group of atoms. [med.L *homologus* f. Gk (as HOMO-, *logos* ratio, proportion)]

ho·mo·logue /hómǝlawg, –log, hó–/ n. (also **ho·mo·log**) a homologous thing. [F f. Gk *homologon* (neut. adj.) (as HOMOLOGOUS)]

ho·mol·o·gy /hǝmólǝjee/ n. a homologous state or relation; correspondence. □□ **ho·mo·log·i·cal** /hómǝlójikǝl/ adj.

ho·mo·mor·phic /hómōmáwrfik, hóm–/ adj. (also **ho·mo·mor·phous**) of the same or similar form. □□ **ho·mo·mor·phi·cal·ly** adv. **ho·mo·mor·phism** n. **ho·mo·mor·phy** n.

hom·o·nym /hómǝnim/ n. 1 a word of the same spelling or sound as another but of different meaning; a homograph or homophone. 2 a namesake. □□ **hom·o·nym·ic** /–nímik/ adj. **ho·mon·y·mous** /hǝmónimǝs/ adj. [L *homonymum* f. Gk *homōnumon* (neut. adj.) (as HOMO-, *onoma* name)]

ho·mo·ou·si·an /hómō-ōōseeǝn, –zee–, –ów–/ n. (also **ho·mo·u·si·an**) *hist.* a person who held that God the Father and God the Son are of the same substance (cf. HOMOIOUSIAN). [eccl.L *homoousianus* f. LL *homousius* f. Gk *homoousios* (as HOMO-, *ousia* essence)]

ho·mo·pho·bi·a /hómǝfóbeeǝ/ n. a hatred or fear of homosexuals. □□ **ho·mo·phobe** /–ǝfōb/ n. **ho·mo·pho·bic** adj.

ho·mo·phone /hómǝfōn, hó–/ n. 1 a word having the same sound as another but of different meaning or origin (e.g., *pair, pare,* and *pear*). 2 a symbol denoting the same sound as another.

ho·mo·phon·ic /hómōfónik, hó–/ adj. *Mus.* in unison; characterized by movement of all parts to the same melody. □□ **ho·mo·phon·i·cal·ly** adv.

ho·moph·o·nous /hǝmófǝnǝs/ adj. 1 (of music) homophonic. 2 (of a word or symbol) that is a homophone. □□ **ho·moph·o·ny** n.

ho·mo·po·lar /hómǝpólǝr, hóm–/ adj. 1 electrically symmetrical. 2 *Electr.* (of a generator) producing direct current without the use of commutators. 3 *Chem.* (of a covalent bond) in which one atom supplies both electrons.

ho·mop·ter·an /hǝmóptǝrǝn/ n. any insect of the suborder Homoptera, including aphids and cicadas, with wings of uniform texture (cf. HETEROPTERAN). □□ **ho·mop·ter·ous** adj. [HOMO- + Gk *pteron* wing]

Ho·mo sa·pi·ens /hómō sáypee-enz/ n. modern humans regarded as a species. [L, = wise man]

ho·mo·sex·u·al /hómǝsékshōōǝl/ adj. & n. ● adj. 1 feeling or involving sexual attraction only to persons of the same sex. 2 concerning homosexual relations or people. 3 relating to the same sex. ● n. a homosexual person. □□ **ho·mo·sex·u·al·i·ty** /–shōōálitee/ n. **ho·mo·sex·u·al·ly** adv.

ho·mo·u·si·an var. of HOMOOUSIAN.

ho·mo·zy·gote /hómōzígōt/ n. *Biol.* 1 an individual with identical alleles determining a particular characteristic. 2 an individual that is homozygous and so breeds true. □□ **ho·mo·zy·gous** adj.

ho·mun·cu·lus /hǝmúngkyǝlǝs/ n. (also **ho·mun·cule** /–kyōōl/) (pl. **ho·mun·cu·li** /–lī/ or **ho·mun·cu·les**) a little man; a manikin. [L *homunculus* f. *homo* –*minis* man]

hom·y var. of HOMEY.

Hon. abbr. 1 Honorary. 2 Honorable.

hon /hun/ n. *colloq.* = HONEY 5. [abbr.]

hon·cho /hónchō/ n. & v. *sl.* ● n. (pl. **·chos**) 1 a leader or manager; the person in charge. 2 an admirable man. ● v.tr. (**·choes, ·choed**) be in charge of; oversee.

| WORD HISTORY | honcho |

1940s: from Japanese *hanchō* 'group leader,' a term brought back to the U.S. by servicemen stationed in Japan during the occupation following World War II.

hone /hōn/ n. & v. ● n. 1 a whetstone, esp. for razors. 2 any of vari-

---

ous stones used as material for this. ● v.tr. sharpen on or as on a hone. [OE *hān* stone f. Gmc]

hon·est /ónist/ adj. & adv. ● adj. 1 fair and just in character or behavior, not cheating or stealing. 2 free of deceit and untruthfulness; sincere. 3 fairly earned (*an honest living*). 4 (of an act or feeling) showing fairness. 5 (with patronizing effect) blameless but undistinguished (cf. WORTHY). 6 (of a thing) unadulterated; unsophisticated. ● adv. *colloq.* genuinely; really. □ **earn** (or **turn**) **an honest penny** (or **dollar**) earn money fairly. **make an honest woman of** *colloq.* marry (esp. a pregnant woman). [ME f. OF (*h*)*oneste* f. L *honestus* f. *honos* HONOR]

hon·est bro·ker n. an impartial mediator in international, industrial or other disputes (with reference to Bismarck, under whom Germany was united).

hon·est·ly /ónistlee/ adv. 1 in an honest way. 2 really (*I don't honestly know; honestly, the nerve of them!*).

hon·est-to-God adj. & adv. (also **honest-to-goodness**) *colloq.* ● adj. genuine; real. ● adv. genuinely; really.

hon·es·ty /ónistee/ n. 1 being honest. 2 truthfulness. 3 a plant of the genus *Lunaria* with purple or white flowers and flat round semitransparent seed pods. [ME f. OF (*h*)*oneste* f. L *honestas* –*tatis* (as HONEST)]

hon·ey /húnee/ n. (pl. **·eys**) 1 a sweet sticky yellowish fluid made by bees and other insects from nectar collected from flowers. 2 the color of this. 3 a sweetness. b a sweet thing. 4 a person or thing excellent of its kind. 5 (usu. as a form of address) darling; sweetheart. [OE *hunig* f. Gmc]

hon·ey badg·er n. a ratel.

hon·ey·bee /húneebee/ n. any of various bees of the genus *Apis*, esp. the common hive bee (*A. mellifera*).

hon·ey buz·zard n. any bird of prey of the genus *Pernis* feeding on the larvae of bees and wasps.

hon·ey·comb /húneekōm/ n. & v. ● n. 1 a structure of hexagonal cells of wax, made by bees to store honey and eggs. 2 a a pattern arranged hexagonally. b fabric made with a pattern of raised hexagons, etc. 3 tripe from the second stomach of a ruminant. 4 a cavernous flaw in metalwork, esp. in guns. ● v.tr. 1 fill with cavities or tunnels; undermine. 2 mark with a honeycomb pattern. [OE *hunigcamb* (as HONEY, COMB)]

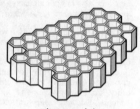

honeycomb 1

hon·ey·dew /húneedōō, –dyōō/ n. 1 a variety of melon with smooth pale skin and sweet green flesh. 2 a sweet sticky substance found on leaves and stems, excreted by aphids, fungus, etc. 3 an ideally sweet substance. 4 tobacco sweetened with molasses.

hon·ey eat·er n. any Australasian bird of the family Meliphagidae with a long tongue that can take nectar from flowers.

hon·eyed /húneed/ adj. (also **hon·ied**) 1 of or containing honey. 2 sweet.

hon·ey guide n. 1 any small bird of the family Indicatoridae which feeds on beeswax and insects. 2 a marking on the corolla of a flower thought to guide bees to nectar.

hon·ey·moon /húneemōōn/ n. & v. ● n. 1 a vacation spent together by a newly married couple. 2 an initial period of enthusiasm or goodwill. ● v.intr. (usu. foll. by *in, at*) spend a honeymoon. □□ **hon·ey·moon·er** n. [HONEY + MOON, orig. with ref. to waning affection, not to a period of a month]

hon·ey sac n. an enlarged part of a bee's gullet where honey is formed.

hon·ey·suck·le /húneesukǝl/ n. any climbing shrub of the genus *Lonicera* with fragrant yellow, pink, or red flowers. [ME *hunisuccle,* –*soukel,* extension of *hunisuce,* –*souke,* f. OE *hunigsūce,* –*sūge* (as HONEY, SUCK)]

hon·ied var. of HONEYED.

honk /hawngk, hongk/ n. & v. ● n. 1 the cry of a wild goose. 2 the harsh sound of a car horn. ● v. 1 intr. emit or give a honk. 2 tr. cause to do this. [imit.]

hon·ky /háwngkee, hóngkee/ n. (pl. **·kies**) *black sl. offens.* 1 a white person. 2 white people collectively. [20th c.: orig. unkn.]

hon·ky-tonk /háwngkeetawngk, hóngkeetongk/ n. *colloq.* 1 ragtime piano music. 2 a cheap or disreputable nightclub, bar, dancehall, etc. [20th c.: orig. unkn.]

hon·or /ónǝr/ n. & v. (Brit. **hon·our**) ● n. 1 high respect; glory; credit; reputation; good name. 2 adherence to what is right or to a conventional standard of conduct. 3 nobleness of mind; magnanimity (*honor among thieves*). 4 a thing conferred as a distinction, esp. an official award for bravery or achievement. 5 (foll. by *of* + verbal noun, or *to* + infin.) privilege; special right (*had the honor of being* *invited*). **6 a** exalted position. **b** (**Honor**) (prec. by *your*, *his*, etc.) a title of a judge, a mayor, or *Ir.* in rustic speech any person of rank. **7** (foll. by *to*) a person or thing that brings honor (*she is an honor to her profession*). **8 a** (of a woman) chastity. **b** the reputation for this. **9** (in *pl.*) **a** special distinction for proficiency in an examination. **b** a course of degree studies more specialized than for a standard course or degree. **10 a** *Bridge* the ace, king, queen, jack, and ten, esp. of trump, or the four aces at no trump. **b** *Whist* the ace, king, queen, and jack, esp. of trump. **11** *Golf* the right of driving off first as having won the last hole (*it is my honor*). • *v.tr.* **1** respect highly. **2** confer honor on. **3** accept or pay (a bill or check) when due. **4** acknowledge. □ **do the honors** perform the duties of a host to guests, etc. **honors are even** *Brit.* there is equality in the contest. **in honor bound** = *on one's honor*. **in honor of** as a celebration of. **on one's honor** (usu. foll. by *to* + infin.) under a moral obligation. **on** (or **upon**) **my honor** an expression of sincerity. [ME f. OF (*h*)*onor* (n.), *onorer* (v.) f. L *honor*, *honarare*]

hon•or•a•ble /ónǝrǝbǝl/ *adj.* **1 a** worthy of honor. **b** bringing honor to its possessor. **c** showing honor; not base. **d** consistent with honor. **e** *colloq.* (of the intentions of a man courting a woman) directed toward marriage. **2** (**Honorable**) a title indicating eminence or distinction, given to certain government officials, members of Congress, and *Brit.* MPs and the children of certain ranks of the nobility. □□ **hon•or•a•ble•ness** *n.* **hon•or•a•bly** *adv.* [ME f. OF *honorable* f. L *honorabilis* (as HONOR)]

hon•or•a•ble men•tion *n.* an award of merit to a candidate in an examination, a work of art, etc., not awarded a prize.

hon•or•and /ónǝrand/ *n.* a person to be honored, esp. with an honorary degree. [L *honorandus* (as HONOR)]

hon•o•rar•i•um /ónǝráireeǝm/ *n.* (*pl.* **hon•o•rar•i•ums** or **hon•o•rar•i•a** /–reeǝ/) a fee, esp. a voluntary payment for professional services rendered without the normal fee. [L, neut. of *honorarius*: see HONORARY]

hon•or•ar•y /ónǝreree/ *adj.* **1 a** conferred as an honor, without the usual requirements, functions, etc. (*honorary degree*). **b** holding such a title or position (*honorary colonel*). **2** (of an office or its holder) unpaid (*honorary secretaryship; honorary treasurer*). **3** (of an obligation) depending on honor, not legally enforceable. [L *honorarius* (as HONOR)]

hon•or bright *int. colloq.*, dated on my honor (*I'll never do it again, honor bright*).

hon•or•if•ic /ónǝrífik/ *adj. & n.* • *adj.* **1** conferring honor. **2** (esp. of forms of speech) implying respect. • *n.* an honorific form of words. □□ **hon•or•if•i•cal•ly** *adv.* [L *honorificus* (as HONOR)]

ho•no•ris cau•sa /ónáwris kówzǝ/ *adv.* (esp. of a degree awarded without examination) as a mark of esteem. [L, = for the sake of honor]

hon•or point *n. Heraldry* the point halfway between the top of a shield and the fesse point.

hon•or roll *n.* a list of people who have attained an honor, esp. a list of students who have received academic honors.

hon•ors list *n.* a list of persons awarded honors.

hon•ors of war *n.* privileges granted to a capitulating force, e.g., that of marching out with colors flying.

hon•or sys•tem *n.* a system of examinations, etc., without supervision, relying on the honor of those concerned.

hon•our *Brit.* var. of HONOR.

Hon. Sec. *abbr.* Honorary Secretary.

hooch /hळch/ *n.* (also **hootch**) *colloq.* alcoholic liquor, esp. inferior or illicit whiskey. [abbr. of Alaskan *hoochinoo*, name of a liquor-making tribe]

hood[1] /hळd/ *n. & v.* • *n.* **1 a** a covering for the head and neck, whether part of a cloak, etc., or separate. **b** a separate hoodlike garment worn over a university gown or a surplice to indicate the wearer's degree. **2** the cover over the engine of a motor vehicle. **3** *Brit.* a folding waterproof top of an automobile, a baby carriage, etc. **4 a** canopy to protect users of machinery or to remove fumes, etc. **5** the

hoodlike part of a cobra, seal, etc. **6** a leather covering for a hawk's head. • *v.tr.* cover with a hood. □□ **hood•less** *adj.* **hood•like** *adj.* [OE *hōd* f. WG, rel. to HAT]

hood[2] *n. sl.* a gangster or gunman. [abbr. of HOODLUM]

hood[3] *n. sl.* a neighborhood, esp. one's own neighborhood. [shortening of NEIGHBORHOOD]

-hood /hळd/ *suffix* forming nouns: **1** of condition or state (*childhood; falsehood*). **2** indicating a collection or group (*sisterhood; neighborhood*). [OE *–hād*, orig. an independent noun, = person, condition, quality]

hood•ed /hळdid/ *adj.* having a hood; covered with a hood. □ **hooded crow** a piebald gray and black crow, *Corvus cornix*, native to Europe.

hood•ie /hळdee/ *n. Sc.* = *hooded crow*.

hood•lum /hळdlǝm, hळd–/ *n.* **1** a street hooligan; a young thug. **2** a gangster. [19th c.: orig. unkn.]

hood mold *n.* (also **hood molding**) *Archit.* a dripstone.

hoo•doo /hळdळ/ *n. & v.* • *n.* **1 a** bad luck. **b** a thing or person that brings or causes this. **2** voodoo. **3** a fantastic rock pinnacle or column of rock formed by erosion, etc. • *v.tr.* (**hoo•doos**, **hoo•dooed**) **1** make unlucky. **2** bewitch. [alt. of VOODOO]

hood•wink /hळdwingk/ *v.tr.* deceive; delude. [orig. 'blindfold,' f. HOOD[1] *n.* + WINK]

hoo•ey /hळ–ee/ *n. & int. sl.* nonsense; humbug. [20th c.: orig. unkn.]

hoof /hळf, hळf/ *n. & v.* • *n.* (*pl.* **hoofs** or **hooves** /hळvz/) the horny part of the foot of a horse, antelope, and other ungulates. • *v.* **1** *tr.* strike with a hoof. **2** *tr. sl.* kick or shove. □ **hoof it** *sl.* **1** go on foot. **2** dance. **on the hoof** (of cattle) not yet slaughtered. □□ **hoofed** *adj.* (also in *comb.*). [OE *hōf* f. Gmc]

hoof•er /hळfǝr, hळfǝr/ *n. sl.* a professional dancer.

hoo-ha /hळhaa/ *n. sl.* a commotion; a row; uproar; trouble. [20th c.: orig. unkn.]

hook /hळk/ *n. & v.* • *n.* **1 a** a piece of metal or other material bent back at an angle or with a round bend, for catching hold or for hanging things on. **b** (in full **fishhook**) a bent piece of wire, usu. barbed and baited, for catching fish. **2** a curved cutting instrument (*reaping hook*). **3 a** a sharp bend, e.g., in a river. **b** a projecting point of land (*Hook of Holland*). **c** a sandspit with a curved end. **4 a** *Cricket & Golf* a hooking stroke (see sense 5 of *v.*). **b** *Boxing* a short swinging blow with the elbow bent and rigid. **5** a trap, a snare. **6 a** a curved stroke in handwriting, esp. as made in learning to write. **b** *Mus.* an added stroke transverse to the stem in the symbol for an eighth-note, etc. **7** (in *pl.*) *sl.* fingers. • *v.* **1** *tr.* **a** grasp with a hook. **b** secure with a hook or hooks. **2** (often foll. by *on*, *up*) **a** *tr.* attach with or as with a hook. **b** *intr.* be or become attached with a hook. **3** *tr.* catch with or as with a hook (*he hooked a fish; she hooked a husband*). **4** *tr. sl.* steal. **5** *tr.* *Cricket* play (the ball) around from the off to the on side with an upward stroke. **b** (also *absol.*) *Golf* strike (the ball) so that it deviates toward the striker. **6** *tr.* *Rugby* secure (the ball) and pass it backward with the foot in the scrum. **7** *tr.* *Boxing* strike (one's opponent) with the elbow bent and rigid. □ **be hooked on** *sl.* be addicted to or captivated by. **by hook or by crook** by one means or another; by fair means or foul. **hook it** *Brit. sl.* make off; run away. **hook, line, and sinker** entirely. **off the hook** **1** *colloq.* no longer in difficulty or trouble. **2** (of a telephone receiver) not on its rest, and so preventing incoming calls. **off the hooks** *Brit. sl.* dead. **on one's own hook** *sl.* on one's own account. **sling** (or **take**) **one's hook** *Brit. sl.* = *hook it*. □□ **hook•less** *adj.* **hook•let** *n.* **hook•like** *adj.* [OE *hōc*: sense 3 of *n.* prob. influenced by Du. *hoek* corner]

hook•ah /hळkǝ/ *n.* an oriental tobacco pipe with a long tube passing through water for cooling the smoke as it is drawn through. [Urdu f. Arab. *ḥukkah* casket]

hook and eye *n.* a small metal hook and loop as a fastener on a garment.

hooked /hळkt/ *adj.* **1** hook-shaped (*hooked nose*). **2** furnished with a hook or hooks. **3** in senses of HOOK *v.* **4** (of a rug or mat) made by pulling woolen yarn through canvas with a hook.

hook and eye

hook•er[1] /hळkǝr/ *n.* **1** *sl.* a prostitute. **2** a person or thing that hooks. **3** *Rugby* the player in the middle of the front row of the scrum who tries to hook the ball.

hook•er[2] /hळkǝr/ *n.* **1** a small Dutch or Irish fishing vessel. **2** *derog.* any ship. [Du. *hoeker* f. *hoek* HOOK]

Hooke's law /hळks/ *n.* the law that the strain in a solid is proportional to the applied stress within the elastic limit of that solid. [R. Hooke, Engl. scientist d. 1703]

hook•nose /hळknōz/ *n.* an aquiline nose. □□ **hook-nosed** *adj.*

hook•up /hळkǝp/ *n.* **1** a connection, esp. an interconnection of broadcasting equipment for special transmissions. **2** a connection to a public water, sewer, electric, etc., line.

hook•worm /hळkwǝrm/ *n.* **1** any of various nematode worms, with hooklike mouthparts for attachment and feeding, infesting humans and animals. **2** a disease caused by one of these, often resulting in severe anemia.

hook·y /hŏŏkee/ *n.* (also **hook·ey**) □ **play hooky** *sl.* play truant. [19th c.: orig. unkn.]

hoo·li·gan /hŏŏligən/ *n.* a young ruffian, esp. a member of a gang. □□ **hoo·li·gan·ism** *n.* [19th c.: orig. unkn.]

hoop[1] /hŏŏp/ *n. & v.* • *n.* **1** a circular band of metal, wood, etc., esp. for binding the staves of casks, etc., or for forming part of a framework. **2 a** a circular usu. wood or plastic band used as a toy. **b** a large ring usu. with paper stretched over it for circus performers to jump through. **3** an arch of iron, etc., through which the balls are hit in croquet; a wicket. **4** (in pl.) the game of basketball. **5** *hist.* **a** a circle of flexible material for expanding a woman's petticoat or skirt. **b** (in full **hoop skirt**) a skirt expanded with this. **6 a** a band of contrasting color on a jockey's blouse, sleeves, or cap. **b** *Austral. colloq.* a jockey. • *v.tr.* **1** bind with a hoop or hoops. **2** encircle with or as with a hoop. □ **be put** (or **go**) **through the hoop** (or **hoops**) undergo an ordeal. [OE *hōp* f. WG]

hoop[2] var. of WHOOP.

hoop iron *n.* flattened iron in long thin strips used for binding together the staves of casks or barrels.

hoop·la /hŏŏplaa/ *n.* **1** *sl.* commotion; excitement. **2** *Brit.* a game in which rings are thrown in an attempt to encircle one of various prizes. **3** *sl.* pretentious nonsense. **4** noisy publicity; ballyhoo.

hoo·poe /hŏŏpoō/ *n.* a salmon-pink bird, *Upupa epops*, with black and white wings and tail, a large erectile crest, and a long decurved bill. [alt. of ME *hoop* f. OF *huppe* f. L *upupa*, imit. of its cry]

hoo·ray /hŏŏráy/ *int.* **1** = HURRAH. **2** *Austral. & NZ* good-bye. [var. of HURRAH]

Hoo·ray Hen·ry /hŏŏray/ *n. Brit. sl.* a rich ineffectual young man, esp. one who is fashionable, extroverted, and conventional.

hoo·roo /hŏŏroō/ *int. & n.* (also **hur·roo**) *Austral. colloq.* = HURRAH. [alt. of HOORAY, HURRAH]

hoose·gow /hŏŏsgow/ *n. sl.* a prison. [Amer. Sp. *juzgao*, Sp. *juzgado* tribunal f. L *judicatum* neut. past part. of *judicare* JUDGE]

hoot /hŏŏt/ *n. & v.* • *n.* **1** an owl's cry. **2** the sound made by a vehicle's horn or a steam whistle. **3** a shout expressing scorn or disapproval; an inarticulate shout. **4** *colloq.* **a** laughter. **b** a cause of this. **5** (also **two hoots**) *sl.* anything at all (*don't care a hoot; don't give a hoot; doesn't matter two hoots*). • *v.* **1** *intr.* **a** (of an owl) utter its cry. **b** (of a vehicle horn or steam whistle) make a hoot. **c** (often foll. by *at*) make loud sounds, esp. of scorn or disapproval or *colloq.* merriment (*hooted with laughter*). **2** *tr.* **a** assail with scornful shouts. **b** (often foll. by *out, away*) drive away by hooting. **3** *tr.* sound (a vehicle horn or steam whistle). [ME *hūten* (v.), perh. imit.]

hootch var. of HOOCH.

hoot·en·an·ny /hŏŏt'nanee/ *n.* (pl. **·nies**) *colloq.* an informal gathering with folk music. [orig. dial., = 'gadget']

hoot·er /hŏŏtər/ *n.* **1** *sl.* a nose. **2** (pl.) *coarse sl.* a women's breasts. **3** a person or animal that hoots. **4** *Brit.* a siren or steam whistle, esp. as a signal for work to begin or cease. **5** *Brit.* the horn of a motor vehicle.

hoots /hŏŏts/ *int. Sc. & No. of Engl.* expressing dissatisfaction or impatience. [natural exclam.: cf. Sw. *hut* begone, Welsh *hwt* away, Ir. *ut* out, all in similar sense]

Hoo·ver /hŏŏvər/ *n. & v.* • *n.* Trademark a vacuum cleaner (properly one made by the Hoover company). • *v.* (**hoover**) **1** *tr.* (also *absol.*) clean (a carpet, etc.) with a vacuum cleaner. **2** (foll. by *up*) **a** *tr.* suck up with or as with a vacuum cleaner (*hoovered up the crumbs*). **b** *absol.* clean a room, etc., with a vacuum cleaner (*decided to hoover up before they arrived*). [W. H. *Hoover*, Amer. manufacturer d. 1932]

hooves pl. of HOOF.

hop[1] /hŏp/ *v. & n.* • *v.* (**hopped, hop·ping**) **1** *intr.* (of a bird, frog, etc.) spring with two or all feet at once. **2** *intr.* (of a person) jump on one foot. **3** *tr.* cross (a ditch, etc.) by hopping. **4** *intr. colloq.* **a** make a quick trip. **b** make a quick change of position or location. **5** *tr. colloq.* **a** jump into (a vehicle). **b** obtain (a ride) in this way. **6** *tr.* (usu. as **hopping** *n.*) (esp. of aircraft) pass quickly from one (place of a specified type) to another (*cloud-hopping; island-hopping*). • *n.* **1** a hopping movement. **2** *colloq.* an informal dance. **3** a short flight in an aircraft; the distance traveled by air without landing; a stage of a flight or journey. □ **hop in** (or **out**) *colloq.* get into (or out of) a car, etc. **hop it** *Brit. sl.* go away. **hopping mad** *colloq.* very angry. **hop the twig** (or **stick**) *Brit. sl.* **1** depart suddenly. **2** die. **on the hop** *Brit. colloq.* **1** unprepared (*caught on the hop*). **2** bustling about. [OE *hoppian*]

hop[2] /hŏp/ *n. & v.* • *n.* **1** a climbing plant, *Humulus lupulus*, cultivated for the cones borne by the female. **2** (in pl.) **a** the ripe cones of this, used to give a bitter flavor to beer. **b** *Austral. & NZ colloq.* beer. **3** *sl.* opium or any other narcotic. • *v.* (**hopped, hop·ping**) **1** *tr.* flavor with hops. **2** *intr.* produce or pick hops. **3** *tr. sl.* (foll. by *up*) stimulate with a drug. □ **hopped up** stimulated through the use of drugs (*he was so hopped up he could barely stand still.*) [ME *hoppe* f. MLG, MDu. *hoppe*]

hope /hŏp/ *n. & v.* • *n.* **1** (in *sing.* or *pl.*; often foll. by *of, that*) expectation and desire combined, e.g., for a certain thing to occur (*hope of getting the job*). **2 a** a person, thing, or circumstance that gives cause for hope. **b** ground of hope; promise. **3** what is hoped for. **4** *archaic* a feeling of trust. • *v.* **1** *intr.* (often foll. by *for*) feel hope. **2** *tr.* expect and desire. **3** *tr.* feel fairly confident. □ **hope against hope** cling to a mere possibility. **not a** (or **some**) **hope!** *colloq.* no chance at all. □□ **hop·er** *n.* [OE *hopa*]

hope chest *n.* **1** a young woman's collection of linens, silver, household goods, etc., in preparation for her marriage. **2** the chest in which it is stored.

hope·ful /hŏpfŏŏl/ *adj. & n.* • *adj.* **1** feeling hope. **2** causing or inspiring hope. **3** likely to succeed; promising. • *n.* (in full **young hopeful**) **1** a person likely to succeed. **2** *iron.* a person likely to be disappointed. □□ **hope·ful·ness** *n.*

hope·ful·ly /hŏpfŏŏlee/ *adv.* **1** in a hopeful manner. **2** *disp.* (qualifying a whole sentence) it is to be hoped (*hopefully, the car will be ready by then*).

▶Some object strongly to the use of **hopefully** as a sentence modifier, with the meaning 'it is to be hoped' (*hopefully, all the details will be in this evening's newspapers*). However, this usage is not only common but long-established in English, as are similar uses of other sentence-modifying adverbs, such as *regrettably, unfortunately,* and *frankly.*

hope·less /hŏplis/ *adj.* **1** feeling no hope. **2** admitting no hope (*a hopeless case*). **3** inadequate; incompetent (*am hopeless at tennis*). **4** without hope of success; futile. □□ **hope·less·ly** *adv.* **hope·less·ness** *n.*

hop·head /hŏp-hed/ *n. sl.* **1** a drug addict. **2** *Austral. & NZ* a drunkard.

Ho·pi /hŏpee/ *n.* **1 a** a N. American people native to northeastern Arizona. **b** a member of this people. **2** the language of this people.

hop·lite /hŏplīt/ *n.* a heavily armed foot soldier of ancient Greece. [Gk *hoplitēs* f. *hoplon* weapon]

hop·per[1] /hŏpər/ *n.* **1** a person who hops. **2** a hopping arthropod, esp. a flea or young locust. **3 a** a container tapering downward (orig. having a hopping motion) through which grain passes into a mill. **b** a similar contrivance in various machines. **4 a** a barge carrying away mud, etc., from a dredging machine and discharging it. **b** a railroad freight car able to discharge coal, etc., through its floor.

hop·per[2] /hŏpər/ *n.* a hop picker.

hop·ple /hŏpəl/ *v. & n.* • *v.tr.* fasten together the legs of (a horse, etc.) to prevent it from straying, etc. • *n.* an apparatus for this. [prob. LG: cf. HOBBLE and early Flem. *hoppelen* = MDu. *hobelen* jump, dance]

hop·sack /hŏpsak/ *n.* (or **sack·ing**) **1 a** a coarse material made from hemp, etc. **b** sacking for hops made from this. **2** a coarse clothing fabric of a loose plain weave.

hop·scotch /hŏpskoch/ *n.* a children's game of hopping over squares or oblongs marked on the ground to retrieve a flat stone, etc. [HOP[1] + SCOTCH[1]]

hop, skip, and jump *n.* **1** a very short distance (*it's just a hop, skip, and jump from my house*). **2** = TRIPLE JUMP.

ho·ra·ry /háwroree/ *adj. archaic* **1** of the hours. **2** occurring every hour; hourly. [med.L *horarius* f. L *hora* HOUR]

horde /hawrd/ *n.* usu. *derog.* **a** a large group; a gang. **b** a moving swarm or pack (of insects, wolves, etc.). **2** a troop of Tartar or other nomads. [Pol. *horda* f. Turki *ordī, ordū* camp: cf. URDU]

hore·hound /háwrhownd/ *n.* (also **hoar·hound**) **1 a** a herbaceous plant, *Marrubium vulgare*, with a white cottony covering on its stem and leaves. **b** its bitter aromatic juice used against coughs, etc. **2 a** a herbaceous plant, *Ballota nigra*, with an unpleasant aroma. [OE *hāre hūne* f. *hār* HOAR + *hūne* a plant]

ho·ri·zon /hərīzən/ *n.* **1 a** the line at which the earth and sky appear to meet. **b** (in full **sensible horizon**) the line at which the earth and sky would appear to meet but for irregularities and obstructions; a circle where the earth's surface touches a cone whose vertex is at the observer's eye. **c** (in full **celestial horizon**) a great circle of the celestial sphere, the plane of which passes through the center of the earth and is parallel to that of the apparent horizon of a place. **2** limit of mental perception, experience, interest, etc. **3** a geological stratum or set of strata, or layer of soil, with particular characteristics. **4** *Archaeol.* the level at which a particular set of remains is found. □ **on the horizon** (of an event) just imminent or becoming apparent. [ME f. OF *orizon(te)* f. LL *horizon –ontis* f. Gk *horizōn (kuklos)* limiting (circle)]

hor·i·zon·tal /háwrizónt'l, hór–/ *adj. & n.* • *adj.* **1 a** parallel to the plane of the horizon; at right angles to the vertical (*horizontal plane*). **b** (of machinery, etc.) having its parts working in a horizontal direction. **2 a** combining firms engaged in the same stage of production (*horizontal integration*). **b** involving social groups of equal status, etc. **3** of or at the horizon. • *n.* a horizontal line, plane, etc. □□ **hor·i·zon·tal·i·ty** /–tálitee/ *n.* **hor·i·zon·tal·ly** *adv.* **hor·i·zon·tal·ness** *n.* [F *horizontal* or mod.L *horizontalis* (as HORIZON)]

hor·i·zon·tal sta·bi·liz·er *n.* a horizontal airfoil at the tail of an aircraft (*Brit.* also **tail·plane**).

hor·mone /háwrmōn/ *n.* **1** *Biochem.* a regulatory substance produced in an organism and transported in tissue fluids such as blood or sap to stimulate cells or tissues into action. **2** a synthetic substance with a similar effect. □□ **hor·mo·nal** /-mốnəl/ *adj.* [Gk *hormōn* part. of *hormaō* impel]

horn /hawrn/ *n. & v.* • *n.* **1 a** a hard permanent outgrowth, often curved and pointed, on the head of cattle, rhinoceroses, giraffes, and other esp. hoofed mammals, found singly, in pairs, or one in front of another. **b** the structure of a horn, consisting of a core of bone encased in keratinized skin. **2** each of two deciduous branched appendages on the head of (esp. male) deer. **3** a hornlike projection on the head of other animals, e.g., a snail's tentacle, the crest of a horned owl, etc. **4** the substance of which horns are composed. **5** anything resembling or compared to a horn in shape. **6** *Mus.* **a** = FRENCH HORN. **b** a wind instrument played by lip vibration, orig. made of horn, now usu. of brass. **c** a horn player. **7** an instrument sounding a warning or other signal (*car horn*; *foghorn*). **8** a receptacle or instrument made of horn, e.g., a drinking vessel or powder flask, etc. **9** a horn-shaped projection. **10** the extremity of the moon or other crescent. **11 a** an arm or branch of a river, bay, etc. **b** (**the Horn**) Cape Horn. **12** a pyramidal peak formed by glacial action. **13** *sl.* the telephone. **14** *coarse sl.* an erect penis. **15** the hornlike emblem of a cuckold. • *v.tr.* **1** (esp. as **horned** *adj.*) provide with horns. **2** gore with the horns. □ **horn** in *sl.* **1** (usu. foll. by *on*) intrude. **2** interfere. **on the horns of a dilemma** faced with a decision involving equally unfavorable alternatives. □□ **horn·ist** *n.* (in sense 6 of *n.*). **horn·less** *adj.* **horn·like** *adj.* [OE f. Gmc, rel. to L *cornu*]

horn·beam /háwrnbeem/ *n.* any tree of the genus *Carpinus*, with a smooth bark and a hard tough wood.

horn·bill /háwrnbil/ *n.* any bird of the family Bucerotidae, with a hornlike excrescence on its large red or yellow curved bill.

horn·blende /háwrnblend/ *n.* a dark brown, black, or green mineral occurring in many igneous and metamorphic rocks, and composed of calcium, magnesium, and iron silicates. [G (as HORN, BLENDE)]

horn·book /háwrnbŏŏk/ *n. hist.* a leaf of paper containing the alphabet, the Lord's Prayer, etc., mounted on a wooden tablet with a handle, and protected by a thin plate of horn.

horned /hawrnd/ *adj.* having a horn.

horned owl *n.* an owl, *Bubo virginianus*, with hornlike feathers over the ears.

horned toad *n.* **1** an American lizard, *Phrynosoma cornutum*, covered with spiny scales. **2** any SE Asian toad of the family Pelobatidae, with horn-shaped extensions over the eyes.

hor·net /háwrnit/ *n.* a large wasp, *Vespa crabro*, with a brown and yellow striped body, and capable of inflicting a serious sting. □ **stir up a hornets' nest** provoke or cause trouble or opposition. [prob. f. MLG, MDu. *horn*(*e*)*te*, corresp. to OE *hyrnet*, perh. rel. to HORN]

horn of plen·ty *n.* a cornucopia.

horn·pipe /háwrnpīp/ *n.* **1** a lively dance, usu. by one person (esp. associated with sailors). **2** the music for this. [name of an obs. wind instrument partly of horn: ME, f. HORN + PIPE]

horn-rimmed *adj.* (esp. of eyeglasses) having rims made of horn, tortoise shell, or a substance resembling these.

horn·stone /háwrnstōn/ *n.* a brittle siliceous rock.

horn·swog·gle /háwrnswogəl/ *v.tr. sl.* cheat; hoax. [19th c.: orig. unkn.]

horn·wort /háwrnwərt/ *n.* any aquatic rootless plant of the genus *Ceratophyllum*, with forked leaves.

horn·y /háwrnee/ *adj.* (**horn·i·er**, **horn·i·est**) **1** of or like horn. **2** hard like horn; callous (*horny-handed*). **3** *sl.* sexually excited or frustrated. □□ **horn·i·ness** *n.*

hor·o·loge /háwrələj, -loj, hór-/ *n. archaic* a timepiece. [ME f. OF *orloge* f. L *horologium* f. Gk *hōrologion* f. *hōra* time + *-logos* *-telling*]

ho·rol·o·gy /hawróləjee/ *n.* the art of measuring time or making clocks, watches, etc.; the study of this. □□ **ho·rol·o·ger** *n.* **hor·o·log·ic** /háwrəlójik/ *adj.* **hor·o·log·i·cal** *adj.* **ho·rol·o·gist** /-róləjist/ *n.* [Gk *hōra* time + -LOGY]

hor·o·scope /háwrəskōp, hór-/ *n. Astrol.* **1** a forecast of a person's future based on a diagram showing the relative positions of the stars and planets at that person's birth. **2** such a diagram (*cast a horoscope*). **3** observation of the sky and planets at a particular moment, esp. at a person's birth. □□ **hor·o·scop·ic** /-skópik/ *adj.* **hor·o·scop·i·cal** *adj.* **ho·ros·co·py** /həróskəpee/ *n.* [F f. L *horoscopus* f. Gk *hōroskopos* f. *hōra* time + *skopos* observer]

hor·ren·dous /həréndəs/ *adj.* horrifying; awful. □□ **hor·ren·dous·ly** *adv.* **hor·ren·dous·ness** *n.* [L *horrendus* gerundive of *horrēre*: see HORRID]

hor·rent /háwrənt, hór-/ *adj. poet.* **1** bristling. **2** shuddering. [L *horrēre*: see HORRID]

hor·ri·ble /háwribəl, hór-/ *adj.* **1** causing or likely to cause horror; hideous; shocking. **2** *colloq.* unpleasant; excessive (*horrible weather*;

horrible noise). □□ **hor·ri·ble·ness** *n.* **hor·ri·bly** *adv.* [ME f. OF (*h*)*orrible* f. L *horribilis* f. *horrēre*: see HORRID]

hor·rid /háwrid, hór-/ *adj.* **1** horrible; revolting. **2** *colloq.* unpleasant; disagreeable (*horrid weather*; *horrid children*). **3** *archaic* rough; bristling. □□ **hor·rid·ly** *adv.* **hor·rid·ness** *n.* [L *horridus* f. *horrēre* bristle, shudder]

hor·rif·ic /hawrífik, hór-/ *adj.* horrifying. □□ **hor·ri·fi·cal·ly** *adv.* [F *horrifique* or L *horrificus* f. *horrēre*: see HORRID]

hor·ri·fy /háwrifī, hór-/ *v.tr.* (**·fies**, **·fied**) arouse horror in; shock; scandalize. □□ **hor·ri·fi·ca·tion** *n.* **hor·ri·fied·ly** /-fidlee/ *adv.* **hor·ri·fy·ing** *adj.* **hor·ri·fy·ing·ly** *adv.* [L *horrificare* (as HORRIFIC)]

hor·rip·i·la·tion /hawrípiláyshən, ho-/ *n.* = GOOSE BUMPS. [LL *horripilatio* f. L *horrēre* to bristle + *pilus* hair]

hor·ror /háwrər, hór-/ *n. & adj.* • *n.* **1** a painful feeling of loathing and fear. **2 a** (often foll. by *of*) intense dislike. **b** (often foll. by *at*) *colloq.* intense dismay. **3 a** a person or thing causing horror. **b** *colloq.* a bad or mischievous person, etc. **4** (in *pl.*; prec. by *the*) a fit of horror, depression, or nervousness, esp. as in delirium tremens. **5** a terrified and revolted shuddering. **6** (in *pl.*) an exclamation of dismay. • *attrib. adj.* (of literature, movies, etc.) designed to attract by arousing pleasurable feelings of horror. [ME f. OF (*h*)*orrour* f. L *horror* *-oris* (as HORRID)]

hor·ror-struck *adj.* (or **hor·ror-strick·en**) horrified; shocked.

hors con·cours /áwr koNkŏŏr/ *adj.* **1** (of an exhibit or exhibitor) not competing for a prize. **2** unrivaled; unequaled. [F, lit. 'outside competition']

hors de com·bat /áwr də kawNbáa/ *adj.* out of the fight; disabled. [F]

hors d'oeu·vre /awrdốrvrə, -dörv/ *n.* an appetizer served at the beginning of a meal or (occasionally) in place of or during a meal. [F, lit. 'outside the work']

horse /hawrs/ *n. & v.* • *n.* **1 a** a solid-hoofed plant-eating quadruped, *Equus caballus*, with flowing mane and tail, used for riding and to carry and pull loads. **b** an adult male horse; a stallion or gelding. **c** a racehorse. **d** any other four-legged mammal of the genus *Equus*, including asses and zebras. **e** (*collect.*; as *sing.*) cavalry. **f** a representation of a horse. **2** a vaulting block. **3** a supporting frame esp. with legs (*clothes-horse*). **4** *sl.* heroin. **5** *colloq.* a unit of horsepower. **6** *Naut.* any of various ropes and bars. **7** *Mining* an obstruction in a vein. • *v.* **1** *intr.* (foll. by *around*) fool around. **2** *tr.* provide (a person or vehicle) with a horse or horses. **3** *intr.* mount or go on horseback. □ **from the horse's mouth** (of information, etc.) from the person directly concerned or another authoritative source. **horses for courses** *Brit.* the matching of tasks and talents. **to horse!** (as a command) mount your horses. □□ **horse·less** *adj.* **horse·like** *adj.* [OE *hors* f. Gmc]

horse-and-bug·gy *adj.* old-fashioned; bygone.

horse·back /háwrsbak/ *n.* the back of a horse, esp. as sat on in riding. □ **on horseback** mounted on a horse.

horse·bean /háwrsbeen/ *n.* a broad bean used as fodder.

horse block *n.* a small platform of stone or wood for mounting a horse.

horse·box /háwrsboks/ *n. Brit.* a closed vehicle for transporting a horse or horses.

horse brass *n.* a round flat brass ornament for the harness of a horse

horse chest·nut *n.* **1** any large ornamental tree of the genus *Aesculus*, with upright conical clusters of white or pink or red flowers. **2** the dark brown fruit of this (like an edible chestnut, but with a coarse bitter taste).

horse-drawn *adj.* (of a vehicle) pulled by a horse or horses.

horse-flesh /háwrsflesh/ *n.* **1** the flesh of a horse, esp. as food. **2** horses collectively.

horse·fly /háwrsflī/ *n.* (*pl.* **·flies**) any of various biting dipterous insects of the family Tabanidae troublesome esp. to horses.

Horse Guards *n.pl.* a mounted brigade from the household troops of the British monarch, used for ceremonial occasions.

horse·hair /háwrs-hair/ *n.* hair from the mane or tail of a horse, used for padding, etc.

horse lat·i·tudes *n.pl.* a belt of calms in each hemisphere between the trade winds and the westerlies.

horse·leech /háwrsleech/ *n.* **1** a large kind of leech feeding by swallowing not sucking. **2** an insatiable person (cf. Prov. 30:15).

horse·less /háwrslis/ *adj.* without a horse.

horse·less car·riage *n. archaic* an automobile.

horse mack·er·el *n.* any large fish of the mackerel type, e.g., the scad or the tuna.

horse·man /háwrsmən/ *n.* (*pl.* **·men**) **1** a rider on horseback. **2** a skilled rider.

horse·man·ship /háwrsmənship/ *n.* the art of riding on horseback; skill in doing this.

horse mush·room *n.* a large edible mushroom, *Agaricus arvensis*.

horse op·er·a *n. sl.* a western movie.

horse pis·tol *n. hist.* a large pistol carried by a horseman.

horse·play /háwrsplay/ *n.* boisterous play.

horse-pond *n.* a pond for watering and washing horses, proverbial as a place for ducking obnoxious persons.

horse·pow·er /háwrspowər/ n. (pl. same) **1** a unit of power equal to 550 foot-pounds per second (about 750 watts). ¶ Abbr.: **hp**. **2** the power of an engine, etc., measured in terms of this.

horse race n. **1** a race between horses with riders. **2** colloq. a close contest. □□ **horse rac·ing** n.

horse·rad·ish /háwrsradish/ n. **1** a cruciferous plant, *Armoracia rusticana*, with long lobed leaves. **2** the pungent root of this scraped or grated as a condiment, often made into a sauce.

horse sense n. colloq. plain common sense.

horse·shoe /háwrs-shōō/ n. **1** an iron shoe for a horse shaped like the outline of the hard part of the hoof. **2** a thing of this shape; an object shaped like C or U (e.g., a magnet, a table, a Spanish or Islamic arch).

horse·shoe crab n. a large marine arthropod, *Xiphosura polyphemus*, with a horseshoe-shaped shell and a long tail-spine. Also called **king crab**.

horseshoe crab

horse sol·dier n. a soldier mounted on a horse.

horse·tail /háwrstayl/ n. **1** the tail of a horse (formerly used in Turkey as a standard, or as an ensign denoting the rank of a pasha). **2** any cryptogamous plant of the genus *Equisetum*, like a horse's tail, with a hollow jointed stem and scalelike leaves. **3** = PONYTAIL.

horse·trad·ing n. **1** dealing in horses. **2** shrewd bargaining.

horse·whip /háwrs-hwip, –wip/ n. & v. • n. a whip for driving horses. • v.tr. (**·whipped**, **·whip·ping**) beat with a horsewhip.

horse·wom·an /háwrswŏŏmən/ n. (pl. **·wom·en**) **1** a woman who rides on horseback. **2** a skilled woman rider.

horst /hawrst/ n. Geol. a raised elongated block of land bounded by faults on both sides. [G, = heap]

hors·y /háwrsee/ adj. (also **hors·ey**) (**hors·i·er**, **hors·i·est**) **1** of or like a horse. **2** concerned with or devoted to horses or horse racing. **3** affectedly using the dress and language of a groom or jockey. **4** colloq. large; clumsy. □□ **hors·i·ly** adv. **hors·i·ness** n.

hor·ta·tive /háwrtətiv/ adj. (also **hor·ta·to·ry** /háwrtətawree/) tending or serving to exhort. □□ **hor·ta·tion** /hawrtáyshən/ n. [L *hortativus* f. *hortari* exhort]

hor·ten·si·a /hawrténseeə/ n. a kind of hydrangea, *Hydrangea macrophylla*, with large rounded infertile flower heads. [mod.L f. *Hortense* Lepaute, 18th-c. Frenchwoman]

hor·ti·cul·ture /háwrtikúlchər/ n. the art of garden cultivation. □□ **hor·ti·cul·tur·al** adj. **hor·ti·cul·tur·ist** n. [L *hortus* garden, after AGRICULTURE]

hortus siccus /háwrtəs síkəs/ n. **1** an arranged collection of dried plants. **2** a collection of uninteresting facts, etc. [L, = dry garden]

Hos. abbr. Hosea (Old Testament).

ho·san·na /hōzánə/ n. & int. a shout of adoration (Matt. 21: 9, 15, etc.). [ME f. LL f. Gk *hōsanna* f. Heb. *hôsa'nā* for *hôsî'a-nnā* save now!]

hose /hōz/ n. & v. • n. **1** (also Brit. **hose-pipe**) a flexible tube conveying water for watering plants, putting out fires, etc. **2 a** (collect.; as pl.) stockings and socks (esp. in trade use). **b** hist. breeches (*doublet and hose*). • v.tr. **1** (often foll. by *down*) water or spray or drench with a hose. **2** provide with hose.

ho·sier /hózhər/ n. a dealer in hosiery.

ho·sier·y /hózhəree/ n. **1** stockings and socks. **2** Brit. knitted or woven underwear.

hosp. abbr. **1** hospital. **2** hospice.

hos·pice /hóspis/ n. **1** a home or system of long-term care for people who are terminally ill. **2** a lodging for travelers, esp. one kept by a religious order. [F f. L *hospitium* (as HOST[2])]

hos·pi·ta·ble /hóspitəbəl, hospít–/ adj. **1** giving or disposed to give welcome and entertainment to strangers or guests. **2** disposed to welcome something readily; receptive. □□ **hos·pi·ta·bly** adv. [F f. *hospiter* f. med.L *hospitare* entertain (as HOST[2])]

hos·pi·tal /hóspit'l/ n. **1** an institution providing medical and surgical treatment and nursing care for ill or injured people. **2** hist. **a** a hospice. **b** an establishment of the Knights Hospitallers. **3** Brit. Law a charitable institution (also in proper names, e.g., *Christ's Hospital*). [ME f. OF f. med.L *hospitale* neut. of L *hospitalis* (adj.) (as HOST[2])]

hos·pi·tal cor·ners n.pl. overlapping folds used to tuck sheets neatly and securely under the mattress at the corners, esp. as used by nurses.

hos·pi·tal·er var. of HOSPITALLER.

hos·pi·tal fe·ver n. a kind of typhus formerly prevalent in crowded hospitals.

hos·pi·tal·ism /hóspit'lizəm/ n. the adverse effects of a prolonged stay in the hospital.

hos·pi·tal·i·ty /hóspitálitee/ n. the friendly and generous reception and entertainment of guests or strangers. [ME f. OF *hospitalité* f. L *hospitalitas –tatis* (as HOSPITAL)]

hos·pi·tal·ize /hóspit'līz/ v.tr. send or admit (a patient) to the hospital. □□ **hos·pi·tal·i·za·tion** n.

hos·pi·tal·ler /hóspit'lər/ n. (also **hos·pi·tal·er**) **1 a** a member of a charitable religious order. **b** (**Hos·pi·tal·ler**) a member of a military religious order, the Knights Hospitaller, established in 11th-c. Jerusalem. **2** a chaplain (in some London hospitals). [ME f. OF *hospitalier* f. med.L *hospitalarius* (as HOSPITAL)]

hos·pi·tal ship n. a ship to receive sick and wounded sailors, or to take sick and wounded soldiers home.

hos·pi·tal train n. a train taking wounded soldiers from a battlefield.

host[1] /hōst/ n. **1** (usu. foll. by *of*) a large number of people or things. **2** archaic an army. **3** (in full **heavenly host**) Bibl. **a** the sun, moon, and stars. **b** the angels. [ME f. OF f. L *hostis* stranger, enemy, in med.L 'army']

host[2] /hōst/ n. & v. • n. **1** a person who receives or entertains another as a guest. **2** the landlord of an inn (*mine host*). **3** Biol. an animal or plant having a parasite or commensal. **4** an animal or person that has received a transplanted organ, etc. **5** the person who introduces and often interviews guests on a show, esp. a television or radio program. • v.tr. act as host to (a person) or at (an event). [ME f. OF *oste* f. L *hospes –pitis* host, guest]

host[3] /hōst/ n. the bread consecrated in the Eucharist. [ME f. OF (h)*oiste* f. L *hostia* victim]

hos·ta /hóstə/ n. any perennial garden plant of the genus *Hosta* (formerly *Funkia*), including the plantain lily, with green or variegated ornamental leaves and loose clusters of tubular lavender or white flowers. [mod.L, f. N. T. *Host*, Austrian physician d. 1834]

hos·tage /hóstij/ n. **1** a person seized or held as security for the fulfillment of a condition. **2** a pledge or security. □□ **hos·tage·ship** n. [ME f. OF (h)*ostage* ult. f. LL *obsidatus* hostageship f. L *obses obsidis* hostage]

hos·tage to for·tune n. an act, commitment, or remark that is regarded as unwise because it invites trouble or could prove difficult to live up to (*restoring full employment was dropped as an impractical hostage to fortune*).

hos·tel /hóst'l/ n. **1** = YOUTH HOSTEL. **2** Brit. **a** a house of residence or lodging for students, nurses, etc. **b** a place providing temporary accommodation for the homeless, etc. **3** archaic an inn. [ME f. OF (h)*ostel* f. med.L (as HOSPITAL)]

hos·tel·ing /hóst'ling/ n. the practice of staying in youth hostels, esp. while traveling. □□ **hos·tel·er** n.

hos·tel·ry /hóst'lree/ n. (pl. **·ries**) archaic or literary an inn. [ME f. OF (h)*ostelerie* f. (h)*ostelier* innkeeper (as HOSTEL)]

host·ess /hóstis/ n. **1** a woman who receives or entertains a guest. **2** a woman employed to welcome and entertain customers at a nightclub, etc. **3** a stewardess on an aircraft, train, etc. (*air hostess*). [ME f. OF (h)*ostesse* (as HOST[2])]

hos·tile /hóstəl, –tīl/ adj. **1** of an enemy. **2** (often foll. by *to*) unfriendly; opposed. □□ **hos·tile·ly** adv. [F *hostile* or L *hostilis* (as HOST[1])]

hos·tile wit·ness n. Law a witness who appears hostile to the party calling him or her and therefore untrustworthy.

hos·til·i·ty /hostílitee/ n. (pl. **·ties**) **1** being hostile; enmity. **2** a state of warfare. **3** (in pl.) acts of warfare. **4** opposition (in thought, etc.). [F *hostilité* or LL *hostilitas* (as HOSTILE)]

hos·tler /hóslər, ós–/ n. **1** = OSTLER. **2** a person who services vehicles or machines, esp. train engines, when they are not in use. [ME f. *hosteler* (as OSTLER)]

hot /hot/ *adj., v., & adv.* • *adj.* (**hot•ter, hot•test**) **1 a** having a relatively or noticeably high temperature. **b** (of food or drink) prepared by heating and served without cooling. **2** producing the sensation of heat (*hot fever; hot flash*). **3** (of pepper, spices, etc.) pungent; piquant. **4** (of a person) feeling heat. **5 a** ardent; passionate; excited. **b** (often foll. by *for, on*) eager; keen (*in hot pursuit*). **c** angry or upset. **d** lustful. **e** exciting. **6 a** (of news, etc.) fresh; recent. **b** *Brit. colloq.* (of Treasury bills) newly issued. **7** *Hunting* (of the scent) fresh and strong, indicating that the quarry has passed recently. **8 a** (of a player) very skillful. **b** (of a competitor in a race or other sporting event) strongly favored to win (*a hot favorite*). **c** (of a hit, return, etc., in ball games) difficult for an opponent to deal with. **d** *colloq.* currently popular or in demand. **9** (of music, esp. jazz) strongly rhythmical and emotional. **10 a** difficult or awkward to deal with. **b** *sl.* (of goods) stolen, esp. easily identifiable and hence difficult to dispose of. **c** *sl.* (of a person) wanted by the police. **11 a** live, at a high voltage. **b** *sl.* radioactive. **12** *colloq.* (of information) unusually reliable (*hot tip*). **13** (of a color, shade, etc.) suggestive of heat; intense; bright. • *v.* (**hot•ted, hot•ting**) (usu. foll. by *up*) *Brit. colloq.* **1** *tr. & intr.* make or become hot. **2** *tr. & intr.* make or become active, lively, exciting, or dangerous. • *adv.* **1** *Brit.* angrily; severely (*give it him hot*). **2** eagerly. □ **go hot and cold 1** feel alternately hot and cold owing to fear, etc. **2** be alternately friendly then aloof. **have the hots for** *sl.* be sexually attracted to. **hot under the collar** angry, resentful, or embarrassed. **make it** (or **things**) **hot for a person** persecute a person. **not so hot** *colloq.* only mediocre. □□ **hot•ly** *adv.* **hot•ness** *n.* **hot•tish** *adj.* [OE *hāt* f. Gmc: cf. HEAT]

hot air *n. sl.* empty, boastful, or excited talk.

hot-air bal•loon *n.* a balloon (see BALLOON *n.* 2) consisting of a bag in which air is heated by burners located below it, causing it to rise.

hot•bed /hótbed/ *n.* **1** a bed of earth heated by fermenting manure. **2** (foll. by *of*) an environment promoting the growth of something, esp. something unwelcome (*hotbed of vice*).

hot-blood•ed *adj.* ardent; passionate.

hot•cake /hótkayk/ *n.* a pancake. □ **like hotcakes** quickly and in great quantity, esp. because of popularity (*the new CD is selling like hotcakes*).

hot cath•ode *n.* a cathode designed to be heated in order to emit electrons.

hotch•potch /hóchpoch/ *n.* (also (in sense 3) **hotch•pot** /–pot/) **1** = HODGEPODGE. **2** a dish of many mixed ingredients, esp. a mutton broth or stew with vegetables. **3** *Law* the reunion and blending of properties for the purpose of securing equal division (esp. of the property of an intestate parent). [ME f. AF & OF *hochepot* f. OF *hocher* shake + POT¹: –*potch* by assim.]

hot cross bun *n.* a bun marked with a cross, traditionally eaten on Good Friday.

hot•dog /hótdawg, –dog/ *v.intr. sl.* show off, esp. one's skills.

hot dog *n. & int.* • *n.* **1 a** = FRANKFURTER. **b** a frankfurter sandwiched in a soft roll. **2** *sl.* a person who is showy or shows off skills. • *int. sl.* expressing approval.

ho•tel /hōtél/ *n.* **1** an establishment providing accommodation and meals for payment. **2** *Austral. & NZ* a public house; a bar. [F *hôtel*, later form of HOSTEL]

ho•te•lier /ótelyáy, hōt'leér/ *n.* a hotel-keeper. [F *hôtelier* f. OF *hostelier*: see HOSTELRY]

hot flash *n.* a sudden sensation of heat, usu. as a symptom of menopause.

hot•foot /hótfŏot/ *adv., v., & adj.* • *adv.* in eager haste. • *v.tr.* hurry eagerly (esp. hotfoot it). • *adj.* acting quickly.

hot gos•pel *n.* the fervent propounding of religious beliefs; zealous evangelism. □□ **hot gos•pel•er** *n.*

hot•head /hót-hed/ *n.* an impetuous person.

hot•head•ed /hót-hédid/ *adj.* impetuous; excitable. □□ **hot•head•ed•ly** *adv.* **hot•head•ed•ness** *n.*

hot•house /hót-hows/ *n. & adj.* • *n.* **1** a heated building, usu. largely of glass, for rearing plants out of season or in a climate colder than is natural for them. **2** an environment that encourages the rapid growth or development of something. • *adj.* (*attrib.*) characteristic of something reared in a hothouse; sheltered; sensitive.

hot line *n.* a direct exclusive line of communication, esp. for emergencies.

hot met•al *n. Printing* using type made from molten metal.

hot mon•ey *n.* capital that is frequently transferred between financial institutions to maximize interest or capital gain.

hot pants *n.* **1** tight, brief women's shorts, worn as a fashion garment. **2** strong sexual desire.

hot plate *n.* a heated metal plate, etc. (or a set of these), for cooking food or keeping it hot.

hot pot *n. Brit.* a casserole of meat and vegetables, usu. with a layer of potato on top.

hot po•ta•to *n. colloq.* a controversial or awkward matter or situation.

hot-press *n. & v.* • *n.* a press of glazed boards and hot metal plates for smoothing paper or cloth or making plywood. • *v.tr.* press (paper, etc.) in this.

hot rod *n.* a motor vehicle modified to have extra power and speed.

hot seat *n. sl.* **1** a position of difficult responsibility. **2** the electric chair.

hot•shot /hótshot/ *n. & adj. colloq.* • *n.* an important or exceptionally able person. • *adj.* (*attrib.*) important; able; expert; suddenly prominent.

hot spot *n.* **1** a small region or area with a relatively hot temperature in comparison to its surroundings. **2** a lively or dangerous place.

hot spring *n.* a spring of naturally hot water, heated by subterranean volcanic activity.

hot•spur /hótspər/ *n.* a rash person. [sobriquet of Sir H. Percy, d. 1403]

hot stuff *n. colloq.* **1** a formidably capable person. **2** an important person or thing. **3** a sexually attractive person. **4** a spirited, strong-willed, or passionate person. **5** a book, movie, etc., with a strongly erotic content.

hot-tempered *adj.* impulsively angry.

Hot•ten•tot /hót'ntot/ *n. & adj.* • *n.* **1** a member of a pastoral black people of SW Africa. **2** their language. • *adj.* of this people. [Afrik., perh. = stammerer, with ref. to their mode of pronunc.]

hot•tie /hótee/ *n.* (also **hot•ty**) (*pl.* •**ties**) *Brit. colloq.* a hot-water bottle.

hot tub *n.* a large tub filled with hot aerated water, used for recreation or physical therapy.

hot war *n.* an open war, with active hostilities.

hot wa•ter *n. colloq.* difficulty, trouble, or disgrace (*be in hot water; get into hot water*).

hot-water bot•tle *n.* (also **hot-water bag**) a flat, oblong container, usu. made of rubber, that is filled with hot water and used for warmth.

hot well *n.* **1** = HOT SPRING. **2** a reservoir in a condensing steam engine.

hot-wire *adj. & v.* • *adj.* (of an electrical instrument) operated by the expansion of heated wire. • *v.tr. sl.* start the engine of a vehicle by bypassing the ignition system, usu. in order to steal it.

Hou•di•ni /hoodéenee/ *n.* **1** an ingenious escape. **2** a person skilled at escaping. [H. *Houdini*, professional name of E. Weiss, American escapologist d. 1926]

hough /hok/ *n. & v. Brit.* • *n.* **1** = HOCK¹. **2** a cut of beef, etc., from this and the leg above it. • *v.tr.* hamstring. □□ **hough•er** *n.* [ME *ho(u)gh* = OE *hōh* (heel) in *hōhsinu* hamstring]

houm•mos var. of HUMMUS.

hound /hownd/ *n. & v.* • *n.* **1 a** a dog used for hunting, esp. one able to track by scent. **b** (**the hounds**) a pack of foxhounds. **2** *colloq.* a despicable man. **3** a runner who follows a trail in hare and hounds. **4** a person keen in pursuit of something (usu. in *comb.*: *newshound*). • *v.tr.* **1** harass or pursue relentlessly. **2** chase or pursue with a hound. **3** (foll. by *at*) set (a dog or person) on (a quarry). **4** urge on or nag (a person). □ **ride to hounds** go fox-hunting on horseback. □□ **hound•er** *n.* **hound•ish** *adj.* [OE *hund* f. Gmc]

hound's tongue *n. Bot.* a tall plant, *Cynoglossum officinale*, with tongue-shaped leaves.

hound's•tooth *n.* a checked pattern with notched corners suggestive of a canine tooth, usu. used in cloth for jackets and suits.

hour /owr/ *n.* **1** a twenty-fourth part of a day and night, 60 minutes. **2** a time of day; a point in time (*a late hour; what is the hour?*). **3** (in *pl.* with preceding numerals in form 18:00, 20:30, etc.) this number of hours and minutes past midnight on the 24-hour clock (*will assemble at 20:00 hours*). **4 a** a period set aside for some purpose (*lunch hour; keep regular hours*). **b** (in *pl.*) a fixed period of time for work, use of a building, etc. (*office hours; opening hours*). **5** a short indefinite period of time (*an idle hour*). **6** the present time (*question of the hour*). **7** a time for action, etc. (*the hour has come*). **8** the distance traversed in one hour by a means of transport stated or implied (*we are an hour from San Francisco*). **9** *RC Ch.* **a** prayers to be said at one of seven fixed times of day (*book of hours*). **b** any of these times. **10** (prec. by *the*) each time o'clock of a whole number of hours (*buses leave on the hour; on the half hour; at quarter past the hour*). **11** *Astron.* 15° of longitude or right ascension. □ **after hours** after closing time. **till all hours** till very late. [ME *ure*, etc. f. AF *ure*, OF *ore, eure* f. L *hora* f. Gk *hōra* season, hour]

hour•glass /ówrglas/ *n. & adj.* • *n.* a reversible device with two connected glass bulbs containing sand that takes an hour to pass from the upper to the lower bulb. • *adj.* hourglass-shaped.

hour hand *n.* the hand on a clock or watch that indicates the hour.

hou•ri /hŏoree/ *n.* a beautiful young woman,

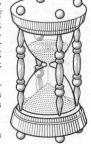

hourglass

esp. in the Muslim Paradise. [F f. Pers. *ḥūrī* f. Arab. *ḥūr* pl. of *ḥawrā'* gazellelike (in the eyes)]

hour·long *adj.* lasting for one hour.

hour·ly /ówrlee/ *adj. & adv.* ● *adj.* **1** done or occurring every hour. **2** frequent; continual. **3** reckoned hour by hour (*hourly wage*). ● *adv.* **1** every hour. **2** frequently; continually.

house *n. & v.* ● *n.* /hows/ (*pl.* /hówziz, –siz/) **1 a** a building for human habitation. **b** (*attrib.*) (of an animal) kept in, frequenting, or infesting houses (*house cat; housefly*). **2** a building for a special purpose (*opera house; summer house*). **3** a building for keeping animals or goods (*henhouse*). **4 a** a religious community. **b** the buildings occupied by it. **5** esp. *Brit.* **a** a body of pupils living in the same building at a boarding school. **b** such a building. **c** a division of a day school for games, competitions, etc. **6** *Brit.* **a** a college of a university. **b** (**the House**) Christ Church, Oxford. **7** a family, esp. a royal family; a dynasty (*House of York*). **8 a** a business or institution. **b** *Brit.* its place of business. **c** (**the House**) *Brit. colloq.* the Stock Exchange. **9 a** a legislative or deliberative assembly. **b** the building where it meets. **c** (**the House**) the House of Representatives. **d** (**the House**) (in the UK) the House of Commons or Lords. **10 a** an audience in a theater, movie theater, etc. **b** *Brit.* a performance in a theater or movie theater (*second house starts at 9 o'clock*). **c** a theater. **11** *Astrol.* a twelfth part of the heavens. **12** (*attrib.*) staying in a hospital as a member of the staff (*house physician; house surgeon*). **13 a** a place of public refreshment; a restaurant or inn (*coffeehouse*). **b** (*attrib.*) (of wine) selected by the management of a restaurant, hotel, etc., to be offered at a special price. **14** a brothel. **15** *Sc.* a dwelling that is one of several in a building. **16** *Brit. sl.* = HOUSEY-HOUSEY. **17** an animal's den, shell, etc. **18** (**the House**) *Brit. hist. euphem.* the workhouse. ● *v.tr.* /howz/ **1** provide (a person, a population, etc.) with a house or houses or other accommodation. **2** store (goods, etc.). **3 a** serve as accommodation for; contain. **b** enclose or encase (a part or fitting). **4** fix in a socket, mortise, etc. □ **as safe as houses** *Brit.* thoroughly or completely safe. **house and home** (as an emphatic) home. **keep house** provide for or manage a household. **keep** (or **make**) **a House** *Brit.* secure the presence of enough members for a quorum in the House of Commons. **keep open house** provide general hospitality. **keep to the house** stay indoors. **like a house on fire 1** vigorously; fast. **2** successfully; excellently. **on the house** at the management's expense; free. **play house** play at being a family in its home. **put** (or **set**) **one's house in order** make necessary reforms. **set up house** begin to live in a separate dwelling. □□ **house·ful** *n.* (*pl.* **·fuls**). **house·less** *adj.* [OE *hūs, hūsian*, f. Gmc]

house ar·rest *n.* detention in one's own house, etc., not in prison.

house·boat /hówsbōt/ *n.* a boat fitted for living in.

house·bound /hówsbownd/ *adj.* unable to leave one's house due to illness, etc.

house·boy /hówsboy/ *n.* a boy or man as a servant in a house.

house·break /hówsbrayk/ *v.tr.* train (a pet living indoors) to excrete outdoors.

house·break·er /hówsbraykər/ *n.* **1** a person guilty of housebreaking. **2** *Brit.* a person who is employed to demolish houses.

house·break·ing /hówsbrayking/ *n.* the act of breaking into a building, esp. in daytime, to commit a crime.

house·bro·ken /hówsbrōkən/ *adj.* **1** (of animals) trained to urinate and defecate outside the house, or only in a special place. **2** *colloq.* well-mannered.

house·carl /hówskaarl/ *n.* (also **house·carle**) *hist.* a member of the bodyguard of a Danish or English king or noble. [OE *húscarl* f. ON *húskarl* f. *hús* HOUSE + *karl* man: cf. CARL]

house church *n. Brit.* **1** a charismatic church independent of traditional denominations. **2** a group meeting in a house as part of the activities of a church.

house·coat /hówskōt/ *n.* a woman's garment for informal wear in the house, usu. a long dresslike coat.

house·craft /hówskraft/ *n. Brit.* skill in household management.

house·dress /hówsdres/ *n.* an inexpensive dress of simple design suitable for wear while doing housework.

house·fa·ther /hówsfaathər/ *n.* a man in charge of a house, esp. of a home for children or a dormitory, etc.

house flag *n.* a flag indicating to what company a ship belongs.

house·fly /hówsflī/ *n.* any fly of the family Muscidae, esp. *Musca domestica*, breeding in decaying organic matter and often entering houses.

house·guest /hówsgest/ *n.* a guest staying for some days in a private home.

house·hold /hóws-hōld/ *n.* **1** the occupants of a house regarded as a unit. **2** a house and its affairs. **3** (prec. by *the*) (in the UK) the royal household.

house·hold·er /hóws-hōldər/ *n.* **1** a person who owns or rents a house. **2** the head of a household.

house·hold gods *n.pl.* **1** gods presiding over a household, esp. (in Roman Antiquity) the lares and penates. **2** the essential possessions of home life.

house·hold name *n.* (also **household word**) **1** a person or thing that is well known by the public (*Elvis is still a household name*). **2** a familiar person or thing.

house·hold troops *n.pl.* (in the UK) troops nominally employed to guard the sovereign.

house·hus·band /hóws-həzbənd/ *n.* a husband who carries out the household duties traditionally performed by a housewife.

house·keep /hówskeep/ *v.intr.* (*past* and *past part.* **·kept**) *colloq.* keep house.

house·keep·er /hówskeepər/ *n.* **1** a person, esp. a woman, employed to manage a household. **2** a person in charge of a house, office, etc.

house·keep·ing /hówskeeping/ *n.* **1** the management of household affairs. **2** money allocated for this. **3** operations of maintenance, record keeping, etc., in an organization.

house·leek /hówsleek/ *n.* a plant, *Sempervivum tectorum*, with pink flowers, growing on walls and roofs.

house lights *n.pl.* the lights in the auditorium of a theater.

house·maid /hówsmayd/ *n.* a female servant in a house.

house·maid's knee *n.* inflammation of the kneecap, often due to excessive kneeling.

house·man /hówsmən/ *n.* (*pl.* **·men**) **1** *Brit.* a resident doctor at a hospital, etc.; a medical intern **2** = HOUSEBOY.

house mar·tin *n.* a black and white swallowlike bird, *Delichon urbica*, which often builds its mud nest on the walls of buildings.

house·mas·ter /hówsmastər/ *n.* (*fem.* **house·mis·tress** /–mistris/) the teacher in charge of a house at a boarding school.

house·moth·er /hówsməthər/ *n.* a woman in charge of a house, esp. of a home for children or a dormitory, etc.

house mu·sic *n.* a style of pop music typically using drum machines and synthesized bass lines with sparse repetitive vocals and a fast beat.

house of cards *n.* **1** an insecure scheme, etc. **2** a structure built (usu. by a child) out of playing cards.

House of Com·mons *n.* (in the UK) the elected chamber of Parliament.

house of God *n.* a church; a place of worship.

house of ill re·pute *n. archaic* a brothel.

House of Lords *n.* **1** (in the UK) the chamber of Parliament composed of peers and bishops. **2** a committee of specially qualified members of this appointed as the ultimate judicial appeal court.

House of Rep·re·sen·ta·tives *n.* the lower house of the US Congress and other legislatures.

house or·gan *n.* a magazine published by a company to be read by its employees and other interested parties and dealing mainly with its own activities.

house·par·ent /hówspərənt/ *n.* a housemother or housefather.

house par·ty *n.* a party at which the guests stay at a house overnight or for a few days.

house·plant /hówsplant/ *n.* a plant grown indoors.

house-proud *adj.* esp. *Brit.* attentive to, or unduly preoccupied with, the care and appearance of the home.

house·room /hówsrōōm, –rŏŏm/ *n.* space or accommodation in one's house. □ **not give houseroom to** *Brit.* not have in any circumstances.

Hous·es of Par·lia·ment *n.pl.* **1** (in the UK) the Houses of Lords and Commons regarded together. **2** the buildings where they meet (the Palace of Westminster).

house spar·row *n.* a common brown and gray sparrow, *Passer domesticus*, which nests in the eaves and roofs of houses.

house style *n.* a particular printer's or publisher's, etc., preferred way of presentation and layout of written material.

house-to-house *adj.* performed at or carried to each house in turn.

house·top /hówstop/ *n.* the roof of a house. □ **proclaim** (or **shout**, etc.) **from the housetops** announce publicly.

house-trained *adj. Brit.* = HOUSEBROKEN.

house·wares /hówswairz/ *n.pl.* small articles for furnishing a home, such as dishware, glassware, and small appliances.

house·warm·ing /hówswawrming/ *n.* a party celebrating a move to a new home.

house·wife /hówswīf/ *n.* (*pl.* **·wives**) **1** a woman (usu. married) managing a household. **2** *Brit.* /húzif/ a case for needles, thread, etc. □□ **house·wife·ly** *adj.* **house·wife·li·ness** *n.* [ME *hus(e)wif* f. HOUSE + WIFE]

house·wif·er·y /hówswīfəree, –wīfree/ *n.* **1** housekeeping. **2** skill in household management and housekeeping.

house·work /hówswərk/ *n.* regular work done in housekeeping, e.g., cleaning and cooking.

house·y-house·y /hówseehówsee, hówzeehówzee/ *n.* (also **hous·ie-hous·ie**) *Brit. sl.* a gambling form of lotto.

hous·ing[1] /hówzing/ *n.* **1 a** dwelling houses collectively. **b** the provision of these. **2** shelter; lodging. **3** a rigid casing, esp. for moving or sensitive parts of a machine. **4** the hole or niche cut in one piece of wood to receive some part of another in order to join them.

hous·ing[2] /hówzing/ n. a cloth covering put on a horse for protection or ornament. [ME = covering, f. obs. *house* f. OF *houce* f. med.L *hultia* f. Gmc]

hous·ing de·vel·op·ment n. (*Brit.* **housing estate**) a residential area in which the houses have all been planned and built at the same time.

HOV abbr. high-occupancy vehicle.

hove past of HEAVE.

hov·el /húvəl, hóv–/ n. **1** a small miserable dwelling. **2** a conical building enclosing a kiln. **3** an open shed or shelter. [ME: orig. unkn.]

hov·er /húvər, hóvər/ v. & n. • v.intr. **1** (of a bird, helicopter, etc.) remain in one place in the air. **2** (often foll. by *about, around*) wait close at hand; linger. **3** remain undecided. • n. **1** hovering. **2** a state of suspense. □□ **hov·er·er** n. [ME f. obs. *hove* hover, linger]

hov·er·craft /húvərkraft, hóv–/ n. (*pl.* same) a vehicle or craft that travels over land or water on a cushion of air provided by a downward blast.

hov·er·port /húvərpawrt, hóv–/ n. a terminal for hovercraft.

hov·er·train /húvərtrayn, hóv–/ n. a train that travels on a cushion of air like a hovercraft.

how /how/ adv., conj., & n. • interrog. adv. **1** by what means; in what way (*how do you do it?; tell me how you do it; how could you behave so disgracefully?; but how to bridge the gap?*). **2** in what condition, esp. of health (*how is the patient?; how do things stand?*). **3 a** used to ask about the extent or degree of something (*how far is it?; how would you like to take my place?; how we laughed!*). **b** used to express a strong feeling such as surprise about the extent of something (*how kind it was of him; how I wish I had been there!*). • rel. adv. in whatever way; as (*do it how you like*). • conj. colloq. that (*told us how he'd been in Canada*). • n. the way a thing is done (*the how and why of it*). □ **and how!** sl. very much so (chiefly used ironically or intensively). **here's how!** *Brit.* I drink to your good health. **how about 1** would you like (*how about a game of chess?*). **2** what is to be done about. **3** what is the news about. **how are you? 1** what is your state of health? **2** = how do you do? **how come?** see COME. **how do?** an informal greeting on being introduced to a stranger. **how do you do?** a formal greeting. **how many** what number. **how much 1** what amount (*how much do I owe you?; did not know how much to take*). **2** what price (*how much is it?*). **3** (as *interrog.*) esp. *Brit. joc.* what? (*"She is a hedonist." "A how much?"*). **how now?** *archaic* what is the meaning of this? **how so?** how can you show that that is so? **how's that?** what is your opinion or explanation of that? [OE *hū* f. WG]

how·be·it /hówbéeit/ adv. archaic nevertheless.

how·dah /hówda/ n. a seat for two or more, usu. with a canopy, for riding on the back of an elephant. [Urdu *hawda* f. Arab. *hawdaj* litter]

how-do-you-do (or **how-d'ye-do**) n. (*pl.* **·dos**) an awkward situation.

how·dy /hówdee/ int. = how do you do? [corrupt.]

how·ev·er /hówévər/ adv. **1 a** in whatever way (*do it however you want*). **b** to whatever extent; no matter how (*must go however inconvenient*). **2** nevertheless. **3** colloq. (as an emphatic) in what way; by what means (*however did that happen?*).

how·itz·er /hówitsər/ n. a short cannon for high-angle firing of shells at low velocities. [Du. *houwitser* f. G *Haubitze* f. Czech *houfnice* catapult]

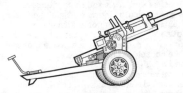

howitzer

howl /howl/ n. & v. • n. **1** a long, loud, doleful cry uttered by a dog, wolf, etc. **2** a prolonged wailing noise, e.g., as made by a strong wind. **3** a loud cry of pain or rage. **4** a yell of derision or merriment. **5** *Electronics* a howling noise in a loudspeaker due to electrical or acoustic feedback. • v. **1** intr. make a howl. **2** intr. weep loudly. **3** tr. utter (words) with a howl. □ **howl down** prevent (a speaker) from being heard by howls of derision. [ME *houle* (v.), prob. imit.: cf. OWL]

howl·er /hówlər/ n. **1** colloq. a glaring mistake. **2** a S. American monkey of the genus *Alouatta*. **3** a person or animal that howls.

howl·ing /hówling/ adj. **1** that howls. **2** sl. extreme (*a howling shame*). **3** archaic dreary (*howling wilderness*).

howl·ing der·vish n. see DERVISH.

how·so·ev·er /hówsō-évər/ adv. (also *poet.* **how·so·e'er** /–sō– áir/) **1** in whatsoever way. **2** to whatsoever extent.

hoy[1] /hoy/ int. & n. • int. used to call attention, drive animals, or

Naut. hail or call aloft. • n. *Austral.* a game of chance resembling bingo, using playing cards. [ME: natural cry]

hoy[2] /hoy/ n. hist. a small vessel, usu. rigged as a sloop, carrying passengers and goods esp. for short distances. [MDu. *hoei, hoede*, of unkn. orig.]

hoy[3] /hoy/ v.tr. *Austral. sl.* throw. [Brit. dial.: orig. unkn.]

hoy·a /hóyə/ n. any climbing shrub of the genus *Hoya*, with pink, white, or yellow waxy flowers. [mod.L f. T. *Hoy*, Engl. gardener d. 1821]

hoy·den /hóyd'n/ n. a boisterous girl. □□ **hoy·den·ish** adj. [orig. = rude fellow, prob. f. MDu. *heiden* (= HEATHEN)]

Hoyle /hoyl/ n. □ **according to Hoyle** adv. correctly; exactly. • adj. correct; exact. [E. *Hoyle*, Engl. writer on card games d. 1769]

h.p. abbr. **1** horsepower. **2** high pressure. **3** *Brit.* hire purchase.

HQ abbr. headquarters.

HR abbr. (also **H.R.**) **1** House of Representatives. **2** home run. **3** home rule.

hr. abbr. hour.

HRH abbr. *Brit.* Her or His Royal Highness.

hrs. abbr. hours.

HS abbr. high school.

Hs symb. *Chem.* the element hassium.

HSH abbr. *Brit.* Her or His Serene Highness.

HST abbr. **1** Hawaii(an) Standard Time. **2** hypersonic transport.

HT abbr. high tension.

hub /hub/ n. **1** the central part of a wheel, rotating on or with the axle, and from which the spokes radiate. **2** a central point of interest, activity, etc. [16th c.: perh. = HOB[1]]

hub·ble-bub·ble /húbəlbúbəl/ n. **1** a rudimentary form of hookah. **2** a bubbling sound. **3** confused talk. [redupl. of BUBBLE]

hub·bub /húbub/ n. **1** a confused din, esp. from a crowd of people. **2** a disturbance or riot. [perh. of Ir. orig.: cf. Gael. *ubub* int. of contempt, Ir. *abú*, used in battle cries]

hub·by /húbee/ n. (*pl.* **·bies**) colloq. a husband. [abbr.]

hub·cap /húbkap/ n. a cover for the hub of a vehicle's wheel.

hu·bris /hyóobris/ n. **1** arrogant pride or presumption. **2** (in Greek tragedy) excessive pride toward or defiance of the gods, leading to nemesis. □□ **hu·bris·tic** adj. [Gk]

huck·a·back /húkəbak/ n. a stout linen or cotton fabric with a rough surface, used for toweling. [17th c.: orig. unkn.]

huck·le·ber·ry /húkəlberee/ n. (*pl.* **·ries**) **1** any low-growing N. American shrub of the genus *Gaylussacia*. **2** the blue or black soft fruit of this plant. [prob. alt. of *hurtleberry*, WHORTLEBERRY]

huck·ster /húkstər/ n. & v. • n. **1** a mercenary person. **2** a publicity agent, esp. for broadcast material. **3** a peddler or hawker. • v. **1** intr. bargain; haggle. **2** tr. carry on a petty traffic in. **3** tr. adulterate. [ME prob. f. LG: cf. dial. *huck* to bargain, HAWKER[1]]

HUD /hud/ abbr. (Department of) Housing and Urban Development.

hud·dle /húd'l/ v. & n. • v. **1** tr. & intr. (often foll. by *up*) crowd together; nestle closely. **2** intr. & refl. (often foll. by *up*) coil one's body into a small space. **3** tr. *Brit.* heap together in a muddle. • n. **1** a confused or crowded mass of people or things. **2** colloq. a close or secret conference (esp. in **go into a huddle**). **3** *Football* a gathering of the players of one team to receive instructions about the next play. **4** confusion; bustle. [16th c.: perh. f. LG and ult. rel. to HIDE[3]]

hue /hyoo/ n. **1 a** a color or tint. **b** a variety or shade of color caused by the admixture of another. **2** the attribute of a color by virtue of which it is discernible as red, green, etc. □□ **–hued** adj. **hue·less** adj. [OE *hīew, hēw* form, beauty f. Gmc: cf. ON *hȳ* down on plants]

hue and cry /hyoo/ n. **1** a loud clamor or outcry. **2** hist. **a** a loud cry raised for the pursuit of a wrongdoer. **b** a proclamation for the capture of a criminal. [AF *hu e cri* f. OF *hu* outcry (f. *huer* shout) + *e* and + *cri* cry]

huff /huf/ v. & n. • v. **1** intr. give out loud puffs of air, steam, etc. **2** intr. bluster loudly or threateningly (*huffing and puffing*). **3** intr. & tr. take or cause to take offense. **4** tr. *Checkers* remove (an opponent's man that could have made a capture) from the board as a forfeit (orig. after blowing on the piece). • n. a fit of petty annoyance. □ **in a huff** annoyed and offended. □□ **huff·ish** adj. [imit. of the sound of blowing]

huff·y /húfee/ adj. (**huff·i·er, huff·i·est**) **1** apt to take offense. **2** offended. □□ **huff·i·ly** adv. **huff·i·ness** n.

hug /hug/ v. & n. • v.tr. (**hugged, hug·ging**) **1** squeeze tightly in one's arms, esp. with affection. **2** (of a bear) squeeze (a person) between its forelegs. **3** keep close to (the shore, curb, etc.). **4** cherish or cling to (prejudices, etc.). **5** refl. congratulate or be pleased with (oneself). • n. **1** a strong clasp with the arms. **2** a squeezing grip in wrestling. □□ **hug·ga·ble** adj. [16th c.: prob. f. Scand.: cf. ON *hugga* console]

huge /hyooj/ adj. **1** extremely large; enormous. **2** (of immaterial things) very great (*a huge success*). □□ **huge·ness** n. [ME *huge* f. OF *ahuge, ahoge*, of unkn. orig.]

huge·ly /hyóojlee/ adv. **1** enormously (*hugely successful*). **2** very much (*enjoyed it hugely*).

hug·ger-mug·ger /húgərmúgər/ adj., adv., n., & v. • adj. & adv. **1** in

secret. 2 confused; in confusion. • *n.* **1** secrecy. **2** confusion. • *v.intr.* proceed in a secret or muddled fashion. [prob. rel. to ME *hoder huddle*, *mokere* conceal: cf. 15th-c. *hoder moder*, 16th-c. *hucker mucker* in the same sense]

Hugh•ie /hyǒo-ee/ *n. Austral. & NZ sl.* the imaginary being responsible for the weather (esp. *send her down, Hughie!*). [male forename *Hugh* + –IE]

Hu•gue•not /hyǒoˈgənot/ *n. hist.* a French Protestant. [F, assim. of *eiguenot* (f. Du. *eedgenot* f. Swiss G *Eidgenoss* confederate) to the name of a Geneva burgomaster *Hugues*]

huh /hə/ *int.* expressing disgust, surprise, etc. [imit.]

hu•la /hǒoˈlə/ *n.* (also **hu•la-hu•la**) a native Hawaiian dance with undulating hips, and gestures symbolizing natural phenomena or historical or mythological subjects, often accompanied by chants and drums. [Hawaiian]

hu•la hoop *n.* a large hoop spun around the body by gyrating the hips, for play or exercise.

hu•la skirt *n.* a long grass skirt.

hulk /hulk/ *n.* **1 a** the body of a dismantled ship, used as a storage vessel, etc. **b** (in *pl.*) *hist.* this used as a prison. **2** an unwieldy vessel. **3** *colloq.* a large clumsy-looking person or thing. [OE *hulc* & MLG, MDu. *hulk*: cf. Gk *holkas* cargo ship]

hulk•ing /húlking/ *adj. colloq.* bulky; large and clumsy.

hull¹ /hul/ *n. & v.* • *n.* the body or frame of a ship, airship, flying boat, etc. • *v.tr.* pierce the hull of (a ship) with gunshot, etc. [ME, perh. rel. to HOLD²]

hull² /hul/ *n. & v.* • *n.* **1** the outer covering of a fruit, esp. the pod of peas and beans, the husk of grain, or the green calyx of a strawberry. **2** a covering. • *v.tr.* remove the hulls from (fruit, etc.). [OE *hulu* ult. f. *helan* cover: cf. HELE]

hul•la•ba•loo /húlǝbǝlǒo/ *n.* (*pl.* **hul•la•ba•loos**) an uproar or clamor. [18th c.: redupl. f. *hallo*, *hullo*, etc.]

hul•lo var. of HELLO.

hum¹ /hum/ *v. & n.* • *v.* (**hummed, hum•ming**) **1** *intr.* make a low steady continuous sound like that of a bee. **2** *tr.* (also *absol.*) sing (a wordless tune) with closed lips. **3** *intr.* utter a slight inarticulate sound. **4** *intr. colloq.* be in an active state (*really made things hum*). **5** *intr. Brit. colloq.* smell unpleasantly. • *n.* **1** a humming sound. **2** an unwanted low-frequency noise caused by variation of electric current, usu. the alternating frequency of a power source, in an amplifier, etc. **3** *Brit. colloq.* a bad smell. □ **hum and haw** (or **ha**) *Brit.* = *hem and haw.* □□ **hum•ma•ble** *adj.* **hum•mer** *n.* [ME, imit.]

hum² /həm/ *int.* expressing hesitation or dissent. [imit.]

hu•man /hyǒomən/ *adj. & n.* • *adj.* **1** of or belonging to the genus *Homo.* **2** consisting of human beings (*the human race*). **3** of or characteristic of people as opposed to God or animals or machines, esp. susceptible to the weaknesses of human beings (*is only human*). **4** showing (esp. the better) qualities of man (*proved to be very human*). • *n.* a human being. □□ **hu•man•ness** *n.* [ME *humai* (*e*) f. OF f. L *humanus* f. *homo* human being]

▶ See note at MAN.

hu•man be•ing *n.* any man or woman or child of the species *Homo sapiens.*

hu•man chain *n.* a line of people formed for passing things along, e.g., buckets of water to the site of a fire.

hu•mane /hyǒomáyn/ *adj.* **1** benevolent; compassionate. **2** inflicting the minimum of pain. **3** (of a branch of learning) tending to civilize or confer refinement. □□ **hu•mane•ly** *adv.* **hu•mane•ness** *n.* [var. of HUMAN, differentiated in sense in the 18th c.]

hu•man en•gi•neer•ing *n.* **1** the management of industrial labor, esp. as regards relationships between humans and machines. **2** the study of this.

hu•man-in•ter•est *adj.* characterizing a story in the media that interests people because it describes the experiences or emotions of individuals (the human-interest angle).

hu•man•ism /hyǒomǝnizǝm/ *n.* **1** an outlook or system of thought concerned with human rather than divine or supernatural matters. **2** a belief or outlook emphasizing common human needs and seeking solely rational ways of solving human problems, and concerned with human beings as responsible and progressive intellectual beings. **3** (often **Humanism**) literary culture, esp. that of the Renaissance humanists.

hu•man•ist /hyǒomǝnist/ *n.* **1** an adherent of humanism. **2** a humanitarian. **3** a student (esp. in the 14th–16th c.) of Roman and Greek literature and antiquities. □□ **hu•man•is•tic** *adj.* **hu•man•is•ti•cal•ly** *adv.* [F *humaniste* f. It. *umanista* (as HUMAN)]

hu•man•i•tar•i•an /hyǒománitáireeǝn/ *n. & adj.* • *n.* **1** a person who seeks to promote human welfare. **2** a person who advocates or practices humane action; a philanthropist. • *adj.* relating to or holding the views of humanitarians. □□ **hu•man•i•tar•i•an•ism** *n.*

hu•man•i•ty /hyǒománitee/ *n.* (*pl.* **-ties**) **1 a** the human race. **b** human beings collectively. **c** the fact or condition of being human. **2** humaneness; benevolence. **3** (in *pl.*) human attributes. **4** (in *pl.*) **a** learning or literature concerned with human culture as opposed to the sciences. **b** the study of Latin and Greek literature and philosophy. [ME f. OF *humanité* f. L *humanitas –tatis* (as HUMAN)]

hu•man•ize /hyǒomǝnīz/ *v.tr.* **1** make human; give a human character to. **2** make humane. □□ **hu•man•i•za•tion** *n.* [F *humaniser* (as HUMAN)]

hu•man•kind /hyǒomǝnkínd/ *n.* human beings collectively.

hu•man•ly /hyǒomǝnlee/ *adv.* **1** by human means (*I will do it if it is humanly possible*). **2** in a human manner. **3** from a human point of view. **4** with human feelings.

hu•man na•ture *n.* the general characteristics and feelings of human beings.

hu•man re•la•tions *n.pl.* relations with or between people or individuals.

hu•man re•sourc•es *n.pl.* = PERSONNEL.

hu•man rights *n.pl.* rights held to be justifiably belonging to any person.

hu•man shield *n.* a person or persons placed in the line of fire in order to discourage attack.

hum•ble /húmbǝl/ *adj. & v.* • *adj.* **1 a** having or showing a low estimate of one's own importance. **b** offered with or affected by such an estimate (*if you want my humble opinion*). **2** of low social or political rank (*humble origins*). **3** (of a thing) of modest pretensions, dimensions, etc. • *v.tr.* **1** make humble; bring low; abase. **2** lower the rank or status of. □ **eat humble pie** make a humble apology; accept humiliation. □□ **hum•ble•ness** *n.* **hum•bly** *adv.* [ME *umble, humble* f. OF *umble* f. L *humilis* lowly f. *humus* ground: *humble pie* f. UMBLES]

SYNONYM TIP humble

ABASE, DEBASE, DEGRADE, DEMEAN, HUMILIATE. While all of these verbs mean to lower in one's own estimation or in the eyes of others, there are subtle distinctions among them. **Humble** and **humiliate** sound similar, but *humiliate* emphasizes shame and the loss of self-respect and usually takes place in public (*humiliated by her tearful outburst*), while *humble* is a milder term implying a lowering of one's pride or rank (*to humble the arrogant professor by pointing out his mistake*). **Abase** suggests groveling or a sense of inferiority and is usually used reflexively (*got down on his knees and abased himself before the king*), while **demean** is more likely to imply a loss of dignity or social standing (*refused to demean herself by marrying a common laborer*). When used to describe things, **debase** implies a deterioration in the quality or value of something (*a currency debased by the country's political turmoil*), but in reference to people it connotes a weakening of moral standards or character (*debased himself by accepting bribes*). **Degrade** is even stronger, suggesting the destruction of a person's character through degenerate or shameful behavior (*degraded by long association with criminals*).

---

hum•ble-bee /húmbǝlbee/ *n.* = BUMBLEBEE. [ME prob. f. MLG *hummelbē*, MDu. *hommel*, OHG *humbal*]

hum•bug /húmbug/ *n. & v.* • *n.* **1** deceptive or false talk or behavior. **2** an impostor. **3** *Brit.* a hard boiled candy usu. flavored with peppermint. • *v.* (**hum•bugged, hum•bug•ging**) **1** *intr.* be or behave like an impostor. **2** *tr.* deceive; hoax. □□ **hum•bug•ger•y** /–búgǝree/ *n.* [18th c.: orig. unkn.]

hum•ding•er /húmdíngǝr/ *n. sl.* an excellent or remarkable person or thing. [20th c.: orig. unkn.]

hum•drum /húmdrum/ *adj. & n.* • *adj.* **1** commonplace; dull. **2** monotonous. • *n.* **1** commonplaceness; dullness. **2** a monotonous routine, etc. [16th c.: prob. f. HUM¹ by redupl.]

hu•mec•tant /hyǒoméktǝnt/ *adj. & n.* • *adj.* retaining or preserving moisture. • *n.* a substance, esp. a food additive, used to reduce loss of moisture. [L (*h*)*umectant-* part. stem of (*h*)*umectare* moisten f. *umēre* be moist]

hu•mer•al /hyǒomǝrǝl/ *adj.* **1** of the humerus or shoulder. **2** worn on the shoulder. [F *huméral* & LL *humeralis* (as HUMERUS)]

hu•mer•us /hyǒomǝrǝs/ *n.* (*pl.* **hu•mer•i** /–rī/) **1** the bone of the upper arm in humans. **2** the corresponding bone in other vertebrates. [L, = shoulder]

hu•mic /hyǒomik/ *adj.* of or consisting of humus.

hu•mid /hyǒomid/ *adj.* (of the air or climate) warm and damp. □□ **hu•mid•ly** *adv.* [F *humide* or L *humidus* f. *umēre* be moist]

hu•mid•i•fi•er /hyǒomídifīǝr/ *n.* a device for keeping the atmosphere moist in a room, etc.

hu•mid•i•fy /hyǒomídifī/ *v.tr.* (**-fies, -fied**) make (air, etc.) humid or damp. □□ **hu•mid•i•fi•ca•tion** *n.*

hu•mid•i•ty /hyǒomíditee/ *n.* (*pl.* **-ties**) **1** a humid state. **2** moisture. **3** the degree of moisture esp. in the atmosphere. [ME f. OF *humidité* or L *humiditas* (as HUMID)]

hu•mi•dor /hyǒomidawr/ *n.* a room or container for keeping cigars or tobacco moist. [HUMID after *cuspidor*]

hu•mi•fy /hyǒomifī/ *v.tr. & intr.* (**-fies, -fied**) make or be made into humus. □□ **hu•mi•fi•ca•tion** *n.*

hu•mil•i•ate /hyǒomílee-ayt/ *v.tr.* make humble; injure the dignity or self-respect of. □□ **hu•mil•i•at•ing** adj. **hu•mil•i•at•ing•ly** adv. **hu•mil•i•a•tion** /–áyshən/ n. **hu•mil•i•a•tor** n. [LL humiliare (as HUMBLE)]

hu•mil•i•ty /hyoōmílitee/ n. **1** humbleness; meekness. **2** a humble condition. [ME f. OF humilité f. L humilitas –tatis (as HUMBLE)]

hum•ming•bird /húmingbərd/ n. any tiny nectar-feeding bird of the family Trochilidae that makes a humming sound by the vibration of its wings when it hovers.

ruby-throated hummingbird

hum•mock /húmək/ n. **1** a hillock or knoll. **2** a piece of rising ground, esp. in a marsh. **3** a hump or ridge in an ice field. □□ **hum•mock•y** adj. [16th c.: orig. unkn.]

hum•mus /hoōmus/ n. (also **houm•mos**) a thick sauce or spread made from ground chickpeas and sesame oil flavored with lemon and garlic. [Turk. humus mashed chickpeas]

hu•mon•gous /hyoōmónggəs, –múng–/ adj. (also **hu•mun•gous**) sl. extremely large or massive. [20th c.: orig. uncert.]

hu•mor /hyoōmər/ n. & v. (Brit. **hu•mour**) • n. **1 a** the condition of being amusing or comic (less intellectual and more sympathetic than wit). **b** the expression of humor in literature, speech, etc. **2** (in full **sense of humor**) the ability to perceive or express humor or take a joke. **3** a mood or state of mind (bad humor). **4** an inclination or whim (in the humor for fighting). **5** (in full **cardinal humor**) hist. each of the four chief fluids of the body (blood, phlegm, choler, melancholy), thought to determine a person's physical and mental qualities. • v.tr. **1** gratify or indulge (a person or taste, etc.). **2** adapt oneself to; make concessions to. □ **out of humor** displeased. □□ **–hu•mored** adj. **hu•mor•less** adj. **hu•mor•less•ly** adv. **hu•mor•less•ness** n.

WORD HISTORY humor

Middle English: via Old French from Latin humor 'moisture', from humere (see HUMID). The original sense was 'bodily fluid' (surviving in aqueous humor and vitreous humor, fluids in the eyeball); it was used specifically for any of the cardinal humors (see sense 5), whence 'mental disposition' (thought to be caused by the relative proportions of the humors). This led, in the 16th cent., to the senses 'state of mind, mood' (see sense 2) and 'whim, fancy', hence to humor someone 'to indulge a person's whim'. Sense 1 dates from the late 16th cent.

hu•mor•al /hyoōmərəl/ adj. **1** hist. of the four bodily humors. **2** Med. relating to body fluids, esp. as distinct from cells. [F humoral or med.L humoralis (as HUMOR)]

hu•mor•esque /hyoōmərésk/ n. a short lively piece of music. [G Humoreske f. Humor HUMOR]

hu•mor•ist /hyoōmərist/ n. **1** a facetious person. **2** a humorous talker, actor, or writer. □□ **hu•mor•is•tic** adj.

hu•mor•ous /hyoōmərəs/ adj. **1** showing humor or a sense of humor. **2** facetious; comic. □□ **hu•mor•ous•ly** adv. **hu•mor•ous•ness** n.

hu•mour Brit. var. of HUMOR.

hu•mous /hyoōməs/ adj. like or consisting of humus.

hump /hump/ n. & v. • n. **1** a rounded protuberance on the back of a camel, etc., or as an abnormality on a person's back. **2** a rounded raised mass of earth, etc. **3** a mound over which railroad cars are pushed so as to run by gravity to the required place in a switchyard. **4** a critical point in an undertaking, ordeal, etc. **5** (prec. by the) Brit. sl. a fit of depression or vexation (it gives me the hump). **6** coarse sl. an act of sexual intercourse; a sexual partner. • v.tr. **1 a** colloq. lift or carry (heavy objects, etc.) with difficulty. **b** esp. Austral. hoist up; shoulder (one's pack, etc.). **2** make hump-shaped. **3** annoy; depress. **4** coarse sl. have sexual intercourse with. □ **live on one's hump** Brit. colloq. be self-sufficient. **over the hump** over the worst; well begun. □□ **humped** adj. **hump•less** adj. [17th c.: perh. rel. to LG humpel hump, LG humpe, Du. homp lump, hunk (of bread)]

hump•back /húmpbak/ n. **1 a** a deformed back with a hump. **b** a person having this. **2** a baleen whale, Megaptera novaeangliae, with a dorsal fin forming a hump. □□ **hump•backed** adj.

hump•back bridge n. Brit. a small bridge with a steep ascent and descent.

humph /humf/ int. & n. an inarticulate sound expressing doubt or dissatisfaction. [imit.]

hump•ty-dump•ty /húmpteedúmptee/ n. (pl. **-ties**) **1** a short dumpy person. **2** a person or thing that once overthrown cannot be restored. [the nursery rhyme Humpty-Dumpty, perh. ult. f. HUMPY[1], DUMPY]

hump•y[1] /húmpee/ adj. (**hump•i•er**, **hump•i•est**) **1** having a hump or humps. **2** humplike.

hump•y[2] /húmpee/ n. (pl. **-ies**) Austral. a primitive hut. [Aboriginal oompi, infl. by HUMP]

hu•mus /hyoōməs/ n. the organic constituent of soil, usu. formed by the decomposition of plants and leaves by soil bacteria. □□ **hu•mus•i•fy** v.tr. & intr. (**-fies**, **-fied**) [L, = soil]

Hun /hun/ n. **1** a member of a warlike Asiatic nomadic people who invaded and ravaged Europe in the 4th–5th c. **2** offens. a German (esp. in military contexts). **3** an uncivilized devastator; a vandal. □□ **Hun•nish** adj. [OE Hūne pl. f. LL Hunni f. Gk Hounnoi f. Turki Hun-yü]

hunch /hunch/ v. & n. • v. **1** tr. bend or arch into a hump. **2** tr. thrust out or up to form a hump. **3** intr. (usu. foll. by up) sit with the body hunched. • n. **1** colloq. an intuitive feeling or conjecture. **2** colloq. a hint. **3** a hump. **4** a thick piece. [16th c.: orig. unkn.]

hunch•back /húnchbak/ n. = HUMPBACK. □□ **hunch•backed** adj.

hun•dred /húndrəd/ n. & adj. • n. (pl. **hun•dreds** or (in sense 1) **hundred**) (in sing., prec. by a or one) **1** the product of ten and ten. **2** a symbol for this (100, c, C). **3** a set of a hundred things. **4** (in sing. or pl.) colloq. a large number. **5** (in pl.) the years of a specified century (the seventeen hundreds). **6** Brit. hist. a subdivision of a county or shire, having its own court. • adj. **1** that amount to a hundred. **2** used to express whole hours in the 24-hour system (thirteen hundred hours). □ **a** (or **one**) **hundred percent** adv. entirely; completely. • adj. **1** entire; complete. **2** (usu. with neg.) fully recovered. □□ **hun•dred•fold** adj. & adv. **hun•dredth** adj. & n. [OE f. Gmc]

hun•dreds and thou•sands n.pl. Brit. tiny colored candies used chiefly for decorating cakes, etc.

hun•dred•weight /húndrədwayt/ n. (pl. same or **-weights**) **1** (in full **short hundredweight**) a unit of weight equal to 100 lb. (about 45.4 kg). **2** (in full **long hundredweight**) Brit. a unit of weight equal to 112 lb. (about 50.8 kg). **3** (in full **metric hundredweight**) a unit of weight equal to 50 kg.

hung past and past part. of HANG.

▶See note at HANG.

Hun•gar•i•an /hunggáireeən/ n. & adj. • n. **1 a** a native or inhabitant of Hungary in E. Europe. **b** a person of Hungarian descent. **2** the Finno-Ugric language of Hungary. • adj. of or relating to Hungary or its people or language. [med.L Hungaria f. Hungari Magyar nation]

hun•ger /húnggər/ n. & v. • n. **1** a feeling of pain or discomfort, or (in extremes) an exhausted condition, caused by lack of food. **2** (often foll. by for, after) a strong desire. • v.intr. **1** (often foll. by for, after) have a craving or strong desire. **2** feel hunger. □ **hunger striker** a person who takes part in a hunger strike. [OE hungor, hyngran f. Gmc]

hun•ger strike n. the refusal of food as a form of protest, esp. by prisoners.

hung ju•ry n. a jury unable to reach unanimous agreement after extended deliberations.

hung-over adj. colloq. suffering from a hangover.

hung par•lia•ment n. (in parliamentary governments) a parliament in which no party has a clear majority.

hun•gry /húnggree/ adj. (**hun•gri•er**, **hun•gri•est**) **1** feeling or showing hunger; needing food. **2** inducing hunger (a hungry air). **3 a** eager; greedy; craving. **b** Austral. mean; stingy. **4** (of soil) poor; barren. □□ **hun•gri•ly** adv. **hun•gri•ness** n. [OE hungrig (as HUNGER)]

hunk /hungk/ n. **1 a** a large piece cut off (a hunk of bread). **b** a thick or clumsy piece. **2** colloq. **a** a sexually attractive man. **b** a very large person. □□ **hunk•y** adj. (**hunk•i•er**, **hunk•i•est**). [19th c.: prob. f. Flem. hunke]

hunk•er /húngkər/ n. & v. • n.pl. the haunches. • v.intr. (foll. by down) **1** squat; crouch. **2** act defensively; hold to a position. [orig. Sc., f. hunker crouch, squat]

hunk•y-do•ry /húngkeedáwree/ adj. colloq. excellent. [19th c.: orig. unkn.]

hunt /hunt/ v. & n. • v. **1** tr. (also absol.) **a** pursue and kill (wild animals, esp. game), Brit. esp. on horseback and with hounds, for sport or food. **b** (of an animal) chase (its prey). **2** intr. (foll. by after, for) seek; search (hunting for a pen). **3** intr. a oscillate. **b** Brit. hist. (of an engine, etc.) run alternately too fast and too slow. **4** tr. (foll. by away, etc.) drive off by pursuit. **5** tr. scour (a district) in pursuit of game. **6** tr. (as **hunted** adj.) (of a look, etc.) expressing alarm or terror as of one being hunted. **7** tr. (foll. by down, up) move the place of (a bell) in ringing the changes. • n. **1** the practice of hunting or an instance of this. **2 a** an association of people engaged in hunting with hounds. **b** an area where hunting takes place. **3** an oscillating motion. □ **hunt down** pursue and capture. **hunt out** find by searching; track down. [OE huntian, weak grade of hentan seize]

hunt•a•way /húntəway/ n. Austral. & NZ a dog trained to drive sheep forward.

hunt•er /húntər/ n. **1 a** (fem. **hunt•ress**) a person or animal that hunts. **b** a horse used in hunting. **2** a person who seeks something. **3** a watch with a hinged cover protecting the glass.

hunt•er's moon n. the first full moon after the harvest moon.

hunt•ing /húnting/ n. the practice of pursuing and killing wild animals, esp. for sport or food. [OE huntung (as HUNT)]

hunt•ing crop n. a short rigid riding whip with a handle at right angles to the stock and a long leather thong.

hunt•ing ground *n.* **1** a place suitable for hunting. **2** a source of information or object of exploitation likely to be fruitful.

hunt•ing horn *n.* a horn blown to give signals during hunting.

hunt•ing pink *n.* see PINK[1].

Hun•ting•ton's cho•re•a /húntingt'nz/ *n.* **1** a hereditary disease marked by degeneration of the brain cells and causing chorea and progressive dementia.. **2** see CHOREA. [G. *Huntington*, Amer. neurologist, d. 1916]

hunts•man /húntsmən/ *n.* (*pl.* •**men**) **1** a hunter. **2** a hunt official in charge of hounds.

hur•dle /hórd'l/ *n. & v.* •*n.* **1** *Track & Field* **a** each of a series of light frames to be cleared by athletes in a race. **b** (in *pl.*) a hurdle race. **2** an obstacle or difficulty. **3 a** a portable rectangular frame strengthened with withes or wooden bars, used as a temporary fence, etc. **4** *Brit. hist.* a frame on which traitors were dragged to execution. •*v.* **1** *Track & Field* **a** *intr.* run in a hurdle race. **b** *tr.* clear (a hurdle). **2** *tr.* fence off, etc., with hurdles. **3** *tr.* overcome (a difficulty). [OE *hyrdel* f. Gmc]

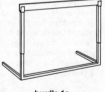

hurdle 1a

hur•dler /hórdlər/ *n.* **1** *Track & Field* a person who runs in hurdle races. **2** a person who makes hurdles.

hur•dy-gur•dy /hórdeegórdee/ *n.* (*pl.* •**dies**) **1** a musical instrument with a droning sound, played by turning a handle, esp. one with a rosined wheel turned by the right hand to sound the drone strings, and keys played by the left hand. **2** *colloq.* a barrel organ. [prob. imit.]

hurl /hórl/ *v. & n.* •*v.* **1** *tr.* throw with great force. **2** *tr.* utter (abuse, etc.) vehemently. **3** *intr.* play hurling. **4** *intr. sl.* vomit. •*n.* **1** a forceful throw. **2** the act of hurling. [ME, prob. imit., but corresp. in form and partly in sense with LG *hurreln*]

Hurl•er's syn•drome /hórlərz/ *n. Med.* a defect in metabolism resulting in mental retardation, a protruding abdomen, and deformities of the bones, including an abnormally large head. Also called **gargoylism**. [G. *Hurler*, Ger. pediatrician]

hurl•ing /hórling/ *n.* (also **hur•ley** /hórlee/) **1** an Irish game somewhat resembling field hockey, played with broad sticks. **2** a stick used in this.

hurl•y-burl•y /hórleebórlee/ *n.* boisterous activity; commotion. [redupl. f. HURL]

Hu•ron /hyóórən, –on/ *n.* **1 a** a N. American people native to the northeastern US. **b** a member of this people. **2** the language of this people.

hur•rah /hoöraá/ *int., n., & v.* (also **hur•ray** /hoöráy/) •*int. & v.* an exclamation of joy or approval. •*v.intr.* cry or shout "hurrah" or "hurray." [alt. of earlier *huzza*, perh. orig. a sailor's cry when hauling]

hur•ri•cane /hórikayn, húr–/ *n.* **1** a storm with a violent wind, esp. a cyclone in the W. Atlantic. **2** *Meteorol.* a wind of 65 knots (75 m.p.h.) or more, force 12 on the Beaufort scale. **3** a violent commotion. [Sp. *huracan* & Port. *furacão* of Carib orig.]

hur•ri•cane bird *n.* a frigate bird.

hur•ri•cane deck *n.* a light upper deck on a ship, etc.

hur•ri•cane lamp *n.* an oil lamp designed to resist a high wind.

hur•ry /hóree, húree/ *n. & v.* •*n.* (*pl.* •**ries**) **1** a great haste. **b** (with *neg.* or *interrog.*) a need for haste (*there is no hurry; what's the hurry?*). **2** (often foll. by *for,* or *to* + infin.) eagerness to get a thing done quickly. •*v.* (•**ries,** •**ried**) **1** *intr.* move or act with great or undue haste. **2** *tr.* (often foll. by *away, along*) cause to move or proceed in this way. **3** *tr.* (as **hurried** *adj.*) hasty; done rapidly owing to lack of time. □ **hurry up** (*or* **along**) make or cause to make haste. **in a hurry 1** hurrying; rushed; in a rushed manner. **2** *colloq.* easily or readily (*you will not beat that in a hurry; shall not ask again in a hurry*). □□ **hur•ried•ly** *adv.* **hur•ried•ness** *n.* [16th c.: imit.]

hur•ry-scur•ry /hóreeskɜree, húreeskúree/ *n., adj., & adv.* •*n.* disorderly haste. •*adj. & adv.* in confusion. [jingling redupl. of HURRY]

hurst /hórst/ *n.* **1** a hillock. **2** a sandbank in the sea or river. **3** a wood or wooded eminence. [OE *hyrst,* rel. to OS, OHG *hurst horst*]

hurt /hórt/ *v, n., & adj.* •*v.* (*past* and *past part.* **hurt**) **1** *tr.* (also *absol.*) cause pain or injury to. **2** *tr.* cause mental pain or distress to (a person, feelings, etc.). **3** *intr.* suffer pain or harm (*my arm hurts*). **4** *tr.* cause damage to; be detrimental to. •*n.* **1** bodily or material injury. **2** harm; wrong. **3** mental pain or distress. •*adj.* expressing emotional pain; distressed; aggrieved. □□ **hurt•less** *adj.* [ME f. OF *hurter, hurt* ult. perh. f. Gmc]

hurt•ful /hórtfool/ *adj.* causing (esp. mental) hurt; causing damage or harm. □□ **hurt•ful•ly** *adv.* **hurt•ful•ness** *n.*

hur•tle /hórt'l/ *v.* **1** *intr. & tr.* move or hurl rapidly or with a clattering sound. **2** *intr.* come with a crash. [HURT in obs. sense 'strike forcibly']

hus•band /húzbənd/ *n. & v.* •*n.* a married man esp. in relation to his wife. •*v. tr.* manage thriftily; use (resources) economically. □□ **hus•band•er** *n.* **hus•band•hood** *n.* **hus•band•less** *adj.* **hus•band•like** *adj.* **hus•band•ly** *adj.* **hus•band•ship** *n.*

hus•band•ry /húzbəndree/ *n.* **1** farming. **2 a** management of resources. **b** careful management.

hush /hush/ *v., int., & n.* •*v.* **1** *tr. & intr.* (often as **hushed** *adj.*) make or become silent, quiet, or muted. **2** *tr.* calm (disturbance, disquiet, etc.); soothe; allay. •*int.* calling for silence. •*n.* an expectant stillness or silence. □ **hush up** suppress public mention of (a scandal). [back-form. f. obs. *husht* int., = quiet!, taken as a past part.]

hush•a•by /húshəbī/ *int.* (also **hush•a•bye**) used to lull a child.

hush-hush /húsh-húsh/ *adj. colloq.* (esp. of an official plan or enterprise, etc.) highly secret or confidential.

hush mon•ey *n.* money paid to someone to prevent them from disclosing embarrassing or discreditable information.

hush pup•py *n.* a deep-fried ball of cornmeal dough.

husk /husk/ *n. & v.* •*n.* **1** the dry outer covering of some fruits or seeds, esp. of a nut or corn. **2** the worthless outside part of a thing. •*v. tr.* remove a husk or husks from. [ME, prob. f. LG *hüske* sheath, dimin. of *hūs* HOUSE]

husk•y[1] /húskee/ *adj.* (**husk•i•er, husk•i•est**) **1** (of a person or voice) dry in the throat; hoarse. **2** of or full of husks. **3** dry as a husk. **4** tough; strong; hefty. □□ **husk•i•ly** *adv.* **husk•i•ness** *n.*

husk•y[2] /húskee/ *n.* (*pl.* •**ies**) **1** a dog of a powerful breed used in the Arctic for pulling sledges. **2** this breed. [perh. contr. f. ESKIMO]

hus•sar /həzaár, –saár/ *n.* **1** a soldier of a light cavalry regiment. **2** a Hungarian light horseman of the 15th c. [Magyar *huszár* f. OSerb. *husar* f. It. *corsaro* CORSAIR]

Huss•ite /húsīt/ *n. hist.* a member or follower of the movement begun by John *Huss*, Bohemian religious and nationalist reformer d. 1415. □□ **Huss•it•ism** *n.*

hus•sy /húsee, –zee/ *n.* (*pl.* •**sies**) *derog.* an impudent or immoral girl or woman. [phonetic reduction of HOUSEWIFE (the orig. sense)]

hust•ings /hústingz/ *n.* **1** political campaigning, esp. the appearances and activities involved with a campaign. **2** *Brit. hist.* a platform from which (before 1872) candidates for Parliament were nominated and addressed electors. [late OE *husting* f. ON *hústhing* house of assembly]

hus•tle /húsəl/ *v. & n.* •*v.* **1** *tr.* push roughly; jostle. **2** *tr.* **a** (foll. by *into, out of,* etc.) force, coerce, or deal with hurriedly or unceremoniously (*hustled them out of the room*). **b** (foll. by *into*) coerce hurriedly (*was hustled into agreeing*). **3** *intr.* push one's way; hurry; bustle. **4** *tr. sl.* obtain by forceful action. **b** swindle. **5** *intr. sl.* engage in prostitution. •*n.* **1 a** an act or instance of hustling. **b** forceful or strenuous activity. **2** *colloq.* a fraud or swindle. [MDu. *husselen* shake, toss, frequent. of *hutsen,* orig. imit.]

hus•tler /húslər/ *n. sl.* **1** an active, enterprising, or unscrupulous individual. **2** a prostitute.

hut /hut/ *n. & v.* •*n.* **1** a small simple or crude house or shelter. **2** *Mil.* a temporary wooden, etc., house for troops. •*v.* (**hut•ted, hut•ting**) **1** *tr.* provide with huts. **2** *tr. Mil.* place (troops, etc.) in huts. **3** *intr.* lodge in a hut. □□ **hut•like** *adj.* [F *hutte* f. MHG *hütte*]

hutch /huch/ *n.* **1** a box or cage, typically with a wire mesh front, for keeping small domesticated animals. **2** a storage chest. **3** a cupboard or dresser typically with open shelves above. [ME, = coffer, f. OF *huche* f. med.L *hutica,* of unkn. orig.]

hut•ment /hútmənt/ *n. Mil.* an encampment of huts.

HWM *abbr.* high-water mark.

hwy. *abbr.* highway.

hwyl /hóöil/ *n. Welsh* an emotional quality inspiring impassioned eloquence. [Welsh]

hy•a•cinth /híəsinth/ *n.* **1** any bulbous plant of the genus *Hyacinthus* with racemes of usu. purplish blue, pink, or white bell-shaped fragrant flowers. **2** = GRAPE HYACINTH. **3** the purplish blue color of the hyacinth flower. **4** an orange variety of zircon used as a precious stone. **5** *poet.* hair or locks like the hyacinth flower (as a Homeric epithet of doubtful sense). □□ **hy•a•cin•thine** /–sínthin, –īn/ *adj.* [F *hyacinthe* f. L *hyacinthus* f. Gk *huakinthos,* flower and gem, also the name of a youth loved by Apollo]

Hy•a•des /híədeez/ *n.pl.* a group of stars in Taurus near the Pleiades, whose heliacal rising was once thought to foretell rain. [ME f. Gk *Huades* (by popular etym. f. *huō* rain, but perh. f. *hus* pig)]

hy•ae•na var. of HYENA.

hy•a•lin /híəlin/ *n.* a clear glassy substance produced as a result of the degeneration of certain body tissues. [Gk *hualos* glass + –IN]

hy•a•line *adj. & n.* •*adj.* /híəlin, –īn/ glasslike; vitreous; transparent. •*n.* /híəleén, –īn/ *literary* a smooth sea, clear sky, etc. [L *hyalinus* f. Gk *hualinos* f. *hualos* glass]

hy·a·line car·ti·lage n. a translucent bluish-white type of cartilage present in the joints and respiratory tract.

hy·a·lite /hī́əlīt/ n. a colorless variety of opal. [Gk *hualos* glass]

hy·a·loid /hī́əloyd/ adj. Anat. glassy. [F *hyaloïde* f. LL *hyaloides* f. Gk *hualoeidēs* (as HYALITE)]

hy·a·loid mem·brane n. a thin transparent membrane enveloping the vitreous humor of the eye.

hy·brid /hī́brid/ n. & adj. ● n. **1** Biol. the offspring of two plants or animals of different species or varieties. **2** often offens. a person of mixed racial or cultural origin. **3** a thing composed of incongruous elements, e.g., a word with parts taken from different languages. ● adj. **1** bred as a hybrid from different species or varieties. **2** Biol. heterogeneous. **3** of mixed character; derived from incongruous elements or unlike sources. □□ **hy·brid·ism** n. **hy·brid·i·ty** /–brídite/ n. [L *hybrida*, (h)*ibrida* offspring of a tame sow and wild boar, child of a freeman and slave, etc.]

hy·brid·ize /hī́bridīz/ v. **1** tr. subject (a species, etc.) to crossbreeding. **2** intr. **a** produce hybrids. **b** (of an animal or plant) interbreed. □□ **hy·brid·iz·a·ble** adj. **hy·brid·i·za·tion** n.

hy·brid vig·or n. heterosis.

hy·da·tid /hī́dətid/ n. Med. **1** a cyst containing watery fluid (esp. one formed by, and containing, a tapeworm larva). **2** a tapeworm larva. □□ **hy·da·tid·i·form** /–tídiform/ adj. [mod.L *hydatis* f. Gk *hudatis* –*idos* watery vesicle f. *hudōr hudatos* water]

hy·dra /hī́drə/ n. **1** a freshwater polyp of the genus *Hydra* with tubular body and tentacles around the mouth. **2** something that is hard to destroy. [ME f. L f. Gk *hudra* water snake, esp. a fabulous one with many heads that grew again when cut off]

hy·dran·gea /hīdráynjə, –dran–/ n. any shrub of the genus *Hydrangea* with large white, pink, or blue flowers. [mod.L f. Gk *hudōr* water + *aggos* vessel (from the cup shape of its seed capsule)]

hy·drant /hī́drənt/ n. a pipe (esp. in a street) with a nozzle to which a hose can be attached for drawing water from a water main. [irreg. f. HYDRO- + –ANT]

hy·drate /hī́drayt/ n. & v. ● n. Chem. a compound of water combined with another compound or with an element. ● v.tr. **1 a** combine chemically with water. **b** (as **hydrated** adj.) chemically bonded to water. **2** cause to absorb water. □□ **hy·drat·a·ble** adj. **hy·dra·tion** /–dráyshən/ n. **hy·dra·tor** n. [F f. Gk *hudōr* water]

hy·drau·lic /hīdráwlik, –drólik/ adj. **1** (of water, oil, etc.) conveyed through pipes or channels usu. by pressure. **2** (of a mechanism, etc.) operated by liquid moving in this manner (*hydraulic brakes*; *hydraulic elevator*). **3** of or concerned with hydraulics (*hydraulic engineer*). **4** hardening under water (*hydraulic cement*). □□ **hy·drau·li·cal·ly** adv. **hy·drau·lic·i·ty** /–lísitee/ n. [L *hydraulicus* f. Gk *hudraulikos* f. *hudōr* water + *aulos* pipe]

hy·drau·lic press n. a device in which the force applied to a fluid creates a pressure that when transmitted to a larger volume of fluid gives rise to a greater force.

hy·drau·lic ram n. an automatic pump in which the kinetic energy of a descending column of water raises some of the water above its original level.

hy·drau·lics /hīdráwliks, –dróliks/ n.pl. (usu. treated as *sing.*) the science of the conveyance of liquids through pipes, etc., esp. as motive power.

hy·dra·zine /hī́drəzeen/ n. Chem. a colorless alkaline liquid which is a powerful reducing agent and is used as a rocket propellant. ¶ Chem. formula: N_2H_4. [HYDROGEN + AZO- + –INE[4]]

hy·dride /hī́drīd/ n. Chem. a binary compound of hydrogen with an element, esp. with a metal.

hy·dri·od·ic ac·id /hī́dreeódik/ n. Chem. a solution of the colorless gas hydrogen iodide in water. ¶ Chem. formula: HI. [HYDROGEN + IODINE]

hy·dro /hī́drō/ n. (pl. **·dros**) colloq. **1** Brit. a hotel or clinic, etc., orig. providing hydropathic treatment; a health spa. **2** a hydroelectric power plant. [abbr.]

hydro- /hī́drō/ comb. form (also **hydr-** before a vowel) **1** having to do with water (*hydroelectric*). **2** Med. affected with an accumulation of serous fluid (*hydrocele*). **3** Chem. combined with hydrogen (*hydrochloric*). [Gk *hudro-* f. *hudōr* water]

hy·dro·bro·mic ac·id /hī́drəbrómik/ n. Chem. a solution of the colorless gas hydrogen bromide in water. ¶ Chem. formula: HBr.

hy·dro·car·bon /hī́drəkaárbən/ n. Chem. a compound of hydrogen and carbon.

hy·dro·cele /hī́drəseel/ n. Med. the accumulation of serous fluid in a body sac.

hy·dro·ceph·a·lus /hī́drəséfələs/ n. Med. an abnormal amount of fluid within the brain, esp. in young children, which makes the head enlarge and can cause mental deficiency. □□ **hy·dro·ce·phal·ic** /–sifálik/ adj.

hy·dro·chlo·ric ac·id /hī́drəkláwrik/ n. Chem. a solution of the colorless gas hydrogen chloride in water. ¶ Chem. formula: HCl.

hy·dro·chlo·ride /hī́drəkláwrīd/ n. Chem. a compound of an organic base with hydrochloric acid.

hy·dro·cor·ti·sone /hī́drəkáwrtizōn/ n. Biochem. a steroid hormone produced by the adrenal cortex, used medicinally to treat inflammation and rheumatism.

hy·dro·cy·an·ic ac·id /hī́drōsiánik/ n. Chem. a highly poisonous volatile liquid with a characteristic odor of bitter almonds. ¶ Chem. formula: HCN. Also called **prussic acid**.

hy·dro·dy·nam·ics /hī́drōdīnámiks/ n. the science of forces acting on or exerted by fluids (esp. liquids). □□ **hy·dro·dy·nam·ic** adj. **hy·dro·dy·nam·i·cal** adj. **hy·dro·dy·nam·i·cist** /–misist/ n. [mod.L *hydrodynamicus* (as HYDRO-, DYNAMIC)]

hy·dro·e·lec·tric /hī́drōiléktrik/ adj. **1** generating electricity by utilization of waterpower. **2** (of electricity) generated in this way. □□ **hy·dro·e·lec·tric·i·ty** /–trísitee/ n.

hy·dro·fluor·ic ac·id /hī́drəflóorik, flăwr–/ n. Chem. a solution of the colorless liquid hydrogen fluoride in water. ¶ Chem. formula: HF.

hy·dro·foil /hī́drəfoyl/ n. **1** a boat equipped with a device consisting of planes for lifting its hull out of the water to increase its speed. **2** this device. [HYDRO-, after AIRFOIL]

hydrofoil

hy·dro·gen /hī́drəjən/ n. Chem. a colorless gaseous element, without taste or odor, the lightest of the elements and occurring in water and all organic compounds. ¶ Symb.: H. □□ **hy·drog·e·nous** /–drójinəs/ adj. [F *hydrogène* (as HYDRO-, –GEN)]

hy·drog·e·nase /hīdrójinays, –nayz/ n. Biochem. any enzyme which catalyzes the oxidation of hydrogen and the reduction of protons.

hy·dro·gen·ate /hīdrójinayt, hī́drəjənayt/ v.tr. charge with or cause to combine with hydrogen. □□ **hy·dro·gen·a·tion** /–náyshən/ n.

hy·dro·gen bomb n. an immensely powerful bomb whose destructive power comes from the rapid release of energy during the nuclear fusion of isotopes of hydrogen (deuterium and tritium), using an atom bomb as a trigger. Also called **H bomb**.

hy·dro·gen bond n. a weak electrostatic interaction between an electronegative atom and a hydrogen atom bonded to a different electronegative atom.

hy·dro·gen per·ox·ide n. Chem. a colorless, viscous, unstable liquid with strong oxidizing properties, commonly used in diluted form in disinfectants and bleaches. ¶ Chem. formula: H_2O_2.

hy·dro·gen sul·fide n. a colorless poisonous gas with a disagreeable smell, formed by rotting animal matter. ¶ Chem. formula: H_2S.

hy·drog·ra·phy /hīdrógrəfee/ n. the science of surveying and charting seas, lakes, rivers, etc. □□ **hy·drog·ra·pher** n. **hy·dro·graph·ic** /hī́drəgráfik/ adj. **hy·dro·graph·i·cal** adj. **hy·dro·graph·i·cal·ly** adv.

hy·droid /hī́droyd/ adj. & n. Zool. any usu. polypoid hydrozoan of the order Hydroida, including hydra.

hy·dro·lase /hī́drōlays, –layz/ n. Biochem. any enzyme which catalyzes the hydrolysis of a substrate.

hy·drol·o·gy /hīdróləjee/ n. the science of the properties of the earth's water, esp. of its movement in relation to land. □□ **hy·dro·log·ic** /hī́drəlójik/ adj. **hy·dro·log·i·cal** adj. **hy·dro·log·i·cal·ly** adv. **hy·drol·o·gist** /–rólɔjist/ n.

hy·drol·y·sis /hīdrólisis/ n. the chemical reaction of a substance with water, usu. resulting in decomposition. □□ **hy·dro·lyt·ic** /hī́drəlítik/ adj.

hy·dro·lyze /hī́drəlīz/ v.tr. & intr. (Brit. **hy·dro·lyse**) subject to or undergo the chemical action of water.

hy·dro·mag·net·ic /hī́drōmagnétik/ adj. involving hydrodynamics and magnetism; magnetohydrodynamic.

hy·dro·ma·ni·a /hī́drəmáyneeə/ n. a craving for water.

hy·dro·me·chan·ics /hī́drōmikániks/ n. the mechanics of liquids; hydrodynamics.

hy·drom·e·ter /hīdrómitər/ n. an instrument for measuring the density of liquids. □□ **hy·dro·met·ric** /hī́drəmétrik/ adj. **hy·drom·e·try** n.

hy·dro·ni·um i·on /hīdróneeəm/ n. Chem. the hydrated hydrogen ion, H_3O^+.

hy·drop·a·thy /hīdrópəthee/ n. the (medically unorthodox) treatment of disease by external and internal application of water. □□ **hy·dro·path·ic** /hī́drəpáthik/ adj. **hy·drop·a·thist** n. [HYDRO-, after HOMEOPATHY, etc.]

hy·dro·phil·ic /hī́drəfilik/ adj. **1** having an affinity for water. **2** wettable by water. [HYDRO- + Gk *philos* loving]

hy·dro·pho·bi·a /hī́drəfóbeeə/ n. **1** a morbid aversion to water, esp. as a symptom of rabies in humans. **2** rabies, esp. in humans. [LL f. Gk *hudrophobia* (as HYDRO-, –PHOBIA)] hy·dro·pho·bic /hídrəfóbik/ adj. 1 of or suffering from hydrophobia. 2 a lacking an affinity for water. b not readily wettable.

hy·dro·phone /hídrəfon/ n. an instrument for the detection of sound waves in water.

hy·dro·phyte /hídrəfīt/ n. an aquatic plant, or a plant which needs much moisture.

hy·dro·plane /hídrəplayn/ n. & v. ● n. 1 a light fast motor boat designed to skim over the surface of water. 2 a finlike attachment which enables a submarine to rise and submerge in water. ● v.intr. 1 (of a boat) skim over the surface of water with its hull lifted. 2 (of a vehicle) glide uncontrollably on the wet surface of a road.

hy·dro·pon·ics /hídrəpóniks/ n. the process of growing plants in sand, gravel, or liquid, without soil and with added nutrients. □□ hy·dro·pon·ic adj. hy·dro·pon·i·cal·ly adv. [HYDRO- + Gk ponos labor]

hy·dro·qui·none /hídrəkwinón/ n. a substance formed by the reduction of quinone, used as a photographic developer.

hy·dro·sphere /hídrəsfeer/ n. the waters of the earth's surface.

hy·dro·stat·ic /hídrəstátik/ adj. of the equilibrium of liquids and the pressure exerted by liquid at rest. □□ hy·dro·stat·i·cal adj. hy·dro·stat·i·cal·ly adv. [prob. f. Gk hudrostatēs hydrostatic balance (as HYDRO-, STATIC)]

hy·dro·stat·ic press n. = HYDRAULIC PRESS.

hy·dro·stat·ics /hídrəstátiks/ n.pl. (usu. treated as sing.) the branch of mechanics concerned with the hydrostatic properties of liquids.

hy·dro·ther·a·py /hídrəthérəpee/ n. the use of water in the treatment of disorders, usu. exercises in swimming pools for arthritic or partially paralyzed patients. □□ hy·dro·ther·a·pist n. hy·dro·ther·a·peu·tic /-pyootik/ adj.

hy·dro·ther·mal /hídrəthérmal/ adj. of the action of heated water on the earth's crust. □□ hy·dro·ther·mal·ly adv.

hy·dro·tho·rax /hídrətháwraks/ n. the condition of having fluid in the pleural cavity.

hy·drot·ro·pism /hīdrótrəpizəm/ adj. a tendency of plant roots, etc., to turn to or from moisture.

hy·drous /hídrəs/ adj. Chem. & Mineral. containing water. [Gk hudōr hudro- water]

hy·drox·ide /hīdróksīd/ n. Chem. a metallic compound containing oxygen and hydrogen either in the form of the hydroxide ion (OH⁻) or the hydroxyl group (–OH).

hydroxy- /hīdróksee/ comb. form Chem. having a hydroxide ion (or ions) or a hydroxyl group (or groups) (hydroxybenzoic acid). [HYDROGEN + OXYGEN]

hy·drox·yl /hīdróksil/ n. Chem. the univalent group containing hydrogen and oxygen, as –OH. [HYDROGEN + OXYGEN + -YL]

hy·dro·zo·an /hídrəzóən/ n. & adj. ● n. any aquatic coelenterate of the class Hydrozoa of mainly marine polyp or medusoid forms, including hydra and Portuguese man-of-war. [mod.L Hydrozoa (as HYDRA, Gk zōion animal)]

hy·e·na /hī-éenə/ n. (also hy·ae·na) any carnivorous mammal of the order Hyaenidae, with hind limbs shorter than forelimbs.

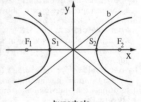
spotted hyena

WORD HISTORY hyena

Middle English: via Latin from Greek *huaina*, feminine of *hus* 'pig.' The transference of the term was probably because the animal's mane was thought to resemble a hog's bristles.

hy·giene /híjeen/ n. 1 a a study, or set of principles, of maintaining health. b conditions or practices conducive to maintaining health. 2 sanitary science. [F hygiène f. mod.L hygieina f. Gk hugieinē (tekhnē) (art) of health f. hugiēs healthy]

hy·gi·en·ic /híjénik, híjéenik/ adj. conducive to hygiene; clean and sanitary. □□ hy·gi·en·i·cal·ly adv.

hy·gi·en·ics /híjéniks, híjéeniks/ n.pl. (usu. treated as sing.) = HYGIENE 1a.

hy·gien·ist /híjénist, -jée-, -híjeenist/ n. a specialist in the promotion and practice of cleanliness for the preservation of health, esp. (den·tal hy·gien·ist) a dental assistant who cleans the teeth.

hygro- /hígro/ comb. form moisture. [Gk hugro- f. hugros wet, moist]

hy·grol·o·gy /hīgróləjee/ n. the study of the humidity of the atmosphere, etc.

hy·grom·e·ter /hīgrómitər/ n. an instrument for measuring the humidity of the air or a gas. □□ hy·gro·met·ric /hígrəmétrik/ adj. hy·grom·e·try n.

hy·groph·i·lous /hīgrófiləs/ adj. (of a plant) growing in a moist environment.

hy·gro·phyte /hígrəfīt/ n. = HYDROPHYTE.

hy·gro·scope /hígrəskōp/ n. an instrument that indicates but does not measure the humidity of the air.

hy·gro·scop·ic /hígrəskópik/ adj. 1 of the hygroscope. 2 (of a substance) tending to absorb moisture from the air. □□ hy·gro·scop·i·cal·ly adv.

479 **hydrophobic ~ hyperbole**

hy·ing pres. part. of HIE.

hy·lic /hílik/ adj. of matter; material. [LL hylicus f. Gk hulikos f. hulē matter]

hylo- /hílō/ comb. form matter. [Gk hulo- f. hulē matter]

hy·lo·mor·phism /híləmáwrfizəm/ n. the theory that physical objects are composed of matter and form. [HYLO- + Gk morphē form]

hy·lo·zo·ism /híləzóizəm/ n. the doctrine that all matter has life. [HYLO- + Gk zōē life]

hy·men /hímən/ n. Anat. a membrane that partially closes the opening of the vagina and is usu. broken at the first occurrence of sexual intercourse. □□ hy·men·al adj. [LL f. Gk humēn membrane]

hy·me·ne·al /híminéeəl/ adj. literary of or concerning marriage. [Hymen (L f. Gk Humēn) Greek and Roman god of marriage]

hy·me·ni·um /híméeneeəm/ n. (pl. hy·me·ni·a /-neeə/) the spore-bearing surface of certain fungi. [mod.L f. Gk humenion dimin. of humēn membrane]

hy·me·nop·ter·an /hímənóptərən/ n. any insect of the order Hymenoptera having four transparent wings, including bees, wasps, and ants. □□ hy·me·nop·ter·ous adj. [mod.L hymenopteros f. Gk humenopteros membrane-winged (as HYMENIUM, pteron wing)]

hymn /him/ n. & v. ● n. 1 a song of praise, esp. to God in Christian worship, usu. a metrical composition sung in a religious service. 2 a song of praise in honor of a god or other exalted being or thing. ● v. 1 tr. praise or celebrate in hymns. 2 intr. sing hymns. □□ hym·nic /hímnik/ adj. [ME ymne, etc. f. OF ymne f. L hymnus f. Gk humnos]

hym·nal /hímnəl/ n. & adj. ● n. a hymnbook. ● adj. of hymns. [ME f. med.L hymnale (as HYMN)]

hym·na·ry /hímnəree/ n. (pl. ·ries) a hymnbook.

hymn·book /hímbook/ n. a book of hymns.

hym·no·dy /hímnədee/ n. (pl. ·dies) 1 a the singing of hymns. b the composition of hymns. 2 hymns collectively. □□ hym·no·dist n. [med.L hymnodia f. Gk humnōidia f. humnos hymn: cf. PSALMODY]

hym·nog·ra·pher /himnógrəfər/ n. a writer of hymns. □□ hym·no·graph·y n. [Gk humnographos f. humnos hymn]

hym·nol·o·gy /himnóləjee/ n. (pl. ·gies) 1 the composition or study of hymns. 2 hymns collectively. □□ hym·nol·o·gist n.

hy·oid /híoyd/ n. & adj. Anat. ● n. (in full hyoid bone) a U-shaped bone in the neck which supports the tongue. ● adj. of or relating to this. [F hyoïde f. mod.L hyoïdes f. Gk huoeidēs shaped like the letter upsilon (hu)]

hy·os·cine /híəseen/ n. a poisonous alkaloid found in plants of the nightshade family, esp. of the genus Scopolia, and used as an antiemetic in motion sickness and a preoperative medication for examination of the eye. Also called scopolamine. [f. HYOSCYAMINE]

hy·os·cy·a·mine /híəsíəmeen/ n. a poisonous alkaloid obtained from henbane, having similar properties to hyoscine. [mod.L hyoscyamus f. Gk huoskuamos henbane f. hus huos pig + kuamos bean]

hy·pae·thral var. of HYPETHRAL.

hy·pal·la·ge /hīpáləjee/ n. Rhet. the transposition of the natural relations of two elements in a proposition (e.g., Melissa shook her doubtful curls). [LL f. Gk hupallagē (as HYPO-, allassō exchange)]

hype¹ /hīp/ n. & v. sl. ● n. 1 extravagant or intensive publicity promotion. 2 cheating; a trick. ● v.tr. 1 promote (a product) with extravagant publicity. 2 cheat; trick. [20th c.: orig. unkn.]

hype² /hīp/ n. sl. 1 a drug addict. 2 a hypodermic needle or injection. □ hyped up stimulated by or as if by a hypodermic injection. [abbr. of HYPODERMIC]

hy·per /hípər/ adj. sl. excessively excited, nervous, stimulated, etc.

hyper- /hípər/ prefix meaning: 1 over; beyond; above (hyperphysical). 2 exceeding (hypersonic). 3 excessively; above normal (hyperbole; hypersensitive). [Gk huper over, beyond]

hy·per·ac·tive /hípəráktiv/ adj. (of a person, esp. a child) abnormally active. □□ hy·per·ac·tiv·i·ty /-tívitee/ n.

hy·per·bar·ic /hípərbárik/ adj. (of a gas) at a pressure greater than normal. [HYPER- + Gk barus heavy]

hy·per·ba·ton /hípárbəton/ n. Rhet. the inversion of the normal order of words, esp. for the sake of emphasis (e.g., this I must see). [L f. Gk huperbaton (as HYPER-, bainō go)]

hy·per·bo·la /hīpárbələ/ n. (pl. hy·per·bo·las or hy·per·bo·lae /-lee/) Geom. the plane curve of two equal branches, produced when a cone is cut by a plane that makes a larger angle with the base than the side of the cone (cf. ELLIPSE). [mod.L f. Gk huperbolē excess (as HYPER-, ballō to throw)]

hyperbola

hy·per·bo·le /hīpárbəlee/ n. Rhet. an exaggerated statement not meant to be taken literally. □□ hy·per·bol·i·cal /hípər-

See page xx for the **Key to Pronunciation.**

bólikəl/ *adj.* **hy•per•bol•i•cal•ly** *adv.* **hy•per•bol•ism** *n.* [L (as HYPER-BOLA)]

hy•per•bol•ic /hípərbólik/ *adj. Geom.* of or relating to a hyperbola.

hy•per•bo•loid /hípərbəloyd/ *n. Geom.* a solid or surface having plane sections that are hyperbolas, ellipses, or circles. □□ **hy•per•bo•loi•dal** *adj.*

hy•per•bo•re•an /hípərbáwreeən, –bəreéən/ *n. & adj.* ● *n.* **1** an inhabitant of the extreme north of the earth. **2** (**Hyperborean**) (in Greek mythology) a member of a race worshiping Apollo and living in a land of sunshine and plenty beyond the north wind. ● *adj.* of the extreme north of the earth. [LL *hyperboreanus* f. L *hyperboreus* f. Gk *huperboreos* (as HYPER-, *Boreas* god of the north wind)]

hy•per•con•scious /hípərkónshəs/ *adj.* (foll. by *of*) acutely or excessively aware.

hy•per•crit•i•cal /hípərkrítikəl/ *adj.* excessively critical, esp. of small faults. □□ **hy•per•crit•i•cal•ly** *adv.*

hy•per•e•mi•a /hípəreémeeə/ *n.* (*Brit.* **hy•per•ae•mi•a**) an excessive quantity of blood in the vessels supplying an organ or other part of the body. □□ **hy•per•e•mic** *adj.* [mod.L (as HYPER-, –EMIA)]

hy•per•es•the•sia /hípəris-theézhə/ *n.* (*Brit.* **hy•per•aes•the•sia**) an excessive physical sensibility, esp. of the skin. □□ **hy•per•es•thet•ic** /–thétik/ *adj.* [mod.L (as HYPER-, Gk –*aisthēsia* f. *aisthanomai* perceive)]

hy•per•fo•cal dis•tance /hípərfókəl/ *n.* the distance on which a camera lens can be focused to bring the maximum range of object distances into focus.

hy•per•ga•my /hípərgəmee/ *n.* marriage to a person of equal or superior caste or class. [HYPER- + Gk *gamos* marriage]

hy•per•gly•ce•mi•a /hípərglíseémeeə/ *n.* an excess of glucose in the bloodstream, often associated with diabetes mellitus. □□ **hy•per•gly•ce•mic** *adj.* [HYPER- + GLYCO- + –EMIA]

hy•per•gol•ic /hípərgólik/ *adj.* (of a rocket propellant) igniting spontaneously on contact with an oxidant, etc. [G *Hypergol* (perh. as HYPO-, ERG[1], –OL)]

hy•per•i•cum /hípérikəm/ *n.* any shrub of the genus *Hypericum* with five-petaled yellow flowers. Also called **St. John's wort**. [L f. Gk *hupereikon* (as HYPER-, *ereikē* heath)]

hy•per•mar•ket /hípərmaarkit/ *n. Brit.* a very large self-service store with a wide range of goods and extensive parking facilities, usu. outside a town. [transl. F *hypermarché* (as HYPER-, MARKET)]

hy•per•me•tro•pi•a /hípərmitrópeeə/ *n.* the condition of being farsighted. □□ **hy•per•me•tro•pic** /–trópik/ *adj.* [mod.L f. HYPER- + Gk *metron* measure, *ōps* eye]

hy•per•on /hípəron/ *n. Physics* an unstable elementary particle which is classified as a baryon apart from the neutron or proton. [HYPER- + –ON]

hy•per•o•pi•a /hípərópeeə/ *n.* = HYPERMETROPIA. □□ **hy•per•op•ic** /–rópik/ *adj.* [mod.L f. HYPER- + Gk *ōps* eye]

hy•per•phys•i•cal /hípərfízikəl/ *adj.* supernatural. □□ **hy•per•phys•i•cal•ly** *adv.*

hy•per•pla•sia /hípərpláyzhə/ *n.* the enlargement of an organ or tissue from the increased production of cells. [HYPER- + Gk *plasis* formation]

hy•per•sen•si•tive /hípərsénsitiv/ *adj.* abnormally or excessively sensitive. □□ **hy•per•sen•si•tive•ness** *n.* **hy•per•sen•si•tiv•i•ty** /–tívitee/ *n.*

hy•per•son•ic /hípərsónik/ *adj.* **1** relating to speeds of more than five times the speed of sound (Mach 5). **2** relating to sound frequencies above about a billion hertz. □□ **hy•per•son•i•cal•ly** *adv.* [HYPER-, after SUPERSONIC, ULTRASONIC]

hy•per•sthene /hípərs-theen/ *n.* a rock-forming mineral, magnesium iron silicate, of greenish color. [F *hyperstène* (as HYPER-, Gk *sthenos* strength, from its being harder than hornblende)]

hy•per•ten•sion /hípərténshən/ *n.* **1** abnormally high blood pressure. **2** a state of great emotional tension. □□ **hy•per•ten•sive** /–ténsiv/ *adj.*

hy•per•text /hípərtekst/ *n. Computing* computer software that links topics on the screen to related information, graphics, etc., usu. by a point-and-click method.

hy•per•ther•mi•a /hípərthérmeeə/ *n. Med.* the condition of having a body temperature greatly above normal. □□ **hy•per•ther•mic** *adj.* [HYPER- + Gk *thermē* heat]

hy•per•thy•roid•ism /hípərthíroydizəm/ *n. Med.* overactivity of the thyroid gland, resulting in rapid heartbeat and an increased rate of metabolism. □□ **hy•per•thy•roid** *n. & adj.* **hy•per•thy•roid•ic** *adj.*

hy•per•ton•ic /hípərtónik/ *adj.* **1** (of muscles) having high tension. **2** (of a solution) having a greater osmotic pressure than another solution. □□ **hy•per•to•ni•a** /–tóneeə/ *n.* (in sense 1). **hy•per•to•nic•i•ty** /–tənísitee/ *n.*

hy•per•tro•phy /hípórtrəfee/ *n.* abnormal enlargement of an organ or part; excessive growth. □□ **hy•per•troph•ic** /–trófik, –trófik/ *adj.* **hy•per•troph•ied** *adj.* [mod.L *hypertrophia* (as HYPER-, Gk –*trophia* nourishment)]

hy•per•ven•ti•la•tion /hípərvént'láyshən/ *n.* breathing at an abnormally rapid rate, resulting in an increased loss of carbon dioxide.

hyp•es•the•sia /hípis-theézhə, –zheeə, –zeeə/ *n.* a diminished capacity for sensation, esp. of the skin. □□ **hyp•es•the•tic** /–thétik/ *adj.* [mod.L (as HYPO-, Gk –*aisthēsia* f. *aisthanomai* perceive)]

hy•pe•thral /hípeéthrəl/ *adj.* (also **hy•pae•thral**) **1** open to the sky; roofless. **2** open-air. [L *hypaethrus* f. Gk *hupaithros* (as HYPO-, *aithēr* air)]

hy•pha /hífə/ *n.* (*pl.* **hy•phae** /–fee/) a filament in the mycelium of a fungus. □□ **hy•phal** *adj.* [mod.L f. Gk *huphē* web]

hy•phen /hífən/ *n. & v.* ● *n.* the sign (-) used to join words semantically or syntactically (as in *pick-me-up*, *rock-forming*), to indicate the division of a word at the end of a line, or to indicate a missing or implied element (as in *man-* and *womankind*). ● *v.tr.* **1** write (a compound word) with a hyphen. **2** join (words) with a hyphen. [LL f. Gk *huphen* together f. *hupo* under + *hen* one]

PUNCTUATION TIP | hyphen

How to Hyphenate. Whenever possible, avoid dividing a word at the end of a line. But when hyphenation is unavoidable, follow these basic rules: **1.** Divide words at syllable breaks. If you're not sure of a word's syllabification, consult the dictionary. **2.** Never divide a one-syllable word. Many words ending in *-ed* (*walked*, *planned*) are still one-syllable words and shouldn't be hyphenated. **3.** Never divide one letter at the beginning or end of a word. Words like *amaze*, *idea*, and *ready* should not be hyphenated. **4.** Avoid dividing words with fewer than six letters. **5.** Never hyphenate acronyms (*YMCA*, *UNICEF*), and avoid dividing abbreviatoins (*assoc.*, *approx.*) and contractions (*haven't*, *shouldn't*).

hy•phen•ate /hífənayt/ *v.tr.* = HYPHEN *v.* □□ **hy•phen•a•tion** /–náyshən/ *n.*

hypno- /hípnō/ *comb. form* sleep; hypnosis. [Gk *hupnos* sleep]

hyp•no•gen•e•sis /hípnōjénisis/ *n.* the induction of a hypnotic state.

hyp•nol•o•gy /hípnóləjee/ *n.* the science of the phenomena of sleep. □□ **hyp•nol•o•gist** *n.*

hyp•no•pe•di•a /hípnōpeédeeə/ *n.* learning by hearing while asleep.

hyp•no•sis /hipnósis/ *n.* **1** a state like sleep in which the subject acts only on external suggestion. **2** artificially produced sleep. [mod.L f. Gk *hupnos* sleep + –OSIS]

hyp•no•ther•a•py /hípnōthérəpee/ *n.* the treatment of disease by hypnosis.

hyp•not•ic /hipnótik/ *adj. & n.* ● *adj.* **1** of or producing hypnosis. **2** (of a drug) soporific. ● *n.* **1** a thing, esp. a drug, that produces sleep. **2** a person under or open to the influence of hypnotism. □□ **hyp•not•i•cal•ly** *adv.* [F *hypnotique* f. LL *hypnoticus* f. Gk *hupnōtikos* f. *hupnoō* put to sleep]

hyp•no•tism /hípnətizəm/ *n.* the study or practice of hypnosis. □□ **hyp•no•tist** *n.*

hyp•no•tize /hípnətīz/ *v.tr.* **1** produce hypnosis in. **2** fascinate; capture the mind of (a person). □□ **hyp•no•tiz•a•ble** *adj.* **hyp•no•tiz•er** *n.*

hy•po[1] /hípō/ *n. Photog.* the chemical sodium thiosulfate (incorrectly called hyposulfite) used as a photographic fixer. [abbr.]

hy•po[2] /hípō/ *n.* (*pl.* **•pos**) *colloq.* = HYPODERMIC *n.* [abbr.]

hypo- /hípō/ *prefix* (usu. **hyp-** before a vowel or *h*) **1** under (*hypodermic*). **2** below normal (*hypoxia*). **3** slightly (*hypomania*). **4** *Chem.* containing an element combined in low valence (*hypochlorous*). [Gk f. *hupo* under]

hy•po•al•ler•gen•ic /hípōalərjénik/ *adj.* having little likelihood of causing an allergic reaction (*hypoallergenic foods*; *hypoallergenic cosmetics*).

hy•po•blast /hípəblast/ *n. Biol.* = ENDODERM. [mod.L *hypoblastus* (as HYPO-, –BLAST)]

hy•po•caust /hípəkawst/ *n.* a hollow space under the floor in ancient Roman houses, into which hot air was sent for heating a room or bath. [L *hypocaustum* f. Gk *hupokauston* place heated from below (as HYPO-, *kaiō*, *kau–* burn)]

hy•po•chon•dri•a /hípəkóndreeə/ *n.* **1** abnormal anxiety about one's health. **2** morbid depression without real cause. [LL f. Gk *hupokhondria* soft parts of the body below the ribs, where melancholy was thought to arise (as HYPO-, *khondros* sternal cartilage)]

hy•po•chon•dri•ac /hípəkóndreeak/ *n. & adj.* ● *n.* a person suffering from hypochondria. ● *adj.* (also **hy•po•chon•dri•a•cal** /–dríəkəl/) of or affected by hypochondria. [F *hypocondriaque* f. Gk *hupokhondriakos* (as HYPOCHONDRIA)]

hy•po•co•ris•tic /hípəkorístik/ *adj. Gram.* of the nature of a pet name. [Gk *hupokoristikos* f. *hupokorizomai* call by pet names]

hy•po•cot•yl /hípəkót'l/ *n. Bot.* the part of the stem of an embryo plant beneath the stalks of the seed leaves or cotyledons and directly above the root.

hy•poc•ri•sy /hipókrisee/ *n.* (*pl.* **•sies**) **1** the assumption or postulation of moral standards to which one's own behavior does not conform; dissimulation, pretense. **2** an instance of this. [ME f. OF *ypocrisie* f. eccl.L *hypocrisis* f. Gk *hupokrisis* acting of a part, pretense (as HYPO-, *krinō* decide, judge)]

hyp•o•crite /hípəkrit/ n. a person given to hypocrisy. □□ **hyp•o•crit•i•cal** /-krítikəl/ adj. **hyp•o•crit•i•cal•ly** adv. [ME f. OF ypocrite f. eccl.L f. Gk hupokritēs actor (as HYPOCRISY)]

hy•po•cy•cloid /hípəsíkloyd/ n. Math. the curve traced by a point on the circumference of a circle rolling on the interior of another circle. □□ **hy•po•cy•cloi•dal** /-síklóyd'l/ adj.

hy•po•der•mic /hípədórmik/ adj. & n. • adj. Med. **1** of or relating to the area beneath the skin. **2 a** (of a drug, etc., or its application) injected beneath the skin. **b** (of a needle, syringe, etc.) used to do this. • n. a hypodermic injection or syringe. □□ **hy•po•der•mi•cal•ly** adv. [HYPO- + Gk derma skin]

hy•po•gas•tri•um /hípəgástreeəm/ n. (pl. **hy•po•gas•tri•a** /-treeə/) the part of the central abdomen which is situated below the region of the stomach. □□ **hy•po•gas•tric** adj. [mod.L f. Gk hupogastrion (as HYPO-, gastēr belly)]

hy•po•ge•an /hípəjeeən/ adj. (also **hy•po•ge•al** /-jeeəl/) **1** (existing or growing) underground. **2** (of seed germination) with the seed leaves remaining below the ground. [LL hypogeus f. Gk hupogeios (as HYPO-, gē earth)]

hy•po•gene /hípəjeen/ adj. Geol. produced under the surface of the earth. [HYPO- + Gk gen- produce]

hy•po•ge•um /hípəjeeəm/ n. (pl. **hy•po•ge•a** /-jeeə/) an underground chamber. [L f. Gk hupogeion neut. of hupogeios: see HYPOGEAN]

hy•po•gly•ce•mi•a /hípōglīseémeeə/ n. a deficiency of glucose in the bloodstream. □□ **hy•po•gly•ce•mic** adj. [HYPO- + GLYCO- + –EMIA]

hy•poid /hípoyd/ n. a gear with the pinion offset from the centerline of the wheel, to connect nonintersecting shafts. [perh. f. HYPERBOLOID]

hy•po•lim•ni•on /hípəlímneeən/ n. (pl. **hy•po•lim•ni•a** /-neeə/) the lower layer of water in stratified lakes. [HYPO- + Gk limnion dimin. of limnē lake]

hy•po•ma•ni•a /hípəmáyneeə/ n. a minor form of mania. □□ **hy•po•man•ic** /-mánik/ adj. [mod.L f. G Hypomanie (as HYPO-, MANIA)]

hy•po•nas•ty /hípənastee/ n. Bot. the tendency in plant organs for growth to be more rapid on the underside. □□ **hy•po•nas•tic** /-nástik/ adj. [HYPO- + Gk nastos pressed]

hy•poph•y•sis /hīpófisis/ n. (pl. **hy•poph•y•ses** /-seez/) Anat. = PITUITARY. □□ **hy•poph•y•se•al** /hípəfizeeəl/ adj. (also **-phy•si•al**). [mod.L f. Gk hupophusis offshoot (as HYPO-, phusis growth)]

hy•pos•ta•sis /hīpóstəsis/ n. (pl. **hy•pos•ta•ses** /-seez/) **1** Med. an accumulation of fluid or blood in the lower parts of the body or organs under the influence of gravity, in cases of poor circulation. **2** Metaphysics an underlying substance, as opposed to attributes or to that which is unsubstantial. **3** Theol. **a** the person of Christ, combining human and divine natures. **b** each of the three persons of the Trinity. □□ **hy•pos•ta•size** v.tr. (in senses 1, 2). [eccl.L f. Gk hupostasis (as HYPO-, STASIS standing, state)]

hy•po•stat•ic /hípəstátik/ adj. (also **hy•po•stat•i•cal**) Theol. relating to the three persons of the Trinity.

hy•po•style /hípəstīl/ adj. Archit. having a roof supported by pillars. [Gk hupostulos (as HYPO-, STYLE)]

hy•po•tax•is /hípətáksis/ n. Gram. the subordination of one clause to another. □□ **hy•po•tac•tic** /-táktik/ adj. [Gk hupotaxis (as HYPO-, taxis arrangement)]

hy•po•ten•sion /hípəténshən/ n. abnormally low blood pressure. □□ **hy•po•ten•sive** adj.

hy•pot•e•nuse /hīpót'noōs, –nyoōs/ n. the side opposite the right angle of a right-angled triangle. [L hypotenusa f. Gk hupoteinousa (grammē) subtending (line) fem. part. of hupoteinō (as HYPO-, teinō stretch)]

hy•po•thal•a•mus /hípətháləməs/ n. (pl. **-mi** /-mī/) Anat. the region of the brain that controls body temperature, thirst, hunger, etc. □□ **hy•po•tha•lam•ic** /-thəlámik/ adj. [mod.L formed as HYPO-, THALAMUS]

hy•poth•ec /hīpóthik/ n. (in Roman and Scottish law) a right established by law over property belonging to a debtor. □□ **hy•poth•e•car•y** /hīpóthikeree/ adj. [F hypothèque f. LL hypotheca f. Gk hupothēkē deposit (as HYPO-, tithēmi place)]

hy•poth•e•cate /hīpóthikayt/ v.tr. **1** pledge; mortgage. **2** hypothesize. □□ **hy•poth•e•ca•tion** /-káyshən/ n. **hy•poth•e•ca•tor** n. [med.L hypothecare (as HYPOTHEC)]

hy•po•ther•mi•a /hípōthórmeeə/ n. Med. the condition of having an abnormally low body temperature. [HYPO- + Gk thermē heat]

hy•poth•e•sis /hīpóthisis/ n. (pl. **hy•poth•e•ses** /-seez/) **1** a proposition made as a basis for reasoning, without the assumption of its truth. **2** a supposition made as a starting point for further investigation from known facts (cf. THEORY). **3** a groundless assumption. [LL f. Gk hupothesis foundation (as HYPO-, THESIS)]

hy•poth•e•size /hīpóthisīz/ v. **1** intr. frame a hypothesis. **2** tr. assume as a hypothesis. □□ **hy•poth•e•sist** /-sist/ n. **hy•poth•e•siz•er** n.

hy•po•thet•i•cal /hípəthétikəl/ adj. **1** of or based on or serving as a hypothesis. **2** supposed but not necessarily real or true. □□ **hy•po•thet•i•cal•ly** adv.

hy•po•thy•roid•ism /hípōthíroydizəm/ n. Med. subnormal activity of the thyroid gland, resulting in cretinism in children, and mental and physical slowing in adults. □□ **hy•po•thy•roid** n. & adj. **hy•po•thy•roid•ic** /-róydik/ adj.

hy•po•ven•ti•la•tion /hípōvént'láyshən/ n. breathing at an abnormally slow rate, resulting in an increased amount of carbon dioxide in the blood.

hy•pox•e•mi•a /hípokseémeeə/ n. Med. an abnormally low concentration of oxygen in the blood. [mod.L (as HYPO-, OXYGEN, –AEMIA)]

hy•pox•i•a /hīpókseeə/ n. Med. a deficiency of oxygen reaching the tissues. □□ **hy•pox•ic** adj. [HYPO- + OX- + –IA[1]]

hypso- /hípsō/ comb. form height. [Gk hupsos height]

hyp•sog•ra•phy /hipsógrəfee/ n. a description or mapping of the contours of the earth's surface. □□ **hyp•so•graph•ic** /-səgráfik/ adj. **hyp•so•graph•i•cal** adj.

hyp•som•e•ter /hipsómitər/ n. **1** a device for calibrating thermometers at the boiling point of water. **2** this instrument when used to estimate height above sea level using barometric pressure. □□ **hyp•so•met•ric** /-səmétrik/ adj.

hy•rax /hírəks/ n. any small mammal of the order Hyracoidea, including the rock rabbit and dassie. [mod.L f. Gk hurax shrew mouse]

hy•son /hísən/ n. a kind of green China tea. [Chin. xichun, lit. 'bright spring']

hys•sop /hísəp/ n. **1** any small bushy aromatic herb of the genus Hyssopus, esp. H. officinalis, formerly used medicinally. **2** Bibl. **a** a plant whose twigs were used for sprinkling in Jewish rites. **b** a bunch of this used in purification. [OE (h)ysope (reinforced in ME by OF ysope) f. L hyssopus f. Gk hyssōpos, of Semitic orig.]

hys•ter•ec•to•my /hístəréktəmee/ n. (pl. **-mies**) the surgical removal of the uterus. □□ **hys•ter•ec•to•mize** v.tr. [Gk hustera uterus + –ECTOMY]

hys•ter•e•sis /hístəreésis/ n. Physics the lagging behind of an effect when its cause varies in amount, etc., esp. of magnetic induction behind the magnetizing force. [Gk husterēsis f. hustereō be behind f. husteros coming after]

hys•te•ri•a /histéreeə, –steér–/ n. **1** a wild uncontrollable emotion or excitement. **2** a functional disturbance of the nervous system, of psychoneurotic origin. [mod.L (as HYSTERIC)]

hys•ter•ic /histérik/ n. & adj. • n. **1** (in pl.) **a** a fit of hysteria. **b** colloq. overwhelming mirth or laughter (we were in hysterics). **2** a hysterical person. • adj. = HYSTERICAL.

WORD HISTORY hysteric

Mid-17th century (as an adjective): via Latin from Greek husterikos 'of the womb,' from hustera 'womb' (hysteria once being thought to be specific to women and associated with the womb).

hys•ter•i•cal /histérikəl/ adj. **1** of or affected with hysteria. **2** morbidly or uncontrolledly emotional. **3** colloq. extremely funny or amusing. □□ **hys•ter•i•cal•ly** adv.

hys•ter•on prot•er•on /hístərən prótərən/ n. Rhet. a figure of speech in which what should come last is put first; an inversion of the natural order (e.g., I die! I faint! I fail!). [LL f. Gk husteron proteron the latter (put in place of) the former]

Hz abbr. hertz.

I

I¹ /ī/ *n.* (also **i**) (*pl.* **Is** or **I's**) **1** the ninth letter of the alphabet. **2** (as a Roman numeral) 1.

I² /ī/ *pron. & n.* ● *pron.* (*obj.* **me**; *poss.* **my, mine**; *pl.* **we**) used by a speaker or writer to refer to himself or herself. ● *n.* (**the I**) *Metaphysics* the ego; the subject or object of self-consciousness. [OE f. Gmc]

I³ *symb. Chem.* the element iodine.

I⁴ *abbr.* (also **I.**) **1** Island(s). **2** Isle(s).

-i¹ /ee, ī/ *suffix* forming the plural of nouns adopted from Latin ending in *–us* (*foci; timpani*) or of nouns adopted from Italian ending in *–e* or *–o* (*dilettanti*).

▶Many nouns with a plural form ending in *-i* can be made plural by adding *-s* or *-es* instead (*syllabuses* or *syllabi*).

-i² /ee/ *suffix* forming adjectives from names of countries or regions in the Near or Middle East (*Israeli; Pakistani*). [adj. suffix in Semitic and Indo-Iranian languages]

-i- a connecting vowel, esp. forming words in *–ana, –ferous, –fic, –form, –fy, –gerous, –vorous* (cf. *–*O-). [from or after F f. L]

IA *abbr.* Iowa (in official postal use).

Ia. *abbr.* Iowa.

-ia¹ /eeə, yə/ *suffix* **1** forming abstract nouns (*mania; utopia*), often in *Med.* (*anemia; pneumonia*). **2** *Bot.* forming names of classes and genera (*dahlia; fuchsia*). **3** forming names of countries (*Australia; India*). [from or after L & Gk]

-ia² /eeə, yə/ *suffix* forming plural nouns or the plural of nouns: **1** from Greek *–ion* or Latin in *–ium* (*paraphernalia; regalia; amnia; labia*). **2** *Zool.* the names of groups (*Mammalia*).

IAA *abbr.* indoleacetic acid.

IAEA *abbr.* International Atomic Energy Agency.

-ial /eeəl, (ch)əl/ *suffix* forming adjectives (*celestial; dictatorial; trivial*). [from or after F *–iel* or L *–ialis:* cf. *–*AL]

i·amb /íamb/ *n. Prosody* a metrical foot consisting of one short (or unstressed) syllable followed by one long (or stressed) syllable. [L f. Gk *iambos* iambus, lampoon, f. *iaptō* assail in words, from its use by Gk satirists]

i·am·bic /íámbik/ *adj. & n. Prosody* ● *adj.* of or using iambs. ● *n.* (usu. in *pl.*) iambic verse. [F *iambique* f. LL *iambicus* f. Gk *iambikos* (as IAMBUS)]

i·am·bus /íámbəs/ *n.* (*pl.* **i·am·bus·es** or **·bi** /-bī/) an iamb.

-ian /eeən/ *suffix* var. of *–*AN. [from or after F *–ien* or L *–ianus*]

-iasis /íəsis/ *suffix* the usual form of *–*ASIS.

IATA /ī-áatə/ *abbr.* International Air Transport Association.

i·at·ro·gen·ic /íátrəjénik/ *adj.* (of a disease, etc.) caused by medical examination or treatment. [Gk *iatros* physician + *–*GENIC]

ib. var. of IBID.

I beam *n.* a girder that has the shape of an I when viewed in section.

I·be·ri·an /ībeéreeən/ *adj. & n.* ● *adj.* of ancient Iberia, the peninsula now comprising Spain and Portugal; of Spain and Portugal. ● *n.* **1** a native of ancient Iberia. **2** any of the languages of ancient Iberia. [L *Iberia* f. Gk *Ibēres* Spaniards]

I·be·ro- /ībáirō/ *comb. form* Iberian; Iberian and (*Ibero-American*).

i·bex /íbeks/ *n.* (*pl.* same or **i·bex·es**) a wild goat, *Capra ibex*, esp. of mountainous areas of Europe, N. Africa, and Asia, with a chin beard and thick curved ridged horns. [L]

ibid. /íbid/ *abbr.* (also **ib.**) in the same book or passage, etc. [L *ibidem* in the same place]

-ibility /íbilitee/ *suffix* forming nouns from, or corresponding to, adjectives in *–ible* (*possibility; credibility*). [F *–ibilité* or L *–ibilitas*]

i·bis /íbis/ *n.* (*pl.* same or **i·bis·es**) any wading bird of the family Threskiornithidae with a curved bill, long neck, and long legs, and nesting in colonies. [ME f. L f. Gk]

-ible /íbəl/ *suffix* forming adjectives meaning 'that may or may be' (see *–*ABLE) (*terrible; forcible; possible*). [F *–ible* or L *–ibilis*]

-ibly /íblee/ *suffix* forming adverbs corresponding to adjectives in *–ible*.

IBM *abbr.* International Business Machines.

I·bo /eébō/ *n.* (also **Ig·bo**) (*pl.* same or **·bos**) **1** a member of a black people of SE Nigeria. **2** the language of this people. [native name]

IBRD *abbr.* International Bank for Reconstruction and Development (also known as the **World Bank**).

i·bu·pro·fen /ibyoōprṓfən/ *n.* an anti-inflammatory medication used to relieve pain and reduce fever.

IC *abbr.* **1** integrated circuit. **2** intensive care.

i/c *abbr.* **1** in charge. **2** in command. **3** internal combustion.

-ic /ik/ *suffix* **1** forming adjectives (*Arabic; classic; public*) and nouns (*critic; epic; mechanic; music*). **2** *Chem.* in higher valence or degree of oxidation (*ferric; sulfuric*) (see also *–*OUS). **3** denoting a particular form or instance of a noun in *–ics* (*aesthetic; tactic*). [from or after F *–ique* or L *–icus* or Gk *–ikos:* cf. *–*ATIC, *–*ETIC, *–*FIC, *–*OTIC]

-ical /íkəl/ *suffix* **1** forming adjectives corresponding to nouns or adjectives, usu. in *–ic* (*classical; comical; farcical; musical*). **2** forming adjectives corresponding to nouns in *–y* (*pathological*).

-ically /íklee/ *suffix* forming adverbs corresponding to adjectives in *–ic* or *–ical* (*comically; musically; tragically*).

ICAO *abbr.* International Civil Aviation Organization.

ICBM *abbr.* intercontinental ballistic missile.

ICC *abbr.* **1** Interstate Commerce Commission. **2** International Claims Commission. **3** Indian Claims Commission.

ice /īs/ *n. & v.* ● *n.* **1 a** frozen water, a brittle transparent crystalline solid. **b** a sheet of this on the surface of water (*fell through the ice*). **2** *Brit.* a portion of ice cream, sherbet, etc. (*would you like an ice?*). **3** *sl.* diamonds. **4** *Austral.* an unemotional or cold-blooded person. ● *v.* **1** *tr.* mix with or cool in ice (*iced drinks*). **2** *tr. & intr.* (often foll. by *over, up*) **a** cover or become covered with ice. **b** freeze. **3** *tr.* cover (a cake, etc.) with icing. **4** *sl.* kill. □ **on ice 1** (of an entertainment, sport, etc.) performed by skaters. **2** *colloq.* held in reserve; awaiting further attention. **on thin ice** in a risky situation. [OE *īs* f. Gmc]

-ice /īs/ *suffix* forming (esp. abstract) nouns (*avarice; justice; service*) (cf. *–*ISE²).

ice age *n.* a glacial period, esp. (the **Ice Age**) in the Pleistocene epoch.

ice ax *n.* a tool used by mountain climbers for cutting footholds.

ice bag *n.* an ice pack.

ice·berg /ísbərg/ *n.* **1** a large floating mass of ice detached from a glacier or ice sheet and carried out to sea. **2** an unemotional or cold-blooded person. □ **the tip of the iceberg** a small perceptible part of something (esp. a difficulty) the greater part of which is hidden. [prob. f. Du. *ijsberg* f. *ijs* ice + *berg* hill]

ice·berg let·tuce *n.* a lettuce of a variety having a dense, round head of crisp, pale leaves.

ice·blink /ísblingk/ *n.* a luminous appearance on the horizon, caused by a reflection from ice.

ice·block /ísblok/ *n. Austral. & NZ* = POPSICLE.

ice·boat /ísbōt/ *n.* **1** a boat mounted on runners for traveling on ice. **2** a boat used for breaking ice on a river, etc.

ice·bound /ísbownd/ *adj.* confined by ice.

ice·box /ísboks/ *n.* **1** a compartment in a refrigerator for making and storing ice. **2** a refrigerator.

ice·break·er /ísbraykər/ *n.* **1** a ship designed for breaking a channel through ice. **2** a thing that serves to relieve inhibitions or tension between people, or start a conversation, etc.

ice buck·et *n.* a bucketlike container with chunks of ice, used to keep a bottle of wine chilled.

ice cap *n.* a permanent covering of ice, e.g., in polar regions.

ice-cold *adj.* as cold as ice.

ice cream *n.* a soft, creamy frozen food made with sweetened and flavored milk fat.

ice cube *n.* a small block of ice made in a freezer, esp. for adding to drinks.

ice·fall /ísfawl/ *n.* a steep part of a glacier like a frozen waterfall.

ice field *n.* an expanse of ice, esp. in polar regions.

ice floe *n.* = FLOE.

ice hock·ey *n.* a fast contact sport played on the ice between two teams of six skaters who try to drive a small rubber disk or puck into the opposing goal with hooked or angled sticks.

ice·house /ís-hows/ *n.* a building often partly or wholly underground for storing ice.

Ice·land·er /ísləndər/ *n.* **1** a native or national of Iceland, an island in the N. Atlantic. **2** a person of Icelandic descent.

Ice·lan·dic /īslándik/ *adj. & n.* ● *adj.* of or relating to Iceland. ● *n.* the language of Iceland.

Ice·land moss /īslənd/ *n.* (also **Ice·land li·chen**) a mountain and moorland lichen, *Cetraria islandica*, with edible branching fronds.

Ice·land pop·py /īslənd/ *n.* an arctic poppy, *Papaver nudicaule*, with red or yellow flowers.

Ice·land spar /īslənd/ *n.* a transparent variety of calcite with the optical property of strong double refraction.

ice lol·ly *n.* (also **iced lolly**) *Brit.* = POPSICLE.

ice·man /īsmən/ *n.* (*pl.* **·men**) **1** a person skilled in crossing ice. **2** a person who sells or delivers ice.

ice pack *n.* a bag filled with ice and applied to the body to reduce swelling or lower temperature.

ice pick *n.* a needlelike implement with a handle for splitting up small pieces of ice.

ice plant *n.* a plant, *Mesembryanthemum crystallinum*, with leaves covered with crystals or vesicles looking like ice specks.

ice rink *n.* = RINK 1.

ice skate *n.* a skate consisting of a boot with a blade beneath, for skating on ice.

ice-skate *v.tr.* skate on ice as a sport or pastime. □□ **ice-skat·er** *n.*

ice sta·tion *n.* a meteorological research center in polar regions.

I Ching /ēē jíng/ *n.* an ancient Chinese manual of divination based on symbolic trigrams and hexagrams, interpreted in terms of the principles of yin and yang. [Chin. *yijing* book of changes]

ich·neu·mon /iknóōmən, –nyōō–/ *n.* **1** (in full **ichneumon fly**) any small hymenopterous insect of the family Ichneumonidae, depositing eggs in or on the larva of another insect as food for its own larva. **2** a mongoose of N. Africa, *Herpestes ichneumon*, noted for destroying crocodile eggs. [L f. Gk *ikhneumōn* spider-hunting wasp f. *ikhneuō* trace f. *ikhnos* footstep]

ich·nog·ra·phy /iknógrəfee/ *n.* (*pl.* **·phies**) **1** the ground-plan of a building, map of a region, etc. **2** a drawing of this. [F *ichnographie* or L *ichnographia* f. Gk *ikhnographia* f. *ikhnos* track: see –GRAPHY]

i·chor /īkawr, íkər/ *n.* **1** (in Greek mythology) fluid flowing like blood in the veins of the gods. **2** *poet.* bloodlike fluid. **3** *hist.* a watery fetid discharge from a wound, etc. □□ **i·chor·ous** /íkərəs/ *adj.* [Gk *ikhōr*]

ichthyo- /íktheeō/ *comb. form* fish. [Gk *ikhthus* fish]

ich·thy·oid /íkthee-oyd/ *adj. & n.* ● *adj.* fishlike. ● *n.* any fishlike vertebrate.

ich·thy·o·lite /íktheeəlīt/ *n.* a fossil fish.

ich·thy·ol·o·gy /íktheeóləjee/ *n.* the study of fishes. □□ **ich·thy·o·log·i·cal** /–theeəlójikəl/ *adj.* **ich·thy·ol·o·gist** *n.*

ich·thy·oph·a·gous /íktheeófəgəs/ *adj.* fish-eating. □□ **ich·thy·oph·a·gy** /–ófəjee/ *n.*

ich·thy·o·saur /íktheeəsáwr/ *n.* (also **ich·thy·o·saur·us** /íktheeəsáwrəs/) any extinct marine reptile of the order Ichthyosauria, with long head, tapering body, four flippers, and usu. a large tail. [ICHTHYO- + Gk *sauros* lizard]

ich·thy·o·sis /íktheeósis/ *n.* a skin disease that causes the epidermis to become dry and horny like fish scales. □□ **ich·thy·ot·ic** /–theeótik/ *adj.* [Gk *ikhthus* fish + –OSIS]

-ician /íshən/ *suffix* forming nouns denoting persons skilled in or concerned with subjects having nouns (usu.) in –*ic* or –*ics* (*magician*; *politician*). [from or after F –*icien* (as –IC, –IAN)]

i·ci·cle /ísikəl/ *n.* a hanging tapering piece of ice, formed by the freezing of dripping water. [ME f. ICE + *ickle* (now dial.) icicle]

ic·ing /ísing/ *n.* **1** a coating of sugar, etc., on a cake or cookie. **2** the formation of ice on a ship or aircraft. □ **icing on the cake** an attractive though inessential addition or enhancement.

-icist /ísist/ *suffix* = –ICIAN (*classicist*). [–IC + –IST]

-icity /ísitee/ *suffix* forming abstract nouns, esp. from adjectives in –*ic* (*authenticity*; *publicity*). [–IC + –ITY]

-ick /ik/ *suffix* archaic var. of –IC.

ick·y /íkkee/ *adj. colloq.* **1** sickly. **2** (as a general term of disapproval) nasty; repulsive. [20th c.: orig. unkn.]

-icle /ikəl/ *suffix* forming nouns which were originally diminutives (*article*; *particle*). [formed as –CULE]

i·con /íkon/ *n.* (also **i·kon**) **1** a devotional painting or carving, usu. on wood, of Christ or another holy figure, esp. in the Eastern Church. **2** a person or thing regarded as a representative symbol of something (*the building is an icon of modernism*). **3** an image or statue. **4** *Computing* a symbol or graphic representation that appears on the monitor in a program, option, or window, esp. one of several for selection. **5** *Linguistics* a sign which has a characteristic in common with the thing it signifies. [L f. Gk *eikōn* image]

i·con·ic /īkónik/ *adj.* **1** of or having the nature of an image or portrait. **2** (of a statue) following a conventional type. **3** *Linguistics* that is an icon. □□ **i·co·nic·i·ty** /íkənísitee/ *n.* (esp. in sense 3). [L *iconicus* f. Gk *eikonikos* (as ICON)]

icono- /īkónō/ *comb. form* an image or likeness. [Gk *eikōn*]

i·con·o·clasm /īkónəklazəm/ *n.* **1** the breaking of images. **2** the assailing of cherished beliefs. [ICONOCLAST after *enthusiasm*, etc.]

i·con·o·clast /īkónəklast/ *n.* **1** a person who attacks cherished beliefs. **2** a person who destroys images used in religious worship, esp. *hist.* during the 8th–9th c. in the churches of the East, or as a Puritan of the 16th–17th c. □□ **i·con·o·clas·tic** /–klástik/ *adj.* **i·con·o·clas·ti·cal·ly** *adv.* [med.L *iconoclastes* f. eccl.Gk *eikonoklastēs* (as ICONO-, *klaō* break)]

i·co·nog·ra·phy /íkənógrəfee/ *n.* (*pl.* **·phies**) **1** the illustration of a subject by drawings or figures. **2 a** the study of portraits, esp. of an individual. **b** the study of artistic images or symbols. **3** a treatise on pictures or statuary. **4** a book whose essence is pictures. □□ **i·co·nog·ra·pher** *n.* **i·con·o·graph·ic** /–nəgráfik/ *adj.* **i·con·o·graph·i·cal** *adj.* **i·con·o·graph·i·cal·ly** *adv.* [Gk *eikonographia* sketch (as ICONO- + –GRAPHY)]

i·co·nol·a·try /íkənólətree/ *n.* the worship of images. □□ **i·co·nol·a·ter** *n.* [eccl.Gk *eikonolatreia* (as ICONO-, –LATRY)]

i·co·nol·o·gy /íkənóləjee/ *n.* **1** an artistic theory developed from iconography (see ICONOGRAPHY 2b). **2** symbolism.

i·co·nos·ta·sis /íkənóstəsis/ *n.* (*pl.* **i·co·nos·ta·ses** /–seez/) (in the Eastern Church) a screen bearing icons and separating the sanctuary from the nave. [mod.Gk *eikonostasis* (as ICONO-, STASIS)]

i·co·sa·he·dron /íkósəheédrən, –ikós–/ *n.* a solid figure with twenty faces. □□ **i·co·sa·he·dral** *adj.* [LL *icosahedrum* f. Gk *eikosaedron* f. *eikosi* twenty + –HEDRON]

-ics /iks/ *suffix* (treated as *sing.* or *pl.*) forming nouns denoting arts or sciences or branches of study or action (*athletics*; *politics*) (cf. –IC 3). [from or after F pl. –*iques* or L pl. –*ica* or Gk pl. –*ika*]

ic·ter·us /íktərəs/ *n. Med.* = JAUNDICE. □□ **ic·ter·ic** /íktérik/ *adj.* [L f. Gk *ikteros*]

ic·tus /íktəs/ *n.* (*pl.* **ic·tus·es** or same) **1** *Prosody* rhythmical or metrical stress. **2** *Med.* a stroke or seizure; a fit. [L, = blow f. *icere* strike]

ICU *abbr.* intensive care unit.

i·cy /īsee/ *adj.* (**i·ci·er**, **i·ci·est**) **1** very cold. **2** covered with or abounding in ice. **3** (of a tone or manner) unfriendly; hostile (*an icy stare*). □□ **i·ci·ly** *adv.* **i·ci·ness** *n.*

ID *abbr.* **1** identification, identity (*ID card*). **2** Idaho (in official postal use).

I'd /īd/ *contr.* **1** I had. **2** I should; I would.

id /id/ *n. Psychol.* the inherited instinctive impulses of the individual as part of the unconscious. [L, = that, transl. G *es*]

id. *abbr.* = IDEM.

i.d. *abbr.* inner diameter.

-id[1] /id/ *suffix* forming adjectives (*arid*; *rapid*). [F –*ide* f. L –*idus*]

-id[2] /id/ *suffix* forming nouns: **1** general (*pyramid*). **2** *Biol.* of structural constituents (*plastid*). **3** *Bot.* of a plant belonging to a family with a name in –*aceae* (*orchid*). [from or after F –*ide* f. L –*is* –*idis* f. Gk –*is* –*ida* or –*idos*]

-id[3] /id/ *suffix* forming nouns denoting: **1** *Zool.* an animal belonging to a family with a name in –*idae* or a class with a name in –*ida* (*canid*; *arachnid*). **2** a member of a person's family (*Seleucid* from *Seleucus*). **3** *Astron.* **a** a meteor in a group radiating from a specified constellation (*Leonid* from Leo). **b** a star of a class like one in a specified constellation (*cepheid*). [from or after L –*ides*, pl. –*idae* or –*ida*]

-id[4] /id/ *suffix* var. of –IDE.

IDA *abbr.* International Development Association.

-ide /īd/ *suffix* (also –**id**) *Chem.* forming nouns denoting: **1** binary compounds of an element (the suffix –*ide* being added to the abbreviated name of the more electronegative element, etc.) (*sodium chloride*; *lead sulfide*; *calcium carbide*). **2** various other compounds (*amide*; *anhydride*; *peptide*; *saccharide*). **3** elements of a series in the periodic table (*actinide*; *lanthanide*). [orig. in OXIDE]

i·de·a /īdéeə/ *n.* **1** a conception or plan formed by mental effort (*have you any ideas?*; *had the idea of writing a book*). **2 a** a mental impression or notion; a concept. **b** a vague belief or fancy (*had an*

---

idea you were married; had no idea where you were). **c** an opinion; an outlook or point of view (*had some funny ideas about marriage).* **3** an intention, purpose, or essential feature (*the idea is to make money).* **4** an archetype or pattern as distinguished from its realization in individual cases. **5** *Philos.* **a** (in Platonism) an eternally existing pattern of which individual things in any class are imperfect copies. **b** a concept of pure reason which transcends experience. □ **get** (or **have**) **ideas** *colloq.* be ambitious, rebellious, etc. **have no idea** *colloq.* **1** not know at all. **2** be completely incompetent. **not one's idea of** *colloq.* not what one regards as (*not my idea of a pleasant evening).* **put ideas into a person's head** suggest ambitions, etc., he or she would not otherwise have had. **that's an idea** *colloq.* that proposal, etc., is worth considering. **the very idea!** *colloq.* an exclamation of disapproval or disagreement. □□ **i·de·aed** *adj.* **i·de·a·less** *adj.* [Gk *idea* form, pattern f. stem *id-* see]

i·de·al /īdéeəl/ *adj. & n.* ● *adj.* **1 a** answering to one's highest conception. **b** perfect or supremely excellent. **2 a** existing only in idea. **b** visionary. **3** embodying an idea. **4** relating to or consisting of ideas; dependent on the mind. ● *n.* **1** a perfect type, or a conception of this. **2 a** an actual thing as a standard for imitation. **b** (often in *pl.*) a moral principle or standard of behavior. □□ **i·de·al·ly** *adv.* [ME f. F *idéal* f. LL *idealis* (as IDEA)]

i·de·al gas *n.* a hypothetical gas consisting of molecules occupying negligible space and without attraction for each other, thereby obeying simple laws.

i·de·al·ism /īdéeəlizəm/ *n.* **1** the practice of forming or following after ideals, esp. unrealistically (cf. REALISM). **2** the representation of things in ideal or idealized form. **3** imaginative treatment. **4** *Philos.* any of various systems of thought in which the objects of knowledge are held to be in some way dependent on the activity of mind (cf. REALISM). □□ **i·de·al·ist** *n.* **i·de·al·is·tic** *adj.* **i·de·al·is·ti·cal·ly** *adv.* [F *idéalisme* or G *Idealismus* (as IDEAL)]

i·de·al·i·ty /īdéeálitee/ *n.* (*pl.* **·ties**) **1** the quality of being ideal. **2** an ideal thing.

i·de·al·ize /īdéeəlīz/ *v.tr.* **1** regard or represent (a thing or person) in ideal form or character. **2** exalt in thought to ideal perfection or excellence. □□ **i·de·al·i·za·tion** *n.* **i·de·al·iz·er** *n.*

i·de·ate /īdeeayt/ *v. Psychol.* **1** *tr.* imagine; conceive. **2** *intr.* form ideas. □□ **i·de·a·tion** /-áyshən/ *n.* **i·de·a·tion·al** /-áyshənəl/ *adj.* **i·de·a·tion·al·ly** /-áyshənəlee/ *adv.* [med.L *ideare* form an idea (as IDEA)]

i·dée fixe /eeday feéks/ *n.* (*pl.* **i·dées fixes** *pronunc.* same) an idea that dominates the mind; an obsession. [F, lit. 'fixed idea']

idée reçue /eeday rəsöő/ *n.* (*pl.* **i·dées re·çues** *pronunc.* same) a generally accepted notion or opinion. [F]

i·dem /ídem/ *adv. & n.* ● *adv.* in the same author. ● *n.* the same word or author. [ME f. L]

i·den·ti·cal /īdéntikəl/ *adj.* **1** (often foll. by *with*) (of different things) agreeing in every detail. **2** (of one thing viewed at different times) one and the same. **3** (of twins) developed from a single fertilized ovum, therefore of the same sex and usu. very similar in appearance. **4** *Logic & Math.* expressing an identity. □□ **i·den·ti·cal·ly** *adv.* **i·den·ti·cal·ness** *n.* [med.L *identicus* (as IDENTITY)]
▶See note at SAME.

i·den·ti·fi·ca·tion /īdéntifikáyshən/ *n.* **1 a** the act or an instance of identifying; recognition; pinpointing. **b** association of oneself with the feelings, situation, characteristics, etc., of another person or group of people. **2** a means of identifying a person. **3** (*attrib.*) serving to identify (esp. the bearer) (*identification card*).

i·den·ti·fi·ca·tion pa·rade *n. Brit.* a police lineup.

i·den·ti·fi·er /īdéntifīər/ *n.* **1** a person or thing that identifies. **2** *Computing* a sequence of characters used to identify or refer to a set of data.

i·den·ti·fy /īdéntifī/ *v.* (**·fies**, **·fied**) **1** *tr.* establish the identity of; recognize. **2** *tr.* establish or select by consideration or analysis of the circumstances (*identify the best method of solving the problem*). **3** *tr.* (foll. by *with*) associate (a person or oneself) inseparably or very closely (with a party, policy, etc.). **4** *tr.* (often foll. by *with*) treat (a thing) as identical. **5** *intr.* (foll. by *with*) **a** regard oneself as sharing characteristics of (another person). **b** associate oneself. □□ **i·den·ti·fi·a·ble** /-fíəbəl/ *adj.* [med.L *identificare* (as IDENTITY)]

I·den·ti-Kit /īdéntikit/ *n.* (often *attrib.*) *Trademark* a reconstructed picture of a person (esp. one sought by the police) assembled from transparent strips showing typical facial features according to witnesses' descriptions. [IDENTITY + KIT[1]]

i·den·ti·ty /īdéntitee/ *n.* (*pl.* **·ties**) **1 a** the quality or condition of being a specified person or thing. **b** individuality; personality (*felt he had lost his identity*). **2** identification or the result of it (*a case of mistaken identity; identity card*). **3** the state of being the same in substance, nature, qualities, etc.; absolute sameness (*no identity of interests between them*). **4** *Algebra* **a** the equality of two expressions for all values of the quantities expressed by letters. **b** an equation expressing this, e.g., $(x + 1)^2 = x^2 + 2x + 1$. **5** *Math.* **a** (in full **i·den·ti·ty el·e·ment**) an element in a set, left unchanged by any operation (or by multiplication). **b** a transformation that leaves an object unchanged. [LL *identitas* f. L *idem* same]

---

485   **ideal ~ idolater**

i·den·ti·ty cri·sis *n.* a temporary period during which an individual experiences feelings of loss or breakdown of identity.

id·e·o·gram /ídeeəgram/ *n.* a character symbolizing the idea of a thing without indicating the sequence of sounds in its name (e.g., a numeral, and many Chinese characters). [Gk *idea* form + –GRAM]

id·e·o·graph /ídeeəgraf/ *n.* = IDEOGRAM. □□ **id·e·o·graph·ic** *adj.* **id·e·og·ra·phy** /ídeeógrəfee/ *n.* [Gk *idea* form + –GRAPH]

i·de·o·logue /ídeeəlawg/ *n.* **1** a theorist; a visionary. **2** an adherent of an ideology. [F *idéologue* f. Gk *idea* (see IDEA) + –LOGUE]

i·de·ol·o·gy /ídeeóləjee, ídee–/ *n.* (*pl.* **·gies**) **1** the system of ideas at the basis of an economic or political theory (*Marxist ideology*). **2** the manner of thinking characteristic of a class or individual (*bourgeois ideology*). **3** visionary speculation. **4** *archaic* the science of ideas. □□ **i·de·o·log·i·cal** /–əlójikəl/ *adj.* **i·de·o·log·i·cal·ly** *adv.* **i·de·ol·o·gist** /–deeól–/ *n.* [F *idéologie* (as IDEOLOGUE)]

ides /īdz/ *n.pl.* the eighth day after the nones in the ancient Roman calendar (the 15th day of March, May, July, October; the 13th of other months). [ME f. OF f. L *idus* (pl.), perh. f. Etruscan]

id·i·o·cy /ídeeəsee/ *n.* (*pl.* **·cies**) **1** utter foolishness; idiotic behavior or an idiotic action. **2** extreme mental imbecility. [ME f. IDIOT, prob. after *lunacy*]

id·i·o·lect /ídeeəlekt/ *n.* the form of language used by an individual person. [Gk *idios* own + –*lect* in DIALECT]

id·i·om /ídeeəm/ *n.* **1** a group of words established by usage and having a meaning not deducible from those of the individual words (as in *at the drop of a hat, see the light*). **2** a form of expression peculiar to a language, person, or group of people. **3 a** the language of a people or country. **b** the specific character of this. **4** a characteristic mode of expression in music, art, etc. [F *idiome* or LL *idioma* f. Gk *idiōma* –*matos* private property f. *idios* own, private]

> **GRAMMAR TIP** **idiom**
>
> An **idiom** is a phrase or expression that is peculiar to a language and that often transcends grammatical rules or literal meanings. For example, when you say that someone has "a skeleton in the closet," you don't literally mean that the person has human bones hidden behind a closed door. Because the meanings of idioms usually cannot be deduced from their individual words, they are among the most difficult features of the English language for a nonnative speaker.

id·i·o·mat·ic /ídeeəmátik/ *adj.* **1** relating to or conforming to idiom. **2** characteristic of a particular language. □□ **id·i·o·mat·i·cal·ly** *adv.* [Gk *idiōmatikos* peculiar (as IDIOM)]

id·i·op·a·thy /ídeeópəthee/ *n. Med.* any disease or condition of unknown cause or that arises spontaneously. □□ **id·i·o·path·ic** /ídeeəpáthik/ *adj.* [mod.L *idiopathia* f. Gk *idiopatheia* f. *idios* own + –PATHY]

id·i·o·syn·cra·sy /ídeeōsíngkrəsee/ *n.* (*pl.* **·sies**) **1** a mental constitution, view or feeling, or mode of behavior, peculiar to a person. **2** anything highly individualized or eccentric. **3** a mode of expression peculiar to an author. **4** *Med.* a physical constitution peculiar to a person. □□ **id·i·o·syn·crat·ic** /–krátik/ *adj.* **id·i·o·syn·crat·i·cal·ly** *adv.* [Gk *idiosugkrasia* f. *idios* own + *sun* together ~ *krasis* mixture]

id·i·ot /ídeeət/ *n.* **1** *colloq.* a stupid person; an utter fool. **2** a person deficient in mind and permanently incapable of rational conduct. □□ **id·i·ot·ic** /ídeeótik/ *adj.* **id·i·ot·i·cal·ly** /ídeeótiklee/ *adv.* [ME f. OF f. L *idiota* ignorant person f. Gk *idiōtēs* private person, layman, ignorant person f. *idios* own, private]

id·i·ot box *n. colloq.* a television set.

i·dle /íd'l/ *adj. & v.* ● *adj.* (**i·dler**, **i·dlest**) **1** lazy; indolent. **2** not in use; not working; unemployed. **3** (of time, etc.) unoccupied. **4** having no special basis or purpose (*idle rumor; idle curiosity*). **5** useless. **6** (of an action, thought, or word) ineffective; worthless; vain. ● *v.* **1 a** *intr.* (of an engine) run slowly without doing any work. **b** *tr.* cause (an engine) to idle. **2** *intr.* be idle. **3** *tr.* (foll. by *away*) pass (time, etc.) in idleness. □□ **i·dle·ness** *n.* **i·dly** *adv.* [OE *īdel* empty, useless]

i·dler /ídlər/ *n.* **1** a habitually lazy person. **2** = IDLE WHEEL.

i·dle wheel *n.* an intermediate wheel between two geared wheels, esp. to allow them to rotate in the same direction.

I·do /éedō/ *n.* an artificial universal language based on Esperanto. [Ido, = offspring]

i·dol /íd'l/ *n.* **1** an image of a deity, etc., used as an object of worship. **2** *Bibl.* a false god. **3** a person or thing that is the object of excessive or supreme adulation (*movie idol*). **4** *archaic* a phantom. [ME f. OF *idole* f. L *idolum* f. Gk *eidōlon* phantom f. *eidos* form]

i·dol·a·ter /īdólətər/ *n.* (*fem.* **i·dol·a·tress** /–tris/) **1** a worshiper of idols. **2** (often foll. by *of*) a devoted admirer. □□ **i·dol·a·trous** *adj.* [ME *idolatrer* f. OF f. L *idolatry* or f. OF *idolâtre*, ult. f. Gk *eidōlolatrēs* (as IDOL, –LATER)]

See page xx for the **Key to Pronunciation.**

i·dol·a·try /īdólətree/ n. **1** the worship of idols. **2** great adulation. [OF *idolatrie* (as IDOLATER)]

i·dol·ize /īd'līz/ v. **1** tr. venerate or love extremely or excessively. **2** tr. make an idol of. **3** intr. practice idolatry. □□ **i·dol·i·za·tion** n. **i·dol·iz·er** n.

IDP abbr. **1** integrated data processing. **2** International Driving Permit.

i·dyll /īd'l/ n. (also **i·dyl**) **1** a short description in verse or prose of a picturesque scene or incident, esp. in rustic life. **2** an episode suitable for such treatment, usu. a love story. □□ **i·dyl·list** n. **i·dyl·ize** v. tr. [L *idyllium* f. Gk *eidullion*, dimin. of *eidos* form]

i·dyl·lic /īdílik/ adj. **1** blissfully peaceful and happy. **2** of or like an idyll. □□ **i·dyl·li·cal·ly** adv.

IE abbr. **1** Indo-European. **2** industrial engineer(ing).

i.e. abbr. that is to say. [L *id est*]

▶See note at VIZ.

-ie /ee/ suffix **1** var. of -Y² (*dearie; nightie*). **2** archaic var. of -Y¹, -Y³ (*litanie; prettie*). [earlier form of -Y]

-ier /eeər, eer/ suffix forming personal nouns denoting an occupation or interest: **1** pronounced with stress on the preceding element (*grazier*). **2** pronounced with stress on the suffix (*cashier; brigadier*). [sense 1 ME of various orig.; sense 2 F *-ier* f. L *-arius*]

IF abbr. intermediate frequency.

if /if/ conj. & n. •conj. **1** introducing a conditional clause: **a** on the condition or supposition that; in the event that (*if he comes I will tell him; if you are tired we will rest*). **b** (with past tense) implying that the condition is not fulfilled (*if I were you; if I knew I would say*). **2** even though (*I'll finish it, if it takes me all day*). **3** whenever (*if I am not sure, I ask*). **4** whether (*see if you can find it*). **5 a** expressing wish or surprise (*if I could just try!; if it isn't my old hat!*). **b** expressing a request (*if you wouldn't mind opening the door?*). **6** with implied reservation, = and perhaps not (*very rarely if at all*). **7** (with reduction of the protasis to its significant word) if there is or it is, etc. (*took little if any*). **8** despite being (*a useful if cumbersome device*). •n. a condition or supposition (*too many ifs about it*). □ **if only 1** even if for no other reason than (*I'll come if only to see her*). **2** (often ellipt.) an expression of regret (*if only I had thought of it; if only I could swim!*). **if so** if that is the case. [OE *gif*]

▶Strictly speaking, **if** should be used to mean 'supposing that' (*if they can't get here on time, we'll have to cancel our reservation*), and **whether** should be used to introduce an alternative (*she hasn't decided whether she's going out to dinner with us or not*). But this distinction is not always maintained; often, *if* is used in place of *whether*, especially informally.

IFC abbr. International Finance Corporation.

iff /if/ conj. Logic & Math. = if and only if. [arbitrary extension of *if*]

if·fy /ífee/ adj. (**if·fi·er, if·fi·est**) colloq. uncertain; doubtful.

Ig·bo var. of IBO.

ig·loo /íglōō/ n. a Eskimo dome-shaped dwelling, esp. one built of snow. [Eskimo, = house]

ig·ne·ous /ígneeəs/ adj. **1** of fire; fiery. **2** Geol. (esp. of rocks) produced by volcanic or magmatic action. [L *igneus* f. *ignis* fire]

ig·nis fat·u·us /ígnis fáchōōəs/ n. (pl. **ig·nes fat·u·i** /ígneez fáchōō-ī/) a will-o'-the-wisp, because of its erratic movement) [mod.L, = foolish fire, because of its erratic movement]

igloo

ig·nite /ígnīt/ v. **1** tr. set fire to; cause to burn. **2** intr. catch fire. **3** tr. Chem. heat to the point of combustion or chemical change. **4** tr. provoke or excite (feelings, etc.). □□ **ig·nit·a·ble** adj. **ig·nit·a·bil·i·ty** /-təbílitee/ n. **ig·nit·i·ble** adj. **ig·nit·i·bil·i·ty** /-tibílitee/ n. [L *ignire* ignit- f. *ignis* fire]

ig·nit·er /ígnītər/ n. **1** a device for igniting a fuel mixture in an engine. **2** a device for causing an electric arc.

ig·ni·tion /ígníshən/ n. **1** a mechanism for, or the action of, starting the combustion of fuel in the cylinder of an internal combustion engine. **2** the act or an instance of igniting or being ignited. [F *ignition* or med.L *ignitio* (as IGNITE)]

ig·ni·tron /ígnítrən, ígni-/ n. Electr. a mercury-arc rectifier able to carry large currents. [IGNITE + -TRON]

ig·no·ble /ígnōbəl/ adj. (**ig·no·bler, ig·no·blest**) **1** dishonorable; mean; base. **2** of low birth, position, or reputation. □□ **ig·no·bil·i·ty** n. **ig·no·bly** adv. [F *ignoble* or L *ignobilis* (as IN-¹, *nobilis* noble)]

ig·no·min·i·ous /ígnəmíneeəs/ adj. **1** causing or deserving ignominy. **2** humiliating. □□ **ig·no·min·i·ous·ly** adv. **ig·no·min·i·ous·ness** n. [ME f. F *ignominieux* or L *ignominiosus*]

ig·no·min·y /ígnəminee/ n. **1** dishonor; infamy. **2** archaic infamous conduct. [F *ignominie* or L *ignominia* (as IN-¹, *nomen* name)]

ig·no·ra·mus /ígnəráyməs/ n. (pl. **ig·no·ra·mus·es** or **ig·no·ra·mi**) an ignorant person.

ig·no·rance /ígnərəns/ n. (often foll. by *of*) lack of knowledge (about a thing). [ME f. OF f. L *ignorantia* (as IGNORANT)]

ig·no·rant /ígnərənt/ adj. **1 a** lacking knowledge or experience. **b** (foll. by *of, in*) uninformed (about a fact or subject). **2** colloq. ill-mannered; uncouth. □□ **ig·no·rant·ly** adv. [ME f. OF f. L *ignorare ignorant-* (as IGNORE)]

ILLITERATE, UNEDUCATED, UNINFORMED, UNLEARNED, UNLETTERED, UNTUTORED. Someone who knows nothing about growing things might be called **ignorant** by a farmer who never went to high school but has spent his life in the fields. Although all of these adjectives refer to a lack of knowledge, *ignorant* refers to a lack of knowledge in general (*a foolish, ignorant person*) or to a lack of knowledge of some particular subject (*ignorant of the fine points of financial management*). A professor of art history might refer to someone who doesn't know how to look at a painting as **uneducated** or **untutored**, both of which refer to a lack of formal education in schools (*she was very bright but basically uneducated, and completely untutored in the fine arts*). Someone who cannot read or write is **illiterate**, a term that may also denote a failure to display civility or cultivated behavior (*the professor routinely referred to his students as illiterate louts*). Someone who is **unlettered** lacks a knowledge of fine literature (*a scientist who was highly trained but unlettered*); it also implies being able to read and write, but with no skill in either of these areas. **Unlearned** is similar to *ignorant* in that it refers to a lack of learning in general or in a specific subject (*an unlearned man who managed to become a millionaire*), but it does not carry the same negative connotations. **Uninformed** refers to a lack of definite information or data. For example, one can be highly intelligent and well educated but still *uninformed* about the latest developments in earthquake prediction.

ig·nore /ígnáwr/ v.tr. **1** refuse to take notice of or accept. **2** intentionally disregard. □□ **ig·nor·er** n. [F *ignorer* or L *ignorare* not know, ignore (as IN-¹, *gno-* know)]

i·gua·na /igwaánə/ n. any of various large lizards of the family Iguanidae native to America, the W. Indies, and the Pacific islands, having a dorsal crest and throat appendages. [Sp. f. Carib *iwana*]

Galápagos land iguana

i·guan·o·don /igwaánədon/ n. a large extinct plant-eating dinosaur of the genus *Iguanodon*, with forelimbs smaller than hind limbs. [IGUANA (from its resemblance to this), and *-odon* after *mastodon*, etc.]

i.h.p. abbr. indicated horsepower.

IHS abbr. Jesus. [ME f. LL, repr. Gk IHΣ = *Iēs(ous)* Jesus: often taken as an abbr. of various Latin words]

i·ke·ba·na /ikəbaánə/ n. the art of Japanese flower arrangement, with formal display according to strict rules. [Jap., = living flowers]

i·kon var. of ICON.

IL abbr. Illinois (in official postal use).

il- /il/ prefix assim. form of IN-¹, IN-² before *l*.

-il /il/ suffix (also **-ile** /īl/) forming adjectives or nouns denoting relation (*civil; utensil*) or capability (*agile; sessile*). [OF f. L *-ilis*]

i·lang-i·lang var. of YLANG-YLANG.

il·e·a pl. of ILEUM.

il·e·os·to·my /íleeóstəmee/ n. (pl. **-mies**) a surgical operation in which the ileum is brought through the abdominal wall to create an artificial opening for the evacuation of the intestinal contents. [ILEUM + Gk *stoma* mouth]

il·e·um /íleeəm/ n. (pl. **il·e·a** /íleeə/) Anat. the third and last portion of the small intestine. □□ **il·e·ac** adj. [var. of ILIUM]

il·e·us /íleeəs/ n. Med. any painful obstruction of the intestine, esp. of the ileum. [L f. Gk (*e*)*ileos* colic]

i·lex /íleks/ n. **1** any tree or shrub of the genus *Ilex*, esp. the common holly. **2** the holm oak. [ME f. L]

il·i·a pl. of ILIUM.

il·i·ac /íleeak/ adj. of the lower body or ilium (*iliac artery*). [LL *iliacus* (as ILIUM)]

il·i·um /íleeəm/ n. (pl. **il·i·a** /íleeə/) **1** the bone forming the upper part of each half of the human pelvis. **2** the corresponding bone in animals. [ME f. L]

ilk /ilk/ n. **1** a family, class, or set (*not of the same ilk as you*). **2** (in of

Late 16th cent. (as the endorsement made by a grand jury on an indictment considered backed by insufficient evidence to bring before a petty jury): Latin, literally 'we do not know' (in legal use 'we take no notice of it'), from *ignorare* (see IGNORE). The modern sense may derive from the name of a character in George Ruggle's *Ignoramus* (1615), a satirical comedy exposing lawyers' ignorance.

that ilk) *Sc.* of the same (landed estate or place) (*Guthrie of that ilk* = of Guthrie). [OE *ilca* same]

Ill. *abbr.* Illinois.

ill. *abbr.* **1** illustrated. **2** illustration. **3** illustrator.

I'll /il/ *contr.* I shall; I will.

ill /il/ *adj., adv., & n.* • *adj.* **1** (usu. *predic.*; often foll. by *with*) out of health; sick (*is ill; was taken ill with pneumonia; mentally ill people*). **2** (of health) unsound; disordered. **3** wretched; unfavorable (*ill fortune; ill luck*). **4** harmful (*ill effects*). **5** hostile; unkind (*ill feeling*). **6** *archaic* morally bad. **7** faulty; unskillful (*ill taste; ill management*). **8** (of manners or conduct) improper. • *adv.* **1** badly; wrongly (*ill-matched*). **2 a** imperfectly (*ill-provided*). **b** scarcely (*can ill afford to do it*). **3** unfavorably (*it would have gone ill with them*). • *n.* **1** injury; harm. **2** evil; the opposite of good. □ **do an ill turn to** harm (a person or a person's interests). **ill at ease** embarrassed; uneasy. **speak ill of** say something unfavorable about. [ME f. ON *illr*, of unkn. orig.]

ill-ad·vised *adj.* **1** (of a person) foolish or imprudent. **2** (of a plan, etc.) not well formed or considered; badly thought out. □□ **ill-ad·vis·ed·ly** /–ədvízidlee/ *adv.*

ill-assorted *adj.* not well matched.

il·la·tion /iláyshən/ *n.* **1 a** deduction or conclusion. **2** a thing deduced. [L *illatio* f. *illatus* past part. of *inferre* INFER]

il·la·tive /iláytiv, íllətiv/ *adj.* **1 a** (of a word) stating or introducing an inference. **b** inferential. **2** *Gram.* (of a case) denoting motion into. □□ **il·la·tive·ly** *adv.* [L *illativus* (as ILLATION)]

ill-be·haved *adj.* having bad manners or conduct.

ill blood *n.* bad feeling; animosity.

ill-bred *adj.* badly brought up; rude.

ill-con·sid·ered *adj.* = ILL-ADVISED.

ill-de·fined *adj.* not clearly defined.

ill-dis·posed *adj.* **1** unfriendly or unsympathetic. **2** inclined to evil; malevolent.

il·le·gal /ileégəl/ *adj.* **1** not legal. **2** contrary to law. □□ **il·le·gal·i·ty** /–gálitee/ *n.* (*pl.* ·**ties**). **il·le·gal·ly** *adv.* [F *illégal* or med.L *illegalis* (as IN-¹, LEGAL)]

il·leg·i·ble /iléjibəl/ *adj.* not legible. □□ **il·leg·i·bil·i·ty** *n.* **il·leg·i·bly** *adv.*

il·le·git·i·mate *adj., n., & v.* • *adj.* /iljítimət/ **1** (of a child) born of parents not married to each other. **2** not authorized by law; unlawful. **3** improper. **4** wrongly inferred. **5** physiologically abnormal. • *n.* /iljítimət/ a person whose position is illegitimate, esp. by birth. • *v.tr.* /iljítimayt/ declare or pronounce illegitimate. □□ **il·le·git·i·ma·cy** /–məsee/ *n.* **il·le·git·i·mate·ly** *adv.* [LL *illegitimus*, after LEGITIMATE]

ill-e·quipped *adj.* not adequately equipped or qualified (*ill-equipped to cope with emergencies*).

ill fame *n.* disrepute.

ill-fat·ed *adj.* destined to or bringing bad fortune.

ill-fa·vored *adj.* unattractive; displeasing; objectionable.

ill feel·ing *n.* bad feeling; animosity.

ill-found·ed *adj.* (of an idea, etc.) not well founded; baseless.

ill-got·ten *adj.* acquired by illegal or unfair means.

ill hu·mor *n.* moroseness; irritability; bad temper. □□ **ill-hu·mored** *adj.*

il·lib·er·al /ilíbərəl/ *adj.* **1** intolerant; narrow-minded. **2** without liberal culture. **3** not generous; stingy. **4** vulgar; sordid. □□ **il·lib·er·al·i·ty** /–álitee/ *n.* (*pl.* ·**ties**). **il·lib·er·al·ly** *adv.* [F *illibéral* f. L *illiberalis* mean, sordid (as IN-¹, LIBERAL)]

il·lic·it /ilísit/ *adj.* **1** unlawful; forbidden (*illicit dealings*). **2** secret; furtive (*an illicit cigarette*). □□ **il·lic·it·ly** *adv.* **il·lic·it·ness** *n.*
▶ See note at ELICIT.

il·lim·it·a·ble /ilímitəbəl/ *adj.* limitless. □□ **il·lim·it·a·bil·i·ty** *n.* **il·lim·it·a·ble·ness** *n.* **il·lim·it·a·bly** *adv.* [LL *illimitatus* f. L *limitatus* (as IN-¹, L *limitatus* past part. of *limitare* LIMIT)]

il·liq·uid /ilíkwid/ *adj.* (of assets) not easily converted into cash. □□ **il·liq·uid·i·ty** /–kwíditee/ *n.*

il·lit·er·ate /ilítərət/ *adj. & n.* • *adj.* **1** unable to read or write. **2** ignorant in a particular subject or activity. **3** uncultured or poorly educated. **4** (esp. of a piece of writing) showing a lack of education, esp. an inability to read or write well. • *n.* an illiterate person. □□ **il·lit·er·a·cy** *n.* **il·lit·er·ate·ly** *adv.* **il·lit·er·ate·ness** *n.* [L *illitteratus* (as IN-¹, *litteratus* LITERATE)]

ill-judged *adj.* unwise; badly considered.

ill-man·nered *adj.* having bad manners; rude.

ill na·ture *n.* churlishness; unkindness. □□ **ill-na·tured** *adj.* **ill-na·tured·ly** *adv.*

ill·ness /ílnis/ *n.* **1** a disease, ailment, or malady. **2** the state of being ill.

il·log·i·cal /ilójikəl/ *adj.* devoid of or contrary to logic. □□ **il·log·i·cal·i·ty** /–kálitee/ *n.* (*pl.* ·**ties**). **il·log·i·cal·ly** *adv.*

ill-o·mened *adj.* attended by bad omens.

ill-starred *adj.* unlucky; destined to failure.

ill tem·per *n.* moroseness. □□ **ill-tem·pered** *adj.*

ill-timed *adj.* done or occurring at an inappropriate time.

ill-treat *v.tr.* act cruelly toward; abuse. □□ **ill-treat·ment** *n.*

il·lude /ilóod/ *v.tr. literary* trick or deceive. [ME, = mock, f. L *illudere* (as ILLUSION)]

il·lume /ilóom/ *v.tr. poet.* light up; make bright. [shortening of ILLUMINE]

il·lu·mi·nant /ilóominənt/ *n. & adj.* • *n.* a means of illumination. • *adj.* serving to illuminate. □□ **il·lu·mi·nance** /–nəns/ *n.* [L *illuminant-* part. stem of *illuminare* ILLUMINATE]

il·lu·mi·nate /ilóominayt/ *v.tr.* **1** light up; make bright. **2** decorate (buildings, etc.) with lights as a sign of festivity. **3** decorate (an initial letter, a manuscript, etc.) with gold, silver, or brilliant colors. **4** help to explain (a subject, etc.). **5** enlighten spiritually or intellectually. **6** shed luster on. □□ **il·lu·mi·nat·ing** *adj.* **il·lu·mi·nat·ing·ly** *adv.* **il·lu·mi·na·tion** /–náyshən/ *n.* **il·lu·mi·na·tive** /–náytiv, –nətiv/ *adj.* **il·lu·mi·na·tor** *n.* [L *illuminare* (as IN-², *lumen luminis* light)]

il·lu·mi·na·ti /ilóominaátee/ *n.pl.* **1** persons claiming to possess special knowledge or enlightenment. **2** (**Illuminati**) *hist.* any of various intellectual movements or societies of illuminati. □□ **il·lu·mi·nism** /ilóominizəm/ *n.* **il·lu·mi·nist** *n.* [pl. of L *illuminatus* or It. *illuminato* past part. (as ILLUMINATE)]

il·lu·mine /ilóomin/ *v.tr. literary* **1** light up; make bright. **2** enlighten spiritually. [ME f. OF *illuminer* f. L (as ILLUMINATE)]

il·lu·sion /ilóozhən/ *n.* **1** deception; delusion. **2** a misapprehension of the true state of affairs. **3 a** the faulty perception of an external object. **b** an instance of this. **4** a figment of the imagination. **5** = OPTICAL ILLUSION. □ **be under the illusion** (foll. by *that* + clause) believe mistakenly. □□ **il·lu·sion·al** *adj.* [ME f. F f. L *illusio* –*onis* f. *illudere* mock (as IN-², *ludere lus-* play)]
▶ See note at ALLUSION.

SPELLING TIP illusion

An *illusion* usually has an *ill*, or negative, impact because it is misleading.
---

il·lu·sion·ist /ilóozhənist/ *n.* a person who produces illusions; a magician. □□ **il·lu·sion·ism** *n.* **il·lu·sion·is·tic** *adj.*

il·lu·sive /ilóosiv/ *adj.* = ILLUSORY. [med.L *illusivus* (as ILLUSION)]

il·lu·so·ry /ilóosəree, –zəree/ *adj.* **1** deceptive (esp. as regards value or content). **2** having the character of an illusion. □□ **il·lu·so·ri·ly** *adv.* **il·lu·so·ri·ness** *n.* [eccl.L *illusorius* (as ILLUSION)]

il·lus·trate /íləstrayt/ *v.tr.* **1 a** provide (a book, newspaper, etc.) with pictures. **b** elucidate (a description, etc.) by drawings or pictures. **2** serve as an example of. **3** explain or make clear, esp. by examples. [L *illustrare* (as IN-², *lustrare* light up)]

il·lus·tra·tion /íləstráyshən/ *n.* **1** a drawing or picture illustrating a book, magazine article, etc. **2** an example serving to elucidate. **3** the act or an instance of illustrating. □□ **il·lus·tra·tion·al** *adj.* [ME f. OF f. L *illustratio* –*onis* (as ILLUSTRATE)]

il·lus·tra·tive /ilústrətiv, íləstray–/ *adj.* (often foll. by *of*) serving as an explanation or example. □□ **il·lus·tra·tive·ly** *adv.*

il·lus·tra·tor /íləstraytər/ *n.* a person who makes illustrations, esp. for magazines, books, advertising copy, etc.

il·lus·tri·ous /ilústreeəs/ *adj.* distinguished; renowned. □□ **il·lus·tri·ous·ly** *adv.* **il·lus·tri·ous·ness** *n.* [L *illustris* (as ILLUSTRATE)]

ill will *n.* bad feeling; animosity.

Il·lyr·i·an /ileéreeən/ *adj. & n.* • *adj.* **1** of or relating to Illyria on the Balkan (east) coast of the Adriatic Sea (corresponding to parts of modern Albania and the former Yugoslavia). **2** of the language group represented by modern Albanian. • *n.* **1** a native of Illyria; a person of Illyrian descent. **2 a** the language of Illyria. **b** the language group represented by modern Albanian.

il·ly·whack·er /íleewakər/ *n. Austral. sl.* a professional trickster. [20th c.: orig. unkn.]

il·men·ite /ílmənit/ *n.* a black ore of titanium. [*Ilmen* mountains in the Urals]

ILO *abbr.* International Labor Organization.

-ily /ilee/ *suffix* forming adverbs corresponding to adjectives in *–y* (see –Y¹, –LY²).

I'm /im/ *contr.* I am.

im- /im/ *prefix* assim. form of IN-¹, IN-² before *b, m, p.*

im·age /ímij/ *n. & v.* • *n.* **1** a representation of the external form of an object, e.g., a statue (esp. of a saint, etc., as an object of veneration). **2** the character or reputation of a person or thing as generally perceived. **3** an optical appearance or counterpart produced by light or other radiation from an object reflected in a mirror, refracted through a lens, etc. **4** semblance; likeness (*God created man in His own image*). **5** a person or thing that closely resembles another (*is the image of his father*). **6** a typical example. **7** a simile or metaphor. **8 a** a mental representation. **b** an idea or conception. **9** *Math.* a set formed by mapping from another set. • *v.tr.* **1** make an image of; portray. **2** reflect; mirror. **3** describe or imagine vividly. **4** typify. □□ **im·age·a·ble** *adj.* **im·age·less** *adj.* [ME f. OF f. L *imago* –*ginis*, rel. to IMITATE]

im·age·ry /ímijree/ *n.* **1** figurative illustration, esp. as used by an author for particular effects. **2** images collectively. **3** statuary; carving. **4** mental images collectively. [ME f. OF *imagerie* (as IMAGE)]

im·ag·i·na·ble /imájinəbəl/ *adj.* that can be imagined (*the greatest difficulty imaginable*). □□ **im·ag·i·na·bly** *adv.* [ME f. LL *imaginabilis* (as IMAGINE)]

i·ma·gi·nal /imájinəl/ *adj.* **1** of an image or images. **2** *Zool.* of an imago. [L *imago imagin-*: see IMAGE]

im·ag·i·nar·y /imájinéree/ *adj.* **1** existing only in the imagination. **2** *Math.* being the square root of a negative quantity, and plotted graphically in a direction usu. perpendicular to the axis of real quantities (see REAL¹). □□ **im·ag·i·nar·i·ly** *adv.* [ME f. L *imaginarius* (as IMAGE)]

▶**Imaginary** means 'product of the imagination; unreal'; **imaginative** means 'showing imagination; original.' Science fiction deals with imaginary people, places, and events; depending on the writer's ability, it may be more or less imaginative. Historical writing should not be imaginary, but the writer's approach, research, etc., may be quite imaginative.

im·ag·i·na·tion /imájináyshən/ *n.* **1** a mental faculty forming images or concepts of external objects not present to the senses. **2** the ability of the mind to be creative or resourceful. **3** the process of imagining. [ME f. OF f. L *imaginatio –onis* (as IMAGINE)]

im·ag·i·na·tive /imájinətiv/ *adj.* **1** having or showing in a high degree the faculty of imagination. **2** given to using the imagination. □□ **im·ag·i·na·tive·ly** *adv.* **im·ag·i·na·tive·ness** *n.* [ME f. OF *imaginatif –ive* f. med.L *imaginativus* (as IMAGINE)]

▶See note at IMAGINARY.

im·ag·ine /imájin/ *v.tr.* **1 a** form a mental image or concept of. **b** picture to oneself (something nonexistent or not present to the senses). **2** (often foll. by *to* + infin.) think or conceive (*imagined them to be soldiers*). **3** guess (*cannot imagine what they are doing*). **4** (often foll. by *that* + clause) suppose; be of the opinion (*I imagine you will need help*). **5** (in *imper.*) as an exclamation of surprise (*just imagine!*). □□ **i·mag·in·er** *n.* [ME f. OF *imaginer* f. L *imaginari* (as IMAGE)]

i·ma·gi·nes *pl.* of IMAGO.

im·ag·in·ings /imájiningz/ *n.pl.* fancies; fantasies.

im·ag·ism /iməjizəm/ *n.* a movement in early 20th-c. poetry which sought clarity of expression through the use of precise images. □□ **im·ag·ist** *n.* **im·ag·is·tic** *adj.*

i·ma·go /imáygō, imaá–/ *n.* (*pl.* **·goes** or **i·ma·gi·nes** /imájineez/) **1** the final and fully developed stage of an insect after all metamorphoses, e.g., a butterfly or beetle. **2** *Psychol.* an idealized mental picture of oneself or others, esp. a parent. [mod.L sense of *imago* IMAGE]

i·mam /imaám/ *n.* **1** a leader of prayers in a mosque. **2** a title of various Muslim leaders, esp. of one succeeding Muhammad as leader of Islam. □□ **i·mam·ate** /–mayt/ *n.* [Arab. *ʿimām* leader f. *ʿamma* precede]

im·bal·ance /imbáləns/ *n.* **1** lack of balance. **2** disproportion.

im·be·cile /imbisil, –səl/ *n. & adj.* ● *n.* **1** a person of abnormally weak intellect, esp. an adult with a mental age of about five. **2** *colloq.* a stupid person. ● *adj.* mentally weak; stupid; idiotic. □□ **im·be·cile·ly** *adv.* **im·be·cil·ic** /–sílik/ *adj.* **im·be·cil·i·ty** /–silitee/ *n.* (*pl.* **·cilies**) [F *imbécil(l)e* f. L *imbecillus* (as IN-¹, *baculum* stick) orig. in sense 'without supporting staff']

im·bed var. of EMBED.

im·bibe /imbíb/ *v.tr.* **1** (also *absol.*) drink (esp. alcoholic liquor). **2 a** absorb or assimilate (ideas, etc.). **b** absorb (moisture, etc.). **3** inhale (air, etc.). □□ **im·bib·er** *n.* **im·bi·bi·tion** /imbibíshən/ *n.* [ME f. L *imbibere* (as IN-², *bibere* drink)]

im·bri·cate *v. & adj.* ● *v.tr. & intr.* /imbrikayt/ arrange (leaves, the scales of a fish, etc.), or be arranged, so as to overlap like roof tiles. ● *adj.* /imbrikət/ having scales, etc., arranged in this way. □□ **im·bri·ca·tion** /–káyshən/ *n.* [L *imbricare imbricat-* cover with rain tiles f. *imbrex –icis* rain tile f. *imber* shower]

im·bro·glio /imbrólyō/ *n.* (*pl.* **·glios**) **1** a confused or complicated situation. **2** a confused heap. [It. *imbrogliare* confuse (as EMBROIL)]

im·brue /imbroo/ *v.tr.* (foll. by *in*, *with*) *literary* stain (one's hand, sword, etc.). [OF *embruer* bedabble (as IN-², *breu* ult. f. Gmc, rel. to BROTH)]

im·bue /imbyoo/ *v.tr.* (**im·bues, im·bued, im·bu·ing**) (often foll. by *with*) **1** inspire or permeate (with feelings, opinions, or qualities). **2** saturate. **3** dye. [orig. as past part., f. F *imbu* or L *imbutus* f. *imbuere* moisten]

IMF *abbr.* International Monetary Fund.

im·ide /ímid/ *n. Chem.* a compound containing the NH group formed by replacing two of the hydrogen atoms in ammonia by acid groups. [orig. F: arbitrary alt. of AMIDE]

i·mine /imeen/ *n. Chem.* a compound containing the group (-NH-) formed by replacing two of the hydrogen atoms in ammonia by other groups. [G *Imin* arbitrary alt. of *Amin* AMINE]

im·i·tate /imitayt/ *v.tr.* **1** follow the example of; copy the action(s) of. **2** mimic. **3** make a copy of; reproduce. **4** be (consciously or not) like. □□ **im·i·ta·ble** *adj.* **im·i·ta·tor** *n.* [L *imitari imitat-*, rel. to *imago* IMAGE]

APE, COPY, IMPERSONATE, MIMIC, MOCK. A young girl might **imitate** her mother by answering the phone in exactly the same tone of voice, while a teenager who deliberately *imitates* the way her mother talks for the purpose of irritating her would more accurately be said to **mimic** her. *Imitate* implies following something as an example or model (*he imitated the playing style of his music teacher*), while *mimic* suggests imitating someone's mannerisms for fun or ridicule (*they liked to mimic the teacher's southern drawl*). To **copy** is to imitate or reproduce something as closely as possible (*he copied the style of dress and speech used by the other gang members*). When someone assumes another person's appearance or mannerisms, sometimes for the purpose of perpetrating a fraud, he or she is said to **impersonate** (*arrested for impersonating a police officer; a comedian well known for impersonating political figures*). **Ape** and **mock** both imply an unflattering imitation. Someone who mimics in a contemptuous way is said to **ape** (*he entertained everyone in the office by aping the boss's phone conversations with his wife*), while someone who imitates with the intention of belittling or irritating is said to **mock** (*the students openly mocked their teacher's attempt to have a serious discussion about sex*).

im·i·ta·tion /imitáyshən/ *n. & adj.* ● *n.* **1** the act or an instance of imitating or being imitated. **2** a copy. **3** *Mus.* the repetition of a phrase, etc., usu. at a different pitch, in another part or voice. ● *adj.* made to appear like something genuine; counterfeit; fake (*imitation leather*). [F *imitation* or L *imitatio* (as IMITATE)]

im·i·ta·tive /imitativ/ *adj.* **1** (often foll. by *of*) imitating; following a model or example. **2** counterfeit. **3** of a word: **a** that reproduces a natural sound (e.g., *fizz*). **b** whose sound is thought to correspond to the appearance, etc., of the object or action described (e.g., *blob*). □□ **im·i·ta·tive·ly** *adv.* **im·i·ta·tive·ness** *n.* [LL *imitativus* (as IMITATE)]

im·mac·u·late /imákyələt/ *adj.* **1** pure; spotless; perfectly clean or neat and tidy. **2** perfectly or extremely well executed (*an immaculate performance*). **3** free from fault; innocent. **4** *Biol.* not spotted. □□ **im·mac·u·la·cy** *n.* **im·mac·u·late·ly** *adv.* **im·mac·u·late·ness** *n.* [ME f. L *immaculatus* (as IN-¹, *maculatus* f. *macula* spot)]

Im·mac·u·late Con·cep·tion *n. RC Ch.* the doctrine that God preserved the Virgin Mary from the taint of original sin from the moment she was conceived.

im·ma·nent /ímənənt/ *adj.* **1** (often foll. by *in*) indwelling; inherent. **2** (of the Supreme Being) permanently pervading the universe (opp. TRANSCENDENT). □□ **im·ma·nence** /–nəns/ *n.* **im·ma·nen·cy** *n.* **im·ma·nent·ism** *n.* **im·ma·nent·ist** *n.* [LL *immanēre* (as IN-², *manēre* remain)]

▶See note at EMINENT.

im·ma·te·ri·al /ímətéereeəl/ *adj.* **1** of no essential consequence; unimportant. **2** not material; incorporeal. □□ **im·ma·te·ri·al·i·ty** /–álitee/ *n.* **im·ma·te·ri·al·ize** *v.tr.* **im·ma·te·ri·al·ly** *adv.* [ME f. LL *immaterialis* (as IN-¹, MATERIAL)]

▶**Immaterial** and **irrelevant** are familiar in legal, especially courtroom, use. **Immaterial** means 'unimportant because not adding anything to the point.' **Irrelevant**, a much more common word, means 'beside the point; not speaking to the point.' Courts have long since ceased to demand precise distinctions, and evidence is often objected to as "immaterial, irrelevant, and incompetent ('offered by a witness who is not qualified to offer it')."

im·ma·te·ri·al·ism /ímətéereeəlizəm/ *n.* the doctrine that matter has no objective existence. □□ **im·ma·te·ri·al·ist** *n.*

im·ma·ture /ímochŏŏr, -tŏŏr, –tyŏŏr/ *adj.* **1** not mature or fully developed. **2** lacking emotional or intellectual development. **3** unripe. □□ **im·ma·ture·ly** *adv.* **im·ma·tur·i·ty** *n.* [L *immaturus* (as IN-¹, MATURE)]

im·meas·ur·a·ble /imézhərəbəl/ *adj.* not measurable; immense. □□ **im·meas·ur·a·bil·i·ty** /–bílitee/ *n.* **im·meas·ur·a·ble·ness** *n.* **im·meas·ur·a·bly** *adv.*

im·me·di·ate /iméedeeət/ *adj.* **1** occurring or done at once or without delay (*an immediate reply*). **2** nearest; next; not separated by others (*the immediate vicinity; the immediate future; my immediate neighbor*). **3** most pressing or urgent; of current concern (*our immediate concern was to get him to the hospital*). **4** (of a relation or action) having direct effect; without an intervening medium or agency (*the immediate cause of death*). **5** (of knowledge, reactions, etc.) intuitive; gained or exhibited without reasoning. □□ **im·me·di·a·cy** *n.* **im·me·di·ate·ness** *n.* [ME f. F *immédiat* or LL *immediatus* (as IN-¹, MEDIATE)]

im·me·di·ate·ly /iméedeeətlee/ *adv. & conj.* ● *adv.* **1** without pause or delay. **2** without intermediary. ● *conj. Brit.* as soon as.

im·med·i·ca·ble /imédikəbəl/ *adj.* that cannot be healed or cured. □□ **im·med·i·ca·bly** *adv.* [L *immedicabilis* (as IN-¹, MEDICABLE)]

im·me·mo·ri·al /imimáwreeəl/ *adj.* **1** ancient beyond memory or record. **2** very old. □□ **im·me·mo·ri·al·ly** *adv.* [med.L *immemorialis* (as IN-[1], MEMORIAL)]

im·mense /iméns/ *adj.* **1** immeasurably large or great; huge. **2** very great; considerable (*made an immense difference*). **3** *colloq.* very good. □□ **im·mense·ness** *n.* **im·men·si·ty** *n.* [ME f. F f. L *immensus* immeasurable (as IN-[1], *mensus* past part. of *metiri* measure)]

im·mense·ly /iménslee/ *adv.* **1** very much (*enjoyed myself immensely*). **2** to an immense degree.

im·merse /imárs/ *v.tr.* **1 a** (often foll. by *in*) dip; plunge. **b** cause (a person) to be completely under water. **2** (often *refl.* or in *passive*; often foll. by *in*) absorb or involve deeply. **3** (often foll. by *in*) bury; embed. [L *immergere* (as IN-[2], *mergere mers-* dip)]

im·mer·sion /imárzhən, -shən/ *n.* **1** the act or an instance of immersing; the process of being immersed. **2** baptism by immersing the whole person in water. **3** mental absorption. **4** *Astron.* the disappearance of a celestial body behind another or in its shadow. [ME f. LL *immersio* (as IMMERSE)]

im·mer·sion heat·er *n.* an electric heater designed for direct immersion in a liquid to be heated, esp. as a fixture in a hot-water tank.

im·mi·grant /ímigrənt/ *n. & adj.* ● *n.* a person who immigrates. ● *adj.* **1** immigrating. **2** of or concerning immigrants.

im·mi·grate /í migrayt/ *v.* **1** *intr.* come as a permanent resident to a country other than one's native land. **2** *tr.* bring in (a person) as an immigrant. □□ **im·mi·gra·tion** /-gráyshən/ *n.* **im·mi·gra·to·ry** *adj.* [L *immigrare* (as IN-[2], MIGRATE)]
▶See note at EMIGRATE.

im·mi·nent /ímənt/ *adj.* **1** (of an event, esp. danger) impending; about to happen. **2** *archaic* overhanging. □□ **im·mi·nence** /-nəns/ *n.* **im·mi·nent·ly** *adv.* [L *imminēre* imminent- overhang, project]
▶See note at EMINENT.

im·mis·ci·ble /imísibəl/ *adj.* (often foll. by *with*) that cannot be mixed. □□ **im·mis·ci·bil·i·ty** *n.* **im·mis·ci·bly** *adv.* [LL *immiscibilis* (as IN-[1], MISCIBLE)]

im·mit·i·ga·ble /imítigəbəl/ *adj.* that cannot be mitigated. □□ **im·mit·i·ga·bly** *adv.* [LL *immitigabilis* (as IN-[1], MITIGATE)]

im·mit·tance /imít'ns/ *n. Electr.* admittance or impedance (when not distinguished). [*impedance* + ad*mittance*]

im·mix·ture /imíks-chər/ *n.* **1** the process of mixing up. **2** (often foll. by *in*) being involved.

im·mo·bile /imóbəl/ *–beel, –bil/ *adj.* **1** not moving. **2** not able to move or be moved. □□ **im·mo·bil·i·ty** /–bílitee/ *n.* [ME f. OF f. L *immobilis* (as IN-[1], MOBILE)]

im·mo·bi·lize /imóbiliz/ *v.tr.* **1** make or keep immobile. **2** make (a vehicle or troops) incapable of being moved. **3** keep (a limb or patient) restricted in movement for healing purposes. **4** restrict the free movement of. **5** withdraw (coins) from circulation to support paper currency. □□ **im·mo·bi·li·za·tion** *n.* **im·mo·bi·liz·er** *n.* [F *immobiliser* (as IMMOBILE)]

im·mod·er·ate /imódərət/ *adj.* excessive; lacking moderation. □□ **im·mod·er·ate·ly** *adv.* **im·mod·er·ate·ness** *n.* **im·mod·er·a·tion** /–ráyshən/ *n.* [ME f. L *immoderatus* (as IN-[1], MODERATE)]

im·mod·est /imódist/ *adj.* **1** lacking modesty; forward; impudent. **2** lacking due decency. □□ **im·mod·est·ly** *adv.* **im·mod·es·ty** *n.* [F *immodeste* or L *immodestus* (as IN-[1], MODEST)]

im·mo·late /íməlayt/ *v.tr.* **1** kill or offer as a sacrifice. **2** *literary* sacrifice (a valued thing). □□ **im·mo·la·tion** /–láyshən/ *n.* **im·mo·la·tor** *n.* [L *immolare* sprinkle with sacrificial meal (as IN-[2], *mola* MEAL[2])]

im·mor·al /imáwrəl, imór–/ *adj.* **1** not conforming to accepted standards of morality. **2** morally wrong (esp. in sexual matters). **3** depraved; dissolute. □□ **im·mo·ral·i·ty** /–álitee/ *n.* (*pl.* **·ties**). **im·mor·al·ly** *adv.*
▶**Immoral** means 'failing to adhere to moral standards'; **amoral** means 'without moral standards.' An *immoral* person commits acts that violate society's moral norms; an *amoral* person has no understanding of these norms, or no sense of right and wrong.

im·mor·tal /imáwrt'l/ *adj. & n.* ● *adj.* **1 a** living forever; not mortal. **b** divine. **2** unfading; incorruptible. **3** likely or worthy to be famous for all time. ● *n.* **1 a** an immortal being. **b** (in *pl.*) the gods of antiquity. **2** a person (esp. an author) of enduring fame. **3** (**Immortal**) a member of the French Academy. □□ **im·mor·tal·i·ty** /–tálitee/ *n.* **im·mor·tal·ize** *v.tr.* **im·mor·tal·i·za·tion** *n.* **im·mor·tal·ly** *adv.* [ME f. L *immortalis* (as IN-[1], MORTAL)]

im·mor·telle /imáwrtél/ *n.* a composite flower of papery texture retaining its shape and color after being dried, esp. a helichrysum. [F, fem. of *immortel* IMMORTAL]

im·mov·a·ble /imóovəbəl/ *adj. & n.* (also **im·move·a·ble**) ● *adj.* **1** that cannot be moved. **2** steadfast; unyielding. **3** emotionless. **4** not subject to change (*immovable law*). **5** motionless. **6** *Law* (of property) consisting of land, houses, etc. ● *n.* (in *pl.*) *Law* immovable property. □□ **im·mov·a·bil·i·ty** *n.* **im·mov·a·ble·ness** *n.* **im·mov·a·bly** *adv.*

im·mune /imyóon/ *adj.* **1 a** (often foll. by *against*, *from*, *to*) protected against an infection owing to the presence of specific antibodies, or through inoculation or inherited or acquired resistance. **b** relating to immunity (*immune mechanism*). **2** (foll. by *from*, *to*) free or exempt from or not subject to (some undesirable factor or circum-

---

stance). [ME f. L *immunis* exempt from public service or charge (as IN-[1], *munis* ready for service): sense 1 f. F *immun*]

im·mune re·sponse *n.* the reaction of the body to the introduction into it of an antigen.

im·mu·ni·ty /imyóonitee/ *n.* (*pl.* **·ties**) **1** *Med.* the ability of an organism to resist infection, by means of the presence of circulating antibodies and white blood cells. **2** freedom or exemption from an obligation, penalty, or unfavorable circumstance. [ME f. L *immunitas* (as IMMUNE): sense 1 f. F *immunité*]

im·mu·nize /ímyəniz/ *v.tr.* make immune, esp. to infection, usu. by inoculation. □□ **im·mu·ni·za·tion** *n.* **im·mu·niz·er** *n.*

immuno- /ímyənō/ *comb. form* immunity to infection.

im·mu·no·as·say /ímyənō-ásay, imyóo–/ *n. Biochem.* the determination of the presence or quantity of a substance, esp. a protein, through its properties as an antigen or antibody.

im·mu·no·chem·is·try /ímyənōkémistree, imyóo–/ *n.* the chemistry of immune systems, esp. in mammalian tissues.

im·mu·no·de·fi·cien·cy /ímyənōdifíshənsee, imyóo–/ *n.* a reduction in a person's normal immune defenses.

im·mu·no·gen·ic /ímyənōjénik, imyóo–/ *adj. Biochem.* of, relating to, or possessing the ability to elicit an immune response.

im·mu·no·glob·u·lin /ímyənōglóbyəlin, imyóo–/ *n. Biochem.* any of a group of structurally related proteins which function as antibodies.

im·mu·nol·o·gy /ímyənóləjee/ *n.* the scientific study of immunity. □□ **im·mu·no·log·ic** /–nəlójik/ *adj.* **im·mu·no·log·i·cal** /–nəlójikəl/ *adj.* **im·mu·no·log·i·cal·ly** *adv.* **im·mu·nol·o·gist** /–nóləjist/ *n.*

im·mu·no·sup·pressed /ímyənōsəprést, imyóo–/ *adj.* (of an individual) rendered partially or completely unable to react immunologically.

im·mu·no·sup·pres·sion /ímyənōsəpréshən, imyóo–/ *n. Biochem.* the partial or complete suppression of the immune response of an individual, esp. to maintain the survival of an organ after a transplant operation. □□ **im·mu·no·sup·pres·sant** *n.*

im·mu·no·sup·pres·sive /ímyənōsəprésiv, imyóo–/ *adj. & n.* ● *adj.* partially or completely suppressing the immune response of an individual. ● *n.* an immunosuppressive drug.

im·mu·no·ther·a·py /ímyənōthérəpee, imyóo–/ *n. Med.* the prevention or treatment of disease with substances that stimulate the immune response.

im·mure /imyóor/ *v.tr.* **1** enclose within walls; imprison. **2** *refl.* shut (oneself) away. □□ **im·mure·ment** *n.* [F *emmurer* or med.L *immurare* (as IN-[2], *murus* wall)]

im·mu·ta·ble /imyóotəbəl/ *adj.* **1** unchangeable. **2** not subject to variation in different cases. □□ **im·mu·ta·bil·i·ty** /–bílitee/ *n.* **im·mu·ta·bly** *adv.* [ME f. L *immutabilis* (as IN-[1], MUTABLE)]

imp /imp/ *n. & v.* ● *n.* **1** a mischievous child. **2** a small mischievous devil or sprite. ● *v.tr.* **1** add feathers to (the wing of a falcon) to restore or improve its flight. **2** *archaic* enlarge; add by grafting.

WORD HISTORY imp

Old English *impa*, *impe* 'young shoot, scion', *impian* 'to graft', based on Greek *emphuein* 'to implant'. In late Middle English, the noun denoted a descendant, especially of a noble family, and later a child of the devil or a person regarded as such; hence a 'little devil' or mischievous child (sense 1, early 17th cent.).

---

im·pact *n. & v.* ● *n.* /ímpakt/ **1** (often foll. by *on*, *against*) the action of one body coming forcibly into contact with another. **2** an effect or influence, esp. when strong. ● *v.* /impákt/ **1** *tr.* (often foll. by *in*, *into*) press or fix firmly. **2** *tr.* (as **impacted** *adj.*) **a** (of a tooth) wedged between another tooth and the jaw. **b** (of a fractured bone) with the parts crushed together. **c** (of feces) lodged in the intestine. **3** *intr.* **a** (foll. by *against*, *on*) come forcibly into contact with a (larger) body or surface. **b** (foll. by *on*) have a pronounced effect. □□ **im·pac·tion** /–pákshən/ *n.* [L *impact-* part. stem of *impingere* IMPINGE]

im·pair /impáir/ *v.tr.* damage or weaken. □□ **im·pair·ment** *n.* [ME *empeire* f. OF *empeirier* (as IN-[2], LL *pejorare* f. L *pejor* worse)]

im·pa·la /impáálə, –pálə/ *n.* (*pl.* same) a small antelope, *Aepyceros melampus*, of S. and E. Africa, capable of long high jumps. [Zulu]

im·pale /impáyl/ *v.tr.* **1** (foll. by *on*, *upon*, *with*) transfix or pierce with a sharp instrument. **2** *Heraldry* combine (two coats of arms) by placing them side by side on one shield separated by a vertical line down the middle. □□ **im·pale·ment** *n.* [F *empaler* or med.L *impalare* (as IN-[2], *palus* stake)]

impala

im·pal·pa·ble /impálpəbəl/ *adj.* **1** not easily grasped by the mind; intangible. **2** imperceptible to the touch. **3** (of powder) very fine; not containing grains that can be felt. □□ **im·pal·pa·bil·i·ty** /–bílitee/ *n.* **im·pal·pa·bly** *adv.* [F *impalpable* or LL *impalpabilis* (as IN-¹, PALPABLE)]

im·pan·el /impán'l/ *v.tr.* (also **em·pan·el**) (·pan·eled, ·pan·el·ing; esp. *Brit.* ·pan·elled, ·pan·el·ling) enroll or enter on a panel (those eligible for jury service). □□ **im·pan·el·ment** *n.* [AF *empaneller* (as EN-¹, PANEL).]

im·park /impaárk/ *v.tr.* **1** enclose (animals) in a park. **2** enclose (land) for a park. [ME f. AF *enparker*, OF *emparquer* (as IN-², *parc* PARK)]

im·part /impaárt/ *v.tr.* (often foll. by *to*) **1** communicate (news, etc.). **2** give a share of (a thing). □□ **im·part·a·ble** *adj.* **im·par·ta·tion** /ímpaartáyshən/ *n.* **im·part·ment** *n.* [ME f. OF *impartir* f. L *impartire* (as IN-², *pars* part)]

im·par·tial /impaárshəl/ *adj.* treating all sides in a dispute, etc., equally; unprejudiced; fair. □□ **im·par·ti·al·i·ty** /–sheeálitee/ *n.* **im·par·tial·ly** *adv.*

im·pas·sa·ble /impásəbəl/ *adj.* that cannot be traversed. □□ **im·pas·sa·bil·i·ty** *n.* **im·pas·sa·ble·ness** *n.* **im·pas·sa·bly** *adv.*

im·passe /ímpas/ *n.* a position from which progress is impossible; deadlock. [F (as IN-¹, *passer* PASS¹)]

im·pas·si·ble /impásibəl/ *adj.* **1** impassive. **2** incapable of feeling or emotion. **3** incapable of suffering injury. **4** *Theol.* not subject to suffering. □□ **im·pas·si·bil·i·ty** *n.* **im·pas·si·ble·ness** *n.* **im·pas·si·bly** *adv.* [ME f. OF f. eccl.L *impassibilis* (as IN-¹, PASSIBLE)]

im·pas·sion /impáshən/ *v.tr.* fill with passion; arouse emotionally. [It. *impassionare* (as IN-², PASSION)]

im·pas·sioned /impáshənd/ *adj.* deeply felt; ardent (*an impassioned plea*).

im·pas·sive /impásiv/ *adj.* **1 a** deficient in or incapable of feeling emotion. **b** undisturbed by passion; serene. **2** without sensation. **3** not subject to suffering. □□ **im·pas·sive·ly** *adv.* **im·pas·sive·ness** *n.* **im·pas·siv·i·ty** /–sívitee/ *n.*

im·pas·to /impástō, –paàs–/ *n. Art* **1** the process of laying on paint thickly. **2** this technique of painting. [It. *impastare* (as IN-², *pastare* paste)]

im·pa·tiens /impáyshənz/ *n.* any plant of the genus *Impatiens*, including several known popularly as touch-me-not. [mod.L f. IMPATIENT]

im·pa·tient /impáyshənt/ *adj.* **1 a** (often foll. by *at, with*) lacking patience or tolerance. **b** (of an action) showing a lack of patience. **2** (often foll. by *for, or* + infin.) restlessly eager. **3** (foll. by *of*) intolerant. □□ **im·pa·tience** /–shəns/ *n.* **im·pa·tient·ly** *adv.* [ME f. OF f. L *impatiens* (as IN-¹, PATIENT)]

im·peach /impéech/ *v.tr.* **1** charge (the holder of a public office) with misconduct. **2** *Brit.* charge with a crime against the government, esp. treason. **3** call in question; disparage (a person's integrity, etc.). □□ **im·peach·a·ble** *adj.* **im·peach·ment** *n.* [ME f. OF *empecher* impede f. LL *impedicare* entangle (as IN-², *pedica* fetter f. *pes pedis* foot)]

im·pec·ca·ble /impékəbəl/ *adj.* **1** (of behavior, performance, etc.) faultless; exemplary. **2** not liable to sin. □□ **im·pec·ca·bil·i·ty** *n.* **im·pec·ca·bly** *adv.* [L *impeccabilis* (as IN-¹, *peccare* sin)]

im·pe·cu·ni·ous /ímpikyóōneeəs/ *adj.* having little or no money. □□ **im·pe·cu·ni·os·i·ty** /–neeósitee/ *n.* **im·pe·cu·ni·ous·ness** *n.* [IN-¹ + obs. *pecunious* having money f. L *pecuniosus* f. *pecunia* money f. *pecu* cattle]

im·ped·ance /imp·éed'ns/ *n.* **1** *Electr.* the total effective resistance of an electric circuit, etc., to alternating current, arising from ohmic resistance and reactance. **2** an analogous mechanical property. [IMPEDE + –ANCE]

▶See note at IMPEDIMENT.

im·pede /impéed/ *v.tr.* retard by obstructing; hinder. [L *impedire* shackle the feet of (as IN-², *pes* foot)]

im·ped·i·ment /impédimənt/ *n.* **1** a hindrance or obstruction. **2** a defect in speech, e.g., a lisp or stammer. □□ **im·ped·i·men·tal** /–mént'l/ *adj.* [ME f. L *impedimentum* (as IMPEDE)]

▶Impedance is a specialized electrical term, while impediment is an everyday term meaning 'a hindrance or obstruction,', e.g., *interpreting his handwriting was an impediment to getting business done.*

im·ped·i·men·ta /impédiméntə/ *n.pl.* **1** encumbrances. **2** traveling equipment, esp. of an army. [L, pl. of *impedimentum*: see IMPEDIMENT]

im·pel /impél/ *v.tr.* (**im·pelled, im·pel·ling**) **1** drive, force, or urge into action. **2** drive forward; propel. □□ **im·pel·lent** *adj. & n.* **im·pel·ler** *n.* [ME f. L *impellere* (as IN-², *pellere puls-* drive)]

im·pend /impénd/ *v.intr.* **1** be about to happen. **2** (often foll. by *over*) **a** (of a danger) be threatening. **b** hang; be suspended. □□ **im·pend·ing** *adj.* [L *impendēre* (as IN-², *pendēre* hang)]

im·pen·e·tra·ble /impénitrəbəl/ *adj.* **1** that cannot be penetrated. **2** inscrutable; unfathomable. **3** inaccessible to ideas, influences, etc. **4** *Physics* (of matter) having the property such that a body is incapable of occupying the same place as another body at the same time. □□ **im·pen·e·tra·bil·i·ty** *n.* **im·pen·e·tra·ble·ness** *n.* **im·pen·e·**

tra·bly *adv.* [ME f. F *impénétrable* f. L *impenetrabilis* (as IN-¹, PENETRATE)]

im·pen·i·tent /impénit'nt/ *adj.* not repentant or penitent. □□ **im·pen·i·tence** *n.* **im·pen·i·ten·cy** *n.* **im·pen·i·tent·ly** *adv.* [eccl.L *impaenitens* (as IN-¹, PENITENT)]

im·per·a·tive /impérətiv/ *adj. & n.* ● *adj.* **1** urgent. **2** obligatory. **3** commanding; peremptory. **4** *Gram.* (of a mood) expressing a command (e.g., *come here!*). ● *n.* **1** *Gram.* the imperative mood. **2** a command. □□ **im·per·a·ti·val** /–ətívəl/ *adj.* **im·per·a·tive·ly** *adv.* **im·per·a·tive·ness** *n.* [LL *imperativus* f. *imperare* command (as IN-², *parare* make ready)]

im·pe·ra·tor /ímpəraátawr/ *n. Rom.Hist.* commander (a title conferred under the Republic on a victorious general and under the Empire on the emperor). □□ **im·per·a·to·ri·al** /ímpérətáwreeəl/ *adj.* [L (as IMPERATIVE)]

im·per·cep·ti·ble /ímpərséptibəl/ *adj.* **1** that cannot be perceived. **2** very slight, gradual, or subtle. □□ **im·per·cep·ti·bil·i·ty** *n.* **im·per·cep·ti·bly** *adv.* [F *imperceptible* or med.L *imperceptibilis* (as IN-¹, PERCEPTIBLE)]

im·per·cip·i·ent /ímpərsípeeənt/ *adj.* lacking in perception. □□ **im·per·cip·i·ence** /–əns/ *n.*

im·per·fect /impórfikt/ *adj. & n.* ● *adj.* **1** not fully formed or done; faulty; incomplete. **2** *Gram.* (of a tense) denoting a (usu. past) action in progress but not completed at the time in question (e.g., *they were singing*). **3** *Mus.* (of a cadence) ending on the dominant chord. ● *n.* the imperfect tense. □□ **im·per·fect·ly** *adv.* [ME *imparfit*, etc., f. OF *imparfait* f. L *imperfectus* (as IN-¹, PERFECT)]

im·per·fec·tion /ímpərfékshən/ *n.* **1** incompleteness. **2 a** faultiness. **b** a fault or blemish. [ME f. OF *imperfection* or LL *imperfectio* (as IMPERFECT)]

im·per·fec·tive /ímpərféktiv/ *adj. & n. Gram.* ● *adj.* (of a verb aspect, etc.) expressing an action without reference to its completion (opp. PERFECTIVE). ● *n.* an imperfective aspect or form of a verb.

im·per·fect rhyme *n. Prosody* a rhyme that only partly satisfies the usual criteria (e.g., *love* and *move*).

im·per·fo·rate /impórfərət/ *adj.* **1** not perforated. **2** *Anat.* lacking the normal opening. **3** (of a postage stamp) lacking perforations.

im·pe·ri·al /impéereeəl/ *adj. & n.* ● *adj.* **1** of or characteristic of an empire or comparable sovereign state. **2 a** of or characteristic of an emperor. **b** supreme in authority. **c** majestic; august. **d** magnificent. **3** (of nonmetric weights and measures) used or formerly used by statute in the UK (*imperial gallon*). **4** a former size of paper, 30 x 22 inches (762 x 559 mm). □□ **im·pe·ri·al·ly** *adv.* [ME f. OF f. L *imperialis* f. *imperium* command, authority]

im·pe·ri·al·ism /impéereeəlizəm/ *n.* **1** an imperial rule or system. **2** usu. *derog.* a policy of acquiring dependent territories or extending a country's influence through trade, diplomacy, etc. □□ **im·pe·ri·al·is·tic** *adj.* **im·pe·ri·al·is·ti·cal·ly** *adv.* **im·pe·ri·al·ize** *v.tr.*

im·pe·ri·al·ist /impéereeəlist/ *n. & adj.* ● *n.* usu. *derog.* an advocate or agent of imperial rule or of imperialism. ● *adj.* of or relating to imperialism or imperialists.

im·per·il /impéril/ *v.tr.* (**im·per·iled, im·per·il·ing**; esp. *Brit.* **im·per·illed, im·per·il·ing**) bring or put into danger.

im·pe·ri·ous /impéereeəs/ *adj.* **1** overbearing; domineering. **2** urgent; imperative. □□ **im·pe·ri·ous·ly** *adv.* **im·pe·ri·ous·ness** *n.* [L *imperiosus* f. *imperium* command, authority]

im·per·ish·a·ble /impérishəbəl/ *adj.* that cannot perish. □□ **im·per·ish·a·bil·i·ty** *n.* **im·per·ish·a·ble·ness** *n.* **im·per·ish·a·bly** *adv.*

im·pe·ri·um /impéereeəm/ *n.* absolute power or authority. [L, = command, authority]

im·per·ma·nent /impórmənənt/ *adj.* not permanent; transient. □□ **im·per·ma·nence** /–nəns/ *n.* **im·per·ma·nen·cy** *n.* **im·per·ma·nent·ly** *adv.*

im·per·me·a·ble /impórmeeəbəl/ *adj.* **1** that cannot be penetrated. **2** *Physics* that does not permit the passage of fluids. □□ **im·per·me·a·bil·i·ty** *n.* [F *imperméable* or LL *impermeabilis* (as IN-¹, PERMEABLE)]

im·per·mis·si·ble /ímpərmísibəl/ *adj.* not allowable. □□ **im·per·mis·si·bil·i·ty** *n.*

im·per·son·al /impórsənəl/ *adj.* **1** having no personality. **2** having no personal feeling or reference. **3** *Gram.* **a** (of a verb) used only with a formal subject (usu. *it*) and expressing an action not attributable to a definite subject (e.g., *it is snowing*). **b** (of a pronoun) = INDEFINITE. □□ **im·per·son·al·i·ty** /–álitee/ *n.* **im·per·son·al·ly** *adv.* [LL *impersonalis* (as IN-¹, PERSONAL)]

im·per·son·ate /impórsənayt/ *v.tr.* **1** pretend to be (another person) for the purpose of entertainment or fraud. **2** act (a character). □□ **im·per·son·a·tion** /–náyshən/ *n.* **im·per·son·a·tor** *n.* [IN-² + L *persona* PERSON]

im·per·ti·nent /impórt'nənt/ *adj.* **1** rude or insolent; lacking proper respect. **2** out of place; absurd. **3** esp. *Law* irrelevant; intrusive. □□ **im·per·ti·nence** /–nəns/ *n.* **im·per·ti·nent·ly** *adv.* [ME f. OF or LL *impertinens* (as IN-¹, PERTINENT)]

im·per·turb·a·ble /ímpərtórbəbəl/ *adj.* not excitable; calm. □□ **im·per·turb·a·bil·i·ty** *n.* **im·per·turb·a·ble·ness** *n.* **im·per·turb·a·bly** *adv.* [ME f. LL *imperturbabilis* (as IN-¹, PERTURB)]

im·per·vi·ous /impórveeəs/ *adj.* (usu. foll. by *to*) **1** not responsive to an argument, etc. **2** not affording passage to a fluid. □□ **im·per·vi·ous·ly** *adv.* **im·per·vi·ous·ness** *n.* [L *impervius* (as IN-¹, PERVIOUS)]

im·pe·ti·go /ímpitígō/ *n.* a contagious bacterial skin infection forming pustules and yellow crusty sores. □□ **im·pe·tig·i·nous** /impitíjinəs/ *adj.* [ME f. L *impetigo* –*ginis* f. *impetere* assail]

im·pet·u·ous /impéchōōəs/ *adj.* **1** acting or done rashly or with sudden energy. **2** moving forcefully or rapidly. □□ **im·pet·u·os·i·ty** /–ósitee/ *n.* **im·pet·u·ous·ly** *adv.* **im·pet·u·ous·ness** *n.* [ME f. OF *impetueux* f. LL *impetuosus* (as IMPETUS)]

im·pe·tus /ímpitəs/ *n.* **1** the force or energy with which a body moves. **2** a driving force or impulse. [L, = assault, force, f. *impetere* assail (as IN-², *petere* seek)]

im·pi /ímpee/ *n.* (*pl.* **im·pies** or **im·pis**) *S.Afr.* **1** a band of armed men. **2** *hist.* an African tribal army or regiment. [Zulu, = regiment, armed band]

im·pi·e·ty /impíətee/ *n.* (*pl.* **·ties**) **1** a lack of piety or reverence. **2** an act, etc. showing this. [ME f. OF *impieté* or L *impietas* (as IN-¹, PIETY)]

im·pinge /impínj/ *v.tr.* (usu. foll. by *on, upon*) **1** make an impact; have an effect. **2** encroach. □□ **im·pinge·ment** *n.* **im·ping·er** *n.* [L *impingere* (a thing) at (as IN-², *pangere* fix, drive)]

im·pi·ous /ímpeeəs, impí–/ *adj.* **1** not pious. **2** wicked; profane. □□ **im·pi·ous·ly** *adv.* **im·pi·ous·ness** *n.* [L *impius* (as IN-¹, PIOUS)]

imp·ish /ímpish/ *adj.* of or like an imp; mischievous. □□ **imp·ish·ly** *adv.* **imp·ish·ness** *n.*

im·plac·a·ble /implákəbəl/ *adj.* that cannot be appeased; inexorable. □□ **im·plac·a·bil·i·ty** *n.* **im·plac·a·bly** *adv.* [ME f. F *implacable* or L *implacabilis* (as IN-¹, PLACABLE)]

im·plant *v. & n.* ●*v.tr.* /implánt/ **1** (often foll. by *in*) insert or fix. **2** (often foll. by *in*) instill (a principle, idea, etc.) in a person's mind. **3** plant. **4** *Med.* **a** insert (tissue, etc.) in a living body. **b** (in *passive*) (of a fertilized ovum) become attached to the wall of the womb. ●*n.* /ímplant/ **1** a thing implanted. **2** a thing implanted in the body, e.g., a piece of tissue or a capsule containing material for radium therapy. □□ **im·plan·ta·tion** *n.* [F *implanter* or LL *implantare* engraft (as IN-², PLANT)]

im·plau·si·ble /impláwzibəl/ *adj.* not plausible. □□ **im·plau·si·bil·i·ty** *n.* **im·plau·si·bly** *adv.*

im·plead /impleéd/ *v.tr. Law* **1** prosecute or take proceedings against (a person). **2** involve (a person, etc.) in a suit. [ME f. AF *empleder*, OF *empleidier* (as EN-¹, PLEAD)]

im·ple·ment *n. & v.* ●*n.* /ímplimənt/ **1** a tool, instrument, or utensil. **2** (in *pl.*) equipment; articles of furniture, dress, etc. **3** *Law* performance of an obligation. ●*v.tr.* /ímpliment/ **1 a** put (a decision, plan, etc.) into effect. **b** fulfill (an undertaking). **2** complete (a contract, etc.). **3** fill up; supplement. □□ **im·ple·men·ta·tion** *n.* [ME f. med.L *implementa* (pl.) f. *implēre* employ (as IN-², L *plēre* *plet*- fill)]

im·pli·cate *v. & n.* ●*v.tr.* /ímplikayt/ **1** (often foll. by *in*) show (a person) to be concerned or involved (in a charge, crime, etc.). **2** (in *passive*; often foll. by *in*) be affected or involved. **3** lead to as a consequence or inference. ●*n.* /ímplikət/ a thing implied. □□ **im·pli·ca·tive** /ímplikaytiv, implíkə–/ *adj.* **im·pli·ca·tive·ly** *adv.*

Late Middle English: from Latin *implicatus* 'folded in', past participle of *implicare* (see IMPLY). The original sense was 'entwine, entangle'; compare with EMPLOY and IMPLY.

IMPUDENT, INSOLENT, INTRUSIVE, MEDDLESOME, OBTRUSIVE. The easiest way to distinguish **impertinent** from these other adjectives that mean exceeding the bounds of propriety is to think of its root: *Impertinent* behavior is not pertinent—in other words, inappropriate or out of place. The *impertinent* individual has a tendency to be rude or presumptuous toward those who are entitled to deference or respect (*it was an impertinent question to ask a woman who had just lost her husband*). The **intrusive** person is unduly curious about other people's affairs (*her constant questions about the state of their marriage were intrusive and unwelcome*), while **obtrusive** implies objectionable actions rather than an objectionable disposition. The *obtrusive* person has a tendency to thrust himself or herself into a position where he or she is conspicuous and apt to do more harm than good (*they tried to keep him out of the meeting because his presence would be obtrusive*). To be **meddlesome** is to have a prying or inquisitive nature and a tendency to interfere in an annoying way in other people's affairs (*a meddlesome neighbor*). **Impudent** and **insolent** are much stronger words for inappropriate behavior. Young people are often accused of being *impudent*, which means to be *impertinent* in a bold and shameless way (*an impudent young man who had a lot to learn about tact*). Anyone who is guilty of insulting and contemptuously arrogant behavior might be called *insolent* (*he was so insolent to the arresting officer that he was handcuffed*).

im·pli·ca·tion /ímplikáyshən/ *n.* **1** what is involved in or implied by something else. **2** the act of implicating or implying. □ **by implication** by what is implied or suggested rather than by formal expression. [ME f. L *implicatio* (as IMPLICATE)]

im·plic·it /implísit/ *adj.* **1** implied though not plainly expressed. **2** (often foll. by *in*) virtually contained. **3** absolute; unquestioning; unreserved (*implicit obedience*). **4** *Math.* (of a function) not expressed directly in terms of independent variables. □□ **im·plic·it·ly** *adv.* **im·plic·it·ness** *n.* [F *implicite* or L *implicitus* (as IMPLICATE)]

▶**Explicit** means 'stated outright' or 'clearly explained.' When you see the word **implicit**, think of something that is *im*plied rather than openly stated.

im·plode /implṓd/ *v.intr. & tr.* burst or cause to burst inward. □□ **im·plo·sion** /–plṓzhən/ *n.* **im·plo·sive** /–plṓsiv/ *adj.* [IN-² + L –*plodere*, after EXPLODE]

im·plore /impláwr/ *v.tr.* **1** (often foll. by *to* + infin.) entreat (a person). **2** beg earnestly for. □□ **im·plor·ing** *adj.* **im·plor·ing·ly** *adv.* [F *implorer* or L *implorare* invoke with tears (as IN-², *plorare* weep)]

im·ply /implí/ *v.tr.* (**·plies**, **·plied**) **1** (often foll. by *that* + clause) strongly suggest the truth or existence of (a thing not expressly asserted). **2** insinuate; hint (*what are you implying?*). **3** signify. □□ **im·plied** *adj.* **im·pli·ed·ly** *adv.*

▶See note at INFER.

Late Middle English: from Old French *emplier*, from Latin *implicare*, from *in-* 'in' + *plicare* 'to fold'. The original sense was ' entwine, entangle'; in the 16th and 17th cents the word also meant 'employ'. Compare with EMPLOY and IMPLICATE.

im·po·lite /ímpəlít/ *adj.* (**im·po·lit·est**) ill-mannered; uncivil; rude. □□ **im·po·lite·ly** *adv.* **im·po·lite·ness** *n.* [L *impolitus* (as IN-¹, POLITE)]

im·pol·i·tic /impólitik/ *adj.* **1** inexpedient; unwise. **2** not politic. □□ **im·pol·i·tic·ly** *adv.*

im·pon·der·a·ble /impóndərəbəl/ *adj. & n.* ●*adj.* **1** that cannot be estimated or assessed in any definite way. **2** very light. **3** *Physics* having no weight. ●*n.* (usu. in *pl.*) something difficult or impossible to assess. □□ **im·pon·der·a·bil·i·ty** *n.* **im·pon·der·a·bly** *adv.*

im·port *v. & n.* ●*v.tr.* /impáwrt, ím–/ **1** bring in (esp. foreign goods or services) to a country. **2** (often foll. by *that* + clause) **a** imply; indicate; signify. **b** express; make known. ●*n.* /ímpawrt/ **1** the process of importing. **2 a** an imported article or service. **b** (in *pl.*) an amount imported (*imports exceeded $50 billion*). **3** what is implied; meaning. **4** importance. □□ **im·port·a·ble** *adj.* **im·por·ta·tion** *n.* **port·er** /–páwrtər/ *n.* (all in sense 1 of *v.*). [ME f. L *importare* bring in, in med.L = imply, be of consequence (as IN-², *portare* carry)]

im·por·tance /impáwrt'ns/ *n.* **1** the state of being important. **2** weight; significance. **3** personal consequence; dignity. [F f. med.L *importantia* (as IMPORT)]

im·por·tant /impáwrt'nt/ *adj.* **1** (often foll. by *to*) of great effect or consequence; momentous. **2** (of a person) having high rank or status, or great authority. **3** pretentious; pompous. **4** (*absol.* in parenthetic construction) what is a more important point or matter (*they are willing and, more important, able*). □□ **im·por·tant·ly** *adv.* (see note below). [F f. med.L (as IMPORT)]

▶The use of *importantly* in place of *important* in sense 4, while common, is considered incorrect by many.

im·por·tu·nate /impáwrchənət/ *adj.* **1** making persistent or pressing requests. **2** (of affairs) urgent. □□ **im·por·tu·nate·ly** *adv.* **im·por·tu·ni·ty** /–pawrtṓōnətee, –tyṓ–/ *n.* [L *importunus* inconvenient (as IN-¹, *portunus* f. *portus* harbor)]

im·por·tune /ímpawrtṓōn, –tyṓōn, impáwrchən/ *v.tr.* **1** solicit (a person) pressingly. **2** solicit for an immoral purpose. [F *importuner* or med.L *importunari* (as IMPORTUNATE)]

im·pose /impṓz/ *v.* **1** *tr.* (often foll. by *on, upon*) require (a tax, duty, charge, or obligation) to be paid or undertaken (by a person, etc.). **2** *tr.* enforce compliance with. **3** *intr. & refl.* (foll. by *on, upon*, or *absol.*) demand the attention or commitment of (a person); take advantage of (*I do not want to impose on you any longer; I did not want to impose*). **4** *tr.* (often foll. by *on, upon*) palm (a thing) off on (a person). **5** *tr. Printing* lay (pages of type) in the proper order ready for printing. **6** *intr.* (foll. by *on, upon*) exert influence by an impressive character or appearance. **7** *intr.* (often foll. by *on, upon*) practice deception. **8** *tr. archaic* (foll. by *upon*) place (a thing). [ME f. F *imposer* f. L *imponere imposit*- inflict, deceive (as IN-², *ponere* put)]

im·pos·ing /impṓzing/ *adj.* impressive or formidable, esp. in appearance. □□ **im·pos·ing·ly** *adv.* **im·pos·ing·ness** *n.*

im·po·si·tion /ímpəzíshən/ *n.* **1** the act or an instance of imposing; the process of being imposed. **2** an unfair or resented demand or burden. **3** a tax or duty. **4** *Brit.* work set as a punishment at school. [ME f. OF *imposition* or L *impositio* f. *imponere*: see IMPOSE]

im·pos·si·bil·i·ty /impósibílitee/ *n.* (*pl.* ·**ties**) **1** the fact or condition of being impossible. **2** an impossible thing or circumstance. [F *impossibilité* or L *impossibilitas* (as IMPOSSIBLE)]

im·pos·si·ble /impósibəl/ *adj.* **1** not possible; that cannot be done, occur, or exist (*it is impossible to alter them*; *such a thing is impossible*). **2** (loosely) not easy; not convenient; not easily believable. **3** *colloq.* (of a person or thing) outrageous; intolerable. □□ **im·pos·si·bly** *adv.* [ME f. OF *impossible* or L *impossibilis* (as IN-¹, POSSIBLE)]

im·post¹ /ímpōst/ *n.* **1** a tax; duty; tribute. **2** a weight carried by a horse in a handicap race. [F f. med.L *impost-* part. stem of L *imponere*: see IMPOSE]

im·post² /ímpōst/ *n.* the upper course of a pillar, carrying an arch. [F *imposte* or It. *imposta* fem. past part. of *imporre* f. L *imponere*: see IMPOSE]

im·pos·tor /impóstər/ *n.* (also **im·post·er**) **1** a person who assumes a false character or pretends to be someone else. **2** a swindler. □□ **im·pos·tor·ous** *adj.* **im·pos·trous** *adj.* [F *imposteur* f. LL *impostor* (as IMPOST¹)]

im·pos·ture /impós-chər/ *n.* the act or an instance of fraudulent deception. [F f. LL *impostura* (as IMPOST¹)]

im·po·tent /ímpət'nt/ *adj.* **1 a** powerless; lacking all strength. **b** helpless. **c** ineffective. **2 a** (esp. of a male) unable, esp. for a prolonged period, to achieve a sexual erection or orgasm. **b** *colloq.* unable to procreate; infertile. □□ **im·po·tence** /–t'ns/ *n.* **im·po·ten·cy** *n.* **im·po·tent·ly** *adv.* [ME f. OF f. L *impotens* (as IN-¹, POTENT¹)]

im·pound /impównd/ *v.tr.* **1** confiscate. **2** take possession of. **3** shut up (animals) in a pound. **4** shut up (a person or thing) as in a pound. **5** (of a dam, etc.) collect or confine (water). □□ **im·pound·a·ble** *adj.* **im·pound·er** *n.* **im·pound·ment** *n.*

im·pov·er·ish /impóvərish/ *v.tr.* (often as **impoverished** *adj.*) **1** make poor. **2** exhaust the strength or natural fertility of. □□ **im·pov·er·ish·ment** *n.* [ME f. OF *empoverir* (as EN-¹, *povre* POOR)]

im·prac·ti·ca·ble /impráktikəbəl/ *adj.* **1** impossible in practice. **2** (of a road, etc.) impassable. **3** (of a person or thing) unmanageable. □□ **im·prac·ti·ca·bil·i·ty** /–bílitee/ *n.* **im·prac·ti·ca·ble·ness** *n.* **im·prac·ti·ca·bly** *adv.*

im·prac·ti·cal /impráktikəl/ *adj.* **1** not practical. **2** not practicable. □□ **im·prac·ti·cal·i·ty** /–kálitee/ *n.* **im·prac·ti·cal·ly** *adv.*

im·pre·cate /imprikayt/ *v.tr.* (often foll. by *upon*) invoke; call down (evil). □□ **im·pre·ca·to·ry** /–kətáwree/ *adj.* [L *imprecari* (as IN-², *precari* pray)]

im·pre·ca·tion /imprikáyshən/ *n.* **1** a spoken curse; a malediction. **2** imprecating.

im·pre·cise /ímprisís/ *adj.* not precise. □□ **im·pre·cise·ly** *adv.* **im·pre·cise·ness** *n.* **im·pre·ci·sion** /–sízhən/ *n.*

im·preg·na·ble /imprégnəbəl/ *adj.* **1** (of a fortified position) unable to be captured or broken into. **2** resistant to attack or criticism. □□ **im·preg·na·bil·i·ty** /–bílitee/ *n.* **im·preg·na·bly** *adv.* [ME f. OF *imprenable* (as IN-¹, *prendre* take)]

im·preg·nate /imprégnayt/ *v. & adj.* ● *v.tr.* **1** (often foll. by *with*) fill or saturate. **2** (often foll. by *with*) imbue; fill (with feelings, moral qualities, etc.). **3 a** make (a female) pregnant. **b** *Biol.* fertilize (a female reproductive cell or ovum). ● *adj.* also /–nət/ **1** pregnant. **2** (often foll. by *with*) permeated. □□ **im·preg·na·tion** /–náyshən/ *n.* [LL *impregnare impregnat-* (as IN-², *pregnare* be pregnant)]

im·pre·sa·ri·o /imprisáareeō, –sáir–/ *n.* (*pl.* ·**os**) an organizer of public entertainments, esp. the manager of an operatic, theatrical, or concert company. [It. f. *impresa* undertaking]

im·pre·scrip·ti·ble /impriskríptibəl/ *adj. Law* (of rights) that cannot be taken away by prescription or lapse of time. [med.L *imprescriptibilis* (as IN-¹, PRESCRIBE)]

im·press¹ *v. & n.* ● *v.tr.* /imprés/ **1** (often foll. by *with*) **a** affect or influence deeply. **b** evoke a favorable opinion or reaction from (a person) (*was most impressed with your efforts*). **2** (often foll. by *on*) emphasize (an idea, etc.) (*must impress on you the need to be prompt*). **3** (often foll. by *on*) imprint or stamp. **b** apply (a mark, etc.) with pressure. **4** make a mark or design on (a thing) with a stamp, seal, etc. **5** *Electr.* apply (voltage, etc.) from outside. ● *n.* /ímpres/ **1** the act or an instance of impressing. **2** a mark made by a seal, stamp, etc. **3** a characteristic mark or quality. **4** = IMPRESSION 3. □□ **im·pres·si·ble** /–présibəl/ *adj.* [ME f. OF *empresser* (as EN-¹, PRESS¹)]

im·press² /ímprés/ *v.tr. hist.* **1** force (men) to serve in the army or navy. **2** seize (goods, etc.) for public service. □□ **im·press·ment** *n.* [IN-² + PRESS²]

im·pres·sion /impréshən/ *n.* **1** an effect produced (esp. on the mind or feelings). **2** a notion or belief (esp. a vague or mistaken one) (*my impression is they are afraid*). **3** an imitation of a person or sound, esp. done to entertain. **4 a** the impressing of a mark. **b** a mark impressed. **5** an unaltered reprint from standing type or plates (esp. as distinct from *edition*). **6 a** the number of copies of a book, newspaper, etc., issued at one time. **b** the printing of these. **7** a print taken from a wood engraving. **8** *Dentistry* a negative copy of the teeth or mouth made by pressing them into a soft substance. □□ **im·**

pres·sion·al *adj.* [ME f. OF f. L *impressio –onis* f. *imprimere* impress- (as IN-², PRESS¹)]

im·pres·sion·a·ble /impréshənəbəl/ *adj.* easily influenced; susceptible to impressions. □□ **im·pres·sion·a·bil·i·ty** /–bílitee/ *n.* **im·pres·sion·a·bly** *adv.* [F *impressionnable* f. *impressionner* (as IMPRESSION)]

im·pres·sion·ism /impréshənizəm/ *n.* **1** a style or movement in art concerned with expression of feeling by visual impression, esp. from the effect of light on objects. **2** a style of music or writing that seeks to describe a feeling or experience rather than achieve accurate depiction or systematic structure. □□ **im·pres·sion·ist** *n.* [F *impressionnisme* (after *Impression*: *Soleil levant*, title of a painting by Monet, 1872)]

im·pres·sion·is·tic /impréshənístik/ *adj.* **1** in the style of impressionism. **2** subjective; unsystematic. □□ **im·pres·sion·is·ti·cal·ly** *adv.*

im·pres·sive /imprésiv/ *adj.* **1** impressing the mind or senses, esp. so as to cause approval or admiration. **2** (of language, a scene, etc.) tending to excite deep feeling. □□ **im·pres·sive·ly** *adv.* **im·pres·sive·ness** *n.*

im·prest /ímprest/ *n.* money advanced to a person, esp. for use in government business. [orig. *in prest* f. OF *prest* loan, advance pay: see PRESS²]

im·pri·ma·tur /ímprimáatər, –máytər, –tōōr/ *n.* **1** *RC Ch.* an official license to print (an ecclesiastical or religious book, etc.). **2** official approval. [L, = let it be printed]

im·pri·ma·tu·ra /impreémətōōrə/ *n.* (in painting) a colored transparent glaze as a primer. [It. *imprimitura* f. *imprimere* IMPRESS¹]

im·print *v. & n.* ● *v.tr.* /imprínt/ **1** (often foll. by *on*) impress or establish firmly, esp. on the mind. **2 a** (often foll. by *on*) make a stamp or impression of (a figure, etc.) on a thing. **b** make an impression on (a thing) with a stamp, etc. ● *n.* /ímprint/ **1** an impression or stamp. **2** the printer's or publisher's name and other details printed in a book. [ME f. OF *empreinter empreint* f. L *imprimere*: see IMPRESSION]

im·print·ing /imprínting/ *n.* **1** in senses of IMPRINT *v.*. **2** *Zool.* the development in a young animal of a pattern of recognition and trust for its own species.

im·pris·on /imprízən/ *v.tr.* **1** put into prison. **2** confine; shut up. □□ **im·pris·on·ment** *n.* [ME f. OF *emprisoner* (as EN-¹, PRISON)]

im·prob·a·ble /impróbəbəl/ *adj.* **1** not likely to be true or to happen. **2** difficult to believe. □□ **im·prob·a·bil·i·ty** *n.* **im·prob·a·bly** *adv.* [F *improbable* or L *improbabilis* (as IN-¹, PROBABLE)]

im·pro·bi·ty /impróbitee/ *n.* (*pl.* ·**ties**) **1** wickedness; lack of moral integrity. **2** dishonesty. **3** a wicked or dishonest act. [L *improbitas* (as IN-¹, PROBITY)]

im·promp·tu /imprómptōō, –tyōō/ *adj., adv., & n.* ● *adj. & adv.* done without being planned, organized, or rehearsed; extempore. ● *n.* **1** an extempore performance or speech. **2** a short piece of instrumental music, esp. a solo, that is reminiscent of an improvisation. [F f. L *in promptu* in readiness: see PROMPT]

im·prop·er /impropər/ *adj.* **1 a** unseemly; indecent. **b** not in accordance with accepted rules of behavior. **2** inaccurate; wrong. **3** not properly so called. □□ **im·prop·er·ly** *adv.* [F *impropre* or L *improprius* (as IN-¹, PROPER)]

im·prop·er frac·tion *n.* a fraction in which the numerator is greater than or equal to the denominator.

im·pro·pri·ate /imprópreeayt/ *v.tr. Brit.* **1** annex (an ecclesiastical benefice) to a corporation or person as property. **2** place (tithes or ecclesiastical property) in lay hands. □□ **im·pro·pri·a·tion** /–áyshən/ *n.* [AL *impropriare* (as IN-², *proprius* own)]

im·pro·pri·a·tor /impróⁿpreeaytər/ *n. Brit.* a person to whom a benefice is impropriated.

im·pro·pri·e·ty /imprəpríətee/ *n.* (*pl.* ·**ties**) **1** lack of propriety; indecency. **2** an instance of improper conduct, etc. **3** incorrectness. **4** unfitness. [F *impropriété* or L *improprietas* (as IN-¹, *proprius* proper)]

im·prov·a·ble /impróⁿvəbəl/ *adj.* **1** that can be improved. **2** suitable for cultivation. □□ **im·prov·a·bil·i·ty** /–bílitee/ *n.*

im·prove /impróⁿv/ *v.* **1 a** *tr. & intr.* make or become better. **b** *intr.* (foll. by *on, upon*) produce something better than. **2** *absol.* (as **improving** *adj.*) giving moral benefit (*improving literature*).

WORD HISTORY improve

Early 16th cent. (as *emprowe* or *improwe*): from Anglo-Norman French *emprower* (based on Old French *prou* 'profit', ultimately from Latin *prodest* 'is of advantage'); *-owe* was changed to *-ove* under the influence of PROVE. The original sense was 'make a profit, increase the value of'; subsequently 'make greater in amount or degree', which led to sense 1 (early 17th cent.).

im·prove·ment /impróⁿvmənt/ *n.* **1** the act or an instance of improving or being improved. **2** something that improves, esp. an addition or alteration that adds to value. **3** something that has been improved. [ME f. AF *emprowement* (as IMPROVE)]

im·prov·er /impróⁿvər/ *n.* **1** a person who improves. **2** *Brit.* a person who works for low wages while acquiring skill and experience in a trade.

im·prov·i·dent /impróvid'nt/ *adj.* **1** lacking foresight or care for the future. **2** not frugal; thriftless. **3** heedless; incautious. □□ **im·prov·i·dence** /–d'ns/ *n.* **im·prov·i·dent·ly** *adv.*

im·pro·vise /ímprəvīz/ *v.tr.* (also *absol.*) **1** compose or perform (music, verse, etc.) extempore. **2** provide or construct (a thing) extempore. □□ **im·prov·i·sa·tion** /–izáyshən/ *n.* **im·prov·i·sa·tion·al** *adj.* **im·prov·i·sa·to·ri·al** /impróvizàtwreeəl/ *adj.* **im·prov·i·sa·to·ry** *adj.* **im·pro·vis·er** *n.* [F *improviser* or It. *improvvisare* f. *improvviso* extempore, f. L *improvisus* past part. (as IN-¹, PROVIDE)]

im·pru·dent /impróod'nt/ *adj.* rash; indiscreet. □□ **im·pru·dence** /–d'ns/ *n.* **im·pru·dent·ly** *adv.* [ME f. L *imprudens* (as IN-¹, PRUDENT)]

im·pu·dent /ímpyəd'nt/ *adj.* **1** insolently disrespectful; impertinent. **2** shamelessly presumptuous. **3** unblushing. □□ **im·pu·dence** /–d'ns/ *n.* **im·pu·dent·ly** *adv.* [ME f. L *impudens* (as IN-¹, *pudēre* be ashamed)]

im·pu·dic·i·ty /ímpyədísitee/ *n.* shamelessness; immodesty. [F *impudicité* f. L *impudicus* (as IMPUDENT)]

im·pugn /impyóon/ *v.tr.* challenge or call in question (a statement, action, etc.). □□ **im·pugn·a·ble** *adj.* **im·pugn·ment** *n.* [ME f. L *impugnare* assail (as IN-², *pugnare* fight)]

im·pu·is·sant /impyóoisənt, impyóo–is–, impwís–/ *adj.* impotent; weak. □□ **im·pu·is·sance** /–səns/ *n.* [F (as IN-¹, PUISSANT)]

im·pulse /ímpuls/ *n.* **1** the act or an instance of impelling; a push. **2** an impetus. **3** *Physics* **a** an indefinitely large force acting for a very short time but producing a finite change of momentum (e.g., the blow of a hammer). **b** the change of momentum produced by this or any force. **4** a wave of excitation in a nerve. **5** mental incitement. **6** a sudden desire or tendency to act without reflection (*did it on impulse*). □ **impulse buying** the unpremeditated buying of goods as a result of a whim or impulse. [L *impulsus* (as IMPEL)]

im·pul·sion /impúlshən/ *n.* **1** the act or an instance of impelling. **2** a mental impulse. **3** impetus. [ME f. OF f. L *impulsio –onis* (as IMPEL)]

im·pul·sive /impúlsiv/ *adj.* **1** (of a person or conduct, etc.) apt to be affected or determined by sudden impulse. **2** tending to impel. **3** *Physics* acting as an impulse. □□ **im·pul·sive·ly** *adv.* **im·pul·sive·ness** *n.* [ME f. F *impulsif –ive* or LL *impulsivus* (as IMPULSION)]

im·pu·ni·ty /impyóonitee/ *n.* exemption from punishment or from the injurious consequences of an action. □ **with impunity** without having to suffer the normal injurious consequences (of an action). [L *impunitas* f. *impunis* (as IN-¹, *poena* penalty)]

im·pure /impyóor/ *adj.* **1** mixed with foreign matter; adulterated. **2 a** dirty. **b** ceremonially unclean. **3** unchaste. **4** (of a color) mixed with another color. □□ **im·pure·ly** *adv.* **im·pure·ness** *n.* [ME f. L *impurus* (as IN-¹, *purus* pure)]

im·pu·ri·ty /impyóoritee/ *n.* (pl. **·ties**) **1** the quality or condition of being impure. **2** an impure thing or constituent. [F *impurité* or L *impuritas* (as IMPURE)]

im·pute /impyóot/ *v.tr.* (foll. by *to*) **1** regard (esp. something undesirable) as being done or caused or possessed by. **2** *Theol.* ascribe (righteousness, guilt, etc.) to (a person) by virtue of a similar quality in another. □□ **im·put·a·ble** *adj.* **im·pu·ta·tion** *n.* **im·pu·ta·tive** /–tətiv/ *adj.* [ME f. OF *imputer* f. L *imputare* enter in the account (as IN-², *putare* reckon)]

im·shi /ímshee/ *int. Austral. colloq.* be off! [colloq. (Egyptian) Arabic]

IN *abbr.* Indiana (in official postal use).

In *symb. Chem.* the element indium.

in /in/ *prep., adv., & adj.* ● *prep.* **1** expressing inclusion or position within limits of space, time, circumstance, etc. (*in Nebraska; in bed; in the rain*). **2** during the time of (*in the night; in 1989*). **3** within the time of (*will be back in two hours*). **4 a** with respect to (*blind in one eye; good in parts*). **b** as a kind of (*the latest thing in luxury*). **5** as a proportionate part of (*one in three failed; a gradient of one in six*). **6** with the form or arrangement of (*packed in tens; falling in folds*). **7** as a member of (*in the army*). **8** concerned with (*is in politics*). **9** as or regarding the content of (*there is something in what you say*). **10** within the ability of (*does he have it in him?*). **11** having the condition of; affected by (*in bad health; in danger*). **12** having a purpose (*in search of; in reply to*). **13** by means of or using as material (*drawn in pencil; modeled in bronze*). **14 a** using as the language of expression (*written in French*). **b** (of music) having as its key (*symphony in C*). **15** (of a word) having as part of its spelling (*words beginning in un–*). **16** wearing as dress (*in blue; in a suit*). **17** with the identity of (*found a friend in Mary*). **18** (of an animal) pregnant with (*in calf*). **19** into (with a verb of motion or change: *put it in the box; cut it in two*). **20** introducing an indirect object after a verb (*believe in; engage in; share in*). **21** forming adverbial phrases (*in any case; in reality; in short*). ● *adv.* expressing position within limits, or motion to such a position: **1** into a room, house, etc. (*come in*). **2** at home, in one's office, etc. (*is not in*). **3** so as to be enclosed or confined (*locked in*). **4** in a publication (*is the advertisement in?*). **5** in or to the inward side (*rub it in*). **6 a** in fashion, season, or office (*long skirts are in; strawberries are not yet in*). **b** elected (*the Democrat got in*). **7** exerting favorable action or influence (*their luck was in*). **8** *Cricket* (of a player or side) batting. **9** (of transport) at the platform, etc. (*the train is in*). **10** (of a season, harvest, order, etc.) hav-

ing arrived or been received. **11** *Brit.* (of a fire) continuing to burn. **12** denoting effective action (*join in*). **13** (of the tide) at the highest point. **14** (in *comb.*) *colloq.* denoting prolonged or concerted action, esp. by large numbers (*sit-in; teach-in*). ● *adj.* **1** internal; living in; inside (*in-patient*). **2** fashionable; esoteric (*the in thing to do*). **3** confined to or shared by a group of people (*in-joke*). □ **in all** see ALL. **in at** present at; contributing to (*in at the kill*). **in between** see BETWEEN *adv.* **in for** **1** about to undergo (esp. something unpleasant). **2** competing in or for. **3** involved in; committed to. **in on** sharing in; privy to (a secret, etc.). **ins and outs** (often foll. by *of*) all the details (of a procedure, etc.). **in that** because; in so far as. **in with** on good terms with. [OE *in, inn,* orig. as adv. with verbs of motion]

in. *abbr.* inch(es).

in-¹ /in/ *prefix* (also **il-, im-, ir-**) added to: **1** adjectives, meaning 'not' (*inedible; insane*). **2** nouns, meaning 'without; lacking' (*inaction*). [L]

in-² /in/ *prefix* (also **il-** before *l,* **im-** before *b, m, p,* **ir-** before *r*) in, on, into, toward, within (*induce; influx; insight; intrude*). [IN, or from or after L *in* in prep.]

-in /in/ *suffix Chem.* forming names of: **1** neutral substances (*gelatin*). **2** antibiotics (*penicillin*). [-INE⁴]

-ina /éenə/ *suffix* denoting: **1** feminine names and titles (*Georgina; tsarina*). **2** names of musical instruments (*concertina*). **3** names of zoological classification categories (*globigerina*). [It. or Sp. or L]

in·a·bil·i·ty /ínəbílitee/ *n.* **1** the state of being unable. **2** a lack of power or means.

in ab·sen·tia /ín absénshə/ *adv.* in (his, her, or their) absence. [L]

in·ac·ces·si·ble /ínaksésibəl/ *adj.* **1** not accessible; that cannot be reached. **2** (of a person) not open to advances or influence; unapproachable. □□ **in·ac·ces·si·bil·i·ty** *n.* **in·ac·ces·si·ble·ness** *n.* **in·ac·ces·si·bly** *adv.* [ME f. F *inaccessible* or LL *inaccessibilis* (as IN-¹, ACCESSIBLE)]

in·ac·cu·rate /inákyərət/ *adj.* not accurate. □□ **in·ac·cu·ra·cy** *n.* (pl. **·cies**). **in·ac·cu·rate·ly** *adv.*

in·ac·tion /inákshən/ *n.* **1** lack of action. **2** sluggishness; inertness.

in·ac·ti·vate /ináktivayt/ *v.tr.* make inactive or inoperative. □□ **in·ac·ti·va·tion** /–váyshən/ *n.*

in·ac·tive /ináktiv/ *adj.* **1** not active or inclined to act. **2** passive. **3** indolent. □□ **in·ac·tive·ly** *adv.* **in·ac·tiv·i·ty** /–tívitee/ *n.*

in·ad·e·quate /inádikwət/ *adj.* (often foll. by *to*) **1** not adequate; insufficient. **2** (of a person) incompetent; unable to deal with a situation. □□ **in·ad·e·qua·cy** /–kwəsee/ *n.* (pl. **·cies**). **in·ad·e·quate·ly** *adv.*

in·ad·mis·si·ble /ínədmísibəl/ *adj.* that cannot be admitted or allowed. □□ **in·ad·mis·si·bil·i·ty** *n.* **in·ad·mis·si·bly** *adv.*

SPELLING TIP inadmissible

Remember the *-ible* ending of this word with the mnemonic: "A *missile* would be inad*missi*ble in court."

in·ad·vert·ent /ínədvórt'nt/ *adj.* **1** (of an action) unintentional. **2 a** not properly attentive. **b** negligent. □□ **in·ad·vert·ence** /–t'ns/ *n.* **in·ad·vert·en·cy** *n.* **in·ad·vert·ent·ly** *adv.* [IN-¹ + obs. *advertent* attentive (as ADVERT²)]

in·ad·vis·a·ble /ínədvízəbəl/ *adj.* not advisable. □□ **in·ad·vis·a·bil·i·ty** *n.* [ADVISABLE]

in·al·ien·a·ble /ínáyleeənəbəl/ *adj.* that cannot be transferred to another; not alienable. □□ **in·al·ien·a·bil·i·ty** *n.* **in·al·ien·a·bly** *adv.*

in·al·ter·a·ble /ináwltərəbəl/ *adj.* not alterable; that cannot be changed. □□ **in·al·ter·a·bil·i·ty** /–bílitee/ *n.* **in·al·ter·a·bly** *adv.* [med.L *inalterabilis* (as IN-¹, *alterabilis* alterable)]

in·am·o·ra·to /ináməràatō/ *n.* (pl. **·tos**; *fem.* **in·am·o·ra·ta** /–tə/) a lover. [It., past part. of *inamorare* enamor (as IN-², *amore* f. L *amor* love)]

in·ane /ináyn/ *adj.* **1** silly; senseless. **2** empty; void. □□ **in·ane·ly** *adv.* **in·ane·ness** *n.* **in·an·i·ty** /–ánitee/ *n.* (pl. **·ties**). [L *inanis* empty, vain]

in·an·i·mate /inánimət/ *adj.* **1** not animate; not endowed with (esp. animal) life. **2** lifeless; showing no sign of life. **3** spiritless; dull. □□ **in·an·i·mate·ly** *adv.* **in·an·i·ma·tion** /–máyshən/ *n.* [LL *inanimatus* (as IN-¹, ANIMATE)]

in·an·i·mate na·ture *n.* everything other than the animal world.

in·a·ni·tion /ínəníshən/ *n.* emptiness, esp. exhaustion from lack of nourishment. [ME f. LL *inanitio* f. L *inanire* make empty (as IN-ANE)]

in·ap·pel·la·ble /ínəpéləbəl/ *adj.* that cannot be appealed against. [obs.F *inappelable* (as IN-¹, *appeler* APPEAL)]

in·ap·pli·ca·ble /ináplikəbəl, ínəplík–/ *adj.* (often foll. by *to*) not applicable; unsuitable. □□ **in·ap·pli·ca·bil·i·ty** *n.* **in·ap·pli·ca·bly** *adv.*

in·ap·po·site /inápəzit/ *adj.* not apposite; out of place. □□ **in·ap·po·site·ly** *adv.* **in·ap·po·site·ness** *n.*

in·ap·pre·ci·a·ble /ínəpreéshəbəl/ adj. **1** imperceptible; not worth reckoning. **2** that cannot be appreciated. □□ **in·ap·pre·ci·a·bly** adv.

in·ap·pre·ci·a·tion /ínəpreesheeáyshən/ n. failure to appreciate. □□ **in·ap·pre·ci·a·tive** /–preéshətiv, –shee-áy-/ adj.

in·ap·pro·pri·ate /ínəpróppreeət/ adj. not appropriate. □□ **in·ap·pro·pri·ate·ly** adv. **in·ap·pro·pri·ate·ness** n.

in·apt /inápt/ adj. **1** not apt or suitable. **2** unskillful. □□ **in·ap·ti·tude** n. **in·apt·ly** adv. **in·apt·ness** n.

in·arch /ináarch/ v.tr. Horticulture graft (a plant) by connecting a growing branch without separating it from its parent stock. [IN-2 + ARCH1 v.]

in·ar·gu·a·ble /ináargyóoəbəl/ adj. that cannot be argued about or disputed. □□ **in·ar·gu·a·bly** adv.

in·ar·tic·u·late /ínaartíkyələt/ adj. **1** unable to speak distinctly or express oneself clearly. **2** (of speech) not articulate; indistinctly pronounced. **3** dumb. **4** esp. Anat. not jointed. □□ **in·ar·tic·u·late·ly** adv. **in·ar·tic·u·late·ness** n. [LL inarticulatus (as IN-1, ARTICULATE)]

in·ar·tis·tic /ínaartístik/ adj. **1** not following the principles of art. **2** lacking skill or talent in art; not appreciating art. □□ **in·ar·tis·ti·cal·ly** adv.

in·as·much /ínəzmúch/ adv. (foll. by as) **1** since; because. **2** to the extent that. [ME, orig. in as much]

in·at·ten·tive /ínəténtiv/ adj. **1** not paying due attention; heedless. **2** neglecting to show courtesy. □□ **in·at·ten·tion** n. **in·at·ten·tive·ly** adv. **in·at·ten·tive·ness** n.

in·au·di·ble /ináwdibəl/ adj. that cannot be heard. □□ **in·au·di·bil·i·ty** n. **in·au·di·bly** adv.

in·au·gu·ral /ináwgyərəl/ adj. & n. ● adj. **1** of inauguration. **2** (of a lecture, etc.) given by a person being inaugurated. ● n. an inaugural speech, etc. [F f. inaugurer (as INAUGURATE)]

in·au·gu·rate /ináwgyərayt/ v.tr. **1** admit (a person) formally to office. **2** initiate the public use of (a building, etc.). **3** begin; introduce. **4** enter with ceremony upon (an undertaking, etc.). □□ **in·au·gu·ra·tion** /–ráyshən/ n. **in·au·gu·ra·tor** n. **in·au·gu·ra·to·ry** /–rətəwree/ adj. [L inaugurare (as IN-2, augurare take omens: see AUGUR)]

in·aus·pi·cious /ínawspíshəs/ adj. **1** ill-omened; unpropitious. **2** unlucky. □□ **in·aus·pi·cious·ly** adv. **in·aus·pi·cious·ness** n.

in-be·tween attrib.adj. colloq. intermediate (at an in-between stage).

in·board /ínbawrd/ adv. & adj. ● adv. within the sides of or toward the center of a ship, aircraft, or vehicle. ● adj. situated inboard.

in·born /ínbáwrn/ adj. existing from birth; implanted by nature.

in-box n. a box or tray on someone's desk for documents, letters, etc., awaiting attention.

in·breathe /ínbreéth/ v.tr. breathe in or absorb.

in·bred /ínbréd/ adj. **1** inborn. **2** produced by inbreeding.

in·breed·ing /ínbreéding/ n. breeding from closely related animals or persons. □□ **in·breed** v.tr. & intr. (past and past part. **in·bred**).

in·built /ínbílt/ adj. incorporated as part of a structure.

inc. abbr. **1** (esp. **Inc.**) Incorporated. **2** incomplete.

In·ca /íngkə/ n. a member of a Native American people in Peru before the Spanish conquest. □□ **In·ca·ic** /ingkáyik/ adj. **In·can** adj. [Quechua, = lord, royal person]

in·cal·cu·la·ble /inkálkyələbəl/ adj. **1** too great for calculation. **2** that cannot be reckoned beforehand. **3** (of a person, character, etc.) uncertain. □□ **in·cal·cu·la·bil·i·ty** n. **in·cal·cu·la·bly** adv.

in cam·er·a see CAMERA.

in·can·desce /ínkandés/ v.intr. & tr. glow or cause to glow with heat. [back-form. f. INCANDESCENT]

in·can·des·cent /ínkandésənt/ adj. **1** glowing with heat. **2** shining brightly. **3** (of an electric or other light) produced by a glowing white-hot filament. □□ **in·can·des·cence** /–səns/ n. **in·can·des·cent·ly** adv. [F f. L incandescere (as IN-2, candescere inceptive of candēre be white)]

in·can·ta·tion /ínkantáyshən/ n. **1 a** a magical formula. **b** the use of this. **2** a spell or charm. □□ **in·can·ta·tion·al** adj. **in·can·ta·to·ry** /–kántətawree/ adj. [ME f. OF f. LL incantatio –onis f. incantare chant, bewitch (as IN-2, cantare sing)]

in·ca·pa·ble /inkáypəbəl/ adj. **1** (often foll. by of) **a** not capable. **b** lacking the required quality or characteristic (favorable or adverse) (incapable of hurting anyone). **2** not capable of rational conduct or of managing one's own affairs (drunk and incapable). □□ **in·ca·pa·bil·i·ty** n. **in·ca·pa·bly** adv. [F incapable or LL incapabilis (as IN-1, capabilis CAPABLE)]

in·ca·pac·i·tate /ínkəpásitayt/ v.tr. **1** render incapable or unfit. **2** disqualify. □□ **in·ca·pac·i·tant** n. **in·ca·pac·i·ta·tion** /–táyshən/ n.

in·ca·pac·i·ty /ínkəpásitee/ n. (pl. **-ties**) **1** inability; lack of the necessary power or resources. **2** legal disqualification. **3** an instance of incapacity. [F incapacité or LL incapacitas (as IN-1, CAPACITY)]

in·car·cer·ate /inkáarsərayt/ v.tr. imprison or confine. □□ **in·car·cer·a·tion** /–ráyshən/ n. **in·car·cer·a·tor** n. [med.L incarcerare (as IN-2, L carcer prison)]

in·car·na·dine /inkáarnədin/ adj. & v. poet. ● adj. flesh-colored or crimson. ● v.tr. dye this color. [F incarnadin –ine f. It. incarnadino (for –tino) f. incarnato INCARNATE adj.]

in·car·nate adj. & v. ● adj. /inkáarnət, –nayt/ **1** (of a person, spirit, quality, etc.) embodied in flesh, esp. in human form (is the devil incarnate). **2** represented in a recognizable or typical form (folly incarnate). ● v.tr. /ínkaárnayt/ **1** embody in flesh. **2** put (an idea, etc.) into concrete form; realize. **3** (of a person, etc.) be the living embodiment of (a quality). [ME f. eccl.L incarnare incarnat- make flesh (as IN-2, L caro carnis flesh)]

PRONUNCIATION TIP | **incarnate**

When used as an adjective, this word is usually pronounced "in-KAR-nit."

---

in·car·na·tion /ínkaarnáyshən/ n. **1 a** embodiment in (esp. human) flesh. **b** (**the Incarnation**) Theol. the embodiment of God the Son in human flesh as Jesus Christ. **2** (often foll. by of) a living type of a quality, etc.). **3** Med. the process of forming new flesh. [ME f. OF f. eccl.L incarnatio –onis (as INCARNATE)]

in·case var. of ENCASE.

in·cau·tious /inkáwshəs/ adj. heedless; rash. □□ **in·cau·tion** n. **in·cau·tious·ly** adv. **in·cau·tious·ness** n.

in·cen·di·ar·y /inséndee-eree/ adj. & n. ● adj. **1** (of a substance or device, esp. a bomb) designed to cause fires. **2 a** of or relating to the malicious setting on fire of property. **b** guilty of this. **3** tending to stir up strife; inflammatory. ● n. (pl. **-ies**) **1** an incendiary bomb or device. **2** an incendiary person. □□ **in·cen·di·a·rism** n. [ME f. L incendiarius f. incendium conflagration f. incendere incens- set fire to]

in·cense1 /ínsens/ n. & v. ● n. **1** a gum or spice producing a sweet smell when burned. **2** the smoke of this, esp. in religious ceremonial. ● v.tr. **1** treat or perfume (a person or thing) with incense. **2** burn incense to (a deity, etc.). **3** suffuse with fragrance. □□ **in·cen·sa·tion** n.

WORD HISTORY | **incense**

Middle English (originally as encense): from Old French encens (noun), encenser (verb), from ecclesiastical Latin incensum 'something burnt, incense', neuter past participle of incendere 'set fire to', from in- 'in' + the base of candere 'to glow'.

---

in·cense2 /inséns/ v.tr. (often foll. by at, with, against) enrage; make angry. [ME f. OF incenser (as INCENDIARY)]

in·cen·so·ry /insénsəree/ n. (pl. **-ries**) = CENSER. [med.L incensorium (as INCENSE1)]

in·cen·tive /inséntiv/ n. & adj. ● n. **1** (often foll. by to) a motive or incitement, esp. to action. **2** a payment or concession to stimulate greater output by workers. ● adj. serving to motivate or incite. [ME f. L incentivus setting the tune f. incinere incent- sing to (as IN-2, canere sing)]

in·cept /insépt/ v. **1** tr. Biol. (of an organism) take in (food, etc.). **2** intr. Brit. hist. take a master's or doctor's degree at a university. □□ **in·cep·tor** n. (in sense 2). [L incipere incept- begin (as IN-2, capere take)]

in·cep·tion /insépshən/ n. a beginning. [ME f. OF inception or L inceptio (as INCEPT)]

in·cep·tive /inséptiv/ adj. & n. ● adj. **1 a** beginning. **b** initial. **2** Gram. (of a verb) that denotes the beginning of an action. ● n. an inceptive verb. [LL inceptivus (as INCEPT)]

in·cer·ti·tude /insértitŏod, –tyŏod/ n. uncertainty; doubt. [F incertitude or LL incertitudo (as IN-1, CERTITUDE)]

in·ces·sant /insésənt/ adj. unceasing; continual; repeated. □□ **in·ces·san·cy** n. **in·ces·sant·ly** adv. **in·ces·sant·ness** n. [F incessant or LL incessans (as IN-1, cessans pres. part. of L cessare CEASE)]

in·cest /ínsest/ n. sexual intercourse between persons regarded as too closely related to marry each other. [ME f. L incestus (as IN-1, castus CHASTE)]

in·ces·tu·ous /inséschŏoəs/ adj. **1** involving or guilty of incest. **2** (of human relations generally) excessively restricted or resistant to wider influence. □□ **in·ces·tu·ous·ly** adv. **in·ces·tu·ous·ness** n. [LL incestuosus (as INCEST)]

inch1 /inch/ n. & v. ● n. **1** a unit of linear measure equal to one-twelfth of a foot (2.54 cm). **2 a** (as a unit of rainfall) a quantity that would cover a horizontal surface to a depth of 1 inch. **b** (of atmospheric or other pressure) an amount that balances the weight of a column of mercury 1 inch high. **3** (as a unit of map scale) so many inches representing 1 mile on the ground (a 4-inch map). **4** a small amount (usu. with neg.: would not yield an inch). ● v.tr. & intr. move gradually in a specified direction (inched forward). □ **every inch 1** entirely (looked every inch a judge). **2** the whole distance or area (combed every inch of the garden). **give a person an inch and he** (or **she**) **will take a mile** a person once conceded to will demand much. **inch by inch** gradually; bit by bit. **within an inch of** almost to the point of. [OE ynce f. L uncia twelfth part: cf. OUNCE1]

inch2 /inch/ n. esp. Sc. a small island (esp. in place-names). [ME f. Gael. innis]

inch•meal /ínchmeel/ *adv.* by inches; little by little; gradually. [f. INCH[1] + MEAL[1]]

in•cho•ate /inkṓit/ *adj. & v.* ● *adj.* **1** just begun. **2** undeveloped; rudimentary; unformed. ● *v.tr.* begin; originate. □□ **in•cho•ate•ly** *adv.* **in•cho•ate•ness** *n.* **in•cho•a•tion** /–áyshən/ *n.* **in•cho•a•tive** /–kṓətiv/ *adj.* [L *inchoatus* past part. of *inchoare* (as IN-[2], *choare* begin)]

▶**Inchoate** is often used incorrectly to mean 'chaotic' or 'incoherent.' The *ch* should be pronounced like a *k*, as in *echo*.

inch•worm /ínchwərm/ *n.* = MEASURING WORM.

in•ci•dence /í nsidəns/ *n.* **1** (often foll. by *of*) the fact, manner, or rate, of occurrence or action. **2** the range, scope, or extent of influence of a thing. **3** *Physics* the falling of a line, or of a thing moving in a line, upon a surface. **4** the act or an instance of coming into contact with a thing. [ME f. OF *incidence* or med.L *incidentia* (as INCIDENT)]

▶**Incidence** and **incidents** sound the same, but **incidence** is more often used in technical contexts, referring to the frequency with which something occurs: *increased UV is likely to cause increased incidence of skin cancer.* **Incidents** is simply the plural of *incident,* an event: *the police are supposed to investigate any incidents of domestic violence.* The form *incidences* should be avoided.

in•ci•dent /í nsidənt/ *n. & adj.* ● *n.* **1 a** an event or occurrence. **b** a minor or detached event attracting general attention or noteworthy in some way. **2** a hostile clash, esp. of troops of countries at war (*a frontier incident*). **3** a distinct piece of action in a play or a poem. **4** *Law* a privilege, burden, etc., attaching to an obligation or right. ● *adj.* **1 a** (often foll. by *to*) apt or liable to happen; naturally attaching or dependent. **b** (foll. by *to*) *Law* attaching to. **2** (often foll. by *on, upon*) (of light, etc.) falling or striking. [ME f. F *incident* or L *incidere* (as IN-[2], *cadere* fall)]

in•ci•den•tal /ínsidéntəl/ *adj.* **1** (often foll. by *to*) **a** having a minor role in relation to a more important thing, event, etc. **b** not essential. **c** casual; happening by chance. **2** (foll. by *to*) liable to happen. **3** (foll. by *on, upon*) following as a subordinate event.

in•ci•den•tal•ly /ínsidént'lee/ *adv.* **1** by the way; as an unconnected remark. **2** in an incidental way.

in•ci•den•tal mu•sic *n.* music used as a background to the action of a play, motion picture, broadcast, etc.

in•cin•er•ate /ínsínərayt/ *v.tr.* **1** consume (a body, etc.) by fire. **2** reduce to ashes. □□ **in•cin•er•a•tion** /–ráyshən/ *n.* [med.L *incinerare* (as IN-[2], *cinis –eris* ashes)]

in•cin•er•a•tor /ínsínəraytər/ *n.* a furnace or apparatus for burning, esp. refuse to ashes.

in•cip•i•ent /ínsípeeənt/ *adj.* **1** beginning. **2** in an initial stage. □□ **in•cip•i•ence** /–əns/ *n.* **in•cip•i•en•cy** *n.* **in•cip•i•ent•ly** *adv.* [L *incipere incipient-* (as INCEPT)]

in•cise /ínsíz/ *v.tr.* **1** make a cut in. **2** engrave. [F *inciser* f. L *incidere incis-* (as IN-[2], *caedere* cut)]

in•ci•sion /ínsízhən/ *n.* **1** a cut; a division produced by cutting; a notch. **2** the act of cutting into a thing. [ME f. OF *incision* or LL *incisio* (as INCISE)]

in•ci•sive /ínsísiv/ *adj.* **1** mentally sharp; acute. **2** clear and effective. **3** cutting; penetrating. □□ **in•ci•sive•ly** *adv.* **in•ci•sive•ness** *n.* [med.L *incisivus* (as INCISE)]

in•ci•sor /ínsízər/ *n.* a cutting tooth, esp. at the front of the mouth. [med.L, = cutter (as INCISE)]

in•cite /ínsít/ *v.tr.* (often foll. by *to*) urge or stir up. □□ **in•ci•ta•tion** *n.* **in•cite•ment** *n.* **in•cit•er** *n.* [ME f. F *inciter* f. L *incitare* (as IN-[2], *citare* rouse)]

in•ci•vil•i•ty /ínsivílitee/ *n.* (*pl.* **-ties**) **1** rudeness; discourtesy. **2** a rude or discourteous act. [F *incivilité* or LL *incivilitas* (as IN-[1], CIVILITY)]

in•clem•ent /ínklémənt/ *adj.* (of the weather or climate) severe, esp. cold or stormy. □□ **in•clem•en•cy** *n.* (*pl.* **-cies**). **in•clem•ent•ly** *adv.* [F *inclément* or L *inclemens* (as IN-[1], CLEMENT)]

in•cli•na•tion /ínklináyshən/ *n.* **1** (often foll. by *to*) a disposition or propensity. **2** (often foll. by *for*) a liking or affection. **3** a leaning, slope, or slant. **4** the difference of direction of two lines or planes, esp. as measured by the angle between them. **5** the dip of a magnetic needle. [ME f. OF *inclination* or L *inclinatio* (as INCLINE)]

in•cline *v. & n.* ● *v.* /ínklín/ **1** *tr.* (usu. in *passive*; often foll. by *to, for,* or *to* + infin.) **a** make (a person, feelings, etc.) willing or favorably disposed (*am inclined to think so; does not incline me to agree*). **b** give a specified tendency to (a thing) (*the door is inclined to bang*). **2** *intr.* **a** be disposed (*I incline to think so*). **b** (often foll. by *to, toward*) tend. **3** *intr. & tr.* lean or turn away from a given direction, esp. the vertical. **4** *tr.* bend (the head, body, or oneself) forward or downward. ● *n.* /ínklín/ **1** a slope. **2** an inclined plane. □ **incline one's ear** (often foll. by *to*) listen favorably. □□ **in•clin•er** *n.* [ME *encline* f. OF *encliner* f. L *inclinare* (as IN-[2], *clinare* bend)]

in•clined plane *n.* a sloping plane (esp. as a means of reducing the force needed to raise a load).

in•cli•nom•e•ter /ínklinómitər/ *n.* **1** an instrument for measuring the angle between the direction of the earth's magnetic field and the horizontal. **2** an instrument for measuring the inclination of an aircraft or ship to the horizontal. **3** an instrument for measuring a slope. [L *inclinare* INCLINE *v.* + –METER]

in•close var. of ENCLOSE.

in•clo•sure var. of ENCLOSURE.

in•clude /ínklŏŏd/ *v.tr.* **1** comprise or reckon in as part of a whole; place in a class or category. **2** (as **including** *prep.*) if we include (*six members, including the chairperson*). **3** treat or regard as so included. **4** (as **included** *adj.*) shut in; enclosed. □□ **in•clud•a•ble** *adj.* **in•clud•i•ble** *adj.* **in•clu•sion** /–klŏŏzhən/ *n.* [ME f. L *includere inclus-* (as IN-[2], *claudere* shut)]

in•clu•sive /ínklŏŏsiv/ *adj.* **1** (often foll. by *of*) including, comprising. **2** with the inclusion of the extreme limits stated (*pages 7 to 26 inclusive*). **3** including all the normal services, etc. (*a hotel offering inclusive terms*). □□ **in•clu•sive•ly** *adv.* **in•clu•sive•ness** *n.* [med.L *inclusivus* (as INCLUDE)]

in•clu•sive lan•guage *n.* language that is deliberately nonsexist, esp. avoiding the use of masculine pronouns to cover both men and women.

in•cog /ínkóg/ *adj., adv., & n. Brit. colloq.* = INCOGNITO. [abbr.]

in•cog•ni•to /ínkogneetō, –kógni–/ *adj., adv., & n.* ● *adj. & adv.* with one's name or identity kept secret (*was traveling incognito*). ● *n.* (*pl.* **-tos**) **1** a person who is incognito. **2** the pretended identity or anonymous character of such a person. [It., = unknown, f. L *incognitus* (as IN-[1], *cognitus* past part. of *cognoscere* know)]

in•cog•ni•zant /ínkógnizənt/ *adj.* (foll. by *of*) unaware; not knowing. □□ **in•cog•ni•zance** /–zəns/ *n.*

in•co•her•ent /ínkōhéerənt/ *adj.* **1** (of a person) unable to speak intelligibly. **2** (of speech, etc.) lacking logic or consistency. **3** *Physics* (of waves) having no definite or stable phase relationship. □□ **in•co•her•ence** /–əns/ *n.* **in•co•her•en•cy** *n.* (*pl.* **-cies**). **in•co•her•ent•ly** *adv.*

in•com•bus•ti•ble /ínkəmbústibəl/ *adj.* that cannot be burned or consumed by fire. □□ **in•com•bus•ti•bil•i•ty** *n.* [ME f. med.L *incombustibilis* (as IN-[1], COMBUSTIBLE)]

in•come /ínkum/ *n.* the money or other assets received, esp. periodically or in a year, from one's business, lands, work, investments, etc. [ME (orig. = arrival), prob. f. ON *innkoma*: in later use f. *come in*]

in•come group *n.* a section of the population determined by income.

in•com•er /ínkumər/ *n.* **1** a person who comes in. **2** *Brit.* a person who arrives to settle in a place; an immigrant. **3** an intruder. **4** a successor.

-incomer /ínkumər/ *comb. form esp. Brit.* earning a specified kind or level of income (*middle-incomer*).

in•come tax *n.* a tax levied on income.

in•com•ing /ínkuming/ *adj. & n.* ● *adj.* **1** coming in (*the incoming tide; incoming telephone calls*). **2** succeeding another person or persons (*the incoming tenant*). **3** *Brit.* immigrant. **4** (of profit) accruing. ● *n.* **1** (usu. in *pl.*) revenue; income. **2** the act of arriving or entering.

in•com•men•su•ra•ble /ínkəménsərəbəl, –shərəbəl/ *adj.* (often foll. by *with*) **1** not comparable in respect of magnitude. **2** incapable of being measured. **3** *Math.* (of a magnitude or magnitudes) having no common factor, integral or fractional. **4** *Math.* irrational. □□ **in•com•men•su•ra•bil•i•ty** *n.* **in•com•men•su•ra•bly** *adv.* [LL *incommensurabilis* (as IN-[1], COMMENSURABLE)]

in•com•men•su•rate /ínkəménsərət, –shərət/ *adj.* **1** (often foll. by *with, to*) out of proportion; inadequate. **2** = INCOMMENSURABLE. □□ **in•com•men•su•rate•ly** *adv.* **in•com•men•su•rate•ness** *n.*

in·com·mode /ínkəmṓd/ v.tr. **1** hinder; inconvenience. **2** trouble; annoy. [F *incommoder* or L *incommodare* (as IN-[1], *commodus* convenient)]

in·com·mo·di·ous /ínkəmṓdeeəs/ adj. not affording good accommodation; uncomfortable. □□ **in·com·mo·di·ous·ly** adv. **in·com·mo·di·ous·ness** n.

in·com·mu·ni·ca·ble /ínkəmyṓónikəbəl/ adj. **1** that cannot be communicated or shared. **2** that cannot be uttered or told. **3** that does not communicate; uncommunicative. □□ **in·com·mu·ni·ca·bil·i·ty** n. **in·com·mu·ni·ca·ble·ness** n. **in·com·mu·ni·ca·bly** adv. [LL *incommunicabilis* (as IN-[1], COMMUNICABLE)]

in·com·mu·ni·ca·do /ínkəmyṓónikáadō/ adj. **1** without or deprived of the means of communication with others. **2** (of a prisoner) in solitary confinement. [Sp. *incomunicado* past part. of *incomunicar* deprive of communication]

in·com·mu·ni·ca·tive /ínkəmyṓónikətiv, –káytiv/ adj. not communicative; taciturn. □□ **in·com·mu·ni·ca·tive·ly** adv. **in·com·mu·ni·ca·tive·ness** n.

in·com·mut·a·ble /ínkəmyṓótəbəl/ adj. **1** not changeable. **2** not commutable. □□ **in·com·mut·a·bly** adv. [ME f. L *incommutabilis* (as IN-[1], COMMUTABLE)]

in·com·pa·ra·ble /inkómpərəbəl/ adj. **1** without an equal; matchless. **2** (often foll. by *with, to*) not to be compared. □□ **in·com·pa·ra·bil·i·ty** n. **in·com·pa·ra·ble·ness** n. **in·com·pa·ra·bly** adv. [ME f. OF f. L *incomparabilis* (as IN-[1], COMPARABLE)]

in·com·pat·i·ble /ínkəmpátibəl/ adj. **1** opposed in character; discordant. **2** (often foll. by *with*) inconsistent. **3** (of persons) unable to live, work, etc., together in harmony. **4** (of drugs) not suitable for taking at the same time. **5** (of equipment, machinery, etc.) not capable of being used in combination. □□ **in·com·pat·i·bil·i·ty** n. **in·com·pat·i·ble·ness** n. **in·com·pat·i·bly** adv. [med.L *incompatibilis* (as IN-[1], COMPATIBLE)]

in·com·pe·tent /inkómpit'nt/ adj. & n. ● adj. **1** (often foll. by *to* + infin.) not qualified or able to perform a particular task or function (*an incompetent builder*). **2** showing a lack of skill (*an incompetent performance*). **3** *Med.* (esp. of a valve or sphincter) not able to perform its function. ● n. an incompetent person. □□ **in·com·pe·tence** /–t'ns/ n. **in·com·pe·ten·cy** n. **in·com·pe·tent·ly** adv. [F *incompétent* or LL *incompetens* (as IN-[1], COMPETENT)]

in·com·plete /ínkəmpleét/ adj. not complete. □□ **in·com·plete·ly** adv. **in·com·plete·ness** n. [ME f. LL *incompletus* (as IN-[1], COMPLETE)]

in·com·pre·hen·si·ble /ínkomprihénsibəl/ adj. (often foll. by *to*) that cannot be understood. □□ **in·com·pre·hen·si·bil·i·ty** n. **in·com·pre·hen·si·ble·ness** n. **in·com·pre·hen·si·bly** adv. [ME f. L *incomprehensibilis* (as IN-[1], COMPREHENSIBLE)]

in·com·pre·hen·sion /ínkomprihénshən/ n. failure to understand.

in·com·press·i·ble /ínkəmprésibəl/ adj. that cannot be compressed. □□ **in·com·press·i·bil·i·ty** n.

in·con·ceiv·a·ble /ínkənseévəbəl/ adj. **1** that cannot be imagined. **2** *colloq.* very remarkable. □□ **in·con·ceiv·a·bil·i·ty** n. **in·con·ceiv·a·ble·ness** n. **in·con·ceiv·a·bly** adv.

in·con·clu·sive /ínkənklṓósiv/ adj. (of an argument, evidence, or action) not decisive or convincing. □□ **in·con·clu·sive·ly** adv. **in·con·clu·sive·ness** n.

in·con·den·sa·ble /ínkəndénsəbəl/ adj. that cannot be condensed, esp. that cannot be reduced to a liquid or solid condition.

in·con·gru·ous /inkóngrṓóəs/ adj. **1** out of place; absurd. **2** (often foll. by *with*) disagreeing; out of keeping. □□ **in·con·gru·i·ty** /–grṓóitee/ n. (pl. **·ties**). **in·con·gru·ous·ly** adv. **in·con·gru·ous·ness** n. [L *incongruus* (as IN-[1], CONGRUOUS)]

in·con·sec·u·tive /ínkənsékyətiv/ adj. lacking sequence; inconsequent. □□ **in·con·sec·u·tive·ly** adv. **in·con·sec·u·tive·ness** n.

in·con·se·quent /inkónsikwənt/ adj. **1** not following naturally; irrelevant. **2** lacking logical sequence. **3** disconnected. □□ **in·con·se·quence** /–kwəns/ n. **in·con·se·quent·ly** adv. [L *inconsequens* (as IN-[1], CONSEQUENT)]

in·con·se·quen·tial /inkónsikwénshəl, ínkon–/ adj. **1** unimportant. **2** = INCONSEQUENT. □□ **in·con·se·quen·ti·al·i·ty** /–sheeálitee/ n. (pl. **·ties**). **in·con·se·quen·tial·ly** adv. **in·con·se·quen·tial·ness** n.

in·con·sid·er·a·ble /ínkənsídərəbəl/ adj. **1** of small size, value, etc. **2** not worth considering. □□ **in·con·sid·er·a·ble·ness** n. **in·con·sid·er·a·bly** adv. [obs. F *inconsidérable* or LL *inconsiderabilis* (as IN-[1], CONSIDERABLE)]

in·con·sid·er·ate /ínkənsídərət/ adj. **1** (of a person or action) thoughtless; rash. **2** lacking in regard for the feelings of others. □□ **in·con·sid·er·ate·ly** adv. **in·con·sid·er·ate·ness** n. **in·con·sid·er·a·tion** /–ráyshən/ n. [L *inconsideratus* (as IN-[1], CONSIDERATE)]

in·con·sis·tent /ínkənsístənt/ adj. **1** acting at variance with one's own principles or former conduct. **2** (often foll. by *with*) not in keeping; discordant; incompatible. **3** (of a single thing) incompatible or discordant; having self-contradictory parts. □□ **in·con·sist·en·cy** n. (pl. **·cies**). **in·con·sist·ent·ly** adv.

in·con·sol·a·ble /ínkənsóləbəl/ adj. (of a person, grief, etc.) that cannot be consoled or comforted. □□ **in·con·sol·a·bil·i·ty** /–bílitee/ n. **in·con·sol·a·ble·ness** n. **in·con·sol·a·bly** adv. [F *inconsolable* or L *inconsolabilis* (as IN-[1], *consolabilis* f. *consolari* CONSOLE[1])]

in·con·so·nant /inkónsənənt/ adj. (often foll. by *with, to*) not harmonious; not compatible. □□ **in·con·so·nance** /–nəns/ n. **in·con·so·nant·ly** adv.

in·con·spic·u·ous /ínkənspíkyṓóəs/ adj. **1** not conspicuous; not easily noticed. **2** *Bot.* (of flowers) small, pale, or green. □□ **in·con·spic·u·ous·ly** adv. **in·con·spic·u·ous·ness** n. [L *inconspicuus* (as IN-[1], CONSPICUOUS)]

in·con·stant /inkónstənt/ adj. **1** (of a person) fickle; changeable. **2** frequently changing; variable; irregular. □□ **in·con·stan·cy** n. (pl. **·cies**). **in·con·stant·ly** adv. [ME f. OF f. L *inconstans –antis* (as IN-[1], CONSTANT)]

in·con·test·a·ble /ínkəntéstəbəl/ adj. that cannot be disputed. □□ **in·con·test·a·bil·i·ty** /–bílitee/ n. **in·con·test·a·ble·ness** n. **in·con·test·a·bly** adv. [F *incontestable* or med.L *incontestabilis* (as IN-[1], *contestabilis* f. L *contestari* CONTEST)]

in·con·ti·nent /inkóntinənt/ adj. **1** unable to control movements of the bowels or bladder or both. **2** lacking self-restraint (esp. in regard to sexual desire). **3** (foll. by *of*) unable to control. □□ **in·con·ti·nence** /–nəns/ n. **in·con·ti·nent·ly** adv. [ME f. OF or L *incontinens* (as IN-[1], CONTINENT[2])]

in·con·tro·vert·i·ble /ínkontrəvórtibəl/ adj. indisputable; indubitable. □□ **in·con·tro·vert·i·bil·i·ty** n. **in·con·tro·vert·i·bly** adv.

in·con·ven·ience /ínkənveényəns/ n. & v. ● n. **1** lack of suitability to personal requirements or ease. **2** a cause or instance of this. ● v.tr. cause inconvenience to. [ME f. OF f. LL *inconvenientia* (as INCONVENIENT)]

in·con·ven·ient /ínkənveényənt/ adj. **1** unfavorable to ease or comfort; not convenient. **2** awkward; troublesome. □□ **in·con·ven·ient·ly** adv. [ME f. OF f. L *inconveniens –entis* (as IN-[1], CONVENIENT)]

in·con·vert·i·ble /ínkənvórtibəl/ adj. **1** not convertible. **2** (esp. of currency) not convertible into another form on demand. □□ **in·con·vert·i·bil·i·ty** n. **in·con·vert·i·bly** adv. [F *inconvertible* or LL *inconvertibilis* (as IN-[1], CONVERTIBLE)]

in·co·or·di·na·tion /inkō–awrd'náyshən/ n. lack of coordination, esp. of muscular action.

in·cor·po·rate v. & adj. ● v. /inkáwrpərayt/ **1** tr. (often foll. by *in, with*) unite; form into one body or whole. **2** intr. become incorporated. **3** tr. combine (ingredients) into one substance. **4** tr. admit as a member of a company, etc. **5** tr. **a** constitute as a legal corporation. **b** (as **incorporated** adj.) forming a legal corporation. ● adj. /inkáwrpərət/ **1** (of a company, etc.) formed into a legal corporation. **2** embodied. □□ **in·cor·po·ra·tion** /–áyshən/ n. **in·cor·po·ra·tor** n. [ME f. LL *incorporare* (as IN-[2], L *corpus –oris* body)]

in·cor·po·re·al /ínkawrpáwreeəl/ adj. **1** not composed of matter. **2** of immaterial beings. **3** *Law* having no physical existence. □□ **in·cor·po·re·al·i·ty** /–reeálitee/ n. **in·cor·po·re·al·ly** adv. **in·cor·po·re·i·ty** /–pərée-itee/ n. [L *incorporeus* (as INCORPORATE)]

in·cor·rect /ínkərékt/ adj. **1** not in accordance with fact; wrong. **2** (of style, etc.) improper; faulty. □□ **in·cor·rect·ly** adv. **in·cor·rect·ness** n. [ME f. OF or L *incorrectus* (as IN-[1], CORRECT)]

in·cor·ri·gi·ble /inkáwrijibəl, –kór–/ adj. **1** (of a person or habit) incurably bad or depraved. **2** not readily improved. □□ **in·cor·ri·gi·bil·i·ty** n. **in·cor·ri·gi·ble·ness** n. **in·cor·ri·gi·bly** adv. [ME f. OF *incorrigible* or L *incorrigibilis* (as IN-[1], CORRIGIBLE)]

in·cor·rupt·i·ble /ínkəróptibəl/ adj. **1** that cannot be corrupted, esp. by bribery. **2** that cannot decay; everlasting. □□ **in·cor·rupt·i·bil·i·ty** /–bílitee/ n. **in·cor·rupt·i·bly** adv. [ME f. OF *incorruptible* or eccl.L *incorruptibilis* (as IN-[1], CORRUPT)]

in·crease v. & n. ● v. /inkreés/ **1** tr. & intr. make or become greater in size, amount, etc., or more numerous. **2** intr. advance (in quality, attainment, etc.). **3** tr. intensify (a quality). ● n. /ínkrees/ **1** the act or process of becoming greater or more numerous; growth; enlargement. **2** (of people, animals, or plants) growth in numbers; multiplication. **3** the amount or extent of an increase. □ **on the increase** increasing, esp. in frequency. □□ **in·creas·a·ble** adj. **in·creas·er** n. **in·creas·ing·ly** adv. [ME f. OF *encreiss-* stem of *encreistre* f. L *increscere* (as IN-[2], *crescere* grow)]

in·cred·i·ble /inkrédibəl/ adj. **1** that cannot be believed. **2** *colloq.* hard to believe; amazing. □□ **in·cred·i·bil·i·ty** n. **in·cred·i·ble·ness** n. **in·cred·i·bly** adv. [ME f. L *incredibilis* (as IN-[1], CREDIBLE)]

in·cred·u·lous /inkréjələs/ adj. (often foll. by *of*) unwilling to believe. □□ **in·cre·du·li·ty** /ínkridṓó litee, –dyṓó–/ n. **in·cred·u·lous·ly** adv. **in·cred·u·lous· ness** n. [L *incredulus* (as IN-[1], CREDULOUS)]

▶ The adjective **incredible** means 'unbelievable' or 'not convincing' and can be applied to a situation, statement, policy, or threat to a person (*I find this testimony incredible*). **Incredulous** means 'disinclined to believe; skeptical' and is usually applied to a person's attitude (*you shouldn't wonder that I'm incredulous after all your lies*).

in·cre·ment /ínkrimənt/ n. **1 a** an increase or addition, esp. one of a series on a fixed scale. **b** the amount of this. **2** *Math.* a small amount by which a variable quantity increases. □□ **in·cre·men·tal** /–ment'l/ adj. [ME f. L *incrementum* f. *increscere* INCREASE]

in·crim·i·nate /inkríminayt/ v.tr. **1** tend to prove the guilt of (*incriminating evidence*). **2** involve in an accusation. **3** charge with a crime.

□□ **in·crim·i·na·tion** /-náyshən/ *n.* **in·crim·i·na·to·ry** /-nətáwree/ *adj.* [LL *incriminare* (as IN-², L *crimen* offense)]

in·crust var. of ENCRUST.

in·crus·ta·tion /inkrustáyshən/ *n.* **1** the process of encrusting or state of being encrusted. **2** a crust or hard coating, esp. of fine material. **3** a concretion or deposit on a surface. **4** a facing of marble, etc., on a building. [F *incrustation* or LL *incrustatio* (as ENCRUST)]

in·cu·bate /íngkyəbayt/ *v.* **1** *tr.* sit on or artificially heat (eggs) in order to bring forth young birds, etc. **2** *tr.* cause the development of (bacteria, etc.) by creating suitable conditions. **3** *intr.* sit on eggs; brood. [L *incubare* (as IN-², *cubare cubit-* or *cubat-* lie)]

in·cu·ba·tion /ingkyəbáyshən/ *n.* **1 a** the act of incubating. **b** brooding. **2** *Med.* **a** a phase through which the germs causing a disease pass before the development of the first symptoms. **b** the period of this. □□ **in·cu·ba·tion·al** *adj.* **in·cu·ba·tive** *adj.* **in·cu·ba·to·ry** /íngkyəbətáwree/ *adj.* [L *incubatio* (as INCUBATE)]

in·cu·ba·tor /íngkyəbaytər/ *n.* **1** an apparatus used to provide a suitable temperature and environment for a premature baby or one of low birthweight. **2** an apparatus used to hatch eggs or grow microorganisms.

in·cu·bus /íngkyəbəs/ *n.* (*pl.* **in·cu·bi** /-bī/ or **in·cu·bus·es**) **1** an evil spirit supposed to descend on sleeping persons. **2** a nightmare. **3** a person or thing that oppresses like a nightmare. [ME f. LL, = L *incubo* nightmare (as INCUBATE)]

in·cu·des pl. of INCUS.

in·cul·cate /ínkúlkayt/ *v.tr.* (often foll. by *upon, in*) urge or impress (a fact, habit, or idea) persistently. □□ **in·cul·ca·tion** /-káyshən/ *n.* **in·cul·ca·tor** *n.* [L *inculcare* (as IN-², *calcare* tread f. *calx calcis* heel)]

in·cul·pate /ínkúlpayt/ *v.tr.* **1** involve in a charge. **2** accuse; blame. □□ **in·cul·pa·tion** /-páyshən/ *n.* **in·cul·pa·tive** /inkúlpətiv/ *adj.* **in·cul·pa·to·ry** /-pətawree/ *adj.* [LL *inculpare* (as IN-², *culpare* blame f. *culpa* fault)]

in·cum·ben·cy /inkúmbənsee/ *n.* (*pl.* **·cies**) the office, tenure, or sphere of an incumbent.

in·cum·bent /inkúmbənt/ *adj. & n.* ● *adj.* **1** (foll. by *on, upon*) resting as a duty (*it is incumbent on you to warn them*). **2** (often foll. by *on*) lying; pressing. **3** in occupation or having the tenure of a post or position. ● *n.* the holder of an office or post, esp. an elected official. [ME f. AL *incumbens* pres. part. of L *incumbere* lie upon (as IN-², *cubare* lie)]

in·cu·na·ble /inkyónəbəl/ *n.* = INCUNABULUM 1. [F, formed as INCUNABULUM]

in·cu·nab·u·lum /inkyənábyələm/ *n.* (*pl.* **in·cu·nab·u·la** /-lə/) **1** a book printed at an early date, esp. before 1501. **2** (in *pl.*) the early stages of the development of a thing. [L *incunabula* swaddling clothes, cradle (as IN-², *cunae* cradle)]

in·cur /inkɔ́r/ *v.tr.* (**in·curred, in·cur·ring**) suffer, experience, or become subject to (something unpleasant) as a result of one's own behavior, etc. (*incurred huge debts*). □□ **in·cur·ra·ble** *adj.* [ME f. L *incurrere incurs-* (as IN-², *currere* run)]

in·cur·a·ble /inkyórəbəl/ *adj. & n.* ● *adj.* that cannot be cured. ● *n.* a person who cannot be cured. □□ **in·cur·a·bil·i·ty** *n.* **in·cur·a·ble·ness** *n.* **in·cur·a·bly** *adv.* [ME f. OF *incurable* or LL *incurabilis* (as IN-¹, CURABLE)]

in·cu·ri·ous /inkyóreeəs/ *adj.* **1** lacking curiosity. **2** heedless; careless. □□ **in·cu·ri·os·i·ty** /-reeósitee/ *n.* **in·cu·ri·ous·ly** *adv.* **in·cu·ri·ous·ness** *n.* [L *incuriosus* (as IN-¹, CURIOUS)]

in·cur·sion /inkɔ́rzhən, -shən/ *n.* an invasion or attack, esp. when sudden or brief. □□ **in·cur·sive** /-kɔ́rsiv/ *adj.* [ME f. L *incursio* (as INCUR)]

in·curve /inkɔ́rv/ *v.tr.* **1** bend into a curve. **2** (as **incurved** *adj.*) curved inward. □□ **in·cur·va·tion** /-váyshən/ *n.* [L *incurvare* (as IN-², CURVE)]

in·cus /íngkəs/ *n.* (*pl.* **in·cudes** /-kyóódeez/) the small anvil-shaped bone in the middle ear, in contact with the malleus and stapes. [L, = anvil]

in·cuse /inkyóóz, -kyóós/ *n., v., & adj.* ● *n.* an impression hammered or stamped on a coin. ● *v.tr.* **1** mark (a coin) with a figure by stamping. **2** impress (a figure) on a coin by stamping. ● *adj.* hammered or stamped on a coin. [L *incusus* past part. of *incudere* (as IN-², *cudere* forge)]

Ind. *abbr.* **1** Independent. **2** Indiana. **3 a** India. **b** Indian.

in·da·ba /indáabə/ *n. S.Afr.* **1** a conference between or with members of S. African native tribes. **2** *colloq.* one's problem or concern. [Zulu, = business]

in·debt·ed /indétid/ *adj.* (usu. foll. by *to*) **1** owing gratitude or obligation. **2** owing money. □□ **in·debt·ed·ness** *n.* [ME f. OF *endetté* past part. of *endetter* involve in debt (as EN-¹, *detter* f. *dette* DEBT)]

in·de·cent /indéesənt/ *adj.* **1** offending against recognized standards of decency. **2** unbecoming; highly unsuitable (*with indecent haste*). □□ **in·de·cen·cy** *n.* (*pl.* **·cies**). **in·de·cent·ly** *adv.* [F *indécent* or L *indecens* (as IN-¹, DECENT)]

in·de·cent ex·po·sure *n.* the intentional act of indecently exposing one's body, esp. the genitals.

in·de·ci·pher·a·ble /indisífərəbəl/ *adj.* that cannot be deciphered.

in·de·ci·sion /indisízhən/ *n.* lack of decision; hesitation. [F *indécision* (as IN-¹, DECISION)]

in·de·ci·sive /indisísiv/ *adj.* **1** not decisive. **2** undecided; hesitating. □□ **in·de·ci·sive·ly** *adv.* **in·de·ci·sive·ness** *n.*

in·de·clin·a·ble /indiklínəbəl/ *adj. Gram.* **1** that cannot be declined. **2** having no inflections. [ME f. F *indéclinable* f. L *indeclinabilis* (as IN-¹, DECLINE)]

in·dec·o·rous /indékərəs/ *adj.* **1** improper. **2** in bad taste. □□ **in·dec·o·rous·ly** *adv.* **in·dec·o·rous·ness** *n.* [L *indecorus* (as IN-¹, *decorus* seemly)]

in·de·co·rum /indikáwrəm/ *n.* **1** lack of decorum. **2** improper behavior. [L, neut. of *indecorus*: see INDECOROUS]

in·deed /indéed/ *adv. & int.* ● *adv.* **1** in truth; really; yes; that is so (*they are, indeed, a remarkable family*). **2** expressing emphasis or intensification (*I shall be very glad indeed; indeed it is; very, indeed inordinately, proud of it*). **3** admittedly (*there are indeed exceptions*). **4** in point of fact (*if indeed such a thing is possible*). **5** expressing an approving or ironic echo (*who is this Mr. Smith? — who is he indeed?*). ● *int.* expressing irony, contempt, incredulity, etc.

indef. *abbr.* indefinite.

in·de·fat·i·ga·ble /indifátigəbəl/ *adj.* (of a person, quality, etc.) that cannot be tired out; unwearying; unremitting. □□ **in·de·fat·i·ga·bil·i·ty** *n.* **in·de·fat·i·ga·bly** *adv.* [obs. F *indéfatigable* or L *indefatigabilis* (as IN-¹, *defatigare* wear out)]

in·de·fea·si·ble /indiféezibəl/ *adj. literary* (esp. of a claim, rights, etc.) that cannot be lost. □□ **in·de·fea·si·bil·i·ty** *n.* **in·de·fea·si·bly** *adv.*

in·de·fect·i·ble /indiféktibəl/ *adj.* **1** unfailing; not liable to defect or decay. **2** faultless. [IN-¹ + *defectible* f. LL *defectibilis* (as DEFECT)]

in·de·fen·si·ble /indifénsibəl/ *adj.* that cannot be defended or justified. □□ **in·de·fen·si·bil·i·ty** *n.* **in·de·fen·si·bly** *adv.*

SPELLING TIP **indefensible**

Remember the *-ible* ending of this word with the mnemonic: "Hitting your *sib*ling is an indefen*sib*le act."

---

in·de·fin·a·ble /indifínəbəl/ *adj.* that cannot be defined or exactly described. □□ **in·de·fin·a·bly** *adv.*

in·def·i·nite /indéfinit/ *adj.* **1** vague; undefined. **2** unlimited. **3** *Gram.* not determining the person, thing, time, etc., referred to. □□ **in·def·i·nite·ness** *n.* [L *indefinitus* (as IN-¹, DEFINITE)]

in·def·i·nite ar·ti·cle *n. Gram.* the word (e.g., *a, an, some* in English) preceding a noun and implying lack of specificity (as in *bought me a book; government is an art; went to a state university*).

in·def·i·nite in·te·gral *n. Math.* an integral expressed without limits, and so containing an arbitrary constant.

in·def·i·nite·ly /indéfinitlee/ *adv.* **1** for an unlimited time (*was postponed indefinitely*). **2** in an indefinite manner.

in·def·i·nite pro·noun *n. Gram.* a pronoun indicating a person, amount, etc., without being definite or particular, e.g., *any, some, anyone*.

in·de·his·cent /indihísənt/ *adj. Bot.* (of fruit) not splitting open when ripe. □□ **in·de·his·cence** /-səns/ *n.*

in·del·i·ble /indélibəl/ *adj.* **1** that cannot be rubbed out or (in abstract senses) removed. **2** (of ink, etc.) that makes indelible marks. □□ **in·del·i·bil·i·ty** *n.* **in·del·i·bly** *adv.* [F *indélébile* or L *indelebilis* (as IN-¹, *delebilis* f. *delēre* efface)]

in·del·i·cate /indélikət/ *adj.* **1** coarse; unrefined. **2** tactless. **3** tending to indecency. □□ **in·del·i·ca·cy** *n.* (*pl.* **·cies**). **in·del·i·cate·ly** *adv.*

in·dem·ni·fy /indémnifī/ *v.tr.* (**·fies, ·fied**) **1** (often foll. by *from, against*) protect or secure (a person) in respect of harm, a loss, etc. **2** (often foll. by *for*) secure (a person) against legal responsibility for actions. **3** (often foll. by *for*) compensate (a person) for a loss, expenses, etc. □□ **in·dem·ni·fi·ca·tion** /-fikáyshən/ *n.* **in·dem·ni·fi·er** *n.* [L *indemnis* unhurt (as IN-¹, *damnum* loss, damage)]

in·dem·ni·ty /indémnitee/ *n.* (*pl.* **·ties**) **1 a** compensation for loss incurred. **b** a sum paid for this, esp. a sum exacted by a victor in war, etc., as one condition of peace. **2** security against loss. **3** legal exemption from penalties, etc., incurred. [ME f. F *indemnité* or LL *indemnitas -tatis* (as INDEMNIFY)]

in·de·mon·stra·ble /indimónstrəbəl, indémən-/ *adj.* that cannot be proved (esp. of primary or axiomatic truths).

in·dene /índeen/ *n. Chem.* a colorless, flammable liquid hydrocarbon obtained from coal tar and used in making synthetic resins. [INDOLE + -ENE]

in·dent¹ /indént/ *v. & n.* ● *v.* **1** *tr.* start (a line of print or writing) further from the margin than other lines, e.g., to mark a new paragraph. **2** *tr.* **a** divide (a document drawn up in duplicate) into its two copies with a zigzag line dividing them and ensuring identification. **b** draw up (usu. a legal document) in exact duplicate. **3** *Brit.* **a** *intr.* (often foll. by *on, upon* a person, *for* a thing) make a requisition (orig. a written order with a duplicate). **b** *tr.* order (goods) by requisition. **4** *tr.* make toothlike notches in. **5** *tr.* form deep recesses in (a coastline, etc.). ● *n.* also /índent/ **1** indentation. **2** an indented line. **3** *Brit.* **a** an order (esp. from abroad) for goods. **b** an official requisition for stores. **4** an indenture. □□ **in•dent•er** *n.* **in•den•tor** *n.* [ME f. AF *endenter* f. AL *indentare* (as IN-², L *dens dentis* tooth)]

in•dent² /índént/ *v.tr.* **1** make a dent in. **2** impress (a mark, etc.). [ME f. IN-² + DENT]

in•den•ta•tion /índentáyshən/ *n.* **1** the act or an instance of indenting; the process of being indented. **2** a cut or notch. **3** a zigzag. **4** a deep recess in a coastline, etc.

in•den•tion /indénshən/ *n.* **1** the indenting of a line in printing or writing. **2** = INDENTATION.

in•den•ture /indénchər/ *n. & v.* ● *n.* **1** an indented document (see INDENT¹ *v.* 2). **2** (usu. in *pl.*) a sealed agreement or contract. **3** a formal list, certificate, etc. ● *v.tr. hist.* bind (a person) by indentures, esp. as an apprentice. □□ **in•den•ture•ship** *n.* [ME (orig. Sc.) f. AF *endenture* (as INDENT¹)]

in•de•pend•ence /índipéndəns/ *n.* **1** (often foll. by *of, from*) the state of being independent. **2** independent income.

In•de•pend•ence Day *n.* a day celebrating the anniversary of national independence; in the US July 4.

in•de•pend•en•cy /índipéndənsee/ *n.* (*pl.* **-cies**) **1** an independent state, territory, etc. **2** = INDEPENDENCE.

in•de•pend•ent /índipéndənt/ *adj. & n.* ● *adj.* **1 a** (often foll. by *of*) not depending on authority or control. **b** self-governing. **2 a** not depending on another person for one's opinion or livelihood. **b** (of income or resources) making it unnecessary to earn one's living. **3** unwilling to be under an obligation to others. **4** *Polit.* (usu. **Independent**) not belonging to or supported by a party. **5** not depending on something else for its validity, efficiency, value, etc. (*independent proof*). **6** (of broadcasting, a school, etc.) not supported by public funds. ● *n.* **1** (usu. **Independent**) a person who is politically independent. **2** (**Independent**) *hist.* a Congregationalist. □□ **in•de•pend•ent•ly** *adv.*

in-depth *adj.* thorough; done in depth.

in-depth see DEPTH.

in•de•scrib•a•ble /índiskríbəbəl/ *adj.* **1** too unusual or extreme to be described. **2** vague; indefinite. □□ **in•de•scrib•a•bil•i•ty** *n.* **in•de•scrib•a•bly** *adv.*

in•de•struct•i•ble /índistrúktibəl/ *adj.* that cannot be destroyed. □□ **in•de•struct•i•bil•i•ty** *n.* **in•de•struct•i•bly** *adv.*

in•de•ter•mi•na•ble /índitérminəbəl/ *adj.* **1** that cannot be ascertained. **2** (of a dispute, etc.) that cannot be settled. □□ **in•de•ter•mi•na•bly** *adv.* [ME f. LL *indeterminabilis* (as IN-¹, L *determinare* DETERMINE)]

in•de•ter•mi•nate /índitérminət/ *adj.* **1** not fixed in extent, character, etc. **2** left doubtful; vague. **3** *Math.* (of a quantity) not limited to a fixed value by the value of another quantity. **4** (of a judicial sentence) such that the convicted person's conduct determines the date of release. □□ **in•de•ter•mi•na•cy** *n.* **in•de•ter•mi•nate•ly** *adv.* **in•de•ter•mi•nate•ness** *n.* [ME f. LL *indeterminatus* (as IN-¹, DETERMINATE)]

in•de•ter•mi•nate vow•el *n.* the obscure vowel /ə/ heard in '*a moment ago*'; a schwa.

in•de•ter•mi•na•tion /índitérmináyshən/ *n.* **1** lack of determination. **2** the state of being indeterminate.

in•de•ter•min•ism /índitérminizəm/ *n.* the belief that human action is not wholly determined by motives. □□ **in•de•ter•min•ist** *n.* **in•de•ter•min•is•tic** *adj.*

in•dex /índeks/ *n. & v.* ● *n.* (*pl.* **in•dex•es** or esp. in technical use **in•di•ces** /índiseez/) **1** an alphabetical list of names, subjects, etc., with references, usu. at the end of a book. **2** = CARD INDEX. **3** (in full **index number**) a number showing the variation of prices or wages as compared with a chosen base period (*retail price index*; *Dow-Jones index*). **4** *Math.* **a** the exponent of a number. **b** the power to which it is raised. **5 a** a pointer, esp. on an instrument, showing a quantity, a position on a scale, etc. **b** an indicator of a trend, direction, tendency, etc. **c** (usu. foll. by *of*) a sign, token, or indication of something. **6** *Physics* a number expressing a physical property, etc., in terms of a standard (*refractive index*). **7** *Computing* a set of items each of which specifies one of the records of a file and contains information about its address. **8** (**Index**) *RC Ch. hist.* a list of books forbidden to Roman Catholics to read. **9** *Printing* a symbol shaped like a pointing hand, used to draw attention to a note, etc. ● *v.tr.* **1** provide (a book, etc.) with an index. **2** enter in an index. **3** relate (wages, etc.) to the value of a price index. □□ **in•dex•a•tion** *n.* **in•**

dex•er *n.* **in•dex•i•ble** /–déksibəl/ *adj.* **in•dex•i•cal** *adj.* **in•dex•less** *adj.*

in•dex fin•ger *n.* the forefinger.

in•dex-linked *adj.* esp. *Brit.* adjusted according to the value of a retail price index.

in•dex of re•frac•tion *n.* the ratio of the velocity of light in a vacuum to its velocity in a specified medium.

in•di•a ink /índeeə/ *n.* (also **In•di•a ink**; *Brit.* **In•di•an ink**) **1** a black pigment made orig. in China and Japan. **2** a dark ink made from this, used esp. in drawing and technical graphics. [*India* in Asia: see INDIAN]

In•di•a•man /índeeəmən/ *n.* (*pl.* **-men**) *Naut. hist.* a ship engaged in trade with India or the East Indies.

In•di•an /índeeən/ *n. & adj.* ● *n.* **1 a** a native or national of India. **b** a person of Indian descent. **2** (in full **American Indian**) a member of the aboriginal peoples of America or their descendants. **3** any of the languages of the aboriginal peoples of America. ● *adj.* **1** of or relating to India, or to the subcontinent comprising India, Pakistan, and Bangladesh. **2** of or relating to the aboriginal peoples of America. [ME f. *India* ult. f. Gk *Indos* the River Indus f. Pers. *Hind*: cf. HINDU]

▶**Indian**, meaning 'native of America before the arrival of Europeans,' is objected to by many who now favor **Native American**. There are others (including many members of this ethnic group), however, who see nothing wrong with *Indian* or *American Indian*, which are long-established terms. The terms *Amerind* and *Amerindian*, once proposed as alternatives to *Indian*, never gained widespread use. Newer alternatives, not widely used or established, include *First Nation* (especially Canadian) and the more generic *aboriginal peoples*. It should be noted that *Indian* is held by many not to include some American groups, e.g., Aleuts and Inuit.

In•di•an clubs *n.pl.* a pair of bottle-shaped clubs swung to exercise the arms in gymnastics.

In•di•an corn *n.* **1** = CORN¹ *n.* 1. **2** any primitive corn with colorful variegated kernels, dried and used for decoration.

In•di•an el•e•phant *n.* the elephant, *Elephas maximus*, of India, which is smaller than the African elephant.

In•di•an file *n.* = SINGLE FILE.

In•di•an hemp *n.* see HEMP 1.

In•di•an ink *n. Brit.* = INDIA INK.

In•di•an O•cean *n.* the ocean between Africa to the west, and Australia to the east.

In•di•an rope trick *n.* a magician's trick, orig. from India, of climbing an upright unsupported length of rope.

In•di•an sum•mer *n.* **1** a period of unusually dry, warm weather sometimes occurring in late autumn. **2** a late period of life characterized by comparative calm.

In•di•a pa•per *n.* **1** a soft absorbent kind of paper orig. imported from China, used for proofs of engravings. **2** a very thin, tough, opaque printing paper.

in•di•a rub•ber /índeeərúbər/ *n.* (also **In•di•a rub•ber**) = RUBBER¹ 2.

In•dic /índik/ *adj. & n.* ● *adj.* of the group of Indo-European languages comprising Sanskrit and its modern descendants. ● *n.* this language group. [L *Indicus* f. Gk *Indikos* INDIAN]

in•di•cate /índikayt/ *v.tr.* (often foll. by *that* + clause) **1** point out; make known; show. **2** be a sign or symptom of; express the presence of. **3** (often in *passive*) suggest; call for; require or show to be necessary (*stronger measures are indicated*). **4** admit to or state briefly (*indicated his disapproval*). **5** (of a gauge, etc.) give as a reading. [L *indicare* (as IN-², *dicare* make known)]

in•di•ca•tion /índikáyshən/ *n.* **1 a** the act or an instance of indicating. **b** something that suggests or indicates; a sign or symptom. **2** something indicated or suggested; esp. in *Med.*, a remedy or treatment that is suggested by the symptoms. **3** a reading given by a gauge or instrument. [F f. L *indicatio* (as INDICATE)]

in•dic•a•tive /indíkətiv/ *adj. & n.* ● *adj.* **1** (foll. by *of*) suggestive; serving as an indication. **2** *Gram.* (of a mood) denoting simple statement of a fact. ● *n. Gram.* **1** the indicative mood. **2** a verb in this mood. □□ **in•dic•a•tive•ly** *adv.* [ME f. F *indicatif –ive* f. LL *indicativus* (as INDICATE)]

in•di•ca•tor /índikaytər/ *n.* **1** a person or thing that indicates. **2** a device indicating the condition of a machine, etc. **3** a recording instrument attached to an apparatus, etc. **4** esp. *Brit.* a board in a railroad station, etc., giving current information. **5** esp. *Brit.* a device (esp. a flashing light) on a vehicle to show that it is about to change direction; turn signal. **6** a substance that changes color at a given stage in a chemical reaction. **7** *Physics & Med.* a radioactive tracer.

in•dic•a•to•ry /indíkətawree/ *adj.* = INDICATIVE *adj.* 1.

in•di•ces *pl.* see INDEX.

in•di•ci•a /indíshə/ *n.pl.* **1** distinguishing or identificatory marks. **2** a stamp or postal mark printed on the envelopes of bulk mail to indicate postage has been paid. [pl. of L *indicium* (as INDEX)]

in•di•cial /indíshəl/ *adj.* **1** of the nature or form of an index. **2** of the nature of indicia; indicative.

in•dict /indít/ *v.tr.* accuse (a person) formally by legal process. □□ **in•**

dict·ee /-tēe/ *n.* **in·dict·er** *n.* [ME f. AF *enditer* indict f. OF *enditi-er* declare f. Rmc *indictare* (unrecorded: as IN-², DICTATE)]

in·dict·a·ble /indítəbəl/ *adj.* **1** (of an offense) rendering the person who commits it liable to be charged with a crime. **2** (of a person) so liable.

in·dict·ment /indítmənt/ *n.* **1** the act of indicting. **2 a** a formal accusation. **b** a legal process in which this is made. **c** a document containing a charge. **3** something that serves to condemn or censure. [ME f. AF *enditement* (as INDICT)]

in·die /índee/ *n. & adj. colloq.* • *n.* an independent record or motion-picture company. • *adj.* (of a pop group or record label) independent, not belonging to one of the major companies.

In·dies /índeez/ *n.pl.* (prec. by *the*) *archaic* India and adjacent regions (see also EAST INDIES, WEST INDIES). [pl. of obs. *Indy* India]

in·dif·fer·ence /indífrəns/ *n.* **1** lack of interest or attention. **2** unimportance (*a matter of indifference*). **3** neutrality. [L *indifferentia* (as INDIFFERENT)]

in·dif·fer·ent /indífrənt/ *adj.* **1** neither good nor bad; average; mediocre. **2 a** not especially good. **b** fairly bad. **3** (often prec. by *very*) decidedly inferior. **4** (foll. by *to*) having no partiality for or against; having no interest in or sympathy for. **5** chemically, magnetically, etc., neutral. □□ **in·dif·fer·ent·ly** *adv.* [ME f. OF *indifferent* or L *indifferens* (as IN-¹, DIFFERENT)]

in·dif·fer·ent·ism /indífrəntizəm/ *n.* an attitude of indifference, esp. in religious matters. □□ **in·dif·fer·ent·ist** *n.*

in·dig·e·nize /indíjiniz/ *v.tr.* **1** make indigenous; subject to native influence. **2** subject to increased use of indigenous people in government, etc. □□ **in·dig·e·ni·za·tion** *n.*

in·dig·e·nous /indíjinəs/ *adj.* **1 a** (esp. of flora or fauna) originating naturally in a region. **b** (of people) born in a region. **2** (foll. by *to*) belonging naturally to a place. □□ **in·dig·e·nous·ly** *adv.* **in·dig·e·nous·ness** *n.* [L *indigena* f. *indi-* = IN-² + *gen-* be born]

in·di·gent /indíjənt/ *adj.* needy; poor. □□ **in·di·gence** /-jəns/ *n.* [ME f. OF f. LL *indigēre* f. *indi-* = IN-² + *egēre* need]

in·di·gest·ed /indijéstid, -dī-/ *adj.* **1** shapeless. **2** ill-considered. **3** not digested.

in·di·gest·i·ble /indijéstibəl/ *adj.* **1** difficult or impossible to digest. **2** too complex or awkward to read or comprehend easily. □□ **in·di·gest·i·bil·i·ty** *n.* **in·di·gest·i·bly** *adv.* [F *indigestible* or LL *indigestibilis* (as IN-¹, DIGEST)]

in·di·ges·tion /indijés-chən/ *n.* **1** difficulty in digesting food. **2** pain or discomfort caused by this. □□ **in·di·ges·tive** *adj.* [ME f. OF *indigestion* or LL *indigestio* (as IN-¹, DIGESTION)]

in·dig·nant /indígnənt/ *adj.* feeling or showing scornful anger or a sense of injured innocence. □□ **in·dig·nant·ly** *adv.* [L *indignari indignant-* regard as unworthy (as IN-¹, *dignus* worthy)]

in·dig·na·tion /indignáyshən/ *n.* scornful anger at supposed unjust or unfair conduct or treatment. [ME f. OF *indignation* or L *indignatio* (as INDIGNANT)]

in·dig·ni·ty /indígnitee/ *n.* (*pl.* **-ties**) **1** unworthy treatment. **2** a slight or insult. **3** the humiliating quality of something (*the indignity of my position*). [F *indignité* or L *indignitas* (as INDIGNANT)]

in·di·go /índigō/ *n.* (*pl.* **-gos**) **1 a** a natural blue dye obtained from the indigo plant. **b** a synthetic form of this dye. **2** any plant of the genus *Indigofera*. **3** (in full **indigo blue**) a color between blue and violet in the spectrum. □□ **in·di·got·ic** /-gótik/ *adj.* [16th-c. *indico* (f. Sp.), *indigo* (f. Port.) f. L *indicum* f. Gk *indikon* INDIAN (dye)]

in·di·rect /indirékt, -dī-/ *adj.* **1** not going straight to the point. **2** (of a route, etc.) not straight. **3** not directly sought or aimed at (*an indirect result*). **4** (of lighting) from a concealed source and diffusely reflected. □□ **in·di·rect·ly** *adv.* **in·di·rect·ness** *n.* [ME f. OF *indirect* or med.L *indirectus* (as IN-¹, DIRECT)]

in·di·rect ob·ject *n. Gram.* a person or thing affected by a verbal action but not primarily acted on (e.g., *him* in *give him the book*).

in·di·rect ques·tion *n. Gram.* a question in reported speech (e.g., *they asked who I was*).

in·di·rect speech *n.* (also **in·di·rect o·ra·tion**) = REPORTED SPEECH.

in·di·rect tax *n.* a tax levied on goods and services and not on income or profits.

in·dis·cern·i·ble /indisə́rnibəl/ *adj.* that cannot be discerned or distinguished from another. □□ **in·dis·cern·i·bil·i·ty** *n.* **in·dis·cern·i·bly** *adv.*

in·dis·ci·pline /indísiplin/ *n.* lack of discipline.

in·dis·creet /indiskréet/ *adj.* **1** not discreet; revealing secrets. **2** injudicious; unwary. □□ **in·dis·creet·ly** *adv.* **in·dis·creet·ness** *n.* [ME f. LL *indiscretus* (as IN-¹, DISCREET)]

in·dis·crete /indiskréet/ *adj.* not divided into distinct parts. [L *indiscretus* (as IN-¹, DISCRETE)]

in·dis·cre·tion /indiskréshən/ *n.* **1** lack of discretion; indiscreet conduct. **2** an indiscreet action, remark, etc. [ME f. OF *indiscretion* or LL *indiscretio* (as IN-¹, DISCRETION)]

in·dis·crim·i·nate /indiskríminət/ *adj.* **1** making no distinctions. **2** confused; promiscuous. □□ **in·dis·crim·i·nate·ly** *adv.* **in·dis·crim·i·nate·ness** *n.* **in·dis·crim·i·na·tion** /-náyshən/ *n.* **in·dis·crim·i·na·tive** *adj.* [IN-¹ + *discriminate* (adj.) f. L *discriminatus* past part. (as DISCRIMINATE)]

in·dis·pen·sa·ble /indispénsəbəl/ *adj.* **1** (often foll. by *to, for*) that cannot be dispensed with; necessary. **2** (of a law, duty, etc.) that is not to be set aside. □□ **in·dis·pen·sa·bil·i·ty** *n.* **in·dis·pen·sa·ble·ness** *n.* **in·dis·pen·sa·bly** *adv.* [med.L *indispensabilis* (as IN-¹, DISPENSABLE)]

in·dis·pose /indispóz/ *v.tr.* **1** (often foll. by *for*, or *to* + infin.) make unfit or unable. **2** (often foll. by *toward*, *from*, or *to* + infin.) make averse.

in·dis·posed /indispózd/ *adj.* **1** slightly unwell. **2** averse or unwilling.

in·dis·po·si·tion /indispəzíshən/ *n.* **1** ill health; a slight or temporary ailment. **2** disinclination. **3** aversion. [F *indisposition* or IN-¹ + DISPOSITION]

in·dis·put·a·ble /indispyóōtəbəl/ *adj.* **1** that cannot be disputed. **2** unquestionable. □□ **in·dis·put·a·bil·i·ty** *n.* **in·dis·put·a·ble·ness** *n.* **in·dis·put·a·bly** *adv.* [LL *indisputabilis* (as IN-¹, DISPUTABLE)]

in·dis·sol·u·ble /indisólyəbəl/ *adj.* **1** that cannot be dissolved or decomposed. **2** lasting; stable (*an indissoluble bond*). □□ **in·dis·sol·u·bil·i·ty** *n.* **in·dis·sol·u·bly** *adv.* [L *indissolubilis* (as IN-¹, DISSOLUBLE)]

in·dis·tinct /indístingkt/ *adj.* **1** not distinct. **2** confused; obscure. □□ **in·dis·tinct·ly** *adv.* **in·dis·tinct·ness** *n.* [ME f. L *indistinctus* (as IN-¹, DISTINCT)]

in·dis·tinc·tive /indístíngktiv/ *adj.* not having distinctive features. □□ **in·dis·tinc·tive·ly** *adv.* **in·dis·tinc·tive·ness** *n.*

in·dis·tin·guish·a·ble /indístínggwishəbəl/ *adj.* (often foll. by *from*) not distinguishable. □□ **in·dis·tin·guish·a·ble·ness** *n.* **in·dis·tin·guish·a·bly** *adv.*

in·dite /indít/ *v.tr. formal* or *joc.* **1** put (a speech, etc.) into words. **2** write (a letter, etc.). [ME f. OF *enditier*: see INDICT]

in·di·um /índeeəm/ *n. Chem.* a soft, silvery-white metallic element occurring naturally in sphalerite, etc., used for electroplating and in semiconductors. ¶ Symb.: **In**. [L *indicum* indigo with ref. to its characteristic spectral lines]

in·di·vert·i·ble /indivə́rtibəl/ *adj.* that cannot be turned aside. □□ **in·di·vert·i·bly** *adv.*

in·di·vid·u·al /indivíjōōəl/ *adj. & n.* • *adj.* **1** single. **2** particular; special; not general. **3** having a distinct character. **4** characteristic of a particular person. **5** designed for use by one person. • *n.* **1 a** single member of a class. **2** a single human being as distinct from a family or group. **3** *colloq.* a person (*a most unpleasant individual*). [ME, = indivisible, f. med.L *individualis* (as IN-¹, *dividuus* f. *dividere* DIVIDE)]

in·di·vid·u·al·ism /indivíjōōəlizəm/ *n.* **1** the habit or principle of being independent and self-reliant. **2** a social theory favoring the free action of individuals. **3** self-centered feeling or conduct; egoism. □□ **in·di·vid·u·al·ist** *n.* **in·di·vid·u·al·is·tic** *adj.* **in·di·vid·u·al·is·ti·cal·ly** *adv.*

in·di·vid·u·al·i·ty /indivíjōō-álitee/ *n.* (*pl.* **-ties**) **1** individual character, esp. when strongly marked. **2** (in *pl.*) individual tastes, etc. **3** separate existence.

in·di·vid·u·al·ize /indivíjōōəlīz/ *v.tr.* **1** give an individual character to. **2** specify. □□ **in·di·vid·u·al·i·za·tion** *n.*

in·di·vid·u·al·ly /indivíjōōəlee/ *adv.* **1** personally; in an individual capacity. **2** in a distinctive manner. **3** one by one; not collectively.

in·di·vid·u·al re·tire·ment ac·count *n.* a savings plan in which money invested and interest earned are not taxed until retirement. ¶ Abbr.: **IRA**.

in·di·vid·u·ate /indivíjōō-ayt/ *v.tr.* individualize; form into an individual. □□ **in·di·vid·u·a·tion** /-áyshən/ *n.* [med.L *individuare* (as INDIVIDUAL)]

in·di·vis·i·ble /indivízibəl/ *adj.* **1** not divisible. **2** not distributable among a number. □□ **in·di·vis·i·bil·i·ty** *n.* **in·di·vis·i·bly** *adv.* [ME f. LL *indivisibilis* (as IN-¹, DIVISIBLE)]

In·do- /índō/ *comb. form* Indian; Indian and. [L *Indus* f. Gk *Indos*]

In·do-Ar·y·an /índō-áireeən/ *n. & adj.* • *n.* **1** a member of any of the Aryan peoples of India. **2** the Indic group of languages. • *adj.* of or relating to the Indo-Aryans or Indo-aryan.

In·do-Chi·nese /índōchīneéz/ *adj. & n.* (also **In·do-chi·nese**) • *adj.* of or relating to Indochina in SE Asia. • *n.* a native of Indochina; a person of Indo-Chinese descent.

in·doc·ile /indósil/ *adj.* not docile. □□ **in·doc·il·i·ty** /-sílitee/ *n.* [F *indocile* or L *indocilis* (as IN-¹, DOCILE)]

in·doc·tri·nate /indóktrinayt/ *v.tr.* **1** teach (a person or group) systematically or for a long period to accept (esp. partisan or tendentious) ideas uncritically. **2** teach; instruct. □□ **in·doc·tri·na·tion** /-náyshən/ *n.* **in·doc·tri·na·tor** *n.* [IN-² + DOCTRINE + -ATE³]

In·do-Eu·ro·pe·an /índō-yŏōrəpeéən/ *adj. & n.* • *adj.* **1** of or relating to the family of languages spoken over the greater part of Europe and Asia as far as N. India. **2** of or relating to the hypothetical parent language of this family. • *n.* **1** the Indo-European family of languages. **2** the hypothetical parent language of all languages belonging to this family. **3** (usu. in *pl.*) a speaker of an Indo-European language.

In·do·I·ra·ni·an /índōiráyneeən/ *adj. & n.* ● *adj.* of or relating to the subfamily of Indo-European languages spoken chiefly in N. India and Iran. ● *n.* this subfamily.

in·dole /índōl/ *n. Chem.* an organic compound with a characteristic odor formed on the reduction of indigo. [INDIGO + L *oleum* oil]

in·dole·a·ce·tic acid /índōləseétik/ *n. Biochem.* any of the several isomeric acetic acid derivatives of indole, esp. one found as a natural growth hormone in plants. ¶ Abbr.: **IAA**. [INDOLE + ACETIC]

in·do·lent /índələnt/ *adj.* **1** lazy; wishing to avoid activity or exertion. **2** *Med.* causing no pain (*an indolent tumor*). □□ **in·do·lence** /–ləns/ *n.* **in·do·lent·ly** *adv.* [LL *indolens* (as IN-¹, *dolēre* suffer pain)]

In·dol·o·gy /indóləjee/ *n.* the study of the history, literature, etc., of India. □□ **In·dol·o·gist** *n.*

in·dom·i·ta·ble /indómitəbəl/ *adj.* **1** that cannot be subdued; unyielding. **2** stubbornly persistent. □□ **in·dom·i·ta·bil·i·ty** *n.* **in·dom·i·ta·ble·ness** *n.* **in·dom·i·ta·bly** *adv.* [LL *indomitabilis* (as IN-¹, L *domitare* tame)]

In·do·ne·sian /índənéezhən, –shən/ *n. & adj.* ● *n.* **1 a** a native or national of Indonesia in SE Asia. **b** a person of Indonesian descent. **2** a member of the chief pre-Malay population of the E. Indies. **3** a language of the group spoken in the E. Indies, esp. the official language of the Indonesian Republic (see also BAHASA INDONESIA). ● *adj.* of or relating to Indonesia or its people or language. [*Indonesia* f. INDIES after *Polynesia*]

in·door /índawr/ *adj.* situated, carried on, or used within a building or under cover (*indoor antenna; indoor games*). [earlier *within-door*. cf. INDOORS]

in·doors /indáwrz/ *adv.* into or within a building. [earlier *within doors*]

in·dorse var. of ENDORSE.

in·draft /índráft/ *n.* (*Brit.* **in·draught**) **1** the drawing in of something. **2** an inward flow or current.

in·drawn /índráwn/ *adj.* **1** (of breath, etc.) drawn in. **2** aloof.

in·dri /índree/ *n.* (*pl.* **in·dris**) a large lemur, *Indri indri*, of Madagascar. [Malagasy *indry* behold, mistaken for its name]

in·du·bi·ta·ble /indōóbitəbəl, –dyōó–/ *adj.* that cannot be doubted. □□ **in·du·bi·ta·bly** *adv.* [F *indubitable* or L *indubitabilis* (as IN-¹, *dubitare* to doubt)]

in·duce /indōós, –dyōós/ *v.tr.* **1** (often foll. by *to* + infin.) prevail on; persuade. **2** bring about; give rise to. **3** *Med.* bring on (labor) artificially, esp. by use of drugs. **4** *Electr.* produce (a current) by induction. **5** *Physics* cause (radioactivity) by bombardment. **6** infer; derive as a deduction. □□ **in·duc·er** *n.* **in·duc·i·ble** *adj.* [ME f. L *inducere induct-* (as IN-², *ducere* lead)]

in·duce·ment /indōósmənt, –dyōós–/ *n.* **1** (often foll. by *to*) an attraction that leads one on. **2** a thing that induces.

in·duct /indúkt/ *v.tr.* (often foll. by *to, into*) **1** introduce formally into possession of a benefice. **2** install into a room, office, etc. **3** introduce; initiate. **4** enlist (a person) for military service. □□ **in·duc·tee** /índuktée/ *n.* [ME (as INDUCE)]

in·duc·tance /indúktəns/ *n. Electr.* the property of an electric circuit that causes an electromotive force to be generated by a change in the current flowing.

in·duc·tion /indúkshən/ *n.* **1** the act or an instance of inducting or inducing. **2** *Med.* the process of bringing on (esp. labor) by artificial means. **3** *Logic* **a** the inference of a general law from particular instances (cf. DEDUCTION). **b** *Math.* a means of proving a theorem by showing that, if it is true of any particular case, it is true of the next case in a series, and then showing that it is indeed true in one particular case. **c** (foll. by *of*) the production of (facts) to prove a general statement. **4** (often *attrib.*) a formal introduction to a new job, position, etc. (*attended an induction course*). **5** *Electr.* **a** the production of an electric or magnetic state by the proximity (without contact) of an electrified or magnetized body. **b** the production of an electric current in a conductor by a change of magnetic field. **6** the drawing of a fuel mixture into the cylinders of an internal combustion engine. **7** enlistment for military service. [ME f. OF *induction* or L *inductio* (as INDUCE)]

in·duc·tion coil *n.* a coil for generating intermittent high voltage from a direct current.

in·duc·tion heat·ing *n.* heating by an induced electric current.

in·duc·tive /indúktiv/ *adj.* **1** (of reasoning, etc.) of or based on induction. **2** of electric or magnetic induction. □□ **in·duc·tive·ly** *adv.* **in·duc·tive·ness** *n.* [LL *inductivus* (as INDUCE)]

in·duc·tor /indúktər/ *n.* **1** *Electr.* a component (in a circuit) which possesses inductance. **2** a person who inducts a member of the clergy. [L (as INDUCE)]

in·due var. of ENDUE.

in·dulge /indúlj/ *v.* **1** *intr.* (often foll. by *in*) take pleasure freely. **2** *tr.* yield freely to (a desire, etc.). **3** *tr.* gratify the wishes of; favor (*indulged them with money*). **4** *intr. colloq.* take alcoholic liquor. □□ **in·dulg·er** *n.* [L *indulgēre indult-* give free rein to]

in·dul·gence /indúljəns/ *n.* **1 a** the act of indulging. **b** the state of

being indulgent. **2** something indulged in. **3** *RC Ch.* the remission of temporal punishment in purgatory, still due for sins after absolution. **4** a privilege granted. [ME f. OF f. L *indulgentia* (as INDULGENT)]

in·dul·gent /indúljənt/ *adj.* **1** ready or too ready to overlook faults, etc. **2** indulging or tending to indulge. □□ **in·dul·gent·ly** *adv.* [F *indulgent* or L *indulgere indulgent-* (as INDULGE)]

in·du·men·tum /índōōméntəm, –dyōō–/ *n.* (*pl.* **in·du·men·ta** /–tə/ or **in·du·men·tums**) *Bot.* the covering of hairs on part of a plant, esp. when dense. [L, = garment]

in·du·na /indōónə/ *n.* **1** *S.Afr.* a tribal councilor or headman. **2 a** an African foreman. **b** a person in authority. [Nguni *inDuna* captain, councilor]

in·du·rate /índərayt, –dyə–/ *v.* **1** *tr. & intr.* make or become hard. **2** *tr.* make callous or unfeeling. **3** *intr.* become inveterate. □□ **in·du·ra·tion** /–ráyshən/ *n.* **in·du·ra·tive** *adj.* [L *indurare* (as IN-², *durus* hard)]

in·du·si·um /indōózeeəm, –zheeəm, –dyōó–/ *n.* (*pl.* **in·du·si·a** /–zeeə/) **1** a membranous shield covering the fruit cluster of a fern. **2** a collection of hairs enclosing the stigma of some flowers. **3** the case of a larva. □□ **in·du·si·al** *adj.* [L, = tunic, f. *induere* put on (a garment)]

in·dus·tri·al /indústreeəl/ *adj. & n.* ● *adj.* **1** of or relating to industry or industries. **2** designed or suitable for industrial use (*industrial alcohol*). **3** characterized by highly developed industries (*the industrial nations*). ● *n.* (in *pl.*) shares in industrial companies. □□ **in·dus·tri·al·ly** *adv.* [INDUSTRY + -AL: in 19th c. partly f. F *industriel*]

in·dus·tri·al ar·chae·ol·o·gy *n.* the study of machines, factories, bridges, etc., formerly used in industry.

in·dus·tri·al es·tate *n. Brit.* = INDUSTRIAL PARK.

in·dus·tri·al·ism /indústreeəlizəm/ *n.* a social or economic system in which manufacturing industries are prevalent.

in·dus·tri·al·ist /indústreeəlist/ *n.* a person engaged in the management of industry.

in·dus·tri·al·ize /indústreeəlīz/ *v.* **1** *tr.* introduce industries to (a country or region, etc.). **2** *intr.* become industrialized. □□ **in·dus·tri·al·i·za·tion** *n.*

in·dus·tri·al park *n.* an area of land developed for a complex of factories and other businesses, usu. separate from an urban center.

in·dus·tri·al re·la·tions *n.pl.* the relations between management and workers in industries.

in·dus·tri·al rev·o·lu·tion *n.* the rapid development of a nation's industry (esp. the **Industrial Revolution**, in the late 18th and early 19th c.).

in·dus·tri·ous /indústreeəs/ *adj.* diligent; hardworking. □□ **in·dus·tri·ous·ly** *adv.* **in·dus·tri·ous·ness** *n.* [F *industrieux* or LL *industriosus* (as INDUSTRY)]

in·dus·try /índəstree/ *n.* (*pl.* **·tries**) **1 a** a branch of trade or manufacture. **b** trade and manufacture collectively (*incentives to industry*). **2** concerted or copious activity (*the building was a hive of industry*). **3 a** diligence. **b** *colloq.* an activity or domain in which a great deal of time or effort is expended (*the Shakespeare industry*). **4** hard work. [ME, = skill, f. F *industrie* or L *industria* diligence]

in·dwell /indwél/ *v.* (*past* and *past part.* **in·dwelt**) *literary* **1** *intr.* (often foll. by *in*) be permanently present as a spirit, principle, etc. **2** *tr.* inhabit spiritually. □□ **in·dwell·er** *n.*

In·dy /índee/ *n. & adj.* ● *n.* a form of automobile racing, usu. at very high speeds on an oval circuit. ● *adj.* relating to or suitable for such a race (*an Indy car; an Indy qualifier*). [short for Indianapolis, Indiana, the city where the principal Indy race is held]

-ine¹ /īn, in/ *suffix* forming adjectives, meaning 'belonging to, of the nature of' (*Alpine; asinine*). [from or after F *–in –ine*, or f. L *–inus*]

-ine² /in/ *suffix* forming adjectives, esp. from names of minerals, plants, etc. (*crystalline*). [L *–inus* from or after Gk *–inos*]

-ine³ /in, een/ *suffix* forming feminine nouns (*heroine; margravine*). [F f. L *–ina* f. Gk *–inē*, or f. G *–in*]

-ine⁴ *suffix* **1** /in/ forming (esp. abstract) nouns (*discipline; medicine*). **2** /een, in/ *Chem.* forming nouns denoting derived substances, esp. alkaloids, halogens, amines, and amino acids. [F f. L *–ina* (fem.) = -INE¹]

in·e·bri·ate *v., adj., & n.* ● *v.tr.* /inéebreeayt/ **1** make drunk; intoxicate. **2** excite. ● *adj.* /inéebreeət/ drunken. ● *n.* /inéebreeət/ a drunken person, esp. a habitual drunkard. □□ **in·e·bri·a·tion** /–áyshən/ *n.* **in·e·bri·e·ty** /inibríətee/ *n.* [ME f. L *inebriatus* past part. of *inebriare* (as IN-², *ebrius* drunk)]

in·ed·i·ble /inédibəl/ *adj.* not edible, esp. not suitable for eating (cf. UNEATABLE). □□ **in·ed·i·bil·i·ty** *n.*

in·ed·it·ed /inéditid/ *adj.* **1** not published. **2** published without editorial alterations or additions.

in·ed·u·ca·ble /inéjəkəbəl/ *adj.* incapable of being educated, esp. through mental retardation. □□ **in·ed·u·ca·bil·i·ty** *n.*

in·ef·fa·ble /inéfəbəl/ *adj.* **1** unutterable; too great for description in words. **2** that must not be uttered. □□ **in·ef·fa·bil·i·ty** *n.* **in·ef·fa·bly** *adv.* [ME f. OF *ineffable* or L *ineffabilis* (as IN-¹, *effari* speak out, utter)]

in·ef·face·a·ble /ínifáysəbəl/ *adj.* that cannot be effaced. ▫▫ **in·ef·face·a·bil·i·ty** *n.* **in·ef·face·a·bly** *adv.*

in·ef·fec·tive /íniféktiv/ *adj.* **1** not producing any effect or the desired effect. **2** (of a person) inefficient; not achieving results. **3** lacking artistic effect. ▫▫ **in·ef·fec·tive·ly** *adv.* **in·ef·fec·tive·ness** *n.*

in·ef·fec·tu·al /inifékchōōəl/ *adj.* **1 a** without effect. **b** not producing the desired or expected effect. **2** (of a person) lacking the ability to achieve results (*an ineffectual leader*). ▫▫ **in·ef·fec·tu·al·i·ty** /–álitee/ *n.* **in·ef·fec·tu·al·ly** *adv.* **in·ef·fec·tu·al·ness** *n.* [ME f. med.L *ineffectualis* (as IN-1, EFFECTUAL)]

in·ef·fi·ca·cious /ínefikáyshəs/ *adj.* (of a remedy, etc.) not producing the desired effect. ▫▫ **in·ef·fi·ca·cious·ly** *adv.* **in·ef·fi·ca·cious·ness** *n.* **in·ef·fi·ca·cy** /inéfikəsee/ *n.*

in·ef·fi·cient /inifíshənt/ *adj.* **1** not efficient. **2** (of a person) not fully capable; not well qualified. ▫▫ **in·ef·fi·cien·cy** *n.* **in·ef·fi·cient·ly** *adv.*

in·e·las·tic /ínilástik/ *adj.* **1** not elastic. **2** unadaptable; inflexible; unyielding. ▫▫ **in·e·las·ti·cal·ly** *adv.* **in·e·las·tic·i·ty** /–lastísitee/ *n.*

in·el·e·gant /inéligənt/ *adj.* **1** ungraceful. **2 a** unrefined. **b** (of a style) unpolished. ▫▫ **in·el·e·gance** /–gəns/ *n.* **in·el·e·gant·ly** *adv.* [F *inélégant* f. L *inelegans* (as IN-1, ELEGANT)]

in·el·i·gi·ble /inélijibəl/ *adj.* **1** not eligible. **2** undesirable. ▫▫ **in·el·i·gi·bil·i·ty** *n.* **in·el·i·gi·bly** *adv.*

in·e·luc·ta·ble /inilúktəbəl/ *adj.* **1** against which it is useless to struggle. **2** that cannot be escaped from. ▫▫ **in·e·luc·ta·bil·i·ty** *n.* **in·e·luc·ta·bly** *adv.* [L *ineluctabilis* (as IN-1, *eluctari* struggle out)]

in·ept /inépt/ *adj.* **1** unskillful. **2** absurd; silly. **3** out of place. ▫▫ **in·ept·i·tude** *n.* **in·ept·ly** *adv.* **in·ept·ness** *n.* [L *ineptus* (as IN-1, APT)]

in·eq·ua·ble /inékwəbəl/ *adj.* **1** not fairly distributed. **2** not uniform. [L *inaequabilis* uneven (as IN-1, EQUABLE)]

in·e·qual·i·ty /inikwólitee/ *n.* (*pl.* **·ties**) **1 a** lack of equality in any respect. **b** an instance of this. **2** the state of being variable. **3** (of a surface) irregularity. **4** *Math.* a formula affirming that two expressions are not equal. [ME f. OF *inequalité* or L *inaequalitas* (as IN-1, EQUALITY)]

▶See note at UNEQUAL.

in·eq·ui·ta·ble /inékwitəbəl/ *adj.* unfair; unjust. ▫▫ **in·eq·ui·ta·bly** *adv.*

in·eq·ui·ty /inékwitee/ *n.* (*pl.* **·ties**) unfairness; bias.

in·e·rad·i·ca·ble /inirádikəbəl/ *adj.* that cannot be rooted out. ▫▫ **in·e·rad·i·ca·bly** *adv.*

in·er·rant /inérənt/ *adj.* not liable to err. ▫▫ **in·er·ran·cy** *n.* [L *inerrans* (as IN-1, ERR)]

in·ert /inə́rt/ *adj.* **1** without inherent power of action, motion, or resistance. **2** without active chemical or other properties. **3** sluggish; slow. ▫▫ **in·ert·ly** *adv.* **in·ert·ness** *n.* [L *iners inert-* (as IN-1, *ars* ART1)]

in·ert gas *n.* = NOBLE GAS.

in·er·tia /inə́rshə/ *n.* **1** *Physics* a property of matter by which it continues in its existing state of rest or uniform motion in a straight line, unless that state is changed by an external force. **2** inertness; sloth. ▫▫ **in·er·tial** *adj.* **in·er·tia·less** *adj.* [L (as INERT)]

in·er·tia reel *n.* esp. *Brit.* a reel device which allows a vehicle seat belt to unwind freely but which locks under force of impact or rapid deceleration.

in·er·tia sell·ing *n.* esp. *Brit.* the sending of unsolicited goods in the hope of making a sale.

in·es·cap·a·ble /iniskáypəbəl/ *adj.* that cannot be escaped or avoided. ▫▫ **in·es·cap·a·bil·i·ty** *n.* **in·es·cap·a·bly** *adv.*

-iness /eenis/ *suffix* forming nouns corresponding to adjectives in *–y* (see *–*Y1, *–*LY2).

in·es·sen·tial /inisénshəl/ *adj. & n.* ● *adj.* **1** not necessary. **2** dispensable. ● *n.* an inessential thing.

in·es·ti·ma·ble /inéstiməbəl/ *adj.* too great, intense, precious, etc., to be estimated. ▫▫ **in·es·ti·ma·bly** *adv.* [ME f. OF f. L *inaestimabilis* (as IN-1, ESTIMABLE)]

in·ev·i·ta·ble /inévitəbəl/ *adj.* **1 a** unavoidable; sure to happen. **b** that is bound to occur or appear. **2** *colloq.* that is tiresomely familiar. **3** (of character drawing, the development of a plot, etc.) so true to nature, etc., as to preclude alternative treatment or solution; convincing. ▫▫ **in·ev·i·ta·bil·i·ty** *n.* **in·ev·i·ta·ble·ness** *n.* **in·ev·i·ta·bly** *adv.* [L *inevitabilis* (as IN-1, *evitare* avoid)]

in·ex·act /ínigzákt/ *adj.* not exact. ▫▫ **in·ex·act·i·tude** /–titōōd, –tyōōd/ *n.* **in·ex·act·ly** *adv.* **in·ex·act·ness** *n.*

in·ex·cus·a·ble /iniskyōōzəbəl/ *adj.* (of a person, action, etc.) that cannot be excused or justified. ▫▫ **in·ex·cus·a·bly** *adv.* [ME f. L *inexcusabilis* (as IN-1, EXCUSE)]

in·ex·haust·i·ble /inigzáwstibəl/ *adj.* **1** that cannot be exhausted or used up. **2** that cannot be worn out. ▫▫ **in·ex·haust·i·bil·i·ty** *n.* **in·ex·haust·i·bly** *adv.*

in·ex·o·ra·ble /inéksərəbəl/ *adj.* **1** relentless. **2** (of a person or attribute) that cannot be persuaded by request or entreaty. ▫▫ **in·ex·o·ra·bil·i·ty** /–bílitee/ *n.* **in·ex·o·ra·bly** *adv.* [F *inexorable* or L *inexorabilis* (as IN-1, *exorare* entreat)]

in·ex·pe·di·ent /ínikspeédeeənt/ *adj.* not expedient. ▫▫ **in·ex·pe·di·en·cy** *n.*

in·ex·pen·sive /ínikspénsiv/ *adj.* **1** not expensive; cheap. **2** offering good value for the price. ▫▫ **in·ex·pen·sive·ly** *adv.* **in·ex·pen·sive·ness** *n.*

in·ex·pe·ri·ence /inikspeéreeəns/ *n.* lack of experience, or of the resulting knowledge or skill. ▫▫ **in·ex·pe·ri·enced** *adj.* [F *inexpérience* f. LL *inexperientia* (as IN-1, EXPERIENCE)]

in·ex·pert /inékspərt/ *adj.* unskillful; lacking expertise. ▫▫ **in·ex·pert·ly** *adv.* **in·ex·pert·ness** *n.* [OF f. L *inexpertus* (as IN-1, EXPERT)]

in·ex·pi·a·ble /inékspeeəbəl/ *adj.* (of an act or feeling) that cannot be expiated or appeased. ▫▫ **in·ex·pi·a·bly** *adv.* [L *inexpiabilis* (as IN-1, EXPIATE)]

in·ex·pli·ca·ble /iniksplíkəbəl, inéks–/ *adj.* that cannot be explained or accounted for. ▫▫ **in·ex·pli·ca·bil·i·ty** *n.* **in·ex·pli·ca·bly** *adv.* [F *inexplicable* or L *inexplicabilis* that cannot be unfolded (as IN-1, EXPLICABLE)]

in·ex·plic·it /iniksplísit/ *adj.* not definitely or clearly expressed. ▫▫ **in·ex·plic·it·ly** *adv.* **in·ex·plic·it·ness** *n.*

in·ex·press·i·ble /iniksprésibəl/ *adj.* that cannot be expressed in words. ▫▫ **in·ex·press·i·bly** *adv.*

in·ex·pres·sive /iniksprésiv/ *adj.* not expressive. ▫▫ **in·ex·pres·sive·ly** *adv.* **in·ex·pres·sive·ness** *n.*

in·ex·pung·i·ble /inikspúnjibəl/ *adj.* that cannot be expunged or obliterated.

in ex·ten·so /in eksténsō/ *adv.* in full; at length. [L]

in·ex·tin·guish·a·ble /inikstínggwishəbəl/ *adj.* **1** not quenchable; indestructible. **2** (of laughter, etc.) irrepressible.

in ex·tre·mis /in ekstreémis, –tré–/ *adj.* **1** at the point of death. **2** in great difficulties. [L]

in·ex·tri·ca·ble /inékstrikəbəl, ínikstrík–/ *adj.* **1** (of a circumstance) that cannot be escaped from. **2** (of a knot, problem, etc.) that cannot be unraveled or solved. **3** intricately confused. ▫▫ **in·ex·tri·ca·bil·i·ty** *n.* **in·ex·tri·ca·bly** *adv.* [ME f. L *inextricabilis* (as IN-1, EXTRICATE)]

inf. *abbr.* **1** infantry. **2** inferior. **3** infinitive.

in·fal·li·ble /infálibəl/ *adj.* **1** incapable of error. **2** (of a method, test, proof, etc.) unfailing; sure to succeed. **3** *RC Ch.* (of the pope) unable to err in pronouncing dogma as doctrinally defined. ▫▫ **in·fal·li·bil·i·ty** /–bílitee/ *n.* **in·fal·li·bly** *adv.* [ME f. F *infaillible* or LL *infallibilis* (as IN-1, FALLIBLE)]

in·fa·mous /ínfəməs/ *adj.* **1** notoriously bad; having a bad reputation. **2** abominable. **3** (in ancient law) deprived of all or some rights of a citizen on account of serious crime. ▫▫ **in·fa·mous·ly** *adv.* **in·fa·my** /ínfəmee/ *n.* (*pl.* **·mies**). [ME f. med.L *infamosus* f. L *infamis* (as IN-1, FAME)]

in·fan·cy /ínfənsee/ *n.* (*pl.* **·cies**) **1** early childhood; babyhood. **2** an early state in the development of an idea, undertaking, etc. **3** *Law* the state of being a minor. [L *infantia* (as INFANT)]

in·fant /ínfənt/ *n.* **1 a** a child during the earliest period of its life. **b** *Brit.* a schoolchild below the age of seven years. **2** (esp. *attrib.*) a thing in an early stage of its development. **3** *Law* a minor; a person under 18. [ME f. OF *enfant* f. L *infans* unable to speak (as IN-1, *fans fantis* pres. part. of *fari* speak)]

in·fan·ta /ínfəntə, –fáan–/ *n. hist.* a daughter of the ruling monarch of Spain or Portugal (usu. the eldest daughter who is not heir to the throne). [Sp. & Port., fem. of INFANTE]

in·fan·te /ínfántee, –fáantay/ *n. hist.* the second son of the ruling monarch of Spain or Portugal. [Sp. & Port. f. L (as INFANT)]

in·fan·ti·cide /infántisīd/ *n.* **1** the killing of an infant soon after birth. **2** the practice of killing newborn infants. **3** a person who kills an infant. ▫▫ **in·fan·ti·cid·al** /–síd'l/ *adj.* [F f. LL *infanticidium*, *–cida* (as INFANT)]

in·fan·tile /ínfəntīl/ *adj.* **1 a** like or characteristic of a child. **b** childish; immature (*infantile humor*). **2** in its infancy. ▫▫ **in·fan·til·i·ty** /–tílitee/ *n.* (*pl.* **·ties**). [F *infantile* or L *infantilis* (as INFANT)]

in·fan·tile pa·ral·y·sis *n.* poliomyelitis.

in·fan·ti·lism /infánt'lizəm/ *n.* **1** childish behavior. **2** *Psychol.* the persistence of infantile characteristics or behavior in adult life.

in·fant mor·tal·i·ty *n.* death before the age of one.

in·fan·try /ínfəntree/ *n.* (*pl.* **·tries**) a body of soldiers who march and fight on foot; foot soldiers collectively. [F *infanterie* f. It. *infanteria* f. *infante* youth, infantryman (as INFANT)]

in·fan·try·man /ínfəntreemən/ *n.* (*pl.* **·men**) a soldier of an infantry unit.

in·farct /ínfaarkt/ *n. Med.* a small localized area of dead tissue caused by an inadequate blood supply. ▫▫ **in·farc·tion** /–fáarkshən/ *n.* [mod.L *infarctus* (as IN-2, L *farcire farct-* stuff)]

in·fat·u·ate /infáchōō-ayt/ *v.tr.* **1** inspire with intense, usu. transitory fondness or admiration. **2** affect with extreme folly. ▫▫ **in·fat·u·a·tion** /–áyshən/ *n.* [L *infatuare* (as IN-2, *fatuus* foolish)]

in·fat·u·at·ed /infáchoŏ-aytid/ *adj.* (often foll. by *with*) affected by an intense fondness or admiration.

in·fau·na /infáwnə/ *n.* the animals living in the sediments of the ocean floor or river or lake beds. [Da. *ifauna* (as IN-², FAUNA)]

in·fea·si·ble /inféezibəl/ *adj.* not feasible; that cannot easily be done. □□ **in·fea·si·bil·i·ty** *n.*

in·fect /infékt/ *v.tr.* **1** contaminate (air, water, etc.) with harmful organisms or noxious matter. **2** affect (a person) with disease, etc. **3** instill bad feeling or opinion into (a person). □□ **in·fec·tor** *n.* [ME f. L *inficere infect-* taint (as IN-², *facere* make)]

in·fec·tion /infékshən/ *n.* **1 a** the process of infecting or state of being infected. **b** an instance of this; an infectious disease. **2** communication of disease, esp. by the agency of air or water, etc. **3 a** moral contamination. **b** the diffusive influence of example, sympathy, etc. [ME f. OF *infection* or LL *infectio* (as INFECT)]

in·fec·tious /infékshəs/ *adj.* **1** infecting with disease. **2** (of a disease) liable to be transmitted by air, water, etc. **3** (of emotions, etc.) apt to spread; quickly affecting others. □□ **in·fec·tious·ly** *adv.* **in·fec·tious·ness** *n.*

in·fec·tious mon·o·nu·cle·o·sis *n.* an infectious viral disease characterized by swelling of the lymph glands and prolonged lassitude.

in·fec·tive /inféktiv/ *adj.* **1** capable of infecting with disease. **2** infectious. □□ **in·fec·tive·ness** *n.* [L *infectivus* (as INFECT)]

in·fe·lic·i·tous /infilísitəs/ *adj.* not felicitous; unfortunate. □□ **in·fe·lic·i·tous·ly** *adv.*

in·fe·lic·i·ty /infilísitee/ *n.* (*pl.* **·ties**) **1 a** inaptness of expression, etc. **b** an instance of this. **2 a** unhappiness. **b** a misfortune. [ME f. L *infelicitas* (as IN-¹, FELICITY)]

in·fer /infér/ *v.tr.* (**in·ferred**, **in·fer·ring**) (often foll. by *that* + clause) **1** deduce or conclude from facts and reasoning. **2** *disp.* imply; suggest. □□ **in·fer·a·ble** *adj.* (also **in·fer(r)ible**). [L *inferre* (as IN-², *ferre* bring)]

▶**Infer** means ' deduce or conclude,' as in *we can infer from the evidence that the car's brakes failed.* Its use in place of **imply**, to mean 'to hint or suggest,' is widely considered incorrect.

in·fer·ence /infərəns/ *n.* **1** the act or an instance of inferring. **2** *Logic* **a** the forming of a conclusion from premises. **b** a thing inferred. □□ **in·fer·en·tial** /-rénshəl/ *adj.* **in·fer·en·tial·ly** *adv.* [med.L *inferentia* as INFER)]

in·fe·ri·or /inféereeər/ *adj. & n.* ● *adj.* **1** (often foll. by *to*) **a** lower; in a lower position. **b** of lower rank, quality, etc. **2** poor in quality. **3** (of a planet, specifically Venus or Mercury) having an orbit within Earth's. **4** *Bot.* situated below an ovary or calyx. **5** (of figures or letters) written or printed below the line. ● *n.* **1** a person inferior to another, esp. in rank. **2** an inferior letter or figure. □□ **in·fe·ri·or·ly** *adv.* [ME f. L, compar. of *inferus* that is below]

in·fe·ri·or·i·ty /inféeree-áwritee, -ór–/ *n.* the state of being inferior.

in·fe·ri·or·i·ty com·plex *n.* an unrealistic feeling of general inadequacy caused by actual or supposed inferiority in one sphere, sometimes marked by aggressive behavior in compensation.

in·fer·nal /infórnəl/ *adj.* **1 a** of hell or the underworld. **b** hellish; fiendish. **2** *colloq.* detestable; tiresome. □□ **in·fer·nal·ly** *adv.*

---

in·fer·no /infórnō/ *n.* (*pl.* **·nos**) **1** a raging fire. **2** a scene of horror or distress. **3** hell, esp. with ref. to Dante's *Divine Comedy*. [It. f. LL *infernus* (as INFERNAL)]

in·fer·tile /infórt'l/ *adj.* not fertile. □□ **in·fer·til·i·ty** /–tílitee/ *n.* [F *infertile* or LL *infertilis* (as IN-¹, FERTILE)]

in·fest /infést/ *v.tr.* (of harmful persons or things, esp. vermin or disease) overrun (a place) in large numbers. □□ **in·fes·ta·tion** *n.* [ME f. F *infester* or L *infestare* assail f. *infestus* hostile]

in·fi·del /infid'l, –del/ *n. & adj.* ● *n.* **1** a person who does not believe in religion or in a particular religion; an unbeliever. **2** usu. *hist.* an adherent of a religion other than Christianity, esp. a Muslim. ● *adj.* **1** that is an infidel. **2** of unbelievers.

---

in·fi·del·i·ty /infidélitee/ *n.* (*pl.* **·ties**) **1 a** disloyalty or unfaithfulness, esp. to a husband or wife. **b** an instance of this. **2** disbelief in Christianity or another religion. [ME f. F *infidélité* or L *infidelitas* (as IN-FIDEL)]

in·field /infeeld/ *n.* **1** *Baseball* **a** the area enclosed by the three bases and home plate. **b** the four fielders stationed near the bases. **2** farmland around or near a homestead. **3 a** arable land. **b** land regularly manured and cropped. □□ **in·field·er** *n.* (in sense 1).

in·fight·ing /infiting/ *n.* **1** hidden conflict or competitiveness within an organization. **2** boxing at closer quarters than arm's length. □□ **in·fight·er** *n.*

in·fill /infil/ *n. & v.* ● *n.* **1** material used to fill a hole, gap, etc. **2** the placing of buildings to occupy the space between existing ones. ● *v.tr.* fill in (a cavity, etc.).

in·fil·trate /infiltrayt/ *v.* **1** *tr.* **a** gain entrance or access to surreptitiously and by degrees (as spies, etc.). **b** cause to do this. **2** *tr.* permeate by filtration. **3** *tr.* (often foll. by *into, through*) introduce (fluid) by filtration. □□ **in·fil·tra·tion** /–tráyshən/ *n.* **in·fil·tra·tor** *n.* [IN-² + FILTRATE]

in·fi·nite /infinit/ *adj. & n.* ● *adj.* **1** boundless; endless. **2** very great. **3** (usu. with *pl.*) innumerable; very many (*infinite resources*). **4** *Math.* **a** greater than any assignable quantity or countable number. **b** (of a series) that may be continued indefinitely. **5** *Gram.* (of a verb part) not limited by person or number, e.g., infinitive, gerund, and participle. ● *n.* **1** (**the Infinite**) God. **2** (**the infinite**) infinite space. □□ **in·fi·nite·ly** *adv.* **in·fi·nite·ness** *n.* [ME f. L *infinitus* (as IN-¹, FINITE)]

in·fin·i·tes·i·mal /infinitésiməl/ *adj. & n.* ● *adj.* infinitely or very small. ● *n.* an infinitesimal amount. □□ **in·fin·i·tes·i·mal·ly** *adv.* [mod.L *infinitesimus* f. INFINITE: cf. CENTESIMAL]

▶Although it is commonly assumed to refer to large numbers, **infinitesimal** describes only very small size. While there may be an *infinite* number of grains of sand on the beach, a single grain may be said to be *infinitesimal*.

in·fin·i·tes·i·mal cal·cu·lus *n.* the differential and integral calculuses regarded as one subject.

in·fin·i·tive / infinitiv/ *n. & adj.* ● *n.* a form of a verb expressing the verbal notion without reference to a particular subject, tense, etc. (e.g., *see* in *we came to see* or *let him see*). ● *adj.* having this form. □□ **in·fin·i·ti·val** /–tívəl/ *adj.* **in·fin·i·ti·val·ly** /–tívəlee/ *adv.* [L *infinitivus* (as IN-¹, *finitivus* definite f. *finire finit-* define)]

GRAMMAR TIP infinitive

Should You Split an Infinitive? Splitting an infinitive means putting an adverb between *to* and the verb form itself. It has been condemned as ungrammatical for centuries, probably on the model of classical Latin, in which the infinitive is a single word and cannot be split. But distinguished writers and speakers of English have been splitting infinitives since the 14th century, and today it is considered not only permissible, but preferable for clarity in many situations. For example, it is better to say, "The company decided to immediately issue a recall of all products containing the faulty material" than to place the adverb *immediately* before the infinitive and cause confusion about what the company did and when.

---

in·fi·ni·tude /infinitoŏd, –tyoŏd/ *n.* **1** the state of being infinite; boundlessness. **2** (often foll. by *of*) a boundless number or extent. [L *infinitus*: see INFINITE, –TUDE]

in·fin·i·ty /infinitee/ *n.* (*pl.* **·ties**) **1** the state of being infinite. **2** an infinite number or extent. **3** infinite distance. **4** *Math.* infinite quantity. ¶ Symb.: ∞ [ME f. OF *infinité* or L *infinitas* (as INFINITE)]

in·firm /infórm/ *adj.* **1** physically weak, esp. through age. **2** (of a person, mind, judgment, etc.) weak; irresolute. □□ **in·fir·mi·ty** *n.* (*pl.* **·ties**). **in·firm·ly** *adv.* [ME f. L *infirmus* (as IN-¹, FIRM¹)]

in·fir·ma·ry /infórməree/ *n.* (*pl.* **·ries**) **1** a hospital. **2** a place for those who are ill in a monastery, school, etc. [med.L *infirmaria* (as IN-FIRM)]

in·fix *v. & n.* ● *v.tr.* /infiks/ **1** (often foll. by *in*) **a** fix (a thing in another). **b** impress (a fact, etc., in the mind). **2** *Gram.* insert (a formative element) into the body of a word. ● *n.* /infiks/ *Gram.* a formative element inserted in a word. □□ **in·fix·a·tion** *n.* [L *infigere infix-* (as IN-², FIX): (n.) after *prefix, suffix*]

in fla·gran·te de·lic·to /in fləgrántee dilíktō/ *adv.* in the very act of committing an offense. [L, = in blazing crime]

in·flame /infláym/ *v.* **1** *tr. & intr.* (often foll. by *with, by*) provoke or become provoked to strong feeling, esp. anger. **2** *Med.* **a** *intr.* become hot, reddened, and sore. **b** *tr.* (esp. as **inflamed**) cause inflammation or fever in (a body, etc.); make hot. **3** *tr.* aggravate. **4** *intr. & tr.* catch or set on fire. **5** *tr.* light up with or as if with flames. □□ **in·flam·er** *n.* [ME f. OF *enflammer* f. L *inflammare* (as IN-², *flamma* flame)]

in·flam·ma·ble /infláməbəl/ *adj. & n.* ● *adj.* **1** easily on fire; flammable. **2** easily excited. ● *n.* (usu. in *pl.*) a flammable substance. □□ **in·flam·ma·bil·i·ty** *n.* **in·flam·ma·ble·ness** *n.* **in·flam·ma·bly** *adv.* [INFLAME after F *inflammable*]

▶Both **inflammable** and **flammable** mean 'easily set on fire.' The opposite is **nonflammable**. Where there is a danger that **inflammable** could be understood to mean its opposite, i.e., 'not easily set on fire, ' **flammable** should be used to avoid confusion.

in·flam·ma·tion /ínfləmáyshən/ n. **1** the act or an instance of inflaming. **2** *Med.* a localized physical condition with heat, swelling, redness, and usu. pain, esp. as a reaction to injury or infection. [L *inflammatio* (as INFLAME)]

in·flam·ma·to·ry /ínflámətáwree/ adj. **1** (esp. of speeches, leaflets, etc.) tending to cause anger, etc. **2** of or tending to inflammation of the body.

in·flat·a·ble /infláytəbəl/ adj. & n. ● adj. that can be inflated. ● n. an inflatable plastic or rubber object.

in·flate /infláyt/ v.tr. **1** distend (a balloon, etc.) with air. **2** (usu. foll. by *with*; usu. in *passive*) puff up (a person with pride, etc.). **3 a** (often *absol.*) bring about inflation (of the currency). **b** raise (prices) artificially. **4** (as **inflated** adj.) (esp. of language, sentiments, etc.) bombastic. □□ **in·flat·ed·ly** adv. **in·flat·ed·ness** n. **in·flat·er** n. **in·fla·tor** n. [L *inflare inflat-* (as IN-², *flare* blow)]

in·fla·tion /infláyshən/ n. **1 a** the act or condition of inflating or being inflated. **b** an instance of this. **2** *Econ.* **a** a general increase in prices and fall in the purchasing value of money. **b** an increase in available currency regarded as causing this. □□ **in·fla·tion·ar·y** adj. **in·fla·tion·ism** n. **in·fla·tion·ist** n. & adj. [ME f. L *inflatio* (as INFLATE)]

in·flect /inflékt/ v. **1** tr. change the pitch of (the voice, a musical note, etc.). **2** *Gram.* **a** tr. change the form of (a word) to express tense, gender, number, mood, etc. **b** intr. (of a word, language, etc.) undergo such change. **3** tr. bend inward; curve. □□ **in·flec·tive** adj. [ME f. L *inflectere inflex-* (as IN-², *flectere* bend)]

in·flec·tion /inflékshən/ n. (also esp. *Brit.* **in·flex·ion**) **1 a** the act or condition of inflecting or being inflected. **b** an instance of this. **2** *Gram.* **a** the process or practice of inflecting words. **b** an inflected form of a word. **c** a suffix, etc., used to inflect, e.g., –*ed.* **3** a modulation of the voice. **4** *Geom.* a change of curvature from convex to concave at a particular point on a curve. □□ **in·flec·tion·al** adj. **in·flec·tion·al·ly** adv. **in·flec·tion·less** adj. [F *inflection* or L *inflexio* (as INFLECT)]

in·flex·i·ble /infléksibəl/ adj. **1** unbendable. **2** stiff; immovable; obstinate (*old and inflexible in his attitudes*). **3** unchangeable; inexorable. □□ **in·flex·i·bil·i·ty** n. **in·flex·i·bly** adv. [L *inflexibilis* as IN-¹, FLEXIBLE)]

in·flict /inflíkt/ v.tr. (usu. foll. by *on, upon*) **1** administer; deal (a stroke, wound, defeat, etc.). **2** (also *refl.*) often *joc.* impose (suffering, a penalty, oneself, one's company, etc.) on (*shall not inflict myself on you any longer*). □□ **in·flict·a·ble** adj. **in·flict·er** n. **in·flic·tor** n. [L *infligere inflict-* (as IN-², *fligere* strike)]

in·flic·tion /inflíkshən/ n. **1** the act or an instance of inflicting. **2** something inflicted, esp. a troublesome or boring experience. [LL *inflictio* (as INFLICT)]

in·flight /ínflīt/ attrib.adj. occurring or provided during an aircraft flight.

in·flo·res·cence /ínflərésəns/ n. **1** *Bot.* **a** the complete flower head of a plant including stems, stalks, bracts, and flowers. **b** the arrangement of this. **2** the process of flowering. [mod.L *inflorescentia* f. LL *inflorescere* (as IN-², FLORESCENCE)]

in·flow /ínflō/ n. **1** a flowing in. **2** something that flows in. □□ **in·flow·ing** n. & adj.

in·flu·ence /ínflooəns/ n. & v. ● n. **1 a** (usu. foll. by *on, upon*) the effect a person or thing has on another. **b** (usu. foll. by *over, with*) moral ascendancy or power. **c** a thing or person exercising such power (*is a good influence on them*). **2** *Astrol.* an ethereal fluid supposedly flowing from the stars and affecting character and destiny. **3** *Electr. archaic* = INDUCTION. ● v.tr. exert influence on; have an effect on. □ **under the influence** *colloq.* affected by alcoholic drink. □□ **in·flu·ence·a·ble** adj. **in·flu·enc·er** n.

Late Middle English: from Old French, or from medieval Latin *influentia* 'inflow', from Latin *influere*, from *in-* 'into' + *fluere* 'to flow'. The word originally had the general sense 'an influx, flowing matter', also specifically (in astrology) 'the flowing in of ethereal fluid (affecting human destiny)'. The sense 'imperceptible or indirect action exerted to cause changes' was established in Scholastic Latin by the 13th cent., but not recorded in English until the late 16th cent.

in·flu·ent /ínflooənt/ adj. & n. ● adj. flowing in. ● n. a tributary stream. [ME f. L (as INFLUENCE)]

in·flu·en·tial /ínfloo-énshəl/ adj. having a great influence or power (*influential in the financial world*). □□ **in·flu·en·tial·ly** adv. [med.L *influentia* INFLUENCE]

in·flu·en·za /ínfloo-énzə/ n. a highly contagious virus infection causing fever, severe aching, and catarrh, often occurring in epidemics. □□ **in·flu·en·zal** adj. [It. f. med.L *influentia* INFLUENCE]

in·flux /ínfluks/ n. **1** a continual stream of people or things (*an influx of complaints*). **2** (usu. foll. by *into*) a flowing in, esp. of a stream, etc. [F *influx* or LL *influxus* (as IN-², FLUX)]

in·fo /ínfō/ n. *colloq.* information. [abbr.]

in·fold var. of ENFOLD.

in·fo·mer·cial /ínfōmɔ́rshəl/ n. a television program promoting a commercial product.

in·form /infáwrm/ v. **1** tr. (usu. foll. by *of, about, on,* or *that, how* + clause) tell (*informed them of their rights; informed us that the train was late*). **2** intr. (usu. foll. by *against, on*) make an accusation. **3** tr. (usu. foll. by *with*) *literary* inspire or imbue (a person, heart, or thing) with a feeling, principle, quality, etc. **4** tr. impart its quality to; permeate. □□ **in·form·ant** n. [ME f. OF *enfo(u)rmer* f. L *informare* give shape to, fashion, describe (as IN-², *forma* form)]

in·for·mal /infáwrməl/ adj. **1** without ceremony or formality (*just an informal chat*). **2** (of language, clothing, etc.) everyday; normal. □□ **in·for·mal·i·ty** /–málitee/ n. (pl. **·ties**). **in·for·mal·ly** adv.

in·for·mat·ics /ínfərmátiks/ n.pl. (usu. treated as *sing.*) the science of processing data for storage and retrieval; information science. [transl. Russ. *informatika* (as INFORMATION, –ICS)]

in·for·ma·tion /ínfərmáyshən/ n. **1 a** something told; knowledge. **b** (usu. foll. by *on, about*) items of knowledge; news (*the latest information on the crisis*). **2** *Law* (usu. foll. by *against*) a charge or complaint lodged with a court or magistrate. **3 a** the act of informing or telling. **b** an instance of this. □□ **in·for·ma·tion·al** adj. **in·for·ma·tion·al·ly** adv. [ME f. OF f. L *informatio –onis* (as INFORM)]

in·for·ma·tion re·triev·al n. *Computing* the tracing and recovery of specific information from stored data.

in·for·ma·tion sci·ence n. the study of the processes for storing and retrieving information.

in·for·ma·tion su·per·high·way n. an extensive electronic network such as the Internet, used for the rapid transfer of information such as sound, video, and graphics in digital form.

in·for·ma·tion the·o·ry n. *Math.* the quantitative study of the transmission of information by signals, etc.

in·for·ma·tive /infáwrmətiv/ adj. (also **in·for·ma·to·ry** /infáwrmətáwree/) giving information; instructive. □□ **in·for·ma·tive·ly** adv. **in·for·ma·tive·ness** n. [med.L *informativus* (as INFORM)]

in·formed /infáwrmd/ adj. **1** knowing the facts; instructed (*his answers show that he is badly informed*). **2** educated; intelligent. □□ **in·form·ed·ly** /infáwrmidlee/ adv. **in·form·ed·ness** /infáwrmidnis/ n.

in·form·er /infáwrmər/ n. **1** a person who informs against another. **2** a person who informs or advises.

in·fo·tain·ment /ínfōtáynmənt/ n. **1** factual information presented in dramatized form on television. **2** a television program mixing news and entertainment.

in·fra /ínfrə/ adv. below, further on (in a book or writing). [L, = below]

infra- /ínfrə/ comb. form **1** below (opp. SUPRA-). **2** *Anat.* below or under a part of the body. [from or after L *infra* below, beneath]

in·frac·tion /infrákshən/ n. esp. *Law* a violation or infringement. □□ **in·fract** v.tr. **in·frac·tor** n. [L *infractio* (as INFRINGE)]

in·fra dig /ínfrə díg/ predic.adj. colloq. beneath one's dignity; unbecoming. [abbr. of L *infra dignitatem*]

in·fran·gi·ble /infránjibəl/ adj. **1** unbreakable. **2** inviolable. □□ **in·fran·gi·bil·i·ty** n. **in·fran·gi·ble·ness** n. **in·fran·gi·bly** adv. [obs.F *infrangible* or med.L *infrangibilis* (as IN-¹, FRANGIBLE)]

in·fra·red /ínfrəréd/ adj. **1** having a wavelength just greater than the red end of the visible light spectrum but less than that of radio waves. **2** of or using such radiation.

in·fra·son·ic /ínfrəsónik/ adj. of or relating to sound waves with a frequency below the lower limit of human audibility. □□ **in·fra·son·i·cal·ly** adv.

in·fra·sound /ínfrəsownd/ n. sound waves with frequencies below the lower limit of human audibility.

in·fra·struc·ture /ínfrəstrukchər/ n. **1 a** the basic structural foundations of a society or enterprise; a substructure or foundation. **b** roads, bridges, sewers, etc., regarded as a country's economic foundation. **2** permanent installations as a basis for military, etc., operations. [F (as INFRA-, STRUCTURE)]

in·fre·quent /infréekwənt/ adj. not frequent. □□ **in·fre·quen·cy** n. **in·fre·quent·ly** adv. [L *infrequens* (as IN-¹, FREQUENT)]

in·fringe /infrínj/ v. **1** tr. **a** act contrary to; violate (a law, an oath, etc.). **b** act in defiance of (another's rights, etc.). **2** intr. (usu. foll. by *on, upon*) encroach; trespass. □□ **in·fringe·ment** n. **in·fring·er** n. [L *infringere infract-* (as IN-², *frangere* break)]

in·fu·la /ínfyələ/ n. (pl. **in·fu·lae** /–lee/) *Eccl.* either of the two ribbons on a bishop's miter. [L, = woolen fillet worn by priest, etc.]

in·fun·dib·u·lar /ínfəndíbyələr/ adj. funnel-shaped. [L *infundibulum* funnel f. *infundere* pour in (as IN-², *fundere* pour)]

in·fu·ri·ate v. & adj. ● v.tr. /infyoóreeayt/ fill with fury; enrage. ● adj. /infyoóreeət/ literary excited to fury; frantic. □□ **in·fu·ri·at·ing** adj. **in·fu·ri·at·ing·ly** adv. **in·fu·ri·a·tion** /–áyshən/ n. [med.L *infuriare infuriat-* (as IN-², L *furia* FURY)]

in·fuse /infyoóz/ v. **1** tr. (usu. foll. by *with*) imbue; pervade (*anger infused with resentment*). **2** tr. steep (herbs, tea, etc.) in liquid to extract the content. **3** tr. (usu. foll. by *into*) instill (grace, spirit, life, etc.). **4** *intr.* undergo infusion (*let it infuse for five minutes*). **5** *tr.* (usu. foll. by *into*) pour (a thing). □□ **in·fus·a·ble** *adj.* **in·fus·er** *n.* **in·fu·sive** /–fyóosiv/ *adj.* [ME f. L *infundere infus-* (as IN-², *fundere* pour)]

in·fu·si·ble /infyóozibǝl/ *adj.* not able to be fused or melted. □□ **in·fu·si·bil·i·ty** /–bílitee/ *n.*

in·fu·sion /infyóozhǝn/ *n.* **1** a liquid obtained by infusing. **2** an infused element; an admixture. **3** *Med.* a slow injection of a substance into a vein or tissue. **4 a** the act of infusing. **b** an instance of this. [ME f. F *infusion* or L *infusio* (as INFUSE)]

in·fu·so·ri·al earth /infyoosáwreeǝl/ *n.* = KIESELGUHR. [mod.L *infusoria*, formerly a class of protozoa found in decaying animal or vegetable matter (as INFUSE)]

-ing¹ /ing/ *suffix* forming gerunds and nouns from verbs (or occas. from nouns), denoting: **1 a** the verbal action or its result (*asking*; *carving*; *fighting*; *learning*). **b** the verbal action as described or classified in some way (*tough going*). **2** material used for or associated with a process, etc. (*piping*; *washing*). **3** an occupation or event (*banking*; *wedding*). **4** a set or arrangement of (*coloring*; *feathering*). [OE *–ung*, *–ing* f. Gmc]

-ing² /ing/ *suffix* **1** forming the present participle of verbs (*asking*; *fighting*), often as adjectives (*charming*; *strapping*). **2** forming adjectives from nouns (*hulking*) and verbs (*balding*). [ME alt. of OE *–ende*, later *–inde*]

-ing³ /ing/ *suffix* forming nouns meaning 'one belonging to' or 'one having the quality of,' surviving esp. in names of coins and fractional parts (*farthing*; *gelding*; *riding*). [OE f. Gmc]

in·gath·er /ín-gáthǝr/ *v.tr.* gather in; assemble.

in·gath·er·ing /ín-gáthǝring/ *n.* the act or an instance of gathering in, esp. of a harvest.

in·gem·i·nate /injéminayt/ *v.tr. literary* repeat; reiterate. □ **ingeminate peace** constantly urge peace. [L *ingeminare ingeminat-* (as IN-², GEMINATE)]

in·gen·ious /inj éenyǝs/ *adj.* **1** clever at inventing, constructing, organizing, etc.; skillful; resourceful. **2** (of a machine, theory, etc.) cleverly contrived. □□ **in·gen·ious·ly** *adv.* **in·gen·ious·ness** *n.* [ME, = talented, f. F *ingénieux* or L *ingeniosus* f. *ingenium* cleverness: cf. ENGINE]

▶Ingenious and ingenuous are often confused. **Ingenious** means 'clever, skillful, or resourceful,' (*an ingenious device*), while **ingenuous** means 'artless' or 'frank,' (*charmed by the ingenuous honesty of the child*).

in·ge·nue /ánzhǝnoo/ *n.* (also **in·gé·nue**) **1** an innocent or unsophisticated young woman. **2** *Theatr.* **a** such a part in a play. **b** the actress who plays this part. [F, fem. of *ingénu* INGENUOUS]

in·ge·nu·i·ty /ínjinóoitee, –nyoo–/ *n.* skill in devising or contriving; ingeniousness. [L *ingenuitas ingenuousness* (as INGENUOUS): Engl. meaning by confusion of INGENIOUS with INGENUOUS]

in·gen·u·ous /injényǝǝs/ *adj.* **1** innocent; artless. **2** open; frank. □□ **in·gen·u·ous·ly** *adv.* **in·gen·u·ous·ness** *n.* [L *ingenuus* free-born, frank (as IN-², root of *gignere* beget)]

in·gest /injést/ *v.tr.* **1** take in (food, etc.); eat. **2** absorb (facts, knowledge, etc.). □□ **in·ges·tion** /injés-chǝn/ *n.* **in·ges·tive** *adj.* [L *ingerere ingest-* (as IN-², *gerere* carry)]

in·gle·nook /ínggǝlnook/ *n.* a space within the opening on either side of a large fireplace; chimney corner. [dial. (orig. Sc.) *ingle* fire burning on a hearth, perh. f. Gael. *aingeal* fire, light + NOOK]

in·glo·ri·ous /in-gláwreeǝs/ *adj.* **1** shameful; ignominious. **2** not famous. □□ **in·glo·ri·ous·ly** *adv.* **in·glo·ri·ous·ness** *n.*

-ingly /inglee/ *suffix* forming adverbs esp. denoting manner of action or nature or condition (*dotingly*; *charmingly*; *slantingly*).

in·go·ing /ín-góing/ *adj.* **1** going in; entering. **2** penetrating; thorough.

in·got /ínggǝt/ *n.* a usu. oblong piece of cast metal, esp. of gold, silver, or steel.

in·graft var. of ENGRAFT.

in·grain *adj. & v.* ● *adj.* /ín-grayn/ **1** inherent; ingrained. **2** (of textiles) dyed in the fiber, before being woven. ● *v.tr.* /in-gráyn/ cause (a dye) to sink deeply into the texture of a fabric; cause to become embedded.

in·grain car·pet *n.* a reversible carpet in which the pattern appears on both sides.

in·grained /ín-gráynd/ *attrib. adj.* ingrate1 deeply rooted; inveterate. **2** thorough. **3** (of dirt, etc.) deeply embedded. □□ **in·grain·ed·ly** /–gráynidlee/ *adv.* [var. of *engrained*: see ENGRAIN]

in·grate /in-grayt/ *n. & adj. formal or literary* ● *n.* an ungrateful person. ● *adj.* ungrateful. [ME f. L *ingratus* (as IN-¹, *gratus* grateful)]

in·gra·ti·ate /in-gráysheeayt/ *v.refl.* (usu. foll. by *with*) bring oneself into favor. □□ **in·gra·ti·at·ing** *adj.* **in·gra·ti·at·ing·ly** *adv.* **in·gra·ti·a·tion** /–áyshǝn/ *n.* [L in *gratiam* into favor]

in·grat·i·tude /in-grátitood, –tyood/ *n.* a lack of due gratitude. [ME f. OF *ingratitude* or LL *ingratitudo* (as INGRATE)]

in·gra·ves·cent /in-grǝvésǝnt/ *adj. Med.* (of a disease, etc.) growing worse. □□ **in·gra·ves·cence** /–sǝns/ *n.* [L *ingravescere* (as IN-², *gravescere* grow heavy f. *gravis* heavy)]

in·gre·di·ent /in-gréedeeǝnt/ *n.* a component part or element in a recipe, mixture, or combination. [ME f. L *ingredi ingress-* enter (as IN-², *gradi* step)]

in·gress /ín-gres/ *n.* **1 a** the act or right of going in or entering. **b** an entrance. **2** *Astron.* the start of an eclipse or transit. □□ **in·gres·sion** /–greshǝn/ *n.* [ME f. L *ingressus* (as INGREDIENT)]

in·group /ín-groop/ *n.* a small exclusive group of people with a common interest.

in·grow·ing /in-gróing/ *adj.* growing inward, esp. (of a toenail) growing into the flesh. □□ **in·grown** *adj.* **in·growth** *n.*

in·gui·nal /ínggwinǝl/ *adj.* of the groin. □□ **in·gui·nal·ly** *adv.* [L *inguinalis* f. *inguen –inis* groin]

in·gulf var. of ENGULF.

in·gur·gi·tate /in-górjitayt/ *v.tr.* **1** swallow greedily. **2** engulf. □□ **in·gur·gi·ta·tion** /–táyshǝn/ *n.* [L *ingurgitare ingurgitat-* (as IN-², *gurges gurgitis* whirlpool)]

in·hab·it /inhábit/ *v.tr.* (of a person or animal) dwell in; occupy (a region, town, house, etc.). □□ **in·hab·it·a·bil·i·ty** /–tǝbílitee/ *n.* **in·hab·it·a·ble** *adj.* **in·hab·it·ant** *n.* **in·hab·i·ta·tion** /–táyshǝn/ *n.* [ME *inhabite, enhabite* f. OF *enhabiter* or L *inhabitare* (as IN-², *habitare* dwell): see HABIT]

in·hab·it·an·cy /inhábit'nsee/ *n.* (also **in·hab·it·ance** /–it'ns/) residence as an inhabitant, esp. during a specified period so as to acquire rights, etc.

in·hal·ant /inháylǝnt/ *n.* a medicinal preparation for inhaling.

in·hale /inháyl/ *v.tr.* (often *absol.*) breathe in (air, gas, tobacco smoke, etc.). □□ **in·ha·la·tion** /–hǝláyshǝn/ *n.* [L *inhalare* breathe in (as IN-², *halare* breathe)]

in·hal·er /inháylǝr/ *n.* a portable device used for relieving esp. asthma by inhaling.

in·har·mon·ic /inhaarmónik/ *adj.* esp. *Mus.* not harmonic.

in·har·mo·ni·ous /inhaarmóneeǝs/ *adj.* esp. *Mus.* not harmonious. □□ **in·har·mo·ni·ous·ly** *adv.*

in·here /inheér/ *v.intr.* (often foll. by *in*) **1** exist essentially or permanently in (*goodness inheres in that child*). **2** (of rights, etc.) be vested in (a person, etc.). [L *inhaerēre inhaes-* (as IN-², *haerēre* to stick)]

in·her·ent /inheérǝnt, inhér–/ *adj.* (often foll. by *in*) **1** existing in something, esp. as a permanent or characteristic attribute. **2** vested in (a person, etc.) as a right or privilege. □□ **in·her·ence** /–rǝns/ *n.* **in·her·ent·ly** *adv.* [L *inhaerēre inhaerent-* (as INHERE)]

SYNONYM TIP inherent

CONGENITAL, ESSENTIAL, INBORN, INGRAINED, INNATE, INTRINSIC. A quality that is **inherent** is a permanent part of a person's nature or essence (*an inherent tendency to fight back*). If it is **ingrained**, it is deeply wrought into his/her substance or character (*ingrained prejudice against women*). **Inborn** and **innate** are nearly synonymous, sharing the basic sense of existing at the time of birth, but *innate* is usually preferred in an abstract or philosophical context (*innate defects, innate ideas*), while *inborn* is reserved for human characteristics that are so deep-seated they seem to have been there from birth (*an inborn aptitude for the piano*). **Congenital** also means from the time of one's birth, but it is primarily used in medical contexts (*congenital color-blindness*) and refers to problems or defects (*a congenital tendency toward schizophrenia*). **Intrinsic** and **essential** are broader terms that can apply to things as well as people. Something that is *essential* is part of the essence or constitution of something (*an essential ingredient, essential revisions in the text*), while *intrinsic* suggests an irreducible minimum, without regard to less *essential* considerations or properties (*her intrinsic fairness, an intrinsic weakness in the design*).

in·her·it /inhérit/ *v.* **1** *tr.* receive (property, rank, title, etc.) by legal descent or succession. **2** *tr.* derive (a quality or characteristic) genetically from one's ancestors. **3** *absol.* succeed as an heir (*a younger son rarely inherits*). □□ **in·her·i·tor** *n.* (fem. **in·her·i·tress** or **in·her·i·trix**). [ME f. OF *enheriter* f. LL *inhereditare* (as IN-², L *heres heredis* heir)]

in·her·it·a·ble /inhéritǝbǝl/ *adj.* **1** capable of being inherited. **2** capable of inheriting. □□ **in·her·it·a·bil·i·ty** /–bílitee/ *n.* [ME f. AF (as INHERIT)]

in·her·it·ance /inhérit'ns/ *n.* **1** something that is inherited. **2 a** the act of inheriting. **b** an instance of this. [ME f. AF *inheritaunce* f. OF *enheriter*: see INHERIT]

in·her·it·ance tax *n.* a tax levied on property, etc., acquired by gift or inheritance.

in·he·sion /inheézhǝn/ *n. formal* the act or fact of inhering. [LL *inhaesio* (as INHERE)]

in·hib·it /inhíbit/ *v.tr.* **1** hinder, restrain, or prevent (an action or progress). **2** (as **inhibited** *adj.*) subject to inhibition. **3 a** (usu. foll. by *from* + verbal noun) forbid or prohibit (a person, etc.). **b** (esp. in ecclesiastical law) forbid (an ecclesiastic) to exercise clerical functions. □□ **in·hib·i·tive** *adj.* **in·hib·i·tor** *n.* **in·hib·i·to·ry** *adj.* [L *inhibēre* (as IN-², *habēre* hold)]

in·hi·bi·tion /inhibíshǝn/ *n.* **1** *Psychol.* a restraint on the direct expression of an instinct. **2** *colloq.* an emotional resistance to a thought, an action, etc. (*has inhibitions about singing in public*). **3** *Law* an order forbidding alteration to property rights. **4 a** the act of inhibiting. **b** the process of being inhibited. [ME f. OF *inhibition* or L *inhibitio* (as INHIBIT)]

in·ho·mo·ge·ne·ous /ínhómǝjéeneeǝs, inhómǝ–/ *adj.* not homogeneous. □□ **in·ho·mo·ge·ne·i·ty** /–jinée-itee/ *n.*

in·hos·pi·ta·ble /ínhospítǝbǝl, inhóspi–/ *adj.* **1** not hospitable. **2** (of a region, coast, etc.) not affording shelter, etc. □□ **in·hos·pi·ta·ble·ness** *n.* **in·hos·pi·ta·bly** *adv.* [obs. F (as IN-¹, HOSPITABLE)]

in·hos·pi·tal·i·ty /inhóspitálitee/ *n.* the act or process of being inhospitable. [L *inhospitalitas* (as IN-¹, HOSPITALITY)]

in-house *adj. & adv.* ● *adj.* /ínhóws/ done or existing within an institution, company, etc. (*an in-house project*). ● *adv.* /inhóws/ internally, without outside assistance.

in·hu·man /inhyōōmǝn/ *adj.* **1** (of a person, conduct, etc.) brutal; unfeeling; barbarous. **2** not of a human type. □□ **in·hu·man·ly** *adv.* [L *inhumanus* (as IN-¹, HUMAN)]

in·hu·mane /ínhyōōmáyn/ *adj.* not humane. □□ **in·hu·mane·ly** *adv.* [L *inhumanus* (see INHUMAN) & f. IN-¹ + HUMANE, orig. = INHUMAN]

in·hu·man·i·ty /ínhyōōmánitee/ *n.* (*pl.* **·ties**) **1** brutality; barbarousness; callousness. **2** an inhumane act.

in·hume /inhyōōm/ *v.tr. literary* bury. □□ **in·hu·ma·tion** *n.* [L *inhumare* (as IN-², *humus* ground)]

in·im·i·cal /inímikǝl/ *adj.* (usu. foll. by *to*) **1** hostile. **2** harmful. □□ **in·im·i·cal·ly** *adv.* [LL *inimicalis* f. L *inimicus* (as IN-¹, *amicus* friend)]

in·im·i·ta·ble /inímitǝbǝl/ *adj.* impossible to imitate. □□ **in·im·i·ta·bil·i·ty** *n.* **in·im·i·ta·ble·ness** *n.* **in·im·i·ta·bly** *adv.* [F *inimitable* or L *inimitabilis* (as IN-¹, *imitabilis* imitable)]

in·iq·ui·ty /iníkwitee/ *n.* (*pl.* **·ties**) **1** wickedness; unrighteousness. **2** a gross injustice. □□ **in·iq·ui·tous** *adj.* **in·iq·ui·tous·ly** *adv.* **in·iq·ui·tous·ness** *n.* [ME f. OF *iniquité* f. L *iniquitas –tatis* f. *iniquus* (as IN-¹, *aequus* just)]

in·i·tial /iníshǝl/ *adj., n., & v.* ● *adj.* of, existing, or occurring at the beginning (*initial stage; initial expenses*). ● *n.* **1** = INITIAL LETTER. **2** (usu. in *pl.*) the first letter or letters of the words of a (esp. a person's) name or names. ● *v.tr.* (**in·i·tialed, in·i·tial·ing**; esp. *Brit.* **in·i·tialled, in·i·tial·ling**) mark or sign with one's initials. □□ **in·i·tial·ly** *adv.* [L *initialis* f. *initium* beginning f. *inire init-* go in]

in·i·tial·ism /iníshǝlizǝm/ *n.* a group of initial letters used as an abbreviation for a name or expression, each letter being pronounced separately (e.g., *CIA*) or the group of letters being pronounced as a word (e.g., *NATO*) (cf. ACRONYM).

in·i·tial·ize /iníshǝliz/ *v.tr. Computing* set to the value or put in the condition appropriate to the start of an operation. □□ **in·i·tial·i·za·tion** *n.*

in·i·tial let·ter *n.* the letter at the beginning of a word.

in·i·tial teach·ing al·pha·bet *n.* a 44-letter phonetic alphabet used to help those beginning to read and write English.

in·i·ti·ate *v., n., & adj.* ● *v.tr.* /inísheeayt/ **1** begin; set going; originate. **2 a** (usu. foll. by *into*) admit (a person) into a society, an office, a secret, etc., esp. with a ritual. **b** (usu. foll. by *in, into*) instruct (a person) in science, art, etc. ● *n.* /inísheeǝt/ a person who has been newly initiated. ● *adj.* /inísheeǝt/ (of a person) newly initiated (*an initiate member*). □□ **in·i·ti·a·tion** /–sheeáyshǝn/ *n.* **in·i·ti·a·tor** *n.* **in·i·ti·a·to·ry** /inísheeǝtáwree/ *adj.* [L *initiare* f. *initium*: see INITIAL]

in·i·ti·a·tive /iníshǝtiv, inísheeǝtiv/ *n. & adj.* ● *n.* **1** the ability to initiate things; enterprise (*I'm afraid he lacks all initiative*). **2** a first step; origination (*a peace initiative*). **3** the power or right to begin something. **4** *Polit.* (esp. in Switzerland and some US states) the right of citizens outside the legislature to originate legislation. ● *adj.* beginning; originating. □ **have the initiative** esp. *Mil.* be able to control the enemy's movements. **on one's own initiative** without being prompted by others. **take the initiative** (usu. foll. by *in* + verbal noun) be the first to take action. [F (as INITIATE)]

in·ject /injékt/ *v.tr. Med.* **1** (usu. foll. by *into*) drive or force (a solution, medicine, etc.) by or as if by a syringe. **b** (usu. foll. by *with*) fill (a cavity, etc.) by injecting. **c** administer medicine, etc., to (a person) by injection. **2** place or insert (an object, a quality, etc.) into something (*may I inject a note of realism?*). □□ **in·ject·a·ble** *adj. & n.* **in·jec·tor** *n.* [L *injicere* (as IN-², *jacere* throw)]

in·jec·tion /injékshǝn/ *n.* **1 a** the act of injecting. **b** an instance of this. **2** a liquid or solution (to be) injected (*prepare a morphine injection*). [F *injection* or L *injectio* (as INJECT)]

in·jec·tion mold·ing *n.* the shaping of rubber or plastic articles by injecting heated material into a mold.

in·ju·di·cious /ínjōōdíshǝs/ *adj.* unwise; ill-judged. □□ **in·ju·di·cious·ly** *adv.* **in·ju·di·cious·ness** *n.*

In·jun /ínjǝn/ *n. offens.* a Native American. [alteration of INDIAN]

in·junc·tion /injúnkshǝn/ *n.* **1** an authoritative warning or order. **2** *Law* a judicial order restraining a person from an act or compelling redress to an injured party. □□ **in·junc·tive** *adj.* [LL *injunctio* f. L *injungere* ENJOIN]

in·jure /ínjǝr/ *v.tr.* **1** do physical harm or damage to; hurt (*was injured in a road accident*). **2** harm or impair (*illness might injure her chances*). **3** do wrong to. □□ **in·jur·er** *n.* [back-form. f. INJURY]

in·jured /ínjǝrd/ *adj.* **1** harmed or hurt (*the injured passengers*). **2** offended; wronged (*in an injured tone*).

in·ju·ri·ous /injóoreeǝs/ *adj.* **1** hurtful. **2** (of language) insulting; libelous. **3** wrongful. □□ **in·ju·ri·ous·ly** *adv.* **in·ju·ri·ous·ness** *n.* [ME f. F *injurieux* or L *injuriosus* (as INJURY)]

in·ju·ry /ínjǝree/ *n.* (*pl.* **·ries**) **1 a** physical harm or damage. **b** an instance of this (*suffered head injuries*). **2** esp. *Law* **a** wrongful action or treatment. **b** an instance of this. **3** damage to one's good name, etc. [ME f. AF *injurie* f. L *injuria* a wrong (as IN-¹, *jus juris* right)]

in·jus·tice /injústis/ *n.* **1** a lack of fairness or justice. **2** an unjust act. □ **do a person an injustice** judge a person unfairly. [ME f. OF f. L *injustitia* (as IN-¹, JUSTICE)]

ink /ingk/ *n. & v.* ● *n.* **1 a** a colored fluid used for writing with a pen, marking with a rubber stamp, etc. **b** a thick paste used in printing, duplicating, in ballpoint pens, etc. **2** *Zool.* a black liquid ejected by a cuttlefish, octopus, etc., to confuse a predator. ● *v.tr.* **1** (usu. foll. by *in, over*, etc.) mark with ink. **2** cover (type, etc.) with ink before printing. **3** apply ink to. **4** (as **inked** *adj.*)*Austral. sl.* drunk. □ **ink out** obliterate with ink. □□ **ink·er** *n.* [ME *enke, inke* f. OF *enque* f. LL *encau(s)tum* f. Gk *egkauston* purple ink used by Roman emperors for signature (as EN-², CAUSTIC)]

ink·blot /ingkblot/ *n.* a spot or patten created by blotted ink. □ **ink·blot test** a psychological test, esp. the Rorschach test, in which subjects must interpret inkblots.

ink·horn /ingkhawrn/ *n. & adj.* ● *n.* a small, portable container for ink, orig. of horn. ● *adj.* pretentiously learned.

ink-jet print·er *n.* a computer-controlled printer in which the characters are formed by minute droplets of ink projected onto the paper.

ink·ling /ingkling/ *n.* (often foll. by *of*) a slight knowledge or suspicion; a hint. [ME *inkle* utter in an undertone, of unkn. orig.]

ink pad *n.* an ink-soaked pad, usu. in a box, used for inking a rubber stamp, etc.

ink·stand /ingkstand/ *n.* a stand for one or more ink bottles, often incorporating a pen tray, etc.

ink·well /ingkwel/ *n.* a pot for ink usu. housed in a hole in a desk.

ink·y /íngkee/ *adj.* (**ink·i·er, ink·i·est**) of, as black as, or stained with ink. □□ **ink·i·ness** *n.*

in·laid *past and past part.* of INLAY.

in·land /ínlǝnd, ínland/ *adj., n., & adv.* ● *adj.* **1** situated in the interior of a country. **2** esp. *Brit.* carried on within the limits of a country; domestic (*inland trade*). ● *n.* the parts of a country remote from the sea or frontiers; the interior. ● *adv.* in or toward the interior of a country. □□ **in·land·er** *n.* **in·land·ish** *adj.*

in·land du·ty *n.* (in the UK) a tax payable on inland trade.

in·land navi·ga·tion *n.* communication by canals and rivers.

In·land Rev·e·nue *n.* (in the UK) the government department responsible for assessing and collecting income taxes, etc.

in·land rev·e·nue *n. Brit.* public revenue consisting of income tax and other direct taxes.

in-law /ínlaw/ *n.* (often in *pl.*) a relative by marriage.

in·lay *v. & n.* ● *v.tr.* /inláy/ (*past* and *past part.* **in·laid** /ínláyd/) **1 a** (usu. foll. by *in*) embed (a thing in another) so that the surfaces are even. **b** (usu. foll. by *with*) ornament (a thing with inlaid work). **2** (as **inlaid** *adj.*) (of a piece of furniture, etc.) ornamented by inlaying. **3** insert (a page, an illustration, etc.) in a space cut in a larger thicker page. ● *n.* /ínlay/ **1** inlaid work. **2** material inlaid. **3** a filling shaped to fit a tooth cavity. □□ **in·lay·er** *n.* [IN-² + LAY¹]

in·let /ínlet, –lit/ *n.* **1** a small arm of the sea, a lake, or a river. **2** a piece inserted, esp. in dressmaking, etc. **3** a way of entry. [ME f. IN + LET¹ *v.*]

in·li·er /ínliǝr/ *n. Geol.* a structure or area of older rocks completely surrounded by newer rocks. [IN, after *outlier*]

in-line /ínlín/ *adj.* **1** having parts arranged in a line. **2** constituting an integral part of a continuous sequence of operations or machines.

in-line skate *n.* a roller skate in which usu. four hard rubber wheels are fixed in a single line along its sole.

in lo·co pa·ren·tis /in lókō pǝréntis/ *adv.* in the place or position of a parent (used of a teacher, etc., responsible for children). [L]

in·ly /ínlee/ *adv. poet.* **1** inwardly; in the heart. **2** intimately; thoroughly. [OE *innlíce* (as IN, –LY²)]

in·mate /ínmayt/ *n.* (usu. foll. by *of*) **1** an occupant of a hospital, prison, institution, etc. **2** an occupant of a house, etc., esp. one of several. [prob. orig. INN + MATE¹, assoc. with IN]

inline skate

in me·di·as res /in meédias ráys/ *adv.* **1** into the midst of things. **2** into the middle of a story, without preamble. [L]

in me·mo·ri·am /in mimáwreeǝm/ *prep. & n.* ● *prep.* in memory of (a dead person). • *n.* a written article or notice, etc., in memory of a dead person; an obituary. [L]

in•most /ínmōst/ *adj.* **1** most inward. **2** most intimate; deepest. [OE *innemest* (as IN, −MOST)]

inn /in/ *n.* **1** an establishment providing accommodations, food, and drink, expecially for travelers. **2** a restaurant or bar, typically one in the country, often with accommodations.

WORD HISTORY inn

Old English (in the sense 'dwelling place, lodging'): of Germanic origin; related to IN. In Middle English the word was used to translate Latin *hospitium* (see HOSPICE), denoting a house of residence for students: this sense is preserved in the names of some British buildings formerly used for this purpose, notably *Gray's Inn* and *Lincoln's Inn*, two buildings in the area of London where many law offices are found. The current sense dates from late Middle English.

---

in•nards /ínardz/ *n.pl. colloq.* **1** entrails. **2** works (of an engine, etc.). [dial. pronunc. of *inwards*, used as a noun]

in•nate /ináyt, ínayt/ *adj.* **1** inborn; natural. **2** *Philos.* originating in the mind. □□ **in•nate•ly** *adv.* **in•nate•ness** *n.* [ME f. L *innatus* (as IN-², *natus* past part. of *nasci* be born)]

in•ner /ínər/ *adj. & n.* • *adj.* (usu. *attrib.*) **1** further in; inside; interior (*the inner compartment*). **2** (of thoughts, feelings, etc.) deeper; more secret. • *n. Archery* esp. *Brit.* **1** a division of the target next to the bull's-eye. **2** a shot that strikes this. □□ **in•ner•ly** *adv.* **in•ner•most** *adj.* **in•ner•ness** *n.* [OE *innera* (adj.), compar. of IN]

in•ner child *n.* a person's supposed original or true self, esp. when regarded as damaged or concealed by negative childhood experiences.

in•ner cir•cle *n.* an intimate, usu. influential small group of people.

in•ner cit•y *n.* the central most densely populated area of a city, esp. when associated with social and economic problems. □□ **inner-city** *adj.*

in•ner-di•rect•ed *adj. Psychol.* governed by standards formed in childhood.

in•ner man *n.* (also **in•ner wom•an** or **in•ner per•son**) **1** the soul or mind. **2** *joc.* the stomach.

in•ner plan•et *n.* any of the four planets closest to the sun (i.e., Mercury, Venus, Earth, and Mars) (cf. OUTER PLANET).

in•ner space *n.* **1** the region between the earth and outer space, or below the surface of the sea. **2** the part of the mind not normally accessible to consciousness.

in•ner•spring /ínərspring/ *adj.* (of a mattress, etc.) with internal springs.

In•ner Tem•ple *n.* one of the two Inns of Court on the site of the Temple in London.

in•ner tube *n.* **1** a separate inflatable tube inside the cover of a pneumatic tire. **2** such a tube inflated and used for sitting in and floating in water.

in•ner•vate /ínərvayt, inór−/ *v.tr.* supply (an organ, etc.) with nerves. □□ **in•ner•va•tion** /−váyshən/ *n.* [IN-² + L *nervus* nerve + −ATE³]

in•ning /íning/ *n.* **1** *Baseball* **a** a division of a game in which the two teams alternate as offense and defense and during which each team is allowed three outs. **b** a single turn at bat for a team until they make three outs. **2** a similar division of play in other games, as horseshoes. **3** a period during which a person, group, etc., can achieve something. [*in* (v.) go in (f. IN)]

in•nings /íningz/ *n.* (*pl.* same; *Brit.* **in•nings•es**) **1** *Cricket* **a** the part of a game during which a side is in or batting. **b** the play of or score achieved by a player during a turn at batting. **2** a period during which a government, party, cause, etc. is in office or effective. **3 a** = INNING 2. **b** *colloq.* a person's life span (*had her innings and died at 94*).

inn•keep•er /ínkeepər/ *n.* a person who keeps an inn.

in•no•cent /ínəsənt/ *adj. & n.* • *adj.* **1** free from moral wrong; sinless. **2** (usu. foll. by *of*) not guilty (of a crime, etc.). **3 a** simple; guileless; naive. **b** pretending to be guileless. **4** harmless. **5** (foll. by *of*) *colloq.* without; lacking (*appeared, innocent of shoes*). • *n.* **1** an innocent person, esp. a young child. **2** (in *pl.*) the young children killed by Herod after the birth of Jesus (Matt. 2:16). □□ **in•no•cence** /−səns/ *n.* **in•no•cen•cy** *n.* **in•no•cent•ly** *adv.* [ME f. OF *innocent* or L *innocens innocent*- (as IN-¹, *nocēre* hurt)]

▶**Innocent** properly means 'harmless' but has long been extended in general language to mean 'not guilty.' The jury (or judge) in a criminal trial does not, strictly speaking, find a defendant 'innocent.' Rather, a defendant may be *guilty* or *not guilty* of the charges brought. In common use, however, owing perhaps to the concept of the *presumption of innocence*, which instructs a jury to consider a defendant free of wrongdoing until proven guilty on the basis of evidence, 'not guilty' and 'innocent' have come to be thought of as synonymous.

In•no•cents' Day *n.* (also **Ho•ly In•no•cents' Day**) a Christian festival commemorating the massacre of the children of Bethlehem by Herod, Dec. 28.

in•noc•u•ous /inókyōōs/ *adj.* **1** not injurious; harmless. **2** inoffensive. □□ **in•no•cu•i•ty** /ínəkyōō-itee/ *n.* **in•noc•u•ous•ly** *adv.* **in•noc•u•ous•ness** *n.* [L *innocuus* (as IN-¹, *nocuus* formed as INNOCENT)]

in•no•mi•nate /inóminət/ *adj.* unnamed. □ **innominate bone** *n. Anat.* the bone formed from the fusion of the ilium, ischium, and pubis; the hipbone. [LL *innominatus* (as IN-¹, NOMINATE)]

in•no•vate /ínəvayt/ *v.intr.* **1** bring in new methods, ideas, etc. **2** (often foll. by *in*) make changes. □□ **in•no•va•tion** /−váyshən/ *n.* **in•no•va•tion•al** /−váyshənəl/ *adj.* **in•no•va•tor** *n.* **in•no•va•tive** *adj.* **in•no•va•tive•ness** *n.* **in•no•va•to•ry** /−vóytáwree/ *adj.* [L *innovare* make new, alter (as IN-², *novus* new)]

in•nox•ious /inókshəs/ *adj.* harmless. □□ **in•nox•ious•ly** *adv.* **in•nox•ious•ness** *n.* [L *innoxius* (as IN-¹, NOXIOUS)]

Inns of Court *n.pl. Brit. Law* **1** the four legal societies having the exclusive right of admitting people to the English bar. **2** any of the sets of buildings in London belonging to these societies. **3** a similar society in Ireland.

in•nu•en•do /ínyōō-éndō/ *n. & v.* • *n.* (*pl.* **•dos** or **•does**) **1** an allusive or oblique remark or hint, usu. disparaging. **2** a remark with a double meaning, usu. suggestive. • *v.intr.* (**•does**, **•doed**) make innuendos. [L, = by nodding at, by pointing to: ablat. gerund of *innuere* nod at (as IN-², *nuere* nod)]

In•nu•it var. of INUIT.

in•nu•mer•a•ble /inōōmərəbəl, inyōō−/ *adj.* too many to be counted. □□ **in•nu•mer•a•bil•i•ty** /−bílitee/ *n.* **in•nu•mer•a•bly** *adv.* [ME f. L *innumerabilis* (as IN-¹, NUMERABLE)]

in•nu•mer•ate /inōōmərət, inyōō−/ *adj.* having no knowledge of or feeling for mathematical operations; not numerate. □□ **in•nu•mer•a•cy** /−rəsee/ *n.* [IN-¹, NUMERATE]

in•nu•tri•tion /ínōōtríshən, −yōō−/ *n.* lack of nutrition. □□ **in•nu•tri•tious** *adj.*

in•ob•serv•ance /ínəbzórvəns/ *n.* **1** inattention. **2** (usu. foll. by *of*) nonobservance (of a law, etc.). [F *inobservance* or L *inobservantia* (as IN-¹, OBSERVANCE)]

in•oc•u•late /inókyəlayt/ *v.tr.* **1 a** treat (a person or animal) with a small quantity of the agent of a disease, in the form of vaccine or serum, usu. by injection, to promote immunity against the disease. **b** implant (a disease) by means of vaccine. **2** instill (a person) with ideas or opinions. □□ **in•oc•u•la•ble** *adj.* **in•oc•u•la•tion** /−láyshən/ *n.* **in•oc•u•la•tive** *adj.* **in•oc•u•la•tor** *n.* [orig. in sense 'insert (a bud) into a plant': L *inoculare inoculat*- engraft (as IN-², *oculus* eye, bud)]

SPELLING TIP inoculate

Inoculate means *inject.* Both words are spelled with only one *n.*

---

in•oc•u•lum /inókyələm/ *n.* (*pl.* **in•oc•u•la** /−lə/) any substance used for inoculation. [mod.L (as INOCULATE)]

in•o•dor•ous /inódərəs/ *adj.* having no smell; odorless.

in•of•fen•sive /ínəfénsiv/ *adj.* not objectionable; harmless. □□ **in•of•fen•sive•ly** *adv.* **in•of•fen•sive•ness** *n.*

in•op•er•a•ble /inópərəbəl/ *adj.* **1** *Surgery* that cannot suitably be operated on (*inoperable cancer*). **2** that cannot be operated; inoperative. □□ **in•op•er•a•bil•i•ty** *n.* **in•op•er•a•bly** *adv.* [F *inopérable* (as IN-¹, OPERABLE)]

in•op•er•a•tive /inópərətiv/ *adj.* not working or taking effect.

in•op•por•tune /inópərtōōn, −tyōōn/ *adj.* not appropriate, esp. as regards time; unseasonable. □□ **in•op•por•tune•ly** *adv.* **in•op•por•tune•ness** *n.* [L *inopportunus* (as IN-¹, OPPORTUNE)]

in•or•di•nate /ináwrd'nət/ *adj.* **1** immoderate; excessive. **2** intemperate. **3** disorderly. □□ **in•or•di•nate•ly** *adv.* [ME f. L *inordinatus* (as IN-¹, *ordinatus* past part. of *ordinare* ORDAIN)]

in•or•gan•ic /ínawrgánik/ *adj.* **1** *Chem.* (of a compound) not organic, usu. of mineral origin (opp. ORGANIC). **2** without organized physical structure. **3** not arising by natural growth; extraneous. **4** *Philol.* not explainable by normal etymology. □□ **in•or•gan•i•cal•ly** *adv.*

in•or•gan•ic chem•is•try *n.* the chemistry of inorganic compounds.

in•os•cu•late /inóskyəlayt/ *v.intr. & tr.* **1** join by running together. **2** join closely. □□ **in•os•cu•la•tion** /−láyshən/ *n.* [IN-² + L *osculare* provide with a mouth f. *osculum* dimin. of *os* mouth]

in•pa•tient /ínpayshənt/ *n.* a patient who stays in the hospital while under treatment.

in pro•pri•a per•so•na /in própreeə pərsónə/ *adv.* in his or her own person. [L]

in•put /ínpŏŏt/ *n. & v.* • *n.* **1** what is put in or taken in, or operated on by any process or system. **2** *Electronics* **a** a place where, or a device through which, energy, information, etc., enters a system (*a tape recorder with inputs for microphone and radio*). **b** energy supplied to a device or system; an electrical signal. **3** the information fed into a computer. **4** the action or process of putting in or feeding in. **5** a contribution of information, etc. • *v.tr.* (**in•put•ting;** *past and past part.* **in•put** or **in•put•ted**) (often foll. by *into*) **1** put in. **2** *Computing* supply (data, programs, etc., to a computer, program, etc.). □ **in•put-out•put** (or **in•put/out•put**) *Computing*, etc. of, relating to, or for input and output. □□ **in•put•ter** *n.*

in·quest /ínkwest, íng–/ n. **1** Law **a** an inquiry by a coroner's court into the cause of a death. **b** a judicial inquiry to ascertain the facts relating to an incident, etc. **c** a coroner's jury. **2** colloq. a discussion analyzing the outcome of a game, an election, etc. [ME f. OF enqueste (as INQUIRE)]

in·qui·e·tude /inkwí-itōod, –tyōod/ n. uneasiness of mind or body. [ME f. OF inquietude or LL inquietudo f. L inquietus (as IN-¹, quietus quiet)]

in·qui·line /ínkwilin, íng–/ n. an animal living in the home of another; a commensal. □□ **in·qui·lin·ous** /–línəs/ adj. [L inquilinus sojourner (as IN-², colere dwell)]

in·quire /inkwír, ing–/ v. **1** intr. (often foll. by of) seek information formally; make a formal investigation. **2** intr. (foll. by about, after, for) ask about a person, a person's health, etc. **3** intr. (foll. by for) ask about the availability of. **4** tr. ask for information as to (inquired whether we were coming). **5** tr. (foll. by into) investigate; look into. □□ **in·quir·er** n. [ME enquere f. OF enquerre ult. f. L inquirere (as IN-², quaerere quaesit– seek)]

in·quir·y /inkwíree, ing–, ínkwəree, íng–/ n. (pl. **·ies**) **1** an investigation, esp. an official one. **2** the act or an instance of asking or seeking information.

in·quir·y a·gent n. Brit. a private detective.

in·qui·si·tion /inkwizíshən, íng–/ n. **1** usu. derog. an intensive search or investigation. **2** a judicial or official inquiry. **3** (**the Inquisition**) RC Ch. hist. an ecclesiastical tribunal for the suppression of heresy, esp. in Spain, operating through torture and execution. □□ **in·qui·si·tion·al** adj. [ME f. OF f. L inquisitio –onis examination (as INQUIRE)]

in·quis·i·tive /inkwízitiv, ing–/ adj. **1** unduly curious; prying. **2** seeking knowledge; inquiring. □□ **in·quis·i·tive·ly** adv. **in·quis·i·tive·ness** n. [ME f. OF inquisitif –ive f. LL inquisitivus (as INQUISITION)]

in·quis·i·tor /inkwízitər, ing–/ n. **1** an official investigator. **2** hist. an officer of the Inquisition. [F inquisiteur f. L inquisitor –oris (as INQUIRE)]

in·quis·i·tor Gen·er·al n. the head of the Spanish Inquisition.

in·quis·i·to·ri·al /inkwízitáwreeəl, ing–/ adj. **1** of or like an inquisitor. **2** offensively prying. **3** Law (of a trial, etc.) in which the judge has a prosecuting role (opp. ACCUSATORIAL). □□ **in·quis·i·to·ri·al·ly** adv. [med.L inquisitorius (as INQUISITOR)]

in·quo·rate /inkwáwrayt, ing–/ adj. not constituting a quorum.

in re /in reé, ráy/ prep. = RE¹. [L, = in the matter of]

INRI abbr. Jesus of Nazareth, King of the Jews. [L Iesus Nazarenus Rex Iudaeorum]

in·road /ínrōd/ n. **1** (often in pl.) **a** (usu. foll. by on, into) an encroachment; a using up of resources, etc. (makes inroads on my time). **b** (often foll. by in, into) progress; an advance (making inroads into a difficult market). **2** a hostile attack; a raid. [IN + ROAD¹ in sense 'riding']

in·rush /ínrush/ n. a rushing in; an influx. □□ **in·rush·ing** adj. & n.

INS abbr. (US) Immigration and Naturalization Service.

ins. abbr. **1** inches. **2** insurance.

in·sa·lu·bri·ous /ínsəlōōbreeəs/ adj. (of a climate or place) unhealthy. □□ **in·sa·lu·bri·ty** n. [L insalubris (as IN-¹, SALUBRIOUS)]

in·sane /insáyn/ adj. **1** not of sound mind; mad. **2** colloq. extremely foolish; irrational. □□ **in·sane·ly** adv. **in·sane·ness** n. **in·san·i·ty** /–sánitee/ n. (pl. **·ties**). [L insanus (as IN-¹, sanus healthy)]

in·san·i·tar·y /insániteree/ adj. not sanitary; dirty or germ-carrying.

in·sa·tia·ble /insáyshəbəl/ adj. **1** unable to be satisfied. **2** (usu. foll. by of) extremely greedy. □□ **in·sa·tia·bil·i·ty** n. **in·sa·tia·bly** adv. [ME f. OF insaciable or L insatiabilis (as IN-¹, SATIATE)]

in·sa·ti·ate /insáysheeət/ adj. never satisfied. [L insatiatus (as IN-¹, SATIATE)]

in·scape /ínskayp/ n. literary the unique inner quality or essence of an object, etc., as shown in a work of art, esp. a poem. [perh. f. IN-² + –SCAPE]

in·scribe /inskríb/ v.tr. **1 a** (usu. foll. by in, on) write or carve (words, etc.) on stone, metal, paper, a book, etc. **b** (usu. foll. by with) mark (a sheet, tablet, etc.) with characters. **2** (usu. foll. by to) write an informal dedication (to a person) in or on (a book, etc.). **3** enter the name of (a person) on a list or in a book. **4** Geom. draw (a figure) within another so that some or all points of it lie on the boundary of the other (cf. CIRCUMSCRIBE). **5** (esp. as **inscribed** adj.) Brit. issue (stock, etc.) in the form of shares with registered holders. □□ **in·scrib·a·ble** adj. **in·scrib·er** n. [L inscribere inscript– (as IN-², scribere write)]

in·scrip·tion /inskrípshən/ n. **1** words inscribed, esp. on a monument, coin, stone, or in a book, etc. **2 a** the act of inscribing, esp. the informal dedication of a book, etc. **b** an instance of this. □□ **in·scrip·tion·al** adj. **in·scrip·tive** adj. [ME f. L inscriptio (as INSCRIBE)]

in·scru·ta·ble /inskrōōtəbəl/ adj. wholly mysterious; impenetrable. □□ **in·scru·ta·bil·i·ty** n. **in·scru·ta·bly** adv. [ME f. eccl.L inscrutabilis (as IN-¹, scrutari search: see SCRUTINY)]

in·sect /ínsekt/ n. **1 a** any arthropod of the class Insecta, having a head, thorax, abdomen, two antennae, three pairs of thoracic legs, and usu. one or two pairs of thoracic wings. **b** (loosely) any other small segmented invertebrate animal. **2** an insignificant or contemptible person or creature. □□ **in·sec·tile** /–séktəl, –tíl/ adj. [L

insectum (animal) notched (animal) f. insecare insect– (as IN-², secare cut)]

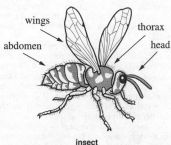

wings *thorax* *abdomen* *head*

insect

in·sec·tar·i·um /insektáireeəm/ n. (also **in·sec·tar·y** /inséktəree/) (pl. **in·sec·tar·i·ums** or **in·sec·tar·ies**) a place for keeping insects.

in·sec·ti·cide /inséktisid/ n. a substance used for killing insects. □□ **in·sec·ti·cid·al** /–síd´l/ adj.

in·sec·ti·vore /inséktivawr/ n. **1** any mammal of the order Insectivora feeding on insects, etc., e.g., a hedgehog or mole. **2** any plant that captures and absorbs insects. □□ **in·sec·tiv·o·rous** /–tívərəs/ adj. [F f. mod.L insectivorus (as INSECT, –VORE: see –VOROUS)]

in·se·cure /ínsikyōōr/ adj. **1** (of a person or state of mind) uncertain; lacking confidence. **2 a** unsafe; not firm or fixed. **b** (of ice, ground, etc.) liable to give way. **c** lacking security; unprotected. □□ **in·se·cure·ly** adv. **in·se·cu·ri·ty** n.

in·sel·berg /ínsəlbərg, –zəl/ n. an isolated hill or mountain rising abruptly from its surroundings; monadnock. [G, = island mountain]

in·sem·i·nate /insémminayt/ v.tr. **1** introduce semen into (a female) by natural or artificial means. **2** sow (seed, etc.). □□ **in·sem·i·na·tion** /–náyshən/ n. **in·sem·i·na·tor** n. [L inseminare (as IN-², SEMEN)]

in·sen·sate /insénsayt/ adj. **1** without physical sensation; unconscious. **2** without sensibility; unfeeling. **3** stupid. □□ **in·sen·sate·ly** adv. [eccl.L insensatus (as IN-¹, sensatus f. sensus SENSE)]

in·sen·si·bil·i·ty /insénsibílitee/ n. **1** unconsciousness. **2** a lack of mental feeling or emotion; hardness. **3** (often foll. by to) indifference. [F insensibilité or LL insensibilitas (as INSENSIBLE)]

in·sen·si·ble /insénsibəl/ adj. **1 a** without one's mental faculties; unconscious. **b** (of the extremities, etc.) numb; without feeling. **2** (usu. foll. by of, to) unaware; indifferent (insensible of her needs). **3** without emotion; callous. **4** too small or gradual to be perceived; inappreciable. □□ **in·sen·si·bly** adv. [ME f. OF insensible or L insensibilis (as IN-¹, SENSIBLE)]

in·sen·si·tive /insénsitiv/ adj. (often foll. by to) **1** unfeeling; boorish; crass. **2** not sensitive to physical stimuli. □□ **in·sen·si·tive·ly** adv. **in·sen·si·tive·ness** n. **in·sen·si·tiv·i·ty** /–tívitee/ n.

in·sen·ti·ent /insénshənt/ adj. not sentient; inanimate. □□ **in·sen·ti·ence** /–shəns/ n.

in·sep·a·ra·ble /insépərəbəl/ adj. & n. • adj. **1** (esp. of friends) unable or unwilling to be separated. **2** Gram. (of a prefix, or a verb in respect of it) unable to be used as a separate word, e.g., dis–, mis–, un–. • n. (usu. in pl.) an inseparable person or thing, esp. a friend. □□ **in·sep·a·ra·bil·i·ty** n. **in·sep·a·ra·bly** adv. [ME f. L inseparabilis (as IN-¹, SEPARABLE)]

in·sert v. & n. • v.tr. /insért/ **1** (usu. foll. by in, into, between, etc.) place, fit, or thrust (a thing) into another. **2** (usu. foll. by in, into)

SYNONYM TIP insert

INJECT, INTERJECT, INTERPOLATE, INTRODUCE, MEDIATE. If you want to put something in a fixed place between or among other things, you can **insert** it (insert a new paragraph in an essay, insert photographs in the text of a book). If it's a liquid, you'll probably want to **inject** it (inject the flu vaccine), although inject can also mean to bring in something new or different (inject some humor into an otherwise dreary speech). If it's a person, you'd better **introduce** him or her, which suggests placing the individual in the midst of a group so as to become part of it. You can also introduce things (introduce a new subject into the curriculum), but if the thing you're introducing doesn't really belong, you may have to **interpolate** it, which pertains to things that are extraneous and often introduced without authorization (to interpolate editorial comments). If you have something to introduce in an abrupt or forced manner, you'll have to **interject**, which usually applies to remarks, statements, or questions (in the midst of his speech, she interjected what she felt were important details). If you interject too often, however, you risk offending the speaker and may have to ask someone to **mediate**, which means to settle a dispute or bring about a compromise by taking a stand midway between extremes.

See page xx for the **Key to Pronunciation.**

introduce (a letter, word, article, advertisement, etc.) into a newspaper, etc. **3** (as **inserted** adj.) *Anat.*, etc., (of a muscle, etc.), attached (at a specific point). ● *n.* /ínsərt/ something inserted, e.g., a loose page in a magazine, a piece of cloth in a garment, a motion-picture cut-in. □□ **in•sert•a•ble** adj. **in•sert•er** n. [L *inserere* (as IN-², *serere sert-* join)]

in•ser•tion /ínsərshən/ n. **1** the act or an instance of inserting. **2** an amendment, etc., inserted in writing or printing. **3** each appearance of an advertisement in a newspaper, etc. **4** an ornamental section of needlework inserted into plain material (*lace insertions*). **5** the manner or place of attachment of a muscle, an organ, etc. **6** the placing of a spacecraft in an orbit. [LL *insertio* (as INSERT)]

in•serv•ice /ínsərvis/ adj. (of training) intended for those actively engaged in the profession or activity concerned.

in•set n. & v. ● n. /ínset/ **1 a** an extra page or pages inserted in a folded sheet or in a book; an insert. **b** a small map, photograph, etc., inserted within the border of a larger one. **2** a piece let into a dress, etc. ● v.tr. /ínset/ (**in•set•ting;** *past* and *past part.* **in•set** or **in•set•ted**) **1** put in as an inset. **2** decorate with an inset. □□ **in•set•ter** n.

in•shore /ínshawr/ adv. & adj. at sea but close to the shore. □ **in•shore of** esp. *Brit.* nearer to shore than.

in•side n., adj., adv., & prep. ● n. /ínsíd/ **1 a** the inner side or surface of a thing. **b** the inner part; the interior. **2** (of a roadway, etc.) the side or lane nearer the center. **3** (usu. in *pl.*) *colloq.* **a** the stomach and bowels (*something wrong with my insides*). **b** the operative part of a machine, etc. **4** *colloq.* a position affording inside information (*knows someone on the inside*). ● adj. /ínsíd/ **1** situated on or in, or derived from, the inside; (of information, etc.) available only to those on the inside. **2** *Baseball* closer to the batter than the near edge of home plate. **3** *Basketball* taking place within the perimeter of the defense. **4** *Soccer & Field Hockey* nearer to the center of the field (*inside forward; inside left; inside right*). ● adv. /ínsíd/ **1** on, in, or to the inside. **2** *sl.* in prison. ● prep. /ínsíd/ **1** on the inner side of; within (*inside the house*). **2** in less than (*inside an hour*). □ **inside of** *colloq.* **1** in less than (a week, etc.). **2** *Brit.* the middle part of. **know a thing inside out** know a thing thoroughly. **turn inside out 1** turn the inner surface of to outward. **2** *colloq.* ransack; cause confusion in. [IN + SIDE]

in•side in•for•ma•tion n. information not accessible to outsiders.

in•side job n. *colloq.* a crime committed by or with the assistance of a person living or working on the premises where it occurred.

in•side out adj. with the inner surface turned outward.

in•sid•er /ínsídər/ n. **1** a person who is within a society, organization, etc. (cf. OUTSIDER). **2** a person privy to a secret, esp. when using it to gain advantage.

in•sid•er trad•ing n. *Stock Exch.* the illegal practice of trading to one's own advantage through having access to confidential information.

in•side track n. **1** the track of a racecourse which is shorter, because of the curve. **2** a position of advantage.

in•sid•i•ous /ínsídeeəs/ adj. **1** proceeding or progressing inconspicuously but harmfully (*an insidious disease*). **2** treacherous; crafty. □□ **in•sid•i•ous•ly** adv. **in•sid•i•ous•ness** n. [L *insidiosus* cunning f. *insidiae* ambush (as IN-², *sedēre* sit)]

in•sight /ínsít/ n. (usu. foll. by *into*) **1** the capacity of understanding hidden truths, etc., esp. of character or situations. **2** an instance of this. □□ **in•sight•ful** adj. **in•sight•ful•ly** adv. [ME, = 'discernment,' prob. of Scand. & Du. orig. (as IN-², SIGHT)]

in•sig•ni•a /ínsígneeə/ n. (treated as *sing.* or *pl.* (formerly with *sing.* **in•sig•ne** /ínsígnee/); usu. foll. by *of*) **1** badges (*wore his insignia of office*). **2** distinguishing marks. [L, pl. of *insigne* neut. of *insignis* distinguished (as IN-², *signis* f. *signum* SIGN)]

▶**Insignia** is the plural of the Latin word *insigne*, and some traditionalists insist that *insigne* is the English singular as well. However, *insignia* as a singular noun and its plural, *insignias*, have long been widely accepted.

in•sig•nif•i•cant /insignífikənt/ adj. **1** unimportant; trifling. **2** (of a person) undistinguished. **3** meaningless. □□ **in•sig•nif•i•cance** /-kəns/ n. **in•sig•nif•i•can•cy** n. **in•sig•nif•i•cant•ly** adv.

in•sin•cere /ínsinseér/ adj. not sincere; not candid. □□ **in•sin•cere•ly** adv. **in•sin•cer•i•ty** /-séritee/ n. (*pl.* **•ties**). [L *insincerus* (as IN-¹, SINCERE)]

in•sin•u•ate /ínsínyoo-ayt/ v.tr. **1** (often foll. by *that* + clause) convey indirectly or obliquely; hint (*insinuated that she was lying*). **2** (often *refl.*; usu. foll. by *into*) **a** introduce (oneself, a person, etc.) into favor, office, etc., by subtle manipulation. **b** introduce (a thing, an idea, oneself, etc.) subtly or deviously into a place (*insinuated himself into their inner circle*). □□ **in•sin•u•a•tion** /-áyshən/ n. **in•sin•u•a•tive** adj. **in•sin•u•a•tor** n. **in•sin•u•a•to•ry** /-sínyōōatáwree/ adj. [L *insinuare insinuat-* (as IN-², *sinuare* to curve)]

in•sip•id /ínsípid/ adj. **1** lacking vigor or interest; dull. **2** lacking flavor; tasteless. □□ **in•si•pid•i•ty** /-píditee/ n. **in•sip•id•ly** adv. **in•sip•id•ness** n. [F *insipide* or LL *insipidus* (as IN-¹, *sapidus* SAPID)]

in•sist /ínsíst/ v.tr. (usu. foll. by *that* + clause; also *absol.*) maintain

or demand positively and assertively (*insisted that he was innocent; give me the bag! I insist!*). □ **insist on** demand or maintain (*I insist on being present; insists on his suitability*). □□ **in•sist•er** n. **in•sist•ing•ly** adv. [L *insistere* stand on, persist (as IN-², *sistere* stand)]

in•sist•ent /insístənt/ adj. **1** (often foll. by *on*) insisting; demanding positively or continually (*is insistent on taking me with him*). **2** obtruding itself on the attention (*the insistent rattle of the window frame*). □□ **in•sist•ence** /-təns/ n. **in•sist•en•cy** n. **in•sist•ent•ly** adv.

in si•tu /ín seetōō, sí-/ adv. **1** in its place. **2** in its original place. [L]

in•so•bri•e•ty /ínsəbrí-itee/ n. intemperance, esp. in drinking.

in•so•far as /ínsōfáar az/ adv. to the extent that.

in•so•la•tion /ínsōláyshən/ n. exposure to the sun's rays, esp. for bleaching. [L *insolatio* f. *insolare* (as IN-², *solare* f. *sol* sun)]

in•sole /ínsōl/ n. **1** a removable sole worn in a boot or shoe for warmth, etc. **2** the fixed inner sole of a boot or shoe.

in•so•lent /ínsələnt/ adj. offensively contemptuous or arrogant; insulting. □□ **in•so•lence** /-ləns/ n. **in•so•lent•ly** adv. [ME, = 'arrogant,' f. L *insolens* (as IN-¹, *solens* pres. part. of *solēre* be accustomed)]

in•sol•u•ble /ínsólyəbəl/ adj. **1** incapable of being solved. **2** incapable of being dissolved. □□ **in•sol•u•bil•i•ty** n. **in•sol•u•bil•ize** /-bilíz/ v.tr. **in•sol•u•ble•ness** n. **in•sol•u•bly** adv. [ME f. OF *insoluble* or L *insolubilis* (as IN-¹, SOLUBLE)]

in•solv•a•ble /ínsólvəbəl/ adj. = INSOLUBLE 1.

in•sol•vent /ínsólvənt/ adj. & n. ● adj. **1** unable to pay one's debts. **2** relating to insolvency (*insolvent laws*). ● n. a debtor. □□ **in•sol•ven•cy** n.

in•som•ni•a /ínsómneeə/ n. habitual sleeplessness; inability to sleep. □□ **in•som•ni•ac** /-neeak/ n. & adj. [L f. *insomnis* sleepless (as IN-¹, *somnus* sleep)]

in•so•much /ínsōmúch/ adv. **1** (foll. by *that* + clause) to such an extent. **2** (foll. by *as*) inasmuch. [ME, orig. *in so much*]

in•sou•ci•ant /ínsóōseeənt, ansōōsyaàN/ adj. carefree; unconcerned. □□ **in•sou•ci•ance** /-seeəns, -syáəns/ n. **in•sou•ci•ant•ly** adv. [F (as IN-¹, *souciant* pres. part. of *soucier* care)]

insp. *abbr.* **1** inspected. **2** inspector.

in•span /ínspán/ v. (**in•spanned, in•span•ning**) *S.Afr.* **1** tr. (also *absol.*) **a** yoke (oxen, etc.) in a team to a vehicle. **b** harness an animal or animals to (a wagon). **2** tr. harness (people or resources) into service. [Du. *inspannen* stretch (as IN-², SPAN²)]

in•spect /ínspékt/ v.tr. **1** look closely at or into. **2** examine (a document, etc.) officially. □□ **in•spec•tion** /-spékshən/ n. [L *inspicere inspect-* (as IN-², *specere* look at), or its frequent. *inspectare*]

in•spec•tor /ínspéktər/ n. **1** a person who inspects. **2** an official employed to supervise a service, a machine, etc., and make reports. **3** a police officer usu. ranking just below a superintendent. □□ **in•spec•tor•ate** /-təreeət/ n. **in•spec•to•ri•al** /-táwreeəl/ adj. **in•spec•tor•ship** n. [L (as INSPECT)]

in•spec•tor gen•er•al n. **1** an official in charge of inspecting a particular institution or activity (*a report by the Pentagon's inspector general*). **2** *Mil.* a staff officer responsible for conducting inspections and investigations.

in•spi•ra•tion /ínspiráyshən/ n. **1 a** a supposed creative force or influence on poets, artists, musicians, etc., stimulating the production of works of art. **b** a person, principle, faith, etc., stimulating artistic or moral fervor and creativity. **c** a similar divine influence supposed to have led to the writing of Scripture, etc. **2** a sudden brilliant, creative, or timely idea. **3** a drawing in of breath; inhalation. □□ **in•spi•ra•tion•al** adj. **in•spi•ra•tion•ism** n. **in•spi•ra•tion•ist** n. [ME f. OF f. LL *inspiratio -onis* (as INSPIRE)]

in•spi•ra•tor /ínspiraytər/ n. an apparatus for drawing in air or vapor. [LL (as INSPIRE)]

in•spire /ínspír/ v.tr. **1** stimulate or arouse (a person) to esp. creative activity, esp. by supposed divine or supernatural agency (*your faith inspired him; inspired by God*). **2 a** (usu. foll. by *with*) animate (a person) with a feeling. **b** (usu. foll. by *into*) instill (a feeling) into a person, etc. **c** (usu. foll. by *in*) create (a feeling) in a person. **3** prompt; give rise to (*the poem was inspired by the autumn*). **4** (as **inspired** adj.) **a** (of a work of art, etc.) as if prompted by or emanating from a supernatural source; characterized by inspiration (*an inspired speech*). **b** (of a guess) intuitive but accurate. **5** (also *absol.*) breathe in (air, etc.); inhale. □□ **in•spir•a•to•ry** /-rətáwree/ adj. **in•spir•ed•ly** /-ridlee/ adv. **in•spir•er** n. **in•spir•ing** n. **in•spir•ing•ly** adv. [ME f. OF *inspirer* f. L *inspirare* breathe in (as IN-², *spirare* breathe)]

in•spir•it /ínspírit/ v.tr. **1** put life into; animate. **2** (usu. foll. by *to, to* + infin.) encourage (a person). □□ **in•spir•it•ing** adj. **in•spir•it•ing•ly** adv.

in•spis•sate /ínspísayt/ v.tr. *literary* thicken; condense. □□ **in•spis•sa•tion** /-sáyshən/ n. [LL *inspissare inspissat-* (as IN-², L *spissus* thick)]

in•spis•sa•tor /ínspisaytər/ n. an apparatus for thickening serum, etc., by heat.

inst. *abbr.* **1** = INSTANT adj. 4 (*the 6th inst.*). **2** instance. **3** institute. **4** institution. **5** instrument.

in•sta•bil•i•ty /ínstəbílitee/ n. (*pl.* **•ties**) **1** a lack of stability. **2** *Psychol.* unpredictability in behavior, etc. **3** an instance of instability. [ME f. F *instabilité* f. L *instabilitas -tatis* f. *instabilis* (as IN-¹, STABLE¹)]

in·stall /instáwl/ v.tr. (also esp. Brit. **in·stal**) (**in·stalled**, **in·stal·ling**) **1** place (equipment, machinery, etc.) in position ready for use. **2** place (a person) in an office or rank with ceremony (installed in the office of attorney general). **3** establish (oneself, a person, etc.) in a place, condition, etc. (installed herself at the head of the table). □□ **in·stall·er** n. [med.L installare (as IN-², stallare f. stallum STALL¹)]

in·stal·la·tion /instəláyshən/ n. **1 a** the act or an instance of installing. **b** the process or an instance of being installed. **2** a piece of apparatus, a machine, etc., installed or the place where it is installed. [med.L installatio (as INSTALL)]

in·stall·ment /instáwlmənt/ n. **1** a sum of money due as one of several usu. equal payments for something, spread over an agreed period of time. **2** any of several parts, esp. of a television or radio serial or a magazine story, published or shown in sequence at intervals. [alt. f. obs. estallment f. AF estalement f. estaler fix: prob. assoc. with INSTALLATION]

in·stall·ment plan n. an arrangement for payment by installments.

in·stance /instəns/ n. & v. • n. **1** an example or illustration of (just another instance of his lack of determination). **2** a particular case (that's not true in this instance). **3** Law a legal suit. • v.tr. cite (a fact, case, etc.) as an instance. □ **at the instance of** at the request or suggestion of. **court of first instance** Law a court of primary jurisdiction. **for instance** as an example. **in the first** (or **second**, etc.) **instance** in the first (or second, etc.) place; at the first (or second, etc.) stage of a proceeding.

WORD HISTORY instance

Middle English: via Old French from Latin instantia 'presence, urgency', from instare 'be present, press upon', from in- 'upon' + stare 'to stand'. The original sense was 'urgency, urgent entreaty', surviving in at the instance of. In the late 16th cent. the word denoted a particular case cited to disprove a general assertion, derived from medieval Latin instantia 'example to the contrary' (translating Greek enstasis 'objection'); hence the meaning 'single occurrence.'

in·stan·cy /instənsee/ n. **1** urgency. **2** pressing nature. [L instantia: see INSTANCE]

in·stant /instənt/ adj. & n. • adj. **1** occurring immediately (gives an instant result). **2 a** (of food, etc.) ready for immediate use, with little or no preparation. **b** prepared hastily and with little effort (I have no instant solution). **3** urgent; pressing. **4** Commerce of the current month (the 6th instant). **5** archaic of the present moment. • n. **1** a precise moment of time, esp. the present (come here this instant; went that instant; told you the instant I heard). **2** a short space of time (was there in an instant; not an instant too soon). [ME f. F f. L instare instant- be present, press upon (as IN-², stare stand)]

in·stan·ta·ne·ous /instəntáyneeəs/ adj. **1** occurring or done in an instant or instantly. **2** Physics existing at a particular instant. □□ **in·stan·ta·ne·i·ty** /instəntənee-itee/ n. **in·stan·ta·ne·ous·ly** adv. **in·stan·ta·ne·ous·ness** n. [med.L instantaneus f. L instans (as INSTANT) after eccl.L momentaneus]

in·stan·ter /instántər/ adv. archaic or joc. immediately; at once. [L f. instans (as INSTANT)]

in·stan·ti·ate /instánsheeayt/ v.tr. represent by an instance. □□ **in·stan·ti·a·tion** /-áyshən/ n. [L instantia: see INSTANCE]

in·stant·ly /instəntlee/ adv. **1** immediately; at once. **2** archaic urgently; pressingly.

in·stant re·play n. the immediate repetition of part of a videotaped sports event, often in slow motion.

in·star /instaar/ n. a stage in the life of an insect, etc., between two periods of molting. [L, = form]

in·state /instáyt/ v.tr. (often foll. by in) install; establish. [IN-² + STATE]

in sta·tu pu·pil·la·ri /in stáytyōō pyōōpiláaree, stáchōō/ adj. **1** under guardianship, esp. as a pupil. **2** in a junior position at a university; not having a master's degree. [L]

in·stau·ra·tion /instawráyshən/ n. formal **1** restoration; renewal. **2** an act of instauration. □□ **in·stau·ra·tor** n. [L instauratio f. instaurare (as IN-²: cf. RESTORE)]

in·stead /instéd/ adv. **1** (foll. by of) as a substitute or alternative to; in place of (instead of this one; stayed instead of going). **2** as an alternative (took me instead) (cf. STEAD). [ME, f. IN + STEAD]

in·step /instep/ n. **1** the inner arch of the foot between the toes and the ankle. **2** the part of a shoe, etc., fitting over or under this. **3** a thing shaped like an instep. [16th c.: ult. formed as IN-² + STEP, but immed. orig. uncert.]

in·sti·gate /instigayt/ v.tr. **1** bring about by incitement or persuasion; provoke (who instigated the inquiry?). **2** (usu. foll. by to) urge on; incite (a person, etc.) to esp. an evil act. □□ **in·sti·ga·tion** /-gáyshən/ n. **in·sti·ga·tive** adj. **in·sti·ga·tor** n. [L instigare instigat-]

in·still /instíl/ v.tr. (esp. Brit. **in·stil**) (**in·stilled**, **in·stil·ling**) (often foll. by into) **1** introduce (a feeling, idea, etc.) into a person's mind, etc., gradually. **2** put (a liquid) into something in drops. □□ **in·stil·la·tion** n. **in·still·er** n. **in·still·ment** n. [L instillare (as IN-², stillare drop): cf. DISTILL]

in·stinct n. & adj. • n. /instingkt/ **1 a** an innate, usu. fixed, pattern of behavior in most animals in response to certain stimuli. **b** a similar propensity in human beings to act without conscious intention; innate impulsion. **2** (usu. foll. by for) unconscious skill; intuition. • predic.adj. /instíngkt/ (foll. by with) imbued; filled (with life, beauty, force, etc.). □□ **in·stinc·tu·al** /-stíngkchōōəl/ adj. **in·stinc·tu·al·ly** adv. [ME, = 'impulse,' f. L instinctus f. instinguere incite (as IN-², stinguere stinct- prick)]

in·stinc·tive /instíngktiv/ adj. **1** relating to or prompted by instinct. **2** apparently unconscious or automatic (an instinctive reaction). □□ **in·stinc·tive·ly** adv.

in·sti·tute /institōōt, -tyōōt/ n. & v. • n. **1 a** a society or organization for the promotion of science, education, etc. **b** a building used by an institute. **2** Law (usu. in pl.) a digest of the elements of a legal subject (Institutes of Justinian). **3** a principle of instruction. **4** a brief course of instruction for teachers, etc. • v.tr. **1** establish; found. **2 a** initiate (an inquiry, etc.). **b** begin (proceedings) in a court. **3** (usu. foll. by to, into) appoint (a person) as a cleric in a church, etc. [ME f. L institutum design, precept, neut. past part. of instituere establish, arrange, teach (as IN-², statuere set up)]

in·sti·tu·tion /institōōshən, -tyōō-/ n. **1** the act or an instance of instituting. **2 a** a society or organization founded esp. for charitable, religious, educational, or social purposes. **b** a building used by an institution. **3** an established law, practice, or custom. **4** colloq. (of a person, a custom, etc.) a familiar object. **5** the establishment of a cleric, etc., in a church. [ME f. OF f. L institutio -onis (as INSTITUTE)]

in·sti·tu·tion·al /institōōshənəl, -tyōō-/ adj. **1** of or like an institution. **2** typical of institutions, esp. in being regimented or unimaginative (the food was dreadfully institutional). **3** (of religion) expressed or organized through institutions (churches, etc.). **4** (of advertising) intended to create prestige rather than immediate sales. □□ **in·sti·tu·tion·al·ism** n. **in·sti·tu·tion·al·ly** adv.

in·sti·tu·tion·al·ize /institōōshənəliz, -tyōō-/ v.tr. **1** (as **institutionalized** adj.) (of a prisoner, a long-term patient, etc.) made apathetic and dependent after a long period in an institution. **2** place or keep (a person) in an institution. **3** convert into an institution; make institutional. □□ **in·sti·tu·tion·al·i·za·tion** n.

in·struct /instrúkt/ v.tr. **1** (often foll. by in) teach (a person) a subject, etc. (instructed her in French). **2** (usu. foll. by to + infin.) direct; command (instructed him to fill in the hole). **3** (often foll. by of, or that, etc. + clause) inform (a person) of a fact, etc. **4** Law (of a judge) give information (esp. clarification of legal principles) to (a jury). [ME f. L instruere instruct- build, teach (as IN-², struere pile up)]

in·struc·tion /instrúkshən/ n. **1** (often in pl.) a direction; an order (gave him his instructions). **2** teaching; education (took a course of instruction). **3** Law (in pl.) directions issued to a jury, etc. **4** Computing a direction in a computer program defining and effecting an operation. □□ **in·struc·tion·al** adj. [ME f. OF f. LL instructio -onis (as INSTRUCT)]

in·struc·tive /instrúktiv/ adj. tending to instruct; conveying a lesson; enlightening (found the experience instructive). □□ **in·struc·tive·ly** adv. **in·struc·tive·ness** n.

in·struc·tor /instrúktər/ n. (fem. **in·struc·tress** /-strúktris/) **1** a person who instructs; a teacher, demonstrator, etc. **2** a university teacher ranking below assistant professor. □□ **in·struc·tor·ship** n.

in·stru·ment /instrəmənt/ n. & v. • n. **1** a tool or implement, esp. for delicate or scientific work. **2** (in full **musical instrument**) a device for producing musical sounds by vibration, wind, percussion, etc. **3 a** a thing used in performing an action (the meeting was an instrument in his success). **b** a person made use of (is merely their instrument). **4** a measuring device, esp. in an airplane, serving to determine its position in darkness, etc. **5** a formal, esp. legal, document. • v.tr. **1** arrange (music) for instruments. **2** equip with instruments (for measuring, recording, controlling, etc.). [ME f. OF instrument or L instrumentum (as INSTRUCT)]

in·stru·men·tal /instrəmént'l/ adj. & n. • adj. **1** (usu. foll. by to, in, or in + verbal noun) serving as an instrument or means (was instrumental in finding the money). **2** (of music) performed on instruments, without singing (cf. VOCAL). **3** of, or arising from, an instrument (instrumental error). **4** Gram. of or in the instrumental. • n. **1** a piece of music performed by instruments, not by the voice. **2** Gram. the case of nouns and pronouns (and words in grammatical agreement with them) indicating a means or instrument. □□ **in·stru·men·tal·ist** n. **in·stru·men·tal·i·ty** /-méntálitee/ n. **in·stru·men·tal·ly** adv. [ME f. F f. med.L instrumentalis (as INSTRUMENT)]

in·stru·men·ta·tion /instrəmentáyshən/ n. **1 a** the arrangement or composition of music for a particular group of musical instruments. **b** the instruments used in any one piece of music. **2 a** the design, provision, or use of instruments in industry, science, etc. **b** such instruments collectively. [F f. instrumenter (as INSTRUMENT)]

in·stru·ment pan·el n. (also **in·stru·ment board**) a surface in front

See page xx for the **Key to Pronunciation**.

of a driver's or pilot's seat, on which the vehicle's or aircraft's instruments are situated.

in·sub·or·di·nate /ínsəbáwrd'nət/ *adj.* disobedient; rebellious. □□ **in·sub·or·di·nate·ly** *adv.* **in·sub·or·di·na·tion** /–náyshən/ *n.*

in·sub·stan·tial /ínsəbstánshəl/ *adj.* **1** lacking solidity or substance. **2** not real. □□ **in·sub·stan·ti·al·i·ty** /–sheeálitee/ *n.* **in·sub·stan·tial·ly** *adv.* [LL *insubstantialis* (as IN-[1], SUBSTANTIAL)]

in·suf·fer·a·ble /insúfərəbəl/ *adj.* **1** intolerable. **2** unbearably arrogant or conceited, etc. □□ **in·suf·fer·a·ble·ness** *n.* **in·suf·fer·a·bly** *adv.*

in·suf·fi·cien·cy /ínsəfíshənsee/ *n.* **1** the condition of being insufficient. **2** *Med.* the inability of an organ to perform its normal function (*renal insufficiency*). [ME f. LL *insufficientia* (as INSUFFICIENT)]

in·suf·fi·cient /ínsəfíshənt/ *adj.* not sufficient; inadequate. □□ **in·suf·fi·cient·ly** *adv.* [ME f. OF f. LL *insufficiens* (as IN-[1], SUFFICIENT)]

in·suf·flate /ínsəflayt/ *v.tr.* **1** *Med.* **a** blow or breathe (air, gas, powder, etc.) into a cavity of the body, etc. **b** treat (the nose, etc.) in this way. **2** *Theol.* blow or breathe on (a person) to symbolize spiritual influence. □□ **in·suf·fla·tion** /–fláyshən/ *n.* [LL *insufflare insufflat-* (as IN-[2], *sufflare* blow upon)]

in·suf·fla·tor /ínsəflaytər/ *n.* **1** a device for blowing powder on to a surface in order to make fingerprints visible. **2** an instrument for insufflating.

in·su·lar /ínsələr, ínsyə–/ *adj.* **1 a** of or like an island. **b** separated or remote, like an island. **2** ignorant of or indifferent to cultures, peoples, etc., outside one's own experience; narrow-minded. **3** of a British variant of Latin handwriting current in the Middle Ages. **4** (of climate) equable. □□ **in·su·lar·ism** *n.* **in·su·lar·i·ty** /–láritee/ *n.* **in·su·lar·ly** *adv.* [LL *insularis* (as INSULATE)]

in·su·late /ínsəlayt, ínsyə–/ *v.tr.* **1** prevent the passage of electricity, heat, or sound from (a thing, room, etc.) by interposing nonconductors. **2** detach (a person or thing) from its surroundings; isolate. **3** *archaic* make (land) into an island. □□ **in·su·la·tion** /–láyshən/ *n.* [L *insula* island + -ATE[3]]

in·su·lat·ing tape *n.* esp. *Brit.* = ELECTRICAL TAPE.

in·su·la·tor /ínsəlaytər, ínsyə–/ *n.* **1** a thing or substance used for insulation against electricity, heat, or sound. **2** an insulating device to support telegraph wires, etc. **3** a device preventing contact between electrical conductors.

in·su·lin /ínsəlin/ *n. Biochem.* a hormone produced in the pancreas by the islets of Langerhans, regulating the amount of glucose in the blood and the lack of which causes diabetes. [L *insula* island + -IN]

in·sult *v. & n.* • *v.tr.* /insúlt/ **1** speak to or treat with scornful abuse or indignity. **2** offend the self-respect or modesty of. • *n.* /ínsult/ **1** an insulting remark or action. **2** *colloq.* something so worthless or contemptible as to be offensive. **3** *Med.* **a** an agent causing damage to the body. **b** such damage. □□ **in·sult·er** *n.* **in·sult·ing·ly** *adv.*

WORD HISTORY   **insult**

Mid 16th cent. (as a verb in the sense 'exult, act arrogantly'): from Latin *insultare* 'jump or trample on', from *in-* 'on' + *saltare*, from *salire* 'to leap'. The noun (in the early 17th cent. denoting an attack) is from French *insulte* or ecclesiastical Latin *insultus*. The main current senses date from the 17th cent., the medical use dating from the early 20th cent.

---

in·su·per·a·ble /ínsoōpərəbəl/ *adj.* **1** (of a barrier) impossible to surmount. **2** (of a difficulty, etc.) impossible to overcome. □□ **in·su·per·a·bil·i·ty** *n.* **in·su·per·a·bly** *adv.* [ME f. OF *insuperable* or L *insuperabilis* (as IN-[1], SUPERABLE)]

in·sup·port·a·ble /ínsəpáwrtəbəl/ *adj.* **1** unable to be endured. **2** unjustifiable. □□ **in·sup·port·a·ble·ness** *n.* **in·sup·port·a·bly** *adv.* [F (as IN-[1], SUPPORT)]

in·sur·ance /inshoōrəns/ *n.* **1** the act or an instance of insuring. **2 a** a sum paid for this; a premium. **b** a sum paid out as compensation for theft, damage, loss, etc. **3** = INSURANCE POLICY. **4** a measure taken to provide for a possible contingency (*take an umbrella as insurance*). [earlier *ensurance* f. OF *enseūrance* (as ENSURE)]

in·sur·ance a·gent *n.* **a** a person authorized to sell insurance policies. **b** *Brit.* a person employed to collect premiums door to door.

in·sur·ance pol·i·cy *n.* **1** a contract of insurance. **2** a document detailing such a policy and constituting a contract.

in·sure /inshoō r/ *v.tr.* **1** (often foll. by *against*; also *absol.*) secure the payment of a sum of money in the event of loss or damage to (property, life, a person, etc.) by regular payments or premiums (*insured the house for $100,000; we have insured against flood damage*). **2** (of the owner of a property, an insurance company, etc.) secure the payment of (a sum of money) in this way. **3** (usu. foll. by *against*) provide for (a possible contingency) (*insured themselves against the rain by taking umbrellas*). **4** = ENSURE. □□ **in·sur·a·ble** *adj.* **in·sur·a·bil·i·ty** /–shoōr əbílitee/ *n.* [ME, var. of ENSURE]

▶**Insure** is widely used in the sense 'protect against loss' (**assure** was formerly used in this sense). For the nontechnical sense 'make

---

sure,' **assure**, **ensure**, and **insure** are all used: *my telephone call will assure you an introduction to the director*; *my telephone call will ensure* (or *insure*) *that you meet the director.*

in·sured /inshoórd/ *adj. & n.* • *adj.* covered by insurance. • *n.* (usu. prec. by *the*) a person, etc., covered by insurance.

in·sur·er /inshoórər/ *n.* **1** a person or company offering insurance policies for premiums; an underwriter. **2** a person that insures.

in·sur·gent /insúrjənt/ *adj. & n.* • *adj.* **1** rising in active revolt. **2** (of the sea, etc.) rushing in. • *n.* a rebel; a revolutionary. □□ **in·sur·gence** /–jəns/ *n.* **in·sur·gen·cy** *n.* (*pl.* **·cies**). [F f. L *insurgere insurrect-* (as IN-[2], *surgere* rise)]

in·sur·mount·a·ble /ínsərmówntəbəl/ *adj.* unable to be surmounted or overcome. □□ **in·sur·mount·a·bly** *adv.*

in·sur·rec·tion /ínsərékshən/ *n.* a rising in open resistance to established authority; a rebellion. □□ **in·sur·rec·tion·ar·y** *adj.* **in·sur·rec·tion·ist** *n.* [ME f. OF f. LL *insurrectio –onis* (as INSURGENT)]

in·sus·cep·ti·ble /ínsəséptibəl/ *adj.* (usu. foll. by *of*, *to*) not susceptible (of treatment, to an influence, etc.). □□ **in·sus·cep·ti·bil·i·ty** *n.*

in·swing·er /ínswingər/ *n.* **1** *Cricket* a ball bowled with a swing toward the batsman. **2** *Soccer* a pass or kick that sends the ball curving toward the goal.

int. *abbr.* **1** interior. **2** internal. **3** international.

in·tact /intákt/ *adj.* **1** entire; unimpaired. **2** untouched. □□ **in·tact·ness** *n.* [ME f. L *intactus* (as IN-[1], *tactus* past part. of *tangere* touch)]

in·tag·li·a·ted /intályaytid/ *adj.* decorated with surface carving. [It. *intagliato* past part. of *intagliare* cut into]

in·tagl·io /intályō, –taál–/ *n. & v.* • *n.* (*pl.* **·ios**) **1** a gem with an incised design (cf. CAMEO). **2** an engraved design. **3** a carving, esp. incised, in hard material. **4** a process of printing from an engraved design. • *v.tr.* (**·ioes**, **·ioed**) **1** engrave (material) with a sunk pattern or design. **2** engrave (such a design). [It. (as INTAGLIATED)]

in·take /íntayk/ *n.* **1 a** the action of taking in. **b** an instance of this. **2** a number or the amount taken in or received. **3** a place where water is taken into a channel or pipe from a river, or fuel or air enters an engine, etc. **4** an airway into a mine.

in·tan·gi·ble /intánjibəl/ *adj. & n.* • *adj.* **1** unable to be touched; not solid. **2** unable to be grasped mentally. • *n.* something that cannot be precisely measured or assessed. □□ **in·tan·gi·bil·i·ty** *n.* **in·tan·gi·bly** *adv.* [F *intangible* or med.L *intangibilis* (as IN-[1], TANGIBLE)]

in·tar·si·a /intaárseeə/ *n.* the craft of using wood inlays, esp. as practiced in 15th-c. Italy. [It. *intarsio*]

in·te·ger /íntijər/ *n.* **1** a whole number. **2** a thing complete in itself. [L (adj.) = untouched, whole: see ENTIRE]

in·te·gral /íntigrəl, intégrəl/ *adj. & n.* • *adj.* **1 a** of a whole or necessary to the completeness of a whole. **b** forming a whole (*integral design*). **c** whole; complete. **2** *Math.* **a** of or denoted by an integer. **b** involving only integers, esp. as coefficients of a function. • *n.* /íntigrəl/ *Math.* **1** a quantity of which a given function is the derivative, either containing an indeterminate additive constant (**indefinite integral**), or calculated as the difference between its values at specified limits (**definite integral**). **2** a function satisfying a given differential equation. □□ **in·te·gral·i·ty** /–grálitee/ *n.* **in·te·gral·ly** *adv.* [LL *integralis* (as INTEGER)]

PRONUNCIATION TIP   **integral**

This word can be pronounced with the stress on either the first or the second syllable, although "IN-te-grul" may be somewhat more common in American English. It is considered careless to say "IN-ter-grul."

---

in·te·gral cal·cu·lus *n.* mathematics concerned with finding integrals, their properties and application, etc. (cf. DIFFERENTIAL CALCULUS).

in·te·grand /íntigrand/ *n. Math.* a function that is to be integrated. [L *integrandus* gerundive of *integrare*: see INTEGRATE]

in·te·grant /íntigrənt/ *adj.* (of parts) making up a whole; component. [F *intégrant* f. *intégrer* (as INTEGRATE)]

in·te·grate *v. & adj.* • *v.* /íntigrayt/ **1** *tr.* **a** combine (parts) into a whole. **b** complete (an imperfect thing) by the addition of parts. **2** *tr. & intr.* bring or come into equal participation in or membership of society, a school, etc. **3** *tr.* desegregate, esp. racially (a school, etc.). **4** *tr. Math.* **a** find the integral of. **b** (as **integrated** *adj.*) indicating the mean value or total sum of (temperature, an area, etc.). • *adj.* /íntigrət/ **1** made up of parts. **2** whole; complete. □□ **in·te·gra·ble** /íntigrəbəl/ *adj.* **in·te·gra·bil·i·ty** *n.* **in·te·gra·tive** /íntigraytiv/ *adj.* [L *integrare integrat-* make whole (as INTEGER)]

in·te·grat·ed cir·cuit *n. Electronics* a small chip, etc., of material replacing several separate components in a conventional electrical circuit.

in·te·gra·tion /íntigráyshən/ *n.* **1** the act or an instance of integrating. **2** the intermixing of persons previously segregated. **3** *Psychol.* the combination of the diverse elements of perception, etc., in a personality. □□ **in·te·gra·tion·ist** *n.* [L *integratio* (as INTEGRATE)]

in·te·gra·tor /íntigraytər/ *n.* **1** an instrument for indicating or registering the total amount or mean value of some physical quality, as area, temperature, etc. **2** a person or thing that integrates.

in·teg·ri·ty /intégritee/ *n.* **1** moral uprightness; honesty. **2** wholeness; soundness. [ME f. F *intégrité* or L *integritas* (as INTEGER)]

in·teg·u·ment /intégyəmənt/ *n.* a natural outer covering, as a skin, husk, rind, etc. □□ **in·teg·u·men·tal** /–mént'l/ *adj.* **in·teg·u·men·ta·ry** /–méntəree/ *adj.* [L *integumentum* f. *integere* (as IN-², *tegere* cover)]

in·tel·lect /intilekt/ *n.* **1 a** the faculty of reasoning, knowing, and thinking, as distinct from feeling. **b** the understanding or mental powers (of a particular person, etc.) (*his intellect is not great*). **2 a** a clever or knowledgeable person. **b** the intelligentsia regarded collectively (*the combined intellect of four universities*). [ME f. OF *intellect* or L *intellectus* understanding (as INTELLIGENT)]

in·tel·lec·tion /intilékshən/ *n.* the action or process of understanding (opp. IMAGINATION). □□ **in·tel·lec·tive** *adj.* [ME f. med.L *intellectio* (as INTELLIGENT)]

in·tel·lec·tu·al /intilékchooəl/ *adj. & n.* ● *adj.* **1** of or appealing to the intellect. **2** possessing a high level of understanding or intelligence; cultured. **3** requiring, or given to the exercise of, the intellect. ● *n.* a person possessing a highly developed intellect. □□ **in·tel·lec·tu·al·i·ty** /–chooálitee/ *n.* **in·tel·lec·tu·al·ize** *v.tr. & intr.* **in·tel·lec·tu·al·ly** *adv.* [ME f. L *intellectualis* (as INTELLECT)]

in·tel·lec·tu·al·ism /intilékchooəlizəm/ *n.* **1** the exercise, esp. when excessive, of the intellect at the expense of the emotions. **2** *Philos.* the theory that knowledge is wholly or mainly derived from pure reason. □□ **in·tel·lec·tu·al·ist** *n.*

in·tel·li·gence /intélijəns/ *n.* **1 a** the intellect; the understanding. **b** (of a person or an animal) quickness of understanding; wisdom. **2 a** the collection of information, esp. of military or political value. **b** people employed in this. **c** information; news. **3** an intelligent or rational being. □□ **in·tel·li·gen·tial** /–jénshəl/ *adj.* [ME f. OF f. L *intelligentia* (as INTELLIGENT)]

in·tel·li·gence a·gen·cy *n.* a usu. government bureau engaged in collecting esp. secret information.

in·tel·li·gence quo·tient *n.* a number denoting the ratio of a person's intelligence to the normal or average. ¶ Abbr.: **IQ**.

in·tel·li·gence test *n.* a test designed to measure intelligence rather than acquired knowledge.

in·tel·li·gent /intélijənt/ *adj.* **1** having or showing intelligence, esp. of a high level. **2** quick of mind; clever. **3 a** (of a device or machine) able to vary its behavior in response to varying situations and requirements and past experience. **b** (esp. of a computer terminal) having its own data-processing capability; incorporating a microprocessor (opp. DUMB). □□ **in·tel·li·gent·ly** *adv.* [L *intelligere intellect*- understand (as INTER-, *legere* gather, pick out, read)]

in·tel·li·gent·si·a /intélijéntseeə/ *n.* **1** the class of intellectuals regarded as possessing culture and political initiative. **2** people doing intellectual work; intellectuals. [Russ. f. Pol. *inteligencja* f. L *intelligentia* (as INTELLIGENT)]

in·tel·li·gi·ble /intélijibəl/ *adj.* **1** (often foll. by *to*) able to be understood; comprehensible. **2** *Philos.* able to be understood only by the intellect, not by the senses. □□ **in·tel·li·gi·bil·i·ty** *n.* **in·tel·li·gi·bly** *adv.* [L *intelligibilis* (as INTELLIGENT)]

In·tel·sat /intelsat/ *n.* an international organization of countries operating a system of commercial communication satellites. [*International Telecommunications Satellite Consortium*]

in·tem·per·ate /intémpərət/ *adj.* **1** (of a person, conduct, or speech) immoderate; unbridled; violent (*used intemperate language*). **2 a** given to excessive indulgence in alcohol. **b** excessively indulgent in one's appetites. □□ **in·tem·per·ance** /–rəns/ *n.* **in·tem·per·ate·ly** *adv.* **in·tem·per·ate·ness** *n.* [ME f. L *intemperatus* (as IN-¹, TEMPERATE)]

in·tend /inténd/ *v.tr.* **1** have as one's purpose; propose (*we intend to go; we intend that it shall be done*). **2** (usu. foll. by *for*, *as*) design or destine (a person or a thing) (*I intend for him to go; I intend it as a

---

AIM, DESIGN, MEAN, PLAN, PROPOSE, PURPOSE. If you **intend** to do something, you may or may not be serious about getting it done (*I intend to clean out the garage some day*), but at least you have a goal in mind. Although **mean** can also imply either a firm resolve (*I mean to go, with or without her permission*) or a vague intention (*I've been meaning to write her for weeks*), it is a less formal word that usually connotes a certain lack of determination or a weak resolve. **Plan**, like *mean* and *intend*, may imply a vague goal (*I plan to tour China some day*), but it is often used to suggest that you're taking active steps (*I plan to leave as soon as I finish packing*). **Aim** indicates that you have an actual goal or purpose in mind (*I aim to be the first woman president*) and that you're putting some effort behind it, without the hint of failure conveyed by *mean*. If you **propose** to do something, you declare your intention ahead of time (*I propose that we set up a meeting next week*), and if you **purpose** to do it, you are even more determined to achieve your goal (*I purpose to write a three-volume history of baseball in America*). **Design** suggests forethought and careful planning in order to bring about a particular result (*to design a strategy that will keep everyone happy*).

---

warning). **3** mean (*what does he intend by that?*). **4** (in *passive*; foll. by *for*) **a** be meant for a person to have or use, etc. (*they are intended for the children*). **b** be meant to represent (*the picture is intended for you*). **5** (as **intending** *adj.*) who intends to be (*an intending visitor*). [ME *entende, intende* f. OF *entendre, intendre* f. L *intendere intent*- or *intens*- strain, direct, purpose (as IN-², *tendere* stretch, tend)]

in·tend·ant /inténdənt/ *n.* **1** (esp. as a title of foreign officials) a superintendent or manager of a department of public business, etc. **2** the administrator of an opera house or theater. □□ **in·tend·an·cy** *n.* [F f. L *intendere* (as INTEND)]

in·tend·ed /inténdid/ *adj. & n.* ● *adj.* **1** done on purpose; intentional. **2** designed; meant. ● *n. colloq.* the person one intends to marry; one's fiancé or fiancée (*is this your intended?*). □□ **in·tend·ed·ly** *adv.*

in·tense /inténs/ *adj.* (**in·tens·er, in·tens·est**) **1** (of a quality, etc.) existing in a high degree; violent; forceful (*intense cold*). **2** (of a person) feeling, or apt to feel, strong emotion (*very intense about her music*). **3** (of a feeling or action, etc.) extreme (*intense joy; intense thought*). □□ **in·tense·ly** *adv.* **in·tense·ness** *n.* [ME f. OF *intens* or L *intensus* (as INTEND)]

▶**Intense** is sometimes wrongly used instead of **intensive** to describe a course of study that covers a large amount of material in a short space of time.

in·ten·si·fi·er /inténsifiər/ *n.* **1** a person or thing that intensifies. **2** *Gram.* = INTENSIVE *n.*

in·ten·si·fy /inténsifī/ *v.* (**·fies, ·fied**) **1** *tr. & intr.* make or become intense or more intense. **2** *tr. Photog.* increase the opacity of (a negative). □□ **in·ten·si·fi·ca·tion** *n.*

in·ten·sion /inténshən/ *n.* **1** *Logic* the internal content of a concept. **2** *formal* the intensity, or high degree, of a quality. **3** *formal* the strenuous exertion of the mind or will. □□ **in·ten·sion·al** *adj.* **in·ten·sion·al·ly** *adv.* [L *intensio* (as INTEND)]

in·ten·si·ty /inténsitee/ *n.* (pl. **·ties**) **1** the quality or an instance of being intense. **2** esp. *Physics* the measurable amount of some quality, e.g., force, brightness, a magnetic field, etc.

in·ten·sive /inténsiv/ *adj. & n.* ● *adj.* **1** thorough; vigorous; directed to a single point, area, or subject (*intensive study; intensive bombardment*). **2** of or relating to intensity as opp. to extent; producing intensity. **3** serving to increase production in relation to costs (*intensive farming methods*). **4** (usu. in *comb.*) *Econ.* making much use of (*a labor-intensive industry*). **5** *Gram.* (of an adjective, adverb, etc.) expressing intensity; giving force, as *really* in *my feet are really cold*. ● *n. Gram.* an intensive adjective, adverb, etc. □□ **in·ten·sive·ly** *adv.* **in·ten·sive·ness** *n.* [F *intensif* –*ive* or med.L *intensivus* (as INTEND)]

▶See note at INTENSE.

in·ten·sive care *n.* special medical treatment of a dangerously ill patient, with constant monitoring.

in·ten·sive-care u·nit *n.* a unit or ward in a hospital devoted to intensive care.

in·tent /intént/ *n. & adj.* ● *n.* (usu. without article) intention; a purpose (*with intent to defraud; my intent to reach the top; with evil intent*). ● *adj.* **1** (usu. foll. by *on*) **a** resolved; bent; determined (*was intent on succeeding*). **b** attentively occupied (*intent on his books*). **2** (esp. of a look) earnest; eager; meaningful. □ **to** (or **for**) **all intents and purposes** practically; virtually. □□ **in·tent·ly** *adv.* **in·tent·ness** *n.* [ME *entent* f. OF f. L *intentus* (as INTEND)]

in·ten·tion /inténshən/ *n.* **1** (often foll. by *to* + infin., or *of* + verbal noun) a thing intended; an aim or purpose (*it was not her intention to interfere; have no intention of staying*). **2** the act of intending (*done without intention*). **3** *colloq.* (usu. in *pl.*) a person's, esp. a man's, designs in respect to marriage (*are his intentions strictly honorable?*). **4** *Logic* a conception. □□ **in·ten·tioned** *adj.* (usu. in *comb.*). [ME *entencion* f. OF f. L *intentio* stretching, purpose (as INTEND)]

in·ten·tion·al /inténshənl/ *adj.* done on purpose. □□ **in·ten·tion·al·i·ty** /–álitee/ *n.* **in·ten·tion·al·ly** *adv.* [F *intentionnel* or med.L *intentionalis* (as INTENTION)]

in·ten·tion trem·or *n. Med.* a trembling of a part of a body when commencing a movement.

in·ter /intór/ *v.tr.* (**in·terred, in·ter·ring**) deposit (a corpse, etc.) in the earth, a tomb, etc.; bury. [ME f. OF *enterrer* f. Rmc (as IN-², L *terra* earth)]

inter. *abbr.* intermediate.

inter- /intər/ *comb. form* **1** between; among (*intercontinental*). **2** mutually; reciprocally (*interbreed*). [OF *entre-* or L *inter* between, among]

in·ter·act /intərákt/ *v.intr.* act reciprocally; act on each other. □□ **in·ter·ac·tant** *adj. & n.*

in·ter·ac·tion /intərákshən/ *n.* **1** reciprocal action or influence. **2** *Physics* the action of atomic and subatomic particles on each other.

in·ter·ac·tive /intəráktiv/ *adj.* **1** reciprocally active; acting upon or influencing each other. **2** (of a computer or other electronic device) allowing a two-way flow of information between it and a user, responding to the user's input. □□ **in·ter·ac·tive·ly** *adv.* [INTER-ACT, after *active*]

in·ter a·li·a /íntər áyleeə, áaleeə/ *adv.* among other things. [L]

in·ter·al·lied /íntərálid/ *adj.* relating to two or more allies (in war, etc.).

in·ter·ar·tic·u·lar /íntəraartíkyələr/ *adj.* between the contiguous surfaces of a joint.

in·ter·a·tom·ic /íntərətómik/ *adj.* between atoms.

in·ter·bank /íntərbangk/ *adj.* agreed, arranged, or operating between banks (*interbank loan*).

in·ter·bed /íntərbéd/ *v.tr.* (·bed·ded, ·bed·ding) embed (one thing) among others.

in·ter·blend /íntərblénd/ *v.* **1** *tr.* (usu. foll. by *with*) mingle (things) together. **2** *intr.* blend with each other.

in·ter·breed /íntərbréed/ *v.* (*past* and *past part.* ·bred /–bréd/) **1** *intr.* & *tr.* breed or cause to breed with members of a different race or species to produce a hybrid. **2** *tr.* breed within one family, etc., in order to produce desired characteristics (cf. CROSSBREED).

in·ter·ca·lar·y /íntərkəléree, íntərkálaree/ *adj.* **1 a** (of a day or a month) inserted in the calendar to harmonize it with the solar year, e.g., Feb. 29 in leap years. **b** (of a year) having such an addition. **2** interpolated; intervening. [L *intercalari(u)s* (as INTERCALATE)]

in·ter·ca·late /íntərkəlayt/ *v.tr.* **1** (also *absol.*) insert (an intercalary day, etc.). **2** interpose (anything out of the ordinary course). **3** (as **intercalated** *adj.*) (of strata, etc.) interposed. □□ **in·ter·ca·la·tion** /–láyshən/ *n.* [L *intercalare intercalat-* (as INTER-, *calare* proclaim)]

in·ter·cede /íntərseéd/ *v.intr.* (usu. foll. by *with*) interpose or intervene on behalf of another; plead (*they interceded with the governor for his life*). □□ **in·ter·ced·er** *n.* [F *intercéder* or L *intercedere intercess-*intervene (as INTER-, *cedere* go)]

in·ter·cel·lu·lar /íntərsélyələr/ *adj.* Biol. located or occurring between cells.

in·ter·cen·sal /íntərsénsəl/ *adj.* between two censuses.

in·ter·cept *v.* & *n.* ● *v.tr.* /íntərsépt/ **1** seize, catch, or stop (a person, message, vehicle, ball, etc.) going from one place to another. **2** (usu. foll. by *from*) cut off (light, etc.). **3** check or stop (motion, etc.). **4** *Math.* mark off (a space) between two points, etc. ● *n.* /íntərsept/ *Math.* the part of a line between two points of intersection with usu. the coordinate axes or other lines. □□ **in·ter·cep·tion** /–sépshən/ *n.* **in·ter·cep·tive** /–séptiv/ *adj.* [L *intercipere intercept-* (as INTER-, *capere* take)]

in·ter·cep·tor /íntərséptər/ *n.* **1** an aircraft used to intercept enemy raiders. **2** a person or thing that intercepts.

in·ter·ces·sion /íntərséshən/ *n.* **1** the act of interceding, esp. by prayer. **2** an instance of this. **3** a prayer. □□ **in·ter·ces·sion·al** *adj.* **in·ter·ces·sor** *n.* **in·ter·ces·so·ri·al** /–sesáwreeəl/ *adj.* **in·ter·ces·so·ry** *adj.* [F *intercession* or L *intercessio* (as INTERCEDE)]

in·ter·change *v.* & *n.* ● *v.tr.* /íntərcháynj/ **1** (of two people) exchange (things) with each other. **2** put each of (two things) in the other's place; alternate. ● *n.* /íntərchaynj/ **1** (often foll. by *of*) a reciprocal exchange between two people, etc. **2** alternation (*the interchange of woods and fields*). **3** a road junction designed so that traffic streams do not intersect. □□ **in·ter·change·a·ble** *adj.* **in·ter·change·a·bil·i·ty** /–cháynjəbílitee/ *n.* **in·ter·change·a·ble·ness** *n.* **in·ter·change·a·bly** *adv.* [ME f. OF *entrechangier* (as INTER-, CHANGE)]

in·ter·cit·y /íntərsítee/ *adj.* existing or traveling between cities.

in·ter·class /íntərklás/ *adj.* existing or conducted between different social classes.

in·ter·col·le·giate /íntərkəleéjət/ *adj.* existing or conducted between colleges or universities.

in·ter·co·lo·ni·al /íntərkəlóneeəl/ *adj.* existing or conducted between colonies.

in·ter·com /íntərkom/ *n. colloq.* a system of intercommunication by radio or telephone between or within offices, aircraft, etc. [abbr.]

in·ter·com·mu·ni·cate /íntərkəmyóonikayt/ *v.intr.* **1** communicate reciprocally. **2** (of rooms, etc.) have free passage into each other; have a connecting door. □□ **in·ter·com·mu·ni·ca·tion** /–káyshən/ *n.* **in·ter·com·mu·ni·ca·tive** /–kaytiv, –kətiv/ *adj.*

in·ter·com·mun·ion /íntərkəmyóonyən/ *n.* **1** mutual communion. **2** a mutual action or relationship, esp. between Christian denominations.

in·ter·com·mu·ni·ty /íntərkəmyóonitee/ *n.* **1** ·the quality of being common to various groups, etc. **2** having things in common.

in·ter·con·nect /íntərkənékt/ *v.tr.* & *intr.* connect with each other. □□ **in·ter·con·nec·tion** /–nékshən/ *n.*

in·ter·con·ti·nen·tal /íntərkóntinént'l/ *adj.* connecting or traveling between continents. □□ **in·ter·con·ti·nen·tal·ly** *adv.*

in·ter·con·vert /íntərkənvért/ *v.tr.* & *intr.* convert into each other. □□ **in·ter·con·ver·sion** /–vórzhən/ *n.* **in·ter·con·vert·i·ble** *adj.*

in·ter·cool·ing /íntərkoóling/ *n.* the cooling of gas between successive compressions, esp. in a car or truck engine. □□ **in·ter·cool** *v.tr.* **in·ter·cool·er** *n.*

in·ter·cor·re·late /íntərkáwrəlayt, –kór/ *v.tr.* & *intr.* correlate with one another. □□ **in·ter·cor·re·la·tion** /–láyshən/ *n.*

in·ter·cos·tal /íntərkóst'l/ *adj.* between the ribs (of the body or a ship). □□ **in·ter·cos·tal·ly** *adv.*

in·ter·coun·ty /íntərkówntee/ *adj.* existing or conducted between counties.

in·ter·course /íntərkawrs/ *n.* **1** communication or dealings between individuals, nations, etc. **2** = SEXUAL INTERCOURSE. **3** communion between human beings and God.

WORD HISTORY intercourse

Late Middle English (denoting communication or dealings): from Old French *entrecours* 'exchange, commerce', from Latin *intercursus*, from *intercurrere* 'intervene', from *inter-* 'between' + *currere* 'run'. The specifically sexual use arose in the late 18th cent.

---

in·ter·crop /íntərkróp/ *v.tr.* (also *absol.*) (·cropped, ·crop·ping) raise (a crop) among plants of a different kind, usu. in the space between rows. □□ **in·ter·crop·ping** *n.*

in·ter·cross /íntərkráws, –krós/ *v.* **1** *tr.* & *intr.* lay or lie across each other. **2 a** *intr.* (of animals) breed with each other. **b** *tr.* cause to do this.

in·ter·cru·ral /íntərkroʻorəl/ *adj.* between the legs.

in·ter·cur·rent /íntərkórənt, –kúr/ *adj.* **1** (of a time or event) intervening. **2** *Med.* **a** (of a disease) occurring during the progress of another. **b** recurring at intervals. □□ **in·ter·cur·rence** /–rəns/ *n.* [L *intercurrere intercurrent-* (as INTERCOURSE)]

in·ter·cut /íntərkút/ *v.tr.* (·cut·ting; *past* and *past part.* ·cut) *Cinematog.* alternate (shots) with contrasting shots by cutting.

in·ter·de·nom·i·na·tion·al /íntərdinómináyshənəl/ *adj.* concerning more than one (religious) denomination. □□ **in·ter·de·nom·i·na·tion·al·ly** *adv.*

in·ter·de·part·men·tal /íntərdeʻepaartmént'l/ *adj.* concerning more than one department. □□ **in·ter·de·part·men·tal·ly** *adv.*

in·ter·de·pend /íntərdipénd/ *v.intr.* depend on each other. □□ **in·ter·de·pend·ence** *n.* **in·ter·de·pend·en·cy** *n.* **in·ter·de·pend·ent** *adj.*

in·ter·dict *n.* & *v.* ● *n.* /íntərdikt/ **1** an authoritative prohibition. **2** *RC Ch.* a sentence debarring a person, or esp. a place, from ecclesiastical functions and privileges. **3** *Sc. Law* an injunction. ● *v.tr.* /íntərdíkt/ **1** prohibit (an action). **2** forbid the use of. **3** (usu. foll. by *from* + verbal noun) restrain (a person). **4** (usu. foll. by *to*) forbid (a thing) to a person. □□ **in·ter·dic·tion** /–díkshən/ *n.* **in·ter·dic·to·ry** /–díktəree/ *adj.*

WORD HISTORY interdict

Middle English *entredite* (in the ecclesi astical sense), from Old French *entredit*, from Latin *interdictum*, past participle of *interdicere* 'interpose, forbid by decree', from *inter-* 'between' + *dicere* 'say'. The spelling change in the 16th cent. was due to association with the Latin form.

---

in·ter·dig·i·tal /íntərdíjit'l/ *adj.* between the fingers or toes. □□ **in·ter·dig·i·tal·ly** *adv.*

in·ter·dig·i·tate /íntərdíjitayt/ *v.intr.* interlock like clasped fingers. [INTER- + L *digitus* finger + –ATE³]

in·ter·dis·ci·pli·nar·y /íntərdísiplinéree/ *adj.* of or between more than one branch of learning.

in·ter·est /íntərist, –trist/ *n.* & *v.* ● *n.* **1 a** a feeling of curiosity or concern (*have no interest in fishing*). **b** a quality exciting curiosity or holding the attention (*this magazine lacks interest*). **c** the power of an issue, action, etc., to hold the attention; noteworthiness; importance (*findings of no particular interest*). **2** a subject, hobby, etc., in which one is concerned (*his interests are gardening and sports*). **3** advantage or profit, esp. when financial (*it is in your interest to go*; *look after your own interests*). **4** money paid for the use of money lent, or for not requiring the repayment of a debt. **5** (usu. foll. by *in*) **a** a financial stake (in an undertaking, etc.). **b** a legal concern, title, or right (in property). **6 a** a party or group having a common interest (*the mining interest*). **b** a principle in which a party or group is concerned. **7** the selfish pursuit of one's own welfare; self-interest. ● *v.tr.* **1** excite the curiosity or attention of (*your story interests me greatly*). **2** (usu. foll. by *in*) cause (a person) to take a personal interest or share (*can I interest you in a weekend cruise?*). **3** (as **interested** *adj.*) having a private interest; not impartial or disinterested (*an interested party*). □ **at interest** (of money borrowed) on the condition that interest is payable. **declare an** (or **one's**) **interest** make known one's financial, etc., interests in an undertaking before it is discussed. **in the interest** (or **interests**) **of** as something that is advantageous to. **lose interest** become bored or boring. **with interest** with increased force, etc. (*returned the blow with interest*). □□ **in·ter·est·ed·ly** *adv.* **in·ter·est·ed·ness** *n.* [ME, earlier *interesse* f. AF f. med.L, alt. app. after OF *interest*, both f. L *interest*, 3rd sing. pres. of *interesse* matter, make a difference (as INTER-, *esse* be)]

in·ter·est·ing /íntristing, –tərésting/ *adj.* causing curiosity; holding the attention. □□ **in·ter·est·ing·ly** *adv.* **in·ter·est·ing·ness** *n.*

in·ter·face /íntərfays/ *n.* & *v.* ● *n.* **1** esp. *Physics* a surface forming a common boundary between two regions. **2** a point where interaction occurs between two systems, processes, subjects, etc. (*the in-*

terface between psychology and education). **3** esp. *Computing* **a** an apparatus for connecting two pieces of equipment so that they can be operated jointly. **b** a means by which a user interacts with a program or utilizes an application. ● *v.tr. & intr.* (often foll. by *with*) connect with (another piece of equipment, etc.) by an interface.

in·ter·fa·cial /íntərfáyshəl/ *adj.* **1** included between two faces of a crystal or other solid. **2** of or forming an interface. □□ **in·ter·fa·cial·ly** *adv.* (esp. in sense 2).

in·ter·fac·ing /íntərfáysing/ *n.* a stiffish material, esp. buckram, between two layers of fabric in collars, etc.

in·ter·fem·o·ral /íntərfémərəl/ *adj.* between the thighs.

in·ter·fere /íntərféer/ *v.intr.* **1** (usu. foll. by *with*) **a** (of a person) meddle; obstruct a process, etc. **b** (of a thing) be a hindrance; get in the way. **2** (usu. foll. by *in*) take part or intervene, esp. without invitation or necessity. **3** (foll. by *with*) *euphem.* molest or assault sexually. **4** *Physics* (of light or other waves) combine so as to cause interference. **5** (of a horse) knock one leg against another. □□ **in·ter·fer·er** *n.* **in·ter·fer·ing** *adj.* **in·ter·fer·ing·ly** *adv.* [OF *s'entreferir* strike each other (as INTER-, *ferir* f. L *ferire* strike)]

in·ter·fer·ence /íntərféerəns/ *n.* **1** (usu. foll. by *with*) **a** the act of interfering. **b** an instance of this. **2** the fading or disturbance of received radio signals by the interference of waves from different sources, or esp. by atmospherics or unwanted signals. **3** *Physics* the combination of two or more wave motions to form a resultant wave in which the displacement is reinforced or canceled. □□ **in·ter·fe·ren·tial** /–fərénshəl/ *adj.*

in·ter·fer·om·e·ter /íntərfərómitər/ *n.* an instrument for measuring wavelengths, etc., by means of interference phenomena. □□ **in·ter·fer·o·met·ric** /–férəmétrik/ *adj.* **in·ter·fer·o·met·ri·cal·ly** *adv.* **in·ter·fer·om·e·try** *n.*

in·ter·fer·on /íntərféeron/ *n.* *Biochem.* any of various proteins that can inhibit the development of a virus in a cell, etc. [INTERFERE + –ON]

in·ter·fi·bril·lar /íntərfíbrilər/ *adj.* between fibrils.

in·ter·file /íntərfíl/ *v.tr.* **1** file (two sequences) together. **2** file (one or more items) into an existing sequence.

in·ter·flow *v. & n.* ● *v.intr.* /íntərflṓ/ flow into each other. ● *n.* /íntərflṓ/ the process or result of this.

in·ter·flu·ent /íntərflṓōənt/ *adj.* flowing into each other. [L *influere interfluent-* (as INTER-, *fluere* flow)]

in·ter·fuse /íntərfyṓōz/ *v.* **1** *tr.* **a** (usu. foll. by *with*) mix (a thing) with; intersperse. **b** blend (things) together. **2** *intr.* (of two things) blend with each other. □□ **in·ter·fu·sion** /–fyṓōzhən/ *n.* [L *interfundere interfus-* (as INTER-, *fundere* pour)]

in·ter·ga·lac·tic /íntərgəláktik/ *adj.* of or situated between two or more galaxies. □□ **in·ter·ga·lac·ti·cal·ly** *adv.*

in·ter·gla·cial /íntərgláyshəl/ *adj.* between glacial periods.

in·ter·gov·ern·men·tal /íntərgúvərnmént'l/ *adj.* concerning or conducted between two or more governments. □□ **in·ter·gov·ern·men·tal·ly** *adv.*

in·ter·gra·da·tion /íntərgrədáyshən/ *n.* the process of merging together by gradual change of the constituents.

in·ter·grade *v. & n.* ● *v.intr.* /íntərgráyd/ pass into another form by intervening grades. ● *n.* /íntərgrayd/ such a grade.

in·ter·growth /íntərgrṓth/ *n.* the growing of things into each other.

in·ter·im /íntərim/ *n., adj., & adv.* ● *n.* the intervening time (*in the interim he had died*). ● *adj.* intervening; provisional; temporary. ● *adv.* *archaic* meanwhile. [L, as INTER- + adv. suffix –*im*]

in·ter·im div·i·dend *n.* a dividend declared on the basis of less than a full year's results.

in·te·ri·or /intéereeər/ *adj. & n.* ● *adj.* **1** inner (opp. EXTERIOR). **2** remote from the coast or frontier; inland. **3** internal; domestic (opp. FOREIGN). **4** (usu. foll. by *to*) situated further in or within. **5** existing in the mind or soul; inward. **6** drawn, photographed, etc., within a building. **7** coming from inside. ● *n.* **1** the interior part; the inside. **2** the interior part of a country or region. **3 a** the home affairs of a country. **b** a department dealing with these (*Secretary of the Interior*). **4** a representation of the inside of a building or a room (*Dutch interior*). **5** the inner nature; the soul. □□ **in·te·ri·or·ize** *v.tr.* **in·te·ri·or·ly** *adv.* [L, compar. f. *inter* among]

in·te·ri·or an·gle *n.* the angle between adjacent sides of a rectilinear figure.

in·te·ri·or de·sign *n.* (also **in·te·ri·or dec·o·ra·tion**) the design or decoration of the interior of a building, a room, etc.

in·te·ri·or mon·o·logue *n.* a form of writing expressing a character's inner thoughts.

interj. *abbr.* interjection.

in·ter·ject /íntərjékt/ *v.tr.* **1** utter (words) abruptly or parenthetical-

ly. **2** interrupt with. □□ **in·ter·jec·to·ry** *adj.* [L *interjicere* (as INTER-, *jacere* throw)]

in·ter·jec·tion /íntərjékshən/ *n.* an exclamation, esp. as a part of speech (e.g., *ah! dear me!*). □□ **in·ter·jec·tion·al** *adj.* [ME f. OF f. L *interjectio –onis* (as INTERJECT)]

in·ter·knit /íntərnít/ *v.tr. & intr.* (·**knit·ting**; *past* and *past part.* ·**knit·ted** or ·**knit**) knit together; intertwine.

in·ter·lace /íntərláys/ *v.* **1** *tr.* bind intricately together; interweave. **2** *tr.* mingle; intersperse. **3** *intr.* cross each other intricately. □□ **in·ter·lace·ment** *n.* [ME f. OF *entrelacier* (as INTER-, LACE *v.*)]

in·ter·lan·guage /íntərlanggwij/ *n.* a language or use of language having features of two others, often a pidgin or dialect form.

in·ter·lap /íntərláp/ *v.intr.* (·**lapped**, ·**lap·ping**) overlap.

in·ter·lard /íntərlaárd/ *v.tr.* (usu. foll. by *with*) mix (writing or speech) with unusual words or phrases. [F *entrelarder* (as INTER-, LARD *v.*)]

in·ter·leaf /íntərleéf/ *n.* (*pl.* ·**leaves**) an extra (usu. blank) leaf between the leaves of a book.

in·ter·leave /íntərleév/ *v.tr.* insert (usu. blank) leaves between the leaves of (a book, etc.).

in·ter·leu·kin /íntərlṓōkin/ *n.* *Biochem.* any of several glycoproteins produced by leukocytes for regulating immune responses. [INTER- + LEUKOCYTE]

in·ter·li·brar·y /íntərlíbreree/ *adj.* between libraries (esp. *interlibrary loan*).

in·ter·line[1] /íntərlín/ *v.tr.* **1** insert words between the lines of (a document, etc.). **2** insert (words) in this way. □□ **in·ter·lin·e·a·tion** /–línee-áyshən/ *n.* [ME f. med.L *interlineare* (as INTER-, LINE[1])]

in·ter·line[2] /íntərlín/ *v.tr.* put an extra lining between the ordinary lining and the fabric of (a garment).

in·ter·lin·e·ar /íntərlíneeər/ *adj.* written or printed between the lines of a text. [ME f. med.L *interlinearis* (as INTER-, LINEAR)]

in·ter·lin·ing /íntərlíning/ *n.* material used to interline a garment.

in·ter·link /íntərlíngk/ *v.tr. & intr.* link or be linked together.

in·ter·lob·u·lar /íntərlóbyələr/ *adj.* situated between lobes.

in·ter·lock /íntərlók/ *v., adj., & n.* ● *v.* **1** *intr.* engage with each other by overlapping or by the fitting together of projections and recesses. **2** *tr.* (usu. in *passive*) lock or clasp within each other. ● *adj.* (of a fabric) knitted with closely interlocking stitches. ● *n.* a device or mechanism for connecting or coordinating the function of different components. □□ **in·ter·lock·er** *n.*

in·ter·loc·u·tor /íntərlókyətər/ *n.* (*fem.* **in·ter·loc·u·trix** /–triks/) a person who takes part in a dialogue or conversation. □□ **in·ter·lo·cu·tion** /–ləkyṓōshən/ *n.* [mod.L f. L *interloqui interlocut-* interrupt in speaking (as INTER-, *loqui* speak)]

in·ter·loc·u·to·ry /íntərlókyətawree/ *adj.* **1** of dialogue or conversation. **2** *Law* (of a decree, etc.) given provisionally in a legal action. [med.L *interlocutorius* (as INTERLOCUTOR)]

in·ter·lop·er /íntərlṓpər/ *n.* **1** an intruder. **2** a person who interferes in others' affairs, esp. for profit. □□ **in·ter·lope** *v.intr.* [INTER- + *loper* as in *landloper* vagabond f. MDu. *landlooper*]

in·ter·lude /íntərlōōd/ *n.* **1 a** a pause between the acts of a play. **b** something performed or done during this pause. **2 a** an intervening time, space, or event that contrasts with what goes before or after. **b** a temporary amusement or entertaining episode. **3** a piece of music played between other pieces, the verses of a hymn, etc. [ME, = a light dramatic item between the acts of a morality play, f. med.L *interludium* (as INTER-, *ludus* play)]

in·ter·mar·riage /íntərmárij/ *n.* **1** marriage between people of different races, castes, families, etc. **2** (loosely) marriage between near relations.

in·ter·mar·ry /íntərmáree/ *v.intr.* (·**ries**, ·**ried**) (foll. by *with*) (of races, castes, families, etc.) become connected by marriage.

in·ter·me·di·ar·y /íntərmeédee-eree/ *n. & adj.* ● *n.* (*pl.* ·**ies**) an intermediate person or thing, esp. a mediator. ● *adj.* acting as mediator; intermediate. [F *intermédiaire* f. It. *intermediario* f. L *intermedius* (as INTERMEDIATE)]

in·ter·me·di·ate *adj., n., & v.* ● *adj.* /íntərmeédeeət/ coming between two things in time, place, order, character, etc. ● *n.* /íntərmeédeeət/ **1** an intermediate thing. **2** a chemical compound formed by one reaction and then used in another, esp. during synthesis. ● *v.intr.* /íntərmeédeeáyt/ (foll. by *between*) act as intermediary; mediate.

□□ **in·ter·me·di·a·cy** /–deeəsee/ *n.* **in·ter·me·di·ate·ly** *adv.* **in·ter·me·di·ate·ness** *n.* **in·ter·me·di·a·tion** /–deeáyshən/ *n.* **in·ter·me·di·a·tor** /–deeaytər/ *n.* [med.L *intermediatus* (as INTER-, *medius* middle)]

in·ter·me·di·ate fre·quen·cy *n.* the frequency to which a radio signal is converted during heterodyne reception.

in·ter·ment /intórmənt/ *n.* the burial of a corpse, esp. with ceremony.
▶**Interment**, which means 'burial,' should not be confused with **internment**, which means 'imprisonment.'

in·ter·mesh /íntərmésh/ *v.tr. & intr.* make or become meshed together.

in·ter·mez·zo /íntərmétsō/ *n.* (*pl.* **in·ter·mez·zi** /–see/ or **·zos**) **1 a** a short connecting instrumental movement in an opera or other musical work. **b** a similar piece performed independently. **c** a short piece for a solo instrument. **2** a short, light dramatic or other performance inserted between the acts of a play. [It. f. L *intermedium* interval (as INTERMEDIATE)]

in·ter·mi·na·ble /intórminəbəl/ *adj.* **1** endless. **2** tediously long or habitual. **3** with no prospect of an end. □□ **in·ter·mi·na·ble·ness** *n.* **in·ter·mi·na·bly** *adv.* [ME f. OF *interminable* or LL *interminabilis* (as IN-¹, TERMINATE)]

in·ter·min·gle /íntərmínggəl/ *v.tr. & intr.* (often foll. by *with*) mix together; mingle.

in·ter·mis·sion /íntərmíshən/ *n.* **1** a pause or cessation. **2** an interval between parts of a play, motion picture, concert, etc. **3** a period of inactivity. [F *intermission* or L *intermissio* (as INTERMIT)]

in·ter·mit /íntərmít/ *v.* (**in·ter·mit·ted, in·ter·mit·ting**) **1** *intr.* esp. *Med.* stop or cease activity briefly (e.g., of a fever, or a pulse). **2** *tr.* suspend; discontinue for a time. [L *intermittere intermiss-* (as INTER-, *mittere* let go)]

in·ter·mit·tent /íntərmít'nt/ *adj.* occurring at intervals; not continuous or steady. □□ **in·ter·mit·tence** /–mít'ns/ *n.* **in·ter·mit·ten·cy** *n.* **in·ter·mit·tent·ly** *adv.* [L *intermittere intermittent-* (as INTERMIT)]

in·ter·mix /íntərmíks/ *v.tr. & intr.* mix together. □□ **in·ter·mix·a·ble** *adj.* **in·ter·mix·ture** *n.* [back-form. f. *intermixed, intermixt* f. L *intermixtus* past part. of *intermiscēre* mix together (as INTER-, *miscēre* mix)]

in·ter·mo·lec·u·lar /íntərməlékyələr/ *adj.* between molecules.

in·tern *n. & v.* • *n.* /íntərn/ (also **in·terne**) a recent graduate or advanced medical student living in a hospital and acting as an assistant physician or surgeon. • *v.* **1** *tr.* /intórn/ confine; oblige (a prisoner, alien, etc.) to reside within prescribed limits. **2** *intr.* /íntərn/ serve as an intern. □□ **in·tern·ment** /–tórn–/ *n.* **in·tern·ship** /íntərn–/ *n.* [F *interne* f. L *internus* internal]
▶See note at INTERMENT.

in·ter·nal /intórnəl/ *adj. & n.* • *adj.* **1** of or situated in the inside or invisible part. **2** relating or applied to the inside of the body (*internal injuries*). **3** of a nation's domestic affairs. **4** (of a student) attending a university, etc., as well as taking its examinations. **5** used or applying within an organization. **6 a** of the inner nature of a thing; intrinsic. **b** of the mind or soul. • *n.* (in *pl.*) intrinsic qualities. □□ **in·ter·nal·i·ty** /–nálitee/ *n.* **in·ter·nal·ize** *v.tr.* **in·ter·nal·i·za·tion** *n.* **in·ter·nal·ly** *adv.* [mod.L *internalis* (as INTERN)]

in·ter·nal com·bus·tion en·gine *n.* an engine that generates motive power by the burning of gasoline, oil, or other fuel with air inside the engine, the hot gases produced being used to drive a piston or do other work as they expand.

in·ter·nal en·er·gy *n.* the energy in a system arising from the relative positions and interactions of its parts.

in·ter·nal ex·ile *n.* penal banishment from a part of one's own country.

in·ter·nal med·i·cine *n.* a branch of medicine specializing in the diagnosis and nonsurgical treatment of diseases.

In·ter·nal Rev·e·nue Ser·vice *n.* (in the US) the government agency responsible for assessing and collecting income taxes, etc. ¶ Abbr.: **IRS.**

in·ter·nal rhyme *n.* a rhyme involving a word in the middle of a line and another at the end of the line or in the middle of the next.

internat. *abbr.* international.

in·ter·na·tion·al /íntərnáshənəl/ *adj. & n.* • *adj.* **1** existing, involving, or carried on between two or more nations. **2** agreed on or used by all or many nations (*international date line; international driver's license*). • *n.* **1 a** a contest, esp. in sport, between teams representing different countries. **b** a member of such a team. **2 a** (**International**) any of four associations founded (1864–1936) to promote socialist or communist action. **b** a member of any of these. □□ **in·ter·na·tion·al·i·ty** /–nálitee/ *n.* **in·ter·na·tion·al·ly** *adv.*

in·ter·na·tion·al date line *n.* (also **International Date Line**) see DATE-LINE 1.

In·ter·na·tio·nale /aNtərnáasyawnáaI/ *n.* (prec. by *the*) an (orig. French) revolutionary song adopted by socialists. [F, fem. of *international* (adj.) f. INTERNATIONAL]

in·ter·na·tion·al·ism /íntərnáshənəlizəm/ *n.* **1** the advocacy of a community of interests among nations. **2** (**Internationalism**) the principles of any of the Internationals. □□ **in·ter·na·tion·al·ist** *n.*

in·ter·na·tion·al·ize /íntərnáshənəlīz/ *v.tr.* **1** make international. **2** bring under the protection or control of two or more nations. □□ **in·ter·na·tion·al·i·za·tion** /–lizáyshən/ *n.*

in·ter·na·tion·al law *n.* a body of rules established by custom or treaty and agreed as binding by nations in their relations with one another.

in·ter·na·tion·al sys·tem of u·nits *n.* a system of physical units based on the meter, kilogram, second, ampere, kelvin, candela, and mole, with prefixes to indicate multiplication or division by a power of ten.

in·ter·na·tion·al u·nit *n.* a standard quantity of a vitamin, etc.

in·terne var. of INTERN *n.*

in·ter·ne·cine /íntərneésən, -néseen/ *adj.* mutually destructive. [orig. = deadly, f. L *internecinus* f. *internecio* massacre f. *internecare* slaughter (as INTER-, *necare* kill)]

in·tern·ee /íntərneé/ *n.* a person interned.

In·ter·net /íntərnét/ *n.* a communications network enabling the linking of computers worldwide for data interchange.

in·tern·ist /íntórnist/ *n. Med.* a specialist in internal medicine.

in·ter·node /íntərnōd/ *n.* **1** *Bot.* a part of a stem between two of the knobs from which leaves arise. **2** *Anat.* a slender part between two joints, esp. the bone of a finger or toe.

in·ter·nu·cle·ar /íntərnoökleeər, –nyoö–/ *adj.* between nuclei.

in·ter·nun·cial /íntərnúnshəl/ *adj.* (of nerves) communicating between different parts of the system. [*internuncio* ambassador f. It. *internunzio*]

in·ter·o·ce·an·ic /íntərósheeánik/ *adj.* between or connecting two oceans.

in·ter·o·cep·tive /íntərōséptiv/ *adj. Biol.* relating to stimuli produced within an organism, esp. in the viscera. [irreg. f. L *internus* interior + RECEPTIVE]

in·ter·os·cu·late /íntəróskyəlayt/ *v.intr.* = INOSCULATE.

in·ter·os·se·ous /íntəróseeəs/ *adj.* between bones.

in·ter·pa·ri·e·tal /íntərpəríət'l/ *adj.* between the right and left parietal bones of the skull. □□ **in·ter·pa·ri·e·tal·ly** *adv.*

in·ter·pel·late /íntórpəlayt/ *v.tr.* (in European parliaments) interrupt the order of the day by demanding an explanation from (the minister concerned). □□ **in·ter·pel·la·tion** /–láyshən/ *n.* **in·ter·pel·la·tor** *n.* [L *interpellare interpellat-* (as INTER-, *pellere* drive)]

in·ter·pen·e·trate /íntərpénitrayt/ *v.* **1** *intr.* (of two things) penetrate each other. **2** *tr.* pervade; penetrate thoroughly. □□ **in·ter·pen·e·tra·tion** /–tráyshən/ *n.* **in·ter·pen·e·tra·tive** *adj.*

in·ter·per·son·al /íntərpórsənəl/ *adj.* (of relations) occurring between persons, esp. reciprocally. □□ **in·ter·per·son·al·ly** *adv.*

in·ter·plait /íntərpláyt, –plát/ *v.tr. & intr.* plait together.

in·ter·plan·e·tar·y /íntərplániteree/ *adj.* **1** between planets. **2** relating to travel between planets.

in·ter·play /íntərplay/ *n.* **1** reciprocal action. **2** the operation of two things on each other.

in·ter·plead /íntərpleéd/ *v.* **1** *intr.* litigate with each other to settle a point concerning a third party. **2** *tr.* cause to do this. □□ **in·ter·plead·er** *n.* [ME f. AF *enterpleder* (as INTER-, PLEAD)]

In·ter·pol /íntərpol, –pol/ *n.* International Criminal Police Organization. [abbr.]

in·ter·po·late /íntórpəlayt/ *v.tr.* **1 a** insert (words) in a book, etc., esp. to give false impressions as to its date, etc. **b** make such insertions in (a book, etc.). **2** interject (a remark) in a conversation. **3** estimate (values) from known ones in the same range. □□ **in·ter·po·la·tion** /–láyshən/ *n.* **in·ter·po·la·tive** /–lótiv/ *adj.* **in·ter·po·la·tor** *n.* [L *interpolare* furbish up (as INTER-, *polire* POLISH)]

in·ter·pose /íntərpóz/ *v.* **1** *tr.* (often foll. by *between*) place or insert (a thing) between others. **2** *tr.* say (words) as an interruption. **3** *tr.* exercise or advance (a veto or objection) so as to interfere. **4** *intr.* (foll. by *between*) intervene (between parties). [F *interposer* f. L *interponere* put (as INTER-, POSE¹)]

in·ter·po·si·tion /íntərpəzíshən/ *n.* **1** the act of interposing. **2** a thing interposed. **3** an interference. [ME f. OF *interposition* or L *interpositio* (as INTER-, POSITION)]

in·ter·pret /intórprit/ *v.* (**in·ter·pret·ed, in·ter·pret·ing**) **1** *tr.* explain the meaning of (foreign or abstruse words, a dream, etc.). **2** *tr.* make out or bring out the meaning of (creative work). **3** *intr.* act as an interpreter, esp. of foreign languages. **4** *tr.* explain or understand (behavior, etc.) in a specified manner (*interpreted his gesture as mocking*). □□ **in·ter·pret·a·ble** *adj.* **in·ter·pret·a·bil·i·ty** *n.* **in·ter·pre·ta·tion** *n.* **in·ter·pre·ta·tion·al** *adj.* **in·ter·pre·ta·tive** /–táytiv/ *adj.* **in·ter·pre·tive** *adj.* **in·ter·pre·tive·ly** *adv.* [ME f. OF *interpreter* or L *interpretari* explain, translate f. *interpres –pretis* agent]

in·ter·pret·er /intórpritər/ *n.* a person who interprets, esp. one who translates speech orally. [ME f. AF *interpretour*, OF *interpreteur* f. LL *interpretator –oris* (as INTERPRET)]

in·ter·pro·vin·cial /íntərprəvínchəl/ *adj.* situated or carried on between provinces.

in·ter·ra·cial /íntəráyshəl/ *adj.* existing between or affecting different races. □□ **in·ter·ra·cial·ly** *adv.*

in·ter·reg·num /íntərrégnəm/ *n.* (*pl.* **in·ter·reg·nums** or **in·ter·reg·na** /–nə/) **1** an interval when the normal government is suspended, esp. between successive reigns or regimes. **2** an interval or pause. [L (as INTER-, *regnum* reign)]

in·ter·re·late /íntəriláyt/ *v.tr.* relate (two or more things) to each other. □□ **in·ter·re·la·tion** /–láyshən/ *n.* **in·ter·re·la·tion·ship** *n.*

interrog. *abbr.* interrogative.

in·ter·ro·gate /intérəgayt/ *v.tr.* ask questions of (a person) esp. closely, thoroughly, or formally. □□ **in·ter·ro·ga·tor** *n.* [ME f. L *interrogare* interrogat- ask (as INTER-, *rogare* ask)]

in·ter·ro·ga·tion /intérəgáyshən/ *n.* **1** the act or an instance of interrogating; the process of being interrogated. **2** a question or inquiry. □□ **in·ter·ro·ga·tion·al** *adj.* [ME f. F *interrogation* or L *interrogatio* (as INTERROGATE)]

in·ter·ro·ga·tion point *n.* (also **interrogation mark**, etc.) = QUESTION MARK.

in·ter·rog·a·tive /íntərógətiv/ *adj. & n.* ● *adj.* **1 a** of or like a question; used in questions. **b** *Gram.* (of an adjective or pronoun) asking a question (e.g., *who?, which?*). **2** having the form or force of a question. **3** suggesting inquiry (*an interrogative tone*). ● *n.* an interrogative word (e.g., *what?, why?*). □□ **in·ter·rog·a·tive·ly** *adv.* [LL *interrogativus* (as INTERROGATE)]

in·ter·rog·a·to·ry /íntərógətáwree/ *adj. & n.* ● *adj.* questioning; of or suggesting inquiry (*an interrogatory eyebrow*). ● *n.* (*pl.* **·ries**) a formal set of questions, esp. *Law* one formally put to an accused person, etc. [LL *interrogatorius* (as INTERROGATE)]

in·ter·rupt /íntərúpt/ *v.tr.* **1** act so as to break the continuous progress of (an action, speech, a person speaking, etc.). **2** obstruct (a person's view, etc.). **3** break or suspend the continuity of. □□ **in·ter·rupt·i·ble** *adj.* **in·ter·rup·tion** /–rúpshən/ *n.* **in·ter·rup·tive** *adj.* **in·ter·rup·to·ry** *adj.* [ME f. L *interrumpere* interrupt- (as INTER-, *rumpere* break)]

in·ter·rupt·er /íntərúptər/ *n.* (also **in·ter·rup·tor**) **1** a person or thing that interrupts. **2** a device for interrupting, esp. an electric circuit.

in·ter·sect /íntərsékt/ *v.* **1** *tr.* divide (a thing) by passing or lying across it. **2** *intr.* (of lines, roads, etc.) cross or cut each other. [L *intersecare* intersect- (as INTER-, *secare* cut)]

in·ter·sec·tion /íntərsékshən/ *n.* **1** the act of intersecting. **2** a place where two roads intersect. **3** a point or line common to lines or planes that intersect. □□ **in·ter·sec·tion·al** *adj.* [L *intersectio* (as INTERSECT)]

in·ter·sep·tal /íntərséptəl/ *adj.* between septa or partitions.

in·ter·sex /íntərseks/ *n.* **1** the abnormal condition of being intermediate between male and female. **2** an individual in this condition.

in·ter·sex·u·al /íntərséksho͞oəl/ *adj.* **1** existing between the sexes. **2** of intersex. □□ **in·ter·sex·u·al·i·ty** /–álitee/ *n.* **in·ter·sex·u·al·ly** *adv.*

in·ter·space *n. & v.* ● *n.* /íntərspáys/ an interval of space or time. ● *v.tr.* /íntərspáys/ put interspaces between.

in·ter·spe·cif·ic /íntərspəsífik/ *adj.* formed from different species.

in·ter·sperse /íntərspórs/ *v.tr.* **1** (often foll. by *between, among*) scatter; place here and there. **2** (foll. by *with*) diversify (a thing or things with others so scattered). □□ **in·ter·sper·sion** /–pérzhən/ *n.* [L *interspergere* interspers- (as INTER-, *spargere* scatter)]

in·ter·spi·nal /íntərspínəl/ *adj.* (also **in·ter·spi·nous** /–spínəs/) between spines or spinous processes.

in·ter·state *adj. & n.* ● *adj.* /íntərstáyt/ existing or carried on between states, esp. of the US. ● *n.* /íntərstayt/ a highway that is part of the US Interstate Highway System.

In·ter·state High·way Sys·tem *n.* a network of divided highways covering the 48 contiguous states, designed for fast intercity and urban travel.

in·ter·stel·lar /íntərstélər/ *adj.* occurring or situated between stars.

in·ter·stice /íntórstis/ *n.* **1** an intervening space. **2** a chink or crevice. [L *interstitium* (as INTER-, *sistere* stit- stand)]

in·ter·sti·tial /íntərstíshəl/ *adj.* of, forming, or occupying interstices. □□ **in·ter·sti·tial·ly** *adv.*

in·ter·tex·tu·al·i·ty /íntərtékscho͞o-álitee/ *n.* the relationship between esp. literary texts.

in·ter·ti·dal /íntərtíd'l/ *adj.* of or relating to the area which is covered at high tide and uncovered at low tide.

in·ter·trib·al /íntərtríbəl/ *adj.* existing or occurring between different tribes.

in·ter·tri·go /íntərtrígō/ *n.* (*pl.* **·gos**) *Med.* inflammation from the rubbing of one area of skin on another. [L f. *interterere* intertrit- (as INTER-, *terere* rub)]

in·ter·twine /íntərtwín/ *v.* **1** *tr.* (often foll. by *with*) entwine (together). **2** *intr.* become entwined. □□ **in·ter·twine·ment** *n.*

in·ter·twist /íntərtwíst/ *v.tr.* twist together.

in·ter·val /íntərvəl/ *n.* **1** an intervening time or space. **2** *Brit.* a pause or break, esp. between the parts of a theatrical or musical performance; intermission. **3** the difference in pitch between two sounds. **4** the distance between persons or things in respect of qualities. □ **at intervals** here and there; now and then. □□ **in·ter·val·lic** /–válik/ *adj.* [ME ult. f. L *intervallum* space between ramparts, interval (as INTER-, *vallum* rampart)]

in·ter·vene /íntərveén/ *v.intr.* (often foll. by *between, in*) **1** occur in time between events. **2** interfere; come between so as to prevent or

---

515 interrelate ~ in toto

modify the result or course of events. **3** be situated between things. **4** come in as an extraneous factor or thing. **5** *Law* interpose in a lawsuit as a third party. □□ **in·ter·ven·er** *n.* **in·ter·ven·ient** *adj.* **in·ter·ve·nor** *n.* [L *intervenire* (as INTER-, *venire* come)]

in·ter·ven·tion /íntərvénshən/ *n.* **1** the act or an instance of intervening. **2** interference, esp. by a state in another's affairs. **3** mediation. [ME f. F *intervention* or L *interventio* (as INTERVENE)]

in·ter·ven·tion·ist /íntərvénshənist/ *n.* a person who favors intervention.

in·ter·ver·te·bral /íntərvórtibrəl, –vərteébrəl/ *adj.* between vertebrae.

in·ter·view /íntərvyo͞o/ *n. & v.* ● *n.* **1** an oral examination of an applicant for employment, a college place, etc. **2** a conversation between a reporter, etc., and a person of public interest, used as a basis of a broadcast or publication. **3** a meeting of persons face to face, esp. for consultation. ● *v.tr.* **1** hold an interview with. **2** question to discover the opinions or experience of (a person). □□ **in·ter·view·ee** /–vyo͞o-eé/ *n.* **in·ter·view·er** *n.* [F *entrevue* f. *s'entrevoir* see each other (as INTER-, *voir* f. L *vidēre* see: see VIEW)]

in·ter·war /íntərwáwr/ *adj.* existing in the period between two wars, esp. the two world wars.

in·ter·weave /íntərweév/ *v.tr.* (*past* **·wove** /–wóv/; *past part.* **·wo·ven** /–wóvən/) **1** (often foll. by *with*) weave together. **2** blend intimately.

in·ter·wind /íntərwínd/ *v.tr. & intr.* (*past* and *past part.* **·wound** /–wównd/) wind together.

in·ter·work /íntərwórk/ *v.* **1** *intr.* work together or interactively. **2** *tr.* interweave.

in·tes·tate /intéstayt, –tət/ *adj. & n.* ● *adj.* (of a person) not having made a will before death. ● *n.* a person who has died intestate. □□ **in·tes·ta·cy** /–téstəsee/ *n.* [ME f. L *intestatus* (as IN-[1], *testari* testat- make a will f. *testis* witness)]

in·tes·tine /intéstin/ *n.* (in *sing.* or *pl.*) the lower part of the alimentary canal from the end of the stomach to the anus. □□ **in·tes·ti·nal** *adj.* [L *intestinum* f. *intestinus* internal]

in·thrall var. of ENTHRALL.

in·ti·fa·da /íntifaádə/ *n.* the Palestinian uprising in the Israeli-occupied West Bank and Gaza Strip, beginning in 1987. [Arab., = uprising]

in·ti·ma·cy /íntiməsee/ *n.* (*pl.* **·cies**) **1** the state of being intimate. **2** an intimate act, esp. sexual intercourse. **3** an intimate remark; an endearment.

in·ti·mate[1] /íntimət/ *adj. & n.* ● *adj.* **1** closely acquainted; familiar; close (*an intimate friend; an intimate relationship*). **2** private and personal (*intimate thoughts*). **3** (usu. foll. by *with*) having sexual relations. **4** (of knowledge) detailed; thorough. **5** (of a relationship between things) close. **6** (of mixing, etc.) thorough. **7** essential; intrinsic. **8** (of a place, etc.) friendly; promoting close personal relationships. ● *n.* a very close friend. □□ **in·ti·mate·ly** *adv.* [L *intimus* inmost]

in·ti·mate[2] /íntimayt/ *v.tr.* **1** (often foll. by *that* + clause) state or make known. **2** imply; hint. □□ **in·ti·mat·er** *n.* **in·ti·ma·tion** /–máyshən/ *n.* [LL *intimare* announce f. L *intimus* inmost]

in·tim·i·date /intímidayt/ *v.tr.* frighten or overawe, esp. to subdue or influence. □□ **in·tim·i·da·tion** /–dáyshən/ *n.* **in·tim·i·da·tor** *n.* [med.L *intimidare* (as IN-[2], *timidare* f. *timidus* TIMID)]

in·tinc·tion /intíngkshən/ *n. Eccl.* the dipping of the Eucharistic bread in the wine so that the communicant receives both together. [LL *intinctio* f. L *intingere* intinct- (as IN-[2], TINGE)]

in·tit·ule /intícho͞ol/ *v.tr. Brit.* entitle (an Act of Parliament, etc.). [OF *intituler* f. LL *intitulare* (as IN-[2], *titulare* f. *titulus* title)]

in·to /íntōō, –tə/ *prep.* **1** expressing motion or direction to a point on or within (*walked into a tree; ran into the house*). **2** expressing direction of attention or concern (*will look into it*). **3** expressing a change of state (*turned into a dragon; separated into groups; forced into cooperation*). **4** *colloq.* interested in; knowledgeable about (*is really into art*). [OE *intō* (as IN, TO)]

in·tol·er·a·ble /intólərəbəl/ *adj.* that cannot be endured. □□ **in·tol·er·a·ble·ness** *n.* **in·tol·er·a·bly** *adv.* [ME f. OF *intolerable* or L *intolerabilis* (as IN-[1], TOLERABLE)]

in·tol·er·ant /intólərənt/ *adj.* not tolerant, esp. of views, beliefs, or behavior differing from one's own. □□ **in·tol·er·ance** /–rəns/ *n.* **in·tol·er·ant·ly** *adv.* [L *intolerans* (as IN-[1], TOLERANT)]

in·to·nate /íntənayt/ *v.tr.* intone. [med.L *intonare*: see INTONE]

in·to·na·tion /íntənáyshən/ *n.* **1** modulation of the voice; accent. **2** the act of intoning. **3** accuracy of pitch in playing or singing (*has good intonation*). **4** the opening phrase of a plainsong melody. □□ **in·to·na·tion·al** *adj.* (as INTONE)]

in·tone /intón/ *v.tr.* **1** recite (prayers, etc.) with prolonged sounds, esp. in a monotone. **2** utter with a particular tone. □□ **in·ton·er** *n.* [med.L *intonare* (as IN-[2], L *tonus* TONE)]

in to·to /in tótō/ *adv.* completely. [L]

See page xx for the **Key to Pronunciation.**

in·tox·i·cant /intóksikənt/ *adj. & n.* • *adj.* intoxicating. • *n.* an intoxicating substance.

in·tox·i·cate /intóksikayt/ *v.tr.* **1** make drunk. **2** excite or elate beyond self-control. □□ **in·tox·i·ca·tion** /-káyshən/ *n.* [med.L *intoxicare* (as IN-², *toxicare* poison f. L *toxicum*): see TOXIC]

in·tox·i·cat·ing /intóksikayting/ *adj.* **1** liable to cause intoxication; alcoholic. **2** exhilarating; exciting. □□ **in·tox·i·cat·ing·ly** *adv.*

intr. *abbr.* intransitive.

intra- /íntrə/ *prefix* forming adjectives usu. from adjectives, meaning 'on the inside, within' (*intramural*). [L *intra* inside]

in·tra·cel·lu·lar /íntrəsélyələr/ *adj.* *Biol.* located or occurring within a cell or cells.

in·tra·cra·ni·al /íntrəkráyneeəl/ *adj.* within the skull. □□ **in·tra·cra·ni·al·ly** *adv.*

in·trac·ta·ble /intráktəbəl/ *adj.* **1** hard to control or deal with. **2** difficult; stubborn. □□ **in·trac·ta·bil·i·ty** *n.* **in·trac·ta·ble·ness** *n.* **in·trac·ta·bly** *adv.* [L *intractabilis* (as IN-¹, TRACTABLE)]

in·tra·dos /íntrədos, –dōs, intráydos, –dōs/ *n.* the lower or inner curve of an arch. [F (as INTRA-, *dos* back f. L *dorsum*)]

in·tra·mo·lec·u·lar /íntrəməlékyələr/ *adj.* within a molecule.

in·tra·mu·ral /íntrəmyóŏrəl/ *adj.* **1** situated or done within the walls of a building. **2** taking place within a single educational institution (*intramural sports*). **3** forming part of normal university or college studies. **4** *Med.* situated within the wall of a hollow organ or a cell. □□ **in·tra·mu·ral·ly** *adv.*

in·tra·mus·cu·lar /íntrəmúskyələr/ *adj.* in or into a muscle or muscles.

in·tra·net /íntrənet/ *n.* *Computing* a local or private network communicating with World Wide Web browsing software.

in·tran·si·gent /intránsijənt, –tránz–/ *adj. & n.* • *adj.* uncompromising; stubborn. • *n.* an intransigent person. □□ **in·tran·si·gence** /–jəns/ *n.* **in·tran·si·gen·cy** *n.* **in·tran·si·gent·ly** *adv.* [F *intransigeant* f. Sp. *los intransigentes* extreme republicans in Cortes, ult. formed as IN-¹ + L *transigere transigent-* come to an understanding (as TRANS-, *agere* act)]

in·tran·si·tive /intránsitiv, –tránz–/ *adj.* (of a verb or sense of a verb) that does not take or require a direct object (whether expressed or implied), e.g., *look* in *look at the sky* (opp. TRANSITIVE). □□ **in·tran·si·tive·ly** *adv.* **in·tran·si·tiv·i·ty** /–tívitee/ *n.* [LL *intransitivus* (as IN-¹, TRANSITIVE)]

in·tra·u·ter·ine /íntrəyóŏtərin, –rīn/ *adj.* within the uterus.

in·tra·u·ter·ine de·vice *n.* a device inserted into the uterus that provides birth control by physically preventing the implantation of fertilized ova. ¶ Abbr.: IUD.

in·tra·ve·nous /íntrəvéenəs/ *adj.* in or into a vein or veins. □□ **in·tra·ve·nous·ly** *adv.* [INTRA- + L *vena* vein]

in·trep·id /intrépid/ *adj.* fearless; very brave. □□ **in·tre·pid·i·ty** /–tripíditee/ *n.* **in·trep·id·ly** *adv.* [F *intrépide* or L *intrepidus* (as IN-¹, *trepidus* alarmed)]

in·tri·cate /íntrikit/ *adj.* very complicated; perplexingly detailed or obscure. □□ **in·tri·ca·cy** /–kəsee/ *n.* (*pl.* **-cies**). **in·tri·cate·ly** *adv.* [ME f. L *intricare intricat-* (as IN-², *tricare* f. *tricae* tricks)]

in·tri·gant /íntrigant/ *n.* (*fem.* **in·tri·gante**) an intriguer. [F *intriguant* f. *intriguer*: see INTRIGUE]

in·trigue *v. & n.* • *v.* /intréeg/ (**in·trigues, in·trigued, in·tri·guing**) **1** *intr.* (foll. by *with*) **a** carry on an underhand plot. **b** use secret influence. **2** *tr.* arouse the curiosity of; fascinate. • *n.* /intréeg, ín–/ **1** an underhand plot or plotting. **2** *archaic* a secret love affair. □□ **in·tri·guer** /intréegər/ *n.* **in·tri·guing** /intréeging/*adj.* (esp. in sense 2 of *v.*). **in·tri·guing·ly** *adv.* [F *intrigue* (n.), *intriguer* (v.) f. It. *intrigo, intrigare* f. L (as INTRICATE)]

in·trin·sic /intrínzik/ *adj.* inherent; essential; belonging naturally (*intrinsic value*). □□ **in·trin·si·cal·ly** *adv.* [ME, = interior, f. F *intrinsèque* f. LL *intrinsecus* (adv.) inwardly]

in·tro /íntrō/ *n.* (*pl.* **·tros**) *colloq.* an introduction. [abbr.]

intro- /íntrō/ *comb. form* into (*introgression*). [L *intro* to the inside]

intro. *abbr.* **1** introduction. **2** introductory.

in·tro·duce /íntrədóŏs, –dyóŏs/ *v.tr.* **1** (foll. by *to*) make (a person or oneself) known by name to another, esp. formally. **2** announce or present to an audience. **3** bring (a custom, idea, etc.) into use. **4** bring (a piece of legislation) before a legislative assembly. **5** (foll. by *to*) draw the attention or extend the understanding of (a person) to a subject. **6** insert; place in. **7** bring in; usher in; bring forward. **8** begin; occur just before the start of. □□ **in·tro·duc·er** *n.* **in·tro·duc·i·ble** *adj.* [ME f. L *introducere introduct-* (as INTRO-, *ducere* lead)]

in·tro·duc·tion /íntrədúkshən/ *n.* **1** the act or an instance of introducing; the process of being introduced. **2** a formal presentation of one person to another. **3** an explanatory section at the beginning of a book, etc. **4** a preliminary section in a piece of music, often thematically different from the main section. **5** an introductory treatise on a subject. **6** a thing introduced. [ME f. OF *introduction* or L *introductio* (as INTRODUCE)]

in·tro·duc·to·ry /íntrədúktəree/ *adj.* serving as an introduction; preliminary. [LL *introductorius* (as INTRODUCTION)]

in·tro·it /íntroyt/ *n.* a psalm or antiphon sung or said while the priest approaches the altar for the Eucharist. [ME f. OF f. L *introitus* f. *introire introit-* enter (as INTRO-, *ire* go)]

in·tro·jec·tion /íntrəjékshən/ *n.* the unconscious incorporation of external ideas into one's mind. [INTRO- after *projection*]

in·tro·mit /íntrəmít/ *v.tr.* (**in·tro·mit·ted, in·tro·mit·ting**) **1** *archaic* (foll. by *into*) let in; admit. **2** insert. □□ **in·tro·mis·sion** /–míshən/ *n.* **in·tro·mit·tent** *adj.* [L *intromittere intromiss-* introduce (as INTRO-, *mittere* send)]

in·tro·spec·tion /íntrəspékshən/ *n.* the examination or observation of one's own mental and emotional processes, etc. □□ **in·tro·spec·tive** *adj.* **in·tro·spec·tive·ly** *adv.* **in·tro·spec·tive·ness** *n.* [L *introspicere introspect-* look inwards (as INTRO-, *specere* look)]

in·tro·vert *n., adj., & v.* • *n.* /íntrəvərt/ **1** *Psychol.* a person predominantly concerned with his or her own thoughts and feelings rather than with external things. **2** a shy, inwardly thoughtful person. • *adj.* /íntrəvərt/ (also **in·tro·vert·ed** /–tid/) typical or characteristic of an introvert. • *v.tr.* /íntrəvórt/ **1** *Psychol.* direct (one's thoughts or mind) inward. **2** *Zool.* withdraw (an organ, etc.) within its own tube or base, like the finger of a glove. □□ **in·tro·ver·sion** /–vórzhən, –shən/ *n.* **in·tro·ver·sive** /–vórsiv/ *adj.* **in·tro·vert·ed** *adj.* **in·tro·ver·tive** /–vərtiv/ *adj.* [INTRO- + *vert* as in INVERT]

in·trude /intróŏd/ *v.* (foll. by *on, upon, into*) **1** *intr.* come uninvited or unwanted; force oneself abruptly on others. **2** *tr.* thrust or force (something unwelcome) on a person. □□ **in·trud·ing·ly** *adv.* [L *intrudere intrus-* (as IN-², *trudere* thrust)]

in·trud·er /intróŏdər/ *n.* a person who intrudes, esp. into a building with criminal intent.

in·tru·sion /intróŏzhən/ *n.* **1** the act or an instance of intruding. **2** an unwanted interruption, etc. **3** *Geol.* an influx of molten rock between or through strata, etc., but not reaching the surface. **4** the occupation of a vacant estate, etc., to which one has no claim. [ME f. OF *intrusion* or med.L *intrusio* (as INTRUDE)]

in·tru·sive /intróŏsiv/ *adj.* **1** that intrudes or tends to intrude. **2** characterized by intrusion. □□ **in·tru·sive·ly** *adv.* **in·tru·sive·ness** *n.*

in·trust var. of ENTRUST.

in·tu·bate /íntoŏbayt, –tyóŏ–/ *v.tr. Med.* insert a tube into the trachea for ventilation, usu. during anesthesia. □□ **in·tu·ba·tion** /–báyshən/ *n.* [IN-² + L *tuba* tube]

in·tu·it /intóŏit, –tyóŏ–/ *v.* **1** *tr.* know by intuition. **2** *intr.* receive knowledge by direct perception. □□ **in·tu·it·a·ble** *adj.* [L *intueri intuit-* consider (as IN-², *tueri* look)]

in·tu·i·tion /íntoŏ-íshən, –tyóŏ–/ *n.* **1** immediate apprehension by the mind without reasoning. **2** immediate apprehension by a sense. **3** immediate insight. □□ **in·tu·i·tion·al** *adj.* [LL *intuitio* (as INTUIT)]

in·tu·i·tion·ism /íntoŏ-íshənizəm, –tyóŏ–/ *n.* (also **in·tu·i·tion·al·ism**) *Philos.* the belief that primary truths and principles (esp. of ethics and metaphysics) are known directly by intuition. □□ **in·tu·i·tion·ist** *n.*

in·tu·i·tive /intóŏitiv, –tyóŏ–/ *adj.* **1** of, characterized by, or possessing intuition. **2** perceived by intuition. □□ **in·tu·i·tive·ly** *adv.* **in·tu·i·tive·ness** *n.* [med.L *intuitivus* (as INTUIT)]

in·tu·i·tiv·ism /intóŏitivizəm, –tyóŏ–/ *n.* the doctrine that ethical principles can be established by intuition. □□ **in·tu·i·tiv·ist** *n.*

in·tu·mesce /íntoŏmés, –tyóŏ–/ *v.intr.* swell up. □□ **in·tu·mes·cence** *n.* **in·tu·mes·cent** *adj.* [L *intumescere* (as IN-², *tumescere* incept. of *tumēre* swell)]

in·tus·sus·cep·tion /íntəsəsépshən/ *n.* **1** *Med.* the inversion of one portion of the intestine within another. **2** *Bot.* the deposition of new cellulose particles in a cell wall, to increase the surface area of the cell. [F *intussusception* or mod.L *intussusceptio* f. L *intus* within + *susceptio* f. *suscipere* take up]

in·twine var. of ENTWINE.

In·u·it /ínyoŏ-it/ *n.* (also **In·nu·it**) (*pl.* same or **In·u·its**) a N. American Eskimo. [Eskimo *inuit* people]

in·un·date /ínəndayt/ *v.tr.* (often foll. by *with*) **1** flood. **2** overwhelm (*inundated with inquiries*). □□ **in·un·da·tion** /–dáyshən/ *n.* [L *inundare* flow (as IN-², *unda* wave)]

in·ure /inyoŏr/ *v.* **1** *tr.* (often in *passive*; foll. by *to*) accustom (a person) to something esp. unpleasant. **2** *intr.* *Law* come into operation; take effect. □□ **in·ure·ment** *n.* [ME f. AF *enuerer* f. phr. *en eure* (both unrecorded) in use or practice, f. *en* in + OF *e(u)vre* work f. L *opera*]

in u·ter·o /in yóŏtərō/ *adv.* in the womb; before birth. [L]

in va·cu·o /in vákyoŏ-ō/ *adv.* in a vacuum. [L]

in·vade /inváyd/ *v.tr.* (often *absol.*) **1** enter (a country, etc.) under arms to control or subdue it. **2** swarm into. **3** (of a disease) attack (a body, etc.). **4** encroach upon (a person's rights, esp. privacy). □□ **in·vad·er** *n.* [L *invadere invas-* (as IN-², *vadere* go)]

in·vag·i·nate /inváijinayt/ *v.tr.* **1** put in a sheath. **2** turn (a tube) inside out. □□ **in·vag·i·na·tion** /–náyshən/ *n.* [IN-² + L *vagina* sheath]

in·va·lid¹ /ínvalid/ *n. & v.* • *n.* **1 a** a person enfeebled or disabled by illness or injury. **2** (*attrib.*) of or for invalids (*invalid car, invalid diet*). **b** being an invalid (*caring for her invalid mother*). • *v.* **1** *tr.* (often foll. by *out*, etc.) remove from active service (one who has become an invalid). **2** *tr.* (usu. in *passive*) disable (a person) by illness. **3** *intr.* become an invalid. □□ **in•va•lid•ism** *n.* [L *invalidus* weak, infirm (as IN-¹, VALID)]

in•val•id² /ínválid/ *adj.* not valid, esp. having no legal force. □□ **in•val•id•ly** *adv.* [L *invalidus* (as INVALID¹)]

PRONUNCIATION TIP   **invalid**

The adjective meaning 'not valid' is pronounced "in-VAL-id." The noun meaning 'a sickly person' is pronounced "IN-vul-id."

---

in•val•i•date /inválidayt/ *v.tr.* **1** make (esp. an argument, etc.) invalid. **2** remove the validity or force of (a treaty, contract, etc.). □□ **in•val•i•da•tion** /–dáyshən/ *n.* [med.L *invalidare invalidat-* (as IN-¹, *validus* VALID)]

in•va•lid•i•ty /ínvəlíditee/ *n.* **1** lack of validity. **2** bodily infirmity. [F *invalidité* or med.L *invaliditas* (as INVALID¹)]

in•val•u•a•ble /invályōōəbəl/ *adj.* above valuation; inestimable. □□ **in•val•u•a•ble•ness** *n.* **in•val•u•a•bly** *adv.*

in•var /inváar, ínvaar/ *n.* an iron-nickel alloy with a negligible coefficient of expansion, used in the manufacture of clocks and scientific instruments. [abbr. of INVARIABLE]

in•var•i•a•ble /inváireeəbəl/ *adj.* **1** unchangeable. **2** always the same. **3** *Math.* constant; fixed. □□ **in•var•i•a•bil•i•ty** /–bílitee/ *n.* **in•var•i•a•ble•ness** *n.* **in•var•i•a•bly** *adv.* [F *invariable* or LL *invariabilis* (as IN-¹, VARIABLE)]

in•var•i•ant /inváireeənt/ *adj. & n.* • *adj.* invariable. • *n. Math.* a function that remains unchanged when a specified transformation is applied. □□ **in•var•i•ance** /–reeəns/ *n.*

in•va•sion /inváyzhən/ *n.* **1** the act of invading or process of being invaded. **2** an entry of a hostile army into a country. □□ **in•va•sive** /–váysiv/ *adj.* [F *invasion* or LL *invasio* (as INVADE)]

in•vec•tive /invéktiv/ *n.* **1 a** strongly attacking words. **b** the use of these. **2** abusive rhetoric. [ME f. OF f. LL *invectivus* attacking (as INVEIGH)]

in•veigh /inváy/ *v.intr.* (foll. by *against*) speak or write with strong hostility. [L *invehi* go into, assail (as IN-², *vehi* passive of *vehere vect-* carry)]

in•vei•gle /inváygəl, –vée–/ *v.tr.* (foll. by *into*, or *to* + infin.) entice; persuade by guile. □□ **in•vei•gle•ment** *n.* [earlier *enve(u)gle* f. AF *envegler*, OF *aveugler* to blind f. *aveugle* blind, f. LL *aboculum*, f. *ab-* away from, without + *ocul-us* eye]

PRONUNCIATION TIP   **inveigle**

The more traditional pronunciation of this word rhymes with *eagle*, but the one that rhymes with *bagel* is more widely accepted in American English.

---

in•vent /invént/ *v.tr.* **1** create by thought; devise; originate (a new method, an instrument, etc.). **2** concoct (a false story, etc.). □□ **in•vent•a•ble** *adj.* [ME, = discover, f. L *invenire invent-* find, contrive (as IN-², *venire vent-* come)]

in•ven•tion /invénshən/ *n.* **1** the process of inventing. **2** a thing invented; a contrivance, esp. one for which a patent is granted. **3** a fictitious story. **4** inventiveness. **5** *Mus.* a short piece for keyboard, developing a simple idea. [ME f. L *inventio* (as INVENT)]

in•ven•tive /invéntiv/ *adj.* **1** able or inclined to invent; original in devising. **2** showing ingenuity of devising. □□ **in•ven•tive•ly** *adv.* **in•ven•tive•ness** *n.* [ME f. F *inventif –ive* or med.L *inventivus* (as INVENT)]

in•ven•tor /invéntər/ *n.* a person who invents, esp. as an occupation.

in•ven•to•ry /ínvəntáwree/ *n. & v.* • *n.* (pl. **·ries**) **1** a complete list of goods in stock, house contents, etc. **2** the goods listed in this. **3** the total of a firm's commercial assets. • *v.tr.* (**·ries**, **·ried**) **1** make an inventory of. **2** enter (goods) in an inventory. [ME f. med.L *inventorium* f. LL *inventarium* (as INVENT)]

in•verse /ínvərs, –və́rs/ *adj. & n.* • *adj.* inverted in position, order, or relation. • *n.* **1** the state of being inverted. **2** (often foll. by *of*) a thing that is the opposite or reverse of another. **3** *Math.* an element which, when combined with a given element in an operation, produces the identity element for that operation. □□ **in•verse•ly** *adv.* [L *inversus* past part. of *invertere*: see INVERT]

in•verse pro•por•tion *n.* (also **in•verse ra•ti•o**) a relation between two quantities such that one increases in proportion as the other decreases.

in•verse square law *n. Physics* a law stating that the intensity of an effect such as illumination or gravitational force changes in inverse proportion to the square of the distance from the source.

in•ver•sion /invə́rzhən, –shən/ *n.* **1** the act of turning upside down or inside out. **2** the reversal of a normal order, position, or relation. **3** the reversal of the order of words, for rhetorical effect. **4** the reversal of the normal variation of air temperature with altitude. **5** the process or result of inverting. **6** the reversal of direction of rotation of a plane of polarized light. **7** homosexuality. □□ **in•ver•sive** /–vórsiv/ *adj.* [L *inversio* (as INVERT)]

in•vert *v. & n.* • *v.tr.* /invórt/ **1** turn upside down. **2** reverse the position, order, or relation of. **3** *Mus.* change the relative position of the notes of (a chord or interval) by placing the lowest note high-

---

er, usu. by an octave. **4** subject to inversion. • *n.* /ínvərt/ **1** a homosexual. **2** an inverted arch, as at the bottom of a sewer. □□ **in•vert•er** *n.* **in•vert•i•ble** *adj.* **in•vert•i•bil•i•ty** *n.* [L *invertere invers-* (as IN-², *vertere* turn)]

in•ver•te•brate /invórtibrət, –brayt/ *adj. & n.* • *adj.* **1** (of an animal) not having a backbone. **2** lacking firmness of character. • *n.* an invertebrate animal. [mod.L *invertebrata* (pl.) (as IN-¹, VERTEBRA)]

in•verted com•ma *n. Brit.* = QUOTATION MARK.

in•verted snob *n. Brit.* a person who likes or takes pride in what a snob might be expected to disapprove of.

in•vert sug•ar /ínvərt shóōgər/ *n.* a mixture of glucose and fructose obtained by the hydrolysis of sucrose.

in•vest /invést/ *v.* **1** *tr.* (often foll. by *in*) apply or use (money), esp. for profit. **2** *intr.* (foll. by *in*) **a** put money for profit (into stocks, etc.). **b** *colloq.* buy (*invested in a new car*). **3** *tr.* **a** (foll. by *with*) provide *or* endue (a person with qualities, insignia, or rank). **b** (foll. by *in*) attribute or entrust (qualities or feelings to a person). **4** *tr.* cover as a garment. **5** *tr.* lay siege to. □□ **in•vest•a•ble** *adj.* **in•vest•i•ble** *adj.* **in•ves•tor** *n.*

WORD HISTORY   **invest**

Mid 16th cent. (in the senses 'clothe', 'clothe with the insignia of a rank', and 'endow with authority'): from French *investir* or Latin *investire*, from *in-* 'into, upon' + *vestire* 'clothe' (from *vestis* 'clothing'). Senses 1 and 2 (early 17th cent.) are influenced by Italian *investire* 'invest.'

---

in•ves•ti•gate /invéstigayt/ *v.* **1** *tr.* **a** inquire into; examine; study carefully. **b** make an official inquiry into. **2** *intr.* make a systematic inquiry or search. □□ **in•ves•ti•ga•tor** *n.* **in•ves•ti•ga•to•ry** /–gətáwree/ *adj.* [L *investigare investigat-* (as IN-², *vestigare* track)]

in•ves•ti•ga•tion /invéstigáyshən/ *n.* **1** the process or an instance of investigating. **2** a formal examination or study.

in•ves•ti•ga•tive /invéstigaytiv/ *adj.* seeking or serving to investigate, esp. (of journalism) inquiring intensively into controversial issues.

in•ves•ti•ture /invéstichōōr, –chər/ *n.* **1** the formal investing of a person with honors or rank, esp. a ceremony at which a sovereign confers honors. **2** (often foll. by *with*) the act of enduing (with attributes). [ME f. med.L *investitura* (as INVEST)]

in•vest•ment /invéstmənt/ *n.* **1** the act or process of investing. **2** money invested. **3** property, etc., in which money is invested. **4** the act of besieging; a blockade.

in•vest•ment trust *n.* a limited company whose business is the investment of shareholders' funds, the shares being traded like those of any other public company.

in•vet•er•ate /invétərət/ *adj.* **1** (of a person) confirmed in an (esp. undesirable) habit, etc. (*an inveterate gambler*). **2 a** (of a habit, etc.) long-established. **b** (of an activity, esp. an undesirable one) habitual. □□ **in•vet•er•a•cy** /–rəsee/ *n.* **in•vet•er•ate•ly** *adv.* [ME f. L *inveterare inveterat-* make old (as IN-², *vetus veteris* old)]

in•vid•i•ous /invídeeəs/ *adj.* (of an action, conduct, attitude, etc.) likely to excite resentment or indignation against the person responsible, esp. by real or seeming injustice (*an invidious position*; *an invidious task*). □□ **in•vid•i•ous•ly** *adv.* **in•vid•i•ous•ness** *n.* [L *invidiosus* f. *invidia* ENVY]

in•vig•i•late /invíjilayt/ *v.intr.* **1** keep watch. **2** *Brit.* supervise candidates at an examination. □□ **in•vig•i•la•tion** /–láyshən/ *n.* **in•vig•i•la•tor** *n.* [orig. = keep watch, f. L *invigilare invigilat-* (as IN-², *vigilare* watch f. *vigil* watchful)]

in•vig•or•ate /invígərayt/ *v.tr.* give vigor or strength to. □□ **in•vig•or•at•ing** *adj.* **in•vig•or•at•ing•ly** *adv.* **in•vig•or•a•tion** /–ráyshən/ *n.* **in•vig•or•a•tive** /–vígərətiv/ *adj.* **in•vig•or•a•tor** *n.* [IN-² + med.L *vigorare vigorat-* make strong]

in•vin•ci•ble /invínsibəl/ *adj.* unconquerable; that cannot be defeated. □□ **in•vin•ci•bil•i•ty** *n.* **in•vin•ci•ble•ness** *n.* **in•vin•ci•bly** *adv.* [ME f. OF f. L *invincibilis* (as IN-¹, VINCIBLE)]

in•vi•o•la•ble /invíoləbəl/ *adj.* not to be violated or profaned. □□ **in•vi•o•la•bil•i•ty** /–bílitee/ *n.* **in•vi•o•la•bly** *adv.* [F *inviolable* or L *inviolabilis* (as IN-¹, VIOLATE)]

in•vi•o•late /invíolət/ *adj.* not violated or profaned. □□ **in•vi•o•la•cy** /–ləsee/ *n.* **in•vi•o•late•ly** *adv.* **in•vi•o•late•ness** *n.* [ME f. L *inviolatus* (as IN-¹, *violare, violat-* treat violently)]

in•vis•i•ble /invízibəl/ *adj.* **1** not visible to the eye, either characteristically or because hidden. **2** too small to be seen or noticed. **3** artfully concealed so as to be imperceptible. □□ **in•vis•i•bil•i•ty** *n.* **in•vis•i•ble•ness** *n.* **in•vis•i•bly** *adv.* [ME f. OF *invisible* or L *invisibilis* (as IN-¹, VISIBLE)]

in•vis•i•ble ex•ports *n.pl.* (also **in•vis•i•ble im•ports**) items, esp. services, involving payment between countries but not constituting tangible commodities.

in•vi•ta•tion /invitáyshən/ *n.* **1 a** the process of inviting or fact of being invited, esp. to a social occasion. **b** the spoken or written form in which a person is invited. **2** the action or an act of enticing; attraction; allurement.

in•vite v. & n. •v. /invít/ **1** tr. (often foll. by to, or to + infin.) ask (a person) courteously to come, or to do something (were invited to lunch; invited them to reply). **2** tr. make a formal courteous request for (invited comments). **3** tr. tend to call forth unintentionally (something unwanted). **4 a** tr. attract. **b** intr. be attractive. •n. /ínvīt/ colloq. an invitation. □□ **in•vi•tee** /–teé/ n. **in•vit•er** n. [F inviter or L invitare]

in•vit•ing /invíting/ adj. **1** attractive. **2** enticing; tempting. □□ **in•vit•ing•ly** adv. **in•vit•ing•ness** n.

in vi•tro /in veétrō/ adv. Biol. (of processes or reactions) taking place in a test tube or other laboratory environment (opp. IN VIVO). [L, = in glass]

in vi•vo /in veévō/ adv. Biol. (of processes) taking place in a living organism. [L, = in a living thing]

in•vo•ca•tion /ínvəkáyshən/ n. **1** the act or an instance of invoking, esp. in prayer. **2** an appeal to a supernatural being or beings, e.g., the Muses, for psychological or spiritual inspiration. **3** Eccl. the words "In the name of the Father," etc., used as the preface to a sermon, etc. □□ **in•voc•a•to•ry** /invókətáwree/ adj. [ME f. OF f. L invocatio –onis (as INVOKE)]

in•voice /ínvoys/ n. & v. •n. a list of goods shipped or sent, or services rendered, with prices and charges; a bill. •v.tr. **1** make an invoice of (goods and services). **2** send an invoice to (a person). [earlier invoyes pl. of invoy = ENVOY²]

in•voke /invók/ v.tr. **1** call on (a deity, etc.) in prayer or as a witness. **2** appeal to (the law, a person's authority, etc.). **3** summon (a spirit) by charms. **4** ask earnestly for (vengeance, help, etc.). □□ **in•vo•ca•ble** adj. **in•vok•er** n. [F invoquer f. L invocare (as IN-², vocare call)]

in•vo•lu•cre /ínvəlóōkər/ n. **1** a covering or envelope. **2** Anat. a membranous envelope. **3** Bot. a whorl of bracts surrounding an inflorescence. □□ **in•vo•lu•cral** /–lóōkrəl/ adj. [F involucre or L involucrum (as INVOLVE)]

in•vol•un•tar•y /invóləntèree/ adj. **1** done without the exercise of the will; unintentional. **2** (of a limb, muscle, or movement) not under the control of the will. □□ **in•vol•un•tar•i•ly** /–térilee/ adv. **in•vol•un•tar•i•ness** n. [LL involuntarius (as IN-², VOLUNTARY)]

in•vo•lute /ínvəlóōt/ adj. & n. •adj. **1** involved; intricate. **2** curled spirally. **3** Bot. rolled inward at the edges. •n. Geom. the locus of a point fixed on a straight line that rolls without sliding on a curve and is in the plane of that curve (cf. EVOLUTE). [L involutus past part. of involvere: see INVOLVE]

in•vo•lut•ed /ínvəlóōtid/ adj. **1** complicated; abstruse. **2** = INVOLUTE adj. 2.

in•vo•lu•tion /ínvəlóōshən/ n. **1** the process of involving. **2** an entanglement. **3** intricacy. **4** curling inward. **5** a part that curls upward. **6** Math. the raising of a quantity to any power. **7** Physiol. the reduction in size of an organ in old age, or when its purpose has been fulfilled (esp. the uterus after childbirth). □□ **in•vo•lu•tion•al** adj. [L involutio (as INVOLVE)]

in•volve /invólv/ v.tr. **1** (often foll. by in) cause (a person or thing) to participate, or share the experience or effect (in a situation, activity, etc.). **2** imply; entail; make necessary. **3** (foll. by in) implicate (a person in a charge, crime, etc.). **4** include or affect in its operations. **5** (as involved adj.) **a** (often foll. by in) concerned or interested. **b** complicated in thought or form. [ME f. L involvere involut- (as IN-², volvere roll)]

in•volve•ment /invólvmənt/ n. **1** the act or an instance of involving; the process of being involved. **2** financial embarrassment. **3** a complicated affair or concern.

in•vul•ner•a•ble /invúlnərəbəl/ adj. that cannot be wounded or hurt, physically or mentally. □□ **in•vul•ner•a•bil•i•ty** n. **in•vul•ner•a•bly** adv. [L invulnerabilis (as IN-¹, VULNERABLE)]

in•ward /ínwərd/ adj. & adv. •adj. **1** directed toward the inside; going in. **2** situated within. **3** mental; spiritual. •adv. (also **in•wards**) **1** (of motion or position) toward the inside. **2** in the mind or soul. [OE innanweard (as IN, –WARD)]

in•ward•ly /ínwərdlee/ adv. **1** on the inside. **2** in the mind or soul. **3** (of speaking) not aloud; inaudibly. [OE inweardlíce (as INWARD)]

in•ward•ness /ínwərdnis/ n. **1** inner nature; essence. **2** the condition of being inward. **3** spirituality.

in•wards var. of INWARD adv.

in•weave /ínweév/ v.tr. (also **en•weave**) (past •wove /–wóv/; past part. •wo•ven /–wóvən/) **1** weave (two or more things) together. **2** intermingle.

in•wrap var. of ENWRAP.

in•wreathe var. of ENWREATHE.

in•wrought /ínráwt/ adj. **1 a** (often foll. by with) (of a fabric) decorated (with a pattern). **b** (often foll. by in, on) (of a pattern) wrought (in or on a fabric). **2** closely blended.

I/O abbr. Computing input/output.

IOC abbr. International Olympic Committee.

i•od•ic /īódik/ adj. Chem. containing iodine in chemical combination (iodic acid). □□ **i•o•date** /íədayt/ n.

i•o•dide /íədīd/ n. Chem. any compound of iodine with another element or group.

i•o•din•ate /íód'nayt, íəd'n–/ v.tr. treat or combine with iodine. □□ **i•o•din•a•tion** /–náyshən/ n.

i•o•dine /íədīn, –din, –deen/ n. **1** Chem. a non-metallic element of the halogen group, forming black crystals and a violet vapor, used in medicine and photography, and important as an essential element for living organisms. ¶ Symb.: **I**. **2** a solution of this in alcohol used as a mild antiseptic. [F iode f. Gk iōdēs violetlike f. ion violet + –INE⁴]

i•o•dism /íədizəm/ n. Med. a condition caused by an overdose of iodides.

i•o•dize /íədīz/ v.tr. treat or impregnate with iodine. □□ **i•o•di•za•tion** n.

iodo- /ī-ódō/ comb. form (usu. **iod-** before a vowel) Chem. iodine.

i•o•do•form /ī-ódəfawrm, –ódə–/ n. a pale yellow, volatile, sweet-smelling solid compound of iodine with antiseptic properties. ¶ Chem. formula: CHI₃. [IODINE after chloroform]

i•on /íən, íon/ n. an atom or group of atoms that has lost one or more electrons (= CATION), or gained one or more electrons (= ANION). [Gk, neut. pres. part. of eimi go]

-ion suffix (usu. as **–sion**, **–tion**, **–xion**; see –ATION, –ITION, –UTION) forming nouns denoting: **1** verbal action (excision). **2** an instance of this (a suggestion). **3** a resulting state or product (vexation; concoction). [from or after F –ion or L –io –ionis]

ion ex•change n. the exchange of ions of the same charge between an insoluble solid and a solution in contact with it, used in water softening and other purification and separation processes.

I•o•ni•an /ī-óneeən/ n. & v. •n. a native or inhabitant of ancient Ionia in W. Asia Minor. •adj. of or relating to Ionia or the Ionians. [L Ionius f. Gk Iōnios]

I•o•ni•an mode n. Mus. the mode represented by the natural diatonic scale C–C.

I•on•ic /īónik/ adj. & n. •adj. **1** of the order of Greek architecture characterized by a column with scroll shapes on either side of the capital. **2** of the ancient Greek dialect used in Ionia. •n. the Ionic dialect. [L Ionicus f. Gk Iōnikos]

i•on•ic /īónik/ adj. of, relating to, or using ions. □□ **i•on•i•cal•ly** adv.

i•on•i•za•tion /íənīzáyshən/ n. the process of producing ions as a result of solvation, heat, radiation, etc.

i•on•i•za•tion cham•ber n. an instrument for detecting ionizing radiation.

i•on•ize /íənīz/ v.tr. & intr. convert or be converted into an ion or ions. □□ **i•on•iz•a•ble** adj.

i•on•iz•er /íənīzər/ n. any thing which produces ionization, esp. a device used to improve the quality of the air in a room, etc.

i•on•iz•ing ra•di•a•tion n. a radiation consisting of particles, X-rays, or gamma rays with sufficient energy to cause ionization in the medium through which it passes.

i•on•o•sphere /íónəsfeer/ n. an ionized region of the atmosphere above the stratosphere, extending to about 600 miles (1,000 km) above the earth's surface and able to reflect radio waves, allowing long-distance transmission around the earth (cf. TROPOSPHERE). □□ **i•on•o•spher•ic** /–sféerik, –sfér–/ adj.

-ior¹ /yər, eeər/ suffix forming adjectives of comparison (senior; ulterior). [L]

-ior² /yər, eeər/ suffix (also esp. Brit. **–iour**) forming nouns (savior; warrior). [-I- (as a stem element) + –OUR, –OR¹]

i•o•ta /ī-ótə/ n. **1** the ninth letter of the Greek alphabet (I, ι). **2** (usu. with neg.) the smallest possible amount. [Gk iōta]

IOU /í-ō-yóō/ n. a signed document acknowledging a debt. [= I owe you]

-iour esp. Brit. var. of –IOR².

-ious /–eeəs, –əs/ suffix forming adjectives meaning 'characterized by, full of,' often corresponding to nouns in –ion (cautious; curious; spacious). [from or after F –ieux f. L –iosus]

IPA abbr. International Phonetic Alphabet (or Association).

ip•e•cac /ípikak/ n. colloq. ipecacuanha. [abbr.]

ip•e•cac•u•an•ha /ípikákyōō-áanə/ n. the root of a S. American shrub, Cephaelis ipecacuanha, used as an emetic and purgative. [Port. f. Tupi-Guarani ipekaaguéne emetic creeper]

ip•o•moe•a /ípəmeéə/ n. any twining plant of the genus Ipomoea, having trumpet-shaped flowers, e.g., the sweet potato and morning glory. [mod.L f. Gk ips ipos worm + homoios like]

ips abbr. (also **i.p.s.**) inches per second.

ip•se dix•it /ípsee díksit/ n. a dogmatic statement resting merely on the speaker's authority. [L, he himself said it (orig. of Pythagoras)]

ip•si•lat•er•al /ípsilátərəl/ adj. belonging to or occurring on the same side of the body. [irreg. f. L ipse self + LATERAL]

ip•sis•si•ma ver•ba /ipsísimə vérbə, –wérbə/ n.pl. the precise words. [L]

ip•so fac•to /ípsō fáktō/ adv. **1** by that very fact or act. **2** thereby. [L]

IQ abbr. intelligence quotient.

-ique *archaic* var. of –IC.

IR *abbr.* infrared.

Ir *symb. Chem.* the element iridium.

ir- /ir/ *prefix* assim. form of IN-[1], IN-[2] before *r*.

IRA *abbr.* **1** individual retirement account. **2** Irish Republican Army.

i·ra·de /iraáde/ *n. hist.* a written decree of the sultan of Turkey. [Turk. f. Arab. 'irāda will]

I·ra·ni·an /iráyneeən/ *adj. & n.* ● *adj.* **1** of or relating to Iran (formerly Persia) in the Middle East. **2** of the Indo-European group of languages including Persian, Pashto, Avestan, and Kurdish. ● *n.* **1** a native or national of Iran. **2** a person of Iranian descent.

I·ra·qi /iraákee/ *adj. & n.* ● *adj.* of or relating to Iraq in the Middle East. ● *n.* (*pl.* **I·ra·qis**) **1 a** a native or national of Iraq. **b** a person of Iraqi descent. **2** the form of Arabic spoken in Iraq.

i·ras·ci·ble /irásibəl/ *adj.* irritable; hot-tempered. □□ **i·ras·ci·bil·i·ty** *n.* **i·ras·ci·bly** *adv.* [ME f. F f. LL *irascibilis* f. L *irasci* grow angry f. *ira* anger]

i·rate /iráyt/ *adj.* angry, enraged. □□ **i·rate·ly** *adv.* **i·rate·ness** *n.* [L *iratus* f. *ira* anger]

IRBM *abbr.* intermediate range ballistic missile.

ire /ir/ *n. literary* anger. □□ **ire·ful** *adj.* [ME f. OF f. L *ira*]

i·ren·ic /irénik, īreénik/ *adj.* (also **i·ren·i·cal**, esp. *Brit.* **ei·ren·ic**) *literary* aiming or aimed at peace. [Gk *eirēnikos* f. *eirēnē* peace]

ir·i·da·ceous /iridáyshəs/ *adj. Bot.* of or relating to the family Iridaceae of plants growing from bulbs, corms, or rhizomes, e.g., iris, crocus, and gladiolus. [mod.L *iridaceus* (as IRIS)]

ir·i·des·cent /iridésənt/ *adj.* **1** showing rainbowlike luminous or gleaming colors. **2** changing color with position. □□ **ir·i·des·cence** /-səns/ *n.* **ir·i·des·cent·ly** *adv.* [L IRIS + –ESCENT]

i·rid·i·um /irídeeəm/ *n. Chem.* a hard, white metallic element of the transition series used esp. in alloys. ¶ Symb.: **Ir.** [mod.L f. L IRIS + –IUM]

i·ris /íris/ *n.* **1** the flat, circular colored membrane behind the cornea of the eye, with a circular opening (pupil) in the center. **2** any herbaceous plant of the genus *Iris*, usu. with tuberous roots, sword-shaped leaves, and showy flowers. **3** (in full **iris diaphragm**) an adjustable diaphragm of thin overlapping plates for regulating the size of a central hole esp. for the admission of light to a lens. [ME f. L *iris iridis* f. Gk *iris iridos* rainbow, iris]

I·rish /írish/ *adj. & n.* ● *adj.* of or relating to Ireland; of or like its people. ● *n.* **1** the Celtic language of Ireland. **2** (prec. by *the*; treated as *pl.*) the people of Ireland. [ME f. OE *Iras* the Irish]

I·rish bull *n.* an expression containing a contradiction in terms or implying ludicrous inconsistency.

I·rish cof·fee *n.* coffee mixed with Irish whiskey and served with cream on top.

I·rish·man /írishmən/ *n.* (*pl.* **-men**) a person who is Irish by birth or descent.

I·rish moss *n.* dried carrageen.

I·rish Sea *n.* the sea between England and Wales and Ireland.

I·rish set·ter *n.* a silky-haired, dark red breed of setter.

I·rish stew *n.* a stew usu. of mutton, potato, and onion.

I·rish ter·ri·er *n.* a rough-haired, light reddish-brown breed of terrier.

I·rish·wom·an /írishwŏŏmən/ *n.* (*pl.* **-wom·en**) a woman who is Irish by birth or descent.

i·ri·tis /irítis/ *n.* inflammation of the iris.

irk /ərk/ *v.tr.* (usu. *impers.*; often foll. by *that* + clause) irritate; bore; annoy. [ME: orig. unkn.]

irk·some /órksəm/ *adj.* tedious; annoying; tiresome. □□ **irk·some·ly** *adv.* **irk·some·ness** *n.* [ME, = tired, etc., f. IRK + –SOME[1]]

IRO *abbr.* International Refugee Organization.

i·ro·ko /iróko/ *n.* (*pl.* **-kos**) **1** either of two African trees, *Chlorophora excelsa* or *C. regia*. **2** the light-colored hardwood from these trees. [Ibo]

i·ron /íərn/ *n., adj., & v.* ● *n.* **1** *Chem.* a silver-white ductile metallic element occurring naturally as hematite, magnetite, etc., much used for tools and implements, and an essential element in all living organisms. ¶ Symb.: **Fe**. **2** this as a type of unyieldingness or a symbol of firmness (*man of iron; will of iron*). **3** a tool or implement made of iron (*branding iron; curling iron*). **4** a household, now usu. electrical, implement with a flat base which is heated to smooth clothes, etc. **5** a golf club with an iron or steel sloping face used for lofting the ball. **6** (usu. in *pl.*) a fetter (*clapped in irons*). **7** (usu. in *pl.*) a stirrup. **8** (often in *pl.*) an iron support for a malformed leg. **9** a preparation of iron as a tonic or dietary supplement (*iron pills*). ● *adj.* **1** made of iron. **2** very robust. **3** unyielding; merciless (*iron determination*). ● *v.tr.* **1** smooth (clothes, etc.) with an iron. **2** furnish or cover with iron. **3** shackle with irons. □ **in irons** handcuffed, chained, etc. **iron in the fire** an undertaking, opportunity, or commitment (usu. in *pl.*: *too many irons in the fire*). **iron out** remove or smooth over (difficulties, etc.). □□ **i·ron·er** *n.* **i·ron·ing** *n.* (in sense 1 of *v.*). **i·ron·less** *adj.* **i·ron·like** *adj.* [OE *īren*, *īsern* f. Gmc, prob. f. Celt.]

I·ron Age *n. Archaeol.* the period following the Bronze Age when iron replaced bronze in the making of implements and weapons.

i·ron·bark /íərnbaark/ *n.* any of various eucalyptus trees with a thick solid bark and hard dense timber.

i·ron·bound /íərnbownd/ *adj.* **1** bound with iron. **2** rigorous; hard and fast. **3** (of a coast) rockbound.

i·ron·clad *adj. & n.* ● *adj.* /íərnklád/ **1** clad or protected with iron. **2** impregnable; rigorous. ● *n.* /íərnklad/ *hist.* an early name for a 19th-c. warship built of iron or protected by iron plates.

I·ron Cross *n.* the highest German military decoration for bravery.

I·ron Cur·tain *n. hist.* a notional barrier to the passage of people and information between the former Soviet bloc and the West.

i·ron hand *n.* firmness or inflexibility (cf. VELVET GLOVE).

i·ron·ic /irónik/ *adj.* (also **i·ron·i·cal**) **1** using or displaying irony. **2** in the nature of irony. □□ **i·ron·i·cal·ly** *adv.* [F *ironique* or LL *ironicus* f. Gk *eirōnikos* dissembling (as IRONY[1])]

i·ron·ing board *n.* a flat surface usu. on legs and of adjustable height on which clothes are ironed.

i·ro·nist /íronist/ *n.* a person who uses irony. □□ **i·ro·nize** *v.intr.* [Gk *eirōn* dissembler f. –IST]

i·ron lung *n.* a rigid case fitted over a patient's body, used for administering prolonged artificial respiration by means of mechanical pumps.

i·ron maid·en *n. hist.* an instrument of torture consisting of a coffin-shaped box lined with iron spikes.

i·ron·mas·ter /íərnmastər/ *n. Brit.* a manufacturer of iron.

i·ron mold *n.* a spot caused by iron rust or an ink stain, esp. on fabric.

i·ron·mon·ger /íərnmunggər, –mong–/ *n. Brit.* a dealer in hardware, etc. □□ **i·ron·mon·ger·y** *n.* (*pl.* **-ies**).

i·ron-on *adj.* able to be fixed to the surface of a fabric by the heat of an iron.

i·ron py·rites *n.* see PYRITES.

i·ron ra·tions *n.pl.* a small emergency supply of food.

i·ron·side /íərnsīd/ *n.* **1** a person of great bravery, strength, or endurance. **2** (usu. **Ironsides**) **a** nickname of Oliver Cromwell. **b** Cromwell's troopers in the English Civil War. **3** (**ironsides**) (usu. treated as *sing.*) an ironclad.

i·ron·stone /íərnstōn/ *n.* **1** any rock containing a substantial proportion of an iron compound. **2** a kind of hard, white, opaque stoneware.

i·ron·ware /íərnwair/ *n.* articles made of iron, esp. domestic implements.

i·ron·wood /íərnwŏŏd/ *n.* **1** any of various tough-timbered trees and shrubs, esp. American hornbeam *Carpinus caroliniana*. **2** the wood from these trees.

i·ron·work /íərnwərk/ *n.* **1** things made of iron. **2** work in iron.

i·ron·works /íərnwərks/ *n.* (as *sing.* or *pl.*) a place where iron is smelted or iron goods are made.

i·ron·y[1] /íronee/ *n.* (*pl.* **-ies**) **1** an expression of meaning, often humorous or sarcastic, by the use of language of a different or opposite tendency. **2** an ill-timed or perverse arrival of an event or circumstance that is in itself desirable. **3** the use of language with one meaning for a privileged audience and another for those addressed or concerned. [L *ironia* f. Gk *eirōneia* simulated ignorance f. *eirōn* dissembler]

i·ron·y[2] /í-ərnee/ *adj.* of or like iron.

Ir·o·quoi·an /írəkwóy–ən/ *n. & adj.* ● *n.* **1** a language family of eastern N. America, including Cherokee and Mohawk. **2** a member of the Iroquois people. ● *adj.* of or relating to the Iroquois or the Iroquoian language family or one of its members.

Ir·o·quois /írəkwoy/ *n. & adj.* ● *n.* (*pl.* same) **1 a** a Native American confederacy of five (later six) peoples formerly inhabiting New York State. **b** a member of any of these peoples. **2** any of the languages of these peoples. ● *adj.* of or relating to the Iroquois or their languages. [F f. Algonquian]

ir·ra·di·ant /iráydeeənt/ *adj. literary* shining brightly. □□ **ir·ra·di·ance** /-əns/ *n.*

ir·ra·di·ate /iráydee-áyt/ *v.tr.* **1** subject to (any form of) radiation. **2** shine upon; light up. **3** throw light on (a subject). □□ **ir·ra·di·a·tive** /-deeətiv/ *adj.* [L *irradiare irradiat-* (as IN-[2], *radiare* f. *radius* RAY[1])]

ir·ra·di·a·tion /iráydee-áyshən/ *n.* **1** the process of irradiating. **2** shining; illumination. **3** the apparent extension of the edges of an illuminated object seen against a dark background. [F *irradiation* or LL *irradiatio* (as IRRADIATE)]

ir·ra·tion·al /iráshənəl/ *adj.* **1** illogical; unreasonable. **2** not endowed with reason. **3** *Math.* (of a root, etc.) not rational; not able to be expressed as a ratio between two integers; not commensurate with the natural numbers (e.g., a nonterminating decimal). □□ **ir·ra·tion·al·i·ty** /-álitee/ *n.* **ir·ra·tion·al·ize** *v.tr.* **ir·ra·tion·al·ly** *adv.* [L *irrationalis* (as IN-[1], RATIONAL)]

ir·re·claim·a·ble /irikláyməbəl/ *adj.* that cannot be reclaimed or reformed. □□ **ir·re·claim·a·bly** *adv.*

ir·rec·on·cil·a·ble /irékənsíləbəl/ *adj. & n.* ● *adj.* **1** implacably hostile. **2** (of ideas, etc.) incompatible. ● *n.* **1** an uncompromising opponent of a political measure, etc. **2** (usu. in *pl.*) any of two or more items, ideas, etc., that cannot be made to agree. □□ **ir·rec·on·cil·a·bil·i·ty** *n.* **ir·rec·on·cil·a·ble·ness** *n.* **ir·rec·on·cil·a·bly** *adv.*

ir·re·cov·er·a·ble /irikúvərəbəl/ *adj.* that cannot be recovered or remedied. □□ **ir·re·cov·er·a·bly** *adv.*

ir·re·cu·sa·ble /irikyōōzəbəl/ *adj.* that must be accepted. [F *irrécusable* or LL *irrecusabilis* (as IN-¹, *recusare* refuse)]

ir·re·deem·a·ble /irideémabəl/ *adj.* **1** that cannot be redeemed. **2** hopeless; absolute. **3 a** (of a government annuity) not terminable by repayment. **b** (of paper currency) for which the issuing authority does not undertake ever to pay coin. □□ **ir·re·deem·a·bil·i·ty** *n.* **ir·re·deem·a·bly** *adv.*

ir·re·den·tist /iridéntist/ *n.* a person, esp. in 19th-c. Italy, advocating the restoration to his or her country of any territory formerly belonging to it. □□ **ir·re·den·tism** *n.* [It. *irredentista* f. (*Italia*) *irredenta* unredeemed (Italy)]

ir·re·duc·i·ble /iridōōsibəl, –dyōō–/ *adj.* **1** that cannot be reduced or simplified. **2** (often foll. by *to*) that cannot be brought to a desired condition. □□ **ir·re·duc·i·bil·i·ty** *n.* **ir·re·duc·i·bly** *adv.*

ir·ref·ra·ga·ble /iréfrəgəbəl/ *adj.* **1** (of a statement, argument, or person) unanswerable; indisputable. **2** (of rules, etc.) inviolable. □□ **ir·ref·ra·ga·bly** *adv.* [LL *irrefragabilis* (as IN-¹, *refragari* oppose)]

ir·re·fran·gi·ble /irifránjibəl/ *adj.* **1** inviolable. **2** *Optics* incapable of being refracted.

ir·ref·u·ta·ble /iréfyətəbəl, irifyōō–/ *adj.* that cannot be refuted. □□ **ir·ref·u·ta·bil·i·ty** *n.* **ir·ref·u·ta·bly** *adv.* [LL *irrefutabilis* (as IN-¹, REFUTE)]

ir·re·gard·less /irigaárdlis/ *adj. & adv. disp.* = REGARDLESS. [prob. blend of IRRESPECTIVE and REGARDLESS]

▶**Irregardless**, with its illogical negative prefix, is widely heard, perhaps arising under the influence of such correct forms as *irrespective*. It is avoided by careful users of English. Use **regardless** to mean 'without regard or consideration for' or 'nevertheless': *I go walking every day regardless of season or weather.*

ir·reg·u·lar /irégyələr/ *adj. & n.* ● *adj.* **1** not regular; unsymmetrical; uneven; varying in form. **2** (of a surface) uneven. **3** contrary to a rule, moral principle, or custom; abnormal. **4** uneven in duration, order, etc. **5** (of troops) not belonging to the regular army. **6** *Gram.* (of a verb, noun, etc.) not inflected according to the usual rules. **7** disorderly. **8** (of a flower) having unequal petals, etc. ● *n.* (in *pl.*) irregular troops. □□ **ir·reg·u·lar·i·ty** /–láritee/ *n.* (*pl.* ·ties). **ir·reg·u·lar·ly** *adv.* [ME f. OF *irreguler* f. LL *irregularis* (as IN-¹, REGULAR)]

ir·rel·a·tive /irélətiv/ *adj.* **1** (often foll. by *to*) unconnected, unrelated. **2** having no relations; absolute. **3** irrelevant. □□ **ir·rel·a·tive·ly** *adv.*

ir·rel·e·vant /irélivənt/ *adj.* (often foll. by *to*) not relevant; not applicable (to a matter in hand). □□ **ir·rel·e·vance** /–vəns/ *n.* **ir·rel·e·van·cy** *n.* **ir·rel·e·vant·ly** *adv.*

▶See note at IMMATERIAL.

ir·re·li·gion /irilíjən/ *n.* disregard of or hostility to religion. □□ **ir·re·li·gion·ist** *n.* [F *irréligion* or L *irreligio* (as IN-¹, RELIGION)]

ir·re·li·gious /irilíjəs/ *adj.* **1** indifferent or hostile to religion. **2** lacking a religion. □□ **ir·re·li·gious·ly** *adv.* **ir·re·li·gious·ness** *n.*

ir·re·me·di·a·ble /írimeédeeəbəl/ *adj.* that cannot be remedied. □□ **ir·re·me·di·a·bly** *adv.* [L *irremediabilis* (as IN-¹, REMEDY)]

ir·re·mis·si·ble /írimísibəl/ *adj.* **1** unpardonable. **2** unalterably obligatory. □□ **ir·re·mis·si·bly** *adv.* [ME f. OF *irremissible* or eccl.L *irremissibilis* (as IN-¹, REMISSIBLE)]

ir·re·mov·a·ble /írimōōvəbəl/ *adj.* that cannot be removed, esp. from office. □□ **ir·re·mov·a·bil·i·ty** *n.* **ir·re·mov·a·bly** *adv.*

ir·rep·a·ra·ble /iréparəbəl/ *adj.* (of an injury, loss, etc.) that cannot be rectified or made good. □□ **ir·rep·a·ra·bil·i·ty** *n.* **ir·rep·a·ra·ble·ness** *n.* **ir·rep·a·ra·bly** *adv.* [ME f. OF f. L *irreparabilis* (as IN-¹, REPARABLE)]

ir·re·place·a·ble /íripláysəbəl/ *adj.* **1** that cannot be replaced. **2** of which the loss cannot be made good. □□ **ir·re·place·a·bly** *adv.*

ir·re·press·i·ble /iriprésibəl/ *adj.* that cannot be repressed or restrained. □□ **ir·re·press·i·bil·i·ty** *n.* **ir·re·press·i·ble·ness** *n.* **ir·re·press·i·bly** *adv.*

ir·re·proach·a·ble /iripróchəbəl/ *adj.* faultless; blameless. □□ **ir·re·proach·a·bil·i·ty** *n.* **ir·re·proach·a·ble·ness** *n.* **ir·re·proach·a·bly** *adv.* [F *irréprochable* (as IN-¹, REPROACH)]

ir·re·sist·i·ble /irizístibəl/ *adj.* **1** too strong or convincing to be resisted. **2** delightful; alluring. □□ **ir·re·sist·i·bil·i·ty** *n.* **ir·re·sist·i·ble·ness** *n.* **ir·re·sist·i·bly** *adv.* [med.L *irresistibilis* (as IN-¹, RESIST)]

ir·res·o·lute /irézəlōōt/ *adj.* **1** hesitant; undecided. **2** lacking in resoluteness. □□ **ir·res·o·lute·ly** *adv.* **ir·res·o·lute·ness** *n.* **ir·res·o·lu·tion** /–lōōshən/ *n.*

ir·re·solv·a·ble /irizólvəbəl/ *adj.* **1** that cannot be resolved into its components. **2** (of a problem) that cannot be solved.

ir·re·spec·tive /irispéktiv/ *adj.* (foll. by *of*) not taking into account; regardless of. □□ **ir·re·spec·tive·ly** *adv.*

ir·re·spon·si·ble /irispónsibəl/ *adj.* **1** acting or done without due sense of responsibility. **2** not responsible for one's conduct. □□ **ir·re·spon·si·bil·i·ty** *n.* **ir·re·spon·si·bly** *adv.*

ir·re·spon·sive /irispónsiv/ *adj.* (often foll. by *to*) not responsive. □□ **ir·re·spon·sive·ly** *adv.* **ir·re·spon·sive·ness** *n.*

ir·re·triev·a·ble /iritreévəbəl/ *adj.* that cannot be retrieved or restored. □□ **ir·re·triev·a·bil·i·ty** *n.* **ir·re·triev·a·bly** *adv.*

ir·rev·er·ent /irévərənt/ *adj.* lacking reverence. □□ **ir·rev·er·ence** /–rəns/ *n.* **ir·rev·er·en·tial** /–rénshəl/ *adj.* **ir·rev·er·ent·ly** *adv.* [L *irreverens* (as IN-¹, REVERENT)]

ir·re·vers·i·ble /irivársibəl/ *adj.* not reversible or alterable. □□ **ir·re·vers·i·bil·i·ty** *n.* **ir·re·vers·i·bly** *adv.*

ir·rev·o·ca·ble /irévəkəbəl, írivōk–/ *adj.* **1** unalterable. **2** gone beyond recall. □□ **ir·rev·o·ca·bil·i·ty** /–bílitee/ *n.* **ir·rev·o·ca·bly** *adv.* [ME f. L *irrevocabilis* (as IN-¹, REVOKE)]

ir·ri·gate /írigayt/ *v.tr.* **1 a** water (land) by means of channels. **b** (of a stream, etc.) supply (land) with water. **2** *Med.* supply (a wound, etc.) with a constant flow of liquid. **3** refresh as with moisture. □□ **ir·**

GRAMMAR TIP   **irregular**

Irregular Verbs. The majority of English verbs form the past tense and the past participle by adding *-d* or *-ed* to the present tense of the verb (as in *walk, walked, have walked*). **Irregular verbs** do not follow this pattern. Some change form in both the past and past participle (*buy, bought, bought*), some retain the same form in all three tenses (*cut, cut, cut*), and some change an internal vowel to form the past tense and add *-n* to the past participle (*break, broke, broken*). Still others follow no discernible pattern. Some of the most common and confusing irregular verbs in English are listed below.

Present	Past	Past Participle
be	was/were	been
bear	bore	borne, born
beat	beat	beaten
become	became	become
begin	began	begun
bend	bent	bent
bite	bit	bitten
blow	blew	blown
bring	brought	brought
buy	bought	bought
catch	caught	caught
choose	chose	chosen
come	came	come
do	did	done
draw	drew	drawn
drink	drank	drunk
drive	drove	driven
eat	ate	eaten
fall	fell	fallen
find	found	found
fly	flew	flown
forget	forgot	forgotten
forgive	forgave	forgiven
freeze	froze	frozen
get	got	got, gotten
give	gave	given
go	went	gone
grown	grew	grown
hear	heard	heard
hide	hid	hidden
keep	kept	kept
know	knew	known
lay	laid	laid
lie	lay	lain
mistake	mistook	mistaken
ride	rode	ridden
ring	rang	rung
rise	rose	risen
see	saw	seen
shake	shook	shaken
shrink	shrank	shrunk
sing	sang	sung
slay	slew	slain
speak	spoke	spoken
spring	sprang	sprung
steal	stole	stolen
swear	swore	sworn
swim	swam	swum
tear	tore	torn
throw	threw	thrown
wake	woke, waked	waked, woken

ri•ga•ble *adj.* ir•ri•ga•tion /–gáyshən/ *n.* ir•ri•ga•tive *adj.* ir•ri•ga•tor *n.* [L *irrigare* (as IN-², *rigare* moisten)]

ir•ri•ta•ble /íritəbəl/ *adj.* **1** easily annoyed or angered. **2** (of an organ, etc.) very sensitive to contact. **3** *Biol.* responding actively to physical stimulus. □□ ir•ri•ta•bil•i•ty *n.* ir•ri•ta•bly *adv.* [L *irritabilis* (as IRRITATE)]

ir•ri•tant /írit'nt/ *adj. & n.* • *adj.* causing irritation. • *n.* an irritant substance. □□ ir•ri•tan•cy *n.*

ir•ri•tate /íritayt/ *v.tr.* **1** excite to anger; annoy. **2** stimulate discomfort or pain in (a part of the body). **3** *Biol.* stimulate (an organ) to action. □□ ir•ri•tat•ed•ly *adv.* ir•ri•tat•ing *adj.* ir•ri•tat•ing•ly *adv.* ir•ri•ta•tion /–táyshən/ *n.* ir•ri•ta•tive *adj.* ir•ri•ta•tor *n.* [L *irritare irritat*–]

ir•rupt /irúpt/ *v.intr.* (foll. by *into*) enter forcibly or violently. □□ ir•rup•tion /irúpshən/ *n.* [L *irrumpere irrupt*- (as IN-², *rumpere* break)]

IRS *abbr.* Internal Revenue Service.

Is. *abbr.* **1 a** Island(s). **b** Isle(s). **2** (also **Isa.**) Isaiah (Old Testament).

is *3rd sing. present of* BE.

i•sa•gog•ic /ísəgójik/ *adj.* introductory. [L *isagogicus* f. Gk *eisagōgikos* f. *eisagōgē* introduction f. *eis* into + *agōgē* leading f. *agō* lead]

i•sa•gog•ics /ísəgójiks/ *n.* an introductory study, esp. of the literary and external history of the Bible.

i•sa•tin /ísətin/ *n. Chem.* a red crystalline derivative of indole used in the manufacture of dyes. [L *isatis* woad f. Gk]

ISBN *abbr.* international standard book number.

is•che•mi•a /iskéemeeə/ *n.* (esp. *Brit.* **is•chae•mi•a**) *Med.* a reduction of the blood supply to part of the body. □□ is•che•mic *adj.* [mod.L f. Gk *iskhaimos* f. *iskhō* keep back]

is•chi•um /iskeeəm/ *n.* (*pl.* **is•chi•a** /–keeə/) the curved bone forming the base of each half of the pelvis. □□ is•chi•al *adj.* [L f. Gk *iskhion* hip joint: cf. SCIATIC]

-ise¹ *suffix* var. of -IZE.

▶See note at -IZE.

-ise² /īz, eez/ *suffix* forming nouns of quality, state, or function (*exercise; expertise; franchise; merchandise*). [from or after F or OF –*ise* f. L –*itia*, etc.]

-ise³ *suffix* var. of -ISH².

i•sen•trop•ic /ísentrópik, –trópik/ *adj.* having equal entropy. [ISO- + ENTROPY]

-ish¹ /ish/ *suffix* forming adjectives: **1** from nouns, meaning: **a** having the qualities or characteristics of (*boyish*). **b** of the nationality of (*Danish*). **2** from adjectives, meaning 'somewhat' (*thickish*). **3** *colloq.* denoting an approximate age or time of day (*fortyish; six-thirtyish*). [OE –*isc*]

-ish² /ish/ *suffix* forming verbs (*vanish, finish*). [from or after F –*iss*- (in extended stems of verbs in –*ir*) f. L –*isc*- incept. suffix]

i•sin•glass /ízinglas/ *n.* **1** a kind of gelatin obtained from fish, esp. sturgeon, and used in making jellies, glue, etc. **2** mica. [corrupt. of obs. Du. *huisenblas* sturgeon's bladder, assim. to GLASS]

isl. *abbr.* island.

Is•lam /íslaam, íz–, islám, iz–/ *n.* **1** the religion of the Muslims, a monotheistic faith regarded as revealed through Muhammad as the Prophet of Allah. **2** the Muslim world. □□ **Is•lam•ic** *adj.* **Is•lam•ism** *n.* **Is•lam•ist** *n.* **Is•lam•ize** *v.tr.* **Is•lam•i•za•tion** /–mizáyshən/ *n.* [Arab. *islām* submission (to God) f. *aslama* resign oneself]

is•land /ílənd/ *n.* **1** a piece of land surrounded by water. **2** anything compared to an island, esp. in being surrounded in some way. **3** = TRAFFIC ISLAND. **4 a** a detached or isolated thing. **b** *Physiol.* a detached portion of tissue or group of cells (cf. ISLET). **5** *Naut.* a ship's superstructure, bridge, etc. [OE *īgland* f. *īg* island + LAND: first syll. infl. by ISLE]

is•land•er /íləndər/ *n.* a native or inhabitant of an island.

isle /īl/ *n. poet.* an island (in place-names) or peninsula, esp. a small one. [ME *ile* f. OF *ile* f. L *insula*: later ME & OF *isle* after L]

is•let /ílit/ *n.* **1** a small island. **2** *Anat.* a portion of tissue structurally distinct from surrounding tissues. **3** an isolated place. [OF, dimin. of ISLE]

is•lets of Lang•er•hans /láanggərhaáns, –haánz/ *n.pl. Physiol.* groups of pancreatic cells secreting insulin and glucagon.

ism /ízəm/ *n. colloq.* usu. *derog.* any distinctive but unspecified doctrine or practice of a kind with a name in –*ism*.

-ism /ízəm/ *suffix* forming nouns, esp. denoting: **1** an action or its result (*baptism; organism*). **2** a system, principle, or ideological movement (*Conservatism; jingoism; feminism*). **3** a state or quality (*heroism; barbarism*). **4** a basis of prejudice or discrimination (*racism; sexism*). **5** a peculiarity in language (*Americanism*). **6** a pathological condition (*alcoholism; Parkinsonism*). [from or after F –*isme* f. L –*ismus* f. Gk –*ismos* or –*isma* f. –*izō* –IZE]

Is•ma•i•li /ismay- eélee, –maa–/ *n.* (*pl.* **Is•ma•i•lis**) a member of a Muslim Shiite sect that arose in the 8th c. [*Ismail* a son of the patriarch Ibrāhim (= Abraham)]

is•n't /íznt/ *contr.* is not.

ISO *abbr.* **1** incentive stock option. **2** International Standardization Organization.

iso- /ísō/ *comb. form* **1** equal (*isometric*). **2** *Chem.* isomeric, esp. of a hydrocarbon with a branched chain of carbon atoms (*isobutane*). [Gk *isos* equal]

---

i•so•bar /ísəbaar/ *n.* **1** a line on a map connecting positions having the same atmospheric pressure at a given time or on average over a given period. **2** a curve for a physical system at constant pressure. **3** one of two or more isotopes of different elements, with the same atomic weight. □□ i•so•bar•ic /–bárik/ *adj.* [Gk *isobarēs* of equal weight (as ISO-, *baros* weight)]

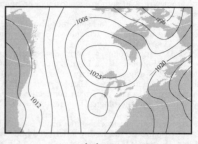

isobars

i•so•cheim /ísəkīm/ *n.* a line on a map connecting places having the same average temperature in winter. [ISO- + Gk *kheima* winter weather]

i•so•chro•mat•ic /ísōkrōmátik/ *adj.* of the same color.

i•soch•ro•nous /ísókrənəs/ *adj.* **1** occurring at the same time. **2** occupying equal time. □□ i•soch•ro•nous•ly *adv.* [ISO- + Gk *khronos* time]

i•so•cli•nal /ísəklín'l/ *adj.* (also i•so•clin•ic /–klínik/) **1** *Geol.* (of a fold) in which the two limbs are parallel. **2** corresponding to equal values of magnetic dip. [ISO- + CLINE]

i•so•clin•ic var. of ISOCLINAL.

i•so•dy•nam•ic /ísōdínámik/ *adj.* corresponding to equal values of (magnetic) force.

i•so•en•zyme /ísō-énzīm/ *n. Biochem.* one of two or more enzymes with identical function but different structure.

i•so•ge•o•therm /ísōjeé-ōthórm/ *n.* a line or surface connecting points in the interior of the earth having the same temperature. □□ i•so•ge•o•ther•mal *adj.*

i•so•gloss /ísəglaws, –glos/ *n.* a line on a map marking an area having a distinct linguistic feature.

i•so•gon•ic /ísəgónik/ *adj.* corresponding to equal values of magnetic declination.

i•so•hel /ísōhel/ *n.* a line on a map connecting places having the same duration of sunshine. [ISO- + Gk *hēlios* sun]

i•so•hy•et /ísōhī-it/ *n.* a line on a map connecting places having the same amount of rainfall in a given period. [ISO- + Gk *huetos* rain]

i•so•late /ísəláyt/ *v.tr.* **1 a** place apart or alone, cut off from society. **b** place (a patient thought to be contagious or infectious) in quarantine. **2 a** identify and separate for attention (*isolated the problem*). **b** *Chem.* separate (a substance) from a mixture. **3** insulate (electrical apparatus). □□ i•so•la•ble /ísələbəl/ *adj.* i•so•lat•a•ble *adj.* i•so•la•tor *n.* [orig. in past part., f. F *isolé* f. It. *isolato* f. LL *insulatus* f. L *insula* island]

i•so•lat•ed /ísəlaytid/ *adj.* **1** lonely; cut off from society or contact; remote (*feeling isolated; an isolated farmhouse*). **2** untypical; unique (*an isolated example*).

i•so•lat•ing /ísəlayting/ *adj.* (of a language) having each element as an independent word without inflections.

i•so•la•tion /ísəláyshən/ *n.* the act or an instance of isolating; the state of being isolated or separated. □ **in isolation** considered singly and not relatively.

i•so•la•tion•ism /ísəláyshənizəm/ *n.* the policy of holding aloof from the affairs of other countries or groups esp. in politics. □□ i•so•la•tion•ist *n.*

i•so•leu•cine /ísōlőőseen/ *n. Biochem.* an amino acid that is a constituent of proteins and an essential nutrient. [G *Isoleucin* (see ISO-, LEUCINE)]

i•so•mer /ísəmər/ *n.* **1** *Chem.* one of two or more compounds with the same molecular formula but a different arrangement of atoms and different properties. **2** *Physics* one of two or more atomic nuclei that have the same atomic number and the same mass number but different energy states. □□ i•so•mer•ic /–mérik/ *adj.* i•som•er•ism /ísómərizəm/ *n.* i•som•er•ize *v.* [G f. Gk *isomerēs* sharing equally (as ISO-, *meros* share)]

i•som•er•ous /ísómərəs/ *adj. Bot.* (of a flower) having the same number of petals in each whorl. [Gk *isomerēs*: see ISOMER]

i•so•met•ric /ísəmétrik/ *adj.* **1** of equal measure. **2** *Physiol.* (of muscle action) developing tension while the muscle is prevented from contracting. **3** (of a drawing, etc.) with the plane of projection at equal angles to the three principal axes of the object shown. **4** *Math.*

(of a transformation) without change of shape or size. □□ **i·so·met·ri·cal·ly** adv. **i·som·e·try** /īsómitree/ n. (in sense 4). [Gk isometria equality of measure (as ISO-, –METRY)]

i·so·met·rics /īsəmétriks/ n.pl. a system of physical exercises in which muscles are caused to act against each other or against a fixed object.

i·so·morph /īsəmawrf/ n. an isomorphic substance or organism. [ISO- + Gk morphē form]

i·so·mor·phic /īsəmáwrfik/ adj. (also **i·so·mor·phous** /–fəs/) **1** exactly corresponding in form and relations. **2** Crystallog. having the same form. □□ **i·so·mor·phism** n.

-ison /isən/ suffix forming nouns, = –ATION (comparison; garrison; jettison; venison). [OF –aison, etc., f. L –atio, etc.: see –ATION]

i·so·phote /īsəfōt/ n. a line (imaginary or in a diagram) of equal brightness or illumination. [ISO- + Gk phōs phōtos light]

i·so·pleth /īsəpleth/ n. a line on a map connecting places having equal incidence of a meteorological feature. [ISO- + Gk plēthos fullness]

i·so·pod /īsəpod/ n. any crustacean of the order Isopoda, including woodlice, often parasitic and having a flattened body with seven pairs of legs. [F isopode f. mod.L Isopoda (as ISO-, Gk pous podos foot)]

i·sos·ce·les /īsósileez/ adj. (of a triangle) having two sides equal. [LL f. Gk isoskelēs (as ISO-, skelos leg)]

i·so·seis·mic /īsósízmik/ adj. & n. (also **i·so·seis·mal** /–məl/) • adj. having equal strength of earthquake shock. • n. a line on a map connecting places having an equal strength of earthquake shock.

i·sos·ta·sy /īsóstəsee/ n. Geol. the general state of equilibrium of the earth's crust, with the rise and fall of land relative to sea. □□ **i·so·stat·ic** /īsəstátik/ adj. [ISO- + Gk stasis station]

i·so·there /īsətheer/ n. a line on a map connecting places having the same average temperature in the summer. [ISO- + Gk theros summer]

i·so·therm /īsətherm/ n. **1** a line on a map connecting places having the same temperature at a given time or on average over a given period. **2** a curve for changes in a physical system at a constant temperature. □□ **i·so·ther·mal** adj. **i·so·ther·mal·ly** adv. [F isotherme (as ISO-, Gk thermē heat)]

i·so·ton·ic /īsətónik/ adj. **1** having the same osmotic pressure. **2** Physiol. (of muscle action) taking place with normal contraction. □□ **i·so·ton·i·cal·ly** adv. **i·so·to·nic·i·ty** /–tónisitee/ n. [Gk isotonos (as ISO-, TONE)]

i·so·tope /īsətōp/ n. Chem. one of two or more forms of an element differing from each other in relative atomic mass, and in nuclear but not chemical properties. □□ **i·so·top·ic** /–tópik/ adj. **i·so·top·i·cal·ly** adv. **i·sot·o·py** /īsótəpee, īsótōpee/ n. [ISO- + Gk topos place (i.e. in the periodic table of elements)]

i·so·trop·ic /īsətrópik, –tróp–/ adj. having the same physical properties in all directions (opp. ANISOTROPIC). □□ **i·so·trop·i·cal·ly** adv. **i·sot·ro·py** /īsótrəpee/ n. [ISO- + Gk tropos turn]

I-spy /ī-spī/ n. a children's game in which one player specifies the first letter of an object they can see, the other players then having to guess the identity of this object.

Is·rae·li /izráylee/ adj. & n. • adj. of or relating to the modern state of Israel in the Middle East. • n. **1** a native or national of Israel. **2** a person of Israeli descent. [Israel, a later name of Jacob, ult. f. Heb. yisrā'ēl he that strives with God (Gen. 32:28) + –I²]

Is·ra·el·ite /ízreeəlīt, –rəlīt/ n. hist. a native of ancient Israel; a Jew.

ISSN abbr. International Standard Serial Number.

is·su·ant /íshooənt/ adj. Heraldry (esp. of a beast with only the upper part shown) rising from the bottom or top of a bearing.

is·sue /íshoo/ n. & v. • n. **1 a** a giving out or circulation of shares, notes, stamps, etc. **b** a quantity of coins, supplies, copies of a newspaper or book, etc., circulated or put on sale at one time. **c** an item or amount given out or distributed. **d** each of a regular series of a magazine, etc. (the May issue). **2 a** an outgoing; an outflow. **b** a way out; an outlet, esp. the place of the emergence of a stream, etc. **3 a** point in question; an important subject of debate or litigation. **4** a result; an outcome; a decision. **5** Law children; progeny (without male issue). **6** archaic a discharge of blood, etc. • v. (**is·sues, is·sued, is·su·ing**) **1** intr. **a** (often foll. by out, forth) literary go or come out. **2** tr. **a** send forth; publish; put into circulation. **b** supply, esp. officially or authoritatively (usu. foll. by to): issued passports to them; issued orders to the staff). **3** intr. **a** (often foll. by from) be derived or result. **b** (foll. by in) end; result. **4** intr. (foll. by from) emerge from a condition. □ **at issue 1** under discussion; in dispute. **2** at variance. **join issue** identify and submit an issue for formal argument (foll. by with, on). **make an issue of** make a fuss about; turn into a subject of contention. **take issue** disagree, esp. on a specific issue (foll. by with, on). □□ **is·su·a·ble** adj. **is·su·ance** n. **is·sue·less** adj. **is·su·er** n. [ME f. OF ult. f. L exitus past part. of exire EXIT]

is·sue of fact n. (also **is·sue of law**) a dispute at law when the significance of a fact or facts is denied or when the application of the law is contested.

-ist /ist/ suffix forming personal nouns (and in some senses related adjectives) denoting: **1** an adherent of a system, etc., in –ism: see –ISM 2 (Marxist; fatalist). **2 a** a member of a profession (pathologist). **b** a person concerned with something (pharmacist). **3** a person who uses a thing (violinist; balloonist; motorist). **4** a person who does something expressed by a verb in –ize (plagiarist). **5** a person who subscribes to a prejudice or practices discrimination (racist; sexist). [OF –iste, L –ista f. Gk –istēs]

isth·mi·an /ísmeeən/ adj. of or relating to an isthmus, esp. (**Isthmian**) to the Isthmus of Corinth in southern Greece.

isth·mus /ísməs/ n. **1** a narrow piece of land connecting two larger bodies of land. **2** Anat. a narrow part connecting two larger parts. [L f. Gk isthmos]

-istic /ístik/ suffix forming adjectives from nouns and other stems generally denoting: of, pertaining to, referring to, or characteristic of that which is denoted by the noun or stem (stylistic, puristic, fatalistic). [F = istique, L = isticus f. Gk = istikos]

is·tle /ístlee/ n. = IXTLE.

IT abbr. information technology.

It. abbr. Italian.

it¹ /it/ pron. (poss. **its**; pl. **they**) **1** the thing (or occas. the animal or child) previously named or in question (took a stone and threw it). **2** the person in question (Who is it? It is I; is it a boy or a girl?). **3** as the subject of an impersonal verb (it is raining; it is winter; it is Tuesday; it is two miles to Denver). **4** as a substitute for a deferred subject or object (it is intolerable, this delay; it is silly to talk like that; I take it that you agree). **5** as a substitute for a vague object (tough it out; run for it!). **6** as the antecedent to a relative word (it was an owl I heard). **7** exactly what is needed (absolutely it). **8** the extreme limit of achievement. **9** colloq. sexual intercourse; sex appeal. **10** (in children's games) a player who has to perform a required feat, esp. to catch the others. □ **that's it** colloq. **1** that is the main point or difficulty. **2** that is enough or the end. **this is it** colloq. **1** the expected event is at hand. **2** this is the difficulty. [OE hit neut. of HE]

it² /it/ n. Brit. colloq. Italian vermouth (gin and it). [abbr.]

i.t.a. abbr. (also **ITA**) Initial Teaching Alphabet.

Ital. abbr. Italian.

ital. abbr. italic (type).

I·tal·ian /itályən/ n. & adj. • n. **1 a** a native or national of Italy. **b** a person of Italian descent. **2** the Romance language used in Italy and parts of Switzerland. • adj. of or relating to Italy or its people or language. [ME f. It. Italiano f. Italia Italy]

I·tal·ian·ate /itályənayt/ adj. of Italian style or appearance. [It. Italianato]

i·tal·ic /itálik/ adj. & n. • adj. **1 a** Printing of the sloping kind of letters now used esp. for emphasis or distinction and in foreign words. **b** (of handwriting) compact and pointed like early Italian handwriting. **2** (**Italic**) of ancient Italy. • n. **1** a letter in italic type. **2** this type. [L italicus f. Gk italikos Italian (because introduced by Aldo Manuzio of Venice)]

i·tal·i·cize /itálisīz/ v.tr. print in italics. □□ **i·tal·i·ci·za·tion** n.

I·tal·i·ot /itáleeət/ n. & adj. • n. an inhabitant of the Greek colonies in ancient Italy. • adj. of or relating to the Italiots. [Gk Italiōtēs f. Italia Italy]

Italo- /itálō/ comb. form Italian; Italian and.

itch /ich/ n. & v. • n. **1** an irritation in the skin. **2** an impatient desire; a hankering. **3** (prec. by the) scabies. • v.intr. **1** feel an irritation in the skin, causing a desire to scratch it. **2** (usu. foll. by to + infin.) (of a person) feel a desire to do something (am itching to tell you the news). [OE gycce, gyccan f. WG]

itch mite n. a parasitic arthropod, Sarcoptes scabiei, which burrows under the skin causing scabies.

itch·y /íchee/ adj. (**itch·i·er, itch·i·est**) having or causing an itch. □ **have itchy feet** colloq. **1** be restless. **2** have a strong urge to travel. □□ **itch·i·ness** n.

it'd /ítəd/ contr. colloq. **1** it had. **2** it would.

-ite¹ /īt/ suffix forming nouns meaning 'a person or thing connected with': **1** in names of persons: **a** as natives of a country (Israelite). **b** often derog. as followers of a movement, etc. (Pre-Raphaelite; Trotskyite). **2** in names of things: **a** fossil organisms (ammonite). **b** minerals (graphite). **c** constituent parts of a body or organ (somite). **d** explosives (dynamite). **e** commercial products (ebonite; vulcanite). **f** salts of acids having names in –ous (nitrite; sulfite). [from or after F –ite f. L –ita f. Gk –itēs]

-ite² /īt, it/ suffix **1** forming adjectives (erudite; favorite). **2** forming nouns (appetite). **3** forming verbs (expedite; unite). [from or after L –itus past part. of verbs in –ēre, –ere, and –īre]

i·tem /ítəm/ n. & adv. • n. **1** any of a number of enumerated or listed things. **b** an entry in an account. **2** an article, esp. one for sale (household items). **3** a separate or distinct piece of news, information, etc. • adv. archaic (introducing the mention of each item) likewise; also. [orig. as adv.: L, = in like manner, also]

i·tem·ize /ítəmīz/ v.tr. state or list item by item. □□ **i·tem·i·za·tion** n. **i·tem·iz·er** n.

it·er·ate /ítərayt/ v.tr. repeat; state repeatedly. □□ **it·er·a·tion** /–áyshən/ n. [L iterare iterat- f. iterum again]

it•er•a•tive /ítəraytiv, –rətiv/ *adj. Gram.* = FREQUENTATIVE. □□ **it•er•a•tive•ly** *adv.*

ith•y•phal•lic /ithifálik/ *adj. Gk Hist.* **1 a** of the phallus carried in Bacchic festivals. **b** (of a statue, etc.) having an erect penis. **2** lewd; licentious. **3** (of a poem or meter) used for Bacchic hymns. [LL *ithyphallicus* f. Gk *ithuphallikos* f. *ithus* straight, *phallos* PHALLUS]

-itic /ítik/ *suffix* forming adjectives and nouns corresponding to nouns in *–ite*, *–itis*, etc. (*Semitic*; *arthritic*; *syphilitic*). [from or after F *–itique* f. L *–iticus* f. Gk *–itikos*: see –IC]

i•tin•er•ant /ítínərənt, itín–/ *adj. & n.* ● *adj.* traveling from place to place (*itinerant traders*). ● *n.* a person who travels from place to place; a tramp. □□ **i•tin•er•a•cy** *n.* **i•tin•er•an•cy** *n.* [LL *itinerari* travel f. L *iter* *itiner-* journey]

i•tin•er•ar•y /ítínəreree, itín–/ *n. & adj.* ● *n.* (*pl.* •ies) **1** a detailed route. **2** a record of travel. **3** a guidebook. ● *adj.* of roads or traveling. [LL *itinerarius* (adj.), *–um* (n.) f. L *iter*: see ITINERANT]

i•tin•er•ate /ítínərayt, itín–/ *v.intr.* travel from place to place or (of a minister, etc.) within a circuit. □□ **i•tin•er•a•tion** /–ráyshən/ *n.* [LL *itinerari*: see ITINERANT]

-ition /ishən/ *suffix* forming nouns, = –ATION (*admonition*; *perdition*; *position*). [from or after F *–ition* or L *–itio* *–itionis*]

-itious[1] /ishəs/ *suffix* forming adjectives corresponding to nouns in *–ition* (*ambitious*; *suppositious*). [L *–itio*, etc. + –OUS]

-itious[2] /ishəs/ *suffix* forming adjectives meaning 'related to, having the nature of' (*adventitious*; *supposititious*). [L *–icius* + –OUS, commonly written with *t* in med.L manuscripts]

-itis /ítis/ *suffix* forming nouns, esp.: **1** names of inflammatory diseases (*appendicitis*; *bronchitis*). **2** *colloq.* in extended uses with ref. to conditions compared to diseases (*electionitis*). [Gk *–itis*, forming fem. of adjectives in *–itēs* (with *nosos* 'disease' implied)]

-itive /itiv/ *suffix* forming adjectives, = –ATIVE (*positive*; *transitive*). [from or after F *–itif* *–itive* or L *–itivus* f. participial stems in *–it-*: see –IVE]

it'll /ít'l/ *contr. colloq.* it will; it shall.

ITO *abbr.* International Trade Organization.

-itor /ítər/ *suffix* forming agent nouns, usu. from Latin words (sometimes via French) (*creditor*). See also –OR[1].

-itory /ítawree/ *suffix* forming adjectives meaning 'relating to or involving (a verbal action)' (*inhibitory*). See also –ORY[2]. [L *–itorius*]

-itous /ítəs/ *suffix* forming adjectives corresponding to nouns in *–ity* (*calamitous*; *felicitous*). [from or after F *–iteux* f. L *–itosus*]

its /its/ *poss.pron.* of it; of itself (*can see its advantages*).

it's /its/ *contr.* **1** it is. **2** it has.

▶Its is an attributive adjective indicating possession, meaning 'of it, belonging to it.' It's is a contraction of 'it is': *It's going to be a good day to tour the city and see its attractions.*

it•self /itsélf/ *pron.* emphatic and refl. form of IT[1]. □ **by itself** apart from its surroundings, automatically, spontaneously. **in itself** viewed in its essential qualities (*not in itself a bad thing*). [OE f. IT[1] + SELF, but often treated as ITS + SELF (cf. *its own self*)]

it•ty-bit•ty /íteebítee/ *adj.* (also **it•sy-bit•sy** /ítseebítsee/) *colloq.* usu. *derog.* tiny; insubstantial; slight. [redupl. of LITTLE, infl. by BIT[1]]

ITU *abbr.* **1** International Telecommunication Union. **2** International Typographical Union.

ITV *abbr.* instructional television.

-ity /itee/ *suffix* forming nouns denoting: **1** quality or condition (*authority*; *humility*; *purity*). **2** an instance or degree of this (*a monstrosity*; *humidity*). [from or after F *–ité* f. L *–itas* *–itatis*]

IU *abbr.* international unit.

IUD *abbr.* **1** intrauterine (contraceptive) device. **2** intra-uterine death (of the fetus before birth).

-ium /eeəm/ *suffix* forming nouns denoting esp.: **1** (also **–um**) names of metallic elements (*uranium*; *tantalum*). **2** a region of the body (*pericardium*; *hypogastrium*). **3** a biological structure (*mycelium*; *prothallium*). [from or after L *–ium* f. Gk *–ion*]

IUPAC /yóōpak/ *abbr.* International Union of Pure and Applied Chemistry.

IV /íveé/ *abbr.* intravenous(ly).

I've /ív/ *contr.* I have.

-ive /iv/ *suffix* forming adjectives meaning 'tending to, having the nature of,' and corresponding nouns (*suggestive*; *corrosive*; *palliative*; *coercive*; *talkative*). □□ **–ively** *suffix* forming adverbs. **–iveness** *suffix* forming nouns. [from or after F *–if –ive* f. L *–ivus*]

IVF *abbr.* in vitro fertilization.

i•vo•ry /ívəree, ívree/ *n.* (*pl.* •ries) **1** a hard, creamy-white substance composing the main part of the tusks of an elephant, hippopotamus, walrus, and narwhal. **2** the color of this. **3** (usu. in *pl.*) **a** an article made of ivory. **b** *sl.* anything made of or resembling ivory, esp. a piano key or a tooth. □□ **i•vo•ried** *adj.* [ME f. OF *yvoire* ult. f. L *ebur eboris*]

i•vo•ry black *n.* black pigment from calcined ivory or bone.

i•vo•ry nut *n.* the seed of a corozo palm, *Phytelephas macrocarpa*, used as a source of vegetable ivory for carving. Also called **corozo nut.**

i•vo•ry tow•er *n.* a state of seclusion or separation from the ordinary world and the harsh realities of life.

i•vy /ívee/ *n.* (*pl.* •vies) **1** a climbing evergreen shrub, *Hedera helix*, with usu. dark-green, shining five-angled leaves. **2** any of various other climbing plants including ground ivy and poison ivy. [OE *ifig*]

I•vy League *n.* a group of universities in the eastern US including Harvard, Yale, Princeton, Columbia, Dartmouth, Cornell, Brown, and the University of Pennsylvania, having high academic and social prestige. [with reference to the ivy traditionally growing over the walls of these establishments] □□ **I•vy Lea•guer** *n.*

IWW *abbr.* Industrial Workers of the World.

ix•i•a /íkseeə/ *n.* any iridaceous plant of the genus *Ixia* of S. Africa, with large showy flowers. [L f. Gk, a kind of thistle]

ix•tle /íkstli/ *n.* (also **is•tle**) (in Mexico and Central America) a plant fiber used for cordage, nets, and carpets, obtained chiefly from agave. [American Sp. from Nahuatl *ixtli*]

iz•ard /ízaard/ *n.* a chamois. [F *isard*, of unkn. orig.]

-ize /íz/ *suffix* (also *Brit.* **-ise**) forming verbs, meaning: **1** make or become such (*Americanize*; *pulverize*; *realize*). **2** treat in such a way (*monopolize*; *pasteurize*). **3 a** follow a special practice (*economize*). **b** have a specified feeling (*sympathize*). **4** affect with, provide with, or subject to (*oxidize*; *hospitalize*). □□ **-ization** /–izá yshən/ *suffix* forming nouns. **-izer** *suffix* forming agent nouns. [from or after F *-iser* f. LL *-izare* f. Gk *-izō*]

▶The form -ize has been in use in English since the 16th c. and is the regular form used in American English. The alternative spelling -ise (reflecting a French influence) is in common use in British English, and is obligatory in certain cases: (*a*) where it forms part of a larger word-element, such as *-mise* ('sending') in *compromise*, and *-prise* ('taking') in *surprise*; and (*b*) in verbs corresponding to nouns with *-i-* in the stem, such as *advertise* and *televise*.

English ivy

J

J¹ /jay/ *n.* (also **j**) (*pl.* **Js** or **J's**) **1** the tenth letter of the alphabet. **2** (as a Roman numeral) = *i* in a final position (*ij; vj*).

J² *abbr.* (also **J.**) **1** *Cards* jack. **2** Jewish. **3** joule(s). **4** Judge. **5** Justice.

jab /jab/ *v. & n.* ● *v.tr.* (**jabbed, jab•bing**) **1 a** poke roughly. **b** stab. **2** (foll. by *into*) thrust (a thing) hard or abruptly. ● *n.* **1** an abrupt blow with one's fist or a pointed implement. **2** *colloq.* a hypodermic injection, esp. a vaccination. [orig. Sc. var. of JOB²]

jab•ber /jábər/ *v. & n.* ● *v.* **1** *intr.* chatter volubly and incoherently. **2** *tr.* utter (words) fast and indistinctly. ● *n.* meaningless jabbering; a gabble. [imit.]

jab•ber•wock•y /jábərwokee/ *n.* (*pl.* **•ies**) a piece of nonsensical writing or speech, esp. for comic effect. [title of a poem in Lewis Carroll's *Through the Looking Glass* (1871)]

jab•i•ru /jábiroo/ *n.* **1** a large stork, *Jabiru mycteria*, of Central and S. America. **2** a black-necked stork, *Xenorhyncus asiaticus*, of Asia and Australia. [Tupi-Guarani *jabirú*]

jab•o•ran•di /jábərándee/ *n.* (*pl.* **jab•o•ran•dis**) **1** any shrub of the genus *Pilocarpus*, of S. America. **2** the dried leaflets of this, having diuretic and diaphoretic properties. [Tupi-Guarani *jaburandi*]

ja•bot /zhabó, ja–/ *n.* an ornamental frill or ruffle of lace, etc., on the front of a shirt or blouse. [F, orig. = crop of a bird]

ja•ca•na /zhaakənaá, –sənaá/ *n.* any of various small tropical wading birds of the family Jacanidae, with elongated toes and hind claws which enable them to walk on floating leaves, etc. [Port. *jaçanã* f. Tupi-Guarani *jasaná*]

jac•a•ran•da /jákərándə/ *n.* **1** any tropical American tree of the genus *Jacaranda*, with trumpet-shaped blue flowers. **2** any tropical American tree of the genus *Dalbergia*, with hard scented wood. [Tupi-Guarani *jacarandá*]

ja•cinth /jáysinth, jás–/ *n.* a reddish-orange variety of zircon used as a gem. [ME *iacynt*, etc., f. OF *iacinte* or med.L *jacint(h)us* f. L *hyacinthus* HYACINTH]

jack¹ /jak/ *n. & v.* ● *n.* **1** a device for lifting heavy objects, esp. the axle of a vehicle, off the ground while changing a wheel, etc. **2** a playing card with a picture of a man, esp. a soldier, page, or knave, etc. **3** a ship's flag, esp. one flown from the bow and showing nationality. **4** a device using a single plug to connect an electrical circuit. **5** in lawn bowling, the small white ball at which the players aim. **6 a** (also **jack•stone**) a small piece of metal, etc., used with others in tossing games. **b** (in *pl.*) a game with a ball and jacks. **7** (**Jack**) the familiar form of *John* esp. typifying the common man or the male of a species (*I'm all right, Jack*). **8** the figure of a man striking the bell on a clock. **9** esp. *Brit. sl.* a detective; a policeman. **10** *sl.* money. **11** = LUMBERJACK. **12** = STEEPLEJACK. **13** a device for turning a spit. **14** any of various marine perchlike fish of the family Carangidae, including the amberjack. **15** a device for plucking the string of a harpsichord, etc., one being operated by each key. ● *v.tr.* **1** (usu. foll. by *up*) raise with or as with a jack (in sense 1). **2** (usu. foll. by *up*) *colloq.* raise, e.g., prices. **3** (foll. by *off*) **a** go away; depart. **b** *coarse sl.* masturbate. □ **before you can say Jack Robinson** *colloq.* very quickly or suddenly. **every man jack** each and every person. **jack in** (or **up**) esp. *Brit. sl.* abandon (an attempt, etc.). **on one's jack** (or **Jack Jones**) *Brit. sl.* alone; on one's own.

WORD HISTORY jack

Late Middle English: from *Jack*, pet form of the given name *John*. The term was used originally to denote an ordinary man (sense 7), also a youth (mid 16th cent.), hence the 'knave' in cards and 'male animal'. The word also denoted various devices saving human labor, as though one had a helper (noun senses 1, 4, 13, and 15, and in compounds such as JACKHAMMER and JACKKNIFE); the general sense 'laborer' arose in the early 18th cent. and survives in CHEAPJACK, LUMBERJACK, STEEPLEJACK, etc. Since the mid 16th cent. a notion of 'smallness' has arisen.

---

jack² /jak/ *n.* **1** = BLACKJACK³. **2** *hist.* a sleeveless padded tunic worn by foot soldiers. [ME f. OF *jaque*, of uncert. orig.]

jack•al /jákəl/ *n.* **1** any of various wild doglike mammals of the genus *Canis*, esp. *C. aureus*, found in Africa and S. Asia, usu. hunting or scavenging for food in packs. **2** *colloq.* **a** a person who does preliminary drudgery for another. **b** a person who assists another's immoral behavior. [Turk. *çakal* f. Pers. *šagāl*]

jack•a•napes /jákənayps/ *n. archaic* **1** a pert or insolent fellow. **2** a mischievous child. **3** a tame monkey. [earliest as *Jack Napes* (1450):

supposed to refer to the Duke of Suffolk, whose badge was an ape's clog and chain]

jack•a•roo var. of JACKEROO.

jack•ass /jákas/ *n.* **1** a male ass. **2** a stupid person.

jack•boot /jákboot/ *n.* **1** a large boot reaching above the knee. **2** this as a symbol of fascism or military oppression. □□ **jack•boot•ed** *adj.*

jack•daw /jákdaw/ *n.* a small gray-headed crow, *Corvus monedula*, often frequenting rooftops and nesting in tall buildings, and noted for its inquisitiveness (cf. DAW).

jack•e•roo /jákəróō/ *n.* (also **jack•a•roo**) *Austral. colloq.* a novice on a sheep or cattle ranch. [JACK¹ + KANGAROO]

jack•et /jákit/ *n. & v.* ● *n.* **1 a** a sleeved, short outer garment. **b** a thing worn esp. around the torso for protection or support (*life jacket*). **2** a casing or covering, e.g., as insulation around a boiler. **3** = *dust jacket*. **4** the skin of a potato, esp. when baked whole. **5** an animal's coat. ● *v.tr.* cover with a jacket. [ME f. OF *ja(c)quet* dimin. of *jaque* JACK²]

jack•et po•ta•to *n. Brit.* a baked potato served with the skin on.

jack•fish /jákfish/ *n.* (*pl.* same) = PIKE¹.

Jack Frost *n.* frost personified.

jack•fruit /jákfroot/ *n.* **1** an East Indian tree, *Artocarpus heterophyllus*, bearing fruit resembling breadfruit. **2** this fruit. [Port. *jaca* f. Malayalam *chakka* + FRUIT]

jack•ham•mer /ják-hamər/ *n.* a pneumatic hammer or drill.

jack-in-of•fice *n. Brit.* a self-important minor official.

jack-in-the-box *n.* a toy figure that springs out of a box when it is opened.

jack-in-the-pul•pit *n.* a N. American plant of the arum family having an upright flower spike and an overarching hoodlike spathe.

jack•knife /jáknif/ *n. & v.* ● *n.* (*pl.* **•knives**) **1** a large pocketknife. **2** a dive in which the body is first bent at the waist and then straightened. ● *v.intr.* (**•knifed**, **•knif•ing**) (of an articulated vehicle) fold against itself in an accidental skidding movement.

jack-of-all-trades *n.* a person who can do many different kinds of work.

jack-o'-lan•tern *n.* **1** a will-o'-the wisp. **2** a lantern made from a hollowed-out pumpkin in which holes are cut to represent facial features, typically made at Halloween.

jack plane *n.* a medium-sized plane for use in rough joinery.

jack-in-the-pulpit

jack plug *n.* a plug consisting of a single shaft used to make a connection that transmits a signal, usu. used in sound equipment.

jack•pot /jákpot/ *n.* a large prize or amount of winnings, esp. accumulated in a game or lottery, etc. □ **hit the jackpot** *colloq.* **1** win a large prize. **2** have remarkable luck or success. [JACK¹ *n.* 2 + POT¹: orig. in a form of poker with two jacks as minimum to open the betting]

jack•rab•bit /jákrabit/ *n.* any of various large prairie hares of the genus *Lepus* with very long ears and hind legs.

Jack Rus•sell /jakrúsəl/ *n.* (also **Jack Rus•sell ter•ri•er**) a terrier of a small working breed with short legs.

jack•shaft /jákshaft/ *n.* = COUNTERSHAFT.

jackal 1

jackrabbit

jack•snipe /jáksnīp/ *n.* a small snipe, *Lymnocryptes minimus*.

jack•staff /jákstaf/ *n. Naut.* **1** a staff at the bow of a ship for a jack. **2** a staff carrying the flag that is to show above the masthead.

jack•stone /jákstōn/ *n.* **1** = JACK[1] 6. **2** (in *pl.*) the game of jacks.

jack•straw /jákstraw/ *n.* **1** a splinter of wood, straw, etc., esp. one of a bundle, pile, etc. **2** (in *pl.*) a game in which a heap of jackstraws is to be removed one at a time without moving the others.

jack-tar *n.* a sailor.

Jack-the-lad *n. Brit. colloq.* a brash, self-assured young man.

Jac•o•be•an /jákəbeéən/ *adj. & n.* • *adj.* **1** of or relating to the reign of James I of England. **2** (of furniture) in the style prevalent then, esp. of the color of dark oak. • *n.* a Jacobean person. [mod.L *Jacobaeus* f. eccl.L *Jacobus* James f. Gk *Iakōbos* Jacob]

Jac•o•bin /jákəbin/ *n.* **1 a** *hist.* a member of a radical democratic club established in Paris in 1789 in the old convent of the Jacobins (see sense 2). **b** any extreme radical. **2** *archaic* a Dominican friar. **3** (**jacobin**) a pigeon with reversed feathers on the back of its neck like a cowl. □□ **Jac•o•bin•ic** /–bínik/ *adj.* **Jac•o•bin•i•cal** *adj.* **Jac•o•bin•ism** /ják–/ *n.* [orig. in sense 2 by assoc. with the Rue St. Jacques in Paris: ME f. F f. med.L *Jacobinus* f. eccl.L *Jacobus*]

Jac•o•bite /jákəbīt/ *n. hist.* a supporter of James II of England after his removal from the throne in 1688, or of his family, the Stuarts. □□ **Jac•o•bit•i•cal** /–bítikəl/ *adj.* **Jac•o•bit•ism** *n.* [L *Jacobus* James: see JACOBEAN]

Ja•cob's lad•der /jáykəbz/ *n.* **1** a plant, *Polemonium caeruleum*, with corymbs of blue or white flowers, and leaves suggesting a ladder. **2** a rope ladder with wooden rungs. [f. Jacob's dream of a ladder reaching to heaven, as described in Gen. 28:12]

Ja•cob's staff *n.* **1** a surveyor's iron-shod rod used instead of a tripod. **2** an instrument for measuring distances and heights. [f. the staffs used by Jacob, as described in Gen. 30:37–43]

jac•o•net /jákənet/ *n.* a cotton cloth like cambric, esp. a dyed waterproof kind for poulticing, etc. [Urdu *jagannāthī* f. *Jagannath* (now Puri) in India, its place of origin: see JUGGERNAUT]

Jac•quard /jákaard, jəkaárd/ *n.* **1** an apparatus using perforated cards that record a pattern and are fitted to a loom to mechanize the weaving of figured fabrics. **2** (in full **Jacquard loom**) a loom fitted with this. **3** a fabric or article made with this, with an intricate variegated pattern. [J. M. *Jacquard*, Fr. inventor d. 1834]

jac•ti•ta•tion /jáktitáyshən/ *n.* **1** *Med.* **a** the restless tossing of the body in illness. **b** the twitching of a limb or muscle. **2** *archaic* the offense of falsely claiming to be a person's wife or husband. [med.L *jactitatio* false declaration f. L *jactitare* boast, frequent. of *jactare* throw: sense 1 f. earlier *jactation*]

Ja•cuz•zi /jəkōōzee/ *n.* (*pl.* **Ja•cuz•zis**) *Trademark* a large bath with underwater jets of water to massage the body. [name of the inventor and manufacturers]

jade[1] /jayd/ *n.* **1** a hard, usu. green stone composed of silicates of calcium and magnesium, or of sodium and aluminum, used for ornaments and implements. **2** the green color of jade. [F: *le jade* for *l'ejade* f. Sp. *piedra de ijada* stone of the flank, i.e., stone for colic (which it was believed to cure)]

jade[2] /jayd/ *n.* **1** an inferior or worn-out horse. **2** *derog.* a disreputable woman. [ME: orig. unkn.]

jad•ed /jáydid/ *adj.* tired or worn out; surfeited. □□ **jad•ed•ly** *adv.* **jad•ed•ness** *n.*

jade•ite /jáydīt/ *n.* a green, blue, or white sodium aluminum silicate form of jade.

jae•ger /yáygər/ *n.* **1** (also **ya•ger**) hunter. **2** (also /jáy–/) any large predatory seabird of the family Stercorariidae that pursues other birds and makes them disgorge the fish they have caught. [G *Jäger* hunter f. *jagen* to hunt]

Jaf•fa /jáfə, jaá–/ *n.* a large, oval, thick-skinned variety of orange. [*Jaffa* in Israel, near where it was first grown]

jag[1] /jag/ *n. & v.* • *n.* a sharp projection of rock, etc. • *v.tr.* (**jagged**, **jag•ging**) **1** cut or tear unevenly. **2** make indentations in. □□ **jag•ger** *n.* [ME, prob. imit.]

jag[2] /jag/ *n. sl.* **1** a drinking bout; a spree. **2** a period of indulgence in an activity, emotion, etc. [orig. 16th c., = load for one horse: orig. unkn.]

jag•ged /jágid/ *adj.* **1** with an unevenly cut or torn edge. **2** deeply indented; with sharp points. □□ **jag•ged•ly** *adv.* **jag•ged•ness** *n.*

jag•gy /jágee/ *adj.* (**jag•gi•er**, **jag•gi•est**) **1** = JAGGED. **2** (also **jag•gie**) *Sc.* prickly.

jag•uar /jágwaar/ *n.* a large, carnivorous spotted feline, *Panthera onca*, of Central and S. America. [Tupi-Guarani *jaguara*]

ja•gua•run•di /jágwərúndee/ *n.* (*pl.* **ja•gua•run•dis**) a long-tailed slender feline, *Felis yaguarondi*, of Central and S. America. [Tupi-Guarani]

jai a•lai /hí lī, əlí/ *n.* an indoor court game somewhat resembling handball in which the ball is propelled with large curved wicker baskets. [Sp. f. Basque *jai* festival + *alai* merry]

jail /jayl/ *n. & v.* (also *Brit.* **gaol** *pronunc.* same) • *n.* **1** a place to which persons are committed by a court for detention. **2** confinement in a jail. • *v.tr.* put in jail. [ME *gayole* f. OF *jaiole, jeole* & ONF *gaole* f. Rmc dimin. of L *cavea* CAGE]

jail•bait /jáylbayt/ *n. sl.* a young woman, or young women collectively, considered in sexual terms but under the age of consent.

jail•bird /jáylbərd/ *n.* (also *Brit.* **gaol•bird**) a prisoner or habitual criminal.

jail•break /jáylbrayk/ *n.* (also *Brit.* **gaol•break**) an escape from jail.

jail•er /jáylər/ *n. Brit.* (also **gaol•er**) a person in charge of a jail or of the prisoners in it.

Jain /jīn/ *n. & adj.* (also **Jai•na** /jínə/) • *n.* an adherent of a nonbrahminical Indian religion. • *adj.* of or relating to this religion. □□ **Jain•ism** *n.* **Jain•ist** *n.* [Hindi f. Skr. *jainas* saint, victor f. *jina* victorious]

jake /jayk/ *adj. sl.* all right; satisfactory. [20th c.: orig. uncert.]

jal•ap /jáləp, jaá–/ *n.* a purgative drug obtained esp. from the tuberous roots of a Mexican climbing plant, *Exogonium purga*. [F f. Sp. *jalapa* f. *Jalapa, Xalapa*, city in Mexico, f. Aztec *Xalapan* sand by the water]

ja•la•pe•ño /halapáynyō, –peén–/ *n.* a variety of hot green chili pepper commonly used in Mexican-style cooking.

ja•lop•y /jəlópee/ *n.* (*pl.* **•ies**) *colloq.* a dilapidated old motor vehicle. [20th c.: orig. unkn.]

jal•ou•sie /jáləsee/ *n.* a blind or shutter made of a row of angled slats to keep out rain, etc., and control the influx of light. [F (as JEALOUSY)]

Jam. *abbr.* **1** Jamaica. **2** James (New Testament).

jam[1] /jam/ *v. & n.* • *v.tr. & intr.* (**jammed**, **jam•ming**) **1 a** *tr.* (usu. foll. by *into*) squeeze or wedge into a space. **b** *intr.* become wedged. **2 a** *tr.* cause (machinery or a component) to become wedged or immovable so that it cannot work. **b** *intr.* become jammed in this way. **3** *tr.* push or cram together in a compact mass. **4** *intr.* (foll. by *in, onto*) push or crowd (*they jammed onto the bus*). **5** *tr.* **a** block (a passage, road, etc.) by crowding or obstructing. **b** (foll. by *in*) obstruct the exit of (*we were jammed in*). **6** *tr.* (usu. foll. by *on*) apply (brakes, etc.) forcefully or abruptly. **7** *tr.* make (a radio transmission) unintelligible by causing interference. **8** *intr. colloq.* (in jazz, etc.) extemporize with other musicians. • *n.* **1** a squeeze or crush. **2** a crowded mass (*traffic jam*). **3** *colloq.* an awkward situation or predicament. **4** a stoppage (of a machine, etc.) due to jamming. **5** (in full **jam session**) *colloq.* improvised playing by a group of jazz musicians. □□ **jam•mer** *n.* [imit.]

jam[2] /jam/ *n. & v.* • *n.* **1** a conserve of fruit and sugar boiled to a thick consistency. **2** *Brit. colloq.* something easy or pleasant (*money for jam*). • *v.tr.* (**jammed**, **jam•ming**) **1** spread jam on. **2** make (fruit, etc.) into jam. [perh. = JAM[1]]

jamb /jam/ *n. Archit.* a side post or surface of a doorway, window, or fireplace. [ME f. OF *jambe* ult. f. LL *gamba* hoof]

jam•ba•lay•a /júmbəlíə/ *n.* a dish of rice with shrimp, chicken, etc. [Louisiana F f. mod. Prov. *jambalaia*]

jam•be•roo /jámbərōō/ *n. Austral.* a spree. [alt. of JAMBOREE]

jam•bo•ree /jámbəreé/ *n.* **1** a celebration or merrymaking. **2** a large rally of Boy Scouts or Girl Scouts. [19th c.: orig. unkn.]

jam•jar /jámjaar/ *n. Brit.* a glass jar for containing jam.

jam•my /jámee/ *adj.* (**jam•mi•er**, **jam•mi•est**) **1** covered with jam. **2** *Brit. colloq.* a lucky. **b** profitable.

jam-packed *adj. colloq.* full to capacity.

jam to•mor•row *n. Brit.* a pleasant thing often promised but usu. never forthcoming.

Jan. *abbr.* January.

jane /jayn/ *n. sl.* a woman (*a plain jane*). [the name *Jane*]

jan•gle /jánggəl/ *v. & n.* • *v.* **1** *intr. & tr.* make, or cause (a bell, etc.) to make, a harsh metallic sound. **2** *tr.* irritate (the nerves, etc.) by discordant sound or speech, etc. • *n.* a harsh metallic sound. [ME f. OF *jangler*, of uncert. orig.]

Jang•lish /jángglish/ *n.* = JAPLISH. [*Japanese* + *English*]

jan•is•sar•y /jániseree/ *n.* (also **jan•i•zar•y** /–zeree/) (*pl.* **•ies**) **1** *hist.* a member of the Turkish infantry forming the Sultan's guard in the 14th–19th c. **2** a devoted follower or supporter. [ult. f. Turk. *yeniçeri* f. *yeni* new + *çeri* troops]

jan•i•tor /jánitər/ *n.* **1** a caretaker of a building. **2** *Brit.* a doorman. □□ **jan•i•to•ri•al** /–táwreeəl/ *adj.* [L f. *janua* door]

jan•i•zar•y var. of JANISSARY.

jank•ers /jángkərz/ *n. Brit. Mil. sl.* punishment for defaulters. [20th c.: orig. unkn.]

Jan•u•ar•y /jányōoeree/ *n.* (*pl.* **•ies**) the first month of the year. [ME f. AF *Jenever* f. L *Januarius* (*mensis*) (month) of Janus the guardian god of doors and beginnings]

Jap /jap/ *n. & adj. colloq. often offens.* = JAPANESE. [abbr.]

ja•pan /jəpán/ *n. & v.* • *n.* **1** a hard, usu. black varnish, esp. of a kind brought orig. from Japan. **2** work in a Japanese style. • *v.tr.* (**ja•panned, ja•pan•ning**) **1** varnish with japan. **2** make black and glossy as with japan. [*Japan* in E. Asia]

Jap•a•nese /jápəneéz/ *n. & adj.* • *n.* (*pl.* same) **1 a** a native or national of Japan. **b** a person of Japanese descent. **2** the language of Japan. • *adj.* of or relating to Japan, its people, or its language.

Jap·a·nese bee·tle *n.* an iridescent green and brown beetle, *Popillia japonica*, that is a garden and crop pest.

Jap·a·nese ce·dar *n.* = CRYPTOMERIA.

Jap·a·nese print *n.* a color print from woodblocks.

Jap·a·nese quince *n.* any flowering shrub of the genus *Chaenomeles*, esp. *C. speciosa*, with round white, green, or yellow edible fruits and bright red flowers. [mod.L, fem. of *japonicus* Japanese]

jape /jayp/ *n. & v.* •*n.* a practical joke. •*v.intr.* play a joke. □□ **jap·er·y** *n.* [ME: orig. uncert.]

Jap·lish /jáplish/ *n.* a blend of Japanese and English, used in Japan. [*Japanese* + *English*]

ja·pon·i·ca /jəpónikə/ *n.* **1** a camellia, *Camellia japonica*, with variously colored waxy flowers. **2** = JAPANESE QUINCE.

jar¹ /jaar/ *n.* **1 a** a container of glass, earthenware, plastic, etc., usu. cylindrical. **b** the contents of this. **2** *Brit. colloq.* a glass of beer. □□ **jar·ful** *n.* (*pl.* **·fuls**). [F *jarre* f. Arab. *jarra*]

jar² /jaar/ *v. & n.* •*v.* (**jarred, jar·ring**) **1** *intr.* (often foll. by *on*) (of sound, words, manner, etc.) sound discordant or grating (on the nerves, etc.). **2 a** *tr.* (foll. by *against, on*) strike or cause to strike with vibration or a grating sound. **b** *intr.* (of a body affected) vibrate gratingly. **3** *tr.* send a shock through (a part of the body) (*the fall jarred his neck*). **4** *intr.* (often foll. by *with*) (of an opinion, fact, etc.) be at variance; be in conflict or in dispute. •*n.* **1** a jarring sound or sensation. **2** a physical shock or jolt. **3** lack of harmony; disagreement. [16th c.: prob. imit.]

jar³ /jaar/ *n.* □ **on the jar** ajar. [late form of obs. *char* turn: see AJAR¹, CHAR¹]

jar·di·niere /jaárd'néer, zhaárdinyáir/ *n.* (also **jar·di·nière**) **1** an ornamental pot or stand for the display of growing plants. **2** a dish of mixed vegetables. [F]

jar·gon¹ /jaárgən/ *n.* **1** words or expressions used by a particular group or profession (*medical jargon*). **2** barbarous or debased language. **3** gibberish. □□ **jar·gon·ic** /–gónik/ *adj.* **jar·gon·is·tic** *adj.* **jar·gon·ize** *v.tr. & intr.* [ME f. OF: orig. unkn.]

jar·gon² var. of JARGOON.

jar·gon·elle /jaárgənél/ *n.* an early-ripening variety of pear. [F, dimin. of JARGON²]

jar·goon /jaargóon/ *n.* (also **jar·gon** /jáargən/) a translucent, colorless, or smoky variety of zircon. [F f. It. *giargone*, prob. ult. formed as ZIRCON]

jarl /yaarl/ *n. hist.* a Norse or Danish chief. [ON, orig. = man of noble birth, rel. to EARL]

jar·rah /járə/ *n.* **1** an Australian hardwood tree, *Eucalyptus marginata*. **2** the durable wood of this. [Aboriginal *djarryl*]

Jas. *abbr.* James (also in New Testament).

jas·mine /jázmin/ *n.* (also **jes·sa·mine** /jésəmin/) any of various fragrant ornamental shrubs of the genus *Jasminum* usu. with white or yellow flowers. [F *jasmin, jessemin* f. Arab. *yās(a)mīn* f. Pers. *yāsamīn*]

jas·mine tea *n.* a tea perfumed with dried jasmine blossoms.

jas·pé /jaspáy, zha–/ *adj.* like jasper; randomly colored (esp. of cotton fabric). [F, past part. of *jasper* marble f. *jaspe* JASPER]

jas·per /jáspər/ *n.* an opaque variety of quartz, usu. red, yellow, or brown in color. [ME f. OF *jasp(r)e* f. L *iaspis* f. Gk, of Oriental orig.]

Jat /jaat/ *n.* a member of an Indo-Aryan people widely distributed in NW India. [Hindi *jāt*]

ja·to /jáytō/ *n.* (*pl.* **·tos**) *Aeron.* **1** jet-assisted takeoff. **2** an auxiliary power unit providing extra thrust at takeoff. [abbr.]

jaun·dice /jáwndis/ *n. & v.* •*n.* **1** *Med.* a condition with yellowing of the skin or whites of the eyes, often caused by obstruction of the bile duct or by liver disease. **2** disordered (esp. mental) vision. **3** envy. •*v.tr.* **1** affect with jaundice. **2** (esp. as **jaundiced** *adj.*) affect (a person) with envy, resentment, or jealousy. [ME *iaunes* f. OF *jaunice* yellowness f. *jaune* yellow]

jaunt /jawnt/ *n. & v.* •*n.* a short excursion for enjoyment. •*v.intr.* take a jaunt. [16th c.: orig. unkn.]

jaunt·ing car *n.* a light, two-wheeled, horse-drawn vehicle formerly used in Ireland.

jaun·ty /jáwntee/ *adj.* (**jaun·ti·er, jaun·ti·est**) **1** cheerful and self-confident. **2** sprightly. □□ **jaun·ti·ly** *adv.* **jaun·ti·ness** *n.* [earlier *jentee* f. F *gentil* GENTLE]

Ja·va Man /jaávə/ *n.* a prehistoric type of man whose remains were found in Java. [*Java* in Indonesia]

Ja·van /jaávən/ *n. & adj.* = JAVANESE.

Jav·a·nese /jávəneéz, jaá–/ *n. & adj.* •*n.* (*pl.* same) **1 a** a native of Java in Indonesia. **b** a person of Javanese descent. **2** the language of Java. •*adj.* of or relating to Java, its people, or its language.

Ja·va spar·row /jaávə/ *n.* a finch, *Padda oryzivora*.

jave·lin /jávəlin, jávlin/ *n.* **1** a light spear thrown in a competitive sport or as a weapon. **2** the athletic event or sport of throwing the javelin. [F *javeline, javelot* f. Gallo-Roman *gabalottus*]

jaw /jaw/ *n. & v.* •*n.* **1 a** each of the upper and lower bony structures in vertebrates forming the framework of the mouth and containing the teeth. **b** the parts of certain invertebrates used for the ingestion of food. **2 a** (in *pl.*) the mouth with its bones and teeth.

b the narrow mouth of a valley, channel, etc. **c** the gripping parts of a tool or machine. **d** gripping power (*jaws of death*). **3** *colloq.* **a** talkativeness; tedious talk. **b** a sermonizing talk; a lecture. •*v. colloq.* **1** *intr.* speak esp. at tedious length. **2** *tr.* **a** persuade by talking. **b** admonish or lecture. [ME f. OF *joe* cheek, jaw, of uncert. orig.]

jaw·bone /jáwbōn/ *n.* **1** each of the two bones forming the lower jaw in most mammals. **2** these two combined into one in other mammals.

jaw·break·er /jáwbraykər/ *n.* **1** *colloq.* a word that is very long or hard to pronounce. **2** a round, very hard candy.

jay /jay/ *n.* **1 a** a noisy chattering European bird, *Garrulus glandarius*, with vivid pinkish-brown, blue, black, and white plumage. **b** any other bird of the subfamily Garrulinae. **2** a person who chatters impertinently. [ME f. OF f. LL *gaius, gaia*, perh. f. L praenomen *Gaius*: cf. JACKDAW, ROBIN]

jay·walk /jáywawk/ *v.intr.* cross or walk in the street or road without regard for traffic. □□ **jay·walk·er** *n.*

jazz /jaz/ *n. & v.* •*n.* **1** music of American origin characterized by improvisation, syncopation, and usu. a regular or forceful rhythm. **2** *sl.* pretentious talk or behavior, nonsensical stuff (*all that jazz*). •*v.intr.* play or dance to jazz. □ **jazz up** brighten or enliven. □□ **jazz·er** *n.* [20th c.: orig. uncert.]

jazz·man /jázman/ *n.* (*pl.* **·men**) a jazz musician.

jazz·y /jázee/ *adj.* (**jazz·i·er, jazz·i·est**) **1** of or like jazz. **2** vivid; unrestrained; showy. □□ **jazz·i·ly** *adv.* **jazz·i·ness** *n.*

J.C.B. *abbr.* Bachelor of Canon Law. [mod.L *Juris Canonici Baccalaureus*]

J.C.D. *abbr. Law* Doctor of Canon Law. [L *Juris Canonici Doctor*]

JCL *abbr. Computing* job control language.

JCS *abbr.* (also **J.C.S.**) Joint Chiefs of Staff.

jct. *abbr.* junction.

jeal·ous /jéləs/ *adj.* **1** (often foll. by *of*) fiercely protective (of rights, etc.). **2** afraid, suspicious, or resentful of rivalry in love or affection. **3** (often foll. by *of*) envious or resentful (of a person or a person's advantages, etc.). **4** (of God) intolerant of disloyalty. **5** (of inquiry, supervision, etc.) vigilant. □□ **jeal·ous·ly** *adv.* [ME f. OF *gelos* f. med.L *zelosus* ZEALOUS]

SYNONYM TIP jealous

COVETOUS, ENVIOUS. A young man who is **jealous** of his girlfriend's admirers cannot tolerate their rivalry and is afraid of being displaced. While *jealous* may merely imply an intense effort to hold on to what one possesses (*jealous of what little time he has to herself*), it is more often associated with distrust, suspicion, anger, and other negative emotions (*a jealous wife*). **Envious**, on the other hand, implies wanting something that belongs to another and to which one has no particular right or claim (*envious of her good fortune*). While jealousy may be either good or bad, depending upon its object, envy is usually bad and often implies a malicious desire to deprive someone else of whatever it is that has made one *envious*. Someone who is **covetous** has fallen prey to an inordinate or wrongful desire, usually for a person or thing that rightfully belongs to another. In other words, a young man might be *jealous* of the other men who flirt with his girlfriend, while they might be *envious* of her obvious preference for him. But if the young man is married, he'd better not be *covetous* of his neighbor's wife.

jeal·ous·y /jéləsee/ *n.* (*pl.* **·ies**) **1** a jealous state or feeling. **2** an instance of this. [ME f. OF *gelosie* (as JEALOUS)]

jean /jeen/ *n.* twilled cotton cloth. [ME, attrib. use of *Jene* f. OF *Janne* f. med.L *Janua* Genoa]

jeans /jeenz/ *n.pl.* pants made of jean or (more usually) denim, for informal wear.

jeep /jeep/ *n.* (also *Trademark* **Jeep**) a small, sturdy, esp. military motor vehicle with four-wheel drive. [orig. US, f. *gp* = *general purposes*, infl. by 'Eugene the Jeep,' an animal in a comic strip]

jee·pers /jeépərz/ *int. sl.* expressing surprise, etc. [corrupt. of *Jesus*]

jeer /jeer/ *v. & n.* •*v.* **1** *intr.* (usu. foll. by *at*) scoff derisively. **2** *tr.* scoff at; deride. •*n.* a scoff or taunt. □□ **jeer·ing·ly** *adv.* [16th c.: orig. unkn.]

jeez /jeez/ *int. sl.* a mild expression of surprise, discovery, etc. (cf. GEE¹). [abbr. of JESUS]

je·had var. of JIHAD.

Je·ho·vah /jəhóvə/ *n.* the Hebrew name of God in the Old Testament. [med.L *Iehoua(h)* f. Heb. *YHVH* (with the vowels of *adonai* 'my lord' included: see YAHWEH)]

Je·ho·vah's Wit·ness *n.* a member of a fundamentalist millenarian Christian sect rejecting the supremacy of government and religious institutions and preaching the Second Coming of Christ.

Je·ho·vist /jəhóvist/ *n.* = YAHWIST.

je·june /jijóon/ *adj.* **1** intellectually unsatisfying; shallow. **2** puerile.

3 (of ideas, writings, etc.) meager; scanty; dry and uninteresting. **4** (of the land) barren, poor. □□ **je•june•ly** adv. **je•june•ness** n. [orig. = fasting, f. L jejunus]

je•ju•num /jijŏŏnəm/ n. Anat. the part of the small intestine between the duodenum and ileum. [L, neut. of jejunus fasting]

Jek•yll and Hyde /jékil ənd híd/ n. a person alternately displaying opposing good and evil personalities. [R. L. Stevenson's story The Strange Case of Dr. Jekyll and Mr. Hyde]

jell /jel/ v.intr. colloq. **1 a** set as a jelly. **b** (of ideas, etc.) take a definite form. **2** (of two different things) cohere. [back-form. f. JELLY]

jel•la•ba var. of DJELLABA.

jel•li•fy /jélifī/ v.tr. & intr. (•fies, •fied) turn into jelly; make or become like jelly. □□ **jel•li•fi•ca•tion** n.

Jell-O /jélō/ n. Trademark (often as jello) a fruit-flavored gelatin dessert made from a commercially prepared powder.

jel•ly /jélee/ n. & v. •n. (pl. •lies) **1 a** a gelatinous preparation of fruit juice, etc., for use as a jam or a condiment (grape jelly). **b** esp. Brit. a soft, stiffish, semitransparent preparation of boiled sugar and fruit juice or milk, etc., often cooled in a mold and eaten as a dessert. **c** a similar preparation derived from meat, bones, etc., and gelatin (marrowbone jelly). **2** any substance of a similar consistency. **3** an inexpensive sandal or shoe made of molded plastic. **4** Brit. sl. gelignite. •v. (•lies, •lied) **1** intr. & tr. set or cause to set as a jelly; congeal. **2** tr. set (food) in a jelly (jellied eels). □□ **jel•ly•like** adj. [ME f. OF gelee frost, jelly, f. Rmc gelata f. L gelare freeze f. gelu frost]

jel•ly ba•by n. Brit. a gelatinous candy in the stylized shape of a baby.

jel•ly bag n. a bag for straining juice from fruit for jelly.

jel•ly bean n. a chewy, gelatinous candy in the shape of a bean with a hard sugar coating.

jel•ly•fish /jéleefish/ n. (pl. usu. same or •fish•es) **1** a free-swimming marine coelenterate of the class Scyphozoa having an umbrella-shaped jellylike body and stinging tentacles. **2** colloq. a feeble person.

jel•ly roll n. a rolled sponge cake with a jelly filling.

je ne sais quoi /zhə nə say kwaá/ n. an indefinable something. [F, = I do not know what]

jen•net /jénit/ n. a small Spanish horse. [F genet f. Sp. jinete light horseman f. Arab. zenāta Berber tribe famous as horsemen]

sea nettle jellyfish

jen•ny /jénee/ n. (pl. •nies) **1** hist. = spinning jenny. **2** a female donkey or ass. **3** a locomotive crane. [pet-form of the name Janet]

jeop•ard•ize /jépərdīz/ v.tr. endanger; put into jeopardy.

jeop•ard•y /jépərdee/ n. **1** danger, esp. of severe harm or loss. **2** Law danger resulting from being on trial for a criminal offense. [ME iuparti f. OF ieu parti divided (i.e., even) game, f. L jocus game + partitus past part. of partire divide f. pars partis part]

Jer. abbr. Jeremiah (Old Testament).

jer•bil esp. Brit. var. of GERBIL.

jer•bo•a /jərbóə/ n. any small desert rodent of the family Dipodidae with long hind legs and the ability to make long jumps. [mod.L f. Arab. yarbū' flesh of loins, jerboa]

jer•e•mi•ad /jérimíad/ n. a doleful complaint or lamentation; a list of woes. [F jérémiade f. Jérémie Jeremiah f. eccl.L Jeremias, with ref. to the Lamentations of Jeremiah in the Old Testament]

Jer•e•mi•ah /jérimíə/ n. a dismal prophet, a denouncer of the times. [with ref. to Jeremiah (as JEREMIAD)]

jerk¹ /jərk/ n. & v. •n. **1** a sharp sudden pull, twist, twitch, start, etc. **2** a spasmodic muscular twitch. **3** (in pl.) Brit. colloq. exercises (physical jerks). **4** sl. a fool; a stupid or contemptible person. •v. **1** intr. move with a jerk. **2** tr. pull, thrust, twist, etc., with a jerk. **3** tr. throw with a suddenly arrested motion. **4** tr. Weightlifting raise (a weight) from shoulder level to above the head. □ **jerk off** coarse sl. masturbate. □□ **jerk•er** n. [16th c.: perh. imit.]

jerk² /jərk/ v.tr. cure (beef) by cutting in long slices and drying it in the sun. [Amer. Sp. charquear f. charqui f. Quechua echarqui dried flesh]

jer•kin /jórkin/ n. **1** a sleeveless jacket. **2** hist. a man's close-fitting jacket, often of leather. [16th c.: orig. unkn.]

jerk•y /jórkee/ adj. (jerk•i•er, jerk•i•est) **1** having sudden abrupt movements. **2** spasmodic. □□ **jerk•i•ly** adv. **jerk•i•ness** n.

jer•o•bo•am /jérəbóəm/ n. a wine bottle four times larger than that of an ordinary bottle. [Jeroboam king of Israel (1 Kings 11:28, 14:16)]

Jer•ry /jéree/ n. (pl. •ries) Brit. sl. **1** a German (esp. in military contexts). **2** the Germans collectively. [prob. alt. of German]

jerkin 1

jer•ry¹ /jéree/ n. (pl. •ries) Brit. sl. a chamber pot.

jer•ry² /jéree/ v.intr. Austral. sl. understand, realize. [20th c.: orig. unkn.]

jer•ry-build•er /jéribildər/ n. a builder of unsubstantial houses, etc., with poor-quality materials. □□ **jer•ry-build•ing** n. **jer•ry-built** adj.

jer•ry can /jérikan/ n. (also **jer•ry•can**, **jer•ri•can**) a flat-sided 5-gallon container (orig. German) for liquids, usu. fuel or water. [JERRY + CAN²]

jer•ry•man•der esp. Brit. var. of GERRYMANDER.

jer•sey /jórzee/ n. (pl. •seys) **1 a** a knitted, usu. woolen pullover or similar garment. **b** a plain-knitted (orig. woolen) fabric. **2** (Jersey) a light brown dairy cow from Jersey. [Jersey, largest of the Channel Islands]

Je•ru•sa•lem ar•ti•choke /jərŏŏsələm/ n. **1** a species of sunflower, Helianthus tuberosus, with edible underground tubers. **2** this tuber used as a vegetable. [corrupt. of It. girasole sunflower]

jess /jes/ n. & v. •n. a short strap of leather, silk, etc., put around the leg of a hawk in falconry. •v.tr. put jesses on (a hawk, etc.). [ME ges f. OF ges, get ult. f. L jactus a throw f. jacere jact- to throw]

jes•sa•mine var. of JASMINE.

jest /jest/ n. & v. •n. **1 a** a joke. **b** fun. **2 a** raillery; banter. **b** an object of derision (a standing jest). •v.intr. **1** joke; make jests. **2** fool about; play or act triflingly. □ **in jest** in fun. □□ **jest•ful** adj.

WORD HISTORY jest

Late Middle English: from earlier gest, from Old French geste, from Latin gesta 'actions, exploits', from gerere 'do'. The original sense was 'exploit, heroic deed', hence 'a narrative of such deeds' (originally in verse); later the term denoted an idle tale, hence a joke (mid 16th cent.).

---

jest•er /jéstər/ n. a professional joker or 'fool' at a medieval court, etc., traditionally wearing a cap with bells on it and carrying a mock scepter.

Jes•u•it /jézhŏŏit, jézŏŏ–, jézyŏŏ–/ n. a member of the Society of Jesus, a Roman Catholic order founded by St. Ignatius Loyola and others in 1534. [F jésuite or mod.L Jesuita f. Jesus: see JESUS]

Jes•u•it•i•cal /jézhŏŏ-itikəl, –yŏŏ–/ adj. **1** of or concerning the Jesuits. **2** often offens. dissembling or equivocating, in the manner once associated with Jesuits. □□ **Jes•u•it•i•cal•ly** adv.

Je•sus /jéezəs/ n. the name of the source of the Christian religion d. c. AD 30.

jet¹ /jet/ n. & v. •n. **1** a stream of water, steam, gas, flame, etc., shot out esp. from a small opening. **2** a spout or nozzle for emitting water, etc., in this way. **3 a** a jet engine. **b** an aircraft powered by one or more jet engines. •v. (**jet•ted**, **jet•ting**) **1** intr. spurt out in jets. **2** tr. & intr. colloq. send or travel by jet plane. [earlier as verb (in sense 1): F jeter throw ult. f. L jactare frequent. of jacere jact- throw]

jet² /jet/ n. **1 a** a hard black variety of lignite capable of being carved and highly polished. **b** (attrib.) made of this. **2** (in full **jet-black**) a deep glossy black color. [ME f. AF geet, OF jaiet f. L gagates f. Gk gagatēs f. Gagai in Asia Minor]

je•té /zhətáy/ n. Ballet a spring or leap with one leg forward and the other stretched backward. [F, past part. of jeter throw: see JET¹]

jet en•gine n. an engine using jet propulsion for forward thrust, esp. of an aircraft.

jet lag n. extreme tiredness and other bodily effects felt after a long flight involving marked differences of local time.

jet-pro•pelled adj. **1** having jet propulsion. **2** (of a person, etc.) very fast.

jet pro•pul•sion n. propulsion by the backward ejection of a high-speed jet of gas or liquid.

jet•sam /jétsəm/ n. discarded material washed ashore, esp. that thrown overboard to lighten a ship, etc. (cf. FLOTSAM). [contr. of JETTISON]

jet set n. colloq. wealthy people frequently traveling by air, esp. for pleasure. □□ **jet-set•ter** n.

jet stream n. **1** a narrow current of very strong winds encircling the globe several miles above the earth. **2** the stream of exhaust from a jet engine.

jet•ti•son /jétisən, –zən/ v. & n. •v.tr. **1 a** throw (esp. heavy material) overboard to lighten a ship, hot-air balloon, etc. **b** drop (goods) from an aircraft. **2** abandon; get rid of (something no longer wanted). •n. the act of jettisoning. [ME f. AF getteson, OF getaison f. L jactatio –onis f. jactare throw: see JET¹]

jet•ton /jét'n/ n. a counter or token with a stamped or engraved design esp. for insertion like a coin to operate a machine, etc. [F jeton f. jeter throw, add up accounts: see JET¹]

jet•ty /jétee/ n. (pl. •ties) **1** a pier or breakwater constructed to protect or defend a harbor, coast, etc. **2** a landing pier. [ME f. OF jetee, fem. past part. of jeter throw: see JET¹]

jeu d'es•prit /zhő despreé/ n. (pl. **jeux d'es•prit** pronunc. same) a witty or humorous (usu. literary) trifle. [F, = game of the spirit]

jeu•nesse do•rée /zhŏnes dawráy/ n. = GILDED YOUTH. [F]

Jew /jŏŏ/ n. & v. •n. **1** a person of Hebrew descent or whose religion is Judaism. **2** sl. offens. (as a stereotype) a person considered

to be parsimonious or to drive a hard bargain in trading. ● *v.tr.* (jew) *sl. offens.* get a financial advantage over. [ME f. OF *giu* f. L *judaeus* f. Gk *ioudaios* ult. f. Heb. *yᵉhûḏî* f. *yᵉhûḏâh* Judah]
▶ The stereotype in sense 2, which is deeply offensive, arose from historical associations of Jews as moneylenders in medieval England.

jew·el /jṓəl/ *n. & v.* ● *n.* **1 a** a precious stone. **b** this as used for its hardness as a bearing in watchmaking. **2** a personal ornament containing a jewel or jewels. **3** a precious person or thing. ● *v.tr.* (**jeweled, jew·el·ing;** esp. *Brit.* **jew·elled, jew·el·ling**) **1** (esp. as **jeweled** *adj.*) adorn or set with jewels. **2** (in watchmaking) set with jewels. □□ **jew·el·like** *adj.* [ME f. AF *juel, jeuel,* OF *joel,* of uncert. orig.]

jew·el box *n.* a plastic case for a compact disk or CD-ROM.

jew·el·er /jṓələr/ *n.* (esp. *Brit.* **jew·el·ler**) a maker of or dealer in jewels or jewelry. [ME f. AF *jueler,* OF *juelier* (as JEWEL)]

jew·el·er's rouge *n.* finely ground rouge for polishing.

jew·el·fish /jṓəlfish/*n.* a scarlet and green tropical cichlid fish, *Hemichromis bimaculatus.*

jew·el·ry /jṓəlree/ *n.* (esp. *Brit.* **jew·el·ler·y** /jṓəlree/) jewels or other ornamental objects, esp. for personal adornment, regarded collectively. [ME f. OF *juelerie* and f. JEWEL, JEWELER]

> **PRONUNCIATION TIP** **jewelry**
> Avoid pronouncing this word "joo-luh-ree."

Jew·ess /jṓo-is/ *n. offens.* a female Jew.

jew·fish /jṓofish/ *n.* **1** a grouper, *Epinephelus itajara,* of N. American, Atlantic, and Pacific coasts. **2** any of various large Australian fish used as food, esp. the mulloway.

Jew·ish /jṓoish/ *adj.* **1** of or relating to Jews. **2** of Judaism. □□ **Jew·ish·ly** *adv.* **Jew·ish·ness** *n.*

Jew·ry /jṓoree/ *n.* (*pl.* **·ries**) **1** Jews collectively. **2** *hist.* a Jews' quarter in a town, etc. [ME f. AF *juerie,* OF *juierie* (as JEW)]

Jew's harp *n.* (also **Jews' harp**) a small lyre-shaped musical instrument held between the teeth and struck with the finger.

Jez·e·bel /jézəbel/ *n.* a shameless or immoral woman. [*Jezebel,* wife of Ahab in the Old Testament (1 Kings 16, 19, 21)]

jg *abbr.* (also **J.G.**) *US Navy* junior grade.

jib[1] /jib/ *n. & v.* ● *n.* **1** a triangular staysail from the outer end of the jibboom to the top of the foremast or from the bowsprit to the masthead. **2** the projecting arm of a crane. ● *v.tr. & intr.* (**jibbed, jib·bing**) (of a sail, etc.) pull or swing around from one side of the ship to the other; jibe. [17th c.: orig. unkn.]

jib[2] /jib/ *v.intr.* (**jibbed, jib·bing**) esp. *Brit.* **1 a** (of an animal, esp. a horse) stop and refuse to go on; move backward or sideways instead of going on. **b** (of a person) refuse to continue. **2** (foll. by *at*) show aversion to (a person or course of action). □□ **jib·ber** *n.* [19th c.: orig. unkn.]

jib·ba /jibə/ *n.* (also **jib·bah**) a long coat worn by Muslims. [Egypt. var. of Arab. *jubba*]

jib·boom /jib-bóom/ *n.* a spar run out from the end of the bowsprit.

jibe[1] var. of GIBE.

jibe[2] /jib/ *v. & n.* (*Brit.* **gybe**) ● *v.* **1** *intr.* (of a fore-and-aft sail or boom) swing across in wearing or running before the winds. **2** *tr.* cause (a sail) to do this. **3** *intr.* (of a ship or its crew) change course so that this happens. ● *n.* a change of course causing jibing. [obs. Du. *gijben*]

jibe[3] /jib/ *v.intr.* (usu. foll. by *with*) *colloq.* agree; be in accord. [19th c.: orig. unkn.]

▶ **Jibe** means 'agree; go together'; **gibe** means 'jeer; deride.' The two words are pronounced identically, and **jibe** is sometimes used in place of **gibe**. **Jive** is a jazz term applied to a style of music and dance, and it can also mean 'misleading or pretentious talk.' **Jive** is sometimes informally substituted for **jibe**.

jiff /jif/ *n.* (also **jif·fy,** *pl.* **·ies**) *colloq.* a short time; a moment (*in a jiffy; half a jiff*). [18th c.: orig. unkn.]

jig /jig/ *n. & v.* ● *n.* **1 a** a lively dance with leaping movements. **b** the music for this, usu. in triple time. **2** a device that holds a piece of work and guides the tools operating on it. ● *v.* (**jigged, jig·ging**) **1** *intr.* dance a jig. **2** *tr. & intr.* move quickly and jerkily up and down. **3** *tr.* work on or equip with a jig or jigs. □ **jig about** (esp. *Brit.*) fidget. **the jig is up** *sl.* all hope is gone, esp. of committing a wrong without being caught. [16th c.: orig. unkn.]

jig·ger[1] /jigər/ *n.* **1** *Naut.* **a** a small tackle consisting of a double and single block with a rope. **b** a small sail at the stern. **c** a small smack having this. **2** *sl.* a gadget. **3** *Golf* an iron club with a narrow face. **4** *Billiards colloq.* a cue rest. **5** a measure of spirits, etc. **b** a small glass holding this. **6** a person or thing that jigs.

jig·ger[2] /jigər/ *n.* **1** = CHIGOE. **2** = CHIGGER 2. [corrupt.]

jig·gered /jigərd/ *adj. colloq.* (as a mild oath) confounded (*I'll be jiggered*). [euphem.]

jig·ger·y-pok·er·y /jigərepókəree/ *n. Brit. colloq.* deceitful or dishonest dealing; trickery. [cf. Sc. *joukery-pawkery* f. *jouk* dodge, skulk]

jig·gle /jigəl/ *v.* (often foll. by *about,* etc.) **1** *tr.* shake lightly; rock jerkily. **2** *intr.* fidget. □□ **jig·gly** *adj.* [JIG or JOGGLE[1]]

jig·saw /jigsaw/ *n.* **1 a** (in full **jigsaw puzzle**) a puzzle consisting of a picture on board or wood, etc., cut into irregular interlocking pieces to be reassembled. **b** a mental puzzle resolvable by assembling various pieces of information. **2** a machine saw with a fine blade enabling it to cut curved lines in a sheet of wood, metal, etc.

ji·had /jihaǎd/ *n.* (also **je·had**) a holy war undertaken by Muslims against unbelievers. [Arab. *jihād*]

Jill /jil/ *n. sl.* (also **Jill**) a young woman. [the name *Jill*]

jil·lion /jílyən/ *n. colloq.* a very large indefinite number.

jilt /jilt/ *v. & n.* ● *v.tr.* abruptly reject or abandon (a lover, etc.). ● *n.* a person (esp. a woman) who jilts a lover. [17th c.: orig. unkn.]

jim crow /jim krṓ/ *n.* (also **Jim Crow**) **1** the practice of segregating blacks. **2** *offens.* a black person. **3** an implement for straightening iron bars or bending rails by screw pressure. □□ **jim crow·ism** *n.* (in sense 1). [mid 19th cent.: the name of a black character in a 19th-cent. plantation song]

jim·jams /jímjamz/ *n.pl.* **1** *sl.* = DELIRIUM TREMENS. **2** *colloq.* a fit of depression or nervousness. [fanciful redupl.]

jim·my /jímee/ *n. & v.* (*Brit.* **jem·mi** /jémee/) ● *n.* (*pl.* **·mies**) a burglar's short crowbar, usu. made in sections. ● *v.tr.* (**·mies, ·mied**) force open with a jimmy. [pet-form of the name *James*]

jim·my·grant /jímeegránt/ *n. Austral. rhyming sl.* an immigrant.

Jim·my Wood·ser /jimee wŏŏdzər/ *n. Austral.* **1** a person who drinks alone. **2** a drink taken on one's own. [*Jimmy Wood,* name of a character in the poem of that name by Barcroft Boake]

jim·son·weed /jímsənweed/ *n.* = THORN APPLE. [*Jamestown* in Virginia]

jin·gle /jínggəl/ *n. & v.* ● *n.* **1** a mixed noise as of bells or light metal objects being shaken together. **2 a** a repetition of the same sound in words, esp. as an aid to memory or to attract attention. **b** a short verse of this kind used in advertising, etc. ● *v.* **1** *intr. & tr.* make or cause to make a jingling sound. **2** *intr.* (of writing) be full of alliterations, rhymes, etc. □□ **jin·gly** *adj.* (**jin·gli·er, jin·gli·est**). [ME: imit.]

jin·go /jínggō/ *n.* (*pl.* **·goes**) a supporter of policy favoring war; a blustering patriot. □ **by jingo!** a mild oath. □□ **jin·go·ism** *n.* **jin·go·ist** *n.* **jin·go·is·tic** /–gō-ístik/ *adj.* [17th c.: orig. a magician's word: polit. sense from use of *by jingo* in a popular song, then applied to any war partisan]

jink /jingk/ *v. & n.* ● *v.* **1** *intr.* move elusively; dodge. **2** *tr.* elude by dodging. ● *n.* an act of dodging or eluding. [orig. Sc.: prob. imit. of nimble motion]

jink·er /jíngkər/ *n. & v. Austral.* ● *n.* **1** a wheeled conveyance for moving heavy logs. **2** a light, two-wheeled cart. ● *v.tr.* convey with a jinker. [Sc. *janker* long pole on wheels used for carrying logs]

jin·ni /jínee, jineé/ *n.* (also **jinn, djinn** /jin/) (*pl.* **jinn** or **jinns, djinn** or **djinns**) (in Muslim mythology) an intelligent being lower than the angels, able to appear in human and animal forms, and having power over people. [Arab. *jinnī,* pl. *jinn:* cf. GENIE]

jinx /jingks/ *n. & v. colloq.* ● *n.* a person or thing that seems to cause bad luck. ● *v.tr.* (often in *passive*) subject (a person) to an unlucky force. [perh. var. of *jynx* wryneck, charm]

jit·ter /jítər/ *n. & v. colloq.* ● *n.* (**the jitters**) extreme nervousness. ● *v.intr.* be nervous; act nervously. □□ **jit·ter·y** *adj.* **jit·ter·i·ness** *n.* [20th c.: orig. unkn.]

jit·ter·bug /jítərbug/ *n. & v.* ● *n.* **1** a nervous person. **2** *hist.* **a** a fast popular dance. **b** a person fond of dancing this. ● *v.intr.* (**·bugged, ·bug·ging**) dance the jitterbug.

jiu·jit·su var. of JUJITSU.

jive /jīv/ *n. & v.* ● *n.* **1** a jerky lively style of dance esp. popular in the 1950s. **2** music for this. **3** *sl.* talk, conversation, esp. when misleading or pretentious. ● *v.intr.* **1** dance the jive. **2** play jive music. □□ **jiv·er** *n.* [20th c.: orig. uncert.]

▶ See note at JIBE.

Jnr. *abbr.* esp. *Brit.* junior.

jo /jō/ *n.* (*pl.* **joes**) *Sc.* a sweetheart or beloved. [var. of JOY]

job[1] /job/ *n. & v.* ● *n.* **1** a piece of work, esp. one done for hire or profit. **2** a paid position of employment. **3** *colloq.* anything one has to do. **4** *colloq.* a difficult task (*had a job to find them*). **5** a product of work, esp. if well done. **6** *Computing* an item of work regarded separately. **7** *sl.* a crime, esp. a robbery. **8** a transaction in which private advantage prevails over duty or public interest. **9** a state of affairs or set of circumstances (*is a bad job*). ● *v.* (**jobbed, job·bing**) **1 a** *intr.* do jobs; do piecework. **2 a** *intr.* deal in stocks. **b** *tr.* buy and sell (stocks or goods) as a middleman. **3 a** *intr.* turn a position of trust to private advantage. **b** *tr.* deal corruptly with (a matter). **4** *tr. sl.* swindle. □ **just the job** esp. *Brit. colloq.* exactly what is wanted. **make a job** (or **good job**) **of** do thoroughly or successfully. **on the job** *colloq.* **1** at work; in the course of doing a piece of work. **2** *coarse* engaged in sexual intercourse. **out of a job** unemployed. [16th c.: orig. unkn.]

job[2] /job/ *v. & n.* ● *v.* (**jobbed, job·bing**) **1** *tr.* prod; stab slightly. **2** *intr.*

(foll. by *at*) thrust. ● *n.* a prod or thrust; a jerk at a horse's bit. [ME, app. imit.: cf. JAB]

job ac·tion *n.* any action, esp. a strike, taken by employees as a protest.

job·ber /jóbər/ *n.* **1 a** a wholesaler. **b** *derog.* a broker (see BROKER 2). **2** *Brit.* a principal or wholesaler dealing on the stock exchange. **3** a person who jobs. [JOB¹]

job·ber·y /jóbəree/ *n.* corrupt dealing.

job·bing /jóbing/ *adj.* esp. *Brit.* working on separate or occasional jobs (esp. of a computer, gardener, or printer).

job con·trol lan·guage *n.* *Computing* a language enabling the user to determine the tasks to be undertaken by the operating system.

job-hunt *v.intr. colloq.* seek employment.

job·less /jóblis/ *adj.* without a job; unemployed. □□ **job·less·ness** *n.*

job lot *n.* a miscellaneous group of articles, esp. bought together.

Job's com·fort·er /jóbz/ *n.* a person who under the guise of comforting aggravates distress. [the patriarch *Job* in the Old Testament (Job 16:2)]

job-shar·ing *n.* an arrangement by which a full-time job is done jointly by several part-time employees who share the remuneration.

Job's tears /jóbz/ *n.pl.* the seeds of a grass, *Coix lacryma-jobi*, used as beads. [the patriarch *Job* in the Old Testament]

Jock /jok/ *n.* *Brit. sl.* a Scotsman. [Sc. form of the name *Jack* (see JACK¹)]

jock¹ /jok/ *n.* *colloq.* a jockey. [abbr.]

jock² /jok/ *n.* *sl.* **1** = JOCKSTRAP. **2** an athlete. [abbr.]

jock·ey /jókee/ *n. & v.* ● *n.* (*pl.* ·**eys**) a rider in horse races, esp. a professional one. ● *v.* (·**eys**, ·**eyed**) **1** *tr.* **a** trick or cheat (a person). **b** outwit. **2** *tr.* (foll. by *away*, *out*, *in*, etc.) draw (a person) by trickery. **3** *intr.* cheat. □ **jockey for position** try to gain an advantageous position esp. by skillful maneuvering or unfair action. □□ **jock·ey·dom** *n.* **jock·ey·ship** *n.*

Late 16th cent.: diminutive of JOCK. Originally the name for an ordinary man, lad, or underling, the word came to mean 'mounted courier', hence the current sense (late 17th cent.). Another early use 'horse-dealer' (long a byword for dishonesty) probably gave rise to the verb sense 'manipulate', whereas the main verb sense probably relates to the behavior of jockeys maneuvering for an advantageous position during a race.

jock·ey cap *n.* a cap with a long visor, as worn by jockeys.

jock·strap /jókstrap/ *n.* a support or protection for the male genitals, worn esp. by athletes. [sl. *jock* genitals + STRAP]

jo·cose /jōkós/ *adj.* **1** playful in style. **2** fond of joking; jocular. □□ **jo·cose·ly** *adv.* **jo·cose·ness** *n.* **jo·cos·i·ty** /–kósitee/ *n.* (*pl.* ·**ties**). [L *jocosus* f. *jocus* jest]

joc·u·lar /jókyələr/ *adj.* **1** merry; fond of joking. **2** of the nature of a joke; humorous. □□ **joc·u·lar·i·ty** /–láritee/ *n.* (*pl.* ·**ties**). **joc·u·lar·ly** *adv.* [L *jocularis* f. *joculus* dimin. of *jocus* jest]

joc·und /jókənd, jó–/ *adj. literary* merry; cheerful; sprightly. □□ **jo·cun·di·ty** /jəkúnditee/ *n.* (*pl.* ·**ties**). **joc·und·ly** *adv.* [ME f. OF f. L *jocundus, jucundus* f. *juvare* delight]

jodh·purs /jódpərz/ *n.pl.* long breeches for riding, etc., close-fitting from the knee to the ankle. [*Jodhpur* in India]

Joe Bloggs /jō blógz/ *n.* *Brit. colloq.* = JOE BLOW.

Joe Blow /jō blō/ *n. colloq.* a hypothetical average man.

jo·ey /jóee/ *n.* (*pl.* ·**eys**) *Austral.* **1** a young kangaroo. **2** a young animal. [Aboriginal *joè*]

jog /jog/ *v. & n.* ● *v.* (**jogged**, **jog·ging**) **1** *intr.* run at a slow pace, esp. as physical exercise. **2** *intr.* (of a horse) move at a jog trot. **3** *intr.* (often foll. by *on*, *along*) proceed laboriously; trudge. **4** *intr.* go on one's way. **5** *intr.* proceed; get through the time (*we must jog on somehow*). **6** *intr.* move up and down with an unsteady motion. **7** *tr.* nudge (a person), esp. to arouse attention. **8** *tr.* shake with a push or jerk. **9** *tr.* stimulate (a person's or one's own memory). ● *n.* **1** a shake, push, or nudge. **2** a slow walk or trot. [ME: app. imit.]

jog·ger /jógər/ *n.* a person who jogs, esp. one who runs for physical exercise.

jog·gle¹ /jógəl/ *v. & n.* ● *v.tr. & intr.* shake or move by or as if by repeated jerks. ● *n.* **1** a slight shake. **2** the act or action of joggling. [frequent. of JOG]

jog·gle² /jógəl/ *n. & v.* ● *n.* **1** a joint of two pieces of stone or lumber, contrived to prevent their sliding on one another. **2** a notch in one of the two pieces, a projection in the other, or a small piece let in between the two, for this purpose. ● *v.tr.* join with a joggle. [perh. f. *jog* = JAG¹]

jog trot *n.* **1** a slow regular trot. **2** a monotonous progression.

john /jon/ *n.* *sl.* a toilet or bathroom. [the name *John*]

John Bull /jon bŏŏl/ *n.* a personification of England or the typical Englishman. [the name of a character repr. the English nation in J. Arbuthnot's satire *Law is a Bottomless Pit* (1712)]

John Do·ry /jon dáwree/ *n.* (*pl.* ·**ries**) a European marine fish, *Zeus faber*, with a laterally flattened body and a black spot on each side.

John Hop /jon hóp/ *n.* *Austral. sl.* a police officer. [rhyming sl. for *cop*]

john·ny /jónee/ *n.* (*pl.* ·**nies**) **1** *colloq.* (also **John·ny**) a fellow; a man. **2** *sl.* a short-sleeved, collarless gown worn by patients in hospitals, examining rooms, etc. [familiar form of the name *John*]

john·ny-come-late·ly *n.* *colloq.* a recently arrived person.

John·so·ni·an /jonsôneeən/ *adj.* **1** of or relating to Samuel Johnson, English man of letters and lexicographer (d. 1784). **2** typical of his style of writing.

joie de vi·vre /zhwaádə veévrə/ *n.* a feeling of healthy and exuberant enjoyment of life. [F. = joy of living]

join /joyn/ *v. & n.* ● *v.* **1** *tr.* (often foll. by *to*, *together*) put together; fasten; unite (one thing or person to another or several together). **2** *tr.* connect (points) by a line, etc. **3** *tr.* become a member of (an association, society, organization, etc.). **4** *tr.* take one's place with or in (a company, group, procession, etc.). **5** *tr.* **a** come into the company of (a person). **b** (foll. by *in*) take part with (others) in an activity, etc. (*joined me in condemnation of the outrage*). **c** (foll. by *for*) share the company of for a specified occasion (*may I join you for lunch?*). **6** *intr.* (often foll. by *with*, *to*) come together; be united. **7** *intr.* (often foll. by *in*) take part with others in an activity, etc. **8** *tr.* be or become connected or continuous with (*the Gila River joins the Colorado at Yuma*). ● *n.* a point, line, or surface at which two or more things are joined. □ **join battle** begin fighting. **join forc·es** combine efforts. **join hands 1 a** clasp each other's hands. **b** clasp one's hands together. **2** combine in an action or enterprise. **join up 1** enlist for military service. **2** (often foll. by *with*) unite; connect. □□ **join·a·ble** *adj.* [ME f. OF *joindre* (stem *joign-*) f. L *jungere junct-*: join: cf. YOKE]

COMBINE, CONJOIN, CONNECT, CONSOLIDATE, LINK, UNITE. It is possible for an individual to **join** an investment club, to **link** up with other people who are interested in putting their money to work, to **consolidate** his or her financial resources, and to **combine** a background in economics with a strong interest in retirement planning. All of these words mean to bring together or to attach two or more things to each other. *Join* is the general term for bringing into contact or conjunction two discrete things (*to join two pieces of wood, to join one's friends in celebration*), while **conjoin** emphasizes both the separateness of the things that are joined and the unity that results (*her innate brilliance, conjoined with a genuine eagerness to learn, made her the ideal candidate for the job*). In contrast, to *combine* is to mix or mingle things together, often to the point where they merge with one another (*to combine the ingredients for a cake*). *Consolidate* also implies a merger of distinct and separate elements, but the emphasis here is on achieving greater compactness, strength, and efficiency (*to consolidate their incomes and buy a new house together*). **Connect** implies a loose or obvious attachment of things to each other, but with each thing's identity or physical separateness preserved (*the two families were connected not only by blood but by where they lived*). In a physical context, it differs from *join* in that it implies an intervening element that permits movement; in other words, the bones are *connected* by ligaments, but bricks are *joined by mortar*. When things are *joined* or *combined* so closely that they form a single thing, they are said to **unite** (*the parties were united in their support of the new law*). ·

join·der /jóyndər/ *n.* *Law* the act of bringing together. [AF f. OF *joindre* to join]

join·er /jóynər/ *n.* **1** a person who makes furniture and light woodwork. **2** *colloq.* a person who readily joins societies, etc. □□ **join·er·y** *n.* (in sense 1). [ME f. AF *joignour*, OF *joigneor* (as JOIN)]

joint /joynt/ *n., adj., & v.* ● *n.* **1 a** a place at which two things are joined together. **b** a point at which, or a contrivance by which, two parts of an artificial structure are joined. **2** a structure in an animal body by which two bones are fitted together. **3 a** any of the parts into which an animal carcass is divided for food. **b** any of the parts of which a body is made up. **4** *sl.* a place of meeting for drinking, etc. **5** *sl.* a marijuana cigarette. **6** the part of a stem from which a leaf or branch grows. **7** a piece of flexible material forming the hinge of a book cover. **8** *Geol.* a fissure in a mass of rock. ● *adj.* **1** held or done by, or belonging to, two or more persons, etc., in conjunction (*a joint mortgage; joint action*). **2** sharing with another in some action, state, etc. (*joint author; joint favorite*). ● *v.tr.* **1** connect by joints. **2** divide (a body or member) at a joint or into joints. **3** fill up the joints of (masonry, etc.) with mortar, etc.; trim the surface of (a mortar joint). **4** prepare (a board, etc.) for being joined to another by planing its edge. □ **joint and several** (of a bond, etc.) signed by more than one person, of whom each is liable for the whole sum. **out of joint 1** (of a bone) dislocated. **2 a** out of order. **b** inappropriate. □□ **joint·less** *adj.* **joint·ly** *adv.* [ME f. OF, past part. of *joindre* JOIN]

joint ac•count *n.* a bank account held by more than one person, each of whom has the right to deposit and withdraw funds.

Joint Chiefs of Staff *n. Mil.* a military advisory group made up of the Army Chief of Staff, the Air Force Chief of Staff, the Marine Corps commandant, and the Chief of Naval Operations.

joint•er /jóyntər/ *n.* **1 a** a plane for jointing. **b** a tool for jointing or pointing masonry. **2** a worker employed in jointing wires, pipes, etc.

joint•ress /jóyntris/ *n.* a widow who holds a jointure. [obs. *jointer* joint possessor]

joint stock *n.* capital held jointly; a common fund.

joint-stock com•pa•ny *n.* a company whose stock is owned jointly by the shareholders.

join•ture /jóynchər/ *n. & v.* • *n.* an estate settled on a wife for the period during which she survives her husband. • *v.tr.* provide (a wife) with a jointure. [ME f. OF f. L *junctura* (as JOIN)]

joist /joyst/ *n.* each of a series of parallel supporting beams of lumber, steel, etc., used in floors, ceilings, etc. □□ **joist•ed** *adj.* [ME f. OF *giste* ult. f. L *jacēre* lie]

jo•jo•ba /hōhṓbə/ *n.* a plant, *Simmondsia chinensis*, with seeds yielding an oily extract used in cosmetics, etc. [Mex. Sp.]

joke /jōk/ *n. & v.* • *n.* **1 a** a thing said or done to excite laughter. **b** a witticism or jest. **2** a ridiculous thing, person, or circumstance. • *v.* **1** *intr.* make jokes. **2** *tr.* poke fun at; banter. □ **no joke** colloq. a serious matter. □□ **jok•ing•ly** *adv.* **jok•ey** *adj.* (also **jok•y**). **jok•i•ly** *adv.* **jok•i•ness** *n.* [17th c. (*joque*), orig. sl.: perh. f. L *jocus* jest]

jok•er /jókər/ *n.* **1** a person who jokes. **2** *sl.* a fellow; a man. **3** a playing card usu. with a figure of a jester, used in some games esp. as a wild card. **4** a clause unobtrusively inserted in a bill or document and affecting its operation in a way not immediately apparent. **5** an unexpected factor or resource.

jok•er in the deck *n.* an unpredictable factor or participant.

joke•smith /jóksmith/ *n.* a skilled user or inventor of jokes.

jo•lie laide /zhōlee láyd/ *n.* (*pl.* **jo•lies laides** *pronunc.* same) a woman whose face is attractive despite having ugly features. [F f. *jolie* pretty + *laide* ugly]

jol•li•fy /jólifi/ *v.tr. & intr.* (**-fies, -fied**) make or be merry, esp. in drinking. □□ **jol•li•fi•ca•tion** *n.*

jol•li•ty /jólitee/ *n.* (*pl.* **-ties**) **1** merrymaking; festiveness. **2** (in *pl.*) festivities. [ME f. OF *joliveté* (as JOLLY¹)]

jol•ly¹ /jólee/ *adj., adv., v., & n.* • *adj.* (**jol•li•er, jol•li•est**) **1** cheerful and good-humored; merry. **2** festive; jovial. **3** slightly drunk. **4** esp. *Brit. colloq.* (of a person or thing) very pleasant; delightful (often *iron.: a jolly shame*). • *adv.* esp. *Brit. colloq.* very (*they were jolly unlucky*). • *v.tr.* (**-lies, -lied**) **1** (usu. foll. by *along*) colloq. coax or humor (a person) in a friendly way. **2** chaff; banter. • *n.* (*pl.* **-lies**) colloq. a party or celebration; an outing. □□ **jol•li•ly** *adv.* **jol•li•ness** *n.* [ME f. OF *jolif* gay, pretty, perh. f. ON *jól* YULE]

jol•ly² /jólee/ *n.* (*pl.* **-lies**) (in full **jolly boat**) a clinker-built ship's boat smaller than a cutter. [18th c.: orig. unkn.: perh. rel. to YAWL]

Jol•ly Rog•er *n.* a pirates' black flag, usu. with the skull and crossbones.

jolt /jōlt/ *v. & n.* • *v.* **1** *tr.* disturb or shake from the normal position (esp. in a moving vehicle) with a jerk. **2** *tr.* give a mental shock to; perturb. **3** *intr.* (of a vehicle) move along with jerks, as on a rough road. • *n.* **1** such a jerk. **2** a surprise or shock. □□ **jolt•y** *adj.* (**jolt•i•er, jolt•i•est**). [16th c.: orig. unkn.]

Jolly Roger

Jon. *abbr.* **1** Jonah (Old Testament). **2** Jonathan.

Jo•nah /jónə/ *n.* a person who seems to bring bad luck. [*Jonah* in the Old Testament]

jon•gleur /zhoNglór/ *n. hist.* an itinerant minstrel. [F, var. of *jougleur* JUGGLER]

jon•quil /jóngkwil/ *n.* a bulbous plant, *Narcissus jonquilla*, with clusters of small fragrant yellow flowers. [mod.L *jonquilla* or F *jonquille* f. Sp. *junquillo* dimin. of *junco*: see JUNCO]

Jor•da•ni•an /jawrdáyneeən/ *adj. & n.* • *adj.* of or relating to the kingdom of Jordan in the Middle East. • *n.* **1** a native or national of Jordan. **2** a person of Jordanian descent. [*Jordan*, river flowing into the Dead Sea]

jo•rum /jáwrəm/ *n.* **1** a large drinking bowl. **2** its contents, esp. punch. [perh. f. *Joram* (2 Sam. 8:10)]

Jos. *abbr.* Joseph.

Josh. *abbr.* Joshua (Old Testament).

josh /josh/ *n. & v. sl.* • *n.* a good-natured or teasing joke. • *v.* **1** *tr.* tease or banter. **2** *intr.* indulge in ridicule. □□ **josh•er** *n.* [19th c.: orig. unkn.]

joss¹ /jos/ *n.* a Chinese idol. [perh. ult. f. Port. *deos* f. L *deus* god]

joss² /jos/ *n. Austral.* a person of influence and importance. [Brit. dial.]

josser /jósər/ *n. Brit. sl.* **1** a fool. **2** a fellow. [JOSS² + -ER¹: cf. Austral. sense 'clergyman']

joss house *n.* a Chinese temple.

joss stick *n.* a stick of fragrant tinder mixed with clay, burned as incense.

jos•tle /jósəl/ *v. & n.* • *v.* **1** *tr.* push against; elbow. **2** *tr.* (often foll. by *away, from,* etc.) push (a person) abruptly or roughly. **3** *intr.* (foll. by *against*) knock or push, esp. in a crowd. **4** *intr.* (foll. by *with*) struggle; have a rough exchange. • *n.* **1** the act or an instance of jostling. **2** a collision. [ME: earlier *justle* f. JOUST + -LE⁴]

jot /jot/ *v. & n.* • *v.tr.* (**jot•ted, jot•ting**) (usu. foll. by *down*) write briefly or hastily. • *n.* (usu. with *neg.* expressed or implied) a very small amount (*not one jot*). [earlier as noun: L f. Gk *iōta*: see IOTA]

jot•ter /jótər/ *n.* a small pad or notebook for making notes, etc.

jot•ting /jóting/ *n.* (usu. in *pl.*) a note; something jotted down.

joule /jōōl/ *n.* the SI unit of work or energy equal to the work done by a force of one newton when its point of application moves one meter in the direction of action of the force, equivalent to a watt-second. ¶ Symb.: **J**. [J. P. *Joule*, Engl. physicist d. 1889]

jounce /jowns/ *v.tr. & intr.* bump; bounce; jolt. [ME: orig. unkn.]

jour•nal /jórnəl/ *n.* **1** a newspaper or periodical. **2** a daily record of events. **3** *Naut.* a logbook. **4** a book in which business transactions are entered, with a statement of the accounts to which each is to be debited and credited. **5** the part of a shaft or axle that rests on bearings. **6** a legislative body's record of daily proceedings. [ME f. OF *jurnal* f. LL *diurnalis* DIURNAL]

jour•nal•ese /jórnəleéz/ *n.* a hackneyed style of language characteristic of some newspaper writing.

jour•nal•ism /jórnəlizəm/ *n.* the business or practice of writing and producing newspapers.

jour•nal•ist /jórnəlist/ *n.* a person employed to report for or edit a newspaper, journal, or newscast. □□ **jour•nal•is•tic** *adj.* **jour•nal•is•ti•cal•ly** /-lístikəlee/ *adv.*

jour•nal•ize /jórnəliz/ *v.tr.* record in a private journal.

jour•ney /jórnee/ *n. & v.* • *n.* (*pl.* **-neys**) **1** an act of going from one place to another, esp. at a long distance. **2** the distance traveled in a specified time (*a day's journey*). **3** the traveling of a vehicle along a route at a stated time. • *v.intr.* (**-neys, -neyed**) make a journey. □□ **jour•ney•er** *n.* [ME f. OF *jornee* day, day's work or travel, ult. f. L *diurnus* daily]

jour•ney•man /jórneemən/ *n.* (*pl.* **-men**) **1** a qualified mechanic or artisan who works for another. **2** *derog.* a reliable but not outstanding worker. **b** a mere hireling. [JOURNEY in obs. sense 'day's work' + MAN]

joust /jowst/ *n. & v. hist.* • *n.* a combat between two knights on horseback with lances. • *v.intr.* engage in a joust. □□ **joust•er** *n.* [ME f. OF *juster* bring together ult. f. L *juxta* near]

Jove /jōv/ *n.* (in Roman mythology) Jupiter. □ **by Jove!** an exclamation of surprise or approval. [ME f. L *Jovis* genit. of OL *Jovis* used as genit. of JUPITER]

jo•vi•al /jóveeəl/ *adj.* **1** merry. **2** convivial. **3** hearty and good-humored. □□ **jo•vi•al•i•ty** /-álitee/ *n.* **jo•vi•al•ly** *adv.* [F f. LL *jovialis* of Jupiter (as JOVE), with ref. to the supposed influence of the planet Jupiter on those born under it]

Jo•vi•an /jóveeən/ *adj.* **1** (in Roman mythology) of or like Jupiter. **2** of the planet Jupiter.

jow•ar /jow-waár/ *n.* = DURRA. [Hindi *jawār*]

jowl¹ /jowl/ *n.* **1** the jaw or jawbone. **2** the cheek (*cheek by jowl*). □□ **-jowled** *adj.* (in *comb.*). [ME *chavel* jaw f. OE *ceafl*]

jowl² /jowl/ *n.* **1** the external loose skin on the throat or neck when prominent. **2** the dewlap of oxen, wattle of a bird, etc. □□ **jowl•y** *adj.* [ME *cholle* neck f. OE *ceole*]

joy /joy/ *n. & v.* ● *n.* **1** (often foll. by *at, in*) a vivid emotion of pleasure; extreme gladness. **2** a thing that causes joy. **3** *Brit. colloq.* satisfaction; success (*got no joy*). ● *v.* esp. *poet.* **1** *intr.* rejoice. **2** *tr.* gladden. □ **wish a person joy of** *Brit. iron.* be gladly rid of (what that person has to deal with). □□ **joy•less** *adj.* **joy•less•ly** *adv.* [ME f. OF *joie* ult. f. L *gaudium* f. *gaudēre* rejoice]

Joyce•e•an /jóyseeən/ *adj. & n.* ● *adj.* of or characteristic of James Joyce, Irish poet and novelist (d. 1941) or his writings. ● *n.* a specialist in or admirer of Joyce's works.

joy•ful /jóyfŏŏl/ *adj.* full of, showing, or causing joy. □□ **joy•ful•ly** *adv.* **joy•ful•ness** *n.*

joy•ous /jóyəs/ *adj.* (of an occasion, circumstance, etc.) characterized by pleasure or joy; joyful. □□ **joy•ous•ly** *adv.* **joy•ous•ness** *n.*

joy•ride /jóyrīd/ *n. & v. colloq.* ● *n.* a ride for pleasure in an automobile, esp. without the owner's permission. ● *v.intr.* (*past* **•rode** /-rōd/; *past part.* **•rid•den** /-rid'n/) go for a joyride. □□ **joy•rid•er** *n.*

joy•stick /jóystik/ *n.* **1** *colloq.* the control column of an aircraft. **2** a lever that can be moved in several directions to control the movement of an image on a computer monitor.

JP *abbr.* **1** justice of the peace. **2** jet propulsion.

Jr. *abbr.* junior.

jt. *abbr.* joint.

ju•bi•lant /jŏŏbilənt/ *adj.* exultant; rejoicing; joyful. □□ **ju•bi•lance** /-ləns/ *n.* **ju•bi•lant•ly** *adv.* [L *jubilare jubilant-* shout for joy]

ju•bi•late /jŏŏbilayt/ *v.intr.* exult; be joyful. □□ **ju•bi•la•tion** /-láyshən/ *n.* [L *jubilare* (as JUBILANT)]

ju•bi•lee /jŏŏbilee/ *n.* **1** a time or season of rejoicing. **2** an anniversary, esp. the 25th or 50th. **3** *Jewish Hist.* a year of emancipation and restoration, kept every 50 years. **4** *RC Ch.* a period of remission from the penal consequences of sin, granted under certain conditions for a year usu. at intervals of 25 years. **5** exultant joy. [ME f. OF *jubilé* f. LL *jubilaeus* (*annus*) (year) of jubilee ult. f. Heb. *yōbēl,* orig. = ram, ram's-horn trumpet]

Jud. *abbr.* Judith (Apocrypha).

Judaeo- esp. *Brit.* var. of JUDEO-.

Ju•da•ic /jŏŏdáyik/ *adj.* of or characteristic of the Jews or Judaism. [L *Judaicus* f. Gk *Ioudaïkos* f. *Ioudaios* JEW]

Ju•da•ism /jŏŏdeeizəm, –day–/ *n.* **1** the religion of the Jews, with a belief in one God and a basis in Mosaic and rabbinical teachings. **2** the Jews collectively. □□ **Ju•da•ist** *n.* [ME f. LL *Judaismus* f. Gk *Ioudaïsmos* (as JUDAIC)]

Ju•da•ize /jŏŏdeeīz, –day–/ *v.* **1** *intr.* follow Jewish customs or rites. **2** *tr.* **a** make Jewish. **b** convert to Judaism. □□ **Ju•da•i•za•tion** *n.* [LL *judaizare* f. Gk *ioudaïzō* (as JUDAIC)]

Ju•das /jŏŏdəs/ *n.* **1** a person who betrays a friend. **2** (*judas*) (in full **judas hole**) a peephole in a door. [*Judas* Iscariot who betrayed Christ (Luke 22)]

Ju•das tree *n.* a Mediterranean tree, *Cercis siliquastrum,* with purple flowers usu. appearing before the leaves.

jud•der /júdər/ *v. & n.* esp. *Brit.* ● *v.intr.* **1** (esp. of a mechanism) vibrate noisily or violently. **2** (of a singer's voice) oscillate in intensity. ● *n.* an instance of juddering. [imit.: cf. SHUDDER]

Judeo- /jŏŏdáy-ō, –dee-ō/ *comb.form* (esp. *Brit.* **Judaeo-**) Jewish; Jewish and. [L *judaeus* Jewish]

Judg. *abbr.* Judges (Old Testament).

judge /juj/ *n. & v.* ● *n.* **1** a public officer appointed to hear and try causes in a court of justice. **2** a person appointed to decide a dispute or contest. **3 a** a person who decides a question. **b** a person regarded in terms of capacity to decide on the merits of a thing or question (*am no judge of that; a good judge of art*). **4** *Jewish Hist.* a leader having temporary authority in Israel in the period between Joshua and the Kings. ● *v.* **1** *tr.* **a** try (a cause) in a court of justice. **b** pronounce sentence on (a person). **2** *tr.* form an opinion about; estimate, appraise. **3** *tr.* act as a judge of (a dispute or contest). **4** *tr.* (often foll. by *to* + infin. or *that* + clause) conclude, consider, or suppose. **5** *intr.* a form a judgment. **b** act as judge. □□ **judge•like** *adj.* **judge•ship** *n.* [ME f. OF *juge* (n.), *juger* (v.) f. L *judex judicis* f. *jus* law + *–dicus* speaking]

judge ad•vo•cate gen•er•al *n.* an officer in supreme control of the courts martial in the armed forces.

judg•ment /júymənt/ *n.* (also **judge•ment**) **1** the critical faculty; discernment (*an error of judgment*). **2** good sense. **3** an opinion or estimate (*in my judgment*). **4** the sentence of a court of justice; a decision by a judge. **5** often *joc.* a misfortune viewed as a deserved recompense (*it is a judgment on you for getting up late*). **6** criticism. □ **against one's better judgment** contrary to what one really feels to be advisable. [ME f. OF *jugement* (as JUDGE)]

judg•men•tal /jujmént'l/ *adj.* (also **judge•men•tal**) **1** of or concerning or by way of judgment. **2** condemning; critical. □□ **judg•men•tal•ly** *adv.*

judg•ment by de•fault *n.* judgment awarded to the plaintiff on the defendant's failure to plead.

Judg•ment Day *n.* the day on which the Last Judgment is believed to take place; doomsday.

ju•di•ca•ture /jŏŏdikəchər/ *n.* **1** the administration of justice. **2** a judge's office or term of office. **3** judges collectively; judiciary. **4** a court of justice. [med.L *judicatura* f. L *judicare* to judge]

ju•di•cial /jŏŏdíshəl/ *adj.* **1** of, done by, or proper to a court of law. **2** having the function of judgment (*a judicial assembly*). **3** of or proper to a judge. **4** expressing a judgment; critical. **5** impartial. **6** regarded as a divine judgment. □□ **ju•di•cial•ly** *adv.* [ME f. L *judicialis* f. *judicium* judgment f. *judex* JUDGE]

▶**Judicial** means 'relating to judgment and the administration of justice': *judicial robes; the judicial system.* Do not confuse it with **judicious,** which means 'prudent' or &oqreasonable': *getting off the highway the minute you felt tired was a judicious choice.*

ju•di•cial sep•a•ra•tion *n.* the separation of man and wife by decision of a court; legal separation.

ju•di•ci•ar•y /jŏŏdíshəree/ *n.* (*pl.* **•ies**) the judges of a nation's judicial branch collectively. [L *judiciarius* (as JUDICIAL)]

ju•di•cious /jŏŏdíshəs/ *adj.* **1** sensible, prudent. **2** sound in discernment and judgment. □□ **ju•di•cious•ly** *adv.* **ju•di•cious•ness** *n.* [F *judicieux* f. L *judicium* (as JUDICIAL)]

▶See note at JUDICIAL.

ju•do /jŏŏdō/ *n.* a sport of unarmed combat derived from jujitsu. □□ **ju•do•ist** *n.* [Jap. f. *jū* gentle + *dō* way]

Ju•dy /jŏŏdee/ *n.* (*pl.* **•dies**) **1** see PUNCH⁴. **2** (also **ju•dy**) esp. *Brit. sl.* a woman. [pet-form of the name *Judith*]

jug /jug/ *n. & v.* ● *n.* **1 a** a deep vessel for holding liquids, with a handle and often with a spout or lip shaped for pouring. **b** the contents of this; a jugful. **2** a large jar with a narrow mouth. **3** *sl.* prison. **4** (in *pl.*) *coarse sl.* a woman's breasts. ● *v.tr.* (**jugged, jug•ging**) **1** (usu. as **jugged** *adj.*) stew or boil (a hare or rabbit) in a covered vessel. **2** *sl.* imprison. □□ **jug•ful** *n.* (*pl.* **•fuls**) [perh. f. *Jug,* pet-form of the name *Joan,* etc.]

Ju•gend•stil /yŏŏgənt-shteel/ *n.* (also **ju•gend•stil**) the German name for art nouveau. [G f. *Jugend* youth + *Stil* style]

jug•ger•naut /júgərnawt/ *n.* **1** esp. *Brit.* a large heavy motor vehicle, esp. a tractor-trailer truck. **2** a huge or overwhelming force or object. **3** (**Juggernaut**) an institution or notion to which persons blindly sacrifice themselves or others. [Hindi *Jagannath* f. Skr. *Jagannātha* = lord of the world: name of an idol of Krishna in Hindu mythol., carried in procession on a huge cart under which devotees are said to have formerly thrown themselves]

jug•gins /júginz/ *n. Brit. sl.* a simpleton. [perh. f. proper name *Juggins* (as JUG): cf. MUGGINS]

jug•gle /júgəl/ *v. & n.* ● *v.* **1 a** *intr.* (often foll. by *with*) perform feats of dexterity, esp. by tossing objects in the air and catching them, keeping several in the air at the same time. **b** *tr.* perform such feats with. **2** *tr.* continue to deal with (several activities) at once, esp. with ingenuity. **3** *intr.* (foll. by *with*) & *tr.* **a** deceive or cheat. **b** misrepresent (facts). **c** rearrange adroitly. ● *n.* **1** a piece of juggling. **2** a fraud. [ME, back-form. f. JUGGLER or f. OF *jogler, jugler* f. L *joculari* jest f. *joculus* dimin. of *jocus* jest]

jug•gler /júglər/ *n.* **1** a person who juggles. **2** a trickster or impostor. □□ **jug•gler•y** *n.* [ME f. OF *jouglere –eor* f. L *joculator –oris* (as JUGGLE)]

Ju•go•slav var. of YUGOSLAV.

jug•u•lar /júgyələr/ *adj. & n.* ● *adj.* **1** of the neck or throat. **2** (of fish) having ventral fins in front of the pectoral fins. ● *n.* = JUGULAR VEIN. [LL *jugularis* f. L *jugulum* collarbone, throat, dimin. of *jugum* YOKE]

jug•u•lar vein *n.* any of several large veins of the neck which carry blood from the head.

ju•gu•late /júgyəlayt/ *v.tr.* **1** kill by cutting the throat. **2** arrest the course of (a disease, etc.) by a powerful remedy. [L *jugulare* f. *jugulum* (as JUGULAR)]

juice /jŏŏs/ *n.* **1** the liquid part of vegetables or fruits. **2** the fluid part of an animal body or substance, esp. a secretion (*gastric juice*). **3** the essence or spirit of anything. **4** *colloq.* gasoline, etc., or electricity as a source of power. **5** *sl.* alcoholic liquor. □□ **juice•less** *adj.* [ME f. OF *jus* f. L *jus* broth, juice]

juic•er /jŏŏsər/ *n.* **1** a kitchen tool or appliance for extracting the juice from fruits and vegetables. **2** *sl.* an alcoholic.

juic•y /jŏŏsee/ *adj.* (**juic•i•er, juic•i•est**) **1** full of juice; succulent. **2** *colloq.* substantial or interesting; racy; scandalous. **3** *colloq.* profitable. □□ **juic•i•ly** *adv.* **juic•i•ness** *n.*

ju•jit•su /jŏŏjítsŏŏ/ *n.* (also **jiu•jit•su**) a Japanese system of unarmed combat and physical training. [Jap. *jūjutsu* f. *jū* gentle + *jutsu* skill]

ju•ju /jŏŏjŏŏ/ *n.* **1** a charm or fetish of some W. African peoples. **2** a supernatural power attributed to this. [perh. f. F *joujou* toy]

ju•jube /jŏŏjŏŏb, –bee/ *n.* **1 a** any plant of the genus *Zizyphus* bearing edible acidic berrylike fruits. **b** this fruit. **2** a small lozenge or candy of gelatin, etc., flavored with or imitating this. [F *jujube* f. med.L *jujuba* ult. f. Gk *zizuphon*]

juke•box /jŏŏkboks/ *n.* a machine that automatically plays a selected musical recording when a coin is inserted. [Gullah *juke* disorderly + BOX¹]

Jul. *abbr.* July.

ju•lep /joōlip/ *n.* **1 a** a sweet drink, esp. as a vehicle for medicine. **b** a medicated drink as a mild stimulant, etc. **2** iced and flavored spirits and water (*mint julep*). [ME f. OF f. Arab. *julāb* f. Pers. *gulāb* f. *gul* rose + *āb* water]

Jul•ian /joōlyən/ *adj.* of or associated with Julius Caesar. [L *Julianus* f. *Julius*]

Jul•ian cal•en•dar *n.* a calendar introduced by Julius Caesar, in which the year consisted of 365 days, every fourth year having 366 (cf. GREGORIAN CALENDAR).

ju•li•enne /joōlee-én/ *n. & adj.* ● *n.* foodstuff, esp. vegetables, cut into short, thin strips. ● *adj.* cut into thin strips. [F f. the name *Jules* or *Julien*]

Ju•li•et cap /joōleeət, –lee-et, joōlee-ét/ *n.* a small network ornamental cap worn by brides, etc. [the heroine of Shakesp. *Romeo & Juliet*]

Ju•ly /joōlí/ *n.* (*pl.* **Ju•lies** or **Ju•lys**) the seventh month of the year. [ME f. AF *julie* f. L *Julius* (*mensis* month), named after Julius Caesar]

jum•ble /júmbəl/ *v. & n.* ● *v.* **1** *tr.* (often foll. by *up*) confuse; mix up. **2** *intr.* move about in disorder. ● *n.* **1** a confused state or heap; a muddle. **2** *Brit.* articles collected for a jumble sale. □□ **jum•bly** *adj.* [prob. imit.]

SYNONYM TIP | jumble

CONFUSION, CONGLOMERATION, DISARRAY, FARRAGO, HODGEPODGE, MÉLANGE, MUDDLE. **Confusion** is a very broad term, applying to any indiscriminate mixing or mingling that makes it difficult to distinguish individual elements or parts (*a confusion of languages*). The typical teenager's bedroom is usually a **jumble** of books, papers, clothing, CDs, and soda cans—*jumble* being a word that suggests physical disorder and a mixture of dissimilar things. If the disorder exists on a figurative level, it is usually called a **hodgepodge** (*a hodgepodge of ideas, opinions, and quotations, with a few facts thrown in for good measure*). **Conglomeration** refers to a collection of dissimilar things, but with a suggestion that the collection is random or inappropriate (*a conglomeration of decorating styles*). **Mélange** carries even stronger connotations of incongruity and is often used in a contemptuous or derogatory way (*a mélange of drug addicts, petty criminals, and street people*). A **farrago** is an irrational or confused mixture of elements and is usually worse than a **conglomeration** (*a farrago of doubts, fears, hopes, and desires*), while a **muddle** is less serious and suggests confused thinking and lack of organization (*their bank records were in a complete muddle*). **Disarray** implies disarrangement and is most appropriately used when order or discipline has been lost (*his unexpected appearance threw the meeting into disarray*).

---

jum•ble sale *n. Brit.* a rummage sale, esp. for charity.

jum•bo /júmbō/ *n. & adj. colloq.* ● *n.* (*pl.* **-bos**) **1** a large animal (esp. an elephant), person, or thing. **2** (in full **jumbo jet**) a large airliner with capacity for several hundred passengers. ● *adj.* **1** very large of its kind. **2** extra large (*jumbo packet*). [19th c. (orig. of a person): orig. unkn.: popularized as the name of a zoo elephant bought by US showman P.T. Barnum in 1882]

jum•buck /júmbuk/ *n. Austral. colloq.* a sheep. [Aboriginal]

jump /jump/ *v. & n.* ● *v.* **1** *intr.* move off the ground or other surface (usu. upward, at least initially) by sudden muscular effort in the legs. **2** *intr.* (often foll. by *up, from, in, out*, etc.) move suddenly or hastily in a specified way (*we jumped into the car*). **3** *intr.* give a sudden bodily movement from shock or excitement, etc. **4** *intr.* undergo a rapid change, esp. an advance in status. **5** *intr.* (often foll. by *about*) change or move rapidly from one idea or subject to another. **6 a** *intr.* rise or increase suddenly (*prices jumped*). **b** *tr.* cause to do this. **7** *tr.* **a** pass over (an obstacle, barrier, etc.) by jumping. **b** move or pass over (an intervening thing) to a point beyond. **8** *tr.* skip or pass over (a passage in a book, etc.). **9** *tr.* cause (a thing, or an animal, esp. a horse) to jump. **10** *intr.* (foll. by *to, at*) reach a conclusion hastily. **11** *tr.* (of a train) leave (the rails) owing to a fault. **12** *tr.* esp. *Brit.* ignore and pass (a red traffic light, etc.). **13** *tr.* get on or off (a train, etc.) quickly, esp. illegally or dangerously. **14** *tr.* pounce on or attack (a person) unexpectedly. **15** *tr.* take summary possession of (a claim allegedly abandoned or forfeit by the former occupant). ● *n.* **1** the act or an instance of jumping. **2 a** a sudden bodily movement caused by shock or excitement. **b** (**the jumps**) *colloq.* extreme nervousness or anxiety. **3** an abrupt rise in amount, price, value, status, etc. **4** an obstacle to be jumped, esp. by a horse. **5 a** a sudden transition. **b** a gap in a series, logical sequence, etc. □ **get** (or **have**) **the jump on** *colloq.* get (or have) an advantage over (a person) by prompt action. **jump at** accept eagerly. **jump bail** see BAIL[1]. **jump down a person's throat** *colloq.* reprimand or contradict a person fiercely. **jump the gun** see GUN. **jump on** *colloq.* attack or criticize severely and without warning. **jump out of one's skin** *colloq.* be extremely startled. **jump the queue** *Brit.* **1** push forward out of one's turn. **2** take unfair precedence over others. **jump ship** (of a seaman) desert. **jump to it** *colloq.* act promptly and energetically. **one jump ahead** one stage further on than a

rival, etc. **on the jump** *colloq.* on the move; in a hurry. □□ **jump•a•ble** *adj.* [16th c.: prob. imit.]

jumped-up *adj. Brit. colloq.* upstart; presumptuously arrogant.

jump•er[1] /júmpər/ *n.* **1** a sleeveless one-piece dress usu. worn over a blouse or shirt. **2** a loose outer jacket of canvas, etc., worn esp. by sailors. **3** *Brit.* a pullover sweater. [prob. f. (17th-c., now dial.) *jump* short coat perh. f. F *jupe* f. Arab. *jubba*]

jumper 1

jump•er[2] /júmpər/ *n.* **1** a person or animal that jumps. **2** *Electr.* a short wire used to make or break a circuit. **3** a rope made fast to keep a yard, mast, etc., from jumping. **4** a heavy chisel-ended iron bar for drilling blast holes.

jump•er ca•bles *n.pl.* a pair of electrical cables attached to a battery and used to start a motor vehicle with a weak or discharged battery.

jump•ing bean /júmping/ *n.* the seed of a Mexican plant that jumps with the movement of the larva inside.

jump•ing jack /júmping/ *n.* **1** a jumping exercise performed by alternating the position of standing feet together with arms at sides with the position of standing feet apart with arms extended and hands above the head. **2** a toy figure of a man, with movable limbs.

jump•ing-off place *n.* (also **jump•ing-off point**, etc.) the place or point of starting.

jump-jet *n.* a jet aircraft that can take off and land vertically.

jump-off *n.* a deciding round in a showjumping competition.

jump rope *n.* a length of rope held at each end and swung over the head and under the feet of the jumper, who must skip over the rope each time it revolves under the feet, used for exercise or a children's game.

jump seat *n.* a folding extra seat in a motor vehicle.

jump-start *v. & n.* ● *v.tr.* **1** start (a car with a dead battery) with jumper cables or by a sudden release of the clutch while it is being pushed. **2** give an added impetus to something that is proceeding slowly or at a standstill (*jump-start the sluggish educational system*). ● *n.* **1** the act of jump-starting a car. **2** an added impetus.

jump•suit /júmpsoōt/ *n.* a one-piece garment for the whole body, of a kind orig. worn by paratroopers.

jump•y /júmpee/ *adj.* (**jump•i•er, jump•i•est**) **1** nervous; easily startled. **2** making sudden movements, esp. of nervous excitement. □□ **jump•i•ly** *adv.* **jump•i•ness** *n.*

Jun. *abbr.* **1** June. **2** Junior.

jun•co /júngkō/ *n.* (*pl.* **·cos** or **·coes**) any small American finch of the genus *Junco*. [Sp. f. L *juncus* rush plant]

junc•tion /júngkshən/ *n.* **1** a point at which two or more things are joined. **2** a place where two or more railroad lines or roads meet, unite, or cross. **3** the act or an instance of joining. **4** *Electronics* a region of transition in a semiconductor between regions where conduction is mainly by electrons and regions where it is mainly by holes. [L *junctio* (as JOIN)]

junc•tion box *n.* a box containing a junction of electric cables, etc.

junc•ture /júngkchər/ *n.* **1** a critical convergence of events; a critical point of time (*at this juncture*). **2** a place where things join. **3** an act of joining. [ME f. L *junctura* (as JOIN)]

June /joōn/ *n.* the sixth month of the year. [ME f. OF *juin* f. L *Junius* var. of *Junonius* sacred to Juno]

June bug *n.* any of several large brown scarab beetles, esp. *Phyllophaga fusca*.

Jung•i•an /yoōngeeən/ *adj. & n.* ● *adj.* of the Swiss psychologist Carl Jung (d. 1961) or his system of analytical psychology. ● *n.* a supporter of Jung or of his system.

jun•gle /júnggəl/ *n.* **1 a** land overgrown with underwood or tangled vegetation, esp. in the tropics. **b** an area of such land. **2** a wild tangled mass. **3** a place of bewildering complexity or confusion, or of a struggle for survival (*blackboard jungle*). □ **law of the jungle** a state of ruthless competition. □□ **jun•gled** *adj.* **jun•gly** *adj.* [Hindi *jangal* f. Skr. *jangala* desert, forest]

jun•gle fe•ver *n.* a severe form of malaria.

jun•gle gym *n.* a playground structure with bars, ladders, etc., on which children can climb.

jun•ior /joōnyər/ *adj. & n.* ● *adj.* **1** less advanced in age. **2** (foll. by *to*) inferior in age, standing, or position. **3** the younger (esp. appended to a name for distinction from an older person of the same name). **4** of less or least standing; of the lower or lowest position (*junior partner*). **5** *Brit.* (of a school) having pupils in a younger age-range, usu. 7–11. **6** of the year before the final year at college, high school, etc. ● *n.* **1** a junior person. **2** one's inferior in length of service, etc. **3** a junior student. **4** *Brit.* a barrister who is not a Queen's Counsel. **5** *colloq.* a young male child, esp. in relation to his family. □□ **jun•ior•i•ty** /–nyáwritee, –yór–/ *n.* [L, compar. of *juvenis* young]

jun·ior col·lege *n.* a college offering a two-year course, esp. in preparation for completion at senior college.

jun·ior com·mon room *n.* (also **jun·ior com·bi·na·tion room**) *Brit.* **1** a room for social use by the junior members of a college. **2** the junior members collectively.

jun·ior high school *n.* school attended between elementary and high school and usu. consisting of grades seven and eight and sometimes nine.

jun·ior light·weight *n.* a weight in professional boxing between a featherweight and a lightweight, with a maximum of 130 pounds.

jun·ior mid·dle·weight *n.* a weight in professional boxing between a welterweight and a middleweight, with a maximum of 154 pounds.

ju·ni·per /jŏŏnipər/ *n.* any evergreen shrub or tree of the genus *Juniperus*, esp. *J. communis* with prickly leaves and dark purple berrylike cones. [ME f. L *juniperus*]

junk¹ /jungk/ *n. & v.* ● *n.* **1** discarded articles; rubbish. **2** anything regarded as of little value. **3** *sl.* a narcotic drug, esp. heroin. **4** old cables or ropes cut up for oakum, etc. **5** *Brit.* a lump or chunk. **6** *Naut.* hard salt meat. **7** a lump of fibrous tissue in the sperm whale's head, containing spermaceti. ● *v.tr.* discard as junk. [ME: orig. unkn.]

junk²

junk² /jungk/ *n.* a flat-bottomed sailing vessel used in the China seas, with a prominent stem and lugsails. [obs. F *juncque*, Port. *junco*, or Du. *jonk*, f. Jav. *djong*]

junk bond *n. Stock Exch.* a high-yield, high-risk security, typically issued by a company seeking to raise capital quickly in order to finance a takeover.

Junk·er /yŏŏngkər/ *n. hist.* **1** a young German nobleman. **2** a member of an exclusive (Prussian) aristocratic party. □□ **junk·er·dom** *n.* [G, earlier *Junkher* f. OHG (as YOUNG, HERR)]

jun·ket /júngkit/ *n. & v.* ● *n.* **1** a dish of sweetened and flavored curds, often served with fruit or cream. **2** a feast. **3** a pleasure outing. **4** an official's tour at public expense. ● *v.intr.* feast; picnic. □□ **jun·ket·ing** *n.* [ME *jonket* f. OF *jonquette* rush-basket (used to carry junket) f. *jonc* rush f. L *juncus*]

junk food *n.* food with low nutritional value, usu. produced in the form of packaged snacks needing little or no preparation.

junk·ie /júngkee/ *n. sl.* **1** a drug addict. **2** a person with a compulsive habit or obsessive dependency on something (*a TV junkie*).

junk mail *n.* unsolicited advertising matter sent through the mail.

junk shop *n.* a store selling inexpensive secondhand goods or antiques.

junk·yard /júngkyard/ *n.* a yard in which junk is collected and sometimes resold.

jun·ta /hŏŏntə, júntə/ *n.* **1 a** a political or military clique or faction taking power after a revolution or coup d'état. **b** a secretive group; a cabal. **2** a deliberative or administrative council in Spain or Portugal. [Sp. & Port. f. L *juncta*, fem. past part. (as JOIN)]

Ju·pi·ter /jŏŏpitər/ *n.* the largest planet of the solar system, orbiting about the sun between Mars and Saturn. [ME f. L *Jupiter* king of the gods f. OL *Jovis pater*]

ju·ral /jŏŏrəl/ *adj.* **1** of law. **2** of rights and obligations. [L *jus juris* law, right]

Ju·ras·sic /jŏŏrásik/ *adj. & n. Geol.* ● *adj.* of or relating to the second period of the Mesozoic era with evidence of many large dinosaurs, the first birds (including Archaeopteryx), and mammals. ● *n.* this era or system. [F *jurassique* f. *Jura* (Mountains): cf. TRIASSIC]

ju·rat¹ /jŏŏrat/ *n.* a statement of the circumstances in which an affidavit was made. [L *juratum* neut. past part. (as JURAT¹)]

ju·rat² /jŏŏrat/ *n. Brit.* **1** a municipal officer (esp. of the Cinque Ports) holding a position similar to that of an alderman. **2** an honorary judge or magistrate in the Channel Islands. [ME f. med.L *juratus* past part. of L *jurare* swear]

ju·rid·i·cal /jŏŏrídikəl/ *adj.* **1** of judicial proceedings. **2** relating to the law. □□ **ju·rid·i·cal·ly** *adv.* [L *juridicus* f. *jus juris* law + *-dicus* saying f. *dicere* say]

ju·ris·con·sult /jŏŏriskónsult/ *n.* a person learned in law; a jurist. [L *jurisconsultus* f. *jus juris* law + *consultus* skilled: see CONSULT]

ju·ris·dic·tion /jŏŏrisdíkshən/ *n.* **1** (often foll. by *over*, *of*) the administration of justice. **2 a** a legal or other authority. **b** the extent of this; the territory it extends over. □□ **ju·ris·dic·tion·al** *adj.* [ME *jurisdiccioun* f. OF *jurediction*, *juridiction*, L *jurisdictio* f. *jus juris* law + *dictio* DICTION]

ju·ris·pru·dence /jŏŏrisprŏŏd'ns/ *n.* **1** the science or philosophy of law. **2** skill in law. □□ **ju·ris·pru·dent** /-dənt/ *adj. & n.* **ju·ris·pru·den·**

tial /-dénshəl/ *adj.* [LL *jurisprudentia* f. L *jus juris* law + *prudentia* knowledge: see PRUDENT]

ju·rist /jŏŏrist/ *n.* **1** an expert in law. **2** a legal writer. **3** a lawyer. □□ **ju·ris·tic** /-rístik/ *adj.* **ju·ris·ti·cal** /-rístikəl/ *adj.* [F *juriste* or med.L *jurista* f. *jus juris* law]

ju·ror /jŏŏrər/ *n.* **1** a member of a jury. **2** a person who takes an oath (cf. NONJUROR). [ME f. AF *jurour*, OF *jureor* f. L *jurator* *-oris* f. *jurare* *jurat-* swear]

ju·ry /jŏŏree/ *n.* (*pl.* **·ries**) **1** a body of persons sworn to render a verdict on the basis of evidence submitted to them in a court of justice. **2** a body of persons selected to award prizes in a competition. [ME f. AF & OF *juree* oath, inquiry, f. *jurata* fem. past part. of L *jurare* swear]

ju·ry box *n.* the enclosure for the jury in a court of law.

ju·ry·man /jŏŏreemən/ *n.* (*pl.* **·men**) a member of a jury.

ju·ry-rigged /jŏŏreerigd/ *adj. Naut.* having temporary makeshift rigging. [perh. ult. f. OF *ajurie* aid]

ju·ry·wom·an /jŏŏreewŏŏmən/ *n.* (*pl.* **·wom·en**) a woman member of a jury.

jus·sive /júsiv/ *adj. Gram.* expressing a command. [L *jubēre juss-* command]

just /just/ *adj. & adv.* ● *adj.* **1** acting or done in accordance with what is morally right or fair. **2** (of treatment, etc.) deserved (*a just reward*). **3** (of feelings, opinions, etc.) well-grounded (*just resentment*). **4** right in amount, etc.; proper. ● *adv.* **1** exactly (*just what I need*). **2** exactly or nearly at this or that moment; a little time ago (*I have just seen them*). **3** *colloq.* simply; merely (*we were just good friends*; *it just doesn't make sense*). **4** barely; no more than (*I just managed it*; *just a minute*). **5** *colloq.* positively (*it is just splendid*). **6** quite (*not just yet*; *it is just as well that I checked*). **7** *colloq.* really; indeed (*won't I just tell him!*). **8** in questions, seeking precise information (*just how did you manage?*). □ **just about** *colloq.* almost exactly; almost completely. **just in case 1** lest. **2** as a precaution. **just now 1** at this moment. **2** a little time ago. **just so 1** exactly arranged (*they like everything just so*). **2** it is exactly as you say. □□ **just·ly** *adv.* **just·ness** *n.* [ME f. OF *juste* f. L *justus* f. *jus* right]

jus·tice /jústis/ *n.* **1** just conduct. **2** fairness. **3** the exercise of authority in the maintenance of right. **4** judicial proceedings (*was duly brought to justice*). **5 a** a magistrate. **b** a judge, esp. of a supreme court. □ **do justice to** treat fairly or appropriately; show due appreciation of. **do oneself justice** perform in a manner worthy of one's abilities. **in justice to** out of fairness to. **with justice** reasonably. □□ **jus·tice·ship** *n.* (in sense 5). [ME f. OF f. L *justitia* (as JUST)]

justice of the peace *n.* a local public official appointed to hear minor cases, grant licenses, perform marriages, etc.

jus·ti·ci·a·ble /jústíshəbəl/ *adj.* liable to legal consideration. [OF f. *justicier* bring to trial f. med.L *justitiare* (as JUSTICE)]

jus·ti·ci·ar·y /justíshee-eree/ *n. & adj.* ● *n.* (*pl.* **·ies**) an administrator of justice. ● *adj.* of the administration of justice. [med.L *justitiarius* f. L *justitia*: see JUSTICE]

jus·ti·fi·a·ble /jústifíəbəl/ *adj.* that can be justified or defended. □□ **jus·ti·fi·a·bil·i·ty** *n.* **jus·ti·fi·a·ble·ness** *n.* **jus·ti·fi·a·bly** *adv.* [F f. *justifier*: see JUSTIFY]

jus·ti·fi·a·ble ho·mi·cide *n.* the killing of a person in circumstances that allow the act to be regarded in law as without criminal guilt.

jus·ti·fy /jústifī/ *v.tr.* (**·fies**, **·fied**) **1** show the justice or rightness of (a person, act, etc.). **2** demonstrate the correctness of (an assertion, etc.). **3** adduce adequate grounds for (conduct, a claim, etc.). **4 a** (esp. in *passive*) (of circumstances) be such as to justify. **b** vindicate. **5** (as **justified** *adj.*) just; right (*am justified in assuming*). **6** *Theol.* declare (a person) righteous. **7** *Printing* adjust (a line of type) to fill a space evenly. □□ **jus·ti·fi·ca·tion** /-fikáyshən/ *n.* **jus·ti·fi·ca·to·ry** /-stif- íkətáwree/ *adj.* **jus·ti·fi·er** *n.* [ME f. F *justifier* f. LL *justificare* do justice to f. L *justus* JUST]

jut /jut/ *v. & n.* ● *v.intr.* (**jut·ted**, **jut·ting**) (often foll. by *out*, *forth*) protrude; project. ● *n.* a projection; a protruding point. [var. of JET¹]

Jute /jo͞ot/ *n.* a member of a Low-German tribe that settled in Britain in the 5th–6th c. □□ **Jut·ish** *adj.* [repr. med.L *Jutae*, *Juti*, in OE *Eotas*, *Iotas* = Icel. *Iótar* people of Jutland in Denmark]

jute /jo͞ot/ *n.* **1** a rough fiber made from the bark of E. Indian plants of the genus *Corchorus*, used for making twine and rope, and woven into sacking, mats, etc. **2** either of two plants *Corchorus capsularis* or *C. olitorius* yielding this fiber. [Bengali *jhōṭo* f. Skr. *jūṭa* = *jaṭā* braid of hair]

ju·ve·nes·cence /jo͞ovinésəns/ *n.* **1** youth. **2** the transition from infancy to youth. □□ **ju·ve·nes·cent** /–sənt/ *adj.* [L *juvenescere* reach the age of youth f. *juvenis* young]

ju·ve·nile /jo͞ovənil, –vinəl/ *adj. & n.* ● *adj.* **1 a** young; youthful. **b** of or for young persons. **2** suited to or characteristic of youth. **3** often *derog.* immature (*behaving in a very juvenile way*). ● *n.* **1** a young

person. **2** *Commerce* a book intended for young people. **3** an actor playing the part of a youthful person. □□ **ju·ve·nile·ly** *adv.* **ju·ve·nil·i·ty** /–nílitee/ *n.* [L *juvenilis* f. *juvenis* young]

ju·ve·nile court *n.* a court for the trial or legal supervision of children usu. under 18.

ju·ve·nile de·lin·quen·cy *n.* offenses committed by a person or persons below the age of legal responsibility. □□ **ju·ve·nile de·lin·quent** *n.*

ju·ve·nil·i·a /jo͞ovəníleeə/ *n.pl.* works produced by an author or artist in youth. [L, neut. pl. of *juvenilis* (as JUVENILE)]

jux·ta·pose /júkstəpōz/ *v.tr.* **1** place (things) side by side. **2** (foll. by *to*, *with*) place (a thing) beside another. □□ **jux·ta·po·si·tion** /–pəzíshən/ *n.* **jux·ta·po·si·tion·al** /–pəzíshənəl/ *adj.* [F *juxtaposer* f. L *juxta* next: see POSE¹]

JV *abbr.* junior varsity.

K

K¹ /kay/ *n.* (also **k**) (*pl.* **Ks** or **K's**) the eleventh letter of the alphabet.

K² *abbr.* (also **K.**) **1** kelvin(s). **2** King, King's. **3** Köchel (catalog of Mozart's works). **4** (also **k**) (prec. by a numeral) **a** *Computing* a unit of 1,024 (i.e., 2¹⁰) bytes or bits, or loosely 1,000. **b** 1,000. **5** *Baseball* strikeout. [sense 4 as abbr. of KILO-]

K³ *symb. Chem.* the element potassium.

k *abbr.* **1** kilo–. **2** knot(s).

Kaa·ba /kȧȧbə/ *n.* (also **Caa·ba**) a sacred building at Mecca, the Muslim Holy of Holies containing the sacred black stone. [Arab. *Ka'ba*]

kab·ba·la var. of CABALA.

ka·bob /kəbób/ *n.* (also **ke·bab, ke·bob**) (usu. in *pl.*) small pieces of meat, vegetables, etc., packed closely on a skewer and cooked. [Urdu f. Arab. *kabāb*]

ka·bu·ki /kəbóokee/ *n.* a form of popular traditional Japanese drama with highly stylized song, acted by males only. [Jap. f. *ka* song + *bu* dance + *ki* art]

ka·chi·na /kəcheénə/ *n.* **1** a Hopi ancestral spirit. **2** (in full **kachina dancer**) a person who represents a kachina in ceremonial dances. [Hopi, = supernatural]

ka·chi·na doll *n.* a wooden doll representing a kachina.

Kad·dish /kȧadish/ *n. Judaism* **1** a Jewish mourner's prayer. **2** a doxology in the synagogue service. [Aram. *kaddīš* holy]

ka·di var. of QADI.

Kaf·fir /ká̇fər/ *n.* **1 a** a member of the Xhosa-speaking peoples of S. Africa. **b** the language of these peoples. **2** *S.Afr. offens.* any black African. [Arab. *kāfir* infidel f. *kafara* not believe]

kaf·fi·yeh /kəfeéə/ *n.* (also **kef·fi·yeh**) a Bedouin Arab's kerchief worn as a headdress. [Arab. *keffiya, kūfiyya,* perh. f. LL *cofea* COIF]

Kaf·ir /ká̇fər/ *n.* a native of the Hindu Kush mountains of NE Afghanistan. [formed as KAFFIR]

Kaf·ka·esque /kȧafkəésk/ *adj.* (of a situation, atmosphere, etc.) impenetrably oppressive, nightmarish, in a manner characteristic of the fictional world of Franz Kafka, German-speaking novelist (d. 1924).

kaf·tan var. of CAFTAN.

kai /ki/ *n. NZ colloq.* food. [Maori]

kail var. of KALE.

kail·yard var. of KALEYARD.

kai·ser /kízər/ *n. hist.* an emperor, esp. the German emperor, the emperor of Austria, or the head of the Holy Roman Empire. □□ **kai·ser·ship** *n.* [in mod. Eng. f. G *Kaiser* and Du. *keizer*; in ME f. OE *cāsere* f. Gmc adoption (through Gk *kaisar*) of L *Caesar*: see CAESAR]

ka·ka /ká̇akaa/ *n.* (*pl.* **ka·kas**) a large New Zealand parrot, *Nestor meridionalis*, with olive-brown plumage. [Maori]

ka·ka·po /kȧakəpó/ *n.* (*pl.* **·pos**) an owllike flightless New Zealand parrot, *Strigops habroptilus*. [Maori, = night kaka]

ka·ke·mo·no /kȧakəmónō/ *n.* (*pl.* **·nos**) a vertical Japanese wall picture, usu. painted or inscribed on paper or silk and mounted on rollers. [Jap. f. *kake-* hang + *mono* thing]

ka·la·a·zar /kȧalə-əzaár/ *n.* a tropical disease caused by the parasitic protozoan *Leishmania donovani,* which is transmitted to humans by sand flies. [Assamese f. *kālā* black + *āzār* disease]

kale /kayl/ *n.* (also **kail**) **1** a variety of cabbage, esp. one with wrinkled leaves and no compact head. Also called **curly kale. 2** *sl.* money. [ME, northern form of COLE]

ka·lei·do·scope /kəlídəskōp/ *n.* **1** a tube containing mirrors and pieces of colored glass, paper, plastic, etc., whose reflections produce changing patterns when the tube is rotated. **2** a constantly changing group of bright or interesting objects. □□ **ka·lei·do·scop·ic** /-skópik/ *adj.* **ka·lei·do·scop·i·cal** *adj.* [Gk *kalos* beautiful + *eidos* form + –SCOPE]

kal·ends var. of CALENDS.

kale·yard /káyl-yaard/ *n.* (also **kail·yard**) *Sc.* a kitchen garden. [KALE + YARD²]

kale·yard school *n.* a group of 19th-c. fiction writers, including J. M. Barrie, who described local town life in Scotland in a romantic vein and with much use of the vernacular.

ka·li /ká̇lee, káylee/ *n.* a glasswort, *Salsola kali,* with fleshy jointed stems, having a high soda content. [Arab. *ḳalī* ALKALI]

kal·mi·a /ká̇lmeeə/ *n.* a N. American evergreen shrub of the genus *Kalmia* with showy flowers, as the mountain laurel. [mod.L f. P. *Kalm,* Sw. botanist d. 1779]

Kal·muck /ká̇lmuk/ *adj. & n. • adj.* of or relating to a people living on the north-western shores of the Caspian Sea. **• n. 1** a member of this people. **2** the language of this people. [Russ. *kalmyk*]

ka·long /ká̇alawng, –long/ *n.* any of various fruit-eating bats of the family Pteropodidae, esp. *Pteropus edulis*; a flying fox. [Malay]

kal·pa /ká̇lpə/ *n. Hinduism & Buddhism* the period between the beginning and the end of the world considered as the day of Brahma (4,320 million human years). [Skr.]

Ka·ma /kȧamə/ *n.* the Hindu god of love. [Skr.]

Ka·ma Su·tra /soótrə/ *n.* an ancient Sanskrit treatise on the art of erotic love.

kame /kaym/ *n.* a short ridge of sand and gravel deposited from the water of a melted glacier. [Sc. form of COMB]

ka·mi·ka·ze /kȧamikȧazee/ *n. & adj. • n. hist.* **1** a Japanese aircraft loaded with explosives and deliberately crashed by its pilot onto its target. **2** the pilot of such an aircraft. **• adj. 1** of or relating to a kamikaze. **2** reckless; dangerous; potentially self-destructive. [Jap. f. *kami* divinity + *kaze* wind]

kam·pong /ká̇ampawng, –póng/ *n.* a Malayan enclosure or village. [Malay: cf. COMPOUND²]

Kam·pu·che·an /ká̇mpoochéeən/ *n. & adj.* = CAMBODIAN. [*Kampuchea,* native name for Cambodia]

Kan. *abbr.* Kansas.

ka·na /kȧanə/ *n.* any of various Japanese syllabaries. [Jap.]

ka·nak·a /kənákə, –naákə/ *n.* **1** a native of Hawaii. **2** a South Sea islander, esp. (formerly) one employed in forced labor in Australia. [Hawaiian, = person]

Ka·na·rese /ká̇nəreéz/ *n.* (*pl.* same) **1** a member of a Dravidian people living in western India. **2** the language of this people. [*Kanara* in India]

kan·ga·roo /ká̇nggəróo/ *n.* a plant-eating marsupial of the genus *Macropus,* native to Australia and New Guinea, with a long tail and strongly developed hindquarters enabling it to travel by jumping. [Aboriginal name]

kangaroo

kan·ga·roo clo·sure *n. Brit. Parl.* a parliamentary closure involving the chairperson of a committee selecting some amendments for discussion and excluding others.

kan·ga·roo court *n.* an unofficial or illegal court held by a mob, etc.

kan·ga·roo mouse *n.* any small rodent of the genus *Microdipodops,* native to N. America, with long hind legs for hopping.

kan·ga·roo paw *n.* any plant of the genus *Angiozanthos,* with green and red wooly flowers.

kan·ga·roo rat *n.* any burrowing rodent of the genus *Dipodomys,* having elongated hind feet.

kan·ga·roo vine *n.* an evergreen climbing plant, *Cissus antarctica,* with tooth-edged leaves.

kan·ji /ká̇anjee/ *n.* Japanese writing using Chinese characters. [Jap. f. *kan* Chinese + *ji* character]

Kan·na·da /ká̇anədə/ *n.* the Kanarese language. [Kanarese *kannaḍa*]

ka·noon /kənóon/ *n.* an instrument like a zither, with fifty to sixty strings. [Pers. or Arab. *kānūn*]

Kans. *abbr.* Kansas.

Kan·sa /ká̇anzə, –sə/ *n.* **1 a** a N. American people native to eastern Kansas. **b** a member of this people. **2** the language of this people. Also called **Kaw.**

ka·o·lin /káyəlin/ *n.* a fine, soft, white clay produced by the decomposition of other clays or feldspar, used esp. for making porcelain and in medicines. Also called **china clay**. □□ **ka·o·lin·ic** /-línik/ *adj.* **ka·o·lin·ize** *v.tr.* [F f. Chin. *gaoling* the name of a mountain f. *gao* high + *ling* hill]

ka·on /káyon/ *n. Physics* a meson having a mass several times that of a pion. [*ka* repr. the letter *K* (as symbol for the particle) + –ON]

ka·pell·meis·ter /kəpélmīstər/ *n.* (*pl.* same) the conductor of an orchestra, opera, choir, etc., esp. in German contexts. [G f. *Kapelle* court orchestra f. It. *cappella* CHAPEL + *Meister* master]

ka·pok /káypok/ *n.* a fine, fibrous, cottonlike substance found surrounding the seeds of a tropical tree, *Ceiba pentandra,* used for stuffing cushions, soft toys, etc. [ult. f. Malay *kāpoq*]

Ka·po·si's sar·co·ma /ká̇pəseez, kapó–/ *n. Med.* a malignant neoplasm of connective tissue marked by bluish-red lesions on the skin; often associated with AIDS. [for Hungarian dermatologist M.K. *Kaposi* (1837–1902)]

kap·pa /kápə/ *n.* the tenth letter of the Greek alphabet (Κ, κ). [Gk]

ka·put /kaapŏŏt/ *predic.adj. sl.* broken, ruined; done for. [G *kaputt*]

kar·a·bi·ner /kárəbeenər/ *n. Brit.* var. of CARABINER.

kar·a·kul /kárəkŏŏl/ *n.* (also **car·a·cul, car·a·cul**) **1** a variety of Asian sheep with a dark curled fleece when young. **2** fur made from or resembling this. Also called **Persian lamb**. [Russ.]

kar·a·o·ke /káreeŏkee, kárə–/ *n.* a form of entertainment offered usu. in bars and clubs, in which people take turns singing popular songs into a microphone over prerecorded backing tracks. [Jap., = empty orchestra]

kar·at /kárət/ *n.* (*Brit.* **car·at**) a measure of purity of gold, pure gold being 24 karats. [cf. CARAT]

ka·ra·te /kəraátee/ *n.* a Japanese system of unarmed combat using the hands and feet as weapons. [Jap. f. *kara* empty + *te* hand]

kar·ma /kaármə/ *n. Buddhism & Hinduism* **1** the sum of a person's actions in previous states of existence, viewed as deciding his or her fate in future existences. **2** destiny. □□ **kar·mic** *adj.* [Skr., = action, fate]

Ka·roo /kərŏŏ́/ *n.* (also **Kar·roo**) an elevated semidesert plateau in S. Africa. [Afrik. f. Hottentot *karo* dry]

kar·ri /káree/ *n.* (*pl.* **kar·ris**) **1** a tall W. Australian tree, *Eucalyptus diversicolor*, with a hard, red wood. **2** the wood from this. [Aboriginal]

Kar·roo var. of KAROO.

karst /kaarst/ *n.* a limestone region with underground drainage and many cavities and passages caused by the dissolution of the rock. [the *Karst*, a limestone region in the northwest of the former Yugoslavia]

karyo- /káreeŏ/ *comb. form Biol.* denoting the nucleus of a cell. [Gk *karuon* kernel]

kar·y·o·ki·ne·sis /káreeŏkineésis/ *n. Biol.* the division of a cell nucleus during mitosis. [KARYO- + Gk *kinēsis* movement f. *kineō* move]

kar·y·o·type /káreeətīp/ *n.* the number and structure of the chromosomes in the nucleus of a cell.

Kas·bah var. of CASBAH.

kat·a·bat·ic /kátəbátik/ *adj. Meteorol.* (of wind) caused by air flowing downward (cf. ANABATIC). [Gk *katabatikos* f. *katabainō* go down]

ka·tab·o·lism esp. *Brit.* var. of CATABOLISM.

ka·ta·ka·na /kátəkaánə/ *n.* an angular form of Japanese kana. [Jap., = side kana]

ka·ty·did /káyteedid/ *n.* any of various green grasshoppers of the family Tettigoniidae, native to the US. [imit. of the sound it makes]

kau·ri /kówree/ *n.* (*pl.* **kau·ris**) a coniferous New Zealand tree, *Agathis australis*, which produces valuable timber and a resin. [Maori]

kau·ri gum *n.* (also **kau·ri res·in**) the resin of the kauri tree, used as a varnish.

ka·va /kaávə/ *n.* **1** a Polynesian shrub, *Piper methysticum*. **2** an intoxicating drink made from the crushed roots of this. Also called **kava kava**. [Polynesian]

kay·ak /kíak/ *n.* **1** an Eskimo canoe for one paddler, consisting of a light wooden frame covered with skins. **2** a small covered canoe resembling this. [Eskimo]

katydid

kayak

kay·o /káyŏ́, káyō/ *v. & n. colloq.* • *v.tr.* (**·oes, ·oed**) knock out; stun by a blow. • *n.* (*pl.* **·os**) a knockout. [repr. pronunc. of *KO*]

ka·zoo /kəzŏŏ́/ *n.* a toy musical instrument into which the player sings or hums. [19th c., app. with ref. to the sound produced]

KB *abbr.* (in the UK) King's Bench.

KBE *abbr.* (in the UK) Knight Commander of the Order of the British Empire.

KC *abbr.* **1** Kansas City. **2** Knights of Columbus. **3** King's Counsel.

kc *abbr.* kilocycle(s).

KCB *abbr.* (in the UK) Knight Commander of the Order of the Bath.

KCMG *abbr.* (in the UK) Knight Commander of the Order of St. Michael and St. George.

kc/s *abbr.* kilocycles per second.

KCVO *abbr.* (in the UK) Knight Commander of the Royal Victorian Order.

KE *abbr.* kinetic energy.

ke·a /ke̍eə, káyə/ *n.* a parrot, *Nestor notabilis*, of New Zealand, with brownish-green and red plumage. [Maori, imit.]

ke·bab var. of KABOB.

ke·bob var. of KABOB.

kedge /kej/ *v. & n.* • *v.* **1** *tr.* move (a ship) by means of a hawser attached to a small anchor that is dropped at some distance away. **2** *intr.* (of a ship) move in this way. • *n.* (in full **kedge anchor**) a small anchor for this purpose. [perh. a specific use of obs. *cagge*, dial. *cadge* bind, tie]

ked·ger·ee /kéjəree/ *n.* **1** an E. Indian dish of rice, lentils, onions, eggs, etc. **2** a European dish of fish, rice, hard-boiled eggs, etc. [Hindi *khichṛī*, Skr. *k'rsara* dish of rice and sesame]

keek /keek/ *v. & n. Sc.* • *v.intr.* peep. • *n.* a peep. [ME *kike*: cf. MDu., MLG *kiken*]

keel[1] /keel/ *n. & v.* • *n.* **1** the lengthwise timber or steel structure along the base of a ship, airship, or some aircraft, on which the framework of the whole is built up. **2** *poet.* a ship. **3** a ridge along the breastbone of many birds; a carina. **4** *Bot.* a prow-shaped pair of petals in a corolla, etc. • *v.* **1** (often foll. by *over*) **a** *intr.* turn over or fall down. **b** *tr.* cause to do this. **2** *tr. & intr.* turn keel upward. □□ **keel·less** *adj.* [ME *kele* f. ON *kjölr* f. Gmc]

keel[2] /keel/ *n. Brit. hist.* **1** a flat-bottomed vessel, esp. of the kind formerly used on the Tyne River, etc., for loading coal ships. **2** an amount carried by such a vessel. [ME *kele* f. MLG *kēl*, MDu. *kiel* ship, boat, f. Gmc]

keel·haul /ke̍elhawl/ *v.tr.* **1** *hist.* drag (a person) through the water under the keel of a ship as a punishment. **2** scold or rebuke severely.

keel·son /ke̍elsən/ *n.* (also **kel·son** /kélsən/) a line of timber fastening a ship's floor timbers to its keel. [ME *kelswayn*, perh. f. LG *kielswīn* f. *kiel* KEEL1 + (prob.) *swīn* SWINE used as the name of a timber]

keen[1] /keen/ *adj.* **1** (of a person, desire, or interest) eager; ardent (*a keen sportsman; keen to be involved*). **2** (foll. by *on*) much attracted by; fond of or enthusiastic about. **3 a** (of the senses) sharp; highly sensitive. **b** (of memory, etc.) clear; vivid. **4** (of a person) intellectually acute; (of a remark, etc.) quick; sharp; biting. **5 a** having a sharp edge or point. **b** (of an edge, etc.) sharp. **6** (of a sound, light, etc.) penetrating; vivid; strong. **7** (of a wind, frost, etc.) piercingly cold. **8** (of a pain, etc.) acute; bitter. **9** *Brit.* (of a price) competitive. **10** *colloq.* excellent. □□ **keen·ly** *adv.* **keen·ness** *n.* [OE *cēne* f. Gmc]

SYNONYM TIP keen

ACUTE, ASTUTE, PENETRATING, PERSPICACIOUS, SHARP, SHREWD. A knife can be **sharp**, even **keen**, but it can't be **astute**. While *keen* and *sharp* mean having a fine point or edge, they also pertain to mental agility and perceptiveness. You might describe someone as having a *keen* mind, which suggests the ability to grapple with complex problems, or to observe details and see them as part of a larger pattern (*a keen appreciation of what victory would mean for the Democratic party*) or a *keen* wit, which suggests an incisive or stimulating sense of humor. Someone who is *sharp* has an alert and rational mind, but is not necessarily well-grounded in a particular field and may in some cases be cunning or devious (*sharp enough to see how the situation might be turned to her advantage*). An **astute** mind, in contrast, is one that has a thorough and profound understanding of a given subject or field (*an astute understanding of the legal principles involved*). Like *sharp*, **shrewd** implies both practicality and cleverness, but with an undercurrent of self-interest (*a shrewd salesperson*). **Acute** is close in meaning to *keen*, but with more emphasis on sensitivity and the ability to make subtle distinctions (*an acute sense of smell*). While a *keen* mind might see only superficial details, a **penetrating** mind would focus on underlying causes (*a penetrating analysis of the plan's feasibility*). **Perspicacious** is the most formal of these terms, meaning both perceptive and discerning (*a perspicacious remark, perspicacious judgment*).

keen[2] /keen/ *n. & v.* • *n.* an Irish funeral song accompanied with wailing. • *v.* **1** *intr.* utter the keen. **2** *tr.* bewail (a person) in this way. **3** *tr.* utter in a wailing tone. □□ **keen·er** *n.* [Ir. *caoine* f. *caoinim* wail]

keep /keep/ *v. & n.* • *v.* (*past and past part.* **kept** /kept/) **1** *tr.* have continuous charge of; retain possession of; save or hold on to. **2** *tr.* (foll. by *for*) retain or reserve for a future occasion or time (*will keep it for tomorrow*). **3** *tr. & intr.* retain or remain in a specified condition, position, course, etc. (*keep cool; keep off the grass; keep them happy*). **4** *tr.* put or store in a regular place (*knives are kept in this drawer*). **5** *tr.* (foll. by *from*) cause to avoid or abstain from something (*will keep you from going too fast*). **6** *tr.* detain; cause to be late (*what kept you?*). **7** *tr.* **a** observe or pay due regard to (a law, custom, etc.). **b** honor or fulfill (a commitment, undertaking, etc.). **c** respect the commitment implied by (a secret, etc.). **d** act fittingly on the occasion of (*keep the Sabbath*). **8** *tr.* own and look after (animals) for amusement or profit (*keeps bees*). **9** *tr.* **a** provide for the sustenance of (a person, family, etc.). **b** (foll. by *in*) maintain (a person) with a supply of. **10** *tr.* manage (a shop, business, etc.). **11 a** *tr.* maintain (accounts, a diary, etc.) by making the requisite entries. **b** *tr.* maintain (a house) in proper order. **12** *tr.* have (a commodity) regularly on sale (*do you keep buttons?*). **13** *tr.* **a** confine or detain (a person, animal, etc.). **b** guard or protect (a person or place, a goal in soccer, etc.). **14** *tr.* preserve in being; continue to have (*keep order*). **15** *intr.* (foll. by verbal noun) continue or do repeatedly or habitually (*why do you keep saying that?*). **16** *tr.* continue to follow (a way or course). **17** *intr.* **a** (esp. of perishable commodities) remain in good condition. **b** (of news or information, etc.) admit of being withheld for a time. **18** *tr.* esp. *Brit.* remain in (one's bed, room, house, etc.). **19** *tr.* retain one's place in (a seat or saddle, one's ground, etc.) against opposition or difficulty. **20** *tr.* maintain (a person) in return for sexual favors (*a kept woman*). • *n.* **1** maintenance or the essentials for this (esp. food) (*hardly earn your keep*). **2** charge or control (*is in your keep*). **3** *hist.* a tower or stronghold. □ **for keeps** *colloq.* (esp. of something received or won) permanently; indefinitely. **keep at** persist or cause to persist with. **keep away** (often foll. by *from*) **1** avoid being near. **2** prevent from being near. **keep back 1** remain or keep at a distance. **2** retard the progress of. **3** conceal; decline to disclose. **4** retain; withhold (*kept back $50*). **keep one's balance 1** remain stable; avoid falling. **2** retain one's composure. **keep down 1** hold in subjection. **2** keep low in amount. **3** lie low; stay hidden. **4** manage not to vomit (food eaten). **keep one's feet** manage not to fall. **keep one's hair on** see HAIR. **keep one's hand in** see HAND. **keep in 1** confine or restrain (one's feelings, etc.). **2** remain or confine indoors. **3** esp. *Brit.* keep (a fire) burning. **keep in mind** take into account having remembered. **keep in with** remain on good terms with. **keep kosher** see KOSHER. **keep off 1** stay or cause to stay away from. **2** ward off; avert. **3** abstain from. **4** avoid (a subject) (*let's keep off religion*). **keep on 1** continue to do something; do continually (*kept on laughing*). **2** continue to use or employ. **3** (foll. by *at*) pester or harass. **keep out 1** keep or remain outside. **2** exclude. **keep state** esp. *Brit.* **1** maintain one's dignity. **2** be difficult of access. **keep to 1** adhere to (a course, schedule, etc.). **2** observe (a promise). **3** confine oneself to. **keep to oneself 1** avoid contact with others. **2** refuse to disclose or share. **keep together** remain or keep in harmony. **keep track of** see TRACK[1] *v.* **keep under** hold in subjection. **keep up 1** maintain (progress, etc.). **2** prevent (prices, one's spirits, etc.) from sinking. **3** keep in repair, in an efficient or proper state, etc. **4** carry on (a correspondence, etc.). **5** prevent (a person) from going to bed, esp. when late. **6** (often foll. by *with*) manage not to fall behind. **keep up with the Joneses** strive to compete socially with one's neighbors. **keep one's word** see WORD. □□ **keep•a•ble** *adj.* [OE *cēpan*, of unkn. orig.]

keep•er /kéepər/ *n.* **1** a person who keeps or looks after something or someone. **2** esp. *Brit.* a custodian of a museum, art gallery, forest, etc. **3 a** = GAMEKEEPER. **b** a person in charge of animals in a zoo. **4 a** = WICKETKEEPER. **b** = GOALKEEPER. **5** a fruit, etc., that remains in good condition. **6** a bar of soft iron across the poles of a horseshoe magnet to maintain its strength. **7 a** a plain ring to preserve a hole in a pierced ear lobe; a sleeper. **b** a ring worn to guard against the loss of a more valuable one. **8 a** a fish large enough to be kept without violating the law. **b** *colloq.* anything worth keeping.

keep•ing /kéeping/ *n.* the action of owning, maintaining, or protecting something (*in safe keeping*). □ **in someone's keeping** in someone's care or custody. **in** (or **out of**) **keeping with** in (or out of) harmony or conformity with.

keep•sake /kéepsayk/ *n.* a thing kept for the sake of or in remembrance of the giver.

kees•hond /káys-hond/ *n.* **1** a dog of a Dutch breed with long, thick hair like a large Pomeranian. **2** this breed. [Du.]

kef /kef, keef/ *n.* (also **kif** /kif/) **1** a drowsy state induced by marijuana, etc. **2** the enjoyment of idleness. **3** a substance smoked to produce kef. [Arab. *kayf* enjoyment, well-being]

kef•fi•yeh var. of KAFFIYEH.

keg /keg/ *n.* a small barrel of less than 30 gallons (usu. 5–10 gallons). [ME *cag* f. ON *kaggi*, of unkn. orig.]

keg beer *n.* beer supplied from a sealed metal container.

keg par•ty *n.* a party at which keg beer is served.

keis•ter /kéestər/ *n. sl.* **1** the buttocks. **2** a suitcase, satchel, handbag, etc. [orig. unkn.]

ke•loid /kéeloyd/ *n.* fibrous tissue formed at the site of a scar or injury. [Gk *khēlē* claw + –OID]

kelp /kelp/ *n.* **1** any of several large, broad-fronded brown seaweeds esp. of the genus *Laminaria*, suitable for use as manure. **2** the calcined ashes of seaweed formerly used in glassmaking and soap manufacture because of their high content of sodium, potassium, and magnesium salts. [ME *cúlp(e)*, of unkn. orig.]

kel•pie /kélpee/ *n. Sc.* **1** a water spirit, usu. in the form of a horse, reputed to delight in the drowning of travelers, etc. **2** an Australian sheepdog orig. bred from a Scottish collie. [18th c.: orig. unkn.]

kel•son var. of KEELSON.

Kelt var. of CELT.

kelt /kelt/ *n.* a salmon or sea trout after spawning. [ME: orig. unkn.]

kel•ter var. of KILTER.

kel•vin /kélvin/ *n.* the SI unit of thermodynamic temperature, equal in magnitude to the degree celsius. ¶ Abbr.: **K**. [Lord *Kelvin*, Brit. physicist d. 1907]

Kel•vin scale *n.* a scale of temperature with absolute zero as zero.

kemp /kemp/ *n.* coarse hair in wool. □□ **kemp•y** *adj.* [ME f. ON *kampr* beard, whisker]

kempt /kempt/ *adj.* combed; neatly kept. [past part. of (now dial.) *kemb* COMB v. f. OE *cemban* f. Gmc]

ken /ken/ *n. & v.* • *n.* range of sight or knowledge (*it's beyond my ken*). • *v.tr.* (**ken•ning**; *past* and *past part.* **kenned** or **kent** *Sc.* & *No. of Engl.* **1** recognize at sight. **2** know. [OE *cennan* f. Gmc]

ken•do /kéndō/ *n.* a Japanese form of fencing with bamboo swords. [Jap., = sword-way]

ken•nel /kénəl/ *n. & v.* • *n.* **1** a small shelter for a dog. **2** (in *pl.*) a breeding or boarding establishment for dogs. **3** a mean dwelling. • *v.* (**ken•neled, ken•nel•ing**; esp. *Brit.* **ken•nelled, ken•nel•ling**) **1** *tr.* put into or keep in a kennel. **2** *intr.* live in or go to a kennel. [ME f. OF *chenil* f. med.L *canile* (unrecorded) f. L *canis* dog]

ken•ning /kéning/ *n.* a compound expression in Old English and Old Norse poetry, e.g., *oar-steed* = ship. [ME, = 'teaching,' etc., f. KEN]

ke•no•sis /kinósis/ *n. Theol.* the doctrine of the renunciation of the divine nature, at least in part, by Christ in the Incarnation. □□ **ke•not•ic** /–nótik/ *adj.* [Gk *kenōsis* f. *kenoō* to empty f. *kenos* empty]

ken•speck•le /kénspekəl/ *adj. Sc.* conspicuous. [*kenspeck* of Scand. orig.: rel. to KEN]

kent *past* and *past part.* of KEN.

Kent•ish /kéntish/ *adj.* of Kent in England. [OE *Centisc* f. *Cent* f. L *Cantium*]

Kent•ish fire *n. Brit.* a prolonged volley of rhythmic clapping, either as applause or as a demonstration of impatience or dissent.

kent•ledge /kéntlij/ *n. Naut.* pig iron, etc., used as permanent ballast. [F *quintelage* ballast, with assim. to *kentle* obs. var. of QUINTAL]

Ken•tuck•y Der•by *n.* a horse race for three-year-olds run annually since 1875 at Louisville, Kentucky.

Ken•yan /kényən, kéen–/ *adj. & n.* • *adj.* of or relating to Kenya in E. Africa. • *n.* **a** a native or national of Kenya. **b** a person of Kenyan descent.

kep•i /képee, káypee/ *n.* (*pl.* **kep•is**) a French military cap with a horizontal peak. [F *képi* f. Swiss G *Käppi* dimin. of *Kappe* cap]

Kep•ler's laws /képlərz/ *n.pl.* three theorems describing orbital motion. □□ **Kep•ler•i•an** /–léeriən/ *adj.* [J. *Kepler* Ger. astronomer d. 1630]

kept *past* and *past part.* of KEEP.

kept wom•an *n.* a woman maintained or supported in return for sexual favors.

ker•a•tin /kérətin/ *n.* a fibrous protein which occurs in hair, feathers, hooves, claws, horns, etc. [Gk *keras keratos* horn + –IN]

kepi

ker•a•tin•ize /kérətiniz/ *v.tr. & intr.* cover or become covered with a deposit of keratin. □□ **ker•a•tin•i•za•tion** *n.*

ker•a•tose /kérətōs/ *adj.* (of sponge) composed of a horny substance. [Gk *keras keratos* horn + –OSE[1]]

kerb *Brit.* var. of CURB 2.

kerb•stone *Brit.* var. of CURBSTONE.

ker•chief /kórchif, –cheef/ *n.* **1** a cloth used to cover the head. **2** *poet.* a handkerchief. □□ **ker•chiefed** *adj.* [ME *curchef* f. AF *courchef*, OF *couvrechief* f. *couvrir* COVER + CHIEF head]

kerf /kərf/ *n.* **1** a slit made by cutting, esp. with a saw. **2** the cut end of a felled tree. [OE *cyrf* f. Gmc (as CARVE)]

ker•fuf•fle /kərfúfəl/ *n.* esp. *Brit. colloq.* a fuss or commotion. [Sc. *curfuffle* f. *fuffle* to disorder: imit.]

ker•mes /kórmeez/ *n.* **1** the female of a bug, *Kermes ilicis*, with a berrylike appearance. **2** (in full **kermes oak**) an evergreen oak, *Quercus coccifera*, of S. Europe and N. Africa, on which this insect feeds. **3** a red dye made from the dried bodies of these insects. **4** (in full **kermes mineral**) a bright red hydrous trisulfide of antimony. [F *kermès* f. Arab. & Pers. *kirmiz*: rel. to CRIMSON]

ker•mis /kórmis/ *n.* **1** a periodical country fair, esp. in the Netherlands. **2** a charity bazaar. [Du., orig. = Mass on the anniversary of the dedication of a church, when yearly fair was held: f. *kerk* formed as CHURCH + *mis, misse* MASS[2]]

kern[1] /kərn/ *n. Printing* the part of a metal type projecting beyond its body or shank. □□ **kerned** *adj.* [perh. f. F *carne* corner f. OF *charne* f. L *cardo cardinis* hinge]

kern² /kərn/ *n.* (also **kerne**) **1** *hist.* a light-armed Irish foot soldier. **2** a peasant; a boor. [ME f. Ir. *ceithern*]

ker·nel /kárnəl/ *n.* **1** a central, softer, usu. edible part within a hard shell of a nut, fruit stone, seed, etc. **2** the whole seed of a cereal. **3** the nucleus or essential part of anything. [OE *cyrnel*, dimin. of CORN¹]

kero /kérō/ *n. Austral.* = KEROSENE. [abbr.]

ker·o·sene /kérəseen/ *n.* (also **ker·o·sine**) a liquid mixture obtained by distillation from petroleum or shale, used esp. as a fuel or solvent. [Gk *kēros* wax f. −ENE]

ker·ry /kéree/ *n.* (also **Kerry**) (*pl.* **·ries**) **1** an animal of a breed of small, black dairy cattle. **2** this breed. [*Kerry* in Ireland]

Ker·ry blue *n.* **1** a terrier of a breed with a silky, wavy, blue-gray coat. **2** this breed.

ker·sey /kárzee/ *n.* (*pl.* **·seys**) **1** a kind of coarse narrow cloth woven from long wool, usu. ribbed. **2** a variety of this. [ME, prob. f. *Kersey* in Suffolk]

ker·sey·mere /kárzeemeer/ *n.* a twilled fine woolen cloth. [alt. of *cassimere*, var. of CASHMERE, assim. to KERSEY]

kes·ki·dee var. of KISKADEE.

kes·trel /késtrəl/ *n.* any small falcon, esp. *Falco tinnunculus*, that hovers while searching for its prey. [ME *castrell*, perh. f. F dial. *casserelle*, F *créc(er)elle*, perh. imit. of its cry]

ketch /kech/ *n.* a two-masted, fore-and-aft rigged sailing boat with a mizzenmast stepped forward of the rudder and smaller than its foremast. [ME *catche*, prob. f. CATCH]

ketch·up /kéchup, káchup/ *n.* (also **catch·up**, **cats·up** /kátsəp/) a spicy sauce made from tomatoes, mushrooms, vinegar, etc., used as a condiment. [Chin. dial. *kōechiap* pickled-fish brine]

ke·tone /keetōn/ *n.* any of a class of organic compounds in which two hydrocarbon groups are linked by a carbonyl group, e.g., propanone (acetone). □□ **ke·ton·ic** /kitónik/ *adj.* [G *Keton* alt. of *Aketon* ACETONE]

ke·tone bod·y *n. Biochem.* any of several ketones produced in the body during the metabolism of fats.

ke·to·nu·ri·a /keetōnŏoreeə, −nyŏor−/ *n.* the excretion of abnormally large amounts of ketone bodies in the urine.

ke·to·sis /keetósis/ *n.* a condition characterized by raised levels of ketone bodies in the body, associated with fat metabolism and diabetes. □□ **ke·tot·ic** /−tótik/ *adj.*

ket·tle /két'l/ *n.* **1** a vessel, usu. of metal with a lid, spout, and handle, for boiling water in. **2** (in full **kettle hole**) a depression in the ground in a glaciated area. □ **a fine** (or **pretty**) **kettle of fish** an awkward state of affairs. □□ **ket·tle·ful** *n.* (*pl.* **·fuls**). [ME f. ON *ketill* ult. f. L *catillus* dimin. of *catinus* deep food-vessel]

ket·tle·drum /két'ldrum/ *n.* a large drum shaped like a bowl with a membrane adjustable for tension (and so pitch) stretched across. □□ **ket·tle·drum·mer** *n.*

keV *abbr.* kilo-electronvolt.

Kev·lar /kévlaar/ *n. Trademark* a synthetic fiber of high tensile strength used esp. as a reinforcing agent in the manufacture of tires and other rubber products and protective gear such as helmets and vests.

kew·pie /kyŏōpee/ *n.* (also **kew·pie doll**) *Trademark* a small, chubby doll with a curl or topknot. [CU-PID + −IE]

key¹ /kee/ *n., adj., & v.* ●*n.* (*pl.* **keys**) **1** an instrument, usu. of metal, for moving the bolt of a lock forward or backward to lock or unlock. **2** a similar implement for operating a switch in the form of a lock. **3** an instrument for grasping screws, pegs, nuts, etc., esp. one for winding a clock, etc. **4** a lever depressed by the finger in playing the organ, piano, flute, concertina, etc. **5** (often in *pl.*) each of several buttons for operating a typewriter, word processor, or computer terminal, etc. **6** what gives or precludes the opportunity for or access to something. **7** a place that by its position gives control of a sea, territory, etc. **8 a** a solution or explanation. **b** a word or system for solving a cipher or code. **c** an explanatory list of symbols used in a map, table, etc. **d** a book of solutions to mathematical problems, etc. **e** a literal translation of a book written in a foreign language. **f** the first move in a chess-problem solution. **9** *Mus.* a system of notes definitely related to each other, based on a particular note, and predominating in a piece of music; tone or pitch (*a study in the key of C major*). **10** a tone or style of thought or expression. **11** a piece of wood or metal inserted between others to secure them. **12** the part of a first coat of wall plaster that passes

kettledrum

between the laths and so secures the rest. **13** the roughness of a surface, helping the adhesion of plaster, etc. **14** the samara of a sycamore, etc. **15** a mechanical device for making or breaking an electric circuit, e.g., in telegraphy. ●*adj.* essential; of vital importance (*the key element in the problem*). ●*v.tr.* (**keys**, **keyed**) **1** (foll. by *in*, *on*, etc.) fasten with a pin, wedge, bolt, etc. **2** (often foll. by *in*) enter (data) by means of a keyboard. **3** roughen (a surface) to help the adhesion of plaster, etc. **4** (foll. by *to*) align or link (one thing to another). **5** regulate the pitch of the strings (of a violin, etc.). **6** word (an advertisement in a particular periodical) so that answers to it can be identified (usu. by varying the form of address given). □ **key up** (often foll. by *to*, or *to* + infin.) make (a person) nervous or tense; excite. □□ **key·er** *n.* **key·less** *adj.* [OE *cǣg*, of unkn. orig.]

key² /kee/ *n.* a low-lying island or reef, esp. off the Florida coast (cf. CAY). [Sp. *cayo* shoal, reef, infl. by QUAY]

key·board /keébawrd/ *n. & v.* ●*n.* **1** a panel of keys that operate a computer, typewriter, piano, etc. **2** an electronic musical instrument with keys arranged as on a piano. ●*v.tr. & intr.* enter (data) by means of a keyboard; work at a keyboard. □□ **key·board·er** *n.* **key·board·ist** *n.*

key card *n.* a plastic card inserted into a door in some hotels instead of a key, bearing magnetically encoded data that is read electronically.

key grip *n.* the person in a movie crew who is in charge of the camera equipment.

key·hole /keéhōl/ *n.* a hole by which a key is put into a lock.

key·hole sur·ger·y *n.* minimally invasive surgery carried out through a very small incision.

key in·dus·try *n.* an industry essential to the functioning of others, such as the manufacture of machine tools.

key lime *n.* a small yellowish lime with a sharp flavor (named after the Florida Keys).

key mon·ey *n.* money paid to a landlord as an inducement by a person wishing to rent a property.

Keynes·i·an /káynzeeən/ *adj. & n.* ●*adj.* of or relating to the economic theories of J. M. Keynes (d. 1946), esp. regarding government control of the economy through money and taxation. ●*n.* an adherent of these theories. □□ **Keynes·i·an·ism** *n.*

key·note /keénōt/ *n.* **1** a prevailing tone or idea (*the keynote of the whole occasion*). **2** (*attrib.*) intended to set the prevailing tone at a meeting or conference (*keynote address*). **3** *Mus.* the note on which a key is based.

key·pad /keépad/ *n.* a miniature keyboard or set of buttons for operating a portable electronic device, telephone, etc.

key·punch /keépunch/ *n. & v.* ●*n.* a device for transferring data by means of punched holes or notches on a series of cards or paper tape. ●*v.tr.* transfer (data) by means of a keypunch. □□ **key·punch·er** *n.*

key ring *n.* a ring for keeping keys on.

key sig·na·ture *n. Mus.* any of several combinations of sharps or flats after the clef at the beginning of each staff indicating the key of a composition.

key·stone /keéstōn/ *n.* **1** the central principle of a system, policy, etc., on which all else depends. **2** a central stone at the summit of an arch locking the whole together.

keystone 2

key·stroke /keéstrōk/ *n.* a single depression of a key on a keyboard, esp. as a measure of work.

key·way /keéway/ *n.* a slot for receiving a machined key.

key·word /keéwərd/ *n.* **1** a word that acts as the key to a cipher or code. **2** a word or concept of great significance. **3** an informative word used in an information retrieval system to indicate the content of a document. **4** a significant word mentioned in an index.

KG *abbr.* (in the UK) Knight of the Order of the Garter.

kg *abbr.* kilogram(s).

KGB *n.* the state security police of the former USSR from 1954. [Russ., abbr. of *Komitet gosudarstvennoĭ bezopasnosti* committee of state security]

Kgs. *abbr.* Kings (Old Testament).

khad·dar /kaádər/ *n.* a homespun cloth of India. [Hindi]

khak·i /kákee, kaá−/ *adj. & n.* ●*adj.* dust-colored; dull brownish-yellow. ●*n.* (*pl.* **khak·is**) **1 a** a khaki fabric of twilled cotton or wool, used esp. in military dress. **b** (in *pl.*) a garment, esp. pants or a military uniform, made of this fabric. **2** the dull brownish-yellow color of this. [Urdu *kākī* dust-colored f. *kāk* dust]

kham·sin /kámsin, kamseén/ *n.* (also **ham·sin** /hám−/) an oppressive hot south or southeast wind occurring in Egypt for about 50 days in March, April, and May. [Arab. *kamsīn* f. *kamsūn* fifty]

khan¹ /kaan, kan/ *n.* **1** a title given to rulers and officials in Central Asia, Afghanistan, etc. **2** *hist.* **a** the supreme ruler of the Turkish, Tartar, and Mongol tribes. **b** the emperor of China in the Middle Ages. □□ **khan·ate** *n.* [Turki *kān* lord]

khan[2] /kaan, kan/ *n.* a caravansary. [Arab. *khān* inn]

khe·dive /kidéev/ *n. hist.* the title of the viceroy of Egypt under Turkish rule 1867–1914. □□ **khe·div·al** *adj.* **khe·div·i·al** *adj.* [F *khédive*, ult. f. Pers. *kadīv* prince]

Khmer /kmair/ *n. & adj.* ● *n.* 1 a native of the ancient Khmer kingdom in SE Asia, or of modern Cambodia. 2 the language of this people. ● *adj.* of the Khmers or their language. [native name]

Khur·ta var. of KURTA.

kHz *abbr.* kilohertz.

ki·ang /keeáng/ *n.* a wild Tibetan ass, *Equus hemionus kiang*, with a thick, furry coat. [Tibetan *kyang*]

kib·ble[1] /kíbəl/ *v. & n.* ● *v.tr.* grind coarsely. ● *n.* coarsely ground pellets of meal, etc.; used as a dry pet food. [18th c.: orig. unkn.]

kib·ble[2] /kíbəl/ *n. Brit.* an iron bucket used in mines for hoisting ore. [G *Kübel* (cf. OE *cyfel*) f. med.L *cupellus*, corn measure, dimin. of *cuppa* cup]

kib·butz /kiboóts/ *n.* (*pl.* **kib·but·zim** /–boótseém/) a communal, esp. farming, settlement in Israel. [mod.Heb. *kibbūs* gathering]

kib·butz·nik /kiboótsnik/ *n.* a member of a kibbutz. [Yiddish (as KIBBUTZ)]

kibe /kib/ *n.* an ulcerated chilblain, esp. on the heel. [ME, prob. f. Welsh *cibi*]

kib·itz /kíbits/ *v.intr. colloq.* act as a kibitzer. [Yiddish f. G *kiebitzen* (as KIBITZER)]

kib·itz·er /kíbitsər/ *n. colloq.* 1 an onlooker at cards, etc., esp. one who offers unwanted advice. 2 a busybody; a meddler. [Yiddish *kibitzer* f. G *Kiebitz* lapwing, busybody]

kib·lah /kíblə/ *n.* (also **qib·la**) 1 the direction of the Kaaba (the sacred building at Mecca), to which Muslims turn at prayer. 2 = MIHRAB. [Arab. *kibla* that which is opposite]

ki·bosh /kíbosh/ *n.* (also *Brit.* **ky·bosh**) *sl.* nonsense. □ **put the kibosh on** put an end to; finally dispose of. [19th c.: orig. unkn.]

kick[1] /kik/ *v. & n.* ● *v.* 1 *tr.* strike or propel forcibly with the foot or hoof, etc. 2 *intr.* (usu. foll. by *at, against*) a strike out with the foot. **b** express annoyance at or dislike of (treatment, a proposal, etc.); rebel against. 3 *tr. sl.* give up (a habit). 4 *tr.* (often foll. by *out*, etc.) expel or dismiss forcibly. 5 *refl.* be annoyed with oneself (*I'll kick myself if I'm wrong*). 6 *tr. Football* score (a goal) by a kick. 7 *intr. Cricket* (of a ball) rise sharply from the field. ● *n.* 1 a a blow with the foot or hoof, etc. **b** the delivery of such a blow. 2 *colloq.* a a sharp stimulant effect, esp. of alcohol (*a cocktail with a kick in it*). **b** (often in *pl.*) a pleasurable thrill (*did it just for kicks; got a kick out of flying*). 3 strength; resilience (*have no kick left*). 4 *colloq.* a specified temporary interest or enthusiasm (*on a jogging kick*). 5 the recoil of a gun when discharged. 6 *Brit. Soccer colloq.* a player of specified kicking ability (*is a good kick*). □ **kick about** (or **around**) *colloq.* 1 a drift idly from place to place. **b** be unused or unwanted. 2 a treat roughly or scornfully. **b** discuss (an idea) unsystematically. **kick the bucket** *sl.* die. **kick one's heels** see HEEL. **kick in** 1 knock down (a door, etc.) by kicking. 2 *sl.* contribute (esp. money); pay one's share. **kick in the pants** (or **teeth**) *colloq.* a humiliating punishment or setback. **kick off** 1 a *Football*, etc., begin or resume play. **b** *colloq.* begin. 2 remove (shoes, etc.) by kicking. **kick over the traces** see TRACE[2]. **kick up** (or **kick up a fuss, dust**, etc.) create a disturbance; object or register strong disapproval. **kick up one's heels** frolic. **kick a person upstairs** shelve a person by giving him or her a promotion or a title. □□ **kick·a·ble** *adj.* **kick·er** *n.* [ME *kike*, of unkn. orig.]

kick[2] /kik/ *n.* an indentation at the bottom of a glass bottle. [19th c.: orig. unkn.]

Kick·a·poo /kíkəpoō/ *n.* 1 a a N. American people native to the upper Midwest. **b** a member of this people. 2 the language of this people.

kick·back /kíkbak/ *n. colloq.* 1 the force of a recoil. 2 payment made to someone who has facilitated a transaction, esp. illicitly.

kick·down *n. Brit.* a device for changing gear in a motor vehicle by full depression of the accelerator.

kick·off /kíkawf/ *n.* 1 *Football & Soccer* the start or resumption of play. 2 the start of something, esp. a campaign, drive, or project.

kick plate *n.* a metal plate attached to the base of a door to protect it from damage or wear.

kick pleat *n.* a pleat at the bottom of a narrow skirt to allow freedom of movement.

kick·shaw /kíkshaw/ *n.* 1 *archaic* a fancy but insubstantial cooked dish, esp. one of foreign origin. 2 something elegant but insubstantial; a toy or trinket. [F *quelque chose* something]

kick·stand /kíkstand/ *n.* a rod attached to a bicycle or motorcycle and kicked into a vertical position to support the vehicle when stationary.

kick-start *v.tr.* 1 start (a motorcycle, etc.) by the downward thrust of a pedal. 2 start or restart (a process, etc.) by providing some initial impetus.

kick start *n.* (also **kick starter**) 1 a device to start the engine of a motorcycle, etc., by the downward thrust of a pedal. 2 a boost or push to start or restart a process, etc.

kick turn *n.* 1 (in skiing) a turn carried out while stationary by lifting first one and then the other ski through 180°. 2 (in skateboarding) a turn performed with the front wheels lifted off the ground.

kid[1] /kid/ *n. & v.* ● *n.* 1 a young goat. 2 the leather made from its skin. 3 *colloq.* a child or young person. ● *v.intr.* (**kid·ded, kid·ding**) (of a goat) give birth. □ **handle with kid gloves** handle in a gentle, delicate, or gingerly manner. [ME *kide* f. ON *kith* f. Gmc]

▶Kid, meaning 'child,' although widely seen in informal contexts, should be avoided in formal writing.

kid[2] /kid/ *v.* (**kid·ded, kid·ding**) *colloq.* 1 *tr. & also refl.* deceive; trick (*don't kid yourself; kidded his mother that he was ill*). 2 *tr. & intr.* tease (*only kidding*). □ **no kidding** (or esp. *Brit.* **kid**) *sl.* that is the truth. □□ **kid·der** *n.* **kid·ding·ly** *adv.* [perh. f. KID[1]]

kid[3] /kid/ *n. hist.* a small wooden tub, esp. a sailor's mess tub for grog or rations. [perh. var. of KIT[1]]

kid broth·er *n.* (also **kid sis·ter**) *sl.* a younger brother or sister.

Kid·der·min·ster /kídərminstər/ *n.* (in full **Kidderminster carpet**) a carpet made of two cloths of different colors woven together so that the carpet is reversible. [*Kidderminster* in S. England]

kid·die /kídee/ *n.* (also **kid·dy**) (*pl.* **·dies**) *sl.* = KID[1] *n.* 3.

kid·dle /kíd'l/ *n.* 1 a barrier in a river with an opening fitted with nets, etc. to catch fish. 2 an arrangement of fishing-nets hung on stakes along the seashore. [ME f. AF *kidel*, OF *quidel, guidel*]

kid·do /kidō/ *n.* (*pl.* **·dos**) *sl.* = KID[1] *n.* 3.

kid·dy var. of KIDDIE.

kid-glove *adj.* used in reference to careful and delicate treatment of a person or situation (*the star is getting kid-glove treatment*).

kid·nap /kídnap/ *v.tr.* (**kid·napped, kid·nap·ping** or **kid·naped, kid·nap·ing**) 1 carry off (a person, etc.) by illegal force or fraud esp. to obtain a ransom. 2 steal (a child). □□ **kid·nap·per** *n.* [back-form. f. *kidnapper* f. KID[1] + *nap* = NAB]

kid·ney /kídnee/ *n.* (*pl.* **·neys**) 1 either of a pair of organs in the abdominal cavity of mammals, birds, and reptiles, which remove nitrogenous wastes from the blood and excrete urine. 2 the kidney of a sheep, ox, or pig as food. 3 temperament; nature; kind (*a man of that kidney; of the right kidney*). [ME *kidnei*, pl. *kidneiren*, app. partly f. *ei* EGG[1]]

kid·ney bean *n.* 1 a dwarf French bean. 2 a scarlet runner bean.

kid·ney ma·chine *n.* = ARTIFICIAL KIDNEY.

kid·ney-shaped *adj.* shaped like a kidney, with one side concave and the other convex.

kid·ney vetch *n.* a herbaceous plant, *Anthyllis vulneraria*.

kid·skin /kídskin/ *n.* = KID[1] *n.* 2.

kid stuff *n. sl.* something very simple.

kid·vid *n. sl.* children's television or video entertainment. [*kids' video*]

kiekie /keékee/ *n.* a New Zealand climbing plant with edible bracts, and leaves that are used for basket-making, etc. [Maori]

kiel·ba·sa /keelbaásə/ *n.* a variety of smoked, seasoned sausage. [Pol., = sausage]

kie·sel·guhr /keezəlgoor/ *n.* diatomaceous earth forming deposits in lakes and ponds and used as a filter, filler, insulator, etc., in various manufacturing processes. [G f. *Kiesel* gravel + dial. *Guhr* earthy deposit]

kif var. of KEF.

kike /kik/ *n. sl. offens.* a Jew. [20th c.: orig. uncert.]

Ki·ku·yu /kikoóyoō/ *n. & adj.* ● *n.* (*pl.* same or **Ki·ku·yus**) 1 a member of an agricultural black African people, the largest Bantu-speaking group in Kenya. 2 the language of this people. ● *adj.* of or relating to this people or their language. [native name]

kil·der·kin /kíldərkin/ *n.* 1 a cask for liquids, etc., holding 18 imperial gallons. 2 *Brit.* this measure. [ME, alt. of *kinderkin* f. MDu. *kinde(r)kin, kinneken*, dimin. of *kintal* QUINTAL]

kill[1] /kil/ *v. & n.* ● *v.tr.* 1 a deprive of life or vitality; put to death; cause the death of. **b** (*absol.*) cause or bring about death (*must kill to survive*). 2 destroy; put an end to (feelings, etc.) (*overwork killed my enthusiasm*). 3 *refl.* (often foll. by *pres. part.*) *colloq.* a overexert oneself (*don't kill yourself lifting them all at once*). **b** laugh heartily. 4 *colloq.* overwhelm (a person) with amusement, delight, etc. (*the things he says really kill me*). 5 switch off (a spotlight, engine, etc.). 6 *colloq.* delete (a line, paragraph, etc.) from a computer file. 7 *colloq.* cause pain or discomfort to (*my feet are killing me*). 8 pass (time, or a specified amount of it) usu. while waiting for a specific event (*had an hour to kill before the interview*). 9 defeat (a bill in Congress, etc.). 10 *colloq.* consume the entire contents of (a bottle of wine, etc.). 11 a *Tennis*, etc., hit (the ball) so skillfully that it cannot be returned. **b** stop (the ball) dead. 12 neutralize or render ineffective (taste, sound, color, etc.) (*thick carpet killed the sound of footsteps*). ● *n.* 1 an act of killing (esp. an animal). 2 an animal or animals killed, esp. by a sportsman. 3 *colloq.* the destruction or disablement of an enemy aircraft, submarine, etc. □ **dressed to kill** dressed showily, alluringly, or impressively. **in at the kill** present at or benefiting from the successful conclusion of an enterprise. **kill off 1** get rid of or destroy completely (esp. a number of persons or things). **2** (of an author) bring about the death of (a fictional character). **kill or cure** (usu. *attrib.*) (of a remedy, etc.) drastic; extreme. **kill two birds with one stone** achieve two aims at once. **kill with kindness** spoil (a person) with overindulgence. [ME *cülle, kille,* perh. ult. rel. to QUELL]

SYNONYM TIP   **kill**

ASSASSINATE, DISPATCH, EXECUTE, MASSACRE, MURDER, SLAUGHTER, SLAY. When it comes to depriving someone or something of life, the options are endless. To **kill** is the most general term, meaning to cause the death of a person, animal, or plant, with no implication or mention required as to the manner of killing, the agent, or the cause (*to be killed in a car accident*). Even inanimate things may be killed (*Congress killed the project when they vetoed the bill*). To **slay** is to **kill** deliberately and violently; it is used more often in written than in spoken English (*a novel about a presidential candidate who is slain by his opponent*). **Murder** implies a malicious and premeditated killing of one person by another (*a gruesome murder carried out by the son-in-law*), while **assassinate** implies that a politically important person has been murdered, often by someone hired to do the job (*to assassinate the head of the guerrilla forces*). Someone who is put to death by a legal or military process is said to be **executed** (*to execute by lethal injection*), but if someone is killed primarily to get rid or him or her, the appropriate verb is **dispatch**, which also suggests speed or promptness (*after delivering the secret documents, the informer was dispatched*). While **slaughter** is usually associated with the killing of animals for food, it can also apply to a mass killing of humans (*the slaughter of innocent civilians provoked a worldwide outcry*). **Massacre** also refers to the brutal *murder* of large numbers of people, but it is used more specifically to indicate the wholesale destruction of a relatively defenseless group of people (*the massacre of Bethlehem's male children by King Herod is commemorated as Holy Innocents' Day*).

---

kill² /kil/ *n.* esp. *New York State dial.* a stream, creek, or tributary river. [Du. *kil* f. MDu. *kille* channel]
kill·deer /kíldeer/ *n.* a large American plover, *Charadrius vociferus,* with a plaintive song. [imit.]
kill·er /kílər/ *n.* **1 a** a person, animal, or thing that kills. **b** a murderer. **2** *colloq.* **a** an impressive, formidable, or excellent thing (*this one is quite difficult, but the next one is a real killer*). **b** a hilarious joke. **c** a decisive blow (*his home run proved to be the killer*).
kill·er bee *n.* a very aggressive honeybee, *Apis mellifera adansonii,* orig. from Africa.
kill·er cell *n. Immunology* a cell that attacks and destroys a cell (as a tumor cell) that bears a specific antigen on its surface.
kill·er in·stinct *n.* **1** an innate tendency to kill. **2** a ruthless streak.
kill·er whale *n.* a predatory cetacean, *Orcinus orca,* with distinctive black and white markings and a prominent dorsal fin.
kil·lick /kílik/ *n.* **1** a heavy stone used by small craft as an anchor. **2** a small anchor. **3** *Brit. Naut. sl.* a leading seaman. [17th c.: orig. unkn.]
kil·li·fish /kíleefish/ *n.* **1** any small fresh- or brackish-water fish of the family Cyprinodontidae, many of which are brightly colored. **2** a brightly colored tropical aquarium fish, *Pterolebias peruensis.* [perh. f. KILL² + FISH¹]
kill·ing /kíling/ *n. & adj.* ● *n.* **1 a** the causing of death. **b** an instance of this. **2** a great (esp. financial) success (*make a killing*). ● *adj. colloq.* **1** overwhelmingly funny. **2** exhausting; very strenuous. □□ **kill·ing·ly** *adv.*
kill·joy /kíljoy/ *n.* a person who throws gloom over or prevents other people's enjoyment.
kiln /kiln, kil–/ *n.* a furnace or oven for burning, baking, or drying, esp. for calcining lime or firing pottery, etc. [OE *cylene* f. L *culina* kitchen]
kiln-dry /kílndrī, kil–/ *v.tr.* (**·dries, ·dried**) dry in a kiln.
ki·lo /kéelo/ *n.* (*pl.* **·los**) **1** a kilogram. **2** a kilometer. [F: abbr.]
kilo- /kílō/ *comb. form* denoting a factor of 1,000 (esp. in metric units). ¶ Abbr.: **k,** or **K** in *Computing.* [F f. Gk *khilioi* thousand]
kil·o·byte /kílōbīt/ *n. Computing* 1,024 (i.e. 2¹⁰) bytes as a measure of memory size.
kil·o·cal·o·rie /kílōkálaree/ *n.* = CALORIE 2.
kil·o·cy·cle /kílōsikəl/ *n.* a former measure of frequency, equivalent to 1 kilohertz. ¶ Abbr.: **kc.**
kil·o·gram /kílōgram/ *n.* (also *Brit.* **kil·o·gramme**) the SI unit of mass, equivalent to the international standard kept at Sèvres near Paris (approx. 2.205 lb.). ¶ Abbr.: **kg.** [F *kilogramme* (as KILO, GRAM¹)]
kil·o·hertz /kílōhərts/ *n.* a measure of frequency equivalent to 1,000 cycles per second. ¶ Abbr.: **kHz.**
kil·o·joule /kílōjōōl/ *n.* 1,000 joules, esp. as a measure of the energy value of foods. ¶ Abbr.: **kJ.**

kil·o·li·ter /kílōleetər/ *n.* (also *Brit.* **kil·o·li·tre**) 1,000 liters (equivalent to 220 imperial gallons). ¶ Abbr.: **kl.**
kil·o·me·ter /kilómitər, kíləmeetər/ *n.* (*Brit.* **kil·o·me·tre**) a metric unit of measurement equal to 1,000 meters (approx. 0.62 miles). ¶ Abbr.: **km.** □□ **kil·o·met·ric** /kíləmétrik/ *adj.* [F *kilomètre* (as KILO-, METER¹)]

PRONUNCIATION TIP   **kilometer**

Although the pronunciation of this word with the stress on the second syllable ("kil-AH-mit-er") originally came about because of a false analogy with *barometer* and *thermometer,* it continues to be the preferred pronunciation in American English. Many people feel that the stress should be on the first syllable, as it is in *millimeter* and *centimeter,* and dictionaries since the 19th century have given both pronunciations.

---

kil·o·ton /kílətun/ *n.* a unit of explosive power equivalent to 1,000 tons of TNT.
kil·o·volt /kílōvōlt/ *n.* 1,000 volts. ¶ Abbr.: **kV.**
kil·o·watt /kílōwot/ *n.* 1,000 watts. ¶ Abbr.: **kW.**
kil·o·watt-hour /kíləwot-ówr/ *n.* a measure of electrical energy equivalent to a power consumption of 1,000 watts for one hour. ¶ Abbr.: **kWh.**
kilt /kilt/ *n. & v.* ● *n.* **1** a skirtlike garment, usu. of pleated tartan cloth and reaching to the knees, as traditionally worn in Scotland by Highland men. **2** a similar garment worn by women and children. ● *v.tr.* **1** tuck up (skirts) around the body. **2** (esp. as **kilted** *adj.*) gather in vertical pleats. □□ **kilt·ed** *adj.* [orig. as verb: ME, of Scand. orig.]
kil·ter /kíltər/ *n.* (also *Brit.* **kel·ter**) (in phrase **out of kilter**) out of harmony or balance. [17th c.: orig. unkn.]
kilt·ie /kíltee/ *n.* a wearer of a kilt, esp. a kilted Highland soldier.
kim·ber·lite /kímbərlīt/ *n. Mineral.* a rare igneous blue-tinged rock sometimes containing diamonds, found in South Africa and Siberia. Also called **blue ground.** [*Kimberley* in S. Africa]
ki·mo·no /kimốnō/ *n.* (*pl.* **·nos**) **1** a long, loose Japanese robe worn with a sash. **2** a dressing gown modeled on this. □□ **ki·mo·noed** *adj.* [Jap.]

kilt 1

kin /kin/ *n. & adj.* ● *n.* one's relatives or family. ● *predic.adj.* (of a person) related (*we are kin; he is kin to me*) (see also AKIN). □ **kith and kin** see KITH. **near of kin** closely related by blood, or in character. **next of kin** see NEXT. □□ **kin·less** *adj.* [OE *cynn* f. Gmc]
-kin /kin/ *suffix* forming diminutive nouns (*catkin; manikin*). [from or after MDu. *-kijn, -ken,* OHG *-chin*]
ki·na /kéenə/ *n.* the monetary unit of Papua New Guinea. [Papuan]
kin·aes·the·sia esp. *Brit.* var. of KINESTHESIA.
kin·cob /kínkob/ *n.* a rich fabric of India embroidered with gold or silver. [Urdu f. Pers. *kamkāb* f. *kamkā* damask]
kind¹ /kīnd/ *n.* **1 a** a race or species (*humankind*). **b** a natural group of animals, plants, etc. (*the wolf kind*). **2** class; type; sort; variety (*what kind of job are you looking for?*). **3** each of the elements of the Eucharist. **4** the manner or fashion natural to a person, etc. (*act after their kind; true to kind*). □ **kind of** *colloq.* to some extent (*felt kind of sorry; I kind of expected it*). **a kind of** used to imply looseness, vagueness, exaggeration, etc., in the term used (*a kind of Jane Austen of our times; I suppose he's a kind of doctor*). **in kind 1** in the same form; likewise (*was insulted and replied in kind*). **2** (of payment) in goods or labor as opposed to money (*received their wages in kind*). **3** in character or quality (*differ in degree but not in kind*). **nothing of the kind 1** not at all like the thing in question. **2** (expressing denial) not at all. **of its kind** within the limitations of its own class (*good of its kind*). **of a kind 1** *derog.* scarcely deserving the name (*a choir of a kind*). **2** similar in some important respect (*they're two of a kind*). **one's own kind** those with whom one has much in common (*he moved to the artists' colony to be with his own kind*). **something of the kind** something like the thing in question. [OE *cynd(e), gecynd (e)* f. Gmc]

▶ **1. Kind of** is sometimes used to be deliberately vague: *it was kind*

kimono 1

of a big evening; I was kind of hoping you'd call. More often, it reveals an inability to speak clearly: he's kind of, like, awesome, you know? Used precisely, it means 'sort' or 'type': a maple is a kind of tree. 2. The plural of **kind** often causes difficulty. With this or that, speaking of one kind, use a singular construction: that kind of fabric doesn't need ironing; with these or those, speaking of more than one kind, use a plural construction: those kinds of animals ought to be left in the wild. Although often encountered, sentences such as "I don't like these kind of things" are incorrect. The same recommendations apply to sort and sorts.

kind² /kīnd/ adj. **1** of a friendly, generous, benevolent, or gentle nature. **2** (usu. foll. by to) showing friendliness, affection, or consideration. **3 a** affectionate. **b** archaic loving. [OE gecynde (as KIND¹): orig. = 'natural, native']

kind·a /kīndə/ colloq. = kind of. [corrupt.]

kin·der·gar·ten /kīndərgaart'n/ n. an establishment or class for pre-school learning. [G, = children's garden]

kind·heart·ed /kīndhaártid/ adj. of a kind disposition. □□ **kind·heart·ed·ly** adv. **kind·heart·ed·ness** n.

kin·dle /kīnd'l/ v. **1** tr. light or set on fire (a flame, fire, substance, etc.). **2** intr. catch fire, burst into flame. **3** tr. arouse or inspire (kindle enthusiasm for the project; kindle jealousy in a rival). **4** intr. (usu. foll. by to) respond; react (to a person, an action, etc.). **5** intr. become animated, glow with passion, etc. (her imagination kindled). **6** tr. & intr. make or become bright (kindle the embers to a glow). □□ **kin·dler** n. [ME f. ON kynda, kindle: cf. ON kindill candle, torch]

kin·dling /kīndling/ n. small sticks, etc., for lighting fires.

kind·ly¹ /kīndlee/ adv. **1** in a kind manner (spoke to the child kindly). **2** often iron. used in a polite request or demand (kindly acknowledge this letter; kindly leave me alone). □ **look kindly upon** regard sympathetically. **take a thing kindly** like or be pleased by it. **take kindly to** be pleased by or endeared to (a person or thing). **thank kindly** thank very much. [OE gecyndelīce (as KIND²)]

kind·ly² /kīndlee/ adj. (**kind·li·er**, **kind·li·est**) **1** kind; kindhearted. **2** (of climate, etc.) pleasant; genial. **3** archaic native-born (a kindly Scot). □□ **kind·li·ly** adv. **kind·li·ness** n. [OE gecyndelic (as KIND¹)]

kind·ness /kīndnis/ n. **1** the state or quality of being kind. **2** a kind act.

kin·dred /kīndrid/ n. & adj. • n. **1** one's relations, referred to collectively. **2** a relationship by blood. **3** a resemblance or affinity in character. • adj. **1** related by blood or marriage. **2** allied or similar in character (other kindred symptoms). [ME f. KIN + -red f. OE ræden condition]

kin·dred spir·it n. a person whose character and outlook have much in common with one's own.

kine /kīn/ archaic pl. of COW¹.

kin·e·mat·ics /kinimátiks/ n.pl. (usu. treated as sing.) the branch of mechanics concerned with the motion of objects without reference to the forces which cause the motion. □□ **kin·e·mat·ic** adj. **kin·e·mat·i·cal·ly** adv. [Gk kinēma -matos motion f. kineō move + -ICS]

kin·e·mat·o·graph var. of CINEMATOGRAPH.

ki·ne·sics /kinéesiks, -ziks/ n.pl. (usu. treated as sing.) **1** the study of body movements and gestures that contribute to communication. **2** these movements; body language. [Gk kinēsis motion (as KINETIC)]

ki·ne·si·ol·o·gy /kinéeseeóləjee, -zee-/ n. the study of the mechanics of body movements.

kin·es·the·sia /kinəs-théezhə/ n. (esp. Brit. **kin·aes·the·sia**) (also **kin·es·the·sis** /kinəs-théesis/) a sense of awareness of the position and movement of the voluntary muscles of the body. □□ **kin·es·thet·ic** /-thétik/ adj. [Gk kineō move + aisthēsis sensation]

ki·net·ic /kinétik, kī-/ adj. of or due to motion. □□ **ki·net·i·cal·ly** adv. [Gk kinētikos f. kineō move]

ki·net·ic art n. a form of art that depends on movement for its effect.

ki·net·ic en·er·gy n. Physics energy that a body possesses by virtue of being in motion.

ki·net·ics /kinétiks, kī-/ n.pl. **1** = DYNAMICS 1a. **2** (usu. treated as sing.) the branch of physical chemistry concerned with measuring and studying the rates of chemical reactions.

ki·net·ic the·o·ry n. a theory which explains the physical properties of matter in terms of the motions of its constituent particles.

ki·ne·tin /kīnitin/ n. Biochem. a synthetic kinin used to stimulate cell division in plants. [as KINETIC + -IN]

kin·folk /kīnfōk/ n.pl. (also **kin·folks**, **kins·folk**) one's relations by blood.

king /king/ n. & v. • n. **1** (as a title usu. **King**) a male sovereign, esp. the hereditary ruler of an independent nation. **2** a person or thing preeminent in a specified field or class (railroad king). **3** a large (or the largest) kind of plant, animal, etc. (king penguin). **4** Chess the piece on each side that the opposing side has to checkmate to win.

5 a piece in checkers with extra capacity of moving, made by crowning an ordinary piece that has reached the opponent's baseline. **6** a playing card bearing a representation of a king and usu. ranking next below an ace. **7** (**the King**) (in the UK) the national anthem when there is a male sovereign. **8** (**Kings** or **Books of Kings**) two Old Testament books dealing with history, esp. of the kingdom of Judah. • v.tr. make (a person) king. □ **king it** play or act the king. **2** (usu. foll. by over) govern; control. □□ **king·hood** n. **king·less** adj. **king·like** adj. **king·ly** adj. **king·li·ness** n. **king·ship** n. [OE cyning, cyng f. Gmc]

king·bird /kíngbərd/ n. any flycatcher of the genus Tyrannus, with olive-gray plumage and long pointed wings.

king·bolt /kíngbōlt/ n. = KINGPIN 1.

King Charles span·iel n. a type of English toy spaniel with a white, black, and tan coat.

king co·bra n. a large and venomous hooded Indian snake, Ophiophagus hannah.

king crab n. (esp. **Alaskan king crab** Paralithodes camtschatia) **1** = HORSESHOE CRAB. **2** any of various large edible spider crabs.

king·craft /kíngkraft/ n. archaic the art of ruling as a king, esp. with reference to the use of clever or crafty diplomacy in dealing with subjects.

king·cup /kíngkup/ n. Brit. a marsh marigold.

king·dom /kíngdəm/ n. **1** an organized community headed by a king. **2** the territory subject to a king. **3 a** the spiritual reign attributed to God (Thy kingdom come). **b** the sphere of this (kingdom of heaven). **4** a domain belonging to a person, animal, etc. **5** a province of nature (the vegetable kingdom). **6** a specified mental or emotional province (kingdom of the heart; kingdom of fantasy). **7** Biol. the highest category in taxonomic classification. □ **come into** (or **to**) **one's kingdom** achieve recognition or supremacy. **kingdom come** colloq. eternity; the next world. **till kingdom come** colloq. forever. □□ **king·domed** adj. [OE cyningdōm (as KING)]

king·fish /kíngfish/ n. any of a number of large sporting fish, esp. the opah or mulloway, many of which are edible.

king·fish·er /kíngfishər/ n. any bird of the family Alcedinidae, esp. Alcedo atthis, with a long sharp beak and brightly colored plumage, which dives for fish in rivers, etc.

kingfisher

King James Bi·ble n. (also **King James Ver·sion**) an English translation of the Bible made in 1611 at the order of James I and still widely used. Also called **Authorized Version**.

king·let /kínglit/ n. **1** a petty king. **2** any of various small birds of the family Regulidae, esp. the goldcrest.

king·mak·er /kíngmaykər/ n. a person who makes kings, leaders, etc., through the exercise of political influence, orig. with ref. to the Earl of Warwick in the reign of Henry VI of England.

king of arms n. Heraldry (in the UK) a title given to certain chief heralds.

king of beasts n. poet. the lion (in reference to the animal's perceived grandeur).

king of birds n. poet. the eagle (in reference to the bird's perceived grandeur).

King of Kings n. **1** God. **2** Jesus Christ.

king of the hill n. (also **king of the moun·tain**) a children's game consisting of trying to displace a rival from an elevated place, such as a mound of earth.

king·pin /kíngpin/ n. **1 a** a main or large bolt in a central position. **b** a vertical bolt used as a pivot. **2** an essential person or thing, esp. in a complex system; the most important person in an organization.

king post n. an upright post from the tie beam of a roof to the apex of a truss.

King's Bench n. (also **Queen's Bench**) (in the UK) a division of the High Court of Justice.

king's bish·op n. (also **king's knight**, etc.) Chess (of pieces that exist in pairs) the piece starting on the king's side of the board.

king's boun·ty n. (also **queen's boun·ty**) Brit. hist. a sum of money given from royal funds to a mother of triplets.

King's Coun·sel n. a senior barrister appointed as counsel to the British Crown. (Also called **Queen's Counsel** during reign of a queen). ¶ Abbr.: KC.

King's Eng·lish n. (also **Queen's Eng·lish**) the English language as written and spoken correctly by the educated people in Britain.

King's ev·i·dence n. (also **Queen's ev·i·dence**) evidence for the prosecution given by a participant in or accomplice to the crime being tried.

king's e•vil *n. hist.* scrofula, formerly held to be curable by the royal touch.

king-size *n.* (also **king-sized**) (esp. of a commerical product) of a larger size than the standard; very large.

king's pawn *n. Chess* the pawn in front of the king at the beginning of a game.

king's ran•som *n.* a fortune.

ki•nin /kínin/ *n.* **1** any of a group of polypeptides present in the blood after tissue damage. **2** any of a group of compounds that promote cell division and inhibit aging in plants. [Gk *kineō* move + –IN]

kink /kingk/ *n. & v.* ● *n.* **1 a** a short backward twist in wire or tubing, etc., such as may cause an obstruction. **b** a tight wave in human or animal hair. **2** a mental twist or quirk. ● *v.intr. & tr.* form or cause to form a kink. [MLG *kinke* (v.) prob. f. Du. *kinken*]

kin•ka•jou /kíngkəjōō/ *n.* a Central and S. American nocturnal fruit-eating mammal, *Potos flavus*, with a prehensile tail and living in trees. [F *quincajou* perh. f. Ojibwa: cf. Algonquian *kwingwaage* wolverine]

kink•y /kíngkee/ *adj.* (**kink•i•er**, **kink•i•est**) **1** *colloq.* **a** given to or involving abnormal sexual behavior. **b** (of clothing, etc.) bizarre in a sexually provocative way. **2** strange; eccentric. **3** having kinks or twists. □□ **kink•i•ly** *adv.* **kink•i•ness** *n.* [KINK + –Y¹]

ki•no /kéenō/ *n.* (*pl.* **-nos**) a catechulike gum produced by various trees and used in medicine and tanning as an astringent. [W. Afr.]

-kins /kinz/ *suffix* = –KIN, often with suggestions of endearment (*babykins*).

kins•folk var. of KINFOLK.

kin•ship /kínship/ *n.* **1** blood relationship. **2** the sharing of characteristics or origins.

kins•man /kínzmən/ *n.* (*pl.* **•men**; *fem.* **kins•wom•an**, *pl.* **•wom•en**) **1** a blood relation or *disp.* a relation by marriage. **2** a member of one's own tribe or people.

ki•osk /kéeosk, –ósk/ *n.* **1** a light, open-fronted booth or cubicle from which food, newspapers, tickets, etc. are sold. **2** *Brit.* a telephone booth. **3** a building in which refreshments are served in a park, zoo, etc. **4** a light, open pavilion in Turkey and Iran. [F *kiosque* f. Turk. *kiūshk* pavilion f. Pers. *guš*]

Ki•o•wa /kíowə/ *n.* **1 a** a N. American people native to the southwest. **b** a member of this people. **2** the language of this people.

kip¹ /kip/ *n. & v. Brit. sl.* ● *n.* **1** a sleep or nap. **2** a bed or cheap motel, etc. **3** (also **kip-house** or **kip-shop**) a brothel. ● *v.intr.* (**kipped**, **kip•ping**) **1** sleep; take a nap. **2** (foll. by *down*) lie or settle down to sleep. [cf. Da. *kippe* mean hut]

kip² /kip/ *n.* the hide of a young or small animal as used for leather. [ME: orig. unkn.]

kip³ /kip/ *n.* (*pl.* same or **kips**) the basic monetary unit of Laos. [Thai]

kip⁴ /kip/ *n. Austral. sl.* a small piece of wood from which coins are spun in the game of two-up. [perh. f. E dial.: cf. *keper* a flat piece of wood preventing a horse from eating the corn, or Ir. dial. *kippeen* f. Ir. *cipin* a little stick]

kip•per /kípər/ *n. & v.* ● *n.* **1** a kippered fish, esp. herring. **2** a male salmon in the spawning season. ● *v.tr.* cure (a herring, etc.) by splitting open, salting, and drying in the open air or smoke. [ME: orig. uncert.]

Kir /keer/ *n.* a drink made from dry white wine and crème de cassis. [Canon Felix *Kir* d. 1968, said to have invented the recipe]

Kir•ghiz /keergeez/ *n. & adj.* ● *n.* (*pl.* same) **1** a member of a Mongol people living in central Asia between the Volga and the Irtysh rivers. **2** the language of this people. ● *adj.* of or relating to this people or their language. [Kirghiz]

kirk /kurk/ *n. Sc. & No. of Engl.* **1** a church. **2** (**the Kirk** or **the Kirk of Scotland**) the Church of Scotland as distinct from the Church of England or from the Episcopal Church in Scotland. [ME f. ON *kirkja* f. OE *cir(i)ce* CHURCH]

kirk•man /kórkmən/ *n.* (*pl.* **•men**) *Sc. & No. of Engl.* a member of the Church of Scotland.

kirsch /keersh/ *n.* (also **kirsch•was•ser** /keershvaasər/) a brandy distilled from the fermented juice of cherries. [G *Kirsche* cherry, *Wasser* water]

kir•tle /kórt'l/ *n. archaic* **1** a woman's gown or outer petticoat. **2** a man's tunic or coat. [OE *cyrtel* f. Gmc, ult. perh. f. L *curtus* short]

kis•ka•dee /kískədee/ *n.* (also **kes•ki•dee** /késkidee/) a tyrant flycatcher, *Pitangus sulphuratus*, of Central and S. America, with brown and yellow plumage. [imit. of its cry]

kis•met /kízmet/ *n.* destiny; fate. [Turk. f. Arab. *kisma(t)* f. *kasama* divide]

kiss /kis/ *v. & n.* ● *v.* **1** *tr.* touch with the lips, esp. as a sign of love, affection, greeting, or reverence. **2** *tr.* express (greeting or farewell) in this way. **3** *absol.* (of two persons) touch each others' lips in this way. **4** *tr.* (also *absol.*) (of a billiard ball, etc., in motion) lightly touch (another ball). ● *n.* **1** a touch with the lips in kissing. **2** the slight impact when one billiard ball, etc., lightly touches another. **3** a usu. droplet-shaped piece of candy or small cookie. □ **kiss and tell** recount one's sexual exploits. **kiss a person's ass** (or **butt**)

coarse sl. act obsequiously toward a person. **kiss away** remove (tears, etc.) by kissing. **kiss the dust** submit abjectly; be overthrown. **kiss good-bye to** *colloq.* accept the loss of. **kiss the ground** prostrate oneself as a token of homage. **kiss off** *sl.* **1** dismiss; get rid of. **2** go away; die. **kiss the rod** *Brit.* accept chastisement submissively. □□ **kiss•a•ble** *adj.* [OE *cyssan* f. Gmc]

kiss curl *n. Brit.* = SPIT CURL.

kiss•er /kísor/ *n.* **1** a person who kisses. **2** (orig. *Boxing*) *sl.* the mouth; the face.

kiss•ing cous•in *n.* (also **kiss•ing kin**) a distant relative (given a formal kiss on occasional meetings).

kiss•ing dis•ease *n.* a disease transmitted by contact with infected saliva, esp. mononucleosis.

kiss•ing gate *n. Brit.* a gate hung in a V- or U-shaped enclosure, to let one person through at a time.

kiss of death *n.* an apparently friendly act which causes ruin.

kiss of life *n.* mouth-to-mouth resuscitation.

kiss of peace *n. Eccl.* a ceremonial kiss, esp. during the Eucharist, as a sign of unity.

kiss•y /kísee/ *adj. colloq.* given to kissing (*not the kissy type*).

kist var. of CIST¹.

Ki•swa•hi•li /kíswaaheélee/ *n.* one of the six languages preferred for use in Africa by the Organization for African Unity. [Swahili *ki-* prefix for an abstract or inanimate object]

kit¹ /kit/ *n. & v.* ● *n.* **1** a set of articles, equipment, or clothing needed for a specific purpose (*first-aid kit*; *bicycle-repair kit*). **2** esp. *Brit.* the clothing, etc., needed for any activity, esp. sports (*hockey kit*). **3** a set of all the parts needed to assemble an item, e.g., a piece of furniture, a model, etc. **4** *Brit.* a wooden tub. ● *v.tr.* (**kit•ted**, **kit•ting**) (often foll. by *out*, *up*) esp. *Brit.* equip with the appropriate clothing or tools. □ **the whole kit and caboodle** see CABOODLE. [ME f. MDu. *kitte* wooden vessel, of unkn. orig.]

kit² /kit/ *n.* **1** a kitten. **2** a young fox, badger, etc. [abbr.]

kit³ /kit/ *n. hist.* a small fiddle esp. as used by a dancing master. [perh. f. L *cithara*; see CITTERN]

kit bag *n.* a large, usu. cylindrical bag used for carrying a soldier's, traveler's, or sportsman's equipment.

kit-cat /kítkat/ *n.* (in full **kit-cat portrait**) a portrait of less than half length, but including one hand; usu. 36 x 28 in. [named after a series of portraits of the members of the *Kit-cat* Club in London, an early 18th-c. Whig society]

kitch•en /kíchin/ *n.* **1** the room or area where food is prepared and cooked. **2** (*attrib.*) of or belonging to the kitchen (*kitchen knife*; *kitchen table*). **3** *sl.* the percussion section of an orchestra. □ **everything but the kitchen sink** everything imaginable. [OE *cycene* f. L *coquere* cook]

kitch•en cab•i•net *n.* a group of unofficial advisers to the holder of an elected office who are thought to be unduly influential.

kitch•en•ette /kíchinét/ *n.* a small kitchen or part of a room fitted as a kitchen.

kitch•en gar•den *n.* a garden where vegetables and sometimes fruit or herbs are grown specifically for household use.

kitch•en mid•den *n.* a prehistoric refuse heap which marks an ancient settlement, chiefly containing bones, seashells, etc.

kitch•en po•lice *n. Mil. sl.* enlisted personnel detailed to help the cook by washing dishes, peeling vegetables, and other kitchen duties. ¶ Abbr.: **KP**.

kitch•en-sink *adj.* (in art forms) depicting extreme realism, esp. drabness or sordidness (*kitchen-sink school of painting*; *kitchen-sink drama*).

kitch•en tea *n. Austral. & NZ* a bridal shower to which guests bring items of kitchen equipment as presents.

kitch•en•ware /kíchinwair/ *n.* the utensils used in the kitchen.

kite /kit/ *n. & v.* ● *n.* **1** a toy consisting of a light framework with thin material stretched over it, flown in the wind at the end of a long string. **2** any of various soaring birds of prey esp. of the genus *Milvus* with long wings and usu. a forked tail. **3** *Brit. sl.* an airplane. **4** *sl.* a fraudulent check, bill, or receipt. **5** *Geom.* a quadrilateral figure symmetrical about one diagonal. **6** *sl.* a letter or note, esp. one that is illicit or surreptitious. **7** (in *pl.*) the highest sail of a ship, set only in a light wind. **8** *archaic* a dishonest person; a sharper. ● *v.* **1** *intr.* soar like a kite. **2** *tr.* (also *absol.*) originate or pass (fraudulent checks, bills, or receipts). **3** *tr.* (also *absol.*) raise (money by dishonest means) (*kite a loan*). [OE *cȳta*, of unkn. orig.]

kith /kith/ *n.* □ **kith and kin** friends and relations. [OE *cȳthth* f. Gmc]

kitsch /kich/ *n.* (often *attrib.*) garish, pretentious, or sentimental art, usu. vulgar and worthless (*kitsch plastic models of the Lincoln Memorial*). □□ **kitsch•y** *adj.* (**kitsch•i•er**, **kitsch•i•est**). **kitsch•i•ness** *n.* [G]

kit•ten /kít'n/ *n. & v.* ● *n.* **1** a young cat. **2** a young ferret, etc. ● *v.intr. & tr.* (of a cat, etc.) give birth or give birth to. □ **have kittens** *colloq.* be extremely upset, anxious, or nervous. [ME *kito(u)n*, *ketoun* f. OF *chitoun*, *chetoun* dimin. of *chat* CAT]

kit•ten•ish /kít'nish/ *adj.* **1** like a young cat; playful and lively. **2** flirtatious. □□ **kit•ten•ish•ly** *adv.* **kit•ten•ish•ness** *n.* [KITTEN]

kit•ti•wake /kíteewayk/ *n.* either of two small gulls, *Rissa tridactyla* and *R. brevirostris*, nesting on sea cliffs. [imit. of its cry]

kit•tle /kít'l/ *adj.* (also **kit•tle-cat•tle** /kít'lkat'l/) **1** *Brit.* (of a person) capricious, rash, or erratic in behavior. **2** difficult to deal with. [ME (now Sc. & dial.) *kittle* tickle, prob. f. ON *kitla*]

kit•ty[1] /kítee/ *n.* (*pl.* **•ties**) **1** a fund of money for communal use. **2** the pool in some card games. [19th c.: orig. unkn.]

kit•ty[2] /kítee/ *n.* (*pl.* **•ties**) a pet name or a child's name for a kitten or cat.

kit•ty-cor•ner var. of CATERCORNERED.

Kit•ty Lit•ter *n. Trademark* a granular clay used in boxes to absorb pet (esp. cat) waste.

ki•wi /kéewee/ *n.* (*pl.* **ki•wis**) **1** a flightless New Zealand bird of the genus *Apteryx* with hairlike feathers and a long bill. Also called **apteryx**. **2** (**Kiwi**) *colloq.* a New Zealander, esp. a soldier or member of a national sports team. [Maori]

ki•wi fruit *n.* (also **ki•wi ber•ry**) the fruit of a climbing plant, *Actinidia chinensis*, having a thin hairy skin, green flesh, and black seeds. Also called **Chinese gooseberry**.

kiwi 1

kJ *abbr.* kilojoule(s).

KKK *abbr.* Ku Klux Klan.

kl *abbr.* kiloliter(s).

Klax•on /kláksən/ *n. Trademark* a horn or warning hooter, orig. on a motor vehicle. [name of the manufacturing company]

Kleen•ex /kléeneks/ *n.* (*pl.* same or **Kleen•ex•es**) *Trademark* an absorbent disposable paper tissue, used esp. as a handkerchief.

Klein bot•tle /klīn/ *n. Math.* a closed surface with only one side, formed by passing the neck of a tube through the side of the tube and joining it to the other end. [F. *Klein*, Ger. mathematician d. 1925]

klepht /kleft/ *n.* **1** a member of the original body of Greeks who refused to submit to the Turks in the 15th c. **2** any of their descendants. **3** a brigand or bandit. [mod. Gk *klephtēs* f. Gk *klephtēs* thief]

klep•to•ma•ni•a /kléptəmáyneeə/ *n.* a recurrent urge to steal, usu. without regard for need or profit. □□ **klep•to•ma•ni•ac** *n. & adj.* [Gk *kleptēs* thief + −MANIA]

klieg /kleeg/ *n.* (also **klieg light**) a powerful lamp in a movie studio, etc. [A. T. & J. H. *Kliegl*, Amer. inventors d. 1927, 1959]

klip•spring•er /klípspringər/ *n.* a S. African dwarf antelope, *Oreotragus oreotragus*, which can bound up and down rocky slopes. [Afrik. f. *klip* rock + *springer* jumper]

Klon•dike /klóndīk/ *n.* a source of valuable material. [*Klondike* in Yukon, Canada, where gold was found in 1896]

kloof /kloof/ *n.* a steep-sided ravine or valley in S. Africa. [Du., = cleft]

kludge /kluj/ *n. sl.* **1** an ill-assorted collection of poorly matching parts. **2** *Computing* a machine, system, or program that has been badly put together.

klutz /kluts/ *n. sl.* **a** a clumsy awkward person. **b** a fool. □□ **klutz•y** *adj.* [Yiddish f. G *Klotz* wooden block]

klys•tron /klístron/ *n.* an electron tube that generates or amplifies microwaves by velocity modulation. [Gk *kluzō klus*- wash over]

km *abbr.* kilometer(s).

K-me•son /kaymézon, –més–, –méezon, –son/ *n.* = KAON. [K (see KAON) + MESON]

kmph *abbr.* kilometers per hour.

kmps *abbr.* kilometers per second.

kn. *abbr. Naut.* knot(s).

knack /nak/ *n.* **1** an acquired or intuitive faculty of doing a thing adroitly. **2** a trick or habit of action or speech, etc. (*has a knack of offending people*). **3** *archaic* an ingenious device (see KNICKKNACK). [ME, prob. identical with *knack* sharp blow or sound f. LG, ult. imit.]

knack•er /nákər/ *n. & v. Brit.* • *n.* **1** a person whose business is the disposal of dead or unwanted animals. **2** a buyer of old houses, ships, etc. for the materials. • *v.tr. sl.* **1** kill. **2** (esp. as **knackered** *adj.*) exhaust; wear out. [19th c.: orig. unkn.]

knack•er•y /nákəree/ *n.* (*pl.* **•ies**) a knacker's yard or business.

knack•wurst var. of KNOCKWURST.

knag /nag/ *n.* **1** a knot in wood; the base of a branch. **2** a short dead branch. **3** esp. *Brit.* a peg for hanging things on. □□ **knag•gy** *adj.* [ME, perh. f. LG *Knagge*]

knap[1] /nap/ *n.* chiefly *dial.* the crest of a hill or of rising ground. [OE *cnæp(p)*, perh. rel. to ON *knappr* knob]

knap[2] /nap/ *v.tr.* (**knapped, knap•ping**) **1** break (stones for roads or building, flints, or *Austral.* ore) with a hammer. **2** *archaic* knock; rap; snap asunder. □□ **knap•per** *n.* [ME, imit.]

knap•sack /nápsak/ *n.* a soldier's or hiker's bag with shoulder straps, carried on the back, and usu. made of canvas or weatherproof material. [MLG, prob. f. *knappen* bite + SACK[1]]

knap•weed /nápweed/ *n.* any of various plants of the genus *Centaurea*, having thistlelike purple flowers. [ME, orig. *knopweed* f. KNOP + WEED]

knar /naar/ *n.* a knot or protuberance in a tree trunk, root, etc. [ME *knarre*, rel. to MLG, M.Du., MHG *knorre* knobbed protuberance]

knave /nayv/ *n.* **1** a rogue; a scoundrel. **2** = JACK[1] *n.* 2. □□ **knav•er•y** *n.* (*pl.* **•ies**). **knav•ish** *adj.* **knav•ish•ly** *adv.* **knav•ish•ness** *n.* [OE *cnafa* boy, servant, f. WG]

knawel /náwəl/ *n.* any low-growing plant of the genus *Scleranthus.* [G *Knauel*]

knead /need/ *v.tr.* **1 a** work (a yeast mixture, clay, etc.) into dough, paste, etc., by pressing and folding. **b** make (bread, pottery, etc.) in this way. **2** blend or weld together (*kneaded them into a unified group*). **3** massage (muscles, etc.) as if kneading. □□ **knead•a•ble** *adj.* **knead•er** *n.* [OE *cnedan* f. Gmc]

knee /nee/ *n. & v.* **1 a** (often *attrib.*) the joint between the thigh and the lower leg in humans. **b** the corresponding joint in other animals. **c** the area around this. **d** the upper surface of the thigh of a sitting person; the lap (*held her on his knee*). **2** the part of a garment covering the knee. **3** anything resembling a knee in shape or position, esp. a piece of wood or iron bent at an angle, a sharp turn in a graph, etc. • *v.tr.* (**knees, kneed, knee•ing**) **1** touch or strike with the knee (*kneed him in the groin*). **2** *colloq.* cause (pants) to bulge at the knee. □ **bend** (or **bow**) **the knee** kneel, esp. in submission. **bring a person to his** (or **her**) **knees** reduce a person to submission. **on** (or **on one's**) **bended knee** (or **knees**) kneeling, esp. in supplication, submission, or worship. [OE *cnēo(w)*]

knee bend *n.* the action of bending the knee, esp. as a physical exercise in which the body is raised and lowered without the use of the hands.

knee breech•es *n.pl. archaic* short trousers worn by men and fastened at or just below the knee.

knee•cap /néekap/ *n. & v.* • *n.* **1** the convex bone in front of the knee joint. **2** a protective covering for the knee. • *v.tr.* (**•capped, •capping**) *colloq.* shoot (a person) in the knee or leg as a punishment, esp. for betraying a terrorist group. □□ **knee•cap•ping** *n.*

knee-deep *adj.* **1** (usu. foll. by *in*) **a** immersed up to the knees. **b** deeply involved. **2** so deep as to reach the knees.

knee-high *adj. & v.* • *adj.* so high as to reach the knees. • *n.* (usu. **knee-highs**) a nylon stocking with an elasticized top that reaches to a person's knee.

knee•hole /néehōl/ *n.* a space for the knees, esp. under a desk.

knee jerk *n.* a sudden involuntary kick caused by a blow on the tendon just below the knee.

knee-jerk *adj.* (of a response) automatic and unthinking (*a knee-jerk reaction*).

kneel /neel/ *v.intr.* (*past* and *past part.* **knelt** /nelt/ or **kneeled**) fall or rest on the knees or a knee. [OE *cnēowlian* (as KNEE)]

knee-length *adj.* reaching the knees.

kneel•er /néelər/ *n.* **1** a hassock or cushion used for kneeling, esp. in church. **2** a person who kneels.

knee-pan /néepan/ *n.* the kneecap.

knee-slap•per *n. colloq.* an uproariously funny joke.

knees-up *n. Brit. colloq.* a lively party or gathering.

knell /nel/ *n. & v.* • *n.* **1** the sound of a bell, esp. when rung solemnly for a death or funeral. **2** an announcement, event, etc., regarded as a solemn warning of disaster. • *v.* **1** *intr.* **a** (of a bell) ring solemnly, esp. for a death or funeral. **b** make a doleful or ominous sound. **2** *tr.* proclaim by or as by a knell (*knelled the death of all their hopes*). □ **ring the knell of** announce or herald the end of. [OE *cnyll, cnyllan*: perh. infl. by *bell*]

knelt *past* and *past part.* of KNEEL.

Knes•set /knéset/ *n.* the parliament of modern Israel. [Heb., lit. gathering]

knew *past* of KNOW.

knick•er•bock•er /níkərbokər/ *n.* **1** (in *pl.*) = KNICKERS 1. **2** (**Knickerbocker**) **a** a New Yorker. **b** a descendant of the original Dutch settlers in New York. [Diedrich *Knickerbocker*, pretended author of W. Irving's *History of New York* (1809)]

knick•ers /níkərz/ *n.pl.* **1** loose-fitting pants gathered at the knee or calf. **2** *Brit.* = PANTIES. **3** (as *int.*) *Brit. sl.* an expression of contempt. [abbr. of KNICKERBOCKER]

knick•knack /níknak/ *n.* **1** a useless and usu. worthless ornament; a trinket. **2** a small, dainty article of furniture, dress, etc. □□ **knick•knack•er•y** *n.* **knick•knack•ish** *adj.* [redupl. of *knack* in obs. sense 'trinket']

knife /nīf/ *n. & v.* • *n.* (*pl.* **knives** /nīvz/) **1 a** a metal blade used as a cutting tool with usu. one long, sharp edge fixed rigidly in a handle or hinged (cf. PENKNIFE). **b** a similar tool used as a weapon. **2** a cutting blade forming part of a machine. • *v.tr.* **1** cut or stab with a knife. **2** *sl.* bring about the defeat of (a person) by underhand means. □ **before you can say knife** *Brit. colloq.* very

knickers 1

quickly or suddenly. **get one's knife into** treat maliciously or vindictively; persecute. **that one could cut with a knife** *colloq.* (of an accent, atmosphere, etc.) very obvious, oppressive, etc. **under the knife** undergoing a surgical operation or operations. □□ **knife‑like** *adj.* **knif‑er** *n.* [OE *cnīf* f. ON *knífr* f. Gmc]

knife‑edge *n.* **1** the edge of a knife. **2** a position of extreme danger or uncertainty. **3** a steel wedge on which a pendulum, etc., oscillates. **4** = ARÊTE.

knife pleat *n.* a narrow flat pleat on a skirt, etc., usu. overlapping another.

knife‑point /nīfpoynt/ *n.* the point of a knife. □ **at knifepoint** threatened with a knife or an ultimatum, etc.

knife rest *n.* a metal or glass support for a knife at the table.

knife‑throwing *n.* a circus, etc., act in which knives are thrown at a target.

knight /nīt/ *n. & v.* ● *n.* **1** a man awarded a non-hereditary title (*Sir*) by a sovereign in recognition of merit or service. **2** *hist.* **a** a man, usu. noble, raised esp. by a sovereign to honorable military rank after service as a page and squire. **b** a military follower or attendant, esp. of a lady as her champion in a war or tournament. **3** a man devoted to the service of a woman, cause, etc. **4** *Chess* a piece usu. shaped like a horse's head. **5 a** *Rom.Hist.* a member of the class of *equites*, orig. the cavalry of the Roman army. **b** *Gk Hist.* a citizen of the second class in Athens. **6** (in full **knight of the shire**) *Brit. hist.* a gentleman representing a shire or county in parliament. ● *v.tr.* confer a knighthood on. □□ **knight‑hood** *n.* **knight‑like** *adj.* **knight‑ly** *adj. & adv. poet.* **knight‑li‑ness** *n.* [OE *cniht* boy, youth, hero f. WG]

knight‑age /nítij/ *n.* **1** knights collectively. **2** a list and account of knights.

knight bach‑e‑lor *n.* (*pl.* **knights bach‑e‑lor**) a knight not belonging to a special order.

knight‑er‑rant *n.* **1** a medieval knight wandering in search of chivalrous adventures. **2** a man of a chivalrous or quixotic nature. □□ **knight‑er‑rant‑ry** *n.*

knight in shin‑ing ar‑mor *n.* a chivalrous rescuer or helper, esp. of a woman.

knight of the road *n. Brit. colloq.* **1** a highwayman. **2** a commercial traveler. **3** a tramp. **4** a truck driver or taxi driver.

Knight Tem‑plar *n.* (*pl.* **Knights Tem‑plars** or **Knights Tem‑plar**) a member of a religious and military order for the protection of pilgrims to the Holy Land, suppressed in 1312.

knish /knish/ *n.* a dumpling of flaky dough filled with potato, meat, cheese, etc., and baked or fried. [Yiddish f. Russ.]

knit /nit/ *v. & n.* ● *v.* (**knit‑ting**; *past* and *past part.* **knit‑ted** or (esp. in senses 2–4) **knit**) **1** *tr.* (also *absol.*) **a** make (a garment, blanket, etc.) by interlocking loops of yarn with knitting needles. **b** make (a garment, etc.) with a knitting machine. **c** make (a plain stitch) in knitting (*knit one, purl one*). **2 a** *tr.* contract (the forehead) in vertical wrinkles. **b** *intr.* (of the forehead) contract; frown. **3** *tr. & intr.* (often foll. by *together*) make or become close or compact esp. by common interests, etc. (*a close-knit group*). **4** *intr.* (often foll. by *together*) (of parts of a broken bone) become joined; heal. ● *n.* knitted material or a knitted garment. □ **knit up** *Brit.* **1** make or repair by knitting. **2** conclude, finish, or end. □□ **knit‑ter** *n.*

WORD HISTORY knit

Old English *cnyttan*, of West Germanic origin; related to German dialect *knütten*, also to KNOT[1]. The original sense was 'tie in or with a knot', hence 'join, unite'; an obsolete Middle English sense 'knot string to make a net' gave rise to sense 1.

knit‑ting /níting/ *n.* **1** a garment, etc., in the process of being knitted. **2 a** the act of knitting. **b** an instance of this.

knit‑ting ma‑chine *n.* a machine used for mechanically knitting garments, etc.

knit‑ting nee‑dle *n.* a thin pointed rod of steel, wood, plastic, etc., used esp. in pairs for knitting.

knit‑wear /nítwair/ *n.* knitted garments.

knives *pl.* of KNIFE.

knob /nob/ *n. & v.* ● *n.* **1 a** a rounded protuberance, esp. at the end or on the surface of a thing. **b** a handle of a door, drawer, etc., shaped like a knob. **c** a knob-shaped attachment for pulling, turning, etc. (*press the knob under the desk*). **2** *Brit.* a small, usu. round, piece (of butter, coal, sugar, etc.). ● *v.* (**knobbed, knob‑bing**) **1** *tr.* provide with knobs. **2** *intr.* (usu. foll. by *out*) bulge. □ **with knobs on** *Brit. sl.* that and more (used as a retort to an insult, in emphatic agreement, etc.) (*and the same to you with knobs on*). □□ **knob‑by** *adj.* **knob‑like** *adj.* [ME f. MLG *knobbe* knot, knob, bud: cf. KNOP, NOB[2], NUB]

knob‑ble /nóbəl/ *n.* a small knob. □□ **knob‑bly** *adj.* [ME, dimin. of KNOB: cf. Du. & LG *knobbel*]

knob‑ker‑rie /nóbkeree/ *n.* a short stick with a knobbed head used as a weapon esp. by S. African tribes. [after Afrik. *knopkierie*]

knock /nok/ *v. & n.* ● *v.* **1 a** *tr.* strike (a hard surface) with an audible sharp blow (*knocked the table three times*). **b** *intr.* strike, esp. a door to gain admittance (*can you hear someone knocking?*; *knocked at the door*). **2** *tr.* make (a hole, a dent, etc.) by knocking (*knock a hole in the fence*). **3** *tr.* (usu. foll. by *in, out, off*, etc.) drive (a thing, a person, etc.) by striking (*knocked the ball into the hole*; *knocked those ideas out of his head*; *knocked her hand away*). **4** *tr. sl.* criticize. **5** *intr.* **a** (of a motor or other engine) make a thumping or rattling noise esp. as the result of a loose bearing. **b** (of a vehicle engine) emit a series of high-pitched explosive sounds caused by faulty combustion. **6** *tr. Brit. sl.* make a strong impression on; astonish. **7** *tr. Brit. coarse sl. offens.* = *knock off* 7. ● *n.* **1** an act of knocking. **2** a sharp rap, esp. at a door. **3** an audible sharp blow. **4** the sound of knocking in esp. a motor engine. □ **knock about** (or **around**) **1** strike repeatedly; treat roughly. **2** lead a wandering adventurous life; wander aimlessly. **3** be present without design or volition (*there's a cup knocking about somewhere*). **4** (usu. foll. by *with*) be associated socially (*knocks about with his brother*). **knock against** *Brit.* **1** collide with. **2** come across casually. **knock back 1** *sl.* eat or drink, esp. quickly. **2** *sl.* disconcert. **3** *Brit. colloq.* refuse; rebuff. **knock the bottom out of** see BOTTOM. **knock down 1** strike (esp. a person) to the ground with a blow. **2** demolish. **3** (usu. foll. by *to*) (at an auction) dispose of (an article) to a bidder by a knock with a hammer (*knocked the Picasso down to him for a million*). **4** *colloq.* lower the price of (an article). **5** take (machinery, furniture, etc.) to pieces for transportation. **6** *sl.* steal. **knock one's head against** come into collision with (unfavorable facts or conditions). **knock into a cocked hat** see COCK[1]. **knock into the middle of next week** *colloq.* send (a person) flying, esp. with a blow. **knock into shape** see SHAPE. **knock off 1** strike off with a blow. **2** *colloq.* **a** finish work (*knocked off at 5:30*). **b** finish (work) (*knocked off work early*). **3** *colloq.* dispatch (business). **4** *colloq.* rapidly produce (a work of art, verses, etc.). **5** (often foll. by *from*) deduct (a sum) from a price, bill, etc. **6** *sl.* steal from (*knocked off a liquor store*). **7** *Brit. coarse sl. offens.* have sexual intercourse with (a woman). **8** *sl.* kill. **knock on the head 1** stun or kill (a person) by a blow on the head. **2** *Brit. colloq.* put an end to (a scheme, etc.). **knock on** (or **knock**) **wood** knock something wooden with the knuckles to avert bad luck. **knock out 1** make (a person) unconscious by a blow on the head. **2** knock down (a boxer) for a count of 10, thereby winning the contest. **3** defeat, esp. in a knockout competition. **4** *sl.* astonish. **5** (*refl.*) *colloq.* exhaust (*knocked themselves out swimming*). **6** *colloq.* make or write (a plan, etc.) hastily. **7** empty (a tobacco pipe) by tapping. **knock sideways** *colloq.* disconcert; astonish. **knock spots off** esp. *Brit.* defeat easily. **knock together** put together or assemble hastily or roughly. **knock under** *Brit.* = *knuckle under*. **knock up 1** make or arrange hastily. **2** damage or mar. **3 a** become exhausted or ill. **b** exhaust or make ill. **4** *Brit.* arouse (a person) by a knock at the door. **5** *coarse sl.* make pregnant. **take a** (or **the**) **knock** esp. *Brit.* be hard hit financially or emotionally. [ME f. OE *cnocian*: prob. imit.]

knock‑a‑bout /nókəbowt/ *adj. & n.* ● *attrib.adj.* **1** (of comedy) boisterous; slapstick. **2** (of clothes) suitable for rough use. **3** *Austral.* of a farm or station handyman. ● *n.* **1** *Austral.* a farm or station handyman. **2** a knockabout performer or performance.

knock‑back *n. Brit. colloq.* a refusal; a rebuff.

knock‑down /nókdown/ *adj. & n.* ● *adj.* **1** (of a blow, misfortune, argument, etc.) overwhelming. **2** *Brit.* (of a price) very low. **3** (of a price at auction) reserve. **4** (of furniture, etc.) easily dismantled and reassembled. ● *n.* **1** a knockdown item. **2** *sl.* an introduction to a person.

knock‑er /nókər/ *n.* **1** a metal or wooden instrument hinged to a door for knocking to call attention. **2** a person or thing that knocks. **3** (in *pl.*) *coarse sl.* a woman's breasts. **4** *Brit.* a person who buys or sells door to door. □ **on the knocker** *Brit.* **1** (buying or selling) from door to door. **2** (obtained) on credit. **up to the knocker** *Brit. sl.* in good condition; to perfection.

knock‑er‑up *n. Brit. hist.* a person employed to rouse early workers by knocking at their doors or windows.

knock‑ing shop *n. Brit. sl.* a brothel.

knock‑knees *n.pl.* a condition in which the legs curve inward at the knee. □□ **knock‑kneed** *adj.*

knock‑on ef‑fect *n. Brit.* a secondary, indirect, or cumulative effect.

knock‑out /nókowt/ *n.* **1** the act of making unconscious by a blow. **2** *Boxing*, etc., a blow that knocks an opponent out. **3** a competition in which the loser in each round is eliminated (also *attrib.*: *a knockout round*). **4** *colloq.* an outstanding or irresistible person or thing.

knock‑out drops *n.pl.* a drug added to a drink to cause unconsciousness.

knock‑wurst /naákwərst/ *n.* a variety of thick, seasoned sausage. [Ger *knackwurst* f. *knacken* to crackle + *wurst* sausage]

knoll[1] /nōl/ *n.* a small hill or mound. [OE *cnoll* hilltop, rel. to MDu., MHG *knolle* clod, ON *knollr* hilltop]

knoll[2] /nōl/ *v. & n. archaic* ● *v.* **1** *tr. & intr.* = KNELL. **2** *tr.* summon by the sound of a bell. ● *n.* = KNELL. [ME, var. of KNELL: perh. imit.]

knop /nop/ *n.* **1** a knob, esp. ornamental. **2** an ornamental loop or tuft in yarn. **3** *archaic* a flower bud. [ME f. MLG, MDu. *knoppe*]

knot[1] /not/ *n. & v.* ● *n.* **1 a** an intertwining of a rope, string, tress of hair, etc., with another, itself, or something else to join or fasten together. **b** a set method of tying a knot (*a reef knot*). **c** a ribbon, etc., tied as an ornament and worn on a dress, etc. **d** a tangle in hair, knitting, etc. **2 a** a unit of a ship's or aircraft's speed equivalent to one nautical mile per hour (see NAUTICAL MILE). **b** a division marked by knots on a log line, as a measure of speed. **c** *colloq.* a nautical mile. **3** (usu. foll. by *of*) a group or cluster (*a small knot of journalists at the gate*). **4** something forming or maintaining a union; a bond or tie, esp. of wedlock. **5** a hard lump of tissue in an animal or human body. **6 a** a knob or protuberance in a stem, branch, or root. **b** a hard mass formed in a tree trunk at the intersection with a branch. **c** a round cross-grained piece in lumber where a branch has been cut through. **d** a node on the stem of a plant. **7** a difficulty; a problem. **8** a central point in a problem or the plot of a story, etc. ● *v.* (**knot·ted, knot·ting**) **1** *tr.* tie (a string, etc.) in a knot. **2** *tr.* entangle. **3** *tr.* esp. *Brit.* knit (the brows). **4** *tr.* unite closely or intricately (*knotted together in intrigue*). **5 a** *intr.* make knots for fringing. **b** *tr.* make (a fringe) with knots. □ **at a rate of knots** *Brit. colloq.* very fast. **get knotted!** *Brit. sl.* an expression of disbelief, annoyance, etc. **tie in knots** *colloq.* baffle or confuse completely. **tie the knot** get married. □□ **knot·less** *adj.* **knot·ter** *n.* **knot·ting** *n.* (esp. in sense 5 of *v.*). [OE *cnotta* f. WG]

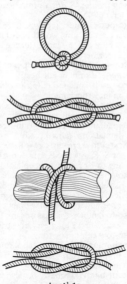

knot[1] 1a

knot[2] /not/ *n.* a small sandpiper, *Calidris canutus*. [ME: orig. unkn.]

knot gar·den *n.* an intricately designed formal garden, esp. of herbs.

knot·grass /nótgras/ *n.* **1** a common weed, *Polygonum aviculare*, with creeping stems and small pink flowers. **2** = POLYGONUM. Also called **knotweed**.

knot·hole /nóthōl/ *n.* a hole in a piece of lumber where a knot has fallen out.

knot·ty /nótee/ *adj.* (**knot·ti·er, knot·ti·est**) **1** full of knots. **2** hard to explain; puzzling (*a knotty problem*). □□ **knot·ti·ly** *adv.* **knot·ti·ness** *n.*

knot·weed /nótweed/ *n.* **1** = POLYGONUM. Also called **knotgrass**.

knot·work /nótwork/ *n.* ornamental work representing or consisting of intertwined cords.

knout /nowt/ *n. & v.* ● *n. hist.* a scourge used in imperial Russia, often causing death. ● *v.tr.* flog with a knout. [F f. Russ. *knut* f. Icel. *knútr*, rel. to KNOT[1]]

know /nō/ *v. & n.* ● *v.* (*past* **knew** /nōō, nyōō/; *past part.* **known** /nōn/) **1** *tr.* (often foll. by *that, how, what*, etc.) **a** have in the mind; have learned; be able to recall (*knows a lot about cars; knows what to do*). **b** (also *absol.*) be aware of (a fact) (*he knows I am waiting; I think she knows*). **c** have a good command of (a subject or language) (*knew German; knows his multiplication tables*). **2** *tr.* be acquainted or friendly with (a person or thing). **3** *tr.* **a** recognize; identify (*I knew him at once; I knew him to be an American*). **b** (foll. by *from* + *infin.*) be aware of (a person or thing) as being or doing what is specified (*knew them to be rogues*). **c** (foll. by *from*) be able to distinguish (one from another) (*did not know him from Adam*). **4** *tr.* be subject to (*her joy knew no bounds*). **5** *tr.* have personal experience of (fear, etc.). **6** *tr.* (as **known** *adj.*) **a** publicly acknowledged (*a known thief; a known fact*). **b** *Math.* (of a quantity, etc.) having a value that can be stated. **7** *intr.* have understanding or knowledge. **8** *tr. archaic* have sexual intercourse with. ● *n.* (in phr. **in the know**) *colloq.* well-informed; having special knowledge. **all one knows** (or **knows how**) **1** all one can (*did all she knew to stop it*). **2** *adv.* to the utmost of one's power (*tried all she knew*). **before one knows where one is** with baffling speed. **be not to know** I have no way of learning (*wasn't to know they'd arrive late*). **2** be not to be told (*she's not to know about the party*). **don't I know it!** *colloq.* an expression of rueful assent. **don't you know** *colloq.* or *joc.* an expression used for emphasis (*such a bore, don't you know*). **for all I know** so far as my knowledge extends. **have been known to** be known to have done (*they have been known to not turn up*). **I knew it!** I was sure that this would happen. **I know what** I have a new idea, suggestion, etc. **know about** have information about. **know best** be or claim to be better informed, etc., than others. **know better than** (foll. by *that*, or *to* + *infin.*) be wise, well-

informed, or well-mannered enough to avoid (specified behavior, etc.). **know by name 1** have heard the name of. **2** be able to give the name of. **know by sight** recognize the appearance (only) of. **know how** know the way to do something. **know of** be aware of; have heard of (*not that I know of*). **know one's own mind** be decisive; not vacillate. **know the ropes** (or **one's stuff**) be fully knowledgeable or experienced. **know a thing or two** be experienced or shrewd. **know what's what** have adequate knowledge of the world, life, etc. **know who's who** be aware of who or what each person is. **not know what hit one** be suddenly injured, killed, disconcerted, etc. **not want to know** refuse to take any notice of. **what do you know?** *colloq.* an expression of surprise. **you know** *colloq.* **1** an expression implying something generally known or known to the hearer (*you know, the store on the corner*). **2** an expression used as a gap-filler in conversation. **you know something** (or **what**)? I am going to tell you something. **you never know** nothing in the future is certain. □□ **know·a·ble** *adj.* **know·er** *n.* [OE (*ge*)*cnāwan*, rel. to CAN[1], KEN]

know-all *n.* esp. *Brit.* = KNOW-IT-ALL.

know-how *n.* **1** practical knowledge or technique; expertise. **2** natural skill or invention.

know·ing /nóing/ *n. & adj.* ● *n.* the state of being aware or informed of any thing. ● *adj.* **1** usu. *derog.* cunning; sly. **2** showing knowledge; shrewd. □ **there is no knowing** no one can tell. □□ **know·ing·ness** *n.*

know·ing·ly /nóinglee/ *adv.* **1** consciously; intentionally (*had never knowingly injured him*). **2** in a knowing manner (*smiled knowingly*).

know-it-all *n. colloq.* a person who acts as if he or she knows everything.

knowl·edge /nólij/ *n.* **1 a** (usu. foll. by *of*) awareness or familiarity gained by experience (of a person, fact, or thing) (*have no knowledge of their character*). **b** a person's range of information (*is not within his knowledge*). **c** specific information; facts or intelligence about something (*received knowledge of their imminent departure*). **2 a** (usu. foll. by *of*) a theoretical or practical understanding of a subject, language, etc. (*has a good knowledge of Greek*). **b** the sum of what is known (*every branch of knowledge*). **c** learning; scholarship. **3** *Philos.* true, justified belief; certain understanding, as opp. to opinion. **4** = CARNAL KNOWLEDGE. □ **come to one's knowledge** become known to one. **to my knowledge 1** so far as I know. **2** as I know for certain. [ME *knaulege*, with earlier *knawlechen* (v.) formed as KNOW + OE –*lēcan* f. *lāc* as in WEDLOCK]

ERUDITION, INFORMATION, LEARNING, PEDANTRY, SCHOLARSHIP, WISDOM. How much do you know? **Knowledge** applies to any body of facts gathered by study, observation, or experience, and to the ideas inferred from these facts (*an in-depth knowledge of particle physics*). **Information** may be no more than a collection of data or facts (*information about vacation resorts*) gathered through observation, reading, or hearsay, with no guarantee of their validity (*false information that led to the arrest*). **Scholarship** emphasizes academic *knowledge* or accomplishment (*a special award for scholarship*), while **learning** is *knowledge* gained not only by study in schools and universities but by individual research and investigation (*a man of education and learning*), which puts it on a somewhat higher plane. **Erudition** is on a higher plane still, implying bookish *knowledge* that is beyond the average person's comprehension (*to exhibit extraordinary erudition in a doctoral dissertation*). **Pedantry**, on the other hand, is a negative term for a slavish attention to obscure facts or details or an undue display of *learning* (*the pedantry of modern literary criticism*). You can have extensive *knowledge* of a subject and even exhibit *erudition*, however, without attaining **wisdom**, the superior judgment and understanding that is based on both *knowledge* and experience.

knowl·edge·a·ble /nólijəbəl/ *adj.* (also **knowl·edg·a·ble**) well-informed; intelligent. □□ **knowl·edge·a·bil·i·ty** *n.* **knowl·edge·a·ble·ness** *n.* **knowl·edge·a·bly** *adv.*

known *past part.* of KNOW.

know-noth·ing *n.* **1** an ignorant person. **2** an agnostic. **3** (**Know-Nothing**) member of the Know-Nothing party.

Know-Noth·ing par·ty *n. US hist.* a short-lived 19th-century political party which was antagonistic toward Roman Catholics and recent immigrants, and whose members preserved its secrecy by denying its existence.

knuck·le /núkəl/ *n. & v.* ● *n.* **1** the bone at a finger joint, esp. that adjoining the hand. **2 a** a projection of the carpal or tarsal joint of a quadruped. **b** a joint of meat consisting of this with the adjoining parts, esp. of bacon or pork. ● *v.tr.* strike, press, or rub with the knuckles. □ **go the knuckle** *Austral. sl.* fight, punch. **knuckle down** (often foll. by *to*) **1** apply oneself seriously (to a task, etc.). **2** give in; submit. **knuckle under** give in; submit. **rap on** (or **over**) **the knuckles** see RAP¹. □□ **knuck‧ly** adj.

WORD HISTORY knuckle

Middle English *knokel* (originally denoting the rounded shape when a joint such as the elbow or knee is bent), from Middle Low German, Middle Dutch *knökel*, diminutive of *knoke* 'bone'. In the mid 18th cent. the verb *knuckle (down)* expressed setting the knuckles down to shoot the taw in a game of marbles, hence the notion of applying oneself with concentration.

---

knuck‧le‧ball /núkəlbawl/ *n. Baseball* a pitch delivered with the ball held by the knuckles or fingernails such that the thrown ball has minimal spin and moves erratically. □□ **knuckleballer** *n.*

knuck‧le‧bone /núkəlbōn/ *n.* **1** bone forming a knuckle. **2** the bone of a sheep or other animal corresponding to or resembling a knuckle. **3** a knuckle of meat. **4** (in *pl.*) animal knucklebones used in the game of jacks. **5** (in *pl.*) the game of jacks.

knuck‧le‧dust‧er *n.* = BRASS KNUCKLES.

knuck‧le‧head /núkəlhed/ *n. colloq.* a slow-witted or stupid person.

knuck‧le sand‧wich *n. sl.* a punch in the mouth.

knur /nər/ *n.* **1** a hard excrescence on the trunk of a tree. **2** a hard concretion. [ME *knorre*, var. of KNAR]

knurl /nərl/ *n.* a small projecting knob, ridge, etc. □□ **knurled** /nərld/ *adj.* [KNUR]

KO *abbr.* **1** knockout. **2** kickoff.

ko‧a /kóə/ *n.* **1** a Hawaiian tree, *Acacia koa*, which produces dark red wood. **2** this wood. [Hawaiian]

ko‧a‧la /kō-áálə/ *n.* an Australian bearlike marsupial, *Phascolarctos cinereus*, having thick, gray fur and feeding on eucalyptus leaves. [Aboriginal *kūl(l)a*]
▶The fuller form *koala bear* is now considered incorrect.

ko‧an /kó-aan/ *n.* a riddle used in Zen Buddhism to demonstrate the inadequacy of logical reasoning. [Jap., = public matter (for thought)]

ko‧bold /kóbawld/ *n.* (in Germanic mythology): **1** a familiar spirit; a brownie. **2** an underground spirit in mines, etc. [G]

koala

Kö‧chel list‧ing /kórshəl, kókhəl/ *n. Mus.* (also **Kö‧chel num‧ber**) a number given to each of Mozart's compositions in the complete catalog of his works compiled by Köchel and his successors. [L. von *Köchel*, Austrian scientist d. 1877]

KO'd /kayōd, káyōd/ *adj.* knocked out. [abbr.]

Ko‧di‧ak /kódeeak/ *n.* (in full **Kodiak bear**) a large Alaskan brown bear, *Ursus arctos middendorffi*. [Kodiak Island, Alaska]

ko‧el /kóəl/ *n.* a dark-colored cuckoo, *Eudynamys scolopacea*. [Hindi *kōīl* f. Skr. *kokila*]

kohl /kōl/ *n.* a black powder, usu. antimony sulfide or lead sulfide, used as eye makeup esp. in Eastern countries. [Arab. *kuḥl*]

kohl‧ra‧bi /kōlraábee/ *n.* (pl. **kohl‧ra‧bies**) a variety of cabbage with an edible turniplike swollen stem. [G f. It. *cavoli rape* (pl.) f. med.L *caulorapa* (as COLE, RAPE²)]

koi‧ne /koynáy, kóynay/ *n.* **1** (usu. **Koine**) the common language of the Greeks from the close of the classical period to the Byzantine era. **2** a common language shared by various peoples; a lingua franca. [Gk *koinē* (*dialektos*) common (language)]

ko‧la var. of COLA.

ko‧lin‧sky /kōlínskee/ *n.* (pl. **‧skies**) **1** the Siberian mink, *Mustela sibirica*, having a brown coat in winter. **2** the fur of this. [Russ. *kolinskiĭ* f. *Kola* in NW Russia]

kol‧khoz /kolkáwz, kulkháws/ *n.* a collective farm in the former USSR. [Russ. f. *kollektivnoe khozyaĭstvo* collective farm]

kohlrabi

kom‧i‧tadj‧i (also **kom‧i‧taj‧i**) var. of COMITADJI.

Ko‧mo‧do drag‧on /kəmódō/ *n.* (also **Ko‧mo‧do liz‧ard**) a large monitor lizard, *Varanus komodoensis*, native to the E. Indies. [Komodo Island in Indonesia]

Kom‧so‧mol /kómsəmáwl/ *n. hist.* **1** an organization for Communist youth in the former Soviet Union. **2** a member of this. [Russ. f. *Kommunisticheskiĭ soyuz molodezhi* Communist League of Youth]

koo‧doo var. of KUDU.

kook /kook/ *n. & adj. sl.* • *n.* a crazy or eccentric person. • *adj.* crazy; eccentric. [20th c.: prob. f. CUCKOO]

kook‧a‧bur‧ra /kóokabərə, –bŭrə/ *n.* any Australian kingfisher of the genus *Dacelo*, esp. *D. novaeguineae*, which makes a harsh cry that sounds like laughter. Also called **laughing jackass**. [Aboriginal]

kook‧y /kóokee/ *adj.* (**kook‧i‧er, kook‧i‧est**) *sl.* crazy or eccentric. □□ **kook‧i‧ly** *adv.* **kook‧i‧ness** *n.*

kop /kop/ *n. S.Afr.* a prominent hill or peak. [Afrik. f. Du., = head: cf. COP²]

ko‧peck /kópek, kópék/ *n.* (also **ko‧pek, co‧peck**) a Russian coin and monetary unit worth one-hundredth of a ruble. [Russ. *Kopeĭka* dimin. of *kop'ĕ* lance (for the lance borne by the figure on the coin in former times)]

kop‧je /kópee/ *n.* (also **kop‧pie**) *S.Afr.* a small hill. [Afrik. *koppie*, Du. *kopje*, dimin. of *kop* head]

ko‧rad‧ji /kəraájee/ *n.* (pl. **ko‧rad‧jis**) *Austral.* an Aboriginal medicine man. [Aboriginal]

Ko‧ran /kərán, –raán, kaw–/ *n.* (also **Qu‧r'an** /kə–/) the Islamic sacred book, believed to be the word of God as dictated to Muhammad and written down in Arabic. □□ **Ko‧ran‧ic** *adj.* [Arab. *ḳur'ān* recitation f. *ḳara'a* read]

Ko‧re‧an /kəréeən, kaw–/ *n. & adj.* • *n.* **1** a native or national of N. or S. Korea in SE Asia. **2** the language of Korea. • *adj.* of or relating to Korea or its people or language.

ko‧sher /kóshər/ *adj. & n.* • *adj.* **1** (of food or premises in which food is sold, cooked, or eaten) fulfilling the requirements of Jewish law. **2** *colloq.* correct; genuine; legitimate. • *n.* kosher food. □ **keep kosher** adhere to kosher practices. [Heb. *kāšēr* proper]

ko‧to /kótō/ *n.* (pl. **‧tos** or same) a Japanese musical instrument with usu. 7 or 13 long esp. silk strings. [Jap.]

ko‧tow var. of KOWTOW.

kou‧miss /kóomis/ *n.* (also **ku‧miss** or **ku‧mis**) a fermented liquor prepared from mare's milk, used as a drink and medicine by Asian nomads. [Tartar *kumiz*]

kour‧bash /kóorbash/ *n.* (also **kur‧bash**) a whip, esp. of hippopotamus hide, used as an instrument of punishment in Turkey and Egypt. [Arab. *kurbāj* f. Turk. *kırbāç* whip]

ko‧whai /kó-wī/ *n.* any of several trees or shrubs of the genus *Sophora*, esp. *S. microphylla*, native to New Zealand, with pendant clusters of yellow flowers. [Maori]

kow‧tow /kowtów/ *n. & v.* (also **ko‧tow** /kōtów/) • *n. hist.* the Chinese custom of kneeling and touching the ground with the forehead in worship or submission. • *v.intr.* **1** *hist.* perform the kowtow. **2** (usu. foll. by *to*) act obsequiously. [Chin. *ketou* f. *ke* knock + *tou* head]

KP *n. Mil. colloq.* **1** enlisted person detailed to help the cooks. **2** kitchen duty. [abbr. of *kitchen police*]

k.p.h. *abbr.* kilometers per hour.

Kr *symb. Chem.* the element krypton.

kraal /kraal/ *n. S.Afr.* **1** a village of huts enclosed by a fence. **2** an enclosure for cattle or sheep. [Afrik. f. Port. *curral*, of Hottentot orig.]

kraft /kraft/ *n.* (in full **kraft paper**) a kind of strong smooth brown wrapping paper. [G f. Sw., = strength]

krait /krīt/ *n.* any venomous snake of the genus *Bungarus* of E. Asia. [Hindi *karait*]

kra‧ken /kraákən/ *n.* a large mythical sea monster said to appear off the coast of Norway. [Norw.]

krans /kraans/ *n. S.Afr.* a precipitous or overhanging wall of rocks. [Afrik. f. Du. *krans* coronet]

kraut /krowt/ *n.* **1** *colloq.* sauerkraut. **2** (also **Kraut**) *sl. offens.* a German. [shortening of SAUERKRAUT]

krem‧lin /krémlin/ *n.* **1** a citadel within a Russian city or town. **2** (**the Kremlin**) **a** the citadel in Moscow. **b** the Russian or former USSR government housed within it. [F, f. Russ. *Kreml'*, of Tartar orig.]

krieg‧spiel /kréegshpeel/ *n.* (also **Krieg‧spiel**) **1** a war game in which blocks representing armies, etc., are moved about on maps. **2** a form of chess with an umpire, in which each player has only limited information about the opponent's moves. [G f. *Krieg* war + *Spiel* game]

krill /kril/ *n.* tiny planktonic crustaceans found in the seas around the Antarctic and eaten by baleen whales. [Norw. *kril* tiny fish]

krim‧mer /krímər/ *n.* a gray or black fur obtained from the wool of young Crimean lambs. [G f. *Krim* Crimea]

kris /krees/ *n.* (also **crease, creese**) a Malay or Indonesian dagger with a wavy blade. [ult. f. Malay *k(i)rīs*]

Krish‧na‧ism /kríshnəizəm/ *n. Hinduism* the worship of Krishna as an incarnation of Vishnu.

kro‧mes‧ky /krəméskee/ *n.* (pl. **‧kies**) a croquette of ground meat or fish, rolled in bacon and fried. [app. f. Pol. *kromeczka* small slice]

kro‧na /krónə/ *n.* **1** (pl. **kro‧nor** /krónər, –nawr/) the chief monetary unit of Sweden. **2** (pl. **kro‧nur** /krónər/) the chief monetary unit of Iceland. [Sw. & Icel., = CROWN]

kro‧ne /krónə/ *n.* (pl. **kro‧ner** /krónər/) the chief monetary unit of Denmark and of Norway. [Da. & Norw., = CROWN]

Kroo var. of KRU.

Kru /kroō/ *n. & adj.* (also **Kroo**) • *n.* (pl. same) a member of a Black seafaring people on the coast of Liberia. • *adj.* of or concerning the Kru. [W. Afr.]

Kru‧ger‧rand /króogərand, –raant/ *n.* (also **kru‧ger‧rand**) a S. African gold coin depicting President Kruger. [S. J. P. *Kruger*, S. Afr. statesman d. 1904, + RAND¹]

krumm•horn /krúmhawrn/ *n.* (also **krum•horn, crum•horn**) a medieval wind instrument with a double reed and a curved end. [G f. *krumm* crooked + *Horn* HORN]

kryp•ton /krípton/ *n. Chem.* an inert gaseous element of the noble gas group, forming a small portion of the earth's atmosphere and used in fluorescent lamps, etc. ¶ Symb.: **Kr**. [Gk *krupton* hidden, neut. adj. f. *kruptō* hide]

KS *abbr.* Kansas (in official postal use).

Kshat•ri•ya /kshátreeə/ *n.* a member of the second of the four great Hindu castes, the military caste. [Skr. f. *kshatra* rule]

KT *abbr.* **1** Knight Templar. **2** (in the UK) Knight of the Order of the Thistle. **3** kiloton(s).

Kt. *abbr.* Knight.

kt. *abbr.* **1** karat(s). **2** kiloton(s). **3** knots.

Ku *symb. Chem.* the element kurchatovium.

ku•dos /kóodōz, –dōs, –dos, kyóo–/ *n. colloq.* glory; renown. [Gk]
▶Kudos, from Greek, is a singular noun meaning 'praise, honor.' However, because of its *-s* ending, it has come to be used as a plural noun meaning 'compliments, congratulations.' As a result, the (etymologically incorrect) singular form *kudo*, also meaning 'praise, honor,' has come into existence.

ku•du /kóodōo/ *n.* (also **koo•doo**) either of two African antelopes, *Tragelaphus strepsiceros* or *T. imberbis*, with white stripes and corkscrew-shaped ridged horns. [Xhosa-Kaffir *iqudu*]

kud•zu /kóodzōo, kúd–/ *n.* (in full **kudzu vine**) a quick-growing climbing plant, *Pueraria thunbergiana*, with reddish-purple flowers. [Jap. *kuzu*]

Ku•fic /kóofik, kyóo–/ *n. & adj.* (also **Cu•fic**) ●*n.* an early angular form of the Arabic alphabet found chiefly in decorative inscriptions. ●*adj.* of or in this type of script. [*Cufa*, a city S. of Baghdad in Iraq]

Ku Klux Klan /kóo kluks klán, kyóo–/ *n.* a secret society founded in the southern US, orig. formed after the Civil War and dedicated to white supremacy. □□ **Ku Klux Klans•man** *n. (pl.* •**men).** [perh. f. Gk *kuklos* circle + CLAN]

kuk•ri /kóokree/ *n. (pl.* **kuk•ris**) a curved knife broadening toward the point, used by Gurkhas. [Hindi *kukrī*]

ku•lak /kóolák, –laàk/ *n. hist.* a peasant working for personal profit in Soviet Russia. [Russ., = fist, tight-fisted person]

ku•lan /kóolən/ *n.* a wild ass of SW Asia, closely related to the kiang. [Tartar]

Kul•tur /kooltóor/ *n. esp. derog.* German civilization and culture (sometimes used to suggest elements of racism, authoritarianism, or militarism). [G f. L *cultura* or F *culture* (see CULTURE)]

Kul•tur•kampf /kooltóorkaampf/ *n. hist.* the conflict in 19th-c. Germany between the civil and ecclesiastical authorities, esp. as regards the control of schools. [G (as KULTUR, *Kampf* struggle)]

ku•ma•ra /kóomərə/ *n. NZ* a sweet potato. [Maori]

ku•miss var. of KOUMISS.

küm•mel /kíməl, kö–/ *n.* a sweet liqueur flavored with caraway and cumin seeds. [G (as CUMIN)]

kum•quat /kúmkwot/ *n.* (also **cum•quat**) **1** an orangelike fruit with a sweet rind and acid pulp, used in preserves. **2** any shrub or small tree of the genus *Fortunella* yielding this. [Cantonese var. of Chin. *kin kü* golden orange]

kung fu /kung fóo, koong/ *n.* the Chinese form of karate. [Chin. *gong-fu* f. *gong* merit + *fu* master]

kur•bash var. of KOURBASH.

kur•cha•tov•i•um /kórchətóveeəm/ *n. Chem.* = RUTHERFORDIUM. ¶ Symb.: **Ku**. [I. V. *Kurchatov*, Russ. physicist d. 1960]

Kurd /kərd/ *n.* a member of a mainly pastoral Aryan Islamic people living in Kurdistan (contiguous areas of Iraq, Iran, and Turkey). [Kurdish]

kur•dait•cha /kərdíchə/ *n. Austral.* **1** the tribal use of a bone in spells intended to cause sickness or death. **2** a man empowered to point the bone at a victim. [Aboriginal]

Kurd•ish /kórdish/ *adj. & n.* ●*adj.* of or relating to the Kurds or their language. ●*n.* the Iranian language of the Kurds.

kur•ra•jong /kórəjawng, –jong, kúr–/ *n.* (also **cur•ra•jong**) an Australian tree, *Brachychiton populneum*, which produces a tough bast fiber. [Aboriginal]

kur•ta /kórtə/ *n.* (also **khur•ta**) a loose shirt or tunic worn by esp. Hindu men and women. [Hind.]

kur•to•sis /kərtósis/ *n. Statistics* the sharpness of the peak of a frequency-distribution curve. [mod.L f. Gk *kurtōsis* bulging f. *kurtos* convex]

kV *abbr.* kilovolt(s).

kvass /kvaas/ *n.* a Russian fermented beverage, low in alcohol, made from rye flour or bread with malt. [Russ. *kvas*]

kvetch /kvech/ *n. & v. sl.* ●*n.* an objectionable person, esp. one who complains a great deal. ●*v.* complain; whine. □□ **kvetch•er** *n.*

kW *abbr.* kilowatt(s).

KWAC /kwak/ *n. Computing,* etc., keyword and context. [abbr.]

kwa•cha /kwaáchə/ *n.* the chief monetary unit of Zambia. [native word, = dawn]

kwash•i•or•kor /kwóshee-áwrkawr/ *n.* a form of malnutrition caused by a protein deficiency of diet, esp. in young children in the tropics. [native name in Ghana]

kWh *abbr.* kilowatt-hour(s).

KY *abbr.* Kentucky (in official postal use).

Ky. *abbr.* Kentucky.

ky•a•nite /kíənit/ *n.* a blue crystalline mineral of aluminum silicate. □□ **ky•a•nit•ic** /–nítik/ *adj.* [Gk *kuanos* dark blue]

ky•an•ize /kíəniz/ *v.tr.* treat (wood) with a solution of corrosive sublimate to prevent decay. [J. H. *Kyan,* Ir. inventor d. 1850]

ky•bosh var. of KIBOSH.

kyle /kil/ *n.* (in Scotland) a narrow channel between islands or between an island and the mainland. [Gael. *caol* strait]

ky•lie /kílee/ *n. W.Austral.* a boomerang. [Aboriginal]

ky•lin /keélin/ *n.* a mythical composite animal figured on Chinese and Japanese ceramics. [Chin. *qilin* f. *qi* male + *lin* female]

Ky•loe /kílō/ *n. Brit.* **1** an animal of a breed of small usu. black longhorned highland cattle. **2** this breed. [*Kyloe* in Northumberland]

ky•mo•graph /kíməgraf/ *n.* an instrument for recording variations in pressure, e.g., in sound waves or in blood within blood vessels. □□ **ky•mo•graph•ic** *adj.* [Gk *kuma* wave + –GRAPH]

ky•pho•sis /kifósis/ *n. Med.* excessive outward curvature of the spine, causing hunching of the back (opp. LORDOSIS). □□ **ky•phot•ic** /–fótik/ *adj.* [mod.L f. Gk *kuphōsis* f. *kuphos* bent]

Kyr•i•e /keéreeay/ (in full **Kyr•i•e e•le•i•son** /iláyizon, –son, eláy–/) *n.* **1 a** a short repeated invocation used in the RC and Greek Orthodox churches, esp. at the beginning of the Mass. **b** a response sometimes used in the Anglican communion service. **2** a musical setting of the Kyrie. [ME f. med.L f. Gk *Kurie eleēson* Lord, have mercy]

L

L¹ /el/ *n.* (also **l**) (*pl.* **Ls** or **L's**) **1** the twelfth letter of the alphabet. **2** (as a Roman numeral) 50. **3** a thing shaped like an L, esp. a joint connecting two pipes at right angles.

L² *abbr.* (also **L.**) **1** Lake. **2** Latin. **3** Liberal. **4** large. **5** *Biol.* Linnaeus. **6** lire.

l *abbr.* (also **l.**) **1** left. **2** line. **3** liter(s). **4** length. **5** *archaic* pound(s) (money).

£ *abbr.* (preceding a numeral) pound or pounds (of money). [L *libra*]

LA *abbr.* **1** Los Angeles. **2** Louisiana (in official postal use). **3** legislative assistant.

La *symb. Chem.* the element lanthanum.

La. *abbr.* Louisiana.

la /laa/ *n. Mus.* **1** (in tonic sol-fa) the sixth note of a major scale. **2** the note A in the fixed-do system. [ME f. L *labii*: see GAMUT]

laa·ger /láagǝr/ *n. & v.* • *n.* **1** esp. *S.Afr.* a camp or encampment, esp. formed by a circle of wagons. **2** *Mil.* a park for armored vehicles. • *v.* **1** *tr.* **a** form (vehicles) into a laager. **b** encamp (people) in a laager. **2** *intr.* encamp. [Afrik. f. Du. *leger*: see LEAGUER²]

Lab. *abbr.* **1** *Brit.* Labour Party. **2** Labrador.

lab /lab/ *n. colloq.* a laboratory. [abbr.]

lab·a·rum /lábǝrǝm/ *n.* **1** a symbolic banner. **2** Constantine the Great's imperial standard, with Christian symbols added to Roman military symbols. [LL: orig. unkn.]

lab·da·num /lábdǝnǝm/ *n.* (also **lad·a·num** /ládǝnǝm/) a gum resin from plants of the genus *Cistus*, used in perfumery, etc. [L f. Gk *ladanon* f. *lēdon* mastic]

lab·e·fac·tion /lábifákshǝn/ *n. literary* a shaking, weakening, or downfall. [L *labefacere* weaken f. *labi* fall + *facere* make]

la·bel /láybǝl/ *n. & v.* • *n.* **1** a usu. small piece of paper, card, linen, metal, etc., for attaching to an object and giving its name, information about it, instructions for use, etc. **2** esp. *derog.* a short classifying phrase or name applied to a person, a work of art, etc. **3 a** a small fabric label sewn into a garment bearing the maker's name. **b** the logo, title, or trademark of esp. a fashion or recording company (*brought it out under their own label*). **c** the piece of paper in the center of a phonograph record describing its contents, etc. **4** an adhesive stamp on a parcel, etc. **5** a word placed before, after, or in the course of a dictionary definition, etc., to specify its subject, register, nationality, etc. **6** *Archit.* a dripstone. **7** *Heraldry* the mark of an eldest son, consisting of a superimposed horizontal bar with usu. three downward projections. • *v.tr.* (**la·beled, la·bel·ing**; esp. *Brit.* **la·belled, la·bel·ling**) **1** attach a label to. **2** (usu. foll. by *as*) assign to a category (*labeled them as irresponsible*). **3 a** replace (an atom) by an atom of a usu. radioactive isotope as a means of identification. **b** replace an atom in (a molecule) or atoms in the molecules of (a substance). **4** (as **labeled** *adj.*) made identifiable by the replacement of atoms. □□ **la·bel·er** *n.* [ME f. OF, = ribbon, prob. f. Gmc (as LAP¹)]

la·bi·a *pl.* of LABIUM.

la·bi·al /láybeeǝl/ *adj. & n.* • *adj.* **1 a** of the lips. **b** *Zool.* of, like, or serving as a lip, a liplike part, or a labium. **2** *Dentistry* designating the surface of a tooth adjacent to the lips. **3** *Phonet.* (of a sound) requiring partial or complete closure of the lips (e.g., *p*, *b*, *f*, *v*, *m*, *w*; and vowels in which lips are rounded, e.g., *oo* in moon). • *n. Phonet.* a labial sound. □□ **la·bi·al·ism** *n.* **la·bi·al·ize** *v.tr.* **la·bi·al·ly** *adv.* [med.L *labialis* f. L *labia* lips]

la·bi·a ma·jo·ra /mǝjáwrǝ/ *n.pl. Anat.* the larger outer folds of the vulva.

la·bi·a mi·no·ra /mináwrǝ/ *n.pl. Anat.* the smaller inner folds of the vulva.

la·bi·ate /láybeeǝt, -ayt/ *n. & adj.* • *n.* any plant of the family Labiatae, including mint and rosemary, having square stems and a corolla or calyx divided into two parts suggesting lips. • *adj.* **1** *Bot.* of or relating to the Labiatae. **2** *Bot. & Zool.* like a lip or labium. [mod.L *labiatus* (as LABIUM)]

la·bile /láybǐl, -bǐl/ *adj. Chem.* (of a compound) unstable; liable to displacement or change, esp. if an atom or group is easily replaced by other atoms or groups. □□ **la·bil·i·ty** /lǝbílitee, lay-/ *n.* [ME f. LL *labilis* f. *labi* to fall]

labio- /láybeeō/ *comb. form* of the lips. [as LABIUM]

la·bi·o·den·tal /láybeeōdént'l/ *adj.* (of a sound) made with the lips and teeth, e.g., *f* and *v*.

la·bi·o·ve·lar /láybeeōvéelǝr/ *adj.* (of a sound) made with the lips and soft palate, e.g., *w*.

la·bi·um /láybeeǝm/ *n.* (*pl.* **la·bi·a** /–beeǝ/) **1** (usu. in *pl.*) *Anat.* each of the two pairs of skin folds that enclose the vulva. **2** the lower lip in the mouthparts of an insect or crustacean. **3** a lip, esp. the lower one of a labiate plant's corolla. [L, = lip]

la·bor /láybǝr/ *n. & v.* (*Brit.* **la·bour**) • *n.* **1 a** physical or mental work; exertion; toil. **b** such work considered as supplying the needs of a community. **2 a** workers, esp. manual, considered as a class or political force (*a dispute between capital and labor*). **b** (in the UK) (**Labour**) the Labour Party. **3** the process of childbirth, esp. the period from the start of uterine contractions to delivery (*has been in labor for three hours*). **4** a particular task, esp. of a difficult nature. • *v.* **1** *intr.* work hard; exert oneself. **2** *intr.* (usu. foll. by *for*, or *to* + infin.) strive for a purpose (*labored to fulfill his promise*). **3** *tr.* **a** treat at excessive length; elaborate needlessly (*I will not labor the point*). **b** (as **labored** *adj.*) done with great effort; not spontaneous or fluent. **4** *intr.* (often foll. by *under*) suffer under (a disadvantage or delusion) (*labored under universal disapproval*). **5** *intr.* proceed with trouble or difficulty (*labored slowly up the hill*). **6** *intr.* (of a ship) roll or pitch heavily. **7** *tr. archaic* or *poet.* till (the ground). □ **labor in vain** make a fruitless effort. **labor of Hercules** a task needing enormous strength or effort. **labor of love** a task done for pleasure, not reward. [ME f. OF *labo(u)r*, *laborer* f. L *labor*, *-oris*, *laborare*]

SYNONYM TIP **labor**

DRUDGERY, GRIND, TOIL, TRAVAIL, WORK. Most people have to **work** for a living, meaning that they have to exert themselves mentally or physically in return for a paycheck. But *work* is not always performed by humans (*a machine that works like a charm*). **Labor** is not only human but usually physical *work* (*the labor required to build a stone wall*), although it can also apply to intellectual *work* of unusual difficulty (*the labor involved in writing a symphony*). Anyone who has been forced to perform **drudgery** knows that it is the most unpleasant, uninspiring, and monotonous kind of *labor* (*a forklift that eliminates the drudgery of stacking boxes; the drudgery of compiling a phone book*). **Grind** is even more intense and unrelenting than *drudgery*, emphasizing *work* that is performed under pressure in a dehumanizing way (*the daily grind of classroom teaching*). **Toil** suggests *labor* that is prolonged and very tiring (*farmers who toil endlessly in the fields*), but not necessarily physical (*mothers who toil to teach their children manners*). Those who **travail** endure pain, anguish, or suffering (*his hours of travail ended in heartbreak*); like *labor*, it is often associated with childbirth.

---

lab·o·ra·to·ry /lábrǝtáwree/ *n.* (*pl.* **·ries**) a room or building fitted out for scientific experiments, research, teaching, or the manufacture of drugs and chemicals. [med.L *laboratorium* f. L *laborare* LABOR]

SPELLING TIP **laboratory**

Remember the correct spelling of *laboratory* with the mnemonic: "People *labor* in a *laboratory*."

---

la·bor camp *n.* a prison camp enforcing a regime of hard labor.

La·bor Day *n.* a public holiday held in honor of working people, on the first Monday in September (or in some other countries on May 1).

la·bor·er /láybǝrǝr/ *n.* **1** a person doing unskilled, usu. manual, work for wages. **2** a person who labors. [ME f. OF *laboureur* (as LABOR)]

la·bor force *n.* all the members of a particular organization or population who are able to work, viewed collectively.

la·bor-in·ten·sive *adj.* (of a form of work) needing a large workforce or a large amount of work in relation to output (*the labor-intensive task of tagging each item in the store*).

la·bo·ri·ous /lǝbáwreeǝs/ *adj.* **1** needing hard work or toil (*a laborious task*). **2** (esp. of literary style) showing signs of toil; pedestrian; not fluent. □□ **la·bo·ri·ous·ly** *adv.* **la·bo·ri·ous·ness** *n.* [ME f. OF *laborieus* f. L *laboriosus* (as LABOR)]

la·bor mar·ket *n.* the supply of available workers with reference to the demand for them.

la·bor-sav·ing /láybǝrsáyving/ *adj.* (of an appliance, etc.) designed to reduce or eliminate work.

la·bor un·ion *n.* an organized association of workers, often in a trade or profession, formed to protect and further their rights and interests.

la·bour, etc. *Brit.* var. of LABOR, etc.

La·bour·ite /láybərīt/ n. (in the UK) a member or follower of the Labour Party.

La·bour Par·ty n. **1** a British political party formed to represent the interests of ordinary working people. **2** any similar political party in other countries.

lab·ra pl. of LABRUM.

Lab·ra·dor /lábrədawr/ n. (in full **Labrador retriever**) **1** a retriever of a breed with a black or golden coat often used as a gun dog or as a guide for a blind person. **2** this breed. [*Labrador* in Canada]

la·bret /láybrit/ n. a piece of shell, bone, etc., inserted in the lip as an ornament. [LABRUM]

la·brum /láybrəm/ n. (pl. **lab·ra** /-brə/) the upper lip in the mouthparts of an insect. [L, = lip: rel. to LABIUM]

la·bur·num /ləbórnəm/ n. any small tree of the genus *Laburnum* with racemes of golden flowers yielding poisonous seeds. Also called **golden chain**. [L]

lab·y·rinth /lábərinth/ n. **1** a complicated irregular network of passages or paths, etc.; a maze. **2** an intricate or tangled arrangement. **3** *Anat.* the complex arrangement of bony and membranous canals and chambers of the inner ear which constitute the organs of hearing and balance. □□ **lab·y·rin·thi·an** /-ríntheeən/ adj. **lab·y·rin·thine** /-rínthin, -thīn/ adj. [F *labyrinthe* or L *labyrinthus* f. Gk *laburinthos*]

labyrinth

lab·y·rinth fish n. a freshwater fish with poorly developed gills and a labyrinthine accessory breathing organ, naive to Africa and Asia.

LAC abbr. leading aircraftsman.

lac[1] /lak/ n. a resinous substance secreted as a protective covering by an Asian insect, and used to make varnish and shellac. [ult. f. Hind. *lākh* f. Prakrit *lakkha* f. Skr. *lākṣā*]

lac[2] var. of LAKH.

lac·co·lith /lákəlith/ n. *Geol.* a lens-shaped intrusion of igneous rock which thrusts the overlying strata into a dome. [Gk *lakkos* reservoir + –LITH]

lace /lays/ n. & v. • n. **1** a fine open fabric, esp. of cotton or silk, made by weaving thread in patterns and used esp. to trim blouses, underwear, etc. **2** a cord or leather strip passed through eyelets or hooks on opposite sides of a shoe, corset, etc., pulled tight and fastened. **3** braid used for trimming esp. dress uniform (*gold lace*). • v. **1** tr. (usu. foll. by up) a fasten or tighten (a shoe, corset, etc.) with a lace or laces. **b** compress the waist of (a person) with a laced corset. **2** tr. flavor or fortify (coffee, beer, etc.) with a dash of liquor. **3** tr. (usu. foll. by with) a streak with color (*cheek laced with blood*). **b** interlace or embroider (fabric) with thread, etc. **4** tr. & (foll. by into) intr. colloq. lash; beat; defeat. **5** tr. (often foll. by through) pass (a shoelace, etc.) through. **6** tr. trim with lace. [ME f. OF *laz*, *las*, *lacier* ult. f. L *laqueus* noose]

lace·mak·er /láysmaykər/ n. a person who makes lace, esp. professionally. □□ **lace·mak·ing** n.

lace pil·low n. a cushion placed on the lap to provide support in lacemaking.

lac·er·ate /lásərayt/ v.tr. **1** mangle or tear (esp. flesh or tissue). **2** distress or cause pain to (the feelings, the heart, etc.). □□ **lac·er·a·ble** adj. **lac·er·a·tion** /-ráyshən/ n. [L *lacerare* f. *lacer* torn]

lac·er·til·i·an /lásərtíleeən/ n. & adj. (also **la·cer·tian** /ləsórshən/, **lac·er·tine** /lásərtīn/) • n. any reptile of the suborder Lacertilia, including lizards. • adj. of or relating to the Lacertilia; lizardlike; saurian. [L *lacerta* lizard]

lace-up adj. & n. • adj. (of a shoe or garment) fastened with laces. • n. a shoe or boot that is fastened with laces.

lace·wing /láyswing/ n. a slender delicate insect of the order Neuroptera, with large clear membranous wings.

lace·wood /láyswʊʊd/ n. the wood of the plane tree.

lach·es /láchiz/ n. *Law* delay in performing a legal duty, asserting a right, claiming a privilege, etc. [ME f. AF *laches(e)*, OF *laschesse* f. *lasche* ult. f. L *laxus* loose]

lach·ry·ma Chris·ti /lákrimə krístee/ n. any of various wines from the slopes of Mt. Vesuvius. [L, = Christ's tear]

lach·ry·mal /lákriməl/ adj. & n. (also **lac·ri·mal**) • adj. **1** literary of or for tears. **2** (usu. as **lacrimal**) *Anat.* concerned in the secretion of tears (*lacrimal canal*; *lacrimal duct*). • n. **1** = *lachrymae vase*. **2** (in pl.) (usu. as **lacrimals**) the lacrimal organs. □ **lachrymal vase** hist. a vial holding the tears of mourners at a funeral. [ME f. med.L *lachrymalis* f. L *lacrima* tear]

lach·ry·ma·tion /lákrimáyshən/ n. (also **lac·ri·ma·tion**) formal the flow of tears. [L *lacrimatio* f. *lacrimare* weep (as LACHRYMAL)]

lach·ry·ma·tor /lákrimaytər/ n. an agent irritating the eyes, causing tears.

lach·ry·ma·to·ry /lákrimətəwree/ adj. & n. • adj. formal of or causing tears. • n. (pl. **·ries**) a name applied to vials of a kind found in ancient Roman tombs and thought to be lachrymal vases.

lach·ry·mose /lákrimōs/ adj. formal given to weeping; tearful. □□ **lach·ry·mose·ly** adv. [L *lacrimosus* f. *lacrima* tear]

lac·ing /láysing/ n. **1** lace trimming, esp. on a uniform. **2** a laced fastening on a shoe or corsets. **3** colloq. a beating. **4** a dash of spirits in a beverage.

lac·ing course n. a strengthening course of bricks built into an arch or wall.

la·cin·i·ate /ləsíneeət, –neeayt/ adj. (also **la·cin·i·at·ed** /-aytid/) *Bot.* & *Zool.* divided into deep narrow irregular segments; fringed. □□ **la·cin·i·a·tion** /-neeáyshən/ n. [L *lacinia* flap of a garment]

lac in·sect n. an Asian scale insect, *Laccifer lacca*, living in trees.

lack /lak/ n. & v. • n. (usu. foll. by of) an absence, want, or deficiency (*a lack of talent; felt the lack of warmth*). • v.tr. be without or deficient in (*lacks courage*). □ **for lack of** owing to the absence of (*went hungry for lack of money*). **lack for** lack. [ME *lac*, *lacen*, corresp. to MDu., MLG *lak* deficiency, MDu. *laken* to lack]

SYNONYM TIP lack

ABSENCE, DEARTH, PRIVATION, SHORTAGE, WANT. To suffer from a **lack** of food means to be partially or totally without it; to be in **want** of food also implies either a partial or complete lack, but with an emphasis on the essential or desirable nature of what is *lacking*; for example, you may experience a complete *lack* of pain following surgery, but you would be in *want* of medication if pain were suddenly to occur. **Absence**, on the other hand, refers to the complete non-existence of something or someone. A *lack* of dairy products in your diet implies that you're not getting enough; an *absence* of dairy products implies that you're not getting any at all. If the scarcity or *lack* of something makes it costly, or if something is in distressingly low supply, the correct word is **dearth** (*a dearth of water in the desert, a dearth of nylon stockings during the war*). A **shortage** of something is a partial insufficiency of an established, required, or accustomed amount (*a shortage of fresh oranges after the late-season frost*), while **privation** is the negative state or absence of a corresponding positive (*they suffered from hunger, cold, and other privations*).

---

lack·a·dai·si·cal /lákədáyzikəl/ adj. **1** unenthusiastic; listless; idle. **2** feebly sentimental and affected. □□ **lack·a·dai·si·cal·ly** adv. **lack·a·dai·si·cal·ness** n. [archaic *lackaday*, –*daisy* (int.): see ALACK]

lack·er var. of LACQUER.

lack·ey /lákee/ n. & v. (also **lac·quey**) • n. (pl. **·eys**) **1** derog. **a** a servile political follower. **b** an obsequious parasitical person. **2** a **a** (usu. liveried) footman or manservant. **b** a servant. • v.tr. (**·eys**, **·eyed**) archaic behave servilely to; dance attendance on. [F *laquais* f. Cat. *alacay* = Sp. ALCALDE]

lack·ing /láking/ adj. **1** absent or deficient (*money was lacking; is lacking in determination*). **2** colloq. deficient in intellect; mentally subnormal.

lack·land /láklənd/ n. & adj. • n. **1** a person having no land. **2** (**Lackland**) a nickname for King John of England. • adj. having no land.

lack·lus·ter /láklustər/ adj. **1** lacking in vitality, force, or conviction. **2** (of the eye) dull.

La·co·ni·an /ləkóneeən/ n. & adj. • n. an inhabitant or the dialect of ancient Laconia. • adj. of the Laconian dialect or people; Spartan. [L *Laconia* Sparta f. Gk *Lakōn* Spartan]

la·con·ic /ləkónik/ adj. **1** (of a style of speech or writing) brief; concise; terse. **2** (of a person) laconic in speech, etc. □□ **la·con·i·cal·ly** adv. **la·con·i·cism** /-sizəm/ n. [L f. Gk *Lakōnikos* f. *Lakōn* Spartan, the Spartans being known for their terse speech]

lac·o·nism /lákənizəm/ n. **1** brevity of speech. **2** a short pithy saying. [Gk *lakōnismos* f. *lakōnizō* behave like a Spartan: see LACONIC]

lac·quer /lákər/ n. & v. (also **lack·er**) • n. **1** a sometimes colored liquid made of shellac dissolved in alcohol, or of synthetic substances, that dries to form a hard protective coating for wood, brass, etc. **2** Brit. = HAIR SPRAY. **3** the sap of the lacquer tree used to varnish wood, etc. • v.tr. coat with lacquer. □□ **lac·quer·er** n. [obs. F *lacre* sealing wax, f. unexpl. var. of Port. *laca* LAC[1]]

lac·quer tree n. an E. Asian tree, *Rhus vernici-flua*, the sap of which is used as a hard-wearing varnish for wood.

lac·quey var. of LACKEY.

lac·ri·mal var. of LACHRYMAL.

lac·ri·ma·tion var. of LACHRYMATION.

la·crosse /ləkráws, –krós/ n. a game like hockey, but with a ball driven by, caught, and carried in a crosse. [F f. *la* the + CROSSE]

lac·tase /láktays/ n. *Biochem.* any of a group of enzymes that catalyze the hydrolysis of lactose to glucose and galactose. [F f. *lactose* LACTOSE]

lac·tate[1] /láktayt/ v.intr. (of mammals) secrete milk. [as LACTATION]

lacrosse stick

lac·tate² /láktayt/ *n. Chem.* any salt or ester of lactic acid.

lac·ta·tion /laktáyshən/ *n.* **1** the secretion of milk by the mammary glands. **2** the suckling of young. [L *lactare* suckle f. *lac lactis* milk]

lac·te·al /lákteeəl/ *adj. & n.* ●*n.* **1** of milk. **2** conveying chyle or other milky fluid. ●*n.* (in *pl.*) the lymphatic vessels of the small intestine which absorb digested fats. [L *lacteus* f. *lac lactis* milk]

lac·tes·cence /laktésəns/ *n.* **1** a milky form or appearance. **2** a milky juice. [L *lactescere* f. *lactēre* be milky (as LACTIC)]

lac·tes·cent /laktésənt/ *adj.* **1** milky. **2** yielding a milky juice.

lac·tic /láktik/ *adj. Chem.* of, relating to, or obtained from milk.

lac·tic ac·id *n.* a clear, odorless, syrupy carboxylic acid formed in sour milk, and produced in the muscle tissues during strenuous exercise. [L *lac lactis* milk]

lac·tif·er·ous /laktífərəs/ *adj.* yielding milk or milky fluid. [LL *lactifer* (as LACTIC)]

lacto- /láktō/ *comb. form* milk. [L *lac lactis* milk]

lac·to·ba·cil·lus /láktōbəsíləs/ *n.* (*pl.* **·bacilli** /-lī/) *Biol.* any grampositive, rod-shaped bacterium of the genus *Lactobacillus*, producing lactic acid from the fermentation of carbohydrates.

lac·tom·e·ter /laktómitər/ *n.* an instrument for testing the density of milk.

lac·tone /láktōn/ *n. Chem.* any of a class of cyclic esters formed by the elimination of water from a hydroxy-carboxylic acid. [G *Lacton*]

lac·to·pro·tein /láktōprṓteen/ *n.* the albuminous constituent of milk.

lac·tose /láktōs/ *n. Chem.* a sugar that occurs in milk, and is less sweet than sucrose. [as LACTO-]

la·cu·na /ləkyōonə/ *n.* (*pl.* **la·cu·nae** /-nee/ or **la·cu·nas**) **1** a hiatus, blank, or gap. **2** a missing portion or empty page, esp. in an ancient manuscript, book, etc. **3** *Anat.* a cavity or depression, esp. in bone. □□ **la·cu·nal** *adj.* **la·cu·nar** *adj.* **la·cu·nar·y** /lákyōonéree/, ləkyōonəree/ *adj.* **la·cu·nose** *adj.* [L, = pool, f. *lacus* LAKE¹]

la·cus·trine /ləkústrin/ *adj. formal* or *Biol.* **1** of or relating to lakes. **2** living or growing in or beside a lake. [L *lacus* LAKE¹, after *palustris* marshy]

LACW *abbr.* leading aircraftswoman.

lac·y /láysee/ *adj.* (**lac·i·er**, **lac·i·est**) of or resembling lace fabric. □□ **lac·i·ly** *adv.* **lac·i·ness** *n.*

lad /lad/ *n.* **1 a** a boy or youth. **b** a young son. **2** (esp. in *pl.*) *Brit. colloq.* a man; a fellow, esp. a workmate, drinking companion, etc. (*he's one of the lads*). **3** *Brit. colloq.* a high-spirited fellow; a rogue (*he's a bit of a lad*). **4** *Brit.* a stableman (regardless of age). [ME *ladde*, of unkn. orig.]

lad·a·num var. of LABDANUM.

lad·der /ládər/ *n. & v.* ●*n.* **1** a set of horizontal bars of wood or metal fixed between two uprights and used for climbing up or down. **2** *Brit.* a run in a stocking or sheer hose. **3 a** a hierarchical structure. **b** such a structure as a means of advancement, promotion, etc. ●*v. Brit.* **1** *intr.* (of a stocking, etc.) develop a ladder. **2** *tr.* cause a ladder in (a stocking, etc.). [OE *hlǣd(d)er*, ult. f. Gmc: cf. LEAN¹]

lad·der-back *n.* an upright chair with a back resembling a ladder.

lad·der stitch *n.* an embroidery stitch consisting of transverse bars.

lad·der tour·na·ment *n.* a sporting contest in which participants are listed in ranking order and can move up by defeating the contestant above.

lad·die /ládee/ *n. colloq.* a young boy or lad.

lade /layd/ *v.* (*past part.* **lad·en** /láyd'n/) **1** *tr.* **a** put cargo on board (a ship). **b** ship (goods) as cargo. **2** *tr.* (of a ship) take on cargo. **3** *tr.* (as **laden** *adj.*) (usu. foll. by *with*) **a** (of a vehicle, donkey, person, tree, table, etc.) heavily loaded. **b** (of the conscience, spirit, etc.) painfully burdened with sin, sorrow, etc. [OE *hladan*]

la-di-da /láadeedáa/ *adj. & n. colloq.* (also **la-de-da**) ●*adj.* pretentious or snobbish, esp. in manner or speech. ●*n.* **1** a la-di-da person. **2** - la-di-da speech or manners. [imit. of an affected manner of speech]

la·dies *pl.* of LADY.

la·dies' man *n.* (also **la·dy's man**) a man who enjoys spending time and flirting with women.

la·dies' night *n.* **1** a function at a men's club, etc., to which women are invited. **2** an evening concert, sports event, session at a nightclub, etc., at which women are admitted free or for a reduced rate, etc.

la·dies' room *n.* a women's restroom in a hotel, office, etc.

la·dy's tress·es *n.* a white-flowered orchid of the genus *Spiranthes*.

La·din /lədéen/ *n.* the Rhaeto-Romanic dialect of the Engadine Valley in Switzerland. [Romansh, f. L *latinus* LATIN]

lad·ing /láyding/ *n.* **1** a cargo. **2** the act or process of lading.

La·di·no / lədéenō/ *n.* (*pl.* **·nos**) **1** the Spanish dialect of the Sephardic Jews. **2** a mestizo or Spanish-speaking white person in Central America. [Sp., orig. = Latin, f. L (as LADIN)]

la·dle /láyd'l/ *n. & v.* ●*n.* **1** a large, long-handled spoon with a cup-shaped bowl used for serving esp. soups and gravy. **2** a vessel for transporting molten metal in a foundry. ●*v.tr.* (often foll. by *out*) transfer (liquid) from one receptacle to another. □ **ladle out** distribute, esp. lavishly. □□ **la·dle·ful** *n.* (*pl.* **·fuls**). **la·dler** *n.* [OE *hlædel* f. *hladan* LADE]

la·dy /láydee/ *n.* (*pl.* **·dies**) **1 a** a woman regarded as being of superior social status or as having the refined manners associated with

this (cf. GENTLEMAN). **b** (**Lady**) a title used by peeresses, female relatives of peers, the wives and widows of knights, etc. **2** (often *attrib.*) a woman; a female person or animal (*ask that lady over there*; *lady butcher*; *lady dog*). **3** *colloq.* **a** a wife. **b** a man's girlfriend. **4** a ruling woman (*lady of the house*; *lady of the manor*). **5** (in *pl.* as a form of address) a female audience or the female part of an audience. **6** *hist.* a woman to whom a man, esp. a knight, is chivalrously devoted; a mistress. □□ **la·dy·hood** *n.*

WORD HISTORY | **lady**

Old English *hlǣfdīge* (denoting a woman to whom homage or obedience is due, such as the wife of a lord or the mistress of a household, also specifically the Virgin Mary), from *hlāf* 'loaf' + a Germanic base meaning 'knead', related to DOUGH; compare with LORD. In LADY DAY and other compounds where it signifies possession, it represents the Old English genitive *hlǣfdīgan* '(Our) Lady's'.

---

la·dy·bird /láydeebərd/ *n. esp. Brit.* = LADYBUG.

La·dy Boun·ti·ful *n.* a patronizingly generous lady of the manor, etc. (a character in Farquhar's *The Beaux' Stratagem*, 1707).

la·dy·bug /láydeebug/ *n.* a coleopterous insect of the family Coccinellidae, with wing covers usu. of a reddish-brown color with black spots.

La·dy chap·el *n.* a chapel in a church or cathedral dedicated to the Virgin Mary.

La·dy Day *n.* the Feast of the Annunciation, March 25.

la·dy fern *n.* a slender fern, *Athyrium filix-femina*.

ladybug

la·dy·fin·ger /láydeefinggər/ *n.* a finger-shaped sponge cake.

la·dy-in-wait·ing *n.* a lady attending a queen or princess.

la·dy-kill·er *n.* **1** an attractive, charming man who habitually seduces women.

la·dy·like /láydeelīk/ *adj.* **1 a** with the modesty, manners, etc., of a lady. **b** befitting a lady. **2** (of a man) effeminate.

la·dy·love /láydeeluv/ *n.* a man's sweetheart.

la·dy of the night *n.* used euphemistically to refer to a prostitute.

la·dy·ship /láydeeship/ *n. archaic* being a lady. □ **her** (or **your** or **their**) **ladyship** (or **ladyships**) **1** a respectful form of reference or address to a titled lady or ladies. **2** *iron.* a form of reference or address to a woman thought to be giving herself airs.

la·dy's maid *n.* a lady's personal maidservant.

la·dy's slip·per *n.* (also **la·dy slip·per**) any orchidaceous plant of the genus *Cypripedium*, with a usu. yellow or pink slipper-shaped lip on its flowers.

laevo- esp. *Brit.* var. of LEVO-.

lae·vo·ro·ta·to·ry esp. *Brit.* var. of LEVOROTATORY.

lae·vu·lose esp. *Brit.* var. of LEVULOSE.

lag¹ /lag/ *v. & n.* ●*v.intr.* (**lagged**, **lag·ging**) **1** (often foll. by *behind*) fall behind; not keep pace. **2** *Billiards* make the preliminary strokes that decide which player shall begin. ●*n.* **1 a** a delay. **2** *Physics* **a** a retardation in a current or movement. **b** the amount of this. □ **lag of tide** the interval by which a tide falls behind mean time at the 1st and 3rd quarters of the moon (cf. PRIMING²). □□ **lag·ger** *n.* [orig. = hindmost person, hang back: perh. f. a fanciful distortion of LAST¹ in a children's game (*fog, seg, lag*, = 1st, 2nd, last, in dial.)]

lady's slipper

lag² /lag/ *v. & n.* ●*v.tr.* (**lagged**, **lag·ging**) enclose or cover in lagging. ●*n.* **1** the non-heat-conducting cover of a boiler, etc.; lagging. **2** a piece of this. [prob. f. Scand.: cf. ON *lögg* barrel-rim, rel. to LAY¹]

lag³ /lag/ *n. & v. Brit. sl.* ●*n.* (esp. as **old lag**) a habitual convict. ●*v.tr.* (**lagged**, **lag·ging**) **1** send to prison. **2** apprehend; arrest. [19th c.: orig. unkn.]

lag·an /lágən/ *n.* goods or wreckage lying on the bed of the sea, sometimes with a marking buoy, etc., for later retrieval. [OF, perh. of Scand. orig., f. root of LIE¹, LAY¹]

la·ger /láagər/ *n.* a kind of beer, effervescent and light in color and body. [G *Lagerbier* beer brewed for keeping f. *Lager* store]

la·ger lout *n. Brit. colloq.* a youth who behaves badly as a result of excessive drinking.

lag·gard /lágərd/ *n. & adj.* ●*n.* a dawdler; a person who lags behind. ●*adj.* dawdling; slow. □□ **lag·gard·ly** *adj. & adv.* **lag·gard·ness** *n.* [LAG¹]

lag·ging /láging/ *n.* material providing heat insulation for a boiler, pipes, etc. [LAG²]

lag·o·morph /lágəmawrf/ *n. Zool.* any mammal of the order Lagomorpha, including hares and rabbits. [Gk *lagōs* hare + *morphē* form]

la·goon /ləgoón/ *n.* **1** a stretch of salt water separated from the sea by a low sandbank, coral reef, etc. **2** the enclosed water of an atoll. **3** a small freshwater lake near a larger lake or river. **4** an artificial pool for the treatment of effluent or to accommodate an overspill from surface drains during heavy rain. [F *lagune* or It. & Sp. *laguna* f. L *lacuna*: see LACUNA]

la·har /laáhaar/ *n.* a mudflow composed mainly of volcanic debris. [Jav.]

la·ic /láyik/ *adj. & n.* ● *adj.* nonclerical; lay; secular; temporal. ● *n. formal* a lay person; a noncleric. □□ **la·i·cal** *adj.* **la·i·cal·ly** *adv.* [LL f. Gk *laïkos* f. *laos* people]

la·ic·i·ty /layísitee/ *n.* the status or influence of the laity.

la·i·cize /láyisīz/ *v.tr.* **1** make (an office, etc.) tenable by lay people. **2** subject (a school or institution) to the control of lay people. **3** secularize. □□ **la·i·ci·za·tion** *n.*

laid *past* and *past part.* of LAY¹.

laid-back *adj. colloq.* relaxed; unbothered; easygoing.

laid pa·per *n.* paper that has a finely ribbed appearance.

laid up *adj.* confined to bed or the house (*laid up with the flu*).

lain *past part.* of LIE¹.

lair¹ /lair/ *n. & v.* ● *n.* **1 a** a wild animal's resting place. **b** a person's hiding place; a den (*tracked him to his lair*). **2** a place where domestic animals lie down. **3** *Brit.* a shed or enclosure for cattle on the way to market. ● *v.* **1** *intr.* go to or rest in a lair. **2** *tr.* place (an animal) in a lair. [OE *leger* f. Gmc: cf. LIE¹]

lair² /lair/ *n. & v. Austral. sl.* ● *n.* a youth or man who dresses flashily and shows off. ● *v.intr.* (often foll. by *up*) behave or dress like a lair. □□ **lair·y** *adj.* [*lair* back-form. f. *lairy*; *lairy* alt. f. LEERY]

laird /laird/ *n. Sc.* a landed proprietor. □□ **laird·ship** *n.* [Sc. form of LORD]

lais·sez-al·ler /lesay-aaláy/ *n.* (also **lais·ser-al·ler**) unconstrained freedom; an absence of constraint. [F, = let go]

lais·sez-faire /lésayfáir/ *n.* (also **lais·ser-faire**) the theory or practice of governmental abstention from interference in the workings of the market, etc. [F, = let act]

lais·sez-pas·ser /lésaypaasáy/ *n.* (also **lais·ser-pas·ser**) a document allowing the holder to pass; a permit. [F, = let pass]

la·i·ty /láy-itee/ *n.* (usu. prec. by *the*; usu. treated as *pl.*) **1** lay people, as distinct from the clergy. **2** nonprofessionals. [ME f. LAY² + -ITY]

lake¹ /layk/ *n.* a large body of water surrounded by land. □□ **lake·less** *adj.* **lake·let** *n.* [ME f. OF *lac* f. L *lacus* basin, pool, lake]

lake² /layk/ *n.* **1** a reddish coloring orig. made from lac (*crimson lake*). **2** a complex formed by the action of dye and mordants applied to fabric to fix color. **3** any insoluble product of a soluble dye and mordant. [var. of LAC¹]

lake dwell·er *n.* a prehistoric inhabitant of lake dwellings.

lake dwell·ings *n.pl.* prehistoric huts built on piles driven into the bed or shore of a lake.

Lake·land ter·ri·er /láyklənd/ *n.* **1** a terrier of a small stocky breed originating in the Lake District of NW England. **2** this breed.

Lake Po·ets *n.pl.* Coleridge, Southey, and Wordsworth, who lived in and were inspired by the Lake District.

lake·side /láyksīd/ *attrib.adj.* beside a lake.

lakh /laak/ *n.* (also **lac**) *Ind.* (usu. foll. by *of*) a hundred thousand (rupees, etc.). [Hind. *lākh* f. Skr. *lakṣa*]

la-la land /laálaaland/ *n.* **1** Los Angeles or Hollywood, esp. with regard to the lifestyle and attitudes of those living there or associated with it. **2** a fanciful state or dreamworld. [*la-la*, reduplication of LA (Los Angeles)]

Lal·lan /lálən/ *n. & adj. Sc.* ● *n.* (now usu. **Lallans**) a Lowland Scots dialect, esp. as a literary language. ● *adj.* of or concerning the Lowlands of Scotland. [var. of LOWLAND]

lal·la·tion /laláyshən/ *n.* **1** the pronunciation of *r* as *l.* **2** imperfect speech, esp. that of young children. [L *lallare lallat-* sing a lullaby]

lal·ly·gag var. of LOLLYGAG.

Lam. *abbr.* Lamentations (Old Testament).

lam¹ /lam/ *v.* (**lammed, lam·ming**) *sl.* **1** *tr.* thrash; hit. **2** *intr.* (foll. by *into*) hit (a person, etc.) hard with a stick, etc. [perh. f. Scand.: cf. ON *lemja* beat so as to LAME]

lam² /lam/ *n.* □ **on the lam** *sl.* in flight, esp. from the police. [20th c.: orig. unkn.]

la·ma /laámə/ *n.* a Tibetan or Mongolian Buddhist monk. □□ **La·ma·ism** *n.* **La·ma·ist** *n. & adj.* [Tibetan *blama* (with silent *b*)]

La·marck·ism /ləmaárkizəm/ *n.* the theory of evolution devised by Lamarck, French botanist and zoologist (d. 1829), based on the inheritance of acquired characteristics. □□ **La·marck·i·an** *n. & adj.*

la·ma·ser·y /laáməseree/ *n.* (*pl.* **·ies**) a monastery of lamas. [F *lamaserie* irreg. f. *lama* LAMA]

La·maze meth·od /ləmaáz/ *n. Med.* a method for childbirth in which breathing exercises and relaxation techniques are used to control pain and facilitate delivery. [for F physician Fernand *Lamaze* (-1890-1957)]

lamb /lam/ *n. & v.* ● *n.* **1** a young sheep. **2** the flesh of a lamb as food. **3** a mild or gentle person, esp. a young child. ● *v.* **1 a** *tr.* (in *passive*) (of a lamb) be born. **b** *intr.* (of a ewe) give birth to lambs. **2** *tr.* tend (lambing ewes). □ **The Lamb** (or **The Lamb of God**) a name for Christ (John 1:29) (cf. AGNUS DEI). **like a lamb** meekly; obediently. □□ **lamb·er** *n.* **lamb·kin** *n.* **lamb·like** *adj.* [OE *lamb* f. Gmc]

lam·ba·da /ləmbaádə/ *n.* a fast erotic Brazilian dance in which couples dance with their hips touching each other.

lam·baste /lambáyst/ *v.tr.* (also **lam·bast** /-bást/) *colloq.* **1** thrash; beat. **2** criticize severely. [LAM¹ + BASTE³]

lamb·da /lámdə/ *n.* **1** the eleventh letter of the Greek alphabet (Λ, λ). **2** (as λ) the symbol for wavelength. [ME f. Gk *la(m)bda*]

lam·bent /lámbənt/ *adj.* **1** (of a flame or a light) playing on a surface with a soft radiance but without burning. **2** (of the eyes, sky, etc.) softly radiant. **3** (of wit, etc.) lightly brilliant. □□ **lam·ben·cy** *n.* **lam·bent·ly** *adv.* [L *lambere* lambent- lick]

lam·bert /lámbərt/ *n.* a former unit of luminance, equal to the emission or reflection of one lumen per square centimeter. [J. H. *Lambert*, Ger. physicist d. 1777]

lam·bre·quin /lámbrikin, lámbər-/ *n.* **1** a short piece of drapery hung over the top of a door or a window or draped on a mantelpiece. **2** *Heraldry* = MANTLING. [F f. Du. (unrecorded) *lamperkin*, dimin. of *lamper* veil]

lamb·skin /lámskin/ *n.* a prepared skin from a lamb with the wool on or as leather.

lamb's let·tuce *n.* esp. *Brit.* = CORN SALAD.

lamb's wool *n.* soft, fine wool from a young sheep used in knitted garments, etc.

lame /laym/ *adj. & v.* ● *adj.* **1** disabled, esp. in the foot or leg; limping; unable to walk normally (*lame in his right leg*). **2 a** (of an argument, story, excuse, etc.) unconvincing; unsatisfactory; weak. **b** (of verse, etc.) halting. ● *v.tr.* **1** make lame; disable. **2** harm permanently. □□ **lame·ly** *adv.* **lame·ness** *n.* **lam·ish** *adj.* [OE *lama* f. Gmc]

la·mé /lamáy/ *n. & adj.* ● *n.* a fabric with gold or silver threads interwoven. ● *adj.* (of fabric, a dress, etc.) having such threads. [F]

lame·brain /láymbrayn/ *n. colloq.* a stupid person. □□ **lame·brained** *adj.*

lame duck *n.* **1** an official (esp. the president) in the final period of office, after the election of a successor. **2** an ineffectual or unsuccessful person or thing. **3** a person who has lost money in the stock market.

la·mel·la /ləmélə/ *n.* (*pl.* **la·mel·lae** /-lee/ or **la·mel·las**) **1** a thin layer, membrane, scale, or platelike tissue or part, esp. in bone tissue. **2** *Bot.* a membranous fold in a chloroplast. □□ **la·mel·lar** *adj.* **la·mel·late** /ləmélayt, lámə-/ *adj.* **la·mel·li·form** *adj.* **la·mel·lose** /-lōs/ *adj.* [L, dimin. of *lamina*: see LAMINA]

la·mel·li·branch /ləmélibrangk/ *n.* any aquatic mollusk having a shell formed of two pieces or valves, e.g., a mussel or oyster. Also called **bivalve.** [LAMELLA + Gk *bragkhia* gills]

la·mel·li·corn /ləmélikawrn/ *n. & adj.* ● *n.* any beetle of the family Lamellicornia, having lamelliform antennae, including the stag beetle, cockchafer, dung beetle, etc. ● *adj.* having lamelliform antennae. [mod.L *lamellicornis* f. L *lamella* (see LAMELLA) + *cornu* horn]

la·ment /ləmént/ *n. & v.* ● *n.* **1** a passionate expression of grief. **2** a song or poem of mourning or sorrow. ● *v.tr.* (also *absol.*) **1** express or feel grief for or about; regret (*lamented the loss of his ticket*). **2** (as **lamented** *adj.*) a conventional expression referring to a recently dead person (*your late lamented father*). □ **lament for** (or **over**) mourn or regret. □□ **la·ment·er** *n.* **la·ment·ing·ly** *adv.* [L *lamentum*]

lam·en·ta·ble /ləméntəbəl, lámənt-/ *adj.* **1** (of an event, fate, condition, character, etc.) deplorable; regrettable. **2** *archaic* mournful. □□ **lam·en·ta·bly** *adv.* [ME f. OF *lamentable* or L *lamentabilis* (as LAMENT)]

lam·en·ta·tion /láməntáyshən/ *n.* **1** the act or an instance of lamenting. **2** a lament. **3** (**Lamentations**) an Old Testament book concerning the destruction of Jerusalem in the 6th c. BC. [ME f. OF *lamentation* or L *lamentatio* (as LAMENT)]

lam·i·na /láminə/ *n.* (*pl.* **lam·i·nae** /-nee/ or **lam·i·nas**) a thin plate or scale, e.g., of bone, stratified rock, or vegetable tissue. □□ **lam·i·nose** *adj.* [L]

lam·i·nar /láminər/ *adj.* **1** consisting of laminae. **2** *Physics* (of a flow) taking place along constant streamlines, not turbulent.

lam·i·nate *v., n., & adj.* ● *v.* /láminayt/ **1** *tr.* beat or roll (metal) into thin plates. **2** *tr.* overlay with metal plates, a plastic layer, etc. **3** *tr.* manufacture by placing layer on layer. **4** *tr. & intr.* split or be split into layers or leaves. ● *n.* /láminət/ a laminated structure or material, esp. of layers fixed together to form rigid or flexible material. ● *adj.* /láminət/ in the form of lamina or laminae. □□ **lam·i·na·tion** /-náyshən/ *n.* **lam·i·na·tor** *n.* [LAMINA + -ATE², -ATE³]

lam·ing·ton /láming tən/ *n. Austral. & NZ* a square of sponge cake coated in chocolate icing and desiccated coconut. [C.W. Ballie, Baron *Lamington*, Governor of Queensland, d. 1940]

Lam·mas /láməs/ *n.* (in full **Lammas Day**) the first day of August, formerly observed as harvest festival. [OE *hlāfmæsse* (as LOAF[1], MASS[2])]

lam·mer·gei·er /lámərgīər/ *n.* (also **lam·mer·gey·er**) a large vulture, *Gypaetus barbatus*, with a very large wingspan (often of 9–10 ft) and dark, beardlike feathers on either side of its beak. [G *Lämmergeier* f. *Lämmer* lambs + *Geier* vulture]

lamp /lamp/ *n. & v.* ● *n.* **1** a device for producing a steady light, esp.: **a** an electric bulb, and usu. its holder and shade or cover (*bedside lamp; bicycle lamp*). **b** an oil lamp. **c** a usu. glass holder for a candle. **d** a gas jet and mantle. **2** a source of spiritual or intellectual inspiration. **3** *poet.* the sun, the moon, or a star. **4** a device producing esp. ultraviolet or infrared radiation as a treatment for various complaints. ● *v.* **1** *intr. poet.* shine. **2** *tr.* supply with lamps; illuminate. **3** *tr. sl.* look at. □□ **lamp·less** *adj.* [ME f. OF *lampe* f. LL *lampada* f. accus. of L *lampas* torch f. Gk]

lamp·black /lámpblak/ *n.* a pigment made from soot.

lamp chim·ney *n.* a glass cylinder enclosing and making a draft for an oil lamp's flame.

lamp·light /lámplīt/ *n.* light given by a lamp or lamps.

lamp·light·er /lámplītər/ *n. hist.* **1** a person employed to light street gaslights by hand.

lam·poon /lampo͞on/ *n. & v.* ● *n.* a satirical attack on a person, etc. ● *v. tr.* satirize. □□ **lam·poon·er** *n.* **lam·poon·er·y** *n.* **lam·poon·ist** *n.* [F *lampon*, conjectured to be f. *lampons* let us drink f. *lamper* gulp down f. *laper* LAP[3]]

lamp·post /lámp-pōst/ *n.* a tall post supporting an outdoor light.

lam·prey /lámpree, –pray/ *n.* (*pl.* **·preys**) any eellike aquatic vertebrate of the family Petromyzonidae, without scales, paired fins, or jaws, but having a sucker mouth with horny teeth and a rough tongue. [ME f. OF *lampreie* f. med.L *lampreda*: cf. LL *lampetra* perh. f. L *lambere* lick + *petra* stone]

lamp·shade /lámpshayd/ *n.* a translucent cover for a lamp used to soften or direct its light.

LAN /lan/ *abbr.* LOCAL AREA NETWORK.

Lan·cas·tri·an /langkástreeən/ *n. & adj.* ● *n.* **1** a native of Lancashire or Lancaster in NW England. **2** *hist.* a follower of the House of Lancaster or of the Red Rose party supporting it in the Wars of the Roses (cf. YORKIST). ● *adj.* of or concerning Lancashire or Lancaster, or the House of Lancaster.

lance /lans/ *n. & v.* ● *n.* **1 a** a long weapon with a wooden shaft and a pointed steel head, used by a horseman in charging. **b** a similar weapon used for spearing a fish, killing a harpooned whale, etc. **2** a metal pipe supplying oxygen to burn metal. **3** = LANCER. ● *v. tr.* **1** *Surgery* prick or cut open with a lancet. **2** pierce with a lance. **3** *poet.* fling; launch. □ **break a lance** (usu. foll. by *for, with*) *Brit.* argue. [ME f. OF *lancier* f. L *lancea: lance corporal* on analogy of obs. *lancepesade* lowest grade of NCO ult. f. It. *lancia spezzata* broken lance]

lance cor·po·ral *n.* **1** marine corps rank between private first class and corporal. **2** *Brit.* lowest ranked corporal in the army.

lance·let /lánslit/ *n.* any small, nonvertebrate fishlike chordate of the family Branchiostomidae, that burrows in sand. [LANCE *n.* + –LET, with ref. to its thin form]

lan·ce·o·late /lánseeəlayt/ *adj.* shaped like a lance head, tapering to each end. [LL *lanceolatus* f. *lanceola* dimin. of *lancea* lance]

lanc·er /lánsər/ *n.* **1** *hist.* a soldier of a cavalry regiment armed with lances. **2** (in *pl.*) **a** a quadrille for 8 or 16 pairs. **b** the music for this. [F *lancier* (as LANCE)]

lan·cet /lánsit/ *n.* a small, broad, two-edged surgical knife with a sharp point. □□ **lan·cet·ed** *adj.* [ME f. OF *lancette* (as LANCE)]

lan·cet arch *n.* (also **lan·cet win·dow**) a narrow arch (or window) with a pointed head.

lance·wood /lánswŏŏd/ *n.* a tough elastic wood from a W. Indian tree *Oxandra lanceolata*, used for carriage shafts, fishing rods, etc.

Land /laant/ *n.* (*pl.* **Länder** /léndər/) a province of Germany or Austria. [G (as LAND)]

land /land/ *n. & v.* ● *n.* **1** the solid part of the earth's surface (opp. SEA, WATER, AIR). **2 a** an expanse of country; ground; soil. **b** such land in relation to its use, quality, etc., or (often prec. by *the*) as a basis for agriculture (*building land; this is good land; works on the land*). **3** a country, nation, or state (*land of hope and glory*). **4** a landed property. **5** (in *pl.*) estates. **5** the space between the rifling grooves in a gun. **6** *Sc.* a building containing several dwellings. **7** *S.Afr.* ground fenced off for tillage. **8** a strip of plow land or pastureland parted from others by drain furrows. ● *v.* **1 a** *tr. & intr.* set or go ashore. **b** *intr.* (often foll. by *at*) disembark (*landed at the harbor*). **2** *tr.* bring (an aircraft, its passengers, etc.) to the ground or the surface of water. **3** *intr.* (of an aircraft, bird, parachutist, etc.) alight on the ground or water. **4** *tr.* bring (a fish) to land. **5** *tr. & intr.* (also *refl.*; often foll. by *up*) *colloq.* bring to, reach, or find oneself in a certain situation, place, or state (*landed himself in jail; landed up in Alaska; landed her in trouble; landed up penniless*). **6** *tr. colloq.* **a** deal (a person, etc.) a blow, etc. (*landed him one in the eye*). **b** (foll. by *with*) present (a person) with (a problem, job, etc.). **7** *tr.* set down (a person, cargo, etc.) from a vehicle, ship, etc. **8** *tr. colloq.* win or obtain (a prize, job, etc.) esp. against strong competi-

tion. □ **how the land lies** what is the state of affairs. **in the land of the living** *joc.* still alive. **land of cakes** *Brit.* Scotland. **land of Nod** sleep (with pun on the phr. in Gen. 4:16). **land on one's feet** attain a good position, job, etc., by luck. □□ **land·less** *adj.* **land·ward** *adj. & adv.* [OE f. Gmc]

land a·gent *n. Brit.* **1** a person employed to manage an estate on behalf of its owners. **2** a person who deals with the sale of land. □□ **land a·gen·cy** *n.*

lan·dau /lándow, –daw/ *n.* a four-wheeled enclosed carriage with a removable front cover and a back cover that can be raised and lowered. [*Landau* near Karlsruhe in Germany, where it was first made]

lan·dau·let /lánd'lét/ *n.* **1** a small landau. **2** *hist.* a car with a folding hood over the rear seats.

land bank *n.* a bank that finances land development esp. for agriculture.

land breeze *n.* a breeze blowing toward the sea from the land, esp. at night.

land bridge *n.* a neck of land joining two large landmasses.

land crab *n.* a crab, *Cardisoma guanhumi*, that lives in burrows inland and migrates in large numbers to the sea to breed.

land·ed /lándid/ *adj.* **1** owning land (*landed gentry*). **2** consisting of, including, or relating to land (*landed property*).

Län·der *pl.* of LAND.

land·er /lándər/ *n.* a spacecraft designed to land on the surface of a planet or moon (*a lunar lander*).

land·fall /lándfawl/ *n.* the approach to land, esp. for the first time on a sea or air journey.

land·fill /lándfil/ *n.* **1** waste material, etc., used to landscape or reclaim areas of ground. **2** the process of disposing of rubbish in this way. **3** a place where rubbish is disposed of by burying it in the ground.

land·form /lándfawrm/ *n.* a natural feature of the earth's surface.

land girl *n. Brit.* a woman doing farmwork, esp. during World War II.

land·grab·ber *n.* a person who seizes and possesses land in an unfair or illegal manner.

land·grave /lándgrayv/ *n.* (*fem.* **land·gra·vine** /–grəveen/) *hist.* **1** a count having jurisdiction over a territory. **2** the title of certain German princes. □□ **land·gra·vi·ate** /–grávveeət, –veeayt/ *n.* [MLG *landgrave*, MHG *lantgrāve* (as LAND, G *Graf* COUNT[2])]

land·hold·er /lándhōldər/ *n.* the proprietor or, esp., the tenant of land. □□ **land·hold·ing** *n. & adj.*

land·ing /lánding/ *n.* **1 a** the act or process of coming to land. **b** an instance of this. **c** (also **land·ing place**) a place where ships, etc., land. **2 a** a platform between two flights of stairs, or at the top or bottom of a flight. **b** a passage leading to upstairs rooms.

land·ing craft *n.* any of several types of craft esp. designed for putting troops and equipment ashore.

land·ing gear *n.* the undercarriage of an aircraft, including the wheels or pontoons on which it rests while not in the air.

land·ing net *n.* a net for landing a large fish which has been hooked.

land·ing stage *n.* a platform, often floating, on which goods and passengers are disembarked.

land·ing strip *n.* an airstrip.

land·la·dy /lándlaydee/ *n.* (*pl.* **·dies**) **1** a woman who rents land, a building, part of a building, etc., to a tenant. **2** a woman who keeps a boardinghouse, an inn, etc.

länd·ler /léndlər/ *n.* (*pl.* same or **länd·lers**) **1** an Austrian dance in triple time, a precursor of the waltz. **2** the music for a ländler. [G f. *Landl* Upper Austria]

land·line /lándlīn/ *n.* conventional telecommunications connection by cable laid across land, either on poles or buried underground.

land·locked /lándlokt/ *adj.* almost or entirely enclosed by land.

land·lop·er /lándlōpər/ *n.* esp. *Sc.* a vagabond. [MDu. *landlooper* (as LAND, *loopen* run, formed as LEAP)]

land·lord /lándlawrd/ *n.* **1** a man who rents land, a building, part of a building, etc., to a tenant. **2** a man who keeps a boardinghouse, an inn, etc.

land·lub·ber /lándlubər/ *n.* a person unfamiliar with the sea or sailing.

land·mark /lándmaark/ *n.* **1 a** a conspicuous object or feature of a landscape or town that is easily seen and recognized from a distance, esp. one that enables someone to establish their location. **b** an object marking the boundary of an estate, country, etc. **2** an event, change, etc., marking a stage or turning point in history, etc. **3** *attrib.* serving as a landmark; signifying an important change, development, etc.

land·mass /lándmas/ *n.* a large area of land.

land mine *n.* **1** an explosive mine laid in or on the ground. **2** a parachute mine.

land of·fice *n.* a government office recording dealings in public land. □ **do a land-office business** do a lot of successful business.

land·own·er /lándōnər/ n. an owner of land. □□ **land·own·ing** adj. & n.

land rail n. = CORN CRAKE.

land·scape /lándskayp/ n. & v. • n. **1** natural or imaginary scenery, as seen in a broad view. **2** (often *attrib.*) a picture representing this; the genre of landscape painting. **3** (in graphic design, etc.) a format in which the width of an illustration, etc., is greater than the height (cf. PORTRAIT). • v.tr. (also *absol.*) improve (a piece of land) by landscape gardening. [MDu. *landscap* (as LAND, –SHIP)]

land·scape gar·den·ing n. (also **land·scape ar·chi·tec·ture**) the laying out of esp. extensive grounds to resemble natural scenery. □□ **land·scape gar·den·er** n.

land·scap·ist /lándskaypist/ n. an artist who paints landscapes.

Land's End n. the westernmost point of Cornwall and the SW tip of England.

land·slide /lándslīd/ n. **1** the sliding down of a mass of land from a mountain, cliff, etc. **2** an overwhelming majority for one side in an election.

land·slip /lándslip/ n. = LANDSLIDE 1.

lands·man /lándzmən/ n. (pl. **·men**) a nonsailor.

land yacht n. **1** a wind-powered wheeled vehicle with sails, for recreation and competition. **2** a large car (*a gas-guzzling land yacht*).

lane /layn/ n. **1** a narrow, often rural, road, street, or path. **2** a division of a road for a stream of traffic (*three-lane highway*). **3** a strip of track or water for a runner, rower, or swimmer in a race. **4** a path or course prescribed for or regularly followed by a ship, aircraft, etc. (*ocean lane*). **5** a gangway between crowds of people, objects, etc. □ **it's a long lane that has no turning** change is inevitable. [OE: orig. unkn.]

lang·lauf /láanglowf/ n. cross-country skiing; a cross-country skiing race. [G, = long run]

lan·gouste /lo͝ngo͞ost, lónggo͞ost/ n. a crawfish or spiny lobster. [F]

lan·gous·tine /lóngo͞osteen, lánggə–/ n. any of several varieties of small lobsters, used as food. [F]

lang syne /lang zīn, sín/ adv. & n. Sc. • adv. in the distant past. • n. the old days (cf. AULD LANG SYNE). [= long since]

lan·guage /lánggwij/ n. **1** the method of human communication, either spoken or written, consisting of the use of words in an agreed way. **2** the language of a particular community or country, etc. (*speaks several languages*). **3 a** the faculty of speech. **b** a style or the faculty of expression; the use of words, etc. (*his language was poetic; hasn't the language to express it*). **c** (also **bad lan·guage**) coarse, crude, or abusive speech (*didn't like his language*). **4** a system of symbols and rules for writing computer programs or algorithms. **5** any method of expression (*the language of mime; sign language*). **6** a professional or specialized vocabulary. **7** literary style. □ **language of flowers** a set of symbolic meanings attached to different flowers. **speak the same language** have a similar outlook, manner of expression, etc. [ME f. OF *langage* ult. f. L *lingua* tongue]

lan·guage lab·o·ra·to·ry n. a room equipped with tape and video recorders, etc., for learning a foreign language.

langue de chat /lóng də sháa/ n. a very thin finger-shaped crisp cookie or piece of chocolate. [F, = cat's tongue]

langue d'oc /long dáwk/ n. the form of medieval French spoken south of the Loire, the basis of modern Provençal. [F *langue* language f. L *lingua* tongue + *de* of + *oc* (f. L *hoc*) the form for *yes*]

langue d'oïl /long dáw-ee, -eel/ n. medieval French as spoken north of the Loire, the basis of modern French. [as LANGUE D'OC + *oïl* (f. L *hoc ille*) the form for *yes*]

lan·guid /lánggwid/ adj. **1** lacking vigor; idle; inert; apathetic. **2** (of ideas, etc.) lacking force; uninteresting. **3** (of trade, etc.) slow-moving; sluggish. **4** faint; weak. □□ **lan·guid·ly** adv. **lan·guid·ness** n. [F *languide* or L *languidus* (as LANGUISH)]

lan·guish /lánggwish/ v.intr. **1** be or grow feeble; lose or lack vitality. **2** put on a sentimentally tender or languid look. □ **languish for** droop or pine for. **languish under** suffer under (esp. depression, confinement, etc.). □□ **lan·guish·er** n. **lan·guish·ing·ly** adv. **lan·guish·ment** n. [ME f. OF *languir*, ult. f. L *languēre*, rel. to LAX]

lan·guor /lánggər/ n. **1** lack of energy or alertness; inertia; idleness; dullness. **2** faintness; fatigue. **3** a soft or tender mood or effect. **4** an oppressive stillness (of the air, etc.). □□ **lan·guor·ous** adj. **lan·guor·ous·ly** adv. [ME f. OF f. L *languor –oris* (as LANGUISH)]

lan·gur /lungo͞or/ n. any of various Asian long-tailed monkeys esp. of the genus *Presbytis*. [Hindi]

la·ni·ar·y /láynee-eree, lán–/ adj. & n. • adj. (of a tooth) adapted for tearing; canine. • n. (pl. **·ies**) a laniary tooth. [L *laniarius* f. *lanius* butcher f. *laniare* to tear]

la·nif·er·ous /lənífərəs/ adj. wool-bearing. [L *lanifer*, –ger f. *lana* wool]

lank /langk/ adj. **1** (of hair, grass, etc.) long, limp, and straight. **2** thin and tall. **3** shrunken; spare. □□ **lank·ly** adv. **lank·ness** n. [OE *hlanc* f. Gmc: cf. FLANK, LINK[1]]

lank·y /lángkee/ adj. (**lank·i·er**, **lank·i·est**) (of limbs, a person, etc.) ungracefully thin and long or tall. □□ **lank·i·ly** adv. **lank·i·ness** n.

lan·ner /lánər/ n. a S. European falcon, *Falco biarmicus*, esp. the female. [ME f. OF *lanier* perh. f. OF *lanier* cowardly, orig. = weaver f. L *lanarius* wool merchant f. *lana* wool]

lan·ner·et /lánərét/ n. a male lanner, smaller than the female. [ME f. OF *laneret* (as LANNER)]

lan·o·lin /lánəlin/ n. a fat found naturally on sheep's wool and used purified for cosmetics, etc. [G f. L *lana* wool + *oleum* oil]

lans·que·net /lánskənət/ n. **1** a card game of German origin. **2** a German mercenary soldier in the 16th–17th c. [F f. G *Landsknecht* (as LAND, *Knecht* soldier f. OHG *kneht*: see KNIGHT)]

lan·ta·na /lantánə/ n. any evergreen shrub of the genus *Lantana*, with usu. yellow or orange flowers. [mod.L]

lan·tern /lántərn/ n. **1 a** a lamp with a transparent usu. glass case protecting a candle flame, etc. **b** a similar electric, etc., lamp. **c** its case. **2 a** a raised structure on a dome, room, etc., glazed to admit light. **b** a similar structure for ventilation, etc. **3** the light chamber of a lighthouse. **4** = MAGIC LANTERN. [ME f. OF *lanterne* f. L *lanterna* f. Gk *lamptēr* torch, lamp]

lan·tern fish n. any marine fish of the family Myctophidae, having small luminous organs on the head and body.

lan·tern fly n. (pl. **flies**) any tropical homopterous insect of the family Fulgoridae, formerly thought to be luminous.

lan·tern jaw n. a long thin jaw and prominent chin. □□ **lan·tern-jawed** adj.

lan·tern slide n. hist. a mounted photographic transparency for projection by a magic lantern.

lan·tha·nide /lánthənīd/ n. Chem. an element of the lanthanide series. [G *Lanthanid* (as LANTHANUM)]

lan·tha·nide se·ries n. a series of 15 metallic elements from lanthanum to lutetium in the periodic table, having similar chemical properties. Also called **rare earth**.

lan·tha·num /lánthənəm/ n. Chem. a silvery metallic element of the lanthanide series which occurs naturally and is used in the manufacture of alloys. ¶ Symb.: **La**. [Gk *lanthanō* escape notice, from having remained undetected in cerium oxide]

la·nu·go /ləno͞ogo, –nyoͦo–/ n. fine, soft hair, esp. that which covers the body and limbs of a human fetus. [L, = down f. *lana* wool]

lan·yard /lányərd/ n. **1** a cord hanging around the neck or looped around the shoulder, esp. of a scout or sailor, etc., to which a knife, a whistle, etc., may be attached. **2** Naut. a short rope or line used for securing, tightening, etc. **3** a cord attached to a breech mechanism for firing a gun. [ME f. OF *laniere, lasniere*: assim. to YARD[1]]

La·od·i·ce·an /layódiseeən/ adj. & n. • adj. lukewarm or halfhearted, esp. in religion or politics. • n. such a person. [L *Laodicea* in Asia Minor (with ref. to the early Christians there: see Rev. 3:16)]

La·o·tian /layóshən, lóushən/ n. & adj. • n. **1 a** a native or national of Laos in SE Asia. **b** a person of Laotian descent. **2** the language of Laos. • adj. of or relating to Laos or its people or language.

lap[1] /lap/ n. **1 a** the front of the body from the waist to the knees of a sitting person (*sat on her lap; caught it in his lap*). **b** the clothing, esp. a skirt, covering the lap. **c** the front of a skirt held up to catch or contain something. **2** a hollow among hills. **3** a hanging flap on a garment, a saddle, etc. □ **in** (or **on**) **a person's lap** as a person's responsibility. **in the lap of the gods** (of an event, etc.) open to chance; beyond human control. **in the lap of luxury** in extremely luxurious surroundings. □□ **lap·ful** n. (pl. **·fuls**).

WORD HISTORY lap

Old English *læppa*, of Germanic origin; related to Dutch *lap*, German *Lappen* 'piece of cloth'. The word originally denoted a fold or flap of a garment (compare with LAPEL), later specifically one that could be used as a pocket or pouch, or the front of a skirt when held up to catch or carry something (Middle English), hence the area between the waist and knees as a place where a child could be nursed or an object held.

---

lap[2] /lap/ n. & v. • n. **1 a** one circuit of a racetrack, etc. **b** a section of a journey, etc. (*finally we were on the last lap*). **2 a** an amount of overlapping. **b** an overlapping or projecting part. **3 a** a layer or sheet (of cotton, etc., being made) wound on a roller. **b** a single turn of rope, silk, thread, etc., around a drum or reel. **4** a rotating disk for polishing a gem or metal. • v. (**lapped, lap·ping**) **1** tr. lead or overtake (a competitor in a race) by one or more laps. **2** tr. (often foll. by *about, around*) coil, fold, or wrap (a garment, etc.) around esp. a person. **3** tr. (usu. foll. by *in*) enfold or wrap (a person) in clothing, etc. **4** tr. (as **lapped** adj.) (usu. foll. by *in*) protectively encircled; enfolded caressingly. **5** tr. surround (a person) with an influence, etc. **6** intr. (usu. foll. by *over*) project; overlap. **7** tr. cause to overlap. **8** tr. polish (a gem, etc.) with a lap. [ME, prob. f. LAP[1]]

lap[3] /lap/ v. & n. • v. (**lapped, lap·ping**) **1** tr. **a** (also *absol.*) (usu. of an animal) drink (liquid) with the tongue. **b** (usu. foll. by *up, down*) consume (liquid) greedily. **c** (usu. foll. by *up*) consume (gossip, praise, etc.) greedily. **2 a** tr. (of water) move or beat upon (a shore) with a rippling sound as of lapping. **b** intr. (of waves, etc.) move in ripples; make a lapping sound. • n. **1** the process or an act of lapping. **b** the amount of liquid taken up. **2** the sound of wavelets on a beach. **3** liquid food for dogs. **4** *sl.* **a** a weak beverage. **b** any liquor. [OE *lapian* f. Gmc]

lap·a·ro·scope /lápərəskṓp/ *n. Surgery* a fiber-optic instrument inserted through the abdominal wall to give a view of the organs in the abdomen. □□ **lap·a·ros·co·py** /-róskəpee/ *n.* (*pl.* **·pies**). [Gk *lapara* flank + –SCOPE]

lap·a·rot·o·my /lápərótəmee/ *n.* (*pl.* **·mies**) a surgical incision into the abdominal cavity for exploration or diagnosis. [Gk *lapara* flank + –TOMY]

lap·dog /lápdawg/ *n.* a small pet dog.

la·pel /ləpél/ *n.* the part of a coat, jacket, etc., folded back against the front around the neck opening. □□ **la·pelled** or **la·peled** *adj.* [LAP¹ + –EL]

lap·i·dar·y /lápideree/ *adj. & n.* ● *adj.* **1** concerned with stone or stones. **2** engraved upon stone. **3** (of writing style) dignified and concise, suitable for inscriptions. ● *n.* (*pl.* **·ies**) a cutter, polisher, or engraver of gems. [ME f. L *lapidarius* f. *lapis* –*idis* stone]

la·pil·li /ləpíli/ *n.pl.* stone fragments ejected from volcanoes. [It. f. L, pl. dimin. of *lapis* stone]

lap·is laz·u·li /lápis lázoolee, lázyə–, lázhə–/ *n.* **1** a blue mineral containing sodium aluminum silicate and sulfur, used as a gemstone. **2** a bright blue pigment formerly made from this. **3** its color. [ME f. L *lapis* stone + med.L *lazuli* genit. of *lazulum* f. Pers. (as AZURE)]

lap joint *n.* the joining of rails, shafts, etc., by halving the thickness of each at the joint and fitting them together.

Lap·land·er /láplandər/ *n.* **1** a native or national of Lapland. **2** a person of this descent. [*Lapland* f. Sw. *Lappland* (as LAPP, LAND)]

Lapp /lap/ *n. & adj.* ● *n.* **1** a member of a nomadic Mongol people of N. Scandinavia. **2** the language of this people. ● *adj.* of or relating to the Lapps or their language. [Sw. *Lapp*, perh. orig. a term of contempt: cf. MHG *lappe* simpleton]

lap·pet /lápit/ *n.* **1** a small flap or fold of a garment, etc. **2** a hanging or loose piece of flesh, such as a lobe or wattle. □□ **lap·pet·ed** *adj.* [LAP¹ + –ET¹]

Lap·pish /lápish/ *adj. & n.* ● *adj.* = LAPP *adj.* ● *n.* the Lapp language.

lap robe *n.* a blanket, etc., used for warmth on a journey.

lapse /laps/ *n. & v.* ● *n.* **1** a slight error; a slip of memory, etc. **2** a weak or careless decline into an inferior state. **3** (foll. by *of*) an interval or passage of time (*after a lapse of three years*). **4** *Law* the termination of a right or privilege through disuse or failure to follow appropriate procedures. ● *v.intr.* **1** fail to maintain a position or standard. **2** (foll. by *into*) fall back into an inferior or previous state. **3** (of a right or privilege, etc.) become invalid because it is not used or claimed or renewed. **4** (as **lapsed** *adj.*) (of a person or thing) that has lapsed. □□ **laps·er** *n.* [L *lapsus* f. *labi laps-* glide, slip, fall]

lapse rate *n. Meteorol.* the rate at which the temperature falls with increasing altitude.

lap·stone /lápstōn/ *n.* a shoemaker's stone held in the lap and used to beat leather on.

lap·strake /lápstrayk/ *n. & adj.* ● *n.* a clinker-built boat. ● *adj.* clinker-built.

lap·sus ca·la·mi /lápsəs káləmī, –mee/ *n.* (*pl.* same) a slip of the pen. [L: see LAPSE]

lap·sus lin·guae /lápsəs línggwee/ *n.* a slip of the tongue. [L: see LAPSE]

lap·top /láptop/ *n.* (often *attrib.*) a microcomputer that is portable and suitable for use while traveling.

lap-weld *v. & n.* ● *v.tr.* weld (something) with overlapping edges. ● *n.* (lap weld) such a weld.

lap·wing /lápwing/ *n.* a plover, *Vanellus vanellus*, with black and white plumage, crested head, and a shrill cry. [OE *hlēapewince* f. *hlēapan* LEAP + WINK: assim. to LAP¹, WING]

lar·board /láarbərd/ *n. & adj. Naut. archaic* = PORT³. [ME *lade-*, *ladde-*, *lathe-* (perh. = LADE + BOARD): later assim. to *starboard*]

lar·ce·ny /láarsənee/ *n.* (*pl.* **·nies**) the theft of personal property. □□ **lar·ce·ner** *n.* **lar·ce·nist** *n.* **lar·ce·nous** *adj.* [OF *larcin* f. L *latrocinium* f. *latro* robber, mercenary f. Gk *latreus*]

larch /laarch/ *n.* **1** a deciduous coniferous tree of the genus *Larix*, with bright foliage and producing tough wood. **2** (in full **larchwood**) its wood. [MHG *larche* ult. f. L *larix* –*icis*]

lard /laard/ *n. & v.* ● *n.* the internal fat of the abdomen of pigs, esp. when rendered and clarified for use in cooking and pharmacy. ● *v.tr.* **1** insert strips of fat or bacon in (meat, etc.) before cooking. **2** (foll. by *with*) embellish (talk or writing) with foreign or technical terms. [ME f. OF *lard* bacon f. L *lardum*, *laridum*, rel. to Gk *larinos* fat]

lar·der /láardər/ *n.* **1** a room or cupboard for storing food. **2** a wild animal's store of food, esp. for winter. [ME f. OF *lardier* f. med.L *lardarium* (as LARD)]

lar·doon /laardoon/ *n.* (also **lar·don** /–d'n/) a strip of fat bacon used to lard meat. [F *lardon* (as LARD)]

lard·y /láardee/ *adj.* like or with lard. □ **lardy-cake** *Brit.* a cake made with lard, currants, etc.

lar·es /láreez, laar–/ *n.pl. Rom.Hist.* the household gods. □ **lares and penates** the home. [L]

large /laarj/ *adj. & n.* ● *adj.* **1** of considerable or relatively great size or extent. **2** of the larger kind (*the large intestine*). **3** of wide range;

comprehensive. **4** pursuing an activity on a large scale (*large farmer*). ● *n.* (**at large**) **1** at liberty. **2** as a body or whole (*popular with the people at large*). **3** (of a narration, etc.) at full length and with all details. **4** without a specific target (*scatters insults at large*). **5** representing a whole area and not merely a part of it (*councilwoman at large*). □ **in large** on a large scale. **large as life** see LIFE. **larger than life** see LIFE. □□ **large·ness** *n.* **larg·ish** *adj.* [ME f. OF f. fem. of L *largus* copious]

large in·tes·tine *n.* the cecum, colon, and rectum collectively.

large·ly /láarjlee/ *adv.* to a great extent; principally (*is largely due to laziness*).

large-mind·ed *adj.* liberal; not narrow-minded.

large-scale *adj.* made or occurring on a large scale or in large amounts.

lar·gesse /laarzhés/ *n.* (also **lar·gess**) **1** money or gifts freely given, esp. on an occasion of rejoicing, by a person in high position. **2** generosity; beneficence. [ME f. OF *largesse* ult. f. L *largus* copious]

lar·ghet·to /laargétō/ *adv., adj., & n. Mus.* ● *adv. & adj.* in a fairly slow tempo. ● *n.* (*pl.* **·tos**) a larghetto passage or movement. [It., dimin. of LARGO]

lar·go /láargō/ *adv., adj., & n. Mus.* ● *adv. & adj.* in a slow tempo and dignified in style. ● *n.* (*pl.* **·gos**) a largo passage or movement. [It., = broad]

lar·i·at /láreeət/ *n.* **1** a lasso. **2** a tethering rope, esp. used by cowboys. [Sp. *la reata* f. *reatar* tie again (as RE–, L *aptare* adjust f. *aptus* APT, fit)]

lark¹ /laark/ *n.* **1** any small bird of the family Alaudidae with brown plumage, elongated hind claws and tuneful song, esp. the skylark. **2** any of various similar birds such as the meadowlark. [OE *lāferce*, *læwerce*, of unkn. orig.]

lark² /laark/ *n. & v. colloq.* ● *n.* **1** a frolic or spree; an amusing incident; a joke. **2** *Brit.* a type of activity, affair, etc. (*fed up with this digging lark*). ● *v.intr.* (foll. by *about*) play tricks; frolic. □□ **lark·y** *adj.* **lark·i·ness** *n.* [19th c.: orig. uncert.]

lark·spur /láarkspur/ *n.* any of various plants of the genus *Consolida*, with a spur-shaped calyx.

larn /laarn/ *v. colloq.* or *joc.* **1** *intr.* = LEARN. **2** *tr.* teach (*that'll larn you*). [dial. form of LEARN]

lar·ri·kin /lárikin/ *n. Austral.* a hooligan. [also Engl. dial.: perh. f. the name *Larry* (pet-form of *Lawrence*) + –KIN]

lar·rup /lárəp/ *v.tr. colloq.* thrash. [dial.: perh. f. LATHER]

lar·va /láarvə/ *n.* (*pl.* **lar·vae** /–vee/) **1** the stage of development of an insect between egg and pupa, e.g., a caterpillar. **2** an immature form of other animals that undergo some metamorphosis, e.g., a tadpole. □□ **lar·val** *adj.* **lar·vi·cide** /–visīd/ *n.* [L, = ghost, mask]

la·ryn·ge·al /lərínjəl, –jeeəl/ *adj.* **1** of or relating to the larynx. **2** *Phonet.* (of a sound) made in the larynx.

lar·yn·gi·tis /lárinjítis/ *n.* inflammation of the larynx. □□ **lar·yn·git·ic** /–jítik/ *adj.*

la·ryn·go·scope /lərínggəskōp, –rínjə–/ *n.* an instrument for examining the larynx, or for inserting a tube through it.

lar·yn·got·o·my /láringgótəmee/ *n.* (*pl.* **·mies**) a surgical incision of the larynx, esp. to provide an air passage when breathing is obstructed.

lar·ynx /láringks/ *n.* (*pl.* **la·ryn·ges** /lərínjeez/ or **lar·ynx·es**) the hollow muscular organ forming an air passage to the lungs and holding the vocal cords in humans and other mammals. [mod.L f. Gk *larugx* –*ggos*]

la·sa·gna /ləzáanyə/ *n.* (also **la·sa·gne**) pasta in the form of sheets or wide ribbons, esp. as cooked and layered with ground meat, cheese, and tomato sauce. [It., pl. of *lasagna* f. L *lasanum* cooking pot]

las·car /láskər/ *n.* an E. Indian sailor. [ult. f. Urdu & Pers. *lashkar* army]

las·civ·i·ous /ləsíveeəs/ *adj.* **1** lustful. **2** inciting to or evoking lust. □□ **las·civ·i·ous·ly** *adv.* **las·civ·i·ous·ness** *n.* [ME f. LL *lasciviosus* f. L *lascivia* lustfulness f. *lascivus* sportive, wanton]

lase /layz/ *v.intr.* **1** function as or in a laser. **2** (of a substance) undergo the physical processes employed in a laser. [back-form. f. LASER]

la·ser /láyzər/ *n.* a device that generates an intense beam of coherent monochromatic radiation in the infrared, visible, or ultraviolet region of the electromagnetic spectrum, by stimulated emission of photons from an excited source. [*light amplification by stimulated emission of radiation*: cf. MASER]

la·ser disc *n.* a disk that resembles a compact disc and functions in a similar manner, but is the size of a long-playing record, used for video and interactive multimedia on computer.

la·ser gun *n.* a hand-held device incorporating a laser beam, used for reading a bar code or for determining the distance or speed of an object.

la·ser print·er *n.* a printer linked to a computer that uses a laser to form a pattern of electrostatically charged dots on a light-sensitive drum, which attract toner or dry ink powder.

La•ser•Vi•sion /láyzərvizhən/ *n. Trademark* a system for the reproduction of video signals recorded on a disk with a laser. [LASER + VISION, after TELEVISION]

lash /lash/ *v. & n.* ● *v.* **1** *intr.* make a sudden whiplike movement with a limb or flexible instrument. **2** *tr.* beat with a whip, rope, etc. **3** *intr.* pour or rush with great force. **4** *intr.* (foll. by *at, against*) strike violently. **5** *tr.* castigate in words. **6** *tr.* urge on as with a lash. **7** *tr.* (foll. by *down, together,* etc.) fasten with a cord, rope, etc. **8** *tr.* (of rain, wind, etc.) beat forcefully upon. ● *n.* **1 a** a sharp blow made by a whip, rope, etc. **b** (prec. by *the*) punishment by beating with a whip, etc. **2** the flexible end of a whip. **3** (usu. in *pl.*) an eyelash. □ **lash out** (often foll. by *at*) speak or hit out angrily. **2** *Brit.* spend money extravagantly; be lavish. □□ **lash•er** *n.* **lash•ing•ly** *adv.* (esp. in senses 4–5 of *v.*). **lash•less** *adj.* [ME: prob. imit.]

lash•ing /láshing/ *n.* **1** a beating. **2** cord used for lashing.

lash•ings /láshingz/ *n.pl. Brit. colloq.* (foll. by *of*) plenty; an abundance.

lash-up *n.* a makeshift or improvised structure or arrangement.

lass /las/ *n.* a girl or young woman. [ME *lasce* ult. f. ON *laskwa* unmarried (fem.)]

Las•sa fe•ver /lásə/ *n.* an acute and often fatal febrile viral disease of tropical Africa. [*Lassa* in Nigeria, where first reported]

las•sie /lásee/ *n. colloq.* = LASS.

las•si•tude /lásitood, –tyood/ *n.* **1** languor; weariness. **2** disinclination to exert or interest oneself. [F *lassitude* or L *lassitudo* f. *lassus* tired]

las•so /láso, lasóo/ *n. & v.* ● *n.* (*pl.* **•sos** or **•soes**) a rope with a noose at one end, used esp. in N. America for catching cattle, etc. ● *v.tr.* (**•soes, •soed**) catch with a lasso. □□ **las•so•er** *n.* [Sp. *lazo* LACE]

last[1] /last/ *adj., adv., & n.* ● *adj.* **1** after all others; coming at or belonging to the end. **2 a** most recent; next before a specified time (*last Christmas; last week*). **b** preceding; previous in a sequence (*got on at the last station*). **3** only remaining (*the last cookie, our last chance*). **4** (prec. by *the*) least likely or suitable (*the last person I'd want; the last thing I'd have expected*). **5** the lowest in rank (*the last place*). ● *adv.* **1** after all others (esp. in *comb.*: *last-mentioned*). **2** on the last occasion before the present (*when did you last see him?*). **3** (esp. in enumerating) lastly. ● *n.* **1** a person or thing that is last, last-mentioned, most recent, etc. **2** (prec. by *the*) the last mention or sight, etc. (*shall never hear the last of it*). **3** the last performance of certain acts (*breathed his last*). **4** (prec. by *the*) **a** the end or last moment. **b** death. □ **at last** (or **long last**) in the end; after much delay. **last post** see POST[3]. **on one's last legs** see LEG. **pay one's last respects** see RESPECT. **to** (or **till**) **the last** till the end; esp. till death. [OE *latost* superl.: see LATE]

▶ In precise usage, **latest** means 'most recent' (*my latest project is wallpapering my dining room*), and **last** means 'final' (*the last day of the school year will be June 18*). But *last* is often used in place of *latest*, especially in informal contexts: *I read his last novel.* See also note at FORMER.

last[2] /last/ *v.intr.* **1** remain unexhausted or adequate or alive for a specified or considerable time; suffice (*enough food to last us a week; the battery lasts and lasts*). **2** continue for a specified time (*the journey lasts an hour*). □ **last out** remain adequate or in existence for the whole of a period previously stated or implied. [OE *lǣstan* f. Gmc]

last[3] /last/ *n.* a shoemaker's model for shaping or repairing a shoe or boot. □ **stick to one's last** not meddle with what one does not understand. [OE *lǣste* last, *lǣst* boot, *lāst* footprint f. Gmc]

last-ditch *adj.* used to denote a final, often desperate act to achieve something in the face of difficulty (*a last-ditch attempt to save the park*).

last•ing /lásting/ *adj.* **1** continuing; permanent. **2** durable. □□ **last•ing•ly** *adv.* **last•ing•ness** *n.*

Last Judg•ment *n.* (in some religions) the judgment of mankind expected to take place at the end of the world.

last•ly /lástlee/ *adv.* finally; in the last place.

last min•ute *n.* the time just before an important event (*canceled at the last minute*). □□ **last-minute** *adj.*

last name *n.* surname.

last rites *n.pl.* (in the Christian Church) sacred rites for a person about to die.

last straw *n.* a slight addition to a burden or difficulty that makes it finally unbearable.

Last Sup•per *n.* the supper eaten by Jesus and his disciples on the eve of the Crucifixion, as recorded in the New Testament.

last word *n.* **1** a final or definitive statement (*always has the last word; is the last word on this subject*). **2** (often foll. by *in*) the latest fashion.

lat. *abbr.* latitude.

latch /lach/ *n. & v.* ● *n.* **1** a bar with a catch and lever used as a fastening for a gate, etc. **2** a springlock preventing a door from being opened from the outside without a key after being shut. ● *v.tr. &*

intr. fasten or be fastened with a latch. □ **latch on** (often foll. by *to*) *colloq.* **1** attach oneself (to). **2** understand. [prob. f. (now dial.) *latch* (v.) seize f. OE *læccan* f. Gmc]

latch•key /láchkee/ *n.* (*pl.* **•keys**) a key of an outer door of a house.

latch•key child *n.* (also **latch•key kid**) a child who is alone at home after school until a parent returns from work.

late /layt/ *adj. & adv.* ● *adj.* **1** after the due or usual time; occurring or done after the proper time (*late for dinner; a late milk delivery*). **2 a** far on in the day or night or in a specified time or period. **b** far on in development. **3** flowering or ripening toward the end of the season (*late strawberries*). **4** (prec. by *the* or *my, his,* etc.) no longer alive or having the specified status (*my late husband; the late president*). **5** of recent date (*the late storms*). **6** (as **latest**, prec. by *the*) fashionable, up to date. ● *adv.* **1** after the due or usual time (*arrived late*). **2** far on in time (*this happened later on*). **3** at or till a late hour. **4** at a late stage of development. **5** formerly but now not (*a family late of New England but now scattered throughout the South*). □ **at the latest** as the latest time envisaged (*will have done it by six at the latest*). **late in the day** *colloq.* at a late stage in the proceedings, esp. too late to be useful. **the latest 1** the most recent news, etc. (*have you heard the latest?*). **2** the current fashion. □□ **late•ness** *n.* [OE *lǣt* (adj.), *late* (adv.) f. Gmc]

▶ For a comparison of **latest** and **last**, see note at LAST[1].

late•com•er /láytkumər/ *n.* a person who arrives late.

la•teen /lətéen/ *n.* (also **la•teen sail**) **1** a triangular sail on a long yard at an angle of 45° to the mast. **2** a ship rigged with such a sail. [F (*voile*) *Latine* Latin (sail), because common in the Mediterranean]

Late Lat•in *n.* Latin of about AD 200–600.

late•ly /láytlee/ *adv.* not long ago; recently; in recent times. [OE *lætlīce* (as LATE, –LY[2])]

La Tène /laa tén/ *adj.* of or relating to the second Iron Age culture of central and W. Europe. [*La Tène* in Switzerland, where remains of it were first identified]

la•tent /láyt'nt/ *adj.* **1** concealed; dormant. **2** existing but not developed or manifest. □□ **la•ten•cy** *n.* **la•tent•ly** *adv.* [L *latēre latent-* be hidden]

lateen sail

SYNONYM TIP latent

ABEYANT, DORMANT, POTENTIAL, QUIESCENT. All of these words refer to what is not currently observable or showing signs of activity. A **latent** talent is one that has not yet manifested itself, while **potential** suggests a talent that exists in an undeveloped state (*a potential concert violinist*). A child may have certain *latent* qualities of which his or her parents are unaware; but teachers are usually quick to spot a *potential* artist or poet in the classroom. **Dormant** and **quiescent** are less frequently associated with people and more often associated with things. A volcano might be described as *dormant*, which applies to anything that is currently inactive, but has been active in the past and is capable of becoming active again in the future. *Dormant* carries the connotation of sleeping (*plants that are dormant in the winter*), while *quiescent* means motionless (*a quiescent sea*), emphasizing inactivity without referring to past or future activity. **Abeyant**, like *dormant*, means suspended or temporarily inactive, but it is most commonly used as a noun (*personal rights and privileges kept in abeyance until the danger had passed*).

la•tent heat *n. Physics* the heat required to convert a solid into a liquid or vapor, or a liquid into a vapor, without change of temperature.

la•tent im•age *n. Photog.* an image not yet made visible by developing.

-later /lətər/ *comb. form* denoting a person who worships a particular thing or person (*idolater*). [Gk: see LATRIA]

lat•er•al /látərəl/ *adj. & n.* ● *adj.* **1** of, at, toward, or from the side or sides. **2** descended from a brother or sister of a person in direct line. ● *n.* a side part, etc., esp. a lateral shoot or branch. □□ **lat•er•al•ly** *adv.* [L *lateralis* f. *latus lateris* side]

lat•er•al line *n. Zool.* a visible line along the side of a fish consisting of a series of sense organs acting as vibration receptors.

lat•er•al think•ing *n.* a method of solving problems indirectly or by apparently illogical methods.

lat•er•ite /látərīt/ *n.* a red or yellow ferruginous clay, friable and hardening in air, used for making roads in the tropics. □□ **lat•er•it•ic** /–rítik/ *adj.* [L *later* brick + –ITE[1]]

la•tex /láyteks/ *n.* (*pl.* **lat•i•ces** /–tiseez/ or **la•tex•es**) **1** a milky fluid of mixed composition found in various plants and trees, esp. the rubber tree, and used for commercial purposes. **2** a synthetic product resembling this. [L, = liquid]

lath /lath/ *n. & v.* ● *n.* (*pl.* **laths** /laths, lathz/) a thin flat strip of wood, esp. each of a series forming a framework or support for the plaster of a wall, etc. ● *v.tr.* attach laths to (a wall or ceiling). [OE *lætt*]

lathe /layth/ *n.* a machine for shaping wood, metal, etc., by means of a rotating drive which turns the piece being worked on against changeable cutting tools. [prob. rel. to ODa. *lad* structure, frame, f. ON *hlath*, rel. to *hlatha* LADE]

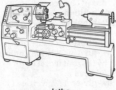

lathe

lath·er /láthər/ *n. & v.* ● *n.* **1** a froth produced by agitating soap, etc., and water. **2** frothy sweat, esp. of a horse. **3** a state of agitation. ● *v.* **1** *intr.* (of soap, etc.) form a lather. **2** *tr.* cover with lather. **3** *intr.* (of a horse, etc.) develop or become covered with lather. **4** *tr. colloq.* thrash. □□ **lath·er·y** *adj.* [OE *lēathor* (n.), *lēthran* (v.)]

la·thi /láatee/ *n.* (*pl.* **la·this**) (in India) a long, heavy, iron-bound bamboo stick used as a weapon, esp. by police. [Hindi *lāṭhī*]

lat·i·ces *pl.* of LATEX.

Lat·in /lát'n/ *n. & adj.* ● *n.* **1** the Italic language of ancient Rome and its empire, originating in Latium. **2** *Rom.Hist.* an inhabitant of ancient Latium in Central Italy. ● *adj.* **1** of or in Latin. **2** of the countries or peoples (e.g., France and Spain) using languages developed from Latin. **3** *Rom.Hist.* of or relating to ancient Latium or its inhabitants. **4** of the Roman Catholic Church. □□ **Lat·in·ism** *n.* **Lat·in·ist** *n.* [ME f. OF *Latin* or L *Latinus* f. *Latium*]

Lat·in A·mer·i·ca *n.* the parts of Central and S. America where Spanish or Portuguese is the main language. □□ **Lat·in A·mer·i·can** *n. & adj.*

Lat·in·ate /lát'nayt/ *adj.* having the character of Latin.

Lat·in Church *n.* the Western Church.

Lat·in·ize /lát'nīz/ *v.* **1** *tr.* give a Latin or Latinate form to. **2** *tr.* translate into Latin. **3** *tr.* make conformable to the ideas, customs, etc., of the ancient Romans, Latin peoples, or Latin Church. **4** *intr.* use Latin forms, idioms, etc. □□ **Lat·in·i·za·tion** *n.* **Lat·in·iz·er** *n.* [LL *latinizare* (as LATIN)]

La·ti·no /lətéenō/ *n.* (*pl.* **La·ti·nos**; *fem.* **La·ti·na** /–nə/, *pl.* **La·ti·nas**) **1** a native or inhabitant of Latin America. **2** a person of Spanish-speaking or Latin-American descent.

lat·ish /láytish/ *adj. & adv.* fairly late.

lat·i·tude /látitōod, –tyōod/ *n.*

1 *Geog.* **a** the angular distance on a meridian north or south of the equator, expressed in degrees and minutes. **b** (usu. in *pl.*) regions or climes, esp. with reference to temperature (*warm latitudes*). **2** freedom from narrowness; liberality of interpretation. **3** tolerated variety of action or opinion (*was allowed much latitude*). **4** *Astron.* the angular distance of a celestial body or point from the ecliptic. □□ **lat·i·tu·di·nal** /–tōod'nəl, –tyōod–/ *adj.* **lat·i·tu·di·nal·ly** *adv.* [ME, = breadth, f. L *latitudo –dinis* f. *latus* broad]

latitude 1a

lat·i·tu·di·nar·i·an /látitōod'náireeən, –tyōod–/ *adj. & n.* ● *adj.* allowing latitude esp. in religion; showing no preference among varying creeds and forms of worship. ● *n.* a person with a latitudinarian attitude. □□ **lat·i·tu·di·nar·i·an·ism** *n.* [L *latitudo –dinis* breadth + –ARIAN]

la·tri·a /lətríə/ *n. Theol.* supreme worship allowed to God alone. [LL f. Gk *latreia* worship f. *latreuō* serve]

la·trine /lətréen/ *n.* a communal toilet, esp. in a camp, barracks, etc. [F f. L *latrina*, shortening of *lavatrina* f. *lavare* wash]

-latry /lətree/ *comb. form* denoting worship (*idolatry*). [Gk *latreia*: see LATRIA]

lat·ten /lát'n/ *n.* an alloy of copper and zinc, often rolled into sheets, and formerly used for monumental brasses and church articles. [ME *latoun* f. OF *laton, leiton*]

lat·ter /látər/ *adj.* **1 a** denoting the second-mentioned of two, or *disp.* the last-mentioned of three or more. **b** (prec. by *the*; usu. *absol.*) the second- or last-mentioned person or thing. **2** nearer to the end (*the latter part of the year*). **3** recent. **4** belonging to the end of a period, of the world, etc. [OE *lætra*, compar. of *læt* LATE]

▶ This word means 'the second-mentioned of two.' Its use to mean 'the last-mentioned of three or more' is common, but considered incorrect by some. *Last* or *last-mentioned* is preferred where three or more things are involved. See also note at FORMER.

lat·ter-day *adj.* modern; newfangled.

Lat·ter-day Saints *n.pl.* the Mormons' name for themselves.

lat·ter·ly /látərlee/ *adv.* **1** in the latter part of life or of a period. **2** recently.

lat·tice /látis/ *n.* **1 a** a structure of strips of wood or metal crossed

---

and fastened together with square or diamond-shaped spaces left between, used as a screen, fence, etc. **b** = LATTICEWORK. **2** *Crystallog.* a regular periodic arrangement of atoms, ions, or molecules in a crystalline solid. □□ **lat·ticed** *adj.* **lat·tic·ing** *n.* [ME f. OF *lattis* f. *latte* lath f. WG]

lat·tice gird·er *n.* a girder or truss made of top and bottom members connected by struts usu. crossing diagonally.

lat·tice win·dow *n.* a window with small panes set in diagonally crossing strips of lead.

lat·tice·work /látiswərk/ *n.* interlacing strips of wood, metal, or other material forming a lattice.

Lat·vi·an /látveeən/ *n. & adj.* ● *n.* **1 a** a native of Latvia, a Baltic republic. **b** a person of Latvian descent. **2** the language of Latvia. ● *adj.* of or relating to Latvia or its people or language.

laud /lawd/ *v. & n.* ● *v.tr.* praise or extol, esp. in hymns. ● *n.* **1** *literary* praise; a hymn of praise. **2** (in *pl.*) the traditional morning prayer of the Roman Catholic Church. [ME: (n.) f. OF *laude*, (v.) f. L *laudare*, f. L *laus laudis* praise]

laud·a·ble /láwdəbəl/ *adj.* commendable; praiseworthy. □□ **laud·a·bil·i·ty** /–bílitee/ *n.* **laud·a·bly** *adv.* [ME f. L *laudabilis* (as LAUD)]

lau·da·num /láwd'nəm/ *n.* a solution containing morphine and prepared from opium, formerly used as a narcotic painkiller. [mod.L, the name given by Paracelsus to a costly medicament, later applied to preparations containing opium: perh. var. of LADANUM]

lau·da·tion /lawdáyshən/ *n. formal* praise. [L *laudatio –onis* (as LAUD)]

laud·a·to·ry /láwdətáwree/ *adj.* (also **laud·a·tive** /–tiv/) expressing praise.

laugh /laf/ *v. & n.* ● *v.* **1** *intr.* make the spontaneous sounds and movements usual in expressing lively amusement, scorn, derision, etc. **2** *tr.* express by laughing. **3** *tr.* bring (a person) into a certain state by laughing (*laughed them into agreeing*). **4** *intr.* (foll. by *at*) ridicule; make fun of (*laughed at us for going*). **5** *intr.* (**be laughing**) *colloq.* be in a fortunate or successful position. **6** *intr.* esp. *poet.* make sounds reminiscent of laughing. ● *n.* **1** the sound or act or manner of laughing. **2** *colloq.* a comical or ridiculous person or thing. □ **have the last laugh** be ultimately the winner. **laugh in a person's face** show open scorn for a person. **laugh off** get rid of (embarrassment or humiliation) with a jest. **laugh out of court** deprive of a hearing by ridicule. **laugh out of the other side of one's mouth** (or **on the other side of one's face**) change from enjoyment or amusement to displeasure, shame, apprehension, etc. **laugh up one's sleeve** be secretly or inwardly amused. □□ **laugh·er** *n.* [OE *hlæhhan, hliehhan* f. Gmc]

laugh·a·ble /láfəbəl/ *adj.* ludicrous; highly amusing. □□ **laugh·a·bly** *adv.*

laugh·ing /láfing/ *n. & adj.* ● *n.* laughter. ● *adj.* in senses of LAUGH *v.* □ **no laughing matter** something serious. □□ **laugh·ing·ly** *adv.*

laugh·ing gas *n.* nitrous oxide as an anesthetic, formerly used without oxygen and causing an exhilarating effect when inhaled.

laugh·ing hy·e·na *n.* = SPOTTED HYENA.

laugh·ing jack·ass *n.* = KOOKABURRA.

laugh·ing·stock /láfingstok/ *n.* a person or thing open to general ridicule.

laugh·ter /láftər/ *n.* the act or sound of laughing. [OE *hleahtor* f. Gmc]

laugh track *n.* recorded laughter added to a comedy show, esp. a television situation comedy.

launce /lans, laans/ *n.* = SAND LANCE. [perh. f. LANCE: cf. *garfish*]

launch[1] /lawnch/ *v. & n.* ● *v.* **1** *tr.* set (a vessel) afloat. **2** *tr.* hurl or send forth (a weapon, rocket, etc.). **3** *tr.* start or set in motion (an enterprise, a person on a course of action, etc.). **4** *tr.* formally introduce (a new product) with publicity, etc. **5** *intr.* (often foll. by *out, into*, etc.) **a** make a start, esp. on an ambitious enterprise. **b** burst into strong language, etc. ● *n.* the act or an instance of launching. □ **launching pad 1** = LAUNCHPAD 2. **2** = SPRINGBOARD 2. [ME f. AF *launcher*, ONF *lancher*, OF *lancier* LANCE *v.*]

launch[2] /lawnch/ *n.* **1** a motorboat, used esp. for pleasure. **2** a man-of-war's largest boat. [Sp. *lancha* pinnace perh. f. Malay *lancharan* f. *lanchār* swift]

launch·er /láwnchər/ *n.* a structure or device to hold a rocket during launching.

launch·pad /láwnchpad/ *n.* a platform with a supporting structure, from which rockets are launched.

laun·der /láwndər, laán–/ *v. & n.* ● *v.tr.* **1** wash and iron (clothes, linen, etc.). **2** *colloq.* transfer (funds) to conceal a dubious or illegal origin. ● *n.* a channel for conveying liquids, esp. molten metal. □□ **laun·der·er** *n.* [ME *launder* (n.) washer of linen, contr. of *lavander* f. OF *lavandier* ult. f. L *lavanda* things to be washed, neut. pl. gerundive of *lavare* wash]

laun·der·ette /lawndərét, laán–/ *n.* (also **laun·drette**) = LAUNDROMAT.

laun·dress /láwndris, laán–/ *n.* a woman who launders clothes, linen, etc., esp. professionally.

laun·dro·mat /láwndrəmat, laán–/ *n. Trademark* an establishment with coin-operated washing machines and dryers for public use.

laun·dry /láwndree, laán–/ *n.* (*pl.* **·dries**) **1** an establishment for washing clothes or linen. **2** clothes or linen for laundering or newly laundered. [contr. f. *lavendry* (f. OF *lavanderie*) after LAUNDER]

laundry list *n. colloq.* a lengthy and often random list of items (*a laundry list of weekend projects; a laundry list of my flaws*).

lau·re·ate /láwreeət, lór–/ *adj. & n.* • *adj.* **1** wreathed with laurel as a mark of honor. **2** consisting of laurel; laurellike. • *n.* **1** a person who is honored for outstanding creative or intellectual achievement (*Nobel laureate*). **2** = POET LAUREATE. □□ **lau·re·ate·ship** *n.* [L *laureatus* f. *laurea* laurel wreath f. *laurus* laurel]

lau·rel /láwrəl, lór–/ *n. & v.* • *n.* **1** = BAY². **2 a** (in *sing.* or *pl.*) the foliage of the bay tree used as an emblem of victory or distinction in poetry, usu. formed into a wreath or crown. **b** (in *pl.*) honor or distinction. **3** any plant with dark-green glossy leaves like a bay tree, e.g., cherry laurel, mountain laurel, spurge laurel. • *v.tr.* (**lau·reled, lau·rel·ing**; esp. *Brit.* **lau·relled, lau·rel·ling**) wreathe with laurel. □ **look to one's laurels** beware of losing one's preeminence. **rest on one's laurels** be satisfied with what one has done and not seek further success. [ME *lorer* f. OF *lorier* f. Prov. *laurier* f. *laur* f. L *laurus*]

lau·rus·ti·nus /láwrəstínəs/ *n.* an evergreen winter-flowering shrub, *Viburnum tinus*, with dense glossy green leaves and white or pink flowers. [mod.L f. L *laurus* laurel + *tinus* wild laurel]

lav /lav/ *n. colloq.* lavatory. [abbr.]

la·va /láavə, lávə/ *n.* **1** the molten matter which flows from a volcano. **2** the solid substance which it forms on cooling. [It. f. *lavare* wash f. L]

la·va·bo /ləvaábō/ *n.* (*pl.* **·bos**) **1** *RC & Anglican Ch.* **a** the ritual washing of the celebrant's hands at the offertory of the Mass. **b** a towel or basin used for this. **2** a monastery washing trough. **3** a washbasin. [L, = I will wash, first word of Psalm 26:6]

la·vage /ləvaázh, lávij/ *n. Med.* the washing out of a body cavity, such as the colon or stomach, with water or a medicated solution. [F f. *laver* wash: see LAVE]

la·va·tion /ləváyshən/ *n. formal* washing. [L *lavatio* f. *lavare* wash]

lav·a·to·ri·al /lávətáwreeəl/ *adj.* esp. *Brit.* (esp. of humor) relating to bathrooms and their use.

lav·a·to·ry /lávətawree/ *n.* (*pl.* **·ries**) **1** a sink or wash basin in a bathroom. **2** a room or compartment with a toilet and wash basin. **3** *Brit.* a flush toilet. [ME, = washing vessel, f. LL *lavatorium* f. L *lavare lavat-* wash]

lave /layv/ *v.tr. literary* **1** wash; bathe. **2** (of water) wash against; flow along. [ME f. OF *laver* f. L *lavare* wash, perh. coalescing with OE *lafian*]

lav·en·der /lávindər/ *n. & v.* • *n.* **1 a** any small evergreen shrub of the genus *Lavandula*, with narrow leaves and blue, purple, or pink aromatic flowers. **b** its flowers and stalks dried and used to scent linen, clothes, etc. **2** a pale blue color with a trace of red. • *v.tr.* put lavender among (linen, etc.). [ME f. AF *lavendre*, ult. f. med.L *lavandula*]

lav·en·der wa·ter *n.* a perfume made from distilled lavender, alcohol, and ambergris.

la·ver¹ /láyvər/ *n.* any of various edible seaweeds, esp. *Porphyra umbilicalis*, having sheetlike fronds. [L]

la·ver² /láyvər/ *n.* **1** *Bibl.* a large brass vessel for Jewish priests' ritual ablutions. **2** *archaic* a washing or fountain basin; a font. [ME *lavo(u)r* f. OF *laveo(i)r* f. LL (as LAVATORY)]

lav·ish /lávish/ *adj. & v.* • *adj.* **1** giving or producing in large quantities; profuse. **2** generous; unstinting. **3** excessive; overabundant. • *v.tr.* (often foll. by *on*) bestow or spend (money, effort, praise, etc.) abundantly. □□ **lav·ish·ly** *adv.* **lav·ish·ness** *n.* [ME f. obs. *lavish, lavas* (n.) profusion f. OF *lavasse* deluge of rain f. *laver* wash]

law /law/ *n.* **1 a** a rule enacted or customary in a community and recognized as enjoining or prohibiting certain actions and enforced by the imposition of penalties. **b** a body of such rules (*the law of the land; forbidden under state law*). **2** the controlling influence of laws; a state of respect for laws (*law and order*). **3** laws collectively as a social system or subject of study (*was reading law*). **4** (with defining word) any of the specific branches or applications of law (*commercial law; law of contract*). **5** binding force or effect (*their word is law*). **6** (prec. by *the*) **a** the legal profession. **b** *colloq.* the police. **7** the statute and common law (opp. EQUITY). **8** (in *pl.*) jurisprudence. **9 a** the judicial remedy; litigation. **b** courts of law as providing this (*go to law*). **10** a rule of action or procedure, e.g., in a game, social context, form of art, etc. **11** a regularity in natural occurrences, esp. as formulated or propounded in particular instances (*the laws of nature; the law of gravity; Parkinson's law*). **12 a** divine commandments as expressed in the Bible or other sources. **b** (**Law of Moses**) the precepts of the Pentateuch. □ **at** (or **in**) **law** according to the laws. **be a law unto oneself** do what one feels is right; disregard custom. **go to law** *Brit.* take legal action; make use of the courts. **lay down the law** be dogmatic or authori-

tarian. **take the law into one's own hands** redress a grievance by one's own means, esp. by force. [OE *lagu* f. ON *lag* something 'laid down' or fixed, rel. to LAY¹]

law-a·bid·ing *adj.* obedient to the laws.

law·break·er /láwbraykər/ *n.* a person who breaks the law. □□ **law·break·ing** *n. & adj.*

law court *n.* a court of law.

law·ful /láwfŏŏl/ *adj.* conforming with, permitted by, or recognized by law; not illegal or (of a child) illegitimate. □□ **law·ful·ly** *adv.* **law·ful·ness** *n.*

law·giv·er /láwgivər/ *n.* a person who lays down laws.

law·less /láwlis/ *adj.* **1** having no laws or enforcement of them. **2** disregarding laws. **3** unbridled; uncontrolled. □□ **law·less·ly** *adv.* **law·less·ness** *n.*

law·mak·er /láwmaykər/ *n.* a legislator.

law·man /láwman/ *n.* (*pl.* **·men**) a law-enforcement officer, esp. a sheriff or policeman.

lawn¹ /lawn/ *n.* an area of short, regularly mown grass in a yard, garden, or park. [ME *laund* glade f. OF *launde* f. OCelt., rel. to LAND]

lawn² /lawn/ *n.* a fine linen or cotton fabric used for clothes. □□ **lawn·y** *adj.* [ME, prob. f. *Laon* in France]

lawn bowl·ing *n.* (also *Brit.* **bowls**) a game played with heavy wooden balls, the object of which is to propel one's ball so that it comes to rest as close as possible to a previously bowled small ball without touching it.

lawn mow·er *n.* a machine for cutting the grass on a lawn.

lawn ten·nis *n. dated* the usual form of tennis, played with a soft ball on outdoor grass or an open court.

law of av·er·ag·es *n.* the principle that if one of two extremes occurs the other will also tend to, so as to maintain the normal average.

law of di·min·ish·ing re·turns *n. Econ.* the fact that the increase of expenditure, investment, taxation, etc., beyond a certain point ceases to produce a proportionate yield.

law of mass ac·tion *n. Chem.* the principle that the rate of a chemical reaction is proportional to the masses of the reacting substances.

law of na·tions *n. Law* international law.

law of na·ture *n.* = NATURAL LAW.

law of par·si·mo·ny *n.* the assertion that no more causes or forces should be assumed than are necessary to account for the facts.

law of suc·ces·sion *n.* the law regulating the inheritance of property.

law·ren·ci·um /lərénseeəm, law–/ *n. Chem.* an artificially made transuranic radioactive metallic element. ¶ Symb.: **Lw**. [E. O. *Lawrence*, Amer. physicist d. 1958]

laws of war *n.pl.* international rules and conventions that limit belligerents' action.

law·suit /láwsŏŏt/ *n.* the process or an instance of making a claim in a court of law.

law·yer /láwyər, lóyər/ *n.* a member of the legal profession. □□ **law·yer·ly** *adj.* [ME *law(i)er* f. LAW]

lax /laks/ *adj.* **1** lacking care, concern, or firmness. **2** loose, relaxed; not compact. **3** *Phonet.* pronounced with the vocal muscles relaxed. □□ **lax·i·ty** *n.* **lax·ly** *adv.* **lax·ness** *n.* [ME, = loose, f. L *laxus*: rel. to SLACK¹]

lax·a·tive /láksətiv/ *adj. & n.* • *adj.* tending to stimulate or facilitate evacuation of the bowels. • *n.* a laxative medicine. [ME f. OF *laxatif –ive* or LL *laxativus* f. L *laxare* loosen (as LAX)]

lay¹ /lay/ *v. & n.* • *v.* (*past* and *past part.* **laid** /layd/) **1** *tr.* place on a surface, esp. horizontally or in the proper or specified place. **2** *tr.* put or bring into a certain or the required position or state (*lay a carpet*). **3** *intr. dial.* or *erron.* lie. **4** *tr.* make by laying (*lay the foundations*). **5** *tr.* (often *absol.*) (of a hen bird) produce (an egg). **6** *tr.* a cause to subside or lie flat. **b** deal with to remove (a ghost, fear, etc.). **7** *tr.* place or present for consideration (a case, proposal, etc.). **8** *tr.* set down as a basis or starting point. **9** *tr.* (usu. foll. by *on*) attribute or impute (blame, etc.). **10** *tr.* locate (a scene, etc.) in a certain place. **11** *tr.* prepare or make ready (a plan or a trap). **12** *tr.* prepare (a table) for a meal. **13** *tr.* place or arrange the material for (a fire). **14** *tr.* put down as a wager; stake. **15** *tr.* (foll. by *with*) coat or strew (a surface). **16** *tr. sl. offens.* have sexual intercourse with (esp. a woman). • *n.* **1** the way, position, or direction in which something lies. **2** *sl. offens.* a partner (esp. female) in sexual intercourse. **3** the direction or amount of twist in rope strands. □ **in lay** (of a hen) laying eggs regularly. **lay about one 1** hit out on all sides. **2** criticize indiscriminately. **lay aside 1** put to one side. **2** cease to practice or consider. **3** save (money, etc.) for future needs. **lay at the door of** see DOOR. **lay back** cause to slope back from the vertical. **lay bare** expose; reveal. **lay a charge** make an accusation. **lay claim to** claim as one's own. **lay down 1** put on the ground. **2** relinquish; give up (an office). **3** formulate or insist on (a rule or principle). **4** pay or wager (money). **5** esp. *Brit.* begin to construct (a ship or railroad). **6** store (wine) in a cellar. **7** set down on paper. **8** sacrifice (one's life). **9** convert (land) into pasture. **10** record (esp. popular music). **lay down the law** see LAW. **lay one's hands on** obtain; acquire; locate. **lay hands on 1** seize or attack. **2** place one's hands on or over, esp. in confirmation, ordination, or spiritual healing. **lay hold of** seize or grasp. **lay in** provide oneself with a stock of. **lay into** *colloq.* punish or scold severely. **lay it on thick** (or **with a trowel**) *colloq.* flatter or exaggerate grossly. **lay low** overthrow, kill, or humble. **lay off 1** discharge (workers) temporarily because of a shortage of work. **2** *colloq.* desist. **lay on 1** spread on (paint, etc.). **2** inflict (blows). **3** impose (a penalty, obligation, etc.). **4** *Brit.* provide (a facility, amenity, etc.). **lay on the table** see TABLE. **lay open 1** break the skin of. **2** (foll. by *to*) expose to criticism, etc.). **lay out 1** spread out. **2** expose to view. **3** prepare (a corpse) for burial. **4** *colloq.* knock unconscious. **5** prepare a layout. **6** expend (money). **7** *refl.* (foll. by *to* + infin.) take pains (to do something) (*laid themselves out to help*). **lay store by** see STORE. **lay to rest** bury in a grave. **lay up 1** store; save. **2** put (a ship, etc.) out of service. **lay waste** see WASTE. [OE *lecgan* f. Gmc]

▶**Lay**, 'to put down on a surface,' is a transitive verb, while **lie**, 'to be horizontal,' is intransitive. Avoid the intransitive use of **lay**, as in "I'm going to lay on the grass at lunchtime" (use *lie* instead). Similarly, avoid the transitive use of **lie**, as in "lie it on the table" (use *lay* instead). These two verbs are often confused, especially because the past of *lie* is *lay*: *we lay on the grass for an hour.* The past of *lay* is *laid*: *I laid down my tools and lay on the grass.*

lay² /lay/ *adj.* **1 a** nonclerical. **b** not ordained into the clergy. **2 a** not professionally qualified, esp. in law or medicine. **b** of or done by such persons. [ME f. OF *lai* f. eccl.L *laicus* f. Gk *laïkos* LAIC]

lay³ /lay/ *n.* **1** a short lyric or narrative poem meant to be sung. **2** a song. [ME f. OF *lai*, Prov. *lais*, of unkn. orig.]

lay⁴ *past* of LIE¹.

lay•a•bout /láyəbowt/ *n.* a habitual loafer or idler.

lay broth•er *n.* (also **lay sis•ter**) a person who has taken the vows of a religious order but is not ordained and is employed in ancillary or manual work.

lay-by /láybí/ *n.* (*pl.* **lay-bys**) **1** *Brit.* an area at the side of an open road where vehicles may stop. **2** a similar arrangement on a canal or railroad. **3** *Austral. & NZ* a system of paying a deposit to secure an article for later purchase.

lay•er /láyər/ *n. & v.* ● *n.* **1** a thickness of matter, esp. one of several, covering a surface. **2** a person or thing that lays. **3** a hen that lays eggs. **4** a shoot fastened down to take root while attached to the parent plant. ● *v.tr.* **1 a** arrange in layers. **b** cut (hair) in layers. **2** propagate (a plant) as a layer. □□ **lay•ered** *adj.* [ME f. LAY¹ + -ER¹]

lay•ette /layét/ *n.* a set of clothing, toilet articles, and bedclothes for a newborn child. [F, dimin. of OF *laie* drawer f. MDu. *laege*]

lay fig•ure /lay/ *n.* **1** a dummy or jointed figure of a human body used by artists. **2** an unrealistic character in a novel, etc. **3** a person lacking in individuality. [*lay* f. obs. *layman* f. Du. *leeman* f. *led* joint]

lay•man /láymən/ *n.* (*pl.* •**men**; *fem.* **lay•wom•an**, *pl.* • **wom•en**) **1** any nonordained member of a church. **2** a person without professional or specialized knowledge in a particular subject.

lay•off /láyawf/ *n.* **1** a temporary discharge of workers. **2** a period when this is in force.

lay of the land *n.* the current state of affairs.

lay•out /láyowt/ *n.* **1** the disposing or arrangement of a site, ground, etc. **2** the way in which plans, printed matter, etc., are arranged or set out. **3** something arranged or set out in a particular way. **4** the make-up of a book, newspaper, etc.

lay•o•ver /láyōvər/ *n.* a period of rest or waiting before a further stage in a journey, etc.; a stopover.

lay read•er *n.* a lay person licensed to conduct some religious services.

laz•ar /lázər, láy-/ *n.* *archaic* a poor and diseased person, esp. a leper. [ME f. med.L *lazarus* f. the name in Luke 16:20]

laz•a•ret•to /lázərétō/ *n.* (also **laz•a•ret** /-rét/) (*pl.* **laz•a•ret•tos** or **laz•a•ret**) **1** a hospital for diseased people, esp. lepers. **2** a building or ship for quarantine. **3** the after part of a ship's hold, used for stores. [(F *lazaret*) f. It. *lazzaretto* f. *lazzaro* LAZAR]

laze /layz/ *v. & n.* ● *v.* **1** *intr.* spend time lazily or idly. **2** *tr.* (often foll. by *away*) pass (time) in this way. ● *n.* a spell of lazing. [back-form. f. LAZY]

laz•u•li /lázəlee, lázyə-, lázhə-/ *n.* = LAPIS LAZULI. [abbr.]

la•zy /láyzee/ *adj.* (**la•zi•er, la•zi•est**) **1** disinclined to work; doing little work. **2** of or inducing idleness. **3** (of a river, etc.) slow-moving. □□ **la•zi•ly** *adv.* **la•zi•ness** *n.* [earlier *laysie, lasie, laesy*, perh. f. LG: cf. LG *lasich* idle]

la•zy•bones /láyzeebōnz/ *n.* (*pl.* same) *colloq.* a lazy person.

la•zy eye *n.* an eye with poor vision that is mainly caused by underuse, esp. the unused eye in strabismus.

la•zy Su•san *n.* a revolving stand or tray on a table, used esp. for holding condiments.

lb. *abbr.* a pound or pounds (weight). [L *libra*]

LC *abbr.* (also **L.C.** or **l.c.**) **1** landing craft. **2** left center. **3** letter of credit. **4** (**LC** or **L.C.**) Library of Congress. **5** lowercase. **6** in the passage, etc., cited. [sense 6 f. L *loco citato*]

LCD *abbr.* **1** liquid crystal display. **2** lowest (or least) common denominator.

LCM *abbr.* lowest (or least) common multiple.

LD *abbr.* lethal dose, usu. with a following numeral indicating the percentage of a group of animals killed by such a dose (LD_{50}).

Ld. *abbr.* Lord.

L-do•pa *n.* /él dópə/ *Biochem.* the levorotatory form of dopa, used to treat Parkinson's disease. Also called **levodopa**.

-le¹ /'l/ *suffix* forming nouns, esp.: **1** names of appliances or instruments (*handle; thimble*). **2** names of animals and plants (*beetle; thistle*). [ult. from or repr. OE –*el*, etc. f. Gmc, with many IE cognates] ▶The suffix has ceased to be syllabic in *fowl, snail*, and *stile*.

-le² /'l/ *suffix* (also **–el**) forming nouns with (or orig. with) diminutive sense, or = –AL (*angle; castle; mantle; syllable; novel; tunnel*). [ME –*el*, –*elle* f. OF ult. f. L forms –*ellus*, –*ella*, etc.]

-le³ /'l/ *suffix* forming adjectives, often with (or orig. with) the sense 'apt or liable to' (*brittle; fickle; little; nimble*). [ME f. OE –*el*, etc. f. Gmc, corresp. to L –*ulus*]

-le⁴ /'l/ *suffix* forming verbs, esp. expressing repeated action or movement or having diminutive sense (*bubble; crumple; wriggle*). [OE –*lian* f. Gmc]

lea /lee, láy/ *n. poet.* (also **ley**) a piece of meadow or pasture or arable land. [OE *lēa(h)* f. Gmc]

leach /leech/ *v.* **1** *tr.* make (a liquid) percolate through some material. **2** *tr.* subject (bark, ore, ash, or soil) to the action of percolating fluid. **3** *tr. & intr.* (foll. by *away, out*) remove (soluble matter) or be removed in this way. □□ **leach•er** *n.* [prob. repr. OE *leccan* to water, f. WG]

lead¹ /leed/ *v., n., & adj.* ● *v.* (*past* and *past part.* **led** /led/) **1** *tr.* cause to go with one, esp. by guiding or showing the way or by going in front and taking a person's hand or an animal's halter, etc. **2** *tr.* **a** direct the actions or opinions of. **b** (often foll. by *to*, or *to* + infin.) guide by persuasion or example or argument (*what led you to that conclusion?; was led to think you may be right*). **3** *tr.* (also *absol.*) provide access to; bring to a certain position or destination (*this door leads you into a small room; the road leads to Atlanta; the path leads uphill*). **4** *tr.* pass or go through (a life, etc., of a specified kind) (*led a miserable existence*). **5** *tr.* **a** have the first place in (*lead the dance; leads the world in sugar production*). **b** (*absol.*) go first; be ahead in a race or game. **c** (*absol.*) be preeminent in some field. **6** *tr.* be in charge of (*leads a team of researchers*). **7** *tr.* **a** direct by example. **b** set (a fashion). **c** be the principal player of (a group of musicians). **8** *tr.* (also *absol.*) begin a round of play at cards by playing (a card) or a card of (a particular suit). **9** *intr.* (foll. by *to*) have as an end or outcome; result in (*what does all this lead to?*). **10** *intr.* (foll. by *with*) *Boxing* make an attack (with a particular hand or blow). **11 a** *intr.* (foll. by *with*) (of a newspaper) use a particular item as the main story (*led with the stock-market crash*). **b** *tr.* (of a story) be the main feature of (a newspaper or part of it) (*the governor's wedding will lead the front page*). **12** *tr.* (foll. by *through*) make (a liquid, strip of material, etc.) pass through a pulley, channel, etc. ● *n.* **1** guidance given by going in front; example. **2 a** a leading place; the leadership (*is in the lead; take the lead*). **b** the amount by which a competitor is ahead of the others (*a lead of ten yards*). **3** a clue, esp. an early indication of the resolution of a problem (*is the first real lead in the case*). **4** a strap or cord for leading a dog, etc. **5** *esp. Brit.* a conductor (usu. a wire) conveying electric current from a source to an appliance. **6 a** the chief part in a play, etc. **b** the person playing this. **7** (in full **lead story**) the item of news given the greatest prominence in a newspaper or magazine. **8 a** the act or right of playing first in a game or round of cards. **b** the card led. **9** the distance advanced by a screw in one turn. **10 a** an artificial watercourse, esp. one leading to a mill. **b** a channel of water in an icefield. ● *attrib.adj.* leading; principal; first. □ **lead astray** see ASTRAY. **lead by the nose** cajole (a person) into compliance. **lead a person a dance** see DANCE. **lead off 1 a** begin; make a start. **b** *Baseball* be the first batter in the batting order or of the inning. **2** *colloq.* lose one's temper. **lead on 1** entice into going further than was intended. **2** mislead or deceive. **lead up the garden path** *colloq.* mislead. **lead up to 1** form an introduction to; precede; prepare for. **2** direct one's talk gradually or cautiously to a particular topic, etc. **lead the way** see WAY. □□ **lead•a•ble** *adj.* [OE *lǣdan* f. Gmc]

lead² /led/ *n. & v.* ● *n.* **1** *Chem.* a heavy, bluish-gray soft ductile metallic element occurring naturally in galena and used in building and the manufacture of alloys. ¶ Symb.: **Pb. 2 a** graphite. **b** a thin length of this for use in a pencil. **3** a lump of lead suspended on a line to determine the depth of water. **4** (in *pl.*) *Brit.* strips of lead covering a roof. **b** a piece of lead-covered roof. **5** (in *pl.*) *Brit.* lead frames holding the glass of a lattice or stained-glass window. **6** *Printing* a blank space between lines of print (orig. with ref. to the metal strip used to give this space). **7** (*attrib.*) made of lead. ● *v.tr.* **1** cover, weight, or frame (a roof or window panes) with lead.

2 *Printing* separate lines of (printed matter) with leads. **3** add a lead compound to (gasoline, etc.). □□ **lead·less** *adj.* [OE *lēad* f. WG]

lead ac·e·tate *n.* a white crystalline compound of lead used in making paints and varnishes.

lead bal·loon *n.* a failure; an unsuccessful venture.

lead·en /léd'n/ *adj.* **1** of or like lead. **2** heavy; slow; burdensome (*leaden limbs*). **3** inert; depressing (*leaden rule*). **4** lead-colored (*leaden skies*). □□ **lead·en·ly** *adv.* **lead·en·ness** *n.* [OE *lēaden* (as LEAD²)]

lead·er /léedər/ *n.* **1 a** a person or thing that leads. **b** a person followed by others. **2 a** the principal player in a music group or of the first violins in an orchestra. **b** a conductor of an orchestra. **3** esp. *Brit.* = LEADING ARTICLE. **4** a short strip of nonfunctioning material at each end of a reel of film or recording tape for connection to the spool. **5** (in full **Leader of the House**) *Brit.* a member of the government officially responsible for initiating business in Parliament. **6** a shoot of a plant at the apex of a stem or of the main branch. **7** (in *pl.*) *Printing* a series of dots or dashes across the page to guide the eye, esp. in tabulated material. **8** the horse placed at the front in a team or pair. □□ **lead·er·less** *adj.* **lead·er·ship** *n.* [OE *lǣdere* (as LEAD¹)]

lead-free *adj.* (of gasoline) without added tetraethyl lead.

lead-in *n.* **1** an introduction, opening, etc. **2** a wire leading in from outside, esp. from an aerial to a receiver or transmitter.

lead·ing¹ /léeding/ *adj. & n.* ● *adj.* chief; most important. ● *n.* guidance; leadership.

lead·ing² /léding/ *n. Printing* = LEAD² n. 6.

lead·ing ar·ti·cle *n. Brit.* a newspaper article giving the editorial opinion.

lead·ing edge *n.* **1** the foremost edge of an airfoil, esp. a wing or propeller blade. **2** *Electronics* the part of a pulse in which the amplitude increases (opp. TRAILING EDGE). **3** *colloq.* the forefront of development, esp. in technology.

lead·ing la·dy *n.* the actress playing the principal part.

lead·ing light *n.* a prominent and influential person.

lead·ing man *n.* the actor playing the principal part.

lead·ing note *n. Mus.* = LEADING TONE.

lead·ing ques·tion *n.* a question that prompts or encourages the desired answer.

▶The phrase **leading question**, originally a legal term, means 'a question that prompts the answer wanted,' or that 'leads' the answerer to the answer. In common use it has come to mean 'a pointed or loaded question,' 'a question that is awkward to answer,' or even 'the most important question,' but these usages are avoided in precise speech and writing.

lead·ing strings *n.pl.* **1** strings for guiding and supporting children learning to walk. **2** oppressive supervision or control.

lead·ing tone *n. Mus.* the seventh note of a diatonic scale of any key. Also called **subtonic**.

lead-off /léedawf/ *n.* **1** an action beginning a process. **2** *Baseball* the first batter in the batting order or the inning.

lead pen·cil *n.* a pencil of graphite enclosed in wood.

lead poi·son·ing *n.* acute or chronic poisoning by absorption of lead into the body. Also called **plumbism**.

lead shot *n.* = SHOT¹ 3b.

lead tet·ra·eth·yl *n.* = TETRAETHYL LEAD.

lead time *n.* the time between the initiation and completion of a production process.

lead·wort /lédwərt, –wawrt/ *n.* = PLUMBAGO 2.

leaf /leef/ *n. & v.* ● *n.* (*pl.* **leaves** /leevz/) **1 a** each of several flattened usu. green structures of a plant, usu. on the side of a stem or branch and the main organ of photosynthesis. **b** other similar plant structures, e.g., bracts, sepals, and petals (*floral leaf*). **2 a** foliage regarded collectively. **b** the state of having leaves out (*a tree in leaf*). **3** the leaves of tobacco or tea. **4** a single thickness of paper, esp. in a book with each side forming a page. **5** a very thin sheet of metal, esp. gold or silver. **6 a** the hinged part or flap of a door, shutter, table, etc. **b** an extra section inserted to extend a table. ● *v.* **1** *intr.* put forth leaves. **2** *tr.* (foll. by *through*) turn over the pages of (a book, etc.). □□ **leaf·age** *n.* **leafed** *adj.* (also in *comb.*). **leaf·less** *adj.* **leaf·less·ness** *n.* **leaf·like** *adj.* [OE *lēaf* f. Gmc]

leaf 1

leaf-green *adj.* the color of green leaves.

leaf·hop·per /léefhopər/ *n.* any homopterous insect of the family Cicadellidae, which sucks the sap of plants and often causes damage and spreads disease.

leaf in·sect *n.* any insect of the family Phylliidae, having a flattened body leaflike in appearance.

leaf·let /léeflit/ *n. & v.* ● *n.* **1** a young leaf. **2** *Bot.* any division of a

compound leaf. **3** a sheet of (usu. printed) paper (sometimes folded but not stitched) giving information, esp. for free distribution. ● *v.tr.* (**leaf·let·ed**, **leaf·let·ing**; **leaf·let·ted**, **leaf·let·ting**) distribute leaflets to.

leaf min·er *n.* any of various larvae burrowing in leaves, esp. moth caterpillars of the family Gracillariidae.

leaf mold *n.* soil consisting chiefly of decayed leaves.

leaf-nosed bat *n.* any of various bats of the families Hipposideridae (Old World) or Phyllostomatidae (New World) with a leaflike appendage on the snout.

leaf spring *n.* a spring made of a number of strips of metal curved slightly upward and clamped together one above the other.

leaf·stalk /léefstawk/ *n.* a petiole.

leaf·y /léefee/ *adj.* (**leaf·i·er**, **leaf·i·est**) **1** having many leaves; (of a place) rich in foliage; verdant. **2** resembling a leaf. □□ **leaf·i·ness** *n.*

league¹ /leeg/ *n. & v.* ● *n.* **1** a collection of people, countries, groups, etc., combining for a particular purpose, esp. mutual protection or cooperation. **2** an agreement to combine in this way. **3** a group of sports organizations that compete over a period for a championship. **4** a class of contestants. ● *v.intr.* (**leagues, leagued, leaguing**) (often foll. by *together*) join in a league. □ **in league** allied; conspiring. [F *ligue* or It. *liga*, var. of *lega* f. *legare* bind f. L *ligare*]

league² /leeg/ *n. archaic* a varying measure of traveling distance by land, usu. about three miles. [ME, ult. f. LL *leuga, leuca*, of Gaulish orig.]

League of Wom·en Vot·ers *n.* an Amer. nonpartisan organization that promotes and sponsors programs, etc., that encourage voter awareness and participations.

lea·guer¹ /léegər/ *n.* a member of a league.

lea·guer² /léegər/ *n. & v.* = LAAGER. [Du. *leger* camp, rel. to LAIR¹]

leak /leek/ *n. & v.* ● *n.* **1 a** a hole in a vessel, pipe, or container, etc., caused by wear or damage, through which matter, esp. liquid or gas, passes accidentally in or out. **b** the matter passing in or out through this. **c** the act or an instance of leaking. **2 a** a similar escape of electrical charge. **b** the charge that escapes. **3** the intentional disclosure of secret information. ● *v.* **1 a** *intr.* (of liquid, gas, etc.) pass in or out through a leak. **b** *tr.* lose or admit (liquid, gas, etc.) through a leak. **2** *tr.* intentionally disclose (secret information). **3** *intr.* (often foll. by *out*) (of a secret, secret information) become known. □ **take a leak** *sl.* urinate. □□ **leak·er** *n.* [ME prob. f. LG]

leak·age /léekij/ *n.* **1** the action or result of leaking. **2** what leaks in or out. **3** an intentional disclosure of secret information.

leak·y /léekee/ *adj.* (**leak·i·er, leak·i·est**) **1** having a leak or leaks. **2** given to letting out secrets. □□ **leak·i·ness** *n.*

leal /leel/ *adj. Sc.* loyal; honest. [ME f. AF *leal*, OF *leel, loial* (as LOYAL)]

lean¹ /leen/ *v. & n.* ● *v.* (*past* and *past part.* **leaned** /leend, lent/ or **leant** /lent/) **1** *intr. & tr.* (often foll. by *across, back, over,* etc.) be or place in a sloping position; incline from the perpendicular. **2** *intr. & tr.* (foll. by *against, on, upon*) rest or cause to rest for support against, etc. **3** *intr.* (foll. by *on, upon*) rely on; derive support from. **4** *intr.* (foll. by *to, toward*) be inclined or partial to; have a tendency toward. ● *n.* a deviation from the perpendicular; an inclination (*has a decided lean to the right*). □ **lean on** *colloq.* put pressure on (a person) to act in a certain way. **lean over backward** see BACKWARD. [OE *hleonian, hlinian* f. Gmc]

lean² /leen/ *adj. & n.* ● *adj.* **1** (of a person or animal) thin; having no superfluous fat. **2** (of meat) containing little fat. **3 a** meager; of poor quality (*lean crop*). **b** not nourishing (*lean diet*). **4** unremunerative. ● *n.* the lean part of meat. □ **lean years** years of scarcity. □□ **lean·ly** *adv.* **lean·ness** *n.* [OE *hlǣne* f. Gmc]

lean·ing /léening/ *n.* a tendency or partiality.

lean-to *n.* (*pl.* **-tos**) **1** a building with its roof leaning against a larger building or a wall. **2** a shed with an inclined roof usu. leaning against trees, posts, etc.

leap /leep/ *v. & n.* ● *v.* (*past* and *past part.* **leaped** /leept, lept/ or **leapt** /lept/) **1** *intr.* jump or spring forcefully. **2** *tr.* jump across. **3** *intr.* (of prices, etc.) increase dramatically. **4** *intr.* hurry; rush; proceed without pausing for thought (*leaped to the wrong conclusion; leapt to their defense*). ● *n.* a forceful jump. □ **by leaps and bounds** with startlingly rapid progress. **leap at** rush toward; pounce upon. **2** accept eagerly. **leap to the eye** be immediately apparent. □□ **leap·er** *n.* [OE *hlȳp, hlēapan* f. Gmc: *leap year* prob. refers to the fact that feast days after Feb. in such a year fall two days later (instead of the normal one day later) than in the previous year]

leap day *n.* the intercalary day in a leap year; February 29.

leap·frog /léepfrawg, –frog/ *n. & v.* ● *n.* a game in which players in turn vault with parted legs over another who is bending down. ● *v.* (**-frogged, -frog·ging**) **1** *intr.* (foll. by *over*) perform such a vault. **2** *tr.* vault over in this way. **3** *tr. & intr.* (of two or more people, vehicles, etc.) overtake alternately.

leap in the dark *n.* a daring step or enterprise whose consequences are unpredictable.

leap of faith *n.* an act or instance of accepting something on the basis of belief or trust, not reason or fact.

white ash
(*Fraxinus americana*)

quaking aspen
(*Populus tremuloides*)

American beech
(*Fagus grandifolia*)

paper beech
(*Betula papyrifera*)

Eastern cottonwood
(*Populus deltoides*)

flowering dogwood
(*Cornus florida*)

American holly
(*Ilex opaca*)

horsechestnut
(*Aesculus hippocastanum*)

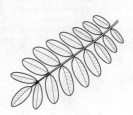

black locust
(*Robinia pseudoacacia*)

silver maple
(*Acer saccharinum*)

sugar maple
(*Acer saccharum*)

pin oak
(*Quercus palustris*)

white oak
(*Quercus alba*)

yellow poplar (tulip tree)
(*Liriodendron tulipifera*)

sycamore
(*Platanus occidentalis*)

leaves of familiar trees of North America

leap year *n.* a year, occurring once in four, with 366 days (including Feb. 29 as an intercalary day).

learn /lərn/ *v.* (*past* and *past part.* **learned** /lərnd, lərnt/ or esp. *Brit.* **learnt** /lərnt/) **1** *tr.* gain knowledge of or skill in by study, experience, or being taught. **2** *tr.* (foll. by *to* + infin.) acquire or develop a particular ability (*learn to swim*). **3** *tr.* commit to memory (*will try to learn your names*). **4** *intr.* (foll. by *of*) be informed about. **5** *tr.* (foll. by *that, how,* etc. + clause) become aware of by information or from observation. **6** *intr.* receive instruction; acquire knowledge or skill. **7** *tr. archaic* or *sl.* teach. □ **learn one's lesson** see LESSON. □□ **learn·a·ble** *adj.* **learn·a·bil·i·ty** /lə́rnəbílitee/ *n.* [OE *leornian* f. Gmc: cf. LORE¹]

learn·ed /lə́rnid/ *adj.* **1** having much knowledge acquired by study. **2** showing or requiring learning (*a learned work*). **3** studied or pursued by learned persons. **4** concerned with the interests of learned persons; scholarly (*a learned journal*). **5** as a courteous description of a lawyer or colleague in certain formal contexts (*my learned friend*). □□ **learn·ed·ly** *adv.* **learn·ed·ness** *n.* [ME f. LEARN in the sense 'teach']

▶**Learn** was once commonly used to mean 'teach, impart knowledge,' but this meaning is no longer generally accepted.

learn·er /lə́rnər/ *n.* **1** a person who is learning a subject or skill. **2** (in full **learner driver**) *Brit.* = STUDENT DRIVER.

learn·ing /lə́rning/ *n.* knowledge acquired by study. [OE *leornung* (as LEARN)]

learn·ing curve *n.* **1** a graph showing the time needed to acquire a new skill, knowledge of a subject, etc. **2** the rate of a person's progress in gaining experience or new skills.

learn·ing dis·a·bil·i·ty *n.* a disorder (such as dyslexia) that interferes with the learning process in a child of usu. normal intelligence.

lease /lees/ *n. & v.* ● *n.* an agreement by which the owner of a building or land allows another to use it for a specified time, usu. in return for payment. ● *v.tr.* grant or take on lease. □ **a new lease on life** a substantially improved prospect of living, or of use after repair. □□ **leas·a·ble** *adj.* **leas·er** *n.* [ME f. AF *les*, OF *lais*, *leis* f. *lesser, laissier* leave f. L *laxare* make loose (*laxus*)]

lease·back /léesbak/ *n.* the leasing of a property back to the vendor.

lease·hold /lées-hōld/ *n. & adj.* ● *n.* **1** the holding of property by lease. **2** property held by lease. ● *adj.* held by lease. □□ **lease·hold·er** *n.*

leash /leesh/ *n. & v.* ● *n.* a thong for holding a dog; a dog's lead. ● *v.tr.* **1** put a leash on. **2** restrain. □ **straining at the leash** eager to begin. [ME f. OF *lesse, laisse* f. specific use of *laisser* let run on a slack lead: see LEASE]

least /leest/ *adj., n., & adv.* ● *adj.* **1** smallest; slightest; most insignificant. **2** (prec. by *the*; esp. with *neg.*) any at all (*it does not make the least difference*). **3** (of a species or variety) very small (*least tern*). ● *n.* the least amount. ● *adv.* in the least degree. □ **at least 1** at all events; anyway; even if there is doubt about a more extended statement. **2** (also **at the least**) not less than. **in the least** (or **the least**) (usu. with *neg.*) in the smallest degree; at all (*not in the least offended*). **to say the least** (or **the least of it**) used to imply the moderation of a statement (*that is doubtful to say the least*). [OE *lǣst, lǣsest* f. Gmc]

least com·mon de·nom·i·na·tor *n.* = LOWEST COMMON DENOMINATOR.

least com·mon mul·ti·ple *n.* = LOWEST COMMON MULTIPLE.

least·ways /léestwayz/ *adv.* (also **least·wise** /–wīz/) *dial.* or at least, or rather.

leat /leet/ *n. Brit.* an open watercourse conducting water to a mill, etc. [OE –*gelǣt* (as Y– + root of LET¹)]

leath·er /léthər/ *n. & v.* ● *n.* **1 a** material made from the skin of an animal by tanning or a similar process. **b** (*attrib.*) made of leather. **2 a** piece of leather for polishing with. **3** the leather part or parts of something. **4** *sl.* a football. **5** (in *pl.*) leather clothes, esp. leggings, breeches, or clothes for wearing on a motorcycle. **6** a thong (*stirrup-leather*). ● *v.tr.* **1** cover with leather. **2** polish or wipe with a leather. **3** beat; thrash (orig. with a leather thong). [OE *lether* f. Gmc]

leath·er·back /léthərbak/ *n.* a large marine turtle, *Dermochelys coriacea*, having a thick leathery carapace.

leath·er·cloth /léthərklawth, –kloth/ *n.* strong fabric coated to resemble leather.

leath·er·ette /léthərét/ *n.* imitation leather.

leath·er·jack·et /léthərjakət/ *n.* **1** any of various tough-skinned marine fish of the family Monacanthidae. **2** any marine fish of the genus *Oligoplites*, family Carangidae, esp. *O. saurus*.

leath·ern /léthərn/ *n. archaic* made of leather.

leath·er·neck /léthərnek/ *n. sl.* a US Marine (with reference to the leather collar formerly worn by them).

leath·er·y /léthəree/ *adj.* **1** like leather. **2** (esp. of meat, etc.) tough. □□ **leath·er·i·ness** *n.*

leave¹ /leev/ *v.* (*past* and *past part.* **left** /left/) **1 a** *tr.* go away from; cease to remain in or on (*left him an hour ago; leave the track; leave here*). **b** *intr.* (often foll. by *for*) depart (*we leave tomorrow; has just left for Denver*). **2** *tr.* cause to or let remain; depart without taking (*has left his gloves; left a slimy trail; left a bad impression; six from seven leaves one*). **3** *tr.* (also *absol.*) cease to reside at or attend or belong to or work for (*has left the school; I am leaving for another firm*). **4** *tr.* abandon; forsake; desert. **5** *tr.* have remaining after one's death (*leaves a wife and two children*). **6** *tr.* bequeath. **7** *tr.* (foll. by *to* + infin.) allow (a person or thing) to do something without interference or assistance (*leave the future to take care of itself*). **8** *tr.* (foll. by *to*) commit or refer to another person (*leave that to me; nothing was left to chance*). **9** *tr.* **a** abstain from consuming or dealing with. **b** (in *passive*; often foll. by *over*) remain over. **10** *tr.* **a** deposit or entrust (a thing) to be attended to, collected, delivered, etc., in one's absence (*left a message with his assistant*). **b** depute (a person) to perform a function in one's absence. **11** *tr.* allow to remain or cause to be in a specified state or position (*left the door open; the performance left them unmoved; left nothing that was necessary undone*). **12** *tr.* pass (an object) so that it is in a specified relative direction (*leave the church on the left*). ● *n.* the position in which a player leaves the balls in billiards, croquet, etc. □ **be left with 1** retain (a feeling, etc.). **be burdened with** (a responsibility, etc.). **be well left** be well provided for by a legacy, etc. **get left** *colloq.* be deserted. **have left** have remaining (*has no friends left*). **leave alone 1** refrain from disturbing; not interfere with. **2** not have dealings with. **leave be** *colloq.* refrain from disturbing; not interfere with. **leave behind 1** go away without. **2** leave as a consequence or a visible sign of passage. **3** pass. **leave a person cold** (or **cool**) not impress or excite a person. **leave go** *colloq.* relax one's hold. **leave hold of** cease holding. **leave it at that** *colloq.* abstain from comment or further action. **leave much** (or **a lot**, etc.) **to be desired** be highly unsatisfactory. **leave off 1** come to or make an end. **2** discontinue (*leave off work; leave off talking*). **3** not wear. **leave out** omit; not include. **leave over** *Brit.* leave to be considered, settled, or used later. **leave a person to himself** or **herself 1** not attempt to control a person. **2** leave a person solitary. **left at the gate** (*post*) beaten from the start of a race. **left for dead** abandoned as being beyond rescue. □□ **leav·er** *n.* [OE *lǣfan* f. Gmc]

▶**Leave** means 'go away from': *we left town together*. The common expression **leave me alone** literally means 'leave (me), so that I can be by myself.' **Let** means 'allow.' Thus *let me be* and *let me alone* mean 'don't bother me.'

leave² /leev/ *n.* **1** (often foll. by *to* + infin.) permission. **2 a** (in full **leave of absence**) permission to be absent from duty. **b** the period for which this lasts. □ **by** (or **with**) **your leave** often *iron.* an expression of apology for taking a liberty or making an unwelcome statement. **on leave** legitimately absent from duty. **take one's leave** bid farewell. **take one's leave of** bid farewell to. **take leave of one's senses** see SENSE. **take leave to** venture or presume to. [OE *lēaf* f. WG: cf. LIEF, LOVE]

leaved /leevd/ *adj.* **1** having leaves. **2** (in *comb.*) having a leaf or leaves of a specified kind or number (*red-leaved maple*).

leav·en /lévən/ *n. & v.* ● *n.* **1** a substance added to dough to make it ferment and rise, esp. yeast, or fermenting dough reserved for the purpose. **2 a** a pervasive transforming influence (cf. Matt. 13:33). **b** (foll. by *of*) a tinge or admixture of a specified quality. ● *v.tr.* **1** ferment (dough) with leaven. **2 a** permeate and transform. **b** (foll. by *with*) modify with a tempering element. [ME f. OF *levain* f. Gallo-roman spec. use of L *levamen* relief f. *levare* lift]

leaves *pl.* of LEAF.

leav·ings /léevingz/ *n.pl.* things left over, esp. as worthless.

Leb·a·nese /lébənéez/ *adj. & n.* ● *adj.* of or relating to Lebanon in the Middle East. ● *n.* (*pl.* same) **1** a native or national of Lebanon. **2** a person of Lebanese descent.

Le·bens·raum /láybənzrowm/ *n.* the territory which a nation believes is needed for its natural development. [G, = living space (orig. with reference to Germany, esp. in the 1930s)]

lech /lech/ *v. & n. colloq.* ● *v.intr.* feel lecherous; behave lustfully. ● *n.* **1** a strong desire, esp. sexual. **2** a lecher. [back-form. f. LECHER: (n.) perh. f. *letch* longing]

lech·er /léchər/ *n.* a lecherous man; a debauchee. [ME f. OF *lecheor, etc.,* f. *lechier* live in debauchery or gluttony f. Frank., rel. to LICK]

lech·er·ous /léchərəs/ *adj.* lustful, having strong or excessive sexual desire. □□ **lech·er·ous·ly** *adv.* **lech·er·ous·ness** *n.* [ME f. OF *lecheros, etc.* f. *lecheur* LECHER]

lech·er·y /léchəree/ *n.* unrestrained indulgence of sexual desire. [ME f. OF *lecherie* f. *lecheur* LECHER]

lec·i·thin /lésithin/ *n.* **1** any of a group of phospholipids found naturally in animals, egg yolk, and some higher plants. **2** a preparation of this used to emulsify foods, etc. [Gk *lekithos* egg yolk + –IN]

lec·tern /léktərn/ *n.* **1** a stand for holding a book in a church or chapel, esp. for a bible from which lessons are to be read. **2** a similar stand for a lecturer, etc. [ME *lettorne* f. OF *let(t)run,* med.L *lectrum* f. *legere lect-* read]

lec·tion /lékshən/ *n.* a reading of a text found in a particular copy or edition. [L *lectio* reading (as LECTERN)]

lec·tion·ar·y /lékshənéree/ *n.* (*pl.* **-ies**) **1** a list of portions of Scripture appointed to be read at divine

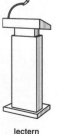

lectern

service. **2** a book containing such portions. [ME f. med.L *lectionarium* (as LECTION)]

lec‧tor /léktər/ *n.* **1** a reader, esp. of lessons in a church service. **2** (esp. *Brit. fem.* **lec‧trice** /lektreés/) a lecturer or reader, esp. one employed in a foreign university to give instruction in his or her native language. [L f. *legere lect-* read]

lec‧ture /lékchər/ *n. & v.* ● *n.* **1** a discourse giving information about a subject to a class or other audience. **2** a long, serious speech, esp. as a scolding or reprimand. ● *v.* **1** *intr.* (often foll. by *on*) deliver a lecture or lectures. **2** *tr.* talk seriously or reprovingly to (a person). **3** *tr.* instruct or entertain (a class or other audience) by a lecture. [ME f. OF *lecture* or med.L *lectura* f. L (as LECTOR)]

lec‧tur‧er /lékchərər/ *n.* a person who lectures, esp. as a teacher in higher education.

lec‧ture‧ship /l ékchərship/ *n.* the office of lecturer.

lec‧y‧thus /lésithəs/ *n.* (*pl.* **lec‧y‧thi** /–thī/) *Gk Antiq.* a thin narrow-necked vase or flask. [Gk *lēkuthos*]

LED *abbr.* light-emitting diode.

led *past* and *past part.* of LEAD[1].

le‧der‧ho‧sen /láydərhózən/ *n.pl.* leather shorts as worn in Bavaria, etc. [G, = leather trousers]

ledge /lej/ *n.* **1** a narrow horizontal surface projecting from a wall, etc. **2** a shelflike projection on the side of a rock or mountain. **3** a ridge of rocks, esp. below water. **4** *Mining* a stratum of metal-bearing rock. □□ **ledged** *adj.* **ledg‧y** *adj.* [perh. f. ME *legge* LAY[1]]

ledg‧er /léjər/ *n.* **1** a tall, narrow book in which a firm's accounts are kept, esp. one which is the principal book of a set and contains debtor-and-creditor accounts. **2** a flat gravestone. **3** a horizontal timber in scaffolding, parallel to the face of the building. [ME f. senses of Du. *ligger* and *legger* (f. *liggen* LIE[1], *leggen* LAY[1]) & pronunc. of ME *ligge, legge*]

ledg‧er line *n.* **1** *Mus.* a short line added for notes above or below the range of a staff. **2** a kind of fishing tackle in which a lead weight keeps the bait on the bottom.

lee /lee/ *n.* **1** shelter given by a neighboring object (*under the lee of*). **2** (in full **lee side**) the sheltered side, the side away from the wind (opp. WEATHER SIDE). [OE *hlēo* f. Gmc]

lee‧board /leébawrd, –bōrd/ *n.* a plank frame fixed to the side of a flat-bottomed vessel and let down into the water to diminish leeway.

leech[1] /leech/ *n.* **1** any freshwater or terrestrial annelid worm of the class *Hirudinea* with suckers at both ends, esp. *Hirudo medicinalis*, a bloodsucking parasite of vertebrates formerly much used medically. **2** a person who extorts profit from or sponges on others. □ **like a leech** persistently or clingingly present. [OE *lǣce*, assim. to LEECH[2]]

leech[2] /leech/ *n. archaic* or *joc.* a physician; a healer. [OE *lǣce* f. Gmc]

leech[3] /leech/ *n.* **1** a perpendicular or sloping side of a square sail. **2** the side of a fore-and-aft sail away from the mast or stay. [ME, perh. rel. to ON *lik*, a nautical term of uncert. meaning]

leech‧craft /leéchkraft/ *n. archaic* the art of healing. [OE *lǣcecræft* (as LEECH[2], CRAFT)]

leek /leek/ *n.* **1** an alliaceous plant, *Allium porrum*, with flat overlapping leaves forming an elongated cylindrical bulb, used as food. **2** this as a Welsh national emblem. [OE *lēac* f. Gmc]

leer[1] /v. & n.* ● *v.intr.* look slyly or lasciviously or maliciously. ● *n.* a leering look. □□ **leer‧ing‧ly** *adv.* [perh. f. obs. *leer* cheek f. OE *hlēor*, as though 'to glance over one's cheek']

leer[2] var. of LEHR.

leer‧y /leéree/ *adj.* (**leer‧i‧er, leer‧i‧est**) *sl.* **1** knowing; sly. **2** (foll. by *of*) wary. □□ **leer‧i‧ness** *n.* [perh. f. obs. *leer* looking askance f. LEER[1] + –Y[1]]

lees /leez/ *n.pl.* **1** the sediment of wine, etc. (*drink to the lees*). **2** dregs; refuse. [pl. of ME *lie* f. OF *lie* f. med.L *lia* f. Gaulish]

lee shore *n.* the shore lying on the leeward side of a ship (and onto which a ship could be blown in foul weather).

leet[1] /leet/ *n. Brit. hist.* **1** (in full **Court leet**) a yearly or half-yearly court of record that lords of certain manors might hold. **2** its jurisdiction or district. [ME f. AF *lete* (= AL *leta*), of unkn. orig.]

leet[2] /leet/ *n. Sc.* a selected list of candidates for some office. □ **short leet** = SHORTLIST. [ME *lite*, etc., prob. f. AF & OF *lit(t)e*, var. of *liste* LIST[1]]

lee‧ward /leéwə rd, *Naut.* loóərd/ *adj., adv., & n.* ● *adj. & adv.* on or toward the side sheltered from the wind (opp. WINDWARD). ● *n.* the leeward region, side, or direction (*to leeward; on the leeward of*).

PRONUNCIATION TIP leeward

Like many nautical words, *leeward* is not pronounced the way it is spelled. Although "LEE-werd" is considered acceptable, the correct pronunciation is "LOO-erd."

---

lee‧ward‧ly /leéwərdlee, loóərdlee/ *adj.* (of a ship) apt to drift to leeward.

565

lee‧way /leéway/ *n.* **1** the sideways drift of a ship to leeward of the desired course. **2 a** allowable deviation or freedom of action. **b** margin of safety. □ **make up leeway** struggle out of a bad position, recover lost time, etc.

left[1] /left/ *adj., adv., & n.* (opp. RIGHT). ● *adj.* **1** on or toward the side of the human body which corresponds to the position of west if one regards oneself as facing north. **2** on or toward the part of an object which is analogous to a person's left side or (with opposite sense) which is nearer to an observer's left hand. **3** (also **Left**) *Polit.* of the Left. ● *adv.* on or to the left side. ● *n.* **1** the left-hand part or region or direction. **2** *Boxing* **a** the left hand. **b** a blow with this. **3 a** (often **Left**) *Polit.* a group or section favoring liberalism, social reform, etc. (orig. the more radical section of a continental legislature, seated on the president's left); such persons collectively. **b** the more advanced or innovative section of any group. **4** the side of a stage which is to the left of a person facing the audience. **5** (esp. in marching) the left foot. **6** the left wing of an army. □ **have two left feet** be clumsy. **left and right** = *right and left*. **marry with the left hand** marry morganatically (see LEFT-HANDED). □□ **left‧ish** *adj.* [ME *lüft, lift, left,* f. OE, orig. sense 'weak, worthless']

left[2] *past* and *past part.* of LEAVE[1].

left bank *n.* the bank of a river on the left facing downstream.

left brain *n.* the left-hand side of the human brain, believed to be associated with linear and analytical thought.

left field *n. Baseball* **1** the part of the outfield to the left of the batter when facing the pitcher. **2** a position or direction that is surprising or unconventional. **3** a position of ignorance, error, or confusion.

left hand *n.* **1** the hand of a person's left side. **2** the region or direction on the left side of a person or thing.

left-hand *adj.* **1** on or toward the left side of a person or thing (*left-hand pocket*). **2** done with the left hand (*left-hand catch*).

left-hand‧ed /léft-hándid/ *adj.* **1** using the left hand by preference as more serviceable than the right. **2** (of a tool, etc.) made to be used with the left hand. **3** (of a blow) struck with the left hand. **4 a** turning to the left; toward the left. **b** (of a racecourse) turning counterclockwise. **c** (of a screw) advanced by turning to the left (counterclockwise). **5** awkward; clumsy. **6 a** (of a compliment) ambiguous. **b** of doubtful sincerity or validity. **7** (of a marriage) morganatic (from a German custom by which the bridegroom gave the bride his left hand in such marriages). □□ **left-hand‧ed‧ly** *adv.* **left-hand‧ed‧ness** *n.*

left-hand‧er /léft-hándər/ *n.* **1** a left-handed person. **2** a left-handed blow.

left‧ie var. of LEFTY.

left‧ism /léftizəm/ *n. Polit.* the principles or policy of the left. □□ **left‧ist** *n. & adj.*

left‧most /léftmōst/ *adj.* furthest to the left.

left‧o‧ver /léftōvər/ *adj. & n.* ● *adj.* remaining over; not used up or disposed of. ● *n.* (in *pl.*) items (esp. of food) remaining after the rest has been used.

left‧ward /léftwərd/ *adv. & adj.* ● *adv.* (also **left‧wards** /–wərdz/) toward the left. ● *adj.* going toward or facing the left.

left wing *n.* **1** the liberal or socialist section of a political party. **2** the left side of a soccer, etc., team on the field. **3** the left side of an army. □□ **left-wing** *adj.* **left-wing‧er** *n.*

left‧y /léftee/ *n.* (also **left‧ie**) (*pl.* **-ies**) *colloq.* **1** *Polit.* a left-winger. **2** a left-handed person.

leg /leg/ *n. & v.* ● *n.* **1 a** each of the limbs on which a person or animal walks and stands. **b** the part of this from the hip to the ankle. **2** a leg of an animal or bird as food. **3** an artificial leg (*wooden leg*). **4** a part of a garment covering a leg or part of a leg. **5 a** a support of a chair, table, bed, etc. **b** a long, thin support or prop, esp. a pole. **6** *Cricket* the half of the field (as divided lengthways through the pitch) in which the striker's feet are placed (opp. OFF). **7 a** a section of a journey. **b** a stage in a relay race. **c** a stage in a competition. **d** one of two or more games constituting a round. **8** one branch of a forked object. **9** *Naut.* a run made on a single tack. **10** *archaic* an obeisance made by drawing back one leg and bending it while keeping the front leg straight. ● *v.tr.* (**legged, leg‧ging**) propel (a boat) through a canal tunnel by pushing with one's legs against the tunnel sides. □ **feel** (or **find**) **one's legs** become able to stand or walk. **give a person a leg up** help a person to mount a horse, etc., or get over an obstacle or difficulty. **have the legs of** esp. *Brit.* be able to go further than. **have no legs** *colloq.* (of a golf ball, etc.) have not enough momentum to reach the desired point. **keep one's legs** not fall. **leg it** *colloq.* walk or run fast. **not have a leg to stand on** be unable to support one's argument by facts or sound reasons. **on one's last legs** near death or the end of one's usefulness, etc. **on one's legs 1** (also **on one's hind legs**) standing, esp. to make a speech. **2** well enough to walk about. **take to one's legs** run away. □□ **legged** /legd, légid/ *adj.* (also in *comb.*). **leg‧ger** *n.* [ME f. ON *leggr* f. Gmc]

leek

leg•a•cy /légəsee/ n. (pl. **•cies**) **1** a gift left in a will. **2** something handed down by a predecessor (*legacy of corruption*). [ME f. OF *legacie* legateship f. med.L *legatia* f. L *legare* bequeath]

le•gal /léegəl/ adj. **1** of or based on law; concerned with law; falling within the province of law. **2** appointed or required by law. **3** permitted by law; lawful. **4** recognized by law, as distinct from equity. **5** *Theol.* **a** of the Mosaic law. **b** of salvation by works rather than by faith. □□ **le•gal•ly** adv. [F *légal* or L *legalis* f. *lex legis* law: cf. LEAL, LOYAL]

le•gal age n. age at which a person assumes adult rights and privileges by law.

le•gal aid n. payment from public funds allowed, in cases of need, to help pay for legal advice or proceedings.

le•gal•ese /léegəleéz/ n. colloq. the technical language of legal documents.

le•gal hol•i•day n. a public holiday established by law.

le•gal•ism /léegəlizəm/ n. **1** excessive adherence to law or formula. **2** *Theol.* adherence to the Law rather than to the Gospel, the doctrine of justification by works. □□ **le•gal•ist** n. **le•gal•is•tic** /–lístik/ adj. **le•gal•is•ti•cal•ly** /–lístikəlee/ adv.

le•gal•i•ty /ligálitee, leegál–/ n. (pl. **•ties**) **1** lawfulness. **2** legalism. **3** (in pl.) obligations imposed by law. [F *légalité* or med.L *legalitas* (as LEGAL)]

le•gal•ize /léegəlíz/ v.tr. **1** make lawful. **2** bring into harmony with the law. □□ **le•gal•i•za•tion** n.

le•gal sep•a•ra•tion n. an arrangement by which a husband or wife remain married but live apart, following a court order.

le•gal ten•der n. currency that cannot legally be refused in payment of a debt (usu. up to a limited amount for coins not made of gold).

le•gate /légət/ n. **1** a member of the clergy representing the Pope. **2** *Rom.Hist.* **a** a deputy of a general. **b** a governor or deputy governor of a province. **3** *archaic* an ambassador or delegate. □□ **leg•ate•ship** n. **leg•a•tine** /–teen, –tīn/ adj. [OE f. OF *legat* f. L *legatus* past part. of *legare* depute, delegate]

leg•a•tee /légətee/ n. the recipient of a legacy. [as LEGATOR + –EE]

le•ga•tion /ligáyshən/ n. **1** a body of deputies. **2 a** the office and staff of a diplomatic minister (esp. when not having ambassadorial rank). **b** the official residence of a diplomatic minister. **3** a legateship. **4** the sending of a legate or deputy. [ME f. OF *legation* or L *legatio* (as LEGATE)]

le•ga•to /ligáto/ adv., adj., & n. Mus. • adv. & adj. in a smooth flowing manner, without breaks between notes (cf. STACCATO, TENUTO). • n. (pl. **•tos**) **1** a legato passage. **2** legato playing. [It., = bound, past part. of *legare* f. L *ligare* bind]

le•ga•tor /ligáytər/ n. the giver of a legacy. [archaic *legate* bequeath f. L *legare* (as LEGACY)]

leg•end /léjənd/ n. **1 a** a traditional story sometimes regarded as historical but unauthenticated; a myth. **b** such stories collectively. **c** a popular but unfounded belief. **d** colloq. a subject of such beliefs (*became a legend in his own lifetime*). **2 a** an inscription, esp. on a coin or medal. **b** *Printing* a caption. **c** wording on a map, etc., explaining the symbols used. **3** hist. **a** the story of a saint's life. **b** a collection of lives of saints or similar stories. □□ **leg•end•ry** n. [ME (in sense 3) f. OF *legende* f. med.L *legenda* what is to be read, neut. pl. gerundive of L *legere* read]

leg•end•ar•y /léjəndəree/ adj. **1** of or connected with legends. **2** described in a legend. **3** colloq. remarkable enough to be a subject of legend. **4** based on a legend. □□ **leg•end•ar•i•ly** adv. [med.L *legendarius* (as LEGEND)]

leg•er•de•main /léjərdəmáyn/ n. **1** sleight of hand; conjuring or juggling. **2** trickery; sophistry. [ME f. F *léger de main* light of hand, dexterous]

leg•er line /lédjər/ n. = LEDGER LINE.

leg•gings /léging/ n.pl. **1** tight-fitting stretch pants worn by women and children. **2** a stout protective outer covering for the leg from the knee to the ankle.

leg•gy /légee/ adj. (**leg•gi•er, leg•gi•est**) **1 a** long-legged. **b** (of a woman) having attractively long legs. **2** long-stemmed. □□ **leg•gi•ness** n.

leg•horn /léghawrn, –ərn/ n. **1 a** fine plaited straw. **b** a hat of this. **2** (also **Leg•horn**) **a** a bird of a small hardy breed of domestic fowl. **b** this breed. [*Leghorn* (Livorno) in Italy, from where the straw and fowls were imported]

leg•i•ble /léjibəl/ adj. (of handwriting, print, etc.) clear enough to read; readable. □□ **leg•i•bil•i•ty** n. **leg•i•bly** adv. [ME f. LL *legibilis* f. *legere* read]

le•gion /léejən/ n. & adj. • n. **1** a division of 3,000–6,000 men, including a complement of cavalry, in the ancient Roman army. **2** a large organized body. **3** a vast host, multitude, or number. • predic.adj. great in number (*his good works have been legion*). [ME f. OF f. L *legio* –onis f. *legere* choose]

le•gion•ar•y /léejənəree/ adj. & n. • adj. of a legion or legions. • n. (pl. **•ies**) a member of a legion. [L *legionarius* (as LEGION)]

le•gioned /léejənd/ adj. poet. arrayed in legions.

le•gion•el•la /léejənélə/ n. the bacterium *Legionella pneumophila*, which causes legionnaires' disease.

le•gion•naire /léejənáir/ n. **1** a member of a foreign legion. **2** a member of the American Legion. [F *légionnaire* (as LEGION)]

le•gion•naires' dis•ease n. a form of bacterial pneumonia first identified after an outbreak at an American Legion meeting in 1976 (cf. LEGIONELLA).

Le•gion of Hon•or n. a French order of distinction founded in 1802.

leg i•ron n. (usu. **leg i•rons**) a metal shackle or chain placed around a prisoner's ankle as a restraint.

leg•is•late /léjislayt/ v.intr. **1** make laws. **2** (foll. by *for*) make provision by law. [back-form. f. LEGISLATION]

leg•is•la•tion /léjisláyshən/ n. **1** the process of making laws. **2** laws collectively. [LL *legis latio* f. *lex legis* law + *latio* proposing f. *lat*- past part. stem of *ferre* bring]

leg•is•la•tive /léjislaytiv/ adj. of or empowered to make legislation. □□ **leg•is•la•tive•ly** adv.

leg•is•la•tor /léjislaytər/ n. **1** a member of a legislative body. **2** a lawgiver. [L (as LEGISLATION)]

leg•is•la•ture /léjislaychər/ n. the legislative body of a nation or state.

le•git /lijít/ adj. & n. colloq. • adj. legitimate. • n. **1** legitimate drama. **2** an actor in legitimate drama. [abbr.]

le•git•i•mate adj. & v. • adj. /lijítimət/ **1 a** (of a child) born of parents lawfully married to each other. **b** (of a parent, birth, descent, etc.) with, of, through, etc., a legitimate child. **2** lawful; proper; regular; conforming to the standard type. **3** logically admissible. **4 a** (of a sovereign's title) based on strict hereditary right. **b** (of a sovereign) having a legitimate title. **5** constituting or relating to serious drama as distinct from musical comedy, revue, etc. • v.tr. /lijítimayt/ **1** make legitimate by decree, enactment, or proof. **2** justify; serve as a justification for. □□ **le•git•i•ma•cy** /–məsee/ n. **le•git•i•mate•ly** /–mətlee/ adv. **le•git•i•ma•tion** /–máyshən/ n. [med.L *legitimare* f. L *legitimus* lawful f. *lex legis* law]

le•git•i•ma•tize /lijítimətíz/ v.tr. legitimize. □□ **le•git•i•ma•ti•za•tion** n.

le•git•i•mism /lijítimizəm/ n. adherence to a sovereign or pretender whose claim is based on direct descent (esp. in French and Spanish history). □□ **le•git•i•mist** n. & adj. [F *légitimisme* f. *légitime* LEGITIMATE]

le•git•i•mize /lijítimíz/ v.tr. **1** make legitimate. **2** serve as a justification for. □□ **le•git•i•mi•za•tion** n.

leg•less /léglis/ adj. **1** having no legs. **2** sl. drunk, esp. too drunk to stand.

leg•man /légman/ n. (pl. **•men**) a person employed to go about gathering news or running errands, etc.

Le•go /légo/ n. Trademark a construction toy consisting of interlocking plastic building blocks. [Da. *leg godt* play well f. *lege* to play]

leg-of-mut•ton sleeve n. a sleeve which is full and loose on the upper arm but close-fitting on the forearm.

leg-pull n. colloq. a hoax.

leg•room /légroom/ n. space for the legs of a seated person.

leg•ume /légyoom/ n. **1** the seedpod of a leguminous plant. **2** any seed, pod, or other edible part of a leguminous plant used as food. [F *légume* f. L *legumen* –minis f. *legere* pick, because pickable by hand]

le•gu•mi•nous /ligyoominəs/ adj. of or like the family Leguminosae, including peas and beans, having seeds in pods and usu. root nodules able to fix nitrogen. [mod.L *leguminosus* (as LEGUME)]

leg warm•er n. either of a pair of tubular knitted garments covering the leg from ankle to thigh.

leg•work /légwərk/ n. work which involves a lot of walking, traveling, or physical activity.

lehr /leer/ n. (also **leer**) a furnace used for the annealing of glass. [17th c.: orig. unkn.]

lei[1] /láy-ee, lay/ n. a garland of flowers usu. worn on the head or shoulders. [Hawaiian]

lei[2] pl. of LEU.

Leib•niz•i•an /líbnítseeən/ adj. & n. • adj. of or relating to the philosophy of G. W. Leibniz, German philosopher (d. 1716), esp. regarding matter as a multitude of monads and assuming a preestablished harmony between spirit and matter. • n. a follower of this philosophy.

Leices•ter /léstər/ n. a kind of mild firm cheese, usu. orange-colored and orig. made in Leicestershire, England.

leish•man•i•a•sis /léeshməníəsis/ n. any of several diseases caused by parasitic protozoans of the genus *Leishmania* transmitted by the bite of sandflies. [W. B. *Leishman*, Brit. physician d. 1926]

leis•ter /léestər/ n. & v. • n. a pronged salmon-spear. • v.tr. pierce with a leister. [ON *ljóstr* f. *ljósta* to strike]

lei•sure /léezhər, lézh–/ n. **1** free time; time at one's own disposal. **2** enjoyment of free time. **3** (usu. foll. by *for*, or *to* + infin.) opportu-

---

PRONUNCIATION TIP leisure

In American English, most people say *leisure* to rhyme with *seizure*, while in British English the pronunciation that rhymes with *pleasure* is preferred.

nity afforded by free time. □ **at leisure 1** not occupied. **2** in an unhurried manner. **at one's leisure** when one has time. □□ **lei·sure·less** *adj.* [ME f. AF *leisour*, OF *leisir* ult. f. L *licēre* be allowed]

lei·sured /lee͞zhərd, lézh–/ *adj.* having ample leisure.

lei·sure·ly /lee͞zhərlee, lézh–/ *adj. & adv.* • *adj.* having leisure; acting or done at leisure; unhurried; relaxed. • *adv.* without hurry. □□ **lei·sure·li·ness** *n.*

lei·sure·wear /lee͞zhərwair, lézh–/ *n.* informal clothes, especially sportswear.

leit·mo·tif /lítmōteef/ *n.* (also **leit·mo·tiv**) a recurrent theme associated throughout a musical, literary, etc., composition with a particular person, idea, or situation. [G *Leitmotiv* (as LEAD¹, MOTIVE)]

lek¹ /lek/ *n.* the chief monetary unit of Albania. [Albanian]

lek² /lek/ *n.* a patch of ground used by groups of certain birds during the breeding season as a setting for the males' display and their meeting with the females. [perh. f. Sw. *leka* to play]

LEM /lem/ *abbr.* lunar excursion module.

lem·an /lémən/ *n.* (*pl.* **lem·ans**) *archaic* **1** a lover or sweetheart. **2** an illicit lover, esp. a mistress. [ME *leofman* (as LIEF, MAN)]

lem·ma /lémə/ *n.* (*pl.* **lem·mas** or **lem·ma·ta** /–mətə/) **1** an assumed or demonstrated proposition used in an argument or proof. **2 a** a heading indicating the subject or argument of a literary composition, a dictionary entry, etc. **b** a heading indicating the subject or argument of an annotation. **3** a motto appended to a picture, etc. [L f. Gk *lēmma* –*matos* thing assumed, f. the root of *lambanō* take]

lem·me /lémee/ *colloq.* let me. [corrupt.]

lem·ming /léming/ *n.* any small arctic rodent of the genus *Lemmus*, esp. *L. lemmus* of Norway which is reputed to rush headlong into the sea and drown during periods of mass migration. [Norw.]

lem·on /lémən/ *n.* **1 a** a pale-yellow, thick-skinned, oval citrus fruit with acidic juice. **b** a tree of the species *Citrus limon* which produces this fruit. **2** a pale-yellow color. **3** *colloq.* a person or thing regarded as feeble or unsatisfactory or disappointing. [ME f. OF *limon* f. Arab. *līma*: cf. LIME²]

lem·on·ade /lémənáyd/ *n.* **1** a beverage made from sweetened lemon juice. **2** a synthetic substitute for this.

lem·on balm *n.* a bushy plant, *Melissa officinalis*, with leaves smelling and tasting of lemon.

lem·on drop *n.* a lemon-flavored hard candy.

lem·on ge·ra·ni·um *n.* a lemon-scented pelargonium, *Pelargonium crispum*.

lem·on·grass /léməngras/ *n.* any fragrant tropical grass of the genus *Cymbopogon*, yielding an oil smelling of lemon.

lem·on sole /lémən/ *n.* a flatfish, *Microstomus kitt*, of the plaice family. [F *limande*]

lem·on squash *n. Brit.* a soft drink made from lemons and other ingredients, often sold in concentrated form.

lem·on thyme *n.* an herb, *Thymus citriodorus*, with lemon-scented leaves used for flavoring.

lem·on ver·be·na *n.* (also **lem·on plant**) a shrub, *Lippia citriodora*, with lemon-scented leaves.

lem·on·y /lémənee/ *adj.* **1** tasting or smelling of lemons. **2** *Austral. & NZ sl.* irritable.

le·mur /leémər/ *n.* any arboreal primate of the family Lemuridae native to Madagascar, with a pointed snout and long tail. [mod.L f. L *lemures* (pl.) spirits of the dead, from its specterlike face]

Len·a·pe /lénəpee, lənaápee/ *n.* see DELAWARE.

lend /lend/ *v.tr.* (*past* and *past part.* **lent** /lent/) **1** (usu. foll. by *to*) grant (to a person) the use of (a thing) on the understanding that it or its equivalent shall be returned. **2** allow the use of (money) at interest. **3** bestow or contribute (something temporary) (*lend assistance*; *lends a certain charm*). □ **lend an ear** or **one's ears**) listen. **lend a hand** see HAND. **lend itself to** (of a thing) be suitable for. **lend oneself to** accommodate oneself to a policy or purpose). □□ **lend·a·ble** *adj.* **lend·er** *n.* **lend·ing** *n.* [ME, earlier *lēne(n)* f. OE *lǣnan* f. *l ǣn* LOAN¹]

▶See note at LOAN.

lend·ing li·brar·y *n.* a library from which books may be borrowed and taken away for a short time.

Lend-lease *n. hist.* an arrangement made in 1941 whereby the US supplied equipment, etc., to the UK and its allies, orig. as a loan in return for the use of British-owned military bases.

length /length, lengkth/ *n.* **1** measurement or extent from end to end; the greater of two or the greatest of three dimensions of a body. **2** extent in, of, or with regard to, time (*a stay of some length*; *the length of a speech*). **3** the distance a thing extends (*at arm's length*; *ships a cable's length apart*). **4** the length of a horse, boat, etc., as a measure of the lead in a race. **5** a long stretch or extent (*a length of*

ring tailed lemur

hair). **6** a degree of thoroughness in action (*went to great lengths*; *prepared to go to any length*). **7** a piece of material of a certain length (*a length of cloth*). **8** *Prosody* the quantity of a vowel or syllable. **9** the extent of a garment in a vertical direction when worn. **10** the full extent of one's body. □ **at length 1** (also **at full** or **great**, etc., **length**) in detail; without curtailment. **2** after a long time; at last. [OE *lengthu* f. Gmc (as LONG¹)]

length·en /léngthən, léngk–/ *v.* **1** *tr. & intr.* make or become longer. **2** *tr.* make (a vowel) long. □□ **length·en·er** *n.*

length·ways /léngthwayz, léngkth–/ *adv.* lengthwise.

length·wise /léngthwīz, léngkth–/ *adv. & adj.* • *adv.* in a direction parallel with a thing's length. • *adj.* lying or moving lengthways.

length·y /léngthee, léngkthee/ *adj.* (**length·i·er, length·i·est**) **1** of unusual length. **2** (of speech, writing, style, a speaker, etc.) tedious; prolix. □□ **length·i·ly** *adv.* **length·i·ness** *n.*

le·ni·ent /leényənt/ *adj.* **1** merciful; tolerant; not disposed to severity. **2** (of punishment, etc.) mild. **3** *archaic* emollient. □□ **le·ni·ence** /–yəns/ *n.* **le·ni·en·cy** *n.* **le·ni·ent·ly** *adv.* [L *lenire lenit-* soothe f. *lenis* gentle]

SYNONYM TIP **lenient**

FOREBEARING, INDULGENT, LAX, MERCIFUL, PERMISSIVE. Not all parents approach discipline in the same way. Someone who is **lenient** is willing to lower his or her standards when it comes to imposing discipline (*the principal was lenient with the students who had been caught playing hookey*). A parent who is **forebearing** struggles against giving in to negative feelings and is therefore able to abstain from hasty or ill-tempered actions, no matter what the provocation (*her father's forebearing attitude meant that she escaped with only a lecture*). **Indulgent** goes beyond *forebearing* and suggests catering to someone's whims (*an indulgent parent who seldom denied her child anything*). **Lax** is a negative kind of leniency involving laziness or indifference (*a lax mother who never imposed a curfew*), while **merciful** suggests a relaxing of standards on the basis of compassion (*a merciful mother who understood her daughter's anger*). To be **permissive** is also to be extremely *lenient*, an approach that connotes tolerance to the point of passivity (*the children's utter disregard for the rules was the result of their permissive upbringing*).

Le·nin·ism /léninizəm/ *n.* Marxism as interpreted and applied by Lenin. □□ **Le·nin·ist** *n. & adj.* **Le·nin·ite** *n. & adj.* [V. I. *Lenin* (name assumed by V. I. Ulyanov), Russian statesman d. 1924]

le·ni·tion /liníshən/ *n.* (in Celtic languages) the process or result of articulating a consonant softly. [L *lenis* soft, after G *Lenierung*]

len·i·tive /lénitiv/ *adj. & n.* • *adj. Med.* soothing. • *n.* **1** *Med.* a soothing drug or appliance. **2** a palliative. [ME f. med.L *lenitivus* (as LENIENT)]

len·i·ty /lénitee/ *n.* (*pl.* **·ties**) *literary* **1** mercifulness; gentleness. **2** an act of mercy. [F *lénité* or L *lenitas* f. *lenis* gentle]

Len·ni Len·a·pe /lénee/ *n.* see DELAWARE.

le·no /leénō/ *n.* (*pl.* **·nos**) an openwork fabric with the warp threads twisted in pairs before weaving. [F *linon* f. *lin* flax f. L *linum*]

lens /lenz/ *n.* **1** a piece of a transparent substance with one or (usu.) both sides curved for concentrating or dispersing light rays, esp. in optical instruments. **2** a combination of lenses used in photography. **3** *Anat.* = CRYSTALLINE LENS. **4** *Physics* a device for focusing or otherwise modifying the direction of movement of light, sound, electrons, etc. □□ **lensed** *adj.* **lens·less** *adj.* [L *lens lentis* lentil (from the similarity of shape)]

Lent /lent/ *n. Eccl.* the period from Ash Wednesday to Holy Saturday, of which the 40 weekdays are devoted to fasting and penitence in commemoration of Christ's fasting in the wilderness. [ME f. LENTEN]

lent *past* and *past part.* of LEND.

-lent /lənt/ *suffix* forming adjectives (*pestilent*; *violent*) (cf. –ULENT). [L –*lentus* –ful]

Lent·en /léntən/ *adj.* of, in, or appropriate to, Lent. [orig. as noun, = spring, f. OE *lencten* f. Gmc, rel. to LONG¹, perh. with ref. to lengthening of the day in spring: now regarded as adj. f. LENT + –EN²]

len·ti·cel /léntisel/ *n. Bot.* any of the raised pores in the stems of woody plants that allow gas exchange between the atmosphere and the internal tissues. [mod.L *lenticella* dimin. of L *lens*: see LENS]

len·tic·u·lar /léntíkyələr/ *adj.* **1** shaped like a lentil or a biconvex lens. **2** of the lens of the eye. [L *lenticularis* (as LENTIL)]

len·til /léntəl/ *n.* **1** a leguminous plant, *Lens culinaris*, yielding edible biconvex seeds. **2** this seed, esp. used as food with the husk removed. [ME f. OF *lentille* f. L *lenticula* (as LENS)]

Lent lil·y *n. Brit.* the European wild daffodil, *Narcissus pseudonarcissus*.

len·to /léntō/ *adj. & adv. Mus.* • *adj.* slow. • *adv.* slowly. [It.]

len·toid /léntoyd/ *adj.* = LENTICULAR 1. [L *lens* (see LENS) + –OID]

Lent term *n. Brit.* the term at a university in which Lent falls.

Le·o /leé-ō/ *n.* (*pl.* **·os**) **1** a constellation, traditionally regarded as contained in the figure of a lion. **2 a** the fifth sign of the zodiac (the Lion). **b** a person born when the sun is in this sign. [OE f. L, = LI-ON]

Le·o·nid /leé·ənid/ *n.* any of the meteors that seem to radiate from the direction of the constellation Leo. [L *leo* (see LEO) *leonis* + –ID³]

Le·o·nine /leé·ənīn/ *adj. & n.* • *adj.* of Pope Leo; made or invented by Pope Leo. • *n.* (in *pl.*) leonine verse. [the name *Leo* (as LEONINE)]

le·o·nine /leé·ənīn/ *adj.* **1** like a lion. **2** of or resembling a lion or lions. [ME f. OF *leonin –ine* or L *leoninus* f. *leo leonis* lion]

le·o·nine verse *n.* **1** medieval Latin verse in hexameter or elegiac meter with internal rhyme. **2** English verse with internal rhyme.

leop·ard /lépərd/ *n.* (*fem.* **leop·ard·ess** /–dis/) **1** a large African or Asian feline, *Panthera pardus*, with either a black-spotted, yellowish-fawn or all black coat. Also called **panther**. **2** *Heraldry* a lion passant guardant as in the arms of England. **3** (*attrib.*) spotted like a leopard (*leopard moth*). [ME f. OF f. LL f. late Gk *leopardos* (as LI-ON, PARD)]

leop·ard's-bane *n.* any plant of the genus *Doronicum*, with large yellow daisylike flowers.

le·o·tard /leé·ōtaard/ *n.* **1** a close-fitting one-piece stretch garment worn by ballet dancers, acrobats, etc. **2** = TIGHTS. [J. *Léotard*, French trapeze artist d. 1870]

lep·er /lépər/ *n.* **1** a person suffering from leprosy. **2** a person shunned on moral grounds. [ME, prob. attrib. use of *leper* leprosy f. OF *lepre* f. L *lepra* f. Gk, fem. use of *lepros* scaly f. *lepos* scale]

lep·i·dop·ter·ous /lépidóptərəs/ *adj.* of the order Lepidoptera of insects, with four scale-covered wings often brightly colored, including butterflies and moths. □□ **lep·i·dop·ter·an** *adj. & n.* **lep·i·dop·ter·ist** *n.* [Gk *lepis –idos* scale + *pteron* wing]

lep·o·rine /lépərīn/ *adj.* of or like hares. [L *leporinus* f. *lepus –oris* hare]

lep·re·chaun /léprəkon, –kawn/ *n.* a small mischievous sprite in Irish folklore. [OIr. *luchorpán* f. *lu* small + *corp* body]

lep·ro·sy /léprəsee/ *n.* **1** a contagious bacterial disease that affects the skin, mucous membranes, and nerves, causing disfigurement. Also called **Hansen's disease**. **2** moral corruption or contagion. [LEPROUS + –Y³]

lep·rous /léprəs/ *adj.* **1** suffering from leprosy. **2** like or relating to leprosy. [ME f. OF f. LL *leprosus* f. *lepra*: see LEPER]

lep·ta *pl.* of LEPTON¹.

lepto- /léptō/ *comb. form* small; narrow. [Gk *leptos* fine, small, thin, delicate]

lep·to·ce·phal·ic /léptəsifálik/ *adj.* (also **lep·to·ceph·a·lous** /–séfələs/) narrow-skulled.

lep·ton¹ /lépton/ *n.* (*pl.* **lep·ta** /–tə/) a Greek coin worth one-hundredth of a drachma. [Gk *lepton* (*nomisma* coin) neut. of *leptos* small]

lep·ton² /lépton/ *n.* (*pl.* **lep·tons**) *Physics* any of a class of elementary particles which do not undergo strong interaction, e.g., an electron, muon, or neutrino. [LEPTO- + –ON]

lep·to·spi·ro·sis /léptōspīrósis/ *n.* an infectious disease caused by bacteria of the genus *Leptospira*, that occurs in rodents, dogs, and other mammals, and can be transmitted to humans. [LEPTO- + SPIRO-¹ + –OSIS]

lep·to·tene /léptəteen/ *n. Biol.* the first stage of the prophase of meiosis in which each chromosome is apparent as two fine chromatids. [LEPTO- + Gk *tainia* band]

les·bi·an /lézbeeən/ *n. & adj.* • *n.* a homosexual woman. • *adj.* **1** of homosexuality in women. **2** (**Lesbian**) of Lesbos. □□ **les·bi·an·ism** *n.* [L *Lesbius* f. Gk *Lesbios* f. *Lesbos*, island in the Aegean Sea, home of Sappho (see SAPPHIC)]

lese maj·es·ty /leez májistee/ *n.* (also **lèse maj·es·té** /layz mázhestay/) **1** treason. **2** an insult to a sovereign or ruler. **3** presumptuous conduct. [F *lèse-majesté* f. L *laesa majestas* injured sovereignty f. *laedere laes-* injure + *majestas* MAJESTY]

le·sion /leézhən/ *n.* **1** damage. **2** injury. **3** *Med.* a morbid change in the functioning or texture of an organ, etc. [ME f. OF f. L *laesio –onis* f. *laedere laes-* injure]

less /les/ *adj., adv., n., & prep.* • *adj.* **1** smaller in extent, degree, duration, number, etc. (*of less importance; in a less degree*). **2** of smaller quantity; not so much (opp. MORE) (*find less difficulty; eat less meat*). **3** *disp.* fewer (*eat less cookies*). **4** of lower rank, etc. (*no less a person than*). • *adv.* to a smaller extent, in a lower degree. • *n.* a smaller amount or quantity or number (*cannot take less; for less than $10; is little less than disgraceful*). • *prep.* minus (*made $1,000 less tax*). □ **in less than no time** *joc.* very quickly or soon. **much less** with even greater force of denial (*do not suspect him of negligence, much less of dishonesty*). [OE *lǣssa* (adj.), *lǣs* (adv.), f. Gmc]

▶See note at FEWER.

-less /lis/ *suffix* forming adjectives and adverbs: **1** from nouns, meaning 'not having, without, free from' (*doubtless; powerless*). **2** from verbs, meaning 'not affected by or doing the action of the verb' (*fathomless; tireless*). □□ **–lessly** *suffix* forming adverbs. **–lessness** *suffix* forming nouns. [OE *–lēas* f. *lēas* devoid of]

les·see /leseé/ *n.* (often foll. by *of*) a person who holds a property by lease. □□ **les·see·ship** *n.* [ME f. AF past part., OF *lessé* (as LEASE)]

less·en /lésən/ *v.tr. & intr.* make or become less; diminish.

less·er /lésər/ *adj.* (usu. *attrib.*) not so great as the other or the rest (*the lesser evil; the lesser celandine*). [double compar., f. LESS + –ER³]

les·son /lésən/ *n. & v.* • *n.* **1 a** an amount of teaching given at one time. **b** the time assigned to this. **2** (in *pl.*; foll. by *in*) systematic instruction (*gives lessons in dancing; took lessons in French*). **3** a thing learned or to be learned by a pupil; an assignment. **4 a** an occurrence, example, rebuke, or punishment, that serves or should serve to warn or encourage (*let that be a lesson to you*). **b** a thing inculcated by experience or study. **5** a passage from the Bible read aloud during a church service. • *v.tr. archaic* **1** instruct. **2** admonish; rebuke. □ **learn one's lesson** profit from or bear in mind a particular (usu. unpleasant) experience. **teach a person a lesson** punish a person, esp. as a deterrent. [ME f. OF *leçon* f. L *lectio –onis*: see LECTION]

les·sor /lésawr/ *n.* a person who lets a property by lease. [AF f. *lesser*: see LEASE]

lest /lest/ *conj.* **1** in order that not; for fear that (*lest we forget*). **2** that (*afraid lest we should be late*). [OE *thȳ lǣs the* whereby less that, later *the lēste*, ME *lest(e)*]

let¹ /let/ *v. & n.* • *v.* (**let·ting**; *past* and *past part.* **let**) **1** *tr.* **a** allow to; not prevent or forbid (*we let them go*). **b** cause to (*let me know; let it be known*). **2** *tr.* (foll. by *into*) **a** allow to enter. **b** make acquainted with (a secret, etc.). **c** inlay in. **3** *tr.* esp. *Brit.* grant the use of (rooms, land, etc.) for rent or hire (*was let to the new tenant for a year*). **4** *tr.* allow or cause (liquid or air) to escape (*let blood*). **5** *tr.* award (a contract for work). **6** *aux.* supplying the first and third persons of the imperative in exhortations (*let us pray*), commands (*let it be done at once; let there be light*), assumptions (*let AB be equal to CD*), and permission or challenge (*let him do his worst*). • *n. Brit.* the act or an instance of letting a house, room, etc. (*a long let*). □ **let alone 1** not to mention (*hasn't got a television, let alone a VCR*). **2** = *let be*. **let be** not interfere with, attend to, or do. **let down 1** lower. **2** fail to support or satisfy; disappoint. **3** lengthen (a garment). **4** *Brit.* deflate (a tire). **let down gently** avoid humiliating abruptly. **let drop** (or **fall**) **1** drop (esp. a word or hint) intentionally or by accident. **2** (foll. by *on, upon, to*) *Geom.* draw (a perpendicular) from an outside point to a line. **let fly 1** (often foll. by *at*) attack physically or verbally. **2** discharge (a missile). **let go 1** release; set at liberty. **2 a** (often foll. by *of*) lose or relinquish one's hold. **b** lose hold of. **3** cease to think or talk about. **let oneself go 1** give way to enthusiasm, impulse, etc. **2** cease to take trouble; neglect one's appearance or habits. **let in 1** allow to enter (*let the dog in; let in a flood of light; this would let in all sorts of evils*). **2** (usu. foll. by *for*) involve (a person, often oneself) in loss or difficulty. **3** (foll. by *on*) allow (a person) to share privileges, information, etc. **4** inlay (a thing) in another. **let oneself in** unassistedly enter another person's home, office, etc., usu. with permission. **let loose** release or unchain (a dog, fury, a maniac, etc.). **let me see** see SEE¹. **let off 1 a** fire (a gun). **b** explode (a bomb or firework). **2** allow or cause (steam, liquid, etc.) to escape. **3** allow to alight from a vehicle, etc. **4 a** not punish or compel. **b** (often foll. by *with*) punish lightly. **5** *Brit.* rent out (part of a house, etc.). **6** *Brit. colloq.* break wind. **let off steam** see STEAM. **let on** *colloq.* **1** reveal a secret. **2** pretend (*let on that he had succeeded*). **let out 1** allow to go out, esp. through a doorway. **2** release from restraint. **3** (often foll. by *that* + clause) reveal (a secret, etc.). **4** make (a garment) looser, esp. by adjustment at a seam. **5** put out to rent, esp. to several tenants, or to contract. **6** exculpate. **7** give vent or expression to; emit (a sound, etc.). **let rip** see RIP¹. **let slip** see SLIP¹. **let through** allow to pass. **let up** *colloq.* **1** become less intense or severe. **2** relax one's efforts. **to let** esp. *Brit.* available for rent. [OE *lǣtan* f. Gmc, rel. to LATE]

▶See note at LEAVE¹.

let² /let/ *n. & v.* • *n.* **1** (in tennis, squash, etc.) an obstruction of a ball or a player in certain ways, requiring the ball to be served again. **2** (*archaic* except in **without let or hindrance**) obstruction; hindrance. • *v.tr.* (**let·ting**; *past* and *past part.* **let·ted** or **let**) *archaic* hinder, obstruct. [OE *lettan* f. Gmc, rel. to LATE]

-let /lit, lət/ *suffix* forming nouns, usu. diminutives (*droplet; leaflet*) or denoting articles of ornament or dress (*anklet*). [orig. corresp. (in *bracelet, crosslet*, etc.) to F *–ette* added to nouns in *–el*]

let·down /létdown/ *n.* a disappointment.

le·thal /leéthəl/ *adj.* causing or sufficient to cause death. □□ **le·thal·i·ty** /–álitee/ *n.* **le·thal·ly** *adv.* [L *let(h)alis* f. *letum* death]

le·thal cham·ber *n.* a chamber in which animals may be killed painlessly with gas.

le·thal dose *n.* the amount of a toxic compound or drug that causes death in humans or animals.

leth·ar·gy /léthərjee/ *n.* **1** lack of energy or vitality; a torpid, inert, or apathetic state. **2** *Med.* morbid drowsiness or prolonged and unnatural sleep. □□ **le·thar·gic** /lithaárjik/ *adj.* **le·thar·gi·cal·ly** *adv.*

[ME f. OF *litargie* f. LL *lethargia* f. Gk *lēthargia* f. *lēthargos* forgetful f. *lēth-, lanthanomai* forget]

Le·the /léethee/ *n.* **1** (in Greek mythology) a river in Hades producing forgetfulness of the past. **2** (also **lethe**) such forgetfulness. □□ **Le·the·an** *adj.* [L, use of Gk *lēthē* forgetfulness (as LETHARGY)]

let-out *n. Brit. colloq.* an opportunity to escape.

let's /lets/ *contr.* let us (*let's go now*).

Lett /let/ *n.* = LATVIAN *n.* 1. [G *Lette* f. Latvian *Latvi*]

let·ter /létər/ *n. & v.* ● *n.* **1 a** a character representing one or more of the simple or compound sounds used in speech; any of the alphabetic symbols. **b** (in *pl.*) *colloq.* the initials of a degree, etc., after the holder's name. **c** a school or college initial as a mark of proficiency in sports, etc. **2 a** a written, typed, or printed communication, usu. sent by mail or messenger. **b** (in *pl.*) an addressed legal or formal document for any of various purposes. **3** the precise terms of a statement; the strict verbal interpretation (opp. SPIRIT *n.* 6) (*according to the letter of the law*). **4** (in *pl.*) **a** literature. **b** acquaintance with books; erudition. **c** authorship (*the profession of letters*). **5** *Printing* **a** types collectively. **b** a fount of type. ● *v.tr.* **1 a** inscribe letters on. **b** impress a title, etc., on (a book cover, etc.). **2** classify with letters. □ **to the letter** with adherence to every detail. □□ **let·ter·er** *n.* **let·ter·less** *adj.* [ME f. OF *lettre* f. L *litera, littera* letter of alphabet, (in *pl.*) epistle, literature]

let·ter car·ri·er *n.* one who delivers mail, usu. as an employee of the postal service.

let·tered /létərd/ *adj.* well-read or educated.

let·ter·head /létərhed/ *n.* **1** a printed heading on stationery stating a person or organization's name and address. **2** stationery with this.

let·ter·ing /létəring/ *n.* **1** the process of inscribing letters. **2** letters inscribed.

let·ter mis·sive *n.* (also **let·ters mis·sive**) a letter from a monarch to a dean and chapter nominating a person to be elected bishop.

let·ter of cred·it *n.* a letter issued by a bank to another bank, usu. in a different country, to serve as a guarantee for payments made to a specified person under specified conditions.

let·ter of marque *n. hist.* **1** a license to fit out an armed vessel and employ it in the capture of an enemy's merchant shipping. **2** (in *sing.*) a ship carrying such a license.

let·ter-per·fect *adj.* **1** *Theatr.* knowing one's part perfectly. **2** accurate; precise.

let·ter·press /létərpres/ *n.* **1** printing from raised type, not from lithography or other planographic processes. **2** *Brit.* the contents of an illustrated book other than the illustrations.

let·ter-qual·i·ty *adj.* of the quality of printing suitable for a business letter; producing print of this quality.

let·ters of ad·min·is·tra·tion *n.pl. Law* authority to administer the estate of someone who has died without making a will.

let·ters pat·ent *n.pl.* an open document from a monarch or government conferring a patent or other right.

Let·tic /létik/ *adj. & n.* ● *adj.* **1** = LATVIAN *adj.* **2** of or relating to the Baltic branch of languages. ● *n.* = LATVIAN *n.* 2.

Let·tish /létish/ *adj. & n.* = LATVIAN *adj., n.* 2.

let·tuce /létis/ *n.* **1** a composite plant, *Lactuca sativa*, with crisp edible leaves used in salads. **2** any of various plants resembling this. [ME *letus(e)*, rel. to OF *laituë* f. L *lactuca* f. *lac lactis* milk, with ref. to its milky juice]

let-up /létup/ *n. colloq.* **1** a reduction in intensity. **2** a relaxation of effort.

leu /láy-oo/ *n.* (*pl.* **lei** /lay/) the basic monetary unit of Romania. [Romanian, = lion]

leu·cine /lóoseen/ *n. Biochem.* an amino acid present in protein and essential in the diet of vertebrates. [F f. Gk *leukos* white + -IN]

leu·ke·mi·a /lookéemeeə/ *n.* (*Brit.* **leu·kae·mi·a**) *Med.* any of a group of malignant diseases in which the bone marrow and other blood-forming organs produce increased numbers of leukocytes. □□ **leu·ke·mic** *adj.* [mod.L f. G *Leukämie* f. Gk *leukos* white + *haima* blood]

leuko- /lóokō/ *comb. form* white. [Gk *leukos* white]

leu·ko·cyte /lóokəsīt/ *n.* (*Brit.* **leu·co·cyte**) **1** a white blood cell. **2** any blood cell that contains a nucleus. □□ **leu·ko·cyt·ic** /-sítik/ *adj.*

leu·ko·ma /lookómə/ *n.* (*Brit.* **leu·co·ma**) a white opacity in the cornea of the eye.

leu·kor·rhe·a /lóokəreeə/ *n.* (*Brit.* **leu·cor·rhoe·a**) a whitish or yellowish discharge of mucus from the vagina.

leu·kot·o·my /lookótəmee/ *n.* (also **leu·cot·o·my**) (*pl.* **-mies**) *Brit.* = *prefrontal lobotomy*.

Lev. *abbr.* Leviticus (Old Testament).

Le·vant /livánt/ *n.* (prec. by *the*) the eastern part of the Mediterranean with its islands and neighboring countries. □ **Levant morocco** high-grade, large-grained morocco leather. [F, pres. part. of *lever* rise, used as noun = point of sunrise, east]

le·vant /livánt/ *v.intr. Brit. sl.* abscond or bolt, esp. with betting or gaming losses unpaid. □□ **le·vant·er** *n.* [perh. f. LEVANT]

le·vant·er[1] /livántər/ *n.* **1** a strong easterly Mediterranean wind. **2** (**Levanter**) a native or inhabitant of the Levant in the eastern Mediterranean.

Le·van·tine /lévəntin, -teen, ləván-/ *adj. & n.* ● *adj.* of or trading to the Levant. ● *n.* a native or inhabitant of the Levant.

le·va·tor /livaytor/ *n.* a muscle that lifts a body part. [L, = one who lifts f. *levare* raise]

lev·ee[1] /lévee, levée/ *n.* **1** an assembly of visitors or guests, esp. at a formal reception. **2** *hist.* (in the UK) an assembly held by the sovereign or sovereign's representative at which men only were received. **3** *hist.* a reception of visitors on rising from bed. [F *levé* var. of *lever* rising f. *lever* to rise: see LEVY]

lev·ee[2] /lévee/ *n.* **1** an embankment against river floods. **2** a natural embankment built up by a river. **3** a landing place; a quay. [F *levée* fem. past part. of *lever* raise]

lev·el /lévəl/ *n., adj., & v.* ● *n.* **1** a horizontal line or plane. **2** a height or value reached, a position on a real or imaginary scale (*eye level; sugar level in the blood; danger level*). **3** a social, moral, or intellectual standard. **4** a plane of rank or authority (*discussions at cabinet level*). **5 a** an instrument giving a line parallel to the plane of the horizon for testing whether things are horizontal. **b** *Surveying* an instrument for giving a horizontal line of sight. **6** a more or less level surface. **7** a flat tract of land. **8** a floor or story in a building, ship, etc. ● *adj.* **1** having a flat and even surface; not bumpy. **2** horizontal; perpendicular to the plumb line. **3** (often foll. by *with*) **a** on the same horizontal plane as something else. **b** having equality with something else. **c** (of a spoonful, etc.) with the contents flat with the brim. **4** even, uniform, equable, or well-balanced in quality, style, temper, judgment, etc. **5** (of a race) having the leading competitors close together. ● *v.* (**lev·eled, lev·el·ing**; esp. *Brit.* **lev·elled, lev·el·ling**) **1** *tr.* make level, even, or uniform. **2** *tr.* (often foll. by *to* (or *with*) *the ground, in the dust*) raze or demolish. **3** *tr.* (also *absol.*) aim (a missile or gun). **4** *tr.* (also *absol.*; foll. by *at, against*) direct (an accusation, criticism, or satire). **5** *tr.* abolish (distinctions). **6** *intr.* (usu. foll. by *with*) *sl.* be frank or honest. **7** *tr.* place on the same level. **8** *tr.* (also *absol.*) *Surveying* ascertain differences in the height of (land). □ **do one's level best** *colloq.* do one's utmost; make all possible efforts. **find one's level 1** reach the right social, intellectual, etc., place in relation to others. **2** (of a liquid) reach the same height in receptacles or regions which communicate with each other. **level down** bring down to a standard. **level off** make or become level or smooth. **level out** make or become level; remove differences from. **level up** esp. *Brit.* bring up to a standard. **on the level** *colloq. adv.* honestly; without deception. ● *adj.* honest; truthful. **on a level with 1** in the same horizontal plane as. **2** equal with. □□ **lev·el·ly** *adv.* **lev·el·ness** *n.* [ME f. OF *livel* ult. f. L *libella* dimin. of *libra* scales, balance]

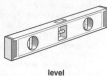

level

lev·el·er /lévələr/ *n.* (esp. *Brit.* **lev·el·ler**) **1** a person who advocates the abolition of social distinctions. **2** (**Leveler**) *hist.* an extreme radical dissenter in 17th-c. England. **3** a person or thing that levels.

lev·el·head·ed /lévəlhédid/ *adj.* mentally well-balanced, cool, sensible. □□ **lev·el·head·ed·ly** *adv.* **lev·el·head·ed·ness** *n.*

lev·el·ing screw *n.* a screw for adjusting parts of a machine, etc., to an exact level.

lev·er /lévər, léev-/ *n. & v.* ● *n.* **1** a bar resting on a pivot, used to help lift a heavy or firmly fixed object. **2** *Mech.* a simple machine consisting of a rigid bar pivoted about a fulcrum (fixed point) which can be acted upon by a force (effort) in order to move a load. **3** a projecting handle moved to operate a mechanism. **4** a means of exerting moral pressure. ● *v.* **1** *intr.* use a lever. **2** *tr.* (often foll. by *away, out, up*, etc.) lift, move, or act on with a lever. [ME f. OF *levier, leveor* f. *lever* raise: see LEVY]

lever 2

lev·er·age /lévərij, léev-/ *n.* **1** the action of a lever; a way of applying a lever. **2** the power of a lever; the mechanical advantage gained by use of a lever. **3** a means of accomplishing a purpose; power; influence. **4** a set or system of levers. **5** *Commerce* the use of a relatively small investment or value in equity to acquire or control a much larger investment.

lev·er·aged buy·out *n.* the purchase of a controlling share in a company by its management, using outside capital.

lev·er es·cape·ment n. a mechanism in a watch connecting the escape wheel and the balance wheel using two levers.

lev·er·et /lévərit/ n. a young hare, esp. one in its first year. [ME f. AF, dimin. of *levre*, OF *lievre* f. L *lepus leporis* hare]

lev·er watch n. a watch with a lever escapement.

lev·i·a·ble see LEVY.

le·vi·a·than /livíəthən/ n. **1** *Bibl.* a sea monster. **2** anything very large or powerful, esp. a ship. **3** an autocratic monarch or state (in allusion to a book by Hobbes, 1651). [ME f. LL f. Heb. *liwyāṯān*]

lev·i·gate /lévigayt/ v.tr. **1** reduce to a fine, smooth powder. **2** make a smooth paste of. □□ **lev·i·ga·tion** /–gáyshən/ n. [L *levigare levigat-* f. *levis* smooth]

lev·in /lévin/ n. *archaic* **1** lightning. **2** a flash of lightning. [ME *leven(e)*, prob. f. ON]

lev·i·rate /lévirət, –rayt, lée–/ n. a custom of the ancient Jews and some other peoples by which a man is obliged to marry his brother's widow. □□ **lev·i·rat·ic** /–rátik/ adj. **lev·i·rat·i·cal** adj. [L *levir* brother-in-law + –ATE¹]

Le·vi's /léeviz/ n.pl. *Trademark* a type of (orig. blue) denim jeans or overalls reinforced with rivets. [*Levi* Strauss, orig. US manufacturer in 1860s]

lev·i·tate /lévitayt/ v. **1** intr. rise and float in the air (esp. with reference to spiritualism). **2** tr. cause to do this. □□ **lev·i·ta·tion** /–táyshən/ n. **lev·i·ta·tor** n. [L *levis* light, after GRAVITATE]

Le·vite /léevit/ n. a member of the tribe of Levi, esp. of that part of it which provided assistants to the priests in the worship in the Jewish temple. [ME f. LL *levita* f. Gk *leuitēs* f. *Leui* f. Heb. *lēwī* Levi]

Le·vit·i·cal /livítikəl/ adj. **1** of the Levites or the tribe of Levi. **2** of the Levites' ritual. **3** of Leviticus. [LL *leviticus* f. Gk *leuitikos* (as LEVITE)]

lev·i·ty /lévitee/ n. **1** humor or frivolity, esp. the treatment of a serious matter with humor or in a manner lacking due respect. **2** *archaic* lightness of weight. [L *levitas* f. *levis* light]

levo- /léevō/ *comb. form* (also esp. *Brit.* **laevo-**) on or to the left. [L *laevus* left]

le·vo·do·pa /léevədópə/ n. = L-DOPA.

le·vo·ro·ta·to·ry /léevə-rótətawree/ adj. (esp. *Brit.* **lae·vo·ro·ta·to·ry**) *Chem.* having the property of rotating the plane of a polarized light ray to the left (counterclockwise facing the oncoming radiation).

lev·u·lose /léevyəlōs/ n. (esp. *Brit.* **laev·u·lose**) = FRUCTOSE. [LEVO- + –ULE + –OSE²]

lev·y /lévee/ v. & n. ● v.tr. (**·ies, ·ied**) **1 a** impose (a rate or toll). **b** raise (contributions or taxes). **c** (also *absol.*) raise (a sum of money) by legal execution or process (*the debt was levied on the debtor's goods*). **d** seize (goods) in this way. **e** extort (*levy blackmail*). **2** enlist or enroll (troops, etc.). **3** (usu. foll. by *upon, against*) wage; proceed to make (war). ● n. (pl. **·ies**) **1 a** the collecting of a contribution, tax, etc., or of property to satisfy a legal judgment. **b** a contribution, tax, etc., levied. **2 a** the act or an instance of enrolling troops, etc. **b** (in pl.) persons enrolled. **c** a body of persons enrolled. **d** the number of persons enrolled. □□ **lev·i·a·ble** adj. [ME f. OF *levee* fem. past part. of *lever* f. L *levare* raise f. *levis* light]

lewd /lōd/ adj. **1** lascivious. **2** indecent; obscene. □□ **lewd·ly** adv. **lewd·ness** n. [OE *lǣwede* LAY², of unkn. orig.]

lew·is /lóis/ n. an iron contrivance for gripping heavy blocks of stone or concrete for lifting. [18th c.: orig. unkn.]

Lew·is gun /lóis/ n. a light machine gun with a magazine, air cooling, and operation by gas from its own firing. [I. N. *Lewis*, Amer. soldier d. 1931, its inventor]

lew·is·ite /lóisit/ n. an irritant gas that produces blisters, developed for use in chemical warfare. [W. L. *Lewis*, Amer. chemist d. 1943 + –ITE¹]

lex dom·i·cil·i·i /léks domisílee-i/ n. *Law* the law of the country in which a person is domiciled. [L]

lex·eme /lékseem/ n. *Linguistics* a basic lexical unit of a language comprising one or several words, the elements of which do not separately convey the meaning of the whole. [LEXICON + –EME]

lex for·i /leks fáwri/ n. *Law* the law of the country in which an action is brought. [L]

lex·i·cal /léksikəl/ adj. **1** of the words of a language. **2** of or as of a lexicon. □□ **lex·i·cal·ly** adv. [Gk *lexikos, lexikon*: see LEXICON]

lex·i·cog·ra·phy /léksikógrəfee/ n. the compiling of dictionaries. □□ **lex·i·cog·ra·pher** n. **lex·i·co·graph·ic** /–kəgráfik/ adj. **lex·i·co·graph·i·cal** adj. **lex·i·co·graph·i·cal·ly** adv.

lex·i·col·o·gy /léksikóləjee/ n. the study of the form, history, and meaning of words. □□ **lex·i·co·log·i·cal** /–kəlójikəl/ adj. **lex·i·co·log·i·cal·ly** adv. **lex·i·col·o·gist** /–kóləjist/ n.

lex·i·con /léksikon/ n. **1** a dictionary, esp. of Greek, Latin, Hebrew, Syriac, or Arabic. **2** the vocabulary of a person, language, branch of knowledge, etc. [mod.L f. Gk *lexikon* (*biblion* book), neut. of *lexikos* f. *lexis* word f. *legō* speak]

lex·is /léksis/ n. **1** words; vocabulary. **2** the total stock of words in a language. [Gk: see LEXICON]

lex lo·ci /leks lósi, –kee, –ki/ n. *Law* the law of the country in which

a transaction is performed, a tort is committed, or a property is situated. [L]

lex ta·li·o·nis /léks taleeónis/ n. the law of retaliation, whereby a punishment resembles the offense committed, in kind and degree. [L]

ley¹ /lay/ n. *Brit.* a field temporarily under grass. [ME (orig. adj.), perh. f. OE, rel. to LAY¹, LIE¹]

ley² /lay, lee/ n. the supposed straight line of a prehistoric track, usu. between hilltops. [var. of LEA]

Ley·den jar /líd'n/ n. an early form of capacitor consisting of a glass jar with layers of metal foil on the outside and inside. [*Leyden* (now *Leiden*) in Holland, where it was invented (1745)]

LF abbr. low frequency.

LH abbr. *Biochem.* luteinizing hormone.

l.h. abbr. left hand.

LI abbr. **1** Long Island. **2** *Brit.* light infantry.

Li symb. *Chem.* the element lithium.

li·a·bil·i·ty /líəbílitee/ n. (pl. **·ties**) **1** the state of being liable. **2** a person or thing that is troublesome as an unwelcome responsibility; a handicap. **3** what a person is liable for, esp. (in pl.) debts or pecuniary obligations.

li·a·ble /líəbəl/ predic.adj. **1** legally bound. **2** (foll. by *to*) subject to (a tax or penalty). **3** (foll. by *to* + infin.) under an obligation. **4** (foll. by *to*) exposed or open to (something undesirable). **5** disp. (foll. by *to* + infin.) apt; likely (*it is liable to rain*). **6** (foll. by *for*) answerable. [ME perh. f. AF f. OF *lier* f. L *ligare* bind]

▶**Liable** is commonly used to mean 'likely (to do something undesirable),' e.g., *without his glasses he's liable to run the car into a tree.* Precisely, however, **liable** means 'legally obligated,' as in *if he runs into another car he may be liable for damages.*

li·aise /lee-áyz/ v.intr. (foll. by *with, between*) colloq. establish cooperation; act as a link. [back-form. f. LIAISON]

li·ai·son /lee-áyzon, lée-ay–/ n. **1 a** communication or cooperation, esp. between military forces or units. **b** a person who initiates such. **2** an illicit sexual relationship. **3** the binding or thickening agent of a sauce. **4** the sounding of an ordinarily silent final consonant before a word beginning with a vowel (or a mute *h* in French). [F f. *lier* bind f. L *ligare*]

li·ai·son of·fi·cer n. a person who is employed to form a working relationship between two organizations to their mutual benefit.

li·a·na /lee-aánə/ n. (also **li·ane** /–aán/) any of several climbing and twining plants of tropical forests. [F *liane, lierne* clematis, of uncert. orig.]

li·ar /líər/ n. a person who tells a lie or lies, esp. habitually. [OE *lēogere* (as LIE², –AR⁴)]

li·as /líəs/ n. **1** (**Lias**) *Geol.* the lower strata of the Jurassic system of rocks, consisting of shales and limestones rich in fossils. **2** a blue limestone rock found in SW England. □□ **li·as·sic** /líásik/ adj. (in sense 1). [ME f. OF *liois* hard limestone, prob. f. Gmc]

Lib. abbr. Liberal.

lib /lib/ n. colloq. liberation (*women's lib*). [abbr.]

li·ba·tion /líbáyshən/ n. **1 a** the pouring out of a drink offering to a god. **b** such a drink offering. **2** joc. a drink. [ME f. L *libatio* f. *libare* pour as offering]

lib·ber /líbər/ n. colloq. an advocate of women's liberation.

li·bel /líbəl/ n. & v. ● n. **1** *Law* **a** a published false statement damaging to a person's reputation (cf. SLANDER). **b** the act of publishing this. **2 a** a false and defamatory written statement. **b** (foll. by *on*) a thing that brings discredit by misrepresentation, etc. (*the portrait is a libel on him; the book is a libel on human nature*). **3 a** (in civil and ecclesiastical law) the plaintiff's written declaration. **b** *Sc. Law* a statement of the grounds of a charge. ● v.tr. (**li·beled, li·bel·ing**; esp. *Brit.* **li·belled, li·bel·ling**) **1** defame by libelous statements. **2** accuse falsely and maliciously. **3** *Law* publish a libel against. **4** (in ecclesiastical law) bring a suit against. □□ **li·bel·er** n. [ME f. OF f. L *libellus* dimin. of *liber* book]

li·bel·ous /líbələs/ adj. containing or constituting a libel. □□ **li·bel·ous·ly** adv.

li·ber /líbər/ n. bast. [L, = bark]

lib·er·al /líbərəl, líbrəl/ adj. & n. ● adj. **1** given freely; ample; abundant. **2** (often foll. by *of*) given freely; generous; not sparing. **3** open-minded; not prejudiced. **4** not strict or rigorous; (of interpretation) not literal. **5** for general broadening of the mind; not professional or technical (*liberal studies*). **6 a** favoring individual liberty and political and social reform. **b** of or characteristic of liberals or a liberal party. **7** *Theol.* regarding many traditional beliefs as dispensable, invalidated by modern thought, or liable to change (*liberal Protestant; liberal Judaism*). ● n. **1** a person of liberal views.

Middle English: via Old French from Latin *liberalis*, from *liber* 'free (man).' The original sense was 'suitable for a free man,' hence 'suitable for a gentleman' (one not tied to a trade), surviving in *liberal arts*. Another early sense 'generous' (compare with sense 1) gave rise to an obsolete meaning 'free from restraint,' leading to senses 3, 4, 6, and 7 (late 18th cent.).

2 a supporter or member of a liberal party. □□ **lib·er·al·ism** *n.* **lib·er·al·ist** *n.* **lib·er·al·is·tic** /–lístik/ *adj.* **lib·er·al·ly** *adv.* **lib·er·al·ness** *n.*

lib·er·al arts *n.pl.* **1** arts subjects such as literature, philosophy, and history, as distinct from science and technology. **2** *hist.* the medieval trivium and quadrivium.

lib·er·al·i·ty /líbərálitee/ *n.* **1** free giving; munificence. **2** freedom from prejudice; breadth of mind. [ME f. OF *liberalite* or L *liberalitas* (as LIBERAL)]

lib·er·al·ize /líbərəlīz, líbrə–/ *v.tr. & intr.* make or become more liberal or less strict. □□ **lib·er·al·i·za·tion** *n.* **lib·er·al·iz·er** *n.*

Lib·er·al Par·ty *n.* a political party advocating liberal policies, esp. a British party that emerged in the 1860s from the old Whig Party.

lib·er·ate /líbərayt/ *v.tr.* **1** (often foll. by *from*) set at liberty; set free. **2** free (a country, etc.) from an oppressor or an enemy occupation. **3** (often as **liberated** *adj.*) free (a person) from rigid social conventions, esp. in sexual behavior. **4** *sl.* steal. **5** *Chem.* release (esp. a gas) from a state of combination. □□ **lib·er·a·tor** *n.* [L *liberare liberat-* f. *liber* free]

lib·er·a·tion /líbəráyshən/ *n.* the act or an instance of liberating; the state of being liberated. □□ **lib·er·a·tion·ist** *n.* [ME f. L *liberatio* f. *liberare*: see LIBERATE]

lib·er·a·tion the·ol·o·gy *n.* a movement in Christian theology that interprets liberation from social, political, and economic oppression as an anticipation of ultimate salvation.

lib·er·tar·i·an /líbərtáireeən/ *n. & adj.* ● *n.* **1** an advocate of liberty. **2** a believer in free will (opp. NECESSITARIAN). ● *adj.* believing in free will. □□ **lib·er·tar·i·an·ism** *n.*

lib·er·tine /líbərteen, –tin/ *n. & adj.* ● *n.* **1** a dissolute or licentious person. **2** a free thinker on religion. **3** a person who follows his or her own inclinations. ● *adj.* **1** licentious; dissolute. **2** freethinking. **3** following one's own inclinations. □□ **lib·er·tin·age** *n.* **lib·er·tin·ism** /–nízəm/ *n.* [L *libertinus* freedman f. *libertus* made free f. *liber* free]

lib·er·ty /líbərtee/ *n.* (*pl.* **·ties**) **1 a** freedom from captivity, imprisonment, slavery, or despotic control. **b** a personification of this. **2 a** the right or power to do as one pleases. **b** (foll. by *to* + infin.) right; power; opportunity; permission. **c** *Philos.* freedom from control by fate or necessity. **3 a** (usu. in *pl.*) a right, privilege, or immunity, enjoyed by prescription or grant. **b** (in *sing.* or *pl.*) *hist.* an area having such privileges, etc., esp. a district controlled by a city though outside its boundary or an area outside a prison where some prisoners might reside. **4** setting aside of rules or convention. □ **at liberty 1** free; not imprisoned (*set at liberty*). **2** (foll. by *to* + infin.) entitled; permitted. **3** available; disengaged. **take liberties 1** (often foll. by *with*) behave in an unduly familiar manner. **2** (foll. by *with*) deal freely or superficially with rules or facts. **take the liberty** (foll. by *to* + infin., or *of* + verbal noun) presume; venture. [ME f. OF *liberté* f. L *libertas –tatis* f. *liber* free]

Lib·er·ty Bell *n.* a bell in Philadelphia first rung on July 8, 1776 to celebrate the first public reading of the Declaration of Independence.

lib·er·ty cap *n. hist.* a conical knit cap worn as a symbol of liberty, esp. by American and French revolutionaries.

lib·er·ty pole *n.* (also **lib·er·ty tree**) *hist.* a pole, flagstaff, or tree atop of which a flag or liberty cap is displayed, esp. as a rallying symbol to American revolutionaries.

Lib·er·ty ship *n. hist.* a prefabricated US-built freighter of World War II.

li·bid·i·nous /libídənəs/ *adj.* lustful. □□ **li·bid·i·nous·ly** *adv.* **li·bid·i·nous·ness** *n.* [ME f. L *libidinosus* f. *libido –dinis* lust]

li·bi·do /libéedō, –bí–/ *n.* (*pl.* **·dos**) **1** sexual desire. **2** *Psychol.* the en-

ergy of the sexual drive as a component of the life instinct. □□ **li·bid·i·nal** /libídənəl/ *adj.* **li·bid·i·nal·ly** *adv.* [L: see LIBIDINOUS]

Li·bra /leébrə, lí–/ *n.* **1** a constellation, traditionally regarded as contained in the figure of scales. **2 a** the seventh sign of the zodiac (the Balance or Scales). **b** a person born when the sun is in this sign. □□ **Li·bran** *n. & adj.* [ME f. L, orig. = pound weight]

li·brar·i·an /lībráireeən/ *n.* a person in charge of, or an assistant in, a library. □□ **li·brar·i·an·ship** *n.* [L *librarius*: see LIBRARY]

li·brar·y /lí breree/ *n.* (*pl.* **·ies**) **1 a** a collection of books, etc., for use by the public or by members of a group. **b** a person's collection of books. **2** a room or building containing a collection of books (for reading or reference rather than for sale). **3 a** a similar collection of films, records, computer software, etc. **b** the place where these are kept. **4** a series of books issued by a publisher in similar bindings, etc., usu. as a set. **5** a public institution charged with the care of a collection of books, films, etc. [ME f. OF *librairie* f. L *libraria* (*taberna* shop), fem. of *librarius* bookseller's, of books, f. *liber libri* book]

li·brar·y e·di·tion *n.* an edition of a book that is of large size and has good-quality print and binding.

li·brar·y sci·ence *n.* the study of librarianship.

li·bra·tion /lībráyshən/ *n.* an apparent oscillation of a heavenly body, esp. the moon, by which the parts near the edge of the disk are alternately in view and out of view. [L *libratio* f. *librare* f. *libra* balance]

li·bret·to /librétō/ *n.* (*pl.* **·tos** or **li·bret·ti** /–tee/) the text of an opera or other long musical vocal work. □□ **li·bret·tist** *n.* [It., dimin. of *libro* book f. L *liber libri*]

Lib·ri·um /líbreeəm/ *n. Trademark* a white crystalline drug used as a tranquilizer.

Lib·y·an /libeeən, líbyən/ *adj. & n.* ● *adj.* **1** of or relating to modern Libya in N. Africa. **2** of ancient N. Africa west of Egypt. **3** of or relating to the Berber group of languages. ● *n.* **1 a** a native or national of modern Libya. **b** a person of Libyan descent. **2** an ancient language of the Berber group.

lice *pl.* of LOUSE.

li·cense /lísəns/ *n. & v.* (esp. *Brit.* **li·cence**) ● *n.* **1** a permit from an authority to own or use something, do a particular thing, or carry on a trade (*gun license; driver's license; liquor license*). **2** formal or official permission to do something (*logging is permitted under license from the Forest Service*). **3** a writer's or artist's freedom to deviate from fact or convention for effect (*artistic license*). **4** freedom to behave as one wishes, esp. in a way that results in unacceptable behavior (*the government was criticized for giving the army too much license*). ● *v.tr.* **1** grant a license to (a person or organization). **2** authorize the use, performance, or release of something (*the drug is already licensed for human use*). **3** dated give permission to someone to do something. □□ **li·cens·a·ble** *adj.* **li·cens·er** *n.* **li·cen·sor** *n.* [ME f. OF f. L *licentia* f. *licēre* be lawful]

li·censed prac·ti·cal nurse *n.* a person licensed to provide basic nursing care. ¶ Abbr.: LPN.

li·cen·see /lísənseé/ *n.* the holder of a license, esp. to sell alcoholic liquor.

li·cense plate *n.* the usu. metal plate affixed to a motor vehicle displaying a series of letters or numbers indicating that the vehicle has been registered with the state.

li·cen·ti·ate /lisénsheeət/ *n.* **1** a holder of a certificate of competence to practice a certain profession. **2** a licensed preacher not yet having an appointment, esp. in a Presbyterian church. [ME f. med.L *licentiatus* past part. of *licentiare* f. L *licentia*: see LICENSE]

li·cen·tious /lisénshəs/ *adj.* **1** immoral in sexual relations. **2** *archaic* disregarding accepted rules or conventions. □□ **li·cen·tious·ly** *adv.* **li·cen·tious·ness** *n.* [L *licentiosus* f. *licentia*: see LICENSE]

li·chee var. of LITCHI.

li·chen /líkən/ *n.* **1** any plant organism of the group Lichenes, composed of a fungus and an alga in symbiotic association, usu. of green, gray, or yellow tint and growing on and coloring rocks, tree trunks, roofs, walls, etc. **2** any of several types of skin disease in which small, round, hard lesions occur close together. □□ **li·chened** *adj.* (in sense 1). **li·chen·ol·o·gy** *n.* (in sense 1). **li·chen·ous** *adj.* (in sense 2). [L f. Gk *leikhēn*]

lich·gate var. of LYCHGATE.

lic·it /lísit/ *adj.* not forbidden; lawful. □□ **lic·it·ly** *adv.* [L *licitus* past part. of *licēre* be lawful]

lick /lik/ *v. & n.* ● *v.tr. & intr.* **1** *tr.* pass the tongue over, esp. to taste, moisten, or (of animals) clean. **2** *tr.* bring into a specified condition or position by licking (*licked it all up; licked it clean*). **3 a** *tr.* (of a flame, waves, etc.) touch; play lightly over. **b** *intr.* move gently or caressingly. **4** *tr. colloq.* **a** defeat; excel. **b** surpass the comprehension of (*has got me licked*). **5** *tr. colloq.* thrash. ● *n.* **1** an act of licking with the tongue. **2** = SALT LICK. **3** *colloq.* a fast pace (*at a lick; at full lick*). **4** *colloq.* **a** a small amount; quick treatment with (foll. by *of*: *a lick of paint*). **b** a quick wash. **5** a smart blow with a stick, etc. □ **a lick and a promise** *colloq.* a hasty performance of a task, esp. of washing oneself. **lick a person's boots** (or **shoes**) toady; be servile. **lick into shape** see SHAPE. **lick one's lips** (or **chops**) **1** look forward with relish. **2** show one's satisfaction. **lick one's wounds** be in retirement after defeat. □□ **lick•er** *n.* (also in *comb.*). [OE *liccian* f. WG]

lick•er•ish /líkərish/ *adj.* (also **liq•uor•ish**) **1** lecherous. **2 a** fond of fine food. **b** greedy; longing. [ME *lickerous* f. OF *lecheros*: see LECH-ER]

lick•e•ty-split /líkəteesplít/ *adv. colloq.* at full speed; headlong. [prob. f. LICK (cf. *at full lick*) + SPLIT]

lick•ing /líking/ *n. colloq.* **1** a thrashing. **2** a defeat.

lick•spit•tle /líkspit'l/ *n.* a toady.

lic•o•rice /líkərish, -ris/ *n.* (also esp. *Brit.* **liq•uo•rice**) **1** a black root extract used as a candy and in medicine. **2** the leguminous plant *Glycyrrhiza glabra* from which it is obtained. [ME f. AF *lycorys*, OF *licoresse* f. LL *liquiritia* f. Gk *glukurrhiza* f. *glukus* sweet + *rhiza* root]

lic•tor /líktər/ *n.* (usu. in *pl.*) *Rom.Hist.* an officer attending the consul or other magistrate, bearing the fasces, and executing sentence on offenders. [ME f. L, perh. rel. to *ligare* bind]

lid /lid/ *n.* **1** a hinged or removable cover, esp. for the top of a container. **2** = EYELID. **3** the operculum of a shell or a plant. **4** *sl.* a hat. □ **put a lid on** be quiet about; keep secret. **take the lid off** *colloq.* expose (a scandal, etc.). □□ **lid•ded** *adj.* (also in *comb.*). **lid•less** *adj.* [OE *hlid* f. Gmc]

li•do /léedō/ *n.* (*pl.* **-dos**) esp. *Brit.* a public open-air swimming pool or beach resort. [It. f. *Lido*, the name of a beach resort near Venice, f. L *litus* shore]

lie[1] /lī/ *v. & n.* ● *v.intr.* (**ly•ing** /lí-ing/; *past* **lay** /lay/; *past part.* **lain** /layn/) **1** be in or assume a horizontal position on a supporting surface; be at rest on something. **2** (of a thing) rest flat on a surface (*snow lay on the ground*). **3** (of abstract things) remain undisturbed or undiscussed, etc. (*let matters lie*). **4 a** be kept or remain or be in a specified, esp. concealed, state or place (*lie hidden; lie in wait; malice lay behind those words; they lay dying; the books lay unread; the money is lying in the bank*). **b** (of abstract things) exist; reside; be in a certain position or relation (foll. by *in, with,* etc.: *the answer lies in education; my sympathies lie with the family*). **5 a** be situated or stationed (*the village lay to the east; the ships are lying off the coast*). **b** (of a road, route, etc.) lead (*the road lies over mountains*). **c** be spread out to view (*the desert lay before us*). **6** (of the dead) be buried in a grave. **7** (foll. by *with*) *archaic* have sexual intercourse. **8** *Law* be admissible or sustainable (*the objection will not lie*). **9** (of a game bird) not rise. ● *n.* **1 a** the way or direction or position in which a thing lies. **b** *Golf* the position of a golf ball when about to be struck. **2** the place of cover of an animal or a bird. □ **as far as in me lies** to the best of my power. **let lie** not raise (a controversial matter, etc.) for discussion, etc. **lie about** (or **around**) be left carelessly out of place. **lie ahead** be going to happen; be in store. **lie back** recline

EQUIVOCATE, FABRICATE, FIB, PREVARICATE, RATIONALIZE. If your spouse asks you if you remembered to mail the tax forms and you say "Yes," even though you know they're still sitting on the passenger seat of your car, you're telling a **lie**, which is a deliberately false statement. If you launch into a lengthy explanation of the day's frustrations and setbacks, the correct word would be **prevaricate**, which is to quibble, dodge the point, or confuse the issue so as to avoid telling the truth. If you tell your spouse that you would have mailed the taxes, but then you started thinking about an important deduction you might be entitled to take and decided it would be unwise to mail them without looking into it, you're **rationalizing**, which is to come up with reasons that put your own behavior in the most favorable possible light. If you say that there was an accident in front of the post office that prevented you from finding a parking space and there really wasn't, **fabricate** is the correct verb, meaning that you've invented a false story or excuse without the harsh connotations of *lie* (*she fabricated an elaborate story about how they got lost on their way home*). **Equivocate** implies saying one thing and meaning another; it usually suggests the use of words that have more than one meaning, or whose ambiguity may be misleading. For example, if your spouse says, "Did you take care of the taxes today?" you might equivocate by saying "Yes," you took care of them—meaning that you finished completing the forms and sealing them in the envelope, but that you didn't actually get them to the post office. To **fib** is to tell a falsehood about something unimportant; it is often used as a euphemism for *lie* (*a child who fibs about eating his vegetables*).

so as to rest. **lie down** assume a lying position; have a short rest. **lie down under** esp. *Brit.* accept (an insult, etc.) without protest. **lie heavy** cause discomfort or anxiety. **lie in 1** remain in bed in the morning. **2** *archaic* be brought to bed in childbirth. **lie in state** (of a deceased great personage) be laid in a public place of honor before burial. **lie low 1** keep quiet or unseen. **2** be discreet about one's intentions. **lie off** *Naut.* stand some distance from shore or from another ship. **lie over** be deferred. **lie to** *Naut.* come almost to a stop facing the wind. **lie up** (of a ship) go into dock or be out of commission. **lie with** (often foll. by *to* + infin.) be the responsibility of (a person) (*it lies with you to answer*). **take lying down** (usu. with *neg.*) accept (defeat, rebuke, etc.) without resistance or protest, etc. [OE *licgan* f. Gmc]

▶See note at LAY[1].

lie[2] /lī/ *n. & v.* ● *n.* **1** an intentionally false statement (*tell a lie; pack of lies*). **2** imposture; false belief (*live a lie*). ● *v.intr. & tr.* (**lies, lied, ly•ing** /lí-ing/) **1** *intr.* **a** tell a lie or lies (*they lied to me*). **b** (of a thing) be deceptive (*the camera cannot lie*). **2** *tr.* (usu. *refl.*; foll. by *into, out of*) get (oneself) into or out of a situation by lying (*lied themselves into trouble; lied my way out of danger*). □ **give the lie to** serve to show the falsity of (a supposition, etc.). [OE *lyge lēogan* f. Gmc]

Lieb•frau•milch /léebfrowmilk/ *n.* a light white wine from the Rhine region. [G f. *Liebfrau* the Virgin Mary, the patroness of the convent where it was first made + *Milch* milk]

lied /leed, leet/ *n.* (*pl.* **lied•er** /léedər/) a type of German song, esp. of the Romantic period, usu. for solo voice with piano accompaniment. [G]

lie de•tec•tor *n.* an instrument for determining whether a person is telling the truth by testing for physiological changes considered to be symptomatic of lying.

lie-down *n.* esp. *Brit.* a short rest.

lief /leef/ *adv. archaic* gladly; willingly. (usu. **had lief, would lief**) [orig. as adj. f. OE *lēof* dear, pleasant, f. Gmc, rel. to LEAVE[2], LOVE]

liege /leej, leezh/ *adj. & n.* usu. *hist.* ● *adj.* (of a superior) entitled to receive or (of a vassal) bound to give feudal service or allegiance. ● *n.* **1** (in full **liege lord**) a feudal superior or sovereign. **2** (usu. in *pl.*) a vassal or subject. [ME f. OF *lige, liege* f. med.L *laeticus*, prob. f. Gmc]

liege•man /léejman, leezh-/ *n.* (*pl.* **-men**) *hist.* a sworn vassal; a faithful follower.

lie-in *n.* **1** *Brit.* a prolonged stay in bed in the morning. **2** an organized protest in which demonstrators lie down (in a public place) refusing to be moved.

lien /leen, léeən/ *n. Law* a right over another's property to protect a debt charged on that property. [F f. OF *loien* f. L *ligamen* bond f. *ligare* bind]

li•erne /leeérn/ *n. Archit.* (in vaulting) a short rib connecting the bosses and intersections of the principal ribs. [ME f. F: see LIANA]

lieu /lōō/ *n.* □ **in lieu 1** instead. **2** (foll. by *of*) in the place of. [ME f. F f. L *locus* place]

lieut. *abbr.* lieutenant.

lieu•ten•ant /lōōténənt/ *n.* **1** a deputy or substitute acting for a superior. **2 a** an army officer next in rank below captain. **b** a naval officer next in rank below lieutenant commander. **3** a police officer next in rank below captain. □□ **lieu•ten•an•cy** *n.* (*pl.* **-cies**) [ME f. OF (as LIEU, TENANT)]

lieu•ten•ant colo•nel *n.* (also **lieu•ten•ant com•man•der** or **lieu•ten•ant gen•er•al**) officers ranking next below colonel, commander, or general.

lieu•ten•ant gov•er•nor *n.* **1** (in the US) the elected official next in rank to a state's governor. **2** *Brit.* a deputy governor.

life /līf/ *n.* (*pl.* **lives** /līvz/) **1** the condition that distinguishes active animals and plants from inorganic matter, including the capacity for growth, functional activity, and continual change preceding death. **2 a** living things and their activity (*insect life; is there life on Mars?*). **b** human presence or activity (*no sign of life*). **3 a** the period during which life lasts, or the period from birth to the present time or from the present time to death (*have done it all my life; will regret it all my life; life membership*). **b** the duration of a thing's existence or of its ability to function; validity, efficacy, etc. (*the battery has a life of two years*). **4 a** a person's state of existence as a living individual (*sacrificed their lives; took many lives*). **b** a living person (*many lives were lost*). **5 a** an individual's occupation, actions, or fortunes; the manner of one's existence (*that would make life easy; start a new life*). **b** a particular aspect of this (*love life; private life*). **6** the active part of existence; the business and pleasures of the world (*travel is the best way to see life*). **7** a human's earthly or supposed future existence. **8 a** energy; liveliness; animation (*full of life; put some life into it!*). **b** an animating influence (*was the life of the party*). **c** (of an inanimate object) power; force; ability to perform its intended function. **9** the living, esp. nude, form or model (*drawn from life*). **10** a written account of a person's life; a biography. **11** *colloq.* a sentence of imprisonment for life (*they were all serving life*). **12** a chance; a fresh start (*cats have nine lives; gave the player three lives*). □ **come to life 1** emerge from unconsciousness or inactivity; begin operating. **2** (of an inanimate object) assume an imaginary animation. **for dear** (or **one's**) **life** as if or in order to escape death; as a matter of extreme urgency (*hanging on for dear life; run for your life*). **for life** for the rest of one's life. **for the life of** (foll. by pers. pron.) even if (one's) life depended on it (*cannot for the life of me remember*). **give one's life 1** (foll. by *for*) die; sacrifice oneself. **2** (foll. by *to*) dedicate oneself. **large as life** *colloq.* in person, esp. prominently (*stood there large as life*). **larger than life 1** exaggerated. **2** (of a person) having an exuberant personality. **lose one's life** be killed. **a matter of life and** (or **and**) **death** a matter of vital importance. **not on your life** *colloq.* most certainly not. **save a person's life 1** prevent a person's death. **2** save a person from serious difficulty. **take one's life in one's hands** take a crucial personal risk. **to the life** true to the original. [OE *līf* f. Gmc]

life-and-death *adj.* vitally important; desperate (*a life-and-death struggle*).

life belt *n.* a belt of buoyant or inflatable material for keeping a person afloat in water.

life·blood /lífblud/ *n.* **1** the blood, as being necessary to life. **2** the vital factor or influence.

life·boat /lífbōt/ *n.* **1** a specially constructed boat launched from land to rescue those in distress at sea. **2** a ship's small boat for use in an emergency.

life bu·oy *n.* a buoyant support (usu. a ring) for keeping a person afloat in water.

lifeboat

life cy·cle *n.* the series of changes in the life of an organism including reproduction.

life ex·pect·an·cy *n.* the average period that a person at a specified age may expect to live.

life force *n.* inspiration or a driving force or influence.

life-form *n.* any living thing.

life-giv·ing *adj.* that sustains life or uplifts and revitalizes.

life·guard /lífgaard/ *n.* an expert swimmer employed to rescue bathers from drowning.

Life Guards *n.pl.* (in the UK) a regiment of the royal household cavalry.

life in·sur·ance *n.* insurance for a sum to be paid on the death of the insured person.

life jack·et *n.* a buoyant or inflatable jacket for keeping a person afloat in water.

life·less /líflis/ *adj.* **1** lacking life; no longer living. **2** unconscious. **3** lacking movement or vitality. □□ **life·less·ly** *adv.* **life·less·ness** *n.* [OE *līflēas* (as LIFE, −LESS)]

life·like /líflīk/ *adj.* closely resembling the person or thing represented. □□ **life·like·ness** *n.*

life jacket

life·line /líflīn/ *n.* **1 a** a rope, etc., used for lifesaving, e.g., that attached to a life buoy. **b** a diver's signaling line. **2** a sole means of communication or transport. **3** a fold in the palm of the hand, regarded as significant in palmistry. **4** an emergency telephone counseling service.

life·long /líflawng, –long/ *adj.* lasting a lifetime.

life peer *n. Brit.* a peer whose title lapses on death.

life pre·serv·er *n.* **1** a life jacket, etc. **2** *Brit.* a short stick with a heavily loaded end; blackjack.

lif·er /lífər/ *n. sl.* **1** a person serving a life sentence in prison. **2** a person committed to a long or lifetime career in a profession, esp. the military.

life raft *n.* an inflatable raft for use in an emergency at sea.

life·sav·er /lífsayvər/ *n.* **1** a person or thing that saves one from serious difficulty. **2** *Austral.* & *NZ* = LIFEGUARD.

life sci·enc·es *n.pl.* biology and related subjects.

life sen·tence *n.* **1** a sentence of imprisonment for life. **2** an illness or commitment, etc., perceived as a continuing threat to one's freedom.

life-size *adj.* (also **life-sized**) of the same size as the person or thing represented.

life·style /lífstīl/ *n.* the particular way of life of a person or group.

life-sup·port *adj.* (of equipment) allowing vital functions to continue in an adverse environment or during severe disablement.

life·time /líftīm/ *n.* **1** the duration of a person's life. **2** the duration of a thing or its usefulness. **3** *colloq.* an exceptionally long time. □ **of a lifetime** such as does not occur more than once in a person's life (*the chance of a lifetime; the journey of a lifetime*).

life·work /lífwórk/ *n.* a task, profession, etc., pursued throughout one's lifetime.

lift /lift/ *v.* & *n.* ● *v.* **1** *tr.* (often foll. by *up*, *off*, *out*, etc.) raise or remove to a higher position. **2** *intr.* go up; be raised; yield to an upward force (*the window will not lift*). **3** *tr.* give an upward direction

to (the eyes or face). **4** *tr.* **a** elevate to a higher plane of thought or feeling (*the news lifted their spirits*). **b** make less heavy or dull; add interest to (something esp. artistic). **c** enhance; improve (*lifted their game after halftime*). **5** *intr.* (of a cloud, fog, etc.) rise; disperse. **6** *tr.* remove (a barrier or restriction). **7** *tr.* transport (supplies, troops, etc.) by air. **8** *tr. colloq.* **a** steal. **b** plagiarize (a passage of writing, etc.). **9** *Phonet.* **a** *tr.* make louder; raise the pitch of. **b** *intr.* (of the voice) rise. **10** *tr.* esp. *Brit.* dig up (esp. potatoes, etc., at harvest). **11** *intr.* (of a floor) swell upward, bulge. **12** *tr.* hold or have on high (*the church lifts its spire*). **13** *tr.* hit (a ball) into the air. **14** *tr.* (usu. in *passive*) perform cosmetic surgery on (esp. the face or breasts) to reduce sagging. ● *n.* **1** the act of lifting or process of being lifted. **2** a free ride in another person's vehicle (*gave them a lift*). **3 a** *Brit.* = ELEVATOR 3a. **b** an apparatus for carrying persons up or down a mountain, etc. (see SKI LIFT). **4 a** transport by air (see AIRLIFT *n.*). **b** a quantity of goods transported by air. **5** the upward pressure that air exerts on an airfoil to counteract the force of gravity. **6** a supporting or elevating influence; a feeling of elation. **7** a layer of leather in the heel of a boot or shoe, esp. to correct shortening of a leg or increase height. **8 a** a rise in the level of the ground. **b** the extent to which water rises in a canal lock. □ **lift a finger** (in *neg.*) make the slightest effort (*didn't lift a finger to help*). **lift up one's head** hold one's head high with pride. **lift up one's voice** sing out. □□ **lift·a·ble** *adj.* **lift·er** *n.* [ME f. ON *lypta* f. Gmc]

lift-off /líftawf/ *n.* the vertical takeoff of a spacecraft or rocket.

lig·a·ment /lígəmənt/ *n.* **1** *Anat.* **a** a short band of tough, flexible, fibrous connective tissue linking bones together. **b** any membranous fold keeping an organ in position. **2** *archaic* a bond of union. □□ **lig·a·men·tal** /–mént'l/ *adj.* **lig·a·men·ta·ry** /–méntoree/ *adj.* **lig·a·men·tous** /–méntəs/ *adj.* [ME f. L *ligamentum* bond f. *ligare* bind]

li·gand /lígond, líg–/ *n. Chem.* an ion or molecule attached to a metal atom by covalent bonding in which both electrons are supplied by one atom. [L *ligandus* gerundive of *ligare* bind]

li·gate /lígayt/ *v.tr. Surgery* tie up (a bleeding artery, etc.). □□ **li·ga·tion** /–gáyshən/ *n.* [L *ligare* ligat-]

lig·a·ture /lígəchər/ *n.* & *v.* ● *n.* **1** a tie or bandage, esp. in surgery for a bleeding artery, etc. **2** *Mus.* a slur; a tie. **3** *Printing* two or more letters joined, e.g., *æ*. **4** a bond; a thing that unites. **5** the act of tying or binding. ● *v.tr.* bind or connect with a ligature. [ME f. LL *ligatura* f. L *ligare* ligat- tie, bind]

li·ger /lígər/ *n.* the offspring of a lion and a tigress (cf. TIGLON). [portmanteau word f. LION + TIGER]

light[1] /līt/ *n., v.,* & *adj.* ● *n.* **1** the natural agent (electromagnetic radiation of wavelength between about 390 and 740 nm) that stimulates sight and makes things visible. **2** the medium or condition of the space in which this is present. **3** an appearance of brightness (*saw a distant light*). **4 a** a source of light, e.g., the sun, or a lamp, fire, etc. **b** (in *pl.*) illuminations. **5** (often in *pl.*) a traffic light (*went through a red light; stop at the lights*). **6 a** the amount or quality of illumination in a place (*bad light stopped play*). **b** one's fair or usual share of this (*you are standing in my light*). **7 a** a flame or spark serving to ignite (*struck a light*). **b** a device producing this (*have you got a light?*). **8** the aspect in which a thing is regarded or considered (*appeared in a new light*). **9 a** mental illumination; elucidation; enlightenment. **b** hope; happiness; a happy outcome. **c** spiritual illumination by divine truth. **10** vivacity, enthusiasm, or inspiration visible in a person's face, esp. in the eyes. **11** (in *pl.*) a person's mental powers or ability (*according to one's lights*). **12** an eminent person (*a leading light*). **13 a** the bright part of a thing; a highlight. **b** the bright parts of a picture, etc., esp. suggesting illumination (*light and shade*). **14 a** a window or opening in a wall to let light in. **b** the perpendicular division of a mullioned window. **c** a pane of glass, esp. in the side or roof of a greenhouse. **15** *Brit.* (in a crossword, etc.) each of the items filling a space and to be deduced from the clues. **16** *Law* the light falling on windows, the obstruction of which by a neighbor is illegal. ● *v.* (*past* lit /lit/; *past part.* lit or (*attrib.*) **lighted**) **1** *tr.* & *intr.* set burning or begin to burn; ignite. **2** *tr.* provide with light or lighting. **3** *tr.* show (a person) the way or surroundings with a light. **4** *intr.* (usu. foll. by *up*) (of the face or eyes) brighten with animation. ● *adj.* **1** well provided with light; not dark. **2** (of a color) pale (*light blue; a light-blue ribbon*). □ **bring** (or **come**) **to light** reveal or be revealed. **in a good** (or **bad**) **light** giving a favorable (or unfavorable) impression. **in** (the) **light of** having regard to; drawing information from. **light of one's life** usu. *joc.* a much-loved person. **light up 1** *colloq.* begin to smoke a cigarette, etc.

WORD HISTORY   light

Old English *lēoht*, *līht* (noun and adjective), *līhtan* (verb), of Germanic origin; related to Dutch *licht* and German *Licht*, from an Indo-European root shared by Greek *leukos* 'white' and Latin *lux* 'light.'

2 switch on lights or lighting; illuminate a scene. **lit up** *colloq.* drunk. **out like a light** deeply asleep or unconscious. **throw** (or **shed**) **light on** help to explain. □□ **light·ish** *adj.* **light·less** *adj.* **light·ness** *n.*

light[2] /līt/ *adj., adv., & v.* • *adj.* **1** of little weight; not heavy; easy to lift. **2** a relatively low in weight, amount, density, intensity, etc. (*light arms; light traffic; light metal; light rain; a light breeze*). **b** deficient in weight (*light coin*). **c** (of an isotope, etc.) having not more than the usual mass. **3 a** carrying or suitable for small loads (*light aircraft; light railroad*). **b** (of a ship) unladen. **c** carrying only light arms, armaments, etc. (*light brigade; light infantry*). **d** (of a locomotive) with no train attached. **4 a** (of food, a meal, etc.) small in amount; easy to digest (*had a light lunch*). **b** (of drink) not heavy on the stomach or strongly alcoholic. **5 a** (of entertainment, music, etc.) intended for amusement, rather than edification; not profound. **b** frivolous; thoughtless; trivial (*a light remark*). **6** (of sleep or a sleeper) easily disturbed. **7** easily borne or done (*light duties*). **8** nimble; quick-moving (*a light step; light of foot; a light rhythm*). **9** (of a building, etc.) graceful; elegant; delicate. **10** (of type) not heavy or bold. **11 a** free from sorrow; cheerful (*a light heart*). **b** giddy (*light in the head*). **12** (of soil) not dense; porous. **13** (of pastry, sponge cake, etc.) fluffy and well-aerated during cooking and with the fat fully absorbed. • *adv.* **1** in a light manner (*tread light; sleep light*). **2** with a minimum load or minimum luggage (*travel light*). • *v.intr.* (*past* and *past part.* **lit** /līt/ or **light·ed**) **1** (foll. by *on, upon*) come upon or find by chance. **2** *archaic* **a** alight; descend. **b** (foll. by *on*) land on (shore, etc.). □ **light into** *colloq.* attack. **light out** *colloq.* depart. **make light of** treat as unimportant. **make light work of** do a thing quickly and easily. □□ **light·ish** *adj.* **light·ness** *n.* [OE *lēoht, līht, līhtan* f. Gmc, the verbal sense from the idea of relieving a horse, etc., of weight]

light·bulb /lītbulb/ *n.* a glass bulb containing an inert gas and a metal filament, providing light when an electric current is passed through.

light·en[1] /līt'n/ *v.* **1 a** *tr. & intr.* make or become lighter in weight. **b** *tr.* reduce the weight or load of. **2** *tr.* bring relief to (the heart, mind, etc.). **3** *tr.* mitigate (a penalty).

light·en[2] /līt'n/ *v.* **1 a** *tr. & intr.* make or grow lighter or brighter. **2** *intr.* **a** shine brightly; flash. **b** emit lightning (*it is lightening*).

light·en·ing /līt'ning/ *n.* a drop in the level of the uterus during the last weeks of pregnancy.

light·er[1] /lītər/ *n.* a device that produces a small flame, usu. for lighting cigarettes.

light·er[2] /lītər/ *n.* a boat, usu. flat-bottomed, for transferring goods from a ship to a wharf or another ship. [ME f. MDu. *lichter* (as LIGHT[2] in the sense 'unload')]

light·er·age /lītərij/ *n.* **1** the transference of cargo by means of a lighter. **2** a charge made for this.

light·er·man /lītərmən/ *n.* (*pl.* **·men**) a person who works on a lighter.

light·er-than-air *adj.* (of an aircraft) weighing less than the air it displaces.

light-fin·gered *adj.* given to stealing.

light fly·weight *n.* **1** a weight in amateur boxing below flyweight. **2** an amateur boxer of this weight.

light-foot·ed *adj.* nimble. □□ **light-foot·ed·ly** *adv.*

light-head·ed *adj.* giddy; frivolous; delirious. □□ **light-head·ed·ly** *adv.* **light-head·ed·ness** *n.*

light-heart·ed /līt-haartid/ *adj.* **1** cheerful. **2** (unduly) casual; thoughtless. □□ **light-heart·ed·ly** *adv.* **light-heart·ed·ness** *n.*

light heav·y·weight *n.* **1** the weight in some sports between middleweight and heavyweight. **2** a sports participant of this weight.

light·house /līt-hows/ *n.* a tower or other structure containing a beacon light to warn or guide ships at sea.

light in·dus·try *n.* the manufacture of small or light articles.

light·ing /līting/ *n.* **1** equipment in a room or street, etc., for producing light. **2** the arrangement or effect of lights.

light·ly /lītlee/ *adv.* in a light (esp. frivolous or unserious) manner. □ **get off lightly** escape with little or no punishment. **take lightly** not be serious about (a thing).

light me·ter *n.* an instrument for measuring the intensity of the light, esp. to show the correct photographic exposure.

light·ning /lītning/ *n. & adj.* • *n.* a flash of bright light produced by an electric discharge between clouds or between clouds and the ground. • *attrib.adj.* very quick (*with lightning speed*). [ME, differentiated from *lightening*, verbal noun f. LIGHTEN[2]]

light·ning bug *n.* = FIREFLY.

lighthouse

light·ning rod *n.* (also **light·ning con·duc·tor**) a metal rod or wire fixed to an exposed part of a building or to a mast to divert lightning into the earth or sea.

light pen *n.* (also **light pencil**) **1** a penlike photosensitive device held to the screen of a computer terminal for passing information on to it. **2** a light-emitting device used for reading bar codes.

light-proof /lītproof/ *adj.* able to block out light completely.

lights /līts/ *n.pl.* the lungs of sheep, pigs, bullocks, etc., used as a food, esp. for pets. [ME, noun use of LIGHT[2]: cf. LUNG]

light·ship /lītship/ *n.* a moored or anchored ship with a beacon light.

light show *n.* a display of changing colored lights for entertainment.

light·some /lītsəm/ *adj.* gracefully light; nimble; merry. □□ **light·some·ly** *adv.* **light·some·ness** *n.*

light touch *n.* delicate or tactful treatment.

light·weight /lītwayt/ *adj. & n.* • *adj.* **1** (of a person, animal, garment, etc.) of below average weight. **2** of little importance or influence. • *n.* **1** a lightweight person, animal, or thing. **2 a** a weight in certain sports intermediate between featherweight and welterweight. **b** a sportsman of this weight.

light·wood /lītwood/ *n.* wood used for kindling, esp. pine.

light-year *n.* **1** *Astron.* the distance light travels in one year, nearly 6 trillion miles. **2** (in *pl.*) *colloq.* a long distance or great amount.

lig·ne·ous /ligneeəs/ *adj.* **1** (of a plant) woody (opp. HERBACEOUS). **2** of the nature of wood. [L *ligneus* (as LIGNI-)]

ligni- /ligni/ *comb. form* wood. [L *lignum* wood]

lig·ni·fy /lignifī/ *v.tr. & intr.* (**·fies, ·fied**) *Bot.* make or become woody by the deposition of lignin.

lig·nin /lignin/ *n. Bot.* a complex organic polymer deposited in the cell walls of many plants making them rigid and woody. [as LIGNI- + -IN]

lig·nite /lignīt/ *n.* a soft brown coal showing traces of plant structure, intermediate between bituminous coal and peat. □□ **lig·nit·ic** /-nitik/ *adj.* [F (as LIGNI-, -ITE[1])]

lig·no·caine /lignəkayn/ *n. Pharm.* a local anesthetic for the gums, mucous membranes, or skin, usu. given by injection. [*ligno-* (as LIGNI-) for XYLO- + COCA + -INE[4]]

lig·num vi·tae /lignəm vītee, veetī/ *n.* = GUAIACUM 2a. [L, = wood of life]

lig·ro·in /ligroïn/ *n. Chem.* a volatile hydrocarbon mixture obtained from petroleum and used as a solvent. [20th c.: orig. unkn.]

lig·u·late /ligyələt, -layt/ *adj. Bot.* having strap-shaped florets. [formed as LIGULE + -ATE[2]]

lig·ule /ligyool/ *n. Bot.* a narrow projection from the sheath of a blade of grass. [L *ligula* strap, spoon f. *lingere* lick]

li·gus·trum /ligústrəm/ *n.* = PRIVET. [L]

lik·a·ble /līkəbəl/ *adj.* (also **like·a·ble**) pleasant; easy to like. □□ **lik·a·ble·ness** *n.* **lik·a·bly** /-blee/ *adv.*

like[1] /līk/ *adj., prep., adv., conj., & n.* • *adj.* (often governing a noun as if a transitive participle such as *resembling*) (**more like, most like**) **1 a** having some or all of the qualities of another or each other or an original; alike (*in like manner; as like as two peas; is very like her brother*). **b** resembling in some way, such as; in the same class as (*good writers like Poe*). **c** (usu. in pairs correlatively) as one is so will the other be (*like mother, like daughter*). **2** characteristic of (*it is not like them to be late*). **3** in a suitable state or mood for (doing or having something) (*felt like working; felt like a cup of coffee*). • *prep.* in the manner of; to the same degree as (*drink like a fish; sell like hotcakes; acted like an idiot*). • *adv.* **1** *archaic* likely (*they will come, like enough*). **2** *archaic* in the same manner (foll. by *as: sang like as a nightingale*). **3** *sl.* so to speak (*did a quick getaway, like; as I said, like, I'm no Shakespeare*). • *conj. colloq. disp.* **1** as (*cannot do it like you do*). **2** as if (*ate like they were starving*). • *n.* **1** a counterpart; an equal; a similar person or thing (*shall not see its like again; compare like with like*). **2** (prec. by *the*) a thing or things of the same kind (*will never do the like again*). □ **and the like** and similar things; et cetera (*music, painting, and the like*). **be nothing like** (usu. with compl.) be in no way similar or comparable or adequate. **like anything** see ANYTHING. **(as) like as not** *colloq.* probably. **like so** *colloq.* like this; in this manner. **the likes of** *colloq.* a person such as. **more like it** *colloq.* nearer what is required. [ME *līc, līk*, shortened form of OE *gelīc* ALIKE]

▶**1.** The use of **like** as a conjunction meaning 'as' or 'as if,' e.g., *I don't have a wealthy set of in-laws like you do* or *they sit up like they're begging for food*, is considered by many to be incorrect. In more precise use, **like** is a preposition, used before nouns and pronouns: *to fly like a bird; a town like ours*. **2.** See note at SAID.

like[2] /līk/ *v. & n.* • *v.tr.* **1 a** find agreeable or enjoyable or satisfactory (*like reading; like the sea; like to dance*). **b** be fond of (a person). **2 a** choose to have; prefer (*like my coffee black; do not like such things discussed*). **b** wish for or be inclined to (*would like a cup of tea*). **3** (usu. in *interrog.*; prec. by *how*) feel about; regard (*how would you like it if it happened to you?*). • *n.* (in *pl.*) the things one likes or prefers. □ **I like that!** *iron.* as an exclamation expressing affront. **like it or not** *colloq.* whether it is acceptable or not. [OE *līcian* f. Gmc]

-like /līk/ *comb. form* forming adjectives from nouns, meaning 'similar to, characteristic of' (*doglike; tortoiselike*).

►In (esp. polysyllabic) formations intended as nonce words, a hyphen is often used (*celebration-like*). Nouns ending in -*ll* always require a hyphen (*shell-like*).

like·a·ble var. of LIKABLE.

like·li·hood /líkleehŏŏd/ *n.* probability; the quality or fact of being likely. □ **in all likelihood** very probably.

like·ly /líklee/ *adj. & adv.* • *adj.* **1** probable; such as well might happen or be true (*it is not likely that they will come; the most likely place is California; a likely story*). **2** (foll. by *to* + infin.) to be reasonably expected (*he is not likely to come now*). **3** promising; apparently suitable (*this is a likely spot; three likely candidates*). • *adv.* probably (*is very likely true*). □ **as likely as not** probably. **not likely!** *colloq.* certainly not; I refuse. □□ **like·li·ness** *n.* [ME f. ON *líkligr* (as LIKE¹, -LY¹)]

like-mind·ed *adj.* having the same tastes, opinions, etc. □□ **like-mind·ed·ly** *adv.* **like-mind·ed·ness** *n.*

lik·en /líkən/ *v.tr.* (foll. by *to*) point out the resemblance of (a person or thing to another). [ME f. LIKE¹ + -EN¹]

like·ness /líknis/ *n.* **1** (foll. by *between*, *to*) resemblance. **2** (foll. by *of*) a semblance or guise (*in the likeness of a ghost*). **3** a portrait or representation (*is a good likeness*). [OE *gelíknes* (as LIKE¹, -NESS)]

SYNONYM TIP likeness

AFFINITY, ANALOGY, RESEMBLANCE, SIMILARITY, SIMILITUDE. Two sisters who are only a year apart in age and who are very similar to each other in terms of appearance and personality would be said to bear a **likeness** to one another. **Similarity** applies to people or things that are merely somewhat alike (*there was a similarity between the two women, both of whom were raised in the Midwest*), while **resemblance** suggests a *similarity* only in appearance or in superficial or external ways (*with their short hair and blue eyes, they bore a strong resemblance to each other*). **Affinity** adds to *resemblance* a natural kinship, temperamental sympathy, common experience, or some other relationship (*to have an affinity for young children*). **Similitude** is a more literary word meaning *likeness* or *similarity* in reference to abstract things (*a similitude of the truth*). An **analogy** is a comparison of things that are basically unlike but share certain attributes or circumstances (*he drew an analogy between the human heart and a bicycle pump*).

like·wise /líkwīz/ *adv.* **1** also; moreover; too. **2** similarly (*do likewise*). [for *in like wise*]

lik·ing /líking/ *n.* **1** what one likes; one's taste (*is it to your liking?*). **2** (foll. by *for*) regard or fondness; taste or fancy (*had a liking for chocolate*). [OE *lícung* (as LIKE², -ING¹)]

li·lac /lílək, -lok, -lak/ *n. & adj.* • *n.* **1** any shrub or small tree of the genus *Syringa*, esp. *S. vulgaris* with fragrant pale pinkish-violet or white blossoms. **2** a pale pinkish-violet color. • *adj.* of this color. [obs. F f. Sp. f. Arab. *lílāk* f. Pers. *lílak*, var. of *nílak* bluish f. *níl* blue]

lil·i·a·ceous /lílee-áyshəs/ *adj.* **1** of or relating to the family Liliaceae of plants with elongated leaves growing from a corm, bulb, or rhizome, e.g., tulip, lily, or onion. **2** lilylike. [LL *liliaceus* f. L *lilium* lily]

lil·li·pu·tian /lílipyŏŏshən/ *n. & adj.* (also **Lil·li·pu·tian**) • *n.* a diminutive person or thing. • *adj.* diminutive. [*Lilliput* in Swift's *Gulliver's Travels*]

lilt /lilt/ *n. & v.* • *n.* **1 a** a light springing rhythm or gait. **b** a song or tune marked by this. **2** (of the voice) a characteristic cadence or inflection; a pleasant accent. • *v.intr.* (esp. as **lilting** *adj.*) move or speak, etc., with a lilt (*a lilting step; a lilting melody*). [ME *lilte*, *lülte*, of unkn. orig.]

lil·y /lílee/ *n.* (*pl.* **-ies**) **1 a** any bulbous plant of the genus *Lilium* with large, trumpet-shaped, often spotted flowers on a tall, slender stem, e.g., the madonna lily and tiger lily. **b** any of several other plants of the family Liliaceae with similar flowers, e.g., the African lily. **c** the water lily. **2** a person or thing of special whiteness or purity. **3** a heraldic fleur-de-lis. **4** (*attrib.*) **a** delicately white (*a lily hand*). **b** pallid. □□ **lil·ied** *adj.* [OE *lilie* f. L *lilium* prob. f. Gk *leirion*]

lil·y-liv·ered *adj.* cowardly.

lil·y of the val·ley *n.* any liliaceous plant of the genus *Convallaria*, with oval leaves in pairs and racemes of white, bell-shaped, fragrant flowers.

lil·y pad *n.* a floating leaf of a water lily.

lil·y-white *adj.* **1** as white as a lily. **2** faultless.

li·ma bean /líma/ *n.* **1** a tropical American bean plant, *Phaseolus limensis*, having large, flat, greenish-white edible seeds. **2** the seed of this plant. [*Lima* in Peru]

limb¹ /lim/ *n.* **1** any of the projecting parts of a person's or animal's body used for contact or movement. **2** a large branch of a tree. **3** a branch of a cross. **4** a spur of a mountain. **5** a clause of a sentence. □ **out on a limb** **1** isolated; stranded. **2** at a disadvantage. **tear limb from limb** violently dismember. **with life and limb** (esp. escape)

lily of the valley

without grave injury. □□ **limbed** *adj.* (also in *comb.*). **limb·less** *adj.* [OE *lim* f. Gmc]

limb² /lim/ *n.* **1** *Astron.* **a** a specified edge of the sun, moon, etc. (*eastern limb; lower limb*). **b** the graduated edge of a quadrant. etc. **2** *Bot.* the broad part of a petal, sepal, or leaf. [F *limbe* or L *limbus* hem, border]

lim·ber¹ /límbər/ *adj. & v.* • *adj.* **1** lithe; agile; nimble. **2** flexible. • *v.* (usu. foll. by *up*) **1** *tr.* make (oneself or a part of the body, etc.) supple. **2** *intr.* warm up in preparation for athletic, etc., activity. □□ **lim·ber·ness** *n.* [16th c.: orig. uncert.]

lim·ber² /límbər/ *n. & v.* • *n.* the detachable front part of a gun carriage, consisting of two wheels, axle, pole, and ammunition box. • *v.* **1** *tr.* attach a limber to (a gun, etc.). **2** *intr.* fasten together the two parts of a gun carriage. [ME *limo(u)r*, app. rel. to med.L *limonarius* f. *limo* -*onis* shaft]

lim·bo¹ /límbō/ *n.* (*pl.* **-bos**) **1** (in some Christian beliefs) the supposed abode of the souls of unbaptized infants, and of the just who died before Christ. **2** an intermediate state or condition of awaiting a decision, etc. **3** prison; confinement. **4** a state of neglect or oblivion. [ME f. med.L phr. *in limbo*, f. *limbus*: see LIMB²]

lim·bo² /límbō/ *n.* (*pl.* **-bos**) a W. Indian dance in which the dancer bends backward to pass under a horizontal bar that is progressively lowered to a position just above the ground. [a W. Indian word, perh. = LIMBER¹]

Lim·burg·er /límbərgər/ *n.* a soft white cheese with a characteristic strong smell, orig. made in Limburg. [Du. f. *Limburg* in Belgium]

lime¹ /lim/ *n. & v.* • *n.* **1** (in full **quicklime**) a white caustic alkaline substance (calcium oxide) obtained by heating limestone and used for making mortar or as a fertilizer or bleach, etc. **2** = BIRDLIME. • *v.tr.* **1** treat (wood, skins, land, etc.) with lime. **2** *archaic* catch (a bird, etc.) with birdlime. □□ **lime·less** *adj.* **lim·y** *adj.* (**lim·i·er**, **lim·i·est**). [OE *lim* f. Gmc, rel. to LOAM]

lime² /lim/ *n.* **1 a** a round citrus fruit like a lemon but greener, smaller, and more acid. **b** the tree, *Citrus aurantifolia*, bearing this. **2** (in full **lime juice**) the juice of limes as a drink and formerly esp. as a cure for scurvy. **3** (in full **lime green**) a pale green color like a lime. [F f. mod.Prov. *limo*, Sp. *lima* f. Arab. *líma*: cf. LEMON]

lime³ /lim/ *n.* **1** (in full **lime tree**) any ornamental tree of the genus *Tilia*, esp. *T. europaea* with heart-shaped leaves and fragrant yellow blossoms. Also called **linden**. **2** the wood of this. [alt. of *line* = OE *lind* = LINDEN]

lime·kiln /límkiln, -kil/ *n.* a kiln for heating limestone to produce lime.

lime·light /límlīt/ *n.* **1** an intense white light obtained by heating a cylinder of lime in an oxyhydrogen flame, used formerly in the theaters. **2** (prec. by *the*) the full glare of publicity; the focus of attention.

lim·er·ick /límərik, límrik/ *n.* a humorous or comic form of five-line stanza with a rhyme scheme *aabba*. [said to be from the chorus "will you come up to Limerick?" sung between improvised verses at a gathering: f. *Limerick* in Ireland]

lime·stone /límstōn/ *n.* *Geol.* a sedimentary rock composed mainly of calcium carbonate, used as building material and in the making of cement.

lime·wash /límwosh, -wawsh/ *n.* a mixture of lime and water for coating walls.

lime·wa·ter /límwawtər/ *n.* an aqueous solution of calcium hydroxide used esp. to detect the presence of carbon dioxide and as an antacid.

lim·ey /límee/ *n.* (also **Lim·ey**) (*pl.* **-eys**) *sl. offens.* a British person (orig. a sailor) or ship. [LIME², because of the former enforced consumption of lime juice in the British Navy to prevent scurvy]

lim·it /límit/ *n. & v.* • *n.* **1** a point, line, or level beyond which something does not or may not extend or pass. **2** (often in *pl.*) the boundary of an area. **3** the greatest or smallest amount permissible or possible (*upper limit; lower limit*). **4** *Math.* a quantity that a function or sum of a series can be made to approach as closely as desired. • *v.tr.* **1** set or serve as a limit to. **2** (foll. by *to*) restrict. □ **be the limit** *colloq.* be intolerable or extremely irritating. **within limits** moderately; with some degree of freedom. **without limit** with no restriction. □□ **lim·it·a·ble** *adj.* **lim·i·ta·tive** /-tətiv/ *adj.* **lim·it·er** *n.* [ME f. L *limes limitis* boundary, frontier]

lim·i·tar·y /límiteree/ *adj.* **1** subject to restriction. **2** of, on, or serving as a limit.

lim·i·ta·tion /límitáyshən/ *n.* **1** the act or an instance of limiting; the process of being limited. **2** a condition of limited ability (often in *pl.*: *know one's limitations*). **3** a limiting rule or circumstance (often in *pl.*: *has its limitations*). **4** a legally specified period beyond which an action cannot be brought, or a property right is not to continue. [ME f. L *limitatio* (as LIMIT)]

lim·it·ed /límitid/ *adj.* **1** confined within limits. **2** not great in scope or talents (*has limited experience*). **3 a** few; scanty; restricted (*lim-*

ited accommodation). **b** restricted to a few examples (*limited edition).* □□ **lim·it·ed·ly** *adv.* **lim·it·ed·ness** *n.*

lim·it·less /límitlis/ *adj.* **1** extending or going on indefinitely (*a limitless expanse).* **2** unlimited (*limitless generosity).* □□ **lim·it·less·ly** *adv.* **lim·it·less·ness** *n.*

limn /lim/ *v.tr.* **1** *archaic* paint (esp. a miniature portrait). **2** *hist.* illuminate (manuscripts). □□ **lim·ner** *n.* [obs. *lumine* illuminate f. OF *luminer* f. L *luminare:* see LUMEN]

lim·nol·o·gy /limnóləjee/ *n.* the study of the physical phenomena of lakes and other fresh waters. □□ **lim·no·log·i·cal** /–nəlójikəl/ *adj.* **lim·nol·o·gist** /–nól–/ *n.* [Gk *limnē* lake + –LOGY]

lim·o /límō/ *n.* (*pl.* **-os**) *colloq.* a limousine. [abbr.]

lim·ou·sine /líməzeén/ *n.* a large, luxurious automobile, often with a partition behind the driver. [F, orig. a caped cloak worn in the former French province of *Limousin*]

> **SPELLING TIP** limousine
>
> To remember the correct spelling of *limousine,* use the mnemonic: "There is a *mouse* in li*mou*sine."

limp[1] /limp/ *v. & n.* ● *v.intr.* **1** walk lamely. **2** (of a damaged ship, aircraft, etc.) proceed with difficulty. **3** (of verse) be defective. ● *n.* a lame walk. □□ **limp·er** *n.* **limp·ing·ly** *adv.* [rel. to obs. *limphalt* lame, OE *lemp-healt*]

limp[2] /limp/ *adj.* **1** not stiff or firm; easily bent. **2** without energy or will. **3** (of a book) having a soft cover. □□ **limp·ly** *adv.* **limp·ness** *n.* [18th c.: orig. unkn.: perh. rel. to LIMP[1] in the sense 'hanging loose']

lim·pet /límpit/ *n.* **1** any of various marine gastropod mollusks, esp. the common limpet *Patella vulgata,* with a shallow conical shell and a broad muscular foot that sticks tightly to rocks. **2** a clinging person. [OE *lempedu* f. med.L *lampreda* limpet, LAMPREY]

lim·pet mine *n.* a mine designed to be attached to a ship's hull and set to explode after a certain time.

lim·pid /límpid/ *adj.* **1** (of water, eyes, etc.) clear, transparent. **2** (of writing) clear and easily comprehended. □□ **lim·pid·i·ty** /–píditee/ *n.* **lim·pid·ly** *adv.* **lim·pid·ness** *n.* [F *limpide* or L *limpidus,* perh. rel. to LYMPH]

limp-wrist·ed *adj. sl. offens.* effeminate; weak; feeble.

lin·age /líníj/ *n.* **1** the number of lines in printed or written matter. **2** payment by the line.

linch·pin /línchpin/ *n.* **1** a pin passed through the end of an axle to keep a wheel in position. **2** a person or thing vital to an enterprise, organization, etc. [ME *linch* f. OE *lynis* + PIN]

Lin·coln green /língkən/ *n. hist.* a bright green woolen cloth orig. made at Lincoln, England.

lin·dane /líndayn/ *n. Chem.* a colorless, crystalline, chlorinated derivative of cyclohexane used as an insecticide. [T. van der *Linden,* Du. chemist b. 1884]

lin·den /líndən/ *n.* a deciduous ornamental tree of the genus *Tilia,* with heart-shaped leaves and fragrant yellow blossoms. [(orig. adj.) f. OE *lind* lime tree: cf. LIME[3]]

line[1] /lin/ *n. & v.* ● *n.* **1** a continuous mark or band made on a surface (*drew a line).* **2** use of lines in art, esp. draftsmanship or engraving (*boldness of line).* **3** a thing resembling such a mark, esp. a furrow or wrinkle. **4** *Mus.* **a** each of (usu. five) horizontal marks forming a stave in musical notation. **b** a sequence of notes or tones forming an instrumental or vocal melody. **5 a** a straight or curved continuous extent of length without breadth. **b** the track of a moving point. **6 a** a contour or outline, esp. as a feature of design (*admired the sculpture's clean lines; this year's line is full at the back; the ship's lines).* **b** a facial feature (*the cruel line of his mouth).* **7 a** (on a map or graph) a curve connecting all points having a specified common property. **b** (**the Line**) the Equator. **8 a** a limit or boundary. **b** a mark limiting the area of play, the starting or finishing point in a race, etc. **c** the boundary between a credit and a debit in an account. **9 a** a row of persons or things. **b** a direction as indicated by them (*line of march).* **c** a queue. **10 a** a row of printed or written words. **b** a portion of verse written in one line. **11** (in *pl.*) **a** a piece of poetry. **b** the words of an actor's part. **c** a specified amount of text, etc., to be written out as a school punishment. **12** a short letter or note (*drop me a line).* **13** (in *pl.*) (in full **marriage lines**) *Brit.* a marriage certificate. **14** a length of cord, rope, wire, etc., usu. serving a specified purpose, esp. a fishing line or clothesline. **15 a** a wire or cable for a telephone or telegraph. **b** a connection by means of this (*am trying to get a line).* **16 a** a single track of a railroad. **b** one branch or route of a railroad system, or the whole system under one management. **17 a** a regular succession of buses, ships, aircraft, etc., plying between certain places. **b** a company conducting this (*shipping line).* **18** a connected series of persons following one another in time (esp. several generations of a family); stock; succession (*a long line of craftsmen; next in line to the throne).* **19 a** a course or manner of procedure, conduct, thought, etc. (*did it along these lines; don't take that line with me).* **b** policy (*the party line).* **c** conformity (*bring them into line).* **20** a direction, course, or channel

(*lines of communication).* **21** a department of activity; a province; a branch of business (*accounting is not my line).* **22** a class of commercial goods (*a new line of hats).* **23** *colloq.* a false or exaggerated account or story; a dishonest approach (*gave me a line about missing the bus).* **24 a** a connected series of military fieldworks, defenses, etc. (*behind enemy lines).* **b** an arrangement of soldiers or ships side by side; a line of battle (*ship of the line).* **c** *Brit.* (prec. by *the*) regular army regiments (not auxiliary forces or guardsmen). **25** each of the very narrow horizontal sections forming a television picture. **26** a narrow range of the spectrum that is noticeably brighter or darker than the adjacent parts. **27** the level of the base of most letters in printing and writing. **28** (as a measure) one twelfth of an inch. ● *v.* **1** *tr.* mark with lines. **2** *tr.* cover with lines (*a face lined with pain).* **3** *tr. & intr.* position or stand at intervals along (*crowds lined the route).* □ **all along the line** at every point. **bring into line** make conform. **come into line** conform. **end of the line** the point at which further effort is unproductive or one can go no further. **get a line on** *colloq.* learn something about. **in line for** likely to receive. **in the line of** in the course of (esp. of duty). **in** (or *out of*) **line with** in (or not in) alignment or accordance with. **lay it on the line** speak frankly. **line up 1** arrange or be arranged in a line or lines. **2** have ready; organize (*had a job lined up).* **on the line 1** at direct risk (*put my reputation on the line).* **2** speaking on the telephone. **3** (of a picture in an exhibition) hung with its center about level with the spectator's eye. **out of line 1** not in alignment; discordant. **2** inappropriate; (of behavior, etc.) improper. **step out of line** behave inappropriately. [ME *line, ligne* f. OF *ligne* ult. f. L *linea* f. *linum* flax, & f. OE *line* rope, series]

line[2] /lin/ *v.tr.* **1 a** cover the inside surface of (a garment, box, etc.) with a layer of usu. different material. **b** serve as a lining for. **2** cover as if with a lining (*shelves lined with books).* **3** *colloq.* fill, esp. plentifully. □ **line** one's **pocket** (or **purse**) make money, usu. by corrupt means. [ME f. obs. *line* flax, with ref. to the use of linen for linings]

lin·e·age /línee-ij/ *n.* lineal descent; ancestry; pedigree. [ME f. OF *linage, lignage* f. Rmc f. L *linea* LINE[1]]

lin·e·al /líneeəl/ *adj.* **1** in the direct line of descent or ancestry. **2** linear; of or in lines. □□ **lin·e·al·ly** *adv.* [ME f. OF f. LL *linealis* (as LINE[1])]

lin·e·a·ment /líneeəmənt/ *n.* (usu. in *pl.*) a distinctive feature or characteristic, esp. of the face. [ME f. L *lineamentum* f. *lineare* make straight f. *linea* LINE[1]]

lin·e·ar /líneeər/ *adj.* **1 a** of or in lines; in lines rather than masses (*linear development).* **b** of length (*linear extent).* **2** long and narrow and of uniform breadth. **3** involving one dimension only. □□ **lin·e·ar·i·ty** /–neeáritee/ *n.* **lin·e·ar·ize** *v.tr.* **lin·e·ar·ly** *adv.* [L *linearis* f. *linea* LINE[1]]

lin·e·ar ac·cel·er·a·tor *n. Physics* an accelerator in which particles travel in straight lines, not in closed orbits.

Lin·e·ar B *n.* a form of Bronze Age writing found in Crete and parts of Greece and recording a form of Mycenaean Greek; an earlier undeciphered form (**Linear A**) also exists.

lin·e·ar e·qua·tion *n.* an equation between two variables that gives a straight line when plotted on a graph.

lin·e·ar mo·tor *n.* a motor producing straight-line (not rotary) motion by means of a magnetic field.

lin·e·a·tion /línee-áyshən/ *n.* **1** a marking with or drawing of lines. **2** a division into lines. [ME f. L *lineatio* f. *lineare* make straight]

line·back·er *n. Football* a defensive player positioned just behind the line of scrimmage.

line danc·ing *n.* a type of country and western dancing in which dancers line up in a row without partners and follow a choreographed pattern of steps to music.

line draw·ing *n.* a drawing in which images are produced from variations of lines.

line drive *n. Baseball* a hard-hit ball that travels nearly parallel to the ground.

line·man /línmən/ *n.* (*pl.* **-men**) **1 a** a person who repairs and maintains telephone or electrical, etc., lines. **b** a person who tests the safety of railroad lines. **2** *Football* a player positioned along the line of scrimmage.

lin·en /línin/ *n. & adj.* ● *n.* **1 a** cloth woven from flax. **b** a particular kind of this. **2** (*collect.*) articles made or orig. made of linen, calico, etc., as sheets, cloths, etc. ● *adj.* made of linen or flax (*linen cloth).* □ **wash one's dirty linen in public** be indiscreet about one's domestic quarrels, etc. [OE *línen* f. WG, rel. to obs. *line* flax]

lin·en·fold /líninfōld/ *n.* (often *attrib.*) a carved or molded ornament representing a fold or scroll of linen (*linenfold paneling).*

line of fire *n.* the expected path of gunfire, a missile, etc.

line of force *n. Physics* an imaginary line that represents the strength and direction of a magnetic, gravitational, or electric field at any point.

line of vi·sion *n.* the straight line along which an observer looks.

line out *v. Baseball* hit a line drive that is caught for an out (*he lined out to the third baseman).*

line print·er *n.* a machine that prints output from a computer a line at a time rather than character by character.

lin·er[1] /línər/ n. a ship or aircraft, etc., carrying passengers on a regular line.

lin·er[2] /línər/ n. a removable lining.

-liner /línər/ comb. form (prec. by a numeral, usu. one or two) colloq. a spoken passage of a specified number of lines in a play, etc. (a one-liner).

lin·er notes n.pl. printed information packaged with records, cassette tapes, and compact disks.

lin·er train n. Brit. a fast freight train with detachable containers on permanently coupled cars.

lines·man /línzmən/ n. (pl. ·men) 1 (in games played on a field or court) an umpire's or referee's assistant who decides whether a ball falls within the playing area or not. 2 Brit. = LINEMAN 1.

line·up /línup/ n. 1 a line of people for inspection or identification. 2 an arrangement of persons on a team, or of nations, etc., in an alliance.

ling[1] /ling/ n. a long slender marine fish, Molva molva, of N. Europe, used as food. [ME leng(e), prob. f. MDu, rel. to LONG[1]]

ling[2] /ling/ n. any of various heathers, esp. Calluna vulgaris. □□ **ling·y** adj. [ME f. ON lyng]

-ling[1] /ling/ suffix 1 denoting a person or thing: **a** connected with (hireling; sapling). **b** having the property of being (weakling; underling) or undergoing (starveling). 2 denoting a diminutive (duckling), often derogatory (lordling). [OE (as -LE[1] + -ING[3]): sense 2 f. ON]

-ling[2] /ling/ suffix forming adverbs and adjectives (darkling) (cf. -LONG). [OE f. Gmc]

lin·gam /línggəm/ n. (also **lin·ga** /línggə/) a phallus, esp. as the Hindu symbol of Siva. [Skr. lingam, lit. 'mark']

lin·ger /línggər/ v.intr. 1 **a** be slow or reluctant to depart. **b** stay about. **c** (foll. by over, on, etc.) dally (lingered over dinner; lingered on what they said). 2 (esp. of an illness) be protracted. 3 (foll. by on) (of a dying person or custom) be slow in dying; drag on feebly. □□ **lin·ger·er** n. **lin·ger·ing·ly** adv. [ME lenger, frequent. of leng f. OE lengan f. Gmc, rel. to LENGTHEN]

lin·ge·rie /laanzhəráy, lánzhəree/ n. women's underwear and nightclothes. [F f. linge linen]

lin·go /línggō/ n. (pl. ·goes) colloq. 1 a foreign language. 2 the vocabulary of a special subject or group of people. [prob. f. Port. lingoa f. L lingua tongue]

lin·gua fran·ca /línggwə frángkə/ n. (pl. **lin·gua fran·cas** or **lin·guae fran·cae** /–gwee frángkee/) 1 a language adopted as a common language between speakers whose native languages are different. 2 a system for mutual understanding. 3 hist. a mixture of Italian with French, Greek, Arabic, and Spanish, used in the Levant. [It., = Frankish tongue]

lin·gual /línggwəl/ adj. 1 of or formed by the tongue. 2 of speech or languages. □□ **lin·gual·ize** v.tr. **lin·gual·ly** adv. [med.L lingualis f. L lingua tongue, language]

lin·gui·form /línggwifawrm/ adj. Bot., Zool., & Anat. tongue-shaped. [L lingua tongue + -FORM]

lin·gui·ne /linggwéenee/ n. (also **lin·gui·ni**) a variety of pasta made in slender flattened strips. [It. dim. of lingua tongue]

lin·guist /línggwist/ n. a person skilled in languages or linguistics. [L lingua language]

lin·guis·tic /linggwístik/ adj. of or relating to language or the study of languages. □□ **lin·guis·ti·cal·ly** adv.

lin·guis·tics /linggwístiks/ n. the scientific study of language and its structure. □□ **lin·guis·ti·cian** /–stíshən/ n. [F linguistique or G Linguistik (as LINGUIST)]

lin·guo·den·tal /línggwōdént'l, línggwə–/ adj. (of a sound) made with the tongue and teeth. [L lingua tongue + DENTAL]

lin·i·ment /línimənt/ n. a liquid or lotion for rubbing on the body to relieve pain, esp. one made with oil. [LL linimentum f. L linire smear]

lin·ing /líning/ n. 1 a layer of material covering the inside surface of something (a lining of fireproof insulation; lining paper). 2 an additional layer of different material attached to the inside of a garment or curtain to make it warmer or hang better.

link[1] /lingk/ n. & v. • n. 1 one loop or ring of a chain, etc. 2 **a** a connecting part, esp. a thing or person that unites or provides continuity; one in a series. **b** a state or means of connection. 3 a means of contact by radio or telephone between two points. 4 a means of travel or transport between two places. 5 = CUFF LINK. 6 a measure equal to one-hundredth of a surveying chain (7.92 inches). • v. 1 tr. (foll. by together, to, with) connect or join (two things or one to another). 2 tr. clasp or intertwine (hands or arms). 3 intr. (foll. by on, to, in to) be joined; attach oneself to (a system, company, etc.). □ **link up** (foll. by with) connect or combine. [ME f. ON f. Gmc]

link[2] /lingk/ n. hist. a torch of pitch and tow for lighting the way in dark streets. [16th c.: perh. f. med.L li(n)chinus wick f. Gk lukhnos light]

link·age /língkij/ n. 1 a connection. 2 a system of links; a linking or link.

link·ing /língking/ adj. connecting or joining something to something else. linkman

link·man /língkmən/ n. (pl. ·men) Brit. 1 a person providing conti-

nuity in a broadcast program. 2 a player between the forwards and halfbacks or strikers and backs in soccer, etc.

links /lingks/ n.pl. 1 (treated as sing. or pl.) a golf course, esp. one having undulating ground, coarse grass, etc. 2 Sc. dial. level or undulating sandy ground near a seashore, with turf and coarse grass. [pl. of link 'rising ground' f. OE hlinc]

link·up /língkup/ n. an act or result of linking up.

linn /lin/ n. Sc. 1 **a** a waterfall. **b** a pool below this. 2 a precipice; a ravine. [Gael. linne]

Lin·nae·an /linéeən, –náyən/ adj. & n. (also **Lin·ne·an**) • adj. of or relating to the Swedish naturalist Linnaeus (Linné, d. 1778) or his system of binary nomenclature in the classification of plants and animals. • n. a follower of Linnaeus.

lin·net /línit/ n. a finch, Acanthis cannabina, with brown and gray plumage. [OF linette f. lin flax (the bird feeding on flax seeds)]

li·no /línō/ n. (pl. ·nos) esp. Brit. linoleum. [abbr.]

li·no·cut /línōkut/ n. 1 a design or form carved in relief on a block of linoleum. 2 a print made from this. □□ **li·no·cut·ting** n.

li·no·le·um /línōleeəm/ n. a material consisting of a canvas backing thickly coated with a preparation of linseed oil and powdered cork, etc., used esp. as a floor covering. □□ **li·no·le·umed** adj. [L linum flax + oleum oil]

Lin·o·type /línətip/ n. Printing Trademark a composing machine producing lines of words as single strips of metal, used esp. for newspapers. [= line o' type]

lin·sang /línsang/ n. any of various civetlike cats, esp. of the genus Poiana of Africa. [Jav.]

lin·seed /línseed/ n. the seed of flax. [OE línsæd f. lín flax + sæd seed]

lin·seed cake n. pressed linseed used as cattle feed.

lin·seed meal n. ground linseed.

lin·seed oil n. oil extracted from linseed and used esp. in paint and varnish.

lin·sey-wool·sey /línzeewoolzee/ n. a fabric of coarse wool woven on a cotton warp. [ME f. linsey coarse linen, prob. f. Lindsey in Suffolk + WOOL, with jingling ending]

lin·stock /línstok/ n. hist. a match-holder used to fire cannon. [earlier lintstock f. Du. lontstok f. lont match + stok stick, with assim. to LINT]

lint /lint/ n. 1 short, fine fibers that separate from the surface of cloth or yarn during processing. 2 Brit. a fabric, orig. of linen, with a raised nap on one side, used for dressing wounds. 3 Sc. flax. □□ **lint·y** adj. [ME lyn(n)et, perh. f. OF linette linseed f. lin flax]

lin·tel /lint'l/ n. Archit. a horizontal supporting piece of wood, stone, etc., across the top of a door or window. □□ **lin·teled** adj. (esp. Brit. **lin·telled**). [ME f. OF lintel threshold f. Rmc limitale (unrecorded), infl. by LL liminare f. L limen threshold]

lint·er /líntər/ n. 1 a machine for removing the short fibers from cottonseed after ginning. 2 (in pl.) these fibers. [LINT + -ER[1]]

lin·y /línee/ adj. (**lin·i·er**, **lin·i·est**) marked with lines; wrinkly.

li·on /líən/ n. 1 (fem. **li·on·ess** /–nis/) a large feline, Panthera leo, of Africa and S. Asia, with a tawny coat and, in the male, a flowing shaggy mane. 2 (**the Lion**) the zodiacal sign or constellation Leo. 3 a brave or celebrated person. 4 the lion as a national emblem of Great Britain or as a representation in heraldry. □□ **li·on·hood** n. **li·on·like** adj. [ME f. AF liun f. L leo -onis f. Gk leōn leontos]

li·on·heart /líənhaart/ n. a courageous and generous person (esp. as a sobriquet of Richard I of England). □□ **li·on·heart·ed** adj.

li·on·ize /líəniz/ v.tr. treat as a celebrity. □□ **li·on·i·za·tion** n. **li·on·iz·er** n.

li·on's share n. the largest or best part.

lip /lip/ n. & v. • n. 1 **a** either of the two fleshy parts forming the edges of the mouth opening. **b** a thing resembling these. **c** = LABIUM. 2 the edge of a cup, vessel, etc., esp. the part shaped for pouring from. 3 colloq. impudent talk (that's enough of your lip!). • v.tr. (**lipped**, **lip·ping**) 1 **a** touch with the lips; apply the lips to. **b** touch

---

GRAMMAR TIP linking

Linking Verbs. A linking verb is one that does not express action, but rather describes a state of existence. Forms of the verb to be are the most common linking verbs, but there are others: seem, appear, become, look, sound, feel, taste, grow, remain, smell. Linking verbs are so called because they link the subject to the word or words that follow it, as in Martha is my sister. Unlike other verbs, linking verbs are never followed by direct objects. They are usually followed by nouns (called **predicate nouns**), such as sister in the sentence above, or adjectives (called **predicate adjectives**), as in the sentence, Dinner tasted wonderful. Some linking verbs can also function as **action verbs**. For example, compare the use of grew in the following two sentences: he grew bored long before the speeches were over (linking verb); he grew almost three inches in one year (action verb).

lightly. **2** *Golf* **a** a hit a ball just to the edge of (the cup). **b** (of a ball) reach the edge of (the cup) but fail to drop in. □ **bite one's lip** repress an emotion; stifle laughter, a retort, etc. **curl one's lip** express scorn. **lick one's lips** see LICK. **pass a person's lips** be eaten, drunk, spoken, etc. **smack one's lips** part the lips noisily in relish or anticipation, esp. of food. □□ **lip·less** *adj.* **lip·like** *adj.* **lipped** *adj.* (also in *comb.*). [OE *lippa* f. Gmc]

li·pase /lípays, líp–/ *n. Biochem.* an enzyme that catalyzes the decomposition of fats. [Gk *lipos* fat + –ASE]

lip·gloss /lípglos, –glaws/ *n.* a cosmetic preparation for adding shine or color to the lips.

lip·id /lípid/ *n. Chem.* any of a group of organic compounds that are insoluble in water but soluble in organic solvents, including fatty acids, oils, waxes, and steroids. [F *lipide* (as LIPASE)]

lip·i·do·sis /lípidósis/ *n.* (also **lip·oi·do·sis** /lípoy–/) (*pl.* **·do·ses** /–seez/) any disorder of lipid metabolism in the body tissues.

Lip·iz·za·ner /lípitsaánər/ *n.* (also **Lip·pi·zan·er**) **1** a horse of a fine white breed used esp. in displays of dressage. **2** this breed. [G f. *Lippiza* in Slovenia]

li·pog·ra·phy /lipógrəfee/ *n.* the omission of letters or words in writing. [Gk *lip-* stem of *leípō* omit + –GRAPHY]

lip·oid /lípoyd/ *adj.* resembling fat.

lip·o·pro·tein /lípópróteen, lí–/ *n. Biochem.* any of a group of proteins that are combined with fats or other lipids. [Gk *lipos* fat + PROTEIN]

lip·o·some /lípósōm, lí–/ *n. Biochem.* a minute artificial spherical sac usu. of a phospholipid membrane enclosing an aqueous core. [G. *Liposom:* see LIPID]

lip·o·suc·tion /lípósúkshən, lí–/ *n.* a technique in cosmetic surgery for removing excess fat from under the skin by suction. [Gk *lipos* fat + SUCTION]

Lip·pi·zan·er var. of LIPIZZANER.

lip·py /lípee/ *adj.* (**lip·pi·er, lip·pi·est**) *colloq.* **1** insolent; impertinent. **2** talkative.

lip·read·ing /lípreeding/ *n.* (esp. of a deaf person) the practice of understanding (speech) entirely from observing a speaker's lip movements.

lip·stick /lípstik/ *n.* a small stick of cosmetic for coloring the lips.

lip-read *v.intr.* (*past* and *past part.* **·read** /–red/) (of a deaf person) understand speech from observing a speaker's lip movements. □□ **lip-read·er** *n.*

lip serv·ice *n.* an insincere expression of support, etc.

lip-sync *n.* synchronize lip movements to recorded sound to appear to be singing or talking.

li·quate /líkwayt/ *v.tr.* separate or purify (metals) by liquefying. □□ **li·qua·tion** /–áyshən/ *n.* [L *liquare* melt, rel. to LIQUOR]

liq·ue·fy /líkwifī/ *v.tr. & intr.* (**·fies, ·fied**) *Chem.* make or become liquid. □□ **liq·ue·fa·cient** /–fáyshənt/ *adj. & n.* **liq·ue·fac·tion** /–fákshən/ *n.* **liq·ue·fac·tive** /–fáktiv/ *adj.* **liq·ue·fi·a·ble** *adj.* **liq·ue·fi·er** *n.* [F *liquéfier* f. L *liquefacere* f. *liquēre* be liquid]

li·ques·cent /líkwésənt/ *adj.* becoming or apt to become liquid. [L *liquescere* (as LIQUEFY)]

li·queur /likór, –kyóor/ *n.* any of several strong, sweet alcoholic liquors, variously flavored, usu. drunk after a meal. [F, = LIQUOR]

liq·uid /líkwid/ *adj. & n.* • *adj.* **1** having a consistency like that of water or oil, flowing freely but of constant volume. **2** having the qualities of water in appearance; translucent (*liquid blue; a liquid luster*). **3** (of a gas, e.g., air, hydrogen) reduced to a liquid state by intense cold. **4** (of sounds) clear and pure; harmonious; fluent. **5** (of assets) easily converted into cash; also, having ready cash or liquid assets. **6** not fixed; fluid (*liquid opinions*). • *n.* **1** a liquid substance. **2** *Phonet.* the sound of *l* or *r*. □□ **liq·uid·ly** *adv.* **liq·uid·ness** *n.* [ME f. L *liquidus* f. *liquēre* be liquid]

li·quid·am·bar /líkwidámbər/ *n.* **1** any tree of the genus *Liquidambar* yielding a resinous gum. **2** this gum. [mod.L app. f. L *liquidus* (see LIQUID) + med.L *ambar* amber]

liq·ui·date /líkwidayt/ *v.* **1 a** *tr.* wind up the affairs of (a company or firm) by ascertaining liabilities and apportioning assets. **b** *intr.* (of a company) be liquidated. **2** *tr.* clear or pay off (a debt). **3** *tr.* put an end to or get rid of (esp. by violent means). [med.L *liquidare* make clear (as LIQUID)]

liq·ui·da·tion /líkwidáyshən/ *n.* the process of liquidating a company, etc. □ **go into liquidation** (of a company, etc.) be wound up and have its assets apportioned.

liq·ui·da·tor /líkwidaytər/ *n.* a person called in to wind up the affairs of a company, etc.

liq·uid crys·tal *n.* a substance that flows like a liquid but has some degree of ordering in the arrangement of its molecules.

liq·uid crys·tal dis·play *n.* a form of visual display in electronic devices, in which the reflectivity of a matrix of liquid crystals changes as a signal is applied.

li·quid·i·ty /líkwíditee/ *n.* (*pl.* **·ties**) **1** the state of being liquid. **2 a** availability of liquid assets. **b** (in *pl.*) liquid assets. [F *liquidité* or med.L *liquiditas* (as LIQUID)]

liq·uid·ize /líkwidīz/ *v.tr.* reduce (esp. food) to a liquid or puréed state.

liq·uid·iz·er /líkwidīzər/ *n.* a machine for liquidizing.

liq·uid meas·ure *n.* a unit for measuring the volume of liquids.

liq·uid par·af·fin *n. Brit.* = MINERAL OIL.

liq·ui·fy var. of LIQUEFY.

liq·uor /líkər/ *n. & v.* • *n.* **1** an alcoholic (esp. distilled) drink. **2** water used in brewing. **3** other liquid, esp. that produced in cooking. **4** *Pharm.* a solution of a specified drug in water. • *v.tr.* **1** dress (leather) with grease or oil. **2** steep (malt, etc.) in water. [ME f. OF *lic(o)ur* f. L *liquor –oris* (as LIQUID)]

liq·uo·rice esp. *Brit.* var. of LICORICE.

liq·uor·ish /líkərish/ *adj.* **1** = LICKERISH. **2** fond of or indicating a fondness for liquor. □□ **liq·uor·ish·ly** *adv.* **liq·uor·ish·ness** *n.* [var. of LICKERISH, misapplied]

li·ra /léerə/ *n.* (*pl.* **li·re** /léere/ or **li·ras**) **1** the chief monetary unit of Italy. **2** the chief monetary unit of Turkey. [It. f. Prov. *liura* f. L *libra* pound (weight, etc.)]

lisle /līl/ *n.* (in full **lisle thread**) a fine, smooth cotton thread for stockings, etc. [*Lisle,* former spelling of *Lille* in France, where orig. made]

lisp /lisp/ *n. & v.* • *n.* **1** a speech defect in which *s* is pronounced like *th* in *thick* and *z* is pronounced like *th* in *this*. **2** a rippling of waters; a rustling of leaves. • *v.intr. & tr.* speak or utter with a lisp. □□ **lisp·er** *n.* **lisp·ing·ly** *adv.* [OE *wlispian* (recorded in *āwlyspian*) f. *wlisp* (adj.) lisping, of uncert. orig.]

lis·some /lísəm/ *adj.* (also **lis·som**) lithe; supple; agile. □□ **lis·some·ly** *adv.* **lis·some·ness** *n.* [ult. f. LITHE + –SOME¹]

list¹ /list/ *n. & v.* • *n.* **1** a number of connected items, names, etc., written or printed together usu. consecutively to form a record or aid to memory (*shopping list*). **2** (in *pl.*) **a** palisades enclosing an area for a tournament. **b** the scene of a contest. **3** *Brit.* a selvage or edge of cloth, usu. of different material from the main body. **b** such edges used as a material. • *v.* **1** *tr.* **a** make a list of. **b** enumerate; name one by one as if in a list. **2** *tr.* enter in a list. **3** *tr.* (as **listed** *adj.*) **a** (of securities) approved for dealings on the stock exchange. **b** (of a building in the UK) officially designated as being of historical importance and having protection from demolition or major alterations. **4** *tr. & intr. archaic* enlist. □□ **list·a·ble** *adj.* [OE *liste* border, strip f. Gmc]

list² /list/ *v. & v.* • *v.intr.* (of a ship, etc.) lean over to one side, esp. owing to a leak or shifting cargo (cf. HEEL²). • *n.* the process or an instance of listing. [17th c.: orig. unkn.]

lis·ten /lísən/ *v.intr.* **1 a** make an effort to hear something. **b** attentively hear a person speaking. **2** (foll. by *to*) **a** give attention with the ear (*listened to my story*). **b** take notice of; respond to advice or a request or to the person expressing it. **3** (also **lis·ten out**) (often foll. by *for*) seek to hear or be aware of by waiting alertly. □ **listen in 1** eavesdrop; tap a private conversation, esp. one by telephone. **2** listen to a radio or television broadcast. **listening post 1 a** a point near an enemy's lines for detecting movements by sound. **b** a station for intercepting electronic communications. **2** a place for the gathering of information from reports, etc. [OE *hlysnan* f. WG]

lis·ten·a·ble /lísənəbəl/ *adj.* easy or pleasant to listen to. □□ **lis·ten·a·bil·i·ty** *n.*

lis·ten·er /lísənər, lísnər/ *n.* **1** a person who listens. **2** a person receiving broadcast radio programs.

list·er /lístər/ *n.* a plow with a double moldboard. [*list* prepare land for a crop + –ER¹]

lis·te·ri·a /listéereeə/ *n.* any motile rodlike bacterium of the genus *Listeria,* esp. *L. monocytogenes* infecting humans and animals eating contaminated food. [mod.L f. J. *Lister,* Engl. surgeon d. 1912]

list·ing /lísting/ *n.* **1** a list or catalog (see LIST¹ 1). **2** the drawing up of a list. **3** *Brit.* selvage (see LIST¹ *n.* 3).

list·less /lístlis/ *adj.* lacking energy or enthusiasm; disinclined for exertion. □□ **list·less·ly** *adv.* **list·less·ness** *n.* [ME f. obs. *list* inclination + –LESS]

list price *n.* the price of something as shown in a list issued by the manufacturer or by the general body of manufacturers of the particular class of goods.

lit *past* and *past part.* of LIGHT¹, LIGHT².

lit·a·ny /lít'nee/ *n.* (*pl.* **·nies**) **1 a** a series of petitions for use in church services or processions, usu. recited by the clergy and responded to in a recurring formula by the people. **b** (**the Litany**) that contained in the Book of Common Prayer. **2** a tedious recital (*a litany of woes*). [ME f. OF *letanie* f. eccl.L *litania* f. Gk *litaneia* prayer f. *litē* supplication]

li·tchi /léechee/ *n.* (also **li·chee, ly·chee**) **1** a sweet, fleshy fruit with a thin, spiny skin. **2** the tree, *Nephelium litchi,* orig. from China, bearing this. [Chin. *lizhi*]

-lite /līt/ *suffix* forming names of minerals (*rhyolite; zeolite*). [F f. Gk *lithos* stone]

li·ter /léetər/ *n.* (*Brit.* **litre**) a metric unit of capacity, formerly defined as the volume of one kilogram of water under standard conditions, now equal to 1 cubic decimeter (about 1.057 quarts). [F f. *litron,* an obs. measure of capacity, f. med.L f. Gk *litra* a Sicilian monetary unit]

lit•er•a•cy /lítərəsee/ *n.* the ability to read and write. [LITERATE + –ACY after *illiteracy*]

lit•er•al /lítərəl/ *adj. & n.* ● *adj.* **1** taking words in their usual or primary sense without metaphor or allegory (*literal interpretation*). **2** following the letter, text, or exact or original words (*literal translation; a literal transcript*). **3** (in full **literal-minded**) (of a person) prosaic; matter-of-fact. **4 a** not exaggerated (*the literal truth*). **b** so called without exaggeration (*a literal extermination*). **5** *colloq. disp.* so called with some exaggeration or using metaphor (*a literal avalanche of mail*). **6** of, in, or expressed by a letter or the letters of the alphabet. **7** *Algebra* not numerical. ● *n. Printing* a misprint of a letter. □□ **lit•er•al•i•ty** /–rálitee/ *n.* **lit•er•al•ize** *v.tr.* **lit•er•al•ly** *adv.* **lit•er•al•ness** *n.* [ME f. OF *literal* or LL *litteralis* f. L *littera* (as LETTER)] ▶**Literally** means 'in fact, not figuratively.' Out of exaggeration, though, many speakers and writers cannot resist saying things such as *we were literally scared to death.*

lit•er•al•ism /lítərəlizəm/ *n.* insistence on a literal interpretation; adherence to the letter. □□ **lit•er•al•ist** *n.* **lit•er•al•is•tic** *adj.*

lit•er•ar•y /lítəreree/ *adj.* **1** of, constituting, or occupied with books or literature or written composition, esp. of the kind valued for quality of form. **2** well informed about literature. **3** (of a word or idiom) used chiefly in literary works or other formal writing. □□ **lit•er•ar•i•ly** /–áirilee/ *adv.* **lit•er•ar•i•ness** *n.* [L *litterarius* (as LETTER)]

lit•er•ar•y ex•ec•u•tor *n.* a person entrusted with a writer's papers, unpublished works, etc.

lit•er•ate /lítərət/ *adj. & n.* ● *adj.* able to read and write. ● *n.* a literate person. □□ **lit•er•ate•ly** *adv.* [ME f. L *litteratus* (as LETTER)]

lit•e•ra•ti /lítəráatee/ *n.pl.* **1** men of letters. **2** the learned class. [L, pl. of *literatus* (as LETTER)]

lit•e•ra•tim /lítəráytim, –raá–/ *adv.* letter for letter; textually; literally. [med.L]

lit•e•ra•tion /lítəráyshən/ *n.* the representation of sounds, etc., by a letter or group of letters. [L *litera* LETTER]

lit•er•a•ture /lítərəchər, –chŏŏr/ *n.* **1** written works, esp. those whose value lies in beauty of language or in emotional effect. **2** the realm of letters. **3** the writings of a country or period. **4** literary production. **5** *colloq.* printed matter, leaflets, etc. **6** the material in print on a particular subject (*there is a considerable literature on geraniums*). [ME, = literary culture, f. L *litteratura* (as LITERATE)]

-lith /lith/ *suffix* denoting types of stone (*laccolith; monolith*). [Gk *lithos* stone]

lith•arge /líthaarj/ *n.* a red or yellow crystalline form of lead monoxide. [ME f. OF *litarge* f. L *lithargyrus* f. Gk *litharguros* f. *lithos* stone + *arguros* silver]

lithe /lith/ *adj.* flexible; supple. □□ **lithe•ly** *adv.* **lithe•ness** *n.* **lithe•some** *adj.* [OE *līthe* f. Gmc]

lith•i•a /lítheeə/ *n.* lithium oxide. [mod.L, alt. of earlier *lithion* f. Gk neut. of *litheios* f. *lithos* stone, after *soda*, etc.]

lith•i•a wa•ter *n.* water containing lithium salts and used against gout.

lith•ic /líthik/ *adj.* **1** of, like, or made of stone. **2** *Med.* of a calculus. [Gk *lithikos* (as LITHIA)]

lith•i•um /lítheeəm/ *n. Chem.* a soft, silver-white metallic element, the lightest metal, used in alloys and in batteries. ¶ Symb.: **Li**. [LITHIA + –IUM]

lith•o /líthō/ *n. & v. colloq.* ● *n.* = LITHOGRAPHY. ● *v.tr.* (•**oes**, •**oed**) produce by lithography. [abbr.]

litho- /líthō/ *comb. form* stone. [Gk *lithos* stone]

lith•o•graph /líthəgraf/ *n. & v.* ● *n.* a lithographic print. ● *v.tr.* **1** print by lithography. **2** write or engrave on stone. [back-form. f. LITHOGRAPHY]

li•thog•ra•phy /lithógrəfee/ *n.* a process of obtaining prints from a stone or metal surface so treated that what is to be printed can be inked but the remaining area rejects ink. □□ **li•thog•ra•pher** *n.* **lith•o•graph•ic** /líthəgráfik/ *adj.* **lith•o•graph•i•cal•ly** *adv.* [G *Lithographie* (as LITHO-, –GRAPHY)]

li•thol•o•gy /lithóləjee/ *n.* the science of the nature and composition of rocks. □□ **lith•o•log•i•cal** /líthəlójikəl/ *adj.*

lith•o•phyte /líthəfīt/ *n. Bot.* a plant that grows on stone.

lith•o•pone /líthəpōn/ *n.* a white pigment of zinc sulfide, barium sulfate, and zinc oxide. [LITHO- + Gk *ponos* work]

lith•o•sphere /líthəsfeer/ *n.* **1** the layer including the earth's crust and upper mantle. **2** solid earth (opp. HYDROSPHERE, ATMOSPHERE). □□ **lith•o•spher•ic** /–sféerik, –sfér–/ *adj.*

li•thot•o•my /lithótəmee/ *n.* (*pl.* •**mies**) the surgical removal of a stone from the urinary tract, esp. the bladder. □□ **li•thot•o•mist** *n.* **li•thot•o•mize** *v.tr.* [LL f. Gk *lithotomia* (as LITHO-, –TOMY)]

lith•o•trip•sy /líthətripsee/ *n.* (*pl.* •**sies**) a treatment using ultrasound to shatter a stone in the bladder into small particles that can be passed through the urethra. □□ **lith•o•trip•ter** /–triptər/ *n.* **lith•o•trip•tic** *adj.* [LITHO- + Gk *tripsis* rubbing f. *tribo* rub]

Lith•u•a•ni•an /líthŏŏ-áyneeən/ *n. & adj.* ● *n.* **1 a** a native of Lithuania, a Baltic republic. **b** a person of Lithuanian descent. **2** the language of Lithuania. ● *adj.* of or relating to Lithuania or its people or language.

lit•i•gant /lítigənt/ *n. & adj.* ● *n.* a party to a lawsuit. ● *adj.* engaged in a lawsuit. [F (as LITIGATE)]

lit•i•gate /lítigayt/ *v.* **1** *intr.* go to law; be a party to a lawsuit. **2** *tr.* contest (a point) in a lawsuit. □□ **lit•i•ga•ble** /–gəbəl/ *adj.* **lit•i•ga•tion** /–gáyshən/ *n.* **lit•i•ga•tor** *n.* [L *litigare litigat-* f. *lis litis* lawsuit]

li•ti•gious /litíjəs/ *adj.* **1** given to litigation; unreasonably fond of going to law. **2** disputable in a court of law; offering matter for a lawsuit. **3** of lawsuits. □□ **li•ti•gious•ly** *adv.* **li•ti•gious•ness** *n.* [ME f. OF *litigieux* or L *litigiosus* f. *litigium* litigation: see LITIGATE]

lit•mus /lítməs/ *n.* a dye obtained from lichens that is red under acid conditions and blue under alkaline conditions. [ME f. ONorw. *litmosi* f. ON *litr* dye + *mosi* moss]

lit•mus pa•per *n.* a paper stained with litmus to be used as a test for acids or alkalis.

lit•mus test *n.* **1** a test for acids and alkalis using litmus paper. **2** a simple test to establish true character.

li•to•tes /lítəteez, līt–, lítóteez/ *n.* ironical understatement, esp. the expressing of an affirmative by the negative of its contrary (e.g., *I won't be sorry for I will be glad*). [LL f. Gk *litotēs* f. *litos* plain, meager]

li•tre *Brit.* var. of LITER.

Litt.D. *abbr.* Doctor of Letters. [L *Litterarum Doctor*]

lit•ter /lítər/ *n. & v.* ● *n.* **1 a** refuse, esp. paper, discarded in an open or public place. **b** odds and ends lying about. **2** a state of untidiness, disorderly accumulation of papers, etc. **3** the young animals brought forth at a birth. **4** a vehicle containing a couch shut in by curtains and carried on men's shoulders or by beasts of burden. **5** a framework with a couch for transporting the sick and wounded. **6 a** straw, rushes, etc., as bedding, esp. for animals. **b** straw and dung in a farmyard. ● *v.tr.* **1** make (a place) untidy with litter. **2** scatter untidily and leave lying about. **3** give birth to (whelps, etc.). **4** (often foll. by *down*) **a** provide (a horse, etc.) with litter as bedding. **b** spread litter or straw on (a floor) or in (a stable). □□ **lit•ter•y** *adj.* (in senses 1, 2 of *n.*). [ME f. AF *litere*, OF *litiere* f. med.L *lectaria* f. L *lectus* bed]

litter 4

lit•te•rae hu•ma•ni•o•res /lítəri hōōmáneeáwrez, litəree/ *n.* the formal study of the humanities.

lit•té•ra•teur /lítərətőr/ *n.* a literary person. [F]

lit•ter•bag /lítərbag/ *n.* a bag used in a motor vehicle, etc., for trash disposal.

lit•ter•bug /lítərbug/ *n.* a person who carelessly leaves litter in a public place.

lit•tle /lít'l/ *adj., n., & adv.* ● *adj.* (**lit•tler**, **lit•tlest**; *less* /les/ or *less•er* /lésər/; *least* /leest/) **1** small in size, amount, degree, etc.; not great or big: often used to convey affectionate or emotional overtones, or condescension, not implied by *small* (*a friendly little guy; a silly little fool; a nice little car*). **2 a** short in stature (*a little man*). **b** of short distance or duration (*will go a little way with you; wait a little while*). **3** (prec. by *a*) a certain though small amount of (*give me a little butter*). **4** trivial; relatively unimportant (*exaggerates every little difficulty*). **5** not much; inconsiderable (*gained little advantage from it*). **6** operating on a small scale (*the little storekeeper*). **7** as a distinctive epithet: **a** of a smaller or the smallest size, etc. (*little finger*). **b** that is the smaller or smallest of the name (*little auk; little grebe*). **8** young or younger (*a little boy; my little sister*). **9** as of a child, evoking tenderness, condescension, amusement, etc. (*we know their little ways*). **10** mean; paltry; contemptible (*you little sneak*). ● *n.* **1** not much; only a small amount (*got very little out of it; did what little I could*). **2** (usu. prec. by *a*) **a** a certain but no great amount (*knows a little of everything; every little bit helps*). **b** a short time or distance (*after a little*). ● *adv.* (**less**, **least**) **1** to a small extent only (*little-known authors; is little more than speculation*). **2** not at all; hardly (*they little thought*). **3** (prec. by *a*) somewhat (*is a little deaf*). □ **little by little** by degrees; gradually. **little or nothing** hardly anything. **no little** considerable; a good deal of (*took no little trouble over it*). **not a little** *n.* much; a great deal. ● *adv.* extremely (*not a little concerned*). □□ **lit•tle•ness** *n.* [OE *lytel* f. Gmc]

lit•tle auk *n.* a small Arctic auk, *Plautus alle.*

Lit•tle Bear *n.* = LITTLE DIPPER.

Lit•tle Dip•per *n.* the constellation of seven bright stars in Ursa Minor in the shape of a dipper.

lit•tle fin•ger *n.* the smallest finger, at the outer end of the hand.

Lit•tle League *n.* an international organization that promotes youth baseball and softball. □□ **Lit•tle Lea•guer** *n.*

lit•tle man *n.* esp. *joc.* (as a form of address) a boy.

lit•tle ones *n.pl.* young children or animals.

lit·tle peo·ple *n.pl.* **1** the ordinary people in a country, organization, etc., who do not have much power. **2** midgets.

Lit·tle Rus·sian *n. & adj. hist.* • *n.* a Ukrainian. • *adj.* Ukrainian.

lit·tle slam *n. Bridge* the winning of 12 tricks.

lit·tle wom·an *n. colloq.* often *derog.* one's wife.

lit·to·ral /lítərəl/ *adj. & n.* • *adj.* of or on the shore of the sea, a lake, etc. • *n.* a region lying along a shore. [L *littoralis* f. *litus litoris* shore]

li·tur·gi·cal /litɔ́rjikəl/ *adj.* of or related to liturgies or public worship. □□ **li·tur·gi·cal·ly** *adv.* **lit·ur·gist** /lítɔrjist/ *n.* [med.L f. Gk *leitourgikos* (as LITURGY)]

lit·ur·gy /lítɔrjee/ *n.* (*pl.* **·gies**) **1 a** a form of public worship. **b** a set of formularies for this. **c** public worship in accordance with a prescribed form. **2** *Brit.* (**the Liturgy**) the Book of Common Prayer. **3** (**the Divine Liturgy**) the Communion office of the Orthodox Church. **4** *Gk. Antiq.* a public office or duty performed voluntarily by a rich Athenian. [F *liturgie* or LL *liturgia* f. Gk *leitourgia* public worship f. *leit-* public + *ergon* work]

liv·a·ble /lívəbəl/ *adj.* (also **live·a·ble**) **1** (of a house, room, climate, etc.) fit to live in. **2** (of a life) worth living. **3** (of a person) companionable; easy to live with. □□ **liv·a·bil·i·ty** *n.* **liv·a·ble·ness** *n.*

live¹ /liv/ *v.* **1** *intr.* have (esp. animal) life; be or remain alive. **2** *intr.* (foll. by *on*) subsist or feed (*lives on fruit*). **3** *intr.* (foll. by *on, off*) depend for subsistence (*lives off the family; lives on income from investments*). **4** *intr.* (foll. by *on, by*) sustain one's position or repute (*live on their reputation; lives by his wits*). **5** *tr.* **a** (with compl.) spend; pass; experience (*lived a happy life*). **b** express in one's life (*was living a lie*). **6** *intr.* conduct oneself in a specified way (*live quietly*). **7** *intr.* arrange one's habits, expenditure, feeding, etc. (*live modestly*). **8** *intr.* make or have one's abode. **9** *intr.* (foll. by *in*) spend the daytime (*the room does not seem to be lived in*). **10** *intr.* (of a person or thing) survive. **11** *intr.* (of a ship) escape destruction. **12** *intr.* enjoy life intensely or to the full (*you haven't lived till you've drunk champagne*). □ **live and let live** condone others' failings so as to be similarly tolerated. **live down** (usu. with *neg.*) cause (past guilt, embarrassment, etc.) to be forgotten by different conduct over a period of time (*you'll never live that down!*). **live in** (of a domestic employee) reside on the premises of one's work. **live it up** *colloq.* live gaily and extravagantly. **live out 1** survive (a danger, difficulty, etc.). **2** (of a domestic employee) reside away from one's place of work. **live through** survive; remain alive at the end of. **live to** survive and reach (*lived to a great age*). **live to oneself** live in isolation. **live together** (esp. of a man and woman not married to each other) share a home and have a sexual relationship. **live up to** honor or fulfill; put into practice (principles, etc.). **live with 1** share a home with. **2** tolerate; find congenial. **long live ...!** an exclamation of loyalty (to a person, etc., specified). [OE *libban, lifian,* f. Gmc]

live² /liv/ *adj.* **1** (*attrib.*) that is alive; living. **2** (of a broadcast) heard or seen at the time of its performance, not from a recording. **3** full of power, energy, or importance; not obsolete or exhausted (*disarmament is still a live issue*). **4** expending or still able to expend energy in various forms, esp.: **a** (of coals) glowing; burning. **b** (of a shell) unexploded. **c** (of a match) unkindled. **d** (of a wire, etc.) connected to a source of electrical power. **5** (of rock) not detached, seeming to form part of the earth's frame. **6** (of a wheel or axle, etc., in machinery) moving or imparting motion. [aphetic form of ALIVE]

live·a·ble var. of LIVABLE.

live bait *n.* small fish used to entice prey.

live-in *attrib.adj.* **1** (of a domestic employee) living in (*live-in maid*). **2** (of a sexual partner) cohabiting.

live·li·hood /lívleehŏŏd/ *n.* a means of living; sustenance. [OE *līflād* f. *līf* LIFE + *lād* course (see LOAD): assim. to obs. *livelihood* liveliness]

live load *n.* the weight of persons or goods in a building or vehicle.

live·long¹ /lívlawng, –long/ *adj. poet.* or *rhet.* in its entire length or apparently so (*the livelong day*). [ME *lefe longe* (as LIEF, LONG¹): assim. to LIVE¹]

live·long² /lívlawng, –long/ *n.* an orpine. [LIVE¹ + LONG¹]

live·ly /lívlee/ *adj.* (**live·li·er, live·li·est**) **1** full of life; vigorous; energetic. **2** brisk (*a lively pace*). **3** vigorous; stimulating (*a lively discussion*). **4** vivacious; jolly; sociable. **5** *joc.* exciting; dangerous; difficult (*the press is making things lively for them*). **6** (of a color) bright and vivid. **7** lifelike; realistic (*a lively description*). **8** (of a boat, etc.) rising lightly to the waves. □□ **live·li·ly** *adv.* **live·li·ness** *n.* [OE *līflic* (as LIFE, –LY¹)]

liv·en /lívən/ *v.tr. & intr.* (often foll. by *up*) *colloq.* brighten; cheer.

live oak *n.* an American evergreen tree, *Quercus virginiana.*

liv·er¹ /lívər/ *n.* **1 a** a large lobed glandular organ in the abdomen of vertebrates, functioning in many metabolic processes including the regulation of toxic materials in the blood, secreting bile, etc. **b** a similar organ in other animals. **2** the flesh of an animal's liver as food. **3** a dark reddish-brown color. □□ **liv·er·less** *adj.* [OE *lifer* f. Gmc]

liv·er² /lívər/ *n.* a person who lives in a specified way (*a clean liver*).

liv·er chest·nut *n.* a horse of a dark chestnut color.

liv·er fluke *n.* either of two types of fluke, esp. *Fasciola hepatica,* the adults of which live within the liver tissues of vertebrates, and the larvae within snails.

liv·er·ish /lívərish/ *adj.* **1** suffering from a disorder of the liver. **2** peevish; glum. **3** resembling liver. □□ **liv·er·ish·ly** *adv.* **liv·er·ish·ness** *n.*

liv·er of sul·fur *n. archaic* a liver-colored mixture of potassium sulfide, used in medicinal ointments.

Liv·er·pud·li·an /lívərpúdleeən/ *n. & adj.* • *n.* a native of Liverpool, England. • *adj.* of or relating to Liverpool. [joc. f. *Liverpool* + PUDDLE]

liv·er sau·sage *n.* = LIVERWURST.

liv·er spot *n.* a small brown pigmentation on the skin, esp. in older people,.

liv·er·wort /lívərwort, –wawrt/ *n.* any small leafy or thalloid bryophyte of the class Hepaticae, of which some have liver-shaped parts.

liv·er·wurst /lívərworst, –vɔrst/ *n.* a sausage containing cooked liver, etc.

liv·er·y¹ /lívəree/ *n.* (*pl.* **·ies**) **1** distinctive clothing worn by a servant or official. **2** a distinctive guise or marking or outward appearance (*birds in their winter livery*). **3** a distinctive color scheme in which the vehicles, aircraft, etc., of a particular company or line are painted. **4** a place where horses can be hired. **5** *hist.* a provision of food or clothing for retainers, etc. **6** *Law* **a** the legal delivery of property. **b** a writ allowing this. □ **at livery** (of a horse) kept for the owner and fed and groomed for a fixed charge. □□ **liv·er·ied** *adj.* (esp. in senses 1, 2).

liv·er·y² /lívəree/ *adj.* **1** of the consistency or color of liver. **2** *Brit.* (of soil) tenacious. **3** *colloq.* liverish.

liv·er·y·man /lívəreemən/ *n.* (*pl.* **·men**) **1** a keeper of or attendant in a livery stable. **2** *Brit.* a member of a livery company.

liv·er·y sta·ble *n.* a stable where horses are kept at livery or let out for hire.

lives *pl.* of LIFE.

live·stock /lívstok/ *n.* (usu. treated as *pl.*) animals, esp. on a farm, regarded as an asset.

live wire *n.* an energetic and forceful person.

liv·id /lívid/ *adj.* **1** *colloq.* furiously angry. **2 a** of a bluish leaden color. **b** discolored as by a bruise. □□ **li·vid·i·ty** /–víditee/ *n.* **liv·id·ly** *adv.* **liv·id·ness** *n.* [F *livide* or L *lividus* f. *livēre* be bluish]

liv·ing /líving/ *n. & adj.* • *n.* **1** a livelihood or means of maintenance (*made my living as a journalist; what does she do for a living?*). **2** *Brit. Eccl.* a position as a vicar or rector with an income or property. • *adj.* **1** contemporary; now existent (*the greatest living poet*). **2** (of a likeness or image of a person) exact. **3** (of a language) still in vernacular use. **4** (of water) perennially flowing. **5** (of rock, etc.) = LIVE² 5. □ **within living memory** within the memory of people still living.

liv·ing room *n.* a room in a house for general everyday use.

liv·ing wage *n.* a wage that affords the means of normal subsistence.

liv·ing will *n.* a written statement of a person's desire not to be kept alive by artificial means in the event of terminal illness or accident.

lix·iv·i·ate /liksívee-ayt/ *v.tr.* separate (a substance) into soluble and insoluble constituents by the percolation of liquid. □□ **lix·iv·i·a·tion** /–áyshən/ *n.* [L *lixivius* made into lye f. *lix* lye]

liz·ard /lízərd/ *n.* any reptile of the suborder Lacertilia, having usu. a long body and tail, four legs, movable eyelids, and a rough or scaly hide. [ME f. OF *lesard(e)* f. L *lacertus*]

LL *abbr.* **1** Late Latin. **2** Low Latin. **3** lower left.

ll. *abbr.* lines.

'll *v.* (usu. after pronouns) shall; will (*I'll; that'll*). [abbr.]

lla·ma /laámə, yaá–/ *n.* **1** a S. American ruminant, *Lama glama,* kept as a beast of burden and for its soft, woolly fleece. **2** the wool from this animal, or cloth made from it. [Sp., prob. f. Quechua]

lla·ne·ro /laanáirō, yaa–/ *n.* (*pl.* **·ros**) an inhabitant of the llanos. [Sp.]

lla·no /laánō, yaá–/ *n.* (*pl.* **·nos**) a treeless grassy plain or steppe, esp. in S. America. [Sp. f. L *planum* plain]

LLB *abbr.* Bachelor of Laws. [L *legum baccalaureus*]

LLD *abbr.* Doctor of Laws. [L *legum doctor*]

llama

LLM *abbr.* Master of Laws. [L *legum magister*]

Lloyd's /loydz/ *n.* an incorporated society of insurance underwriters in London. [after the orig. meeting in a coffeehouse established in 1688 by Edward *Lloyd*]

Lloyd's List *n.* a daily publication devoted to shipping news.

Lloyd's Reg·is·ter *n.* **1** an annual alphabetical list of ships assigned to various classes. **2** a society that produces this.

LM *abbr.* **1** long meter. **2** lunar module.

lm *abbr.* lumen(s).

ln *abbr.* natural logarithm. [mod.L *logarithmus naturalis*]

lo /lō/ *int. archaic* calling attention to an amazing sight. □ **lo and behold** *joc.* a formula introducing a surprising or unexpected fact. [OE *lā* int. of surprise, etc., & ME *lō* = *lōke* LOOK]

loach /lōch/ *n.* any small edible freshwater fish of the family Cobitidae. [ME f. OF *loche*, of unkn. orig.]

load /lōd/ *n. & v.* ●*n.* **1 a** what is carried or is to be carried; a burden. **b** an amount usu. or actually carried (often in *comb.*: *a busload of tourists*; *a truckload of bricks*). **2** a unit of measure or weight of certain substances. **3** a burden or commitment of work, responsibility, care, grief, etc. **4** (in *pl.*; often foll. by *of*) *colloq.* plenty; a lot. **5 a** *Electr.* the amount of power supplied by a generating system at any given time. **b** *Electronics* an impedance or circuit that receives or develops the output of a transistor or other device. **6** the weight or force borne by the supporting part of a structure. **7** a material object or force acting as a weight or clog. **8** the resistance of machinery to motive power. ●*v.* **1** *tr.* **a** put a load on or aboard (a person, vehicle, ship, etc.). **b** place (a load or cargo) aboard a ship, on a vehicle, etc. **2** *intr.* (often foll. by *up*) (of a ship, vehicle, or person) take a load aboard, pick up a load. **3** *tr.* (often foll. by *with*) **a** add weight to; be a weight or burden upon. **b** oppress. **4** *tr.* strain the bearing-capacity of (*a table loaded with food*). **5** *tr.* (also **load up**) (foll. by *with*) **a** supply overwhelmingly (*loaded us with work*). **b** assail overwhelmingly (*loaded us with abuse*). **6** *tr.* charge (a firearm) with ammunition. **7** *tr.* insert (the required operating medium) in a device, e.g., film in a camera, magnetic tape in a tape recorder, a program into a computer, etc. **8** *tr.* add an extra charge to (an insurance premium) in the case of a poorer risk. **9** *tr.* **a** weight with lead. **b** give a bias to (dice, a roulette wheel, etc.) with weights. □ **get a load of** *sl.* listen attentively to; notice. [OE *lād* way, journey, conveyance, f. Gmc: rel. to LEAD[1], LODE]

load·ed /lódid/ *adj.* **1** bearing or carrying a load. **2** *sl.* **a** wealthy. **b** drunk. **c** drugged. **3** (of dice, etc.) weighted or given a bias. **4** (of a question or statement) charged with some hidden or improper implication.

load·er /lódər/ *n.* **1** a loading machine. **2** (in *comb.*) a gun, machine, truck, etc., loaded in a specified way (*breechloader*). **3** an attendant who loads guns at a shoot. □□ **–load·ing** *adj.* (in *comb.*) (in sense 2).

load·ing /lóding/ *n.* **1** *Electr.* the maximum current or power taken by an appliance. **2** an increase in an insurance premium due to a factor increasing the risk involved (see LOAD *v.* 8).

load line *n.* = PLIMSOLL LINE.

load·star var. of LODESTAR.

load·stone var. of LODESTONE.

loaf[1] /lōf/ *n.* (*pl.* **loaves** /lōvz/) **1** a portion of baked bread, usu. of a standard size or shape. **2** (often in *comb.*) a quantity of other food formed into a particular shape (*sugarloaf*; *meat loaf*). **3** *Brit. sl.* the head, esp. as a source of common sense (*use your loaf*). [OE *hlāf* f. Gmc]

loaf[2] /lōf/ *v. & n.* ●*v.* **1** *intr.* (often foll. by *about, around*) spend time idly; hang about. **2** *tr.* (foll. by *away*) waste (time) idly (*loafed away the morning*). **3** *intr.* saunter. ●*n.* an act or spell of loafing. [prob. a back-form. f. LOAFER]

loaf·er /lófər/ *n.* **1** an idle person. **2** (**Loafer**) *Trademark* a leather shoe shaped like a moccasin with a flat heel. [perh. f. G *Landläufer* vagabond]

loam /lōm/ *n.* **1** a fertile soil of clay and sand containing decayed vegetable matter. **2** a paste of clay and water with sand, chopped straw, etc., used in making bricks, plastering, etc. □□ **loam·y** *adj.* **loam·i·ness** *n.* [OE *lām* f.WG, rel. to LIME[1]]

loan[1] /lōn/ *n. & v.* ●*n.* **1** something lent, esp. a sum of money to be returned normally with interest. **2** the act of lending or state of being lent. **3** a word, custom, etc., adopted by one people from another. ●*v.tr.* lend (esp. money). □ **on loan** acquired or given as a loan. □□ **loan·a·ble** *adj.* **loan·ee** /lōnée/ *n.* **loan·er** *n.* [ME *lan* f. ON *lán* f. Gmc: cf. LEND]

▶Traditionally, **loan** was a noun and **lend** was a verb: *I went to ask for a loan*; *can you lend me twenty dollars?* But **loan** is now widely used as a verb, especially in financial contexts.

loan[2] /lōn/ *n.* (also **loan·ing** /lóning/) *Sc.* **1** a lane. **2** an open place where cows are milked. [ME var. of LANE]

loan shark *n. colloq.* a person who lends money at exorbitant rates of interest.

loan trans·la·tion *n.* an expression adopted by one language from another in a more or less literally translated form.

loan·word /lónwərd/ *n.* a word adopted usu. with little modification, from a foreign language.

loath /lōth, lōth/ *adj.* (also esp. *Brit.* **loth**) (usu. foll. by *to* + infin.) disinclined; reluctant; unwilling (*was loath to admit it*). [OE *lāth* f. Gmc]

loathe /lōth/ *v.tr.* regard with disgust; abominate; detest. □□ **loath·er** *n.* **loath·ing** *n.* [OE *lāthian* f. Gmc, rel. to LOATH]

loath·some /lóthsəm, lóth–/ *adj.* arousing hatred or disgust; offensive; repulsive. □□ **loath·some·ly** *adv.* **loath·some·ness** *n.* [ME f. *loath* disgust f. LOATHE]

loaves *pl.* of LOAF[1].

lob /lob/ *v. & n.* ●*v.tr.* (**lobbed**, **lob·bing**) **1** hit or throw (a ball or missile, etc.) slowly or in a high arc. **2** send (an opponent) a lobbed ball. ●*n.* **1** a ball struck in a high arc. **2** a stroke producing this result. [earlier as noun, prob. f. LG or Du.]

lo·bar /lóbər, –baar/ *adj.* **1** of the lungs (*lobar pneumonia*). **2** of, relating to, or affecting a lobe.

lo·bate /lóbayt/ *adj. Biol.* having a lobe or lobes. □□ **lo·ba·tion** /–áyshən/ *n.*

lob·by /lóbee/ *n. & v.* ●*n.* (*pl.* **·bies**) **1** a porch, anteroom, entrance hall, or corridor. **2** *Brit.* **a** (in the House of Commons) a large hall used esp. for interviews between members of Parliament and the public. **b** (also **division lobby**) each of two corridors to which members of Parliament retire to vote. **3** a body of persons seeking to influence legislators on behalf of a particular interest (*the tobacco lobby*). **4** (prec. by *the*) (in the UK) a group of journalists who receive unattributable briefings from the government (*lobby correspondent*). ●*v.* (**·bies**, **·bied**) **1** *tr.* solicit the support of (an influential person). **2** *tr.* (of members of the public) seek to influence (the members of a legislature). **3** *intr.* frequent a parliamentary lobby. **4** *tr.* (foll. by *through*) get (a bill, etc.) through a legislature, by interviews, etc., in the lobby. □□ **lob·by·er** *n.* **lob·by·ism** *n.* **lob·by·ist** *n.* [med.L *lobia*, *lobium* LODGE]

lobe /lōb/ *n.* **1** a roundish and flattish projecting or pendulous part, often each of two or more such parts divided by a fissure (*lobes of the brain*). **2** = EARLOBE. □□ **lobed** *adj.* **lobe·less** *adj.* [LL f. Gk *lobos* lobe, pod]

lo·bec·to·my /lōbéktəmee/ *n.* (*pl.* **·mies**) *Surgery* the excision of a lobe of an organ such as the thyroid gland, lung, etc.

lo·bel·ia /lōbéelyə/ *n.* any plant of the genus *Lobelia*, with blue, scarlet, white, or purple flowers having a deeply cleft corolla. [M. de *Lobel*, Flemish botanist in England d. 1616]

lo·bot·o·my /ləbótəmee/ *n.* (*pl.* **·mies**) *Surgery* see PREFRONTAL LOBOTOMY. [LOBE + –TOMY]

lob·scouse /lóbskows/ *n.* a sailor's dish of meat stewed with vegetables and ship's biscuit. [18th c.: orig. unkn.: cf. Du. *lapskous*, Da., Norw., G *Lapskaus*]

lob·ster /lóbstər/ *n. & v.* ●*n.* **1** any large marine crustacean of the family Nephropidae, with stalked eyes and two pincerlike claws as the first pair of ten limbs. **2** its flesh as food. ●*v.intr.* catch lobsters. [OE *lopustre*, corrupt. of L *locusta* crustacean, locust: *thermidor* f. the name of the 11th month of the Fr. revolutionary calendar]

lobster

lob·ster pot *n.* a basket in which lobsters are trapped.

lob·ster ther·mi·dor /thórmidawr/ *n.* a mixture of lobster meat, mushrooms, cream, egg yolks, and sherry, cooked in a lobster shell.

lob·ule /lóbyōol/ *n.* a small lobe. □□ **lob·u·lar** *adj.* **lob·u·late** /–layt/ *adj.* [LOBE]

lob·worm /lóbwərm/ *n.* **1** a large earthworm used as fishing bait. **2** = LUGWORM. [LOB in obs. sense 'pendulous object']

lo·cal /lókəl/ *adj. & n.* ●*adj.* **1** belonging to or existing in a particular place or places. **2** peculiar to or only encountered in a particular place or places. **3** of or belonging to the neighborhood (*the local doctor*). **4** of or affecting a part and not the whole, esp. of the body (*local pain*; *a local anesthetic*). **5** in regard to place. ●*n.* a local person or thing, esp.: **1** an inhabitant of a particular place regarded with reference to that place. **2** a local train, bus, etc. **3** (often prec. by *the*) *Brit. colloq.* a pub. **4** a local anesthetic. **5** a local branch of a labor union. □□ **lo·cal·ly** *adv.* **lo·cal·ness** *n.* [ME f. OF f. LL *localis* f. L *locus* place]

lo·cal an·es·thet·ic *n.* an anesthetic that affects a restricted area of the body.

lo·cal ar·e·a net·work *n. Computing* a system for linking telecommunications or computer equipment in several offices, a group of buildings, etc. ¶ Abbr.: **LAN**.

lo·cal col·or *n.* the customs, manner of speech, dress, or other features of a place that contribute to its particular character.

lo•cale /lōkál/ *n.* a scene or locality, esp. with reference to an event or occurrence taking place there. [F *local* (n.) (as LOCAL), respelled to indicate stress: cf. MORALE]

lo•cal gov•ern•ment *n.* a system of administration of a county, etc., by the elected representatives of those who live there.

lo•cal•ism /lōkəlizəm/ *n.* **1** preference for what is local. **2** a local idiom, custom, etc. **3 a** attachment to a place. **b** a limitation of ideas, etc., resulting from this.

lo•cal•i•ty /lōkálitee/ *n.* (*pl.* •ties) **1** a district or neighborhood. **2** the site or scene of something, esp. in relation to its surroundings. **3** the position of a thing; the place where it is. [F *localité* or LL *localitas* (as LOCAL)]

lo•cal•ize /lōkəlīz/ *v.tr.* **1** restrict or assign to a particular place. **2** invest with the characteristics of a particular place. **3** attach to districts; decentralize. □□ **lo•cal•iz•a•ble** *adj.* **lo•cal•i•za•tion** *n.*

lo•cal op•tion *n.* a choice available to a local administration to accept or reject national legislation (e.g., concerning the sale of alcoholic liquor).

lo•cal time *n.* **1** time measured from the sun's transit over the meridian of a place. **2** the time as reckoned in a particular place, esp. with reference to an event recorded there.

lo•cal train *n.* a train stopping at all the stations on its route.

lo•cate /lōkayt, lōkáyt/ *v.* **1** *tr.* discover the exact place or position of (*locate the enemy's camp*). **2** *tr.* establish or install in a place or in its proper place. **3** *tr.* state the locality of. **4** *tr.* (in *passive*) be situated. **5** *intr.* (often foll. by *in*) take up residence or business (in a place). □□ **lo•cat•a•ble** *adj.* **lo•cat•er, lo•ca•tor** *n.*
▶In formal English one should avoid using **locate** to mean 'find' (*it drives him out of his mind when he can't locate something*). In precise usage, **locate** means 'fix the position of, put in place' (*the studio should be located on a north-facing slope*).

WORD HISTORY locate

Early 16th cent.: from Latin *locat-* 'placed,' from the verb *locare*, from *locus* 'place.' The original sense was as a legal term meaning 'let out on hire', later (late 16th cent.) 'assign to a particular place,' then (particularly in North American usage) 'establish in a place.' The sense 'discover the exact position of' dates from the late 19th cent.

lo•ca•tion /lōkáyshən/ *n.* **1** a particular place; the place or position in which a person or thing is. **2** the act of locating or process of being located. **3** an actual place or natural setting featured in a motion picture, etc., as distinct from a simulation in a studio (*filmed entirely on location*). [L *locatio* (as LOCATE)]

loc•a•tive /lōkətiv/ *n. & adj. Gram.* • *n.* the case of nouns, pronouns, and adjectives, expressing location. • *adj.* of or in the locative. [formed as LOCATE + –IVE, after *vocative*]

loc. cit. /lók sít/ *abbr.* in the passage already cited. [L *loco citato*]

loch /lok, lokh/ *n. Sc.* **1** a lake. **2** an arm of the sea, esp. when narrow or partially landlocked. [ME f. Gael.]

lo•chi•a /lókeeə, ló–/ *n.* a discharge from the uterus after childbirth. □□ **lo•chi•al** *adj.* [mod.L f. Gk *lokhia* neut. pl. of *lokhios* of childbirth]

lo•ci *pl.* of LOCUS.

lo•ci clas•si•ci *pl.* of LOCUS CLASSICUS.

lock[1] /lok/ *n. & v.* • *n.* **1** a mechanism for fastening a door, lid, etc., with a bolt that requires a key of a particular shape, or a combination of movements (see COMBINATION LOCK), to work it. **2** a confined section of a canal or river where the water level can be changed for raising and lowering boats between adjacent sections by the use of gates and sluices. **3 a** the turning of the front wheels of a vehicle to change its direction of motion. **b** (in full **full lock**) the maximum extent of this. **4** an interlocked or jammed state. **5** *Wrestling* a hold that keeps an opponent's limb fixed. **6** an appliance to keep a wheel from revolving or slewing. **7** a mechanism for exploding the charge of a gun. **8** = AIRLOCK 2. • *v.* **1 a** *tr.* fasten with a lock. **b** *tr.* (foll. by *up*) shut and secure (esp. a building) by locking. **c** *intr.* (of a door, window, box, etc.) have the means of being locked. **2** *tr.* (foll. by *up, in, into*) enclose (a person or thing) by locking or as if by locking. **3** *tr.* (often foll. by *up, away*) store or allocate inaccessibly (*capital locked up in land*). **4** *tr.* (foll. by *in*) hold fast (in sleep or enchantment, etc.). **5** *tr.* (usu. in *passive*) (of land, hills, etc.) enclose. **6** *tr. & intr.* make or become rigidly fixed or immovable. **7** *intr. & tr.* become or cause to become jammed or caught. **8** *tr.* (often in *passive*; foll. by *in*) entangle in an embrace or struggle. **9** *tr.* provide (a canal, etc.) with locks. **10** *tr.* (foll. by *up, down*) convey (a boat) through a lock. **11** *intr.* go through a lock on a canal, etc. □ **lock on** to locate or cause to locate by radar, etc., and then track. **lock out 1** keep (a person) out by locking the door. **2** (of an employer) submit (employees) to a lockout. **lock, stock, and barrel** *n.* the whole of a thing. • *adv.* completely. **under lock and key** securely locked up. □□ **lock•a•ble** *adj.* **lock•less** *adj.* [OE *loc* f. Gmc]

lock[2] /lok/ *n.* **1 a** a portion of hair that coils or hangs together. **b** (in *pl.*) the hair of the head. **2** a tuft of wool or cotton. □□ **–locked** *adj.* (in *comb.*). [OE *locc* f. Gmc]

lock•age /lókij/ *n.* **1** the amount of rise and fall effected by canal locks. **2** a toll for the use of a lock. **3** the construction or use of locks. **4** locks collectively; the aggregate of locks constructed.

lock•er /lókər/ *n.* **1** a small lockable cupboard or compartment, esp. each of several for public use. **2** *Naut.* a chest or compartment for clothes, stores, ammunition, etc. **3** a person or thing that locks.

lock•er room *n.* a room containing lockers for the storage of personal belongings, esp. in schools or gymnasiums.

lock•et /lókit/ *n.* **1** a small ornamental case holding a portrait, lock of hair, etc., and usu. hung from the neck. **2** a metal plate or band on a scabbard. [OF *locquet* dimin. of *loc* latch, lock, f. WG (as LOCK[1])]

lock•fast /lókfast/ *adj. Sc.* secured with a lock.

lock•jaw /lókjaw/ *n.* = TRISMUS.

lock•keep•er /lók-keepər/ *n.* a keeper of a lock on a river or canal.

lock•knit *adj.* knitted with an interlocking stitch.

lock•nut /lóknut/ *n. Mech.* a nut screwed down on another to keep it tight.

lock•out /lókowt/ *n.* the exclusion of employees by their employer from their place of work until certain terms are agreed to.

lock•smith /lóksmith/ *n.* a maker and repairer of locks.

lock•step /lókstep/ *n.* marching with each person as close as possible to the one in front.

lock•stitch /lókstich/ *n.* a stitch made by a sewing machine by firmly locking together two threads or stitches.

lock•up /lókup/ *n. & adj.* • *n.* **1** a house or room for the temporary detention of prisoners. **2** *Brit.* nonresidential premises, etc., that can be locked up, esp. a small store or storehouse. **3 a** the locking up of premises for the night. **b** the time of doing this. **4 a** the unrealizable state of invested capital. **b** an amount of capital locked up. • *attrib.adj. Brit.* that can be locked up (*lockup shop*).

lo•co[1] /lókō/ *adj. & n.* • *adj. sl.* crazy. • *n.* (*pl.* •cos or •coes) **1** *colloq.* = LOCOWEED. **2** *sl.* a crazy person; maniac.

lo•co[2] /lókō/ *n.* (*pl.* •cos) *colloq.* a locomotive engine. [abbr.]

lo•co•mo•tion /lókəmóshən/ *n.* **1** motion or the power of motion from one place to another. **2** travel; a means of traveling, esp. an artificial one. [L *loco* ablat. of *locus* place + *motio* MOTION]

lo•co•mo•tive /lókəmótiv/ *n. & adj.* • *n.* (in full **locomotive engine**) an engine powered by steam, diesel fuel, or electricity, used for pulling trains. • *adj.* **1** of or relating to or effecting locomotion (*locomotive power*). **2** having the power of or given to locomotion; not stationary.

lo•co•mo•tor /lókəmótər/ *adj.* of or relating to locomotion. [LOCOMOTION + MOTOR]

lo•co•weed /lókōweed/ *n.* a poisonous leguminous plant of the southwestern US, causing brain disease in cattle eating it. [Sp., = insane]

loc•u•lus /lókyələs/ *n.* (*pl.* **loc•u•li** /–lī/) *Zool., Anat., & Bot.* each of a number of small separate cavities. □□ **loc•u•lar** *adj.* [L, dimin. of *locus*: see LOCUS]

lo•cum /lókəm/ *n. colloq.* = LOCUM TENENS. [abbr.]

lo•cum te•nens /teenenz, tén–/ *n.* (*pl.* **lo•cum te•nen•tes** /tinénteez/) esp. *Brit.* a deputy acting esp. for a clergyman or doctor. □□ **lo•cum te•nen•cy** /ténənsee/ *n.* [med.L, one holding a place: see LOCUS, TENANT]

lo•cus /lókəs/ *n.* (*pl.* **lo•ci** /lósī, –kee, –kī/) **1** a position or point, esp. in a text, treatise, etc. **2** *Math.* a curve, etc., formed by all the points satisfying a particular equation of the relation between coordinates, or by a point, line, or surface moving according to mathematically defined conditions. **3** *Biol.* the position of a gene, mutation, etc., on a chromosome. [L, = place]

lo•cus clas•si•cus /lókəs-kláskəs/ *n.* (*pl.* **lo•ci clas•si•ci** /klásísī, –kī/) the best known or most authoritative passage on a subject. [L]

lo•cus stan•di /lókəs-stándī/ *n.* a recognized or identifiable (esp. legal) status.

lo•cust /lókəst/ *n.* **1** any of various African and Asian grasshoppers of the family Acrididae, migrating in swarms and destroying vegetation. **2** a cicada. **3** (in full **locust bean**) a carob. **4** (in full **locust tree**) **a** a carob tree. **b** = ACACIA 2. **c** = KOWHAI. [ME f. OF *locuste* f. L *locusta* lobster, locust]

lo•cust-bird *n.* (also **lo•cust-eat•er**) any of various birds that feed on locusts.

lo•cu•tion /lōkyóōshən/ *n.* **1** a word or phrase, esp. considered in regard to style or idiom. **2** style of speech. [ME f. OF *locution* or L *locutio* f. *loqui locut–* speak]

lode /lōd/ *n.* a vein of metal ore. [var. of LOAD]

lo•den /lód'n/ *n.* **1** a thick, waterproof woolen cloth. **2** the dark green color in which this is often made. [G]

lode•star /lódstaar/ *n.* (also **load•star**) **1** a star that a ship, etc., is steered by, esp. the pole star. **2 a** a guiding principle. **b** an object of pursuit. [LODE in obs. sense 'way, journey' + STAR]

lode•stone /lódstōn/ *n.* (also **load•stone**) **1** magnetic oxide of iron, magnetite. **2 a** a piece of this used as a magnet. **b** a thing that attracts.

lodge /loj/ *n. & v.* • *n.* **1** a small house at the gates of a park or on the grounds of a large house, occupied by a gatekeeper, gardener, etc. **2** any large house or hotel, esp. in a resort. **3** a house occupied in the hunting or shooting season. **4 a** a porter's room or quarters at the gate of a college or other large building. **b** the residence of a head of a college, esp. at Cambridge University in England. **5** the members or the meeting place of a branch of a society such as the Freemasons. **6** *Brit.* a local branch of a labor union. **7** a beaver's or otter's lair. **8** a type of Native American dwelling; a wigwam. • *v.* **1** *tr.* deposit in court or with an official a formal statement of (complaint or information). **2** *tr.* deposit (money, etc.) for security. **3** *tr.* bring forward (an objection, etc.). **4** *tr.* (foll. by *in, with*) place (power, etc.) in a person or group. **5** *tr. & intr.* make or become fixed or caught without further movement (*the bullet lodged in his brain; the tide lodges mud in the cavities*). **6** *tr.* **a** provide with sleeping quarters. **b** receive as a guest or inmate. **c** establish as a resident in a house or room or rooms. **7** *intr.* reside or live, esp. as a guest paying for accommodation. **8** *tr.* serve as a habitation for; contain. **9** *tr.* (in *passive*; foll. by *in*) be contained in. **10 a** *tr.* (of wind or rain) flatten (crops). **b** *intr.* (of crops) be flattened in this way. [ME *loge* f. OF *loge* arbor, hut, f. med.L *laubia, lobia* (see LOBBY) f. Gmc]

lodg•er /lójər/ *n.* a person receiving accommodation in another's house for payment.

lodg•ing /lójing/ *n.* **1** temporary accommodation (*a lodging for the night*). **2** (in *pl.*) esp. *Brit.* a room or rooms (other than in a hotel) rented for lodging in. **3** a dwelling place. **4** *Brit.* (in *pl.*) the residence of a head of a college at Oxford. □ **lodging house** a house in which lodgings are let.

lodg•ment /lójmənt/ *n.* (also esp. *Brit.* **lodge•ment**) **1** a place in which a person or thing is located, deposited, or lodged. **2** the depositing of money in a particular bank, account, etc. **3** *Mil.* a temporary defensive work made on a captured part of an enemy's fortifications to make good a position and provide protection. [F *logement* (as LODGE)]

lod•i•cule /lódiky l/ *n. Bot.* a small green or white scale below the ovary of a grass flower. [L *lodicula* dimin. of *lodix* coverlet]

lo•ess /lóis, les, lus/ *n.* a deposit of fine, light-colored windblown dust found esp. in the basins of large rivers and very fertile when irrigated. □□ **lo•ess•i•al** /ló-éseeəl, léseeəl, lús–/ *adj.* [G *Löss* f. Swiss G *lösch* loose f. *lösen* loosen]

loft /lawft, loft/ *n. & v.* • *n.* **1** the space under the roof of a house, above the ceiling of the top floor; an attic. **2** a room over a stable, esp. for hay and straw. **3** a gallery in a church or hall (*organ loft*). **4** an upstairs room. **5** a pigeon house. **6** *Golf* a backward slope in a club head. **b** a lofting stroke. • *v.tr.* **1 a** send (a ball, etc.) high up. **b** clear (an obstacle) in this way. **2** (esp. as **lofted** *adj.*) give a loft to (a golf club). [OE f. ON *lopt* air, sky, upper room, f. Gmc (as LIFT)]

loft•er /láwftər, lóf–/ *n.* a golf club for lofting the ball.

loft•y /láwftee, lóf–/ *adj.* (**loft•i•er, loft•i•est**) **1** *literary* (of things) of imposing height; towering; soaring (*lofty heights*). **2** consciously haughty, aloof, or dignified (*lofty contempt*). **3** exalted or noble; sublime (*lofty ideals*). □□ **loft•i•ly** *adv.* **loft•i•ness** *n.* [ME f. LOFT as in *aloft*]

log[1] /lawg, log/ *n. & v.* • *n.* **1** an unhewn piece of a felled tree, or a similar rough mass of wood, esp. cut for firewood. **2 a** a float attached to a line wound on a reel for gauging the speed of a ship. **b** any other apparatus for the same purpose. **3** a record of events occurring during and affecting the voyage of a ship or aircraft (including the rate of a ship's progress shown by a log: see sense 2). **4** any systematic record of things done, experienced, etc. **5** = LOGBOOK. • *v.tr.* (**logged, log•ging**) **1 a** enter (the distance made or other details) in a ship's logbook. **b** enter details about (a person or event) in a logbook. **c** (of a ship) achieve (a certain distance). **2 a** enter (information) in a regular record. **b** attain (a cumulative total of time, etc., recorded in this way) (*logged 50 hours on the computer*). **3** cut into logs. □ **like a log 1** in a helpless or stunned state (*fell like a log under the left hook*). **2** without stirring (*slept like a log*). **log in** = *log on.* **log on** (or *off*) go through the procedures to begin (or conclude) use of a computer system. [ME: orig. unkn.]

log[2] /lawg, log/ *n.* a logarithm (esp. prefixed to a number or algebraic symbol whose logarithm is to be indicated). [abbr.]

-log var. of –LOGUE.

lo•gan /lógən/ *n.* (in full **logan stone**) a poised heavy stone rocking at a touch. [= *logging* f. dial. *log* to rock + STONE]

lo•gan•ber•ry /lógənberee/ *n.* (*pl.* **-ries**) **1** a hybrid, *Rubus loganobaccus,* between a blackberry and a raspberry with dull red acid fruits. **2** the fruit of this plant. [J. H. *Logan,* Amer. horticulturalist d. 1928 + BERRY]

log•a•rithm /láwgərithəm, lóg–/ *n.* **1** one of a series of arithmetic exponents tabulated to simplify computation by making it possible to use addition and subtraction instead of multiplication and division. **2** the power to which a fixed number or base (see BASE[1] 7) must be raised to produce a given number (*the logarithm of 1,000 to base 10 is 3*). ¶ Abbr.: **log.** □□ **log•a•rith•mic** /–ríthmik/ *adj.* **log•a•rith•mi•cal•ly** *adv.* [mod.L *logarithmus* f. Gk *logos* reckoning, ratio + *arithmos* number]

log•book /láwgb k, lóg–/ *n.* a book containing a detailed record or log.

loge /lózh/ *n.* (in a theater, etc.) **1** the front section of the first balcony. **2** a private box or enclosure. [F]

-loger /ləjər/ *comb. form* forming nouns, = –LOGIST. [after *astrologer*]

log•ger /láwgər, lóg–/ *n.* a lumberjack.

log•ger•head /láwgərhed, lóg–/ *n.* **1** an iron instrument with a ball at the end heated for melting tar, etc. **2** any of various large-headed animals, esp. a turtle (*Caretta caretta*) or shrike (*Lanius ludovicianus*). **3** *archaic* a blockhead or fool. □ **at loggerheads** (often foll. by *with*) disagreeing or disputing. [prob. f. dial. *logger* block of wood for hobbling a horse + HEAD]

log•gia /lójeeə, láwj–/ *n.* **1** an open-sided gallery or arcade. **2** an open-sided extension of a house. [It., = LODGE]

log•ging /láwging, lóg–/ *n.* the work of cutting and preparing forest timber.

lo•gi•a *pl.* of LOGION.

log•ic /lójik/ *n.* **1 a** the science of reasoning, proof, thinking, or inference. **b** a particular scheme of or treatise on this. **2 a** a chain of reasoning (*I don't follow your logic*). **b** the correct or incorrect use of reasoning (*your logic is flawed*). **c** ability in reasoning (*argues with great learning and logic*). **d** arguments (*is not governed by logic*). **3 a** the inexorable force or compulsion of a thing (*the logic of events*). **b** the necessary consequence of (an argument, decision, etc.). **4 a** a system or set of principles underlying the arrangements of elements in a computer or electronic device so as to perform a specified task. **b** logical operations collectively. □□ **lo•gi•cian** /ləjíshən/ *n.* [ME f. OF *logique* f. LL *logica* f. Gk *logikē* (*tekhnē*) (art) of reason: see LOGOS]

-logic /lójik/ *comb. form* (also **–logical** /lójikəl/) forming adjectives corresponding esp. to nouns in –*logy* (*analogic; theological*). [from or after Gk –*logikos*: see –IC, –ICAL]

log•i•cal /lójikəl/ *adj.* **1** of logic or formal argument. **2** not contravening the laws of thought; correctly reasoned. **3** deducible or defensible on the grounds of consistency; reasonably to be believed or done. **4** capable of correct reasoning. □□ **log•i•cal•i•ty** /–kálitee/ *n.* **log•i•cal•ly** *adv.* [med.L *logicalis* f. LL *logica* (as LOGIC)]

log•i•cal at•om•ism *n. Philos.* the theory that all propositions can be analyzed into simple independent elements.

log•i•cal ne•ces•si•ty *n.* the compulsion to believe that of which the opposite is inconceivable.

log•i•cal pos•i•tiv•ism *n.* (also **log•i•cal em•pir•i•cism**) a form of positivism in which symbolic logic is used and linguistic problems of meaning are emphasized.

lo•gi•on /lógeeon, –jee–/ *n.* (*pl.* **lo•gi•a** /–geeə/) a saying attributed to Christ, esp. one not recorded in the canonical Gospels. [Gk, = oracle f. *logos* word]

-logist /ləjist/ *comb. form* forming nouns denoting a person skilled or involved in a branch of study, etc., with a name in –*logy* (*archaeologist; etymologist*).

lo•gis•tics /ləjístiks/ *n.pl.* **1** the organization of moving, lodging, and supplying troops and equipment. **2** the detailed organization and implementation of a plan or operation. □□ **lo•gis•tic** *adj.* **lo•gis•ti•cal** *adj.* **lo•gis•ti•cal•ly** *adv.* [F *logistique* f. *loger* lodge]

log•jam /láwgjam, lóg–/ *n.* **1** a crowded mass of logs in a river. **2** a deadlock.

lo•go /lógō/ *n.* (*pl.* **-gos**) *colloq.* **1** = LOGOTYPE 2. **2** a motto, esp. of a commercial product, etc. [abbr.]

log•o•gram /láwgəgram, lóg–/ *n.* a sign or character representing a word, esp. in shorthand. [Gk *logos* word + –GRAM]

lo•gom•a•chy /ləgóməkee/ *n.* (*pl.* **-chies**) *literary* a dispute about words; controversy turning on merely verbal points. [Gk *logomakhia* f. *logos* word + *makhia* fighting]

log•or•rhe•a /láwgəreeə, lóg–/ *n.* (*Brit.* **log•or•rhoe•a**) an excessive flow of words, esp. in mental illness. □□ **log•or•rhe•ic** *adj.* [Gk *logos* word + *rhoia* flow]

Lo•gos /lógōs, lógos/ *n. Theol.* the Word of God, associated with the second person of the Trinity. [Gk, = word, reason]

log•o•type /láwgətip, lóg–/ *n.* **1** *Printing* a single piece of type that prints a word or group of separate letters. **2 a** an emblem or device used as the badge of an organization in display material. **b** *Printing* a single piece of type that prints this. [Gk *logos* word + TYPE]

log•roll•ing /láwgrōling, lóg–/ *n.* **1** *colloq.* the practice of exchanging favors, esp. (in politics) of exchanging votes to mutual benefit. **2** a sport in which two contestants stand on a floating log and try to knock each other off. □□ **log•roll** *v.intr. & tr.* **log•roll•er** *n.* [polit. sense f. phr. *you roll my log and I'll roll yours*]

log ta•ble *n.* (usu. in *pl.*) a table of logarithms.

-logue /lawg, log/ *comb. form* (also **–log**) **1** forming nouns denoting talk (*dialogue*) or compilation (*catalog*). **2** = –LOGIST (*ideologue*). [from or after F –*logue* f. Gk –*logos, –logon*]

log·wood /láwgwo͝od, lóg–/ *n.* **1** a W. Indian tree, *Haematoxylon campechianum.* **2** the wood of this, producing a substance used in dyeing.

-logy /ləjee/ *comb. form* forming nouns denoting: **1** (usu. as **–ology**) a subject of study or interest (*archaeology; zoology*). **2** a characteristic of speech or language (*tautology*). **3** discourse (*trilogy*). [F *–logie* or med.L *–logia* f. Gk (as LOGOS)]

loin /loyn/ *n.* **1** (in *pl.*) the part of the body on both sides of the spine between the false ribs and the hipbones. **2** a cut of meat that includes the loin vertebrae. [ME f. OF *loigne* ult. f. L *lumbus*]

loin·cloth /lóynklawth, –kloth/ *n.* a cloth worn around the loins, esp. as a sole garment.

loi·ter /lóytər/ *v.* **1** *intr.* hang around; linger idly. **2** *intr.* travel indolently and with long pauses. **3** *tr.* (foll. by *away*) pass (time, etc.) in loitering. □□ **loi·ter·er** *n.* [ME f. MDu. *loteren* wag about]

loll /lol/ *v.* **1** *intr.* stand, sit, or recline in a lazy attitude. **2** *intr.* (foll. by *out*) (of the tongue) hang out. **3** *tr.* (foll. by *out*) hang (one's tongue) out. **4** *tr.* let (one's head or limbs) rest lazily on something. □□ **loll·er** *n.* [ME: prob. imit.]

Lol·lard /lólərd/ *n.* any of the followers of the 14th-c. religious reformer John Wyclif. □□ **Lol·lard·ism** *n.* [MDu. *lollaerd* f. *lollen* mumble]

lol·li·pop /lóleepop/ *n.* a large, usu. flat, round candy on a small stick. [perh. f. dial. *lolly* tongue + POP[1]]

lol·lop /lóləp/ *v.intr. colloq.* **1** flop about. **2** esp. *Brit.* move or proceed in a lounging or ungainly way. [prob. f. LOLL, assoc. with TROLLOP]

lol·ly /lólee/ *n.* (*pl.* **·lies**) *colloq.* **a** a lollipop. **b** *Austral.* a piece of candy. **c** (in full **ice lol·ly**) *Brit.* = POPSICLE. **2** *Brit. sl.* money. [abbr. of LOLLIPOP]

lol·ly·gag /lóleegag/ *v.intr.* (also **lal·ly·gag** /láleegag/) (**·gagged**, **·gagging**) *sl.* **1** loiter. **2** cuddle amorously. [20th c.: orig. unkn.]

Lom·bard /lómbaard, –bərd, lúm–/ *n. & adj.* ●*n.* **1** a member of a Germanic people who conquered Italy in the 6th c. **2** a native of Lombardy in N. Italy. **3** the dialect of Lombardy. ●*adj.* of or relating to the Lombards or Lombardy. □□ **Lom·bar·dic** /–bárdik/ *adj.* [ME f. OF *lombard* or MDu. *lombaerd*, f. It. *lombardo* f. med.L *Longobardus* f. L *Langobardus* f. Gmc]

Lom·bard·y pop·lar /lómberdee, lúm–/ *n.* a variety of poplar with an especially tall slender form.

lo·ment /lómént/ *n. Bot.* a kind of pod that breaks up when mature into one-seeded joints. □□ **lo·men·ta·ceous** /–táyshəs/ *adj.* [L *lomentum* bean meal (orig. cosmetic) f. *lavare* wash]

Lon·don·er /lúndənər/ *n.* a native or inhabitant of London.

Lon·don plane /lúndən/ *n.* a hybrid plane tree resistant to air pollution and therefore often planted in cities.

lone /lōn/ *attrib.adj.* **1** (of a person) solitary; without a companion or supporter. **2** (of a place) unfrequented; uninhabited; lonely. **3** *literary* feeling or causing to feel lonely. [ME, f. ALONE]

lone hand *n.* **1** a hand played or a player playing against the rest in certain card games. **2** a person or action without allies.

lone·li·ness /lónleenis/ *n.* a feeling of sadness because one is without friends or company.

lone·ly /lónlee/ *adj.* (**lone·li·er, lone·li·est**) **1** solitary; companionless; isolated. **2** (of a place) unfrequented. **3** sad because without friends or company.

lone·ly-hearts *adj.* of or relating to people looking for a lover or friend by advertising in a newspaper (*lonely hearts column*).

lon·er /lónər/ *n.* a person or animal that prefers not to associate with others.

lone·some /lónsəm/ *adj.* **1** solitary; lonely. **2** feeling lonely or forlorn. **3** causing such a feeling. □ **by** (or **on**) **one's lonesome** all alone. □□ **lone·some·ly** *adv.* **lone·some·ness** *n.*

lone wolf *n.* a person who prefers to act alone.

long[1] /lawng, long/ *adj., n., & adv.* ●*adj.* (**long·er** /láwnggər, lóng–/; **long·est** /láwnggist, lóng–/) **1** measuring much from end to end in space or time; not soon traversed or finished (*a long line; a long journey; a long time ago*). **2** (following a measurement) in length or duration (*three miles long; the vacation is two months long*). **3** relatively

great in extent or duration (*a long meeting*). **4 a** consisting of a large number of items (*a long list*). **b** seemingly more than the stated amount; tedious; lengthy (*ten long miles; tired after a long day*). **5** of elongated shape. **6 a** lasting or reaching far back or forward in time (*a long friendship*). **b** (of a person's memory) retaining things for a long time. **7** far-reaching; acting at a distance; involving a great interval or difference. **8** *Phonet. & Prosody* of a vowel or syllable: **a** having the greater of the two recognized durations. **b** stressed. **c** (of a vowel in English) having the pronunciation shown in the name of the letter (as in *pile* and *cute*, which have a long *i* and *u*, as distinct from *pill* and *cut*) (cf. SHORT *adj.* 6). **9** (of odds or a chance) reflecting or representing a low level of probability. **10** *Stock Exch.* **a** (of stocks) bought in large quantities in advance, with the expectation of a rise in price. **b** (of a broker, etc.) buying, etc., on this basis. **11** (of a bill of exchange) maturing at a distant date. **12** (of a cold drink) large and refreshing. **13** *colloq.* (of a person) tall. **14** (foll. by *on*) *colloq.* well supplied with. ●*n.* **1** a long interval or period (*shall not be away for long; it will not take long*). **2** *Phonet.* **a** a long syllable or vowel. **b** a mark indicating that a vowel is long. **3 a** long-dated stock. **b** a person who buys this. ●*adv.* (**long·er** /lónggər/; **long·est** /lónggist/) **1** by or for a long time (*long before; long ago; long live the king!*). **2** (following nouns of duration) throughout a specified time (*all day long*). **3** (in *compar.*; with *neg.*) after an implied point of time (*shall not wait any longer*). ● **as** (or **so**) **long as 1** during the whole time that. **2** provided that; only if. **at long last** see LAST[1]. **before long** fairly soon (*shall see you before long*). **be long** (often foll. by *pres. part.* or *in* + verbal noun) take a long time; be slow (*was long finding it out; the chance was long in coming; I won't be long*). **by a long chalk** *Brit.* see CHALK. **in the long run 1** over a long period. **2** eventually; finally. **long ago** in the distant past. **the long and the short of it 1** all that can or need be said. **2** the eventual outcome. **long in the tooth** rather old (orig. of horses, from the recession of the gums with age). **not by a long shot** by no means. □□ **long·ish** *adj.* [OE *long, lang*]

long[2] /lawng, long/ *v.intr.* (foll. by *for* or *to* + infin.) have a strong wish or desire for. [OE *langian* seem long to]

long. *abbr.* longitude.

-long /lawng, long/ *comb. form* forming adjectives and adverbs: **1** for the duration of (*lifelong*). **2** = –LING[2] (*headlong*).

long-a·go *adj.* that is in the distant past.

long·board /láwngbawrd, lóng–/ *n.* a type of surfboard.

long·boat /láwngbōt, lóng–/ *n.* a sailing ship's largest boat.

long·bow /láwngbō, lóng–/ *n.* a bow drawn by hand and shooting a long feathered arrow.

long-case clock *n.* a grandfather clock.

long-chain *adj.* (of a molecule) containing a chain of many carbon atoms.

long-day *adj.* (of a plant) needing a long daily period of light to cause flowering.

long-dis·tance *adj.* **1** (of a telephone call, public transport, etc.) between distant places. **2** (of a weather forecast) long-range.

long di·vi·sion *n.* arithmetical division in which the divisor has two or more figures, and the details of the calculations are written down.

long doz·en *n.* thirteen; baker's dozen.

long-drawn *adj.* (also **long-drawn-out**) prolonged, esp. unduly.

longe /lonj/ *n. & v.* (also **lunge** /lunj/) ●*n.* **1** a long rope on which a horse is held and made to move in a circle around its trainer. **2** a circular exercise ground for training horses. ● *v. tr.* exercise (a horse) with or in a lunge. [F *longe, allonge* (as LUNGE[1])]

lon·ge·ron /lónjərən/ *n.* a longitudinal member of a plane's fuselage. [F, = girder]

lon·gev·i·ty /lonjévitee, lawn–/ *n.* long life. [LL *longaevitas* f. L *longus* long + *aevum* age]

long face *n.* a dismal or disappointed expression. □□ **long-faced** *adj.*

long·hair /láwnghair, lóng–/ *n.* a person characterized by the associations of long hair, esp. a hippie or intellectual.

long·hand /láwnghand, lóng–/ *n.* ordinary handwriting (as opposed to shorthand or typing or printing).

long haul *n.* **1** the transport of goods or passengers over a long distance. **2** a prolonged effort or task.

long-head·ed /láwnghedid, lóng–/ *adj.* shrewd; far-seeing; sagacious. □□ **long-head·ed·ness** *n.*

long·horn /láwnghawrn, lóng–/ *n.* **1** one of a breed of cattle with long horns. **2** any beetle of the family Cerambycidae with long antennae.

long·house /láwnghows, lóng–/ *n.* a tribal communal dwelling, esp. in N. America and the Far East.

long hun·dred·weight *n.* see HUNDREDWEIGHT.

lon·gi·corn /lónjikawrn/ *n.* a longhorn beetle. [mod.L *longicornis* f. L *longus* long + *cornu* horn]

long·ing /láwnging, lóng–/ *n. & adj.* ● *n.* a feeling of intense desire. ● *adj.* having or showing this feeling. □□ **long·ing·ly** *adv.*

lon·gi·tude /lónjitōōd, –tyōōd, láwn–/ *n.* **1** *Geog.* the angular distance east or west from a standard meridian such as Greenwich to the meridian of any place. ¶ Symb.: λ. **2** *Astron.* the angular distance of a celestial body north or south of the ecliptic measured along a great circle through the body and the poles of the ecliptic. [ME f. L *longitudo –dinis* f. *longus* long]

longitude

lon·gi·tu·di·nal /lónjitōōd'nəl, –tyōōd–, láwn–/ *adj.* **1** of or in length. **2** running lengthwise. **3** of longitude. □□ **lon·gi·tu·di·nal·ly** *adv.*

lon·gi·tu·di·nal wave *n.* a wave vibrating in the direction of propagation.

long johns *n. pl. colloq.* = LONG UNDERWEAR.

long jump *n.* a track-and-field contest of jumping as far as possible along the ground in one leap.

long-life *adj. Brit.* (of consumable goods) treated to preserve freshness.

long-lived *adj.* having a long life; durable.

PRONUNCIATION TIP | **long-lived**

In compound words such as *long-lived* and *short-lived*, the historically correct pronunciation of *-lived* is with a "long i," since it is derived from the noun *life* rather than the verb *live*. But the "short i" pronunciation, a 20th-century variant, has now taken hold. Both pronunciations are considered acceptable.

---

long me·ter *n. Mus.* **1** a hymn stanza of four lines with eight syllables each. **2** a quatrain of iambic tetrameters with alternate lines rhyming.

long-play·ing *adj.* (of a phonograph record) playing for about 20–30 minutes on each side.

long-range *adj.* **1** (of a missile, etc.) having a long range. **2** of or relating to a period of time far into the future.

long-run·ning *adj.* continuing for a long time.

long·ship /láwngship, lóng–/ *n. hist.* a long, narrow warship with many rowers, used esp. by the Vikings.

long·shore /láwngshawr, lóng–/ *adj.* **1** existing on or frequenting the shore. **2** directed along the shore. [*along shore*]

long·shore·man /láwngshawrmən, lóng–/ *n.* (pl. **·men**) a person employed to load and unload ships.

long shot *n.* **1** a wild guess or venture. **2** a bet at long odds. **3** *Cinematog.* a shot including objects at a distance.

long·sight·ed /láwngsítid, lóng–/ *adj.* **1** = FARSIGHTED. **2** having imagination or foresight. □□ **long·sight·ed·ly** *adv.* **long·sight·ed·ness** *n.*

long-stand·ing *adj.* having existed or continued for a long time.

long-suf·fer·ing *adj.* bearing provocation patiently. □□ **long-suf·fer·ing·ly** *adv.*

long suit *n.* **1** many cards of one suit in a hand (esp. more than 3 or 4 in a hand of 13). **2** a thing at which one excels.

long-term *adj.* occurring in or relating to a long period of time (*-long-term plans*).

long·time /láwngtīm, lóng–/ *adj.* that has been such for a long time.

long ton *n.* see TON[1].

lon·gueur /lawNgǿÆr, long–/ *n.* **1** a tedious passage in a book, etc. **2** a tedious stretch of time. [F, = length]

long un·der·wear *n.* a warm, close-fitting undergarment with ankle-length legs and often a long-sleeved top.

long va·ca·tion *n. Brit.* the summer vacation of law courts and universities.

long waist *n.* a low or deep waist on a dress or a person's body.

long wave *n.* a radio wave of frequency less than 300 kHz.

long·ways /láwngwayz, lóng–/ *adv.* (also **long·wise** /–wīz/) = LENGTHWAYS.

long-wind·ed /láwngwíndid, lóng–/ *adj.* **1** (of speech or writing) tediously lengthy. **2** able to run a long distance without rest. □□ **long-wind·ed·ly** *adv.* **long-wind·ed·ness** *n.*

lo·nic·e·ra /lənísərə/ *n.* **1** a dense evergreen shrub, *Lonicera nitidum*, much used as hedging. **2** = HONEYSUCKLE. [A. *Lonicerus*, Ger. botanist d. 1586]

loo[1] /lōō/ *n. Brit. colloq.* a toilet. [20th c.: orig. uncert.]

loo[2] /lōō/ *n.* **1** a card game with penalties paid to the pool. **2** this penalty. [abbr. of obs. *lanterloo* f. F *lanturlu*, refrain of a song]

loof var. of LUFF.

loo·fah /lōōfə/ *n.* (also **luf·fa** /lúfə/) **1** a climbing gourdlike plant, *Luffa cylindrica*, native to Asia, producing edible marrowlike fruits. **2** the dried fibrous vascular system of this fruit used as a sponge. [Egypt. Arab. *lūfa*, the plant]

look /lŏŏk/ *v., n., & int.* ● *v.* **1 a** *intr.* (often foll. by *at*) use one's sight; turn one's eyes in some direction. **b** *tr.* turn one's eyes on; contemplate or examine (*looked me in the eyes*). **2** *intr.* **a** make a visual or mental search (*I'll look in the morning*). **b** (foll. by *at*) consider; examine (*we must look at the facts*). **3** *intr.* (foll. by *for*) **a** search for. **b** hope or be on the watch for. **c** expect. **4** *intr.* inquire (*when one looks deeper*). **5** *intr.* have a specified appearance; seem (*look a fool*; *look foolish*). **6** *intr.* (foll. by *to*) **a** consider; take care of; be careful about (*look to the future*). **b** rely on (a person or thing) (*you can look to me for support*). **c** expect. **7** *intr.* (foll. by *into*) investigate or examine. **8** *tr.* (foll. by *what, where,* etc. + clause) ascertain or observe by sight (*look where we are*). **9** *intr.* (of a thing) face or be turned, or have or afford an outlook, in a specified direction. **10** *tr.* express, threaten, or show (an emotion, etc.) by one's looks. **11** *intr.* (foll. by *that* + clause) take care; make sure. **12** *intr.* (foll. by *to* + infin.) expect (*am looking to finish this today*). ● *n.* **1** an act of looking; the directing of the eyes to look at a thing or person; a glance (*a scornful look*). **2** (in *sing.* or *pl.*) the appearance of a face; a person's expression or personal aspect. **3** the (esp. characteristic) appearance of a thing (*the place has a European look*). **4** (also **look here!**) calling attention, expressing a protest, etc. □ **look after 1** attend to; take care of. **2** follow with the eye. **3** seek for. **look one's age** appear to be as old as one really is. **look alive** (or **lively**) *colloq.* be brisk and alert. **look around 1** look in every or another direction. **2** examine the objects of interest in a place (*you must come and look around sometime*). **3** examine the possibilities, etc., with a view to deciding on a course of action. **look as if** suggested by appearance the belief (*it looks as if he's gone*). **look back 1** (foll. by *on, upon, to*) turn one's thoughts to (something past). **2** (usu. with *neg.*) cease to progress (*since then we have never looked back*). **3** *Brit.* make a further visit later. **look before you leap** avoid precipitate action. **look daggers** see DAGGER. **look down on** (or **upon** or **look down one's nose at**) regard with contempt or a feeling of superiority. **look for trouble** see TROUBLE. **look forward to** await (an expected event) eagerly or with specified feelings. **look in** make a short visit or call. **look a person in the eye** (or **eyes** or **face**) look directly and unashamedly at him or her. **look like 1** have the appearance of. **2** *Brit.* seem to be (*they look like winning*). **3** threaten or promise (*it looks like rain*). **4** indicate the presence of (*it looks like woodworm*). **look on 1** (often foll. by *as*) regard (*looks on you as a friend; looked on them with disfavor*). **2** be a spectator; avoid participation. **look oneself** appear in good health (esp. after illness, etc.). **look out 1** direct one's sight or put one's head out of a window, etc. **2** (often foll. by *for*) be vigilant or prepared. **3** (foll. by *on, over,* etc.) have or afford a specified outlook. **4** search for and produce (*shall look one out for you*). **look over 1** inspect or survey (*looked over the house*). **2** examine (a document, etc.), esp. cursorily (*I'll look it over*). **look sharp** act promptly; make haste (orig. = keep strict watch). **look small** see SMALL. **look through 1** examine the contents of, esp. cursorily. **2** penetrate (a pretense or pretender) with insight. **3** ignore by pretending not to see (*I waved, but you just looked through me*). **look up 1** search for (esp. information in a book). **2** *colloq.* go to visit (a person) (*had intended to look them up*). **3** raise one's eyes (*looked up when I went in*). **4** improve, esp. in price, prosperity, or well-being (*things are looking up*). **look a person up and down** scrutinize a person keenly or contemptuously. **look up to** respect or venerate. **not like the look of** find alarming or suspicious. □□ **–look•ing** *adj.* (in *comb.*). [OE *lōcian* f. WG]

look-a•like *n.* a person or thing closely resembling another (*an Elvis look-alike*).

look•er /lŏŏkər/ *n.* **1** a person having a specified appearance (*a good-looker*). **2** *colloq.* an attractive person.

look•er-on *n.* a person who is a mere spectator.

look-in *n. colloq.* **1** an informal call or visit. **2** *esp. Brit.* a chance of participation or success (*never gets a look-in*). **3** *Football* a short pass pattern in which the receiver runs diagonally toward the center of the field.

look•ing glass /lŏŏking glas/ *n.* a mirror for looking at oneself.

look•out /lŏŏkowt/ *n.* **1** a watch or looking out (*on the lookout for bargains*). **2 a** a post of observation. **b** a person or party or boat stationed to keep watch. **3** a view over a landscape. **4** *esp. Brit.* a prospect of luck (*it's a bad lookout for them*). **5** *colloq.* a person's own concern.

look-see *n. colloq.* a survey or inspection.

loom[1] /lŏŏm/ *n.* an apparatus for weaving yarn or thread into fabric. [ME *lōme* f. OE *gelōma* tool]

loom[2] /lŏŏm/ *v. & n.* ●*v.intr.* (often foll. by *up*) **1** come into sight dimly, esp. as a vague and often magnified or threatening shape. **2** (of an event or prospect) be ominously close. ●*n.* a vague often exaggerated first appearance of land at sea, etc. [prob. f. LG or Du.: cf. E Fris. *lōmen* move slowly, MHG *lüemen* be weary]

loom[1]

loon /lŏŏn/ *n.* **1** any aquatic diving bird of the family Gaviidae, with a long, slender body and a sharp bill; a diver. **2** *colloq.* a crazy person (cf. LOONY). [alt. f. *loom* f. ON *lómr*]

loon•y /lŏŏnee/ *n. & adj. sl.* ●*n.* (*pl.* **-ies**) a mad or silly person; a lunatic. ●*adj.* (**loon•i•er**, **loon•i•est**) crazy; silly. □□ **loon•i•ness** *n.* [abbr. of LUNATIC]

loon•y bin *n. sl.* a mental home or hospital.

loop /lŏŏp/ *n. & v.* ●*n.* **1 a** a figure produced by a curve, or a doubled thread, etc., that crosses itself. **b** anything forming this figure. **2** a similarly shaped attachment or ornament formed of cord or thread, etc., and fastened at the crossing. **3** a ring or curved piece of material as a handle, etc. **4** a contraceptive coil. **5** a railroad or telegraph line that diverges from a main line and joins it again. **6** a maneuver in which an airplane describes a vertical loop. **7** *Skating* a maneuver describing a curve that crosses itself, made on a single edge. **8** *Electr.* a complete circuit for a current. **9** an endless strip of tape or film allowing continuous repetition. **10** *Computing* a programmed sequence of instructions that is repeated until or while a particular condition is satisfied. ●*v.* **1** *tr.* form (thread, etc.) into a loop or loops. **2** *tr.* enclose with or as with a loop. **3** *tr.* (often foll. by *up*, *back*, *together*) fasten or join with a loop or loops. **4** *intr.* **a** form a loop. **b** move in looplike patterns. **5** *intr.* (also **loop the loop**) *Aeron.* perform an aerobatic loop. [ME: orig. unkn.]

loop•er /lŏŏpər/ *n.* **1** a caterpillar of the geometer moth, which progresses by arching itself into loops. **2** a device for making loops. **3** *Baseball* a shallow fly ball to the outfield.

loop•hole /lŏŏp-hōl/ *n. & v.* ●*n.* **1** a means of evading a rule, etc., without infringing the letter of it. **2** a narrow vertical slit in a wall for shooting or looking through or to admit light or air. ●*v.tr.* make loopholes in (a wall, etc.). [ME *loop* in the same sense + HOLE]

loop•y /lŏŏpee/ *adj.* (**loop•i•er**, **loop•i•est**) **1** *sl.* crazy. **2** having many loops.

loose /lŏŏs/ *adj., n., & v.* ●*adj.* **1 a** not or no longer held by bonds or restraint. **b** (of an animal) not confined or tethered, etc. **2** detached or detachable from its place (*has come loose*). **3** not held together or contained or fixed. **4** not specially fastened or packaged (*loose papers; had her hair loose*). **5** hanging partly free (*a loose end*). **6** slack; relaxed; not tense or tight. **7** not compact or dense (*loose soil*). **8** (of language, concepts, etc.) inexact; conveying only the general sense. **9** (preceding an agent noun) doing the expressed action in a loose or careless manner (*a loose thinker*). **10** morally lax; dissolute (*loose living*). **11** (of the tongue) likely to speak indiscreetly. **12** (of the bowels) tending to diarrhea. **13** *Sports* **a** (of a ball) in play but not in any player's possession. **b** (of play, etc.) with the players not close together. **14** *Cricket* **a** (of bowling) inaccurately pitched. **b** (of fielding) careless or bungling. **15** (in *comb.*) loosely (*loose-flowing; loose-fitting*). ●*n.* **1** a state of freedom or unrestrainedness. **2** loose play in soccer (*in the loose*). **3** free expression. ●*v.tr.* **1** release; set free; free from constraint. **2** untie or undo (something that constrains). **3** detach from moorings. **4** relax (*loosed my hold on it*). **5** discharge (a bullet or arrow, etc.). □ **at loose ends** (of a person) unoccupied, esp. temporarily. **on the loose 1** es-

caped from captivity. **2** having a free enjoyable time. **play fast and loose** ignore one's obligations; be unreliable; trifle. □□ **loose•ly** *adv.* **loose•ness** *n.* **loos•ish** *adj.* [ME *lōs* f. ON *lauss* f. Gmc]

loose-leaf *adj. &n.* ●*adj.* (of a notebook, manual, etc.) having each sheet of paper separate and removable. ●*n.* a loose-leaf notebook, etc.

▶The adjective **loose**, meaning 'not tight,' should not be confused with the verb **loose**, which means 'let go' (*they loosed the reins and let the horse gallop*). This verb in turn should not be confused with the verb **lose**, which means 'be deprived of, fail to keep' (*I will lose my keys if I don't mend the hole in my pocket; the neighbors will lose their house if the mortgage is not paid*).

loose-limbed *adj.* having supple limbs.

loos•en /lŏŏsən/ *v.* **1** *tr. & intr.* make or become less tight or compact or firm. **2** *tr.* make (a regime, etc.) less severe. **3** *tr.* release (the bowels) from constipation. **4** *tr.* relieve (a cough) from dryness. □ **loosen a person's tongue** make a person talk freely. **loosen up** = *limber up* (see LIMBER[1]). □□ **loos•en•er** *n.*

loose•strife /lŏŏs-strīf/ *n.* **1** any marsh plant of the genus *Lysimachia*, esp. the golden or yellow loosestrife, *L. vulgaris*. **2** any plant of the genus *Lythrum*, esp. the purple loosestrife, *L. salicaria*, with racemes of star-shaped purple flowers. [LOOSE + STRIFE, taking the Gk name *lusimakhion* (f. *Lusimakhos*, its discoverer) as if directly f. *luō* undo + *makhē* battle]

loot /lŏŏt/ *n. & v.* ●*n.* **1** goods taken from an enemy; spoil. **2** booty; illicit gains made by an official. **3** *sl.* money. ●*v.* **1** *tr.* rob (premises) or steal (goods) left unprotected, esp. after riots or other violent events. **2** plunder or sack (a city, building, etc.). **3** carry off as booty. □□ **loot•er** *n.* [Hindi *lūt*]

lop[1] /lop/ *n. & v.* ●*v.* (**lopped**, **lop•ping**) **1** *tr.* **a** (often foll. by *off*, *away*) cut or remove (a part or parts) from a whole, esp. branches from a tree. **b** remove branches from (a tree). **2** *tr.* (often foll. by *off*, *away*) remove (items) as superfluous. **3** *intr.* (foll. by *at*) make lopping strokes on (a tree, etc.). ●*n.* parts lopped off, esp. branches and twigs of trees. □□ **lop•per** *n.* [ME f. OE *loppian* (unrecorded): cf. obs. *lip* to prune]

lop[2] /lop/ *v.* (**lopped**, **lop•ping**) **1** *intr. & tr.* hang limply. **2** *intr.* (foll. by *about*) slouch; dawdle; hang about. **3** *intr.* move with short bounds. **4** *tr.* (of an animal) let (the ears) hang. □ **lop-eared** (of an animal) having drooping ears. □□ **lop•py** *adj.* [rel. to LOB]

lope /lōp/ *v. & n.* ●*v.intr.* (esp. of animals) run with a long bounding stride. ●*n.* a long bounding stride. [ME, var. of Sc. *loup* f. ON *hlaupa* LEAP]

lopho- /lófŏ, lófō/ *comb. form Zool.* crested. [Gk *lophos* crest]

loph•o•branch /lófəbrangk, lō–/ *adj.* (of a fish) having the gills arranged in tufts. [LOPHO- + BRANCHIA]

loph•o•dont /lófədont, lō–/ *n. & adj.* ●*adj.* having transverse ridges on the grinding surface of molar teeth. ●*n.* an animal with these teeth. [LOPHO- + Gk *odous odont-* tooth]

loph•o•phore /lófəfawr, lō–/ *n.* a tentacled disk at the mouth of bryozoans and brachiopods.

lop•o•lith /lópəlith/ *n. Geol.* a large, saucer-shaped intrusion of igneous rock. [Gk *lopas* basin + –LITH]

lop-sid•ed /lópsídid/ *adj.* with one side lower or smaller than the other; unevenly balanced. □□ **lop-sid•ed•ly** *adv.* **lop-sid•ed•ness** *n.* [LOP[2] + SIDE]

lo•qua•cious /lōkwáyshəs/ *adj.* **1** talkative. **2** (of birds or water) chattering; babbling. □□ **lo•qua•cious•ly** *adv.* **lo•qua•cious•ness** *n.* **lo•quac•i•ty** /–kwásitee/ *n.* [L *loquax –acis* f. *loqui* talk]

lo•quat /lókwot/ *n.* **1** a rosaceous tree, *Eriobotrya japonica*, bearing small, yellow egg-shaped fruits. **2** this fruit. [Chin. dial. *luh kwat* rush orange]

lo•qui•tur /lókwitŏŏr/ *v.intr.* (abbrev. **loq.**) (he or she) speaks (with the speaker's name following, as a stage direction or to inform the reader). [L, from *loqui* talk, speak]

lor /lawr/ *int. Brit. sl.* an exclamation of surprise or dismay. [abbr. of LORD]

lo•ran /láwran/ *n.* a system of long-distance navigation in which position is determined from the intervals between signal pulses received from widely spaced radio transmitters. [*long-range navigation*]

lord /lawrd/ *n., int., & v.* ●*n.* **1** a master or ruler. **2** *hist.* a feudal superior, esp. of a manor. **3** (in the UK) a peer of the realm or a person entitled to the title *Lord*, esp. a marquess, earl, viscount, or baron. **4** (**Lord**) (often prec. by *the*) a name for God or Christ. **5** (**Lord**) **a** prefixed as the designation of a marquess, earl, viscount, or baron. **b** prefixed to the Christian name of the younger son of a duke or marquess. **c** (**the Lords**) = HOUSE OF LORDS. **6** *Astrol.* the ruling planet (of a sign, house, or chart). ●*int.* (**Lord**) expressing surprise, dismay, etc. ●*v.tr.* confer the title of Lord upon. □ **live like a lord** live sumptuously. **lord it over** domineer. **lord over** (usu. in *passive*) domineer; rule over. □□ **lord•less** *adj.* **lord•like** *adj.* [OE *hlāford* f. *hlāfweard* = loaf-keeper (as LOAF[1], WARD)]

Lord Chan•cel•lor *n.* (also **Lord High Chan•cel•lor**) (in the UK) the highest officer of the Crown, presiding in the House of Lords, etc.

Lord Chief Jus•tice *n.* (in the UK) the president of the Queen's Bench Division.

lord•ling /láwrdling/ n. usu. *derog.* a minor lord.

lord•ly /láwrdlee/ adj. (**lord•li•er**, **lord•li•est**) **1** haughty; imperious. **2** suitable for a lord. □□ **lord•li•ness** n. [OE *hláfordlic* (as LORD)]

lord may•or n. the title of the mayor in London and some other large cities.

lor•do•sis /lawrdósis/ n. *Med.* inward curvature of the spine (opp. KYPHOSIS). □□ **lor•dot•ic** /–dótik/ adj. [mod.L f. Gk *lordōsis* f. *lordos* bent backward]

Lord Priv•y Seal n. (in the UK) a senior cabinet minister without official duties.

Lord's Day n. Sunday.

lord•ship /láwrdship/ n. **1** (usu. **Lordship**) a title used in addressing or referring to a man with the rank of Lord or (in the UK) a judge or a bishop (*Your Lordship*; *His Lordship*). **2** (foll. by *of*, *over*) dominion, rule, or ownership. **3** the condition of being a lord. [OE *hláfordscipe* (as LORD, -SHIP)]

Lord's Prayer n. the prayer taught by Jesus to his disciples.

Lords spir•it•u•al n.pl. the bishops in the House of Lords.

Lord's Sup•per n. the Eucharist.

Lords tem•po•ral n.pl. the members of the House of Lords other than the bishops.

Lord•y /láwrdee/ int. = LORD int.

lore[1] /lawr/ n. a body of traditions and knowledge on a subject or held by a particular group (*herbal lore*; *gypsy lore*). [OE *lār* f. Gmc, rel. to LEARN]

lore[2] /lawr/ n. *Zool.* a straplike surface between the eye and upper mandible in birds, or between the eye and nostril in snakes. [L *lorum* strap]

lor•gnette /lawrnyét/ n. (in *sing.* or *pl.*) a pair of eyeglasses or opera glasses held by a long handle. [F f. *lorgner* to squint]

lor•i•cate /láwrikayt, –kit, lór–/ adj. & n. *Zool.* ● adj. having a defensive armor of bone, plates, scales, etc. ● n. an animal with this. [L *loricatus* f. *lorica* breastplate f. *lorum* strap]

lor•i•keet /láwrikeet, lór–/ n. any of various small, brightly colored parrots of the subfamily Loriinae, including the rainbow lorikeet. [dimin. of LORY, after *parakeet*]

lorgnette

lo•ris /láwris/ n. (*pl.* same) either of two small, tailless nocturnal primates, *Loris tardigradus* of S. India (**slender loris**), and *Nycticebus coucang* of the E. Indies (**slow loris**). [F perh. f. obs. Du. *loeris* clown]

lorn /lawrn/ adj. *literary* desolate; forlorn; abandoned. [past part. of obs. *leese* f. OE *-lēosan* lose]

lor•ry /láwree, lór–/ n. (*pl.* **•ries**) **1** a large strong motor vehicle for transporting goods, etc.; a truck. **2** a long flat low wagon. **3** a railway freight car. [19th c.: orig. uncert.]

lo•ry /láwree/ n. (*pl.* **•ries**) any of various brightly colored Australasian parrots of the subfamily Loriinae. [Malay *lūrī*]

lose /lōōz/ v. (*past* and *past part.* **lost** /lawst, lost/) **1** *tr.* be deprived of or cease to have, esp. by negligence or misadventure. **2** *tr.* **a** be deprived of (a person, esp. a close relative) by death. **b** suffer the loss of (a baby) in childbirth. **3** *tr.* become unable to find; fail to keep in sight or follow or mentally grasp (*lose one's way*). **4** *tr.* let or have pass from one's control or reach (*lose one's chance*; *lose one's bearings*). **5** *tr.* be defeated in (a game, race, lawsuit, battle, etc.). **6** *tr.* evade; get rid of (*lost our pursuers*). **7** *tr.* fail to obtain, catch, or perceive (*lose a train*; *lose a word*). **8** *tr.* forfeit (a stake, deposit, right to a thing, etc.). **9** *tr.* spend (time, efforts, etc.) to no purpose (*lost no time in raising the alarm*). **10** *intr.* **a** suffer loss or detriment; incur a disadvantage. **b** be worse off, esp. financially. **11** *tr.* cause (a person) the loss of (*will lose you your job*). **12** *intr.* & *tr.* (of a timepiece) become slow; become slow by (a specified amount of time). **13** *tr.* (in *passive*) **a** disappear; perish; be dead (*was lost in the war*). **b** fall, sin; be damned (*souls lost to drunkenness and greed*). **14** (as **lost** adj.) **a** gone; stray; mislaid; forgotten (*lost valuables*; *a lost art*). **b** dead; destroyed (*lost comrades*). **c** damned; fallen (*lost souls in hell*). □ **be lost** (or **lose oneself**) **in** be engrossed in. **be lost on** be wasted on, or not noticed or appreciated by. **be lost to** be no longer affected by or accessible to (*is lost to pity*; *is lost to the world*). **be lost without** have great difficulty if deprived of (*am lost without my diary*). **get lost** *sl.* (usu. in *imper.*) go away. **lose one's balance 1** fail to remain stable; fall. **2** fail to retain one's composure. **lose one's cool** *colloq.* lose one's composure. **lose face** be humiliated; lose one's credibility. **lose ground** see GROUND[1]. **lose one's head** see HEAD. **lose heart** be discouraged. **lose one's head** see HEART. **lose one's nerve** become timid or irresolute. **lose out** (often foll. by *on*) *colloq.* be unsuccessful; not get a fair chance or advantage (in). **lose sleep over a thing** lie awake worrying about a thing. **lose one's temper** become angry. **lose time** allow time to pass with something unachieved, etc. **lose touch** see TOUCH. **lose track of** see TRACK[1].

lose one's way become lost; fail to reach one's destination. [OE *losian* perish, destroy f. *los* loss]

▶ See note at LOOSE.

los•er /lōōzər/ n. **1** a person or thing that loses or has lost (esp. a contest or game) (*is a poor loser*; *the loser pays*). **2** *colloq.* a person who regularly fails.

los•ing bat•tle n. a contest or effort in which failure seems certain.

loss /laws, los/ n. **1** the act or an instance of losing; the state of being lost. **2** a person, thing, or amount lost. **3** the detriment or disadvantage resulting from losing (*that is no great loss*). □ **at a loss** (sold, etc.) for less than was paid for it. **be at a loss** be puzzled or uncertain. **be at a loss for words** not know what to say. [ME *los*, *loss* prob. back-form. f. *lost*, past part. of LOSE]

loss lead•er n. an item sold at a loss to attract customers.

lost *past* and *past part.* of LOSE.

lost cause n. **1** an enterprise, etc., with no chance of success. **2** a person one can no longer hope to influence.

lost gen•er•a•tion n. **1** (**Lost Generation**) a generation reaching maturity during and just after World War I, a high proportion of whose men were killed during those years. **2** an unfulfilled generation coming to maturity during a period of instability. [phrase applied by Gertrude Stein to disillusioned young American writers such as Ernest Hemingway and F. Scott Fitzgerald, who went to live in Paris in the 1920s.]

lost wax proc•ess n. a method of bronze casting using a clay core and a wax coating placed in a mold: the wax is melted in the mold and bronze poured into the space left, producing a hollow bronze figure when the core is discarded. [F, = lost wax]

lot /lot/ n. & v. ● n. **1** *colloq.* (prec. by *a* or in *pl.*) **a** a large number or amount (*a lot of people*; *lots of chocolate*). **b** *colloq.* much (*a lot warmer*; *smiles a lot*; *is lots better*). **2 a** each of a set of objects used in making a chance selection. **b** this method of deciding (*chosen by lot*). **3** a share, or the responsibility resulting from it. **4** a person's destiny, fortune, or condition. **5** a plot; an allotment of land (*parking lot*). **6** an article or set of articles for sale at an auction, etc. **7** a number or quantity of associated persons or things. ● v. tr. (**lot•ted**, **lot•ting**) divide into lots. □ **cast** (or **draw**) **lots** decide by means of lots. **throw in one's lot with** decide to share the fortunes of. **the** (or **the whole**) **lot** the whole number or quantity. **a whole lot** *colloq.* very much (*is a whole lot better*). [OE *hlot* portion, choice f. Gmc]

▶ There is no such single word as "alot." Always spell it as two words (*she accomplished a lot in two days*).

loth var. of LOATH.

lo•thar•i•o /lōtháireeō/ n. (also **Lo•thar•i•o**) (*pl.* **•os**) a rake or libertine. [a character in Rowe's *Fair Penitent* (1703)]

lo•tion /lóshən/ n. a medicinal or cosmetic liquid preparation applied externally. [ME f. OF *lotion* or L *lotio* f. *lavare lot-* wash]

lot•ter•y /lótəree/ n. (*pl.* **•ies**) **1** a means of raising money by selling numbered tickets and giving prizes to the holders of numbers drawn at random. **2** an enterprise, process, etc., whose success is governed by chance (*life is a lottery*). [prob. f. Du. *loterij* (as LOT)]

lot•to /lótō/ n. a lottery in which players choose or are assigned numbers that they attempt to match against numbers randomly drawn. [It.]

lo•tus /lótəs/ n. **1** (in Greek mythology) a legendary plant inducing luxurious languor when eaten. **2 a** any water lily of the genus *Nelumbo*, esp. *N. nucifera* of India, with large pink flowers. **b** this flower used symbolically in Hinduism and Buddhism. **3** an Egyptian water lily, *Nymphaea lotus*, with white flowers. **4** any plant of the genus *Lotus*, e.g., bird's-foot trefoil. [L f. Gk *lōtos*, of Semitic orig.]

American lotus

lo•tus-eat•er n. a person given to indolent enjoyment.

lo•tus-land /lótəsland/ n. a place of indolent enjoyment. [the land of lotus-eaters in Homer's *Odyssey*]

lo•tus po•si•tion n. a cross-legged position of meditation with the feet resting on the thighs.

louche /lōōsh/ adj. disreputable; shifty. [F, = squinting]

loud /lowd/ adj. & adv. ● adj. **1 a** strongly audible, esp. noisily or oppressively so. **b** able or liable to produce loud sounds (*a loud engine*). **c** clamorous; insistent (*loud complaints*). **2** (of colors, design, etc.) gaudy; obtrusive. **3** (of behavior) aggressive and noisy. ● adv. in a loud manner. □ **out loud 1** aloud. **2** loudly (*laughed out loud*). □□ **loud•en** v.tr. & intr. **loud•ish** adj. **loud•ly** adv. **loud•ness** n. [OE *hlūd* f. WG]

loud•mouth /lówdmowth/ n. *colloq.* a noisily self-assertive, vociferous person. □□ **loud•mouthed** adj.

loud•speak•er /lówdspeekər/ n. an apparatus that converts electrical impulses into sound, esp. music and voice.

Lou Gehr·ig's dis·ease /lōō gérigz/ *n.* see AMYOTROPHIC LATERAL SCLEROSIS.

lough /lok, lokh/ *n. Ir.* = LAKE[1]. [Ir. *loch* LAKE[1], assim. to the related obs. ME form *lough*]

lou·is /lōō-ee/ *n.* (*pl.* same /lōō-eez/) *hist.* (in full **louis d'or** /dawr/) a former French gold coin worth about 20 francs. [*Louis*, the name of kings of France]

lounge /lownj/ *v. & v.intr.* **1** recline comfortably and casually; loll. **2** stand or move about idly. ● *n.* **1** a place for lounging, esp.: **a** a public room (e.g., in a hotel). **b** a place in an airport, etc., with seats for waiting passengers. **c** *Brit.* a sitting room in a house; living room. **2** a spell of lounging. [perh. f. obs. *lungis* lout]

lounge liz·ard *n. colloq.* **1** a person, esp. a man, who frequents bars, etc. **2** an idler in fashionable society.

loupe /lōōp/ *n.* a small magnifying glass used by jewelers, etc. [F]

lour var. of LOWER[3].

louse /lows/ *n. & v.* ● *n.* **1** (*pl.* **lice** /līs/) **a** a parasitic insect, *Pediculus humanus*, infesting the human hair and skin and transmitting various diseases. **b** any insect of the order Anoplura or Mallophaga parasitic on mammals, birds, fish, or plants. **2** *sl.* (*pl.* **lous·es**) a contemptible or unpleasant person. ● *v.tr.* remove lice from. □ **louse up** *sl.* make a mess of. [OE *lūs*, pl. *lȳs*]

louse·wort /lówswərt, –wawrt/ *n.* any plant of the genus *Pedicularis* with purple-pink flowers found in marshes and wet places.

louse (magnified)

lous·y /lówzee/ *adj.* (**lous·i·er, lous·i·est**) **1** infested with lice. **2** *colloq.* very bad; disgusting (also as a term of general disparagement). **3** *colloq.* (often foll. by *with*) well supplied; teeming (with). □□ **lous·i·ly** *adv.* **lous·i·ness** *n.*

lout /lowt/ *n.* a rough, crude, or ill-mannered person (usu. a man). □□ **lout·ish** *adj.* **lout·ish·ly** *adv.* **lout·ish·ness** *n.* [perh. f. archaic *lout* to bow]

lou·ver /lōōvər/ *n.* (also esp. *Brit.* **lou·vre**) **1** each of a set of overlapping slats designed to admit air and some light and exclude rain. **2** a domed structure on a roof with side openings for ventilation, etc. □□ **lou·vered** *adj.* [ME f. OF *lover, lovier* skylight, prob. f. Gmc]

lou·ver boards *n.pl.* the slats or boards making up a louver.

louver 1

lov·a·ble /lúvəbəl/ *adj.* (also **love·a·ble**) inspiring or deserving love or affection. □□ **lov·a·bil·i·ty** *n.* **lov·a·ble·ness** *n.* **lov·a·bly** *adv.*

lov·age /lúvij/ *n.* **1** a S. European herb, *Levisticum officinale*, used for flavoring, etc. **2** a white-flowered umbelliferous plant, *Ligusticum scoticum.* [ME *loveache* alt. f. OF *levesche* f. LL *levisticum* f. L *ligusticum* neut. of *ligusticus* Ligurian]

lov·at /lúvət/ *n.* (also *attrib.*) a muted green color found esp. in tweed and woolen garments. [*Lovat* in Scotland]

love /luv/ *n. & v.* ● *n.* **1** an intense feeling of deep affection or fondness for a person or thing; great liking. **2** sexual passion. **3** sexual relations. **4** a beloved one; a sweetheart (often as a form of address). **b** *Brit. colloq.* a form of address regardless of affection. **5** *colloq.* a person of whom one is fond. **6** affectionate greetings (*give him my love*). **7** (often **Love**) a representation of Cupid. **8** (in some games) no score; nil. ● *v.tr.* **1** (also *absol.*) feel love or deep fondness for. **2** delight in; admire; greatly cherish. **3** *colloq.* like very much (*loves books*). **4** (foll. by verbal noun, or *to* + infin.) be inclined, esp. as a habit; greatly enjoy; find pleasure in (*children love dressing up; loves to find fault*). □ **fall in love** (often foll. by *with*) develop a great (esp. sexual) love (for). **for love** for pleasure not profit. **for the love of** for the sake of. **in love** (often foll. by *with*) deeply enamored (of). **make love** (often foll. by *to*) **1** have sexual intercourse (with). **2** *archaic* pay amorous attention (to). **not for love or money** not in any circumstances. **out of love** no longer in love. □□ **love·wor·thy** *adj.* [OE *lufu* f. Gmc]

love·a·ble var. of LOVABLE.

love af·fair *n.* a romantic or sexual relationship between two people in love; a passion for something.

love ap·ple *n. archaic* a tomato.

love·bird /lúvbərd/ *n.* **1** any of various African and Madagascan parrots, esp. *Agapornis personata.* **2** (in *pl.*) a pair of lovers who display much affection.

love·bite /lúvbīt/ *n. esp. Brit.* = HICKEY 2.

love child *n.* a child born to parents who are not married to each other.

love feast *n. hist.* **1** a meal affirming brotherly love among early Christians. **2** a religious service or gathering imitating this, esp. among early Methodists.

love game *n.* (in tennis and similar sports) a game in which the loser makes no score.

love-hate re·la·tion·ship *n.* an intensely emotional relationship in which one or each party has ambivalent feelings of love and hate for the other.

love-in-a-mist *n.* a blue-flowered garden plant, *Nigella damascena*, with many delicate green bracts.

love·less /lúvlis/ *adj.* without love; unloving or unloved or both. □□ **love·less·ly** *adv.* **love·less·ness** *n.*

love-lies-bleed·ing *n.* a South American garden plant, *Amaranthus caudatus*, with long, drooping tassels of crimson flowers.

love life *n.* one's amorous or sexual relationships.

love·lock /lúvlok/ *n. archaic* a curl or lock of hair worn on the temple or forehead.

love·lorn /lúvlawrn/ *adj.* pining from unrequited love.

love·ly /lúvlee/ *adj. & n.* ● *adj.* (**love·li·er, love·li·est**) **1** exquisitely beautiful. **2** *colloq.* pleasing; delightful. ● *n.* (*pl.* **·lies**) *colloq.* a pretty woman. □□ **love·li·ness** *n.* [OE *luflic* (as LOVE)]

love·mak·ing /lúvmayking/ *n.* **1** amorous sexual activity, esp. sexual intercourse. **2** *archaic* courtship.

love match *n.* a marriage made for love's sake.

love nest *n.* a place where two lovers spend time together, esp. in secret.

lov·er /lúvər/ *n.* **1** a person in love with another. **2** a person with whom another is having sexual relations. **3** (in *pl.*) a couple in love or having sexual relations. **4** a person who likes or enjoys something specified (*a music lover; a lover of words*). □□ **lov·er·less** *adj.*

love seat *n.* an armchair or small sofa for two.

love·sick /lúvsik/ *adj.* languishing with romantic love. □□ **love·sick·ness** *n.*

love·some /lúvsəm/ *adj. literary* lovely; lovable.

lov·ey /lúvee/ *n.* (*pl.* **·eys**) esp. *Brit. colloq.* love; sweetheart (esp. as a form of address).

lov·ey-dov·ey /lúveedúvee/ *adj. colloq.* fondly affectionate, esp. unduly sentimental.

lov·ing /lúving/ *adj. & n.* ● *adj.* feeling or showing love; affectionate. ● *n.* affection; active love. □□ **lov·ing·ly** *adv.* **lov·ing·ness** *n.* [OE *lufiende* (as LOVE)]

lov·ing cup *n.* **1** a two-handled drinking cup passed around at banquets for each guest to drink from in turn.

low[1] /lō/ *adj., n., & adv.* ● *adj.* **1** of less than average height; not high or tall or reaching far up (*a low wall*). **2 a** situated close to ground or sea level, etc.; not elevated in position (*low altitude*). **b** (of the sun) near the horizon. **c** (of latitude) near the equator. **3** of or in humble rank or position (*of low birth*). **4** of small or less than normal amount or extent or intensity (*low price; low temperature; low in calories*). **5** small and reduced in quantity (*stocks are low*). **6** coming below the normal level (*a dress with a low neck*). **7 a** dejected; lacking vigor (*feeling low; in low spirits*). **b** poorly nourished; indicative of poor nutrition. **8** (of a sound) not shrill or loud or high-pitched. **9** not exalted or sublime; commonplace. **10** unfavorable (*a low opinion*). **11** abject; mean; vulgar (*low cunning; low slang*). **12** (in *compar.*) situated on less high land or to the south. **13** (of a geographical period) earlier. ● *n.* **1** a low or the lowest level or number (*the dollar has reached a new low*). **2** an area of low pressure. ● *adv.* **1** in or to a low position or state. **2** in a low tone (*speak low*). **3** (of a sound) at or to a low pitch. □□ **low·ish** *adj.* **low·ness** *n.* [ME *lāh* f. ON *lágr* f. Gmc]

low[2] /lō/ *n. & v.* ● *n.* a sound made by cattle; a moo. ● *v.intr.* utter this sound. [OE *hlōwan* f. Gmc]

low-ball *n. & v.* ● *n. Cards* a type of poker. ● *v.* underestimate or underbid a price (usu. for a service) deliberately.

low beam *n.* an automobile headlight providing short-range illumination.

low-born /lóbawrn/ *adj.* born to a family that has a low social status.

low·boy /lóboy/ *n.* a low chest or table with drawers and short legs.

low·brow /lóbrow/ *adj. & n.* ● *adj.* not highly intellectual or cultured. ● *n.* a lowbrow person. □□ **low·browed** *adj.*

Low Church *adj.* the section of the Church of England giving little emphasis to ritual, priestly authority, and the sacraments.

low-class *adj.* of low or inferior standard, quality, or social class.

low com·e·dy *n.* that in which the subject and the treatment border on farce.

Low Coun·tries *n.pl.* the Netherlands, Belgium, and Luxembourg.

low-cut *adj.* (of a dress, etc.) made with a low neckline.

low-down *adj. & n.* ● *adj.* abject; mean; dishonorable. ● *n. colloq.* (usu. foll. by *on*) the relevant information (about).

low·er[1] /lóər/ *adj. & adv.* ● *adj.* (*compar.* of LOW[1]). **1** less high in position or status. **2** situated below another part (*lower lip; lower atmosphere*). **3 a** situated on less high land (*Lower Egypt*). **b** situated to the south (*Lower California*). **4** (of a mammal, plant, etc.) evolved to a relatively small degree (e.g., a platypus or fungus). ● *adv.* in or to a lower position, status, etc. □□ **low·er·most** *adj.*

low·er[2] /lóər/ *v.* **1** *tr.* let or haul down. **2** *tr. & intr.* make or become lower. **3** *tr.* reduce the height or pitch of (*lower your voice; lower one's eyes*). **4** *tr.* degrade. **5** *tr. & intr.* diminish.

low·er[3] /lówər/ *v. & n.* (also **lour**) ● *v.intr.* **1** frown; look sullen. **2** (of the sky, etc.) look dark and threatening. ● *n.* **1** a scowl. **2** a gloomy look (of the sky, etc.). □□ **low•er•ing•ly** *adv.* **low•er•y** *adj.* [ME *loure*, of unkn. orig.]

low•er•case /lṓərkays/ *n., adj., & v.* ● *n.* small letters (as in contrast to capital letters). ● *adj.* of or having small letters. ● *v.tr.* print or write in lowercase.

low•er class *n.* working-class people and their families. □□ **low•er-class** *adj.*

low•er crit•i•cism *n.* textual criticism of the Bible.

low•er deck *n.* **1** the deck of a ship situated immediately over the hold. **2** the petty officers and men of a ship collectively.

low•er house *n.* the usu. larger body in a legislature, esp. in Britain, the House of Commons.

low•er re•gions *n.* (also **low•er world**) *archaic* hell or the underworld.

low•est com•mon de•nom•i•na•tor *n. Math.* the lowest common multiple of the denominators of several fractions.

low•est com•mon mul•ti•ple *n. Math.* the lowest quantity that is a multiple of two or more given quantities (e.g., 12 is the lowest common multiple of 2, 3, and 4).

low fre•quen•cy *n.* (in radio) 30–300 kilohertz.

Low Ger•man *n.* a vernacular language spoken in much of northern Germany, more closely related to Dutch than to standard German.

low-grade *adj.* of low quality or strength.

low-key *adj.* lacking intensity or prominence; restrained.

low•land /lṓlənd/ *n. & adj.* ● *n.* **1** (usu. in *pl.*) low-lying country. **2** (**Lowland**) (usu. in *pl.*) the region of Scotland lying south and east of the Highlands. ● *adj.* of or in lowland or the Scottish Lowlands. □□ **low•land•er** *n.* (also **Low•land•er**).

Low Lat•in *n.* medieval and later forms of Latin.

low lat•i•tudes *n.pl.* regions near the equator.

low-lev•el *adj.* **1** showing a small degree of some measurable quantity (*low-level radioactive waste*). **2** *Computing* (of a programming language) close in form to machine code.

low•life *n.* people or activities characterized as being disreputable and often criminal.

low•light /lṓlīt/ *n.* **1** a monotonous or dull period; a feature of little prominence (*one of the lowlights of the evening*). **2** (usu. in *pl.*) a dark tint in the hair produced by dyeing. [after HIGHLIGHT]

low•ly /lṓlee/ *adj.* (**low•li•er**, **low•li•est**) **1** humble in feeling, behavior, or status. **2** modest; unpretentious. **3** (of an organism) evolved to only a slight degree. □□ **low•li•ly** *adv.* **low•li•ness** *n.*

low-ly•ing *adj.* at low altitude (above sea level, etc.).

low Mass *n.* Mass with no music and a minimum of ceremony.

low-mind•ed /lṓmíndid/ *adj.* vulgar or ignoble in mind or character. □□ **low-mind•ed•ness** *n.*

low-pitched *adj.* **1** (of a sound) low. **2** (of a roof) having only a slight slope.

low pro•file *n.* avoidance of attention or publicity. □□ **low-pro•file** *adj.* **1** having a low profile. **2** (of a motor-vehicle tire) having a greater width than usual in relation to height.

low re•lief *n.* = BAS-RELIEF.

low-rise *adj.* (of a building) having few stories.

low spir•its *n.pl.* dejection; depression. □□ **low-spir•it•ed** *adj.* **low-spir•it•ed•ness** *n.*

Low Sun•day *n.* the Sunday after Easter.

low tide *n.* the time or level of the tide at its ebb.

low-wa•ter mark *n.* **1** the level reached by the sea at low tide, or by a lake or river during a drought or dry season. **2** a minimum recorded level or value, etc.

lox¹ /loks/ *n.* liquid oxygen. [abbr.]

lox² /loks/ *n.* smoked salmon. [Yiddish *laks*]

loy•al /lóyəl/ *adj.* **1** (often foll. by *to*) true or faithful (to duty, love, or obligation). **2** steadfast in allegiance; devoted to the legitimate sovereign or government of one's country. **3** showing loyalty. □□ **loy•al•ly** *adv.* [F f. OF *loial*, etc. f. L *legalis* LEGAL]

loy•al•ist /lóyəlist/ *n.* **1** a person who remains loyal to the legitimate sovereign, etc., esp. in the face of rebellion or usurpation. **2** (**Loy•alist**) **a** *hist.* a resident of N. America who supported Great Britain during the American Revolution. **b** a supporter of Parliamentary union between Great Britain and Northern Ireland. □□ **loy•al•ism** *n.*

loy•al•ty /lóyəltee/ *n.* (*pl.* **•ties**) **1** the state of being loyal. **2** (often in *pl.*) a feeling or application of loyalty.

loz•enge /lózinj/ *n.* **1** a rhombus or diamond figure. **2** a small medicinal tablet, originally of this shape, taken for sore throats and dissolved in the mouth. **3** *Heraldry* a charge in the shape of a solid diamond, in particular, one on which the arms of an unmarried or widowed woman are displayed. [ME f. OF *losenge*, ult. of Gaulish or Iberian orig.]

LP *abbr.* **1** long-playing (phonograph record). **2** low pressure.

LPG *abbr.* liquefied petroleum gas.

LPN *abbr.* licensed practical nurse.

LSAT *abbr.* Law School Admissions Test.

LSD *abbr.* lysergic acid diethylamide.

l.s.d. *n.* (also **£.s.d.**) *Brit.* **1** pounds, shillings, and pence (in former British currency). **2** money; riches. [L *librae, solidi, denarii*]

Lt. *abbr.* **1** lieutenant. **2** light.

LTA *abbr.* (of aircraft) lighter-than-air.

Ltd. *abbr.* limited.

Lu *symb. Chem.* the element lutetium.

lub•ber /lúbər/ *n.* a big clumsy fellow; a lout. □□ **lub•ber•like** *adj.* **lub•ber•ly** *adj. & adv.* [ME, perh. f. OF *lobeor* swindler, parasite f. *lober* deceive]

lub•ber line *n. Naut.* a line marked on a compass, showing the ship's forward direction.

lu•bra /lṓbrə/ *n. Austral.* sometimes *derog.* an Aboriginal woman. [F *loubra* f. Tasmanian]

lu•bri•cant /lṓbrikənt/ *n. & adj.* ● *n.* a substance used to reduce friction. ● *adj.* lubricating.

lu•bri•cate /lṓbrikayt/ *v.tr.* **1** reduce friction in (machinery, etc.) by applying oil or grease, etc. **2** make slippery or smooth with oil or grease. □□ **lu•bri•ca•tion** /–káyshən/ *n.* **lu•bri•ca•tive** *adj.* **lu•bri•ca•tor** *n.* [L *lubricare lubricat-* f. *lubricus* slippery]

lu•bri•cious /lṓbríshəs/ *adj.* (also **lu•bri•cous** /lṓbrikəs/) **1** slippery; smooth; oily. **2** lewd; prurient; evasive. □□ **lu•bric•i•ty** /–brísitee/ *n.* [L *lubricus* slippery]

Lu•can /lṓkən/ *adj.* of or relating to St. Luke. [eccl.L *Lucas* f. Gk *Loukas* Luke]

luce /lṓs/ *n.* a pike (fish), esp. when full-grown. [ME f. OF *lus, luis* f. LL *lucius*]

lu•cent /lṓsənt/ *adj. literary* **1** shining; luminous. **2** translucent. □□ **lu•cen•cy** *n.* **lu•cent•ly** *adv.* [L *lucēre* shine (as LUX)]

lu•cerne /lṓsŕn/ *n.* (also **lu•cern**) *Brit.* = ALFALFA. [F *luzerne* f. mod. Prov. *luzerno* glowworm, with ref. to its shiny seeds]

lu•cid /lṓsid/ *adj.* **1** expressing or expressed clearly; easy to understand. **2** of or denoting intervals of sanity between periods of insanity or dementia. **3** *Bot.* with a smooth shining surface. **4** *poet.* bright. □□ **lu•cid•i•ty** /–síditee/ *n.* **lu•cid•ly** *adv.* **lu•cid•ness** *n.* [L *lucidus* (perh. through F *lucide* or It. *lucido*) f. *lucēre* shine (as LUX)]

Lu•ci•fer /lṓsifər/ *n.* **1** Satan. **2** *poet.* the morning star (the planet Venus). **3** (**lucifer**) *archaic* a match struck by rubbing it on a rough surface. [OE f. L, = light-bringing, morning star (as LUX, *–fer* f. *ferre* bring)]

luck /luk/ *n.* **1** chance regarded as the bringer of good or bad fortune. **2** circumstances of life (beneficial or not) brought by this. **3** good fortune; success due to chance (*in luck; out of luck*). □ **for luck** to bring good fortune. **no such luck** *colloq.* unfortunately not. **try one's luck** make a venture. **with luck** if all goes well. **worse luck** *colloq.* unfortunately. [ME f. LG *luk* f. MLG *geluke*]

luck•i•ly /lúkilee/ *adv.* **1** (qualifying a whole sentence or clause) fortunately (*luckily there was enough food*). **2** in a lucky or fortunate manner.

luck•less /lúklis/ *adj.* having no luck; unfortunate. □□ **luck•less•ly** *adv.* **luck•less•ness** *n.*

luck•y /lúkee/ *adj.* (**luck•i•er**, **luck•i•est**) **1** having or resulting from good luck, esp. as distinct from skill or design or merit. **2** bringing good luck (*a lucky mascot*). **3** fortunate; appropriate (*a lucky guess*). □□ **luck•i•ness** *n.*

lu•cra•tive /lṓkrətiv/ *adj.* profitable; yielding financial gain. □□ **lu•cra•tive•ly** *adv.* **lu•cra•tive•ness** *n.* [ME f. L *lucrativus* f. *lucrari* to gain]

lu•cre /lṓkər/ *n. derog.* financial profit or gain. [ME f. F *lucre* or L *lucrum*]

lu•cu•brate /lṓkyoobráyt/ *v.intr. literary* **1** write or study, esp. by night. **2** express one's meditations in writing. □□ **lu•cu•bra•tor** *n.* [L *lucubrare lucubrat-* work by lamplight (as LUX)]

lu•cu•bra•tion /lṓkyoobráyshən/ *n. literary* **1** nocturnal study or meditation. **2** (usu. in *pl.*) literary writings, esp. of a pedantic or elaborate character. [L *lucubratio* (as LUCUBRATE)]

Lu•cul•lan /lṓkúlən/ *adj.* profusely luxurious. [L. Licinius *Lucullus*, Roman general of 1st c. BC famous for his lavish banquets]

Lud•dite /lúdīt/ *n. & adj.* ● *n.* **1** *hist.* a member of any of the bands of English artisans who rioted against mechanization and destroyed machinery (1811–16). **2** a person opposed to increased industrialization or new technology. ● *adj.* of the Luddites or their beliefs. □□ **Lud•dism** *n.* **Lud•dit•ism** *n.* [perh. f. Ned *Lud*, who destroyed machinery c. 1779]

lu•di•crous /lṓdikrəs/ *adj.* absurd or ridiculous; laughable. □□ **lu•di•crous•ly** *adv.* **lu•di•crous•ness** *n.* [L *ludicrus* prob. f. *ludicrum* stage play]

lues /lṓ-eez/ *n.* (in full **lues venerea** /vinéereeə/) syphilis. □□ **lu•et•ic** /loo-étik/ *adj.* [L]

luff /luf/ *n. & v.* (also **loof** /lṓf/) *Naut.* ● *n.* **1** the edge of the fore-and-aft sail next to the mast or stay. **2** *Brit.* the broadest part of the ship's bow where the sides begin to curve in. ● *v.tr.* (also *absol.*) **1** steer (a ship) nearer the wind. **2** turn (the helm) so as to achieve this. **3** obstruct (an opponent in yacht racing) by sailing closer to

See inside front cover for the **Pronunciation Guide** & **Symbols Key.**

the wind. **4** raise or lower (the jib of a crane or derrick). [ME *lo*(*o*)*f* f. OF *lof*, prob. f. LG]

luf·fa var. of LOOFAH.

Luft·waf·fe /lŏoftvaafə/ *n. hist.* the German air force. [G f. *Luft* air + *Waffe* weapon]

lug[1] /lug/ *v. & n.* ● *v.* (**lugged, lug·ging**) **1** *tr.* **a** drag or tug (a heavy object) with effort or violence. **b** (usu. foll. by *around, about*) carry (something heavy) around with one. **2** *tr.* (usu. foll. by *in, into*) introduce (a subject, etc.) irrelevantly. **3** *tr.* (usu. foll. by *along, to*) force (a person) to join in an activity. **4** *intr.* (usu. foll. by *at*) pull hard. ● *n.* **1** a hard or rough pull. **2** (in *pl.*) affectation (*put on lugs*). [ME, prob. f. Scand.: cf. Sw. *lugga* pull a person's hair f. *lugg* forelock]

lug[2] /lug/ *n.* **1** *Sc.* or *colloq.* an ear. **2** a projection on an object by which it may be carried, fixed in place, etc. **3** *sl.* a lout; a sponger; a stupid person. [prob. f. Scand. orig.: cf. LUG[1]]

lug[3] /lug/ *n.* = LUGWORM. [17th c.: orig. unkn.]

lug[4] /lug/ *n.* = LUGSAIL. [abbr.]

luge /lŏozh/ *n. & v.* ● *n.* a light toboggan for one or two people, ridden (usu. raced) in a supine position down a chute. ● *v.intr.* ride on a luge. [Swiss F]

Lu·ger /lŏogər/ *n.* a type of German automatic pistol. [G. *Luger*, German firearms expert d. 1922]

lug·gage /lúgij/ *n.* suitcases, bags, etc., to hold a traveler's belongings. [LUG[1] + -AGE]

lug·ger /lúgər/ *n.* a small ship carrying two or three masts with a lugsail on each. [LUGSAIL + -ER[1]]

lug nut *n.* a nut that attaches to a heavy bolt, esp. as used to attach a wheel to a motor vehicle.

lug·sail /lúgsayl, -səl/ *n. Naut.* a quadrilateral sail that is bent on and hoisted from a yard. [prob. f. LUG[2]]

lu·gu·bri·ous /lŏogŏobreeəs, -gyŏo-/ *adj.* doleful; mournful; dismal. □□ **lu·gu·bri·ous·ly** *adv.* **lu·gu·bri·ous·ness** *n.* [L *lugubris* f. *lugēre* mourn]

lug·worm /lúgwərm/ *n.* any polychaete worm of the genus *Arenicola*, living in muddy sand and leaving characteristic worm-casts on lower shores, and often used as bait by fishermen. [LUG[3]]

luke·warm /lŏokwáwrm/ *adj.* **1** moderately warm; tepid. **2** unenthusiastic; indifferent. □□ **luke·warm·ly** *adv.* **luke·warm·ness** *n.* [ME f. (now dial.) *luke, lew* f. OE]

lull /lul/ *v. & n.* ● *v.* **1** *tr.* soothe or send to sleep gently. **2** *tr.* (usu. foll. by *into*) deceive (a person) into confidence (*lulled into a false sense of security*). **3** *tr.* allay (suspicions, etc.) usu. by deception. **4** *intr.* (of noise, a storm, etc.) abate or fall quiet. ● *n.* a temporary quiet period in a storm or in any activity. [ME, imit. of sounds used to quiet a child]

lull·a·by /lúləbī/ *n. & v.* ● *n.* (*pl.* **-bies**) **1** a soothing song to send a child to sleep. **2** the music for this. ● *v.tr.* (**·bies, ·bied**) sing to sleep. [as LULL + -*by* as in BYE-BYE[2]]

lu·lu /lŏolŏo/ *n. sl.* a remarkable or excellent person or thing. [19th c., perh. f. *Lulu*, pet form of *Louise*]

lum·ba·go /lumbáygō/ *n.* rheumatic pain in the muscles of the lower back. [L *lumbus* loin]

lum·bar /lúmbər, -baar/ *adj. Anat.* relating to the loin, esp. the lower back area. [med.L *lumbaris* f. L *lumbus* loin]

lum·bar punc·ture *n.* the withdrawal of spinal fluid from the lower back with a hollow needle, usu. for diagnosis.

lum·ber[1] /lúmbər/ *v.intr.* (usu. foll. by *along, past, by*, etc.) move in a slow, clumsy, noisy way. □□ **lum·ber·ing** *adj.* [ME *lomere*, perh. imit.]

lum·ber[2] /lúmbər/ *n. & v.* ● *n.* **1** logs or timber cut and prepared for use. **2 a** disused articles of furniture, etc., inconveniently taking up space. **b** useless or cumbersome objects. ● *v.* **1** *intr.* cut and prepare forest timber for transport. **2** *tr.* **a** (usu. foll. by *with*) leave (a person, etc.) with something unwanted or unpleasant (*always lumbering me with the cleaning*). **b** (as **lumbered** *adj.*) in an unwanted or inconvenient situation (*afraid of being lumbered*). **3** *tr.* (usu. foll. by *together*) heap or group together carelessly. **4** *tr.* (usu. foll. by *up*) obstruct. □□ **lum·ber·er** *n.* (in sense 1 of *v.*). **lum·ber·ing** *n.* (in sense 1 of *v.*). [perh. f. LUMBER[1]: later assoc. with obs. *lumber* pawnbroker's shop]

lum·ber·jack /lúmbərjak/ *n.* (also **lum·ber·man** /-mən/ *pl.* **·men**) one who fells, prepares, or conveys lumber.

lum·ber jack·et *n.* a warm thick jacket, usu. in a bright color with a check pattern, of the kind worn by lumberjacks.

lum·ber·some /lúmbərsəm/ *adj.* unwieldy; awkward.

lum·bri·cal mus·cle /lúmbrikəl/ *n.* any of the muscles flexing the fingers or toes. [mod.L *lumbricalis* f. L *lumbricus* earthworm, with ref. to its shape]

lu·men /lŏomən/ *n.* **1** *Physics* the SI unit of luminous flux, equal to the amount of light emitted per second in a unit solid angle of one steradian from a uniform source of one candela. ¶ Abbr.: **lm**. **2** *Anat.* (*pl.* **lu·mi·na** /-minə/) a cavity within a tube, cell, etc. □□ **lu·mi·nal** /-minəl/ *adj.* [L *lumen luminis* a light, an opening]

Lu·mi·nal /lŏominəl/ *n. Trademark* phenobarbital. [as LUMEN + *-al* as in *veronal*]

lu·mi·nance /lŏominəns/ *n. Physics* the intensity of light emitted from a surface per unit area in a given direction. [L *luminare* illuminate (as LUMEN)]

lu·mi·nar·y /lŏomineree/ *n.* (*pl.* **·ies**) **1** *literary* a natural light-giving body, esp. the sun or moon. **2** a person as a source of intellectual light or moral inspiration. **3** a prominent member of a group or gathering (*a host of show-business luminaries*). [ME f. OF *luminarie* or LL *luminarium* f. L LUMEN]

lu·mi·nes·cence /lŏominésəns/ *n.* the emission of light by a substance other than as a result of incandescence. □□ **lu·mi·nes·cent** /-sənt/ *adj.* [as LUMEN + *-escence* (-ESCENT)]

lu·mi·nif·er·ous /lŏominífərəs/ *adj.* producing or transmitting light.

lu·mi·nous /lŏominəs/ *adj.* **1** full of or shedding light; radiant; bright; shining. **2** phosphorescent; visible in darkness (*luminous paint*). **3** (esp. of a writer or a writer's work) throwing light on a subject. **4** of visible radiation (*luminous intensity*). □□ **lu·mi·nos·i·ty** /-nósitee/ *n.* **lu·mi·nous·ly** *adv.* **lu·mi·nous·ness** *n.* [ME f. OF *lumineux* or L *luminosus*]

lum·mox /lúməks/ *n. colloq.* a clumsy or stupid person. [19th c. in US & dial.: orig. unkn.]

lump[1] /lump/ *n. & v.* ● *n.* **1** a compact shapeless or unshapely mass. **2** *sl.* a quantity or heap. **3** a tumor, swelling, or bruise. **4** a heavy, dull, or ungainly person. **5** (prec. by *the*) *Brit.* casual workers in the building and other trades. ● *v.* **1** *tr.* (usu. foll. by *together, with, in with, under*, etc.) mass together or group indiscriminately. **2** *tr.* carry or throw carelessly (*lumping crates around the yard*). **3** *intr.* become lumpy. **4** *intr.* (usu. foll. by *along*) proceed heavily or awkwardly. **5** *intr.* (usu. foll. by *down*) sit down heavily. □ **in the lump** taking things as a whole; in a general manner. **lump in the throat** a feeling of pressure there, caused by emotion. □□ **lump·er** *n.* (in sense 2 of *v.*). [ME, perh. of Scand. orig.]

lump[2] /lump/ *v.tr. colloq.* endure or suffer (a situation) ungraciously. □ **like it or lump it** put up with something whether one likes it or not. [imit.: cf. *dump, grump*, etc.]

lump·ec·to·my /lumpéktəmee/ *n.* (*pl.* **·mies**) the surgical removal of a usu. cancerous lump from the breast.

lum·pen·pro·le·tar·i·at /lúmpənprōlitáireeət/ *n.* (esp. in Marxist terminology) the unorganized and unpolitical lower orders of society, not interested in revolutionary advancement. □□ **lum·pen** *adj.* [G f. *Lumpen* rag, rogue: see PROLETARIAT]

lump·fish /lúmpfish/ *n.* (*pl.* **·fish·es** or **·fish**) a spiny-finned fish, *Cyclopterus lumpus*, of the N. Atlantic with modified pelvic fins for clinging to objects. [MLG *lumpen*, MDu. *lumpe* (perh. = LUMP[1]) + FISH[1]]

lump·ish /lúmpish/ *adj.* **1** heavy and clumsy. **2** stupid; lethargic. □□ **lump·ish·ly** *adv.* **lump·ish·ness** *n.*

lump sum *n.* **1** a sum covering a number of items. **2** money paid down at once (opp. INSTALLMENT).

lump·y /lúmpee/ *adj.* (**lump·i·er, lump·i·est**) **1** full of or covered with lumps. **2** (of water) cut up by the wind into small waves. □□ **lump·i·ly** *adv.* **lump·i·ness** *n.*

lu·na·cy /lŏonəsee/ *n.* (*pl.* **·cies**) **1** insanity (orig. referring to insanity of an intermittent kind attributed to changes of the moon); the state of being a lunatic. **2** *Law* such mental unsoundness as interferes with civil rights or transactions. **3** great folly or eccentricity; a foolish act.

lu·na moth /lŏonə/ *n.* a N. American moth, *Actias luna*, with crescent-shaped spots on its pale green wings. [L *luna*, = moon (from its markings)]

lu·nar /lŏonər/ *adj.* **1** of, relating to, or determined by the moon. **2** concerned with travel to the moon and related research. **3** (of light, glory, etc.) pale; feeble. **4** crescent-shaped; lunate. **5** of or containing silver (from alchemists' use of *luna* (= moon) for 'silver'). [L *lunaris* f. *luna* moon]

lu·nar caus·tic *n.* silver nitrate, esp. in stick form.

lu·nar cy·cle *n.* = METONIC CYCLE.

lu·nar dis·tance *n.* the angular distance of the moon from the sun, a planet, or a star, used in finding longitude at sea.

lu·nar mod·ule *n.* a small craft used for traveling between the moon's surface and a spacecraft in orbit around the moon.

lu·nar month *n.* **1** the period of the moon's revolution, esp. the interval between new moons of about 29½ days. **2** (in general use) a period of four weeks.

lu·nar nodes *n.pl.* the points at which the moon's orbit cuts the ecliptic.

lu·nar ob·ser·va·tion *n.* a measurement of the position of the moon in order to calculate longitude from lunar distance.

lu·nar or·bit *n.* **1** the orbit of the moon around the earth. **2** an orbit around the moon.

lu·nar year *n.* a period of 12 lunar months.

lu·nate /lŏonayt/ *adj. & n.* ● *adj.* crescent-shaped. ● *n.* a crescent-shaped prehistoric implement, etc. [L *lunatus* f. *luna* moon]

lu·nate bone *n.* a crescent-shaped bone in the wrist.

lu·na·tic /lŏonətik/ *n. & adj.* ● *n.* **1** an insane person. **2** someone foolish or eccentric. ● *adj.* mad; foolish. [ME f. OF *lunatique* f. LL *lunaticus* f. L *luna* moon]

lu·na·tic a·sy·lum *n. hist.* a mental home or hospital.

lu·na·tic fringe *n.* an extreme or eccentric minority group.

lu·na·tion /loonáyshən/ *n.* the interval between new moons, about 29½ days. [ME f. med.L *lunatio* (as LUNATIC)]

lunch /lunch/ *n. & v.* ● *n.* **1** the meal eaten in the middle of the day. **2** a light meal eaten at any time. ● *v.* **1** *intr.* eat one's lunch. **2** *tr.* provide lunch for. □ **out to lunch** *sl.* unaware; incompetent. □□ **lunch·er** *n.* [LUNCHEON]

lunch·box /lúnchboks/ *n.* a container for a packed lunch.

lunch·eon /lúnchən/ *n. formal* lunch. [17th c.: orig. unkn.]

lunch·eon·ette /lúnchənét/ *n.* a small restaurant or snack bar serving light lunches.

lunch·time /lúnchtīm/ *n.* the time (usu. around noon) at which lunch is eaten.

lune /loon/ *n. Geom.* a crescent-shaped figure formed on a sphere or plane by two arcs intersecting at two points. [F f. L *luna* moon]

lu·nette /loonét/ *n.* **1** an arched aperture in a domed ceiling to admit light. **2** a crescent-shaped or semicircular space or alcove that contains a painting, statue, etc. **3** a watch crystal of flattened shape. **4** a ring through which a hook is placed to attach a vehicle to the vehicle towing it. **5** a temporary fortification with two faces forming a salient angle, and two flanks. **6** *RC Ch.* a holder for the consecrated host in a monstrance. [F, dimin. of *lune* (see LUNE)]

lung /lung/ *n.* either of the pair of respiratory organs, which bring air into contact with the blood in humans and many other vertebrates. □□ **lunged** *adj.* **lung·ful** *n. (pl.* **·fuls**). **lung·less** *adj.* [OE *lungen* f. Gmc, rel. to LIGHT[2]]

lunge[1] /lunj/ *n. & v.* ● *n.* **1** a sudden movement forward. **2** a thrust with a sword, etc., esp. the basic attacking move in fencing. **3** a movement forward by bending the front leg at the knee while keeping the back leg straight. ● *v.* **1** *intr.* make a lunge. **2** *intr.* (usu. foll. by *at, out*) deliver a blow from the shoulder in boxing. **3** *tr.* drive (a weapon, etc.) violently in some direction. [earlier *allonge* f. F *allonger* lengthen f. *à* to + *long* LONG[1]]

lunge[2] var. of LONGE.

lung·fish /lúngfish/ *n.* any freshwater fish of the order Dipnoi, having gills and a modified swim bladder used as lungs, and able to estivate to survive drought.

lun·gi /lóonggee/ *n. (pl.* **lun·gis**) a length of cotton cloth, usu. worn as a loincloth in India, or as a skirt in Burma where it is the national dress for both sexes. [Urdu]

lung·wort /lúngwərt, –wawrt/ *n.* **1** any herbaceous plant of the genus *Pulmonaria*, esp. *P. officinalis* with white-spotted leaves likened to a diseased lung. **2** a lichen, *Lobaria pulmonaria*, used as a remedy for lung disease.

lu·ni·so·lar /lóonisólər/ *adj.* of or concerning the sun and moon. [L *luna* moon + *sol* sun]

lu·ni·so·lar pe·ri·od *n.* a period of 532 years between the repetitions of both solar and lunar cycles.

lu·ni·so·lar year *n.* a year with divisions regulated by changes of the moon and an average length made to agree with the solar year.

lu·nu·la /lóonyələ/ *n. (pl.* **lu·nu·lae** /–lee/) **1** a crescent-shaped mark, esp. the white area at the base of the fingernail. **2** a crescent-shaped Bronze Age ornament. [L, dimin. of *luna* moon]

lu·pine[1] /lóopin/ *n.* (also **lu·pin**) **1** any plant of the genus *Lupinus*, with long tapering spikes of blue, purple, pink, white, or yellow flowers. **2** (in *pl.*) seeds of the lupine. [ME f. L *lupinus*]

lu·pine[2] /lóopīn/ *adj.* of or like a wolf or wolves. [L *lupinus* f. *lupus* wolf]

lu·pus /lóopəs/ *n.* any of various ulcerous skin diseases, esp. tuberculosis of the skin. □□ **lu·poid** *adj.* **lu·pous** *adj.* [L, = wolf]

lu·pus vul·ga·ris /vulgáiris/ *n.* direct infection of the skin with tuberculosis, causing dark red patches.

lur /loor/ *n.* (also **lure** /lyoor/) a bronze S-shaped trumpet of prehistoric times, still used in Scandinavia to call cattle. [Da. & Norw.]

lurch[1] /lərch/ *n. & v.* ● *n.* a stagger; a sudden unsteady movement or leaning. ● *v.intr.* stagger; move suddenly and unsteadily. [orig. Naut., *lee-lurch* alt. of *lee-latch* drifting to leeward]

lurch[2] /lərch/ *n.* □ **leave in the lurch** desert (a friend, etc.) in difficulties. [orig. = a severe defeat in a game, f. F *lourche* (also the game itself, like backgammon)]

lurch·er /lérchər/ *n.* **1** *Brit.* a crossbred dog, usu. a retriever, collie, or sheepdog crossed with a greyhound, used esp. for hunting and by poachers. **2** *archaic* a petty thief, swindler, or spy. [f. obs. *lurch* (v.) var. of LURK]

lure /loor/ *v. & n.* ● *v.tr.* **1** (usu. foll. by *away, into*) entice (a person, an animal, etc.) usu. with some form of bait. **2** attract back again or recall (a person, animal, etc.) with the promise of a reward. ● *n.* **1** a thing used to entice. **2** (usu. foll. by *of*) the attractive or compelling qualities (of a pursuit, etc.). **3** a falconer's apparatus for recalling a hawk, consisting of a bunch of feathers attached to a thong, within which the hawk finds food while being trained. □□ **lur·ing** *adj.* **lur·ing·ly** *adv.* [ME f. OE *luere* f. Gmc]

Lur·ex /lóoreks/ *n. Trademark* **1** a type of yarn that incorporates a glittering metallic thread. **2** fabric made from this yarn.

lu·rid /lóorid/ *adj.* **1** vivid or glowing in color (*lurid orange*). **2** of an unnatural glare (*lurid nocturnal brilliance*). **3** sensational, horrifying, or terrible (*lurid details*). **4** showy; gaudy (*paperbacks with lurid covers*). **5** ghastly; wan (*lurid complexion*). **6** *Bot.* of a dingy yellowish brown. □ **cast a lurid light on** explain or reveal (facts or character) in a horrific, sensational, or shocking way. □□ **lu·rid·ly** *adv.* **lu·rid·ness** *n.* [L *luridus* f. *luror* wan or yellow color]

lurk /lərk/ *v. & n.* ● *v.intr.* **1** linger furtively or unobtrusively. **2 a** lie in ambush. **b** (usu. foll. by *in, under, about*, etc.) hide, esp. for sinister purposes. **3** (as **lurking** *adj.*) latent; semiconscious (*a lurking suspicion*). ● *n. Austral. colloq.* a dodge, racket, or scheme; a method of profitable business. □□ **lurk·er** *n.* [ME perh. f. LOUR with frequent. *–k* as in TALK]

lus·cious /lúshəs/ *adj.* **1 a** richly sweet in taste or smell. **b** *colloq.* delicious. **2** (of literary style, music, etc.) overrich in sound, imagery, or voluptuous suggestion. **3** voluptuously attractive. □□ **lus·cious·ly** *adv.* **lus·cious·ness** *n.* [ME perh. alt. of obs. *licious* f. DELICIOUS]

lush[1] /lush/ *adj.* **1** (of vegetation, esp. grass) luxuriant and succulent. **2** luxurious. □□ **lush·ly** *adv.* **lush·ness** *n.* [ME, perh. var. of obs. *lash* soft, f. OF *lasche* lax (see LACHES): assoc. with LUSCIOUS]

lush[2] /lush/ *n. & v. sl.* ● *n.* **1** (*also pl.*) liquor. **2** an alcoholic; a drunkard. ● *v.* **1** *tr. & intr.* drink (alcohol). **2** *tr.* ply with alcohol. [18th c.: perh. joc. use of LUSH[1]]

lust /lust/ *n. & v.* ● *n.* **1** strong sexual desire. **2 a** (usu. foll. by *for, of*) a passionate desire for (*a lust for power*). **b** (usu. foll. by *of*) a passionate enjoyment of (*the lust of battle*). **3** (usu. in *pl.*) a sensuous appetite regarded as sinful (*the lusts of the flesh*). ● *v.intr.* (usu. foll. by *after, for*) have a strong or excessive (esp. sexual) desire. □□ **lust·ful** *adj.* **lust·ful·ly** *adv.* **lust·ful·ness** *n.* [OE f. Gmc]

lus·ter[1] /lústər/ *n. & v.* ● *n.* **1** gloss, brilliance, or sheen. **2** a shining or reflective surface. **3 a** a thin metallic coating giving an iridescent glaze to ceramics. **b** = LUSTERWARE. **4** a radiance or attractiveness; splendor; glory; distinction (of achievements, etc.) (*add luster to; shed luster on*). **5 a** a prismatic glass pendant on a chandelier, etc. **b** a cut-glass chandelier or candelabra. **6 a** *Brit.* a thin dress material with a cotton warp, woolen weft, and a glossy surface. **b** any fabric with a sheen or gloss. ● *v.tr.* put luster on (pottery, a cloth, etc.). □□ **lus·ter·less** *adj.* **lus·trous** *adj.* **lus·trous·ly** *adv.* **lus·trous·ness** *n.* [F f. It. *lustro* f. *lustrare* f. L *lustrare* illuminate]

lus·ter[2] /lústər/ *n.* (*Brit.* **lus·tre**) = LUSTRUM. [ME, Anglicized f. LUSTRUM]

lus·ter·ware /lústərwair/ *n.* (*Brit.* **lus·tre·ware**) ceramics with an iridescent glaze. [LUSTER[1]]

lus·tra *pl.* of LUSTRUM.

lus·tral /lústrəl/ *adj.* relating to or used in ceremonial purification. [L *lustralis* (as LUSTRUM)]

lus·trate /lústrayt/ *v.tr.* purify by expiatory sacrifice, ceremonial washing, or other such rite. □□ **lus·tra·tion** /–tráyshən/ *n.* [L *lustrare* (as LUSTRUM)]

lus·tre *Brit.* var. of LUSTER.

lus·trum /lústrəm/ *n.* (*pl.* **lus·tra** /lústrə/ or **lus·trums**) a period of five years. [L, an orig. purificatory sacrifice after a quinquennial census]

lust·y /lústee/ *adj.* (**lust·i·er**, **lust·i·est**) **1** healthy and strong. **2** vigorous or lively. □□ **lust·i·ly** *adv.* **lust·i·ness** *n.* [ME f. LUST + –Y[1]]

lu·sus /lóosəs/ *n.* (in full **lusus naturae** /nətóoree, –tyóoree/) a freak of nature. [L]

lu·ta·nist var. of LUTENIST.

lute[1] /loot/ *n.* a guitarlike instrument with a long neck and a pear-shaped body, much used in the 14th–17th c. [ME f. F *lut, leüt*, prob. f. Prov. *laüt* f. Arab. *al-'ūd*]

lute[2] /loot/ *n. & v.* ● *n.* **1** clay or cement used to stop a hole, make a joint airtight, coat a crucible, protect a graft, etc. **2** a rubber seal for a jar, etc. ● *v.tr.* apply lute to. [ME f. OF *lut* f. L *lutum* mud, clay]

lu·te·ci·um var. of LUTETIUM.

lu·te·in /lóoteein/ *n. Chem.* a pigment of a deep yellow color found in egg yolk, etc. [L *luteum* yolk of egg, neut. of *luteus* yellow]

lute[1]

lu·te·in·iz·ing hor·mone /lóoteeinīzing/ *n. Biochem.* a hormone secreted by the anterior pituitary gland that in females stimulates ovulation and in males stimulates the synthesis of androgen. ¶ Abbr.: **LH**. [LUTEIN]

lu•te•nist /lŏŏt'nist/ *n.* (also **lu•ta•nist**) a lute player. [med.L *lutanista* f. *lutana* LUTE¹]

luteo- /lŏŏteeō/ *comb. form* orange-colored. [as LUTEOUS + –O–]

lu•te•o•ful•vous /lŏŏteeōfúlvəs/ *adj.* orange-tawny.

lu•te•ous /lŏŏteeəs/ *adj.* of a deep orange yellow or greenish yellow. [L *luteus* f. *lutum* WELD²]

lute•string /lŏŏtstring/ *n. archaic* a glossy silk fabric. [app. f. *lustring* f. F *lustrine* or It. *lustrino* f. *lustro* LUSTER¹]

lu•te•ti•um /lŏŏteéshəm/ *n.* (also **lu•te•ci•um**) *Chem.* a silvery metallic element of the lanthanide series. ¶ Symb.: **Lu**. [F *lutécium* f. L *Lutetia* the ancient name of Paris]

Lu•ther•an /lŏŏthərən/ *n. & adj.* ●*n.* **1** a follower of Martin Luther, Ger. religious reformer d. 1546. **2** a member of the Lutheran Church, which accepts the Augsburg confession of 1530, with justification by faith alone as a cardinal doctrine. ●*adj.* of or characterized by the theology of Martin Luther. □□ **Lu•ther•an•ism** *n.* **Lu•ther•an•ize** *v.tr. & intr.*

Lu•tine bell /lŏŏteen/ *n.* a bell kept at Lloyd's in London and rung whenever there is an important announcement to be made to the underwriters. [HMS *Lutine*, which sank in 1799, whose bell it was]

lut•ing /lŏŏting/ *n.* = LUTE² *n.*

lutz /luts/ *n.* a jump in figure skating in which the skater takes off from the outside back edge of one skate and lands, after a complete rotation in the air, on the outside back edge of the opposite skate. [prob. f. Swiss figure skater Gustave *Lussi* b. 1898, who invented it]

lux /luks/ *n.* (*pl.* same or **lux•es**) *Physics* the SI unit of illumination, equivalent to one lumen per square meter. ¶ Abbr.: **lx**. [L *lux lucis* light]

luxe /lŏŏks, luks/ *n.* luxury (cf. DELUXE). [F f. L *luxus*]

Lux•em•bourg•er /lúksəmbərgər/ *n.* **1** a native or national of Luxembourg. **2** a person of Luxembourg descent.

lux•u•ri•ant /lugzhŏŏreeənt, lukshŏŏr–/ *adj.* **1** (of vegetation, etc.) lush; profuse in growth. **2** prolific; exuberant; rank (*luxuriant imagination*). **3** (of literary or artistic style) florid; richly ornate. □□ **lux•u•ri•ance** /–eeəns/ *n.* **lux•u•ri•ant•ly** *adv.* [L *luxuriare* grow rank f. *luxuria* LUXURY]

▶See note at LUXURIOUS.

lux•u•ri•ate /lugzhŏŏreeayt, lukshŏŏr–/ *v.intr.* **1** (foll. by *in*) take self-indulgent delight in; enjoy in a luxurious manner. **2** take one's ease; relax in comfort.

lux•u•ri•ous /lugzhŏŏreeəs, lukshŏŏr–/ *adj.* **1** supplied with luxuries. **2** extremely comfortable. **3** fond of luxury; self-indulgent; voluptuous. □□ **lux•u•ri•ous•ly** *adv.* **lux•u•ri•ous•ness** *n.* [ME f. OF *luxurios* f. L *luxuriosus* (as LUXURY)]

▶**Luxuriant** and **luxurious** are sometimes confused. **Luxuriant** means 'lush, profuse, prolific ' (*forests of dark luxuriant foliage; luxuriant black eyelashes*). **Luxurious**, a much commoner word, means 'supplied with luxuries, extremely comfortable' (*a luxurious mansion*).

lux•u•ry /lúgzhəree, lúkshəree/ *n.* (*pl.* **-ries**) **1** choice or costly surroundings, possessions, food, etc.; luxuriousness (*a life of luxury*). **2** something desirable for comfort or enjoyment, but not indispensable. **3** (*attrib.*) providing great comfort; expensive (*a luxury apartment; a luxury vacation*). [ME f. OF *luxurie, luxure* f. L *luxuria* f. *luxus* abundance]

Lw *symb. Chem.* the element lawrencium.

LWM *abbr.* low-water mark.

LWV *abbr.* League of Women Voters.

lx *abbr.* lux.

LXX *abbr.* Septuagint.

-ly¹ /lee/ *suffix* forming adjectives esp. from nouns, meaning: **1** having the qualities of (*princely; manly*). **2** recurring at intervals of (*daily; hourly*). [from or after OE *–lic* f. Gmc, rel. to LIKE¹]

-ly² /lee/ *suffix* forming adverbs from adjectives, denoting esp. manner or degree (*boldly; happily; miserably; deservedly; amusingly*). [from or after OE *–līce* f. Gmc (as –LY¹)]

ly•can•thrope /líkənthrōp, líkán–/ *n.* **1** a werewolf. **2** an insane person who believes that he or she is an animal, esp. a wolf. [mod.L *lycanthropus* f. Gk (as LYCANTHROPY)]

ly•can•thro•py /líkánthrəpee/ *n.* **1** the mythical transformation of a person into a wolf (see also WEREWOLF). **2** a form of madness involving the delusion of being a wolf, with changed appetites, voice, etc. [mod.L *lycanthropia* f. Gk *lukanthrōpia* f. *lukos* wolf + *anthrōpos* man]

ly•cée /leesáy/ *n.* (*pl.* **ly•cées**) a government-sponsored secondary school, esp. in France. [F f. L (as LYCEUM)]

Ly•ce•um /líseéəm/ *n.* **1 a** the garden at Athens in which Aristotle taught philosophy. **b** Aristotelian philosophy and its followers. **2** (**lyceum**) a literary institution, lecture hall, concert hall, etc. [L f. Gk *Lukeion* neut. of *Lukeios* epithet of Apollo (from whose neighboring temple the Lyceum was named)]

ly•chee var. of LITCHI.

lych•gate /líchgayt/ *n.* (also **lich•gate**) a roofed gateway to a churchyard, formerly used at burials for sheltering a coffin until a clergyman's arrival. [ME f. OE *līc* corpse f. Gmc + GATE¹]

lych•nis /líknis/ *n.* any herbaceous plant of the genus *Lychnis*, including ragged robin. [L f. Gk *lukhnis* a red flower f. *lukhnos* lamp]

ly•co•pod /líkəpod/ *n.* any of various club mosses, esp. of the genus *Lycopodium*. [Anglicized form of LYCOPODIUM]

ly•co•po•di•um /líkəpódeeəm/ *n.* **1** = LYCOPOD. **2** a fine powder of spores from this, used as an absorbent in surgery, and in making fireworks, etc. [mod.L f. Gk *lukos* wolf + *pous podos* foot]

Ly•cra /líkrə/ *n. Trademark* an elastic polyurethane fiber or fabric used esp. for close-fitting sports clothing.

Lyd•i•an /lídeeən/ *n. & adj.* ●*n.* **1** a native or inhabitant of ancient Lydia in W. Asia Minor. **2** the language of this people. ●*adj.* of or relating to the people of Lydia or their language. [L *Lydius* f. Gk *Ludios* of Lydia]

Lyd•i•an mode *n. Mus.* the mode represented by the natural diatonic scale F–F.

lye /lī/ *n.* **1** water that has been made alkaline by lixiviation of vegetable ashes. **2** any strong alkaline solution, esp. of potassium hydroxide used for washing or cleansing. [OE *lēag* f. Gmc: cf. LATHER]

ly•ing¹ /lí-ing/ *pres. part.* of LIE¹. ●*n.* a place to lie (*a dry lying*).

ly•ing² /lí-ing/ *pres. part.* of LIE². *adj.* deceitful; false. □□ **ly•ing•ly** *adv.*

lyke-wake /líkwayk/ *n. Brit.* a night watch over a dead body. [perh. f. ON: cf. LICH(–GATE), WAKE¹]

Lyme dis•ease /līm/ *n.* a disease transmitted by ticks, usually characterized by rash, fever, fatigue, and joint pain. [for Lyme, Connecticut, where first described]

lymph /limf/ *n.* **1** *Physiol.* a colorless fluid containing white blood cells, drained from the tissues and conveyed through the body in the lymphatic system. **2** this fluid used as a vaccine. **3** exudation from a sore, etc. **4** *poet.* pure water. □□ **lym•phoid** *adj.* **lym•phous** *adj.* [F *lymphe* or L *lympha, limpa* water]

lym•phat•ic /limfátik/ *adj. & n.* ●*adj.* **1** of or secreting or conveying lymph (*lymphatic gland*). **2** (of a person) pale, flabby, or sluggish. ●*n.* a veinlike vessel conveying lymph. [orig. = frenzied, f. L *lymphaticus* mad f. Gk *numpholēptos* seized by nymphs: now assoc. with LYMPH (on the analogy of *spermatic*, etc.)]

lym•phat•ic sys•tem *n.* a network of vessels conveying lymph.

lymph node *n.* (also **lymph gland**) a small mass of tissue in the lymphatic system where lymph is purified and lymphocytes are formed.

lym•pho•cyte /límfəsīt/ *n.* a form of leukocyte occurring in the blood, in lymph, etc. □□ **lym•pho•cyt•ic** /–sítik/ *adj.*

lym•pho•ma /limfōmə/ *n.* (*pl.* **lym•pho•mas** or **lym•pho•ma•ta** /–mətə/) any malignant tumor of the lymph nodes, excluding leukemia.

lyn•ce•an /linseéən/ *adj.* lynx-eyed; keen-sighted. [L *lynceus* f. Gk *lugkeios* f. *lugx* LYNX]

lynch /linch/ *v.tr.* (of a mob) put (a person) to death for an alleged offense without a legal trial, esp. by hanging. □□ **lynch•er** *n.* **lynch•ing** *n.* [*Lynch's law*, after Capt. W. *Lynch* of Virginia *c.* 1780]

lyn•chet /línchit/ *n.* (in the UK) a ridge or ledge formed by ancient plowing on a slope. [*linch* f. OE *hlinc*: cf. LINKS]

lynch mob *n.* a group of people intent on lynching someone.

lynch•pin var. of LINCHPIN.

lynx /lingks/ *n.* **1** a medium-sized feline, *Lynx lynx*, with short tail, spotted fur, and tufted ear tips. **2** its fur. □□ **lynx•like** *adj.* [ME f. L f. Gk *lugx*]

lynx-eyed *adj.* keen-sighted.

ly•o•phil•ic /líəfílik/ *adj.* (of a colloid) readily dispersed by a solvent. [Gk *luō* loosen, dissolve + Gk *philos* loving]

lynx

ly•oph•i•lize /líófilīz/ *v.tr.* freeze-dry.

ly•o•pho•bic /líəfóbik/ *adj.* (of a colloid) not lyophilic. [Gk *luō* loosen, dissolve + *–phobic* (–PHOBIA)]

ly•rate /lírayt, –rət/ *adj. Biol.* lyre-shaped.

lyre /līr/ *n. Gk. Antiq.* an ancient stringed instrument like a small U-shaped harp, played usu. with a plectrum and accompanying the voice. [ME f. OF *lire* f. L *lyra* f. Gk *lura*]

lyre•bird /lírbərd/ *n.* any Australian bird of the family Menuridae, the male of which has a lyre-shaped tail display.

lyr•ic /lírik/ *adj. & n.* ●*adj.* **1** (of poetry) expressing the writer's emotions, usu. briefly and in stanzas or recognized forms. **2** (of a poet) writing in this manner. **3** of or for the lyre. **4** meant to be sung; fit to be expressed in song; songlike (*lyric drama; lyric opera*). ●*n.* **1** a lyr-

lyre

ic poem or verse. **2** (in *pl.*) lyric verses. **3** (usu. in *pl.*) the words of a song. [F *lyrique* or L *lyricus* f. Gk *lurikos* (as LYRE)]

lyr·i·cal /lírikəl/ *adj.* **1** = LYRIC *adj.* 1, 2. **2** resembling, couched in, or using language appropriate to, lyric poetry. **3** *colloq.* highly enthusiastic (*wax lyrical about*). □□ **lyr·i·cal·ly** *adv.* **lyr·i·cal·ness** *n.*

lyr·i·cism /lírisizəm/ *n.* **1** the character or quality of being lyric or lyrical. **2** a lyrical expression. **3** high-flown sentiments.

lyr·i·cist /lírisist/ *n.* a person who writes the words to a song.

lyr·ist *n.* **1** /lírist/ a person who plays the lyre. **2** /lírist/ a lyric poet. [L *lyrista* f. Gk *luristēs* f. *lura* lyre]

lyse /līs/ *v.tr. & intr. Biol.* bring about or undergo lysis. [back-form. f. LYSIS]

ly·ser·gic ac·id /līsérjik/ *n.* a crystalline acid extracted from ergot or prepared synthetically. [hydro*lysis* + *erg*ot + –IC]

ly·ser·gic ac·id di·eth·yl·am·ide *n.* /dī-éthilámid/ a powerful hallucinogenic drug. ¶ Abbr.: **LSD.**

ly·sin /lísin/ *n. Biol.* a protein in the blood able to cause lysis. [G *Lysine*]

ly·sine /líseen/ *n. Biochem.* an amino acid present in protein and essential in the diet of vertebrates. [G *Lysin*, ult. f. LYSIS]

ly·sis /lísis/ *n.* (*pl.* **ly·ses** /–seez/) *Biol.* the disintegration of a cell. [L f. Gk *lusis* loosening f. *luō* loosen]

-lysis /lisis/ *comb. form* forming nouns denoting disintegration or decomposition (*electrolysis*; *hemolysis*).

ly·so·some /lísəsōm/ *n. Biol.* a cytoplasmic organelle in eukaryotic cells containing degradative enzymes enclosed in a membrane. [LYSIS + –SOME³]

ly·so·zyme /lísəzīm/ *n. Biochem.* an enzyme found in tears and egg white that catalyzes the destruction of cell walls of certain bacteria. [LYSIS + ENZYME]

lyt·ic /lítik/ *adj.* of, relating to, or causing lysis.

-lytic /lítik/ *comb. form* forming adjectives corresponding to nouns in –*lysis*. [Gk *lutikos* (as LYSIS)]

Oxford
Language
Guide

Oxford Language Guide Contents

Oxford Language Guide: How to Use English Most Effectively

Speaking and writing are critically important forms of communication, and make a strong impression on people. Yet, you may not always express your thoughts and ideas as clearly as you would like to, or you may be unsure of which words to choose to convey exactly what you mean. Many people have problems with spelling, grammar, or punctuation. The **Oxford Language Guide** provides information that will help you use these mechanical aspects of English with confidence and grace.

If you know something about the history of English, you will have a better understanding of your language. **Where English Comes From** is an overview of how and why words become part of English; why the meaning or spelling of some words changes; why and how new words are invented; and why some words that were once popular are now old-fashioned or obsolete.

Making Words will help you understand the structure of words. This section explains roots, prefixes, suffixes, and combining forms. It explains how an understanding of these word parts can help you increase your vocabulary and avoid spelling errors. It lists the most commonly used prefixes, suffixes, and combining forms, gives their meanings, and illustrates how each is used.

Learning to Spell Correctly will help you with spelling problems that may arise when a word is inflected, that is, changed to show number, person, tense, or comparison. It lists spelling rules and exceptions to the rules. A section on **commonly misspelled words** lists words commonly misspelled because of confusing pronunciations or because they contain "silent letters."

Writing and Spelling Traps is a representative list of words that have different meanings, but may be misused because they sound alike or are similar in form.

Choosing the Right Word will show you how to add power and vitality to your use of English.

Parts of Speech explains the traditional approach to grammar. Here, the eight parts of speech are defined and the use of each is explained and illustrated.

Capitalization and **Punctuation** show how to use these aspects of language to make your writing easier and your meaning clearer.

Using Correct Forms of Address details the formally correct ways to offer greetings and address correspondence when communicating with various officials, dignitaries, and members of the clergy.

The final section, **Increasing Your Word Power**, explains why a good vocabulary is an asset.

Where English Comes From

The English language has existed for many hundreds of years, with a written history traceable to at least AD 800. Aside from its core Germanic word stock, many other words came into English from various European languages. For example, St. Augustine and other Latin-speaking missionaries to England introduced such words as *bishop* and *priest*. Latin was the language of scholarship and religion, and wherever Latin scholars, missionaries, and government officials exerted influence, Latin words came into use. When Scandinavians invaded and settled in Britain in the ninth and tenth centuries, some words beginning with *sk-* were adopted into English, such as *skill*, *skirt*, and *sky*. The Scandinavian influence also contributed important pronouns such as *their*, *them*, and *they*. There are thousands of words of French origin, many introduced from the time of the Norman conquest of England in 1066. These include *army*, *blue*, *chair*, *dinner*, *government*, *jolly*, *mayor*, *paper*, and *towel*. Other European languages contributed more indirectly, via commercial contacts and cultural and literary influence. *Balcony*, *piano*, and *pizza* come from Italy; *fiesta* and *siesta* from Spain; *orchestra* and many others from Greek. The influence of Greek roots, prefixes, and suffixes is profound on English, owing mainly to words introduced by scholars and translators of Greek works. Much of the familiar English vocabulary was in place by the seventeenth century, yet the foreign influx continued, as English-speaking people colonized places around the world and increased contact with other cultures via trade. English took in words from many languages: *boomerang* from Aboriginal Australian; *vodka* from Russia; and *igloo* from the Inuit peoples. This growth is ongoing and seemingly never-ending.

English is always growing and changing; words constantly are being added and falling into disuse. Many words that you hear, speak, and read today were not part of the language your grandparents used. Look in a dictionary published at that time and you will not find such words as *carjack*, *miniskirt*, *pay-per-view*, *yuppie*, and *VCR*. Every time new inventions, scientific discoveries, art forms, or fashions appear that do not have names to identify them, new words must be invented or old words given new applications, or taken from other languages.

On the other hand, when words are not used, they become obsolete. Many obsolete words are still included in the dictionary because they are part of our history and our culture. They may not be in everyday use, but people need to know what they mean when they read them in old books or hear them used in plays written a long time ago. Before the automobile was a common form of transportation, people traveled in buggies drawn by horses. Now when you hear or see the word *buggy* you are inclined to think of something old-fashioned, yet the word was in common use less than one hundred years ago, and is common in the writing of that time and earlier.

Many words have changed their meanings over time, such that their most familiar sense today is quite different from their earlier sense. For example, sly or crafty people were once described as *pretty*. At one time, when people wanted to describe someone as stupid or ignorant, they referred to that person as *nice*. Today, if someone is said to be nice or pretty, it is usually a complement, not criticism.

These are only a few of the ways in which language changes and grows. By knowing how words become part of the language, you discover important clues to social, political, and cultural roots that take trace the history and growth of a country using that language.

How English began

English ultimately derives from a common ancestral language believed to have been in existence about 3000 BC. This language, called *Indo-European*, was used by people inhabiting an area of modern-day southeastern Russia, north and east of the Black Sea. About 4,500 years ago, the people who spoke this language split into groups that migrated into Europe and parts of Asia. Different speech communities developed as these migrating groups became widespread and isolated, eventually giving rise to several separate (yet related) language families, including Italic and its descendant Latin, from which many of the languages spoken in Europe today developed. Another family of Indo-European languages is known as Germanic, and this is the primary parent language of both English and German, as well as Dutch and the Scandinavian languages.

Warrior-adventurers, who spoke Germanic, invaded what is now Great Britain about AD 450. The invaders—called Angles, Saxons, and Jutes—all spoke similar Germanic dialects. The people they conquered, known as Britons, spoke Celtic, another branch of Indo-European. The Celtic language of the native Britons included Latin words because conquering Roman troops occupied Britain from AD 43 until the 400s. The Romans eventually returned home to defend Rome against invading armies. The Germanic Angles, Saxons, and Jutes conquered Britain after the Romans left.

As the invading tribes took over and settled in Britain, the Celtic language speakers gradually retreated. Since the Celtic people were forced to communicate with their Germanic rulers, the history of the English language begins with the takeover of Britain by the Germanic tribes. As a result, Celtic made only a small contribution to the English vocabulary, with words such as *crag* and *bin*. However, many place names were adopted from the Celtic. Among them are *Avon*, *Kent*, *London*, *Aberdeen*, and *Thames*. Small groups of people living in Ireland, Wales, and the Scottish Highlands still speak varieties of Celtic, such as Scots Gaelic, Welsh, Breton, and the recently revived Irish Gaelic.

Old English

The Angles and Saxons occupied a large part of Britain. The name of one of these Germanic-speaking tribes eventually became the name of the land they occupied, *England*. Their Anglo-Saxon language, now usually called Old English, became firmly established in Britain in the period from AD 500 to 1066.

Even as this happened, changes were taking place. Latin-speaking Roman and Celtic missionaries under St. Augustine began spreading Christianity in Britain. The introduction of Christianity exerted a great impact on the English language. Religion brought with it many new ideas and customs. And Christianity used Latin as its official language. In their attempt to identify and deal with all these new influences, the Anglo-Saxons did not hesitate to borrow from Latin the special vocabulary needed for religious affairs. Among the words taken from Church Latin which still survive are:

Latin	Old English	Modern English
abbatis (Aramaic, via Greek)	abbod	abbot
altaria	altar	altar
amen (from Greek)	amen	amen
apostolus (from Greek)	apostol	apostle
candela	candel	candle

However, users of Old English did not borrow as heavily from Latin and other languages in this early period as they did later when there was greater communication with the European continent. Sometimes they changed the meanings of native words. The word for Easter (*eastron*) originally was the name for the spring festival honoring the goddess of dawn. *Geōl* (Yule), the name of the festival held to celebrate the passing of the shortest day of the year in late December, came to denote Christmas.

Native ingenuity was shown in creating new words by combining two native words in much the same way as we now combine words such as *space* and *worthy* to form *spaceworthy*. Old English words such as *lǣcecraft* (leech-craft), meaning 'medicine,' and *handbōc* (handbook), meaning 'manual,' illustrate this practice.

The growth of the Old English vocabulary during this period of language history reflects the growth of English culture. Because of the Church's influence, scholarship was encouraged and Britain began its rise as one of the intellectual leaders of Europe.

Toward the end of the 700s, Vikings from Denmark, Norway, and Sweden began invading and settling in many parts of Britain. By the 1000s, a Danish king ruled Britain. As a result of the invasions from the Danish peninsula, many Scandinavian words became part of English. These did not identify new ideas and objects, but were everyday words for which English already had terms and expressions.

The Scandinavian invaders were Germanic people like the Anglo-Saxons. Their cultures were similar and their languages enough alike to that they understood one another. Many words were exactly alike, such as *father, husband, house, life, man, mother, summer, wife*, and *winter*. Other words were so much alike they were used interchangeably.

Although the Scandinavians and the English fought each other, still many Scandinavians settled peacefully in Britain, intermarried with the English, and raised families. Often both languages were spoken in the same household. Where different words existed for the same thing, the English word usually won out, but there were some exceptions. The results of this absorption of language through close contact is seen in the histories of such words from Scandinavia as *skirt, skill, window, leg, gasp, birth, glitter, they, their, them, egg*. Scholars believe that at least 900 words of Scandinavian origin have survived into Modern English. Many more are still in use in Great Britain, in dialects spoken in English regions heavily settled by Scandinavians one thousand years ago.

Middle English

Old English began to undergo a great change when the Normans invaded England from France in 1066. Until that time, in spite of the Latin brought in by the introduction of Christianity to England, the vocabulary of English was still overwhelmingly Germanic. The Normans began a process that brought many French words into the English language, many of these being ultimately from Latin. The Norman conquerors replaced the English as rulers, chief landholders, and church officials, and Norman French became the language of the ruling class in England. However, the common people continued to speak English.

Norman French and English existed side by side until political and social changes began to favor the use of English by all classes. The Normans ruling in England lost control of their territory in France in the early 1200s. Confined to Britain, the Normans began to learn English. Eventually, it replaced French as the language of the ruling class, the schools, and the courts. By the end of what is known as the Middle English period (1100-1500), English again had established itself as the major language in Britain.

During this period, English borrowed thousands of words from French and from Latin. In the English we now speak, more than half of the words in common use come from these two sources. Many words from Old English and Anglo-French that are roughly synonymous exist side by side today, for example, *dress* and *clothes*, *aid* and *help*, *royal* and *kingly*. In addition, trade between Britain and the Low Countries, especially Holland, accounts for the inclusion of perhaps as many as 2,500 words of Dutch origin in the English language. Some examples are: *boom* (at the bottom of a sail), *deck, easel, etch, freight, furlough*, and *stoop* (porch or entrance).

Before the Norman invasion, a great change in English was beginning to shift grammatical and pronunciation patterns. The coming of the Normans accelerated these changes. Everyday use, growth of dialects, and contact with foreign languages caused inflections (word endings) to lose their distinctive meanings and their usefulness. Instead of depending on word endings to indicate grammatical relationships in a sentence, as had been the case in Old English, word order became the important indicator.

In Old English, for example, *To his þeowum se fæder cwæð*, meaning 'The father said to his servants' or 'To his servants the father said,' would have the same meaning no matter how the words were placed in the sentence. The *-um* ending on þeow(um) would always indicate who was being spoken to. In modern English, if we shift word order to make the sentence read *His servants said to the father*, the meaning becomes quite different. English still retains some inflections, including plurals of nouns and verb endings. But even Middle English had far fewer inflections than Old English.

Modern English

The Modern English period, starting about 1500, has seen a great deal of regularization and standardization of the language, largely under the influence of printing and widespread education. But attempts to fix English into a permanent form have generally failed, despite efforts by some writers and scholars. English is a living, growing language, and usage always produces change.

However, fixing a language and freezing its usages into a form that tolerates no change is different from trying to standardize spellings so that writing is easy and effective. Several factors contributed to establishing standard English spellings, as well as some accepted forms of usage and many of the common traits that exist in modern English. These factors included the printing press (introduced into England in 1477 by William Caxton), the revival of interest in literature, and the growth of popular education.

The need for standardization was recognized as early as the mid-1300s. From that time, the London dialect of English (called East Midland) was gradually adopted from the four main dialects in existence (Northern, East and West Midland, and Southern) as the basis for standard English. The choice was made because the London dialect was the language of contracts and commerce and the speech of the English royal court, and all official documents originating there were written in the London dialect. Furthermore, the translation of the Book of Common Prayer and the King James version of the Bible became tremendous forces for standardizing English.

Before Caxton and the printing press, literary works were written for the most part in the dialect of the author. Spoken dialects continued for a long time and, indeed, still exist. But by the end of the 1400s, the London dialect was becoming accepted in English literary usage.

By the early part of the 1600s, more than 20,000 different works were printed in England alone. Books were available to all who could read and afford them. The printed word helped to make spelling more uniform. Up until that time spelling usually varied from region to region.

From the 1500s through the 1700s, many English writers experimented with words. During this period over 10,000 new words entered the English language. Many of these were taken from Latin and Greek by scholars who wanted to replace the forms earlier adopted from French. English translators and writers believed their native language was rough, unpolished, and incapable of doing what Latin and Greek had done, and what Italian could do. They set about enlarging the vocabulary, chiefly by translating or borrowing and adapting words from Greek and Latin. Largely because of the borrowings in this period, more than twenty-five percent of modern English words come almost directly from the classical languages. Very often we have two words that go back to the same Latin original—one brought in by the Normans, and one taken in directly. Examples include words such as *painting* and *picture, certainty* and *certitude*. The adoption of Greek and Latin forms became so abundant, and sometimes so outrageous, that these borrowings were dubbed "inkhorn terms," in reference to their scholarly origin. However, some of these terms were useful and necessary, and many have survived to this day. Among them are *conduct, dexterity, extinguish, scientific*, and *spurious*.

American English and British English

After the British colonized America, the English language used by Americans began to diverge from that used in the old country, and began its own, separate history. One important factor in this change was the need to create or adopt new words to identify unfamiliar objects. Animals, trees, food, and the physical features of the land were different. The English-speaking Americans took words from native American Indians to refer to a raccoon, a tomahawk, a papoose, and a wigwam. When there were no appropriate words, they did what their ancestors had done—they combined words and gave old words new meanings. The combination of *garter* and *snake* produced a word to describe a crawling creature they had never seen before. They named the sweet, edible root of a vine belonging to the morning glory family a *sweet potato*. They adapted from the Narragansett Indians the name for the fruit of a plant of the gourd family, the *squash*.

The growth of American nationalism led to a desire for cultural as well as political independence from the mother country. This, too, influenced American English, as in conscious attempts to reform spelling so that in time, *musick* became *music*, and *labour* became *labor*. New ideas in the arts and sciences and the coming to America of people from many different countries also had powerful effects on American English.

Changes have not been so extensive that we speak a new language, although we generally can detect a "British accent" very quickly, largely by differences in intonational patterns and the pronunciation of certain words (e.g., *garage, vitamin*). In vocabulary, Americans may not know that when the British say *vest* they mean an *undershirt* (in British English, *waistcoat* is the term for what Americans call a *vest*), and that the British *goods wagon* is the American *freight car*. But for the most part, Americans and Britons communicate easily because basic grammatical and phonetic patterns have not changed, though many words and their pronunciation are different in these two main varieties of English. In formal written English, the most apparent differences are merely different spellings, as in the British use of *centre* and *practise* (for the verb).

English has also changed in other countries where it is used. Canadians, Australians, New Zealanders, and others have adapted English to fit their own needs. Although all English-speaking people can generally understand each other, each English-speaking country has developed distinctive ways of using the language. For example, New Zealanders refer to a *section* (a building lot in a city), Australians to a *mob* (a group of animals), and Canadians to a *chesterfield* (an overstuffed sofa).

As long as travel and trade exist between nations, as long as large groups of people continue to settle in countries other than their native lands, and as long as the sciences and the arts progress, new ideas, new words, and new usages of words will continue to keep language changing and growing.

Making Words

You can often learn the spelling and meaning of words more easily when you know how they are put together. Three parts or elements go into the making of many words: *roots, affixes* (which includes both *prefixes* and *suffixes*), and *combining forms.*

A root gives a word its basic or etymological meaning. It may be a word in itself or a word part. *View*, meaning 'sight' or 'to look at' is a root word. The root *port*, which is from Latin, means 'carry.' It is found in Anglicized Latin borrowings as in the words *portable, porter,* and *import.*

Affixes are added before (prefixes) or after (suffixes) words or word parts to modify the meaning of a root. The prefix *re-* is added before *view* to make the word *review,* meaning 'to look at again.' The suffix *-er* can be added to *view,* to make a word meaning 'a person who looks at,' or to *review* to make a word meaning 'a person who looks at again.' Prefixes and suffixes may be one or more syllables, and sometimes look the same as a word.

The root word *fold* means 'to bend or double over.' Add the prefix *un-*, meaning 'the opposite,' and you have *unfold,* which means 'to open up what has been doubled over.' Add the suffix *-er,* meaning 'performer of an act,' and you have *folder,* 'something or someone that folds.'

A list of prefixes and suffixes commonly used in word building follows below. *Attachable, attaching, reattach,* and *unattached* have the same root. Try to analyze and identify the root, prefixes, and suffixes. Then look up the prefixes and suffixes in the lists that follow and see how they modify the meaning of the root.

Suffixes often change a word's part of speech. The adjective *sad* is made into a noun by adding *-ness,* which means 'the state of being.' The noun *courage* is changed into an adjective by adding the suffix *-ous,* meaning 'full of.' Writers commonly use the suffix *-ly* to make adverbs: *glad, gladly; correct, correctly.* Suffixes also are used with adjectives and adverbs to indicate increasing degree. The suffix *-er* forms the comparative, and *-est* forms the superlative for many words: *greater, greatest; faster, fastest; prettier, prettiest.*

Another element used in building words is called a combining form. This is a special form of a word joined with another word or word part to make a combined or compound word. *Tele-*, meaning 'having to do with or operating over a long distance' (from Greek *têle,* meaning 'far off'), and *-phone,* meaning 'sound' (from the Greek *phōnéē,* meaning 'sound'), combine to make *telephone. Bio-*, meaning 'life or living things' (from Greek *bios,* meaning 'life'), and *-logy,* meaning 'science of' (from Greek *lógos,* meaning 'deal with or discuss'), combine to form *biology. Cosmology, geology,* and *hydrology* are made the same way. Another example is the combining form *auto-*, which can be used with other combining forms and words such as *biography, graph,* and *mobile.* Many combining forms are well-established in English, but are borrowed from Latin or Green words, or may originate from other languages, such as French or German.

A list of combining forms that can be used with other word elements to create thousands of words follows below.

Word parts and spelling

Understanding the building of words helps with understanding of words, remembering their meanings, and spelling. Those who realize that *tele-* is a combining form meaning 'operating over long distances' are unlikely to make errors in spelling *telephone* or *telecommunications* with an *a* instead of the *e* at the end of the prefix *tele-.* Often, the addition of a suffix does not change the spelling of a root word: *heiress, greenish, brighten, joyful.* In some cases, however, the suffix requires a variation in the spelling of the root word: *desirable, victorious, truly.* At times, the prefix calls for insertion of a hyphen before the rest of the word: *anti-inflammatory.* See the section on Basic Spelling Rules in the Language Guide for tips on spelling words made by adding prefixes or suffixes.

Understanding unfamiliar words

Understanding something about the function of roots, affixes, and combining forms will often help you recognize many new or unfamiliar words. If you know the meanings of such combining forms as *photo-* (meaning 'light'); *-meter* (meaning 'device for measuring'); *chrono-* (meaning 'time'); and *-graph* (meaning 'something written, drawn, or pictured' and 'an instrument that writes, draws or pictures, or records'), you can construct and determine the meaning of many words, such as the following:

> photochemistry
> photocopy
> photometer
> photograph
> photochronograph
> chronometer
> chronophotograph
> chronograph

Once you know that words are made up of elements in predictable positions, you can break down a word into its parts. You may know the meanings of these parts, or you can easily look them up. The lists of prefixes, suffixes, and combining forms help you do this. Many English words are made up of roots and affixes that are derived from Latin and Greek. For example, consider the word *interplanetary.* It is composed of the prefix *inter-* (from the Latin *inter,* meaning 'among; between'); the root word, *planet* (from the Greek *planéētēs [astérēs],* meaning 'wandering stars'); and the suffix *-ary* (from the Latin *-ărius,* meaning 'place for; belonging to'). Thus, the definition of the word *interplanetary* is 'situated between the planets; in the region of the planets.' Sometimes two combining forms are joined to make a word. For example, *Anglo-* (from the Latin *Anglī,* meaning 'English') and *-phile* (from the Greek *philos,* meaning 'lover of') are two combining forms joined to make the word *Anglophile,* which is defined as 'a friend or admirer of England and the English.'

Knowing word organization can enrich your vocabulary. Once you understand unfamiliar words, you will be able to use them in speaking and writing. The greater the variety of words that you can use with confidence, the better your ideas and opinions will be accepted and understood by others.

Following are lists of selected prefixes, suffixes, and combining forms. Any element listed may change its form when being used to make a word. For example, the combining form *auto* sometimes drops the final *o* when added to word parts beginning with vowels: *autism, autarchy*.

Prefixes

Prefix	Meaning	Example
a-	on, in, into	afire, abed
	in the act of	aflutter
	not	apolitical
ab-; a-	from, away, off	abdicate; avert
ad-; a-; ac-	to, toward	adverb; ascribe; accede
	at, near	adjacent
an-	not	anastigmatic
	without	anarchy
ana-	back, again	anachronism
	up, upward	anode
ante-	before	antebellum
anti-	against, opposed to	antiaircraft
	not, opposite of	antisocial
apo-	from, away, off	apocryphal
arch-	chief, principal	archbishop; architect
	extreme, ultra	archconservative
bi-	two	bisect
	twice, once every two	biannual
cata-	down, downward	cataract
	against	catapult
circum-	around, on all sides	circumlocution
cis-	on this side of	cislunar
co-	with, together	cooperate
	joint, fellow	coauthor
com-; col-; con-	with, together, altogether	combine; collaborate; congress
contra-	against	contradict
de-	to do the opposite of	decentralize
	down, lower	depress
	away, off	derail
	to remove, take away	defrost
demi-	half, partial	demigod
	smaller than ordinary	demitasse
di-	twice, double, two	diphthong; dissyllable
dia-; di-	through, across	diameter; diocese
dis-	opposite, lack of	dishonest
	apart, away	dismiss
dys-	bad, defective	dysfunctional
en-; em-	to cause to be, make	enable; employ
	to put in, put on	enthrone; emblem
epi-; ep-	on, upon, above, in addition, toward	epidemic; epitaph; ephemeral
eu-	good, well, true	euphoria

Prefix	Meaning	Example
ex-; e-	former, formerly	ex-president
	out of, from, out	exhale; emerge
	thoroughly, utterly	exterminate; evaporate
extra-	outside, beyond	extraordinary
fore-	front, in front	forepaw
	before, beforehand	foregoing
hemi-	half	hemisphere
hyper-	over, excessive, above, exceedingly	hypercritical, hypersensitive
hypo-	under, beneath	hypodermic
	to a lesser degree	hypothyroid
in-; il-; im-; ir-	not, lack of, opposite of	incorrect; illegal; impatient; irregular
	in, into, on, upon	inscribe;illuminate; imbibe; irrigate
infra-	below, beneath	infrastructure
inter-	one with the other	intercommunicate
	between, among	interpose
intra-	within, inside	intramural
intro-	inward, within, into	introduce
meta-	between, among	metacarpus
	change of state	metabolism
	behind, after	metathorax
mis-	bad, badly	misgovern
	wrong, wrongly	mispronounce
non-	not, opposite of, lack of, failure	nonbreakable, nonliving
ob-; op-; of-; o-	against, in the way, hindering	obstruct; oppose; offend; omit
	inversely, contrary	oblate
	toward, to	obvert; offer
	on, over	obtuse
para-	beside, near	parathyroid
	beyond	parapsychology
	related to, subordinate to	paramedical, paralegal
per-	throughout	perpetual
peri-	around, surrounding	perimeter
post-	after, in time	postwar
	after, in space	postnasal
pre-	before	prewar
pro-	forward	proceed
	forth, out	proclaim
	on the side of	pro-British
	in place of, acting as	proconsul
	before, preceding	prologue
	in front of	proscenium
quasi-	partly, as if	quasi-judicial
re-	again, anew	reappear
	back	repay

Prefix	Meaning	Example	Prefix	Meaning	Example
semi-	exactly half	semicircle	trans-	across, over, through	transcontinental
	about half, partly	semicivilized			
sub-	under, below	subnormal		beyond, on the other side of	transcend, transoceanic
	down, further, again	subdivide		to or into a different condition	transform, transmigration
	near, nearly	subtropical			
	lower, subordinate	subhead	ultra-	beyond	ultraviolet
super-	over, above	superimpose		extremely	ultramodern
	besides, further	superadd	un-	not	unequal
	in high proportion	superabundant		the opposite of	ungodly
	surpassing	supernatural	uni-	one, a single	unicellular
syn-; syl-; sym-	with, together, jointly	synagogue; syllogism; symbol	up-	up	update
			vice-	one who acts in place of another	vice president, viceroy

Suffixes

Suffix	Meaning	Example	Suffix	Meaning	Example
-able	that can be	obtainable	-ed	having, or having characteristics of	long-legged, bigoted, honeyed
	suitable for; giving	comfortable			
	inclined to	peaceable	-en	cause to be; make	blacken
	fit to; deserving of	wearable, lovable		cause to have	strengthen
-age	action; process	breakage		to become	sicken
	group; collection of	baggage		made of; have look of	silken
	state or rank of	peerage		plural	oxen
	cost of; fee for	postage	-ence	state of being	indifference
	house or place of	orphanage, anchorage	-ent	one who	president
-al, -ial	having the nature of	ornamental; facial	-er, -ier, -yer	one who does or is concerned with	reporter, cashier; lawyer
	act of	arrival		person living in	New Yorker
-an; -ean; -ian	native of	American; European		more (comparative)	smarter
	having to do with	Shakespearean		action or process of	waiver
-ana; -iana	collection of; about	Americana; Burnsiana	-ery	the art of	cookery
-ance; -ancy	act of	resistance		the condition of	slavery
				quality or action of	knavery
	thing that	conveyance		a place where	bindery
	quality or state of	buoyancy	-ese	having to do with	Chinese
-ant	state or condition of	defiant	-esque	in the style of	Romanesque
				like a	statuesque
	one who	assistant	-ess	female	heiress
-ary	place for	infirmary	-est	most (superlative)	smartest
	collection of	statuary	-et	little, small	owlet
	having to do with	legendary	-ette	little, small	dinette
-ate	having to do with	collegiate	-ful	full of	cupful, playful
	make or cause to be	alienate	-fy	make or cause to be	electrify, simplify
	produce	ulcerate	-hood	state of being	childhood
	supply or treat with	aerate	-ible	can be, able to be	divisible
	combine with	oxygenate	-ic	having to do with	atmospheric
-ation	act or process of	computation		having the nature of	heroic
-cle, -cule	little, small	particle; molecule		containing	alcoholic
-cy	state of being	bankruptcy		made or caused by	volcanic
	position or rank	captaincy		like; similar to	meteoric
-dom	rank or realm of	kingdom	-ical	of the nature of	critical, political
	condition of	freedom	-ing	act of person or thing	acting, running

Suffix	Meaning	Example	Suffix	Meaning	Example
-ion	act or process of	admission	-ment	act or state of	enjoyment
	state or condition	subjection		condition of being	amazement
-ish	somewhat	sweetish		product or result of	pavement
	like a	childish	-most	most (superlative)	uppermost
	having to do with	English	-ness	state or quality of	greatness
	tending to	bookish	-oid	like, similar to	adenoid, spheroid
-ism	act or practice of	baptism	-or	person or thing	auditor, actor,
	quality or condition	heroism		that does something	elevator
	doctrine or theory	Darwinism		act, state, quality,	error, horror,
-ist	expert in	botanist		or condition	labor, terror
	one who believes in	socialist	-ory	place for	conservatory
-ite	native of	Denverite		tending or inclined to	conciliatory
	descendant of	Israelite			
	follower of	Jacobite	-osis	abnormal condition	psychosis
-itis	inflammation of	tonsillitis			
-ity	state of	acidity	-ous	full of	poisonous
-ive	having to do with	sportive	-ry	occupation or work of	dentistry
-ize	become or resemble	Americanize		collection of	citizenry
	treat or combine with	oxidize	-ship	condition of being	partnership
				office or occupation	authorship
-less	without	meatless		act, power, or skill	horsemanship
	that does not	tireless	-some	tending to	meddlesome
	that cannot be	countless	-ster	person who	trickster
-let	little, small	booklet	-tion	act or state of	locomotion
-like	like; similar to	homelike	-ule	little, small	capsule, globule
-ling	little, small	duckling	-ure	act or process of	closure
-ly	in a manner	cheerfully	-ward	toward; leading to	homeward
	like a	ghostly			

Combining forms

Form	Meaning	Example	Form	Meaning	Example
aero-	atmosphere	aerospace	deca-	ten	decade
agro-	field, soil	agrology	deci-	one tenth	decibel
ambi-	both	ambidextrous	dextro-	toward the right	dextrorotatory
amphi-	around; on both sides	amphitheater	ecto-	to or on the outside	ectoderm
archaeo-	primitive, ancient	archaeology	electro-	electric	electromagnet
astro-	star; heavenly body	astrophysics	endo-	inner	endoderm
			equi-	equal	equivalence
atmo-	vapor, steam	atmosphere	ethno-	race, nation	ethnology
auto-	self	autobiography	ferro-	contains iron	ferronickel
baro-	atmospheric pressure	barometer	fibro-	fiber, fibrous	fibrovascular
			-gamous	marrying, joining	bigamous
biblio-	books	bibliography	-gamy	marriage	polygamy
bio-	life; of living things	biochemistry	geo-	earth	geology
			giga-	one billion	gigabyte
calci-	lime, calcium	calciferous	-gram	something written	telegram
cardio-	heart	cardiology	-graph	instrument that writes	seismograph
centi-	one hundred	centipede			
	one hundredth	centimeter	-graphy	to write	biography
centro-	center, central	centrobaric	-gynous	woman, female	misogynous
chromato-,	color, pigment	chromatology,	gyro-	circle	gyroscope
chromo-		chromoplast	hecto-	a hundred	hectogram
chrono-	time	chronometer	helio-	the sun	helioscope
-cide	killer	insecticide	hema-,	blood	hemachrome,
cosmo-	world, universe	cosmological	hemo-		hemolymph
counter-	against	counteract	hepta-	seven	heptagon
cranio-	skull	craniology	hexa-	six	hexagon
crypto-	hidden, secret	cryptography	holo-	whole	holocaust
cyclo-	circle	cyclotron	homo-	the same; equal	homogenous
cyto-	cell	cytogenesis	hydro-	water	hydroplane

Form	Meaning	Example	Form	Meaning	Example
hypno-	sleep, hypnosis	hypnology	phil-, philo-	loving; fond of	philanthropy, philobiblic
hypo-	under, below	hypodermic			
ideo-	idea	ideograph	-phobia	fear, hatred	acrophobia
iso-	equal, alike	isobar	phon-, phono-	sound	phonics, phonometer
kilo-	one thousand	kilometer			
lacto-	milk	lactoprotein	photo-	light	photograph
leuko-	without color	leukocyte	phyto-	plant	phytochemistry
levo-	toward the left	levorotatory	pico-	one trillionth	picofarad
litho-	stone, stony	lithography	poly-	many	polynomial
-logy	science of	biology	pyro-	having to do with fire	pyromania
macro-	large	macrocosm			
mal-	bad, poor	maladjusted	quadr-, quadri-	four	quadrangle, quadrilateral
mega-	large	megaphone			
	one million	megabyte	schizo-	split, divided	schizophrenic
-meter	a device for measuring	chronometer	sept-	seven	septangular
			sex-	six	sexangular
micro-	small	microcosm	spectro-	spectrum	spectroscope
	one millionth	microfarad	spermato-	seed, sperm	spermatocyte
mid-	middle	midnight	sporo-	spore	sporogenesis
milli-	one thousandth	millimeter	-stat	stabilizing instrument	thermostat
mini-	smaller or less than normal	miniskirt	stereo-	solid	stereobate
				three dimensional	stereoscopic
-monger	dealer, seller	fishmonger			
mono-	one, single	monorail	tel-, tele-	operating over long distances	telectric, telescope
multi-	many, much	multiform			
nano-	one billionth	nanosecond	tera-	one trillion	terabyte
neo-	new, recent	neoplasm	tetra-	four	tetrahedron
neuro-	nerve	neurosurgery	theo-	a god or gods	theology
nitro-	nitric acid	nitrocellulose	thermo-	heat	thermodynamics
oct-, octa-, octo-	eight	octet, octachord, octopus	topo-	place	topography
			tri-	three	triangle
omni-	all, completely	omnipotent	tricho-	hair, hairlike	trichosis
ortho-	straight, correct	orthopedics	vaso-	blood vessel	vasoconstrictor
paleo-	old, ancient	paleography	xeno-	stranger	xenophobia
pan-	all	Pan-American	xero-	dry	xeroderma
-pathy	feeling	antipathy	xylo-	wood, woody	xylophone
	disease	psychopathy	zoo-	animal	zoology
pedo-	child, children	pedodontics	zygo-	yoke, paired	zygomorphic
penta-	five	pentameter			

Learning to Spell Correctly

The best way to learn how to spell any word correctly is by looking up the word in a dictionary. If you are not sure of the spelling, you might still try to find it, ask someone, or look on a list of commonly misspelled words (like the one in this Language Guide).

Once you have looked it up, make the word yours by following these steps:

1. Write the word out neatly and clearly.
2. Close your eyes and visualize the word in your mind.
3. Spell the word out loud. It is important that you say it out loud.
4. Study the syllables if it has more than one.
5. Pronounce the word out loud.
6. Study its meaning; it may have more than one.
7. Make up a sentence using the word. Say the sentence.
8. Use the word at the next opportunity in writing or talking.

If you know how to spell the basic forms of words, most other spelling problems arise when the word is inflected, that is, changed to show number, person, tense, or comparison.

To help you with these problems, a list of spelling rules is given below. Don't try to memorize the rules. Remember that they can be found on these pages. When you have a spelling problem look it up here, and learn the rules and exceptions by using them.

Basic spelling rules

Rules for Plural Nouns

dogs, bills, receipts; handkerchiefs. RULE: Most singular words are made plural by simply adding *s*. Exceptions: Some nouns ending in *f* or *fe* form the plural by changing the *f* or *fe* to *ve* and adding *s: knives, elves, halves, calves, leaves, loaves, sheaves, shelves, wives.*

churches. RULE: Words ending in *ch, j, s, ss, sh, x,* or *z* are made plural by adding *es*. Also following this rule: *buses, bosses, bushes, boxes, topazes*

potatoes, tomatoes. RULE: Nouns ending in *o* preceded by a consonant form the plural by adding *es*. Exceptions: Some words add *s* only: *silos, dittos.* In other cases, either *s* or *es* is correct: *buffalos* or *buffaloes; volcanoes* or *volcanos.* Check the dictionary if you are not sure.

armies. RULE: Nouns ending in *y* preceded by a consonant form the plural by changing *y* to *i* and adding *es*. Exceptions: Proper names ending in *y* form the plural by adding *s*. Example: "There are four *Marys* in this class."

monkeys. RULE: Nouns ending in *y* preceded by a vowel form the plural by adding *s*. Also following this rule: *keys, bays.* Exception: *soliloquy,* plural *soliloquies.*

cameos. RULE: Nouns ending in *o* preceded by a vowel form the plural by adding *s*. Also following this rule: *radios, stereos.*

Other Spelling Rules

believe. RULE: Use *i* before *e* except after *c* or when sounded as "ay" as in *neighbor* and *weigh*. Also following this rule: *relieve, sleigh*—Exceptions: *counterfeit, either, foreign, forfeit, height, leisure, seize, weird.*

desirable. RULE: For words ending in *e*, drop the final *e* before adding a suffix beginning with a vowel. Also following this rule: *caring.* Exceptions: *mileage, saleable.*

humaneness. RULE: For words ending in *e*, keep the final *e* before adding a suffix beginning with a *consonant*.

canoeing. RULE: For words ending in *e* preceded by a vowel, keep the *e* before adding a suffix, except a suffix beginning with *e*. Also following this rule: *lovely.*

dying. RULE: For words ending in *ie*, change the *ie* to *y* before adding a suffix. Also following this rule: *lying.*

supplied. RULE: For words ending in *y* preceded by a consonant, change *y* to *i* before a suffix, unless suffix begins with *i.*

shyly. RULE: For words of one syllable ending in *y*, keep the *y* before a suffix: *shy, shyly; dry, dryly.*

stayed. For words ending in *y* preceded by a vowel, retain the *y* before a suffix. Exceptions: *daily, laid, paid, said, slain.*

changeable. RULE: For words ending in soft-sounding *ce* or *ge*, retain the final *e* when adding suffixes. Also following this rule: *advantageous.*

preferred. RULE: For words ending in a consonant preceded by a single vowel, double the consonant before adding a vowel suffix. Also following this rule: *beginning.* Exceptions: *crocheting, ricocheted, filleted.*

benefiting. RULE: For words ending in a consonant preceded by more than one vowel, or not accented on the last syllable, do not double the final consonant. Also following this rule: *revealing; boiling.*

accidentally. RULE: For words ending in one *l*, keep the final *l* before a suffix beginning with *l.*

fully. RULE: For words ending in *ll*, drop one *l* before adding an *ly* suffix. Also following this rule: *hilly.*

brothers-in-law. RULE: For compound nouns, add *s* to the main word to form a plural. Exceptions: *cupfuls;* for words ending in *ful*, add the simple plural *-s.*

Commonly misspelled words

How many times have you heard people say, "if you do not know how to spell a word, look it up in the dictionary"? But how do you find a word that you cannot spell? First, try checking the spelling rules and exceptions on the previous pages in the Language Guide. You might have switched an *e* and *i*, or added a prefix or suffix without making the correct change in the root. You can also try different ways of pronouncing and spelling a word, then look for these varieties in the dictionary. One of the most common reasons for misspelling is mispronunciation. For example, you may develop the habit of saying *government* without the *n,* and spelling it that way. Some words have confusing sounds or silent letters. You might spell *maritime* with an *a* instead of the first *i,* or *fasten* without the *t.* Words that sound alike but have different meanings can be tricky. You might use *principal* when you mean *principle,* or *affect* instead of *effect.* Becoming familiar with the words listed below, and with the next section of the Language Guide, **Writing and spelling traps,** can help you avoid this.

Following is a list of commonly misspelled words. These words are problematic for many people, and are frequently used in school spelling bees.

abscess
acceptance
accommodate
according
accustomed
achievement
acquaintance
acquire
adequate
adjourned
affidavit
analysis
anesthetic
Antarctic
anticipation
anxiety
appetite
approximately
arctic
artificial
assassin
assess
athletics
attorneys
auxiliary

bankruptcy
benefit
bought
brief
bureau

cafeteria
campaign
cancellation
candidate
capacity
casserole
census
cessation
challenge
characteristic
circuit
civilized
collateral
colloquial
colonel

commitment
committee
comparatively
complaint
condemn
condescend
confidential
conscience
conscious
consensus
consequently
continuous
controversy
convenience
corporation
correlate
correspondence
counsel
counterfeit
courteous
crisis
criticism
curiosity
cylinder

debtor
definitely
descend
despair
diaphragm
dilemma
dining
disappear
disappoint
discipline
dissipate
distinguish
dormitory

effervescent
efficacy
efficiency
eligible
eliminate
ellipse
encouraging
enthusiasm

equipped
esteemed
exaggerating
except
exceptionally
excessive
executive
exhibition
exhilarating
existence

facilities
fallacy
fascinating
feasible
fictitious
financial
foliage
forego
fortunately

gauge
guarantee

handkerchief
haphazard
harass
height
hemorrhage
hydraulic
hygiene
hypocrisy

icicle
immediately
immense
inalienable
incidentally
inconvenience
indelible
indictment
indispensable
inevitable
inferred
initial
installation
intellectual

intermittent
intimate
irrelevant
irresistible

jeopardize
journal

laboratory
leisure
license
lieutenant
livelihood

maintenance
management
manufacturer
mathematics
miniature
molecule
monotonous
mortgage
murmur
mutual

necessarily
ninety
noticeable

occasion
occasionally
occurred
offense
official
omitted
opportunities
ordinarily

pamphlet
paradise
parallel
parenthesis
partial
participate
peaceable
peculiar
perceive

peril
perpendicular
perseverance
petition
philosophy
physician
plateau
plausible
pneumonia
politician
possess
practically
precisely
predecessor
prior
probability
privilege
psychology
pursuit

receipt
receiving
recommend
referred
reign
relevant
remembrance
reminisce
remiss
remittance
rendezvous
representative
requisition
restaurant
reticence
ridiculous

satisfactorily
schedule
scissors
seize
separate
shepherd
sheriff
simultaneous
skiing
solemn

sorority
specific
spontaneous
statistics
statutes
strength
substantial
succeeded
succession
sufficient
supplement
surveillance
suspicion
sustenance
sympathy
synchronous

temporarily
tentative
terrestrial
thoroughly
tournament
tourniquet
tragedy
transferred

unanimous
undoubtedly
unique
unison
unmanageable
unnecessary
utilize

vacancy
vague
veil

warrant
weird
wretched
wrought

Writing and Spelling Traps

In English, there are many words that sound alike or look alike, but have different meanings. There are also a number of words and phrases that are sometimes used incorrectly. Such words and phrases are often confusing and lead to errors in usage or spelling. The following list has been compiled from many sources. It is representative, but not exhaustive. The usage notes and spelling tips included under entries in this dictionary offer additional examples and more details on many of the words and phrases below.

ability, capability. *Ability* is the skill to perform; *capability* is the ability of a person to learn or to do something or of a thing to do something. The captain has the *ability* to steer the ship. The ship has a *capability* of thirty knots.

accept, except. The first, always a verb, means to take or receive; the second, sometimes a verb, means to exclude; as preposition, it means excluding. She will *accept* the conditions *except* those that deal with her personal life.

adapt, adept, adopt. *Adapt* means to make suitable; *adept* to be skilled or expert; *adopt* to take for one's own.

adjoin, adjourn. The first means to be next to; the second, to put off until later.

advice, advise. The first means an opinion. The second means to give counsel. He *advised* me about buying that house, but I didn't take his *advice*.

affect, effect. Usually *affect* is a verb meaning to influence. *Effect* used as a noun means result; as a verb it means to bring to pass. The new law *affected* the crime rate, and this *effect* was largest in the cities.

agree to, agree with. You *agree to* a plan, but *agree with* another person.

aid, aide. *Aid* means to give help; an *aide* is an assistant.

air, heir. *Air* is the gas we breathe; *heir* is someone who inherits property.

allay, ally. *Allay* means to put at rest, *ally* to unite. The countries *allied* (became *allies*) to *allay* the possibility of attack.

all right, alright. *All right* is always all right, but *alright* (a nonstandard spelling) is not all right.

all together, altogether. *All together* means everyone in a group. *Altogether* means completely or entirely. *Altogether* there are 14 persons when the group is *all together*.

allude, elude. You *allude* to (refer indirectly to) a book, but you *elude* (slip away from) a bore.

allusion, illusion. You make an *allusion* by referring indirectly to a person or thing, while an *illusion* is an unreal or misleading appearance.

although, though. *Although* usually introduces a clause that precedes the main clause, *though* usually introduces one that follows. *Although* many have succeeded, he failed completely, *though* he tried hard.

amiable, amicable. *Amiable* describes a friendly, good-natured person; *amicable* describes a peaceful, friendly relationship.

among, between. *Among* usually refers to more than two and *between* refers to two. The main pieces were divided *among* the group. The remainder was split *between* Tom and Bill. However, where there are more than two parties involved, *between* may be used to emphasize the relationship of pairs within the group.

ante, anti. *Ante* means before; *anti* means against.

anyplace, anywhere. Use *anywhere*. This same holds true for *everywhere, nowhere,* and *somewhere.*

appraise, apprise. The former means to estimate value; the latter, to inform. He *appraised* the vase, then *apprised* the owner of its value.

arms, alms. The first refers to part of the body or weapons; the second, to gifts to the poor.

as large as, larger than. The first is used when you want to say that something is two or more times bigger than something else; the latter, compares two things. Colorado is three times *as large as* Maine, but Texas is *larger than* Colorado.

as, like. Use *as* to introduce a clause, *like* to introduce a phrase. Do *as* I do, and you'll find the work will be *like* play.

ascent, assent. The first refers to going up; the second, to agreement or consent.

assay, essay. He wrote an *essay* (composition) on how to *assay* (analyze) gold ore.

averse, adverse. You are probably *averse* (opposed) to *adverse* (bad) weather conditions.

bases, basis. The *bases* (underlying supports, or series of stations) were built on the *basis* (groundwork) of a survey.

beau, bough, bow. He *bowed* and extended his hand to his sister's *beau* (suitor) when they met under the *bough* (main branch) of the tree.

bell, belle. As the *bells* rang, the *belles* (beautiful women) came into the hall.

beside, besides. *Beside* means by the side of; *besides* means also or in addition to. *Besides* his hat and coat, he left his shoes *beside* the river.

biannual, biennial. *Biannual* means twice a year; *biennial* means every two years.

block, bloc. *Block* means many things, but a *bloc* means only a group of persons combined for a purpose.

born, borne. *Born* means bring into life; *borne* to carry or support.

bouillon, bullion. The first is soup; the second refers to gold and silver.

breach, breech. *Breach* refers to an opening; *breech* refers to the lower or back part of something.

bring, take. *Bring* indicates motion toward a speaker; *take* indicates motion away. *Bring* the soup to him and *take* the plates from the table.

calendar, calender. The first is a table showing the divisions of a year; the second, a machine that presses cloth or paper.

callous, callus. *Callous* is an adjective meaning hard or unfeeling; *callus* is a noun referring to a hard, thickened place on the skin. Only a *callous* person would not feel pity when they saw the *calluses* on his skin.

can, may. *Can* implies ability; *may* implies permission. Mary *may* drive the car, if she *can*.

cannon, canon. The first is an artillery weapon; the second, a church rule or law.

canvas, canvass. *Canvas* is a type of cloth; *canvass* means to examine, discuss, or solicit.

capital, capitol. A *capital* is the city or town in which the government of a country, state, or province is located. A *capitol* is the building in which a legislative body meets.

casual, causal. The former means uncertain or informal in manner; the latter refers to the cause of.

censor, censure. As a verb, the former means to act as a censor (one who suppresses objectionable material); the latter means to blame or criticize. He *censured* him for *censoring* the letter.

cents, scents, sense. *Cents* refers to money, *scents* to smells, and *sense* to the mind.

cession, session. *Cession* means handing over to another; *session* is a meeting or time period.

charted, charter. *Charted* involves maps. *Charter* concerns a written grant or order.

choral, coral, corral. *Choral* refers to a chorus; *coral* to tiny sea animals and the reefs they build; *corral* to an animal pen.

cite, sight, site. *Cite* means to quote or refer to; *sight* deals with seeing; *site* is a position or place.

clench, clinch. *Clench* means to close tightly; *clinch* is to fasten or settle decisively. She *clenched* her teeth as she *clinched* the deal.

click, clique. *Click* is a sound; *clique* is a group of people.

climactic, climatic. *Climactic* refers to a climax; *climatic* to the climate.

coarse, course. *Coarse* means rough or vulgar; *course* can be onward movement, a track, or a series of studies.

compare, contrast. *Compare* is commonly used in two senses: (1) to point out likenesses (compare to) and (2) to examine two or more objects to find both likenesses and differences (compare with). *Contrast* means to point out differences.

compare to, compare with. *Compare to* means to point out general or metaphorical resemblances. *Compare with* means to note specific similarities or differences between persons or things of the same kind. He *compared* the sea *to* a woman, and his painting of waves were tranquil *compared with* those of Jones.

complement, compliment. The first is something that completes; the second refers to praise.

compose, comprise. The parts *compose* the whole; the whole is *comprised* of the parts.

confidant, confident. The first is a trusted person; the second refers to firm belief.

core, corps. *Core* refers to the central part; *corps* is a group of people.

corespondent, correspondent. The first involves a divorce; the second involves letters or journalism. The *correspondent* wrote about the divorce case in which Smith was named *corespondent*.

council, counsel. *Council* is an assemblage of people; *counsel* means advice.

continual, continuous. *Continual* implies a recurrence at frequent intervals; *continuous* means extending uninterruptedly. The *continual* hammering gave him a *continuous* headache.

coward, cowered. The first is someone who lacks courage; the second refers to crouching from danger, or in fear.

credible, creditable. The first means believable; the second bringing honor or praise.

cue, queue. You receive a *cue* as a hint, but you wait in a *queue* (line of people) or wear your hair in one (a braid).

currant, current. *Currants* are seedless raisins or tart berries. *Current* refers to flow or to present time.

decree, degree. *Decree* is something ordered by authority, while *degree* is a stage in a process or an academic award.

defer, differ. The first means to put off or yield; the second, to be unlike or disagree.

descent, dissent. *Descent* refers to coming or going down; *dissent* means to disagree.

desert, dessert. Do not confuse *desert* (a place of little rainfall) with *dessert* (sweets or the like served at the end of a meal).

desolate, dissolute. A desert is *desolate* (barren); people who have no morals are *dissolute.*

disburse, disperse. You *disburse* (pay out) money, but you *disperse* (distribute) handbills.

discomfit, discomfort. *Discomfit* means to overthrow, defeat, or embarrass; *discomfort* refers to uneasiness.

discreet, discrete. The former means careful and sensible, the latter means distinct or separate from others. It was a *discreet* action consisting of two *discrete* maneuvers.

distract, detract. *Distract* means to draw away or confuse; *detract,* to take away from. The defect *distracts* your attention and *detracts* from the value.

ecology, environment. *Ecology* is the study of the relationship of living things to each other and their *environment* (surrounding conditions). Pollution affects the *environment; ecology* attempts to determine how.

either means one or the other, not both. Do not say, There are lions behind *either* door when there are lions behind *both* doors. Either is followed by *or,* not *nor.*

elicit, illicit. *Elicit* is a verb meaning to draw out something that is hidden or held back; *illicit* is an adjective meaning unlawful or improper. The police *elicited* from him the hiding place of the *illicit* drug.

emigrate, immigrate. A person *emigrates,* or moves out of, one country and *immigrates,* or moves into, a new place or another country. The *emigrant* from Poland was finally given permission to *immigrate* to the U.S.

eminent, imminent. Do not say something is *eminent* (distinguished) when you mean his arrival is *imminent* (about to occur).

ensure, insure. Both words mean *to make certain,* but *insure* usually is confined to the meaning *guarantee against loss.* His house was *insured* against fire to *ensure* that he would have money to buy another if it burned down.

envelop, envelope. The first is a verb meaning to wrap or cover; the second, a noun referring to stationery or an enclosing covering.

equable, equitable. *Equable* means uniform; *equitable* means fair. *Equable* distribution is the only *equitable* way.

errand, errant. Do not refer to a short trip, or the purpose of the trip, as an *errant,* which means wandering or incorrect.

exalt, exult. *Exalt* means to raise in rank or to fill with pride; *exult* means to rejoice.

extant, extent. *Extant* means still existing; *extent* means the amount to which something extends. The animal is *extant* and roams the whole *extent* of the range.

fair, fare. *Fare* refers to a price for travel or to food; *fair* means just, not bad, or not dark.

farther, further. *Farther* refers to physical distance; *further,* to abstract relationships of degree or quantity. Smithville was *farther* from the capital than Johnstown and it was *further* behind Johnstown in cultural development.

feint, faint. *Feint* refers to a false appearance or movement; *faint* means not clear or weak, or to lose consciousness.

fewer, less. *Fewer* refers to number, *less* to degree or quantity. There were *fewer* fans and *less* enthusiasm.

fish, fishes. *Fish* is the plural for many of one kind, but *fishes* is used when writing of different species. Halibut, mackerel, and salmon are the most abundant *fishes* in those waters.

flair, flare. The first refers to perception or talent; the second, to flaming up or spreading out.

flew, flu, flue. The insect *flew* down the *flue* (chimney passage) and bit the man with the *flu* (influenza).

flounder, founder. As a verb the first means to struggle; the second, to stumble or sink. They *floundered* for life jackets, as the boat began to *founder.*

flout, flaunt. He *flouts* (treats with contempt) his work, but *flaunts* (displays boldly) his clothes.

fondling, foundling. The first refers to treating lovingly; the second is a noun meaning a deserted child.

foreword, forward. A *foreword* is an introduction or preface; *forward* means ahead or onward.

formally, formerly. *Formally* means in a formal manner. *Formerly* means in the past.

frees, freeze, frieze. Jonathan *frees* the captives tied below the *frieze* (ornamental band around a building or room), so they do not *freeze* to death.

fulsome means disgusting or offensive, not ample or abundant.

gait, gate. He had a swinging *gait* (way of walking) as he came through the *gate*.

gamble, gambol. You may *gambol* (frolic) if you win a risky *gamble* (game of chance).

gamut, gantlet, gauntlet. *Gamut* refers to the whole range of something. *Gantlet* is a method of punishment. *Gauntlet* is a glove.

gild, guild. *Gild* means to cover with gold; *guild* is a society or union.

grate, great. It is not so *great* to have to clean the *grate* (fireplace). It *grates* on your nerves.

grisly, gristly, grizzly. The *grisly* (frightening) *grizzly* (grayish) bear gnawed on the *gristly* (tough) gazelle.

hail, hale. Besides small pieces of ice, *hail* means to shout in welcome. *Hale* means strong and well.

hallow, hollow. *Hallow* refers to holy or sacred; *hollow* means empty inside.

hangar, hanger. A *hangar* is a shelter for airplanes; a *hanger* is someone who hangs things or a device for hanging clothes.

hoard, horde. *Hoard* means to save or store away; *horde* is a crowd or swarm.

hoarse, horse. Do not confuse *hoarse* (a rough, deep voice) with *horse* (an animal).

hospitable, hospital. *Hospitable* refers to friendly treatment; *hospital* is a place for sick or injured persons.

idle, idol. *Idle* means doing nothing; *idol* is an object that is worshipped.

imply, infer. A speaker *implies*. A hearer *infers*. He *implied* that he would be late; I *inferred* that he meant very late.

incite, insight. Do not confuse *incite* (the act of stirring up) with *insight* (understanding or wisdom).

incredible, incredulous. The former means unbelievable; the latter means unbelieving. They felt *incredulous* about his *incredible* story.

inequity, iniquity. *Inequity* refers to unfairness; *iniquity*, to wickedness.

ingenious, ingenuous. *Ingenious* means clever, skillful; *ingenuous* means frank, simple, sincere.

insolate, insulate. The former means to expose to the sun; the latter means to keep from losing heat or cold, or to set apart.

intense, intents. *Intense* means very strong; *intents* means purposes. She felt *intense* about her career *intents*.

interment, internment. Do not confuse *interment* (burial) and *internment* (confinement).

interstate, intrastate, intestate. *Interstate* means between states; *intrastate* means within a state; *intestate* means without a will.

its, it's. *It's* is a contraction of it is. *Its* name is Fido; *it's* a special breed.

jam, jamb. He was *jammed* (squeezed) against the door *jamb* (side of the door) by the fat man eating *jam* (food).

key, quay, cay. *Key* refers to a locking device. *Key* and *cay* both refer to a low island or reef. *Quay* is a landing place for ships.

knead, need. *Knead* is to mix by pressing; *need* refers to a lack of something.

knight, night. *Knight* is an honorable rank. *Night* is the dark time of a day.

later, latter. *Later* means more late, *latter* means the second of two. John and Joe were *late*, but the *latter* was *later*.

lay, lie. *Lay* is the action word. *Lie* is the state of laying. However, the past tense of *lie* is *lay*. *Lay* the medicine on the table. It is for the boy who *lay* (not laid) in the wet grass so long that he will have to *lie* in bed for a few days.

lean, lien. *Lean* means to incline, rest against, or without fat. *Lien* means a legal right on another's property.

leave, let. *Leave alone* means to depart from, or allow (cause) to be in solitude. *Let alone* means to be undisturbed. He talked the robber into *letting her alone;* later he had to go home and *leave her alone*.

less, fewer. *Less* refers to degree or quantity; *fewer*, to number. The Bears have *fewer* good linemen than the Vikings and these linemen have *less* experience.

lesser, lessor. *Lesser* means the less important of two. *Lessor* is a person who grants a lease.

liable, libel. *Liable* means likely or bound by law; *libel* refers to a false or damaging statement.

load, lode. You *load* a truck, but you mine a *lode* (vein) of metal ore.

loath, loathe. *Loath* means unwilling; *loathe* is to feel a strong dislike.

lose, loose. *Lose* means to stop having. *Loose* (verb) means to set free, or (adjective) not fastened.

main, mane. *Main* refers to the most important; *mane* refers to long neck hair on a horse and lion.

manner, manor. *Manner* refers to a way of behaving or happening; *manor* is part of an estate where the owner lives.

mantel, mantle. You put things on the *mantel* of a fireplace, but you wear a *mantle*.

maybe, may be. *Maybe* is an adverb or noun; *may be* is a verb form. *Maybe* you will have better luck next spring when you *may be* stronger.

mean, mien. *Mean* refers to the significance of something or to quality or grade. *Mien* refers to a way of acting or looking. He had a stern *mien*, but this did not *mean* he lacked compassion.

median, mean, average. *Median* refers to the middle. *Mean* and *average* refer to the total of all components divided by number of components. The *median* income of Springfield is $18,500; its *mean* summer temperature is 72°F.

medal, meddle. *Medal* refers to an award or commemorative coin; *meddle* refers to interfering in another's affairs.

metal, mettle. *Metals* are elements and alloys such as iron and steel. *Mettle* is the quality of a disposition; a person's spirit.

moat, mote. *Moat* is a protective ditch; *mote* is a speck of dust.

moral, morale. Do not write *moral* (concerning right conduct) when you mean *morale* (mental condition as regards courage and confidence).

morning, mourning. Do not write *morning* (the early part of the day) when you mean *mourning* (sorrow or wearing black).

naval, navel. *Naval* refers to warships and the navy; *navel* is the depression in the middle surface of the abdomen below the waist.

neither should be followed by *nor*, not *or*.

ordinance, ordnance. Do not confuse *ordinance* (a rule or law) with *ordnance* (military weapons).

over, more than. *Over* refers to relationships in space; *more than* is used with numbers. The airplane flew *over* a city with a population of *more than* 500,000.

pail, pale. Do not write *pail* (a bucket) when you want to refer to *pale* (something without much color or light, a narrow pointed board, or an enclosure).

pain, pane. You suffer *pain* as a hurt, but *pane* usually refers to a single division of a window or door.

pair, pairs. *Pair* is singular, but can be used as a plural after a numeral or an adjective of number such as several. She bought a *pair* of gloves and six *pairs* (or *pair*) of socks.

palate, palette, pallet. *Palate* is the roof of the mouth or the sense of taste. *Palette* is a set of colors or the thin board on which colors are mixed. *Pallet* may mean *palette*, or a poor bed, or a potter's blade, or a low platform on which loads are stacked.

passed, past. The past tense and past participle of *pass* are *passed*. *Past* is the adjective, adverb, and preposition. As he *passed* the house, he thought of *past* troubles and good times.

peak, peek, pique. He was *piqued* (angry) because he could not reach the *peak* (top); in fact he did not even get close enough to *peek* (look) at the summit (*peak*).

peddle, pedal. When you sell something, you *peddle* it. When you ride a bicycle, you *pedal* it.

peer, pier. *Peer* refers to a person equal in ability, age, and so on, or to look closely. *Pier* is a structure extending out into the water.

personal, personnel. *Personal* has to do with a person's private affairs; *personnel* refers to people employed in an organization.

plane, plain. *Plane* is a level, a flat surface, or a carpenter's tool. *Plain* means uncomplicated, or a flat stretch of land.

pole, poll. You can raise a flag on a *pole*, but you count the opinions or votes in a *poll*.

poor, pore, pour. *Poor* means having little or nothing: Some families are very *poor*. *Pore*[2] means to look over carefully: The editor *pored* over the manuscript. *Pore*[1] is a small opening: You have *pores* in your skin. *Pour* means to cause to flow: *Pour* the milk carefully.

practical, practicable. The former means having to do with action rather than theory; the latter means capable of being done. My *practical* scheme was to make the job *practicable* by removing several obstacles.

pray, prey. Man *prays* (communicates) to God, but *preys* on (hunts) animals.

preceding, previous. *Preceding* means to come before; *previous* means to come before at other times. In 1925, we made more money than in the *preceding* year, but not as much as in *previous* years.

prescribe, proscribe. You *prescribe* when you order or direct something; you *proscribe* when you prohibit or condemn something.

pretense, pretext. A *pretext* is put forward to conceal a truth. A *pretense* is intended to conceal personal feelings.

principle, principal. The former is a basic truth or guiding rule; the latter, a dominant or leading person or thing.

rain, reign, rein. Be sure to distinguish between *rain* (water falling from the clouds), *reign* (a period of power or rule), and *rein* (a strap to control an animal).

raise, raze. Do not write *raise* (lift up) when you mean *raze* (tear down).

reluctant, reticent. If you do not want to act you are *reluctant*. If you do not want to speak, you are *reticent*.

respectfully, respectively. The former means in a courteous manner, the latter in the order given. The soldiers took their *respective* positions and *respectfully* saluted the old captain.

role, roll. We play a *role* in life, but we *roll* objects along or into a ball.

root, route. *Root* refers to part of a plant; *route* means a road or way to go. (*Route* is sometimes pronounced like *rout*, which means a defeat and disorderly retreat.)

sac, sack. *Sac* refers to a baglike part in an animal or plant; *sack* usually means a bag of cloth or paper.

sail, sale. A *sail* goes on a boat; a *sale* involves exchanging money and goods.

serge, surge. *Serge* is a type of cloth; *surge* refers to a rising of waves or feelings.

set, sit. *Set* means to cause to sit; *sit* means to be seated. I *set* the projector on the table, then chose to *sit* in the big chair.

species, specie. *Species* refers to a kind or class; *specie*, to money in the form of coin.

shear, sheer. *Shear* means to cut or break; *sheer* can mean very thin, a steep grade, or to turn from a course.

sloe, slough, slow. If you *slow* down and think, you will not confuse *sloe* (a fruit) with *slough* (a muddy, swampy place or skin that is cast off).

soar, sore. When you *soar* you rise to great heights, but when you are *sore* you feel hurt or angry.

speciality, specialty. Use *speciality* when you mean the special character off something; use *specialty* when referring to a special line of work or business. American history is the *speciality* of that college and his *specialty* is the Civil War period.

stationary, stationery. *Stationary* means fixed, *stationery* means writing materials.

straight, strait. *Straight* means direct or without a curve; *strait* is a narrow channel or passage between two larger bodies of water.

such as, like. Use *such as* for examples; *like* for resemblances. Some ships, *such as* ocean liners, are *like* small cities.

tail, tale. Do not confuse *tail* (the hindmost part of an animal, or object), with *tale* (the story of an event).

team, teem. Do not write *team* (a group of people) when you mean *teem* (to be full).

tear, tier. You cry *tears* or *tear* a piece of paper, but *tiers* are a series of rows arranged one above the other.

temperatures get higher or lower, not warmer or cooler.

tenant, tenet. A *tenant* is an occupant or renter; a *tenet* is a doctrine or belief.

that, which. *That* is preferred in clauses that restrict a thought. *Which* is nonrestrictive, adding subsidiary information. The river *that* forms the boundary between Texas and Mexico is the Rio Grande, *which* has its source in Colorado.

then, than. Use *than* in comparisons; *then* when time is involved, or you mean also. This train is faster *than* that one, but *then* it has a more powerful locomotive.

their, there, they're. *Their* is the possessive form of *they* and means belong to. *There* means in or at that place. *They're* means they are. *They're* going to buy *their* equipment *there*.

tic, tick. Do not confuse *tic* (an involuntary twitch) with *tick* (the sound of a timepiece, or a blood-sucking insect).

timber, timbre. Use *timber* when writing about wood; *timbre* when referring to sound or resonance.

tortuous, torturous. The first means full of twists and turns; the second refers to inflicting pain. The sun was *torturous* as he rode through the *tortuous* ravines.

track, tract. *Track* refers to a patch, or a sport; *tract* to a stretch of land or water.

unique means the only one of its kind. Something cannot be very unique, quite unique, somewhat unique, or rather unique; but it can be rare, odd, or unusual.

vain, vane. *Vain* refers to having too much pride, or to not succeeding; *vane* is a blade or flag that moves with wind or water.

vial, vile. *Vial* refers to a small container or to an outpouring of wrath; *vile* means bad or foul.

waive, wave. *Waive* refers to giving something up; *wave* refers to movements like the surge or swell of water.

weather, whether. You should not confuse *weather* (the condition of the atmosphere) with an expression of choice or alternative.

were, was. *Were* is used when a statement is contrary to fact, expresses a wish, or states a doubtful situation. *Was* is used for statements of facts in the past. If he *were* here, he would be as wise as he *was* during the war.

wet, whet. *Wet* is the opposite of dry; *whet* is to sharpen by rubbing or to make keen.

whither, wither. Use *whither* to mean to what place; *wither* to mean a loss of freshness or vigor.

who, whom. *Whom* refers to someone who has been the object of an action. *Who* is used for the person who is the actor. We cannot determine *who* is cheating *whom*.

who's, whose. *Who's* means who is; *whose* is the possessive. I do not know *who's* putting *whose* things in the closet.

wrack, rack. Use *wrack* when you mean ruin or destruction; *rack* when you refer to strain, or torture, or to a frame.

wrest, rest. *Wrest* means to pull away, or take by force; *rest* refers to ease, or lack of activity.

wry, rye. *Rye* is a cereal grain, while *wry* refers to twisted or distorted. He made a *wry* face when he tasted the drink made from fermented *rye*.

Choosing the Right Word

English contains more words than most languages. Because it is a rich blend of words from Latin, French, Greek, and other languages, English has many words with similar meanings. These words are called *synonyms.*

Using words with different shades of meaning adds richness, color, variety, and excitement to your language. The careful use of synonyms helps you communicate accurately and effectively. But wrong choices among words of similar meaning may leave a listener, or reader, with unclear or mistaken impressions.

Repetition of the same words makes reading and conversation dull and monotonous. Instead of always saying a person, thing, or event is *nice,* you can substitute more precise words such as *pleasant, enjoyable, delightful, attractive, lovely, charming, engaging, fascinating, thrilling, enchanting.* Rather than repeatedly describing a food that you like as *delicious,* you can call the food *savory, tasty, palatable, piquant, delectable, elegant, scrumptious, flavorful, appetizing, mouth-watering, luscious.*

The word *said* is often overworked in writing that includes conversation. Take this paragraph, for example:

> "What kind of entertainment shall we have for our class party?" Joan *said.* Tim and David thought for a while. "How about a Punch-and-Judy show?" Tim *said.* "That's a good idea!" David *said.* "Oh, no, that's too silly!" Joan *said.* "Why don't we act out a mystery instead?" Tim thought hard. Then he *said,* "Let's write our own play."

The paragraph would be clearer and more interesting written this way:

> "What kind of entertainment shall we have for our class party?" Joan *asked.* Tim and David thought for a while. "How about a Punch-and-Judy show?" Tim *suggested.* "That's a good idea!" David *shouted.* "Oh, no, that's too silly!" Joan *objected.* "Why don't we act out a mystery instead?" Tim thought hard. Then he *replied,* "Let's write our own play."

Some synonyms are interchangeable; either word can be used in a sentence without changing the meaning of the sentence. There is no difference in meaning between "The *small* boy with the *little* dog lives in the red house," and "The *little* boy with the *small* dog lives in the red house." Other synonyms are the same in one meaning of the words, but they differ in other meanings. You might say that a classmate is *dull* or *stupid.* You would not say that a knife is *stupid,* or that a jackass is *dull.* You could *mislay* or *misplace* your wallet, but you only *misplace* your trust.

Using the "Synonym Tip" Sections in the Dictionary

This dictionary includes feature sections in the A–Z text (headed "Synonym Tip") which give a full treatment, with illustrative example sentences, of a set of closely related synonyms. They explain the shades of meaning for each of the synonyms in the set, to help you to decide when a related word can appropriately be substituted for another word you have in mind.

Parts of Speech

Every word in this dictionary belongs to one of eight parts of speech; nouns, pronouns, adjectives, verbs, adverbs, prepositions, conjunctions, and interjections.

In fact, many words belong to more than one part of speech, depending on how they are used. A noun is a word used as the name of a person, place, thing, event, or quality. *Cream* is a noun when you speak of cream for coffee. An adjective describes or modifies a noun, so that *cream* becomes an adjective when you speak of banana cream pie. A verb is a word that expresses action. *Cream* becomes a verb when you cream butter and sugar together to make a cake.

You have to know how a word is used in a sentence to label it properly. But that's not has hard as it sounds. Once you get the hang of it, you can sort words into their categories with little trouble.

Nouns

Nouns are the easiest to recognize. A noun is a word for a person, place, or thing: *Susan, man, Mrs. Smith, England, Michigan, ocean, truck, car, Golden Gate Bridge.*

There are two kinds of nouns: common and proper. Proper nouns name particular persons, places, or things: *Susan, England,* and *Golden Gate Bridge* are proper nouns. Common nouns do not tell us the particular person, place, or thing, and they are not capitalized: *man, ocean,* and *truck* are common nouns.

Common nouns are divided into three groups: abstract, concrete, and collective.

Abstract nouns name qualities, actions, and ideas: *courage, helpfulness, loyalty.* Most of the time, you use *the* before abstract nouns, but not *a.* Ordinarily, you would not say *a* helpfulness.

Concrete nouns name things that you can see or touch: *door, pencil, car.* Most of the time, you use either *a* or *the* before a concrete noun, depending on the meaning you want to convey. Also, concrete nouns can be plural—*doors, pencils, cars*—whereas you would not ordinarily say *courages* or *helpfulnesses.*

Collective nouns are singular, but they refer to a group of persons or things: *team, class, herd, set.* Collective nouns are usually followed by singular verbs: "Our *team was* defeated." But they can be followed by a plural verb, especially where they emphasize the individuals more than the group: "The *people were* discontented."

Pronouns

Pronouns take the place of nouns. Our language would be cumbersome without them. You could say, "Mrs. Smith asked John to be careful with Mrs. Smith's car when John borrowed the car to take John's date home." But it is easier to say, "Mrs. Smith asked John to be careful with her car when he borrowed it to take his date home."

The noun that is replaced or referred to by the pronoun is called the antecedent. Every pronoun must have an antecedent, either stated or understood. In our example, *Mrs. Smith, John,* and *car* are antecedents, and the pronouns *her, he, his,* and *it* relieve you of the necessity of repeating the nouns.

There are five kinds of pronouns: personal, relative, interrogative, demonstrative (definite), and indefinite.

Personal pronouns state for the name of a person, a place, or a thing. English has seven personal pronouns: *I, you, he, she, it, we,* and *they.* All seven are subject form. They "do" the action. Any one will take the place of a noun in the sentence: " . . . saw Mary."

Each of the seven personal pronouns has an object form. The object forms are: *me, you, him, her, it, us,* and *them.* They receive some kind of action. Some action happens "to" them. Any one will take the place of a noun in the sentence: "Mary saw. . . . "

In speaking and writing, people often misuse personal pronouns in sentences with verbs such as *is, are, am, was, were,* and *to be.* After such verbs, the subject form of the personal pronoun is always used: "It is *I.*" Choosing the right pronoun to follow a preposition—such as *to, for, at, between*—can be troublesome, too. Prepositions call for the object form of the pronoun. "She talked to Mary and *me.*" (Not Mary and *I*).

If we add *self* or *selves* to a personal pronoun, it becomes a compound form: *myself, yourself, herself, itself, ourselves, themselves.* This form may be intensive (giving emphasis) or reflexive (expressing action turned back on the subject). Do not use the compound form when you should use a simple personal pronoun. It is wrong to say "My brother and *myself* are going." You may say "I *myself* am going" (intensive), and you may also say "He shaves *himself*" (reflexive).

Relative pronouns serve a double purpose. First, they connect two clauses (groups of words containing a subject and a verb); "She did not buy the same book *that* he did." Second, they relate back to a noun or a pronoun in a preceding clause. "She went with the boy *who* lives on Oak Street." Words frequently used as relative pronouns are *that, what, which, who, whom, whose.* Compound relative pronouns in common use are *whatever, whichever,* and *whoever.*

Interrogative pronouns—*what, which,* and *who*—are used to ask questions. They ask the identity, the nature, or the possessor of whatever is in question. "*Who* was there?" "*Which* of the books is yours?"

Demonstrative pronouns. *That, these, this,* and *those* answer the question "Which?" by pointing out a particular person or thing. They are sometimes called definite pronouns. "*That* is all wrong." "*This* is the one I want." "*Those* are too expensive." "*These* are just perfect."

Indefinite pronouns also answer the question "Which?" But in so doing, they do not refer to definite persons or things. "*Somebody* took my pencil." "*Neither* will do the job." Other indefinite pronouns include *both, each, many, one, other.* Like demonstrative pronouns, many indefinite pronouns are adjectives. "*Both* boys were absent." "*Neither* book is mine."

Adjectives

An *old* man; a *black* cat; a *long* bill. *Old, black,* and *long* are adjectives. Each is used to modify, or to give a more exact meaning to, a noun. It is not just any man, it is an *old* man; it is not just any cat, it is a *black* cat; it is not just any bill, it is a *long* bill.

Descriptive adjectives describe a quality or condition of a noun: a *short* stick, a *sad* girl, a *grassy* slope. Limiting adjectives single out the object talked about or indicate quantity: *this* book, *that* ring, *two* words. Notice that some limiting adjectives are regularly used as pronouns (*that, these, this, those*). *A, an,* and *the,* also limiting adjectives, are sometimes called articles.

Phrases and clauses may also serve as adjectives. "The man *with the green hat* saw me." In addition to modifying nouns, adjectives modify a word or group of words that is acting as a noun: "*Going to school* (noun) is *necessary* (adjective)."

Verbs

The most important word in a sentence is the verb. A verb expresses action or a state of being. In "John the ball," we have a subject, *John,* and we have an object, *ball.* But only after adding a verb, such as *threw,* do we have an action, and a sentence. "John threw the ball." Sometimes the action is mental rather than physical. "She *believed* the story."

Not all verbs express action. Those that do not may be either linking verbs or auxiliary verbs. Linking verbs join the subject of the sentence to another word, in order to make a statement. "Sara *felt* ill." The verb *felt* links the subject *Sara,* with the word *ill,* to make a statement about Sara's health. Some linking verbs regularly used are *appear, be, grow, look, remain, seem, smell, stay, taste.*

Auxiliary verbs are used with other verbs to form a verb tense, voice, or mood. "I studied" becomes "I *have* studied," with the addition of the helping, or auxiliary verb, *have.* Other common auxiliary verbs are *be, do, may, will.*

Verbs may be either transitive or intransitive. A transitive verb takes an object. "He *lifted* the hammer." An intransitive verb does not take an object. "They *ran* fast." Many verbs are transitive in some sentences and intransitive in others. "She *sang* the song." (transitive) "She could not *sing.*" (intransitive)

Adverbs

Adverbs, like adjectives, give a more exact meaning to other words. But adjectives modify only nouns, and words acting as nouns. Adverbs modify verbs, adjectives, other adverbs, entire sentences, or clauses. "The boat was *absolutely* waterproof." (Adverb modifying adjective) "The radio worked *unusually* well." (Adverb modifying adverb) "I went to school *yesterday.*" (Adverb modifying sentence)

An adverb *usually* answers the questions: *How? When? Where?* or *To what extent?* "He ran *quickly* down the road." (How?) "She went to school *today.*" (When?) "She dropped the ball *there.*" (Where?) "John sang *loudly.*" (To what extent?)

Interrogative adverbs ask questions. "*Where* did she go?" "*Why* did she go?" Other common interrogative adverbs are *when* and *how.*

Conjunctive adverbs appear between clauses and serve the double function of connecting the two clauses and modifying one. "You signed a contract; *therefore,* we demand payment." Other conjunctive adverbs are *however, moreover, nevertheless, otherwise, still.*

Words commonly used as adverbs are *almost, fast, very,* and most words ending in -ly: *badly, sorely.*

Prepositions

Prepositions may be short words (*in, for, on, to*), long words (*alongside, concerning*), or groups of words (*in spite of, as far as*). But they all do the same thing. They show the relation of one word (usually a noun or a pronoun) to some other word in the sentence. Some of the relations are:

Position—"The book is *on* the table."
Direction—"He walked *toward* the door."
Time—"She left *before* him."

Words frequently used as prepositions are *at, between, by, down, fore, in, of, on, over, toward, up, with.*

Conjunctions

Conjunctions join together words or word groups. There are coordinating, correlative, and subordinating conjunctions.

Coordinating conjunctions are the simplest, linking two words or word groups that are grammatically the same. "She bought meat *and* potatoes." Other coordinating conjunctions are *but* and *yet.*

When two coordinating conjunctions are used together, they are called correlative conjunctions. "*Both* Henry *and* Bill are gone." Other correlative conjunctions are *either . . . or, though . . . yet.*

Subordinating conjunctions connect a subordinate clause to the main clause of a sentence. In the following instance, the subordinating conjunction *because* introduces the subordinate clause. "Mary was happy *because* she found her mother at home." Other subordinating conjunctions include *as, before, if, since, unless.*

Interjections

Ah! Alas! Oh! Ouch! These are interjections. A unique characteristic of interjections is that they bear no grammatical relation to other words in a sentence. They neither affect other words—as do adjectives—nor are they affected by other words—as are nouns. A second property held in common by interjections is that they all express emotion. *Ouch!* It hurts. *Alas!* It is a shame. *Ah!* Here comes Mary.

Capitalization

Capital (large) letters are used in writing to make reading easier. They distinguish specific or proper names from general or common names. They signal the beginning of new sentences, quotes, and thoughts. English has many rules for using capitals. The main ones follow:

What to capitalize	Examples
Proper nouns	John Jones Chicago the Bill of Rights
Proper adjectives	Paris fashions the Clinton administration Persian rugs
Personified nouns	All Nature sang. Let not Evil triumph.
The first word of a sentence, a phrase, or a word that has the force of a sentence	What are you doing? Nothing. Stop!
The first word of a direct quotation	Bob called out, "Hurry up."
The first word of a complete statement following a colon (:)	This is our conclusion: The trial was fair.
The first words and all important words in titles of books, magazines, newspapers, songs, and other writings. (Capitalize *a; an; and; the;* prepositions, and conjunctions only when they come at the beginning or end of a title or when they consist of five or more letters.)	*Business Week* *The Evening News* "America the Beautiful"
The pronoun *I* and the interjection *O*	I was right. Rejoice, O ye people.
The days of the week, months, and holidays	Tuesday February Easter Ramadan
Words used instead of, or as part of, a family member's name	I asked Father for a dollar. He called Uncle Bob.
Nicknames, titles, and their abbreviations	Old Hickory Senator Brown Dr. Ph.D.
Specific political, geographical, and cultural subdivisions	Sacramento Cook County the Sioux people
Specific rivers, mountains, and other geographical features	Amazon River Rocky Mountains Atlantic Ocean
Specific streets, highways, buildings, and other locations	Michigan Avenue Empire State Bldg. the Washington Monument
Political parties, religious denominations, and their members	Democratic Party Baptist Church Republicans
Organizations, business firms, and institutions	Red Cross General Motors Columbia University
Sacred writings and words that refer to a Supreme Being	Bible Holy Writ In God We Trust Vishnu
Specific historical events, wars, treaties, documents, etc.	Louisiana Purchase World War II Treaty of Ghent
Branches, departments, and other divisions of government	U.S. Congress Parliament Department of State
Specific trains, planes, ships, satellites, submarines, and other vehicles	Golden State Limited Concorde Titanic Apollo XIII
Stars, planets, constellations, and other heavenly bodies	Sirius Mars Big Dipper Milky Way
Creeds and confessions of faith	Nicene Creed Augsburg Confession

Specific historical periods	Age of Reason Renaissance
Military decorations	Purple Heart Navy Cross Victoria Cross
Preface, contents, chapter, index, and other parts of a book when referred to specifically	This point is explained in Chapter Three and is listed both in the Index and Contents

Punctuation

Punctuation is used to make written language clearer. The following rules will show you the main uses for each punctuation mark. The punctuation marks follow in alphabetical order.

Use the Apostrophe:

1. To show omission of one or more letters, one or more words, or figures in a number.

can't (cannot)   'cause (because)
'45 (1745)   five o'clock (five of the clock)

2. To show possession by means of the possessive case of nouns.

Singular	**Plural**
a cat's paws	the girls' lunches
Jack's coat	the Browns' home

But:
Do not use the apostrophe with possessives of personal pronouns.

The dog broke *its* leg.   Here is *your* book.

Use Brackets:

1. For parentheses within parentheses.

(That was the color [red] he preferred.)

2. To correct a mistake in a direct quote.

"The artist Le[o]nardo painted it."

3. To indicate explanations of your own comments within quotations.

He replied, "That's [Cleveland] where I was born."

4. To indicate stage and acting directions.

CHARLES [waving his arms] Away with you!

Use the Colon:

1. After a statement followed by a list.

Campers must take these items: bedding, linen, and cooking utensils.

2. After a statement followed by a clause that extends, explains, or amplifies the statement.

Judges have a double duty: They must protect the innocent and punish the guilty.

3. After the salutation of a business letter.

Dear Sir: Gentlemen: Dear Ms. Harris:

4. To separate hours from minutes in indicating time.

2:40 P.M.

5. To separate parts of a citation.

Elementary English XLIV:114-123   Exodus 4:1

Use the Comma:

1. To separate the day of the month, or a special day, from the year.

July 20, 1969   Independence Day, 1776

2. To separate the parts of an address.

He lives at 230 Lake Street, Oak Park, Illinois 60302.
ABC Company, 200 Mark Ave., New York, NY 10017

3. After the greeting of an informal letter.

Dear Alice,   Dear Uncle John,

4. After the closing of a letter.

Affectionately,   Sincerely yours,

5. Before any title or its abbreviation that follows a person's name.

H. W. McDowell, M.D.   Byron Phelps, Dean of
the College
Sarah Caldwell, Secretary   Melvin Brown, Ph.D.

6. Between words or phrases in a series.

Go up the road, across the river, and into the park.
The paper can be white, yellow, or blue.

7. To set off the name of a person spoken to.

Bill, here is your cap.   Here, Bill, is your cap.

8. To set off words or phrases that suggest a break in thought, such as *however, of course,* and *moreover.*

You find, however, that small ones are rare.
The winner, of course, received the blue ribbon.

9. To set off *first, second, no, yes, oh,* and similar words when they introduce a sentence.

Yes, the letter came.   First, who is not coming?

10. To set off groups of digits in large numbers.

4,342   65,001   210,563,270

11. To separate unrelated numbers in a sentence.

By 1960, 30,000 people lived in the city.

12. To set off words that explain or define other words (apposition).

Janet Jones, my cousin, won a speech award.
The ball ricocheted, or bounced, off a brick wall.

13. To set off phrases and dependent clauses preceding the main clause of a sentence.

By the end of the week, most of the work was done.
To be a good jumper, a person needs strong legs.
Although the children were poorly dressed, they looked healthy.

14. To set off phrases or clauses that add to the main thought of a sentence but are not essential to it.

Climbing, Joe skinned his leg.
The girls, busy as they were, found time to help.
The final reports, which were completed today, give all totals.

15. To separate long coordinate clauses of a compound sentence.

The building collapsed, but no one was hurt.
Snow fell during the night, and the ground froze.
But:
He sang and he danced.
The thunder rumbled and the lightning flashed.

16. To set off coordinate phrases modifying the same noun.

This lake is as deep as, but smaller than, Lake Erie.

17. Between parts of a sentence that suggest contrast or comparison.

The more people he met, the lonelier he felt.
The sooner we get started, the sooner we'll finish.
The more he saw of her, the more he liked her.

18. To indicate the omission of one or more words.

The first game was exciting; the second, dull.
For:
The first game was exciting; the second game was dull.

19. To separate identical or similar words in a sentence.

Who he was, is a mystery.
Let them go in, in pairs.

20. To separate adjacent words that might be mistakenly joined in reading a sentence.

To an Asian, Americans are foreigners.
Just as we walked in, the window broke.

Use the En-Dash:

1. In place of *to* between numbers or dates.

You will find helpful information on pages 27–36.
The years 1930–1936 were hard ones for the family.

2. Between proper names showing terminals of airplanes, buses, ships, and trains.

The New York–Chicago flight was late.

Use the Em-Dash:

1. Before a summarizing statement introduced by *all*, *this*, or similar words.

Bob, Bill, Harry—all found summer jobs.
To defeat every opponent—this was his ambition.

2. Before a repeated word or expression.

He was a gentleman—a gentleman of the old school.

3. To emphasize or define a part of a sentence.

The Declaration of Independence—that historic document—was written in 1776.

4. To indicate an "aside" or a point of view of the speaker.

You may—though I doubt it—enjoy this book.

5. To suggest halting or hesitant speech.

"Well—I—ah—I didn't know," he stammered.

6. To indicate a sudden break or interruption in a sentence.

"I'm sorry, sir, but—" He was already through the gate.

Use Ellipses:

1. Within a quotation to indicate places where a word or words have been omitted.

"The house . . . was built in 1935."
For:
"The house on Elm Street was built in 1935."

2. At the end of a quotation to indicate words omitted before the period. Be sure to include the period.

"He was a giant of a man. . . . "
For:
"He was a giant of a man and was highly respected."

Use the Exclamation Mark:

1. After a word, phrase, or sentence that expresses strong or sudden feeling.

> Ouch! That hurts!
> Good for you!

2. To emphasize a command or strong point of view.

> Come here at once!
> We won't discuss this again!

3. To show sarcasm, irony, or amusement.

> You are a fine one to talk about lazy people!
> That should be an easy job for you!

Use the Hyphen:

1. To mark the division of a word at the end of a line. Here are some general rules for using the hyphen in this way.

You may divide a word only between syllables. Divide it in such a way that each part of the hyphenated word contains at least two letters. If you are uncertain where to break a word into syllables, consult the dictionary. Avoid dividing a word in a way that might lead to incorrect pronunciation. For example, *omnipotent* is pronounced /om nip'ɔ tent/. Do not hyphenate omnipo-tent; the correct way is omnip-otent. Remember that pronunciation is not an accurate guide to syllabication. For instance, the word *babble*, pronounced /bab'əl/, is broken into syllables as *bab-ble*.

Avoid dividing a word in a place where either part of the hyphenated word forms a word by itself; for example, tartan.

Do not divide a word that is a number or a figure, a contraction, an abbreviation, a word of one syllable, or a word of five letters or less. For example, eighty-five, wouldn't, UNESCO, joint, flora.

Here are specific rules for hyphenating words at the end of a line. You may divide:

a. Between double consonants unless the root ends in the double consonant.

> run-ning   remit-tance   col-lection
> *But:*
> Divide after a double consonant if the root ends in the double consonant.
> roll-ing   bless-edly   miss-ing

b. Before a suffix only if it has three or more letters.

> port-able   transi-tion   argu-ment
> *But not:*
> writ-er   person-al   horri-fy

c. After a prefix only if it has three or more letters.

> trans-mission   anti-climax   pro-logue

But not:
> a-symmetry   bi-cycle   en-circle

d. A compound word only where a hyphen already occurs in the word.

> first-class   self-reliant
> *Not:*
> self-re-liant   ep-och-making

2. To join word parts and to separate words parts, use a hyphen:

a. In compound numbers between 21 and 99.

> thirty-six   thirty-sixth   ninety-one

b. Between the two parts of fractions when used as modifiers, unless one part of the fraction contains a hyphen.

> two-thirds vote   one twenty-second piece
> one-fourth capacity   twenty-one thirtieths
> *But:*
> Do not use the hyphen between the numerator and denominator when the fraction is a noun.
> He bought one half.   He took three tenths.

c. After the prefix *re-* to prevent confusion with other words with the same spelling.

> re-lay a carpet   re-cover a chair
> *But:*
> a relay race   recover from an illness

d. After a prefix: when the prefix ends with the same letter with which the root word begins; when the root word begins with *w* or *y*; or when the root word begins with a capital letter.

> de-emphasize   co-worker   pre-Columbian

Exceptions occur when the dictionary shows that the preferred spelling is without the hyphen, as in *cooperate*.

e. Between the parts of a compound adjective when it appears before the word it modifies.

> drive-in movie   would-be actor   foreign-born person
> *But:*
> The client was foreign born.

Do not hyphenate a compound adjective that includes an adverb ending in *ly* even when the adjective is used before the word or phrase it modifies.

> It was a slowly moving train.
> *Not:*
> It was a slowly-moving train.
> *But:*
> It was a slow-moving train.

f. In compounds containing a prepositional phrase, unless the dictionary shows that the preferred spelling is without the hyphen, as in *coat of arms*.

> mother-in-law   man-about-town

g. After any prefix that precedes a proper noun or adjective.

un-American   pre-Revolutionary
pro-Communists

h. After each item in a series when the last item requires a hyphen.

first-, second-, and third-grade pupils.

i. After *great* in describing generations or descent.

great-great-grandfather   great-grandmother

j. To spell out a word or a name.

s-e-p-a-r-a-t-e   D-i-s-r-a-e-l-i

Check your dictionary for words beginning with the prefixes *ante, after, non, pro, pre, super, ultra,* and *well.* Some of these words are hyphenated; some are not. Also check compound words beginning or ending with the words *book, boy, child, dealer, girl, like, maker, man, mill, payer, shop, store,* and *work.* Examples:

man-hours of work   man in white   manslaughter

Use Parentheses:

1. Around explanatory material in a sentence when this material has no essential connection with the rest of the sentence.

To make holes, use an awl (a sharp, pointed tool).

2. To enclose sources of information within a sentence.

The population of Boise is 74,990 (1970 census).

3. Around numbers or letters that indicate subdivisions of a sentence.

This committee has three duties: (a) to solicit members, (b) to collect dues, and (c) to send receipts.

4. Around figures which repeat a number written out.

Enclosed is five dollars ($5.00).

Put marks of punctuation inside the parentheses when they belong with the parenthetical matter.

Carol's question ("Whom did you take to the dance?") produced a chill in the air.
But:
John walked to the store in all that snow (even though I asked him not to).

Use the Period:

1. After a sentence.

It is cold outside.

2. After a command given without emphasis.

Please hurry.

3. After initials.

J. P. Jones

4. After an abbreviation or each part of many abbreviations. (Exceptions are listed in the dictionary entry for the word or abbreviation.)

A.M. C.O.D. lbs. Mr. Mrs. Ph.D. Prof. yds.
But:
AFL-CIO AWOL ICBM NAACP NBC

5. After each number or letter that begins a heading in an outline.

Why I Like to Read
I. Satisfies my curiosity
   A. About people
   B. About things

Use the Question Mark:

1. After a direct question.

How old is Bill?

2. After a statement followed by a short question.

It's cold outside, isn't it?

3. After a word that indicates a question.

What?   How?   Why?

Use Quotation Marks:

1. To enclose the exact words of a speaker.

Mary exclaimed, "I refuse to go!"

2. Around each part of a direct quotation when explanatory words come between the parts.

"This material," said the clerk, "washes easily."
"It will not fade," he added. "The colors are fast."

3. To enclose quoted words or phrases within a sentence.

The leader told us we must "put our shoulders to the wheel."

Enclose a quotation within a quotation in single quotation marks.

"I do not understand your statement: 'He obtained the stock illegally.' "

British usage is opposite, with single quotation marks for most uses and double ones for quotations within quotations.

4. Around the titles of songs or poems.

We all sang "America."
The child recited "Little Miss Muffet."

5. Around the titles of lectures, sermons, pamphlets, handbooks, chapters of a book, magazine articles, and other titled material that is less than a whole book.

"Rescued" was the longest chapter in the book.

6. Around a word or phrase explained or defined by the rest of the sentence.

The "crib" in cribbage is made up of discards from players' hands.

7. Around a word to which attention is called in general writing. (In formal writing, underscore or italicize the word.)

You have spelled "parallel" incorrectly.

8. Around a technical or trade name.

Many people use "Jell-Right."

9. Before each paragraph of continuous quoted material and after the last paragraph. They are not used at the end of intermediate paragraphs.

"Green told us that the venture turned out to be a complete failure.
"Upon hearing this, Smith knew he was a ruined man. He quickly left the room."
"We have not heard from him since that night. Not even his wife knows where he is. I don't know if he is dead or alive."

Commas and periods are placed inside closing quotation marks (in United States usage).

We all sang "America."

Semicolons and colons are placed outside closing quotation marks.

John said, "I'll call you tomorrow"; but I haven't heard from him.
Here's what he did when he said, "I'll go":
He closed the window and walked out the door.

Question marks and exclamation points are placed inside the closing quotation marks if they belong to the quotation.

"Get out!" she shouted.
But:
How surprised I was to hear her say, "You have written the best essay in the class"!
"Are you going to the movies tonight?" he asked.
But:
What did he mean when he said, "I didn't know you were here"?

;

Use the Semicolon:

1. Between parts of a compound sentence when they are not joined by the conjunctions *and, but, for, nor,* or *or.*

I must leave you now; you can visit me later.

2. Before a conjunction connecting independent clauses when either clause contains commas.

During the summer, he accomplished nothing; but during the winter, he finished writing his book.

3. After each clause in a series of three or more clauses.

Bells rang; whistles shrieked; horns blared; and people screamed.

4. Before words like *therefore, however,* and *nevertheless* when they connect two independent clauses.

Mr. Black is a busy man; nevertheless, he has agreed to help us with our fund-raising project.

5. After listings when commas occur within the list.

You will need to call Mr. H. H. Hall, of the First Ward; Mr. Henry Griffin, of the Third Ward; and Mr. R. J. Troy of the Council.

6. Before explanatory expressions such as *for example, for instance, that is,* and *namely.*

There are several reasons why this is a good factory site; namely, proximity to fuel, availability of raw materials, good shipping facilities, and an abundance of skilled labor.

Use Underlining:
In manuscript, for words that should appear in italics when set in type, underline:

1. The name of any book or complete volume.

<u>Tom Sawyer</u> describes boyhood near the Mississippi River.

2. The name of a magazine or periodical.

There are amusing cartoons in <u>The New Yorker.</u>

3. Any foreign word that is not commonly used in English.

The treasurer made an <u>ad interim</u> report.

4. The names of ships, paintings, and works of art.

<u>Titanic</u>
<u>The Last Supper</u>
Rodin's sculpture <u>The Thinker</u>

5. Any words considered not for their grammatical meaning but as words.

<u>But</u>, <u>for</u>, and <u>or</u> are all conjunctions.

Use the Slash (Virgule):

1. Between two words to indicate that the meaning of either word pertains.

The man and/or his wife may cash the check.

2. As a dividing line in dates, fractions, and abbreviations.

4/4/76   3/4   1/2   c/o   B/L

3. When recording bibliographical information to indicate the ends of lines in a title or subtitle.

The/Oxford/English/Dictionary/Volume 1

4. With a run-in passage of poetry to indicate where one line ends and another begins.

"This above all: to thine own self be true,/ And it must follow, as the night the day,/ Thou canst not then be false to any man."

Using Correct Forms of Address

The following pages include a listing of some titled persons and the forms you use to address them in writing and speaking. Not every dignitary you might have occasion to address is included. Nor are the forms necessarily the only correct ones. Address forms for women are the same as for men, except where indicated. A safe form for closing business, or formal, letters is "Very truly yours." Personal, or informal, letters can be closed with "Sincerely yours."

United States Officials
President

In speaking: Mr. *or* Madam President *or* Sir *or* Madam

In writing:
The President
The White House
Washington, DC 20500

Mr. *or* Madam President: *(business)*
Dear Mr. *or* Madam President: *(personal)*
The President and Mrs. [Mr.] Green *(address)*

Closing: Respectfully,

Vice President

In speaking: Mr. *or* Madam Vice President *or* Sir *or* Madam
In writing:
The Vice President
United States Senate
Washington, DC 20510

Mr. *or* Madam Vice President: *(business)*
Dear Mr. *or* Madam Vice President: *(personal)*
The Vice President and Mrs. [Mr.] Green *(address)*

Cabinet Member (except Attorney General)

In speaking: Mr. Secretary *or* Mr. Green *or*
Madam Secretary *or* Miss, Mrs., *or* Ms. Green

In writing:
The Honorable John Green
The Honorable Mary Green
Secretary of State

Sir: *or* Madam: *(business)*
Dear Mr. *or* Madam Secretary: *(personal)*
The Secretary of State and Mrs. [Mr.] Green *(address)*

Attorney General

In writing:
The Attorney General
Sir: *or* Madam: *(business)*
Dear Mr. *or* Madam Attorney General: *(personal)*
(The other forms are the same as for Cabinet members.)

Chief Justice of the United States

In speaking: Mr. *or* Madam Chief Justice
In writing:

The Chief Justice of the United States
Supreme Court Building
Washington, DC 20543

Sir: *or* Madam: *(business)*
Dear Mr. *or* Madam Chief Justice: *(personal)*
The Chief Justice and Mrs. [Mr.] Green *(address)*

Associate Justice of the Supreme Court

In speaking: Mr. *or* Madam Justice *or* Mr. *or* Madam Justice Green

In writing:
Mr. (Miss, Mrs., *or* Ms.) Justice Green

Sir: *or* Madam: *(business)*
Dear Mr. *or* Madam Justice: (personal)
Mr. [Madam] Justice and Mrs. [Mr.] Green *(address)*

Speaker of the House of Representatives

In speaking: Mr. *or* Madam Speaker *or* Mr. *or* Madam Green
In writing:
The Honorable John Green
The Honorable Mary Green
Speaker of the House of Representatives

Sir: *or* Madam: *(business)*
Dear Mr. *or* Madam Green: *(personal)*
The Speaker of the House of Representatives and Mrs. [Mr.] Green *(address)*

United States Senator

In speaking: Senator Green
In writing:
The Honorable John Green
The Honorable Mary Green
United States Senate
Washington, DC 20510

Sir: *or* Madam: *(business)*
Dear Senator Green: *(personal)*
The Honorable and Mrs. John Green *(address)*
The Honorable Mary Green and Mr. Green *(address)*

United States Representative

In speaking: Mr. Green *or* Miss, Mrs., *or* Ms. Green

In writing: The Honorable John Green
The Honorable Mary Green
House of Representatives
Washington, DC 20515

Sir: *or* Madam: *(business)*
Dear Mr. *or* Miss, Mrs., *or* Ms. Green: *(personal)*
The Honorable and Mrs. John Green *(address)*
The Honorable Mary Green and Mr. Green *(address)*

Ambassador

In speaking: Mr. *or* Madam Ambassador

In writing:
The Honorable John Green
The Honorable Mary Green
Ambassador of the United States of America

Sir: *or* Madam: *(business)*
Dear Mr. *or* Madam Ambassador: *(personal)*
The Honorable and Mrs. John Green *(address)*
The Honorable Mary Green and Mr. Green *(address)*

(Although it is permissible to refer to United States ambassadors as "American" ambassadors, it is wise not to do so, because other Western Hemisphere ambassadors are also very conscious of being Americans.)

Governor of a State

In speaking: Governor Green

In writing:
The Honorable John Green
The Honorable Mary Green
Governor of New York

Sir: *or* Madam: *(business)*
Dear Governor Green: *(personal)*
The Honorable John Green and Mrs. Green *(address)*
The Honorable Mary Green and Mr. Green *(address)*

State Senator or Representative

(State legislators are addressed in the same manner as United States Senators and Representatives. Official letters are sent to them at their seats of government.)

Mayor or City Manager

In speaking: Mayor Green *or* Mr. *or* Madam Mayor

In writing:
The Honorable John Green
The Honorable Mary Green

Sir: *or* Madam: *(business)*
Dear Mayor Green: *(personal)*
The Honorable and Mrs. [Mr.] Green *(address)*

(City managers do not use "Honorable" except at ceremonies. They are addressed "Mr. John Green" or "Miss, Mrs., or Ms. Mary Green" and "Dear Mr. Green" or "Dear Miss Green:".)

Judge

In speaking: Mr. *or* Madam Justice

In writing:
The Honorable John Green
The Honorable Mary Green

Sir: *or* Madam: *(business)*
Dear Mr. *or* Madam Justice *(personal)*
The Honorable and Mrs. [Mr.] Green *(address)*

President or Chancellor of a University or College

In speaking: President Green *or* Chancellor Green

In writing:
President *or* Chancellor John Green
President *or* Chancellor Mary Green
Dear Sir: *or* Madam: *(business)*
Dear President Green: *or* Chancellor Green: *(personal)*

Canadian Officials

Governor General

In speaking: Your Excellency

In writing:
His *or* Her Excellency
The Right Honourable John Green
The Right Honourable Mary Green
Governor General of Canada
Government House Ottawa, ON K1A 0A1

Sir: *or* Madam: *or* Dear Sir: *or* Madam:

(The wife [husband] of the Governor General is called Her [His] Excellency.)
(Their Excellencies Governor General and Mrs. [Mr. or other title] Green)

Closing: I have the honour to be, Sir, (Madam,)
Your Excellency's obedient servant

Prime Minister

In speaking: Your Excellency *or* Mr. *or* Madam Prime Minister

In writing:
The Right Honourable John Green, P.C., M.P.
The Right Honourable Mary Green, P.C., M.P.
Prime Minister of Canada
Ottawa, ON K1A 0A2

Sir: *or* Madam: *or* Dear Sir *or* Madam: *(business)*
Dear Mr. *or* Madam Green: *or* My Dear Mr. *or* Madam Green *(personal)*
Closing: Very truly yours, *(business)*
Sincerely yours, *(personal)*

Senator

In speaking: Sir *or* Madam *or* Senator Green

In writing:
The Honorable John Green
The Honorable Mary Green
The Senate
Ottawa, ON K1A 0A4

Dear Sir: *or* Madam:
Closing: Sincerely yours,

Member of the House of Commons

In speaking: Sir *or* Madam *or* Mr. Green

In writing:
John H. Green, M.P.
Mary Green, M.P.
House of Commons
Ottawa, ON K1A 0A6

Dear Sir *or* Madam:
Closing: Sincerely yours,

Other Commonwealth Officials
Reigning King or Queen

In speaking: Your Majesty *or* Sir *or* Madam

In writing:
  His Majesty the King
  Her Majesty the Queen
  Buckingham Palace
  London,
  England *(on cables and envelopes only)*

  May it please Your Majesty:

Closing: Yours very respectfully, *or* Yours respectfully,

Nonreigning Members of the Royal Family
In speaking: Your Royal Highness

In writing:
  H.R.H. The Prince of Wales
  Sir:
  H.R.H. The Duchess of Trent
  Madam:

Closing: Yours very respectfully, *or* Respectfully yours,

Prime Minister

In speaking: Mr. *or* Madam Green

In writing:
  The Right Honourable John *or* Mary Green
  Prime Minister
  Sir *or* Madam: *or* Dear Sir *or* Madam:

Closing: Respectfully

Member of the House of Lords

In speaking: My Lord

In writing:
  The Right Honourable
  The Viscount (Duke, Earl) Green
  The House of Lords

  My Lord: *(business)*
  Dear Lord Green: *(personal)*
  (Do not use the abbreviation "M.P." for members of the House of Lords.)

Member of the House of Commons

In speaking: Sir *or* Mr. *or* Madam Green

In writing:
  Sir John Green, Bt., M.P. (with title)
  John Green, Esq., M.P. (without title)
  Mary Smith, M.P.
  House of Commons

  Dear Sir *or* Madam: *(business)*
  Dear Mr. *or* Madam Green: *(personal)*

Closing: Yours very truly, *(business)*
  Sincerely yours, *(personal)*

Foreign Officials in the United States
Ambassador to the United States

In speaking: Mr. *or* Madam Ambassador

In writing:
  His (Her) Excellency
  Ambassador of Australia

  Sir: *or* Madam: *(business)*
  My dear Mr. *or* Madam Ambassador: *(personal)*
  His [Her] Excellency, the Ambassador of Australia, and
  Mrs. [Mr.] Green *(address)*

Closing: Yours very truly, *(business)*
  Sincerely yours, *(personal)*

Secretary-General of the United Nations

In speaking: Mr. *or* Madam Secretary-General

In writing:
  His (Her) Excellency
  John Green
  Secretary-General of the United Nations

  Sir *or* Madam: *or* Dear Mr. *or* Madam Secretary-General:

Representatives to the United Nations

(Ambassadors and representatives to the United Nations use the form "Representative of Brazil to the United Nations.")

Clergy
The correct form for closing all business letters to the clergy is "Respectfully yours," and for closing personal letters, "Sincerely yours." These terms are preceded by another sentence, where indicated. When writing to the clergy, use a precise street address.

Protestant Clergy

Most Protestant clergy are addressed as ministers with or without doctorate; see below. Exceptions for the Protestant Episcopal and Methodist churches, the Anglican Church of Canada, and the Church of England are listed.

Protestant Episcopal Bishop

In speaking: Bishop Green

In writing:
  The Right Reverend John Green

  Right Reverend Sir: *(business)*
  My dear Bishop: *(personal)*

Protestant Episcopal Archdeacon

In speaking: Sir *or* Archdeacon

In writing:
  The Venerable John Green, D.D.

  Venerable Sir: *(business)*
  My dear Archdeacon: *(personal)*

Protestant Episcopal Dean

In speaking: Sir, Dean, *or* Dean Green

In writing:
  The Very Reverend

John Green, D.D., S.T.D.
Very Reverend Sir: *(business)*
My dear Dean Green: *(personal)*

Protestant Episcopal Canon

In speaking: Sir *or* Canon Green

In writing:
The Reverend John Green

Reverend Sir: *(business)*
My dear Canon Green: *(personal)*

Methodist Bishop

In speaking: Bishop Green

In writing:
The Reverend John Green

Reverend Sir: *(business)*
My dear Bishop: *(personal)*

Anglican Church of Canada

The forms of address are similar to the addresses for equivalent clergy of the Protestant Episcopal Church. The primate and archbishops of the Canadian Church are addressed as "The Most Reverend" rather than "The Right Reverend." In informal situations, "Mr." is often placed before the title, such as, "Mr. Dean." Canons are referred to as "The Reverend Canon."

Church of England Archbishop

In speaking: Your Grace

In writing:
The Most Reverend
The Lord Archbishop of Canterbury

Your Grace: *(business)*
My dear Archbishop: *(personal)*

Closing: I have the honour to be,
Most Reverend Sir,
Your obedient servant, *etc.*

Church of England Bishop

In speaking: My Lord

In writing:
The Right Reverend
The Lord Bishop of Bristol

My Lord: *or* My Lord Bishop:

Closing: I am, Right Reverend Sir, *etc.*

Church of England Dean and Canon

These clergy are addressed the same as their counterparts the Anglican Church of Canada.

Protestant Clergy
In speaking: Sir, *or* Doctor Green

In writing:
The Reverend John Green, (D.D.)

Reverend Sir: *(business)*
My dear Mr. *or* Dr. Green: *(personal)*

Roman Catholic Clergy

Pope

In speaking: Your Holiness *or* Most Holy Father

In writing:
His Holiness, the Pope *or*
His Holiness
Pope John Paul II

Your Holiness:

Closing: Your Holiness, Most Humble Servant, *etc.*

Cardinal

In speaking: Your Eminence

In writing:
His Eminence
John Cardinal Green

Your Eminence: *or less formally,*
My dear Cardinal Green:

Closing: I have the honor to be,
Your Eminence, *etc.*

Roman Catholic Archbishop

In speaking: Your excellency
or Archbishop Green

In writing:
The Most Reverend John Green
Your Excellency: *or*
Most Reverend Sir: *(business)*
My dear Archbishop; *or*
Dear Archbishop Green: *(personal)*

Closing: I have the honor to be,
Your Excellency, *etc.*

Roman Catholic Bishop
In speaking: Your Excellency
or Bishop Green

In writing:
The Most Reverend *(in America)*
The Right Reverend *(in Canada and Britain)*

Your Excellency: *or*
Most Reverend Sir: *(business)*
My dear Bishop: *or*
Dear Bishop Green: *(personal)*

Closing: I have the honor to be;
Your Excellency, *etc.*

Roman Catholic Priest

In speaking: Father Green

In writing:
The Reverend Father John Green,

Reverend Father: *(business)*
Dear Father Green: *(personal)*

Closing: I am, Reverend Father, *etc.*

Jewish Clergy

Rabbi with Doctorate
In speaking: Doctor Green or Rabbi Green

In writing:
Rabbi John H. Green, D.D.

Sir: *(business)*
My dear Rabbi Green: *(personal)*

Rabbi without Doctorate

In speaking: Rabbi Green

In writing:
Rabbi John Green,
Sir: *(business)*
My dear Rabbi Green: *(personal)*

Cantor

In speaking: Cantor Green

In writing:
Cantor John Green
Sir: *(business)*
My dear Cantor Green: *(personal)*

Greek Orthodox Clergy

Patriarch

In speaking: Your Holiness

In writing:
His Holiness

The Ecumenical Patriarch of Constantinople
Your Holiness:

Greek Orthodox Archbishop

In speaking: Your Eminence

In writing:
The Most Reverend John
Archbishop of North America
Your Eminence:

Greek Orthodox Bishop

In speaking: Your Grace

In writing:
The Right Reverend John
Bishop of Olympus
Right Reverend Sir: *(business)*
My dear Bishop: *(personal)*

Greek Orthodox Priest

In speaking: Father *or* Father Green

In writing:
The Very Reverend John Green
My dear Father Green

Increasing Your Word Power

A strong and varied vocabulary goes hand in hand with your ability to think logically and to retain knowledge easily and quickly. Language helps you to understand yourself and the world around you. Your ability to use words correctly and effectively can be your passport to new worlds of interest and opportunity. You can travel in the past, in the present, and in the future through the words you read or hear. You can learn to use words to help transport others to the worlds you have discovered.

Words can help you achieve the poise and popularity that come with self-confidence. A good vocabulary makes any school work easier and more rewarding. Your skill in expressing your opinions and ideas helps you get a good job, and to grow and progress in your career. Words are important socially, too. Everyone enjoys the company of an interesting and articulate person.

Your vocabulary can grow and mature throughout your life. Have you ever wondered *how* your vocabulary grows?

In your preschool years, all the things around you, plus the effort your parents and family made to sound out words and introduce new experiences to you and to identify objects for you, were the most important elements in laying the foundation for a good vocabulary. Even before you could talk, you learned words by hearing them and remembering what they meant. This listening vocabulary was your first vocabulary. Long before you were able to utter a single understandable word, you had begun to recognize some of the words you heard. You repeated words that your parents and other members of your family used and you realized that words are very useful. You did not have to point to objects or cry to get what you wanted. Words were a more efficient way to make yourself understood. You had taken the first steps in acquiring a speaking vocabulary.

The first words you spoke were the names of things. You learned words relating to food and people. You used words to show action and to describe how you felt. Your earliest vocabulary probably contained words like *mama, dada, baby, dog, cat, bad, good, hot, cold, give, go,* and *cry.*

These words seem short and simple, and you might think that you used all short words when you were just learning to use words at all. In fact, you used short words of only three kinds—*nouns,* the names of things; *adjectives,* to describe the nouns; and *verbs,* to express action. If you were like most children, you did not properly use a group of words that are short and seem simple, such as *I* and *me, we* and *us, him* and *her, you* and *they.* These words, called *pronouns,* stand for the names of people or things. They are among the trickiest words in our language. When you first used them, you may have said such things as "Me want it." Gradually you learned to pick the right word, such as *she, her,* or *hers,* until you could use the main pronouns in their proper contexts. As you grew older, your thoughts and your needs were becoming more and more complex. You constantly needed more and more words to express your ideas. You listened and learned.

As your vocabulary grew, you began to understand that things could be separated into *general* and *specific* categories. This awareness of differences added many more words to your vocabulary. For example, you learned that although all dogs are called *dogs,* there are many varieties (*poodle, collie, greyhound*) just as there are many kinds of flowers, buildings, trees, birds, and people. At about the same time you learned that *apples, bananas,* and *cherries* are all kinds of *fruit;* that *corn* and *spinach* are both *vegetables;* and that *meat, fruit,* and *vegetables,* as well as *bread, cake,* and *milk,* are all forms of *food.*

By the time you were ready to enter school, you already had a stock of more than 2,000 words in your vocabulary.

When you entered the first grade, you could probably recognize such words as *cat, dog,* and *ball* in print. In school, you were taught to read by associating the words you already knew with the printed or written symbols (letters) that make up words. In time, you began to read words that may not have related at all to any of your firsthand experiences. You may never have ridden in an *airplane,* or seen a *barn,* or been on a *train,* but when you learned to read, these new words became part of your vocabulary.

As you read, your vocabulary was made even larger by all the words you saw around you—in advertisements, on labels, on road signs, on television, and anything else in print that caught your eye and interested you.

While you were learning to read, you were also learning to write. You began to understand how words are put together and how to recognize the names of things (nouns), action words (verbs), descriptive words (adjectives and adverbs), and words that have no meaning themselves but help to make sentences by relating words to each other (conjunctions and function words such as prepositions). You began to understand the importance of putting words in a particular order in a sentence if you wanted to communicate exactly what you meant. You discovered that the English language has interesting peculiarities. For example, some words look and sound exactly alike, but do not have the same meaning. The word *chest* may be a box for storing things, a piece of furniture, or part of the body. Other words sound alike, but have neither the same spelling nor the same meaning; words like *mail* and *male.*

As you listened and read, you found also that words die out when they are not used and that some words even change meanings. You learned that new words constantly join the thousands that already exist in English because each time a new thing is discovered or invented, a new word has to be created to help you identify it.

When you entered the intermediate grades and began to write compositions, you were suddenly made aware of how important it was to be able to express what you wanted to say with precision. You learned that some words are different in sound and spelling but have the same or nearly the same meanings. These words, called synonyms, are invaluable additions to your vocabulary. They not only help you to express yourself with exactness, they make your writing and conversation more interesting by adding variety. You knew now that the simple, easy-to-spell words were not always the ones you wanted to use. Perhaps your teacher suggested rules, such as the following, to help you increase your vocabulary.

1. Be alert for new words in everything you hear.
2. Keep a vocabulary notebook. In it, list new words and their meanings. Be sure you know how to pronounce them.

3. Read widely. Newspapers, books, encyclopedias, and magazines will all give you new words.

4. Use your dictionary to make sure you can pronounce, spell, and use correctly any of the new words you have discovered.

5. Try out new words when you speak and write.

6. Set yourself a vocabulary goal. Try to learn and use at least one new word a day.

In junior high school, your social and school activities continue to expand. They open up many opportunities for an increased vocabulary. You make new friends who have talents and interests that differ from your own. They introduce new words to your vocabulary.

Your hobbies, the school trips you take, your participation in after-school activities also expose you to new words. For example, if you play in the school band, you learn the names of band instruments and musical terms such as *coda* and *diminuendo.* In art class, you may learn such words as *chiaroscuro, easel,* and *patina.*

In high school, you read and write more than ever before. And when you read, you ask questions about the author's words. Does the author use the proper words to express an idea? Do the words make what is said more interesting and colorful? Is there a rhythm and tone when certain words are used that disappears if they are changed or are put in a different order?

You go through the same process when you hear speeches. Is the speaker using "empty words," that is, words that sound fine, but mean little or nothing? Are the words organized properly? Do the words persuade you to the speaker's way of thinking? What words would you have used to make the ideas clearer and more meaningful?

All of these questions you then apply to your own writing.

A broad and varied vocabulary and your ability to use words with discrimination make up a large part of almost any exam or report you are likely to encounter either in school or in industry. By improving your vocabulary, by making your vocabulary grow as you grow older, you improve your chances for success in school, in college entrance tests, and in succeeding at any job that interests you.

M

M¹ /em/ *n.* (*pl.* **Ms** or **M's**) **1** the thirteenth letter of the alphabet. **2** (as a Roman numeral) 1,000.

M² *abbr.* (also **M.**) **1** Master. **2** *Monsieur.* **3** mega–. **4** *Chem.* molar. **5** Mach. **6** *Mus.* major.

m *abbr.* (also **m.**) **1 a** masculine. **b** male. **2** married. **3** mile(s). **4** meter(s). **5** million(s). **6** minute(s). **7** *Physics* mass. **8** *Currency* mark(s). **9** milli–.

'm *n. colloq.* madam (in *yes'm,* etc.).

MA *abbr.* **1** Master of Arts. **2** Massachusetts (in official postal use).

ma /maa/ *n. colloq.* mother. [abbr. of MAMA]

ma'am /mam/ *n.* madam. [contr.]

Mac /mak/ *n. colloq.* man (esp. as a form of address).

mac /mak/ *n.* (also **mack**) *colloq.* mackintosh. [abbr.]

ma•ca•bre /məkáabər/ *adj.* (also **ma•ca•ber**) grim, gruesome. [ME f. OF *macabré* perh. f. *Macabé* a Maccabee, with ref. to a miracle play showing the slaughter of the Maccabees]

mac•ad•am /məkádəm/ *n.* **1** material for making roads with successive layers of compacted broken stone. **2** a road made from such material. □□ **mac•ad•am•ize** *v.tr.* [J. L. *McAdam,* Brit. surveyor d. 1836, who advocated using this material]

mac•a•da•mi•a /mákədáymeeə/ *n.* any Australian evergreen tree of the genus *Macadamia,* esp. *M. ternifolia,* bearing edible nutlike seeds. [J. *Macadam,* Austral. chemist d. 1865]

ma•caque /məkák/ *n.* any monkey of the genus *Macaca,* including the rhesus monkey and Barbary ape, having prominent cheek pouches and usu. a long tail. [F f. Port. *macaco* f. Bantu *makaku* some monkeys f. *kaku* monkey]

mac•a•ro•ni /mákərónee/ *n.* **1** a tubular variety of pasta. **2** (*pl.* **mac•a•ro•nies**) *hist.* an 18th-c. British dandy affecting Continental fashions. [It. *maccaroni* f. late Gk *makaria* food made from barley]

mac•a•ron•ic /mákərónik/ *n. & adj.* ● *n.* (in *pl.*) burlesque verses containing Latin (or other foreign) words and vernacular words with Latin, etc., terminations. ● *adj.* (of verse) of this kind. [mod.L *macaronicus* f. obs. It. *macaronico,* joc. formed as MACARONI]

mac•a•roon /mákəróon/ *n.* a small light cake or cookie made with egg white, sugar, and ground almonds or coconut. [F *macaron* f. It. (as MACARONI)]

Ma•cas•sar /məkásər/ *n.* (in full **Macassar oil**) a kind of oil formerly used as a dressing for the hair. [*Macassar,* now in Indonesia, from where its ingredients were said to come]

ma•caw /məkáw/ *n.* any long-tailed brightly colored parrot of the genus *Ara* or *Anodorhynchus,* native to S. and Central America. [Port. *macao,* of unkn. orig.]

Macc. *abbr.* Maccabees (Apocrypha).

Mac•ca•bees /mákəbeez/ *n.pl.* (in full **Books of the Maccabees**) four books of Jewish history and theology, of which the first and second are in the Apocrypha. □□ **Mac•ca•be•an** /–béeən/ *adj.* [the name of a Jewish family that led a revolt *c.*170 BC under Judas *Maccabaeus*]

Mace /mays/ *n. Trademark* a chemical spray used to disable an attacker temporarily. □□ **mace** *v.*

mace¹ /mays/ *n.* **1** a heavy club usu. having a metal head and spikes used esp. in the Middle Ages. **2** a ceremonial staff of office. **3** a stick used in the game of bagatelle. **4** = MACEBEARER. [ME f. OF *mace, masse* f. Rmc *mattea* (unrecorded) club]

mace² /mays/ *n.* the fibrous layer between a nutmeg's shell and its husk, dried and ground as a spice. [ME *macis* (taken as pl.) f. OF *macis* f. L *macir* a red spicy bark]

mace•bear•er /máysbairər/ *n.* an official who carries a mace on ceremonial occasions.

mac•é•doine /másidwaan/ *n.* mixed vegetables or fruit, esp. cut up small or in jelly. [F, = Macedonia, with ref. to the mixture of peoples there]

mac•er•ate /másərayt/ *v.* **1** *tr. & intr.* make or become soft by soaking. **2** *intr.* waste away, as by fasting. □□ **mac•er•a•tion** /–ráyshən/ *n.* **mac•er•a•tor** *n.* [L *macerare macerat*]

Mach /maak, mak/ *n.* (in full **Mach number**) the ratio of the speed of a body to the speed of sound in the surrounding medium. □ **Mach one** (or **two,** etc.) the speed (or twice the speed) of sound. [E. *Mach,* Austrian physicist d. 1916]

ma•chet•e /məshétee, məchétee/ *n.* a broad heavy knife used in Central America and the W. Indies as an implement and weapon. [Sp. f. *macho* hammer f. LL *marcus*]

machete

Mach•i•a•vel•li•an /mákeeəvélee-

—ən/ *adj.* elaborately cunning; scheming, unscrupulous. □□ **Mach•i•a•vel•li•an•ism** *n.* [N. dei *Machiavelli,* Florentine statesman and political writer d. 1527, who advocated resort to morally questionable methods in the interests of the state]

ma•chic•o•late /məchíkəlayt/ *v.tr.* (usu. as **machicolated** *adj.*) furnish (a parapet, etc.) with openings between supporting corbels for dropping stones, etc., on attackers. □□ **ma•chic•o•la•tion** /–láyshən/ *n.* [OF *machicoler,* ult. f. Prov. *machacol* f. *macar* crush + *col* neck]

ma•chin•a•ble /məsheenəbəl/ *adj.* capable of being cut by machine tools. □□ **ma•chin•a•bil•i•ty** *n.*

mach•i•na•tion /makináyshən, mash–/ *n.* the laying of plots; intrigue. □□ **mach•i•nate** /mákinayt/ *v.* **mach•i•na•tor** *n.* [L *machinari* contrive (as MACHINE)]

ma•chine /məsheen/ *n. & v.* ● *n.* **1** an apparatus using or applying mechanical power, having several parts each with a definite function and together performing certain kinds of work. **2** a particular kind of machine, esp. a vehicle, a piece of electrical or electronic apparatus, etc. **3** an instrument that transmits a force or directs its application. **4** the controlling system of an organization, etc. (*the party machine*). **5** a person who acts mechanically and with apparent lack of emotion. ● *v.tr.* make or operate on with a machine (esp. in sewing or manufacturing). **2** (of artistic presentation, etc.) precise, slick, esp. excessively so. [F f. L *machina* f. Gk *makhana* Doric form of *mēkhanē* f. *mēkhos* contrivance]

ma•chine code *n.* (also **ma•chine lan•guage**) a computer language to which a particular computer can respond directly.

ma•chine gun *n.* an automatic gun giving continuous fire.

ma•chine pis•tol *n.* a pistol designed to fire automatically.

ma•chine-read•a•ble *adj.* in a form that a computer can process.

ma•chin•er•y /məsheenəree/ *n.* (*pl.* **-ies**) **1** machines collectively. **2** the components of a machine; a mechanism. **3** (foll. by *of*) an organized system. **4** (foll. by *for*) the means devised or available (*the machinery for decision making*).

ma•chine tool *n.* a mechanically operated tool for working on metal, wood, or plastics. □□ **ma•chine-tooled** *adj.* **1** shaped by a machine tool.

ma•chin•ist /məsheenist/ *n.* **1** a person who operates a machine, esp. a machine tool. **2** a person who makes machinery.

ma•chis•mo /məcheezmō, –chízmō/ *n.* exaggeratedly assertive manliness; a show of masculinity. [Sp. f. *macho* MALE f. L *masculus*]

ma•cho /maachō/ *adj. & n.* ● *adj.* showily manly or virile. ● *n.* (*pl.* **chos**) **1** a macho man. **2** = MACHISMO. [Mex. Sp., 'masculine or vigorous.']

mac•in•tosh var. of MACKINTOSH.

mack var. of MAC.

mack•er•el /mákərəl, mákrəl/ *n.* (*pl.* same or **mack•er•els**) a N. Atlantic marine fish, *Scomber scombrus,* with a greenish-blue body, used for food. [ME f. AF *makerel,* OF *maquerel*]

mack•er•el shark *n.* any of the sharks of the family Lamnidae, incl. the mako and the great white.

mack•er•el sky *n.* a sky dappled with rows of small white fleecy clouds, like the pattern on a mackerel's back.

mack•in•tosh /mákintosh/ *n.* (also **mac•in•tosh**) **1** a waterproof, esp. rubberized, coat. **2** cloth waterproofed with rubber. [C. *Macintosh,* Sc. inventor d. 1843, who orig. patented the cloth]

mack•le /mákəl/ *n.* a blurred impression in printing. [F *macule* f. L *macula* blemish: see MACULA]

ma•cle /mákəl/ *n.* **1** a twin crystal. **2** a dark spot in a mineral. [F f. L (as MACKLE)]

mac•ra•mé /mákrəmáy/ *n.* **1** the art of knotting cord or string in patterns to make decorative articles. **2** articles made in this way. [Turk. *makrama* bedspread f. Arab. *mikrama*]

mac•ro /mákrō/ *n.* (also **mac•ro•in•struc•tion**) *Computing* a series of abbreviated instructions expanded automatically when required.

macro- /mákrō/ *comb. form* **1** long. **2** large; large-scale. [Gk *makro-* f. *makros* long, large]

mac·ro·bi·ot·ic /mákrōbíótik/ *adj. & n.* ● *adj.* relating to or following a diet intended to prolong life, comprising pure vegetable foods, brown rice, etc. ● *n.* (in *pl.*; treated as *sing.*) the use or theory of such a dietary system.

mac·ro·ce·phal·ic /mákrōsifálik/ *adj.* (also **mac·ro·ceph·a·lous** /–séfələs/) having a long or large head. □□ **mac·ro·ceph·a·ly** /–séfəlee/ *n.*

mac·ro·cosm /mákrōkozəm/ *n.* **1** the universe. **2** the whole of a complex structure. □□ **mac·ro·cos·mic** /–kózmik/ *adj.* **mac·ro·cos·mi·cal·ly** /–kózmiklee/ *adv.*

mac·ro·ec·o·nom·ics /mákrō-eékənómiks, -ék-/ *n.* the study of large-scale or general economic factors, e.g., national productivity. □□ **mac·ro·ec·o·nom·ic** *adj.*

mac·ro·in·struc·tion /mákrō-instrúkshən/ *n.* = MACRO.

mac·ro·mol·e·cule /mákrōmólikyool/ *n. Chem.* a molecule containing a very large number of atoms. □□ **mac·ro·mo·lec·u·lar** /–məlékyələr/ *adj.*

ma·cron /máykraan, mák-/ *n.* a diacritical mark (‾) over a long or stressed vowel. [Gk *makron* neut. of *makros* large]

mac·ro·phage /mákrəfayj/ *n.* a large phagocytic white blood cell usu. occurring at points of infection.

mac·ro·pho·tog·ra·phy /mákrōfətógrəfee/ *n.* photography producing photographs larger than life.

mac·ro·pod /mákrəpod/ *n.* any plant-eating mammal of the family Macropodidae native to Australia and New Guinea, including kangaroos and wallabies. [MACRO- + Gk *pous podos* foot]

mac·ro·scop·ic /mákrəskópik/ *adj.* **1** visible to the naked eye. **2** regarded in terms of large units. □□ **mac·ro·scop·i·cal·ly** *adv.*

mac·u·la /mákyələ/ *n.* (*pl.* **mac·u·lae** /–lee/) a dark spot, esp. a permanent one, in the skin. **2** (in full **macula lutea** /lóoteeə/) the region of greatest visual acuity in the retina. □□ **mac·u·lar** *adj.* **mac·u·la·tion** /–láyshən/ *n.* [L, = spot, mesh]

mad /mad/ *adj. & v.* ● *adj.* (**mad·der, mad·dest**) **1** insane; having a disordered mind. **2** (of a person, conduct, or an idea) wildly foolish. **3** (often foll. by *about, Brit. on*) wildly excited or infatuated (*mad about football; is chess-mad*). **4** *colloq.* angry. **5** (of an animal) rabid. **6** wildly lighthearted. ● *v.* (**mad·ded, mad·ding**) **1** *intr. archaic* be mad; act madly (*the madding crowd*). □ **as mad as a hatter** see HATTER. **like mad** *colloq.* with great energy, intensity, or enthusiasm. □□ **mad·ness** *n.* [OE *gemǣded* part. form f. *gemād* mad]

mad·am /mádəm/ *n.* **1** a polite or respectful form of address or mode of reference to a woman. **2** a woman brothel-keeper. **3** *Brit. colloq.* a conceited or precocious girl or young woman. [ME f. OF *ma dame* my lady]

Mad·ame /mədáam, mádəm/ *n.* **1** (*pl.* **Mes·dames** /maydáam, –dám/) a title or form of address used of or to a French-speaking woman, corresponding to Mrs. or madam. **2** (**madame**) = MADAM 1. [F (as MADAM)]

mad·cap /mádkap/ *adj. & n.* ● *adj.* **1** wildly impulsive. **2** undertaken without forethought. ● *n.* a wildly impulsive person.

MADD /mad/ *abbr.* Mothers Against Drunk Driving.

mad·den /mád'n/ *v.* **1** *tr. & intr.* make or become mad. **2** *tr.* irritate intensely. □□ **mad·den·ing** *adj.* **mad·den·ing·ly** *adv.*

mad·der /mádər/ *n.* **1** a herbaceous plant, *Rubia tinctorum*, with yellowish flowers. **2** a red dye obtained from the root of the madder, or its synthetic substitute. [OE *mædere*]

made /mayd/ **1** *past* and *past part.* of MAKE. **2** *adj.* (usu. in *comb.*) **a** (of a person or thing) built or formed (*well-made; strongly made*). **b** successful (*a self-made man*). □ **have it made** *colloq.* be sure of success. **made for** ideally suited to. **made of** consisting of. **made of money** *colloq.* very rich.

Ma·dei·ra /mədeérə/ *n.* an amber-colored fortified white wine from the island of Madeira off the coast of N. Africa.

mad·e·leine /mádəlin/ *n.* a small shell-shaped sponge cake. [F, probably named after *Madeleine* Paulmier, 19th-cent. F pastry cook]

Mad·e·moi·selle /mádəmŭzél, mádmwə–/ *n.* (*pl.* **-s** or **Mes·de·moi·selles**) /máydmwə–/ **1** a title or form of address used of or to an unmarried French-speaking woman, corresponding to Miss. **2** (**mademoiselle**) **a** a young Frenchwoman. **b** a French governess. [F f. *ma* my + *demoiselle* DAMSEL]

mad·house /mádhows/ *n.* **1** *archaic* or *colloq.* a home or hospital for the mentally disturbed. **2** *colloq.* a scene of extreme confusion or uproar.

mad·ly /mádlee/ *adv.* **1** in a mad manner. **2** *colloq.* **a** passionately. **b** extremely.

mad·man /mádmən, -man/ *n.* (*pl.* **·men**) a man who is insane or who behaves insanely.

Ma·don·na /mədónə/ *n. Eccl.* **1** (prec. by *the*) a name for the Virgin Mary. **2** a picture or statue of the Madonna. [It. f. *ma* = *mia* my + *donna* lady f. L *domina*]

Ma·don·na lil·y *n.* the white *Lilium candidum*, as shown in many pictures of the Madonna.

mad·ras /mádrəs, mədrás/ *n.* a strong, lightweight cotton fabric with colored or white stripes, checks, etc. [*Madras* in India]

mad·re·pore /mádripawr/ *n.* any perforated reef-building coral of the genus *Madrepora*. □□ **mad·re·por·ic** /–páwrik/ *adj.* [F *madrépore* or mod.L *madrepora* f. It. *madrepora* f. *madre* mother + *poro* PORE[1]]

mad·ri·gal /mádrigəl/ *n.* **1** a usu. 16th-c. or 17th-c. part song for several voices, usu. arranged in elaborate counterpoint and without instrumental accompaniment. **2** a short love poem. □□ **mad·ri·gal·i·an** /–gáyleeən/ *adj.* **mad·ri·gal·esque** /–gəlésk/ *adj.* **mad·ri·gal·ist** *n.* [It. *madrigale* f. med.L *matricalis* mother (church), formed as MATRIX]

mad·wom·an /mádwŏomən/ *n.* (*pl.* **·wom·en**) a woman who is insane or who behaves insanely.

Mae·ce·nas /mīseénəs/ *n.* a generous patron, esp. of literature, art, or music. [Gaius *Maecenas*, Roman statesman d. 8 BC, the patron of Horace and Virgil]

mael·strom /máylstrəm/ *n.* **1** a great whirlpool. **2** a state of confusion. [early mod.Du. f. *malen* grind, whirl + *stroom* STREAM]

mae·nad /meénad/ *n.* **1** a bacchante. **2** a frenzied woman. □□ **mae·nad·ic** /–nádik/ *adj.* [L *Maenas Maenad-* f. Gk *Mainas –ados* f. *mainomai* rave]

maes·to·so /mīstósō/ *adj., adv., & n. Mus.* ● *adj. & adv.* to be performed majestically. ● *n.* (*pl.* **·sos**) a piece of music to be performed in this way. [It.]

maes·tro /místrō/ *n.* (*pl.* **maes·tri** /–stree/ or **·tros**) (often as a respectful form of address) **1** a distinguished musician, esp. a conductor or performer. **2** a great performer in any sphere, esp. artistic. [It., = master]

Mae West /may wést/ *n. sl.* an inflatable life jacket. [for the movie actress d. 1980, noted for her large bust]

Ma·fi·a /máafeeə, máf–/ *n.* **1** an organized international body of criminals, orig. in Sicily, now also in Italy, the US, and elsewhere. **2** (**mafia**) a group regarded as exerting a hidden sinister influence. [It. dial. (Sicilian), = bragging]

Ma·fi·o·so /máafeeósō, máf–/ *n.* (*pl.* **Ma·fi·o·si** /–see/) a member of the Mafia. [It. (as MAFIA)]

mag[1] /mag/ *n. colloq.* a magazine (periodical). [abbr.]

mag[2] /mag/ *v. & n. esp. Austral.* ● *v.intr.* chatter or talk incessantly. ● *n.* a chatterbox. [f. MAGPIE]

mag. *abbr.* **1** magazine. **2** magnesium. **3** magneto. **4** magnetic.

mag·a·zine /mágəzeén/ *n.* **1** a periodical publication containing articles, stories, etc., usu. with photographs, illustrations, etc. **2** a chamber for holding a supply of cartridges to be fed automatically to the breech of a gun. **3** a similar device feeding a camera, slide projector, etc. **4** a store for arms, ammunition, and provisions for use in war. **5** a store for explosives.

WORD HISTORY magazine

Late 16th century: from French *magasin*, from Italian *magazzino*, from Arabic *makzin*, *makzan* 'storehouse,' from *kazana* 'store up.' The original sense was 'store'; this was often used from the mid-17th century onward in the title of books providing information useful to particular groups of people, and from it arose sense 1 (mid-18th century). Sense 4, a contemporary specialization of the original meaning, gave rise to sense 2 in the mid-18th century.

Mag·da·le·ni·an /mágdəleéneeən/ *adj. & n. Archaeol.* ● *adj.* of the final Paleolithic period in Europe, characterized by horn and bone tools. ● *n.* the culture of this period. [F *Magdalénien* of La *Madeleine*, Dordogne, France, where remains were found]

mage /mayj/ *n. archaic* **1** a magician. **2** a wise and learned person. [ME, Anglicized f. MAGUS]

Mag·el·lan·ic cloud /mágəlánik/ *n.* each of two galaxies visible in the southern sky. [F. *Magellan*, Port. explorer d. 1521]

ma·gen·ta /məjéntə/ *n. & adj.* **1** a brilliant mauvish-crimson shade. **2** an aniline dye of this color; fuchsin. ● *adj.* of or colored with magenta. [*Magenta* in N. Italy, site of a battle (1859) fought shortly before the dye was discovered]

mag·got /mágət/ *n.* **1** the soft-bodied larva of a dipterous insect, esp. the housefly or bluebottle. **2** *archaic* a whimsical fancy. □□ **mag·got·y** *adj.* [ME perh. alt. f. *maddock*, earlier *mathek* f. ON *mathkr*: cf. MAWKISH]

ma·gi *pl.* of MAGUS.

ma·gi·an /máyjeeən/ *adj. & n.* ● *adj.* of the magi or Magi. ● *n.* **1** a magus or Magus. **2** a magician. □□ **ma·gi·an·ism** *n.* [L *magus*: see MAGUS]

mag·ic /májik/ *n., adj., & v.* ● *n.* **1 a** the supposed art of influencing the course of events by the occult control of nature or of the spirits. **b** witchcraft. **2** conjuring tricks or sleight of hand. **3** an inexplicable or remarkable influence producing surprising results. **4** an enchanting quality or phenomenon. ● *adj.* **1** of or resulting from magic. **2** producing surprising results. **3** *colloq.* wonderful, exciting. ● *v.tr.* (**mag·icked, mag·ick·ing**) change or create by magic, or apparently so. □ **like magic** very effectively or rapidly. [ME f. OF *magique* f. L *magicus* adj., LL *magica* n., f. Gk *magikos* (as MAGUS)]

mag·i·cal /májikəl/ *adj.* **1** of or relating to magic. **2** resembling magic; produced as if by magic. **3** wonderful, enchanting. □□ **mag·i·cal·ly** *adv.*

mag·ic bul·let *n.* a medicine or treatment that is curative without incurring adverse side effects.

mag·ic car·pet *n.* a mythical carpet able to transport a person on it to any desired place.

ma·gi·cian /məjíshən/ *n.* **1** a person skilled in or practicing magic. **2** a person who performs magic tricks for entertainment. **3** a person with exceptional skill. [ME f. OF *magicien* f. LL *magica* (as MAGIC)]

mag·ic lan·tern *n.* a simple form of image projector used for showing photographic slides.

Mag·ic Mark·er *Trademark* a felt-tipped marking pen with a wide tip.

mag·ic mush·room *n. sl.* a mushroom producing psilocybin.

mag·ic square *n.* a square divided into smaller squares each containing a number such that the sums of all vertical, horizontal, or diagonal rows are equal.

ma·gilp var. of MEGILP.

Ma·gi·not line /mázhinō/ *n.* **1** a line of fortifications along the NE border of France begun in 1929, overrun by the German army in 1940 in World War II. **2** a line of defense on which one relies blindly. [A. *Maginot*, Fr. minister of war d. 1932]

mag·is·te·ri·al /májistéereeəl/ *adj.* **1** imperious. **2** invested with authority. **3** of or conducted by a magistrate. **4** (of a work, opinion, etc.) highly authoritative. □□ **mag·is·te·ri·al·ly** *adv.* [med.L *magisterialis* f. LL *magisterius* f. L *magister* MASTER]

mag·is·te·ri·um /májistéereeəm/ *n. RC Ch.* the official teaching of a bishop or pope. [L, = the office of a master (as MAGISTERIAL)]

mag·is·tra·cy /májistrəsee/ *n.* (*pl.* **·cies**) **1** the office or authority of a magistrate. **2** magistrates collectively.

mag·is·tral /májistrəl/ *adj.* **1** of a master or masters. **2** *Pharm.* (of a remedy, etc.) devised and made up for a particular case (cf. OFFICINAL). [F *magistral* or L *magistralis* f. *magister* MASTER]

mag·is·trate /májistrayt, –strət/ *n.* **1** a civil officer administering the law. **2** an official conducting a court for minor cases and preliminary hearings (*magistrates' court*). □□ **mag·is·trate·ship** *n.* **mag·is·tra·ture** /–chər/ *n.* [ME f. L *magistratus* (as MAGISTRAL)]

Mag·le·mo·si·an /mágləmōzeeən/ *n. & adj.* • *n.* a N. European Mesolithic culture, characterized by bone and stone implements. • *adj.* of or relating to this culture. [*Maglemose* in Denmark, where articles from it were found]

mag·lev /máglev/ *n.* (usu. *attrib.*) magnetic levitation, a system in which trains glide above the track in a magnetic field. [abbr.]

mag·ma /mágmə/ *n.* (*pl.* **mag·ma·ta** /–mətə/ or **mag·mas**) **1** fluid or semifluid material from which igneous rock is formed by cooling. **2** a crude pasty mixture of mineral or organic matter. □□ **mag·mat·ic** /–mátik/ *adj.* [ME, = a solid residue f. L f. Gk *magma* –atos f. the root of *massō* knead]

Mag·na Car·ta /mágnə kaártə/ *n.* (also **Mag·na Char·ta**) **1** a charter of liberty and political rights obtained from King John of England in 1215. **2** any similar document of rights. [med.L, = great charter]

mag·nan·i·mous /magnánimos/ *adj.* nobly generous; not petty in feelings or conduct. □□ **mag·na·nim·i·ty** /mágnənimítee/ *n.* **mag·nan·i·mous·ly** *adv.* [L *magnanimus* f. *magnus* great + *animus* soul]

mag·nate /mágnayt, –nət/ *n.* a wealthy and influential person, esp. in business (*shipping magnate*; *financial magnate*). [ME f. LL *magnas –atis* f. L *magnus* great]

mag·ne·sia /magnéezhə, –shə, –zyə/ *n.* **1** *Chem.* magnesium oxide. **2** (in general use) hydrated magnesium carbonate, a white powder used as an antacid and laxative. □□ **mag·ne·sian** *adj.* [ME f. med.L f. Gk *Magnēsia* (*lithos*) (stone) of Magnesia in Asia Minor, orig. referring to lodestone]

mag·ne·site /mágnisīt/ *n.* a white or gray mineral form of magnesium carbonate.

mag·ne·si·um /magnéezeeəm/ *n. Chem.* a silvery metallic element occurring naturally in magnesite and dolomite, used for making light alloys and important as an essential element in living organisms. ¶ Symb.: **Mg**.

mag·ne·si·um light (also **mag·ne·si·um flare**) *n.* a blinding white light produced by burning magnesium wire.

mag·net /mágnit/ *n.* **1** a piece of iron, steel, alloy, ore, etc., usu. in the form of a bar or horseshoe, having properties of attracting or repelling iron. **2** a lodestone. **3** a person or thing that attracts. [ME f. L *magnes magnetis* f. Gk *magnēs = Magnēs –ētos* (*lithos*) (stone) of Magnesia: cf. MAGNESIA]

mag·net·ic /magnétik/ *adj.* **1 a** having the properties of a magnet. **b** producing, produced by, or acting by magnetism. **2** capable of being attracted by or acquiring the properties of a magnet. **3** very attractive or alluring (*a magnetic personality*). □□ **mag·net·i·cal·ly** *adv.* [LL *magneticus* (as MAGNET)]

mag·net·ic com·pass *n.* = COMPASS 1.

mag·net·ic disk *n.* see DISK.

mag·net·ic e·qua·tor *n.* an imaginary line, near the equator, on which a magnetic needle has no dip.

mag·net·ic field *n.* a region of variable force around magnets, magnetic materials, or current-carrying conductors.

mag·net·ic in·cli·na·tion *n.* = DIP *n.* 8.

mag·net·ic mine *n.* a submarine mine detonated by the proximity of a magnetized body such as that of a ship.

mag·net·ic mo·ment *n.* the property of a magnet that interacts with an applied field to give a mechanical moment.

mag·net·ic nee·dle *n.* a piece of magnetized steel used as an indicator on the dial of a compass and in magnetic and electrical apparatus, esp. in telegraphy.

mag·net·ic north *n.* the point indicated by the north end of a compass needle.

mag·net·ic pole *n.* **1** each of the points near the extremities of the axis of rotation of the earth or another body where a magnetic needle dips vertically. **2** each of the regions of an artificial or natural magnet, from which the magnetic forces appear to originate.

mag·net·ic res·o·nance im·ag·ing *n.* a noninvasive diagnostic technique employing a scanner to obtain computerized images of internal body tissue. ¶ Abbr.: **MRI**.

mag·net·ic storm *n.* a disturbance of the earth's magnetic field caused by charged particles from the sun, etc.

mag·net·ic tape *n.* a tape coated with magnetic material for recording sound or pictures or for the storage of information.

mag·net·ism /mágnitizəm/ *n.* **1 a** magnetic phenomena and their study. **b** the property of producing these phenomena. **2** attraction; personal charm. [mod.L *magnetismus* (as MAGNET)]

mag·net·ite /mágnitīt/ *n.* magnetic iron oxide. [G *Magnetit* (as MAGNET)]

mag·net·ize /mágnitīz/ *v.tr.* **1** give magnetic properties to. **2** make into a magnet. **3** attract as or like a magnet. □□ **mag·net·iz·a·ble** *adj.* **mag·ne·ti·za·tion** *n.* **mag·net·iz·er** *n.*

mag·ne·to /magnéetō/ *n.* (*pl.* **·tos**) an electric generator using permanent magnets and producing high voltage, esp. for the ignition of an internal combustion engine. [abbr. of MAGNETOELECTRIC]

magneto- /magnéetō/ *comb. form* indicating a magnet or magnetism. [Gk *magnēs*: see MAGNET]

mag·ne·to·e·lec·tric /magnéetō-iléktrik/ *adj.* (of an electric generator) using permanent magnets. □□ **mag·ne·to·e·lec·tric·i·ty** /–trísitee/ *n.*

mag·ne·to·graph /magnéetəgraf/ *n.* an instrument for recording measurements of magnetic quantities.

mag·ne·tom·e·ter /mágnitómitər/ *n.* an instrument measuring magnetic forces, esp. the earth's magnetism. □□ **mag·ne·tom·e·try** *n.*

mag·ne·to·mo·tive /magnéetōmōtiv/ *adj.* (of a force) being the sum of the magnetizing forces along a circuit.

mag·ne·ton /mágniton/ *n.* a unit of magnetic moment in atomic and nuclear physics. [F *magnéton* (as MAGNETIC)]

mag·ne·to·sphere /magnéetəsfeer/ *n.* the region surrounding a planet, star, etc., in which its magnetic field is effective.

mag·ne·tron /mágnitron/ *n.* an electron tube for amplifying or generating microwaves, with the flow of electrons controlled by an external magnetic field. [MAGNET + –TRON]

mag·net school *n.* a public school that draws students from throughout a district, offering superior facilities, specialized courses, etc.

mag·nif·i·cat /magnífikat/ *n.* **1** a song of praise. **2** (**Magnificat**) the hymn of the Virgin Mary (Luke 1: 46–55) used as a canticle. [f. the opening words *magnificat anima mea Dominum* my soul magnifies the Lord]

mag·ni·fi·ca·tion /mágnifikáyshən/ *n.* **1** the act or an instance of magnifying; the process of being magnified. **2** the amount or degree of magnification. **3** the apparent enlargement of an object by a lens.

mag·nif·i·cent /magnífisənt/ *adj.* **1** splendid, stately. **2** sumptuously or lavishly constructed or adorned. **3** *colloq.* fine, excellent. □□ **mag·nif·i·cence** /–səns/ *n.* **mag·nif·i·cent·ly** *adv.* [F *magnificent* or L *magnificus* f. *magnus* great]

mag·nif·i·co /magnífikō/ *n.* (*pl.* **·coes**) a magnate or grandee. [It., = MAGNIFICENT: orig. with ref. to Venice]

mag·ni·fy /mágnifī/ *v.tr.* (**·fies**, **·fied**) **1** make (a thing) appear larger than it is, as with a lens. **2** exaggerate. **3** intensify. **4** *archaic* extol, glorify. □□ **mag·ni·fi·a·ble** *adj.* **mag·ni·fi·er** *n.* [ME f. OF *magnifier* or L *magnificare* (as MAGNIFICENT)]

mag·ni·fy·ing glass *n.* a lens used to produce an enlarged image.

mag·nil·o·quent /magnílokwənt/ *adj.* **1** grand or grandiose in speech. **2** boastful. □□ **mag·nil·o·quence** /–kwəns/ *n.* **mag·nil·o·quent·ly** *adv.* [L *magniloquus* f. *magnus* great + *–loquus* -speaking]

mag·ni·tude /mágnitōod, –tyōod/ *n.* **1** largeness. **2** size. **3** importance. **4 a** the degree of brightness of a star (see also ABSOLUTE MAGNITUDE, APPARENT MAGNITUDE). **b** a class of stars arranged according to this (*of the third magnitude*). □ **of the first magnitude** very important. [ME f. L *magnitudo* f. *magnus* great]

mag·no·lia /magnólyə/ *n.* **1** any tree or shrub of the genus *Magnolia*, cultivated for its dark-green foliage and large waxlike flowers in spring. **2** a pale creamy-pink color. [mod.L f. P. *Magnol*, Fr. botanist d. 1715]

mag·num /mágnəm/ *n.* (*pl.* **mag·nums**) **1** a wine bottle of about twice the standard size. **2 a** a cartridge or shell that is especially powerful or large. **b** (often *attrib.*) a cartridge or gun adapted so as to be more powerful than its caliber suggests. [L, neut. of *magnus* great]

mag·num o·pus /mágnəmópəs/ *n.* **1** a great and usu. large work of art, literature, etc. **2** the most important work of an artist, writer, etc. [L, = great work: see OPUS]

mag·pie /mágpī/ *n.* **1** a Eurasian crow (*Pica pica*) or a N. American crow (*P. nuttalli*) with a long pointed tail, black-and-white plumage, and noisy behavior. **2** any of various birds with plumage like a magpie, esp. *Gymnorhina tibicen* of Australia. **3** an idle chatterer. **4** a person who collects things indiscriminately. **5** *colloq.* a black-and-white cow or steer, esp. a Holstein. [*Mag*, abbr. of *Margaret* + PIE²]

mags·man /mágzmən/ *n. Austral. sl.* **1** a confidence man. **2** a storyteller, a raconteur.

mag·uey /mágway/ *n.* an agave plant, esp. one yielding pulque. [Sp. f. Haitian]

ma·gus /máygəs/ *n.* (*pl.* **ma·gi** /máyjī/) **1** a member of a priestly caste of ancient Persia. **2** a sorcerer. **3** (**the Magi**) the "wise men" from the East who brought gifts to the infant Christ (Matt. 2:1). [ME f. L f. Gk *magos* f. OPers. *magus*]

Mag·yar /mágyaar/ *n. & adj.* •*n.* **1** a member of a Ural-Altaic people now predominant in Hungary. **2** the language of this people. •*adj.* of or relating to this people or language. [native name]

ma·ha·ra·ja /maáhəraájə, –zhə/ *n.* (also **ma·ha·ra·jah**) *hist.* a title of some princes of India, esp. a ruler of one of the former states. [Hindi *mahārājā* f. *mahā* great + RAJA]

ma·ha·ra·ni /maáhəraanee/ *n.* (also **ma·ha·ra·nee**) *hist.* a maharaja's wife or widow. [Hindi *mahārānī* f. *mahā* great + RANI]

ma·ha·ri·shi /maáhəreeshi/ *n.* a great Hindu sage or spiritual leader. [Hindi f. *mahā* great + RISHI]

ma·hat·ma /məhaátmə, –hát–/ *n.* **1 a** (esp. in India) a person regarded with reverence. **b** a sage. **2** each of a class of persons in India and Tibet supposed by some to have preternatural powers. [Skr. *mahātman* f. *mahā* great + *ātman* soul]

Ma·ha·ya·na /maáhəyaánə/ *n.* a school of Buddhism practiced in China, Japan, and Tibet. [Skr. f. *mahā* great + *yāna* vehicle]

Mah·di /maádee/ *n.* (*pl.* **Mah·dis**) **1** a spiritual and temporal messiah expected by Muslims. **2** esp. *hist.* a leader claiming to be this messiah. □□ **Mah·dism** *n.* **Mah·dist** *n.* [Arab. *mahdīy* he who is guided right, past part. of *hadā* guide]

Ma·hi·can /məheékən/ *n. & adj.* (also **Mo·hi·can** /mō–/) •*n.* **1** a N. American people native to the upper Hudson River Valley of New York state. **2** a member of this people. •*adj.* of or relating to this people.

mah-jongg /maajóng, –jáwng, –zhóng, -zháwng/ *n.* (also **mahjong**) a Chinese game for four resembling rummy and played with 136 or 144 pieces called tiles. [Chin. dial. *ma-tsiang*, lit. sparrows]

mahl·stick var. of MAULSTICK.

ma·hog·a·ny /məhógənee/ *n.* (*pl.* **-nies**) **1 a** a reddish-brown wood used for furniture. **b** the color of this. **2** any tropical tree of the genus *Swietenia*, esp. *S. mahagoni*, yielding this wood. [17th c.: orig. unkn.]

ma·ho·ni·a /məhóneeə/ *n.* any evergreen shrub of the genus *Mahonia*, with yellow bell-shaped or globular flowers. [F *mahonne*, Sp. *mahona*, It. *maona*, Turk. *māwuna*]

ma·hout /məhówt/ *n.* (esp. in India) an elephant driver or keeper. [Hindi *mahāut* f. Skr. *mahāmātra* high official, lit. "great in measure"]

Mah·rat·ta var. of MARATHA.

Mah·rat·ti var. of MARATHI.

maid /mayd/ *n.* **1** a female domestic servant. **2** *archaic* or *poet.* a girl or young woman. □□ **maid·ish** *adj.* [ME, abbr. of MAIDEN]

mai·dan /mídaán/ *n. Anglo-Ind.* **1** an open space in or near a town. **2** a parade ground. [Urdu f. Arab. *maydān*]

maid·en /máyd'n/ *n. & adj.* •*n.* **1** *archaic* or *poet.* a girl; a young unmarried woman. **2** (often *attrib.*) **a** a horse that has never won a race. **b** a race open only to such horses. •*adj.* **1** unmarried (*maiden aunt*). **2** being or involving the first attempt or occurrence (*maiden speech*; *maiden voyage*). **3** (of a female animal) unmated. □□ **maid·en·hood** *n.* **maid·en·ish** *adj.* **maid·en·like** *adj.* **maid·en·ly** *adj.* [OE *mægden*, dimin. f. *mægeth* f. Gmc]

maid·en·hair /máyd'nhair/ *n.* (in full **maidenhair fern**) a fern of the genus *Adiantum*, esp. *A. capillus-veneris*, with fine hairlike stalks and delicate fronds.

maid·en·hair tree *n.* = GINKGO.

maid·en·head /máyd'nhed/ *n.* **1** virginity. **2** the hymen.

maid·en name *n.* a wife's surname before marriage.

maid of hon·or *n.* **1** a principal bridesmaid. **2** *Brit.* a kind of small custard tart. **3** an unmarried lady attending a queen or princess.

maid·serv·ant /máydservənt/ *n.* a female domestic servant.

ma·ieu·tic /may-oótik/ *adj.* (of the Socratic mode of inquiry) serving to bring a person's latent ideas into clear consciousness. [Gk *maieutikos* f. *maieuomai* act as a midwife f. *maia* midwife]

mai·gre /máygər/ *adj. RC Ch.* **1** (of a day) on which abstinence from meat is ordered. **2** (of food) suitable for eating on maigre days. [F, lit. lean: cf. MEAGER]

mail¹ /mayl/ *n. & v.* •*n.* **1 a** letters and parcels, etc., conveyed by the postal system. **b** the postal system. **c** one complete delivery or collection of mail. **d** one delivery of letters to one place, esp. to a business on one occasion. **2** (usu. **the mails**) the system that delivers the mail. **3** a vehicle carrying mail. **4** *hist.* a bag of letters for conveyance by mail. •*v.tr.* send (a letter, etc.) by mail. [ME f. OF *male* wallet f. WG]

mail² /mayl/ *n. & v.* •*n.* **1** armor made of rings, chains, or plates, joined together flexibly. **2** the protective shell, scales, etc., of an animal. •*v.tr.* clothe with or as if with mail. □□ **mailed** *adj.* [ME f. OF *maille* f. L *macula* spot, mesh]

mail·a·ble /máyləbəl/ *adj.* acceptable for conveyance by mail.

mail·bag /máylbag/ *n.* a large sack or bag for carrying mail.

mail·boat *n.* a boat carrying mail.

mail·box /máylboks/ *n.* **1** a public receptacle for depositing mail. **2** a private receptacle for at-home pickup and delivery of mail. **3** a computer file in which electronic mail is stored.

mail car·ri·er *n.* a person who delivers mail.

mail drop *n.* a receptacle for mail.

mailed fist *n.* physical force.

mail·ing list *n.* a list of people to whom advertising matter, information, etc., is to be mailed.

mail·lot /maayó/ *n.* **1** a woman's close-fitting one-piece bathing suit. **2** tights for dancing, gymnastics, etc. **3** a jersey or top, esp. one worn in sports. [F]

mail·man /máylmən/ *n.* (*pl.* **·men**) a mail carrier.

mail or·der *n.* an order for goods sent by mail.

mail·room /máylroōm, –room/ *n.* a room for sorting incoming and outgoing mail in a business or an organization.

maim /maym/ *v.tr.* **1** cripple, disable, mutilate. **2** harm, impair (*emotionally maimed by neglect*). [ME *maime*, etc., f. OF *mahaignier*, etc., of unkn. orig.]

main¹ /mayn/ *adj. & n.* •*adj.* **1** chief in size, importance, extent, etc.; principal (*the main part*; *the main point*). **2** exerted to the full (*by main force*). •*n.* **1** a principal channel, duct, etc., for water, sewage, etc. (*water main*). **2** *Brit.* (usu. in *pl.*; prec. by *the*) **a** the central distribution network for electricity, gas, water, etc. **b** a domestic electricity supply as distinct from batteries. **3** *archaic* or *poet.* **a** the ocean or oceans (*the Spanish Main*). **b** the mainland. □ **in the main** for the most part. **2** *Naut.* the mainsail. **with might and main** with all one's force. [ME, partly f. ON *megenn*, *megn* (adj.), partly f. OE *mægen*- f. Gmc: (n.) orig. = physical force]

main² /mayn/ *n.* a match between fighting cocks. [16th c.: prob. orig. *main chance*: see MAIN¹]

main brace *n. Naut.* the brace attached to the main yard.

main course *n.* **1** the most substantial course of a meal.

main deck *n. Naut.* **1** the deck below the spar deck in a man-of-war. **2** the upper deck between the poop and the forecastle in a merchantman.

main drag *n. US colloq.* = MAIN STREET.

Maine coon *n.* (also **Maine coon cat**) a large domestic cat with long hair and a bushy tail, native to America.

main·frame /máynfraym/ *n.* **1** the central processing unit and primary memory of a computer. **2** (often *attrib.*) a large computer system.

main·land /máynlənd/ *n.* a large continuous extent of land, excluding neighboring islands, etc. □□ **main·land·er** *n.*

main·line /máynlin/ *v. sl.* **1** *intr.* take drugs intravenously. **2** *tr.* inject (drugs) intravenously. □□ **main·lin·er** *n.*

main line *n.* **1** a chief railway line. **2** *sl.* a principal vein, esp. as a site for a drug injection (cf. MAINLINE). **3** a chief road or street.

main·ly /máynlee/ *adv.* for the most part; chiefly.

main man *n. sl.* **1** best male friend **2** man who is most admired, relied upon, etc.

main·mast /máynmast, –məst/ *n. Naut.* the principal mast of a ship.

main·sail /máynsayl, –səl/ *n. Naut.* **1** (in a square-rigged vessel) the lowest sail on the mainmast. **2** (in a fore-and-aft rigged vessel) a sail set on the after part of the mainmast.

main·spring /máynspring/ *n.* **1** the principal spring of a mechanical watch, clock, etc. **2** a chief motive power; an incentive.

main·stay /máynstay/ *n.* **1** a chief support (*has been his mainstay since his trouble*). **2** *Naut.* a stay from the maintop to the foot of the foremast.

main·stream /máynstreem/ *n.* **1** (often *attrib.*) the prevailing trend in opinion, fashion, etc. **2** a type of jazz based on the 1930s swing style and consisting esp. of solo improvisation on chord sequences. **3** the principal current of a river.

main street *n.* the principal street of a town.

Main Street *n. US* used in reference to the materialism, mediocrity, or parochialism regarded as typical of small-town life (after Sinclair Lewis's novel, 1920).

main·tain /mayntáyn/ v.tr. **1** cause to continue; keep up, preserve (a state of affairs, an activity, etc.) (*maintained friendly relations*). **2** (often foll. by *in*; often *refl.*) support (life, a condition, etc.) by work, nourishment, expenditure, etc. (*maintained him in comfort; maintained themselves by fishing*). **3** (often foll. by *that* + clause) assert (an opinion, statement, etc.) as true (*maintained that she was the best; his story was true, he maintained*). **4** preserve or provide for the preservation of (a building, machine, road, etc.) in good repair. **5** give aid to (a cause, party, etc.). **6** provide means for (a garrison, etc., to be equipped). □□ **main·tain·er** n. **main·tain·a·ble** adj. **main·tain·a·bil·i·ty** n. [ME f. OF *maintenir* ult. f. L *manutenēre* hold in the hand]

main·te·nance /máyntənəns/ n. **1** the process of maintaining or being maintained. **2** the provision of the means to support life, esp. by work, etc. **3** *Law hist.* the offense of aiding a party in litigation without lawful cause. [ME f. OF f. *maintenir*: see MAINTAIN]

main·top /máyntop/ n. *Naut.* a platform above the head of the lower mainmast.

main·top·mast /mayntópmast, –məst/ n. *Naut.* a mast above the head of the lower mainmast.

main yard n. *Naut.* the yard on which the mainsail is extended.

ma·iol·i·ca var. of MAJOLICA.

mai·son·ette /máyzənét/ n. (also **mai·son·nette**) **1** a part of a house, apartment building, etc., forming separate living accommodation, usu. on two floors and having a separate entrance. **2** a small house. [F *maisonnette* dimin. of *maison* house]

maî·tre d'hô·tel /métrədōtél, máyt–/ n. (pl. **maî·tres d'hô·tel** pronunc. same) **1** (also **maitre d'**) a headwaiter. **2** the manager, head steward, etc., of a hotel. [F, = master of (the) house]

maize /mayz/ n. **1** esp. *Brit.* = CORN¹ n. 1. **2** a pale golden-yellow color. [F *maïs* or Sp. *maiz*, of Carib orig.]

Maj. abbr. Major.

ma·jes·tic /məjéstik/ adj. showing majesty; stately and dignified; grand, imposing. □□ **ma·jes·ti·cal·ly** adv.

maj·es·ty /májistee/ n. (pl. **·ties**) **1** impressive stateliness, dignity, or authority, esp. of bearing, language, the law, etc. **2 a** royal power. **b** (**Majesty**) part of several titles given to a sovereign or a sovereign's wife or widow or used in addressing them (*Your Majesty; Her Majesty the Queen Mother*). **3** (also **Christ in Majesty**) a picture of God or Christ enthroned within an aureole. □ **Her** (or **His**) **Majesty's** *Brit.* part of the title of several government institutions (*Her Majesty's Stationery Office*). [ME f. OF *majesté* f. L *majestas –tatis* (as MAJOR)]

maj·lis /májlis/ n. *Polit.* the parliament of various N. African or Middle Eastern countries, esp. Iran. [Pers., = assembly]

ma·jol·i·ca /məyólikə, məjól–/ n. (also **ma·iol·i·ca**) **1** a 19th-c. trade name for earthenware with colored decoration on an opaque white glaze. **2** a white tin-glazed earthenware decorated with metallic colors, orig. popular in the Mediterranean area during the Renaissance. [It. f. former name of Majorca]

ma·jor /máyjər/ adj., n., & v. ● adj. **1** important, large, serious, significant (*a major road; a major war; the major consideration must be their health*). **2** (of an operation) serious or life-threatening. **3** *Mus.* **a** (of a scale) having intervals of a semitone between the third and fourth, and seventh and eighth degrees. **b** (of an interval) greater by a semitone than a minor interval (*major third*). **c** (of a key) based on a major scale, tending to produce a bright or joyful effect (*D major*). **4** of full legal age. **5** *Logic* **a** (of a term) occurring in the predicate or conclusion of a syllogism. **b** (of a premise) containing a major term. **6** *Brit.* (appended to a surname, esp. in public schools) the elder of two brothers or the first to enter the school (*Smith major*). ● n. **1 a** an army officer next below lieutenant colonel and above captain. **b** a person in charge of a section of band instruments (*drum major*). **2** a person of full legal age. **3** *US* **a** a student's most emphasized subject or course. **b** a student specializing in a specified subject (*a philosophy major*). **4** *Logic* a major term or premise. ● v.intr. (foll. by *in*) study or qualify in a special subject (*majored in theology*). □□ **ma·jor·ship** n. [ME f. L, compar. of *magnus* great]

ma·jor ax·is n. the axis of an ellipse, passing through its foci.

ma·jor·do·mo /máyjərdómō/ n. (pl. **·mos**) **1** the chief official of an Italian or Spanish princely household. **2** a house steward; a butler. [orig. *mayordome* f. Sp. *mayordomo*, It. *maggiordomo* f. med.L *major domus* highest official of the household (as MAJOR, DOME)]

ma·jor·ette /máyjərét/ n. = DRUM MAJORETTE. [abbr.]

ma·jor gen·er·al n. an officer next below a lieutenant general./se> majority

ma·jor·i·ty /məjáwritee, –jór–/ n. (pl. **·ties**) **1** (usu. foll. by *of*) the greater number or part. **2** *Polit.* **a** the number by which the votes cast for one party, candidate, etc., exceed those of the next in rank (*won by a majority of 151*). **b** a party, etc., receiving the greater number of votes. **3** full legal age (*attained his majority*). **4** the rank of major. □ **the great majority 1** much the greater number. **2** *euphem.* the dead (*has joined the great majority*). **in the majority**

esp. *Polit.* belonging to or constituting a majority party, etc. [F *majorité* f. med.L *majoritas –tatis* (as MAJOR)]

ma·jor·i·ty rule n. the principle that the greater number should exercise greater power.

ma·jor·i·ty ver·dict n. a verdict given by more than half of the jury, but not unanimous.

ma·jor league n. **1** a professional baseball league, either the American League or the National League. **2** a professional league in another sport.

ma·jor piece n. *Chess* a rook or queen.

ma·jor plan·et n. *Astron.* any of the nine large planets that revolve around the sun: Mercury, Venus, Earth, Mars, Jupiter, Saturn, Uranus, Neptune, or Pluto.

ma·jor proph·et n. any of the prophets after whom the longer prophetic books of the Bible are named; Isaiah, Jeremiah, or Ezekiel.

ma·jor suit n. *Bridge* spades or hearts.

ma·jus·cule /májəskyool/ n. & adj. ● n. *Paleog.* **1** a large letter, whether capital or uncial. **2** large lettering. ● adj. of, written in, or concerning majuscules. □□ **ma·jus·cu·lar** /məjúskyələr/ adj. [F f. L *majuscula* (*littera* letter), dimin. of MAJOR]

make /mayk/ v. & n. ● v. (*past* and *past part.* made /mayd/) **1** tr. construct; create; form from parts or other substances (*made a table; made it out of cardboard; made him a sweater*). **2** tr. (often foll. by *to* + infin.) cause or compel (a person, etc.) to do something (*make him repeat it; was made to confess*). **3** tr. **a** cause to exist; create; bring about (*made a noise; made an enemy*). **b** cause to become or seem (*made an exhibition of myself; made him angry*). **c** appoint; designate (*made him a cardinal*). **4** tr. compose; prepare; draw up (*made her will; made a film about Japan*). **5** tr. constitute; amount to (*makes a difference; 2 and 2 make 4; this makes the tenth time*). **6** tr. **a** undertake or agree to (an aim or purpose) (*made a promise; make an effort*). **b** execute or perform (a bodily movement, a speech, etc.) (*made a face; made a bow*). **7** tr. gain, acquire, procure (money, a profit, etc.) (*made $20,000 on the deal*). **8** tr. prepare (tea, coffee, a dish, etc.) for consumption (*made apple pie*). **9** tr. **a** arrange bedding neatly on (a bed). **b** arrange and ignite materials for (a fire). **10** intr. **a** proceed (*made toward the river*). **b** (foll. by *to* + infin.) begin an action (*he made to go*). **11** tr. colloq. **a** arrive at (a place) or in time for (a train, etc.) (*made the border before dark; made the six o'clock train*). **b** manage to attend; manage to attend on (a certain day) or at (a certain time) (*couldn't make the meeting last week; can make any day except Friday*). **c** achieve a place in (*made the first team; made the six o'clock news*). **d** achieve the rank of (*made colonel in three years*). **12** tr. establish or enact (a distinction, rule, law, etc.). **13** tr. consider to be; estimate as (*I'd make the time to be 7:00 o'clock; do you make that a 1 or a 7?*). **14** tr. secure the success or advancement of (*his mother made him; it made my day*). **15** tr. accomplish (a distance, speed, score, etc.) (*made 60 m.p.h. on the freeway*). **16** tr. **a** become by development or training (*made a great leader*). **b** serve as (*a log makes a useful seat*). **17** tr. (usu. foll. by *out*) represent as; cause to appear as (*makes him out a liar*). **18** tr. form in the mind; feel (*I make no judgment*). **19** tr. (foll. by *it* + compl.) **a** determine, establish, or choose (*let's make it Tuesday; made it my business to know*). **b** bring to (a chosen value, etc.) (*decided to make it a dozen*). **20** tr. sl. have sexual relations with. **21** tr. *Cards* **a** win (a trick). **b** play (a card) to advantage. **c** win the number of tricks that fulfills (a contract). **d** shuffle (a pack of cards) for dealing. **22** tr. *Cricket* score (runs). **23** tr. *Electr.* complete or close (a circuit) (opp. BREAK¹). **24** intr. (of the tide) begin to flow or ebb. ● n. **1** (esp. of a product) a type, origin, brand, etc., of manufacture (*different make of car; our own make*). **2** a kind of mental, moral, or physical structure or composition. **3** an act of shuffling cards. **4** *Electr.* **a** the making of contact. **b** the position in which this is made. □ **be made for** be ideally suited to. **be made of** consist of (*cake made of marzipan*). **have it made** colloq. be sure of success; be successful. **made of money** colloq. very rich. **made to measure** (of a suit, etc.) made to a specified customer's measurements. **made to order** see ORDER. **make as if** (or **though**) (foll. by *to* + infin. or conditional) act as if the specified circumstances applied (*made as if to leave; made as if he would hit me; made as if I had not noticed*). **make conversation** talk politely. **make a day** (or **night**, etc.) **of it** devote a whole day (or night, etc.) to an activity. **make do 1** manage with the limited or inadequate means available. **2** (foll. by *with*) manage with (something) as an inferior substitute. **make an entrance** see ENTRANCE¹. **make an example of** punish as a warning to others. **make a fool of** see FOOL¹. **make for 1** tend to result in (happiness, etc.). **2** proceed toward (a place). **3** assault; attack. **4** confirm (an opinion). **make friends** (often foll. by *with*) become friendly. **make fun of** see FUN. **make good** see GOOD. **make a habit of** see HABIT. **make a hash of** see HASH¹. **make hay** see HAY¹. **make head or tail** (or **heads or tails**) **of** see HEAD. **make headway** advance, progress. **make it 1** colloq. succeed in reaching, esp. in time. **2** colloq. be successful. **3** (usu. foll. by *with*) *sl.* have sexual intercourse (with). **make it up** fill in a deficit. **make it up to** remedy negligence, an injury, etc., to (a person). **make light of** see LIGHT². **make love** see LOVE. **make a meal of** see MEAL¹. **make merry** see MERRY. **make the most of** see MOST. **make much** (or **little** or **the best**) **of 1** derive much (or little, etc.) advantage from. **2** give much (or little, etc.) attention, importance, etc., to. **make a name for oneself** see NAME. **make no bones about** see BONE. **make nothing of 1** do without hesitation. **2** treat as a trifle. **3** be unable to understand, use, or deal with. **make of 1** construct from. **2** conclude to be the meaning or character of (*can you make anything of it?*). **make off** (or **away**) **with** carry away; steal. **make oneself scarce** see SCARCE. **make or break** cause the success or ruin of. **make out 1 a** distinguish by sight or hearing. **b** decipher (handwriting, etc.). **2** understand (*can't make him out*). **3** assert; pretend (*made out he liked it*). **4** *colloq.* make progress; fare (*how did you make out?*). **5** (usu. foll. by *to, in favor of*) draw up; write out (*made out a check to her*). **6** prove or try to prove (*how do you make that out?*). **7** (often foll. by *with*). *colloq.* engage in kissing and caressing. **make over 1** transfer the possession of (a thing) to a person. **2** refashion, restyle. **make a point of** see POINT. **make sail** *Naut.* **1** spread a sail or sails. **2** start a voyage. **make shift** see SHIFT. **make so bold as to** see BOLD. **make time 1** (usu. foll. by *for* or *to* + infin.) find an occasion when time is available. **2** (usu. foll. by *with*) *sl.* make sexual advances (to a person). **make up 1** serve or act to overcome (a deficiency). **2** complete (an amount, a party, etc.). **3** compensate. **4** be reconciled. **5** put together; compound; prepare (*made up the medicine*). **6** sew (parts of a garment, etc.) together. **7** get (a sum of money, a company, etc.) together. **8** concoct (a story). **9** (of parts) compose (a whole). **10 a** apply cosmetics. **b** apply cosmetics to. **11** settle (a dispute). **12** prepare (a bed) for use with fresh sheets, etc. **13** *Printing* arrange (type) in pages. **14** compile (a list, an account, a document, etc.). **15** arrange (a marriage, etc.). **make up one's mind** decide, resolve. **make water 1** urinate. **2** (of a ship) take in water. **make way 1** (often foll. by *for*) allow room for others to proceed. **2** achieve progress. **make one's way** proceed. **make with** *colloq.* use; proceed with (*made with the feet and left in a hurry*). **on the make** *colloq.* **1** intent on gain. **2** looking for sexual partners. ▫▫ **mak•a•ble** *adj.* [OE *macian* f. WG: rel. to MATCH¹]

make-be•lieve *n. & adj.* ● *n.* the action of pretending or imagining. ● *adj.* imitating something real; pretend (*shooting a make-believe gun*).

make•o•ver /máykōvər/ *n.* a complete transformation or restyling.

mak•er /máykər/ *n.* **1** (often in *comb.*) a person or thing that makes. **2** (**our, the**, etc., Maker) God. **3** *archaic* a poet.

make•shift /máykshift/ *adj. & n.* ● *adj.* temporary; serving for the time being (*a makeshift arrangement*). ● *n.* a temporary substitute or device.

make•up /máykəp/ *n.* **1** cosmetics such as lipstick or powder applied to the face for enhancing or altering the appearance. **2** the appearance of the face, etc., when cosmetics have been applied (*his make-up was not convincing*). **3** *Printing* the making up of a type. **4** *Printing* the type made up. **5** a person's character, temperament, etc. **6** the composition or constitution of a thing.

make•weight /máykwayt/ *n.* **1** a small quantity or thing added to make up the full weight. **2** an unimportant extra person. **3** an unimportant point added to make an argument seem stronger.

mak•ing /máyking/ *n.* **1** in senses of MAKE *v.* **2** (in *pl.*) **a** earnings; profit. **b** (foll. by *of*) essential qualities or ingredients (*has the makings of a general; we have the makings of a meal*). **c** *US & Austral. colloq.* paper and tobacco for rolling a cigarette. ▫ **be the making of** ensure the success or favorable development of. **in the making** in the course of being made or formed. [OE *macung* (as MAKE)]

ma•ko¹ /máykō, maákō/ *n.* (*pl.* •**kos**) a blue shark, *Isurus oxyrinchus.* [Maori]

ma•ko² /mákō/ *n.* (*pl.* •**kos**) a small New Zealand tree, *Aristotelia serrata*, with clusters of dark-red berries and large racemes of pink flowers. Also called wineberry. [Maori]

Mal. *abbr.* Malachi (Old Testament).

mal- /mal/ *comb. form* **1 a** bad, badly (*malpractice; maltreat*). **b** faulty, faultily (*malfunction*). **2** not (*maladroit*). [F *mal* badly f. L *male*]

mal•ab•sorp•tion /máləbsáwrpshən, -záwrp-/ *n.* imperfect absorption of food material by the small intestine.

ma•lac•ca /məlákə/ *n.* (in full **malacca cane**) a rich-brown cane from the stem of the palm tree *Calamus scipionum*, used for walking sticks, etc. [*Malacca* in Malaysia]

mal•a•chite /máləkīt/ *n.* a bright-green mineral of hydrous copper carbonate, taking a high polish and used for ornament. [OF *melochite* f. L *molochites* f. Gk *molokhitis* f. *molokhē* = *malakhē* mallow]

malaco- /máləkō/ *comb. form* soft. [Gk *malakos* soft]

mal•a•col•o•gy /máləkóləjee/ *n.* the study of mollusks.

mal•a•cos•tra•can /máləkóstrəkən/ *n. & adj.* ● *n.* any crustacean of the class Malacostraca, including crabs, shrimps, lobsters, and krill. ● *adj.* of or relating to this class. [MALACO- + Gk *ostrakon* shell]

mal•a•dap•tive /málədáptiv/ *adj.* (of an individual, species, etc.) failing to adjust adequately to the environment, and undergoing emotional, behavioral, physical, or mental repercussions. ▫▫ **mal•ad•ap•ta•tion** /máladaptáyshən/ *n.*

mal•ad•just•ed /máləjústid/ *adj.* **1** not correctly adjusted. **2** (of a person) unable to adapt to or cope with the demands of a social environment. ▫▫ **mal•ad•just•ment** *n.*

mal•ad•min•is•ter /máládmínistər/ *v.tr.* manage or administer inefficiently, badly, or dishonestly. ▫▫ **mal•ad•min•is•tra•tion** /-stráyshən/ *n.*

mal•a•droit /máládróyt/ *adj.* clumsy; bungling. ▫▫ **mal•a•droit•ly** *adv.* **mal•a•droit•ness** *n.* [F (as MAL-, ADROIT)]

mal•a•dy /máladee/ *n.* (*pl.* •**dies**) **1** an ailment; a disease. **2** a morbid or depraved condition; something requiring a remedy. [ME f. OF *maladie* f. *malade* sick ult. f. L *male* ill + *habitus* past part. of *habēre* have]

ma•la fi•de /máylə fídee, maálaa feédé/ *adj. & adv.* ● *adj.* acting or done in bad faith. ● *adv.* in bad faith. [L]

Ma•la•ga /máləgə/ *n.* a sweet fortified wine from Málaga in S. Spain.

Mal•a•gas•y /máləgásee/ *adj. & n.* ● *adj.* of or relating to Madagascar, an island in the Indian Ocean. ● *n.* the language of Madagascar. [orig. *Malegass, Madegass* f. *Madagascar*]

ma•la•gue•ña /máləgáynyə/ *n.* **1** a Spanish dance resembling the fandango. **2** a piece of music for or in the style of a fandango. [Sp. (as MALAGA)]

ma•laise /məláyz/ *n.* **1** a non-specific bodily discomfort not associated with the development of a disease. **2** a feeling of uneasiness. [F f. OF *mal* bad + *aise* EASE]

mal•a•mute /máləmyōōt/ *n.* (also **mal•e•mute**) any of an Alaskan breed of large sled dogs. [name of a native Alaskan people]

mal•an•ders /máləndərz/ *n.pl.* (also **mal•len•ders**) a dry scabby eruption behind a horse's knee. [ME f. OF *malandre* (sing.) f. L *malandria* (pl.) neck pustules]

mal•a•pert /máləpert/ *adj. & n. archaic* ● *adj.* impudent; saucy. ● *n.* an impudent or saucy person. [ME f. OF (as MAL-, *apert* = *espert* EXPERT)]

mal•a•prop•ism /máləpropizəm/ *n.* (also **mal•a•prop** /máləprop/) the use of a word in mistake for one sounding similar, to comic effect, e.g., *allegory* for *alligator*. [Mrs. *Malaprop* (f. MALAPROPOS) in Sheridan's *The Rivals* (1775)]

mal•a•pro•pos /máláprəpṓ/ *adv., adj., & n.* ● *adv.* inopportunely; inappropriately. ● *adj.* inopportune; inappropriate. ● *n.* something inappropriately said, done, etc. [F *mal à propos* f. *mal* ill: see APROPOS]

ma•lar /máylər/ *adj. & n.* ● *adj.* of the cheek. ● *n.* (also **malar bone**) a bone of the cheek. [mod.L *malaris* f. L *mala* jaw]

ma•lar•i•a /məláireeə/ *n.* **1** a recurrent fever caused by a protozoan parasite of the genus *Plasmodium*, introduced by the bite of a mosquito. **2** *archaic* an unwholesome atmosphere caused by the exhalations of marshes, to which this fever was formerly attributed. ▫▫ **ma•lar•i•al** *adj.* **ma•lar•i•an** *adj.* **ma•lar•i•ous** *adj.* [It. *mal' aria* bad air]

ma•lar•key /məláarkee/ *n. colloq.* humbug; nonsense. [20th c.: orig. unkn.]

mal•a•thi•on /máləthíon/ *n.* an insecticide containing phosphorus, with low toxicity to plants. [diethyl *maleate* + *thio-* acid + –ON]

Ma•lay /máylay, məláy/ *n. & adj.* ● *n.* **1 a** a member of a people predominating in Malaysia and Indonesia. **b** a person of Malay descent. **2** the language of this people, the official language of Malaysia. ● *adj.* of or relating to this people or language. ▫▫ **Ma•lay•an** *n. & adj.* [Malay *malāyu*]

Mal•a•ya•lam /máləyaáləm/ *n.* the Dravidian language of the state of Kerala in S. India. [native]

Malayo- /məláyō/ *comb. form* Malayan and (*Malayo-Chinese*). [MALAY]

mal•con•tent /málkəntent/ *n. & adj.* ● *n.* a discontented person; a rebel. ● *adj.* discontented or rebellious. [F (as MAL-, CONTENT¹)]

mal de mer /mál də máir/ *n.* seasickness. [F, = sickness of (the) sea]

male /mayl/ *adj. & n.* ● *adj.* **1** of the sex that can beget offspring by fertilization or insemination (*male child; male dog*). **2** of men or male animals, plants, etc.; masculine (*the male sex; a male-voice choir*). **3 a** (of plants or their parts) containing only fertilizing organs. **b** (of plants) thought of as male because of color, shape, etc. **4** (of parts of machinery, etc.) designed to enter or fill the corresponding female part (*a male plug*). ● *n.* a male person or animal. ▫▫ **male•ness** *n.* [ME f. OF *ma(s)le*, f. L *masculus* f. *mas* a male]

male chau•vin•ist *n.* (also **male chau•vin•ist pig**) a man who is prejudiced against women or regards women as inferior.

mal•e•dic•tion /málidíkshən/ *n.* **1** a curse. **2** the utterance of a curse. ▫▫ **mal•e•dic•tive** *adj.* **mal•e•dic•to•ry** *adj.* [ME f. L *maledictio* f. *maledicere* speak evil of f. *male* ill + *dicere dict-* speak]

mal•e•fac•tor /málifaktər/ *n.* a criminal; an evildoer. ▫▫ **mal•e•fac•tion** /–fákshən/ *n.* [ME f. L *malefacere malefact-* f. *male* ill + *facere* do]

male fern *n.* a common lowland fern, *Dryopteris filix-mas.*

ma•lef•ic /məléfik/ *adj. literary* (of magical arts, etc.) harmful; baleful. [L *maleficus* f. *male* ill]

ma·lef·i·cent /məléfisənt/ *adj. literary* **1** (often foll. by *to*) hurtful. **2** criminal. □□ **ma·lef·i·cence** /–səns/ *n.* [*maleficence* formed as MALEFIC after *malevolence*]

ma·le·ic ac·id /məláyik/ *n.* a colorless crystalline organic acid used in making synthetic resins. [F *maléique* (as MALIC ACID)]

male men·o·pause *n.* a crisis of potency, confidence, etc., supposed to afflict men in middle life.

mal·e·mute var. of MALAMUTE.

ma·lev·o·lent /məlévələnt/ *adj.* wishing evil to others. □□ **ma·lev·o·lence** /–ləns/ *n.* **ma·lev·o·lent·ly** *adv.* [OF *malivolent* or f. L *malevolens* f. *male* ill + *volens* willing, part. of *velle*]

mal·fea·sance /malféezəns/ *n. Law* evildoing. □□ **mal·fea·sant** /–zənt/ *n. & adj.* [AF *malfaisance* f. OF *malfaisant* (as MAL-, *faisant* part. of *faire* do f. L *facere*): cf. MISFEASANCE]

mal·for·ma·tion /málformáyshən/ *n.* faulty formation. □□ **mal·formed** /–fáwrmd/ *adj.*

mal·func·tion /málfúngkshən/ *n. & v.* ● *n.* a failure to function in a normal or satisfactory manner. ● *v.intr.* fail to function normally or satisfactorily.

mal·ic ac·id /málik/ *n.* an organic acid found in unripe apples and other fruits. [F *malique* f. L *malum* apple]

mal·ice /mális/ *n.* **1 a** the intention to do evil. **b** a desire to tease, esp. cruelly. **2** *Law* wrongful intention, esp. as increasing the guilt of certain offenses. [ME f. OF f. L *malitia* f. *malus* bad]

mal·ice a·fore·thought *n. Law* the deliberate intention to commit a crime, esp. murder.

ma·li·cious /məlíshəs/ *adj.* characterized by malice; intending or intended to do harm. □□ **ma·li·cious·ly** *adv.* **ma·li·cious·ness** *n.* [OF *malicius* f. L *malitiosus* (as MALICE)]

ma·lign /məlín/ *adj. & v.* ● *adj.* **1** (of a thing) injurious. **2** (of a disease) malignant. **3** malevolent. ● *v.tr.* speak ill of; slander. □□ **ma·lign·er** *n.* **ma·lig·ni·ty** /məlígnitee/ *n. (pl.* **·ties**). **ma·lign·ly** /–línlee/ *adv.* [ME f. OF *malin maligne, malignier* f. LL *malignare* contrive maliciously f. L *malignus* f. *malus* bad: cf. BENIGN]

ma·lig·nant /məlígnənt/ *adj.* **1 a** (of a disease) very virulent or infectious (*malignant cholera*). **b** (of a tumor) tending to invade normal tissue and recur after removal; cancerous. **2** harmful; feeling or showing intense ill will. □□ **ma·lig·nan·cy** *n. (pl.* **n-cies**). **ma·lig·nant·ly** *adv.* [LL *malignare* (as MALIGN)]

ma·lin·ger /məlínggər/ *v.intr.* exaggerate or feign illness in order to escape duty, work, etc. □□ **ma·lin·ger·er** *n.* [back-form. f. *malingerer* app. f. F *malingre*, perh. formed as MAL- + *haingre* weak]

mall /mawl/ *n.* **1** a sheltered walk or promenade. **2** an enclosed shopping center. **3** *hist.* **a** = PALL-MALL. **b** an alley used for this. [var. of MAUL: applied to *The Mall* in London (orig. a pall-mall alley)]

mal·lard /málərd/ *n. (pl.* same or **mallards**) **1 a** wild duck or drake, *Anas platyrhynchos*, of the northern hemisphere. **2** the flesh of the mallard. [ME f. OF prob. f. *maslart* (unrecorded, as MALE)]

mallard

mal·le·a·ble /máleeəbəl/ *adj.* **1** (of metal, etc.) able to be hammered or pressed permanently out of shape without breaking or cracking. **2** adaptable; pliable, flexible. □□ **mal·le·a·bil·i·ty** *n.* **mal·le·a·bly** *adv.* [ME f. OF f. med.L *malleabilis* f. L *malleare* to hammer f. *malleus* hammer]

mal·lee /málee/ *n. Austral.* **1** any of several types of eucalyptus, esp. *Eucalyptus dumosa*, that flourish in arid areas. **2** a scrub formed by mallee. [Aboriginal]

mal·lee fowl *n.* (also **mal·lee bird** or **mal·lee hen**) a megapode, *Leipoa ocellata*, resembling a turkey.

mal·lei *pl.* of MALLEUS.

mal·le·muck var. of MOLLYMAWK.

mal·len·ders var. of MALANDERS.

mal·le·o·lus /məleeéeləs/ *n. (pl.* **mal·le·o·li** /–lī/) *Anat.* a bone with the shape of a hammerhead, esp. each of those forming a projection on either side of the ankle. [L, dimin. of *malleus* hammer]

mal·let /málit/ *n.* **1** a hammer, usu. of wood. **2** a long-handled wooden hammer for striking a croquet or polo ball. [ME f. OF *maillet* f. *mailler* to hammer f. *mail* hammer f. L *malleus*]

mal·le·us /máleeəs/ *n. (pl.* **mallei** /–lee-ī/) *Anat.* a small bone in the middle ear transmitting the vibrations of the tympanum to the incus. [L, = hammer]

mallet 1

mal·low /málō/ *n.* **1** a herbaceous plant of the genus *Malva*, with hairy stems and leaves and pink or purple flowers. **2** any of several other plants of the family Malvaceae, including marsh mallow and hollyhock. [OE *meal(u)we* f. L *malva*]

malm /maam/ *n.* **1** a soft chalky rock. **2** a loamy soil produced by the disintegration of this rock. **3** a fine-quality brick made originally from malm, marl, or a similar chalky clay. [OE *mealm-* (in compounds) f. Gmc]

malm·sey /máamzee/ *n.* a strong sweet wine orig. from Greece, now chiefly from Madeira. [ME f. MDu., MLG *malmesie, –eye*, f. *Monemvasia* in S. Greece: cf. MALVOISIE]

mal·nour·ished /málnərisht, –núr–/ *adj.* suffering from malnutrition.

mal·nour·ish·ment /málnərishmənt, –núr–/ *n.* = MALNUTRITION.

mal·nu·tri·tion /málnōotríshən, –nyōō–/ *n.* a dietary condition resulting from the absence of some foods or essential elements necessary for health; insufficient nutrition.

mal·oc·clu·sion /málōklōôzhən/ *n. Dentistry* faulty contact of opposing teeth when the jaws are closed. [MAL- + OCCLUSION]

mal·o·dor·ous /málódərəs/ *adj.* having an unpleasant smell.

Mal·pi·ghi·an lay·er /malpígeeən/ *n.* a layer of proliferating cells in the epidermis. [M. *Malpighi*, It. physician d. 1694]

mal·prac·tice /malpráktis/ *n.* **1** improper or negligent professional treatment, as by a medical practitioner. **2 a** criminal wrongdoing; misconduct. **b** an instance of this.

malt /mawlt/ *n. & v.* ● *n.* **1** barley or other grain that is steeped, germinated, and dried, esp. for brewing or distilling and vinegar making. **2** *colloq.* esp. *Brit.* malt whiskey; malt liquor. ● *v.* **1** *tr.* convert (grain) into malt. **2** *intr.* (of seeds) become malt when germination is checked by drought. [OE *m(e)alt* f. Gmc, rel. to MELT]

malt·ase /mawltáys, –táyz/ *n. Biochem.* an enzyme found esp. in the small intestine that converts maltose to glucose.

malt·ed milk *n.* **1** a drink combining milk, a malt preparation, and ice cream or flavoring. **2** the powdered malt preparation used to make this.

Mal·tese /máwltéez, –tées/ *n. & adj.* ● *n.* **1** (*pl.* same) **a** a native or national of Malta, an island in the W. Mediterranean. **b** a person of Maltese descent. **2** the language of Malta. ● *adj.* of or relating to Malta or its people or language.

Mal·tese cat *n.* a variety of domestic cat with a blue-gray coat.

Mal·tese cross *n.* a cross with arms of equal length broadening from the center, often indented at the ends.

Mal·tese dog *n.* a breed of toy dog having a long, straight, white coat that hangs almost to the ground.

mal·tha /máltha/ *n.* a cement made of pitch and wax or other ingredients. [L f. Gk]

Mal·thu·sian /malthóōzhən, -zeeən/ *adj. & n.* ● *adj.* of or relating to T. R. Malthus, English clergyman and economist (d. 1834) or his theories, esp. that sexual restraint should be exercised as a means of preventing an increase of the population beyond its means of subsistence. ● *n.* a follower of Malthus. □□ **Mal·thu·sian·ism** *n.*

malt·ing /máwlting/ *n.* the process or an instance of brewing or distilling with malt.

malt liq·uor *n.* a kind of strong beer.

malt·ose /máwltōs, -tōz/ *n. Chem.* a sugar produced by the hydrolysis of starch under the action of the enzymes in malt, saliva, etc. [F (as MALT)]

mal·treat /máltreét/ *v.tr.* ill-treat. □□ **mal·treat·er** *n.* **mal·treat·ment** *n.* [F *maltraiter* (as MAL-, TREAT)]

malt·ster /máwltstər/ *n.* a person who makes or deals in malt.

malt whis·key *n.* whiskey made from malted barley.

malt·y /máwltee/ *adj.* (**malt·i·er, malt·i·est**) of, containing, or resembling malt. □□ **malt·i·ness** *n.*

mal·va·ceous /malváyshəs/ *adj. Bot.* of or relating to the Malvaceae, the mallow family. [L *malvaceus* f. *malva* MALLOW]

mal·ver·sa·tion /málvərsáyshən/ *n. formal* 1 corrupt behavior in a position of trust. 2 (often foll. by *of*) corrupt administration (of public money, etc.). [F f. *malverser* f. L *male* badly + *versari* behave]

mal·voi·sie /málvwəzeé/ *n.* = MALMSEY. [ME f. OF *malvesie* f. F form of *Monemvasia*: see MALMSEY]

ma·ma /máamə, məmáa/ *n. colloq.* (esp. as a child's term) mother. [imit. of child's *ma, ma*]

mam·ba /máambə/ *n.* any venomous African snake of the genus *Dendroaspis*, esp. the green mamba (*D. angusticeps*) or black mamba (*D. polylepis*). [Zulu *imamba*]

mam·bo /máambō/ *n. & v.* ● *n.* (*pl.* **·bos**) 1 a Latin American dance like the rumba. 2 the music for this. ● *v.intr.* (**·boes, ·boed**) perform the mambo. [Amer. Sp. prob. f. Haitian]

Mam·e·luke /mámələōk/ *n. hist.* a member of the military class (orig. Caucasian slaves) that ruled Egypt 1254–1811. [F *mameluk*, ult. f. Arab. *mamlūk* slave f. *malaka* possess]

ma·mil·la /məmílə/ *n.* var of MAMMILLA.

mam·ma¹ /máamə/ *n.* (also **mom·ma**) *colloq.* (esp. as a child's term) MAMA.

mam·ma² /máamə/ *n.* (*pl.* **mam·mae** /-mee/) 1 a milk-secreting organ of female mammals. 2 a corresponding nonsecretory structure in male mammals. □□ **mam·mi·form** *adj.* [OE f. L]

mam·mal /máməl/ *n.* any vertebrate of the class Mammalia, usu. a warm-blooded quadruped with hair or fur, the females of which possess milk-secreting mammae for the nourishment of the young, and including humans, dogs, rabbits, whales, etc. □□ **mam·ma·li·an** /-máyliən/ *adj. & n.* **mam·mal·o·gy** /-mólijee/ *n.* [mod.L *mammalia* neut. pl. of L *mammalis* (as MAMMA²)]

mam·ma·lif·er·ous /máməlífərəs/ *adj. Geol.* containing mammalian remains.

mam·ma·ry /máməree/ *adj.* of the human female breasts or milk-secreting organs of other mammals. [MAMMA² + -ARY¹]

mam·ma·ry gland *n.* the milk-producing gland of female mammals.

mam·mee /mamée/ *n.* a tropical American tree, *Mammea americana*, with large red-rinded yellow-pulped fruit. [Sp. *mamei* f. Haitian]

mam·mil·la /məmílə/ *n.* (*pl.* **mam·mil·lae** /-lee/) 1 the nipple of a woman's breast. 2 a nipple-shaped organ, etc. □□ **mam·mil·lar·y** /mámmileree/ *adj.* **mam·mil·late** /mámilayt/ *adj.* [L, dimin. of MAMMA²]

mam·mog·ra·phy /mamógrəfee/ *n. Med.* an X-ray technique of diagnosing and locating abnormalities (esp. tumors) of the breasts. [MAMMA² + -GRAPHY]

mam·mon /mámən/ *n.* (also **Mam·mon**) 1 wealth regarded as a god or as an evil influence. 2 the worldly rich. □□ **mam·mon·ish** *adj.* **mam·mon·ism** *n.* **mam·mon·ist** *n.* **mam·mon·ite** *n.* [ME f. LL *Mam(m)ona* f. Gk *mamōnas* f. Aram. *māmōn* riches: see Matt. 6:24, Luke 16: 9–13]

mam·moth /máməth/ *n. & adj.* ● *n.* any large extinct elephant of the genus *Mammuthus*, with a hairy coat and curved tusks. ● *adj.* huge. [Russ. *mamo(n)t*]

mam·my /mámee/ *n.* (*pl.* **·mies**) 1 a child's word for

mammoth

mother. 2 *formerly southern US* an African-American nursemaid or nanny in charge of white children. [formed as MAMMA¹]

Man. *abbr.* Manitoba.

man /man/ *n. & v.* ● *n.* (*pl.* **men** /men/) 1 an adult human male, esp. as distinct from a woman or boy. 2 a a human being; a person (*no man is perfect*). b human beings in general; the human race (*man is mortal*). 3 a person showing characteristics associated with males (*she's more of a man than he is*). 4 a worker; an employee (*the manager spoke to the men*). b esp. *Brit.* a manservant or valet. c *hist.* a vassal. 5 a (usu. in *pl.*) soldiers, sailors, etc., esp. nonofficers (*was in command of 200 men*). b an individual, usu. male, person (*fought to the last man*). c (usu. prec. by *the*, or *poss. pron.*) a person regarded as suitable or appropriate in some way; a person fulfilling requirements (*I'm your man; not the man for the job*). 6 a a husband (*man and wife*). b *colloq.* a boyfriend or lover. 7 a a human being of a specified historical period or character (*Renaissance man*). b a type of prehistoric man named after the place where the remains were found (*Peking man*). 8 any one of a set of pieces used in playing chess, checkers, etc. 9 (as second element in *comb.*) a man of a specified nationality, profession, skill, etc. (*Dutchman; clergyman; horseman; gentleman*). 10 a an expression of impatience, etc., used in addressing a male (*nonsense, man!*). b *colloq.* a general mode of address (*blew my mind, man!*). 11 (prec. by *a*) a person; one (*what can a man do?*). 12 a person pursued; an opponent, etc. (*the police have so far not caught their man*). 13 (**the Man**) *sl.* a the police. b *sl.* esp. *Afr.-Amer.* a person with power or authority. 14 (in *comb.*) a ship of a specified type (*merchantman; Indiaman*). ● *v.tr.* (**manned, man·ning**) 1 supply (a ship, fort, factory, etc.) with a person or people for work or defense, etc. 2 work or service or defend (a specified piece of equipment, a fortification, etc.) (*man the pumps*). 3 *Naut.* place men at (a part of a ship). 4 fill (a post or office). 5 (usu. *refl.*) fortify the spirits or courage of (*manned herself for the task*). □ **as one man** in unison; in agreement. **be a man** be courageous; not show fear. **be one's own man** 1 be free to act; be independent. 2 be in full possession of one's faculties, etc. **men's room** a usu. public restroom for men. **my** (or **my good**) **man** a patronizing mode of address to a man. **separate** (or **sort out**) **the men from the boys** *colloq.* find those who are truly virile, competent, etc. **to a man** all without exception. □□ **man·less** *adj.* [OE *man(n)*, pl. *men*, *mannian*, f. Gmc]

▶Many consider the use of **man** to mean 'human being' or 'the human race' offensive and sexist.

ma·na /máanə/ *n.* 1 power; authority; prestige. 2 supernatural or magical power. [Maori]

man a·bout town *n.* a fashionable man of leisure.

man·a·cle /mánəkəl/ *n. & v.* ● *n.* (usu. in *pl.*) 1 a fetter or shackle for the hand; a handcuff. 2 a restraint. ● *v.tr.* fetter with manacles. [ME f. OF *manicle* handcuff f. L *manicula* dimin. of *manus* hand]

man·age /mánij/ *v. & n.* ● *v.* 1 *tr.* organize; regulate; be in charge of (a business, household, team, a person's career, etc.). 2 *tr.* (often foll. by *to* + infin.) succeed in achieving; contrive (*managed to arrive on time; managed a smile; managed to ruin the day*). 3 *intr.* a (often foll. by *with*) succeed in one's aim, esp. against heavy odds (*managed with one assistant*). b meet one's needs with limited resources, etc. (*just about manages on a pension*). 4 *tr.* gain influence with or maintain control over (a person, etc.) (*cannot manage their teenage son*). 5 *tr.* (also *absol.*; often prec. by *can*, *be able to*) a cope with; make use of (*couldn't manage another bite; can you manage by yourself?*). b be free to attend on (a certain day) or at (a certain time) (*can you manage Thursday?*). 6 *tr.* handle or wield (a tool, weapon, etc.). 7 *tr.* take or have charge or control of (an animal or animals, esp. cattle). ● *n. archaic* 1 a the training of a horse. b the trained movements of a horse. 2 a riding school (cf. MANÈGE). [It. *maneggiare, maneggio* ult. f. L *manus* hand]

man·age·a·ble /mánijəbəl/ *adj.* able to be easily managed, controlled, or accomplished, etc. □□ **man·age·a·bil·i·ty** *n.* **man·age·a·ble·ness** *n.* **man·age·a·bly** *adv.*

man·aged care *n.* health care administered by a health maintenance organization or similar system, intended to limit hospital and practitioner fees.

man·age·ment /mánijmənt/ *n.* 1 the process or an instance of managing or being managed. 2 a the professional administration of business concerns, public undertakings, etc. b the people engaged in this. c (prec. by *the*) a governing body; a board of directors or the people in charge of running a business, regarded collectively. 3 (usu. foll. by *of*) *Med.* the technique of treating a disease, etc. 4 trickery; deceit.

man·age·ment in·for·ma·tion sys·tem *n. Computing* a computer system used in business for processing data related to management activities. ¶ Abbr.: MIS.

man·ag·er /mánijər/ *n.* 1 a person controlling or administering a business or part of a business. 2 a person controlling the affairs, training, etc., of a person or team in sports, entertainment, etc. 3 a person regarded in terms of skill in household or financial or other management (*a good manager*). □□ **man·a·ge·ri·al** /mánijeéreeəl/ *adj.* **man·a·ge·ri·al·ly** /-jeéreeəlee/ *adv.* **man·a·ger·ship** *n.*

man·ag·ing /mánijing/ *adj.* **1** (in *comb.*) having executive control or authority (*managing partner*). **2** (*attrib.*) fond of controlling affairs, etc. **3** *archaic* economical.

man·a·kin /mánəkin/ *n.* any small bird of the family Pipridae of Central and S. America, the males of which are often brightly colored. [var. of MANIKIN]

ma·ña·na /mənyaánə/ *adv. & n.* ● *adv.* in the indefinite future (esp. to indicate procrastination). ● *n.* an indefinite future time. [Sp., = tomorrow]

man-at-arms *n.* (*pl.* **men-at-arms**) *archaic* a soldier, esp. when heavily armed and mounted.

man·a·tee /mánətee/ *n.* any large aquatic plant-eating mammal of the genus *Trichechus*, with paddlelike forelimbs, no hind limbs, and a powerful tail. [Sp. *manati* f. Carib *manattoui*]

man·chi·neel /mánchineel/ *n.* a W. Indian tree, *Hippomane mancinella*, with a poisonous and caustic milky sap and acrid applelike fruit. [F *mancenille* f. Sp. *manzanilla* dimin. of *manzana* apple]

manatee

Man·chu /manchoo/ *n. & adj.* ● *n.* **1** a member of a people in China, descended from a Tartar people, who formed the last imperial dynasty (1644–1912). **2** the language of the Manchus, now spoken in part of NE China. ● *adj.* of or relating to the Manchu people or their language. [Manchu, = pure]

man·ci·ple /mánsipəl/ *n.* esp. *Brit.* an officer who buys provisions for a college, an Inn of Court, etc. [ME f. AF & OF f. L *mancipium* purchase f. *manceps* buyer f. *manus* hand + *capere* take]

Man·cu·ni·an /mangkyooneeən/ *n. & adj.* ● *n.* a native of Manchester in NW England. ● *adj.* of or relating to Manchester. [L *Mancunium* Manchester]

-mancy /mansee/ *comb. form* forming nouns meaning 'divination by' (*geomancy*; *necromancy*). □□ **-mantic** *comb. form* forming adjectives. [OF *-mancie* f. LL *-mantia* f. Gk *manteia* divination]

Man·dae·an /mandeeən/ *n. & adj.* (also **Mandean**) ● *n.* **1** a member of a Gnostic sect surviving in Iraq and claiming descent from John the Baptist. **2** the language of this sect. ● *adj.* of or concerning the Mandaeans or their language. □□ **Man·dae·an·ism** *n.* [Aram. *mandaiia* Gnostics f. *manda* knowledge]

man·da·la /mándələ, mún–/ *n.* **1** a symbolic circular figure representing the universe in various religions. **2** *Psychol.* such a symbol in a dream, representing the dreamer's search for completeness and self-unity. [Skr. *máṇḍala* disk]

man·da·mus /mandáyməs/ *n. Law* a judicial writ issued as a command to an inferior court, or ordering a person to perform a public or statutory duty. [L, = we command]

man·da·rin¹ /mándərin/ *n.* **1** (**Mandarin**) the most widely spoken form of Chinese and the official language of China. **2** *hist.* a Chinese official in any of nine grades of the pre-communist civil service. **3 a** a party leader; a bureaucrat. **b** a powerful member of the establishment. **4 a** a nodding Chinese figure, usu. of porcelain. **b** porcelain, etc., decorated with Chinese figures in mandarin dress. □□ **man·da·rin·ate** *n.* [Port. *mandarim* f. Malay f. Hindi *mantrī* f. Skr. *mantrin* counselor]

man·da·rin² /mándərin/ *n.* (in full **mandarin orange**) **1** a small flattish deep-colored orange with a loose skin. **2** the tree, *Citrus reticulata*, yielding this. Also called **tangerine**. [F *mandarine* (perh. as MANDARIN¹, with ref. to the official's yellow robes)]

man·da·rin col·lar *n.* a small close-fitting upright collar.

man·da·rin duck *n.* a small Chinese duck, *Aix galericulata*, noted for its bright plumage.

man·da·rin sleeve *n.* a wide loose sleeve.

man·da·tar·y /mándətéree/ *n.* (*pl.* **-ies**) esp. *hist.* a person or country receiving a mandate. [LL *mandatarius* (as MANDATE)]

man·date /mándayt/ *n. & v.* ● *n.* **1** an official command or instruction by an authority. **2** support for a policy or course of action, regarded by a victorious party, candidate, etc., as derived from the wishes of the people in an election. **3** a commission to act for another. **4** *Law* a commission by which a party is entrusted to perform a service, often gratuitously and with indemnity against loss by that party. **5** *hist.* a commission from the League of Nations to a member country to administer a territory. **6** a papal decree or decision. ● *v.tr.* **1** instruct (a delegate) to act or vote in a certain way. **2** (usu. foll. by *to*) *hist.* commit (a territory, etc.) to a mandatary. □□ **man·da·tor** *n.* [L *mandatum*, neut. past part. of *mandare* command f. *manus* hand + *dare* give: sense 2 of n. after F *mandat*]

man·da·to·ry /mándətáwree/ *adj. & n.* ● *adj.* **1** of or conveying a command. **2** compulsory. ● *n.* (*pl.* **-ies**) = MANDATARY. □□ **man·da·to·ri·ly** *adv.* [LL *mandatorius* f. L (as MANDATE)]

man·di·ble /mándibəl/ *n.* **1** the jaw, esp. the lower jaw in mammals and fishes. **2** the upper or lower part of a bird's beak. **3** either half of the crushing organ in an arthropod's mouthparts. □□ **man·dib**-

u·lar /–díbyələr/ *adj.* **man·dib·u·late** /–díbyələt/ *adj.* [ME f. OF *mandible* or LL *mandibula* f. *mandere* chew]

man·do·lin /mándəlin/ *n.* (also **man·do·line**) a musical instrument resembling a lute, having paired metal strings plucked with a plectrum. □□ **man·do·lin·ist** *n.* [F *mandoline* f. It. *mandolino* dimin. of *mandola* a large lute]

man·dor·la /mandawrlə/ *n.* = VESICA 2. [It., = almond]

man·drag·o·ra /mandrágərə/ *n. hist.* the mandrake, esp. as a type of narcotic (Shakesp. *Othello* III. iii. 334). [OE f. med.L f. L f. Gk *mandragoras*]

man·drake /mándrayk/ *n.* **1** a poisonous plant, *Mandragora officinarum*, with white or purple flowers and large yellow fruit, having emetic and narcotic properties and possessing a root once thought to resemble the human form and to shriek when plucked. **2** = MAYAPPLE. [ME *mandrag(g)e*, prob. f. MDu. *mandrag(r)e* f. med.L (as MANDRAGORA) assoc. with MAN + *drake* dragon (cf. DRAKE)]

mandolin

man·drel /mándrəl/ *n.* **1 a** a shaft in a lathe to which work is fixed while being turned. **b** a cylindrical rod around which metal or other material is forged or shaped. **2** *Brit.* a miner's pick. [16th c.: orig. unkn.]

man·drill /mándril/ *n.* a large W. African baboon, *Papio* (or *Mandrillus*) *sphinx*, the adult of which has a brilliantly colored face and blue-colored buttocks. [prob. f. MAN + DRILL³]

man·du·cate /mánjookayt/ *v.tr. literary* chew; eat. □□ **man·du·ca·tion** /–káyshən/ *n.* **man·du·ca·to·ry** /–kətáwree/ *adj.* [L *manducare* manducat- chew f. *manduco* guzzler f. *mandere* chew]

mane /mayn/ *n.* **1** long hair growing in a line on the neck of a horse, lion, etc. **2** *colloq.* a person's long hair. □□ **maned** *adj.* (also in *comb.*). **mane·less** *adj.* [OE *manu* f. Gmc]

ma·nège /manézh/ *n.* (also **ma·nege**) **1** a riding school. **2** the movements of a trained horse. **3** horsemanship. [F *manège* f. It. (as MANAGE)]

ma·nes /maánayz, máyneez/ *n.pl.* **1** the deified souls of dead ancestors. **2** (as *sing.*) the revered ghost of a person. [ME f. L]

ma·neu·ver /mənoovər/ *n. & v.* ● *n.* **1** a planned and controlled movement or series of moves. **2** (in *pl.*) a large-scale exercise of troops, warships, etc. **3 a** an often deceptive planned or controlled action designed to gain an objective. **b** a skillful plan. ● *v.* **1** *intr. & tr.* perform or cause to perform a maneuver (*maneuvered the car into the space*). **2** *intr. & tr.* perform or cause (troops, etc.) to perform military maneuvers. **3** *a tr.* (usu. foll. by *into*, *out*, *away*) force, drive, or manipulate (a person, thing, etc.) by scheming or adroitness. **b** *intr.* use artifice. □□ **ma·neu·ver·a·ble** *adj.* **ma·neu·ver·a·bil·i·ty** /–vrəbílitee, –vrə–/ *n.* **ma·neu·ver·er** *n.* [F *manœuvre*, *manœuvrer* f. med.L *manuoperare* f. L *manus* hand + *operari* to work]

man Fri·day *n.* a helper or follower (after *Man Friday* in Defoe's *Robinson Crusoe*).

man·ful /mánfool/ *adj.* brave; resolute. □□ **man·ful·ly** *adv.* **man·ful·ness** *n.*

man·ga·bey /mánggəbay/ *n.* any small long-tailed W. African monkey of the genus *Cercocebus*. [*Mangabey*, a region of Madagascar]

man·ga·nese /mánggəneez/ *n.* **1** *Chem.* a gray brittle metallic transition element used with steel to make alloys. ¶ Symb.: **Mn. 2** (in full **manganese oxide**) the black mineral oxide of this used in the manufacture of glass. □□ **man·gan·ic** /–gánik/ *adj.* **man·ga·nous** /mánggənəs/ *adj.* [F *manganèse* f. It. *manganese*, alt. f. MAGNESIA]

mange /maynj/ *n.* a skin disease in hairy and woolly animals, caused by an arachnid parasite and occasionally communicated to people. [ME *mangie*, *maniewe* f. OF *manjue*, *mangeue* itch f. *mangier* *manju-* eat f. L *manducare* chew]

man·gel /mánggəl/ *n.* esp. *Brit.* (also **man·gold** /mánggōld/) (in full **mangel-wurzel**, **mangold-wurzel** /–wúrzəl/) a large kind of beet, *Beta vulgaris*, used as cattle food. [G *Mangoldwurzel* f. *Mangold* beet + *Wurzel* root]

man·ger /máynjər/ *n.* a long open box or trough in a stable, etc., for horses or cattle to eat from. [ME f. OF *mangeoire*, *mangeure* ult. f. L (as MANDUCATE)]

man·gle¹ /mánggəl/ *v.tr.* **1** hack, cut, or mutilate by blows, etc. **2** spoil (a quotation, text, etc.) by misquoting, mispronouncing, etc. **3** cut roughly so as to disfigure. □□ **man·gler** *n.* [AF *ma(ha)ngler*, app. frequent. of *mahaignier* MAIM]

man·gle² /mánggəl/ *n. & v.* ● *n.* a machine having two or more heated, revolving cylinders between which clothes, sheets, etc., are smoothed and pressed. ● *v.tr.* press (clothes, etc.) in a mangle. [Du.

mangel(stok) f. *mangelen* to mangle, ult. f. Gk *magganon* + *stok* staff, STOCK]

man•go /mánggō/ *n.* (*pl.* •**goes** or •**gos**) **1** a fleshy yellowish-red fruit, eaten ripe or used green for pickles, etc. **2** the E. Indian evergreen tree, *Mangifera indica*, bearing this. [Port. *manga* f. Malay *mangā* f. Tamil *mānkāy* f. *mān* mango tree + *kāy* fruit]

man•gold (also **man•gold-wur•zel**) var. of MANGEL.

man•go•nel /mánggonəl/ *n. Mil. hist.* a military engine for throwing stones, etc. [ME f. OF *mangonel(le)*, f. med.L *manganellus* dimin. of LL *manganum* f. Gk *magganon*]

man•go•steen /mánggəsteen/ *n.* **1** a white juicy-pulped fruit with a thick reddish-brown rind. **2** the E. Indian tree, *Garcinia mangostana*, bearing this. [Malay *manggustan*]

man•grove /mánggrōv/ *n.* any tropical tree or shrub of the genus *Rhizophora*, growing in tidal-shore mud with many tangled roots above ground. [17th c.: orig. uncert.: assim. to GROVE]

man•gy /máynjee/ *adj.* (**man•gi•er, man•gi•est**) **1** (esp. of a domestic animal) having mange. **2** squalid; shabby. □□ **man•gi•ly** *adv.* **man•gi•ness** *n.*

man•han•dle /mánhánd'l/ *v.tr.* **1** move (heavy objects) by hand with great effort. **2** *colloq.* handle (someone or something) roughly.

man•hat•tan /manhátən/ *n.* (also **Manhattan**) a cocktail made of vermouth and whiskey, usu. flavored with bitters. [*Manhattan*, borough of New York City]

man•hole /mánhōl/ *n.* a covered opening in a floor, pavement, sewer, etc., for workers to gain access.

man•hood /mánhŏod/ *n.* **1** the state of being a man rather than a child or woman. **2 a** manliness; courage. **b** a man's sexual potency. **3** the men of a country, etc. **4** the state of being human.

man-hour *n.* an hour regarded in terms of the amount of work that could be done by one person within this period.

man•hunt /mánhunt/ *n.* an organized search for a person, esp. a criminal.

ma•ni•a /máyneeə/ *n.* **1** *Psychol.* mental illness marked by periods of great excitement and violence. **2** (often foll. by *for*) excessive enthusiasm; an obsession (*has a mania for jogging*). [ME f. LL f. Gk, = madness f. *mainomai* be mad, rel. to MIND]

-mania /máyneeə/ *comb. form* **1** *Psychol.* denoting a special type of mental abnormality or obsession (*megalomania*). **2** denoting extreme enthusiasm or admiration (*bibliomania*; *Anglomania*).

ma•ni•ac /máyneeak/ *n. & adj.* ● *n.* **1** *colloq.* a person exhibiting extreme symptoms of wild behavior, etc.; a madman. **2** *colloq.* an obsessive enthusiast. **3** *Psychol. archaic* a person suffering from mania. ● *adj.* of or behaving like a maniac. □□ **ma•ni•a•cal** /məníəkəl/ *adj.* **ma•ni•a•cal•ly** /məníəklee/ *adv.* [LL *maniacus* f. late Gk *maniakos* (as MANIA)]

-maniac /máyneeak/ *comb. form* forming adjectives and nouns meaning 'affected with –mania' or 'a person affected with –mania' (*kleptomaniac*).

man•ic /mánik/ *adj.* of or affected by mania. □□ **man•i•cal•ly** *adv.*

man•ic-de•pres•sive *n. Psychol. adj.* affected by or relating to a mental disorder with alternating periods of elation and depression. ● *n.* a person having such a disorder.

Man•i•chee /mánikee/ *n.* **1** an adherent of a religious system of the 3rd–5th c., representing Satan in a state of everlasting conflict with God. **2** *Philos.* a dualist (see DUALISM). □□ **Man•i•che•an** /–kéeən/ *adj. & n.* (also **Man•i•chae•an**). **Man•i•che•ism** /–kée-izəm/ *n.* (also **Man•i•chae•ism**). [LL *Manichaeus* f. late Gk *Manikhaios*, f. *Manes* or *Manichaeus* Persian founder of the sect]

man•i•cure /mánikyŏor/ *n. & v.* ● *n.* a cosmetic treatment of the hands involving cutting, shaping, and often painting of the nails, removal of the cuticles, and softening of the skin. ● *v.tr.* give a manicure to (the hands or a person). □□ **man•i•cur•ist** *n.* [F f. L *manus* hand + *cura* care]

man•i•cur•ist /mánikyŏorist/ *n.* a person who gives manicures professionally.

man•i•fest¹ /mánifest/ *adj. & v.* ● *adj.* clear or obvious to the eye or mind (*his distress was manifest*). ● *v.* **1** *tr.* display or show (a quality, feeling, etc.) by one's acts, etc. **2** *tr.* show plainly to the eye or mind. **3** *tr.* be evidence of; prove. **4** *refl.* (of a thing) reveal itself. **5** *intr.* (of a ghost) appear. □□ **man•i•fes•ta•tion** /–stáyshən/ *n.* **man•i•fes•ta•tive** /–fést ətiv/ *adj.* **man•i•fest•ly** *adv.* [ME f. OF *manifeste* (adj.), *manifester* (v.) or L *manifestus, manifestare* f. *manus* hand + *festus* (unrecorded) struck]

man•i•fest² /mánifest/ *n. & v.* ● *n.* **1** a cargo list for the use of customs officers. **2** a list of passengers in an aircraft or of cars, etc., in a freight train. ● *v.tr.* record (names, cargo, etc.) in a manifest. [It. *manifesto*: see MANIFESTO]

Man•i•fest Des•ti•ny *n.* 19th-c. doctrine asserting that the United States was destined to expand westward to the Pacific and to exert economic and social control throughout N. America.

man•i•fes•to /mániféstō/ *n.* (*pl.* •**tos** or •**toes**) **1** a public declaration of policy and aims esp. political or social. **2** *Brit.* the platform of a political party or candidate. [It. f. *manifestare* f. L (as MANIFEST¹)]

man•i•fold /mánifōld/ *adj. & n.* ● *adj. literary* **1** many and various (*manifold vexations*). **2** having various forms, parts, applications, etc. **3** performing several functions at once. ● *n.* **1** a thing with many different forms, parts, applications, etc. **2** *Mech.* a pipe or chamber branching into several openings. □□ **man•i•fold•ly** *adv.* **man•i•fold•ness** *n.* [OE *manigfeald* (as MANY, –FOLD)]

man•i•kin /mánikin/ *n.* (also **man•ni•kin**) **1** a little man; a dwarf. **2** an artist's lay figure. **3** an anatomical model of the body. **4** (usu. **mannikin**) any small finchlike bird of the genus *Lonchura*, native to Africa and Australasia. [Du. *manneken*, dimin. of *man* MAN]

Ma•nil•a /mənílə/ *n.* (also **Ma•nil•la**) **1** (in full **Manila hemp**) the strong fiber of a Philippine tree, *Musa textilis*, used for rope, etc. **2** (also **manila**) a strong brown paper made from Manila hemp or other material and used for wrapping paper, envelopes, etc. **3** a cigar or cheroot made in Manila. [*Manila* in the Philippines]

ma•nil•la /mənílə/ *n.* a metal bracelet used by African tribes as a medium of exchange. [Sp., prob. dimin. of *mano* hand f. L *manus*]

man in the moon *n.* the semblance of a face seen on the surface of a full moon.

man in the street *n.* (also **man on the street**) an ordinary average person, as distinct from an expert.

man•i•oc /máneeok/ *n.* **1** cassava. **2** the flour made from it. [Tupi *mandioca*]

man•i•ple /mánipəl/ *n.* **1** *Rom.Hist.* a subdivision of a legion, containing 120 or 60 men. **2** a Eucharistic vestment consisting of a strip folded over the left arm. [OF *maniple* or L *manipulus* handful, troop f. *manus* hand]

ma•nip•u•late /mənípyəlayt/ *v.tr.* **1** handle, treat, or use, esp. skillfully (a tool, question, material, etc.). **2** manage (a person, situation, etc.) to one's own advantage, esp. unfairly or unscrupulously. **3** manually examine and treat (a part of the body). **4** *Computing* alter, edit, or move (text, data, etc.). □□ **ma•nip•u•la•ble** /–ləbəl/ *adj.* **ma•nip•u•la•bil•i•ty** /–ləbílitee/ *n.* **ma•nip•u•lat•a•ble** *adj.* **ma•nip•u•la•tion** /–láyshən/ *n.* **ma•nip•u•la•tor** /–lətawree/ *adj.* [back-form. f. *manipulation*. F *manipulation* f. mod.L *manipulatio* (as MANIPLE), after F *manipuler*]

ma•nip•u•la•tive /mənípyələtiv/ *adj.* **1** characterized by unscrupulous exploitation of a situation, person, etc., for one's own ends. **2** of or concerning manipulation. □□ **ma•nip•u•la•tive•ly** *adv.* **ma•nip•u•la•tive•ness** *n.*

Manit. *abbr.* Manitoba.

man•i•tou /mánitŏo/ *n.* **1** a good or evil spirit as an object of reverence. **2** something regarded as having supernatural power. [Algonquian *manito, –tu* he has surpassed]

man•kind *n.* **1** /mánkínd/ the human species. **2** /mánkínd/ male people, as distinct from female.

man•like /mánlīk/ *adj.* **1** having the qualities of a man. **2** (of a woman) mannish. **3** (of an animal, shape, etc.) resembling a human being.

man•ly /mánlee/ *adj.* (**man•li•er, man•li•est**) **1** having qualities regarded as admirable in a man, such as courage, frankness, etc. **2** (of a woman) mannish. **3** (of things, qualities, etc.) befitting a man. □□ **man•li•ness** *n.*

man-made *adj.* (esp. of a textile fiber) artificial; synthetic.

man•na /mánə/ *n.* **1** the substance miraculously supplied as food to the Israelites in the wilderness (Exod. 16). **2** an unexpected benefit (esp. manna from heaven). **3** spiritual nourishment, esp. the Eucharist. **4** the sweet dried juice from the manna ash and other related plants, used as a mild laxative. [OE f. LL f. Gk f. Aram. *mannā* f. Heb. *mān*, explained as = *mān hū* what is it?, but prob. = Arab. *mann* exudation of common tamarisk (*Tamarix gallica*)]

man•na ash *n.* an ash tree native to S. Europe, *Fraxinus ornus*.

man•na grass *n.* any N. American marsh grass of the genus *Glyceria*.

manned /mand/ *adj.* (of an aircraft, spacecraft, etc.) having a human crew. [past part. of MAN]

man•ne•quin /mánikin/ *n.* **1** a model employed by a dressmaker, etc., to show clothes to customers. **2** a model of the human form, for fitting or displaying garments. **3** an artist's lay figure. [F, = MANIKIN]

man•ner /mánər/ *n.* **1** a way a thing is done or happens (*always dresses in that manner*). **2** (in *pl.*) **a** social behavior (*it is bad manners to stare*). **b** polite or well-bred behavior (*he has no manners*). **c** modes of life; conditions of society. **3** a person's outward bearing, way of speaking, etc. (*has an imperious manner*). **4 a** a style in literature, art, etc. (*in the manner of Rembrandt*). **b** = MANNERISM 2a. **5** *archaic* a kind or sort (*what manner of man is he?*). □ **all manner of** many different kinds of. **in a manner of speaking** in some sense; to some extent; so to speak. **to the manner born 1** *colloq.* naturally at ease in a specified job, situation, etc. **2** destined by birth to follow a custom or way of life (Shakesp. *Hamlet* I. iv. 17). □□ **man•ner•less** *adj.* (in sense 2b of *n.*). [ME f. AF *manere*, OF *maniere* ult. f. L *manuarius* of the hand (*manus*)]

man•nered /mánərd/ *adj.* **1** (in *comb.*) behaving in a specified way (-*ill-mannered; well-mannered*). **2** (of a style, artist, writer, etc.) showing idiosyncratic mannerisms. **3** (of a person) eccentrically affected in behavior.

man·ner·ism /mánərizəm/ n. **1** a habitual gesture or way of speaking, etc.; an idiosyncrasy. **2 a** excessive addiction to a distinctive style in art or literature. **b** a stylistic trick. **3** a style of Italian art preceding the Baroque, characterized by lengthened figures. □□ **man·ner·ist** n. **man·ner·is·tic** /-rístik/ adj. **man·ner·is·ti·cal** /-rístikəl/ adj. **man·ner·is·ti·cal·ly** /-rístiklee/ adv. [MANNER]

man·ner·ly /mánərlee/ adj. & adv. ● adj. well-mannered; polite. ● adv. politely. □□ **man·ner·li·ness** n.

man·ni·kin var. of MANIKIN.

man·nish /mánish/ adj. **1** usu. derog. (of a woman) masculine in appearance or manner. **2** characteristic of a man. □□ **man·nish·ly** adv. **man·nish·ness** n. [OE mennisc f. (and assim. to) MAN]

man·oeu·vre Brit. var. of MANEUVER.

man of the cloth n. a clergyman.

man of God n. **1** a clergyman. **2** a male saint.

man of hon·or n. a man whose word can be trusted.

man of let·ters n. (also **woman of letters**) a scholar or author.

man-of-war n. an armed ship, esp. of a specified country.

ma·nom·e·ter /mənómitər/ n. a pressure gauge for gases and liquids. □□ **man·o·met·ric** /mánəmétrik/ adj. [F manomètre f. Gk manos thin]

ma non trop·po adv. (see TROPPO¹). manor

man·or /mánər/ n. **1** (also **man·or house**) **a** a large country house with lands. **b** the house of the lord of the manor. **2** Brit. **a** a unit of land consisting of a lord's demesne and lands rented to tenants, etc. **b** hist. a feudal lordship over lands. **3** Brit. colloq. the district covered by a police station. □□ **ma·no·ri·al** /mənáwreeəl/ adj. [ME f. AF maner, OF maneir, f. L manēre remain]

man·pow·er /mánpowr/ n. **1** the power generated by a person working. **2** the number of people available or required for work, service, etc.

man·qué /maaNkáy/ adj. (placed after noun) that might have been but is not; unfulfilled (a comic actor manqué). [F, past part. of manquer lack]

man·sard /mánsaard/ n. a roof that has four sloping sides, each of which becomes steeper halfway down. [F mansarde f. F. Mansart, Fr. architect d. 1666]

manse /mans/ n. **1** the house of a minister, esp. a Presbyterian **2** a mansion. □ **son** (or **daughter**) of the manse the child of a Presbyterian, etc., minister. [ME f. med.L mansus, -sa, -sum, house f. manēre mans- remain]

man·serv·ant /mánservənt/ n. (pl. **men·serv·ants**) a male servant.

-manship /mənship/ suffix forming nouns denoting skill in a subject or activity (craftsmanship; gamesmanship).

man·sion /mánshən/ n. **1** a large house. **2** (usu. in pl.) Brit. a large building divided into apartments. [ME f. OF f. L mansio -onis a staying (as MANSE)]

man-sized adj. (also **man-size**) **1** of the size of a man (man-sized plants). **2** big enough for a man.

man·slaugh·ter /mánslawtər/ n. **1** the killing of one human being by another. **2** Law the unlawful killing of a human being without malice aforethought.

man·sue·tude /mánswitŏod, -tyŏod/ n. archaic meekness, docility, gentleness. [ME f. OF mansuetude or L mansuetudo f. mansuetus gentle, tame f. manus hand + suetus accustomed]

man·ta /mántə/ n. **1** esp. SW US & Latin Amer. a cloak or shawl made from a square cloth. **2** any large ray of the family Mobulidae, esp. Manta birostris, having winglike pectoral fins and a whiplike tail. [Amer. Sp., = large blanket]

man·tel /mánt'l/ n. **1** = MANTELPIECE 1. **2** = MANTELSHELF. [var. of MANTLE]

man·tel·et /mánt'lit/ n. (also **mant·let** /mántlit/) **1** hist. a woman's short loose sleeveless mantle. **2** a protective screen for gunners, etc. [ME f. OF, dimin. of mantel MANTLE]

man·tel·piece /mánt'lpees/ n. **1** a structure of wood, marble, etc., above and around a fireplace. **2** = MANTELSHELF.

man·tel·shelf /mánt'lshelf/ n. a shelf above a fireplace.

man·tic /mántik/ adj. formal of or concerning divination or prophecy. [Gk mantikos f. mantis prophet]

man·tid /mántid/ n. = MANTIS.

man·til·la /mantílə, -téeə/ n. a lace scarf worn by Spanish women over the hair and shoulders. [Sp., dimin. of manta MANTLE]

mantilla

man·tis /mántis/ n. (pl. same or **man·tis·es**) any insect of the family Mantidae, feeding on other insects, etc. [Gk, = prophet]

man·tis·sa /mantísə/ n. the part of a logarithm after the decimal point. [L, = makeweight]

man·tle /mánt'l/ n. & v. ● n. **1** a loose sleeveless

mantis

cloak. **2** a covering of a specified sort (a mantle of snow). **3** a fragile lacelike tube fixed around a gas jet to give an incandescent light. **4** an outer fold of skin enclosing a mollusk's viscera. **5** a bird's back, scapulars, and wing coverts, esp. if of a distinctive color. **6** the region between the crust and the core of the earth. ● v. **1** tr. clothe in or as if in a mantle; cover; conceal; envelop. **2** intr. **a** (of the blood) suffuse the cheeks. **b** (of the face) glow with a blush. **3** intr. (of a liquid) become covered with a coating or scum. [ME f. OF f. L mantellum cloak]

mant·let var. of MANTELET.

man·tling /mántling/ n. Heraldry **1** ornamental drapery, etc. behind and around a shield. **2** a representation of this. [MANTLE + -ING¹]

man-to-man adj. with candor; honestly.

man·tra /mántrə, maán-, mún-/ n. **1** a word or sound repeated to aid concentration in meditation, orig. in Hinduism and Buddhism. **2** a Vedic hymn. [Skr., = instrument of thought f. man think]

man·trap /mántrap/ n. a trap for catching poachers, trespassers, etc.

man·tu·a /mánchŏoə/ n. hist. a woman's loose gown of the 17th–18th c. [corrupt. of manteau (F, as MANTLE) after Mantua in Italy]

man·u·al /mányŏoəl/ adj. & n. ● adj. **1** of or done with the hands (manual labor). **2** (of a machine, etc.) worked by hand, not automatically. ● n. **1 a** a book of instructions, esp. for operating a machine or learning a subject; a handbook (a computer manual). **b** any small book. **2** a nonelectric typewriter. **3** an organ keyboard played only with the hands. **4** Mil. an exercise in handling a rifle, etc. **5** hist. a book of the forms to be used by priests in the administration of the sacraments. □□ **man·u·al·ly** adv. [ME f. OF manuel, f. (and later assim. to) L manualis f. manus hand]

man·u·al al·pha·bet n. set of sign-language symbols used in finger-spelling.

man·u·fac·to·ry /mányəfáktəree/ n. (pl. **·ries**) archaic = FACTORY. [MANUFACTURE, after factory]

man·u·fac·ture /mányəfákchər/ n. & v. ● n. **1 a** the making of articles, esp. in a factory, etc. **b** a branch of an industry (woolen manufacture). **2** esp. derog. the merely mechanical production of literature, art, etc. ● v. tr. **1** make (articles), esp. on an industrial scale. **2** invent or fabricate (evidence, a story, etc.). **3** esp. derog. make or produce (literature, art, etc.) in a mechanical way. □□ **man·u·fac·tur·a·ble** adj. **man·u·fac·tur·a·bil·i·ty** /-chərəbílitee/ n. **man·u·fac·tur·er** n. [F f. It. manifattura & L manufactum made by hand]

ma·nu·ka /manŏŏkə, maánəkə/ n. Austral. & NZ a small tree, Leptospermum scoparium, with aromatic leaves and hard timber. [Maori]

man·u·mit /mányəmít/ v.tr. (**man·u·mit·ted, man·u·mit·ting**) hist. set (a slave) free. □□ **man·u·mis·sion** /-míshən/ n. [ME f. L manumittere manumiss- f. manus hand + emittere send forth]

ma·nure /mənŏŏr, -nyŏŏr/ n. & v. ● n. **1** animal dung used for fertilizing land. **2** any compost or artificial fertilizer. ● v.tr. (also absol.) apply manure to (land, etc.). □□ **ma·nu·ri·al** adj. [ME f. AF mainoverer = OF manouvrer MANEUVER]

man·u·script /mányəskript/ n. & adj. ● n. **1** a book, document, etc., written by hand. **2** an author's handwritten or typed text, submitted for publication. **3** handwritten form (produced in manuscript). ● adj. written by hand. [med.L manuscriptus f. manu by hand + scriptus past part. of scribere write]

Manx /mangks/ adj. & n. ● adj. of or relating to the Isle of Man. ● n. **1** the now extinct Celtic language formerly spoken in the Isle of Man. **2** (prec. by the; treated as pl.) the Manx people. [ON f. OIr. Manu Isle of Man]

Manx·man /mángksmən/ n. (pl. **·men**; fem. **Manx·wom·an**, pl. **·wom·en**) a native of the Isle of Man.

Manx cat n. a breed of tailless cat.

man·y /ménee/ adj. & n. ● adj. (**more** /mawr/; **most** /mōst/) great in number; numerous (many times; many people; many a person; his reasons were many). ● n. (as pl.) **1** a large number (many like skiing; many went). **2** (prec. by the) the multitude of esp. working people. □ **as many** the same number of (six mistakes in as many lines). **as many again** the same number additionally (sixty here and as many again there). **be too** (or **one too**) **many for** outwit, baffle. **a good** (or **great**) **many** a large number. **many's the time** often (many's the time we saw it). **many a time** many times. [OE manig, ult. f. Gmc]

man·y-sid·ed adj. having many sides, aspects, interests, capabilities, etc. □□ **man·y-sid·ed·ness** n.

man·za·nil·la /mánzəneélyə, -nee-ə/ n. a pale very dry Spanish sherry. [Sp., lit. 'camomile']

man·za·ni·ta /mánzəneétə/ n. any of several evergreen shrubs of the genus Arctostaphylos, esp. A. manzanita, native to western N. America. [Sp., dimin. of manzana apple]

Mao·ism /mówizəm/ n. the Communist doctrines of Mao Zedong (d. 1976), Chinese statesman. □□ **Mao·ist** n. & adj.

Ma·o·ri /mówree/ n. & adj. ● n. (pl. same or **Ma·o·ris**) **1** a member of the Polynesian aboriginal people of New Zealand. **2** the language of the Maori. ● *adj.* of or concerning the Maori or their language. [native name]

map /map/ *n. & v.* ● *n.* **1 a** a usu. flat representation of the earth's surface, or part of it, showing physical features, cities, etc. (cf. GLOBE). **b** a diagrammatic representation of a route, etc. (*drew a map of the journey*). **2** a two-dimensional representation of the stars, the heavens, etc., or of the surface of a planet, the moon, etc. **3** a diagram showing the arrangement or components of a thing. **4** *sl.* the face. ● *v.tr.* (**mapped, map•ping**) **1** represent (a country, etc.) on a map. **2** *Math.* associate each element of (a set) with one element of another set. □ **map out** arrange in detail; plan (a course of conduct, etc.). **off the map** *colloq.* **1** of no account; obsolete. **2** very distant. **on the map** *colloq.* prominent, important. **wipe off the map** *colloq.* obliterate. □□ **map•less** *adj.* **map•pa•ble** *adj.* **map•per** *n.* [L *mappa* napkin: in med.L *mappa (mundi)* map (of the world)]

ma•ple /máypəl/ *n.* **1** any tree or shrub of the genus *Acer* grown for shade, ornament, wood, or its sugar. **2** the wood of the maple. [ME *mapul*, etc., f. OE *mapeltrēow, mapulder*]

ma•ple leaf *n.* the leaf of the maple, used as an emblem of Canada.

ma•ple sug•ar *n.* a sugar produced by evaporating the sap of certain maples, esp. the sugar maple.

ma•ple syr•up *n.* syrup produced from the sap of certain maples, esp. the sugar maple.

ma•quette /məkét/ *n.* **1** a sculptor's small preliminary model in wax, clay, etc. **2** a preliminary sketch. [F f. It. *machietta* dimin. of *macchia* spot]

ma•quil•lage /mákeeyáazh/ *n.* **1** makeup; cosmetics. **2** the application of makeup. [F f. *maquiller* make up f. OF *masquiller* stain]

Ma•quis /makée/ *n.* **1** the French resistance movement during the German occupation (1940–45). **2** a member of this. [F, = brushwood, f. Corsican It. *macchia* thicket]

Mar. *abbr.* March.

mar /maar/ *v.tr.* (**marred, mar•ring**) **1** ruin. **2** impair the perfection of; spoil; disfigure. [OE *merran* hinder]

mar•a•bou /márəbōo/ *n.* (also **mar•a•bout**) **1** a large W. African stork, *Leptoptilos crumeniferus.* **2** a tuft of down from the wing or tail of the marabou used as a trimming for hats, etc. [F f. Arab. *murābiṭ* holy man (see MARABOUT), the stork being regarded as holy]

mar•a•bout /márəbōot, –bōō/ *n.* **1** a Muslim hermit or monk, esp. in N. Africa. **2** a shrine marking a marabout's burial place. [F f. Port. *marabuto* f. Arab. *murābiṭ* holy man f. *ribāṭ* frontier station, where he acquired merit by combat against the infidel]

ma•rac•a /məraákə/ *n.* a hollow clublike gourd or gourd-shaped container filled with beans, etc., and usu. shaken in pairs as a percussion instrument in Latin American music. [Port. *maracá*, prob. f. Tupi]

mar•a•schi•no /márəskeenō, –shee–/ *n.* (*pl.* **•nos**) a strong, sweet liqueur made from a small black Dalmatian cherry. [It. f. *marasca* small black cherry, for *amarasca* f. *amaro* bitter f. L *amarus*]

mar•a•schi•no cher•ry *n.* a cherry preserved in or flavored with maraschino and used to decorate cocktails and desserts.

ma•ras•mus /mərázməs/ *n.* undernourishment causing a child's weight to be significantly low for their age. □□ **ma•ras•mic** *adj.* [mod.L f. Gk *marasmos* f. *marainō* wither]

Ma•ra•tha /məraátə, –rátə/ *n.* (also **Mah•rat•ta**) a member of a warrior people native to the modern Indian state of Maharashtra. [Hindi *Marhaṭṭa* f. Skr. *Māhārāshṭra* great kingdom]

Ma•ra•thi /məraátee, –rátee/ *n.* (also **Mah•rat•ti**) the language of the Marathas. [MARATHA]

mar•a•thon /márəthon/ *n.* **1** a long-distance running race, usu. of 26 miles 385 yards (42.195 km). **2** a long-lasting or difficult task, operation, etc. (often *attrib.*: *a marathon shopping expedition*). □□ **mar•a•thon•er** *n.* [*Marathon* in Greece, scene of a victory over the Persians in 490 BC: a messenger was said to have run to Athens with the news, but the account has no authority]

ma•raud /məráwd/ *v.* **1** *intr.* **a** make a plundering raid. **b** pilfer systematically; plunder. **2** *tr.* plunder (a place). □□ **ma•raud•er** *n.* [F *marauder* f. *maraud* rogue]

mar•ble /maárbəl/ *n. & v.* ● *n.* **1** limestone in a metamorphic crystalline (or granular) state, and capable of taking a polish, used in sculpture and architecture. **2** (often *attrib.*) **a** anything made of marble (*a marble clock*). **b** anything resembling marble in hardness, coldness, durability, etc. (*her features were marble*). **3 a** a small ball of marble, glass, clay, etc., used as a toy. **b** (in *pl.*; treated as *sing.*) a game using these. **4** (in *pl.*) *sl.* one's mental faculties (*he's lost his marbles*). **5** (in *pl.*) a collection of sculptures (*Roman marbles*). ● *v.tr.* **1** (esp. as **marbled** *adj.*) stain or color (paper, the edges of a book, soap, etc.) to look like variegated marble. **2** (as **marbled** *adj.*) (of meat) streaked with alternating layers of lean and fat. □□ **mar•bly** *adj.* [ME f. OF *marbre, marble*, f. L *marmor* f. Gk *marmaros* shining stone]

mar•ble cake *n.* a cake with a streaked appearance, made of light and dark batter.

mar•bling /maárbling/ *n.* **1** coloring or marking like marble. **2** streaks of fat in lean meat.

marc /maark/ *n.* **1** the refuse of pressed grapes, etc. **2** a brandy made from this. [F f. *marcher* tread, MARCH[1]]

Mar•can /maárkən/ *adj.* of or relating to St. Mark. [L *Marcus* Mark]

mar•ca•site /maárkəsīt/ *n.* **1** a yellowish crystalline iron sulfide mineral. **2** these bronze-yellow crystals used in jewelry. [ME f. med.L *marcasita*, f. Arab. *markaṣīṭā* f. Pers.]

mar•cat•o /maarkaátō/ *adv. & adj. Mus.* played with emphasis. [It., = marked]

mar•cel /maarsél/ *n. & v.* ● *n.* (in full **marcel wave**) a deep wave in the hair. ● *v.tr.* (**mar•celled, mar•cel•ling**) wave (hair) with a deep wave. [*Marcel* Grateau, Paris hairdresser d. 1936, who invented the method]

mar•ces•cent /maarsésənt/ *adj.* (of part of a plant) withering but not falling. □□ **mar•ces•cence** /–səns/ *n.* [L *marcescere* incept. of *marcēre* wither]

March /maarch/ *n.* the third month of the year. [ME f. OF *march(e)*, dial. var. of *marz, mars*, f. L *Martius (mensis)* (month) of Mars]

march[1] /maarch/ *v. & n.* ● *v.* **1** *intr.* (usu. foll. by *away, off, out*, etc.) walk in a military manner with a regular measured tread. **2** *tr.* (often foll. by *away, on, off*, etc.) cause to march or walk (*marched the army to Moscow; marched him out of the room*). **3** *intr.* **a** walk or proceed steadily, esp. across country. **b** (of events, etc.) continue unrelentingly (*time marches on*). **4** *intr.* take part in a protest march. ● *n.* **1 a** the act or an instance of marching. **b** the uniform step of troops, etc. (*a slow march*). **2** a long difficult walk. **3** a procession as a protest or demonstration. **4** (usu. foll. by *of*) progress or continuity (*the march of events*). **5 a** a piece of music composed to accompany a march. **b** a composition of similar character and form. □ **march on 1** advance toward (a military objective). **2** proceed. **march past** *n.* the marching of troops past a saluting point at a review. ● *v.intr.* (of troops) carry out a march past. **on the march 1** marching. **2** in steady progress. □□ **march•er** *n.* [F *marche* (n.), *marcher* (v.), f. LL *marcus* hammer]

march[2] /maarch/ *n. & v.* ● *n. hist.* **1** (usu. in *pl.*) a boundary, a frontier (esp. of the borderland between England and Scotland or Wales). **2** a tract of often disputed land between two countries. ● *v.intr.* (foll. by *upon, with*) (of a country, an estate, etc.) have a common frontier with, border on. [ME f. OF *marche, marchir* ult. f. Gmc: cf. MARK[1]]

march•er /maárchər/ *n.* an inhabitant of a march or border district.

March hare *n.* a hare in the breeding season, characterized by excessive leaping, strange behavior, etc. (*mad as a March hare*).

march•ing or•ders *n.pl.* **1** *Mil.* the instructions from a superior officer for troops to depart for war, etc. **2** a dismissal (*gave him his marching orders*).

mar•chion•ess /maárshənés/ *n.* **1** the wife or widow of a marquess. **2** a woman holding the rank of marquess in her own right (cf. MARQUISE). [med.L *marchionissa* f. *marchio –onis* captain of the marches (as MARCH[2])]

march•pane /maárchpayn/ *n. archaic* var. of MARZIPAN.

Mar•di Gras /maárdee graá/ *n.* a carnival held in some countries on the last day before Lent (Shrove Tuesday), most famously in New Orleans. [F, = fat Tuesday]

mare[1] /mair/ *n.* the female of any equine animal, esp. the horse. [ME f. OE *mearh* horse f. Gmc: cf. MARSHAL]

mare[2] /maáray/ *n.* (*pl.* **ma•ri•a** /maáreeə/ or **mares**) **1** (in full **mare clausum** /klówsŏom/) *Law* the sea under the jurisdiction of a particular country. **2** (in full **mare liberum** /leébərŏom/) *Law* the sea open to all nations. **3 a** any of a number of large dark flat areas on the surface of the moon, once thought to be seas. **b** a similar area on Mars. [L, = sea]

ma•rem•ma /mərémə/ *n.* (*pl.* **ma•rem•me** /–mee/) low marshy land near a seashore. [It. f. L *maritima* (as MARITIME)]

mare's nest *n.* **1** an illusory discovery; a hoax. **2** a muddle.

mare's tail *n.* **1** a tall slender marsh plant, *Hippuris vulgaris.* **2** (in *pl.*) long straight streaks of cirrus cloud.

mar•ga•rine /maárjərin/ *n.* a butter substitute made from vegetable oils or animal fats with milk, etc. [F, misapplication of a chem. term, f. *margarique* f. Gk *margaron* pearl]

mar•ga•ri•ta /maárgəréetə/ *n.* a cocktail made with tequila, lime or lemon juice, and orange-flavored liqueur, usu. served in a salt-rimmed glass.

mar•gay /maárgay/ *n.* a small wild S. American cat, *Felis wiedii.* [F f. Tupi *mbaracaïa*]

marge[2] /maarj/ *n. poet.* a margin or edge. [F f. L *margo* (as MARGIN)]

mar•gin /maárjin/ *n. & v.* ● *n.* **1** an edge or border. **2 a** the blank border on each side of the print on a page, etc. **b** a line or rule, as on paper, marking off a margin. **3** an amount (of time, money, etc.) by which a thing exceeds, falls short, etc. (*won by a narrow margin; a margin of profit*). **4** the lower limit of possibility, success, etc. (*his effort fell below the margin*). **5** an amount deposited with a stockbroker by the customer when borrowing from the broker to purchase securities. **6** in banking, the difference between the current market value of a loan's collateral and the face value of the loan.

7 *Austral.* an increment to a basic wage, paid for skill. ● *v.tr.* (**margined, margining**) provide with a margin or marginal notes. [ME f. L *margo –ginis*]

mar·gin·al /maárjinəl/ *adj.* **1 a** of or written in a margin. **b** having marginal notes. **2 a** of or at the edge; not central. **b** not significant or decisive (*the work is of merely marginal interest*). **3** close to the limit, esp. of profitability. **4** (of the sea) adjacent to the shore of a state. **5** (of land) difficult to cultivate; unprofitable. **6** barely adequate; unprovided for. **7** *Brit.* (of a parliamentary seat or constituency) having a small majority at risk in an election. □□ **mar·gin·al·i·ty** /–nálitee/ *n.* **mar·gin·al·ly** *adv.* [med.L *marginalis* (as MARGIN)]

mar·gin·al cost *n.* the cost added by producing one extra item of a product.

mar·gi·na·li·a /maárjináyleeə/ *n.pl.* marginal notes. [med.L, neut. pl. of *marginalis*]

mar·gin·al·ize /maárjinəliz/ *v.tr.* make or treat as insignificant. □□ **mar·gin·al·i·za·tion** *n.*

mar·gin·ate *v. & adj.* ● *v.tr.* /maárjinayt/ **1** = MARGINALIZE. **2** provide with a margin or border. ● *adj.* /maárjinət/ *Biol.* having a distinct margin or border. □□ **mar·gin·a·tion** /–náyshən/ *n.*

mar·gin of er·ror *n.* a usu. small difference allowed for miscalculation, change of circumstances, etc.

mar·gin re·lease *n.* a device on a typewriter allowing a word to be typed beyond the margin normally set.

mar·grave /maárgrayv/ *n. hist.* the hereditary title of some princes of the Holy Roman Empire (orig. of a military governor of a border province). □□ **mar·gra·vate** /maárgrəvət/ *n.* [MDu. *markgrave* border count (as MARK[1], *grave* COUNT[2] f. OLG *grēve*]

mar·gra·vine /maárgrəveen/ *n. hist.* the wife of a margrave. [Du. *markgravin* (as MARGRAVE)]

mar·gue·rite /maárgəreét/ *n.* an oxeye daisy. [F f. L *margarita* f. Gk *margaritēs* f. *margaron* pearl]

ma·ri·a *pl.* of MARE[2].

ma·ri·a·chi /maareeaáchee, mar–/ *n.* **1** a Mexican band of strolling street musicians. **2** the music played by such a band. [Mex. Sp.]

mar·i·age de con·ve·nance /máriaázh də kawnvənóns/ *n.* = MARRIAGE OF CONVENIENCE. [F]

Mar·i·an /máireeən/ *adj. RC Ch.* of or relating to the Virgin Mary (*Marian vespers*). [L *Maria* Mary]

mar·i·gold /márigōld/ *n.* any plant of the genus *Tagetes* or *Calendula*, with bright yellow, orange, or maroon flowers. [ME f. *Mary* (prob. the Virgin) + dial. *gold*, OE *golde*, prob. rel. to GOLD]

ma·ri·jua·na /máriwaánə/ *n.* (also **ma·ri·hua·na**) **1** the dried leaves, flowering tops, and stems of the hemp, used as a drug, often smoked in cigarettes. **2** the plant yielding these (cf. HEMP). [Amer. Sp.]

ma·rim·ba /mərímbə/ *n.* **1** a xylophone of Africa and Central America. **2** a modern orchestral instrument derived from this. [Congo]

ma·ri·na /məreénə/ *n.* a specially designed harbor with moorings for pleasure yachts, etc. [It. & Sp. fem. adj. f. *marino* f. L (as MARINE)]

mar·i·nade /márináyd/ *n. & v.* ● *n.* **1** a mixture of wine, vinegar, oil, spices, etc., in which meat, fish, etc., is soaked before cooking. **2** meat, fish, etc., soaked in this liquid. ● *v.tr.* = MARINATE. [F f. Sp. *marinada* f. *marinar* pickle in brine f. *marino* (as MARINE)]

ma·ri·na·ra /marináárə/ *adj.* (of a pasta sauce) made with tomatoes, spices, etc., usu. without meat. [It. *alla marinara* in sailor's style f. L (MARINE)]

mar·i·nate /márinayt/ *v.tr.* soak (meat, fish, etc.) in a marinade. □□ **mar·i·na·tion** /–náyshən/ *n.* [It. *marinare* or F *mariner* (as MARINE)]

ma·rine /məreén/ *adj. & n.* ● *adj.* **1** of, found in, or produced by the sea. **2** of or relating to shipping or naval matters (*marine insurance*). **b** for use at sea. ● *n.* **1** a country's shipping, fleet, or navy (*merchant marine*). **2 a** a member of the US Marine Corps. **b** a member of a body of troops trained to serve on land or sea. **3** a picture of a scene at sea. □ **tell that to the marines** *colloq.* an expression of disbelief. [ME f. OF *marin marine* f. L *marinus* f. *mare* sea]

mar·i·ner /márinər/ *n.* a seaman. [ME f. AF *mariner*, OF *marinier* f. med.L *marinarius* f. L (as MARINE)]

mar·i·ner's com·pass *n.* a compass showing magnetic or true north and the bearings from it.

Mar·i·ol·a·try /máireeólətree/ *n. derog.* idolatrous worship of the Virgin Mary. [L *Maria* Mary + –LATRY, after *idolatry*]

mar·i·on·ette /máreeənét/ *n.* a puppet worked by strings. [F *marionnette* f. *Marion* dimin. of *Marie* Mary]

Mar·ist /márist, mair–/ *n.* a member of the Roman Catholic Society of Mary. [F *Mariste* f. *Marie* Mary]

mar·i·tal /máritəl/ *adj.* **1** of marriage or the relations between husband and wife. **2** of

marionette

or relating to a husband. □□ **mar·i·tal·ly** *adv.* [L *maritalis* f. *maritus* husband]

mar·i·time /máritīm/ *adj.* **1** connected with the sea or seafaring (*maritime insurance*). **2** living or found near the sea. [L *maritimus* f. *mare* sea]

mar·jo·ram /maárjərəm/ *n.* an aromatic culinary herb of the genus *Origanum*, esp. *O. majorana* (**sweet marjoram**), the fresh or dried leaves of which are used as a flavoring in cooking. [ME & OF *majorane* f. med.L *majorana*, of unkn. orig.]

mark[1] /maark/ *n. & v.* ● *n.* **1** a trace, sign, stain, scar, etc., on a surface, page, face, etc. **2** (esp. *in comb.*) **a** a written or printed symbol (*punctuation mark*; *question mark*). **b** a numerical or alphabetical award denoting excellence, conduct, proficiency, etc. (*got a good mark for effort*; *gave him a black mark*). **3** (usu. foll. by *of*) a sign or indication of quality, character, feeling, etc. (*took off his hat as a mark of respect*). **4 a** a sign, seal, etc., used for distinction or identification. **b** a cross, etc., made in place of a signature by an illiterate person. **5 a** a target, object, goal, etc. (*missed the mark with his first shot*). **b** a standard for attainment (*his work falls below the mark*). **6** a line, etc., indicating a position; a marker. **7** (usu. **Mark**) (followed by a numeral) a particular design, model, etc., of a car, aircraft, etc. (*this is the Mark 2 model*). **8** a runner's starting point in a race. **9** *Naut.* a piece of material, etc., used to indicate a position on a sounding line. **10 a** *Rugby* a heel mark on the ground made by a player who has caught the ball direct from a kick or forward throw by an opponent. **b** *Austral. Rules Football* the catching before it reaches the ground of a ball kicked at least ten meters; the spot from which the subsequent kick is taken. **11** *sl.* the intended victim of a swindler, etc. **12** *Boxing* the pit of the stomach. **13** *hist.* a tract of land held in common by a Teutonic or medieval German village community. ● *v.tr.* **1 a** make a mark on (a thing or person), esp. by writing, cutting, scraping, etc. **b** put a distinguishing or identifying mark, initials, name, etc., on (clothes, etc.) (*marked the tree with their initials*). **2 a** allot marks to; correct (a student's work, etc.). **b** record (the points gained in games, etc.). **3** attach a price to (goods, etc.) (*marked the doll at $2*). **4** (often foll. by *by*) show or manifest (displeasure, etc.) (*marked his anger by leaving early*). **5** notice or observe (*she marked his agitation*). **6 a** characterize or be a feature of (*the day was marked by storms*). **b** acknowledge, recognize, celebrate (*marked the occasion with a toast*). **7** name or indicate (a place on a map, the length of a syllable, etc.) by a sign or mark. **8** characterize (a person or a thing) as (*marked them as weak*). **9 a** *Brit.* keep close to so as to prevent the free movement of (an opponent in sport). **b** *Austral. Rules Football* catch (the ball). **10** (as **marked** *adj.*) having natural marks (*is marked with silver spots*). **11** (of a graduated instrument) show, register (so many degrees, etc.). **12** *US & Austral.* castrate (a lamb). □ **beside** (or **off** or **wide of**) **the mark 1** not to the point; irrelevant. **2** not accurate. **make one's mark** attain distinction. **mark down 1** mark (goods, etc.) at a lower price. **2** make a written note of. **3** choose (a person) as one's victim. **mark my words** heed my warning or prediction. **mark off** (often foll. by *from*) separate (one thing from another) by a boundary, etc. (*marked off the subjects for discussion*). **mark out 1** plan (a course of action, etc.). **2** destine (*marked out for success*). **3** trace out boundaries, a course, etc. **mark time 1** *Mil.* march on the spot, without moving forward. **2** act routinely; go through the motions. **3** await an opportunity to advance. **mark up 1** mark (goods, etc.) at a higher price. **2** mark or correct (text, etc.) for typesetting or alteration. **mark you** esp. *Brit.* please note (*without obligation, mark you*). **off the mark 1** having made a start. **2** = *beside the mark* (see above). **of mark** noteworthy. **on the mark** ready to start. **on your mark** (or **marks**) (as an instruction) get ready to start (esp. a race). **up to the mark** reaching the usual or normal standard, esp. of health. [OE *me(a)rc* (n.), *mearcian* (v.), f. Gmc]

mark[2] /maark/ *n.* **1 a** = DEUTSCH MARK. **b** *hist.* = OSTMARK. **2** *hist.* **a** a European denomination of weight for gold and silver. **b** English money of account. [OE *marc*, prob. rel. to med.L *marca, marcus*]

mark·down /maárkdown/ *n.* a reduction in price.

marked /maarkt/ *adj.* **1** having a visible mark. **2** clearly noticeable; evident (*a marked difference*). **3** (of playing cards) having distinctive marks on their backs to assist cheating. □□ **mark·ed·ly** /–kidlee/ *adv.* **mark·ed·ness** /–kidnis/ *n.* [OE (past part. of MARK[1])]

marked man *n.* **1** a person whose conduct is watched with suspicion or hostility. **2** a person destined to succeed.

mark·er /maárkər/ *n.* **1** a stone, post, etc., used to mark a position, place reached, etc. **2** a person or thing that marks. **3** a felt-tipped pen with a broad tip. **4** a person who records a score, esp. in billiards. **5** a place, etc., used to direct a pilot to a target. **6** a bookmark. **7** *US sl.* a promissory note; an IOU.

mar·ket /maárkit/ *n. & v.* ● *n.* **1** the gathering of people for the purchase and sale of merchandise, esp. with a number of different vendors. **2** an open space or covered building where vendors convene to sell their goods. **3** (often foll. by *for*) a demand for a particular commodity or service (*there is a market for lawn ornaments*). **4** a place or group providing such a demand. **5** conditions or opportunity for buying or selling; the state of trade at a particular time or in a particular context (*the bottom's fallen out of the market*). **6** the rate of purchase and sale, market value (*the market fell*). **7** (prec. by *the*) the trade in a specified commodity (*the grain market*). **8** (**the Market**) *Brit.* the European Union (formerly known as the Common Market). ● *v.* **1** *tr.* sell. **2** *tr.* offer for sale. **3** *intr.* buy or sell goods in a market. □ **be in the market for** wish to buy. **be on** (or **come into**) **the market** be offered for sale. **make a market** *Stock Exch.* induce active dealing in a stock or shares. **put on the market** offer for sale. □□ **mar·ket·er** *n.* [ME ult. f. L *mercatus* f. *mercari* buy: see MERCHANT]

mar·ket·a·ble /maárkitəbəl/ *adj.* able or fit to be sold. □□ **mar·ket·a·bil·i·ty** /–bílitee/ *n.*

mar·ket·eer /maárkiteér/ *n.* **1** *Brit.* a supporter of the European Union and British membership in it. **2** a marketer.

mar·ket·ing /maárkiting/ *n.* **1** selling or buying in a market. **2** the activity or process involving research, promotion, sales, and distribution of a product or service.

mar·ket·place /maárkitpláys/ *n.* **1** an open space where a market is held in a town. **2** the scene of actual dealings. **3** a forum or sphere for the exchange of ideas, etc.

mar·ket price *n.* the price when sold in a given market.

mar·ket re·search *n.* the study of consumers' needs and preferences.

mar·ket val·ue *n.* the amount for which something can be sold on a given market (cf. BOOK VALUE).

mar·khor /maárkawr/ *n.* a large spiral-horned wild goat, *Capra falconeri*, of N. India. [Pers. *mār-ḵwār* f. *mār* serpent + *ḵwār* –eating]

mark·ing /maárking/ *n.* (usu. in *pl.*) **1** an identification mark, esp. a symbol on an aircraft. **2** the coloring of an animal's fur, feathers, skin, etc.

marks·man /maárksmən/ *n.* (*pl.* **·men**; *fem.* **·woman**, *pl.* **·women**) a person skilled in shooting, esp. with a pistol or rifle. □□ **marks·man·ship** *n.*

mark·up /maárkup/ *n.* **1** the amount added to the cost of goods to cover overhead charges, profit, etc. **2** the process or result of correcting text in preparation for printing.

marl[1] /maarl/ *n. & v.* ● *n.* soil consisting of clay and lime, with fertilizing properties. ● *v.tr.* apply marl to (the ground). □□ **marl·y** *adj.* [ME f. OF *marle* f. med.L *margila* f. L *marga*]

marl[2] /maarl/ *n. Brit.* **1** a mottled yarn of differently colored threads. **2** the fabric made from this. [shortening of *marbled*: see MARBLE]

mar·lin /maárlin/ *n. US* any of various large long-nosed marine fish of the family Istophoridae, esp. the blue marlin *Makaira nigricans*. [MARLINSPIKE, with ref. to its pointed snout]

mar·line /maárlin/ *n. Naut.* a light rope of two strands. □ **marline-spike** = MARLINSPIKE. [ME f. Du. *marlijn* f. *marren* bind + *lijn* LINE[1]]

mar·lin·spike /maárlinspík/ *n. Naut.* a pointed iron tool used to separate strands of rope or wire. [orig. app. *marling-spike* f. *marl* fasten with marline (f. Du. *marlen* frequent. of MDu. *marren* bind) + –ING[1] + SPIKE[1]]

mar·ma·lade /maárməlayd/ *n.* a preserve of citrus fruit, usu. bitter oranges, made like jam. [F *marmelade* f. Port. *marmelada* quince jam f. *marmelo* quince f. L *melimelum* f. Gk *melimēlon* f. *meli* honey + *mēlon* apple]

mar·mo·re·al /maarmáwreeəl/ *adj. poet.* of or like marble. □□ **mar·mo·re·al·ly** *adv.* [L *marmoreus* (as MARBLE)]

mar·mo·set /maárməset, –zet/ *n.* any of several small tropical American monkeys of the family Callitricidae, having a long bushy tail. [OF *marmouset* grotesque image, of unkn. orig.]

mar·mot /maármət/ *n.* any burrowing rodent of the genus *Marmota*, with a heavyset body and short bushy tail. [F *marmotte* prob. f. Romansh *murmont* f. L *murem* (nominative *mus*) *montis* mountain mouse]

mar·o·cain /márəkayn/ *n.* a dress fabric of ribbed crepe. [F, = Moroccan f. *Maroc* Morocco]

Mar·o·nite /márənit/ *n.* a member of a sect of Syrian Christians dwelling chiefly in Lebanon. [med.L *Maronita* f. *Maro* the 5th-c. Syrian founder]

ma·roon[1] /mərón/ *adj. & n.* ● *adj.* brownish-crimson. ● *n.* **1** this color. **2** esp. *Brit.* an explosive device giving a loud report. [F *marron* chestnut f. It. *marrone* f. med.Gk *maraon*]

ma·roon[2] /mərón/ *v. & n.* ● *v.tr.* **1** leave (a person) isolated in a desolate place (esp. an island). **2** (of a person or a natural phenomenon) cause (a person) to be unable to leave a place. ● *n.* **1** a person descended from a group of fugitive slaves in the remoter parts of Suriname and the W. Indies. **2** a marooned person. [F *marron* f. Sp. *cimarrón* wild f. *cima* peak]

mar·que[1] /maark/ *n.* a make of a product, as a sports car (*the Jaguar marque*). [F, = MARK[1]]

mar·quee /maárkée/ *n.* **1** a rooflike projection over the entrance to a theater, hotel, etc. **2** *Brit.* a large tent used for social or commercial functions. [MARQUISE, taken as pl. & assim. to –EE]

mar·quess /maárkwis/ *n.* a British nobleman ranking between a duke and an earl (cf. MARQUIS). □□ **mar·quess·ate** /–kwisət/ *n.* [var. of MARQUIS]

mar·que·try /maárkitree/ *n.* (also **mar·que·te·rie**) inlaid work in wood, ivory, etc. [F *marqueterie* f. *marqueter* variegate f. MARQUE[1]]

mar·quis /maárkwis, –kée/ *n.* a nobleman ranking between a duke and a count (cf. MARQUESS). □□ **mar·quis·ate** /–kwisət/ *n.* [ME f. OF *marchis* f. Rmc (as MARCH[2], –ESE)]

mar·quise /maarkéez, –kée/ *n.* **1 a** the wife or widow of a marquis. **b** a woman holding the rank of marquis in her own right (cf. MARCHIONESS). **2 a** a finger ring set with a pointed oval cluster of gems. **b** (also **marquise cut**) an oval cut gem with many facets. **3** *archaic* = MARQUEE. [F, fem. of MARQUIS]

mar·qui·sette /maárkizét/ *n.* a fine light cotton, rayon, or silk fabric for net curtains, etc. [F, dimin. of MARQUISE]

mar·ram /márəm/ *n.* a shore grass, *Ammophila arenaria*, that binds sand with its tough rhizomes. [ON *marálmr* f. *marr* sea + *hálmr* HAULM]

mar·riage /márij/ *n.* **1** the legal union of a man and a woman in order to live together and often to have children. **2** an act or ceremony establishing this union. **3** one particular union of this kind (*by a previous marriage*). **4** an intimate union (*the marriage of true minds*). **5** *Cards* the union of a king and queen of the same suit. □ **by marriage** as a result of a marriage (*related by marriage*). **in marriage** as husband or wife (*give in marriage; take in marriage*). [ME f. OF *mariage* f. *marier* MARRY[1]]

mar·riage·a·ble /márijəbəl/ *adj.* **1** fit for marriage, esp. old or rich enough to marry. **2** (of age) fit for marriage. □□ **mar·riage·a·bil·i·ty** /–bílitee/ *n.*

mar·riage cer·tif·i·cate *n.* a certificate certifying the completion of a marriage ceremony.

mar·riage li·cense *n.* a license to marry.

mar·riage of con·ven·ience *n.* a marriage concluded to achieve some practical purpose, esp. financial or political.

mar·ried /máreed/ *adj. & n.* ● *adj.* **1** united in marriage. **2** of or relating to marriage (*married name; married life*). ● *n.* (usu. in *pl.*) a married person (*young marrieds*).

mar·ron gla·cé /maróⁿ glaasáy/ *n.* (*pl.* **mar·rons glacés** *pronunc.* same) a chestnut preserved in and coated with sugar. [F, = iced chestnut: cf. GLACÉ]

mar·row /márō/ *n.* **1** a soft fatty substance in the cavities of bones, in which blood cells are produced. **2** the essential part of something. **3** *Brit.* (in full **vegetable marrow**) = SUMMER SQUASH. □ **to the marrow** to one's most innermost being. □□ **mar·row·less** *adj.* **mar·row·y** *adj.* [OE *mearg, mærg* f. Gmc]

mar·row·bone /márōbōn/ *n.* a bone containing edible marrow.

mar·row·fat /márōfat/ *n.* a kind of large pea.

mar·ry[1] /máree/ *v.* (**·ries**, **·ried**) **1** *tr.* **a** take as one's wife or husband in marriage. **b** (often foll. by *to*) (of a priest, etc.) join (persons) in marriage. **c** (of a parent or guardian) give (a son, daughter, etc.) in marriage. **2** *intr.* **a** enter into marriage. **b** (foll. by *into*) become a member of (a family) by marriage. **3** *tr.* **a** unite intimately. **b** correlate (things) as a pair. **c** *Naut.* splice (rope ends) together without increasing their girth. □ **marry off** find a wife or husband for. [ME f. OF *marier* f. L *maritare* f. *maritus* husband]

mar·ry[2] /máree/ *int. archaic* expressing surprise, asseveration, indignation, etc. [ME, = (the Virgin) *Mary*]

mar·ry·ing /máree-ing/ *adj.* likely or inclined to marry (*not a marrying man*).

Mars /maarz/ *n.* a reddish planet, fourth in order of distance from the sun and next beyond the earth. [L *Mars Martis* the Roman god of war]

Mar·sa·la /maarsaálə/ *n.* a dark sweet fortified wine. [*Marsala* in Sicily, where orig. made]

Marseillaise /maársayéz, maársəláyz/ *n.* the national anthem of France, first sung in Paris by Marseilles patriots. [F, fem. adj. f. *Marseille* Marseilles]

marsh /maarsh/ *n.* **1** low land flooded in wet weather and usu. watery at all times. **2** (*attrib.*) of or inhabiting marshland. □□ **marsh·y** *adj.* (**marsh·i·er, marsh·i·est**). **marsh·i·ness** *n.* [OE *mer(i)sc* f. WG]

mar·shal /maárshəl/ *n. & v.* ● *n.* **1** (in the US) an officer of a judicial district, similar to a sheriff. **2** (in the US) the head of a fire department. **3 a** a high-ranking officer in the armed forces of certain countries (*air marshal; field marshal*). **b** (in the UK) a high-ranking officer of state (*earl marshal*). **4** an officer arranging ceremonies, controlling procedure at races, etc. **5** (in full **judge's marshal**) (in the UK) an official accompanying a judge on circuit,

---

WORD HISTORY   **marshal**

Middle English (denoting a high-ranking officer of state): from Old French *mareschal* 'farrier, commander,' from late Latin *mariscalcus*, from Germanic elements meaning 'horse' (related to *mare*) and 'servant.'

with secretarial and social duties. **6** (in the US) a court officer who assists a judge. ● *v.* (**mar•shaled, mar•shal•ing;** *Brit.* **mar•shalled, mar•shal•ling**) **1** *tr.* arrange (soldiers, facts, one's thoughts, etc.) in due order. **2** *tr.* (often foll. by *into, to*) conduct (a person) ceremoniously. **3** *tr. Heraldry* combine (coats of arms). **4** *intr.* take up positions in due arrangement. □□ **mar•shal•er** *n.* **mar•shal•ship** *n.*

mar•shal•ing yard *n.* a railroad yard in which freight is sorted onto trains.

Mar•shal of the Roy•al Air Force *n.* (in the UK) an officer of the highest rank in the Royal Air Force.

marsh fe•ver *n.* malaria.

marsh gas *n.* methane.

marsh hawk *n.* the northern harrier, *Circus cyaneus* (see HARRIER³).

marsh•land /maárshland/ *n.* land consisting of marshes.

marsh•mal•low /maárshmélō, –málō/ *n.* a soft, spongy confection made of sugar, albumen, and gelatin.

marsh mal•low *n.* a shrubby herbaceous plant, *Althaea officinalis*, the roots of which were formerly used to make marshmallow.

marsh mar•i•gold *n.* a golden-flowered ranunculaceous plant, *Caltha palustris*, growing in moist meadows, etc. Also called **cow-slip** or **kingcup**.

marsh tre•foil *n.* the buckbean.

mar•su•pi•al /maarsoopeeəl/ *n. & adj.* ● *n.* any mammal of the order Marsupialia, characterized by being born incompletely developed and usu. carried and suckled in a pouch on the mother's belly. ● *adj.* **1** of or belonging to this order. **2** of or like a pouch (*marsupial muscle*). [mod.L *marsupialis* f. L *marsupium* f. Gk *marsupion* pouch, dimin. of *marsipos* purse]

mart /maart/ *n.* **1** a trade center. **2** an auction room. **3 a** a market. **b** a marketplace. [ME f. obs. Du. *mart*, var. of *markt* MARKET]

Mar•ta•gon lil•y /maártəgən/ *n.* = TURK'S-CAP LILY.

Mar•tel•lo /maartélō/ *n.* (*pl.* **•los**) (also **Mar•tel•lo tower**) a small circular fort, usu. on the coast to prevent a hostile landing. [alt. f. Cape *Mortella* in Corsica, where such a tower proved difficult to capture in 1794]

mar•ten /maárt'n/ *n.* a semi-arboreal weasellike mammal of the genus *Martes*, hunted for its fur in many northern countries. [ME f. MDu. *martren* f. OF (*peau*) *martrine* marten (fur) f. *martre* f. WG]

mar•ten•site /maárt'nzīt/ *n.* the chief constituent of hardened steel. [A. *Martens*, German metallurgist d. 1914 + –ITE¹]

mar•tial /maárshəl/ *adj.* **1** of or appropriate to warfare. **2** warlike; brave; fond of fighting. □□ **mar•tial•ly** *adv.* [ME f. OF *martial* or L *martialis* of the Roman god Mars: see MARS]

mar•tial arts *n.pl.* fighting sports such as judo and karate.

mar•tial law *n.* military government, involving the suspension of ordinary law.

Mar•tian /maárshən/ *adj. & n.* ● *adj.* of the planet Mars. ● *n.* a hypothetical inhabitant of Mars. [ME f. OF *martien* or L *Martianus* f. *Mars*: see MARS]

mar•tin /maárt'n/ *n.* any of several swallows of the family Hirundinidae, esp. the house martin and purple martin. [prob. f. St. *Martin*: see MARTINMAS]

mar•ti•net /maárt'nét/ *n.* a strict (esp. military or naval) disciplinarian. □□ **mar•ti•net•tish** *adj.* (also **mar•ti•net•ish**). [J. *Martinet*, 17th-c. French drillmaster]

mar•tin•gale /maárt'ngayl/ *n.* **1** a strap, or set of straps, fastened at one end to the noseband of a horse and at the other end to the girth, to prevent rearing, etc. **2** *Naut.* a rope for holding down the jib boom. **3** a gambling system of continually doubling the stakes after each loss. [F, of uncert. orig.]

mar•ti•ni /maarteénee/ *n.* a cocktail made of gin or vodka with dry vermouth, usu. garnished with a green olive or lemon peel. [*Martini* & Rossi, Italian firm selling vermouth]

Mar•tin•mas /maárt'nməs/ *n.* St. Martin's day, Nov. 11 [ME f. St. *Martin*, bishop of Tours in the 4th c., + MASS²]

mart•let /maártlit/ *n.* **1** *Heraldry* a bird like a swallow without feet, used as a bearing for a fourth son. **2** *archaic* **a** a swift. **b** a house martin. [F *martelet* alt. f. *martinet* dimin. f. MARTIN]

mar•tyr /maártər/ *n. & v.* ● *n.* **1 a** a person who is put to death for refusing to renounce a faith or belief. **b** a person who suffers for adhering to a principle, cause, etc. **2** a person who feigns or complains of suffering to gain sympathy. **3** (foll. by *to*) a constant sufferer from (an ailment). ● *v.tr.* **1** put to death as a martyr. **2** torment. □ **make a martyr of oneself** accept or pretend to accept unnecessary discomfort, etc. [OE *martir* f. eccl.L *martyr* f. Gk *martur, martus –uros* witness]

mar•tyr•dom /maártərdəm/ *n.* **1** the sufferings and death of a martyr. **2** torment. [OE *martyrdōm* (as MARTYR, –DOM)]

mar•tyr•ize /maártərīz/ *v.tr. & refl.* make a martyr of. □□ **mar•tyr•i•za•tion** *n.*

mar•tyr•ol•o•gy /maártərólōjee/ *n.* (*pl.* **•gies**) **1** a list or register of martyrs. **2** the history of martyrs. □□ **mar•tyr•o•log•i•cal** /–rəlójikəl/ *adj.* **mar•tyr•ol•o•gist** /–rólə–/ *n.* [med.L *martyrologium* f. eccl.Gk *marturologion* (as MARTYR, *logos* account)]

mar•tyr•y /maártəree/ *n.* (*pl.* **•ies**) a shrine or church erected in hon-

or of a martyr. [ME f. med.L *martyrium* f. Gk *marturion* martyrdom (as MARTYR)]

mar•vel /maárvəl/ *n. & v.* ● *n.* **1** a wonderful thing or person. **2** (often foll. by *of*) a wonderful example (*a marvel of engineering; she's a marvel of patience*). ● *v.intr.* (**mar•veled, mar•vel•ing;** *Brit.* **mar•velled, mar•vel•ling;**) *literary* **1** (foll. by *at*, or *that* + clause) feel surprise or wonder. **2** (foll. by *how, why*, etc. + clause) wonder. □□ **mar•vel•er** *n.* [ME f. OF *merveille, merveiller* f. LL *mirabilia* neut. pl. of L *mirabilis* f. *mirari* wonder at: see MIRACLE]

mar•vel•ous /maárvələs/ *adj.* (*Brit.* **mar•vel•lous**) **1** extraordinary; excellent; extremely good. **2** causing great wonder; astonishing. **3** extremely improbable. □□ **mar•vel•ous•ly** *adv.* **mar•vel•ous•ness** *n.* [ME f. OF *merveillos* f. *merveille*: see MARVEL]

Marx•ism /maárksizəm/ *n.* the political and economic theories of Karl Marx, German political philosopher (d. 1883), predicting the overthrow of capitalism and the eventual attainment of a classless society with the state controlling the means of production. □□ **Marx•ist** *n. & adj.*

Marx•ism-Le•nin•ism *n.* the doctrines of Marx as interpreted and put into effect by Lenin. □□ **Marx•ist Le•nin•ist** *n. & adj.*

mar•zi•pan /maárzipan/ *n. & v.* ● *n.* **1** a paste of ground almonds, sugar, etc., made up into small cakes, etc., or used to coat large cakes. **2** a piece of marzipan. ● *v.tr.* (**mar•zi•panned, mar•zi•pan•ning**) cover with or as with marzipan. [G f. It. *marzapane*]

Ma•sai /maasí, maási/ *n. & adj.* ● *n.* (*pl.* same or **Ma•sais**) **1 a** a pastoral people of mainly Hamitic stock living in Kenya and Tanzania. **b** a member of this people. **2** the Nilotic language of the Masai. ● *adj.* of or relating to the Masai or their language. [Bantu]

mas•car•a /maskárə/ *n.* a cosmetic for darkening the eyelashes. [It. *mascara, maschera* MASK]

mas•cle /máskəl/ *n. Heraldry* a lozenge with a central lozenge-shaped aperture. [ME f. AF f. AL *ma(s)cula* f. L MACULA]

mas•con /máskon/ *n. Astron.* a concentration of dense matter below the moon's surface, producing a gravitational pull. [*mass concentration*]

mas•cot /máskot/ *n.* a person, animal, or thing that is supposed to bring good luck. [F *mascotte* f. mod. Prov. *mascotto* fem. dimin. of *masco* witch]

mas•cu•line /máskyəlin/ *adj. & n.* ● *adj.* **1** of or characteristic of men. **2** manly; vigorous. **3** (of a woman) having qualities considered appropriate to a man. **4** *Gram.* of or denoting the gender proper to men's names (e.g., *he, his*.) **5** *Prosody* (as of rhyme) occurring in a stressed final syllable. ● *n. Gram.* the masculine gender; a masculine word. □□ **mas•cu•line•ly** *adv.* **mas•cu•line•ness** *n.* **mas•cu•lin•i•ty** /–línitee/ *n.* [ME f. OF *masculin –ine* f. L *masculinus* (as MALE)]

ma•ser /máyzər/ *n.* a device using the stimulated emission of radiation by excited atoms to amplify or generate coherent monochromatic electromagnetic radiation in the microwave range (cf. LASER). [*microwave amplification by stimulated emission of radiation*]

MASH /mash/ *abbr.* Mobile Army Surgical Hospital.

mash /mash/ *n. & v.* ● *n.* **1** a soft mixture. **2** a mixture of boiled grain, bran, etc., given warm to horses, etc. **3** a mixture of malt or other grain and hot water used in brewing, distilling, etc. **4** *Brit. colloq.* mashed potatoes (*sausage and mash*). **5** a soft pulp made by crushing, mixing with water, etc. ● *v.tr.* **1** reduce (potatoes, etc.) to a uniform mass by crushing. **2** crush or pound to a pulp. **3** mix (malt) with hot water to form wort. □□ **mash•er** *n.* [OE *māsc* f.WG, perh. rel. to MIX]

mash•ie /máshee/ *n. Golf* former name of an iron used for lofting or for medium distances; five iron. [perh. f. F *massue* club]

mask /mask/ *n. & v.* ● *n.* **1** a covering for all or part of the face: **a** worn as a disguise, or to appear grotesque and amuse or terrify. **b** made of wire, gauze, etc., and worn for protection (e.g., by a fencer) or by a surgeon to prevent infection of a patient. **c** worn to conceal the face at masquerades, etc. **2** a respirator used to filter inhaled air or to supply gas for inhalation. **3** a likeness of a person's face, esp. one made by taking a mold from the face (*death mask*). **4** a disguise or pretense (*throw off the mask*). **5** a hollow model of a human head worn by ancient Greek and Roman actors. **6** *Photog.* a screen used to exclude part of an image. **7** the face or head of an animal, esp. a fox. **8** a cosmetic preparation spread on the face and left to dry before removal. ● *v.tr.* **1** cover (the face, etc.) with a mask. **2** disguise or conceal (a taste, one's feelings, etc.). **3** protect from a process. **4** *Mil.* **a** conceal (a battery, etc.) from the enemy's view. **b** hinder (an army, etc.) from action by observing with adequate force. **c** hinder (a friendly force) by standing in its line of fire. □□ **mask•er** *n.* [F *masque* f. It. *maschera* f. Arab. *maskara* buffoon f. *sakira* to ridicule]

masked /maskt/ *adj.* wearing or disguised with a mask.

masked ball *n.* a ball at which participants wear masks to conceal their faces.

mask·ing tape *n.* adhesive tape used in painting to cover areas on which paint is not wanted.

mas·ki·nonge /máskinonj/ *n.* = MUSKELLUNGE.

mas·och·ism /másəkizəm/ *n.* **1** a form of (esp. sexual) perversion characterized by gratification derived from one's own pain or humiliation (cf. SADISM). **2** *colloq.* the enjoyment of what appears to be painful or tiresome. □□ **mas·och·ist** *n.* **mas·och·is·tic** *adj.* **mas·och·is·ti·cal·ly** *adv.* [L. von Sacher- *Masoch*, Austrian novelist d. 1895, who described cases of it]

ma·son /máysən/ *n. & v.* •*n.* **1** a person who builds with stone or brick. **2** (**Mason**) a Freemason. •*v.tr.* build or strengthen with masonry. [ME f. OF *masson, maçonner*, ONF *machun*, prob. ult. f. Gmc]

Ma·son–Dix·on line /máysən-díksən/ *n.* the boundary between Maryland and Pennsylvania, taken as the northern limit of the slave-owning states before the abolition of slavery. [C. *Mason* & J. *Dixon*, 18th-c. English astronomers who surveyed it]

Ma·son·ic /məsónik/ *adj.* of or relating to Freemasons.

ma·son jar /máysən/ *n.* (also **Mason jar**) a glass jar with a wide mouth and tight-sealing lid, used for canning. [for J. *Mason*, 19th-c. US inventor]

ma·son·ry /máysənree/ *n.* **1 a** the work of a mason. **b** stonework; brickwork. **2** (**Masonry**) Freemasonry. [ME f. OF *maçonerie* (as MA-SON)]

ma·son's mark *n.* a device carved on stone by the mason who dressed it.

Ma·so·rah /məsáwrə/ *n.* (also **Mas·so·rah**) a body of traditional information and comment on the text of the Hebrew Bible. [Heb. *māsōret*, perh. = bond]

Ma·so·rete /másərəet/ *n.* (also **Mas·so·rete**) a Jewish scholar contributing to the Masorah. □□ **Mas·o·ret·ic** /–rétik/ *adj.* [F *Massoret* & mod.L *Massoreta*, orig. a misuse of Heb. (see MASORAH), assim. to –ETE]

masque /mask/ *n.* **1** a dramatic and musical entertainment esp. of the 16th and 17th c., orig. of pantomime, later with metrical dialogue. **2** a dramatic composition for this. □□ **mas·quer** *n.* [var. of MASK]

mas·quer·ade /máskəráyd/ *n. & v.* •*n.* **1** a false show or pretense. **2** a masked ball. •*v.intr.* (often foll. by *as*) appear in disguise, assume a false appearance. □□ **mas·quer·ad·er** *n.* [F *mascarade* f. Sp. *mascarada* f. *máscara* mask]

Mass. *abbr.* Massachusetts.

mass¹ /mas/ *n. & v.* •*n.* **1** a coherent body of matter of indefinite shape. **2** a dense aggregation of objects (*a mass of fibers*). **3** (in *sing.* or *pl.*; foll. by *of*) a large number or amount. **4** (usu. foll. by *of*) an unbroken expanse (of color, etc.). **5** (prec. by *a*; foll. by *of*) covered or abounding in (*was a mass of cuts and bruises*). **6** a main portion (of a painting, etc.) as perceived by the eye. **7** (prec. by *the*) **a** the majority. **b** (in *pl.*) the ordinary people. **8** *Physics* the quantity of matter a body contains. **9** (*attrib.*) relating to, done by, or affecting large numbers of people or things; large-scale (*mass audience; mass action; mass murder*). •*v.tr. & intr.* **1** assemble into a mass or as one body (*the bands massed at dawn*). **2** *Mil.* (with ref. to troops) concentrate or be concentrated. □ **in the mass** in the aggregate. □□ **mass·less** *adj.* [ME f. OF *masse, masser* f. L *massa* f. Gk *maza* barley cake: perh. rel. to *massō* knead]

mass² /mas/ *n.* (often **Mass**) **1** the Eucharist, esp. in the Roman Catholic Church. **2** a celebration of this. **3** the liturgy used in the Mass. **4** a musical setting of parts of this. [OE *mæsse* f. eccl.L *missa* f. L *mittere miss-* dismiss, perh. f. the concluding dismissal *Ite, missa est* Go, it is the dismissal]

Mas·sa·chu·set /masəchŏŏsət, –zət/ *n. & adj.* •*n.* **1 a** a N. American people, no longer in existence as a separate people, who occupied eastern Massachusetts in colonial times. **b** a member of this people. **2** the language of this people. •*adj.* of or relating to this people or their language.

mas·sa·cre /másəkər/ *n. & v.* •*n.* **1** an indiscriminate slaughter of people. **2** an utter defeat or destruction. •*v.tr.* **1** make a massacre of. **2** murder (esp. a large number of people) cruelly or violently. [OF, of unkn. orig.]

mas·sage /məsáázh, –sáaj/ *n. & v.* •*n.* **1** the rubbing, kneading, etc., of muscles and joints of the body with the hands for therapeutic benefit. **2** an instance of this. •*v.tr.* **1** apply massage to. **2** manipulate (statistics) to give an acceptable result. □□ **mas·sag·er** *n.* [F f. *masser* treat with massage, perh. f. Port. *amassar* knead, f. *massa* dough: see MASS¹]

mas·sage par·lor *n.* **1** an establishment providing massage. **2** *euphem.* a brothel.

mas·sa·sau·ga /másəsáwgə/ *n.* a small N. American rattlesnake, *Sistrurus catenatus*. [irreg. f. *Mississagi* River, Ontario]

mas·sé /masáy/ *n. Billiards* a stroke made with the cue held nearly vertical. [F, past part. of *masser* make such a stroke (as MACE¹)]

mass de·fect *n.* the difference between the mass of an isotope and its mass number.

mass en·er·gy *n.* a body's ability to do work according to its mass.

mas·se·ter /maseétər/ *n.* either of two chewing muscles which run from the temporal bone to the lower jaw. [Gk *masētēr* f. *masaomai* chew]

mas·seur /masör/ *n.* (*fem.* **mas·seuse** /masöz/) a person who provides massage professionally. [F f. *masser*: see MASSAGE]

mas·si·cot /másikət/ *n.* yellow lead monoxide, used as a pigment. [F, perh. rel. to It. *marzacotto* unguent prob. f. Arab. *mashaḵūnyā*]

mas·sif /maseéf, máseef/ *n.* a compact group of mountain heights. [F *massif* used as noun: see MASSIVE]

mas·sive /másiv/ *adj.* **1** large and heavy or solid. **2** (of the features, head, etc.) relatively large; of solid build. **3** exceptionally large (*took a massive overdose*). **4** substantial; impressive (*a massive reputation*). **5** *Mineral.* not visibly crystalline. **6** *Geol.* without structural divisions. □□ **mas·sive·ly** *adv.* **mas·sive·ness** *n.* [ME f. F *massif –ive* f. OF *massiz* ult. f. L *massa* MASS¹]

mass-mar·ket *n.* intended to be widely distributed through a variety of retail outlets.

mass me·di·a *n.pl.* = MEDIA¹ 2.

mass noun *n. Gram.* a noun that is not countable and cannot be used with the indefinite article or in the plural (e.g., *happiness*).

mass num·ber *n.* the total number of protons and neutrons in a nucleus.

Mas·so·rah var. of MASORAH.

Mas·so·rete var. of MASORETE.

mass pro·duc·tion *n.* the production of large quantities of a standardized article by a standardized mechanical process. □□ **mass-pro·duce** *v.* produce by mass production.

mass spec·tro·graph *n.* an apparatus separating isotopes, molecules, and molecular fragments according to mass by their passage in ionic form through electric and magnetic fields.

mass spec·trom·e·ter *n.* a device similar to a mass spectrograph but employing electrical detection.

mass spec·trum *n.* the distribution of ions shown by the use of a mass spectrograph or mass spectrometer.

mast¹ /mast/ *n. & v.* •*n.* **1** a long upright post of timber, iron, etc., set up from a ship's keel or deck, esp. to support sails. **2** a post or latticework upright for supporting a radio or television antenna. **3** a flagpole (*half-mast*). •*v.tr.* furnish (a ship) with masts. □ **before the mast** serving as an ordinary seaman (quartered in the forecastle). □□ **mast·ed** *adj.* (also in *comb.*). **mas·ter** *n.* (also in *comb.*). [OE *mæst* f. WG]

mast¹ 1

mast² /mast/ *n.* the fruit of the beech, oak, chestnut, and other forest trees, esp. as food for pigs. [OE *mæst* f. WG, prob. rel. to MEAT]

mas·ta·ba /mástəbə/ *n.* **1** *Archaeol.* an ancient Egyptian tomb with sloping sides and a flat roof. **2** a bench, usu. of stone, attached to a house in Islamic countries. [Arab. *maṣṭabah*]

mas·tec·to·my /mastéktəmee/ *n.* (*pl.* **-mies**) *Surgery* the removal of all or part of a breast. [Gk *mastos* breast + –ECTOMY]

mas·ter /mástər/ *n., adj., & v.* •*n.* **1 a** a person having control of persons or things. **b** an employer, esp. of a servant. **c** a male head of a household (*master of the house*). **d** the owner of a dog, horse, etc. **e** the owner of a slave. **f** *Naut.* the captain of a merchant ship. **g** *Hunting* the person in control of a pack of hounds, etc. **2** esp. *Brit.* a male teacher or tutor, esp. a schoolmaster. **3 a** the head of a private school, etc. **b** the presiding officer of a Masonic lodge, etc. **4** a person who has or gets the upper hand (*we shall see which of us is master*). **5** a person skilled in a particular trade and able to teach others (often *attrib.*: *master carpenter*). **6** a holder of a university degree orig. giving authority to teach in the university (*Master of Arts; Master of Science*). **7** a great artist. **8** *Chess*, etc., a player of proven ability at international level. **9** an original version (e.g., of a film or audio recording) from which a series of copies can be made. **10** (**Master**) **a** a title prefixed to the name of a boy not old enough to be called *Mr.* (*Master T. Jones; Master Tom*). **b** *archaic* a title for a man of high rank, learning, etc. **12** a machine or device directly controlling another (cf. SLAVE). •*adj.* **1** showing very great skill or proficiency (*a master painter*). **2** main, principal (*master bedroom*). **3** controlling others (*master plan*). •*v.tr.* **1** overcome, defeat. **2** reduce to subjection. **3** acquire complete knowledge of (a subject) or facility in using (an instrument, etc.). **4** rule as a master. □ **be master of 1** have at one's disposal. **2** know how to control. **be one's own master** be independent or free to do as one wishes. **make oneself master of** acquire a thorough knowledge of or facility in using. □□ **mas·ter·dom** *n.* **mas·ter·hood** *n.* **mas·ter·less** *adj.* [OE *mægester* (later also f. OF *maistre*) f. L *magister*, prob. rel. to *magis* more]

mas·ter-at-arms *n.* (*pl.* **mas·ters-at-arms**) a petty officer who enforces discipline aboard a naval vessel.

mas•ter class *n.* a class given by a person of distinguished skill, esp. in music.

mas•ter•ful /mástərfŏŏl/ *adj.* **1** imperious, domineering. **2** masterly. □□ **mas•ter•ful•ly** *adv.* **mas•ter•ful•ness** *n.*

▶Masterful and masterly overlap in meaning and are sometimes confused. Leaving aside masterful's meaning of 'domineering,' it also means 'very skillful, masterly.' However, **masterful** used in this sense generally describes a person, e.g., *he has limited talent but he's masterful at exploiting it*, while **masterly** usually describes an achievement or action, e.g., *that was a masterly response to our opponents' arguments*.

mas•ter hand *n.* **1** a person having commanding power or great skill. **2** the action of such a person.

mas•ter key *n.* a key that opens several locks, each of which also has its own key.

mas•ter•ly /mástərlee/ *adj.* worthy of a master; very skillful (*a masterly piece of work*). □□ **mas•ter•li•ness** *n.*

mas•ter mar•i•ner *n.* **1** the captain of a merchant ship. **2** a seaman certified competent to be captain.

mas•ter ma•son *n.* **1** a skilled mason, or one in business on his or her own account. **2** a fully qualified Freemason, who has passed the third degree.

mas•ter•mind /mástərmīnd/ *n. & v.* ●*n.* **1 a** a person with an outstanding intellect. **b** such an intellect. **2** the person directing an intricate operation. ●*v.tr.* plan and direct (a scheme or enterprise).

master of ceremonies *n.* **1** (also **MC** or **emcee**) a person introducing speakers at a banquet, entertainers in a variety show, contestants in a game show, etc. **2** a person in charge of ceremonies at a state or public occasion.

mas•ter•piece /mástərpees/ *n.* **1** an outstanding piece of artistry or workmanship. **2** a person's best work.

mas•ter•ship /mástərship/ *n.* **1** the position or function of a master, esp. a schoolmaster. **2** dominion, control.

mas•ter•sing•er /mástərsingər/ *n.* = MEISTERSINGER.

mas•ter•stroke /mástərstrōk/ *n.* an outstandingly skillful act of policy, etc.

mas•ter switch *n.* a switch controlling the supply of electricity, etc., to an entire system.

mas•ter•work /mástərwərk/ *n.* a masterpiece.

mas•ter•y /mástəree/ *n.* **1** comprehensive knowledge or skill in a subject or accomplishment (*she played with some mastery*). **2** the action or process of mastering a subject or accomplishment (*mastery of language*). **3** control over someone or something. [ME f. OF *maistrie* (as MASTER)]

mast•head /mást-hed/ *n. & v.* ●*n.* **1** the highest part of a ship's mast, esp. that of a lower mast as a place of observation or punishment. **2 a** the title of a newspaper, etc., at the head of the front or editorial page. **b** the printed notice in a newspaper, magazine, etc., giving details of staff, ownership, etc. ●*v.tr.* send (a sailor) to the masthead. **2** raise (a sail) to its position on the mast.

mas•tic /mástik/ *n.* **1** a gum or resin exuded from the bark of the mastic tree, used in making varnish. **2** (in full **mastic tree**) the evergreen tree, *Pistacia lentiscus*, yielding this. **3** a waterproof filler and sealant used in building. **4** a liquor flavored with mastic gum. [ME f. OF f. LL *masticum* f. L *mastiche* f. Gk *mastikhē*, perh. f. *mastikhaō* (see MASTICATE) with ref. to its use as chewing gum]

mas•ti•cate /mástikayt/ *v.tr.* grind or chew (food) with one's teeth. □□ **mas•ti•ca•tion** /-káyshən/ *n.* **mas•ti•ca•tor** *n.* **mas•ti•ca•to•ry** /-kətáwree/ *adj.* [LL *masticare masticat-* f. Gk *mastikhaō* gnash the teeth]

mas•tiff /mástif/ *n.* **1** a dog of a large strong breed with a short, thick coat and drooping ears. **2** this breed of dog. [ME ult. f. OF *mastin* ult. f. L *mansuetus* tame; see MANSUETUDE]

mas•ti•tis /mástítis/ *n.* an inflammation of the mammary gland (the breast or udder). [Gk *mastos* breast + –ITIS]

mas•to•don /mástədon/ *n.* a large extinct mammal of the genus *Mammut*, resembling the elephant but having nipple-shaped tubercles on the crowns of its molar teeth. □□ **mas•to•don•tic** /-dóntik/ *adj.* [mod.L f. Gk *mastos* breast + *odous odontos* tooth]

mastodon

mas•toid /mástoyd/ *adj. & n.* ●*adj.* shaped like a woman's breast. ●*n.* **1** = MASTOID PROCESS. **2** *colloq.* mastoiditis. [F *mastoïde* or mod.L *mastoides* f. Gk *mastoeidēs* f. *mastos* breast]

mas•toid•i•tis /mástoydítis/ *n.* inflammation of the mastoid process.

mastoid proc•ess *n.* a conical prominence on the temporal bone behind the ear, to which muscles are attached.

mas•tur•bate /mástərbayt/ *v.intr. & tr.* arouse oneself sexually or cause (another person) to be aroused by manual stimulation of the genitals. □□ **mas•tur•ba•tion** /-báyshən/ *n.* **mas•tur•ba•tor** *n.* **mas•tur•ba•to•ry** /-tərbətáwree/ *adj.* [L *masturbat-* masturbated, from the verb *masturbari*]

mat¹ /mat/ *n. & v.* ●*n.* **1** a piece of coarse material for wiping shoes on, esp. a doormat. **2** a piece of cork, rubber, plastic, etc., to protect a surface from the heat or moisture of an object placed on it. **3** a piece of resilient material for landing on in gymnastics, wrestling, etc. **4** a piece of coarse fabric of plaited rushes, straw, etc., for lying on, packing furniture, etc. **5** a small rug. ●*v.* (**mat•ted, mat•ting**) **1 a** *tr.* (esp. as **matted** *adj.*) entangle in a thick mass (*matted hair*). **b** *intr.* become matted. **2** *tr.* cover or furnish with mats. □ **on the mat** esp. *Brit. sl.* being reprimanded (orig. in the army, on the orderly-room mat before the commanding officer). [OE *m(e)att(e)* f. WG f. LL *matta*]

mat² var. of MATTE¹.

mat³ /mat/ *n.* = MATRIX 1. [abbr.]

mat•a•dor /mátədawr/ *n.* **1** a bullfighter whose task is to kill the bull. **2** a principal card in omber, quadrille, etc. **3** a domino game in which the piece played must make a total of seven. [Sp. f. *matar* kill f. Pers. *māt* dead]

Ma•ta Ha•ri /máátə hááree/ *n.* a beautiful and seductive female spy. [name taken by Dutch spy M. G. Zelle, d. 1917, f. Malay *mata* eye + *hari* day]

match¹ /mach/ *n. & v.* ●*n.* **1** a contest or game of skill, etc., in which persons or teams compete against each other. **2 a** a person able to contend with another as an equal (*meet one's match; be more than a match for*). **b** a person equal to another in some quality (*we shall never see his match*). **c** a person or thing exactly like or corresponding to another. **3** a marriage. **4** a person viewed in regard to his or her eligibility for marriage, esp. as to rank or fortune (*an excellent match*). ●*v.* **1 a** *tr.* be equal to or harmonious with; correspond to in some essential respect (*the curtains match the wallpaper*). **b** *intr.* (often foll. by *with*) correspond; harmonize (*his socks do not match; does the ribbon match with your hat?*). **c** (as **matching** *adj.*) having correspondence in some essential respect (*matching curtains*). **2** *tr.* (foll. by *against, with*) place (a person, etc.) in conflict, contest, or competition with (another). **3** *tr.* find material, etc., that matches (another) (*can you match this silk?*). **4** *tr.* find a person or thing suitable for another (*matching unemployed workers to available jobs*). **5** *tr.* prove to be a match for. **6** *tr. Electronics* produce or have an adjustment of (circuits) such that maximum power is transmitted between them. **7** *tr.* (usu. foll. by *with*) *archaic* join (a person) with another in marriage. □ **make a match** bring about a marriage. **to match** corresponding in some essential respect with what has been mentioned (*yellow dress with a scarf to match*). □□ **match•a•ble** *adj.* [OE *gemæcca* mate, companion, f. Gmc]

match² /mach/ *n.* **1** a short thin piece of flammable material tipped with a composition that can be ignited by friction. **2** a piece of wick, cord, etc., designed to burn at a uniform rate, for firing a cannon, etc. [ME f. OF *mesche, meiche*, perh. f. L *myxa* lamp nozzle]

match•board /máchbawrd/ *n.* a board with a tongue cut along one edge and a groove along another, so as to fit with similar boards.

match•box /máchboks/ *n.* a box for holding matches.

match•less /máchlis/ *adj.* without an equal, incomparable. □□ **match•less•ly** *adv.*

match•lock /máchlok/ *n. hist.* **1** an old type of gun with a lock in which a match was placed for igniting the powder. **2** such a lock.

match•mak•er /máchmaykər/ *n.* a person who tries to arrange an agreement or relationship between two parties, esp. a marriage partnership. □□ **match•mak•ing** *n.*

match play *n. Golf* play in which the score is reckoned by counting the holes won by each side (cf. STROKE PLAY).

match point *n.* **1** *Tennis*, etc. **a** the state of a game when one side needs only one more point to win the match. **b** this point. **2** *Bridge* a unit of scoring in matches and tournaments.

match•stick /máchstik/ *n.* the stem of a match.

match•wood /máchwŏŏd/ *n.* **1** wood suitable for matches. **2** minute splinters. □ **make matchwood of** smash utterly.

mate¹ /mayt/ *n. & v.* ●*n.* **1** a friend or fellow worker. **2** *Brit.*, etc. *colloq.* a general form of address, esp. to another man. **3 a** each of a pair, esp. of animals, birds, or socks. **b** *colloq.* a partner in marriage. **c** (in *comb.*) a fellow member or joint occupant of (*teammate; roommate*). **4** *Naut.* an officer on a merchant ship subordinate to the master. **5** an assistant to a skilled worker (*plumber's mate*). ●*v.* (often foll. by *with*) **1 a** *tr.* bring (animals or birds) together for breeding. **b** *intr.* (of animals or birds) come together for breeding. **2 a** *tr.* join (persons) in marriage. **b** *intr.* (of persons) be joined in marriage. **3** *intr. Mech.* fit well. □□ **mate•less** *adj.* [ME f. MLG *mate* f. *gemate* messmate f. WG, rel. to MEAT]

mate² /mayt/ *n. & v.tr. Chess* = CHECKMATE. [ME f. F *mat(er)*: see CHECKMATE]

ma•té /máatay/ *n.* **1** a beverage made from the leaves of a S. American shrub, *Ilex paraguayensis*. **2** this shrub, or its leaves. **3** a vessel in which these leaves are infused. [Sp. *mate* f. Quechua *mati*]

mate·lot /mátlō/ n. (also **mat·low, mat·lo**) Brit. sl. a sailor. [F mate-lot]

mat·e·lote /mátəlōt/ n. a dish of fish, etc., with a sauce of wine and onions. [F (as MATELOT)]

ma·ter /máytər/ n. Brit. sl. mother.[L] ▶Now only in jocular or affected use.

ma·ter·fa·mil·i·as /máytərfəmíleeəs/ n. the woman head of a family or household (cf. PATERFAMILIAS). [L f. mater mother + familia FAMILY]

ma·te·ri·al /mətéereeəl/ n. & adj. ● n. 1 the matter from which a thing is made. 2 cloth, fabric. 3 (in pl.) things needed for an activity (building materials; cleaning materials; writing materials). 4 a person or thing of a specified kind or suitable for a purpose (officer material). 5 (in sing. or pl.) information, etc., to be used in writing a book, etc. (experimental material; materials for a biography). 6 (in sing. or pl., often foll. by of) the elements or constituent parts of a substance. ● adj. 1 of matter; corporeal. 2 concerned with bodily comfort, etc. (material well-being). 3 (of conduct, points of view, etc.) not spiritual. 4 (often foll. by to) important, essential, relevant (at the material time). 5 concerned with the matter, not the form, of reasoning. □□ **ma·te·ri·al·i·ty** /–reeálitee/ n. [ME f. OF materiel, –al, f. LL materialis f. L (as MATTER)]

ma·te·ri·al·ism /mətéereeəlizəm/ n. 1 a tendency to prefer material possessions and physical comfort to spiritual values. 2 Philos. a the opinion that nothing exists but matter and its movements and modifications. b the doctrine that consciousness and will are wholly due to material agency. 3 Art a tendency to lay stress on the material aspect of objects. □□ **ma·te·ri·al·ist** n. **ma·te·ri·al·is·tic** /–lístik/ adj. **ma·te·ri·al·is·ti·cal·ly** /–lístiklee/ adv.

ma·te·ri·al·ize /mətéereeəlīz/ v. 1 intr. become actual fact. 2 a tr. cause (a spirit) to appear in bodily form. b intr. (of a spirit) appear in this way. 3 intr. colloq. appear or be present when expected. 4 tr. represent or express in material form. 5 tr. make materialistic. □□ **ma·te·ri·al·i·za·tion** n.

ma·te·ri·al·ly /mətéereeəlee/ adv. 1 substantially, considerably. 2 in respect of matter.

ma·ter·i·a med·i·ca /matéereeə médikə/ n. 1 the remedial substances used in the practice of medicine. 2 the study of the origin and properties of these substances. [mod.L, transl. Gk hulē iatrikē healing material]

ma·té·ri·el /mətéeree-él/ n. available means, esp. materials and equipment in warfare (opp. PERSONNEL). [F (as MATERIAL)]

ma·ter·nal /mətə́rnəl/ adj. 1 of or like a mother. 2 motherly. 3 related through the mother (maternal uncle). 4 of the mother in pregnancy and childbirth. □□ **ma·ter·nal·ism** n. **ma·ter·nal·is·tic** /–lístik/ adj. **ma·ter·nal·ly** adv. [ME f. OF maternel or L maternus f. mater mother]

ma·ter·ni·ty /mətə́rnitee/ n. 1 motherhood. 2 motherliness. 3 (attrib.) a for women during and just after childbirth (maternity hospital; maternity leave). b suitable for a pregnant woman (maternity dress; maternity wear). [F maternité f. med.L maternitas –tatis f. L maternus f. mater mother]

mate·ship /máytship/ n. Austral. companionship, fellowship.

mate·y /máytee/ adj. & n. ● adj. Brit. (**mat·i·er, mat·i·est**) (often foll. by with) sociable; familiar and friendly. ● n. Brit. (pl. **·eys**) colloq. (usu. as a form of address) mate, companion. □□ **mate·y·ness** n. (also **mat·i·ness**). **mate·i·ly** adv.

math /math/ n. US colloq. mathematics (cf. MATHS). [abbr.]

math·e·mat·i·cal /máthimátikəl/ adj. 1 of or relating to mathematics. 2 (of a proof, etc.) rigorously precise. □□ **math·e·mat·i·cal·ly** adv. [ME f. L mathematicus or L mathematicus f. Gk mathēmatikos f. mathēma –matos science f. manthanō learn]

math·e·mat·i·cal in·duc·tion n. = INDUCTION 3b.

math·e·mat·i·cal ta·bles n.pl. tables of logarithms and trigonometric values, etc.

math·e·mat·ics /máthimátiks/ n.pl. 1 (also treated as sing.) the abstract science of number, quantity, and space studied in its own right (**pure mathematics**), or as applied to other disciplines such as physics, engineering, etc. (**applied mathematics**). 2 (as pl.) the use of mathematics in calculation, etc. □□ **math·e·ma·ti·cian** /–mətíshən/ n. [prob. f. F mathématiques pl. f. L mathematica f. Gk mathēmatika: see MATHEMATICAL]

PRONUNCIATION TIP **mathematics**

Many people pronounce this word as if it had only three syllables. Pronounce all four syllables ("MATH-i-MAT-iks") and you'll be less likely to misspell it.

---

maths /maths/ n. Brit. colloq. mathematics (cf. MATH). [abbr.]

Ma·til·da /mətíldə/ n. Austral. sl. a bushman's bundle; a swag. □ **waltz** (or **walk**) **Matilda** carry a swag. [the name Matilda]

mat·i·née /mat'náy/ n. (US also **mat·i·nee**) an afternoon performance in a theater, etc. [F, = what occupies a morning f. matin morning (as MATINS)]

mat·i·née i·dol n. a handsome actor admired esp. by women.

mat·ins /mát'nz/ n. (also **mat·tins**) (as sing. or pl.) 1 a service of morning prayers in various churches, esp. the Angelican Church. 2 a service forming part of the traditional Divine Office of the Western Christian Church, originally said at or after midnight, but historically often held with lauds on the previous evening. 2 (also **mat·in**) poet. the morning song of birds. [ME f. OF matines f. eccl.L matutinas, accus. fem. pl. adj. f. L matutinus of the morning f. Matuta dawn goddess]

mat·lo (also **mat·low**) var. of MATELOT.

mat·rass /mátrəs/ n. hist. a long-necked glass vessel with a round or oval body, used for distilling, etc. [F matras, of uncert. orig.]

ma·tri·arch /máytreeaark/ n. a woman who is the head of a family or tribe. □□ **ma·tri·ar·chal** /–áarkəl/ adj. [L mater mother, on the false analogy of PATRIARCH]

ma·tri·ar·chy /máytreeaarkee/ n. (pl. **·chies**) a form of social organization in which the mother is the head of the family and descent is reckoned through the female line.

ma·tri·ces pl. of MATRIX.

mat·ri·cide /mátrisīd, máy–/ n. 1 the killing of one's mother. 2 a person who does this. □□ **mat·ri·cid·al** adj. [L matricida, matricidium f. mater matris mother]

ma·tric·u·late /mətríkyəlayt/ v. 1 intr. be enrolled at a college or university. 2 tr. admit (a student) to membership of a college or university. □□ **ma·tric·u·la·to·ry** /–lətáwree/ adj. [med.L matriculare matriculat- enroll f. LL matricula register, dimin. of L MATRIX]

ma·tric·u·la·tion /mətríkyəláyshən/ n. 1 the act or an instance of matriculating. 2 an examination to qualify for this.

mat·ri·lin·e·al /mátrilíneeəl/ adj. of or based on kinship with the mother or the female line. □□ **mat·ri·lin·e·al·ly** adv. [L mater matris mother + LINEAL]

mat·ri·lo·cal /mátrilókəl/ adj. of or denoting a custom in marriage where the husband goes to live with the wife's community. [L mater matris mother + LOCAL]

mat·ri·mo·ny /mátrimōnee/ n. (pl. **·nies**) 1 the rite of marriage. 2 the state of being married. □□ **mat·ri·mo·ni·al** /–móneeəl/ adj. **mat·ri·mo·ni·al·ly** /–móneeəlee/ adv. [ME f. AF matrimonie, OF matremoi(g)ne f. L matrimonium f. mater matris mother]

ma·trix /máytriks/ n. (pl. **ma·tri·ces** /–triseez/ or **ma·trix·es**) 1 a mold in which a thing is cast or shaped, such as a phonograph record, printing type, etc. 2 a an environment or substance in which a thing is developed. b archaic a womb. 3 a mass of fine-grained rock in which gems, fossils, etc., are embedded. 4 Math. a rectangular array of elements in rows and columns that is treated as a single element. 5 Biol. the substance between cells or in which structures are embedded. 6 Computing a gridlike array of interconnected circuit elements. [L, = breeding female, womb, register f. mater matris mother]

ma·tron /máytrən/ n. 1 a married woman, esp. a dignified and sober one. 2 a woman managing the domestic arrangements of a school, prison, etc. 3 Brit. dated a woman in charge of the nursing in a hospital. □□ **ma·tron·hood** n. [ME f. OF matrone f. L matrona f. mater matris mother]

ma·tron·ly /máytrənlee/ adj. like or characteristic of a matron, esp. in respect of staidness or portliness.

ma·tron of hon·or n. a married woman attending the bride at a wedding.

Matt. abbr. Matthew (esp. in the New Testament).

matte[1] /mat/ adj., n., & v. (also **matt** or **mat**) ● adj. (of a color, surface, etc.) dull, without luster. ● n. 1 a border of dull gold around a framed picture. 2 (in full **matte paint**) paint formulated to give a dull flat finish (cf. GLOSS[1]). 3 the appearance of unburnished gold. ● v.tr. (**mat·ted, mat·ting**) 1 make (gilding, etc.) dull. 2 frost (glass). [F mat, mater, identical with mat MATE[2]]

matte[2] /mat/ n. an impure product of the smelting of sulfide ores, esp. those of copper or nickel. [F]

matte[3] /mat/ n. Cinematog. a mask to obscure part of an image and allow another image to be superimposed, giving a combined effect. [F]

mat·ter /mátər/ n. & v. ● n. 1 a physical substance in general, as distinct from mind and spirit. b that which has mass and occupies space. 2 a particular substance (coloring matter). 3 (prec. by the; often foll. by with) the thing that is amiss (what is the matter?; there is something the matter with him). 4 material for thought or expression. 5 a the substance of a book, speech, etc., as distinct from its manner or form. b Logic the particular content of a proposition, as distinct from its form. 6 a thing or things of a specified kind (printed matter; reading matter). 7 an affair or situation being considered, esp. in a specified way (a serious matter; a matter for concern; the matter of your overdraft). 8 Physiol. a any substance in or discharged from the body (fecal matter; gray matter). b pus. 9 (foll. by of, for) what is or may be a good reason for (complaint, regret, etc.). 10 Printing the body of a printed work, as type or as printed sheets. ● v.intr. 1 (often foll. by to) be of importance; have significance (it does not matter to me when it happened). 2 secrete or discharge pus. □ **as a matter of fact** in reality (esp. to correct a falsehood or misunderstanding). **for that matter 1** as far as that is concerned. **2** and indeed also. **in the matter of** as regards. **a matter of 1** approximately (*for a matter of 40 years*). **2** a thing that relates to, depends on, or is determined by (*a matter of habit*; *only a matter of time before they agree*). **no matter 1** (foll. by *when, how,* etc.) regardless of (*will do it no matter what the consequences*). **2** it is of no importance. **what is the matter** with surely there is no objection to. **what matter?** esp. *Brit.* that need not worry us. [ME f. AF *mater(i)e*, OF *matiere* f. L *materia* timber, substance, subject of discourse]

mat·ter of fact 1 what belongs to the sphere of fact as distinct from opinion, etc. **2** *Law* the part of a judicial inquiry concerned with the truth of alleged facts (see also MATTER-OF-FACT).

mat·ter-of-fact /mátərəfákt/ *adj.* **1** unimaginative, prosaic. **2** unemotional. □□ **mat·ter-of-fact·ly** *adv.* **mat·ter-of-fact·ness** *n.*

mat·ter of form *n.* a mere routine.

mat·ter of law *n.* *Law* the part of a judicial inquiry concerned with the interpretation of the law.

mat·ting /máting/ *n.* **1** fabric of hemp, bast, grass, etc., for mats (*coconut matting*). **2** in senses of MAT[1] *v.*

mat·tins var. of MATINS.

mat·tock /mátək/ *n.* an agricultural tool shaped like a pickax, with an adze and a chisel edge as the ends of the head. [OE *mattuc*, of unkn. orig.]

mat·toid /mátoyd/ *n.* a person of erratic mind, a mixture of genius and fool. [It. *mattoide* f. *matto* insane]

mat·tress /mátris/ *n.* a fabric case stuffed with soft, firm, or springy material, or a similar case filled with air or water, used on or as a bed. [ME f. OF *materas* f. It. *materasso* f. Arab. *almatrah* the place, the cushion f. *taraha* throw]

mat·u·rate /máchərayt/ *v.intr.* **1** *Med.* (of a boil, etc.) come to maturation. **2** mature [L *maturatus* (asMATURE *v.*)]

mat·u·ra·tion /máchəráyshən/ *n.* **1 a** the act or an instance of maturing; the state of being matured. **b** the ripening of fruit. **2** *Med.* **a** the formation of purulent matter. **b** the causing of this. □□ **tur·a·tive** /məchŏŏrətiv/ *adj.* [ME f. F *maturation* or med.L *maturatio* f. L (as MATURE *v.*)]

mattock

ma·ture /məchŏŏr, –tyŏŏr, –tŏŏr/ *adj. & v.* ● *adj.* (**ma·tur·er, ma·tur·est**) **1** with fully developed powers of body and mind; adult. **2** complete in natural development; ripe. **3** (of thought, intentions, etc.) duly careful and adequate. **4** (of a bond, etc.) due for payment. ● *v.* **1 a** *tr. & intr.* develop fully. **b** *tr. & intr.* ripen. **c** *intr.* come to maturity. **2** *tr.* perfect (a plan, etc.). **3** *intr.* (of a bond, etc.) become due for payment. □□ **ma·ture·ly** *adv.* **ma·ture·ness** *n.* **ma·tu·ri·ty** *n.* [ME f. L *maturus* timely, early]

SYNONYM TIP mature

AGE, DEVELOP, MELLOW, RIPEN. Most of us would prefer to **mature** rather than simply to **age**. *Mature* implies gaining wisdom, experience, or sophistication as well as adulthood; when applied to non-human living things, it indicates fullness of growth and readiness for normal functioning (*a mature crop of strawberries*). *Age*, on the other hand, refers to the changes that result from the passage of time, often with an emphasis on the negative or destructive changes that accompany growing old (*the tragedy aged him five years*). **Develop** is like *mature* in that it means to go through a series of positive changes to attain perfection or effectiveness, but it can refer to a part as well as a whole organism (*the kitten's eyesight had begun to develop at three weeks*). **Ripen** is a less formal word meaning to *mature*, but it usually applies to fruit (*the apples ripened in the sun*). **Mellow** suggests the tempering, moderation, or reduction in harshness that comes with time or experience. With its connotations of warmth, mildness, and sweetness, it is a more positive word than *mature* or *age* (*to mellow as one gets older*).

ma·tu·ti·nal /mətŏŏt'n'l, –tyŏŏt–, máchŏŏtinəl/ *adj.* **1** of or occurring in the morning. **2** early. [LL *matutinalis* f. L *matutinus*: see MATINS]

mat·zo /máatsə/ *n.* (also **mat·zoh**; *pl.* **·zos** or **zohs** or **mat·zoth** /–sŏt/) **1** a wafer of unleavened bread for the Passover. **2** such bread collectively. [Yiddish f. Heb. *maṣṣāh*]

maud /mawd/ *n.* **1** a Scots shepherd's gray-striped plaid. **2** a traveling robe or rug like this. [18th c.: orig. unkn.]

maud·lin /máwdlin/ *adj. & n.* ● *adj.* weakly or tearfully sentimental, esp. in a tearful and effusive stage of drunkenness. ● *n.* weak or mawkish sentiment. [ME f. OF *Madeleine* f. eccl.L *Magdalena* Magdalen, with ref. to pictures of Mary Magdalen weeping]

maul /mawl/ *v. & n.* ● *v.tr.* **1** beat and bruise. **2** handle roughly or

carelessly. **3** damage by criticism. ● *n.* **1** a special heavy hammer, commonly of wood, esp. for driving in wedges or stakes. **2** *Rugby* a loose scrum with the ball off the ground. **3** *Brit.* a brawl. □□ **maul·er** *n.* [ME f. OF *mail* f. L *malleus* hammer]

maul·stick /máwlstik/ *n.* (also **mahl·stick**) a light stick with a padded leather ball at one end, held against work by a painter to support and steady the brush hand. [Du. *maalstok* f. *malen* to paint + *stok* stick]

maun·der /máwndər/ *v.intr.* **1** talk in a dreamy or rambling manner. **2** move or act listlessly or idly. [perh. f. obs. *maunder* beggar, to beg]

maund·y /máwndee/ *n.* the ceremony of washing the feet of the poor, in commemoration of Jesus' washing of the disciples' feet at the Last Supper. [ME f. OF *mandé* f. L *mandatum* MANDATE, commandment (see John 13: 34)]

maun·dy mon·ey *n.* alms distributed on Maundy Thursday or as part of the maundy ceremony.

Maun·dy Thurs·day *n.* the Thursday before Easter.

mau·so·le·um /máwsəleéəm/ *n.* a large and grand tomb. [L f. Gk *Mausōleion* f. *Mausōlos* Mausolus king of Caria (4th c. BC), to whose tomb the name was orig. applied]

mauve /mōv/ *adj. & n.* ● *adj.* pale purple. ● *n.* **1** this color. **2** a bright but delicate pale purple dye from coal-tar aniline. □□ **mauv·ish** *adj.* [F, lit. = mallow, f. L *malva*]

ma·ven /máyvən/ *n.* (also **ma·vin**) *colloq.* an expert or connoisseur. [Yiddish *meyvn* f. Heb. *mēbīn*]

mav·er·ick /mávərik, mávrik/ *n.* **1** an unbranded calf or yearling. **2** an unorthodox or independent-minded person. [S. A. *Maverick*, Texas engineer and rancher d. 1870, who did not brand his cattle]

ma·vis /máyvis/ *n.* esp. *Brit. poet.* or *dial.* a song thrush. [ME f. OF *mauvis* of uncert. orig.]

maw /maw/ *n.* **1 a** the stomach of an animal. **b** the jaws or throat of a voracious animal. **2** *colloq.* the stomach of a greedy person. [OE *maga* f. Gmc]

mawk·ish /máwkish/ *adj.* **1** sentimental in a feeble or sickly way. **2** having a faint sickly flavor. □□ **mawk·ish·ly** *adv.* **mawk·ish·ness** *n.* [obs. *mawk* maggot f. ON *mathkr* f. Gmc]

max *abbr.* maximum. □ **to the max** *sl.* to the utmost, to the fullest extent.

max·i /máksee/ *n.* (*pl.* **max·is**) *colloq.* a maxiskirt or other garment with a long skirt. [abbr.]

maxi- /máksee/ *comb. form* very large or long (*maxicoat, maxiskirt*). [abbr. of MAXIMUM: cf. MINI-]

max·il·la /maksílə/ *n.* (*pl.* **max·il·lae** /–lee/ or **max·il·las**) **1** the jaw or jawbone, esp. the upper jaw in most vertebrates. **2** the mouthpart of many arthropods used in chewing. □□ **max·il·lar·y** /máksəléree/ *adj.* [L, = jaw]

max·im /máksim/ *n.* a general truth or rule of conduct expressed in a sentence. [ME f. F *maxime* or med.L *maxima (propositio)*, fem. adj. (as MAXIMUM)]

max·i·ma *pl.* of MAXIMUM.

max·i·mal /máksiməl/ *adj.* being or relating to a maximum; the greatest possible in size, duration, etc. □□ **max·i·mal·ly** *adv.*

max·i·mal·ist /máksiməlist/ *n.* a person who rejects compromise and expects a full response to (esp. political) demands. [MAXIMAL, after Russ. *maksimalist*]

max·i·mize /máksimīz/ *v.tr.* increase or enhance to the utmost. □□ **max·i·mi·za·tion** *n.* **max·i·miz·er** *n.* [L *maximus*: see MAXIMUM]

max·i·mum /máksiməm/ *n. & adj.* ● *n.* (*pl.* **max·i·ma** /–mə/) the highest possible or attainable amount. ● *adj.* that is a maximum. [mod.L, neut. of L *maximus*, superl. of *magnus* great]

max·well /mákswel/ *n.* a unit of magnetic flux in the centimeter-gram-second system, equal to that induced through one square centimeter by a perpendicular magnetic field of one gauss. [J. C. *Maxwell*, Brit. physicist d. 1879]

May /may/ *n.* **1** the fifth month of the year. **2** (**may**) esp. *Brit.* the hawthorn or its blossom. **3** *poet.* bloom, prime. [ME f. OF *mai* f. L *Maius (mensis)* (month) of the goddess *Maia*]

may /may/ *v.aux.* (*3rd sing. present* **may**; *past* **might** /mīt/) **1** (often foll. by *well* for emphasis) expressing possibility (*it may be true; I may have been wrong; you may well lose your way*). **2** expressing permission (*you may not go; may I come in?*). **3** expressing a wish (*may he live to regret it*). **4** expressing uncertainty or irony in questions (*who may you be?; who are you, may I ask?*). **5** in purpose clauses and after *wish, fear,* etc. (*take such measures as may avert disaster; hope he may succeed*). □ **be that as it may** despite that; nevertheless (*be that as it may, I still want to go*). [OE *mæg* f. Gmc, rel. to MAIN[1], MIGHT[2]]

▶Traditionalists insist that one should distinguish between **may** (present tense) and **might** (past tense) in expressing possibility: *I may have some dessert after dinner if I'm still hungry; I might have known that the highway would be closed because of the storm.* In casual use, though, **may** and **might** are generally interchangeable: *They might take a vacation next month*; *He may have called earlier, but the answering machine was broken.* For **may** vs. **can**, see note at CAN[1].

Ma·ya /maáyə/ *n.* **1** (*pl.* same or **Ma·yas**) a member of an ancient native people of Central America. **2** the language of this people. □□ **Ma·yan** *adj. & n.* [native name]

ma·ya /maáyə/ *n. Hinduism* a marvel or illusion, esp. in the phenomenal universe. [Skr. *māyā*]

may·ap·ple /máyapəl/ *n.* (also **man·drake**) an American herbaceous plant, *Podophyllum peltatum*, bearing a yellow egg-shaped fruit in May.

may·be /máybee/ *adv.* perhaps, possibly. [ME f. *it may be*]

May·day /máyday/ *n.* an international radio-telephone distress signal used esp. by ships and aircraft. [repr. pronunc. of F *m'aidez* help me]

May Day *n.* May 1, celebrated in many countries as a festival, or as an international holiday honoring workers.

may·est /máyist/ *archaic* = MAYST.

May·flow·er *n.* the ship on which the Pilgrims traveled from England to N. America in 1620.

may·flow·er /máyflowər/ *n.* any of various flowers that bloom in May, esp. the trailing arbutus, *Epigaea repens.*

may·fly /máyflī/ *n.* (*pl.* **·flies**) **1** any insect of the order Ephemeroptera, living briefly in spring in the adult stage. **2** an imitation mayfly used by anglers.

may·hap /máyháp/ *adv. archaic* perhaps, possibly. [ME f. *it may hap*]

may·hem /máyhem/ *n.* **1** violent or damaging action. **2** rowdy confusion, chaos. **3** *hist.* the crime of maiming a person so as to render him or her partly or wholly defenseless. [AF *mahem*, OF *mayhem* (as MAIM)]

may·ing /máying/ *n.* (also **Maying**) participation in May Day festivities. [ME f. MAY]

may·n't /máyənt/ *contr.* may not.

may·on·naise /máyənáyz/ *n.* a thick creamy dressing made of egg yolks, oil, vinegar, etc. [F, perh. f. *mahonnais –aise* of Port *Mahon* on Minorca]

may·or /máyər, mair/ *n.* the chief executive of a city or town. □□ **may·or·ship** *n.* [ME f. OF *maire* f. L (as MAJOR)]

may·or·al /máyərəl, máyáwrəl/ *of* or relating to a mayor.

PRONUNCIATION TIP mayoral

Although the most widely accepted pronunciation of the word *mayoral* places the stress on the first syllable, pronouncing it with the stress on the second syllable is also acceptable.

may·or·al·ty /máyərəltee, máir–/ *n.* (*pl.* **·ties**) **1** the office of mayor. **2** a mayor's period of office. [ME f. OF *mairalté* (as MAYOR)]

may·or·ess /máyəris, máir–/ *n.* **1** a woman holding the office of mayor. **2** the wife of a mayor.

may·pole /máypōl/ *n.* (also **May·pole**) a pole painted and decked with flowers and ribbons, for dancing around on May Day.

May queen *n.* a girl chosen to preside over celebrations on May Day.

mayst /mayst/ *archaic 2nd sing. present* of MAY.

may·weed /máyweed/ *n.* the stinking chamomile, *Anthemis cotula*. [earlier *maidwede* f. obs. *maithe(n)* f. OE *magothe*, *mægtha* + WEED]

maz·a·rine /mázəreen/ *n. & adj.* a rich deep blue. [17th c., perh. f. the name of Cardinal *Mazarin*, French statesman d. 1661, or Duchesse de *Mazarin*, French noblewoman d. 1699]

maze /mayz/ *n. & v.* ● *n.* **1** a network of paths and hedges designed as a puzzle for those who try to penetrate it. **2** a complex network of paths or passages; a labyrinth. **3** confusion, a confused mass, etc. ● *v.tr. Brit.* (esp. as **mazed** *adj.*) bewilder, confuse. □□ **ma·zy** *adj.* (**ma·zi·er**, **ma·zi·est**). [ME, orig. as *mased* (adj.): rel. to AMAZE]

ma·zer /máyzər/ *n. hist.* a hardwood drinking-bowl, usu. silver-mounted. [ME f. OF *masere* f. Gmc]

ma·zur·ka /məzúrkə/ *n.* **1** a usu. lively Polish dance in triple time. **2** the music for this. [F *mazurka* or G *Masurka*, f. Pol. *mazurka* woman of the province *Mazovia*]

maz·zard /mázərd/ *b.* the wild sweet cherry, *Prunus avum*, of Europe. [alt. of MAZER]

MB *abbr.* **1** *Computing* megabyte(s). **2** esp. *Brit.* Bachelor of Medicine. [sense 2 f. L *Medicinae Baccalaureus*]

MBA *abbr.* Master of Business Administration.

MBE *abbr.* Member of the Order of the British Empire.

MC *abbr.* **1** master of ceremonies. **2** Marine Corps. **3** Medical Corps. **4** Member of Congress. **5** (in the UK) Military Cross.

Mc *abbr.* **1** megacurie(s). **2** megacycle(s).

Mc·Car·thy·ism /məkáarthee-izəm/ *n.* the policy of hunting out suspected subversives or esp. Communists, usu. on the basis of weak evidence or false allegations. [J. R. *McCarthy*, US senator d. 1957]

Mc·Coy /məkóy/ *n. colloq.* □ **the real McCoy** the real thing; the genuine article. [19th c.: orig. uncert.]

mCi *abbr.* millicurie(s).

MCP *abbr. colloq.* male chauvinist pig.

MCR *abbr.* Master of Comparative Religion.

MD *abbr.* **1** Doctor of Medicine. **2** Maryland (in official postal use). **3** Managing Director. **4** muscular dystrophy. [sense 1 f. L *Medicinae Doctor*]

Md *symb. Chem.* the element mendelevium.

Md. *abbr.* Maryland.

MDA *abbr.* methylene dioxymethamphetamine, an amphetamine-based drug that causes euphoric and hallucinatory effects, originally produced as an appetite suppressant (see ECSTASY 3).

ME *abbr.* **1** Maine (in official postal use). **2** Middle East. **3** middle English.

Me. *abbr.* **1** Maine. **2** *Maître* (title of a French advocate).

me[1] /mee/ *pron.* **1** objective case of I[2] (*he saw me*). **2** *colloq.* = I[2] (*it's me all right*; *is taller than me*). **3** *colloq.* myself, to or for myself (*I got me a gun*). **4** *colloq.* used in exclamations (*ah me!*; *dear me!*; *silly me!*). □ **me and mine** me and my relatives. [OE *me*, *mē* accus. & dative of I[2] f. Gmc]

me[2] var. of MI.

me·a cul·pa /máyə kóŏlpə, meéə kúlpə/ *n. & int.* ● *n.* an acknowledgment of one's fault or error. ● *int.* expressing such an acknowledgment. [L, = by my fault]

mead[1] /meed/ *n.* an alcoholic drink of fermented honey and water. [OE *me(o)du* f. Gmc]

mead[2] /meed/ *n. poet.* or *archaic* = MEADOW. [OE *mǣd* f. Gmc, rel. to MOW[1]]

mead·ow /médō/ *n.* **1** a piece of grassland, esp. one used for hay. **2** a piece of low well-watered ground, esp. near a river. □□ **mead·ow·y** *adj.* [OE *mǣdwe*, oblique case of *mǣd*: see MEAD[2]]

mead·ow grass *n.* a perennial creeping grass, esp. the Kentucky bluegrass, *Poa pratensis.*

mead·ow·lark /médōlaark/ *n.* any songbird of the genus *Sturnella*, esp. the yellow-breasted *S. magna* of N. America.

mead·ow rue *n.* any ranunculaceous plant of the genus *Thalictrum*, esp. *T. dioicum*, with drooping greenish white flowers.

mead·ow saf·fron *n.* a perennial plant, *Colchicum autumnale*, abundant in meadows, with lilac flowers. Also called autumn crocus.

Eastern meadowlark

mead·ow·sweet /médōsweet/ *n.* **1** any of several rosaceous plants of the genus *Spiraea*, native to N. America. **2** a rosaceous plant, *Filipendula ulmaria*, common in meadows and damp places, with creamy-white fragrant flowers.

mea·ger /meégər/ *adj.* (*Brit.* **mea·gre**) **1** lacking in amount or quality (*a meager salary*). **2** (of literary composition, ideas, etc.) lacking fullness, unsatisfying. **3** (of a person or animal) lean, thin. □□ **mea·ger·ly** *adv.* **mea·ger·ness** *n.* [ME f. AF *megre*, OF *maigre* f. L *macer*]

meal[1] /meel/ *n.* **1** any of the regular occasions in a day when food is eaten, such as breakfast, lunch, or dinner. **2** the food eaten on such an occasion.

WORD HISTORY meal[1]

Old English *mæl* (also in the sense 'measure,' surviving in words such as *piecemeal* 'measure taken at one time'), of Germanic origin. The early sense of *meal* involved a notion of 'fixed time'; compare with Dutch *maal* 'meal, (portion of) time' and German *Mal* 'time,' *Mahl* 'meal,' from an Indo-European root meaning 'to measure.'

meal[2] /meel/ *n.* **1** the edible part of any grain or pulse (usu. other than wheat) ground to powder. **2** *Sc.* oatmeal. **3** any powdery substance made by grinding. [OE *melu* f. Gmc]

meal·time /meéltīm/ *n.* any of the usual times of eating.

meal bee·tle *n.* an insect, *Tenebrio molitor*, infesting granaries, etc.

meals on wheels *n.pl.* a service by which meals are delivered to the elderly, invalids, etc.

meal tick·et *n.* **1** a ticket entitling one to a meal, esp. at a specified place with reduced cost. **2** a person or thing that is a source of food or income.

meal·worm /meélwórm/ *n.* the larva of the meal beetle.

meal·y /meélee/ *adj.* (**meal·i·er**, **meal·i·est**) **1 a** of or like meal; soft and powdery. **b** containing meal. **2** (of a complexion) pale. **3** (of a horse) spotty. **4** (in full **mealy-mouthed**) not outspoken; ingratiating; afraid to use plain expressions. □□ **meal·i·ness** *n.*

meal·y·bug /meéleebúg/ *n.* any insect of the genus *Pseudococcus*, infesting plants, etc., whose body is covered with white powder.

mean[1] /meen/ *v.tr.* (*past* and *past part.* **meant** /ment/) **1 a** (often foll. by *to* + infin.) have as one's purpose or intention; have in mind (*they really mean mischief*; *I didn't mean to break it*). **b** (foll. by *by*) have as a motive in explanation (*what do you mean by that?*). **2** (often in *passive*) design or destine for a purpose (*mean it to be used*;

mean it for a stopgap; is meant to be a gift). **3** intend to convey or indicate or refer to (a particular thing or notion) (*I mean we cannot go; I mean Springfield in Ohio*). **4** entail, involve (*it means catching the early train*). **5** (often foll. by *that* + clause) portend, signify (*this means trouble; your refusal means that we must look elsewhere*). **6** (of a word) have as its explanation in the same language or its equivalent in another language. **7** (foll. by *to*) be of some specified importance to (a person), esp. as a source of benefit or object of affection, etc. (*that means a lot to me*). □ **mean business** be in earnest. **mean it** not be joking or exaggerating. **mean to say** really admit (usu. in interrog.: *do you mean to say you have lost it?*). **mean well** (often foll. by *to, toward, by*) have good intentions. [OE *mǽnan* f. WG, rel. to MIND]

mean² /meen/ *adj.* **1** unwilling to share, esp. money; not generous. **2** (of an action) ignoble, small-minded. **3** (of a person's capacity, understanding, etc.) inferior, poor. **4** (of housing) not imposing in appearance; shabby. **5 a** malicious, ill-tempered. **b** vicious or aggressive in behavior. **6** *colloq.* skillful, formidable (*is a mean fighter*). **7** *colloq.* ashamed (*feel mean*). □ **no mean** a very good (*that is no mean achievement*). □□ **mean·ly** *adv.* **mean·ness** *n.*

mean³ /meen/ *n. & adj.* ● *n.* **1** a condition, quality, virtue, or course of action equally removed from two opposite (usu. unsatisfactory) extremes. **2** *Math.* **a** the term or one of the terms midway between the first and last terms of an arithmetical or geometrical, etc., progression (*2 and 8 have the arithmetic mean 5 and the geometric mean 4*). **b** the quotient of the sum of several quantities and their number, the average. ● *adj.* **1** (of a quantity) equally far from two extremes. **2** calculated as a mean. [ME f. AF *meen* f. OF *meien, moien* f. L *medianus* MEDIAN]

▶ The difference between *median* and *mean* is most clearly expressed in numbers: **Mean**, or *average*, refers to the result obtained by dividing the sum of a set of quantities by the number of quantities in the set: *The mean or average of 3, 11, 9, and 5 is 28 divided by 4, or 7.* The **median** is the middle number in a sequence or, if the sequence has an even number of quantities, the average between the two middle numbers: *The median of 3, 4, 5, 8, and 14 is 5. The median of 2, 9, 10, and 35 is 9.5, that is, the mean or the average of 9 and 10.*

me·an·der /meeándər/ *v. & n.* ● *v.intr.* **1** wander at random. **2** (of a stream) wind about. ● *n.* **1 a** a curve in a winding river, etc. **b** a crooked or winding path or passage. **2** a circuitous journey. **3** an ornamental pattern of lines winding in and out; a fret. □□ **me·an·drous** *adj.* [L *maeander* f. Gk *Maiandros*, the name of a winding river in Phrygia]

me·an·drine /meeándrin/ *adj.* full of windings (esp. of corals of the genus *Meandrina*, with a surface like a human brain). [MEANDER + −INE¹]

mean free path *n.* the average distance traveled by a gas molecule, etc., between collisions.

mean·ie /meenee/ *n.* (also **mean·y**) (*pl. ·ies*) *colloq.* a mean, ungenerous, or small-minded person.

mean·ing /meening/ *n. & adj.* ● *n.* **1** what is meant by a word, action, idea, etc. **2** significance. **3** importance. ● *adj.* expressive, significant (*a meaning glance*). □□ **mean·ing·ly** *adv.*

mean·ing·ful /meeningfool/ *adj.* **1** full of meaning; significant. **2** *Logic* able to be interpreted. □□ **mean·ing·ful·ly** *adv.* **mean·ing·ful·ness** *n.*

mean·ing·less /meeninglis/ *adj.* having no meaning or significance. □□ **mean·ing·less·ly** *adv.* **mean·ing·less·ness** *n.*

means /meenz/ *n.pl.* **1** (often treated as *sing.*) that by which a result is brought about (*a means of quick travel*). **2 a** money resources (*live beyond one's means*). **b** wealth (*a man of means*). □ **by all means** of course; certainly. **by any means** at all; in any way (*I'm not rich by any means*). **by means of** with the help or agency of (*supplying water by means of aqueducts*). **by no means** not at all; certainly not. [pl. of MEAN³]

mean sea lev·el *n.* the sea level halfway between the mean levels of high and low water.

means test *n.* an official inquiry to establish need before financial assistance from public funds is given.

mean sun *n.* an imaginary sun moving in the celestial equator at the mean rate of the real sun, used in calculating solar time.

meant past and past part. of MEAN¹.

mean·time /meentīm/ *adv. & n.* ● *adv.* = MEANWHILE. ● *n.* the intervening period (esp. in the meantime). [MEAN³ + TIME]

mean time *n.* the time based on the movement of the mean sun. See also GREENWICH MEAN TIME.

mean·while /meenwil, –hwil/ *adv. & n.* ● *adv.* **1** in the intervening

period of time. **2** at the same time. ● *n.* the intervening period (esp. in the meanwhile). [MEAN³ + WHILE]

mean·y var. of MEANIE.

mea·sles /meezəlz/ *n.pl.* (also treated as *sing.*) **1 a** an acute infectious viral disease marked by red spots on the skin. **b** the spots of measles. **2** a tapeworm disease of pigs. [ME *masele(s)* prob. f. MLG *masele*, MDu. *masel* pustule (cf. Du. *mazelen* measles), OHG *masala*: change of form prob. due to assim. to ME *meser* leper]

mea·sly /meezlee/ *adj.* (**mea·sli·er, mea·sli·est**) **1** *colloq.* inferior, contemptible, worthless. **2** *colloq. derog.* ridiculously small in size, amount, or value. **3** of or affected with measles. **4** (of pork) infested with tapeworms. [MEASLES + −Y¹]

meas·ur·a·ble /mézhərəbəl/ *adj.* that can be measured. □□ **meas·ur·a·bil·i·ty** /–bílitee/ *n.* **meas·ur·a·bly** *adv.* [ME f. OF *mesurable* f. LL *mensurabilis* f. L *mensurare* (as MEASURE)]

meas·ure /mézhər/ *n. & v.* ● *n.* **1** a size or quantity found by measuring. **2** a system of measuring (*liquid measure; linear measure*). **3** a rod or tape, etc., for measuring. **4** a vessel of standard capacity for transferring or determining fixed quantities of liquids, etc. (*a pint measure*). **5 a** the degree, extent, or amount of a thing. **b** (foll. by *of*) some degree of (*there was a measure of wit in her remark*). **6 a** unit of capacity, e.g., a bushel (*20 measures of wheat*). **7** a factor by which a person or thing is reckoned or evaluated (*their success is a measure of their determination*). **8** (usu. in *pl.*) suitable action to achieve some end (*took measures to ensure a good profit*). **9** a legislative act. **10** a quantity contained in another an exact number of times. **11** a prescribed extent or quantity. **12** *Printing* the width of a page or column of type. **13 a** poetical rhythm; meter. **b** a metrical group of a dactyl or two iambs, trochees, spondees, etc. **14** *US Mus.* a bar or the time content of a bar. **15** *archaic* a dance. **16** a mineral stratum (*coal measures*). ● *v.* **1** *tr.* ascertain the extent or quantity of (a thing) by comparison with a fixed unit or with an object of known size. **2** *intr.* be of a specified size (*it measures six inches*). **3** *tr.* ascertain the size and proportion of (a person) for clothes. **4** *tr.* estimate (a quality, person's character, etc.) by some standard or rule. **5** *tr.* (often foll. by *off*) mark (a line, etc., of a given length). **6** *tr.* (foll. by *out*) deal or distribute (a thing) in measured quantities. **7** *tr.* (foll. by *with, against*) bring (oneself or one's strength, etc.) into competition with. **8** *tr. poet.* traverse (a distance). □ **beyond measure** excessively. **for good measure** as something beyond the minimum; as a finishing touch. **in a** (or **some**) **measure** partly. **measure up 1 a** determine the size, etc., of by measurement. **b** take comprehensive measurements. **2** (often foll. by *to*) have the necessary qualifications (for). [ME f. OF *mesure* f. L *mensura* f. *metiri mens–* measure]

meas·ured /mézhərd/ *adj.* **1** rhythmical; regular in movement (*a measured tread*). **2** (of language) carefully considered. □□ **meas·ured·ly** *adv.*

meas·ure·less /mézhərlis/ *adj.* not measurable; infinite. □□ **meas·ure·less·ly** *adv.*

meas·ure·ment /mézhərmənt/ *n.* **1** the act or an instance of measuring. **2** an amount determined by measuring. **3** (in *pl.*) detailed dimensions.

meas·ur·ing cup *n.* a cup marked to measure its contents.

meas·ur·ing worm *n.* looper, the caterpillar of the geometer moth.

meat /meet/ *n.* **1** the flesh of animals (esp. mammals) as food. **2** (foll. by *of*) the essence or chief part of. **3** the edible part of fruits, nuts, eggs, shellfish, etc. **4** *archaic* a food of any kind. **b** a meal. □□ **meat·less** *adj.* [OE *mete* food f. Gmc]

meat-and-po·ta·toes *n.* ordinary but fundamental things.

meat-ax *n.* **1** a butcher's cleaver. **2** drastic method of reducing something, esp. expenses.

meat·ball /meetbawl/ *n.* seasoned ground meat formed into a small round ball.

meat·hooks *n.pl.* sl. a person's hands or fists.

meat loaf *n.* seasoned ground meat molded into the shape of a loaf and baked.

meat mar·ket *n. colloq.* a place such as a bar or nightclub for people seeking sexual encounters.

meat·pack·ing /meetpaking/ *n.* the business of slaughtering animals and processing the meat for sale as food.

me·a·tus /meeáytəs/ *n.* (*pl.* same or **me·a·tus·es**) *Anat.* a channel or passage in the body or its opening. [L, = passage f. *meare* flow, run]

meat·y /meetee/ *adj.* (**meat·i·er, meat·i·est**) **1** full of meat; fleshy. **2** of or like meat. **3** full of substance. □□ **meat·i·ly** *adv.* **meat·i·ness** *n.*

Mec·ca /mékə/ *n.* **1** a place one aspires to visit. **2** the birthplace of a faith, policy, pursuit, etc. [Mecca in Arabia, birthplace of Muhammad and chief place of Muslim pilgrimage]

me·chan·ic /mikánik/ *n.* a skilled worker, esp. one who makes or uses or repairs machinery. [ME (orig. as adj.) f. OF *mecanique* or L *mechanicus* f. Gk *mēkhanikos* (as MACHINE)]

me·chan·i·cal /mikánikəl/ *adj.* **1** of or relating to machines or mechanisms. **2** working or produced by machinery. **3** (of a person or action) like a machine; automatic; lacking originality. **4 a** (of an agency, principle, etc.) belonging to mechanics. **b** (of a theory, etc.) explaining phenomena by the assumption of mechanical action. **5** of or relating to mechanics as a science. □□ **me•chan•i•cal•ism** *n.* (in sense 4). **me•chan•i•cal•ly** *adv.* **me•chan•i•cal•ness** *n.* [ME f. L *mechanicus* (as MECHANIC)]

me•chan•i•cal ad•van•tage *n.* the ratio of exerted to applied force in a machine.

me•chan•i•cal draw•ing *n.* a scale drawing of machinery, etc., done with precision instruments.

me•chan•i•cal en•gi•neer *n.* a person skilled in the branch of engineering dealing with the design, construction, and repair of machines.

mech•a•ni•cian /mékəníshən/ *n.* a person skilled in constructing machinery.

me•chan•ics /mikániks/ *n.pl.* (usu. treated as *sing.*) **1** the branch of applied mathematics dealing with motion and tendencies to motion. **2** the science of machinery. **3** the method of construction or routine operation of a thing.

mech•an•ism /mékənizəm/ *n.* **1** the structure or adaptation of parts of a machine. **2** a system of mutually adapted parts working together in or as in a machine. **3** the mode of operation of a process. **4** *Art* mechanical execution; technique. **5** *Philos.* the doctrine that all natural phenomena, including life, allow mechanical explanation by physics and chemistry. [mod.L *mechanismus* f. Gk (as MACHINE)]

mech•a•nist /mékənist/ *n.* **1** a mechanician. **2** an expert in mechanics. **3** *Philos.* a person who holds the doctrine of mechanism. □□ **mech•a•nis•tic** /–nístik/ *adj.* **mech•a•nis•ti•cal•ly** /–nístiklee/ *adv.*

mech•a•nize /mékəniz/ *v.tr.* **1** give a mechanical character to. **2** introduce machines in. **3** *Mil.* equip with tanks, armored cars, etc. (orig. as a substitute for horse-drawn vehicles and cavalry). □□ **mech•a•ni•za•tion** *n.* **mech•a•niz•er** *n.*

mechano- /mékənō/ *comb. form* mechanical. [Gk *mēkhano-* f. *mēkhanē* machine]

mech•a•no•re•cep•tor /mékənōriséptər/ *n. Biol.* a sensory receptor that responds to mechanical stimuli such as touch or sound.

mech•a•tron•ics /mékətróniks/ *n.* the science of the combination of electronics and mechanics in developing new manufacturing techniques. [*mech*anics + elec*tronics*]

Mech•lin /méklin/ *n.* (in full **Mechlin lace**) a fine lace originally made at Mechlin (now Mechelen or Malines) in Belgium.

M.Econ. *abbr.* Master of Economics.

me•co•ni•um /mikóneeəm/ *n. Med.* a dark substance forming the first feces of a newborn infant. [L, lit. poppy juice, f. Gk *mēkónion* f. *mēkōn* poppy]

M.Ed. *abbr.* Master of Education.

Med /med/ *n.* esp. *Brit. colloq.* the Mediterranean Sea. [abbr.]

med /med/ *adj.* medical (*med school*).

med. *abbr.* **1** medium. **2** medical. **3** medicine. **4** medieval.

med•al /méd'l/ *n.* a piece of metal, usu. in the form of a disk, struck or cast with an inscription or device to commemorate an event, etc., or awarded as a distinction to a soldier, scholar, athlete, etc., for services rendered, for proficiency, etc. □□ **med•aled** *adj.* **me•dal•lic** /midálik/ *adj.* [F *médaille* f. It. *medaglia* ult. f. L *metallum* METAL]

SPELLING TIP medal/metal

A me*d*al is an awar*d*; both have a *d* in them. *T*in is a me*t*al; both have a *t*.

med•al•ist /méd'list/ *n.* (also esp. *Brit.* **med•al•list**) **1** a recipient of a (specified) medal (*gold medalist*). **2** an engraver or designer of medals.

me•dal•lion /midályən/ *n.* **1** a large medal. **2** a thing shaped like this, e.g., a decorative panel or tablet, portrait, etc. [F *médaillon* f. It. *medaglione* augment. of *medaglia* (as MEDAL)]

med•al play *n. Golf* = STROKE PLAY.

Med•al of Free•dom *n.* (also **Presidential Medal of Freedom**) medal awarded by the US president for achievement in various fields.

Med•al of Hon•or *n.* (also **Congressional Medal of Honor**) the highest US military decoration, awarded by Congress for exceptional bravery.

med•dle /méd'l/ *v.intr.* (often foll. by *with, in*) interfere in or busy oneself unduly with others' concerns. □□ **med•dler** *n.* [ME f. OF *medler*, var. of *mesler* ult. f. L *miscēre* mix]

med•dle•some /méd'lsəm/ *adj.* fond of meddling; interfering. □□ **med•dle•some•ly** *adv.* **med•dle•some•ness** *n.*

Mede /meed/ *n. hist.* a member of an Indo-European people who established an empire in Media in Persia (modern Iran) in the 7th c. BC. □□ **Me•di•an** *adj.* [ME f. L *Medi* (pl.) f. Gk *Mēdoi*]

med•e•vac /médəvak/ *n.* the evacuation of military or other casualties to the hospital in a helicopter or airplane. [from me*d*ical *evac*uation]

me•di•a[1] /méedeeə/ *n.pl.* **1** *pl.* of MEDIUM. **2** (usu. prec. by *the*) the main means of mass communication (esp. newspapers and broadcasting) regarded collectively. □ **media event** an event primarily intended to attract publicity.

▶The Latin-derived noun **medium**, 'means for distributing information,' is singular. Its plural is **media**: *The newspaper is a powerful advertising medium; The government used all media to reach voters; some media are more influential than others.* Many speakers now use the plural as singular: *The media is only as good as the integrity of the people who report the stories.*

me•di•a[2] /méedeeə/ *n.* (*pl.* **me•di•ae** /–dee-ée/) **1** *Phonet.* a voiced stop, e.g., *g*, *b*, *d*. **2** *Anat.* a middle layer of the wall of an artery or other vessel. [L, fem. of *medius* middle]

me•di•ae•val var. of MEDIEVAL.

me•di•al /méedeeəl/ *adj.* **1** situated in the middle. **2** of average size. □□ **me•di•al•ly** *adv.* [LL *medialis* f. L *medius* middle]

me•di•an /méedeeən/ *adj. & n.* ● *adj.* situated in the middle. ● *n.* **1** *Anat.* a median artery, vein, nerve, etc. **2** *Geom.* a straight line drawn from any vertex of a triangle to the middle of the opposite side. **3** *Math.* the middle value of a series of values arranged in order of size. **4** (also **median strip**) center divider separating opposing lanes on a divided highway. □□ **me•di•an•ly** *adv.* [F *mé diane* or L *medianus* (as MEDIAL)]

▶See note at MEAN[3].

me•di•ant /méedeeənt/ *n. Mus.* the third note of a diatonic scale of any key. [F *médiante* f. It. *mediante* part. of obs. *mediare* come between, f. L (as MEDIATE)]

me•di•as•ti•num /méedeeəstínəm/ *n.* (*pl.* **me•di•as•ti•na** /–nə/) *Anat.* a membranous middle septum, esp. between the lungs. □□ **me•di•as•ti•nal** *adj.* [mod.L f. med.L *mediastinus* medial, after L *mediastinus* drudge f. *medius* middle]

me•di•ate *v. & adj.* ● *v.* /méedeeayt/ **1** *intr.* (often foll. by *between*) intervene (between parties in a dispute) to produce agreement or reconciliation. **2** *tr.* be the medium for bringing about (a result) or for conveying (a gift, etc.). **3** *tr.* form a connecting link between. ● *adj.* /méedeeət/ **1** connected not directly but through some other person or thing. **2** involving an intermediate agency. □□ **me•di•ate•ly** /–ətlee/ *adv.* **me•di•a•tion** /–áyshən/ *n.* **me•di•a•tor** /méedeeaytər/ *n.* **me•di•a•to•ry** /méedeeətáwree/ *adj.* [LL *mediare mediat-* f. L *medius* middle]

med•ic[1] /médik/ *n. colloq.* a medical practitioner or student, esp. a member of a military medical corps. [L *medicus* physician f. *medēri* heal]

med•ic[2] /médik/ *n.* (also **med•ick**) any leguminous plant of the genus *Medicago*, esp. alfalfa. [ME f. L *medica* f. Gk *Mēdikē poa* Median grass]

med•i•ca•ble /médikəbəl/ *adj.* able to be treated or cured. [L *medicabilis* (as MEDICATE)]

Med•i•caid /médikayd/ *n.* a federal system of health insurance for those requiring financial assistance. [MEDICAL + AID]

med•i•cal /médikəl/ *adj. & n.* ● *adj.* **1** of or relating to the science of medicine in general. **2** of or relating to conditions requiring medical and not surgical treatment (*medical ward*). ● *n. colloq.* = MEDICAL EXAMINATION. □□ **med•i•cal•ly** *adv.* [F *médical* or med.L *medicalis* f. L *medicus*: see MEDIC[1]]

med•i•cal ex•am•in•a•tion *n.* an examination to determine a person's physical fitness.

med•i•cal ex•am•in•er *n.* a person, usu. a physician, employed by a city, county, etc., to conduct autopsies and determine the cause of death.

med•i•cal ju•ris•pru•dence *n.* the law relating to medicine.

me•dic•a•ment /médikəmənt, midíkə–/ *n.* a substance used for medical treatment. [F *médicament* or L *medicamentum* (as MEDICATE)]

Med•i•care /médikair/ *n.* US federal government program for health insurance for persons esp. over 65 years of age. [MEDICAL + CARE]

med•i•cate /médikayt/ *v.tr.* **1** treat medically. **2** impregnate with a medicinal substance. □□ **med•i•ca•tive** /médikáytiv/ *adj.* [L *medicari medicat-* administer remedies to f. *medicus*: see MEDIC[1]]

med•i•ca•tion /médikáyshən/ *n.* **1** a substance used for medical treatment. **2** treatment using drugs.

Med•i•ce•an /médichéeən, –sée–/ *adj.* of the Medici family, rulers of Florence in the 15th c. [mod.L *Mediceus* f. It. *Medici*]

me•dic•i•nal /mədísinəl/ *adj. & n.* ● *adj.* (of a substance) having healing properties. ● *n.* a medicinal substance. □□ **me•dic•i•nal•ly** *adv.* [ME f. OF f. L *medicinalis* (as MEDICINE)]

med•i•cine /médisin/ *n.* **1** the science or practice of the diagnosis, treatment, and prevention of disease, esp. as distinct from surgical methods. **2** any drug or preparation used for the treatment or prevention of disease, esp. one taken by mouth. **3** a spell, charm, or fetish which is thought to cure afflictions. □ **a dose** (or **taste**) **of one's own medicine** treatment such as one is accustomed to giving others. **take one's medicine** submit to something disagreeable. [ME f. OF *medecine* f. L *medicina* f. *medicus*: see MEDIC[1]]

med•i•cine ball *n.* a stuffed leather ball thrown and caught for exercise.

med·i·cine man *n.* a person believed to have magical powers of healing, esp. among Native Americans.

med·i·cine show *n.* a traveling show offering entertainment to entice a crowd to whom patent medicines, etc., would be sold.

med·ick var. of MEDIC[2].

med·i·co /médikō/ *n.* (*pl.* **·cos**) *colloq.* a medical practitioner or student. [It. f. L (as MEDIC[1])]

medico- /médikō/ *comb. form* medical; medical and (*medicolegal*). [L *medicus* (as MEDIC[1])]

me·di·e·val /méedee-éevəl, méd–, míd–/ *adj.* (also **me·di·ae·val**) **1** of, or in the style of, the Middle Ages. **2** *colloq.* old-fashioned, archaic. □ **medieval history** the history of the 5th– 15th c. **medieval Latin** Latin of about AD 600–1500. □□ **me·di·e·val·ism** *n.* **me·di·e·val·ist** *n.* **me·di·e·val·ize** *v.tr. & intr.* **me·di·e·val·ly** *adv.* [mod.L *medium aevum* f. L *medius* middle + *aevum* age]

me·di·o·cre /méedeeókər/ *adj.* **1** of middling quality, neither good nor bad. **2** second-rate. [F *médiocre* or f. L *mediocris* of middle height or degree f. *medius* middle + *ocris* rugged mountain]

me·di·oc·ri·ty /méedeeókritee/ *n.* (*pl.* **·ties**) **1** the state of being mediocre. **2** a mediocre person or thing.

med·i·tate /méditayt/ *v.* **1** *intr.* **a** exercise the mind in (esp. religious) contemplation. **b** (usu. foll. by *on, upon*) focus on a subject in this manner. **2** *tr.* plan mentally; design. □□ **med·i·ta·tion** /–táyshən/ *n.* **med·i·ta·tor** *n.* [L *meditari* contemplate]

med·i·ta·tive /méditaytiv/ *adj.* **1** inclined to meditate. **2** indicative of meditation. □□ **med·i·ta·tive·ly** *adv.* **med·i·ta·tive·ness** *n.*

Med·i·ter·ra·ne·an /méditərάyneeən/ *n. & adj.* **1** a large land-locked sea bordered by S. Europe, SW Asia, and N. Africa. **2** a native of a country bordering on the Mediterranean Sea. • *adj.* **1** of or characteristic of the Mediterranean or its surrounding region (*Mediterranean climate*; *Mediterranean cooking*). **2** (of a person) dark-complexioned and not tall. [L *mediterraneus* inland f. *medius* middle + *terra* land]

me·di·um /méé deeəm/ *n. & adj.* • *n.* (*pl.* **me·di·a** or **me·di·ums**) **1** the middle quality, degree, etc., between extremes (*find a happy medium*). **2** the means by which something is communicated (*the medium of sound*; *the medium of television*). **3** the intervening substance through which impressions are conveyed to the senses, etc. (*light passing from one medium into another*). **4** *Biol.* the physical environment or conditions of growth, storage, or transport of a living organism (*the shape of a fish is ideal for its fluid medium*; *growing mold on the surface of a medium*). **5** an agency or means of doing something (*the medium through which money is raised*). **6** the material or form used by an artist, composer, etc. (*language as an artistic medium*). **7** the liquid (e.g., oil or gel) with which pigments are mixed for use in painting. **8** (*pl.* **me·di·ums**) a person claiming to be in contact with the spirits of the dead and to communicate between the dead and the living. • *adj.* **1** between two qualities, degrees, etc. **2** average; moderate (*of medium height*). □□ **me·di·um·ism** *n.* (in sense 8 of *n.*). **me·di·um·is·tic** /–mí stik/ *adj.* (in sense 8 of *n.*). **me·di·um·ship** *n.* (in sense 8 of *n.*). [L, = middle, neut. of *medius*]

▶See note at MEDIA.

me·di·um fre·quen·cy *n.* a radio frequency between 300 kHz and 3 MHz.

me·di·um of cir·cu·la·tion *n.* something that serves as an instrument of commercial transactions, e.g., coin.

med·lar /médlər/ *n.* **1** a rosaceous tree, *Mespilus germanica*, bearing small brown applelike fruits. **2** the fruit of this tree that is eaten when decayed. [ME f. OF *medler* f. L *mespila* f. Gk *mespilē, –on*]

med·ley /médlee/ *n., adj., & v.* • *n.* (*pl.* **·leys**) **1** a varied mixture; a miscellany. **2** a collection of songs, parts of songs, or other musical items from one work or various sources performed as a continuous piece (*a medley of Beatles songs*). • *adj. archaic* mixed; motley. • *v.tr.* (**·leys**, **·leyed**) *archaic* make a medley of; intermix. [ME f. OF *medlee* var. of *meslee* f. Rmc (as MEDDLE)]

med·ley re·lay *n.* a relay race between teams in which each member runs a different distance, swims a different stroke, etc.

Me·doc /maydók/ *n.* a fine red claret from the Médoc region of SW France.

me·dul·la /midúlə/ *n.* **1** the inner region of certain organs or tissues, usu. when it is distinguishable from the outer region or cortex, as in hair or a kidney. **2** the myelin layer of certain nerve fibers. **3** the soft internal tissue of plants. □□ **med·ul·lar·y** /méd'léree, mejə–, mədúləree/ *adj.* [L, = pith, marrow, prob. rel. to *medius* middle]

me·dul·la ob·long·a·ta *n.* /óblonggáátə/ the continuation of the spinal cord within the skull, forming the lowest part of the brain stem.

me·du·sa /midóósə, –zə, –dyóő–/ *n.* (*pl.* **me·du·sae** /–see/ or **me·du·sas**) **1** a jellyfish. **2** a free-swimming form of any coelenterate, having tentacles around the edge of a usu. umbrella-shaped jellylike body, e.g., a jellyfish. □□ **me·du·san** *adj.* [L f. Gk *Medousa*, name of a Gorgon with snakes instead of hair]

meed /meed/ *n. literary* or *archaic* **1** reward. **2** merited portion (of praise, etc.). [OE *mēd* f. WG, rel. to Goth. *mizdō*, Gk *misthos* reward]

meek /meek/ *adj.* **1** humble and submissive; suffering injury, etc.,

tamely. **2** piously gentle in nature. □□ **meek·ly** *adv.* **meek·ness** *n.* [ME *me(o)c* f. ON *mjúkr* soft, gentle]

meer·kat /méerkat/ *n.* the suricate. [Du., = sea cat]

meer·schaum /méershəm, –shawm/ *n.* **1** a soft white form of hydrated magnesium silicate, found chiefly in Turkey, which resembles clay. **2** a tobacco pipe with the bowl made from this. [G, = sea foam f. *Meer* sea + *Schaum* foam, transl. Pers. *kef-i-daryā*, with ref. to its frothiness]

meet[1] /meet/ *v. & n.* • *v.* (*past* and *past part.* **met** /met/) **1 a** *tr.* encounter (a person or persons) by accident or design; come face to face with. **b** *intr.* (of two or more people) come into each other's company by accident or design (*decided to meet on the bridge*). **2** *tr.* go to a place to be present at the arrival of (a person, train, etc.). **3** *a tr.* (of a moving object, line, feature of landscape, etc.) come together or into contact with (*where the road meets the river*). **b** *intr.* come together or into contact with (*where the sea and the sky meet*). **4** *a tr.* make the acquaintance of (*delighted to meet you*). **b** *intr.* (of two or more people) make each other's acquaintance. **5** *intr. & tr.* come together or come into contact with for the purposes of conference, business, worship, etc. (*the committee meets every week*; *the union met management yesterday*). **6** *tr.* **a** (of a person or a group) deal with or answer (a demand, objection, etc.) (*met the original proposal with hostility*). **b** satisfy or conform with (proposals, deadlines, a person, etc.) (*agreed to meet the new terms*; *did my best to meet them on that point*). **7** *tr.* pay (a bill, etc.); provide the funds required by (*meet the cost of the move*). **8** *tr. &* (foll. by *with*) *intr.* experience, encounter, or receive (success, disaster, a difficulty, etc.) (*met their death*; *met with many problems*). **9** *tr.* oppose in battle, contest, or confrontation. • *n.* **1** the assembly of competitors for various sporting activities, as track, swimming, etc. **2** the assembly of riders and hounds for a hunt. □ **make ends meet** see END. **meet the eye** (or **the ear**) be visible (or audible). **meet a person's eye** check if another person is watching and look into his or her eyes in return. **meet a person halfway** make a compromise, respond in a friendly way to the advances of another person. **meet up** *colloq.* happen to meet. **meet with** receive (a reaction) (*met with the committee's approval*). **more than meets the eye** possessing hidden qualities or complications. □□ **meet·er** *n.* [OE *mētan* f. Gmc: cf. MOOT]

meet[2] /meet/ *adj. archaic* suitable; fit; proper. □□ **meet·ly** *adv.* **meet·ness** *n.* [ME (*i*)*mete* repr. OE *gemēte* f. Gmc, rel. to METE[1]]

meet·ing /méeting/ *n.* **1** in senses of MEET[1]. **2** an assembly of people, esp. the members of a society, committee, etc., for discussion or entertainment. **3** an assembly (esp. of Quakers) for worship. **4** the persons assembled (*address the meeting*).

meet·ing·house /méetinghows/ *n.* a place of worship, esp. of Quakers, etc.

meet·ing of minds *n.* accord; agreement.

meg·a /mégə/ *adj. & adv. sl.* • *adj.* **1** excellent. **2** enormous. • *adv.* extremely. [Gk f. as MEGA–]

mega- /mégə/ *comb. form* **1** large. **2** denoting a factor of one million (10[6]) in the metric system of measurement. ¶ Abbr.: **M**. [Gk f. *megas* great]

meg·a·buck /mégəbuk/ *n.* (usu. **megabucks**) *colloq.* **1** a million dollars. **2** great sums of money.

meg·a·byte /mégəbit/ *n. Computing* 1,048,576 (i.e., 2[20]) bytes as a measure of data capacity, or loosely 1,000,000 bytes. ¶ Abbr.: **MB**.

meg·a·death /mégədeth/ *n.* the death of one million people (esp. as a unit in estimating the casualties of war).

meg·a·hertz /mégəhərts/ *n.* one million hertz, esp. as a measure of frequency of radio transmissions. ¶ Abbr.: **MHz**.

meg·a·lith /mégəlith/ *n. Archaeol.* a large stone, esp. one placed upright as a monument or part of one. [MEGA- + Gk *lithos* stone]

meg·a·lith·ic /mégəlíthik/ *adj. Archaeol.* made of or marked by the use of large stones.

megalo- /mégəlō/ *comb. form* great (*megalomania*). [Gk f. *megas megal-* great]

meg·a·lo·ma·ni·a /mégəlōmáyneeə/ *n.* **1** a mental disorder producing delusions of grandeur. **2** a passion for grandiose schemes. □□ **meg·a·lo·ma·ni·ac** *adj. & n.* **meg·a·lo·ma·ni·a·cal** /–məníəkəl/ *adj.* **meg·a·lo·man·ic** /–mánik/ *adj.*

meg·a·lop·o·lis /mégəlópəlis/ *n.* **1** a great city or its way of life. **2** an urban complex consisting of a city and its environs. □□ **meg·a·lo·pol·i·tan** /–ləpólit'n/ *adj. & n.* [MEGA- ;pl Gk *polis* city]

meg·a·lo·sau·rus /mégələsáwrəs/ *n.* a large flesh-eating dinosaur of the genus *Megalosaurus*, with stout hind legs and small forelimbs. [MEGALO- + Gk *sauros* lizard]

meg·a·phone /mégəfōn/ *n.* a large funnel-shaped device for amplifying the sound of the voice.

megaphone

meg·a·plex /mégəpleks/ *n.* a complex of movie theaters in a single facility, offering a variety of different feature-length films at any one time.

meg·a·pode /mégəpōd/ *n.* (also **meg·a·pod** /–pod/) any bird of the family Megapodidae, native to Australasia, that builds a mound of debris for the incubation of its eggs, e.g., a mallee fowl. [mod.L *Megapodius* (genus name) formed as MEGA- + Gk *pous podos* foot]

meg·a·ron /mégəron/ *n.* the central hall of a large Mycenaean house. [Gk, = hall]

meg·a·spore /mégəspawr/ *n.* the larger of the two kinds of spores produced by some ferns (cf. MICROSPORE).

meg·a·star /mégəstaar/ *n.* a very famous person, esp. in the world of entertainment.

meg·a·ton /mégətun/ *n.* a unit of explosive power equal to one million tons of TNT.

meg·a·volt /mégəvōlt/ *n.* one million volts, esp. as a unit of electromotive force. ¶ Abbr.: **MV**.

meg·a·watt /mégəwot/ *n.* one million watts, esp. as a measure of electrical power as generated by power stations. ¶ Abbr.: **MW**.

me·gilp /məgílp/ *n.* (also **ma·gilp**) a mixture of mastic resin and linseed oil, added to oil paints, much used in the 19th c. [18th c.: orig. unkn.]

meg·ohm /mégōm/ *n. Electr.* one million ohms. [MEGA- + OHM]

me·grim[1] /méegrim/ *n.* **1** *archaic* migraine. **2** a whim, a fancy. **3** (in *pl.*) **a** a depression; low spirits. **b** vertigo in horses, etc. [ME *mygrane* f. OF MIGRAINE]

me·grim[2] /mégrim/ *n.* any deepwater flatfish of the family *Lepidorhombus*, esp. *L. whiffiagonis*. Also called **sail fluke**. [19th c.: orig. unkn.]

mei·o·sis /mīṓsis/ *n.* **1** *Biol.* a type of cell division in reproductive cells (e.g., egg or sperm) that results in daughter cells with half the chromosome number of the parent cell (cf. MITOSIS). **2** = LITOTES. □□ **mei·ot·ic** /mīótik/ *adj.* **mei·ot·i·cal·ly** /mīótiklee/ *adv.* [mod.L f. Gk *meiōsis* f. *meioō* lessen f. *meiōn* less]

Meis·sen /mísən/ *n.* a hard-paste porcelain made since 1710. [*Meissen* near Dresden in Germany]

Mei·ster·sing·er /místərsingər/ *n.* (*pl.* same) a member of one of the 14th–16th-c. German guilds for lyric poets and musicians. [G f. *Meister* MASTER + *Singer* singer (see SING)]

meit·ner·i·um /mītnəreeəm/ *n. Chem.* an artificially produced chemical element, atomic number 109. ¶ Symb.: **Mt**. [for Austrian physicist Lise *Meitner* (1878–1968)]

mel·a·mine /méləmeen/ *n.* **1** a white crystalline compound that can be copolymerized with methanal to give thermosetting resins. **2** (in full **melamine resin**) a plastic made from melamine and used esp. for laminated coatings. [*melam* (arbitrary) + AMINE]

mel·an·cho·li·a /mélənkóleeə/ *n.* a mental condition marked by depression and ill-grounded fears. [LL: see MELANCHOLY]

mel·an·chol·y /mélənkolee/ *n. & adj.* • *n.* (*pl.* **-ies**) **1** a pensive sadness. **2** a mental depression. **b** a habitual or constitutional tendency to this. **3** *hist.* one of the four humors; black bile (see HUMOR *n.* 5). • *adj.* (of a person) sad, gloomy; (of a thing) saddening, depressing; (of words, a tune, etc.) expressing sadness. □□ **mel·an·chol·ic** /–kólik/ *adj.* **mel·an·chol·i·cal·ly** /–kóliklee/ *adv.* [ME f. OF *melancolie* f. LL *melancholia* f. Gk *melagkholia* f. *melas melanos* black + *kholē* bile]

Mel·a·ne·sian /mélənéezhən, –shən/ *n. & adj.* • *n.* **1** a member of the dominant Negroid people of Melanesia, an island group in the W. Pacific. **2** the language of this people. • *adj.* of or relating to this people or their language. [*Melanesia* f. Gk *melas* black + *nēsos* island]

mé·lange /maylóNzh/ *n.* a mixture, a medley. [F f. *mêler* mix (as MEDDLE)]

mel·a·nin /mélənin/ *n.* a dark-brown to black pigment occurring in the hair, skin, and iris of the eye that is responsible for tanning of the skin when exposed to sunlight. [Gk *melas melanos* black + –IN]

mel·a·nism /mélənizəm/ *n.* an unusual darkening of body tissues caused by excessive production of melanin.

mel·a·no·ma /mélənṓmə/ *n.* a malignant tumor of melanin-forming cells, usu. in the skin. [MELANIN + –OMA]

mel·a·no·sis /mélənṓsis/ *n.* **1** = MELANISM. **2** a disorder in the body's production of melanin. □□ **mel·a·not·ic** /–nótik/ *adj.* [mod.L f. Gk (as MELANIN)]

mel·a·to·nin /mélətṓnin/ *n.* a hormone secreted by the pineal gland that inhibits melanin formation.

Mel·ba /mélbə/ *n.* □ **do a Melba** *Austral. sl.* **1** return from retirement. **2** make several farewell appearances. [Dame Nellie *Melba*, Austral. operatic soprano d. 1931]

Mel·ba sauce *n.* a sauce made from puréed raspberries thickened with confectioners' sugar.

Mel·ba toast *n.* very thin crisp toast.

meld[1] /meld/ *v. & n.* • *v.tr.* (also *absol.*) (in rummy, canasta, etc.) lay down or declare (one's cards) in order to score points. • *n.* a completed set or run of cards in any of these games. [G *melden* announce]

meld[2] /meld/ *v.tr. & intr.* merge, blend, combine. [perh. f. MELT + WELD[1]]

me·lee /máyláy/ *n.* (also **mê·lée**) **1** a confused fight, skirmish, or scuffle. **2** a muddle. [F (as MEDLEY)]

mel·ic /mélik/ *adj.* (of a poem, esp. a Gk lyric) meant to be sung. [L *melicus* f. Gk *melikos* f. *melos* song]

mel·io·rate /méelyərayt, méeleeə–/ *v.tr. & intr. literary* improve (cf. AMELIORATE). □□ **mel·io·ra·tion** /–ráyshən/ *n.* **mel·io·ra·tive** /–ráytiv, –rətiv/ *adj.* [LL *meliorare* (as MELIORISM)]

mel·io·rism /méelyərizəm, méeleeə–/ *n.* a doctrine that the world may be made better by human effort. □□ **mel·io·rist** *n.* [L *melior* better + –ISM]

me·lis·ma /milízmə/ *n.* (*pl.* **me·lis·ma·ta** /–mətə/ or **me·lis·mas**) *Mus.* a group of notes sung to one syllable of text. □□ **mel·is·mat·ic** /–mátik/ *adj.* [Gk]

mel·lif·er·ous /məlífərəs/ *adj.* yielding or producing honey. [L *mellifer* f. *mel* honey]

mel·lif·lu·ous /məlíflōōəs/ *adj.* (of a voice or words) pleasing, musical, flowing. □□ **mel·lif·lu·ence** *n.* **mel·lif·lu·ent** *adj.* **mel·lif·lu·ous·ly** *adv.* **mel·lif·lu·ous·ness** *n.* [ME f. OF *melliflue* or LL *mellifluus* f. *mel* honey + *fluere* flow]

mel·low /mélō/ *adj. & v.* • *adj.* **1** (of sound, color, light) soft and rich, free from harshness. **2** (of character) softened or matured by age or experience. **3** genial, jovial. **4** partly intoxicated. **5** (of fruit) soft, sweet, and juicy. **6** (of wine) well-matured, smooth. **7** (of earth) rich, loamy. • *v.tr. & intr.* make or become mellow. □ **mellow out** *sl.* relax. □□ **mel·low·ly** *adv.* **mel·low·ness** *n.* [ME, perh. f. attrib. use of OE *melu, melw-* MEAL[2]]

me·lo·de·on /məlṓdeeən/ *n.* (also **me·lo·di·on**) **1** a small organ popular in the 19th c., similar to the harmonium. **2** a small German accordion, played esp. by folk musicians. [MELODY + HARMONIUM with Graecized ending]

me·lod·ic /məlódik/ *adj.* **1** of or relating to melody. **2** having or producing melody. □□ **me·lod·i·cal·ly** *adv.* [F *mélodique* f. LL *melodicus* f. Gk *melōidikos* (as MELODY)]

me·lod·ic mi·nor *n.* a scale with the sixth and seventh degrees raised when ascending and lowered when descending.

me·lo·di·ous /məlṓdeeəs/ *adj.* **1** of, producing, or having melody. **2** sweet-sounding. □□ **me·lo·di·ous·ly** *adv.* **me·lo·di·ous·ness** *n.* [ME f. OF *melodieus* (as MELODY)]

mel·o·dist /mélədist/ *n.* **1** a composer of melodies. **2** a singer.

mel·o·dize /mélədīz/ *v.* **1** *intr.* make a melody or melodies; make sweet music. **2** *tr.* make melodious. □□ **mel·o·diz·er** *n.*

mel·o·dra·ma /mélədraamə, –dramə/ *n.* **1** a sensational dramatic piece with exaggerated characters and exciting events intended to appeal to the emotions. **2** the genre of drama of this type. **3** language, behavior, or an occurrence suggestive of this. **4** *hist.* a play with songs interspersed and with orchestral music accompanying the action. □□ **mel·o·dra·mat·ic** /–drəmátik/ *adj.* **mel·o·dra·mat·i·cal·ly** /–drəmátiklee/ *adv.* **mel·o·dra·ma·tist** /–drámətist/ *n.* **mel·o·dram·a·tize** /–drámətīz/ *v.tr.* [earlier *melodrame* f. F *mélodrame* f. Gk *melos* music + F *drame* DRAMA]

mel·o·dra·mat·ics /mélədrəmátiks/ *n.pl.* melodramatic behavior, action, or writing.

mel·o·dy /mélədee/ *n.* (*pl.* **-dies**) **1** an arrangement of single notes in a musically expressive succession. **2** the principal part in harmonized music. **3** a musical arrangement of words. **4** sweet music, tunefulness. [ME f. OF *melodie* f. LL *melodia* f. Gk *melōidia* f. *melos* song]

mel·on /mélən/ *n.* **1** the sweet fruit of various gourds. **2** the gourd producing this (*honeydew melon; watermelon*). [ME f. OF f. LL *melo –onis* abbr. of L *melopepo* f. Gk *mēlopepōn* f. *mēlon* apple + *pepōn* gourd f. *pepōn* ripe]

melt[1] /melt/ *v. & n.* • *v.* **1** *intr.* become liquefied by heat. **2** *tr.* change to a liquid condition by heat. **3** *tr.* (as **molten** *adj.*) (usu. of materials that require a great deal of heat to melt) liquefied by heat (*molten lava; molten lead*). **4 a** *intr. & tr.* dissolve. **b** *intr.* (of food) be easily dissolved in the mouth. **5** *intr.* **a** (of a person, feelings, the heart, etc.) be softened as a result of pity, love, etc. **b** dissolve into tears. **6** *tr.* soften (a person, feelings, the heart, etc.) (*a look to melt a heart of stone*). **7** *intr.* (usu. foll. by *into*) change or merge imperceptibly into another form or state (*night melted into dawn*). **8** *intr.* (often foll. by *away*) (of a person) leave or disappear unobtrusively (*melted into the background; melted away into the crowd*). **9** *intr.* (usu. as **melting** *adj.*) (of sound) be soft and liquid (*melting chords*). **10** *intr. colloq.* (of a person) suffer extreme heat (*I'm melting in this thick sweater*). • *n.* **1** liquid metal, etc. **2** an amount melted at any one time. **3** the process or an instance of melting. □ **melt away** disappear or make disappear by liquefaction. **melt down** **1** melt (esp. metal articles) in order to reuse the raw material. **2** become liquid and lose structure (cf. MELTDOWN). □□ **melt·a·ble** *adj. & n.* **melt·er** *n.* **melt·ing·ly** *adv.* [OE *meltan, mieltan* f. Gmc, rel. to MALT]

melt[2] /melt/ *n.* (also **milt**) the spleen in mammals, esp. cows, pigs, and other livestock.

melt·down /méltdown/ *n.* **1** the melting of (and consequent damage to) a structure, esp. the overheated core of a nuclear reactor. **2** a disastrous event, esp. a rapid fall in share prices.

melt·ing point *n.* the temperature at which any given solid will melt.

melt·ing pot *n.* **1** a pot in which metals, etc., are melted and mixed. **2** a place where races, theories, etc., are mixed, or an imaginary pool where ideas are mixed together.

mel·ton /méltən/ *n.* cloth with a close-cut nap, used for overcoats, etc. [*Melton Mowbray* in central England]

melt·wa·ter /méltwawtər/ *n.* water formed by the melting of snow and ice, esp. from a glacier.

mem·ber /mémbər/ *n.* **1** a person, animal, plant, etc., belonging to a society, team, taxonomic group, etc. **2** a person formally elected to take part in the proceedings of certain organizations (*Member of Congress*). **3** (also *attrib.*) a part or branch of a political body (*member state; a member of the United Nations*). **4** a constituent portion of a complex structure. **5** a part of a sentence, equation, group of figures, mathematical set, etc. **6 a** any part or organ of the body, esp. a limb. **b** = PENIS. □□ **mem·bered** *adj.* (also in *comb.*). **mem·ber·less** *adj.* [ME f. OF *membre* f. L *membrum* limb]

mem·ber·ship /mémbərship/ *n.* **1** being a member. **2** the number of members. **3** the body of members.

mem·brane /mémbrayn/ *n.* **1** any pliable sheetlike structure acting as a boundary, lining, or partition in an organism. **2** a thin pliable sheet or skin of various kinds. □□ **mem·bra·na·ceous** /–brənáyshəs/ *adj.* **mem·bran·e·ous** /–bráyneeəs/ *adj.* **mem·bra·nous** /–brənəs/ *adj.* [L *membrana* skin of body, parchment (as MEMBER)]

me·men·to /miméntō/ *n.* (*pl.* **·tos** or **·toes**) an object kept as a reminder or a souvenir of a person or an event. [L, imper. of *meminisse* remember]

me·men·to mo·ri /məméntō máwree, –rí/ *n.* (*pl.* same) a warning or reminder of death (e.g., a skull). [L, = remember you must die]

mem·o /mémō/ *n.* (*pl.* **·os**) *colloq.* memorandum. [abbr.]

mem·oir /mémwaar/ *n.* **1** a historical account or biography written from personal knowledge or special sources. **2** (in *pl.*) an autobiography or a written account of one's memory of certain events or people. **3 a** an essay on a learned subject specially studied by the writer. **b** (in *pl.*) the proceedings or transactions of a learned society (*Memoirs of the American Mathematical Society*). □□ **mem·oir·ist** *n.* [F *mémoire* (masc.), special use of *mémoire* (fem.) MEMORY]

mem·o·ra·bil·i·a /mémərəbileeə, –bílyə/ *n.pl.* **1** souvenirs of memorable events. **2** *archaic* memorable or noteworthy things. [L, neut. pl. (as MEMORABLE)]

mem·o·ra·ble /mémərəbəl/ *adj.* **1** worth remembering, not to be forgotten. **2** easily remembered. □□ **mem·o·ra·bil·i·ty** /–bílitee/ *n.* **mem·o·ra·ble·ness** *n.* **mem·o·ra·bly** *adv.* [ME f. F *mémorable* or L *memorabilis* f. *memorare* bring to mind f. *memor* mindful]

mem·o·ran·dum /mémərándəm/ *n.* (*pl.* **mem·o·ran·da** /–də/ or **mem·o·ran·dums**) **1** a note or record made for future use. **2** an informal written message, esp. in business, diplomacy, etc. **3** *Law* a document recording the terms of a contract or other legal details. [ME f. L neut. sing. gerundive of *memorare*: see MEMORABLE]

me·mo·ri·al /məmáwreeəl/ *n. & adj.* ● *n.* **1** an object, institution, or custom established in memory of a person or event (*the Albert Memorial*). **2** (often in *pl.*) *hist.* a statement of facts as the basis of a petition, etc.; a record; an informal diplomatic paper. ● *adj.* intending to commemorate a person or thing (*memorial service*). □□ **me·mo·ri·al·ist** *n.* [ME f. OF *memorial* or L *memorialis* (as MEMORY)]

Me·mo·ri·al Day *n.* (in the US) a holiday on which those who died in war are remembered, usu. the last Monday in May.

me·mo·ri·al·ize /məmáwreeəlíz/ *v.tr.* **1** commemorate. **2** address a memorial to (a person or body).

mem·o·rize /méməríz/ *v.tr.* commit to memory. □□ **mem·o·riz·a·ble** *adj.* **mem·o·ri·za·tion** *n.* **mem·o·riz·er** *n.*

mem·o·ry /méməree/ *n.* (*pl.* **·ries**) **1** the faculty by which things are recalled to or kept in the mind. **2 a** this faculty in an individual (*my memory is beginning to fail*). **b** one's store of things remembered (*buried deep in my memory*). **3** a recollection or remembrance (*the memory of better times*). **4** the storage capacity of a computer or other electronic machinery. **5** the remembrance of a person or thing (*his mother's memory haunted him*). **6 a** the reputation of a dead person (*his memory lives on*). **b** in formulaic phrases used of a dead sovereign, etc. (*of blessed memory*). **7** the length of time over which the memory or memories of any given person or group extends (*within living memory; within the memory of anyone still working here*). **8** the act of remembering (*a deed worthy of memory*). □ **commit to memory** learn (a thing) so as to be able to recall it. **from memory** without verification in books, etc. **in memory of** to keep alive the remembrance of. [ME f. OF *memorie, memoire* f. L *memoria* f. *memor* mindful, remembering, rel. to MOURN]

mem·o·ry lane *n.* (usu. prec. by *down, along*) an imaginary and sentimental journey into the past.

mem·sa·hib /mémsaa-íb, –saáb/ *n. Anglo-Ind. hist.* form of address for a European married woman in India. [MA'AM + SAHIB]

men *pl.* of MAN.

men·ace /ménis/ *n. & v.* ● *n.* **1** a threat. **2** a dangerous or obnoxious

thing or person. **3** *joc.* a pest, a nuisance. ● *v.tr. & intr.* threaten, esp. in a malignant or hostile manner. □□ **men·ac·er** *n.* **men·ac·ing** *adj.* **men·ac·ing·ly** *adv.* [ME ult. f. L *minax –acis* threatening f. *minari* threaten]

mé·nage /maynaázh/ *n.* the members of a household. [OF *manaige* ult. f. L (as MANSION)]

mé·nage à trois /maynaázh aa trwaá/ *n.* an arrangement in which three people live together, usu. a married couple and the lover of one of them. [F, = household of three (as MÉNAGE)]

me·nag·er·ie /mənájəree, –názh–/ *n.* **1** a collection of wild animals in captivity for exhibition, etc. **2** the place where these are housed. [F *ménagerie* (as MÉNAGE)]

men·ar·che /menáarkee/ *n.* the onset of first menstruation. [mod.L formed as MENO- + Gk *arkhē* beginning]

mend /mend/ *v. & n.* ● *v.* **1** *tr.* restore to a sound condition; repair (a broken article, a damaged road, torn clothes, etc.). **2** *intr.* regain health; heal (as a bone). **3** *tr.* improve (*mend matters*). **4** *tr.* add fuel to (a fire). ● *n.* a darn or repair in material, etc. (*a mend in my shirt*). □ **mend one's fences** make peace with a person. **mend one's ways** reform, improve one's habits. **on the mend** improving in health or condition. □□ **mend·a·ble** *adj.* **mend·er** *n.* [ME f. AF *mender* f. *amender* AMEND]

men·da·cious /mendáyshəs/ *adj.* lying, untruthful. □□ **men·da·cious·ly** *adv.* **men·da·cious·ness** *n.* **men·dac·i·ty** /–dásitee/ *n.* (*pl.* **·ties**). [L *mendax –dacis* perh. f. *mendum* fault]

men·de·le·vi·um /méndəleeveeəm/ *n. Chem.* an artificially made transuranic radioactive metallic element. ¶ Symb.: **Md**. [D. I. *Mendeleev*, Russ. chemist d. 1907]

Men·del·ism /méndəlizəm/ *n.* the theory of heredity based on the recurrence of certain inherited characteristics transmitted by genes. □□ **Men·de·li·an** /–deéleeən/ *adj. & n.* [G. J. *Mendel*, Austrian botanist d. 1884 + –ISM]

men·di·cant /méndikənt/ *adj. & n.* ● *adj.* **1** begging. **2** (of a friar) living solely on alms. ● *n.* **1** a beggar. **2** a mendicant friar. □□ **men·di·can·cy** *n.* **men·dic·i·ty** /–dísitee/ *n.* [L *mendicare* beg f. *mendicus* beggar f. *mendum* fault]

mend·ing /ménding/ *n.* **1** the action of a person who mends. **2** things, esp. clothes, to be mended.

men·folk /ménfōk/ *n.pl.* **1** men in general. **2** the men of one's family.

men·ha·den /menháyd'n/ *n.* (*pl.* same) any large herringlike fish of the genus *Brevoortia*, of the E. coast of N. America, yielding valuable oil and used for manure. [Algonquian: cf. Narragansett *munnawhatteaûg*]

men·hir /ménheer/ *n. Archaeol.* a tall upright usu. prehistoric monumental stone. [Breton *men* stone + *hir* long]

me·ni·al /meéneeəl/ *adj. & n.* ● *adj.* **1** (esp. of unskilled domestic work) degrading, servile. **2** usu. *derog.* (of a servant) domestic. ● *n.* **1** a menial servant. **2** a servile person. □□ **me·ni·al·ly** *adv.* [ME f. OF *meinee* household]

men·in·gi·tis /méninjítis/ *n.* an inflammation of the meninges due to infection by viruses or bacteria. □□ **men·in·git·ic** /–jítik/ *adj.*

me·ninx /meéningks/ *n.* (*pl.* **me·nin·ges** /mənínjeez/) (usu. in *pl.*) any of the three membranes that line the skull and vertebral canal and enclose the brain and spinal cord (dura mater, arachnoid, pia mater). □□ **me·nin·ge·al** /minínjeeəl/ *adj.* [mod.L f. Gk *mēnigx –iggos* membrane]

me·nis·cus /mənískəs/ *n.* (*pl.* **me·nis·ci** /–nísī/ or **me·nis·cus·es**) **1** *Physics* the curved upper surface of a liquid in a tube. **2** a lens that is convex on one side and concave on the other. **3** *Math.* a crescent-shaped figure. **4** *Anat.* a cartilaginous disk within a joint, esp. the knee. □□ **me·nis·coid** *adj.* [mod.L f. Gk *mēniskos* crescent, dimin. of *mēnē* moon]

Men·non·ite /ménənīt/ *n.* a member of a Protestant sect originating in Friesland in the 16th c., emphasizing adult baptism and rejecting church organization, military service, and public office. [*Menno* Simons, its founder, d. 1561]

meno- /ménō/ *comb. form* menstruation. [Gk *mēn mēnos* month]

me·nol·o·gy /minóləjee/ *n.* (*pl.* **·gies**) a calendar, esp. that of the Greek Church, with biographies of the saints. [mod.L *menologium* f. eccl.Gk *mēnologion* f. *mēn* month + *logos* account]

men·o·pause /ménəpawz/ *n.* **1** the ceasing of menstruation. **2** the period in a woman's life (usu. between 45 and 50) when this occurs (see also MALE MENOPAUSE). □□ **men·o·pau·sal** /–páwzəl/ *adj.* [mod.L *menopausis* (as MENO-, PAUSE)]

me·nor·ah /mənáwrə, –nórə/ *n.* a candelabrum used in Jewish worship, originally one with seven branches, now often replicated as a nine-branched candelabrum used at Hanukkah. [Heb., = candlestick]

menorah

men·or·rha·gi·a /ménəráyjeeə/ *n.* abnormally heavy bleeding at menstruation. [MENO- + stem of Gk *rhēgnumi* burst]

men·ses /ménseez/ *n.pl.* **1** blood and other materials discharged from the uterus at menstruation. **2** the time of menstruation. [L, pl. of *mensis* month]

Men·she·vik /ménshəvik/ *n. hist.* a member of the non-Leninist wing of the Russian Social Democratic Workers' Party (cf. BOLSHEVIK). [Russ. *Men'shevik* a member of the minority (*men'she* less)]

mens rea /menz reeə/ *n.* criminal intent; the knowledge of wrongdoing. [L, = guilty mind]

men·stru·al /ménstrŏŏəl/ *adj.* of or relating to the menses or menstruation. [ME f. L *menstrualis* f. *mensis* month]

men·stru·al cy·cle *n.* the process of ovulation and menstruation in woman and othe female primates.

men·stru·ate /ménstrŏŏ-ayt/ *v.intr.* undergo menstruation. [LL *menstruare menstruat-* (as MENSTRUAL)]

men·stru·a·tion /ménstrŏŏ-áyshən/ *n.* the process of discharging blood and other materials from the uterus in sexually mature nonpregnant women at intervals of about one lunar month until the menopause.

men·stru·ous /ménstrŏŏəs/ *adj.* **1** of or relating to the menses. **2** menstruating. [ME f. OF *menstrueus* or LL *menstruosus* (as MENSTRUAL)]

men·stru·um /ménstrŏŏəm/ *n.* (*pl.* **men·stru·ums** or **men·stru·a** /-strŏŏə/) a solvent. [ME f. L, neut. of *menstruus* monthly f. *mensis* month f. the alchemical parallel between transmutation into gold and the supposed action of menses on the ovum]

men·sur·a·ble /ménshərəbəl, -sŏ-/ *adj.* **1** measurable, having fixed limits. **2** *Mus.* = MENSURAL 2. [F *mensurable* or LL *mensurabilis* f. *mensurare* to measure f. L *mensura* MEASURE]

men·su·ral /ménshərəl, -sŏ-/ *adj.* **1** of or involving measure. **2** *Mus.* of or involving a fixed rhythm or notes of definite duration (cf. PLAINSONG). [L *mensuralis* f. *mensura* MEASURE]

men·su·ra·tion /ménshəráyshən, -sŏ-/ *n.* **1** measuring. **2** *Math.* the measuring of geometric magnitudes such as the lengths of lines, areas of surfaces, and volumes of solids. [LL *mensuratio* (as MENSURABLE)]

mens·wear /ménzwair/ *n.* clothes for men.

-ment /mənt/ *suffix* **1** forming nouns expressing the means or result of the action of a verb (*abridgment; embankment*). **2** forming nouns from adjectives (*merriment; oddment*). [from or after F f. L *–mentum*]

men·tal /mént'l/ *adj. & n.* ● *adj.* **1** of or in the mind. **2** done by the mind. **3** *colloq.* **a** insane. **b** crazy, wild, eccentric (*is mental about pop music*). □□ **men·tal·ly** *adv.* [ME f. OF *mental* or LL *mentalis* f. L *mens –ntis* mind]

men·tal age *n.* the degree of a person's mental development expressed as an age at which the same degree is attained by an average person.

men·tal block *n.* (or **psy·cho·log·i·cal block**) a particular mental inability due to subconscious emotional factors.

men·tal cru·el·ty *n.* the infliction of suffering on another's mind, esp. *Law* as grounds for divorce.

men·tal ill·ness *n.* a condition that causes abnormality or disorder in a person's behavior or thinking.

men·tal·ism /mént'lizəm/ *n.* **1** *Philos.* the theory that physical and psychological phenomena are ultimately only explicable in terms of a creative and interpretative mind. **2** *Psychol.* the primitive tendency to personify in spirit form the forces of nature, or endow inert objects with the quality of "soul." □□ **men·tal·ist** *n.* **men·tal·is·tic** /-lístik/ *adj.*

men·tal·i·ty /mentálitee/ *n.* (*pl.* **·ties**) **1** mental character or disposition. **2** kind or degree of intelligence. **3** what is in or of the mind.

men·ta·tion /mentáyshən/ *n.* **1** mental action. **2** state of mind. [L *mens –ntis* mind]

men·thol /ménthawl/ *n.* a mint-tasting organic alcohol found in oil of peppermint, etc., used as a flavoring and to relieve local pain. [G f. L *mentha* MINT[1]]

men·tho·lat·ed /ménthəlaytid/ *adj.* treated with or containing menthol.

men·tion /ménshən/ *v. & n.* ● *v.tr.* **1** refer to briefly. **2** specify by name. **3** reveal or disclose (*do not mention this to anyone*). **4** *Brit.* (in dispatches) award (a person) an honor for meritorious, usu. gallant, military service. ● *n.* **1** a reference, esp. by name, to a person or thing. **2** *Brit.* (in dispatches) a military honor awarded for outstanding conduct. □ **don't mention it** said in polite dismissal of an apology or thanks. **make mention** (or **no mention**) **of** refer (or not refer) to. **not to mention** introducing a fact or thing of secondary or (as a rhetorical device) of primary importance. □□ **men·tion·a·ble** *adj.* [OF f. L *mentio -onis* f. the root of *mens* mind]

men·tor /méntawr/ *n.* an experienced and trusted adviser. [F f. L f. Gk *Mentōr* adviser of the young Telemachus in Homer's *Odyssey* and Fénelon's *Télémaque*]

men·u /ményŏŏ/ *n.* **1 a** a list of dishes available in a restaurant, etc.

b a list of items to be served at a meal. **2** *Computing* a list of options showing the commands or facilities available. [F, = detailed list, f. L *minutus* MINUTE[2]]

men·u-driv·en *adj.* (of a program or computer) used by making selections from menus.

me·ow /mee-ów/ *n. & v.* ● *n.* the characteristic cry of a cat. ● *v.intr.* make this cry. [imit.]

me·per·i·dine /məpérədeen/ *n.* a narcotic compound, $C_{15}H_{21}NO_2$, used as an analgesic, sedative, and antispasmodic.

Meph·i·stoph·e·les /méfistófəleez/ *n.* **1** an evil spirit to whom Faust, in the German legend, sold his soul. **2** a fiendish person. □□ **Meph·is·to·phe·le·an** /-léeən/ *adj.* **Meph·is·to·phe·li·an** /-féeleeən/ *adj.* [G (16th c.), of unkn. orig.]

me·phi·tis /məfítis/ *n.* **1** a noxious emanation, esp. from the earth. **2** a foul-smelling or poisonous stench. □□ **me·phit·ic** /-fítik/ *adj.* [L]

-mer /mər/ *comb. form* denoting a substance of a specified class, esp. a polymer (*dimer; isomer; tautomer*). [Gk *meros* part, share]

mer·can·tile /mórkəntil/ *adj.* **1** of trade, trading. **2** commercial. **3** mercenary, fond of bargaining. [F f. It. f. *mercante* MERCHANT]

mer·can·til·ism /mórkəntilizəm/ *n.* **1** belief in the benefits of profitable trading; commercialism. **2** *hist.* the economic theory that trade generates wealth and is stimulated by the accumulation of profitable balances, which a government should encourage by means of protectionism. □□ **mer·can·til·ist** *n. & adj.*

mer·cap·tan /mərkáptən/ *n.* = THIOL. [mod.L *mercurium captans* capturing mercury]

Mer·ca·tor pro·jec·tion /mərkáytər/ *n.* (also **Mer·ca·tor's pro·jec·tion**) a projection of a map of the world onto a cylinder so that all the parallels of latitude have the same length as the equator, first published in 1569 and esp. for marine charts and certain climatological maps. [G. *Mercator* (Latinized f. Kremer), Flemish-born geographer d. 1594]

mer·ce·nar·y /mórsəneree/ *adj. & n.* ● *adj.* primarily concerned with money or other reward (*mercenary motives*). ● *n.* (*pl.* **·ies**) a hired soldier in foreign service. □□ **mer·ce·nar·i·ness** *n.* [ME f. L *mercenarius* f. *merces –edis* reward]

mer·cer /mórsər/ *n. Brit.* a dealer in textile fabrics, esp. silk and other costly materials. □□ **mer·cer·y** *n.* (*pl.* **·ies**). [ME f. AF *mercer*, OF *mercier* ult. f. L *merx mercis* goods]

mer·cer·ize /mórsəriz/ *v.tr.* treat (cotton fabric or thread) under tension with caustic alkali to give greater strength and impart luster. □□ **mer·cer·i·za·tion** *n.* [J. *Mercer*, alleged inventor of the process d. 1866]

mer·chan·dise /mórchəndiz/ *n. & v.* ● *n.* goods for sale. ● *v.* **1** *tr.* put on the market, promote the sale of (goods), esp. by their presentation in retail outlets. **2** advertise, publicize (an idea or person). □□ **mer·chan·dis·a·ble** *adj.* **mer·chan·dis·er** *n.* [ME f. OF *marchandise* f. *marchand*: see MERCHANT]

mer·chant /mórchənt/ *n.* **1** a retail trader; dealer; storekeeper. **2** esp. *Brit.* a wholesale trader, esp. with foreign countries. **3** *colloq.* usu. *derog.* a person showing a partiality for a specified activity or practice (*speed merchant*). [ME f. OF *marchand, marchant* ult. f. L *mercari* trade f. *merx mercis* merchandise]

mer·chant·a·ble *adj.* salable; marketable. [ME f. *merchant* (v.) f. OF *marchander* f. *marchand*: see MERCHANT]

mer·chant·man /mórchəntmən/ *n.* (*pl.* **·men**) a ship used in commerce.

mer·chant ma·rine *n.* a nation's commercial shipping.

mer·chant ship *n.* = MERCHANTMAN.

mer·ci·ful /mórsifŏŏl/ *adj.* having, showing, or feeling mercy. □□ **mer·ci·ful·ness** *n.*

mer·ci·ful·ly /mórsifŏŏlee/ *adv.* **1** in a merciful manner. **2** (qualifying a whole sentence) fortunately (*mercifully, the sun came out*).

mer·ci·less /mórsilis/ *adj.* **1** pitiless. **2** showing no mercy. □□ **mer·ci·less·ly** *adv.* **mer·ci·less·ness** *n.*

mer·cu·ri·al /mərkyŏŏreeəl/ *adj. & n.* ● *adj.* **1** (of a person) sprightly, ready-witted, volatile. **2** of or containing mercury. **3** (**Mercurial**) of the planet Mercury. ● *n.* a drug containing mercury. □□ **mer·cu·ri·al·ism** *n.* **mer·cu·ri·al·i·ty** /-reeálitee/ *n.* **mer·cu·ri·al·ly** *adv.* [ME f. OF *mercuriel* or L *mercurialis* (as MERCURY)]

mer·cu·ry /mórkyəree/ *n.* **1** *Chem.* a silvery-white heavy liquid metallic element occurring naturally in cinnabar and used in barometers, thermometers, and amalgams; quicksilver. ¶ Symb.: **Hg.** **2** (**Mercury**) the planet nearest to the sun. **3** any plant of the genus *Mercurialis*, esp. *M. perenne*. □□ **mer·cu·ric** /-kyŏŏrik/ *adj.* **mer·cu·rous** *adj.* [ME f. L *Mercurius* messenger of the gods and god of traders f. *merx mercis* merchandise]

mer·cu·ry va·por lamp *n.* a lamp in which light is produced by an electric discharge through mercury vapor.

mer·cy /mórsee/ *n. & int.* ● *n.* (*pl.* **·cies**) **1** compassion or forbearance shown to enemies or offenders in one's power. **2** the quality of compassion. **3** an act of mercy. **4** (*attrib.*) administered or performed out of mercy or pity for a suffering person (*mercy killing*). **5** something to be thankful for (*small mercies*). ● *int.* expressing surprise or fear. □ **at the mercy of 1** wholly in the power of. **2** liable to danger or harm from. **have mercy on** show mercy to. [ME f. OF *merci* f. L *merces –edis* reward, in LL pity, thanks]

mer·cy kill·ing n. = EUTHANASIA.

mere[1] /meer/ *attrib.adj.* (**mer·est**) that is solely or no more or better than what is specified (*a mere boy*; *no mere theory*). □□ **mere·ly** *adv.* [ME f. AF *meer*, OF f. L *merus* unmixed]

mere[2] /meer/ *n. archaic* or *poet.* a lake or pond. [OE f. Gmc]

mer·e·tri·cious /méritríshəs/ *adj.* **1** (of decorations, literary style, etc.) showily but falsely attractive. **2** *archaic* of or befitting a prostitute. □□ **mer·e·tri·cious·ly** *adv.* **mer·e·tri·cious·ness** *n.* [L *meretricius* f. *meretrix –tricis* prostitute f. *merēri* be hired]

mer·gan·ser /mərgánsər/ *n.* any of various diving fish-eating northern ducks of the genus *Mergus*, with a long narrow serrated hooked bill. [mod.L f. L *mergus* diver f. *mergere* dive + *anser* goose]

merge /mərj/ *v.* **1** *tr. & intr.* (often foll. by *with*) **a** combine or be combined. **b** join or blend gradually. **2** *intr. & tr.* (foll. by *in*) lose or cause to lose character and identity in (something else). **3** *tr.* (foll. by *in*) embody (a title or estate) in (a larger one). □□ **mer·gence** *n.* [L *mergere mers-* dip, plunge, partly through legal AF *merger*]

merg·er /mə́rjər/ *n.* **1** the combining of two commercial companies, etc., into one. **2** a merging, esp. of one estate in another. **3** *Law* the absorbing of a minor offense in a greater one. [AF (as MERGE)]

me·rid·i·an /mərídeeən/ *n. & adj.* ● *n.* **1** a circle passing through the celestial poles and zenith of any place on the earth's surface. **2 a** a circle of constant longitude, passing through a given place and the terrestrial poles. **b** the corresponding line on a map. **3** *archaic* the point at which a sun or star attains its highest altitude. **4** prime; full splendor. ● *adj.* **1** of noon. **2** of the period of greatest splendor, vigor, etc. [ME f. OF *meridien* or L *meridianus* (adj.) f. *meridies* midday f. *medius* middle + *dies* day]

me·rid·i·o·nal /mərídeeənəl/ *adj. & n.* ● *adj.* **1** of or in the south (esp. of Europe). **2** of or relating to a meridian. ● *n.* an inhabitant of the south (esp. of France). [ME f. OF f. LL *meridionalis* irreg. f. L *meridies*: see MERIDIAN]

me·ringue /məráng/ *n.* **1** a confection of sugar, egg whites, etc., baked crisp. **2** a small cake or shell of this, usu. decorated or filled with whipped cream, etc. [F, of unkn. orig.]

me·ri·no /məréenō/ *n.* (pl. **-nos**) **1** (in full **merino sheep**) a variety of sheep with long fine wool. **2** a soft woolen or wool-and-cotton material like cashmere, orig. of merino wool. **3** a fine woolen yarn. [Sp., of uncert. orig.]

mer·i·stem /méristem/ *n. Bot.* a plant tissue consisting of actively dividing cells forming new tissue. □□ **mer·i·ste·mat·ic** /-stəmátik/ *adj.* [Gk *meristos* divisible f. *merizō* divide f. *meros* part, after *xylem*]

mer·it /mérit/ *n. & v.* ● *n.* **1** the quality of deserving well. **2** excellence, worth. **3** (usu. in *pl.*) **a** a thing that entitles one to reward or gratitude. **b** esp. *Law* intrinsic rights and wrongs (*the merits of a case*). **4** *Theol.* good deeds as entitling to a future reward. ● *v.tr.* deserve or be worthy of (reward, punishment, consideration, etc.). □ **judge something on its merits** with regard only to its intrinsic worth. [ME f. OF *merite* f. L *meritum* price, value, = past part. of *merēri* earn, deserve]

mer·i·toc·ra·cy /méritókrəsee/ *n.* (pl. **-cies**) **1** government by persons selected competitively according to merit. **2** a group of persons selected in this way. **3** a society governed by meritocracy.

mer·i·to·ri·ous /méritáwreeəs/ *adj.* **1** (of a person or act) having merit; deserving reward, praise, or gratitude. **2** deserving commendation for thoroughness, etc. □□ **mer·i·to·ri·ous·ly** *adv.* **mer·i·to·ri·ous·ness** *n.* [ME f. L *meritorius* f. *merēri* merit- earn]

mer·it sys·tem *n.* a policy of hiring and promoting (esp. public)

employees based on their abilities rather than political favoritism, seniority, etc.

merle /mərl/ *n.* (also **merl**) *Sc.* or *archaic* a blackbird. [ME f. F f. L *merula*]

mer·lin /mə́rlin/ *n.* a small European or N. American falcon, *Falco columbarius*, that hunts small birds. [ME f. AF *merilun* f. OF *esmerillon* augment. f. *esmeril* f. Frank.]

mer·lon /mə́rlən/ *n.* the solid part of an embattled parapet between two embrasures. [F f. It. *merlone* f. *merlo* battlement]

mer·maid /mə́rmayd/ *n.* an imaginary half-human sea creature, with the head and trunk of a woman and the tail of a fish. [ME f. MERE[2] in obs. sense 'sea' + MAID]

mer·man /mə́rman/ *n.* (pl. **-men**) the male equivalent of a mermaid.

mero- /mérō/ *comb. form* partly, partial. [Gk *meros* part]

-merous /mərəs/ *comb. form* esp. Bot. having so many parts (*dimerous*). [Gk (as MERO-)]

Mer·o·vin·gi·an /mérəvínjeeən, –jən/ *adj. & n.* ● *adj.* of or relating to the Frankish dynasty founded by Clovis and reigning in Gaul and Germany *c.*500–750. ● *n.* a member of this dynasty. [F *mérovingien* f. med.L *Merovingi* f. L *Meroveus* name of the reputed founder]

mer·ri·ment /mérimənt/ *n.* **1** exuberant enjoyment; being merry. **2** mirth, fun.

mer·ry /méree/ *adj.* (**mer·ri·er**, **mer·ri·est**) **1 a** joyous. **b** full of laughter or gaiety. **2** *Brit. colloq.* slightly drunk. □ **make merry 1** be festive; enjoy oneself. **2** (foll. by *over*) make fun of. □□ **mer·ri·ly** *adv.* **mer·ri·ness** *n.* [OE *myrige* f. Gmc]

mer·ry-go-round /méreegōrownd/ *n.* **1** a revolving machine with wooden horses or other animals, etc., for riding on at an amusement park, etc. **2** a cycle of bustling activities.

mer·ry·mak·ing /méreemayking/ *n.* festivity, fun. □□ **mer·ry·mak·er** *n.*

mer·ry·thought /méreethawt/ *n. dated, esp. Brit.* the wishbone of a cooked chicken, etc.

me·sa /máysə/ *n.* an isolated flat-topped hill with steep sides, found in landscapes with horizontal strata. [Sp., lit. table, f. L *mensa*]

mé·sal·li·ance /mayzáleeəns, máyzalyaàNs/ *n.* a marriage with a person of a lower social position. [F (as MIS-[2], ALLIANCE)]

mes·cal /méskal/ *n.* **1 a** maguey. **b** liquor obtained from this. **2** a peyote cactus. [Sp. *mezcal* f. Nahuatl *mexcalli*]

mes·cal but·tons *n.pl.* disk-shaped dried tops from the peyote cactus, eaten or chewed as an intoxicant and hallucinogen.

mes·ca·line /méskəleen, –lin/ *n.* (also **mes·ca·lin** /–lin/) a hallucinogenic alkaloid present in mescal buttons.

mes·dames *pl.* of MADAME.

mes·de·moi·selles *pl.* of MADEMOISELLE.

me·sem·bry·an·the·mum /mizémbreeánthiməm/ *n.* any of various succulent plants of the genus *Mesembryanthemum* of S. Africa, having daisylike flowers in a wide range of bright colors that open fully in sunlight. [mod.L f. Gk *mesembria* noon + *anthemon* flower]

mes·en·ceph·a·lon /mésenséfələn, méz–/ *n.* the part of the brain developing from the middle of the primitive or embryonic brain. Also called **midbrain**. [Gk *mesos* middle + *encephalon* brain: see ENCEPHALIC]

mes·en·ter·y /mésəntéree, méz–/ *n.* (pl. **-ies**) a double layer of peritoneum attaching the stomach, small intestine, pancreas, spleen, and other abdominal organs to the posterior wall of the abdomen. □□ **mes·en·ter·ic** /–térik/ *adj.* **mes·en·ter·i·tis** /–rítis/ *n.* [med.L *mesenterium* f. Gk *mesenterion* (as MESO-, *enteron* intestine)]

mesh /mesh/ *n. & v.* ● *n.* **1** a network fabric or structure. **2** each of the open spaces or interstices between the strands of a net or sieve, etc. **3** (in *pl.*) **a** a network. **b** a snare. **4** (in *pl.*) *Physiol.* an interlaced structure. ● *v.* **1** *intr.* (often foll. by *with*) (of the teeth of a wheel) be engaged (with others). **2** *intr.* be harmonious. **3** *tr.* catch in or as in a net. □ **in mesh** (of the teeth of wheels) engaged. [earlier *meish*, etc. f. MDu. *maesche* f. Gmc]

me·si·al /méezeeəl/ *adj.* of, in, or directed toward the middle line of a body. □□ **me·si·al·ly** *adv.* [irreg. f. Gk *mesos* middle]

mes·mer·ism /mézmərizəm/ *n.* **1** *Psychol.* **a** a hypnotic state produced in a person by another's influence over the will and nervous system. **b** a doctrine concerning this. **c** an influence producing this. **2** fascination. □□ **mes·mer·ic** /mezmérik/ *adj.* **mes·mer·i·cal·ly** /–mériklee/ *adv.* **mes·mer·ist** *n.* [F.A. *Mesmer*, Austrian physician d. 1815]

mes·mer·ize /mézmərīz/ *v.tr.* **1** *Psychol.* hypnotize; exercise mesmerism on. **2** fascinate, spellbind. □□ **mes·mer·i·za·tion** *n.* **mes·mer·i·zer** *n.* **mes·mer·i·zing·ly** *adv.*

mesne /meen/ *adj. Law* intermediate. [ME f. law F, var. of AF *meen*, MEAN[3]: cf. DEMESNE]

mesne lord *n. Engl. hist.* a lord holding an estate from a superior feudal lord.

mesne prof•its *n.pl.* profits received from an estate by a tenant between two dates.

meso- /méso, méz–/ *comb. form* middle, intermediate. [Gk *mesos* middle]

mes•o•blast /mésəblast, méz–/ *n. Biol.* the middle germ layer of an embryo.

mes•o•derm /mésəderm, méz–/ *n. Biol.* = MESOBLAST. [MESO- + Gk *derma* skin]

mes•o•lith•ic /mézəlíthik, més–/ *adj. Archaeol.* of or concerning the Stone Age between the Paleolithic and Neolithic periods. [MESO- + Gk *lithos* stone]

mes•o•morph /mézəmawrf, més–/ *n.* a person with a compact and muscular build of body (cf. ECTOMORPH, ENDOMORPH). □□ **mes•o•mor•phic** /–máwrfik/ *adj.* [MESO- + Gk *morphē* form]

me•son /mézon, més–, meezon, –son/ *n. Physics* any of a class of elementary particles believed to participate in the forces that hold nucleons together in the atomic nucleus. □□ **me•sic** /mézik, més–, meezik, –sik/ *adj.* **me•son•ic** /mezónik/ *adj.* [earlier *mesotron*: cf. MESO-, –ON]

mes•o•phyll /mésəfil, méz–/ *n.* the inner tissue of a leaf. [MESO- + Gk *phullon* leaf]

mes•o•phyte /mésəfīt, méz–/ *n.* a plant needing only a moderate amount of water.

mes•o•sphere /mésəsfeer, méz–/ *n.* the region of the atmosphere extending from the top of the stratosphere to an altitude of about 50 miles.

Mes•o•zo•ic /mésəzó-ik, méz–/ *adj. & n. Geol.* • *adj.* of or relating to an era of geological time marked by the development of dinosaurs, and with evidence of the first mammals, birds, and flowering plants. • *n.* this era (cf. CENOZOIC, PALEOZOIC). [MESO- + Gk *zōion* animal]

mes•quite /meskéet/ *n.* **1** any N. American leguminous tree of the genus *Prosopis*, esp. *P. juliflora.* **2** the wood of the mesquite, as used in grilling food. [Mex. Sp. *mezquite*]

mes•quite bean *n.* a pod from the mesquite, used as fodder.

mess /mes/ *n. & v.* • *n.* **1** a dirty or untidy state of things (*the room is a mess*). **2** a state of confusion, embarrassment, or trouble. **3** something causing a mess, e.g., spilled liquid, etc. **4** a domestic animal's excreta. **5 a** a company of persons who take meals together, esp. in the armed forces. **b** a place where such meals or recreation take place communally. **c** a meal taken there. **6** *derog.* a disagreeable concoction or medley. **7** *Brit.* a liquid or mixed food for hounds, etc. **8** a portion of liquid or pulpy food. • *v.* **1** *tr.* (often foll. by *up*) **a** make a mess of; dirty. **b** muddle; make into a state of confusion. **2** *intr.* (foll. by *with*) interfere with. **3** *intr.* take one's meals. **4** *intr. colloq.* defecate. □ **make a mess of** bungle (an undertaking). **mess around** (or **about**) **1** interfere with; make things awkward for; cause arbitrary inconvenience to (a person). **2** pass time aimlessly. **3** engage in a sexual relationship with someone.

WORD HISTORY mess

Middle English: from Old French *mes* 'portion of food,' from late Latin *missum* 'something put on the table,' past participle of *mittere* 'send, put.' The original sense was 'a serving of food,' also 'a serving of liquid or partly liquid food,' and later 'liquid or mixed food for an animal'; this gave rise, in the early 19th century, to the senses 'unappetizing concoction' and 'predicament,' on which the present senses 1 and 2 are based. In late Middle English there was also a sense 'one of the small groups into which the company at a banquet was divided' (who were served from the same dishes); hence, 'a group who regularly eat together' (recorded in military use from the mid-16th century).

---

mes•sage /mésij/ *n. & v.* • *n.* **1** an oral or written communication sent by one person to another. **2 a** an inspired or significant communication from a prophet, writer, or preacher. **b** the central import or meaning of an artistic work, etc. **3** a mission or errand. • *v.tr.* **1** send as a message. **2** transmit (a plan, etc.) by signaling, etc. □ **get the message** *colloq.* understand what is meant. [ME f. OF ult. f. L *mittere miss-* send]

mes•sei•gneurs *pl.* of MONSEIGNEUR.

mes•sen•ger /mésinjər/ *n.* **1** a person who carries a message. **2** a person employed to carry messages. [ME & OF *messager* (as MESSAGE): *-n-* as in *harbinger, passenger,* etc.]

mes•sen•ger RNA *n.* a form of RNA carrying genetic information from DNA to a ribosome. ¶ Abbr.: **mRNA.**

mess hall *n.* a communal, esp. military, dining area.

Mes•si•ah /misíə/ *n.* **1** (also **messiah**) a liberator or would-be liberator of an oppressed people or country. **2 a** the promised deliverer of the Jews. **b** (usu. prec. by *the*) Christ regarded as this. □□ **Mes•si•ah•ship** *n.* [ME f. OF *Messie* ult. f. Heb. *māšīaḥ* anointed]

Mes•si•an•ic /méseeánik/ *adj.* **1** of the Messiah. **2** inspired by hope or belief in a Messiah. □□ **Mes•si•a•nism** /mesíənizəm/ *n.* [F *messianique* (as MESSIAH) after *rabbinique* rabbinical]

mes•sieurs *pl.* of MONSIEUR.

mess•mate /mésmayt/ *n.* a person with whom one regularly takes meals, esp. in the armed forces.

mess jack•et *n.* a short close-fitting coat worn by a military officer on formal occasions.

mess kit *n.* a soldier's cooking and eating utensils.

messrs. /mésərz/ *pl.* of MR. [abbr. of MESSIEURS]

mes•suage /méswij/ *n. Law* a dwelling house with outbuildings and land assigned to its use. [ME f. AF: perh. an alternative form of *mesnage* dwelling]

mess•y /mésee/ *adj.* (**mess•i•er, mess•i•est**) **1** untidy or dirty. **2** causing or accompanied by a mess. **3** difficult to deal with; full of awkward complications. □□ **mess•i•ly** *adv.* **mess•i•ness** *n.*

mes•ti•zo /mesteézó/ *n.* (*pl.* **·zos**; *fem.* **mes•ti•za** /–zə/, *pl.* **·zas**) a Spaniard or Portuguese of mixed race, esp. the offspring of a Spaniard and a Native American. [Sp. ult. f. L *mixtus* past part. of *miscēre* mix]

Met /met/ *n.* (in full **the Met**) *colloq.* **1** the Metropolitan Opera House in New York. **2** the Metrolpolitan Museum of Art in New York. [abbr.]

met *past* and *past part.* of MEET[1].

met. /met/ *abbr.* **1** meteorology; meteorological. **2** metropolitan. **3** metaphor; metaphoric.

meta- /métə/ *comb. form* (usu. **met-** before a vowel or *h*) **1** denoting change of position or condition (*metabolism*). **2** denoting position: **a** behind. **b** after or beyond (*metaphysics; metacarpus*). **c** of a higher or second-order kind (*metalanguage*). **3** *Chem.* **a** relating to two carbon atoms separated by one another in a benzene ring. **b** relating to a compound formed by dehydration (*metaphosphate*). [Gk *meta-, met-, meth-* f. *meta* with, after]

me•tab•o•lism /mətábəlizəm/ *n.* all the chemical processes that occur within a living organism, resulting in energy production (CATABOLISM) and growth (ANABOLISM). □□ **met•a•bol•ic** /métəbólik/ *adj.* **met•a•bol•i•cal•ly** /métəbóliklee/ *adv.* [Gk *metabolē* change (as META-, *bolē* f. *ballō* throw)]

me•tab•o•lite /mətábəlīt/ *n. Physiol.* a substance formed in or necessary for metabolism.

me•tab•o•lize /mətábəlīz/ *v.tr. & intr.* process or be processed by metabolism. □□ **me•tab•o•liz•a•ble** *adj.*

met•a•car•pus /métəkaárpəs/ *n.* (*pl.* **met•a•car•pi** /–pī/) **1** the set of five bones of the hand that connects the wrist to the fingers. **2** this part of the hand. □□ **met•a•car•pal** *adj.* [mod.L f. Gk *metakarpon* (as META-, CARPUS)]

met•a•cen•ter /métəsentər/ *n.* the point of intersection between a line (vertical in equilibrium) through the center of gravity of a floating body and a vertical line through the center of pressure after a slight angular displacement, which must be above the center of gravity to ensure stability. □□ **met•a•cen•tric** /–séntrik/ *adj.* [F *métacentre* (as META-, CENTER)]

met•age /méetij/ *n.* **1** the official measuring of a load of coal, etc. **2** the duty paid for this. [METE[1] + –AGE]

met•a•gen•e•sis /métəjénisis/ *n.* the alternation of generations between sexual and asexual reproduction. □□ **met•a•ge•net•ic** /–jinétik/ *adj.* [mod.L (as META-, GENESIS)]

met•al /mét'l/ *n., adj., & v.* • *n.* **1 a** any of a class of chemical elements such as gold, silver, iron, and tin, usu. lustrous ductile solids and good conductors of heat and electricity and forming basic oxides. **b** an alloy of any of these. **2** material used for making glass, in a molten state. **3** *Heraldry* gold or silver as tincture. **4** (in *pl.*) the rails of a railroad line. • *v.tr.* (**met•aled, met•al•ing;** esp. *Brit.* **met•alled, met•al•ling**) provide or fit with metal. [ME f. OF *metal* or L *metallum* f. Gk *metallon* mine]

SPELLING TIP metal

See note at MEDAL.

---

met•a•lan•guage /métəlanggwij/ *n.* **1** a form of language used to discuss a language. **2** a system of propositions about propositions.

met•al de•tec•tor *n.* an electronic device giving a signal when it locates metal.

met•al•ize /mét'līz/ *v.tr.* (esp. *Brit.* **met•al•lize**) **1** render metallic. **2** coat with a thin layer of metal. □□ **met•al•i•za•tion** *n.*

me•tal•lic /mətálik/ *adj.* **1** of, consisting of, or characteristic of metal or metals. **2** sounding sharp and ringing, like struck metal. **3** having the sheen or luster of metals. □□ **me•tal•li•cal•ly** *adv.* [L *metallicus* f. Gk *metallikos* (as METAL)]

met•al•lif•er•ous /mét'lífərəs/ *adj.* bearing or producing metal. [L *metallifer* (as METAL, –FEROUS)]

met•al•log•ra•phy /mét'lógrəfee/ *n.* the descriptive science of the structure and properties of metals. □□ **met•al•lo•graph•ic** /metáləgráfik/ *adj.* **met•al•lo•graph•i•cal** *adj.* **met•al•lo•graph•i•cal•ly** *adv.*

met•al•loid /mét'loyd/ *adj. & n.* • *adj.* having the form or appearance of a metal. • *n.* any element intermediate in properties between metals and nonmetals, e.g., boron, silicon, and germanium.

met•al•lur•gy /mét'lərjee/ *n.* the science concerned with the production, purification, and properties of metals and their application.

□□ **met·al·lur·gic** /mét'lərjik/ *adj.* **met·al·lur·gi·cal** *adj.* **met·al·lur·gi·cal·ly** *adv.* **met·al·lur·gist** *n.* [Gk *metallon* metal + *–ourgia* working]

met·al·work /mét'lwərk/ *n.* **1** the art of working in metal. **2** metal objects collectively. □□ **met·al·work·er** *n.*

met·a·mere /métəmeer/ *n. Zool.* each of several similar segments, that contain the same internal structures, of an animal body. [META- + Gk *meros* part]

met·a·mer·ic /métəmérik/ *adj.* **1** *Chem.* having the same proportional composition and molecular weight, but different functional groups and chemical properties. **2** *Zool.* of or relating to metameres. □□ **met·a·mer** /métəmər/ *n.* **me·tam·er·ism** /metámərizəm/ *n.*

met·a·mor·phic /métəmáwrfik/ *adj.* **1** of or marked by metamorphosis. **2** *Geol.* (of rock) that has undergone transformation by natural agencies such as heat and pressure. □□ **met·a·mor·phism** *n.* [META- + Gk *morphē* form]

met·a·mor·phose /métəmawrfōz/ *v.tr.* **1** change in form. **2** (foll. by *to, into*) **a** turn (into a new form). **b** change the nature of. [F *métamorphoser* f. *métamorphose* METAMORPHOSIS]

met·a·mor·pho·sis /métəmáwrfəsis/ *n.* (*pl.* **met·a·mor·pho·ses** /-seez/) **1** a change of form (by natural or supernatural means). **2** a changed form. **3** a change of character, conditions, etc. **4** *Zool.* the transformation between an immature form and an adult form, e.g., from a pupa to an insect, or from a tadpole to a frog. [L f. Gk *metamorphōsis* f. *metamorphoō* transform (as META-, *morphoō* f. *morphē* form)]

met·a·phase /métəfayz/ *n. Biol.* the stage of meiotic or mitotic cell division when the chromosomes become attached to the spindle fibers.

met·a·phor /métəfawr/ *n.* **1** the application of a name or descriptive term or phrase to an object or action to which it is imaginatively but not literally applicable (e.g., *killing him with kindness*). **2** an instance of this. □□ **met·a·phor·ic** /-fáwrik, -fórik/ *adj.* **met·a·phor·i·cal** /-fáwrikəl, -fórikəl/ *adj.* **met·a·phor·i·cal·ly** /-fáwriklee, -fórik-lee/ *adv.* [F *métaphore* or L *metaphora* f. Gk *metaphora* f. *metapherō* transfer]

met·a·phrase /métəfrayz/ *n. & v.* ● *n.* literal translation. ● *v.tr.* put into other words. □□ **met·a·phras·tic** /-frástik/ *adj.* [mod.L *metaphrasis* f. Gk *metaphrasis* f. *metaphrazō* translate]

met·a·phys·ic /métəfízik/ *n.* a system of metaphysics.

met·a·phys·i·cal /métəfízikəl/ *adj. & n.* ● *adj.* **1** of or relating to metaphysics. **2** based on abstract general reasoning. **3** excessively subtle or theoretical. **4** incorporeal; supernatural. **5** visionary. **6** (of poetry, esp. in the 17th c. in England) characterized by subtlety of thought and complex imagery. ● *n.* (**the Metaphysicals**) the metaphysical poets. □□ **met·a·phys·i·cal·ly** *adv.*

met·a·phys·ics /métəfíziks/ *n.pl.* (usu. treated as *sing.*) **1** the theoretical philosophy of being and knowing. **2** the philosophy of mind. **3** *colloq.* abstract or subtle talk; mere theory. □□ **met·a·phy·si·cian** /-zíshən/ *n.* **met·a·phys·i·cize** /-fízisiz/ *v.intr.* [ME *metaphysic* f. OF *metaphysique* f. med.L *metaphysica* ult. f. Gk *ta meta ta phusika* the things after the Physics, from the sequence of Aristotle's works]

met·a·pla·sia /métəpláyzhə, -zeeə/ *n. Physiol.* an abnormal change in the nature of a tissue. □□ **met·a·plas·tic** /-plástik/ *adj.* [mod.L f. G *Metaplase* f. Gk *metaplasis* (as META-, *plasis* f. *plassō* to mold)]

met·a·psy·chol·o·gy /métəsīkóləjee/ *n.* the study of the nature and functions of the mind beyond what can be studied experimentally. □□ **met·a·psy·cho·log·i·cal** /-kəlójikəl/ *adj.*

met·a·sta·ble /métəstáybəl/ *adj.* **1** (of a state of equilibrium) stable only under small disturbances. **2** passing to another state so slowly as to seem stable. □□ **met·a·sta·bil·i·ty** /-stəbílitee/ *n.*

me·tas·ta·sis /metástəsis/ *n.* (*pl.* **me·tas·ta·ses** /-seez/) *Physiol.* **1** the transference of a bodily function, disease, etc., from one part or organ to another. **2** the transformation of chemical compounds into others in the process of assimilation by an organism. □□ **me·tas·ta·size** *v.intr.* **met·a·stat·ic** /métəstátik/ *adj.* [LL f. Gk f. *methistēmi* change]

met·a·tar·sus /métətaársəs/ *n.* (*pl.* **met·a·tar·si** /-sī/) **1** the part of the foot between the ankle and the toes. **2** the set of bones in this. □□ **met·a·tar·sal** *adj.* [mod.L (as META-, TARSUS)]

me·tath·e·sis /mitáthisis/ *n.* (*pl.* **me·tath·e·ses** /-seez/) **1** *Gram.* the transposition of sounds or letters in a word. **2** *Chem.* the interchange of atoms or groups of atoms between two molecules. **3** an instance of either of these. □□ **met·a·thet·ic** /métəthétik/ *adj.* **met·a·thet·i·cal** /métəthétikəl/ *adj.* [LL f. Gk *metatithēmi* transpose]

met·a·zo·an /métəzóən/ *n. & adj. Zool.* ● *n.* any animal of the subkingdom Metazoa, having multicellular and differentiated tissues. ● *adj.* of or relating to the Metazoans. [*Metazoa* f. Gk META- + *zōia* pl. of *zōion* animal]

mete[1] /meet/ *v.tr.* **1** (usu. foll. by *out*) *literary* apportion or allot (a punishment or reward). **2** *poet.* or *Bibl.* measure. [OE *metan* f. Gmc., rel. to MEET[1]]

mete[2] /meet/ *n.* a boundary or boundary stone. [ME f. OF f. L *meta* boundary, goal]

me·tem·psy·cho·sis /mətémsīkósis, métəm-/ *n.* (*pl.* **·psy·cho·ses** /-seez/) **1** the supposed transmigration of the soul of a human being or animal at death into a new body of the same or a different species. **2** an instance of this. □□ **me·tem·psy·cho·sist** *n.* [LL f. Gk *metempsukhōsis* (as META-, EN-[2], *psukhē* soul)]

me·te·or /meeteeər, –eeawr/ *n.* **1** a small body of matter from outer space that becomes incandescent as a result of friction with the earth's atmosphere. **2** a streak of light emanating from a meteor. [ME f. mod.L *meteorum* f. Gk *meteōron* neut. of *meteōros* lofty, (as META-, *aeirō* raise)]

me·te·or·ic /meetee-áwrik, –ór–/ *adj.* **1 a** of or relating to the atmosphere. **b** dependent on atmospheric conditions. **2** of meteors. **3** rapid like a meteor; dazzling, transient (*meteoric rise to fame*). □□ **me·te·or·i·cal·ly** *adv.*

me·te·or·ite /meeteeərit/ *n.* a fallen meteor, or fragment of natural rock or metal, that reaches the earth's surface from outer space. □□ **me·te·or·it·ic** /-rítik/ *adj.*

me·te·or·o·graph /meeteeərəgraf/ *n.* an apparatus that records several meteorological phenomena at the same time. [F *météorographe* (as METEOR, –GRAPH)]

me·te·or·oid /meeteeəróyd/ *n.* any small body moving in the solar system that becomes visible as it passes through the earth's atmosphere as a meteor. □□ **me·te·or·oid·al** /-róyd'l/ *adj.*

me·te·or·ol·o·gy /meeteeəróləjee/ *n.* **1** the study of the processes and phenomena of the atmosphere, esp. as a means of forecasting the weather. **2** the atmospheric character of a region. □□ **me·te·or·o·log·i·cal** /-rəlójikəl/ *adj.* **me·te·or·o·log·i·cal·ly** *adv.* **me·te·or·ol·o·gist** *n.* [Gk *meteōrologia* (as METEOR)]

me·te·or show·er *n.* a group of meteors appearing to radiate from one point in the sky at a particular date each year, due to the earth regularly passing through them at that position in its orbit.

me·ter[1] /meetər/ *n.* (*Brit.* **me·tre**) a metric unit and the base SI unit of linear measure, equal to about 39.4 inches, and reckoned as the length of the path traveled by light in a vacuum during $1/299{,}792{,}458$ of a second. □□ **me·ter·age** /meetərij/ *n.* [F *mètre* f. Gk *metron* measure]

me·ter[2] /meetər/ *n.* (*Brit.* **me·tre**) **1 a** any form of poetic rhythm, determined by the number and length of feet in a line. **b** a metrical group or measure. **2** the basic pulse and rhythm of a piece of music. [OF *metre* f. L *metrum* f. Gk *metron* MEASURE]

me·ter[3] /meetər/ *n. & v.* ● *n.* **1** an instrument that measures, esp. one for recording a quantity of gas, electricity, postage, etc., supplied, present, or needed. **2** = PARKING METER. ● *v.tr.* measure by means of a meter. [ME f. METE[1] + –ER[1]]

-meter /mitər, meetər/ *comb. form* **1** forming nouns denoting measuring instruments (*barometer*). **2** *Prosody* forming nouns denoting lines of poetry with a specified number of measures (*pentameter*).

me·ter-kil·o·gram-sec·ond *adj.* denoting a system of measure using the meter, kilogram, and second as the basic units of length, mass, and time. ¶ Abbr.: **mks**.

meth·a·done /méthədōn/ *n.* a powerful synthetic analgesic drug that is similar to morphine and is used as a substitute drug in the treatment of morphine and heroin addiction. [6-dimethylamino-4,4-diphenyl-3-heptan*one*]

meth·am·phet·a·mine /méthamfétəmin, –meen/ *n.* an amphetamine derivative with quicker and longer action, used as a stimulant. [METHYL + AMPHETAMINE]

meth·a·nal /méthənal/ *n. Chem.* = FORMALDEHYDE. [METHANE + ALDEHYDE]

meth·ane /méthayn/ *n. Chem.* a colorless, odorless, flammable, gaseous hydrocarbon, the simplest in the alkane series, and the main constituent of natural gas. ¶ Chem. formula: CH_4. [METHYL + –ANE[2]]

meth·a·nol /méthənawl, -nol/ *n. Chem.* a colorless, volatile, flammable liquid, used as a solvent. ¶ Chem. formula: CH_3OH. Also called **methyl alcohol**. [METHANE + ALCOHOL]

me·thinks /mithíngks/ *v.intr.* (*past* **me·thought** /mitháwt/) *archaic* it seems to me. [OE *mē thyncth* f. *mē* dative of ME[1] + *thyncth* 3rd sing. of *thyncan* seem, THINK]

me·thi·o·nine /methíəneen/ *n. Biochem.* an amino acid containing sulfur and an important constituent of proteins. [METHYL + Gk *theion* sulfur]

meth·od /méthəd/ *n.* **1** a special form of procedure esp. in any branch of mental activity. **2** orderliness; regular habits. **3** the orderly arrangement of ideas. **4** a scheme of classification. **5** *Theatr.* a technique of acting based on the actor's thorough emotional identification with the character. □ **method in** (or **to**) **one's madness** sense in what appears to be foolish or strange behavior. [F *méthode* or L *methodus* f. Gk *methodos* pursuit of knowledge (as META-, *hodos* way)]

me·thod·i·cal /mithódikəl/ *adj.* (also **me·thod·ic**) characterized by method or order. □□ **me·thod·i·cal·ly** *adv.* [LL *methodicus* f. Gk *methodikos* (as METHOD)]

Meth·od·ist /méthədist/ *n.* **1** a member of any of several Protestant religious bodies (now united) originating in the 18th-c. evangelistic movement of Charles and John Wesley and George Whitefield.

2 (**methodist**) a person who follows or advocates a particular method or system of procedure. □□ **Meth·od·ism** *n.* **Meth·od·is·tic** /–dístik/ *adj.* **Meth·od·is·ti·cal** /–dístikəl/ *adj.* [mod.L *methodista* (as METHOD): sense 1 prob. from following a specified "method" of devotional study]

meth·od·ize /méthədīz/ *v.tr.* **1** reduce to order. **2** arrange in an orderly manner. □□ **meth·od·iz·er** *n.*

meth·od·ol·o·gy /méthədóləjee/ *n.* (*pl.* **·gies**) **1** the science of method. **2** a body of methods used in a particular branch of activity. □□ **meth·od·o·log·i·cal** /–dəlójikəl/ *adj.* **meth·od·o·log·i·cal·ly** *adv.* **meth·od·ol·o·gist** *n.* [mod.L *methodologia* or F *méthodologie* (as METHOD)]

me·thought *past* of METHINKS.

Me·thu·se·lah /mithóózələ/ *n.* **1** a very old person or thing. **2** (also **methuselah**) a large wine bottle with a capacity of approx. 6 liters. [ME: the name of a patriarch said to have lived 969 years (Gen. 5:27)]

meth·yl /méthil/ *n.* *Chem.* the univalent hydrocarbon radical CH_3, present in many organic compounds. □ **methyl alcohol** = METHANOL. **methyl benzene** = TOLUENE. □□ **me·thyl·ic** /methílik/ *adj.* [G *Methyl* or F *méthyle*, back-form. f. G *Methylen*, F *méthylène*: see METHYLENE]

meth·yl·ate /méthilayt/ *v.tr.* **1** mix or impregnate with methanol. **2** introduce a methyl group into (a molecule or compound). □□ **meth·yl·a·tion** /–láyshən/ *n.*

meth·yl·at·ed spir·its *n.pl.* alcohol for general use that has been made unfit for drinking by the addition of methanol.

meth·yl·ene /méthileen/ *n.* *Chem.* the highly reactive divalent group of atoms CH_2. [F *méthylène* f. Gk *methu* wine + *hulē* wood + –ENE]

met·ic /métik/ *n.* *Gk Antiq.* an alien living in a Greek city with some privileges of citizenship. [irreg. f. Gk *metoikos* (as META-, *oikos* dwelling)]

me·tic·u·lous /mətíkyələs/ *adj.* **1** giving great or excessive attention to details. **2** very careful and precise. □□ **me·tic·u·lous·ly** *adv.* **me·tic·u·lous·ness** *n.* [L *meticulosus* f. *metus* fear]

mé·tier /métyáy/ *n.* (also **me·tier**) **1** one's trade, profession, or department of activity. **2** one's forte. [F ult. f. L *ministerium* service]

mé·tis /maytées/ *n.* (*pl.* **mé·tis**; *fem.* **mé·tisse**, *pl.* **mé·tisses**) a person of mixed race, esp. the offspring of a white person and a Native American in Canada. [F *métis*, OF *mestis* f. Rmc, rel. to MESTIZO]

Me·tol /méetawl/ *n.* *Trademark* a white soluble powder used as a photographic developer. [G, arbitrary name]

Me·ton·ic cy·cle /mitónik/ *n.* a period of 19 years (235 lunar months) covering all the changes of the moon's position relative to the sun and the earth. [Gk *Metōn*, Athenian astronomer of the 5th c. BC]

met·o·nym /métənim/ *n.* a word used in metonymy. [back-form. f. METONYMY, after *synonym*]

me·ton·y·my /mitónimee/ *n.* the substitution of the name of an attribute or adjunct for that of the thing meant (e.g., *White House* for *president*, *the turf* for *horse racing*). □□ **met·o·nym·ic** /métənímik/ *adj.* **met·o·nym·i·cal** /métənímikəl/ *adj.* [LL *metonymia* f. Gk *metōnumia* (as META-, *onoma*, *onuma* name)]

met·o·pe /métəpee, métōp/ *n.* *Archit.* a square space between triglyphs in a Doric frieze. [L *metopa* f. Gk *metopē* (as META-, *opē* hole for a beam end)]

me·tre *Brit.* var. of METER.

met·ric /métrik/ *adj.* of or based on the meter. [F *métrique* (as METER[1])]

-metric /métrik/ *comb. form* (also **–metrical**) forming adjectives corresponding to nouns in *–meter* and *–metry* (*thermometric*; *geometric*). □□ **–metrically** *comb. form* forming adverbs. [from or after F *–métrique* f. L (as METRICAL)]

met·ri·cal /métrikəl/ *adj.* **1** of, relating to, or composed in meter (*metrical psalms*). **2** of or involving measurement (*metrical geometry*). □□ **met·ri·cal·ly** *adv.* [ME f. L *metricus* f. Gk *metrikos* (as METER[2])]

met·ri·cate /métrikayt/ *v.intr.* & *tr.* change or adapt to a metric system of measurement. □□ **met·ri·ca·tion** /–káyshən/ *n.* **met·ri·cize** /–trisiz/ *v.tr.*

met·ric sys·tem *n.* the decimal measuring system with the meter, liter, and gram (or kilogram) as units of length, capacity, and weight or mass (see also SI).

met·ric ton *n.* (also **met·ric tonne**) a unit of weight equal to 1,000 kilograms (2,205 lb.).

me·tri·tis /mitrítis/ *n.* inflammation of the uterus. [Gk *mētra* womb + –ITIS]

met·ro /métrō/ *n.* (*pl.* **·ros**) a subway system in a city, esp. Paris. [F *métro*, abbr. of *métropolitain* METROPOLITAN]

me·trol·o·gy /mitróləjee/ *n.* the scientific study of measurement. □□ **me·tro·log·ic** /métrəlójik/ *adj.* **me·tro·log·i·cal** /métrəlójikəl/ *adj.* [Gk *metron* measure + –LOGY]

met·ro·nome /métrənōm/ *n.* *Mus.* an instrument marking time at a

selected rate by giving a regular tick. □□ **met·ro·nom·ic** /–nómik/ *adj.* [Gk *metron* measure + *nomos* law]

me·tro·nym·ic /métrənímik/ *adj.* & *n.* • *adj.* (of a name) derived from the name of a mother or female ancestor. • *n.* a metronymic name. [Gk *mētēr mētros* mother, after *patronymic*]

me·trop·o·lis /mitrópəlis/ *n.* **1** the chief city of a country; a capital city. **2** a metropolitan bishop's see. **3** a center of activity. [LL f. Gk *mētropolis* parent state f. *mētēr mētros* mother + *polis* city]

met·ro·pol·i·tan /métrəpólit'n/ *adj.* & *n.* • *adj.* **1** of or relating to a metropolis, esp. as distinct from its environs (*metropolitan New York*). **2** belonging to, forming or forming part of, a mother country as distinct from its colonies, etc. (*metropolitan France*). **3** of an ecclesiastical metropolis. • *n.* **1** (in full **metropolitan bishop**) a bishop having authority over the bishops of a province, in the Western Church equivalent to archbishop, in the Orthodox Church ranking above archbishop and below patriarch. **2** an inhabitant of a metropolis. □□ **met·ro·pol·i·tan·ate** *n.* (in sense 1 of *n.*). **met·ro·pol·i·tan·ism** *n.* [ME f. LL *metropolitanus* f. Gk *mētropolitēs* (as METROPOLIS)]

me·tror·rha·gi·a /meetrō-ráyjeeə, –jə/ *n.* abnormal bleeding from the womb. [mod.L f. Gk *mētra* womb + *–rrhage* as HEMORRHAGE]

-metry /mitree/ *comb. form* forming nouns denoting procedures and systems corresponding to instruments in *–meter* (*calorimetry*; *thermometry*). [after *geometry*, etc., f. Gk *–metria* f. *–metrēs* measurer]

met·tle /mét'l/ *n.* **1** the quality of a person's disposition or temperament (*a chance to show your mettle*). **2** natural ardor. **3** spirit, courage. □ **on one's mettle** incited to do one's best. □□ **met·tled** *adj.* (also in *comb.*). **met·tle·some** *adj.* [var. of METAL *n.*]

meu·niè·re /mónyáir/ *adj.* (esp. of fish) cooked or served in lightly browned butter with lemon juice and parsley (*sole meunière*). [F (*à la*) *meunière* (in the manner of) a miller's wife]

MeV *abbr.* megaelectronvolt(s).

mew[1] /myōo/ *v.* & *n.* • *v.intr.* (of a cat, gull, etc.) utter its characteristic cry. • *n.* this sound, esp. of a cat. [ME: imit.]

mew[2] /myōo/ *n.* a gull, esp. the common gull, *Larus canus*. Also called **mew gull**. [OE *mǣw* f. Gmc]

mew[3] /myōo/ *n.* & *v.* • *n.* a cage for hawks, esp. while molting. • *v.tr.* **1** put (a hawk) in a cage. **2** (often foll. by *up*) shut up; confine. [ME f. OF *mue* f. *muer* molt f. L *mutare* change]

mewl /myōol/ *v.intr.* **1** cry feebly; whimper. **2** mew like a cat. [imit.]

mews /myōoz/ *n.* esp. *Brit.* a set of stables around an open yard or along a lane, now often converted into dwellings. [pl. (now used as sing.) of MEW[3], orig. of the royal stables on the site of hawks' mews at Charing Cross, London]

Mex·i·can /méksikən/ *n.* & *adj.* • *n.* **1 a** a native or national of Mexico, a country in southern N. America. **b** a person of Mexican descent. **2** a language spoken in Mexico, esp. Nahuatl. • *adj.* **1** of or relating to Mexico or its people. **2** of Mexican descent. [Sp. *mexicano*]

me·ze·re·on /mizéereeən/ *n.* (also **me·ze·re·um**) a small European and Asian shrub, *Daphne mezereum*, with fragrant purplish red flowers and red berries. [med.L f. Arab. *māzaryūn*]

me·zu·zah /mezóózə, –zóozaá/ *n.* (also **me·zu·za**; *pl.* **-s**; also **me·zu·zot** or **me·zu·zoth** /–zoozót/) a parchment inscribed with religious texts and attached in a case to the doorpost of a Jewish house as a sign of faith. [Heb. *mʿzûzāh* doorpost]

mez·za·nine /mézəneen/ *n.* **1** a low story between two others (usu. between the first and second floors). **2 a** the lowest balcony in a theater. **b** the first several rows of this balcony. [F f. It. *mezzanino* dimin. of *mezzano* middle f. L *medianus* MEDIAN]

mez·za vo·ce /métsə vóchay/ *adv. Mus.* with less than the full strength of the voice or sound. [It., = half voice]

mez·zo /métsō/ *adj.* & *n. Mus.* half, moderately. • *n.* (in full **mezzo-soprano**) (*pl.* **·zos**) **1 a** a female singing voice between soprano and contralto. **b** a singer with this voice. **2** a part written for mezzo-soprano. [It., f. L *medius* middle]

mez·zo for·te *adj.* fairly loud.

mez·zo pi·a·no *adj.* fairly soft.

mez·zo-re·lie·vo /métsō-rileevō/ *n.* (also **mez·zo-ri·lie·vo** /–rilyáyvō/) (*pl.* **·vos**) a raised surface in the form of half-relief, in which the figures project half their true proportions. [It. *mezzo-rilievo* = half-relief]

mez·zo-ri·lie·vo var. of MEZZO–RELIEVO.

mez·zo·tint /métsōtint/ *n.* & *v.* • *n.* **1** a method of printing or engraving in which the surface of a plate is roughened by scraping so that it produces tones and halftones. **2** a print produced by this proc-

metronome

ess. • *v. tr.* engrave in mezzotint. □□ **mez•zo•tint•er** *n.* [It. *mezzotin-to* f. *mezzo* half + *tinto* tint]

MF *abbr.* medium frequency.

mf *abbr.* mezzo forte.

M.F.A. *abbr.* Master of Fine Arts.

mfg. *abbr.* manufacturing.

m.f.n. *abbr.* most favored nation.

mfr. *abbr.* **1** manufacture. **2** manufacturer.

MG *abbr.* **1** machine gun. **2** major general. **3** myasthenia gravis.

Mg *symb. Chem.* the element magnesium.

mg *abbr.* milligram(s).

Mgr. *abbr.* **1** Manager. **2** Monseigneur. **3** Monsignor.

mho /mō/ *n. (pl.* **mhos)** *Electr.* the reciprocal of an ohm, a former unit of conductance. [OHM reversed]

MHR *abbr.* (in the US and Australia) Member of the House of Representatives.

MHz *abbr.* megahertz.

MI *abbr.* **1** Michigan (in official postal use). **2** myocardial infarction.

M.I.5 *abbr.* (in the UK) the department of Military Intelligence concerned with government security.
▶Neither *M.I.5* nor *M.I.6* is in official use.

M.I.6 *abbr.* (in the UK) the department of Military Intelligence concerned with espionage.

mi /mee/ *n.* (also **me**) *Mus.* **1** the third tone of the diatonic scale. **2** the note E in the fixed solmization system. [ME f. L *mira*: see GAMUT]

mi. *abbr.* mile(s).

MIA *abbr.* missing in action.

Mi•am•i /mīámee/ *n. & adj.* • *n.* **1 a** a N. American people native to the midwestern United States. **b** a member of this people. **2** the language of this people. • *adj.* of or relating to this people or their language.

mi•as•ma /mī-ázmə, mee-/ *n. (pl.* **mi•as•ma•ta** /-mətə/ or **mi•as•mas**) *archaic* an infectious or noxious vapor. □□ **mi•as•mal** *adj.* **mi•as•mat•ic** /-mátik/ *adj.* **mi•as•mic** *adj.* **miasmically** *adv.* [Gk, = defilement, f. *miainō* pollute]

Mic. *abbr.* Micah (Old Testament).

mi•ca /mīkə/ *n.* any of a group of silicate minerals with a layered structure, esp. muscovite. □□ **mi•ca•ceous** /-káyshəs/ *adj.* [L, = crumb]

mice *pl.* of MOUSE.

mi•celle /misél, mī-/ *n. Chem.* an aggregate of molecules in a colloidal solution, as occurs, e.g., when soap dissolves in water. [mod.L *micella* dimin. of L *mica* crumb]

Mich. *abbr.* **1** Michigan. **2** Michaelmas.

Mich•ael•mas /míkəlməs/ *n.* the feast of St. Michael, September 29. [OE *sancte Micheles mæsse* Saint Michael's mass: see MASS[2]]

Mich•ael•mas dai•sy *n.* an autumn-flowering aster.

Mich•ael•mas term *n. Brit.* (in some universities) the autumn term.

mick /mik/ *n. sl. offens.* an Irishman. [pet form of the name *Michael*]

Mick•ey Finn /míkee fín/ (often **Mickey**) *n. sl.* **1** an alcoholic drink, adulterated with a narcotic or laxative. **2** the adulterant itself. [20th c.: orig. uncert.]

mick•le /míkəl/ *adj. & n. archaic* or *Sc.* • *adj.* much, great. • *n.* a large amount. □ **many a little makes a mickle** many small amounts accumulate to make a large amount. [ME f. ON *mikell* f. Gmc]

mi•cro /míkrō/ *n. (pl.* **•cros)** *colloq.* **1** = MICROCOMPUTER. **2** = MICROPROCESSOR.

micro- /míkrō/ *comb. form* **1** small (*microchip*). **2** denoting a factor of one millionth (10^{-6}) (*microgram*). ¶ Symb.: μ. [Gk *mikro-* f. *mikros* small]

mi•cro•a•nal•y•sis /míkrōənálisis/ *n.* the quantitative analysis of chemical compounds using a sample of a few milligrams.

mi•crobe /míkrōb/ *n.* a minute living being; a microorganism (esp. bacteria causing disease and fermentation). □□ **mi•cro•bi•al** /-krṓbeeəl/ *adj.* **mi•cro•bic** /-krṓbik/ *adj.* [F f. Gk *mikros* small + *bios* life]

mi•cro•bi•ol•o•gy /míkrōbīóləjee/ *n.* the scientific study of microorganisms, e.g., bacteria, viruses, and fungi. □□ **mi•cro•bi•o•log•i•cal** /-bīəlójikəl/ *adj.* **mi•cro•bi•o•log•i•cal•ly** /-bīəlójiklee/ *adv.* **mi•cro•bi•ol•o•gist** *n.*

mi•cro•brew•er•y /míkrōbrṓʻəree/ *n.* a limited-production brewery, often selling only locally.

mic•ro•burst /míkrōbərst/ *n.* a particularly violent wind shear, esp. during a thunderstorm.

mi•cro•ceph•a•ly /míkrōséfəlee/ *n.* an abnormal smallness of the head in relation to the rest of the body. □□ **mi•cro•ce•phal•ic** /-sifálik/ *adj. & n.* **mi•cro•ceph•a•lous** /-séfələs/ *adj.*

mi•cro•chip /míkrōchip/ *n.* a small piece of semiconductor (usu. silicon) used to carry electronic circuits.

mi•cro•cir•cuit /míkrōsərkit/ *n.* an integrated circuit on a microchip. □□ **mi•cro•cir•cuit•ry** *n.*

mi•cro•cli•mate /míkrōklīmit/ *n.* the climate of a small local area, e.g., inside a greenhouse. □□ **mi•cro•cli•mat•ic** /-mátik/ *adj.* **mi•cro•cli•mat•i•cal•ly** /-mátiklee/ *adv.*

mi•cro•code /míkrōkōd/ *n.* **1** = MICROINSTRUCTION. **2** = MICROPROGRAM.

Mi•cro•com•pu•ter /míkrōkəmpyŏótər/ *n.* a small computer that contains a microprocessor as its central processor.

mi•cro•cop•y /míkrōkópee/ *n. & v.* • *n. (pl.* **•ies)** a copy of printed matter that has been reduced by microphotography. • *v. tr.* (**•ies,** • **ied)** make a microcopy of.

mi•cro•cosm /míkrəkozəm/ *n.* **1** (often foll. by *of*) a miniature representation. **2** mankind viewed as the epitome of the universe. **3** any community or complex unity viewed in this way. □□ **mi•cro•cos•mic** /-kózmik/ *adj.* **mi•cro•cos•mi•cal•ly** /-kózmiklee/ *adv.* [ME f. F *microcosme* or med.L *microcosmus* f. Gk *mikros kosmos* little world]

mi•cro•dot /míkrōdot/ *n.* a microphotograph of a document, etc., reduced to the size of a dot.

mi•cro•ec•o•nom•ics /míkrō-éekənómiks, –ék–/ *n.* the branch of economics dealing with individual commodities, producers, etc.

mi•cro•e•lec•tron•ics /míkrō-ílektróniks/ *n.* the design, manufacture, and use of microchips and microcircuits.

mi•cro•fiche /míkrōfeesh/ *n. (pl.* same or **mi•cro•fich•es**) a flat rectangular piece of film bearing microphotographs of the pages of a printed text or document.

mi•cro•film /míkrəfilm/ *n. & v.* • *n.* a length of film bearing microphotographs of documents, etc. • *v. tr.* photograph (a document, etc.) on microfilm.

mi•cro•form /míkrōfawrm/ *n.* microphotographic reproduction on film or paper of a manuscript, etc.

mi•cro•gram /míkrōgram/ *n.* one-millionth of a gram.

mi•cro•graph /míkrōgraf/ *n.* a photograph taken by means of a microscope.

mi•cro•in•struc•tion /míkrō-instrúkshən/ *n.* a machine-code instruction that effects a basic operation in a computer system.

mi•cro•light /míkrōlit/ *n.* a kind of motorized hang glider.

mi•cro•lith /míkrōlith/ *n. Archaeol.* a minute worked flint usu. as part of a composite tool. □□ **mi•cro•lith•ic** /-líthik/ *adj.*

mi•cro•man•age /míkrōmánij/ *v.* control every part, no matter how detailed, of an enterprise.

mi•cro•mesh /míkrōmesh/ *n.* (often *attrib.*) material, esp. nylon, consisting of a very fine mesh.

mi•crom•e•ter[1] /mikrómitər/ *n.* a gauge for accurately measuring small distances, thicknesses, etc. □□ **mi•crom•e•try** *n.*

mi•cro•me•ter[2] /míkrōméetər/ *n.* = MICRON.

mi•cro•min•i•a•tur•i•za•tion /míkrōmínee-əchərīzáyshən/ *n.* the manufacture of very small electronic devices by using integrated circuits.

mi•cron /míkron/ *n.* one-millionth of a meter. Also called **micrometer**. [Gk *mikron* neut. of *mikros* small: cf. MICRO-]

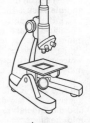

micrometer

Mi•cro•ne•sian /míkrəneé́ezhən/ *adj. & n.* • *adj.* of or relating to Micronesia, an island group in the W. Pacific. • *n.* a native of Micronesia. [*Micronesia*, formed as MICRO- + Gk *nēsos* island]

mi•cro•or•gan•ism /míkrō-áwrgənizəm/ *n.* any of various microscopic organisms, including algae, bacteria, fungi, protozoa, and viruses.

mi•cro•phone /míkrəfōn/ *n.* an instrument for converting sound waves into electrical energy variations that may be reconverted into sound after transmission by wire or radio or after recording. □□ **mi•cro•phon•ic** /-fónik/ *adj.*

mi•cro•pho•to•graph /míkrōfṓtəgraf/ *n.* a photograph reduced to a very small size.

mi•cro•phyte /míkrōfīt/ *n.* a microscopic plant.

mi•cro•proc•es•sor /míkrōprósesər/ *n.* an integrated circuit that contains all the functions of a central processing unit of a computer.

mi•cro•pro•gram /míkrōprógram/ *n.* a microinstruction program that controls the functions of a central processing unit of a computer.

mi•cro•pyle /míkrōpīl/ *n. Bot.* a small opening in the surface of an ovule, through which pollen passes. [MICRO- + Gk *pulē* gate]

mi•cro•scope /míkrəskōp/ *n.* an instrument magnifying small objects by means of a lens or lenses so as to reveal details invisible to the naked eye. [mod.L *microscopium* (as MICRO-, –SCOPE)]

mi•cro•scop•ic /míkrəskópik/ *adj.* **1** so small as to be visible only with a microscope. **2** extremely small. **3** regarded in terms of small units. **4** of the microscope. □□ **mi•cro•scop•i•cal** *adj.* (in sense 4). **mi•cro•scop•i•cal•ly** *adv.*

mi•cros•co•py /míkróskəpee/ *n.* the use of the microscope. □□ **mi•cros•co•pist** *n.*

mi•cro•sec•ond /míkrōsekənd/ *n.* one-millionth of a second.

microscope

mi•cro•some /míkrəsōm/ n. Biol. a small particle of organelle fragments obtained by centrifugation of homogenized cells. [MICRO- + –SOME³]

mi•cro•spore /míkrəspawr/ n. the smaller of the two kinds of spore produced by some ferns.

mi•cro•struc•ture /míkrōstrúkchər/ n. (in a metal or other material) the arrangement of crystals, etc., that can be made visible and examined with a microscope.

mi•cro•sur•ger•y /míkrōsúrjəree/ n. intricate surgery performed using microscopes, enabling the tissue to be operated on with miniaturized precision instruments. □□ **mi•cro•sur•gi•cal** /–súrjikəl/ adj.

mi•cro•switch /míkrōswich/ n. a switch that can be operated rapidly by a small movement.

mic•ro•tome /míkrətōm/ n. an instrument for cutting extremely thin sections of material for examination under a microscope. [MICRO- + –TOME]

mi•cro•tone /míkrətōn/ n. Mus. an interval smaller than a semitone.

mi•cro•tu•bule /míkrōtooˌbyool, –tyoo–/ n. Biol. a minute protein filament occurring in cytoplasm and involved in forming the spindles during cell division, etc.

mi•cro•wave /míkrəwayv/ n. & v. • n. 1 an electromagnetic wave with a wavelength in the range 0.001–0.3m. 2 (in full **microwave oven**) an oven that uses microwaves to cook or heat food quickly. • v. tr. (•ing) cook in a microwave oven.

mic•tu•ri•tion /míkchəríshən/ n. formal or Med. urination. [L micturire micturit-, desiderative f. mingere mict- urinate]

mid¹ /mid/ attrib.adj. 1 (usu. in comb.) that is the middle of (in mid-air; from mid-June to mid-July). 2 that is in the middle; medium, half. 3 Phonet. (of a vowel) pronounced with the tongue neither high nor low. [OE midd (recorded only in oblique cases), rel. to L medius, Gk mesos]

mid² /mid/ prep. poet. = AMID. [abbr. f. AMID]

mid•air /midáir/ n. a place or point in the air far removed from the ground or other solid surface.

Mi•das touch /mídəs/ n. the ability to turn one's activities to financial advantage. [Midas, king of Phrygia, whose touch was said to turn all things to gold]

mid•brain /mídbrayn/ n. the part of the brain developing from the middle of the primitive or embryonic brain.

mid•day /míd-dáy/ n. the middle of the day; noon. [OE middæg (as MID¹, DAY)]

mid•den /míd'n/ n. 1 a dunghill. 2 a refuse heap near a dwelling. 3 = KITCHEN MIDDEN. [ME myddyng, of Scand. orig.: cf. Da. mødding muck heap]

mid•dle /míd'l/ adj., n., & v. • attrib.adj. 1 at an equal distance from the extremities of a thing. 2 (of a member of a group) so placed as to have the same number of members on each side. 3 intermediate in rank, quality, etc. 4 average (of middle height). 5 (of a language) of the period between the old and modern forms. 6 Gram. designating the voice of (esp. Greek) verbs that expresses reciprocal or reflexive action. • n. 1 (often foll. by of) the middle point or position or part. 2 a person's waist. 3 Gram. the middle form or voice of a verb. 4 = MIDDLE TERM. • v. tr. 1 place in the middle. 2 Soccer return (the ball) from the wing to the midfield. 3 Naut. fold in the middle. □ **in the middle of** (often foll. by verbal noun) in the process of; during. [OE middel f. Gmc]

mid•dle age n. the period between youth and old age, about 45 to 60. □□ mid•dle-aged adj.

Mid•dle Ag•es n.pl. the period of European history from the fall of the Roman Empire in the West (5th c.) to the fall of Constantinople (1453), or more narrowly from c.1000 to 1453.

Mid•dle A•mer•i•ca n. 1 the N. American region that includes Mexico and Central America, and often the West Indies. 2 the middle class in the US, esp. as a conservative political force. 3 the US Middle West.

mid•dle•brow /míd'lbrow/ adj. & n. colloq. • adj. claiming to be or regarded as only moderately intellectual. • n. a middlebrow person.

mid•dle C n. Mus. the C near the middle of the piano keyboard, the note between the treble and bass staves, at about 260 Hz.

mid•dle class n. the class of society between the upper and the lower, including professional and business workers and their families. □□ mid•dle-class adj.

mid•dle dis•tance n. 1 (in a painting, drawing, or actual landscape) the part between the foreground and the background. 2 Track a race distance of esp. 800 or 1500 meters.

mid•dle ear n. the cavity of the central part of the ear behind the eardrum.

Mid•dle East n. the area covered by countries from Egypt to Iran inclusive. □□ **Mid•dle East•ern** adj. of or in the Middle East.

Mid•dle Eng•lish n. the English language from c.1150 to 1500.

mid•dle fin•ger n. the finger between the forefinger and the ring finger.

mid•dle game n. the central phase of a chess game, when strategies are developed.

mid•dle ground n. a neutral position between two opposing extremes.

mid•dle-in•come adj. of the wages earned by the middle class.

mid•dle man•age•ment n. in business and industry, the mid-level positions in administration.

mid•dle name n. 1 a person's name placed after the first name and before the surname. 2 a person's most characteristic quality (sobriety is my middle name).

mid•dle-of-the-road adj. (of a person, course of action, etc.) moderate; avoiding extremes.

mid•dle pas•sage n. the sea journey between W. Africa and the W. Indies (with ref. to the slave trade).

mid•dle school n. a school for children from about 10 to 13 years old (grades 5–8).

Mid•dle Tem•ple n. one of the two Inns of Court on the site of the Temple in London (cf. INNER TEMPLE).

mid•dle term n. Logic the term common to both premises of a syllogism.

mid•dle watch n. the watch from midnight to 4 a.m. on board a ship.

mid•dle•man /míd'lman/ n. (pl. •men) 1 any of the traders who handle a commodity between its producer and its consumer. 2 an intermediary.

mid•dle•weight /míd'lwayt/ n. 1 a weight in certain sports intermediate between welterweight and light heavyweight. 2 a sportsman of this weight.

Mid•dle West n. = MIDWEST

mid•dling /mídling/ adj., n., & adv. • adj. 1 a moderately good (esp. fair to middling). b second-rate. 2 (of goods) of the second of three grades. • n. (in pl.) middling goods, esp. flour of medium fineness. • adv. 1 fairly or moderately (middling good). 2 colloq. fairly well (esp. in health). □□ **mid•dling•ly** adv. [ME, of Sc. orig.: prob. f. MID¹ + –LING²]

mid•dy¹ /mídee/ n. (pl. •dies) 1 colloq. a midshipman. 2 (in full **middy blouse**) a woman's or child's loose blouse with a collar like that worn by sailors.

mid•dy² /mídee/ n. (pl. •dies) Austral. sl. a measure of beer of varying size, often a half a pint. [20th c.: orig. unkn.]

Mid•east /mídeest/ n. = MIDDLE EAST.

mid•field /mídfeeld/ n. in certain sports, esp. football and soccer, the area of the field midway between the two goals. □□ **mid•field•er** n.

midge /mij/ n. 1 colloq. a a gnatlike insect. b a small person. 2 a any dipterous nonbiting insect of the family Chironomidae. b any similar insect of the family Ceratopogonidae with piercing mouthparts for sucking blood or eating smaller insects. [OE mycg(e) f. Gmc]

mid•get /míjit/ n. 1 an extremely small person or thing. 2 (attrib.) very small. [MIDGE + –ET¹]

mid•gut /mídgút/ n. the middle part of the alimentary canal, including the small intestine.

MIDI /mídee/ n. a system for using combinations of electronic equipment, esp. audio and computer equipment. [acronym of musical instrument digital interface]

mi•di /mídee/ n. (pl. **mi•dis**) a garment of medium length, usu. reaching to mid-calf. [MID¹ after MINI]

mid•i•nette /mídinét/ n. a Parisian shopgirl, esp. a milliner's assistant. [F f. midi midday + dînette light dinner]

mid•land /mídlənd/ n. & adj. • n. 1 the middle part of a country. 2 the dialect of American English spoken in the east-central US, from southern New Jersey and northern Delaware west across the Appalachians and the Ohio and Mississippi river valleys. 3 (the Midlands) the inland counties of central England. • adj. of or in the midland or Midlands. □□ **mid•land•er** n.

mid•life /mídlīf/ n. middle age.

mid•life cri•sis n. an emotional crisis of self-confidence that can occur in early middle age.

mid•line /mídlīn/ n. a median line, or plane of bilateral symmetry.

mid•most /mídmōst/ adj. & adv. in the very middle.

mid•night /mídnīt/ n. 1 the middle of the night; 12 o'clock at night. 2 intense darkness. [OE midniht (as MID¹, NIGHT)]

mid•night sun n. the sun visible at midnight during the summer in polar regions.

mid•rash /mídraash/ n. (pl. **mid•ra•shim** /–shím/) an ancient commentary on part of the Hebrew scriptures. [Bibl. Heb. midrāš commentary]

mid•rib /mídrib/ n. the central rib of a leaf.

mid•riff /mídrif/ n. 1 a the region of the front of the body between the thorax and abdomen. b the diaphragm. 2 a garment or part of a garment covering the abdomen. [OE midhrif (as MID¹, hrif belly)]

mid•ship /mídship/ n. the middle part of a ship or boat.

mid•ship•man /mídshipmən/ n. (pl. •men) 1 a cadet in the U.S. Naval Academy. 2 Brit. a naval officer of rank between naval cadet and sublieutenant.

mid•ships /mídships/ adv. = AMIDSHIPS.

midst /midst/ prep. & n. • prep. poet. amidst. • n. middle (now only in phrases as below). □ **in the midst of** among; in the middle of. in our (or **your** or **their**) midst among us (or you or them). [ME *mid-dest*, *middes* f. *in middes*, *in middan* (as IN, MID¹)]

mid·sum·mer /mídsúmər/ *n.* the period of or near the summer solstice, around June 21. [OE *midsumor* (as MID¹, SUMMER¹)]

Mid·sum·mer Day *n.* (also **Mid·sum·mer's Day**) (in England, Wales, and Ireland) June 24, originally coinciding with the summer solstice and in some countries marked by a summer festival.

mid·town /mídtown/ *n.* the central part of a city between the downtown and uptown areas.

mid·way /mídwáy/ *n. & adv.* • *n.* area for concessions and amusements at a carnival, fair, etc. • *adv.* in or toward the middle of the distance between two points.

Mid·west /mídwést/ *n.* region of northern US states from Ohio west to the Rocky Mountains.

mid·wife /mídwíf/ *n.* (*pl.* **·wives** /–wīvz/) **1** a person (usu. a woman) trained to assist women in childbirth. **2** a person who helps in producing or bringing something forth. □□ **mid·wife·ry** /mídwífəree, –wífəree/ *n.* [ME, prob. f. obs. prep. *mid* with + WIFE woman, in the sense of 'one who is with the mother']

PRONUNCIATION TIP midwife/midwifery

Although *midwife* is pronounced with a "long i" in the second syllable, *midwifery* is often pronounced with a "short i," rhyming with *whiff*.

mid·win·ter /mídwíntər/ *n.* the period of or near the winter solstice, around Dec. 22 [OE (as MID¹, WINTER)]

mien /meen/ *n. literary* a person's look or bearing, as showing character or mood. [prob. f. obs. *demean* f. DEMEAN², assim. to F *mine* expression]

miff /mif/ *v. & n. colloq.* • *v.tr.* (usu. in *passive*) put out of humor; offend. • *n.* **1** a petty quarrel. **2** a huff. [perh. imit.: cf. G *muff*, exclam. of disgust]

might¹ /mīt/ *past* of MAY, used esp.: **1** in reported speech, expressing possibility (*said he might come*) or permission (*asked if I might leave*) (cf. MAY 1, 2). **2** expressing a possibility based on a condition not fulfilled (*if you'd looked you might have found it; but for the radio we might not have known*). **3** expressing complaint that an obligation or expectation is not or has not been fulfilled (*he might offer to help; they might have asked; you might have known they wouldn't come*). **4** expressing a request (*you might call in at the butcher's*). **5** *colloq.* **a** = MAY 1 (*it might be true*). **b** (in tentative questions) = MAY 2 (*might I have the pleasure of this dance?*). **c** = MAY 4 (*who might you be?*). □ **might as well** expressing that it is probably at least as desirable to do a thing as not to do it (*finished the work and decided they might as well go to lunch; won't win but might as well try*).
▶See note at MAY.

might² /mīt/ *n.* **1** great bodily or mental strength. **2** power to enforce one's will (usu. in contrast with *right*). □ **with all one's might** to the utmost of one's power. **with might and main** see MAIN ¹. [OE *miht*, *mieht* f. Gmc, rel. to MAY]

might-have-been *n. colloq.* **1** a past possibility that no longer applies. **2** a person who could have been more eminent.

mightn't /mít'nt/ *contr.* might not.

might·y /mítee/ *adj. & adv.* • *adj.* (**might·i·er**, **might·i·est**) **1** powerful or strong, in body, mind, or influence. **2** *colloq.* great, considerable. • *adv. colloq.* very (*a mighty difficult task*). □□ **might·i·ly** *adv.* **might·i·ness** *n.* [OE *mihtig* (as MIGHT²)]

mi·gnon·ette /mínyənét/ *n.* **1 a** any of various plants of the genus *Reseda*, esp. *R. odorata*, with fragrant greenish-white flowers. **b** the color of these. **2** a light, fine, narrow pillow lace. [F *mignonnette* dimin. of *mignon* small]

mi·graine /mígrayn/ *n.* a recurrent throbbing headache that usually affects one side of the head, often accompanied by nausea and disturbance of vision. □□ **mi·grain·ous** /–gráynis/ *adj.* [F f. LL *hem-icrania* f. Gk *hēmikrania* (as HEMI-, CRANIUM): orig. of a headache confined to one side of the head]

mi·grant /mígrənt/ *adj. & n.* • *adj.* that migrates. • *n.* **1** a person who moves regularly, as for work. **2** an animal that changes habitats, as with the seasons.

mi·grate /mígráyt/ *v.intr.* **1** (of people) move from one place of abode to another, esp. in a different country. **2** (of a bird or fish) change its area of habitation with the seasons. **3** move under natural forces. □□ **mi·gra·tion** /–gráyshən/ *n.* **mi·gra·tion·al** /–gráyshənəl/ *adj.* **mi·gra·tor** *n.* **mi·gra·to·ry** /–grətáwree/ *adj.* [L *migrare migrat–*]

mih·rab /meeraab/ *n.* a niche or slab in a mosque, used to show the direction of Mecca. [Arab. *miḥrāb* praying place]

mi·ka·do /mikaado/ *n.* (*pl.* **·dos**) *hist.* the emperor of Japan. [Jap. f. *mi* august + *kado* door]

mike /mīk/ *n. colloq.* a microphone. [abbr.]

mil /mil/ *n.* one-thousandth of an inch, as a unit of measure for the diameter of wire, etc. [L *millesimum* thousandth f. *mille* thousand]

mi·la·dy /miláydee/ *n.* (*pl.* **·dies**) **1** an English noblewoman or great lady. **2** a form used in speaking of or to such a person. [F f. E *my lady*: cf. MILORD]

mil·age var. of MILEAGE.

Mi·lan·ese /mílənéez/ *adj. & n.* • *adj.* of or relating to Milan in N. Italy. • *n.* (*pl.* same) a native of Milan.

milch /milch/ *adj.* (of a domestic mammal) giving or kept for milk. [ME *m(i)elche* repr. OE *mielce* (unrecorded) f. Gmc: see MILK]

mild /mīld/ *adj.* **1** (esp. of a person) gentle and conciliatory. **2** (of a rule, punishment, illness, feeling, etc.) moderate; not severe. **3** (of the weather, esp. in winter) moderately warm. **4** (of food, tobacco, etc.) not sharp or strong in taste, etc. **5** (of medicine) operating gently. **6** tame; feeble; lacking energy or vivacity. □□ **mild·en** *v.tr. & intr.* **mild·ish** *adj.* **mild·ness** *n.* [OE *milde* f. Gmc]

mil·dew /míldoo, –dyoo/ *n. & v.* • *n.* **1** a destructive growth of minute fungi on plants. **2** a similar growth on paper, leather, etc., exposed to damp. • *v.tr. & intr.* taint or be tainted with mildew. □□ **mil·dew·y** *adj.* [OE *mildēaw* f. Gmc]

mild·ly /míldlee/ *adv.* in a mild fashion. □ **to put it mildly** as an understatement (implying the reality is more extreme).

mild steel *n.* steel containing a small percentage of carbon, strong and tough but not readily tempered.

mile /mīl/ *n.* **1** (also **stat·ute mile**) a unit of linear measure equal to 1,760 yards (approx. 1.609 kilometers). **2** *hist.* a Roman measure of 1,000 paces (approx. 1,620 yards). **3** (in *pl.*) *colloq.* a great distance or amount (*miles better; beat them by miles*). **4** a race extending over a mile. [OE *mīl* ult. f. L *mil(l)ia* pl. of *mille* thousand (see sense 2)]

mile·age /mílij/ *n.* (also **mil·age**) **1 a** a number of miles traveled, used, etc. **b** the number of miles traveled by a vehicle per unit of fuel. **2** traveling expenses (per mile). **3** *colloq.* benefit, profit, advantage (*we got a lot of mileage out of that old chair*).

mile·post /mílpōst/ *n.* **1** a post or sign giving distance in miles, as along a highway. **2** a post one mile from the finish line of a race, etc.

mil·er /mílər/ *n. colloq.* a person or horse qualified or trained specially to run a mile.

mile·stone /mílstōn/ *n.* **1** a stone set up beside a road to mark a distance in miles. **2** a significant event or stage in a life, history, project, etc.

mil·foil /mílfoyl/ *n.* the common yarrow, *Achillea millefolium*, with small white flowers and finely divided leaves. [ME f. OF f. L *mille-folium* f. *mille* thousand + *folium* leaf, after Gk *muriophullon*]

mil·i·ar·y /mílee-éree, mílyəree/ *adj.* **1** like a millet seed in size or form. **2** (of a disease) having as a symptom a rash with lesions resembling millet seed. [L *miliarius* f. *milium* millet]

mi·lieu /milyṓ, meélyō/ *n.* (*pl.* **mi·lieus** or **mi·lieux** /–lyṓz/) one's environment or social surroundings. [F f. *mi* MID¹ + *lieu* place]

mil·i·tant /mílit'nt/ *adj. & n.* • *adj.* **1** combative; aggressively active, esp. in support of a (usu. political) cause. **2** engaged in warfare. • *n.* **1** a militant person, esp. a political activist. **2** a person engaged in warfare. □□ **mil·i·tan·cy** *n.* **mil·i·tant·ly** *adv.* [ME f. OF f. L (as MILITATE)]

mil·i·ta·rism /mílitərizəm/ *n.* **1** the spirit or tendencies of a professional soldier. **2** undue prevalence of the military spirit or ideals. □□ **mil·i·ta·ris·tic** /–rístik/ *adj.* **mil·i·ta·ris·ti·cal·ly** /–rístiklee/ *adv.* [F *militarisme* (as MILITARY)]

mil·i·ta·rist /mílitərist/ *n.* **1** a person dominated by militaristic ideas. **2** a student of military science.

mil·i·ta·rize /mílitərīz/ *v.tr.* **1** equip with military resources. **2** make military or warlike. **3** imbue with militarism. □□ **mil·i·ta·ri·za·tion** *n.*

mil·i·tar·y /mílitéree/ *adj. & n.* • *adj.* of, relating to, or characteristic of soldiers or armed forces. • *n.* (as *sing.* or *pl.*; prec. by *the*) members of the armed forces, as distinct from civilians and the police. □□ **mil·i·tar·i·ly** /–táirəlee/ *adv.* **mil·i·tar·i·ness** *n.* [F *militaire* or L *militaris* f. *miles militis* soldier]

mil·i·tar·y hon·ors *n.pl.* marks of respect paid by troops at the burial of a soldier, to royalty, etc.

mil·i·tar·y po·lice *n.* a corps responsible for police and disciplinary duties in the army.

mil·i·tate /mí litayt/ *v.intr.* (usu. foll. by *against*) (of facts or evidence) have force or effect (*what you say militates against our opinion*). [L *militare militat–* f. *miles militis* soldier]
▶**Militate**, a word usually followed by *against*, means 'have a profound effect or force': *Overeagerness on our part would militate against success in negotiation*. Do not confuse it with **mitigate**, which means 'make less intense or severe': *Tension can lead to headaches unless mitigated by some form of regular relaxation.*.

mi·li·tia /milíshə/ *n.* **1** a military force, esp. one raised from the civil population and supplementing a regular army in an emergency. **2** a military force that engages in rebel or terrorist activities, typically in opposition to a regular army. [L, = military service f. *miles militis* soldier]

mi·li·tia·man /milíshəmən/ *n.* (*pl.* **·men**) a member of a militia.

milk /milk/ *n. & v.* • *n.* **1** an opaque white fluid secreted by female mammals for the nourishment of their young. **2** the milk of cows, goats, or sheep as food. **3** the milklike juice of plants, e.g., in the coconut. **4** a milklike preparation of herbs, drugs, etc. ● *v. tr.* **1** draw milk from (a cow, ewe, goat, etc.). **2 a** exploit (a person) esp. financially. **b** get all possible advantage from (a situation). **3** extract sap, venom, etc., from. **4** *sl.* tap (telegraph or telephone wires, etc.). □ **cry over spilled milk** lament an irremediable loss or error. **in milk** secreting milk. □□ **milk·er** *n.* [OE *milc, milcian* f. Gmc]

milk and hon·ey *n.* abundant means of prosperity.

milk choc·o·late *n.* solid chocolate made in a similar way to plain chocolate but with the addition of milk.

milk leg *n.* a painful swelling of the leg after giving birth, caused by thrombophlebitis in the femoral vein.

milk·maid /mílkmayd/ *n.* a girl or woman who milks cows or works in a dairy.

milk of mag·ne·sia *n.* a white suspension of magnesium hydroxide usu. in water as an antacid or laxative.

milk·man /mílkman/ *n.* (*pl.* **·men**) a person who sells or delivers milk.

milk route *n.* **1** a fixed route on which milk is delivered regularly. **2** a regular trip or tour involving calls at several places.

milk run *n.* a routine expedition or service journey.

milk shake *n.* a drink of milk, flavoring, and usu. ice cream, mixed by shaking or blending.

milk snake *n.* any of various harmless snakes, *Lampropeltis triangulum*, common to N. America, with colorful markings on a grayish or tan body.

milk·sop /mílksop/ *n.* a spiritless or meek person, esp. a man.

milk sug·ar *n.* lactose.

milk-toast *adj. & n.* ● *adj.* lacking assertiveness; timid. ● *n.* = MILQUETOAST.

milk tooth *n.* a temporary tooth in young mammals.

milk vetch *n.* any leguminous yellow-flowered plant of the genus *Astragalus*.

milk·weed /mílkweed/ *n.* any of various wild plants with milky juice.

milk·wort /mílkwərt/ *n.* any plant of the genus *Polygala*, formerly supposed to increase women's milk.

milk·y /mílkee/ *adj.* (**milk·i·er, milk·i·est**) **1** of, like, or mixed with milk. **2** (of a gem or liquid) cloudy; not clear. **3** effeminate; weakly amiable. □ **Milky Way** a faintly luminous band of light emitted by countless stars encircling the heavens; the Galaxy. □□ **milk·i·ness** *n.*

mill[1] /mil/ *n. & v.* ● *n.* **1 a** a building fitted with a mechanical apparatus for grinding grain. **b** such an apparatus. **2** an apparatus for grinding any solid substance to powder or pulp (*pepper mill*). **3 a** a building fitted with machinery for manufacturing processes, etc. (*cotton mill*). **b** such machinery. **4 a** a boxing match. **b** a fistfight. **5** a place that processes things or people in a mechanical way (*diploma mill*). ● *v.* **1** *tr.* grind (grain), produce (flour), or hull (seeds) in a mill. **2** *tr.* produce regular ribbed markings on the edge of (a coin). **3** *tr.* cut or shape (metal) with a rotating tool. **4** *intr.* (often foll. by *about, around*) (of people or animals) move in an aimless manner, esp. in a confused mass. **5** *tr.* thicken (cloth, etc.) by fulling. **6** *tr.* beat (chocolate, etc.) to froth. **7** *tr. sl.* beat, strike, fight. □ **go** (or **put**) **through the mill** undergo (or cause to undergo) intensive work or training, etc. □□ **mill·a·ble** *adj.* [OE *mylen* ult. f. LL *molinum* f. L *mola* grindstone, mill f. *molere* grind]

mill[2] /mil/ *n.* one-thousandth of a US dollar as money of account. [L *millesimum* thousandth: cf. CENT]

mill·board /mílbawrd/ *n.* stout pasteboard for bookbinding, etc.

mille-feuille /meelfő-yə/ *n.* a rich confection of puff pastry split and filled with custard, whipped cream, etc. [F, = thousand-leaf]

mil·le·nar·i·an /mílináireeən/ *adj. & n.* ● *adj.* **1** of or related to the millennium. **2** believing in the millennium. ● *n.* a person who believes in the millennium. [as MILLENARY]

mil·le·nar·y /mílənéree/ *n. & adj.* ● *n.* (*pl.* **·ies**) **1** a period of 1,000 years. **2** the festival of the 1,000th anniversary of a person or thing. **3** a person who believes in the millennium. ● *adj.* of or relating to a millenary. [LL *millenarius* consisting of a thousand f. *milleni* distrib. of *mille* thousand]

mil·len·ni·um /míléneeəm/ *n.* (*pl.* **mil·len·ni·a** /–neeə/ or **mil·len·ni·ums**) **1** a period of a thousand years, esp. when calculated from the traditional date of the birth of Christ. **2** an anniversary of a

SPELLING TIP milmium

The spelling of **millennium** is less difficult if you remember that it comes ultimately from two Latin words containing double letters: *mille*, 'thousand,' and *annum*, 'year.'

---

thousand years. **3** *Christian Theology* the prophesied thousand-year reign of Christ at the end of the age (Rev. 20:1-5). **4** a utopian period of good government, happiness, and prosperity. □□ **mil·len·ni·al** *adj.* **mil·len·ni·al·ist** *n. & adj.* [mod.L f. L *mille* thousand after BIENNIUM]

mil·le·pede var. of MILLIPEDE.

mil·le·pore /mílipawr/ *n.* a reef-building coral of the order Milleporina, with polyps protruding through pores in the calcareous exoskeleton. [F *millépore* or mod.L *millepora* f. L *mille* thousand + *porus* PORE[1]]

mill·er /mílər/ *n.* **1** the proprietor or tenant of a mill. **2** a person who works or owns a mill. [ME *mylnere*, prob. f. MLG, MDu. *molner, mulner*, OS *mulineri* f. LL *molinarius* f. *molina* MILL[1], assim. to MILL[1]]

mill·er's-thumb *n.* a small spiny freshwater fish, *Cottus gobio*. Also called **bullhead**.

mil·les·i·mal /mílésiməl/ *adj. & n.* ● *adj.* **1** thousandth. **2** of or belonging to a thousandth. **3** of or dealing with thousandths. ● *n.* a thousandth part. □□ **mil·les·i·mal·ly** *adv.* [L *millesimus* f. *mille* thousand]

mil·let /mílit/ *n.* **1** any of various cereal plants, esp. *Panicum miliaceum*, bearing a large crop of small nutritious seeds. **2** the seed of this. [ME f. F, dimin. of *mil* f. L *milium*]

mil·let grass *n.* a tall woodland grass, *Milium effusum*.

milli- /mílee, –i, –ə/ *comb. form* a thousand, esp. denoting a factor of one thousandth. ¶ Abbr.: **m.** [L *mille* thousand]

mil·li·am·me·ter /míleeámitər/ *n.* an instrument for measuring electrical current in milliamperes.

mil·li·am·pere /míleeámpir/ *n.* one-thousandth of an ampere, a measure for small electrical currents.

mil·liard /mílyərd, –yaard/ *n. Brit.* one thousand million. ▶This word has been largely superseded by *billion*. [F f. *mille* thousand]

mil·li·bar /míləbaar/ *n.* one-thousandth of a bar, the cgs unit of atmospheric pressure equivalent to 100 pascals.

mil·li·gram /míligram/ *n.* one-thousandth of a gram.

mil·li·li·ter /míleeetər/ *n.* one-thousandth of a liter (0.002 pint).

mil·li·me·ter /mílimeetər/ *n.* one-thousandth of a meter (0.039 in.).

mil·li·ner /mílinər/ *n.* a person who makes or sells women's hats. □□ **mil·li·ner·y** /–eree/ *n.* [orig. = vendor of goods from *Milan*]

mil·lion /mílyən/ *n. & adj.* ● *n.* (*pl.* same or (in sense 2) **mil·lions**) (in *sing.* prec. by *a* or *one*) **1** a thousand thousand. **2** (in *pl.*) *colloq.* a very large number (*millions of years*). **3** (prec. by *the*) the bulk of the population. **4** (prec. by *a*) a million dollars. ● *adj.* that amount to a million. □ **gone a million** *Austral. sl.* completely defeated. □□ **mil·lion·fold** *adj. & adv.* **mil·lionth** *adj. & n.* [ME f. OF, prob. f. It. *millione* f. *mille* thousand + *–one* augment. suffix]

mil·lion·aire /mílyənáir/ *n.* (*fem.* **mil·lion·air·ess** /–ris/) **1** a person whose assets are worth at least one million dollars, pounds, etc. **2** a person of great wealth. [F *millionnaire* (as MILLION)]

mil·li·pede /míləpeed/ *n.* (also **mil·le·pede**) any arthropod of the class Diplopoda, having a long segmented body with two pairs of legs on each segment. [L *millepeda* wood louse f. *mille* thousand + *pes pedis* foot]

mil·li·sec·ond /mílisekənd/ *n.* one-thousandth of a second.

mill·pond /mílpond/ *n.* a pool of water retained by a dam for the operation of a mill. □ **like a millpond** (of a stretch of water) very calm.

mill·race /mílrays/ *n.* a current of water that drives a mill wheel.

mill·stone /mílstōn/ *n.* **1** each of two circular stones used for grinding grain. **2** a heavy burden or responsibility (cf. Matt. 18: 6).

mill·wright /mílrīt/ *n.* a person who designs, builds, or operates a mill or milling machinery.

mi·lom·e·ter /mílómitər/ *n. Brit.* an instrument for measuring the number of miles traveled by a vehicle.

mi·lord /miláwrd/ *n. hist.* an English gentleman, esp. one traveling in Europe in aristocratic style. [F f. E *my lord*: cf. MILADY]

milque·toast /mílktōst/ *n.* a meek, unassertive person. [for Casper *Milquetoast*, character in comic strip by US cartoonist H.T. Webster (1885–1952)]

milt /milt/ *n.* **1** a sperm-filled reproductive gland of a male fish. **2** the sperm-filled secretion of this gland. **3** var. of MELT[2]. [OE *milt(e)* f. Gmc, perh. rel. to MELT]

milt·er /míltər/ *n.* a male fish in spawning time.

mim·bar /mímbaar/ *n.* (also **min·bar** /mín–/) a stepped platform for preaching in a mosque. [Arab. *minbar*]

mime /mīm/ *n. & v.* ● *n.* **1** the theatrical technique of suggesting action, character, etc., by gesture and expression without using words. **2** a theatrical performance using this technique. **3** *Gk & Rom. Antiq.* a simple farcical drama including mimicry. **4** (also **mime art·ist**) a practitioner of mime. ● *v.* **1** *tr.* (also *absol.*) convey (an idea or emotion) by gesture without words. **2** *intr.* esp. *Brit.* (often foll. by *to*) (of singers, etc.) mouth the words of a song, etc., along with a recording or another's voice; lip-sync (*mime to a record*). □□ **mim·er** *n.* [L *mimus* f. Gk *mimos*]

mim·e·o·graph /mímeeəgraf/ *n. & v.* ● *n.* **1** (often *attrib.*) a duplicating machine that produces copies from a stencil. **2** a copy produced in this way. ● *v. tr.* reproduce (text or diagrams) by this process. [irreg. f. Gk *mimeomai* imitate: see −GRAPH]

mi•me•sis /mimḗesis, mī-/ *n. Biol.* a close external resemblance of an animal to another that is distasteful or harmful to predators of the first. [Gk *mimēsis* imitation]

mi•met•ic /mimétik/ *adj.* **1** relating to or habitually practicing imitation or mimicry. **2** *Biol.* of or exhibiting mimesis. □□ **mi•met•i•cal•ly** *adv.* [Gk *mimētikos* imitation (as MIMESIS)]

mim•ic /mímik/ *v., n., & adj.* ● *v. tr.* (**mim•icked, mim•ick•ing**) **1** imitate (a person, gesture, etc.) esp. to entertain or ridicule. **2** copy minutely or servilely. **3** (of a thing) resemble closely. ● *n.* a person skilled in imitation. ● *adj.* having an aptitude for mimicry; imitating; imitative of a thing, esp. for amusement. □□ **mim•ick•er** *n.* [L *mimicus* f. Gk *mimikos* (as MIME)]

mim•i•cry /mímikree/ *n.* (*pl.* **-cries**) **1** the act or art of mimicking. **2** a thing that mimics another. **3** *Zool.* mimesis.

mi•mo•sa /mimṓsə, -zə/ *n.* **1** any leguminous shrub of the genus *Mimosa*, esp. *M. pudica*, having globular usu. yellow flowers and sensitive leaflets that droop when touched. **2** any of various acacia plants with showy yellow flowers. **3** a cocktail of champagne and orange juice. [mod.L, app. f. L (as MIME, from being as sensitive as animals) + −*osa* fem. suffix]

mim•u•lus /mímyələs/ *n.* any flowering plant of the genus *Mimulus*, including musk and the monkey flower. [mod.L, app. dimin. of L (as MIME, perh. with ref. to its masklike flowers)]

Min /min/ *n.* any of the Chinese languages or dialects spoken in the Fukien province in SE China. [Chin.]

Min. *abbr.* esp. *Brit.* **1** Minister. **2** Ministry.

min. *abbr.* **1** minute(s). **2** minimum. **3** minim (fluid measure).

mi•na var. of MYNAH.

min•a•ret /mínərét/ *n.* a slender turret connected to a mosque and having a balcony from which the muezzin calls at hours of prayer. □□ **min•a•ret•ed** *adj.* [F *minaret* or Sp. *minarete* f. Turk. *minare* f. Arab. *manār(a)* lighthouse, minaret f. *nār* fire, light]

min•a•to•ry /mínətáwree/ *adj.* threatening, menacing. [LL *minatorius* f. *minari minat-* threaten]

min•bar var. of MIMBAR.

mince /mins/ *v. & n.* ● *v.* **1** *tr.* cut up or grind into very small pieces. **2** *tr.* (usu. with *neg.*) restrain (one's words, etc.) within the bounds of politeness. **3** *intr.* (usu. as **mincing** *adj.*) speak or walk with an affected delicacy. ● *n.* esp. *Brit.* ground meat. □ **mince matters** (usu. with *neg.*) use polite expressions, etc. □□ **minc•er** *n.* **minc•ing•ly** *adv.* (in sense 3 of *v.*). [ME f. OF *mincier* ult. f. L (as MINUTIA)]

mince•meat /mínsmeet/ *n.* a mixture of currants, raisins, sugar, apples, candied peel, spices, often suet, and sometimes meat. □ **make mincemeat of** utterly defeat (a person, argument, etc.).

mind /mīnd/ *n. & v.* ● *n.* **1 a** the element of a person that enables them to be aware of the world and their experiences, to think and feel; the faculty of consciousness; thought, volition, and feeling. **b** attention, concentration (*my mind keeps wandering*). **2** the intellect; intellectual powers; aptitude. **3** remembrance, memory (*it went out of my mind; I can't call it to mind*). **4** one's opinion (*we're of the same mind*). **5** a way of thinking or feeling (*shocking to the Victorian mind*). **6** the focus of one's thoughts or desires (*put one's mind to it*). **7** the state of normal mental functioning (*lose one's mind; in one's right mind*). **8** a person as embodying mental faculties (*a great mind*). ● *v. tr.* **1** (usu. with *neg.* or *interrog.*) object to (*do you mind if I smoke?; I don't mind your being late*). **2 a** remember; take care to (*mind you come on time*). **b** (*Brit.* often foll. by *out*) take care; be careful. **3** have charge of temporarily (*mind the house while I'm away*). **4** apply oneself to, concern oneself with (business, affairs, etc.) (*I try to mind my own business*). **5** give heed to; notice (*mind the step; don't mind the expense; mind how you go*). **6** be obedient to (*mind what your mother says*). □ **be of two minds** be undecided. **be of a mind** (often foll. by *to* + infin.) be prepared or disposed. **cast one's mind back** think back; recall an earlier time. **come into a person's mind** occur to one. **come to mind** (of a thought, idea, etc.) suggest itself. **cross one's mind** happen to occur to one. **don't mind me** *iron.* do as you please. **do you mind!** *iron.* an expression of annoyance. **give a person a piece of one's mind** scold or reproach a person. **have a good** (or **half a**) **mind to** (often as a threat, usu. unfulfilled) feel tempted to (*I've a good mind to report you*). **have in mind** intend. **have a mind of one's own** be capable of independent opinion. **have on one's mind** be troubled by the thought of. **in one's mind's eye** in one's imagination or mental view. **mind one's Ps & Qs** be careful in one's behavior. **mind the store** have charge of affairs temporarily. **mind you** an expression used to qualify a previous

minaret

statement (*I found it quite quickly—mind you, it wasn't easy*). **never mind 1** an expression used to comfort or console. **2** (also **never you mind**) an expression used to evade a question. **3** disregard (*never mind the cost*). **open** (or **close**) **one's mind to** be receptive (or unreceptive) to (changes, new ideas, etc.). **out of one's mind** crazy. **put** (or **set**) **a person's mind at rest** reassure a person. **put a person** (or **thing**) **out of one's mind** deliberately forget. **read a person's mind** discern a person's thoughts. **to my mind** in my opinion. [ME *mynd* f. OE *gemynd* f. Gmc]

mind-bend•ing *adj. colloq.* (esp. of a psychedelic drug) influencing or altering one's state of mind.

mind-blow•ing *adj. sl.* **1** overwhelmingly impressing. **2** confusing, shattering. **3** (esp. of drugs, etc.) inducing hallucinations.

mind-bog•gling *adj. colloq.* intellectually overwhelming or startling.

mind•ed /míndid/ *adj.* **1** (in *comb.*) **a** inclined to think in some specified way (*mathematically minded; fair-minded*). **b** having a specified kind of mind (*high-minded*). **c** interested in or enthusiastic about a specified thing (*car-minded*). **2** (usu. foll. by *to* + infin.) disposed or inclined (to an action).

mind•er /míndər/ *n.* **1 a** a person whose job it is to attend to a person or thing. **b** (in *comb.*) *Brit.* (*child-minder; machine-minder*). **2** esp. *Brit. sl.* **a** a bodyguard, esp. a person employed to protect a criminal. **b** a thief's assistant.

mind-ex•pand•ing *adj.* causing heightened perceptions, as from psychedelic drugs.

mind•ful /míndfŏŏl/ *adj.* (often foll. by *of*) taking heed or care; being conscious. □□ **mind•ful•ly** *adv.* **mind•ful•ness** *n.*

mind game *n.* a series of deliberate actions or responses planned for psychological effect on another, typically for amusement or competitive advantage.

mind•less /míndlis/ *adj.* **1** lacking intelligence; stupid. **2** not requiring thought or skill (*totally mindless work*). **3** (usu. foll. by *of*) heedless (of advice, etc.). □□ **mind•less•ly** *adv.* **mind•less•ness** *n.*

mind read•er *n.* a person who can supposedly discern what another person is thinking. □□ **mind read•ing** *n.*□□

mind•set /míndset/ *n.* **1** a mental attitude that can influence one's interpretation of events or situations. **2** an inclination or a fixed way of thinking.

mine[1] /mīn/ *poss. pron.* **1** the one or ones belonging to or associated with me (*it is mine; mine are over there*). **2** (*attrib.* before a vowel) *archaic* = MY (*mine eyes have seen; mine host*). □ **of mine** of or belonging to me (*a friend of mine*). [OE *mīn* f. Gmc]

mine[2] /mīn/ *n. & v.* ● *n.* **1** an excavation in the earth for extracting metal, coal, salt, etc. **2** an abundant source (of information, etc.). **3** a receptacle filled with explosive and placed in the ground or in the water for destroying enemy personnel, ships, etc. **4 a** a subterranean gallery in which explosive is placed to blow up fortifications. **b** *hist.* a subterranean passage under the wall of a besieged fortress. ● *v. tr.* **1** obtain (metal, coal, etc.) from a mine. **2** (also *absol.*, often foll. by *for*) dig in (the earth, etc.) for ore, etc. **3 a** dig or burrow in (usu. the earth). **b** delve into (an abundant source) for information, etc. **c** make (a hole, passage, etc.) underground. **4** lay explosive mines under or in. **5** = UNDERMINE. □□ **min•ing** *n.* [ME f. OF *mine, miner*, perh. f. Celt.]

mine de•tec•tor *n.* an instrument for detecting explosive mines.

mine•field /mínfeeld/ *n.* **1** an area planted with explosive mines. **2** a subject or situation presenting unseen hazards.

mine•lay•er /mínlayər/ *n.* a ship or aircraft for laying mines.

min•er /mínər/ *n.* **1** a person who works in a mine. **2** any burrowing insect or grub. [ME f. OF *minĕor, minour* (as MINE[2])]

min•er•al /mínərəl/ *n. & adj.* ● *n.* **1** any of the species into which inorganic substances are classified. **2** a substance obtained by mining. **3** (often in *pl.*) *Brit.* an artificial mineral water or other effervescent drink. ● *adj.* **1** of or containing a mineral or minerals. **2** obtained by mining. [ME f. OF *mineral* or med.L *mineralis* f. *minera* ore f. OF *miniere* mine]

min•er•al•ize /mínərəlīz/ *v.* **1** *v. tr. & intr.* change wholly or partly into a mineral. **2** *v. tr.* impregnate (water, etc.) with a mineral substance.

min•er•al•o•gy /mínərólɔjee/ *n.* the scientific study of minerals. □□ **min•er•al•og•i•cal** /-rəlójikəl/ *adj.* **min•er•al•o•gist** *n.*

min•er•al oil *n. Pharm.* a colorless, odorless, oily liquid obtained from petroleum and used as a laxative, in manufacturing cosmetics, etc.

min•er•al wa•ter *n.* **1** water found in nature with some dissolved salts present. **2** an artificial imitation of this, esp. soda water. **3** *Brit.* any effervescent nonalcoholic drink.

min•er•al wax *n.* a fossil resin, esp. ozocerite.

min•er•al wool *n.* a woollike substance made from inorganic material, used for packing or insulation.

min•e•stro•ne /mínistrṓnee/ *n.* a soup containing vegetables and pasta, beans, or rice. [It.]

See page xx for the **Key to Pronunciation**.

mine•sweep•er /mínsweepər/ n. a ship for clearing away floating and submarine mines.

min•e•ver var. of MINIVER.

mine•work•er /mínwərkər/ n. a person who works in a mine.

Ming /ming/ n. 1 the dynasty ruling China 1368–1644. 2 Chinese porcelain made during the rule of this dynasty. [Chin.]

min•gle /mínggəl/ v. 1 tr. & intr. mix, blend. 2 intr. (often foll. by with) (of a person) move about, associate. □ **mingle their** (etc.) tears literary weep together. □□ **min•gler** n. [ME mengel f. obs. meng f. OE mengan, rel. to AMONG]

min•gy /mínjee/ adj. (**min•gi•er**, **min•gi•est**) colloq. mean, stingy. □□ **min•gi•ly** adv. [perh. f. MEAN² and STINGY]

min•i /mínee/ n. (pl. **min•is**) colloq. a miniskirt, minidress, etc.

mini- /mínee/ comb. form miniature; very small or minor of its kind (minivan; minicomputer). [abbr. of MINIATURE]

min•i•a•ture /míneeəchər, mínichər/ adj., n., & v. ● adj. 1 much smaller than normal. 2 represented on a small scale. ● n. 1 any object reduced in size. 2 a small-scale minutely finished portrait. 3 this branch of painting (portrait in miniature). 4 a picture or decorated letters in an illuminated manuscript. ● v.tr. represent on a smaller scale. □ **in miniature** on a small scale. □□ **min•i•a•tur•ist** n. (in senses 2 and 3 of n.). [It. miniatura f. med.L miniatura f. L miniare rubricate, illuminate f. L minium red lead, vermilion]

min•i•a•ture golf n. a game similar to golf, played with a golf ball and putter, on a confined, usu. carpeted course featuring obstacles, etc.

min•i•a•tur•ize /míneeəchəriz, mínichə–/ v.tr. produce in a smaller version; make small. □□ **min•i•a•tur•i•za•tion** n.

min•i•bike /míneebik/ n. a motorbike designed for off-road use, esp. with elevated handlebars.

min•i•bus /míneebus/ n. a small bus or van.

min•i•cab /míneekab/ n. Brit. a small car used as a taxi.

min•i•cam /míneekam/ n. a portable lightweight video camera.

min•i•com•pu•ter /míneekəmpyóotər/ n. a computer of medium power, more than a microcomputer but less than a mainframe.

min•i•kin /mínikin/ adj. & n. ● adj. 1 small; insignificant. 2 affected, mincing. ● n. a diminutive creature. [obs. Du. minneken f. minne love + –ken, –kijn –KIN]

min•im /mínim/ n. 1 one-sixtieth of a fluid dram, about a drop. 2 Mus. esp. Brit. = HALF NOTE. 3 an object or portion of the smallest size or importance. 4 a single downstroke of the pen. [ME f. L minimus smallest]

min•i•ma pl. of MINIMUM.

min•i•mal /mínimal/ adj. 1 very minute or slight. 2 being or related to a minimum. 3 the least possible in size, duration, etc. 4 Art, etc., characterized by the use of simple or primary forms or structures, etc., often geometric or massive (huge minimal forms in a few colors). □□ **min•i•mal•ism** n. (in sense 4). **min•i•mal•ly** adv. (in senses 1–3). [L minimus smallest]

min•i•mal•ist /mínimalist/ n. 1 (also attrib.) a person advocating small or moderate reform in politics (opp. MAXIMALIST). 2 = MEN-SHEVIK. 3 a person who advocates or practices minimal art. □□ **min•i•mal•ism** n.

min•i•max /míneemaks/ n. 1 Math. the lowest of a set of maximum values. 2 (usu. attrib.) **a** a strategy that minimizes the greatest risk to a participant in a game, etc. **b** the theory that in a game with two players, a player's smallest possible maximum loss is equal to the same player's greatest possible minimum gain. [MINIMUM + MAX-IMUM]

min•i•mize /mínimiz/ v. 1 tr. reduce to, or estimate at, the smallest possible amount or degree. 2 tr. estimate or represent at less than the true value or importance. 3 intr. attain a minimum value. □□ **min•i•mi•za•tion** n. **min•i•miz•er** n.

min•i•mum /míniməm/ n. & adj. (pl. **min•i•ma** /–mə/) ● n. the least possible or attainable amount (reduced to a minimum). ● adj. that is a minimum. [L, neut. of minimus least]

min•i•mum wage n. the lowest wage permitted by law.

min•i•on /mínyən/ n. 1 derog. a servile agent; a slave. 2 a favorite servant, animal, etc. 3 a favorite of a sovereign, etc. [F mignon, OF mignot, of Gaulish orig.]

min•i•se•ries /míneeseereez/ n. a short series of television programs on a common theme.

min•i•skirt /míneeskərt/ n. a very short skirt.

min•is•ter /mínistər/ n. & v. ● n. 1 a member of the clergy; a person authorized to officiate in religious worship. 2 a head of a government department (in some countries). 3 a diplomatic agent, usu. ranking below an ambassador. 4 (usu. foll. by of) a person employed in the execution of (a purpose, will, etc.) (a minister of justice). 5 (in full **minister general**) the superior of some religious orders. ● v. 1 intr. (usu. foll. by to) render aid or service (to a person, cause, etc.). 2 tr. (usu. foll. by with) archaic furnish, supply, etc. □□ **min•is•tra•ble** adj. [ME f. OF ministre f. L minister servant f. minus less]

min•is•te•ri•al /mínistéereeəl/ adj. 1 of a minister of religion or a min-

ister's office. 2 instrumental or subsidiary in achieving a purpose (ministerial in bringing about a settlement). 3 of a government minister. □□ **min•is•te•ri•al•ist** n. (in sense 3b). **min•is•te•ri•al•ly** adv. [F ministériel or LL ministerialis f. L (as MINISTRY)]

Min•is•ter of the Crown n. Brit. Parl. a member of the Cabinet.

min•is•tra•tion /mínistráyshən/ n. 1 (usu. in pl.) aid or service (the kind ministrations of his neighbors). 2 ministering, esp. in religious matters. 3 (usu. foll. by of) the supplying (of help, justice, etc.). □□ **min•is•trant** /mínistrənt/ adj. & n. **min•is•tra•tive** /mínistráytiv/ adj. [ME f. OF ministration or L ministratio (as MINISTER)]

min•is•try /mínistree/ n. (pl. **-tries**) 1 **a** (prec. by the) the vocation or profession of a religious minister (called to the ministry). **b** the office of a religious minister, priest, etc. **c** the period of tenure of this. 2 (prec. by the) the body of ministers of a government or of a religion. 3 **a** a government department headed by a minister. **b** the building which it occupies (the Ministry of Transportation). 4 a period of government under one Prime Minister. 5 ministering, ministration. [ME f. L ministerium (as MINISTER)]

min•i•van /míneevan/ n. a vehicle, smaller than a full-sized van, for passengers, cargo, etc.

min•i•ver /mínivər/ n. (also **min•e•ver**) plain white fur used in ceremonial costume. [ME f. AF menuver, OF menu vair (as MENU, VAIR)]

mink /mingk/ n. 1 either of two small semiaquatic stoatlike animals of the genus Mustela, M. vison of N. America and M. intreola of Europe. 2 the thick brown fur of these. 3 a coat made of this. [cf. Sw. mänk, menk]

minke /míngkə/ n. a small baleen whale, Balaenoptera acutorostrata, with a pointed snout. [prob. f. Meincke, the name of a Norw. whaler]

Minn. abbr. Minnesota.

min•ne•sing•er /mínisíngər/ n. a German lyric poet and singer of the 12th–14th c. [G, = love-singer]

min•now /mínō/ n. any of various small freshwater fish of the carp family, esp. Phoxinus phoxinus. [late ME menow, perh. repr. OE mynwe (unrecorded), myne: infl. by ME menuse, menise f. OF menuise, ult. rel. to MINUTIA]

Mi•no•an /minóən/ adj. & n. Archaeol. ● adj. of or relating to the Bronze Age civilization centered on Crete (c.3000–1100 BC). ● n. 1 an inhabitant of Minoan Crete or the Minoan world. 2 the language or scripts associated with the Minoans. [named after the legendary Cretan king Minos (Gk Minōs), to whom the palace excavated at Knossos was attributed]

mi•nor /mínər/ adj., n., & v. ● adj. 1 lesser or comparatively small in size or importance (minor poet; minor operation). 2 Mus. **a** (of a scale) having intervals of a semitone between the second and third, fifth and sixth, and seventh and eighth degrees. **b** (of an interval) less by a semitone than a major interval. **c** (of a key) based on a minor scale, tending to produce a melancholy effect. 3 pertaining to a student's secondary field of study. 4 Logic **a** (of a term) occurring as the subject of the conclusion of a categorical syllogism. **b** (of a premise) containing the minor term in a categorical syllogism. 5 (**Minor**) Brit. (in schools) indicating the younger of two children from the same family or the second to enter the school (usu. put after the name). ● n. 1 a person under the legal age limit or majority (no unaccompanied minors). 2 Mus. a minor key, etc. 3 a student's subsidiary subject or course (cf. MAJOR). 4 Logic a minor term or premise. ● v.intr. (foll. by in) (of a student) undertake study in (a subject) as a subsidiary to a main subject. □ **in a minor key** (of novels, events, people's lives, etc.) understated, uneventful. [L, = smaller, less, rel. to minuere lessen]

mi•nor ax•is n. Geom. the shorter axis of an ellipse that is perpendicular to its major axis.

mi•nor can•on n. a cleric who is not a member of the chapter, who assists in daily cathedral services.

mi•nor•i•ty /mináwritee, –nór–/ n. (pl. **-ties**) 1 (often foll. by of) a smaller number or part, esp. within a political party or structure. 2 the number of votes cast for this (a minority of two). 3 the state of having less than half the votes or of being supported by less than half of the body of opinion (in the minority). 4 a relatively small group of people differing from others in the society of which they are a part in race, religion, language, political persuasion, etc. 5 (attrib.) relating to or done by the minority (minority interests). 6 **a** the state of being under full legal age. **b** the period of this. [F minorité or med.L minoritas f. L minor: see MINOR]

mi•nor•i•ty lead•er n. the leader of the minority political party in a legislature.

mi•nor key n. Mus. a key based on a minor scale.

mi•nor league n. (in baseball, basketball, etc.) a league of professional clubs other than the major leagues.

mi•nor or•ders n.pl. RC Ch. hist. the grades of members of the clergy below that of deacon.

mi•nor piece n. Chess a bishop or a knight.

mi•nor plan•et n. an asteroid.

Mi•nor Proph•et n. any of the twelve Old Testament prophets from Hosea to Malachi, whose surviving writings are not lengthy.

mi·nor scale n. Mus. a scale with half steps between the second and third, fifth and sixth, and seventh and eighth degrees.

mi·nor suit n. Bridge diamonds or clubs.

Min·o·taur /mínətawr/ n. (in Greek mythology) a man with a bull's head, kept in a Cretan labyrinth and fed with human flesh. [ME f. OF f. L Minotaurus f. Gk Minōtauros f. Minōs, legendary king of Crete (see MINOAN) + tauros bull]

min·ox·i·dil /mənóksədil/ n. a vasodilator drug taken orally to treat hypertension or applied topically to stimulate hair growth in certain types of baldness.

min·ster /mínstər/ n. 1 a large or important church (York Minster). 2 the church of a monastery. [OE mynster f. eccl.L monasterium f. Gk monastērion MONASTERY]

min·strel /mínstrəl/ n. 1 a medieval singer or musician, esp. singing or reciting poetry. 2 hist. a person who entertained patrons with singing, buffoonery, etc. 3 (usu. in pl.) a member of a band of public entertainers with blackened faces, etc., performing songs and music ostensibly of African-American origin. [ME f. OF menestral entertainer, servant, f. Prov. menest(ai)ral officer, employee, musician, f. LL ministerialis official, officer: see MINISTERIAL]

min·strel·sy /mínstrəlsee/ n. (pl. ·sies) 1 the minstrel's art. 2 a body of minstrels. 3 minstrel poetry. [ME f. OF menestralsie (as MINSTREL)]

mint[1] /mint/ n. 1 any aromatic plant of the genus Mentha. 2 a peppermint sweet or lozenge. □□ **mint·y** adj. (**mint·i·er, mint·i·est**). [OE minte ult. f. L ment(h)a f. Gk minthē]

mint[2] /mint/ n. & v. ● n. 1 a place where money is coined, usu. under government authority. 2 a vast sum of money (making a mint). 3 a source of invention, etc. (a mint of ideas). ● v.tr. 1 make (coin) by stamping metal. 2 invent, coin (a word, phrase, etc.). □ **in mint condition** (of an object) new or like new. □□ **mint·er** n. [OE mynet f. WG f. L moneta MONEY]

mint ju·lep n. a sweet iced alcoholic drink of bourbon flavored with mint.

min·u·end /mínyoo-énd/ n. Math. a quantity or number from which another is to be subtracted. [L minuendus gerundive of minuere diminish]

min·u·et /mínyoo-ét/ n. & v. ● n. 1 a slow stately dance for two in triple time. 2 Mus. the music for this, or music in the same rhythm and style, often as a movement in a suite, sonata, or symphony. ● v.intr. (**min·u·et·ed, min·u·et·ing**) dance a minuet. [F menuet, orig. adj. = fine, delicate, dimin. of menu: see MENU]

mi·nus /mínəs/ prep., adj., & n. ● prep. 1 with the subtraction of (7 minus 4 equals 3). ¶ Symb.: –. 2 (of temperature) below zero (minus 2°). 3 colloq. lacking; deprived of (returned minus their dog). ● adj. 1 Math. negative. 2 Electronics having a negative charge. ● n. 1 = MINUS SIGN. 2 Math. a negative quantity. 3 a disadvantage. [L, neut. of minor less]

mi·nus·cule /mínəskyōōl/ n. & adj. ● n. 1 Paleog. a kind of cursive script developed in the 7th c. 2 a lowercase letter. ● adj. 1 lowercase. 2 colloq. extremely small or unimportant. □□ **mi·nus·cu·lar** /mínúskyōōlər/ adj. [F f. L minuscula (littera letter) dimin. of minor: see MINOR]

SPELLING TIP minuscule

Avoid the common misspelling of **minuscule** as "miniscule."

mi·nus sign n. the symbol (–) indicating subtraction or a negative value.

min·ute[1] /mínit/ n. & v. ● n. 1 the sixtieth part of an hour. 2 a distance covered in one minute (twenty minutes from the station). 3 a a moment; an instant; a point of time (expecting her any minute; the train leaves in a minute). b (prec. by this) colloq. the present time (what are you doing at this minute?). c (foll. by clause) as soon as (call me the minute you get back). 4 the sixtieth part of an angular degree. 5 (in pl.) a brief summary of the proceedings at a meeting. 6 an official memorandum authorizing or recommending a course of action. ● v.tr. 1 record (proceedings) in the minutes. 2 send the minutes to (a person). □ **just** (or **wait**) **a minute** 1 a request to wait for a short time. 2 as a prelude to a query or objection.

WORD HISTORY minute

Late Middle English (in the singular in the sense 'note or memorandum'): from French minute, from the notion of a rough copy of a manuscript in 'small writing' (Latin scriptura minuta) as distinct from the finished copy in carefully formed book hand. The verb dates from the mid-16th century.

mi·nute[2] /mīnōōt, –yōōt/ adj. (**mi·nut·est**) 1 very small. 2 trifling, petty. 3 (of an inquiry, inquirer, etc.) accurate, detailed, precise. □□ **mi·nute·ly** adv. **mi·nute·ness** n. [ME f. L minutus past part. of minuere lessen]

min·ute hand n. the hand on a watch or clock that indicates minutes.

min·ute·man /mínitman/ n. (pl. ·**men**) 1 US hist. (also **Minuteman**) an American militiaman of the Revolutionary War period (ready

to march at a minute's notice). 2 a type of three-stage intercontinental ballistic missile.

min·ute steak n. a thin slice of steak to be cooked quickly.

mi·nu·ti·a /minōōsheeə, –shə, –nyōō–/ n. (pl. ·**iae** /–shee-ee/) (usu. in pl.) a precise, trivial, or minor detail. [L, = smallness, in pl. trifles f. minutus: see MINUTE[2]]

minx /mingks/ n. a pert, sly, or playful girl. □□ **minx·ish** adj. **minx·ish·ly** adv. [16th c.: orig. unkn.]

Mi·o·cene /míəseen/ adj. & n. Geol. ● adj. of or relating to the fourth epoch of the Tertiary period with evidence for the diversification of primates, including early apes. ● n. this epoch or system. [irreg. f. Gk meiōn less + kainos new]

mi·o·sis /míósis/ n. (also **my·o·sis**) (pl. ·**ses** /–seez/) excessive constriction of the pupil of the eye. □□ **mi·ot·ic** /míótik/ adj. [Gk muō shut the eyes + –OSIS]

mir·a·belle /mírəbél/ n. 1 a a European variety of plum tree, Prunus insititia, bearing small round yellow fruit. b a fruit from this tree. 2 a liqueur distilled from this fruit. [F]

mir·a·cle /mírəkəl/ n. 1 an extraordinary event attributed to some supernatural agency. 2 a any remarkable occurrence. b a remarkable development in some specified area (an economic miracle; the German miracle). 3 (usu. foll. by of) a remarkable or outstanding specimen (the plan was a miracle of ingenuity). [ME f. OF f. L miraculum object of wonder f. mirari wonder f. mirus wonderful]

mir·a·cle drug n. a drug that represents a breakthrough in medical science.

mir·a·cle play n. a medieval play based on the Bible or the lives of the saints.

mi·rac·u·lous /mirákyələs/ adj. 1 of the nature of a miracle. 2 supernatural. 3 remarkable, surprising. □□ **mi·rac·u·lous·ly** adv. **mi·rac·u·lous·ness** n. [F miraculeux or med.L miraculosus f. L (as MIRACLE)]

mir·a·dor /mírədáwr/ n. a turret or tower, etc., attached to a building and commanding an excellent view. [Sp. f. mirar to look at]

mi·rage /miráazh/ n. 1 an optical illusion caused by atmospheric conditions, esp. the appearance of a sheet of water in a desert or on a hot road from the reflection of light. 2 an illusory thing. [F f. se mirer be reflected, f. L mirare look at]

mire /mīr/ n. & v. ● n. 1 a stretch of swampy or boggy ground. 2 mud, dirt. ● v. 1 tr. & intr. plunge or sink in a mire. 2 tr. involve in difficulties. □ **in the mire** in difficulties. [ME f. ON mýrr f. Gmc, rel. to MOSS]

mire·poix /meerpwáa/ n. (also **mire·pois**) sautéed diced vegetables, used in sauces, etc. [F, f. Duc de Mirepoix, Fr. general d. 1757]

mirk var. of MURK.

mirk·y var. of MURKY.

mir·ror /mírər/ n. & v. ● n. 1 a polished surface, usu. of amalgam-coated glass or metal, which reflects an image; a looking glass. 2 anything regarded as giving an accurate reflection or description of something else. ● v.tr. reflect as in a mirror. [ME f. OF mirour ult. f. L mirare look at]

mir·ror im·age n. an identical image, but with the structure reversed, as in a mirror.

mir·ror-writ·ing n. backward writing, like ordinary writing reflected in a mirror.

mirth /mərth/ n. merriment, laughter. □□ **mirth·ful** adj. **mirth·ful·ly** adv. **mirth·ful·ness** n. **mirth·less** adj. **mirth·less·ly** adv. **mirth·less·ness** n. [OE myrgth (as MERRY)]

MIRV /mərv/ abbr. multiple independently targeted reentry vehicle (a type of missile).

MIS abbr. Computing management information system.

mis-[1] /mis/ prefix added to verbs and verbal derivatives: meaning 'amiss,' 'badly,' 'wrongly,' 'unfavorably' (mislead; misshapen; mistrust). [OE f. Gmc]

mis-[2] /mis/ prefix occurring in a few words adopted from French meaning 'badly,' 'wrongly,' 'amiss,' 'ill-,' or having a negative force (misadventure; mischief). [OF mes- ult. f. L minus (see MINUS): assim. to MIS-[1]]

mis·ad·dress /mísədrés/ v.tr. 1 address (a letter, etc.) wrongly. 2 address (a person) wrongly, esp. impertinently.

mis·ad·ven·ture /mísədvénchər/ n. 1 Law an accident without concomitant crime or negligence (death by misadventure). 2 bad luck. 3 a misfortune. [ME f. OF mesaventure f. mesavenir turn out badly (as MIS-[2], ADVENT: cf. ADVENTURE)]

mis·a·lign /mísəlín/ v.tr. give the wrong alignment to. □□ **mis·a·lign·ment** n.

mis·al·li·ance /mísəlíəns/ n. an unsuitable alliance, esp. an unsuitable marriage. □□ **mis·al·ly** /–əlí/ v.tr. (·**lies**, ·**lied**) [MIS-[1] + ALLIANCE, after MÉSALLIANCE]

mis·an·thrope /mísənthrōp, míz–/ n. (also **mis·an·thro·pist** /mísánthrəpist/) 1 a person who hates mankind. 2 a person who avoids human society. □□ **mis·an·throp·ic** /–thrópik/ adj. **mis·an·throp·i·cal** adj. **mis·an·throp·i·cal·ly** adv. **mis·an·thro·py** /mísánthrəpee/ n.

mis·an·throp·ize /misánthrəpīz/ *v.intr.* [F f. Gk *misanthrōpos* f. *misos* hatred + *anthrōpos* man]

mis·ap·ply /mísəplí/ *v.tr.* (**·plies, ·plied**) apply (esp. funds) wrongly. □□ **mis·ap·pli·ca·tion** /mísaplikáyshən/ *n.*

mis·ap·pre·hend /mísaprihénd/ *v.tr.* misunderstand (words, a person). □□ **mis·ap·pre·hen·sion** /–hénshən/ *n.* **mis·ap·pre·hen·sive** *adj.*

mis·ap·pro·pri·ate /mísəprópreeayt/ *v.tr.* apply (usu. another's money) to one's own use, or to a wrong use. □□ **mis·ap·pro·pri·a·tion** /–áyshən/ *n.*

mis·be·got·ten /mísbigót'n/ *adj.* **1** badly conceived, designed, or planned (*a misbegotten journey*). **2** contemptible, disreputable. **3** *archaic* (of a child) illegitimate.

mis·be·have /mísbiháyv/ *v.intr. & refl.* (of a person) fail to conduct oneself in a way that is acceptable to others; behave badly. □□ **mis·be·hav·er** *n.* **mis·be·hav·ior** *n.*

mis·be·lief /mísbileéf/ *n.* a wrong or false belief or opinion.

misc. *abbr.* miscellaneous.

mis·cal·cu·late /mískálkyəlayt/ *v.tr.* (also *absol.*) calculate (amounts, results, etc.) wrongly. □□ **mis·cal·cu·la·tion** /–láyshən/ *n.*

mis·call /mískáwl/ *v.tr.* **1** call by a wrong or inappropriate name. **2** *archaic* or *dial.* call (a person) names.

mis·car·riage /mískárij/ *n.* **1** a spontaneous abortion, esp. before the 28th week of pregnancy. **2** the failure (of a plan, letter, etc.) to reach completion or its destination. [MISCARRY, after CARRIAGE]

mis·car·riage of jus·tice *n.* any failure of the judicial system to attain the ends of justice.

mis·car·ry /mískáree/ *v.intr.* (**·ries, ·ried**) **1** (of a woman) have a miscarriage. **2** (of a letter, etc.) fail to reach its destination. **3** (of a business, plan, etc.) fail, be unsuccessful.

mis·cast /mískást/ *v.tr.* (*past* and *past part.* **·cast**) allot an unsuitable part to (an actor).

mis·ceg·e·na·tion /miséjináyshən, mísəjə–/ *n.* the interbreeding of races, esp. of whites and nonwhites. [irreg. f. L *miscēre* mix + *genus* race]

mis·cel·la·ne·a /mísəláyneeə/ *n.pl.* **1** a literary miscellany. **2** a collection of miscellaneous items. [L neut. pl. (as MISCELLANEOUS)]

mis·cel·la·ne·ous /mísəláyneeəs/ *adj.* **1** of mixed composition or character. **2** (foll. by pl. noun) of various kinds. **3** (of a person) many-sided. □□ **mis·cel·la·ne·ous·ly** *adv.* **mis·cel·la·ne·ous·ness** *n.* [L *miscellaneus* f. *miscellus* mixed f. *miscēre* mix]

mis·cel·la·ny /mísəláynee/ *n.* (*pl.* **·nies**) **1** a mixture, a medley. **2** a book containing a collection of stories, etc., or various literary compositions. □□ **mis·cel·la·nist** *n.* [F *miscellanées* (fem. pl.) or L MIS-CELLANEA]

mis·chance /míscháns/ *n.* **1** bad luck. **2** an instance of this. [ME f. OF *mesch(e)ance* f. *mescheoir* (as MIS-², CHANCE)]

mis·chief /míschif/ *n.* **1** conduct that is troublesome, but not malicious, esp. in children. **2** pranks, scrapes (*get into mischief*; *keep out of mischief*). **3** playful malice; archness; satire (*eyes full of mischief*). **4** harm or injury caused by a person or thing. **5** a person or thing responsible for harm or annoyance (*that loose connection is the mischief*). **6** (prec. by *the*) the annoying part or aspect (*the mischief of it is that*, etc.). [ME f. OF *meschief* f. *meschever* (as MIS-², *chever* come to an end f. *chef* head: see CHIEF)]

mis·chie·vous /míschivəs/ *adj.* **1** (of a person) disposed to mischief. **2** (of conduct) playfully malicious. **3** (of a thing) having harmful effects. □□ **mis·chie·vous·ly** *adv.* **mis·chie·vous·ness** *n.*

WORD HISTORY mischievous

Middle English: from Anglo-Norman French *meschevous*, from Old French *meschever* 'come to an unfortunate end.' The early sense was 'unfortunate or calamitous,' later 'having harmful effects'; the sense of 'playfully malicious' dates from the late 17th century.

PRONUNCIATION TIP mischievous

Do not pronounce this word with an extra syllable, "mis-CHEE-vee-uhs."

---

misch met·al /mish/ *n.* an alloy of lanthanide metals, usu. added to iron to improve its malleability. [G *mischen* mix + *Metall* metal]

mis·ci·ble /mísibəl/ *adj.* (often foll. by *with*) capable of being mixed. □□ **mis·ci·bil·i·ty** /–bílitee/ *n.* [med.L *miscibilis* f. L *miscēre* mix]

mis·con·ceive /mískənseév/ *v.* **1** *intr.* (often foll. by *of*) have a wrong idea or conception. **2** *tr.* (as **misconceived** *adj.*) badly planned, organized, etc. **3** *tr.* misunderstand (a word, person, etc.). □□ **mis·con·ceiv·er** *n.* **mis·con·cep·tion** /–sépshən/ *n.*

mis·con·duct *n. & v.* /–/ /mískóndukt/ **1** improper or unprofessional behavior. **2** bad management. ● *v.* /mískəndúkt/ **1** *refl.* misbehave. **2** *tr.* mismanage.

mis·con·strue /mískənstroó/ *v.tr.* (**·construes, ·construed, ·con-**

struing) **1** interpret (a word, action, etc.) wrongly. **2** mistake the meaning of (a person). □□ **mis·con·struc·tion** /–strúkshən/ *n.*

mis·cop·y /mískópee/ *v.tr.* (**·ies, ·ied**) copy (text, etc.) incorrectly.

mis·count /mískównt/ *v. & n.* ● *v.tr.* (also *absol.*) count wrongly. ● *n.* a wrong count.

mis·cre·ant /mískreeənt/ *n. & adj.* ● *n.* **1** a person who behaves badly or breaks the law. **2** *archaic* a heretic. ● *adj.* **1** behaving badly or in a way that breaks the law (*her miscreant husband*). **2** *archaic* heretical. [ME f. OF *mescreant* (as MIS-², *creant* part. of *croire* f. L *credere* believe)]

mis·cue /mískyoō/ *n. & v.* ● *n.* (in billiards, etc.) the failure to strike the ball properly with the cue. ● *v.intr.* (**·cues, ·cued, ·cueing** or **·cuing**) make a miscue.

mis·date /misdáyt/ *v.tr.* date (an event, a letter, etc.) wrongly.

mis·deal /místeél/ *v. & n.* ● *v.tr.* (also *absol.*) (*past* and *past part.* **·dealt** /–délt/) make a mistake in dealing (cards). ● *n.* **1** a mistake in dealing cards. **2** a misdealt hand.

mis·deed /misdeéd/ *n.* an evil deed, a wrongdoing; a crime. [OE *misdēd* (as MIS-¹, DEED)]

mis·de·mean·ant /mísdimeénənt/ *n.* a person convicted of a misdemeanor or guilty of misconduct. [archaic *misdemean* misbehave]

mis·de·mean·or /mísdimeénər/ *n.* **1** a minor wrongdoing, a misdeed. **2** *Law* an offense less serious than a felony.

mis·di·ag·nose /misdíəgnōs, –nōz/ *v.tr.* diagnose incorrectly. □□ **mis·di·ag·no·sis** /–nōsis/ *n.*

mis·di·al /misdíəl/ *v.tr.* (also *absol.*) (**·dialed, ·dialing;** esp. *Brit.* **·dialled, ·dialling**) dial (a telephone number, etc.) incorrectly.

mis·di·rect /mísdirékt, –dī–/ *v.tr.* **1** direct (a person, letter, blow, etc.) wrongly. **2** (of a judge) instruct (the jury) wrongly. □□ **mis·di·rec·tion** /–rékshən/ *n.*

mis·do·ing /misdoōing/ *n.* a misdeed.

mis·doubt /misdówt/ *v.tr.* **1** have doubts or misgivings about the truth or existence of. **2** be suspicious about; suspect that.

mis·ed·u·ca·tion /mísejəkáyshən/ *n.* wrong or faulty education. □□ **mis·ed·u·cate** /–éjəkayt/ *v.tr.*

mise-en-scène /meéz ON sén/ *n.* **1** *Theatr.* the scenery and properties of a play. **2** the setting or surroundings of an event. [F]

mis·em·ploy /mísemplóy/ *v.tr.* employ or use wrongly or improperly. □□ **mis·em·ploy·ment** *n.*

mi·ser /mízər/ *n.* **1** a person who hoards wealth and lives miserably. **2** an avaricious person. [L, = wretched]

mis·er·a·ble /mízərəbəl/ *adj.* **1** wretchedly unhappy or uncomfortable (*felt miserable*). **2** unworthy, inadequate (*a miserable hovel*); contemptible. **3** causing wretchedness or discomfort (*miserable weather*). **4** stingy; mean. □□ **mis·er·a·ble·ness** *n.* **mis·er·a·bly** *adv.* [ME f. F *misérable* f. L *miserabilis* pitiable f. *miserari* to pity f. *miser* wretched]

mis·e·re·re /mízəráiree, –reéree/ *n.* **1** (**Miserere**) Psalm 50 (in the Vulgate) and 51 (in the Authorized Version). **2** a cry for mercy. **3** = MISERICORD 1. [ME f. L, imper. of *miserēri* have mercy (as MISER); first word of Ps. 50 in Latin]

mis·er·i·cord /mízərikawrd, –mízér–/ *n.* **1** a shelving projection on the underside of a hinged seat in a choir stall serving (when the seat is turned up) to help support a person standing. **2** an apartment in a monastery in which some relaxations of discipline are permitted. **3** a dagger for dealing the death stroke. [ME f. OF *misericorde* f. L *misericordia* f. *misericors* compassionate f. stem of *miserēri* pity + *cor cordis* heart]

mi·ser·ly /mízərlee/ *adj.* characteristic of a miser; stingy. □□ **mi·ser·li·ness** *n.* [MISER]

mis·er·y /mízəree/ *n.* (*pl.* **·ies**) **1** a state or feeling of great distress or discomfort of mind or body. **2** a thing causing this. □ **put (something) out of its misery 1** release (a person, animal, etc.) from suffering or suspense. **2** kill (an animal in pain). [ME f. OF *misere* or L *miseria* (as MISER)]

mis·fea·sance /mísfeézəns/ *n. Law* a transgression, esp. the wrongful exercise of lawful authority. [ME f. OF *mesfaisance* f. *mesfaire* misdo (as MIS-², *faire* do f. L *facere*): cf. MALFEASANCE]

mis·fire /mísfír/ *v. & n.* ● *v.intr.* **1** (of a gun, motor engine, etc.) fail to go off or start or function regularly. **2** (of an action, etc.) fail to have the intended effect. ● *n.* a failure of function or intention.

mis·fit /misfit/ *n.* **1** a person unsuited to a particular kind of environment, occupation, etc. **2** a garment, etc., that does not fit.

mis·for·tune /misfáwrchən/ *n.* **1** bad luck. **2** an instance of this.

mis·give /misgív/ *v.tr.* (*past* **·gave** /–gáyv/; *past part.* **·given** /–gívən/) (often foll. by *about, that*) (of a person's mind, heart, etc.) fill (a person) with suspicion or foreboding.

mis·giv·ing /misgíving/ *n.* (usu. in *pl.*) a feeling of mistrust or apprehension.

mis·gov·ern /misgúvərn/ *v.tr.* govern (a state, a nation, etc.) badly. □□ **mis·gov·ern·ment** *n.*

mis·guide /misgíd/ *v.tr.* **1** (as **misguided** *adj.*) mistaken in thought or action. **2** mislead, misdirect. □□ **mis·guid·ance** *n.* **mis·guid·ed·ly** *adv.* **mis·guid·ed·ness** *n.*

mis·han·dle /mis-hánd'l/ *v.tr.* **1** deal with incorrectly or ineffectively. **2** handle (a person or thing) roughly or rudely; ill-treat.

mis·hap /mís-háp/ *n.* an unlucky accident.

mis·hear /mis-heér/ *v.tr.* (*past* and *past part.* **·heard** /–hérd/) hear incorrectly or imperfectly.

mis·hit *v. & n.* /mis-hít/ (**·hitting**; *past* and *past part.* **·hit**) hit (a tennis ball, etc.) faultily. ● *n.* /mís-hit/ a faulty or bad hit.

mish·mash /míshmash, –maash/ *n.* a confused mixture. [ME, reduplication of MASH]

Mish·nah /míshnə/ *n.* a collection of precepts forming the basis of the Talmud, and embodying Jewish oral law. □□ **Mish·na·ic** /–náyik/ *adj.* [Heb. *mišnāh* (teaching by) repetition]

mis·i·den·ti·fy /mísidéntifí/ *v.tr.* (**·fies, ·fied**) identify erroneously. □□ **mis·i·den·ti·fi·ca·tion** /–fikáyshən/ *n.*

mis·in·form /mísinfórm/ *v.tr.* give wrong information to; mislead. □□ **mis·in·for·ma·tion** /–fərmáyshən/ *n.*

mis·in·ter·pret /mísintə́rprit/ *v.tr.* (**·in·ter·pret·ed, ·in·ter·pret·ing**) **1** interpret wrongly. **2** draw a wrong inference from. □□ **mis·in·ter·pre·ta·tion** /–táyshən/ *n.* **mis·in·ter·pret·er** *n.*

mis·judge /mísjúj/ *v.tr.* (also *absol.*) **1** judge wrongly. **2** have a wrong opinion of. □□ **mis·judg·ment** *n.* (also **mis·judge·ment**).

mis·key /mískee/ *v.tr.* (**·keys, ·keyed**) key (data) wrongly.

mis·lay /mísláy/ *v.tr.* (*past* and *past part.* **·laid** /–láyd/) **1** unintentionally put (a thing) where it cannot readily be found. **2** *euphem.* lose.

mis·lead /misleéd/ *v.tr.* (*past* and *past part.* **·led** /–léd/) **1** cause (a person) to go wrong, in conduct, belief, etc. **2** lead astray or in the wrong direction. □□ **mis·lead·er** *n.*

mis·lead·ing /misleéding/ *adj.* causing to err or go astray; imprecise; confusing. □□ **mis·lead·ing·ly** *adv.* **mis·lead·ing·ness** *n.*

mis·like /mislík/ *v.tr. & n. archaic* dislike. [OE *mislícian* (as MIS-[1], LIKE[2])]

mis·man·age /mismánij/ *v.tr.* manage badly or wrongly. □□ **mis·man·age·ment** *n.*

mis·mar·riage /mísmárij/ *n.* an unsuitable marriage or alliance. [MIS-[1] + MARRIAGE]

mis·match *v. & n.* ● *v.tr.* /mismách/ (usu. as **mismatched** *adj.*) match unsuitably or incorrectly, esp. in marriage. ● *n.* /mísmach/ a bad match.

mis·mat·ed /mismáytid/ *adj.* **1** (of people) not suited to each other, esp. in marriage. **2** (of objects) not matching.

mis·meas·ure /mismézhər/ *v.tr.* measure or estimate incorrectly. □□ **mis·meas·ure·ment** *n.*

mis·name /misnáym/ *v.tr.* = MISCALL.

mis·no·mer /misnómər/ *n.* **1** a name or term used wrongly. **2** the wrong use of a name or term. [ME f. AF f. OF *mesnom(m)er* (as MIS-[2], *nommer* name f. L *nominare* formed as NOMINATE)]

mi·sog·a·my /misógəmee/ *n.* the hatred of marriage. □□ **mi·sog·a·mist** *n.* [Gk *misos* hatred + *gamos* marriage]

mi·sog·y·ny /misójinee/ *n.* the hatred of women. □□ **mi·sog·y·nist** *n.* **mi·sog·y·nous** *adj.* [Gk *misos* hatred + *gunē* woman]

mis·pick·el /míspikəl/ *n. Mineral.* arsenical pyrite. [G]

mis·place /mispláys/ *v.tr.* **1** put in the wrong place. **2** bestow (affections, confidence, etc.) on an inappropriate object. **3** time (words, actions, etc.) badly. □□ **mis·place·ment** *n.*

mis·play *v. & n.* ● *v.tr.* /mispláy/ play (a ball, card, etc.) in a wrong or ineffective manner. ● *n.* /mispláy, mísplay/ an instance of this.

mis·print *n. & v.* ● *n.* /mísprint/ a mistake in printing. ● *v.tr.* /misprínt/ print wrongly.

mis·pri·sion[1] /mispríprízhən/ *n. Law* **1** (in full **misprision of a felony** or **of treason**) the deliberate concealment of one's knowledge of a crime, treason, etc. **2** a wrong action or omission. [ME f. AF *mesprisioun* f. OF *mesprison* error f. *mesprendre* to mistake (as MIS-[2], *prendre* take)]

mis·pri·sion[2] /mispríprízhən/ *n.* **1** a misreading, misunderstanding, etc. **2** (usu. foll. by *of*) a failure to appreciate the value of a thing. **3** *archaic* contempt. [MISPRIZE after MISPRISION[1]]

mis·prize /mispríz/ *v.tr. literary* despise, scorn; fail to appreciate. [ME f. OF *mesprisier* (as MIS-[1], PRIZE[1])]

mis·pro·nounce /mísprənówns/ *v.tr.* pronounce (a word, etc.) wrongly. □□ **mis·pro·nun·ci·a·tion** /–nunseeáyshən/ *n.*

mis·quote /mískwót/ *v.tr.* quote wrongly. □□ **mis·quo·ta·tion** /–táyshən/ *n.*

mis·read /mísreéd/ *v.tr.* (*past* and *past part.* **·read** /–réd/) read or interpret (text, a situation, etc.) wrongly.

mis·re·mem·ber /mísrimémbər/ *v.tr.* remember imperfectly or incorrectly.

mis·re·port /mísripáwrt/ *v. & n.* ● *v.tr.* give a false or incorrect report of. ● *n.* a false or incorrect report.

mis·rep·re·sent /mísreprizént/ *v.tr.* represent wrongly; give a false or misleading account or idea of. □□ **mis·rep·re·sen·ta·tion** /–táyshən/ *n.* **mis·rep·re·sen·ta·tive** *adj.*

mis·rule /mísroól/ *n. & v.* ● *n.* bad government; disorder. ● *v.tr.* govern badly.

Miss. *abbr.* Mississippi.

miss[1] /mis/ *v. & n.* ● *v.* **1** (also *absol.*) fail to hit, reach, find, catch, etc. (an object or goal). **2** *tr.* fail to catch (a bus, train, etc.). **3** *tr.* fail to experience, see, or attend (an occurrence or event). **4** *tr.* fail to meet (a person); fail to keep (an appointment). **5** *tr.* fail to seize

(an opportunity, etc.) (*I missed my chance*). **6** *tr.* fail to hear or understand (*I'm sorry, I missed what you said*). **7** *tr.* **a** regret the loss or absence of (a person or thing) (*did you miss me while I was away?*). **b** notice the loss or absence of (an object) (*bound to miss the key if it isn't there*). **8** *tr.* avoid (*go early to miss the traffic*). **9** *tr.* = miss out 1. **10** *intr.* (of an engine, etc.) fail, misfire. ● *n.* **1** a failure to hit, reach, attain, connect, etc. **2** *colloq.* = MISCARRIAGE 1. □ **be missing** see MISSING *adj.* **give(a thing) a miss** esp. *Brit.* avoid, leave alone (*gave the party a miss*). **miss the boat** (or **bus**) lose an opportunity. **miss fire** (of a gun) fail to go off or hit the mark (cf. MISFIRE). **a miss is as good as a mile** the fact of failure or escape is not affected by the narrowness of the margin. **miss out 1** (usu. foll. by *on*) *colloq.* fail to get or experience (*always misses out on the good times*). **2** *Brit.* omit, leave out (*missed out my name from the list*). **not miss much** be alert. **not miss a trick** never fail to seize an opportunity, advantage, etc. □□ **miss·a·ble** *adj.* [OE *missan* f. Gmc]

miss[2] /mis/ *n.* **1** a girl or unmarried woman. **2** (**Miss**) **a** a respectful title of an unmarried woman or girl, or of a married woman retaining her maiden name for professional purposes (cf. **Ms.**). **b** the title of a beauty queen (*Miss World*). **3** usu. *derog.* or *joc.* a girl, esp. a schoolgirl. **4** the title used to address a young woman or girl. □□ **miss·ish** *adj.* (in sense 3). [abbr. of MISTRESS]

mis·sal /mísəl/ *n. RC Ch., Anglican Ch.* **1** a book containing the texts used in the service of the Mass throughout the year. **2** a book of prayers, esp. an illuminated one. [ME f. med.L *missale* neut. of eccl.L *missalis* of the mass f. *missa* MASS[2]]

mis·shape /mís-sháyp/ *v.tr.* give a bad shape or form to; distort.

mis·shap·en /mís-sháypən/ *adj.* ill-shaped, deformed, distorted. □□ **mis·shap·en·ly** *adv.* **mis·shap·en·ness** *n.*

mis·sile /mísəl/ *n.* **1** an object or weapon suitable for throwing at a target or for discharge from a machine. **2** a weapon directed by remote control or automatically. □□ **mis·sile·ry** /–ə lree/ *n.* [L *missilis* f. *mittere miss-* send]

SPELLING TIP | **missile**

Try the mnemonic: "To be accurate, a *missile* must have two *eyes* (*i*'s)."

---

miss·ing /mísing/ *adj.* **1** not in its place; lost. **2** (of a person) not yet traced or confirmed as alive but not known to be dead. **3** not present.

miss·ing link *n.* **1** a thing lacking to complete a series. **2** a hypothetical intermediate type, esp. between humans and apes.

mis·sion /míshən/ *n.* **1 a** a particular task or goal assigned to a person or group. **b** a journey undertaken as part of this. **c** a person's vocation (*mission in life*). **2** a military or scientific operation or expedition for a particular purpose. **3** a body of persons sent, esp. to a foreign country, to conduct negotiations, etc. **4 a** a body sent to propagate a religious faith. **b** a field of missionary activity. **c** a missionary post or organization. **d** a place of worship attached to a mission. **5** a particular course or period of preaching, services, etc., undertaken by a parish or community. [F *mission* or L *missio* f. *mittere miss-* send]

mis·sion·ar·y /míshəneree/ *adj. & n.* ● *adj.* of, concerned with, or characteristic of, religious missions. ● *n.* (*pl.* **·ies**) a person doing missionary work. [mod.L *missionarius* f. L (as MISSION)]

mis·sion·ar·y po·si·tion *n. colloq.* a position for sexual intercourse with the woman lying on her back and the man lying on top and facing her.

mis·sion·er /míshənər/ *n.* **1** a missionary. **2** a person in charge of a religious mission.

mis·sis var. of MISSUS.

mis·sive /mísiv/ *n.* **1** *joc.* a letter, esp. a long and serious one. **2** an official letter. [ME f. med.L *missivus* f. L (as MISSION)]

Mis·sour·i /mizoóree, –zoórə/ *n.* **1 a** N. American tribe native to the Missouri River valley. **2** a member of this people. ● *adj.* of or relating to this people.

mis·spell /mís-spél/ *v.tr.* (*past* and *past part.* **·spelled** or esp. *Brit.* **·spelt**) spell wrongly.

mis·spel·ling /mís-spéling/ *n.* a wrong spelling.

mis·spend /mís-spénd/ *v.tr.* (*past* and *past part.* **·spent** /–spént/) (esp. as **misspent** *adj.*) spend amiss or wastefully.

mis·state /mís-stáyt/ *v.tr.* state wrongly or inaccurately.

mis·state·ment /mís-stáytmənt/ *n.* a wrong or inaccurate statement.

mis·step /mís-stép/ *n.* **1** a wrong step or action. **2** a faux pas.

mis·sus /mísəz/ *n.* (also **mis·sis** /–siz/) *sl.* or *joc.* **1** a form of address to a woman. **2** a wife. □ **the missus** my or your wife. [corrupt. of MISTRESS: cf. MRS.]

miss·y /mísee/ *n.* (*pl.* **·ies**) an affectionate or derogatory form of address to a young girl.

mist /mist/ *n. & v.* ● *n.* **1 a** water vapor near the ground in minute droplets limiting visibility. **b** condensed vapor settling on a surface and obscuring glass, etc. **2** dimness or blurring of the sight caused by tears, etc. **3** a cloud of particles resembling mist. ● *v.tr. & intr.* (usu. foll. by *up, over*) cover or become covered with mist or as with mist. □□ **mist·ful** *adj.* **mist·like** *adj.* [OE f. Gmc]

mis·take /mistáyk/ *n. & v.* ● *n.* **1** an incorrect idea or opinion; a thing incorrectly done or thought. **2** an error of judgment. ● *v.tr.* (*past* **mis·took** /–tŏŏk/; *past part.* **mis·tak·en** /–táykən/) **1** misunderstand the meaning or intention of (a person, a statement, etc.). **2** (foll. by *for*) wrongly take or identify (*mistook me for you*). **3** choose wrongly (*mistake one's vocation*). □ **and** (or **make**) **no mistake** *colloq.* undoubtedly. **by mistake** accidentally; in error. **there is no mistaking** one is sure to recognize (a person or thing). □□ **mis·tak·a·ble** *adj.* **mis·tak·a·bly** *adv.* [ME f. ON *mistaka* (as MIS-[1], TAKE)]

> **SYNONYM TIP** mistake
>
> BLOOPER, BLUNDER, ERROR, FAUX PAS, GOOF, SLIP. It would be a **mistake** to argue with your boss the day before he or she evaluates your performance, but to forget an important step in a task that has been assigned to you would be an **error**. Although both of these nouns are used interchangeably in many contexts, a *mistake* is usually caused by poor judgment or a disregard of rules or principles (*it was a mistake not to tell the truth at the outset*), while an *error* implies an unintentional deviation from standards of accuracy or right conduct (*a mathematical error*). A **blunder** is a careless, stupid, or blatant *mistake* involving behavior or judgment; it suggests awkwardness or ignorance on the part of the person who makes it (*a blunder that ruined the evening*). A **slip** is a minor and usually accidental *mistake* that is the result of haste or carelessness (*a slip of the tongue spoiled the surprise*), while a **faux pas** (which means "false step" in French) is an embarrassing breach of etiquette (*it was a faux pas to have meat at the table when so many of the guests were vegetarians*). **Goof** and **blooper** are humorous *mistakes*. A *blooper* is usually a mix-up in speech, while a *goof* is a careless *error* that is honestly admitted (*when confronted with the evidence, she shrugged her shoulders and said, "It was a goof!"*).

mis·tak·en /mistáykən/ *adj.* **1** wrong in opinion or judgment. **2** based on or resulting from this (*mistaken loyalty; mistaken identity*). □□ **mis·tak·en·ly** *adv.* **mis·tak·en·ness** *n.*

mis·teach /mís-teéch/ *v.tr.* (*past* and *past part.* ·**taught** /–táwt/) teach wrongly or incorrectly.

mis·ter /místər/ *n.* **1** (**Mister**) respectful title for a man, usu. abbr. (as **Mr.**). **2** *sl.* or *joc.* sir; a form of address to a man (*Hey, mister!*). **3** a husband. [weakened form of MASTER in unstressed use before a name: cf. MR.]

mis·time /mís-tím/ *v.tr.* say or do at the wrong time. [OE *mistīmian* (as MIS-[1], TIME)]

mis·ti·tle /mís-tít'l/ *v.tr.* give the wrong title or name to.

mis·tle·toe /mísəltō/ *n.* **1** a parasitic plant, *Viscum album*, growing on apple and other trees and bearing white glutinous berries in winter. **2** a similar plant, genus *Phoradendron*, native to N. America. [OE *misteltān*]

mis·took *past* of MISTAKE.

mis·tral /místrəl, mistraál/ *n.* a cold northerly wind that blows down the Rhône valley and S. France into the Mediterranean. [F & Prov. f. L (as MAGISTRAL)]

mis·trans·late /místranzláyt, –trans–, mistránzlayt, –tráns–/ *v.tr.* translate incorrectly. □□ **mis·trans·la·tion** /–láyshən/ *n.*

mis·treat /místreét/ *v.tr.* treat badly. □□ **mis·treat·ment** *n.*

mis·tress /místris/ *n.* **1** a female head of a household. **2 a** a woman in authority over others. **b** the female owner of a pet. **3** a woman with power to control, etc. (often foll. by *of: mistress of the situation*). **4** *Brit.* **a** a female teacher (*music mistress*). **b** a female head of a college, etc. **5 a** a woman (other than his wife) with whom a married man has a (usu. prolonged) sexual relationship. **b** *archaic* or *poet.* a woman loved and courted by a man. **6** *archaic* or *dial.* (as a title) = MRS. [ME f. OF *maistresse* f. *maistre* MASTER]

mis·tri·al /mís-tríəl/ *n.* **1** a trial rendered invalid through some error in the proceedings. **2** a trial in which the jury cannot agree on a verdict.

mis·trust /mís-trúst/ *v. & n.* ● *v.tr.* **1** be suspicious of. **2** feel no confidence in (a person, oneself, one's powers, etc.). ● *n.* **1** suspicion. **2** lack of confidence.

mis·trust·ful /mís-trústfŏŏl/ *adj.* **1** (foll. by *of*) suspicious. **2** lacking confidence or trust. □□ **mis·trust·ful·ly** *adv.* **mis·trust·ful·ness** *n.*

mist·y /místee/ *adj.* (**mist·i·er, mist·i·est**) **1** of or covered with mist. **2** indistinct or dim in outline. **3** obscure, vague (*a misty idea*). □□ **mist·i·ly** *adv.* **mist·i·ness** *n.* [OE *mistig* (as MIST)]

mis·type /mís-típ/ *v.tr.* type wrongly. [MIS-[1] + TYPE]

mis·un·der·stand /mísundərstánd/ *v.tr.* (*past* and *past part.* ·**un·der·stood** /–stŏŏd/) **1** fail to understand correctly. **2** (usu. as **misunderstood** *adj.*) misinterpret the words or actions of (a person).

mis·un·der·stand·ing /mísundərstánding/ *n.* **1** a failure to understand correctly. **2** a slight disagreement or quarrel.

mis·us·age /mísyŏŏsij/ *n.* **1** wrong or improper usage. **2** ill-treatment.

mis·use *v. & n.* ● *v.tr.* /mísyŏŏz/ **1** use wrongly; apply to the wrong purpose. **2** ill-treat. ● *n.* /mísyŏŏs/ wrong or improper use or application. □□ **mis·us·er** *n.*

MIT *abbr.* Massachusetts Institute of Technology.

mite[1] /mīt/ *n.* any small arachnid of the order Acari, having four pairs of legs when adult. □□ **mit·y** *adj.* [OE *mīte* f. Gmc]

mite[2] /mīt/ *n. & adv.* ● *n.* **1** *hist.* a Flemish copper coin of small value. **2** any small monetary unit. **3** a small object or person, esp. a child. **4** a modest contribution; the best one can do (*offered my mite of comfort*). ● *adv.* (usu. prec. by *a*) *colloq.* somewhat (*is a mite shy*). [ME f. MLG, MDu. *mīte* f. Gmc: prob. the same as MITE[1]]

mi·ter /mítər/ *n. & v.* (*Brit.* **mi·tre**) ● *n.* **1** a tall deeply-cleft headdress worn by bishops and abbots, esp. as a symbol of office. **2** the joint of two pieces of wood or other material at an angle of 90°, such that the line of junction bisects this angle. **3** a diagonal join of two pieces of fabric that meet at a corner, made by folding. ● *v.* **1** *tr.* bestow the miter on. **2** *tr. & intr.* join with a miter. □□ **mi·tered** *adj.* [ME f. OF f. L *mitra* f. Gk *mitra* girdle, turban]

mi·ter box *n.* a guide to enable a saw to cut miter joints at the desired angle.

Mith·ra·ism /míthrayizəm/ *n.* the cult of the ancient Persian god Mithras associated with the sun. □□ **Mith·ra·ic** /–ráyik/ *adj.* **Mith·ra·ist** *n.* [L *Mithras* f. Gk *Mithras* f. OPers. *Mithra* f. Skr. *Mitra*]

mith·ri·da·tize /mithrídətīz/ *v.tr.* render proof against a poison by administering gradually increasing doses of it. □□ **mith·ri·dat·ic** /–dátik/ *adj.* **mith·ri·da·tism** /–dətizəm/ *n.* [f. *mithridate* a supposed universal antidote attributed to *Mithridates* VI, king of Pontus d. 63 BC]

mit·i·gate /mí tigayt/ *v.tr.* make milder or less intense or severe; moderate (*your offer certainly mitigated their hostility*). □□ **mit ·i·ga·ble** *adj.* **mit·i·ga·tion** /–gáyshən / *n.* **mit·i·ga·tor** *n.* **mit·i·ga·to·ry** /–gətáwree/ *adj.* [ME f. L *mitigare mitigat-* f. *mitis* mild]
▶ See note at MILITATE.

mit·i·gat·ing cir·cum·stanc·es *n.pl. Law* circumstances permitting greater leniency.

mi·to·chon·dri·on /mítəkóndreeən/ *n.* (*pl.* **mi·to·chon·dri·a** /–dreeə/) *Biol.* an organelle found in most eukaryotic cells, containing enzymes for respiration and energy production. [mod.L f. Gk *mitos* thread + *khondrion* dimin. of *khondros* granule]

mi·to·sis /mītṓsis/ *n. Biol.* a type of cell division that results in two daughter cells each having the same number and kind of chromosomes as the parent nucleus (cf. MEIOSIS). □□ **mi·tot·ic** /–tótik/ *adj.* [mod.L f. Gk *mitos* thread]

mi·tral /mítrəl/ *adj.* of or like a miter. [mod.L *mitralis* f. L *mitra* girdle]

mi·tral valve *n.* a two-cusped valve between the left atrium and the left ventricle of the heart.

mi·tre *Brit.* var. of MITER.

mitt /mit/ *n.* **1** a baseball glove for catching the ball. **2** = MITTEN. **3** *sl.* a hand or fist. **4** a glove leaving the fingers and thumb-tip exposed. [abbr. of MITTEN]

mit·ten /mít'n/ *n.* a glove with two sections, one for the thumb and the other for all four fingers. □□ **mit·tened** *adj.* [ME f. OF *mitaine* ult. f. L *medietas* half: see MOIETY]

mit·ti·mus /mítiməs/ *n.* a warrant committing a person to prison. [ME f. L, = we send]

mitz·vah /mítsvə/ *n.* (*pl.* **mitz·voth** /–vōt/ or **mitz·vahs**) in Judaism: **1** a precept or commandment. **2** a good deed done from religious duty. [Heb. *miṣwāh* commandment]

mix /miks/ *v. & n.* ● *v.* **1** *tr.* combine or put together (two or more substances or things) so that the constituents of each are diffused among those of the other(s). **2** *tr.* prepare (a compound, cocktail, etc.) by combining the ingredients. **3** *tr.* combine an activity, etc., with another simultaneously (*mix business and pleasure*). **4** *intr.* **a** join, be mixed, or combine, esp. readily (*oil and water will not mix*). **b** be compatible. **c** be sociable (*must learn to mix*). **5** *intr.* **a** (foll. by *with*) (of a person) be harmonious or sociable with; have regular dealings with. **b** (foll. by *in*) participate in. **6** *tr.* drink different kinds of (alcoholic liquor) in close succession. ● *n.* **1 a** the act or an instance of mixing; a mixture. **b** the proportion of materials, etc., in a mixture. **2** *colloq.* a group of persons of different types (*social mix*). **3** the ingredients prepared commercially for making a cake, etc., or for a process such as making concrete. **4** the merging of film pictures or sound. □ **be mixed up in** (or **with**) be involved in or with (esp. something undesirable). **mix in** be harmonious or sociable. **mix it** (usu. foll. by *up*) *colloq.* start fighting. **mix up 1** mix thoroughly. **2** confuse; mistake the identity of. □□ **mix·a·ble** *adj.* [back-form. f. MIXED (taken as past part.)]

mixed /mikst/ *adj.* **1** of diverse qualities or elements. **2** containing persons from various backgrounds, etc. **3** for or involving persons of both sexes (*a mixed school; mixed swimming*). □□ **mixed·ness** /mík-sidnis/ *n.* [ME *mixt* f. OF *mixte* f. L *mixtus* past part. of *miscēre* mix]

mixed bag *n.* a diverse assortment of things or persons.

mixed bless·ing *n.* a thing having advantages and disadvantages.

mixed crys·tal *n.* a crystal formed from more than one substance.

mixed dou·bles *n.pl. Tennis* a game or competition with a man and a woman on each side.

mixed drink *n.* an alcoholic beverage containing two or more ingredients, esp. one made according to a standard recipe.

mixed e·con·o·my *n.* an economic system combining private and public enterprise.

mixed farm·ing *n.* farming of both crops and livestock.

mixed grill *n.* a dish of various grilled meats and vegetables, etc.

mixed mar·riage *n.* a marriage between persons of different races or religions.

mixed met·a·phor *n.* a combination of inconsistent metaphors (e.g., *this tower of strength will forge ahead*).

mixed num·ber *n.* an integer and a proper fraction.

mixed-up *adj. colloq.* mentally or emotionally confused; socially ill-adjusted.

mix·er /míksər/ *n.* **1** a device for mixing foods, etc. or for processing other materials. **2** a person who manages socially in a specified way (*a good mixer*). **3** a (usu. soft) drink to be mixed with another. **4** *Broadcasting & Cinematog.* **a** a device for merging input signals to produce a combined output in the form of sound or pictures. **b** a person who operates this.

mix·ol·o·gy /miksólojee/ *n.* the art or skill of preparing mixed drinks. □□ **mix·ol·o·gist** *n.*

mix·ture /míks-chər/ *n.* **1** the process of mixing or being mixed. **2** the result of mixing; something mixed; a combination. **3** *Chem.* the product of the random distribution of one substance through another without any chemical reaction taking place between the components, as distinct from a chemical compound. **4** ingredients mixed together to produce a substance, esp. a medicine (*cough mixture*). **5** a person regarded as a combination of qualities and attributes. **6** gas or vaporized gasoline or oil mixed with air, forming an explosive charge in an internal-combustion engine. [ME f. F *mixture* or L *mixtura* (as MIXED)]

mix-up *n.* a confusion, misunderstanding, or mistake.

miz·zen /mízən/ *n.* (also **miz·en**) *Naut.* (in full **mizzen sail**) the lowest fore-and-aft sail of a fully rigged ship's mizzen-mast. [ME f. F *misaine* f. It. *mezzana* mizen-sail, fem. of *mezzano* middle: see MEZZANINE]

miz·zen·mast /mízənmast/ *n.* the mast next aft of a ship's mainmast.

miz·zen yard *n.* the spar on which the mizzen is extended.

miz·zle¹ /mízəl/ *n. & v.intr.* drizzle. □□ **miz·zly** *adj.* [ME, prob. f. LG *miseln*: cf. MDu. *miezelen*]

miz·zle² /mízəl/ *v.intr. Brit. sl.* run away; decamp. [18th c.: orig. unkn.]

Mk. *abbr.* **1** the German mark. **2** Mark (esp. in the New Testament).

mks *abbr.* meter-kilogram-second.

mkt. *abbr.* market.

ml *abbr.* milliliter(s).

MLA *abbr.* Modern Language Association (of America).

MLD *abbr.* minimum lethal dose.

M.Litt. *abbr.* Master of Letters. [L *Magister Litterarum*]

Mlle. *abbr.* (*pl.* **Mlles.**) Mademoiselle.

MM *abbr.* **1** (as **MM.**) Messieurs. **2** (in the UK) Military Medal.

mm *abbr.* millimeter(s).

Mme. *abbr.* (*pl.* **Mmes.**) Madame.

m.m.f. *abbr.* magnetomotive force.

MN *abbr.* Minnesota (in official postal use).

Mn *symb. Chem.* the element manganese.

mne·mon·ic /nimónik/ *adj. & n.* ● *adj.* of or designed to aid the memory. ● *n.* a mnemonic device. □□ **mne·mon·i·cal·ly** *adv.* **mne·mon·ist** /néemənist/ *n.* [med.L *mnemonicus* f. Gk *mnēmonikos* f. *mnēmōn* mindful]

mne·mon·ics /nimóniks/ *n.pl.* (usu. treated as *sing.*) **1** the art of improving memory. **2** a system for this.

MO *abbr.* **1** Missouri (in official postal use). **2** money order.

Mo *symb. Chem.* the element molybdenum.

Mo. *abbr.* Missouri.

mo. *abbr.* month.

m.o. *abbr.* modus operandi.

mo·a /móə/ *n.* an extinct, flightless bird of the family Dinornithidae, resembling the ostrich, formerly found in New Zealand. [Maori]

moan /mōn/ *n. & v.* ● *n.* **1** a long murmur expressing physical or mental suffering. **2** a low plaintive sound of wind, etc. **3** a complaint; a grievance. ● *v.* **1** *intr.* make a moan or moans. **2** *intr. colloq.* complain or grumble. **3** *tr.* **a** utter with moans. **b** lament.

□□ **moan·er** *n.* **moan·ful** *adj.* **moan·ing·ly** *adv.* [ME f. OE *mān* (unrecorded) f. Gmc]

moat /mōt/ *n. & v.* ● *n.* a deep defensive ditch around a castle, town, etc., usu. filled with water. ● *v.tr.* surround with or as with a moat. [ME *mot(e)* f. OF *mote, motte* mound]

mob /mob/ *n. & v.* ● *n.* **1** a disorderly crowd; a rabble. **2** (prec. by *the*) usu. *derog.* the populace. **3** *colloq.* a gang; an associated group of persons. **4** = MAFIA. **5** esp. *Austral.* a flock or herd. ● *v.tr. & intr.* (**mobbed, mobbing**) **1** *tr.* crowd around in order to attack or admire. **b** (of a mob) attack. **c** crowd into (a building). **2** *intr.* assemble in a mob. □□ **mob·ber** *n. & adj.* [abbr. of *mobile*, short for L *mobile vulgus* excitable crowd: see MOBILE]

mob·cap /móbkap/ *n. hist.* a woman's large indoor cap covering all the hair, worn in the 18th and early 19th c. [obs. (18th-c.) *mob*, orig. = slut f. CAP]

mo·bile /móbəl, –beel, –bīl/ *adj. & n.* ● *adj.* **1** movable; not fixed; free or able to move or flow easily. **2** (of the face, etc.) readily changing its expression. **3** (of a shop, library, etc.) accommodated in a vehicle so as to serve various places. **4** (of a person) able to change his or her social status. ● *n.* /–beel/ a decorative structure that may be hung so as to turn freely. □□ **mo·bil·i·ty** /mōbílitee/ *n.* [ME f. F f. L *mobilis* f. *movēre* move]

mo·bile home *n.* a large, transportable house trailer, usu. parked in one place and used as a residence.

mo·bile sculp·ture *n.* a sculpture having moving parts.

mo·bi·lize /móbiliz/ *v.* **1 a** *tr.* organize for service or action (esp. troops in time of war). **b** *intr.* be organized in this way. **2** *tr.* render movable; bring into circulation. □□ **mo·bi·liz·a·ble** *adj.* **mo·bi·li·za·tion** *n.* **mo·bi·liz·er** *n.* [F *mobiliser* (as MOBILE)]

mob rule *n.* law or rule imposed and enforced by a mob.

Mö·bi·us strip /móbīəs, máy–, mó–/ *n. Math.* a one-sided surface formed by joining the ends of a rectangle after twisting one end through 180°. [A. F. *Möbius*, Ger. mathematician d. 1868]

mob·oc·ra·cy /mobókrəsee/ *n.* (*pl.* **·cies**) *colloq.* **1** rule by a mob. **2** a ruling mob.

mob·ster /móbstər/ *n. sl.* a gangster.

moc·ca·sin /mókəsin/ *n.* **1** a type of soft leather slipper or shoe with combined sole and heel, as orig. worn by Native Americans. **2** (in full **water moccasin**) a poisonous American snake of the genus *Agkistrodon*, esp. the cottonmouth, *A. piscivorus*. [Algonquian *mockasin, makisin*]

mo·cha /mókə/ *n.* **1** a coffee of fine quality. **2** a beverage or flavoring made with this, often with chocolate added. **3** a soft kind of sheepskin. [*Mocha*, a port on the Red Sea, from where the coffee first came]

mock /mok/ *v., adj., & n.* ● *v.* **1 a** *tr.* ridicule; scoff at. **b** *intr.* (foll. by *at*) act with scorn or contempt for. **2** *tr.* mimic contemptuously. **3** *tr.* jeer, defy, or delude contemptuously. ● *attrib.adj.* sham, imitation (esp. without intention to deceive); pretended (*a mock battle; mock cream*). ● *n.* **1** a thing deserving scorn. **2** (in *pl.*) *colloq.* mock examinations. □ **make mock** (or **a mock**) **of** ridicule. □□ **mock·a·ble** *adj.* **mock·er** *n.* **mock·ing·ly** *adv.* [ME *mokke, mocque* f. OF *mo(c)quer* deride f. Rmc]

mock·er·y /mókəree/ *n.* (*pl.* **·ies**) **1 a** derision, ridicule. **b** a subject or occasion of this. **2** (often foll. by *of*) a counterfeit or absurdly inadequate representation. **3** a ludicrously or insultingly futile action, etc. [ME f. OF *moquerie* (as MOCK)]

mock-he·ro·ic *adj. & n.* ● *adj.* (of a literary style) imitating the style of heroic literature to satirize an unheroic subject. ● *n.* a burlesque imitation of the heroic character or literary style.

mock·ing·bird /mókingbird/ *n.* a bird that mimics the notes of other birds, esp. the American songbird *Mimus polyglottos*.

mock moon *n.* paraselene.

mock or·ange *n.* a white-flowered heavy-scented shrub, *Philadelphus coronarius*.

mock sun *n.* parhelion.

mock tur·tle soup *n.* soup made from a calf's head, etc., to resemble turtle soup.

mock-up *n.* **1** a model or replica of a machine or structure, used for instructional or experimental purposes. **2** an arrangement of text and pictures to be printed (*a mock-up of the following day's front page*).

mod /mod/ *adj. & n. colloq.* ● *adj.* modern, esp. in style of dress. ● *n. Brit.* a young person (esp. in the 1960s) of a group aiming at sophistication and smart modern dress.

mod·al /mód'l/ *adj.* **1** of or relating to mode or form as opposed to substance. **2** *Gram.* **a** of or denoting the mood of a verb. **b** (of an auxiliary verb, e.g., *would*) used to express the mood of another verb. **c** (of a particle) denoting manner. **3** *Statistics* of or relating to a mode; occurring most frequently in a sample or population. **4** *Mus.* denoting a style of music using a particular mode. **5** *Logic* (of a proposition) in which the predicate is affirmed of the subject with some qualification, or which involves the affirmation of possibility, impossibility, necessity, or contingency. □□ **mod•al•ly** *adv.* [med.L *modalis* f. L (as MODE)]

mo•dal•i•ty /mōdálitee/ *n.* (*pl.* •ties) **1** the state of being modal. **2** (in *sing.* or *pl.*) a prescribed method of procedure. [med.L *modalitas* (as MODAL)]

mode /mōd/ *n.* **1** a way or manner in which a thing is done; a method of procedure. **2** a prevailing fashion or custom. **3** *Computing* a way of operating or using a system (*print mode*). **4** *Statistics* the value that occurs most frequently in a given set of data. **5** *Mus.* **a** each of the scale systems that result when the white notes of the piano are played consecutively over an octave (*Lydian mode*). **b** each of the two main modern scale systems, the major and minor (*minor mode*). **6** *Logic* **a** the character of a modal proposition. **b** = MOOD[2]. **7** *Physics* any of the distinct kinds or patterns of vibration of an oscillating system. **8** *Gram.* = MOOD[2]. [F *mode* and L *modus* measure]

mod•el /mód'l/ *n. & v.* • *n.* **1** a representation in three dimensions of an existing person or thing or of a proposed structure, esp. on a smaller scale (often *attrib.: a model train*). **2** a simplified (often mathematical) description of a system, etc., to assist calculations and predictions. **3** a figure in clay, wax, etc., to be reproduced in another material. **4** a particular design or style of a structure or commodity, esp. of a car. **5** a system or thing used as an example to follow or imitate (*the law became a model for dozens of laws banning nondegradable products*). **6 a** an exemplary person or thing (*a model of self-discipline*). **b** (*attrib.*) ideal, exemplary (*a model student*). **7** a person employed to pose for an artist, photographer, or sculptor. **8** a person, usu. a woman, employed to display clothes by wearing them. • *v.* (**mod•eled, mod•el•ing**; *Brit.* **mod•elled, mod•el•ling**) **1** *tr.* fashion or shape (a figure) in clay, wax, etc. **b** (foll. by *after, on*, etc.) form (a thing in imitation of). **2 a** *intr.* act or pose as a model. **b** *tr.* (of a person acting as a model) display (a garment). **3** *tr.* devise a (usu. mathematical) model of (a phenomenon, system, etc.). **4** *tr. Painting* cause to appear three-dimensional. □□ **mod•el•er** *n.* [F *modelle* f. It. *modello* ult. f. L *modulus*: see MODULUS]

SYNONYM TIP model

ARCHETYPE, EXAMPLE, IDEAL, PARADIGM, PATTERN, PROTOTYPE. Most parents try to set a good **example** for their children, although they may end up setting a bad one. An *example*, in other words, is a precedent for imitation, either good or bad. Most parents would do better to provide a **model** for their children, which refers to a person or thing that is to be followed or imitated because of its excellence in conduct or character; *model* also connotes a physical shape to be copied closely (*a ship's model, a model airplane*). Not all children regard their parents as an **ideal** to which they aspire, a word that suggests an imagined perfection or a standard based upon a set of desirable qualities (*the ideal gentleman, the ideal of what an artist should be*); but young people's lives often end up following the **pattern** established by their parents, meaning that their lives follow the same basic configuration or design. While **prototype** and **archetype** are often used interchangeably, they really mean quite different things. An *archetype* is a perfect and unchanging form that existing things or people can approach but never duplicate (*the archetype of a mother*), while a *prototype* is an early, usually unrefined version that later versions reflect but may depart from (*the prototype for today's gas-guzzling cars*). **Paradigm** can refer to an example that serves as a *model*, but today its use is primarily confined to a grammatical context, where it means a set giving all the various forms of a word, such as the conjugation of a verb.

mo•dem /mṓdem/ *n.* a combined device for modulation and demodulation, e.g., between a computer and a telephone line. [*modulator + demodulator*]

mod•er•ate *adj., n., & v.* • *adj.* /mṓdərət/ **1** avoiding extremes; temperate in conduct or expression. **2** fairly or tolerably large or good. **3** (of the wind) of medium strength. **4** (of prices) fairly low. • *n.* /mṓdərət/ a person who holds moderate views, esp. in politics. • *v.* /mṓdərayt/ **1** *tr. & intr.* make or become less violent, intense, rigorous, etc. **2** *tr.* (also *absol.*) act as a moderator of or to. **3** *tr. Physics* retard (neutrons) with a moderator. □□ **mod•er•ate•ly** /–rətlee/ *adv.* **mod•er•ate•ness** /–rətnis/ *n.* **mod•er•a•tism** /mṓdərətizəm/ *n.* [ME f. L *moderatus* past part. of *moderare* reduce, control: rel. to MODEST]

mod•er•a•tion /mṓdəráyshən/ *n.* **1** the process or an instance of moderating. **2** the quality of being moderate. **3** *Physics* the retardation of neutrons by a moderator (see MODERATOR 4). □ **in moderation** in a moderate manner or degree. [ME f. OF f. L *moderatio –onis* (as MODERATE)]

mod•e•ra•to /mṓdəráàtō/ *adj., adv., & n. Mus.* • *adj. & adv.* performed at a moderate pace. • *n.* (*pl.* •tos) a piece of music to be performed in this way. [It. (as MODERATE)]

mod•er•a•tor /mṓdəraytər/ *n.* **1** an arbitrator or mediator. **2** a pre-

siding officer. **3** *Eccl.* a Presbyterian minister presiding over an ecclesiastical body. **4** *Physics* a substance used in a nuclear reactor to retard neutrons. □□ **mod•er•a•tor•ship** *n.* [ME f. L (as MODERATE)]

mod•ern /mṓdərn/ *adj. & n.* • *adj.* **1** of the present and recent times. **2** in current fashion; not antiquated. • *n.* (usu. in *pl.*) a person living in modern times. □□ **mo•der•ni•ty** /–dérnitee/ *n.* **mod•ern•ly** *adv.* **mod•ern•ness** *n.* [F *moderne* or LL *modernus* f. L *modo* just now]

mod•ern Eng•lish *n.* English from about 1500 onward.

mod•ern his•to•ry *n.* history from the end of the Middle Ages to the present day.

mod•ern•ism /mṓdərnizəm/ *n.* **1 a** modern ideas or methods. **b** the tendency of religious belief to harmonize with modern ideas. **2** a modern term or expression. □□ **mod•ern•ist** *n.* **mod•ern•is•tic** /–nístik/ *adj.* **mod•ern•is•ti•cal•ly** /–nístiklee/ *adv.*

mod•ern•ize /mṓdərnīz/ *v.* **1** *tr.* make modern; adapt to modern needs or habits. **2** *intr.* adopt modern ways or views. □□ **mod•ern•i•za•tion** /–záyshən/ *n.* **mod•ern•iz•er** *n.*

mod•est /mṓdist/ *adj.* **1** having or expressing a humble or moderate estimate of one's own merits or achievements. **2** diffident, bashful, retiring. **3** decorous in manner and conduct. **4** moderate or restrained in amount, extent, severity, etc.; not excessive or exaggerated (*a modest sum*). **5** (of a thing) unpretentious in appearance, etc. □□ **mod•est•ly** *adv.* [F *modeste* f. L *modestus* keeping due measure]

mod•es•ty /mṓdistee/ *n.* the quality of being modest.

mod•i•cum /mṓdikəm/ *n.* (foll. by *of*) a small quantity. [L, = short distance or time, neut. of *modicus* moderate f. *modus* measure]

mod•i•fi•ca•tion /mṓdifikáyshən/ *n.* **1** the act or an instance of modifying or being modified. **2** a change made. [F or f. L *modificatio* (as MODIFY)]

mod•i•fi•er /mṓdifīər/ *n.* **1** a person or thing that modifies. **2** *Gram.* a word, esp. an adjective or noun used attributively, that qualifies the sense of another word (e.g., *good* and *family* in *a good family house*).

▶A modifier is said to be *misplaced* if it has no clear grammatical connection to another part of the sentence. Thus, in the sentence *Having seen the movie, my views were offered* the meaning may be clear, but the first phrase appears to modify *views*. The sentence would be better worded as: *Having seen the movie, I offered my views.* Careful writers avoid such lapses in syntax, which can cause ludicrous images, especially in the case of **dangling participles** such as the one in the sentence *Filled with wine, the fireworks delighted us.*

mod•i•fy /mṓdifī/ *v.tr.* (•fies, •fied) **1** make less severe or extreme; tone down (*modify one's demands*). **2** make partial changes in; make different. **3** *Gram.* qualify or expand the sense of (a word, etc.). **4** *Phonet.* change (a vowel) by umlaut. **5** *Chem.* change or replace all the substituent radicals of a polymer, thereby changing its physical properties such as solubility, etc. (*modified starch*). □□ **mod•i•fi•a•ble** *adj.* **mod•i•fi•ca•to•ry** /–fikətáwree/ *adj.* [ME f. OF *modifier* f. L *modificare* (as MODE)]

mo•dil•lion /mədílyən/ *n. Archit.* a projecting bracket under the corona of a cornice in the Corinthian and other orders. [F *modillon* f. It. *modiglione* ult. f. L *mutulus* mutule]

mod•ish /mṓdish/ *adj.* fashionable. □□ **mod•ish•ly** *adv.* **mod•ish•ness** *n.*

mo•diste /mōdéest/ *n.* a milliner; a dressmaker. [F (as MODE)]

mod•u•lar /mṓjələr/ *adj.* using a module or modules as the basis of design or construction (*modular housing units*). □□ **mod•u•lar•i•ty** /–láritee/ *n.* [mod.L *modularis* f. L *modulus*: see MODULUS]

mod•u•late /mṓjəlayt/ *v.* **1** *tr.* **a** regulate or adjust. **b** moderate. **2** *tr.* adjust or vary the tone or pitch of (the speaking voice). **3** *tr.* alter the amplitude or frequency of (a wave) by a wave of a lower frequency to convey a signal. **4** *intr. & tr. Mus.* (often foll. by *from, to*) change or cause to change from one key to another. □□ **mod•u•la•tion** /–láyshən/ *n.* **mod•u•la•tor** *n.* [L *modulari modulat-* to measure f. *modus* measure]

mod•ule /mṓjo͞ol/ *n.* **1** a standardized part or independent unit used in construction, esp. of furniture, a building, or an electronic system. **2** an independent self-contained unit of a spacecraft (*lunar module*). **3** a unit or period of training or education. **4 a** a standard or unit of measurement. **b** *Archit.* a unit of length for expressing proportions, e.g., the semidiameter of a column at the base. [F *module* or L *modulus*: see MODULUS]

mod•u•lo /mṓjəlō/ *prep. & adj. Math.* using, or with respect to, a modulus (see MODULUS 2). [L, ablat. of MODULUS]

mod•u•lus /mṓjələs/ *n.* (*pl.* **mod•u•li** /–lī/) *Math.* **1 a** the magnitude of a real number without regard to its sign. **b** the positive square root of the sum of the squares of the real and imaginary parts of a complex number. **2** a constant factor or ratio. **3** (in number theory) a number used as a divisor for considering numbers in sets giving the same remainder when divided by it. **4** a constant indicating the relation between a physical effect and the force producing it. [L, = measure, dimin. of *modus*]

mo•dus op•e•ran•di /mṓdəsópərándee, –dī/ *n.* (*pl.* **mo•di op•e•ran•di** /mṓdee, –dī/) **1** the particular way in which a person performs a task or action. **2** the way a thing operates. [L, = way of operating: see MODE]

mo•dus vi•ven•di /módəs vivéndee, –dī/ *n.* (*pl.* **mo•di vi•ven•di** /módee, –dī/) **1 a** a way of living or coping. **2 a** an arrangement whereby those in dispute can carry on pending a settlement. **b** an arrangement between people who agree to differ. [L, = way of living: see MODE]

mo•fette /mōfét/ *n.* **1** a fumarole. **2** an exhalation of vapor from this. [F *mofette* or Neapolitan It. *mofetta*]

mo•gul /mógəl/ *n.* **1** *colloq.* an important or influential person. **2** (**Mogul**) *hist.* **a** = MUGHAL. **b** (often **the Great Mogul**) any of the emperors of Delhi in the 16th–19th c. [Pers. *mugūl*: see MUGHAL]

mo•hair /móhair/ *n.* **1** the hair of the angora goat. **2** a yarn or fabric from this, either pure or mixed with wool or cotton. [ult. f. Arab. *mukayyar,* lit. choice, select]

Mo•ham•med•an var. of MUHAMMADAN.

Mo•hawk /móhawk/ *n.* **1 a** a member of a Native American people of New York State. **b** the language of this people. **2** (of a hairstyle) with the head shaved except for a strip of hair from the middle of the forehead to the back of the neck, often worn in tall spikes.

Mo•he•gan /mōhéegən/ *n. & adj.* • *n.* a member of a Native American people of Connecticut. • *adj.* of or relating to this people.

Mo•hi•can var. of MAHICAN.

mo•ho /móhō/ *n.* (*pl.* **•hos**) *Geol.* a boundary of discontinuity separating the earth's crust and mantle. [A. *Mohorovičić,* Yugoslav seismologist d. 1936]

moi•dore /móydawr/ *n. hist.* a Portuguese gold coin, current in England in the 18th c. [Port. *moeda d'ouro* money of gold]

moi•e•ty /móyətee/ *n.* (*pl.* **•ties**) *Law* or *literary* **1** a half. **2** each of the two parts into which a thing is divided. [ME f. OF *moité, moitié* f. L *medietas –tatis* middle f. *medius* (adj.) middle]

moil /moyl/ *v. & n. archaic* • *v.intr.* drudge (esp. toil and moil). • *n.* drudgery. [ME f. OF *moillier* moisten, paddle in mud, ult. f. L *mollis* soft]

moire /mwaar, mawr/ *n.* (in full **moire antique**) watered fabric, orig. mohair, now usu. silk. [F (earlier *mouaire*) f. MOHAIR]

moi•ré /mwaaráy, máwray/ *adj. & n.* • *adj.* **1** (of silk) watered. **2** (of metal) having a patterned appearance like watered silk. • *n.* **1** this patterned appearance. **2** = MOIRE. [F, past part. of *moirer* (as MOIRE)]

moist /moyst/ *adj.* **1 a** slightly wet; damp. **b** (of the season, etc.) rainy. **2** (of a disease) marked by a discharge of matter, etc. **3** (of the eyes) wet with tears. □□ **moist•ly** *adv.* **moist•ness** *n.* [ME f. OF *moiste,* ult. from or rel. to L *mucidus* (see MUCUS) and *musteus* fresh (see MUST²)]

mois•ten /móysən/ *v.tr. & intr.* make or become moist.

mois•ture /móys-chər/ *n.* water or other liquid diffused in a small quantity as vapor, or within a solid, or condensed on a surface. □□ **mois•ture•less** *adj.* [ME f. OF *moistour* (as MOIST)]

mois•tur•ize /móys-chərīz/ *v.tr.* make less dry (esp. the skin by use of a cosmetic). □□ **mois•tur•iz•er** *n.*

Mo•ja•ve /mōhaávee/ *n. & adj.* (also **Mo•ha•ve**) • *n.* **1** a N. American people native to Arizona and California. **2** a member of this people. • *adj.* of or relating to this people.

moke /mōk/ *n. sl.* **1** *Brit.* a donkey. **2** *Austral.* a very poor horse. [19th c.: orig. unkn.]

mo•ksha /mókshə/ *n.* (also **mo•ksa**) *Hinduism,* etc., release from the cycle of rebirth imprel. [Skr. *mokṣa*]

mol /mōl/ *abbr.* = MOLE⁴.

mo•lal /móləl/ *adj. Chem.* (of a solution) containing one mole of solute per kilogram of solvent. □□ **mo•lal•i•ty** /məlálitee/ *n.* [MOLE⁴ + –AL]

mo•lar¹ /mólər/ *adj. & n.* • *adj.* (usu. of a mammal's back teeth) serving to grind. • *n.* a molar tooth. [L *molaris* f. *mola* millstone]

mo•lar² /mólər/ *adj.* **1** of or relating to mass. **2** acting on or by means of large masses or units. [L *moles* mass]

mo•lar³ /mólər/ *adj. Chem.* **1** of a mass of substance usu. per mole (*molar latent heat*). **2** (of a solution) containing one mole of solute per liter of solvent. □□ **mo•lar•i•ty** /məláritee/ *n.* [MOLE⁴ + –AR¹]

mo•las•ses /məlásiz/ *n.pl.* (treated as *sing.*) uncrystallized syrup extracted from raw sugar during refining. [Port. *melaço* f. LL *mellaceum* MUST² f. *mel* honey]

mold¹ /mōld/ *n. & v.* (*Brit.* **mould**) • *n.* **1** a hollow container into which molten metal, etc., is poured or soft material is pressed to harden into a required shape. **2 a** a metal or earthenware vessel used to give shape to cakes, etc. **b** a dessert, etc., made in this way. **3** a form or shape, esp. of an animal body. **4** *Archit.* a molding or group of moldings. **5** a frame or template for producing moldings. **6** character or disposition (*in heroic mold*). • *v.tr.* **1** make (an object) in a required shape or from certain ingredients (*was molded out of clay*). **2** give a shape to. **3** influence the formation or development of (*consultation helps to mold policies*). **4** (esp. of clothing) fit closely to (*the gloves molded his hands*). □□ **mold•a•ble** *adj.* **mold•er** *n.* [ME *mold(e),* app. f. OF *modle* f. L *modulus:* see MODULUS]

mold² /mōld/ *n.* (*Brit.* **mould**) a woolly or furry growth of minute fungi occurring esp. in moist warm conditions. [ME prob. f. obs. *mold* adj.; past part. of *moul* grow moldy f. ON *mygla*]

mold³ /mōld/ *n.* (*Brit.* **mould**) **1** loose earth. **2** the upper soil of cultivated land, esp. when rich in organic matter.

mold•er /móldər/ *v.intr.* (*Brit.* **mould•er**) **1** decay to dust. **2** (foll. by *away*) rot or crumble. **3** deteriorate. [perh. f. MOLD³, but cf. Norw. dial. *muldra* crumble]

mold•ing /mólding/ *n.* (*Brit.* **mould•ing**) **1 a** an ornamentally shaped outline as an architectural feature, esp. in a cornice. **b** a strip of material in wood or stone, etc., for use as molding. **2** similar material in wood or plastic, etc., used for other decorative purposes, e.g., in picture framing.

mold•y /móldee/ *adj.* (*Brit.* **mould•y**) (**•i•er,** **•i•est**) **1** covered with mold. **2** stale; out of date. **3** *colloq.* (as a general term of disparagement) dull, miserable, boring. □□ **mold•i•ness** *n.*

mole¹ /mōl/ *n.* **1** any small burrowing insect-eating mammal of the family Talpidae, esp. *Talpa europaea,* with dark velvety fur and very small eyes. **2** *colloq.* **a** a spy established deep within an organization and usu. dormant for a long period while attaining a position of trust. **b** a betrayer of confidential information. [ME *molle,* prob. f. MDu. *moll(e), mol,* MLG *mol, mul*]

Eastern mole 1

mole² /mōl/ *n.* a small often slightly raised dark blemish on the skin caused by a high concentration of melanin. [OE *māl* f. Gmc]

mole³ /mōl/ *n.* **1** a massive structure serving as a pier, breakwater, or causeway. **2** an artificial harbor. [F *môle* f. L *moles* mass]

mole⁴ /mōl/ *n. Chem.* the SI unit of amount of substance equal to the quantity containing as many elementary units as there are atoms in 0.012 kg of carbon 12. [G *Mol* f. *Molekül* MOLECULE]

mole⁵ /mōl/ *n. Med.* an abnormal mass of tissue in the uterus. [F *môle* f. L *mola* millstone]

mo•lec•u•lar /məlékyələr/ *adj.* of, relating to, or consisting of molecules. □□ **mo•lec•u•lar•i•ty** /–láritee/ *n.* **mo•lec•u•lar•ly** *adv.*

mo•lec•u•lar bi•ol•o•gy *n.* the study of the structure and function of large molecules associated with living organisms.

mo•lec•u•lar sieve *n.* a crystalline substance with pores of molecular dimensions that permit the entry of certain molecules but are impervious to others.

mo•lec•u•lar weight *n.* the ratio of the average mass of one molecule of an element or compound to one twelfth of the mass of an atom of carbon-12. Also called **relative molecular mass.**

mol•e•cule /mólikyōōl/ *n.* **1** *Chem.* the smallest fundamental unit (usu. a group of atoms) of a chemical compound that can take part in a chemical reaction. **2** (in general use) a small particle. [F *molécule* f. mod.L *molecula* dimin. of L *moles* mass]

mole•hill /mólhil/ *n.* a small mound thrown up by a mole in burrowing. □ **make a mountain out of a molehill** exaggerate the importance of a minor difficulty.

mole•skin /mólskin/ *n.* **1** the skin of a mole used as fur. **2 a** a thick, strong cotton fabric with a shaved pile surface. **b** (*in pl.*) clothes, esp. trousers, made of this. **3** (*in pl.*) a soft fabric with adhesive backing used as a foot bandage.

mo•lest /məlést/ *v.tr.* **1** assault or abuse (a person), esp. sexually. **2** annoy or pester (a person) in a hostile or injurious way. □□ **mo•les•ta•tion** /mólestáyshən, mól–/ *n.* **mo•lest•er** *n.* [OF *molester* or L *molestare* annoy f. *molestus* troublesome]

mo•line /məlín/ *adj. Heraldry* (of a cross) having each extremity broadened and curved back. [prob. f. AF *moliné* f. *molin* MILL¹, because of the resemblance to the iron support of a millstone]

moll /mol/ *n. sl.* **1** a gangster's female companion. **2** a prostitute. [pet form of the name *Mary*]

mol•li•fy /mólifī/ *v.tr.* (**•fies,** **•fied**) **1** appease, pacify. **2** reduce the severity of; soften. □□ **mol•li•fi•ca•tion** /–fikáyshən/ *n.* **mol•li•fi•er** *n.* [ME f. F *mollifier* or L *mollificare* f. *mollis* soft]

mol•lusk /móləsk/ *n.* (also esp. *Brit.* **mol•lusc**) any invertebrate of the phylum Mollusca, with a soft body and usu. a hard shell, including limpets, snails, cuttlefish, oysters, mussels, etc. □□ **mol•lus•kan** or **mol•lus•can** /məlúskən/ *adj.* **mol•lusk•like** *adj.* [mod.L *mollusca* neut. pl. of L *molluscus* f. *mollis* soft]

mol•ly•cod•dle /móleekodəl/ *v. & n.* • *v.tr.* coddle, pamper. • *n.* an effeminate man or boy; a milksop. [formed as MOLL + CODDLE]

mol•ly•mawk /móleemawk/ *n.* (also **mal•le•muck** /málimuk/) any of various small kinds of albatross or similar birds. [Du. *mallemok* f. *mal* foolish + *mok* gull]

Mo•loch /mólok, mólok/ *n.* **1 a** a Canaanite idol to whom children were sacrificed. **b** a tyrannical object of sacrifices. [LL f. Gk *Molokh* f. Heb. *mōlek*]

mo•loch /mólok, mólək/ *n.* a harmless spiny lizard, *Moloch horridus,* that feeds chiefly on ants and is found in arid inland Australia.

Mo•lo•tov cock•tail /mólətáwf/ *n.* a crude incendiary device usu. consisting of a bottle filled with flammable liquid. [V. M. *Molotov*, Russian statesman d. 1986]

molt /mōlt/ *v. & n.* (*Brit.* **moult**) • *v.* **1** *intr.* shed feathers, hair, a shell, etc., in the process of renewing plumage, a coat, etc. **2** *tr.* (of an animal) shed (feathers, hair, etc.). • *n.* the act or an instance of molting (*is in molt once a year*). □□ **molt•er** *n.* [ME *moute* f. OE *mutian* (unrecorded) f. L *mutare* change: –*l*- after *fault*, etc.]

mol•ten /móltən/ *adj.* melted, esp. made liquid by heat. [past part. of MELT]

mol•to /móltō/ *adv. Mus.* very (*molto sostenuto; allegro molto*). [It. f. L *multus* much]

mo•ly /mólee/ *n.* (*pl.* •**lies**) **1** an alliaceous plant, *Allium moly*, with small yellow flowers. **2** a mythical herb with white flowers and black roots, endowed with magic properties. [L f. Gk *mōlu*]

mo•lyb•de•nite /məlíbdinīt/ *n.* molybdenum disulfide as an ore.

mo•lyb•de•num /məlíbdinəm/ *n. Chem.* a silver-white brittle metallic transition element occurring naturally in molybdenite and used in steel to give strength and resistance to corrosion. ¶ Symb.: **Mo**. [mod.L, earlier *molybdena*, orig. = molybdenite, lead ore: L *molybdena* f. Gk *molubdaina* plummet f. *molubdos* lead]

mom /mom/ *n. colloq.* mother. [abbr. of MOMMA]

mom-and-pop (store) *n.* of or pertaining to a small retail business, as a grocery store, owned and operated by members of a family.

mo•ment /mómənt/ *n.* **1** a very brief portion of time; an instant. **2** a short period of time (*wait a moment*) (see also MINUTE[1]). **3** an exact or particular point of time (*at last the moment arrived; I came the moment you called*). **4** importance (*of no great moment*). **5** *Physics & Mech.*, etc. **a** the turning effect produced by a force acting at a distance on an object. **b** this effect expressed as the product of the force and the distance from its line of action to a point. □ **at the moment** at this time; now. **in a moment 1** very soon. **2** instantly. **not for a** (or **one**) **moment** never; not at all. **of the moment** currently popular, famous, or important. **this moment** immediately; at once (*come here this moment*). [ME f. OF f. L *momentum*: see MOMENTUM]

mo•men•ta *pl.* of MOMENTUM.

mo•men•tar•i•ly /móməntairilee/ *adv.* **1** for a moment. **2 a** at any moment. **b** instantly.

mo•men•tar•y /mómənteree/ *adj.* **1** lasting only a moment. **2** short-lived; transitory. □□ **mo•men•tar•i•ness** *n.* [L *momentarius* (as MOMENT)]

mo•ment•ly /móməntlee/ *adv. literary* **1** from moment to moment. **2** every moment. **3** for a moment.

mo•ment of in•er•tia *n. Physics* the quantity by which the angular acceleration of a body must be multiplied to give corresponding torque.

mo•ment of truth *n.* a time of crisis or test (orig. the final sword thrust in a bullfight).

mo•men•tous /móméntəs/ *adj.* having great importance. □□ **mo•men•tous•ly** *adv.* **mo•men•tous•ness** *n.*

mo•men•tum /mōméntəm/ *n.* (*pl.* **mo•men•ta** /–tə/) **1** *Physics* the quantity of motion of a moving body, measured as a product of its mass and velocity. **2** the impetus gained by movement. **3** strength or continuity derived from an initial effort. [L f. *movimentum* f. *movēre* move]

mom•ma /mómə/ *n.* var. of MAMMA[1].

mom•my /mómee/ *n.* (*pl.* •**mies**) *colloq.* mother. [imit. of a child's pronunc.: cf. MAMMA[1]]

Mon. *abbr.* Monday.

mon•ad /mónad, mó–/ *n.* **1** the number one; a unit. **2** *Philos.* any ultimate unit of being (e.g., a soul, an atom, a person, God). **3** *Biol.* a simple organism, e.g., one assumed as the first in the genealogy of living beings. □□ **mo•nad•ic** /mənádik/ *adj.* **mon•ad•ism** *n.* (in sense 2). [F *monade* or LL *monas monad*- f. Gk *monas –ados* unit f. *monos* alone]

mon•a•del•phous /mónədélfəs/ *adj. Bot.* **1** (of stamens) having filaments united into one bundle. **2** (of a plant) with such stamens. [Gk *monos* one + *adelphos* brother]

mo•nad•nock /mənádnok/ *n.* a steep-sided isolated hill resistant to erosion and rising above a plain. [Mount *Monadnock* in New Hampshire]

mo•nan•dry /mənándree/ *n.* **1** the custom of having only one husband at a time. **2** *Bot.* the state of having a single stamen. □□ **mo•nan•drous** *adj.* [MONO- after *polyandry*]

mon•arch /mónərk, –aark/ *n.* **1** a sovereign with the title of king, queen, emperor, empress, or the equivalent. **2** a supreme ruler. **3** a powerful or preeminent person. **4** a large orange and black butterfly, *Danaus plexippus*. □□ **mon•ar•chal** /mənáarkəl/ *adj.* **mo•nar•chic** /mənáarkik/ *adj.* **mo•nar•chi•cal** /mənáarkikəl/ *adj.* **mo•nar•chi•cal•ly** /mənáarkiklee/ *adv.* [ME f. F *monarque* or LL *monarcha* f. Gk *monarkhēs, –os*, f. *monos* alone + *arkhō* to rule]

mon•ar•chism /mónərkizəm/ *n.* the advocacy of or the principles of monarchy. □□ **mon•ar•chist** *n.* [F *monarchisme* (as MONARCHY)]

mon•ar•chy /mónərkee/ *n.* (*pl.* •**chies**) **1** a form of government with a monarch at the head. **2** a nation with this. □□ **mo•nar•chi•al** /monáarkeeəl/ *adj.* [ME f. OF *monarchie* f. LL *monarchia* f. Gk *monarkhia* the rule of one (as MONARCH)]

mon•as•ter•y /mónəsteree/ *n.* (*pl.* •**ies**) the residence of a religious community, esp. of monks living in seclusion. [ME f. eccl.L *monasterium* f. eccl.Gk *monastērion* f. *monazō* live alone f. *monos* alone]

mo•nas•tic /mənástik/ *adj. & n.* • *adj.* **1** of or relating to monasteries or the religious communities living in them. **2** resembling these or their way of life; solitary and celibate. • *n.* a monk or other follower of a monastic rule. □□ **mo•nas•ti•cal•ly** *adv.* **mo•nas•ti•cism** /–tisizəm/ *n.* **mo•nas•ti•cize** /–tisīz/ *v.tr.* [F *monastique* or LL *monasticus* f. Gk *monastikos* (as MONASTERY)]

mon•a•tom•ic /mónətómik/ *adj. Chem.* **1** (esp. of a molecule) consisting of one atom. **2** having one replaceable atom or radical.

mon•au•ral /mónáwrəl/ *adj.* **1** = MONOPHONIC. **2** of or involving one ear. □□ **mon•au•ral•ly** *adv.* [MONO- + AURAL[1]]

mon•a•zite /mónəzīt/ *n.* a phosphate mineral containing rare-earth elements and thorium. [G *Monazit* f. Gk *monazō* live alone (because of its rarity)]

Mon•day /múnday, –dee/ *n. & adv.* • *n.* the second day of the week, following Sunday. • *adv. colloq.* **1** on Monday. **2** (**Mondays**) on Mondays; each Monday. [OE *mōnandæg* day of the moon, transl. LL *lunae dies*]

Mo•nel /mōnél/ *n.* (in full **Monel metal**) *Trademark* a nickel-copper alloy with high tensile strength and resisting corrosion. [A. *Monell*, US businessman d. 1921]

mon•e•ta•rism /mónitərizəm, mún–/ *n.* the theory or practice of controlling the supply of money as the chief method of stabilizing the economy.

mo•ne•tar•ist /mónitərist, mún–/ *n. & adj.* • *n.* an advocate of monetarism. • *adj.* in accordance with the principles of monetarism.

mon•e•tar•y /móniteree, –mún/ *adj.* **1** of the currency in use. **2** of or consisting of money. □□ **mon•e•tar•i•ly** /–táirəlee/ *adv.* [F *monétaire* or LL *monetarius* f. L (as MONEY)]

mon•e•tize /mónitīz, mún–/ *v.tr.* **1** give a fixed value as currency. **2** put (a metal) into circulation as money. □□ **mon•e•ti•za•tion** *n.* [F *monétiser* f. L (as MONEY)]

mon•ey /múnee/ *n.* **1 a** a current medium of exchange in the form of coins and paper currency. **b** a particular form of this (*silver money*). **2** (*pl.* •**eys** or •**ies**) (in *pl.*) sums of money. **3 a** wealth; property viewed as convertible into money. **b** wealth as giving power or influence (*money speaks*). **c** a rich person or family (*has married into money*). **4 a** money as a resource (*time is money*). **b** profit, remuneration (*in it for the money*). □ **for my money** in my opinion or judgment; for my preference (*is too aggressive for my money*). **have money to burn** see BURN[1]. **in the money** *colloq.* having or winning a lot of money. **money for jam** (or **old rope**) *Brit. colloq.* profit for little or no trouble. **put money into** invest in. □□ **mon•ey•less** *adj.* [ME f. OF *moneie* f. L *moneta* mint, money, orig. a title of Juno, in whose temple at Rome money was minted]

mon•ey•bags /múneebagz/ *n.pl.* (treated as *sing.*) *colloq.* usu. *derog.* a wealthy person.

mon•ey chang•er *n.* a person whose business it is to change money, esp. at an official rate.

mon•eyed /múneed/ *adj.* **1** having much money; wealthy. **2** consisting of money (*moneyed assistance*).

mon•ey-grub•ber *n. colloq.* a person greedily intent on amassing money. □□ **mon•ey-grub•bing** *n.* this practice. • *adj.* given to this.

mon•ey•lend•er /múneelendər/ *n.* a person who lends money, esp. as a business, at interest. □□ **mon•ey•lend•ing** *n. & adj.*

mon•ey•mak•er /múneemaykər/ *n.* **1** a person who earns much money. **2** a thing, idea, etc., that produces much money. □□ **mon•ey•mak•ing** *n. & adj.*

mon•ey mar•ket *n. Stock Exch.* the trade in short-term loans between banks and other financial institutions.

mon•ey of ac•count *n.* see ACCOUNT.

mon•ey or•der *n.* an order for payment of a specified sum, issued by a bank or post office.

mon•ey-spin•ner *n.* esp. *Brit.* a thing that brings in a profit.

mon•ey•wort /múneewərt/ *n.* a trailing evergreen plant, *Lysimachia nummularia*, with round glossy leaves and yellow flowers.

mon•ger /múnggər, móng–/ *n.* (usu. in *comb.*) **1** esp. *Brit.* a dealer or trader (*fishmonger; ironmonger*). **2** usu. *derog.* a person who promotes or deals in something specified (*warmonger; scaremonger*). [OE *mangere* f. *mangian* to traffic f. Gmc, ult. f. L *mango* dealer]

Mon•gol /mónggəl, –gōl/ *adj. & n.* • *adj.* **1** of or relating to the Asian people now inhabiting Mongolia in Central Asia. **2** resembling this people, esp. in appearance. • *n.* **1** a Mongolian. [native name: perh. f. *mong* brave]

Mon•go•li•an /monggóleeən/ *n. & adj.* • *n.* a native or inhabitant of Mongolia; the language of Mongolia. • *adj.* of or relating to Mongolia or its people or language.

mon•gol•ism /mónggəlizəm/ *n.* = DOWN'S SYNDROME. [MONGOL + –ISM, because its physical characteristics were thought to be reminiscent of Mongolians]

▶The term *Down's syndrome* is now preferred.

Mon·gol·oid /móngɡəloyd/ *adj. & n.* ● *adj.* **1** characteristic of the Mongolians, esp. in having a broad flat yellowish face. **2** (**mongoloid**) often *offens.* having the characteristic symptoms of Down's syndrome. ● *n.* a Mongoloid or mongoloid person.

mon·goose /móngɡoos/ *n.* (*pl.* **mon·goos·es** or **mon·geese**) a small carnivorous mammal of the family Viverridae, esp. of the genus *Herpestes*, with a long body and tail and a grizzled or banded coat, native to Africa and Asia. [Marathi *mangūs*]

mongoose

mon·grel /múnggrəl, móng–/ *n. & adj.* ● *n.* **1** a dog of no definable type or breed. **2** any other animal or plant resulting from the crossing of different breeds or types. **3** *derog.* a person of mixed race. ● *adj.* of mixed origin, nature, or character. □□ **mon·grel·ism** *n.* **mon·grel·ize** *v.tr.* **mon·grel·i·za·tion** /–lizáyshən/ *n.* **mon·grel·ly** *adj.* [earlier *meng-, mang-* f. Gmc: prob. rel. to MINGLE]

'mongst *poet.* var. of AMONG. [see AMONG]

mo·ni·al /móneeəl/ *n.* a mullion. [ME f. OF *moinel* middle f. *moien* MEAN³]

mon·ick·er var. of MONIKER.

mon·ies see MONEY 2.

mon·i·ker /mónikər/ *n.* (also **mon·ick·er**) *sl.* a name. [19th c.: orig. unkn.]

mo·nil·i·form /mónílifawrm/ *adj.* with a form suggesting a string of beads. [F *moniliforme* or mod.L *moniliformis* f. L *monile* necklace]

mon·ism /mónizəm, mó–/ *n.* **1** any theory denying the duality of matter and mind. **2** the doctrine that only one ultimate principle or being exists. □□ **mon·ist** *n.* **mo·nis·tic** /–nístik/ *adj.* [mod.L *monismus* f. Gk *monos* single]

mo·ni·tion /məníshən/ *n.* **1** (foll. by *of*) *literary* a warning (of danger). **2** *Eccl.* a formal notice from a bishop or ecclesiastical court admonishing a person not to commit an offense. [ME f. OF f. L *monitio –onis* (as MONITOR)]

mon·i·tor /mónitər/ *n. & v.* ● *n.* **1** any of various persons or devices for checking or warning about a situation, operation, etc. (*a heart monitor*). **2** a school student with special duties, such as helping to keep order. **3** a cathode-ray tube used as a television receiver or computer display device. **4** a person who listens to and reports on foreign broadcasts, etc. **5** a detector of radioactive contamination. **6** *Zool.* any tropical lizard of the genus *Varanus*, supposed to give warning of the approach of crocodiles. **7** a heavily armed shallow-draft warship. ● *v.tr.* **1** act as a monitor of. **2** maintain regular surveillance over. **3** regulate the strength of (a recorded or transmitted signal). □□ **mon·i·to·ri·al** /–táwreeəl/ *adj.* **mon·i·tor·ship** *n.* [L f. *monēre monit-* warn]

mon·i·to·ry /mónitawree/ *adj. & n.* ● *adj. literary* giving or serving as a warning. ● *n.* (*pl.* **·ies**) *Eccl.* a letter of admonition from the pope or a bishop. [L *monitorius* (as MONITION)]

monk /mungk/ *n.* a member of a religious community of men living under certain vows, esp. of poverty, chastity, and obedience. □□ **monk·ish** *adj.* [OE *munuc* ult. f. Gk *monakhos* solitary f. *monos* alone]

mon·key /múngkee/ *n. & v.* ● *n.* (*pl.* **·keys**) **1** any of various New World and Old World primates esp. of the families Cebidae (including capuchins), Callitrichidae (including marmosets and tamarins), and Cercopithecidae (including baboons and apes). **2** a mischievous person, esp. a child (*young monkey*). **3** *Brit.* sl. £500. **4** (in full **monkey engine**) a machine hammer for pile driving, etc. ● *v.* (**·keys, ·keyed**) **1** *tr.* mimic or mock. **2** *intr.* (often foll. by *with*) tamper or play mischievous tricks. **3** *intr.* (foll. by *around, about*) fool around. □ **have a monkey on one's back 1** *sl.* be a drug addict. **2** have a persistent problem or hindrance. **make a monkey of** humiliate by making appear ridiculous. □□ **mon·key·ish** *adj.* [16th c.: orig. unkn. (perh. LG)]

mon·key busi·ness *n. colloq.* mischief.

mon·key jack·et *n.* a short close-fitting jacket worn by sailors, etc., or at a mess.

mon·key puz·zle *n.* a coniferous tree, *Araucaria araucana*, native to Chile, with downward-pointing branches and small close-set leaves.

mon·key·shine /múngkeeshīn/ *n.* (usu. in *pl.*) *US colloq.* = MONKEY BUSINESS.

mon·key suit *n. colloq.* formal attire, esp. a tuxedo.

mon·key tricks *n. Brit. colloq.* mischief.

mon·key wrench *n.* a wrench with an adjustable jaw.

monk·fish /múnkfish/ *n.* an anglerfish, esp. *Lophius piscatorius*, often used as food.

monks·hood /múngks-hŏŏd/ *n. Bot.* a poisonous garden plant *Aconitum napellus*, with hood-shaped blue or purple flowers.

mon·o¹ /mónō/ *n. colloq.* infectious mononucleosis. [abbr.]

mon·o² /mónō/ *adj. & n. colloq.* ● *adj.* monophonic. ● *n.* (*pl.* **·os**) a monophonic record, reproduction, etc. [abbr.]

mono- /mónō/ *comb. form* (usu. **mon-** before a vowel) **1** one, alone, single. **2** *Chem.* (forming names of compounds) containing one atom or group of a specified kind. [Gk f. *monos* alone]

mon·o·ac·id /mónōásid/ *adj. Chem.* (of a base) having one replaceable hydroxide ion.

mon·o·ba·sic /mónōbáysik/ *adj. Chem.* (of an acid) having one replaceable hydrogen atom.

mon·o·car·pic /mónōkáarpik/ *adj.* (also **mon·o·car·pous** /–káarpəs/) *Bot.* bearing fruit only once. [MONO- + Gk *karpos* fruit]

mon·o·caus·al /mónōkáwzəl/ *adj.* in terms of a sole cause.

mon·o·ceph·a·lous /mónōséfələs/ *adj. Bot.* having only one head.

mon·o·chord /mónōkawrd/ *n. Mus.* an instrument with a single string and a movable bridge, used esp. to determine intervals. [ME f. OF *monocorde* f. LL *monochordon* f. Gk *monokhordon* (as MONO-, CHORD¹)]

mon·o·chro·mat·ic /mónəkrəmátik/ *adj.* **1** *Physics* (of light or other radiation) of a single wavelength or frequency. **2** containing only one color. □□ **mon·o·chro·mat·i·cal·ly** *adv.*

mon·o·chro·ma·tism /mónōkrṓmətizəm/ *n.* complete color blindness in which all colors appear as shades of one color.

mon·o·chrome /mónōkrōm/ *n. & adj.* ● *n.* a photograph or picture done in one color or different tones of this, or in black and white only. ● *adj.* having or using only one color or in black and white only. □□ **mon·o·chro·mic** /–krṓmik/ *adj.* [ult. f. Gk *monokhrōmatos* (as MONO-, *khrōmatos* f. *khrōma* color)]

mon·o·cle /mónəkəl/ *n.* a single eyeglass. □□ **mon·o·cled** *adj.* [F, orig. *adj.* f. LL *monoculus* one-eyed (as MONO-, *oculus* eye)]

mon·o·cline /mónōklīn/ *n. Geol.* a bend in rock strata that are otherwise uniformly dipping or horizontal. □□ **mon·o·cli·nal** /–klín'l/ *adj.* [MONO- + Gk *klinō* lean, dip]

mon·o·clin·ic /mónōklínik/ *adj.* (of a crystal) having one axial intersection oblique. [MONO- + Gk *klinō* lean, slope]

mon·o·clo·nal /mónōklónəl/ *adj.* forming a single clone; derived from a single individual or cell.

mon·o·clo·nal an·ti·bod·ies *n.* antibodies produced artificially by a single clone and consisting of identical antibody molecules.

mon·o·coque /mónəkok/ *n. Aeron.* an aircraft or vehicle structure in which the chassis is integral with the body. [F (as MONO-, *coque* shell)]

mon·o·cot /mónōkot, –kōt/ *n.* = MONOCOTYLEDON. [abbr.]

mon·o·cot·y·le·don /mónəkót'lee'd'n/ *n. Bot.* any flowering plant with a single cotyledon. □□ **mon·o·cot·y·le·don·ous** *adj.*

mon·oc·ra·cy /mónókrəsee/ *n.* (*pl.* **·cies**) government by one person only. □□ **mon·o·crat·ic** /mónəkrátik/ *adj.*

mon·oc·u·lar /mənókyələr/ *adj.* with or for one eye. □□ **mo·noc·u·lar·ly** *adj.* [LL *monoculus* having one eye]

mon·o·cul·ture /mónōkulchər/ *n.* the cultivation of a single crop.

mon·o·cy·cle /mónōsíkəl/ *n.* a one-wheeled vehicle, esp. a unicycle.

mon·o·cyte /mónəsīt/ *n. Biol.* a large type of leukocyte.

mon·o·dac·ty·lous /mónədáktiləs/ *adj.* having one finger, toe, or claw.

mon·o·dra·ma /mónōdraamə, –dramə/ *n.* a dramatic piece for one performer.

mon·o·dy /mónədee/ *n.* (*pl.* **·dies**) **1** an ode sung by a single actor in a Greek tragedy. **2** a poem lamenting a person's death. **3** *Mus.* a composition with only one melodic line. □□ **mo·nod·ic** /mənódik/ *adj.* **mon·o·dist** /móna–/ *n.* [LL *monodia* f. Gk *monōidia* f. *monōidos* singing alone (as MONO-, ODE)]

mon·oe·cious /mənéeshəs/ *adj.* **1** *Bot.* with unisexual male and female organs on the same plant. **2** *Zool.* hermaphroditic. [mod.L *Monoecia* the class of such plants (Linnaeus) f. Gk *monos* single + *oikos* house]

mon·o·fil·a·ment /mónōfíləmənt/ *n.* **1** a single strand of man-made fiber. **2** a type of fishing line using this.

mo·nog·a·my /mənógəmee/ *n.* **1** the practice or state of being married to one person at a time. **2** *Zool.* the habit of having only one mate at a time. □□ **mo·nog·a·mist** *n.* **mo·nog·a·mous** *adj.* **mo·nog·a·mous·ly** *adv.* [F *monogamie* f. eccl.L f. Gk *monogamia* (as MONO-, *gamos* marriage)]

mon·o·gen·e·sis /mónōjénisis/ *n.* (also **mo·nog·e·ny** /mənójinee/) **1** the theory of the development of all beings from a single cell. **2** the theory that mankind descended from one pair of ancestors. □□ **mon·o·ge·net·ic** /–jinétik/ *adj.*

mon·o·glot /mónəglot/ *adj. & n.* ● *adj.* using only one language. ● *n.* a monoglot person.

mon·o·gram /mónəgram/ *n. & v.* ● *n.* a motif of two or more interwoven letters, esp. a person's initials, used as a logo or to identify a personal possession. ● *v.* decorate with a monogram. □□ **mon·o·gram·mat·ic** /–grəmátik/ *adj.* **mon·o·grammed** *adj.* [F *monogramme* f. LL *monogramma* f. Gk (as MONO-, –GRAM)]

mon•o•graph /mónəgraf/ *n. & v.* ● *n.* a separate treatise on a single subject or an aspect of it. ● *v. tr.* write a monograph on. □□ **mo•nog•ra•pher** /mənógrəfər/ *n.* **mo•nog•ra•phist** /mənógrəfist/ *n.* **mon•o•graph•ic** /mónəgráfik/ *adj.* [earlier *monography* f. mod.L *monographia* f. *monographus* writer on a single genus or species (as MONO-, –GRAPH, –GRAPHY)]

mo•nog•y•nous /mənójinəs/ *adj. Bot.* having only one pistil.

mo•nog•y•ny /mənójinee/ *n.* the custom of having only one wife at a time.

mon•o•hull /mónōhul/ *n.* a boat with a single hull.

mon•o•hy•brid /mónōhíbrid/ *n.* a hybrid with respect to only one allele.

mon•o•hy•dric /mónōhídrik/ *adj. Chem.* containing one hydroxyl group.

mon•o•ki•ni /mónōke̅enee/ *n.* a woman's bathing suit equivalent to the lower half of a bikini. [MONO- + BIKINI, by false assoc. with BI-]

mon•o•lay•er /mónōlayər/ *n. Chem.* a layer only one molecule in thickness.

mon•o•lin•gual /mónōlínggwəl/ *adj.* speaking or using only one language.

mon•o•lith /mónəlith/ *n.* **1** a single block of stone, esp. shaped into a pillar or monument. **2** a person or thing like a monolith in being massive, immovable, or solidly uniform. **3** a large block of concrete. □□ **mon•o•lith•ic** /–líthik/ *adj.* [F *monolithe* f. Gk *monolithos* (as MONO-, *lithos* stone)]

mon•o•logue /mónəlawg, –log/ *n.* **1 a** a scene in a drama in which a person speaks alone. **b** a dramatic composition for one performer. **2** a long speech by one person in a conversation, etc. □□ **mon•o•log•ic** /–lójik/ *adj.* **mon•o•log•i•cal** /–lójikəl/ *adj.* **mon•o•log•ist** /mənóləjist/ *n.* (also –logu•ist). **mo•nol•o•gize** /mənóləjīz/ *v.intr.* [F f. Gk *monologos* speaking alone (as MONO-, –LOGUE)]

mon•o•ma•ni•a /mónəmáyneeə/ *n.* obsession of the mind by one idea or interest. □□ **mon•o•ma•ni•ac** *n. & adj.* **mon•o•ma•ni•a•cal** /–məníəkəl/ *adj.* [F *monomanie* (as MONO-, –MANIA)]

mon•o•mer /mónəmər/ *n. Chem.* **1** a unit in a dimer, trimer, or polymer. **2** a molecule or compound that can be polymerized. □□ **mon•o•mer•ic** /–mérik/ *adj.*

mo•no•mi•al /mənómeeəl/ *adj. & n. Math.* ● *adj.* (of an algebraic expression) consisting of one term. ● *n.* a monomial expression. [MONO- after *binomial*]

mon•o•mo•lec•u•lar /mónōmələkyələr/ *adj. Chem.* (of a layer) only one molecule in thickness.

mon•o•mor•phic /mónəmáwrfik/ *adj.* (also **mon•o•mor•phous** /–máwrfəs/) *Biochem.* not changing form during development. □□ **mon•o•mor•phism** *n.*

mon•o•nu•cle•o•sis /mónōno̅oklee-ósis, –nyo̅o–/ *n.* an abnormally high proportion of monocytes in the blood, esp. = INFECTIOUS MONONUCLEOSIS. [MONO- + NUCLEO- + –OSIS]

mon•o•pet•al•ous /mónəpétləs/ *adj. Bot.* having the corolla in one piece, or the petals united into a tube.

mon•o•phon•ic /mónəfónik/ *adj.* **1** (of sound reproduction) using only one channel of transmission (cf. STEREOPHONIC). **2** *Mus.* homophonic. □□ **mon•o•phon•i•cal•ly** *adv.* [MONO- + Gk *phōnē* sound]

mon•oph•thong /mónəf-tháwng, –thong/ *n. Phonet.* a single vowel sound. □□ **mon•oph•thon•gal** /–thónggəl/ *adj.* [Gk *monophthoggos* (as MONO-, *phthoggos* sound)]

Mo•noph•y•site /mənófisīt/ *n.* a person who holds that there is only one nature (partly divine, partly and subordinately human) in the person of Christ. [eccl.L *monophysita* f. eccl.Gk *monophusitēs* (as MONO-, *phusis* nature)]

mon•o•plane /mónōplayn/ *n.* an airplane with one set of wings (cf. BIPLANE).

mo•nop•o•list /mənópəlist/ *n.* a person who has or advocates a monopoly. □□ **mo•nop•o•lis•tic** /–lístik/ *adj.*

mo•nop•o•lize /mənópəlīz/ *v.tr.* **1** obtain exclusive possession or control of (a trade or commodity, etc.). **2** dominate or prevent others from sharing in (a conversation, person's attention, etc.). □□ **mo•nop•o•li•za•tion** *n.* **mo•nop•o•liz•er** *n.*

mo•nop•o•ly /mənópəlee/ *n.* (*pl.* **·lies**) **1 a** the exclusive possession or control of the trade in a commodity or service. **b** this conferred as a privilege by the government. **2 a** a commodity or service that is subject to a monopoly. **b** a company, etc., that possesses a monopoly. **3** (foll. by *on*) exclusive possession, control, or exercise. [L *monopolium* f. Gk *monopōlion* (as MONO-, *pōleō* sell)]

mon•o•rail /mónōrayl/ *n.* a railway in which the track consists of a single rail, usu. elevated with the cars suspended from it.

mon•o•sac•cha•ride /mónōsákərīd/ *n. Chem.* a sugar that cannot be hydrolyzed to give a simpler sugar, e.g., glucose.

mon•o•so•di•um glu•ta•mate /mónōsódiəm glo̅otəmayt/ *n. Chem.* a sodium salt of glutamic acid used to flavor food (cf. GLUTAMATE).

mon•o•sper•mous /mónóspə́rməs/ *adj. Bot.* having one seed. [MONO- + Gk *sperma* seed]

mon•o•stich•ous /mənóstikəs/ *adj. Bot. & Zool.* arranged in or consisting of one layer or row. [MONO- + Gk *stikhos* row]

mon•o•syl•lab•ic /mónəsilábik/ *adj.* **1** (of a word) having one syllable. **2** (of a person or statement) using or expressed in monosyllables. □□ **mon•o•syl•lab•i•cal•ly** *adv.*

mon•o•syl•la•ble /mónəsiləbəl/ *n.* a word of one syllable. □ **in monosyllables** in simple direct words.

mon•o•the•ism /mónətheèizəm/ *n.* the doctrine that there is only one God. □□ **mon•o•the•ist** *n.* **mon•o•the•is•tic** /–ístik/ *adj.* **mon•o•the•is•ti•cal•ly** /–ístiklee/ *adv.* [MONO- + Gk *theos* god]

mon•o•tint /mónōtint/ *n.* = MONOCHROME.

mon•o•tone /mónətōn/ *n. & adj.* ● *n.* **1** a sound or utterance continuing or repeated on one note without change of pitch. **2** sameness of style in writing. ● *adj.* without change of pitch. [mod.L *monotonus* f. late Gk *monotonos* (as MONO-, TONE)]

mon•o•ton•ic /mónətónik/ *adj.* **1** uttered in a monotone. **2** *Math.* (of a function or quantity) varying in such a way that it either never decreases or never increases. □□ **mon•o•ton•i•cal•ly** *adv.*

mo•not•o•nous /mənót'nəs/ *adj.* **1** lacking in variety; tedious through sameness. **2** (of a sound or utterance) without variation in tone or pitch. □□ **mo•not•o•nize** *v.tr.* **mo•not•o•nous•ly** *adv.* **mo•not•o•nous•ness** *n.*

mo•not•o•ny /mənót'nee/ *n.* **1** the state of being monotonous. **2** dull or tedious routine.

mon•o•treme /mónətreem/ *n.* any mammal of the order Monotremata, native to Australia and New Guinea, including the duckbill and spiny anteater, laying large yolky eggs through a common opening for urine, feces, etc. [MONO- + Gk *trēma –matos* hole]

mon•o•type /mónətīp/ *n.* **1** (**Monotype**) *Printing Trademark* a typesetting machine that casts and sets up types in individual characters. **2** an impression on paper made from an inked design painted on glass or metal.

mon•o•typ•ic /mónətípik/ *adj.* having only one type or representative.

mon•o•va•lent /mónəváylənt/ *adj. Chem.* having a valence of one; univalent. □□ **mon•o•va•lence** /–ləns/ *n.* **mon•o•va•len•cy** *n.*

mon•ox•ide /mənóksīd/ *n. Chem.* an oxide containing one oxygen atom (*carbon monoxide*). [MONO- + OXIDE]

Mon•roe doc•trine /munrō/ *n.* the US policy of objecting to intervention by European powers in the affairs of the Western Hemisphere. [J. *Monroe*, US president d. 1831, who formulated it]

Mon•sei•gneur /máwNsenyŕ/ *n.* (*pl.* **Mes•sei•gneurs** /mésenyŕ/) a title given to an eminent French person, esp. a prince, cardinal, archbishop, or bishop. [F f. *mon* my + *seigneur* lord]

Mon•sieur /məsyŕ/ *n.* (*pl.* **Mes•sieurs** /mesyŕ/) **1** the title or form of address used of or to a French-speaking man, corresponding to Mr. or sir. **2** a Frenchman. [F f. *mon* my + *sieur* lord]

Mon•si•gnor /monséenyər/ *n.* (*pl.* **Mon•si•gnors** or **Mon•si•gno•ri** /–nyáwree/) the title of various Roman Catholic prelates, officers of the papal court, etc. [It., after MONSEIGNEUR: see SIGNOR]

mon•soon /monso̅ón, món–/ *n.* **1** a wind in S. Asia, esp. in the Indian Ocean, blowing from the southwest in summer (**wet monsoon**) and the northeast in winter (**dry monsoon**). **2** a rainy season accompanying a wet monsoon. **3** any wind with periodic alternations. □□ **mon•soon•al** *adj.* [obs. Du. *monssoen* f. Port. *monção* f. Arab. *mawsim* fixed season f. *wasama* to mark]

mons pu•bis /monz pyo̅óbis/ *n.* a rounded mass of fatty tissue lying over the joint of the pubic bones. [L, = mount of the pubes]

mon•ster /mónstər/ *n.* **1** an imaginary creature, usu. large and frightening, compounded of incongruous elements. **2** an inhumanly cruel or wicked person. **3** a misshapen animal or plant. **4** a large hideous animal or thing (e.g., a building). **5** (*attrib.*) huge; extremely large of its kind. [ME f. OF *monstre* f. L *monstrum* portent, monster f. *monēre* warn]

mon•ster•a /mónstərə/ *n.* any tropical American climbing plant of the genus *Monstera*, esp. *M. deliciosa*. [mod.L, perh. f. L *monstrum* monster (from the odd appearance of its leaves)]

mon•strance /mónstrəns/ *n. RC Ch.* a vessel in which the consecrated Host is displayed for veneration. [ME, = demonstration, f. med.L *monstrantia* f. L *monstrare* show]

mon•stros•i•ty /monstrósitee/ *n.* (*pl.* **·ties**) **1** a huge or outrageous thing. **2** monstrousness. **3** = MONSTER 3. [LL *monstrositas* (as MONSTROUS)]

mon•strous /mónstrəs/ *adj.* **1** like a monster; abnormally formed. **2** huge. **3 a** outrageously wrong or absurd. **b** atrocious. □□ **mon•strous•ly** *adv.* **mon•strous•ness** *n.* [ME f. OF *monstreux* or L *monstrosus* (as MONSTER)]

mons ve•ne•ris /monz vénəris/ *n.* the human female's mons pubis. [L, = mount of Venus]

Mont. *abbr.* Montana.

mon•tage /montaázh, mawn–/ *n.* **1 a** a process of selecting, editing, and piecing together separate sections of movie or television film to form a continuous whole. **b** a sequence of such film as a section of a longer film. **2 a** the technique of producing a new composite whole from fragments of pictures, words, music, etc. **b** a composition produced in this way. [F f. *monter* MOUNT[1]]

mon•tane /móntayn/ *adj.* of or inhabiting mountainous country. [L *montanus* (as MOUNT[2], –ANE[1])]

mont·bre·tia /monbreeshə/ *n.* a hybrid plant of the genus *Crocosmia*, with bright orange-yellow trumpet-shaped flowers. [mod.L f. A. F. E. Coquebert de *Montbret*, Fr. botanist d. 1801]

mon·te /móntee/ *n. Cards* **1** (also **monte bank**) a Spanish game of chance, played with 40 cards. **2** (in full **three-card monte**) a game of Mexican origin played with three cards. [Sp., = mountain, heap of cards]

Mon·te Car·lo meth·od /móntee kaárlō/ *n. Statistics* a method of using the random sampling of numbers in order to estimate the solution to a numerical problem. [*Monte Carlo* in Monaco, famous for its gambling casino]

Mon·tes·so·ri /móntisáwree/ *n.* (usu. *attrib.*) a system of education (esp. of young children) that seeks to develop natural interests and activities rather than use formal teaching methods. [Maria *Montessori*, It. educationist d. 1952, who initiated it]

month /munth/ *n.* **1** (in full **calendar month**) **a** each of usu. twelve periods into which a year is divided. **b** a period of time between the same dates in successive calendar months. **2** a period of 28 days or of four weeks. **3** = LUNAR MONTH. [OE *mōnath* f. Gmc, rel. to MOON]

month·ly /múnthlee/ *adj., adv., & n.* ● *adj.* done, produced, or occurring once a month. ● *adv.* once a month; from month to month. ● *n.* (*pl.* **·lies**) **1** a monthly periodical. **2** (in *pl.*) *colloq.* a menstrual period.

month of Sun·days *n.phr.* a very long period.

mon·ti·cule /móntikyōol/ *n.* **1** a small hill. **2** a small mound caused by a volcanic eruption. [F f. LL *monticulus* dimin. of *mons* MOUNT²]

mon·u·ment /mónyəmənt/ *n.* **1** anything enduring that serves to commemorate or make celebrated, esp. a structure or building. **2** a stone or other structure placed over a grave or in a church, etc., in memory of the dead. **3** an ancient building or site, etc., that has survived or been preserved. **4** (foll. by *of, to*) a typical or outstanding example (*a monument of indiscretion*). **5** a written record. [ME f. F f. L *monumentum* f. *monēre* remind]

mon·u·men·tal /mónyəmént'l/ *adj.* **1 a** extremely great; stupendous (*a monumental achievement*). **b** (of a literary work) massive and permanent. **2** of or serving as a monument. **3** *colloq.* (as an intensifier) very great; calamitous (*a monumental blunder*). □□ **mon·u·men·tal·i·ty** /-tálitee/ *n.* **mon·u·men·tal·ly** *adv.*

mon·u·men·tal·ize /mónyəmént'līz/ *v.tr.* record or commemorate by or as by a monument.

mon·u·men·tal ma·son *n.* a maker of tombstones, etc.

-mony /mōnee/ *suffix* forming nouns, esp. denoting an abstract state or quality (*acrimony; testimony*). [L *-monia, -monium*, rel. to -MENT]

moo /mōō/ *v. & n.* ● *v.intr.* (**moos, mooed**) make the characteristic vocal sound of cattle; = LOW². ● *n.* (*pl.* **moos**) this sound. [imit.]

mooch /mōōch/ *v. colloq.* **1** borrow (an item, service, etc.) with no intention of making repayment. **2** beg. **3** steal. **4** sneak around; skulk. **5** *intr.* loiter or saunter desultorily. □□ **mooch·er** *n.* [ME, prob. f. OF *muchier* hide, skulk]

moo-cow *n.* a childish name for a cow.

mood¹ /mōōd/ *n.* **1** a state of mind or feeling. **2** (in *pl.*) fits of melancholy or bad temper. **3** (*attrib.*) inducing a particular mood (*mood music*). □ **in the** (or **no**) **mood** (foll. by *for*, or *to* + infin.) inclined (or disinclined) (*was in no mood to agree*). [OE *mōd* mind, thought, f. Gmc]

mood² /mōōd/ *n.* **1** *Gram.* **a** a form or set of forms of a verb serving to indicate whether it is to express fact, command, wish, etc. (*subjunctive mood*). **b** the distinction of meaning expressed by different moods. **2** *Logic* any of the classes into which each of the figures of a valid categorical syllogism is subdivided. [var. of MODE, assoc. with MOOD¹]

mood·swing /mōōdswing/ *n.* a marked change in temperament, as from euphoria to depression.

mood·y /mōōdee/ *adj. & n.* ● *adj.* (**mood·i·er, mood·i·est**) given to changes of mood; gloomy, sullen. ● *n. colloq.* a bad mood; a tantrum. □□ **mood·i·ly** *adv.* **mood·i·ness** *n.* [OE *mōdig* brave (as MOOD¹)]

Moog /mōōg/ *n.* (in full **Moog synthesizer**) *Trademark* an electron-

ic instrument with a keyboard, for producing a wide variety of musical sounds: see SYNTHESIZER. [R. A. *Moog*, Amer. engineer b. 1934, who invented it]

moo·la /mōōlə/ *n. sl.* money. [20th c.: orig. unkn.]

moon /mōōn/ *n. & v.* ● *n.* **1 a** the natural satellite of the earth, orbiting it monthly, illuminated by the sun and reflecting some light to the earth. **b** this regarded in terms of its waxing and waning in a particular month (*new moon*). **c** the moon when visible (*there is no moon tonight*). **2** a satellite of any planet. **3** (prec. by *the*) something desirable but unattainable (*promised them the moon*). **4** *poet.* a month. ● *v.* **1** *intr.* (often foll. by *about, around*, etc.) move or look listlessly. **2** *tr.* (foll. by *away*) spend (time) in a listless manner. **3** *intr.* (foll. by *over*) act aimlessly or inattentively from infatuation for (a person). **4** *tr. sl.* expose one's naked buttocks publicly as a joke, sign of disrespect, etc. □ **over the moon** esp. *Brit.* extremely happy or delighted. □□ **moon·less** *adj.*

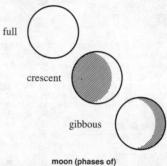

full

crescent

gibbous

moon (phases of)

moon·beam /mōōnbeem/ *n.* a ray of moonlight.

moon·calf /mōōnkaf/ *n.* a born fool.

moon-faced *adj.* having a round face.

moon·fish /mōōnfish/ *n.* = OPAH.

Moon·ie /mōōnee/ *n. sl.* a member of the Unification Church. [Sun Myung *Moon*, its founder]

moon·light /mōōnlit/ *n. & v.* ● *n.* **1** the light of the moon. **2** (*attrib.*) lighted by the moon. ● *v.intr.* (**·light·ed**) *colloq.* have two paid occupations, one by day and one by night. □□ **moon·light·er** *n.*

moon·light flit *n. Brit.* a hurried departure by night, esp. to avoid paying a debt.

moon·lit /mōōnlit/ *adj.* lighted by the moon.

moon·quake /mōōnkwayk/ *n.* a tremor of the moon's surface.

moon·rise /mōōnriz/ *n.* **1** the rising of the moon. **2** the time of this.

moon·scape /mōōnskayp/ *n.* **1** the surface or landscape of the moon. **2** an area resembling this; a wasteland.

moon·set /mōōnset/ *n.* **1** the setting of the moon. **2** the time of this.

moon·shine /mōōnshin/ *n.* **1** foolish or unrealistic talk or ideas. **2** *sl.* illicitly distilled or smuggled alcoholic liquor. **3** moonlight.

moon·shin·er /mōōnshinər/ *n. sl.* an illicit distiller or smuggler of alcoholic liquor.

moon·shot /mōōnshot/ *n.* the launching of a spacecraft to the moon.

moon·stone /mōōnstōn/ *n.* feldspar of pearly appearance.

moon·struck /mōōnstruk/ *adj.* **1** mentally deranged. **2** romantically distracted.

moon·y /mōōnee/ *adj.* (**moon·i·er, moon·i·est**) **1** listless; stupidly dreamy. **2** of or like the moon.

Moor /mōōr/ *n.* a member of a Muslim people of mixed Berber and Arab descent, inhabiting NW Africa. [ME f. OF *More* f. L *Maurus* f. Gk *Mauros* inhabitant of Mauretania, a region of N. Africa]

moor¹ /mōōr/ *n.* **1** a tract of open uncultivated upland, esp. when covered with heather. **2** a tract of ground preserved for shooting. **3** a marsh. □□ **moor·ish** *adj.* **moor·y** *adj.* [OE *mōr* waste land, marsh, mountain, f. Gmc]

moor² /mōōr/ *v.* **1** *tr.* make fast (a boat, buoy, etc.) by attaching a cable, etc., to a fixed object. **2** *intr.* (of a boat) be moored. □□ **moor·age** *n.* [ME *more*, prob. f. LG or MLG *mōren*]

moor·hen /mōōrhen/ *n.* **1** = GALLINULE 1. **2** esp. *Brit.* a female red grouse.

moor·ing /mōōring/ *n.* **1 a** a fixed object to which a boat, buoy, etc., is moored. **b** (often in *pl.*) a place where a boat, etc., is moored. **2** (in *pl.*) a set of permanent anchors and chains laid down for ships to be moored to.

Moor·ish /móorish/ *adj.* of or relating to the Moors.

Moor·ish i·dol *n.* a brightly colored Pacific fish of the genus *Zanclus*.

moor·land /móorlənd/ *n.* an extensive area of moor.

moose /moōs/ *n.* (*pl.* same) largest variety of N. American deer. [Narragansett *moos*]

moot /moōt/ *adj.*, *v.*, & *n.* • *adj.* (orig. the noun used *attrib.*) **1** debatable, undecided (*a moot point*). **2** *Law* having no practical significance. • *v.tr.* raise (a question) for discussion. • *n.* **1** *hist.* an assembly. **2** *Law* a discussion of a hypothetical case as an academic exercise. [OE *mōt*, and *mōtian* converse, f. Gmc, rel. to MEET[1]]

moose

mop /mop/ *n.* & *v.* • *n.* **1** a wad or bundle of cotton or synthetic material fastened to the end of a stick, for cleaning floors, etc. **2** a similarly shaped large or small implement for various purposes. **3** anything resembling a mop, esp. a thick mass of hair. **4** an act of mopping or being mopped (*gave it a mop*). • *v.tr.* (**mopped, mop·ping**) **1** wipe or clean with or as with a mop. **2 a** wipe tears or sweat, etc., from (one's face or brow, etc.). **b** wipe away (tears, etc.). □ **mop up 1** wipe up with or as with a mop. **2** *colloq.* absorb (profits, etc.). **3** dispatch; make an end of. **4** *Mil.* **a** complete the occupation of (a district, etc.) by capturing or killing enemy troops left there. **b** capture or kill (stragglers). □□ **mop·py** *adj.* [ME *mappe*, perh. ult. rel. to L *mappa* napkin]

mope /mōp/ *v.* & *n.* • *v.intr.* be gloomily depressed or listless; behave sulkily. • *n.* **1** a person who mopes. **2** (**the mopes**) low spirits. □□ **mop·er** *n.* **mop·ish** *adj.* **mop·y** *adj.* (**mop·i·er, mop·i·est**). **mop·i·ly** *adv.* **mop·i·ness** *n.* [16th c.: prob. rel. to *mope, mopp(e)* fool]

mo·ped /mōped/ *n.* a low-power, lightweight motorized bicycle with pedals. [Sw. (as MOTOR, PEDAL[1])]

mop·head /móp-hed/ *n.* a person with thick matted hair.

mop·pet /mópit/ *n. colloq.* (esp. as a term of endearment) a baby or small child. [obs. *moppe* baby, doll]

mo·quette /mōkét/ *n.* a thick pile or looped material used for carpets and upholstery. [F, perh. f. obs. It. *mocaiardo* mohair]

mo·raine /məráyn/ *n.* an area covered by rocks and debris carried down and deposited by a glacier. □□ **mo·rain·al** *adj.* **mo·rain·ic** *adj.* [F f. It. dial. *morena* f. F dial. *mor(re)* snout f. Rmc]

mor·al /máwrəl, mór–/ *adj.* & *n.* • *adj.* **1 a** concerned with goodness or badness of human character or behavior, or with the distinction between right and wrong. **b** concerned with accepted rules and standards of human behavior. **2 a** conforming to accepted standards of general conduct. **b** capable of moral action (*man is a moral agent*). **3** (of rights or duties, etc.) founded on moral law. **4 a** concerned with morals or ethics (*moral philosophy*). **b** (of a literary work, etc.) dealing with moral conduct. **5** concerned with or leading to a psychological effect associated with confidence in a right action (*moral courage; moral support; moral victory*). • *n.* **1 a** a moral lesson (esp. at the end) of a fable, story, event, etc. **b** a moral maxim or principle. **2** (in *pl.*) moral behavior, e.g., in sexual conduct. □□ **mor·al·ly** *adv.*

▶**Moral vs. Morale. Moral** has two basic meanings: as an adjective it refers to ethics or correct behavior (*a nation in need of moral guidance*) and as a noun it means 'the main point' or 'a lesson' (*the moral of the story*). **Morale** is a noun referring to spirit, especially in the face of opposition or hardship (*employee morale was at an all-time low after the layoffs*).

WORD HISTORY moral

Late Middle English: from Latin *moralis*, from *mos, mor-* 'custom,' (plural) *mores* 'morals.' As a noun the word was first used to translate late Latin *Moralia*, the title of St. Gregory the Great's moral exposition of the biblical Book of Job, and was subsequently applied to the works of various classical writers.

mor·al cer·tain·ty *n.* probability so great as to allow no reasonable doubt.

mo·rale /mərál/ *n.* the mental attitude or bearing of a person or group, esp. as regards confidence, discipline, etc. [F *moral* respelled to preserve the pronunciation]

▶See note at MORAL.

mor·al·ism /máwrəlizəm, mór–/ *n.* **1** a natural system of morality. **2** religion regarded as moral practice.

mor·al·ist /máwrəlist, mór–/ *n.* **1** a person who practices or teaches morality. **2** a person who follows a natural system of ethics. □□ **mor·al·is·tic** /–lístik/ *adj.* **mor·al·is·ti·cal·ly** /–lístiklee/ *adv.*

mo·ral·i·ty /mərálitee/ *n.* (*pl.* **·ties**) **1** the degree of conformity of an idea, practice, etc., to moral principles. **2** right moral conduct. **3** a lesson in morals. **4** the science of morals. **5** a particular system of morals (*commercial morality*). **6** (in *pl.*) moral principles; points of ethics. **7** (in full **morality play**) *hist.* a kind of drama with personified abstract qualities as the main characters and inculcating a moral lesson, popular in the 16th c. [ME f. OF *moralité* or LL *moralitas* f. L (as MORAL)]

mor·al·ize /máwrəlīz, mór–/ *v.* **1** *intr.* (often foll. by *on*) indulge in moral reflection or talk. **2** *tr.* interpret morally; point the moral of. **3** *tr.* make moral or more moral. □□ **mor·al·i·za·tion** *n.* **mor·al·iz·er** *n.* **mor·al·iz·ing·ly** *adv.* [F *moraliser* or med.L *moralizare* f. L (as MORAL)]

mor·al law *n.* the conditions to be satisfied by any right course of action.

mor·al ma·jor·i·ty *n.* the majority of people, regarded as favoring firm moral standards (orig. *Moral Majority*, name of a right-wing movement).

mor·al phi·los·o·phy *n.* the branch of philosophy concerned with ethics.

mor·al pres·sure *n.* persuasion by appealing to a person's moral sense.

mor·al sci·ence *n.* systematic knowledge as applied to morals.

mor·al sense *n.* the ability to distinguish right and wrong.

mo·rass /mərás/ *n.* **1** an entanglement; a disordered situation, esp. one impeding progress. **2** *literary* a bog or marsh. [Du. *moeras* (assim. to *moer* MOOR[1]) f. MDu. *marasch* f. OF *marais* marsh f. med.L *mariscus*]

mor·a·to·ri·um /máwrətáwreeəm, mór–/ *n.* (*pl.* **mor·a·to·ri·ums** or **mor·a·to·ri·a** /–reeə/) **1** (often foll. by *on*) a temporary prohibition or suspension (of an activity). **2 a** a legal authorization to debtors to postpone payment. **b** the period of this postponement. [mod.L, neut. of LL *moratorius* delaying f. L *morari* morat- to delay f. *mora* delay]

Mo·ra·vi·an /məráyveeən/ *n.* & *adj.* • *n.* **1** a native of Moravia, now part of the Czech Republic. **2** a member of a Protestant sect founded in Saxony by emigrants from Moravia, holding views derived from the Hussites and accepting the Bible as the only source of faith. • *adj.* of, relating to, or characteristic of Moravia or its people.

mo·ray /máwray/ *n.* any tropical eellike fish of the family Muraenidae, esp. *Muraena helena* found in Mediterranean waters. [Port. *moreia* f. L f. Gk *muraina*]

mor·bid /máwrbid/ *adj.* **1 a** (of the mind, ideas, etc.) unwholesome; sickly; macabre. **b** given to morbid feelings. **2** *colloq.* melancholy. **3** *Med.* of the nature of or indicative of disease. □□ **mor·bid·i·ty** /–bíditee/ *n.* **mor·bid·ly** *adv.* **mor·bid·ness** *n.* [L *morbidus* f. *morbus* disease]

mor·bid a·nat·o·my *n.* the anatomy of diseased organs, tissues, etc.

mor·bif·ic /mawrbífik/ *adj.* causing disease. [F *morbifique* or mod.L *morbificus* f. L *morbus* disease]

mor·bil·li /mawrbíli/ *n.pl.* **1** measles. **2** the spots characteristic of measles. [L, pl. of *morbillus* pustule f. *morbus* disease]

mor·dant /máwrd'nt/ *adj.* & *n.* • *adj.* **1** (of sarcasm, etc.) caustic; biting. **2** pungent; smarting. **3** corrosive; cleansing. **4** (of a substance) serving to fix coloring matter or gold leaf on another substance. • *n.* a mordant substance (in senses 3, 4 of *adj.*). □□ **mor·dan·cy** *n.* **mor·dant·ly** *adv.* [ME f. F, part. of *mordre* bite f. L *mordēre*]

mor·dent /máwrd'nt/ *n. Mus.* **1** an ornament consisting of one rapid alternation of a written note with the note immediately below it. **2** a pralltriller. [G f. It. *mordente* part. of *mordēre* bite]

more /mawr/ *adj.*, *n.*, & *adv.* • *adj.* **1** existing in a greater or additional quantity, amount, or degree (*more problems than last time; bring some more water*). **2** greater in degree (*more's the pity; the more*

SYNONYM TIP moral

ETHICAL, HONORABLE, RIGHTEOUS, SANCTIMONIOUS, VIRTUOUS. You can be an **ethical** person without necessarily being a **moral** one, since *ethical* implies conformity with a code of fair and honest behavior, particularly in business or in a profession (*an ethical legislator who didn't believe in cutting deals*), while *moral* refers to generally accepted standards of goodness and rightness in character and conduct—especially sexual conduct (*the moral values she'd learned from her mother*). In the same way, you can be **honorable** without necessarily being **virtuous**, since *honorable* suggests dealing with others in a decent and *ethical* manner, while *virtuous* implies the possession of *moral* excellence in character (*many honorable businesspeople fail to live a virtuous private life*). **Righteous** is similar in meaning to *virtuous* but also implies freedom from guilt or blame (*righteous anger*), but the *righteous* person can also be somewhat intolerant and narrow-minded, in which case "self-righteous" might be a better adjective. Someone who makes a hypocritical show of being *righteous* is often described as **sanctimonious**—in other words, acting like a saint without having a saintly character.

fool you). ● *n.* a greater quantity, number, or amount (*more than three people; more to it than meets the eye*). ● *adv.* **1** in a greater degree (*do it more carefully*). **2** to a greater extent (*people like to walk more these days*). **3** forming the comparative of adjectives and adverbs, esp. those of more than one syllable (*more absurd; more easily*). **4** again (*once more; never more*). **5** moreover. □ **more and more** in an increasing degree. **more like it** see LIKE¹. **more of** to a greater extent (*more of a poet than a musician*). **more or less 1** in a greater or less degree. **2** approximately; as an estimate. **more so of** the same kind to a greater degree. [OE *māra* f. Gmc]

mo•reen /mawreen/ *n.* a strong ribbed woolen or cotton material for curtains, etc. [perh. fanciful f. MOIRE]

mo•rel¹ /mərél/ *n.* an edible fungus of the genus *Morchella*, esp. *M. esculenta*, with ridged mushroom caps. [F *morille* f. Du. *morilje*]

mo•rel² /mərél/ *n.* (also **mo•relle**) a nightshade, esp. the black nightshade. [ME f. OF *morele* fem. of *morel* dark brown ult. f. L *Maurus* MOOR]

mo•rel•lo /mərélō/ *n.* (*pl.* **•los**) a sour kind of dark cherry. [It. *morello* blackish f. med.L *morellus* f. L (as MOREL¹)]

more•o•ver /máwrṓvər/ *adv.* (introducing or accompanying a new statement) further, besides.

mo•res /máwrayz, –reez/ *n.pl.* customs or conventions regarded as essential to or characteristic of a community. [L, pl. of *mos* custom]

Mo•res•co var. of MORISCO.

Mo•resque /mawrésk/ *adj.* (of art or architecture) Moorish in style or design. [F f. It. *moresco* f. *Moro* MOOR]

mor•ga•nat•ic /máwrgənátik/ *adj.* **1** (of a marriage) between a person of high rank and another of lower rank, the spouse and children having no claim to the possessions or title of the person of higher rank. **2** (of a wife) married in this way. □□ **mor•ga•nat•i•cal•ly** *adv.* [F *morganatique* or G *morganatisch* f. med.L *matrimonium ad morganaticam* 'marriage with a morning gift,' the husband's gift to the wife after consummation being his only obligation in such a marriage]

morgue /mawrg/ *n.* **1** a mortuary. **2** (in a newspaper office, etc.) a room or file of miscellaneous information, esp. for future obituaries. [F, orig. the name of a Paris mortuary]

mor•i•bund /máwribund, mór–/ *adj.* **1** at the point of death. **2** lacking vitality. **3** on the decline, stagnant. □□ **mor•i•bun•di•ty** /–búnditee/ *n.* [L *moribundus* f. *mori* die]

Mo•ris•co /mərískō/ *n. & adj.* (also **Mo•res•co** /–réskō/) ● *n.* (*pl.* **•cos** or **•coes**) **1** a Moor, esp. in Spain. **2** a morris dance. ● *adj.* Moorish. [Sp. f. *Moro* MOOR]

Mor•mon /máwrmən/ *n.* a member of the Church of Jesus Christ of Latter-day Saints, a millenary religion founded in 1830 by Joseph Smith on the basis of revelations in the Book of Mormon. □□ **Mormon•ism** *n.*

morn /mawrn/ *n. poet.* morning. [OE *morgen* f. Gmc]

mor•nay /mawrnáy/ *n.* a cheese-flavored white sauce. [20th c.: orig. uncert.]

morn•ing /máwrning/ *n. & int.* ● *n.* **1** the early part of the day, esp. from sunrise to noon (*this morning; during the morning; morning coffee*). **2** this time spent in a particular way (*had a busy morning*). **3** sunrise, daybreak. **4** a time compared with the morning, esp. the early part of one's life, etc. ● *int.* = *good morning* (see GOOD *adj.* 14). □ **in the morning 1** during or in the course of the morning. **2** *colloq.* tomorrow. [ME *mor(we)ning* f. *morwen* MORN + –ING¹ after *evening*]

morn•ing af•ter *n. colloq.* a hangover.

morn•ing-af•ter pill *n.* a contraceptive pill effective when taken some hours after intercourse.

morn•ing coat *n.* a coat with tails, and with the front cut away below the waist.

morn•ing dress *n.* a man's morning coat and striped trousers.

morn•ing glo•ry *n.* any of various twining plants of the genus *Ipomoea*, with trumpet-shaped flowers.

morn•ing sick•ness *n.* nausea felt in the morning in pregnancy.

morn•ing star *n.* a planet or bright star, usu. Venus, seen in the east before sunrise.

morn•ing watch *n. Naut.* the 4–8 a.m. watch.

Mo•ro /máwrō/ *n.* (*pl.* **•ros**) a Muslim living in the Philippines. [Sp., = MOOR]

Mo•roc•can /mərókən/ *n. & adj.* ● *n.* **1** a native or national of Morocco in N. Africa. **2** a person of Moroccan descent. ● *adj.* of or relating to Morocco.

mo•roc•co /mərókō/ *n.* (*pl.* **•cos**) **1** a fine flexible leather made (orig. in Morocco) from goatskins tanned with sumac, used esp. in bookbinding and shoemaking. **2** an imitation of this in grained calf, etc.

mo•ron /máwron/ *n.* **1** *colloq.* a very stupid or foolish person. **2** an adult with a mental age of about 8–12. □□ **mo•ron•ic** /mərónik/ *adj.* **mo•ron•i•cal•ly** /məróniklee/ *adv.* **mo•ron•ism** *n.* [Gk *mōron*, neut. of *mōros* foolish]

mo•rose /mərṓs/ *adj.* sullen and ill-tempered. □□ **mo•rose•ly** *adv.* **mo•rose•ness** *n.* [L *morosus* peevish, etc. f. *mos moris* manner]

morph¹ /mawrf/ *n.* = ALLOMORPH. [back-form.]

morph² /mawrf/ *v. intr. Cinematog.* change form or appearance, as from person to animal, by computer-controlled special effects.

mor•pheme /máwrfeem/ *n. Linguistics* **1** a morphological element considered in respect of its functional relations in a linguistic system. **2** a meaningful morphological unit of a language that cannot be further divided (e.g., *in, come, –ing*, forming *incoming*). □□ **mor•phe•mic** /–feémik/ *adj.* **mor•phe•mi•cal•ly** /–feémiklee/ *adv.* [F *morphème* f. Gk *morphē* form, after PHONEME]

mor•phe•mics /mawrfeémiks/ *n.pl.* (usu. treated as *sing.*) *Linguistics* the study of word structure.

mor•phi•a /máwrfeeə/ *n.* = MORPHINE.

mor•phine /máwrfeen/ *n.* an analgesic and narcotic drug obtained from opium and used medicinally to relieve pain. □□ **mor•phin•ism** /–finizəm/ *n.* [G *Morphin* & mod.L *morphia* f. *Morpheus* god of sleep]

morph•ing /máwrfing/ *n.* a computer graphics technique used in filmmaking, whereby an image is apparently transformed into another by a smooth progression; the act or process of changing one image into another using this technique. [shortened f. META-MORPHOSIS + –ING¹]

mor•pho•gen•e•sis /máwrfəjénisis/ *n. Biol.* the development of form in organisms. □□ **mor•pho•ge•net•ic** /–jinétik/ *adj.* **mor•pho•gen•ic** *adj.* [mod.L f. Gk *morphē* form + GENESIS]

mor•phol•o•gy /mawrfóləjee/ *n.* the study of the forms of things, esp.: **1** *Biol.* the study of the forms of organisms. **2** *Philol.* **a** the study of the forms of words. **b** the system of forms in a language. □□ **mor•pho•log•i•cal** /mawrfəlójikəl/ *adj.* **mor•pho•log•i•cal•ly** /–fəlójiklee/ *adv.* **mor•phol•o•gist** *n.* [Gk *morphē* form + –LOGY]

Mor•ris chair /máwris, móris/ *n.* a type of plain easy chair with an adjustable back. [William Morris, Engl. poet and craftsman d. 1896]

mor•ris dance /máwris, mór–/ *n.* a traditional English dance by groups of people in fancy costume, usu. as characters in legend, with ribbons and bells. □□ **mor•ris danc•er** *n.* **mor•ris danc•ing** *n.* [*morys*, var. of MOORISH]

mor•row /máwrō, mór–/ *n.* (usu. prec. by *the*) *literary* **1** the following day. **2** the time following an event. [ME *morwe, moru* (as MORN)]

Morse /mawrs/ *n. & v.* ● *n.* (in full **Morse code**) an alphabet or code in which letters are represented by combinations of long and short light or sound signals. ● *v.tr. & intr.* signal by Morse code. [S. F. B. *Morse*, Amer. inventor d. 1872, who devised it]

mor•sel /máwrsəl/ *n.* a mouthful; a small piece (esp. of food). [ME f. OF, dimin. of *mors* a bite f. *mordēre mors-* to bite]

mort /mawrt/ *n. Hunting* a note sounded when the quarry is killed. [ME f. OF f. L *mors mortis* death]

mor•ta•del•la /mawrtədélə/ *n.* (*pl.* **mor•ta•del•le** /–déle/) a large spiced pork sausage. [It. dimin., irreg. f. L *murtatum* seasoned with myrtle berries]

mor•tal /máwrt'l/ *adj. & n.* ● *adj.* **1 a** (of a living being, esp. a human) subject to death. **b** (of material or earthly existence) temporal, ephemeral. **2** (often foll. by *to*) causing death; fatal. **3** (of a battle) fought to the death. **4** associated with death (*mortal agony*). **5** (of an enemy) implacable. **6** (of pain, fear, an affront, etc.) intense, very serious. **7** *colloq.* **a** very great (*in a mortal hurry*). **b** long and tedious (*for two mortal hours*). **8** *colloq.* conceivable, imaginable (*every mortal thing; of no mortal use*). ● *n.* **1** a mortal being, esp. a human. **2** *joc.* a person described in some specified way (*a thirsty mortal*). □□ **mor•tal•ly** *adv.* [ME f. OF *mortal, mortel* or L *mortalis* f. *mors mortis* death]

mor•tal•i•ty /mawrtálitee/ *n.* (*pl.* **•ties**) **1** the state of being subject to death. **2** loss of life on a large scale. **3 a** the number of deaths in a given period, etc. **b** (in full **mortality rate**) a death rate. [ME f. OF *mortalité* f. L *mortalitas –tatis* (as MORTAL)]

mor•tal sin *n. Theol.* a grave sin that is regarded as depriving the soul of divine grace.

mor•tar /máwrtər/ *n. & v.* ● *n.* **1** a mixture of lime with cement, sand, and water, used in building to bond bricks or stones. **2** a short large-bore cannon for firing shells at high angles. **3** a contrivance for firing a lifeline or firework. **4** a vessel made of hard material, in which ingredients are pounded with a pestle. ● *v.tr.* **1** plaster or join with mortar. **2** attack or bombard with mortar shells. □□ **mor•tar•less** *adj.* (in sense 1). **mor•tar•y** *adj.* (in sense 1). [ME f. AF *morter*, OF *mortier* f. L *mortarium*: partly from LG]

mor•tar•board /máwrtərbawrd/ *n.* **1** an ac-

mortar 2

mortar 4 with pestle

mortarboard

ademic cap with a stiff, flat square top. **2** a flat board with a handle on the undersurface, for holding mortar in bricklaying, etc.

mort•gage /máwrgij/ *n. & v.* ● *n.* **1 a** a conveyance of property by a debtor to a creditor as security for a debt (esp. one incurred by the purchase of the property), on the condition that it shall be returned on payment of the debt within a certain period. **b** a deed effecting this. **2 a** a debt secured by a mortgage. **b** a loan resulting in such a debt. ● *v.tr.* **1** convey (a property) by mortgage. **2** (often foll. by *to*) pledge (oneself, one's powers, etc.). □□ **mort•gage•a•ble** *adj.* [ME f. OF, = dead pledge f. *mort* f. L *mortuus* dead + *gage* GAGE[1]]

mort•ga•gee /máwrgijée/ *n.* the creditor in a mortgage, usu. a bank or other lending institution.

mortgage rate *n.* the rate of interest charged by a mortgagee.

mort•ga•gor /máwrgijər/ *n.* (also **mort•ga•ger** /–jər/) the debtor in a mortgage.

mor•tice var. of MORTISE.

mor•ti•cian /mawrtíshən/ *n.* an undertaker; a manager of funerals. [L *mors mortis* death + –ICIAN]

mor•ti•fy /máwrtifī/ *v.* (**•fies, •fied**) **1** *tr.* **a** cause (a person) to feel shamed or humiliated. **b** wound (a person's feelings). **2** *tr.* bring (the body, the flesh, the passions, etc.) into subjection by self-denial or discipline. **3** *intr.* (of flesh) be affected by gangrene or necrosis. □□ **mor•ti•fi•ca•tion** /–fikáyshən/ *n.* **mor•ti•fy•ing** *adj.* **mor•ti•fy•ing•ly** *adv.* [ME f. OF *mortifier* f. eccl.L *mortificare* kill, subdue f. *mors mortis* death]

mor•tise /máwrtis/ *n. & v.* (also **mor•tice**) ● *n.* a hole in a framework designed to receive the end of another part, esp. a tenon. ● *v.tr.* **1** join securely, esp. by mortise and tenon. **2** cut a mortise in. [ME f. OF *mortoise* f. Arab. *murtazz* fixed in]

mor•tise lock *n.* a lock recessed into a mortise in the frame of a door or window, etc.

mort•main /máwrtmayn/ *n. Law* **1** the status of lands or tenements held inalienably by an ecclesiastical or other corporation. **2** the land or tenements themselves. [ME f. AF, OF *mortemain* f. med.L *mortua manus* dead hand, prob. in allusion to impersonal ownership]

mor•tu•a•ry /máwrchōō–eree/ *n. & adj.* ● *n.* (pl. **•ies**) a room or building in which dead bodies may be kept until burial or cremation. ● *adj.* of or concerning death or burial. [ME f. AF *mortuarie* f. med.L *mortuarium* f. L *mortuarius* f. *mortuus* dead]

mor•u•la /máwryələ, máwrə–/ *n.* (pl. **mor•u•lae** /–lee/) a fully segmented ovum from which a blastula is formed. [mod.L, dimin. of L *morum* mulberry]

Mo•sa•ic /mōzáyik/ *adj.* of or associated with Moses (in the Old Testament). [F *mosaïque* or mod.L *Mosaicus* f. *Moses* f. Heb. *Mōšeh*]

mo•sa•ic /mōzáyik/ *n. & v.* ● *n.* **1 a** a picture or pattern produced by an arrangement of small variously colored pieces of glass or stone, etc. **b** work of this kind as an art form. **2** a diversified thing. **3** an arrangement of photosensitive elements in a television camera. **4** *Biol.* a chimera. **5** (in full **mosaic disease**) a virus disease causing leaf-mottling in plants, esp. tobacco, corn, and sugar cane. **6** (*attrib.*) **a** of or like a mosaic. **b** diversified. ● *v.tr.* (**mo•sa•icked, mo•sa•ick•ing**) **1** adorn with mosaics. **2** combine into or as into a mosaic. □□ **mo•sa•i•cist** /–záyisist/ *n.* [ME f. F *mosaïque* f. It. *mosaico* f. med.L *mosaicus, musaicus* f. Gk *mous(e)ion* mosaic work f. *mousa* MUSE[1]]

Mo•sa•ic Law *n.* the laws attributed to Moses and listed in the Pentateuch.

mo•sa•ic gold *n.* **1** tin disulfide. **2** an alloy of copper and zinc used in cheap jewelry, etc.

mo•sa•saur•us /mōsəsáwrəs/ *n.* any large extinct marine reptile of the genus *Mosasaurus*, with a long slender body and flipperlike limbs. [mod.L f. *Mosa* river Meuse (near which it was first discovered) + Gk *sauros* lizard]

mos•cha•tel /móskətél/ *n.* a small plant, *Adoxa moschatellina*, with pale-green flowers and a musky smell. [F *moscatelle* f. It. *moscatella* f. *moscato* musk]

Mo•selle /mōzél/ *n.* a light medium-dry white wine produced in the valley of the Moselle River in Germany.

mo•sey /mōzee/ *v.intr.* (**•seys, •seyed**) (often foll. by *along*) *sl.* walk in a leisurely or aimless manner. [19th c.: orig. unkn.]

mo•shav /mōshaáv/ *n.* (pl. **mo•sha•vim**) a cooperative association of Israeli farmers. [Heb. *mošāb*, lit. 'dwelling']

Mos•lem var. of MUSLIM.

▶See note at MUSLIM.

mosque /mosk/ *n.* a Muslim place of worship. [F *mosquée* f. It. *moschea* f. Arab. *masjid*]

mos•qui•to /məskéetō/ *n.* (pl. **•toes** or **•tos**) any of various slender biting insects, esp. of the genus *Culex*, *Anopheles*, or *Aedes*, the female of which punctures the skin of humans and other animals with a long proboscis to suck their blood and transmits diseases such as filariasis and malaria. [Sp. & Port., dimin. of *mosca* f. L *musca* fly]

mos•qui•to boat *n.* a motor torpedo-boat.

mos•qui•to net *n.* a net designed to keep out mosquitoes.

moss /maws/ *n. & v.* ● *n.* **1** any small cryptogamous plant of the class Musci, growing in dense clusters on the surface of the ground, in bogs, on trees, stones, etc. **2** *Sc. & No. of Engl.* a bog, esp. a peatbog. ● *v.tr.* cover with moss. □□ **moss•like** *adj.* [OE *mos* bog, moss f. Gmc]

moss ag•ate *n.* agate with mosslike dendritic markings.

moss-grown *adj.* overgrown with moss.

moss hag *n. Sc.* broken ground from which peat has been taken.

mos•sie /mózee/ *n.* esp. *Austral. sl.* = MOSQUITO.

mos•so /máwsō/ *adv. Mus.* with animation or speed. [It., past part. of *muovere* move]

moss•troop•er /máws-trōōpər/ *n.* **1** a freebooter of the Scottish-English border in the 17th c. **2** any such freebooter.

moss•y /máwsee/ *adj.* (**moss•i•er, moss•i•est**) **1** covered in or resembling moss. **2** *sl.* antiquated, old-fashioned. □□ **moss•i•ness** *n.*

most /mōst/ *adj., n., & adv.* ● *adj.* **1** existing in the greatest quantity or degree (*you have made the most mistakes*; *see who can make the most noise*). **2** the majority of; nearly all of (*most people think so*). ● *n.* **1** the greatest quantity or number (*this is the most I can do*). **2** (**the most**) *sl.* the best of all. **3** the majority (*most of them are missing*). ● *adv.* **1** in the highest degree (*this is most interesting*; *what most annoys me*). **2** forming the superlative of adjectives and adverbs, esp. those of more than one syllable (*most certain*; *most easily*). **3** *colloq.* almost. □ **at most** no more or better than (*this is at most a makeshift*). **at the most 1** as the greatest amount. **2** not more than. **for the most part 1** as regards the greater part. **2** usually. **make the most of 1** employ to the best advantage. **2** represent at its best or worst. [OE *māst* f. Gmc]

-most /mōst/ *suffix* forming superlative adjectives and adverbs from prepositions and other words indicating relative position (*foremost*; *uttermost*). [OE *–mest*]

most•ly /mōstlee/ *adv.* **1** as regards the greater part. **2** usually.

Most Rev•er•end *adj.* a title given to archbishops and to Roman Catholic bishops.

mot /mō/ *n.* (pl. **mots** *pronunc.* same) a witty saying. [F, = word, ult. f. L *muttum* uttered sound f. *muttire* murmur]

mote /mōt/ *n.* a speck of dust. [OE *mot*, corresp. to Du. *mot* dust, sawdust, of unkn. orig.]

mo•tel /mōtél/ *n.* a roadside hotel providing accommodation for motorists and parking for their vehicles. [portmanteau word f. MOTOR + HOTEL]

mo•tet /mōtét/ *n. Mus.* a short sacred choral composition. [ME f. OF, dimin. of *mot*: see MOT]

moth /mawth, moth–/ *n.* **1** any usu. nocturnal insect of the order Lepidoptera excluding butterflies, having a stout body and without clubbed antennae. **2** any small lepidopterous insect of the family Tineidae breeding in cloth, etc., on which its larva feeds. [OE *moththe*]

moth•ball /máwthbawl, móth–/ *n. & v.* ● *n.* a ball of naphthalene, etc. placed in stored clothes to keep away moths. ● *v.tr.* **1** place in mothballs. **2** leave unused. □ **in mothballs** stored unused for a considerable time.

moth-eat•en *adj.* **1** damaged or destroyed by moths. **2** antiquated, timeworn.

moth•er /múthər/ *n. & v.* ● *n.* **1 a** a woman in relation to a child or children to whom she has given birth. **b** (in full **adoptive mother**) a woman who has continuous care of a child, esp. by adoption. **2** any female animal in relation to its offspring. **3** a quality or condition, etc., that gives rise to another (*necessity is the mother of invention*). **4** (in full **Mother Superior**) the head of a female religious community. **5** *archaic* (esp. as a form of address) an elderly woman. **6** (*attrib.*) **a** designating an institution, etc., regarded as having maternal authority (*Mother Church*; *mother earth*). **b** designating the main ship, spacecraft, etc., in a convoy or mission (*the mother craft*). ● *v.tr.* **1** give birth to; be the mother of. **2** protect as a mother. **3** give rise to; be the source of. **4** acknowledge or profess oneself the mother of. □□ **moth•er•less** *adj.* **moth•er•less•ness** *n.* **moth•er•like** *adj. & adv.* [OE *mōdor* f. Gmc]

moth•er•board /múthərbawrd/ *n.* a computer's main circuit board, into which other boards can be plugged or wired.

Moth•er Car•ey's chick•en *n.* a storm petrel, esp. Wilson's storm petrel (see STORM PETREL).

moth•er coun•try *n.* a country in relation to its colonies.

moth•er fig•ure *n.* an older woman who is regarded as a source of nurture, support, etc.

Moth•er Goose rhyme *n.* a nursery rhyme.

moth•er•hood /múthərhŏŏd/ *n.* **1** the condition or fact of being a mother. **2** (*attrib.*) (of an issue, report, etc.) protective, withholding the worst aspects.

Moth•er•ing Sun•day /múthəring/ *n. Brit.* the fourth Sunday in Lent, traditionally a day for honoring mothers.

moth•er-in-law *n.* (pl. **moth•ers-in-law**) the mother of one's husband or wife.

moth•er•land /múthərland/ *n.* one's native country.

moth•er lode *n. Mining* the main vein of a system.

moth•er•ly /múthərlee/ *adj.* **1** like or characteristic of a mother in affection, care, etc. **2** of or relating to a mother. □□ **moth•er•li•ness** *n.* [OE *mōdorlic* (as MOTHER)]

moth•er-of-pearl *n.* a smooth iridescent substance forming the inner layer of the shell of some mollusks.

Moth•er's Day *n.* **1** the second Sunday in May, traditionally a day for honoring mothers. **2** *Brit.* = MOTHERING SUNDAY.

mother's son *n. colloq.* a man (*every mother's son of you*).

mother tongue *n.* **1** one's native language. **2** a language from which others have evolved.

mother wit *n.* native wit; common sense.

moth•proof /máwthpr<del>oo</del>f, móth–/ *adj. & v.* ● *adj.* (of clothes) treated so as to repel moths. ● *v.tr.* treat (clothes) in this way.

moth•y /máwthee, móthee/ *adj.* (**moth•i•er, moth•i•est**) infested with moths.

mo•tif /mōtéef/ *n.* **1** a distinctive feature or dominant idea in artistic or literary composition. **2** *Mus.* = FIGURE *n.* 10. **3** an ornament of lace, etc., sewn separately on a garment. **4** *Brit.* an ornament on a vehicle identifying the maker, model, etc. [F (as MOTIVE)]

mo•tile /mōt'l, –tīl, –til/ *adj. Zool. & Bot.* capable of motion. □□ **mo•til•i•ty** /–tílitee/ *n.* [L *motus* motion (as MOVE)]

mo•tion /mōshən/ *n. & v.* ● *n.* **1** the act or process of moving or of changing position. **2** a particular manner of moving the body in walking, etc. **3** a change of posture. **4** a gesture. **5** a formal proposal put to a committee, legislature, etc. **6** *Law* an application for a rule or order of court. **7** *esp. Brit.* **a** an evacuation of the bowels. **b** (in *sing.* or *pl.*) feces. **8** a piece of moving mechanism. ● *v.* (often foll. by *to* + infin.) **1** *tr.* direct (a person) by a sign or gesture. **2** *intr.* (often foll. by *to* a person) make a gesture directing (*motioned to me to leave*). □ **go through the motions 1** make a pretense; do something perfunctorily or superficially. **2** simulate an action by gestures. **in motion** moving; not at rest. **put** (or **set**) **in motion** set going or working. □□ **mo•tion•al** *adj.* **mo•tion•less** *adj.* [ME f. OF f. L *motio –onis* (as MOVE)]

mo•tion pic•ture *n.* (often with hyphen) *attrib.*) a film or movie with the illusion of movement (see FILM *n.* 3).

mo•ti•vate /mōtivayt/ *v.tr.* **1** supply a motive to; be the motive of. **2** cause (a person) to act in a particular way. **3** stimulate the interest of (a person in an activity). □□ **mo•ti•va•tion** /–váyshən/ *n.* **mo•ti•va•tion•al** /–váyshənəl/ *adj.* **mo•ti•va•tion•al•ly** /–váyshənəlee/ *adv.*

mo•tive /mōtiv/ *n., adj., & v.* ● *n.* **1** a factor or circumstance that induces a person to act in a particular way. **2** = MOTIF. ● *adj.* **1** tending to initiate movement. **2** concerned with movement. ● *v.tr.* = MOTIVATE. □□ **mo•tive•less** *adj.* **mo•tive•less•ly** *adv.* **mo•tive•less•ness** *n.* **mo•tiv•i•ty** /–tívitee/ *n.* [ME f. OF *motif* (adj. & n.) f. LL *motivus* (adj.) (as MOVE)]

mo•tive pow•er *n.* a moving or impelling power, esp. a source of energy used to drive machinery.

mot juste /mō zhŸst/ *n.* (*pl.* **mots justes** *pronunc.* same) the most appropriate expression.

mot•ley /mótlee/ *adj. & n.* ● *adj.* (**mot•li•er, mot•li•est**) **1** diversified in color. **2** of varied character (*a motley crew*). ● *n.* **1** an incongruous mixture. **2** *hist.* the parti-colored costume of a jester. □ **wear motley** play the fool. [ME *mottelay,* perh. ult. rel. to MOTE]

mo•to•cross /mótōkraws, –kros/ *n.* cross-country racing on motorcycles. [MOTOR + CROSS]

mo•to per•pet•u•o /mótō pərpétyōō-ō/ *n. Mus.* a usu. fast-moving instrumental composition consisting mainly of notes of equal value. [It., = perpetual motion]

mo•tor /mótər/ *n., adj., & v.* ● *n.* **1** a thing that imparts motion. **2** a machine (esp. one using electricity or internal combustion) supplying motive power for a vehicle, etc., or for some other device with moving parts. **3** *Brit.* = CAR 1. ● *adj.* **1** giving, imparting, or producing motion. **2** driven by a motor. **3** of or for motor vehicles. **4** *Anat.* relating to muscular movement or the nerves activating it. ● *v.intr. & tr. esp. Brit.* go or convey in a motor vehicle. □□ **mo•tor•i•al** /mótáwreeəl/ *adj.* (in sense 4a of *n.*). **mo•tor•y** *adj.* (in sense 4a of *n.*). [L, = mover (as MOVE)]

▶See note at ENGINE.

mo•tor•a•ble /mótərəbəl/ *adj. Brit.* (of a road) that can be used by motor vehicles.

mo•tor ar•e•a *n.* the part of the frontal lobe of the brain associated with the initiation of muscular action.

mo•tor bi•cy•cle *n.* a motor cycle or moped.

mo•tor•bike /mótərbīk/ *n.* **1** lightweight motorcycle. **2** motorized bicycle.

mo•tor•boat /mótərbōt/ *n.* a motor-driven boat, esp. a recreational boat. *v.* travel by motorboat.

mo•tor•bus /mótərbus/ *n.* = BUS 1.

mo•tor•cade /mótərkayd/ *n.* a procession of motor vehicles. [MOTOR, after *cavalcade*]

mo•tor•car /mótərkaar/ *n. esp. Brit.* see CAR 1.

mo•tor•cy•cle /mótərsíkəl/ *n.* two-wheeled motor-driven road vehicle without pedal propulsion. □□ **mo•tor•cy•clist** *n.*

mo•tor home *n.* a vehicle built on a truck frame that includes kitchen facilities, beds, etc. (see also TRAILER or MOBILE HOME).

mo•tor•ist /mótərist/ *n.* the driver or passenger of an automobile.

mo•tor•ize /mótəriz/ *v.tr.* **1** equip (troops, etc.) with motor transport. **2** provide with a motor for propulsion, etc. □□ **mo•tor•i•za•tion** *n.*

mo•tor•man /mótərmən/ *n.* (*pl.* **•men**) the driver of a subway train, streetcar, etc.

mo•tor•mouth /mótərmówth/ *n. sl.* a person who talks incessantly and trivially.

mo•tor neu•ron *n.* a nerve carrying impulses from the brain or spinal cord to a muscle.

mo•tor pool *n.* a group of vehicles maintained by a government agency, military installation, etc., for use by personnel as needed.

mo•tor scoot•er *n.* see SCOOTER.

mo•tor ve•hi•cle *n.* a road vehicle powered by an internal-combustion engine.

mo•tor•way /mótərwáy/ *n. Brit.* an expressway.

Mo•town /mótown/ *n.* music with rhythm and blues elements, associated with Detroit. [a nickname for Detroit, shortening of *Motor Town*]

motte /mot/ *n.* **1** a mound forming the site of a castle, camp, etc. **2** *SW US* (also **mott**) clump of trees; grove. [ME f. OF *mote* (as MOAT)]

mot•tle /mót'l/ *v. & n.* ● *v.tr.* (esp. as **mottled** *adj.*) mark with spots or smears of color. ● *n.* **1** an irregular arrangement of spots or patches of color. **2** any of these spots or patches. [prob. back-form. f. MOTLEY]

mot•to /mótō/ *n.* (*pl.* **•toes** or **•tos**) **1** a maxim adopted as a rule of conduct. **2** a phrase or sentence accompanying a coat of arms or crest. **3** a sentence inscribed on some object and expressing an appropriate sentiment. **4** quotation prefixed to a book or chapter. [It. (as MOT)]

moue /mōō/ *n.* = POUT[1] *n.* [F]

mouf•lon /mōōflon/ *n.* (also **mouf•flon**) a wild mountain sheep, *Ovis musimon,* of S. Europe. [F *mouflon* f. It. *muflone* f. Rmc]

mouil•lé /mōō-yáy/ *adj. Phonet.* (of a consonant) palatalized. [F, = wetted]

mou•jik var. of MUZHIK.

mould *Brit.* var. of MOLD[1], MOLD[2], MOLD[3].

mould•er *Brit.* var. of MOLDER.

mould•ing *Brit.* var. of MOLDING.

mould•y *Brit.* var. of MOLDY.

mou•lin /mōōlán/ *n.* a nearly vertical shaft in a glacier, formed by surface water percolating through a crack in the ice. [F, lit. = mill]

moult *Brit.* var. of MOLT.

mound[1] /mownd/ *n. & v.* ● *n.* **1** a raised mass of earth, stones, or other compacted material. **2** a heap or pile. **3** a hillock. ● *v.tr.* **1** heap up in a mound or mounds. **2** enclose with mounds. [16th c. (orig. = hedge or fence): orig. unkn.]

mound[2] /mownd/ *n. Heraldry* a ball of gold, etc., representing the earth, and usu. surmounting a crown. [ME f. OF *monde* f. L *mundus* world]

Mound Build•ers /mownd bíldərz/ *n.* prehistoric Native American peoples of the Mississippi River Valley who left behind earthworks and burial mounds.

mount[1] /mownt/ *v. & n.* ● *v.* **1** *tr.* ascend or climb (a hill, stairs, etc.). **2** *tr.* **a** get up on (an animal, esp. a horse) to ride it. **b** set (a person) on horseback. **c** provide (a person) with a horse. **d** (as **mounted** *adj.*) serving on horseback (*mounted police*). **3** *tr.* go up or climb on to (a raised surface). **4** *intr.* **a** move upward. **b** (often foll. by *up*) increase, accumulate. **c** (of a feeling) become stronger or more intense (*excitement was mounting*). **d** (of the blood) rise into the cheeks. **5** *tr.* (esp. of a male animal) get on to (a female) to copulate. **6** *tr.* (often foll. by *on*) place (an object) on an elevated support. **7** *tr.* **a** set in or attach to a backing, setting, or other support. **b** attach (a picture, etc.) to a mount or frame. **c** fix (an object for viewing) on a microscope slide. **8** *tr.* **a** arrange (a play, exhibition, etc.) or present for public view or display. **b** take action to initiate (a program, campaign, etc.). **9** *tr.* prepare (specimens) for preservation. **10** *tr.* **a** bring into readiness for operation. **b** raise (guns) into position on a fixed mounting. **11** *intr.* rise to a higher level of rank, power, etc. ● *n.* **1** a backing, setting, or other support on which a picture, etc., is set or displayed. **2** the margin surrounding a picture or photograph. **3 a** a horse available for riding. **b** an opportunity to ride a horse, esp. as a jockey. □ **mount guard** *esp. Brit.* (often foll. by *over*) perform the duty of guarding; take up sentry duty. □□ **mount•a•ble** *adj.* **mount•er** *n.* [ME f. OF *munter, monter* ult. f. L (as MOUNT[2])]

mount[2] /mownt/ *n. archaic* (except before a name): mountain, hill (*Mount Everest; Mount of Olives*). [ME f. OE *munt* & OF *mont* f. L *mons montis* mountain]

moun•tain /mównt'n/ *n.* **1** a large natural elevation of the earth's surface rising abruptly from the surrounding level; a large or high and steep hill. **2** a large heap or pile; a huge quantity (*a mountain of work*). **3** a large surplus stock of a commodity (*butter mountain*). □ **make a mountain out of a molehill** see MOLEHILL. **move mountains 1** achieve spectacular results. **2** make every possible effort. □□ **moun·tain·y** *adj.* [ME f. OF *montaigne* ult. f. L (as MOUNT²)]

moun·tain ash *n.* **1** a tree, *Sorbus aucuparia*, with delicate pinnate leaves and scarlet berries. Also called **rowan. 2** any of several Australian eucalypti.

mountain avens *n.* an arctic-alpine plant, *Dryas octopetala*, with white flowers and glossy leaves.

moun·tain bike *n.* a bicycle with a light sturdy frame, broad deep-treaded tires, and multiple gears, originally designed for riding on mountainous terrain.

moun·tain·eer /mównt'neér/ *n. & v.* ●*n.* **1** a person skilled in mountain climbing. **2** a person living in an area of high mountains. ●*v.intr.* climb mountains as a sport. □□ **moun·tain·eer·ing** *n.*

moun·tain goat *n.* a white goatlike animal, *Oreamnos americanus*, of the Rocky Mountains, etc.

moun·tain lau·rel *n.* a N. American shrub, *Kalmia latifolia*.

moun·tain li·on *n.* a puma.

moun·tain·ous /mównt'nəs/ *adj.* **1** (of a region) having many mountains. **2** huge.

moun·tain pan·ther *n.* = OUNCE².

moun·tain range *n.* a line of mountains connected by high ground.

moun·tain sick·ness *n.* a sickness caused by the rarefaction of the air at great heights.

moun·tain·side /mównt'nsīd/ *n.* the slope of a mountain below the summit.

moun·tain time *n.* (also **Mountain Standard Time**) the standard time of parts of Canada and the US in or near the Rocky Mountains.

moun·te·bank /mówntibángk/ *n.* **1** a swindler; a charlatan. **2** a clown. **3** *hist.* an itinerant quack appealing to an audience from a platform. □□ **moun·te·bank·er·y** *n.* [It. *montambanco = monta in banco* climb on bench: see MOUNT¹, BENCH]

Moun·tie /mówntee/ *n. colloq.* a member of the Royal Canadian Mounted Police.

mount·ing /mównting/ *n.* **1** = MOUNT¹ *n.* 1. **2** in senses of MOUNT¹ *v.*

mount·ing block *n.* a block of stone placed to help a rider mount a horse.

mourn /mawrn/ *v.* **1** *tr. &* (foll. by *for*) intr. feel or show deep sorrow or regret for (a dead person, a lost thing, a past event, etc.). **2** *intr.* show conventional signs of grief for a period after a person's death. [OE *murnan*]

SYNONYM TIP mourn

BEMOAN, GRIEVE, LAMENT, RUE, SORROW. Not everyone exhibits unhappiness in the same way. **Grieve** is the strongest of these verbs, implying deep mental anguish or suffering, often endured alone and in silence (*She grieved over the loss of her unborn baby for years*). **Mourn** is more formal and often more public; although it implies deep emotion felt over a period of time, that emotion may be more ceremonial than sincere (*The people mourned the loss of their leader*). **Lament** comes from the Latin word meaning to wail or weep, and it therefore suggests a vocal or verbal expression of loss (*The woman lamented her husband's death by shrieking and tearing her clothes*). **Bemoan** also suggests suppressed or inarticulate sounds of *grief*, often expressing regret or disapproval (*to bemoan one's fate*). **Sorrow** combines deep sadness with regret and often pertains to a less tragic loss than *grieve* or *mourn* (*to sorrow over missed opportunities*), while **rue** has even stronger connotations of regret and repentance (*She rued the day she was born*).

mourn·er /mawrnər/ *n.* **1** a person who mourns, esp. at a funeral. **2** a person hired to attend a funeral.

mourn·ful /máwrnfŏŏl/ *adj.* **1** doleful, sad, sorrowing. **2** expressing or suggestive of mourning. □□ **mourn·ful·ly** *adv.* **mourn·ful·ness** *n.*

mourn·ing /mawrning/ *n.* **1** the expression of deep sorrow, esp. for a dead person, by the wearing of solemn dress. **2** the clothes worn in mourning. □ **in mourning** assuming the signs of mourning, esp. in dress.

mourn·ing band *n.* a band of black crepe, etc., around a person's sleeve or hat as a token of mourning.

mourn·ing dove *n.* an American dove with a plaintive note, *Zenaida macroura*.

mou·sa·ka var. of MOUSSAKA.

mouse /mows/ *n. & v.* ●*n.* (*pl.* **mice** /mīs/) **1 a** any of various small rodents of the family Muridae, esp. of the genus *Mus*. **b** any of several similar rodents such as a small shrew or vole. **2** a timid or feeble person. **3** *Computing* a small hand-held device that controls the cursor on a computer monitor. **4** *sl.* a black eye. ●*v.intr.* (also /mowz/) **1** (esp. of a cat, owl, etc.) hunt for or catch mice. **2** (foll. by *about*) search industriously; prowl about as if searching. □□ **mouse·like** *adj. & adv.* **mous·er** *n.* [OE *mūs*, pl. *mȳs* f. Gmc]

mouse-col·ored *adj.* **1** dark gray with a yellow tinge. **2** nondescript light brown.

mouse deer *n.* a chevrotain.

mouse hare *n.* esp. *Brit.* a pika.

mouse·trap /mówstrap/ *n.* a spring trap with bait for catching and usu. killing mice.

mous·sa·ka /mōōsáaka, –saakáa/ *n.* (also **mou·sa·ka**) a Greek dish of ground meat, eggplant, etc., with a cheese sauce. [mod. Gk or Turk.]

mousse /mōōs/ *n.* **1 a** a dessert of whipped cream, eggs, etc., usu. flavored with fruit or chocolate. **b** a meat or fish purée made with whipped cream, etc. **2** a preparation applied to the hair enabling it to be styled more easily. **3** a mixture of oil and seawater which forms a froth on the surface of the water after an oil spill. [F, = moss, froth]

mousse·line /mōōsleén/ *n.* **1** a muslinlike fabric of silk, etc. **2** a sauce lightened by the addition of whipped cream or eggs. [F: see MUSLIN]

mous·tache var. of MUSTACHE.

Mous·te·ri·an /mōōsteéreeən/ *adj. Archaeol.* of or relating to the flint workings of the Middle Paleolithic epoch, dated to *c.*70,000–30,000 BC, and attributed to Neanderthal peoples. [F *moustérien* f. *Le Moustier* in SW France, where remains were found]

mous·y /mówsee/ *adj.* (**mous·i·er, mous·i·est**) **1** of or like a mouse. **2** (of a person) shy or timid; ineffectual. **3** = MOUSE-COLORED. □□ **mous·i·ly** *adv.* **mous·i·ness** *n.*

mouth *n. & v.* ●*n.* /mowth/ (*pl.* **mouths** /mowthz/) **1 a** an external opening in the head, through which most animals admit food and emit communicative sounds. **b** (in humans and some animals) the cavity behind it containing the means of biting and chewing and the vocal organs. **2 a** the opening of a container such as a bag or sack. **b** the opening of a cave, volcano, etc. **c** the open end of a woodwind or brass instrument. **d** the muzzle of a gun. **3** the place where a river enters the sea. **4** *colloq.* a talkativeness. **b** impudent talk; cheek. **5** an individual regarded as needing sustenance (*an extra mouth to feed*). **6** a horse's readiness to feel and obey the pressure of the bit. **7** an expression of displeasure; a grimace ●*v.* /mowth/ **1** *tr. &* intr. utter or speak solemnly or with affectations; rant, declaim (*mouthing platitudes*). **2** *tr.* utter very distinctly. **3** *intr.* **a** move the lips silently. **b** grimace. **4** *tr.* take (food) in the mouth. **5** *tr.* touch with the mouth. **6** *tr.* train the mouth of (a horse). □ **keep one's mouth shut** *colloq.* not reveal a secret. **put words into a person's mouth** represent a person as having said something in a particular way. **take the words out of a person's mouth** say what another was about to say. □□ **mouthed** /mowthd/ *adj.* (also in *comb.*). **mouth·er** /mówthər/ *n.* **mouth·less** /mówthlis/ *adj.* [OE *mūth* f. Gmc]

mouth·ful /mówthfŏŏl/ *n.* (*pl.* **·fuls**) **1** a quantity, esp. of food, that fills the mouth. **2** a small quantity. **3** a long or complicated word or phrase. **4** *colloq.* something important said.

mouth or·gan *n.* = HARMONICA.

mouth·piece /mówthpees/ *n.* **1 a** the part of a musical instrument placed between or against the lips. **b** the part of a telephone for speaking into. **c** the part of a tobacco pipe placed between the lips. **2 a** a person who speaks for another or others. **b** *colloq.* a lawyer. **3** a part attached as an outlet.

mouth-to-mouth *adj.* (of resuscitation) in which a person breathes into a subject's lungs through the mouth.

mouth·wash /mówthwosh, –wawsh/ *n.* **1** a liquid antiseptic, etc., for rinsing the mouth or gargling. **2** esp. *Brit. colloq.* nonsense.

mouth·wa·ter·ing /mówthwawtəring/ *adj.* **1** (of food, etc.) having a delicious smell or appearance. **2** tempting; alluring. □□ **mouth·wa·ter·ing·ly** *adv.*

mouth·y /mówthee, –thee/ *adj.* (**mouth·i·er, mouth·i·est**) **1** ranting, railing. **2** bombastic.

mov·a·ble /mōōvəbəl/ *adj. & n.* (also **move·a·ble**) ●*adj.* **1** that can be moved. **2** *Law* (of property) of the nature of a chattel, as distinct from land or buildings. **3** (of a feast or festival) variable in date from year to year. ●*n.* **1** an article of furniture that can be removed from a house, as distinct from a fixture. **2** (in *pl.*) personal property. □□ **mov·a·bil·i·ty** /–bílitee/ *n.* **mov·a·ble·ness** *n.* **mov·a·bly** *adv.* [ME f. OF (as MOVE)]

mov·a·ble-do *n. Mus.* applied to a system of sight-singing in which do is the keynote of any major scale (cf. FIXED-DO).

mov·a·ble type *n.* type in which each character is on a separate piece of metal.

move /mōōv/ *v. & n.* ●*v.* **1** *intr. &* tr. change one's position or posture, or cause to do this. **2** *tr. &* intr. put or keep in motion; rouse, stir. **3 a** *intr.* make a move in a board game. **b** *tr.* change the position of (a piece) in a board game. **4** *intr.* (foll. by *about, away, etc.*) go or pass from place to place. **5** *intr.* take action, esp. promptly (*moved to reduce unemployment*). **6** *intr.* make progress (*the project is moving fast*). **7** *intr.* **a** change one's place of residence. **b** (of a business, etc.) change to new premises (also *tr.*: *move offices*). **8** *intr.* (foll. by *in*) live or be socially active in (a specified place or group, etc.) (*moves in the best circles*). **9** *tr.* affect (a person) with (usu. tender or sympathetic) emotion. **10** *tr.* **a** (foll. by *in*) stimulate (laughter, anger, etc., in a person). **b** (foll. by *to*) provoke (a person to laughter, etc.). **11** *tr.* (foll. by *to*, or *to* + *infin.*) prompt or incline (a person to a feeling or action). **12 a** *tr.* cause (the bowels) to be evacuated. **b** *intr.* (of the bowels) be evacuated. **13** *tr.* (often foll. by *that* + clause) propose in a meeting, deliberative assembly, etc. **14** *intr.* (foll. by *for*) make a formal request or application. **15** *intr.* (of merchandise) be sold. • *n.* **1** the act or an instance of moving. **2** a change of house, business premises, etc. **3** a step taken to secure some action or effect; an initiative. **4 a** the changing of the position of a piece in a board game. **b** a player's turn to do this. □ **get a move on** *colloq.* **1** hurry up. **2** make a start. **make a move** take action. **move along** (or **on**) change to a new position, esp. to avoid crowding, getting in the way, etc. **move heaven and earth** see HEAVEN. **move in 1** take possession of a new house. **2** get into a position of influence, interference, etc. **3** get into a position of readiness or proximity (for an offensive action, etc.). **move mountains** see MOUNTAIN. **move out 1** leave one's home; change one's place of residence. **2** leave a position, job, etc. **move over** (or **up**) adjust one's position to make room for another. **on the move 1** progressing. **2** moving about. [ME f. AF *mover*, OF *moveir* f. L *movēre mot–*]

move•a•ble var. of MOVABLE.

move•ment /mōōvmənt/ *n.* **1** the act or an instance of moving or being moved. **2 a** the moving parts of a mechanism (esp. a clock or watch). **b** a particular group of these. **3 a** a body of persons with a common object (*the peace movement*). **b** a campaign undertaken by such a body. **4** (usu. in *pl.*) a person's activities and whereabouts, esp. at a particular time. **5** *Mus.* a principal division of a longer musical work, self-sufficient in terms of key, tempo, structure, etc. **6** the progressive development of a poem, story, etc. **7** motion of the bowels. **8 a** an activity in a market for some commodity. **b** a rise or fall in price. **9** a mental impulse. **10** a development of position by a military force or unit. **11** a prevailing tendency in the course of events or conditions; trend. [ME f. OF f. med.L *movimentum* (as MOVE)]

mov•er /mōōvər/ *n.* **1** a person or thing that moves. **2** a person or company that moves household goods, etc., from one location to another as a business. **3** the author of a fruitful idea.

mov•ie /mōōvee/ *n.* esp. *colloq.* **1** a motion picture. **2** (**the movies**) **a** the motion-picture industry or medium. **b** the showing of a movie (*going to the movies*). □ **movie house** a theater that shows movies [abbr. of moving picture]

mov•ie•dom /mōōveedəm/ *n.* the movie industry and its associated businesses, personnel, etc.

mov•ing /mōōving/ *adj.* **1** that moves or causes to move. **2** affecting with emotion.□□ **mov•ing•ly** *adv.* (in sense 2).

SYNONYM TIP moving

AFFECTING, PATHETIC, POIGNANT, TOUCHING. A film about the Holocaust might be described as **moving**, since it arouses emotions or strong feelings, particularly feelings of pathos. A film about a young girl's devotion to her dog might more accurately be described as **touching**, which means arousing tenderness or compassion, while a film dealing with a young girl's first experience with love would be **poignant**, since it pierces one's heart or keenly affects one's sensibilities. *Poignant* implies a bittersweet response that combines pity and longing or other contradictory emotions, but **pathetic** means simply moving one to pity (*a pathetic scene in which the dog struggled to save his drowning mistress*). Almost any well-made film can be **affecting**, a more general term that suggests moving one to tears or some other display of feeling (*the affecting story of a daughter's search for her birth mother*).

---

mov•ing pic•ture *n.* a continuous picture of events obtained by projecting a sequence of photographs taken at very short intervals.

mov•ing stair•case *n.* esp. *Brit.* an escalator.

mov•ing van *n.* a large van used to move furniture, household goods, etc., from one house to another.

mow[1] /mō/ *v.tr.* (*past part.* **mowed** or **mown**) **1** cut down (grass, hay, etc.) with a scythe or machine. **2** cut down the produce of (a field) or the grass, etc., of (a lawn) by mowing. □ **mow down** kill or destroy randomly or in great numbers. □□ **mow•a•ble** *adj.* **mow•er** *n.* [OE *māwan* f. Gmc, rel. to MEAD[2]]

mow[2] /mow/ *n.* dial. **1** a stack of hay, wheat, etc. **2** a place in a barn where hay, etc., is heaped. [OE *mūga*]

mox•a /móksə/ *n.* a downy substance from the dried leaves of *Artemisia moxa*, burned on the skin in Eastern medicine as a counterirritant. [Jap. *mogusa* f. *moe kusa* burning herb]

mox•ie /móksee/ *n. sl.* energy, courage, daring. [trade name of a drink]

moz•za•rel•la /mótsəréllə/ *n.* an Italian semisoft cheese. [It.]

moz•zle /mózəl/ *n.* Austral. *colloq.* luck, fortune. [Heb. *mazzā*]

MP *abbr.* **1 a** military police. **b** military policeman. **2** Member of Parliament.

mp *abbr.* mezzo piano.

m.p. *abbr.* melting point.

m.p.g. *abbr.* miles per gallon.

---

m.p.h. *abbr.* miles per hour.

Mr. /místər/ *n.* (*pl.* **Messrs.**) **1** the respectful title of a man without a higher title (*Mr. Jones*). **2** a title prefixed to a designation of office, etc. (*Mr. President; Mr. Speaker*). [abbr. of MISTER]

Mr. Big *n. sl.* the head of an organization; any important person.

MRI *abbr.* magnetic resonance imaging.

mRNA *abbr. Biol.* messenger RNA.

Mr. Right *n. joc.* a woman's destined husband.

Mrs. /mísiz/ *n.* (*pl.* same or **Mes•dames**) the respectful title of a married woman without a higher title (*Mrs. Jones*). [abbr. of MISTRESS: cf. MISSUS]

MS *abbr.* **1** Mississippi (in official postal use). **2** Master of Science. **3** multiple sclerosis. **4** (also **ms.**) manuscript.

Ms. /miz/ *n.* form of address for a woman, used regardless of marital status. [combination of MRS., MISS[2]]

M.Sc. *abbr.* Master of Science.

MS-DOS /émesdáws, –dós/ *abbr. Trademark* a microcomputer disk operating system.

MSG *abbr.* monosodium glutamate.

Msgr. *abbr.* **1** Monseigneur. **2** Monsignor.

MSS *abbr.* (also **mss.**) manuscripts.

MST *abbr.* Mountain Standard Time.

MT *abbr.* **1** Montana (in official postal use). **2** Mountain Time. **3** mechanical transport.

Mt *abbr.* MEITNERIUM.

Mt. *abbr.* **1** mount. **2** mountain

mu /myōō, mōō/ *n.* **1** the twelfth Greek letter (M, μ). **2** (μ, as a symbol) = MICRO- 2.[Gk]

much /much/ *adj., n., & adv.* • *adj.* **1** existing or occurring in a great quantity (*much trouble; not much rain; too much noise*). **2** (prec. by *as, how, that*, etc.) with relative rather than distinctive sense (*I don't know how much money you want*). • *n.* **1** a great quantity (*much of that is true*). **2** (prec. by *as, how, that*, etc.) with relative rather than distinctive sense (*we do not need that much*). **3** (usu. in *neg.*) a noteworthy or outstanding example (*not much to look at; not much of a party*). • *adv.* **1 a** in a great degree (*much to my surprise; is much the same*). **b** (qualifying a verb or past participle) greatly (*they much regret the mistake; I was much annoyed*). **c** qualifying a comparative or superlative adjective (*much better; much the most likely*). **2** for a large part of one's time (*is much away from home*). □ **as much** the extent or quantity just specified; the idea just mentioned (*I thought as much; as much as that?*). **a bit much** *colloq.* somewhat excessive or immoderate. **make much of** see MAKE. **much as** even though (*cannot come, much as I would like to*). **much less** see LESS. **not much** *colloq.* **1** *iron.* very much. **2** certainly not. **not much in it** see IN. **too much** *colloq.* an intolerable situation, etc. (*that really is too much*). **too much for 1** more than a match for. **2** beyond what is endurable by. □□ **much•ly** *adv. joc.* [ME f. *muchel* MICKLE: for loss of *el* cf. BAD, WENCH]

much•ness /múchnis/ *n.* greatness in quantity or degree. □ **much of a muchness** very nearly the same or alike.

much o•bliged *n.* see OBLIGE.

mu•ci•lage /myōōsilij/ *n.* **1** a viscous substance obtained from plant seeds, etc., by maceration. **2** a solution of gum, glue, etc. □□ **mu•ci•lag•i•nous** /–lájinəs/ *adj.* [ME f. F f. LL *mucilago –ginis* musty juice (MUCUS)]

muck /muk/ *n. & v.* • *n.* **1** farmyard manure. **2** *colloq.* dirt or filth; anything disgusting. **3** *colloq.* an untidy state; a mess. • *v.tr.* **1** (usu. foll. by *up*) *colloq.* bungle (a job). **2** (often foll. by *out*) remove muck from. **3** make dirty or untidy. **4** manure with muck. □ **make a muck of** *colloq.* bungle. **muck about** (or **around**) esp. *Brit. colloq.* **1** putter or fool about. **2** (foll. by *with*) fool or interfere with. [ME *muk* prob. f. Scand.: cf. ON *myki* dung, rel. to MEEK]

muck•le var. of MICKLE.

muck•rake /múkrayk/ *v.intr.* search out and reveal scandal, esp. among famous people. □□ **muck•rak•er** *n.* **muck•rak•ing** *n.*

muck•y /múkee/ *adj.* (**muck•i•er, muck•i•est**) **1** covered with muck. **2** dirty. □□ **muck•i•ness** *n.*

muco- /myōōkō/ *comb. form Biochem.* mucus, mucous.

mu•co•pol•y•sac•cha•ride /myōōkōpóleesákərid/ *n. Biochem.* any of a group of polysaccharides whose molecules contain sugar residues and are often found as components of connective tissue.

mu•co•sa /myōōkósə/ *n.* (*pl.* **mu•co•sae** /–see/) a mucous membrane. [mod.L, fem. of *mucosus*: see MUCOUS]

mu•cous /myōōkəs/ *adj.* of or covered with mucus.□□ **mu•cos•i•ty** /–kósitee/ *n.* [L *mucosus* (as MUCUS)]

mu•cous mem•brane *n.* a mucus-secreting epithelial tissue lining many body cavities and tubular organs.

mu•cro /myōōkrō/ *n.* (*pl.* **mu•cro•nes** /–krōneez/) *Bot. & Zool.* a sharp-pointed part or organ. □□ **mu•cro•nate** /–krənət, –nayt/ *adj.* [L *mucro –onis* sharp point]

mu•cus /myōōkəs/ *n.* **1** a slimy substance secreted by a mucous membrane. **2** a gummy substance found in all plants. **3** a slimy substance exuded by some animals, esp. fishes. [L]

mud /mud/ *n.* **1** wet, soft, earthy matter. **2** hard ground from the drying of an area of this. **3** what is worthless or polluting. □ **as clear as mud** *colloq.* not at all clear. **fling** (or **sling** or **throw**) **mud** speak disparagingly or slanderously. **here's mud in your eye!** *colloq.* a drinking toast. **one's name is mud** one is unpopular or in disgrace. [ME *mode, mudde*, prob. f. MLG *mudde*, MHG *mot* bog]

mud bath *n.* **1** a bath in the mud of mineral springs, esp. to relieve rheumatism, etc. **2** a muddy scene or occasion.

mud brick *n.* a brick made from baked mud; adobe.

mud·dle /múd'l/ *v. & n.* ● *v.* **1** *tr.* (often foll. by *up, together*) bring into disorder. **2** *tr.* bewilder, confuse. **3** *tr.* mismanage (an affair). **4** *tr.* crush and mix (the ingredients for a drink). **5** *intr.* (often foll. by *with*) busy oneself in a confused and ineffective way. ● *n.* **1** disorder. **2** a muddled condition. □ **make a muddle of 1** bring into disorder. **2** bungle. **muddle along** (or **on**) progress in a haphazard way. **muddle through** succeed by perseverance rather than skill or efficiency. **muddle up** confuse (two or more things). □□ **mud·dler** *n.* **mud·dling·ly** *adv.*

WORD HISTORY   **muddle**

Late Middle English (in the sense 'wallow in mud'): perhaps from Middle Dutch *moddelen*, derived from *modden* 'dabble in mud' (related to *mud*). The sense 'confuse' was initially associated with alcoholic drink (late 17th century), giving rise to 'busy oneself in a confused way' and 'jumble up' (mid-19th century).

---

mud·dle-head·ed *adj.* stupid, confused. □□ **mud·dle-head·ed·ness** *n.* stupidity; a confused state.

mud·dy /múdee/ *adj. & v.* ● *adj.* (**mud·di·er, mud·di·est**) **1** like mud. **2** covered in or full of mud. **3** (of liquid) turbid. **4** mentally confused. **5** obscure. **6** (of light) dull. **7** (of color) impure. ● *v.tr.* (**·dies, ·died**) make muddy. □□ **mud·di·ly** *adv.* **mud·di·ness** *n.*

mud·fish /múdfish/ *n.* any fish that burrows in mud, as the bowfin.

mud·flap /múdflap/ *n.* a flap hanging behind the wheel of a vehicle, to catch mud and stones, etc., thrown up from the road.

mud flat *n.* a stretch of muddy land left uncovered at low tide.

mud·guard /múdgaard/ *n.* a curved strip or cover over a wheel of a bicycle or motorcycle to reduce the amount of mud, etc., thrown up from the road.

mud·lark /múdlaark/ *n. Brit.* **1** *hist.* a destitute person, esp. a child, searching in river mud for objects of value. **2** *hist.* a street urchin.

mud pup·py *n.* a large nocturnal salamander, *Necturus maculosus*, of eastern US.

mud·stone /múdstōn/ *n.* a dark clay rock.

mud vol·ca·no *n.* a volcano discharging mud.

mues·li /móoslee, myóoz–/ *n.* a breakfast food of crushed cereals, dried fruits, nuts, etc., eaten with milk. [Swiss G]

mu·ez·zin /myoo-ézin, moo–/ *n.* a Muslim crier who proclaims the hours of prayer, usu. from a minaret. [Arab. *mu'addin* part. of *'addana* proclaim]

muff[1] /muf/ *n.* a fur or other covering, usu. in the form of a tube with an opening at each end for the hands to be inserted for warmth. [Du. *mof*, MDu. *moffel, muffel* f. med.L *muff(u)la*, of unkn. orig.]

muff[2] /muf/ *v. & n.* ● *v.tr.* **1** bungle; deal clumsily with. **2** fail to catch or receive (a ball, etc.). **3** blunder in (a theatrical part, etc.). ● *n.* **1** esp. *Brit.* a person who is awkward or stupid, orig. in some athletic sport. **2** a failure, esp. to catch a ball in baseball, etc. □□ **muff·ish** *adj.* [19th c.: orig. unkn.]

muf·fin /múfin/ *n.* a small cake or quick bread made from batter or dough and baked in a muffin pan. [18th c.: orig. unkn.]

muf·fle[1] /múfəl/ *v. & n.* ● *v.tr.* **1** (often foll. by *up*) wrap or cover for warmth. **2** cover or wrap up (a source of sound) to reduce its loudness. **3** (usu. as **muffled** *adj.*) stifle (an utterance, e.g., a curse). **4** prevent from speaking. ● *n.* **1** a receptacle in a furnace where substances may be heated without contact with combustion products. **2** a similar chamber in a kiln for baking painted pottery. [ME: (n.) f. OF *moufle* thick glove; (v.) perh. f. OF *enmoufler* f. *moufle*]

muf·fle[2] /múfəl/ *n.* the thick part of the upper lip and nose of ruminants and rodents. [F *mufle*, of unkn. orig.]

muf·fler /múflər/ *n.* **1** a wrap or scarf worn for warmth. **2** a noise-reducing device on a motor vehicle's exhaust system. **3 a** *Brit.* any of various devices used to deaden sound in musical instruments. **b** a mute.

muf·ti[1] /múftee/ *n.* a Muslim legal expert empowered to give rulings on religious matters. [Arab. *muftī*, part. of *'aftā* decide a point of law]

muf·ti[2] /múftee/ *n.* plain clothes worn by a person who also wears (esp. military) uniform (*in mufti*). [19th c.: perh. f. MUFTI[1]]

mug[1] /mug/ *n. & v.* ● *n.* **1 a** a drinking vessel, usu. cylindrical and with a handle and used without a saucer. **b** its contents. **2** *sl.* the face or mouth of a person. **3** *sl.* a hoodlum or thug. **4** *Brit. sl.* **a** a simpleton. **b** a gullible person. ● *v.* (**mugged, mug·ging**) **1** *tr.* rob

(a person) with violence, esp. in a public place. **2** *tr.* fight; thrash. **3** *tr.* strangle. **4** *intr. sl.* make faces, esp. before an audience, a camera, etc. □ **a mug's game** *colloq.* a foolish or unprofitable activity. □□ **mug·ger** *n.* (esp. in sense 1 of *v.*). **mug·ful** *n.* (*pl.* **·fuls**). **mug·ging** *n.* (in sense 1 of *v.*). [prob. f. Scand.: sense 2 of *n.* prob. f. the representation of faces on mugs, and sense 3 prob. from this]

mug[2] /mug/ *v.tr.* (**mugged, mug·ging**) *Brit.* (usu. foll. by *up*) *sl.* learn (a subject) by concentrated study. [19th c.: orig. unkn.]

mug·ger[1] see MUG[1].

mug·ger[2] /múgər/ *n.* a broad-nosed E. Indian crocodile, *Crocodylus palustris*, venerated by many Hindus. [Hindi *magar*]

mug·gins /múginz/ *n. Brit.* (*pl.* same or **mug·gins·es**) **1** *colloq.* **a** a simpleton. **b** a person who is easily outwitted (often with allusion to oneself: so muggins had to pay). **2** a card game like snap. [perh. the surname *Muggins*, with allusion to MUG[1]]

mug·gy /múgee/ *adj.* (**mug·gi·er, mug·gi·est**) (of the weather, a day, etc.) oppressively damp and warm; humid. □□ **mug·gi·ness** *n.* [dial. *mug* mist, drizzle f. ON *mugga*]

Mu·ghal /móogaal/ *n.* **1** a Mongolian. **2** (*attrib.*) denoting the Muslim dynasty in India in the 16th–19th c. (cf. MOGUL 2b.) [Pers. *mugūl* MONGOL]

mug shot *n. sl.* a photograph of a face, esp. for official purposes.

mug·wort /múgwort, –wawrt/ *n.* any of various plants of the genus *Artemisia*, esp. *A. vulgaris*, with silver-gray aromatic foliage. [OE *mucgwyrt* (as MIDGE, WORT)]

mug·wump /múgwump/ *n.* **1** a great man; a boss. **2** a person who remains aloof, esp. from party politics. [Algonquian *mugquomp* great chief]

Mu·ham·mad·an /məháməd'n/ *n. & adj.* (also **Mo·ham·med·an**) = MUSLIM. □□ **Mu·ham·mad·an·ism** *n.* [*Muhammad*, Arabian prophet d. 632]

▶This term is not used or favored by Muslims, and is often regarded as offensive.

mu·ja·hi·din /móojaahideén/ *n.pl.* (also **mu·ja·he·din, –deen**) guerrilla fighters in Islamic countries, esp. supporting Muslim fundamentalism. [Pers. & Arab. *mujāhidīn* pl. of *mujāhid* one who fights a JIHAD]

mu·lat·to /məolátō, –laá–, myoo–/ *n. & adj.* ● *n.* (*pl.* **·toes** or **·tos**) a person of mixed white and black parentage. ● *adj.* of the color of mulattoes; tawny. [Sp. *mulato* young mule, *mulatto*, irreg. f. *mulo* MULE[1]]

mul·ber·ry /múlberee, –bəree/ *n.* (*pl.* **·ries**) **1** any deciduous tree of the genus *Morus*, grown originally for feeding silkworms, and now for its fruit and ornamental qualities. **2** its dark-red or white berry. **3** a dark-red or purple color. [ME *mol-, mool-, mulberry*, dissim. f. *murberie* f. OE *mōrberie*, f. L *morum*: see BERRY]

mulch /mulch/ *n. & v.* ● *n.* a mixture of straw, leaves, etc., spread around or over a plant to enrich or insulate the soil. ● *v.tr.* treat with mulch. [prob. use as noun of *mulsh* soft: cf. dial. *melsh* mild f. OE *melsc*]

mulct /mulkt/ *v. & n.* ● *v.tr.* **1** extract money from by fine or taxation. **2 a** (often foll. by *of*) deprive by fraudulent means; swindle. **b** obtain by swindling. ● *n.* a fine. [earlier *mult(e)* f. L *multa, mulcta*: (v.) through F *mulcter* & L *mulctare*]

mule[1] /myool/ *n.* **1** the offspring (usu. sterile) of a male donkey and a female horse, or (in general use) of a female donkey and a male horse (cf. HINNY[1]), used as a beast of burden. **2** a stupid or obstinate person. **3** (often *attrib.*) a hybrid and usu. sterile plant or animal (*mule canary*). **4** (in full **spinning mule**) a kind of spinning machine producing yarn on spindles. [ME f. OF *mul(e)* f. L *mulus mula*]

mule[2] /myool/ *n.* a light shoe or slipper without a back. [F]

mu·le·teer /myóoliteér/ *n.* a mule driver. [F *muletier* f. *mulet* dimin. of OF *mul* MULE[1]]

mul·ga /múlgə/ *n. Austral.* **1** a small spreading tree, *Acacia aneura.* **2** the wood of this tree. **3** scrub or bush. **4** *colloq.* the outback. [Aboriginal]

mu·li·eb·ri·ty /myóolee-ébritee/ *n. literary* **1** womanhood. **2** the normal characteristics of a woman. **3** softness, effeminacy. [LL *muliebritas* f. L *mulier* woman]

mul·ish /móolish/ *adj.* **1** like a mule. **2** stubborn. □□ **mul·ish·ly** *adv.* **mul·ish·ness** *n.*

mull[1] /mul/ *v.tr. & intr.* (often foll. by *over*) ponder or consider. [perh. f. *mull* grind to powder, ME *mul* dust f. MDu.]

mull[2] /mul/ *v.tr.* warm (wine or beer) with added sugar, spices, etc. [17th c.: orig. unkn.]

mull[3] /mul/ *n. Sc.* a promontory. [ME: cf. Gael. *maol*, Icel. *múli*]

mull[4] /mul/ *n.* humus formed under nonacid conditions. [G f. Da. *muld*]

mull[5] /mul/ *n.* a thin, soft, plain muslin. [abbr. of *mulmull* f. Hindi *malmal*]

mul·lah /múlə, móol–/ *n.* a Muslim learned in Islamic theology and sacred law. [Pers., Turk., Urdu *mullā* f. Arab. *mawlā*]

mul·lein /múlin/ *n.* any herbaceous plant of the genus *Verbascum*, with woolly leaves and yellow flowers. [ME f. OF *moleine* f. Gaulish]

mul·ler /múlər/ *n.* a stone or other heavy weight used for grinding material on a slab. [ME, perh. f. AF *moldre* grind]

mul·let /múlit/ *n.* any fish of the family Mullidae (**red mullet**) or Mugilidae (**gray mullet**), usu. with a thick body and a large blunt-nosed head, commonly used as food. [ME f. OF *mulet* dimin. of L *mullus* red mullet f. Gk *mollos*]

mul·li·ga·taw·ny /múligətáwnee/ *n.* a highly seasoned soup orig. from India. [Tamil *milagutannir* pepper water]

mul·lion /múlyən/ *n.* (also **mun·nion** /mún–/) a vertical bar dividing the panes in a window (cf. TRANSOM). □□ **mul·lioned** *adj.* [prob. an altered form of MONIAL]

mul·lo·way /múləway/ *n. Austral.* a large marine fish, *Sciaena antarctica*, used as food. [19th c.: orig. unkn.]

mul·tan·gu·lar /multánggyələr/ *adj.* having many angles. [med.L *multangularis* (as MULTI-, ANGULAR)]

multi- /múltee, –tī/ *comb. form* many; more than one. [L f. *multus* much, many]

mul·ti·ac·cess /múlteeáksess, –tī–/ *n.* (often *attrib.*) the simultaneous connection to a computer of a number of terminals.

mul·ti·ax·i·al /múlteeákseeəl/ *adj.* of or involving several axes.

mul·ti·cel·lu·lar /múlteesélyələr, –tī–/ *adj. Biol.* having many cells.

mul·ti·chan·nel /múlteechánəl, –tī–/ *adj.* employing or possessing many communication or television channels.

mul·ti·col·or /múltikúlər/ *adj.* (also **mul·ti·col·ored**) of many colors.

mul·ti·cul·tur·al /múlteekúlchərəl/ *adj.* of or relating to or constituting several cultural or ethnic groups within a society. □□ **mul·ti·cul·tur·al·ism** *n.* **mul·ti·cul·tur·al·ly** *adv.*

mul·ti·di·men·sion·al /múlteediménshənəl, –dī–/ *adj.* of or involving more than three dimensions. □□ **mul·ti·di·men·sion·al·i·ty** /–nálitee/ *n.* **mul·ti·di·men·sion·al·ly** *adv.*

mul·ti·di·rec·tion·al /múlteedirékshənəl, –dī–, –tī–/ *adj.* of, involving, or operating in several directions.

mul·ti·fac·et·ed /múlteefásitid, –tī–/ *adj.* having several facets.

mul·ti·far·i·ous /múltifáireeəs/ *adj.* 1 (foll. by pl. noun) many and various. 2 having great variety. □□ **mul·ti·far·i·ous·ly** *adv.* **mul·ti·far·i·ous·ness** *n.* [L *multifarius*]

mul·ti·fid /múltifid/ *adj. Bot. & Zool.* divided into many parts. [L *multifidus* (as MULTI-, *fid–* stem of *findere* cleave)]

mul·ti·foil /múltifoyl/ *n. Archit.* an ornament consisting of more than five foils.

mul·ti·form /múltifawrm/ *n.* (usu. *attrib.*) 1 having many forms. 2 of many kinds. □□ **mul·ti·for·mi·ty** /–fáwrmitee/ *n.*

mul·ti·func·tion·al /múlteefúngkshənəl, –tī–/ *adj.* having or fulfilling several functions.

mul·ti·grade /múltigrayd/ *n.* (usu. *attrib.*) an engine oil, etc., meeting the requirements of several standard grades.

mul·ti·lat·er·al /múltilátərəl/ *adj.* 1 a (of an agreement, treaty, conference, etc.) in which three or more parties participate. b performed by more than two parties (*multilateral disarmament*). 2 having many sides. □□ **mul·ti·lat·er·al·ly** *adv.*

mul·ti·lin·gual /múlteelínggwəl, –tī–/ *adj.* in or using several languages. □□ **mul·ti·lin·gual·ly** *adv.*

mul·ti·me·di·a /múltimeédeeə/ *adj. & n.* ● *attrib. adj.* involving several media. ● *n.* the combined use of several media, such as film, print, sound, etc.

mul·ti·mil·lion /múlteemílyən, –tī–/ *attrib.adj.* costing or involving several million (dollars, pounds, etc.) (*multimillion-dollar fraud*).

mul·ti·mil·lion·aire /múlteemílyənáir, –tī–/ *n.* a person with a fortune of several millions.

mul·ti·na·tion·al /múlteenáshənəl, –tī–/ *adj. & n.* ● *adj.* 1 (of a business organization) operating in several countries. 2 relating to or including several nationalities or ethnic groups. ● *n.* a multinational company. □□ **mul·ti·na·tion·al·ly** *adv.*

mul·ti·no·mi·al /múltinómeeəl/ *adj. & n. Math.* = POLYNOMIAL. [MULTI-, after *binomial*]

mul·tip·a·rous /multípərəs/ *adj.* 1 bringing forth many young at a birth. 2 having borne more than one child. [MULTI- + –PAROUS]

mul·ti·par·tite /múltipaártit/ *adj.* divided into many parts.

mul·ti·phase /múltifayz/ *n. Electr.* = POLYPHASE.

mul·ti·ple /múltipəl/ *adj. & n.* ● *adj.* 1 having several or many parts, elements, or individual components. 2 (foll. by pl. noun) many and various. 3 *Bot.* (of fruit) collective. ● *n.* a number that may be divided by another a certain number of times without a remainder (*56 is a multiple of 7*). □□ **mul·ti·ply** *adv.* [F f. LL *multiplus* f. L (as MULTIPLEX)]

mul·ti·ple-choice *n.* (of a question in an examination) accompanied by several possible answers from which the correct one has to be chosen.

mul·ti·ple per·son·al·i·ty *n. Psychol.* the apparent existence of two or more distinct personalities in one individual.

mul·ti·ple scle·ro·sis *n.* see SCLEROSIS.

mul·ti·ple shop (also **mul·ti·ple store**) *n. Brit.* = CHAIN STORE.

mul·ti·ple stand·ard *n.* see STANDARD.

mul·ti·ple star *n.* several stars so close as to seem one, esp. when forming a connected system.

mul·ti·plex /múltipleks/ *adj., v., & n.* ● *adj.* 1 manifold; of many elements. 2 involving simultaneous transmission of several messages along a single channel of communication. ● *v. tr.* incorporate into a multiplex signal or system. ● *n.* a building that houses several movie theaters □□ **mul·ti·plex·er** *n.* (also **mul·ti·plex·or**). [L (as MULTI-, –plex –plicis –fold)]

mul·ti·pli·a·ble /múltipliəbəl/ *adj.* that can be multiplied.

mul·ti·plic·a·ble /múltiplíkəbəl/ *adj.* = MULTIPLIABLE. [OF *multiplicable* or med.L *multiplicabilis* f. L (as MULTIPLY)]

mul·ti·pli·cand /múltiplikánd/ *n.* a quantity to be multiplied by a multiplier. [med.L *multiplicandus* gerundive of L *multiplicare* (as MULTIPLY)]

mul·ti·pli·ca·tion /múltiplikáyshən/ *n.* 1 the arithmetical process of multiplying. 2 the act or an instance of multiplying. □□ **mul·ti·pli·ca·tive** /–plíkətiv/ *adj.* [ME f. OF *multiplication* or L *multiplicatio* (as MULTIPLY)]

mul·ti·pli·ca·tion sign *n.* the sign (×) to indicate that one quantity is to be multiplied by another, as in $2 \times 3 = 6$.

mul·ti·pli·ca·tion table *n.* a list of multiples of a particular number, usu. from 1 to 12.

mul·ti·plic·i·ty /múltiplísitee/ *n.* (*pl.* **·ties**) 1 manifold variety. 2 (foll. by *of*) a great number. [LL *multiplicitas* (as MULTIPLEX)]

mul·ti·pli·er /múltiplīər/ *n.* 1 a quantity by which a given number is multiplied. 2 *Econ.* a factor by which an increment of income exceeds the resulting increment of saving or investment. 3 *Electr.* an instrument for increasing by repetition the intensity of a current, force, etc.

mul·ti·ply /múltipli/ *v.* (**·plies, ·plied**) 1 *tr.* (also *absol.*) obtain from (a number) another that is a specified number of times its value (*multiply 6 by 4 and you get 24*). 2 *intr.* increase in number esp. by procreation. 3 *tr.* produce a large number of (instances, etc.). 4 *tr.* **a** breed (animals). **b** propagate (plants). [ME f. OF *multiplier* f. L *multiplicare* (as MULTIPLEX)]

mul·ti·po·lar /múltipólər/ *adj.* having many poles (see POLE²).

mul·ti·proc·ess·ing /múlteeprósesing/ *n. Computing* processing by a number of processors sharing a common memory and common peripherals.

mul·ti·pro·gram·ming /múlteeprógraming/ *n. Computing* the execution of two or more independent programs concurrently.

mul·ti·pur·pose /múlteepórpəs, –tī–/ *n.* (*attrib.*) having several purposes.

mul·ti·ra·cial /múlteeráyshəl, –tī–/ *adj.* relating to or made up of many human races. □□ **mul·ti·ra·cial·ly** *adv.*

mul·ti·role /múlteeról/ *n.* (*attrib.*) having several roles or functions.

mul·ti·stage /múltistayj/ *n.* (*attrib.*) (of a rocket, etc.) having several stages of operation.

mul·ti·sto·ry /múltistáwree/ *n.* (*attrib.*) (of a building) having several (esp. similarly designed) stories.

mul·ti·tude /múltitood, –tyood/ *n.* 1 (often foll. by *of*) a great number. 2 a large gathering of people; a crowd. 3 (**the multitude**) the common people. 4 the state of being numerous. [ME f. OF f. L *multitudo –dinis* f. *multus* many]

mul·ti·tu·di·nous /múltitóod′nəs, –tyood–/ *adj.* 1 very numerous. 2 consisting of many individuals or elements. 3 (of an ocean, etc.) vast. □□ **mul·ti·tu·di·nous·ly** *adv.* **mul·ti·tu·di·nous·ness** *n.* [L (as MULTITUDE)]

mul·ti·us·er /múltiyóōzər/ *n.* (*attrib.*) (of a computer system) having a number of simultaneous users (cf. MULTI-ACCESS).

mul·ti·va·lent /múltiváylənt, multívə–/ *adj. Chem.* 1 having a valence of more than two. 2 having a variable valency. □□ **mul·ti·va·len·cy** *n.*

mul·ti·valve /múltivalv/ *n.* (*attrib.*) (of a shell, etc.) having several valves.

mul·ti·ver·si·ty /múltivérsitee/ *n.* (*pl.* **·ties**) a large university with many different departments. [MULTI- + UNIVERSITY]

mul·tiv·o·cal /multívəkəl/ *adj.* having many meanings.

mum¹ /mum/ *adj. colloq.* silent (*keep mum*). □ **mum's the word** say nothing. [ME: imit. of closed lips]

mum² /mum/ *v. intr.* (**mummed, mum·ming**) act in a traditional masked mime. [cf. MUM² and MLG *mummen*]

mum³ /mum/ *n.* = CHRYSANTHEMUM.

mum⁴ /mum/ *n. Brit. colloq.* mother. [abbr. of MUMMY¹]

mum·ble /múmbəl/ *v. & n.* ● *v.* 1 *intr. & tr.* speak or utter indistinctly. 2 *tr.* bite or chew with or as with toothless gums. ● *n.* an indistinct utterance. □□ **mum·bler** *n.* **mum·bling·ly** *adv.* [ME *momele*, as MUM²: cf. LG *mummelen*]

mum·bo jum·bo /múmbōjúmbō/ *n.* (*pl.* **jum·bos**) 1 meaningless or ignorant ritual. 2 language or action intended to mystify or confuse. 3 an object of senseless veneration. [*Mumbo Jumbo*, a supposed African idol]

mu-me·son *n.* = MUON.

mum·mer /múmər/ *n.* 1 an actor in a traditional masked mime.

2 *archaic* or *derog.* an actor in the theater. [ME f. OF *momeur* f. *momer* MUM³]

mum·mer·y /múmɔree/ *n.* (*pl.* **·ies**) **1** ridiculous (esp. religious) ceremonial. **2** a performance by mummers. [OF *momerie* (as MUMMER)]

mum·mi·fy /múmifī/ *v.tr.* (**·fies**, **·fied**) **1** embalm and preserve (a body) in the form of a mummy (see MUMMY²). **2** (usu. as **mummified** *adj.*) shrivel or dry up (tissues, etc.). □□ **mum·mi·fi·ca·tion** /-fikáyshɔn/.

mum·my¹ /múmee/ *n.* (*pl.* **·mies**) esp. *Brit.* = MOMMY.

mum·my² /múmee/ *n.* (*pl.* **·mies**) **1** a body of a human being or animal embalmed for burial, esp. in ancient Egypt. **2** a dried-up body. **3** *Brit.* a pulpy mass (*beat it to a mummy*). **4** a rich brown pigment. [F *momie* f. med.L *mumia* f. Arab. *mūmiyā* f. Pers. *mūm* wax]

mumps /mumps/ *n.pl.* **1** (treated as *sing.*) a contagious and infectious viral disease with swelling of the parotid salivary glands in the face. **2** *Brit.* a fit of sulks. □□ **mump·ish** *adj.* (in sense 2). [archaic *mump* be sullen]

munch /munch/ *v.tr.* eat steadily with a marked action of the jaws. [ME, imit.: cf. CRUNCH]

munch·ies /múncheez/ *n.pl. colloq.* **1** snack foods. **2** the urge to snack.

mun·dane /múndáyn/ *adj.* **1** dull, routine. **2** of this world; worldly. □□ **mun·dane·ly** *adv.* **mun·dane·ness** *n.* **mun·dan·i·ty** /-dánitee/ *n.* (*pl.* **·ties**). [ME f. OF *mondain* f. LL *mundanus* f. L *mundus* world]

mung /mung/ *n.* (in full **mung bean**) a leguminous plant, *Phaseolus aureus*, native to India and used as food. [Hindi *mūng*]

mun·go /múnggō/ *n.* (*pl.* **·gos**) the short fibers recovered from heavily felted material. [19th c.: orig. uncert.]

mu·nic·i·pal /myoonísipɔl/ *adj.* of or concerning a municipality or its self-government. □□ **mu·nic·i·pal·ize** *v.tr.* **mu·nic·i·pal·i·za·tion** /-lizáyshɔn/ *n.* **mu·nic·i·pal·ly** *adv.* [L *municipalis* f. *municipium* free city f. *municeps –cipis* citizen with privileges f. *munia* civic offices + *capere* take]

mu·nic·i·pal bond *n.* a bond issued by a city, county, state, etc., to finance public projects.

mu·nic·i·pal·i·ty /myoonisipálitee/ *n.* (*pl.* **·ties**) **1** a town or district having local government. **2** the governing body of this area. [F *municipalité* f. *municipal* (as MUNICIPAL)]

mu·nif·i·cent /myoonífisɔnt/ *adj.* (of a giver or a gift) splendidly generous, bountiful. □□ **mu·nif·i·cence** *n.* **mu·nif·i·cent·ly** *adv.* [L *munificent-*, var. stem of *munificus* f. *munus* gift]

mu·ni·ment /myoonimɔnt/ *n.* (usu. in *pl.*) **1** a document kept as evidence of rights or privileges, etc. **2** an archive. [ME f. OF f. L *munimentum* defense, in med.L title deed f. *munire munit-* fortify]

mu·ni·tion /myoonishɔn/ *n. & v.* ● *n.* (usu. in *pl.*) military weapons, ammunition, equipment, and stores. ● *v.tr.* supply with munitions. [F f. L *munitio –onis* fortification (as MUNIMENT)]

mu·ni·tion·er /myoonishɔnɔr/ *n.* a person who makes or supplies munitions.

mun·nion var. of MULLION.

munt·jac /múntjak/ *n.* (also **munt·jak**) any small deer of the genus *Muntiacus* native to SE Asia, the male having tusks and small antlers. [Sundanese *minchek*]

Muntz met·al /munts/ *n.* an alloy (approx. 60% copper, 40% zinc) used for sheathing ships, etc. Also called **alpha-beta brass**. [G. F. *Muntz*, Engl. manufacturer d. 1857]

mu·on /myóō-on/ *n. Physics* an unstable elementary particle like an electron, but with a much greater mass. [μ (MU), as the symbol for it]

mu·rage /myoorij/ *n. Brit. hist.* a tax levied for building or repairing the walls of a town. [ME f. OF, in med.L *muragium* f. OF *mur* f. L *murus* wall]

mu·ral /myoorɔl/ *n. & adj.* ● *n.* a painting executed directly on a wall. ● *adj.* **1** of or like a wall. **2** on a wall. □□ **mu·ral·ist** *n.* [F f. L *muralis* f. *murus* wall]

mu·ral crown *n. Rom. Antiq.* a crown or garland given to the soldier who was first to scale the wall of a besieged town.

mur·der /mórdɔr/ *n. & v.* ● *n.* **1** the unlawful premeditated killing of a human being by another (cf. MANSLAUGHTER). **2** *colloq.* an unpleasant, troublesome, or dangerous state of affairs (*it was murder here on Saturday*). ● *v.tr.* **1** kill (a human being) unlawfully, esp. wickedly or inhumanly. **2** *Law* kill (a human being) with a premeditated motive. **3** *colloq.* utterly defeat or spoil by a bad performance, mispronunciation, etc. (*murdered the soliloquy in the second act*). □ **cry bloody murder** *sl.* make an extravagant outcry. **get away with murder** *colloq.* do whatever one wishes and escape punishment. **murder will out** murder cannot remain undetected. □□ **mur·der·er** *n.* **mur·der·ess** *n.* [OE *morthor* & OF *murdre* f. Gmc]

mur·der·ous /mórdɔrɔs/ *adj.* **1** (of a person, weapon, action, etc.) capable of, intending, or involving murder or great harm. **2** *colloq.* extremely troublesome, unpleasant, or dangerous. □□ **mur·der·ous·ly** *adv.* **mur·der·ous·ness** *n.*

mure /myoor/ *v.tr. archaic* **1** immure. **2** (foll. by *up*) wall up or shut up in an enclosed space. [ME f. OF *murer* f. *mur*: see MURAGE]

mu·rex /myóōreks/ *n.* (*pl.* **mu·ri·ces** /–riseez/ or **mu·rex·es**) any gastropod mollusk of the genus *Murex*, yielding a purple dye. [L]

mu·rine /myóōrīn/ *adj.* of or like a mouse or mice. [L *murinus* f. *mus muris* mouse]

murk /mɔrk/ *n. & adj.* (also **mirk**) ● *n.* **1** darkness, poor visibility. **2** air obscured by fog, etc. ● *adj. archaic* (of night, day, place, etc.) = MURKY. [prob. f. Scand.: cf. ON *myrkr*]

murk·y /mórkee/ *adj.* (also **mirk·y**) (**·i·er**, **·i·est**) **1** dark, gloomy. **2** (of darkness) thick, dirty. **3** suspiciously obscure (*murky past*). □□ **murk·i·ly** *adv.* **murk·i·ness** *n.*

mur·mur /mórmɔr/ *n. & v.* ● *n.* **1** a subdued continuous sound, as made by waves, a brook, etc. **2** a softly spoken or nearly inarticulate utterance. **3** *Med.* a recurring sound heard in the auscultation of the heart and usu. indicating abnormality. **4** a subdued expression of discontent. ● *v.* **1** *intr.* make a subdued continuous sound. **2** *tr.* utter (words) in a low voice. **3** *intr.* (usu. foll. by *at*, *against*) complain in low tones, grumble. □□ **mur·mur·er** *n.* **mur·mur·ing·ly** *adv.* **mur·mur·ous** *adj.* [ME f. OF *murmurer* f. L *murmurare*: cf. Gk *mormurō* (of water) roar, Skr. *marmaras* noisy]

mur·phy /mórfee/ *n.* (*pl.* **·phies**) *sl.* a potato. [Ir. surname]

Mur·phy's Law /mórfeez/ *n. joc.* any of various maxims about the perverseness of things.

mur·rain /mórin/ *n.* **1** an infectious disease of cattle, carried by parasites. **2** *archaic* a plague, esp. the potato blight during the Irish famine in the mid-19th c. [ME f. AF *moryn*, OF *morine* f. *morir* f. L *mori* die]

mur·rey /mɔree/ *n. & adj. archaic* ● *n.* the color of a mulberry; a deep red or purple. ● *adj.* of this color. [ME f. OF *moré* f. med.L *moratus* f. *morum* mulberry]

mur·ther /mórthɔr/ *archaic* var. of MURDER.

Mus.B. *abbr.* (also **Mus. Bac.**) Bachelor of Music. [L *Musicae Baccalaureus*]

mus·ca·del var. of MUSCATEL.

Mus·ca·det /múskɔday/ *n.* **1** a white wine from the Loire region of France. **2** a variety of grape from which the wine is made. [*Muscadet* variety of grape]

mus·ca·dine /múskɔdin, –dīn/ *n.* a variety of grape with a musk flavor, used chiefly in wine making. [perh. Engl. form f. Prov. MUSCAT]

mus·ca·rine /múskɔrin/ *n.* a poisonous alkaloid from the fungus *Amanita muscaria*. [L *muscarius* f. *musca* fly]

mus·cat /múskat, –kɔt/ *n.* **1** = MUSCATEL. **2** a muscadine. [F f. Prov. *muscat muscade* (adj.) f. *musc* MUSK]

mus·ca·tel /múskɔtél/ *n.* (also **mus·ca·del** /–dél/) **1** a sweet fortified white wine made from muscadines. **2** a raisin from a muscadine grape. [ME f. OF f. Prov. dimin. of *muscat*: see MUSCAT]

mus·cle /músɔl/ *n. & v.* ● *n.* **1** a fibrous tissue with the ability to contract, producing movement in or maintaining the position of an animal body. **2** the part of an animal body that is composed of muscles. **3** physical power or strength. ● *v.intr.* (usu. foll. by *in*) *colloq.* force oneself on others; intrude by forceful means. □ **not move a muscle** be completely motionless. □□ **mus·cled** *adj.* (usu. in *comb.*). **mus·cle·less** *adj.* **mus·cly** *adj.* [F f. L *musculus* dimin. of *mus* mouse, from the fancied mouselike form of some muscles]

mus·cle-bound *adj.* having well-developed or overdeveloped muscles.

mus·cle man *n.* a man with highly developed muscles, esp. one employed as an intimidator.

mus·col·o·gy /muskólɔjee/ *n.* the study of mosses. □□ **mus·col·o·gist** *n.* [mod.L *muscologia* f. L *muscus* moss]

mus·co·va·do /múskɔvaádō/ *n.* (*pl.* **·dos**) an unrefined sugar made from the juice of sugar cane by evaporation and draining off the molasses. [Sp. *mascabado* (sugar) of the lowest quality]

Mus·co·vite /múskɔvīt/ *n. & adj.* ● *n.* **1** a native or citizen of Moscow. **2** *archaic* a Russian. ● *adj.* **1** of or relating to Moscow. **2** *archaic* of or relating to Russia. [mod.L *Muscovita* f. *Muscovia* = MUSCOVY]

mus·co·vite /múskɔvīt/ *n.* a silver-gray form of mica with a sheetlike crystalline structure that is used in the manufacture of electrical equipment, etc. [obs. MUSCOVY *glass* (in the same sense) + –ITE¹]

Mus·co·vy /múskɔvee/ *n. archaic* Russia. [obs. F *Muscovie* f. mod.L *Moscovia* f. Russ. *Moskva* Moscow]

Mus·co·vy duck *n.* a tropical American duck, *Cairina moschata*, having a small crest and red markings on its head.

mus·cu·lar /múskyɔlɔr/ *adj.* **1** of or affecting the muscles. **2** having well-developed muscles. □□ **mus·cu·lar·i·ty** /–láritee/ *n.* **mus·cu·lar·ly** *adv.* [earlier *musculous* (as MUSCLE)]

mus·cu·lar Chris·ti·an·i·ty *n.* a Christian life of cheerful physical activity as described in the writings of Charles Kingsley.

mus·cu·lar dys·tro·phy *n.* a hereditary progressive weakening and wasting of the muscles.

mus·cu·lar rheu·ma·tism *n.* = MYALGIA.

mus·cu·lar stomach *n.* see STOMACH.

mus·cu·la·ture /múskyɔlɔchɔr/ *n.* the muscular system of a body or organ. [F f. L (as MUSCLE)]

mus·cu·lo·skel·e·tal /məskyəlōskélətʹl/ *adj.* of or involving both the muscles and the skeleton.

Mus.D. *abbr.* (also **Mus. Doc.**) Doctor of Music. [L *Musicae Doctor*]

muse[1] /myōz/ *n.* **1** (as **the Muses**) (in Greek and Roman mythology) nine goddesses, the daughters of Zeus and Mnemosyne, who inspire poetry, music, drama, etc. **2** (usu. prec. by *the*) **a** a poet's inspiring goddess. **b** a poet's genius. [ME f. OF *muse* or L *musa* f. Gk *mousa*]

muse[2] /myōz/ *v. & n.* • *v. literary* **1** *intr.* **a** (usu. foll. by *on, upon*) ponder, reflect. **b** (usu. foll. by *on*) gaze meditatively (on a scene, etc.). **2** *tr.* say meditatively. • *n. archaic* a fit of abstraction. [ME f. OF *muser* to waste time f. Rmc perh. f. med.L *musum* muzzle]

mu·sette /myōzét/ *n.* **1 a** a kind of small bagpipe with bellows, common in the French court in the 17th–18th c. **b** a tune imitating the sound of this. **2** a small oboelike double-reed instrument in 19th-c. France. **3** a popular dance in the courts of Louis XIV and XV. **4** a small knapsack. [ME f. OF, dimin. of *muse* bagpipe]

mu·se·um /myōzéeəm/ *n.* a building used for storing and exhibiting objects of historical, scientific, or cultural interest. □ **museum piece 1** a specimen of art, etc., fit for a museum. **2** *often derog.* an old-fashioned or quaint person or object. □□ **mu·se·ol·o·gy** /myōozeeóləjee/ *n.* [L f. Gk *mouseion* seat of the Muses: see MUSE[1]]

mush[1] /mush/ *n.* **1** soft pulp. **2** feeble sentimentality. **3** a boiled cornmeal dish. **4** *sl.* the mouth; the face. □□ **mush·y** *adj.* (**mush·i·er, mush·i·est**). **mush·i·ly** *adv.* **mush·i·ness** *n.* [app. var. of MASH]

mush[2] /mush/ *v. & n.* • *v.intr.* **1** (in *imper.*) used as a command to dogs pulling a sled to urge them forward. **2** go on a journey across snow with a dogsled. • *n.* a journey across snow with a dogsled. [prob. corrupt. f. F *marchons* imper. of *marcher* advance]

mush·room /múshrŏŏm, –rŏŏm/ *n. & v.* • *n.* **1** the usu. edible, spore-producing body of various fungi, esp. *Agaricus campestris*, with a stem and domed cap, proverbial for its rapid growth. **2** the pinkish-brown color of this. **3** any item resembling a mushroom in shape (*darning mushroom*). **4** (usu. *attrib.*) something that appears or develops suddenly or is ephemeral; an upstart. • *v.intr.* **1** appear or develop rapidly. **2** expand and flatten like a mushroom cap. **3** gather mushrooms. □□ **mush·room·y** *adj.* [ME f. OF *mousseron* f. LL *mussirio –onis*]

mush·room cloud *n.* a cloud suggesting the shape of a mushroom, esp. from a nuclear explosion.

mush·room growth *n.* **1** a sudden development or expansion. **2** anything undergoing this.

mu·sic /myōzik/ *n.* **1** the art of combining vocal or instrumental sounds (or both) to produce beauty of form, harmony, and expression of emotion. **2** the sounds so produced. **3** musical compositions. **4** the written or printed score of a musical composition. **5** certain pleasant sounds, e.g., birdsong, the sound of a stream, etc. □ **music to one's ears** something very pleasant to hear. [ME f. OF *musique* f. L *musica* f. Gk *mousikē* (*tekhnē* art) of the Muses (*mousa* Muse: see MUSE[1])]

mu·si·cal /myōzikəl/ *adj. & n.* • *adj.* **1** of or relating to music. **2** (of sounds, a voice, etc.) melodious, harmonious. **3** fond of or skilled in music (*the musical one of the family*). **4** set to or accompanied by music. • *n.* a movie or drama that features songs. □□ **mu·si·cal·i·ty** /–kálitee/ *n.* **mu·si·cal·ize** *v.tr.* **mu·si·cal·ly** *adv.* **mu·si·cal·ness** *n.* [ME f. OF f. med.L *musicalis* f. L *musica*: see MUSIC]

mu·si·cal box *n. Brit.* = MUSIC BOX.

mu·si·cal bumps *n. Brit.* a game similar to musical chairs, with players sitting on the floor and the one left standing eliminated.

mu·si·cal chairs *n.* **1** a party game in which the players compete in successive rounds for a decreasing number of chairs. **2** a series of changes or political maneuvering, etc., after the manner of the game.

mu·si·cale /myōzikál/ *n.* a musical party. [F fem. adj. (as MUSICAL)]

mu·sic box *n.* a mechanical instrument playing a tune by causing a toothed cylinder to strike a comblike metal plate within a box.

mu·sic cen·ter *n. Brit.* = ENTERTAINMENT CENTER.

mu·sic dra·ma *n.* Wagnerian-type opera without formal arias, etc., and governed by dramatic considerations.

mu·sic hall *n. Brit.* a theater featuring variety entertainment, esp. singing, dancing, and novelty acts.

mu·si·cian /myōzíshən/ *n.* a person who plays a musical instrument, esp. professionally, or is otherwise musically gifted. □□ **mu·si·cian·ly** *adj.* **mu·si·cian·ship** *n.* [ME f. OF *musicien* f. *musique* (as MUSIC, –ICIAN)]

mu·sic of the spheres *n.* see SPHERE.

mu·sic pa·per *n.* paper printed with staves for writing music.

mu·sic stand *n.* a rest or frame on which sheet music or a score is supported.

mu·sic the·a·ter *n.* in late 20th-c. music, the combination of elements from music and drama in new forms distinct from traditional opera, esp. as designed for small groups of performers.

mu·si·col·o·gy /myōzikóləjee/ *n.* the study of music other than that directed to proficiency in performance or composition. □□ **mu·si·col·o·gist** *n.* **mu·si·co·log·i·cal** /–kəlójikəl/ *adj.* [F *musicologie* or MUSIC + –LOGY]

mu·sique con·crète /myzéek kawNkrét/ *n.* music constructed by mixing recorded sounds. [F]

musk /musk/ *n.* **1** a strong-smelling reddish-brown substance produced by a gland in the male musk deer and used as an ingredient in perfumes. **2** the plant, *Mimulus moschatus*, with pale-green ovate leaves and yellow flowers (orig. with a smell of musk that is no longer perceptible in modern varieties). □□ **musk·y** *adj.* (**musk·i·er, musk·i·est**). **musk·i·ness** *n.* [ME f. LL *muscus* f. Pers. *mušk*, perh. f. Skr. *muṣka* scrotum (from the shape of the musk deer's gland)]

musk deer *n.* any small Asian deer of the genus *Moschus*, having no antlers and in the male having long protruding canine teeth. musk duck

musk duck *n.* the Australian duck *Biziura lobata*, having a musky smell.

musk·keg /múskeg/ *n.* a level swamp or bog in Canada. [Cree]

mus·kel·lunge /múskəlunj/ *n.* (also **mas·ki·nonge**) a large N. American pike, *Esox masquinongy*, found esp. in the Great Lakes. [ult. f. Ojibwa 'great fish']

mus·ket /múskit/ *n. hist.* an infantryman's (esp. smooth-bored) light gun, often supported on the shoulder. [F *mousquet* f. It. *moschetto* crossbow bolt f. *mosca* fly]

mus·ket·eer /múskitéer/ *n. hist.* a soldier armed with a musket.

mus·ket·ry /múskitree/ *n.* **1** muskets, or soldiers armed with muskets, referred to collectively. **2** the knowledge of handling muskets.

mus·ket-shot *n.* **1** a shot fired from a musket. **2** the range of this shot.

musk·mel·on /múskmelən/ *n.* the common yellow or green melon, *Cucumis melo*, usu. with a raised network of markings on the skin.

musk ox *n.* a large goat-antelope, *Ovibos moschatus*, native to N. America, with a thick shaggy coat and small curved horns.

musk·rat /múskrat/ *n.* **1** a large aquatic rodent, *Ondatra zibethica*, native to N. America, having a musky smell. Also called **musquash**. **2** the fur of this.

musk rose *n.* a rambling rose, *Rosa moschata*, with large white flowers smelling of musk.

musk this·tle *n.* a nodding thistle, *Carduus nutans*, whose flowers have a musky fragrance.

Mus·lim /múzlim, mŏŏz–, mŏŏs–/ *n. & adj.* (also **Mos·lem** /mózləm/) • *n.* a follower of the Islamic religion. • *adj.* of or relating to the Muslims or their religion. [Arab. *muslim*, part. of *aslama*: see IsLAM]

▶**Muslim** is the preferred term for 'follower of Islam,' although *Moslem* is also widely used. Avoid 'Mohammedan.'

mus·lin /múzlin/ *n.* **1** a fine delicately woven cotton fabric. **2** a cotton cloth in plain weave. □□ **mus·lined** *adj.* [F *mousseline* f. It. *mussolina* f. *Mussolo* Mosul in Iraq, where it was made]

mus·mon /múzmən/ *n. Zool.* = MOUFLON. [L *musimo* f. Gk *mousmōn*]

mus·quash /múskwosh/ *n.* = MUSKRAT. [Algonquian]

muss /mus/ *v. & n. colloq.* • *v.tr.* (often foll. by *up*) disarrange; throw into disorder. • *n.* a state of confusion; untidiness, mess. □□ **muss·y** *adj.* [app. var. of MESS]

mus·sel /músəl/ *n.* **1** any bivalve mollusk of the genus *Mytilus*, living in seawater and often used for food. **2** any similar freshwater mollusk of the genus *Margaritifer* or *Anodonta*, forming pearls. [ME f. OE *mus(c)le* & MLG *mussel*, ult. rel. to L *musculus* (as MUSCLE)]

Mus·sul·man /músəlmən/ *n. & adj. archaic* • *n.* (*pl.* **·mans** or **·men**) a Muslim. • *adj.* of or concerning Muslims. [Pers. *musulmān* orig. adj. f. *muslim* (as MUSLIM)]

must[1] /must/ *v. & n.* • *v.aux.* (*3rd sing.* present **must**; *past* **had to** or in indirect speech **must**) (foll. by infin., or *absol.*) **1 a** be obliged to (*you must go to school; must we leave now?; said he must go; I must away*). **b** in ironic questions (*must you slam the door?*). **2** be certain to (*we must win in the end; you must be her sister; he must be mad; they must have left by now; seemed as if the roof must blow off*). **3** ought to (*we must see what can be done; it must be said that*). **4** expressing insistence (*I must ask you to leave*). **5** (foll. by *not* + infin.) **a** not be permitted to, be forbidden to (*you must not smoke*). **b** ought not; need not (*you mustn't think he's angry; you must not worry*). **c** expressing insistence that something should not be done (*they must not be told*). **6** (as past or historic present) expressing the perversity of destiny (*what must I but break my leg*). • *n. colloq.* a thing that cannot or should not be overlooked or missed (*if you go to London, St. Paul's is a must*). □ **I must say** often *iron.* I cannot refrain from saying (*I must say he made a good attempt; a fine way to behave, I must say*). **must needs** see NEEDS. [OE *mōste* past of *mōt* may]

▶The negative (i.e., lack of obligation) is expressed by *not have to* or *need not*; *must not* denotes positive forbidding, as in *you must not smoke*.

must[2] /must/ *n.* grape juice before fermentation is complete. [OE f. L *mustum* neut. of *mustus* new]

must[3] /must/ *n.* mustiness, mold. [back-form. f. MUSTY]

must[4] var. of MUSTH.

mus•tache /mústash, məstásh/ n. (also **mous•tache**) **1** hair left to grow on a man's upper lip. **2** a similar growth around the mouth of some animals. □□ **mus•tached** adj. [F f. It. mostaccio f. Gk mustax –akos]

mus•tache cup n. a cup with a partial cover to protect the mustache when drinking.

mus•ta•chio /məstaásheeō, –stásheeō, –shō/ n. (pl. **•chios**) (often in pl.) archaic a mustache. □□ **mus•ta•chioed** adj. [Sp. mostacho & It. mostaccio (as MUSTACHE)]

mus•tang /mústang/ n. a small wild horse native to Mexico and California. [Sp. mestengo f. mesta company of graziers, & Sp. mostrenco]

mus•tang grape n. a grape from the wild vine Vitis candicans, of the southern US, used for making wine.

mus•tard /mústərd/ n. **1 a** any of various plants of the genus Brassica with slender pods and yellow flowers, esp. B. nigra. **b** any of various plants of the genus Sinapis, esp. S. alba, eaten at the seedling stage, often with cress. **2** the seeds of these which are crushed, made into a paste, and used as a spicy condiment. **3** the brownish-yellow color of this condiment. **4** sl. a thing that adds piquancy or zest. □ **cut the mustard** sl. be able to reach an expected level of performance. [ME f. OF mo(u)starde: orig. the condiment as prepared with MUST²]

mus•tard gas n. a colorless oily liquid whose vapor is a powerful irritant and vesicant.

mus•tard plas•ter n. a poultice made with mustard.

mus•tard seed n. **1** the seed of the mustard plant. **2** a small thing capable of great development (Matt. 13: 31).

mus•ter /mústər/ v. & n. **1** tr. collect (orig. soldiers) for inspection, to check numbers, etc. **2** tr. & intr. collect, gather together. **3** tr. Austral. round up (livestock). •n. **1** the assembly of persons for inspection. **2** an assembly, a collection. **3** Austral. a rounding up of livestock. **4** Austral. sl. the number of people attending (a meeting, etc.) (had a good muster). **5** = MUSTER ROLL. □ **muster in** enroll (recruits). **muster out** discharge (soldiers, etc.). **muster up** collect or summon (courage, strength, etc.). **pass muster** be accepted as adequate. □□ **mus•ter•er** n. (in sense 3 of n. & v.). [ME f. OF mo(u)stre ult. f. L monstrare show]

mus•ter book n. a book for registering military personnel.

mus•ter roll n. an official list of officers and men in a regiment or ship's company.

musth /must/ adj. & n. (also **must**) •adj. (of a male elephant or camel) in a state of frenzy. •n. this state. [Urdu f. Pers. mast intoxicated]

must•n't /músənt/ contr. must not.

mus•ty /mústee/ adj. (**mus•ti•er**, **mus•ti•est**) **1** moldy. **2** of a moldy or stale smell or taste. **3** stale, antiquated (musty old books). □□ **mus•ti•ly** adv. **mus•ti•ness** n. [perh. alt. f. moisty (MOIST) by assoc. with MUST²]

mu•ta•ble /myoٓotəbəl/ adj. literary **1** liable to change. **2** fickle. □□ **mu•ta•bil•i•ty** /–bílitee/ n. [L mutabilis f. mutare change]

mu•ta•gen /myoٓotəjən/ n. an agent promoting mutation, e.g., radiation. □□ **mu•ta•gen•ic** /–jénik/ adj. **mu•ta•gen•e•sis** /–jénisis/ n. [MUTATION + –GEN]

mu•tant /myoٓot'nt/ adj. & n. •adj. resulting from mutation. •n. a mutant form. [L mutant- part. f. mutare change]

mu•tate /myoٓotáyt/ v.intr. & tr. undergo or cause to undergo mutation. [back-form. f. MUTATION]

mu•ta•tion /myoٓotáyshən/ n. **1** the process or an instance of change or alteration. **2** a genetic change which, when transmitted to offspring, gives rise to heritable variations. **3** a mutant. **4 a** an umlaut. **b** (in a Celtic language) a change of a consonant, etc., determined by a preceding word. □□ **mu•ta•tion•al** adj. **mu•ta•tion•al•ly** adv. [L mutatio f. L mutatio f. mutare change]

mu•ta•tis mu•tan•dis /moٓotaátis moٓotaándis, myoٓo–/ adv. (in comparing cases) making the necessary alterations. [L]

mutch /much/ n. Brit. dial. a woman's or child's linen cap. [ME f. MDu. mutse MHG mütze f. med.L almucia AMICE²]

mute /myoٓot/ adj., n., & v. •adj. **1** silent, refraining from or temporarily bereft of speech. **2** not emitting articulate sound. **3** (of a person or animal) dumb; speechless. **4** not expressed in speech (mute protest). **5 a** (of a letter) not pronounced. **b** (of a consonant) plosive. **6** (of hounds) not giving tongue. •n. **1** a dumb person (a deaf mute). **2** Mus. **a** a clamp for damping the resonance of the strings of a violin, etc. **b** a pad or cone for damping the sound of a wind instrument. **3** an unsounded consonant. **4** an actor whose part is in a dumb show. **5** a hired mourner. •v.tr. **1** deaden, muffle, or soften the sound of (a thing, esp. a musical instrument). **2** alleviate (a tone down, make less intense. **b** (as **muted** adj.) (of colors, etc.) subdued (a muted green). □□ **mute•ly** adv. **mute•ness** n. [ME f. OF muet, dimin. of mu f. L mutus, assim. to L]

mute but•ton n. a device on a telephone, etc., to temporarily prevent the caller from hearing what is being said at the receiver's end.

mute swan n. the common white swan, Cygnus olor.

mu•ti•late /myoٓot'layt/ v.tr. **1 a** deprive (a person or animal) of a limb or organ. **b** destroy the use of (a limb or organ). **2** render (a book, etc.) imperfect by excision or some act of destruction. □□ **mu•ti•la•tion** /–láyshən/ n. **mu•ti•la•tive** /–láytiv/ adj. **mu•ti•la•tor** n. [L mutilare f. mutilus maimed]

mu•ti•neer /myoٓot'neer/ n. a person who mutinies. [F mutinier f. mutin rebellious f. muete movement ult. f. L movēre move]

mu•ti•nous /myoٓot'nəs/ adj. rebellious; tending to mutiny. □□ **mu•ti•nous•ly** adv. [obs. mutine rebellion f. F mutin: see MUTINEER]

mu•ti•ny /myoٓot'nee/ n. & v. •n. (pl. **•nies**) an open revolt against constituted authority, esp. by soldiers or sailors against their officers. •v.intr. (**•nies**, **•nied**) (often foll. by against) revolt; engage in mutiny. [obs. mutine (as MUTINOUS)]

mut•ism /myoٓotizəm/ n. muteness; silence; dumbness. [F mutisme f. L (as MUTE)]

mu•ton /myoٓoton/ n. Biol. the smallest element of genetic material capable of giving rise to a mutant individual.

mutt /mut/ n. **1** a dog. **2** sl. an ignorant, stupid, or blundering person. [abbr. of muttonhead]

mut•ter /mútər/ v. & n. •v. **1** intr. speak low in a barely audible manner. **2** intr. (often foll. by against, at) murmur or grumble about. **3** tr. utter (words, etc.) in a low tone. **4** tr. say in secret. •n. **1** muttered words or sounds. **2** muttering. □□ **mut•ter•er** n. **mut•ter•ing•ly** adv. [ME, rel. to MUTE]

mut•ton /mút'n/ n. **1** the flesh of sheep used for food. **2** joc. a sheep. □ **mutton dressed as lamb** Brit. colloq. a usu. middle-aged or elderly woman dressed or made up to appear younger. □□ **mut•ton•y** adj. [ME f. OF moton f. med.L multo –onis prob. f. Gaulish]

mut•ton bird n. Austral. **1** any bird of the genus Puffinus, esp. the short-tailed shearwater, P. tenuirostris. **2** any of various petrels.

mut•ton-chops /mút'nchops/ n. side whiskers trimmed narrow at the temples and broad along the cheeks.

mu•tu•al /myoٓochoٓoəl/ adj. **1** (of feelings, actions, etc.) experienced or done by each of two or more parties with reference to the other or others (mutual affection). **2** colloq. disp. common to two or more persons (a mutual friend; a mutual interest). **3** standing in (a specified) relation to each other (mutual well-wishers; mutual beneficiaries). □□ **mu•tu•al•i•ty** /–choٓo-álitee, –tyoٓo-álitee/ n. **mu•tu•al•ly** adv. [ME f. OF mutuel f. L mutuus mutual, borrowed, rel. to mutare change]

▶ Traditionalists consider using **mutual** to mean 'common to two or more people,' as in a mutual friend; a mutual interest, to be incorrect, holding that the sense of reciprocity is necessary: mutual respect; mutual need. However, both senses are well established and acceptable in standard English.

SYNONYM TIP mutual

COMMON, INTERCHANGEABLE, JOINT, RECIPROCAL, SHARED. In the 15th century, **mutual** was synonymous with **reciprocal**; both adjectives suggested—and still do—a relationship between two parties in which the same thing is given and taken on both sides (mutual admiration, a mutual misunderstanding). Since the 16th century, however, it has also been used to mean **shared** or having in common (Their mutual objective was peace). Nowadays, reciprocal is more commonly used in official or technical contexts (a reciprocal lowering of taxes by both states, a reciprocal trade agreement), while mutual is used to describe any similarity of interests, opinions, or feelings, even if the relationship is not a reciprocal one (a mutual interest in bird watching). **Common** is a much vaguer term, used to describe anything that is shared by others or by all members of a group (a common language), while joint emphasizes the possession of something by two people (a joint business venture). Shared implies more emotional warmth than joint, mutual, or reciprocal (a shared passion for classical music); it is also used to describe something that is actually divided up and used by two or more people (a shared meal). Unlike all of the above, interchangeable applies to elements that can be used in place of one another (interchangeable parts, interchangeable terms); it has more to do with function and less to do with human relationships.

---

mu•tu•al fund n. an investment program funded by shareholders that trades in diversified holdings and is professionally managed.

mu•tu•al in•duct•ance n. the property of an electric circuit that causes an electromotive force to be generated in it by change in the current flowing through a magnetically linked circuit.

mu•tu•al in•duc•tion n. the production of an electromotive force between adjacent circuits that are magnetically linked.

mu•tu•al in•sur•ance n. insurance in which some or all of the profits are divided among the policyholders.

mu•tu•al•ism /myoٓochoٓoəlizəm/ n. **1** the doctrine that mutual dependence is necessary to social well-being. **2** mutually beneficial symbiosis. □□ **mu•tu•al•ist** n. & adj. **mu•tu•al•is•tic** /–lístik/ adj. **mu•tu•al•is•ti•cal•ly** /–lístiklee/ adv.

mu•tu•el /myoٓochoٓoəl/ n. a totalizator; a pari-mutuel. [abbr. of PARI-MUTUEL]

mu·tule /myṓ́ochōōl/ n. Archit. a block derived from the ends of wooden beams projecting under a Doric cornice. [F f. L mutulus]

muu·muu /mṓ́omōo/ n. a woman's loose brightly colored dress. [Hawaiian]

Mu·zak /myṓ́ozak/ n. 1 Trademark a system of music transmission for playing in public places. 2 (**muzak**) recorded light background music. [alt. f. MUSIC]

mu·zhik /mṓózhik/ n. (also **moujik**) hist. a Russian peasant. [Russ. muzhik]

muz·zle /múzəl/ n. & v. • n. 1 the projecting part of an animal's face, including the nose and mouth. 2 a guard, usu. made of straps or wire, fitted over an animal's nose and mouth to stop it biting or feeding. 3 the open end of a firearm. • v.tr. 1 put a muzzle on (an animal, etc.). 2 impose silence upon. 3 Naut. take in (a sail). □□ **muz·zler** n. [ME f. OF musel ult. f. med.L musum: cf. MUSE²]

muz·zle ve·loc·i·ty n. the velocity with which a projectile leaves the muzzle of a gun.

muz·zy /múzee/ adj. (**muz·zi·er**, **muz·zi·est**) 1 a mentally hazy; dull, spiritless. b esp. Brit. stupid from drinking alcohol. 2 blurred, indistinct. □□ **muz·zi·ly** adv. **muz·zi·ness** n. [18th c.: orig. unkn.]

MV abbr. 1 megavolt(s). 2 motor vessel. 3 muzzle velocity.

MVP abbr. Sports most valuable player.

MW abbr. 1 megawatt(s). 2 medium wave.

mW abbr. milliwatt(s).

Mx. abbr. maxwell(s).

my /mī/ poss.pron. (attrib.) 1 of or belonging to me or myself (my house; my own business). 2 as a form of address in affectionate, sympathetic, jocular, or patronizing contexts (my dear boy). 3 in various expressions of surprise (my God!; oh my!). 4 colloq. indicating the speaker's husband, wife, child, etc. (my Johnny's ill again). □ **my Lady** (or **Lord**) the form of address to certain titled persons. [ME mī, reduced f. mīn MINE¹]

my- comb. form var. of MYO-.

my·al·gi·a /mīáljə/ n. a pain in a muscle or group of muscles. □□ **my·al·gic** adj. [mod.L f. Gk mus muscle]

my·al·ism /mīəlizəm/ n. a kind of sorcery akin to obeah, practiced esp. in the W. Indies. [myal, prob. of W.Afr. orig.]

my·all /mīəl/ n. 1 a any tree of the genus Acacia, esp. A. pendula, native to Australia. b the hard scented wood of this, used for fences and tobacco pipes. 2 an Aboriginal living in a traditional way. [Aboriginal maiāl]

my·as·the·ni·a /mīəs-theeneeə/ n. a condition causing abnormal weakness of certain muscles. [mod.L f. Gk mus muscle: cf. ASTHENIA]

my·as·the·ni·a gra·vis n. a disease characterized by fatigue and muscle weakness, caused by an autoimmune attack on acetylcholine receptors.

my·ce·li·um /mīséeleeəm/ n. (pl. **my·ce·li·a** /–leeə/) the vegetative part of a fungus, consisting of microscopic threadlike hyphae. □□ **my·ce·li·al** adj. [mod.L f. Gk mukēs mushroom, after EPITHELIUM]

My·ce·nae·an /mīsineeən/ adj. & n. • adj. Archaeol. of or relating to the late Bronze Age civilization in Greece (c.1580–1100 BC), depicted in the Homeric poems and represented by finds at Mycenae and elsewhere. • n. an inhabitant of Mycenae or the Mycenaean world. [L Mycenaeus]

-mycin /mísin/ comb. form used to form the names of antibiotic compounds derived from fungi. [Gk mukēs fungus + –IN]

my·col·o·gy /mīkóləjee/ n. 1 the study of fungi. 2 the fungi of a particular region. □□ **my·co·log·i·cal** /–kəlójikəl/ adj. **my·co·log·i·cal·ly** /–kəlójiklee/ adv. **my·col·o·gist** n. [Gk mukēs mushroom + –LOGY]

my·cor·rhi·za /mīkərízə/ n. (pl. **my·cor·rhi·zae** /–zee/) a symbiotic association of a fungus and the roots of a plant. □□ **my·cor·rhi·zal** adj. [mod.L f. Gk mukēs mushroom + rhiza root]

my·co·sis /mīkósis/ n. any disease caused by a fungus, e.g., ringworm. □□ **my·cot·ic** /–kótik/ adj. [Gk mukēs mushroom + –OSIS]

my·co·tox·in /mīkətóksin/ n. any toxic substance produced by a fungus.

my·cot·ro·phy /mīkótrəfee/ n. the condition of a plant which has mycorrhizae and is perhaps helped to assimilate nutrients as a result. [G Mykotrophie f. Gk mukēs mushroom + trophē nourishment]

my·dri·a·sis /midríəsis/ n. excessive dilation of the pupil of the eye. [L f. Gk mudriasis]

my·e·lin /mī-ilin/ n. a white substance which forms a sheath around certain nerve fibers. □□ **my·e·li·na·tion** n. [Gk muelos marrow + –IN]

my·e·li·tis /mī-ilítis/ n. inflammation of the spinal cord. [mod.L f. Gk muelos marrow]

my·e·loid /mí-iloyd/ adj. of or relating to bone marrow or the spinal cord. [Gk muelos marrow]

my·e·lo·ma /mī-ilómə/ n. (pl. **my·e·lo·mas** or **my·e·lo·ma·ta** /–mətə/) a malignant tumor of the bone marrow. [mod.L, as MYELITIS +–OMA]

My·lar /mílaar/ n. Trademark an extremely strong polyester film made in thin sheets and used for recording tapes, insulation, etc.

my·lo·don /mílədon/ n. an extinct gigantic ground sloth of the ge-

nus Mylodon, with cylindrical teeth and found in deposits formed during the ice age of the Pleistocene epoch in South America. [mod.L f. Gk mulē mill, molar + odous odontos tooth]

my·nah /mínə/ n. (also **my·na**, **mi·na**) any of various SE Asian starlings, esp. those such as Gracula religiosa, which are able to mimic the human voice. [Hindi mainā]

myo- /mío/ comb. form (also **my-** before a vowel) muscle. [Gk mus muos muscle]

mynah

my·o·car·di·um /míokaárdeeəm/ n. (pl. **my·o·car·di·a** /–deeə/) the muscular tissue of the heart. □□ **my·o·car·di·ac** adj. **my·o·car·di·al** adj. [MYO- + Gk kardia heart]

my·o·car·di·al in·farc·tion n. a heart attack.

my·o·fi·bril /míofíbril/ n. any of the elongated contractile threads found in striated muscle cells.

my·o·gen·ic /míəjénik/ adj. originating in muscle tissue.

my·o·glo·bin /míəglóbin/ n. an oxygen-carrying protein containing iron and found in muscle cells.

my·ol·o·gy /mīóləjee/ n. the study of the structure and function of muscles.

my·ope /míop/ n. a myopic person. [F f. LL myops f. Gk muōps f. muō shut + ōps eye]

my·o·pi·a /míopeeə/ n. 1 nearsightedness. 2 lack of imagination or intellectual insight. □□ **my·op·ic** /míópik/ adj. **my·op·i·cal·ly** /míópiklee/ adv. [mod.L (as MYOPE)]

my·o·sis var. of MIOSIS.

my·o·so·tis /míəsótis/ n. (also **my·o·sote** /míəsōt/) any plant of the genus Myosotis with blue, pink, or white flowers, esp. a forget-me-not. [L f. Gk muosōtis f. mus muos mouse + ous ōtos ear]

my·o·to·ni·a /míətóneeə/ n. the inability to relax voluntary muscle after vigorous effort. □□ **my·o·ton·ic** /–tónik/ adj. [MYO- + Gk tonos tone]

myr·i·ad /míreeəd/ n. & adj. literary • n. 1 an indefinitely great number. 2 ten thousand. • adj. of an indefinitely great number. [LL mirias miriad- f. murias –ados f. murioi 10,000]

myr·i·a·pod /míreeəpód/ n. & adj. • n. any land-living arthropod of the group Myriapoda, with numerous leg-bearing segments, e.g., centipedes and millipedes. • adj. of or relating to this group. [mod.L Myriapoda (as MYRIAD, Gk pous podos foot)]

myr·mi·don /mármid'n, –don/ n. 1 a hired ruffian. 2 a base servant. [L Myrmidones (pl.) f. Gk Murmidones, warlike Thessalian people who went with Achilles to Troy]

my·rob·a·lan /miróbələn/ n. 1 (in full **myrobalan plum**) = CHERRY PLUM. 2 (in full **myrobalan nut**) the fruit of an Asian tree, Terminalia chebula, used in medicines, for tanning leather, and to produce inks and dyes. [F myrobolan or L myrobalanum f. Gk murobalanos f. muron unguent + balanos acorn]

myrrh¹ /mər/ n. a gum resin from several trees of the genus Commiphora used, esp. in the Near East, in perfumery, medicine, incense, etc. □□ **myrrh·ic** adj. **myrrh·y** adj. [OE myrra, myrre f. L myrr(h)a f. Gk murra, of Semitic orig.]

myrrh² /mər/ n. = SWEET CICELY. [L myrris f. Gk murris]

myr·ta·ceous /mərtáyshəs/ adj. of or relating to the plant family Myrtaceae, including myrtles.

myr·tle /mártəl/ n. 1 an evergreen shrub of the genus Myrtus with aromatic foliage and white flowers, esp. M. communis, bearing purple-black ovoid berries. 2 = PERIWINKLE¹. [ME f. med.L myrtilla, –us dimin. of L myrta, myrtus f. Gk murtos]

my·self /mīsélf/ pron. 1 emphat. form of I² or ME¹ (I saw it myself; I like to do it myself). 2 refl. form of ME¹ (I was angry with myself; able to dress myself; as bad as myself). 3 in my normal state of body and mind (I'm not myself today). 4 poet. = I². □ **by myself** see by oneself. **I myself** I for my part (I myself am doubtful). [ME¹ + SELF: my- partly after herself with her regarded as poss. pron.]

mys·te·ri·ous /mistéereeəs/ adj. 1 full of or wrapped in mystery. 2 (of a person) delighting in mystery. □□ **mys·te·ri·ous·ly** adv. **mys·te·ri·ous·ness** n. [F mystérieux f. mystère f. OF (as MYSTERY¹)]

mys·ter·y¹ /místəree/ n. (pl. **-ies**) 1 a secret, hidden, or inexplicable matter (the reason remains a mystery). 2 secrecy or obscurity (wrapped in mystery). 3 (attrib.) secret, undisclosed (mystery guest). 4 the practice of making a secret of (esp. unimportant) things (engaged in mystery and intrigue). 5 (in full **mystery story**) a fictional work dealing with a puzzling event, esp. a crime (a well-known mystery writer). 6 a a religious truth divinely revealed, esp. one beyond human reason. b RC Ch. a decade of the rosary. 7 (in pl.) a the secret religious rites of the ancient Greeks, Romans, etc. b archaic the Eucharist. □ **make a mystery of** treat as an impressive secret. [ME f. OF mistere or L mysterium f. Gk mustērion, rel. to MYSTIC]

mys•ter•y² /místəree/ *n.* (*pl.* **•ies**) *archaic* a handicraft or trade, esp. as referred to in indentures, etc. (*art and mystery*). [ME f. med.L *misterium* contr. of *ministerium* MINISTRY, assoc. with MYSTERY¹]

mys•ter•y play *n.* a miracle play.

mys•ter•y tour *n.* (also **mys•ter•y trip**) *Brit.* a pleasure excursion to an unspecified destination.

mys•tic /místik/ *n. & adj.* ● *n.* a person who seeks by contemplation and self-surrender to obtain unity or identity with or absorption into the Deity or the ultimate reality, or who believes in the spiritual apprehension of truths that are beyond the understanding. ● *adj.* **1** mysterious and awe-inspiring. **2** spiritually allegorical or symbolic. **3** occult, esoteric. **4** of hidden meaning. □□ **mys•ti•cism** /-tisizəm/ *n.*

> **WORD HISTORY** mystic
>
> Middle English (in the sense 'mystical meaning'): from Old French *mystique*, or via Latin from Greek *mustikos*, from *mustēs* 'initiated person' from *muein* 'close the eyes or lips,' also used to mean 'initiate,' as of initiations into ancient mystery religious. The current sense of the noun dates from the late 17th century.

mys•ti•cal /místikəl/ *adj.* of mystics or mysticism. □□ **mys•ti•cal•ly** *adv.*

mys•ti•fy /místifī/ *v.tr.* (**•fies**, **•fied**) **1** bewilder, confuse. **2** hoax, take advantage of the credulity of. **3** wrap up in mystery. □□ **mys•ti•fi•ca•tion** /-fikáyshən/ *n.* [F *mystifier* (irreg. formed as MYSTIC or MYSTERY¹)]

mys•tique /mistéek/ *n.* **1** an atmosphere of mystery and veneration attending some activity or person. **2** any skill or technique impressive or mystifying to the layman. [F f. OF (as MYSTIC)]

myth /mith/ *n.* **1** a traditional narrative usu. involving supernatural or imaginary persons and embodying popular ideas on natural or social phenomena, etc. **2** such narratives collectively. **3** a widely held but false notion. **4** a fictitious person, thing, or idea. **5** an allegory (*the Platonic myth*). □□ **myth•ic** *adj.* **myth•i•cal** *adj.* **myth•i•cal•ly** *adv.* [mod.L *mythus* f. LL *mythos* f. Gk *muthos*]

myth•i•cize /míthisīz/ *v.tr.* treat (a story, etc.) as a myth; interpret mythically. □□ **myth•i•cism** /-sizəm/ *n.* **myth•i•cist** /-sist/ *n.*

mytho- /míthō/ *comb. form* myth.

myth•o•gen•e•sis /míthōjénisis/ *n.* the production of myths.

myth•og•ra•pher /mithógrəfər/ *n.* a compiler of myths.

myth•og•ra•phy /mithógrəfee/ *n.* the representation of myths in plastic art.

myth•oi *pl.* of MYTHOS.

my•thol•o•gy /mithóləjee/ *n.* (*pl.* **•gies**) **1** a body of myths (*Greek mythology*). **2** the study of myths. □□ **my•thol•o•ger** *n.* **myth•o•log•ic** /-thəlójik/ *adj.* **myth•o•log•i•cal** /-thəlójikəl/ *adj.* **myth•o•log•i•cal•ly** /-thəlójiklee/ *adv.* **my•thol•o•gist** *n.* **my•thol•o•gize** *v.tr. & intr.* **my•thol•o•giz•er** *n.* [ME f. F *mythologie* or LL *mythologia* f. Gk *muthologia* (as MYTHO-, -LOGY)]

myth•o•ma•ni•a /míthōmáyneeə/ *n.* an abnormal tendency to exaggerate or tell lies. □□ **myth•o•ma•ni•ac** /-neeak/ *n. & adj.*

myth•o•poe•ia /míthōpeeə/ *n.* the making of myths. □□ **myth•o•poe•ic** *adj.* (also **myth•o•po•et•ic** /-pō-étik/).

myth•os /míthos/ *n.* (*pl.* **myth•oi** /-thoy/) *literary* a myth. [mod.L: see MYTH]

myx•e•de•ma /míksədeemə/ *n.* a syndrome caused by hypothyroidism, resulting in thickening of the skin, weight gain, mental dullness, loss of energy, and sensitivity to cold.

myxo- /míksō/ *comb. form* (also **myx-** before a vowel) mucus. [Gk *muxa* mucus]

myx•o•ma /míksōmə/ *n.* (*pl.* **myx•o•mas** or **myx•o•ma•ta** /-mətə/) a benign tumor of mucous or gelatinous tissue. □□ **myx•om•a•tous** /-sómətəs/ *adj.* [mod.L (as MYXO-, -OMA)]

myx•o•ma•to•sis /míksəmətósis/ *n.* an infectious usu. fatal viral disease in rabbits, causing swelling of the mucous membranes.

myx•o•my•cete /míksōmīseet/ *n.* any of a group of small acellular organisms inhabiting damp areas.

myx•o•vi•rus /míksōvīrəs/ *n.* any of a group of viruses including the influenza virus.

N

N¹ /en/ *n.* (also **n**) (*pl.* **Ns** or **N's**) **1** the fourteenth letter of the alphabet. **2** *Printing* en. **3** *Math.* (*n*) an indefinite number. □ **to the nth** (or **nth degree**) **1** *Math.* to any required power. **2** to any extent; to the utmost.

N² *abbr.* (also **N.**) **1** north; northern. **2** newton(s). **3** *Chess* knight. **4** New. **5** nuclear.

N³ *symb. Chem.* the element nitrogen.

n *abbr.* (also **n.**) **1** name. **2** nano-. **3** neuter. **4** noon. **5** note. **6** noun.

'n *conj.* (also **'n'**) *colloq.* and. [abbr.]

-n¹ *suffix* see –EN².

-n² *suffix* see –EN³.

Na *symb. Chem.* the element sodium.

na /nə/ *adv. Sc.* (in *comb.*; usu. with an auxiliary verb) = NOT (*I canna do it; they didna go*).

N.A. *abbr.* North America.

n/a *abbr.* **1** not applicable. **2** not available.

NAACP /endəbəláyseepee/ *abbr.* National Association for the Advancement of Colored People.

NAAFI /náfee/ *abbr. Brit.* **1** Navy, Army, and Air Force Institutes. **2** a canteen for servicemen run by the NAAFI.

nab /nab/ *v.tr.* (**nabbed**, **nab·bing**) *sl.* **1** arrest; catch in wrongdoing. **2** seize, grab. [17th c., also *napp*, as in KIDNAP: orig. unkn.]

na·bob /náybob/ *n.* **1** *hist.* a Muslim official or governor under the Mogul empire. **2** (formerly) a conspicuously wealthy person, esp. one returned from India with a fortune. **3** any wealthy person of influence. [Port. *nababo* or Sp. *nabab*, f. Urdu (as NAWAB)]

nac·a·rat /nákərat/ *n.* a bright orange-red color. [F, perh. f. Sp. & Port. *nacardo* (*nacar* NACRE)]

na·celle /nəsél/ *n.* **1** the outer casing of the engine of an aircraft. **2** the car of an airship. [F, f. LL *navicella* dimin. of L *navis* ship]

na·cho /naáchō/ *n.* (*pl.* **·chos**) (usu. in *pl.*) a tortilla chip, usu. topped with melted cheese and spices, etc. [20th c.: orig. uncert.]

na·cre /náykər/ *n.* mother-of-pearl from any shelled mollusk. □□ **na·cred** *adj.* **na·cre·ous** /náykreeəs/ *adj.* **na·crous** /-krəs/ *adj.* [F]

na·dir /náydər, –deer/ *n.* **1** the part of the celestial sphere directly below an observer (opp. ZENITH). **2** the lowest point in one's fortunes; a time of deep despair. [ME f. OF f. Arab. *naẓīr* (*as-samt*) opposite (to the zenith)]

naff¹ /naf/ *v.intr. Brit. sl.* **1** (in *imper.*, foll. by *off*) go away. **2** (as **naffing** *adj.*) used as an intensive to express annoyance, etc.

naff² /naf/ *adj. Brit. sl.* **1** unfashionable; socially awkward. **2** worthless, rubbishy. [20th c.: orig. unkn.]

NAFTA /náftə/ *abbr.* North American Free Trade Agreement.

nag¹ /nag/ *v. & n.* ● *v.* (**nagged**, **nag·ging**) **1 a** *tr.* annoy or irritate (a person) with persistent faultfinding or continuous urging. **b** *intr.* (often foll. by *at*) find fault, complain, or urge, esp. persistently. **2** *intr.* (of a pain) ache dully but persistently. **3 a** *tr.* worry or preoccupy (a person, the mind, etc.) (*his mistake nagged him*). **b** *intr.* (often foll. by *at*) worry or gnaw. **c** (as **nagging** *adj.*) persistently worrying or painful. ● *n.* a persistently nagging person. □□ **nag·ger** *n.* **nag·ging·ly** *adv.* [of dial., perh. Scand. or LG, orig.: cf. Norw. & Sw. *nagga* gnaw, irritate, LG (g)*naggen* provoke]

nag² /nag/ *n.* **1** *colloq.* a horse. **2** a small riding horse or pony. [ME: orig. unkn.]

Nah. *abbr.* Nahum (Old Testament).

Na·hua·tl /naáwaát'l/ *n. & adj.* ● *n.* **1** a member of a group of peoples native to S. Mexico and Central America, including the Aztecs. **2** the language of these people. ● *adj.* of or concerning the Nahuatl peoples or language. □□ **Na·hua·tlan** *adj.* [Sp. f. Nahuatl]

nai·ad /níad/ *n.* (*pl.* **nai·ads** or **·a·des** /níədeez/) **1** *Mythol.* a water nymph. **2** the larva of a dragonfly, etc. **3** any aquatic plant of the genus *Najas*, with narrow leaves and small flowers. [L *Naïas Naïad-* f. Gk *Naias –ados* f. *naō* flow]

nail /nayl/ *n. & v.* ● *n.* **1** a small usu. sharpened metal spike with a broadened flat head, driven in with a hammer to join things together or to serve as a peg, protection (cf. HOBNAIL), or decoration. **2 a** a horny covering on the upper surface of the tip of the human finger or toe. **b** a claw or talon. **c** a hard growth on the upper mandible of some soft-billed birds. **3** *hist.* a measure of cloth length (equal to 2¼ inches). ● *v.tr.* **1** fasten with a nail or nails (*nailed it to the beam; nailed the planks together*). **2** fix or keep (a person, attention, etc.) fixed. **3 a** secure, catch, or get hold of (a person or thing). **b** expose or discover (a lie or a liar). □ **hard as nails 1** callous; unfeeling. **2** in good physical condition. **nail one's colors to the mast** persist; refuse to give in. **nail down 1** bind (a person) to a promise, etc. **2** define precisely. **3** fasten (a thing) with nails. **nail in a person's coffin** something thought to increase the risk of death. **nail up 1** close (a door, etc.) with nails. **2** fix (a thing) at a height with nails. **on the nail** (esp. of payment) without delay (*cash on the nail*). □□ **nailed** *adj.* (also in *comb.*). **nail·less** *adj.* [OE *nægel, næglan* f. Gmc]

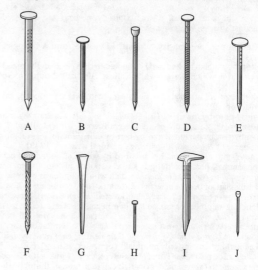

A common nail   F screw nail
B box nail   G cut *or* flooring nail
C finish nail   H wire nail
D ring *or* anchor nail   I wrought nail
E roofing nail   J brad

nail 1

nail-bit·ing *adj.* causing severe anxiety or tension.

nail e·nam·el *n.* = NAIL POLISH.

nail·er /náylər/ *n.* a nail driver, esp. an automatic device.

nail file *n.* a roughened metal or emery strip used for smoothing the nails.

nail pol·ish *n.* a varnish applied to the nails to color them or make them shiny.

nail scis·sors *n.* small curved scissors for trimming the nails.

nail set *n.* a tool for sinking the head of a nail below a surface.

nail var·nish *n. Brit.* = NAIL POLISH.

nain·sook /náynsŏok/ *n.* a fine soft cotton fabric, orig. from India. [Hindi *nainsukh* f. *nain* eye + *sukh* pleasure]

nai·ra /nírə/ *n.* the chief monetary unit of Nigeria. [contr. of *Nigeria*]

na·ïve /naa-éev/ *adj.* (also **na·ive**) **1** artless; innocent; unaffected. **2** foolishly credulous; simple. □□ **na·ïve·ly** *adv.* **na·ïve·ness** *n.* [F, fem. of *naïf* f. L *nativus* NATIVE]

na·ïve·té /naa-eevtáy, –éevtáy/ *n.* (also **na·ive·te, na·ive·té** esp. *Brit.* **na·ïve·ty** /naa-eevətee/) **1** the state or quality of being naïve. **2** a naïve action. [F *naïveté* (as NAÏVE)]

na·ked /náykid/ *adj.* **1** without clothes; nude. **2** plain; undisguised; exposed (*the naked truth; his naked soul*). **3** (of a light, flame, etc.) unprotected from the wind, etc.; unshaded. **4** defenseless. **5** without addition, comment, support, evidence, etc. (*his naked word; naked assertion*). **6 a** (of landscape) barren; treeless. **b** (of rock) exposed; without soil, etc. **7** (of a sword, etc.) unsheathed. **8** (usu. foll. by *of*) devoid; without. **9** without leaves, hairs, scales, shell, etc. **10** (of a room, wall, etc.) without decoration, furnishings, etc.; empty; plain. □□ **na·ked·ly** *adv.* **na·ked·ness** *n.* [OE *nacod* f. Gmc]

SYNONYM TIP naked

BALD, BARE, BARREN, NUDE. Someone who isn't wearing any clothes is **naked**; this adjective is usually associated with revealing a part or all of the body (*They found her naked and weak with hunger*). A *naked* person who appears in a painting or photograph is called a **nude**, a euphemistic but more socially acceptable term referring to the unclothed human body. **Bare** can describe the branches of a tree as well as human limbs; it implies the absence of the conventional or appropriate covering (*a bare wooden floor; bare legs; four bare walls*). **Bald** also suggests a lack of covering, but it refers particularly to lack of natural covering, esp. hair (*a bald head*). **Barren**, like *bald*, implies a lack of natural covering, especially vegetation, but it also connotes destitution and fruitlessness (*a barren wasteland that could barely support life*). A bald artist might paint a *nude* woman whose *bare* arms are extended against a *barren* winter landscape.

---

na·ked ape *n.* present-day humans, as viewed from a biological perspective.

na·ked boys (also **na·ked la·dy** or **na·ked la·dies**) *n. Brit.* the meadow saffron, which flowers while leafless. Also called **autumn crocus**.

na·ked eye *n.* unassisted vision, e.g., without a telescope, microscope, etc.

nam·by-pam·by /námbeepámbee/ *adj. & n.* ● *adj.* **1** lacking vigor or drive; weak. **2** insipidly pretty or sentimental. ● *n.* (*pl.* **·bies**) **1** a namby-pamby person. **2** namby-pamby talk. [fanciful formulation on name of *Ambrose* Philips, Engl. pastoral writer d. 1749]

name /naym/ *n. & v.* ● *n.* **1 a** the word by which an individual person, animal, place, or thing is known, spoken of, etc. (*mentioned him by name; her name is Joanna*). **b** all who go under one name; a family, clan, or people in terms of its name (*the Scottish name*). **2 a** a usu. abusive term used of a person, etc. (*called him names*). **b** a word denoting an object or esp. a class of objects, ideas, etc. (*what is the name of that kind of vase?; that sort of behavior has no name*). **3** a famous person (*many great names were there*). **4** a reputation, esp. a good one (*has a name for honesty; their name is guarantee enough*). **5** something existing only nominally (opp. FACT, REALITY). **6** (*attrib.*) widely known (*a name brand of shampoo*). ● *v.tr.* **1** give a usu. specified name to (*named the dog Spot*). **2** call (a person or thing) by the right name (*named the man in the photograph*). **3** mention; specify; cite (*named her requirements*). **4** nominate, appoint, etc. (*was named the new chairman*). **5** specify as something desired (*named it as her dearest wish*). **6** *Brit. Parl.* (of the Speaker) mention (an MP) as disobedient to the chair. □ **by name** called (*Tom by name*). **have to one's name** possess. **in all but name** virtually. **in name** (or **name only**) as a mere formality; hardly at all (*is the leader in name only*). **in a person's name** = *in the name of*. **in the name of** calling to witness; invoking (*in the name of goodness*). **in one's own name** independently; without authority. **make a name for oneself** become famous. **name after** (also **for**) call (a person) by the name of (a specified person) (*named him after his uncle Roger*). **name the day** arrange a date (esp. of a woman fixing the date for her wedding). **name names** mention specific names, esp. in accusation. **name of the game** *colloq.* the purpose or essence of an action, etc. **of** (or **by**) **the name of** called. **put one's name down for 1** apply for. **2** promise to subscribe (a sum). **what's in a name?** names are arbitrary labels. **you name it** *colloq.* no matter what; whatever you like. □□ **name·a·ble** *adj.* [OE *nama, noma,* (*ge*)*namian* f. Gmc, rel. to L *nomen,* Gk *onoma*]

name-call·ing *n.* abusive language.

name-drop·ping *n.* the practice of casually mentioning famous people one knows or pretends to know as a form of boasting. □□ **name-drop** *v.* **name-drop·per** *n.*

name·less /náymlis/ *adj.* **1** having no name or name inscription. **2** inexpressible; indefinable (*a nameless sensation*). **3** unnamed; anonymous, esp. deliberately (*our informant, who shall be nameless*). **4** too loathsome or horrific to be named (*nameless vices*). **5** obscure; inglorious. **6** illegitimate. □□ **name·less·ly** *adv.* **name·less·ness** *n.*

name·ly /náymlee/ *adv.* that is to say; in other words.

name·sake /náymsayk/ *n.* a person or thing having the same name as another (*was her aunt's namesake*). [prob. f. phr. *for the name's sake*]

name tape *n.* a tape fixed to a garment, etc., and bearing the name of the owner.

nam·ma var. of GNAMMA.

nan·a /nánə/ *n. colloq.* **1** grandmother. **2** godmother. **3** nursemaid. [f. NANNY]

nance /nans/ *n. & adj.* (also **nan·cy** /nánsee/) *derog. sl.* ● *n.* (*pl.* **·cies**) (in full **nancy boy**) an effeminate man, esp. a homosexual. ● *adj.* effeminate. [f. name *Nancy*]

---

nan·keen /nangkeén/ *n.* **1** a yellowish cotton cloth. **2** a yellowish buff color. **3** (in *pl.*) trousers of nankeen. [*Nankin(g)* in China, where orig. made]

nan·ny /nánee/ *n. & v.* ● *n.* (*pl.* **·nies**) **1 a** a child's nursemaid. **b** *Brit.* an unduly protective person, institution, etc. (*the nanny state*). **2** (in full **nanny goat**) a female goat. ● *v.tr.* (**·nies, ·nied**) be unduly protective toward. [pet form of name *Ann*]

nano- /nánō, náynō/ *comb. form* denoting a factor of 10^{-9} (*nanosecond*). [L f. Gk *nanos* dwarf]

nan·o·me·ter /nánōmeetər/ *n.* one billionth of a meter. ¶ Abbr.:**nm**.

nan·o·sec·ond /nánōsekənd/ *n.* one billionth of a second. ¶ Abbr.: **ns**.

na·os /náyos/ *n.* (*pl.* **na·oi** /náyoy/) *Gk Hist.* the inner part of a temple. [Gk, = temple]

nap¹ /nap/ *v. & n.* ● *v.intr.* (**napped, nap·ping**) sleep lightly or briefly. ● *n.* a short sleep or doze, esp. by day (*took a nap*). □ **catch a person napping 1** find a person asleep or off guard. **2** detect in negligence or error. [OE *hnappian,* rel. to OHG (*h*)*naffezan* to slumber]

nap² /nap/ *n. & v.* ● *n.* **1** the raised pile on textiles, esp. velvet. **2** a soft downy surface. **3** *Austral. colloq.* blankets, bedding, swag. ● *v.tr.* (**napped, nap·ping**) raise a nap on (cloth). □□ **nap·less** *adj.* [ME *noppe* f. MDu., MLG *noppe* nap, *noppen* trim nap from]

nap³ /nap/ *n. & v.* ● *n.* **1 a** a form of whist in which players declare the number of tricks they expect to take, up to five. **b** a call of five in this game. **2** *Brit.* **a** the betting of all one's money on one horse, etc. **b** a tipster's choice for this. ● *v.tr. Brit.* (**napped, nap·ping**) name (a horse, etc.) as a probable winner. □ **go nap** *Brit.* **1** attempt to take all five tricks in nap. **2** risk everything in one attempt. **3** win all the matches, etc., in a series. **not go nap on** *Austral. colloq.* not be too keen on; not care much for. [abbr. of orig. name of game NAPOLEON]

na·pa var. of NAPPA.

na·palm /náypaam/ *n. & v.* ● *n.* **1** a thickening agent produced from naphthenic acid, other fatty acids, and aluminum. **2** a jellied substance made from this, used in incendiary bombs. ● *v.tr.* attack with napalm bombs. [NAPHTHENIC + *palmitic acid* in coconut oil]

nape /nayp/ *n.* the back of the neck. [ME: orig. unkn.]

na·per·y /náypəree/ *n. Sc.* or *archaic* household linen, esp. table linen. [ME f. OF *naperie* f. *nape* (as NAPKIN)]

naph·tha /náf-thə, náp–/ *n.* a flammable oil obtained by the dry distillation of organic substances such as coal, shale, or petroleum. [L f. Gk, = flammable volatile liquid issuing from the earth, of Oriental origin]

naph·tha·lene /náf-thəleen, náp–/ *n.* a white crystalline aromatic substance produced by the distillation of coal tar and used in mothballs and the manufacture of dyes, etc. □□ **naph·thal·ic** /–thálik/ *adj.* [NAPHTHA + –ENE]

naph·thene /náf-theen, náp–/ *n.* any of a group of cycloalkanes. [NAPHTHA + –ENE]

naph·then·ic /naf-theénik, náp–/ *adj.* of a naphthene or its radical.

naph·then·ic ac·id *n.* any carboxylic acid resulting from the refining of petroleum.

Na·pier·i·an log·a·rithm /naypeéreeən, nə–/ *n.* = NATURAL LOGARITHM. [J. *Napier,* Sc. mathematician d. 1617]

nap·kin /nápkin/ *n.* **1** (in full **ta·ble nap·kin**) a square piece of linen, paper, etc. used for wiping the lips, fingers, etc., at meals; a serviette. **2** *Brit.* a baby's diaper. **3** a small towel. [ME f. OF *nappe* f. L *mappa* (MAP)]

nap·kin ring *n.* a ring used to hold (and distinguish) a person's table napkin when not in use.

na·po·le·on /nəpóleeən/ *n.* **1** *hist.* a gold twenty-franc piece minted in the reign of Napoleon I. **2** *hist.* a 19th-c. high boot. **3** = NAP³. **4** = MILLE-FEUILLE. [F *napoléon* f. *Napoléon,* name of 19th-c. French emperors]

Na·po·le·on·ic /nəpóleeónik/ *adj.* of, relating to, or characteristic of Napoleon I or his time.

nap·pa /nápə/ *n.* (also **na·pa**) a soft leather made by a special process from the skin of sheep or goats. [*Napa* in California]

nappe /nap/ *n. Geol.* a sheet of rock that has moved sideways over neighboring strata, usu. as a result of overthrust. [F *nappe* tablecloth]

nap·py /nápee/ *n.* (*pl.* **·pies**) *Brit.* a baby's diaper. [abbr. of NAPKIN]

narc /nark/ *n.* (also **nark**) *sl.* a federal agent or police officer who enforces the laws regarding illicit sale or use of drugs and narcotics.

nar·ce·ine /naárseeeen, –in/ *n.* a narcotic alkaloid obtained from opium. [F *narcéine* f. Gk *narkē* numbness]

nar·cis·sism /naársisizəm/ *n. Psychol.* excessive or erotic interest in oneself, one's physical features, etc. □□ **nar·cis·sist** *n.* **nar·cis·sis·tic** *adj.* **nar·cis·sis·ti·cal·ly** *adv.* [*Narcissus* (Gk *Narkissos*), youth who fell in love with his reflection in water]

nar·cis·sus /naársisəs/ *n.* (*pl.* **nar·cis·si** /–sī/ or **nar·cis·sus·es**) any bulbous plant of the genus *Narcissus,* esp. *N. poeticus* bearing a heavily scented single flower with an undivided corona edged with crimson and yellow. [L f. Gk *narkissos,* perh. f. *narkē* numbness, with ref. to its narcotic effects]

nar·co·lep·sy /naárkəlepsee/ *n. Med.* a disease with fits of sleepiness and drowsiness. □□ **nar·co·lep·tic** /–léptik/ *adj. & n.* [Gk *narkoō* make numb, after EPILEPSY]

nar·co·sis /naarkósis/ *n.* **1** *Med.* the working or effects of soporific narcotics. **2** a state of insensibility. [Gk *narkōsis* f. *narkoō* make numb]

nar·co·ter·ror·ism /náarkōtérərizəm/ *n.* violent crime associated with illicit drugs. □□ **nar·co·ter·ror·ist** *adj. & n.* [NARCOTIC + *terrorism*]

nar·cot·ic /naarkótik/ *adj. & n.* ● *adj.* **1** (of a substance) inducing drowsiness, sleep, stupor, or insensibility. **2** (of a drug) affecting the mind. **3** of or involving narcosis. **4** soporific. ● *n.* a narcotic substance, drug, or influence. □□ **nar·cot·i·cal·ly** *adv.* **nar·co·tism** /náarkətizəm/ *n.* **nar·co·tize** /náarkətīz/ *v.tr.* **nar·co·ti·za·tion** /–tizáyshən/ *n.* [ME f. OF *narcotique* or med.L f. Gk *narkōtikos* (as NARCOSIS)]

nard /naard/ *n.* **1** any of various plants yielding an aromatic balsam used by the ancients. **2** = SPIKENARD. [ME f. L *nardus* f. Gk *nardos* ult. f. Skr.]

nar·es /náireez/ *n.pl. Anat.* the nostrils. □□ **nar·i·al** *adj.* [pl. of L *naris*]

nar·ghi·le /náargilee/ *n.* a Middle Eastern tobacco pipe with the smoke drawn through water; a hookah. [Pers. *nārgīleh* (*nārgīl* coconut)]

nark /naark/ *n. & v. sl.* *n.* **1** *Brit.* a police informer or decoy. **2** *Austral.* an annoying person or thing. *v.tr.* (usu. in *passive*) *Brit.* annoy; infuriate (*was narked by their attitude*). □ **nark it!** *Brit.* stop that! [Romany *nāk* nose]

Nar·ra·gan·sett /narəgánsət, -gánt-/ *n.* **1 a** a N. American people native to Rhode Island. **b** a member of this people. **2** the language of this people.

nar·rate /nárayt, naráyt/ *v.tr.* (also *absol.*) **1** give a continuous story or account of. **2** provide a spoken commentary or accompaniment for (a film, etc.). □□ **nar·rat·a·ble** *adj.* **nar·ra·tion** /–ráyshən/*n.* [L *narrare narrat*–]

nar·ra·tive /nárətiv/ *n. & adj.* ● *n.* **1** a spoken or written account of connected events in order of happening. **2** the practice or art of narration. ● *adj.* in the form of, or concerned with, narration (*narrative verse*). □□ **nar·ra·tive·ly** *adv.* [F *narratif –ive* f. LL *narrativus* (as NARRATE)]

nar·ra·tor /náraytər/ *n.* **1** an actor, announcer, etc., who delivers a commentary in a film, broadcast, etc. **2** a person who narrates. [L (as NARRATE)]

nar·row /nárō/ *adj., n., & v.* ● *adj.* (**nar·row·er, nar·row·est**) **1 a** of small width in proportion to length; lacking breadth. **b** confined or confining; constricted (*within narrow bounds*). **2** of limited scope; restricted (*in the narrowest sense*). **3** with little margin (*a narrow escape*). **4** searching; precise; exact (*a narrow examination*). **5** = NARROW-MINDED. **6** (of a vowel) tense. **7** of small size. ● *n.* **1** (usu. in *pl.*) the narrow part of a strait, river, sound, etc. **2** a narrow pass or street. ● *v.* **1** *intr.* become narrow; diminish; contract; lessen. **2** *tr.* make narrow; constrict; restrict. □□ **nar·row·ish** *adj.* **nar·row·ly** *adv.* **nar·row·ness** *n.* [OE *nearu nearw-* f. Gmc]

nar·row cir·cum·stanc·es *n.* poverty.

nar·row gauge *n.* a railroad track that has a smaller gauge than the standard one.

nar·row-mind·ed /nárōmíndid/ *adj.* rigid or restricted in one's views; intolerant; prejudiced; illiberal. □□ **nar·row-mind·ed·ly** *adv.* **nar·row-mind·ed·ness** *n.*

nar·row seas *n. Brit.* the English Channel and the Irish Sea.

nar·row squeak *n. Brit.* **1** a narrow escape. **2** a success barely attained.

nar·thex /náartheks/ *n.* **1** a railed-off antechamber or porch, etc., at the western entrance of some early Christian churches, used by catechumens, penitents, etc. **2** a similar antechamber in a modern church. [L f. Gk *narthēx* giant fennel, stick, casket, narthex]

nar·whal /náarwəl/*n.* an Arctic white whale, *Monodon monoceros*, the male of which has a long straight spirally fluted tusk developed from one of its teeth. Also called *beluga*. [Du. *narwal* f. Da. *narhval* f. hval whale: cf. ON *náhvalr* (perh. f. *nár* corpse, with ref. to its skin color)]

nar·y /náiree/ *adj. colloq.* or *dial.* not any; no (*nary a one*). [f. *ne'er a*]

NAS *abbr.* National Academy of Sciences.

NASA /násə/ *abbr.* National Aeronautics and Space Administration.

na·sal /náyzəl/ *adj. & n.* ● *adj.* **1** of, for, or relating to the nose. **2** *Phonet.* (of a letter or a sound) pronounced with the breath passing through the nose, e.g., *m, n, ng,* or French *en, un,* etc. **3** (of the voice or speech) having an intonation caused by breathing through the nose. ● *n.* **1** *Phonet.* a nasal letter or sound. **2** *hist.* a nosepiece on a helmet. □□ **na·sal·i·ty** /–zálitee/ *n.* **na·sal·ize** *v.intr. & tr.* **na·sal·i·za·tion** *n.* **na·sal·ly** *adv.* [F *nasal* or med.L. *nasalis* f. L *nasus* nose]

nas·cent /násənt, náy–/ *adj.* **1** in the act of being born. **2** just beginning to be; not yet mature. **3** *Chem.* just being formed and therefore unusually reactive (*nascent hydrogen*). □□ **nas·cen·cy** /násənsee, náy–/ *n.* [L *nasci nascent-* be born]

NASDAQ /názdak, nás–/ *abbr.* National Association of Securities Dealers Automated Quotations.

nase·ber·ry /náyzberee/ *n.* (*pl.* **·ries**) a sapodilla. [Sp. & Port. *néspera* medlar f. L (see MEDLAR): assim. to BERRY]

naso- /náyzō/ *comb. form* nose. [L *nasus* nose]

na·so·front·al /náyzōfrúnt'l/ *adj.* of or relating to the nose and forehead.

nas·tic /nástik/ *adj. Bot.* (of the movement of plant parts) not determined by an external stimulus. [Gk *nastos* squeezed together f. *nassō* to press]

nas·tur·tium /nəstórshəm/ *n.* **1** (in general use) a trailing plant, *Tropaeolum majus*, with rounded edible leaves and bright orange, yellow, or red flowers. **2** any cruciferous plant of the genus *Nasturtium*, including watercress. [L]

nas·ty /nástee/ *adj. & n.* ● *adj.* (**nas·ti·er, nas·ti·est**) **1 a** highly unpleasant (*a nasty experience*). **b** annoying; objectionable (*the car has a nasty habit of breaking down*). **2** difficult to negotiate; dangerous, serious (*a nasty fence; a nasty question; a nasty illness*). **3** (of a person or animal) ill-natured, ill-tempered, spiteful; violent, offensive (*nasty to his mother; turns nasty when he's drunk*). **4** (of the weather) foul, wet, stormy. **5 a** disgustingly dirty, filthy. **b** unpalatable; disagreeable (*nasty smell*). **c** (of a wound) septic. **6 a** obscene. **b** delighting in obscenity. ● *n. Brit.* (*pl.* **·ties**) *colloq.* a horror film, esp. one on video and depicting cruelty or killing. □ **a nasty bit** (or **piece**) **of work** esp. *Brit. colloq.* an unpleasant or contemptible person. □□ **nas·ti·ly** *adv.* **nas·ti·ness** *n.* [ME: orig. unkn.]

nat. *abbr.* **1** national. **2** native. **3** natural.

na·tal /náytəl/ *adj.* of or from one's birth. [ME f. L *natalis* (as NATION)]

na·tal·i·ty /naytálitee, nə–/ *n.* (*pl.* **·ties**) birth rate. [F *natalité* (as NATAL)]

na·ta·tion /naytáyshən, na–/ *n. formal* or *literary* the act or art of swimming. [L *natatio* f. *natare* swim]

na·ta·to·ri·al /náytətáwreeəl, nát–/ *adj.* (also **na·ta·to·ry** /–táwree/) *formal* **1** swimming. **2** of or concerning swimming. [LL *natatorius* f. L *natator* swimmer (as NATATION)]

na·ta·to·ri·um /náytətawreeəm/ *n.* (*pl.* **·ums** or **·ri·a** /–ree-ə/) a swimming pool, esp. indoors. [LL neut. of *natatorius* (see NATATORIAL)]

natch /nach/ *adv. colloq.* = NATURALLY. [abbr.]

Natch·ez /náchiz / *n.* **1 a** a N. American people native to Mississippi. **b** a member of this people. **2** the language of this people.

na·tes /náyteez/ *n.pl. Anat.* the buttocks.[L]

nathe·less /náythlis/ *adv.* (also **nath·less**) *archaic* nevertheless. [ME f. OE *nā* not (f. *ne* not + *ā* ever) + THE + *lǣs* LESS]

na·tion /náyshən/ *n.* **1** a community of people of mainly common descent, history, language, etc., forming a unified government or inhabiting a territory. **2** a tribe or confederation of tribes of Native Americans. □□ **na·tion·hood** *n.* [ME f. OF f. L *natio –onis* f. *nasci nat-* be born]

na·tion·al /náshənəl/ *adj. & n.* ● *adj.* **1** of or common to a nation or the nation. **2** peculiar to or characteristic of a particular nation. ● *n.* **1** a citizen of a specified country, usu. entitled to hold that country's passport (*French nationals*). **2** a fellow countryman. **3** (**the National**) *Brit.* = GRAND NATIONAL. □□ **na·tion·al·ly** *adv.* [F (as NATION)]

na·tion·al an·them *n.* a song adopted by a nation, expressive of its identity, etc., and intended to inspire patriotism.

Na·tion·al As·sem·bly *n.* **1** an elected house of legislature in various countries. **2** *hist.* the elected legislature in France 1789–91.

na·tion·al bank *n.* a bank chartered under the federal government.

na·tion·al debt *n.* the money owed by a country because of loans to it.

na·tion·al foot·ball *n. Austral.* Australian Rules football.

Na·tion·al Front *n.* a UK political party with extreme reactionary views on immigration, etc.

na·tion·al grid *n. Brit.* **1** the network of high-voltage electric power lines between major power stations. **2** the metric system of geographical coordinates used in maps of the British Isles.

Na·tion·al Guard *n.* the primary reserve force partly maintained by the states of the United States but available for federal use.

Na·tion·al Health *n.* (also **Na·tion·al Health Serv·ice**) (in the UK) a system of national medical care paid for mainly by taxation and started in 1948.

na·tion·al in·come *n.* the total money earned within a nation.

na·tion·al·ism /náshənəlizəm/ *n.* **1 a** a patriotic feeling, principles, etc. **b** an extreme form of this; chauvinism. **2** a policy of national independence. □□ **na·tion·al·ist** *n. & adj.* **na·tion·al·is·tic** *adj.* **na·tion·al·is·ti·cal·ly** *adv.*

na·tion·al·i·ty /náshənálitee/ *n.* (*pl.* **·ties**) **1 a** the status of belonging to a particular nation (*what is your nationality?; has Austrian nationality*). **b** a nation (*people of all nationalities*). **2** the condition of being national; distinctive national qualities. **3** an ethnic group forming a part of one or more political nations. **4** existence as a nation; nationhood. **5** patriotic sentiment.

na·tion·al·ize /náshənəlīz/ *v.tr.* **1** take over (railroads, health care, the steel industry, land, etc.) from private ownership on behalf of the government. **2 a** make national. **b** make into a nation. **3** naturalize (a foreigner). □□ **na·tion·al·i·za·tion** n. **na·tion·al·iz·er** n. [F *nationaliser* (as NATIONAL)]

na·tion·al park n. an area of natural beauty protected by the government for the use of the general public.

na·tion·al serv·ice n. Brit. hist. service in the army, etc., under conscription.

Na·tion·al So·cial·ism n. hist. the doctrines of nationalism, racial purity, etc., adopted by the Nazis. □□ **Na·tion·al So·cial·ist** n. hist. a member of the fascist party implementing National Socialism in Germany, 1933–45.

Na·tion·al Trust n. an organization for maintaining and preserving historic buildings, etc.

na·tion·wide /náyshənwíd/ adj. extending over the whole nation.

na·tive /náytiv/ n. & adj. • n. **1 a** (usu. foll. by of) a person born in a specified place, or whose parents are domiciled in that place at the time of the birth (a native of Chicago). **b** a local inhabitant. **2** often offens. a member of a nonwhite indigenous people, as regarded by the colonial settlers. **3** (usu. foll. by of) an indigenous animal or plant. • adj. **1** (usu. foll. by to) belonging to a person or thing by nature; inherent; innate (spoke with the facility native to him). **2** of one's birth or birthplace (native dress; native country). **3** belonging to one by right of birth. **4** (usu. foll. by to) belonging to a specified place (the anteater is native to S. America). **5 a** (esp. of a non-European) indigenous; born in a place. **b** of the natives of a place (native customs). **6** in a natural state; unadorned; simple. **7** Geol. (of metal, etc.) found in a pure or uncombined state. □ **go native** esp. Brit. (of a settler) adopt the local way of life, esp. in a non-European country. □□ **na·tive·ly** adv. **na·tive·ness** n. [ME (earlier as adj.) f. OF natif –ive or L nativus f. nasci nat– be born]

SYNONYM TIP native

ABORIGINAL, ENDEMIC, INDIGENOUS. A *native* New Yorker is probably not *indigenous*, although both words apply to persons or things that belong to or are associated with a particular place by birth or origin. **Native** means born or produced in a specific region or country (native plants; native dances), but it can also apply to persons or things that were introduced from elsewhere some time ago—which is the case with most New Yorkers who consider themselves *natives*. **Indigenous**, on the other hand, is more restricted in meaning; it applies only to something or someone that is not only *native* but was not introduced from elsewhere (the pumpkin is indigenous to America). Generally speaking, *native* applies to individual organisms, while *indigenous* applies to races or species. Something that is **endemic** is prevalent in a particular region because of special conditions there that favor its growth or existence (heather is endemic in the Scottish Highlands; malaria is endemic in Central America). There are no longer any **aboriginal** New Yorkers, a word that refers to the earliest known inhabitants of a place or to ancient peoples who have no known ancestors and have inhabited a region since its earliest historical time. Australia is known for its *aboriginal* culture, which was preserved for centuries through geographical isolation.

Na·tive A·mer·i·can n. & adj. • n. a member of the aboriginal peoples of America or their descendants. • adj. of or relating to these people.

na·tive bear n. Austral. & NZ = KOALA.

na·tive rock n. rock in its original place.

na·tiv·ism /náytivizəm/ n. Philos. the doctrine of innate ideas. □□ **na·tiv·ist** n.

na·tiv·i·ty /nətívitee, nay-/ n. (pl. **-ties**) **1** (esp. **the Nativity**) **a** the birth of Christ. **b** the festival of Christ's birth; Christmas. **2** a picture of the Nativity. **3** birth. **4** the horoscope at a person's birth. **5 a** the birth of the Virgin Mary or St. John the Baptist. **b** the festival of the nativity of the Virgin (Sept. 8) or St. John (June 24). [ME f. OF nativité f. LL nativitas –tatis f. L (as NATIVE)]

na·tiv·i·ty play n. a play usu. performed by children at Christmas dealing with the birth of Christ.

natl. abbr. national.

NATO /náytō/ abbr. North Atlantic Treaty Organization.

na·tron /náytrən/ n. a mineral form of hydrated sodium salts found in dried lake beds. [F f. Sp. natrón f. Arab. naṭrūn f. Gk nitron NITER]

nat·ter /nátər/ v. & n. colloq. • v.intr. esp. Brit. **1** chatter idly. **2** grumble; talk fretfully. • n. **1** aimless chatter. **2** grumbling talk. □□ **nat·ter·er** n. [orig. Sc., imit.]

nat·ter·jack /nátərjak/ n. a European toad, Bufo calamita, with a bright yellow stripe down its back, and moving by running not hopping. [perh. f. NATTER, from its loud croak, + JACK¹]

nat·tier blue /náteeər/ n. a soft shade of blue. [much used by J. M. Nattier, Fr. painter d. 1766]

nat·ty /nátee/ adj. (**nat·ti·er**, **nat·ti·est**) colloq. **1 a** smartly or neatly

---

dressed, dapper. **b** spruce; trim; smart (a natty blouse). **2** deft. □□ **nat·ti·ly** adv. **nat·ti·ness** n. [orig. sl., perh. rel. to NEAT¹]

nat·u·ral /náchərəl/ adj. & n. • adj. **1 a** existing in or caused by nature; not artificial (natural landscape). **b** uncultivated; wild (existing in its natural state). **2** in the course of nature; not exceptional or miraculous (died of natural causes; a natural occurrence). **3** (of human nature, etc.) not surprising; to be expected (natural for her to be upset). **4 a** (of a person or a person's behavior) unaffected, easy, spontaneous. **b** (foll. by to) spontaneous; easy (friendliness is natural to him). **5 a** (of qualities, etc.) inherent; innate (a natural talent for music). **b** (of a person) having such qualities (a natural linguist). **6** not disguised or altered (as by makeup, etc.). **7** lifelike; as if in nature (the portrait looked very natural). **8** likely by its or their nature to be such (natural enemies; the natural antithesis). **9** having a physical existence as opposed to what is spiritual, intellectual, etc. (the natural world). **10 a** related by nature, out of wedlock, esp. in a specified manner (her natural son). **b** illegitimate (a natural child). **11** based on the innate moral sense; instinctive (natural justice). **12** Mus. **a** (of a note) not sharpened or flattened (B natural). **b** (of a scale) not containing any sharps or flats. **13** not enlightened or communicated by revelation (the natural man). • n. **1** colloq. (usu. foll. by for) a person or thing naturally suitable, adept, expert, etc. (a natural for the championship). **2** archaic a person mentally deficient from birth. **3** Mus. **a** a sign (♮) denoting a return to natural pitch after a sharp or a flat. **b** a natural note. **c** a white key on a piano. **4 a** Cards a hand with no wild card or joker. **b** Cards a hand making 21 in the first deal in blackjack. **c** a throw of 7 or 11 at craps. **5** a pale fawn color. □□ **nat·u·ral·ness** n. [ME f. OF naturel f. L naturalis (as NATURE)]

nat·u·ral-born adj. having a character or position by birth.

nat·u·ral child·birth n. Med. childbirth with minimal medical or technological intervention.

nat·u·ral clas·si·fi·ca·tion n. a scientific classification according to natural features.

nat·u·ral death n. death by age or disease, not by accident, poison, violence, etc.

nat·u·ral food n. food without preservatives, etc.

nat·u·ral gas n. a flammable mainly methane gas found in the earth's crust, not manufactured.

nat·u·ral his·to·ry n. **1** the study of animals or plants esp. as set forth for popular use. **2** an aggregate of the facts concerning the flora and fauna, etc., of a particular place or class (a natural history of the Florida Keys).

nat·u·ral·ism /náchərəlizəm/ n. **1** the theory or practice in art and literature of representing nature, character, etc. realistically and in great detail. **2 a** Philos. a theory of the world that excludes the supernatural or spiritual. **b** any moral or religious system based on this theory. **3** action based on natural instincts. **4** indifference to conventions. [NATURAL, in Philos. after F naturalisme]

nat·u·ral·ist /náchərəlist/ n. & adj. • n. **1** an expert in natural history. **2** a person who believes in or practices naturalism. • adj. = NATURALISTIC.

nat·u·ral·is·tic /náchərəlístik/ adj. **1** imitating nature closely; lifelike. **2** of or according to naturalism. **3** of natural history. □□ **nat·u·ral·is·ti·cal·ly** adv.

nat·u·ral·ize /náchərəlīz/ v. **1** tr. admit (a foreigner) to the citizenship of a country. **2** tr. introduce (an animal, plant, etc.) into another region so that it flourishes in the wild. **3** tr. adopt (a foreign word, custom, etc.). **4** intr. become naturalized. **5** tr. Philos. exclude from the miraculous; explain naturalistically. **6** tr. free from conventions; make natural. **7** tr. cause to appear natural. **8** intr. study natural history. □□ **nat·u·ral·i·za·tion** n. [F naturaliser (as NATURAL)]

nat·u·ral key (also **nat·u·ral scale**) n. Mus. a key or scale having no sharps or flats, i.e., C major and A minor.

nat·u·ral lan·guage n. a language that has developed naturally.

nat·u·ral law n. **1** Philos. unchanging moral principles common to all people by virtue of their nature as human beings. **2** a correct statement of an invariable sequence between specified conditions and a specified phenomenon. **3** the laws of nature; regularity in nature (where they saw chance, we see natural law).

nat·u·ral life n. the duration of one's life on earth.

nat·u·ral log·a·rithm n. (also **Na·pier·i·an log·a·rithm**) a logarithm to the base of the irrational number e (2.71828.....). ¶ Abbr.: **ln** or $\log_e$.

nat·u·ral·ly /náchərəlee, náchrə-/ adv. **1** in a natural manner. **2** as a natural result. **3** (qualifying a whole sentence) as might be expected; of course.

nat·u·ral mag·ic n. magic involving the supposed invocation of impersonal spirits.

nat·u·ral note n. Mus. a note that is neither sharp nor flat.

nat·u·ral num·bers n.pl. the integers 1, 2, 3, etc.

nat·u·ral phi·los·o·pher n. archaic a physicist.

nat·u·ral phi·los·o·phy n. archaic physics.

nat·u·ral re·li·gion n. a religion based on reason (opp. REVEALED RELIGION); deism.

nat·u·ral re·sources *n.pl.* materials or conditions occurring in nature and capable of economic exploitation.

nat·u·ral sci·ence *n.* the sciences used in the study of the physical world, e.g., physics, chemistry, geology, biology, botany.

nat·u·ral se·lec·tion *n.* the Darwinian theory of the survival and propagation of organisms best adapted to their environment.

nat·u·ral the·ol·o·gy *n.* the knowledge of God as gained by the light of natural reason.

nat·u·ral u·ra·ni·um *n.* unenriched uranium.

nat·u·ral vir·tues *n. Philos.* justice, prudence, temperance, fortitude.

nat·u·ral year *n.* the time taken by one revolution of the earth around the sun, 365 days 5 hours 48 minutes.

na·ture /náychər/ *n.* 1 a thing's or person's innate or essential qualities or character (*not in their nature to be cruel*; *is the nature of iron to rust*). 2 (often **Nature**) **a** the physical power causing all the phenomena of the material world (*Nature is the best physician*). **b** these phenomena, including plants, animals, landscape, etc. (*nature gives him comfort*). 3 a kind, sort, or class (*things of this nature*). 4 = HUMAN NATURE. 5 **a** a specified element of human character (*the rational nature*; *our animal nature*). **b** a person of a specified character (*even strong natures quail*). 6 **a** an uncultivated or wild area, condition, community, etc. **b** the countryside, esp. when picturesque. 7 inherent impulses determining character or action. 8 heredity as an influence on or determinant of personality (opp. NURTURE). 9 a living thing's vital functions or needs (*such a diet will not support nature*). □ **against nature** unnatural; immoral. **against** (or **contrary to**) **nature** miraculous; miraculously. **back to nature** returning to a precivilized or natural state. **by nature** innately. **from nature** *Art* using natural objects as models. **in nature 1** actually existing. **2** anywhere; at all. **in** (or **of**) **the nature of** characteristically resembling or belonging to the class of (*the answer was in the nature of an excuse*). **in a state of nature 1** in an uncivilized or uncultivated state. **2** totally naked. **3** in an unregenerate state. [ME f. OF f. L *natura* f. *nascinat-* be born]

na·ture cure *n.* = NATUROPATHY.

na·tured /náychərd/ *adj.* (in *comb.*) having a specified disposition (*good-natured*; *ill-natured*).

na·ture print·ing *n.* a method of producing a print of leaves, etc., by pressing them on a prepared plate.

na·ture re·serve *n.* a tract of land managed so as to preserve its flora, fauna, physical features, etc.

na·ture stud·y *n.* the practical study of plant and animal life, etc., as a school subject.

na·ture trail *n.* a signposted path through the countryside designed to draw attention to natural phenomena.

na·tur·ism /náychərizəm/ *n.* 1 nudism. 2 naturalism in regard to religion. 3 the worship of natural objects. □□ **na·tur·ist** *n.*

na·tur·op·a·thy /náychərópəthee/ *n.* 1 the treatment of disease, etc., without drugs, usu. involving diet, exercise, massage, etc. 2 this regimen used preventively. □□ **na·tur·o·path** /-əpáth/ *n.* **na·tur·o·path·ic** *adj.*

naught /nawt/ *n. & adj.* (also **nought**) • *n.* 1 *archaic* or *literary* nothing; nothingness. 2 zero; cipher. • *adj.* (usu. *predic.*) *archaic* or *literary* worthless; useless. □ **bring to naught** ruin; baffle. **come to naught** be ruined or baffled. **set at naught** disregard; despise. [OE *nāwiht*, *-wuht* f. *nā* (see NO²) + *wiht* WIGHT]

naugh·ty /náwtee/ *adj.* (**naugh·ti·er**, **naugh·ti·est**) 1 (esp. of children) disobedient; badly behaved. 2 *colloq. joc.* indecent. 3 *archaic* wicked. □□ **naugh·ti·ly** *adv.* **naugh·ti·ness** *n.* [ME f. NAUGHT + -Y¹]

nau·pli·us /náwpleeəs/ *n.* (*pl.* **nau·pli·i** /-n-plee-ī/) the first larval stage of some crustaceans. [L, = a kind of shellfish, or f. Gk *Nauplios* son of Poseidon]

nau·se·a /náwzeeə, -zhə, -seeə, -shə/ *n.* 1 a feeling of sickness with an inclination to vomit. 2 loathing; revulsion. [L f. Gk *nausia* f. *naus* ship]

nau·se·ate /náwzeeayt, -zhee, -see, -shee/ *v.* 1 *tr.* affect with nausea (*was nauseated by the smell*); disgust. 2 *intr.* (usu. foll. by *at*) loathe food, an occupation, etc.; feel sick. □□ **nau·se·at·ing** *adj.* **nau·se·at·ing·ly** *adv.* [L *nauseare* (as NAUSEA)]

▶A distinction has traditionally been drawn between **nauseated**, meaning 'affected with nausea,' and **nauseous**, meaning 'causing nausea.' Today, however, the use of **nauseous** to mean 'affected with nausea' is so common that it is generally considered to be standard.

nau·seous /náwshəs, -zeeəs/ *adj.* 1 affected with nausea; sick. 2 causing nausea; offensive to the taste or smell. 3 disgusting; loathsome. □□ **nau·seous·ly** *adv.* **nau·seous·ness** *n.* [L *nauseosus* (as NAUSEA)]

▶See note at NAUSEATE.

nautch /nawch/ *n.* a performance of professional dancing girls from India. [Urdu (Hindi) *nāch* f. Prakrit *nachcha* f. Skr. *nṛitja* dancing]

nautch girl *n.* a professional dancing girl from India.

nau·ti·cal /náwtikəl/ *adj.* of or concerning sailors or navigation; naval; maritime. □□ **nau·ti·cal·ly** *adv.* [F *nautique* or f. L *nauticus* f. Gk *nautikos* f. *nautēs* sailor f. *naus* ship]

nau·ti·cal al·ma·nac *n.* a yearbook containing astronomical and tidal information for navigators, etc.

nau·ti·cal mile *n.* a unit of approx. 2,025 yards (1,852 meters). Also called **sea mile**.

nau·ti·lus /náwt'ləs/ *n.* (*pl.* **nau·ti·lus·es** or **nau·ti·li** /-lī/) 1 any cephalopod of the genus *Nautilus* with a light brittle spiral shell, esp. (**pearly nautilus**) one having a chambered shell with nacreous septa. 2 (in full **paper nautilus**) any small floating octopus of the genus *Argonauta*, of which the female has a very thin shell and webbed saillike arms. [L f. Gk *nautilos*, lit. sailor (as NAUTICAL)]

nautilus 1

Nav·a·jo /návəhō, náa-/ *n.* (also **Nav·a·ho**) (*pl.* **·jos**) 1 a member of a N. American people native to New Mexico and Arizona. 2 the language of this people. [Sp., = pueblo]

na·val /náyvəl/ *adj.* 1 of, in, for, etc., the navy or a navy. 2 of or concerning ships (*a naval battle*). □□ **na·val·ly** *adv.* [L *navalis* f. *navis* ship]

na·val a·cad·e·my *n.* a college for training naval officers.

na·val ar·chi·tect *n.* a designer of ships.

na·val ar·chi·tec·ture *n.* the designing of ships.

na·val of·fi·cer *n.* an officer in a navy.

na·val stores *n.* all materials used in shipping.

nave¹ /nayv/ *n.* the central part of a church, usu. from the west door to the chancel and excluding the side aisles. [med.L *navis* f. L *navis* ship]

nave² /nayv/ *n.* the hub of a wheel. [OE *nafu*, *nafa* f. Gmc, rel. to NAVEL]

na·vel /náyvəl/ *n.* 1 a depression in the center of the belly caused by the detachment of the umbilical cord. 2 a central point.

na·vel or·ange *n.* a large seedless orange with a navellike formation at the top.

na·vel·wort /n áyvəlwərt/ *n.* a pennywort.

na·vic·u·lar /n əvíkyələr/ *adj. & n.* • *adj.* boat-shaped. • *n.* (in full **navicular bone**) a boat-shaped bone in the foot or hand. [F *naviculaire* or LL *navicularis* f. L *navicula* dimin. of *navis* ship]

na·vic·u·lar dis·ease *n.* an inflammatory disease of the navicular bone in horses, causing lameness.

nav·i·ga·ble /návigəbəl/ *adj.* 1 (of a river, the sea, etc.) affording a passage for ships. 2 (of a ship, etc.) seaworthy (*in navigable condition*). 3 (of a balloon, aircraft, etc.) steerable. □□ **nav·i·ga·bil·i·ty** *n.* [F *navigable* or L *navigabilis* (as NAVIGATE)]

nav·i·gate /návigayt/ *v.* 1 *tr.* manage or direct the course of (a ship, aircraft, etc.). 2 *tr.* **a** sail on (a sea, river, etc.). **b** travel or fly through (the air). 3 *intr.* (of a passenger in a vehicle) assist the driver by map-reading, etc. 4 *intr.* sail a ship; sail in a ship. 5 *tr.* (often *refl.*) *colloq.* steer (oneself, a course, etc.) through a crowd, etc. [L *navigare* f. *navis* ship + *agere* drive]

nav·i·ga·tion /návigáyshən/ *n.* 1 the act or process of navigating. 2 any of several methods of determining or planning a ship's or aircraft's position and course by geometry, astronomy, radio signals, etc. 3 a voyage. □□ **nav·i·ga·tion·al** *adj.* [F or f. L *navigatio* (as NAVIGATE)]

nav·i·ga·tion light *n. Brit.* = RUNNING LIGHT 1.

nav·i·ga·tor /návigaytər/ *n.* 1 a person skilled or engaged in navigation. 2 an explorer by sea. [L (as NAVIGATE)]

nav·vy /návee/ *n. & v. Brit.* • *n.* (*pl.* **·vies**) a laborer employed in building or excavating roads, canals, etc. • *v.intr.* (**·vies**, **·vied**) work as a navvy. [abbr. of NAVIGATOR]

na·vy /náyvee/ *n.* (*pl.* **·vies**) 1 (often **the Navy**) **a** the whole body of a nation's ships of war, including crews, maintenance systems, etc. **b** the officers, men, and women of a navy. 2 (in full **navy blue**) a dark-blue color. 3 *poet.* a fleet of ships. [ME, = fleet f. OF *navie* ship, fleet f. Rmc & pop.L *navia* ship f. L *navis*]

na·vy bean *n.* a small white kidney bean, usu. dried for storage and then soaked and cooked before being eaten.

Na·vy Cross *n.* a US Navy decoration awarded for extraordinary heroism against an enemy.

na·vy yard *n.* a government shipyard where naval vessels are built, maintained, etc., and where naval supplies are stored.

na·wab /nəwaáb, –waáwb/ *n.* **1** the title of a distinguished Muslim in Pakistan. **2** *hist.* the title of a governor or nobleman in India. [Urdu *nawwāb* pl. f. Arab. *nā'ib* deputy: cf. NABOB]

nay /nay/ *adv. & n.* ● *adv.* **1** or rather; and even; and more than that (*impressive, nay, magnificent*). **2** *archaic* = NO² *adv.* 1. ● *n.* **1** the word 'nay'. **2** a negative vote (*counted 16 nays*). **3** a person who votes nay. [ME f. ON *nei* f. *ne* not + *ei* AYE²]

nay·say /náysay/ *v.* (*3rd sing. present* **·says**; *past* and *past part.* **·said**) **1** *intr.* utter a denial or refusal. **2** *tr.* refuse or contradict. □□ **nay·say·er** *n.*

Naz·a·rene /názərēen/ *n. & adj.* ● *n.* **1 a** (*prec. by the*) Christ. **b** (esp. in Jewish or Muslim use) a Christian. **2** a native or inhabitant of Nazareth. **3** a member of an early Jewish-Christian sect. ● *adj.* of or concerning Nazareth, the Nazarenes, etc. [ME f. LL *Nazarenus* f. Gk *Nazarēnos* f. *Nazaret* Nazareth]

Naz·a·rite /názərīt/ *n.* (also **Naz·i·rite**) *hist.* a Hebrew who had taken certain vows of abstinence; an ascetic (Num. 6). [LL *Nazaraeus* f. Heb. *nāzīr* f. *nāzar* to separate or consecrate oneself]

Na·zi /naátsee, nát–/ *n. & adj.* ● *n.* (*pl.* **Na·zis**) **1** *hist.* a member of the German National Socialist party. **2** *derog.* a person holding extreme racist or authoritarian views or behaving brutally. **3** a person belonging to any organization similar to the Nazis. ● *adj.* of or concerning the Nazis, Nazism, etc. □□ **Na·zi·dom** *n.* **Na·zi·fy** /–sifī/ *v.tr.* (**·fies, ·fied**). **Na·zi·ism** /–see–izəm/ *n.* **Na·zism** /naátsizəm, nát–/ *n.* [repr. pronunc. of *Nati–* in G *Nationalsozialist*]

Naz·i·rite var. of NAZARITE.

NB *abbr.* **1** New Brunswick. **2** nota bene. **3** Scotland (North Britain).

Nb *symb. Chem.* the element niobium.

NBC *abbr.* National Broadcasting Company.

NbE *abbr.* north by east.

NbW *abbr.* north by west.

NC *abbr.* North Carolina (also in official postal use).

NCO *abbr.* noncommissioned officer.

ND *abbr.* North Dakota (in official postal use).

Nd *symb. Chem.* the element neodymium.

n.d. *abbr.* no date.

-nd *suffix* see –AND, –END.

N.Dak. *abbr.* North Dakota.

NE *abbr.* **1** Nebraska (in official postal use). **2** northeast. **3** northeastern.

Ne *symb. Chem.* the element neon.

né /nay/ *adj.* born (indicating a man's previous name) (*Lord Beaconsfield, né Benjamin Disraeli*). [F, past part. of *naître* be born: cf. NÉE]

NEA *abbr.* National Education Association.

Ne·an·der·thal /neeándərthawl, –tawl, –taal/ *adj.* (also **Ne·an·der·tal**) of or belonging to the type of human widely distributed in Paleolithic Europe, with a retreating forehead and massive brow ridges. [*Neanderthal,* a region in Germany where remains were found]

neap /neep/ *n. & v.* ● *n.* (in full **neap tide**) a tide just after the first and third quarters of the moon when there is least difference between high and low water. ● *v.* **1** *intr.* (of a tide) tend toward or reach the highest point of a neap tide. **2** *tr.* (in *passive*) (of a ship) be kept aground, in harbor, etc., by a neap tide. [OE *nēpflōd* (cf. FLOOD), of unkn. orig.]

Ne·a·pol·i·tan /neeəpólitən/ *n. & adj.* ● *n.* a native or citizen of Naples in Italy. ● *adj.* of or relating to Naples. [ME f. L *Neapolitanus* f. L *Neapolis* Naples f. Gk f. *neos* new + *polis* city]

Ne·a·pol·i·tan ice cream *n.* ice cream made in layers of different colors and flavors, esp. vanilla, chocolate, and strawberry.

Ne·a·pol·i·tan vi·o·let *n.* a sweet-scented double viola.

near /neer/ *adv., prep., adj., & v.* ● *adv.* **1** (often foll. by *to*) to or at a short distance in space or time; close by (*the time drew near; dropped near to them*). **2** closely (*as near as one can guess*). **3** *archaic* almost, nearly (*very near died*). **4** *archaic* parsimoniously; meanly (*lives very near*). ● *prep.* (compar. & superl. also used) **1** to or at a short distance (in space, time, condition, or resemblance) from (*stood near the back* ; *occurs nearer the end; the sun is near setting*). **2** (in comb.) **a** that is almost (*near-hysterical; a near-Communist*). **b** intended as a substitute for; resembling (*near beer*). ● *adj.* **1** (usu. *predic.*) close at hand; close to, in place or time (*the man nearest you; in the near future*). **2 a** closely related (*a near relation*). **b** intimate (*a near friend*). **3** (of a part of a vehicle, animal, or road) left (*the near foreleg; near side front wheel* [orig. of the side from which one mounted]) (opp. OFF). **4** close; narrow (*a near escape; a near guess*). **5** (of a road or way) direct. **6** niggardly, mean. ● *v.* **1** *tr.* approach; draw near to (*neared the harbor*). **2** *intr.* draw near (*could distinguish them as they neared*). □ **come** (or **go**) **near** (foll. by verbal noun, or *to* +

verbal noun) be on the point of, almost succeed in (*came near to falling*). **go near** (foll. by *to* + infin.) narrowly fail. **near at hand 1** within easy reach. **2** in the immediate future. **near go** *Brit. colloq.* a narrow escape. **near the knuckle** *Brit. colloq.* verging on the indecent. **near upon** *archaic* not far in time from. □□ **near·ish** *adj.* **near·ness** *n.* [ME f. ON *nær*, orig. compar. of *ná* = OE *nēah* NIGH]

near·by /néerbī/ *adj. & adv.* ● *adj.* situated in a near position (*a nearby hotel*). ● *adv.* close; not far away.

Ne·arc·tic /neeaárktik/ *adj.* of or relating to the Arctic and the temperate parts of N. America as a zoogeographical region. [NEO- + ARCTIC]

Near East *n.* the region comprising the countries of the eastern Mediterranean. □□ **Near East·ern** *adj.*

near·ly /néerlee/ *adv.* **1** almost (*we are nearly there*). **2** closely (*they are nearly related*). □ **not nearly** nothing like; far from (*not nearly enough*).

near miss *n.* **1** a bomb, etc., that is close to the target. **2** a situation in which a collision is narrowly avoided. **3** an attempt that is almost but not quite successful.

near·sight·ed /néersítid/ *adj.* having the inability to focus the eyes except on comparatively near objects. □□ **near·sight·ed·ly** *adv.* **near·sight·ed·ness** *n.*

neat¹ /neet/ *adj.* **1** tidy and methodical. **2** elegantly simple in form, etc.; well-proportioned. **3** (of language, style, etc.) brief, clear, and pointed; epigrammatic. **4 a** cleverly executed (*a neat piece of work*). **b** deft; dexterous. **5** (of esp. alcoholic liquor) undiluted. **6** *sl.* (as a general term of approval) good, pleasing, excellent. □□ **neat·ly** *adv.* **neat·ness** *n.* [F *net* f. L *nitidus* shining f. *nitēre* shine]

neat² /neet/ *n. archaic* **1** a bovine animal. **2** (as *pl.*) cattle. [OE *nēat* f. Gmc]

neat·en /néet'n/ *v.tr.* make neat.

neath /neeth/ *prep. poet.* beneath. [BENEATH]

neat's-foot oil *n.* oil made from boiled cow heel and used to dress leather.

NEB *abbr.* New English Bible.

Neb. *abbr.* Nebraska.

neb /neb/ *n. Sc. & No. of Engl.* **1** a beak or bill. **2** a nose; a snout. **3** a tip, spout, or point. [OE *nebb* ult. f. Gmc: cf. NIB]

neb·bish /nébish/ *n. & adj. colloq.* ● *n.* a submissive or timid person. ● *adj.* submissive; timid. [Yiddish *nebach* poor thing!]

Nebr. *abbr.* Nebraska.

Neb·u·chad·nez·zar /nébəkədnézər, nébyōō–/ *n.* a wine bottle of about 20 times the standard size. [name of a king of Babylonia (6th c. BC)]

neb·u·la /nébyələ/ *n.* (*pl.* **neb·u·lae** /–lee/ or **neb·u·las**) **1** *Astron.* **a** a cloud of gas and dust, sometimes glowing and sometimes appearing as a dark silhouette against other glowing matter. **b** a bright area caused by a galaxy, or a large cloud of distant stars. **2** *Med.* a clouded spot on the cornea causing defective vision. [L, = mist]

neb·u·lar /nébyələr/ *adj.* of or relating to a nebula or nebulae.

neb·u·lar the·o·ry (also **neb·u·lar hy·poth·e·sis**) *n.* the theory that the solar and stellar systems were developed from a primeval nebula.

neb·u·lous /nébyələs/ *adj.* **1** cloudlike. **2 a** formless, clouded. **b** hazy, indistinct, vague (*put forward a few nebulous ideas*). **3** *Astron.* of or like a nebula or nebulae. □□ **neb·u·los·i·ty** /–lósitee/ *n.* **neb·u·lous·ly** *adv.* **neb·u·lous·ness** *n.* [ME f. F *nébuleux* or L *nebulosus* (as NEBULA)]

neb·u·lous star *n.* a small cluster of indistinct stars, or a star in a luminous haze.

neb·u·ly /nébyəlee/ *adj. Heraldry* wavy in form; cloudlike. [F *nébulé* f. med.L *nebulatus* f. L NEBULA]

nec·es·sar·i·an /nésisáireeən/ *n. & adj.* = NECESSITARIAN. □□ **nec·es·sar·i·an·ism** *n.*

nec·es·sar·i·ly /nésəsérilee/ *adv.* as a necessary result; inevitably.

nec·es·sar·y /nésəseree/ *adj. & n.* ● *adj.* **1** requiring to be done, achieved, etc.; requisite; essential (*it is necessary to work; lacks the necessary documents*). **2** determined, existing, or happening by natural laws, predestination, etc., not by free will; inevitable (*a neces-*

SYNONYM TIP *necessary*

ESSENTIAL, INDISPENSABLE, REQUISITE. Food is **essential** to human life, which means that we must have it to survive. *Essential* can also apply to something that makes up the *essence*, or necessary qualities or attributes, of a thing (*good brakes are essential to safe driving*). Clothing is **indispensable** in Northern climates, which means that it cannot be done without if the specified or implied purpose—in this case, survival—is to be achieved. **Necessary** applies to something without which a condition cannot be fulfilled (*cooperation was necessary to gather the harvest*), although it generally implies a pressing need rather than absolute indispensability. **Requisite** refers to that which is required by the circumstances (*the requisite skills for a botanist*) and generally describes a requirement that is imposed from the outside rather than an inherent need.

sary evil). **3** Philos. (of a concept or a mental process) inevitably resulting from or produced by the nature of things, etc., so that the contrary is impossible. **4** Philos. (of an agent) having no independent volition. ● n. (pl. ·ies) (usu. in pl.) any of the basic requirements of life, such as food, warmth, etc. □ **the necessary** colloq. **1** money. **2** an action, item, etc., needed for a purpose (they will do the necessary). [ME f. OF necessaire f. L necessarius f. necesse needful]

ne·ces·si·tar·i·an /nisésitáireeən/ n. & adj. Philos. ● n. a person who holds that all action is predetermined and that free will is impossible. ● adj. of or concerning such a person or theory (opp. LIBERTARIAN). □□ **ne·ces·si·tar·i·an·ism** n.

ne·ces·si·tate /nisésitayt/ v.tr. **1** make necessary (esp. as a result) (will necessitate some sacrifice). **2** (usu. foll. by to + infin.) force or compel (a person) to do something. [med.L necessitare compel (as NECESSITY)]

ne·ces·si·tous /nisésitəs/ adj. poor; needy. [F nécessiteux or f. NECESSITY + -OUS]

ne·ces·si·ty /nisésitee/ n. (pl. ·ties) **1 a** an indispensable thing; a necessary thing (central heating is a necessity). **b** (usu. foll. by of) indispensability (the necessity of a warm overcoat). **2** a state of things or circumstances enforcing a certain course (there was a necessity to hurry). **3** imperative need (necessity is the mother of invention). **4** want; poverty; hardship (stole because of necessity). **5** constraint or compulsion regarded as a natural law governing all human action. □ **of necessity** unavoidably. [ME f. OF necessité f. L necessitas –tatis f. necesse needful]

neck /nek/ n. & v. ● n. **1 a** the part of the body connecting the head to the shoulders. **b** the part of a shirt, dress, etc., around or close to the neck. **2 a** something resembling a neck, such as the narrow part of a cavity or vessel, a passage, channel, pass, isthmus, etc. **b** the narrow part of a bottle near the mouth. **3** the part of a violin, etc., bearing the fingerboard. **4** the length of a horse's head and neck as a measure of its lead in a race. **5** the flesh of an animal's neck (neck of lamb). **6** Geol. solidified lava or igneous rock in an old volcano crater or pipe. **7** Archit. the lower part of a capital. **8** Brit. sl. impudence (you've got a neck, asking that). ● v. **1** intr. & tr. colloq. kiss and caress amorously. **2 a** tr. form a narrowed part in. **b** intr. form a narrowed part. □ **get it in the neck** colloq. **1** receive a severe reprimand or punishment. **2** suffer a fatal or severe blow. **neck and neck** running even in a race, etc. **neck or nothing** risking everything on success. **up to one's neck** (often foll. by in) colloq. very deeply involved; very busy. □□ **necked** adj. (also in comb.). **neck·er** n. (in sense 1 of v.). **neck·less** adj. [OE hnecca ult. f. Gmc]

neck·band /nékband/ n. a strip of material around the neck of a garment.

neck·cloth /nék-klawth, –kloth/ n. hist. a cravat.

neck·er·chief /nékərchif, –cheef/ n. a square of cloth worn around the neck.

neck·ing /néking/ n. Archit. = NECK n. 7.

neck·lace /nékləs/ n. a chain or string of beads, precious stones, links, etc., worn as an ornament around the neck.

neck·let /néklit/ n. **1** = NECKLACE. **2** a strip of fur worn around the neck.

neck·line /néklin/ n. the edge or shape of the opening of a garment at the neck (a square neckline).

neck of the woods n. colloq. **1** region; neighborhood. **2** esp. Brit. a usu. remote locality.

neck·tie /néktí/ n. = TIE n. 2.

neck·tie par·ty n. sl. a lynching or hanging.

neck·wear /nékwair/ n. collars, ties, etc.

necro- /nékrō/ comb. form corpse. [from or after Gk nekro- f. nekros corpse]

nec·ro·bi·o·sis /nékrōbīósis/ n. decay in the tissues of the body, esp. swelling of the collagen bundles in the dermis. □□ **nec·ro·bi·ot·ic** /–biótik/ adj.

ne·crol·a·try /nekrólətree/ n. worship of or excessive reverence toward the dead.

ne·crol·o·gy /nekróləjee/ n. (pl. ·gies) **1** a list of recently dead people. **2** an obituary notice. □□ **nec·ro·log·i·cal** /–rəlójikəl/ adj.

nec·ro·man·cy /nékrōmansee/ n. **1** the prediction of the future by the supposed communication with the dead. **2** witchcraft. □□ **nec·ro·man·cer** n. **nec·ro·man·tic** /–mántik/ adj. [ME f. OF nigromancie f. med.L nigromantia changed (by assoc. with L niger nigri black) f. LL necromantia f. Gk nekromanteia (as NECRO-, –MANCY)]

nec·ro·phil·i·a /nékrəfileeə/ n. (also **nec·ro·phil·y** /nikrófilee/) a morbid and esp. erotic attraction to corpses. □□ **nec·ro·phil·i·ac** /–fileeak/ n. **nec·ro·phil·ic** adj. **nec·roph·i·lism** /–krófilizəm/ n. **nec·roph·i·list** /–krófilist/ n. [NECRO- + Gk –philia loving]

nec·ro·pho·bi·a /nékrəfóbeeə/ n. an abnormal fear of death or dead bodies.

ne·crop·o·lis /nekrópəlis/ n. an ancient cemetery or burial place.

nec·rop·sy /nékropsee/ n. (also **nec·ros·co·py** /–króskəpee/) (pl. ·pies) = AUTOPSY 1. [NECRO- after AUTOPSY, or + –SCOPY]

ne·cro·sis /nekrósis/ n. Med. & Physiol. the death of tissue caused

by disease or injury, esp. as one of the symptoms of gangrene or pulmonary tuberculosis. □□ **ne·crose** v.intr. **ne·crot·ic** /–krótik/ adj. **nec·ro·tize** /nékrətiz/ v.intr. [mod.L f. Gk nekrōsis (as NECRO-, –OSIS)]

nec·tar /néktər/ n. **1** a sugary substance produced by plants and made into honey by bees. **2** (in Greek and Roman mythology) the drink of the gods. **3** a drink compared to this. □□ **nec·tar·e·an** /–táireeən/ adj. **nec·tar·e·ous** /–táireeəs/ adj. **nec·tar·if·er·ous** /–rífərəs/ adj. **nec·tar·ous** adj. [L f. Gk nektar]

nec·tar·ine /néktəreen/ n. **1** a variety of peach with a thin brightly colored smooth skin and firm flesh. **2** the tree bearing this. [orig. as adj., = nectarlike, f. NECTAR + –INE⁴]

nec·ta·ry /néktəree/ n. (pl. ·ries) the nectar-secreting organ of a flower or plant. [mod.L nectarium (as NECTAR)]

ned·dy /nédee/ n. (pl. ·dies) Brit. colloq. a donkey. [dimin. of Ned, pet form of the name Edward]

Ned Kel·ly /ned kélee/ n. Austral. a person of reckless courage or unscrupulous business dealings. [the name of the most famous Australian bushranger (1857–80)]

née /nay/ adj. (also **nee**) (used in adding a married woman's maiden name after her surname) born (Mrs. Ann Smith, née Jones). [F, fem. past part. of naître be born]

need /need/ v. & v. ● v. **1** tr. stand in want of; require (needs a new coat). **2** tr. (foll. by to + infin.; 3rd sing. present neg. or interrog. need without to) be under the necessity or obligation (it needs to be done carefully; he need not come; need you ask?). **3** intr. archaic be necessary. ● n. **1 a** a want or requirement (my needs are few; the need for greater freedom). **b** a thing wanted (my greatest need is a car). **2** circumstances requiring some course of action; necessity (there is no need to worry; if need arise). **3** destitution; poverty. **4** a crisis; an emergency (failed them in their need). □ **at need** in time of need. **had need** archaic ought to (had need remember). **have need of** require; want. **have need to** require to (has need to be warned). **in need** requiring help. **in need of** requiring. **need not have** did not need to (but did). [OE nēodian, nēd f. Gmc]

need·ful /néedfool/ adj. **1** requisite; necessary; indispensable. **2** (prec. by the) **a** what is necessary. **b** colloq. money or action needed for a purpose. □□ **need·ful·ly** adv. **need·ful·ness** n.

nee·dle /néed'l/ n. & v. ● n. **1 a** a very thin small piece of smooth steel, etc., pointed at one end and with a slit (eye) for thread at the other, used in sewing. **b** a larger plastic, wooden, etc., slender stick without an eye, used in knitting. **c** a slender hooked stick used in crochet. **2** a pointer on a dial (see MAGNETIC NEEDLE). **3** any of several small thin pointed instruments, esp.: **a** a surgical instrument for stitching. **b** the end of a hypodermic syringe. **c** = STYLUS 1. **d** an etching tool. **e** a steel pin exploding the cartridge of a breechloading gun. **4 a** an obelisk (Cleopatra's Needle). **b** a pointed rock or peak. **5** the leaf of a fir or pine tree. **6** a beam used as a temporary support during underpinning. **7** Brit. sl. a fit of bad temper or nervousness (got the needle while waiting). ● v.tr. **1** colloq. incite or irritate; provoke (the silence needled him). **2** sew, pierce, or operate on with a needle. [OE nēdl f. Gmc]

nee·dle·craft /néed'lkraft/ n. skill in needlework.

nee·dle·fish /néed'lfish/ n. a garfish.

nee·dle in a hay·stack n. something almost impossible to find because it is concealed by so many other things, etc.

nee·dle·point /néed'lpoynt/ n. decorative needlework or lace made with a needle.

nee·dle's eye (also **eye of a nee·dle**) n. the least possible aperture, esp. with ref. to Matt. 19:24.

need·less /néedlis/ adj. **1** unnecessary. **2** uncalled-for; gratuitous. □ **needless to say** of course; it goes without saying. □□ **need·less·ly** adv. **need·less·ness** n.

nee·dle time n. Brit. an agreed maximum allowance of time for broadcasting music from records.

nee·dle valve n. a valve closed by a thin tapering part.

nee·dle·wom·an /néed'lwoomən/ n. (pl. ·wom·en) **1** a seamstress. **2** a woman or girl with specified sewing skill (a good needlewoman).

nee·dle·work /néed'lwərk/ n. sewing or embroidery.

needs /needz/ adv. archaic (usu. prec. or foll. by must) of necessity (must needs decide). [OE nēdes (as NEED, –S³)]

need·y /néedee/ adj. (need·i·er, need·i·est) **1** (of a person) poor; destitute. **2** (of circumstances) characterized by poverty. **3** emotionally impoverished or demanding. □□ **need·i·ness** n.

neep /neep/ n. Sc. & No. of Engl. a turnip. [OE nǣp f. L napus]

ne'er /nair/ adv. poet. = NEVER. [ME contr. of NEVER]

ne'er-do-well n. n. a good-for-nothing person. ● adj. good-for-nothing.

ne·far·i·ous /nifáireeəs/ adj. wicked; iniquitous. □□ **ne·far·i·ous·ly** adv. **ne·far·i·ous·ness** n. [L nefarius f. nefas wrong f. ne- not + fas divine law]

neg. abbr. negative.

ne·gate /nigáyt/ v.tr. **1** nullify; invalidate. **2** imply, involve, or assert the nonexistence of. **3** be the negation of. □□ **ne•ga•tor** *n.* [L *negare negat-* deny]

ne•ga•tion /nigáyshən/ *n.* **1** the absence or opposite of something actual or positive. **2 a** the act of denying. **b** an instance of this. **3** (usu. foll. by *of*) a refusal, contradiction, or denial. **4** a negative statement or doctrine. **5** a negative or unreal thing; a nonentity. **6** *Logic* the assertion that a certain proposition is false. □□ **neg•a•tory** /négətáwree/ *adj.* [F *negation* or L *negatio* (as NEGATE)]

neg•a•tive /négətiv/ *adj., n., & v.* • *adj.* **1** expressing or implying denial, prohibition, or refusal (*a negative vote; a negative answer*). **2** (of a person or attitude): **a** lacking positive attributes; apathetic; pessimistic. **b** opposing or resisting; uncooperative. **3** marked by the absence of qualities (*a negative reaction ; a negative result from the test*). **4** of the opposite nature to a thing regarded as positive (*debt is negative capital*). **5** *Algebra* (of a quantity) less than zero, to be subtracted from others or from zero (opp. POSITIVE). **6** *Electr.* **a** of the kind of charge carried by electrons (opp. POSITIVE). **b** containing or producing such a charge. • *n.* **1** a negative statement, reply, or word (*hard to prove a negative*). **2** *Photog.* **a** an image with black and white reversed or colors replaced by complementary ones, from which positive pictures are obtained. **b** a developed film or plate bearing such an image. **3** a negative quality; an absence of something. **4** (prec. by *the*) a position opposing the affirmative. **5** *Logic* = NEGATION 6. • *v.tr.* **1** refuse to accept or countenance; veto; reject. **2** disprove (an inference or hypothesis). **3** contradict (a statement). **4** neutralize (an effect). □ **in the negative** with negative effect; so as to reject a proposal, etc.; no (*the answer was in the negative*). □□ **neg•a•tive•ly** *adv.* **neg•a•tive•ness** *n.* **neg•a•tiv•i•ty** /–tívitee/ *n.* [ME f. OF *negatif –ive* or LL *negativus* (as NEGATE)]

━━━━━━━━━━━━━━━━━
GRAMMAR TIP | negative
━━━━━━━━━━━━━━━━━
Two Negatives Make a Positive. Negative words include *no, nobody, nothing, nowhere, none, never, nor, neither,* and *not,* as well as the negative contractions that are formed by combining a verb with *not* (*can't, won't, wouldn't,* etc.). Generally speaking, only one negative expression should appear in a sentence. But using a double negative may be a more effective way of expressing a positive thought than a straightforward, positive statement. For example, in the sentence "I couldn't just stand there and do nothing," the double negative gives the sentence a positive meaning. However, if the sentence is intended to have a negative meaning, it should have only a single negative (*I stood there and did nothing*).

neg•a•tive ev•i•dence (also **neg•a•tive in•stance**) *n.* evidence of the nonoccurrence of something.

neg•a•tive feed•back *n.* **1** the return of part of an output signal to the input, tending to decrease the amplification, etc. **2** feedback that tends to diminish or counteract the process giving rise to it.

negative geotropism *n.* the tendency of stems, etc., to grow away from the center of the earth.

neg•a•tive in•come tax *n.* an amount credited as allowance to a taxed income, and paid as benefit when it exceeds debited tax.

neg•a•tive pole *n.* the south-seeking pole of a magnet.

neg•a•tive prop•o•si•tion *n.* *Logic* = NEGATION 6.

neg•a•tive quan•ti•ty *n.* *joc.* nothing.

neg•a•tive sign *n.* a symbol (-) indicating subtraction or a value less than zero.

neg•a•tive vir•tue *n.* abstention from vice.

neg•a•tiv•ism /négətivizəm/ *n.* **1** a negative position or attitude; extreme skepticism, criticism, etc. **2** denial of accepted beliefs. □□ **neg•a•tiv•ist** *n.* **neg•a•tiv•is•tic** /–vístik/ *adj.*

ne•glect /niglékt/ *v. & n.* • *v.tr.* **1** fail to care for or to do; be remiss about (*neglected their duty; neglected his children*). **2** (foll. by verbal noun, or *to* + infin.) fail; overlook or forget the need to (*neglected to inform them; neglected telling them*). **3** not pay attention to; disre-

━━━━━━━━━━━━━━━━━
SYNONYM TIP | neglect
━━━━━━━━━━━━━━━━━
DISREGARD, IGNORE, OVERLOOK, SLIGHT. One of the most common reasons why people fail to arrive at work on time is that they **neglect** to set their alarm clocks, a verb that implies a failure to carry out some expected or required action, either intentionally or through carelessness. Some people, of course, choose to **disregard** their employers' rules pertaining to tardiness, which implies a voluntary, and sometimes deliberate, inattention. Others hear the alarm go off and simply **ignore** it, which suggests not only a deliberate decision to *disregard* something but a stubborn refusal to face the facts. No doubt they hope their employers will **overlook** their frequent late arrivals, which implies a failure to see or to take action, which can be either intentional or due to haste or lack of care (*to overlook minor errors*). But they also hope no one will **slight** them for their conduct when it comes to handing out raises and promotions, which means to *disregard* or *neglect* in a disdainful way.

gard (*neglected the obvious warning*). • *n.* **1** lack of caring; negligence (*the house suffered from neglect*). **2 a** the act of neglecting. **b** the state of being neglected (*the house fell into neglect*). **3** (usu. foll. by *of*) disregard. □□ **ne•glect•ful** *adj.* **ne•glect•ful•ly** *adv.* **ne•glect•ful•ness** *n.* [L *neglegere* neglect- f. *neg-* not + *legere* choose, pick up]

neg•li•gee /néglizháy/ *n.* (also **neg•li•gée**, **nég•ligé**) **1** a woman's dressing gown of sheer fabric. **2** unceremonious or informal attire. [F, past part. of *négliger* NEGLECT]

neg•li•gence /néglijəns/ *n.* **1 a** a lack of proper care and attention; carelessness. **b** an act of carelessness. **2** *Law* = CONTRIBUTORY NEGLIGENCE. **3** *Art* freedom from restraint or artificiality. □□ **neg•li•gent** /–jənt/ *adj.* **neg•li•gent•ly** *adv.* [ME f. OF *negligence* or L *negligentia* f. *negligere = neglegere*: see NEGLECT]

neg•li•gi•ble /néglijibəl/ *adj.* not worth considering; insignificant. □□ **neg•li•gi•bil•i•ty** *n.* **neg•li•gi•bly** *adv.* [obs. F f. *négliger* NEGLECT]

ne•go•ti•a•ble /nigóshəbəl, –sheeə–/ *adj.* **1** open to discussion or modification. **2** able to be negotiated. □□ **ne•go•ti•a•bil•i•ty** *n.*

ne•go•ti•ate /nigósheeayt, –seeayt/ *v.* **1** *intr.* (usu. foll. by *with*) confer with others in order to reach a compromise or agreement. **2** *tr.* arrange (an affair) or bring about (a result) by negotiating (*negotiated a settlement*). **3** *tr.* find a way over, through, etc. (an obstacle, difficulty, fence, etc.). **4** *tr.* **a** transfer (a check, etc.) to another for a consideration. **b** convert (a check, etc.) into cash or notes. **c** get or give value for (a check, etc.) in money. □□ **ne•go•ti•ant** /–sheeənt, –seeənt/ *n.* **ne•go•ti•a•tion** /–áyshən/ *n.* **ne•go•ti•a•tor** *n.* [L *negotiari* f. *negotium* business f. *neg-* not + *otium* leisure]

Ne•gress /neégris/ *n.* often *offens.* a female Negro (black person).

Ne•gril•lo /nigriló/ *n.* (*pl.* **•los**) a member of a very small Negroid people native to Central and S. Africa. [Sp., dimin. of NEGRO]

Ne•gri•to /nigreetó/ *n.* (*pl.* **•tos**) a member of a small Negroid people native to the Malayo-Polynesian region. [as NEGRILLO]

neg•ri•tude /neégritood, –tyood, nég–/ *n.* (also **Neg•ri•tude**) *n.* **1** the quality or state of being a Negro (black person). **2** the affirmation or consciousness of the value of Negro (black) culture. [F *négritude* NIGRITUDE]

Ne•gro /neégró/ *n. & adj.* • *n.* (*pl.* **•groes**) a member of a dark-skinned race orig. native to Africa. • *adj.* **1** of or concerning Negroes (black people). **2** (as **negro**) *Zool.* black or dark (*negro ant*). [Sp. & Port., f. L *niger nigri* black]

▶The term *black* or *African American* is usually preferred when referring to people.

Ne•groid /neégroyd/ *adj. & n.* • *adj.* **1** (of features, etc.) characterizing a member of the Negro (black) race, esp. in having dark skin, tightly curled hair, and a broad flattish nose. **2** of or concerning Negroes (black people). • *n.* a Negro (black person). [NEGRO]

Ne•gus /neégəs/ *n.* *hist.* the title of the ruler of Ethiopia. [Amh. *n'gus* king]

ne•gus /neégəs/ *n.* *hist.* a hot drink of port, sugar, lemon, and spice. [Col. F. *Negus* d. 1732, its inventor]

Neh. *abbr.* Nehemiah (Old Testament).

neigh /nay/ *n. & v.* • *n.* **1** the high whinnying sound of a horse. **2** any similar sound, e.g., a laugh. • *v.* **1** *intr.* make such a sound. **2** *tr.* say, cry, etc., with such a sound. [OE *hnægan*, of imit. orig.]

neigh•bor /náybər/ *n. & v.* • *n.* **1** a person living next door to or near or nearest another (*my next-door neighbor; his nearest neighbor is 12 miles away; they are neighbors*). **2 a** a person regarded as having the duties or claims of friendliness, consideration, etc., of a neighbor. **b** a fellow human being, esp. as having claims on friendship. **3** a person or thing near or next to another (*my neighbor at dinner*). **4** (*attrib.*) neighboring. • *v.* **1** *tr.* border on; adjoin. **2** *intr.* (often foll. by *on, upon*) border; adjoin. □□ **neigh•bor•ing** *adj.* **neigh•bor•less** *adj.* **neigh•bor•ship** *n.* [OE *nēahgebūr* (as NIGH: *gebūr*, cf. BOOR)]

neigh•bor•hood /náybərhood/ *n.* **1 a** a district, esp. one forming a community within a town or city. **b** the people of a district; one's neighbors. **2** neighborly feeling or conduct. □ **in the neighborhood of** roughly; about (*paid in the neighborhood of $100*).

neigh•bor•hood watch *n.* systematic local vigilance by householders to discourage crime, esp. against children and property.

neigh•bor•ly /náybərlee/ *adj.* characteristic of a good neighbor; friendly; kind. □□ **neigh•bor•li•ness** *n.*

nei•ther /neéthər, níth–/ *adj., pron., adv., & conj.* • *adj. & pron.* (foll. by sing. verb) **1** not the one nor the other (of two things); not either (*neither of the accusations is true; neither of them knows; neither wish was granted; neither went to the fair*). **2** *disp.* none of any number of specified things. • *adv.* **1** not either; not on the one hand (foll. by *nor*; introducing the first of two or more things in the negative: *neither knowing nor caring; would neither come in nor go out; neither the teachers nor the parents nor the children*). **2** not either; also not (*if you do not, neither shall I*). **3** (with *neg.*) *disp.* either (*I don't know that neither*). • *conj.* archaic nor yet; nor (*I know not, neither can I guess*). [ME *naither, neither* f. OE *nōwther* contr. of *nōhwæther* (as NO[2], WHETHER): assim. to EITHER]

━━━━━━━━━━━━━━━━━
GRAMMAR TIP | neither
━━━━━━━━━━━━━━━━━
See note at EITHER.

nek·ton /néktən/ *n. Zool.* any aquatic animal able to swim and move independently. [G f. Gk *nekton* neut. of *nēktos* swimming f. *nēkhō* swim]

nel·lie /nélee/ *n.* a silly or effeminate person. □ **not on your nellie** *Brit. sl.* certainly not. [perh. f. the name *Nelly*: idiom f. rhyming sl. *Nelly Duff* = puff = breath: cf. *not on your life*]

nel·son /nélsən/ *n.* a wrestling hold in which one arm is passed under the opponent's arm from behind and the hand is applied to the neck (**half nelson**), or both arms and hands are applied (**full nelson**). [app. f. the name *Nelson*]

ne·lum·bo /nilúmbō/ *n.* (*pl.* **·bos**) any water lily of the genus *Nelumbo*, native to India and China, bearing small pink flowers. Also called **lotus**. [mod.L f. Sinh. *neḷum(bu)*]

nem·a·to·cyst /nímátəsist, némə–/ *n.* a specialized cell in a jellyfish, etc., containing a coiled thread that can be projected as a sting. [as NEMATODE + CYST]

nem·a·tode /nématōd/ *n.* any parasitic or free-living worm of the phylum Nematoda, with a slender unsegmented cylindrical shape. Also called **roundworm**. [Gk *nēma –matos* thread + –ODE[1]]

Nem·bu·tal /némbyətawl, –taal/ *n. Trademark* a sodium salt of pentobarbitone, used as a sedative and anticonvulsant. [*N*a (= sodium) + 5-*e*thyl-5-(1-methyl*bu*tyl) barbiturate + –AL]

nem. con. *abbr.* with no one dissenting. [L *nemine contradicente*]

ne·mer·te·an /nimórteeən/ *n. & adj.* (also **ne·mer·tine** /–tīn/) • *n.* any marine ribbon worm of the phylum Nemertea, often very long and brightly colored, found in tangled knots in coastal waters of Europe and the Mediterranean. • *adj.* of or relating to this class. [mod.L *Nemertes* f. Gk *Nēmertēs* name of a sea nymph]

nem·e·sia /nimée̱zhə/ *n.* any S. African plant of the genus *Nemesia*, cultivated for its variously colored and irregular flowers. [mod.L f. Gk *nemesion*, the name of a similar plant]

nem·e·sis /némisis/ *n.* (*pl.* **nem·e·ses** /–seez/) **1** retributive justice. **2 a** a downfall caused by this. **b** an agent of such a downfall. [Gk, = righteous indignation, personified as goddess of retribution f. *nemō* give what is due]

neo- /née-ō/ *comb. form* **1** new, modern. **2** a new or revived form of. [Gk f. *neos* new]

ne·o·clas·si·cal /née-ōklásikəl/ *adj.* (also **ne·o·clas·sic** /–ik/) of or relating to a revival of a classical style or treatment in art, literature, music, etc. □□ **ne·o·clas·si·cism** /–sisizəm/ *n.* **ne·o·clas·si·cist** *n.*

ne·o·co·lo·ni·al·ism /née-ōkəlóneeəlizəm/ *n.* the use of economic, political, or other pressures to control or influence other countries, esp. former dependencies. □□ **ne·o·co·lo·ni·al·ist** *n. & adj.*

ne·o·dym·i·um /née-ədímeeəm/ *n. Chem.* a silver-gray naturally occurring metallic element of the lanthanide series used in coloring glass, etc. ¶ Symb.: **Nd**. [NEO- + DIDYMIUM]

ne·o·lith·ic /née-əlíthik/ *adj.* of or relating to the later Stone Age, when ground or polished stone weapons and implements prevailed. [NEO- + Gk *lithos* stone]

ne·ol·o·gism /nee-óləjizəm/ *n.* **1** a new word or expression. **2** the coining or use of new words. □□ **ne·ol·o·gist** *n.* **ne·ol·o·gize** /–jīz/ *v.intr.* [F *néologisme* (as NEO-, –LOGY, –ISM)]

ne·o·my·cin /née-ōmísin/ *n.* an antibiotic related to streptomycin.

ne·on /née-on/ *n. Chem.* an inert gaseous element occurring in traces in the atmosphere and giving an orange glow when electricity is passed through it in a sealed low-pressure tube, used in lights and illuminated advertisements (*neon light; neon sign*). ¶ Symb.: **Ne**. [Gk, neut. of *neos* new]

ne·o·nate /née-ənayt/ *n.* a newborn child. □□ **ne·o·na·tal** /–náyt'l/ *adj.* [mod.L *neonatus* (as NEO-, L *nasci nat–* be born)]

ne·o·phyte /née-əfīt/ *n.* **1** a new convert, esp. to a religious faith. **2** *RC Ch.* **a** a novice of a religious order. **b** a newly ordained priest. **3** a beginner; a novice. [eccl.L *neophytus* f. NT Gk *neophutos* newly planted (as NEO- + *phuton* plant)]

ne·o·plasm /née-əplazəm/ *n.* a new and abnormal growth of tissue in some part of the body, esp. a tumor. □□ **ne·o·plas·tic** /–plástik/ *adj.* [NEO- + Gk *plasma* formation: see PLASMA]

Ne·o·pla·to·nism /née-ōpláyt'nizəm/ *n.* a philosophical and religious system developed by the followers of Plotinus in the third c., combining Platonic thought with oriental mysticism. □□ **Ne·o·pla·ton·ic** /–plətónik/ *adj.* **Ne·o·pla·to·nist** *n.*

ne·o·prene /née-əpreen/ *n.* a synthetic rubberlike polymer. [NEO- + *chloroprene*, etc. (perh. f. PROPYL + –ENE)]

ne·ot·e·ny /neeót'nee/ *n.* the retention of juvenile features in the adult form of some animals, e.g., an axolotl. □□ **ne·ot·e·nic** /née-ōténik/ *adj.* **ne·ot·e·nous** *adj.* [G *Neotenie* (as NEO- + Gk *teinō* extend)]

ne·o·ter·ic /née-ətérik/ *adj. literary* recent; newfangled; modern. [LL *neotericus* f. Gk *neōterikos* (*neōteros* compar. of *neos* new)]

ne·o·trop·i·cal /née-ōtrópikəl/ *adj.* of or relating to tropical and S. America as a biogeographical region.

Nep·a·lese /népəleéz, –leés/ *adj. & n.* (*pl.* same) = NEPALI.

Ne·pal·i /nipáwlee/ *n. & adj.* • *n.* (*pl.* same or **Ne·pa·lis**) **1 a** a native or national of Nepal in Central Asia. **b** a person of Nepali descent. **2** the language of Nepal. • *adj.* of or relating to Nepal or its language or people.

ne·pen·the /nipénthee/ *n.* = NEPENTHES 1. [var. of NEPENTHES, after It. *nepente*]

ne·pen·thes /nipéntheez/ *n.* **1** *poet.* a drug causing forgetfulness of grief. **2** any pitcher plant of the genus *Nepenthes*. [L f. Gk *nēpenthes* (*pharmakon* drug), neut. of *nēpenthēs* f. *nē–* not + *penthos* grief]

neph·ew /néfyoo/ *n.* a son of one's brother or sister, or of one's brother-in-law or sister-in-law. [ME f. OF *neveu* f. L *nepos nepotis* grandson, nephew]

ne·phol·o·gy /nefóləjee/ *n.* the study of clouds. [Gk *nephos* cloud + –LOGY]

neph·rite /néfrīt/ *n.* a green, yellow, or white calcium magnesium silicate form of jade. [G *Nephrit* f. Gk *nephros* kidney, with ref. to its supposed efficacy in treating kidney disease]

ne·phrit·ic /nəfrítik/ *adj.* **1** of or in the kidneys; renal. **2** of or relating to nephritis. [LL *nephriticus* f. Gk *nephritikos* (as NEPHRITIS)]

ne·phri·tis /nefrítis/ *n.* inflammation of the kidneys. Also called **Bright's disease**. [LL f. Gk *nephros* kidney]

nephro- /néfrō/ *comb. form* (usu. **nephr-** before a vowel) kidney. [Gk f. *nephros* kidney]

ne plus ul·tra /náyplooʊsóoltraa, nēplus últrə/ *n.* (**the ne plus ul·tra**) **1** the farthest attainable point. **2** the culmination, acme, or perfection. [L, = not farther beyond, the supposed inscription on the Pillars of Hercules (the Strait of Gibraltar) prohibiting passage by ships]

nep·o·tism /népətizəm/ *n.* favoritism shown to relatives in conferring offices or privileges. □□ **nep·o·tist** *n.* **nep·o·tis·tic** *adj.* [F *népotisme* f. It. *nepotismo* f. *nepote* NEPHEW: orig. with ref. to popes with illegitimate sons called nephews]

Nep·tune /néptōon, –tyōon/ *n.* a distant planet of the solar system, eighth from the sun, discovered in 1846 from mathematical computations. [ME f. F *Neptune* or L *Neptunus* god of the sea]

nep·tu·ni·um /neptōoneeəm, –tyōo–/ *n. Chem.* a radioactive transuranic metallic element produced when uranium atoms absorb bombarding neutrons. ¶ Symb.: **Np**. [NEPTUNE, as the next planet beyond Uranus, + –IUM]

nerd /nərd/ *n.* (also **nurd**) *sl.* **1** a foolish, feeble, or uninteresting person. **2** a person academically or intellectually talented but socially unskilled. □□ **nerd·y** *adj.* [20th c.: orig. uncert.]

ne·re·id /néereeid/ *n. Mythol.* a sea nymph. [L *Nereïs Nereïd–* f. Gk *Nēreïs –idos* daughter of the sea god Nereus]

ne·ri·ne /nirínee/ *n.* any S. African plant of the genus *Nerine*, bearing flowers with usu. six narrow strap-shaped petals, often crimped and twisted. [mod.L f. the L name of a water nymph]

ner·o·li /nérəlee, néer–/ *n.* (in full **neroli oil**) an essential oil from the flowers of the Seville orange, used in perfumery. [F *néroli* f. It. *neroli*, perh. f. the name of an Italian princess]

ner·vate /nórvayt/ *adj.* (of a leaf) having veins. □□ **ner·va·tion** /–váyshən/ *n.* [NERVE + –ATE[2]]

nerve /nərv/ *n. & v.* • *n.* **1 a** a fiber or bundle of fibers that transmits impulses of sensation or motion between the brain or spinal cord and other parts of the body. **b** the material constituting these. **2 a** coolness in danger; bravery; assurance. **b** *colloq.* impudence; audacity (*they've got a nerve*). **3** (in *pl.*) **a** the bodily state in regard to physical sensitiveness and the interaction between the brain and other parts. **b** a state of heightened nervousness or sensitivity; a condition of mental or physical stress (*need to calm my nerves*). **4** a rib of a leaf, esp. the midrib. **5** *poet. archaic* a sinew or tendon. • *v.tr.* **1** (usu. *refl.*) brace (oneself) to face danger, suffering, etc. **2** give strength, vigor, or courage to. □ **get on a person's nerves** irritate or annoy a person. **have nerves of iron** (or **steel**) (of a person, etc.) be not easily upset or frightened. □□ **nerved** *adj.* (also in *comb.*). [ME, = sinew, f. L *nervus*, rel. to Gk *neuron*]

nerve cell *n.* an elongated branched cell transmitting impulses in nerve tissue.

nerve cen·ter *n.* **1** a group of closely connected nerve cells associated in performing some function. **2** the center of control of an organization, etc.

nerve gas *n.* a poisonous gas affecting the nervous system.

nerve·less /nórvlis/ *adj.* **1** inert; lacking vigor or spirit. **2** confident; not nervous. **3** (of style) diffuse. **4** *Bot. & Entomol.* without nervures. **5** *Anat. & Zool.* without nerves. □□ **nerve·less·ly** *adv.* **nerve·less·ness** *n.*

nerve-rack·ing *adj.* (also **nerve-wrack·ing**) stressful, frightening; straining the nerves.

nerv·ine /nórvīn/ *adj. & n.* • *adj.* relieving nerve disorders. • *n.* a nervine drug. [F *nervin* (as NERVE)]

nervo- /nórvō/ *comb. form* (also **nerv-** before a vowel) a nerve or the nerves.

nerv·ous /nórvəs/ *adj.* **1** having delicate or disordered nerves. **2** timid or anxious. **3 a** excitable; highly strung; easily agitated. **b** resulting from this temperament (*nervous tension; a nervous headache*). **4** affecting or acting on the nerves. **5** (foll. by *about* + verbal noun) reluctant; afraid (*am nervous about meeting them*). □□ **nerv‧ous‧ly** *adv.* **nerv‧ous‧ness** *n.* [ME f. L *nervosus* (as NERVE)]

nerv‧ous break‧down *n.* a period of mental illness, usu. resulting from severe depression or anxiety.

nerv‧ous sys‧tem *n.* the body's network of specialized cells that transmit nerve impulses between parts of the body (cf. CENTRAL NERVOUS SYSTEM, PERIPHERAL NERVOUS SYSTEM).

nerv‧ous wreck *n. colloq.* a person suffering from mental stress, exhaustion, etc.

ner‧vure /nɔ́rvyǝr/ *n.* **1** each of the hollow tubes that form the framework of an insect's wing; a venule. **2** the principal vein of a leaf. [F *nerf* nerve]

nerv‧y /nɔ́rvee/ *adj.* (**nerv‧i‧er**, **nerv‧i‧est**) **1** bold, impudent, pushy. **2** esp. *Brit.* nervous; easily excited or disturbed. **3** *archaic* sinewy, strong. □□ **nerv‧i‧ly** *adv.* **nerv‧i‧ness** *n.*

nes‧cient /néshǝnt, –eeǝnt/ *adj. literary* (foll. by *of*) lacking knowledge; ignorant. □□ **nesc‧ience** *n.* [LL *nescientia* f. L *nescire* not know f. *ne-* not + *scire* know]

ness /nes/ *n.* a headland or promontory. [OE *næs*, rel. to OE *nasu* NOSE]

-ness /nis/ *suffix* forming nouns from adjectives and occas. other words, expressing: **1** state or condition, or an instance of this (*bitterness; conceitedness; happiness; a kindness*). **2** something in a certain state (*wilderness*). [OE *-nes*, *-ness* f. Gmc]

nest /nest/ *n. & v.* ● *n.* **1** a structure or place where a bird lays eggs and shelters its young. **2** an animal's or insect's breeding place or lair. **3** a snug or secluded retreat or shelter. **4** (often foll. by *of*) a place fostering something undesirable (*a nest of vice*). **5** a brood or swarm. **6** a group or set of similar objects, often of different sizes and fitting together for storage (*a nest of tables*). ● *v.* **1** *intr.* use or build a nest. **2** *intr.* take wild birds' nests or eggs. **3** *intr.* (of objects) fit together or one inside another. **4** *tr.* (usu. as **nested** *adj.*) establish in or as in a nest. □□ **nest‧ful** *n.* (*pl.* **‧fuls**). **nest‧ing** *n.* (in sense 2 of *v.*). **nest‧like** *adj.* [OE *nest*]

nest egg *n.* **1** a sum of money saved for the future. **2** a real or artificial egg left in a nest to induce hens to lay eggs there.

nes‧tle /nésǝl/ *v.* **1** *intr.* (often foll. by *down*, *in*, etc.) settle oneself comfortably. **2** *intr.* press oneself against another in affection, etc. **3** *tr.* (foll. by *in*, *into*, etc.) push (a head or shoulder, etc.) affectionately or snugly. **4** *intr.* lie half hidden or embedded. [OE *nestlian* (as NEST)]

nest‧ling /nésling, nést–/ *n.* a bird that is too young to leave its nest.

net[1] /net/ *n. & v.* ● *n.* **1** an open-meshed fabric of cord, rope, fiber, etc.; a structure resembling this. **2** a piece of net used esp. to restrain, contain, or delimit, or to catch fish or other animals. **3** a structure with net to enclose an area of ground, esp. in sport. **4 a** a structure with net used in various games, esp. forming the goal in soccer, hockey, etc., and dividing the court in tennis, etc. **b** (often in *pl.*) a practice ground in cricket, surrounded by nets. **5** a system or procedure for catching or entrapping a person or persons. **6** = NETWORK. ● *v.* (**net‧ted**, **net‧ting**) **1** *tr.* **a** cover, confine, or catch with a net. **b** procure as with a net. **2** *tr.* hit (a ball) into the net, esp. of a goal. **3** *intr.* make netting. **4** *tr.* make (a purse, hammock, etc.) by knotting, etc.; threads together to form a net. **5** *tr.* fish with nets, or set nets, in (a river). **6** *tr.* (usu. as **netted** *adj.*) mark with a netlike pattern; reticulate. □□ **net‧ful** *n.* (*pl.* **‧fuls**). [OE *net*, *nett*]

net[2] /net/ *adj. & v.* ● *adj.* **1** (esp. of money) remaining after all necessary deductions, or free from deductions. **2** (of a price) to be paid in full; not reducible. **3** (of a weight) excluding that of the packaging or container, etc. **4** (of an effect, result, etc.) ultimate, effective. ● *v.tr.* (**net‧ted**, **net‧ting**) gain or yield (a sum) as net profit. [F *net* NEAT[1]]

neth‧er /néthǝr/ *adj. archaic* = LOWER[1]. □□ **neth‧er‧most** *adj.* [OE *nithera*, etc. f. Gmc]

Neth‧er‧land‧er /néthǝrlandǝr/ *n.* **1** a native or national of the Netherlands. **2** a person of Dutch descent. □□ **Neth‧er‧land‧ish** *adj.* [Du. *Nederlander*, *Nederlandsch*]

Neth‧er‧lands /néthǝrlǝndz/ *n.* **1** (usu. prec. by *the*) Holland. **2** *hist.* the Low Countries. [Du. *Nederland* (as NETHER, LAND)]

neth‧er re‧gions *n.pl.* (also **neth‧er world**) hell; the underworld.

net prof‧it *n.* the effective profit; the actual gain after expenses have been paid.

net ton *n.* see TON[1].

ne‧tsu‧ke /nétsookee/ *n.* (*pl.* same or **ne‧tsu‧kes**) (in Japan) a carved buttonlike ornament, esp. of ivory or wood, formerly worn to suspend articles from a girdle. [Jap.]

net‧ting /néting/ *n.* **1** netted fabric. **2** a piece of this.

net‧tle /nétl/ *n. & v.* ● *n.* **1** any plant of the genus *Urtica*, esp. *U. dioica*, with jagged leaves covered with stinging hairs. **2** any of various plants resembling this. ● *v.tr.* **1** irritate; provoke; annoy. **2** sting with nettles. [OE *netle*, *netele*]

net‧tle‧rash *n.* = URTICARIA (for its resemblance to the sting of a nettle).

net‧tle‧some /nétl'sǝm/ *adj.* **1** awkward, difficult. **2** causing annoyance.

net‧work /nétwǝrk/ *n. & v.* ● *n.* **1** an arrangement of intersecting horizontal and vertical lines, like the structure of a net. **2** a complex system of railways, roads, canals, etc. **3** a group of people who exchange information, contacts, and experience for professional or social purposes. **4** a chain of interconnected computers, machines, or operations. **5** a system of connected electrical conductors. **6** a group of broadcasting stations connected for a simultaneous broadcast of a program. ● *v.* **1** *tr.* link (machines, esp. computers) to operate interactively. **2** *intr.* establish a network. **3** *Brit. tr.* broadcast on a network. **4** *intr.* be a member of a network (see sense 3 of *n.*).

net‧work‧er /nétwǝrkǝr/ *n.* **1** *Computing* a member of an organization or computer network who operates from home, from an external office, or from one of several computer terminals within an office. **2** a member of a professional or social network.

neume /noom, nyoom/ *n.* (also **neum**) *Mus.* a sign in plainsong indicating a note or group of notes to be sung to a syllable. [ME f. OF *neume* f. med.L *neu(p)ma* f. Gk *pneuma* breath]

neu‧ral /noorǝl, nyoor–/ *adj.* of or relating to a nerve or the central nervous system. □□ **neu‧ral‧ly** *adv.* [Gk *neuron* nerve]

neu‧ral‧gia /nooráljǝ, nyoo–/ *n.* an intense intermittent pain along the course of a nerve, esp. in the head or face. □□ **neu‧ral‧gic** *adj.* [as NEURAL + –ALGIA]

neu‧ral net‧work *n.* (also **neu‧ral net**) *Computing* a computer system modeled on the human brain and nervous system.

neur‧as‧the‧ni‧a /noorǝstheéneeǝ, nyoo–/ *n.* a general term for fatigue, anxiety, listlessness, etc. (not in medical use). □□ **neur‧as‧then‧ic** /–thénik/ *adj. & n.* [Gk *neuron* nerve + ASTHENIA]

neu‧ri‧tis /noorítis, nyoo–/ *n.* inflammation of a nerve or nerves. □□ **neu‧rit‧ic** /–rítik/ *adj.* [formed as NEURO- + –ITIS]

neuro- /noorō, nyoorō/ *comb. form* a nerve or the nerves. [Gk *neuron* nerve]

neu‧ro‧gen‧e‧sis /noorōjénisis, nyoor–/ *n.* the growth and development of nervous tissue.

neu‧ro‧gen‧ic /noorōjénik, nyoor–/ *adj.* caused by or arising in nervous tissue.

neu‧rog‧li‧a /nooráagleeǝ, nyoor–/ *n.* the connective tissue supporting the central nervous system. [NEURO- + Gk *glia* glue]

neu‧ro‧hor‧mone /noorōháwrmōn, nyoor–/ *n.* a hormone produced by nerve cells and secreted into the circulation.

neu‧rol‧o‧gy /nooráalǝjee, nyoo–/ *n.* the branch of medicine or biology that deals with the anatomy, functions, and organic disorders of nerves and the nervous system. □□ **neu‧ro‧log‧i‧cal** /–rǝlójikǝl/ *adj.* **neu‧ro‧log‧i‧cal‧ly** *adv.* **neu‧rol‧o‧gist** *n.* [mod.L *neurologia* f. mod. Gk (as NEURO-, –LOGY)]

neu‧ro‧ma /noorōmǝ, nyoo–/ *n.* (*pl.* **neu‧ro‧mas** or **neu‧ro‧ma‧ta** /–mǝtǝ/) a tumor on a nerve or in nerve tissue. [Gk *neuron* nerve + –OMA]

neu‧ro‧mus‧cu‧lar /noorōmúskyǝlǝr, nyoor–/ *adj.* of or relating to nerves and muscles.

neu‧ron /nooron, nyoor–/ *n.* (also **neu‧rone** /–ōn/) a specialized cell transmitting nerve impulses; a nerve cell. □□ **neu‧ron‧al** *adj.* **neu‧ron‧ic** /–rónik/ *adj.* [Gk *neuron* nerve]

neu‧ro‧path /noorōpath, nyoor–/ *n.* a person affected by nervous disease, or with an abnormally sensitive nervous system. □□ **neu‧ro‧path‧ic** *adj.* **neu‧rop‧a‧thy** /–rópǝthee/ *n.*

neu‧ro‧pa‧thol‧o‧gy /noorōpathólǝjee, nyoor–/ *n.* the pathology of the nervous system. □□ **neu‧ro‧pa‧thol‧o‧gist** *n.*

neu‧ro‧phys‧i‧ol‧o‧gy /noorōfizeeólǝjee, nyoor–/ *n.* the physiology of the nervous system. □□ **neu‧ro‧phys‧i‧o‧log‧i‧cal** /–zeeǝlójikǝl/ *adj.* **neu‧ro‧phys‧i‧ol‧o‧gist** *n.*

neu‧rop‧ter‧an /nooróptǝrǝn, nyoo–/ *n.* any insect of the order Neuroptera, including lacewings, having four finely veined membranous leaflike wings. □□ **neu‧rop‧ter‧ous** *adj.* [NEURO- + Gk *pteron* wing]

neu‧ro‧sis /noorósis, nyoo–/ *n.* (*pl.* **neu‧ro‧ses** /–seez/) a mental illness characterized by irrational or depressive thought or behavior, caused by a disorder of the nervous system usu. without organic change (cf. PSYCHOSIS). [mod.L (as NEURO-, –OSIS)]

neu‧ro‧sur‧ger‧y /noorōsórjǝree, nyoor–/ *n.* surgery performed on the nervous system, esp. the brain and spinal cord. □□ **neu‧ro‧sur‧geon** *n.* **neu‧ro‧sur‧gi‧cal** *adj.*

neu‧rot‧ic /noorótik, nyoo–/ *adj. & n.* ● *adj.* **1** caused by or relating to neurosis. **2** (of a person) suffering from neurosis. **3** *colloq.* abnormally sensitive or obsessive. ● *n.* a neurotic person. □□ **neu‧rot‧ic‧al‧ly** *adv.* **neu‧rot‧i‧cism** /–isizǝm/ *n.*

neu‧rot‧o‧my /noorótǝmee, nyoo–/ *n.* (*pl.* **‧mies**) the operation of cutting a nerve, esp. to produce sensory loss.

neu‧ro‧trans‧mit‧ter /noorōtránsmitǝr, –tránz–, nyoor–/ *n. Biochem.* a chemical substance released from a nerve fiber that effects the transfer of an impulse to another nerve or muscle.

neut. *abbr.* NEUTER.

neu‧ter /nóotǝr, nyóo–/ *adj., n., & v.* ● *adj.* **1** *Gram.* (of a noun, etc.) neither masculine nor feminine. **2** (of a plant) having neither pistils nor stamen. **3** (of an insect, animal, etc.) **a** sexually undeveloped. **b** castrated or spayed. ● **n. 1** *Gram.* a neuter word. **2 a** a nonfertile insect, esp. a worker bee or ant. **b** a castrated animal. ● *v.tr.* castrate or spay. [ME f. OF *neutre* or L *neuter* neither f. *ne-* not + *uter* either]

neu·tral /nōōtrəl, nyōō–/ *adj. & n.* ● *adj.* **1** not helping or supporting either of two opposing sides, esp. nations at war or in dispute; impartial. **2** belonging to a neutral party, nation, etc. (*neutral ships*). **3** indistinct, vague, indeterminate. **4** (of a gear) in which the engine is disconnected from the driven parts. **5** (of colors) not strong nor positive; gray or beige. **6** *Chem.* neither acid nor alkaline. **7** *Electr.* neither positive nor negative. **8** *Biol.* sexually undeveloped; asexual. ● *n.* **1 a** a neutral nation, person, etc. **b** a subject of a neutral nation. **2** a neutral gear. □□ **neu·tral·i·ty** /–trálitee/ *n.* **neu·tral·ly** *adv.* [ME f. obs. F *neutral* or L *neutralis* of neuter gender (as NEUTER)]

neu·tral·ism /nōōtrəlizəm, nyōō–/ *n.* a policy of political neutrality. □□ **neu·tral·ist** *n.*

neu·tral·ize /nōōtrəliz, nyōō–/ *v.tr.* **1** make neutral. **2** counterbalance; render ineffective by an opposite force or effect. **3** exempt or exclude (a place) from the sphere of hostilities. □□ **neu·tral·i·za·tion** *n.* **neu·tral·iz·er** *n.* [F *neutraliser* f. med.L *neutralizare* (as NEUTRAL)]

neu·tri·no /nōōtreenō, nyōō–/ *n.* (*pl.* **·nos**) any of a group of stable elementary particles with zero electric charge and probably zero mass, which travel at the speed of light. [It., dimin. of *neutro* neutral (as NEUTER)]

neu·tron /nōōtron, nyōō–/ *n.* an elementary particle of about the same mass as a proton but without an electric charge, present in all atomic nuclei except those of ordinary hydrogen. [NEUTRAL + –ON]

neu·tron bomb *n.* a nuclear bomb producing neutrons and little blast, causing damage to life but little destruction to property.

neu·tron star *n.* a very dense star composed mainly of neutrons.

Nev. *abbr.* Nevada.

né·vé /nayváy/ *n.* an expanse of granular snow not yet compressed into ice at the head of a glacier. [Swiss F, = glacier, ult. f. L *nix nivis* snow]

nev·er /névər/ *adv.* **1 a** at no time; on no occasion; not ever (*have never been to Paris; never saw them again*). **b** *colloq.* as an emphatic negative (*I never heard you come in*). **2** not at all (*never fear*). **3** *Brit. colloq.* (expressing surprise) surely not (*you never left the key in the lock!*). □ **never a one** none. **never say die** see DIE[1]. **well I never!** expressing great surprise. [OE *næfre* f. *ne* not + *æfre* EVER]

nev·er-end·ing *adj.* eternal, undying; immeasurable.

nev·er·more /névərmáwr/ *adv.* at no future time.

nev·er-nev·er *n.* (often prec. by *the*) *Brit. colloq.* a system by which a buyer pays for an item in regular installment payments while having the use of it.

nev·er-nev·er land *n.* an imaginary utopian place.

nev·er·the·less /névərthəlés/ *adv.* in spite of that; notwithstanding; all the same.

ne·vus /néevəs/ *n.* (*pl.* **ne·vi** /–vī/) **1** a birthmark in the form of a raised red patch on the skin. **2** = MOLE[2]. □□ **ne·void** *adj.* [L]

new /nōō, nyōō/ *adj. & adv.* ● *adj.* **1** of recent origin or arrival. **b** made, invented, discovered, acquired, or experienced recently or now for the first time (*a new star; has many new ideas*). **2** in original condition; not worn or used. **3 a** renewed or reformed (*a new life; the new order*). **b** reinvigorated (*felt like a new person*). **4** different from a recent previous one (*has a new job*). **5** in addition to others already existing (*have you been to the new supermarket?*). **6** (often foll. by *to*) unfamiliar or strange (*a new sensation; the idea was new to me*). **7** (often foll. by *at*) (of a person) inexperienced, unaccustomed (to doing something) (*am new at this business*). **8** (usu. prec. by *the*) often *derog.* **a** later, modern. **b** newfangled. **c** given to new or modern ideas (*the new man*). **d** recently affected by social change (*the new rich*). **9** (often prec. by *the*) advanced in method or theory (*the new formula*). **10** (in place names) discovered or founded later than and named after (*New York; New Zealand*). ● *adv.* (usu. in *comb.*) **1** newly, recently (*new-fashioned; new-baked*). **2** anew, afresh. □□ **new·ish** *adj.* **new·ness** *n.*

> **WORD HISTORY**   **new**
>
> Old English *nīwe*, *nēowe*, of Germanic origin; related to Dutch *nieuw* and German *neu*, from an Indo-European root shared by Sanskrit *nava*, Latin *novus*, and Greek *neos* 'new.'

New Age *n.* a set of beliefs intended to replace traditional Western Culture, with alternative approaches to religion, medicine, the environment, music, etc. □□ **New Ag·er** *n.* **New Ag·ey** *adj.*

new birth *n.* *Theol.* spiritual regeneration.

new·born /nōōbawrn, nyōō–/ *adj.* **1** (of a child, etc.) recently born. **2** spiritually reborn; regenerated.

new broom *n.* see BROOM.

new·com·er /nōōkumər, nyōō–/ *n.* **1** a person who has recently arrived. **2** a beginner in some activity.

new deal *n.* new arrangements or conditions, esp. when better than the earlier ones.

---

new·el /nōōəl, nyōō–/ *n.* **1** the supporting central post of winding stairs. **2** the top or bottom supporting post of a stair rail. [ME f. OF *noel, nouel*, knob f. med.L *nodellus* dimin. of L *nodus* knot]

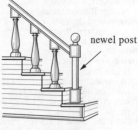

newel post

newel post 2

new·fan·gled /nōōfánggəld, nyōō–/ *adj. derog.* different from what one is used to; objectionably new. [ME *newfangle* (now dial.) liking what is new f. *newe* NEW *adv.* + *–fangel* f. OE *fangol* (unrecorded) inclined to take]

New·found·land /nōōfəndlənd, noofówndlənd, nyōō–, –land, –fənd–, nyōō–/ *n.* (in full **Newfoundland dog**) **1** a dog of a very large breed with a thick, usu. black, coarse coat. **2** this breed. [the name of a Canadian province, an island at the mouth of the St. Lawrence River]

new look *n.* a new or revised appearance or presentation, esp. of something familiar.

new·ly /nōōlee, nyōō–/ *adv.* **1** recently (*a friend newly arrived; a newly discovered country*). **2** afresh, anew (*newly painted*). **3** in a new or different manner (*newly arranged*).

new·ly·wed /nōōleewed, nyōō–/ *n.* a recently married person.

new math·e·mat·ics *n.* (also *Brit.* **new maths**) a system of teaching mathematics to children, with emphasis on investigation by them and on set theory.

new moon *n.* **1** the moon when first seen as a crescent after conjunction with the sun. **2** the time of its appearance.

new one *n.* (often foll. by *on*) *colloq.* an account or idea not previously encountered (by a person).

new po·ta·toes *n.pl.* the earliest potatoes of a new crop.

news /nōōz, nyōōz/ *n.pl.* (usu. treated as *sing.*) **1** information about important or interesting recent events, esp. when published or broadcast. **2** (prec. by *the*) a broadcast report of news. **3** newly received or noteworthy information. **4** (foll. by *to*) *colloq.* information not previously known (to a person) (*that's news to me*). □□ **news·less** *adj.* [ME, pl. of NEW after OF *noveles* or med.L *nova* neut. pl. of *novus* new]

news a·gen·cy *n.* an organization that collects and distributes news items.

news·a·gent /nōōzayjənt, nyōōz–/ *n. Brit.* a seller of or shop selling newspapers and usu. related items, e.g., stationery.

news·boy /nōōzboy, nyōōz–/ *n.* a boy who sells or delivers newspapers.

news brief *n.* a short item of news, esp. on television; a news flash.

news bul·le·tin *n.* **1** *US* brief item of news broadcast almost as soon as received. **2** *Brit.* a collection of items of news, esp. for broadcasting.

news·cast /nōōzkast, nyōōz–/ *n.* a radio or television broadcast of news reports.

news·cast·er /nōōzkastər, nyōōz–/ *n.* a person who reads the news broadcast on radio or television.

news con·fer·ence *n.* a press conference.

news·deal·er /nōōzdeelər, nyōōz–/ *n.* a person who sells newspapers, magazines, etc.

news flash *n.* a single item of important news, broadcast separately and often interrupting other programs.

news·girl /nōōzgərl, nyōōz–/ *n.* a girl who sells or delivers newspapers.

news·let·ter /nōōzletər, nyōōz–/ *n.* an informal printed report issued periodically to the members of a society, business, organization, etc.

news·man /nōōzman, –mən, nyōōz–/ *n.* (*pl.* **·men**) a newspaper reporter; a journalist.

news·mong·er /nōōzmonggər, nyōōz–/ *n.* a gossip.

news·pa·per /nōōzpaypər, nyōōz–, nōōs–, nyōōs–/ *n.* **1** a printed publication (usu. daily or weekly) containing news, advertisements, correspondence, etc. **2** the sheets of paper forming this (*wrapped in newspaper*).

news·pa·per·man /nōōzpaypərman, –mən, nyōōz–, nōōs–, nyōōs–/ *n.* (*pl.* **·men**) a journalist.

news·speak /nōōspeek, nyōō–/ *n.* (also **New·speak**) ambiguous euphemistic language used esp. in political propaganda. [an artificial official language in George Orwell's *Nineteen Eighty-Four* (1949)]

news·print /nōōzprint, nyōōz–/ *n.* a type of low-quality paper on which newspapers are printed.

news·read·er /nōōzreedər, nyōōz–/ *n. Brit.* = NEWSCASTER.

news·reel /nōōzreel, nyōōz–/ *n.* a short movie of recent events.

news•room /nŏŏzroom, nyŏŏz–/ *n.* a room in a newspaper or broad-castingoffice where news stories are prepared.

news•stand /nŏŏzstand, nyŏŏz–/ *n.* a stall for the sale of newspapers, magazines, etc.

new star *n.* a nova.

New Style *n.* dating reckoned by the Gregorian Calendar.

news•week•ly /nŏŏzweeklee, nyŏŏz–/ *n.* a periodical published weekly that summarizes current events.

news•wor•thy /nŏŏzwɔrthee, nyŏŏz–/ *adj.* topical; noteworthy as news. □□ **news•wor•thi•ness** *n.*

news•y /nŏŏzee, nyŏŏ–/ *adj.* (**news•i•er**, **news•i•est**) *colloq.* full of news.

newt /nŏŏt, nyŏŏt/ *n.* any of various small amphibians, esp. of the genus *Triturus*, having a well-developed tail. [ME f. *ewt*, with *n* from *an* (cf. NICKNAME): var. of *evet* EFT]

New Test. *abbr.* New Testament.

New Tes•ta•ment *n.* the part of the Bible concerned with the life and teachings of Christ and his earliest followers.

new•ton /nŏŏt'n, nyŏŏ–/ *n. Physics* the SI unit of force that, acting on a mass of one kilogram, increases its velocity by one meter per second every second along the direction that it acts. ¶ Abbr.: **N**. [Sir Isaac *Newton*, Engl. scientist d. 1727]

New•to•ni•an /nŏŏtóneeən, nyŏŏ–/ *adj.* of or devised by Isaac Newton (see NEWTON).

New•to•ni•an me•chan•ics *n.* the system of mechanics that relies on Newton's laws of motion concerning the relations between forces acting and motions occurring.

New•to•ni•an tel•e•scope *n.* a reflecting telescope with a small secondary mirror at 45° to the main beam of light to reflect it into a magnifying eyepiece.

new town *n.* a self-sufficient, planned town established as a completely new settlement.

new wave *n.* **1** = NOUVELLE VAGUE. **2** a style of rock music popular in the 1970s.

New World *n.* N. and S. America regarded collectively in relation to Europe.

new year *n.* **1** the calendar year just begun or about to begin. **2** the first few days of a year.

New Year's Day *n.* January 1.

New Year's Eve December 31.

New Zea•land•er /nŏŏzeéləndər, nyŏŏ–/ *n.* **1** a native or national of New Zealand, an island group in the Pacific. **2** a person of New Zealand descent.

next /nekst/ *adj., adv., n.,* & *prep.* • *adj.* **1** (often foll. by *to*) being or positioned or living nearest (*in the next house; the chair next to the fire*). **2** the nearest in order of time; the first or soonest encountered or considered (*next Friday; ask the next person you see*). • *adv.* **1** (often foll. by *to*) in the nearest place or degree (*put it next to mine; came next to last*). **2** on the first or soonest occasion (*when we next meet*). • *n.* the next person or thing. • *prep. colloq.* next to. **next to** almost (*next to nothing left*). [OE *nēhsta* superl. (as NIGH)]

next-best *adj.* the next in order of preference.

next door *adv., adj.,* & *n.* • *adj.* in or to the next house or room. • *adj.* (**next-door**) living or situated next door. • *n.* the building, room, or people next door. □ **next door to 1** in the next house or room to. **2** nearly, almost, near to.

next of kin *n.* the closest living relative or relatives.

next world *n.* see WORLD.

nex•us /néksəs/ *n.* (*pl.* same) **1** a connected group or series. **2** a bond; a connection. [L f. *nectere nex*- bind]

Nez Per•cé /náypersáy/ *n.* (also **Nez Perce** /néz pɔ́rs, nés pérs/) **1 a** a N. American people native to the northwestern US. **b** a member of this people. **2** the language of this people.

Nfld. *abbr.* (also **NF**) Newfoundland.

n.g. *abbr.* no good.

NH *abbr.* New Hampshire (also in official postal use).

NHS *abbr.* (in the UK) National Health Service.

NI *abbr.* Northern Ireland.

Ni *symb. Chem.* the element nickel.

ni•a•cin /nīsin/ *n.* = NICOTINIC ACID. [*ni*cotinic *ac*id + –IN]

nib /nib/ *n.* & *v.* • *n.* **1** the point of a pen, which touches the writing surface. **2** (in *pl.*) shelled and crushed coffee or cocoa beans. **3** the point of a tool, etc. • *v.* (**nibbed**, **nib•bing**) **1** *tr.* provide with a nib. **2** *tr.* mend the nib of. **3** *tr.* & *intr.* nibble. [prob. f. MDu. *nib* or MLG *nibbe*, var. of *nebbe* NEB]

nib•ble /níbəl/ *v.* & *n.* • *v.* **1** *tr.* & (foll. by *at*) intr. **a** take small bites at. **b** eat in small amounts. **c** bite at gently or cautiously or playfully. **2** *intr.* (foll. by *at*) show cautious interest in. • *n.* **1** an instance of nibbling. **2** a very small amount of food. **3** *Computing* half a byte, i.e., 4 bits. □□ **nib•bler** *n.* [prob. f. LG or Du. orig.: cf. LG *nibbeln* gnaw]

nib•lick /níblik/ *n. Golf* an iron with a large round heavy head, used esp. for playing out of bunkers. [19th c.: orig. unkn.]

nibs /nibz/ *n.* □ **his nibs** *joc. colloq.* a mock title used with reference to an important or self-important person. [19th c.: orig. unkn. (cf. earlier *nabs*)]

ni•cad /nícad/ *adj.* & *n.* • *adj.* nickel and cadmium. • *n.* a nickel and cadmium battery. [NICKEL + CADMIUM]

nice /nīs/ *adj.* **1** pleasant, agreeable, satisfactory. **2** (of a person) kind, good-natured. **3** *iron.* bad or awkward (*a nice mess you've made*). **4 a** fine or subtle (*a nice distinction*). **b** requiring careful thought or attention (*a nice problem*). **5** fastidious; delicately sensitive. **6** punctilious, scrupulous (*were not too nice about their methods*). **7** (foll. by an adj., often with *and*) satisfactory or adequate in terms of the quality described (*a nice long time; nice and warm*). □ **nice work** a task well done. □□ **nice•ly** *adv.* **nice•ness** *n.*

▶Nice originally had a number of meanings, including 'fine, subtle, discriminating'; 'refined in taste, fastidious'; and 'precise, strict': *they are not very nice in regard to the company they keep; she has a nice sense of decorum.* The popular overuse of **nice** to mean 'pleasant, agreeable, satisfactory,' etc., has rendered the word trite: *we had a very nice time; this is a nice room; he's a nice boy.*

Ni•cene Creed /níseén/ *n.* a formal statement of Christian belief based on that adopted at the first Council of Nicaea in 325. [*Nicene* ME f. LL *Nicenus* of Nicaea in Asia Minor]

ni•ce•ty /nísitee/ *n.* (*pl.* **•ties**) **1** a subtle distinction or detail. **2** precision, accuracy. **3** intricate or subtle quality (*a point of great nicety*). **4** (in *pl.*) **a** minutiae; fine details. **b** refinements, trimmings. □ **to a nicety** with exactness. [ME f. OF *niceté* (as NICE)]

niche /nich, neesh/ *n.* & *v.* • *n.* **1** a shallow recess, esp. in a wall to contain a statue, etc. **2** a comfortable or suitable position in life or employment. **3** an appropriate combination of conditions for a species to thrive. • *v.tr.* (often as **niched** *adj.*) **1** place in a niche. **2** ensconce (esp. oneself) in a recess or corner. [F f. *nicher* make a nest, ult. f. L *nidus* nest]

Ni•chrome /níkrōm/ *n. Trademark* a group of nickel-chromium alloys used for making wire in heating elements, etc. [NICKEL + CHROME]

nick /nik/ *n.* & *v.* • *n.* **1** a small cut or notch. **2** *Brit. sl.* **a** a prison. **b** a police station. **3** (prec. by *in* with adj.) *Brit. colloq.* condition (*in reasonable nick*). **4** the junction between the floor and walls in a squash court. • *v.tr.* **1** make a nick or nicks in. **2** *Brit. sl.* **a** steal. **b** arrest, catch. □ **in the nick of time** only just in time; just at the right moment. [ME: orig. uncert.]

nick•el /níkəl/ *n.* & *v.* • *n.* **1** *Chem.* a malleable ductile silver-white metallic transition element, occurring naturally in various minerals and used in special steels, in magnetic alloys, and as a catalyst. ¶ Symb.: **Ni**. **2** a five-cent coin. • *v.tr.* (**nick•eled**, **nick•el•ing**) coat with nickel. [abbr. of G *Kupfernickel* copper-colored ore, from which nickel was first obtained, f. *Kupfer* copper + *Nickel* demon, with ref. to the ore's failure to yield copper]

nick•el-and-dime *adj.* & *v.tr.* • *adj.* involving a small amount of money; insignificant; trivial. • *v.tr.* weaken (one's financial position) by continued small expenses, bills, etc.

nick•el brass *n.* an alloy of copper, zinc, and a small amount of nickel.

nick•el•o•de•on /níkəlódeeən/ *n. colloq.* **1** an early movie theater, esp. one with admission priced at 5 cents. **2** a jukebox. [NICKEL + MELODEON]

nick•el-plat•ed *adj.* coated with nickel by plating.

nick•el sil•ver *n.* = GERMAN SILVER.

nick•el steel *n.* a type of stainless steel with chromium and nickel.

nick•nack var. of KNICKKNACK.

nick•name /níknaym/ *n.* & *v.* • *n.* a familiar or humorous name given to a person or thing instead of or as well as the real name. • *v.tr.* **1** give a nickname to. **2** call (a person or thing) by a nickname. [ME f. *eke-name*, with *n* from *an* (cf. NEWT): *eke* = addition, f. OE *ēaca* (as EKE)]

Nic•ol /níkəl/ *n.* (in full **Nic•ol prism**) a device for producing plane-polarized light, consisting of two pieces of cut calcite cemented together with Canada balsam. [W. *Nicol*, Sc. physicist d. 1851, its inventor]

nic•o•tine /níkəteén/ *n.* a colorless poisonous alkaloid present in tobacco. [F f. mod.L *nicotiana* (*herba*) tobacco plant, f. J. *Nicot*, Fr. diplomat & introducer of tobacco into France in the 16th c.]

nic·o·tin·ic ac·id /níkətínik/ *n.* a vitamin of the B complex, found in milk, liver, and yeast, a deficiency of which causes pellagra. Also called **niacin**.

nic·ti·tate /níktitayt/ *v.intr.* close and open the eyes; blink or wink. □□ **nic·ti·ta·tion** /-táyshən/ *n.* [med.L *nictitare* frequent. of L *nictare* blink]

nic·ti·tat·ing mem·brane *n.* a clear membrane forming a third eyelid in amphibians, birds, and some other animals, that can be drawn across the eye to give protection without loss of vision.

nide /nīd/ *n.* (*Brit.* **nye** /nī/) a brood of pheasants. [F *nid* or L *nidus*: see NIDUS]

nid·i·fi·cate /nídifikayt/ *v.intr.* (of a bird) build a nest. □□ **nid·i·fi·ca·tion** /-fikáyshən/ *n.* [L *nidificare* f. NIDUS nest]

nid·i·fy /nídifī/ *v.intr.* (·**fies**, ·**fied**) = NIDIFICATE.

ni·dus /nídəs/ *n.* (*pl.* **ni·di** /-dī/ or **ni·dus·es**) **1** a place in which an insect, etc., deposits its eggs, or in which spores or seeds develop. **2** a place in which something is nurtured or developed. [L, rel. to NEST]

niece /nees/ *n.* a daughter of one's brother or sister, or of one's brother-in-law or sister-in-law. [ME f. OF ult. f. L *neptis* granddaughter]

ni·el·lo /nee-élō/ *n.* (*pl.* **ni·el·li** /-lee/ or **·los**) **1** a black composition of sulfur with silver, lead, or copper, for filling engraved lines in silver or other metal. **2 a** such ornamental work. **b** an object decorated with this. □□ **ni·el·loed** *adj.* [It. f. L *nigellus* dimin. of *niger* black]

niels·bohr·i·um /neelzbáwreeəm/ *n.* an artificially produced radioactive element; atomic number 107. ¶ Symb.: **Ns**. [for Danish physicist *Niels Bohr* (1885–1962)]

nif·ty /níftee/ *adj.* (**nif·ti·er, nif·ti·est**) *colloq.* **1** clever, adroit. **2** smart, stylish. □□ **nif·ti·ly** *adv.* **nif·ti·ness** *n.* [19th c.: orig. uncert.]

nig·gard /nígərd/ *n. & adj.* • *n.* a mean or stingy person. • *adj.* archaic = NIGGARDLY. [ME, alt. f. earlier (obs.) *nigon*, prob. of Scand. orig.: cf. NIGGLE]

nig·gard·ly /nígərdlee/ *adj. & adv.* • *adj.* **1** stingy, parsimonious. **2** meager, scanty. • *adv.* in a stingy or meager manner. □□ **nig·gard·li·ness** *n.*

nig·ger /nígər/ *n.* **1** *offens.* a contemptuous term used of a black or dark-skinned person. **2** (in black English) a fellow person. [earlier *neger* f. F *nègre* f. Sp. *negro* NEGRO]
▶In sense 1, this term is considered a highly inflammatory expression of racial bigotry.

nig·gle /nígəl/ *v. & n.* • *v.* **1** *intr.* be overattentive to details. **2** *intr.* find fault in a petty way. **3** *tr. colloq.* irritate; nag pettily. • *n.* a trifling complaint or criticism; a worry or annoyance. [app. of Scand. orig.: cf. Norw. *nigla*]

nig·gling /nígling/ *adj.* **1** troublesome or irritating in a petty way. **2** trifling or petty. □□ **nig·gling·ly** *adv.*

nigh /nī/ *adv., prep., & adj. archaic* or *dial.* near. □ **nigh on** nearly, almost. [OE *nēh*, *nēah*]

night /nīt/ *n.* **1** the period of darkness between one day and the next; the time from sunset to sunrise. **2** nightfall (*shall not reach home before night*). **3** the darkness of night (*as black as night*). **4** a night or evening appointed for some activity, or spent or regarded in a certain way (*last night of the performance; a great night out*). □□ **night·less** *adj.* [OE *neaht, niht* f. Gmc]

night·bird /nítbərd/ *n. Brit. colloq.* = NIGHT OWL.

night blind·ness *n.* = NYCTALOPIA.

night·cap /nítkap/ *n.* **1** *hist.* a cap worn in bed. **2** a hot or alcoholic drink taken at bedtime.

night·clothes /nítklōz, -klōthz/ *n.* clothes worn in bed.

night·club /nítklub/ *n.* a club that is open at night and provides refreshment and entertainment.

night·dress /nítdres/ *n.* = NIGHTGOWN.

night·fall /nítfawl/ *n.* the onset of night; the end of daylight.

night fight·er *n.* an airplane used for interception at night.

night·gown /nítgown/ *n.* **1** a woman's or child's loose garment worn in bed. **2** *hist.* a dressing gown.

night·hawk /níthawk/ *n.* an American nightjar with sharply pointed wings.

night·ie /nítee/ *n. colloq.* a nightgown. [abbr.]

night·in·gale /nít'ngayl/ *n.* any small reddish-brown bird of the genus *Luscinia*, esp. *L. megarhynchos*, of which the male sings melodiously, esp. at night. [OE *nihtegala* (whence obs. *nightgale*) f. Gmc: for *-n-* cf. FARTHINGALE]

night·jar /nítjaar/ *n.* any nocturnal bird of the family Caprimulgidae, having a characteristic harsh cry.

night·life /nítlīf/ *n.* entertainment available at night in a town or city.

night-light *n.* (also **night·light** or **night light**) a dim light kept on in a bedroom at night.

night·long /nítlawng/ *adj. & adv.* • *adj.* lasting all night. • *adv.* throughout the night.

night·ly /nítlee/ *adj. & adv.* • *adj.* **1** happening, done, or existing in the night. **2** recurring every night. • *adv.* every night. [OE *nihtlic* (as NIGHT)]

night·mare /nítmair/ *n.* **1** a frightening or unpleasant dream. **2** *colloq.* a terrifying or very unpleasant experience or situation. **3** a

haunting or obsessive fear. □□ **night·mar·ish** *adj.* **night·mar·ish·ly** *adv.* [an evil spirit (incubus) once thought to lie on and suffocate sleepers: OE *mære* incubus]

night nurse *n.* a nurse on duty during the night.

night owl *n. colloq.* a person active at night.

night safe *n. Brit.* a safe with access from the outer wall of a bank for the deposit of money, etc., when the bank is closed.

night school *n.* an institution providing evening classes for those working by day.

night·shade /nítshayd/ *n.* any of various poisonous plants, esp. of the genus *Solanum*, including *S. nigrum* (**black nightshade**) with black berries, and *S. dulcamara* (**woody nightshade** or **bittersweet**) with red berries. [OE *nihtscada* app. formed as NIGHT + SHADE, prob. with ref. to its poisonous properties]

night shift *n.* a shift of workers employed during the night.

night·shirt /nítshərt/ *n.* a long shirt worn in bed.

night·spot /nítspot/ *n.* a nightclub.

night·stick /nítstik/ *n.* a policeman's club.

night soil *n.* the contents of cesspools, etc., removed at night, esp. for use as manure.

night·time /níttīm/ *n.* the time of darkness.

night watch·man *n.* **1** a person whose job is to keep watch by night. **2** *Cricket* an inferior batsman sent in when a wicket falls near the close of a day's play.

ni·gres·cent /nígrésənt/ *adj.* blackish. □□ **ni·gres·cence** /-səns/ *n.* [L *nigrescere* grow black f. *niger nigri* black]

nig·ri·tude /nígritōōd, -tyōōd, nī-/ *n.* blackness. [L *nigritudo* (as NIGRESCENT)]

NIH *abbr.* National Institutes of Health.

ni·hil·ism /ní-ilizəm, nee-/ *n.* **1** the rejection of all religious and moral principles. **2** an extreme form of skepticism maintaining that nothing has a real existence. □□ **ni·hil·ist** *n.* **ni·hil·is·tic** *adj.* [L *nihil* nothing]

ni·hil·i·ty /nihílitee, nee-/ *n.* (*pl.* ·**ties**) **1** nonexistence, nothingness. **2** a mere nothing; a trifle. [med.L *nihilitas* (as NIHILISM)]

nihil obstat /níhil óbstat, nee-/ *n.* **1** *RC Ch.* a certificate that a book is not open to objection on doctrinal or moral grounds. **2** an authorization or official approval. [L, = nothing hinders]

-nik /nik/ *suffix* forming nouns denoting a person associated with a specified thing or quality (*beatnik; refusenik*). [Russ. (as SPUTNIK) and Yiddish]

nil /nil/ *n.* nothing; no number or amount (esp. *Brit.* as a score in games). [L, = *nihil* nothing]

Nile /nīl/ *n. & adj.* (in full **Nile blue, Nile green**) pale greenish blue or green. [the river *Nile* in NE Africa]

nil·gai /nílgī/ *n.* a large short-horned E. Indian antelope, *Boselaphus tragocamelus*. [Hindi *nīlgāī* f. *nīl* blue + *gāī* cow]

Ni·lot·ic /nīlótik/ *adj.* **1** of or relating to the Nile or the Nile region of Africa. **2** of or relating to a group of E. African Negroid peoples, or the languages spoken by them. [L *Niloticus* f. Gk *Neilōtikos* f. *Neilos* Nile]

nim /nim/ *n.* a game in which two players must alternately take one or more objects from one of several heaps and seek either to avoid taking or to take the last remaining object. [20th c.: perh. f. archaic *nim* take (as NIMBLE), or G *nimm* imper. of *nehmen* take]

nim·ble /nímbəl/ *adj.* (**nim·bler, nim·blest**) **1** quick and light in movement or action; agile. **2** (of the mind) quick to comprehend; clever, versatile. □□ **nim·ble·ness** *n.* **nim·bly** *adv.* [OE *nǣmel* quick to seize f. *niman* take, f. Gmc, with *-b-* as in THIMBLE]

nim·bo·stra·tus /nímbōstráytəs, -strátəs/ *n.* (*pl.* **nim·bo·stra·ti** /-tī/) *Meteorol.* a low dark-gray layer of cloud. [mod.L, f. NIMBUS + STRATUS]

nim·bus /nímbəs/ *n.* (*pl.* **nim·bi** /-bī/ or **nim·bus·es**) **1 a** a bright cloud or halo investing a deity or person or thing. **b** the halo of a saint, etc. **2** *Meteorol.* a rain cloud. □□ **nim·bused** *adj.* [L, = cloud, aureole]

NIMBY /nímbee/ *abbr. colloq.* not in my backyard.

nim·i·ny-pim·i·ny /nímineepíminee/ *adj.* feeble, affected; lacking in vigor. [cf. NAMBY-PAMBY]

Nim·rod /nímrod/ *n.* a great hunter or sportsman. [Heb. *Nimrōd* valiant: see Gen. 10:8-9]

nin·com·poop /nínkəmpōōp/ *n.* a simpleton; a fool. [17th c.: orig. unkn.]

nine /nīn/ *n. & adj.* • *n.* **1** one more than eight, or one less than ten; the sum of five units and four units. **2** a symbol for this (9, ix, IX). **3** a size, etc., denoted by nine. **4** a set or team of nine individuals. **5** the time of nine o'clock (*is it nine yet?*). **6** a card with nine pips. **7** (**the Nine**) the nine muses. • *adj.* that amount to nine. □ **dressed** (*Brit.* **up**) **to the nines** dressed very elaborately. **nine days' wonder** a person or thing that is briefly famous. **nine times out of ten** nearly always. **nine to five** a designation of typical office hours. [OE *nigon* f. Gmc]

See page xx for the **Key to Pronunciation**.

nine·fold /nínfōld/ *adj. & adv.* **1** nine times as much or as many. **2** consisting of nine parts.

nine·pin /nínpin/ *n.* **1** (in *pl.*; usu. treated as *sing.*) a game in which nine pins are set up at the end of an alley and bowled at in an attempt to knock them down. **2** a pin used in this game.

nine points *n.* nine tenths, i.e. nearly the whole (esp. *possession is nine points of the law*).

nine·teen /nínteen/ *n. & adj.* ● *n.* **1** one more than eighteen, nine more than ten. **2** the symbol for this (19, xix, XIX). **3** a size, etc., denoted by nineteen. ● *adj.* that amount to nineteen. □ *talk nineteen to the dozen* see DOZEN. □□ **nine·teenth** *adj. & n.* [OE *nigontȳne*]

nine·ty /níntee/ *n. & adj.* ● *n.* (*pl.* **·ties**) **1** the product of nine and ten. **2** a symbol for this (90, xc, XC). **3** (in *pl.*) the numbers from 90 to 99, esp. the years of a century or of a person's life. ● *adj.* that amount to ninety. □□ **nine·ti·eth** *adj. & n.* **nine·ty·fold** *adj. & adv.* [OE *nigontig*]

nine·ty-first, –second, etc. *adj.* the ordinal numbers between ninetieth and hundredth.

nine·ty-one, –two, etc. *n.* the cardinal numbers between ninety and one hundred.

nin·ja /nínjə/ *n.* a person skilled in ninjutsu. [Jap.]

nin·jut·su /ninjŏŏtsōō/ *n.* one of the Japanese martial arts, characterized by stealthy movement and camouflage. [Jap.]

nin·ny /nínee/ *n.* (*pl.* **·nies**) a foolish or simpleminded person. [perh. f. *innocent*]

ni·non /neénon, neenáwN/ *n.* a lightweight silk dress fabric. [F]

ninth /nīnth/ *n. & adj.* ● *n.* **1** the position in a sequence corresponding to the number 9 in the sequence 1–9. **2** something occupying this position. **3** each of nine equal parts of a thing. **4** *Mus.* **a** an interval or chord spanning nine consecutive notes in the diatonic scale (e.g., C to D an octave higher). **b** a note separated from another by this interval. ● *adj.* that is the ninth. □□ **ninth·ly** *adv.*

ni·o·bi·um /nīóbeeəm/ *n. Chem.* a rare gray-blue metallic transition element occurring naturally in several minerals and used in alloys for superconductors. ¶ Symb.: **Nb**. Also called **columbium**. □□ **ni·o·bic** *adj.* **ni·o·bous** *adj.* [*Niobe* daughter of Tantalus: so-called because first found in TANTALITE]

Nip /nip/ *n. sl. offens.* a Japanese person. [abbr. of NIPPONESE]

nip[1] /nip/ *v. & n.* ● *v.* (**nipped, nip·ping**) **1** *tr.* pinch, squeeze, or bite sharply. **2** *tr.* (often foll. by *off*) remove by pinching, etc. **3** *tr.* (of the cold, frost, etc.) cause pain or harm to. **4** *intr.* (foll. by *in, out*, etc.) *Brit. colloq.* go nimbly or quickly. **5** *tr. sl.* steal, snatch. ● *n.* **1 a** a pinch, a sharp squeeze. **b** a bite. **2 a** biting cold. **b** a check to vegetation caused by this. □ *nip and tuck* neck and neck. *nip in the bud* suppress or destroy (esp. an idea) at an early stage. □□ **nip·ping** *adj.* [ME, prob. f. LG or Du. orig.]

nip[2] /nip/ *n. & v.* ● *n.* a small quantity of liquor. ● *v.intr.* (**nipped, nip·ping**) drink liquor. [prob. abbr. of *nipperkin* small measure: cf. LG, Du. *nippen* to sip]

ni·pa /neépə/ *n.* **1** an E. Indian palm tree, *Nipa fruticans*, with a creeping trunk and large feathery leaves. **2** an alcoholic drink made from its sap. [Sp. & Port. f. Malay *nīpah*]

nip·per /nípər/ *n.* **1** a person or thing that nips. **2** the claw of a crab, lobster, etc. **3** *Brit. colloq.* a young child. **4** (in *pl.*) any tool for gripping or cutting, e.g., forceps or pincers.

nip·ple /nípəl/ *n.* **1** a small projection in which the mammary ducts of either sex of mammals terminate and from which in females milk is secreted for the young. **2** the mouthpiece of a feeding bottle or pacifier. **3** a device like a nipple in function, e.g., the tip of a grease gun. **4** a nipplelike protuberance. **5** a short section of pipe with a screw thread at each end for coupling. [16th c., also *neble, nible*, perh. dimin. f. *neb*]

Nip·pon·ese /nípənéez, –née′s/ *n. & adj.* ● *n.* (*pl.* same) a Japanese person. ● *adj.* Japanese. [Jap. *Nippon* Japan, lit. "land of the rising sun"]

nip·py /nípee/ *adj.* (**nip·pi·er, nip·pi·est**) *colloq.* **1** esp. *Brit.* quick, nimble, active. **2** chilly, cold. **3** tending to nip, as a dog. □□ **nip·pi·ly** *adv.* [NIP[1] + –Y[1]]

nir·va·na /nərvaánə, neer–/ *n.* (in Buddhism) perfect bliss and release from karma, attained by the extinction of individuality. [Skr. *nirvāṇa* f. *nirvā* be extinguished f. *nis* out + *vā*– to blow]

ni·sei /neésay, neesáy/ (also **Ni·sei**) *n.* an American whose parents were immigrants from Japan. [Jap., lit. 'second generation']

ni·si /nísī/ *adj. Law* that takes effect only on certain conditions (*decree nisi*). [L, = 'unless']

Nis·sen hut /nísən/ *n.* a tunnel-shaped hut of corrugated iron with a cement floor. [P. N. *Nissen*, British engineer d. 1930, its inventor]

nit /nit/ *n.* **1** the egg or young form of a louse or other parasitic insect, esp. of human head lice or body lice. **2** *Brit. sl.* a stupid person. [OE *hnitu* f. WG]

ni·ter /nítər/ *n.* (*Brit.* **ni·tre**) saltpeter, potassium nitrate. [ME f. OF f. L *nitrum* f. Gk *nitron*, of Semitic orig.]

ni·ti·nol /nít′nawl, –nōl/ *n.* an alloy of nickel and titanium. [*Ni* + *Ti* + *N*aval *O*rdnance *L*aboratory, Maryland]

nit·pick /nítpik/ *v.intr. colloq.* find fault in a petty manner; criticize. □□ **nit·pick·er** *n.* **nit·pick·ing** *n.*

ni·trate /nítrayt/ *n. & v.* ● *n.* **1** any salt or ester of nitric acid. **2** potassium or sodium nitrate when used as a fertilizer. ● *v.tr. Chem.* treat, combine, or impregnate with nitric acid. □□ **ni·tra·tion** /–áyshən/ *n.* [F (as NITER, –ATE[1])]

ni·tre *Brit.* var. of NITER.

ni·tric /nítrik/ *adj.* of or containing nitrogen, esp. in the quinquevalent state. [F *nitrique* (as NITER)]

ni·tric ac·id *n.* a colorless corrosive poisonous liquid. ¶ Chem. formula: HNO_3.

ni·tric ox·ide *n.* a colorless gas. ¶ Chem. formula: NO.

ni·tride /nítrīd/ *n. Chem.* a binary compound of nitrogen with a more electropositive element. [NITER + –IDE]

ni·tri·fy /nítrifī/ *v.tr.* (**·fies, ·fied**) **1** impregnate with nitrogen. **2** convert (nitrogen, usu. in the form of ammonia) into nitrites or nitrates. □□ **ni·tri·fi·a·ble** *adj.* **ni·tri·fi·ca·tion** /–fikayshən/ *n.* [F *nitrifier* (as NITER)]

ni·trile /nítrīl/ *n. Chem.* an organic compound consisting of an alkyl radical bound to a cyanide radical.

ni·trite /nítrīt/ *n.* any salt or ester of nitrous acid.

nitro- /nítrō/ *comb. form* **1** of or containing nitric acid, niter, or nitrogen. **2** made with or by use of any of these. **3** of or containing the monovalent $-NO_2$ group (*the nitro groups in TNT*). [Gk (as NITER)]

ni·tro·ben·zene /nítrōbénzeen/ *n.* a yellow oily liquid made by the nitration of benzene and used to make aniline, etc.

ni·tro·cel·lu·lose /nítrōsélyələs/ *n.* a highly flammable material made by treating cellulose with concentrated nitric acid, used in the manufacture of explosives and celluloid.

ni·tro·gen /nítrəjən/ *n. Chem.* a colorless, tasteless, odorless gaseous element that forms four-fifths of the atmosphere and is an essential constituent of proteins and nucleic acids. ¶ Symb.: **N**. □□ **ni·trog·e·nous** /–trójinəs/ *adj.* [F *nitrogène* (as NITRO-, –GEN)]

ni·tro·gen cy·cle *n.* the interconversion of nitrogen and its compounds, usu. in the form of nitrates, in nature.

ni·tro·gen fix·a·tion *n.* a chemical process in which atmospheric nitrogen is assimilated into organic compounds in living organisms and hence into the nitrogen cycle.

ni·tro·glyc·er·in /nítrōglísərin/ *n.* (also **ni·tro·glyc·er·ine**) an explosive yellow liquid made by reacting glycerol with a mixture of concentrated sulfuric and nitric acids.

ni·trous /nítrəs/ *adj.* of, like, or impregnated with nitrogen, esp. in the tervalent state. [L *nitrosus* (as NITER), partly through F *nitreux*]

ni·trous ac·id *n.* a weak acid existing only in solution and in the gas phase. ¶ Chem. formula: HNO_2.

ni·trous ox·ide *n.* a colorless gas used as an anesthetic (= LAUGHING GAS) and as an aerosol propellant. ¶ chem. formula: N_2O.

nit·ty-grit·ty /níteegríteé/ *n. sl.* the realities or practical details of a matter. [20th c.: orig. uncert.]

nit·wit /nítwit/ *n. colloq.* a stupid person. □□ **nit·wit·ter·y** /–witəree/ *n.* [perh. f. NIT + WIT[1]]

nit·wit·ted /nítwítid/ *adj.* stupid. □□ **nit·wit·ted·ness** /–wítidnis/ *n.*

nix[1] /niks/ *n. & v. sl.* ● *n.* **1** nothing. **2** a denial or refusal. ● *v.tr.* **1** cancel. **2** reject. [G, colloq. var. of *nichts* nothing]

nix[2] /niks/ *n.* (*fem.* **nix·ie** /níksee/) a water spirit of German folklore. [G (fem. *Nixe*)]

nix[3] /niks/ *int. esp. Brit. sl.* giving warning to confederates, etc., that a person in authority is approaching. [19th c.: perh. = NIX[1]]

NJ *abbr.* New Jersey (also in official postal use).

NLRB *abbr.* National Labor Relations Board.

NM *abbr.* New Mexico (in official postal use).

nm *abbr.* nanometer.

n.m. *abbr.* nautical mile.

N.Mex. *abbr.* New Mexico.

NMR *abbr.* (also **nmr**) nuclear magnetic resonance.

NNE *abbr.* north-northeast.

NNW *abbr.* north-northwest.

No[1] *symb. Chem.* the element nobelium.

No[2] /nō/ *n.* (also **Noh**) traditional Japanese drama with dance and song, evolved from Shinto rites. [Jap. *nō*]

No. *abbr.* **1** number. **2** North. [sense 1 f. L *numero*, ablat. of *numerus* number]

no[1] /nō/ *adj.* **1** not any (*there is no excuse; no circumstances could justify it; no two of them are alike*). **2** not a, quite other than (*is no fool; is no part of my plan; caused no slight inconvenience*). **3** hardly any (*in no distance; did it in no time*). **4** used elliptically as a slogan, notice, etc., to forbid, reject, or deplore the thing specified (*no parking; no surrender*). □ **by no means** see MEANS. **no ball** *Cricket n.* an illegally delivered ball. ● *v.tr.* pronounce (a bowler) to have bowled a no ball. **no dice** see DICE. **no doubt** see DOUBT. **no end** seeEND. **no entry** (of a notice) prohibiting vehicles or persons from entering a road or place. **no fear** see FEAR. **no joke** see JOKE. **no joy** see JOY *n.* 3. **no little** see LITTLE. **no man** no person, nobody. **no side** *Rugby* 1 the end of a game. 2 the referee's announcement of this. **no small** see SMALL. **no sweat** *colloq.* no bother, no trouble. **no thoroughfare** *Brit.* an indication that passage along a street, path, etc., is blocked or prohibited. **no time** see TIME. **no trumps** (or **trump**) *Bridge* a declaration or bid involving playing without a trump suit. **no way** *colloq.* 1 it is impossible. 2 I will not agree, etc. **no whit** see WHIT. **no wonder** see WONDER. **... or no ...** regardless of the ... (*rain or no rain, I shall go out*). **there is no ... ing** it is impossible to ... (*there is no accounting for tastes; there was no mistaking what he meant*). [ME f. *nān, nōn* NONE[1], orig. only before consonants]

no[2] /nō/ *adv. & n.* • *adv.* 1 equivalent to a negative sentence: the answer to your question is negative; your request or command will not be complied with; the statement made or course of action intended or conclusion arrived at is not correct or satisfactory; the negative statement made is correct. 2 (foll. by *compar.*) by no amount; not at all (*no better than before*). 3 *Sc.* not (*will ye no come back again?*). • *n.* (*pl.* **noes** or **nos**) 1 an utterance of the word *no*. 2 a denial or refusal. 3 a negative vote. □ **is no more** has died or ceased to exist. **no can do** *colloq.* I am unable to do it. **the noes have it** the negative voters are in the majority. **no less** (often foll. by *than*) 1 as much (*gave me $50, no less; gave me no less than $50; is no less than a scandal; a no less fatal victory*). 2 as important (*no less a person than the president*). 3 *disp.* no fewer (*no less than ten people have told me*). **no longer** not now or henceforth as formerly. **no more** *n.* nothing further (*have no more to say; want no more of it*). • *adj.* not any more (*no more wine?*). • *adv.* 1 no longer. 2 never again. 3 to no greater extent (*is no more an authority than I am; could no more do it than fly in the air*). 4 just as little, neither (*you did not come, and no more did he*). **no, no** an emphatic equivalent of a negative sentence (cf. sense 1 of *adv.*). **no sooner ... than** see SOON. **not take no for an answer** persist in spite of refusals. **or no** or not (*pleasant or no, it is true*). **whether or no** (or **not**) 1 in either case. 2 (as an indirect question) which is the case and its negative (*tell me whether or no*). [OE *nō, nā* f. *ne* not + *ō, ā* ever]

NOAA /nóə/ *abbr.* National Oceanic and Atmospheric Administration.

no-ac•count *adj.* unimportant; worthless.

No•ah's ark /nóəz/ *n.* 1 a the ship in which (according to the Bible) Noah, his family, and the animals were saved. b an imitation of this as a child's toy. 2 a large or cumbrous or old-fashioned trunk or vehicle. 3 a bivalve mollusk, *Arca noae*, with a boat-shaped shell. [*Noah*, Hebrew patriarch in Gen. 6]

nob[1] /nob/ *n. sl.* the head. □ **his nob** *Cribbage* a score of one point for holding the jack of the same suit as a card turned up by the dealer. [perh. var. of KNOB]

nob[2] /nob/ *n. Brit. sl.* a person of wealth or high social position. [orig. Sc. *knabb, nab*; 18th c., of unkn. orig.]

nob•ble /nóbəl/ *v.tr. Brit. sl.* 1 tamper with (a racehorse) to prevent its winning. 2 get hold of (money, etc.) dishonestly. 3 catch (a criminal). 4 secure the support of or weaken (a person) esp. by underhand means. 5 seize, grab. 6 try to influence (e.g., a judge) unfairly. [prob. = dial. *knobble, knubble* knock, beat, f. KNOB]

nob•bler /nóblər/ *n. Austral. sl.* a glass or drink of liquor. [19th c.: orig. unkn.]

No•bel•ist /nóbélist/ *n.* a winner of a Nobel prize.

no•bel•i•um /nōbéeleeəm/ *n. Chem.* a radioactive transuranic metallic element. ¶ Symb.: **No**. [*Nobel* (see NOBEL PRIZE) + –IUM]

No•bel prize /nóbél/ *n.* any of six international prizes awarded annually for physics, chemistry, physiology or medicine, literature, economics, and the promotion of peace. [Alfred *Nobel* (d. 1896), Swedish chemist and engineer, who endowed them]

no•bil•i•ar•y /nóbílee-eree, –bílyəree/ *adj.* of the nobility. [F *nobiliaire* (as NOBLE)]

no•bil•i•ar•y par•ti•cle *n.* a preposition forming part of a title of nobility (e.g., French *de*, German *von*).

no•bil•i•ty /nóbílitee/ *n.* (*pl.* **•ties**) 1 nobleness of character, mind, birth, or rank. 2 (prec. by *a, the*) a class of nobles; an aristocracy. [ME f. OF *nobilité* or L *nobilitas* (as NOBLE)]

no•ble /nóbəl/ *adj. & n.* • *adj.* (**no•bler, no•blest**) 1 belonging by rank, title, or birth to the aristocracy. 2 of excellent character; having lofty ideals; free from pettiness and meanness; magnanimous. 3 of imposing appearance; splendid; magnificent; stately. 4 excellent, admirable (*noble horse; noble cellar*). • *n.* 1 a nobleman or noblewoman. 2 *hist.* a former English gold coin first issued in 1351. □□ **no•ble•ness** *n.* **no•bly** *adv.* [ME f. OF f. L (*g*)*nobilis*, rel. to KNOW]

noble gas *n.* any one of a group of gaseous elements that almost never combine with other elements.

no•ble•man /nóbəlmən/ *n.* (*pl.* **•men**) a man of noble rank or birth; a peer.

noble metal *n.* a metal (e.g., gold, silver, or platinum) that resists chemical action, does not corrode or tarnish in air or water, and is not easily attacked by acids.

noble sav•age *n.* primitive man idealized as in Romantic literature.

noble sci•ence *n.* = BOXING.

no•blesse /nóblés/ *n.* the class of nobles (as of France, etc.). □ **noblesse oblige** /óbleezh/ privilege entails responsibility. [ME = nobility, f. OF (as NOBLE)]

no•ble•wom•an /nóbəlwʊmən/ *n.* (*pl.* **•wom•en**) a woman of noble rank or birth; a peeress.

no•bod•y /nóbodee, –budee, –bədee/ *pron. & n.* • *pron.* no person. • *n.* (*pl.* **•ies**) a person of no importance, authority, or position. □ **like nobody's business** see BUSINESS. **nobody's fool** see FOOL. [ME f. NO[1] + BODY (= person)]

no-brain•er *n.* a problem, question, examination, etc., that requires very little thought.

nock /nok/ *n. & v.* • *n.* 1 a notch at either end of a bow for holding the string. 2 a a notch at the butt end of an arrow for receiving the bowstring. b a notched piece of horn serving this purpose. • *v.tr.* set (an arrow) on the string. [ME, perh. = *nock* forward upper corner of some sails, f. MDu. *nocke*]

noc•tam•bu•list /noktámbyəlist/ *n.* a sleepwalker. □□ **noc•tam•bu•lism** *n.* [L *noxnoctis* night + *ambulare* walk]

noc•tule /nókchool/ *n.* a large W. European bat, *Nyctalus noctula*. [F f. It. *nottola* bat]

noc•turn /nóktərn/ *n. RC Ch.* a part of matins orig. said at night. [ME f. OF *nocturne* or eccl.L *nocturnum* neut. of L *nocturnus*: see NOCTURNAL]

noc•tur•nal /noktə́rnəl/ *adj.* of or in the night; done or active by night. □□ **noc•tur•nal•ly** *adv.* [LL *nocturnalis* f. L *nocturnus* of the night f. *nox noctis* night]

noc•tur•nal e•mis•sion *n.* involuntary emission of semen during sleep.

noc•turne /nóktərn/ *n.* 1 *Mus.* a short composition of a romantic nature, usu. for piano. 2 a picture of a night scene. [F (as NOCTURN)]

noc•u•ous /nókyōōəs/ *adj. literary* noxious, harmful. [L *nocuus* f. *nocēre* hurt]

nod /nod/ *v. & n.* • *v.* (**nod•ded, nod•ding**) 1 *intr.* incline one's head slightly and briefly in greeting, assent, or command. 2 *intr.* let one's head fall forward in drowsiness; be drowsy. 3 *tr.* incline (one's head). 4 *tr.* signify (assent, etc.) by a nod. 5 *intr.* (of flowers, plumes, etc.) bend downward and sway, or move up and down. 6 *intr.* make a mistake due to a momentary lack of alertness or attention. 7 *intr.* (of a building, etc.) incline from the perpendicular (*nodding to its fall*). • *n.* a nodding of the head, esp. as a sign to proceed, etc. □ **get the nod** be chosen or approved. **nod off** *colloq.* fall asleep. **on the nod** *colloq.* 1 with merely formal assent and no discussion. 2 *Brit. sl.* on credit. □□ **nod•ding•ly** *adv.* [ME *nodde*, of unkn. orig.]

nod•ding ac•quaint•ance *n.* (usu. foll. by *with*) a very slight acquaintance with a person or subject.

nod•dle[1] /nód'l/ *n. colloq.* the head. [ME *nodle*, of unkn. orig.]

nod•dle[2] /nód'l/ *v.tr. colloq.* nod or wag (one's head). [NOD + –LE[4]]

nod•dy /nódee/ *n.* (*pl.* **•dies**) 1 a simpleton. 2 any of various tropical seabirds of the genus *Anous*, resembling terns. [prob. f. obs. *noddy* foolish, which is perh. f. NOD]

node /nōd/ *n.* 1 *Bot.* a the part of a plant stem from which one or more leaves emerge. b a knob on a root or branch. 2 *Anat.* a natural swelling or bulge in an organ or part of the body. 3 *Astron.* either of two points at which a planet's orbit intersects the plane of the ecliptic or the celestial equator. 4 *Physics* a point of minimum disturbance in a standing wave system. 5 *Electr.* a point of zero current or voltage. 6 *Math.* a a point at which a curve intersects itself. b a vertex in a graph. 7 a component in a computer network. □□ **nod•al** *adj.* **nod•i•cal** *adj.* (in sense 3). [L *nodus* knot]

no•di *pl.* of NODUS.

no•dose /nódōs/ *adj.* (also **no•dous**) knotty, knotted. □□ **no•dos•i•ty** /–dósitee/ *n.* [L *nodosus* (as NODE)]

nod•ule /nójool/ *n.* 1 a small, rounded lump of anything, e.g., flint in chalk, carbon in cast iron, or a mineral on the seabed. 2 a small swelling or aggregation of cells, e.g., a small tumor, node, or ganglion, or a swelling on a root of a legume containing bacteria. □□ **nod•u•lar** /–jələr/ *adj.* **nod•u•lat•ed** /–jəlaytid/ *adj.* **nod•u•la•tion** /–jəlayshən/ *n.* **nod•u•lose** /–jolōs/ *adj.* **nod•u•lous** /–jələs/ *adj.* [L *nodulus* dimin. of *nodus*: see NODUS]

no•dus /nódəs/ *n.* (*pl.* **no•di** /–dī/) a knotty point, a difficulty, a complication in the plot of a story, etc. [L, = knot]

No•el /nō-él/ *n.* 1 Christmas (esp. as a refrain in carols); the Christmas season. 2 (also **noel**) a Christmas carol. [F f. L (as NATAL)]

no•et•ic /nō-étik/ *adj. & n.* • *adj.* 1 of the intellect. 2 purely intellectual or abstract. 3 given to intellectual speculation. • *n.* (in *sing.* or *pl.*) the science of the intellect. [Gk *noētikos* f. *noētos* intellectual f. *noeō* apprehend]

no-fault *adj.* 1 (of insurance) valid regardless of the allocation of blame for an accident, etc. 2 denoting a form of divorce granted without requiring one party to prove that the other is to blame for the breakdown of the marriage.

no-frills *adj.* without ornament or embellishment.

nog[1] /nog/ *n. & v. • n.* **1** a small block or peg of wood. **2** a snag or stump on a tree. **3** nogging. • *v.tr.* (**nogged, nog•ging**) **1** secure with nogs. **2** build in the form of nogging. [17th c.: orig. unkn.]

nog[2] /nog/ *n.* **1** = EGGNOG. **2** *Brit.* a strong beer formerly brewed in Norfolk, England. [17th c.: orig. unkn.]

nog•gin /nógin/ *n.* **1** a person's head. **2** a small quantity of liquor, usu. a quarter of a pint. **3** *sl.* the head. [17th c.: orig. unkn.]

nog•ging /nóging/ *n.* brickwork or timber braces in a timber frame. [NOG[1] + −ING[1]]

no-go *adj.* impossible, hopeless.

no-good *adj. & n.* • *adj.* useless. • *n.* a useless thing or person.

no-hit•ter *n. Baseball* a game in which a pitcher allows no hits.

Noh var. of NO[2].

no-hop•er *n. sl.* esp. *Brit.* a useless person.

no•how /nóhow/ *adv.* **1** in no way; by no means. **2** *dial.* out of order; out of sorts.

noil /noyl/ *n.* (in *sing.* or *pl.*) short wool-combings. [perh. f. OF *noel* f. med.L *nodellus* dimin. of L *nodus* knot]

noise /noyz/ *n. & v.* • *n.* **1** a sound, esp. a loud or unpleasant or undesired one. **2** a series of loud sounds, esp. shouts; a confused sound of voices and movements. **3** irregular fluctuations accompanying a transmitted signal but not relevant to it. **4** (in *pl.*) conventional remarks, or speechlike sounds without actual words (*made sympathetic noises*). • *v.* **1** *tr.* (usu. in *passive*) make public; spread abroad (a person's fame or a fact). **2** *intr. archaic* make much noise. □ **make a noise 1** (usu. foll. by *about*) talk or complain much. **2** be much talked of; attain notoriety. **noises off** esp. *Brit.* sounds made offstage to be heard by the audience of a play. [ME f. OF, = outcry, disturbance, f. L *nausea*: see NAUSEA]

noise•less /nóyzlis/ *adj.* **1** silent. **2** making no avoidable noise. □□ **noise•less•ly** *adv.* **noise•less•ness** *n.*

noise•mak•er /nóyzmàkər/ *n.* a device for making a loud noise at a party, etc.

noise pol•lu•tion *n.* harmful or annoying noise.

noi•sette /nwaazét/ *n.* a small, lean, usu. round piece of meat, etc. [F, dimin. of *noix* nut]

noi•some /nóysəm/ *adj. literary* **1** harmful, noxious. **2** evil-smelling. **3** objectionable, offensive. □□ **noi•some•ness** *n.* [ME f. obs. *noy* f. ANNOY]

▶Noisome means 'bad-smelling.' It has no relation to the word *noise*.

nois•y /nóyzee/ *adj.* (**nois•i•er, nois•i•est**) **1** full of or attended with noise. **2** making or given to making much noise. **3** clamorous; turbulent. **4** (of a color, garment, etc.) loud; conspicuous. □□ **nois•i•ly** *adv.* **nois•i•ness** *n.*

no•lens vo•lens /nólenz vólenz, nólens wólens/ *adv. literary* willy-nilly; perforce. [L participles, = unwilling, willing]

nol•le pros•e•qui /nólee prósikwì, −kwee/ *n. Law* **1** the relinquishment by a plaintiff or prosecutor of all or part of a suit. **2** the entry of this on record. ¶ Abbr.: **nol pros**. [L, = refuse to pursue]

nom. *abbr.* nominal.

no•mad /nómad/ *n. & adj.* • *n.* **1** a member of a tribe roaming from place to place for pasture. **2** a wanderer. • *adj.* **1** living as a nomad. **2** wandering. □□ **no•mad•ic** /−mádik/ *adj.* **no•mad•i•cal•ly** *adv.* **no•mad•ism** *n.* **no•mad•ize** *v.intr.* [F *nomade* f. L *nomas nomad-* f. Gk *nomas −ados* f. *nemō* to pasture]

no man's land *n.* **1** *Mil.* the space between two opposing armies. **2** an area not assigned to any owner. **3** an area not clearly belonging to any one subject, etc.

nom•bril /nómbril/ *n. Heraldry* the point halfway between fess point and the base of the shield. [F, = navel]

nom de guerre /nóm də gáir/ *n.* (*pl.* **noms de guerre** *pronunc.* same) an assumed name under which a person fights, plays, writes, etc. [F, = war name]

nom de plume /nóm də plóom/ *n.* (*pl.* **noms de plume** *pronunc.* same) an assumed name under which a person writes. [formed in E of F words, = pen name, after NOM DE GUERRE]

no•men /nómen/ *n.* (*pl.* **nom•i•na** /nóminə/) an ancient Roman's second name, indicating the gens, as in Marcus *Tullius* Cicero. [L, = name]

no•men•cla•ture /nóménklaychər, nōménklɒchər/ *n.* **1** a person's or community's system of names for things. **2** the terminology of a science, etc. **3** systematic naming. **4** a catalog or register. □□ **no•men•cla•tive** *adj.* **no•men•cla•tur•al** /−kláchərəl/ *adj.* [F f. L *nomenclatura* f. *nomen* + *calare* call]

nom•i•nal /nóminəl/ *adj.* **1** existing in name only; not real or actual (*nominal and real prices; nominal ruler*). **2** (of a sum of money, rent, etc.) virtually nothing; much below the actual value of a thing. **3** of or in names (*nominal and essential distinctions*). **4** consisting of or giving the names (*nominal list of officers*). **5** of or as or like a noun. □□ **nom•i•nal•ly** *adv.* [ME f. F *nominal* or L *nominalis* f. *nomen −inis* name]

nom•i•nal def•i•ni•tion *n.* a statement of all that is connoted in the name of a concept.

nom•i•nal•ism /nóminəlizəm/ *n. Philos.* the doctrine that universals or general ideas are mere names (opp. REALISM). □□ **nom•i•nal•ist** *n.* **nom•i•nal•is•tic** *adj.* [F *nominalisme* (as NOMINAL)]

nom•i•nal•ize /nóminəlìz/ *v.tr.* form a noun from (a verb, adjective, etc.), e.g., *output, truth*, from *put out, true.* □□ **nom•i•nal•i•za•tion** *n.*

nom•i•nal val•ue *n.* the face value (of a coin, shares, etc.).

nom•i•nate /nóminayt/ *v.tr.* **1** propose (a candidate) for election. **2** appoint to an office (*a board of six nominated and six elected members*). **3** name or appoint (a date or place). **4** mention by name. **5** call by the name of, designate. □□ **nom•i•na•tor** *n.* [L *nominare nominat-* (as NOMINAL)]

nom•i•na•tion /nóminȧyshən/ *n.* **1** the act or an instance of nominating; the state of being nominated. **2** the right of nominating for an appointment (*have a nomination at your disposal*). [ME f. OF *nomination* or L *nominatio* (as NOMINATE)]

nom•i•na•tive /nóminətiv/ *n. & adj.* • *n. Gram.* **1** the case of nouns, pronouns, and adjectives, expressing the subject of a verb. **2** a word in this case. • *adj.* **1** *Gram.* of or in this case. **2** /−naytiv/ of, or appointed by, nomination (as distinct from election). □□ **nom•i•na•tiv•al** /−tívəl/ *adj.* [ME f. OF *nominatif −ive* or L *nominativus* (as NOMINATE), transl. Gk *onomastikē* (*ptōsis* case)]

nom•i•nee /nóminée/ *n.* **1** a person who is nominated for an office or as the recipient of a grant, etc. **2** *Commerce* a person (not necessarily the owner) in whose name a stock, etc., is registered. [NOMINATE]

nom•o•gram /nóməgram, nó−/ *n.* (also **nom•o•graph** /−graf/) a graphical presentation of relations between quantities whereby the value of one may be found by simple geometrical construction (e.g., drawing a straight line) from those of others. □□ **nom•o•graph•ic** *adj.* **nom•o•graph•i•cal•ly** *adv.* **no•mog•ra•phy** /nəmógrəfee/ *n.* [Gk *nomo-* f. *nomos* law + −GRAM]

nom•o•thet•ic /nóməthétik, nó−/ *adj.* **1** stating (esp. scientific) laws. **2** legislative. [obs. *nomothete* legislator f. Gk *nomothetēs*]

-nomy /nəmee/ *comb. form* denoting an area of knowledge or the laws governing it (*astronomy; economy*).

non- /non/ *prefix* giving the negative sense of words with which it is combined, esp.: **1** not doing or having or involved with (*nonattendance; nonpayment; nonproductive*). **2 a** not of the kind or class described (*nonalcoholic; nonmember; nonevent*). **b** forming terms used adjectivally (*nonunion; nonparty*). **3** a lack of (*nonaccess*). **4** (with adverbs) not in the way described (*nonaggressively*). **5** forming adjectives from verbs, meaning 'that does not' or 'that is not meant to (or to be)' (*nonskid; noniron*). **6** used to form a neutral negative sense when a form in *in-* or *un-* has a special sense or (usu. unfavorable) connotation (*noncontroversial; noneffective; nonhuman*). [from or after ME *no* (*u*)*n-* f. AF *noun-*, OF *non-*, *nom-* f. L *non* not]

▶The number of words that can be formed with this prefix is unlimited; consequently only a selection, considered the most current or semantically noteworthy, can be given here.

nona- /nónə/ *comb. form* nine. [L f. *nonus* ninth]

non•ab•stain•er /nónəbstáynər/ *n.* a person who does not abstain (esp. from alcohol).

non•ac•cept•ance /nónəkséptəns/ *n.* a lack of acceptance.

non•ac•cess /nónákses/ *n.* a lack of access.

non•ad•dic•tive /nónədíktiv/ *adj.* (of a drug, habit, etc.) not causing addiction.

non•age /nónij, nó−/ *n.* **1** *hist.* the state of being under full legal age, minority. **2** a period of immaturity. [ME f. AF *nounage*, OF *nonage* (as NON-, AGE)]

non•a•ge•nar•i•an /nónəjináireeən, nó−/ *n. & adj.* • *n.* a person from 90 to 99 years old. • *adj.* of this age. [L *nonagenarius* f. *nonageni* distributive of *nonaginta* ninety]

non•ag•gres•sion /nónəgréshən/ *n.* lack of or restraint from aggression (often *attrib.*: *nonaggression pact*).

non•a•gon /nónəgon/ *n.* a plane figure with nine sides and angles. [L *nonus* ninth, after HEXAGON]

non•al•co•hol•ic /nónalkəhólik/ *adj.* (of a drink, etc.) not containing alcohol.

non•a•ligned /nónəlínd/ *adj.* (of nations, etc.) not aligned with another (esp. major) power. □□ **non•a•lign•ment** *n.*

non•al•ler•gic /nónəlɔ́rjik/ *adj.* not causing allergy; not allergic.

non•am•big•u•ous /nónambígyōoəs/ *adj.* not ambiguous.

non•ap•pear•ance /nónəpeerəns/ *n.* failure to appear or be present.

non•art /nónaart/ *n.* something that avoids the normal forms of art.

no•na•ry /nónəree/ *adj. & n.* • *adj. Math.* (of a scale of notation) having nine as its base. • *n.* (*pl.* **-ries**) a group of nine. [L *nonus* ninth]

non-Ar•y•an /nónáireeən/ *adj. & n.* • *adj.* (of a person or language) not Aryan or of Aryan descent. • *n.* a non-Aryan person.

non•at•tached /nónətácht/ *adj.* not attached.

▶Neutral in sense: see NON- 6, UNATTACHED.

non•at•ten•dance /nónəténdəns/ *n.* failure to attend.

non•at•trib•ut•a•ble /nónətríbyŏotəbəl/ *adj.* that cannot or may not be attributed to a particular source, etc. □□ **non•at•trib•ut•a•bly** *adv.*

non•a•vail•a•bil•i•ty /nónəváyləbílitee/ *n.* a state of not being available.

non·be·liev·er /nónbileévər/ *n.* a person who does not believe or has no (esp. religious) faith.

non·bel·lig·er·en·cy /nónbəlíjərənsee/ *n.* a lack of belligerency.

non·bel·lig·er·ent /nónbəlíjərənt/ *adj. & n.* • *adj.* not engaged in hostilities. • *n.* a nonbelligerent nation, etc.

non·bi·o·log·i·cal /nónbiəlójikəl/ *adj.* not concerned with biology or living organisms.

non·black /nónblák/ *adj. & n.* • *adj.* **1** (of a person) not black. **2** of or relating to nonblack people. • *n.* a nonblack person.

non·break·a·ble /nónbráykəbəl/ *adj.* not breakable.

non·cap·i·tal /nónkápit'l/ *adj.* (of an offense) not punishable by death.

non·Cath·o·lic /nónkáthəlik, –káthlik/ *adj. & n.* • *adj.* not Roman Catholic. • *n.* a non-Catholic person.

nonce /nons/ *n.* □ **for the nonce** for the time being; for the present occasion. [ME *for than anes* (unrecorded) = for the one, altered by wrong division (cf. NEWT)]

nonce word *n.* a word coined for one occasion.

non·cha·lant /nónshəlaánt/ *adj.* calm and casual, unmoved, unexcited, indifferent. □□ **non·cha·lance** /–aáns/ *n.* **non·cha·lant·ly** *adv.* [F, part. of *nonchaloir* f. *chaloir* be concerned]

non-Chris·tian /nónkrís-chən/ *adj. & n.* • *adj.* not Christian. • *n.* a non-Christian person.

non·cit·i·zen /nónsítizən/ *n.* a person who is not a citizen (of a particular nation, town, etc.).

non·clas·si·fied /nónklásifid/ *adj.* (esp. of information) that is not classified.
▶Neutral in sense: see NON- 6, UNCLASSIFIED.

non·cler·i·cal /nónklérikəl/ *adj.* not doing or involving clerical work.

non·col·le·giate /nónkəleéjət/ *adj.* **1** not attached to a college. **2** not having colleges.

non·com /nónkom/ *n. colloq.* a noncommissioned officer. [abbr.]

non·com·bat·ant /nónkəmbát'nt,–kómbət'nt/ *n.* a person not fighting in a war, esp. a civilian, army chaplain, etc.

non·com·mis·sioned /nónkəmíshənd/ *adj. Mil.* (of an officer) not holding a commission. ¶ Abbr.: **NCO**.

non·com·mit·tal /nónkəmít'l/ *adj.* avoiding commitment to a definite opinion or course of action. □□ **non·com·mit·tal·ly** *adv.*

non·com·mu·ni·cant /nónkəmyoÓonikənt/ *n.* a person who is not a communicant (esp. in the religious sense).

non·com·mu·ni·cat·ing /nónkəmyoÓonikayting/ *adj.* that does not communicate.

non·com·mu·nist /nónkómyənist/ *adj. & n.* (also **non-Com·mu·nist** with ref. to a particular party) • *adj.* not advocating or practicing communism. • *n.* a noncommunist person.

non·com·pli·ance /nónkəmplíəns/ *n.* failure to comply; a lack of compliance.

non com·pos men·tis /nón kompəs méntis/ *adj.* (also **non com·pos**) not in one's right mind. [L, = not having control of one's mind]

non·con·duc·tor /nónkəndúktər/ *n.* a substance that does not conduct heat or electricity. □□ **non·con·duct·ing** *adj.*

non·con·fi·den·tial /nónkonfidénshəl/ *adj.* not confidential. □□ **non·con·fi·den·tial·ly** *adv.*

non·con·form·ist /nónkənfáwrmist/ *n.* **1** a person who does not conform to the doctrine or discipline of an established Church, esp. (**Nonconformist**) a member of a (usu. Protestant) sect dissenting from the Anglican Church. **2** a person who does not conform to a prevailing principle. □□ **non·con·form·ism** *n.* **Non·con·form·ism** *n.*

non·con·form·i·ty /nónkənfáwrmitee/ *n.* **1 a** nonconformists as a body, esp. (**Nonconformity**) Protestants dissenting from the Anglican Church. **b** the principles or practice of nonconformists, esp. (**Nonconformity**) Protestant dissent. **2** (usu. foll. by *to*) failure to conform to a rule, etc. **3** lack of correspondence between things.

non·con·ta·gious /nónkəntáyjəs/ *adj.* not contagious.

non·con·ten·tious /nónkənténshəs/ *adj.* not contentious.

non·con·trib·u·to·ry /nónkəntríbyətawree/ *adj.* not contributing or (esp. of a pension plan) involving contributions.

non·con·tro·ver·sial /nónkóntrəvərshəl/ *adj.* not controversial.

non·co·op·er·a·tion /nónkō-ópəráyshən/ *n.* failure to cooperate; a lack of cooperation.

non·de·liv·er·y /nóndilívəree/ *n.* failure to deliver.

non·de·nom·i·na·tion·al /nóndinóminnáyshənəl/ *adj.* not restricted as regards religious denomination.

non·de·script /nóndiskript/ *adj. & n.* • *adj.* lacking distinctive characteristics; not easily classified; neither one thing nor another. • *n.* a nondescript person or thing. □□ **non·de·script·ly** *adv.* **non·de·script·ness** *n.* [NON- + *descript* described f. L *descriptus* (as DESCRIBE)]

non·de·struc·tive /nóndistrúktiv/ *adj.* that does not involve destruction or damage.

non·drink·er /nóndríngkər/ *n.* a person who does not drink alcoholic liquor.

non·driv·er /nóndrívər/ *n.* a person who does not drive a motor vehicle.

none[1] /nun/ *pron., adj., & adv.* • *pron.* **1** (foll. by *of*) **a** not any of (*none of this concerns me; none of them has found it; none of your im-*

pudence!). **b** not any one of (*none of them has come; none were recovered*). **2 a** no persons (*none but fools have ever believed it*). **b** no person (*none can tell*). • *adj.* (usu. with a preceding noun implied) **1** no; not any (*you have money and I have none; would rather have a bad reputation than none at all*). **2** not to be counted in a specified class (*his understanding is none of the clearest ; if a linguist is wanted, I am none*). • *adv.* (foll. by *the* + compar., or *so, too*) by no amount; not at all (*am none the wiser ; are none too fond of him*). □ **none other** (usu. foll. by *than*) no other person. [OE *nān* f. *ne* not + *ān* ONE]
▶The verb following *none* in the sense of "not any one of" can be singular or plural according to the sense: *none have arrived yet; none has come forward.*

none[2] /non/ *n.* (also in *pl.*) **1** the office of the fifth of the canonical hours of prayer, orig. said at the ninth hour (3 p.m.). **2** this hour. [F f. L *nona* fem. sing. of *nonus* ninth: cf. NOON]

non·earn·ing /non-órning/ *adj.* not earning (esp. a regular wage or salary).

non·ef·fec·tive /nóniféktiv/ *adj.* that does not have an effect.

non·e·go /nóneégō/ *n. Philos.* all that is not the conscious self.

non·en·ti·ty /nonéntitee/ *n.* (*pl.* **·ties**) **1** a person or thing of no importance. **2 a** nonexistence. **b** a nonexistent thing, a figment. [med.L *nonentitas* nonexistence]

nones /nonz/ *n.pl.* in the ancient Roman calendar, the ninth day before the ides by inclusive reckoning—i.e., the 7th day of March, May, July, and October, and the 5th of other months. [OF *nones* f. L *nonae* fem. pl. of *nonus* ninth]

non·es·sen·tial /nónisénshəl/ *adj.* not essential.

none·such /núnsuch/ *n.* (also **non·such**) **1** a person or thing that is unrivaled, a paragon. **2** a leguminous plant, *Medicago lupulina*, with black pods. [NONE[1] + SUCH, usu. now assim. to NON-]

no·net /nonét/ *n.* **1** *Mus.* **a** a composition for nine voices or instruments. **b** the performers of such a piece. **2** a group of nine. [It. *nonetto* f. *nono* ninth f. L *nonus*]

none·the·less /núnthəlés/ *adv.* nevertheless.

non-Eu·clid·e·an /nónyooklídeeən/ *adj.* denying or going beyond Euclidean principles in geometry.

non·e·vent /nónivént/ *n.* an unimportant or anticlimactic occurrence.

non·ex·ist·ent /nónigzístənt/ *adj.* not existing. □□ **non·ex·ist·ence** /–təns/ *n.*

non·ex·plo·sive /nóniksplósiv/ *adj.* (of a substance) that does not explode.

non·fat·ten·ing /nónfát'ning/ *adj.* (of food) that does not fatten.

non·fea·sance /nónfeézəns/ *n.* failure to perform an act required by law. [NON-: see MISFEASANCE]

non·fer·rous /nónférəs/ *adj.* (of a metal) other than iron or steel.

non·fic·tion /nónfíkshən/ *n.* literary work other than fiction, including biography and reference books. □□ **non·fic·tion·al** *adj.*

non·flam·ma·ble /nónflámməbəl/ *adj.* not flammable.
▶See note at INFLAMMABLE.

non·ful·fill·ment /nónfoolfílmənt/ *n.* failure to fulfill (an obligation).

non·func·tion·al /nónfúngkshənəl/ *adj.* not having a function.

nong /nong/ *n. Austral. sl.* a foolish or stupid person. [20th c.: orig. unkn.]

non·gov·ern·men·tal /nón-guvərnmént'l/ *adj.* not belonging to or associated with a government.

non·hu·man /nónhyoÓomən/ *adj. & n.* • *adj.* (of a being) not human. • *n.* a nonhuman being.
▶Neutral in sense: see NON- 6, INHUMAN, UNHUMAN.

non·in·fec·tious /nóninfékshəs/ *adj.* (of a disease) not infectious.

non·in·flect·ed /nóninfléktid/ *adj.* (of a language) not having inflections.

non·in·ter·fer·ence /nónintərfeéərəns/ *n.* a lack of interference.

non·in·ter·ven·tion /nónintərvénshən/ *n.* the principle or practice of not becoming involved in others' affairs, esp. by one nation in regard to another.

non·in·tox·i·cat·ing /nónintóksikayting/ *adj.* (of drink) not causing intoxication.

non·i·ron /nóníərn/ *adj. Brit.* (of a fabric) that needs no ironing.

non·join·der /nónjóyndər/ *n. Law* the failure of a partner, etc., to become a party to a suit.

non·ju·ror /nónjoÓorər/ *n.* a person who refuses to take an oath, esp. *hist.* (also **Nonjuror**) a member of the clergy refusing to take the oath of allegiance to King William and Queen Mary of Great Britain in 1689. □□ **non·jur·ing** *adj.*

non·ju·ry /nónjoÓoree/ *adj.* (of a trial) without a jury.

non·lin·e·ar /nónlíneeər/ *adj.* not linear, esp. with regard to dimension.

non·lit·er·ar·y /nónlítəreree/ *adj.* (of writing, a text, etc.) not literary in character.

non·log·i·cal /nónlójikəl/ *adj.* not involving logic.
▶Neutral in sense: see NON- 6, ILLOGICAL.

non·mag·net·ic /nónmagnétik/ *adj.* (of a substance) not magnetic.

non·mem·ber /nónmémbər/ *n.* a person who is not a member (of a particular association, club, etc.). □□ **non·mem·ber·ship** *n.*

non·met·al /nónmét'l/ *adj.* not made of metal. □□ **non·me·tal·lic** /–mətálik/ *adj.*

non·mil·i·tant /nónmílitənt/ *adj.* not militant.

non·mil·i·tar·y /nónmíliteree/ *adj.* not military; not involving armed forces; civilian.

non·min·is·te·ri·al /nónministeéreeəl/ *adj.* not ministerial (esp. in political senses).

non·mor·al /nónmáwrəl, –mór–/ *adj.* not concerned with morality. □□ **non·mor·al·ly** *adv.*
▶Neutral in sense: see NON- 6, AMORAL, IMMORAL.

non·nat·u·ral /nón-náchərəl/ *adj.* not involving natural means nor processes.
▶Neutral in sense: see NON- 6, UNNATURAL.

non·ne·go·ti·a·ble /nón-nigóshəbəl, –sheeə–/ *adj.* that cannot be negotiated (esp. in financial senses).

non·nu·cle·ar /nón-nookleeər, –nyoo–/ *adj.* **1** not involving nuclei nor nuclear energy. **2** (of a nation, etc.) not having nuclear weapons.

no-no *n. colloq.* a thing not possible or acceptable.

non·ob·serv·ance /nónəbzórvəns/ *n.* failure to observe (esp. an agreement, requirement, etc.).

non·non·sense *adj.* serious, without flippancy.

non·op·er·a·tion·al /nónopəráyshənəl/ *adj.* **1** that does not operate. **2** out of order.

non·or·gan·ic /nóawrgánik/ *adj.* not organic.
▶Neutral in sense: see NON- 6, INORGANIC.

non·pa·reil /nónpərél/ *adj. & n.* ● *adj.* unrivaled or unique. ● *n.* **1** such a person or thing. **2** a candy made from a chocolate disk, decorated with sugar pellets. [F f. *pareil* equal f. pop.L *pariculus* dimin. of L *par*]

non·par·tic·i·pat·ing /nónpaartísipayting/ *adj.* not taking part.

non·par·ti·san /nónpaartizən/ *adj.* not partisan.

non·par·ty /nónpaártee/ *adj.* independent of political parties.

non·pay·ment /nónpáymənt/ *n.* failure to pay; a lack of payment.

non·per·son /nónpórsən/ *n.* a person regarded as nonexistent or insignificant (cf. UNPERSON).

non·per·son·al /nónpórsənəl/ *adj.* not personal.
▶Neutral in sense: see NON- 6, IMPERSONAL.

non·phys·i·cal /nónfízikəl/ *adj.* not physical. □□ **non·phys·i·cal·ly** *adv.*

non pla·cet /non pláyset/ *n.* a negative vote in a church or university assembly. [L, = it does not please]

non·play·ing /nónpláying/ *adj.* that does not play or take part (in a game, etc.).

non·plus /nonplús/ *v. & n.* ● *v.tr.* (**non·plussed** or **non·plused**, **non·plus·sing** or **non·plus·ing**) completely perplex. ● *n.* a state of perplexity, a standstill (*at a nonplus; reduce to a nonplus*). [L *non plus* not more]

non·poi·son·ous /nónpóyzənəs/ *adj.* (of a substance) not poisonous.

non·po·lit·i·cal /nónpəlítikəl/ *adj.* not political; not involved in politics.

non·po·rous /nónpáwrəs/ *adj.* (of a substance) not porous.

non pos·su·mus /nonpósəməs/ *n.* a statement of inability to act in a matter. [L, = we cannot]

non·pro·duc·tive /nónprədúktiv/ *adj.* not productive. □□ **non·pro·duc·tive·ly** *adv.*

non·pro·fes·sion·al /nónprəféshənəl/ *adj.* not professional (esp. in status).
▶Neutral in sense: see NON- 6, UNPROFESSIONAL.

non·prof·it /nónprófit/ *adj.* not involving nor making a profit.

non·pro·lif·er·a·tion /nónprəlifəráyshən/ *n.* the prevention of an increase in something, esp. possession of nuclear weapons.

non·ra·cial /nónráyshəl/ *adj.* not involving race or racial factors.

non·read·er /nónreédər/ *n.* a person who cannot or does not read.

non·res·i·dent /nónrézidənt/ *adj. & n.* ● *adj.* **1** not residing in a particular place, esp. (of a member of the clergy) not residing where his or her duties require. **2** (of a post) not requiring the holder to reside at the place of work. ● *n.* a nonresident person. □□ **non·res·i·dence** /–dəns/ *n.* **non·res·i·den·tial** /–dénshəl/ *adj.*

non·re·sis·tance /nónrizístəns/ *n.* failure to resist; a lack of resistance.

non·re·turn·a·ble /nónritórnəbəl/ *adj.* that may or will not be returned.

non·rig·id /nónríjid/ *adj.* (esp. of materials) not rigid.

non·sci·en·tif·ic /nónsiəntifik/ *adj.* not involving science or scientific methods. □□ **non·sci·en·tist** /–síəntist/ *n.*
▶Neutral in sense: see NON- 6, UNSCIENTIFIC.

non·sec·tar·i·an /nónsektáireeən/ *adj.* not sectarian.

non·sense /nónsens, –səns/ *n.* **1 a** (often as *int.*) absurd or meaningless words or ideas; foolish or extravagant conduct. **b** an in-

stance of this. **2** a scheme, arrangement, etc., that one disapproves of. **3** (often *attrib.*) a form of literature meant to amuse by absurdity (*nonsense verse*). □□ **non·sen·si·cal** /–sénsikəl/ *adj.* **non·sen·si·cal·i·ty** /nónsensikálitee/ *n.* (*pl.* **·ties**). **non·sen·si·cal·ly** /–sénsiklee/ *adv.*

SYNONYM TIP   nonsense

BULL, BUNK, DRIVEL, POPPYCOCK, TWADDLE. If you write or speak in an obscure, senseless, or ponderous manner, you'll probably be accused of producing **nonsense**. It is the most general of these nouns and may refer to behavior as well as to what is said (*the demonstrators were told in no uncertain terms to give up this nonsense or leave the room*). **Twaddle** refers to silly, empty utterances from people who know nothing about a subject but who write or talk about it anyway (*I was sick of her twaddle about the dangers of electromagnetic fields*). **Bunk** (short for *bunkum*) is more specific; it applies to an utterance that strikes the popular fancy even though it is lacking in worth or substance (*the speech, which received enthusiastic applause, was pure bunk*). **Poppycock** applies to nonsense that is full of complex, confused, or clichéd ideas (*the report was a strange combination of logical thinking and outright poppycock*). **Bull** is a slang term for deceitful and often boastful writing or speech (*he gave them a line of bull*). Perhaps the most insulting of these terms is **drivel**, which implies a steady flow of inane, idle, or nonsensical speech or writing similar to what might be expected from a very young child or an idiot (*his first novel was full of romantic drivel*).

---

non se·qui·tur /nonsékwitər/ *n.* a conclusion that does not logically follow from the premises. [L, = it does not follow]

non·sex·u·al /nónsékshooəl/ *adj.* not based on or involving sex. □□ **non·sex·u·al·ly** *adv.*

non·skid /nónskíd/ *adj.* **1** that does not skid. **2** that inhibits skidding.

non·slip /nónslíp/ *adj.* **1** that does not slip. **2** that inhibits slipping.

non·smok·er /nónsmókər/ *n.* **1** a person who does not smoke. **2** a train compartment, etc., in which smoking is forbidden. □□ **non·smok·ing** *adj. & n.*

non·sol·u·ble /nónsólyəbəl/ *adj.* (esp. of a substance) not soluble.

non·spe·cial·ist /nónspéshəlist/ *n.* a person who is not a specialist (in a particular subject).

non·spe·cif·ic /nónspisífik/ *adj.* that cannot be specified.

non·stand·ard /nónstándərd/ *adj.* **1** not standard. **2** *Gram.* not conforming to standard usage.

non·start·er /nónstaártər/ *n.* **1** a person or animal that does not start in a race. **2** *colloq.* a person or thing that is unlikely to succeed or be effective.

non·stick /nónstík/ *adj.* **1** that does not stick. **2** that does not allow things to stick to it.

non·stop /nónstóp/ *adj., adv., & n.* ● *adj.* **1** (of a train, etc.) not stopping at intermediate places. **2** (of a journey, performance, etc.) done without a stop or intermission. ● *adv.* without stopping or pausing (*flying nonstop to Chicago*). ● *n.* a nonstop train, etc.

non·sub·scrib·er /nónsəbskríbər/ *n.* a person who is not a subscriber.

non·such var. of NONESUCH.

non·suit /nónsóot , –syóot/ *n. & v. Law* ● *n.* the stoppage of a suit by the judge when the plaintiff fails to make out a legal case or to bring sufficient evidence. ● *v.tr.* subject (a plaintiff) to a nonsuit. [ME f. AF *no(u)nsuit*]

non·swim·mer /nónswímər/ *n.* a person who cannot swim.

non·tech·ni·cal /nóntéknikəl/ *adj.* **1** not technical. **2** without technical knowledge.

non·tox·ic /nóntóksik/ *adj.* not toxic.

non·trans·fer·a·ble /nóntransfórəbəl/ *adj.* that may not be transferred.

non-U /nónyoo/ *adj.* esp. *Brit. colloq.* not characteristic of the upper class. [NON- + U²]

non·un·i·form /nónyoónifawrm/ *adj.* not uniform.

non·un·ion /nónyoónyən/ *adj.* **1** not belonging to a labor union. **2** not done or produced by members of a labor union.

non·us·age /nónyoósij, –yoózij/ *n.* failure to use.

non·use /nónyoós/ *n.* failure to use.

non·us·er /nónyoósər/ *n. Law* the failure to use a right, by which it may be lost. [AF *nounuser* (unrecorded) (as NON-, USER)]

non·ver·bal /nónvórbəl/ *adj.* not involving words or speech. □□ **non·ver·bal·ly** *adv.*

non·vin·tage /nónvíntij/ *adj.* (of wine, etc.) not vintage.

non·vi·o·lence /nónvíələns/ *n.* the avoidance of violence, esp. as a principle. □□ **non·vi·o·lent** /–lənt/ *adj.*

non·vol·a·tile /nónvólət'l, –til/ *adj.* (esp. of a substance) not volatile.

non·vot·ing /nónvóting/ *adj.* not having or using a vote. □□ **non·vot·er** *n.*

non·white /nónhwit, –wit/ *adj. & n.* ● *adj.* **1** (of a person) not white. **2** of or relating to nonwhite people. ● *n.* a non-white person.

non·word /nónwərd/ *n.* an unrecorded or unused word.

noo·dle¹ /noód'l/ *n.* a strip or ring of pasta. [G *Nudel*]

noo•dle[2] /noॕod'l/ *n.* **1** a simpleton. **2** *sl.* the head. [18th c.: orig. unkn.]

nook /noॕok/ *n.* a corner or recess; a secluded place. □ **in every nook and cranny** everywhere. [ME *nok(e)* corner, of unkn. orig.]

nook•y /noॕokee/ *n.* (also **nook•ie**) *coarse sl.* sexual intercourse. [20th c.: perh. f. NOOK]

noon /noॕon/ *n.* **1** twelve o'clock in the day; midday. **2** the culminating point. [OE *nōn* f. L *nona* (*hora*) ninth hour: orig. = 3 p.m. (cf. NONE[2])]

noon•day /noॕonday/ *n.* midday.

no one /nॕo wun/ *n.* no person; nobody.

noon•time /noॕontīm/ *n.* (also **noon•tide** /–tīd/) midday.

noose /noॕos/ *n. & v.* ● *n.* **1** a loop with a running knot, tightening as the rope or wire is pulled, esp. in a snare, lasso, or hangman's halter. **2** a snare or bond. **3** *joc.* the marriage tie. ● *v.tr.* **1** catch with or enclose in a noose, ensnare. **2 a** make a noose on (a cord). **b** (often foll. by *around*) arrange (a cord) in a noose. □ **put one's head in a noose** bring about one's own downfall. [ME *nose*, perh. f. OF *no(u)s* f. L *nodus* knot]

no•pal /nॕopəl, –paॕl/ *n.* any American cactus of the genus *Nopalea*, esp. *N. cochinellifera* grown in plantations for breeding cochineal. [F & Sp. f. Nahuatl *nopalli* cactus]

nope /nōp/ *adv. colloq.* = NO[2] *adv.* **1**. [NO[2]]

nor /nawr, nər/ *conj.* **1** and not; and not either (*neither one thing nor the other; not a man nor a child was to be seen; I said I had not seen it, nor had I; can neither read nor write*). **2** and no more; neither ("*I cannot go*"—"*Nor can I*"). ● **nor . . . nor . . .** *poet.* or *archaic* neither . . . nor . . . [ME, contr. f. obs. *nother* f. OE *nawther, nāhwæther* (as NO[2], WHETHER)]

nor' /nawr/ *n., adj., & adv.* (esp. in compounds) = NORTH (*nor'ward*; *nor'wester*). [abbr.]

nor•a•dren•a•line /nawrədrénəlin/ *n.* (also **nor•a•dren•a•lin**) = NOR-EPINEPHRINE. [*normal* + ADRENALIN]

Nor•dic /nॕawrdik/ *adj. & n.* ● *adj.* **1** of or relating to the tall blond dolichocephalic Germanic people found in N. Europe, esp. in Scandinavia. **2** of or relating to Scandinavia or Finland. **3** (of skiing) with cross-country work and jumping. ● *n.* a Nordic person, esp. a native of Scandinavia or Finland. [F *nordique* f. *nord* north]

nor'east•er /noreॕestər/ *n.* a northeaster.

nor•ep•i•neph•rine /nॕawrepinéfrin, –reen/ *n.* a hormone released by the adrenal medulla and by sympathetic nerve endings as a neurotransmitter. Also called **noradrenaline**. [*normal* + EPINEPHRINE]

Nor•folk jack•et /nॕawrfək/ *n.* a man's loose belted jacket, with box pleats. [*Norfolk* in S. England]

nor•land /nॕawrlənd/ *n. Brit.* a northern region. [contr. of NORTHLAND]

norm /nawrm/ *n.* **1** a standard or pattern or type. **2** a standard quantity to be produced or amount of work to be done. **3** customary behavior, etc. [L *norma* carpenter's square]

nor•mal /nॕawrməl/ *adj. & n.* ● *adj.* **1** conforming to a standard; regular; usual; typical. **2** free from mental or emotional disorder. **3** *Geom.* (of a line) at right angles; perpendicular. **4** *Chem.* (of a solution) containing one gram-equivalent of solute per liter. ● *n.* **1 a** the normal value of a temperature, etc., esp. that of blood. **b** the usual state, level, etc. **2** *Geom.* a line at right angles. □□ **nor•mal•cy** *n.* **nor•mal•i•ty** /–málitee / *n.* [F *normal* or L *normalis* (as NORM)]

▶ **Normalcy** has been criticized as an uneducated alternative to **normality**, but actually is a common American usage and can be taken as standard.

AVERAGE, NATURAL, ORDINARY, REGULAR, TYPICAL, USUAL. Most of us want to be regarded as **normal**, an adjective that implies conformity with established norms or standards and is the opposite of *abnormal* (*a normal body temperature; normal intelligence*). **Regular**, like *normal*, is usually preferred to its opposite (*irregular*) and implies conformity to prescribed standards or established patterns (*their regular monthly meeting; a regular guy*), but *normal* carries stronger connotations of conformity within prescribed limits and sometimes allows for a wider range of differences. Few of us think of ourselves as **ordinary**, a term used to describe what is commonplace or unexceptional (*an ordinary person wearing ordinary clothes*), although many people are ordinary in some ways and extraordinary in others. **Average** also implies conformity with what is regarded as normal or ordinary (*a woman of average height*), although it tends to emphasize the middle ground and to exclude both positive and negative extremes. **Typical** applies to persons or things possessing the representative characteristics of a type or class (*a typical teenager; a typical suburban mother*). Someone or something described as **natural** behaves or operates in accordance with his/her/its inherent nature or character (*his fears were natural for one so young*), while **usual** applies to that which conforms to common or ordinary use or occurrence (*we paid the usual price*).

nor•mal dis•tri•bu•tion *n. Statistics* a function that represents the distribution of many random variables as a symmetrical bell-shaped graph.

nor•mal•ize /nॕawrməlīz/ *v.* **1** *tr.* make normal. **2** *intr.* become normal. **3** *tr.* cause to conform. □□ **nor•mal•i•za•tion** *n.* **nor•mal•iz•er** *n.*

nor•mal•ly /nॕawrməlee/ *adv.* **1** in a normal manner. **2** usually.

nor•mal school *n.* (in the US, France, etc.) formerly, a school or college for training teachers.

Nor•man /nॕawrmən/ *n. & adj.* ● *n.* **1** a native or inhabitant of medieval Normandy (now part of France). **2** a descendant of the people of mixed Scandinavian and Frankish origin established there in the 10th c., who conquered England in 1066. **3** Norman French. **4** *Archit.* the style of Romanesque architecture found in Britain under the Normans. **5** any of the English kings from William I to Stephen. ● *adj.* **1** of or relating to the Normans. **2** of or relating to the Norman style of architecture. □□ **Nor•man•esque** /–nésk/ *adj.* **Nor•man•ism** *n.* **Nor•man•ize** *v.tr. & intr.* [OF *Normans* pl. of *Normant* f. ON *Northmathr* (as NORTH, MAN)]

Nor•man Con•quest *n.* see CONQUEST.

Nor•man Eng•lish *n.* English as spoken or influenced by the Normans.

Nor•man French *n.* French as spoken by the Normans or (after 1066) in English courts of law.

nor•ma•tive /nॕawrmətiv/ *adj.* of or establishing a norm. □□ **nor•ma•tive•ly** *adv.* **nor•ma•tive•ness** *n.* [F *normatif* *–ive* f. L *norma* (see NORM)]

Norn /nawrn/ *n.* any of three goddesses of destiny in Scandinavian mythology. [ON: orig. unkn.]

Norse /nawrs/ *n. & adj.* ● *n.* **1 a** the Norwegian language. **b** the Scandinavian language group. **2** (prec. by *the*; treated as *pl.*) **a** the Norwegians. **b** the Vikings. ● *adj.* of ancient Scandinavia, esp. Norway. □□ **Norse•man** *n.* (*pl.* •**men**). [Du. *noor(d)sch* f. *noord* north]

north /nawrth/ *n., adj., & adv.* ● *n.* **1 a** the point of the horizon 90° counterclockwise from east. **b** the compass point corresponding to this. **c** the direction in which this lies. **2** (usu. **the North**) **a** the part of the world or a country or a town lying to the north. **b** the northern part of the United States, esp. the northeastern states that fought to preserve the Union during the Civil War. **c** the arctic. **3** (**North**) *Bridge* a player occupying the position designated "north." ● *adj.* **1** toward, at, near, or facing north. **2** coming from the north (*north wind*). ● *adv.* **1** toward, at, or near the north. **2** (foll. by *of*) farther north than. ● **north and south** lengthwise along a line from north to south. **north by east** (or **west**) between north and north-northeast (or north-northwest). **to the north** (often foll. by *of*) in a northerly direction. [OE f. Gmc]

North A•mer•i•can *adj. & n.* ● *adj.* of North America. ● *n.* a native or inhabitant of North America, esp. a citizen of the US or Canada.

north•bound /nॕawrthbownd/ *adj.* traveling or leading northward.

North Coun•try *n.* **1** a name for any of various geographical regions, including Alaska and the Canadian Yukon, northern New York State, northern Vermont, etc. **2** the northern part of England (north of the Humber estuary).

north•east /nawrtheॕest/ *n., adj., & adv.* ● *n.* **1** the point of the horizon midway between north and east. **2** the compass point corresponding to this. **3** the direction in which this lies. ● *adj.* of, toward, or coming from the northeast. ● *adv.* toward, at, or near the northeast.

north•east•er /nॕawrtheॕestər, náwreॕestər/ *n.* (also **nor'easter**) **1** a northeast wind. **2** a strong storm from the northeast, esp. in New England.

north•er /nॕawrthər/ *n.* a strong cold north wind blowing in autumn and winter, esp. over Texas, Florida, and the Gulf of Mexico.

north•er•ly /nॕawrthərlee/ *adj., adv., & n.* ● *adj. & adv.* **1** in a northern position or direction. **2** (of wind) blowing from the north. ● *n.* (*pl.* •**lies**) (usu. in *pl.*) a wind blowing from the north.

north•ern /nॕawrthərn/ *adj.* **1** of or in the north; inhabiting the north. **2** lying or directed toward the north. □□ **north•ern•most** *adj.* [OE *northerne* (as NORTH, –ERN)]

north•ern•er /nॕawrthərnər/ *n.* a native or inhabitant of the north.

north•ern har•ri•er *n.* (also **north•en har•ri•er**) a hawk, *Circus cyaneus*, that inhabits marshy regions of N. America and Europe.

north•ern hem•i•sphere *n.* (also **North•ern Hem•i•sphere**) the half of the earth north of the equator.

north•ern lights *n.pl.* the aurora borealis.

north•ern states *n.pl.* the states in the north of the US.

North Germanic *n.* the Scandinavian languages.

north•ing /nॕawrthing, –thing/ *n. Naut.* the distance traveled or measured northward.

north•land /nॕawrthlənd/ *n. poet.* (also **Northland**) the northern lands; the northern part of a country. [OE (as NORTH, LAND)]

north light *n.* light from the north, esp. as desired by painters and in factory design.

North•man /nॕawrthmən/ *n.* (*pl.* •**men**) a native of Scandinavia, esp. of Norway. [OE]

north-north•east *n.* the point or direction midway between north and northeast.

north-north•west *n.* the point or direction midway between north and northwest.

north pole *n.* (also **North Pole**) **1** the northernmost point of the earth's axis of rotation. **2** the northernmost point about which the stars appear to revolve.

North Star *n.* the polestar.

North•um•bri•an /nawrthúmbreeən/ *adj. & n.* ● *adj.* of or relating to ancient Northumbria (England north of the Humber) or modern Northumberland. ● *n.* **1** a native of ancient Northumbria or modern Northumberland. **2** the dialect of ancient Northumbria or modern Northumberland. [obs. *Northumber*, persons living beyond the Humber, f. OE *Northhymbre*]

north•ward /náwrthwərd/ *adj., adv., & n.* ● *adj. & adv.* (also **north•wards**) toward the north. ● *n.* a northward direction or region.

north•west /náwrthwést/ *n., adj., & adv.* ● *n.* **1** the point of the horizon midway between north and west. **2** the compass point corresponding to this. **3** the direction in which this lies. ● *adj.* of, toward, or coming from the northwest. ● *adv.* toward, at, or near the northwest.

north•west•er /náwrthwéstər, náwrwés–/ *n.* (also **nor'wester**) a northwest wind.

Nor•way rat /náwrway/ *n.* the common brown rat, *Rattus norvegicus.*

Nor•we•gian /nawrweéjən/ *n. & adj.* ● *adj.* **1 a** a native or national of Norway. **b** a person of Norwegian descent. **2** the language of Norway. ● *adj.* of or relating to Norway or its people or language. [med.L *Norvegia* f. ON *Norvegr* (as NORTH, WAY), assim. to *Norway*]

Nos. *abbr.* (also **nos.**) numbers. [cf. No.]

nose /nōz/ *n. & v.* ● *n.* **1** an organ above the mouth on the face or head of a human or animal, containing nostrils and used for smelling and breathing. **2 a** the sense of smell (*dogs have a good nose*). **b** the ability to detect a particular thing (*a nose for scandal*). **3** the odor or perfume of wine, tea, tobacco, hay, etc. **4** the open end or nozzle of a tube, pipe, pair of bellows, retort, etc. **5 a** the front end or projecting part of a thing, e.g., of a car or aircraft. **b** = NOSING. **6** *Brit. sl.* an informer for the police. ● *v.* **1** *tr.* (often foll. by *out*) **a** perceive the smell of, discover by smell. **b** detect. **2** *tr.* thrust or rub one's nose against or into, esp. in order to smell. **3** *intr.* (usu. foll. by *about, around,* etc.) pry or search. **4 a** *intr.* make one's way cautiously forward. **b** *tr.* make (one's or its way). □ **as plain as the nose on your face** easily seen. **by a nose** by a very narrow margin (*won the race by a nose*). **count noses** count those present, one's supporters, etc.; decide a question by mere numbers. **cut off one's nose to spite one's face** disadvantage oneself in the course of trying to disadvantage another. **get up a person's nose** *Brit. sl.* annoy a person. **keep one's nose clean** *sl.* stay out of trouble; behave properly. **keep one's nose to the grindstone** see GRINDSTONE. **on the nose 1** *sl.* precisely. **2** *Austral. sl.* annoying. **3** *Austral. sl.* stinking. **put a person's nose out of joint** *colloq.* embarrass, disconcert, frustrate, or supplant a person. **rub a person's nose in it** see RUB. **see no farther than one's nose** be shortsighted, esp. in foreseeing the consequences of one's actions, etc. **speak through one's nose** pronounce words with a nasal twang. **turn up one's nose** (usu. foll. by *at*) *colloq.* show disdain. **under a person's nose** *colloq.* right before a person (esp. of defiant or unnoticed actions). **with one's nose in the air** haughtily. □□ **nosed** *adj.* (also in *comb.*). **nose•less** *adj.* [OE *nosu*]

nose•bag /nózbag/ *n.* a bag containing fodder, hung on a horse's head.

nose•band /nózband/ *n.* the lower band of a bridle, passing over the horse's nose.

nose•bleed /nózbleed/ *n.* an instance of bleeding from the nose.

nose cone *n.* the cone-shaped nose of a rocket, etc.

nose•dive /nózdīv/ *n. & v.* ● *n.* **1** a steep downward plunge by an airplane. **2** a sudden plunge or drop. ● *v.intr.* make a nosedive.

no-see-um *n.* (also **–em**) a small bloodsucking insect, esp. a midge of the family Ceratopogonidae.

nose flute *n.* a musical instrument blown with the nose.

nose•gay /nózgay/ *n.* a bunch of flowers, esp. a sweet-scented posy. [NOSE + GAY in obs. use = ornament]

nose job *n. sl.* surgery on the nose, esp. for cosmetic reasons; rhinoplasty.

nose leaf *n.* a fleshy part on the nostrils of some bats, used for echo location.

nose•piece /nózpees/ *n.* **1** = NOSEBAND. **2** the part of a helmet, etc., protecting the nose. **3** the part of a microscope to which the objective is attached. **4** the bridge on the frame of eyeglasses.

nose rag *n. Brit. sl.* a pocket handkerchief.

nose ring *n.* a ring fixed in the nose.

nos•ey *adj. & v.* var. of NOSY.

nosh /nosh/ *v. & n. sl.* ● *v.tr. & intr.* **1** eat or drink. **2** eat between meals. ● *n.* **1** food or drink. **2** a snack. [Yiddish]

nosh•er•y /nóshəree/ *n.* (*pl.* **•ies**) *sl.* a restaurant or snack bar.

no-show *n.* a person who has reserved a seat, etc., but neither uses it nor cancels the reservation.

nosh-up *n. Brit.* a large meal.

nos•ing /nózing/ *n.* a rounded edge of a step, molding, etc., or a metal shield for it.

no•sog•ra•phy /nósógrəfee/ *n.* the systematic description of diseases. [Gk *nosos* disease + –GRAPHY]

no•sol•o•gy /nósóləjee/ *n.* the branch of medical science dealing with the classification of diseases. □□ **nos•o•log•i•cal** /nósəlójikəl/ *adj.* [Gk *nosos* disease + –LOGY]

nos•tal•gia /nostáljə, –jeeə, nə–/ *n.* **1** (often foll. by *for*) sentimental yearning for a period of the past. **2** regretful or wistful memory of an earlier time. **3** severe homesickness. □□ **nos•tal•gic** *adj.* **nos•tal•gi•cal•ly** *adv.* [mod.L f. Gk *nostos* return home]

nos•toc /nóstok/ *n.* any gelatinous blue-green unicellular alga of the genus *Nostoc*, which fix nitrogen from the atmosphere. [name invented by Paracelsus]

Nos•tra•da•mus /nóstrədáaməs, –dáy–, nó–/ *n.* a person who claims to foretell future events. [Latinized form of the name of M. de *Nostredame*, French astrologer and physician d. 1566]

nos•tril /nóstrəl/ *n.* either of two external openings of the nasal cavity in vertebrates that admit air to the lungs and smells to the olfactory nerves. □□ **nos•trilled** *adj.* (also in *comb.*). [OE *nosthyrl, nosterl* f. *nosu* NOSE + *thȳr(e)l* hole: cf. THRILL]

nos•trum /nóstrəm/ *n.* **1** a quack remedy, a patent medicine, esp. one prepared by the person recommending it. **2** a panacean plan or scheme, esp. for political or social reform. [L, neut. of *noster* our, used in sense "of our own make"]

nos•y /nózee/ *adj. & n.* (also **nos•ey**) ● *adj.* (**nos•i•er, nos•i•est**) **1** *colloq.* inquisitive, prying. **2** *Brit.* having a large nose. **3** *Brit.* having a distinctive (good or bad) smell. ● *n.* (*pl.* **•ies**) a person with a large nose. □□ **nos•i•ly** *adv.* **nos•i•ness** *n.*

Nos•y Par•ker *n.* esp. *Brit. colloq.* (also **Nos•ey Par•ker**) a busybody.

not /not/ *adv.* expressing negation, esp.: **1** (also **n't** joined to a preceding verb) following an auxiliary verb or *be* or (in a question) the subject of such a verb (*she isn't there; didn't you tell me?; am I not right?; aren't we smart?*). **2** used elliptically for a negative sentence or verb or phrase (*Is she coming? — I hope not; Do you want it? — Certainly not!*). **3** used to express the negative of other words (*not a single one was left; Are they pleased? — Not they; he is not my cousin, but my nephew*). □ **not at all** (in polite reply to thanks) there is no need for thanks. **not but what** *archaic* **1** all the same; nevertheless (*I cannot do it, not but what a stronger man might*). **2** not such . . . or so . . . that . . . not (*not such a fool but what he can see it*). **not half** see HALF. **not least** with considerable importance, notably. **not much** see MUCH. **not quite 1** almost (*am not quite there*). **2** noticeably not (*not quite proper*). **not that** (foll. by clause) it is not to be inferred that (*if he said so — not that he ever did — he lied*). **not a thing** nothing at all. **not very** see VERY. [ME contr. of NOUGHT]

▶Use with verbs other than auxiliary verbs or *be* is now archaic (*fear not*), except with participles and infinities (*not knowing; I cannot say; we asked them not to come*).

no•ta be•ne /nótə bénay/ *v.tr.* (as *imper.*) observe what follows, take notice (usu. drawing attention to a following qualification of what has preceded). [L, = note well]

no•ta•bil•i•ty /nótəbílitee/ *n.* (*pl.* **•ties**) **1** the state of being notable (*names of no historical notability*). **2** a prominent person. [ME f. OF *notabilité* or LL *notabilitas* (as NOTABLE)]

no•ta•ble /nótəbəl/ *adj. & n.* ● *adj.* worthy of note; striking; remarkable; eminent. ● *n.* an eminent person. □□ **no•ta•ble•ness** *n.* **no•ta•bly** *adv.* [ME f. OF f. L *notabilis* (as NOTE)]

no•ta•rize /nótəriz/ *v.tr.* certify (a document) as a notary.

no•ta•ry /nótəree/ *n.* (*pl.* **•ries**) (in full **notary public**) a person authorized to perform certain legal formalities, esp. to draw up or certify contracts, deeds, etc. □□ **no•tar•i•al** /nótáireeəl/ *adj.* **no•tar•i•al•ly** /nótáireeəlee/ *adv.* [ME f. L *notarius* secretary (as NOTE)]

no•tate /nótayt/ *v.tr.* write in notation. [back-form. f. NOTATION]

no•ta•tion /nōtáyshən/ *n.* **1 a** the representation of numbers, quantities, pitch and duration, etc., of musical notes, etc., by symbols. **b** any set of such symbols. **2** a set of symbols used to represent chess moves, dance steps, etc. **3 a** a note or annotation. **b** a record. **4** = *scale of notation* (see SCALE³). □□ **no•ta•tion•al** *adj.* [F *notation* or L *notatio* (as NOTE)]

notch /noch/ *n. & v.* ● *n.* **1** a V-shaped indentation on an edge or surface. **2** a nick made on a stick, –etc., in order to keep count. **3** *colloq.* a step or degree (*move up a notch*). **4** a deep, narrow mountain pass or gap. ● *v.tr.* **1** make notches in. **2** (foll. by *up*) record or score with or as with notches. **3** secure or insert by notches. □□ **notched** *adj.* **notch•er** *n.* **notch•y** *adj.* (**notch•i•er, notch•i•est**). [AF *noche* perh. f. a verbal form *nocher* (unrecorded), of uncert. orig.]

note /nōt/ *n. & v.* ● *n.* **1** a brief record of facts, topics, thoughts, etc., as an aid to memory, for use in writing, public speaking, etc. (often in *pl.*: *make notes; spoke without notes*). **2** an observation, usu. unwritten, of experiences, etc. (*compare notes*). **3** a short or informal letter. **4** a formal diplomatic or parliamentary communication. **5** a short annotation or additional explanation in a book, etc.; a footnote. **6 a** *Brit.* = BANKNOTE (*a five-pound note*). **b** a written promise or notice of payment of various kinds. **7 a** notice, attention (*worthy of note*). **b** distinction, eminence (*a person of note*). **8 a** a written sign representing the pitch and duration of a musical sound. **b** a single tone of definite pitch made by a musical instrument, the human voice, etc. **c** a key of a piano, etc. **9 a** a bird's song or call. **b** a single tone in this. **10** a quality or tone of speaking, expressing mood or attitude, etc.; a hint or suggestion (*sound a note of warning*; *ended on a note of optimism*). **11** a characteristic; a distinguishing feature. • *v.tr.* **1** observe, notice; give or draw attention to. **2** record as a thing to be remembered or observed. **3** (in *passive*; often foll. by *for*) be famous or well known (for a quality, activity, etc.) (*were noted for their generosity*). □ **hit** (or **strike**) **the right note** speak or act in exactly the right manner. **of note** important, distinguished (*a person of note*). **take note** (often foll. by *of*) observe; pay attention (to). □□ **not·ed** *adj.* (in sense 3 of *v.*). **note·less** *adj.* [ME f. OF *note* (n.), *noter* (v.) f. L *nota* mark]

note·book /nốtbŏŏk/ *n.* a small book for making or taking notes.

note·book com·pu·ter *n.* a lightweight computer that closes to notebook size for portability.

note·case /nốtkays/ *n. Brit.* a billfold.

note·let /nốtlit/ *n. Brit.* a small folded sheet of paper, usu. with a decorative design, for an informal letter; note paper.

note·pa·per /nốtpaypər/ *n.* paper for writing notes.

note·wor·thy /nốtwərthee/ *adj.* worthy of attention; remarkable. □□ **note·wor·thi·ness** *n.*

noth·ing /núthing/ *n. & adv.* • *n.* **1** not anything (*nothing has been done*; *have nothing to do*). **2** no thing (often foll. by compl.: *I see nothing that I want*; *can find nothing useful*). **3 a** a person or thing of no importance or concern; a trivial event or remark (*was nothing to me*; *the little nothings of life*). **b** (*attrib.*) *colloq.* of no value; indeterminate (*a nothing sort of day*). **4** nonexistence; what does not exist. **5** (in calculations) no amount; naught (*a third of nothing is nothing*). • *adv.* **1** not at all, in no way (*is nothing like what we expected*). **2** *colloq.* not at all (*Is he ill? — Ill nothing, he's dead.*). □ **be nothing to 1** not concern. **2** not compare with. **be** (or **have**) **nothing to do with 1** have no connection with. **2** not be involved or associated with. **for nothing 1** at no cost; without payment. **2** to no purpose. **have nothing on 1** be naked. **2** have no engagements. **3** have no evidence against. **no nothing** *colloq.* (concluding a list of negatives) nothing at all. **nothing doing** *colloq.* **1 a** there is no prospect of success or agreement. **b** I refuse. **2** nothing is happening. **nothing (or nothing else) for it** (often foll. by *but to* + infin.) *Brit.* no alternative (*nothing for it but to pay up*). **nothing** (or **not much**) **in it** (or **to it**) **1** untrue or unimportant. **2** simple to do. **3** no (or little) advantage to be seen in one possibility over another. **nothing less than** at least (*nothing less than a disaster*). **think nothing of it** do not apologize or feel bound to show gratitude. [OE *nān thing* (as NO¹, THING)]

noth·ing·ness /núthingnis/ *n.* **1** nonexistence; the nonexistent. **2** worthlessness, triviality, insignificance.

no·tice /nốtis/ *n. & v.* • *n.* **1** attention; observation (*it escaped my notice*). **2** a displayed sheet, etc., bearing an announcement or other information. **3 a** an intimation or warning, esp. a formal one to allow preparations to be made (*give notice*; *at a moment's notice*). **b** (often foll. by *to* + infin.) a formal announcement or declaration of intention to end or leave employment at a specified time (*hand in one's notice*; *notice to quit*). **4** a short published review or comment about a new play, book, etc. • *v.tr.* **1** (often foll. by *that, how*, etc., + clause) perceive; observe; take notice of. **2** remark upon; speak of. □ **at short** (or **a moment's**) **notice** with little warning. **put a person on notice** alert or warn a person. **take notice** (or **no notice**) show signs (or no signs) of interest. **take notice of 1** observe; pay attention to. **2** act upon. **under notice** served with a formal notice. [ME f. OF f. L *notitia* being known f. *notus* past part. of *noscere* know]

no·tice·a·ble /nốtisəbəl/ *adj.* **1** easily seen or noticed; perceptible. **2** noteworthy. □□ **no·tice·a·bly** *adv.*

SPELLING TIP noticeable

This word means *able* to be *notice*d.

no·tice-board *n. Brit.* a board for displaying notices; bulletin board.

no·ti·fi·a·ble /nốtifīəbəl/ *adj.* (of a disease) that must be reported to the health authorities.

no·ti·fy /nốtifī/ *v.tr.* (**·fies**, **·fied**) **1** (often foll. by *of*, or *that* + clause) inform or give notice to (a person). **2** make known; announce or report (a thing). □□ **no·ti·fi·ca·tion** /–fikáyshən/ *n.* [ME f. OF *notifier* f. L *notificare* f. *notus* known: see NOTICE]

no·tion /nốshən/ *n.* **1 a** a concept or idea; a conception (*it was an absurd notion*). **b** an opinion (*has the notion that people are honest*). **c** a vague view or understanding (*have no notion what you mean*). **2** an inclination, impulse, or intention (*has no notion of conforming*). **3** (in *pl.*) small, useful articles, esp. thread, needles, buttons, etc.; sundries. [L *notio* idea f. *notus* past part. of *noscere* know]

no·tion·al /nốshənəl/ *adj.* **1 a** hypothetical, imaginary. **b** (of knowledge, etc.) speculative; not based on experiment, etc. **2** *Gram.* (of a verb) conveying its own meaning; not auxiliary. □□ **no·tion·al·ly** *adv.* [obs. F *notional* or med.L *notionalis* (as NOTION)]

no·to·chord /nốtəkawrd/ *n.* a cartilaginous skeletal rod supporting the body in all embryo and some adult chordate animals. [Gk *nōton* back + CHORD²]

no·to·ri·ous /nốtáwreeəs/ *adj.* well-known, esp. unfavorably (*a notorious criminal*; *notorious for its climate*). □□ **no·to·ri·e·ty** /–təríʃtee/ *n.* **no·to·ri·ous·ly** *adv.* [med.L *notorius* f. L *notus* (as NOTION)]

no·tor·nis /nətáwrnis/ *n.* a rare flightless New Zealand bird, *Porphyrio mantelli*, with a large bill and brightly colored plumage. Also called **takahe**. [Gk *notos* south + *ornis* bird]

no-trump·er *n. Bridge* a hand on which a no-trump bid can suitably be, or has been, made.

not·with·stand·ing /nốtwithstánding, –with–/ *prep., adv., & conj.* • *prep.* in spite of; without prevention by (*notwithstanding your objections*; *this fact notwithstanding*). • *adv.* nevertheless; all the same. • *conj.* (usu. foll. by *that* + clause) although. [ME, orig. absol. part. f. NOT + WITHSTAND + –ING²]

nou·gat /nốŏgət/ *n.* a usu. chewy candy made from sugar or honey, nuts, egg white, and often fruit pieces. [F f. Prov. *nogat* f. *noga* nut]

nought var. of NAUGHT.

noughts and cross·es *n. Brit.* tick-tack-toe.

noun /nown/ *n. Gram.* a word (other than a pronoun) or group of words used to name or identify any of a class of persons, places, things, or qualities (**common noun**), or a particular one of these (**proper noun**). □□ **noun·al** *adj.* [ME f. AF f. L *nomen* name]

GRAMMAR TIP noun

Types of Nouns. A **noun** is a word for a person, place, thing, or quality: *Susan, man, Mrs. Smith, England, honor, ocean, truck, Golden Gate Bridge*. There are two kinds of nouns: *common* and *proper*. **Proper nouns** name particular persons, places, or things: *Susan, Fido, England*, and *Golden Gate Bridge* are proper nouns. **Common nouns** do not refer to a particular person, place, or thing, and they are generally not capitalized: *cat, ocean*, and *truck* are common nouns. Common nouns are divided into three groups: *abstract, concrete*, and *collective*. **Abstract nouns** name qualities, actions, and ideas: *courage, helpfulness, loyalty*. Most of the time, *the* is used before abstract nouns, but not *a* (ordinarily, you would not say *a helpfulness*). **Concrete nouns** name things that you can see or touch: *door, pencil, car*. Either *a* or *the* is generally used before a concrete noun, depending on the meaning you want to convey. Also, concrete nouns can be plural—*doors, pencils, cars*—whereas you would not ordinarily say *courages* or *helpfulnesses*. **Collective nouns** are singular, but they refer to a group of persons or things: *team, class, herd, set*. Collective nouns are usually followed by singular verbs: "our team *was* defeated." But they can sometimes be followed by a plural verb, especially where they emphasize the individuals more than the group: "the people *were* discontented."

nour·ish /nŕish, núr–/ *v.tr.* **1 a** sustain with food. **b** enrich; promote the development of (the soil, etc.). **c** provide with intellectual or emotional sustenance or enrichment. **2** foster or cherish (a feeling, etc.). □□ **nour·ish·er** *n.* [ME f. OF *norir* f. L *nutrire*]

nour·ish·ing /nŕishing, núr–/ *adj.* (esp. of food) containing much nourishment; sustaining. □□ **nour·ish·ing·ly** *adv.*

nour·ish·ment /nŕishmənt, núr–/ *n.* sustenance, food.

nous *n.* **1** /nŏŏs/ *Philos.* the mind or intellect. **2** /nows/ *Brit. colloq.* common sense; gumption. [Gk]

SYNONYM TIP noticeable

CONSPICUOUS, OUTSTANDING, PROMINENT, REMARKABLE, STRIKING. A scratch on someone's face might be **noticeable**, while a scar that runs from cheekbone to chin would be **conspicuous**. When it comes to describing the things that attract our attention, *noticeable* means readily noticed or unlikely to escape observation (*a noticeable facial tic*; *a noticeable aversion to cocktail parties*), while *conspicuous* implies that the eye (or mind) cannot miss it (*her absence was conspicuous*). Use **prominent** when you want to describe something that literally or figuratively stands out from its background (*a prominent nose*). It can also apply to persons or things that stand out so clearly that they are generally known or recognized (*a prominent citizen*; *a prominent position on the committee*). Something or someone who is **outstanding** rises above or beyond others and is usually superior to them (*an outstanding student*). **Remarkable** applies to whatever is *noticeable* because it is extraordinary or exceptional (*remarkable blue eyes*). **Striking** is an even stronger word, used to describe something so out of the ordinary that it makes a deep and powerful impression on the observer's mind or vision (*a striking young woman over six feet tall*).

nou·veau riche /nōōvō reésh/ *n.* (*pl.* **nou·veaux riches** *pronunc.* same) a person who has recently acquired (usu. ostentatious) wealth. [F, = new rich]

nou·velle cui·sine /nōōvél kwizee'en/ *n.* a modern style of cookery avoiding heaviness and emphasizing presentation. [F, = new cookery]

nou·velle vague /nōōvél vaág/ *n.* a new trend, esp. in French filmmaking of the early 1960s. [F, fem. of *nouveau* new + *vague* wave]

Nov. *abbr.* November.

no·va /nóvə/ *n.* (*pl.* **no·vas** or **no·vae** /–vee/) a star showing a sudden large increase of brightness that then subsides. [L, fem. of *novus* new, because orig. thought to be a new star]

nov·el[1] /nóvəl/ *n.* **1** a fictitious prose story of book length. **2** (prec. by *the*) this type of literature.

WORD HISTORY novel[1]

Mid-16th century: from Italian *novella* (*storia*) 'new (story),' feminine of *novello* 'new,' from Latin *novellus*, from *novus* 'new.' The word is also found from late Middle English until the 18th century in the sense 'a novelty, a piece of news,' from Old French *novelle*, also from Latin *novellus* and the source of NOVEL[2].

nov·el[2] /nóvəl/ *adj.* of a new kind or nature; strange; previously unknown. [ME f. OF f. L *novellus* f. *novus* new]

nov·el·ette /nóvəlét/ *n.* **1 a** a short novel. **b** esp. *Brit. derog.* a light romantic novel. **2** *Mus.* a piano piece in free form with several themes.

nov·el·ist /nóvəlist/ *n.* a writer of novels. ▫▫ **nov·el·is·tic** *adj.*

nov·el·ize /nóvəlīz/ *v.tr.* make into a novel, as a screenplay. ▫▫ **nov·el·i·za·tion** *n.*

no·vel·la /nəvélə/ *n.* (*pl.* **no·vel·las** or **no·vel·le**) a short novel or narrative story; a tale. [It.: see NOVEL[1]]

nov·el·ty /nóvəltee/ *n.* (*pl.* **·ties**) **1 a** a newness; new character. **b** originality. **2** a new or unusual thing or occurrence. **3** a small toy or decoration, etc., of novel design. **4** (*attrib.*) having novelty (*novelty toys*). [ME f. OF *novelté* (as NOVEL[2])]

No·vem·ber /nōvémbər/ *n.* the eleventh month of the year. [ME f. OF *novembre* f. L *November* f. *novem* nine (orig. the ninth month of the Roman year)]

no·ve·na /nōvée'nə, nə–/ *n.* *RC Ch.* a devotion consisting of special prayers or services on nine successive days. [med.L f.L *novem* nine]

nov·ice /nóvis/ *n.* **1 a** a probationary member of a religious order, before the taking of vows. **b** a new convert. **2** a beginner; an inexperienced person. **3** an animal that has not won a major prize in a competition. [ME f. OF f. L *novicius* f. *novus* new]

SYNONYM TIP novice

APPRENTICE, BEGINNER, NEOPHYTE, PROBATIONER. All of these nouns are used to describe someone who has not yet acquired the skills and experience needed to qualify for a trade, a career, a profession, or a sphere of life. **Beginner** is the most general and informal term, used to describe someone who has begun to acquire the necessary skills but has not yet mastered them (*violin lessons for beginners*). An **apprentice** is a *beginner*, usually a young person, who is serving under a more experienced master or teacher to learn the skills of a trade or profession (*he served as an apprentice to one of the great Renaissance painters*); in a broad sense, *apprentice* refers to any *beginner* whose efforts are unpolished. **Novice** implies that the person lacks training and experience (*a novice when it came to writing fiction*), while **neophyte** is a less negative term, suggesting that the person is eagerly learning the ways, methods, or principles of something (*a neophyte who worshipped the world's most famous mountaineer*). A **probationer** is a *beginner* who is undergoing a trial period, during which he must prove an aptitude for a certain type of work or life (*she was a lowly probationer, with no privileges or status*).

no·vi·ti·ate /nōvísheeət, –ayt/ *n.* (also **no·vi·ci·ate**) **1** the period of being a novice. **2** a religious novice. **3** novices' quarters. [F *noviciat* or med.L *noviciatus* (as NOVICE)]

No·vo·caine /nóvəkayn/ *n.* (also **no·vo·caine**) *Trademark* a local anesthetic derived from benzoic acid. [L *novus* new + COCAINE]

now /now/ *adv., conj., & n.* ● *adv.* **1** at the present or mentioned time. **2** immediately (*I must go now*). **3** by this or that time (*it was now clear*). **4** under the present circumstances (*I cannot now agree*). **5** on this further occasion (*what do you want now?*). **6** in the immediate past (*just now*). **7** (esp. in a narrative or discourse) then, next (*the police now arrived; now to consider the next point*). **8** (without reference to time, giving various tones to a sentence) surely, I insist, I wonder, etc. (*now what do you mean by that?; oh come now!*). ● *conj.* (often foll. by *that* + clause) as a consequence of the fact (*now that I am older, now you mention it*). ● *n.* this time; the present (*should be there by now; has happened before now*). ▫ **as of now** from or at this time. **for now** until a later time (*goodbye for now*). **now and again**

(or **then**) from time to time; intermittently. **now or never** an expression of urgency. [OE *nū*]

now·a·days /nówədayz/ *adv. & n.* ● *adv.* at the present time or age; in these times. ● *n.* the present time.

no·way /nóway/ *adv.* (also **no·ways**) = NOWISE; see *no way* at NO.

now·el (also **now·ell**) *archaic* var. of NOEL.

no·where /nó hwair, –wair/ *adv. & pron.* ● *adv.* in or to no place. ● *pron.* no place. ▫ **be** (or **come in**) **nowhere** esp. *Brit.* be unplaced in a race or competition. **come from nowhere** be suddenly evident or successful. **get nowhere** make or cause to make no progress. **in the middle of nowhere** *colloq.* remote from urban life. **nowhere near** not nearly. [OE *nāhwēr* (as NO[1], WHERE)]

▶See note at ANYWAY.

no-win *adj.* of or designating a situation in which success is impossible.

no·wise /nówīz/ *adv.* in no manner; not at all.

nowt /nowt/ *n. Brit. colloq.* or *dial.* nothing. [var. of NOUGHT]

nox·ious /nókshəs/ *adj.* harmful, unwholesome. ▫▫ **nox·ious·ly** *adv.* **nox·ious·ness** *n.* [f. L *noxius* f. *noxa* harm]

noz·zle /nózəl/ *n.* a spout on a hose, etc., from which a jet issues. [NOSE + -LE[2]]

NP *abbr.* **1** notary public. **2** nurse-practitioner.

Np *symb. Chem.* the element neptunium.

n.p. *abbr.* **1** new paragraph. **2** no place of publication.

nr. *abbr.* near.

NRC *abbr.* Nuclear Regulatory Commission.

NS *abbr.* **1** new style. **2** new series. **3** Nova Scotia.

Ns *abbr.* NIELSBOHRIUM.

ns *abbr.* nanosecond.

NSA *abbr.* National Security Agency.

NSC *abbr.* National Security Council.

NSF *abbr.* **1** National Science Foundation. **2** not sufficient funds.

NSPCA *abbr. Brit.* National Society for the Prevention of Cruelty to Animals.

NSW *abbr.* New South Wales.

NT *abbr.* **1** New Testament. **2** Northern Territory (of Australia). **3** Northwest Territories (of Canada). **4** *Cards* no trump.

–n't /ənt/ *adv.* (in *comb.*) = NOT (usu. with *is, are, have, must*, and the auxiliary verbs *can, do, should, would*: *isn't; mustn't*) (see also CAN'T, DON'T, WON'T). [contr.]

nth see N[1].

NTP *abbr.* normal temperature and pressure.

nt. wt. *abbr.* net weight.

nu /nōō, nyōō/ *n.* the thirteenth letter of the Greek alphabet (N, ν). [Gk]

nu·ance /nōō-aáns, nyōō–/ *n. & v.* ● *n.* a subtle difference in or shade of meaning, feeling, color, etc. ● *v.tr.* give a nuance or nuances to. [F f. *nuer* to shade, ult. f. L *nubes* cloud]

nub /nub/ *n.* **1** the point or gist (of a matter or story). **2** a small lump, esp. of coal. **3** a stub; a small residue. ▫▫ **nub·by** *adj.* [app. var. of *knub*, f. MLG *knubbe, knobbe* KNOB]

nub·ble /núbəl/ *n.* a small knob or lump. ▫▫ **nub·bly** *adj.* [dimin. of NUB]

nu·bile /nóōbil, –bil, nyóō–/ *adj.* (of a woman) marriageable or sexually attractive. ▫▫ **nu·bil·i·ty** /–bilitee/ *n.* [L *nubilis* f. *nubere* become the wife of]

nu·chal /nóōkəl, nyōō–/ *adj.* of or relating to the nape of the neck. [*nucha* nape f. med.L *nucha* medulla oblongata f. Arab. *nuka* 'spinal marrow']

nuci- /nóōsee, nyōō–/ *comb. form* nut. [L *nux nucis* nut]

nu·cif·er·ous /nōōsifərəs, nyōō–/ *adj. Bot.* bearing nuts.

nu·civ·o·rous /nōōsívərəs, nyōō–/ *adj.* nut-eating.

nu·cle·ar /nóōkleeər, nyōō–/ *adj.* **1** of, relating to, or constituting a nucleus. **2** using nuclear energy (*nuclear reactor*). **3** having nuclear weapons. [NUCLEUS + -AR[1]]

PRONUNCIATION TIP nuclear

Though widespread, the pronunciation "NOO-kyoo-lur" is reviled by careful speakers, and is best avoided.

nu·cle·ar bomb *n.* a bomb involving the release of energy by nuclear fission or fusion or both.

nu·cle·ar dis·ar·ma·ment *n.* the gradual or total reduction by a nation or nations of stocks of nuclear weapons.

nu·cle·ar en·er·gy *n.* energy obtained by nuclear fission or fusion.

nu·cle·ar fam·i·ly *n.* a couple and their children, regarded as a basic social unit.

nu·cle·ar fis·sion *n.* a nuclear reaction in which a heavy nucleus splits spontaneously or on impact with another particle, with the release of energy.

nu·cle·ar force *n.* a strong attractive force between nucleons in the atomic nucleus that holds the nucleus together.

nu·cle·ar-free *adj.* free from nuclear weapons, power, etc.

nu·cle·ar fu·el *n.* a substance that will sustain a fission chain reaction so that it can be used as a source of nuclear energy.

nu·cle·ar fu·sion *n.* a nuclear reaction in which atomic nuclei of low atomic number fuse to form a heavier nucleus with the release of energy.

nu·cle·ar mag·net·ic res·o·nance *n.* the absorption of electromagnetic radiation by a nucleus having a magnetic moment when in an external magnetic field, used mainly as an analytical technique and in body imaging for diagnosis. ¶ Abbr.: **NMR, nmr.**

nu·cle·ar med·i·cine *n. Med.* a specialty that uses radioactive materials for diagnosis and treatment.

nu·cle·ar phys·ics *n.* the physics of atomic nuclei and their interactions, esp. in the generation of nuclear energy.

nu·cle·ar pow·er *n.* **1** electric or motive power generated by a nuclear reactor. **2** a country that has nuclear weapons.

nu·cle·ar re·ac·tor *n.* a device in which a nuclear fission chain reaction is sustained and controlled in order to produce energy.

nu·cle·ar war·fare *n.* warfare in which nuclear weapons are used.

nu·cle·ar waste *n.* any radioactive waste material from the reprocessing of spent nuclear fuel.

nu·cle·ar win·ter *n.* obstruction of sunlight as a potential result of nuclear warfare, causing extreme cold.

nu·cle·ase /nóōkleeays, –ayz, nyóō–/ *n.* an enzyme that catalyzes the breakdown of nucleic acids.

nu·cle·ate /nóōkleeayt, nyóō–/ *adj. & v.* ● *adj.* having a nucleus. ● *v. intr. & tr.* form or form into a nucleus. □□ **nu·cle·a·tion** /–áyshən/ *n.* [LL *nucleare nucleat*– form a kernel (as NUCLEUS)]

nu·cle·i *pl.* of NUCLEUS.

nu·cle·ic acid /nóōkleéik, –kláyik, nyóō–/ *n.* either of two complex organic molecules (DNA and RNA), consisting of many nucleotides linked in a long chain, and present in all living cells.

nucleo- /nóōkleeō, nyóō–/ *comb. form* nucleus; nucleic acid (*nucleoprotein*).

nu·cle·o·lus /nóōkleéələs, nyóō–/ *n.* (*pl.* **nu·cle·o·li** /–lī/) a small dense spherical structure within a nondividing nucleus. □□ **nu·cle·o·lar** *adj.* [LL, dimin. of L *nucleus*: see NUCLEUS]

nu·cle·on /nóōkleeon, nyóō–/ *n. Physics* a proton or neutron.

nu·cle·on·ics /nóōkleeóniks, nyóō–/ *n.pl.* (treated as *sing.*) the branch of science and technology concerned with atomic nuclei and nucleons, esp. the exploitation of nuclear power. □□ **nu·cle·on·ic** *adj.* [NUCLEAR, after *electronics*]

nu·cle·o·pro·tein /nóōkleeōpróteen, nyóō–/ *n.* a complex of nucleic acid and protein.

nu·cle·o·side /nóōkleeəsīd, nyóō–/ *n. Biochem.* an organic compound consisting of a purine or pyrimidine base linked to a sugar, e.g., adenosine.

nu·cle·o·tide /nóōkleeōtīd, nyóō–/ *n. Biochem.* an organic compound consisting of a nucleoside linked to a phosphate group.

nu·cle·us /nóōkleeəs/ *n.* (*pl.* **nu·cle·i** /–lee-ī/) **1 a** the central part or thing around which others are collected. **b** the kernel of an aggregate or mass. **2** an initial part meant to receive additions. **3** *Astron.* the solid part of a comet's head. **4** *Physics* the positively charged central core of an atom that contains most of its mass. **5** *Biol.* a large dense organelle of eukaryotic cells, containing the genetic material. **6** a discrete mass of gray matter in the central nervous system. [L, = kernel, inner part, dimin. of *nux nucis* nut]

nu·clide /nóōklīd, nyóō–/ *n. Physics* a certain type of atom characterized by the number of protons and neutrons in its nucleus. □□ **nu·clid·ic** /nóōklídik, nyóō–/ *adj.* [NUCLEUS + Gk *eidos* form]

nude /nóōd, nyóōd/ *adj. & n.* ● *adj.* naked, bare, unclothed. ● *n.* **1** a painting, sculpture, photograph, etc., of a nude human figure; such a figure. **2** a nude person. **3** (prec. by *the*) **a** an unclothed state. **b** the representation of an undraped human figure as a genre in art. [L *nudus*]

nudge /nuj/ *v. & n.* ● *v.tr.* **1** prod gently with the elbow to attract attention. **2** push gently or gradually. **3** give a gentle reminder or encouragement to (a person). ● *n.* the act or an instance of nudging; a gentle push. □□ **nudg·er** *n.* [17th c.: orig. unkn.: cf. Norw. dial. *nugga, nyggja* to push, rub]

nud·ist /nóōdist, nyóō–/ *n.* a person who advocates or practices going unclothed. □□ **nud·ism** *n.*

nu·di·ty /nóōditee, nyóō–/ *n.* the state of being nude; nakedness.

nu·ga·to·ry /nóōgətáwree, nyóō–/ *adj.* **1** futile; trifling; worthless. **2** inoperative; not valid. [L *nugatorius* f. *nugari* to trifle f. *nugae* jests]

nug·get /núgit/ *n.* **1 a** a lump of gold, platinum, etc., as found in the earth. **b** a lump of anything compared to this. **2** something valuable for its size (often abstract in sense: *a little nugget of information*). [app. f. dial. *nug* lump, etc.]

nui·sance /nóōsəns, nyóō–/ *n.* **1** a person, thing, or circumstance causing trouble or annoyance. **2** anything harmful or offensive to the community or a member of it and for which a legal remedy exists. [ME f. OF, = hurt, f. *nuire nuis*– f. L *nocēre* to hurt]

nui·sance value *n.* esp. *Brit.* an advantage resulting from the capacity to harass or frustrate.

nuke /nóōk, nyóōk/ *n. & v. colloq.* ● *n.* a nuclear weapon. ● *v.tr.* **1** *colloq.* bomb or destroy with nuclear weapons. **2** *colloq.* to cook (something) in a microwave oven. [abbr.]

null /nul/ *adj. & n.* ● *adj.* **1** (esp. **null and void**) invalid; not binding.

2 nonexistent; amounting to nothing. **3** having or associated with the value zero. **4** *Computing* **a** empty; having no elements (*null list*). **b** all the elements of which are zeros (*null matrix*). **5** without character or expression. ● *n. Brit.* a dummy letter in a code. [F *nul nulle* or L *nullus* none f. *ne* not + *ullus* any]

nul·lah /núlə/ *n. Anglo-Ind.* a dry riverbed or ravine. [Hindi *nālā*]

nul·la-nul·la /núlənulə/ *n.* (also **nul·la**) *Austral.* a hardwood club used by Aborigines. [Aboriginal]

null char·ac·ter *n. Computing* a character denoting nothing, usu. represented by a zero.

null hy·poth·e·sis *n.* a hypothesis suggesting that the difference between statistical samples does not imply a difference between populations.

nul·li·fid·i·an /núlifídeeən/ *n. & adj.* (a person) having no religious faith or belief. [med.L *nullifidius* f. L *nullus* none + *fides* faith]

nul·li·fy /núlifī/ *v.tr.* (**-fies, -fied**) make null; neutralize; invalidate; cancel. □□ **nul·li·fi·ca·tion** /–fikáyshən/ *n.* **nul·li·fi·er** *n.*

nul·lip·a·ra /nulípərə/ *n.* a woman who has never borne a child. □□ **nul·lip·a·rous** *adj.* [mod.L f. L *nullus* none + –*para* fem. of –*parus* f. *parere* bear children]

nul·li·pore /núlipawr/ *n.* any of various seaweeds able to secrete lime. [L *nullus* none + PORE¹]

nul·li·ty /núlitee/ *n.* (*pl.* **-ties**) **1** *Law* being null; invalidity, esp. of marriage. **b** an act, document, etc., that is null. **2 a** nothingness. **b** a mere nothing; a nonentity. [F *nullité* or med.L *nullitas* f. L *nullus* none]

null link *n. Computing* a reference incorporated into the last item in a list to indicate there are no further items in the list.

Num. *abbr.* Numbers (Old Testament).

num. *abbr.* **1** number. **2** numerical.

numb /num/ *adj. & v.* ● *adj.* (often foll. by *with*) deprived of feeling or the power of motion (*numb with cold*). ● *v.tr.* **1** make numb. **2** stupefy; paralyze. □□ **numb·ly** *adv.* **numb·ness** *n.* [ME *nome* (*n*) past part. of *nim* take: for –*b* cf. THUMB]

num·bat /númbat/ *n.* a small Australian marsupial, *Myrmecobius fasciatus*, with a bushy tail and black and white striped back. [Aboriginal]

num·ber /númbə r/ *n. & v.* ● *n.* **1 a** an arithmetical value representing a particular quantity and used in counting and making calculations. **b** a word, symbol, or figure representing this; a numeral. **c** an arithmetical value showing position in a series, esp. for identification, reference, etc. (*registration number*). **2** (often foll. by *of*) the total count or aggregate (*the number of accidents has decreased; twenty in number*). **3 a** the study of the behavior of numbers; numerical reckoning (*the laws of number*). **b** (in *pl.*) arithmetic (*not good at numbers*). **4** (in *sing.* or *pl.*) a quantity or amount; a total; a count (*a large number of people; only in small numbers*). **b** (in *pl.*) numerical preponderance (*force of numbers; there is safety in numbers*). **5 a** a person or thing having a place in a series, esp. a single issue of a magazine, an item in a program, etc. **b** a song, dance, musical item, etc. **6** company, collection, group (*among our number*). **7** *Gram.* **a** the classification of words by their singular or plural forms. **b** a particular such form. **8** *colloq.* a person or thing regarded familiarly or affectionately (usu. qualified in some way: *an attractive little number*). **9** (**Numbers**) the Old Testament book containing a census. ● *v.tr.* **1** include (*I number you among my friends*). **2** assign a number or numbers to. **3** have or amount to (a specified number). **4 a** count. **b** comprise (*numbering forty thousand men*). □ **a number of** some, several. **by numbers** following simple instructions (as if) identified by numbers. **do a number on** sl. injure, cheat, criticize, or humiliate. **one's days are numbered** one does not have long to live. **have a person's number** *colloq.* understand a person's real motives, character, etc. **have a person's number on it** (of a bomb, bullet, etc.) be destined to hit a specified person. **one's number is up** *colloq.* one is finished or doomed to die.. **without number** innumerable. [me F. of *nombre* (N.), *nombrer* (v.) f. L *numerus, numerare*]

▶1. The use of *number* with a plural verb is now standard: *a number of problems remain; a number of people are coming to the party.* 2. See note at AMOUNT.

num·ber crunch·er *n. Computing & Math. sl.* a machine or person capable of complex calculations, etc.

num·ber crunch·ing *n. Computing & Math. sl.* the act or process of making complex calculations.

num·ber·less /númbərlis/ *adj.* innumerable.

num·ber one *n. colloq.* oneself (*always takes care of number one*). ● *adj.* most important (*the number-one priority*).

num·ber plate *n. Brit.* = LICENSE PLATE.

num·bers game *n.* an illegal lottery based on the occurrence of unpredictable numbers in the results of races, etc.

num·ber two *n.* a second in command.

num·bles /númbəlz/ *n.pl.* (also **nom·bles**) the edible entrails of a deer, etc. [ME f. OF *numbles*, *nombles* loin, etc., f. L *lumbulus* dimin. of *lumbus* loin: cf. UMBLES]

numb·skull var. of NUMSKULL.

nu·men /nóōmən, nyóō–/ *n.* (*pl.* **nu·mi·na** /–minə/) a presiding deity or spirit. [L *numen* –*minis*]

nu·mer·a·ble /nóōmərəbəl, nyóō–/ *adj.* that can be counted. □□ **nu·mer·a·bly** *adv.* [L *numerabilis* f. *numerare* NUMBER *v.*]

nu·mer·al /nóōmərəl, nyóō–/ *n. & adj.* ● *n.* a word, figure, or group of figures denoting a number. ● *adj.* of or denoting a number. [LL *numeralis* f. L (as NUMBER)]

nu·mer·ate *v. & adj.* ● *v.tr.* /nóōmərayt, nyóō–/ **1** = ENUMERATE. **2.** represent numbers by numerals. ● *adj.* /nóōmərət, nyóō–/ acquainted with the basic principles of mathematics. □□ **nu·mer·a·cy** /–əsee/ *n.* [L *numerus* number + –ATE[2] after *literate*]

nu·mer·a·tion /nóōməráyshən, nyóō–/ *n.* **1 a** a method or process of numbering or computing. **b** calculation. **2** the expression in words of a number written in figures. [ME f. L *numeratio* payment, in LL numbering (as NUMBER)]

nu·mer·a·tor /nóōmərayter, nyóō–/ *n.* **1** the number above the line in a common fraction showing how many of the parts indicated by the denominator are taken (e.g., 2 in $^2/_3$). **2** a person or device that numbers. [F *numérateur* or LL *numerator* (as NUMBER)]

nu·mer·i·cal /nóōmérikəl, nyóō–/ *adj.* (also **nu·mer·ic**) of or relating to a number or numbers (*numerical superiority*). □□ **nu·mer·i·cal·ly** *adv.* [med.L *numericus* (as NUMBER)]

nu·mer·i·cal a·nal·y·sis *n.* the branch of mathematics that deals with the development and use of numerical methods for solving problems.

nu·mer·ol·o·gy /nóōməróləjee, nyóō–/ *n.* (*pl.* **·gies**) the study of the supposed occult significance of numbers. □□ **nu·mer·o·log·i·cal** /–rəlójikəl/ *adj.* **nu·mer·ol·o·gist** *n.* [L *numerus* number + –LOGY]

nu·mer·ous /nóōmərəs, nyóō–/ *adj.* **1** (with *pl.*) great in number (*received numerous gifts*). **2** consisting of many (*the rose family is a numerous one*). □□ **nu·mer·ous·ly** *adv.* **nu·mer·ous·ness** *n.* [L *numerosus* (as NUMBER)]

nu·mi·na *pl.* of NUMEN.

nu·mi·nous /nóōminəs, nyóō–/ *adj.* **1** indicating the presence of a divinity. **2** spiritual. **3** awe-inspiring. [L *numen*: see NUMEN]

nu·mis·mat·ic /nóōmizmátik, nyóō–/ *adj.* of or relating to coins or medals. □□ **nu·mis·mat·i·cal·ly** *adv.* [F *numismatique* f. L *numisma* f. Gk *nomisma* –*atos* current coin f. *nomizō* use currently]

nu·mis·mat·ics /nóōmizmátiks, nyóō–/ *n.pl.* (usu. treated as *sing.*) the study of coins or medals. □□ **nu·mis·ma·tist** /nóōmízmətist, nyóō–/ *n.*

nu·mis·ma·tol·o·gy /nóōmízmətóləjee, nyóō–/ *n.* = NUMISMATICS.

num·mu·lite /númyəlit/ *n.* a disk-shaped fossil shell of a foraminiferous protozoan found in Tertiary strata. [L *nummulus* dimin. of *nummus* coin]

num·skull /númskul/ *n.* (also **numb·skull**) a stupid or foolish person. [NUMB + SKULL]

nun /nun/ *n.* a member of a community of women living apart from society under religious vows. □□ **nun·hood** *n.* **nun·like** *adj.* **nun·nish** *adj.* [ME f. OE *nunne* and OF *nonne* f. eccl.L *nonna* fem. of *nonnus* monk, orig. a title given to an elderly person]

nun·a·tak /núnətak/ *n.* an isolated peak of rock projecting above a surface of glaciated land, e.g., in Greenland. [Inuit]

nun buoy /nún boy, bōóee/ *n.* a conical buoy. [obs. *nun* child's top + BUOY]

Nunc Di·mit·tis /núngk dimítis/ *n.* the song of Simeon (Luke 2:29–32) used as a canticle. [f. the opening words *nunc dimittis* now let (your servant) depart]

nun·ci·a·ture /núnsheeəchoor, –chər, nóōn–/ *n. RC Ch.* the office or tenure of a nuncio. [It. *nunziatura* (as NUNCIO)]

nun·ci·o /núnsheeō/ *n.* (*pl.* **·os**) *RC Ch.* a papal ambassador. [It. f. L *nuntius* messenger]

nun·cu·pate /núngkyəpayt/ *v.tr.* declare (a will or testament) orally, not in writing. □□ **nun·cu·pa·tion** /–páyshən/ *n.* **nun·cu·pa·tive** /–páytiv/ *adj.* [L *nuncupare nuncupat*- name]

nun·ner·y /núnəree/ *n.* (*pl.* **·ies**) a religious house of nuns; a convent.

nup·tial /núpshəl/ *adj. & n.* ● *adj.* of or relating to marriage or weddings. ● *n.* (usu. in *pl.*) a wedding. [F *nuptial* or L *nuptialis* f. *nuptiae* wedding f. *nubere nupt*- wed]

nurd var. of NERD.

nurse /nərs/ *n. & v.* ● *n.* **1** a person trained to care for the sick or infirm. **2** (formerly) a person employed or trained to take charge of young children. **3** *archaic* = WET NURSE. **4** *Forestry* a tree planted as a shelter to others. **5** *Zool.* a nonreproductive bee, ant, etc., caring for a young brood; a worker. ● *v.* **1 a** *intr.* work as a nurse. **b** *tr.* attend to (a sick person). **c** *tr.* give medical attention to (an illness or injury). **2** *tr. & intr.* feed or be fed at the breast. **3** *tr.* (in *passive*; foll. by *in*) be brought up in (a specified condition) (*nursed in poverty*). **4** *tr.* esp. *Brit.* hold or treat carefully or caressingly (*sat nursing my feet*). **5** *tr.* **a** foster; promote the development of (the arts,

plants, etc.). **b** harbor or nurture (a grievance, hatred, etc.). **c** esp. *Brit.* pay special attention to (*nursed the voters*). **6** *tr.* consume slowly or over a long time.

nurse·ling var. of NURSLING.

nurse·maid /nərsmayd/ *n. & v.* ● *n.* **1** a woman in charge of a child or children. **2** a person who watches over or guides another carefully. ● *v.tr.* act as nursemaid to.

nurse-mid·wife *n.* a registered nurse who assists women during childbirth.

nurse-prac·ti·tion·er *n.* a registered nurse who has received advanced training in diagnosing and treating illness.

nurs·er·y /nərsəree/ *n.* (*pl.* **·ies**) **1 a** a room or place equipped for young children. **b** = DAY NURSERY. **2** a place where plants, trees, etc., are reared for sale or transplantation. **3** any sphere or place in or by which qualities or types of people are fostered or bred.

nurs·er·y·man /nərsəreemən/ *n.* (*pl.* **·men**) an owner of or worker in a plant nursery.

nurs·er·y rhyme *n.* a simple traditional song or story in rhyme for children.

nurs·er·y school *n.* a school for children from the age of about three to five.

nurs·ing /nərsing/ *n.* **1** the practice or profession of caring for the sick as a nurse. **2** (*attrib.*) concerned with or suitable for nursing the sick or elderly, etc. (*nursing home*).

nurs·ing of·fi·cer *n. Brit.* a senior nurse.

nurs·ling /nərsling/ *n.* (also **nurse·ling**) an infant that is being suckled.

nur·ture /nərchər/ *n. & v.* ● *n.* **1** the process of bringing up or training (esp. children); fostering care. **2** nourishment. **3** sociological factors as an influence on or determinant of personality (opp. NATURE). ● *v.tr.* **1** bring up; rear. **2** nourish. □□ **nur·tur·er** *n.* [ME f. OF *nour(e) ture* (as NOURISH)]

nut /nut/ *n. & v.* ● *n.* **1 a** a fruit consisting of a hard or tough shell around an edible kernel. **b** this kernel. **2** a pod containing hard seeds. **3** a small usu. square or hexagonal flat piece of metal or other material with a threaded hole through it for screwing on the end of a bolt to secure it. **4** *sl.* a person's head. **5** *sl.* **a** a crazy or eccentric person. **b** an obsessive enthusiast or devotee (*a health-food nut*). **6** esp. *Brit.* small lump of coal, butter, etc. **7 a** a device fitted to the bow of a violin for adjusting its tension. **b** the fixed ridge on the neck of a stringed instrument over which the strings pass. **8** (in *pl.*) *coarse sl.* the testicles. ● *v.intr.* (**nut·ted, nut·ting**) seek or gather nuts (*go nutting*). □ **do one's nut** *Brit. sl.* be extremely angry or agitated. **for nuts** *Brit. colloq.* even tolerably well (*cannot sing for nuts*). **off one's nut** *sl.* crazy. □□ **nut·like** *adj.* [OE *hnutu* f. Gmc]

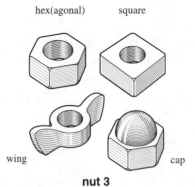

hex(agonal)   square

wing   cap

nut 3

nu·tant /nóōt'nt, nyóō–/ *adj. Bot.* nodding, drooping. [L *nutare* nod]

nu·ta·tion /nóōtáyshən, nyóō–/ *n.* **1** the act or an instance of nodding. **2** *Astron.* a periodic oscillation of the earth's poles. **3** oscillation of a spinning top. **4** the spiral movement of a plant organ during growth. [L *nutatio* (as NUTANT)]

nut case /nútkays/ *n.* (also **nut·case**) *sl.* a crazy or foolish person.

nut·crack·er /nútkrakər/ *n.* a device for cracking nuts.

nut cut·let *n. Brit.* a cutlet-shaped portion of meat substitute, made from nuts, etc.

nut·gall /nútgawl/ *n.* a gall found esp. on oak, often used as a dye-stuff.

nut·hatch /nút-hach/ *n.* any small bird of the family Sittidae, climbing up and down tree trunks and feeding on nuts, insects, etc. [NUT + *hatch* rel. to HATCH[2]]

nut·house /núthows/ *n. sl.* a mental home or hospital.

nut·let /nútlit/ *n.* a small nut or nutlike fruit.

nut·meg /nútmeg/ *n.* **1** an evergreen E. Indian tree, *Myristica fragrans*, yielding a hard aromatic spheroidal seed. **2** the seed of this used as a spice and in medicine. [ME: partial transl. of OF *nois mug* (*u*)*ede* ult. f. L *nux* nut + LL *muscus* MUSK]

nut oil *n.* an oil obtained from hazelnuts and walnuts and used in paints and varnishes.

nu·tri·a /nóõtreeə, nyóõ–/ *n.* **1** an aquatic beaverlike rodent, *Myocastor Coypus*, native to S. America and bred in captivity for its fur. **2** its skin or fur. [Sp., = otter]

nuthatch

nu·tri·ent /nóõtreeənt, nyóõ–/ *n. & adj.* ● *n.* any substance that provides essential nourishment for the maintenance of life. ● *adj.* serving as or providing nourishment. [L *nutrire* nourish]

nu·tri·ment /nóõtrimənt, nyóõ–/ *n.* **1** nourishing food. **2** an intellectual or artistic, etc., nourishment or stimulus. □□ **nu·tri·men·tal** /–mént'l/ *adj.* [L *nutrimentum* (as NUTRIENT)]

nu·tri·tion /nóõtríshən, nyóõ–/ *n.* **1 a** the process of providing or receiving nourishing substances. **b** food, nourishment. **2** the study of nutrients and nutrition. □□ **nu·tri·tion·al** *adj.* [F *nutrition* or LL *nutritio* (as NUTRIENT)]

nu·tri·tion·ist /nóõtríshənist, nyóõ–/ *n.* a person who studies or is an expert on the processes of human nourishment.

nu·tri·tious /nóõtríshəs, nyóõ–/ *adj.* efficient as food; nourishing. □□ **nu·tri·tious·ly** *adv.* **nu·tri·tious·ness** *n.* [L *nutritius* (as NURSE)]

nu·tri·tive /nóõtritiv, nyóõ–/ *adj. & n.* ● *adj.* **1** of or concerned in nutrition. **2** serving as nutritious food. ● *n.* a nutritious article of food. [ME f. F *nutritif* *–ive* f. med.L *nutritivus* (as NUTRIENT)]

nuts /nuts/ *adj. & int.* ● *adj. sl.* crazy, mad, eccentric. ● *int. sl.* an expression of contempt or derision (*nuts to you*). □ **be nuts about** (or *Brit.* on) *colloq.* be enthusiastic about or very fond of.

nuts and bolts *n.pl. colloq.* the practical details.

nut·shell /nútshel/ *n.* the hard exterior covering of a nut. □ **in a nutshell** in a few words.

nut·ter /nútər/ *n. Brit. sl.* a crazy or eccentric person.

nut tree *n.* any tree bearing nuts.

nut·ty /nútee/ *adj.* (**nut·ti·er, nut·ti·est**) **1 a** full of nuts. **b** tasting like nuts. **2** *sl.* = NUTS *adj.* □□ **nut·ti·ness** *n.*

nux vom·i·ca /nuks vómikə/ *n.* **1** an E. Indian tree, *Strychnos nux-vomica*, yielding a poisonous fruit. **2** the seeds of this tree, containing strychnine. [med.L f. L *nux* nut + *vomicus* f. *vomere* vomit]

nuz·zle /núzəl/ *v.* **1** *tr.* prod or rub gently with the nose. **2** *intr.* (foll. by *into, against, up to*) press the nose gently. **3** *tr.* (also *refl.*) nestle; lie snug. [ME f. NOSE + –LE[4]]

NV *abbr.* Nevada (in official postal use).

NW *abbr.* **1** northwest. **2** northwestern.

NWT *abbr.* Northwest Territories (in Canada).

NY *abbr.* New York (also in official postal use).

nya·la /nyaálə/ *n.* (also **in·ya·la** /in–/) (*pl.* **nya·las** or same) a large antelope, *Tragelaphus angasi*, native to S. Africa, with curved horns having a single complete turn. [Zulu]

NYC *abbr.* New York City.

nyc·ta·lo·pi·a /níktəlópeeə/ *n.* the inability to see in dim light or at night. Also called **night blindness**. [LL f. Gk *nuktalōps* f. *nux nuktos* night + *alaos* blind + *ōps* eye]

nyc·ti·trop·ic /níktitrópik, –tróp–/ *adj. Bot.* (of plant movements) occurring at night and caused by changes in light and temperature. [Gk *nukti–* comb. form of *nux nuktos* night + *tropos* turn]

nyl·ghau /nílgaw/ *n.* = NILGAI. [Hind. f. Pers. *nīlgāw* f. *nīl* blue + *gāw* cow]

ny·lon /nílon/ *n.* **1** any of various synthetic polyamide fibers having a proteinlike structure, with tough, lightweight, elastic properties, used in industry and for textiles, etc. **2** a nylon fabric. **3** (in *pl.*) stockings made of nylon. [invented word, after *cotton, rayon*]

nymph /nimf/ *n.* **1** any of various mythological semidivine spirits regarded as maidens and associated with aspects of nature, esp. rivers and woods. **2** *poet.* a beautiful young woman. **3 a** an immature form of some insects. **b** a young dragonfly or damselfly. □□ **nymph·al** *adj.* **nym·phe·an** /–féeən/ *adj.* **nymph·like** *adj.* [ME f. OF *nimphe* f. L *nympha* f. Gk *numphē*]

nym·phae /nímfee/ *n.pl. Anat.* the labia minora. [L, pl. of *nympha*: see NYMPH]

nym·phet /nímfét/ *n.* **1** a young nymph. **2** *colloq.* a sexually precocious or provocative young woman.

nym·pho /nímfō/ *n.* (*pl.* **·phos**) *colloq.* a nymphomaniac. [abbr.]

nym·pho·lep·sy /nímfəlepsee/ *n.* ecstasy or frenzy caused by desire of the unattainable. [NYMPHOLEPT after *epilepsy*]

nym·pho·lept /nímfəlept/ *n.* a person inspired by violent enthusiasm, esp. for an ideal. □□ **nym·pho·lep·tic** /–léptik/ *adj.* [Gk *numpholēptos* caught by nymphs (as NYMPH, *lambanō* take)]

nym·pho·ma·ni·a /nímfəmáyneeə/ *n.* excessive sexual desire in women. □□ **nym·pho·ma·ni·ac** *n. & adj.* [mod.L (as NYMPH, –MANIA)]

NYSE *abbr.* New York Stock Exchange.

nys·tag·mus /nistágməs/ *n.* rapid involuntary movements of the eyes. □□ **nys·tag·mic** *adj.* [Gk *nustagmos* nodding f. *nustazō* nod]

NZ *abbr.* New Zealand.

O

O¹ /ō/ *n.* (also **o**) (*pl.* **Os** or **O's**) **1** the fifteenth letter of the alphabet. **2** (**0**) naught; zero (in a sequence of numerals, esp. when spoken). **3** a human blood type of the ABO system.

O² *abbr.* (also **O.**) Old.

O³ *symb. Chem.* the element oxygen.

O⁴ /ō/ *int.* **1** var. of OH¹. **2** prefixed to a name in the vocative (*O God*). [ME, natural excl.]

O' /ō, ə/ *prefix* of Irish patronymic names (*O'Connor*). [Ir. *ó*, *ua*, descendant]

o' /ə/ *prep.* of, on (esp. in phrases: o'clock; *will-o'-the-wisp*). [abbr.]

-o /ō/ *suffix* forming usu. *sl.* or *colloq.* variants or derivatives (*weirdo*; *wino*). [perh. OH¹ as joc. suffix]

-o- /ō/ *suffix* the terminal vowel of combining forms (*spectro-*; *chemico-*; *Franco-*). [orig. Gk]

▶This suffix is often elided before a vowel, as in *neuralgia*.

oaf /ōf/ *n.* (*pl.* **oafs**) **1** an awkward lout. **2** a stupid person. □□ **oaf‑ish** *adj.* **oaf‑ish‑ly** *adv.* **oaf‑ish‑ness** *n.* [orig. = elf's child, var. of obs. *auf* f. ON *álfr* elf]

oak /ōk/ *n.* **1** any tree or shrub of the genus *Quercus* usu. having lobed leaves and bearing acorns. **2** the durable wood of this tree, used esp. for furniture and in building. **3** (*attrib.*) made of oak (*oak table*). **4** *Brit.* a heavy outer door of a set of university college rooms. **5** (**the Oaks**) (treated as *sing.*) an annual race at Epsom Downs (in Surrey, England) for three-year-old fillies (from the name of a nearby estate). □□ **oak‑en** *adj.* [OE *āc* f. Gmc]

oak ap‑ple *n.* (also **oak gall**) an applelike gall containing larvae of certain wasps, found on oak trees.

oa‑kum /ōkəm/ *n.* a loose fiber obtained by picking old rope to pieces and used esp. in caulking. [OE *ǣcumbe*, *ācumbe*, lit. "off-combings"]

oar /awr/ *n.* **1** a pole with a blade used for rowing or steering a boat by leverage against the water. **2** a rower. □ **put** (or **stick**) **one's oar in** interfere; meddle. **rest on one's oars** relax one's efforts. □□ **oared** *adj.* (also in *comb.*). **oar‑less** *adj.* [OE *ār* f. Gmc, perh. rel. to Gk *eretmos* oar]

oar‑fish /áwrfish/ *n.* a ribbonfish, esp. *Regalecus glesne*.

oar‑lock /áwrlok/ *n.* a device on a boat's gunwale, esp. a pair of tholepins, serving as a fulcrum for an oar and keeping it in place. [OE *ārloc*]

oars‑man /áwrzmən/ *n.* (*pl.* **‑men**; *fem.* **oars‑wom‑an**, *pl.* **‑wom‑en**) a rower. □□ **oars‑man‑ship** *n.*

OAS *abbr.* Organization of American States.

o‑a‑sis /ō-áysis/ *n.* (*pl.* **o‑a‑ses** /‑seez/) **1** a fertile spot in a desert, where water is found. **2** an area or period of calm in the midst of turbulence. [LL f. Gk, app. of Egypt. orig.]

oast /ōst/ *n.* a kiln for drying hops. [OE *āst* f. Gmc]

oast-house *n.* esp. *Brit.* a building containing a kiln for drying hops.

oat /ōt/ *n.* **1 a** a cereal plant, *Avena sativa*, cultivated in cool climates. **b** (in *pl.*) the grain yielded by this, used as food. **2** any other cereal of the genus *Avena*, esp. the wild oat, *A. fatua*. **3** *poet.* the oat stem used as a musical pipe by shepherds, etc., usu. in pastoral or bucolic poetry. **4** (in *pl.*) esp. *Brit. sl.* sexual gratification. □ **feel one's oats** *colloq.* **1** be lively. **2** feel self-important. **off one's oats** *colloq.* not hungry. **sow one's oats** (or **wild oats**) indulge in youthful excess or promiscuity. □□ **oat‑en** *adj.* [OE *āte*, pl. *ātan*, of unkn. orig.]

oat‑cake /ōtkayk/ *n.* a thin unleavened cake made of oatmeal, common in Scotland and the north of England.

oat grass *n.* any of various grasses, esp. of the genus *Arrhenatherum*.

oath /ōth/ *n.* (*pl.* **oaths** /ōthz, ōths/) **1** a solemn declaration or undertaking (often naming God) as to the truth of something or as a commitment to future action. **2** a statement or promise contained in an oath (*oath of allegiance*). **3** a profane or blasphemous utterance; a curse. □ **under** (or **on**) **oath** having sworn a solemn oath. **take** (or **swear**) **an oath** make such a declaration or undertaking. [OE *āth* f. Gmc]

oat‑meal /ōtmeel/ *n.* **1** meal made from ground or rolled oats used esp. in breakfast cereal, cookies, etc. **2** a cooked breakfast cereal made from this. **3** a grayish-fawn color flecked with brown.

OAU *abbr.* Organization of African Unity.

OB *abbr.* **1 a** obstetric. **b** obstetrician. **c** obstetrics. **2** off Broadway.

ob. *abbr.* he or she died. [L *obiit*]

ob- /ob/ *prefix* (also **oc-** before *c*, **of-** before *f*, **op-** before *p*) occurring mainly in words of Latin origin, meaning: **1** exposure, openness (*object*; *obverse*). **2** meeting or facing (*occasion*; *obvious*). **3** direction (*oblong*; *offer*). **4** opposition, hostility, or resistance (*obstreperous*; *opponent*; *obstinate*). **5** hindrance, blocking, or concealment (*obese*; *obstacle*; *occult*). **6** finality or completeness (*obsolete*; *occupy*). **7** (in modern technical words) inversely; in a direction or manner contrary to the usual (*obconical*; *obovate*). [L f. *ob* toward, against, in the way of]

Obad. *abbr.* Obadiah (Old Testament).

ob‑bli‑ga‑to /óbligáatō/ *n.* (*pl.* **‑tos**) *Mus.* an accompaniment, usu. special and unusual in effect, forming an integral part of a composition (*with violin obbligato*). [It., = obligatory, f. L *obligatus* past part. (as OBLIGE)]

ob‑con‑i‑cal /obkónikəl/ *adj.* (also **ob‑con‑ic**) in the form of an inverted cone.

ob‑cor‑date /obkáwrdayt/ *adj. Biol.* in the shape of a heart and attached at the pointed end.

ob‑du‑rate /óbdoorit, ‑dyoor‑/ *adj.* **1** stubborn. **2** hardened against persuasion or influence. □□ **ob‑du‑ra‑cy** /‑doorəsee, ‑dyoor‑/ *n.* **ob‑du‑rate‑ly** *adv.* **ob‑du‑rate‑ness** *n.* [ME f. L *obduratus* past part. of *obdurare* (as OB-, *durare* harden f. *durus* hard)]

OBE *abbr.* (in the UK) Officer (of the Order) of the British Empire.

o‑be‑ah /óbeeə/ *n.* (also **o‑bi** /óbee/) a kind of sorcery practiced esp. in the West Indies. [W. Afr.]

o‑be‑che /ōbeéchee/ *n.* **1** a West African tree, *Triplochiton scleroxylon*. **2** the light-colored timber from this. [Nigerian name]

o‑be‑di‑ence /ōbeédeeəns/ *n.* **1** obeying as an act or practice or quality. **2** submission to another's rule or authority. **3** compliance with a law or command. **4** *Eccl.* **a** compliance with a monastic rule. **b** a sphere of authority (*the Roman obedience*). □ **in obedience to** actuated by or in accordance with. [ME f. OF f. L *obedientia* (as OBEY)]

o‑be‑di‑ent /ōbeédeeənt/ *adj.* **1** obeying or ready to obey. **2** (often foll. by *to*) submissive to another's will; dutiful (*obedient to the law*). □□ **o‑be‑di‑ent‑ly** *adv.* [ME f. OF f. L *obediens* *-entis* (as OBEY)]

o‑bei‑sance /ōbáysəns, ōbée‑/ *n.* **1** a bow, curtsy, or other respectful, or submissive gesture (*make an obeisance*). **2** homage; submission; deference (*pay obeisance*). □□ **o‑bei‑sant** /‑sənt/ *adj.* **o‑bei‑sant‑ly** *adv.* [ME f. OF *obeissance* (as OBEY)]

ob‑e‑li *pl.* of OBELUS.

ob‑e‑lisk /óbəlisk/ *n.* **1 a** a tapering, usu. four-sided stone pillar set up as a monument or landmark, etc. **b** a mountain, tree, etc., of similar shape. **2** = OBELUS. [L *obeliscus* f. Gk *obeliskos* dimin. of *obelos* SPIT²]

ob‑e‑lize /óbəlīz/ *v.tr.* mark with an obelus as spurious, etc. [Gk *obelizō* f. *obelos*: see OBELISK]

ob‑e‑lus /óbələs/ *n.* (*pl.* **ob‑e‑li** /‑lī/) **1** a dagger-shaped reference mark in printed matter. **2** a mark (− or ÷) used in ancient manuscripts to mark a word or passage, esp. asspurious. [L f. Gk *obelos* SPIT²]

o‑bese /ōbée's/ *adj.* very fat; corpulent. □□ **o‑bese‑ness** *n.* **o‑be‑si‑ty** *n.* [L *obesus* (as OB-, *edere* eat)]

o‑bey /ōbáy/ *v.* **1** *tr.* **a** carry out the command of (*you will obey me*). **b** carry out (a command) (*obey orders*). **2** *intr.* do what one is told to do. **3** *tr.* be actuated by (a force or impulse). □□ **o‑bey‑er** *n.* [ME f. OF *obeir* f. L *obedire* (as OB-, *audire* hear)]

ob‑fus‑cate /óbfuskayt/ *v.tr.* **1** obscure or confuse (a mind, topic, etc.). **2** stupefy, bewilder. □□ **ob‑fus‑ca‑tion** /‑káyshən/ *n.* **ob‑fus‑ca‑to‑ry** /obfúskətawree/ *adj.* [LL *obfuscare* (as OB-, *fuscus* dark)]

ob-gyn /óbee-jeewíen/ *abbr.* **1** obstetrician-gynecologist. **2** obstetrics-gynecology.

o‑bi¹ var. of OBEAH.

o‑bi² /óbee/ *n.* (*pl.* same or **o‑bis**) a broad sash worn with a Japanese kimono. [Jap. *obi* belt]

o‑bit /óbit, ōbít/ *n. colloq.* an obituary. [abbr.]

ob‑i‑ter dic‑tum /óbitərdíktəm/ *n.* (*pl.* **ob‑i‑ter dic‑ta** /‑tə/) **1** a judge's

obelisk 1a

oarlock

expression of opinion uttered in court or giving judgment, but not essential to the decision and therefore without binding authority. **2** an incidental remark. [L f. *obiter* by the way + *dictum* a thing said]

o·bit·u·ar·y /ōbíchōō–eree/ *n.* (*pl.* **·ies**) **1** a notice of a death or deaths esp. in a newspaper. **2** an account of the life of a deceased person. **3** (*attrib.*) of or serving as an obituary. □□ **o·bit·u·ar·i·al** /–áireeəl/ *adj.* **o·bit·u·ar·ist** *n.* [med.L *obituarius* f. L *obitus* death f. *obire* obit- die (as OB–, *ire* go)]

obj. *abbr.* **1** object. **2** objective. **3** objection.

ob·ject *n. & v.* ● *n.* /óbjikt, –jekt/ **1** a material thing that can be seen or touched. **2** (foll. by *of*) a person or thing to which action or feeling is directed (*the object of attention; the object of our study*). **3** a thing sought or aimed at; a purpose. **4** *Gram.* a noun or its equivalent governed by an active transitive verb or by a preposition. **5** *Philos.* a thing external to the thinking mind or subject. **6** *derog.* a person or thing of esp. a pathetic or ridiculous appearance. **7** *Computing* a package of information and a description of its manipulation. ● *v.* /əbjékt/ **1** *intr.* (often foll. by *to*) express or feel opposition, disapproval, or reluctance; protest (*I object to being treated like this*). **2** *tr.* (foll. by *that* + clause) state as an objection (*objected that they were kept waiting*). **3** *tr.* (foll. by *to* or *that* + clause) adduce (a quality or fact) as contrary or damaging (to a case). □ **no object** not forming an important or restricting factor (*money is no object*). □□ **object·less** /óbjiktlis/ *adj.* **ob·jec·tor** /əbjéktər/ *n.* [ME f. med.L *objectum* thing presented to the mind, past part. of L *objicere* (as OB–, *jacere ject*- throw)]

ob·ject ball *n. Billiards* the ball at which a player aims the cue ball.

ob·ject glass *n.* the lens in a telescope, etc., nearest to the object observed.

ob·jec·ti·fy /əbjéktifī/ *v.tr.* (**·fies, ·fied**) **1** make objective; embody. **2** present as an object of perception. □□ **ob·jec·ti·fi·ca·tion** /–fikáyshən/ *n.*

ob·jec·tion /əbjékshən/ *n.* **1** an expression or feeling of opposition or disapproval. **2** the act of objecting. **3** an adverse reason or statement. [ME f. OF *objection* or LL *objectio* (as OBJECT)]

ob·jec·tion·a·ble /əbjékshənəbəl/ *adj.* **1** open to objection. **2** unpleasant, offensive. □□ **ob·jec·tion·a·ble·ness** *n.* **ob·jec·tion·a·bly** *adv.*

ob·jec·tive /əbjéktiv/ *adj. & n.* ● *adj.* **1** external to the mind; actually existing; real. **2** (of a person, writing, art, etc.) dealing with outward things or exhibiting facts uncolored by feelings or opinions; not subjective. **3** *Gram.* (of a case or word) constructed as or appropriate to the object of a transitive verb or preposition (cf. ACCUSATIVE). **4** aimed at (*objective point*). **5** (of symptoms) observed by another and not only felt by the patient. ● *n.* **1** something sought or aimed at; an objective point. **2** *Gram.* the objective case. **3** = OBJECT GLASS. □□ **ob·jec·ti·val** /óbjektívəl/ *adj.* **ob·jec·tive·ly** *adv.* **ob·jec·tive·ness** *n.* **ob·jec·tiv·i·ty** /–tívitee/ *n.* **ob·jec·tiv·ize** *v.tr.* **ob·jec·ti·vi·za·tion** /med.L *objectivus* (as OBJECT)]

ob·jec·tiv·ism /əbjéktivizəm/ *n.* **1** the tendency to lay stress on what is objective. **2** *Philos.* the belief that certain things (esp. moral truths) exist apart from human knowledge or perception of them. □□ **ob·jec·tiv·ist** *n.* **ob·jec·ti·vis·tic** *adj.*

ob·ject lan·guage *n.* **1** a language described by means of another language (see METALANGUAGE). **2** *Computing* a language into which a program is translated by means of a compiler or assembler.

ob·ject les·son *n.* a striking practical example of some principle.

ob·ject of the ex·er·cise *n.* the main point of an activity.

ob·jet d'art /áwbzhay daár/ *n.* (*pl.* **ob·jets d'art** *pronunc.* same) a small decorative object. [F, lit. 'object of art']

ob·jur·gate /óbjərgayt, objór–/ *v.tr. literary* chide or scold. □□ **ob·jur·ga·tion** /–gáyshən/ *n.* **ob·jur·ga·to·ry** /–jórgətáwree/ *adj.* [L *objurgare objurgat-* (as OB–, *jurgare* quarrel f. *jurgium* strife)]

ob·lan·ce·o·late /oblánseeəlayt/ *adj. Bot.* (esp. of leaves) lanceolate with the more pointed end at the base.

ob·late[1] /óblayt/ *n.* a person dedicated to a monastic or religious life or work. [F f. med.L *oblatus* f. *offerre oblat-* offer (as OB–, *ferre* bring)]

ob·late[2] /óblayt/ *adj. Geom.* (of a spheroid) flattened at the poles (cf. PROLATE). [mod.L *oblatus* (as OBLATE[1])]

ob·la·tion /əbláyshən, ob–/ *n. Relig.* **1** a thing offered to a divine being. **2** the presentation of bread and wine to God in the Eucharist.

□□ **ob·la·tion·al** *adj.* **ob·la·to·ry** /óblətáwree/ *adj.* [ME f. OF *oblation* or LL *oblatio* (as OBLATE[1])]

ob·li·gate *v. & adj.* ● *v.tr.* /óbligayt/ **1** (usu. in *passive*; foll. by *to* + infin.) bind (a person) legally or morally. **2** commit (assets) as security. ● *adj.* /óbligət/ *Biol.* that has to be as described (*obligate parasite*). □□ **ob·li·ga·tor** *n.* [L *obligare obligat-* (as OBLIGE)]

ob·li·ga·tion /óbligáyshən/ *n.* **1** the constraining power of a law, precept, duty, contract, etc. **2** a duty; a burdensome task. **3** a binding agreement, esp. one enforceable under legal penalty; a written contract or bond. **4 a** a service or benefit; a kindness done or received (*repay an obligation*). **b** indebtedness for this (*be under an obligation*). □ **of obligation** obligatory. □□ **ob·li·ga·tion·al** *adj.* [ME f. OF f. L *obligatio –onis* (as OBLIGE)]

ob·lig·a·to·ry /əblígətáwree/ *adj.* **1** legally or morally binding. **2** compulsory and not merely permissive. **3** constituting an obligation. □□ **ob·lig·a·to·ri·ly** *adv.* [ME f. LL *obligatorius* (as OBLIGE)]

o·blige /əblíj/ *v.* **1** *tr.* (foll. by *to* + infin.) constrain; compel. **2** *tr.* be binding on. **3** *tr.* **a** make indebted by conferring a favor. **b** (foll. by *with*, or *by* + verbal noun) gratify (*oblige me by leaving*). **c** perform a service for (often *absol.*: *will you oblige?*). **4** *tr.* (in *passive*; foll. by *to*) be indebted (*am obliged to you for your help*). **5** *intr. colloq.* (foll. by *with*) make a contribution of a specified kind (*Doris obliged with a song*). **6** *tr. archaic* or *Law* (foll. by *to*, or *to* + infin.) bind by oath, promise, contract, etc. □ **much obliged** an expression of thanks. □□ **o·blig·er** *n.* [ME f. OF *obliger* f. L *obligare* (as OB–, *ligare* bind)]

ob·li·gee /óblijee/ *n. Law* a person to whom another is bound by contract or other legal procedure (cf. OBLIGOR).

o·blig·ing /əblíjing/ *adj.* courteous, accommodating; ready to do a service or kindness. □□ **o·blig·ing·ly** *adv.* **o·blig·ing·ness** *n.*

ob·li·gor /óbligáwr/ *n. Law* a person who is bound to another by contract or other legal procedure (cf. OBLIGEE).

o·blique /əbleék/ *adj., n., & v.* ● *adj.* **1 a** slanting; declining from the vertical or horizontal. **b** diverging from a straight line or course. **2** not going straight to the point; roundabout; indirect. **3** *Geom.* **a** (of a line, plane figure, or surface) inclined at other than a right angle. **b** (of an angle) acute or obtuse. **c** (of a cone, cylinder, etc.) with an axis not perpendicular to the plane of its base. **4** *Anat.* neither parallel nor perpendicular to the long axis of a body or limb. **5** *Bot.* (of a leaf) with unequal sides. **6** *Gram.* denoting any case other than the nominative or vocative. ● *n.* **1** an oblique muscle. **2** *Brit.* an oblique stroke (|/|). ● *v.intr.* (**o·bliques, o·bliqued, o·bliqu·ing**) esp. *Mil.* advance obliquely. □□ **o·blique·ly** *adv.* **o·blique·ness** *n.* **o·bliq·ui·ty** /əblíkwitee/ *n.* [ME f. F f. L *obliquus*]

o·blique sphere *n.* see SPHERE.

ob·lit·er·ate /əblítərayt/ *v.tr.* **1 a** blot out; efface; erase; destroy. **b** leave no clear traces of. **2** deface (a postage stamp, etc.) to prevent further use. □□ **ob·lit·er·a·tion** /–ráyshən/ *n.* **ob·lit·er·a·tive** /–rətiv/ *adj.* **ob·lit·er·a·tor** *n.* [L *obliterare* (as OB–, *litera* LETTER)]

ob·liv·i·on /əblíveeən/ *n.* **1 a** the state of having or being forgotten. **b** disregard; an unregarded state. **2** an amnesty or pardon. □ **fall into oblivion** be forgotten or disused. [ME f. OF f. L *oblivio –onis* f. *oblivisci* forget]

ob·liv·i·ous /əblíveeəs/ *adj.* **1** (often foll. by *of*) forgetful; unmindful. **2** (foll. by *to*, *of*) unaware or unconscious of. □□ **ob·liv·i·ous·ly** *adv.* **ob·liv·i·ous·ness** *n.* [ME f. L *obliviosus* (as OBLIVION)]

ob·long /óblawng/ *adj. & n.* ● *adj.* **1** deviating from a square form by having one long axis, esp. rectangular with adjacent sides unequal. **2** greater in breadth than in height. ● *n.* an oblong figure or object. [ME f. L *oblongus* longish (as OB–, *longus* long)]

ob·lo·quy /óbləkwee/ *n.* **1** the state of being generally ill spoken of. **2** abuse, detraction. [ME f. LL *obloquium* contradiction f. L *obloqui* deny (as OB–, *loqui* speak)]

ob·nox·ious /əbnókshəs/ *adj.* offensive, objectionable, disliked. □□ **ob·nox·ious·ly** *adv.* **ob·nox·ious·ness** *n.* [orig. = vulnerable (to harm), f. L *obnoxiosus* or *obnoxius* (as OB–, *noxa* harm: assoc. with NOXIOUS)]

o·boe /ōbō/ *n.* **1 a** a woodwind double-reed instrument of treble pitch and plaintive incisive tone. **b** its player. **2** an organ stop with a quality resembling an oboe. □□ **o·bo·ist** /ōbō-ist/ *n.* [It. *oboe* or F *hautbois* f. *haut* high + *bois* wood: F *d'amour* = of love]

o·boe d'a·mour /dəmoŏr/ *n.* an oboe with a pear-shaped bell and mellow tone, pitched a minor third below a normal oboe, commonly used in baroque music.

ob·ol /óbol/ *n.* an ancient Greek coin, equal to one-sixth of a drachma. [L *obolus* f. Gk *obolos*, var. of *obelos* OBELUS]

ob·o·vate /obóvayt/ *adj. Biol.* (of a leaf) ovate with the narrower end at the base.

oboe

ob·scene /əbseẻn/ *adj.* **1** offensively or repulsively indecent, esp. by offending accepted sexual morality. **2** *colloq.* highly offensive or repugnant (*an obscene accumulation of wealth*). **3** esp. *Brit. Law* (of a publication) tending to deprave or corrupt. □□ **ob·scene·ly** *adv.* **ob·scene·ness** *n.* [F *obscène* or L *obsc(a)enus* ill-omened, abominable]

ob·scen·i·ty /əbsénitee/ *n.* (*pl.* **·ties**) **1** the state or quality of being obscene. **2** an obscene action, word, etc. [L *obscaenitas* (as OBSCENE)]

ob·scu·rant·ism /əbskyōōrəntizəm, óbskyōōrán–/ *n.* opposition to knowledge and enlightenment. □□ **ob·scu·rant** /əbskyōōrənt/ *n.* **ob·scu·rant·ist** *n.* [*obscurant* f. G f. L *obscurans* f. *obscurare*: see OBSCURE]

ob·scure /əbskyōōr/ *adj.* & *v.* ● *adj.* **1** not clearly expressed nor easily understood. **2** unexplained; doubtful. **3** dark; dim. **4** indistinct; not clear. **5** hidden; remote from observation. **6 a** unnoticed. **b** (of a person) undistinguished; hardly known. **7** (of a color) dingy; dull; indefinite. ● *v.tr.* **1** make obscure, dark, indistinct, or unintelligible. **2** dim the glory of; outshine. **3** conceal from sight. □□ **ob·scu·ra·tion** *n.* **ob·scure·ly** *adv.* [ME f. OF *obscur* f. L *obscurus* dark]

ob·scu·ri·ty /əbskyōōritee/ *n.* (*pl.* **·ties**) **1** the state of being obscure. **2** an obscure person or thing. [F *obscurité* f. L *obscuritas* (as OBSCURE)]

ob·se·cra·tion /óbsikráyshən/ *n.* earnest entreaty. [ME f. L *obsecratio* f. *obsecrare* entreat (as OB–, *sacrare* f. *sacer sacri* sacred)]

ob·se·quies /óbsikweez/ *n.pl.* **1** funeral rites. **2** a funeral. □□ **ob·se·qui·al** /əbseẻkweeəl/ *adj.* [ME, pl. of obs. *obsequy* f. AF *obsequie*, OF *obseque* f. med.L *obsequiae* f. L *exsequiae* funeral rites (see EXEQUIES): assoc. with *obsequium* (see OBSEQUIOUS)]

ob·se·qui·ous /əbseẻkweeəs/ *adj.* servilely obedient or attentive. □□ **ob·se·qui·ous·ly** *adv.* **ob·se·qui·ous·ness** *n.* [ME f. L *obsequiosus* f. *obsequium* compliance (as OB–, *sequi* follow)]

SYNONYM TIP *obsequious*

MENIAL, SERVILE, SLAVISH, SUBSERVIENT. If you want to get ahead with your boss, you might trying being **obsequious**, which suggests an attitude of inferiority that may or may not be genuine, but that is assumed in order to placate a superior in hopes of getting what one wants (*a "goody two shoes" whose obsequious behavior made everyone in the class cringe*). While **subservient** may connote similar behavior, it is more often applied to those who are genuinely subordinate or dependent and act accordingly (*a timid, subservient child who was terrified of making a mistake*). **Servile** is a stronger and more negative term, suggesting a cringing submissiveness (*the dog's servile obedience to her master*), while **slavish** suggests the status or attitude of a slave (*a slavish adherence to the rules of etiquette*). **Menial** refers to occupations that are ranked low in terms of economic or social status or that require no special skill or intellectual attainment (*he was qualified to perform only menial jobs*).

---

ob·serv·ance /əbzérvəns/ *n.* **1** the act or process of keeping or performing a law, duty, custom, ritual, etc. **2** an act of a religious or ceremonial character; a customary rite. **3** the rule of a religious order. **4** *archaic* respect; deference. **5** *archaic* the act of observing or watching; observation. [ME f. OF f. L *observantia* (as OBSERVE)]

ob·serv·ant /əbzérvənt/ *adj.* & *n.* ● *adj.* **1 a** acute or diligent in taking notice. **b** (often foll. by *of*) carefully particular; heedful. **2** attentive in esp. religious observances (*an observant Jew*). ● *n.* (**Observant**) a member of the branch of the Franciscan order that observes the strict rule. □□ **ob·serv·ant·ly** *adv.* [F (as OBSERVE)]

ob·ser·va·tion /óbzərváyshən/ *n.* **1** the act or an instance of noticing; the condition of being noticed. **2** perception; the faculty of taking notice. **3** a remark or statement, esp. one that is of the nature of a comment. **4 a** the accurate watching and noting of phenomena as they occur in nature with regard to cause and effect or mutual relations. **b** the noting of the symptoms of a patient, the behavior of a suspect, etc. **5** the taking of the sun's or another heavenly body's altitude to find a latitude or longitude. **6** *Mil.* the watching of a fortress or hostile position or movements. □ **under observation** being watched. □□ **ob·ser·va·tion·al** *adj.* **ob·ser·va·tion·al·ly** *adv.* [ME f. L *observatio* (as OBSERVE)]

ob·ser·va·tion car *n.* esp. *US* a railroad car built so as to afford good views.

ob·ser·va·tion post *n. Mil.* a post for watching the effect of artillery fire, etc.

ob·serv·a·to·ry /əbzérvətawree/ *n.* (*pl.* **·ries**) a room or building equipped for the observation of natural, esp. astronomical or meteorological, phenomena. [mod.L *observatorium* f. L *observare* (as OBSERVE)]

ob·serve /əbzérv/ *v.* **1** *tr.* (often foll. by *that* or *how* + clause) perceive; note; take notice of; become conscious of. **2** *tr.* watch carefully. **3** *tr.* **a** follow or adhere to (a law, command, method, principle, etc.). **b** keep or adhere to (an appointed time). **c** maintain (silence). **d** duly perform (a rite). **e** celebrate (an anniversary). **4** *tr.* examine and note (phenomena) without the aid of experiment. **5** *tr.* (often foll. by *that* + clause) say, esp. by way of comment. **6** *intr.* (foll. by *on*) make a remark or remarks about. □□ **ob·serv·a·**

ble *adj.* **ob·serv·a·bly** *adv.* [ME f. OF *observer* f. L *observare* watch (as OB–, *servare* keep)]

ob·serv·er /əbzérvər/ *n.* **1** a person who observes. **2** an interested spectator. **3** a person who attends a conference, etc., to note the proceedings but does not participate. **4 a** a person trained to notice and identify aircraft. **b** a person carried in an airplane to note the enemy's position, etc.

ob·sess /əbsés/ *v.tr.* & *intr.* (often in *passive*) preoccupy; haunt; fill the mind of (a person) continually. □□ **ob·ses·sive** *adj.* & *n.* **ob·ses·sive·ly** *adv.* **ob·ses·sive·ness** *n.* [L *obsidēre obsess-* (as OB–, *sedēre* sit)]

ob·ses·sion /əbséshən/ *n.* **1** the act of obsessing or the state of being obsessed. **2** a persistent idea or thought dominating a person's mind. **3** a condition in which such ideas are present. □□ **ob·ses·sion·al** *adj.* **ob·ses·sion·al·ism** *n.* **ob·ses·sion·al·ly** *adv.* [L *obsessio* (as OBSESS)]

ob·ses·sive-com·pul·sive *adj.* relating to a neurosis characterized by the persistence of an obsessive thought and the desire to engage in compulsive behavior, such as repeated hand washing.

ob·sid·i·an /əbsídeeən/ *n.* a dark glassy volcanic rock formed from hardened lava. [L *obsidianus*, error for *obsianus* f. *Obsius*, the name (in Pliny) of the discoverer of a similar stone]

ob·so·les·cent /óbsəlésənt/ *adj.* becoming obsolete; going out of use or date. □□ **ob·so·les·cence** /–səns/ *n.* [L *obsolescere obsolescent-* (as OB–, *solēre* be accustomed)]

ob·so·lete /óbsəleẻt/ *adj.* **1** disused; discarded; antiquated. **2** *Biol.* less developed than formerly or than in a cognate species; rudimentary. □□ **ob·so·lete·ly** *adv.* **ob·so·lete·ness** *n.* **ob·so·let·ism** *n.* [L *obsoletus* past part. (as OBSOLESCENT)]

ob·sta·cle /óbstəkəl/ *n.* a person or thing that obstructs progress. [ME f. OF f. L *obstaculum* f. *obstare* impede (as OB–, *stare* stand)]

ob·sta·cle course *n.* **1** a training course through which a series of obstacles (walls, ditches, etc.) must be overcome in succession. **2** any situation that presents a series of challenges or obstacles.

ob·stet·ric /əbstétrik, ob–/ *adj.* (also **ob·stet·ri·cal**) of or relating to childbirth and associated processes. □□ **ob·stet·ri·cal·ly** *adv.* **ob·ste·tri·cian** /–stətríshən/ *n.* [mod.L *obstetricus* for L *obstetricius* f. *obstetrix* midwife f. *obstare* be present (as OB–, *stare* stand)]

ob·stet·rics /əbstétriks, ob–/ *n.pl.* (usu. treated as *sing.*) the branch of medicine and surgery concerned with childbirth and midwifery.

ob·sti·nate /óbstinət/ *adj.* **1** stubborn, intractable. **2** firmly adhering to one's chosen course of action or opinion despite dissuasion. **3** inflexible, self-willed. **4** unyielding; not readily responding to treatment, etc. □□ **ob·sti·na·cy** *n.* **ob·sti·nate·ly** *adv.* [ME f. L *obstinatus* past part. of *obstinare* persist (as OB–, *stare* stand)]

ob·strep·er·ous /əbstrépərəs/ *adj.* **1** turbulent; unruly; noisily resisting control. **2** noisy; vociferous. □□ **ob·strep·er·ous·ly** *adv.* **ob·strep·er·ous·ness** *n.* [L *obstreperus* f. *obstrepere* (as OB–, *strepere* make a noise)]

ob·struct /əbstrúkt/ *v.tr.* **1** block up; make hard or impossible to pass. **2** prevent or retard the progress of; impede. □□ **ob·struc·tor** *n.* [L *obstruere obstruct-* (as OB–, *struere* build)]

ob·struc·tion /əbstrúkshən/ *n.* **1** the act or an instance of blocking; the state of being blocked. **2** the act of making or the state of becoming more or less impassable. **3** an obstacle or blockage. **4** the retarding of progress by deliberate delays, esp. within a legislative assembly. **5** *Sports* the act of unlawfully obstructing another player. **6** *Med.* a blockage in a bodily passage, esp. in an intestine. □□ **ob·struc·tion·ism** *n.* (in sense 4). **ob·struc·tion·ist** *n.* (in sense 4). [L *obstructio* (as OBSTRUCT)]

ob·struc·tive /əbstrúktiv/ *adj.* & *n.* ● *adj.* causing or intended to cause an obstruction. ● *n.* an obstructive person or thing. □□ **ob·struc·tive·ly** *adv.* **ob·struc·tive·ness** *n.*

ob·tain /əbtáyn/ *v.* **1** *tr.* acquire; secure; have granted to one. **2** *intr.* be prevalent or established or in vogue. □□ **ob·tain·a·ble** *adj.* **ob·tain·a·bil·i·ty** *n.* **ob·tain·er** *n.* **ob·tain·ment** *n.* **ob·ten·tion** /əbténshən/ *n.* [ME f. OF *obtenir* f. L *obtinēre obtent-* keep (as OB–, *tenēre* hold)]

ob·trude /əbtrōōd/ *v.* **1** *intr.* be or become obtrusive. **2** *tr.* (often foll. by *on, upon*) thrust forward (oneself, one's opinion, etc.) importunately. □□ **ob·trud·er** *n.* **ob·tru·sion** /–trō̄ōzhən/ *n.* [L *obtrudere obtrus-* (as OB–, *trudere* push)]

ob·tru·sive /əbtrōōsiv/ *adj.* **1** unpleasantly or unduly noticeable. **2** obtruding oneself. □□ **ob·tru·sive·ly** *adv.* **ob·tru·sive·ness** *n.* [as OBTRUDE]

ob·tund /əbtúnd/ *v.tr.* blunt or deaden (a sense or faculty). [ME f. L *obtundere obtus-* (as OB–, *tundere* beat)]

ob·tuse /əbt ōōs, –tyōōs/ *adj.* **1** dull-witted; slow to understand. **2** of blunt form; not sharp-pointed nor sharp-edged. **3** (of an angle) more than 90 ° and less than 180°. **4** (of pain or the senses) dull; not acute. □□ **ob·tuse·ly** *adv.* **ob·tuse·ness** *n.* **ob·tus·i·ty** *n.* [L *obtusus* past part. (as OBTUND)]

ob·verse /óbvərs/ *n. & v.* •*n.* **1 a** the side of a coin or medal, etc., bearing the head or principal design. **b** this design (cf. REVERSE). **2** the front or proper or top side of a thing. **3** the counterpart of a fact or truth. •*adj.* **1** *Biol.* narrower at the base or point of attachment than at the apex or top (see OB- 7). **2** answering as the counterpart to something else. □□ **ob·verse·ly** *adv.* [L *obversus* past part. (as OBVERT)]

ob·vert /əbv órt/ *v. tr. Logic* alter (a proposition) so as to infer another proposition with a contradictory predicate, e.g., *no men are immortal* to *all men are mortal.* □□ **ob·ver·sion** /–zhən/ *n.* [L *obvertere obvers-* (as OB-, *vertere* turn)]

ob·vi·ate /óbveeayt/ *v. tr.* get around or do away with (a need, inconvenience, etc.). □□ **ob·vi·a·tion** /–áyshən/ *n.* [LL *obviare* oppose (as OB-, *via* way)]

ob·vi·ous /óbveeəs/ *adj.* easily seen or recognized or understood; palpable; indubitable. □□ **ob·vi·ous·ly** *adv.* **ob·vi·ous·ness** *n.* [L *obvius* f. *ob viam* in the way]

OC *abbr.* officer candidate.

oc- /ok/ *prefix* assim. form of OB- before *c*.

o.c. *abbr.* in the work cited. [L *opere citato*]

oc·a·ri·na /ókəreénə/ *n.* a small egg-shaped ceramic (usu. terracotta) or metal wind instrument. [It. f. *oca* goose (from its shape)]

Oc·cam's ra·zor /ókəmz/ *n.* the principle attributed to the English philosopher William of Occam (d. *c.*1350) that the fewest possible assumptions are to be made in explaining a thing.

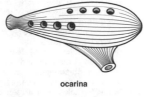

ocarina

oc·ca·sion /əkáyzhən/ *n. & v.* •*n.* **1 a** a special or noteworthy event or happening (*dressed for the occasion*). **b** the time or occurrence of this (*on the occasion of their marriage*). **2** (often foll. by *for*, or *to* + infin.) a reason, ground, or justification (*there is no occasion to be angry*). **3** a juncture suitable for doing something; an opportunity. **4** an immediate but subordinate or incidental cause (*the assassination was the occasion of the war*). •*v. tr.* **1** be the occasion or cause of; bring about esp. incidentally. **2** (foll. by *to* + infin.) cause (a person or thing to do something). □ **on occasion** now and then; when the need arises. **rise to the occasion** produce the necessary will, energy, ability, etc., in unusually demanding circumstances. **take occasion** (foll. by *to* + infin.) make use of the opportunity. [ME f. OF *occasion* or L *occasio* juncture, reason, f. *occidere occas-* go down (as OB-, *cadere* fall)]

oc·ca·sion·al /əkáyzhənəl/ *adj.* **1** happening irregularly and infrequently. **2 a** made or meant for, or associated with, a special occasion. **b** (of furniture, etc.) made or adapted for infrequent and varied use. **3** acting on a special occasion. □□ **oc·ca·sion·al·i·ty** /–náliteé/ *n.* **oc·ca·sion·al·ly** *adv.*

oc·ca·sion·al cause *n.* a secondary cause; an occasion (see OCCASION *n.* 4).

oc·ca·sion·al ta·ble *n.* a small table for infrequent and varied use.

Oc·ci·dent /óksidənt/ *n. poet.* or *rhet.* **1** (prec. by *the*) the West. **2** western Europe. **3** Europe, America, or both, as distinct from the Orient. **4** European, in contrast to Oriental, civilization. [ME f. OF f. L *occidens* –*entis* setting, sunset, west (as OCCASION)]

oc·ci·den·tal /óksidént'l/ *adj. & n.* •*adj.* **1** of the Occident. **2** western. **3** of Western nations. •*n.* (**Occidental**) a native of the Occident. □□ **oc·ci·den·tal·ism** *n.* **oc·ci·den·tal·ist** *n.* **oc·ci·den·tal·ize** *v. tr.* **oc·ci·den·tal·ly** *adv.* [ME f. OF *occidental* or L *occidentalis* (as OCCIDENT)]

occipito- /oksípitō/ *comb. form* the back of the head. [as OCCIPUT]

oc·ci·put /óksiput/ *n.* the back of the head. □□ **oc·cip·i·tal** /–sípit'l/ *adj.* [ME f. L *occiput* (as OB-, *caput* head)]

Oc·ci·tan /óksitan/ *n.* (also *attrib.*) the Provençal language. [F: cf. LANGUE D'OC]

oc·clude /əkl óód/ *v. tr.* **1** stop up or close (pores or an orifice). **2** *Chem.* absorb and retain (gases or impurities). [L *occludere occlus-* (as OB-, *claudere* shut)]

oc·clud·ed front *n. Meteorol.* a front resulting from occlusion.

oc·clu·sion /əkl óózhən/ *n.* **1** the act or process of occluding. **2** *Meteorol.* a phenomenon in which the cold front of a depression overtakes the warm front, causing upward displacement of warm air between them. **3** *Dentistry* the position of the teeth when the jaws are closed. **4** the blockage or closing of a hollow organ, etc. (*coronary occlusion*). **5** *Phonet.* the momentary closure of the vocal passage. □□ **oc·clu·sive** *adj.*

oc·cult /əkúlt, ókult/ *adj. & v.* •*adj.* **1** involving the supernatural; mystical; magical. **2** kept secret; esoteric. **3** recondite; mysterious; beyond the range of ordinary knowledge. **4** *Med.* not obvious on inspection. •*v. tr. Astron.* (of a concealing body much greater in size than the concealed body) hide from view by passing in front; conceal by being in front. □ **the occult** occult phenomena generally. □□ **oc·cul·ta·tion** /–táyshən/ *n.* **oc·cult·ism** *n.* **oc·cult·ist** *n.* **oc·cult·ly** *adv.* **oc·cult·ness** *n.* [L *occulere occult-* (as OB-, *celare* hide)]

oc·cult·ing light *n.* a light, esp. of a lighthouse, that is cut off at regular intervals.

oc·cu·pant /ókyəpənt/ *n.* **1** a person who occupies, resides in, or is in a place, etc. (*both occupants of the car were unhurt*). **2** a person holding property, esp. land, in actual possession. **3** a person who establishes a title by taking possession of something previously without an established owner. □□ **oc·cu·pan·cy** /–pənsee/ *n.* (*pl.* **-cies**). [F *occupant* or L *occupans* –*antis* (as OCCUPY)]

oc·cu·pa·tion /ókyəpáyshən/ *n.* **1** what occupies one; a means of passing one's time. **2** a person's temporary or regular employment; a business, calling, or pursuit. **3** the act of occupying or state of being occupied. **4 a** the act of taking or holding possession of (a country, district, etc.) by military force. **b** the state or time of this. **5** tenure, occupancy. **6** (*attrib.*) for the sole use of the occupiers of the land concerned (*occupation road*). [ME f. AF *ocupacioun*, OF *occupation* f. L *occupatio* –*onis* (as OCCUPY)]

oc·cu·pa·tion·al /ókyəpáyshənəl/ *adj.* **1** of or in the nature of an occupation or occupations. **2** (of a disease, hazard, etc.) rendered more likely by one's occupation.

oc·cu·pa·tion·al ther·a·py *n.* mental or physical activity designed to assist recovery from disease or injury.

oc·cu·pi·er /ókyəpīər/ *n. Brit.* a person residing in a property as its owner or tenant.

oc·cu·py /ókyəpī/ *v. tr.* (**·pies**, **·pied**) **1** reside in; be the tenant of. **2** take up or fill (space or time or a place). **3** hold (a position or office). **4** take military possession of (a country, region, town, strategic position). **5** place oneself in (a building, etc.) forcibly or without authority. **6** (usu. in *passive*; often foll. by *in* or *with*) keep busy or engaged. [ME f. OF *occuper* f. L *occupare* seize (as OB-, *capere* take)]

oc·cur /əkór/ *v. intr.* (**oc·curred, oc·cur·ring**) **1** come into being as an event or process at or during some time; happen. **2** exist or be encountered in some place or conditions. **3** (foll. by *to*; usu. foll. by *that* + clause) come into the mind of, esp. as an unexpected or casual thought (*it occurred to me that you were right*). [L *occurrere* go to meet, present itself (as OB-, *currere* run)]

oc·cur·rence /əkórəns, əkúr–/ *n.* **1** the act or an instance of occurring. **2** an incident or event. □ **of frequent occurrence** often occurring. [*occurrent* that occurs f. F f. L *occurrens* –*entis* (as OCCUR)]

o·cean /óshən/ *n.* **1 a** a large expanse of sea, esp. each of the main areas called the Atlantic, Pacific, Indian, Arctic, and Antarctic Oceans. **b** these regarded cumulatively as the body of water surrounding the land of the globe. **2** (usu. prec. by *the*) the sea. **3** (often in *pl.*) a very large expanse or quantity of anything (*oceans of time*). □□ **o·cean·ward** *adv.* (also esp. *Brit.* **–wards**). [ME f. OF *occean* f. L *oceanus* f. Gk *ōkeanos* stream encircling the earth's disk, Atlantic]

o·cea·nar·i·um /óshənáireeəm/ *n.* (*pl.* **o·cea·nar·i·ums** or **·nar·i·a** /–reeə/) a large seawater aquarium for keeping sea animals. [OCEAN + –ARIUM, after *aquarium*]

o·cean-go·ing /óshən-góing/ *adj.* (of a ship) able to cross oceans.

O·ce·a·ni·a /ósheeáneeə, –áaneeə/ *n.* the islands of the Pacific and adjacent seas. □□ **O·ce·an·i·an** *adj. & n.* [mod.L f. F *Océanie* f. L (as OCEAN)]

o·ce·an·ic /ósheeánik/ *adj.* **1** of, like, or near the ocean. **2** (of a climate) governed by the ocean. **3** of the part of the ocean distant from the continents. **4** (**Oceanic**) of Oceania.

O·ce·a·nid /óseeənid/ *n.* (*pl.* **O·ce·a·nids** or **·ides** /óseeánideez/) (in Greek mythology) an ocean nymph. [Gk *ōkeanis* –*idos* daughter of Oceanus]

o·cea·nog·ra·phy /óshənógrəfee/ *n.* the study of the oceans. □□ **o·cea·nog·ra·pher** *n.* **o·cea·no·graph·ic** /–nəgráfik/ *adj.* **o·cea·no·graph·i·cal** *adj.*

o·cean tramp *n. Brit.* = TRAMP *n.* 6.

o·cel·lus /ōséləs/ *n.* (*pl.* **o·cel·li** /–lī/) **1** each of the simple, as opposed to compound, eyes of insects, etc. **2** a spot of color surrounded by a ring of a different color on the wing of a butterfly, etc. □□ **o·cel·lar** *adj.* **o·cel·late** /ósilayt/ *adj.* **o·cel·lat·ed** *adj.* [L, dimin. of *oculus* eye]

oc·e·lot /ósilot, ósi–/ *n.* **1** a medium-sized feline, *Felis pardalis*, native to S. and Central America, having a deep yellow or orange coat with black striped and spotted markings. **2** its fur. [F f. Nahuatl *ocelotl* jaguar]

och /okh/ *int. Sc. & Ir.* expressing surprise or regret. [Gael. & Ir.]

o·cher /ókər/ *n.* (*Brit.* **o·chre**) **1** a mineral of clay and ferric oxide, used as a pigment varying from light yellow to brown or red. **2** a pale brownish yellow. □□ **o·cher·ous** *adj.* **o·cher·y** *adj.* [ME f. OF *ocre* f. L *ochra* f. Gk *ōkhra* yellow ocher]

och·loc·ra·cy /oklókrəsee/ *n.* (*pl.* **·cies**) mob rule. □□ **och·lo·crat** /óklökrat/ *n.* **och·lo·crat·ic** /óklökrátik/ *adj.* [F *ochlocratie* f. Gk *okhlokratia* f. *okhlos* mob]

o·chone /okhón/ *int.* (also **o·hone**) *Sc. & Ir.* expressing regret or lament. [Gael. & Ir. *ochóin*]

o·chre *Brit.* var. of OCHER.

-ock /ək/ *suffix* forming nouns orig. with diminutive sense (*hillock*; *bullock*). [from or after OE *–uc*, *–oc*]

ock•er /ókər/ *n. Austral. sl.* a boorish or aggressive Australian (esp. as a stereotype). [20th c.: orig. uncert.]

o'clock /əklók/ *adv.* of the clock (used to specify the hour) (6 *o'clock*).

OCR *abbr.* optical character recognition.

OCS *abbr.* officer candidate school.

Oct. *abbr.* October.

oct. *abbr.* octavo.

oct- /okt/ *comb. form* assim. form of OCTA-, OCTO- before a vowel.

octa- /óktə/ *comb. form* (also **oct-** before a vowel) eight. [Gk *okta-* f. *oktō* eight]

oc•tad /óktad/ *n.* a group of eight. [LL *octas octad-* f. Gk *oktas –ados* f. *oktō* eight]

oc•ta•gon /óktəgon, –gən/ *n.* **1** a plane figure with eight sides and angles. **2** an object or building with this cross section. □□ **oc•tag•o•nal** /-tágənəl/ *adj.* **oc•tag•o•nal•ly** *adv.* [L *octagonos* f. Gk *octagōnos* (as OCTA-, –GON)]

oc•ta•he•dron /óktəheédrən/ *n.* (*pl.* **oc•ta•he•drons** or **oc•ta•he•dra** /-drə/) **1** a solid figure contained by eight (esp. triangular) plane faces. **2** a body, esp. a crystal, in the form of a regular octahedron. □□ **oc•ta•he•dral** *adj.* [Gk *oktaedron* (as OCTA-, –HEDRON)]

oc•tal /óktəl/ *adj.* reckoning or proceeding by eights (*octal scale*).

oc•tam•er•ous /oktámərəs/ *adj.* **1** esp. Bot. having eight parts. **2** *Zool.* having organs arranged in eights.

oc•tane /óktayn/ *n.* a colorless flammable hydrocarbon of the alkane series. ¶ Chem. formula: C_8H_{18}. [OCT- + –ANE[2]]

octahedron

oc•tane num•ber *n.* (also **oc•tane rat•ing**) a figure indicating the antiknock properties of a fuel.

oc•tant /óktənt/ *n.* **1** an arc of a circle equal to one-eighth of the circumference. **2** such an arc with two radii, forming an area equal to one eighth of the circle. **3** each of eight parts into which three planes intersecting (esp. at right angles) at a point divide the space or the solid body round it. **4** *Astron.* a point in a body's apparent course 45° distant from a given point, esp. a point at which the moon is 45° from conjunction or opposition with the sun. **5** an instrument in the form of a graduated eighth of a circle, used in astronomy and navigation. [L *octans octant-* half-quadrant f. *octo* eight]

oc•ta•roon var. of OCTOROON.

oc•ta•style /óktəstīl/ *adj. & n.* • *adj.* having eight columns at the end or in front. • *n.* an octastyle portico or building. [L *octastylus* f. Gk *oktastulos* (as OCTA- + *stulos* pillar)]

oc•ta•va•lent /óktəváylənt/ *adj.* Chem. having a valence of eight. [OCTA- + VALENCE[1]]

oc•tave /óktiv, –tayv/ *n.* **1** *Mus.* **a** a series of eight notes occupying the interval between (and including) two notes, one having twice or half the frequency of vibration of the other. **b** this interval. **c** each of the two notes at the extremes of this interval. **d** these two notes sounding together. **2** a group or stanza of eight lines; an octet. **3 a** the seventh day after a festival. **b** a period of eight days including a festival and its octave. **4** a group of eight. **5** the last of eight parrying positions in fencing. **6** esp. *Brit.* a wine cask holding an eighth of a pipe. [ME f. OF f. L *octava dies* eighth day (reckoned inclusively)]

oc•ta•vo /óktáyvō, oktaávō/ *n.* (*pl.* **•vos**) **1** a size of book or page given by folding a standard sheet three times to form a quire of eight leaves. **2** a book or sheet of this size. ¶ Abbr.: **8vo.** [L *in octavo* in an eighth f. *octavus* eighth]

oc•ten•ni•al /okténeeəl/ *adj.* **1** lasting eight years. **2** occurring every eight years. [LL *octennium* period of eight years (as OCT-, *annus* year)]

oc•tet /oktét/ *n.* (also **oc•tette**) **1** *Mus.* **a** a composition for eight voices or instruments. **b** the performers of such a piece. **2** a group of eight. **3** the first eight lines of a sonnet. **4** Chem. a stable group of eight electrons. [It. *ottetto* or G *Oktett*: assim. to OCT-, DUET, QUARTET]

octo- /óktō/ *comb. form* (also **oct-** before a vowel) eight. [L *octo* or Gk *oktō* eight]

Oc•to•ber /októbər/ *n.* the tenth month of the year. [OE f. L (as OCTO-): cf. DECEMBER, SEPTEMBER]

Oc•to•brist /októbrist/ *n. hist.* a member of the moderate party in the Russian Duma, supporting the Imperial Constitutional Manifesto of Oct. 30, 1905. [OCTOBER, after Russ. *oktyabrist*]

oc•to•cen•ten•ar•y /óktōsénténəree, –sént'neree/ *n. & adj.* • *n.* (*pl.* **•ies**) **1** an eight-hundredth anniversary. **2** a celebration of this. • *adj.* of or relating to an octocentenary.

oc•to•dec•i•mo /óktōdésimō/ *n.* (*pl.* **•mos**) **1** a size of book or page given by folding a standard sheet into eighteen leaves. **2** a book or sheet of this size. [*in octodecimo* f. L *octodecimus* eighteenth]

oc•to•ge•nar•i•an /óktəjináireeən/ *n. & adj.* • *n.* a person from 80 to 89 years old. • *adj.* of this age. [L *octogenarius* f. *octogeni* distributive of *octoginta* eighty]

oc•to•pod /óktəpod/ *n.* any cephalopod of the order Octopoda, with eight arms usu. having suckers, and a round saclike body, including octopuses. [Gk *oktōpous –podos* f. *oktō* eight + *pous* foot]

oc•to•pus /óktəpəs/ *n.* (*pl.* **oc•to•pus•es**) **1** any cephalopod mollusk of the genus *Octopus* having eight suckered arms, a soft saclike body, and strong beaklike jaws. **2** an organized and usu. harmful ramified power or influence. [Gk *oktō-pous*: see OCTOPOD]

octopus

oc•to•roon /óktərōŏn/ *n.* (also **oc•ta•roon**) the offspring of a quadroon and a white person; a person of one-eighth black ancestry. [OCTO- after QUADROON]

oc•to•syl•lab•ic /óktōsilábik/ *adj. & n.* • *adj.* having eight syllables. • *n.* an octosyllabic verse. [LL *octosyllabus* (as OCTO-, SYLLABLE)]

oc•to•syl•la•ble /óktəsíləbəl/ *n. & adj.* • *n.* an octosyllabic verse or word. • *adj.* = OCTOSYLLABIC.

oc•troi /óktroi, áwktrwaa/ *n.* **1** a duty levied in some European countries on goods entering a town. **2 a** the place where this is levied. **b** the officials by whom it is levied. [F f. *octroyer* grant, f. med.L *auctorizare*: see AUTHORIZE]

oc•tu•ple /óktəpəl, oktōō–, –tyōō–/ *adj., n., & v.* • *adj.* eightfold. • *n.* an eightfold amount. • *v.tr. & intr.* multiply by eight. [F *octuple* or L *octuplus* (adj.) f. *octo* eight: cf. DOUBLE]

oc•u•lar /ókyoolər/ *adj. & n.* • *adj.* of or connected with the eyes or sight; visual. • *n.* the eyepiece of an optical instrument. □□ **oc•u•lar•ly** *adv.* [F *oculaire* f. LL *ocularis* f. L *oculus* eye]

oc•u•list /ókyəlorist/ *n.* a maker of artificial eyes. [F *oculariste* (as OCULAR)]

oc•u•lar spec•trum *n.* see SPECTRUM.

oc•u•late /ókyəlayt/ *adj.* = ocellate (see OCELLUS). [L *oculatus* f. *oculus* eye]

oc•u•list /ókyəlist/ *n. formerly* **1** an ophthalmologist. **2** an optometrist. □□ **oc•u•lis•tic** /–lístik/ *adj.* [F *oculiste* f. L *oculus* eye]

oculo- /ókyəlō/ *comb. form* eye (*oculonasal*). [L *oculus* eye]

OD[1] *abbr.* **1** doctor of optometry. **2** *oculus dexter* (right eye). **3** officer of the day. **4 a** overdraft. **b** overdrawn.

OD[2] /ōd eé/ *n. & v. sl.* • *n.* an overdose, esp. of a narcotic drug. • *v.intr.* (**OD's, OD'd, OD'ing**) take an overdose. [abbr.]

od[1] /od/ *n.* a hypothetical power once thought to pervade nature and account for various scientific phenomena. [arbitrary term coined in G by Baron von Reichenbach, Ger. scientist d. 1869]

od[2] /od/ *n.* (as *int.* or in oaths) *archaic* = GOD. [corruption]

o.d. *abbr.* outside diameter.

o•da•lisque /ōdəlisk/ *n. hist.* an Eastern female slave or concubine, esp. in the Turkish sultan's seraglio. [F f. Turk. *odalik* f. *oda* chamber + *lik* function]

odd /od/ *adj. & n.* • *adj.* **1** extraordinary, strange, queer, remarkable, eccentric. **2** casual, occasional, unconnected (*odd jobs*; *odd moments*). **3** not normally noticed or considered; unpredictable (*in some odd corner*; *picks up odd bargains*). **4** additional; besides the calculated amount (*a few odd cents*). **5 a** (of numbers) not integrally divisible by two. **b** (of things or persons numbered consecutively) bearing such a number (*no parking on odd dates*). **6** left over when the rest have been distributed or divided into pairs (*have got an odd sock*). **7** detached from a set or series (*a few odd volumes*). **8** (appended to a number, sum, weight, etc.) somewhat more than (*forty odd*; *forty-odd people*). **9** by which a round number, given sum, etc., is exceeded (*we have 102 — what shall we do with the odd 2?*). • *n.* Golf one stroke more than the opponent's. **2** *Brit.* a handicap of one stroke at each hole. □□ **odd•ish** *adj.* **odd•ly** *adv.* **odd•ness** *n.* [ME f. ON *odda-* in *odda-mathr* third man, odd man, f. *oddi* angle]

odd•ball /ódbawl/ *n. colloq.* **1** an odd or eccentric person. **2** (*attrib.*) strange, bizarre.

Odd Fel•low /ód fellō/ *n.* a member of a fraternity similar to the Freemasons.

odd•i•ty /óditee/ *n.* (*pl.* **•ties**) **1** a strange person, thing, or occurrence. **2** a peculiar trait. **3** the state of being odd.

odd job *n.* a casual isolated piece of work.

odd job man *n.* (also **odd job•ber**) a person who does odd jobs.

odd man out *n.* **1** a person or thing differing from all the others in a group in some respect. **2** a method of selecting one of three or more persons, e.g., by tossing a coin.

odd•ment /ódmənt/ *n.* **1** an odd article; something left over. **2** (in *pl.*) miscellaneous articles. **3** *Printing* matter other than the main text.

odds /odz/ *n.pl.* **1** the ratio between the amounts staked by the parties to a bet, based on the expected probability either way. **2** the chances or balance of probability in favor of or against some result (*the odds are against it; the odds are that it will rain*). **3** the balance of advantage (*the odds are in your favor; won against all the odds*). **4** an equalizing allowance to a weaker competitor. **5** a difference giving an advantage (*makes no odds*). □ **at odds** (often foll. by *with*) in conflict or at variance. **by all odds** certainly. **lay** (or **give**) **odds** offer a bet with odds favorable to the other bettor. **take odds** offer a bet with odds unfavorable to the other bettor. **what's** (or **what are**) **the odds?** *colloq.* what are the chances? (implying a slim likelihood). [app. pl. of ODD *n.*: cf. NEWS]

odds and ends *n.* miscellaneous articles or remnants.

odds-on *adj.* a state when success is more likely than failure, esp. as indicated by the betting odds.

ode /ōd/ *n.* **1** a lyric poem, usu. rhymed and in the form of an address, in varied or irregular meter. **2** *hist.* a poem meant to be sung. [F f. LL *oda* f. Gk *ōidē* Attic form of *aoidē* song f. *aeidō* sing]

-ode[1] /ōd/ *suffix* forming nouns meaning 'thing of the nature of' (*geode; trematode*). [Gk *-ōdēs* adj. ending]

-ode[2] /ōd/ *comb. form Electr.* forming names of electrodes, or devices having them (*cathode; diode*). [Gk *hodos* way]

o•de•um /ódeeəm/ *n.* (*pl.* **o•de•a** /–deeə/ or **o•de•ums**) a building for musical performances, esp. among the ancient Greeks and Romans. [F *odéum* or L *odeum* f. Gk *ōideion* (as ODE)]

o•di•ous /ódeeəs/ *adj.* hateful; repulsive. □□ **o•di•ous•ly** *adv.* **o•di•ous•ness** *n.* [ME f. OF *odieus* f. L *odiosus* (as ODIUM)]

o•di•um /ódeeəm/ *n.* a general or widespread dislike or reprobation incurred by a person or associated with an action. [L, = hatred f. *odi* to hate]

o•dom•e•ter /ōdómitər/ *n.* an instrument for measuring the distance traveled by a wheeled vehicle. □□ **o•dom•e•try** *n.* [F *odomètre* f. Gk *hodos* way: see –METER]

odonto- /ōdóntō/ *comb. form* tooth. [Gk *odous odont-* tooth]

o•don•to•glos•sum /ōdóntəglósəm/ *n.* any of various orchids bearing flowers with jagged edges like tooth marks. [ODONTO- + Gk *glōssa* tongue]

o•don•toid /ōd óntoyd/ *adj.* toothlike. [Gk *odontoeidēs* (as ODONTO- + Gk *eidos* form)]

o•don•toid proc•ess *n.* a projection from the second cervical vertebra.

o•don•tol•o•gy /ódontólǝjee/ *n.* the scientific study of the structure and diseases of teeth. □□ **o•don•to•log•i•cal** /–təlójikəl/ *adj.* **o•don•tol•o•gist** *n.*

o•dor /ódər/ *n.* (*Brit.* **o•dour**) **1** the property of a substance that has an effect on the nasal sense of smell. **2** a lasting quality or trace attaching to something (*an odor of intolerance*). **3** regard, repute (*in bad odor*). □□ **o•dor•less** *adj.* (in sense 1). [ME f. AF *odour*, OF *odor* f. L *odor –oris* smell, scent]

o•dor•if•er•ous /ódərífərəs/ *adj.* diffusing a scent, esp. an agreeable one; fragrant. □□ **o•dor•if•er•ous•ly** *adv.* [ME f. L *odorifer* (as ODOR)]

o•dor•ous /ódərəs/ *adj.* **1** having a scent. **2** = ODORIFEROUS. □□ **o•dor•ous•ly** *adv.* [L *odorus* fragrant (as ODOR)]

o•dour *Brit.* var. of ODOR.

od•ys•sey /ódisee/ *n.* (*pl.* **•seys**) a series of wanderings; a long adventurous journey. □□ **Od•ys•se•an** *adj.* [L *Odyssea* f. Gk *Odusseia*, title of an epic poem attributed to Homer describing the adventures of Odysseus (Ulysses) on his journey home from Troy]

OECD *abbr.* Organization for Economic Cooperation and Development.

OED *abbr.* Oxford English Dictionary.

oe•de•ma *Brit.* var. of EDEMA.

Oed•i•pus com•plex /édipəs, éedi–/ *n. Psychol.* (according to Freud, etc.) the complex of emotions aroused in a young (esp. male) child by a subconscious sexual desire for the parent of the opposite sex and by a wish to exclude the parent of the same sex. □□ **Oed•i•pal** *adj.* [Gk *Oidipous*, legendary king of Thebes who unknowingly killed his father and married his mother]

OEM *abbr.* original equipment manufacturer.

oe•nol•o•gy var. of ENOLOGY.

oe•no•phile /éenəfil/ *n.* a connoisseur of wines. □□ **oe•noph•i•list** /eenófilist/ *n.* [as ENOLOGY]

o'er /óər/ *adv. & prep. poet.* = OVER. [contr.]

oer•sted /órsted/ *n.* a unit of magnetic field strength equivalent to 79.58 amperes per meter. [H. C. *Oersted*, Da. physicist d. 1851]

oe•soph•a•gus *Brit.* var. of ESOPHAGUS.

oes•tro•gen *Brit.* var. of ESTROGEN.

oes•trus *Brit.* var. of ESTRUS.

oeu•vre /óvrə/ *n.* the works of an author, composer, painter, etc., esp. regarded collectively. [F, = work, f. L *opera*]

of /uv, ov, əv/ *prep.* connecting a noun (often a verbal noun) or pronoun with a preceding noun, adjective, adverb, or verb, expressing a wide range of relations broadly describable as follows: **1** origin, cause, or authorship (*paintings of Turner; people of Rome; died of malnutrition*). **2** the material or substance constituting or identifying a thing (*a house of cards; was built of bricks*). **3** belonging, connection, or possession (*a thing of the past; articles of clothing; the head of the business; the tip of the iceberg*). **4** identity or close relation (*the city of Rome; a pound of apples; a fool of a man*). **5** removal, separation, or privation (*north of the city; got rid of them; robbed us of $500*). **6** reference, direction, or respect (*beware of the dog; suspected of lying; very good of you; short of money; the selling of goods*). **7** objective relation (*love of music; in search of peace*). **8** partition, classification, or inclusion (*no more of that; part of the story; a friend of mine; this sort of book; some of us will stay*). **9** description, quality, or condition (*the hour of prayer; a person of tact; a girl of ten; on the point of leaving*). **10** time in relation to the following hour (*a quarter of three*). □ **be of** possess intrinsically; give rise to (*is of great interest*). **of all** designating the (nominally) least likely or expected example (*you of all people!*). **of all the nerve** (or *Brit.* **cheek**, etc.) an exclamation of indignation at a person's impudence, etc. **of an evening** (or **morning**, etc.) *colloq.* **1** on most evenings (or mornings, etc.). **2** at some time in the evenings (or mornings, etc.). **of late** recently. **of old** formerly; long ago. [OE, unaccented form of *æf*, f. Gmc]

of- /of/ *prefix* assim. form of OB- before *f.*

o•fay /ófay/ *n. US sl. offens.* a white person (esp. used by black persons). [20th c.: prob. of Afr. orig.]

off /awf/ *adv., prep., adj., & n.* ● *adv.* **1 a** away; at or to a distance (*drove off; is three miles off*). **b** distant or remote in fact, nature, likelihood, etc. **2** out of position; not on or touching or attached; loose; separate; gone (*has come off; take your coat off*). **3** so as to be rid of (*sleep it off*). **4** so as to break continuity or continuance; discontinued; stopped (*turn off the radio; take a day off; the game is off*). **5** esp. *Brit.* not available as a choice, e.g., on a menu (*swordfish is off*). **6** to the end; entirely; so as to be clear (*clear off; finish off; pay off*). **7** situated as regards money, supplies, etc. (*is badly off; is not very well off*). **8** esp. *Brit.* offstage (*noises off*). **9** esp. *Brit.* (with preceding numeral) denoting a quantity produced or made at one time (esp. one-off). **10** away or free from a regular commitment (*How about tomorrow? I'm off then*). ● *prep.* **1 a** from; away or down or up from (*fell off the chair; took something off the price; jumped off the edge*). **b** not on (*was already off the pitch*). **2 a** (temporarily) relieved of or abstaining from (*off duty; am off my diet*). **b** not attracted by for the time being (*off their food; off smoking*). **c** not achieving or doing one's best in (*off form; off one's game*). **3** using as a source or means of support (*live off the land*). **4** leading from; not far from (*a street off 1st Avenue*). **5** at a short distance to sea from (*sank off Cape Horn*). ● *adj.* **1** far, further (*the off side of the wall*). **2** (of a part of a vehicle, animal, or road) right (*the off front wheel*). **3 a** (of food, etc.) beginning to decay. **b** in error; abnormal; odd. ● *n. Brit.* the start of a race. □ **a bit off** *Brit. colloq.* **1** rather annoying or unfair. **2** somewhat unwell (*am feeling a bit off*). **off and on** intermittently; now and then. **off one's feet** see FOOT. **off form** see FORM. **off guard** see GUARD. **off of** *sl. disp.* = OFF *prep.* (*picked it off of the floor*). **off the record** see RECORD. **off the point** *adj.* irrelevant. ● *adv.* irrelevantly. [orig. var. of OF, to distinguish the sense]

▶Avoid using the redundant colloquialisms *off of*, *from off*, or *off from*. Say, "The paperweight rolled off the desk" (not "off of the desk") or "I bought the car from my uncle" (not "from off my uncle").

off. *abbr.* **1** office. **2** officer.

of•fal /áwfəl, óf–/ *n.* **1** the less valuable edible parts of a carcass, esp. the entrails and internal organs. **2** refuse or waste stuff. **3** carrion; putrid flesh. [ME f. MDu. *afval* f. *af* OFF + *vallen* FALL]

off•beat *adj. & n.* ● *adj.* /áwfb eét, óf–/ **1** not coinciding with the beat. **2** eccentric; unconventional. ● *n.* /ófbeet/ any of the unaccented beats in a bar.

off-cen•ter *adj.* not quite coinciding with a central position.

off chance *n.* a slight possibility.

off-col•or *adj.* **1** somewhat indecent. **2** *Brit.* not in good health.

off day *n.* a day when one is not at one's best.

off•cut /áwfkut, óf–/ *n.* esp. *Brit.* a remnant of lumber, paper, etc., after cutting.

of•fence *Brit.* var. of OFFENSE .

of•fend /əfénd/ *v.* **1** *tr.* cause offense to or resentment in; wound the feelings of. **2** *tr.* displease or anger. **3** *intr.* (often foll. by *against*) do wrong; transgress. □□ **of•fend•ed•ly** *adv.* **of•fend•er** *n.* **of•fend•ing** *adj.* [ME f. OF *offendre* f. L (as OFFENSE)]

of•fense /əféns/ *n.* (*Brit.* **of•fence**) **1** an illegal act; a transgression or misdemeanor. **2** a wounding of the feelings; resentment or um-

---

WORD HISTORY **offense**

Late Middle English: from Old French *offens* 'misdeed,' from Latin *offensus* 'annoyance,' reinforced by French *offense*, from Latin *offensa* 'a striking against, a hurt, or displeasure'; based on Latin *offendere* 'strike against.'

brage (*no offense was meant*). **3** /áwfens, óf–/ the act of attacking or taking the offensive; aggressive action. **4** /áwfens, óf–/ *Sports* the team in possession of the ball, puck, etc. □ **give offense** cause hurt feelings. **take offense** suffer hurt feelings. □□ **of·fense·less** *adj.*

of·fen·sive /əfénsiv/ *adj. & n.* ● *adj.* **1** giving or meant or likely to give offense; insulting (*offensive language*). **2** disgusting, foul-smelling, nauseous, repulsive. **3 a** aggressive, attacking. **b** (of a weapon) meant for use in attack. **4** *Sports* designating the team in possession of the ball, puck, etc. ● *n.* **1** an aggressive action or attitude (*take the offensive*). **2** an attack; an offensive campaign or stroke. **3** aggressive or forceful action in pursuit of a cause (*a peace offensive*). □□ **of·fen·sive·ly** *adv.* **of·fen·sive·ness** *n.* [F *offensif –ive* or med.L *offensivus* (as OFFENSE)]

SYNONYM TIP offensive

ABHORRENT, ABOMINABLE, DETESTABLE, ODIOUS, REPUGNANT. Looking for just the right word to express your dislike, distaste, disgust, or aversion to something? **Offensive** is a relatively mild adjective, used to describe anyone or anything that is unpleasant or disagreeable (*she found his remarks offensive; the offensive sight of an open kitty litter box*). If you want to express strong dislike for someone or something that deserves to be disliked, use **detestable** (*a detestable man who never had a kind word for anyone*). If something is so **offensive** that it provokes a physical as well as a moral or intellectual response, use **odious** (*the odious treatment of women during the war in Bosnia*), and if you instinctively draw back from it, use **repugnant** (*the very thought of piercing one's nose was repugnant to her*). If your **repugnance** is extreme, go one step further and use **abhorrent** (*an abhorrent act that could not go unpunished*). Save **abominable** for persons and things that are truly loathsome or terrifying (*an abominable act of desecration; abominable taste in clothes; the Abominable Snowman*).

of·fer /áwfər, óf–/ *v. & n.* ● *v.* **1** *tr.* present for acceptance or refusal or consideration (*offered me a drink; was offered a ride; offer one's services; offer no apology*). **2** *intr.* (foll. by *to* + infin.) express readiness or show intention (*offered to take the children*). **3** *tr.* provide; give an opportunity for. **4** *tr.* make available for sale. **5** *tr.* (of a thing) present to one's attention or consideration (*each day offers new opportunities*). **6** *tr.* present (a sacrifice, prayer, etc.) to a deity. **7** *intr.* present itself; occur (*as opportunity offers*). **8** *tr.* give an opportunity for (battle) to an enemy. **9** *tr.* attempt, or try to show (violence, resistance, etc.). ● *n.* **1** an expression of readiness to do or give if desired, or to buy or sell (for a certain amount). **2** an amount offered. **3** a proposal (esp. of marriage). **4** a bid. □ **on offer** *Brit.* for sale at a certain (esp. reduced) price. □□ **of·fer·er** *n.* **of·fer·or** *n.* [OE *offrian* in religious sense, f. L *offerre* (as OB–, *ferre* bring)]

of·fer·ing /áwfəring, óf–/ *n.* **1** a contribution, esp. of money, to a church. **2** a thing offered as a religious sacrifice or token of devotion. **3** anything, esp. money, contributed or offered.

of·fer·to·ry /áwfərtawree, óf–/ *n.* (*pl.* **·ries**) **1** *Eccl.* **a** the offering of the bread and wine at the Eucharist. **b** an anthem accompanying this. **2 a** the collection of money at a religious service. **b** the money collected. [ME f. eccl.L *offertorium* offering f. LL *offert-* for L *oblat-* past part. stem of *offerre* OFFER]

off·hand /áwfhánd, óf–/ *adj. & adv.* ● *adj.* curt or casual in manner. ● *adv.* **1** in an offhand manner. **2** without preparation or premeditation. □□ **off·hand·ed** *adj.* **off·hand·ed·ly** *adv.* **off·hand·ed·ness** *n.*

of·fice /áwfis, óf–/ *n.* **1** a room or building used as a place of business, esp. for clerical or administrative work. **2** a room or department or building for a particular kind of business (*ticket office; post office*). **3** the local center of a large business (*our Honolulu office*). **4** the consulting room of a professional person. **5** a position with duties attached to it; a place of authority or trust or service, esp. of a public nature. **6** tenure of an official position, esp. that of government (*hold office; out of office for 13 years*). **7** (**Office**) *Brit.* the quarters or staff or collective authority of a government department, etc. (*Foreign Office*). **8** a duty attaching to one's position; a task or function. **9** (usu. in *pl.*) a piece of kindness or attention; a service (esp. *through the good offices of*). **10** *Eccl.* **a** an authorized form of worship (*Office for the Dead*). **b** (in full **divine office**) the daily service of the Roman Catholic breviary (*say the office*). **11** a ceremonial duty. **12** (in *pl.*) *Brit.* the parts of a house devoted to household work, storage, etc. **13** *sl.* a hint or signal. [ME f. OF f. L *officium* performance of a task (in med.L also office, divine service), f. *opus* work + *facere* fic– do]

of·fice block *n. Brit.* a large building designed to contain business offices.

of·fice boy *n.* (also **of·fice girl**) a young man (or woman) employed to do minor jobs in a business office.

of·fice hours *n.* the hours during which business is normally conducted.

of·fice park *n.* a commercial property with usu. several office buildings situated in or near a parklike setting.

of·fi·cer /áwfisər, óf–/ *n. & v.* ● *n.* **1** a person holding a position of

authority or trust, esp. one with a commission in the armed services, in the merchant marine, or on a passenger ship. **2** a policeman or policewoman. **3** a holder of a post in a society or business enterprise (e.g., the president or secretary). **4** a holder of a public, civil, or ecclesiastical office; a sovereign's minister; an appointed or elected functionary (usu. with a qualifying word: *medical officer; probation officer; returning officer*). **5** a bailiff (*the sheriff's officer*). **6** a member of the grade below commander in the Order of the British Empire, etc. ● *v.tr.* **1** provide with officers. **2** act as the commander of. [ME f. AF *officer*, OF *officier* f. med.L *officiarius* f. L *officium*: see OFFICE]

of·fi·cer of arms *n.* a herald or pursuivant.

of·fice work·er *n.* an employee in a business office.

of·fi·cial /əfíshəl/ *adj. & n.* ● *adj.* **1** of or relating to an office (see OFFICE *n.* 5, 6) or its tenure or duties. **2** characteristic of officials and bureaucracy. **3** emanating from or attributable to a person in office; properly authorized. **4** holding office; employed in a public capacity. **5** *Med.* according to the pharmacopoeia; officinal. ● *n.* **1** a person holding office or engaged in official duties. **2** *Brit.* (in full **official principal**) the presiding officer or judge of an archbishop's, bishop's, or esp. archdeacon's court. □□ **of·fi·cial·dom** *n.* **of·fi·cial·ism** *n.* **of·fi·cial·ly** *adv.* [ME (as noun) f. OF f. L *officialis* (as OFFICE)]

of·fi·cial birth·day *n. Brit.* a day in June chosen for the observance of the sovereign's birthday.

of·fi·cial·ese /əfíshəleéz/ *n. derog.* the formal precise language characteristic of official documents.

of·fi·cial se·crets *n.pl. Brit.* confidential information involving national security.

of·fi·ci·ant /əfíshənt/ *n.* a person who officiates at a religious ceremony.

of·fi·ci·ate /əfísheeáyt/ *v.intr.* **1** act in an official capacity, esp. on a particular occasion. **2** perform a divine service or ceremony. □□ **of·fi·ci·a·tion** /–áyshən/ *n.* **of·fi·ci·a·tor** *n.* [med.L *officiare* perform a divine service (*officium*): see OFFICE]

of·fic·i·nal /əfísinəl/ *adj.* **1 a** (of a medicine) kept ready for immediate dispensing. **b** made from the pharmacopoeia recipe (cf. MAGISTRAL). **c** (of a name) adopted in the pharmacopoeia. **2** (of an herb or drug) used in medicine. □□ **of·fic·i·nal·ly** *adv.* [med.L *officinalis* f. L *officina* workshop]

of·fi·cious /əfíshəs/ *adj.* **1** asserting one's authority aggressively; domineering. **2** intrusive or excessively enthusiastic in offering help, etc.; meddlesome. **3** *Diplomacy* informal, unofficial. □□ **of·fi·cious·ly** *adv.* **of·fi·cious·ness** *n.* [L *officiosus* obliging f. *officium*: see OFFICE]

off·ing /áwfing, óf–/ *n.* the more distant part of the sea in view. □ **in the offing** not far away; likely to appear or happen soon. [perh. f. OFF + –ING[1]]

off·ish /áwfish, óf–/ *adj. colloq.* inclined to be aloof. □□ **off·ish·ly** *adv.* **off·ish·ness** *n.* [OFF: cf. *uppish*]

off-key *adj. & adv.* **1** out of tune. **2** not quite suitable or fitting.

off-li·cence *n. Brit.* a shop selling alcoholic drink for consumption elsewhere.

off limits *adj.* not to be frequented or used, out of bounds.

off-line *adj. Computing* (of a computer terminal or process) not directly controlled by or connected to a central processor.

off-load *v.* = UNLOAD.

off-peak *adj. & adv.* used or for use at times other than those of greatest demand.

off-price /áwfprís, óf–/ *adj.* involving merchandise sold at a lower price than that recommended by the manufacturer.

off·print /áwfprint, óf–/ *n.* a printed copy of an article, etc., originally forming part of a larger publication.

off-put·ting *adj.* disconcerting; repellent. □□ **off-put·ting·ly** *adv.*

off-road *attrib.adj.* **1** away from the road, on rough terrain. **2** (of a vehicle, etc.) designed for rough terrain or for cross-country driving.

off-road·ing *n.* driving on dirt tracks and other unpaved surfaces as a sport or leisure activity. □□ **off-road·er** *n.*

off-screen /áwfskr eén, óf–/ *adj. & adv.* ● *adj.* not appearing on a movie, television, or computer screen. ● *adv.* **1** without use of a screen. **2** outside the view presented by a filmed scene.

off-sea·son *n.* (also **off-sea·son** or **off sea·son**) a time when business, etc., is slack.

off·set *n. & v.* ● *n.* /áwfset, óf–/ **1** a side shoot from a plant serving for propagation. **2** an offshoot or scion. **3** a compensation; a consideration or amount diminishing or neutralizing the effect of a contrary one. **4** *Archit.* a sloping ledge in a wall, etc., where the thickness of the part above is diminished. **5** a mountain spur. **6** a bend in a pipe, etc., to carry it past an obstacle. **7** (often *attrib.*) a method of printing in which ink is transferred from a plate or stone to a uniform rubber surface and from there to paper, etc. (*offset* *lithography*). **8** *Surveying* a short distance measured perpendicularly from the main line of measurement. ● *v. tr.* /áwfsét, óf–/ (**·set·ting**; *past* and *past part.* **·set**) **1** counterbalance, compensate. **2** place out of line. **3** print by the offset process.

off·shoot /áwfshoot, óf–/ *n.* **1 a** a side shoot or branch. **b** a collateral branch or descendant of a family. **2** something derivative.

off·shore /áwfsháwr, óf–/ *adj.* **1** situated at sea some distance from the shore. **2** (of the wind) blowing seaward. **3** (of goods, funds, etc.) made or registered abroad.

off·side *adj. & n.* ● *adj.* /áwfsíd, óf–/ *Sports* (of a player in a field game or ice hockey) in a position, usu. ahead of the ball, that is not allowed if it affects play. ● *n.* /áwfsíd, óf–/ (often *attrib.*) esp. *Brit.* the right side of a vehicle, animal, etc.

off·sid·er /awfsídər, of–/ *n.* *Austral. colloq.* a partner, assistant, or deputy.

off·spring /áwfspring, óf–/ *n.* (*pl.* same) **1** a person's child or children or descendant(s). **2** an animal's young or descendant(s). **3** a result. [OE *ofspring* f. OF from + *springan* SPRING *v.*]

off·stage /áwfstayj, óf–/ *adj. & adv.* *Theatr.* not on the stage and so not visible to the audience.

off-the-cuff *adj. colloq.* without preparation; spontaneous.

off-the-rack *adj.* (of clothes) ready-made.

off the wall *adj.* see WALL.

off time *n.* a time when business, etc., is slack.

off-white *n.* white with a gray or yellowish tinge.

oft /awft, oft/ *adv. archaic* or *literary* often (usu. in *comb.*: *oft-recurring*). [OE]

of·ten /áwfən, áwftən, óf–/ *adv.* (**of·ten·er, of·ten·est**) **1 a** frequently; many times. **b** at short intervals. **2** in many instances. □ **as often as not** in roughly half the instances. [ME: extended f. OFT, prob. after *selden* = SELDOM]

of·ten·times /áwfəntimz, óf–/ *adv.* (also **oft·times**) often.

og·am var. of OGHAM.

og·do·ad /ógdō-ad/ *n.* a group of eight. [LL *ogdoas ogdoad-* f. Gk *ogdoas –ados* f. *ogdoos* eighth f. *oktō* eight]

o·gee /ōjée, ōjee/ *adj. & n. Archit.* ● *adj.* showing in section a double continuous S-shaped curve. ● *n.* an S-shaped line or molding. □□ **o·gee'd** *adj.* [app. f. OGIVE, as being the usu. molding in groin ribs]

o·gee arch *n.* an arch with two ogee curves meeting at the apex.

og·ham /ógəm, áw–/ *n.* (also **og·am**) **1** an ancient British and Irish alphabet of twenty characters formed by parallel strokes on either side of or across a continuous line. **2** an inscription in this alphabet. **3** each of its characters. [OIr. *ogam*, referred to the Irish god *Ogma*, its supposed inventor]

o·give /ōjīv, ōjív/ *n.* **1** a pointed or Gothic arch. **2** one of the diagonal groins or ribs of a vault. **3** an S-shaped line. **4** *Statistics* a cumulative frequency graph. □□ **o·gi·val** *adj.* [ME f. F, of unkn. orig.]

o·gle /ōgəl/ *v. & n.* ● *v.* **1** *tr.* eye amorously or lecherously. **2** *intr.* look amorously. ● *n.* an amorous or lecherous look. □□ **o·gler** *n.* [prob. LG or Du.: cf. LG *oegeln*, frequent. of *oegen* look at]

o·gre /ógər/ *n.* (*fem.* **o·gress** /ógris/) **1** a human-eating giant in folklore, etc. **2** a terrifying person. □□ **o·gre·ish** *adj.* (also **o·grish**). [F, first used by Perrault in 1697, of unkn. orig.]

OH *abbr.* Ohio (in official postal use).

oh[1] /ō/ *int.* (also **O**) expressing surprise, pain, entreaty, etc. (*oh, what a mess; oh for a holiday*). □ **oh boy** expressing surprise, excitement, etc. **oh well** expressing resignation. [var. of O[4]]

oh[2] /ō/ *n.* = O[1] (sense 2).

o.h.c. *abbr.* overhead camshaft.

ohm /ōm/ *n. Electr.* the SI unit of resistance, transmitting a current of one ampere when subjected to a potential difference of one volt. ¶ Symb.: Ω. □□ **ohm·age** *n.* [G. S. *Ohm*, Ger. physicist d. 1854]

ohm·me·ter /óm-meetər/ *n.* an instrument for measuring electrical resistance.

OHMS *abbr.* on Her (or His) Majesty's Service.

Ohm's law /ōmz/ *n. Electr.* a law stating that current is proportional to voltage and inversely proportional to resistance. [see OHM]

oho /ōhō/ *int.* expressing surprise or exultation. [ME f. O[4] + HO]

–oholic var. of –AHOLIC.

o·hone var. of OCHONE.

oi var. of OY.

-oid /oyd/ *suffix* forming adjectives and nouns, denoting form or resemblance (*asteroid; rhomboid; thyroid*). □□ **-oidal** *suffix* forming adjectives. **-oidally** *suffix* forming adverbs. [mod.L *-oides* f. Gk *-oeidēs* f. *eidos* form]

o·id·i·um /ō-ídeeəm/ *n.* (*pl.* **o·id·i·a** /–eeə/) spores formed by the breaking up of fungal hyphae into cells. [mod.L f. Gk *ōion* egg + *–idion* dimin. suffix]

oil /oyl/ *n. & v.* ● *n.* **1** any of various thick, viscous, usu. flammable liquids insoluble in water but soluble in organic solvents (see also ESSENTIAL OIL, FIXED OIL, MINERAL OIL, VOLATILE OIL). **2** petroleum. **3** using oil as fuel (*oil heater*). **4 a** (usu. in *pl.*) = OIL PAINT. **b** *colloq.* a picture painted in oil paints. **5** (in *pl.*) = OILSKIN. ● *v.* **1** *tr.* apply oil to; lubricate. **2** *tr.* impregnate or treat with oil (*oiled silk*). **3** *tr. & intr.* supply with or take on oil as fuel. **4** *tr. & intr.* make (butter, grease, etc.) into or (of butter, etc.) become an oily liquid. □ **oil a person's palm** (or **hand**) bribe a person. **oil the wheels** help make things go smoothly. **well-oiled 1** operating smoothly. **2** *colloq.* drunk. □□ **oil·less** *adj.* [ME *oli, oile* f. AF, ONF *olie* = OF *oile*, etc. f. L *oleum* (olive) oil f. *olea* olive]

oil·bird /óylbərd/ *n.* n.a. a guacharo.

oil cake *n.* a mass of compressed linseed, etc., left after oil has been extracted, used as fodder or manure.

oil·can /óylkan/ *n.* a can containing oil, esp. one with a long spout for oiling machinery.

oil·cloth /óylklawth, –kloth/ *n.* **1** a fabric waterproofed with oil. **2** an oilskin. **3** a canvas coated with linseed or other oil and used to cover a table or floor.

oiled silk *n.* silk made waterproof with oil.

oil·er /óylər/ *n.* **1** an oilcan for oiling machinery. **2** an oil tanker. **3 a** an oil well. **b** (in *pl.*) oilskin.

oil-fired *adj.* using oil as fuel.

oil lamp *n.* a lamp using oil as fuel.

oil·man /óylmən/ *n.* (*pl.* **·men**) a person who deals in oil.

oil meal *n.* ground oil cake.

oil of juniper *n.* oil from juniper cones used in medicine and in flavoring gin, etc.

oil of turpentine *n.* a volatile pungent oil distilled from turpentine, used in mixing paints and varnishes, and in medicine.

oil of vit·ri·ol *n.* concentrated sulfuric acid.

oil paint *n.* (also **oil col·or**) a mix of ground color pigment and oil.

oil paint·ing *n.* **1** the art of painting in oil paints. **2** a picture painted in oil paints.

oil palm *n.* either of two trees, *Elaeis guineensis* of W. Africa, or *E. oleifera* of the US, from which palm oil is extracted.

oil pan *n.* the bottom section of an internal combustion engine's crankcase.

oil·pa·per /óylpáypər/ *n.* a paper made transparent or waterproof by soaking in oil.

oil press *n.* an apparatus for pressing oil from seeds, etc.

oil rig *n.* esp. *Brit.* = DRILL RIG.

oil sand *n.* a stratum of porous rock yielding petroleum.

oil·seed /óylseed/ *n.* any of various seeds from cultivated crops yielding oil, e.g., rape, peanut, or cotton.

oil shale *n.* a fine-grained rock from which oil can be extracted.

oil·skin /óylskin/ *n.* **1** cloth waterproofed with oil. **2 a** a garment made of this. **b** (in *pl.*) a suit made of this.

oil slick *n.* a smooth patch of oil, esp. one on the sea.

oil·stone /óylstōn/ *n.* a fine-grained flat stone used with oil for sharpening flat tools, e.g., chisels, planes, etc. (cf. WHETSTONE).

oil tank·er *n.* a ship designed to carry oil in bulk.

oil well *n.* a well from which petroleum is drawn.

oil·y /óylee/ *adj.* (**oil·i·er, oil·i·est**) **1** of, like, or containing much oil. **2** covered or soaked with oil. **3** (of a manner, etc.) fawning, insinuating, unctuous. □□ **oil·i·ly** *adv.* **oil·i·ness** *n.*

oink /oyngk/ *v. intr.* (of a pig) make its characteristic grunt. [imit.]

oint·ment /óyntmənt/ *n.* a smooth greasy healing or cosmetic preparation for the skin. [ME *oignement, ointment,* f. OF *oignement* ult. f. L (as UNGUENT): *oint-* after obs. *oint* anoint f. OF, past part. of *oindre* ANOINT]

Oir·each·tas /awráwkhtəs/ *n.* the legislature of the Irish Republic: the president, the Dáil, and the Seanad. [Ir.]

O·jib·wa /ōjíbway/ *n. & adj.* ● *n.* **1 a** a N. American people native to Canada and the eastern and central northern United States. **b** a member of this people. **2** the language of this people. ● *adj.* of or relating to this people or their language. Also called **Chippewa**.

OK[1] /ōkáy/ *adj., adv., n., & v.* (also **o·kay**) *colloq.* ● *adj.* (often as *int.* expressing agreement or acquiescence) all right; satisfactory. ● *adv.* well; satisfactorily (*that worked out OK*). ● *n.* (*pl.* **OKs**) approval, sanction. ● *v. tr.* (**OK's, OK'd, OK'ing**) give an OK to; approve, sanction.

OK[2] *abbr.* Oklahoma (in official postal use).

o·ka·pi /ōkáapee/ *n.* (*pl.* same or **o·ka·pis**) a ruminant mammal, *Okapia johnstoni*, native to N. and NE Zaïre, with a head resembling that of a giraffe and a body resembling that of a zebra, having a dark chestnut coat and transverse stripes on the hindquarters and upper legs only. [Mbuba]

o•kay var. of OK[1].

o•key-doke /ṓkeedṓk/ *adj. & adv.* (also **o•key•do•key** /-dṓkee/) *sl.* = OK[1]. [redupl.]

Okla. *abbr.* Oklahoma.

o•kra /ṓkrə/ *n.* **1** a malvaceous African plant, *Abelmoschus esculentus,* yielding long ridged seedpods. **2** the seedpods eaten as a vegetable and used to thicken soups and stews. Also called **gumbo**. [W.Afr. native name]

-ol[1] /awl, ol/ *suffix Chem.* the termination of *alcohol,* used in names of alcohols or analogous compounds (*methanol; phenol*).

-ol[2] /ol/ *comb. form* = -OLE. [L *oleum* oil]

old /ōld/ *adj.* (**old•er, old•est**) (cf. ELDER, ELDEST). **1 a** advanced in age; far on in the natural period of existence. **b** not young or near its beginning. **2** made long ago. **3** long in use. **4** worn or dilapidated or shabby from the passage of time. **5** having the characteristics (experience, feebleness, etc.) of age (*the child has an old face*). **6** practiced, inveterate (*an old offender; old in crime*). **7** belonging only or chiefly to the past; lingering on; former (*old times; haunted by old memories*). **8** dating from far back; long established or known; ancient; primeval (*old as the hills; old friends; an old family*). **9** (appended to a period of time) of age (*is four years old; a four-year-old boy; a four-year-old*). **10** (of language) as used in former or earliest times. **11** *colloq.* as a term of affection or casual reference (*good old Charlie; old shipmate; wants his old job back*). **12** the former or first of two or more similar things (*our old house; wants his old job back*). □ **an old one** a familiar joke. □□ **old•ish** *adj.* **old•ness** *n.* [OE *ald* f. WG]

▶**Older vs. Oldest.** Where two, and no more, are involved, they may be **older** and **younger:** *The older of the twins, by ten minutes, is Sam; the younger is Pamela.* Where there are more than two, one may be the *oldest* or *youngest: I have four siblings, of whom Jane is the oldest.*

SYNONYM TIP old

AGED, ANCIENT, ANTEDILUVIAN, ANTIQUATED, ARCHAIC, OBSOLETE. No one likes to be thought of as **old,** which means having been in existence or use for a relatively long time (*an old washing machine*). But those who are **aged,** indicating a longer life span than *old* and usually referring to persons of very advanced years, are often proud of the fact that they have outlived most of their peers. Children may exaggerate and regard their parents as **ancient,** which very often means dating back to the remote past, specifically the time before the end of the Roman Empire (*ancient history*), and their attitudes as **antediluvian,** which literally means dating back to the period before the biblical Great Flood and Noah's ark (*an antediluvian transportation system*), even though the parents in question have barely reached middle age. Some people seem older than they really are, simply because their ideas are **antiquated,** which means out of vogue or no longer practiced (*antiquated ideas about dating*). Things rather than people are usually described as **archaic,** which means having the characteristics of an earlier, sometimes primitive, period (*archaic words like "thou" and "thine"*). **Obsolete** also refers to things, implying that they have gone out of use or need to be replaced by something newer (*an obsolete textbook; a machine that will be obsolete within the decade*).

---

old age *n.* the later part of normal life.

Old Bai•ley *n.* the Central Criminal Court in London.

Old Bill *n. Brit. sl.* the police.

old bird *n.* a wary person.

old boy *n.* **1** *Brit.* a former male pupil of a school. **2** *colloq.* **a** an elderly man. **b** an affectionate form of address to a boy or man.

old-boy net•work *n.* preferment in employment of those from a similar social background, esp. fellow alumni.

Old Church Sla•von•ic *n.* the Slavic language of *c.* 800 –1000, as found in the Biblical translations of Cyril and Methodius.

old coun•try *n.* the native country of colonists, etc.

old•en /ṓldən/ *adj. archaic* of old; of a former age (esp. in olden times).

Old Eng•lish *n.* the English language up to *c.* 1150.

old-fash•ioned *adj.* in or according to a fashion or tastes no longer current; antiquated.

Old French *n.* the French language of the period before *c.*1400.

old fustic *n.* **1** a tropical tree, *Chlorophora tinctoria,* native to America. **2** the wood of this tree.

old girl *n.* **1** *colloq.* **a** an elderly woman. **b** an affectionate term of address to a girl or woman. **2** *Brit.* a former female pupil of a school.

Old Glo•ry *n.* the US national flag.

old gold *n.* a dull brownish-gold color.

old guard *n.* the original or past or conservative members of a group.

old hand *n.* a person with much experience.

old hat *n. & adj. colloq.* ● *adj.* tediously familiar or out-of-date. ● *n.* something tediously familiar or out-of-date.

Old High Ger•man *n.* High German (see GERMAN) up to *c.*1200.

old•ie /ṓldee/ *n. colloq.* an old person or thing.

old la•dy *n. colloq.* one's mother or wife.

old lag *n. Brit.* see LAG[3].

old maid *n.* **1** *derog.* an elderly unmarried woman. **2** a prim and fussy person. **3** a card game in which players try not to be left with an unpaired queen.

old-maid•ish *adj.* like an old maid.

old man *n. colloq.* **1** one's husband or father. **2** one's employer or other person in authority over one. **3** esp. *Brit.* an affectionate form of address to a boy or man.

old-man's beard *n.* a wild clematis, *Clematis vitalba,* with gray fluffy hairs around the seeds. Also called **traveler's-joy.**

old mas•ter *n.* **1** a great artist of former times, esp. of the 13th–17th c. in Europe. **2** a painting by such a master.

old moon *n.* the moon in its last quarter, before the new moon.

Old Nick *n.* the Devil.

Old Norse *n.***1** the Germanic language from which the Scandinavian languages are derived. **2** the language of Norway and its colonies until the 14th c.

Old Pre•tend•er *n.* James Stuart (1688–1766), son of James II and claimant to the British throne.

Old Prussian *n.* the language spoken in Prussia until the 17th c.

old school *n.* (usu. **of** or **from the old school**) **1** traditional attitudes. **2** people having such attitudes.

old school tie *n.*esp. *Brit.* **1** a necktie with a characteristic pattern worn by the pupils of a particular school. **2** the principle of excessive loyalty to traditional values.

old sol•dier *n.* an experienced person, esp. in an arduous activity.

old stag•er *n.* an experienced person, an old hand.

old•ster /ṓldstər/ *n.* an old person. [OLD + -STER, after *youngster*]

old style *n.* of a date reckoned by the Julian calendar.

Old Tes•ta•ment *n.* the part of the Christian Bible containing the scriptures of the Hebrews.

old-time *adj.* belonging to former times.

old-tim•er *n.* a person with long experience or standing.

old wives' tale *n.* a foolish or unscientific tradition or belief.

old wom•an *n. colloq.* **1** one's wife or mother. **2** a fussy or timid man.

old-wom•an•ish *adj.* fussy and timid.

Old World *n.* Europe, Asia, and Africa.

old-world *adj.* belonging to or associated with old times.

-ole /ōl/ *comb. form* forming names of esp. heterocyclic compounds (*indole*). [L *oleum* oil]

o•le•a•ceous /ōleeáyshəs/ *adj.* of the plant family Oleaceae, including olive and jasmine. [mod.L *Oleaceae* f. L *olea* olive tree]

o•le•ag•i•nous /ōleeájinəs/ *adj.* **1** having the properties of or producing oil. **2** oily, greasy. **3** obsequious, ingratiating. [F *oléagineux* f. L *oleaginus* f. *oleum* oil]

o•le•an•der /ṓleeándər/ *n.* an evergreen poisonous shrub, *Nerium oleander,* native to the Mediterranean and bearing clusters of white, pink, or red flowers. [med.L]

o•le•as•ter /ṓleeástər/ *n.* any of various trees of the genus *Elaeagnus,* often thorny and with evergreen leathery foliage, esp. *E. angustifolia* bearing olive-shaped yellowish fruits. Also called **Russian olive.** [ME f. L f. *olea* olive tree: see -ASTER]

o•lec•ra•non /ōlékrənon, ṓlikráynən/ *n.* a bony prominence on the upper end of the ulna at the elbow. [Gk *ōle(no)kranon* f. *ōlenē* elbow + *kranion* head]

o•le•fin /ṓlifin/ *n.* (also **o•le•fine**) *Chem.* = ALKENE. [F *oléfiant* oil-forming (with ref. to oily ethylene dichloride)]

o•le•ic ac•id /ōleéik/ *n.* an unsaturated fatty acid present in many fats and soaps. □□ **o•le•ate** /ṓleeət/ *n.* [L *oleum* oil]

o•le•if•er•ous /ṓleeífərəs/ *adj.* yielding oil. [L *oleum* oil + -FEROUS]

oleo- /ṓleeō/ *comb. form* oil. [L *oleum* oil]

o•le•o•graph /ṓleeəgraf/ *n.* a print made to resemble an oil painting.

o•le•o•mar•ga•rine /ṓleeōmaárjərin/ *n.* **1** a margarine made from vegetable oils. **2** a fatty substance extracted from beef fat and used in margarine.

o•le•om•e•ter /ṓleeómitər/ *n.* an instrument for determining the density and purity of oils.

o•le•o•res•in /ṓleeōrézin/ *n.* a natural or artificial mixture of essential oils and a resin, e.g., balsam.

o•le•um /ṓleeəm/ *n.* concentrated sulfuric acid containing excess sulfur trioxide in solution forming a dense corrosive liquid. [L, = oil]

ol•fac•tion /olfákshən, ōl-/ *n.* the act or capacity of smelling; the sense of smell. □□ **ol•fac•tive** *adj.* [L *olfactus* a smell f. *olēre* to smell + *facere* fact- make]

ol•fac•to•ry /olfáktəree, ōl-/ *adj.* of or relating to the sense of smell (*olfactory nerves*). [L *olfactare* frequent. of *olfacere* (as OLFACTION)]

o•lib•a•num /ōlíbənəm/ *n.* an aromatic gum resin from any tree of the genus *Boswellia,* used as incense. [ME f. med.L f. LL *libanus* f. Gk *libanos* frankincense, of Semitic orig.]

ol•i•garch /óligaark, óli-/ *n.* a member of an oligarchy. [Gk *oligarkhēs* f. *oligoi* few + *arkhō* to rule]

ol·i·gar·chy /óligaarkee, óli–/ n. (pl. **·chies**) **1** government by a small group of people. **2** a nation governed in this way. **3** the members of such a government. □□ **ol·i·gar·chic** /–gaárkik/ adj. **ol·i·gar·chi·cal** adj. **ol·i·gar·chi·cal·ly** adv. [F oligarchie or med.L oligarchia f. Gk oligarkhia (as OLIGARCH)]
▶See note at ARISTOCRACY.

oligo- /óligō, óli–/ comb. form few, slight. [Gk oligos small, oligoi few]

Ol·i·go·cene /óligəseen, óli–/ adj. & n. Geol. adj. of or relating to the third epoch of the Tertiary period, with evidence of the first primates. • n. this epoch or system. [as OLIGO- + Gk kainos new]

ol·i·gop·o·ly /óligópəlee, óli–/ n. (pl. **·lies**) a state of limited competition between a small number of producers or sellers. □□ **ol·i·gop·o·list** n. **ol·i·gop·o·lis·tic** /–lístik/ adj. [OLIGO-, after MONOPOLY]

ol·i·go·sac·cha·ride /óligōsákərīd, óli–/ n. any carbohydrate whose molecules are composed of a relatively small number of monosaccharide units.

ol·i·go·troph·ic /óligōtrófik, –tróf–, óli–/ adj. (of a lake, etc.) relatively poor in plant nutrients. □□ **ol·i·got·ro·phy** /–igótrəfee/ n.

o·li·o /óleeō/ n. (pl. **·os**) **1** a mixed dish; a stew of various meats and vegetables. **2** a hodgepodge or miscellany. [Sp. olla stew f. L olla cooking pot]

ol·i·va·ceous /óliváyshəs/ adj. olive-green; of a dusky yellowish green.

ol·i·va·ry /óliveree/ adj. Anat. olive-shaped; oval. [L olivarius (as OLIVE)]

ol·ive /óliv/ n. & adj. • n. **1** (in full **olive tree**) any evergreen tree of the genus Olea, having dark-green, lance-shaped leathery leaves with silvery undersides, esp. O. europaea of the Mediterranean, and O. africana native to S. Africa. **2** the small oval fruit of this, having a hard stone and bitter flesh, green when unripe and bluish-black when ripe. **3** (in full **olive-green**) the grayish-green color of an unripe olive. **4** the wood of the olive tree. **5** Anat. each of a pair of olive-shaped swellings in the medulla oblongata. **6 a** any olive-shaped gastropod of the genus Oliva. **b** the shell of this. **7** Brit. a slice of beef or veal made into a roll with stuffing inside and stewed. • adj. **1** colored like an unripe olive. **2** (of the complexion) yellowish-brown, sallow. [ME f. OF f. L oliva f. Gk elaia f. elaion oil]

ol·ive branch n. **1** the branch of an olive tree as a symbol of peace. **2** a gesture of reconciliation or friendship.

ol·ive drab n. the dull olive color of US Army uniforms.

ol·ive oil n. an oil extracted from olives used esp. in cookery.

ol·i·vine /óliveen/ n. Mineral. a naturally occurring form of magnesium-iron silicate, usu. olive-green and found in igneous rocks.

ol·la po·dri·da /óləpədréedə, ólyə/ n. = OLIO. [Sp., lit. 'rotten pot' (as OLIO + L putridus: cf. PUTRID]

Ol·mec /ólmek, ól–/ n. & adj. • n. **1** a N. American people native to the Gulf coast of Mexico. **2** a member of this people. • adj. of or relating to this people.

-ology /ólәjee/ comb. form see –LOGY.

o·lo·ro·so /ōlərōsō/ n. (pl. **·sos**) a heavy dark medium-sweet sherry. [Sp., lit. 'fragrant']

O·lym·pi·ad /ólimpeead/ n. **1 a** a period of four years between Olympic games, used by the ancient Greeks in dating events. **b** a celebration of the ancient Olympic Games held every four years in Greece. **2** a celebration of the modern Olympic Games. **3** a regular international contest in chess, etc. [ME f. F Olympiade f. L Olympias Olympiad- f. Gk Olumpias Olumpiad- f. Olumpios: see OLYMPIAN, OLYMPIC]

O·lym·pi·an /əlímpeeən, ōlím–/ adj. & n. • adj. **1 a** of or associated with Mount Olympus in NE Greece, traditionally the home of the Greek gods. **b** celestial; godlike. **2** (of manners, etc.) magnificent; condescending; superior. **3 a** of or relating to ancient Olympia in S. Greece. **b** = OLYMPIC. • n. **1** any of the pantheon of twelve gods regarded as living on Olympus. **2** a person of great attainments or of superhuman calm and detachment. [L Olympus or Olympia: see OLYMPIC]

O·lym·pic /əlímpik, ōlím–/ adj. & n. • adj. of ancient Olympia or the Olympic games. • n.pl. (**the Olympics**) the Olympic games. [L Olympicus f. Gk Olumpikos of Olympus or Olympia (the latter being named from the games held in honor of Zeus of Olympus)]

O·lym·pic Games n. (also **the O·lym·pics**) **1** an ancient Greek festival held at Olympia every four years, with athletic, literary, and musical competitions. **2** a modern international revival of this as a sports festival usu. held every four years since 1896 in different venues.

OM abbr. (in the UK) Order of Merit.

-oma /ṓmə/ n. forming nouns denoting tumors and other abnormal growths (carcinoma). [mod.L f. Gk –ṓma suffix denoting the result of verbal action]

O·ma·ha /ṓmәhaw, –haa/ n. & adj. • n. **1 a** a N. American people native to Nebraska. **b** a member of this people. **2** the language of this people. • adj. of or relating to this people or their language.

o·ma·sum /ōmáysəm/ n. (pl. **o·ma·sa** /–sə/) the third stomach of a ruminant. [L, = bullock's tripe]

OMB abbr. Office of Management and Budget.

om·bre /ómbər/ n. (also **hom·bre**) a card game for three, popular in Europe in the 17th–18th c. [Sp. hombre man, with ref. to one player seeking to win the pool]

om·bré /awmbráy/ adj. (of a fabric, etc.) having gradual shading of color from light to dark. [F, past part. of ombrer to shadow (as UMBER)]

ombro- /ómbrō/ comb. form rain. [Gk ombros rain shower]

om·buds·man /ómbŏŏdzmən/ n. (pl. **·men**) an official appointed by a government to investigate individuals' complaints against public authorities, etc. [Sw., = legal representative]

-ome /ōm/ suffix forming nouns denoting objects or parts of a specified nature (rhizome; trichome). [var. of –OMA]

o·me·ga /ōmáygə, ómeegə, ōmégə/ n. **1** the last (24th) letter of the Greek alphabet (Ω, ω). **2** the last of a series; the final development. [Gk, ōmega = great O]

om·e·lette /ómlit/ n. (also **om·e·let**) a dish of beaten eggs cooked in a frying pan and served plain or with a savory or sweet filling. [F omelette, obs. amelette by metathesis f. alumette var. of alumelle f. lemele knife blade f. L lamella: see LAMELLA]

o·men /ṓmən/ n. & v. • n. **1** an occurrence or object regarded as portending good or evil. **2** prophetic significance (of good omen). • v.tr. (usu. in passive) portend; foreshow. □□ **o·mened** (also in comb.). [L omen ominis]

o·men·tum /ōméntəm/ n. (pl. **o·men·ta** /–tə/) a fold of peritoneum connecting the stomach with other abdominal organs. □□ **o·men·tal** adj. [L]

omertà /ómairtáa/ n. a code of silence, esp. as practiced by the Mafia. [It., = conspiracy of silence]

om·i·cron /ómikron, ómi–/ n. the fifteenth letter of the Greek alphabet (O, o). [Gk, o mikron = small o]

om·i·nous /ómines/ adj. **1** threatening; indicating disaster or difficulty. **2** of evil omen; inauspicious. **3** giving or being an omen. □□ **om·i·nous·ly** adv. **om·i·nous·ness** n. [L ominosus (as OMEN)]

SYNONYM TIP ominous

FATEFUL, FORBIDDING, FOREBODING, PORTENTOUS, PREMONITORY. A sky filled with low, dark clouds might look **ominous**, but it wouldn't be considered **portentous**, even though the root words omen and portent are nearly synonymous. What is ominous is usually threatening and may imply impending disaster (an ominous silence), while portentous is more often used to describe something that provokes awe or amazement (a portentous show of military strength), or a very important outcome (a portentous moment for the American people). Like ominous, **foreboding** implies that something evil is coming (a foreboding expression), while **forbidding** suggests an ominous appearance that promises to be unfriendly or threatening (a dark, forbidding castle). **Fateful** and **premonitory** are less frightening words. What is fateful appears to have been inevitable or decreed by fate (a fateful meeting with her ex-boyfriend), with an emphasis on decisive importance (a battle that would prove fateful). Anything that serves to warn beforehand is premonitory, whether or not the warning concerns something negative (a premonitory dream about her father's death; a premonitory feeling about the exam).

---

o·mis·sion /ōmíshən/ n. **1** the act or an instance of omitting or being omitted. **2** something that has been omitted or overlooked. □□ **o·mis·sive** /–siv/ adj. [ME f. OF omission or LL omissio (as OMIT)]

o·mit /ōmít/ v.tr. (**o·mit·ted**, **o·mit·ting**) **1** leave out; not insert or include. **2** leave undone. **3** (foll. by verbal noun or to + infin.) fail or neglect (omitted saying anything; omitted to say). □□ **o·mis·si·ble** /–místəbəl/ adj. [ME f. L omittere omiss- (as OB-, mittere send)]

om·ma·tid·i·um /ómətídeeəm/ n. (pl. **om·ma·tid·i·a** /–eeə/) a structural element in the compound eye of an insect. [mod.L f. Gk ommatidion dimin. of omma ommat- eye]

omni- /ómnee/ comb. form **1** all; of all things. **2** in all ways or places. [L f. omnis all]

om·ni·bus /ómnibəs/ n. & adj. • n. **1** formal = BUS. **2** a volume containing several novels, etc., previously published separately. • adj. **1** serving several purposes at once. **2** comprising several items. [F f. L (dative pl. of omnis), = for all]

om·ni·com·pe·tent /ómnikómpit'nt/ adj. **1** able to deal with all matters. **2** having jurisdiction in all cases. □□ **om·ni·com·pe·tence** /–t'ns/ n.

om·ni·di·rec·tion·al /ómneedirékshən'l/ adj. (of an antenna, etc.) receiving or transmitting in all directions.

om·ni·far·i·ous /ómnifáireeəs/ adj. of all sorts or varieties. [LL omnifarius (as OMNI-): cf. MULTIFARIOUS]

om·nip·o·tent /ómnípət'nt/ adj. **1** having great or absolute power. **2** having great influence. □□ **om·nip·o·tence** /–t'ns/ n. **om·nip·o·tent·ly** adv. [ME f. OF f. L omnipotens (as OMNI-, POTENT[1])]

om·ni·pres·ent /ómniprézənt/ adj. **1** present everywhere at the same time. **2** widely or constantly encountered. □□ **om·ni·pres·ence** /–zəns/ n. [med.L omnipraesens (as OMNI-, PRESENT[1])]

om·nis·cient /omníshənt/ *adj.* knowing everything or much. □□ **om·nis·cience** /–shəns/ *n.* **om·nis·cient·ly** *adv.* [med.L *omnisciens –entis* (as OMNI-, *scire* know)]

om·ni·um gath·er·um /ómneeəm gáthərəm/ *n. colloq.* a miscellany or strange mixture. [mock L f. L *omnium* of all + GATHER]

om·niv·o·rous /omnívərəs/ *adj.* **1** feeding on many kinds of food, esp. on both plants and flesh. **2** making use of everything available. □□ **om·ni·vore** /ómnivawr/ *n.* **om·niv·o·rous·ly** *adv.* **om·niv·o·rous·ness** *n.* [L *omnivorus* (as OMNI-, –VOROUS)]

omphalo- /ómfəlō/ *comb. form* navel. [Gk (as OMPHALOS)]

om·pha·los /ómfəlos/ *n. Gk Antiq.* **1** a conical stone (esp. that at Delphi) representing the navel of the earth. **2** a boss on a shield. **3** a center or hub. [Gk, = navel, boss, hub]

on /on, awn/ *prep., adv., & adj.* ● *prep.* **1** (so as to be) supported by or attached to or covering or enclosing (*sat on a chair; stuck on the wall; rings on her fingers; leaned on his elbow*). **2** carried with; about the person of (*do you have a pen on you?*). **3** (of time) exactly at; during; contemporaneously with (*on May 29; on the hour; on schedule; working on Tuesday*). **4** immediately after or before (*I saw them on my return*). **5** as a result of (*on further examination I found this*). **6** (so as to be) having membership, etc., of or residence at or in (*she is on the board of directors; lives on the waterfront*). **7** supported financially by (*lives on $200 a week; lives on his wits*). **8** close to; just by (*a house on the sea; lives on the main road*). **9** in the direction of; against. **10** so as to threaten; touching or striking (*advanced on him; pulled a knife on me; a punch on the nose*). **11** having as an axis or pivot (*turned on his heels*). **12** having as a basis or motive (*works on a transmission; arrested on suspicion*). **13** having as a standard, confirmation, or guarantee (*had it on good authority; did it on purpose; I promise you on my word*). **14** concerning or about (*writes on finance*). **15** using or engaged with (*is on the pill; here on business*). **16** so as to affect (*walked out on her*). **17** at the expense of (*the drinks are on me; the joke is on him*). **18** added to (*disaster on disaster*). **19** in a specified manner or style (often foll. by the + adj. or noun: *on the cheap; on the run*). ● *adv.* **1** (so as to be) covering or in contact with something, esp. of clothes (*put your boots on*). **2** in the appropriate direction; toward something (*look on*). **3** further forward; in an advanced position or state (*is getting on in years; it happened later on*). **4** with continued movement or action (*went plodding on; keeps on complaining*). **5** in operation or activity (*the light is on; the chase was on*). **6** due to take place as planned (*is the party still on?*). **7** *colloq.* **a** (of a person) willing to participate or approve, or make a bet. **b** esp. *Brit.* (of an idea, proposal, etc.) practicable or acceptable (*that's just not on*). **8** being shown or performed (*a good movie on tonight*). **9** (of an actor) on stage. **10** (of an employee) on duty. **11** forward (*head on*). ● *adj. Baseball* positioned at a base as a runner. □ **be on about** refer to or discuss esp. tediously or persistently (*what are they on about?*). **be on at** *colloq.* nag or grumble at. **be on to 1** realize the significance or intentions of. **2** get in touch with (esp. by telephone). **on and off** intermittently; now and then. **on and on** continually; at tedious length. **on time 1** punctual; punctually; in good time. **2** by means of installment payments (*buying new furniture on time*). **on to** to a position or state on or in contact with (cf. ONTO). [OE *on, an* f. Gmc]

-on /on/ *suffix Physics, Biochem., & Chem.* forming nouns denoting: **1** elementary particles (*meson; neutron*). **2** quanta (*photon*). **3** molecular units (*codon*). **4** substances (*interferon; parathion*). [ION, orig. in *electron*]

on·a·ger /ónəgər/ *n.* **1** a wild ass, esp. *Equus hemionus* of Central Asia. **2** *hist.* an ancient military engine for throwing rocks. [ME f. L f. Gk *onagros* f. *onos* ass + *agrios* wild]

o·nan·ism /ónənizəm/ *n.* **1** masturbation. **2** coitus interruptus. □□ **o·nan·ist** *n.* **o·nan·is·tic** /–nístik/ *adj.* [F *onanisme* or mod.L *onanismus* f. *Onan* (Gen. 38:9)]

once /wuns/ *adv., conj., & n.* ● *adv.* **1** on one occasion or for one time only (*did not once say please; have read it once*). **2** at some point or period in the past (*could once play chess*). **3** ever or at all (*if you once forget it*). **4** multiplied by one; by one degree. ● *conj.* as soon as (*once they have gone we can relax*). ● *n.* one time or occasion (*just the once*). □ **all at once 1** without warning; suddenly. **2** all together. **at once 1** immediately. **2** simultaneously. **for once** on this (or that) occasion, even if at no other. **once again** (or **more**) another time. **once and for all** (or **once for all**) (done) in a final or conclusive manner, esp. so as to end hesitation or uncertainty. **once** (or **every once**) **in a while** from time to time; occasionally. **once or twice** a few times. **once upon a time** at some vague time in the past. [ME *ānes, ōnes,* genit. of ONE]

once-o·ver *n. colloq.* **1** a rapid preliminary inspection or piece of work. **2** an appraising glance.

oncer /wúnsər/ *n.* **1** *Brit. hist. sl.* a one-pound note. **2** *Brit. colloq.* a thing that occurs only once. **3** *Austral. colloq.* an election of an MP likely to serve only one term.

on·cho·cer·ci·a·sis /óngkōsərkíəsis/ *n.* a tropical disease of the skin caused by a parasitic worm, the larvae of which can migrate into the eye and cause blindness. Also called **river blindness**.

onco- /óngkō/ *comb. form Med.* tumor. [Gk *onkos* mass]

on·co·gene /óngkəjeen/ *n.* a gene that can transform a cell into a tumor cell. □□ **on·co·gen·ic** /–jénik/ *adj.* **on·co·gen·ous** /–kójinəs/ *adj.*

on·col·o·gy /ongkóləjee/ *n. Med.* the study of tumors.

on·com·ing /ónkuming, áwn–/ *adj. & n.* ● *adj.* approaching from the front. ● *n.* an approach or onset.

on·cost /ónkawst, áwn–/ *n. Brit.* an overhead expense.

one /wun/ *adj., n., & pron.* ● *adj.* **1** single and integral in number. **2** (with a noun implied) a single person or thing of the kind expressed or implied (*one of the best; a nasty one*). **3 a** a particular but undefined, esp. as contrasted with another (*that is one view; one thing after another*). **b** *colloq.* (as an emphatic) a noteworthy example of (*that is one difficult question*). **4** only such (*the one man who can do it*). **5** forming a unity (*one and undivided*). **6** identical; the same (*of one opinion*). ● *n.* **1 a** the lowest cardinal number. **b** a thing numbered with it. **2** unity; a unit (*one is half of two; came in ones and twos*). **3** a single thing or person or example (often referring to a noun previously expressed or implied: *the big dog and the small one*). **4** *colloq.* an alcoholic drink (*have a quick one; have one on me*). **5** a story or joke (*the one about the frog*). ● *pron.* **1** a person of a specified kind (*loved ones; like one possessed*). **2** any person, as representing people in general (*one is bound to lose in the end*). **3** I, me (*one would like to help*). □ **all one** (often foll. by *to*) a matter of indifference. **at one** in agreement. **for one** being one, even if the only one (*I for one do not believe it*). **for one thing** as a single consideration, ignoring others. **one and the same** the same; (the) identical. **one another** each the other or others (as a formula of reciprocity: love one another). **one by one** singly, successively. **one day 1** on an unspecified day. **2** at some unspecified future date. **one or two** see OR[1]. **one up** (often foll. by *on*) *colloq.* having a particular advantage. [OE *ān* f. Gmc]

▶The use of **one** to mean *I* or *me* is often regarded as an affectation.

-one /ōn/ *suffix Chem.* forming nouns denoting various compounds, esp. ketones (*acetone*). [Gk –*ōn ē* fem. patronymic]

one-armed ban·dit *n. colloq.* a slot machine worked by a long handle at the side.

one·fold /wúnfōld/ *adj.* consisting of only one member or element; simple.

one-horse *adj.* **1** using a single horse. **2** *colloq.* small, poorly equipped.

O·nei·da /ōnídə/ *n. & adj.* ● *n.***1a** a N. American people native to New York state. **b** a member of this people. **2** the language of this people. ● *adj.* of or relating to this people or their language.

o·nei·ric /ōnírik/ *adj.* of or relating to dreams or dreaming. [Gk *oneiros* dream]

oneiro- /ōnírō/ *comb. form* dream. [Gk *oneiros* dream]

o·nei·ro·man·cy /óniʳəmansee/ *n.* the interpretation of dreams.

one-lin·er *n. colloq.* a single brief sentence, often witty or apposite.

one-man *adj.* involving, done, or operated by only one person.

one·ness /wún-nis/ *n.* **1** the fact or state of being one; singleness. **2** uniqueness. **3** agreement; unity of opinion. **4** identity; sameness.

one-night stand *n.* **1** a single performance of a play, etc., in a place. **2** *colloq.* a sexual liaison lasting only one night.

one-off *adj.* esp. *Brit. colloq. adj.* made or done as the only one; not repeated. ● *n.* the only example of a manufactured product; something not repeated.

one-on-one *adj.* **1** of or involving a direct confrontation or communication between two persons. **2** *Sports* playing directly against one opposing player.

one-piece *adj.* (of a bathing suit, etc.) made as a single garment.

on·er /wúnər/ *n. Brit. sl.* **1** one pound (of money). **2** a remarkable person or thing.

on·er·ous /ónərəs, ón–/ *adj.* **1** burdensome; causing or requiring trouble. **2** *Law* involving heavy obligations. □□ **on·er·ous·ly** *adv.* **on·er·ous·ness** *n.* [ME f. OF *onereus* f. L *onerosus* f. *onus oneris* burden]

one·self /wunsélf/ *pron.* the reflexive and (in apposition) emphatic form of *one* (*kill oneself; one has to do it oneself*).

one-sid·ed *adj.* **1** favoring one side in a dispute; unfair; partial. **2** having or occurring on one side only. **3** larger or more developed on one side. □□ **one-sid·ed·ly** *adv.* in a one-sided manner. **one-sid·ed·ness** *n.* the act or state of being one-sided.

one-step *n. Dancing* a vigorous kind of foxtrot in three-quarter time.

one·time /wúntīm/ *adj. & adv.* former.

one-to-one *adj.* with one member of one group corresponding to one of another.

one-track mind *n.* a mind preoccupied with one subject.

one-two *n. colloq.* **1** *Boxing* the delivery of two punches in quick succession. **2** *Soccer,* etc. a series of reciprocal passes between two advancing players.

one·up·man·ship *n. colloq.* the art of maintaining a psychological advantage.

one-way *n.* allowing movement or travel in one direction only.

on·go·ing /ón-góing, áwn–/ *adj.* **1** continuing to exist or be operative, etc. **2** that is or are in progress (*ongoing discussions*). □□ **on·go·ing·ness** *n.*

on·ion /únyən/ *n.* **1** a liliaceous plant, *Allium cepa*, having a short stem and bearing greenish-white flowers. **2** the swollen bulb of this with many concentric skins used in cooking, pickling, etc. □ **know one's onions** *colloq.* be fully knowledgeable or experienced. □□ **on·ion·y** *adj.* [ME f. AF *union*, OF *oignon* ult. f. L *unio –onis*]

on·ion dome *n.* a bulbous dome on a church, palace, etc.

on·ion·skin /únyənskín/ *n.* **1** the brown outermost skin or any outer skin of an onion. **2** a type of thin, smooth, translucent paper.

on·kus /óngkəs/ *adj. Austral. colloq.* unpleasant; disorganized. [20th c.: orig. unkn.]

on-line *adj. Computing* (of equipment or a process) directly controlled by or connected to a central processor.

on·look·er /ónlŏŏkər, áwn–/ *n.* a nonparticipating observer; a spectator. □□ **on·look·ing** *adj.*

on·ly /ónlee/ *adv., adj., & conj.* ● *adv.* **1** solely, merely, exclusively; and no one or nothing more besides (*I only want to sit down; will only make matters worse; needed six only; is only a child*). **2** no longer ago than (*saw them only yesterday*). **3** not until (*arrives only on Tuesday*). **4** with no better result than (*hurried home only to find her gone*). ● *attrib.adj.* **1** existing alone of its or their kind (*their only son*). **2** best or alone worth knowing (*the only place to eat*). ● *conj. colloq.* **1** except that; but for the fact that (*I would go, only I feel ill*). **2** but then (as an extra consideration) (*he always makes promises, only he never keeps them*). □ **only too** extremely (*is only too willing*). [OE *ānlic*, *ǣnlic*, ME *onliche* (as ONE, –LY²)]

▶In informal English *only* is usually placed between the subject and verb regardless of what it refers to (*I only want to talk to you*); in more formal English it is often placed more exactly, esp. to avoid ambiguity (*I want to talk only to you*). In speech, intonation usually serves to clarify the sense.

on·ly-be·got·ten *adj. literary* begotten as the only child.

on-off *adj.* **1** (of a switch) having two positions, 'on' and 'off.' **2** = *on and off.*

on·o·mas·tic /ónəmástik/ *adj.* relating to names or nomenclature. [Gk *onomastikos* f. *onoma* name]

on·o·mas·tics /ónəmástiks/ *n.pl.* (treated as *sing.*) the study of the origin and formation of (esp. personal) proper names.

on·o·mat·o·poe·ia /ónəmátəpéeə, –maátə–/ *n.* **1** the formation of a word from a sound associated with what is named (e.g., *cuckoo*, *sizzle*). **2** the use of such words. □□ **on·o·mat·o·poe·ic** *adj.* **on·o·mat·o·poe·i·cal·ly** *adv.* [LL f. Gk *onomatopoiia* word making f. *onoma –matos* name + *poieō* make]

On·on·da·ga /aanəndáwgə, –day–, –daa–/ *n. & adj.* ● *n.* **1 a** a N. American people native to New York state. **b** a member of these people. **2** the language of these people. ● *adj.* of or relating to these people or their language.

on·rush /ónrush, áwn–/ *n.* an onward rush.

on·set /ónset, áwn–/ *n.* **1** an attack. **2** a beginning, esp. an energetic or determined one.

on-screen *adj.* appearing in a movie or on television. ● *adv.* **1** on or by means of a screen. **2** within the view presented by a filmed scene.

on·shore /ónsháwr, áwn–/ *adj. & adv.* ● *adj.* **1** on the shore. **2** (of the wind) blowing from the sea toward the land. ● *adv.* ashore.

on·side /ónsíd, áwn–/ *adj.* (of a player in a field or ice hockey game) in a lawful position; not offside.

on·slaught /ónslawt, áwn–/ *n.* a fierce attack. [earlier *anslaight* f. MDu. *aenslag* f. *aen* on + *slag* blow, with assim. to obs. *slaught* slaughter]

on·stage /ónstáyj/ *Theatr. adj. & adv.* on the stage; visible to the audience.

Ont. *abbr.* Ontario.

-ont /ont/ *comb. form Biol.* denoting an individual of a specified type (*symbiont*). [Gk *ōn* *ont-* being]

on·to /óntoo, áwn–/ *prep.* to a position or state on or in contact with (cf. *on to*).

▶It is important to maintain a distinction between the preposition *onto* and the use of the adverb *on* followed by the preposition *to*: *she climbed onto the roof* but *let's go on to the next point.*

on·to·gen·e·sis /óntəjénisis/ *n.* the origin and development of an individual (cf. PHYLOGENESIS). □□ **on·to·ge·net·ic** /–jinétik/ *adj.* **on·to·ge·net·i·cal·ly** /–jinétiklee/ *adv.* [formed as ONTOGENY + Gk *genesis* birth]

on·tog·e·ny /óntójənee/ *n.* = ONTOGENESIS. □□ **on·to·gen·ic** /–təjénik/ *adj.* **on·to·gen·i·cal·ly** *adv.* [Gk *ōn* *ont-* being, pres. part. of *eimi* be + –GENY]

on·tol·o·gy /óntóləjee/ *n.* the branch of metaphysics dealing with the nature of being. □□ **on·to·log·i·cal** /–təlójikəl/ *adj.* **on·to·log·i·**

cal·ly *adv.* **on·tol·o·gist** *n.* [mod.L *ontologia* f. Gk *ōn* *ont-* being + –LOGY]

o·nus /ónəs/ *n.* (*pl.* **o·nus·es**) a burden, duty, or responsibility. [L]

on·ward /ónwərd, áwn–/ *adv. & adj.* ● *adv.* (also **on·wards**) **1** further on. **2** toward the front. **3** with advancing motion. ● *adj.* directed onward.

on·yx /óniks/ *n.* a semiprecious variety of agate with different colors in layers. [ME f. OF *oniche*, *onix* f. L f. Gk *onux* fingernail, onyx]

on·yx mar·ble *n.* banded calcite, etc., used as a decorative material.

oo- /ŏə/ *comb. form Biol.* egg, ovum. [Gk *ōion* egg]

o·o·cyte /ŏəsít/ *n.* an immature ovum in an ovary.

oo·dles /ŏŏd'lz/ *n.pl. colloq.* a very great amount. [19th-c. US: orig. unkn.]

oof /ŏŏf/ *n.* esp. *Brit. sl.* money, cash. [Yiddish *ooftisch*, G *auf dem Tische* on the table (of money in gambling)]

oof·y /ŏŏfee/ *adj. Brit. sl.* rich, wealthy. □□ **oof·i·ness** *n.*

o·og·a·mous /ō-ógəməs/ *adj.* reproducing by the union of mobile male and immobile female cells. □□ **o·og·a·my** *n.*

o·og·en·e·sis /ŏəjénisis/ *n.* the production or development of an ovum.

ooh /ŏŏ/ *int.* expressing surprise, delight, pain, etc. [natural exclam.]

o·o·lite /ŏəlīt/ *n.* **1** a sedimentary rock, usu. limestone, consisting of rounded grains made up of concentric layers. **2** = OOLITH. □□ **o·o·lit·ic** /–lítik/ *adj.* [F *oölithe* (as OO-, –LITE)]

o·o·lith /ŏəlith/ *n.* any of the rounded grains making up oolite.

o·ol·o·gy /ō-óləjee/ *n.* the study or collecting of birds' eggs. □□ **o·o·log·i·cal** /ŏəlójikəl/ *adj.* **o·ol·o·gist** *n.*

oo·long /ŏŏlawng, –long/ *n.* a dark kind of cured China tea. [Chin. *wulong* black dragon]

oom·pah /ŏŏmpaa/ *n. colloq.* the rhythmical sound of deep-toned brass instruments in a band. [imit.]

oomph /ŏŏmf/ *n. sl.* **1** energy; enthusiasm. **2** attractiveness, esp. sexual appeal. [20th c.: orig. uncert.]

-oon /ŏŏn/ *suffix* forming nouns, orig. from French words having the stressed syllable *-on* (*balloon*; *buffoon*). [L *-o –onis*, sometimes via It. *-one*]

▶This suffix is replaced by *-on* in recent borrowings and those with unstressed *-on* (*baron*).

oops /ŏŏps, ŏŏps/ *int. colloq.* expressing surprise or apology, esp. on making an obvious mistake. [natural exclam.]

o·o·sperm /ŏəspərm/ *n.* a fertilized ovum.

ooze[1] /ŏŏz/ *v. & n.* ● *v.* **1** *intr.* (of fluid) pass slowly through the pores of a body. **2** *intr.* trickle or leak slowly out. **3** *intr.* (of a substance) exude moisture. **4** *tr.* exude or exhibit (a feeling) liberally (*oozed sympathy*). ● *n.* **1** a sluggish flow or exudation. **2** an infusion of oak bark or other vegetable matter, used in tanning. □□ **ooz·y** *adj.* **ooz·i·ly** *adv.* **ooz·i·ness** *n.* [orig. as noun (sense 2), f. OE *wōs* juice, sap]

ooze[2] /ŏŏz/ *n.* **1** a deposit of wet mud or slime, esp. at the bottom of a river, lake, or estuary. **2** a bog or marsh; soft muddy ground. □□ **ooz·y** *adj.* [OE *wāse*]

OP *abbr.* **1** *RC Ch.* Order of Preachers (Dominican). **2** observation post. **3** *Brit.* opposite prompt.

op. /op/ *abbr.* **1** *Mus.* opus. **2** operator.

o.p. *abbr.* **1** out of print. **2** overproof.

op- /op/ *prefix* assim. form of OB- before *p*.

o·pac·i·fy /ōpásifí/ *v.tr. & intr.* (·**fies**, ·**fied**) make or become opaque. □□ **o·pac·i·fi·er** *n.*

o·pac·i·ty /ōpásitee/ *n.* **1 a** the state of being opaque. **b** degree to which something is opaque. **2** obscurity of meaning. **3** obtuseness of understanding. [F *opacité* f. L *opacitas –tatis* (as OPAQUE)]

o·pah /ópə/ *n.* a large rare deep-sea fish, *Lampris guttatus*, usu. having a silver-blue back with white spots and crimson fins. Also called **moonfish**. [W. Afr. name]

o·pal /ópəl/ *n.* a quartzlike form of hydrated silica, usu. white or colorless and sometimes showing changing colors, often used as a gemstone. [F *opale* or L *opalus* prob. ult. f. Skr. *upalas* precious stone]

o·pal·es·cent /ópəlésənt/ *adj.* showing changing colors like an opal. □□ **o·pal·esce** *v.intr.* **o·pal·es·cence** /–səns/ *n.*

o·pal glass *n.* a semitranslucent white glass.

o·pal·ine /ópəlin, –leen, –lín/ *adj. & n.* ● *adj.* opallike; opalescent; iridescent. ● *n.* opal glass.

o·paque /ōpáyk/ *adj. & n.* ● *adj.* (**o·paqu·er**, **o·paqu·est**) **1** not transmitting light. **2** impenetrable to sight. **3** obscure; not lucid. **4** obtuse; dull-witted. ● *n.* **1** an opaque thing or substance. **2** a substance for producing opaque areas on negatives.

OPEC *abbrev.* Organization of the Petroleum Exporting Countries.

o·pen /ópən/ *adj., v., & n.* ● *adj.* **1** not closed nor locked nor blocked up; allowing entrance or passage or access. **2 a** (of a room, field, or other area) having its door or gate in a position allowing access, or part of its confining boundary removed. **b** (of a container) not fastened nor sealed; in a position or with the lid, etc., in a position allowing access to the inside part. **3** unenclosed; unconfined; unobstructed (*the open road*; *open views*). **4 a** uncovered, bare, exposed (*open drain*; *open wound*). **b** *Sports* (of a goal or other object of attack) unprotected; vulnerable. **5** undisguised; public; manifest; not exclusive nor limited (*open scandal*; *open hostilities*). **6** expanded, unfolded, or spread out (*had the map open on the table*). **7** (of a fabric) not close; with gaps or intervals. **8 a** (of a person) frank and communicative. **b** (of the mind) accessible to new ideas; unprejudiced or undecided. **c** generous. **9 a** (of an exhibition, shop, etc.) accessible to visitors or customers; ready for business. **b** (of a meeting) admitting all, not restricted to members, etc. **10 a** (of a race, competition, scholarship, etc.) unrestricted as to who may compete. **b** (of a champion, scholar, etc.) having won such a contest. **11** (of government) conducted in an informative manner receptive to inquiry, criticism, etc., from the public. **12** (foll. by *to*) **a** willing to receive (*is open to offers*). **b** (of a choice, offer, or opportunity) still available (*there are three courses open to us*). **c** likely to suffer from or be affected by (*open to abuse*). **13 a** (of the mouth) with lips apart, esp. in surprise or incomprehension. **b** (of the ears or eyes) eagerly attentive. **14** *Mus.* **a** (of a string) allowed to vibrate along its whole length. **b** (of a pipe) unstopped at each end. **c** (of a note) sounded from an open string or pipe. **15** (of an electrical circuit) having a break in the conducting path. **16** (of the bowels) not constipated. **17** (of a return ticket) not restricted as to day of travel. **18** (of a boat) without a deck. **19** (of a river or harbor) free of ice. **20** (of the weather or winter) free of frost. **21** *Phonet.* **a** (of a vowel) produced with a relatively wide opening of the mouth. **b** (of a syllable) ending in a vowel. **22** (of a town, city, etc.) not defended even if attacked. ● *v.* **1** *tr.* & *intr.* make or become open or more open. **2 a** *tr.* change from a closed or fastened position so as to allow access (*opened the door; opened the box*). **b** *intr.* (of a door, lid, etc.) have its position changed to allow access (*the door opened slowly*). **3** *tr.* remove the sealing or fastening element of (a container) to get access to the contents (*opened the envelope*). **4** *intr.* (foll. by *into, on to,* etc.) (of a door, room, etc.) afford access as specified (*opened on to a large garden*). **5 a** *tr.* start or establish or set going (a business, activity, etc.). **b** *intr.* be initiated; make a start (*the session opens tomorrow; the story opens with a murder*). **c** *tr.* (of a counsel in a court of law) make a preliminary statement in (a case) before calling witnesses. **6** *tr.* **a** spread out or unfold (a map, newspaper, etc.). **b** (often *absol.*) refer to the contents of (a book). **7** *intr.* (often foll. by *with*) (of a person) begin speaking, writing, etc. (*he opened with a warning*). **8** *intr.* (of a prospect) come into view; be revealed. **9** *tr.* **a** reveal or communicate (one's feelings, intentions, etc.). **b** make available, provide. **10** *tr.* make (one's mind, heart, etc.) more sympathetic or enlightened. **11** *tr.* ceremonially declare (a building, etc.) to be completed and in use. **12** *tr.* break up (ground) with a plow, etc. **13** *tr.* cause evacuation of (the bowels). **14** *Naut.* **a** *tr.* get a view of by change of position. **b** *intr.* come into full view. ● *n.* **1** (prec. by *the*) **a** open space or country or air. **b** public notice or view; general attention (esp. into the open). **2** an open championship, competition, or scholarship. □ **be open with** speak frankly to. **keep open house** see HOUSE. **open the door to** see DOOR. **open a person's eyes** see EYE. **open out 1** unfold; spread out. **2** develop, expand. **3** *Brit.* become communicative. **4** *Brit.* accelerate. **open up 1** unlock (premises). **2** make accessible. **3** reveal; bring to notice. **4** accelerate, esp. a motor vehicle. **5** begin shooting or sounding. **6** become communicative. **with open arms** see ARM[1]. □□ **o•pen•a•ble** *adj.* **o•pen•ness** *n.* [OE *open*]

o•pen air *n.* (usu. prec. by *the*) a free or unenclosed space outdoors. □□ **o•pen-air** (*attrib.*) *adj.* out of doors.

o•pen-and-shut *adj.* (of an argument, case, etc.) straightforward and conclusive.

o•pen-armed *adj.* cordial; warmly receptive.

o•pen book *n.* a person who is easily understood.

o•pen•cast /ópənkast/ *adj. Brit.* (of a mine or mining) with removal of the surface layers and working from above, not from shafts.

o•pen door *n.* free admission of foreign trade and immigrants. □□ **o•pen-door** *adj.* open, accessible, public.

o•pen-end•ed *adj.* having no predetermined limit or boundary.

o•pen•er /ópənər/ *n.* **1** a device for opening cans, bottles, etc. **2** *colloq.* the first item on a program, etc. □ **for openers** *colloq.* to start with.

o•pen-eyed *adj.* **1** with the eyes open. **2** alert; watchful.

o•pen-faced *adj.* having a frank or ingenuous expression.

o•pen-hand•ed /ópənhandid/ *adj.* generous. □□ **o•pen-hand•ed•ly** *adv.* **o•pen-hand•ed•ness** *n.*

o•pen-heart•ed *adj.* frank and kindly. □□ **o•pen-heart•ed•ness** *n.* an open-hearted quality.

o•pen-hearth proc•ess *n.* a process of steel manufacture, using a shallow reverberatory furnace.

o•pen-heart sur•ger•y *n.* surgery with the heart exposed and the blood made to bypass it.

o•pen house *n.* **1** welcome or hospitality for all visitors. **2** time when real estate offered for sale is open to prospective buyers.

o•pen ice *n.* ice through which navigation is possible.

o•pen•ing /ópəning/ *n. & adj.* ● *n.* **1** an aperture or gap, esp. allowing access. **2** a favorable situation or opportunity. **3** a beginning; an initial part. **4** *Chess* a recognized sequence of moves at the beginning

of a game. **5** a counsel's preliminary statement of a case in a court of law. ● *adj.* initial; first.

o•pen let•ter *n.* a letter, esp. of protest, addressed to an individual and published in a newspaper or journal.

o•pen•ly /ópənlee/ *adv.* **1** frankly; honestly. **2** publicly; without concealment. [OE *openlīce* (as OPEN, -LY [2])]

o•pen mar•ket *n.* an unrestricted market with free competition of buyers and sellers.

o•pen-mind•ed *adj.* accessible to new ideas; unprejudiced. □□ **o•pen-mind•ed•ly** *adv.* **o•pen-mind•ed•ness** *n.*

o•pen-mouthed *adj.* with the mouth open, esp. in surprise.

o•pen-plan *adj.* (usu. *attrib.*) (of a house, office, etc.) having large undivided rooms.

o•pen ques•tion *n.* a matter on which differences of opinion are legitimate.

o•pen-reel *adj.* (of a tape recorder) having reels of tape requiring individual threading, as distinct from a cassette.

o•pen sand•wich *n.* a sandwich without a top slice of bread.

o•pen sea *n.* an expanse of sea away from land.

o•pen sea•son *n.* the season when restrictions on the hunting of game, etc., are lifted.

o•pen se•cret *n.* a supposed secret that is known to many people.

o•pen ses•a•me *n.* see SESAME.

o•pen shop *n.* **1** a business, etc., where employees do not have to be members of a labor union (opp. CLOSED SHOP). **2** this system.

o•pen so•ci•e•ty *n.* a society with wide dissemination of information and freedom of belief.

open-toed *adj.* (of a shoe) leaving the toes partly bare.

o•pen ver•dict *n.* esp. *Brit.* a verdict affirming that a crime has been committed but not specifying the criminal or (in case of violent death) the cause.

o•pen•work /ópənwərk/ *n.* a pattern with intervening spaces in metal, leather, lace, etc.

op•er•a[1] /ópərə, óprə/ *n.* **1 a** a dramatic work in one or more acts, set to music for singers (usu. in costume) and instrumentalists. **b** this as a genre. **2** a building for the performance of opera. [It. f. L, = labor, work]

o•pe•ra[2] *pl.* of OPUS.

op•er•a•ble /ópərəbəl/ *adj.* **1** that can be operated. **2** suitable for treatment by surgical operation. □□ **op•er•a•bil•i•ty** /-bílitee/ *n.* [LL *operabilis* f. L (as OPERATE)]

o•pe•ra buf•fa /ópərəbóofə, óprə, áwperaa bóofaa/ *n.* (esp. Italian) comic opera, esp. with characters drawn from everyday life. [It.]

o•pé•ra co•mique /áwperaákawmeék/ *n.* (esp. French) opera on a lighthearted theme, with spoken dialogue. [F]

o•pe•ra glass•es *n.pl.* (also **op•er•a glass**) small binoculars for use at the opera or theater.

o•pe•ra hat *n.* a man's tall collapsible top hat.

op•er•a house *n.* a theater for the performance of opera.

op•er•and /ópərand/ *n. Math.* the quantity, etc., on which an operation is to be done. [L *operandum* neut. gerundive of *operari*: see OPERATE]

o•pe•ra se•ri•a /ópərəseéreeə, óprə/ *n.* (esp. 18th-c. Italian) opera on a serious, usu. classical or mythological theme. [It.]

op•er•ate /ópərayt/ *v.* **1** *tr.* manage; work; control; put or keep in a functional state. **2** *intr.* be in action; function. **3** *intr.* produce an effect; exercise influence (*the tax operates to our disadvantage*). **4** *intr.* (often foll. by *on*) **a** perform a surgical operation. **b** conduct a military or naval action. **c** be active in business, etc., esp. dealing in stocks and shares. **5** *intr.* (foll. by *on*) influence or affect (feelings, etc.). **6** *tr.* bring about; accomplish. [L *operari* to work f. *opus operis* work]

op•er•at•ing sys•tem *n.* the basic software that enables the running of a computer program.

op•er•at•ing room *n.* a room for surgical operations.

op•er•at•ic /ópərátik/ *adj.* **1** of or relating to opera. **2** resembling or characteristic of opera. □□ **op•er•at•i•cal•ly** *adv.* [irreg. f. OPERA[1], after *dramatic*]

op•er•at•ics /ópərátiks/ *n.pl.* the production and performance of operas.

op•er•a•tion /ópəráyshən/ *n.* **1 a** the action or process or method of working or operating. **b** the state of being active or functioning (*not yet in operation*). **c** the scope or range of effectiveness of a thing's activity. **2** an active process; a discharge of a function (*the operation of breathing*). **3** a piece of work, esp. one in a series (often in *pl.*: *begin operations*). **4** an act of surgery performed on a patient. **5 a** a strategic movement of troops, ships, etc., for military action. **b** preceding a code name (*Operation Desert Storm*). **6** a financial transaction. **7** *Math.* the subjection of a number or quantity or function to a process affecting its value or form, e.g., multiplication, differentiation. [ME f. OF f. L *operatio -onis* (as OPERATE)]

op•er•a•tion•al /ópəráyshənəl/ *adj.* **1 a** of or used for operations.

b engaged or involved in operations. **2** able or ready to function. □□ **op·er·a·tion·al·ly** adv.

op·er·a·tion·al re·search n. the application of scientific principles to business management, providing a quantitative basis for complex decisions.

op·er·a·tions re·search n. = OPERATIONAL RESEARCH.

op·er·a·tive /ópərətiv, óprə–/ adj. & n. ● adj. **1** in operation; having effect. **2** having the principal relevance (*"may" is the operative word*). **3** of or by surgery. **4** Law expressing an intent to perform a transaction. ● n. **1** a worker, esp. a skilled one. **2** an agent employed by a detective agency or secret service. □□ **op·er·a·tive·ly** adv. **op·er·a·tive·ness** n. [LL *operativus* f. L (as OPERATE)]

op·er·a·tor /ópəraytər/ n. **1** a person operating a machine, etc., esp. making connections of lines in a telephone exchange. **2** a person operating or engaging in business. **3** colloq. a person acting in a specified way (*a smooth operator*). **4** Math. a symbol or function denoting an operation (e.g., x, +). [LL f. L *operari* (as OPERATE)]

o·per·cu·lum /ópérkyələm/ n. (pl. **o·per·cu·la** /–lə/) **1** Zool. **a** a flaplike structure covering the gills in a fish. **b** a platelike structure closing the aperture of a gastropod mollusk's shell when the organism is retracted. **c** any of various other parts covering or closing an aperture, such as a flap over the nostrils in some birds. **2** Bot. a lidlike structure of the spore-containing capsule of mosses. □□ **o·per·cu·lar** adj. **o·per·cu·late** /–lət/ adj. **o·per·cu·li-** comb.form. [L f. *operire* cover]

op·er·et·ta /ópərétə/ n. **1** a one-act or short opera. **2** a light opera. [It., dimin. of *opera*: see OPERA]

oph·i·cleide /ófiklid/ n. **1** an obsolete usu. bass brass wind instrument developed from the serpent. **2** a powerful organ reed stop. [F *ophicléide* f. Gk *ophis* serpent + *kleis kleidos* key]

o·phid·i·an /ōfídeeən/ n. & adj. ● n. any reptile of the suborder Serpentes (formerly Ophidia), including snakes. ● adj. **1** of or relating to this group. **2** snakelike. [mod.L *Ophidia* f. Gk *ophis* snake]

ophio- /ófeeō/ comb.form snake. [Gk *ophis* snake]

oph·thal·mi·a /of-thálmeeə, op–/ n. an inflammation of the eye, esp. conjunctivitis. [LL f. Gk f. *ophthalmos* eye]

oph·thal·mic /of-thálmik, op–/ adj. of or relating to the eye and its diseases. [L *ophthalmicus* f. Gk *ophthalmikos* (as OPHTHALMIA)]

oph·thal·mic op·ti·cian n. Brit. **1** ophthalmologist. **2** optometrist.

ophthalmo- /of-thálmō, op–/ comb.form Optics denoting the eye. [Gk *ophthalmos* eye]

oph·thal·mol·o·gist /óf-thalmóləjist, –thə–, op–/ n. a medical doctor who specializes in ophthalmology.

PRONUNCIATION TIP ophthalmologist

Careful speakers articulate the first *l* in this word, and pronounce the *ph* like *f* rather than *p*. But because so many people say "OP-tha-MOL-a-jist," this pronunciation is widely accepted.

oph·thal·mol·o·gy /óf-thalmóləjee, –thə–, op–/ n. the scientific study of the eye. □□ **oph·thal·mo·log·i·cal** /–məlójikəl/ adj.

oph·thal·mo·scope /of-thálməskōp, op–/ n. an instrument for inspecting the retina and other parts of the eye. □□ **oph·thal·mo·scop·ic** /–skópik/ adj.

-opia /ópeeə/ comb.form denoting a visual disorder (*myopia*). [Gk f. *ōps* eye]

o·pi·ate adj., n., & v. ● adj. /ópeeət/ **1** containing opium. **2** narcotic, soporific. ● n. /ópeeət/ **1** a drug containing opium, usu. to ease pain or induce sleep. **2** a thing which soothes or stupefies. ● v.tr. /ópeeayt/ **1** mix with opium. **2** stupefy. [med.L *opiatus, –um, opiare* f. L *opium*: see OPIUM]

o·pine /ópín/ v.tr. (often foll. by *that* + clause) hold or express as an opinion. [L *opinari* think, believe]

o·pin·ion /əpínyən/ n. **1** a belief or assessment based on grounds short of proof. **2** a view held as probable. **3** (often foll. by *on*) what one thinks about a particular topic or question (*my opinion on capital punishment*). **4 a** a formal statement of professional advice (*will get a second opinion*). **b** Law a formal statement of reasons for a judgment given. **5** an estimation (*had a low opinion of it*). □ **be of the opinion that** believe or maintain that. **in one's opinion** according to one's view or belief. **a matter of opinion** a disputable point. [ME f. OF f. L *opinio –onis* (as OPINE)]

o·pin·ion·at·ed /əpínyənaytid/ adj. conceitedly assertive or dogmatic in one's opinions. □□ **o·pin·ion·at·ed·ly** adv. **o·pin·ion·at·ed·ness** n. [obs. *opinionate* in the same sense f. OPINION]

o·pin·ion poll n. an assessment of public opinion by questioning a representative sample, as for forecasting the results of voting, etc.

o·pi·um /ópeeəm/ n. **1** a reddish-brown heavy-scented addictive drug prepared from the juice of the opium poppy, used in medicine as an analgesic and narcotic. **2** anything regarded as soothing or stupefying. [ME f. L f. Gk *opion* poppy juice f. *opos* juice]

o·pi·um den n. a haunt of opium smokers.

o·pi·um pop·py n. a poppy, *Papaver somniferum*, native to Europe and E. Asia, with white, red, pink, or purple flowers.

o·pos·sum /əpósəm/ n. **1 a** any mainly tree-living marsupial of the family Didelphidae, native to America, having a prehensile tail and hind feet with an opposable thumb. **b** (in full **water opossum**) an opossum, *Chironectes minimus*, suited to an aquatic habitat and having webbed hind feet. Also called **yapok**. **2** Austral. & NZ = POSSUM 2. [Virginian Ind. *āpassūm*]

opossum

opp. abbr. opposite.

op·po·nent /əpónənt/ n. & adj. ● n. a person who opposes or belongs to an opposing side. ● adj. opposing; contrary; opposed. □□ **op·po·nen·cy** n. [L *opponere opponent-* (as OB-, *ponere* place)]

op·po·nent muscle n. a muscle enabling the thumb to be placed front to front against a finger of the same hand.

op·por·tune /ópərtōōn, –tyōōn/ adj. **1** (of a time) well-chosen or especially favorable or appropriate (*an opportune moment*). **2** (of an action or event) well-timed; done or occurring at a favorable or useful time. □□ **op·por·tune·ly** adv. **op·por·tune·ness** n. [ME f. OF *opportun –une* f. L *opportunus* (as OB-, *portus* harbor), orig. of the wind driving toward the harbor]

op·por·tun·ism /ópərtōōnizəm, –tyōō–/ n. **1** the adaptation of policy or judgment to circumstances or opportunity, esp. regardless of principle. **2** the seizing of opportunities when they occur. □□ **op·por·tun·ist** n. & adj. **op·por·tun·is·tic** adj. **op·por·tun·is·ti·cal·ly** adv. [OPPORTUNE after It. *opportunismo* and F *opportunisme* in political senses]

op·por·tu·ni·ty /ópərtōōnitee, –tyōō–/ n. (pl. **·ties**) **1** a good chance; a favorable occasion. **2** a chance or opening offered by circumstances. **3** good fortune. □ **opportunity knocks** an opportunity occurs. [ME f. OF *opportunité* f. L *opportunitas –tatis* (as OPPORTUNE)]

op·pos·a·ble /əpózəbəl/ adj. **1** able to be opposed. **2** Zool. (of the thumb in primates) capable of facing and touching the other digits on the same hand.

op·pose /əpóz/ v.tr. (often absol.) **1** set oneself against; resist; argue against. **2** be hostile to. **3** take part in a game, sport, etc., against (another competitor or team). **4** (foll. by *to*) place in opposition or contrast. □ **as opposed to** in contrast with. □□ **op·pos·er** n. [ME f. OF *opposer* f. L *opponere*: see OPPONENT]

op·po·site /ópəzit/ adj., n., adv., & prep. ● adj. **1** (often foll. by *to*) having a position on the other or further side, facing or back to

SYNONYM TIP opposite

ANTITHETICAL, CONTRADICTORY, CONTRARY, REVERSE. All of these adjectives are usually applied to abstractions and are used to describe ideas, statements, qualities, forces, etc., that are so far apart as to seem irreconcilable. **Opposite** refers to ideas or things that are symmetrically opposed in position, direction, or character—in other words, that are set against each other in such a way that the contrast or conflict between them is highlighted (*they sat opposite each other at the table*). **Contradictory** goes a little further, implying that if one of two opposing statements, propositions, or principles is true, the other must be false. *Contradictory* elements are mutually exclusive; for example, "alive " and "dead" are *contradictory* terms because logically they cannot both be applied to the same thing. **Antithetical** implies that the two things being contrasted are diametrically opposed—as far apart or as different from each other as is possible (*their interests were antithetical*). **Contrary** adds connotations of conflict or antagonism (*a contrary view of the situation*), while **reverse** applies to that which moves or faces in the *opposite* direction (*the reverse side*).

SYNONYM TIP opinion

BELIEF, CONVICTION, PERSUASION, SENTIMENT, VIEW. When you give your **opinion** on something, you offer a conclusion or a judgment that, although it may be open to question, seems true or probable to you at the time (*she was known for her strong opinions on women in the workplace*). A **view** is an *opinion* that is affected by your personal feelings or biases (*his views on life were essentially optimistic*), while a **sentiment** is a more or less settled *opinion* that may still be colored by emotion (*her sentiments on aging were shared by many other women approaching fifty*). A **belief** differs from an *opinion* or a view in that it is not necessarily the creation of the person who holds it; the emphasis here is on the mental acceptance of an idea, a proposition, or a doctrine and on the assurance of its truth (*religious beliefs; his belief in the power of the body to heal itself*). A **conviction** is a firmly-held and unshakable *belief* whose truth is not doubted (*she could not be swayed in her convictions*), while a **persuasion** (in this sense) is a strong *belief* that is unshakable because you want to believe that it's true rather than because there is evidence proving it so (*she was of the persuasion that he was innocent*).

back. **2** (often foll. by *to, from*) **a** of a contrary kind; diametrically different. **b** being the other of a contrasted pair. **3** (of angles) between opposite sides of the intersection of two lines. **4** *Bot.* (of leaves, etc.) placed at the same height on the opposite sides of the stem, or placed straight in front of another organ. ● *n.* an opposite thing or person or term. ● *adv.* **1** in an opposite position (*the tree stands opposite*). **2** (of a leading theatrical, etc., part) in a complementary role to (another performer). ● *prep.* in a position opposite to (*opposite the house is a tree*). □□ **op•po•site•ly** *adv.* **op•po•site•ness** *n.* [ME f. OF f. L *oppositus* past part. of *opponere*: see OPPONENT]

op•po•site num•ber *n.* a person holding an equivalent position in another group or organization.

op•po•site prompt *n. Brit.* the side of a theater stage usually to an actor's right.

op•po•site sex *n.* women in relation to men or vice versa.

op•po•si•tion /ópəzíshən/ *n.* **1** resistance, antagonism. **2** the state of being hostile or in conflict or disagreement. **3** contrast or antithesis. **4 a** a group or party of opponents or competitors. **b** (**the Opposition**) the principal political party opposed to that in office. **5** the act of opposing or placing opposite. **6 a** diametrically opposite position. **b** *Astrol. & Astron.* the position of two heavenly bodies when their longitude differs by 180°, as seen from the earth. □□ **op•po•si•tion•al** *adj.* [ME f. OF f. L *oppositio* (as OB-, POSITION)]

op•press /əprés/ *v.tr.* **1** keep in subservience by coercion. **2** govern or treat harshly or with cruel injustice. **3** weigh down (with cares or unhappiness). □□ **op•pres•sor** *n.* [ME f. OF *oppresser* f. med.L *oppressare* (as OB-, PRESS¹)]

op•pres•sion /əpréshən/ *n.* **1** the act or an instance of oppressing; the state of being oppressed. **2** prolonged harsh or cruel treatment or control. **3** mental distress. [OF f. L *oppressio* (as OPPRESS)]

op•pres•sive /əprésiv/ *adj.* **1** oppressing; harsh or cruel. **2** difficult to endure. **3** (of weather) close and sultry. □□ **op•pres•sive•ly** *adv.* **op•pres•sive•ness** *n.* [F *oppressif –ive* f. med.L *oppressivus* (as OPPRESS)]

op•pro•bri•ous /əprṓbreeəs/ *adj.* (of language) severely scornful; abusive. □□ **op•pro•bri•ous•ly** *adv.* [ME f. LL *opprobriosus* (as OPPROBRIUM)]

op•pro•bri•um /əprṓbreeəm/ *n.* **1** disgrace or bad reputation attaching to some act or conduct. **2** a cause of this. [L f. *opprobrum* (as OB-, *probrum* disgraceful act)]

op•pugn /əpyṓn/ *v.tr. literary* call into question; controvert. □□ **op•pugn•er** *n.* [ME f. L *oppugnare* attack, besiege (as OB-, L *pugnare* fight)]

op•pug•nant /əpúgnənt/ *adj. formal* attacking; opposing. □□ **op•pug•nance** /–nəns/ *n.* **op•pug•nan•cy** *n.* **op•pug•na•tion** /–náyshən/ *n.*

op•so•nin /ópsənin/ *n.* an antibody that assists the action of phagocytes. □□ **op•son•ic** /opsónik/ *adj.* [Gk *opsōnion* victuals + –IN]

opt /opt/ *v.intr.* (usu. foll. by *for, between*) exercise an option; make a choice. □ **opt out** (often foll. by *of*) choose not to participate (*opted out of these*). [F *opter* f. L *optare* choose, wish]

op•ta•tive /optáytiv, óptətiv/ *adj. & n. Gram.* ● *adj.* expressing a wish. ● *n.* the optative mood. □□ **op•ta•tive•ly** *adv.* [F *optatif –ive* f. LL *optativus* (as OPT)]

op•ta•tive mood *n.* a set of verb forms expressing a wish, etc., distinct esp. in Sanskrit and Greek.

op•tic /óptik/ *adj. & n.* ● *adj.* of or relating to the eye or vision (*optic nerve*). ● *n.* **1** a lens, etc., in an optical instrument. **2** *archaic or joc.* the eye. [F *optique* or med.L *opticus* f. Gk *optikos* f. *optos* seen]

op•ti•cal /óptikəl/ *adj.* **1** of sight; visual. **2 a** of or concerning sight or light in relation to each other. **b** belonging to optics. **3** (esp. of a lens) constructed to assist sight or on the principles of optics. □□ **op•ti•cal•ly** *adv.*

op•ti•cal ac•tiv•i•ty *n. Chem.* the property of rotating the plane of polarization of plane-polarized light.

op•ti•cal art *n.* a style of painting that gives the illusion of movement by the precise use of pattern and color.

op•ti•cal char•ac•ter rec•og•ni•tion *n.* the identification of printed characters using photoelectric devices.

op•ti•cal fi•ber *n.* thin glass fiber through which light can be transmitted.

op•ti•cal glass *n.* a very pure kind of glass used for lenses, etc.

op•ti•cal il•lu•sion *n.* **1** a thing having an appearance so resembling something else as to deceive the eye. **2** an instance of mental misapprehension caused by this.

op•ti•cal mi•cro•scope *n.* a microscope using the direct perception of light (cf. ELECTRON MICROSCOPE).

op•tic ax•is *n.* **1** a line passing through the center of curvature of a lens or spherical mirror and parallel to the axis of symmetry. **2** the direction in a doubly refracting crystal for which no double refraction occurs.

op•ti•cian /optíshən/ *n.* **1** a maker or seller of optical instruments, esp. eyeglasses and contact lenses. **2** a person trained in the detection and correction of poor eyesight (see OPHTHALMOLOGIST, OPTOMETRIST). [F *opticien* f. med.L *optica* (as OPTIC)]

op•tic lobe *n.* the dorsal lobe in the brain from which the optic nerve arises.

op•tics /óptiks/ *n.pl.* (treated as *sing.*) the scientific study of sight and the behavior of light, or of other radiation or particles (*electron optics*).

op•ti•ma *pl.* of OPTIMUM.

op•ti•mal /óptiməl/ *adj.* best or most favorable, esp. under a particular set of circumstances. □□ **op•ti•mal•ly** *adv.* [L *optimus* best]

op•ti•mism /óptimizəm/ *n.* **1** an inclination to hopefulness and confidence (opp. PESSIMISM). **2** *Philos.* **a** the doctrine, esp. as set forth by Leibniz, that this world is the best of all possible worlds. **b** the theory that good must ultimately prevail over evil in the universe. □□ **op•ti•mist** *n.* **op•ti•mis•tic** *adj.* **op•ti•mis•ti•cal•ly** *adv.* [F *optimisme* f. L OPTIMUM]

op•ti•mize /óptimīz/ *v.* **1** *tr.* make the best or most effective use of (a situation, an opportunity, etc.). **2** *intr.* be an optimist. □□ **op•ti•mi•za•tion** *n.* [L *optimus* best]

op•ti•mum /óptiməm/ *n. & adj.* ● *n.* (*pl.* **op•ti•ma** /–mə/ or **op•ti•mums**) **1 a** the most favorable conditions (for growth, reproduction, etc.). **b** the best or most favorable situation. **2** the best possible compromise between opposing tendencies. ● *adj.* = OPTIMAL. [L, neut. (as n.) of *optimus* best]

op•tion /ópshən/ *n.* **1 a** the act or an instance of choosing; a choice. **b** a thing that is or may be chosen (*those are the options*). **2** the liberty of choosing; freedom of choice. **3** *Stock Exch.*, etc., the right, obtained by payment, to buy, sell, etc., specified stocks, etc., at a specified price within a set time. □ **have no option but to** must. **keep** (or **leave**) **one's options open** not commit oneself. [F or f. L *optio*, stem of *optare* choose]

op•tion•al /ópshənəl/ *adj.* being an option only; not obligatory. □□ **op•tion•al•i•ty** /–álitee/ *n.* **op•tion•al•ly** *adv.*

op•tom•e•ter /optómitər/ *n.* an instrument for testing the refractive power and visual range of the eye. □□ **op•to•met•ric** /óptəmétrik/ *adj.* **op•tom•e•try** *n.* [Gk *optos* seen + –METER]

op•tom•e•trist /optómitrist/ *n.* a person who practices optometry.

op•tom•e•try /optómitree/ *n.* the practice or profession of testing the eyes for defects in vision and prescribing corrective lenses or exercises.

op•to•phone /óptəfōn/ *n.* an instrument converting light into sound, and so enabling the blind to read print, etc., by ear. [Gk *optos* seen + –PHONE]

op•u•lent /ópyələnt/ *adj.* **1** ostentatiously rich; wealthy. **2** luxurious (*opulent surroundings*). **3** abundant; profuse. □□ **op•u•lence** /–ləns/ *n.* **op•u•lent•ly** *adv.* [L *opulens, opulent-* f. *opes* wealth]

o•pun•ti•a /ōpúnsheeə, –shə/ *n.* any cactus of the genus *Opuntia*, with jointed cylindrical or elliptical stems and barbed bristles. Also called **prickly pear**. [L plant name f. *Opus –untis* in Locris in ancient Greece]

o•pus /ópəs/ *n.* (*pl.* **o•pe•ra** /ópərə/ or **o•pus•es**) **1** *Mus.* **a** a separate musical composition or set of compositions of any kind. **b** (also **op.**) used before a number given to a composer's work, usu. indicating the order of publication (*Beethoven, op. 15*). **2** any artistic work (cf. MAGNUM OPUS). [L, = work]

o•pus•cule /ōpúskyōōl/ *n.* (also **o•pus•cu•lum** /əpúskyələm/) (*pl.* **o•pus•cules** or **o•pus•cu•la** /–lə/) a minor (esp. musical or literary) work. [F f. L *opusculum* dimin. of OPUS]

o•pus De•i /dáyee/ *n. Eccl.* **1** liturgical worship regarded as man's primary duty to God. **2** (**Opus Dei**) a Roman Catholic organization of laymen and priests founded in Spain in 1928 with the aim of reestablishing Christian ideals in society.

OR *abbr.* **1** operational research. **2** Oregon (in official postal use). **3** operating room.

or¹ /awr, ər/ *conj.* **1 a** introducing the second of two alternatives (*white*

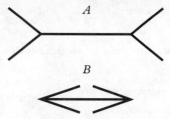

OPTICAL ILLUSION

(horizontal line *A* appears to be longer
than horizontal line *B*, but in fact,
they are of equal length)

or black). **b** introducing all but the first, or only the last, of any number of alternatives (*white or gray or black; white, gray, or black*). **2** (often prec. by *either*) introducing the only remaining possibility or choice given (*take it or leave it; either come in or go out*). **3** (prec. by *whether*) introducing the second part of an indirect question or conditional clause (*ask him whether he was there or not; must go whether I like or dislike it*). **4** introducing a synonym or explanation of a preceding word, etc. (*suffered from vertigo or dizziness*). **5** introducing a significant afterthought (*he must know—or is he bluffing?*). **6** otherwise (*run or you'll be late*). **7** *poet.* each of two; either (*or in the heart or in the head*). □ **not A or B** not A, and also not B. **one or two** (or two or three, etc.) *colloq.* a few. **or else 1** otherwise (*do it now, or else you will have to do it tomorrow*). **2** *colloq.* expressing a warning or threat (*hand over the money or else*). **or rather** introducing a rephrasing or qualification of a preceding statement, etc. (*he was there, or rather I heard that he was*). **or so** (after a quantity or a number) or thereabouts (*send me ten or so*). [reduced form of obs. *other* conj. (which superseded OE *oththe* or), of uncert. orig.]

or² /awr/ *n. & adj. Heraldry* ● *n.* a gold or yellow color. ● *adj.* (usu. following noun) gold or yellow (*a crescent or*). [F f. L *aurum* gold]

-or¹ /ər/ *suffix* forming nouns denoting a person or thing performing the action of a verb, or an agent more generally (*actor, escalator; tailor*) (see also –ATOR, –ITOR). [L –*or*, –*ator*, etc., sometimes via AF –*eour*, OF –*ëor*, –*ëur*]

-or² /ər/ *suffix* forming nouns denoting state or condition (*error, horror*). [L –*or* –*oris*, sometimes via (or after) OF –*or*, –*ur*]

-or³ /ər/ *suffix* forming adjectives with comparative sense (*major, senior*). [AF –*our* f. L –*or*]

or·ache /áwrich, ór–/ *n.* (also **or·ach**) = SALTBUSH. [ME *arage* f. AF *arasche* f. L *atriplex* f. Gk *atraphaxus*]

or·a·cle /áwrəkəl, ór–/ *n.* **1 a** a place at which advice or prophecy was sought from the gods in classical antiquity. **b** the usu. ambiguous or obscure response given at an oracle. **c** a prophet or prophetess at an oracle. **2 a** a person or thing regarded as an infallible guide to future action, etc. **b** a saying, etc., regarded as infallible guidance. **3** divine inspiration or revelation. [ME f. OF f. L *oraculum* f. *orare* speak]

o·rac·u·lar /awrákyələr/ *adj.* **1** of or concerning an oracle or oracles. **2** (esp. of advice, etc.) mysterious or ambiguous. **3** prophetic. □□ **o·rac·u·lar·i·ty** /–láritee/ *n.* **o·rac·u·lar·ly** *adv.* [L (as ORACLE)]

o·ra·cy /áwrəsee/ *n.* the ability to express oneself fluently in speech. [L *os oris* mouth, after *literacy*]

o·ral /áwrəl/ *adj. & n.* ● *adj.* **1** by word of mouth; spoken; not written (*the oral tradition*). **2** done or taken by the mouth (*oral contraceptive*). **3** of the mouth. **4** *Psychol.* of or concerning a supposed development of infant emotional and sexual development, in which the mouth is of central interest. ● *n. colloq.* a spoken examination, test, etc. □□ **o·ral·ly** *adv.* [LL *oralis* f. L *os oris* mouth]

oral sex *n.* sexual activity in which the genitals of one partner are stimulated by the mouth of the other.

o·ral so·ci·e·ty *n.* a society that has not reached the stage of literacy.

Or·ange /áwrinj, ór–/ *adj.* of or relating to Orangemen or their activities. □□ **Or·ange·ism** *n.*

or·ange /áwrinj, ór–/ *n. & adj.* ● *n.* **1 a** a large roundish juicy citrus fruit with a bright reddish-yellow tough rind. **b** any of various trees or shrubs of the genus *Citrus*, esp. *C. sinensis* or *C. aurantium*, bearing fragrant white flowers and yielding this fruit. **2** a fruit or plant resembling this. **3 a** the reddish-yellow color of an orange. **b** orange pigment. ● *adj.* orange-colored; reddish-yellow. [ME f. OF *orenge*, ult. f. Arab. *nāranj* f. Pers. *nārang*]

or·ange·ade /áwrinjáyd, ór–/ *n.* a usu. carbonated nonalcoholic drink flavored with orange.

or·ange blos·som *n.* the flowers of the orange tree, traditionally worn by the bride at a wedding.

or·ange flow·er wa·ter *n.* a solution of neroli in water.

Or·ange·man /áwrinjmən, ór–/ *n.* (*pl.* **·men**) a member of a political society formed in 1795 to support Protestantism in Ireland. [after William of *Orange* (William III)]

or·ange peel *n.* **1** the skin of an orange. **2** a rough surface resembling this.

or·ange pe·koe *n.* tea made from very small leaves.

or·ange·ry /áwrinjree, ór–/ *n.* (*pl.* **·ries**) a place, esp. a special structure, where orange trees are cultivated.

or·ange stick *n.* a thin stick, pointed at one end and usu. of orangewood, for manicuring the fingernails.

or·ange·wood /áwrinjwŏŏd/ *n.* the wood of the orange tree.

o·rang·u·tan /awrángətán, əráng–/ *n.* (also **o·rang·ou·tang**) /–tang/) a large red long-haired tree-living ape, *Pongo pygmaeus*, native to

orangutan

Borneo and Sumatra, with characteristic long arms and hooked hands and feet. [Malay *ōrangūtan* wild man]

o·rate /awráyt, áwrayt/ *v.intr.* esp. *joc.* or *derog.* make a speech or speak, esp. pompously or at length. [back-form. f. ORATION]

o·ra·tion /awráyshən, ōráy–/ *n.* **1** a formal speech, discourse, etc., esp. when ceremonial. **2** *Gram.* a way of speaking; language. [ME f. L *oratio* discourse, prayer f. *orare* speak, pray]

or·a·tor /áwrətər, ór–/ *n.* **1** a person making a speech. **2** an eloquent public speaker. □□ **or·a·to·ri·al** /–táwreeəl/ *adj.* [ME f. AF *oratour*, OF *orateur* f. L *orator* –*oris* speaker, pleader (as ORATION)]

or·a·to·ri·o /áwrətáwreeō, ór–/ *n.* (*pl.* **·os**) a semidramatic work for orchestra and voices, esp. on a sacred theme, performed without costume, scenery, or action. □□ **or·a·to·ri·al** *adj.* [It. f. eccl.L *oratorium*, orig. use of musical services at church of Oratory of St. Philip Neri in Rome]

or·a·to·ry /áwrətawree, ór–/ *n.* (*pl.* **·ries**) **1** the art or practice of formal speaking, esp. in public. **2** exaggerated, eloquent, or highly colored language. **3** a small chapel, esp. for private worship. **4** (**Oratory**) *RC Ch.* **a** a religious society of priests without vows founded in Rome in 1564 and providing plain preaching and popular services. **b** a branch of this in England, etc. □□ **or·a·to·ri·an** /–táwreeən/ *adj. & n.* **or·a·to·ri·cal** /–táwrikəl/ *adj.* [senses 1 and 2 f. L *ars oratoria* art of speaking; senses 3 and 4 ME f. AF *oratorie*, OF *oratoire* f. eccl.L *oratorium*: both f. L *oratorius* f. *orare* pray, speak]

orb /awrb/ *n. & v.* ● *n.* **1** a globe surmounted by a cross, esp. carried by a sovereign at a coronation. **2** a sphere; a globe. **3** *poet.* a heavenly body. **4** *poet.* an eyeball; an eye. ● *v.* **1** *tr.* enclose in (an orb); encircle. **2** *intr.* form or gather into an orb. [L *orbis* ring]

or·bic·u·lar /awrbíkyələr/ *adj. formal* **1** circular and flat; disk-shaped; ring-shaped. **2** spherical; globular; rounded. **3** forming a complete whole. □□ **or·bic·u·lar·i·ty** /–láritee/ *n.* **or·bic·u·lar·ly** *adv.* [ME f. LL *orbicularis* f. L *orbiculus* dimin. of *orbis* ring]

or·bic·u·late /awrbíkyəlit, –layt/ *adj. Bot.* (of a leaf, etc.) almost circular.

or·bit /áwrbit/ *n. & v.* ● *n.* **1 a** the curved, usu. closed course of a planet, satellite, etc. **b** (prec. by *in, into, out of*, etc.) the state of motion in an orbit. **c** one complete passage around an orbited body. **2** the path of an electron around an atomic nucleus. **3** a range or sphere of action. **4 a** the eye socket. **b** the area around the eye of a bird or insect. ● *v.* (**or·bit·ed, or·bit·ing**) **1** *intr.* **a** (of a satellite, etc.) go around in orbit. **b** fly in a circle. **2** *tr.* move in orbit around. **3** *tr.* put into orbit. □□ **or·bit·er** *n.* [L *orbita* course, track (in med.L eye cavity): fem. of *orbitus* circular f. *orbis* ring]

or·bit·al /áwrbitəl/ *adj. & n.* ● *adj.* **1** *Anat., Astron., & Physics* of an orbit or orbits. **2** *Brit.* (of a road) passing around the outside of a town. ● *n. Physics* a state or function representing the possible motion of an electron around an atomic nucleus.

or·bit·al sand·er *n.* a sander having a circular and not oscillating motion.

or·ca /áwrkə/ *n.* **1** any of various whales, esp. the killer whale. **2** any other large sea creature. [F *orque* or L *orca* a kind of whale]

Or·ca·di·an /awrkáydeeən/ *adj. & n.* ● *adj.* of or relating to the Orkney Islands off the N. coast of Scotland. ● *n.* a native of the Orkney Islands. [L *Orcades* Orkney Islands]

orch. *abbr.* **1** orchestra. **2** orchestrated by.

or·chard /áwrchərd/ *n.* a piece of land with fruit trees. □□ **or·chard·ist** *n.* [OE *ortgeard* f. L *hortus* garden + YARD²]

or·chard·ing /áwrchərding/ *n.* the cultivation of fruit trees.

or·chard·man /áwrchərdmən/ *n.* (*pl.* **·men**) a fruit grower.

or·ches·tra /áwrkəstrə/ *n.* **1** a usu. large group of instrumentalists, esp. combining strings, woodwinds, brass, and percussion (*symphony orchestra*). **2 a** (in full **orchestra pit**) the part of a theater, opera house, etc., where the orchestra plays, usu. in front of the stage and on a lower level. **b** the main-floor seating area in a theater. **3** the semicircular space in front of an ancient Greek theater stage where the chorus danced and sang. □□ **or·ches·tral** /–késtrəl/ *adj.* **or·ches·tral·ly** *adv.* [L f. Gk *orkhēstra* f. *orkheomai* to dance (in sense 3)]

or·ches·trate /áwrkəstrayt/ *v.tr.* **1** arrange, score, or compose for orchestral performance. **2** combine, arrange, or build up (elements of a situation, etc.) for maximum effect. □□ **or·ches·tra·tion** /–tráyshən/ *n.* **or·ches·tra·tor** *n.*

or·chid /áwrkid/ *n.* **1** any usu. epiphytic plant of the family Orchidaceae, bearing flowers in fantastic shapes and brilliant colors, usu. having one petal larger than the others and variously spurred, lobed, pouched, etc. **2** a flower of any of these plants. □□ **or·chi·da·ceous** /–dáyshəs/ *adj.* **or·chid·ist** *n.* **or·chid·ol·o·gy** /–dóləjee/ *n.* [mod.L *Orchid(ac)eae* irreg. f. L *orchis*: see ORCHIS]

or·chil /áwrkil, –chil/ *n.* (also **ar·chil** /áarkil, –chil/) **1** a red or violet dye from lichen, esp. from *Roccella tinctoria*, often used in litmus. **2** the tropical lichen yielding this. [ME f. OF *orcheil*, etc. perh. ult. f. L *herba urceolaris* a plant for polishing glass pitchers]

or·chis /áwrkis/ *n.* **1** any orchid of the genus *Orchis*, with a tuberous root and an erect fleshy stem having a spike of usu. purple or red flowers. **2** any of various wild orchids. [L f. Gk *orkhis*, orig. = testicle (with ref. to the shape of its tuber)]

or•chi•tis /awrkítis/ *n.* inflammation of the testicles. [mod.L f. Gk *orkhis* testicle]

or•ci•nol /áwrsinawl, –ol/ *n.* (also **or•cin** /áwrsin/) a crystalline substance, becoming red in air, extracted from any of several lichens and used to make dyes. [mod.L *orcina* f. It. *orcello* orchil]

ord. *abbr.* ordinary.

or•dain /awrdáyn/ *v.tr.* **1** confer holy orders on; appoint to the Christian ministry (*ordained him priest; was ordained in 1970*). **2 a** (often foll. by *that* + clause) decree (*ordained that he should go*). **b** (of God, fate, etc.) destine; appoint (*has ordained us to die*). □□ **or•dain•er** *n.*

or•dain•ment *n.* [ME f. AF *ordeiner*, OF *ordein-* stressed stem of *ordener* f. L *ordinare* f. *ordo –inis* order]

or•deal /awrdéel/ *n.* **1** a painful or horrific experience; a severe trial. **2** *hist.* (in full **trial by ordeal**) an ancient esp. Germanic test of guilt or innocence by subjection of the accused to severe pain or torture, survival of which was taken as divine proof of innocence. [OE *ordāl*, *ordēl* f. Gmc: cf. DEAL[1]]

or•der /áwrdər/ *n. & v.* • *n.* **1 a** the condition in which every part, unit, etc., is in its right place; tidiness (*restored some semblance of order*). **b** a usu. specified sequence, succession, etc. (*alphabetical order; the order of events*). **2** (in *sing.* or *pl.*) an authoritative command, direction, instruction, etc. (*only obeying orders; gave orders for it to be done; the judge made an order*). **3** a state of peaceful harmony under a constituted authority (*order was restored; law and order*). **4** (in the UK; esp. in *pl.*) a social class, rank, etc., constituting a distinct group in society (*the lower orders; the order of baronets*). **5** a kind; a sort (*talents of a high order*). **6 a** usu. written direction to a manufacturer, tradesman, waiter, etc., to supply something. **b** the quantity of goods, etc., supplied. **7** the constitution or nature of the world, society, etc. (*the moral order; the order of things*). **8** *Biol.* a taxonomic rank below a class and above a family. **9** (esp. **Order**) a fraternity of monks and friars, or formerly of knights, bound by a common rule of life (*the Franciscan order; the Order of Templars*). **10 a** any of the grades of the Christian ministry. **b** (in *pl.*) the status of a member of the clergy (*Anglican orders*). **11 a** any of the five classical styles of architecture (Doric, Ionic, Corinthian, Tuscan, and Composite) based on the proportions of columns, amount of decoration, etc. **b** any style or mode of architecture subject to uniform established proportions. **12** (in the UK; esp. **Order**) **a** a company of distinguished people instituted esp. by a sovereign to which appointments are made as an honor or reward (*Order of the Garter; Order of Merit*). **b** the insignia worn by members of an order. **13** *Math.* **a** a degree of complexity of a differential equation (*equation of the first order*). **b** the order of the highest derivative in the equation. **14** *Math.* **a** the size of a matrix. **b** the number of elements of a finite group. **15** *Eccl.* the stated form of divine service (*the order of confirmation*). **16** the principles of procedure, decorum, etc., accepted by a meeting, legislative assembly, etc., or enforced by its president. **17** *Mil.* **a** a style of dress and equipment (*review order*). **b** (prec. by *the*) the position of a company, etc., with arms ordered (see *order arms*). **18** a Masonic or similar fraternity. **19** any of the nine grades of angelic beings (seraphim, cherubim, thrones, dominations, principalities, powers, virtues, archangels, angels). **20** *Brit.* a pass admitting the bearer to a theater, museum, etc., free or at a reduced rate or as a privilege. • *v.tr.* **1** (usu. foll. by *to* + infin., or *that* + clause) command; bid; prescribe (*ordered him to go; ordered that they should be sent*). **2** command or direct (a person) to a specified destination (*was ordered to Singapore; ordered them home*). **3** direct a manufacturer, waiter, tradesman, etc., to supply (*ordered a new suit; ordered dinner*). **4** put in order; regulate (*ordered her affairs*). **5** (of God, fate, etc.) ordain (*fate ordered it otherwise*). **6** command (a thing) done or (a person) dealt with (*ordered it settled; ordered him expelled*). □ **by order** according to the proper authority. **in bad** (or **good**, etc.) **order** not working (or working properly, etc.). **in order 1** one after another according to some principle. **2** ready or fit for use. **3** according to the rules (of procedure at a meeting, etc.). **in order that** with the intention; so that. **in order to** with the purpose of doing; with a view to. **keep order** enforce orderly behavior. **made to order 1** made according to individual requirements, measurements, etc. (opp. READY-MADE). **2** exactly what is wanted. **not in order** not working properly. **of** (or **in** or **on**) **the order of 1** approximately. **2** having the order of magnitude specified by (*of the order of one in a million*). **on order** (of goods, etc.) ordered but not yet received. **order about 1** dominate; command officiously. **2** send here and there. **order arms** *Mil.* hold a rifle with its butt on the ground close to one's right side. **out of order 1** not working properly. **2** not according to the rules (of a meeting, organization, etc.). **3** not in proper sequence. **take orders 1** accept commissions. **2** accept and carry out commands. **3** (also **take holy orders**) be ordained. □□ **or•der•er** *n.* [ME f. OF *ordre* f. L *ordo ordinis* row, array, degree, command, etc.]

or•der form *n.* a printed form in which details are entered by a customer.

or•der•ly /áwrd'rlee/ *adj. & n.* • *adj.* **1** methodically arranged; regular. **2** obedient to discipline; well-behaved; not unruly. **3** *Mil.* **a** of or concerned with orders. **b** charged with the conveyance or execution of orders. • *n.* (*pl.* **•lies**) **1** a hospital attendant with nonmedical duties, esp. cleaning, moving equipment, escorting patients, etc. **2** a soldier who carries orders for an officer, etc. □□ **or•der•li•ness** *n.*

or•der•ly of•fi•cer *n. Brit. Mil.* the officer of the day.

or•der•ly room *n.Brit. Mil.* a room in a barracks used for company business.

Or•der of the Gar•ter *n. Brit.* the highest order of knighthood.

or•der of the day *n.* **1** the prevailing state of things. **2** a principal topic of action or a procedure decided upon. **3** business set down for discussion; a program.

or•der of mag•ni•tude *n.* a class in a system of classification determined by size, usu. by powers of 10.

or•di•nal /áwrd'nəl/ *n. & adj.* • *n.* **1** (in full **ordinal number**) a number defining a thing's position in a series, e.g., "first," "second," "third," etc. (cf. CARDINAL). **2** *Eccl.* a service book, esp. one with the forms of service used at ordinations. • *adj.* **1 a** of or relating to an ordinal number. **b** defining a thing's position in a series, etc. **2** *Biol.* of or concerning an order (see ORDER *n.* 8). [ME f. LL *ordinalis* & med.L *ordinale* neut. f. L (as ORDER)]

or•di•nance /áwrd'nəns/ *n.* **1** an authoritative order; a decree. **2** an enactment by a local authority. **3** a religious rite. **4** *archaic* = ORDONNANCE. [ME f. OF *ordenance* f. med.L *ordinantia* f. L *ordinare*: see ORDAIN]

or•di•nand /áwrd'nand/ *n. Eccl.* a candidate for ordination. [L *ordinandus*, gerundive of *ordinare* ORDAIN]

or•di•nar•y /áwrd'neree/ *adj. & n.* • *adj.* **1 a** regular; normal; customary; usual (*in the ordinary course of events*). **b** boring; commonplace (*an ordinary man*). **2** (of a judge) having immediate or ex officio jurisdiction. • *n.* (*pl.* **•ies**) **1** a person, esp. a judge, having immediate or ex officio jurisdiction. **2** (**the Ordinary**) **a** an archbishop in a province. **b** a bishop in a diocese. **3** (usu. **Ordinary**) *RC Ch.* **a** those parts of a service, esp. the mass, that do not vary from day to day. **b** a rule or book laying down the order of divine service. **4** *Heraldry* a charge of the earliest, simplest, and commonest kind (esp. chief, pale, bend, fess, bar, chevron, cross, saltire). **5** (prec. by *the*) *colloq.* the customary or usual condition, course, or degree. **6** an early type of bicycle with one large and one very small wheel. **7** *Brit. hist.* **a** a public meal provided at a fixed time and price at an inn, etc. **b** an establishment providing this. □ **in ordinary** *Brit.* by permanent appointment (esp. to the royal household) (*physician in ordinary*). **in the ordinary way** if the circumstances are or were not exceptional. **out of the ordinary** unusual. □□ **or•di•nar•i•ly** /–áirəlee/ *adv.* **or•di•nar•i•ness** *n.* [ME f. L *ordinarius* orderly (as ORDER)]

or•di•nar•y sea•man *n.* a sailor of the lowest rank, that below ablebodied seaman.

or•di•nate /áwrd'nit/ *n. Math.* a straight line from any point drawn parallel to one coordinate axis and meeting the other, usually a coordinate measured parallel to the vertical (cf. ABSCISSA). [L *linea ordinata applicata* line applied parallel f. *ordinare*: see ORDAIN]

or•di•na•tion /áwrd'náyshən/ *n.* **1 a** the act of conferring holy orders, esp. on a priest or deacon. **b** the admission of a priest, etc., to church ministry. **2** the arrangement of things, etc., in ranks; classification. **3** the act of decreeing or ordaining. [ME f. OF *ordination* or L *ordinatio* (as ORDAIN)]

ord•nance /áwrdnəns/ *n.* **1** mounted guns; cannon. **2** a branch of the armed forces dealing esp. with military stores and materials. [ME var. of ORDINANCE]

Ord•nance Sur•vey *n. Brit.* (in the UK) an official survey organization, orig. under the Master of the Ordnance, preparing large-scale detailed maps of the whole country.

or•don•nance /áwrdənəns/ *n.* the systematic arrangement, esp. of literary or architectural work. [F f. OF *ordenance*: see ORDINANCE]

Or•do•vi•cian /áwrdəvíshən/ *adj. & n. Geol.* • *adj.* of or relating to the second period of the Paleozoic era, with evidence of the first vertebrates and an abundance of marine invertebrates. • *n.* this period or system. [L *Ordovices* ancient British tribe in N. Wales]

or•dure /áwrjər, –dyoor/ *n.* **1** excrement; dung. **2** obscenity; filth; foul language. [ME f. OF f. *ord* foul f. L *horridus*: see HORRID]

Ore. *abbr.* Oregon.

ore /awr/ *n.* a naturally occurring solid material from which metal or other valuable minerals may be extracted. [OE *ōra* unwrought metal, *ār* bronze, rel. to L *aes* crude metal, bronze]

ö•re /órə/ *n.* (also **ø•re**) a Scandinavian monetary unit equal to one-hundredth of a krona or krone. [Swedish]

o•re•ad /áwreead/ *n.* (in Greek and Roman mythology) a mountain nymph. [ME f. L *oreas –ados* f. Gk *oreias* f. *oros* mountain]

o•rec•tic /awréktik/ *adj. Philos. & Med.* of or concerning desire or appetite. [Gk *orektikos* f. *oregō* stretch out]

Oreg. *abbr.* Oregon.

o•reg•a•no /ərégənō, awrég–/ *n.* an aromatic herb, *Origanum vulgare*, the fresh or dried leaves of which are used as a flavoring in cooking. Also called **wild marjoram**. (cf. MARJORAM). [Sp., = ORIGAN]

or·gan /áwrgən/ n. **1 a** a usu. large musical instrument having pipes supplied with air from bellows, sounded by keys, and distributed into sets or stops that form partial organs, each with a separate keyboard (*choir organ*; *pedal organ*). **b** a smaller instrument without pipes, producing similar sounds electronically. **c** a smaller keyboard wind instrument with metal reeds; a harmonium. **d** = BARREL ORGAN. **2 a** a usu. self-contained part of an organism having a special vital function (*vocal organs*; *digestive organs*). **b** esp. *joc.* the penis. **3** a medium of communication, esp. a newspaper, sectarian periodical, etc. **4** *archaic* a professionally trained singing voice. **5** *Phrenol. archaic* a region of the brain held to be the seat of a particular faculty. [ME f. OE *organa* & OF *organe*, f. L *organum* f. Gk *organon* tool]

or·gan·dy /áwrgəndee/ n. (also **or·gan·die**) (*pl.* **·dies**) a fine translucent cotton muslin, usu. stiffened. [F *organdi*, of unkn. orig.]

or·gan·elle /áwrgənél/ n. *Biol.* any of various organized or specialized structures that form part of a cell. [mod.L *organella* dimin.; see ORGAN, –LE]

or·gan-grind·er n. the player of a barrel organ.

or·gan·ic /awrgánik/ adj. **1 a** *Physiol.* of or relating to a bodily organ or organs. **b** *Med.* (of a disease) affecting the structure of an organ. **2** (of a plant or animal) having organs or an organized physical structure. **3** *Agriculture* produced or involving production without the use of chemical fertilizers, pesticides, etc. (*organic crop*; *organic farming*). **4** *Chem.* (of a compound, etc.) containing carbon (opp. INORGANIC). **5 a** structural; inherent. **b** constitutional; fundamental. **6** organized; systematic; coordinated (*an organic whole*). □□ **or·gan·i·cal·ly** adv. [F *organique* f. L *organicus* f. Gk *organikos* (as ORGAN)]

or·gan·ic chem·is·try n. the chemistry of carbon compounds.

or·gan·ic law n. a law stating the formal constitution of a country.

or·gan·ism /áwrgənizəm/ n. **1** a living individual consisting of a single cell or of a group of interdependent parts sharing the life processes. **2 a** an individual live plant or animal. **b** the material structure of this. **3** a whole with interdependent parts compared to a living being. [F *organisme* (as ORGANIZE)]

or·gan·ist /áwrgənist/ n. the player of an organ.

or·gan·i·za·tion /áwrgənizáyshən/ n. **1** the act or an instance of organizing; the state of being organized. **2** an organized body, esp. a business, government department, charity, etc. **3** systematic arrangement; tidiness. □□ **or·gan·i·za·tion·al** adj. **organ·i·za·tion·al·ly** adv.

or·gan·i·za·tion man n. a man who subordinates his individuality and his personal life to the organization he serves.

or·gan·ize /áwrgəniz/ v.tr. **1 a** give an orderly structure to; systematize. **b** bring the affairs of (another person or oneself) into order; make arrangements for (a person). **2** *Brit.* **a** arrange for or initiate (a plan, etc.). **b** provide; take responsibility for (*organized some sandwiches*). **3** (often *absol.*) **a** enroll (new members) in a labor union, political party, etc. **b** form (a labor union or other political group). **4 a** form (different elements) into an organic whole. **b** form (an organic whole). **5** (esp. as **organized** adj.) make organic; make into a living being or tissue. □□ **or·gan·iz·a·ble** adj. **or·gan·iz·er** n. [ME f. OF *organiser* f. med.L *organizare* f. L (as ORGAN)]

or·gan·ized crime n. **1** an organization of people who carry out illegal activities for profit. **2** the people involved in this.

or·gan loft n. a gallery in a church or concert room for an organ.

organo- /áwrgənō/ *comb. form* **1** esp. *Biol.* organ. **2** *Chem.* organic. [Gk (as ORGAN)]

or·gan of Cor·ti /káwrtee/ n. *Anat.* a structure in the inner ear of mammals, responsible for converting sound signals into nerve impulses. [A. *Corti*, It. anatomist d. 1876]

or·ga·no·lep·tic /áwrgənōléptik, awrgánō–/ adj. affecting the organs of sense. [ORGANO- + Gk *lēptikos* disposed to take f. *lambanō* take]

or·ga·no·me·tal·lic /áwrgənōmitálik, awrgánō–/ adj. (of a compound) organic and containing a metal.

or·ga·non /áwrgənon/ n. (also **or·ga·num** /órgənəm/) an instrument of thought, esp. a means of reasoning or a system of logic. [Gk *organon* & L *organum* (as ORGAN): *Organon* was the title of Aristotle's logical writings, and *Novum* (new) *Organum* that of Bacon's]

or·ga·no·ther·a·py /áwrgənōthérəpee, awrgánō–/ n. the treatment of disease with extracts of organs.

or·gan pipe n. any of the pipes on an organ.

or·gan screen n. an ornamental screen usu. between the choir and the nave of a church, cathedral, etc., on which the organ is placed.

or·gan stop n. **1** a set of pipes of a similar tone in an organ. **2** the handle of the mechanism that brings it into action.

or·gan·za /awrgánzə/ n. a thin stiff transparent silk or synthetic dress fabric. [prob. f. *Lorganza* (trade name)]

or·gan·zine /áwrgənzeen/ n. a silk thread in which the main twist is in a contrary direction to that of the strands. [F *organsin* f. It. *organzino*, of unkn. orig.]

or·gasm /áwrgazəm/ n. & v. • n. **1 a** the climax of sexual excitement, esp. during sexual intercourse. **b** an instance of this. **2** violent excitement; rage. • v.intr. experience a sexual orgasm. □□ **or·gas·mic** /–gázmik/ adj. **or·gas·mic·al·ly** adv. **or·gas·tic** /–gástik/ adj. **or·gas·ti·cal·ly** adv. [F *orgasme* or mod.L f. Gk *orgasmos* f. *orgaō* swell, be excited]

or·geat /awrzhát, áwrjat/ n. a cooling drink made from barley or almonds and orange flower water. [F f. Prov. *orjat* f. *ordi* barley f. L *hordeum*]

or·gi·as·tic /áwrjeeástik/ adj. of or resembling an orgy. □□ **or·gi·as·ti·cal·ly** adv. [Gk *orgiastikos* f. *orgiastēs* agent-noun f. *orgiazō* hold an orgy]

or·gu·lous /áwrgyələs/ adj. *archaic* haughty; splendid. [ME f. OF *orguillus* f. *orguill* pride f. Frank.]

or·gy /áwrjee/ n. (*pl.* **·gies**) **1** a wild drunken festivity, esp. one at which indiscriminate sexual activity takes place. **2** excessive indulgence in an activity. **3** (usu. in *pl.*) *Gk & Rom. Hist.* secret rites used in the worship of esp. Bacchus, celebrated with dancing, drunkenness, singing, etc. [orig. pl., f. F *orgies* f. L *orgia* f. Gk *orgia* secret rites]

or·i·bi /áwribee, ór–/ n. (*pl.* same or **or·i·bis**) a small S. African grazing antelope, *Ourebia ourebi*, having a reddish fawn back and white underparts. [prob. Khoisan]

o·ri·el /áwreeəl/ n. **1** a large polygonal recess built out usu. from an upper story and supported from the ground or on corbels. **2** (in full **oriel window**) **a** any of the windows in an oriel. **b** the projecting window of an upper story. [ME f. OF *oriol* gallery, of unkn. orig.]

oriel

o·ri·ent n., adj., & v. • n. /áwreeənt/ **1** (**the Orient**) a *poet.* the east. **b** the countries E. of the Mediterranean, esp. E. Asia. **2** an orient pearl. • adj. /áwreeənt/ **1** *poet.* oriental. **2** (of precious stones and esp. the finest pearls coming orig. from the East) lustrous; sparkling; precious. **3** *archaic* **a** radiant. **b** (of the sun, daylight, etc.) rising. • v. /áwree–ent/ **1** tr. **a** place or exactly determine the position of with the aid of a compass; settle or find the bearings of. **b** (often foll. by *toward*) bring (oneself, different elements, etc.) into a clearly understood position or relationship; direct. **2** tr. **a** place or build (a church, building, etc.) facing toward the East. **b** bury (a person) with the feet toward the East. **3** intr. turn eastward or in a specified direction. □ **orient oneself** determine how one stands in relation to one's surroundings. [ME f. OF *orient*, *orienter* f. L *oriens* –*entis* rising, sunrise, east, f. *oriri* rise]

▶When you're talking about helping someone or something adjust to new surroundings or circumstances, **orient** is preferable to **orientate**.

o·ri·en·tal /áwree-éntəl/ adj. & n. • adj. **1** (often **Oriental**) **a** of or characteristic of Eastern civilization, etc. **b** of or concerning the East, esp. E. Asia. **2** (of a pearl, etc.) orient. • n. (esp. **Oriental**) a native of the Orient. □□ **o·ri·en·tal·ism** n. **o·ri·en·tal·ist** n. **o·ri·en·tal·ize** v.intr. & tr. **o·ri·en·tal·ly** adv. [ME f. OF *oriental* or L *orientalis* (as ORIENT)]

▶The term **Oriental**, which has many associations with European imperialism in Asia, is regarded as offensive by many Asians, especially Asian Americans. **Asian** or, if appropriate, **East Asian** is preferred.

o·ri·en·tate /áwree-entayt/ v.tr. & intr. = ORIENT v. [prob. back-form. f. ORIENTATION]

o·ri·en·ta·tion /áwree-entáyshən/ n. **1** the act or an instance of orienting; the state of being oriented. **2 a** a relative position. **b** a person's attitude or adjustment in relation to circumstances, esp. politically or psychologically. **3** an introduction to a subject or situation;

a briefing. **4** the faculty by which birds, etc., find their way home from a distance. □□ **o·ri·en·ta·tion·al** *adj.* [app. f. ORIENT]

o·ri·en·ta·tion course *n.* a course giving information to newcomers to a university, etc.

o·ri·en·teer·ing /áwree-entéering/ *n.* a competitive sport in which runners cross open country with a map, compass, etc. □□ **o·ri·en·teer** *n. & v.intr.* [Sw. *orientering*]

or·i·fice /áwrifis, ór–/ *n.* an opening, esp. the mouth of a cavity, a bodily aperture, etc. [F f. LL *orificium* f. *os oris* mouth + *facere* make]

or·i·flamme /áwriflam, ór–/ *n.* **1** *hist.* the sacred scarlet silk banner of St. Denis given to early French kings by the abbot of St. Denis on setting out for war. **2** a standard, a principle, or an ideal as a rallying point in a struggle. **3** a bright conspicuous object, color, etc. [ME f. OF f. L *aurum* gold + *flamma* flame]

orig. *abbr.* **1** original. **2** originally.

o·ri·ga·mi /áwrigaámee/ *n.* the Japanese art of folding paper into decorative shapes and figures. [Jap. f. *ori* fold + *kami* paper]

or·i·gan /áwrigən, ór–/ *n.* (also **origanum** /əríganəm/) any plant of the genus *Origanum*, esp. oregano. [(ME f. OF *origan*) f. L *origanum* f. Gk *origanon*]

origami

or·i·gin /áwrijin, ór–/ *n.* **1** a beginning or starting point; a derivation; a source (*a word of Latin origin*). **2** (often in *pl.*) a person's ancestry (*what are his origins?*). **3** *Anat.* **a** a place at which a muscle is firmly attached. **b** a place where a nerve or blood vessel begins or branches from a main nerve or blood vessel. **4** *Math.* a fixed point from which coordinates are measured. [F *origine* or f. L *origo –ginis* f. *oriri* rise]

SYNONYM TIP origin

INCEPTION, PROVENANCE, ROOT, SOURCE. The **origin** of something is the point from which it starts or sets out, or the person or thing from which it is ultimately derived (*the origin of the custom of carving pumpkins at Halloween; the origin of a word*). It often applies to causes that were in operation before the thing itself was brought into being. **Source**, on the other hand, applies to that which provides a first and continuous supply (*the source of the river; an ongoing source of inspiration and encouragement*). **Root**, more often than *source*, applies to what is regarded as the first or final cause of something; it suggests an origin so fundamental as to be the ultimate cause from which something stems (*money is the root of all evil*). **Inception** refers specifically to the beginning of an undertaking, project, institution, or practice (*she was in charge of the organization from its inception*). **Provenance** is similarly restricted in meaning, referring to the specific place, or sometimes the race or people, from which something is derived or by whom it was invented or constructed (*in digging, they uncovered an artifact of unknown provenance*).

o·rig·i·nal /əríjinəl/ *adj. & n.* ● *adj.* **1** existing from the beginning; innate. **2** novel; inventive; creative (*has an original mind*). **3** serving as a pattern; not derivative or imitative; firsthand (*in the original Greek; has an original Rembrandt*). ● *n.* **1** an original model, pattern, picture, etc., from which another is copied or translated (*kept the copy and destroyed the original*). **2** an eccentric or unusual person. **3 a** a garment specially designed for a fashion collection. **b** a copy of such a garment made to order. □□ **o·rig·i·nal·ly** *adv.* [ME f. OF *original* or L *originalis* (as ORIGIN)]

o·rig·i·nal in·stru·ment *n.* a musical instrument, or a copy of one, dating from the time the music played on it was composed.

o·rig·i·nal·i·ty /əríjinálitee/ *n.* (*pl.* **·ties**) **1** the power of creating or thinking creatively. **2** newness or freshness (*this vase has originality*). **3** an original act, thing, trait, etc.

o·rig·i·nal print *n.* a print made directly from an artist's own woodcut, etching, etc., and printed under the artist's supervision.

o·rig·i·nal sin *n.* the innate depravity of all humankind held to be a consequence of the Fall of Adam.

o·rig·i·nate /əríjinayt/ *v.* **1** *tr.* cause to begin; initiate. **2** *intr.* (usu. foll. by *from, in, with*) have as an origin; begin. □□ **o·rig·i·na·tion** /–náyshən/ *n.* **o·rig·i·na·tive** *adj.* **o·rig·i·na·tor** *n.* [med. L *originare* (as ORIGIN)]

o·ri·na·sal /áwrináyzəl, ór–/ *adj.* (esp. of French nasalized vowels) sounded with both the mouth and the nose. [L *os oris* mouth + NASAL]

O-ring /ó-ring/ *n.* a gasket in the form of a ring with a circular cross section.

o·ri·ole /áwreeōl/ *n.* **1** any Old World bird of the genus *Oriolus*, many of which have brightly colored plumage (see GOLDEN ORIOLE). **2** any New World bird of the genus *Icterus*, with similar coloration. [med. L *oriolus* f. OF *oriol* f. L *aureolus* dimin. of *aureus* golden f. *aurum* gold]

O·ri·on /əríən/ *n.* a brilliant constellation on the celestial equator visible from most parts of the earth. [ME f. L f. Gk *Oríōn*, name of a legendary hunter]

O·ri·on's belt *n.* three bright stars in a short line across the middle of the constellation Orion.

O·ri·on's hound *n.* Sirius, the brightest star in the sky.

or·i·son /áwrizən, ór–/ *n.* (usu. in *pl.*) *archaic* a prayer. [ME f. AF *ureison*, OF *oreison* f. L (as ORATION)]

-orium /áwreeəm/ *suffix* forming nouns denoting a place for a particular function (*auditorium; crematorium*). [L, neut. of adjectives in *–orius*: see –ORY[1]]

O·ri·ya /áwreeə/ *n.* **1** a native of the state of Orissa in India. **2** the Indo-European language of this people. [Hindi]

orle /awrl/ *n.* *Heraldry* a narrow band or border of charges near the edge of a shield. [Fo(u)*rle* f. *ourler* to hem, ult. f. L *ora* edge]

Or·lon /áwrlon/ *n. Trademark* a synthetic fiber and fabric for textiles and knitwear. [invented word, after NYLON]

or·lop /áwrlop/ *n.* the lowest deck of a ship with three or more decks. [ME f. MDu. *overloop* covering f. *overloopen* run over (as OVER-, LEAP)]

or·mer /áwrmər/ *n.* an edible univalve mollusk, *Haliotis tuberculata*, having a flattened shell with a series of holes of increasing size along the outer margin. Also called **sea ear.** [Channel Islands F f. F *ormier* f. L *auris maris* ear of sea]

or·mo·lu /áwrməlōō/ *n.* **1** (often *attrib.*) **a** a gilded bronze or gold-colored alloy of copper, zinc, and tin used to decorate furniture, make ornaments, etc. **b** articles made of or decorated with these. **2** showy trash. [F *or moulu* powdered gold (for use in gilding)]

or·na·ment *n. & v.* ● *n.* /áwrnəmənt/ **1 a** a thing used or serving to adorn, esp. a small trinket, vase, figure, etc. (*a mantelpiece crowded with ornaments; her only ornament was a brooch*). **b** a quality or person conferring adornment, grace, or honor (*an ornament to her profession*). **2** decoration added to embellish, esp. a building (*a tower rich in ornament*). **3** (in *pl.*) *Mus.* embellishments and decorations made to a melody. **4** (usu. in *pl.*) the accessories of worship, e.g., the altar, chalice, sacred vessels, etc. ● *v.tr.* /áwrnəmənt/ adorn; beautify. □□ **or·na·men·ta·tion** /–táyshən/ *n.* [ME f. AF *urnement*, OF *o(u)rnement* f. L *ornamentum* equipment f. *ornare* adorn]

or·na·men·tal /áwrnəmént'l/ *adj. & n.* ● *adj.* serving as an ornament; decorative. ● *n.* a thing considered to be ornamental, esp. a cultivated plant. □□ **or·na·men·tal·ism** *n.* **or·na·men·tal·ist** *n.* **or·na·men·tal·ly** *adv.*

or·nate /awrnáyt/ *adj.* **1** elaborately adorned; highly decorated. **2** (of literary style) convoluted; flowery. □□ **or·nate·ly** *adv.* **or·nate·ness** *n.* [ME f. L *ornatus* past part. of *ornare* adorn]

or·ner·y /áwrnəree/ *adj. colloq.* **1** cantankerous; unpleasant. **2** of poor quality. □□ **or·ner·i·ness** *n.* [var. of ORDINARY]

or·nith·ic /awrníthik/ *adj.* of or relating to birds. [Gk *ornithikos* birdlike (as ORNITHO-)]

ornitho- /áwrnithō/ *comb. form* bird. [Gk f. *ornis ornithos* bird]

or·ni·thol·o·gy /áwrnithóləjee/ *n.* the scientific study of birds. □□ **or·ni·tho·log·i·cal** /–thəlójikəl/ *adj.* **or·ni·tho·log·i·cal·ly** *adv.* **or·ni·thol·o·gist** *n.* [mod.L *ornithologia* f. Gk *ornithologos* treating of birds (as ORNITHO-, –LOGY)]

or·nith·o·rhyn·chus /áwrnithəríngkəs/ *n.* = PLATYPUS. [ORNITHO- + Gk *rhugkhos* bill]

oro- /áwrō/ *comb. form* mountain. [Gk *oros* mountain]

o·rog·e·ny /awrójinee/ *n.* (also **o·ro·gen·e·sis** /áwrōjénisis/) the process of the formation of mountains. □□ **or·o·ge·net·ic** /áwrōjinétik/ *adj.* **or·o·gen·ic** /áwrəjénik/ *adj.*

o·rog·ra·phy /áwrógrəfee/ *n.* the branch of physical geography dealing with mountains. □□ **or·o·graph·ic** *adj.* **or·o·graph·i·cal** *adj.*

o·ro·tund /áwrətund/ *adj.* **1** (of the voice or phrasing) full and round; imposing. **2** (of writing, style, expression, etc.) pompous; pretentious. [L *ore rotundo* with rounded mouth]

or·phan /áwrfən/ *n. & v.* ● *n.* (often *attrib.*) **1** a child bereaved of a parent or usu. both parents. **2** a young animal that has lost its mother. **3** a person or thing bereft of previous protection, support, advantages, etc. ● *v.tr.* bereave (a child) of its parents or a parent. □□ **or·phan·hood** *n.* **or·phan·ize** *v.tr.* [ME f. LL *orphanus* f. Gk *orphanos* bereaved]

or·phan·age /áwrfənij/ *n.* **1** a usu. residential institution for the care and education of orphans. **2** orphanhood.

Or·phe·an /áwrféeən, áwrfeeən/ *adj.* like the music of Orpheus, a legendary Greek poet and lyre player; melodious; entrancing. [L *Orpheus* (adj.) f. Gk *Orpheios* f. *Orpheus*]

Or·phic /áwrfik/ *adj.* **1** of or concerning Orpheus or the mysteries, doctrines, etc., associated with him; oracular; mysterious. **2** = ORPHEAN. □□ **Or·phism** /–fizəm/ *n.* [L *Orphicus* f. Gk *Orphikos* f. *Orpheus*]

or·phrey /áwrfree/ *n.* (*pl.* **·phreys**) an ornamental stripe or border or separate piece of ornamental needlework, esp. on ecclesiastical vestments. [ME *orfreis* (taken as pl.) (gold) embroidery f. OF f. med.L *aurifrisium*, etc. f. L *aurum* gold + *Phrygius* Phrygian, also ' embroidered']

or·pi·ment /áwrpimənt/ *n.* **1** a mineral form of arsenic trisulfide, formerly used as a dye and artist's pigment. Also called **yellow arsenic**. **2** (in full **red orpiment**) = REALGAR. [ME f. OF f. L *auripigmentum* f. *aurum* gold + *pigmentum* pigment]

or·pine /áwrpin/ *n.* (also **or·pin**) a succulent herbaceous purple-flowered plant, *Sedum telephium*. [ME f. OF *orpine*, prob. alt. of ORPIMENT, orig. of a yellow-flowered species of the same genus]

or·ra /áwrə, órə/ *adj. Sc.* **1** not matched; odd. **2** occasional; extra. [18th c.: orig. unkn.]

or·rer·y /áwrəree, ór–/ *n.* (*pl.* **·ies**) a clockwork model of the solar system. [named after the fourth Earl of *Orrery* d. 1731, for whom one was made]

or·ris /áwris, ór–/ *n.* **1** any plant of the genus *Iris*, esp. *I. florentina*. **2** = ORRISROOT. [16th c.: app. an unexpl. alt. of IRIS]

or·ris pow·der *n.* powdered orrisroot.

or·ris·root /áwrisrōot, –rŏŏ t, ór–/ *n.* the fragrant rootstock of the orris, used in perfumery and formerly in medicine.

or·tan·ique /áwrtənéek/ *n. Brit.* a citrus fruit produced by crossing an orange and a tangerine. [*orange* + *tangerine* + un*ique*]

ortho- /áwrthō/ *comb. form* **1 a** straight, rectangular, upright. **b** right, correct. **2** *Chem.* **a** relating to two adjacent carbon atoms in a benzene ring. **b** relating to acids and salts (e.g., *orthophosphates*) giving *meta-* compounds on removal of water. [Gk *orthos* straight]

or·tho·ce·phal·ic /áwrthōsifálik/ *adj.* having a head with a medium ratio of breadth to height.

or·tho·chro·mat·ic /áwrthōkrōmátik/ *adj.* giving fairly correct relative intensity to colors in photography by being sensitive to all except red.

or·tho·clase /áwrthəklays, –klayz/ *n.* a common alkali feldspar usu. occurring as variously colored crystals, used in ceramics and glassmaking. [ORTHO- + Gk *klasis* breaking]

or·tho·don·tics /áwrthədóntiks/ *n.pl.* (treated as *sing.*) (also **or·tho·don·tia** /–dónshə/) the treatment of irregularities in the teeth and jaws. □□ **or·tho·don·tic** *adj.* **or·tho·don·tist** *n.* [ORTHO- + Gk *odous odont-* tooth]

or·tho·dox /áwrthədoks/ *adj.* **1 a** holding correct or currently accepted opinions, esp. on religious doctrine, morals, etc. **b** not independent-minded; unoriginal; unheretical. **2** (of religious doctrine, standards of morality, etc.) generally accepted as right or true; authoritatively established; conventional. **3** (also **Orthodox**) (of Judaism) strictly keeping to traditional doctrine and ritual. □□ **or·tho·dox·ly** *adv.* [eccl. L *orthodoxus* f. Gk *orthodoxos* f. *doxa* opinion]

Or·tho·dox Church *n.* the Eastern Christian Church, separated from the Western Christian Church in the 11th c., having the Patriarch of Constantinople as its head, and including the national churches of Russia, Romania, Greece, etc.

or·tho·dox·y /áwrthədoksee/ *n.* (*pl.* **·ies**) **1** the state of being orthodox. **2 a** the orthodox practice of Judaism. **b** the body of orthodox Jews. **3** esp. Relig. an authorized or generally accepted theory, doctrine, etc. [LL *orthodoxia* f. late Gk *orthodoxia* sound doctrine (as ORTHODOX)]

or·tho·epy /awrthō-ipee, áwrthōepee/ *n.* the study of the (correct) pronunciation of words. □□ **or·tho·ep·ic** /–thōépik/ *adj.* **or·tho·e·pist** *n.* [Gk *orthoepeia* correct speech (as ORTHO-, *epos* word)]

or·tho·gen·e·sis /áwrthōjénisis/ *n.* a theory of evolution that proposes that variations follow a defined direction and are not merely sporadic and fortuitous. □□ **or·tho·ge·net·ic** /–jənétik/ *adj.* **or·tho·ge·net·i·cal·ly** *adv.*

or·thog·na·thous /awrthógnəthəs/ *adj.* (of mammals, including humans) having a jaw that does not project forward and a facial angle approaching a right angle. [ORTHO- + Gk *gnathos* jaw]

or·thog·o·nal /awrthógənəl/ *adj.* of or involving right angles. [F f. *orthogone* (as ORTHO-, –GON)]

or·thog·ra·phy /awrthógrəfee/ *n.* (*pl.* **·phies**) **1 a** correct or conventional spelling. **b** spelling with reference to its correctness (*dreadful orthography*). **c** the study or science of spelling. **2 a** perspective projection used in maps and elevations in which the projection lines are parallel. **b** a map, etc., so projected. □□ **or·thog·ra·pher** *n.* **or·tho·graph·ic** /áwrthəgráfik/ *adj.* **or·tho·graph·i·cal** *adj.* **or·tho·graph·i·cal·ly** *adv.* [ME f. OF *ortografie* f. L *orthographia* f. Gk *orthographia* (as ORTHO-, –GRAPHY)]

or·tho·pe·dics /áwrthəpéediks/ *n.pl.* (treated as *sing.*) (*Brit.* **–pae·dics**) the branch of medicine dealing with the correction of deformities of bones or muscles, orig. in children. □□ **or·tho·pe·dic** *adj.* **or·tho·pe·dist** *n.* [F *orthopédie* (as ORTHO–, *pédie* f. Gk *paideia* rearing of children)]

or·thop·ter·an /awrthóptərən/ *n.* any insect of the order Orthoptera, with straight narrow forewings, and hind legs modified for jumping, etc., including grasshoppers and crickets. □□ **or·thop·ter·ous** *adj.* [ORTHO- + Gk *pteros* wing]

or·thop·tic /awrthóptik/ *adj.* relating to the correct or normal use of the eyes. □□ **or·thop·tist** *n.* [ORTHO- + Gk *optikos* of sight: see OPTIC]

or·thop·tics /awrthóptiks/ *n. Med.* the study or treatment of irregularities of the eyes, esp. with reference to the eye muscles.

or·tho·rhom·bic /áwrthōrómbik/ *adj. Crystallog.* (of a crystal) characterized by three mutually perpendicular axes that are unequal in length, as in topaz and talc.

or·thot·ics /awrthaátiks/ *n.* **1** *Med.* the science of treating joint, bone, or muscle disorders with mechanical support, braces, etc. **2** devices, such as inserts for athletic shoes, used for such treatment.

or·tho·tone /áwrthətōn/ *adj. & n.* • *adj.* (of a word) having an independent stress pattern, not enclitic nor proclitic. • *n.* a word of this kind.

or·to·lan /áwrt'lən/ *n.* (in full **or·to·lan bun·ting**) *Zool.* a small European bird, *Emberiza hortulana*, eaten as a delicacy. [F f. Prov., lit. gardener, f. L *hortulanus* f. *hortulus* dimin. of *hortus* garden]

Or·well·i·an /awrwéleeən/ *adj.* of or characteristic of the writings of George Orwell (E. A. Blair), English writer d. 1950, esp. with reference to the totalitarian development of the state as depicted in *1984* and *Animal Farm*.

-ory[1] /áwree, əree/ *suffix* forming nouns denoting a place for a particular function (*dormitory; refectory*). □□ **–orial** /áwreeəl, óreeəl/ *suffix* forming adjectives. [L *–oria, –orium*, sometimes via ONF and AF *–orie*, OF *–oire*]

-ory[2] /əree/ *suffix* forming adjectives (and occasionally nouns) relating to or involving a verbal action (*accessory; compulsory; directory*). [L *–orius*, sometimes via AF *–ori(e)*, OF *–oir(e)*]

oryx /áwriks, ór–/ *n.* any large straight-horned antelope of the genus *Oryx*, native to Africa and Arabia. [ME f. L f. Gk *orux* stonemason's pickax, f. its pointed horns]

OS *abbr.* **1** old style. **2** ordinary seaman. **3** *oculus sinister* (left eye). **4** outsize. **5** out of stock.

Os *symb. Chem.* the element osmium.

O·sage /ōsáyj, ó–/ *n. & adj.* • *n.* **1 a** a N. American people native to Missouri. **b** a member of this people. **2** the language of this people. • *adj.* of or relating to this people or their language.

O·sage or·ange *n.* **1** a hardy thorny tree, *Maclura pomifera*, of the US, bearing inedible wrinkled orangelike fruit. **2** the durable orange-colored wood from this.

Os·can /óskən/ *n. & adj.* • *n.* the ancient language of Campania in Italy, related to Latin and surviving only in inscriptions. • *adj.* relating to or written in Oscan. [L *Oscus*]

Os·car /óskər/ *n.* any of the statuettes awarded by the Academy of Motion Picture Arts and Sciences for excellence in motion-picture acting, directing, etc. [the name *Oscar*]

os·cil·late /ósilayt/ *v.* **1** *intr. & tr.* **a** swing back and forth like a pendulum. **b** move back and forth between points. **2** *intr.* vacillate; vary between extremes of opinion, action, etc. **3** *intr. Physics* move with periodic regularity. **4** *intr. Electr.* (of a current) undergo high-frequency alternations as across a spark gap or in a valve-transmitter circuit. **5** *intr.* (of a radio receiver) radiate electromagnetic waves owing to faulty operation. □□ **os·cil·la·tion** /–áyshən/ *n.* **os·cil·la·tor** *n.* **os·cil·la·to·ry** /–ətáwree/ *adj.* [L *oscillare oscillat-* swing]

oscillo- /əsílō/ *comb. form* oscillation, esp. of electric current.

os·cil·lo·gram /əsíləgram/ *n.* a record obtained from an oscillograph.

os·cil·lo·graph /əsíləgraf/ *n.* a device for recording oscillations. □□ **os·cil·lo·graph·ic** *adj.* **os·cil·log·ra·phy** /ósilógrəfee/ *n.*

os·cil·lo·scope /əsíləskōp/ *n.* a device for viewing oscillations by a display on the screen of a cathode-ray tube. □□ **os·cil·lo·scop·ic** /–skópik/ *adj.*

os·cine /ósin, –in/ *adj.* (also **os·cin·ine** /ósineen/) of or relating to the suborder Oscines of passerine birds including many of the songbirds. [L *oscen –cinis* songbird (as OB–, *canere* sing)]

os·ci·ta·tion /ósitáyshən/ *n. formal* **1** yawning; drowsiness. **2** inattention; negligence. [L *oscitatio* f. *oscitare* gape f. *os* mouth + *citare* move]

os·cu·la *pl.* of OSCULUM.

os·cu·lar /óskyələr/ *adj.* **1** of or relating to the mouth. **2** of or relating to kissing. [L *osculum* mouth, kiss, dimin. of *os* mouth]

os·cu·late /óskyəlayt/ *v.* **1** *tr. Math.* (of a curve or surface) have contact of at least the second order with; have two branches with a common tangent, with each branch extending in both directions of the tangent. **2** *v.intr. & tr. joc.* kiss. **3** *intr. Biol.* (of a species, etc.) be related through an intermediate species; have common characteristics with another or with each other. □□ **os·cu·lant** *adj.* **os·cu·la·tion** /–láyshən/ *n.* **os·cu·la·to·ry** /–lətáwree/ *adj.* [L *osculari* kiss (as OSCULAR)]

os·cu·lum /óskyələm/ *n.* (*pl.* **os·cu·la** /–lə/) a mouthlike aperture, esp. of a sponge. [L: see OSCULAR]

-ose[1] /ōs/ *suffix* forming adjectives denoting possession of a quality (*grandiose; verbose*). □□ **–osely** *suffix* forming adverbs. **–oseness** *suffix* forming nouns (cf. –OSITY). [from or after L *–osus*]

-ose[2] /ōs/ *suffix Chem.* forming names of carbohydrates (*cellulose; sucrose*). [after GLUCOSE]

OSHA /óshə/ *abbr.* Occupational Safety and Health Administration.

o·sier /ózhər/ *n.* **1** any of various willows, esp. *Salix viminalis*, with long flexible shoots used in basketwork. **2** a shoot of a willow. [ME f. OF: cf. med.L *auseria* osier bed]

-osis /ósis/ *suffix* (*pl.* **·oses** /óseez/) denoting a process or condition (*apotheosis*; *metamorphosis*), esp. a pathological state (*acidosis*; *neurosis*; *thrombosis*). [L f. Gk *–ōsis* suffix of verbal nouns]

-osity /ósitee/ *suffix* forming nouns from adjectives in *–ose* (see *–*OSE[1]) and *–ous* (*verbosity*; *curiosity*). [F *–osité* or L *–ositas –ositatis*: cf. *–*ITY]

Os·man·li /ozmánlee, os–/ *adj. & n.* = OTTOMAN. [Turk. f. *Osman* f. Arab. *'u ṯmān* (see OTTOMAN) + *–li* adj. suffix]

os·mic /ózmik/ *adj.* of or relating to odors or the sense of smell. □□ **os·mi·cal·ly** *adv.* [Gk *osm ē* smell, odor]

os·mi·um /ózmeeəm/ *n. Chem.* a hard, bluish-white transition element, the heaviest known metal, occurring naturally in association with platinum and used in certain alloys. ¶ Symb.: **Os**. [Gk *osmē* smell (from the pungent smell of its tetroxide)]

os·mo·sis /ozmósis, os–/ *n.* **1** *Biochem.* the passage of a solvent through a semipermeable partition into a more concentrated solution. **2** any process by which something is acquired by absorption. □□ **os·mot·ic** /–mótik/ *adj.* **os·mot·i·cal·ly** /–mótikəlee/ *adv.* [orig. *osmose*, after F f. Gk *ōsmos* push]

os·mund /ózmənd/ *n.* (also **os·mun·da** /ozmúndə/) any fern of the genus *Osmunda*, esp. the royal fern, having large divided fronds. [ME f. AF, of uncert. orig.]

os·prey /óspray, –pree/ *n.* (*pl.* **·preys**) **1** a large bird of prey, *Pandion haliaetus*, with a brown back and white markings, feeding on fish. Also called **fish hawk**. **2** a plume on a woman's hat. [ME f. OF *ospres* app. ult. f. L *ossifraga* osprey f. *os* bone + *frangere* break]

OSS *abbr.* Office of Strategic Services.

os·se·in /óseein/ *n.* the collagen of bones. [L *osseus* (as OSSEOUS)]

os·se·ous /óseeəs/ *adj.* **1** consisting of bone. **2** having a bony skeleton. **3** ossified. [L *osseus* f. *os ossis* bone]

os·si·cle /ósikəl/ *n.* **1** *Anat.* any small bone, esp. of the middle ear. **2** a small piece of bonelike substance. [L *ossiculum* dimin. (as OSSEOUS)]

os·si·fy /ósifi/ *v.tr. & intr.* (**·fies, ·fied**) **1** turn into bone; harden. **2** make or become rigid, callous, or unprogressive. □□ **os·sif·ic** /ósifik/ *adj.* **os·si·fi·ca·tion** /–fikáyshən/ *n.* [F *ossifier* f. L *os ossis* bone]

os·so bu·co /áwsōbóōkō/ *n.* (also **os·so buc·co**) shank of veal stewed in wine with vegetables. [It., = marrowbone]

os·su·ar·y /óshŏōeree, ósyŏō–/ *n.* (*pl.* **·ies**) **1** a receptacle for the bones of the dead; a charnel house; a bone urn. **2** a cave in which ancient bones are found. [LL *ossuarium* irreg. f. *os ossis* bone]

os·te·i·tis /osteeítis/ *n.* inflammation of the substance of a bone. [Gk *osteon* bone + *–*ITIS]

os·ten·si·ble /osténsibəl/ *adj.* apparent but not necessarily real; professed (*his ostensible function was that of interpreter*). □□ **os·ten·si·bly** *adv.* [F f. med.L *ostensibilis* f. L *ostendere ostens-* stretch out to view (as OB-, *tendere* stretch)]

SYNONYM TIP ostensible

APPARENT, ILLUSORY, SEEMING. The **apparent** reason for something is not necessarily the real reason. In this sense the word applies to what appears only on the surface, not to what is borne out by scientific investigation or an examination of the relevant facts and circumstances (*the apparent cause was only an illusion*). The **ostensible** reason for something is the reason that is expressed, declared, or avowed; but it implies that the truth is being concealed (*the ostensible purpose of the meeting was to give the two men a chance to get acquainted*). **Seeming** usually refers to the character of the thing observed rather than to a defect in the observation; it implies even more doubt than *apparent* or *ostensible* (*her seeming innocence fooled no one*). That which is **illusory** is always deceptive; it has a character or appearance that doesn't really exist (*an illusory beauty that faded quickly in the bright light*).

---

os·ten·sive /osténsiv/ *adj.* **1** directly demonstrative. **2** (of a definition) indicating by direct demonstration that which is signified by a term. □□ **os·ten·sive·ly** *adv.* **os·ten·sive·ness** *n.* [LL *ostensivus* (as OSTENSIBLE)]

os·ten·so·ry /osténsəree/ *n.* (*pl.* **·ries**) *RC Ch.* a receptacle for displaying the host to the congregation; a monstrance. [med.L *ostensorium* (as OSTENSIBLE)]

os·ten·ta·tion /óstentáyshən/ *n.* **1** a pretentious and vulgar display, esp. of wealth and luxury. **2** the attempt or intention to attract notice; showing off. □□ **os·ten·ta·tious** *adj.* **os·ten·ta·tious·ly** *adv.* [ME f. OF f. L *ostentatio –onis* f. *ostentare* frequent. of *ostendere*: see OSTENSIBLE]

osteo- /ósteeō/ *comb. form* bone. [Gk *osteon*]

os·te·o·ar·thri·tis /ósteeōaarthrítis/ *n.* a degenerative disease of joint cartilage, esp. in the elderly. □□ **os·te·o·ar·thrit·ic** /–thrítik/ *adj.*

os·te·o·gen·e·sis /ósteeōjénisis/ *n.* the formation of bone. □□ **os·te·o·ge·net·ic** /–jinétik/ *adj.*

os·te·ol·o·gy /ósteeóləjee/ *n.* the study of the structure and func-

---

tion of the skeleton and bony structures. □□ **os·te·o·log·i·cal** /–teeəlójikəl/ *adj.* **os·te·o·log·i·cal·ly** *adv.* **os·te·ol·o·gist** *n.*

os·te·o·ma·la·cia /ósteeōməláyshə/ *n.* softening of the bones, often through a deficiency of vitamin D and calcium. □□ **os·te·o·ma·lac·ic** /–lásik/ *adj.* [mod.L (as OSTEO–, Gk *malakos* soft)]

os·te·o·my·e·li·tis /ósteeōmī-ilítis/ *n.* inflammation of the bone or of bone marrow, usu. due to infection.

os·te·op·a·thy /ósteeópəthee/ *n.* the treatment of disease through the manipulation of bones, esp. the spine, displacement of these being the supposed cause. □□ **os·te·o·path** /ósteeəpath/ *n.* **os·te·o·path·ic** *adj.*

os·te·o·po·ro·sis /ósteeōpərósis/ *n.* a condition of brittle and fragile bones caused by loss of bony tissue, esp. as a result of hormonal changes, or deficiency of calcium or vitamin D. [OSTEO- + Gk *poros* passage, pore]

os·ti·na·to /óstinaàtō/ *n.* (*pl.* **·tos**) (often *attrib.*) *Mus.* a persistent phrase or rhythm repeated through all or part of a piece. [It., = OBSTINATE]

ost·ler /óslər/ *n. Brit. hist.* a stableman at an inn. [f. earlier HOSTLER, *hosteler* f. AF *hostiler*, OF *(h)ostelier* (as HOSTEL)]

Ost·mark /áwstmaark, óst–/ *n. hist.* the chief monetary unit of the former Democratic Republic of Germany. [G, = east mark: see MARK[2]]

Ost·po·li·tik /áwstpawliteěk/ *n. hist.* the foreign policy of many western European countries with reference to the former Communist bloc. [G f. *Ost* east + *Politik* politics]

os·tra·cize /óstrəsiz/ *v.tr.* **1** exclude (a person) from a society, favor, common privileges, etc.; refuse to associate with. **2** (esp. in ancient Athens) banish (a powerful or unpopular citizen) for five or ten years by popular vote. □□ **os·tra·cism** /–sizəm/ *n.* [Gk *ostrakizō* f. *ostrakon* shell, potsherd (used to write a name on in voting)]

os·trich /óstrich, áw–/ *n.* **1** a large African swift-running flightless bird, *Struthio camelus*, with long legs and two toes on each foot. **2** a person who refuses to accept facts (from the belief that ostriches bury their heads in the sand when pursued). [ME f. OF *ostric(h)e* f. L *avis* bird + LL *struthio* f. Gk *strouthiōn* ostrich f. *strouthos* sparrow, ostrich]

os·trich farm *n.* a place that breeds ostriches for their eggs, meat, and feathers.

os·trich plume *n.* a feather or bunch of feathers of an ostrich.

ostrich

Os·tro·goth /óstrəgoth/ *n. hist.* a member of the Eastern branch of the Goths, who conquered Italy in the 5th–6th c. □□ **Os·tro·goth·ic** /–góthik/ *adj.* [LL *Ostrogothi* (pl.) f. Gmc *austro-* (unrecorded) east + LL *Gothi* Goths: see GOTH]

OT *abbr.* Old Testament.

o.t. *abbr.* (also **O.T.**) **1** occupational therapist. **2** occupational therapy. **3** overtime.

-ot[1] /ət/ *suffix* forming nouns, orig. diminutives (*ballot*; *chariot*; *parrot*). [F]

-ot[2] /ət/ *suffix* forming nouns denoting persons (*patriot*), e.g., natives of a place (*Cypriot*). [F *–ote*, L *–ota*, Gk *–ōtēs*]

OTB *abbr.* off-track betting.

OTC *abbr.* **1** over-the-counter. **2** *Brit.* Officers' Training Corps.

oth·er /úthər/ *adj., n.* or *pron.*, & *adv.* ● *adj.* **1** not the same as one or some already mentioned or implied; separate in identity or distinct in kind (*other people*; *use other means*). **2 a** further; additional (*a few other examples*). **b** alternative of two (*open your other eye*) (cf. *every other*). **3** (prec. by *the*) that remains after all except the one or ones in question have been considered, eliminated, etc. (*must be in the other pocket*; *where are the other two?*; *the other three left*). **4** (foll. by *than*) apart from; excepting (*any person other than you*). ● *n.* or *pron.* (orig. an ellipt. use of the adj., now with pl. in *–s*) **1** an additional, different, or extra person, thing, example, etc. (*some others have come*) (see also ANOTHER, EACH OTHER). **2** (in *pl.*; prec. by *the*) the ones remaining (*where are the others?*). ● *adv.* (usu. foll. by *than*) *disp.* otherwise (*cannot react other than angrily*). □ **no other** *archaic* nothing else (*I can do no other*). **of all others** out of the many possible or likely (*on this night of all others*). **on the other hand** see HAND. **the other day** (or **night** or **week**, etc.) a few days, etc., ago (*heard from him the other day*). **other things being equal** if conditions are or were alike in all but the point in question. **someone** (or **something** or **somehow**, etc.) **or other** some unspecified person, thing, manner, etc. [OE *ōther* f. Gmc]

▶As an adverb, **other** is used informally; **otherwise** is standard in more formal use.

oth·er-di·rect·ed *adj.* governed by external circumstances and trends.

oth·er half *n. colloq.* one's wife or husband.

oth·er·ness /úthərnis/ *n.* **1** the state of being different; diversity. **2** a thing or existence other than the thing mentioned and the thinking subject.

oth·er place *n. Brit. joc.* Oxford University as regarded by Cambridge, and vice versa.

oth·er ranks *n. Brit.* soldiers other than commissioned officers.

oth·er·where /úthərhwáir, –wáir/ *adj. archaic* or *poet.* elsewhere.

oth·er·wise /úthərwiz/ *adv. & adj.* ●*adv.* **1** else; or else; in the circumstances other than those considered, etc. (*bring your umbrella, otherwise you will get wet*). **2** in other respects (*he is somewhat unkempt, but otherwise very suitable*). **3** (often foll. by *than*) in a different way (*could not have acted otherwise; cannot react otherwise than angrily*). **4** as an alternative (*otherwise known as Jack*). ●*adj.* **1** (*predic.*) in a different state (*the matter is quite otherwise*). **2** archaic that would otherwise exist (*their otherwise dullness*). □ **and** (or **or**) **otherwise** the negation or opposite (of a specified thing) (*the merits or otherwise of the proposal; experiences pleasant and otherwise*). [OE *onōthre wisan* (as OTHER, WISE[2])]

oth·er wom·an *n.* a married man's mistress.

oth·er world *n.* see WORLD.

oth·er·world·ly /úthərwórldlee/ *adj.* **1** unworldly; impractical. **2** concerned with life after death, etc. □□ **oth·er·world·li·ness** *n.*

o·tic /ótik, ótik/ *adj.* of or relating to the ear. [Gk *ōtikos* f. *ousōtos* ear]

-otic /ótik/ *suffix* forming adjectives and nouns corresponding to nouns in *–osis*, meaning 'affected with or producing or resembling a condition in *–osis*' or 'a person affected with this' (*narcotic; neurotic; osmotic*). □□ **–otically** *suffix* forming adverbs. [from or after F *–otique* f. L f. Gk *–ōtikos* adj. suffix]

o·ti·ose /ósheeōs, ótee–/ *adj.* **1** serving no practical purpose; not required; functionless. **2** *archaic* indolent; futile. □□ **o·ti·ose·ly** *adv.* **o·ti·ose·ness** *n.* [L *otiosus* f. *otium* leisure]

o·ti·tis /ōtítis/ *n.* inflammation of the ear. [mod.L (as OTO-)]

oto- /ótō/ *comb. form* ear. [Gk *ōto-* f. *ousōtos* ear]

o·to·lar·yn·gol·o·gy /ótōláringgóləjee/ *n.* the study of diseases of the ear and throat. □□ **o·to·la·ryn·go·log·i·cal** /–gəlójikəl/ *adj.* **o·to·lar·yn·gol·o·gist** *n.*

o·to·lith /ótəlith/ *n.* any of the small particles of calcium carbonate in the inner ear. □□ **o·to·lith·ic** *adj.*

o·tol·o·gy /ōtóləjee/ *n.* the study of the anatomy and diseases of the ear. □□ **o·to·log·i·cal** /ótəlójikəl/ *adj.* **o·tol·o·gist** *n.*

o·to·rhi·no·lar·yn·gol·o·gy /ótōrínōláringgóləjee/ *n.* the study of diseases of the ear, nose, and throat.

o·to·scope /ótəskōp/ *n.* an apparatus for examining the eardrum and the passage leading to it from the ear. □□ **o·to·scop·ic** /–skópik/ *adj.*

ot·ta·va ri·ma /ōtaávəreemə/ *n.* a stanza of eight lines of 10 or 11 syllables, rhyming *abababcc*. [It., lit. eighth rhyme]

Ot·ta·wa /aátəwə, –waa, –waw/ *n. & adj.* ●*n.* **1 a** a N. American people native to Canada and the great Lakes region. **b** a member of this people. **2** the language of this people. ●*adj.* of or relating to this people or their language.

ot·ter /ótər/ *n.* **1 a** any of several aquatic fish-eating mammals of the family Mustelidae, esp. of the genus *Lutra*, having strong claws and webbed feet. **b** its fur or pelt. **2** = SEA OTTER. **3** a piece of board used to carry fishing bait in water. **4** *Brit.* a type of paravane, esp. as used on nonnaval craft. [OE *otr, ot(t)or* f. Gmc]

ot·ter board *n.* a device for keeping the mouth of a trawl net open.

ot·ter hound *n.* (also **ot·ter dog**) a dog of a breed used in otter hunting.

ot·to var. of ATTAR.

Ot·to·man /ótəmən/ *adj. & n.* ●*adj. hist.* **1** of or concerning the dynasty of Osman or Othman I, the branch of the Turks to which he belonged, or the empire ruled by his descendants. **2** Turkish. ●*n.* (*pl.* **Ot·to·mans**) an Ottoman person; a Turk. [F f. Arab. *'u ṭmānī* adj. of Othman (*' uṭmān*)]

ot·to·man /ótəmən/ *n.* (*pl.* **ot·to·mans**) **1 a** an upholstered seat, usu. square and without a back or arms, sometimes a box with a padded top. **b** a footstool of similar design. **2** a heavy silken fabric with a mixture of cotton or wool. [F *ottomane* fem. (as OTTOMAN)]

Ot·to·man Porte see PORTE.

ou·bli·ette /óobliee-ét/ *n.* a secret dungeon with access only through a trapdoor. [F f. *oublier* forget]

ouch /owch/ *int.* expressing pain or annoyance. [imit.: cf. G *autsch*]

ought[1] /awt/ *v.aux.* (usu. foll. by *to* + infin.; present and past indicated by the following infin.) **1** expressing duty or rightness (*we ought to love our neighbors*). **2** expressing shortcoming (*it ought to have been done long ago*). **3** expressing advisability or prudence (*you

river otter

ought to go for your own good*). **4** expressing esp. strong probability (*he ought to be there by now*). □ **ought not** the negative form of *ought* (*he ought not to have stolen it*). [OE *āhte*, past of *āgan* OWE]

ought[2] var. of AUGHT[2].

ought[3] var. of AUGHT[1].

ought·n't /áwt'nt/ *contr.* ought not.

Oui·ja /weéjə, –jee/ *n.* (in full **Ouija board**) *Trademark* a board having letters or signs at its rim to which a planchette, movable pointer, or upturned glass points in answer to questions from attenders at a seance, etc. [F *oui* ycs + G *ja* ycs]

ounce[1] /owns/ *n.* **1 a** a unit of weight of one-sixteenth of a pound avoirdupois (approx. 28 grams). ¶ Abbr.: **oz. b** a unit of one-twelfth of a pound troy or apothecaries' measure, equal to 480 grains (approx. 31 grams). **2** a small quantity. [ME & OF *unce* f. L *uncia* twelfth part of pound or foot: cf. INCH[1]]

ounce[2] /owns/ *n.* a large Asian feline, *Panthera uncia*, with leopardlike markings on a cream-colored coat. Also called **mountain panther** or **snow leopard**. [ME f. OF *once* (earlier *lonce*) = It. *lonza* ult. f. L *lynx*: see LYNX]

our /owr, aar/ *poss.pron.* (*attrib.*) **1** of or belonging to us or ourselves (*our house; our own business*). **2** of or belonging to all people (*our children's future*). **3** (esp. as **Our**) of Us the king or queen, emperor or empress, etc. (*given under Our seal*). **4** of us, the editorial staff of a newspaper, etc. (*a foolish adventure in our view*). **5** *colloq.* indicating a relative, acquaintance, or colleague of the speaker (*our Barry works there*). [OE *ūre* orig. genit. pl. of 1st pers. pron. = of us, later treated as possessive adj.]

-our /ər/ *suffix Brit.* **1** var. of –OR[1] (*saviour*). **2** var. of –OR[2] (*ardour; colour; valour*).

Our Fa·ther *n.* **1** the Lord's Prayer. **2** God.

Our La·dy *n.* the Virgin Mary.

ours /owrz, aars/ *poss.pron.* the one or ones belonging to or associated with us (*it is ours; ours are over there*). □ **of ours** of or belonging to us (*a friend of ours*).

Our Sav·ior *n.* Jesus Christ.

our·self /owrsélf, aar–/ *pron. archaic* a word formerly used instead of *myself* by a sovereign, newspaper editorial staff, etc. (cf. OUR 3, 4).

our·selves /owrsélvz, aar–/ *pron.* **1 a** *emphat. form* of WE or US (*we ourselves did it; made it ourselves; for our friends and ourselves*). **b** *refl. form* of US (*are pleased with ourselves*). **2** in our normal state of body or mind (*not quite ourselves today*). □ **be ourselves** act in our normal unconstrained manner. **by ourselves** see *by oneself* (see BY).

-ous /əs/ *suffix* **1** forming adjectives meaning 'abounding in, characterized by, of the nature of' (*envious; glorious; mountainous; poisonous*). **2** *Chem.* denoting a state of lower valence than the corresponding word in *–ic* (*ferrous*). □□ **–ously** *suffix* forming adverbs. **–ousness** *suffix* forming nouns. [from or after AF *–ous*, OF *–eus*, f. L *–osus*]

ou·sel var. of OUZEL.

oust /owst/ *v.tr.* **1** (usu. foll. by *from*) drive out or expel, esp. by forcing oneself into the place of. **2** (usu. foll. by *of*) *Law* put (a person) out of possession; deprive. [AF *ouster*, OF *oster* take away, f. L *obstare* oppose, hinder (as OB–, *stare* stand)]

oust·er /ówstər/ *n.* **1** ejection as a result of physical action, judicial process, or political upheaval. **2** dismissal; expulsion.

out /owt/ *adv., prep., n., adj., int., & v.* ●*adv.* **1** away from or not in or at a place, etc. (*keep him out; get out of here; my son is out in California*). **2** (forming part of phrasal verbs) **a** indicating dispersal away from a center, etc. (*hire out; share out; board out*). **b** indicating coming or bringing into the open for public attention, etc. (*call out; send out; shine out; stand out*). **c** indicating a need for attentiveness (*watch out; look out*). **3 a** not in one's house, office, etc. (*went out for a walk*). **b** no longer in prison. **4** to or at an end; completely (*tired out; die out; out of bananas; fight it out; typed it out*). **5** (of a fire, candle, etc.) not burning. **6** in error. **7** *colloq.* unconscious (*she was out for five minutes*). **8 a** (of a tooth) extracted. **b** (of a joint, bone, etc.) dislocated (*put his shoulder out*). **9** (of a party, politician, etc.) not in office. **10** (of a jury) considering its verdict in secrecy. **11** (of workers) on strike. **12** (of a secret) revealed. **13** (of a flower) blooming, open. **14** (of a book) published. **15** (of a star) visible after dark. **16** unfashionable (*wide lapels are out*). **17** *Sports* (of a batter, baserunner, etc.) no longer taking part as such, having been tagged, struck out, caught, etc. **18 a** not worth considering; rejected (*that idea is out*). **b** not allowed. **19** *colloq.* (prec. by *superl.*) known to exist (*the best game out*). **20** (of a stain, mark, etc.) not visible; removed (*painted out the sign*). **21 a** (of time) not spent working (*took five minutes out*). **b** into the future (*let's look five years out*). **22** (of a rash, bruise, etc.) visible. **23** (of the tide) at the lowest point. **24** *Boxing* unable to rise from the floor (*out for the count*). **25** *archaic* (of a young upper-class woman) introduced into society. **26** (in a radio conversation, etc.) transmission ends (*over and out*). ●*prep.* **1** out of (*looked out the window*). **2** *archaic* outside; beyond the limits of. ●*n.* **1** *colloq.* a way of escape; an excuse. **2** (**the outs**) the political party out of office. **3** *Baseball* play in which a batter or baserunner is retired from an inning. ●*adj.* **1** esp. *Brit.* (of a match) played away. **2** (of an island) away from the mainland. • *int.* a peremptory dismissal, reproach, etc. (*out, you scoundrel!*). • *v.* **1** *tr.* **a** put out. **b** *colloq.* eject forcibly. **2** *intr.* come or go out; emerge (*murder will out*). **3** *tr. Boxing* knock out. **4** *tr. colloq.* expose the homosexuality of (esp. a prominent person). □ **at outs** at variance or enmity. **out and about** (of a person, esp. after an illness) engaging in normal activity. **out for** having one's interest or effort directed to; intent on. **out of 1** from within (*came out of the house*). **2** not within (*I was never out of the city*). **3** from among (*nine people out of ten; must choose out of these*). **4** beyond the range of (*is out of reach*). **5** without or so as to be without (*was swindled out of his money; out of breath; out of sugar*). **6** from (*get money out of him*). **7** owing to; because of (*asked out of curiosity*). **8** by the use of (material) (*what did you make it out of?*). **9** at a specified distance from (a town, port, etc.) (*seven miles out of Topeka*). **10** beyond (*something out of the ordinary*). **11** *Racing* (of an animal, esp. a horse) born of. **out of bounds** see BOUND². **out of the closet** see CLOSET. **out of doors** see DOOR. **out of drawing** see DRAWING. **out of hand** see HAND. **out of it 1** not included; forlorn. **2** *sl.* extremely drunk or otherwise disoriented. **out of order** see ORDER. **out of pocket** see POCKET. **out of the question** see QUESTION. **out of sorts** see SORT. **out of temper** see TEMPER. **out of this world** see WORLD. **out of the way** see WAY. **out to** keenly striving to do. **out to lunch** *colloq.* crazy; mad. **out with** an exhortation to expel or dismiss (an unwanted person). **out with it** say what you are thinking. [OE *ūt*, OHG *ūz*, rel. to Skr. *ud*–]

out- /owt/ *prefix* added to verbs and nouns, meaning: **1** so as to surpass or exceed (*outdo; outnumber*). **2** external; separate (*outline; outhouse; outdoors*). **3** out of; away from; outward (*outspread; outgrowth*).

out·act /ówtákt/ *v.tr.* surpass in acting or performing.

out·age /ówtij/ *n.* a period of time during which a power supply, etc., is not operating.

out-and-out *adj.* thorough; surpassing. • *adv.* thoroughly; surpassingly.

out-and-out·er /ówtənówtər/ *n. sl.* **1** a thorough or supreme person or thing. **2** an extremist.

out·back /ówtbak/ *n.* esp. *Austral.* the remote and usu. uninhabited inland districts. □□ **out·back·er** *n.*

out·bal·ance /ówtbáləns/ *v.tr.* **1** count as more important than. **2** outweigh.

out·bid /ówtbíd/ *v.tr.* (**·bid·ding;** *past* and *past part.* **·bid**) **1** bid higher than (another person) at an auction. **2** surpass in exaggeration, etc.

out·board /ówtbawrd/ *adj., adv., & n.* • *adj.* **1** (of a motor) portable and attachable to the outside of the stern of a boat. **2** (of a boat) having an outboard motor. • *adj. & adv.* on, toward, or near the outside of esp. a ship, an aircraft, etc. • *n.* **1** an outboard engine. **2** a boat with an outboard engine.

out·bound /ówtbownd/ *adj.* outward bound.

out-box *n.* a box, tray, basket, etc., usu. on a desk, for holding finished work, outgoing correspondence, etc.

out·brave /ówtbráyv/ *v.tr.* **1** outdo in bravery. **2** face defiantly.

out·break /ówtbrayk/ *n.* **1** a usu. sudden eruption of war, disease, rebellion, etc. **2** an outcrop.

out·breed·ing /ówtbreeding/ *n.* the theory or practice of breeding from animals not closely related. □□ **out·breed** *v.intr. & tr.* (*past* and *past part.* **·bred**).

out·build·ing /ówtbilding/ *n.* a detached shed, barn, garage, etc., within the grounds of a main building.

out·burst /ówtbərst/ *n.* **1** an explosion of anger, etc., expressed in words. **2** an act or instance of bursting out. **3** an outcrop.

out·cast /ówtkast/ *n. & adj.* • *n.* **1** a person cast out from or rejected by his or her home, country, society, etc. **2** a tramp or vagabond. • *adj.* rejected; homeless; friendless.

out·caste *n. & v.* • *n.* /ówtkast/ (also *attrib.*) **1** a person who has no caste, esp. in Hindu society. **2** a person who has lost his or her caste. • *v.tr.* /ówtkást/ cause (a person) to lose his or her caste.

out·class /ówtklás/ *v.tr.* **1** belong to a higher class than. **2** defeat easily.

out·come /ówtkum/ *n.* a result; a visible effect.

out·crop /ówtkrop/ *n. & v.* • *n.* **1 a** the emergence of a stratum, vein, or rock, at the surface. **b** a stratum, etc., emerging. **2** a noticeable manifestation or occurrence. • *v.intr.* (**·cropped, ·crop·ping**) appear as an outcrop; crop out.

out·cry /ówtkrī/ *n.* (*pl.* **·cries**) **1** the act or an instance of crying out. **2** an uproar. **3** a noisy or prolonged public protest.

out·dance /ówtdáns/ *v.tr.* surpass in dancing.

out·dare /ówtdáir/ *v.tr.* **1** outdo in daring. **2** overcome by daring.

out·dat·ed /ówtdáytid/ *adj.* out of date; obsolete.

out·dis·tance /ówtdístəns/ *v.tr.* leave (a competitor) behind completely.

out·do /ówtdoo/ *v.tr.* (*3rd sing. present* **·does;** *past* **·did;** *past part.* **·done**) exceed or excel in doing or performance; surpass.

out·door /ówtdawr/ *adj.* done, existing, or used out of doors.

out·doors /ówtdáwrz/ *adv. & n.* • *adv.* in or into the open air; out of doors. • *n.* the world outside buildings; the open air.

out·doors·man /owtdórzmən, –dáwrz–/ *n.* a person who spends much time in outdoor activities, as fishing, camping, etc.

out·doors·y /owtdórzee, –dáwrz–/ *adj.* **1** relating to or suitable for the outdoors. **2** having a fondness for the outdoors.

out·er /ówtər/ *adj. & n.* • *adj.* **1** outside; external (*pierced the outer layer*). **2** farther from the center or inside; relatively far out. **3** objective or physical, not subjective or psychical. • *n.* **1** *Brit.* **a** the division of a target furthest from the bull's-eye. **b** a shot that strikes this. **2** esp. *Brit.* an outer garment or part of one. **3** *Austral. sl.* the part of a racecourse outside the enclosure. **4** *Brit.* an outer container for transport or display. [ME f. OUT, replacing UTTER¹]

out·er bar *n.* see BAR¹.

out·er man *n.* (also **out·er wom·an**) personal appearance; dress.

out·er·most /ówtərmōst/ *adj.* furthest from the inside; the most far out.

out·er plan·et *n.* a planet with an orbit outside that of Mars: Jupiter, Saturn, Uranus, Neptune, or Pluto.

out·er space *n.* the universe beyond the earth's atmosphere.

out·er world *n.* people outside one's own circle.

out·er·wear /ówtərwair/ *n.* clothes worn over other clothes, esp. for warmth, protection, etc.

out·face /ówtfáys/ *v.tr.* disconcert or defeat by staring or by a display of confidence.

out·fall /ówtfawl/ *n.* the mouth of a river, drain, etc., where it empties into the sea, etc.

out·field /ówtfeeld/ *n.* **1** the outer part of a playing area, esp. a baseball field. **2** outlying land. □□ **out·field·er** *n.*

out·fight /ówtfīt/ *v.tr.* fight better than; beat in a fight.

out·fit /ówtfit/ *n. & v.* • *n.* **1** a set of clothes worn or esp. designed to be worn together. **2** a complete set of equipment, etc., for a specific purpose. **3** *colloq.* a group of people regarded as a unit, organization, etc.; a team. • *v.tr.* (also *refl.*) (**·fit·ted, ·fit·ting**) provide with an outfit, esp. of clothes.

out·fit·ter /ówtfitər/ *n.* **1** a business that supplies outdoor equipment, arranges tours, etc. **2** a supplier of men's clothing; a haberdasher.

out·flank /ówtflángk/ *v.tr.* **1 a** extend one's flank beyond that of (an enemy). **b** outmaneuver (an enemy) in this way. **2** get the better of; confound (an opponent).

out·flow /ówtflō/ *n.* **1** an outward flow. **2** the amount that flows out.

out·fly /ówtflī/ *v.tr.* (**·flies;** *past* **·flew;** *past part.* **·flown**) **1** surpass in flying. **2** fly faster or farther than.

out·fox /ówtfóks/ *v.tr. colloq.* outwit.

out·gen·er·al /ówtjénərəl/ *v.tr.* **1** outdo in generalship. **2** get the better of by superior strategy or tactics.

out·go *v. & n.* • *v.tr.* /ówtgō/ (*3rd sing. present* **·goes;** *past* **·went;** *past part.* **·gone**) *archaic* go faster than; surpass. • *n.* /ówtgō/ (*pl.* esp. *Brit.* **·goes**) expenditure of money, effort, etc.

out·go·ing *adj. & n.* • *adj.* /ówtgóing/ **1** friendly; sociable; extrovert. **2** retiring from office. **3** going out or away. • *n.* /ówtgóing/ **1** the act or an instance of going out. **2** *Brit.* (in *pl.*) expenditure.

out·grow /ówtgrō/ *v.tr.* (*past* **·grew;** *past part.* **·grown**) **1** grow too big for (one's clothes). **2** leave behind (a childish habit, taste, ailment, etc.) as one matures. **3** grow faster or taller than (a person, plant, etc.). □ **outgrow one's strength** esp. *Brit.* become lanky and weak through too rapid growth.

out·growth /ówtgrōth/ *n.* **1** something that grows out. **2** an offshoot; a natural product. **3** the process of growing out.

out·guess /ówtgés/ *v.tr.* guess correctly what is intended by (another person).

out·gun /ówtgún/ *v.tr.* (**·gunned, ·gun·ning**) **1** surpass in military or other power or strength. **2** shoot better than.

out·house /ówt-hows/ *n.* **1** a building, esp. a shed, lean-to, barn, etc., built next to or in the grounds of a house. **2** an outbuilding used as a toilet, usu. with no plumbing.

out·ing /ówting/ *n.* **1** a short vacation away from home, esp. of one day or part of a day; a pleasure trip; an excursion. **2** any brief journey from home. **3** an appearance in an athletic contest, race, etc. **4** *colloq.* the practice or policy of exposing the homosexuality of a prominent person. [OUT *v.* = put out, go out + –ING¹]

out·jock·ey /ówtjókee/ *v.tr.* (**·eys, ·eyed**) outwit by adroitness or trickery.

out·jump /ówtjúmp/ *v.tr.* surpass in jumping.

out·land·er /ówtlandər/ *n.* a foreigner, alien, or stranger.

out·land·ish /owtlándish/ *adj.* **1** looking or sounding foreign. **2** bizarre; strange; unfamiliar. □□ **out·land·ish·ly** *adv.* **out·land·ish·ness** *n.* [OE *ūtlendisc* f. *ūtland* foreign country f. OUT + LAND]

out·last /ówtlást/ *v.tr.* last longer than (a person, thing, or duration) (*outlasted its usefulness*).

out·law /ówtlaw/ *n. & v.* • *n.* **1** a fugitive from the law. **2** *hist.* a person deprived of the protection of the law. • *v.tr.* **1** declare (a person) an outlaw. **2** make illegal; proscribe (a practice, etc.).

□□ **out·law·ry** n. [OE *ūtlaga, ūtlagian* f. ON *útlagi* f. *útlagr* outlawed, rel. to OUT, LAW]

out·law strike n. *Brit.* = WILDCAT STRIKE.

out·lay /ówtlay/ n. what is spent on something.

out·let /ówtlet, –lit/ n. 1 a means of exit or escape. 2 (usu. foll. by *for*) a means of expression (of a talent, emotion, etc.) (*find an outlet for tension*). 3 an agency, distributor, or market for goods (*a new retail outlet in China*). 4 US an electrical power receptacle. [ME f. OUT- + LET[1]]

out·li·er /ówtlīər/ n. 1 (also *attrib.*) an outlying part or member. 2 *Geol.* a younger rock formation isolated in older rocks. 3 *Statistics* a result differing greatly from others in the same sample.

out·line /ówtlīn/ n. & v. ● n. 1 a rough draft of a diagram, plan, proposal, etc. 2 a a précis of a proposed novel, article, etc. b a verbal description of essential parts only; a summary. 3 a sketch containing only contour lines. 4 (in *sing.* or *pl.*) a lines enclosing or indicating an object (*the outline of a shape under the blankets*). b a contour. c an external boundary. 5 (in *pl.*) the main features or general principles (*the outlines of a plan*). 6 the representation of a word in shorthand. ● v.tr. 1 draw or describe in outline. 2 mark the outline of. □ **in outline** sketched or represented as an outline.

out·live /ówtlív/ v.tr. 1 live longer than (another person). 2 live beyond (a specified date or time). 3 live through (an experience).

out·look /ówtlŏŏk/ n. 1 the prospect for the future (*the outlook is bleak*). 2 one's mental attitude or point of view (*narrow in their outlook*). 3 what is seen on looking out.

out·ly·ing /ówtlī-ing/ adj. situated far from a center; remote.

out·ma·neu·ver /ówtmənōōvər/ v.tr. (*Brit.* **–ma·noeu·vre**) 1 use skill and cunning to secure an advantage over (a person). 2 outdo in maneuvering.

out·match /ówtmách/ v.tr. be more than a match for (an opponent, etc.); surpass.

out·meas·ure /ówtmézhər/ v.tr. exceed in quantity or extent.

out·mod·ed /ówtmódid/ adj. 1 no longer in fashion. 2 obsolete. □□ **out·mod·ed·ly** adv. **out·mod·ed·ness** n.

out·most /ówtmōst/ adj. 1 outermost; furthest. 2 uttermost. [ME, var. of *utmost* UTMOST]

out·num·ber /ówtnúmbər/ v.tr. exceed in number.

out of date adj. (*attrib.* **out-of-date**) old-fashioned; obsolete.

out-of-pocket expenses n. expenses paid for directly rather than being put on account or charged to some other person or organization.

out·pace /ówtpáys/ v.tr. 1 go faster than. 2 outdo in a contest.

out·pa·tient /ówtpayshənt/ n. a hospital patient whose treatment does not require overnight hospitalization.

out·per·form /ówtpərfáwrm/ v.tr. 1 perform better than. 2 surpass in a specified field or activity. □□ **out·per·for·mance** n.

out·place·ment /ówtplaysmənt/ n. the act or process of finding new employment for workers who have been dismissed.

out·play /ówtpláy/ v.tr. surpass in playing; play better than.

out·point /ówtpóynt/ v.tr. (in various sports, esp. boxing) score more points than.

out·port /ówtpawrt/ n. 1 esp. *Brit.* a subsidiary port. 2 *Can.* a small remote fishing village.

out·post /ówtpōst/ n. 1 a detachment set at a distance from the main body of an army, esp. to prevent surprise. 2 a distant branch or settlement. 3 the furthest territory of an (esp. the British) empire.

out·pour·ing /ówtpawring/ n. 1 (usu. in *pl.*) a copious spoken or written expression of emotion. 2 what is poured out.

out·put /ówtpŏŏt/ n. & v. ● n. 1 the product of a process, esp. of manufacture, of mental or artistic work. 2 the quantity or amount of this. 3 the printout, results, etc., supplied by a computer. 4 the power, etc., delivered by an apparatus. 5 a place where energy, information, etc., leaves a system. ● v.tr. (**putting**; *past* and *past part.* **put** or **put·ted**) 1 put or send out. 2 (of a computer) supply (results, etc.).

out·rage /ówt-rayj/ n. & v. ● n. 1 an extreme or shocking violation of others' rights, sentiments, etc. 2 a gross offense or indignity. 3 fierce anger or resentment (*a feeling of outrage*). ● v.tr. 1 subject to outrage. 2 injure, insult, etc., flagrantly. 3 shock and anger. [ME f. OF *outrage* f. *outrer* exceed f. *outre* f. L *ultra* beyond]

out·ra·geous /owt-ráyjəs/ adj. 1 immoderate. 2 shocking. 3 grossly cruel. 4 immoral; offensive. □□ **out·ra·geous·ly** adv. **out·ra·geous·ness** n. [ME f. OF *outrageus* (as OUTRAGE)]

SPELLING TIP outrageous

To remember the *-geous* ending of *outrageous*, use the mnemonic: "Out*rageou*s behavior puts people in a *rage*."

out·ran *past* of OUTRUN.

out·range /ówt-ráynj/ v.tr. (of a gun or its user) have a longer range than.

out·rank /ówt-rángk/ v.tr. 1 be superior in rank to. 2 take priority over.

ou·tré /ōōtráy/ adj. 1 outside the bounds of what is usual or proper. 2 eccentric or indecorous. [F, past part. of *outrer*: see OUTRAGE]

out·reach v. & n. ● v.tr. /ówt-réech/ 1 reach further than. 2 surpass. 3 *poet.* stretch out (one's arms, etc.). ● n. /ówtreech/ 1 a any organization's involvement with or influence in the community, esp. in the context of social welfare. b the extent of this. 2 the extent or length of reaching out (*an outreach of 38 feet*).

out·ride /ówt-ríd/ v.tr. (*past* **rode**; *past part.* **rid·den**) 1 ride better, faster, or further than. 2 (of a ship) come safely through (a storm, etc.).

out·rid·er /ówt-rīdər/ n. 1 a mounted attendant riding ahead of, or with, a carriage, etc. 2 a motorcyclist acting as a guard in a similar manner. 3 a cowhand, etc., keeping cattle, etc., within bounds. □□ **out·rid·ing** n.

out·rigged /ówt-rigd/ adj. (of a boat, etc.) having outriggers.

out·rig·ger /ówt-rigər/ n. 1 a beam, spar, or framework, rigged out and projecting from or over a ship's side for various purposes. 2 a similar projecting beam, etc., in a building. 3 a log, etc., fixed parallel to a canoe to stabilize it. 4 esp. *Brit.* a an extension of the crossbar of a carriage, etc., to enable another horse to be harnessed outside the shafts. b a horse harnessed in this way. 5 a an iron bracket bearing an oarlock attached horizontally to a boat's side to increase the leverage of the oar. b a boat fitted with these. [OUT- + RIG[1]: perh. partly after obs. (Naut.) *outligger*]

outrigger 3

out·right adv. & adj. ● adv. /ówt-rít/ 1 altogether; entirely (*proved outright*). 2 not gradually, nor by degrees, nor by installments (*bought it outright*). 3 without reservation; openly (*denied the charge outright*). ● adj. /ówt-rít/ 1 downright; direct; complete (*their resentment turned to outright anger*). 2 undisputed; clear (*the outright winner*). □□ **out·right·ness** n.

out·ri·val /ówt-rívəl/ v.tr. outdo as a rival.

out·rode *past* of OUTRIDE.

out·run v.tr. /ówt-rún/ (**run·ning**; *past* **ran**; *past part.* **run**) 1 a run faster or farther than. b escape from. 2 go beyond (a specified point or limit).

out·rush /ówt-rush/ n. 1 a rushing out. 2 a violent overflow.

out·sail /ówtsáyl/ v.tr. sail better or faster than.

out·sat *past* and *past part.* of OUTSIT.

out·sell /ówtsél/ v.tr. (*past* and *past part.* **sold**) 1 sell more than. 2 be sold in greater quantities than.

out·set /ówtset/ n. the start; the beginning. □ **at** (or **from**) **the outset** at or from the beginning.

out·shine /ówtshín/ v.tr. (*past* and *past part.* **shone**) shine brighter than; surpass in ability, excellence, etc.

out·shoot /ówtshŏŏt/ v.tr. (*past* and *past part.* **shot**) 1 shoot better or further than (another person). 2 attempt or score more goals, points, etc., than (another player or team).

out·side n., adj., adv., & prep. ● n. /ówtsíd/ 1 the external side or surface; the outer parts (*painted blue on the outside*). 2 the external appearance; the outward aspect of a building, etc. 3 (of a roadway, etc.) the side or lane farthest from the center. 4 (also *attrib.*) all that is without; the world as distinct from the thinking subject (*learn about the outside world*; *viewed from the outside the problem is simple*). 5 a position on the outer side (*the gate opens from the outside*). 6 *colloq.* the highest computation (*it is a mile at the outside*). 7 an outside player in soccer, etc. 8 (in *pl.*) the outer sheets of a ream of paper. ● adj. /ówtsíd/ 1 of or on or nearer the outside; outer. 2 a not of or belonging to some circle or institution (*outside help*; *outside work*). b (of a broker) not a member of the stock exchange. 3 (of a chance, etc.) remote; very unlikely. 4 (of an estimate, etc.) the greatest or highest possible (*the outside price*). 5 (of a player in soccer, etc.) positioned nearest to the edge of the field. 6 *Baseball* (of a pitched ball) missing the strike zone by passing home plate on the side away from the batter. ● adv. /ówtsíd/ 1 on or to the outside. 2 in or to the open air. 3 not within or enclosed or included. 4 *sl.* not in prison. ● prep. /ówtsíd/ (also *disp.* foll. by *of*) 1 not in; to or at the exterior of (*meet me outside the post office*). 2 external to; not included in; beyond the limits of (*outside the law*). 3 *colloq.* other than; apart from. □ **at the outside** (of an estimate, etc.) at the most. **outside and in** outside and inside.

▶Avoid using *of* after **outside**. Say "The submarine was located outside the 100-mile buffer zone," not *outside of*.

out·side edge n. (on an ice skate) each of the edges facing outward when both feet are together.

outside in adv. & adj. = INSIDE OUT.

out·side in·ter·est n. a hobby; an interest not connected with one's work or normal way of life.

out·sid·er /ówtsídər/ n. 1 a a nonmember of some circle, party, profession, etc. b an uninitiated person; a layman. 2 a person without special knowledge, breeding, etc., or not fit to mix with good society. **3** a competitor, applicant, etc., thought to have little chance of success.

out·side seat *n.* a seat nearer the end of a row.

out·side track *n.* the outside lane of a sports track, etc., which is longer because of the curve.

out·sit /ówtsít/ *v.tr.* (·**sit·ting**; *past* and *past part.* ·**sat**) sit longer than (another person or thing).

out·size /ówtsíz/ *adj. & n.* ● *adj.* **1** unusually large. **2** (of garments, etc.) of an exceptionally large size. ● *n.* an exceptionally large person or thing, esp. a garment.

out·skirts /ówtskərts/ *n.pl.* the outer border or fringe of a town, district, subject, etc.

out·smart /ówtsm áart/ *v.tr. colloq.* outwit; be cleverer than.

out·sold *past* and *past part.* of OUTSELL.

out·span /ówtspan/ *v. & n. S.Afr.* ● *v.* (·**spanned**, ·**span·ning**) **1** *tr.* (also *absol.*) unharness (animals) from a cart, plow, etc. **2** *intr.* make a rest stop during a wagon journey. ● *n.* a place for grazing or encampment. [S.Afr. Du. *uitspannen* unyoke]

out·spend /ówtspénd/ *v.tr.* (*past* and *past part.* ·**spent**) spend more than (one's resources or another person).

out·spo·ken /ówtspókən/ *adj.* given to or involving plain speaking; frank in stating one's opinions. □□ **out·spo·ken·ly** *adv.* **out·spo·ken·ness** *n.*

out·spread /ówtspréd/ *adj. & v.* ● *adj.*, spread out; fully extended or expanded. ● *v.tr. & intr.* (*past* and *past part.* ·**spread**) spread out; expand.

out·stand·ing /ówtstánding/ *adj.* **1 a** conspicuous; eminent, esp. because of excellence. **b** (usu. foll. by *at, in*) remarkable in (a specified field). **2** (esp. of a debt) not yet settled (*$200 still outstanding*). □□ **out·stand·ing·ly** *adv.*

out·stare /ówtstáir/ *v.tr.* **1** outdo in staring. **2** abash by staring.

out·sta·tion /ówtstayshən/ *n.* **1** a branch of an organization, enterprise, or business in a remote area or at a considerable distance from headquarters. **2** esp. *Austral. & NZ* part of a farming estate separate from the main estate.

out·stay /ówtstáy/ *v.tr.* **1** stay beyond the limit of (one's welcome, invitation, etc.). **2** stay or endure longer than (another person, etc.).

out·step /ówtstép/ *v.tr.* (·**stepped**, ·**step·ping**) step outside or beyond.

out·stretch /ówtstréch/ *v.tr.* **1** (usu. as **outstretched** *adj.*) reach out or stretch out (esp. one's hands or arms). **2** reach or stretch further than.

out·strip /ówtstríp/ *v.tr.* (·**stripped**, ·**strip·ping**) **1** pass in running, etc. **2** surpass in competition or relative progress or ability.

out·take /ówt-tayk/ *n.* a length of film or tape rejected in editing.

out·talk /ówt-táwk/ *v.tr.* outdo or overcome in talking.

out·think /ówt-thíngk/ *v.tr.* (*past* and *past part.* ·**thought**) outwit; outdo in thinking.

out·thrust *adj., v., & n.* ● *adj.* /ówt-thrúst/ extended; projected (*ran forward with outthrust arms*). ● *v.tr.* /ówt-thrúst/ (*past* and *past part.* ·**thrust**) thrust out. ● *n.* /ówt-thrust/ **1** the act or an instance of thrusting forcibly outward. **2** the act or an instance of becoming prominent or noticeable.

out·top /ówt-tóp/ *v.tr.* (·**topped**, ·**top·ping**) surmount, surpass in height, extent, etc.

out·turn /ówt-tərn/ *n.* **1** the quantity produced. **2** the result of a process or sequence of events.

out·val·ue /ówtvályoō/ *v.tr.* (·**val·ues**, ·**val·ued**, ·**val·u·ing**) be of greater value than.

out·vote /ówtvót/ *v.tr.* defeat by a majority of votes.

out·walk /ówt-wáwk/ *v.tr.* **1** outdo in walking. **2** walk beyond.

out·ward /ówt-wərd/ *adj., adv., & n.* ● *adj.* **1** situated on or directed toward the outside. **2** going out (*on the outward voyage*). **3** bodily; external; apparent; superficial (*in all outward respects*). **4** *archaic* outer (*the outward man*). ● *adv.* (also **out·wards**) in an outward direction; toward the outside. ● *n.* the outward appearance of something; the exterior. □ **to outward seeming** esp. *Brit.* apparently. □□ **out·ward·ly** *adv.* [OE *ūtweard* (as OUT, –WARD)]

out·ward-bound *adj.* (of a ship, passenger, etc.) going away from home.

Out·ward Bound *n.* an organization that provides adventure training and other outdoor activities.

out·ward form *n.* appearance.

out·ward·ness /ówt-wərdnis/ *n.* **1** external existence; objectivity. **2** an interest or belief in outward things; objectivity.

out·wards var. of OUTWARD *adv.*

out·ward things *n.pl.* the world around us.

out·wash /ówt-wosh, –wawsh/ *n.* the material carried from a glacier by meltwater and deposited beyond the moraine.

out·watch /ówt-wóch/ *v.tr.* **1** watch more than or longer than. **2** *archaic* keep awake beyond the end of (night, etc.).

out·wear *v. & n.* ● *v.tr.* /ówt-wáir/ (*past* ·**wore**; *past part.* ·**worn**) **1** exhaust; wear out; wear away. **2** live or last beyond the duration of. **3** (as **outworn** *adj.*) out of date; obsolete. ● *n. Brit.* /ówt–wair/ outer clothing.

out·weigh /ówt-wáy/ *v.tr.* exceed in weight, value, importance, or influence.

out·went *past* of OUTGO.

out·wit /ówt-wít/ *v.tr.* (·**wit·ted**, ·**wit·ting**) be too clever or crafty for; deceive by greater ingenuity.

out·with /ówt-wíth/ *prep. Sc.* outside, beyond.

out·wore *past* of OUTWEAR.

out·work /ówt-wərk/ *v. & n.* ● *v.* work harder, faster, or longer than. ● *n.* **1** an advanced or detached part of a fortification. **2** *Brit.* work done outside the shop or factory that supplies it. □□ **out·work·er** *n.* (in sense 2).

out·worn *past part.* of OUTWEAR.

ou·zel /oōzəl/ *n.* (also **ou·sel**) **1** = RING OUZEL. **2** (in full **water ouzel**) = DIPPER. **3** *archaic* a blackbird. [OE *ōsle* blackbird, of unkn. orig.]

ou·zo /oōzō/ *n.* (*pl.* ·**zos**) a Greek anise-flavored liqueur. [mod.Gk]

o·va *pl.* of OVUM.

o·val /óvəl/ *adj. & n.* ● *adj.* **1** egg-shaped; ellipsoidal. **2** having the outline of an egg; elliptical. ● *n.* **1** an egg-shaped or elliptical closed curve. **2** any object with an oval outline. **3** *Austral.* a field for Australian Rules football. □□ **o·val·i·ty** /ōválitee/ *n.* **o·val·ly** *adv.* **o·val·ness** *n.* [med.L *ovalis* (as OVUM)]

O·val Of·fice *n.* the office of the US president in the White House.

o·va·ry /óvəree/ *n.* (*pl.* ·**ries**) **1** each of the female reproductive organs in which ova are produced. **2** the hollow base of the carpel of a flower, containing one or more ovules. □□ **o·var·i·an** /ōváireeən/ *adj.* **o·var·i·ec·to·my** /–ree-éktəmee/ *n.* (*pl.* ·**mies**) (in sense 1). **o·var·i·ot·o·my** /–reeótəmee/ *n.* (*pl.* ·**mies**) (in sense 1). **o·va·ri·tis** /–rítis/ *n.* (in sense 1). [mod.L *ovarium* (as OVUM)]

o·vate /óvayt/ *adj. Biol.* egg-shaped as a solid or in outline; oval. [L *ovatus* (as OVUM)]

o·va·tion /ōváyshən/ *n.* **1** an enthusiastic reception, esp. spontaneous and sustained applause. **2** *Rom. Antiq.* a lesser form of triumph. □□ **o·va·tion·al** *adj.* [L *ovatio* f. *ovare* exult]

ov·en /úvən/ *n.* **1** an enclosed compartment of brick, stone, or metal for cooking food. **2** a chamber for heating or drying. **3** a small furnace or kiln used in chemistry, metallurgy, etc. [OE *ofen* f. Gmc]

ov·en·bird /úvənbərd/ *n.* **1** an American warbler, *Seiurus aurocapillus*, noted for the oven-shaped nest it builds on or near the ground. **2** any Central or S. American bird of the family Furnariidae, many of which make domed nests.

ov·en·proof /úvənproōf/ *adj.* suitable for use in an oven; heat-resistant.

ov·en-read·y *adj.* esp. *Brit.* (of food) prepared before sale so as to be ready for immediate cooking in the oven.

ov·en·ware /úvənwair/ *n.* dishes that can be used for cooking food in the oven.

o·ver /óvər/ *adv., prep., n., & adj.* ● *adv.* expressing movement or position or state above or beyond something stated or implied: **1** outward and downward from a brink or from any erect position (*knocked the man over*). **2** so as to cover or touch a whole surface (*paint it over*). **3** so as to produce a fold, or reverse a position; with the effect of being upside down. **4 a** across a street or other space (*decided to cross over; came over from England*). **b** for a visit, etc. (*invited them over last night*). **5** with transference or change from one hand or part to another (*went over to the enemy; handed them over*). **6** with motion above something; so as to pass across something (*climb over; fly over; boil over*). **7 a** from beginning to end with repetition or detailed concentration (*think it over; did it six times over*). **b** again, once more. **8** in excess; more than is right or required (*left over*). **9** for or until a later time (*hold it over*). **10** at an end; settled (*the crisis is over; all is over between us*). **11** (in full **over to you**) (as *int.*) (in radio conversations, etc.) said to indicate that it is the other person's turn to speak. **12** (as *int.*) Cricket an umpire's call to change ends. ● *prep.* **1** above, in, or to a position higher than; upon. **2** out and down from; down from the edge of (*fell over the cliff*). **3** so as to cover (*a hat over his eyes*). **4** above and across; so as to clear (*flew over the North Pole; a bridge over the Hudson*). **5** concerning; engaged with; as a result of; while occupied with (*laughed over a good joke; fell asleep over the newspaper*). **6 a** in superiority of; superior to; in charge of (*a victory over the enemy; reign over three kingdoms*). **b** in preference to. **7** divided by. **8 a** throughout; covering the extent of (*traveled over most of Africa; a blush spread over his face*). **b** so as to deal with completely (*went over the plans*). **9 a** for the duration of (*stay over Saturday night*). **b** at any point during the course of (*I'll do it over the weekend*). **10** beyond; more than (*bids of*

WORD HISTORY over

Old English *ofer*, of Germanic origin; related to Dutch *over* and German *über*, from an Indo-European word (originally a comparative of the word element represented by -*ove* in *above*) that is also the base of Latin *super* and Greek *huper*.

over $50; are you over 18?). **11** transmitted by (*heard it over the radio*). **12** in comparison with (*gained 20 percent over last year*). **13** having recovered from (*am now over my cold; will get over it in time*). • *n. Cricket* **1** a sequence of balls (now usu. six), bowled from one end of the field. **2** play resulting from this (*a maiden over*). • *adj.* (see also OVER-). **1** upper, outer. **2** superior. **3** extra. □ **begin** (or **start,** etc.) **over** begin again. **get it over with** do or undergo something unpleasant, etc., so as to be rid of it. **not over** not very; not at all (*not over friendly*). **over again** once again; again from the beginning. **over against** in an opposite situation to; adjacent to, in contrast with. **over and above** in addition to; not to mention (*$100 over and above the asking price*). **over and over** so that the same thing or the same point comes up again and again (*said it over and over; rolled it over and over*). **over the fence** *Austral.* & *NZ sl.* unreasonable; unfair; indecent. **over one's head** see HEAD. **over the hill** see HILL. **over the moon** see MOON. **over the way** *Brit.* (in a street, etc.) facing or opposite.

over- /óvər/ *prefix* added to verbs, nouns, adjectives, and adverbs, meaning: **1** excessively; to an unwanted degree (*overheat; overdue*). **2** upper; outer; extra (*overcoat; overtime*). **3** 'over' in various senses (*overhang; overshadow*). **4** completely; utterly (*overawe; overjoyed*).

o•ver•a•bun•dant /óvərəbúndənt/ *adj.* in excessive quantity. □□ **o•ver•a•bound** /–əbównd/ *v. intr.* **o•ver•a•bun•dance** *n.* **o•ver•a•bun•dant•ly** *adv.*

o•ver•a•chieve /óvərəcheev/ *v.* **1** *intr.* do more than might be expected (esp. scholastically). **2** *tr.* achieve more than (an expected goal or objective, etc.). □□ **o•ver•a•chieve•ment** *n.* **o•ver•a•chiev•er** *n.*

o•ver•act /óvərákt/ *v. tr.* & *intr.* act in an exaggerated manner.

o•ver•ac•tive /óvəráktiv/ *adj.* excessively active. □□ **o•ver•ac•tiv•i•ty** /–tívitee/ *n.*

o•ver•age¹ /óvəráyj/ *adj.* **1** having attained a certain age limit. **2** too old.

o•ver•age² /óvərij/ *n.* a surplus or excess, esp. an amount greater than estimated.

o•ver•all *adj., adv.,* & *n.* • *adj.* /óvərawl/ **1** from end to end (*overall length*). **2** total; inclusive of all (*overall cost*). • *adv.* /óvəráwl/ in all parts; taken as a whole (*overall, the performance was excellent*). • *n.* /óvərawl/ **1** (in *pl.*) protective trousers, or a combination suit, worn by workmen, etc. **2** *Brit.* an outer garment worn to keep out dirt, wet, etc. **3** *Brit.* close-fitting trousers worn as part of army uniform. □□ **o•ver•alled** /óvərawld/ *adj.*

o•ver•am•bi•tious /óvərambíshəs/ *adj.* excessively ambitious. □□ **o•ver•am•bi•tion** *n.* **o•ver•am•bi•tious•ly** *adv.*

o•ver•anx•ious /óvərángkshəs/ *adj.* excessively anxious. □□ **o•ver•anx•i•e•ty** /–angzí-itee/ *n.* **o•ver•anx•ious•ly** *adv.*

o•ver•arch /óvəráarch/ *v. tr.* form an arch over.

o•ver•arch•ing /óvəráarching/ *adj.* **1** forming an arch. **2** dominating or encompassing everything else.

o•ver•arm /óvəraarm/ *adj.* & *adv.* **1** thrown with the hand above the shoulder (*pitch it overarm; an overarm tennis serve*). **2** *Swimming* with one or both arms lifted out of the water during a stroke.

o•ver•ate *past of* OVEREAT.

o•ver•awe /óvər-áw/ *v. tr.* **1** restrain by awe. **2** keep in awe.

o•ver•bal•ance /óvərbáləns/ *v.* & *n.* • *v.* **1** *tr.* outweigh. **2** *intr.* fall over, capsize. **3** *tr.* esp. *Brit.* cause (a person or thing) to lose its balance and fall. • *n.* **1** an excess. **2** the amount of this.

o•ver•bear /óvərbáir/ *v. tr.* (*past* **bore;** *past part.* **borne**) **1** bear down; upset by weight, force, or emotional pressure. **2** put down or repress by power or authority. **3** surpass in importance, etc.; outweigh.

o•ver•bear•ing /óvərbéring/ *adj.* **1** domineering; masterful. **2** overpowering; of critical import. □□ **o•ver•bear•ing•ly** *adv.* **o•ver•bear•ing•ness** *n.*

o•ver•bid *v.* & *n.* • *v.* /óvərbíd/ (**-bid•ding;** *past* and *past part.* **bid**) **1** *tr.* make a higher bid than. **2** *tr.* (also *absol.*) *Bridge* **a** bid more on (one's hand) than warranted. **b** overcall. • *n.* /óvərbid/ a bid that is higher than another, or higher than is justified. □□ **o•ver•bid•der** *n.*

o•ver•bite /óvərbīt/ *n.* a condition in which the teeth of the upper jaw project forward over those of the lower jaw.

o•ver•blouse /óvərblows, –blowz/ *n.* a garment like a blouse, but worn without tucking it into a skirt or slacks.

o•ver•blown /óvərblón/ *adj.* **1** excessively inflated or pretentious. **2** (of a flower or a woman's beauty, etc.) past its prime.

o•ver•board /óvərbáwrd/ *adv.* from on a ship into the water (*fall overboard*). □ **go overboard 1** be highly enthusiastic. **2** behave immoderately; go too far. **throw overboard** abandon; discard.

o•ver•bold /óvərbóld/ *adj.* excessively bold.

o•ver•book /óvərbook/ *v. tr.* (also *absol.*) make too many bookings for (an aircraft, hotel, etc.).

o•ver•boot /óvərboot/ *n.* a boot worn over another boot or shoe.

o•ver•bore *past of* OVERBEAR.

o•ver•borne *past part. of* OVERBEAR.

o•ver•bought *past* and *past part. of* OVERBUY.

o•ver•build /óvərbíld/ *v. tr.* (*past* and *past part.* **built**) **1** build over or upon. **2** place too many buildings on (land, etc.).

o•ver•bur•den /óvərbárd'n/ *v.* & *n.* • *v. tr.* burden (a person, thing, etc.) to excess. • *n.* **1** rock, etc., that must be removed prior to mining the mineral deposit beneath it. **2** an excessive burden. □□ **o•ver•bur•den•some** *adj.*

o•ver•bus•y /óvərbízee/ *adj.* excessively busy.

o•ver•buy /óvərbí/ *v. tr.* & *intr.* (*past* and *past part.* **bought**) buy (a commodity, etc.) in excess of immediate need.

o•ver•call *v.* & *n.* • *v. tr.* /óvərkáwl/ (also *absol.*) *Bridge* **1** make a higher bid than (a previous bid or opponent). **2** *Brit.* = OVERBID *v.* 2b. • *n.* /óvərkawl/ an act or instance of overcalling.

o•ver•came *past of* OVERCOME.

o•ver•ca•pac•i•ty /óvərkəpásitee/ *n.* a state of saturation or an excess of productive capacity.

o•ver•cap•i•tal•ize /óvərkápit'līz/ *v. tr.* fix or estimate the capital of (a company, etc.) too high.

o•ver•care•ful /óvərkáirfool/ *adj.* excessively careful. □□ **o•ver•care•ful•ly** *adv.*

o•ver•cast /óvərkást/ *adj., v.,* & *n.* • *adj.* **1** (of the sky, weather, etc.) covered with cloud; dull and gloomy. **2** (in sewing) edged with stitching to prevent fraying. • *v. tr.* (*past* and *past part.* **cast**) **1** cover (the sky, etc.) with clouds or darkness. **2** stitch over (a raw edge, etc.) to prevent fraying. • *n.* /óvərkast/ a cloud covering part of the sky.

o•ver•cau•tious /óvərkáwshəs/ *adj.* excessively cautious. □□ **o•ver•cau•tion** *n.* **o•ver•cau•tious•ly** *adv.* **o•ver•cau•tious•ness** *n.*

o•ver•charge /óvərchaárj/ *v.* & *n.* • *v. tr.* **1 a** charge too high a price to (a person) or for (a thing). **b** charge (a specified sum) beyond the right price. **2** put too much charge into (a battery, gun, etc.). **3** put exaggerated or excessive detail into (a description, picture, etc.). • *n.* an excessive charge (of explosive, money, etc.).

o•ver•check /óvərchek/ *n.* **1** a combination of two different-sized check patterns. **2** a cloth with this pattern.

o•ver•cloud /óvərklówd/ *v. tr.* **1** cover with cloud. **2** mar, spoil, or dim, esp. as the result of anxiety, etc. (*overclouded by uncertainties*). **3** make obscure.

o•ver•coat /óvərkōt/ *n.* **1** a heavy coat, esp. one worn over indoor clothes for warmth outdoors in cold weather. **2** a protective coat of paint, etc.

o•ver•come /óvərkúm/ *v.* (*past* **came;** *past part.* **come**) **1** *tr.* prevail over; master; conquer. **2** *tr.* (as **overcome** *adj.*) **a** exhausted; made helpless. **b** (usu. foll. by *with, by*) affected by (emotion, etc.). **3** *intr.* be victorious. [OE *ofercuman* (as OVER-, COME)]

o•ver•com•pen•sate /óvərkómpensayt/ *v.* **1** *tr.* (usu. foll. by *for*) compensate excessively for (something). **2** *intr. Psychol.* strive for power, etc., in an exaggerated way, esp. to make allowance or amends for a real or fancied grievance, defect, handicap, etc. □□ **o•ver•com•pen•sa•tion** /–áyshən/ *n.* **o•ver•com•pen•sa•to•ry** /–kəmpénsitawree/ *adj.*

o•ver•con•fi•dent /óvərkónfidənt/ *adj.* excessively confident. □□ **o•ver•con•fi•dence** *n.* **o•ver•con•fi•dent•ly** *adv.*

o•ver•cook /óvərkook/ *v. tr.* cook too much or for too long. □□ **o•ver•cooked** *adj.*

o•ver•crit•i•cal /óvərkrítikəl/ *adj.* excessively critical; quick to find fault.

o•ver•crop /óvərkróp/ *v. tr.* (**cropped, crop•ping**) exhaust (the land) by the continuous growing of crops.

o•ver•crowd /óvərkrówd/ *v. tr.* (often as **overcrowded** *adj.*) fill a space, object, etc.) beyond what is usual or comfortable. □□ **o•ver•crowd•ing** *n.*

o•ver•cu•ri•ous /óvərkyooréeəs/ *adj.* excessively curious. □□ **o•ver•cu•ri•os•i•ty** /–reeósitee/ *n.* **o•ver•cu•ri•ous•ly** *adv.*

o•ver•del•i•cate /óvərdélikət/ *adj.* excessively delicate. □□ **o•ver•del•i•ca•cy** *n.*

o•ver•de•vel•op /óvərdivéləp/ *v. tr.* **1** develop too much. **2** *Photog.* treat with developer for too long.

o•ver•do /óvərdōō/ *v. tr.* (*3rd sing. present* **does;** *past* **did;** *past part.* **done**) **1** carry to excess; take too far; exaggerate (*I think you overdid the sarcasm*). **2** (esp. as **overdone** *adj.*) overcook. □ **overdo it** (or **things**) exhaust oneself. [OE *ofercuman* (as OVER-, DO¹)]

o•ver•dose /óvərdōs/ *n.* & *v.* • *n.* an excessive dose (of a drug, etc.). • *v.* **1** *tr.* give an excessive dose of (a drug, etc.) or to (a person). **2** *intr.* take an excessive dose (of a drug, etc.). **3** *sl.* (usu. foll. by *on*) have or experience an excessive amount of (*we overdosed on movies this weekend*). □□ **o•ver•dos•age** /óvərdósij/ *n.*

o•ver•draft /óvərdraft/ *n.* **1** a deficit in a bank account caused by drawing more money than is credited to it. **2** the amount of this.

o•ver•draw /óvərdráw/ *v.* (*past* **drew;** *past part.* **drawn**) **1** *tr.* **a** draw a sum of money in excess of the amount credited to (one's bank account). **b** (as **overdrawn** *adj.*) have overdrawn one's account. **2** *intr.* overdraw one's account. **3** *tr.* exaggerate in describing or depicting. □□ **o•ver•draw•er** *n.* (in senses 1 & 2).

o•ver•dress *v.* & *n.* • *v.* /óvərdrés/ **1** *tr.* dress with too much display or formality. **2** *intr.* overdress oneself. ● *n.* /óvərdres/ a dress worn over another dress or a blouse, etc.

o•ver•drink /óvərdríngk/ *v.intr. & refl.* (*past* •**drank**; *past part.* •**drunk**) drink too much, esp. of alcoholic beverages.

o•ver•drive /óvərdriv/ *n.* **1 a** a mechanism in a motor vehicle providing a gear ratio higher than that of the usual gear. **b** an additional speed-increasing gear. **2** (usu. prec. by *in, into*) a state of high or excessive activity.

o•ver•dub *v. & n.* ● *v.tr.* /óvərdúb/ (•**dubbed**, •**dub•bing**) (also *absol.*) impose (additional sounds) on an existing recording. ● *n.* /óvərdub/ the act or an instance of overdubbing.

o•ver•due /óvərdóō, –dyóō/ *adj.* **1** past the time when due or ready. **2** not yet paid, arrived, born, etc., although after the expected time. **3** (of a library book, etc.) retained longer than the period allowed.

o•ver•ea•ger /óvəreegər/ *adj.* excessively eager. □□ **o•ver•ea•ger•ly** *adv.* **o•ver•ea•ger•ness** *n.*

o•ver•eat /óvəreet/ *v.intr. & refl.* (*past* •**ate**; *past part.* •**eat•en**) eat too much.

o•ver•e•lab•o•rate /óvərilábərət/ *adj.* excessively elaborate. □□ **o•ver•e•lab•o•rate•ly** *adv.*

o•ver•e•mo•tion•al /óvərimóshənəl/ *adj.* excessively emotional. □□ **o•ver•e•mo•tion•al•ly** *adv.*

o•ver•em•pha•sis /óvərémfəsis/ *n.* excessive emphasis. □□ **o•ver•em•pha•size** /–fəsiz/ *v.tr. & intr.*

o•ver•en•thu•si•asm /óvərinthóōzeeazəm, –thyóō–/ *n.* excessive enthusiasm. □□ **o•ver•en•thu•si•as•tic** /–zeeástik/ *adj.* **o•ver•en•thu•si•as•ti•cal•ly** *adv.*

o•ver•es•ti•mate *v. & n.* ● *v.tr.* (also *absol.*) /óvəréstimayt/ form too high an estimate of (a person, ability, cost, etc.). ● *n.* /óvəréstimit/ too high an estimate. □□ **o•ver•es•ti•ma•tion** /–áyshən/ *n.*

o•ver•ex•cite /óvəriksít/ *v.tr.* excite excessively. □□ **o•ver•ex•cite•ment** *n.*

o•ver•ex•er•cise /óvəréksərsiz/ *v. & n.* ● *v.* **1** *tr.* use or exert (a part of the body, one's authority, etc.) too much. **2** *intr.* do too much exercise; overexert oneself. ● *n.* excessive exercise.

o•ver•ex•ert /óvərigzórt/ *v.tr. & refl.* exert too much. □□ **o•ver•ex•er•tion** /–zérshən/ *n.*

o•ver•ex•pose /óvərikspóz/ *v.tr.* (also *absol.*) **1** expose too much, esp. to the public eye. **2** *Photog.* expose (film) for too long a time. □□ **o•ver•ex•po•sure** /–spózhər/ *n.*

o•ver•ex•tend /óvəriksténd/ *v.tr.* **1** extend (a thing) too far. **2** (also *refl.*) take on (oneself) or impose on (another person) an excessive burden of work.

o•ver•falls /óvərfawlz/ *n.* **1** a turbulent stretch of sea, etc., caused by a strong current or tide over a submarine ridge, or by a meeting of currents. **2** a place provided on a dam, weir, etc., for the overflow of surplus water.

o•ver•fa•mil•iar /óvərfəmílyər/ *adj.* excessively familiar.

o•ver•fa•tigue /óvərfəteeg/ *n.* excessive fatigue.

o•ver•feed /óvərfeed/ *v.tr.* (*past and past part.* •**fed**) feed excessively.

o•ver•fill /óvərfil/ *v.tr. & intr.* fill to excess or to overflowing.

o•ver•fine /óvərfin/ *adj.* excessively fine; too precise.

o•ver•fish /óvərfish/ *v.tr.* deplete (a stream, etc.) by too much fishing.

o•ver•flow *v. & n.* ● *v.* /óvərfló/ **1** *tr.* **a** flow over (the brim, limits, etc.). **b** flow over the brim or limits of. **2** *intr.* **a** (of a receptacle, etc.) be so full that the contents overflow it (*until the cup was overflowing*). **b** (of contents) overflow a container. **3** *tr.* (of a crowd, etc.) extend beyond the limits of (a room, etc.). **4** *tr.* flood (a surface or area). **5** *intr.* (foll. by *with*) be full of. **6** *intr.* (of kindness, a harvest, etc.) be very abundant. ● *n.* /óvərflō/ (also *attrib.*) **1** what overflows or is superfluous (*mop up the overflow; put the audience overflow in another room*). **2** an instance of overflowing (*overflow occurs when both systems are run together*). **3** (esp. in a bath or sink) an outlet for excess water, etc. **4** *Computing* the generation of a number having more digits than the assigned location. □ **overflow meeting** esp. *Brit.* a meeting for those who cannot be accommodated at the main gathering. [OE *oferflōwan* (as OVER-, FLOW)]

o•ver•fly /óvərflí/ *v.tr.* (•**flies**; *past* •**flew**; *past part.* •**flown**) fly over or beyond (a place or territory). □□ **o•ver•flight** /óvərflīt/ *n.*

o•ver•fold /óvərfold/ *n.* a series of strata folded so that the middle part is upside down.

o•ver•fond /óvərfónd/ *adj.* (often foll. by *of*) having too great an affection or liking (for a person or thing) (*overfond of chocolate; an overfond parent*). □□ **o•ver•fond•ly** *adv.* **o•ver•fond•ness** *n.*

o•ver•ful•fill /óvərfōōlfíl/ *v.tr.* fulfill (a plan, quota, etc.) beyond expectation or before the appointed time. □□ **o•ver•ful•fill•ment** *n.*

o•ver•full /óvərfōōl/ *adj.* filled excessively or to overflowing.

o•ver•gen•er•al•ize /óvərjénərəlīz/ *v.* **1** *intr.* draw general conclusions from inadequate data, etc. **2** *intr.* argue more widely than is justified by the available evidence, by circumstances, etc. **3** *tr.* draw an overgeneral conclusion from (data, circumstances, etc.). □□ **o•ver•gen•er•al•i•za•tion** *n.*

o•ver•gen•er•ous /óvərjénərəs/ *adj.* excessively generous. □□ **o•ver•gen•er•ous•ly** *adv.*

o•ver•glaze /óvərglayz/ *n. & adj.* ● *n.* **1** a second glaze applied to ce-

ramic ware. **2** decoration on a glazed surface. ● *adj.* (of painting, etc.) done on a glazed surface.

o•ver•ground /óvərgrownd/ *adj.* **1** raised above the ground. **2** not underground.

o•ver•grow /óvərgró/ *v.tr.* (*past* •**grew**; *past part.* •**grown**) **1** (as **overgrown** *adj.* /óvərgrón/) **a** abnormally large (*an overgrown eggplant*). **b** wild; grown over with vegetation (*an overgrown pond*). **2** grow over, overspread, esp. so as to choke (*brambles have overgrown the pathway*). **3** esp. *Brit.* grow too big for (one's strength, etc.). □□ **o•ver•growth** *n.*

o•ver•hand /óvərhand/ *adj. & adv.* **1** (in tennis, baseball, etc.) thrown or played with the hand above the shoulder; overarm. **2** *Swimming* = OVERARM. **3 a** with the palm of the hand downward or inward. **b** with the hand above the object held.

o•ver•hand knot *n.* a simple knot made by forming a loop and passing the free end through it.

o•ver•hang *v. & n.* ● *v.* /óvərháng/ (*past and past part.* •**hung**) **1** *tr. & intr.* project or hang over. **2** *tr.* menace; preoccupy; threaten. ● *n.* /óvərhang/ **1** the overhanging part of a structure or rock formation. **2** the amount by which this projects.

o•ver•haste /óvərháyst/ *n.* excessive haste. □□ **o•ver•hast•y** *adj.* **o•ver•hast•i•ly** *adv.*

o•ver•haul *v. & n.* ● *v.tr.* /óvərháwl/ **1 a** take to pieces in order to examine. **b** examine the condition of (and repair if necessary). **2** overtake. ● *n.* /óvərhawl/ a thorough examination, with repairs if necessary. [orig. Naut., = release (rope tackle) by slackening]

o•ver•head *adv., adj., & n.* ● *adv.* /óvərhéd/ **1** above one's head. **2** in the sky or on the floor above. ● *adj.* /óvərhed/ **1** (of a driving mechanism, etc.) above the object driven. **2** (of expenses) arising from general operating costs, as distinct from particular business transactions. ● *n.* /óvərhed/ overhead expenses.

o•ver•head pro•jec•tor *n.* a device that projects an enlarged image of a transparency onto a surface above and behind the user.

o•ver•hear /óvərheer/ *v.tr.* (*past and past part.* •**heard**) (also *absol.*) hear as an eavesdropper or as an unperceived or unintentional listener.

o•ver•heat /óvərheet/ *v.* **1** *tr. & intr.* make or become too hot; heat to excess. **2** *tr.* (as **overheated** *adj.*) too passionate about a matter.

o•ver•in•dulge /óvərindúlj/ *v.tr. & intr.* indulge to excess. □□ **o•ver•in•dul•gence** *n.* **o•ver•in•dul•gent** *adj.*

o•ver•in•sure /óvərinshóōr/ *v.tr.* insure (property, etc.) for more than its real value; insure excessively. □□ **o•ver•in•sur•ance** *n.*

o•ver•is•sue /óvərishóō/ *v. & n.* ● *v.tr.* (•**is•sues**, •**is•sued**, •**is•su•ing**) issue (notes, shares, etc.) beyond the authorized amount, or the ability to pay. ● *n.* the notes, shares, etc., or the amount so issued.

o•ver•joyed /óvərjóyd/ *adj.* (often foll. by *at, to hear*, etc.) filled with great joy.

o•ver•kill /óvərkil/ *n. & v.* ● *n.* **1** the amount by which destruction or the capacity for destruction exceeds what is necessary for victory or annihilation. **2** excess; excessive behavior. ● *v.tr. & intr.* kill or destroy to a greater extent than necessary.

o•ver•lad•en /óvərláyd'n/ *adj.* bearing or carrying too large a load.

o•ver•laid *past and past part.* of OVERLAY[1].

o•ver•lain *past part.* of OVERLIE.

o•ver•land /óvərland, –lənd/ *adj., adv., & v.* ● *adj. & adv.* also /óvərlánd/ **1** by land. **2** not by sea. ● *v. Austral.* **1** *tr.* drive (livestock) overland. **2** *intr.* go a long distance overland.

o•ver•land•er /óvərlandər/ *n. Austral. & NZ* **1** a person who drives livestock overland. **2** *sl.* a tramp; a sundowner.

o•ver•lap *v. & n.* ● *v.* /óvərláp/ (•**lapped**, •**lap•ping**) **1** *tr.* (of part of an object) partly cover (another object). **2** *tr.* cover and extend beyond. **3** *intr.* (of two things) partly coincide; not be completely separate (*where psychology and philosophy overlap*). ● *n.* /óvərlap/ **1** an instance of overlapping. **2** the amount of this.

o•ver•lay[1] *v. & n.* ● *v.tr.* /óvərláy/ (*past and past part.* •**laid**) **1** lay over. **2** (foll. by *with*) cover the surface of (a thing) with (a coating, etc.). **3** overlie. ● *n.* /óvərlay/ **1** a thing laid over another. **2** (in printing, map reading, etc.) a transparent sheet to be superimposed on another sheet. **3** *Computing* **a** the process of transferring a block of data, etc., to replace what is already stored. **b** a section so transferred. **4** a coverlet, small tablecloth, etc.

o•ver•lay[2] *past* of OVERLIE.

o•ver•leaf /óvərleef/ *adv.* on the other side of the leaf (of a book) (*see the diagram overleaf*).

o•ver•leap /óvərleep/ *v.tr.* (*past and past part.* •**leaped** or •**leapt**) **1** leap over; surmount. **2** omit; ignore. [OE *oferhlēapan* (as OVER, LEAP)]

o•ver•lie /óvərlí/ *v.tr.* (•**ly•ing**; *past* •**lay**; *past part.* •**lain**) lie on top of.

o•ver•load *v. & n.* ● *v.tr.* /óvərlód/ load excessively; force (a person, thing, etc.) beyond normal or reasonable capacity. ● *n.* /óvərlōd/ an excessive quantity; a demand, etc., that surpasses capability or capacity.

o•ver•look *v. & n.* ● *v.tr.* /óvərlóōk/ **1** fail to notice; ignore, condone (an offense, etc.). **2** have a view from above; be higher than. **3** supervise; oversee. **4** bewitch with the evil eye. • *n.* /ṓvərlŏŏk/ a commanding position or view. □□ **o•ver•look•er** *n.*

o•ver•lord /ṓvərlawrd/ *n. & v.* • *n.* **1** a supreme lord. **2** a powerful authoritarian; a highly influential person (*the overlords of technology*). • *v.* **1** rule as a tyrant. **2** domineer. □□ **o•ver•lord•ship** *n.*

o•ver•ly /ṓvərlee/ *adv.* excessively; too.

o•ver•ly•ing *pres. part.* of OVERLIE.

o•ver•man *v. & n.* • *v.tr.* /ṓvərmán/ (•**manned**, •**man•ning**) provide with too large a crew, staff, etc. • *n.* /ṓvərman, –mən/ (*pl.* •**men**) esp. *Brit.* an overseer in a coal-mining operation.

o•ver•man•tel /ṓvərmant'l/ *n.* ornamental shelves, etc., over a mantelpiece.

o•ver•mas•ter /ṓvərmástər/ *v.tr.* master completely; conquer. □□ **o•ver•mas•ter•ing** *adj.* **o•ver•mas•ter•y** *n.*

o•ver•match /ṓvərmách/ *v.tr.* be more than a match for; defeat by superior strength, etc.

o•ver•meas•ure /ṓvərmezhər/ *n.* an amount beyond what is proper or sufficient.

o•ver•much /ṓvərmúch/ *adv. & adj.* • *adv.* to too great an extent; excessively. • *adj.* excessive; superabundant.

o•ver•nice /ṓvərnís/ *adj.* excessively fussy, punctilious, particular, etc. □□ **o•ver•nice•ness** *n.* **o•ver•ni•ce•ty** *n.*

o•ver•night *adv. & adj.* • *adv.* /ṓvərnít/ **1** for the duration of a night (*stay overnight*). **2** during the course of a night. **3** suddenly; immediately (*the situation changed overnight*). • *adj.* /ṓvərnít/ **1** for use overnight (*an overnight bag*). **2** done, etc., overnight (*an overnight stop*).

o•ver•night•er /ṓvərnítər/ *n.* **1** a person who stops at a place overnight. **2** an overnight bag.

o•ver•paid *past* and *past part.* of OVERPAY.

o•ver•par•tic•u•lar /ṓvərpərtíkyələr, –pətík–/ *adj.* excessively particular or fussy.

o•ver•pass *n. & v.* • *n.* /ṓvərpas/ a road or railroad line that passes over another by means of a bridge. • *v.tr.* /ṓvərpás/ **1** pass over or across or beyond. **2** get to the end of; surmount. **3** (as **overpassed** or **overpast** *adj.*) that has gone by; past.

o•ver•pay /ṓvərpáy/ *v.tr.* (*past* and *past part.* •**paid**) recompense (a person, service, etc.) too highly. □□ **o•ver•pay•ment** *n.*

o•ver•pitch /ṓvərpích/ *v.tr. Brit.* exaggerate.

o•ver•play /ṓvərpláy/ *v.tr.* play (a part) to excess; give undue importance to; overemphasize. □ **overplay one's hand 1** be unduly optimistic about one's capabilities. **2** spoil a good case by exaggerating its value.

o•ver•plus /ṓvərplus/ *n.* a surplus; a superabundance. [ME, partial transl. of AF *surplus* or med.L *su(pe)rplus*]

o•ver•pop•u•lat•ed /ṓvərpópyəlaytid/ *adj.* having too large a population. □□ **o•ver•pop•u•la•tion** /–láyshən/ *n.*

o•ver•pow•er /ṓvərpówr/ *v.tr.* **1** reduce to submission; subdue. **2** make (a thing) ineffective or imperceptible by greater intensity. **3** (of heat, emotion, etc.) be too intense for; overwhelm. □□ **o•ver•pow•er•ing** *adj.* **o•ver•pow•er•ing•ly** *adv.*

o•ver•price /ṓvərprís/ *v.tr.* price (a thing) too highly.

o•ver•print *v. & n.* • *v.tr.* /ṓvərprínt/ **1** print further matter on (a surface already printed, esp. a postage stamp). **2** print (further matter) in this way. **3** *Photog.* print (a positive) darker than was intended. **4** (also *absol.*) print too many copies of (a work). • *n.* /ṓvərprint/ **1** the words, etc., overprinted. **2** an overprinted postage stamp.

o•ver•pro•duce /ṓvərprədóŏs, –dyóŏs/ *v.tr.* (usu. *absol.*) **1** produce more of (a commodity) than is wanted. **2** produce to an excessive degree. □□ **o•ver•pro•duc•tion** /–dúkshən/ *n.*

o•ver•proof /ṓvərpróŏf/ *adj.* containing more alcohol than proof spirit does.

o•ver•pro•tec•tive /ṓvərprətéktiv/ *adj.* excessively protective, esp. of a person in one's charge.

o•ver•qual•i•fied /ṓvərkwólifíd/ *adj.* too highly qualified (esp. for a particular job, etc.).

o•ver•ran *past* of OVERRUN.

o•ver•rate /ṓvəráyt/ *v.tr.* assess too highly.

o•ver•reach /ṓvəréech/ *v.tr.* circumvent; outwit; get the better of by cunning or artifice. □ **overreach oneself 1** strain oneself by reaching too far. **2** defeat one's object by going too far.

o•ver•re•act /ṓvəreeákt/ *v.intr.* respond more forcibly, etc., than is justified. □□ **o•ver•re•ac•tion** /–ákshən/ *n.*

o•ver•re•fine /ṓvərifín/ *v.tr.* (also *absol.*) **1** refine too much. **2** make too subtle distinctions in (an argument, etc.).

o•ver•ride *v. & n.* • *v.tr.* /ṓvəríd/ (*past* •**rode**; *past part.* •**rid•den**) **1** (often as **overriding** *adj.*) have or claim precedence or superiority over (*an overriding consideration*). **2 a** intervene and make ineffective. **b** interrupt the action of (an automatic device), esp. to take manual control. **3 a** trample down or underfoot. **b** supersede arrogantly. **4** extend over, esp. (of a part of a fractured bone) overlap (another part). **5** ride over (enemy country). **6** exhaust (a horse,

etc.) by hard riding. • *n.* /ṓvərīd/ **1** the action or process of suspending an automatic function. **2** a device for this.

o•ver•ripe /ṓvəríp/ *adj.* (esp. of fruit, etc.) past its best; excessively ripe; full-blown.

o•ver•rode *past* of OVERRIDE.

o•ver•ruff *v. & n. Cards* • *v.tr.* /ṓvərúf/ (also *absol.*) overtrump. • *n.* /ṓvəruf/ an instance of this.

o•ver•rule /ṓvərŏŏl/ *v.tr.* **1** set aside (a decision, argument, proposal, etc.) by exercising a superior authority. **2** annul a decision by or reject a proposal of (a person) in this way.

o•ver•run *v. & n.* • *v.tr.* /ṓvərún/ (•**run•ning**; *past* •**ran**; *past part.* •**run**) **1** (of pests, weeds, etc.) swarm or spread over. **2** conquer or ravage (territory) by force. **3** (of time, expenditure, production, etc.) exceed (a fixed limit). **4** *Printing* carry over (a word, etc.) to the next line or page. **5** *Mech.* rotate faster than. **6** flood (land). • *n.* /ṓvərun/ **1** an instance of overrunning. **2** the amount of this. **3** the movement of a vehicle at a speed greater than is imparted by the engine. [OE *oferyrnan* (as OVER-, RUN)]

o•ver•saw *past* of OVERSEE.

o•ver•scru•pu•lous /ṓvərskróŏpyələs/ *adj.* excessively scrupulous or particular.

o•ver•seas *adv. & adj.* • *adv.* /ṓvərseéz/ (also *Brit.* **oversea**) abroad (*was sent overseas for training; came back from overseas*). • *adj.* /ṓvərseez/ (also *Brit.* **o•ver•sea**) **1** foreign; across or beyond the sea. **2** of or connected with movement or transport over the sea (*overseas postage rates*).

o•ver•see /ṓvərseé/ *v.tr.* (•**sees**; *past* •**saw**; *past part.* •**seen**) officially supervise (workers, work, etc.). [OE *ofersēon* look at from above (as OVER-, SEE[1])]

o•ver•se•er /ṓvərseer, –seéər/ *n.* a person who supervises others, esp. workers. [OVERSEE]

o•ver•sell /ṓvərsél/ *v.tr.* (*past* and *past part.* •**sold**) (also *absol.*) **1** sell more of (a commodity, etc.) than one can deliver. **2** exaggerate the merits of.

o•ver•sen•si•tive /ṓvərsénsitiv/ *adj.* excessively sensitive; easily hurt by, or too quick to react to, outside influences. □□ **o•ver•sen•si•tive•ness** *n.* **o•ver•sen•si•tiv•i•ty** /–tívitee/ *n.*

o•ver•set /ṓvərsét/ *v.tr.* (•**set•ting**; *past* and *past part.* •**set**) **1** overturn; upset. **2** *Printing* set up (type) in excess of the available space.

o•ver•sew /ṓvərsṓ/ *v.tr.* (*past part.* •**sewn** or •**sewed**) **1** sew (two edges) with every stitch passing over the join. **2** join the sections of (a book) by a stitch of this type.

o•ver•sexed /ṓvərsékst/ *adj.* having unusually strong sexual desires.

o•ver•shad•ow /ṓvərshádō/ *v.tr.* **1** appear much more prominent or important than. **2 a** cast into the shade; shelter from the sun. **b** cast gloom over; mar; spoil. [OE *ofersceadwian* (as OVER-, SHADOW)]

o•ver•shoe /ṓvərshŏŏ/ *n.* a shoe of rubber, felt, etc., worn over another as protection from wet, cold, etc.

o•ver•shoot *v. & n.* • *v.tr.* /ṓvərshŏŏt/ (*past* and *past part.* •**shot**) **1** pass or send beyond (a target or limit). **2** (of an aircraft) fly beyond or taxi too far along (the runway) when landing or taking off. • *n.* /ṓvərshŏŏt/ **1** the act of overshooting. **2** the amount of this. □ **overshoot the mark** go beyond what is intended or proper; go too far.

o•ver•shot wheel *n.* a waterwheel operated by the weight of water falling into buckets attached to its periphery.

o•ver•side /ṓvərsíd/ *adv.* over the side of a ship (into a smaller boat, or into the sea).

o•ver•sight /ṓvərsīt/ *n.* **1** a failure to notice something. **2** an inadvertent mistake. **3** supervision.

o•ver•sim•pli•fy /ṓvərsímplifī/ *v.tr.* (•**fies**, •**fied**) (also *absol.*) distort (a problem, etc.) by stating it in too simple terms. □□ **o•ver•sim•pli•fi•ca•tion** *n.*

o•ver•size /ṓvərsíz/ *adj.* (also –**sized** /–sīzd/) of more than the usual size.

o•ver•skirt /ṓvərskərt/ *n.* an outer or second skirt.

o•ver•slaugh /ṓvərslaw/ *n. & v.* • *n. Brit. Mil.* the passing over of one's turn of duty. • *v.tr.* **1** *Brit. Mil.* pass over (one's duty) in consideration of another duty that takes precedence. **2** pass over in favor of another. **3** omit to consider. [Du. *overslag* (n.) f. *overslaan* omit (as OVER, *slaan* strike)]

o•ver•sleep /ṓvərsleép/ *v.intr. & refl.* (*past* and *past part.* •**slept**) **1** continue sleeping beyond the intended time of waking. **2** sleep too long.

o•ver•sleeve /ṓvərsleev/ *n.* a protective sleeve covering an ordinary sleeve.

o•ver•sold *past* and *past part.* of OVERSELL.

o•ver•so•lic•i•tous /ṓvərsəlísitəs/ *adj.* excessively worried, anxious, eager, etc. □□ **o•ver•so•lic•i•tude** /–sitŏŏd, –tyŏŏd/ *n.*

o•ver•soul /ṓvərsōl/ *n.* God as a spirit animating the universe and including all human souls.

o•ver•spe•cial•ize /ṓvərspéshəliz/ *v.intr.* concentrate too much on one aspect or area. □□ **o•ver•spe•cial•i•za•tion** *n.*

o•ver•spend /ṓvərspénd/ *v.* (*past* and *past part.* •**spent**) **1** *intr. & refl.* spend too much. **2** *tr.* spend more than (a specified amount).

o·ver·spill /ốvərspil/ n. **1** what is spilled over or overflows. **2** Brit. the surplus population leaving a country or city to live elsewhere.

o·ver·spread /ôvərspréd/ v.tr. (past and past part. **·spread**) **1** become spread or diffused over. **2** cover or occupy the surface of. **3** (as **overspread** adj.) (usu. foll. by with) covered (high mountains overspread with trees). [OE ofersprǣdan (as OVER-, SPREAD)]

o·ver·staff /ốvərstáf/ v.tr. provide with too large a staff.

o·ver·state /ốvərstáyt/ v.tr. **1** state (esp. a case or argument) too strongly. **2** exaggerate. □□ **o·ver·state·ment** n.

o·ver·stay /ốvərstáy/ v.tr. stay longer than (one's welcome, a time limit, etc.).

o·ver·steer /ốvərsteér/ v. & n. ● v.intr. (of a motor vehicle) have a tendency to turn more sharply than was intended. ● n. this tendency.

o·ver·step /ốvərstép/ v.tr. (**·stepped**, **·step·ping**) **1** pass beyond (a boundary or mark). **2** violate (certain standards of behavior, etc.).

o·ver·stock /ốvərstók/ v. & n. ● v.tr. stock excessively. ● n. stock that is in excess of need or demand.

o·ver·strain /ốvərstráyn/ v.tr. strain too much.

o·ver·stress /ốvərstrés/ v. & n. ● v.tr. stress too much. ● n. an excessive degree of stress.

o·ver·stretch /ốvərstréch/ v.tr. **1** stretch too much. **2** (esp. as **overstretched** adj.) make excessive demands on (resources, a person, etc.).

o·ver·strung adj. **1** /ốvərstrúng/ (of a person, disposition, etc.) intensely strained, highly strung. **2** /ốvərstrúng/ (of a piano) with strings in sets crossing each other obliquely.

o·ver·stud·y /ốvərstúdee/ v.tr. (**·ies**, **·ied**) **1** study beyond what is necessary or desirable. **2** (as **overstudied** adj.) excessively deliberate; affected.

o·ver·stuff /ốvərstúf/ v.tr. **1** stuff more than is necessary. **2** (as **overstuffed** adj.) (of furniture) made soft and comfortable by thick upholstery.

o·ver·sub·scribe /ốvərsəbskríb/ v.tr. (usu. as **o·ver·sub·scribed** adj.) subscribe for more than the amount available of (a commodity offered for sale, etc.) (the offer was oversubscribed).

o·ver·sub·tle /ốvərsút'l/ adj. excessively subtle; not plain or clear.

o·ver·sup·ply /ốvərsəplí/ v. & n. ● v.tr. (**·ies**, **·ied**) supply with too much. ● n. an excessive supply.

o·ver·sus·cep·ti·ble /ốvərsəséptibəl/ adj. too susceptible or vulnerable.

o·vert /ốvərt, ốvərt/ adj. unconcealed; done openly. □□ **o·vert·ly** adv. **o·vert·ness** n. [ME f. OF past part. of ovrir open f. L aperire]

o·ver·take /ốvərtáyk/ v.tr. (past **·took**; past part. **·tak·en**) **1** (esp. Brit. also absol.) catch up with and pass in the same direction. **2** (of a storm, misfortune, etc.) come suddenly or unexpectedly upon. **3** become level with and exceed (a compared value, etc.).

o·ver·task /ốvərtásk/ v.tr. **1** give too heavy a task to. **2** be too heavy a task for.

o·ver·tax /ốvərtáks/ v.tr. **1** make excessive demands on (a person's strength, etc.). **2** tax too heavily.

over the counter adj. **1** (of stock) sold through a broker directly, not on an exchange **2** by ordinary retail purchase.

o·ver·the·coun·ter adj. **1** (of medicine) sold without a prescription. **2** (of stocks, etc.) not listed on or traded by an organized securities exchange.

o·ver·the·top adj. Brit. colloq. (esp. of behavior, dress, etc.) outrageous, excessive.

o·ver·throw v. & n. ● v.tr. /ốvərthrố/ (past **o·ver·threw**; past part. **o·ver·thrown**) **1** remove forcibly from power. **2** put an end to (an institution, etc.). **3** conquer; overcome. **4** knock down; upset. **5** Baseball **a** (of a fielder) throw beyond the intended place. **b** (of a pitcher) throw too vigorously. ● n. /ốvərthrō/ **1** a defeat or downfall. **2** Archit. a panel of decorated wrought-iron work in an arch or gateway.

o·ver·thrust /ốvərthrust/ n. Geol. the thrust of esp. lower strata on one side of a fault over those on the other side.

o·ver·time /ốvərtīm/ n. & adv. ● n. **1** the time during which a person works at a job in addition to the regular hours. **2** payment for this. **3** Sports an additional period of play at the end of a game when the scores are equal. ● adv. in addition to regular hours.

o·ver·tire /ốvərtír/ v.tr. & refl. exhaust or wear out (esp. an invalid, etc.).

o·ver·tone /ốvərtōn/ n. **1** Mus. any of the tones above the lowest in a harmonic series. **2** a subtle or elusive quality or implication (sinister overtones). [OVER- + TONE, after G Oberton]

o·ver·top /ốvərtóp/ v.tr. (**·topped**, **·top·ping**) **1** be or become higher than. **2** surpass.

o·ver·train /ốvərtráyn/ v.tr. & intr. subject to or undergo too much (esp. athletic) training with a consequent loss of proficiency.

o·ver·trick /ốvərtrik/ n. Bridge a trick taken in excess of one's contract.

o·ver·trump /ốvərtrúmp/ v.tr. (also absol.) play a higher trump than (another player).

o·ver·ture /ốvərchər, –chōor/ n. **1** an orchestral piece opening an opera, etc. **2** a one-movement composition in this style. **3** (usu. in pl.)

a an opening of negotiations. **b** a formal proposal or offer (esp. make overtures to). **4** the beginning of a poem, etc. [ME f. OF f. L apertura APERTURE]

o·ver·turn v. & n. ● v. /ốvərtórn/ **1** tr. cause to turn over; upset. **2** tr. reverse; subvert; abolish; invalidate. **3** intr. turn over; fall over. ● n. /ốvərtərn/ a subversion, an act of upsetting.

o·ver·use v. & n. ● v.tr. /ốvəryōoz/ use too much. ● n. /ốvəryōos/ excessive use.

o·ver·val·ue /ốvərvályōo/ v.tr. (**·val·ues**, **·val·ued**, **·val·u·ing**) value too highly; have too high an opinion of.

o·ver·view /ốvəryōo/ n. a general survey.

o·ver·ween·ing /ốvərweéning/ adj. arrogant, presumptuous, conceited, self-confident. □□ **o·ver·ween·ing·ly** adv. **o·ver·ween·ing·ness** n.

o·ver·weight adj., n., & v. ● adj. /ốvərwáyt/ beyond an allowed or suitable weight. ● n. /ốvərwayt/ excessive or extra weight; preponderance. ● v.tr. /ốvərwáyt/ (usu. foll. by with) load unduly.

o·ver·whelm /ốvərhwélm, –wélm/ v.tr. **1** overpower with emotion. **2** (usu. foll. by with) overpower with an excess of business, etc. **3** bring to sudden ruin or destruction; crush. **4** bury or drown beneath a huge mass; submerge utterly.

o·ver·whelm·ing /ốvərhwélming, –wél–/ adj. irresistible by force of numbers, influence, amount, etc. □□ **o·ver·whelm·ing·ly** adv. **o·ver·whelm·ing·ness** n.

o·ver·wind v. & n. ● v.tr. /ốvərwínd/ (past and past part. **·wound**) wind (a mechanism, esp. a watch) beyond the proper stopping point. ● n. /ốvərwind/ an instance of this.

o·ver·win·ter /ốvərwíntər/ v. **1** intr. (usu. foll. by at, in) spend the winter. **2** intr. (of insects, fungi, etc.) live through the winter. **3** tr. keep (animals, plants, etc.) alive through the winter.

o·ver·work /ốvərwórk/ v. & n. ● v. **1** intr. work too hard. **2** tr. cause (another person) to work too hard. **3** tr. weary or exhaust with too much work. **4** tr. make excessive use of. ● n. excessive work.

o·ver·wound past and past part. of OVERWIND.

o·ver·write /ốvərít/ v. (past **·wrote**; past part. **·writ·ten**) **1** tr. write on top of (other writing). **2** tr. Computing destroy (data) in (a file, etc.) by entering new data. **3** intr. (esp. as **overwritten** adj.) write too elaborately or too ornately. **4** intr. & refl. write too much; exhaust oneself by writing. **5** tr. write too much about. **6** intr. (esp. as **overwriting** n.) in shipping insurance, accept more risk than the premium income limits allow.

o·ver·wrought /ốvəráwt/ adj. **1** overexcited; nervous; distraught. **2** overdone; too elaborate.

o·ver·zeal·ous /ốvərzéləs/ adj. too zealous in one's attitude, behavior, etc.; excessively enthusiastic. □□ **o·ver·zeal** /–zeél/ n.

ovi-¹ /ốvee/ comb. form egg, ovum. [L ovum egg]

ovi-² /ốvee/ comb. form sheep. [L ovis sheep]

o·vi·bo·vine /ốvibōvīn, –veen/ adj. & n. Zool. ● adj. having characteristics intermediate between a sheep and an ox. ● n. such an animal, e.g., a musk ox.

o·vi·duct /ốvidukt/ n. the tube through which an ovum passes from the ovary. □□ **o·vi·du·cal** /–dóokəl, –dy óo–/ adj. **o·vi·duc·tal** /–dúktəl/ adj.

o·vi·form /ốvifawrm/ adj. egg-shaped.

o·vine /ốvīn/ adj. of or like sheep. [LL ovinus f. L ovis sheep]

o·vip·a·rous /ōvípərəs/ adj. Zool. producing young by means of eggs expelled from the body before they are hatched (cf. VIVIPAROUS). □□ **o·vi·par·i·ty** /–páritee/ n. **o·vip·a·rous·ly** adv.

o·vi·pos·it /ốvipózit/ v.intr. lay an egg or eggs, esp. with an ovipositor. □□ **o·vi·po·si·tion** /–pəzíshən/ n. [OVI-¹ f. L ponere posit- to place]

o·vi·pos·i·tor /ốvipózitər/ n. a pointed tubular organ with which a female insect deposits her eggs. [mod.L f. OVI-¹ + L positor f. ponere posit- to place]

o·void /ốvoyd/ adj. & n. ● adj. **1** (of a solid or of a surface) egg-shaped. **2** oval, with one end more pointed than the other. ● n. an ovoid body or surface. [F ovoïde f. mod.L ovoides (as OVUM)]

o·vo·lo /ốvolō/ n. (pl. **o·vo·li** /–lee/) Archit. a rounded convex molding. [It. dimin. of ovo egg f. L OVUM]

o·vo·tes·tis /ốvotéstis/ n. (pl. **·tes·tes** /–teez/) Zool. an organ producing both ova and spermatozoa. [OVUM + TESTIS]

o·vo·vi·vip·a·rous /ốvovívipərəs/ adj. Zool. producing young by means of eggs hatched within the body (cf. OVIPAROUS, VIVIPAROUS). □□ **o·vo·vi·vi·par·i·ty** /–páritee/ n. [OVUM + VIVIPAROUS]

ov·u·late /ốvyəlayt, óvyə–/ v.intr. produce ova or ovules, or discharge them from the ovary. □□ **ov·u·la·tion** /–láyshən/ n. **ov·u·la·to·ry** /–lətáwree/ adj. [mod.L ovulum (as OVULE)]

ov·ule /ákvy ōol, óvyōol/ n. the part of the ovary of seed plants that contains the germ cell; an unfertilized seed. □□ **ov·u·lar** adj. [F f. med.L ovulum, dimin. of OVUM]

o·vum /ốvəm/ n. (pl. **o·va** /ốvə/) **1** a mature reproductive cell of female animals, produced by the ovary. **2** the egg cell of plants. [L, = egg]

ow /ow/ *int.* expressing sudden pain. [natural exclam.]

owe /ō/ *v.tr.* **1 a** be under obligation (to a person, etc.) to pay or repay (money, etc.) (*we owe you five dollars; owe more than I can pay*). **b** (*absol.*, usu. foll. by *for*) be in debt (*still owe for my car*). **2** (often foll. by *to*) be under obligation to render (gratitude, honor, etc.) (*owe grateful thanks to*). **3** (usu. foll. by *to*) be indebted to a person or thing for (*we owe to Newton the principle of gravitation*). □ **owe it to oneself** (often foll. by *to* + infin.) need (to do) something to protect one's own interests. [OE *āgan* (see OUGHT¹) f. Gmc]

ow·ing /ó-ing/ *predic.adj.* **1** owed; yet to be paid (*the balance owing*). **2** (foll. by *to*) **a** caused by; attributable to (*the cancellation was owing to ill health*). **b** (as *prep.*) because of (*trains are delayed owing to bad weather*).

owl /owl/ *n.* **1** any nocturnal bird of prey of the order Strigiformes, with large eyes and a hooked beak, including barn owls, great horned owls, etc. **2** *colloq.* a person compared to an owl, esp. in looking solemn or wise. □□ **owl·ish** *adj.* **owl·ish·ly** *adv.* **owl·ish·ness** *n.* (in sense 2). **owl·like** *adj.* [OE *ūle* f. Gmc]

owl·et /ówlit/ *n.* a small or young owl.

owl mon·key *n.* (*pl.* **·keys**) a douroucouli.

own /ōn/ *adj. & v.* ● *adj.* (prec. by possessive) **1 a** belonging to oneself or itself; not another's (*saw it with my own eyes*). **b** individual; peculiar; particular (*a charm all of its own*). **2** used to emphasize identity rather than possession (*cooks his own meals*). (*absol.*) a private property (*is it your own?*). **b** kindred (*among my own*). ● *v.* **1** *tr.* have as property; possess. **2 a** *tr.* confess; admit as valid, true, etc. (*own their faults; owns he did not know*). **b** *intr.* (foll. by *to*) confess to (*owned to a prejudice*). **3** *tr.* acknowledge paternity, authorship, or possession of. □ **come into one's own 1** receive one's due. **2** achieve recognition. **get one's own back** (often foll. by *on*) *colloq.* get revenge. **hold one's own** maintain one's position; not be defeated or lose strength. **of one's own** belonging to oneself alone. **on one's own 1** alone. **2** independently, without help. **own up** (often foll. by *to*) confess frankly. □□ **–owned** *adj.* (in comb.). [OE *āgen, āgnian*: see OWE]

own brand *n.* esp. *Brit.* (often *attrib.*) goods manufactured specially for a retailer and bearing the retailer's name.

own·er /ónər/ *n.* **1** a person who owns something. **2** *sl.* the captain of a ship. □□ **own·er·less** *adj.* **own·er·ship** *n.*

own·er·oc·cu·pi·er *adj.* esp. *Brit.* a person who owns the house, etc., he or she lives in.

own goal *n. Brit.* **1** a goal scored (usu. by mistake) against the scorer's own side. **2** an act or initiative that has the unintended effect of harming one's own interests.

ox /oks/ *n.* (*pl.* **ox·en** /óksən/) **1** any bovine animal, esp. a large usu. horned domesticated ruminant used for draft, for supplying milk, and for eating as meat. **2** a castrated male of a domesticated species of cattle, *Bos taurus.* [OE *oxa* f. Gmc]

ox- var. of OXY-².

ox·al·ic ac·id /oksálik/ *n. Chem.* a very poisonous and sour acid found in sorrel and rhubarb leaves. ¶ *Chem.* formula: $(COOH)_2$. □□ **ox·a·late** /óksəlayt/ *n.* [F *oxalique* f. L *oxalis* f. Gk *oxalis* wood sorrel]

ox·a·lis /óksəlis, oksál–/ *n.* any plant of the genus *Oxalis*, with trifoliate leaves and white or pink flowers. [L f. Gk f. *oxus* sour]

ox·bow /óksbō/ *n.* **1** a U-shaped collar of an ox yoke. **2 a** a loop formed by a horseshoe bend in a river. **b** a lake formed when the river cuts across the narrow end of the loop.

Ox·bridge /óksbrij/ *n. Brit.* **1** (also *attrib.*) Oxford and Cambridge universities regarded together, esp. in contrast to newer institutions. **2** (often *attrib.*) the characteristics of these universities. [portmanteau word f. *Ox*(ford) + (*Cam*)*bridge*]

ox·en *pl.* of OX.

ox·eye /óksī/ *n.* a plant with a flower like the eye of an ox. □□ **ox·eyed** *adj.*

ox·eye dai·sy *n.* a daisy, *Leucanthemum vulgare*, having flowers with white petals and a yellow center.

Ox·fam /óksfam/ *abbr.* Oxford Committee for Famine Relief.

ox·ford /óksfərd/ *n.* **1** a low-heeled shoe that laces over the instep. **2** a fabric of cotton or a cotton blend made in a basket weave, used for shirts and sportswear. [for *Oxford*, England]

Ox·ford Group /óksfərd/ *n.* a religious movement founded at Oxford, England, in 1921, with discussion of personal problems by groups.

Ox·ford move·ment /óksfərd/ *n.* an Anglican High Church movement started in Oxford, England, in 1833, advocating traditional forms of worship.

ox·hide /óks-hīd/ *n.* **1** the hide of an ox. **2** leather made from this.

ox·i·dant /óksidənt/ *n.* an oxidizing agent. □□ **ox·i·da·tion** /–dáyshən/ *n.* **ox·i·da·tion·al** *adj.* **ox·i·da·tive** /–daytiv/ *adj.* [F, part. of *oxider* (as OXIDE)]

great horned owl

ox·ide /óksīd/ *n.* a binary compound of oxygen. [F f. *oxygène* OXYGEN + *–ide* after *acide* ACID]

ox·i·dize /óksidīz/ *v.* **1** *intr. & tr.* combine or cause to combine with oxygen. **2** *tr. & intr.* cover (metal) or (of metal) become covered with a coating of oxide; make or become rusty. **3** *intr. & tr.* undergo or cause to undergo a loss of electrons. □□ **ox·i·diz·a·ble** *adj.* **ox·i·di·za·tion** *n.* **ox·i·diz·er** *n.*

ox·i·dized sil·ver *n.* esp. *Brit.* a popular name for silver covered with a dark coat of silver sulfide.

ox·i·diz·ing a·gent *n. Chem.* a substance that brings about oxidation by being reduced and gaining electrons.

ox·lip /ókslip/ *n.* **1** a woodland primula, *Primula elatior*. **2** (in general use) a natural hybrid between a primrose and a cowslip.

Oxon. /óksən/ *abbr.* **1** Oxfordshire. **2** of Oxford University or the diocese of Oxford. [abbr. of med.L *Oxoniensis* f. *Oxonia*: see OXONIAN]

Ox·o·ni·an /oksóneeən/ *adj. & n.* ● *adj.* of or relating to Oxford or Oxford University. ● *n.* **1** a member of Oxford University. **2** a native or inhabitant of Oxford. [*Oxonia* Latinized name of *Ox* (*en*) *ford*]

ox·peck·er /ókspekər/ *n.* any African bird of the genus *Buphagus*, feeding on skin parasites living on animals.

ox·tail /ókstayl/ *n.* the tail of an ox, often used in making soup.

ox·ter /ókstər/ *n. Sc. & No. of Engl.* the armpit. [OE *ōhsta, ōxta*]

ox·tongue /ókstung/ *n.* **1** the tongue of an ox, esp. cooked as food. **2** any composite plant of the genus *Picris*, with bright yellow flowers.

oxy-¹ /óksee/ *comb. form* denoting sharpness (*oxytone*). [Gk *oxu-* f. *oxus* sharp]

oxy-² /óksee/ *comb. form* (also **ox-** /oks/) *Chem.* oxygen (*oxyacetylene*). [abbr.]

ox·y·a·cet·y·lene /ókseeəsét'leen/ *adj.* of or using a mixture of oxygen and acetylene, esp. in cutting or welding metals (*oxyacetylene burner*).

ox·y·ac·id /ókseeásid/ *n. Chem.* an acid containing oxygen.

ox·y·gen /óksijən/ *n. Chem.* a colorless, tasteless, odorless gaseous element, occurring naturally in air, water, and most minerals and organic substances, and essential to plant and animal life. ¶ Symb.: **O.** □□ **ox·yg·e·nous** /oksíjinəs/ *adj.* [F *oxygène* acidifying principle (as OXY-²): it was at first held to be the essential principle in the formation of acids]

ox·y·gen·ate /óksijənayt/ *v.tr.* **1** supply, treat, or mix with oxygen; oxidize. **2** charge (blood) with oxygen by respiration. □□ **ox·y·gen·a·tion** /–náyshən/ *n.* [F *oxygéner* (as OXYGEN)]

ox·y·gen·a·tor /óksijənaytər/ *n.* an apparatus for oxygenating the blood.

ox·y·gen·ize /óksijənīz/ *v.tr.* = OXYGENATE.

ox·y·gen mask *n.* a mask placed over the nose and mouth and connected to a supply of oxygen, used when the body is not able to gain enough oxygen by breathing air.

ox·y·gen tent *n.* a tentlike enclosure supplying a patient with air rich in oxygen.

ox·y·he·mo·glo·bin /ókseehee'məglóbin/ *n. Biochem.* a bright red complex formed when hemoglobin combines with oxygen.

ox·y·mo·ron /ókseemáwron/ *n. rhet.* a figure of speech in which apparently contradictory terms appear in conjunction (e.g., *faithful kept him falsely true*). [Gk *oxumōron* neut. of *oxumōros* pointedly foolish f. *oxus* sharp + *mōros* foolish]

ox·y·to·cin /óksitósin/ *n.* **1** a hormone released by the pituitary gland that causes increased contraction of the womb during labor and stimulates the ejection of milk into the ducts of the breasts. **2** a synthetic form of this used to induce labor, etc. [*oxytocic* accelerating parturition f. Gk *oxutokia* sudden delivery (as OXY-¹, *tokos* childbirth)]

ox·y·tone /óksitōn/ *adj. & n.* ● *adj.* (esp. in ancient Greek) having an acute accent on the last syllable. ● *n.* a word of this kind. [Gk *oxutonos* (as OXY-¹, *tonos* tone)]

oy /oy/ *int.* calling attention or expressing alarm, etc. [var. of HOY¹]

o·yer and ter·mi·ner /óyər ənd términər/ *n.* **1** (in some US states) a high criminal court. **2** *hist.* a commission issued to judges on a circuit to hold courts. [ME f. AF *oyer et terminer* f. L *audire* hear + *et* and + *terminare* determine]

o·yes /ō-yés, ō-yéz/ *int.* (also **o·yes**) uttered, usu. three times, by a public crier or a court officer to command silence and attention. [ME f. AF, OF *oiez, oyez*, imper. pl. of *oïr* hear f. L *audire*]

oys·ter /óystər/ *n.* **1** any of various bivalve mollusks of the family Ostreidae or Aviculidae, esp. edible kinds. **2** an oyster-shaped morsel of meat in a fowl's back. **3** something regarded as containing all that one desires (*the world is my oyster*). **4** (in full **oyster white**) a white color with a gray tinge. [ME & OF *oistre* f. L *ostrea, ostreum* f. Gk *ostreon*]

oys·ter bed *n.* a part of the sea bottom where oysters breed or are bred.

oyster

oys·ter farm *n.* an area of the seabed used for breeding oysters.

oys·ter plant *n.* **1** = SALSIFY. **2** a blue-flowered plant, *Mertensia maritima*, growing on beaches.

Oz /oz/ *n. Austral. sl.* Australia. [abbr.]

oz. *abbr.* ounce(s). [It. f. *onza* ounce]

o·zo·ce·rite /ōzőkərit/ *n.* (also **o·zo·ke·rite**) a waxlike fossil paraffin used for candles, insulation, etc. [G *Ozokerit* f. Gk *ozō* smell + *kēros* wax]

o·zone /ózōn/ *n.* **1** *Chem.* a colorless unstable gas with a pungent odor and powerful oxidizing properties, used for bleaching, etc. ¶ Chem. formula: O₃. **2** *colloq.* **a** invigorating air at the seaside, etc. **b** *Brit.* exhilarating influence. □□ **o·zon·ic** /ōzónik/ *adj.* **o·zon·ize**

v.tr. **o·zon·i·za·tion** *n.* **o·zon·iz·er** *n.* [G *Ozon* f. Gk, neut. pres. part. of *ozō* smell]

o·zone de·ple·tion *n.* a reduction of ozone concentration in the stratosphere, caused by atmospheric pollution.

o·zone-friend·ly *adj.* (of manufactured articles) containing chemicals that are not destructive to the ozone layer.

o·zone hole *n.* an area of the ozone layer in which depletion has occurred.

o·zone lay·er *n.* a layer of ozone in the stratosphere that absorbs most of the sun's ultraviolet radiation.

P

P¹ /pee/ *n.* (also **p**) (*pl.* **Ps** or **P's**) the sixteenth letter of the alphabet.

P² *abbr.* (also **P.**) **1** (on road signs) parking. **2** *Chess* pawn. **3** *Physics* poise (unit).

P³ *symb. Chem.* the element phosphorus.

p *abbr.* (also **p.**) **1** page. **2** piano (softly). **3** pico–. **4** *Brit.* penny; pence.

PA *abbr.* **1** Pennsylvania (in official postal use). **2** public address (esp. PA system). **3** Press Association. **4** *Brit.* personal assistant.

Pa *symb. Chem.* the element protactinium.

pa /paa/ *n. colloq.* father. [abbr. of PAPA]

p.a. *abbr.* per annum.

PABA *abbr. Biochem.* PARA-AMINOBENZOIC ACID.

Pab·lum /páblǝm/ *n.* **1** *Trademark* a bland cereal food for infants. **2** (**pablum**) simplistic or unimaginative writing, speech, or ideas.

pab·u·lum /pábyǝlǝm/ *n.* **1** food, esp. for the mind (*mental pabulum*). **2** insipid or bland ideas, writings, etc. [L f. *pascere* feed]

PAC /pak/ *abbr.* POLITICAL ACTION COMMITTEE.

pa·ca /pákǝ/ *n.* any tailless rodent of the genus *Cuniculus*, esp. the spotted cavy of S. and Central America. [Sp. & Port., f. Tupi]

pace¹ /pays/ *n. & v.* ● *n.* **1 a** a single step in walking or running. **b** the distance covered in this (about 30 in. or 75 cm). **c** the distance between two successive stationary positions of the same foot in walking. **2** speed in walking or running. **3** *Theatr. & Mus.* speed or tempo in theatrical or musical performance (*played with great pace*). **4** a rate of progression. **5 a** a manner of walking or running; a gait. **b** any of various gaits, esp. of a trained horse, etc. (*rode at an ambling pace*). ● *v.* **1** *intr.* walk (esp. repeatedly or methodically) with a slow or regular pace (*pacing up and down*). **b** (of a horse) = AMBLE. **2** *tr.* traverse by pacing. **3** *tr.* set the pace for (a rider, runner, etc.). **4** *tr.* (often foll. by *out*) measure (a distance) by pacing. □ **keep pace** (often foll. by *with*) advance at an equal rate (as). **put a person through his** (or **her**) **paces** test a person's qualities in action, etc. **set the pace** determine the speed, esp. by leading. **stand** (or **stay**) **the pace** be able to keep up with others. □□ **paced** *adj.* **pac·er** *n.* [ME f. OF *pas* f. L *passus* f. *pandere* pass- stretch]

pa·ce² /paáchay, –kay, páysee/ *prep.* (in stating a contrary opinion) with due deference to the person named). [L, ablat. of *pax* peace]

pace·mak·er /páysmaykǝr/ *n.* **1** a natural or artificial device for stimulating the heart muscle and determining the rate of its contractions. **2** a competitor who sets the pace in a race.

pace·set·ter /páys-setǝr/ *n.* a leader.

pa·cha var. of PASHA.

pa·chin·ko /pǝchíngkō/ *n.* a Japanese form of pinball. [Jap.]

pa·chi·si /pǝcheézee/ *n.* a four-handed board game orig. from India historically using six cowries like dice. [Hindi, = of 25 (the highest throw)]

pach·y·derm /pákidǝrm/ *n.* any thick-skinned mammal, esp. an elephant or rhinoceros. □□ **pach·y·der·ma·tous** /–dérmǝtǝs/ *adj.* [F *pachyderme* f. Gk *pakhudermos* f. *pakhus* thick + *derma* –*matos* skin]

pach·y·san·dra /pakisándrǝ/ *n.* any low-growing evergreen plant of the genus *Pachysandra*, used as a ground cover.

pa·cif·ic /pǝsífik/ *adj. & n.* ● *adj.* **1** characterized by or tending to peace; tranquil. **2** (**Pacific**) of or adjoining the Pacific. ● *n.* (**the Pacific**) the expanse of ocean between N. and S. America to the east and Asia to the west. □□ **pa·cif·i·cal·ly** *adv.* [F *pacifique* or L *pacificus* f. *pax pacis* peace]

pac·i·fi·ca·tion /pásifikáyshǝn/ *n.* the act of pacifying or the process of being pacified. □□ **pa·cif·i·ca·to·ry** /pǝsífikǝtáwree/ *adj.* [F f. L *pacificatio –onis* (as PACIFY)]

Pa·cif·ic Time *n.* the standard time used in the Pacific region of Canada and the US.

pac·i·fi·er /pásifiǝr/ *n.* **1** a person or thing that pacifies. **2** a rubber or plastic nipple for a baby to suck on.

pac·i·fism /pásifizǝm/ *n.* the belief that war and violence are morally unjustified and that all disputes can be settled by peaceful means. □□ **pac·i·fist** *n. & adj.* [F *pacifisme* f. *pacifier* PACIFY]

pac·i·fy /pásifí/ *v.tr.* (**·fies**, **·fied**) **1** appease (a person, anger, etc.). **2** bring (a country, etc.) to a state of peace. [ME f. OF *pacifier* or L *pacificare* (as PACIFY)]

pack¹ /pak/ *n. & v.* ● *n.* **1 a** a collection of things wrapped up or tied together for carrying. **b** = BACKPACK. **2** a set of items packaged for use or disposal together. **3** usu. *derog.* a lot or set (of similar things or persons) (*a pack of lies; a pack of thieves*). **4** a set of playing cards. **5 a** a group of hounds esp. for foxhunting. **b** a group of wild animals, esp. wolves, hunting together. **6** an organized group of Cub

Scouts or Brownies. **7** *Rugby* a team's forward. **8 a** a medicinal or cosmetic substance applied to the skin. **b** a hot or cold pad of absorbent material for treating a wound, etc. **9** = PACK ICE. **10** a quantity of fish, fruit, etc., packed in a season, etc. **11** *Med.* **a** the wrapping of a body or part of a body in a wet sheet, etc. **b** a sheet, etc., used for this. ● *v.* **1** *tr.* (often foll. by *up*) **a** fill (a suitcase, bag, etc.) with clothes and other items. **b** put (things) together in a bag or suitcase, esp. for traveling. **2** *intr. & tr.* come or put closely together; crowd or cram (*packed a lot into a few hours; passengers packed like sardines*). **3** *tr.* (in *passive*; often foll. by *with*) be filled (with); contain extensively (*the restaurant was packed; the book is packed with information*). **4** *tr.* fill (a hall, theater, etc.) with an audience, etc. **5** *tr.* cover (a thing) with something pressed tightly around. **6** *intr.* be suitable for packing. **7** *tr. colloq.* **a** carry (a gun, etc.). **b** be capable of delivering (a punch) with skill or force. **8** *intr.* (of animals, etc.) form a pack. □ **packed out** *Brit. colloq.* full; crowded. **pack it in** (or **up**) *colloq.* end or stop it. **pack off** send (a person) away, esp. abruptly or promptly. **pack up** *Brit. colloq.* **1** (esp. of a machine) stop functioning; break down. **2** retire from an activity, contest, etc. **send packing** *colloq.* dismiss (a person) summarily. □□ **pack·a·ble** *adj.* [ME f. MDu., MLG *pak*, *pakken*, of unkn. orig.]

pack² /pak/ *v.tr.* select (a jury, etc.) or fill (a meeting) so as to secure a decision in one's favor. [prob. f. obs. verb *pact* f. PACT]

pack·age /pákij/ *n. & v.* ● *n.* **1 a** a bundle of things packed. **b** a box, parcel, etc., in which things are packed. **2** (in full **package deal**) a set of proposals or items offered or agreed to as a whole. **3** *Computing* a piece of software suitable for various applications rather than one which is custom-built. **4** *colloq.* = PACKAGE TOUR. ● *v.tr.* make up into or enclose in a package. □□ **pack·ag·er** *n.* [PACK¹ + –AGE]

pack·age store *n.* a retail store selling alcoholic beverages in sealed containers.

pack·age tour *n.* (also *Brit.* **pack·age hol·i·day**) a tour with all arrangements made at an inclusive price.

pack·ag·ing /pákijing/ *n.* **1** a wrapping or container for goods. **2** the process of packing goods.

pack an·i·mal *n.* an animal used for carrying packs.

pack drill *n.* a military punishment of marching up and down carrying full equipment.

packed lunch *n.* a lunch carried in a bag, box, etc., esp. to work, school, etc.

pack·er /pákǝr/ *n.* a person or thing that packs, esp. a dealer who processes and packs food for transportation and sale.

pack·et /pákit/ *n.* **1** a small package. **2** esp. *Brit. colloq.* a large sum of money won, lost, or spent. **3** (in full **packet boat**) *hist.* a mail boat or passenger ship. [PACK¹ + –ET¹]

pack·horse /pák-hawrs/ *n.* a horse for carrying loads.

pack ice *n.* an area of large crowded pieces of floating ice in the sea.

pack·ing /páking/ *n.* **1** the act or process of packing. **2** material used as padding to pack esp. fragile articles. **3** material used to seal a joint or assist in lubricating an axle.

pack·ing case *n.* (also **pack·ing box**) a case (usu. wooden) or crate for packing goods in.

pack rat *n.* **1** a large hoarding rodent. **2** a person who hoards unneeded things.

pack·thread /pákthred/ *n.* strong thread for sewing or tying up packs.

pact /pakt/ *n.* an agreement or a treaty. [ME f. OF *pact(e)* f. L *pactum*, neut. past part. of *pacisci* agree]

pad¹ /pad/ *n. & v.* • *n.* **1** a piece of soft material used to reduce friction or jarring, fill out hollows, hold or absorb liquid, etc. **2** a number of sheets of blank paper fastened together at one edge, for writing or drawing on. **3** the fleshy underpart of an animal's foot or of a human finger. **4** a soft guard for the limbs or joints protecting them from injury, esp. in sports. **5** a flat surface for helicopter take-off or rocket launching. **6** *colloq.* an apartment or bedroom. **7** the floating leaf of a water lily. • *v.tr.* (**pad·ded, pad·ding**) **1** provide with a pad or padding; stuff. **2 a** (foll. by *out*) lengthen or fill out (a book, etc.) with unnecessary material. **b** to increase fraudulently, as an expense account. [prob. of LG or Du. orig.]

pad² /pad/ *v. & n.* • *v.* (**pad·ded, pad·ding**) **1** *intr.* walk with a soft dull steady step. **2 a** *tr.* hike along (a road, etc.) on foot. **b** *intr.* travel on foot. • *n.* the sound of soft steady steps. [LG *padden* tread, *pad* PATH]

pad·ded cell *n.* a room with padded walls in a mental hospital.

pad·ding /páding/ *n.* soft material used to pad or stuff with.

pad·dle¹ /pád'l/ *n. & v.* • *n.* **1** a short broad-bladed oar used without an oarlock. **2** a paddle-shaped instrument. **3** *Zool.* a fin or flipper. **4** each of the boards fitted around the circumference of a paddle wheel or mill wheel. **5** esp. *Brit.* the action or a period of paddling. • *v.* **1** *intr. & tr.* move on water or propel a boat by means of paddles. **2** *intr. & tr.* row gently. **3** *tr. colloq.* spank. □□ **pad·dler** *n.* [15th c.: orig. unkn.]

pad·dle² /pád'l/ *v. & n.* esp. *Brit.* • *v.intr.* walk barefoot or dabble the feet or hands in shallow water. • *n.* the action or a period of paddling. □□ **pad·dler** *n.* [prob. of LG or Du. orig.: cf. LG *paddeln* tramp about]

pad·dle·ball /pád'lbawl/ *n.* a game played on an enclosed court with short-handled perforated paddles and a ball similar to a tennis ball.

pad·dle·boat /pád'lbōt/ *n.* a boat propelled by a paddle wheel.

pad·dle wheel *n.* a wheel for propelling a ship, with boards around the circumference so as to press backward against the water.

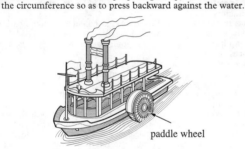

paddle wheel

pad·dock /pádək/ *n.* **1** a small field, esp. for keeping horses in. **2** an enclosure adjoining a racecourse where horses or cars are assembled before a race. **3** *Austral. & NZ* a field; a plot of land. [app. var. of (now dial.) *parrock* (OE *pearruc*): see PARK]

Pad·dy /pádee/ *n.* (*pl.* ·**dies**) *colloq.* often *offens.* **1** an Irishman. **2** (**pad·dy**) a policeman. [nickname for the Irish name *Padraig* (= Patrick)]

pad·dy¹ /pádee/ *n.* (*pl.* ·**dies**) **1** a field where rice is grown. **2** rice before threshing or in the husk. [Malay *pādī*]

pad·dy wag·on *n. colloq.* a police van for transporting those under arrest.

pad·dy² /pádee/ *n.* (*pl.* ·**dies**) *Brit. colloq.* a rage; a fit of temper. [PADDY]

pad·e·mel·on /pádeeméllən/ *n.* any small wallaby of the genus *Thylogale*, inhabiting the coastal scrub of Australia. [corrupt. of an Aboriginal name]

pad·lock /pádlok/ *n. & v.* • *n.* a detachable lock hanging by a pivoted hook on the object fastened. • *v.tr.* secure with a padlock. [ME f. LOCK¹: first element unexpl.]

pa·douk /pədóok/ *n.* **1** any timber tree of the genus *Pterocarpus*, esp. *P. indicus*. **2** the wood of this tree, resembling rosewood. [Burmese]

pa·dre /paádray, –dree/ *n.* **1** a clergyman, esp. a priest. **2** a chaplain in any of the armed services. [It., Sp., & Port., = father, priest, f. L *pater patris* father]

pae·an /péeən/ *n.* a song of praise or triumph. [L f. Doric Gk *paian* hymn of thanksgiving to Apollo (under the name of *Paian*)]

paedo- *Brit.* var. of PEDO-.

pa·el·la /pī-élə, paa-áyaa/ *n.* a Spanish dish of rice, saffron, chicken, seafood, etc., cooked and served in a large shallow pan. [Catalan f. OF *paele* f. L *patella* pan]

pae·on /péeən/ *n.* a metrical foot of one long syllable and three short syllables in any order. □□ **pae·on·ic** /pee-ónik/ *adj.* [L f. Gk *paiōn*, the Attic form of *paian* PAEAN]

pa·gan /páygən/ *n. & adj.* • *n.* **1** a person not subscribing to any of the main religions of the world. **2** a person following a polytheistic or pantheistic religion. **3** a hedonist. • *adj.* **1 a** of or relating to or associated with pagans. **b** irreligious. **2** identifying divinity or spirituality in nature; pantheistic. □□ **pa·gan·ish** *adj.* **pa·gan·ism** *n.* **pa·gan·ize** *v.tr. & intr.* [ME f. L *paganus* villager, rustic f. *pagus* country district: in Christian L = civilian, heathen]

page¹ /payj/ *n. & v.* • *n.* **1 a** a leaf of a book, periodical, etc. **b** each side of this. **c** what is written or printed on this. **2 a** an episode that might fill a page in written history, etc.; a record. **b** a memorable event. **3** *Computing* a section of computer memory of specified size, esp. one that can be readily transferred between main and auxiliary memories. • *v.tr.* paginate. [F f. L *pagina* f. *pangere* fasten]

page² /payj/ *n. & v.* • *n.* **1** a person employed to run errands, attend to a door, etc. **2** a boy employed as a personal attendant of a bride, etc. **3** *hist.* a boy in training for knighthood and attached to a knight's service. • *v.tr.* **1** (in hotels, airports, etc.) summon by making an announcement or by sending a messenger. **2** summon by means of a pager.

WORD HISTORY   page

Middle English (in the sense 'youth, male of uncouth manners'): from Old French, perhaps from Italian *paggio*, from Greek *paidion*, diminutive of *pais*, *paid-* 'boy.' Early use of the verb (mid-16th century) was in the sense 'follow as or like a page'; its current noun sense 1 dates from the early 20th century.

pag·eant /pájənt/ *n.* **1 a** an elaborate parade or spectacle. **b** a spectacular procession, or play performed in the open, illustrating historical events. **c** a tableau, etc., on a fixed stage or moving vehicle. **2** an empty or specious show. [ME *pagyn*, of unkn. orig.]

SPELLING TIP   pageant

To spell *pageant* correctly, try the mnemonic: "There is a *page* and an *ant* in *pageant*."

pag·eant·ry /pájəntree/ *n.* (*pl.* ·**ries**) **1** elaborate or sumptuous show or display. **2** an instance of this.

page boy *n.* **1** = PAGE² *n.* 2. **2** a hairstyle with the hair reaching to the shoulder and rolled under at the ends.

pag·er /páyjər/ *n.* a radio device with a beeper, activated from a central point to alert the person wearing it.

pag·i·nal /pájinəl/ *adj.* **1** of pages (of books, etc.). **2** corresponding page for page. □□ **pag·i·nar·y** *adj.* [LL *paginalis* (as PAGE¹)]

pag·i·nate /pájinayt/ *v.tr.* assign numbers to the pages of a book, etc. □□ **pag·i·na·tion** /–náyshən/ *n.* [F *paginer* f. L *pagina* PAGE¹]

pa·go·da /pəgódə/ *n.* **1** a Hindu or Buddhist temple or sacred building, esp. a many-tiered tower, in India and the Far East. **2** an ornamental imitation of this. [Port. *pagode*, prob. ult. f. Pers. *butkada* idol temple]

pa·go·da tree *n.* any of various trees, esp. *Sophora japonica*, resembling a pagoda in shape.

pah /paa/ *int.* expressing disgust or contempt. [natural utterance]

Pah·la·vi /paáləvee/ *n.* (also **Peh·le·vi** /páylovee/) the writing system of Persia from the 2nd c. BC to the advent of Islam in the 7th c. AD. [Pers. *pahlawī* f. *pahlav* f. *parthava* Parthia]

paid *past* and *past part.* of PAY¹.

paid va·ca·tion *n.* an agreed period of time off from work for which wages are paid as normal.

pail /payl/ *n.* **1** a bucket. **2** an amount contained in this. □□ **pail·ful** *n.* (*pl.* ·**fuls**). [OE *pægel* gill (cf. MDu. *pegel* gauge), assoc. with OF *paelle*: see PAELLA]

pagoda

pail·lasse esp. *Brit.* var. of PALLIASSE.

pail·lette /pīyét, pəlét/ *n.* **1** a piece of bright metal used in enamel painting. **2** a spangle. [F, dimin. of *paille* f. L *palea* straw, chaff]

pain /payn/ *n. & v.* • *n.* **1 a** the range of unpleasant bodily sensations produced by illness or by harmful physical contact, etc. **b** a particular kind or instance of this (often in *pl.*: *suffering from stomach pains*). **2** mental suffering or distress. **3** (in *pl.*) careful effort; trouble taken (*take pains*; *got nothing for my pains*). **4** (also **pain in the neck**, etc.) *colloq.* a troublesome person or thing; a nuisance. • *v.tr.*

1 cause pain to. **2** (as **pained** *adj.*) expressing pain (*a pained expression*). □ **in pain** suffering pain. **on** (or **under**) **pain of** with (death, etc.) as the penalty. [ME f. OF *peine* f. L *poena* penalty]

pain·ful /páynfŏol/ *adj.* **1** causing bodily or mental pain or distress. **2** (esp. of part of the body) suffering pain. **3** causing trouble or difficulty; laborious (*a painful climb*). □□ **pain·ful·ly** *adv.* **pain·ful·ness** *n.*

pain·kil·ler /páynkilər/ *n.* a medicine or drug for alleviating pain. □□ **pain·kil·ling** *adj.*

pain·less /páynlis/ *adj.* not causing or suffering pain. □□ **pain·less·ly** *adv.* **pain·less·ness** *n.*

pain·stak·ing /páynztayking/ *adj.* careful, industrious, thorough. □□ **pain·stak·ing·ly** *adv.* **pain·stak·ing·ness** *n.*

paint /paynt/ *n. & v.* ● *n.* **1 a** coloring matter, esp. in liquid form for imparting color to a surface. **b** this as a dried film or coating (*the paint peeled off*). **2** cosmetic makeup, esp. rouge or nail polish. **3** = PINTO. ● *v.tr.* **1 a** cover the surface of (a wall, object, etc.) with paint. **b** apply paint of a specified color to (*paint the door green*). **2** depict (an object, scene, etc.) with paint; produce (a picture) by painting. **3** describe vividly as if by painting (*painted a gloomy picture of the future*). **4 a** apply liquid or cosmetic to (the face, skin, etc.). **b** apply (a liquid to the skin, etc.). □ **paint out** efface with paint. **paint the town red** *colloq.* enjoy oneself flamboyantly; celebrate. □□ **paint·a·ble** *adj.* [ME f. *peint* past part. of OF *peindre* f. L *pingere* *pict-* paint]

paint·box /páyntboks/ *n.* a box holding dry paints for painting pictures.

paint·brush /páyntbrush/ *n.* a brush for applying paint.

paint·ed la·dy *n.* **1** an orange-red butterfly, esp. *Vanessa cardui*, with black and brown markings. **2** (also **paint·ed wom·an**) = PROSTITUTE 1a.

paint·er[1] /páyntər/ *n.* a person who paints, esp. an artist or decorator. [ME f. OF *peintour* ult. f. L *pictor* (as PAINT)]

paint·er[2] /páyntər/ *n.* a rope attached to the bow of a boat for tying it to a pier, dock, etc. [ME, prob. f. OF *penteur* rope from a masthead: cf. G *Pentertakel* f. *pentern* fish the anchor]

paint·er·ly /páyntərlee/ *adj.* **1 a** using paint well; artistic. **b** characteristic of a painter or paintings. **2** (of a painting) lacking clearly defined outlines.

paint·ing /páynting/ *n.* **1** the process or art of using paint. **2** a painted picture.

paint shop *n.* **1** a store selling paint (for building interiors and exteriors) and painting supplies. **2** the part of a factory where goods are painted, esp. by spraying.

paint stick *n.* a stick of water-soluble paint used like a crayon.

paint·work /páyntwərk/ *n.* **1** a painted surface or area in a building, etc. **2** the work of painting.

paint·y /páyntee/ *adj.* (**paint·i·er**, **paint·i·est**) **1** of or covered with paint. **2** (of a picture, etc.) overcharged with paint.

pair /pair/ *n. & v.* ● *n.* **1** a set of two persons or things used together or regarded as a unit (*a pair of gloves; a pair of eyes*). **2** an article (e.g., scissors, pants, or pajamas) consisting of two joined or corresponding parts not used separately. **3 a** a romantically involved couple. **b** a mated couple of animals. **4** two horses harnessed side by side (*a coach and pair*). **5** the second member of a pair in relation to the first (*cannot find its pair*). **6** two playing cards of the same denomination. **7** either or both of two members of a legislative assembly on opposite sides absenting themselves from voting by mutual arrangement. ● *v.tr. & intr.* **1** (often foll. by *off* or *up*) arrange or be arranged in couples. **2 a** join or be joined in marriage. **b** (of animals) mate. **3** form a legislative pair. □ **in pairs** in twos. [ME f. OF *paire* f. L *paria* neut. pl. of *par* equal]

pair pro·duc·tion *n.* *Physics* the conversion of a radiation quantum into an electron and a positron.

pair roy·al *n.* *Cribbage* a set of three cards of the same denomination.

pai·sa /pīsaá/ *n.* (*pl.* **pai·se** /–sáy/) a coin and monetary unit of India, Pakistan, Nepal, and Bangladesh, equal to one hundredth of a rupee or taka. [Hindi]

Pais·ley /páyzlee/ *n.* (also **pais·ley**) (often *attrib.*) **1** a distinctive detailed pattern of curved feather-shaped figures. **2** a soft woolen garment or fabric having this pattern. [*Paisley* in Scotland]

Pai·ute /pīyŏot/ *n.* (also **Pi·ute**) **1 a** a N. American people native to the southwestern US. **b** a member of this people. **2** the language of this people.

pa·ja·mas /pəjaámən, –jám–/ *n.pl.* **1** a suit of loose pants and jacket for sleeping in. **2** loose pants tied at the waist, worn by both sexes in some Asian countries. **3** (**pajama**) (*attrib.*) designating parts of a suit of pajamas (*pajama top; pajama pants; pajama bottoms*). [Urdu *pā(e)jāma* f. Pers. *pae, pay* leg + Hindi *jāma* clothing]

pa·ke·ha /paákihaa/ *n.* NZ a white person as opposed to a Maori. [Maori]

Pak·i /pákee/ *n.* (*pl.* **Pak·is**) *Brit. sl. offens.* a Pakistani, esp. an immigrant in Britain. [abbr.]

Pa·ki·sta·ni /pákistánee, paákistaáanee/ *n. & adj.* ● *n.* **1** a native or national of Pakistan. **2** a person of Pakistani descent. ● *adj.* of or relating to Pakistan. [Hindu]

pa·ko·ra /pəkáwrə/ *n.* a piece of cauliflower, carrot, or other vegetable, coated in seasoned batter and deep-fried. [Hind.]

pal /pal/ *n. & v.* ● *n. colloq.* a friend or comrade. ● *v.intr.* (**palled**, **pal·ling**) (usu. foll. by *up*) associate; form a friendship. [Romany = brother, friend, ult. f. Skr. *bhrātr* BROTHER]

pal·ace /pális/ *n.* **1 a** the official residence of a president or sovereign. **b** esp. *Brit.* the official residence of an archbishop or bishop. **2** a mansion; a spacious building. [ME f. OF *palais* f. L *Palatium* Palatine (hill) in Rome where the house of the emperor was situated]

pal·ace rev·o·lu·tion *n.* (also **pal·ace coup**) the (usu. nonviolent) overthrow of a sovereign, government, etc. at the hands of senior officials.

pal·a·din /páladin/ *n. hist.* **1** any of the twelve peers of Charlemagne's court, of whom the Count Palatine was the chief. **2** a knight errant; a champion. [F *paladin* f. It. *paladino* f. L *palatinus*: see PALATINE[1]]

palaeo- *comb. form Brit.* var. of PALEO-.

Pa·lae·o·zo·ic *Brit.* var. of PALEOZOIC.

pal·aes·tra /pəléstrə/ *n.* (also **pa·les·tra**) *Gk & Rom. Antiq.* a wrestling school or gymnasium. [ME f. L *palaestra* f. Gk *palaistra* f. *palaiō* wrestle]

pa·lais /paláy/ *n. Brit. colloq.* a public hall for dancing. [F *palais (de danse)* (dance) hall]

pal·an·quin /pálənkéen/ *n.* (also **pal·an·keen**) (in India and Asia) a covered litter for one passenger. [Port. *palanquim*: cf. Hindi *pālkī* f. Skr. *palyanka* bed, couch]

pal·at·a·ble /pálətəbəl/ *adj.* **1** pleasant to taste. **2** (of an idea, suggestion, etc.) acceptable, satisfactory. □□ **pal·at·a·bil·i·ty** *n.* **pal·at·a·ble·ness** *n.* **pal·at·a·bly** *adv.*

pal·a·tal /pálət'l/ *adj. & n.* ● *adj.* **1** of the palate. **2** (of a sound) made by placing the blade of the tongue against or near the hard palate (e.g., *y* in *yes*). ● *n.* a palatal sound. □□ **pal·a·tal·ize** *v.tr.* **pal·a·tal·i·za·tion** *n.* **pal·a·tal·ly** *adv.* [F (as PALATE)]

pal·ate /pálət/ *n.* **1** a structure closing the upper part of the mouth cavity in vertebrates. **2** the sense of taste. **3** a mental taste or inclination; liking. [ME f. L *palatum*]

SPELLING TIP palate/palette

You use your *palate* to taste food served on a *plate*. An artist uses a *palette* to mix a *pale* tint.

---

pa·la·tial /pəláyshəl/ *adj.* (of a building) like a palace, esp. spacious and magnificent. □□ **pa·la·tial·ly** *adv.* [L (as PALACE)]

pa·lat·i·nate /pəlát'nayt/ *n.* territory under the jurisdiction of a Count Palatine.

pal·a·tine[1] /pálətīn/ *adj.* (also **Pal·a·tine**) *hist.* **1** (of an official or feudal lord) having local authority that elsewhere belongs only to a sovereign (*Count Palatine*). **2** (of a territory) subject to this authority. [ME f. F *palatin –ine* f. L *palatinus* of the PALACE]

pal·a·tine[2] /pálətīn/ *adj. & n.* ● *adj.* of or connected with the palate. ● *n.* (in full **palatine bone**) each of two bones forming the hard palate. [F *palatin –ine* (as PALATE)]

pa·la·ver /pəlávər, –laávər/ *n. & v.* ● *n.* **1** fuss and bother, esp. prolonged. **2** profuse or idle talk. **3** cajolery. **4** *colloq.* a prolonged or tiresome business. **5** esp. *hist.* a parley between European traders and Africans or other indigenous peoples. ● *v.* **1** *intr.* talk profusely. **2** *tr.* flatter, wheedle. [Port. *palavra* word f. L (as PARABLE)]

pale[1] /payl/ *adj. & v.* ● *adj.* **1** (of a person or complexion) diminished in coloration; of a whitish or ashen appearance. **2 a** (of a color) faint; not dark or deep. **b** faintly colored. **3** of faint luster; dim. **4** lacking intensity, vigor, or strength (*pale imitation*). ● *v.* **1** *intr. & tr.* grow or make pale. **2** *intr.* (often foll. by *before, beside*) become feeble in comparison (with). □□ **pale·ly** *adv.* **pale·ness** *n.* **pal·ish** *adj.* [ME f. OF *pale, palir* f. L *pallidus* f. *pallēre* be pale]

SYNONYM TIP pale[1]

ASHEN, LIVID, PALLID, WAN. Someone of fair complexion who usually stays indoors and spends very little time in the sun is apt to be *pale*, referring to an unnaturally-white or colorless complexion; one can also become *pale* out of fear or illness. Someone who has lost color from being ill or under stress may be described as **pallid**, which suggests a paleness that is the result of weakness, weariness, faintness, or some other abnormal condition (*she appeared pallid when she left the police station*). **Wan** also connotes an unhealthy condition or sickly paleness (*her wan face smiled at him from the hospital bed*). Someone who is **ashen** has skin the *pale* grayish color of ashes (*ashen with fear*), while **livid** can mean bluish to describe loss of normal coloring (*the livid face of a drowned corpse*), or can mean reddish or flushed (*livid with rage*).

---

pale[2] /payl/ *n.* **1** a pointed piece of wood for fencing, etc.; a stake. **2** a boundary or enclosed area. **3** *Heraldry* a vertical stripe in the middle of a shield. □ **beyond the pale** outside the bounds of acceptable behavior. **in pale** *Heraldry* arranged vertically. [ME f. OF *pal* f. L *palus* stake]

pa·le·a /páyleeə/ *n.* (*pl.* **pa·le·ae** /–lee-ee/) *Bot.* a chafflike bract, esp. in a flower of grasses. [L, = chaff]

paled /payld/ *adj.* having palings.

pale·face /páylfays/ *n.* a white person.

paleo- /páyleeō/ *comb. form* ancient; old; of ancient (esp. prehistoric) times. [Gk *palaios* ancient]

pa·le·o·bot·a·ny /páyleeōbót'nee/ *n.* the study of fossil plants.

Pa·le·o·cene /páyleeəseén/ *adj. & n. Geol.* ● *adj.* of or relating to the earliest epoch of the Tertiary period with evidence of the emergence and development of mammals. ● *n.* this epoch or system. [PALEO- + Gk *kainos* new]

pa·le·o·cli·ma·tol·o·gy /páyleeōklímətóləjee/ *n.* (*Brit.* **pa·lae·o·cli·ma·tol·o·gy**) the study of the climate in geologically past times.

pa·le·o·ge·og·ra·phy /páyleeōjeeógrəfee/ *n.* (*Brit.* **pa·lae·o·ge·og·ra·phy**) the study of the geographical features at periods in the geological past.

pa·le·og·ra·phy /páyleeógrəfee/ *n.* (*Brit.* **pa·lae·og·ra·phy**) the study of writing and documents from the past. □□ **pa·le·og·ra·pher** *n.* **pa·le·o·graph·ic** /–leeəgráfik/ *adj.* **pa·le·o·graph·i·cal** *adj.* **pa·le·o·graph·i·cal·ly** *adv.* [F *paléographie* f. mod.L *paleographia* (as PALEO-, –GRAPHY)]

pa·le·o·lith·ic /páyleeəlíthik/ *adj.* (*Brit.* **pa·lae·o·lith·ic**) *Archaeol.* of or relating to the early part of the Stone Age. [PALEO- + Gk *lithos* stone]

pa·le·o·mag·net·ism /páyleeōmágnitizəm/ *n.* (*Brit.* **pa·lae·o·mag·net·ism**) the study of the magnetism remaining in rocks.

pa·le·on·tol·o·gy /páyleeóntóləjee/ *n.* (*Brit.* **pa·lae·on·tol·o·gy**) the study of life in the geological past. □□ **pa·le·on·to·log·i·cal** *adj.* **pa·le·on·tol·o·gist** *n.* [PALEO- + Gk *onta* neut. pl. of *ōn* being, part. of *eimi* be + –LOGY]

Pa·le·o·zo·ic /páyleeəzóik/ *adj. & n. Geol.* ● *adj.* of or relating to an era of geological time marked by the appearance of marine and terrestrial plants and animals, esp. invertebrates. ● *n.* this era (cf. CENOZOIC, MESOZOIC). [PALEO- + Gk *zōē* life, *zōos* living]

Pal·es·tin·i·an /pálistíneeən/ *adj. & n.* ● *adj.* of or relating to Palestine, a region (in ancient and modern times) and former British territory on the E. Mediterranean coast. ● *n.* **1** a native of Palestine in ancient or modern times. **2** an Arab, or a descendant of one, born or living in the area called Palestine.

pa·les·tra var. of PALAESTRA.

pal·ette /pálit/ *n.* **1** a thin board or slab or other surface, usu. with a hole for the thumb, on which an artist holds and mixes colors. **2** the range of colors, etc., used by an artist. [F, dimin. of *pale* shovel f. L *pala* spade]

SPELLING TIP **palette**

See note at PALATE.

pal·ette knife *n.* **1** a thin steel blade with a handle for mixing colors or applying or removing paint. **2** *Brit.* a kitchen knife with a long blunt round-ended flexible blade.

pal·frey /páwlfree/ *n.* (*pl.* **·freys**) *archaic* a horse for ordinary riding, esp. for women. [ME f. OF *palefrei* f. med.L *palefredus*, LL *paraveredus* f. Gk *para* beside, extra, + L *veredus* light horse, of Gaulish orig.]

Pa·li /páalee/ *n.* an Indic language used in the canonical books of Buddhists. [Skr. *pāli-bhāsā* f. *pāli* canon + *bhāsā* language]

pal·i·mo·ny /pálimōnee/ *n. colloq.* usu. court-ordered allowance made by one member of an unmarried couple to the other after separation. [PAL + ALIMONY]

pal·imp·sest /pálimpsest/ *n.* **1** a piece of writing material or manuscript on which the original writing has been erased to make room for other writing. **2** a place, etc., showing layers of history, etc. **3** a monumental brass turned and re-engraved on the reverse side. [L *palimpsestus* f. Gk *palimpsēstos* f. *palin* again + *psēstos* rubbed smooth]

pal·in·drome /pálindrōm/ *n.* a word or phrase that reads the same backward as forward (e.g., *rotator, nurses run*). □□ **pal·in·drom·ic** /–drómik, –dró/ *adj.* **pa·lin·dro·mist** *n.* [Gk *palindromos* running back again f. *palin* again + *drom-* run]

pal·ing /páyling/ *n.* **1** a fence of pales. **2** a pale.

pal·in·gen·e·sis /pálinjénisis/ *n.* **1** *Biol.* the exact reproduction of ancestral characteristics in ontogenesis. **2** transmigration of souls. □□ **pal·in·ge·net·ic** /–jənétik/ *adj.* [Gk *palin* again + *genesis* birth, GENESIS]

pal·i·node /pálinōd/ *n.* **1** a poem in which the writer retracts a view or sentiment expressed in a former poem. **2** a recantation. [F *palinode* or LL *palinodia* f. Gk *palinōidia* f. *palin* again + *ōidē* song]

pal·i·sade /pálisáyd/ *n. & v.* ● *n.* **1 a** a fence of pales or iron railings. **b** a strong pointed wooden stake used in a close row for defense. **2** (in *pl.*) a line of high cliffs. ● *v.tr.* enclose or provide with a pali-

sade. [F *palissade* f. Prov. *palissada* f. *palissa* paling ult. f. L *palus* stake]

pal·i·sade lay·er *n. Bot.* a layer of elongated cells below the epidermis.

pall[1] /pawl/ *n.* **1** a cloth spread over a coffin, hearse, or tomb. **2** a shoulder band with pendants, worn as an ecclesiastical vestment and sign of authority. **3** a dark covering (*a pall of darkness; a pall of smoke*). **4** *Heraldry* a Y-shaped bearing charged with crosses representing the front of an ecclesiastical pall. [OE *pæll*, f. L *pallium* cloak]

pall[2] /pawl/ *v.* **1** *intr.* (often foll. by *on*) become uninteresting (to). **2** *tr.* satiate; cloy. [ME, f. APPALL]

pal·la·di·a *pl.* of PALLADIUM[2].

Pal·la·di·an /pəládeeən/ *adj. Archit.* in the neoclassical style of Palladio. □□ **Pal·la·di·an·ism** *n.* [A. *Palladio*, It. architect d. 1580]

pal·la·di·um[1] /pəláydeeəm/ *n. Chem.* a white ductile metallic element occurring naturally in various ores and used in chemistry as a catalyst and for making jewelry. ¶ Symb.: **Pd**. [mod.L f. *Pallas*, an asteroid discovered (1803) just before the element, + –IUM; cf. CERIUM]

pal·la·di·um[2] /pəláydeeəm/ *n.* (*pl.* **pal·la·di·a** /–deeə/) a safeguard or source of protection. [ME f. L f. Gk *palladion* image of Pallas (Athene), a protecting deity]

pall·bear·er /páwlbairər/ *n.* a person helping to carry or officially escorting a coffin at a funeral.

pal·let[1] /pálit/ *n.* **1** a straw mattress. **2** a mean or makeshift bed. [ME *pailet, paillet* f. AF *paillete* straw f. OF *paille* f. L *palea*]

pal·let[2] /pálit/ *n.* **1** a flat wooden blade with a handle, used in ceramics to shape clay. **2** = PALETTE. **3** a portable platform for transporting and storing loads. **4** a projection in a timepiece transmitting motion from an escapement to a pendulum, etc. **5** a projection on a machine part, serving to change the mode of motion of a wheel. □□ **pal·let·ize** *v.tr.* (in sense 3). [F *palette*: see PALETTE]

pal·li·a *pl.* of PALLIUM.

pal·liasse /palyás/ *n.* (also esp. *Brit.* **pail·lasse**) a straw mattress. [F *paillasse* f. It. *pagliaccio* ult. f. L *palea* straw]

pal·li·ate /páleeayt/ *v.tr.* **1** alleviate (disease) without curing it. **2** excuse; extenuate. □□ **pal·li·a·tion** /–áyshən/ *n.* **pal·li·a·tor** *n.* [LL *palliare* to cloak f. *pallium* cloak]

pal·li·a·tive /páleeətiv/ *n. & adj.* ● *n.* anything used to alleviate pain, anxiety, etc. ● *adj.* serving to alleviate. □□ **pal·li·a·tive·ly** *adv.* [F *palliatif –ive* or med.L *palliativus* (as PALLIATE)]

pal·lid /pálid/ *adj.* pale, esp. from illness. □□ **pal·lid·i·ty** /–líditee/ *n.* **pal·lid·ly** *adv.* **pal·lid·ness** *n.* [L *pallidus* PALE[1]]

pal·li·um /páleeəm/ *n.* (*pl.* **pal·li·ums** or **pal·li·a** /–leeə/) **1** an ecclesiastical pall, esp. that sent by the Pope to an archbishop as a symbol of authority. **2** *hist.* a man's large rectangular cloak, esp. as worn in antiquity. **3** *Zool.* the mantle of a mollusk or brachiopod. [L]

pall-mall /pélmél, pálmál, páwlmáwl/ *n. hist.* a game in which a ball was driven through an iron ring suspended in a long alley. [obs. F *pallemaille* f. It. *pallamaglio* f. *palla* ball + *maglio* mallet]

pal·lor /pálər/ *n.* pallidness; paleness. [L f. *pallēre* be pale]

pal·ly /pálee/ *adj.* (**pal·li·er, pal·li·est**) *colloq.* like a pal; friendly.

palm[1] /paam, paw(l)m/ *n.* **1** any usu. tropical tree of the family Palmae, with no branches and a mass of large pinnate or fan-shaped leaves at the top. **2 a** the leaf of this tree as a symbol of victory. **b** a military decoration shaped like a palm leaf. **3 a** supreme excellence. **b** a prize for this. **4** a branch of various trees used instead of a palm in non-tropical countries, esp. in celebrating Palm Sunday. □□ **pal·ma·ceous** /palmáyshəs, paa(l)–/ *adj.* [OE *palm(a)* f. Gmc f. L *palma* PALM[2], its leaf being likened to a spread hand]

palm[2] /paam, paw(l)m/ *n. & v.* ● *n.* **1** the inner surface of the hand between the wrist and fingers. **2** the part of a glove, etc., that covers this. **3** the palmate part of an antler. ● *v.tr.* **1** conceal in the hand. **2** *Basketball* to hold (the ball) in one hand. □ **in the palm of one's hand** under one's control or influence. **palm off 1** (often foll. by *on*) **a** impose or thrust fraudulently (on a person). **b** cause a person to accept unwillingly or unknowingly (*palmed my old typewriter off on him*). **2** (often foll. by *with*) cause (a person) to accept unwillingly or unknowingly (*palmed him off with my old typewriter*). □□ **pal·mar** /pálmər, páa(l)–/ *adj.* **palmed** *adj.* **palm·ful** *n.* (*pl.* **·fuls**). [ME *paume* f. OF *paume* f. L *palma*: later assim. to L]

pal·mate /pálmayt, paál–, páamayt/ *adj.* **1** shaped like an open hand. **2** having lobes, etc., like spread fingers. [L *palmatus* (as PALM[2])]

palm·er /páamər, páal–/ *n.* **1** *hist.* **a** a pilgrim returning from the Holy Land with a palm branch or leaf. **b** an itinerant monk under a vow of poverty. **2** a hairy artificial fly used in fishing. [ME f. AF *palmer*, OF *palmier* f. med.L *palmarius* pilgrim]

palm·er·worm /páamərwərm/ *n.* a destructive hairy caterpillar of a moth, *Dichomeris ligulella*, of the eastern US.

pal·mette /palmét/ *n. Archaeol.* an ornament of radiating petals like a palm leaf. [F, dimin. of *palme* PALM[1]]

pal·met·to /palméttō/ n. (pl. **·tos**) **1** a small palm tree, e.g., any of various fan palms of the genus Sabal. **2** palm fronds used in weaving. [Sp. palmito, dimin. of palma PALM[1], assim. to It. words in *-etto*]

pal·mi·ped /pálmiped/ adj. & n. (also **pal·mi·pede** /-peed/) • adj. web-footed. • n. a web-footed bird. [L palmipes –pedis (as PALM[2], pes pedis foot)]

palm·is·try /páamistree/ n. supposed divination from lines and other features on the palm of the hand. □□ **palm·ist** n. [ME (orig. palmestry) f. PALM[2]: second element unexpl.]

palm oil n. oil from the fruit of any of various palms.

Palm Sun·day n. the Sunday before Easter, celebrating Christ's entry into Jerusalem.

cabbage palmetto

palm wine n. an alcoholic drink made from fermented palm sap.

palm·y /páamee/ adj. (**palm·i·er, palm·i·est**) **1** of or like or abounding in palms. **2** triumphant; flourishing (palmy days).

pal·my·ra /palmírə/ n. an Asian palm, Borassus flabellifer, with fan-shaped leaves used for matting, etc. [Port. palmeira palm tree, assim. to Palmyra in Syria]

pal·o·mi·no /páləmeenō/ n. (pl. **·nos**) a golden or tan-colored horse with a light-colored mane and tail, orig. bred in the southwestern US. [Amer. Sp. f. Sp. palomino young pigeon f. paloma dove f. L palumba]

pa·lo·ver·de /pálōvórdee, –várd/ n. a thorny tree of the genus Cercidium having greenish bark and yellow flowers, found in the southwestern US. [Amer. Sp., = green tree]

palp /palp/ n. (also **pal·pus** /pálpəs/) (pl. **palps** or **pal·pi** /-pī/) a segmented sensory organ at the mouth of an arthropod; a feeler. □□ **pal·pal** adj. [L palpus f. palpare feel]

pal·pa·ble /pálpəbəl/ adj. **1** that can be touched or felt. **2** readily perceived by the senses or mind. □□ **pal·pa·bil·i·ty** n. **pal·pa·bly** adv. [ME f. LL palpabilis (as PALPATE)]

pal·pate /pálpáyt/ v.tr. examine (esp. medically) by touch. □□ **pal·pa·tion** /-páyshən/ n. [L palpare palpat- touch gently]

pal·pe·bral /palpeébrəl, pálpibrəl/ adj. of or relating to the eyelids. [LL palpebralis f. L palpebra eyelid]

pal·pi·tate /pálpitayt/ v.intr. **1** pulsate; throb. **2** tremble. □□ **pal·pi·tant** adj. [L palpitare frequent. of palpare touch gently]

pal·pi·ta·tion /pálpitáyshən/ n. **1** throbbing; trembling. **2** (often in pl.) increased activity of the heart due to exertion, agitation, or disease. [L palpitatio (as PALPITATE)]

pal·pus var. of PALP.

pals·grave /páwlzgrayv/ n. a Count Palatine. [Du. paltsgrave f. palts palatinate + grave count]

pal·stave /páwlstayv/ n. Archaeol. a type of chisel made of bronze, etc., shaped to fit into a split handle. [Da. paalstav f. ON pálstavr f. páll hoe (cf. L palus stake) + stafr STAFF[1]]

pal·sy /páwlzee/ n. & v. • n. (pl. **·sies**) **1** paralysis, esp. with involuntary tremors. **2 a** a condition of utter helplessness. **b** a cause of this. • v.tr. (**·sies, ·sied**) **1** affect with palsy. **2** render helpless. [ME pa(r)lesi f. OF paralisie ult. f. L paralysis: see PARALYSIS]

pal·ter /páwltər/ v.intr. **1** haggle or equivocate. **2** trifle. □□ **pal·ter·er** n. [16th c.: orig. unkn.]

pal·try /páwltree/ adj. (**pal·tri·er, pal·tri·est**) worthless; contemptible; trifling. □□ **pal·tri·ness** n. [16th c.: f. paltry trash app. f. palt, pelt rubbish + –RY (cf. trumpery): cf. LG paltrig ragged]

pa·lu·dal /pəlóód'l, pályə–/ adj. **1** of a marsh. **2** malarial. □□ **pa·lu·dism** /pályədizəm/ n. (in sense 2). [L palus –udis marsh + –AL]

pal·y·nol·o·gy /pálinóləjee/ n. the study of pollen, spores, etc., for rock dating and the study of past environments. □□ **pal·y·no·log·i·cal** /-nəlójikəl/ adj. **pal·y·nol·o·gist** n. [Gk palunō sprinkle + –LOGY]

pam·pas /pámpəs/ n.pl. large treeless plains in S. America. [Sp. f. Quechua pampa plain]

pam·pas grass n. a tall grass, Cortaderia selloana, from S. America, with silky flowering plumes.

pam·per /pámpər/ v.tr. **1** overindulge (a person, taste, etc.); cosset. **2** spoil (a person) with luxury. □□ **pam·per·er** n. [ME, prob. of LG or Du. orig.]

pam·pe·ro /pampáirō/ n. (pl. **·ros**) a strong cold SW wind in S. America, blowing from the Andes to the Atlantic. [Sp. (as PAMPAS)]

pam·phlet /pámflit/ n. & v. • n. a small, unbound booklet or leaflet containing information or a short treatise. • v.tr. (**pam·phlet·ed, pam·phlet·ing**) distribute pamphlets. [ME f. Pamphilet, the familiar name of the 12th-c. Latin love poem Pamphilus seu de Amore]

pam·phlet·eer /pámfliteér/ n. & v. • n. a writer of (esp. political) pamphlets. • v.intr. write pamphlets.

pan[1] /pan/ n. & v. • n. **1 a** a vessel of metal, earthenware, etc., usu. broad and shallow, used for cooking and other domestic purposes. **b** the contents of this. **2** a panlike vessel in which substances are heated, etc. **3** any similar shallow container such as the bowl of a pair of scales or that used for washing gravel, etc., to separate gold. **4** Brit. toilet bowl. **5** part of the lock that held the priming in old guns. **6** a hollow in the ground (salt pan). **7** a hard substratum of soil. **8** sl. the face. **9** a negative or unfavorable review. • v. (**panned, pan·ning**) **1** tr. colloq. criticize severely. **2 a** tr. (often foll. by off, out) wash (gold-bearing gravel) in a pan. **b** intr. search for gold by panning gravel. **c** intr. (foll. by out) (of gravel) yield gold. □ **pan out** (of an action, etc.) turn out well or in a specified way. □□ **pan·ful** n. (pl. **·fuls**). **pan·like** adj. [OE panne, perh. ult. f. L patina dish]

pan[2] /pan/ v. & n. • v. (**panned, pan·ning**) **1** tr. swing (a video or movie camera) horizontally to give a panoramic effect or to follow a moving object. **2** intr. (of a video or movie camera) be moved in this way. • n. a panning movement. [abbr. of PANORAMA]

pan[3] /paan/ n. Bot. **1** a leaf of the betel. **2** this enclosing lime and areca-nut parings, chewed in India, etc. [Hindi f. Skr. parna feather, leaf]

pan- /pan/ comb. form **1** all; the whole of. **2** relating to the whole or all the parts of a continent, racial group, religion, etc. (pan-American; pan-African; pan-Hellenic; pan-Anglican). [Gk f. pan neut. of pas all]

pan·a·ce·a /pánəseéə/ n. a universal remedy. □□ **pan·a·ce·an** adj. [L f. Gk panakeia f. panakēs all-healing (as PAN–, akos remedy)]

pa·nache /pənásh, –náash/ n. **1** assertiveness or flamboyant confidence of style or manner. **2** hist. a tuft or plume of feathers, esp. as a headdress or on a helmet. [F f. It. pennacchio f. LL pinnaculum dimin. of pinna feather]

pa·na·da /pənaádə/ n. **1** a thick paste of flour, etc., used as a sauce base or binder. **2** bread boiled to a pulp and flavored. [Sp. ult. f. L panis bread]

pan·a·ma /pánəmaa/ n. a hat of strawlike material made from the leaves of a palmlike tropical plant. [Panama in Central America]

Pan·a·ma·ni·an /pánəmáyneeən/ n. & adj. • n. **1** a native or national of the Republic of Panama in Central America. **2** a person of Panamanian descent. • adj. of or relating to Panama.

pan·a·tel·la /pánətélə/ n. a long thin cigar. [Amer. Sp. panatela, = long thin biscuit f. It. panatella dimin. of panata (as PANADA)]

pan·cake /pánkayk/ n. & v. • n. **1** a thin flat cake of batter usu. fried and turned in a pan or on a griddle. **2** a flat cake of makeup, etc. • v. **1** intr. make a pancake landing. **2** tr. cause (an aircraft) to pancake. □ **flat as a pancake** completely flat. [ME f. PAN[1] + CAKE]

pan·cake land·ing n. an emergency landing by an aircraft with its landing gear still retracted, in which the pilot attempts to keep the aircraft in a horizontal position throughout.

Pan·chen la·ma /páanchən laámə/ n. a Tibetan lama ranking next after the Dalai lama. [Tibetan panchen great learned one]

pan·chro·mat·ic /pánkrōmátik/ adj. Photog. (of film, etc.) sensitive to all visible colors of the spectrum.

pan·cre·as /pángkreeəs/ n. a gland near the stomach supplying the duodenum with digestive fluid and secreting insulin into the blood. □□ **pan·cre·at·ic** /-kreeátik/ adj. **pan·cre·a·ti·tis** /-kreeətítis/ n. [mod.L f. Gk pagkreas (as PAN–, kreas –atos flesh)]

pan·cre·a·tin /pánkreeətən, páng–/ n. a digestive extract containing pancreatic enzymes, prepared from animal pancreases.

pan·da /pándə/ n. **1** (also **gi·ant pan·da**) a large bearlike mammal, Ailuropoda melanoleuca, native to China and Tibet, having characteristic black and white markings. **2** (also **red pan·da**) a Himalayan raccoonlike mammal, Ailurus fulgens, with reddish-brown fur and a long bushy tail. [Nepali name]

pan·da car n. Brit. a police patrol car (orig. white with black stripes on the doors).

panda 1

pan·dect /pándekt/ n. (usu. in pl.) **1** a complete body of laws. **2** hist. a compendium in 50 books of the Roman civil law made by order of Justinian in the 6th c. [F pandecte or L pandecta pandectes f. Gk pandektēs all-receiver (as PAN–, dektēs f. dekhomai receive)]

pan·dem·ic /pandémik/ adj. & n. • adj. (of a disease) prevalent over a whole country or the world. • n. a pandemic disease. [Gk pandēmos (as PAN–, dēmos people)]

pan·de·mo·ni·um /pándimōneeəm/ n. **1** uproar; utter confusion. **2** a scene of this. [mod.L (place of all demons in Milton's Paradise Lost) f. PAN– + Gk daimōn DEMON[1]]

pan·der /pándər/ v. & n. • v.intr. (foll. by to) gratify or indulge a person, a desire or weakness, etc. • n. (also **pan·der·er**) **1** a go-between in illicit love affairs; a procurer. **2** a person who encourages licentiousness. [*Pandare*, a character in Boccaccio and in Chaucer's *Troilus and Criseyde*, f. L *Pandarus* f. Gk *Pandaros*]

pan·dit var. of PUNDIT 1.

Pan·do·ra's box /pandáwrəz/ *n.* a process that once activated will generate many unmanageable problems. [in Gk Mythol. the box from which the ills of humankind were released, hope alone remaining: f. Gk *Pandōra* all-gifted (as PAN-, *dōron* gift)]

pane /payn/ *n.* **1** a single sheet of glass in a window or door. **2** a rectangular division of a checkered pattern, etc. **3** a sheet of postage stamps. [ME f. OF *pan* f. L *pannus* piece of cloth]

pan·e·gyr·ic /pánijírik, –jírik/ *n.* a laudatory discourse; a eulogy. □□ **pan·e·gyr·i·cal** *adj.* [F *panégyrique* f. L *panegyricus* f. Gk *panēgurikos* of public assembly (as PAN-, *ēguris* = *agora* assembly)]

pan·e·gy·rize /pánijiríz/ *v.tr.* speak or write in praise of; eulogize. □□ **pan·e·gyr·ist** /–jírist/ *n.* [Gk *panēgurizō* (as PANEGYRIC)]

pan·el /pánəl/ *n. & v.* ● *n.* **1 a** a distinct, usu. rectangular, section of a surface (e.g., of a wall or door). **b** a control panel (see CONTROL *n.* 5). **c** = INSTRUMENT PANEL. **2** a strip of material as part of a garment. **3** a group of people gathered to form a team in a broadcast game, for a discussion, etc. **4** *Brit. hist.* a list of medical practitioners registered in a district as accepting patients under the National Insurance Act. **5 a** a list of available jurors; a jury. **b** *Sc.* a person or persons accused of a crime. **6** a comic strip or one frame of a comic strip. ● *v.tr.* (**pan·eled** or **pan·elled, pan·el·ing** or **pan·el·ing**) **1** fit or provide with panels. **2** cover or decorate with panels.

WORD HISTORY panel

Middle English: from Old French, literally 'piece of cloth,' based on Latin *pannus* '(piece of) cloth.' An early sense, 'piece of parchment,' was extended to mean 'list,' whence the notion 'advisory group.' Sense 1 derives from the late Middle English sense 'distinct (usually framed) section of a surface.'

---

pan·el game *n.* a quiz show, etc., played by a panel.

pan·el heat·ing *n.* the heating of rooms by panels in the wall, etc., containing the sources of heat.

pan·el·ing /pánəling/ *n.* (also **pan·el·ling**) **1** paneled work. **2** wood for making panels.

pan·el·ist /pánəlist/ *n.* (also **pan·el·list**) a member of a panel (esp. in broadcasting).

pan·el saw *n.* a saw with small teeth for cutting thin wood for panels.

pan·el truck *n.* a small enclosed delivery truck.

pang /pang/ *n.* (often in *pl.*) a sudden sharp pain or painful emotion. [16th c.: var. of earlier *prange* pinching f. Gmc]

pan·ga /pánggə/ *n.* a bladed African tool like a machete. [native name in E. Africa]

pan·go·lin /pánggəlin, panggó–/ *n.* any scaly anteater of the genus *Manis*, native to Asia and Africa, having a small head with elongated snout and tongue, and a tapering tail. [Malay *peng-gōling* roller (from its habit of rolling itself up)]

pan·han·dle /pánhand'l/ *n. & v.* ● *n.* a narrow strip of territory extending from one state into another. ● *v.tr. & intr. colloq.* beg for money in the street. □□ **pan·han·dler** *n.*

pan·ic[1] /pánik/ *n. & v.* ● *n.* **1 a** sudden uncontrollable fear or alarm. **b** (*attrib.*) characterized or caused by panic (*panic buying*). **2** infectious apprehension or fright esp. in commercial dealings. ● *v.tr. & intr.* (**pan·icked, pan·ick·ing**) (often foll. by *into*) affect or be affected with panic (*was panicked into buying*). □□ **pan·ick·y** *adj.* [F *panique* f. mod.L *panicus* f. Gk *panikos* f. *Pan* a rural god causing terror]

pan·ic[2] /pánik/ *n.* any grass of the genus *Panicum*, including various cereals. [OE f. L *panicum* f. *panus* thread on bobbin, millet ear f. Gk *pēnos* web]

pan·ic but·ton *n.* a button for summoning help in an emergency. □ **hit** (or **press** or **push**) **the panic button** respond to a situation by panicking or taking emergency measures.

pan·i·cle /pánikəl/ *n. Bot.* a loose branching cluster of flowers, as in oats. □□ **pan·i·cled** *adj.* [L *paniculum* dimin. of *panus* thread]

pan·ic-mon·ger *n.* a person who fosters a panic.

pan·ic sta·tions *n. Brit.* a state of emergency.

pan·ic-strick·en *adj.* (also **pan·ic-struck**) affected with panic; very apprehensive.

pan·jan·drum /panjándrəm/ *n.* **1** a mock title for an important person. **2** a pompous or pretentious official, etc. [app. invented in nonsense verse by S. Foote 1755]

panne /pan/ *n.* (in full **panne velvet**) a silk or rayon velvet fabric with a flattened pile. [F]

pan·nier /pányər/ *n.* **1** a basket, esp. one of a pair carried by a beast of burden. **2** each of a pair of bags or boxes on either side of the rear wheel of a bicycle or motorcycle. **3** *hist* also /panyáy/ **a** part of a skirt looped up around the hips. **b** a frame supporting this. [ME f. OF *panier* f. L *panarium* bread basket f. *panis* bread]

---

pan·ni·kin /pánikin/ *n.* **1** *Brit.* a small metal drinking cup. **2** *Brit.* the contents of this. **3** *Austral. sl.* the head (esp. *off one's pannikin*). □ **pannikin boss** *Austral. sl.* a minor overseer or foreman. [PAN[1] + –KIN, after *cannikin*]

pan·o·ply /pánəplee/ *n.* (*pl.* **·plies**) **1** a complete or magnificent array. **2** a complete suit of armor. □□ **pan·o·plied** *adj.* [F *panoplie* or mod.L *panoplia* full armor f. Gk (as PAN-, *oplia* f. *hopla* arms)]

pan·op·tic /panóptik/ *adj.* showing or seeing the whole at one view. [Gk *panoptos* seen by all, *panoptēs* all-seeing]

pan·o·ram·a /pánərámə, –ráa–/ *n.* **1** an unbroken view of a surrounding region. **2** a complete survey or presentation of a subject, sequence of events, etc. **3** a picture or photograph containing a wide view. **4** a continuous passing scene. □□ **pan·o·ram·ic** *adj.* **pan·o·ram·i·cal·ly** *adv.* [PAN- + Gk *horama* view f. *horaō* see]

pan·pipes /pánpips/ *n.pl.* a musical instrument orig. associated with the Greek rural god Pan, made of a series of short pipes graduated in length and fixed together with the mouthpieces in line.

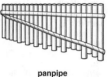

panpipe

pan·sy /pánzee/ *n.* (*pl.* **·sies**) **1** any garden plant of the genus *Viola*, with flowers of various rich colors. **2** *colloq. derog.* **a** an effeminate man. **b** a male homosexual. [F *pensée* thought, pansy f. *penser* think f. L *pensare* frequent. of *pendere* pensweigh]

pant /pant/ *v. & n.* ● *v.* **1** *intr.* breathe with short quick breaths. **2** *tr.* (often foll. by *out*) utter breathlessly. **3** *intr.* (often foll. by *for*) yearn or crave. **4** *intr.* (of the heart, etc.) throb violently. ● *n.* **1** a panting breath. **2** a throb. □□ **pant·ing·ly** *adv.* [ME f. OF *pantaisier* ult. f. Gk *phantasioō* cause to imagine (as FANTASY)]

pan·ta·lets /pántəléts/ *n.pl.* (also **pan·ta·lettes**) *hist.* long underpants worn by women and girls in the 19th c., with a frill at the bottom of each leg. [dimin. of PANTALOON]

pan·ta·loon /pántəloᴐ́n/ *n.* **1** (in *pl.*) *hist.* men's close-fitting breeches fastened below the calf or at the foot. **2** (**Pantaloon**) a character in Italian comedy wearing pantaloons. [F *pantalon* f. It. *pantalone*, a character in Italian comedy]

pan·tech·ni·con /pantéknikon/ *n. Brit.* a large van for transporting furniture. [PAN- + TECHNIC orig. as the name of a bazaar and then a furniture warehouse]

pan·the·ism /pántheeizəm/ *n.* **1** the belief that God is identifiable with the forces of nature and with natural substances. **2** worship that admits or tolerates all gods. □□ **pan·the·ist** *n.* **pan·the·is·tic** *adj.* **pan·the·is·ti·cal** *adj.* **pan·the·is·ti·cal·ly** *adv.* [PAN- + Gk *theos* god]

pan·the·on /pántheeon, –ən/ *n.* **1** a building in which illustrious dead are buried or have memorials. **2** the deities of a people collectively. **3** a temple dedicated to all the gods, esp. the circular one at Rome. **4** a group of esteemed persons. [ME f. L f. Gk *pantheion* (as PAN-, *theion* holy f. *theos* god)]

pan·ther /pánthər/ *n.* **1** a leopard, esp. with black fur. **2** a cougar. [ME f. OF *pantere* f. L *panthera* f. Gk *panthēr*]

pant·ie gir·dle /pánteegərd'l/ *n.* (also **panty girdle**) a woman's girdle with a crotch.

pant·ies /pánteez/ *n.pl. colloq.* short-legged or legless underpants worn by women and girls. [dimin. of PANTS]

pan·tile /pántil/ *n.* a roofing tile curved to form an S-shaped section, fitted to overlap. [PAN[1] + TILE]

pan·to /pántō/ *n.* (*pl.* **·tos**) *Brit. colloq.* = PANTOMIME 2. [abbr.]

panto- /pántō/ *comb.form* all; universal. [Gk *pas pantos* all]

pan·to·graph /pántəgraf/ *n.* **1** *Art & Painting* an instrument for copying a plan or drawing, etc., on a different scale by a system of jointed rods. **2** a jointed framework conveying a current to an electric vehicle from overhead wires. □□ **pan·to·graph·ic** *adj.* [PANTO- + Gk –*graphos* writing]

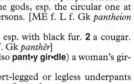

pantile

pan·to·mime /pántəmīm/ *n. & v.* ● *n.* **1** the use of gestures and facial expression to convey meaning without speech, esp. in drama and dance. **2** *Brit.* a theatrical entertainment based on a fairy tale, with music, topical jokes, etc., usu. produced around Christmas. **3** *colloq.* an absurd or outrageous piece of behavior. ● *v.* to convey meaning without speech using only gestures. □□ **pan·to·mim·ic** /–mímik/ *adj.* [F *pantomime* or L *pantomimus* f. Gk *pantomimos* (as PANTO-, MIME)]

pan·to·then·ic ac·id /pántəthénik/ *n.* a vitamin of the B complex, found in rice, bran, and many other foods, and essential for the oxidation of fats and carbohydrates. [Gk *pantothen* from every side]

pan·try /pántree/ *n.* (*pl.* **·tries**) **1** a small room or cupboard in which dishes, silverware, table linen, etc., are kept. **2** a small room or cupboard in which groceries, etc., are kept. [ME f. AF *panetrie*, OF *paneterie* f. *panetier* baker ult. f. LL *panarius* bread seller f. L *panis* bread]

pan·try·man /pántreemən/ n. (pl. **·men**) a person who works in a pantry, esp. in a hotel or hospital.

pants /pants/ n.pl. **1** an outer garment reaching from the waist usu. to the ankles, divided into two parts to cover the legs. **2** Brit. underpants. □ **bore** (or **scare**, etc.) **the pants off** colloq. bore, scare, etc., to an intolerable degree. **wear the pants** be the dominant partner in a marriage. **with one's pants down** colloq. in an embarrassingly unprepared state. [abbr. of PANTALOON(S)]

pant·suit /pántsoot/ n. (also **pants suit**) a woman's suit with pants and a jacket.

pant·y gir·dle var. of PANTIE GIRDLE.

pant·y hose /pánteehōz/ n. (usu. treated as pl.) usu. sheer one-piece garment combining panties and stockings. [PANTIES + HOSE]

pan·zer /pánzər, paánts–/ n. **1** (in pl.) armored troops. **2** (attrib.) heavily armored (panzer division). [G, = coat of mail]

pap[1] /pap/ n. **1 a** a soft or semiliquid food for infants or invalids. **b** a mash or pulp. **2** light or trivial reading matter; nonsense. □□ **pap·py** adj. [ME prob. f. MLG, MDu. pappe, prob. ult. f. L pappare eat]

pap[2] /pap/ n. archaic or dial. the nipple of a breast or something shaped like a nipple. [ME, of Scand. orig.: ult. imit. of sucking]

pa·pa /paápə, pəpaá/ n. father (esp. as a child's word). [F f. LL f. Gk papas]

pa·pa·cy /páypəsee/ n. (pl. **·cies**) **1** a pope's office or tenure. **2** the papal system. [ME f. med.L papatia f. papa pope]

Pap·a·go /paápəgō, pá–/ n. **1 a** a N.American people native to southwestern Arizona and adjoining parts of Mexico. **b** a member of this people. **2** the language of this people.

pa·pa·in /pəpáyin, –pí-in/ n. an enzyme obtained from unripe papaya, used to tenderize meat and as a food supplement to aid digestion. [PAPAYA + –IN]

pa·pal /páypəl/ adj. of or relating to a pope or to the papacy. □□ **pa·pal·ly** adv. [ME f. OF f. med.L papalis f. eccl.L papa POPE[1]]

Pa·pal States n. hist. the temporal dominions belonging to the Pope, esp. in central Italy.

pa·pa·raz·zo /paápəraátsō/ n. (pl. **pa·pa·raz·zi** /–see/) a freelance photographer who pursues celebrities to get photographs of them. [It.]

pa·pav·er·ous /pəpávərəs/ adj. like or related to the poppy. □□ **pa·ver·a·ceous** /–ráyshəs/ adj. [L papaver poppy]

pa·paw var. of PAWPAW.

pa·pa·ya /pəpíə/ n. **1** an elongated melon-shaped fruit with edible orange flesh and small black seeds. **2** a tropical tree, Carica papaya, bearing this and producing a milky sap from which papain is obtained. [earlier form of PAWPAW]

pa·per /páypər/ n. & v. • n. **1** a material manufactured in thin sheets from the pulp of wood or other fibrous substances, used for writing or drawing or printing on, or as wrapping material, etc. **2** (attrib.) **a** made of or using paper. **b** flimsy like paper. **3** = NEWSPAPER. **4 a** a document printed on paper. **b** (in pl.) documents attesting identity or credentials. **c** (in pl.) documents belonging to a person or relating to a matter. **5** Commerce **a** a negotiable documents, e.g., bills of exchange. **b** (attrib.) recorded on paper though not existing (paper profits). **6 a** a set of questions to be answered at one session in an examination. **b** the written answers to these. **7** = WALLPAPER. **8** an essay or dissertation, esp. one read to a learned society or published in a learned journal. **9** a piece of paper, esp. as a wrapper, etc. **10** Theatr. sl. free tickets or the people admitted by them (the house is full of paper). • v.tr. **1** apply paper to, esp. decorate (a wall, etc.) with wallpaper. **2** (foll. by over) **a** cover (a hole or blemish) with paper. **b** disguise or try to hide (a fault, etc.). **3** Theatr. sl. fill (a theater) by giving free passes. **4** distribute flyers, pamphlets, etc., as in a neighborhood. □ **on paper 1** in writing. **2** in theory; to judge from written or printed evidence. □□ **pa·per·er** n. **pa·per·less** adj. [ME f. AF papir, = OF papier f. L papyrus: see PAPYRUS]

pa·per·back /páypərbak/ (also **pa·per·bound**) adj. & n. • adj. (of a book) bound in stiff paper. • n. a paperback book.

pa·per·boy /páypərboy/ n. (fem. **pa·per·girl** /–gərl/) a boy or girl who delivers or sells newspapers.

pa·per clip n. a clip of bent wire or of plastic for holding several sheets of paper together.

pa·per knife n. a blunt knife for opening letters, etc.

pa·per mill n. a mill in which paper is made.

pa·per mon·ey n. money in the form of bills.

pa·per mul·ber·ry n. a small Asiatic tree, Broussonetia papyrifera, of the mulberry family, whose bark is used for making paper and cloth.

pa·per nau·ti·lus n. see NAUTILUS 2.

pa·per route n. (also Brit. **pa·per round**) **1** a job of regularly delivering newspapers. **2** a route taken doing this.

pa·per tape n. Computing tape made of paper, esp. that on which data or instructions are represented by means of holes punched in it, for conveying to a processor, etc.

pa·per ti·ger n. an apparently threatening, but ineffectual, person or thing.

pa·per trail n. documentation of transactions, etc.

pa·per·weight /páypərwayt/ n. a small heavy object for keeping loose papers in place.

pa·per·work /páypərwərk/ n. **1** routine clerical or administrative work. **2** documents, esp. for a particular purpose.

pa·per·y /páypəree/ adj. like paper in thinness or texture.

pa·pier-mâ·ché /páypər məsháy, papyáy/ n. paper pulp used for molding into boxes, trays, etc. [F, = chewed paper]

pa·pil·i·o·na·ceous /pəpíleeənáyshəs/ adj. (of a plant) with a corolla like a butterfly. [mod.L papilionaceus f. L papilio –onis butterfly]

pa·pil·la /pəpílə/ n. (pl. **pa·pil·lae** /–pílee/) **1** a small nipplelike protuberance in a part or organ of the body. **2** Bot. a small fleshy projection on a plant. □□ **pap·il·lar·y** adj. **pa·pil·late** /pápilayt/ adj. **pap·il·lose** /pápilōs/ adj. [L, = nipple, dimin. of papula: see PAPULA]

pap·il·lo·ma /pápilōmə/ n. (pl. **pap·il·lo·mas** or **pap·il·lo·ma·ta** /–mətə/) a wartlike usu. benign tumor.

pap·il·lon /paapeeyóN, pá–/ n. **1** a toy dog of a breed with ears suggesting the form of a butterfly. **2** this breed. [F, = butterfly, f. L papilio –onis]

pa·pist /páypist/ n. & adj. often derog. • n. **1** a Roman Catholic. **2** hist. an advocate of papal supremacy. • adj. of or relating to Roman Catholics. □□ **pa·pis·tic** adj. **pa·pis·ti·cal** adj. **pa·pist·ry** n. [F papiste or mod.L papista f. eccl.L papa POPE[1]]

pa·poose /papóos, pə–/ n. a young Native American child. [Algonquian]

pap·pus /pápəs/ n. (pl. **pap·pi** /–pī/) a group of hairs on the fruit of thistles, dandelions, etc. □□ **pap·pose** adj. [L f. Gk pappos]

pap·ri·ka /pəpreékə, páprikə/ n. **1** Bot. a red pepper. **2** a condiment made from it. [Magyar]

Pap smear /pap/ n. (also **Pap test**) n. a test for cervical cancer, etc., done by a cervical smear. [abbr. of G. N. Papanicolaou, US scientist d. 1962]

pap·u·la /pápyələ/ n. (also **pap·ule** /pápyool/) (pl. **pap·u·lae** /–lee/) **1** a pimple. **2** a small fleshy projection on a plant. □□ **pap·u·lar** adj. **pap·u·lose** adj. **pap·u·lous** adj. [L]

pap·y·rol·o·gy /pápiróləjee/ n. the study of ancient papyri. □□ **pa·py·ro·log·i·cal** /–rəlójikəl/ adj. **pap·y·rol·o·gist** n.

pa·py·rus /pəpírəs/ n. (pl. **pa·py·ri** /–rī/) **1** an aquatic plant, Cyperus papyrus, with dark green stems topped with fluffy inflorescence. **2 a** a writing material prepared in ancient Egypt from the pithy stem of this. **b** a document written on this. [ME f. L papyrus f. Gk papyros]

par[1] /paar/ n. & v. • n. **1** the average or normal amount, degree, condition, etc. (be up to par). **2** equality; an equal status or footing (on a par with). **3** Golf the number of strokes a skilled player should normally require for a hole or course. **4** Stock Exch. the face value of stocks and shares, etc. (at par). **5** (in full **par of exchange**) the recognized value of one country's currency in terms of another's. • v. Golf to score par. □ **above par** Stock Exch. at a premium. **at par** Stock Exch. at face value. **below par 1** less good than usual in health or other quality. **2** Stock Exch. at a discount. **par for the course** colloq. what is normal or expected in any given circumstances. [L (adj. & n.) = equal, equality]

par[2] /paar/ n. Brit. esp. Journalism colloq. paragraph. [abbr.]

par. abbr. (also **para**.) paragraph.

par- /pər, par, paar/ prefix var. of PARA-[1] before a vowel or h; (paraldehyde; parody; parhelion).

pa·ra /párə/ n. colloq. **1** a paratrooper. **2** a paraprofessional. **3** Brit. a paragraph. [abbr.]

para-[1] /párə/ prefix (also **par-**) **1** beside (paramilitary). **2** beyond (paranormal). **3** Chem. a modification of (paraldehyde). **b** relating to diametrically opposite carbon atoms in a benzene ring (paradichlorobenzene). [from or after Gk para- f. para beside, past, beyond]

para-[2] /párə/ comb. form protect; ward off (parachute; parasol). [F f. It. f. L parare defend]

par·a·a·mi·no·ben·zo·ic ac·id /parə-əmeénōbenzóik/ n. Biochem. a yellow crystalline compound, often used in suntan lotions and sunscreens to absorb ultraviolet light. ¶ Abbr.: **PABA**.

par·a·bi·o·sis /párəbiósis/ n. Biol. the natural or artificial joining of two individuals. □□ **par·a·bi·ot·ic** /–bíotik/ adj. [mod.L, formed as PARA-[1] + Gk biōsis mode of life f. bios life]

par·a·ble /párəbəl/ n. **1** a narrative of imagined events used to illustrate a moral or spiritual lesson. **2** an allegory. [ME f. OF parabole f. LL sense 'allegory, discourse' of L parabola comparison]

pa·rab·o·la /pərábələ/ n. an open plane curve formed by the intersection of a cone with a plane parallel to its side, resembling the path of a projectile under the action of gravity. [mod.L f. Gk parabolē placing side by side, comparison (as PARA-[1], bolē a throw f. ballō)]

par·a·bol·ic /párəbólik/ adj. **1** of or expressed in a parable. **2** of or like a parabola. □□ **par·a·bol·i·cal·ly** adv. [LL parabolicus f. Gk parabolikos (as PARABOLA)]

par·a·bol·i·cal /párəbólikəl/ *adj.* = PARABOLIC 1.

pa·rab·o·loid /pərábəloyd/ *n.* **1** (in full **paraboloid of revolution**) a solid generated by the rotation of a parabola about its axis of symmetry. **2** a solid having two or more non-parallel parabolic cross sections. □□ **pa·rab·o·loi·dal** *adj.*

par·a·ce·ta·mol /párəsétəmawl, –mol, –se̅e̅tə–/ *n. Brit.* ACETAMINOPHEN. [*para-acetyl*amino*phenol*]

pa·rach·ro·nism /pərákrənizəm/ *n.* an error in chronology, esp. by assigning too late a date. [PARA-[1] + Gk *khronos* time, perh. after *anachronism*]

par·a·chute /párəshoo̅t/ *n. & v.* ● *n.* **1** a rectangular or umbrella-shaped canopy allowing a person or heavy object attached to it to descend slowly from a height, esp. from an aircraft, or to retard motion in other ways. **2** (*attrib.*) dropped or to be dropped by parachute (*parachute drop*). ● *v.tr. & intr.* convey or descend by parachute. [F (as PARA-[2], CHUTE[1])]

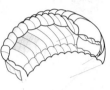

par·a·chut·ist /párəshoo̅tist/ *n.* **1** a person who uses a parachute. **2** (in *pl.*) parachute troops.

parachute

Par·a·clete /párəkleet/ *n.* the Holy Spirit as advocate or counselor. [ME f. OF *paraclet* f. LL *paracletus* f. Gk *paraklētos* called in aid (as PARA-[1], *klētos* f. *kaleō* call)]

pa·rade /pəráyd/ *n. & v.* ● *n.* **1 a** a formal or ceremonial muster of troops for inspection. **b** = PARADE GROUND. **2** a public procession. **3** ostentatious display (*made a parade of their wealth*). **4** *Brit.* a public square, promenade, or row of shops. ● *v.* **1** *intr.* assemble for parade. **2 a** *tr.* march through (streets, etc.) in procession. **b** *intr.* march ceremonially. **3** *tr.* display ostentatiously. □ **on parade 1** taking part in a parade. **2** on display. □□ **pa·rad·er** *n.* [F, = show, f. Sp. *parada* and It. *parata* ult. f. L *parare* prepare, furnish]

pa·rade ground *n.* a place for the muster of troops.

par·a·did·dle /párədid'l/ *n.* a drum roll with alternate beating of sticks. [imit.]

par·a·digm /párədīm/ *n.* **1** an example or pattern. **2** *Gram.* a representative set of the inflections of a noun, verb, etc. □□ **par·a·dig·mat·ic** /–digmátik/ *adj.* **par·a·dig·mat·i·cal·ly** *adv.* [LL *paradigma* f. Gk *paradeigma* f. *paradeiknumi* show side by side (as PARA-[1], *deiknumi* show)]

par·a·dise /párədīs/ *n.* **1** (in some religions) heaven as the ultimate abode of the just. **2** a place or state of complete happiness. **3** (in full **earthly paradise**) the abode of Adam and Eve in the biblical account of the Creation; the garden of Eden. □□ **par·a·di·sa·i·cal** /–disáyikəl/ *adj.* **par·a·dis·al** /párədīsəl/ *adj.* **par·a·di·si·a·cal** /–disíəkəl/ *adj.* **par·a·di·si·cal** /–disíkəl/ *adj.* [ME f. OF *paradis* f. LL *paradisus* f. Gk *paradeisos* f. Avestan *pairidaēza* park]

par·a·dos /párədos/ *n.* an elevation of earth behind a fortified place as a protection against attack from the rear, esp. a mound along the back of a trench. [F (as PARA-[2], *dos* back f. L *dorsum*)]

par·a·dox /párədoks/ *n.* **1 a** a seemingly absurd or contradictory statement, even if actually well-founded. **b** a self-contradictory or essentially absurd statement. **2** a person or thing conflicting with a preconceived notion of what is reasonable or possible. **3** a paradoxical quality or character. [orig. = a statement contrary to accepted opinion, f. LL *paradoxum* f. Gk *paradoxon* neut. adj. (as PARA-[1], *doxa* opinion)]

par·a·dox·i·cal /párədóksikəl/ *adj.* **1** of or like or involving paradox. **2** fond of paradox. □□ **par·a·dox·i·cal·ly** *adv.*

par·af·fin /párəfin/ *n.* **1** (also **par·af·fin wax**) a waxy mixture of hydrocarbons used in candles, waterproofing, etc. **2** *Brit.* = KEROSENE. **3** *Chem.* = ALKANE. [G (1830) f. L *parum* little + *affinis* related, from the small affinity it has for other substances]

par·a·go·ge /párəgójee/ *n.* the addition of a letter or syllable to a word in some contexts or as a language develops (e.g., *t* in *peasant*). □□ **par·a·gog·ic** /–gójik/ *adj.* [LL f. Gk *paragōgē* derivation (as PARA-[1], *agōgē* f. *agō* lead)]

par·a·gon /párəgon, –gən/ *n.* **1 a** a model of excellence. **b** a supremely excellent person or thing. **2** (foll. by *of*) a model (of virtue, etc.). **3** a perfect diamond of 100 carats or more. [obs. F f. It. *paragone* touchstone, f. med.Gk *parakonē* whetstone]

par·a·graph /párəgraf/ *n. & v.* ● *n.* **1** a distinct section of a piece of writing, beginning on a new usu. indented line. **2** a symbol (usu. ¶) used to mark a new paragraph, and also as a reference mark. **3** a short item in a newspaper, usu. of only one paragraph. ● *v.tr.* arrange (a piece of writing) in paragraphs. □□ **par·a·graph·ic** /–gráfik/ *adj.* [F *paragraphe* or med.L *paragraphus* f. Gk *paragraphos* short stroke marking a break in sense (as PARA-[1], *graphō* write)]

par·a·keet /párəkeet/ *n.* any of various small usu. long-tailed parrots. [OF *paroquet*, It. *parrocchetto*, Sp. *periquito*, perh. ult. f. dimin. of *Pierre*, etc. Peter: cf. PARROT]

par·a·lan·guage /párəlanggwij/ *n.* elements or factors in communication that are ancillary to language proper, e.g., intonation and gesture.

par·al·de·hyde /pəráldihīd/ *n.* a cyclic polymer of acetaldehyde, used as a narcotic and sedative. [PARA-[1] + ALDEHYDE]

par·a·le·gal /párəle̅e̅gəl/ *adj. & n.* ● *adj.* of or relating to auxiliary aspects of the law. ● *n.* a person trained in subsidiary legal matters. [PARA-[1] + LEGAL]

par·a·li·pom·e·na /párəlipómǐnə/ *n. pl.* (also **–lei·pom·e·na** /párəlī–/) **1** things omitted from a work and added as a supplement. **2** *Bibl.* the books of Chronicles in the Old Testament, containing particulars omitted from Kings. [ME f. eccl.L f. Gk *paraleipomena* f. *paraleipō* omit (as PARA-[1], *leipō* leave)]

par·a·lip·sis /párəlípsis/ *n.* (also **–leip·sis** /–lípsis/) (*pl.* **·ses** /–seez/) *Rhet.* **1** the device of giving emphasis by professing to say little or nothing of a subject, as in *not to mention their unpaid debts of several million dollars.* **2** an instance of this. [LL f. Gk *paraleipsis* passing over (as PARA-[1], *leipsis* f. *leipō* leave)]

par·al·lax /párəlaks/ *n.* **1** the apparent difference in the position or direction of an object caused when the observer's position is changed. **2** the angular amount of this. □□ **par·al·lac·tic** /–láktik/ *adj.* [F *parallaxe* f. mod.L *parallaxis* f. Gk *parallaxis* change f. *parallassō* to alternate (as PARA-[1], *allassō* exchange f. *allos* other)]

par·al·lel /párəlel/ *adj., n., & v.* ● *adj.* **1 a** (of lines or planes) side by side and having the same distance continuously between them. **b** (foll. by *to, with*) (of a line or plane) having this relation (to another). **2** (of circumstances, etc.) precisely similar, analogous, or corresponding. **3 a** (of processes, etc.) occurring or performed simultaneously. **b** *Computing* involving the simultaneous performance of operations. ● *n.* **1** a person or thing precisely analogous or equal to another. **2** a comparison (*drew a parallel between the two situations*). **3** (in full **parallel of latitude**) *Geog.* **a** each of the imaginary parallel circles of constant latitude on the earth's surface. **b** a corresponding line on a map (*the 49th parallel*). **4** *Printing* two parallel lines (||) as a reference mark. ● *v.tr.* (**par·al·leled, par·al·lel·ing**) **1** be parallel to; correspond to. **2** represent as similar; compare. **3** adduce as a parallel instance. □ **in parallel** (of electric circuits) arranged so as to join at common points at each end. □□ **par·al·lel·ism** *n.* [F *parallèle* f. L *parallelus* f. Gk *parallēlos* (as PARA-[1], *allēlos* one another)]

par·al·lel bars *n.* a pair of parallel rails on posts for gymnastics.

par·al·lel·e·pi·ped /párəlelləpípid, –pípid/ *n. Geom.* a solid body of which each face is a parallelogram. [Gk *parallēlepipedon* (as PARALLEL, *epipedon* plane surface)]

par·al·lel·o·gram /párəleləgram/ *n. Geom.* a four-sided plane rectilinear figure with opposite sides parallel. [F *parallélogramme* f. LL *parallelogrammum* f. Gk *parallēlogrammon* (as PARALLEL, *grammē* line)]

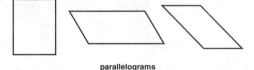

parallelograms

par·al·lel·o·gram of forc·es *n.* **1** a parallelogram illustrating the theorem that if two forces acting at a point are represented in magnitude and direction by two sides of a parallelogram meeting at that point, their resultant is represented by the diagonal drawn from that point. **2** this theorem.

pa·ral·o·gism /pərálǝjizǝm/ *n. Logic* **1** a fallacy. **2** illogical reasoning (esp. of which the reasoner is unconscious). □□ **pa·ral·o·gist** *n.* **pa·ral·o·gize** *v.intr.* [F *paralogisme* f. LL *paralogismus* f. Gk *paralogismos* f. *paralogizomai* reason falsely f. *paralogos* contrary to reason (as PARA-[1], *logos* reason)]

pa·ral·y·sis /pərálisis/ *n.* (*pl.* **pa·ral·y·ses** /–seez/) **1** impairment or loss of esp. the motor function of the nerves. **2** a state of utter powerlessness. [L f. Gk *paralusis* f. *paraluō* disable (as PARA-1, *luō* loosen)]

par·a·lyt·ic /párəlítik/ *adj. & n.* ● *adj.* **1** affected by paralysis. **2** esp. *Brit. sl.* very drunk. ● *n.* a person affected by paralysis. □□ **par·a·lyt·i·cal·ly** *adv.* [ME f. OF *paralytique* f. L *paralyticus* f. Gk *paralutikos* (as PARALYSIS)]

par·a·lyze /párəlīz/ *v.tr.* (also *Brit.* **par·a·lyse**) **1** affect with paralysis. **2** render powerless; cripple. □□ **par·a·ly·za·tion** *n.* **par·a·lyz·ing·ly** *adv.* [F *paralyser* f. *paralysie*: cf. PALSY]

par·a·mag·net·ic /párəmagnétik/ *adj.* (of a body or substance) tending to become weakly magnetized so as to lie parallel to a magnetic field force. □□ **par·a·mag·net·ism** /–mágnitizəm/ *n.*

par·a·mat·ta var. of PARRAMATTA.

par·a·me·ci·um /párəmée̊seeəm/ *n.* (also *Brit.* **par·a·moe·ci·um**) any freshwater protozoan of the genus *Paramecium*, of a characteristic slipperlike shape covered with cilia. [mod.L f. Gk *paramēkēs* oval (as PARA-1, *mēkos* length)]

par·a·med·ic /párəmédik/ *n.* **1** a paramedical worker. **2** a person trained in emergency medical procedures.

par·a·med·i·cal /párəmédikəl/ *adj.* (of services, etc.) supplementing and supporting medical work.

pa·ram·e·ter /pərámitər/ *n.* **1** *Math.* a quantity constant in the case considered but varying in different cases. **2 a** an (esp. measurable or quantifiable) characteristic or feature. **b** (loosely) a constant element or factor, esp. serving as a limit or boundary. □□ **par·a·met·ric** /párəmétrik/ *adj.* **pa·ram·e·trize** *v.tr.* [mod.L f. Gk *para* beside + *metron* measure]

par·a·mil·i·tar·y /párəmílitеree/ *adj.* (of forces) ancillary to and similarly organized to military forces.

par·am·ne·sia /páramnée̊zhə/ *n. Psychol.* = DÉJÀ VU. [PARA-1 + AMNESIA]

par·a·mo /párəmō, páar–/ *n.* (*pl.* **-mos**) a high treeless plateau in tropical S. America. [Sp. & Port. f. L *paramus*]

par·a·moe·ci·um *Brit.* var. of PARAMECIUM.

par·a·mount /párəmownt/ *adj.* **1** supreme; requiring first consideration; preeminent (*of paramount importance*). **2** in supreme authority. □□ **par·a·mount·cy** *n.* **par·a·mount·ly** *adv.* [AF *paramont* f. OF *par* by + *amont* above: cf. AMOUNT]

par·a·mour /párəmoor/ *n.* an illicit lover, esp. of a married person. [ME f. OF *par amour* by love]

pa·rang /párang/ *n.* a large heavy Malayan knife used for clearing vegetation, etc. [Malay]

par·a·noi·a /párənóyə/ *n.* **1** a personality disorder esp. characterized by delusions of persecution and self-importance. **2** an abnormal tendency to suspect and mistrust others. □□ **par·a·noi·ac** *adj. & n.* **par·a·noi·a·cal·ly** *adv.* **par·a·no·ic** /–nóyik, –nó-ik/ *adj.* **par·a·no·i·cal·ly** *adv.* **par·a·noid** /–noyd/ *adj. & n.* [mod.L f. Gk f. *paranoos* distracted (as PARA-1, *noos* mind)]

par·a·nor·mal /páranórməl/ *adj.* beyond the scope of normal objective investigation or explanation. □□ **par·a·nor·mal·ly** *adv.*

par·a·pet /párəpit/ *n.* **1** a low wall at the edge of a roof, balcony, etc., or along the sides of a bridge. **2** a defense of earth or stone to conceal and protect troops. □□ **par·a·pet·ed** *adj.* [F *parapet* or It. *parapetto* breast-high wall (as PARA-2, *petto* breast f. L *pectus*)]

par·aph /párəf/ *n.* a flourish after a signature, orig. as a precaution against forgery. [ME f. F *paraphe* f. med.L *paraphus* for *paragraphus* PARAGRAPH]

par·a·pher·na·lia /párəfərnáylyə/ *n.pl.* (also treated as *sing.*) miscellaneous belongings, items of equipment, accessories, etc. [orig. = property owned by a married woman, f. med.L *paraphernalia* f. LL *parapherna* f. Gk *parapherna* property apart from a dowry (as PARA-1, *pherna* f. *phernē* dower)]

par·a·phrase /párəfrayz/ *n. & v.* ● *n.* a free rendering or rewording of a passage. ● *v.tr.* express the meaning of (a passage) in other words. □□ **par·a·phras·tic** /–frástik/ *adj.* [F *paraphrase* or L *paraphrasis* f. Gk *paraphrasis* f. *paraphrazō* (as PARA-1 *phrazō* tell)]

par·a·ple·gi·a /párəplée̊jə/ *n.* paralysis of the legs and part or the whole of the trunk. □□ **par·a·ple·gic** *adj. & n.* [mod.L f. Gk *paraplēgia* f. *paraplēssō* (as PARA-1, *plēssō* strike)]

par·a·psy·chol·o·gy /párəsīkóləjee/ *n.* the study of mental phenomena outside the sphere of ordinary psychology (hypnosis, telepathy, etc.). □□ **par·a·psy·cho·log·i·cal** /–sīkəlójikəl/ *adj.* **par·a·psy·chol·o·gist** *n.*

par·a·quat /párəkwot/ *n.* a quick-acting herbicide, becoming inactive on contact with the soil. [PARA-1 + QUATERNARY (from the position of the bond between the two parts of the molecule relative to quaternary nitrogen atom)]

par·a·sail·ing /párəsayling/ *n.* a sport in which participants wearing open parachutes are towed behind a vehicle or motor boat to gain height, sometimes releasing for a conventional descent, usu. toward a predetermined target. □□ **par·a·sail·er** *n.* **par·a·sail·or** *n.*

par·a·se·le·ne /párəsileénee/ *n.* (*pl.* **par·a·se·le·nae** /–nee/) a bright spot, esp. an image of the moon, on a lunar halo. Also called **mock moon.** [mod.L (as PARA-1, Gk *selēne* moon)]

par·a·site /párəsīt/ *n.* **1** an organism living in or on another and benefiting at the expense of the other. **2** a person who lives off or exploits another or others. **3** *Philol.* an inorganic sound or letter developing from an adjacent one. □□ **par·a·sit·ic** /–sítik/ *adj.* **par·a·sit·i·cal** /–sítikəl/ *adj.* **par·a·sit·i·cal·ly** *adv.* **par·a·sit·i·cide** /–sítisīd/ *n.* **par·a·sit·ism** /–sítizəm/ *n.* **par·a·si·tol·o·gy** /–tólə̊jee/ *n.* **par·a·si·tol·o·gist** /–tóləjist/ *n.* [L *parasitus* f. Gk *parasitos* one who eats at another's table (as PARA-1, *sitos* food)]

par·a·si·tize /párəsitīz/ *v.tr.* infest as a parasite. □□ **par·a·sit·i·za·tion** *n.*

par·a·sol /párəsawl, –sol/ *n.* a light umbrella used to give shade from the sun. [F f. It. *parasole* (as PARA-2, *sole* sun f. L *sol*)]

par·a·sym·pa·thet·ic /párəsímpəthétik/ *adj. Anat.* relating to the part of the nervous system that consists of nerves leaving the lower end of the spinal cord and connecting with those in or near the viscera (cf. SYMPATHETIC 9). [PARA-1 + SYMPATHETIC, because some of these nerves run alongside sympathetic nerves]

par·a·syn·the·sis /párəsínthisis/ *n. Philol.* **1** a derivation from a compound, e.g., *black-eyed* from *black eye*(*s*) + *–ed.* **2** a word formed by adding both a prefix and a derivational ending. □□ **par·a·syn·thet·ic** /–thétik/ *adj.* [Gk *parasunthesis* (as PARA-1, SYNTHESIS)]

par·a·tax·is /párətáksis/ *n. Gram.* the placing of clauses, etc., one after another, without words to indicate coordination or subordination, e.g., *Tell me, how are you?* □□ **par·a·tac·tic** /–táktik/ *adj.* **par·a·tac·ti·cal·ly** *adv.* [Gk *parataxis* (as PARA-1, *taxis* arrangement f. *tassō* arrange)]

par·a·thi·on /párəthíon/ *n.* a highly toxic agricultural insecticide. [PARA-1 + THIO- + –ON]

par·a·thy·roid /párəthýroyd/ *n. & adj. Anat.* ● *n.* a gland next to the thyroid, secreting a hormone that regulates calcium levels in the body. ● *adj.* of or associated with this gland.

par·a·troop /párətroop/ *n.* (*attrib.*) of or consisting of paratroops (*paratroop regiment*).

par·a·troop·er /párətroopər/ *n.* a member of a body of paratroops.

par·a·troops /párətroops/ *n.pl.* troops equipped to be dropped by parachute from aircraft. [contr. of PARACHUTE + TROOP]

par·a·ty·phoid /párətífoyd/ *n. & adj.* ● *n.* a fever resembling typhoid but caused by various different though related bacteria. ● *adj.* of, relating to, or caused by this fever.

par·a·vane /párəvayn/ *n.* a torpedo-shaped device towed at a depth regulated by its vanes or planes to cut the moorings of submerged mines.

par a·vion /páar avyáwN/ *adv.* by airmail. [F, = by airplane]

par·boil /páarboyl/ *v.tr.* partly cook by boiling. [ME f. OF *parbo*(*u*)*illir* f. LL *perbullire* boil thoroughly (as PER-, *bullire* boil: confused with PART)]

par·buck·le /páarbukəl/ *n. & v.* ● *n.* a rope arranged like a sling, for raising or lowering casks and cylindrical objects. ● *v.tr.* raise or lower with this. [earlier *parbunkle*, of unkn. orig.: assoc. with BUCKLE]

par·cel /páarsəl/ *n. & v.* ● *n.* **1 a** goods, etc., wrapped up in a single package. **b** a bundle of things wrapped up, usu. in paper. **2** a piece of land, esp. as part of a larger lot. **3** a quantity dealt with in one commercial transaction. **4** a group or collection of things, people, etc. **5** part. ● *v.tr.* (**par·celed, par·cel·ing** or **par·celled, par·cel·ling**) **1** (foll. by *out*) divide into portions **2** (foll. by *up*) wrap as a parcel. **3** cover (rope) with strips of canvas. [ME f. OF *parcelle* ult. f. L *particula* (as PART)]

par·cel post *n.* **1** a mail service dealing with parcels. **2** a postage rate for parcels.

parch /paarch/ *v.* **1** *tr. & intr.* make or become hot and dry. **2** *tr.* roast (peas, grain, etc.) slightly. [ME *perch, parche*, of unkn. orig.]

parched /paarcht/ *adj.* **1** hot and dry; dried out with heat. **2** *colloq.* thirsty.

Par·chee·si /paarchée̊zee, pər–, -see/ *n. Trademark* a board game, played with dice, similar to pachisi.

parch·ment /páarchmənt/ *n.* **1 a** an animal skin, esp. that of a sheep or goat, prepared as a writing or painting surface. **b** a manuscript written on this. **c** a diploma, esp. one written on this. **2** (in full **vegetable parchment**) high-grade paper made to resemble parchment. [ME f. OF *parchemin*, ult. a blend of LL *pergamina* writing material from Pergamum (in Asia Minor) with *Parthica pellis* Parthian skin (leather)]

par·close /páarklōz/ *n.* a screen or railing in a church, separating a side chapel. [ME f. OF *parclos –ose* past part. of *parclore* enclose]

pard /paard/ *n. archaic* or *poet.* a leopard. [ME f. OF f. L *pardus* f. Gk *pardos*]

pard·ner /páardnər/ *n. US dial. colloq.* a partner or comrade. [corrupt.]

par·don /páard'n/ *n., v., & int.* ● *n.* **1** the act of excusing or forgiving an offense, error, etc. **2** (in full **full pardon**, *Brit.* **free pardon**) a remission of the legal consequences of a crime or conviction. **3** *RC Ch.* an indulgence. ● *v.tr.* **1** release from the consequences of an offense, error, etc. **2** forgive or excuse a person for (an offense, etc.). **3** make (esp. courteous) allowances for; excuse. ● *int.* (also **par•don me** or **I beg your par•don**) **1** a formula of apology or disagreement. **2** a request to repeat something said. □□ **par•don•a•ble** *adj.* **par•don•a•bly** *adv.* [ME f. OF *pardun*, *pardoner* f. med.L *perdonare* concede, remit (as PER-, *donare* give)]

par•don•er /paárd'nər/ *n. hist.* a person licensed to sell papal pardons or indulgences. [ME f. AF (as PARDON)]

pare /pair/ *v.tr.* **1 a** trim (esp. fruit and vegetables) by cutting away the surface or edge. **b** (often foll. by *off*, *away*) cut off (the surface or edge). **2** (often foll. by *away*, *down*) diminish little by little. □□ **par•er** *n.* [ME f. OF *parer* adorn, peel (fruit), f. L *parare* prepare]

par•e•gor•ic /párigáwrik, –gór–/ *n.* a camphorated tincture of opium used to reduce pain or relieve diarrhea. [LL *paregoricus* f. Gk *parēgorikos* soothing (as PARA-¹, *–agoros* speaking f. *agora* assembly)]

pa•rei•ra /pəráirə/ *n.* a drug from the root of a Brazilian shrub, *Chondrodendron tomentosum*, used as a muscle relaxant in surgery, etc. [Port. *parreira* vine trained against a wall]

pa•ren•chy•ma /pəréngkimə/ *n.* **1** *Anat.* the functional part of an organ as distinguished from the connective and supporting tissue. **2** *Bot.* the cellular material, usu. soft and succulent, found esp. in the softer parts of leaves, pulp of fruits, bark and pith of stems, etc. □□ **pa•ren•chy•mal** *adj.* **pa•ren•chym•a•tous** /–kímətəs/ *adj.* [Gk *paregkhuma* something poured in besides (as PARA-¹, *egkhuma* infusion f. *egkheō* pour in)]

par•ent /páirənt, pár–/ *n. & v.* ● *n.* **1** a person who has begotten or borne offspring; a father or mother. **2** a person who holds the position or exercises the functions of such a parent. **3** an ancestor. **4** an animal or plant from which others are derived. **5** a source or origin. **6** an initiating organization or enterprise. ● *v.tr.* (also *absol.*) be a parent of. □□ **pa•ren•tal** /pərént'l/ *adj.* **pa•ren•tal•ly** /pəréntəlee/ *adv.* **par•ent•hood** *n.* [ME f. OF f. L *parens parentis* f. *parere* bring forth]

par•ent•age /páirəntij, pár–/ *n.* lineage; descent from or through parents (*their parentage is unknown*). [ME f. OF (as PARENT)]

parent com•pa•ny *n.* a company of which other companies are subsidiaries.

par•en•ter•al /pəréntərəl/ *adj. Med.* administered or occurring elsewhere than in the alimentary canal. □□ **par•en•ter•al•ly** *adv.* [PARA-¹ + Gk *enteron* intestine]

pa•ren•the•sis /pərénthəsis/ *n.* (*pl.* **pa•ren•the•ses** /–seez/) **1 a** a word, clause, or sentence inserted as an explanation or afterthought into a passage which is grammatically complete without it, and usu. marked off by brackets or dashes or commas. **b** (in *pl.*) a pair of rounded brackets ( ) used for this. **2** an interlude or interval. □ **in parenthesis** as a parenthesis or afterthought. [LL f. Gk *parenthesis* f. *parentithēmi* put in beside]

pa•ren•the•size /pərénthəsīz/ *v.tr.* **1** (also *absol.*) insert as a parenthesis. **2** put into brackets or similar punctuation.

par•en•thet•ic /párənthétik/ *adj.* **1** of or by way of a parenthesis. **2** interposed. □□ **par•en•thet•i•cal** *adj.* **par•en•thet•i•cal•ly** *adv.* [PARENTHESIS after *synthesis*, *synthetic*, etc.]

par•ent•ing /páirənting, pár–/ *n.* the occupation or concerns of parents.

Parent–Teach•er As•so•ci•a•tion *n.* (abbrev.: **PTA**) a local organization of parents and teachers for promoting closer relations and improving educational facilities at a school.

par•er•gon /pərérgən/ *n.* (*pl.* **par•er•ga** /–gə/) **1** work subsidiary to one's main employment. **2** an ornamental accessory. [L f. Gk *parergon* (as PARA-¹, *ergon* work)]

pa•re•sis /pəréesis, párisis/ *n.* (*pl.* **pa•re•ses** /–seez/) *Med.* partial paralysis. □□ **pa•ret•ic** /pərétik/ *adj.* [mod.L f. Gk f. *pariēmi* let go (as PARA-¹, *hiēmi* let go)]

pa•reve /paárəvə, paárvə/ *adj.* made without milk or meat and thus suitable for kosher use.

par ex•cel•lence /paár eksəlóns/ *adv.* as having special excellence; being the supreme example of its kind (*the short story par excellence*). [F, = by excellence]

par•fait /paarfáy/ *n.* **1** a rich frozen custard of whipped cream, eggs, etc. **2** layers of ice cream, meringue, etc., served in a tall glass. [F *parfait* PERFECT adj.]

par•get /paárjit/ *v. & n.* ● *v.tr.* (**par•get•ed**, **par•get•ing**) **1** plaster (a wall, etc.) esp. with an ornamental pattern. **2** roughcast. ● *n.* **1** plaster applied in this way; ornamental plasterwork. **2** roughcast. [ME f. OF *pargeter*, *parjeter* f. *par* all over + *jeter* throw]

par•he•li•on /paarhéeleeən/ *n.* (*pl.* **par•he•li•a** /–leeə/) a bright spot on the solar halo. Also called **mock sun** or **sundog**. □□ **par•he•li•a•cal** /–hílíəkəl/ *adj.* **par•he•lic** *adj.* [L *parelion* f. Gk (as PARA-¹, *hēlios* sun)]

pa•ri•ah /pəríə/ *n.* **1** a social outcast. **2** *hist.* a member of a low caste or of no caste in S. India. [Tamil *paṟaiyar* pl. of *paṟaiyan* hereditary drummer f. *paṟai* drum]

pa•ri•e•tal /pəríətəl/ *adj.* **1** *Anat.* of the wall of the body or any of its cavities. **2** *Bot.* of the wall of a hollow structure, etc. **3** relating to

residence and visitation rules in a college dormitory. [F *pariétal* or LL *parietalis* f. L *paries –etis* wall]

pa•ri•e•tal bone *n.* either of a pair of bones forming the central part of the sides and top of the skull.

pari-mu•tu•el /párimyōōchōōəl/ *n.* **1** a form of betting in which those backing the first three places divide the losers' stakes (less the operator's commission). **2 a** a device showing the number and amount of bets staked on a race, to facilitate the division of the total among those backing the winner. **b** a system of betting based on this. [F, = mutual stake]

par•ing /páiring/ *n.* a strip or piece cut off.

pa•ri pas•su /paáree pásōō, páree/ *adv.* **1** with equal speed. **2** simultaneously and equally. [L]

Par•is Com•mune see COMMUNE¹.

Par•is green /páris/ *n.* a poisonous chemical used as a pigment and insecticide. [*Paris* in France]

par•ish /párish/ *n.* **1** an area having its own church and clergy. **2** a county in Louisiana. **3** *Brit.* (in full **civil parish**) a district constituted for purposes of local government. **4** the inhabitants of a parish. [ME *paroche*, *parosse* f. OF *paroche*, *paroisse* f. eccl.L *parochia*, *paroechia* f. Gk *paroikia* sojourning f. *paroikos* (as PARA-¹, *–oikos* –dwelling f. *oikeō* dwell)]

parish clerk *n.* an official performing various duties concerned with the church.

par•ish coun•cil *n. Brit.* the administrative body in a civil parish.

pa•rish•ion•er /pərishənər/ *n.* an inhabitant or member of a parish. [obs. *parishen* ME f. OF *parossien*, formed as PARISH]

parish reg•is•ter *n.* a book recording christenings, marriages, and burials, at a parish church.

Pa•ri•sian /pəréezhən, –rízhən, –rízeeən/ *adj. & n.* ● *adj.* of or relating to Paris in France. ● *n.* **1** a native or inhabitant of Paris. **2** the kind of French spoken in Paris. [F *parisien*]

par•i•son /párisən/ *n.* a rounded mass of glass formed by rolling immediately after taking it from the furnace. [F *paraison* f. *parer* prepare f. L *parare*]

par•i•ty¹ /páritee/ *n.* **1** equality or equal status, esp. as regards status or pay. **2** parallelism or analogy (*parity of reasoning*). **3** equivalence of one currency with another; being at par. **4 a** (of a number) the fact of being even or odd. **b** *Computing* mathematical parity used for error detection. **5** *Physics* (of a quantity) the fact of changing its sign or remaining unaltered under a given transformation of coordinates, etc. [F *parité* or LL *paritas* (as PAR¹)]

par•i•ty² /páritee/ *n. Med.* **1** the fact or condition of having borne children. **2** the number of children previously borne. [formed as –PAROUS + –ITY]

park /paark/ *n. & v.* ● *n.* **1** a large public area in a town, used for recreation. **2** a large enclosed piece of ground, usu. with woodland and pasture, attached to a country house, etc. **3 a** a large area of land kept in its natural state for public recreational use. **b** esp. *Brit.* a large enclosed area of land used to accommodate wild animals in captivity (*wildlife park*). **4** esp. *Brit.* an area for motor vehicles, etc., to be left in (*car park*). **5** the gear position or function in an automatic transmission in which the gears are locked, preventing the vehicle's movement. **6** an area devoted to a specified purpose (*industrial park*). **7** a sports arena or stadium. ● *v.* **1** *tr.* (also *absol.*) leave (a vehicle) temporarily, in a parking lot, by the side of the road, etc. **2** *tr. colloq.* deposit and leave, usu. temporarily. **3** *intr. sl.* engage in petting or kissing in a parked car. □ **park oneself** *colloq.* sit down.

WORD HISTORY park

Middle English: from Old French *parc*, from medieval Latin *parricus*, of Germanic origin; related to German *Pferch* 'pen, fold,' also to *paddock*. The word was originally a legal term designating land held by royal grant for keeping game animals: this was enclosed and therefore distinct from a *forest* or *chase*, and (also unlike a *forest*) had no special laws or officers. A military sense 'space occupied by artillery, wagons, stores, etc., in an encampment' (late 17th century) is the origin of the verb sense (mid-19th century) and of senses 4 and 6 (early 20th century).

par•ka /paárkə/ *n.* **1** a skin jacket with hood, worn by Eskimos. **2** a similar windproof fabric garment worn in cold weather. [Aleutian]

par•kin /paárkin/ *n. Brit.* a cake or cookie made with oatmeal, ginger, and sugar syrup or molasses. [perh. f. the name *Parkin*, dimin. of *Peter*]

park•ing lot *n.* an area for parking vehicles.

park•ing me•ter *n.* a coin-operated meter that receives payment for vehicles parked in the street and indicates the time available.

parking ticket *n.* a notice, usu. attached to a vehicle, of a penalty imposed for parking illegally.

Par•kin•son•ism /paárkinsənizəm/ *n.* = PARKINSON'S DISEASE.

Par•kin•son's dis•ease /paárkinsənz/ *n.* a progressive disease of the nervous system with tremor, muscular rigidity, and emaciation. Also called **Parkinsonism**. [J. *Parkinson*, Engl. surgeon d. 1824]

Par•kin•son's law /paárkinsənz/ *n.* the notion that work expands so as to fill the time available for its completion. [C. N. *Parkinson*, Engl. writer b. 1909]

park·land /paárkland/ *n.* open grassland with clumps of trees, etc.

park·way /paárkway/ *n.* **1** an open landscaped highway. **2** *Brit.* a railroad station with extensive parking facilities.

Parl. *abbr. Brit.* **1** Parliament. **2** Parliamentary.

par·lance /paárləns/ *n.* a particular way of speaking, esp. as regards choice of words, idiom, etc. [OF f. *parler* speak, ult. f. L *parabola* (see PARABLE): in LL = 'speech']

par·lay /paárlay/ *v. & n.* •*v.tr.* **1** use (money won on a bet) as a further stake. **2** increase in value by or as if by parlaying. •*n.* **1** an act of parlaying. **2** a bet made by parlaying. [F *paroli* f. It. f. *paro* like f. L *par* equal]

par·ley /paárlee/ *n. & v.* •*n.* (*pl.* •**leys**) a conference for debating points in a dispute, esp. a discussion of terms for an armistice, etc. •*v.intr.* (•**leys**, •**leyed**) (often foll. by *with*) hold a parley. [perh. f. OF *parlee*, fem. past part. of *parler* speak: see PARLANCE]

par·lia·ment /paárləmənt/ *n.* **1** (**Parliament**) **a** (in the UK) the highest legislature, consisting of the Sovereign, the House of Lords, and the House of Commons. **b** the members of this legislature for a particular period, esp. between one dissolution and the next. **2** a similar legislature in other nations. [ME f. OF *parlement* speaking (as PARLANCE)]

par·lia·men·tar·i·an /paárləməntáireeən/ *n. & adj.* •*n.* **1** a member of a parliament. **2** a person who is well-versed in parliamentary procedures. **3** *hist.* an adherent of Parliament in the English Civil War of the 17th c. •*adj.* = PARLIAMENTARY.

par·lia·men·ta·ry /paárləméntəree, -tree/ *adj.* **1** of or relating to a parliament. **2** enacted or established by a parliament. **3** (of language) admissible in a parliament; polite.

par·lor /paárlər/ *n.* (*Brit.* **par·lour**) **1** a sitting room in a private house. **2** a room in a hotel, club, etc., for the private use of residents. **3** a store providing specified goods or services (*beauty parlor; ice cream parlor*). **4** a room or building equipped for milking cows. **5** (*attrib.*) *derog.* denoting support for esp. political views by those who do not try to practice them (*parlor socialist*). [ME f. AF *parlur*, OF *parleor*, *parleur*: see PARLANCE]

par·lor game *n.* an indoor game, esp. a word game.

par·lous /paárləs/ *adj. & adv.* •*adj.* **1** dangerous or difficult. **2** *archaic* clever; cunning. •*adv.* extremely. □□ **par·lous·ly** *adv.* **par·lous·ness** *n.* [ME, = PERILOUS]

Par·ma vi·o·let /paármə/ *n.* a variety of sweet violet with heavy scent and lavender-colored flowers. [*Parma* in Italy]

Par·me·san /paármizaán, -zán, -zən/ *n.* a kind of hard dry cheese made orig. at Parma and used esp. in grated form. [F f. It. *parmegiano* of Parma in Italy]

Par·nas·si·an /paarnáseeən/ *adj. & n.* •*adj.* **1** of Parnassus, a mountain in central Greece, in antiquity sacred to the Muses. **2** poetic. **3** of or relating to a group of French poets in the late 19th c., emphasizing strictness of form, named from the anthology *Le Parnasse contemporain* (1866). •*n.* a member of this group.

pa·ro·chi·al /pərókeeəl/ *adj.* **1** of or concerning a parish. **2** (of affairs, views, etc.) merely local, narrow or restricted in scope. □□ **pa·ro·chi·al·ism** *n.* **pa·ro·chi·al·i·ty** /-álitee/ *n.* **pa·ro·chi·al·ly** *adv.* [ME f. AF *parochiel*, OF *parochial* f. eccl.L *parochialis* (as PARISH)]

pa·ro·chi·al school *n.* a private elementary or high school maintained by a religious organization, esp. the Roman Catholic Church.

par·o·dy /párədee/ *n. & v.* •*n.* (*pl.* •**dies**) **1** a humorous exaggerated imitation of an author, literary work, style, etc. **2** a feeble imitation; a travesty. •*v.tr.* (•**dies**, •**died**) **1** compose a parody of. **2** mimic humorously. □□ **pa·rod·ic** /pəródik/ *adj.* **par·o·dist** *n.* [LL *parodia* or Gk *parōidia* burlesque poem (as PARA-¹, *ōidē* ode)]

pa·rol /pəról/ *adj. & n.* *Law* •*adj.* given orally. •*n.* an oral declaration. [OF *parole* (as PAROLE)]

pa·role /pəról/ *n. & v.* •*n.* **1 a** the release of a prisoner temporarily for a special purpose or completely before the fulfillment of a sentence, on the promise of good behavior. **b** such a promise. **2** a word of honor. •*v.tr.* put (a prisoner) on parole. □ **on parole** released on the terms of parole. □□ **pa·rol·ee** /-lee/ *n.* [F, = PARLANCE]

par·o·no·ma·sia /páronōmáyzhə, -zheeə/ *n.* a play on words; a pun. [L f. Gk *paronomasia* (as PARA-¹, *onomasia* naming f. *onomazō* to name f. *onoma* a name)]

par·o·nym /párənim/ *n.* **1** a word cognate with another. **2** a word formed from a foreign word. □□ **pa·ron·y·mous** /pəróniməs/ *adj.* [Gk *parōnumon*, neut. of *parōnumos* (as PARA-¹, *onuma* name)]

pa·rot·id /pərótid/ *adj. & n.* •*adj.* (in full **parotid gland**) a salivary gland in front of the ear. [F *parotide* or L *parotis parotid-* f. Gk *parōtis -idos* (as PARA-¹, *ous ōtos* ear)]

pa·rot·id duct *n.* a duct opening from the parotid gland into the mouth.

pa·ro·ti·tis /párətítis/ *n.* **1** inflammation of the parotid gland. **2** mumps. [PAROTID + -ITIS]

-parous /pərəs/ *comb. form* bearing offspring of a specified number or kind (*multiparous; viviparous*). [L *-parus* -bearing f. *parere* bring forth]

Par·ou·si·a /paarōoseéə, pərōόzeeə/ *n.* *Theol.* the supposed second coming of Christ. [Gk, = presence, coming]

par·ox·ysm /párəksizəm/ *n.* **1** (often foll. by *of*) a sudden attack or outburst (of rage, laughter, etc.). **2** a fit of disease. □□ **par·ox·ys·mal** /-sízməl/ *adj.* [F *paroxysme* f. med.L *paroxysmus* f. Gk *paroxusmos* f. *paroxunō* exasperate (as PARA-¹, *oxunō* sharpen f. *oxus* sharp)]

par·pen /paárpən/ *n.* (also **per·pend**) a stone passing through a wall from side to side, with two smooth vertical faces. [ME f. OF *parpain*, prob. ult. f. L *per* through + *pannus* piece of cloth, in Rmc 'piece of wall']

par·quet /paárkáy/ *n. & v.* •*n.* **1** a flooring of wooden blocks arranged in a pattern. **2** the main-floor seating area of a theater. •*v.tr.* (**par·queted** /-káyd/; **par·quet·ing** /-káying/) furnish (a room) with a parquet floor. [F, = small compartment, floor, dimin. of *parc* PARK]

par·quet cir·cle *n.* the rear seating area of a theater, esp. the section under the balcony.

par·quet·ry /paárkitree/ *n.* the use of wooden blocks to make floors or inlay for furniture.

parr /paar/ *n.* a young salmon with blue-gray fingerlike markings on its sides, younger than a smolt. [18th c.: orig. unkn.]

par·ra·mat·ta /párəmátə/ *n.* (also **par·a·mat·ta**) a light dress fabric of wool and silk or cotton. [*Parramatta* in New South Wales, Australia]

par·ri·cide /párisīd/ *n.* **1** the killing of a near relative, esp. of a parent. **2** an act of parricide. **3** a person who commits parricide. □□ **par·ri·cid·al** /-síd'l/ *adj.* [F *parricide* or L *parricida* (= sense 3), *parricidium* (= sense 1), of uncert. orig., assoc. in L with *pater* father and *parens* parent]

par·rot /párət/ *n. & v.* •*n.* **1** any of various mainly tropical birds of the order Psittaciformes, with a short hooked bill, often having vivid plumage and able to mimic the human voice. **2** a person who mechanically repeats the words or actions of another. •*v.tr.* (**par·rot·ed, par·rot·ing**) repeat mechanically. [prob. f. obs. or dial. F *perrot* parrot, dimin. of *Pierre* Peter: cf. PARAKEET]

parrot 1

par·rot fish *n.* any fish of the genus *Scarus*, with a mouth like a parrot's bill.

par·ry /páree/ *v. & n.* •*v.tr.* (•**ries**, •**ried**) **1** avert or ward off (a weapon or attack), esp. with a countermove. **2** deal skillfully with (an awkward question, etc.). •*n.* (*pl.* •**ries**) an act of parrying. [prob. repr. F *parez* imper. of *parer* f. It. *parare* ward off]

parse /paars/ *v.tr.* **1** describe (a word in context) grammatically, stating its inflection, relation to the sentence, etc. **2** resolve (a sentence) into its component parts and describe them grammatically. □□ **pars·er** *n.* esp. *Computing.* [perh. f. ME *pars* parts of speech f. OF *pars*, pl. of *part* PART, infl. by L *pars* part]

par·sec /paársek/ *n.* a unit of stellar distance, equal to about 3.25 light years (3.08 x 10¹⁶ meters), the distance at which the mean radius of the earth's orbit subtends an angle of one second of arc. [PARALLAX + SECOND²]

Par·see /paársee/ *n.* **1** an adherent of Zoroastrianism. **2** a descendant of the Persians who fled to India from Muslim persecution in the 7th–8th c. **3** = PAHLAVI. □□ **Par·see·ism** *n.* [Pers. *pārsī* Persian f. *pārs* Persia]

par·si·mo·ny /paársimōnee/ *n.* **1** carefulness in the use of money or other resources. **2** stinginess. □□ **par·si·mo·ni·ous** /-mōneeəs/ *adj.* **par·si·mo·ni·ous·ly** *adv.* **par·si·mo·ni·ous·ness** *n.* [ME f. L *parsimonia*, *parcimonia* f. *parcere* *pars-* spare]

pars·ley /paárslee/ *n.* a biennial herb, *Petroselinum crispum*, with white flowers and crinkly aromatic leaves, used for seasoning and garnishing food. [ME *percil*, *per(e)sil* f. OF *peresil*, and OE *petersilie* ult. f. L *petroselinum* f. Gk *petroselinon*; *parsley piert* prob. corrupt. of F *perce-pierre* pierce stone]

pars·ley fern *n.* a fern, *Cryptogramma crispa*, with leaves like parsley.

pars·ley piert *n.* a dwarf annual herb, *Aphanes arvensis*.

pars·nip /paársnip/ *n.* **1** a biennial umbelliferous plant, *Pastinaca sativa*, with yellow flowers and a large pale yellow tapering root. **2** this root eaten as a vegetable. [ME *pas(se)nep* (with assim. to *nep* turnip) f. OF *pasnaie* f. L *pastinaca*]

par·son /paársən/ *n.* **1** a rector. **2** any (esp. Protestant) member of the clergy. □□ **par·son·i·cal** /-sónikəl/ *adj.* [ME *person(e)*, *parson* f. OF *persone* f. L *persona* PERSON (in med.L rector)]

par·son·age /paársənij/ *n.* a church house provided for a parson.

par·son's nose *n.* the piece of fatty flesh at the rump of a fowl.

part /paart/ *n., v., & adv.* •*n.* **1** some but not all of a thing or number of things. **2** an essential member or constituent of anything (*part of the family; a large part of the job*). **3** a component of a machine, etc. (*spare parts; needs a new part*). **4 a** a portion of a human or animal body. **b** (in *pl.*) *colloq.* = PRIVATE PARTS. **5** a division of a book, broadcast serial, etc., esp. as much as is issued or broadcast at one time. **6** each of several equal portions of a whole (*the recipe has 3 parts sugar to 2 parts flour*). **7 a** a portion allotted; a share. **b** a person's share in an action or enterprise (*will have no part in it*). **c** one's duty (*was not my part to interfere*). **8 a** a character assigned to an actor on stage. **b** the words spoken by an actor on stage. **c** a copy of these. **9** *Mus.* a melody or other constituent of harmony assigned to a particular voice or instrument. **10** each of the sides in an agreement or dispute. **11** (in *pl.*) a region or district (*am not from these parts*). **12** (in *pl.*) abilities (*a man of many parts*). **13** a dividing line in combed hair. • *v.* **1** *tr.* & *intr.* divide or separate into parts (*the crowd parted to let them through*). **2** *intr.* **a** leave one another's company (*they parted the best of friends*). **b** (foll. by *from*) say goodbye to. **3** *tr.* cause to separate (*they fought hard and had to be parted*). **4** *intr.* (foll. by *with*) give up possession of; hand over. **5** *tr.* separate (the hair of the head on either side of the part) with a comb. • *adv.* to some extent; partly (*is part iron and part wood; a lie that is part truth*). □ **for the most part** see MOST. **for one's part** as far as one is concerned. **in part** (or **parts**) to some extent; partly. **look the part** appear suitable for a role. **on the part of** on the behalf or initiative of (*no objection on my part*). **part and parcel** (foll. by *of*) an essential part. **part company** see COMPANY. **play a part 1** be significant or contributory. **2** act deceitfully. **3** perform a theatrical role. **take part** (often foll. by *in*) assist or have a share (in). **take the part of 1** support; back up. **2** perform the role of. **three parts** three quarters. [ME f. OF f. L *pars partis* (n.), *partire, partiri* (v.)]

par·take /paartáyk/ *v.intr.* (*past* **par·took** /–tŏŏk/; *past part.* **par·tak·en** /–táykən/) **1** (foll. by *of, in*) take a share or part. **2** (foll. by *of*) eat or drink some or *colloq.* all (of a thing). **3** (foll. by *of*) have some (of a quality, etc.) (*their manner partook of insolence*). □□ **par·tak·a·ble** *adj.* **par·tak·er** *n.* [16th c.: back-form. f. *partaker, partaking* = partaker, etc.]

par·terre /paartáir/ *n.* **1** a level space in a garden occupied by flower beds arranged formally. **2** = PARQUET CIRCLE. [F, = *par terre* on the ground]

part-ex·change *n.* *Brit.* a transaction in which goods are given as part of the payment for other goods, with the balance in money. • *v.tr.* give (goods) in such a transaction.

par·the·no·gen·e·sis /paárthinōjénisis/ *n.* *Biol.* reproduction by a female gamete without fertilization, esp. as a normal process in invertebrates and lower plants. □□ **par·the·no·ge·net·ic** /–jinétik/ *adj.* **par·the·no·ge·net·i·cal·ly** *adv.* [mod.L f. Gk *parthenos* virgin + *genesis* as GENESIS]

Par·thi·an shot /paártheeən/ *n.* a remark or glance, etc., reserved for the moment of departure. [*Parthia*, an ancient kingdom in W. Asia: from the custom of a retreating Parthian horseman firing a shot at the enemy]

par·tial /paárshəl/ *adj.* & *n.* • *adj.* **1** not complete; forming only part (*a partial success*). **2** biased; unfair. **3** (foll. by *to*) having a liking for. • *n.* **1** *Mus.* any of the component tones of a complex tone. **2** a denture for replacing one or several, but not all, of the teeth. □□ **par·tial·ly** *adv.* **par·tial·ness** *n.* [ME f. OF *parcial* f. LL *partialis* (as PART)]

▶**Partial, Partly, and Partially.** In the sense 'to some extent, not entirely' traditionalists prefer **partly** to **partially**: *The piece was written partly in poetry; What we decide will depend partly on the amount of the contract.* The form **partial**, however, appears in many phrases as the adjectival form of **part**: *partial blindness, partial denture, partial paralysis, partial payment, partial shade, partial vacuum,* etc. **Partially** is therefore widely used, with the same sense as **partly**: *partially blind in one eye.*

par·tial e·clipse *n.* an eclipse in which only part of the luminary is covered or darkened.

par·ti·al·i·ty /paársheeálitee/ *n.* **1** bias; favoritism. **2** (foll. by *for*) fondness. [ME f. OF *parcialité* f. med.L *partialitas* (as PARTIAL)]

par·tial ver·dict *n.* a verdict finding a person guilty of part of a charge.

par·tic·i·pant /paartísipənt/ *n.* someone who or something that participates.

par·tic·i·pate /paartísipayt/ *v.intr.* **1** (often foll. by *in*) take a part or share (in). **2** *literary* or *formal* (foll. by *of*) have a certain quality (*the speech participated of wit*). □□ **par·tic·i·pa·tion** /–páyshən/ *n.* **par·tic·i·pa·tor** *n.* **par·tic·i·pa·to·ry** /–tísəpətáwree/ *adj.* [L *participare* f. *participes –cipis* taking part, formed as PART + *–cip– = cap–* stem of *capere* take]

par·ti·ci·ple /paártisipəl/ *n.* *Gram.* a word formed from a verb (e.g., *going, gone, being, been*) and used in compound verb forms (e.g., *is going, has been*) or as an adjective (e.g., *working woman, burned toast*). □□ **par·ti·cip·i·al** /–sípeeəl/ *adj.* **par·ti·cip·i·al·ly** /–sípeeəlee/ *adv.* [ME f. OF, by-form of *participe* f. L *participium* (as PARTICIPATE)]

▶**Dangling Participle.** See note at MODIFIER.

par·ti·cle /paártikəl/ *n.* **1** a minute portion of matter. **2** the least possible amount (*not a particle of sense*). **3** *Gram.* **a** a minor part of speech, esp. a short indeclinable one. **b** a common prefix or suffix such as *in–, –ness.* [ME f. L *particula* (as PART)]

par·ti·cle·board /paártikəlbŏrd, –bawrd/ *n.* a building material made in flat sheets from scrap wood bonded with adhesive.

par·ti·col·ored /paárteekúlərd/ *adj.* partly of one color, partly of another or others. [PARTY² + COLORED]

par·tic·u·lar /pərtíkyələr, pətík–/ *adj.* & *n.* • *adj.* **1** relating to or considered as one thing or person as distinct from others; individual (*in this particular instance*). **2** more than is usual; special; noteworthy (*took particular trouble*). **3** scrupulously exact; fastidious. **4** detailed (*a full and particular account*). **5** *Logic* (of a proposition) in which something is asserted of some but not all of a class (opp. UNIVERSAL *adj.* 2). • *n.* **1** a detail; an item. **2** (in *pl.*) points of information; a detailed account. □ **in particular** especially; specifically. [ME f. OF *particuler* f. L *particularis* (as PARTICLE)]

par·tic·u·lar·ism /pərtíkyələrízəm, pətík–/ *n.* **1** exclusive devotion to one party, sect, etc. **2** the principle of leaving political independence to each state in an empire or federation. **3** the theological doctrine of individual election or redemption. □□ **par·tic·u·lar·ist** *n.* [F *particularisme*, mod.L *particularismus*, and G *Partikularismus* (as PARTICULAR)]

par·tic·u·lar·i·ty /pərtíkyəláritee, pətík–/ *n.* **1** the quality of being individual or particular. **2** fullness or minuteness of detail in a description.

par·tic·u·lar·ize /pərtíkyələrīz, pətík–/ *v.tr.* (also *absol.*) **1** name specifically or one by one. **2** specify (items). □□ **par·tic·u·lar·i·za·tion** *n.* [F *particulariser* (as PARTICULAR)]

par·tic·u·lar·ly /pərtíkyələrlee, pətík–/ *adv.* **1** especially; very. **2** specifically (*they particularly asked for you*). **3** in a particular or fastidious manner.

par·tic·u·late /pərtíkyəlayt, –lət, paar–/ *adj.* & *n.* • *adj.* in the form of separate particles. • *n.* matter in this form. [L *particula* PARTICLE]

part·ing /paárting/ *n.* **1** a leave-taking or departure (often *attrib.*: *parting words*). **2** *Brit.* = PART n. 13. **3** a division; an act of separating.

part·ing shot *n.* = PARTHIAN SHOT.

par·ti pris /paártee preé/ *n.* a preconceived view; a bias. • *adj.* prejudiced; biased. [F, = side taken]

par·ti·san /paártizən/ *n.* & *adj.* (also **par·ti·zan**) • *n.* **1** a strong, esp. unreasoning, supporter of a party, cause, etc. **2** *Mil.* a guerrilla in wartime. • *adj.* **1** of or characteristic of partisans. **2** loyal to a particular cause; biased. □□ **par·ti·san·ship** *n.* [F f. It. dial. *partigiano,* etc. f. *parte* PART]

par·ti·ta /paarteétə/ *n.* (*pl.* **par·tite** /–tay/) *Mus.* **1** a suite. **2** an air with variations. [It., fem. past part. of *partire* divide, formed as PART]

par·tite /paártit/ *adj.* **1** divided (esp. in *comb.*: *tripartite*). **2** *Bot.* & *Zool.* divided to or nearly to the base. [L *partitus* past part. of *partiri* PART v.]

par·ti·tion /paartíshən/ *n.* & *v.* • *n.* **1** division into parts, esp. *Polit.* of a country with separate areas of government. **2** a structure dividing a space into two parts, esp. a light interior wall. • *v.tr.* **1** divide into parts. **2** (foll. by *off*) separate (part of a room, etc.) with a partition. □□ **par·ti·tioned** *adj.* **par·ti·tion·er** *n.* **par·ti·tion·ist** *n.* [ME f. OF f. L *partitio –onis* (as PARTITE)]

par·ti·tive /paártitiv/ *adj.* & *n.* *Gram.* • *adj.* (of a word, form, etc.) denoting part of a collective group or quantity. • *n.* a partitive word (e.g., *some, any*) or form. □□ **par·ti·tive·ly** *adv.* [F *partitif –ive* or med.L *partitivus* (as PARTITE)]

par·ti·tive gen·i·tive *n.* a genitive used to indicate a whole divided into or regarded in parts, expressed in English by *of* as in *most of us.*

par·ti·zan var. of PARTISAN.

part·ly /paártlee/ *adv.* **1** with respect to a part or parts. **2** to some extent.

▶See note at PARTIAL.

part·ner /paártnər/ *n.* & *v.* • *n.* **1** a person who shares or takes part with another or others, esp. in a business firm with shared risks and profits. **2** a companion in dancing. **3** a player (esp. one of two) on the same side in a game. **4** either member of a married couple, or of an unmarried couple living together. • *v.tr.* be the partner of. **2** associate as partners. □□ **part·ner·less** *adj.* [ME, alt. of *parcener* joint heir, after PART]

part·ner·ship /paártnərship/ *n.* **1** the state of being a partner or partners. **2** a joint business. **3** a pair or group of partners.

part of speech *n.* each of the categories to which words are assigned in accordance with their grammatical and semantic functions (in English esp. noun, pronoun, adjective, adverb, verb, preposition, conjunction, and interjection).

par·took *past* of PARTAKE.

par·tridge /paártrij/ *n.* (*pl.* same or **par·tridg·es**) **1** any game bird of the genus *Perdix,* esp. *P. perdix* of Europe and Asia. **2** any other of various similar birds of Europe or N. America, including the snow partridge, ruffed grouse, and bobwhite. [ME *partrich,* etc. f. OF *perdriz,* etc. f. L *perdix –dicis:* for *–dge* cf. CABBAGE]

part-song *n.* a song with three or more voice parts, often without accompaniment, and harmonic rather than contrapuntal in character.

part time *adv.* less than the full time required by an activity.

part-time *adj.* occupying or using only part of one's working time. □□ **part-tim·er** *n.*

par·tu·ri·ent /paartŏŏreeənt, –tyŏŏr–/ *adj.* about to give birth. [L *parturire* be in labor, incept. f. *parere part–* bring forth]

par·tu·ri·tion /páartŏŏríshən, –tyŏŏ–, –chŏŏ–/ *n. Med.* the act of bringing forth young; childbirth. [LL *parturitio* (as PARTURIENT)]

par·ty[1] /páartee/ *n. & v. •n.* (*pl.* **·ties**) **1** a social gathering, usu. of invited guests. **2** a body of persons engaged in an activity or traveling together (*fishing party; search party*). **3** a group of people united in a cause, opinion, etc., esp. an organized political group. **4** a person or persons forming one side in an agreement or dispute. **5** (foll. by *to*) *Law* an accessory (to an action). **6** *colloq.* a person. **•** *v. tr. & intr.* (**·ties, ·tied**) entertain at or attend a party. [ME f. OF *partie* ult. f. L *partire*: see PART]

par·ty[2] /páartee/ *adj. Heraldry* divided into parts of different colors. [ME f. OF *parti* f. L (as PARTY[1])]

par·ty line *n.* **1** the policy adopted by a political party. **2** a telephone line shared by two or more subscribers.

par·ty poop·er *n. sl.* a person whose manner or behavior inhibits other people's enjoyment; a killjoy.

par·ty wall *n.* a wall common to two adjoining buildings or rooms.

par·ve·nu /paarvənŏŏ/ *n. & adj. •n.* (*fem.* **par·ve·nue**) **1** a person who has recently gained wealth or position. **2** an upstart. **•** *adj.* **1** associated with or characteristic of such a person. **2** upstart. [F, past part. of *parvenir* arrive f. L *pervenire* (as PER-, *venire* come)]

par·vis /paarvis/ *n.* (also **par·vise**) **1** an enclosed area in front of a cathedral, church, etc. **2** a room over a church porch. [ME f. OF *parvis* ult. f. LL *paradisus* PARADISE, a court in front of St. Peter's, Rome]

pas /paa/ *n.* (*pl.* same) a step in dancing, esp. in classical ballet.

pas·cal /paskál, paaskáal/ *n.* **1** a standard unit of pressure, equal to one newton per square meter. **2** (**Pascal** or **PASCAL**) *Computing* a programming language esp. used in education. [B. *Pascal*, Fr. scientist d. 1662: sense 2 so named because he built a calculating machine]

pas·chal /páskəl/ *adj.* **1** of or relating to the Jewish Passover. **2** of or relating to Easter. [ME f. OF *pascal* f. eccl.L *paschalis* f. *pascha* f. Gk *paskha* f. Aram. *pasha*, rel. to Heb. *pesah* PASSOVER]

pas·chal lamb *n.* **1** a lamb sacrificed at Passover. **2** Christ.

pas de chat /də shaá/ *n.* a leap in which each foot in turn is raised to the opposite knee.

pas de deux /də dố/ *n.* a dance for two persons.

pas glis·sé /gleesáy/ *n.* a gliding step.

pash /pash/ *n.* esp. *Brit. sl.* a brief infatuation. [abbr. of PASSION]

pa·sha /paashə/ *n.* (also **pa·cha**) *hist.* the title (placed after the name) of a Turkish officer of high rank, e.g., a military commander, the governor of a province, etc. [Turk. *paşa*, prob. = *başa* f. *baş* head, chief]

pashm /páshəm/ *n.* the underfur of some Tibetan animals, esp. that of goats as used for cashmere shawls.

Pash·to /póshtō/ *n. & adj. •n.* the official language of Afghanistan, also spoken in areas of Pakistan. **•** *adj.* of or in this language. [Pashto]

pa·so do·ble /páso dóblay/ *n.* **1** a ballroom dance based on a quick march played at bullfights. **2** a quick style of marching. [Sp., = double step]

pasque·flow·er /páskflowər/ *n.* a ranunculaceous plant, genus *Anemone*, with bell-shaped purple flowers and fernlike foliage. Al-

---

GRAMMAR TIP   **part of speech**

The Eight Parts of Speech. The English language has eight grammatical types of words, based on their function in a sentence:

Noun—names a person, place, thing, or quality: *Mrs. Jones, city, job, fairness*

Pronoun—takes the place of a noun or a group of words functioning as a noun: *he , she, it, they, who, myself, this, somebody*

Verb—expresses an action, an occurrence, or a state of being: *run, happen, seem*

Adjective—describes or modifies a noun or pronoun: *hot room, outrageous fortune, lucky few*

Adverb—describes or modifies a verb, adjective, or another adverb; answers when? where? how? or to what extent?: *act quickly, highly sensitive, very carefully done*

Preposition—shows the relationship between a noun or pronoun and another word, which the preposition introduces in a prepositional phrase: *above the clouds, despite the weather, against the tide*

Conjunction—joins two words, phrases, or clauses: *you and I, under the table or in the closet, you can run but you can't hide*

Interjection—expresses strong emotion (usually followed by an exclamation point): *holy cow! nonsense! bravo!*

As is clear by looking through the entries in a dictionary, many words can function as more than one part of speech, for example, *cool* in: *cool the bath water* (verb); *a cool shower* (adjective); and *he tried to act cool* (adverb).

---

so called **anemone**. [earlier *passe-flower* f. F *passe-fleur*. assim. to *pasque* = obs. *pasch* (as PASCHAL), Easter]

pas·quin·ade /páskwináyd/ *n.* a lampoon or satire, orig. one displayed in a public place. [It. *pasquinata* f. *Pasquino*, a statue in Rome on which abusive Latin verses were annually posted]

pass[1] /pas/ *v. & n.* **•** *v.* (*past part.* **passed**) (see also PAST). **1** *intr.* (often foll. by *along, by, down, on,* etc.) move onward; proceed, esp. past some point of reference (*saw the procession passing*). **2** *tr.* **a** go past; leave (a thing, etc.) on one side or behind in proceeding. **b** overtake, esp. in a vehicle. **c** go across (a frontier, mountain range, etc.). **3** *intr.* **a** be transferred or cause to be transferred from one person or place to another (*pass the butter; the estate passes to his son*). **4** *tr.* surpass; be too great for (*it passes my comprehension*). **5** *intr.* get through; effect a passage. **6** *intr.* **a** be accepted as adequate; go uncensured (*let the matter pass*). **b** (foll. by *as, for*) be accepted or currently known as. **c** (of a person with some African-American ancestry) be accepted as white. **7** *tr.* move; cause to go (*passed her hand over her face; passed a rope round it*). **8** *a tr.* (of a candidate in an examination) be successful. **b** *tr.* be successful in (an examination). **c** *tr.* (of an examiner) judge the performance of (a candidate) to be satisfactory. **9** *a tr.* (of a bill) be approved by a parliamentary body or process). **b** *tr.* cause or allow (a bill) to proceed to further legislative processes. **c** *intr.* (of a bill or proposal) be approved. **10** *intr.* **a** occur; elapse (*the remark passed unnoticed; time passes slowly*). **b** happen; be done or said (*heard what passed between them*). **11** *a intr.* circulate; be current. **b** *tr.* put into circulation (*was passing forged checks*). **12** *tr.* spend or use up (a certain time or period) (*passed the afternoon reading*). **13** *tr.* (also *absol.*) *Sports* send (the ball) to another player of one's own team. **14** *intr.* forgo one's turn or chance in a game, etc. **15** *intr.* (foll. by *to, into*) change from one form (to another). **16** *intr.* come to an end. **17** *tr.* discharge from the body as or with excreta. **18** *tr.* (foll. by *on, upon*) **a** utter (criticism) about. **b** pronounce (a judicial sentence) on. **19** *intr.* (often foll. by *on, upon*) adjudicate. **20** *tr.* not declare or pay (a dividend). **21** *tr.* cause (troops, etc.) to go by, esp. ceremonially. **•** *n.* **1** an act or instance of passing. **2** *Brit.* **a** success in an examination. **b** the status of a university degree without honors. **3** written permission to pass into or out of a place, or to be absent from quarters. **4** a ticket or permit giving free entry or access, etc. **5** *Sports* a transference of the ball to another player on the same side. **6** *Baseball* a base on balls. **7** a thrust in fencing. **8** a juggling trick. **9** an act of passing the hands over anything, as in conjuring or hypnotism. **10** a critical position (*has come to a fine pass*). □ **in passing 1** by the way. **2** in the course of speech, conversation, etc. **make a pass at** *colloq.* make amorous or sexual advances to. **pass around 1** distribute. **2** send or give to each of a number in turn. **pass away 1** *euphem.* die. **2** cease to exist; come to an end. **pass the buck** *colloq.* deny or shift responsibility. **pass by 1** go past. **2** disregard; omit. **pass (or run) one's eye over** see EYE. **pass muster** see MUSTER. **pass off 1** (of feelings, etc.) disappear gradually. **2** (of proceedings) be carried through (in a specified way). **3** (foll. by *as*) misrepresent (a person or thing) as something else. **4** evade or lightly dismiss (an awkward remark, etc.). **pass on 1** proceed on one's way. **2** *euphem.* die. **3** transmit to the next person in a series. **pass out 1** become unconscious. **2** *Brit. Mil.* complete one's training as a cadet. **3** distribute. **pass over 1** omit, ignore, or disregard. **2** ignore the claims of (a person) to promotion or advancement. **3** *euphem.* die. **pass through** experience. **pass the time of day** see TIME. **pass up** *colloq.* refuse or neglect (an opportunity, etc.). **pass water** urinate. □□ **pass·er** *n.* [ME f. OF *passer* ult. f. L *passus* PACE[1]]

pass[2] /pas/ *n.* **1** a narrow passage through mountains. **2** a navigable channel, esp. at the mouth of a river. □ **sell the pass** *Brit.* betray a cause. [ME, var. of PACE[1], infl. by F *pas* and by PASS[1]]

pass·a·ble /pásəbəl/ *adj.* **1** barely satisfactory; just adequate. **2** (of a road, pass, etc.) that can be passed. □□ **pass·a·ble·ness** *n.* **pass·a·bly** *adv.* [ME f. OF (as PASS[1])]

pas·sa·ca·glia /paasəkaalyə, pásəkalyə/ *n. Mus.* an instrumental piece usu. with a ground bass. [It. f. Sp. *pasacalle* f. *pasar* pass + *calle* street: orig. often played in the streets]

pas·sage[1] /pásij/ *n.* **1** the process or means of passing; transit. **2** = PASSAGEWAY. **3** the liberty or right to pass through. **4 a** the right of conveyance as a passenger by sea or air. **b** a journey by sea or air. **5** a transition from one state to another. **6 a** a short extract from a book, etc. **b** a section of a piece of music. **c** a detail or section of a painting. **7** the passing of a bill, etc., into law. **8** (in *pl.*) an interchange of words, etc. **9** *Anat.* a duct, etc., in the body. □ **work one's passage** earn a right (orig. of passage) by working for it. [ME f. OF (as PASS[1])]

pas·sage[2] /pásij/ *v.* **1** *intr.* (of a horse or rider) move sideways, by the pressure of the rein on the horse's neck and of the rider's leg on the opposite side. **2** *tr.* make (a horse) do this. [F *passager*, earlier *passéger* f. It. *passeggiare* to walk, pace f. *passeggio* walk f. L *passus* PACE[1]]

pas·sage of arms *n.* (also **pas·sage at arms**) a fight or dispute.

pas·sage·way /pásijway/ *n.* a narrow way for passing along, esp. with walls on either side; a corridor.

pas·sant /pásənt/ *adj.* *Heraldry* (of an animal) walking and looking to the dexter side, with three paws on the ground and the right forepaw raised. [ME f. OF, part. of *passer* PASS[1]]

pass·band /pásband/ *n.* a frequency band within which signals are transmitted by a filter without attenuation.

pass·book /pásbŏŏk/ *n.* a book issued by a bank, etc., to an account holder for recording amounts deposited and withdrawn.

pas·sé /pasáy/ *adj.* **1** behind the times; out-of-date. **2** past its prime. [F, past part. of *passer* PASS[1]]

passed pawn *n.* *Chess* a pawn that has advanced beyond the pawns on the other side.

passe·men·terie /pasméntree/ *n.* a trimming of gold or silver lace, braid, beads, etc. [F f. *passement* gold lace, etc. f. *passer* PASS[1]]

pas·sen·ger /pásinjər/ *n.* **1** a traveler in or on a public or private conveyance (other than the driver, pilot, crew, etc.). **2** *colloq.* a member of a team, crew, etc., who does no effective work. **3** (*attrib.*) for the use of passengers (*passenger seat*). [ME f. OF *passager* (adj.) passing (as PASSAGE[1]): *-n-* as in *messenger*, etc.]

pas·sen·ger mile *n.* one mile traveled by one passenger, as a unit of traffic.

pas·sen·ger pi·geon *n.* an extinct wild migratory pigeon of N. America.

passe-par·tout /páspaartŏŏ/ *n.* **1** a master key. **2** a picture frame (esp. for mounted photographs) consisting of two pieces of glass or one piece of glass and a backing of cardboard, etc., stuck together at the edges with adhesive paper or tape. **3** adhesive tape or paper used for this. [F, = passes everywhere]

pass·er·by /pásərbí/ *n.* (*pl.* **pass·ers·by**) a person who goes past, esp. by chance.

pas·ser·ine /pásərīn, –reen/ *n. & adj.* *•n.* any perching bird of the order Passeriformes, having feet with three toes pointing forward and one pointing backward, including sparrows and most land birds. *•adj.* **1** of or relating to this order. **2** of the size of a sparrow. [L *passer* sparrow]

pas seul /sŏl/ *n.* a solo dance. [F, = step]

pas·si·ble /pásibəl/ *adj.* capable of feeling or suffering. □□ **pas·si·bil·i·ty** *n.* [ME f. OF *passible* or LL *passibilis* f. L *pati* pass- suffer]

pas·sim /pásim/ *adv.* (of allusions or references in a published work) to be found at various places throughout the text. [L f. *passus* scattered f. *pandere* spread]

pass·ing /pásing/ *adj., adv., & n.* *•adj.* **1** in senses of PASS[1] *v.* **2** transient; fleeting (*a passing glance*). **3** cursory; incidental (*a passing reference*). *•adv.* exceedingly; very. *•n.* in senses of PASS[1] *v.* **2** *euphem.* the death of a person (*mourned his passing*). □□ **pass·ing·ly** *adv.*

pass·ing note *n.* *Mus.* a note not belonging to the harmony but interposed to secure a smooth transition.

pass·ing shot *n.* *Tennis* a shot aiming the ball beyond and out of reach of the other player.

pas·sion /páshən/ *n.* **1** strong barely controllable emotion. **2** an outburst of anger (*flew into a passion*). **3 a** intense sexual love. **b** a person arousing this. **4 a** strong enthusiasm (*has a passion for football*). **b** an object arousing this. **5** (**the Passion**) **a** *Relig.* the suffering of Christ during his last days. **b** a narrative of this from the Gospels. **c** a musical setting of any of these narratives. **6** *archaic* the suffering of any martyr. □□ **pas·sion·less** *adj.* [ME f. OF f. LL *passio –onis* f. L *pati* pass- suffer]

pas·sion·al /páshənəl/ *adj. & n.* *•adj.* of or marked by passion. *•n.* a book of the sufferings of saints and martyrs.

pas·sion·ate /páshənət/ *adj.* **1** dominated by or easily moved to strong feeling, esp. love or anger. **2** showing or caused by passion. □□ **pas·sion·ate·ly** *adv.* **pas·sion·ate·ness** *n.* [ME f. med.L *passionatus* (as PASSION)]

pas·sion·flow·er /páshənflowr, –flowr/ *n.* any climbing plant of the genus *Passiflora*, with a flower that was supposed to suggest the instruments of the Crucifixion.

pas·sion fruit *n.* the edible fruit of some species of passionflower, esp. *Passiflora edulis*. Also called **granadilla**.

pas·sion play *n.* a miracle play representing Christ's Passion.

Pas·sion Sun·day *n.* *Eccl.* formerly the fifth Sunday in Lent, now used synonymously for Palm Sunday.

Pas·sion·tide /páshəntīd/ *n.* the last two weeks of Lent.

Pas·sion Week *n.* *Eccl.* formerly the week between the fifth Sunday in Lent and Palm Sunday, now used synonymously for Holy Week.

pas·si·vate /pásivayt/ *v.tr.* make (esp. metal) passive (see PASSIVE). □□ **pas·si·va·tion** /–váyshən/ *n.*

pas·sive /pásiv/ *adj.* **1** suffering action; acted upon. **2** offering no opposition; submissive. **3 a** not active; inert. **b** (of a metal) abnormally unreactive. **4** *Gram.* designating the voice in which the subject undergoes the action of the verb (e.g., in *they were killed*). **5** (of a

debt) incurring no interest payment. **6** collecting or distributing the sun's energy without use of machinery (*passive solar heating*). □□ **pas·sive·ly** *adv.* **pas·sive·ness** *n.* **pas·siv·i·ty** /–sívətee/ *n.* [ME f. OF *passif –ive* or L *passivus* (as PASSION)]

pas·sive o·be·di·ence *n.* **1** surrender to another's will without cooperation. **2** compliance with commands irrespective of their nature.

pas·sive re·sist·ance *n.* a nonviolent refusal to cooperate.

pas·sive smok·ing *n.* the involuntary inhaling, esp. by a nonsmoker, of smoke from others' cigarettes, etc.

pass·key /páskee/ *n.* **1** a private key to a gate, etc., for special purposes. **2** a skeleton key or master key.

Pass·o·ver /pásōvər/ *n.* **1** the Jewish spring festival commemorating the liberation of the Israelites from Egyptian bondage, held from the 14th to the 21st day of the seventh month of the Jewish year. **2** = PASCHAL LAMB. [*pass over* = pass without touching, with ref. to the exemption of the Israelites from the death of the firstborn (Exod. 12)]

pass·port /páspawrt/ *n.* **1** an official document issued by a government certifying the holder's identity and citizenship, and entitling the holder to travel under its protection to and from foreign countries. **2** (foll. by *to*) a thing that ensures admission or attainment (*a passport to success*). [F *passeport* (as PASS[1], PORT[1])]

pass·word /páswərd/ *n.* **1** a selected word or phrase securing recognition, admission, etc., when used by those to whom it is disclosed. **2** *Computing* a word or string of characters securing access to an account or file for those authorized.

past /past/ *adj., n., prep., & adv.* *•adj.* **1** gone by in time and no longer existing (*in past years; the time is past*). **2** recently completed or gone by (*the past month; for some time past*). **3** relating to a former time (*past president*). **4** *Gram.* expressing a past action or state. *•n.* **1** (prec. by *the*) **a** a past time. **b** what has happened in past time (*cannot undo the past*). **2** a person's past life or career, esp. if discreditable (*a man with a past*). **3** a past tense or form. *•prep.* **1** beyond in time or place (*is past two o'clock; ran past the house*). **2** beyond the range, duration, or compass of (*past belief; past endurance*). *•adv.* so as to pass by (*hurried past*). □ **not put it past a person** believe it possible of a person. **past it** *colloq.* incompetent or unusable through age. [past part. of PASS[1] *v.*]

pas·ta /páastə/ *n.* **1** a dried flour paste used in various shapes in cooking (e.g., lasagna, spaghetti). **2** a cooked dish made from this. [It., = PASTE]

paste /payst/ *n. & v.* *•n.* **1** any moist fairly stiff mixture, esp. of powder and liquid. **2** a dough of flour with fat, water, etc., used in baking. **3** an adhesive of flour, water, etc., esp. for sticking paper and other light materials. **4** an easily spread preparation of ground meat, fish, etc. (*anchovy paste*). **5** a hard vitreous composition used in making imitation gems. **6** a mixture of clay, water, etc., used in making ceramic ware, esp. a mixture of low plasticity used in making porcelain. *•v.tr.* **1** fasten or coat with paste. **2** *sl.* **a** beat soundly. **b** bomb or bombard heavily. □□ **past·ing** *n.* (esp. in sense 2 of *v.*). [ME f. OF f. LL *pasta* small square medicinal lozenge f. Gk *pastē* f. *pastos* sprinkled]

paste·board /páystbawrd/ *n.* **1** a sheet of stiff material made by pasting together sheets of paper. **2** (*attrib.*) **a** flimsy; unsubstantial. **b** fake.

pas·tel /pastél/ *n.* **1** a crayon consisting of powdered pigments bound with a gum solution. **2** a work of art in pastel. **3** a light and subdued shade of a color. □□ **pas·tel·ist** *n.* **pas·tel·list** *n.* [F *pastel* or It. *pastello*, dimin. of *pasta* PASTE]

pas·tern /pástərn/ *n.* **1** the part of a horse's foot between the fetlock and the hoof. **2** a corresponding part in other animals. [ME *pastron* f. OF *pasturon* f. *pasture* hobble ult. f. L *pastorius* of a shepherd: see PASTOR]

paste-up *n.* a document prepared for copying, etc., by combining and pasting various sections on a backing.

pas·teur·ize /páschərīz, pástyə–/ *v.tr.* subject (milk, etc.) to the process of partial sterilization by heating. □□ **pas·teur·i·za·tion** /–záyshən/ *n.* **pas·teur·iz·er** *n.* [L. *Pasteur*, Fr. chemist d. 1895]

pas·tic·cio /pasteéchō, –cheéō/ *n.* (*pl.* **·cios**) = PASTICHE. [It.: see PASTICHE]

pas·tiche /pasteésh/ *n.* **1** a medley, esp. a picture or a musical composition, made up from or imitating various sources. **2** a literary or other work of art composed in the style of a well-known author. [F f. It. *pasticcio* ult. f. LL *pasta* PASTE]

pas·tille /pasteél, –tíl/ *n.* **1** a small candy or medicated lozenge. **2** a small roll of aromatic paste burned as a fumigator, etc. [F f. L *pastillus* little loaf, lozenge f. *panis* loaf]

pas·time /pástīm/ *n.* **1** a pleasant recreation or hobby. **2** a sport or game. [PASS[1] + TIME]

pas·tis /pasteés/ *n.* an aniseed-flavored liqueur. [F]

past mas·ter *n.* **1** a person who is especially adept or expert in an activity, subject, etc. **2** a person who has been a master in a guild, lodge, etc.

pas·tor /pástər/ *n.* **1** a priest or minister in charge of a church or a congregation. **2** a person exercising spiritual guidance. **3** a pink

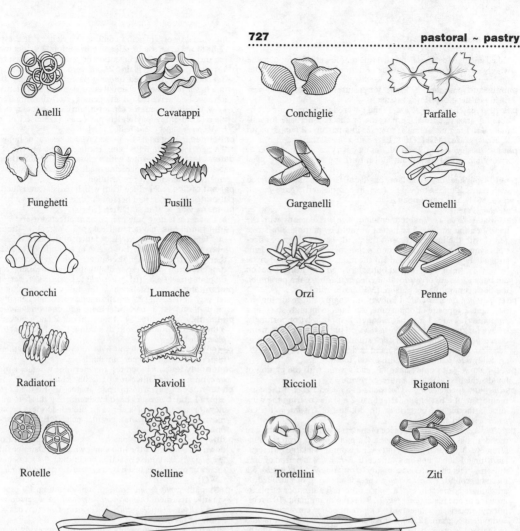

Anelli   Cavatappi   Conchiglie   Farfalle

Funghetti   Fusilli   Garganelli   Gemelli

Gnocchi   Lumache   Orzi   Penne

Radiatori   Ravioli   Riccioli   Rigatoni

Rotelle   Stelline   Tortellini   Ziti

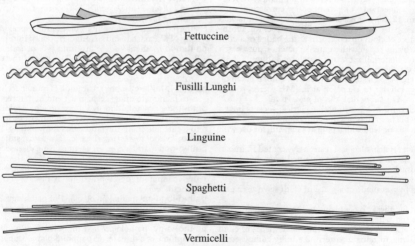

Fettuccine

Fusilli Lunghi

Linguine

Spaghetti

Vermicelli

pasta shapes

starling, *Sturnus roseus*, of Europe and Asia. □□ **pas•tor•ship** *n*. [ME f. AF & OF *pastour* f. L *pastor –oris* shepherd f. *pascere past-* feed, graze]

pas•to•ral /pástərəl/ *adj. & n.* ●*adj.* **1** of, relating to, or associated with shepherds or flocks and herds. **2** (of land) used for pasture. **3** (of a poem, picture, etc.) portraying country life, usu. in a romantic or idealized form. **4** of or appropriate to a pastor. ●*n.* **1** a pastoral poem, play, picture, etc. **2** a letter from a pastor (esp. a bishop) to the clergy or people. □□ **pas•to•ral•ism** *n.* **pas•to•ral•i•ty** /–álitee/ *n.* **pas•to•ral•ly** *adv.* [ME f. L *pastoralis* (as PASTOR)]

pas•to•rale /pástəraál, –rál, –raálee/ *n.* (*pl.* **pas•to•rales** or **pas•to•ra•li** /–lee/) **1** a slow instrumental composition in compound time,

usu. with drone notes in the bass. **2** a simple musical play with a rural subject. [It. (as PASTORAL)]

pas•to•ral staff *n.* a bishop's crosier.

pas•to•ral the•ol•o•gy *n.* that considering religious truth in relation to spiritual needs.

pas•tor•ate /pástərət/ *n.* **1** the office or tenure of a pastor. **2** a body of pastors.

past per•fect *n.* = PLUPERFECT.

pas•tra•mi /pəstraámee/ *n.* seasoned smoked beef. [Yiddish]

pas•try /páystree/ *n.* (*pl.* **•tries**) **1** a dough of flour, fat, and water

See page xx for the **Key to Pronunciation**.

baked and used as a base and covering for pies, etc. **2 a** food, made wholly or partly of this. **b** a piece or item of this food. [PASTE after OF *pastaierie*]

pas·tur·age /páschərij/ *n.* **1** land for pasture. **2** the process of pasturing cattle, etc. [OF (as PASTURE)]

pas·ture /páschər/ *n. & v.* ●*n.* **1** land covered with grass, etc., suitable for grazing animals, esp. cattle or sheep. **2** herbage for animals. ●*v.* **1** *tr.* put (animals) to graze in a pasture. **2** *intr. & tr.* (of animals) graze. [ME f. OF f. LL *pastura* (as PASTOR)]

past·y[1] /pástee/ *n.* esp. *Brit.* (*pl.* **·ies**) a pastry case with a sweet or savory filling, baked without a dish to shape it. [ME f. OF *pasté* ult. f. LL *pasta* PASTE]

pas·ty[2] /páystee/ *adj.* (**pas·ti·er, pas·ti·est**) **1** of or like or covered with paste. **2** unhealthily pale (esp. in complexion) (*pasty-faced*). □□ **past·i·ly** *adv.* **past·i·ness** *n.*

Pat. *abbr.* Patent.

pat[1] /pat/ *v. & n.* ●*v.* (**pat·ted, pat·ting**) **1** *tr.* strike gently with the hand or a flat surface. **2** *tr.* flatten or mold by patting. **3** *tr.* strike gently with the inner surface of the hand, esp. as a sign of affection, sympathy, or congratulation. **4** *intr.* beat lightly. ●*n.* **1** a light stroke or tap, esp. with the hand in affection, etc. **2** the sound made by this. **3** a small mass (esp. of butter) formed by patting. □ **pat on the back** a gesture of approval or congratulation. **pat a person on the back** congratulate a person. [ME, prob. imit.]

pat[2] /pat/ *adj. & adv.* ●*adj.* **1** known thoroughly and ready for any occasion. **2** apposite or opportune, esp. unconvincingly so (*gave a pat answer*). ●*adv.* **1** in a pat manner. **2** appositely; opportunely. □ **have** (or **know**) **down pat** (*Brit.* **have off pat**) know or have memorized perfectly. **stand pat 1** stick stubbornly to one's opinion or decision. **2** *Poker* retain one's hand as dealt; not draw other cards. □□ **pat·ly** *adv.* **pat·ness** *n.* [16th c.: rel. to PAT[1]]

pat-a-cake *n.* (also **pat·ty-cake**) a child's game with the patting of hands (the first words of a nursery rhyme).

pa·ta·gi·um /pətáyjeeəm/ *n.* (*pl.* **pa·ta·gi·a** /–jeeə/) *Zool.* **1** the wing membrane of a bat or similar animal. **2** a scale covering the wing joint in moths and butterflies. [med.L use of L *patagium* f. Gk *patageion* gold edging]

patch /pach/ *n. & v.* ●*n.* **1** a piece of material or metal, etc., used to mend a hole or as reinforcement. **2** a pad worn to protect an injured eye. **3** a dressing, etc., put over a wound. **4** a large or irregular distinguishable area on a surface. **5** *Brit. colloq.* a period of time in terms of its characteristic quality (*went through a bad patch*). **6** a piece of ground. **7** *Brit. colloq.* an area assigned to or patrolled by an authorized person, esp. a police officer. **8** a number of plants growing in one place (*brier patch*). **9** a scrap or remnant. **10** a temporary electrical connection. **11** a temporary correction in a computer program. **12** *hist.* a small disk, etc., of black silk attached to the face, worn esp. by women in the 17th–18th c. for adornment. **13** *Mil.* a piece of cloth on a uniform as the badge of a unit. ●*v.tr.* **1** (often foll. by *up*) repair with a patch or patches; put a patch or patches on. **2** (of material) serve as a patch to. **3** (often foll. by *up*) put together, esp. hastily or in a makeshift way. **4** (foll. by *up*) settle (a quarrel, etc.) esp. hastily or temporarily. □ **not a patch on** *Brit. colloq.* greatly inferior to. □□ **patch·er** *n.* [ME *pacche, patche,* perh. var. of *peche* f. OF *pieche* dial. var. of *piece* PIECE]

patch·board /páchbawrd/ *n.* a board with electrical sockets linked to enable changeable permutations of connection.

patch cord *n.* an insulated lead with a plug at each end, for use with a patchboard.

patch·ou·li /pəchoolee, páchoolee/ *n.* **1** a strongly scented E. Indian plant, *Pogostemon cablin.* **2** the perfume obtained from this. [a native name in Madras]

patch pan·el *n.* = PATCHBOARD.

patch pock·et *n.* a pocket made of a piece of cloth sewn on a garment.

patch test *n.* a test for allergy by applying to the skin patches containing allergenic substances.

patch·work /páchwərk/ *n.* **1** sewn work using small pieces of cloth with different designs, forming a pattern. **2** a thing composed of various small pieces or fragments.

patch·y /páchee/ *adj.* (**patch·i·er, patch·i·est**) **1** uneven in quality. **2** having or existing in patches. □□ **patch·i·ly** *adv.* **patch·i·ness** *n.*

pate /payt/ *n. colloq.* or *joc.* **1** the top of the head **2** the head, esp. representing the seat of intellect. [ME: orig. unkn.]

pâ·té /paatáy, pa–/ *n.* a rich paste or spread of finely chopped and spiced meat or fish, etc. [F f. OF *pasté* (as PASTY[1])]

pâte /paat/ *n.* the paste of which porcelain is made. [F, = PASTE]

pâ·té de foie gras /də fwaa graá/ *n.* a paste of fatted goose liver.

pa·tel·la /pətélə/ *n.* (*pl.* **pa·tel·lae** /–lee/) the kneecap. □□ **pa·tel·lar** *adj.* **pa·tel·late** /–lət/ *adj.* [L, dimin. of *patina:* see PATEN]

pat·en /pátən/ *n.* **1** a shallow dish used for the bread at the Eucharist. **2** a thin circular plate of metal. [ME ult. f. OF *patene* or L *patena, patina* shallow dish f. Gk *patanē* a plate]

pat·ent /pát'nt/ *n., adj., & v.* ●*n.* **1** a government authority to an

individual or organization conferring a right or title, esp. the sole right to make or use or sell some invention. **2** a document granting this authority. **3** an invention or process protected by it. ●*adj.* **1** /páyt'nt/ obvious; plain. **2** conferred or protected by patent. **3 a** made and marketed under a patent; proprietary. **b** to which one has a proprietary claim. **4** such as might be patented; ingenious; well-contrived. **5** (of an opening, etc.) allowing free access. ●*v.tr.* obtain a patent for (an invention). □□ **pa·ten·cy** *n.* **pat·ent·a·ble** *adj.* **pat·ent·ly** /páytəntlee, pát–/ *adv.* (in sense 1 of *adj.*). [ME f. OF *patent* and L *patēre* lie open]

pat·en·tee /pát'ntee/ *n.* **1** a person who takes out or holds a patent. **2** a person for the time being entitled to the benefit of a patent.

pat·ent leath·er *n.* leather with a glossy varnished surface.

pat·ent med·i·cine *n.* medicine made and marketed under a patent and available without prescription.

pat·ent of·fice *n.* an office from which patents are issued.

pat·en·tor /pát'ntər/ *n.* a person or body that grants a patent.

pa·ter /páytər/ *n. Brit. sl.* father. [L]

▶This term is now only in jocular or affected use.

pa·ter·fa·mil·i·as /páytərfəmíleeas, paá–, pátər–/ *n.* the male head of a family or household. [L, = father of the family]

pa·ter·nal /pətə́rnəl/ *adj.* **1** of or like or appropriate to a father. **2** fatherly. **3** related through the father. **4** (of a government, etc.) limiting freedom and responsibility by well-meaning regulations. □□ **pa·ter·nal·ly** *adv.* [LL *paternalis* f. L *paternus* f. *pater* father]

pa·ter·nal·ism /pətə́rnəlizəm/ *n.* the policy of governing in a paternal way, or behaving paternally to one's associates or subordinates. □□ **pa·ter·nal·ist** *n.* **pa·ter·nal·is·tic** *adj.* **pa·ter·nal·is·ti·cal·ly** *adv.*

pa·ter·ni·ty /pətə́rnitee/ *n.* **1** fatherhood. **2** one's paternal origin. **3** the source or authorship of a thing. [ME f. OF *paternité* or LL *paternitas*]

pa·ter·ni·ty suit *n.* a lawsuit held to determine whether a certain man is the father of a certain child.

pa·ter·ni·ty test *n.* a blood test to determine whether a man may be or cannot be the father of a particular child.

pa·ter·nos·ter /páytərnóstər, paá–, pátər–/ *n.* **1 a** the Lord's Prayer, esp. in Latin. **b** a rosary bead indicating that this is to be said. **2** an elevator consisting of a series of linked doorless compartments moving continuously on a circular belt. [OE f. L *pater noster* our father]

path /path/ *n.* (*pl.* **paths** /paathz/) **1** a way or track laid or trodden down for walking. **2** the line along which a person or thing moves (*flight path*). **3** a course of action or conduct. **4** a sequence of movements or operations taken by a system. □□ **path·less** *adj.* [OE *pæth* f. WG]

-path /path/ *comb. form* forming nouns denoting: **1** a practitioner of curative treatment (*homoeopath; osteopath*). **2** a person who suffers from a disease (*psychopath*). [back-form. f. –PATHY, or f. Gk –*pathēs* –sufferer (as PATHOS)]

Pa·than /pətaán/ *n.* a member of a Pashto-speaking people inhabiting NW Pakistan and SE Afghanistan. [Hindi]

pa·thet·ic /pəthétik/ *adj.* **1** arousing pity or sadness or contempt. **2** *colloq.* miserably inadequate. **3** *archaic* of the emotions. □□ **pa·thet·i·cal·ly** *adv.* [F *pathétique* f. LL *patheticus* f. Gk *pathētikos* (as PATHOS)]

pa·thet·ic fal·la·cy *n.* the attribution of human feelings and responses to inanimate things, esp. in art and literature.

path·find·er /páthfindər/ *n.* **1** a person who explores new territory, investigates a new subject, etc. **2** an aircraft or its pilot sent ahead to locate and mark the target area for bombing.

patho- /páthō/ *comb. form* disease. [Gk *pathos* suffering: see PATHOS]

path·o·gen /páthəjən/ *n.* an agent causing disease. □□ **path·o·gen·ic** /–jénik/ *adj.* **pa·thog·e·nous** /–thójənəs/ *adj.* [PATHO- + –GEN]

path·o·gen·e·sis /páthəjénisis/ *n.* (also **pa·thog·e·ny** /pəthójənee/) the manner of development of a disease. □□ **path·o·ge·net·ic** /–jinétik/ *adj.*

path·o·log·i·cal /páthəlójikəl/ *adj.* **1** of pathology. **2** of or caused by a physical or mental disorder (*a pathological fear of spiders*). □□ **path·o·log·i·cal·ly** *adv.*

pa·thol·o·gy /pəthóləjee/ *n.* **1** the science of bodily diseases. **2** the symptoms of a disease. □□ **pa·thol·o·gist** *n.* [F *pathologie* or mod.L *pathologia* (as PATHO-, –LOGY)]

pa·thos /páythos, –thaws, –thōs/ *n.* a quality in speech, writing, events, etc., that evokes pity or sadness. [Gk *pathos* suffering, rel. to *paskhō* suffer, *penthos* grief]

path·way /páthway/ *n.* **1** a path or its course. **2** *Biochem.*, etc., a sequence of reactions undergone in a living organism.

-pathy /pəthee/ *comb. form* forming nouns denoting: **1** curative treatment (*allopathy; homeopathy*). **2** feeling (*telepathy*). [Gk *patheia* suffering]

pa·tience /páyshəns/ *n.* **1** calm endurance of hardship, provocation, pain, delay, etc. **2** tolerant perseverance or forbearance. **3** the capacity for calm self-possessed waiting. **4** esp. *Brit.* = SOLITAIRE 3. □ **have no patience with 1** be unable to tolerate. **2** be irritated by. [ME f. OF f. L *patientia* (as PATIENT)]

pa·tient /páyshənt/ *adj. & n.* ●*adj.* having or showing patience. ●*n.*

a person receiving or registered to receive medical treatment. □□ **pa·tient·ly** *adv.* [ME f. OF f. L *patiens –entis* pres. part. of *pati* suffer]

pat·i·na /pǎteĕnǝ, pǎt'nǝ/ *n.* (*pl.* **pat·i·nas**) **1** a film, usu. green, formed on the surface of old bronze. **2** a similar film on other surfaces. **3** a gloss produced by age on woodwork. □□ **pat·i·nat·ed** /pǎt'-naytid/ *adj.* **pat·i·na·tion** *n.* [It. f. L *patina* dish]

pat·i·o /pǎteeō/ *n.* (*pl.* **·os**) **1** a paved usu. roofless area adjoining and belonging to a house. **2** an inner court open to the sky esp. in a Spanish or Spanish-American house. [Sp.]

pa·tis·se·rie /pǝtísǝree, paateesreé/ *n.* **1** a shop where pastries are made and sold. **2** pastries collectively. [F *pâtisserie* f. med.L *pasticium* pastry f. *pasta* PASTE]

pat·ois /patwáa, pátwaa/ *n.* (*pl.* same, *pronunc.* /-waaz/) the dialect of the common people in a region, differing fundamentally from the literary language. [F, = rough speech, perh. f. OF *patoier* treat roughly f. *patte* paw]

pa·tri·arch /páytreeaark/ *n.* **1** the male head of a family or tribe. **2** (often in *pl.*) *Bibl.* any of those regarded as fathers of the human race, esp. Adam and his descendants, including Noah; Abraham, Isaac, and Jacob; or the sons of Jacob, founders of the tribes of Israel. **3** *Eccl.* **a** the title of a chief bishop, esp. those presiding over the Churches of Antioch, Alexandria, Constantinople, and (formerly) Rome; now also the title of the heads of certain autocephalous Orthodox Churches. **b** (in the Roman Catholic Church) a bishop ranking next above primates and metropolitans, and immediately below the pope. **c** the head of a Uniate community. **d** a high dignitary of the Mormon church. **4 a** the founder of an order, science, etc. **b** a venerable old man. **c** the oldest member of a group. □□ **pa·tri·ar·chal** /–áarkǝl/ *adj.* **pa·tri·ar·chal·ly** /–áarkǝlee/ *adv.* [ME f. OF *patriarche* f. eccl.L *patriarcha* f. Gk *patriarkhēs* f. *patria* family f. *patēr* father + *–arkhēs* ruler]

pa·tri·arch·ate /páytreeaarkǝt, –kayt/ *n.* **1** the office, see, or residence of an ecclesiastical patriarch. **2** the rank of a tribal patriarch. [med.L *patriarchatus* (as PATRIARCH)]

pa·tri·arch·y /páytreeaarkee/ *n.* (*pl.* **·ies**) a system of society, government, etc., ruled by a man or men and with descent through the male line. □□ **pa·tri·arch·ism** *n.* [med.L *patriarchia* f. Gk *patriarkhia* (as PATRIARCH)]

pa·tri·cian /pǝtríshǝn/ *n. & adj.* **●** *n.* **1** *hist.* a member of the ancient Roman nobility (cf. PLEBEIAN). **2** *hist.* a nobleman in some Italian republics. **3** an aristocrat. **4** a person of educated or refined tastes and upbringing. **●** *adj.* **1** noble; aristocratic; well-bred. **2** *hist.* of the ancient Roman nobility. [ME f. OF *patricien* f. L *patricius* having a noble father f. *pater patris* father]

pa·tri·ci·ate /pǝtrísheeǝt, –ayt/ *n.* **1** a patrician order; an aristocracy. **2** the rank of patrician. [L *patriciatus* (as PATRICIAN)]

pat·ri·cide /pátrisíd/ *n.* = PARRICIDE (esp. with reference to the killing of one's father). □□ **pat·ri·cid·al** /–síd'l/ *adj.* [LL *patricida, patricidium,* alt. of L *parricida, parricidium* (see PARRICIDE) after *pater* father]

pat·ri·lin·e·al /pátrilíneeǝl/ *adj.* of or relating to, or based on kinship with, the father or descent through the male line. [L *pater patris* father + LINEAL]

pat·ri·mo·ny /pátrimōnee/ *n.* (*pl.* **·nies**) **1** property inherited from one's father or ancestor. **2** a heritage. **3** the endowment of a church, etc. □□ **pat·ri·mo·ni·al** *adj.* [ME *patrimoigne* f. OF *patrimoine* f. L *patrimonium* f. *pater patris* father]

pa·tri·ot /páytreeǝt, –ot/ *n.* a person who is devoted to and ready to support or defend his or her country. □□ **pa·tri·ot·ic** /–reeótik/ *adj.* **pa·tri·ot·i·cal·ly** *adv.* **pa·tri·ot·ism** *n.* [F *patriote* f. LL *patriota* f. Gk *patriōtēs* f. *patrios* of one's fathers f. *patēr patros* father]

pa·tris·tic /pǝtrístik/ *adj.* of the early Christian writers or their work. □□ **pa·tris·tics** *n.pl.* (usu. treated as *sing.*). [G *patristisch* f. L *pater patris* father]

pa·trol /pǝtról/ *n. & v.* **●** *n.* **1** the act of walking or traveling around an area, esp. at regular intervals, in order to protect or supervise it. **2** one or more persons or vehicles assigned or sent out on patrol, esp. a detachment of guards, police, etc. **3 a** a detachment of troops sent out to reconnoiter. **b** such reconnaissance. **4** a routine operational voyage of a ship or aircraft. **5** a routine monitoring of astronomical or other phenomena. **6** *Brit.* an official controlling traffic where children cross the road. **7** a unit of Boy or Girl Scouts. **●** *v.* (**pa·trolled, pa·trol·ling**) **1** *tr.* carry out a patrol of. **2** *intr.* act as a patrol. □□ **pa·trol·ler** *n.* [F *patrouiller* paddle in mud f. *patte* paw: (n.) f. G *Patrolle* f. F *patrouille*]

pa·trol car *n.* a police car used in patrolling roads and streets.

pa·trol·man /pǝtrólmǝn/ *n.* (*pl.* **·men**) a police officer assigned to or patrolling a specific route.

pa·trol·o·gy /pǝtrólǝjee/ *n.* (*pl.* **·gies**) **1** the study of the writings of the Fathers of the Church. **2** a collection of such writings. □□ **pat·ro·log·i·cal** /pátrǝlójikǝl/ *adj.* **pa·trol·o·gist** *n.* [Gk *patēr patros* father]

pa·trol wag·on *n.* a police van for transporting prisoners.

pa·tron /páytrǝn/ *n.* (*fem.* **pa·tron·ess**) **1** a person who gives financial or other support to a person, cause, work of art, etc., esp. one who buys works of art. **2** a usu. regular customer of a store, etc. **3** *Rom. Antiq.* **a** the former owner of a freed slave. **b** the protector

729 **patina ~ pauper**

of a client. **4** *Brit.* a person who has the right of presenting a member of the clergy to a benefice. [ME f. OF f. L *patronus* protector of clients, defender f. *pater patris* father]

pa·tron·age /pátrǝnij/ *n.* **1** the support, promotion, or encouragement given by a patron. **2** a patronizing or condescending manner. **3 a** the power to appoint others to government jobs. **b** the distribution of such jobs. **4** *Rom. Antiq.* the rights and duties or position of a patron. **5** *Brit.* the right of presenting a member of the clergy to a benefice, etc. **6** a customer's support for a store, etc. [ME f. OF (as PATRON)]

pa·tron·ize /páytrǝnīz, pát–/ *v.tr.* **1** treat condescendingly. **2** act as a patron toward (a person, cause, artist, etc.); support; encourage. **3** frequent (a store, etc.) as a customer. □□ **pa·tron·i·za·tion** *n.* **pa·tron·iz·er** *n.* **pa·tron·iz·ing** *adj.* **pa·tron·iz·ing·ly** *adv.* [obs. F *patroniser* or med.L *patronizare* (as PATRON)]

pa·tron saint *n.* the protecting or guiding saint of a person, place, etc.

pat·ro·nym·ic /pátrǝnímik/ *n. & adj.* **●** *n.* a name derived from the name of a father or ancestor, e.g., *Johnson, O'Brien, Ivanovich.* **●** *adj.* (of a name) so derived. [LL *patronymicus* f. Gk *patrōnumikos* f. *patrōnumos* f. *patēr patros* father + *onuma, onoma* name]

pa·troon /pǝtrōn/ *n.* *hist.* a landowner with manorial privileges under the Dutch governments of New York and New Jersey. [Du., = PATRON]

pat·sy /pátsee/ *n.* (*pl.* **·sies**) *sl.* a person who is deceived, ridiculed, tricked, etc. [20th c.: orig. unkn.]

pat·ten /pát'n/ *n.* *hist.* a shoe or clog with a raised sole or set on an iron ring, for walking in mud, etc. [ME f. OF *patin* f. *patte* paw]

pat·ter¹ /pátǝr/ *v. & v.* **●** *v.* **1** *intr.* make a rapid succession of taps, as of rain on a windowpane. **2** *intr.* run with quick short steps. **3** *tr.* cause (water, etc.) to patter. **●** *n.* a rapid succession of taps, short light steps, etc. [PAT¹]

pat·ter² /pátǝr/ *n. & v.* **●** *n.* **1 a** the rapid speech used by a comedian or introduced into a song. **b** the words of a comic song. **2** the words used by a person selling or promoting a product; a sales pitch. **3** the special language or jargon of a profession, class, etc. **4** *colloq.* mere talk; chatter. **●** *v.* **1** *tr.* repeat (prayers, etc.) in a rapid mechanical way. **2** *intr.* talk glibly or mechanically. [ME f. *pater* = PATERNOSTER]

pat·tern /pátǝrn/ *n. & v.* **●** *n.* **1** a repeated decorative design on wallpaper, cloth, a carpet, etc. **2** a regular or logical form, order, or arrangement of parts (*behavior pattern; the pattern of one's daily life*). **3** a model or design, e.g., of a garment, from which copies can be made. **4** an example of excellence; an ideal; a model (*a pattern of elegance*). **5** the prescribed flight path for an airplane taking off or esp. landing at an airport. **6** a wooden or metal figure from which a mold is made for a casting. **7** a sample (of cloth, wallpaper, etc.). **8** the marks made by shots, bombs, etc. on a target or target area. **9** a random combination of shapes or colors. **●** *v.tr.* **1** (usu. foll. by *after, on*) model (a thing) on a design, etc. **2** decorate with a pattern. [ME *patron* (see PATRON): differentiated in sense and spelling since the 16th–17th c.]

pat·tern bomb·ing *n.* bombing over a large area, not on a single target.

pat·ty /pátee/ *n.* (*pl.* **·ties**) **1** a small flat cake of ground meat, etc., sometimes breaded and fried. **2** esp. *Brit.* a little pie or pastry. [F *pâté* PASTY¹]

pat·ty·pan /páteepan/ *n.* **1** a flattish summer squash having a scalloped edge. **2** a pan for baking a patty.

pat·u·lous /páchǝlǝs/ *adj.* **1** (of branches, etc.) spreading. **2** open; expanded. □□ **pat·u·lous·ly** *adj.* **pat·u·lous·ness** *n.* [L *patulus* f. *patēre* be open]

pau·a /pówǝ/ *n.* **1** a large edible New Zealand shellfish of the genus *Haliotis.* **2** its ornamental shell. **3** a fishhook made from this. [Maori]

pau·ci·ty /páwsitee/ *n.* smallness of number or quantity. [ME f. OF *paucité* or f. L *paucitas* f. *paucus* few]

Pau·li ex·clu·sion prin·ci·ple /páwlee, pów–/ *n.* *Physics* the assertion that no two fermions can have the same quantum number. [W. *Pauli,* Austrian physicist d. 1958]

Pau·line /páwlīn, –leen/ *adj.* of or relating to St. Paul (*the Pauline epistles*). [ME f. med.L *Paulinus* f. L *Paulus* Paul]

pau·low·ni·a /pawlṓneeǝ/ *n.* any Asian tree of the genus *Paulownia,* with fragrant purple flowers. [Anna *Paulovna,* Russian princess d. 1865]

paunch /pawnch/ *n.* **1** the belly or stomach, esp. when protruding. **2** a ruminant's first stomach; the rumen. □□ **paunch·y** *adj.* (**paunch·i·er, paunch·i·est**). **paunch·i·ness** *n.* [ME f. AF *pa(u)nche,* ONF *panche* ult. f. L *pantex panticis* bowels]

pau·per /páwpǝr/ *n.* **1** a person without means; a beggar. **2** a person dependent on private or government charity. □□ **pau·per·dom** /–pǝrdǝm/ *n.* **pau·per·ism** /–rizǝm/ *n.* **pau·per·ize** *v.tr.* **pau·per·i·za·tion** /–rízáysh'n/ *n.* [L, = poor]

pause /pawz/ *n. &v.* •*n.* **1** an interval of inaction, esp. when due to hesitation; a temporary stop. **2** a break in speaking or reading; a silence. **3** *Mus.* a fermata. •*v.* **1** *intr.* make a pause; wait. **2** *intr.* (usu. foll. by *upon*) linger over (a word, etc.). **3** *tr.* cause to hesitate or pause. □ **give pause to** cause (a person) to hesitate. [ME f. OF *pause* or L *pausa* f. Gk *pausis* f. *pauō* stop]

pa·vane /pəváan, –ván/ *n.* (also **pav·an**) *hist.* **1** a stately dance in elaborate clothing. **2** the music for this. [F *pavane* f. Sp. *pavana*, perh. f. *pavon* peacock]

pave /payv/ *v.tr.* **1** cover (a street, floor, etc.) with paving, etc. **2** cover or strew (a floor, etc.) with anything (*paved with flowers*). □ **pave the way for** prepare for; facilitate. □□ **pav·er** *n.* **pav·ing** *n.* [ME f. OF *paver*, back-form. (as PAVEMENT)]

pa·vé /paváy, pávay/ *n.* **1** a paved street, road, or path. **2** a setting of jewels placed closely together. [F, past part. of *paver*: see PAVE]

pave·ment /páyvmənt/ *n.* **1** the hard, durable covering of a street, driveway, etc., as of asphalt or concrete. **2** esp. *Brit.* = SIDEWALK. **3** a roadway. **4** *Zool.* a pavementlike formation of close-set teeth, scales, etc. [ME f. OF f. L *pavimentum* f. *pavire* beat, ram]

pa·vil·ion /pəvílyən/ *n. & v.* •*n.* **1** a usu. open building at a fairground, park, etc., used for exhibits, refreshments, etc. **2** a decorative building in a garden. **3** a tent, esp. a large one at a show, fair, etc. **4** a building used for entertainments. **5** a temporary stand at an exhibition. **6** a detached building that is part of a connected set of buildings, as at a hospital. **7** the part of a cut gemstone below the girdle. •*v.tr.* enclose in or provide with a pavilion. [ME f. OF *pavillon* f. L *papilio –onis* butterfly, tent]

pav·ing stone *n.* a large flat usu. rectangular piece of stone, etc., for paving.

pav·ior *n.* (also *Brit.* **pav·iour**) see PAVE.

pa·vlo·va /pavlóvə/ *n.* esp. *Austral. & NZ* a meringue dessert served with cream and fruit. [A. *Pavlova*, Russ. ballerina d. 1931]

Pav·lov·i·an /pavlóviən/ *adj.* of or relating to I. P. Pavlov, Russian physiologist d. 1936, or his work, esp. on conditioned reflexes.

paw /paw/ *n. & v.* •*n.* **1** a foot of an animal having claws or nails. **2** *colloq.* a person's hand. •*v.* **1** *tr.* strike or scrape with a paw or foot. **2** *intr.* scrape the ground with a paw or hoof. **3** *tr. colloq.* handle awkwardly or indecently. [ME *pawe, powe* f. OF *poue*, etc. ult. f. Frank.]

pawk·y /páwkee/ *adj.* (**pawk·i·er, pawk·i·est**) *Sc. & Brit. dial.* **1** dryly humorous. **2** shrewd. □□ **pawk·i·ly** *adv.* **pawk·i·ness** *n.* [Sc. & North Engl. dial. *pawk* trick, of unkn. orig.]

pawl /pawl/ *n. & v.* •*n.* **1** a lever with a catch for the teeth of a wheel or bar. **2** *Naut.* a short bar used to lock a capstan, windlass, etc., to prevent it from recoiling. •*v.tr.* secure (a capstan, etc.) with a pawl. [perh. f. LG & Du. *pal*, rel. to *pal* fixed]

pawn[1] /pawn/ *n.* **1** *Chess* a piece of the smallest size and value. **2** a person used by others for their own purposes. [ME f. AF *poun*, OF *peon* f. med.L *pedo –onis* foot soldier f. L *pes pedis* foot: cf. PEON]

pawn[2] /pawn/ *v. & v.* •*v.tr.* **1** deposit an object, esp. with a pawnbroker, as security for money lent. **2** pledge or wager (one's life, honor, word, etc.). •*n.* **1** an object left as security for money, etc., lent. **2** anything or any person left with another as security, etc. [ME f. OF *pan, pand, pant*, pledge, security f. WG]

pawn·bro·ker /páwnbrōkər/ *n.* a person who lends money at interest on the security of personal property pawned. □□ **pawn·bro·king** *n.*

Paw·nee /pawnee, paa–/ *n.* **1 a** a N. American people native to Kansas and Nebraska. **b** a member of this people. **2** the language of this people.

pawn·shop /páwnshop/ *n.* a shop where pawnbroking is conducted.

paw·paw /páwpaw/ *n.* (also **pa·paw**) a N. American tree, *Asimina triloba*, with purple flowers and edible fruit. [earlier *papay(a)* f. Sp. & Port. *papaya*, of Carib orig.]

pax /paks, paaks/ *n.* **1** the kiss of peace. **2** (as *int.*) *Brit. sl.* a call for a truce (used esp. by schoolchildren). **3** (also **Pax**) a historical period of peace, usu. enforced by a dominant military power (*Pax Romana*). [ME f. L, = peace]

pay[1] /pay/ *v., n., & adj.* •*v.tr.* (*past* and *past part.* **paid** /payd/) **1** (also *absol.*) give (a person, etc.) what is due for services done, goods received, debts incurred, etc. (*paid him in full; I assure you I have paid*). **2 a** give (a usu. specified amount) for work done, a debt, a ransom, etc. (*they pay $6 an hour*). **b** (foll. by *to*) hand over the amount of (a debt, wages, recompense, etc.) to (*paid the money to the assistant*). **3 a** give, bestow, or express (attention, respect, etc.) (*paid them no heed*). **b** make (a visit, a call, etc.) (*paid a visit to their uncle*). **4** (also *absol.*) (of a business, undertaking, attitude, etc.) be profitable or advantageous to (a person, etc.). **5** reward or punish (*can never pay you for what you have done for us; I shall pay you for that*). **6** (usu. as **paid** *adj.*) recompense (work, time, etc.) (*paid holiday*). **7** (usu. foll. by *out, away*) let out (a rope) by slackening it. •*n.* wages; payment. •*adj.* **1** requiring payment for (a service, etc.) **2** requiring payment of a coin for use (*pay phone*). □ **in the pay of** employed by. **pay dearly** (usu. foll. by *for*) **1** obtain

at a high cost, great effort, etc. **2** suffer for a wrongdoing, etc. **pay for 1** hand over the price of. **2** bear the cost of. **3** suffer or be punished for (a fault, etc.). **pay in** pay (money) into a bank account. **pay its** (or **one's**) **way** cover costs; not be indebted. **pay one's dues** earn status or respect from hard effort. **pay one's last respects** show respect toward a dead person by attending the funeral. **pay off 1** dismiss (workers) with a final payment. **2** *colloq.* yield good results; succeed. **3** pay (a debt) in full. **4** (of a ship) turn to leeward through the movement of the helm. **pay out 1** spend; hand out (money). **2** = PAY BACK. **3** let out (a rope). **pay the piper 1** bear a cost or consequence. **2** (**pay the piper and call the tune**) pay for, and therefore have control over, a proceeding. **pay one's respects 1** make a polite visit. **2** attend someone's funeral. **pay through the nose** *colloq.* pay much more than a fair price. **pay up** pay the full amount, or the full amount of. **put paid to** esp. *Brit. colloq.* **1** deal effectively with (a person). **2** terminate (hopes, etc.). □□ **pay·ee** /payée/ *n.* **pay·er** *n.*

████ **WORD HISTORY** pay[1]

Middle English (in the sense 'pacify'): from Old French *paie* (noun), *payer* (verb), from Latin *pacare* 'appease,' from *pax, pac-* 'peace.' The notion of 'payment' arose from the sense of 'pacifying' a creditor.

pay[2] /pay/ *v.tr.* (*past* and *past part.* **payed**) *Naut.* smear (a ship) with pitch, tar, etc., as waterproofing. [OF *peier* f. L *picare* f. *pix picis* PITCH[2]]

pay·a·ble /páyəbəl/ *adj.* **1** that must be paid; due (*payable in April*). **2** that may be paid. **3** (of a mine, etc.) profitable.

pay·back /páybak/ *n.* **1** a financial return or reward, esp. profit from an investment equal to the initial outlay. **2** an act of revenge or retaliation.

pay·back pe·ri·od *n.* the length of time required for an investment to pay for itself in terms of profits or savings.

pay·day /páyday/ *n.* a day on which salary or wages are paid.

pay dirt *n.* **1** *Mineral.* ground worth working for ore. **2** a financially promising situation.

pay·ing guest *n.* a boarder.

pay·load /páylōd/ *n.* **1** the part of an aircraft's load from which revenue is derived, as paying passengers. **2 a** the explosive warhead carried by an aircraft or rocket. **b** the instruments, etc., carried by a spaceship.

pay·mas·ter /páymastər/ *n.* **1** an official who pays troops, workers, etc. **2** a person, organization, etc., to whom another owes duty or loyalty because of payment given. **3** (in full **Paymaster General**) *Brit.* the minister at the head of the Treasury department responsible for payments.

pay·ment /páymənt/ *n.* **1** the act or an instance of paying. **2** an amount paid. **3** reward; recompense. [ME f. OF *paiement* (as PAY[1])]

pay·nim /páynim/ *n. archaic* **1** a pagan. **2** a non-Christian, esp. a Muslim. [ME f. OF *pai(e)nime* f. eccl.L *paganismus* heathenism (as PAGAN)]

pay·off /páyawf/ *n. sl.* **1** an act of payment. **2** a climax. **3** a final reckoning. **4** *colloq.* a bribe; bribery.

pay·o·la /payólə/ *n.* **1** a bribe offered in return for unofficial promotion of a product, etc., in the media. **2** the practice of such bribery. [PAY[1] + –*ola* as in *Victrola*, make of gramophone]

pay phone *n.* a telephone, usu. in a public place, requiring payment by coin, credit card, etc., for use.

pay·roll /páyrōl/ *n.* a list of employees receiving regular pay.

Pb *symb. Chem.* the element lead. [L *plumbum*]

PBS *abbr.* Public Broadcasting Service.

PBX *abbr.* private branch exchange (private telephone switchboard).

PC *abbr.* **1** personal computer. **2** political correctness; politically correct. **3** Peace Corps. **4** (in the UK) police constable.

p.c. *abbr.* **1** percent. **2** postcard.

PCB *abbr.* **1** *Computing* printed circuit board. **2** *Chem.* polychlorinated biphenyl, any of several toxic compounds containing two benzene molecules in which hydrogens have been replaced by chlorine atoms, formed as waste in industrial processes.

PCP *n.* **1** *sl.* an illicit hallucinogenic drug, phencyclidine hydrochloride (phenyl cyclohexyl piperidine). **2** pneumocystis carinii pneumonia. **3** primary care physician.

pct. *abbr.* percent.

PD *abbr.* Police Department.

Pd *symb. Chem.* the element palladium.

pd. *abbr.* paid.

p.d.q. *abbr. colloq.* pretty damn quick.

PDT *abbr.* Pacific Daylight Time.

PE *abbr.* physical education.

p/e *abbr.* price/earnings (ratio).

pea /pee/ *n.* **1 a** a hardy climbing plant, *Pisum sativum*, with seeds growing in pods and used for food. **b** its seed. **2** any of several similar plants (*sweet pea; chickpea*). [back-form. f. PEASE (taken as pl.): cf. CHERRY]

pea brain *n. colloq.* a stupid or dim-witted person.

peace /pees/ n. **1 a** quiet; tranquillity (*needs peace to work well*). **b** mental calm; serenity (*peace of mind*). **2 a** (often *attrib.*) freedom from or the cessation of war (*peace talks*). **b** (esp. **Peace**) a treaty of peace between two nations, etc., at war. **3** freedom from civil disorder. **4** *Eccl.* a ritual liturgical greeting. □ **at peace 1** in a state of friendliness. **2** serene. **3** *euphem.* dead. **hold one's peace** keep silent. **keep the peace** prevent, or refrain from, strife. **make one's peace** (often foll. by *with*) reestablish friendly relations. **make peace** bring about peace; reconcile. **the peace** (or *Brit.* **the queen's peace**) peace existing within a realm; civil order. [ME f. AF *pes*, OF *pais* f. L *pax pacis*]

peace·a·ble /peesəbəl/ adj. **1** disposed to peace; unwarlike. **2** free from disturbance; peaceful. □□ **peace·a·ble·ness** n. **peace·a·bly** adv. [ME f. OF *peisible, plaisible* f. LL *placibilis* pleasing f. L *placēre* please]

Peace Corps n. a federal governmental organization sending people to work as volunteers in developing countries.

peace div·i·dend n. public money that becomes available when defense spending is reduced.

peace·ful /peesfool/ adj. **1** characterized by peace; tranquil. **2** not violating or infringing peace (*peaceful coexistence*). **3** belonging to a state of peace. □□ **peace·ful·ly** adv. **peace·ful·ness** n.

peace·mak·er /peesmaykər/ n. a person who brings about peace. □□ **peace·mak·ing** n. & adj.

peace of·fer·ing n. **1** a propitiatory or conciliatory gift. **2** *Bibl.* an offering presented as a thanksgiving to God.

peace pipe n. a tobacco pipe smoked as a token of peace among some Native Americans.

peace·time /peestim/ n. a period when a country is not at war.

peach[1] /peech/ n. **1 a** a round juicy fruit with downy cream or yellow skin flushed with red. **b** the tree, *Prunus persica*, bearing it. **2** the yellowish pink color of a peach. **3** *colloq.* **a** a person or thing of superlative quality. **b** often *offens.* an attractive young woman. □ **peaches and cream 1** (of a complexion) creamy skin with downy pink cheeks. **2** fine; satisfactory (*it wasn't all peaches and cream*). □□ **peach·y** adj. (**peach·i·er, peach·i·est**). **peach·i·ness** n. [ME f. OF *peche, pesche*, f. med.L *persica* f. L *persicum* (*malum*), lit. Persian apple]

peach[2] /peech/ v. **1** intr. (usu. foll. by *against, on*) colloq. turn informer; inform. **2** tr. inform against. [ME f. *appeach* f. AF *enpecher*, OF *empechier* IMPEACH]

peach bloom n. an oriental porcelain glaze of reddish pink, usu. with green markings.

pea·chick /peechik/ n. a young peafowl. [formed as PEACOCK + CHICK[1]]

peach Mel·ba n. a dish of ice cream and peaches with liqueur or sauce.

pea·coat /peecōt/ n. = PEA JACKET.

pea·cock /peekok/ n. **1 a** male peafowl, having brilliant plumage and a tail (with eyelike markings) that can be expanded erect in display like a fan. **2** an ostentatious strutting person. [ME *pecock* f. OE *pēa* f. L *pavo* + COCK[1]]

pea·cock blue n. the lustrous greenish blue of a peacock's neck.

pea·cock but·ter·fly n. a butterfly, *Inachis io*, with eyelike markings on its wings.

pea·fowl /peefowl/ n. **1** a peacock or peahen. **2** a pheasant of the genus *Pavo*.

peacock 1

pea green n. bright green.

pea·hen /peehen/ n. a female peafowl.

pea jack·et /pee jakit/ n. a sailor's short double-breasted woolen overcoat. Also called **peacoat**. [prob. f. Du. *pijjakker* f. *pij* coat of coarse cloth + *jekker* jacket: assim. to JACKET]

peak[1] /peek/ n. & v. • n. **1** a projecting usu. pointed part, esp.: **a** the pointed top of a mountain. **b** a mountain with a peak. **c** a stiff brim at the front of a cap. **d** a pointed beard. **e** the narrow part of a ship's hold at the bow or stern. **f** *Naut.* the upper outer corner of a sail extended by a gaff. **2 a** the highest point in a curve (*on the peak of the wave*). **b** the time of greatest success (*in a career, etc.*). **c** the highest point on a graph, etc. **3** = WIDOW'S PEAK. • v. intr. reach the highest value, quality, etc. (*output peaked in September*). □□ **peaked** adj. **peak·i·ness** n. [prob. back-form. f. *peaked* var. of dial. *picked* pointed (PICK[2])]

peak[2] /peek/ v.intr. **1** waste away. **2** (as **peaked** /peekid/ adj.) pale; sickly. [16th c.: orig. unkn.]

pea jacket

peak hour n. the time of the most intense traffic, greatest demand for electrical power, etc.

peak load n. the maximum of electric power demand, etc.

peal /peel/ n. & v. • n. **1 a** the loud ringing of a bell or bells, esp. a series of changes. **b** a set of bells. **2** a loud repeated sound, esp. of thunder, laughter, etc. • v. **1** intr. sound forth in a peal. **2** tr. utter sonorously. **3** tr. ring (bells) in peals. [ME *pele* f. *apele* APPEAL]

pe·an /peen/ n. *Heraldry* fur represented as sable spotted with or. [16th c.: orig. unkn.]

pea·nut /peenut/ n. **1** a leguminous plant, *Arachis hypogaea*, bearing pods that ripen underground and contain seeds used as food and yielding oil. **2** the seed of this plant. **3** (in pl.) colloq. a paltry or trivial thing or amount, esp. of money.

pea·nut brit·tle n. a candy made with peanuts and caramelized sugar.

pea·nut but·ter n. a paste of ground roasted peanuts.

pear /pair/ n. **1** a yellowish or brownish green fleshy fruit, tapering toward the stalk. **2** any of various trees of the genus *Pyrus* bearing it, esp. *P. communis*. [OE *pere, peru* ult. f. L *pirum*]

pear drop n.a small candy in the shape of a pear.

pearl[1] /pərl/ n. & v. • n. **1 a** (often *attrib.*) a usu. white or bluish gray hard mass formed within the shell of a pearl oyster or other bivalve mollusk, highly prized as a gem for its luster (*pearl necklace*). **b** an imitation of this. **c** (in pl.) a necklace of pearls. **d** = MOTHER-OF-PEARL (cf. SEED PEARL). **2** a precious thing; the finest example. **3** anything resembling a pearl, e.g., a dewdrop, tear, etc. • v. **1** tr. poet. **a** sprinkle with pearly drops. **b** make pearly in color, etc. **2** adorn with pearls. **3** tr. reduce (barley, etc.) to small rounded grains. **4** intr. fish for pearl oysters. **5** intr. poet. form pearllike drops. □ **cast pearls before swine** offer a treasure to a person unable to appreciate it. □□ **pearl·er** n. [ME f. OF *perle* prob. f. L *perna* leg (applied to leg-of-mutton-shaped bivalve)]

pearl[2] /pərl/ n. *Brit.* [var. of PURL[1]].

pearl ash n. commercial potassium carbonate.

pearl bar·ley n. barley reduced to small round grains by grinding.

pearl bulb n. *Brit.* a translucent electric light bulb.

pearl but·ton n. a button made of mother-of-pearl or an imitation of it.

pearl div·er n. a person who dives for pearl oysters.

pearled /pərld/ adj. **1** adorned with pearls. **2** formed into pearl-like drops or grains. **3** pearl colored.

pearl·es·cent /pərlésənt/ adj. having or producing the appearance of mother-of-pearl.

pearl·ite /pərlīt/ n. a ferrite and cementite mixture occurring in iron and carbon steel.

pearl·ized /pərlīzd/ adj. treated so as to resemble mother-of-pearl.

pearl mil·let n. any of several tall cereals of the genus *Pennisetum*.

pearl on·ion n. a very small onion used esp. in pickles.

pearl oys·ter n. any of various marine bivalve mollusks of the genus *Pinctada*, bearing pearls.

pearl·y /pərlee/ adj. (**pearl·i·er, pearl·i·est**) **1** resembling a pearl; lustrous. **2** containing pearls or mother-of-pearl. **3** adorned with pearls. □□ **pearl·i·ness** n.

Pearl·y Gates n. colloq. the gates of Heaven.

pearl·y nau·ti·lus see NAUTILUS.

pearl·y whites n.pl. a person's teeth.

peart /pərt/ adj. dial. lively; cheerful. [var. of PERT]

peas·ant /pézənt/ n. **1** esp. colloq. a rural person; a rustic. **2 a** a worker on the land, esp. a laborer or farmer. **b** hist. a member of an agricultural class dependent on subsistence farming. **3** derog. a boorish or unsophisticated person. □□ **peas·ant·ry** n. (pl. **·ies**). **peas·ant·y** adj. [ME f. AF *paisant*, OF *païsent*, earlier *païsence* f. *païs* country ult. f. L *pagus* canton]

pease /peez/ n.pl. archaic peas. [OE *pise* pea, pl. *pisan*, f. LL *pisa* f. L *pisum* f. Gk *pison*: cf. PEA]

pease pud·ding n. esp. *Brit.* boiled split peas (served esp. with boiled ham).

pea·shoot·er /peeshootər/ n. a small tube for blowing dried peas through as a toy.

pea-soup·er n. esp. *Brit.* colloq. a thick fog.

peat /peet/ n. **1** vegetable matter decomposed in water and partly carbonized, used for fuel, in horticulture, etc. **2** a cut piece of this. □□ **peat·y** adj. [ME f. AL *peta*, perh. f. Celt.: cf. PIECE]

peat·bog /peetbawg, –bog/ n. a bog composed of peat.

peat·moss /peetmaws, –mos/ n. **1** a peatbog. **2** any of various mosses of the genus *Sphagnum*, which grow in damp conditions and form peat as they decay.

peau-de-soie /pōdəswaá/ n. a smooth ribbed satiny fabric of silk or rayon. [F, = skin of silk]

peb·ble /pébəl/ n. **1** a small smooth stone worn by the action of water. **2 a** a type of colorless transparent rock crystal used for eyeglasses. **b** a lens of this. **c** (*attrib.*) colloq. (of a lens) very thick and convex. **3** an agate or other gem, esp. when found as a pebble in a stream, etc. **4** an irregular or grainy surface, as on paper, leather, etc. □□ **peb·bly** *adj.* [OE *papel-stān* pebble-stone, *pyppelrīpig* pebble-stream, of unkn. orig.]

peb·ble dash *n.* esp. *Brit.* mortar with pebbles in it used as a coating for external walls.

pec /pek/ *abbr.* pectoral (muscle).

pe·can /pikaán, –kán, peékan/ *n.* **1** a pinkish brown smooth nut with an edible kernel. **2** a hickory, *Carya illinoensis*, of the southern US, producing this. [earlier *paccan*, of Algonquian orig.]

pec·ca·ble /pékəbəl/ *adj.* liable to sin. □□ **pec·ca·bil·i·ty** *n.* [F, f. med.L *peccabilis* f. *peccare* sin]

pec·ca·dil·lo /pékədílō/ *n.* (*pl.* **·loes** or **·los**) a trifling offense; a venial sin. [Sp. *pecadillo*, dimin. of *pecado* sin f. L (as PECCANT)]

pec·cant /pékənt/ *adj.* **1** sinning. **2** faulty. □□ **pec·can·cy** *n.* [F *peccant* or L *peccare* sin]

pec·ca·ry /pékəree/ *n.* (*pl.* **·ries**) any American wild pig of the family Tayassuidae, esp. *Tayassu tajacu* and *T. pecavз3ri.* [Carib *pakira*]

pec·ca·vi /pekaávee, –wee, –káyvī/ *int.* & *v.* expressing guilt. ● *n.* (*pl.* **pec·ca·vis**) a confession of guilt. [L, = I have sinned]

peccary

peck[1] /pek/ *v.* & *n.* ● *v.tr.* **1** strike or bite (something) with a beak. **2** kiss (esp. a person's cheek) hastily or perfunctorily. **3 a** make (a hole) by pecking. **b** (foll. by *out*, *off*) remove or pluck out by pecking. **4** *colloq.* (also *absol.*) eat (food) listlessly; nibble at. **5** mark with short strokes. ● *n.* **1 a** a stroke or bite with a beak. **b** a mark made by this. **2** a hasty or perfunctory kiss. **3** *Brit. sl.* food. □ **peck at 1** eat (food) listlessly; nibble. **2** carp at; nag. **3** strike (a thing) repeatedly with a beak. [ME prob. f. MLG *pekken*, of unkn. orig.]

peck[2] /pek/ *n.* **1** a measure of capacity for dry goods, equal to 2 gallons or 8 quarts. **2** a vessel used to contain this amount. □ **a peck of** a large number or amount of (troubles, dirt, etc.). [ME f. AF *pek*, of unkn. orig.]

peck·er /pékər/ *n.* **1** a bird that pecks (*woodpecker*). **2** *coarse sl.* the penis. □ **keep your pecker up** *Brit. colloq.* remain cheerful.

peck·ing or·der *n.* a social hierarchy, orig. as observed among hens.

peck·ish /pékish/ *adj. colloq.* **1** esp. *Brit.* hungry. **2** irritable.

pe·co·ri·no /pékəreénō/ *n.* (*pl.* **·nos**) an Italian cheese made from sheep's milk. [It. f. *pecorino* f. *pecora* sheep]

pec·ten /péktin/ *n.* (*pl.* **pec·tens** or **pec·tines** /–tineez/) *Zool.* **1** a comblike structure of various kinds in animal bodies. **2** any bivalve mollusk of the genus *Pecten*. Also called **scallop**. □□ **pec·ti·nate** /–nət/ *adj.* **pec·ti·nat·ed** /–naytid/ *adj.* **pec·ti·na·tion** /–tináyshən/ *n.* (all in sense 1). [L *pecten pectinis* comb]

pec·tin /péktin/ *n. Biochem.* any of various soluble gelatinous polysaccharides found in ripe fruits, etc., and used as a gelling agent in jams and jellies. □□ **pec·tic** *adj.* [Gk *pēktos* congealed f. *pēgnumi* make solid]

pec·to·ral /péktərəl/ *adj.* & *n.* ● *adj.* **1** of or relating to the breast or chest; thoracic (*pectoral fin*; *pectoral muscle*). **2** worn on the chest (*pectoral cross*). ● *n.* **1** (esp. in *pl.*) a pectoral muscle. **2** a pectoral fin. **3** an ornamental breastplate esp. of a Jewish high priest. [ME f. OF f. L *pectorale* (n.), *pectoralis* (adj.) f. *pectus pectoris* breast, chest]

pec·tose /péktōs/ *n. Biochem.* an insoluble polysaccharide derivative found in unripe fruits and converted into pectin by ripening, heating, etc. [*pectic* (see PECTIN) + –OSE[2]]

pec·u·late /pékyəlayt/ *v.tr.* & *intr.* embezzle (money). □□ **pec·u·la·tion** /–láyshən/ *n.* **pec·u·la·tor** *n.* [L *peculari* rel. to *peculium*: see PE-CULIAR]

pe·cu·liar /pikyōōlyər/ *adj.* & *n.* ● *adj.* **1** strange; odd; unusual (*a peculiar flavor*; *is a little peculiar*). **2 a** (usu. foll. by *to*) belonging exclusively (*a fashion peculiar to the time*). **b** belonging to the individual (*in their own peculiar way*). **3** particular; special (*a point of peculiar interest*). ● *n.* **1** a peculiar property, privilege, etc. **2** esp. *Brit.* a parish or church exempt from the jurisdiction of the diocese in which it lies.

WORD HISTORY peculiar

late Middle English (in the sense 'particular, special'): from Latin *peculiaris* 'of private property,' from *peculium* 'property,' from *pecu* 'cattle' (cattle being private property). The sense 'odd' dates from the early 17th century.

---

pe·cu·li·ar·i·ty /pikyōōleeáritee/ *n.* (*pl.* **·ties**) **1 a** idiosyncrasy; oddity. **b** an instance of this. **2** a characteristic or habit (*meanness is his peculiarity*). **3** the state of being peculiar.

pe·cu·liar·ly /pikyōōlyərlee/ *adv.* **1** more than usually; especially (*peculiarly annoying*). **2** oddly. **3** as regards oneself alone; individually (*does not affect him peculiarly*).

pe·cu·ni·ar·y /pikyōōnee-eree/ *adj.* **1** of, concerning, or consisting

of, money (*pecuniary aid*; *pecuniary considerations*). **2** (of an offense) entailing a money penalty or fine. □□ **pe·cu·ni·ar·i·ly** *adv.* [L *pecuniarius* f. *pecunia* money f. *pecu* cattle]

ped·a·gogue /pédəgog, –gawg/ *n.* a schoolmaster or teacher, esp. a pedantic one. □□ **ped·a·gog·ic** /–gójik, –gójik/ *adj.* **ped·a·gog·i·cal** *adj.* **ped·a·gog·i·cal·ly** *adv.* **ped·a·gog·ism** *n.* (also **ped·a·gogu·ism**). [ME f. L *paedagogus* f. Gk *paidagōgos* f. *pais paidos* boy + *agōgos* guide]

ped·a·go·gy /pédəgōjee, –gojee/ *n.* the science of teaching. □□ **ped·a·gog·ics** /–gójiks, –gójiks/ *n.* [F *pédagogie* f. Gk *paidagōgia* (as PEDAGOGUE)]

ped·al[1] /péd'l/ *n.* & *v.* ● *n.* **1** any of several types of foot-operated levers or controls for mechanisms, esp.: **a** either of a pair of levers for transmitting power to a bicycle or tricycle wheel, etc. **b** any of the foot-operated controls in a motor vehicle. **c** any of the foot-operated keys of an organ used for playing notes, or for drawing out several stops at once, etc. **d** each of the foot-levers on a piano, etc., for making the tone fuller or softer. **e** each of the foot-levers on a harp for altering the pitch of the strings. **2** (in full **pedal point**) a note sustained in one part, usu. the bass, through successive harmonies, some of which are independent of it. ● *v.* (**pedaled** or **pedalled**, **pedaling** or **pedalling**) **1** *intr.* operate a cycle, organ, etc., by using the pedals. **2** *tr.* work (a bicycle, etc.) with the pedals. [F *pédale* f. It. *pedale* f. L (as PEDAL[2])]

ped·al[2] /péd'l, pée–/ *adj. Zool.* of the foot or feet (esp. of a mollusk). [L *pedalis* f. *pes pedis* foot]

ped·a·lo /péd'lō/ *n. Brit.* (*pl.* **·los**) a pedal-operated pleasure boat.

ped·al push·ers *n.pl.* women's and girls' calf-length pants.

ped·ant /péd'nt/ *n.* **1** a person who insists on strict adherence to formal rules or literal meaning at the expense of a wider view. **2** a person who rates academic learning or technical knowledge above everything. **3** a person who is obsessed by a theory; a doctrinaire. □□ **pe·dan·tic** /pidántik/ *adj.* **pe·dan·ti·cal·ly** *adv.* **ped·ant·ize** *v.intr.* & *tr.* **ped·ant·ry** *n.* (*pl.* **·ries**). [F *pédant* f. It. *pedante*: app. formed as PEDAGOGUE]

ped·ate /pédayt/ *adj.* **1** *Zool.* having feet. **2** *Bot.* (of a leaf) having divisions like toes or a bird's claws. [L *pedatus* f. *pes pedis* foot]

ped·dle /péd'l/ *v.* **1** *tr.* **a** sell (goods), esp. in small quantities, as a peddler. **b** advocate or promote (ideas, a philosophy, a way of life, etc.). **2** *tr.* sell (drugs) illegally. **3** *intr.* engage in selling, esp. as a peddler. [back-form. f. PEDDLER]

ped·dler /pédlər/ *n.* **1** a traveling seller of small items esp. carried in a pack, etc. **2** (usu. foll. by *of*) a dealer in gossip, influence, etc. **3** a person who sells drugs illegally. □□ **ped·dler·y** *n.* [ME *pedlere* alt. of *pedder* f. *ped* pannier, of unkn. orig.]

ped·er·ast /pédərast/ *n.* a man who performs pederasty.

ped·er·as·ty /pédərastee/ *n.* anal intercourse esp. between a man and a boy. [mod.L *paederastia* f. Gk *paiderastia* f. *pais paidos* boy + *erastēs* lover]

ped·es·tal /pédistəl/ *n.* & *v.* ● *n.* **1** a base supporting a column or pillar. **2** the stone, etc., base of a statue, etc. **3** either of the two supports of a desk or table, usu. containing drawers. ● *v.tr.* (**pedestaled**, **ped·es·tal·ing** or **pedestalled**, **ped·es·tal·ling**) set or support on a pedestal. □ **put** (or **set**) **on a pedestal** regard as highly admirable, important, etc.; venerate. [F *piédestal* f. It. *piedestallo* f. *piè pes pedis* + *di* of + *stallo* STALL[1]]

pe·des·tri·an /pidéstreeən/ *n.* & *adj.* ● *n.* (often *attrib.*) a person who is walking, esp. in a town (*pedestrian crossing*). ● *adj.* prosaic; dull; uninspired. □□ **pe·des·tri·an·ism** *n.* **pe·des·tri·an·ize** *v.tr.* & *intr.* **pe·des·tri·an·i·za·tion** *n.* [F *pédestre* or L *pedester* –*tris*]

pe·des·tri·an cross·ing *n.* a specified part of a road or street where pedestrians have the right of way to cross.

pe·di·at·rics /peedeeátriks/ *n.pl.* (treated as *sing.*) the branch of medicine dealing with children and their diseases. □□ **pe·di·at·ric** *adj.* **pe·di·a·tri·cian** /–deeətríshən/ *n.* [PEDO– + Gk *iatros* physician]

ped·i·cab /pédikab/ *n.* a pedal-operated rickshaw.

ped·i·cel /pédisəl/ *n.* (also **ped·i·cle** /pédikəl/) **1** a small (esp. subordinate) stalklike structure in a plant or animal (cf. PEDUNCLE). **2** *Surgery* part of a graft left temporarily attached to its original site. □□ **ped·i·cel·late** /–sélət, –layt/ *adj.* **pe·dic·u·late** /pidíkyələt, –layt/ *adj.* [mod.L *pedicellus* & L *pediculus* dimin. of *pes pedis* foot]

pe·dic·u·lar /pidíkyələr/ *adj.* (also **pe·dic·u·lous** /–ləs/) infested with lice. □□ **pe·dic·u·lo·sis** /–lósis/ *n.* [L *pedicularis*, –*losus* f. *pediculus* louse]

ped·i·cure /pédikyoor/ *n.* & *v.* ● *n.* **1** the care or treatment of the feet, esp. of the toenails. **2** a person practicing this, esp. professionally. ● *v.tr.* treat (the feet) by removing corns, etc. [F *pédicure* f. L *pes pedis* foot + *curare*: see CURE]

ped·i·gree /pédigree/ *n.* **1** (often *attrib.*) a recorded line of descent of a person or esp. a pure-bred domestic or pet animal. **2** the derivation of a word. **3** a genealogical table. **4** *Brit. colloq.* the 'life history' of a person, thing, idea, etc. □□ **ped·i·greed** *adj.* [ME *pedegru* etc. f. AF f. OF *pie de grue* (unrecorded) crane's foot, a mark denoting succession in pedigrees]

ped·i·ment /pédimənt/ *n.* **1 a** the triangular front part of a building in Grecian style, surmounting esp. a portico of columns. **b** a similar part of a building in Roman or Renaissance style. **2** *Geol.* a broad flattish rock surface at the foot of a mountain slope. □□ **ped·i·men·tal** /–mént'l/ *adj.* **ped·i·ment·ed** *adj.* [earlier *pedament, periment*, perh. corrupt. of PYRAMID]

pediment 1

ped·lar var. of PEDDLER.

pedo- /pédō/ *comb. form* (*Brit.* **paedo-**) child. [Gk *paid- pais* = child]

pe·dol·o·gy /pidóləjee/ *n.* the scientific study of soil, esp. its formation, nature, and classification. □□ **pe·do·log·i·cal** /pédəlójikəl/ *adj.* **pe·dol·o·gist** *n.* [Russ. *pedologiya* f. Gk *pedon* ground]

pe·dom·e·ter /pidómitər/ *n.* an instrument for estimating the distance traveled on foot by recording the number of steps taken. [F *pédomètre* f. L *pes pedis* foot]

pe·do·phile /peedəfil, péd–/ *n.* a person who displays pedophilia.

pe·do·phil·i·a /peedəfileeə, pédə–/ *n.* sexual desire directed toward children.

pe·dun·cle /pedúngkəl, peedung–/ *n.* **1** *Bot.* the stalk of a flower, fruit, or cluster, esp. a main stalk bearing a solitary flower or subordinate stalks (cf. PEDICEL). **2** *Zool.* a stalklike projection in an animal body. □□ **pe·dun·cu·lar** /–kyələr/ *adj.* **pe·dun·cu·late** /–kyələt/ *adj.* [mod.L *pedunculus* f. L *pes pedis* foot: see –UNCLE]

pee /pee/ *v. & n. colloq.* or *coarse* ● *v.* (**pees, peed**) **1** *intr.* urinate. **2** *tr.* pass (urine, blood, etc.) from the bladder. ● *n.* **1** urination. **2** urine. [initial letter of PISS]

peek /peek/ *v. & n.* ● *v.intr.* (usu. foll. by *in, out, at*) look quickly or slyly; peep. ● *n.* a quick or sly look. [ME *pike, pyke*, of unkn. orig.]

peek·a·boo /peekəbōō/ *adj. & n.* ● *adj.* **1** (of a garment, etc.) transparent or having a pattern of small holes. **2** (of a hairstyle) concealing one eye with the bangs or a wave. ● *n.* game of hiding and suddenly reappearing, played with a young child. [PEEK + BOO]

peel[1] /peel/ *v. & n.* ● *v.* **1** *tr.* **a** strip the skin, rind, bark, wrapping, etc., from (a fruit, vegetable, tree, etc.). **b** (usu. foll. by *off*) strip (skin, peel, wrapping, etc.) from a fruit, etc. **2** *intr.* **a** (of a tree, an animal's or person's body, a painted surface, etc.) become bare of bark, skin, paint, etc. **b** (often foll. by *off*) (of bark, a person's skin, paint, etc.) flake off. **3** *intr.* (often foll. by *off*) *colloq.* (of a person) strip for exercise, etc. **4** *tr. Croquet* send (another player's ball) through a wicket. ● *n.* the outer covering of a fruit, vegetable, shrimp, etc.; rind. □ **peel off 1** veer away and detach oneself from a group of marchers, a formation of aircraft, etc. **2** *colloq.* strip off one's clothes. □□ **peel·er** *n.* (in sense 1 of *v.*) [earlier *pill, pele* (orig. = plunder) f. ME *pilien*, etc. f. OE *pilian* (unrecorded) f. L *pilare* f. *pilus* hair]

peel[2] /peel/ *n.* a shovel, esp. a baker's shovel for bringing loaves, etc., into or out of an oven. [ME & OF *pele* f. L *pala*, rel. to *pangere* fix]

peel[3] /peel/ *n.* (also **pele**) *hist.* a small square tower built in the 16th c. in the border counties of England and Scotland for defense against raids. [ME *pel* stake, palisade, f. AF & OF *pel* f. L *palus* stake: cf. PALE[2]]

peel·er /peelər/ *n. Brit. archaic sl.* or *dial.* a policeman. [Sir Robert *Peel*, Engl. statesman d. 1850]

peel·ing /peeling/ *n.* a strip of the outer skin of a vegetable, fruit, etc. (*potato peelings*).

peen /peen/ *n. & v.* ● *n.* the wedge-shaped or thin or curved end of a hammer head (opp. FACE n. 5a). ● *v.tr.* **1** hammer with a peen. **2** treat (sheet metal) with a stream of metal shot in order to shape it. [17th c.: also *pane*, app. f. F *panne* f. Du. *pen* f. L *pinna* point]

peep[1] /peep/ *v. & n.* ● *v.intr.* **1** (usu. foll. by *at, in, out, into*) look through a narrow opening; look furtively. **2** (usu. foll. by *out*) **a** (of daylight, a flower beginning to bloom, etc.) come slowly into view; emerge. **b** (of a quality, etc.) show itself unconsciously. ● *n.* **1** a furtive or peering glance. **2** the first appearance (*at peep of day*). [ME: cf. PEEK, PEER[1]]

peep[2] /peep/ *v. & n.* ● *v.intr.* make a shrill feeble sound as of young birds, mice, etc.; squeak; chirp. ● *n.* **1** such a sound; a cheep. **2** the slightest sound or utterance, esp. of protest, etc. [imit.: cf. CHEEP]

peep·er /peepər/ *n.* **1** a person who peeps. **2** *colloq.* an eye. **3** *NE US* any of several species of frogs with a high peeping cry.

peep·hole /peephōl/ *n.* a tiny hole in a solid door, fence, etc., to look through.

peep·ing Tom *n.* a furtive voyeur.

peep show *n.* **1** a small exhibition of pictures, etc., viewed through a lens or hole set into a box, etc. **2** an erotic movie or picture viewed through a usu. coin-operated machine.

peep sight *n.* the aperture backsight of some rifles.

pee·pul /peepəl/ *n.* (also **pi·pal**) = BO-TREE. [Hindi *pīpal* f. Skr. *pippala*]

peer[1] /peer/ *v.intr.* **1** (usu. foll. by *into, at*, etc.) look keenly or with difficulty (*peered into the fog*). **2** appear; peep out. **3** *archaic* come into view. [var. of *pire*, LG *pīren*; perh. partly f. APPEAR]

peer[2] /peer/ *n. & v.* ● *n.* **1** a person who is equal in ability, standing, rank, or value; a contemporary (*tried by a jury of his peers*). **2 a** (*fem.* **peer·ess**) a member of one of the degrees of the nobility in Britain, i.e. a duke, marquis, earl, viscount, or baron. **b** a noble of any country. ● *v.intr. & tr.* (usu. foll. by *with*) rank or cause to rank equally. □□ **peer·less** *adj.* [ME f. AF & OF *pe(e)r, perer* f. LL *pariare* f. L *par* equal]

peer·age /peerij/ *n.* **1** peers as a class; the nobility. **2** the rank of peer or peeress (*was given a life peerage*). **3** a book containing a list of peers with their genealogy, etc.

peer group *n.* a group of people of the same age, status, interests, etc.

peer of the realm *n.* (also **peer of the U·nit·ed King·dom**) any of the class of peers (in the UK) whose adult members may all sit in the House of Lords.

peeve /peev/ *v. & n. colloq.* ● *v.tr.* (usu. as **peeved** *adj.*) annoy; vex; irritate. ● *n.* **1** a cause of annoyance. **2** vexation. [back-form. f. PEEVISH]

pee·vish /peevish/ *adj.* querulous; irritable. □□ **pee·vish·ly** *adv.* **pee·vish·ness** *n.* [ME, = foolish, mad, spiteful, etc., of unkn. orig.]

pee·wit /peewit/ *n.* (also **pe·wit**) **1** a lapwing. **2** its cry. [imit.]

peg /peg/ *n. & v.* ● *n.* **1 a** a usu. cylindrical pin or bolt of wood or metal, often tapered at one end, and used for holding esp. two things together. **b** such a peg attached to a wall, etc., and used for hanging garments, etc., on. **c** a peg driven into the ground and attached to a rope for holding up a tent. **d** a bung for stoppering a cask, etc. **e** each of several pegs used to tighten or loosen the strings of a violin, etc. **f** a small peg, matchstick, etc., stuck into holes in a board for calculating the scores at cribbage. **2** *Brit.* = CLOTHES-PIN. **3** *Brit.* a measure of spirits or wine. ● *v.tr.* (**pegged, peg·ging**) **1** (usu. foll. by *down, in, out*, etc.) fix (a thing) with a peg. **2** *Econ.* **a** stabilize (prices, wages, exchange rates, etc.). **b** prevent the price of (stock, etc.) from falling or rising by freely buying or selling at a given price. **3** mark (the score) with pegs on a cribbage board. **4** throw. □ **off the peg** esp. *Brit.* (of clothes) ready-made. **peg away** (often foll. by *at*) work consistently and esp. for a long period. **peg down** restrict (a person, etc.) to rules, a commitment, etc. **peg on** = *peg away*. **peg out 1** mark the boundaries of (land, etc.). **2** score the winning point at cribbage. **3** *Croquet* hit the peg with the ball as the final stroke in a game. **4** *Brit. sl.* die. **a peg to hang an idea**, etc., **on** a suitable occasion or pretext, etc., for it. **a round** (or **square**) **peg in a square** (or **round**) **hole** a misfit. **take a person down a peg or two** humble a person. [ME, prob. of LG or Du. orig.: cf. MDu. *pegge*, Du. dial. *peg*, LG *pigge*]

peg·board /pégbawrd/ *n.* a board having a regular pattern of small holes for pegs, used for commercial displays, games, etc.

peg leg *n.* **1** an artificial leg. **2** *offens.* a person with an artificial leg.

peg·ma·tite /pégmətīt/ *n.* a coarsely crystalline type of granite. [Gk *pēgma –atos* thing joined together f. *pēgnumi* fasten]

peg top /pég top/ *n.* a pear-shaped spinning top with a metal pin or peg forming the point, spun by the rapid uncoiling of a string wound around it.

Peh·le·vi var. of PAHLAVI.

PEI *abbr.* Prince Edward Island.

peign·oir /paynwáar, pen–, páynwaar, pén–/ *n.* a woman's loose dressing gown. [F f. *peigner* to comb]

pe·jo·ra·tive /pijáwrətiv, –jór–, péjərə–, pee–/ *adj. & n.* ● *adj.* (of a word, an expression, etc.) depreciatory. ● *n.* a depreciatory word. □□ **pe·jo·ra·tive·ly** *adv.* [F *péjoratif –ive* f. LL *pejorare* make worse (*pejor*)]

pek·an /pékən/ = FISHER 1.

peke /peek/ *n. colloq.* a Pekingese dog. [abbr.]

Pe·king·ese /peekineez, –ees/ *n. & adj.* (also **Pe·kin·ese**) ● *n.* (*pl.* same) **1 a** a lapdog of a short-legged breed with long hair and a snub nose. **b** this breed. **2** a citizen of Peking (Beijing) in China. **3** the form of the Chinese language used in Beijing. ● *adj.* of or concerning Beijing or its language or citizens.

pe·koe /peekō/ *n.* a superior kind of black tea. [Chin. dial. *pek–ho* f. *pek* white + *ho* down, leaves being picked young with down on them]

pel·age /pélij/ *n.* the fur, hair, wool, etc., of a mammal. [F f. *poil* hair]

Pe·la·gi·an /pil:áyjeeən/ *adj. & n.* ● *adj.* of or concerning the monk

Pelagius (4th–5th c.) or his theory denying the doctrine of original sin. • *n.* a follower of Pelagius. □□ **Pe·la·gi·an·ism** *n.* [eccl.L *Pelagianus* f. *Pelagius*]

pe·la·gi·an /pilǽyeeən/ *adj. & n.* • *adj.* inhabiting the open sea. • *n.* an inhabitant of the open sea. [L *pelagius* f. Gk *pelagios* of the sea (*pelagos*)]

pe·lag·ic /pilájik/ *adj.* **1** of or performed on the open sea (*pelagic whaling*). **2** of marine life) belonging to the upper layers of the open sea. [L *pelagicus* f. Gk *pelagikos* (as PELAGIAN)]

pel·ar·go·ni·um /pélərgóneeəm/ *n.* any plant of the genus *Pelargonium*, with red, pink, or white flowers and fragrant leaves. Also called **geranium**. [mod.L f. Gk *pelargos* stork: cf. GERANIUM]

pele var. of PEEL³.

pelf /pelf/ *n. derog.* or *joc.* money; wealth. [ME f. ONF f. OF *pelfre*, *peufre* spoils, of unkn. orig.: cf. PILFER]

pel·ham /péləm/ *n.* a horse's bit combining a curb and a snaffle. [the surname *Pelham*]

pel·i·can /pélikən/ *n.* any large gregarious waterfowl of the family Pelecanidae with a large bill and a pouch in the throat for storing fish. [OE *pellican* & OF *pelican* f. LL *pelicanus* f. Gk *pelekan* prob. f. *pelekus* axe, with ref. to its bill]

pel·i·can cross·ing *n.* (in the UK) a pedestrian crossing with traffic lights operated by pedestrians.

pel·i·can hook *n.* a hinged hook with a sliding ring by which it can be quickly secured or released.

pelican

pe·lisse /pilées/ *n. hist.* **1** a woman's cloak with armholes or sleeves, reaching to the ankles. **2** a fur-lined cloak, esp. as part of a hussar's uniform. [F f. med.L *pellicia* (*vestis*) (garment) of fur f. *pellis* skin]

pe·lite /péelīt/ *n.* a rock composed of claylike sediment. [Gk *pēlos* clay, mud]

pel·la·gra /pilágrə, –láygrə, –laá–/ *n.* a disease caused by deficiency of nicotinic acid, characterized by cracking of the skin and often resulting in insanity. □□ **pel·la·grous** *adj.* [It. f. *pelle* skin, after PO-DAGRA]

pel·let /pélit/ *n. & v.* • *n.* **1** a small compressed ball of paper, bread, etc. **2** a pill. **3 a** a small mass of bones, feathers, etc., regurgitated by a bird of prey. **b** a small hard piece of animal, usu. rodent, excreta. **4 a** a piece of small shot. **b** an imitation bullet for a toy gun. • *v.tr.* (**pel·let·ed, pel·let·ing**) **1** make into a pellet or pellets. **2** hit with (esp. paper) pellets. □□ **pel·let·ize** *v.tr.* [ME f. OF *pelote* f. L *pila* ball]

pel·li·cle /pélikəl/ *n.* a thin skin, membrane, or film. □□ **pel·lic·u·lar** /–líkyōolər/ *adj.* [F *pellicule* f. L *pellicula*, dimin. of *pellis* skin]

pel·li·to·ry /pélitawree/ *n.* any of several wild plants, esp.: **1** (in full **pellitory of Spain**) a composite plant, *Anacyclus pyrethrum*, with a pungent flavored root, used as a local irritant, etc. **2** (in full **pellitory of the wall**) a low bushy plant, *Parietaria judaica*, with greenish flowers growing on or at the foot of walls. [(sense 1) alt. f. ME f. OF *peletre*, *peretre* f. L *pyrethrum* f. Gk *purethron* feverfew: (sense 2) ult. f. OF *paritaire* f. LL *parietaria* f. L *paries* –*etis* wall]

pell-mell /pélmél/ *adv., adj., & n.* • *adv.* **1** headlong; recklessly (*rushed pell-mell out of the room*). **2** in disorder or confusion (*stuffed the papers together pell-mell*). • *adj.* confused; tumultuous. • *n.* confusion; a mixture. [F *pêle-mêle*, OF *pesle mesle*, *mesle pesle*, etc., redupl. of *mesle* f. *mesler* mix]

pel·lu·cid /pilóosid/ *adj.* **1** (of water, light, etc.) transparent; clear. **2** (of style, speech, etc.) not confused; clear. **3** mentally clear. □□ **pel·lu·cid·i·ty** /–síditee/ *n.* **pel·lu·cid·ly** *adv.* [L *pellucidus* f. *perlucēre* (as PER–, *lucēre* shine)]

pel·met /pélmit/ *n.* a narrow border of cloth, wood, etc., above esp. a window, concealing the curtain rail. [prob. F f. PALMETTE]

pe·lo·rus /piláwrəs/ *n.* a sighting device like a ship's compass for taking bearings. [perh. f. *Pelorus*, reputed name of Hannibal's pilot]

pe·lo·ta /pilótə/ *n.* **1** a Basque or Spanish game similar to jai alai played in a walled court with a ball and basketlike rackets attached to the hand. **2** the ball used in jai alai. [Sp., = ball, augment. of *pella* f. L *pila*]

pelt¹ /pelt/ *v. & n.* • *v.* **1 tr.** (usu. foll. by *with*) **a** hurl many small missiles at. **b** strike repeatedly with missiles. **c** assail (a person, etc.) with insults, abuse, etc. **2** *intr.* (usu. foll. by *down*) (of rain, etc.) fall quickly and torrentially. **3** *intr.* run fast. **4** *intr.* (often foll. by *at*) fire repeatedly. • *n.* the act or an instance of pelting. □ **at full pelt** esp. *Brit.* as fast as possible. [16th c.: orig. unkn.]

pelt² /pelt/ *n.* **1** the undressed skin of a fur-bearing mammal. **2** the skin of a sheep, goat, etc., with short wool, or stripped ready for tanning. **3** *joc.* the human skin. □□ **pelt·ry** *n.* hist. [ME f. obs. *pelt* skin, dimin. of *pel* f. AF *pell*, OF *pel*, or back-form. f. *peltry*, AF *pelterie*, OF *peleterie* f. *peletier* furrier, ult. f. L *pellis* skin]

pel·ta /péltə/ *n.* (*pl.* **pel·tae** /–tee/) **1** a small light shield used by the

ancient Greeks, Romans, etc. **2** *Bot.* a shieldlike structure. □□ **pel·tate** *adj.* [L f. Gk *peltē*]

pel·vic /pélvik/ *adj.* of or relating to the pelvis.

pel·vic gir·dle *n.* the bony or cartilaginous structure in vertebrates to which the posterior limbs are attached.

pel·vis /pélvis/ *n.* (*pl.* **pel·vis·es** or **pel·ves** /–veez/) **1** a basin-shaped cavity at the lower end of the torso of most vertebrates, formed from the innominate bones with the sacrum and other vertebrae. **2** the basinlike cavity of the kidney. [L, = basin]

pem·mi·can /pémikən/ *n.* **1** a cake of dried pounded meat mixed with melted fat, orig. made by Native Americans. **2** beef so treated and flavored with dried fruit, etc., for use by Arctic travelers, etc. [Cree *pimecan* f. *pime* fat]

pem·phi·gus /pémfigəs/ *n. Med.* the formation of watery blisters or eruptions on the skin. □□ **pem·phi·goid** *adj.* **pem·phi·gous** *adj.* [mod.L f. Gk *pemphix* –*igos* bubble]

PEN *abbr.* International Association of Poets, Playwrights, Editors, Essayists, and Novelists.

Pen. *abbr.* Peninsula.

pen¹ /pen/ *n. & v.* • *n.* **1** an instrument for writing or drawing with ink, orig. consisting of a shaft with a sharpened quill or metal nib, now more widely applied. **2 a** (usu. prec. by *the*) the occupation of writing. **b** a style of writing. **3** *Zool.* the internal feather-shaped cartilaginous shell of certain cuttlefish, esp. squid. • *v.tr.* (**penned, pen·ning**) **1** write. **2** compose and write. □ **put pen to paper** begin writing. [ME f. OF *penne* f. L *penna* feather]

pen² /pen/ *n. & v.* • *n.* **1** a small enclosure for cows, sheep, poultry, etc. **2** a place of confinement. **3** an enclosure for sheltering submarines. • *v.tr.* (**penned, pen·ning**) (often foll. by *in, up*) enclose or shut in a pen. [OE *penn*, of unkn. orig.]

pen³ /pen/ *n.* a female swan. [16th c.: orig. unkn.]

pen⁴ /pen/ *n. sl.* = PENITENTIARY *n.* 1. [abbr.]

pe·nal /péenəl/ *adj.* **1 a** of or concerning punishment or its infliction (*penal laws; a penal sentence; a penal colony*). **b** (of an offense) punishable, esp. by law. **2** extremely severe (*penal taxation*). □□ **pe·nal·ly** *adv.* [ME f. OF *penal* or L *poenalis* f. *poena* PAIN]

PRONUNCIATION TIP   **penal**

Both *penal* and *penalize* are traditionally pronounced with a "long e" ("PEE-nul, " "PEE-nul-ize"), but the related word *penalty* is pronounced with a "short e" ("PEN-ul-tee"). *Penalize* is sometimes pronounced with a "short e" in American English, probably on analogy to *penalty*.

---

pe·nal·ize /péenəlīz, pénəl–/ *v.tr.* **1** subject (a person) to a penalty or comparative disadvantage. **2** make or declare (an action) penal. □□ **pe·nal·i·za·tion** *n.*

pe·nal ser·vi·tude *n. hist.* imprisonment with compulsory labor.

pen·al·ty /pé nəltee/ *n.* (*pl.* **·ties**) **1 a** a punishment, esp. a fine, for a breach of law, contract, etc. **b** a fine paid. **2** a disadvantage, loss, etc., esp. as a result of one's own actions (*paid the penalty for his carelessness*). **3 a** a disadvantage imposed on a competitor or team in a game, etc., for a breach of the rules, etc. **b** (*attrib.*) awarded against a side incurring a penalty (*clipping penalty; penalty kick*). **4** *Bridge*, etc., points gained by opponents when a contract is not fulfilled. □ **the penalty of** a disadvantage resulting from (a quality, etc.). **under** (or **on**) **penalty of** under the threat of (dismissal, etc.). [AF *penalte* (unrecorded), F *pénalité* f. med.L *penalitas* (as PENAL)]

pen·al·ty ar·e·a *n. Soccer* the area in front of the goal in which a foul by defenders involves the award of a penalty kick.

pen·al·ty box *n. Ice Hockey* an area reserved for penalized players and some officials.

pen and ink *n. & adj.* • *n.* **1** the instruments of writing. **2** writing. • *adj.* (**pen-and-ink**) drawn or written with ink.

pen·ance /pénəns/ *n. & v.* • *n.* **1** an act of self-punishment as reparation for guilt. **2 a** (esp. in the RC and Orthodox Church) a sacrament including confession of and absolution for a sin. **b** a penalty imposed esp. by a priest, or undertaken voluntarily, for a sin. • *v.tr.* impose a penance on. □ **do penance** perform a penance. [ME f. OF f. L *paenitentia* (as PENITENT)]

pen·an·nu·lar /penányəlᵊr/ *adj.* almost ringlike. [L *paene* almost + ANNULAR]

pe·na·tes /pináyteez, pináa–/ *n.pl.* (often **Pe·na·tes**) (in Roman mythology) the household gods, esp. of the storeroom (see LARES). [L f. *penus* provision of food]

pence *Brit. pl.* of PENNY.

pen·chant /pénchənt/ *n.* an inclination or liking (*has a penchant for old films*). [F, pres. part. of *pencher* incline]

pen·cil /pénsil/ *n. & v.* • *n.* **1** (often *attrib.*) **a** an instrument for writing or drawing, usu. consisting of a thin rod of graphite, etc., enclosed in a wooden cylinder (*a pencil sketch*). **b** a similar instrument with a metal or plastic cover and retractable lead. **c** a cosmetic in pencil form. **2** (*attrib.*) resembling a pencil in shape (*pencil skirt*). **3** *Optics* a set of rays meeting at a point. **4** *Geom.* a figure formed by a set of straight lines meeting at a point. **5** a draftsman's or artist's art or style. • *v.tr.* (**pen·ciled, pen·cil·ing** or **pen·cilled, pen·cil·**

ling) **1** tint or mark with or as if with a pencil. **2** (usu. foll. by *in*) **a** write, esp. tentatively or provisionally (*have penciled in the 29th for our meeting*). **b** (esp. as **penciled** *adj.*) fill (an area) with soft pencil strokes (*penciled in her eyebrows*). □□ **pen·cil·er** or *Brit.* **pen·cil·ler** *n.* [ME f. OF *pincel* ult. f. L *penicillum* paintbrush, dimin. of *peniculus* brush, dimin. of *penis* tail]

pen·cil case *n.* (also **pen·cil box**) a container for pencils, etc.

pen·cil push·er *n. colloq. derog.* a clerical worker or one who does considerable paperwork.

pen·cil push·ing *n. colloq. derog.* clerical work.

pend·ant /péndənt/ *n.* (also **pend·ent**) **1** a hanging jewel, etc., esp. one attached to a necklace, bracelet, etc. **2** a light fitting, ornament, etc., hanging from a ceiling. **3** *Naut.* **a** a short rope hanging from the head of a mast, etc., used for attaching tackles. **b** *Brit.* = PENNANT 1. **4** the shank and ring of a pocket watch by which it is suspended. **5** /péndənt, póNDoN/ (usu. foll. by *to*) a match, companion, parallel, complement, etc. [ME f. OF f. *pendre* hang f. L *pendere*]

pend·ent /péndənt/ *adj.* (also **pend·ant**) **1 a** hanging. **b** overhanging. **2** undecided; pending. **3** *Gram.* (esp. of a sentence) incomplete; not having a finite verb (*pendent nominative*). □□ **pen·den·cy** *n.* [ME (as PENDANT)]

pen·den·te li·te /pendéntee lítee/ *adv. Law* during the progress of a suit. [L]

pen·den·tive /pendéntiv/ *n. Archit.* a curved triangle of vaulting formed by the intersection of a dome with its supporting arches. [F *pendentif –ive* (adj.) (as PENDANT)]

pend·ing /pénding/ *adj. & prep. • predic.adj.* **1** awaiting decision or settlement; undecided (*a settlement was pending*). **2** about to come into existence (*patent pending*). • *prep.* **1** during (*pending these negotiations*). **2** until (*pending his return*). [after F *pendant* (see PENDENT)]

pend·ing-tray *n.* esp. *Brit.* = IN-BOX.

pen·drag·on /pendrágon/ *n. hist.* an ancient British or Welsh prince (often as a title). [Welsh, = chief war leader, f. *pen* head + *dragon* standard]

pen·du·line /pénjəlin, péndə–, –dyə–/ *adj.* **1** (of a nest) suspended. **2** (of a bird) of a kind that builds such a nest. [F (as PENDULOUS)]

pen·du·lous /pénjələs, péndə–, –dyə–/ *adj.* **1** (of ears, breasts, flowers, bird's nests, etc.) hanging down; drooping and esp. swinging. **2** oscillating. □□ **pen·du·lous·ly** *adv.* [L *pendulus* f. *pendere* hang]

pen·du·lum /pénjələm, péndə–, –dyə–/ *n.* a weight suspended so as to swing freely, esp. a rod with a weighted end regulating the movement of a clock's works. [L neut. adj. (as PENDULOUS)]

pe·ne·plain /péeniplayn/ *n. Geol.* a fairly flat area of land produced by erosion. [L *paene* almost + PLAIN[1]]

pen·e·tra·li·a /pénitráyleeə/ *n.pl.* **1** innermost shrines or recesses. **2** secret or hidden parts; mysteries. [L, neut. pl. of *penetralis* interior (as PENETRATE)]

pen·e·trate /pénitrayt/ *v.* **1** *tr.* **a** find access into or through, esp. forcibly. **b** (usu. foll. by *with*) imbue (a person or thing) with; permeate. **2** *tr.* see into, find out, or discern (a person's mind, the truth, a meaning, etc.). **3** *tr.* see through (darkness, fog, etc.) (*could not penetrate the gloom*). **4** *intr.* be absorbed by the mind (*my hint did not penetrate*). **5** *tr.* (as **penetrating** *adj.*) **a** having or suggesting sensitivity or insight (*a penetrating remark*). **b** (of a voice, etc.) easily heard through or above other sounds; piercing. **c** (of a smell) sharp; pungent. **6** *tr.* (of a man) put the penis into the vagina of (a woman). **7** *intr.* (usu. foll. by *into, through, to*) make a way. □□ **pen·e·tra·ble** *adj.* **pen·e·tra·bil·i·ty** *n.* **pen·e·trant** *adj. & n.* **pen·e·trat·ing·ly** *adv.* **pen·e·tra·tion** *n.* **pen·e·tra·tive** /–trətiv/ *adj.* **pen·e·tra·tor** *n.* [L *penetrare* place or enter within f. *penitus* interior]

pen-feath·er *n.* a quill-feather of a bird's wing.

pen-friend *n. Brit.* = PEN PAL.

pen·guin /pénggwin/ *n.* any flightless sea bird of the family Spheniscidae of the southern hemisphere, with black upperparts and white underparts, and wings developed into scaly flippers for swimming underwater. [16th c., orig. = great auk: orig. unkn.]

pen·hold·er /pénhóldər/ *n.* **1** the esp. wooden shaft of a pen with a metal nib. **2** a rack for storing pens or nibs.

pen·i·cil·late /pénisílit, –ayt/ *adj. Biol.* **1** having or forming a small tuft or tufts.

pendulum

Adélie penguin

2 marked with streaks as of a pencil or brush. [L *penicillum*: see PENCIL]

pen·i·cil·lin /pénisílin/ *n.* any of various antibiotics produced naturally by molds of the genus *Penicillium*, or synthetically, and able to prevent the growth of certain disease-causing bacteria. [mod.L *Penicillium* genus name f. L *penicillum*: see PENCIL]

pe·nile /péenil, –nəl/ *adj.* of or concerning the penis. [mod.L *penilis*]

pe·nil·lion /penílyən/ *n.pl.* (also **pen·nil·lion**) an improvised stanza sung to a harp accompaniment at an eisteddfod, etc. [Welsh f. *penn* head]

pen·in·su·la /pənínsələ, –syələ/ *n.* a piece of land almost surrounded by water or projecting far into a sea or lake, etc. □□ **pen·in·su·lar** *adj.* [L *paeninsula* f. *paene* almost + *insula* island]

pe·nis /péenis/ *n.* (*pl.* **pe·nis·es** or **pe·nes** /–neez/) **1** the male organ of copulation and (in mammals) urination. **2** the male copulatory organ in lower vertebrates. [L, = tail, penis]

pen·i·tent /pénitənt/ *adj. & n.* • *adj.* regretting and wishing to atone for sins, etc.; repentant. • *n.* **1** a repentant sinner. **2** a person doing penance under the direction of a confessor. **3** (in *pl.*) various RC orders associated for mutual discipline, etc. □□ **pen·i·tence** *n.* **pen·i·tent·ly** *adv.* [ME f. OF f. L *paenitens* f. *paenitēre* repent]

pen·i·ten·tial /péniténshəl/ *adj.* of or concerning penitence or penance. □□ **pen·i·ten·tial·ly** *adv.* [OF *penitencial* f. LL *paenitentialis* f. *paenitentia* penitence (as PENITENT)]

pen·i·ten·tia·ry /péniténshəree/ *n. & adj.* • *n.* (*pl.* **-ries**) **1** a reformatory prison, esp. a state or federal prison. **2** an office in the papal court deciding questions of penance, dispensations, etc. • *adj.* **1** of or concerning penance. **2** of or concerning reformatory treatment. **3** (of an offense) making a culprit liable to a prison sentence. [ME f. med.L *paenitentiarius* (adj. & n.) (as PENITENT)]

pen-knife /pén-nif/ *n.* a small folding knife, esp. for carrying in a pocket.

pen-light /pénlit/ *n.* a pen-sized flashlight.

pen-man /pénmən/ *n.* (*pl.* **-men**) **1** a person who writes by hand with a specified skill (*a good penman*). **2** an author. □□ **pen-man-ship** *n.*

Penn. *abbr.* (also **Penna.**) Pennsylvania.

pen name *n.* a literary pseudonym.

pen·nant /pénənt/ *n.* **1** *Naut.* a tapering flag, esp. that flown at the masthead of a vessel in commission. **2** = PENDANT 3a. **3** = PENNON. **4 a** a flag denoting a sports championship, etc. **b** (by extension) a sports championship. [blend of PENDANT and PENNON]

pen·ni·less /pénilis/ *adj.* having no money; destitute. □□ **pen·ni·less·ly** *adv.* **pen·ni·less·ness** *n.*

pen·non /pénən/ *n.* **1** a long narrow flag, triangular or swallow-tailed, esp. as the military ensign of lancer regiments. **2** *Naut.* a long pointed streamer on a ship. **3** a flag. □□ **pen·noned** *adj.* [ME f. OF f. L *penna* feather]

Penn·syl·va·nia Dutch /pénsilváynyə/ *n.* **1** a dialect of High German spoken by descendants of 17th–18th-c. German and Swiss immigrants to Pennsylvania, etc. **2** (as *pl.*) these settlers or their descendants.

Penn·syl·va·nian /pénsilváynyən/ *n. & adj.* • *n.* **1** a native or inhabitant of Pennsylvania. **2** (prec. by *the*) *Geol.* the upper Carboniferous period or system in N. America. • *adj.* **1** of or relating to Pennsylvania. **2** *Geol.* of or relating to the upper Carboniferous period or system in N. America.

pen·ny /pénee/ *n.* (*pl.* for separate coins **·nies**, *Brit.* for a sum of money **pence** /pens/) **1** (in the US, Canada, etc.) a one-cent coin. **2** a British coin and monetary unit equal to one hundredth of a pound. ¶ Abbr.: **p. 3** *hist.* a former British bronze coin and monetary unit equal to one two-hundred-and-fortieth of a pound. ¶ Abbr.: **d. 4** *Bibl.* a denarius. □ **in for a penny, in for a pound** an exhortation to total commitment to an undertaking. **like a bad penny** continually returning when unwanted. **pennies from heaven** unexpected benefits. **the penny drops** *Brit. colloq.* one begins to understand at last. **a penny for your thoughts** a request to a thoughtful person to confide in the speaker. **penny wise and pound foolish** frugal in small expenditures but wasteful of large amounts. **a pretty penny** a large sum of money. **two a penny** almost worthless though easily obtained. [OE *penig, penning* f. Gmc, perh. rel. to PAWN[2]]

-penny *comb. form* **1** /pénee/ denoting a size of nail (based on former price per hundred) (*tenpenny nail*). **2** /pəni/ *Brit.* forming attributive adjectives meaning 'costing .|.|. pence' (esp. in pre-decimal currency) (*fivepenny*).

pen·ny-a-lin·er *n.* esp. *Brit.* a hack writer.

pen·ny dread·ful *n.* a cheap sensational adventure story or comic.

pen·ny-pinch·er *n.* a very frugal person.

pen·ny-pinch·ing *n. & adj.* • *n.* frugality; cheapness. • *adj.* frugal.

pen·ny·roy·al /péneeróyəl/ *n.* **1** a European creeping mint, *Mentha pulegium*, cultivated for its supposed medicinal properties. **2** an aromatic N. American plant, *Hedeoma pulegioides*. [app. f. earlier *puliol(e) ryall* f. AF *puliol*, OF *pouliol* ult. f. L *pulegium* + *real* ROYAL]

See page xx for the **Key to Pronunciation**.

pen·ny·weight /péneewayt/ *n.* a unit of weight, 24 grains or one twentieth of an ounce troy.

pen·ny whis·tle *n.* a tin pipe with six holes giving different notes.

pen·ny·wort /péneewərt, –wawrt/ *n.* any of several wild plants with rounded leaves, esp.: **1** (**wall pennywort**) *Umbilicus rupestris*, growing in crevices. **2** (**marsh** or **water pennywort**) *Hydrocotyle vulgaris*, growing in marshy places. [ME, f. PENNY + WORT]

pen·ny·worth /péneewərth/ *n.* esp. *Brit.* (also **penn'orth** /pénərth/) **1** as much as can be bought for a penny. **2** a bargain of a specified kind (*a bad pennyworth*). □ **not a pennyworth** not the least bit.

Pe·nob·scot /pənóbskot, –skət/ *n.* **1 a** a N. American people native to Maine. **b** a member of this people. **2** the language of this people.

pe·nol·o·gy /peenólə jee/ *n.* the study of the punishment of crime and of prison management. □□ **pe·no·log·i·cal** /–nəlójikəl/ *adj.* **pe·nol·o·gist** *n.* [L *poena* penalty + –LOGY]

pen pal *n. colloq.* a friend communicated with by letter only.

pen·sée /ponsáy/ *n.* a thought or reflection put into literary form; an aphorism. [F]

pen·sile /pénsil/ *adj.* **1** hanging down; pendulous. **2** (of a bird, etc.) building a pensile nest. [L *pensilis* f. *pendēre pens-* hang]

pen·sion[1] /pénshən/ *n. & v.* ● *n.* **1** a regular payment made by an employer, etc., after the retirement of an employee. **2** a similar payment made by a government to people above a specified age, to the disabled, etc. ● *v.tr.* **1** grant a pension to. **2** bribe with a pension. □ **pension off** dismiss with a pension. □□ **pen·sion·less** *adj.* [ME f. OF f. L *pensio –onis* payment f. *pendere pens-* pay]

pen·sion[2] /paaNsyóN/ *n.* a European, esp. French, boardinghouse providing full or half board at a fixed rate. □ **en pension** /oN/ as a boarder. [F: see PENSION[1]]

pen·sion·a·ble /pénshənəbəl/ *adj.* **1** entitled to a pension. **2** (of a service, job, etc.) entitling an employee to a pension. □□ **pen·sion·a·bil·i·ty** *n.*

pen·sion·ar·y /pénshəneree/ *adj. & n.* ● *adj.* of or concerning a pension. ● *n.* (*pl.* **-ies**) **1** a pensioner. **2** a creature; a hireling. [med.L *pensionarius* (as PENSION[1])]

pen·sion·er /pénshənər/ *n.* a recipient of a pension, esp. a retirement pension. [ME f. AF *pensionner*, OF *pensionnier* (as PENSION[1])]

pen·sive /pénsiv/ *adj.* **1** deep in thought. **2** sorrowfully thoughtful. □□ **pen·sive·ly** *adv.* **pen·sive·ness** *n.* [ME f. OF *pensif, –ive* f. *penser* think f. L *pensare* frequent. of *pendere pens-* weigh]

pen·ste·mon /penstéemən, pénstəmən/ *n.* (also **pent·ste·mon** /pentstéemən/) any American herbaceous plant of the genus *Penstemon*, with showy flowers and five stamens, one of which is sterile. [mod.L, irreg. f. PENTA- + Gk *stēmōn* warp, used for 'stamen']

pen·stock /pénstok/ *n.* **1** a sluice; a floodgate. **2** a channel for conveying water to a waterwheel, etc. [PEN[2] in sense 'mill dam' + STOCK]

pent /pent/ *adj.* (often foll. by *in*, *up*) closely confined; shut in (*pent-up feelings*). [past part. of *pend* var. of PEN[2] *v.*]

penta- /péntə/ *comb. form* **1** five. **2** *Chem.* (forming the names of compounds) containing five atoms or groups of a specified kind (*pentachloride; pentoxide*). [Gk f. *pente* five]

pen·ta·cle /péntəkəl/ *n.* a figure used as a symbol, esp. in magic, e.g., a pentagram. [med.L *pentaculum* (as PENTA-)]

pen·tad /péntad/ *n.* **1** the number five. **2** a group of five. [Gk *pentas –ados* f. *pente* five]

pen·ta·dac·tyl /péntədáktil/ *adj. Zool.* having five toes or fingers.

pen·ta·gon /péntəgon/ *n.* **1** a plane figure with five sides and angles. **2** (**the Pentagon**) **a** the pentagonal headquarters building of the US armed forces, located near Washington, D.C. **b** the US Department of Defense; the leaders of the US armed forces. □□ **pen·tag·o·nal** /–tágənəl/ *adj.* [F *pentagone* or f. LL *pentagonus* f. Gk *pentagōnon* (as PENTA-, –GON)]

pen·ta·gram /péntəgram/ *n.* a five-pointed star formed by extending the sides of a pentagon both ways until they intersect, formerly used as a mystic symbol. [Gk *pentagrammon* (as PENTA-, –GRAM)]

pen·tag·y·nous /pentájinəs/ *adj. Bot.* having five pistils.

pen·ta·he·dron /péntəhéedrən/ *n.* a solid figure with five faces. □□ **pen·ta·he·dral** *adj.*

pen·tam·er·ous /pentámərəs/ *adj.* **1** *Bot.* having five parts in a flower whorl. **2** *Zool.* having five joints or parts.

pen·tam·e·ter /pentámitər/ *n.* **1** a verse of five feet, e.g., English iambic verse of ten syllables. **2** a form of Gk or Latin dactylic verse composed of two halves each of two feet and a long syllable, used in elegiac verse. [L f. Gk *pentametros* (as PENTA-, –METER)]

pen·tan·drous /pentándrəs/ *adj. Bot.* having five stamens.

pen·tane /péntayn/ *n. Chem.* a hydrocarbon of the alkane series. ¶ Chem. formula: C_5H_{12}. [Gk *pente* five + ALKANE]

pen·tan·gle /péntanggəl/ *n.* = PENTAGRAM. [med.L *pentaculum* PENTACLE, assim. to L *angulus* ANGLE[1]]

pen·ta·prism /péntəprizəm/ *n.* a five-sided prism with two silvered surfaces used in a viewfinder to obtain a constant deviation of all rays of light through 90°.

Pen·ta·teuch /péntətook, –tyook/ *n.* the first five books of the Old Testament, traditionally ascribed to Moses. □□ **pen·ta·teuch·al** *adj.* [eccl.L *pentateuchus* f. eccl.Gk *pentateukhos* (as PENTA-, *teukhos* implement, book)]

pen·tath·lon /pentáthlən, –laan/ *n.* an athletic event comprising five different events for each competitor. □□ **pen·tath·lete** /–táthleet/ *n.* [Gk f. *pente* five + *athlon* contest]

pen·ta·ton·ic /péntətónik/ *adj. Mus.* **1** consisting of five notes. **2** relating to such a scale.

pen·ta·va·lent /péntəváylənt/ *adj. Chem.* having a valence of five; quinquevalent.

Pen·te·cost /péntikawst, –kost/ *n.* **1 a** Whitsunday. **b** a festival celebrating the descent of the Holy Spirit on Whitsunday, fifty days after Easter. **2 a** the Jewish harvest festival, on the fiftieth day after the second day of Passover (Lev. 23:15–16). **b** a synagogue ceremony on the anniversary of the giving of the Law on Mount Sinai. [OE *pentecosten* & OF *pentecoste*, f. eccl.L *pentecoste* f. Gk *pentēkostē (hēmera)* fiftieth (day)]

Pen·te·cos·tal /péntikóst'l, –káwst'l/ *adj. & n.* ● *adj.* (also **pen·te·cos·tal**) **1** of or relating to Pentecost. **2** of or designating Christian sects and individuals who emphasize the gifts of the Holy Spirit, are often fundamentalist in outlook, and express religious feelings by clapping, shouting, dancing, etc. ● *n.* a Pentecostalist. □□ **Pen·te·cos·tal·ism** *n.* **Pen·te·cos·tal·ist** *adj. & n.*

pent·house /pént-hows/ *n.* **1** a house or apartment on the roof or the top floor of a tall building. **2** a sloping roof, esp. of an outhouse built on to another building. **3** an awning; a canopy. [ME *pentis* f. OF *apentis, –dis*, f. med.L *appendicium*, in LL = appendage, f. L (as APPEND): infl. by HOUSE]

pen·ti·men·to /péntiméntō/ *n.* (*pl.* **pen·ti·men·ti** /–tee/) the phenomenon of earlier painting showing through a layer or layers of paint on a canvas. [It., = repentance]

pen·to·bar·bi·tal /péntəbáárbitawl, –tal/ *n.* (also **pen·to·bar·bi·tone** /–tōn/) a narcotic and sedative barbiturate drug formerly used to relieve insomnia. [PENTA-, BARBITAL]

pen·tode /péntōd/ *n.* a thermionic valve having five electrodes. [Gk *pente* five + *hodos* way]

pen·tose /péntōs, –tōz/ *n. Biochem.* any monosaccharide containing five carbon atoms, including ribose. [PENTA- + –OSE[2]]

Pen·to·thal /péntəthawl/ *n. Trademark* an intravenous anesthetic, thiopental sodium.

pent-roof /péntroof, –roof/ *n.* a roof sloping in one direction only. [PENTHOUSE + ROOF]

pent·ste·mon var. of PENSTEMON.

pen·tyl /péntil/ *n.* = AMYL. [PENTANE + –YL]

pe·nult /pinúlt, peénult/ *n. & adj.* ● *n.* the last but one (esp. syllable). ● *adj.* last but one. [abbr. of L *paenultimus* (see PENULTIMATE) or of PENULTIMATE]

pe·nul·ti·mate /pinúltimət/ *adj. & n.* ● *adj.* last but one. ● *n.* **1** the last but one. **2** the last syllable but one. [L *paenultimus* f. *paene* almost + *ultimus* last, after *ultimate*]

pe·num·bra /pinúmbrə/ *n.* (*pl.* **pe·num·brae** /–bree/ or **pe·num·bras**) **1 a** the partly shaded region around the shadow of an opaque body, esp. that around the total shadow of the moon or earth in an eclipse. **b** the less dark outer part of a sunspot. **2** a partial shadow. □□ **pe·num·bral** *adj.* [mod.L f. L *paene* almost + UMBRA shadow]

pe·nu·ri·ous /pinóoreeəs, pinyóor–/ *adj.* **1** poor; destitute. **2** stingy; grudging. **3** scanty. □□ **pe·nu·ri·ous·ly** *adv.* **pe·nu·ri·ous·ness** *n.* [med.L *penuriosus* (as PENURY)]

pen·u·ry /pényəree/ *n.* (*pl.* **-ies**) **1** destitution; poverty. **2** a lack; scarcity. [ME f. L *penuria*, perh. rel. to *paene* almost]

pe·on /péeon, péeən/ *n.* **1** a Spanish American day laborer or farmworker. **2** an unskilled worker; drudge. **3** *hist.* a worker held in servitude in the southwestern US. **4** also *Brit.* /pyóon/ (in India) an office messenger, attendant, or orderly. **5** a bullfighter's assistant. □□ **pe·on·age** *n.* [Port. *peão* & Sp. *peon* f. med.L *pedo –onis* walker f. L *pes pedis* foot: cf. PAWN[1]]

pe·o·ny /péeənee/ *n.* (*pl.* **-nies**) any herbaceous plant of the genus *Paeonia*, with large globular red, pink, or white flowers, often double in cultivated varieties. [OE *peonie* f. L *peonia* f. Gk *paiōnia* f. *Paiōn*, physician of the gods]

peo·ple /péepəl/ *n. & v.* ● *n.* **1** (usu. as *pl.*) **a** persons composing a community, tribe, race, nation, etc. (*the American people; a warlike people*). **b** a group of persons of a usu. specified kind (*the chosen people; these people here; right-thinking people*). (prec. by *the*; treated as *pl.*) **a** the mass of people in a country, etc., not having special rank or position. **b** these considered as an electorate (*the people will reject it*). **3** parents or other relatives. **4 a** subjects, armed followers, a retinue, etc. **b** a congregation of a parish priest, etc. **5** persons in general (*people do not like rudeness*). ● *v.tr.* (usu. foll. by *with*) **1** fill with people, animals, etc.; populate. **2** (esp. as **peopled** *adj.*) inhabit; occupy; fill (*thickly peopled*). [ME f. AF *poeple, people*, OF *pople, peuple*, f. L *populus*]

▶See note at PERSON.

pep /pep/ *n. & v. colloq.* ● *n.* vigor; go; spirit. ● *v.tr.* (**pepped, pepping**) (usu. foll. by *up*) fill with vigor. [abbr. of PEPPER]

pep·er·i·no /pépəréenō/ *n.* a light porous (esp. brown) volcanic rock formed of small grains of sand, cinders, etc. [It. f. *pepere* pepper]

pep·er·o·ni var. of PEPPERONI.

pep·lum /pépləm/ n. **1** a short flounce, ruffle, etc., at waist level, esp. of a blouse or jacket over a skirt. **2** *Gk Antiq.* a woman's outer garment. [L f. Gk *peplos*]

pe·po /peépō/ n. (*pl.* **·pos**) any fleshy fruit of the melon, squash, or cucumber type, with numerous seeds and surrounded by a hard skin. [L, = pumpkin, f. Gk *pepōn* abbr. of *pepōn sikuos* ripe gourd]

pep·per /pépər/ n. & v. ● n. **1 a** a hot aromatic condiment from the dried berries of certain plants used whole or ground. **b** any climbing vine of the genus *Piper*, esp. *P. nigrum*, yielding these berries. **2** anything hot or pungent. **3 a** any plant of the genus *Capsicum*, esp. *C. annuum*. **b** the fruit of this used esp. as a vegetable or salad ingredient. **4** = CAYENNE. ● v. tr. **1** sprinkle or treat with or as if with pepper. **2 a** pelt with missiles. **b** hurl abuse, etc., at. **3** punish severely. [OE *piper, pipor* f. L *piper* f. Gk *peperi* f. Skr. *pippalī*- berry, peppercorn]

pep·per·corn /pépərkawrn/ n. **1** the dried berry of *Piper nigrum* as a condiment. **2** *Brit.* (in full **peppercorn rent**) a nominal rent.

pep·per mill n. a device for grinding pepper by hand.

pep·per·mint /pépərmint/ n. **1 a** a mint plant, *Mentha piperita*, grown for the strong-flavored oil obtained from its leaves. **b** the oil from this. **2** a candy flavored with peppermint. **3** *Austral.* any of various eucalyptuses yielding oil with a similar flavor. □□ **pep·per·mint·y** adj.

pep·per·mint stick n. a hard usu. cylindrical stick of peppermint-flavored candy.

pep·per·o·ni /pépərōnee/ n. (also **pep·er·o·ni**) beef and pork sausage seasoned with pepper. [It. *peperone* chilli]

pep·per pot n. **1** a W. Indian dish of meat, etc., stewed with cayenne pepper. **2** (also **Phil·a·del·phi·a pep·per pot**) a thick soup containing tripe, meat, vegetables, and seasonings, esp. pepper.

pep·per·wort /pépərwərt, –wawrt/ n. any cruciferous plant of the genus *Lepidium*, esp. garden cress.

pep·per·y /pépəree/ adj. **1** of, like, or containing much pepper. **2** - hot-tempered. **3** pungent; stinging. □□ **pep·per·i·ness** n.

pep pill n. a pill containing a stimulant drug.

pep·py /pépee/ adj. (**pep·pi·er**, **pep·pi·est**) *colloq.* vigorous; energetic; bouncy. □□ **pep·pi·ly** adv. **pep·pi·ness** n.

pep·sin /pépsin/ n. an enzyme contained in the gastric juice that hydrolyzes proteins. [G f. Gk *pepsis* digestion]

pep talk n. a usu. short talk intended to enthuse, encourage, etc.

pep·tic /péptik/ adj. concerning or promoting digestion. [Gk *peptikos* able to digest (as PEPTONE)]

pep·tic glands n.pl. glands secreting gastric juice.

pep·tic ul·cer n. an ulcer in the stomach or duodenum.

pep·tide /péptīd/ n. *Biochem.* any of a group of organic compounds consisting of two or more amino acids bonded in sequence. [G *Peptid*, back-form. (as POLYPEPTIDE)]

pep·tone /péptōn/ n. a protein fragment formed by hydrolysis in the process of digestion. □□ **pep·to·nize** /–tənīz/ v.tr. [G *Pepton* f. Gk *peptos*, neut. *pepton* cooked]

Pe·quot /peékwot/ n. **1 a** a N. American people native to eastern Connecticut. **b** a member of this people. **2** the language of this people.

per /pər/ prep. & adv. ● prep. **1** for each; for every (*two cupcakes per child; five miles per hour*). **2** by means of; by; through (*per rail*). **3** (in full **as per**) in accordance with (*as per instructions*). **4** *Heraldry* in the direction of. ● adv. *colloq.* each; apiece. □ **as per usual** *colloq.* as usual. [L]

▶Per is the Latin word meaning 'for every.' Although business correspondence frequently uses the expression, *As per your letter,* meaning "In reference to your letter," this usage is not universally accepted.

per- /pər/ prefix **1** forming verbs, nouns, and adjectives meaning: **a** through; all over (*perforate; perforation; pervade*). **b** completely; very (*perfervid; perturb*). **c** to destruction; to the bad (*pervert; perdition*). **2** *Chem.* having the maximum of some element in combination, esp.: **a** in the names of binary compounds in *–ide* (*peroxide*). **b** in the names of oxides, acids, etc., in *–ic* (*perchloric; permanganic*). **c** in the names of salts of these acids (*perchlorate; permanganate*). [L *per-* (as PER)]

per·ad·ven·ture /pərədvénchər, pér–/ adv. & n. archaic or joc. ● adv. perhaps. ● n. uncertainty; chance; conjecture; doubt (esp. beyond or without peradventure). [ME f. OF *per* or *par auenture* by chance (as PER, ADVENTURE)]

per·am·bu·late /pərámbyəlayt/ v. **1** tr. walk through, over, or about (streets, the country, etc.). **2** intr. walk from place to place. **3** tr. **a** travel through and inspect (territory). **b** formally establish the boundaries of (a parish, etc.) by walking around them. □□ **per·am·bu·la·tion** /–láyshən/ n. **per·am·bu·la·to·ry** /–lətáwree/ adj. [L *perambulare perambulat-* (as PER-, *ambulare* walk)]

per·am·bu·la·tor /pərámbyəlaytər/ n. *Brit. formal* = PRAM¹. [PERAMBULATE]

per an·num /pər ánəm/ adv. for each year. [L]

per·cale /pərkáyl/ n. a closely woven cotton fabric like calico. [F, of uncert. orig.]

per cap·i·ta /pər kápitə/ adv. & adj. (also **per ca·put** /kápoot/) for each person. [L, = by heads]

per·ceive /pərseév/ v.tr. **1** apprehend, esp. through the sight; observe. **2** (usu. foll. by *that, how,* etc., + clause) apprehend with the mind; understand. **3** regard mentally in a specified manner (*perceives the universe as infinite*). □□ **per·ceiv·a·ble** adj. **per·ceiv·er** n. [ME f. OF *perçoivre,* f. L *percipere* (as PER-, *capere* take)]

per·cent /pərsént/ adv. & n. (also **per cent**) ● adv. in every hundred. ● n. **1** percentage. **2** one part in every hundred (*half a percent*). **3** (in *pl.*) *Brit.* public securities yielding interest of so much percent (*three percents*).

per·cent·age /pərséntij/ n. **1** a rate or proportion percent. **2** a proportion. **3** *colloq.* personal benefit or advantage.

per·cen·tile /pərséntil/ n. *Statistics* one of 99 values of a variable dividing a population into 100 equal groups as regards the value of that variable.

per·cept /pérsept/ n. *Philos.* **1** an object of perception. **2** a mental concept resulting from perceiving, esp. by sight. [L *perceptum* perceived (thing), neut. past part. of *percipere* PERCEIVE, after *concept*]

per·cep·ti·ble /pərséptibəl/ adj. capable of being perceived by the senses or intellect. □□ **per·cep·ti·bil·i·ty** /–bilitee/ n. **per·cep·ti·bly** adv. [OF *perceptible* or LL *perceptibilis* f. L (as PERCEIVE)]

per·cep·tion /pərsépshən/ n. **1 a** the faculty of perceiving. **b** an instance of this. **2** (often foll. by *of*) **a** the intuitive recognition of a truth, aesthetic quality, etc. **b** an instance of this (*a sudden perception of the true position*). **3** *Philos.* the ability of the mind to refer sensory information to an external object as its cause. □□ **per·cep·tion·al** adj. **per·cep·tu·al** /–chōōəl/ adj. **per·cep·tu·al·ly** adv. [ME f. L *perceptio* (as PERCEIVE)]

per·cep·tive /pərséptiv/ adj. **1** capable of perceiving. **2** sensitive; discerning; observant (*a perceptive remark*). □□ **per·cep·tive·ly** adv. **per·cep·tive·ness** n. **per·cep·tiv·i·ty** /–séptivitee/ n. [med.L *perceptivus* (as PERCEIVE)]

perch¹ /pərch/ n. & v. ● n. **1** a usu. horizontal bar, branch, etc., used by a bird to rest on. **2** a usu. high or precarious place for a person or thing to rest on. **3** esp. *Brit.* a measure of length, esp. for land, of 5½ yards. ● v.intr. & tr. (usu. foll. by *on*) settle or rest, or cause to settle or rest on or as if on a perch, etc. (*the bird perched on a branch; a town perched on a hill*). □ **knock a person off his** (or **her**) **perch 1** vanquish; destroy. **2** make less confident or secure. [ME f. OF *perche, percher* f. L *pertica* pole]

perch² /pərch/ n. (*pl.* same or **perch·es**) **1** any spiny-finned freshwater edible fish of the genus *Perca*, esp. *P. flavescens* of N. America or *P. fluviatilis* of Europe. **2** any fish of several similar or related species. [ME f. OF *perche* f. L *perca* f. Gk *perkē*]

per·chance /pərcháns/ adv. **1** by chance. **2** possibly; maybe. [ME f. AF *par chance* f. *par* by, CHANCE]

perch·er /pérchər/ n. any bird with feet adapted for perching; a passerine.

per·che·ron /pérchəron, –shə–/ n. a powerful breed of draft horse. [F, orig. bred in le *Perche*, a district of N. France]

per·chlo·rate /pərkláwrayt/ n. *Chem.* a salt or ester of perchloric acid.

per·chlo·ric ac·id /pərkláwrik/ n. *Chem.* a strong liquid acid containing heptavalent chlorine. [PER- f CHLORINE]

per·cip·i·ent /pərsípeeənt/ adj. & n. ● adj. **1** able to perceive; conscious. **2** discerning; observant. ● n. a person who perceives, esp. something outside the range of the senses. □□ **per·cip·i·ence** n. **per·cip·i·ent·ly** adv. [L (as PERCEIVE)]

per·co·late /pérkəlayt/ v. **1** intr. (often foll. by *through*) **a** (of liquid, etc.) filter or ooze gradually (esp. through a porous surface). **b** (of an idea, etc.) permeate gradually. **2** tr. prepare (coffee) by repeatedly passing boiling water through ground beans. **3** tr. ooze through; permeate. **4** tr. strain (a liquid, powder, etc.) through a fine mesh, etc. **5** intr. colloq. become livelier, more active, etc. □□ **per·co·la·tion** /–láyshən/ n. [L *percolare* (as PER-, *colare* strain f. *colum* strainer)]

per·co·la·tor /pérkəlaytər/ n. a machine for making coffee by circulating boiling water through ground beans.

per con·tra /per kóntrə/ adv. on the opposite side (of an account, assessment, etc.); on the contrary. [It.]

per·cuss /pərkús/ v.tr. *Med.* tap (a part of the body) gently with a finger or an instrument as part of a diagnosis. [L *percutere percuss-* strike (as PER-, *cutere* = *quatere* shake)]

per·cus·sion /pərkúshən/ n. **1** *Mus.* **a** (often *attrib.*) the playing of music by striking instruments with sticks, etc. (*a percussion band*).

b the section of such instruments in an orchestra or band (*asked the percussion to stay behind*). **2** *Med.* the act or an instance of percussing. **3** the forcible striking of one esp. solid body against another. □□ **per•cus•sion•ist** *n.* **per•cus•sive** *adj.* **per•cus•sive•ly** *adv.* **per•cus•sive•ness** *n.* [F *percussion* or L *percussio* (as PERCUSS)]

per•cus•sion cap *n.* a small amount of explosive powder contained in metal or paper and exploded by striking, used esp. in toy guns and formerly in some firearms.

per•cu•ta•ne•ous /pérkyōōtáyneeəs/ *adj.* esp. *Med.* made or done through the skin. [L *per cutem* through the skin]

per di•em /pər deé-em, díem/ *adv., adj., & n.* ● *adv. & adj.* for each day. ● *n.* an allowance or payment for each day. [L]

per•di•tion /pərdíshən/ *n.* eternal death; damnation. [ME f. OF *perdiciun* or eccl.L *perditio* f. L *perdere* destroy (as PER-, *dere dit-* = *dare* give)]

per•dur•a•ble /pərdōōrəbəl, –dyōōr–/ *adj. formal* permanent; eternal; durable. □□ **per•dur•a•bil•i•ty** /–bílitee/ *n.* **per•dur•a•bly** *adv.* [ME f. OF f. LL *perdurabilis* (as PER-, DURABLE)]

père /pair/ *n.* (added to a surname to distinguish a father from a son) the father; senior (cf. FILS). [F, = father]

Père Da•vid's deer /páir daavéedz, dáyvidz/ *n.* a large slender-antlered deer, *Elaphurus davidianus.* [after Father A. *David,* Fr. missionary d. 1900]

per•e•gri•nate /périgrinayt/ *v.intr.* travel; journey, esp. extensively or at leisure. □□ **per•e•gri•na•tion** /–náyshən/ *n.* **per•e•gri•na•tor** *n.* [L *peregrinari* (as PEREGRINE)]

per•e•grine /périgrin, –green/ *n. & adj.* ● *n.* (in full **peregrine falcon**) a widely distributed falcon, *Falco peregrinus,* much used for falconry. ● *adj.* **1** imported from abroad; foreign; outlandish. **2** inclined to wander. [L *peregrinus* f. *peregre* abroad f. *per* through + *ager* field]

per•emp•to•ry /pərémptəree/ *adj.* **1** (of a statement or command) admitting no denial or refusal. **2** (of a person, a person's manner, etc.) dogmatic; imperious; dictatorial. **3** *Law* not open to appeal or challenge; final. **4** absolutely fixed; essential. □□ **per•emp•to•ri•ly** *adv.* **per•emp•to•ri•ness** *n.* [AF *peremptorie,* OF *peremptoire* f. L *peremptorius* deadly, decisive, f. *perimere perempt-* destroy, cut off (as PER-, *emere* take, buy)]

▶Peremptory and preemptive can be confused, as both involve stopping something. A **peremptory** act or statement is absolute; it cannot be denied: *He issued a peremptory order.* A **preemptive** action is one taken before an adversary can act: *Preemptive air strikes stopped the enemy from launching the new warship.*

per•emp•to•ry chal•lenge *n.Law* a defendant's objection to a proposed juror, made without needing to give a reason.

per•en•ni•al /pəréneeəl/ *adj. & n.* ● *adj.* **1** lasting through a year or several years. **2** (of a plant) lasting several years (cf. ANNUAL). **3** lasting a long time or for ever. **4** (of a stream) flowing through all seasons of the year. ● *n.* a perennial plant (*a herbaceous perennial*). □□ **per•en•ni•al•i•ty** /–neeálitee/ *n.* **per•en•ni•al•ly** *adv.* [L *perennis* (as PER-, *annus* year)]

pe•re•stroi•ka /pérestróykə/ *n. hist.* (in the former Soviet Union) the policy or practice of restructuring or reforming the economic and political system. [Russ. *perestroĭka* = restructuring]

per•fect *adj., v., & n.* ● *adj.* /pə́ rfikt/ **1** complete; not deficient. **2 a** faultless (*a perfect diamond*). **b** blameless in morals or behavior. **3 a** very satisfactory (*a perfect evening*). **b** (often foll. by *for*) most appropriate; suitable. **4** exact; precise (*a perfect circle*). **5** entire; unqualified (*a perfect stranger*). **6** *Math.* (of a number) equal to the sum of its divisors. **7** *Gram.* (of a tense) denoting a completed action or event in the past, formed in English with *have* or *has* and the past participle, as in *they have eaten.* **8** *Mus.* (of pitch) absolute. **9** *Bot.* **a** (of a flower) having all four types of whorl. **b** (of a fungus) in the stage where the sexual spores are formed. **10** (often foll. by *in*) thoroughly trained or skilled (*is perfect in geometry*). ● *v.tr.* /pərfékt/ **1** make perfect; improve. **2** carry through; complete. **3** complete (a sheet) by printing the other side. ● *n.* /pé rfikt/ *Gram.* the perfect tense. □□ **per•fect•er** *n.* **per•fect•i•ble** *adj.* **per•fect•i•bil•i•ty** *n.* **per•fect•ness** *n.* [ME and OF *parfit, perfet* f. L *perfectus* past part. of *perficere* complete (as PER- , *facere* do)]

GRAMMAR TIP perfect

Perfect Tenses. The **perfect tenses** of a verb —known as the **present perfect,** the **past perfect,** and the **future perfect** —show a completed state or action. The **present perfect,** formed by adding *has* or *have* to the past participle of the verb, is used to describe a state or action that started in the past and may continue to the present (*we have lived here for over 20 years*). The **past perfect,** formed by adding *had* to the past participle of the verb, describes a state or action that occurred before something else in the past (*they had lived in California until the earthquake*). The **future perfect** describes a state or action that will occur before something else in the future (*she will have lived on the East Coast for most of her life*).

▶Literally, **perfect, unique,** etc., are absolute words and should not be modified, as they often are in such phrases as "most perfect, " "quite unique," etc.

per•fec•ta /pərféktə/ *n.* a form of betting in which the first two places in a race must be predicted in the correct order. [Amer. Sp. *quiniela perfecta* perfect quinella]

per•fect bind•ing *n.* a form of bookbinding in which the leaves are attached to the spine by gluing rather than sewing.

per•fect in•ter•val *n. Mus.* a fourth or fifth as it would occur in a major or minor scale starting on the lower note of the interval, or octave.

per•fec•tion /pərfékshən/ *n.* **1** the act or process of making perfect. **2** the state of being perfect; faultlessness; excellence. **3** a perfect person, thing, or example. **4** an accomplishment. **5** full development; completion. □ **to perfection** exactly; completely. [ME f. OF f. L *perfectio –onis* (as PERFECT)]

per•fec•tion•ism /pərfékshənizəm/ *n.* **1** the uncompromising pursuit of excellence. **2** *Philos.* the belief that religious or moral perfection is attainable. □□ **per•fec•tion•ist** *n. & adj.* [PERFECT]

per•fec•tive /pərféktiv/ *adj. & n. Gram.* ● *adj.* (of an aspect of a verb, etc.) expressing the completion of an action (opp. IMPERFECTIVE). ● *n.* the perfective aspect or form of a verb. [med.L *perfectivus* (as PERFECT)]

per•fect•ly /pérfiktlee/ *adv.* **1** completely; absolutely (*I understand you perfectly*). **2** quite; completely (*is perfectly capable of doing it*). **3** in a perfect way. **4** very (*you know perfectly well*).

per•fec•to /pərféktō/ *n. (pl.* **·tos**) a large thick cigar pointed at each end. [Sp., = perfect]

perfect pitch *n.* = ABSOLUTE PITCH 1.

perfect square *n.* = SQUARE NUMBER.

per•fer•vid /pərfə́rvid/ *adj.* very fervid. □□ **per•fer•vid•ly** *adv.* **per•fer•vid•ness** *n.* [mod.L *perfervidus* (as PER-, FERVID)]

per•fi•dy /pə́rfidee/ *n.* breach of faith; treachery. □□ **per•fid•i•ous** /–fídeeəs/ *adj.* **per•fid•i•ous•ly** *adv.* [L *perfidia* f. *perfidus* treacherous (as PER-, *fidus* f. *fides* faith)]

per•fo•li•ate /pərfṓleeət/ *adj.* (of a plant) having the stalk apparently passing through the leaf. [mod.L *perfoliatus* (as PER-, FOLIATE)]

per•fo•rate *v. & adj.* ● *v.* /pə́rfərayt/ **1** *tr.* make a hole or holes through; pierce. **2** *tr.* make a row of small holes in (paper, etc.) so that a part may be torn off easily. **3** *tr.* make an opening into; pass into or extend through. **4** *intr.* (usu. foll. by *into, through,* etc.) penetrate. ● *adj.* /pə́rfərət/ perforated. □□ **per•fo•ra•tion** /–ráyshən/ *n.* **per•fo•ra•tive** /pə́rfərətiv/ *adj.* **per•fo•ra•tor** /pə́rfəraytər/ *n.* [L *perforare* (as PER-, *forare* pierce)]

per•force /pərfáwrs/ *adv. archaic* unavoidably; necessarily. [ME f. OF *par force* by FORCE[1]]

per•form /pərfawrm/ *v.* **1** *tr.* (also *absol.*) carry into effect; be the agent of; do (a command, promise, task, etc.). **2** *tr.* (also *absol.*) go through; execute (a public function, play, piece of music, etc.). **3** *intr.* act in a play; play an instrument or sing, etc., (*likes performing*). **4** *intr.* (of a trained animal) execute tricks, etc., at a public show. **5** *intr.* operate; function. □□ **per•form•a•ble** *adj.* **per•form•a•bil•i•ty** *n.* **per•form•a•to•ry** *adj. & n. (pl.* **·ries**). **per•form•er** *n.* **per•form•ing** *adj.* [ME f. AF *parfourmer* f. OF *parfournir* (assim. to *forme* FORM) f. *par* PER- + *fournir* FURNISH]

per•for•mance /pərfáwrməns/ *n.* **1** (usu. foll. by *of*) **a** the act or process of performing or carrying out. **b** the execution or fulfillment (of a duty, etc.). **2** a staging or production (of a drama, piece of music, etc.) (*the afternoon performance*). **3** a person's achievement under test conditions, etc. (*put up a good performance*). **4** *colloq.* a fuss; a scene; a public exhibition (*made such a performance about leaving*). **5 a** the capabilities of a machine, esp. a car or aircraft. **b** (*attrib.*) of high capability (*a performance car*).

per•for•ma•tive /pərfáwrmətiv/ *adj. & n.* ● *adj.* **1** of or relating to performance. **2** denoting an utterance that effects an action by being spoken or written (e.g., *I bet, I apologize*). ● *n.* a performative utterance.

per•form•ing arts /pərfáwrming/ *n.pl.* the arts, such as drama, music, and dance, that require performance for their realization.

per•fume /pə́rfyoōm/ *n. & v.* ● *n.* **1** a sweet smell. **2** fluid containing the essence of flowers, etc.; scent. ● *v.tr.* (also /pərfyoōm/) (usu. as **perfumed** *adj.*) impart a sweet scent to; impregnate with a sweet smell. □□ **per•fum•y** *adj.* [F *parfum, parfumer* f. obs. It. *parfumare, perfumare* (as PER-, *fumare* smoke, FUME): orig. of smoke from a burning substance]

per•fum•er /pərfyoōmər/ *n.* a maker or seller of perfumes. □□ **per•fum•er•y** *n. (pl.* **·ies**).

per•func•to•ry /pərfúngktəree/ *adj.* **1 a** done merely for the sake of getting through a duty. **b** done in a cursory or careless manner. **2** superficial; mechanical. □□ **per•func•to•ri•ly** *adv.* **per•func•to•ri•ness** *n.* [LL *perfunctorius* careless f. L *perfungi perfunct-* (as PER-, *fungi* perform)]

per•fuse /pərfyoōz/ *v.tr.* **1** (often foll. by *with*) **a** sprinkle (with water, etc.). **b** cover or suffuse (with radiance, etc.). **2** pour or diffuse (water, etc.) through or over. **3** *Med.* cause a fluid to pass through (an organ, etc.). □□ **per•fu•sion** /-fyőőzhən/ *n.* **per•fu•sive** /-fyőősiv/ *adj.* [L *perfundere perfus-* (as PER-, *fundere* pour)]

per•go•la /pórgələ/ *n.* an arbor or covered walk, formed of growing plants trained over a trellis. [It. f. L *pergula* projecting roof f. *pergere* proceed]

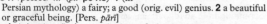

pergola

per•haps /pərháps/ *adv.* **1** it may be; possibly (*perhaps it is lost*). **2** introducing a polite request (*perhaps you would open the window?*). [PER + HAP]

pe•ri /péeree/ *n.* (*pl.* **pe•ris**) **1** (in Persian mythology) a fairy; a good (*orig.* evil) genius. **2** a beautiful or graceful being. [Pers. *parī*]

peri- /péree/ *prefix* **1** around; about. **2** *Astron.* the point nearest to (*perigee*; *perihelion*). [Gk *peri* around, about]

per•i•anth /péreeánth/ *n.* the outer part of a flower. [F *périanthe* f. mod.L *perianthium* (as PERI- + Gk *anthos* flower)]

per•i•apt /péreeápt/ *n.* a thing worn as a charm; an amulet. [F *périapte* f. Gk *periapton* f. *haptō* fasten]

per•i•car•di•um /périkaárdeeəm/ *n.* (*pl.* **per•i•car•di•a** /-deeə/) the membranous sac enclosing the heart. □□ **per•i•car•di•ac** /-deeak/ *adj.* **per•i•car•di•al** *adj.* **per•i•car•di•tis** /-dítis/ *n.* [mod.L f. Gk *perikardion* (as PERI- + *kardia* heart)]

per•i•carp /périkaarp/ *n.* the part of a fruit formed from the wall of the ripened ovary. [F *péricarpe* f. Gk *perikarpion* pod, shell (as PE-RI-, *karpos* fruit)]

per•i•chon•dri•um /périkóndreeəm/ *n.* the membrane enveloping cartilage tissue (except at the joints). [PERI- + Gk *khondros* cartilage]

per•i•clase /périklays/ *n.* a pale mineral consisting of magnesia. [mod.L *periclasia*, erron. f. Gk *peri* exceedingly + *klasis* breaking, from its perfect cleavage]

per•i•cli•nal /périklínəl/ *adj. Geol.* (of a mound, etc.) sloping down in all directions from a central point. [Gk *periklinēs* sloping on all sides (as PERI-, CLINE)]

pe•ric•o•pe /pəríkəpee/ *n.* a short passage or paragraph, esp. a portion of Scripture read in public worship. [LL f. Gk *perikopē* (as PE-RI-, *kopē* cutting f. *koptō* cut)]

per•i•cra•ni•um /périkráyneeəm/ *n.* the membrane enveloping the skull. [mod.L f. Gk (as PERI-, *kranion* skull)]

per•i•dot /péridot/ *n.* a green variety of olivine, used esp. as a semi-precious stone. [ME f. OF *peritot*, of unkn. orig.]

per•i•gee /périjee/ *n.* the point in an orbit where the orbiting body is nearest the center of the body it is orbiting. (opp. APOGEE). □□ **per•i•ge•an** /périjéeən/ *adj.* [F *périgée* f. mod.L f. Gk *perigeion* around the earth (as PERI-, *gē* earth)]

per•i•gla•cial /périgláyshəl/ *adj.* of or relating to a region adjoining a glacier.

pe•rig•y•nous /pəríjinəs/ *adj.* (of stamens) situated around the pistil or ovary. [mod.L *perigynus* (as PERI-, –GYNOUS)]

per•i•he•li•on /périhéelyən/ *n.* (*pl.* **per•i•he•li•a** /-lyə/) the point of a planet's or comet's orbit nearest to the sun's center. [Graecized f. mod.L *perihelium* (as PERI-, Gk *hēlios* sun)]

per•il /péril/ *n. & v.* • *n.* serious and immediate danger. • *v.tr.* (**per•iled, per•il•ing** or **per•illed, per•il•ling**) threaten; endanger. □ **at one's peril** at one's own risk. **in peril of** with great risk to (*in peril of your life*). [ME f. OF f. L *peric(u)lum*]

per•il•ous /périləs/ *adj.* **1** full of risk; dangerous; hazardous. **2** exposed to imminent risk of destruction, etc. □□ **per•il•ous•ly** *adv.* **per•il•ous•ness** *n.* [ME f. OF *perillous* f. L *periculosus* f. *periculum*: see PERIL]

per•i•lune /périlōōn/ *n.* the point in a body's lunar orbit where it is closest to the moon's center (opp. APOLUNE). [PERI- + L *luna* moon, after *perigee*]

per•i•lymph /périlimf/ *n.* the fluid in the labyrinth of the ear.

pe•rim•e•ter /pərímitər/ *n.* **1 a** the circumference or outline of a closed figure. **b** the length of this. **2 a** the outer boundary of an enclosed area. **b** a defended boundary. **3** an instrument for measuring a field of vision. □□ **per•i•met•ric** /périmétrik/ *adj.* [F *périmètre* or f. L *perimetrus* f. Gk *perimetros* (as PERI-, *metros* f. *metron* measure)]

per•i•na•tal /pérináyt'l/ *adj.* of or relating to the time immediately before and after birth.

per•i•ne•um /périnéeəm/ *n.* the region of the body between the anus and the scrotum or vulva. □□ **per•i•ne•al** *adj.* [LL f. Gk *perinaion*]

pe•ri•od /péereeəd/ *n. & adj.* • *n.* **1** a length or portion of time (*periods of rain*). **2** a distinct portion of history, a person's life, etc. (*the Federal period*; *Picasso's Blue Period*). **3** *Geol.* a time forming part of a geological era (*the Quaternary period*). **4 a** an interval between recurrences of an astronomical or other phenomenon. **b** the time taken by a planet to rotate about its axis. **5** the time allowed for a lesson in school. **6** an occurrence of menstruation. **7 a** a complete sentence, esp. one consisting of several clauses. **b** (in *pl.*) rhetorical language. **8 a** a punctuation mark (.) used at the end of a sentence or an abbreviation. **b** used at the end of a sentence, etc., to indicate

---

finality, absoluteness, etc. (*we want the best, period*). **9 a** a set of figures repeated in a recurring decimal. **b** the smallest interval over which a function takes the same value. **10** *Chem.* a sequence of elements between two noble gases forming a row in the periodic table. **11** *Music* a discrete division of a musical composition, containing two or more phrases and ending in a cadence. • *adj.* belonging to or characteristic of some past period (*period furniture*). □ **of the period** of the era under discussion (*the custom of the period*).

per•i•o•date /pəríədayt/ *n. Chem.* a salt or ester of periodic acid.

pe•ri•od•ic /péereeódik/ *adj.* **1** appearing or occurring at regular intervals. **2** of or concerning the period of a celestial body (*periodic motion*). **3** (of diction, etc.) expressed in periods (see PERIOD *n.* 7a). □□ **pe•ri•o•dic•i•ty** /-reedísitee/ *n.* [F *périodique* or L *periodicus* f. Gk *periodikos* (as PERIOD)]

per•i•od•ic ac•id /pəríódik/ *n. Chem.* a hygroscopic solid acid containing heptavalent iodine. [PER- + IODINE]

pe•ri•od•i•cal /péereeódikəl/ *n. & adj.* • *n.* a newspaper, magazine, etc., issued at regular intervals, usu. monthly or weekly. • *adj.* **1** published at regular intervals. **2** periodic; occasional. □□ **pe•ri•od•i•cal•ly** *adv.*

pe•ri•od•ic dec•i•mal *n. Math.* a set of figures repeated in a recurring decimal.

per•i•od•ic func•tion *n. Math.* a function returning to the same value at regular intervals.

pe•ri•od•ic ta•ble *n.* an arrangement of elements in order of increasing atomic number and in which elements of similar chemical properties appear at regular intervals.

pe•ri•od•i•za•tion /péereeədízáyshən/ *n.* the division of history into periods.

per•i•o•don•tics /péreeədóntiks/ *n.pl.* (treated as *sing.*) the branch of dentistry concerned with the structures surrounding and supporting the teeth. □□ **per•i•o•don•tal** *adj.* **per•i•o•don•tist** *n.* [PERI- + Gk *odous odont-* tooth]

per•i•o•don•tol•o•gy /péreeədontóləjee/ *n.* = PERIODONTICS.

pe•ri•od piece *n.* an object or work whose main interest lies in its historical, etc., associations.

per•i•os•te•um /péreeósteeəm/ *n.* (*pl.* **per•i•os•te•a** /-teeə/) a membrane enveloping the bones where no cartilage is present. □□ **per•i•os•te•al** *adj.* **per•i•os•ti•tis** /-stítis/ *n.* [mod.L f. Gk *periosteon* (as PERI-, *osteon* bone)]

per•i•pa•tet•ic /péripətétik/ *adj. & n.* • *adj.* **1** (of a teacher) working in more than one school or college, etc. **2** going from place to place; itinerant. **3** (**Peripatetic**) Aristotelian (from Aristotle's habit of walking in the Lyceum while teaching). • *n.* a peripatetic person, esp. a teacher. □□ **per•i•pa•tet•i•cal•ly** *adv.* **per•i•pa•tet•i•cism** *n.* [ME f. OF *peripatetique* or L *peripateticus* f. Gk *peripatētikos* f. *peripateō* (as PERI-, *pateō* walk)]

per•i•pe•tei•a /péripiteeə, -tíə/ *n.* a sudden change of fortune in a drama or in life. [Gk (as PERI-, *pet-* f. *piptō* fall)]

pe•riph•er•al /pərífərəl/ *adj. & n.* • *adj.* **1** of minor importance; marginal. **2** of the periphery; on the fringe. **3** *Anat.* near the surface of the body, with special reference to the circulation and nervous system. **4** (of equipment) used with a computer, etc., but not an integral part of it. • *n.* a peripheral device or piece of equipment. □□ **pe•riph•er•al•ly** *adv.*

pe•riph•er•al nerv•ous sys•tem *n. Anat.* the nervous system outside the brain and spinal cord.

pe•riph•er•al vi•sion *n.* **1** area seen around the outside of one's field of vision. **2** ability to perceive in this area (*contact lenses offered better peripheral vision than glasses*).

pe•riph•er•y /pərífəree/ *n.* (*pl.* **-ies**) **1** the boundary of an area or surface. **2** an outer or surrounding region (*built on the periphery of the old town*). [LL *peripheria* f. Gk *periphereia* circumference (as PERI-, *phereia* f. *phero* bear)]

pe•riph•ra•sis /pərífrəsis/ *n.* (*pl.* **pe•riph•ra•ses** /-seez/) **1** a roundabout way of speaking; circumlocution. **2** a roundabout phrase. [L f. Gk f. *periphrazō* (as PERI-, *phrazō* declare)]

per•i•phras•tic /périfrástik/ *adj.* **1** of or involving periphrasis. **2** *Gram.* (of a case, tense, etc.) formed by combination of words rather than by inflection (*e.g., did go, of the people* rather than *went, the people's*). □□ **per•i•phras•ti•cal•ly** *adv.* [Gk *periphrastikos* (as PE-RIPHRASIS)]

pe•rip•ter•al /pəríptərəl/ *adj.* (of a temple) surrounded by a single row of columns. [Gk *peripteron* (as PERI-, Gk *pteron* wing)]

per·i·scope /périskōp/ n. an apparatus with a tube and mirrors or prisms, by which an observer in a trench, submerged submarine, or at the rear of a crowd, etc., can see things otherwise out of sight.

per·i·scop·ic /périskópik/ adj. of a periscope. □□ **per·i·scop·i·cal·ly** adv.

per·i·scop·ic lens n. a lens allowing distinct vision over a wide angle.

per·ish /pérish/ v. 1 intr. be destroyed; suffer death or ruin. 2 Brit. a intr. (esp. of rubber, a rubber object, etc.) lose its normal qualities; deteriorate; rot. b tr. cause to rot or deteriorate. 3 Brit. tr. (in passive) suffer from cold or exposure (we were perished standing outside). □ **perish the thought** an exclamation of horror against an unwelcome idea. □□ **per·ish·less** adj. [ME f. OF perir f. L perire pass away (as PER-, ire go)]

periscope

per·ish·a·ble /périshəbəl/ adj. & n. ● adj. liable to perish; subject to decay. ● n. a thing, esp. a foodstuff, subject to speedy decay. □□ **per·ish·a·bil·i·ty** /–bílitee/ n. **per·ish·a·ble·ness** n.

per·ish·ing /périshing/ adj. & adv. Brit. colloq. ● adj. 1 confounded. 2 freezing cold; extremely chilly. ● adv. confoundedly. □□ **per·ish·ing·ly** adv.

per·i·sperm /périspərm/ n. a mass of nutritive material outside the embryo in some seeds. [PERI- + Gk sperma seed]

per·i·stal·sis /péristáwlsis, –stál–/ n. an involuntary muscular wavelike movement by which the contents of the alimentary canal, etc., are propelled along. □□ **per·i·stal·tic** adj. **per·i·stal·ti·cal·ly** adv. [mod.L f. Gk peristellō wrap around (as PERI-, stellō place)]

per·i·stome /péristōm/ n. 1 Bot. a fringe of small teeth around the mouth of a capsule in mosses and certain fungi. 2 Zool. the parts surrounding the mouth of various invertebrates. [mod.L peristoma f. PERI- + Gk stoma mouth]

per·i·style /péristīl/ n. a row of columns surrounding a temple, court, cloister, etc.; a space surrounded by columns. [F péristyle f. L peristylum f. Gk peristulon (as PERI-, stulos pillar)]

per·i·to·ne·um /périt'nééəm/ n. (pl. **per·i·to·ne·ums** or **per·i·to·ne·a** /–nééə/) the serous membrane lining the cavity of the abdomen. □□ **per·i·to·ne·al** adj. [LL f. Gk peritonaion (as PERI-, tonaion f. –tonos stretched)]

per·i·to·ni·tis /périt'nítis/ n. an inflammatory disease of the peritoneum.

per·i·wig /périwig/ n. esp. hist. a wig. □□ **per·i·wigged** adj. [alt. of PERUKE, with –wi- for F –u- sound]

per·i·win·kle[1] /périwingkəl/ n. 1 any plant of the genus Vinca, esp. an evergreen trailing plant with blue or white flowers. 2 a tropical shrub, Catharanthus roseus, native to Madagascar. [ME f. AF pervenke, OF pervenche f. LL pervinca, assim. to PERIWINKLE[2]]

per·i·win·kle[2] /périwingkəl/ n. any edible marine gastropod mollusk of the genus Littorina; a winkle. [16th c.: orig. unkn.]

per·jure /pórjər/ v.refl. Law 1 willfully tell an untruth when under oath. 2 (as **perjured** adj.) guilty of or involving perjury. □□ **per·jur·er** n. [ME f. OF parjurer f. L perjurare (as PER-, jurare swear)]

per·ju·ry /pórjəree/ n. (pl. **-ries**) Law 1 a breach of an oath, esp. the act of willfully telling an untruth when under oath. 2 the practice of this. □□ **per·ju·ri·ous** /–jŏoreeəs/ adj. [ME f. AF perjurie f. OF parjurie f. L perjurium (as PERJURE)]

perk[1] /pərk/ v. & adj. ● v.tr. raise (one's head, etc.) briskly. ● adj. perky; pert. □ **perk up 1** recover confidence, courage, life, or zest. 2 restore confidence or courage or liveliness in (esp. another person). 3 freshen up. [ME, perh. f. var. of PERCH[1]]

perk[2] /pərk/ n. colloq. a perquisite. [abbr.]

perk[3] /pərk/ v. colloq. 1 intr. (of coffee) percolate, make a bubbling sound in the percolator. 2 tr. percolate (coffee). [abbr. of PERCOLATE]

perk·y /pórkee/ adj. (**perk·i·er**, **perk·i·est**) 1 self-assertive; cocky; pert. 2 lively; cheerful. □□ **perk·i·ly** adv. **perk·i·ness** n.

per·lite /pórlīt/ n. (also **pear·lite**) a glassy type of vermiculite, expandable to a solid form by heating, used for insulation, etc. [F f. perle pearl]

perm /pərm/ n. & v. ● n. a permanent wave. ● v.tr. give a permanent wave to (a person or a person's hair). [abbr.]

per·ma·frost /pórməfrawst, –frost/ n. subsoil that remains frozen throughout the year, as in polar regions. [PERMANENT + FROST]

perm·al·loy /pórməloy, pərmálloy/ n. an alloy of nickel and iron that is easily magnetized and demagnetized. [PERMEABLE + ALLOY]

per·ma·nent /pórmənənt/ adj. & n. ● adj. lasting, or intended to last or function, indefinitely (opp. TEMPORARY). ● n. = PERMANENT WAVE. □□ **per·ma·nence** n. **per·ma·nen·cy** n. **per·ma·nent·ize** v.tr. **per·ma·nent·ly** adv. [ME f. OF permanent or L permanēre (as PER-, manēre remain)]

per·ma·nent mag·net n. a magnet retaining its magnetic properties without continued excitation.

per·ma·nent press n. a process applied to a fabric to make it wrinkle-free.

Per·ma·nent Sec·re·tar·y n. (also **Un·der·sec·re·tar·y**, etc.) (in the UK) a senior grade in the Civil Service, often a permanent adviser to a minister.

per·ma·nent tooth n. a tooth succeeding a baby tooth in a mammal, and lasting most of the mammal's life.

per·ma·nent wave n. an artificial wave in the hair, intended to last for some time.

per·ma·nent way n. Brit. the finished roadbed of a railroad.

per·man·ga·nate /pərmánggənayt/ n. Chem. any salt of permanganic acid, esp. potassium permanganate.

per·man·gan·ic ac·id /pórmanggánik/ n. Chem. an acid containing heptavalent manganese. [PER- + manganic: see MANGANESE]

per·me·a·bil·i·ty /pérmeeəbílitee/ n. 1 the state or quality of being permeable. 2 a quantity measuring the influence of a substance on the magnetic flux in the region it occupies.

per·me·a·ble /pórmeeəbəl/ adj. capable of being permeated. [L permeabilis (as PERMEATE)]

per·me·ate /pórmeeayt/ v. 1 tr. penetrate throughout; pervade; saturate. 2 intr. (usu. foll. by through, among, etc.) diffuse itself. □□ **per·me·ance** n. **per·me·ant** adj. **per·me·a·tion** /–áyshən/ n. **per·me·a·tor** n. [L permeare permeat- (as PER-, meare pass, go)]

Per·mi·an /pórmeeən/ adj. & n. Geol. ● adj. of or relating to the last period of the Paleozoic era with evidence of the development of reptiles and amphibians, and deposits of sandstone. ● n. this period or system. [Perm in Russia]

per mill /per mil/ adv. (also **per mil**) in every thousand. [L]

per·mis·si·ble /pərmísibəl/ adj. allowable. □□ **per·mis·si·bil·i·ty** n. **per·mis·si·bly** adv. [ME f. F or f. med.L permissibilis (as PERMIT)]

per·mis·sion /pərmíshən/ n. (often foll. by to + infin.) consent; authorization. [ME f. OF or f. L permissio (as PERMIT)]

per·mis·sive /pərmísiv/ adj. 1 tolerant; liberal, esp. in sexual matters (the permissive society). 2 giving permission. □□ **per·mis·sive·ly** adv. **per·mis·sive·ness** n. [ME f. OF (-if –ive) or med.L permissivus (as PERMIT)]

per·mit v. & n. ● v. /pərmít/ (**per·mit·ted**, **per·mit·ting**) 1 tr. give permission or consent to; authorize (permit me to say). 2 a tr. allow as possible; give an opportunity to (permit the traffic to flow again). b intr. give an opportunity (circumstances permitting). 3 intr. (foll. by of) admit; allow for. ● n. /pórmit/ 1 a a document giving permission to act in a specified way (was granted a work permit). b a document, etc., that allows entry into a specified zone. 2 permission. □□ **per·mit·tee** /pórmitee/ n. **per·mit·ter** n. [L permittere (as PER-, mittere miss- let go)]

per·mit·tiv·i·ty /pórmitívitee/ n. Electr. a quantity measuring the ability of a substance to store electrical energy in an electric field.

per·mu·tate /pórmyootayt/ v.tr. change the order or arrangement of. [as PERMUTE, or back-form. f. PERMUTATION]

per·mu·ta·tion /pórmyootáyshən/ n. 1 a an ordered arrangement or grouping of a set of numbers, items, etc. b any one of the range of possible groupings. 2 any combination or selection of a specified number of things from a larger group. □□ **per·mu·ta·tion·al** adj. [ME f. OF or f. L permutatio (as PERMUTE)]

per·mute /pərmyóot/ v.tr. alter the sequence or arrangement of. [ME f. L permutare (as PER-, mutare change)]

per·ni·cious /pərníshəs/ adj. destructive; ruinous; fatal. □□ **per·ni·cious·ly** adv. **per·ni·cious·ness** n. [L perniciosus f. pernicies ruin f. nex necis death]

per·ni·cious a·ne·mi·a n. a defective formation of red blood cells through a lack of vitamin B_{12} or folic acid.

per·nick·et·y /pərníkitee/ Brit. var. of PERSNICKETY.

per·o·ne·al /pérənééəl/ adj. Anat. relating to or near the fibula. [mod.L peronaeus peroneal muscle f. perone fibula f. Gk peronē pin, fibula]

per·o·rate /pérərayt/ v.intr. 1 sum up and conclude a speech. 2 speak at length. [L perorare perorat- (as PER-, orare speak)]

per·o·ra·tion /pérəráyshən/ n. 1 the concluding part of a speech, forcefully summing up what has been said. 2 a long or overly rhetorical speech.

per·ox·i·dase /pəróksidays, –dayz/ n. Biochem. any of a class of enzymes found esp. in plants, which catalyze the oxidation of a substrate by hydrogen peroxide.

per·ox·ide /pəróksīd/ n. & v. ● n. Chem. 1 a = HYDROGEN PEROXIDE. b (often attrib.) a solution of hydrogen peroxide used to bleach the hair or as an antiseptic. 2 a compound of oxygen with another element containing the greatest possible proportion of oxygen. 3 any salt or ester of hydrogen peroxide. ● v.tr. bleach (the hair) with peroxide. [PER- + OXIDE]

per·pend var. of PARPEN.

per·pen·dic·u·lar /pórpəndíkyələr/ adj. & n. ● adj. 1 a at right angles to the plane of the horizon. b (usu. foll. by to) Geom. at right angles (to a given line, plane, or surface). 2 upright; vertical. 3 (of a slope, etc.) very steep. 4 (**Perpendicular**) Archit. of the third stage of English Gothic (15th–16th c.) with vertical tracery in large windows. **5** in a standing position. ● *n.* **1** a perpendicular line. **2** a plumb rule or a similar instrument. **3** (prec. by *the*) a perpendicular line or direction (*is out of the perpendicular*). □□ **per•pen•dic•u•lar•i•ty** /–dikyōōláritee/ *n.* **per•pen•dic•u•lar•ly** *adv.* [ME f. L *perpendicularis* f. *perpendiculum* plumb line f. PER- + *pendēre* hang]

per•pe•trate /pə́rpitrayt/ *v.tr.* commit or perform (a crime, blunder, or anything outrageous). □□ **per•pe•tra•tion** /–tráyshən/ *n.* **per•pe•tra•tor** *n.*

▶**Perpetrate vs. Perpetuate.** To **perpetrate** something is to commit it: *The gang perpetrated outrages against several citizens.* To **perpetuate** something is to cause it to continue or to keep happening: *The stories only serve to perpetuate the myth that the house is haunted.*

WORD HISTORY   perpetrate

mid-16th century: from Latin *perpetrat-* 'performed,' from the verb *perpetrare*, from *per-* 'to completion' + *patrare* 'bring about.' In Latin the act perpetrated might be good or bad; in English the verb was first used in statutes referring to crime, hence it acquired a negative association.

per•pet•u•al /pərpéchōōəl/ *adj.* **1** eternal; lasting for ever or indefinitely. **2** continuous; uninterrupted. **3** *colloq.* frequent; much repeated (*perpetual interruptions*). **4** (of an office, etc.) held for life (*perpetual secretary*). □□ **per•pet•u•al•ism** *n.* **per•pet•u•al•ly** *adv.* [ME f. OF *perpetuel* f. L *perpetualis* f. *perpetuus* f. *perpes -etis* continuous]

per•pet•u•al cal•en•dar *n.* a calendar which can be adjusted to show any combination of day, month, and year.

per•pet•u•al check *n. Chess* the position of play when a draw is obtained by repeated checking of the king.

per•pet•u•al mo•tion *n.* the motion of a hypothetical machine which once set in motion would run forever unless subject to an external force or to wear.

per•pet•u•ate /pərpéchōō-ayt/ *v.tr.* **1** make perpetual. **2** preserve from oblivion. □□ **per•pet•u•ance** *n.* **per•pet•u•a•tion** /–áyshən/ *n.* **per•pet•u•a•tor** *n.* [L *perpetuare* (as PERPETUAL)]

▶See note at PERPETRATE.

per•pe•tu•i•ty /pə́rpitōō-itee, –tyōō–/ *n.* (*pl.* **•ties**) **1** the state or quality of being perpetual. **2** a perpetual annuity. **3** a perpetual possession or position. □ **in** (or **to** or **for**) **perpetuity** forever. [ME f. OF *perpetuité* f. L *perpetuitas -tatis* (as PERPETUAL)]

per•plex /pərpléks/ *v.tr.* **1** puzzle, bewilder, or disconcert (a person, a person's mind, etc.). **2** complicate or confuse (a matter). **3** (as **perplexed** *adj.*) *archaic* entangled; intertwined. □□ **per•plex•ed•ly** /–pléksidlee/ *adv.* **per•plex•ing** *adj.* **per•plex•ing•ly** *adv.* [back-form. f. *perplexed* f. obs. *perplex* (adj.) f. OF *perplexe* or L *perplexus* (as PER-, *plexus* past part. of *plectere* plait)]

per•plex•i•ty /pərpléksitee/ *n.* (*pl.* **•ties**) **1** bewilderment; the state of being perplexed. **2** a thing which perplexes. **3** the state of being complicated. **4** *archaic* an entangled state. [ME f. OF *perplexité* f. LL *perplexitas* (as PERPLEX)]

per pro. /pər prṓ/ *abbr.* through the agency of (used in signatures). [L *per procurationem*]

▶The correct sequence is A per pro. B, where B is signing on behalf of A.

per•qui•site /pə́rkwizit/ *n.* **1** an extra profit or allowance additional to a main income, etc. **2** a customary extra right or privilege. **3** an incidental benefit attached to employment, etc. **4** a thing which has served its primary use and to which a subordinate or servant has a customary right. [ME f. med.L *perquisitum* f. L *perquirere* search diligently for (as PER-, *quaerere* seek)]

▶**Perquisite** and **prerequisite** are sometimes confused. **Perquisite** usually means 'an extra allowance or privilege' (*he had all the perquisites of a movie star, including a stand-in*). **Prerequisite** means 'something required as a precondition' (*passing the examination was one of the prerequisites for a teaching position*).

Per•ri•er /péreeay/ *n. Trademark* a carbonated natural mineral water. [the name of a spring at Vergèze, France, its source]

per•ron /pérən/ *n.* an exterior staircase leading up to a main entrance to a church or other (usu. large) building. [ME f. OF ult. f. L *petra* stone]

per•ry /péree/ *n.* (*pl.* **•ries**) a drink like cider, made from the fermented juice of pears. [ME *pereye*, etc. f. OF *peré*, ult. f. L *pirum* pear]

per se /pər sáy/ *adv.* by or in itself; intrinsically. [L]

per•se•cute /pə́rsikyōōt/ *v.tr.* **1** subject (a person, etc.) to hostility or ill-treatment, esp. on the grounds of political or religious belief. **2** harass; worry. **3** (often foll. by *with*) bombard (a person) with questions, etc. □□ **per•se•cu•tor** *n.* **per•se•cu•to•ry** *adj.* [ME f. OF *persecuter* back-form. f. *persecuteur* persecutor f. LL *persecutor* f. L *persequi* (as PER-, *sequi secut-* follow, pursue)]

per•se•cu•tion /pérsikyōōshən/ *n.* the act or an instance of persecuting; the state of being persecuted.

per•se•cu•tion com•plex *n.* (also **per•se•cu•tion ma•ni•a**) an irrational obsessive fear that others are scheming against one.

per•se•ver•ance /pə́rsivéerəns/ *n.* **1** the steadfast pursuit of an objec-

tive. **2** (often foll. by *in*) constant persistence (in a belief, etc.). [ME f. OF f. L *perseverantia* (as PERSEVERE)]

per•sev•er•ate /pərsévərayt/ *v.intr.* **1** continue action, etc., for an unusually or excessively long time. **2** *Psychol.* tend to prolong or repeat a response after the original stimulus has ceased. □□ **per•sev•er•a•tion** /–ráyshən/ *n.* [L *perseverare* (as PERSEVERE)]

per•se•vere /pə́rsiveér/ *v.intr.* (often foll. by *in, at, with*) continue steadfastly or determinedly; persist. [ME f. OF *perseverer* f. L *perseverare* persist f. *perseverus* very strict (as PER-, *severus* severe)]

Per•sian /pérzhən, –shən/ *n. & adj.* ● *n.*
1 a a native or inhabitant of ancient or modern Persia (now Iran). **b** a person of Persian descent. **2** the language of ancient Persia or modern Iran. **3** (in full **Persian cat**) **a** a cat of a breed with long silky hair and a thick tail. **b** this breed. ● *adj.* of or relating to Persia or its people or language. [ME f. OF *persien* f. med.L]

Persian cat 3

▶With modern reference the preferred terms are *Iranian* for the people and *Farsi* for the language (which is one of several languages belonging to the Iranian family of languages).

Per•sian car•pet *n.* (also **Per•sian rug**) a carpet or rug of a tradiational pattern made in Persia.

Per•sian lamb *n.* the silky tightly curled fur of a young karakul, used in clothing.

per•si•ennes /pórzee-énz/ *n.pl.* window shutters, or outside blinds, with louvers. [F, fem. pl. of obs. *persien* Persian]

per•si•flage /pórsiflaazh/ *n.* light raillery; banter. [F *persifler* banter, formed as PER- + *siffler* whistle]

per•sim•mon /pərsímən/ *n.* **1** any usu. tropical evergreen tree of the genus *Diospyros* bearing edible tomatolike fruits. **2** the fruit of this. [corrupt. of an Algonquian word]

per•sist /pərsíst/ *v.intr.* **1** (often foll. by *in*) continue firmly or obstinately (in an opinion or a course of action) esp. despite obstacles, remonstrance, etc. **2** (of an institution, custom, phenomenon, etc.) continue in existence; survive. [L *persistere* (as PER-, *sistere* stand)]

per•sist•ent /pərsístənt/ *adj.* **1** continuing obstinately; persisting. **2** enduring. **3** constantly repeated (*persistent nagging*). **4** *Biol.* (of horns, leaves, etc.) remaining instead of falling off in the normal manner. □□ **per•sist•ence** *n.* **per•sist•en•cy** *n.* **per•sist•ent•ly** *adv.*

per•snick•et•y /pərsníkitee/ *adj. colloq.* (also **per•nick•et•y**) **1** fastidious. **2** precise or overprecise. **3** requiring tact or careful handling. [19th-c. Sc.: orig. unkn.]

per•son /pórsən/ *n.* **1** an individual human being (*a cheerful and forthright person*). **2** the living body of a human being (*hidden about your person*). **3** *Gram.* any of three classes of personal pronouns, verb forms, etc.: the person speaking (**first person**); the person spoken to (**second person**); the person spoken of (**third person**). **4** (in *comb.*) used to replace –*man* in words referring to either sex (*salesperson*). **5** (in Christianity) God as Father, Son, or Holy Ghost (*three persons in one God*). **6** *Brit. euphem.* the genitals (*expose one's person*). **7** a character in a play or story. □ **in one's own person** oneself; as oneself. **in person** physically present. [ME f. OF *persone* f. L *persona* actor's mask, character in a play, human being]

▶Some prefer the plural **persons** to **people**, considering the former more formal and specific, and holding **people** to be more general and indefinite. General usage, however, does not support this distinction. In some contexts, **persons**, by pointing to the individual, may sound less friendly than **people**: *The number should not be disclosed to any unauthorized persons.*

per•so•na /pərsṓnə/ *n.* (*pl.* **per•so•nae** /–nee/) **1** an aspect of the personality as shown to or perceived by others (opp. ANIMA). **2** *Literary criticism* an author's assumed character in his or her writing. [L (as PERSON)]

per•son•a•ble /pórsənəbəl/ *adj.* pleasing in appearance and behavior. □□ **per•son•a•ble•ness** *n.* **per•son•a•bly** *adv.*

per•son•age /pórsənij/ *n.* **1** a person, esp. of rank or importance. **2** a character in a play, etc. [ME f. PERSON + -AGE, infl. by med.L *personagium* effigy & F *personnage*]

per•so•na gra•ta *n.* /gráätə/ a person, esp. a diplomat, acceptable to certain others.

per•son•al /pórsənəl/ *adj.* **1** one's own; individual; private. **2** done or made in person (*made a personal appearance*; *my personal attention*). **3** directed to or concerning an individual (*a personal letter*). **4 a** referring (esp. in a hostile way) to an individual's private life or concerns (*making personal remarks*; *no need to be personal*). **b** close; intimate (*a personal friend*). **5** of the body and clothing (*personal hygiene*; *personal appearance*). **6** existing as a person, not as an abstraction or thing (*a personal God*). **7** *Gram.* of or denoting one of the three persons (*personal pronoun*). [ME f. OF f. L *personalis* (as PERSON)]

per·son·al col·umn *n.* (also **per·son·als**) the part of a newspaper devoted to private messages or advertisements, esp. those in which a romantic partner is sought.

per·son·al com·pu·ter *n.* a computer designed for use by a single individual. ¶ Abbr.: PC

per·son·al e·qua·tion *n.* 1 the allowance for an individual person's time of reaction in making observations, esp. in astronomy. 2 a bias or prejudice.

per·son·al i·den·ti·fi·ca·tion num·ber *n.* a number allocated to an individual, serving as a password esp. for an ATM, computer, etc. ¶ Abbr.: PIN.

per·son·al·i·ty /pórsənálitee/ *n.* (*pl.* **·ties**) 1 the distinctive character or qualities of a person, often as distinct from others (*an attractive personality*). 2 a famous person; a celebrity (*a TV personality*). 3 a person who stands out from others by virtue of his or her character (*is a real personality*). 4 personal existence or identity; the condition of being a person. 5 (usu. in *pl.*) personal remarks. □ **have personality** have a lively character or noteworthy qualities. [ME f. OF *personalité* f. LL *personalitas* –*tatis* (as PERSONAL)]

per·son·al·i·ty cult *n.* the extreme adulation of an individual.

per·son·al·i·ty trait *n.* a set pattern of perceiving, relating to, and thinking about one's environment.

per·son·al·ize /pórsənəliz/ *v.tr.* 1 make personal, esp. by marking with one's name, etc. 2 personify. □□ **per·son·al·i·za·tion** *n.*

per·son·al·ly /pórsənəlee/ *adv.* 1 in person (*see to it personally*). 2 for one's own part (*speaking personally*). 3 in the form of a person (*a god existing personally*). 4 in a personal manner (*took the criticism personally*). 5 as a person; on a personal level.

per·son·al or·gan·iz·er *n.* 1 a loose-leaf notebook with sections for various kinds of information, including a diary, etc. 2 a handheld microcomputer serving the same purpose.

per·son·al pro·noun *n.* a pronoun replacing the subject, object, etc., of a clause, etc., e.g., *I, we, you, them, us*.

per·son·al prop·er·ty *n.* (also **per·son·al es·tate**) *Law* all one's property except land and those interests in land that pass to one's heirs (cf. REAL[1] *adj.* 3).

per·son·al serv·ice *n.* individual service given to a customer.

per·son·al ster·e·o *n.* a small portable audio cassette or CD player, often with radio, used with lightweight headphones.

per·son·al touch *n.* an element or feature contributed by an individual to make something less impersonal.

per·son·al·ty /pórsənəltee/ *n.* (*pl.* **·ties**) *Law* one's personal property or estate (opp. REALTY). [AF *personalté* (as PERSONAL)]

per·so·na non gra·ta *n.* /non gráatə, grátə/ a person not acceptable or not welcome.

per·son·ate /pórsənayt/ *v.tr.* 1 play the part of (a character in a drama, etc.; another type of person). 2 pretend to be (another person), esp. for fraudulent purposes; impersonate. □□ **per·son·a·tion** /–náyshən/ *n.* **per·son·a·tor** *n.* [LL *personare personat-* (as PERSON)]

per·son·hood /pórsənhŏod/ *n.* the quality or condition of being an individual person.

per·son·i·fi·ca·tion /pərsónifikáyshən/ *n.* 1 the act of personifying. 2 (foll. by *of*) a person or thing viewed as a striking example of (a quality, etc.) (*the personification of ugliness*).

per·son·i·fy /pərsónifi/ *v.tr.* (**·fies**, **·fied**) 1 attribute a personal nature to (an abstraction or thing). 2 symbolize (a quality, etc.) by a figure in human form. 3 (usu. as **personified** *adj.*) embody (a quality in one's own person); exemplify typically (*has always been kindness personified*). □□ **per·son·i·fi·er** *n.* [F *personnifier* (as PERSON)]

per·son·nel /pórsənél/ *n.pl.* 1 people employed in an organization or engaged in an organized undertaking such as military service. 2 short for PERSONNEL DEPARTMENT. [F, orig. adj. = personal]

per·son·nel car·ri·er *n.* an armored vehicle for transporting troops, etc.

per·son·nel de·part·ment, etc., *n.* the part of an organization concerned with the appointment, training, and welfare of employees.

per·son-to-per·son *adj.* 1 between individuals. 2 (of a phone call) booked through the operator to a specified person.

per·spec·tive /pərspéktiv/ *n. & adj.* ● *n.* 1 **a** the art of drawing solid objects on a two-dimensional surface so as to give the right impression of relative positions, size, etc. **b** a picture drawn in this way. 2 the apparent relation between visible objects as to position, distance, etc. 3 a mental view of the relative importance of things (*keep the right perspective*). 4 a geographical or imaginary prospect. ● *adj.* of or in perspective. □ **in perspective** 1 drawn or viewed according to the rules of perspective. 2 correctly regarded in terms of relative importance. □□ **per·spec·tiv·al** *adj.* **per·spec·tive·ly** *adv.* [ME f. med.L *perspectiva* (*ars* art) f. *perspicere perspect-* (as PER-, *specere spect-* look)]

Per·spex /pórspeks/ *n. Brit. Trademark* = PLEXIGLAS. [L *perspicere* look through (as PER-, *specere* look)]

per·spi·ca·cious /pórspikáyshəs/ *adj.* having mental penetration or

discernment. □□ **per·spi·ca·cious·ly** *adv.* **per·spi·ca·cious·ness** *n.* **per·spi·cac·i·ty** /–kásitee/ *n.* [L *perspicax* –*acis* (as PERSPEX)]

per·spic·u·ous /pərspíkyŏŏəs/ *adj.* 1 easily understood; clearly expressed. 2 (of a person) expressing things clearly. □□ **per·spi·cu·i·ty** /pórspikyŏŏ-itee/ *n.* **per·spic·u·ous·ly** *adv.* **per·spic·u·ous·ness** *n.* [ME, = transparent f. L *perspicuus* (as PERSPECTIVE)]

per·spi·ra·tion /pórspiráyshən/ *n.* 1 = SWEAT. 2 sweating. □□ **per·spir·a·to·ry** /pərspírətawree, pórspirə–/ *adj.* [F (as PERSPIRE)]

per·spire /pərspír/ *v.* 1 *intr.* sweat or exude perspiration, esp. as the result of heat, exercise, anxiety, etc. 2 *tr.* sweat or exude (fluid, etc.). [F *perspirer* f. L *perspirare* (as PER-, *spirare* breathe)]

per·suade /pərswáyd/ *v.tr. & refl.* 1 (often foll. by *of*, or *that* + clause) cause (another person or oneself) to believe; convince (*persuaded them that it would be helpful; tried to persuade me of its value*). 2 **a** (often foll. by *to* + infin.) induce (another person or oneself) (*persuaded us to join them; managed to persuade them at last*). **b** (foll. by *away from, down to*, etc.) lure, attract, entice, etc. (*persuaded them away from the pub*). □□ **per·suad·a·ble** *adj.* **per·suad·a·bil·i·ty** *n.* **per·sua·si·ble** *adj.* [L *persuadēre* (as PER-, *suadēre suas-* advise)]

per·suad·er /pərswáydər/ *n.* 1 a person who persuades. 2 *sl.* a gun or other weapon.

per·sua·sion /pərswáyzhən/ *n.* 1 persuading (*yielded to persuasion*). 2 persuasiveness (*use all your persuasion*). 3 a belief or conviction (*my private persuasion*). 4 a religious belief, or the group or sect holding it (*of a different persuasion*). 5 *colloq.* any group or party (*the male persuasion*). [ME f. L *persuasio* (as PERSUADE)]

per·sua·sive /pərswáysiv, –ziv/ *adj.* able to persuade. □□ **per·sua·sive·ly** *adv.* **per·sua·sive·ness** *n.* [F *persuasif* –*ive* or med.L *persuasivus*, (as PERSUADE)]

PERT *abbr.* program evaluation and review technique.

pert /pərt/ *adj.* 1 saucy or impudent, esp. in speech or conduct. 2 (of clothes, etc.) neat and jaunty. 3 = PEART. □□ **pert·ly** *adv.* **pert·ness** *n.* [ME f. OF *apert* f. L *apertus* past part. of *aperire* open & f. OF *aspert* f. L *expertus* EXPERT]

pert. *abbr.* pertaining.

per·tain /pərtáyn/ *v.intr.* 1 (foll. by *to*) **a** relate or have reference to. **b** belong to as a part or appendage or accessory. 2 (usu. foll. by *to*) be appropriate to. [ME f. OF *partenir* f. L *pertinēre* (as PER-, *tenēre* hold)]

per·ti·na·cious /pórt'náyshəs/ *adj.* stubborn; persistent; obstinate (in a course of action, etc.). □□ **per·ti·na·cious·ly** *adv.* **per·ti·na·cious·ness** *n.* **per·ti·nac·i·ty** /–násitee/ *n.* [L *pertinax* –*acis*, as PER-, *tenax* tenacious)]

per·ti·nent /pórt'nənt/ *adj.* 1 (often foll. by *to*) relevant to the matter in hand; apposite. 2 to the point. □□ **per·ti·nence** *n.* **per·ti·nen·cy** *n.* **per·ti·nent·ly** *adv.* [ME f. OF *pertinent* or L *pertinēre* (as PERTAIN)]

per·turb /pərtórb/ *v.tr.* 1 throw into confusion or disorder. 2 disturb mentally; agitate. 3 *Physics & Math.* subject (a physical system, or a set of equations, or its solution) to a perturbation. □□ **per·turb·a·ble** *adj.* **per·tur·ba·tive** /pərtúrbətiv, pórtərbáytiv/ *adj.* **per·turb·ing·ly** *adv.* [ME f. OF *perturber* f. L (as PER-, *turbare* disturb)]

per·tur·ba·tion /pórtərbáyshən/ *n.* 1 the act or an instance of perturbing; the state of being perturbed. 2 a cause of disturbance or agitation. 3 *Physics* a slight alteration of a physical system, e.g., of the electrons in an atom, caused by a secondary influence. 4 *Astron.* a minor deviation in the course of a celestial body, caused by the attraction of a neighboring body.

per·tus·sis /pərtúsis/ *n.* whooping cough. [mod.L f. PER- + L *tussis* cough]

pe·ruke /pərŏŏk/ *n. hist.* a wig. [F *perruque* f. It. *perrucca parrucca*, of unkn. orig.]

pe·ruse /pərŏŏz/ *v.tr.* 1 (also *absol.*) read or study, esp. thoroughly or carefully. 2 examine (a person's face, etc.) carefully. □□ **pe·rus·al** *n.* **pe·rus·er** *n.* [ME, orig. = use up, prob. f. AL f. Rmc (as PER-, USE)]

Pe·ru·vi·an /pərŏŏveeən/ *n. & adj.* ● *n.* 1 a native or national of Peru. 2 a person of Peruvian descent. ● *adj.* of or relating to Peru. [mod.L *Peruvia* Peru]

Pe·ru·vi·an bark *n.* the bark of the cinchona tree.

peruke

perv /pərv/ *n. & v.* (also **perve**) *sl.* ● *n.* 1 *Brit.* a sexual pervert. 2 *Austral.* an erotic gaze. ● *v.intr.* 1 *Brit.* act like a sexual pervert. 2 (foll. by *at, on*) *Austral.* gaze with erotic interest. [abbr.]

per·vade /pərváyd/ *v.tr.* 1 spread throughout; permeate. 2 (of influences, etc.) become widespread among or in. 3 be rife among or through. □□ **per·va·sion** /–váyzhən/ *n.* [L *pervadere* (as PER-, *vadere vas-* go)]

per·va·sive /pərváysiv, –ziv/ *adj.* 1 pervading. 2 able to pervade. □□ **per·va·sive·ly** *adv.* **per·va·sive·ness** *n.*

perve var. of PERV.

per·verse /pərvə́rs/ *adj.* **1** (of a person or action) deliberately or stubbornly departing from what is reasonable or required. **2** persistent in error. **3** wayward; intractable; peevish. **4** perverted; wicked. **5** (of a verdict, etc.) against the weight of evidence or the judge's direction. □□ **per·verse·ly** *adv.* **per·verse·ness** *n.* **per·ver·si·ty** *n.* (*pl.* **·ties**). [ME f. OF *pervers perverse* f. L *perversus* (as PERVERT)]

per·ver·sion /pərvə́rzhən, –shən/ *n.* **1** an act of perverting; the state of being perverted. **2** a perverted form of an act or thing. **3 a** preference for an abnormal form of sexual activity. **b** such an activity. [ME f. L *perversio* (as PERVERT)]

per·vert *v. & n.* ● *v.tr.* /pərvə́rt/ **1** turn (a person or thing) aside from its proper use or nature. **2** misapply or misconstrue (words, etc.). **3** lead astray (a person, a person's mind, etc.) from right opinion or conduct, or esp. religious belief. **4** (as **perverted** *adj.*) showing perversion. ● *n.* /pə́rvərt/ **1** a perverted person. **2** a person showing sexual perversion. □□ **per·ver·sive** /–və́rsiv/ *adj.* **per·vert·ed·ly** /–və́rtidlee/ *adv.* **per·vert·er** /–və́rtər/ *n.* [ME f. OF *pervertir* or f. L *pervertere* (as PER-, *vertere vers-* turn): cf. CONVERT]

per·vi·ous /pə́rveeəs/ *adj.* **1** permeable. **2** (usu. foll. by *to*) **a** affording passage. **b** accessible (to reason, etc.). □□ **per·vi·ous·ness** *n.* [L *pervius* (as PER-, *vius* f. *via* way)]

Pe·sach /páysaakh, pé–/ *n.* the Passover festival. [Heb. *Pesaḥ*]

pe·se·ta /pəsáytə/ *n.* the chief monetary unit of Spain, orig. a silver coin. [Sp., dimin. of *pesa* weight f. L *pensa* pl. of *pensum*: see POISE¹]

pes·ky /péskee/ *adj.* (**pes·ki·er, pes·ki·est**) *colloq.* troublesome; annoying. □□ **pes·ki·ly** *adv.* **pes·ki·ness** *n.* [18th c.: f. PEST]

pe·so /páysō/ *n.* (*pl.* **·sos**) **1** the chief monetary unit of several Latin American countries and of the Philippines. **2** a note or coin worth one peso. [Sp., = weight, f. L *pensum*: see POISE¹]

pes·sa·ry /pésəree/ *n.* (*pl.* **·ries**) *Med.* **1** a device worn in the vagina to support the uterus or as a contraceptive. **2** a vaginal suppository. [ME f. LL *pessarium, pessulum* f. *pessum, pessus* f. Gk *pessos* oval stone]

pes·si·mism /pésimizəm/ *n.* **1** a tendency to take the worst view or expect the worst outcome. **2** *Philos.* a belief that this world is as bad as it could be or that all things tend to evil (opp. OPTIMISM). □□ **pes·si·mist** *n.* **pes·si·mis·tic** *adj.* **pes·si·mis·ti·cal·ly** *adv.* [L *pessimus* worst, after OPTIMISM]

pest /pest/ *n.* **1** a troublesome or annoying person or thing; a nuisance. **2** a destructive animal, esp. an insect which attacks crops, livestock, etc. **3** *archaic* a pestilence; a plague. [F *peste* or L *pestis* plague]

pes·ter /péstər/ *v.tr.* trouble or annoy, esp. with frequent or persistent requests. □□ **pes·ter·er** *n.* [prob. f. *impester* f. F *empestrer* encumber: infl. by PEST]

pes·ti·cide /péstisīd/ *n.* a substance used for destroying insects or other organisms harmful to cultivated plants or to animals. □□ **pes·ti·cid·al** /–síd'l/ *adj.*

pes·tif·er·ous /pestífərəs/ *adj.* **1** noxious; pestilent. **2** harmful; pernicious; bearing moral contagion. [L *pestifer, –ferus* (as PEST)]

pes·ti·lence /péstiləns/ *n.* **1** a fatal epidemic disease, esp. bubonic plague. **2** something evil or destructive. [ME f. OF f. L *pestilentia* (as PESTILENT)]

pes·ti·lent /péstilənt/ *adj.* **1** destructive to life; deadly. **2** harmful or morally destructive. **3** *colloq.* troublesome; annoying. □□ **pes·ti·lent·ly** *adv.* [L *pestilens, pestilentus* f. *pestis* plague]

pes·ti·len·tial /péstilénshəl/ *adj.* **1** of or relating to pestilence. **2** dangerous; troublesome. □□ **pes·ti·len·tial·ly** *adv.* [ME f. med.L *pestilentialis* f. L *pestilentia* (as PESTILENT)]

pes·tle /pésəl/ *n. & v.* ● *n.* **1** a club-shaped instrument for pounding substances in a mortar. **2** an appliance for pounding, etc. ● *v.* **1** *tr.* pound with a pestle or in a similar manner. **2** *intr.* use a pestle. [ME f. OF *pestel* f. L *pistillum* f. *pinsare pist-* to pound]

pes·to /péstō/ *n.* a sauce made of fresh chopped basil, garlic, olive oil, and Parmesan cheese, used for pasta, fish, etc. [It., f. *pestare* to pound]

Pet. *abbr.* Peter (New Testament).

pet¹ /pet/ *n., adj., & v.* ● *n.* **1** a domestic or tamed animal kept for pleasure or companionship. **2** a darling; a favorite (often as a term of endearment). ● *attrib.adj.* **1** kept as a pet (*pet lamb*). **2** of or for pet animals (*pet food*). **3** often *joc.* favorite or particular (*pet aversion*). **4** expressing fondness or familiarity (*pet name*). ● *v.tr.* (**pet·ted, pet·ting**) **1** treat as a pet. **2** (also *absol.*) fondle, esp. erotically. □□ **pet·ter** *n.* [16th-c. Sc. & No. of Engl. dial.: orig. unkn.]

pet² /pet/ *n.* a feeling of petty resentment or ill-humor (esp. be in a pet). [16th c.: orig. unkn.]

peta- /pétə/ *comb. form* denoting a factor of 10¹⁵. [perh. f. PENTA-]

pet·al /pét'l/ *n.* each of the parts of the corolla of a flower. □□ **pet·al·ine** /–līn, –lin/ *adj.* **pet·alled** (also *in comb.*). **pet·al·like** *adj.* **pet·al·oid** *adj.* [mod.L *petalum*, in LL metal plate f. Gk *petalon* leaf f. *petalos* outspread]

pe·tard /pitáard/ *n. hist.* **1** a small bomb used to blast down a door, etc. **2** a kind of firework. □ **hoist with** (or **by**) **one's own petard** affected oneself by one's schemes against others. [F *pétard* f. *péter* break wind]

pet·a·sus /pétəsəs/ *n.* an ancient Greek hat with a low crown and broad brim, esp. (in Greek mythology) as worn by Hermes. [L f. Gk *petasos*]

pe·tau·rist /pətáwrist/ *n.* any flying squirrel of the genus *Petaurista*, native to E. Asia. [Gk *petauristēs* performer on a springboard (*petauron*)]

pe·te·chi·a /piteékeeə/ *n.* (*pl.* **pe·te·chi·ae** /–kee-ee/) *Med.* a small red or purple spot as a result of bleeding into the skin. □□ **pe·te·chi·al** *adj.* [mod.L f. It. *petecchia* a freckle or spot on one's face]

pe·ter¹ /peétər/ *v. & n.* ● *v.intr.* **1** (foll. by *out*) (orig. of a vein of ore, etc.) diminish; come to an end. **2** *Bridge* play an echo. ● *n. Bridge* an echo. [19th c.: orig. unkn.]

pe·ter² /peétər/ *n. sl.* **1** a prison cell. **2** a safe. **3** *coarse sl.* penis. [perh. f. the name *Peter*]

pe·ter·man /peétərmən/ *n.* (*pl.* **·men**) (also **pete·man**) *sl.* a safecracker.

Pe·ter Pan /peétər pán/ *n.* a person who retains youthful features, or who is immature. [hero of J. M. Barrie's play of the same name (1904)]

Pe·ter Prin·ci·ple /peétər/ *n. joc.* the principle that members of a hierarchy are promoted until they reach the level at which they are no longer competent. [L. J. *Peter*, its propounder, b. 1919]

pe·ter·sham /peétərshəm/ *n.* thick corded silk ribbon used for belts, etc. [Lord *Petersham*, Engl. army officer d. 1851]

Pe·ter's pence /peétərz/ *n.pl. RC Ch.* **1** *hist.* an annual tax of one penny, formerly paid to the papal see by English landowners. **2** (since 1860) a voluntary payment to the papal treasury. [St. *Peter*, as first pope]

pet·i·ole /péteeōl/ *n.* the slender stalk joining a leaf to a stem. □□ **pet·i·o·lar** *adj.* **pet·i·o·late** /pétiəláyt/ *adj.* [F *pétiole* f. L *petiolus* little foot, stalk]

pet·it /pétee/ *adj.* esp. *Law* petty; small; of lesser importance. □ **pet·it jury** a jury of 12 persons who try the final issue of fact in civil or criminal cases and pronounce a verdict. [ME f. OF, = small, f. Rmc, perh. imit. of child's speech]

pe·tit bour·geois /pétee bŏŏrzhwaa, bŏŏrzhwáa, pətée/ *n.* (*pl.* **petits bour·geois** *pronunc.* same) a member of the lower middle classes. [F]

pe·tite /pətéet/ *adj. & n.* ● *adj.* (of a woman) of small and dainty build. ● *n.* a clothing size for petite women. [F, fem. of PETIT]

pe·tite bour·geoi·sie *n.* the lower middle classes.

pe·tit four /pətée fáwr/ *n.* (*pl.* **pe·tits fours** /fórz/) a very small fancy frosted cake. [F, = little oven]

pe·ti·tion /pətíshən/ *n. & v.* ● *n.* **1** a supplication or request. **2** a formal written request, esp. one signed by many people, appealing to authority in some cause. **3** *Law* an application to a court for a writ, etc. ● *v.* **1** *tr.* make or address a petition to (*petition the court*). **2** *intr.* (often foll. by *for, to*) appeal earnestly or humbly. □□ **pe·ti·tion·a·ble** *adj.* **pe·ti·tion·ar·y** *adj.* **pe·ti·tion·er** *n.* [ME f. OF f. L *petitio –onis*]

Pe·ti·tion of Right *n.* **1** *Brit. hist.* a parliamentary declaration of rights and liberties of the people assented to by Charles I in 1628. **2** *Brit. Law* a common-law remedy against the crown for the recovery of property.

pe·ti·ti·o prin·ci·pi·i /pitísheeō prinkípee-ee, –sípee-ī/ *n.* a logical fallacy in which a conclusion is taken for granted in the premise; begging the question. [L, = assuming a principle: see PETITION]

pe·tit-maî·tre /pəteemáytrə/ *n.* a dandy or fop. [F, = little master]

pe·tit mal /pétee maál, mál/ *n.* a mild form of epilepsy with only momentary loss of consciousness (cf. GRAND MAL). [F, = little sickness]

pet·it point /pétee póynt, pətée pwáṅ/ *n.* **1** embroidery on canvas using small stitches. **2** tent stitch. [F, = little point]

pet peeve *n. colloq.* something especially annoying to an individual.

Pe·trar·chan /pitraárkən/ *adj.* denoting a sonnet of the kind used by the Italian poet Petrarch (d. 1374), with an octave rhyming *abbaabba*, and a sestet usu. rhyming *cdcdcd* or *cdecde*.

pet·rel /pétrəl/ *n.* any of various sea birds of the family Procellariidae or Hydrobatidae, usu. flying far from land. [17th c. (also *pitteral*), of uncert. orig.: later assoc. with St. Peter (Matt. 14:30)]

Pe·tri dish /peetree/ *n.* a shallow covered dish used for the culture of bacteria, etc. [J. R. *Petri*, Ger. bacteriologist d. 1921]

pet·ri·fac·tion /pétrifákshən/ *n.* **1** the process of fossilization whereby organic matter is turned into a stony substance. **2** a petrified substance or mass. **3** a state of extreme fear or terror. [PETRIFY after *stupefaction*]

pet·ri·fy /pétrifī/ *v.* (**·fies, ·fied**) **1** *tr.* (also as **petrified** *adj.*) paralyze with fear, astonishment, etc. **2** *tr.* change (organic matter) into a stony substance. **3** *intr.* become like stone. **4** *tr.* deprive (the mind, a doctrine, etc.) of vitality; deaden. [F *pétrifier* f. med.L *petrificare* f. L *petra* rock f. Gk]

petro- /pétrō/ *comb. form* **1** rock. **2** petroleum (*petrochemistry*). [Gk *petros* stone or *petra* rock]

pet·ro·chem·i·cal /pétrōkémikəl/ *n. & adj.* ● *n.* a substance industrially obtained from petroleum or natural gas. ● *adj.* of or relating to petrochemistry or petrochemicals.

pet·ro·chem·is·try /pétrōkémistree/ *n.* **1** the chemistry of rocks. **2** the chemistry of petroleum.

pet·ro·dol·lar /pétrōdolər/ *n.* a notional unit of currency earned by a petroleum-exporting country.

pet·ro·glyph /pétrəglif/ *n.* a rock carving, esp. a prehistoric one. [PETRO- + Gk *glyphē* carving]

pe·trog·ra·phy /petrógrəfee/ *n.* the scientific description of the composition and formation of rocks. □□ **pe·trog·ra·pher** *n.* **pet·ro·graph·ic** /–rəgráfik/ *adj.* **pet·ro·graph·i·cal** *adj.*

pet·rol /pétrəl/ *n. Brit.* **1** refined petroleum used as a fuel in motor vehicles, aircraft, etc.; gasoline. **2** (*attrib.*) concerned with the supply of petrol (*petrol pump; petrol station*). [F *pétrole* f. med.L *petroleum*: see PETROLEUM]

pet·ro·la·tum /pétrəláytəm/ *n.* petroleum jelly. [mod.L f. PETROL + –*atum*]

pet·rol bomb *n. Brit.* a simple bomb made of a bottle filled with petrol (gasoline) and a wick; a Molotov cocktail.

pe·tro·le·um /pətróleeəm/ *n.* a hydrocarbon oil found in the upper strata of the earth, refined for use as a fuel for heating and in internal combustion engines, for lighting, dry cleaning, etc. [med.L f. L *petra* rock f. Gk + L *oleum* oil]

pe·tro·le·um e·ther *n.* a volatile liquid distilled from petroleum, consisting of a mixture of hydrocarbons.

pe·tro·le·um jel·ly *n.* a translucent solid mixture of hydrocarbons used as a lubricant, ointment, etc.

pe·trol·ic /petrólik/ *adj.* of or relating to petrol or petroleum.

pe·trol·o·gy /petróləjee/ *n.* the study of the origin, structure, composition, etc., of rocks. □□ **pet·ro·log·ic** /pétrəlójik/ *adj.* **pet·ro·log·i·cal** *adj.* **pe·trol·o·gist** *n.*

pet·rous /pétrəs/ *adj.* **1** *Anat.* denoting the hard part of the temporal bone protecting the inner ear. **2** *Geol.* of, like, or relating to rock. [L *petrosus* f. L *petra* rock f. Gk]

pet·ti·coat /péteekōt/ *n.* **1** a woman's or girl's skirted undergarment hanging from the waist or shoulders. **2** often *derog. sl.* **a** a woman or girl. **b** (in *pl.*) the female sex. **3** (*attrib.*) often *derog.* feminine; associated with women (*petticoat pedantry*). □□ **pet·ti·coat·ed** *adj.* **pet·ti·coat·less** *adj.* [ME f. *petty coat*]

pet·ti·fog /péteefawg, –fog/ *v.intr.* (**pet·ti·fogged, pet·ti·fog·ging**) **1** practice legal deception or trickery. **2** quibble or wrangle about petty points. back-form. f. PETTIFOGGER]

pet·ti·fog·ger /péteefáwgər, –fóg–/ *n.* **1** a rascally lawyer; an inferior legal practitioner. **2** a petty practitioner in any activity. □□ **pet·ti·fog·ger·y** *n.* **pet·ti·fog·ging** *adj.* [PETTY + *fogger* underhanded dealer, prob. f. *Fugger* family of German merchants in the 15th–16th c.]

pet·tish /pétish/ *adj.* peevish, petulant; easily put out. □□ **pet·tish·ly** *adv.* **pet·tish·ness** *n.* [PET² + –ISH¹]

pet·ty /pétee/ *adj.* (**pet·ti·er, pet·ti·est**) **1** unimportant; trivial. **2** mean; small-minded; contemptible. **3** minor; inferior; on a small scale (*petty princes*). **4** *Law* (of a crime) of lesser importance (*petty sessions*) (cf. COMMON, GRAND). □□ **pet·ti·ly** *adv.* **pet·ti·ness** *n.* [ME *pety*, var. of PETIT]

pet·ty bour·geois *n.* = PETIT BOURGEOIS.

pet·ty bour·geoi·sie *n.* = PETITE BOURGEOISIE.

pet·ty cash *n.* money from or for small items of receipt or expenditure.

pet·ty of·fi·cer *n.* a naval NCO.

pet·u·lant /péchələnt/ *adj.* peevishly impatient or irritable. □□ **pet·u·lance** *n.* **pet·u·lant·ly** *adv.* [F *pétulant* f. L *petulans –antis* f. *petere* seek]

pe·tu·nia /pitōónyə, –tyóōn–/ *n.* **1** any plant of the genus *Petunia* with white, purple, red, etc., funnel-shaped flowers. **2** a dark violet or purple color. [mod.L f. F *petun* f. Guarani *petỹ* tobacco]

pe·tun·tse /pitōóntsee/ *n.* a white variable feldspathic mineral used for making porcelain. [Chin. *baidunzi* f. *bai* white + *dun* stone + suffix –*zi*]

pew /pyōō/ *n. & v.* ● *n.* **1** (in a church) a long bench with a back; an enclosed compartment. **2** *Brit. colloq.* a seat (esp. *take a pew*). ● *v.tr.* furnish with pews. □□ **pew·age** *n.* **pew·less** *adj.* [ME *pywe, puwe* f. OF *puye* balcony f. L *podia* pl. of PODIUM]

pe·wit var. of PEEWIT.

pew·ter /pyóōtər/ *n.* **1** a gray alloy of tin with lead, copper, antimony, or various other metals. **2** utensils made of this. **3** *Brit. sl.* a tankard, etc., as a prize. □□ **pew·ter·er** *n.* [ME f. OF *peutre, peualtre* f. Rmc, of unkn. orig.]

pe·yo·te /payōtee/ *n.* **1** any Mexican cactus of the genus *Lophophora*, esp. *L. williamsii* having no spines and buttonlike tops when dried. **2** a hallucinogenic drug containing mescaline prepared from this. [Amer. Sp. f. Nahuatl *peyotl*]

Pf. *abbr.* pfennig.

Pfc. *abbr.* (also **PFC**) Private First Class.

pfen·nig /fénig, pfénikh/ *n.* a small German coin, worth one hundredth of a mark. [G, rel. to PENNY]

PG *abbr.* (of movies) classified as suitable for children subject to parental guidance.

pg. *abbr.* page.

PGA *abbr.* Professional Golfers' Association.

PG-13 *abbr.* (of a film) classified as suitable for children under age 13 subject to parental guidance.

pH /pée-áych/ *n. Chem.* a logarithm of the reciprocal of the hydrogen-ion concentration in moles per liter of a solution, giving a measure of its acidity or alkalinity. [G, f. *Potenz* power + *H* (symbol for hydrogen)]

pha·e·ton /fáyit'n, fáyt'n/ *n.* **1** a light open four-wheeled carriage, usu. drawn by a pair of horses. **2** a vintage touring car. [F *phaéton* f. L *Phaethon* f. Gk *Phaethōn*, son of Helios the sun god who was allowed to drive the sun-chariot for a day, with disastrous results]

phage /fayj/ *n.* = BACTERIOPHAGE. [abbr.]

phaeton 1

phag·o·cyte /fágəsīt/ *n.* a type of cell capable of engulfing and absorbing foreign matter, esp. a leukocyte ingesting bacteria in the body. □□ **phag·o·cyt·ic** /–sítik/ *adj.* [Gk *phag-* eat + –CYTE]

phag·o·cy·to·sis /fágəsītósis/ *n.* the ingestion of bacteria, etc., by phagocytes. □□ **phag·o·cyt·ize** *v.tr.* **phag·o·cy·tose** *v.tr.*

-phagous /fəgəs/ *comb. form* that eats (as specified) (*ichthyophagous*). [L –*phagus* f. Gk –*phagos* f. *phagein* eat]

-phagy /fəjee/ *comb. form* the eating of (specified food) (*ichthyophagy*). [Gk –*phagia* (as –PHAGOUS)]

phal·ange /fálanj, fəlánj/ *n.* **1** *Anat.* = PHALANX 3. **2** (**Phalange**) a right-wing activist Maronite party in Lebanon (cf. FALANGE). [F f. L *phalanx*: see PHALANX]

pha·lan·ge·al /fəlánjeeəl/ *adj. Anat.* of or relating to a phalanx.

pha·lan·ger /fəlánjər/ *n.* any of various marsupials of the family Phalangeridae, including cuscuses and possums. [F f. Gk *phalaggion* spider's web, f. the webbed toes of its hind feet]

pha·lanx /fálangks/ *n.* (*pl.* **pha·lanx·es** or **pha·lan·ges** /fəlánjeez/) **1** *Gk Antiq.* a line of battle, esp. a body of Macedonian infantry drawn up in close order. **2** a set of people, etc., forming a compact mass, or banded for a common purpose. **3** a bone of the finger or toe. **4** *Bot.* a bundle of stamens united by filaments. [L f. Gk *phalagx –ggos*]

phal·a·rope /fálərōp/ *n.* any small wading or swimming bird of the subfamily Phalaropodidae, with a straight bill and lobed feet. [F f. mod.L *Phalaropus*, irreg. f. Gk *phalaris* coot + *pous podos* foot]

phal·li *pl.* of PHALLUS.

phal·lic /fálik/ *adj.* **1** of, relating to, or resembling a phallus. **2** *Psychol.* denoting the stage of male sexual development characterized by preoccupation with the genitals. □□ **phal·li·cal·ly** *adv.* [F *phallique* & Gk *phallikos* (as PHALLUS)]

phal·lo·cen·tric /fálōséntrik/ *adj.* centered on the phallus or on male attitudes. □□ **phal·lo·cen·tric·i·ty** /–sentrísitee/ *n.* **phal·lo·cen·trism** /–trizəm/ *n.*

phal·lus /fáləs/ *n.* (*pl.* **phal·li** /–lī/ or **phal·lus·es**) **1** the (esp. erect) penis. **2** an image of this as a symbol of generative power in nature. □□ **phal·li·cism** /–lisízəm/ *n.* **phal·lism** *n.* [LL f. Gk *phallos*]

pha·nar·i·ot /fənáreeət/ *n. hist.* a member of a class of Greek officials in Constantinople under the Ottoman Empire. [mod.Gk *phanariōtēs* f. *Phanar* the part of the city where they lived f. Gk *phanarion* lighthouse (on the Golden Horn)]

phan·er·o·gam /fánərəgám/ *n. Bot.* a plant that has stamens and pistils, a flowering plant (cf. CRYPTOGAM). □□ **phan·er·o·gam·ic** /–gámik/ *adj.* **phan·er·og·a·mous** /–rógəməs/ *adj.* [F *phanérogame* f. Gk *phaneros* visible + *gamos* marriage]

phan·tasm /fántazəm/ *n.* **1** an illusion; a phantom. **2** (usu. foll. by *of*) an illusory likeness. **3** a supposed vision of an absent (living or dead) person. □□ **phan·tas·mal** /–tázm'l/ *adj.* **phan·tas·mic** /–tázmik/ *adj.* [ME f. OF *fantasme* f. L f. Gk *phantasma* f. *phantazō* make visible f. *phainō* show]

phan·tas·ma·go·ri·a /fántazməgáwreeə/ *n.* **1** a shifting series of real or imaginary figures as seen in a dream. **2** an optical device for rapidly varying the size of images on a screen. □□ **phan·tas·ma·gor·ic** /–gáwrik, –gór–/ *adj.* **phan·tas·ma·gor·i·cal** *adj.* [prob. f. F *fantasmagorie* (as PHANTASM + fanciful ending)]

phan·tom /fántəm/ *n. & adj.* ● *n.* **1** a ghost; an apparition; a specter. **2** a form without substance or reality; a mental illusion. **3** *Med.* a model of the whole or part of the body used to practice or demonstrate operative or therapeutic methods. ● *adj.* merely apparent; illusory. *Med.* [ME f. OF *fantosme* ult. f. Gk *phantasma* (as PHANTASM)]

phan·tom cir·cuit *n.* an arrangement of telegraph or other electrical wires equivalent to an extra circuit.

phan·tom limb *n.* a continuing sensation of the presence of a limb that has been amputated.

phan·tom preg·nan·cy *n.* the symptoms of pregnancy in a person not actually pregnant.

phar. *abbr.* (also **pharm.** or **Pharm.**) **1** pharmaceutical. **2** pharmacist. **3** pharmacy.

Phar·aoh /fáirō, fárō, fáyrō/ *n.* **1** the ruler of ancient Egypt. **2** the title of this ruler. □□ **Phar·a·on·ic** /fáirayónik/ *adj.* [OE f. eccl.L *Pharao* f. Gk *Pharaō* f. Heb. *par'ōh* f. Egypt. *pr-'o* great house]

Phar·i·see /fárisee/ (also **phar·i·see**) *n.* **1** a member of an ancient Jewish sect, distinguished by strict observance of the traditional and written law. **2** a person of the spirit or disposition attributed to the Pharisees in the New Testament; a self-righteous person; a hypocrite. □□ **Phar·i·sa·ic** /fárisáyik/ *adj.* **Phar·i·sa·i·cal** /fárisáyikəl/ *adj.* **Phar·i·sa·ism** /fárisayizəm/ *n.* [OE *fariseus* & OF *pharise* f. eccl.L *pharisaeus* f. Gk *Pharisaios* f. Aram. *p'rišayyā* pl. f. Heb. *pārûš* separated]

phar·ma·ceu·ti·cal /faárməsoótikəl/ *adj. & n.* ● *adj.* **1** of or engaged in pharmacy. **2** of the use or sale of medicinal drugs. ● *n.* a medicinal drug. □□ **phar·ma·ceu·ti·cal·ly** *adv.* **phar·ma·ceu·tics** *n.* [LL *pharmaceuticus* f. Gk *pharmakeutikos* f. *pharmakeutēs* druggist f. *pharmakon* drug]

phar·ma·cist /faárməsist/ *n.* a person qualified to prepare and dispense drugs.

phar·ma·cog·no·sy /faárməkógnəsee/ *n.* the science of drugs, esp. relating to medicinal products in their natural or unprepared state. [Gk *pharmakon* drug + *gnōsis* knowledge]

phar·ma·col·o·gy /faárməkóləjee/ *n.* the science of the action of drugs on the body. □□ **phar·ma·co·log·i·cal** *adj.* **phar·ma·co·log·i·cal·ly** *adv.* **phar·ma·col·o·gist** *n.* [mod.L *pharmacologia* f. Gk *pharmakon* drug]

phar·ma·co·poe·ia /faárməkəpeéə/ *n.* **1** a book, esp. one officially published, containing a list of drugs with directions for use. **2** a stock of drugs. □□ **phar·ma·co·poe·ial** *adj.* [mod.L f. Gk *pharmakopoiia* f. *pharmakopoios* drug maker (as PHARMACOLOGY + *-poios* making)]

phar·ma·cy /faárməsee/ *n.* (*pl.* **-cies**) **1** the preparation and the (esp. medicinal) dispensing of drugs. **2** a drugstore; a dispensary. [ME f. OF *farmacie* f. med.L *pharmacia* f. Gk *pharmakeia* practice of the druggist f. *pharmakeus* f. *pharmakon* drug]

pha·ros /fáiros/ *n.* a lighthouse or a beacon to guide sailors. [L f. Gk *Pharos* island off Alexandria where a famous lighthouse stood]

pharyngo- /fəringgō/ *comb. form* denoting the pharynx.

phar·yn·got·o·my /fáringgótəmee/ *n.* (*pl.* **-mies**) an incision into the pharynx.

phar·ynx /fáringks/ *n.* (*pl.* **pha·ryn·ges** /fərínjeez/) a cavity, with enclosing muscles and mucous membrane, behind the nose and mouth, and connecting them to the esophagus. □□ **pha·ryn·gal** /-ríngaal/ *adj.* **pha·ryn·ge·al** /fərínjeeəl, -jəl, fáringjeéəl/ *adj.* **phar·yn·gi·tis** /-rinjítis/ *n.* [mod.L f. Gk *pharugx -ggos*]

phase /fayz/ *n. & v.* ● *n.* **1** a distinct period or stage in a process of change or development. **2** each of the aspects of the moon or a planet, according to the amount of its illumination, esp. the new moon, the first quarter, the last quarter, and the full moon. **3** *Physics* a stage in a periodically recurring sequence, esp. of alternating electric currents or light vibrations. **4** a difficult or unhappy period, esp. in adolescence. **5** a genetic or seasonal variety of an animal's coloration, etc. **6** *Chem.* a distinct and homogeneous form of matter separated by its surface from other forms. ● *v.tr.* carry out (a program, etc.) in phases or stages. □ **in phase** having the same phase at the same time. **out of phase** not in phase. **phase in** (or **out**) bring gradually into (or out of) use. □□ **pha·sic** *adj.* [F *phase* & f. earlier *phasis* f. Gk *phasis* appearance f. *phainō* phan- show]

phase rule *n. Chem.* a rule relating the possible numbers of phases, constituents, and degrees of freedom in a chemical system.

phat·ic /fátik/ *adj.* (of speech, etc.) used to convey general sociability rather than to communicate a specific meaning, e.g., "How do you do?" [Gk *phatos* spoken f. *phēmi* phan- speak]

Ph.D. *abbr.* Doctor of Philosophy. [L *philosophiae doctor*]

pheas·ant /fézənt/ *n.* any of several long-tailed game birds of the family Phasianidae, orig. from Asia. □□ **pheas·ant·ry** *n.* (*pl.* **-ries**). [ME f. AF *fesaunt* f. OF *faisan* f. L *phasianus* f. Gk *phasianos* (bird) of the river *Phasis* in Asia Minor]

ring-necked pheasant

phe·nac·e·tin /finásitin/ *n.* an acetyl derivative of phenol used to treat fever, etc. [PHENO- + ACETYL + -IN]

pheno- /feénō/ *comb. form* **1** *Chem.* derived from benzene (*phenol*; *phenyl*). **2** showing (*phenocryst*). [Gk *phainō* shine (with ref. to substances used for illumination), show]

phe·no·bar·bi·tone /feénōbaárbitawl, -tal/ *n.* (*Brit.* **phe·no·bar·bi·tone** /-bitōn/) a narcotic and sedative barbiturate drug used esp. to treat epilepsy.

phe·no·cryst /feénəkrist/ *n.* a large or conspicuous crystal in porphyritic rock. [F *phénocryste* (as PHENO-, CRYSTAL)]

phe·nol /feénawl, -nol/ *n. Chem.* **1** the monohydroxyl derivative of benzene used in dilute form as an antiseptic and disinfectant. Also called **carbolic.** ¶ Chem. formula: C_6H_5OH. **2** any hydroxyl derivative of an aromatic hydrocarbon. □□ **phe·no·lic** /finólik/ *adj.* [F *phénole* f. *phène* benzene (formed as PHENO-)]

phe·nol·phthal·ein /feénolthályeen/ *n. Chem.* a white crystalline solid used in solution as an acid-base indicator and medicinally as a laxative. [PHENOL + *phthal* f. NAPHTHALENE + -IN]

phe·nom·e·na *pl.* of PHENOMENON.

phe·nom·e·nal /finóminəl/ *adj.* **1** of the nature of a phenomenon. **2** extraordinary; remarkable; prodigious. **3** perceptible by, or perceptible only to, the senses. □□ **phe·nom·e·nal·ize** *v.tr.* **phe·nom·e·nal·ly** *adv.*

phe·nom·e·nal·ism /finóminəlizəm/ *n. Philos.* **1** the doctrine that human knowledge is confined to the appearances presented to the senses. **2** the doctrine that appearances are the foundation of all our knowledge. □□ **phe·nom·e·nal·ist** *n.* **phe·nom·e·nal·is·tic** *adj.*

phe·nom·e·nol·o·gy /finóminóləjee/ *n. Philos.* **1** the science of phenomena. **2** the description and classification of phenomena. □□ **phe·nom·e·no·log·i·cal** /-nəlójikəl/ *adj.* **phe·nom·e·no·log·i·cal·ly** *adv.*

phe·nom·e·non /finóminən/ *n.* (*pl.* **phe·nom·e·na** /-nə/) **1** a fact or occurrence that appears or is perceived, esp. one of which the cause is in question. **2** a remarkable person or thing. **3** *Philos.* the object of a person's perception; what the senses or the mind notice. [LL f. Gk *phainomenon* neut. pres. part. of *phainomai* appear f. *phainō* show]

▶The singular of this Greek word is **phenomenon**, the plural **phenomena:** *Halley's Comet is a rare phenomenon, one of the most spectacular of celestial phenomena.*

phe·no·type /feénōtīp/ *n. Biol.* a set of observable characteristics of an individual or group as determined by its genotype and environment. □□ **phe·no·typ·ic** /-típik/ *adj.* **phe·no·typ·i·cal** *adj.* **phe·no·typ·i·cal·ly** *adv.* [G *Phaenotypus* (as PHENO-, TYPE)]

phen·yl /fénil, feé-/ *n. Chem.* the univalent radical formed from benzene by the removal of a hydrogen atom. [PHENE- + -YL]

phen·yl·a·la·nine /féniláləneen, feé-/ *n. Biochem.* an amino acid widely distributed in plant proteins and essential in the human diet. [PHENYL + *alanine* a simple amino acid]

phen·yl·ke·to·nu·ri·a /fénilkeétōnóōreeə, -yóōr-, feé-/ *n.* an inherited inability to metabolize phenylalanine, ultimately leading to mental deficiency if untreated. [PHENYL + KETONE + -URIA]

pher·o·mone /férəmōn/ *n.* a chemical substance secreted and released by an animal for detection and response by another usu. of the same species. □□ **pher·o·mo·nal** /-mōn'l/ *adj.* [Gk *pherō* convey + HORMONE]

phew /fyoō/ *int.* an expression of impatience, discomfort, relief, astonishment, or disgust. [imit. of puffing]

phi /fī/ *n.* the twenty-first letter of the Greek alphabet (Φ, φ). [Gk]

phi·al /fīəl/ *n.* a small glass bottle, esp. for liquid medicine; vial. [ME f. OF *fiole* f. L *phiola phiala* f. Gk *phialē*, a broad flat vessel: cf. VIAL]

Phi Be·ta Kap·pa *n.* **1** an intercollegiate honorary society to which distinguished scholars may be elected (from the initial letters of a Greek motto, = philosophy is the guide to life). **2** a member of this society.

Phil. *abbr.* **1** Philharmonic. **2** Philippians (New Testament). **3** Philippines. **4** Philosophy.

phil- *comb. form* var. of PHILO-.

-phil *comb. form* var. of -PHILE.

phil·a·del·phus /filədélfəs/ *n.* any highly-scented deciduous flowering shrub of the genus *Philadelphus*, esp. the mock orange. [mod.L f. Gk *philadelphon*]

phi·lan·der /filándər/ *v.intr.* (often foll. by *with*) flirt or have casual affairs with women; womanize. □□ **phi·lan·der·er** *n.* [*philander* (n.) used in Gk literature as the proper name of a lover, f. Gk *philandros* fond of men f. *anēr* male person: see PHIL-]

phil·an·thrope /filənthrōp/ *n.* = *philanthropist* (see PHILANTHROPY). [Gk *philanthrōpos* (as PHIL-, *anthrōpos* human being)]

phil·an·throp·ic /filənthrópik/ *adj.* loving one's fellow people; benevolent. □□ **phil·an·throp·i·cal·ly** *adv.* [F *philanthropique* (as PHILANTHROPE)]

phi·lan·thro·py /filánthrəpee/ *n.* **1** a love of humankind. **2** practical benevolence, esp. charity on a large scale. □□ **phi·lan·thro·pism** *n.* **phi·lan·thro·pist** *n.* **phi·lan·thro·pize** *v.tr. & intr.* [LL *philanthropia* f. Gk *philanthrōpia* (as PHILANTHROPE)]

phi·lat·e·ly /filát'lee/ *n.* the collection and study of postage stamps. □□ **phil·a·tel·ic** /filətélik/ *adj.* **phil·a·tel·i·cal·ly** *adv.* **phi·lat·e·list** *n.* [F *philatélie* f. Gk *ateleia* exemption from payment f. *a-* not + *telos* toll, tax]

-phile /fīl/ *comb. form* (also **–phil** /fil/) forming nouns and adjectives denoting fondness for what is specified (*bibliophile*; *Francophile*). [Gk *philos* dear, loving]

Philem. *abbr.* Philemon (New Testament).

phil·har·mon·ic /fílhaarmónik/ *adj.* **1** fond of music. **2** used characteristically in the names of orchestras, choirs, etc. (*New York Philharmonic Orchestra*). [F *philharmonique* f. It. *filarmonico* (as PHIL-, HARMONIC)]

phil·hel·lene /fílhéleen/ *n.* (often *attrib.*) **1** a lover of Greece and Greek culture. **2** *hist.* a supporter of the cause of Greek independence. □□ **phil·hel·len·ic** /–helénik/ *adj.* **phil·hel·len·ism** /–hélinizəm/ *n.* **phil·hel·len·ist** /–hélinist/ *n.* [Gk *philellēn* (as PHIL-, HELLENE)]

-philia /fíleeə/ *comb. form* **1** denoting (esp. abnormal) fondness or love for what is specified (*necrophilia*). **2** denoting undue inclination (*hemophilia*). □□ **–philiac** /–leeak/ *comb. form* forming nouns and adjectives. **–philic** /–ik/ *comb. form* forming adjectives. **–philous** /–əs/ *comb. form* forming adjectives. [Gk f. *philos* loving]

phi·lip·pic /filípik/ *n.* a bitter verbal attack or denunciation. [L *philippicus* f. Gk *philippikos* the name of Demosthenes' speeches against Philip II of Macedon and Cicero's against Mark Antony]

Phil·ip·pine /fílipeen/ *adj.* of or relating to the Philippine Islands or their people; Filipino. [*Philip II* of Spain]

Phil·is·tine /fílisteen, –stīn, fílistin, –teen/ *n. & adj.* • *n.* **1** a member of a people opposing the Israelites in ancient Palestine. **2** (usu. **philistine**) a person who is hostile or indifferent to culture, or one whose interests or tastes are commonplace or material. • *adj.* hostile or indifferent to culture; commonplace; prosaic. □□ **phil·is·tin·ism** /fílistinízəm/ *n.* [ME f. F *Philistin* or LL *Philistinus* f. Gk *Philistinos* = *Palaistinos* f. Heb. *pᵉlištî*]

Phil·lips /fílips/ *n.* (usu. *attrib.*) *Trademark* denoting a screw with a cross-shaped slot for turning, or a corresponding screwdriver. [H. M. *Phillips* d. 1935, original US manufacturer]

phil·lu·men·ist /filóomənist/ *n.* a collector of matchboxes or matchbox labels. □□ **phil·lu·me·ny** *n.* [PHIL- + L *lumen* light]

Phil·ly /fílee/ *n. sl.* Philadelphia. [abbr.]

philo- /fílō/ *comb. form* (also **phil-** before a vowel or *h*) denoting a liking for what is specified.

phi·lo·den·dron /fílədéndrən/ *n.* (*pl.* **phil·o·den·drons** or **phil·o·den·dra** /–drə/) any tropical American climbing plant of the genus *Philodendron*, with bright foliage. [PHILO- + Gk *dendron* tree]

phi·log·y·nist /filójənist/ *n.* a person who likes or admires women. [PHILO- + Gk *gunē* woman]

phi·lol·o·gy /filóləjee/ *n.* **1** the science of language, esp. in its historical and comparative aspects. **2** the love of learning and literature. □□ **phi·lo·lo·gi·an** /–lǝlójeeən/ *n.* **phi·lol·o·gist** *n.* **phil·o·log·i·cal** /–lǝlójikəl/ *adj.* **phil·o·log·i·cal·ly** /–lǝlójiklee/ *adv.* **phi·lol·o·gize** *v.intr.* [F *philologie* f. L *philologia* love of learning f. Gk (as PHILO-, –LOGY)]

Phil·o·mel /fíləmel/ *n.* (also **phil·o·mel, Phil·o·me·la** /fíləméélə/) *poet.* the nightingale. [earlier *philomene* f. med.L *philomena* f. L *philomela* nightingale f. Gk *philomēla*: cap. with ref. to the myth of *Philomela*]

phil·o·pro·gen·i·tive /fílōprōjénitiv/ *adj.* **1** prolific. **2** loving one's offspring.

phi·los·o·pher /filósəfər/ *n.* **1** a person engaged or learned in philosophy or a branch of it. **2** a person who lives by philosophy. **3** a person who shows philosophic calmness in trying circumstances. [ME f. AF *philosofre* var. of OF, *philosophe* f. L *philosophus* f. Gk *philosophos* (as PHILO-, *sophos* wise)]

phi·los·o·phers' stone *n.* (also **phi·los·o·pher's stone**) the supreme object of alchemy, a substance supposed to change other metals into gold or silver.

phil·o·soph·i·cal /fíləsófikəl/ *adj.* (also **phil·o·soph·ic**) **1** of or according to philosophy. **2** skilled in or devoted to philosophy or learning; learned (*philosophical society*). **3** wise; serene; temperate. **4** calm in adverse circumstances. □□ **phil·o·soph·i·cal·ly** *adv.* [LL *philosophicus* f. L *philosophia* (as PHILOSOPHY)]

phi·los·o·phize /filósəfīz/ *v.* **1** *intr.* reason like a philosopher. **2** *intr.* moralize. **3** *intr.* speculate; theorize. **4** *tr.* render philosophic. □□ **phi·los·o·phiz·er** *n.* [app. f. F *philosopher*]

phi·los·o·phy /filósəfee/ *n.* (*pl.* **–phies**) **1** the use of reason and argument in seeking truth and knowledge of reality, esp. of the causes and nature of things and of the principles governing existence, the material universe, perception of physical phenomena, and human behavior. **2 a** a particular system or set of beliefs reached by this. **b** a personal rule of life. **3** advanced learning in general (*doctor of philosophy*). **4** serenity; calmness; conduct governed by a particular philosophy. [ME f. OF *filosofie* f. L *philosophia* wisdom f. Gk (as PHILO-, *sophos* wise)]

phil·ter /fíltər/ *n.* (also **phil·tre**) a drink supposed to excite sexual love in the drinker. [F *philtre* f. L *philtrum* f. Gk *philtron* f. *phileō* to love]

-phily /fílee/ *comb. form* = –PHILIA.

phi·mo·sis /fīmósis/ *n.* a constriction of the foreskin, making it dif-

ficult to retract. □□ **phi·mot·ic** /–mótik/ *adj.* [mod.L f. Gk, = muzzling]

phiz /fiz/ *n.* (also **phizog** /fízog/) *colloq.* **1** the face. **2** the expression on a face. [abbr. of *phiznomy* = PHYSIOGNOMY]

phle·bi·tis /flibítis/ *n.* inflammation of the walls of a vein. □□ **phle·bit·ic** /–bítik/ *adj.* [mod.L f. Gk f. *phleps phlebos* vein]

phle·bot·o·my /flibótəmee/ *n.* **1** the surgical opening or puncture of a vein. **2** esp. *hist.* bloodletting as a medical treatment. □□ **phle·bot·o·mist** *n.* **phle·bot·o·mize** *v.tr.* [ME f. OF *flebothomi* f. LL *phlebotomia* f. Gk f. *phleps phlebos* vein + –TOMY]

phlegm /flem/ *n.* **1** the thick viscous substance secreted by the mucous membranes of the respiratory passages, discharged by coughing. **2 a** coolness and calmness of disposition. **b** sluggishness or apathy (supposed to result from too much phlegm in the constitution). **3** *archaic* phlegm regarded as one of the four bodily humors. □□ **phlegm·y** *adj.*

WORD HISTORY phlegm

Middle English *fleem*, *fleume*, from Old French *fleume*, from late Latin *phlegma* 'clammy moisture (of the body),' from Greek *phlegma* 'inflammation,' from *phlegein* 'to burn.' The spelling change in the 16th century was due to association with the Latin and Greek forms.

---

phleg·mat·ic /flegmátik/ *adj.* stolidly calm; unexcitable; unemotional. □□ **phleg·mat·i·cal·ly** *adv.*

phlo·em /flóem/ *n. Bot.* the tissue conducting food material in plants (cf. XYLEM). [Gk *phloos* bark]

phlo·gis·ton /flōjíston/ *n.* a substance formerly supposed to exist in all combustible bodies, and to be released in combustion. [mod.L f. Gk *phlogizō* set on fire f. *phlox phlogos* flame]

phlox /floks/ *n.* any cultivated plant of the genus *Phlox*, with scented clusters of esp. white, blue, and red flowers. [L f. Gk *phlox*, the name of a plant (lit. flame)]

-phobe /fōb/ *comb. form* forming nouns and adjectives denoting a person having a fear or dislike of what is specified (*xenophobe*). [F f. L *–phobus* f. Gk *–phobos* f. *phobos* fear]

pho·bi·a /fóbeeə/ *n.* an abnormal or morbid fear or aversion. □□ **pho·bic** *adj. & n.* [-PHOBIA used as a separate word]

-phobia /fóbeeə/ *comb. form* forming abstract nouns denoting a fear or dislike of what is specified (*agoraphobia*; *xenophobia*). □□ **–pho·bic** *comb. form* forming adjectives. [L f. Gk]

phoe·be /feébee/ *n.* any American flycatcher of the genus *Sayornis*. [imit.: infl. by the name]

Phoe·ni·cian /fəneéeshən, fəní–/ *n. & adj.* • *n.* a member of a Semitic people of ancient Phoenicia in S. Syria or of its colonies. • *adj.* of or relating to Phoenicia. [ME f. OF *phenicien* f. L *Phoenicia* f. L *Phoenice* f. Gk *Phoinikē* Phoenicia]

phoe·nix /feéniks/ *n.* **1** a mythical bird, the only one of its kind, that after living for five or six centuries in the Arabian desert, burned itself on a funeral pyre and rose from the ashes with renewed youth to live through another cycle. **2 a** a unique person or thing. **b** a person or thing having recovered, esp. seemingly miraculously, from a disaster. [OE & OF *fenix* f. L *phoenix* f. Gk *phoinix* Phoenician, purple, phoenix]

phon /fon/ *n.* a unit of the perceived loudness of sounds. [Gk *phōnē* sound]

pho·nate /fónayt/ *v.intr.* utter a vocal sound. □□ **pho·na·tion** /–náyshən/ *n.* **pho·na·to·ry** /fónatawree/ *adj.* [Gk *phōnē* voice]

phone¹ /fōn/ *n. & v.tr. & intr. colloq.* = TELEPHONE. [abbr.]

phone² /fōn/ *n.* a simple vowel or consonant sound. [formed as PHONEME]

-phone /fōn/ *comb. form* forming nouns and adjectives meaning: **1** an instrument using or connected with sound (*telephone*; *xylophone*). **2** a person who uses a specified language (*anglophone*). [Gk *phōnē* voice, sound]

phone book *n.* = TELEPHONE BOOK.

phone-in *adj.* (esp. of a broadcast program) denoting a program during which the listeners or viewers can telephone the studio, etc., and participate.

pho·neme /fóneem/ *n.* any of the units of sound in a specified language that distinguish one word from another (e.g., *p, b, d, t* as in pad, pat, bad, bat, in English). □□ **pho·ne·mic** /–neémik/ *adj.* **pho·ne·mics** /–neémiks/ *n.* [F *phonème* f. Gk *phōnēma* sound, speech f. *phōneō* speak]

pho·net·ic /fənétik/ *adj.* **1** representing vocal sounds. **2** (of a system of spelling, etc.) having a direct correspondence between symbols and sounds. **3** of or relating to phonetics. □□ **pho·net·i·cal·ly** *adv.* **pho·net·i·cism** /–nétəsizəm/ *n.* **pho·net·i·cist** /–nétəsist/ *n.* **pho·net·i·cize** /–nétəsīz/ *v.tr.* [mod.L *phoneticus* f. Gk *phōnētikos* f. *phōneō* speak]

pho·net·ics /fənétiks/ *n.pl.* (usu. treated as *sing.*) **1** vocal sounds and their classification. **2** the study of these. □□ **pho·ne·ti·cian** /fónitíshən/ *n.*

pho·ne·tist /fónitist/ *n.* an advocate of phonetic spelling.

phon·ic /fónik/ *adj. & n.* • *adj.* of sound; acoustic; of vocal sounds.

● *n.* (in *pl.*) a method of teaching reading based on sounds. □□ **phon•i•cal•ly** *adv.* [Gk *phōnē* voice]

phono- /fōnō/ *comb. form* denoting sound. [Gk *phōnē* voice, sound]

pho•no•gram /fōnəgram/ *n.* a symbol representing a spoken sound.

pho•no•graph /fōnəgraf/ *n.* an instrument that reproduces recorded sound by a stylus that is in contact with a rotating grooved disk. ►Now more usually called a RECORD PLAYER.

pho•nog•ra•phy /fənógrəfee/ *n.* **1** writing in esp. shorthand symbols, corresponding to the sounds of speech. **2** the recording of sounds by phonograph. □□ **pho•no•graph•ic** /fōnəgráfik/ *adj.*

pho•nol•o•gy /fənóləjee/ *n.* the study of sounds in a language. □□ **pho•no•log•i•cal** /fōnəlójikəl/ *adj.* **pho•no•log•i•cal•ly** *adv.* **pho•nol•o•gist** /fənóləjist/ *n.*

pho•non /fōnon/ *n. Physics* a quantum of sound or elastic vibrations. [Gk *phōnē* sound, after PHOTON]

pho•ny /fōnee/ *adj. & n.* (also **pho•ney**) *colloq.* ● *adj.* (**pho•ni•er, pho•ni•est**) **1** sham; counterfeit. **2** fictitious; fraudulent. ● *n.* (*pl.* **•nies** or **•neys**) a phony person or thing. □□ **pho•ni•ly** *adv.* **pho•ni•ness** *n.* [20th c.: orig. unkn.]

phoo•ey /fōo-ee/ *int.* an expression of disgust or disbelief. [imit.]

-phore /fawr/ *comb. form* forming nouns meaning 'bearer' (*ctenophore; semaphore*). □□ **-phorous** /fərəs/ *comb. form* forming adjectives. [mod.L f. Gk *–phoros –phoron* bearing, bearer f. *pherō* bear]

phor•e•sy /fáwrəsee/ *n. Biol.* an association in which one organism is carried by another, without being a parasite. □□ **phor•et•ic** /fawrétik/ *adj.* [F *phorésie* f. Gk *phorēsis* being carried]

phos•gene /fósjeen, fóz–/ *n.* a colorless poisonous gas (carbonyl chloride), formerly used in warfare. ¶ Chem. formula: $COCl_2$. [Gk *phōs* light + –GEN, with ref. to its orig. production by the action of sunlight on chlorine and carbon monoxide]

phos•pha•tase /fósfətays, –tayz/ *n. Biochem.* any enzyme that catalyzes the synthesis or hydrolysis of an organic phosphate.

phos•phate /fósfayt/ *n.* **1** any salt or ester of phosphoric acid, esp. used as a fertilizer. **2** a flavored effervescent drink containing a small amount of phosphate. □□ **phos•phat•ic** /–fátik/ *adj.* [F f. *phosphore* PHOSPHORUS]

phos•phene /fósfeen/ *n.* the sensation of rings of light produced by pressure on the eyeball due to irritation of the retina. [irreg. f. Gk *phōs* light + *phainō* show]

phos•phide /fósfid/ *n. Chem.* a binary compound of phosphorus with another element or group.

phos•phine /fósfeen/ *n. Chem.* a colorless ill-smelling gas, phosphorus trihydride. ¶ Chem. formula: PH_3. □□ **phos•phin•ic** /–fínik/ *adj.* [PHOSPHO- + –INE[4], after *amine*]

phos•phite /fósfīt/ *n. Chem.* any salt or ester of phosphorous acid. [F (as PHOSPHO-)]

phospho- /fósfō/ *comb. form* denoting phosphorus. [abbr.]

phos•pho•lip•id /fósfəlípid/ *n. Biochem.* any lipid consisting of a phosphate group and one or more fatty acids.

phos•phor /fósfər/ *n.* **1** = PHOSPHORUS. **2** a synthetic fluorescent or phosphorescent substance esp. used in cathode-ray tubes. [G f. L *phosphorus* PHOSPHORUS]

phos•pho•rate /fósfərayt/ *v.tr.* combine or impregnate with phosphorus.

phos•phor bronze *n.* a tough hard bronze alloy containing a small amount of phosphorus, used esp. for bearings.

phos•pho•res•cence /fósfərésəns/ *n.* **1** radiation similar to fluorescence but detectable after excitation ceases. **2** the emission of light without combustion or perceptible heat. □□ **phos•pho•resce** *v.intr.* **phos•pho•res•cent** *adj.*

phos•pho•rite /fósfərīt/ *n.* a noncrystalline form of apatite.

phos•pho•rus /fósfərəs/ *n. Chem.* a nonmetallic element occurring naturally in various phosphate rocks and existing in allotropic forms, esp. as a poisonous whitish waxy substance burning slowly at ordinary temperatures and so appearing luminous in the dark, and a reddish form used in matches, fertilizers, etc. ¶ Symb.: **P**. □□ **phos•phor•ic** /–fórik/ *adj.* **phos•pho•rous** *adj.* [L, = morning star, f. Gk *phōsphoros* f. *phōs* light + *–phoros –*bringing]

phos•pho•ryl•ate /fósfərīláyt, fosfáwr–/ *v.tr. Chem.* introduce a phosphate group into (an organic molecule, etc.). □□ **phos•pho•ryl•a•tion** /–láyshən/ *n.*

phot /fot, fōt/ *n.* a unit of illumination equal to one lumen per square centimeter. [Gk *phōs phōtos* light]

pho•tic /fótik/ *adj.* **1** of or relating to light. **2** (of ocean layers) reached by sunlight.

pho•tism /fótizəm/ *n.* a hallucinatory sensation or vision of light. [Gk *phōtismos* f. *phōtizō* shine f. *phōs phōtos* light]

pho•to /fótō/ *n. & v.* ● *n.* (*pl.* **•tos**) = PHOTOGRAPH *n.* ● *v.tr.* (**•toes, •toed**) = PHOTOGRAPH *v.* [abbr.]

photo- /fótō/ *comb. form* denoting: **1** light (*photosensitive*). **2** photography (*photocomposition*). [Gk *phōs phōtos* light, or as abbr. of PHOTOGRAPH]

pho•to•bi•ol•o•gy /fótōbīóləjee/ *n.* the study of the effects of light on living organisms.

pho•to•call *n. Brit.* = PHOTO OPPORTUNITY.

pho•to•cell /fótōsel/ *n.* = PHOTOELECTRIC CELL.

pho•to•chem•is•try /fótōkémistree/ *n.* the study of the chemical effects of light. □□ **pho•to•chem•i•cal** *adj.*

pho•to•com•po•si•tion /fótōkómpəzíshən/ *n. Printing* a typesetting process in which characters, etc., are projected onto a light-sensitive material such as photographic film.

pho•to•con•duc•tiv•i•ty /fótōkónduktívitee/ *n.* conductivity due to the action of light. □□ **pho•to•con•duc•tive** /–dúktiv/ *adj.* **pho•to•con•duc•tor** /–dúktər/ *n.*

pho•to•cop•i•er /fótōkópeeər/ *n.* a machine for producing photocopies.

pho•to•cop•y /fótōkópee/ *n. & v.* ● *n.* (*pl.* **•ies**) a photographic copy of printed or written material produced by a process involving the action of light on a specially prepared surface. ● *v.tr.* (**•ies, •ied**) make a photocopy of. □□ **pho•to•cop•i•a•ble** *adj.*

pho•to•di•ode /fótōdíōd/ *n.* a semiconductor diode responding electrically to illumination.

pho•to•e•lec•tric /fótōiléktrik/ *adj.* marked by or using emissions of electrons from substances exposed to light. □□ **pho•to•e•lec•tric•i•ty** /–trísitee/ *n.*

pho•to•e•lec•tric cell *n.* a device using a photoelectric effect to generate current.

pho•to•e•lec•tron /fótōiléktron/ *n.* an electron emitted from an atom by interaction with a photon, esp. one emitted from a solid surface by the action of light.

pho•to•e•mis•sion /fótōimíshən/ *n.* the emission of electrons from a surface by the action of light incident on it. □□ **pho•to•e•mit•ter** *n.*

pho•to fin•ish *n.* a close finish of a race or contest, esp. one where the winner is only distinguishable on a photograph.

pho•to•fin•ish•ing /fótōfinishing/ *n.* the process of developing and printing photographic film.

pho•to•gen•ic /fótōjénik/ *adj.* **1** (esp. of a person) having an appearance that looks pleasing in photographs. **2** *Biol.* producing or emitting light. □□ **pho•to•gen•i•cal•ly** *adv.*

pho•to•gram /fótəgram/ *n.* **1** a picture produced with photographic materials but without a camera. **2** *archaic* a photograph.

pho•to•gram•me•try /fótōgrámitree/ *n.* the use of photography for surveying. □□ **pho•to•gram•me•trist** *n.*

pho•to•graph /fótəgraf/ *n. & v.* ● *n.* a picture taken by means of the chemical action of light or other radiation on sensitive film. ● *v.tr.* (also *absol.*) take a photograph (of a person, etc.). □□ **pho•to•graph•a•ble** *adj.* **pho•tog•ra•pher** /fətógrəfər/ *n.* **pho•to•graph•i•cal•ly** /–gráfiklee/ *adv.*

pho•to•graph•ic /fótəgráfik/ *adj.* **1** of, used in, or produced by photography. **2** having the accuracy of a photograph (*photographic likeness*).

pho•tog•ra•phy /fətógrəfee/ *n.* the taking and processing of photographs.

pho•to•gra•vure /fótōgrəvyŏŏr/ *n.* **1** an image produced from a photographic negative transferred to a metal plate and etched in. **2** this process. [F (as PHOTO-, *gravure* engraving)]

pho•to•jour•nal•ism /fótōjórnəlizəm/ *n.* the art or practice of relating news by photographs, with or without an accompanying text, esp. in magazines, etc. □□ **pho•to•jour•nal•ist** *n.*

pho•to•li•thog•ra•phy /fótōlithógrəfee/ *n.* (*Brit.* also **pho•to•lith•o** /–líthō/) lithography using plates made photographically. □□ **pho•to•li•thog•ra•pher** *n.* **pho•to•lith•o•graph•ic** /–thəgráfik/ *adj.* **pho•to•lith•o•graph•i•cal•ly** *adv.*

pho•tol•y•sis /fótólisis/ *n.* decomposition or dissociation of molecules by the action of light. □□ **pho•to•lyze** /fótəlīz/ *v.tr. & intr.* **pho•to•lyt•ic** /–təlítik/ *adj.*

pho•tom•e•ter /fótómitər/ *n.* an instrument for measuring light. □□ **pho•to•met•ric** /fótōmétrik/ *adj.* **pho•tom•e•try** /–tómitree/ *n.*

pho•to•mi•cro•graph /fótōmíkrəgraf/ *n.* a photograph of an image produced by a microscope. □□ **pho•to•mi•crog•ra•phy** /–krógrəfee/ *n.*

pho•ton /fóton/ *n.* **1** a quantum of electromagnetic radiation energy, proportional to the frequency of radiation. **2** a unit of luminous intensity as measured at the retina. [Gk *phōs phōtos* light, after *electron*]

pho•to•nov•el /fótōnóvəl/ *n.* a novel told in a series of photographs with superimposed speech bubbles.

pho•to•off•set /fótō-áwfset, –óf–/ *n.* offset printing with plates made photographically.

pho•to op•por•tu•ni•ty *n.* (also **pho•to-op**) an occasion on which actors, politicians, famous personalities, etc., pose for photographers by arrangement.

pho•to•pe•ri•od /fótōpéereeəd/ *n.* the period of daily illumination which an organism receives. □□ **pho•to•pe•ri•od•ic** /–ee-ódik/ *adj.*

pho•to•pe•ri•od•ism /fótōpéereeədizəm/ *n.* the response of an organism to changes in the lengths of the daily periods of light.

pho•to•pho•bi•a /fótōfóbeeə/ *n.* an abnormal fear of or aversion to light. □□ **pho•to•pho•bic** *adj.*

pho·to·re·cep·tor /fōtōriséptər/ n. any living structure that responds to incident light.

pho·to·sen·si·tive /fótōsénsitiv/ adj. reacting chemically, electrically, etc., to light. □□ **pho·to·sen·si·tiv·i·ty** /–tívitee/ n.

pho·to·set·ting /fótōseting/ n. = PHOTOCOMPOSITION. □□ **pho·to·set** v. tr. (past and past part. ·set). **pho·to·set·ter** n.

pho·to·sphere /fótəsfeer/ n. the luminous envelope of a star from which its light and heat radiate. □□ **pho·to·spher·ic** /–sférik/ adj.

Pho·to·stat /fótəstat/ n. & v. • n. Trademark 1 a type of machine for making photocopies. 2 a copy made by this means. • v.tr. (photostat) (·stat·ted, ·stat·ting) make a Photostat of. □□ **pho·to·stat·ic** /–státik/ adj.

pho·to·syn·the·sis /fótōsínthisis/ n. the process in which the energy of sunlight is used by organisms, esp. green plants, to synthesize carbohydrates from carbon dioxide and water. □□ **pho·to·syn·the·size** v.tr. & intr. **pho·to·syn·thet·ic** /–thétik/ adj. **pho·to·syn·thet·i·cal·ly** adv.

pho·to·tran·sis·tor /fótōtranzístər/ n. a transistor that responds to incident light by generating and amplifying an electric current.

pho·tot·ro·pism /fətótrəpízəm, fótōtrópizəm/ n. the tendency of a plant, etc., to bend or turn toward or away from a source of light. □□ **pho·to·trop·ic** /–trópik/ adj.

pho·to·vol·ta·ic /fótōvoltáyik, –vōl–/ adj. relating to the production of electric current at the junction of two substances exposed to light.

phras·al /fráyzəl/ adj. Gram. consisting of a phrase.

phras·al verb n. an idiomatic phrase consisting of a verb and an adverb (e.g., break down), a verb and a preposition (e.g., see to), or a combination of both (e.g., look down on).

phrase /frayz/ n. & v. • n. 1 a group of words forming a conceptual unit, but not a sentence. 2 an idiomatic or short pithy expression. 3 a manner or mode of expression (a nice turn of phrase). 4 Mus. a group of notes forming a distinct unit within a larger piece. • v.tr. 1 express in words (phrased the reply badly). 2 (esp. when reading aloud or speaking) divide (sentences, etc.) into units so as to convey the meaning of the whole. 3 Mus. divide (music) into phrases, etc., in performance. □□ **phras·ing** n. [earlier phrasis f. L f. Gk f. phrazō declare, tell]

phrase book n. a book for tourists, etc., listing useful expressions with their equivalents in a foreign language.

phra·se·o·gram /fráyzeeəgrám/ n. a written symbol representing a phrase, esp. in shorthand.

phra·se·ol·o·gy /fráyzeeóləjee/ n. (pl. ·gies) 1 a choice or arrangement of words. 2 a mode of expression. □□ **phra·se·o·log·i·cal** /–əlójikəl/ adj. [mod.L phraseologia f. Gk phraseōn genit. pl. of phrasis PHRASE]

phre·at·ic /freeátik/ adj. Geol. 1 (of water) situated underground in the zone of saturation; ground water. 2 (of a volcanic eruption or explosion) caused by the heating and expansion of underground water. [Gk phrear phreatos well]

phre·net·ic /frənétik/ adj. (also **fre·net·ic**) 1 frantic. 2 fanatic. □□ **phre·net·i·cal·ly** adv. [ME, var. of FRENETIC]

phren·ic /frénik/ adj. Anat. of or relating to the diaphragm. [F phrénique f. Gk phrēn phrenos diaphragm, mind]

phre·nol·o·gy /frinóləjee/ n. hist. the study of the shape and size of the cranium as a supposed indication of character and mental faculties. □□ **phre·no·log·i·cal** /–nəlójikəl/ adj. **phre·nol·o·gist** n.

Phryg·i·an /fríjeeən/ n. & adj. • n. 1 a native or inhabitant of ancient Phrygia in central Asia Minor. 2 the language of this people. • adj. of or relating to Phrygia or its people or language.

Phryg·i·an cap n. (also **Phryg·i·an bon·net**) an ancient conical cap with the top bent forward, now identified with the liberty cap.

Phryg·i·an mode n. Mus. the mode represented by the natural diatonic scale E–E.

phthal·ic ac·id /thálik, fthál–/ n. Chem. one of three isomeric dicarboxylic acids derived from benzene. □□ **phthal·ate** /–layt/ n. [abbr. of naphthalic: see NAPHTHALENE]

phthi·sis /thísis, tí–/ n. any progressive wasting disease, esp. pulmonary tuberculosis. □□ **phthis·ic** /tízik, thíz–/ adj. **phthis·i·cal** adj. [L f. Gk f. phthinō to decay]

phut /fut/ n. esp. Brit. a dull abrupt sound as of an impact or explosion. □ **go phut** colloq. (esp. of a scheme or plan) collapse; break down. [perh. f. Hindi phaṭnā to burst]

phy·col·o·gy /fīkóləjee/ n. the study of algae. □□ **phy·co·log·i·cal** /–kəlójikəl/ adj. **phy·col·o·gist** n. [Gk phukos seaweed + –LOGY]

phy·co·my·cete /fīkōmíseet, –mīseé't/ n. any of various fungi that typically resemble algae. [Gk phukos seaweed + pl. of Gk mukēs mushroom]

phy·la pl. of PHYLUM.

phy·lac·ter·y /filáktəree/ n. (pl. ·ies) 1 a small leather box containing Hebrew texts on vellum, worn by Jewish men at morning prayer as a reminder to keep the law. 2 an amulet; a charm. [ME f. OF f. LL phylacterium f. Gk phulaktērion amulet f. phulassō guard]

phy·let·ic /fīlétik/ adj. Biol. of or relating to the development of a species or other group. [Gk phuletikos f. phuletēs tribesman f. phulē tribe]

phyllo- /fílō/ comb. form leaf. [Gk phullo- f. phullon leaf]

phyl·lode /fílōd/ n. a flattened leafstalk resembling a leaf. [mod.L phyllodium f. Gk phullōdēs leaflike (as PHYLLO-)]

phyl·loph·a·gous /filófəgəs/ adj. feeding on leaves.

phyl·lo·qui·none /fílōkwinón, –kwínon/ n. one of the K vitamins, found in cabbage, spinach, and other leafy green vegetables, and essential for the blood clotting process. Also called **vitamin K₁**.

phyl·lo·stome /fílōstōm/ n. any bat of the family Phyllostomatidae having a nose leaf. [PHYLLO- + Gk stoma mouth]

phyl·lo·tax·is /fílōtáksis/ n. (also **phyl·lo·tax·y** /–táksee/) the arrangement of leaves on an axis or stem. □□ **phyl·lo·tac·tic** adj.

phyl·lox·e·ra /filóksərə/ n. any plant louse of the genus Phylloxera, esp. of a species attacking vines. [mod.L f. Gk phullon leaf + xēros dry]

phylo- /fílō/ comb. form Biol. denoting a race or tribe. [Gk phulon, phulē]

phy·lo·gen·e·sis /fīlōjénisis/ n. (also **phy·log·e·ny** /fīlójənee/) 1 the evolutionary development of an organism or groups of organisms. 2 a history of this. □□ **phy·lo·ge·net·ic** /–jinétik/ adj. **phy·lo·gen·ic** /–jénik/ adj.

phy·lum /fíləm/ n. (pl. **phy·la** /–lə/) Biol. a taxonomic rank below kingdom comprising a class or classes and subordinate taxa. [mod.L f. Gk phulon race]

phys·ic /fizik/ n. & v. esp. archaic • n. 1 a a medicine or drug. b a laxative; cathartic (a dose of physic). 2 the art of healing. 3 the medical profession. • v.tr. (**phys·icked, phys·ick·ing**) dose with physic. [ME f. OF fisique medicine f. L physica f. Gk phusikē (epistēmē) (knowledge) of nature]

phys·i·cal /fízikəl/ adj. & n. • adj. 1 of or concerning the body (physical exercise; physical education). 2 of matter; material (both mental and physical force). 3 a of, or according to, the laws of nature (a physical impossibility). b belonging to physics (physical science). 4 rough; violent. • n. (in full **physical examination**) a medical examination to determine physical fitness. □□ **phys·i·cal ther·a·pist** n. **phys·i·cal·i·ty** /–kálitee/ n. **phys·i·cal·ly** adv. **phys·i·cal·ness** n. [ME f. med.L physicalis f. L physica (as PHYSIC)]

phys·i·cal chem·is·try n. the application of physics to the study of chemical behavior.

phys·i·cal ed·u·ca·tion n. instruction in physical exercise and games, esp. in schools. ¶ Abbr.: PE & Phys. Ed.

phys·i·cal ge·og·ra·phy n. geography dealing with natural features.

phys·i·cal sci·ence n. the sciences used in the study of inanimate natural objects, e.g., physics, chemistry, astronomy, etc.

phys·i·cal ther·a·py n. the treatment of disease, injury, deformity, etc., by physical methods including manipulation, massage, infrared heat treatment, remedial exercise, etc., not by drugs.

phys·ic gar·den n. Brit. a garden for cultivating medicinal herbs, etc.

phy·si·cian /fizíshən/ n. 1 a a person legally qualified to practice medicine and surgery. b a specialist in medical diagnosis and treatment. c any medical practitioner. 2 a healer (work is the best physician). [ME f. OF fisicien (as PHYSIC)]

phys·i·cist /fízisist/ n. a person skilled or qualified in physics.

physico- /fízikō/ comb. form 1 physical (and). 2 of physics (and). [Gk phusikos (as PHYSIC)]

phys·i·co·chem·i·cal /fízikōkémikəl/ adj. relating to physics and chemistry or to physical chemistry.

phys·ics /fíziks/ n. the science dealing with the properties and interactions of matter and energy. [pl. of physic physical (thing), after L physica, Gk phusika natural things f. phusis nature]

physio- /fízeeō/ comb. form nature; what is natural. [Gk phusis nature]

phys·i·oc·ra·cy /fízeeókrəsee/ n. (pl. ·cies) hist. 1 government according to the natural order, esp. as advocated by some 18th-c. economists. 2 a society based on this. □□ **phys·i·o·crat** /–zeeəkrát/ n. **phys·i·o·crat·ic** adj. [F physiocratie (as PHYSIO-, –CRACY)]

phys·i·og·no·my /fízeeógnəmee, –ónəmee/ n. (pl. ·mies) 1 a the cast or form of a person's features, expression, body, etc. b the art of supposedly judging character from facial characteristics, etc. 2 the external features of a landscape, etc. 3 a characteristic, esp. moral, aspect. □□ **phys·i·og·nom·ic** /–ognómik, –ənómik/ *adj.* **phys·i·og·nom·i·cal** *adj.* **phys·i·og·nom·i·cal·ly** *adv.* **phys·i·og·no·mist** *n.* [ME *fisnomie*, etc. f. OF *phisonomie* f. med.L *phisonomia* f. Gk *phusiognōmonia* judging of a man's nature (by his features) (as PHYSIO-, *gnōmōn* judge)]

phys·i·og·ra·phy /fízeeógrəfee/ *n.* the description of nature, of natural phenomena, or of a class of objects; physical geography. □□ **phys·i·og·ra·pher** *n.* **phys·i·o·graph·ic** /–zeeəgráfik/ *adj.* **phys·i·o·graph·i·cal** *adj.* **phys·i·o·graph·i·cal·ly** *adv.* [F *physiographie* (as PHYSIO-, –GRAPHY)]

phys·i·o·log·i·cal /fízeeəlójikəl/ *adj.* (also **phys·i·o·log·ic**) of or concerning physiology. □□ **phys·i·o·log·i·cal·ly** *adv.*

phys·i·o·log·i·cal salt so·lu·tion *n.* (also **phys·i·o·log·i·cal sa·line so·lu·tion**) a saline solution having a concentration about equal to that of body fluids.

phys·i·ol·o·gy /fízeeóləjee/ *n.* **1** the science of the functions of living organisms and their parts. **2** these functions. □□ **phys·i·ol·o·gist** *n.* [F *physiologie* or L *physiologia* f. Gk *phusiologia* (as PHYSIO-, –LOGY)]

phys·i·o·ther·a·py /fízeeōthérəpee/ = PHYSICAL THERAPY.

phy·sique /fizéek/ *n.* the bodily structure, development, and organization of an individual (*an athletic physique*). [F, orig. adj. (as PHYSIC)]

-phyte /fīt/ *comb. form* forming nouns denoting a vegetable or plantlike organism (*saprophyte; zoophyte*). □□ **–phytic** /fítik/ *comb. form* forming adjectives. [Gk *phuton* plant f. *phuō* come into being]

phyto- /fítō/ *comb. form* denoting a plant.

phy·to·chem·is·try /fítōkémistree/ *n.* the chemistry of plant products. □□ **phy·to·chem·i·cal** *adj.* **phy·to·chem·ist** *n.*

phy·to·chrome /fítəkrōm/ *n.* Biochem. a blue-green pigment found in many plants, and regulating various developmental processes according to the nature and timing of the light it absorbs. [PHYTO- + Gk *khrōma* color]

phy·to·gen·e·sis /fítōjénisis/ *n.* (also **phy·tog·e·ny** /–tójinee/) the science of the origin or evolution of plants.

phy·to·ge·og·ra·phy /fítōjeeógrəfee/ *n.* the geographical distribution of plants.

phy·to·pa·thol·o·gy /fítōpəthóləjee/ *n.* the study of plant diseases.

phy·toph·a·gous /fítófəgəs/ *adj.* feeding on plants.

phy·to·plank·ton /fítōplángktən/ *n.* plankton consisting of plants.

phy·tot·o·my /fítótəmee/ *n.* the dissection of plants.

phy·to·tox·ic /fítōtóksik/ *adj.* poisonous to plants.

phy·to·tox·in /fítōtóksin/ *n.* **1** any toxin derived from a plant. **2** a substance poisonous or injurious to plants, esp. one produced by a parasite.

pi[1] /pī/ *n.* **1** the sixteenth letter of the Greek alphabet (Π, π). **2** (as π) the symbol of the ratio of the circumference of a circle to its diameter (approx. 3.14159). [Gk: sense 2 f. Gk *periphereia* circumference]

pi[2] /pī/ *adj. Brit. sl.* pious. [abbr.]

pi[3] /pī/ *n. & v.* (also **pie**) *•n.* **1** a confused mass of printers' type. **2** chaos. *•v.tr.* (**pie·ing**) muddle up (type). [perh. transl. F PÂTÉ = PIE[1]]

pi·ac·u·lar /piákyələr/ *adj.* **1** expiatory. **2** needing expiation. [L *piacularis* f. *piaculum* expiation f. *piare* appease]

piaffe /pyáf/ *v.intr.* (of a horse, etc.) move as in a trot, but slower. [F *piaffer* to strut]

piaff·er /pyáfər/ *n.* the action of piaffing.

pi·a ma·ter /píəmáytər, peéə/ *n. Anat.* the delicate innermost membrane enveloping the brain and spinal cord (see MENINX). [med.L, = tender mother, transl. of Arab. *al-'umm al-rakīka*: cf. DURA MATER]

pi·a·ni *pl.* of PIANO[2].

pi·a·nism /peéənizəm/ *n.* **1** the art or technique of piano playing. **2** the skill or style of a composer of piano music. □□ **pi·a·nis·tic** /–nístik/ *adj.* **pi·a·nis·ti·cal·ly** /–nístiklee/ *adv.*

pi·a·nis·si·mo /peéənísimó/ *adj., adv., & n. Mus. •adj.* performed very softly. *•adv.* very softly. *•n.* (*pl.* **·mos** or **pi·a·nis·si·mi** /–mee/) a passage to be performed very softly. [It., superl. of PIANO[2]]

pi·an·ist /peéənist, pee-án–/ *n.* the player of a piano. [F *pianiste* (as PIANO[1])]

pi·an·o[1] /peeánō, pyánó/ *n.* (*pl.* **·os**) a large musical instrument played by pressing down keys on a keyboard and causing hammers to strike metal strings, the vibration from which is stopped by dampers when the keys are released. [It., abbr. of PIANOFORTE]

pi·a·no[2] /pyaánō/ *adj., adv., & n. •adj.* **1** Mus. performed softly. **2** subdued. *•adv.* **1** Mus. softly. **2** in a subdued manner. *•n.* (*pl.* **·nos** or **pi·a·ni** /–nee/) Mus. a piano passage. [It. f. L *planus* flat, (of sound) soft]

pi·an·o ac·cor·di·on *n.* an accordion with the melody played on a small vertical keyboard like that of a piano.

pi·an·o·forte /pyánōfáwrt, –fáwrtee/

piano[1]

n. Mus. a piano. [It., earlier *piano e forte* soft and loud, expressing its gradation of tone]

Pi·a·no·la /peéənólə/ *n.* **1** Trademark a kind of automatic piano; a player piano. **2** (**pianola**) Bridge an easy hand needing no skill. **3** (**pianola**) an easy task. [app. dimin. of PIANO[1]]

pia·no no·bi·le /pyaáanō nōbilay/ *n. Archit.* the main story of a large house. [It., = noble floor]

pi·an·o or·gan *n.* a mechanical piano constructed like a barrel organ.

pi·an·o play·er *n.* **1** a pianist. **2** a contrivance for playing a piano automatically.

pi·as·sa·va /peéəsaávə/ *n.* **1** a stout fiber obtained from the leafstalks of various American and African palm trees. **2** any of these trees. [Port. f. Tupi *piaçába*]

pi·as·ter /peeástər/ *n.* (also **pi·as·tre**) a monetary unit of several Middle Eastern countries, equal to one hundredth of a pound. [F *piastre* f. It. *piastra* (*d'argento*) plate (of silver), formed as PLASTER]

pi·az·za *n.* /pee-aátsə, –saal/ **1** a public square or marketplace esp. in an Italian town. **2** /peeázə, –aázə/ *dial.* the veranda of a house. [It., formed as PLACE]

pi·broch /peébrokh, –brawkh/ *n.* a series of esp. martial or funerary variations on a theme for the bagpipes. [Gael. *piobaireachd* art of piping f. *piobar* piper f. *piob* f. E PIPE]

pic /pik/ *n. colloq.* a picture, esp. a movie. [abbr.]

pi·ca[1] /píkə/ *n. Printing* **1** a unit of type size ($^1/_6$ inch). **2** a size of letters in typewriting (10 per inch). [app. dimin. of PIANO[1]] [AL *pica* 15th-c. book of rules about church feasts, perh. formed as PIE[2]]

pi·ca[2] /píkə/ *n. Med.* the eating of substances other than normal food. [mod.L or med.L, = magpie]

pi·ca·dor /píkədawr/ *n.* a mounted man with a lance who goads the bull in a bullfight. [Sp. f. *picar* prick]

pic·a·resque /píkərésk/ *adj.* (of a style of fiction) dealing with the episodic adventures of rogues, etc. [F f. Sp. *picaresco* f. *picaro* rogue]

pic·a·roon /píkəróōn/ *n.* **1 a** a rogue. **b** a thief. **2 a** a pirate. **b** a pirate ship. [Sp. *picarón* (as PICARESQUE)]

pic·a·yune /píkəyóōn/ *n. & adj. •n.* **1** *colloq.* a small coin of little value, esp. a 5-cent piece. **2** an insignificant person or thing. *•adj.* **1** of little value; trivial. **2** mean; contemptible; petty. [F *picaillon* Piedmontese coin, cash, f. Prov. *picaioun*, of unkn. orig.]

pic·ca·lil·li /píkəlílee/ *n.* (*pl.* **pic·ca·lil·lis**) a pickle of chopped vegetables, mustard, and hot spices. [18th c.: perh. f. PICKLE + CHILI]

pic·ca·nin·ny var. of PICKANINNY.

pic·co·lo /píkəlō/ *n. & adj. •n.* (*pl.* **·los**) **1** a small flute sounding an octave higher than the ordinary one. **2** its player. *•adj.* (esp. of a musical instrument) smaller or having a higher range than usual. [It., = small (flute)]

pick[1] /pik/ *v. & n. •v.tr.* **1** (also *absol.*) choose carefully from a number of alternatives (*picked the pink one; picked a team; picked the right moment to intervene*). **2** detach or pluck (a flower, fruit, etc.) from a stem, tree, etc. **3 a** probe (the teeth, nose, ears, a pimple, etc.) with the finger, an instrument, etc., to remove unwanted matter. **b** clear (a bone, carcass, etc.) of scraps of meat, etc. **4** (also *absol.*) (of a person) eat (food, a meal, etc.) in small bits; nibble without appetite. **5** (also *absol.*) pluck the strings of (a banjo, etc.). **6** remove stalks, etc., from (esp. soft fruit) before cooking. **7 a** select (a route or path) carefully over difficult terrain by foot. **b** place (one's steps, etc.) carefully. **8** pull apart. **9** (of a bird) take up (grains, etc.) in the beak. **10** open (a lock) with an instrument other than the proper key. *•n.* **1** the act or an instance of picking. **2 a** a selection or choice. **b** the right to select (*had first pick of the prizes*). **3** (usu. foll. by *of*) the best (*the pick of the bunch*). □ **pick and choose** select carefully or fastidiously. **pick at 1** eat (food) without interest; nibble. **2** = *pick on* 1 (PICK[1]). **pick a person's brains** extract ideas, information, etc., from a person for one's own use. **pick holes (or a hole) in 1** make holes in (material, etc.) by plucking, poking, etc. **2** find fault with (an idea, etc.). **pick off 1** pluck (leaves, etc.) off. **2** shoot (people, etc.) one by one without haste. **3** eliminate (opposition, etc.) singly. **4** *Baseball* put out a base runner caught off base. **pick on 1** find fault with; nag at. **2** select, as for special attention. **pick out 1** take from a larger number (*picked him out from the others*). **2** distinguish from surrounding objects or at a distance (*can just pick out the church spire*). **3** play (a tune) by ear on the piano, etc. **4** (often foll. by *in, with*) **a** highlight (a painting, etc.) with touches of another color. **b** accentuate (decoration, a painting, etc.) with a contrasting color (*picked out the handles in red*). **5** make out (the meaning of a passage, etc.). **pick over** select the best from. **pick a person's pockets** steal the contents of a person's pockets. **pick a quarrel (or fight)** start an argument or a fight deliberately. **pick to pieces** = *take to pieces* (see PIECE). **pick up 1 a** grasp and raise (from the ground, etc.) (*picked up his hat*). **b** clean up; straighten up. **2** gain or acquire by chance or without effort (*picked up a cold*). **3 a** fetch (a person, animal, or thing) left in another person's charge. **b** stop for and take along with one, esp. in a vehicle (*pick me up on the corner*). **4** make the acquaintance of (a person) casually, esp. as a sexual overture. **5** (of one's health, the weather, stock prices, etc.) recover; prosper; improve. **6** (of an engine, etc.) recover speed; accelerate. **7** (of the police, etc.) take into custody; arrest. **8** detect by scrutiny or with a telescope, searchlight, radio, etc. (*picked up most of the mistakes; picked up a distress signal*). **9** (often foll. by *with*) form or renew a friendship. **10** accept the responsibility of paying (a bill, etc.). **11** (*refl.*) raise (oneself, etc.) after a fall, etc. **12** raise (the feet, etc.) clear of the ground. **13** *Golf* pick up one's ball, esp. when conceding a hole. **take one's pick** make a choice. ▫▫ **pick·a·ble** *adj.* [ME, earlier *pike*, of unkn. orig.]

pick² /pik/ *n. & v.* • *n.* **1** a long-handled tool having a usu. curved iron bar pointed at one or both ends, used for breaking up hard ground, masonry, etc. *colloq.* **3** any instrument for picking, such as a toothpick. • *v.tr.* **1** break the surface of (the ground, etc.) with or as if with a pick. **2** make (holes, etc.) in this way. [ME, app. var. of PIKE²]

pick·a·back var. of PIGGYBACK.

pick·a·nin·ny /píkəninee/ *n. & adj.* (also **pic·ca·nin·ny**) • *n.* (*pl.* **·nies**) *offens.* a small African-American child. • *adj. archaic* very small. [W.Ind. Negro f. Sp. *pequeño* or Port. *pequeno* little]

pick·ax /píkaks/ *n. & v.* (also **pick·axe**) • *n.* = PICK² *n.* 1. • *v.* **1** *tr.* break (the ground, etc.) with a pickax. **2** *intr.* work with a pickax. [ME *pikois* f. OF *picois*, rel. to PIKE²; assim. to AX]

pick·er /píkər/ *n.* **1** a person or thing that picks. **2** (often in *comb.*) a person who gathers or collects (*grape-picker; rag-picker*).

pick·er·el /píkərəl/ *n.* (*pl.* same or **pick·er·els**) **1** any of various species of N. American pike of the genus *Esox*. **2** = WALLEYE. **3** esp. *Brit.* a young pike. [ME, dimin. of PIKE¹]

pick·et /píkit/ *n. & v.* • *n.* **1** a person or group of people outside a place of work, intending to persuade esp. workers not to enter during a strike, etc. **2** a pointed stake or peg driven into the ground to form a fence or palisade, to tether a horse, etc. **3** (also **pic·quet, pi·quet**) *Mil.* **a** a small body of troops or a single soldier sent out to watch for the enemy, held in readiness, etc. **b** a party of sentries. **c** an outpost. **d** a camp guard on police duty in a garrison town, etc. • *v.* (**pick·et·ed, pick·et·ing**) **1 a** *tr. & intr.* station or act as a picket. **b** *tr.* beset or guard (a factory, workers, etc.) with a picket or pickets. **2** *tr.* secure with stakes. **3** *tr.* tether (an animal). ▫▫ **pick·et·er** *n.* [F *piquet* pointed stake f. *piquer* prick, f. *pic* PICK²]

pick·et line *n.* a boundary established by workers on strike, esp. at the entrance to the place of work, which others are asked not to cross.

pick·ings /píkingz/ *n.pl.* **1** perquisites; pilferings (*rich pickings*). **2** remaining scraps; gleanings.

pick·le /píkəl/ *n. & v.* • *n.* **1 a** (often in *pl.*) vegetables, esp. cucumbers, preserved in brine, vinegar, mustard, etc., and used as a relish. **b** the brine, vinegar, etc., in which food is preserved. **2** *colloq.* a plight (*a fine pickle we are in!*). **3** *Brit. colloq.* a mischievous child. **4** an acid solution for cleaning metal, etc. • *v.tr.* **1** preserve in pickle. **2** treat with pickle. **3** (as **pickled** *adj.*) *sl.* drunk. [ME *pekille, pykyl*, f. MDu., MLG *pekel*, of unkn. orig.]

pick·ler /píklər/ *n.* **1** a person who pickles vegetables, etc. **2** a vegetable suitable for pickling.

pick·lock /píklok/ *n.* **1** a person who picks locks. **2** an instrument for this.

pick-me-up *n.* **1** a restorative tonic, as for the nerves, etc. **2** a good experience, good news, etc., that cheers.

pick·pock·et /píkpókit/ *n.* a person who steals from the pockets of others.

pick·up /píkəp/ *n.* **1** *sl.* a person met casually, esp. for sexual purposes. **2** a small truck with an enclosed cab and open back. **3 a** the part of a record player carrying the stylus. **b** a detector of vibrations, etc. **4 a** the act of picking up. **b** something picked up. **5** the capacity for acceleration. **6** = PICK-ME-UP.

Pick·wick·i·an /pikwikeeən/ *adj.* **1** of or like Mr. Pickwick in Dickens's *Pickwick Papers*. esp. in being jovial, plump, etc. **2** (of words or their sense) misunderstood or misused, esp. to avoid offense.

pick·y /píkee/ *adj.* (**pick·i·er, pick·i·est**) *colloq.* excessively fastidious; choosy. ▫▫ **pick·i·ness** *n.*

pick-your-own *adj.* (usu. *attrib.*) (of commercially grown fruit and vegetables) dug or picked by the customer at the place of production.

pic·nic /píknik/ *n. & v.* • *n.* **1** an outing or excursion including a packed meal eaten out of doors. **2** any meal eaten out of doors or without preparation, tables, chairs, etc. **3** (usu. with *neg.*) *colloq.* something agreeable or easily accomplished, etc. (*it was no picnic organizing the meeting*). • *v.intr.* (**pic·nicked, pic·nick·ing**) take part in a picnic. ▫▫ **pic·nick·er** *n.* **pic·nick·y** *adj. colloq.* [F *pique-nique*, of unkn. orig.]

pico- /péekō, píkō/ *comb. form* denoting a factor of 10^{-12} (*picometer*). [Sp. *pico* beak, peak, little bit]

pi·cot /péekō, peekó/ *n.* a small loop of twisted thread in a lace edging, etc. [F, dimin. of *pic* peak, point]

pic·o·tee /píkətee/ *n.* a type of carnation of which the flowers have light petals with darker edges. [F *picoté* –*ée* past part. of *picoter* prick (as PICOT)]

pic·quet var. of PICKET 3.

pic·ric ac·id /píkrik/ *n.* a very bitter yellow compound used in dyeing and surgery and in explosives. ▫▫ **pic·rate** /-rayt/ *n.* [Gk *pikros* bitter]

Pict /pikt/ *n.* a member of an ancient people of northern Britain. ▫▫ **Pict·ish** *adj.* [ME f. LL *Picti* perh. f. *pingere pict-* paint, tattoo]

pic·to·graph /píktəgraf/ *n.* (also **pic·to·gram** /píktəgram/) **1 a** a pictorial symbol for a word or phrase. **b** an ancient record consisting of these. **2** a pictorial representation of statistics, etc., on a chart, graph, etc. ▫▫ **pic·to·graph·ic** *adj.* **pic·tog·ra·phy** /-tógrəfee/ *n.* [L *pingere pict-* paint]

pic·to·ri·al /piktáwreeəl/ *adj. & n.* • *adj.* **1** of or expressed in a picture or pictures. **2** illustrated. **3** picturesque. • *n.* a journal, postage stamp, etc., with a picture or pictures as the main feature. ▫▫ **pic·to·ri·al·ly** *adv.* [LL *pictorius* f. L *pictor* painter (as PICTURE)]

pic·ture /píkchər/ *n. & v.* • *n.* **1 a** (often *attrib.*) a painting, drawing, photograph, etc., esp. as a work of art (*picture frame*). **b** a portrait, esp. a photograph, of a person (*does not like to have her picture taken*). **c** a beautiful object (*her hat is a picture*). **2 a** a total visual or mental impression produced; a scene (*the picture looks bleak*). **b** a written or spoken description (*drew a vivid picture of moral decay*). **3 a** a movie. **b** (in *pl.*) a showing of movies at a movie theater (*went to the pictures*). **c** (in *pl.*) movies in general. **4** an image on a television screen. **5** *colloq.* **a** esp. *iron.* a person or thing exemplifying something (*he was the picture of innocence*). **b** a person or thing resembling another closely (*the picture of her aunt*). • *v.tr.* **1** represent in a picture. **2** (also *refl.*; often foll. by *to*) imagine, esp. visually or vividly (*pictured it to herself*). **3** describe graphically. □ **get the picture** *colloq.* grasp the tendency or drift of circumstances, information, etc. **in the picture** fully informed or noticed. **out of the picture** uninvolved; inactive; irrelevant. [ME f. L *pictura* f. *pingere pict-* paint]

pic·ture book *n.* a book containing many illustrations, esp. one intended for small children.

pic·ture card *n.* a face card.

pic·ture gal·ler·y *n.* a place containing an exhibition or collection of pictures.

pic·ture mold·ing *n.* (also **pic·ture mold** or **pic·ture rail**) **1** woodwork, etc., used for framing pictures. **2** a rail on a wall used for hanging pictures from.

pic·ture post·card *n.* a postcard with a picture on one side.

pic·tur·esque /píkchərésk/ *adj.* **1** (of landscape, etc.) beautiful or striking, as in a picture. **2** (of language, etc.) strikingly graphic; vivid. ▫▫ **pic·tur·esque·ly** *adv.* **pic·tur·esque·ness** *n.* [F *pittoresque* f. It. *pittoresco* f. *pittore* painter f. L (as PICTORIAL): assim. to PICTURE]

pic·ture tube *n.* the cathode-ray tube of a television set.

pic·ture win·dow *n.* a very large window consisting of one pane of glass.

pic·ture writ·ing *n.* a mode of recording events, etc., by pictorial symbols as in early hieroglyphics, etc.

pid·dle /píd'l/ *v. & n.* • *v.intr.* **1** *colloq.* urinate (used esp. to or by children). **2** work or act in a trifling way. **3** (as **piddling** *adj.*) *colloq.* trivial; trifling. • *n. colloq.* **1** urination. **2** urine (used esp. to or by children). ▫▫ **pid·dler** *n.* [sense 1 prob. f. PISS + PUDDLE: sense 2 perh. f. PEDDLE]

pid·dock /pídək/ *n.* any rock-boring bivalve mollusk of the family Pholadidae, used for bait. [18th c.: orig. unkn.]

pidg·in /píjin/ *n.* a simplified language containing vocabulary from two or more languages, used for communication between people not having a common language. [corrupt. of *business*]

pidg·in Eng·lish *n.* a pidgin in which the chief language is English, used esp. between Chinese and Europeans.

pi-dog var. of PYE-DOG.

pie¹ /pī/ *n.* **1** a baked dish of fruit, meat, custard, etc., usu. with a top and base of pastry. **2** anything resembling a pie in form (*a mud pie*). □ **easy as pie** very easy. **pie in the sky** an unrealistic prospect of future happiness after present suffering; a misleading promise. [ME, perh. = PIE² f. miscellaneous contents compared to objects collected by a magpie]

pie² /pī/ *n. archaic* **1** a magpie. **2** a pied animal. [ME f. OF f. L *pica*]

pie³ /pī/ var. of PI³.

pie⁴ /pī/ *n. hist.* a former monetary unit of India equal to one twelfth of an anna. [Hind., etc. *pā'ī* f. Skr. *pad, padī* quarter]

pie·bald /píbawld/ *adj. & n.* • *adj.* **1** (usu. of an animal, esp. a horse) having irregular patches of two colors, esp. black and white. **2** motley; mongrel. • *n.* a piebald animal, esp. a horse.

piece /pees/ *n. & v.* • *n.* **1 a** (often foll. by *of*) one of the distinct portions forming part of or broken off from a larger object; a bit; a part (*a piece of string*). **b** each of the parts of which a set or category is composed (*a five-piece band; a piece of furniture*). **2** a coin of specified value (*50-cent piece*). **3 a** a usu. short literary or musical composition or a picture. **b** a theatrical play. **4** an item, instance, or example (*a piece of news*). **5 a** any of the objects used to make moves in board games. **b** a chessman (strictly, other than a pawn). **6** a definite quantity in which a thing is sold. **7** (often foll. by *of*) an enclosed portion (of land, etc.). **8** *sl. derog.* a woman. **9** (foll. by *of*) a financial share or investment in (*has a piece of the new production*). **10** *colloq.* a short distance. **11** *sl.* = PISTOL. • *v.tr.* **1** (usu. foll. by *together*) form into a whole; put together; join (*finally pieced his story together*). **2** (usu. foll. by *out*) **a** eke out. **b** form (a theory, etc.) by combining parts, etc. **3** (usu. foll. by *up*) patch. **4** join (threads) in spinning. □ **break to pieces** break into fragments. **by the piece** (paid) according to the quantity of work done. **go to pieces** collapse emotionally; suffer a breakdown. **in one piece 1** unbroken. **2** unharmed. **in pieces** broken. **of a piece** (often foll. by *with*) uniform; consistent; in keeping. **a piece of the action** *sl.* a share of the profits; a share in the excitement. **piece of ass** *sl. offens.* a person regarded as a sexual partner. **a piece of cake** see CAKE. **a piece of one's mind** a sharp rebuke or lecture. **say one's piece** give one's opinion or make a prepared statement. **take to pieces 1** break up or dismantle. **2** criticize harshly. □□ **piec•er** *n.* (in sense 4 of *v.*). [ME f. AF *pece*, OF *piece* f. Rmc, prob. of Gaulish orig.: cf. PEAT]

pièce de ré•sis•tance /pyés də rayzeéstons/ *n.* (*pl.* **pièces de ré•sis•tance** *pronunc.* same) **1** the most important or remarkable item. **2** the most substantial dish at a meal. [F]
piece goods *n.* fabrics woven in standard lengths.
piece•meal /peésmeel/ *adv. & adj.* • *adv.* piece by piece; gradually. • *adj.* partial; gradual; unsystematic. [ME f. PIECE + *–meal* f. OE *mǣlum* (instr. dative pl. of *mǣl* MEAL¹)]
piece of eight *n. hist.* a Spanish dollar, equivalent to 8 reals.
piece of wa•ter *n. Brit.* a small lake, etc.
piece of work *n.* **1** a thing made by working. **2** a remarkable person or thing.
piece rates *n.pl.* a rate paid according to the amount produced.
piece work *n.* work paid for by the amount produced.
pie chart *n.* a circle divided into sections to represent relative quantities.
pie•crust /píkrust/ *n.* the baked pastry crust of a pie.
pie•crust ta•ble *n.* a table with an indented edge like a piecrust.
pied /pīd/ *adj.* particolored. [ME f. PIE², orig. of friars]
pied-à-terre /pyáydaatáir/ *n.* (*pl.* **pieds-à-terre** *pronunc.* same) a usu. small apartment, house, etc., kept for occasional use. [F, lit. 'foot to earth']
pied•mont /peédmont/ *n.* a gentle slope leading from the foot of mountains to a region of flat land. [It. *piemonte* mountain foot, name of a region at the foot of the Alps]
pie-dog var. of PYE-DOG.
Pied Pip•er *n.* a person enticing followers, esp. to their doom.
pie-eat•er *n. Austral. sl.* a person of little account.
pie-eyed *adj. sl.* drunk.
pier /peer/ *n.* **1 a** a structure of iron or wood raised on piles and leading out to sea, a lake, etc., used as a promenade and landing place. **b** a breakwater; a mole. **2 a** a support of an arch or of the span of a bridge; a pillar. **b** solid masonry between windows, etc. [ME *per* f. AL *pera*, of unkn. orig.]
pierce /peers/ *v.* **1** *tr.* **a** (of a sharp instrument, etc.) penetrate the surface of. **b** (often foll. by *with*) prick with a sharp instrument, esp. to make a hole in. **c** make (a hole, etc.) (*pierced a hole in the belt*). **d** (of cold, grief, etc.) affect keenly or sharply. **e** (of a light, glance, sound, etc.) penetrate keenly or sharply. **2** (as **piercing** *adj.*) (of a glance, intuition, high noise, bright light, etc.) keen, sharp, or unpleasantly penetrating. **3** *tr.* force (a way, etc.) through or into (something) (*pierced their way through the jungle*). **4** *intr.* (usu. foll. by *through, into*) penetrate. □□ **pierc•er** *n.* **pierc•ing•ly** *adv.* [ME f. OF *percer* f. L *pertundere* bore through (as PER-, *tundere* tus- thrust)]
pier glass *n.* a large mirror, used orig. to fill wall space between windows.
pie-ro•gi /pərógee, pee–/ *n.* (also **pi•ro•gi**) (*pl.* **·gi** or **·gies**) small pastry envelopes filled with mashed potatoes, cabbage, or chopped meat. [Pol. pl. of *pieróg* dumpling]
Pi•er•rot /peérō, pyeró/ *n. Theatr.* a French pantomime character dressed in a loose white clown's costume. [F, dimin. of Pierre Peter]
pie•tà /pyetaá/ *n.* a picture or sculpture of the Virgin Mary holding

the dead body of Christ on her lap or in her arms. [It. f. L (as PIETY)]
pi•e•tas /píotaas/ *n.* respect due to an ancestor, a forerunner, etc. [L: see PIETY]
pi•e•tism /píotizəm/ *n.* **1 a** pious sentiment. **b** an exaggerated or affected piety. **2** (esp. as **Pietism**) *hist.* a movement for the revival of piety in the Lutheran Church in the 17th c. □□ **pi•e•tist** *n.* **pi•e•tis•tic** *adj.* **pi•e•tis•ti•cal** *adj.* [G *Pietismus* (as PIETY)]
pi•e•ty /pí-itee/ *n.* (*pl.* **·ties**) **1** the quality of being pious. **2** a pious act. [ME f. OF *pieté* f. L *pietas –tatis* dutifulness (as PIOUS)]
pi•e•zo•e•lec•tric•i•ty /pī-eézõĭlektrísitee, pee-áyzō–/ *n.* electric polarization in a substance resulting from the application of mechanical stress, esp. in certain crystals. □□ **pi•e•zo•e•lec•tric** /–iléktrik/ *adj.* **pi•e•zo•e•lec•tri•cal•ly** *adv.* [Gk *piezō* press + ELECTRIC]
pi•e•zom•e•ter /pí-izómitər, peéi–/ *n.* an instrument for measuring the magnitude or direction of pressure.
pif•fle /pífəl/ *n. & v. colloq.* • *n.* nonsense; empty speech. • *v.intr.* talk or act feebly; trifle. □□ **pif•fler** *n.* [imit.]
pif•fling /pífling/ *adj. colloq.* trivial; worthless.
pig /pig/ *n. & v.* • *n.* **1 a** any omnivorous hoofed bristly mammal of the family Suidae, esp. a domesticated kind, *Sus scrofa.* **b** a young pig; a piglet. **c** (often in *comb.*) any similar animal (*guinea pig*). **2** the flesh of esp. a young or suckling pig as food (*roast pig*). **3** *colloq.* **a** a greedy, dirty, obstinate, sulky, or annoying person. **b** a person who eats too much or too fast. **c** an unpleasant, awkward, or difficult thing, task, etc. **4** an oblong mass of metal (esp. iron or lead) from a smelting furnace. **5** *sl. derog.* a policeman. **6** *sl. derog.* a sexist or racist person. • *v.* (**pigged, pig•ging**) **1** *tr.* (also *absol.*) (of a sow) bring forth (piglets). **2** *tr. colloq.* eat (food) greedily. **3** *intr.* herd together or behave like pigs. □ **bleed like a pig** (or **stuck pig**) bleed copiously. **buy a pig in a poke** buy, accept, etc., something without knowing its value or esp. seeing it. **in a pig's eye** *colloq.* certainly not. **make a pig of oneself** overeat. **make a pig's ear of** *Brit. colloq.* make a mess of; bungle. **pig it** live in a disorderly, untidy, or filthy fashion. **pig out** (often foll. by *on*) *sl.* eat gluttonously. **when pigs fly** *iron.* an expression of disbelief. □□ **pig•gish** *adj.* **pig•gish•ly** *adv.* **pig•gish•ness** *n.* **pig•let** *n.* **pig•like** *adj.* **pig•ling** *n.* [ME *pigge* f. OE *pigga* (unrecorded)]

pig 1

pi•geon¹ /píjin/ *n.* **1** any of several large usu. gray and white birds of the family Columbidae, esp. *Columba livia*, often domesticated and bred and trained to carry messages, etc.; a dove (cf. ROCK DOVE). **2** a person easily swindled; a simpleton. □□ **pi•geon•ry** *n.* (*pl.* **·ries**). [ME f. OF *pijon* f. LL *pipio –onis* (imit.)]
pi•geon² /píjin/ *n.* **1** = PIDGIN. **2** *colloq.* a particular concern, job, or business (*that's not my pigeon*).
pi•geon breast *n.* (also **pi•geon chest**) a deformed human chest with a projecting breastbone. □□ **pi•geon breast•ed** (or **chest•ed**) *adj.*
pi•geon fan•ci•er *n.* a person who keeps and breeds fancy pigeons. □□ **pi•geon fan•cy•ing** *n.*
pi•geon hawk *n.* = MERLIN.
pi•geon•hole /píjinhōl/ *n. & v.* • *n.* **1** each of a set of compartments in a cabinet or on a wall for papers, letters, etc. **2** a small recess for a pigeon to nest in. • *v.tr.* **1** deposit (a document) in a pigeonhole. **2** put (a matter) aside for future consideration or to forget it. **3** assign (a person or thing) to a preconceived category.
pi•geon pair *n. Brit.* **1** boy and girl twins. **2** a boy and girl as sole children.
pi•geon's milk *n.* **1** a secretion from the esophagus with which pigeons feed their young. **2** esp. *Brit.* an imaginary article for which children are sent on a fool's errand.
pi•geon-toed *adj.* (of a person) having the toes turned inward.
pig•ger•y /pígəree/ *n.* (*pl.* **·ies**) **1** a pig-breeding farm, etc. **2** = PIGSTY. **3** piggishness.
pig•gy /pígee/ *n. & adj.* (also **pig•gie**) *colloq.* **1** a little pig. **2 a** a child's word for a pig. **b** a child's word for a toe. **3** *Brit.* the game of tipcat. • *adj.* (**pig•gi•er, pig•gi•est**) **1** like a pig. **2** (of features, etc.) like those of a pig (*little piggy eyes*).
pig•gy•back /pígeebak/ *n. & adv.* (also **pick•a•back** /píkəbak/) • *n.* a ride on the back and shoulders of another person. • *adv.* **1** on the back and shoulders of another person. **2 a** on the back or top of a larger object. **b** in addition to; along with. [16th c.: orig. unkn.]
pig•gy bank *n.* a pig-shaped box for coins.
pig•gy in the mid•dle *n.* = PIG IN THE MIDDLE.
pig•head•ed /píg-hédid/ *adj.* obstinate. □□ **pig•head•ed•ly** *adv.* **pig•head•ed•ness** *n.*

pig in the mid·dle *n.* esp. *Brit.* a person who is placed in an awkward situation between two others (after a ball game for three with one in the middle).

pig i·ron *n.* crude iron from a smelting furnace.

Pig Is·land *n. Austral.* & *NZ sl.* New Zealand.

pig Lat·in *n.* a jargon based on alternation of English sounds (e.g., "igpay atinlay" for *pig Latin*).

pig-meat *n. Brit.* pork, ham, or bacon.

pig·ment /pígmənt/ *n. & v.* ● *n.* **1** coloring matter used as paint or dye, usu. as an insoluble suspension. **2** the natural coloring matter of animal or plant tissue, e.g., chlorophyll, hemoglobin. ● *v.tr.* color with or as if with pigment. □□ **pig·men·tal** /–mént'l/ *adj.* **pig·men·tar·y** /–məntéree/ *adj.* [ME f. L *pigmentum* f. *pingere* paint]

pig·men·ta·tion /pígməntáyshən/ *n.* **1** the natural coloring of plants, animals, etc. **2** the excessive coloring of tissue by the deposition of pigment.

pig·my var. of PYGMY.

pig·nut /pígnut/ *n.* one of two species of hickory trees or their nuts.

pig·pen /pígpen/ *n.* = PIGSTY.

pig·skin /pígskin/ *n.* **1** the hide of a pig. **2** leather made from this. **3** a football.

pig·stick·ing /pígstiking/ *n.* **1** the hunting of wild boar with a spear on horseback. **2** the butchering of pigs.

pig·sty /pígsti/ *n.* (*pl.* **·sties**) **1** a pen or enclosure for a pig or pigs. **2** a filthy house, room, etc.

pig's wash *n.* = PIGSWILL.

pig·swill /pígswil/ *n.* kitchen refuse and scraps fed to pigs.

pig·tail /pígtayl/ *n.* **1** a braid or gathered hank of hair hanging from the back of the head, or either of a pair at the sides. **2** a thin twist of tobacco. □□ **pig·tailed** *adj.*

pig·wash /pígwawsh, –wosh/ *n.* = PIGSWILL.

pig·weed /pígweed/ *n.* any herb of the genus *Amaranthus*, grown for grain or fodder.

pi·ka /peékə, píkə/ *n.* any small rabbitlike mammal of the genus *Ochotona*, with small ears and no tail. [Tungus *piika*]

pike¹ /pik/ *n.* (*pl.* same) **1** a large voracious freshwater fish, *Esox lucius*, with a long narrow snout and sharp teeth. **2** any other fish of the family Esocidae. [ME, = PIKE² (because of its pointed jaw)]

pike² /pik/ *n. & v.* ● *n.* **1** *hist.* an infantry weapon with a pointed steel or iron head on a long wooden shaft. **2** *Northern Engl.* the peaked top of a hill, esp. in place names. ● *v.tr.* thrust through or kill with a pike. □ **pike on** *Brit. colloq.* withdraw timidly from. [OE *píc* point, prick: sense 2 perh. f. ON]

pike³ /pik/ *n.* a turnpike. □ **come down the pike** *colloq.* appear; occur. [abbr. of TURNPIKE]

pike⁴ /pik/ *n.* a jackknife position in diving or gymnastics. [20th c.: orig. unkn.]

pik·er /píkər/ *n.* a cautious, timid, or cheap person.

pike perch *n.* any of various pikelike perches of the genus *Lucioperca* or *Stizostedion*.

pike·staff /píkstaf/ *n.* **1** the wooden shaft of a pike. **2** a walking stick with a metal point. □ **plain as a pikestaff** quite plain or obvious (orig. *packstaff*, a smooth staff used by a peddler).

pi·laf /pilaáf, peélaaf/ *n.* (also **pi·laff; pi·law, pi·lau** /–láw, –lów/) a dish of spiced rice or wheat with meat, fish, vegetables, etc. [Turk. *piláv*]

pi·las·ter /pilástər/ *n.* a rectangular column, esp. one projecting from a wall. □□ **pi·las·tered** *adj.* [F *pilastre* f. It. *pilastro* f. med.L *pilastrum* f. L *pila* pillar]

pil·chard /pílchərd/ *n.* a small marine fish, *Sardinia pilchardus*, of the herring family (see SARDINE). [16th-c. *pilcher*, etc.: orig. unkn.]

pile¹ /pil/ *n. & v.* ● *n.* **1** a heap of things used or gathered upon one another (*a pile of leaves*). **2 a** a large imposing building (*a stately pile*). **b** a large group of tall buildings. **3** *colloq.* **a** a large quantity. **b** a large amount of money; a fortune (*made his pile*). **4 a** a series of plates of dissimilar metals laid one on another alternately to produce an electric current. **b** = ATOMIC PILE. **5** a funeral pyre. ● *v.* **1 a** (often foll. by *up, on*) heap up (*piled the plates on the table*). **b** (foll. by *with*) load (*piled the bed with coats*). **2** *intr.* (usu. foll. by *in, into, on, out of,* etc.) crowd hurriedly or tightly (*all piled into the car; piled out of the restaurant*). □ **pile arms** *hist.* place (usu. four) rifles with their butts on the ground and the muzzles together. **pile it on** *colloq.* exaggerate. **pile on the agony** *colloq.* exaggerate for effect or to gain sympathy, etc. **pile up 1** accumulate; heap up. **2** *colloq.* run (a ship) aground or cause (a vehicle, etc.) to crash. [ME f. OF f. L *pila* pillar, pier, mole]

pile² /pil/ *n. & v.* ● *n.* **1** a heavy beam driven vertically into the bed of a river, soft ground, etc., to support the foundations of a superstructure. **2** a pointed stake or post. **3** *Heraldry* a wedge-shaped device. ● *v.tr.* **1** provide with piles. **2** drive (piles) into the ground, etc. [OE *píl* f. L *pilum* javelin]

pile³ /pil/ *n.* **1** the soft projecting surface on velvet, plush, etc., or esp. on a carpet; nap. **2** soft hair or down, or the wool of a sheep. [ME prob. f. AF *pyle, peile,* OF *poil* f. L *pilus* hair]

pi·le·at·ed /pílee-aytəd/ *adj.* (of birds) having a crest on the top of the head.

pi·le·at·ed wood·peck·er *n.* a black-and-white N. American woodpecker, *Dryocopus pileatus*, with a red crest.

pile driv·er *n.* a machine for driving piles into the ground.

pile dwell·ing *n.* a dwelling built on piles, esp. in a lake.

piles /pilz/ *n.pl. colloq.* hemorrhoids. [ME prob. f. L *pila* ball, f. the globular form of external piles]

pile-up /pilup/ *n.* **1** a collision of (esp. several) motor vehicles. **2** any mass or pile resulting from accumulation.

pi·le·us /píleeəs/ *n.* (*pl.* **pi·le·i** /–lee-í/) the caplike part of a mushroom or other fungus. □□ **pi·le·ate** /–leeət/ *adj.* **pi·le·at·ed** /–leeaytid/ *adj.* [L, = felt cap]

pile·wort /pílwərt, –wawrt/ *n.* the lesser celandine. [PILES, f. its reputed efficacy against piles]

pil·fer /pílfər/ *v.tr.* (also *absol.*) steal (objects) esp. in small quantities. □□ **pil·fer·age** /–fərij/ *n.* **pil·fer·er** *n.* [ME f. AF & OF *pelfrer* pillage, of unkn. orig.: assoc. with archaic *pill* plunder: PELF]

pil·grim /pílgrim/ *n. & v.* ● *n.* **1** a person who journeys to a sacred place for religious reasons. **2** a person regarded as journeying through life, etc. **3** a traveler. **4** (Pilgrim) one of the English Puritans who founded the colony of Plymouth, Massachusetts, in 1620. ● *v.intr.* (**pil·grimed, pil·grim·ing**) wander like a pilgrim. □□ **pil·grim·ize** *v.intr.* [ME *pilegrim* f. Prov. *pelegrin* f. L *peregrinus* stranger: see PEREGRINE]

pil·grim·age /pílgrimij/ *n. & v.* ● *n.* **1** a pilgrim's journey (*go on a pilgrimage*). **2** life viewed as a journey. **3** any journey taken for nostalgic or sentimental reasons. ● *v.intr.* go on a pilgrimage. [ME f. Prov. *pilgrinatge* (as PILGRIM)]

Pil·i·pi·no /pílipeénō/ *n.* the national language of the Philippines. [Tagalog f. Sp. *Filipino*]

pill /pil/ *n.* **1 a** solid medicine formed into a ball or a flat disk for swallowing whole. **b** (usu. prec. by *the*) *colloq.* a contraceptive pill. **2** an unpleasant or painful necessity; a humiliation (*a bitter pill; must swallow the pill*). **3** *colloq.* or *joc.* a ball. **4** *sl.* a difficult or unpleasant person. □ **sweeten** (or **sugar**) **the pill** make an unpleasant necessity acceptable. [MDu., MLG *pille* prob. f. L *pilula* dimin. of *pila* ball]

pil·lage /pílij/ *v. & n.* ● *v.tr.* (also *absol.*) plunder; sack (a place or a person). ● *n.* **1** the act or an instance of pillaging, esp. in war. **2** *hist.* goods plundered. □□ **pil·lag·er** *n.* [ME f. OF f. *piller* plunder]

pil·lar /pílər/ *n.* **1 a** a usu. slender vertical structure of wood, metal, or esp. stone used as a support for a roof, etc. **b** a similar structure used for ornament. **c** a post supporting a structure. **2** a person regarded as a mainstay or support (*a pillar of the faith; a pillar of strength*). **3** an upright mass of air, water, rock, etc. (*pillar of salt*). **4** a solid mass of coal, etc., left to support the roof of a mine. □ **from pillar to post** (driven, etc.) from one place to another; to and fro. □□ **pil·lared** *adj.* **pil·lar·et** *n.* [ME & AF *piler*, OF *pilier* ult. f. L *pila* pillar]

pil·lar-box *n. Brit.* a public mailbox shaped like a pillar.

pil·lar-box red *n. Brit.* a bright red color, as of pillar-boxes.

Pil·lars of Her·cu·les *n.* **1** two rocks on either side of the Strait of Gibraltar. **2** the ultimate limit.

pill·box /pílboks/ *n.* **1** a small shallow cylindrical box for holding pills. **2** a hat of a similar shape. **3** *Mil.* a small partly underground enclosed concrete fort used as an outpost.

pil·lion /pílyən/ *n.* **1** esp. *Brit.* seating for a passenger behind a cyclist. **2** *hist.* **a** a woman's light saddle. **b** a cushion attached to the back of a saddle for a usu. female passenger. □ **ride pillion** esp. *Brit.* travel seated behind a motorcyclist, etc. [Gael. *pillean, pillin* dimin. of *pell* cushion f. L *pellis* skin]

pil·li·winks /píliwingks/ *n. hist.* an instrument of torture used for squeezing the fingers. [ME *pyrwykes, pyrewinkes,* of unkn. orig.]

pil·lock /pílək/ *n. Brit. sl.* a stupid person; a fool. [16th c., = penis (var. of *pillcock*): 20th c. in sense defined]

pil·lo·ry /píloree/ *n. & v.* ● *n.* (*pl.* **·ries**) *hist.* a wooden framework with holes for the head and hands, enabling the public to assault or ridicule a person so imprisoned. ● *v.tr.* (**·ries, ·ried**) **1** expose (a person) to ridicule or public contempt. **2** *hist.* put in the pillory. [ME f. AL *pillorium* f. OF *pilori*, etc.: prob. f. Prov. *espilori* of uncert. orig.]

pil·low /pílō/ *n. & v.* ● *n.* **1 a** a usu. oblong support for the head, esp. in bed, with a cloth cover stuffed with feathers, down, foam rubber, etc. **b** any pillow-shaped block or support. **2** = LACE PILLOW. ● *v.tr.* **1** rest (the head, etc.) on or as if on a pillow (*pillowed his head on his arms*). **2** serve as a pillow for (*moss pillowed her head*). □□ **pil·low·y** *adj.* [OE *pyle, pylu,* ult. f. L *pulvinus* cushion]

pillory

pil·low·case /pílōkays/ *n.* a washable cotton, etc., cover for a pillow.

pil·low fight *n.* a mock fight with pillows, esp. by children.

pil·low lace *n.* lace made on a lace pillow.

pil·low la·va *n.* lava forming rounded masses.

pil·low·slip /pílōslip/ *n.* = PILLOWCASE.

pil·low talk *n.* romantic or intimate conversation in bed.

pill pop·per *n. colloq.* a person who takes pills freely; a drug addict.

pill push·er *n. colloq.* a drug pusher.

pil·lule var. of PILULE.

pill·wort /pílwərt, –wawrt/ *n.* an aquatic fern, *Pilularia globulifera*, with small globular spore-producing bracts.

pi·lose /pílōs/ *adj.* (also **pi·lous** /–ləs/) covered with hair. □□ **pi·los·i·ty** /pílósitee/ *n.* [L *pilosus* f. *pilus* hair]

pi·lot /pílət/ *n. & v.* • *n.* **1** a person who operates the flying controls of an aircraft. **2** a person qualified to take charge of a ship entering or leaving a harbor. **3** (usu. *attrib.*) an experimental undertaking or test, esp. in advance of a larger one (*a pilot project*). **4** a guide; a leader. **5** = PILOT LIGHT. **6** *archaic* a steersman. • *v.tr.* (**pi·lot·ed**, **pi·lot·ing**) **1** act as a pilot on (a ship) or of (an aircraft). **2** conduct, lead, or initiate as a pilot (*piloted the new scheme*). □□ **pi·lot·age** *n.* **pi·lot·less** *adj.* [F *pilote* f. med.L *pilotus*, *pedot(t)a* f. Gk *pēdon* oar]

pi·lot bal·loon *n.* a small balloon used to track air currents, etc.

pi·lot bird *n.* a rare dark-brown Australian babbler, *Pycnoptilus floccosus*, with a distinctive loud cry.

pi·lot chute *n.* a small parachute used to bring the main one into operation.

pi·lot-cloth *n.* thick blue woolen cloth for seamen's coats, etc.

pi·lot fish *n.* a small fish, *Naucrates ductor*, said to act as a pilot leading a shark to food.

pi·lot·house /pílət-hows/ *n.* an enclosed area on a vessel for the helmsman, etc.

pi·lot light *n.* **1** a small gas burner kept alight to light another. **2** an electric indicator light or control light.

pi·lot of·fi·cer *n. Brit.* the lowest commissioned rank in the RAF.

Pils·ner /pílznər, pils–/ *n.* (also **Pil·sen·er**) **1** a lager beer brewed or like that brewed at *Pilsen* (*Plzeň*) in the Czech Republic. **2** (usu. **pil·sner**) a tall tapered glass used for serving beer, etc.

pil·ule /pílyōōl/ *n.* (also **pil·lule**) a small pill. □□ **pil·u·lar** /–yələr/ *adj.* **pil·u·lous** *adj.* [F f. L *pilula*: see PILL]

Pi·ma /peémə/ *n.* **1 a** a N. American people native to southern Arizona and adjoining parts of Mexico. **b** a member of this people. **2** the language of this people. □□ **Pi·man** *adj.*

pi·men·to /piméntō/ *n.* (*pl.* **·tos**) **1** a small tropical tree, *Pimenta dioica*, native to Jamaica. **2** the unripe dried berries of this, usu. crushed for culinary use. Also called **allspice**. **3** = PIMIENTO. [Sp. *pimiento* (as PIMIENTO)]

pi·me·son *n.* = PION.

pi·mien·to /piméntō, pímyéntō/ *n.* (also **pi·men·to**) (*pl.* **·tos**) **1** = SWEET PEPPER. **2** a sweet red pepper used as a garnish, esp. in stuffed inside a pitted olive. [Sp. f. L *pigmentum* PIGMENT, in med.L = spice]

pimp /pimp/ *n. & v.* • *n.* a man who lives off the earnings of a prostitute or a brothel; a pander. • *v.intr.* act as a pimp. [17th c.: orig. unkn.]

pim·per·nel /pímpərnel/ *n.* any plant of the genus *Anagallis*, esp. = SCARLET PIMPERNEL. [ME f. OF *pimpernelle*, *piprenelle* ult. f. L *piper* PEPPER]

pimp·ing /pímping/ *adj.* **1** small or insignificant. **2** esp. *dial.* sickly. [17th c.: orig. unkn.]

pim·ple /pímpəl/ *n.* **1** a small hard inflamed spot on the skin. **2** anything resembling a pimple, esp. in relative size. □□ **pim·pled** *adj.* **pim·ply** *adj.* [ME nasalized f. OE *piplian* break out in pustules]

PIN /pin/ *n.* personal identification number (as issued by a bank, etc., to validate electronic transactions). [abbr.]

pin /pin/ *n. & v.* • *n.* **1 a** a small thin pointed piece of esp. steel wire with a round or flattened head used (esp. in sewing) for holding things in place, attaching one thing to another, etc. **b** any of several types of pin (*safety pin; hairpin*). **c** a small brooch (*diamond pin*). **d** a badge fastened with a pin. **2** a peg of wood or metal for various purposes, e.g., one of the slender rods making up part of an electrical connector. **3** something of small value (*don't care a pin*). **4** (in *pl.*) *colloq.* legs (*quick on his pins*). **5** *Med.* a steel rod used to join the ends of fractured bones while they heal. **6** *Chess* a position in which a piece is pinned to another. **7** *Golf* a stick with a flag placed in a hole to mark its position. **8** *Mus.* a peg around which one string of a musical instrument is fastened. • *v.tr.* (**pinned**, **pin·ning**) **1 a** (often foll. by *to*, *up*, *together*) fasten with a pin or pins (*pinned up the hem; pinned the fabrics together*). **b** transfix with a pin, lance, etc. **2** (usu. foll. by *on*) fix (blame, responsibility, etc.) on a person, etc. (*pinned the blame on his friend*). **3** (often foll. by *against*, *on*, etc.) seize and hold fast. **4** *Chess* prevent (an opposing piece) from moving except by exposing a more valuable piece to capture. **5** *US* show affection for a woman by giving her a fraternity pin. □ **on pins and needles** in an agitated state of suspense. **pin down 1** (often foll. by *to*) bind (a person, etc.) to a promise, arrangement, etc. **2** force (a person) to declare his or her intentions. **3** restrict the actions or movement of (an enemy, etc.). **4** specify (a thing) precisely (*could not pin down his reason for leaving*). **5** hold (a person, etc.) down by force. **pin one's faith** (or **hopes**, etc.) **on** rely

---

implicitly on. [OE *pinn* f. L *pinna* point, etc., assoc. with *penna* PEN[1]]

pi·na co·la·da /peénəkəláadə/ *n.* (also **pi·ña co·la·da** /peényə/) a drink made from pineapple juice, rum, and cream of coconut. [Sp., lit. 'strained pineapple']

pin·a·fore /pínəfawr/ *n.* **1 a** *Brit.* an apron, esp. with a bib. **b** a woman's sleeveless, wraparound, washable covering for the clothes, tied at the back. **2** (in full **pinafore dress**) a collarless sleeveless dress worn over a blouse or sweater. [PIN + AFORE (because orig. pinned on the front of a dress)]

PINAFORE

pin·as·ter /pínástər/ *n.* = CLUSTER PINE. [L, = wild pine f. *pinus* pine + –ASTER]

pi·ña·ta /peenyáatə/ *n.* a decorated container, often of papier mâché, filled with toys, candy, etc., that is used in a game in which it is suspended at a height and attempts are made to break it open with a stick while blindfolded. [Sp., lit., pot f. It. *pignatta* perh. f. *pigna* pinecone]

pinafore 1

pin·ball /pínbawl/ *n.* a game in which small metal balls are shot across a sloping board, scoring points by striking various targets.

pince-nez /pánsnáy, píns–/ *n.* (*pl.* same) a pair of eyeglasses with a nose-clip instead of earpieces. [F, lit. = pinch-nose]

pince nez

pin·cers /pínsərz/ *n.pl.* **1** (also **pair of pincers**) a gripping tool resembling scissors but with blunt usu. concave jaws to hold a nail, etc., for extraction. **2** the front claws of lobsters and some other crustaceans. [ME *pinsers*, *pinsours* f. AF f. OF *pincier* PINCH]

pin·cer move·ment *n. Mil.* a movement by two wings of a military unit converging on the enemy.

pinch /pinch/ *v. & n.* • *v.* **1** *tr.* **a** a grip (esp. the skin of part of the body or of another person) tightly, esp. between finger and thumb (*pinched my finger in the door; stop pinching me*). **b** (often *absol.*) (of a shoe, garment, etc.) constrict (the flesh) painfully. **2** *tr.* (of cold, hunger, etc.) grip (a person) painfully (*she was pinched with cold*). **3** *tr. sl.* **a** steal; take without permission. **b** arrest (a person) (*pinched him for loitering*). **4** (as **pinched** *adj.*) (of the features) drawn, as with cold, hunger, worry, etc. **5 a** *tr.* (usu. foll. by *in*, *of*, *for*, etc.) stint (a person). **b** *intr.* be niggardly with money, food, etc. **6** *tr.* (usu. foll. by *out*, *back*, *down*) *Hort.* remove (leaves, buds, etc.) to encourage bushy growth. **7** *intr.* sail very close to the wind. • *n.* **1** the act or an instance of pinching, etc., the flesh. **2** an amount that can be taken up with fingers and thumb (*a pinch of snuff*). **3** the stress or pain caused by poverty, cold, hunger, etc. **4** *sl.* **a** an arrest. **b** a theft. □ **at** (or **in**) **a pinch** in an emergency; if necessary. **feel the pinch** experience the effects of poverty. [ME f. AF & ONF *pinchier* (unrecorded), OF *pincier*, ult. f. L *pungere punct-* prick]

pinch·beck /pínchbek/ *n. & adj.* • *n.* an alloy of copper and zinc resembling gold and used in cheap jewelry, etc. • *adj.* **1** counterfeit; sham. **2** cheap; tawdry. [C. *Pinchbeck*, Engl. watchmaker d. 1732]

pinch-hit *v.* **1** *Baseball* bat instead of another player. **2** fill in as a substitute, esp. at the last minute.

pinch hit·ter *n.* **1** *Baseball* a baseball player who bats instead of another. **2** a person acting as a substitute.

pinch·pen·ny /pínchpenee/ *n.* (*pl.* **·nies**) (also *attrib.*) a miserly person.

pin·cush·ion /pínkŏŏshən/ *n.* a small cushion for holding pins.

pine[1] /pīn/ *n.* **1** any evergreen tree of the genus *Pinus* native to northern temperate regions, with needle-shaped leaves growing in clusters. **2** the soft timber of this, often used to make furniture. Also called **deal**. **3** (*attrib.*) made of pine. **4** = PINEAPPLE. □□ **pin·er·y** *n.* (*pl.* **·ies**). [ME f. OE *pīn* & OF *pin* f. L *pinus*]

pine[2] /pīn/ *v.intr.* **1** (often foll. by *away*) decline or waste away, esp. from grief, disease, etc. **2** (usu. foll. by *for*, *after*, or *to* + infin.) long eagerly; yearn. [OE *pīnian*, rel. to obs. E *pine* punishment, f. Gmc f. med.L *pena*, L *poena*]

pin·e·al /píneeəl, pī–/ *adj.* shaped like a pine cone. [F *pinéal* f. L *pinea* pine cone: see PINE[1]]

pin·e·al gland *n.* (also **pin·e·al bod·y**) a pea-sized conical mass of tissue behind the third ventricle of the brain, secreting a hormonelike substance in some mammals.

pine·ap·ple /pínapəl/ *n.* **1** a tropical plant, *Ananas comosus*, with a spiral of sword-shaped leaves and a thick stem bearing a large fruit developed from many flowers. **2** the fruit of this, consisting of

yellow flesh surrounded by a tough segmented skin and topped with a tuft of stiff leaves.
□ **the rough end of the pineapple** *Austral. colloq.* a raw deal. [PINE[1], from the fruit's resemblance to a pine cone]

pine cone *n.* the cone-shaped fruit of the pine
tree.

pine mar·ten *n.* a weasellike mammal, *Martes
martes*, native to Europe and America, with a
dark brown coat and white throat and stomach.

pine nut *n.* the edible seed of various pine trees.

pi·ne·tum /pīnēétəm/ *n.* (*pl.* **pi·ne·ta** /-tə/) a
plantation of pine trees or other conifers for
scientific or ornamental purposes. [L f.
pinus pine]

pine·y var. of PINY.

pin·fold /pínfōld/ *n. & v.* ●*n.* **1** a pound for
stray cattle, etc. **2** any place of confinement.
●*v.tr.* confine (cattle) in a pinfold. [OE
pundfald (as POUND[3], FOLD[2])]

ping /ping/ *n. & v.* ●*n.* **1** a single short high ringing sound. ●*v.intr.* **1** make a ping. **2** = KNOCK
5b. [imit.]

ping·er /píngər/ *n.* **1** a device that transmits
pings at short intervals for purposes of detection or measurement, etc. **2** a device to
ring a bell.

pin·go /pínggō/ *n.* (*pl.* **-gos**) *Geol.* a dome-shaped mound found in
permafrost areas. [Eskimo]

Ping-Pong /píngpong/ *n. Trademark* = TABLE TENNIS. [imit. f. the
sound of a paddle striking a ball]

pin·guid /pínggwid/ *adj.* fat, oily, or greasy. [L *pinguis* fat]

pin·head /pínhed/ *n.* **1** the flattened head of a pin. **2** a very small
thing. **3** *colloq.* a stupid or foolish person.

pin·head·ed /pínhédid/ *adj. colloq.* stupid; foolish. □□ **pin·head·ed·
ness** *n.*

pin·hole /pínhōl/ *n.* **1** a hole made by a pin. **2** a hole into which a
peg fits.

pin·hole cam·er·a *n.* a camera with a pinhole aperture and no
lens.

pin·ion[1] /pínyən/ *n. & v.* ●*n.* **1** the outer part of a bird's wing, usu.
including the flight feathers. **2** *poet.* a wing; a flight feather. ●*v.tr.*
1 cut off the pinion of (a wing or bird) to prevent flight. **2 a** bind
the arms of (a person). **b** (often foll. by *to*) bind (the arms, a
person, etc.) esp. to a thing. [ME f. OF *pignon* ult. f. L *pinna*: see
PIN]

pin·ion[2] /pínyən/ *n.* **1** a small toothed gear engaging with a larger
one. **2** a toothed spindle engaging with a wheel. [F *pignon* alt. f.
obs. *pignol* f. L *pinea* pine cone (as PINE[1])]

pink[1] /pingk/ *n. & adj.* ●*n.* **1** a pale red color (*decorated in pink*).
2 a any cultivated plant of the genus *Dianthus*, with sweet-smelling
white, pink, crimson, etc., flowers. **b** the flower of this plant.
3 (prec. by *the*) the most perfect condition, etc. (*the pink of health*).
4 (also **hunt·ing pink**) **a** a foxhunter's red coat. **b** the cloth for this.
c a foxhunter. ●*adj.* **1** (often in *comb.*) of a pale red color of any of
various shades (*rose pink; salmon pink*). **2** esp. *derog.* tending to socialism. □ **in the pink** *colloq.* in very good health. □□ **pink·ish** *adj.*
pink·ly *adv.* **pink·ness** *n.* **pink·y** *adj.* [perh. f. dial. *pink-eyed* having small eyes]

pink[2] /pingk/ *v.tr.* **1** pierce slightly with a sword, etc. **2** cut a scalloped or zigzag edge on. **3** (often foll. by *out*) ornament (leather,
etc.) with perforations. **4** adorn; deck. [ME, perh. f. LG or Du.:
cf. LG *pinken* strike, peck]

pink[3] /pingk/ *v.intr. Brit.* = KNOCK 5b.

pink[4] /pingk/ *n. hist.* a sailing ship, esp. with a narrow stern, orig.
small and flatbottomed. [ME f. MDu. *pin(c)ke*, of unkn. orig.]

pink-col·lar *adj.* (usu. *attrib.*) (of a profession, etc.) traditionally held
by women (cf. WHITE-COLLAR, BLUE-COLLAR).

pink el·e·phants *n. colloq.* hallucinations
caused by alcoholism.

pink·eye /píngkī/ *n.* acute conjunctivitis.

pink gin *n. Brit.* gin flavored with angostura bitters.

pink·ie[1] /píngkee/ *n.* (also **pink·y**) esp. *US &
Sc.* the little finger. [cf. dial. *pink* small,
half-shut (eye)]

pink·ie[2] /píngkee/ *n.* (also **pink·y**) esp. *Austral. sl.* cheap red wine.

pink·ing shears *n.pl.* (also **pink·ing scis·
sors**) a dressmaker's serrated shears for
cutting a zigzag edge.

pink slip *n.* a notice of layoff or termination
from one's job.

pineapple 2

pine cone

pinking shears

---

pink·ster flow·er *n.* the pink azalea, *Rhododendron nudiflorum*.

pink·y[1] var. of PINKIE[1].

pink·y[2] var. of PINKIE[2].

pin mon·ey *n.* **1** *hist.* an allowance to a woman for clothing, etc.,
from her husband. **2** a very small sum of money, esp. for spending
on inessentials (*only works for pin money*).

pin·na /pínə/ *n.* (*pl.* **pin·nae** /-nee/ or **pin·nas**) **1** the auricle; the external part of the ear. **2** a primary division of a pinnate leaf. **3** a fin or
finlike structure, feather, wing, etc. [L, = *penna* feather, wing, fin]

pin·nace /pínis/ *n. Naut.* a warship's or other ship's small boat, usu.
motor-driven, orig. schooner-rigged or eight-oared. [F *pinnace,
pinasse* ult. f. L *pinus* PINE[1]]

pin·na·cle /pínəkəl/ *n. & v.* ●*n.* **1** the culmination or climax (of endeavor, success, etc.). **2** a natural peak. **3** a small ornamental turret usu. ending in a pyramid or cone, crowning a buttress, roof,
etc. ●*v.tr.* **1** set on or as if on a pinnacle. **2** form the pinnacle of.
3 provide with pinnacles. [ME *pinacle* f. OF *pin(n)acle* f. LL *pinnaculum* f. *pinna* wing, point (as PIN, –CULE)]

pin·nae *pl.* of PINNA.

pin·nate /pínayt/ *adj.* **1** (of a compound leaf) having leaflets arranged
on either side of the stem, usu. in pairs opposite each other. **2** having branches, tentacles, etc., on each side of an axis. □□ **pin·nat·ed**
adj. **pin·nate·ly** *adv.* **pin·na·tion** /-náyshən/ *n.* [L *pinnatus* feathered
(as PINNA)]

pinni- /pínee/ *comb. form* wing; fin. [L *pinna*]

pin·ni·ped /píniped/ *adj. & n.* ●*adj.* denoting any aquatic mammal
with limbs ending in fins. ●*n.* a pinniped mammal. [L *pinna* fin +
pes ped- foot]

pin·nule /pínyool/ *n.* **1** the secondary division of a pinnate leaf. **2** a
part or organ like a small wing or fin. □□ **pin·nu·lar** *adj.* [L *pinnu-
la* dimin. of *pinna* fin, wing]

pin·ny /pínee/ *n.* (*pl.* **·nies**) *Brit. colloq.* a pinafore. [abbr.]

pi·noch·le /péenokəl/ *n.* **1** a card game with a double pack of 48
cards (nine to ace only). **2** the combination of queen of spades and
jack of diamonds in this game. [19th c.: orig. unkn.]

pi·no·le /pínōlee/ *n.* flour made from parched cornflour, esp. mixed
with sweet flour made of mesquite beans, sugar, etc. [Amer. Sp. f.
Aztec *pinolli*]

pi·ñon /peenyón, pínyən/ *n.* **1** a pine, *Pinus cembra*, bearing edible
seeds. **2** the seed of this, a type of pine nut. [Sp. f. L *pinea* pine
cone]

pin·point /pínpoynt/ *n. & v.* ●*n.* **1** the point of a pin. **2** something
very small or sharp. **3** (*attrib.*) **a** very small. **b** precise; accurate.
●*v.tr.* locate with precision (*pinpointed the target*).

pin·prick /pínprik/ *n.* **1** a prick caused by a pin. **2** a trifling irritation.

pins and nee·dles *n.pl.* a tingling sensation in a limb recovering
from numbness.

pin·stripe /pínstrīp/ *n.* **1** a very narrow stripe in cloth. **2** a fabric or
garment with this.

pint /pīnt/ *n.* **1** a measure of capacity for liquids, etc., one eighth of
a gallon or 20 fluid oz. (0.47 liter). **2** esp. *Brit.* **a** *colloq.* a pint of
beer. **b** a pint of a liquid, esp. milk. **3** *Brit.* a measure of shellfish,
being the amount containable in a pint mug (*bought a pint of whelks*).
[ME f. OF *pinte*, of unkn. orig.]

pin·ta /píntə/ *n. Brit. colloq.* a pint of milk. [corrupt. of *pint of*]

pin·ta·ble *n. Brit.* a pinball machine.

pin·tail /píntayl/ *n.* a duck, esp. *Anas acuta*, or a grouse with a pointed tail.

pin·tle /pínt'l/ *n.* a pin or bolt, esp. one on which some other part
turns. [OE *pintel* penis, of unkn. orig.: cf. OFris., etc., *pint*]

pin·to /píntō/ *adj. & n.* ●*adj.* piebald. ●*n.* (*pl.* **·tos**) a piebald horse.
[Sp., = mottled, ult. f. L *pictus* past part. of *pingere* paint]

pin·to bean *n.* a variety of bean with a mottled or spotted appearance, grown mainly in the southwestern US.

pint·pot *n.* a mug, esp. of pewter, holding one pint, esp. of beer.

pint-sized *adj.* (also **pint-size**) *colloq.* very small, esp. of a person.

pin·up /pínup/ *n.* **1** a photograph of a movie star, etc., for display.
2 a person in such a photograph.

pin·wheel /pínhweel/ *n.* **1** a fireworks device that whirls and emits
colored fire. **2** a child's toy consisting of a stick with vanes that twirl
in the wind.

pin·worm /pínwərm/ *n.* a small parasitic nematode worm, *Enterobius
vermicularis*, of which the female has a pointed tail.

pin·y /pínee/ *adj.* (also **pine·y**) of, like, or full of pines.

Pin·yin /pínyín/ *n.* a system of romanized spelling for transliterating
Chinese. [Chin. *pīnyīn*, lit. 'spell sound']

pi·o·let /peeəláy/ *n.* a two-headed ice ax for mountaineering. [F]

pi·on /píon/ *n. Physics* a meson having a mass approximately 270
times that of an electron. Also called **pi-meson**. □□ **pi·on·ic** /píónik/
adj. [PI[1] (the letter used as a symbol for the particle) + –ON]

pi·o·neer /píəneer/ *n. & v.* ●*n.* **1** an initiator of a new enterprise, an
inventor, etc. **2** an explorer or settler; a colonist. **3** *Mil.* a member
of an infantry group preparing roads, terrain, etc., for the main
body of troops. ●*v.* **1 a** *tr.* initiate or originate (an enterprise, etc.).
b *intr.* act or prepare the way as a pioneer. **2** *tr. Mil.* open up (a

road, etc.) as a pioneer. **3** *tr.* go before, lead, or conduct (another person or persons). [F *pionnier* foot soldier, pioneer, OF *paonier, peon(n)ier* (as PEON)]

pi•ous /píəs/ *adj.* **1** devout; religious. **2** hypocritically virtuous; sanctimonious. **3** dutiful. □□ **pi•ous•ly** *adv.* **pi•ous•ness** *n.* [L *pius* dutiful, pious]

pi•ous fraud *n.* a deception intended to benefit those deceived, esp. religiously.

pip[1] /pip/ *n. & v.* ● *n.* **1** the seed of an apple, pear, orange, grape, etc. **2** an extraordinary person or thing. ● *v.tr.* (**pipped, pip•ping**) remove the pips from (fruit, etc.). □□ **pip•less** *adj.* [abbr. of PIPPIN]

pip[2] /pip/ *n. Brit.* a short high-pitched sound, usu. mechanically produced, esp. as a radio time signal. [imit.]

pip[3] /pip/ *n.* **1** any of the spots on playing cards, dice, or dominos. **2** *Brit.* a star (1–3 according to rank) on the shoulder of an army officer's uniform. **3** a single blossom of a clustered head of flowers. **4** a diamond-shaped segment of the surface of a pineapple. **5** an image of an object on a radar screen. [16th c. *peep*, of unkn. orig.]

pip[4] /pip/ *n.* **1** a disease of poultry, etc., causing thick mucus in the throat and white scale on the tongue. **2** esp. *Brit. colloq.* a fit of disgust or bad temper (esp. *give one the pip*). [ME f. MDu. *pippe*, MLG *pip* prob. ult. f. corrupt. of L *pituita* slime]

pip[5] /pip/ *v.tr.* (**pipped, pip•ping**) *Brit. colloq.* **1** hit with a shot. **2** defeat. **3** blackball. □ **pip at the post** defeat at the last moment. **pip out** die. [PIP[2] or PIP[1]]

pi•pa /pípə/ *n.* an aquatic S. American toad, *Pipa pipa*, having a flat body with long webbed feet, the female of which carries her eggs and tadpoles in pockets on her back. Also called **Surinam toad**. [Surinam *pipál* (masc.), *pipá* (fem.)]

pi•pal var. of PEEPUL.

pipe /pīp/ *n. & v.* ● *n.* **1** a tube of metal, plastic, wood, etc., used to convey water, gas, etc. **2 a** (also **to•bac•co pipe**) a narrow wooden or clay, etc., tube with a bowl at one end containing burning tobacco, etc., the smoke from which is drawn into the mouth. **b** the quantity of tobacco held by this (*smoked a pipe*). **c** a hookah. **3** *Mus.* **a** a wind instrument consisting of a single tube. **b** any of the tubes by which sound is produced in an organ. **c** (in *pl.*) = BAGPIPE(S). **d** (in *pl.*) a set of pipes joined together, e.g., panpipes. **4** a tubal organ, vessel, etc., in an animal's body. **5** a high note or song, esp. of a bird. **6** a cylindrical vein of ore. **7** a cavity in cast metal. **8 a** a boatswain's whistle. **b** the sounding of this. **9** a cask for wine, esp. as a measure of two hogsheads, usu. equivalent to 105 gallons (about 477 liters). **10** *colloq.* (also in *pl.*) the voice, esp. in singing. ● *v.tr.* **1** (also *absol.*) play (a tune, etc.) on a pipe or pipes. **2 a** convey (oil, water, gas, etc.) by pipes. **b** provide with pipes. **3** transmit (music, a radio program, etc.) by wire or cable. **4** (usu. foll. by *up, on, to,* etc.) *Naut.* **a** summon (a crew) to a meal, work, etc. **b** signal the arrival of (an officer, etc.) on board. **5** utter in a shrill voice; whistle. **6 a** arrange (icing, etc.) in decorative lines or twists on a cake, etc. **b** ornament (a cake, etc.) with piping. **7** trim (a dress, etc.) with piping. **8** lead or bring (a person, etc.) by the sound of a pipe. **9** propagate (pinks, etc.) by taking cuttings at the joint of a stem. □ **pipe away** give a signal for (a boat) to start. **pipe down 1** *colloq.* be quiet or less insistent. **2** *Naut.* dismiss from duty. **pipe up** begin to play, sing, speak, etc. **put that in your pipe and smoke it** *colloq.* a challenge to another to accept something frank or unwelcome. □□ **pipe•ful** *n.* (*pl.* **-fuls**). **pipe•less** *adj.* **pip•y** *adj.* [OE *pīpe, pīpian* & OF *piper* f. Gmc ult. f. L *pipare* peep, chirp]

pipe clay /pípˈklay/ *n. & v.* ● *n.* a fine white clay used for tobacco pipes, whitening leather, etc. ● *v.tr.* (**pipe-clay**) **1** whiten (leather, etc.) with this. **2** put in order.

pipe clean•er *n.* a piece of flexible covered wire for cleaning a tobacco pipe.

pipe dream /pípˈdreem/ *n.* an unattainable or fanciful hope or scheme. [orig. as experienced when smoking an opium pipe]

pipe•fit•ter /pípfitər/ *n.* a person who installs and repairs pipes.

pipe•fit•ting /pípfiting/ *n.* **1** a coupling, elbow, etc., used as a connector in a pipe system. **2** the work of a pipefitter.

pipe•line /pípˈlīn/ *n.* **1** a long, usu. underground, pipe for conveying esp. oil. **2** a channel supplying goods, information, etc. □ **in the pipeline** awaiting completion or processing.

pip em•ma /pip émə/ *adv. & n. Brit. colloq.* = P.M. [formerly signalers' names for letters PM]

pipe or•gan *n. Mus.* an organ using pipes instead of or as well as reeds.

pip•er /pípər/ *n.* **1** a bagpipe player. **2** a person who plays a pipe, esp. an itinerant musician. [OE *pīpere* (as PIPE)]

pipe rack *n.* a rack for holding tobacco pipes.

pi•per•i•dine /pipérideen, pi–/ *n. Chem.* a peppery-smelling liquid formed by the reduction of pyridine. [L *piper* pepper + –IDE + –INE[4]]

pi•pette /pīpét/ *n. & v.* ● *n.* a slender tube for transferring or measuring small quantities of liquids esp. in chemistry. ● *v.tr.* transfer or measure (a liquid) using a pipette. [F, dimin. of *pipe* PIPE]

pip•ing /píping/ *n. & adj.* ● *n.* **1** the act or an instance of piping, esp.

whistling or singing. **2** a thin pipelike fold used to edge hems or frills on clothing, seams on upholstery, etc. **3** ornamental lines of icing, potato, etc., on a cake or other dish. **4** lengths of pipe, or a system of pipes, esp. in domestic use. ● *adj.* (of a noise) high; whistling.

pip•ing hot *adj.* very or suitably hot (esp. as required of food, water, etc.).

pip•i•strelle /pípistrél/ *n.* any bat of the genus *Pipistrellus*, native to temperate regions and feeding on insects. [F f. It. *pipistrello, vip-,* f. L *vespertilio* bat f. *vesper* evening]

pip•it /pípit/ *n.* any of various birds of the family Motacillidae, esp. of the genus *Anthus*, found worldwide and having brown plumage often heavily streaked with a lighter color. [prob. imit.]

pip•kin /pípkin/ *n.* a small earthenware pot or pan. [16th c.: orig. unkn.]

pip•pin /pípin/ *n.* **1 a** an apple grown from seed. **b** a red and yellow dessert apple. **2** *colloq.* an excellent person or thing; a beauty. [ME f. OF *pepin* f. unkn. orig.]

pip•squeak /pípskweek/ *n. colloq.* an insignificant or contemptible person or thing. [imit.]

pi•quant /péekənt, –kaant, peekaˈant/ *adj.* **1** agreeably pungent, sharp, or appetizing. **2** pleasantly stimulating, or disquieting, to the mind. □□ **pi•quan•cy** *n.* **pi•quant•ly** *adv.* [F, pres. part. of *piquer* (as PIQUE[1])]

pique[1] /peek/ *v. & n.* ● *v.tr.* (**piques, piqued, piqu•ing**) **1** wound the pride of; irritate. **2** arouse (curiosity, interest, etc.). **3** (*refl.*; usu. foll. by *on*) pride or congratulate oneself. ● *n.* ill-feeling; enmity; resentment (*in a fit of pique*). [F *piquer* prick, irritate, f. Rmc]

pique[2] /peek/ *n. & v.* ● *n.* the winning of 30 points on cards and play in piquet before one's opponent scores anything. ● *v.* (**piques, piqued, piqu•ing**) **1** *tr.* score a pique against. **2** *intr.* score a pique. [F *pic*, of unkn. orig.]

pi•qué /peekáy/ *n.* a stiff ribbed cotton or other fabric. [F, past part. of *piquer*: see PIQUE[1]]

pi•quet[1] /pikáy, –két/ *n.* a game for two players with a pack of 32 cards (seven to ace only). [F, of unkn. orig.]

pi•quet[2] var. of PICKET 3.

pi•ra•cy /pírəsee/ *n.* (*pl.* **•cies**) **1** the practice or an act of robbery of ships at sea. **2** a similar practice or act in other forms, esp. hijacking. **3** the infringement of copyright. [med.L *piratia* f. Gk *pirateia* (as PIRATE)]

pi•ra•gua /piraágwə, –rág–/ *n.* **1** a long narrow canoe made from a single tree trunk; a pirogue. **2** a two-masted sailing barge. [Sp. f. Carib, = dug-out]

pi•ra•nha /piraánə, –ránə, –raˈanyə, –rányə/ *n.* any of various freshwater predatory fish of the genera *Pygocentrus, Rooseveltiella,* or *Serrasalmus*, native to S. America and having sharp cutting teeth. [Port. f. Tupi, var. of *piraya* scissors]

pi•rate /pírət/ *n. & v.* ● *n.* **1 a** a person who commits piracy. **b** a ship used by pirates. **2** a person who infringes another's copyright or other business rights; a plagiarist. **3** (often *attrib.*) a person, organization, etc., that broadcasts without official authorization (*pirate radio station*). ● *v.tr.* **1** appropriate or reproduce (the work or ideas, etc., of another) without permission, for one's own benefit. **2** plunder. □□ **pi•rat•ic** /–rátik/ *adj.* **pi•rat•i•cal** *adj.* **pi•rat•i•cal•ly** *adv.* [ME f. L *pirata* f. Gk *peiratēs* f. *peiraō* attempt, assault]

pi•rogue /piróg/ *n.* = PIRAGUA. [F, prob. f. Galibi]

pir•ou•ette /píroo-ét/ *n. & v.* ● *n.* a dancer's spin on one foot or the point of the toe. ● *v.intr.* perform a pirouette. [F, = spinning top]

pis al•ler /peez aláy/ *n.* a course of action followed as a last resort. [F f. *pis* worse + *aller* go]

pis•ca•ry /pískəree/ *n.* (in phrase **common of piscary**) the right of fishing in another's waters in common with the owner and others. [ME f. med.L *piscaria* f. *piscis* fish]

pis•ca•to•ri•al /pískətáwreeəl/ *adj.* = PISCATORY 1. □□ **pis•ca•to•ri•al•ly** *adv.*

pis•ca•to•ry /pískətawree/ *adj.* **1** of or concerning fishermen or fishing. **2** addicted to fishing. [L *piscatorius* f. *piscator* fisherman f. *piscis* fish]

Pis•ces /píseez/ *n.* (*pl.* same) **1** a constellation, traditionally regarded as contained in the figure of fishes. **2 a** the twelfth sign of the zodiac (the Fishes). **b** a person born when the sun is in this sign. □□ **Pis•ce•an** /píseeən/ *n. & adj.* [ME f. L, pl. of *piscis* fish]

pis•ci•cul•ture /písikulchər/ *n.* the artificial rearing of fish. □□ **pis•ci•cul•tur•al** *adj.* **pis•ci•cul•tur•ist** *n.* [L *piscis* fish, after *agriculture,* etc.]

pis•ci•na /piseénə, –sínə/ *n.* (*pl.* **pis•ci•nae** /–nee/ or **pis•ci•nas**) **1** a basin near the altar in some churches for draining water from liturgical ablutions. **2** a fishpond. **3** *hist.* a Roman bathing pool. [L f. *piscis* fish]

pis•cine[1] /píseen, písīn/ *adj.* of or concerning fish. [L *piscis* fish]

pis•cine[2] /piseén/ *n.* a swimming pool. [F (as PISCINA)]

pis•civ•o•rous /pisívərəs, pī–/ *adj.* fish-eating. [L *piscis* fish + –VOROUS]

pish /pish/ *int. & n.* • *int.* an expression of contempt, impatience, or disgust. • *n.* nonsense; rubbish. [imit.]

pi•si•form /písifawrm/ *adj.* pea-shaped. [mod.L *pisiformis* f. *pisum* pea]

pi•si•form bone *n.* a small bone in the wrist in the upper row of the carpus.

pis•mire /písmīr/ *n. dial.* an ant. [ME f. PISS (from smell of anthill) + obs. *mire* ant]

piss /pis/ *v. & n. coarse sl.* • *v.* **1** *intr.* urinate. **2** *tr.* **a** discharge (blood, etc.) when urinating. **b** wet with urine. **3** *tr.* (as **pissed** *adj.*) **a** esp. *Brit.* drunk. **b** angry; annoyed. • *n.* **1** urine. **2** an act of urinating. □ **piss off 1** (often as **pissed off** *adj.*) annoy; depress. **2** *Brit.* go away. [ME f. OF *pisser* (imit.)]

pis•soir /peeswaár/ *n.* a public urinal, esp. in Europe. [F]

pis•tach•i•o /pistásheeō, –staásheeō/ *n.* (*pl.* **-os**) **1** an evergreen tree, *Pistacia vera,* bearing small brownish green flowers and ovoid reddish fruit. **2** (in full **pistachio nut**) the edible pale green seed of this. **3** a pale green color. [It. *pistaccio* and Sp. *pistacho* f. L *pistacium* f. Gk *pistakion* f. Pers. *pistah*]

piste /peest/ *n.* a ski run of compacted snow. [F, = racetrack]

pis•til /pístil/ *n.* the female organs of a flower, comprising the stigma, style, and ovary. □□ **pis•til•lar•y** *adj.* **pis•til•lif•er•ous** /–lífərəs/ *adj.* **pis•til•line** /–līn/ *adj.* [F *pistile* or L *pistillum* PESTLE]

pis•til•late /pístilət, –layt/ *adj.* **1** having pistils. **2** having pistils but no stamens.

pis•tol /pístəl/ *n. & v.* • *n.* **1** a small hand-held firearm. **2** anything of a similar shape. • *v.tr.* (**pis•toled, pis•tol•ing** or **pis•tolled, pis•tol•ling**) shoot with a pistol.

WORD HISTORY   pistol

mid-16th century: from obsolete French *pistole,* from German *Pistole,* from Czech *pišt'ala,* of which the original meaning was 'whistle, fife,' hence 'a firearm' because of the resemblance in shape of the barrel to a fife or pipe.

---

pis•tole /pistól/ *n. hist.* a foreign (esp. Spanish) gold coin. [F *pistole* abbr. of *pistolet,* of uncert. orig.]

pis•to•leer /pístəleér/ *n.* a soldier armed with a pistol.

pis•tol grip *n.* a handle shaped like a pistol butt.

pis•tol shot *n.* **1** the range of a pistol. **2** a shot fired from a pistol.

pis•tol-whip *v.tr.* (**-whipped, -whip•ping**) beat with a pistol.

pis•ton /pístən/ *n.* **1** a disk or short cylinder fitting closely within a tube in which it moves up and down against a liquid or gas, used in an internal combustion engine to impart motion, or in a pump to receive motion. **2** a sliding valve in a trumpet, etc. [F f. It. *pistone* var. of *pestone* augment. of *pestello* PESTLE]

pis•ton ring *n.* a ring on a piston sealing the gap between the piston and the cylinder wall.

piston 1

pis•ton rod *n.* a rod or crankshaft attached to a piston to drive a wheel or to impart motion.

pit¹ /pit/ *n. & v.* • *n.* **1 a** a usu. large deep hole in the ground. **b** a hole made in digging for industrial purposes, esp. for coal (*chalk pit; gravel pit*). **c** a covered hole as a trap for esp. wild animals. **2 a** an indentation left after smallpox, acne, etc. **b** a hollow in a plant or animal body or on any surface. **3** *Theatr.* **a** = *orchestra pit.* **b** usu. *hist.* seating behind the orchesta seats. **c** the people in the pit. **4 a** (**the pit** or **bottomless pit**) hell. **b** (**the pits**) *sl.* the worst imaginable place, situation, person, etc. **5 a** an area at the side of a track where racing cars are serviced and refueled. **b** a sunken area in a workshop floor for access to a car's underside. **6** the part of the floor of an exchange allotted to special trading (*wheat pit*). **7** = COCKPIT. **8** *Brit. sl.* a bed. • *v.* (**pit•ted, pit•ting**) **1** *tr.* (usu. foll. by *against*) **a** set (one's wits, strength, etc.) in opposition or rivalry. **b** set (a cock, dog, etc.) to fight, orig. in a pit, against another. **2** *tr.* (usu. as **pitted** *adj.*) make pits, esp. scars, in. **3** *intr.* (of the flesh, etc.) retain the impression of a finger, etc., when touched. **4** *tr.* put (esp. vegetables, etc., for storage) into a pit. □ **dig a pit for** try to ensnare. [OE *pytt* ult. f. L *puteus* well]

pit² /pit/ *n. & v.* • *n.* the stone of a fruit. • *v.tr.* (**pit•ted, pit•ting**) remove pits from (fruit). [perh. Du., rel. to PITH]

pi•ta /peetə/ *n.* (also **pit•ta**) a flat, hollow, unleavened bread that can be split and filled with salad, etc. [mod.Gk, = a cake]

pit-a-pat /pítəpát/ *adv. & n.* (also **pit•ter-pat•ter** /pítərpátər/) • *adv.* **1** with a sound like quick light steps. **2** with a faltering sound (*heart went pit-a-pat*). • *n.* such a sound. [imit.]

pit bull *n.* (in full **pit bull ter•ri•er**) a strong, compact breed of American dog noted for its ferocity.

pitch¹ /pich/ *v. & n.* • *v.* **1** *tr.* (also *absol.*) erect and fix (a tent, camp, etc.). **2** *tr.* **a** throw; fling. **b** (in games) throw (an object) toward a mark. **3** *tr.* fix or plant (a thing) in a definite position. **4** *tr.* express in a particular style or at a particular level (*pitched his argument at the most basic level*). **5** *intr.* (often foll. by *against, into,* etc.) fall heavily, esp. headlong. **6** *intr.* (of a ship, aircraft, etc.) plunge in a longitudinal direction (cf. ROLL *v.* 8a). **7** *tr. Mus.* set at a particular pitch. **8** *intr.* (of a roof, etc.) slope downwards. **9** *intr.* (often foll. by *about*) move with a vigorous jogging motion, as in a train, carriage, etc. **10 a** *tr. Baseball* deliver (the ball) to the batter. **b** *intr. Baseball* play at the position of pitcher. **c** *tr. Cricket* cause (a bowled ball) to strike the ground at a specified point, etc. **d** *intr. Cricket* (of a bowled ball) strike the ground. **11** *tr. colloq.* tell (a yarn or a tale). **12** *tr. Golf* play (a ball) with a pitch shot. **13** *tr.* pave (a road) with stones. • *n.* **1 a** *Brit.* the area of play in a field game. **b** *Cricket* the area between the creases. **2** height, degree, intensity, etc. (*the pitch of despair; nerves were strung to a pitch*). **3 a** the steepness of a slope, esp. of a roof, stratum, etc. **b** the degree of such a pitch. **4** *Mus.* that quality of a sound which is governed by the rate of vibrations producing it; the degree of highness or lowness of a tone. **b** = CONCERT PITCH 1. **5** the pitching motion of a ship, etc. **6** the delivery of a baseball by a pitcher. **7** *colloq.* a salesman's advertising or selling approach. **8** *Brit.* a place where a street vendor sells wares, has a stall, etc. **9** (also **pitch shot**) *Golf* a high approach shot with a short run. **10** *Mech.* the distance between successive corresponding points or lines, e.g., between the teeth of a cogwheel, etc. **11** the height to which a falcon, etc., soars before swooping on its prey. **12** *Cricket* the act or mode of delivery in bowling, or the spot where the ball bounces. □ **pitch in** *colloq.* **1** set to work vigorously. **2** assist; cooperate. **pitch into** *colloq.* **1** attack forcibly with blows, words, etc. **2** assail (food, work, etc.) vigorously. **pitch on** (or **upon**) *Brit.* happen to select. [ME *pic(c)he,* perh. f. OE *picc(e)an* (unrecorded: cf. *picung* stigmata)]

pitch² /pich/ *n. & v.* • *n.* **1** a sticky resinous black or dark brown substance obtained by distilling tar or turpentine, semiliquid when hot, hard when cold, and used for caulking the seams of ships, etc. **2** any of various bituminous substances including asphalt. • *v.tr.* cover, coat, or smear with pitch. [OE *pic* f. Gmc f. L *pix picis*]

pitch-and-toss *n.* a gambling game in which coins are pitched at a mark and then tossed.

pitch-black *adj.* (also **pitch-dark**) very or completely dark; as black as pitch.

pitch•blende /píchblend/ *n.* a mineral form of uranium oxide occurring in pitchlike masses and yielding radium. [G *Pechblende* (as PITCH², BLENDE)]

pitched bat•tle *n.* **1** a vigorous argument, etc. **2** *Mil.* a battle planned beforehand and fought on chosen ground.

pitched roof *n.* a sloping roof.

pitch•er¹ /píchər/ *n.* **1** a large usu. earthenware or glass jug with a lip and a handle, for holding liquids. **2** a modified leaf in pitcher form. □□ **pitch•er•ful** *n.* (*pl.* **-fuls**). [ME f. OF *pichier, pechier,* f. Frank.]

pitch•er² /píchər/ *n.* **1** a person or thing that pitches. **2** *Baseball* a player who delivers the ball to the batter. **3** a stone used for paving.

pitch•er plant *n.* any of various plants, esp. of the family Nepenthaceae or Sarraceniaceae, with pitcher leaves that can hold liquids, trap insects, etc.

pitch•fork /píchfawrk/ *n. & v.* • *n.* a long-handled two-pronged fork for pitching hay, etc. • *v.tr.* **1** throw with or as if with a pitchfork. **2** (usu. foll. by *into*) thrust (a person) forcibly into a position, office, etc. [in ME *pickfork,* prob. f. PICK¹ + FORK, assoc. with PITCH¹]

pitch•man /píchmən/ *n.* **1** a salesperson who uses overly aggressive selling tactics. **2** a person who delivers commercial messages on radio or television. **3** a person who sells small goods from a portable stand, as at a fair or on the street.

pitch pine *n.* any of various pine trees, esp. *Pinus rigida* or *P. palustris,* yielding much resin.

pitch pipe *n. Mus.* a small pipe blown to set the pitch for singing or tuning.

pitch•stone /píchstōn/ *n.* obsidian, etc., resembling pitch.

pitch•y /píchee/ *adj.* (**pitch•i•er, pitch•i•est**) of, like, or dark as pitch.

pit•e•ous /píteeəs/ *adj.* deserving or causing pity; wretched. □□ **pit•e•ous•ly** *adv.* **pit•e•ous•ness** *n.* [ME *pito(u)s,* etc., f. AF *pitous,* OF *pitos* f. Rmc (as PIETY)]

pit•fall /pítfawl/ *n.* **1** an unsuspected snare, danger, or drawback. **2** a covered pit for trapping animals, etc.

pith /pith/ *n. & v.* • *n.* **1** spongy white tissue lining the rind of an orange, lemon, etc. **2** the essential part; the quintessence (*came to the pith of his argument*). **3** *Bot.* the spongy cellular tissue in the stems and branches of dicotyledonous plants. **4 a** physical strength; vigor. **b** force; energy. **5** importance; weight. **6** *archaic* spinal cord. • *v.tr.* **1** remove the pith or marrow from. **2** slaughter or immobilize (an animal) by severing the spinal cord. □□ **pith•less** *adj.* [OE *pitha* f. WG]

pith•e•can•thrope /píthikánthrōp/ *n.* any prehistoric apelike human of the extinct genus *Pithecanthropus*, now considered to be part of the genus *Homo* (see also JAVA MAN). [Gk *pithēkos* ape + *anthrōpos* man]

pith hel·met *n.* a lightweight sun helmet made from the dried pith of the sola, etc.

pi·thos /píthos, pí–/ *n.* (*pl.* **pi·thoi** /–thoy/) *Archaeol.* a large storage jar. [Gk]

pith·y /píthee/ *adj.* (**pith·i·er, pith·i·est**) **1** (of style, speech, etc.) condensed, terse, and forceful. **2** of, like, or containing much pith. □□ **pith·i·ly** *adv.* **pith·i·ness** *n.*

pit·i·a·ble /píteeəbəl/ *adj.* **1** deserving or causing pity. **2** contemptible. □□ **pit·i·a·ble·ness** *n.* **pit·i·a·bly** *adv.* [ME f. OF *piteable, pitoiable* (as PITY)]

pit·i·ful /pítifŏŏl/ *adj.* **1** causing pity. **2** contemptible. **3** *archaic* compassionate. □□ **pit·i·ful·ly** *adv.* **pit·i·ful·ness** *n.*

pit·i·less /pítilis/ *adj.* showing no pity (*the pitiless heat of the desert*). □□ **pit·i·less·ly** *adv.* **pit·i·less·ness** *n.*

pit·man /pítmən/ *n.* **1** (*pl.* **·men**) a person who works in a pit, as a miner. **2** (*pl.* **·mans**) a connecting rod in machinery.

pit of the stom·ach *n.* **1** the floor of the stomach. **2** the depression below the bottom of the breastbone.

pi·ton /peeton/ *n.* a peg or spike driven into a rock or crack to support a climber or a rope. [F, = eye-bolt]

Pi·tot tube /péetō, peetō/ *n.* a device consisting of an open-ended right-angled tube used to measure the speed or flow of a fluid. [H. Pitot, Fr. physicist d. 1771]

pit po·ny *n. Brit. hist.* a pony kept underground for haulage in coal mines.

pit prop *n.* a beam of wood used to support the roof of a coal mine.

pit saw *n.* a large saw for use in a saw pit.

pit stop *n.* **1** a brief stop at the pit by a racing car for servicing or refueling. **2** *colloq.* **a** a stop, as during a long journey, for food, rest, etc. **b** the place where such a stop is made.

pit·ta var. of PITA.

pit·tance /pít'ns/ *n.* **1** a scanty or meager allowance, remuneration, etc. (*paid him a mere pittance*). **2** a small number or amount. **3** *hist.* a pious bequest to a religious house for extra food, etc. [ME f. OF *pitance* f. med.L *pi(e)tantia* f. L *pietas* PITY]

pit·ter-pat·ter var. of PIT-A-PAT.

pit·tos·po·rum /pitóspərəm, pítospáwrəm/ *n.* any evergreen shrub of the family Pittosporaceae, chiefly native to Australasia with many species having fragrant foliage. [Gk *pitta* PITCH² + *sporos* seed]

pi·tu·i·tar·y /pitōō-iteree, –tyōō–/ *n. & adj.* ● *n.* (*pl.* **·ies**) (also **pi·tu·i·tar·y gland** or **pi·tu·i·tar·y bod·y**) a small ductless gland at the base of the brain secreting various hormones essential for growth and other bodily functions. ● *adj.* of or relating to this gland. [L *pituitarius* secreting phlegm f. *pituita* phlegm]

pit vi·per *n.* any venomous snake of the family Crotalidae of the US and Asia with a pit between the eye and the nostril.

pit·y /pítee/ *n. & v.* ● *n.* (*pl.* **·ies**) **1** sorrow and compassion aroused by another's condition (*felt pity for the child*). **2** something to be regretted; grounds for regret (*what a pity!*). ● *v.tr.* (**·ies, ·ied**) feel (often contemptuous) pity for (*they are to be pitied; I pity you if you think that*). □ **for pity's sake** an exclamation of urgent supplication, anger, etc. **more's the pity** so much the worse. **take pity on** feel or act compassionately toward. □□ **pit·y·ing** *adj.* **pit·y·ing·ly** *adv.* [ME f. OF *pité* f. L *pietas* (as PIETY)]

pit·y·ri·a·sis /pítiríəsis/ *n.* any of a group of skin diseases characterized by the shedding of branlike scales. [mod.L f. Gk *pituriasis* f. *pituron* bran]

più /pyŏŏ/ *adv. Mus.* more (*più piano*). [It.]

Pi·ute /píŏŏt, píŏŏt/ *n.* = PAIUTE.

piv·ot /pívət/ *n. & v.* ● *n.* **1** a short shaft or pin on which something turns or oscillates. **2** a crucial or essential person, point, etc., in a scheme or enterprise. **3** *Mil.* the man or men about whom a body of troops wheels. ● *v.* (**piv·ot·ed, piv·ot·ing**) **1** *intr.* turn on or as if on a pivot. **2** *intr.* (foll. by *on, upon*) hinge on; depend on. **3** *tr.* provide with or attach by a pivot. □□ **piv·ot·a·ble** *adj.* **piv·ot·a·bil·i·ty** *n.* **piv·ot·al** *adj.* [F, of uncert. orig.]

pix¹ /piks/ *n.pl. colloq.* pictures, esp. photographs. [abbr.: cf. PIC]

pix² var. of PYX.

pix·el /píksəl/ *n. Electronics* any of the minute areas of uniform illumination of which an image on a display screen is composed. [abbr. of *picture element*: cf. PIX¹]

pix·ie /píksee/ *n.* (also **pix·y**) (*pl.* **·ies**) a being like a fairy; an elf. [17th c.: orig. unkn.]

pix·ie hat *n.* (also **pix·ie hood**) a child's hat with a pointed crown.

pix·i·lat·ed /píksilaytid/ *adj.* (also **pix·il·lat·ed**) **1** bewildered; crazy. **2** drunk. [var. of *pixie-led* (as PIXIE, LED)]

piz·za /péetsə/ *n.* a flat round base of dough baked with a topping of tomatoes, cheese, onions, etc. [It., = pie]

piz·zazz /pizáz/ *n.* (also **pi·zazz**) *sl.* verve; energy; liveliness; sparkle. (as PIZZA)]

piz·ze·ri·a /péetsəréeə/ *n.* a place where pizzas are made or sold. [It. (as PIZZA)]

piz·zi·ca·to /pítsikaátō/ *adv., adj., & n. Mus.* ● *adv.* plucking the strings of a violin, etc., with the finger. ● *adj.* (of a note, passage,

etc.) performed pizzicato. ● *n.* (*pl.* **piz·zi·ca·tos** or **piz·zi·ca·ti** /–tee/) a note, passage, etc., played pizzicato. [It., past part. of *pizzicare* twitch f. *pizzare* f. *pizza* edge]

piz·zle /pízəl/ *n.* the penis of an animal, esp. a bull, formerly used as a whip. [LG *pesel*, dimin. of MLG *pēse*, MDu. *pēze*]

pk. *abbr.* **1** park. **2** peak. **3** peck(s). **4** pack.

pkg. *abbr.* (also **pkge.**) package.

pl. *abbr.* **1** plural. **2** place. **3** plate. **4** esp. *Mil.* platoon.

plac·a·ble /plákəbəl, pláy–/ *adj.* easily placated; mild; forgiving. □□ **plac·a·bil·i·ty** *n.* **plac·a·bly** *adv.* [ME f. OF *placable* or L *placabilis* f. *placare* appease]

plac·ard /plákaard, –kərd/ *n. & v.* ● *n.* a printed or handwritten poster esp. for advertising. ● *v.tr.* **1** set up placards on (a wall, etc.). **2** advertise by placards. **3** display (a poster, etc.) as a placard. [ME f. OF *placquart* f. *plaquier* to plaster f. MDu. *placken*]

pla·cate /pláykayt, plák–/ *v.tr.* pacify; conciliate. □□ **pla·cat·ing·ly** *adv.* **pla·ca·tion** /–áyshən/ *n.* **pla·ca·to·ry** /–kətawree/ *adj.* [L *placare* placat–]

place /plays/ *n. & v.* ● *n.* **1 a** a particular portion of space. **b** a portion of space occupied by a person or thing (*it has changed its place*). **c** a proper or natural position (*he is out of his place; take your places*). **d** situation; circumstances (*put yourself in my place*). **2 a** a city, town, village, etc. (*was born in this place*). **3** a residence; a dwelling (*has a place in the country; come around to my place*). **4 a** a group of houses in a town, etc., esp. a square. **b** a country house with its surroundings. **5** a person's rank or status (*know their place; a place in history*). **6** a space, esp. a seat, for a person (*two places in the coach*). **7** a building or area for a specific purpose (*place of worship; fireplace*). **8 a** a point reached in a book, etc. (*lost my place*). **b** a passage in a book. **9** a particular spot on a surface, esp. of the skin (*a sore place on his wrist*). **10 a** employment or office (*lost his place at the university*). **b** the duties or entitlements of office, etc. (*is his place to hire staff*). **11** a position as a member of a team, a student in a college, etc. **12 a** *US* the second finishing position, esp. in a horse race. **b** *Brit.* any of the first three or sometimes four positions in a race, esp. other than the winner (*backed it for a place*). **13** the position of a number in a series indicated in decimal or similar notation (*calculated to 5 decimal places*). ● *v.tr.* **1** put (a thing, etc.) in a particular place or state; arrange. **2** identify, classify, or remember correctly (*cannot place him*). **3** assign to a particular place; locate. **4 a** appoint (a person, esp. a member of the clergy) to a post. **b** find a job, clerical post, etc., for. **c** (usu. foll. by *with*) consign to a person's care, etc. (*placed her with her aunt*). **5** assign rank, importance, or worth to (*place him among the best teachers*). **6 a** dispose of (goods) to a customer. **b** make (an order for goods, etc.). **7** (often foll. by *in, on*, etc.) have (confidence, etc.). **8** invest (money). **9** *Brit.* state the position of (any of the first three or sometimes four runners) in a race. **10** *tr.* (as **placed** *adj.*) **a** *US* second in a race. **b** *Brit.* among the first three or sometimes four in a race. □ **all over the place** in disorder; chaotic. **give place to 1** make room for. **2** yield precedence to. **3** be succeeded by. **go places** *colloq.* be successful. **in place** in the right position; suitable. **in place of** in exchange for; instead of. **in places** at some places or in some parts, but not others. **keep a person in his** (or her) **place** suppress a person's esp. social pretensions. **out of place 1** in the wrong position. **2** unsuitable. **put oneself in another's place** imagine oneself in another's position. **put a person in his** (or her) **place** deflate or humiliate a person. **take place** occur. **take one's place** go to one's correct position, be seated, etc. **take the place of** be substituted for; replace. □□ **place·less** *adj.* **place·ment** *n.* [ME f. OF f. L *platea* f. Gk *plateia* (*hodos*) broad (way)]

place bet *n.* **1** *US* a bet on a horse to come in second. **2** *Brit.* a bet on a horse to come first, second, third, or sometimes fourth in a race.

pla·ce·bo /pləséebō/ *n.* (*pl.* **·bos**) **1 a** a pill, medicine, etc., prescribed more for psychological reasons than for any physiological effect. **b** a placebo used as a control in testing new drugs, etc. **2** *RC Ch.* the opening antiphon of the vespers for the dead. [L, = I shall be acceptable or pleasing f. *placēre* please, first word of Ps. 114: 9]

place card *n.* a card marking a person's place at a table, etc.

place in the sun *n.* a favorable situation, position, etc.

place·kick /pláykik/ *n. Football* a kick made with the ball held on the ground or on a tee.

place mat *n.* a small mat on a table underneath a person's plate.

place-name *n.* the name of a geographic location, as a city, town, hill, lake, etc.

pla·cen·ta /pləséntə/ *n.* (*pl.* **pla·cen·tae** /–tee/ or **pla·cen·tas**) **1** a flattened circular organ in the uterus of pregnant mammals nourishing and maintaining the fetus through the umbilical cord and expelled after birth. **2** (in flowers) part of the ovary wall carrying the ovules. □□ **pla·cen·tal** *adj.* [L f. Gk *plakous –ountos* flat cake f. the root of *plax plakos* flat plate]

plac·er /plásər/ *n.* a deposit of sand, gravel, etc., in the bed of a stream, etc., containing valuable minerals in particles. [Amer. Sp., rel. to *placel* sandbank f. *plaza* PLACE]

place set·ting *n.* a set of plates, silverware, etc., for one person at a meal.

pla·cet /pláyset/ *n.* esp. *Brit.* an affirmative vote in a church or university assembly. [L, = it pleases]

plac·id /plásid/ *adj.* **1** (of a person) not easily aroused or disturbed; peaceful. **2** mild; calm; serene. □□ **pla·cid·i·ty** /pləsíditee/ *n.* **plac·id·ly** *adv.* **plac·id·ness** *n.* [F *placide* or L *placidus* f. *placēre* please]

plack·et /plákit/ *n.* **1** an opening or slit in a garment, for fastenings or access to a pocket. **2** the flap of fabric under this. [var. of PLACARD]

plac·oid /plákoyd/ *adj. & v.* ● *adj.* **1** (of a fish scale) consisting of a hard base embedded in the skin and a spiny backward projection (cf. CTENOID). **2** (of a fish) covered with these scales. ● *n.* a placoid fish, e.g., a shark. [Gk *plax plakos* flat plate]

pla·fond /plafón/ *n.* **1 a** an ornately decorated ceiling. **b** such decoration. **2** an early form of contract bridge. [F f. *plat* flat + *fond* bottom]

pla·gal /pláygəl/ *adj.* *Mus.* (of a church mode) having sounds between the dominant and its octave (cf. AUTHENTIC). [med.L *plagalis* f. *plaga* plagal mode f. L *plagius* f. med. Gk *plagios* (in anc. Gk = oblique) f. Gk *plagos* side]

pla·gal ca·dence *n.* a cadence in which the chord of the subdominant immediately precedes that of the tonic.

plage /plaazh/ *n.* **1** *Astron.* an unusually bright region on the sun. **2** a seaside beach, esp. at a fashionable resort. [F, = beach]

pla·gia·rism /pláyjərizəm/ *n.* **1** the act or an instance of plagiarizing. **2** something plagiarized. □□ **pla·gia·rist** *n.* **pla·gia·ris·tic** *adj.*

pla·gia·rize /pláyjərīz/ *v.tr.* (also *absol.*) **1** take and use (the thoughts, writings, inventions, etc., of another person) as one's own. **2** pass off the thoughts, etc., of (another person) as one's own. □□ **pla·gia·riz·er** *n.* [L *plagiarius* kidnapper f. *plagium* a kidnapping f. Gk *plagion*]

plagio- /pláyjeeō/ *comb. form* oblique. [Gk *plagios* oblique f. *plagos* side]

pla·gi·o·clase /pláyjeeōkláys/ *n.* a series of feldspar minerals forming glassy crystals. [PLAGIO- + Gk *klasis* cleavage]

plague /playg/ *n., v., & int.* ● *n.* **1** a deadly contagious disease spreading rapidly over a wide area. **2** (foll. by *of*) an unusual infestation of a pest, etc. (*a plague of frogs*). **3 a** great trouble. **b** an affliction, esp. as regarded as divine punishment. **4** *colloq.* a nuisance. ● *v.tr.* (**plagues, plagued, plagu·ing**) **1** affect with plague. **2** *colloq.* pester or harass continually. ● *int. joc.* or *archaic* a curse, etc. (*a plague on it!*). □□ **plague·some** *adj.* [ME f. L *plaga* stroke, wound prob. f. Gk *plaga*, *plēgē*]

plaice /plays/ *n.* (*pl.* same) **1** a European flatfish, *Pleuronectes platessa*, having a brown back with orange spots and a white underside, much used for food. **2** (in full **American plaice**) a N. Atlantic fish, *Hippoglossoides platessoides*. [ME f. OF *plaïz* f. LL *platessa* app. f. Gk *platus* broad]

plaid /plad/ *n.* **1 a** (often *attrib.*) tartan usu. woolen twilled cloth (*a plaid skirt*). **b** any cloth with a tartan pattern. **2** a long piece of plaid worn over the shoulder as part of Highland Scottish costume. □□ **plaid·ed** *adj.* [Gael. *plaide*, of unkn. orig.]

plain¹ /playn/ *adj., adv., & n.* ● *adj.* **1** clear; evident (*is plain to see*). **2** readily understood; simple (*in plain words*). **3 a** (of food, sewing, decoration, etc.) uncomplicated; not elaborate; unembellished; simple. **b** without a decorative pattern. **4** (esp. of a woman or girl) not good-looking; homely. **5** outspoken; straightforward. **6** (of manners, dress, etc.) unsophisticated; homely (*a plain man*). **7** (of drawings, etc.) not colored. **8** not in code. ● *adv.* **1** clearly; unequivocally (*to speak plain, I don't approve*). **2** simply (*that is plain stupid*). ● *n.* **1** a level tract of esp. treeless country. **2** a basic knitting stitch made by putting the needle through the back of the stitch and passing the wool round the front of the needle (opp. PURL¹). □ **as plain as day** obvious. **be plain with** speak bluntly to. □□ **plain·ly** *adv.* **plain·ness** /pláyn-nis/ *n.* [ME f. OF *plain* (adj. & n.) f. L *planus* (adj.), *planum* (n.)]

plain² /playn/ *v.intr.* *archaic* or *poet.* **1** mourn. **2** complain. **3** make a plaintive sound. [ME f. OF *plaindre* (stem *plaign-*) f. L *plangere planct-* lament]

plain card *n.* neither a trump nor a face card.

plain·chant /pláynchant/ *n.* = PLAINSONG.

plain choc·o·late *n.* *Brit.* dark chocolate without added milk.

plain·clothes·man /playnklózmən, klóthz-, -man/ *n.* a police officer who wears civilian clothes while on duty.

plain cook *n.* *Brit.* a person competent in plain English cooking.

plain deal·ing *n.* honest and straightforward behavior toward others.

plain sail·ing *n.* **1** sailing a straightforward course. **2** an uncomplicated situation or course of action.

plain serv·ice *n.* *Eccl.* a church service without music.

plains·man /pláynzmən/ *n.* (*pl.* **·men**) a person who lives on a plain, esp. in N. America.

plain·song /pláynsawng, –song/ *n.* unaccompanied church music sung in unison in medieval modes and in free rhythm corresponding to the accentuation of the words (cf. GREGORIAN CHANT).

plain-speak·ing *adj.* outspoken; blunt.

plain-spo·ken *adj.* (also **plain·spo·ken**) outspoken; blunt. □□ **plain-spo·ken·ness** *n.*

plain suit *n.* a suit that is not trumps.

plaint /playnt/ *n.* **1** *Brit.* *Law* an accusation; a charge. **2** *literary* or *archaic* a complaint; a lamentation. [ME f. OF *plainte* fem. past part. of *plaindre*, and OF *plaint* f. L *planctus* (as PLAIN²)]

plain text *n.* a text not in cipher or code.

plain·tiff /pláyntif/ *n.* *Law* a person who brings a case against another into court (opp. DEFENDANT). [ME f. OF *plaintif* (adj.) (as PLAINTIVE)]

plain time *n.* *Brit.* time not paid for at overtime rates.

plain·tive /pláyntiv/ *adj.* **1** expressing sorrow; mournful. **2** mournful-sounding. □□ **plain·tive·ly** *adv.* **plain·tive·ness** *n.* [ME f. OF (*-if, –ive*) f. *plainte* (as PLAINT)]

plain weav·ing *n.* weaving with the weft alternately over and under the warp.

plait /playt, plat/ *n. & v.* ● *n.* **1** = BRAID 2. **2** = PLEAT. ● *v.tr.* = BRAID 1. [ME f. OF *pleit* fold ult. f. L *plicare* fold]

plan /plan/ *n. & v.* ● *n.* **1 a** a formulated and esp. detailed method by which a thing is to be done; a design or scheme. **b** an intention or proposed proceeding (*my plan was to distract them; plan of campaign*). **2** a drawing or diagram made by projection on a horizontal plane, esp. showing a building or one floor of a building (cf. ELEVATION). **3** a large-scale detailed map of a town or district. **4 a** a table, etc., indicating times, places, etc., of intended proceedings. **b** a scheme or arrangement (*prepared the seating plan*). **5** an imaginary plane perpendicular to the line of vision and containing the objects shown in a picture. ● *v.* (**planned, plan·ning**) **1** *tr.* (often foll. by *that* + clause or *to* + infin.) arrange (a procedure, etc.) beforehand; form a plan (*planned to catch the evening ferry*). **2** *tr.* **a** design (a building, new town, etc.). **b** make a plan of (an existing building, an area, etc.). **3** *tr.* (as **planned** *adj.*) in accordance with a plan (*his planned arrival*). **4** *intr.* make plans. □ **plan on** *colloq.* aim at doing; intend. □□ **plan·ning** *n.* [F f. earlier *plant*, f. It. *pianta* plan of building: cf. PLANT]

pla·nar /pláynər/ *adj.* *Math.* of, relating to, or in the form of a plane.

pla·nar·i·an /plənáireeən/ *n.* any flatworm of the class Turbellaria, usu. living in fresh water. [mod.L *Planaria* the genus name, fem. of L *planarius* lying flat]

planch·et /plánchit/ *n.* a plain metal disk, esp. one from which a coin is made. [dimin. of *planch* slab of metal f. OF *planche*: see PLANK]

plan·chette /planshét/ *n.* a small usu. heart-shaped board on casters with a pencil that is supposedly caused to write spirit messages when a person's fingers rest lightly on it. [F, dimin. of *planche* PLANK]

Planck's con·stant /plangks/ *n.* (also **Planck con·stant**) a fundamental constant, equal to the energy of quanta of electromagnetic radiation divided by its frequency, with a value of 6.626×10^{-34} joules. [M. Planck, Ger. physicist d. 1947]

plane¹ /playn/ *n., adj., & v.* ● *n.* **1 a** a flat surface on which a straight line joining any two points on it would wholly lie. **b** an imaginary flat surface through or joining, etc., material objects. **2** a level surface. **3** *colloq.* = AIRPLANE. **4** a flat surface producing lift by the action of air or water over and under it (usu. in *comb.*: *hydroplane*). **5** (often foll. by *of*) a level of attainment, thought, knowledge, etc. **6** a flat thin object such as a tabletop. ● *adj.* **1** (of a surface, etc.) perfectly level. **2** (of an angle, figure, etc.) lying in a plane. ● *v.intr.* **1** (often foll. by *down*) travel or glide in an airplane. **2** (of a speedboat, etc.) skim over water. **3** soar. [L *planum* flat surface, neut. of *planus* PLAIN¹ (different. f. PLAIN¹ in 17th c.): adj. after F *plan*, *plane*]

plane² /playn/ *n. & v.* ● *n.* **1 a** tool consisting of a wooden or metal block with a projecting steel blade, used to smooth a wooden surface by paring shavings from it. **2** a similar tool for smoothing metal. ● *v.tr.* **1** smooth (wood, metal, etc.) with a plane. **2** (often foll. by *away, down*) pare (irregularities) with a plane. **3** *archaic* level (*plane the way*). [ME f. OF var. of *plaine* f. LL *plana* f. L *planus* PLAIN¹]

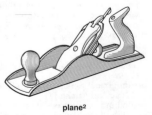

plane²

plane³ /playn/ *n.* (in full **plane tree**) any tree of the genus *Platanus* often growing to great heights, with maplelike leaves and bark which peels in uneven patches. [ME f. OF f. L *platanus* f. Gk *platanos* f. *platus* broad]

plane chart *n.* a chart on which meridians and parallels of latitude are represented by equidistant straight lines, used in plane sailing.

plane po·lar·i·za·tion *n.* a process restricting the vibrations of electromagnetic radiation, esp. light, to one direction.

plane sail·ing *n.* **1** the practice of determining a ship's position on the theory that she is moving on a plane. **2** = PLAIN SAILING.

plan·et /plánit/ *n.* **1 a** a celestial body moving in an elliptical orbit around a star. **b** the earth. **2** esp. *Astrol. hist.* a celestial body distinguished from the fixed stars by having an apparent motion of its own (including the moon and sun), esp. with reference to its supposed influence on people and events. □□ **plan·e·tol·o·gy** /-tóləjee/ *n.* [ME f. OF *planete* f. LL *planeta, planetes* f. Gk *planētēs* wanderer, planet f. *planaomai* wander]

plane ta·ble *n.* a surveying instrument used for direct plotting in the field, with a circular drawing board and pivoted alidade.

plan·e·tar·i·um /plánitáireeəm/ *n.* (*pl.* **plan·e·tar·i·ums** or **plan·e·tar·i·a** /-reeə/) **1** a domed building in which images of stars, planets, constellations, etc., are projected for public entertainment or education. **2** the device used for such projection. **3** = ORRERY. [mod.L (as PLANET)]

plan·e·tar·y /plániteree/ *adj.* **1** of or like planets (*planetary influence*). **2** terrestrial; mundane. **3** wandering; erratic. [LL *planetarius* (as PLANET)]

plan·e·tar·y neb·u·la *n.* a ring-shaped nebula formed by an expanding shell of gas around a star.

plan·e·tes·i·mal /plánitésiməl/ *n.* any of a vast number of minute planets or planetary bodies. [PLANET, after *infinitesimal*]

plan·e·tes·i·mal hy·poth·e·sis *n.* the theory that planets were formed by the accretion of planetesimals in a cold state.

plan·et·oid /plánitoyd/ *n.* = ASTEROID.

plan·gent /plánjənt/ *adj.* **1** (of a sound) loud and reverberating. **2** (of a sound) plaintive; sad. □□ **plan·gen·cy** *n.* [L *plangere plangent-* lament]

pla·nim·e·ter /plənímitər/ *n.* an instrument for mechanically measuring the area of a plane figure. □□ **plan·i·met·ric** /plánimétrik/ *adj.* **plan·i·met·ri·cal** *adj.* **pla·nim·e·try** /-mətree/ *n.* [F *planimètre* f. L *planus* level]

plan·ish /plánish/ *v.tr.* flatten (sheet metal, coining metal, etc.) with a smooth-faced hammer or between rollers. □□ **plan·ish·er** *n.* [ME f. OF *planir* smooth f. *plain* PLANE[1] *adj.*]

plan·i·sphere /plánisfeer/ *n.* a map formed by the projection of a sphere or part of a sphere on a plane, esp. to show the appearance of the heavens at a specific time or place. □□ **plan·i·spher·ic** /-sférik/ *adj.* [ME f. med.L *planisphaerium* (as PLANE[1], SPHERE): infl. by F *planisphère*]

plank /plangk/ *n. & v.* • *n.* **1** a long flat piece of timber used esp. in building, flooring, etc. **2** an item of a political or other program (cf. PLATFORM). • *v.tr.* **1** provide, cover, or floor, with planks. **2** cook and serve (fish, steak, etc.) on a plank. **3** (usu. foll. by *down*; also *absol.*) *colloq.* **a** put (a thing, person, etc.) down roughly or violently. **b** pay (money) on the spot or abruptly (*planked down $5*). □ **walk the plank** *hist.* (of a pirate's captive, etc.) be made to walk blindfold along a plank over the side of a ship to one's death in the sea. [ME f. ONF *planke*, OF *planche* f. LL *planca* board f. *plancus* flat-footed]

plank bed *n.* a bed of boards without a mattress, esp. in prison.

plank·ing /plángking/ *n.* planks as flooring, etc.

plank·ton /plángktən/ *n.* the chiefly microscopic organisms drifting or floating in the sea or fresh water (see BENTHOS, NEKTON). □□ **plank·ton·ic** /-tónik/ *adj.* [G f. Gk *plagktos* wandering f. *plazomai* wander]

plan·ner /plánər/ *n.* **1** a person who controls or plans the development of towns, designs buildings, etc. **2** a person who makes plans. **3** a list, table, booklet, etc., with information helpful in planning.

plan·ning per·mis·sion *n. Brit.* formal permission for building development, etc., esp. from a local authority.

plano- /plánō/ *comb. form* level; flat. [L *planus* flat]

plan·o·con·cave /playnōkónkayv, -konkáyv/ *adj.* (of a lens, etc.) with one surface plane and the other concave.

plan·o·con·vex /playnōkónveks, -konvéks/ *adj.* (of a lens, etc.) with one surface plane and the other convex.

pla·no·graph·ic /playnəgráfik/ *adj.* relating to or produced by a process in which printing is done from a plane surface. □□ **pla·nog·ra·phy** /plənógrəfee/ *n.*

pla·nom·e·ter /plənómitər/ *n.* a flat plate used as a gauge for plane surfaces in metalwork.

plant /plant/ *n. & v.* • *n.* **1 a** any living organism of the kingdom Plantae, usu. containing chlorophyll enabling it to live wholly on inorganic substances and lacking specialized sense organs and the power of voluntary movement. **b** a small organism of this kind, as distinguished from a shrub or tree. **2 a** machinery, fixtures, etc., used in industrial processes. **b** a factory. **c** buildings, fixtures, equipment, etc., of an institution. **3 a** *colloq.* something, esp. incriminating or compromising, positioned or concealed so as to be discovered later. **b** *sl.* a spy or detective; hidden police officers. • *v.tr.* **1** place (a seed, bulb, or growing thing) in the ground so that it may take root and flourish. **2** (often foll. by *in, on*, etc.) put or fix

in position. **3** deposit (young fish, spawn, oysters, etc.) in a river or lake. **4** station (a person, etc.), esp. as a spy or source of information. **5** *refl.* take up a position (*planted myself by the door*). **6** cause (an idea, etc.) to be established esp. in another person's mind. **7** deliver (a blow, kiss, etc.) with a deliberate aim. **8 a** *colloq.* position or conceal (something incriminating or compromising) for later discovery. **b** *sl.* post or infiltrate (a person) as a spy. **9 a** settle or people (a colony, etc.). **b** found or establish (a city, community, etc.). **10** bury. □ **plant out** transfer (a plant) from a pot or frame to the open ground; set out (seedlings) at intervals. □□ **plant·a·ble** *adj.* **plant·let** *n.* **plant·like** *adj.* [OE *plante* & F *plante* f. L *planta* sprout, slip, cutting]

Plan·tag·e·net /plantájinit/ *adj. & n.* • *adj.* of or relating to the kings of England from Henry II to Richard II (1154– 1485). • *n.* any of these kings. [f. L *planta genista* sprig of broom, worn as a distinctive mark, the origin of their surname]

plan·tain[1] /plántin/ *n.* any shrub of the genus *Plantago*, with broad flat leaves spread out close to the ground and seeds used as food for birds and as a mild laxative. [ME f. OF f. L *plantago –ginis* f. *planta* sole of the foot (from its broad prostrate leaves)]

plan·tain[2] /plántin/ *n.* **1** a banana plant, *Musa paradisiaca*, widely grown for its fruit. **2** the starchy fruit of this containing less sugar than a banana and chiefly used in cooking. [earlier *platan* f. Sp. *plá(n)tano* plane tree, prob. assim. f. Galibi *palatana*, etc.]

plan·tain lil·y *n.* = HOSTA.

plan·tar /plántər/ *adj.* of or relating to the sole of the foot. [L *plantaris* f. *planta* sole]

plan·ta·tion /plantáyshən/ *n.* **1** an estate on which cotton, tobacco, etc., is cultivated esp. by resident (formerly slave) labor. **2** an area planted with trees, etc., for cultivation. **3** *hist.* a colony; colonization. [ME f. OF *plantation* or L *plantatio* (as PLANT)]

plan·ta·tion song *n.* a song of the kind formerly sung by African-American slaves on American plantations.

plant·er /plántər/ *n.* **1** a person who cultivates the soil. **2** the manager or occupier of a coffee, cotton, tobacco, etc., plantation. **3** a large container for decorative plants. **4** a machine for planting seeds, etc.

plan·ti·grade /plántigrayd/ *adj. & n.* • *adj.* (of an animal) walking on the soles of its feet. • *n.* a plantigrade animal, e.g., humans or bears (cf. DIGITIGRADE). [F f. mod.L *plantigradus* f. L *planta* sole + *–gradus* –walking]

plant louse *n.* a small insect that infests plants, esp. an aphid.

plaque /plak/ *n.* **1** an ornamental tablet of metal, porcelain, etc., esp. affixed to a building in commemoration. **2** a deposit on teeth where bacteria proliferate. **3** *Med.* **a** a patch or eruption of skin, etc., as a result of damage. **b** a fibrous lesion in atherosclerosis. **4** a small badge of rank in an honorary order. □□ **pla·quette** /plakét/ *n.* [F f. Du. *plak* tablet f. *plakken* stick]

plash[1] /plash/ *n. & v.* • *n.* **1** a splash; a plunge. **2 a** a marshy pool. **b** a puddle. • *v.* **1** *tr. & intr.* splash. **2** *tr.* strike the surface of (water). □□ **plash·y** *adj.* [OE *plæsc*, prob. imit.]

plash[2] /plash/ *v.tr.* esp. *Brit.* **1** bend down and interweave (branches, twigs, etc.) to form a hedge. **2** make or renew (a hedge) in this way. [ME f. OF *pla(i)ssier* ult. f. L *plectere* plait: cf. PLEACH]

plas·ma /plázmə/ *n.* (also **plasm** /plázəm/) **1** the colorless fluid part of blood, lymph, or milk, in which corpuscles or fat globules are suspended. **2** = PROTOPLASM. **3** a gas of positive ions and free electrons with an approximately equal positive and negative charge. **4** a green variety of quartz used in mosaic and for other decorative purposes. □□ **plas·mat·ic** /-mátik/ *adj.* **plas·mic** *adj.* [LL, = mold f. Gk *plasma –atos* f. *plassō* to shape]

plas·mo·des·ma /plázmədézmə/ *n.* (*pl.* **plas·mo·des·ma·ta** /-mətə/) a narrow thread of cytoplasm that passes through cell walls and affords communication between plant cells. [PLASMA + Gk *desma* bond, fetter]

plas·mo·di·um /plazmódeeəm/ *n.* (*pl.* **plas·mo·di·a** /-deeə/) **1** any parasitic protozoan of the genus *Plasmodium*, including those causing malaria in man. **2** a form within the life cycle of various microorganisms including slime molds, usu. consisting of a mass of naked protoplasm containing many nuclei. □□ **plas·mo·di·al** *adj.* [mod.L f. PLASMA + *–odium*: see –ODE[1]]

plas·mol·y·sis /plazmólisis/ *n.* contraction of the protoplast of a plant cell as a result of loss of water from the cell. [mod.L (as PLASMA, –LYSIS)]

plas·mo·lyze /plázməliz/ *v.intr. & tr.* (*Brit.* **plas·mo·lyse**) undergo or subject to plasmolysis.

plas·ter /plástər/ *n. & v.* • *n.* **1** a soft pliable mixture esp. of lime putty with sand or Portland cement, etc., for spreading on walls, ceilings, etc., to form a smooth hard surface when dried. **2** *Brit.* = STICKING PLASTER. **3** *hist.* a curative or protective substance spread on a bandage, etc., and applied to the body (*mustard plaster*). • *v.tr.* **1** cover (a wall, etc.) with plaster or a similar substance. **2** (often foll. by *with*) coat thickly or to excess; bedaub (*plastered the bread with jam; the wall was plastered with slogans*). **3** stick or apply (a thing) thickly like plaster (*plastered glue all over it*). **4** (often foll. by *down*) make (esp. hair) smooth with water, gel, etc.; fix flat. **5** (as **plastered** *adj.*) *sl.* drunk. **6** apply a medical plaster or plaster cast to. **7** *sl.* bomb or shell heavily. □□ **plas·ter·er** *n.* **plas·ter·y** *adj.* [ME f. OE & OF *plastre* or F *plastrer* f. med.L *plastrum* f. L *emplastrum* f. Gk *emplastron*]

plas·ter·board /plástərbawrd/ *n.* a type of board with a center filling of plaster, used to form or line the inner walls of houses, etc.

plas·ter cast *n.* **1** a bandage stiffened with plaster of Paris and applied to a broken limb, etc. **2** a statue or mold made of plaster.

plas·ter of Par·is *n.* fine white plaster made of gypsum and used for making plaster casts, etc.

plas·ter saint *n. iron.* a person regarded as being without moral faults or human frailty.

plas·tic /plástik/ *n. & adj.* ● *n.* **1** any of a number of synthetic polymeric substances that can be given any required shape. **2** (*attrib.*) made of plastic (*plastic bag*); made of cheap materials. **3** = PLASTIC MONEY. ● *adj.* **1 a** capable of being molded; pliant; supple. **b** susceptible; impressionable. **c** artificial; unsincere. **2** molding or giving form to clay, wax, etc. **3** *Biol.* exhibiting an adaptability to environmental changes. **4** (esp. in philosophy) formative; creative. □□ **plas·ti·cal·ly** *adv.* **plas·tic·i·ty** /–tísitee/ *n.* **plas·ti·cize** /–tisīz/ *v.tr.* **plas·ti·ci·za·tion** /–tisīzáyshən/ *n.* **plas·ti·ciz·er** *n.* **plas·tick·y** *adj.* [F *plastique* or L *plasticus* f. Gk *plastikos* f. *plassō* mold]

plas·tic arts *n.* art forms involving modeling or molding, e.g., sculpture and ceramics, or art involving the representation of solid objects with three-dimensional effects.

plas·tic bomb *n.* a bomb containing plastic explosive.

plas·tic ex·plo·sive *n.* a puttylike explosive capable of being molded by hand.

Plas·ti·cine /plástiseen/ *n. Trademark* a soft plastic material used, esp. by children, for modeling. [PLASTIC + –INE⁴]

plas·tic mon·ey *n. colloq.* a credit card, charge card, or other plastic card that can be used in place of money.

plas·tic sur·ger·y *n.* the process of reconstructing or repairing parts of the body by the transfer of tissue, either in the treatment of injury or for cosmetic reasons. □□ **plas·tic sur·geon** *n.*

plas·tid /plástid/ *n.* any small organelle in the cytoplasm of a plant cell, containing pigment or food. [G f. Gk *plastos* shaped]

plas·tron /plástrən, –tron/ *n.* **1 a** a fencer's leather-covered breastplate. **b** a lancer's breast-covering of facings cloth. **2 a** an ornamental front on a woman's bodice. **b** a man's starched shirt front. **3 a** the ventral part of the shell of a tortoise or turtle. **b** the corresponding part in other animals. **4** *hist.* a steel breastplate. □□ **plas·tral** *adj.* [F f. It. *piastrone* augment. of *piastra* breastplate, f. L *emplastrum* PLASTER]

plat¹ /plat/ *n.* **1** a plot of land. **2** a plan of an area of land. [16th c.: collateral form of PLOT]

plat² /plat/ *n. & v.* ● *n.* = PLAIT *n.* **1.** ● *v.tr.* (**plat·ted, plat·ting**) = PLAIT *v.*

plat·an /pláton/ *n.* = PLANE³. [ME f. L *platanus*: see PLANE³]

plat du jour /pláà dəzhŏŏr/ *n.* a dish specially featured on a day's menu. [F, = dish of the day]

plate /playt/ *n. & v.* ● *n.* **1 a** a shallow vessel, usu. circular and of earthenware or china, from which food is eaten or served. **b** the contents of this (*ate a plate of sandwiches*). **2** a similar vessel usu. of metal or wood, used esp. for making a collection in a church, etc. **3** a main course of a meal, served on one plate. **4** food and service for one person (*a fundraiser with a $30 per plate dinner*). **5 a** (*collect.*) utensils of silver, gold, or other metal. **b** (*collect.*) objects of plated metal. **c** = PLATING. **6 a** a piece of metal with a name or inscription for affixing to a door, container, etc. **b** = LICENSE PLATE. **7** an illustration on special paper in a book. **8** a thin sheet of metal, glass, etc., coated with a sensitive film for photography. **9** a flat thin usu. rigid sheet of metal, etc., with an even surface and uniform thickness, often as part of a mechanism. **10 a** a smooth piece of metal, etc., for engraving. **b** an impression made from this. **11** *Brit.* **a** a silver or gold cup as a prize for a horse race, etc. **b** a race with this as a prize. **12 a** a thin piece of plastic material, molded to the shape of the mouth and gums, to which artificial teeth or another orthodontic appliance are attached. **b** *colloq.* a complete denture or orthodontic appliance. **13** *Geol.* each of several rigid sheets of rock thought to form the earth's outer crust. **14** *Biol.* a thin flat organic structure or formation. **15** a light shoe for a racehorse. **16** a stereotype, electrotype, or plastic cast of a page of composed movable types, or a metal or plastic copy of filmset matter, from which sheets are printed. **17** *Baseball* a flat five-sided piece of whitened rubber at which the batter stands and by stepping on which a runner scores. **18** the anode of a thermionic valve. **19** a horizontal timber laid along the top of a wall to support the ends of joists or rafters. ● *v.tr.* **1** apply a thin coat esp. of silver, gold, or tin to (another metal). **2** cover (esp. a ship) with plates of metal,

esp. for protection. **3** make a plate of (type, etc.) for printing. □ **on a plate** *colloq.* available with little trouble to the recipient. **on one's plate** for one to deal with or consider. □□ **plate·ful** *n.* (*pl.* **·fuls**). **plate·less** *adj.* **plat·er** *n.*

plate ar·mor *n.* armor of metal plates, for a man, ship, etc.

pla·teau /platố/ *n. & v.* ● *n.* (*pl.* **pla·teaux** /–tốz/ or **pla·teaus**) **1** an area of fairly level high ground. **2** a state of little variation after an increase. ● *v.intr.* (**pla·teaus, pla·teaued**) (often foll. by *out*) reach a level or stable state after an increase. [F f. OF *platel* dimin. of *plat* flat surface]

plate glass *n.* thick fine-quality glass for storefront windows, etc., orig. cast in plates.

plate·lay·er /pláytlayər/ *n. Brit.* a person employed in fixing and repairing railroad rails.

plate·let /pláytlit/ *n.* a small colorless disk of protoplasm found in blood and involved in clotting.

plate mark *n.* a hallmark.

plat·en /plát'n/ *n.* **1** a plate in a printing press which presses the paper against the type. **2** a cylindrical roller in a typewriter against which the paper is held. [OF *platine* a flat piece f. *plat* flat]

plate rack *n. Brit.* a rack in which plates are placed to drain.

plat·er·esque /plátorésk/ *adj.* richly ornamented in a style suggesting silverware. [Sp. *plateresco* f. *platero* silversmith f. *plata* silver]

plate tec·ton·ics *n. Geol.* the study of the earth's surface based on the concept of moving plates (see sense 13 of *n.*) forming its structure.

plate trac·er·y *n. Archit.* tracery with perforations in otherwise continuous stone.

plat·form /plátfawrm/ *n.* **1** a raised level surface; a natural or artificial terrace. **2** a raised surface from which a speaker addresses an audience. **3** a raised elongated structure along the side of a track in a railroad, subway station, etc. **4** the floor area at the entrance to a bus. **5** a thick sole of a shoe. **6** the declared policy of a political party. [F *plateforme* flat plan f. *plate* flat + *forme* FORM]

plat·form tick·et *n. Brit.* a ticket allowing a nontraveler access to a station platform.

plat·ing /pláyting/ *n.* **1** a coating of gold, silver, etc. **2** an act of plating.

pla·tin·ic /plətínik/ *adj.* of or containing (esp. tetravalent) platinum.

plat·i·nize /plát'nīz/ *v.tr.* coat with platinum. □□ **plat·i·ni·za·tion** *n.*

plat·i·noid /plát'noyd/ *n.* an alloy of copper, zinc, nickel, and tungsten.

plat·i·num /plát'nəm/ *n. Chem.* a ductile malleable silvery-white metallic element occurring naturally in nickel and copper ores, unaffected by simple acids and fusible only at a very high temperature, used in making jewelry and laboratory apparatus. ¶ Symb.: **Pt**. [mod.L f. earlier *platina* f. Sp., dimin. of *plata* silver]

plat·i·num black *n.* platinum in powder form like lampblack.

plat·i·num blonde *adj. & n.* (also **plat·i·num blond**) ● *adj.* silvery-blond. ● *n.* a person with esp. bleached or dyed silvery-blond hair.

plat·i·num met·al *n.* any metallic element found with and resembling platinum, e.g., osmium, iridium, and palladium.

plat·i·tude /plátitŏŏd, –tyŏŏd/ *n.* **1** a trite or commonplace remark, esp. one solemnly delivered. **2** the use of platitudes; dullness; insipidity. □□ **plat·i·tu·di·nize** /–tŏŏd'nīz,–tyŏŏ–/ *v.intr.* **plat·i·tu·di·nous** /–tŏŏdənəs/ *adj.* [F f. *plat* flat, after *certitude, multitudinous*, etc.]

Pla·ton·ic /plətónik/ *adj.* **1** of or associated with the Greek philosopher Plato (d. 347 BC) or his ideas. **2** (**platonic**) (of love or friendship) purely spiritual; not sexual. **3** (**platonic**) confined to words or theory; not leading to action; harmless. □□ **Pla·ton·i·cal·ly** *adv.* [L *Platonicus* f. Gk *Platōnikos* f. *Platōn* Plato]

Pla·ton·ic sol·id *n.* (also **Pla·ton·ic bod·y**) any of the five regular solids (tetrahedron, cube, octahedron, dodecahedron, icosahedron).

Pla·to·nism /pláyt'nizəm/ *n.* the philosophy of Plato or his followers. □□ **Pla·to·nist** *n.*

pla·toon /plətŏŏn/ *n.* **1** *Mil.* a subdivision of a company, a tactical unit commanded by a lieutenant and usu. divided into three sections. **2** a group of persons acting together. [F *peloton* small ball, dimin. of *pelote*: see PELLET, –OON]

plat·ter /plátər/ *n.* **1** a large flat dish or plate, esp. for food. **2** *colloq.* a phonograph record. □ **on a platter** = *on a plate* (see PLATE). [ME & AF *plater* f. AF *plat* PLATE]

platy- /pláti, –tee/ *comb. form* broad; flat. [Gk *platu-* f. *platus* broad, flat]

plat·y·hel·minth /plátihélminth/ *n.* any invertebrate of the phylum Platyhelminthes, including flatworms, flukes, and tapeworms.

plat·y·pus /plátipəs/ *n.* an Australian aquatic egg-laying mammal,

Ornithorhynchus anatinus, having a pliable ducklike bill, webbed feet, and sleek gray fur. Also called **duckbill**.

duck-billed platypus

plat·yr·rhine /plátirin/ *adj. & n.* ● *adj.* (of primates) having nostrils far apart and directed forward or sideways (cf. CATARRHINE). ● *n.* such an animal. [PLATY- + Gk *rhis rhin-* nose]

plau·dit /pláwdit/ *n.* (usu. in *pl.*) **1** a round of applause. **2** an emphatic expression of approval. [shortened f. L *plaudite* applaud, imper. pl. of *plaudere plaus-* applaud, said by Roman actors at the end of a play]

plau·si·ble /pláwzibəl/ *adj.* **1** (of an argument, statement, etc.) seeming reasonable or probable. **2** (of a person) persuasive but deceptive. □□ **plau·si·bil·i·ty** /–bilitee/ *n.* **plau·si·bly** *adv.* [L *plausibilis* (as PLAUDIT)]

play /play/ *v. & n.* ● *v.* **1** *intr.* (often foll. by *with*) occupy or amuse oneself pleasantly with some recreation, game, exercise, etc. **2** *intr.* (foll. by *with*) act lightheartedly or flippantly (with feelings, etc.). **3** *tr.* **a** perform on or be able to perform on (a musical instrument). **b** perform (a piece of music, etc.). **c** cause (a record, record player, etc.) to produce sounds. **4 a** *intr.* (foll. by *in*) perform a role in (a drama, etc.). **b** perform (a drama or role) on stage, or in a movie or broadcast. **c** *tr.* give a dramatic performance at (a particular theater or place). **5** *tr.* act in real life the part of (*play truant*; *play the fool*). **6** *tr.* (foll. by *on*) perform (a trick or joke, etc.) on (a person). **7** *tr.* (foll. by *for*) regard (a person) as (something specified) (*played me for a fool*). **8** *intr. colloq.* participate; cooperate; do what is wanted (*they won't play*). **9** *intr.* gamble. **10** *tr.* gamble on. **11** *tr.* **a** take part in (a game or recreation). **b** compete with (another player or team) in a game. **c** occupy (a specified position) in a team for a game. **d** (foll. by *in, on, at,* etc.) assign (a player) to a position. **12** *tr.* move (a piece) or display (a playing card) in one's turn in a game. **13** *tr.* (also *absol.*) strike or catch (a ball, etc.) or execute (a stroke) in a game. **14** *intr.* move about in a lively or unrestrained manner. **15** *intr.* (often foll. by *on*) **a** touch gently. **b** emit light, water, etc. (*fountains gently playing*). **16** *tr.* allow (a fish) to exhaust itself pulling against a line. **17** *intr.* (often foll. by *at*) **a** engage in a half-hearted way (in an activity). **b** pretend to be. **18** *intr.* (of a court, field, etc.) be conducive to play as specified (*the greens are playing fast*). **19** *intr. colloq.* act or behave as specified (*play fair*). **20** *tr.* (foll. by *in, out,* etc.) accompany (a person) with music (*were played out with bagpipes*). ● *n.* **1** recreation, amusement, esp. as the spontaneous activity of children and young animals. **2 a** the playing of a game. **b** the action or manner of this. **c** the status of the ball, etc., in a game as being available to be played according to the rules (*in play*; *out of play*). **3** a dramatic piece for the stage, etc. **4** activity or operation (*are in full play*; *brought into play*). **5 a** freedom of movement. **b** space or scope for this. **6** brisk, light, or fitful movement. **7** gambling. **8** an action or maneuver, esp. in or as in a game. □ **at play** engaged in recreation. **in play** for amusement; not seriously. **make play** *Brit.* act effectively. **make a play for** *colloq.* make a conspicuous attempt to acquire or attract. **make play with** use ostentatiously. **play along** pretend to cooperate. **play around** (or **about**) **1** behave irresponsibly. **2** philander. **play back** play (sounds recently recorded), esp. to monitor recording quality, etc. **play ball** see BALL[1]. **play by ear 1** perform (music) previously heard without having or having seen a score. **2** (also **play it by ear**) proceed instinctively or step by step according to results and circumstances. **play one's cards right** (or **well**) make good use of opportunities; act shrewdly. **play down** minimize the importance of. **played out** exhausted of energy or usefulness. **play false** act, or treat (a person), deceitfully or treacherously. **play fast and loose** act unreliably; ignore one's obligations. **play the field** see FIELD. **play for time** seek to gain time by delaying. **play the game** see GAME[1]. **play God** see GOD. **play havoc with** see HAVOC. **play hell with** see HELL. **play hooky** see HOOKY. **play into a person's hands** act so as unwittingly to give a person an advantage. **play it cool** *colloq.* **1** affect indifference. **2** be relaxed or unemotional. **play the market** speculate in stocks, etc. **play off** (usu. foll. by *against*) **1** oppose (one person against another), esp. for one's own advantage. **2** play an extra match to decide a draw or tie. **play on 1** continue to play. **2** take advantage of (a person's feelings, etc.). **play on words** a pun. **play possum** see POSSUM. **play safe** (or **for safety**) avoid risks. **play to the gallery** see GALLERY. **play up 1** make the most of; emphasize. **2** *Brit.* cause trouble; be irritating (*my rheumatism is playing up again*). **3** *Brit.* obstruct or annoy in this way (*played the teacher up*). **4** *Brit.* put all one's energy into a game. **5** *Brit.* behave mischievously. **play up to** flatter, esp. to win favor. **play with fire** take foolish risks. □□ **play·a·ble** *adj.* **play·a·bil·i·ty** /pláyəbílitee/ *n.* [OE *plega* (n.), *pleg(i)an* (v.), orig. = (to) exercise]

pla·ya /pláayə/ *n.* a flat dried-up area, esp. a desert basin from which water evaporates quickly. [Sp., = beach, f. LL *plagia*]

play·act /pláyakt/ *v.* **1** *intr.* act in a play. **2** *intr.* behave affectedly or

insincerely. **3** *tr.* act (a scene, part, etc.). □□ **play·act·ing** *n.* **play·ac·tor** *n.*

play·back /pláybak/ *n.* an act or instance of replaying recorded audio or video from a tape, etc.

play·bill /pláybil/ *n.* **1** a poster announcing a theatrical performance. **2** a theater program.

play·boy /pláyboy/ *n.* an irresponsible pleasure-seeking man, esp. a wealthy one.

play-by-play *adj. & n.* ● *adj.* pertaining to a description, esp. of a sports event, with continuous commentary. ● *n.* such a description (*he called the play-by-play for the big game*).

play·er /pláyər/ *n.* **1 a** a person taking part in a sport or game. **b** a gambler. **2** a person playing a musical instrument. **3** a person who plays a part on the stage; an actor. **4** = RECORD PLAYER. [OE *plegere* (as PLAY)]

play·er pi·an·o *n.* a piano fitted with an apparatus enabling it to be played automatically.

play·fel·low /pláyfelō/ *n.* a playmate.

play·ful /pláyfŏŏl/ *adj.* **1** fond of or inclined to play. **2** done in fun; humorous; jocular. □□ **play·ful·ly** *adv.* **play·ful·ness** *n.*

play·go·er /pláygōr/ *n.* a person who goes often to the theater.

play·ground /pláygrownd/ *n.* an outdoor area set aside for children to play.

play·group /pláygrŏŏp/ *n.* a group of preschool children who play regularly together at a particular place under supervision.

play·house /pláyhows/ *n.* **1** a theater. **2** a toy house for children to play in.

play·ing card /pláying/ *n.* each of a set of usu. 52 rectangular pieces of card or other material with an identical pattern on one side and different values represented by numbers and symbols on the other, used to play various games.

play·ing field /pláying/ *n.* a field used for outdoor team games.

play·let /pláylit/ *n.* a short play or dramatic piece.

play·mate /pláymayt/ *n.* a child's companion in play.

play-off *n. Sports* a game played to break a tie.

play·pen /pláypen/ *n.* a portable enclosure for young children to play in.

play·thing /pláything/ *n.* **1** a toy or other thing to play with. **2** a person treated as a toy.

play·time /pláytīm/ *n.* time for play or recreation.

play·wright /pláyrīt/ *n.* a person who writes plays.

pla·za /pláazə/ *n.* **1** a marketplace or open square (esp. in a town). **2** a public area beside an expressway with facilities such as restaurants or service stations. [Sp., = place]

plc *Brit. abbr.* (also **PLC**) Public Limited Company.

plea /plee/ *n.* **1** an earnest appeal or entreaty. **2** *Law* a formal statement by or on behalf of a defendant. **3** an argument or excuse. [ME & AF *ple, plai,* OF *plait, plaid* agreement, discussion f. L *placitum* a decree, neut. past part. of *placēre* to please]

plea bar·gain *n. & v.* **1** (also **plea bar·gain·ing**) an arrangement between prosecutor and defendant whereby the defendant pleads guilty to a lesser charge in the expectation of leniency. ● *v.* (**plea-bar·gain**) negotiate a plea bargain agreement.

pleach /pleech/ *v.tr.* entwine or interlace (esp. branches to form a hedge). [ME *pleche* f. OF (as PLASH[2])]

plead /pleed/ *v.* (*past* and *past part.* **plead·ed** or **pled** /pled/) **1** *intr.* (foll. by *with*) make an earnest appeal to. **2** *intr. Law* address a court of law as an advocate on behalf of a party. **3** *tr.* maintain (a cause) esp. in a court of law. **4** *tr. Law* declare to be one's state as regards guilt in or responsibility for a crime (*plead guilty*; *plead insanity*). **5** *tr.* offer or allege as an excuse (*pleaded forgetfulness*). **6** *intr.* make an appeal or entreaty. □ **plead** (or **take**) **the Fifth** refuse to incriminate oneself legally, in accordance with the Fifth Amendment to the Constitution. □□ **plead·a·ble** *adj.* **plead·er** *n.* **plead·ing·ly** *adv.* [ME f. AF *pleder,* OF *plaidier* (as PLEA)]

plead·ing /pléeding/ *n.* (usu. in *pl.*) a formal statement of the cause of an action or defense.

plea of ten·der *n. Law* a plea that the defendant has always been ready to satisfy the plaintiff's claim and now brings the sum into court.

pleas·ance /plézəns/ *n.* a secluded enclosure or part of a garden, esp. one attached to a large house. [ME f. OF *plaisance* (as PLEAS-ANT)]

pleas·ant /plézənt/ *adj.* (**pleas·ant·er, pleas·ant·est**) pleasing to the mind, feelings, or senses. □□ **pleas·ant·ly** *adv.* **pleas·ant·ness** *n.* [ME f. OF *plaisant* (as PLEASE)]

SYNONYM TIP *pleasant*

AGREEABLE, ATTRACTIVE, CONGENIAL, ENJOYABLE, GRATIFYING, PLEASING. One might have a **pleasant** smile and a **pleasing** personality, since the former suggests something that is naturally appealing while the latter suggests a conscious attempt to please. Something that is **enjoyable** is able to give enjoyment or pleasure (*a thoroughly enjoyable evening*), while **agreeable** describes something that is in harmony with one's personal mood or wishes (*an agreeable afternoon spent relaxing in the sun*). **Gratifying** is more intense, suggesting that deeper expectations or needs have been met (*the awards ceremony was particularly gratifying for parents*). Something that is **attractive** gives pleasure because of its appearance or manner (*an attractive house in a wooded setting*), while **congenial** has more to do with compatibility (*a congenial couple*).

pleas·ant·ry /plézəntree/ *n.* (*pl.* **·ries**) **1** a pleasant or amusing remark, esp. made in casual conversation. **2** a humorous manner of speech. **3** jocularity. [F *plaisanterie* (as PLEASANT)]

please /pleez/ *v.* **1** *tr.* (also *absol.*) be agreeable to; make glad; give pleasure to (*the gift will please them; anxious to please*). **2** *tr.* (in passive) **a** (foll. by *to* + infin.) be glad or willing to (*am pleased to help*). **b** (often foll. by *about, at, with*) derive pleasure or satisfaction (from). **3** *tr.* (with *it* as subject; usu. foll. by *to* + infin.) be the inclination or wish of (*it did not please them to attend*). **4** *intr.* think fit; have the will or desire (*take as many as you please*). **5** *tr.* (short for **may it please you**) used in polite requests (*come in, please*). □ **if you please** if you are willing, esp. *iron.* to indicate unreasonableness (*then, if you please, we had to pay*). **pleased as Punch** see PUNCH[4]. **please oneself** do as one likes. □□ **pleased** *adj.* **pleas·ing** *adj.* **pleas·ing·ly** *adv.* [ME *plaise* f. OF *plaisir* f. L *placēre*]

pleas·ur·a·ble /plézhərəbəl/ *adj.* causing pleasure; agreeable. □□ **pleas·ur·a·ble·ness** *n.* **pleas·ur·a·bly** *adv.* [PLEASURE + –ABLE, after *comfortable*]

pleas·ure /plézhər/ *n. & v.* ● *n.* **1** a feeling of satisfaction or joy. **2** enjoyment. **3** a source of pleasure or gratification (*painting was my chief pleasure; it is a pleasure to take a rest*). **4** *formal* a person's will or desire (*what is your pleasure?*). **5** sensual gratification or enjoyment (*a life of pleasure*). **6** (*attrib.*) done or used for pleasure (*pleasure ground*). ● *v.* **1** *tr.* give (esp. sexual) pleasure to. **2** *intr.* (often foll. by *in*) take pleasure. □ **take pleasure in** take doing. **with pleasure** gladly. [ME & OF *plesir, plaisir* PLEASE, used as a noun]

pleat /pleet/ *n. & v.* ● *n.* a fold or crease, esp. a flattened fold in cloth doubled upon itself. ● *v.tr.* make a pleat or pleats in. [ME, var. of PLAIT]

pleb /pleb/ *n. colloq.* usu. *derog.* an ordinary insignificant person. □□ **pleb·by** *adj.* [abbr. of PLEBEIAN]

plebe /pleeb/ *n.* a first-year student at a military academy.

ple·be·ian /plibéeən/ *n. & adj.* ● *n.* a commoner, esp. in ancient Rome. ● *adj.* **1** of low birth; of the common people. **2** uncultured. **3** coarse; ignoble. □□ **ple·be·ian·ism** *n.* [L *plebeius* f. *plebs plebis* the common people]

pleb·i·scite /plébisit, –sīt/ *n.* **1** the direct vote of all the electors of a nation, etc., on an important public question, e.g., a change in the constitution. **2** the public expression of a community's opinion, with or without binding force. **3** *Rom.Hist.* a law enacted by the plebeians' assembly. □□ **ple·bi·sci·ta·ry** /pləbísiteree, plebísit–/ *adj.*

WORD HISTORY plebiscite

mid-16th century (referring to Roman history): from French *plébiscite*, from Latin *plebiscitum*, from *plebs, pleb-* 'the common people' + *scitum* 'decree' (from *sciscere* 'vote for'). The sense 'direct vote of the whole electorate' dates from the mid-19th century.

---

plec·trum /pléktrəm/ *n.* (*pl.* **plec·trums** or **plec·tra** /–trə/) **1** a thin flat piece of plastic or horn, etc., held in the hand and used to pluck a string, esp. of a guitar. **2** the corresponding mechanical part of a harpsichord, etc. [L f. Gk *plēktron* f. *plēssō* strike]

pled *past* of PLEAD.

pledge /plej/ *n. & v.* ● *n.* **1** a solemn promise or undertaking. **2** a thing given as security for the fulfillment of a contract, the payment of a debt, etc., and liable to forfeiture in the event of failure. **3** a thing put in pawn. **4** a thing given as a token of love, favor, or something to come. **5** the drinking to a person's health; a toast. **6** a solemn undertaking to abstain from alcohol (*sign the pledge*). **7** a person who has promised to join a fraternity or sorority. ● *v.tr.* **1 a** deposit as security. **b** pawn. **2** promise solemnly by the pledge of (one's honor, word, etc.). **3** (often *refl.*) bind by a solemn promise. **4** drink to the health of. □ **pledge one's troth** see TROTH. □□ **pledge·a·ble** *adj.* **pledg·er** *n.* **pledg·or** *n.* [ME *plege* f. OF *plege* f. LL *plebium* f. *plebire* assure]

pledg·ee /plejée/ *n.* a person to whom a pledge is given.

pledg·et /pléjit/ *n.* a small wad of lint, cotton, etc., used as a bandage or compress. [16 c.: orig. unkn.]

ple·iad /pléeəd, pláy–/ *n.* a brilliant group of (usu. seven) persons or things. [named after PLEIADES]

Ple·ia·des /pléeədeez, pláy–/ *n.pl.* a cluster of six visible stars in the

---

constellation Taurus, usu. known as the Seven Sisters after seven sisters in Greek mythology. [ME f. L *Pleïas* f. Gk *Plēïas –ados*]

Pleis·to·cene /plístəseen/ *adj. & n. Geol.* ● *adj.* of or relating to the first epoch of the Quaternary period marked by great fluctuations in temperature with glacial periods followed by interglacial periods. ● *n.* this epoch or system. Also called **Ice Age**. [Gk *pleistos* most + *kainos* new]

ple·na·ry /pléenəree, plén–/ *adj.* **1** entire; unqualified; absolute (*plenary indulgence*). **2** (of an assembly) to be attended by all members. [LL *plenarius* f. *plenus* full]

plen·i·po·ten·ti·a·ry /plénipəténshəree, –shee-eree/ *n. & adj.* ● *n.* (*pl.* **·ies**) a person (esp. a diplomat) invested with the full power of independent action. ● *adj.* **1** having this power. **2** (of power) absolute. [med.L *plenipotentiarius* f. *plenus* full + *potentia* power]

plen·i·tude /plénitōod, –tyōod/ *n.* **1** fullness; completeness. **2** abundance. [ME f. OF f. LL *plenitudo* f. *plenus* full]

plen·te·ous /plénteeəs/ *adj.* plentiful. □□ **plen·te·ous·ly** *adv.* **plen·te·ous·ness** *n.* [ME f. OF *plentivous* f. *plentif –ive* f. *plenté* PLENTY: cf. *bounteous*]

plen·ti·ful /pléntifōol/ *adj.* abundant; copious. □□ **plen·ti·ful·ly** *adv.* **plen·ti·ful·ness** *n.*

plen·ty /pléntee/ *n., adj., & adv.* ● *n.* **1** (often foll. by *of*) a great or sufficient quantity or number (*we have plenty; plenty of time*). **2** abundance (*in great plenty*). ● *adj. colloq.* existing in an ample quantity. ● *adv. colloq.* fully; entirely (*it is plenty large enough*). [ME *plenteth, plente* f. OF *plentet* f. L *plenitas –tatis* f. *plenus* full]

ple·num /pléenəm, plénəm/ *n.* **1** a full assembly of people or a committee, etc. **2** *Physics* space filled with matter. [L, neut. of *plenus* full]

ple·o·chro·ic /pléeəkróik/ *adj.* showing different colors when viewed in different directions. □□ **ple·och·ro·ism** *n.* [Gk *pleiōn* more + –*khroos* f. *khrōs* color]

ple·o·mor·phism /pléeəmáwrfizəm/ *n. Biol., Chem., & Mineral.* the occurrence of more than one distinct form. □□ **ple·o·mor·phic** *adj.* [Gk *pleiōn* more + *morphē* form]

ple·o·nasm /pléeənazəm/ *n.* the use of more words than are needed to give the sense (e.g., *see with one's eyes*). □□ **ple·o·nas·tic** /–nástik/ *adj.* **ple·o·nas·ti·cal·ly** *adv.* [LL *pleonasmus* f. Gk *pleonasmos* f. *pleonazō* be superfluous]

ple·si·o·sau·rus /pléeseeəsáwrəs/ *n.* (also **ple·si·o·saur** /–sawr/) any of a group of extinct marine reptiles with a broad flat body, short tail, long flexible neck, and large paddlelike limbs. [mod.L f. Gk *plēsios* near + *sauros* lizard]

ples·sor var. of PLEXOR.

pleth·o·ra /pléthərə/ *n.* **1** an oversupply, glut, or excess. **2** *Med.* **a** an abnormal excess of red corpuscles in the blood. **b** an excess of any body fluid. □□ **ple·thor·ic** /plətháwrik, –thór–/ *adj.* **ple·thor·i·cal·ly** *adv.* [LL f. Gk *plēthōrē* f. *plēthō* be full]

pleu·ra[1] /plŏorə/ *n.* (*pl.* **pleu·rae** /–ree/) **1** each of a pair of serous membranes lining the thorax and enveloping the lungs in mammals. **2** lateral extensions of the body wall in arthropods. □□ **pleu·ral** *adj.* [med.L f. Gk, = side of the body, rib]

pleu·ra[2] *pl.* of PLEURON.

pleu·ri·sy /plŏorisee/ *n.* inflammation of the pleura, marked by pain in the chest or side, fever, etc. □□ **pleu·rit·ic** /–ritik/ *adj.* [ME f. OF *pleurisie* f. LL *pleurisis* alt. f. L *pleuritis* f. Gk (as PLEURA[1])]

pleuro- /plŏorō/ *comb. form* **1** denoting the pleura. **2** denoting the side.

pleu·ron /plŏoron/ *n.* (*pl.* **pleu·ra** /–rə/) = PLEURA[1] 2. [Gk, = side of the body, rib]

pleu·ro·pneu·mo·nia /plŏorōnŏomṓnyə, –nyŏo–/ *n.* pneumonia complicated with pleurisy.

Plex·i·glas /pléksiglas/ *n. Trademark* tough, clear thermoplastic used instead of glass. [formed as PLEXOR + GLASS]

plex·or /pléksər/ *n.* (also **ples·sor** /plésər/) *Med.* a small hammer used to test reflexes and in percussing. [irreg. f. Gk *plēxis* percussion + –OR[1]]

plex·us /pléksəs/ *n.* (*pl.* same or **plex·us·es**) **1** *Anat.* a network of nerves or vessels in an animal body (*gastric plexus*). **2** any network or weblike formation. □□ **plex·i·form** *adj.* [L f. *plectere plex-* braid]

pli·a·ble /plíəbəl/ *adj.* **1** bending easily; supple. **2** yielding; compliant. □□ **pli·a·bil·i·ty** *n.* **pli·a·ble·ness** *n.* **pli·a·bly** *adv.* [F f. *plier* bend: see PLY[1]]

pli·ant /plíənt/ *adj.* = PLIABLE 1. □□ **pli·an·cy** *n.* **pli·ant·ly** *adv.* [ME f. OF (as PLIABLE)]

pli·cate /plíkayt/ *adj. Biol. & Geol.* folded; crumpled; corrugated. □□ **pli·cat·ed** *adj.* [L *plicatus* past part. of *plicare* fold]

pli·ca·tion /plikáyshən/ *n.* **1** the act of folding. **2** a fold, or folded condition. [ME f. med.L *plicatio* or L *plicare* fold, after *complication*]

pli·é /plee-áy/ *n. Ballet* a bending of the knees with the feet on the ground. [F, past part. of *plier* bend: see PLY[1]]

pli·ers /plíərz/ *n.pl.* pincers with parallel flat

pliers

usu. serrated surfaces for holding small objects, bending wire, etc. [(dial.) *ply* bend (as PLIABLE)]

plight[1] /plīt/ *n.* a condition or state, esp. an unfortunate one. [ME & AF *plit* = OF *pleit* fold: see PLAIT: *–gh-* by confusion with PLIGHT[2]]

plight[2] /plīt/ *v. & n. archaic* ● *v.tr.* **1** pledge or promise solemnly (one's faith, loyalty, etc.). **2** (foll. by *to*) engage, esp. in marriage. ● *n.* an engagement or act of pledging. □ **plight one's troth** see TROTH. [orig. as noun, f. OE *pliht* danger f. Gmc]

plim·soll /plímsəl, –sōl/ *n.* (also **plim·sole**) *Brit.* a kind of sneaker with a canvas upper. [prob. from the resemblance of the side of the sole to a PLIMSOLL LINE]

Plim·soll line /plímsəl, –sōl/ *n.* (also **Plim·soll mark**) a marking on a ship's side showing the limit of legal submersion under various conditions. [S. *Plimsoll*, Engl. politician d. 1898]

plinth /plinth/ *n.* **1** the lower square slab at the base of a column. **2** a base supporting a vase or statue, etc. [F *plinthe* or L *plinthus* f. Gk *plinthos* tile, brick, squared stone]

Pli·o·cene /plíəseen/ *adj. & n. Geol.* ● *adj.* of or relating to the last epoch of the Tertiary period with evidence of the extinction of many mammals, and the development of hominids. ● *n.* this epoch or system. [Gk *pleiōn* more + *kainos* new]

plis·sé /pleesáy, plī–/ *adj. & n.* ● *adj.* (of cloth, etc.) treated so as to cause permanent puckering. ● *n.* material treated in this way. [F, past part. of *plisser* pleat]

PLO *abbr.* Palestine Liberation Organization.

plod /plod/ *v. & n.* ● *v.* (**plod·ded, plod·ding**) **1** *intr.* (often foll. by *along, on,* etc.) walk doggedly or laboriously; trudge. **2** *intr.* (often foll. by *at*) work slowly and steadily. **3** *tr.* tread or make (one's way) laboriously. ● *n.* the act or a spell of plodding. □□ **plod·der** *n.* **plod·ding·ly** *adv.* [16th c.: prob. imit.]

-ploid /ployd/ *comb. form Biol.* forming adjectives denoting the number of sets of chromosomes in a cell (*diploid; polyploid*). [after HAPLOID]

ploi·dy /plóydee/ *n.* the number of sets of chromosomes in a cell. [after DIPLOIDY, *polyploidy,* etc.]

plonk[1] var. of PLUNK.

plonk[2] /plongk/ *n.* esp. *Brit. colloq.* cheap or inferior wine. [orig. Austral.: prob. corrupt. of *blanc* in F *vin blanc* white wine]

plonk·er /plóngkər/ *n. coarse Brit. sl.* a stupid person.

plon·ko /plóngkō/ *n.* (*pl.* **·kos**) *Austral. sl.* an excessive drinker of cheap wine; an alcoholic.

plop /plop/ *n., v., & adv.* ● *n.* **1** a sound as of a smooth object dropping into water without a splash. **2** an act of falling with this sound. ● *v.* (**plopped, plop·ping**) *intr. & tr.* fall or drop with a plop. ● *adv.* with a plop. [19th c.: imit.]

plo·sion /plṓzhən/ *n. Phonet.* the sudden release of breath in the pronunciation of a stop consonant. [EXPLOSION]

plo·sive /plṓsiv/ *adj. & n. Phonet.* ● *adj.* pronounced with a sudden release of breath. ● *n.* a plosive sound. [EXPLOSIVE]

plot /plot/ *n. & v.* ● *n.* **1** a defined and usu. small piece of ground. **2** the interrelationship of the main events in a play, novel, movie, etc. **3** a conspiracy or secret plan, esp. to achieve an unlawful end. **4** a graph or diagram. **5** a graph showing the relation between two variables. ● *v.* (**plot·ted, plot·ting**) *tr.* **1** make a plan or map of (an existing object, a place or thing to be laid out, constructed, etc.). **2** (also *absol.*) plan or contrive secretly (a crime, conspiracy, etc.). **3** mark (a point or course, etc.) on a chart or diagram. **4 a** mark out or allocate (points) on a graph. **b** make (a curve, etc.) by marking out a number of points. □□ **plot·less** *adj.* **plot·less·ness** *n.* **plot·ter** *n.* [OE and f. OF *complot* secret plan: both of unkn. orig.]

plough *n. & v.* esp. *Brit.* var. of PLOW. □ **the Plough** *Brit.* = BIG DIPPER.

plough·man's lunch *n. Brit.* a meal of bread and cheese with pickle or salad.

Plough Mon·day *n. Brit.* the first Monday after the Epiphany.

plov·er /plúvər, plṓ–/ *n.* any plump-breasted shorebird of the family Charadriidae, including the lapwing, sandpiper, etc., usu. having a short bill. [ME & AF f. OF *plo(u)vier* ult. f. L *pluvia* rain]

plow /plow/ *n. & v.* (also *Brit.* **plough**) ● *n.* **1** an implement with a cutting blade fixed in a frame drawn by a tractor or by horses, for

cutting furrows in the soil and turning it up. **2** an implement resembling this and having a comparable function (*snowplow*). **3** plowed land. ● *v.* **1** *tr.* (also *absol.*) turn up (the earth) with a plow, esp. before sowing. **2** *tr.* (foll. by *out, up, down,* etc.) turn or extract (roots, weeds, etc.) with a plow. **3 a** *tr.* furrow, or scratch (a surface) as if with a plow. **b** move through or break the surface of (water). **4** *tr.* produce (a furrow, line, or wake) in this way. **5** *intr.* (foll. by *through*) advance laboriously, esp. through work, a book, etc. **6** *intr.* (foll. by *through, into*) move like a plow steadily or violently. **7** (**plough**) *intr. & tr. Brit. colloq.* fail in an examination. □ **plow back 1** plow (grass, etc.) into the soil to enrich it. **2** reinvest (profits) in the business producing them. **put one's hand to the plow** undertake a task (Luke 9:62). □□ **plow·a·ble** *adj.* **plow·er** *n.* [OE *plōh* f. ON *plógr* f. Gmc]

plow·man /plówmən/ *n.* (also *Brit.* **plough·man**) (*pl.* **·men**) a person who uses a plow.

plow·share /plówshair/ *n.* the cutting blade of a plow.

ploy /ploy/ *n. colloq.* a stratagem; a cunning maneuver to gain an advantage. [orig. Sc., 18th c.: orig. unkn.]

pluck /pluk/ *v. & n.* ● *v.* **1** *tr.* (often foll. by *out, off,* etc.) remove by picking or pulling out or away. **2** *tr.* strip (a bird) of feathers. **3** *tr.* pull at; twitch. **4** *intr.* (foll. by *at*) tug or snatch at. **5** *tr.* sound (the string of a musical instrument) with the finger or plectrum, etc. **6** *tr.* plunder. **7** *tr.* swindle. ● *n.* **1** courage; spirit. **2** an act of plucking; a twitch. **3** the heart, liver, and lungs of an animal as food. □ **pluck up** summon up (one's courage, spirits, etc.). □□ **pluck·er** *n.* **pluck·less** *adj.* [OE *ploccian, pluccian,* f. Gmc]

pluck·y /plúkee/ *adj.* (**pluck·i·er, pluck·i·est**) brave; spirited. □□ **pluck·i·ly** *adv.* **pluck·i·ness** *n.*

plug /plug/ *n. & v.* ● *n.* **1** a piece of solid material fitting tightly into a hole, used to fill a gap or cavity or act as a wedge or stopper. **2 a** a device of metal pins in an insulated casing fitting into holes in a socket for making an electrical connection, esp. between an appliance and a power supply. **b** *colloq.* an electric socket. **3** = SPARK PLUG. **4** *colloq.* a piece of (often free) publicity for an idea, product, etc. **5** a mass of solidified lava filling the neck of a volcano. **6** a cake or stick of tobacco; a piece of this for chewing. **7** = FIREPLUG. ● *v.* (**plugged, plug·ging**) **1** *tr.* (often foll. by *up*) stop up (a hole, etc.) with a plug. **2** *tr. sl.* shoot or hit (a person, etc.). **3** *tr. colloq.* seek to popularize (an idea, product, etc.) by constant recommendation. **4** *intr. colloq.* (often foll. by *at*) work steadily away (at). □ **plug away (at)** work steadily (at). **plug in** connect electrically by inserting a plug in a socket. **plug into** connect with, as by means of a plug. □□ **plug·ger** *n.* [MDu. & MLG *plugge,* of unkn. orig.]

plug-in *adj.* able to be connected by means of a plug.

plug·o·la /plugṓlə/ *n. colloq.* **1** a bribe offered in return for incidental or surreptitious promotion of a person or product, esp. on radio or television. **2** the practice of such bribery. [PLUG + *–ola,* prob. after PAYOLA]

plug-ug·ly *n. & adj. sl. n.* (*pl.* **·lies**) a thug or ruffian. ● *adj.* villainous-looking; ugly.

plum /plum/ *n.* **1 a** an oval fleshy fruit, usu. purple or yellow when ripe, with sweet pulp and a flattish pointed stone. **b** any deciduous tree of the genus *Prunus* bearing this. **2** a reddish-purple color. **3** a dried grape or raisin used in cooking. **4** *colloq.* the best of a collection; something especially prized (often *attrib.: a plum job*). [OE *plūme* f. med.L *pruna* f. L *prunum*]

plum·age /plṓmij/ *n.* a bird's feathers. □□ **plum·aged** *adj.* (usu. in *comb.*). [ME f. OF (as PLUME)]

plumb[1] /plum/ *n., adv., adj., & v.* ● *n.* a ball of lead or other heavy material, esp. one attached to the end of a line for finding the depth of water or determining the vertical on an upright surface. ● *adv.* **1** exactly (*plumb in the center*). **2** vertically. **3** *sl.* quite; utterly (*plumb crazy*). ● *adj.* **1** vertical. **2** downright; sheer (*plumb nonsense*). **3** *Cricket* (of the wicket) level; true. ● *v.tr.* **1 a** measure the depth of (water) with a plumb. **b** determine (a depth). **2** test (an upright surface) to determine the vertical. **3** reach or experience in extremes (*plumb the depths of fear*). **4** learn in detail the facts about (a matter). □ **out of plumb** not vertical. [ME, prob. ult. f. L *plumbum* lead, assim. to OF *plomb* lead]

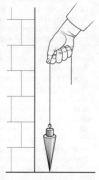

plumb

plumb[2] /plum/ *v.* **1** *tr.* provide (a building or room, etc.) with plumbing. **2** *tr.* (often foll. by *in*) fit as part of a plumbing system. **3** *intr.* work as a plumber. [back-form. f. PLUMBER]

plum·ba·go /plumbáygō/ *n.* (*pl.* **·gos**) **1** = GRAPHITE. **2** any plant of the genus *Plumbago*, with gray or blue flowers. Also called **lead-wort**. [L f. *plumbum* LEAD²]

plum·be·ous /plúmbeeəs/ *adj.* **1** of or like lead. **2** lead-glazed. [L *plumbeus* f. *plumbum* LEAD²]

plumb·er /plúmər/ *n.* a person who fits and repairs the apparatus of a water supply system. [ME *plummer*, etc. f. OF *plommier* f. L *plumbarius* f. *plumbum* LEAD²]

plum·bic /plúmbik/ *adj.* **1** *Chem.* containing lead esp. in its tetravalent form. **2** *Med.* due to the presence of lead. □□ **plum·bism** *n.* (in sense 2). [L *plumbum* lead]

plumb·ing /plúming/ *n.* **1** the system or apparatus of water supply, heating, etc., in a building. **2** the work of a plumber. **3** *colloq.* any system of tubes, vessels, etc., that carry fluids.

plumb·less /plúmlis/ *adj.* (of a depth of water, etc.) that cannot be plumbed.

plumb line *n.* a line with a plumb attached.

plum·bous /plúmbəs/ *n. Chem.* containing lead in its divalent form.

plumb rule *n.* a plumb line attached to a board for determining the vertical.

plum cake *n.* esp. *Brit.* a cake containing raisins, currants, etc.

plum duff *n. Brit.* a plain flour pudding with raisins or currants.

plume /ploom/ *n. & v.* ● *n.* **1** a feather, esp. a large one used for ornament. **2** an ornament of feathers, etc., attached to a helmet or hat or worn in the hair. **3** something resembling this (*a plume of smoke*). **4** *Zool.* a featherlike part or formation. ● *v.* **1** *tr.* decorate or provide with a plume or plumes. **2** *refl.* (foll. by *on, upon*) pride (oneself on esp. something trivial). **3** *tr.* (of a bird) preen (itself or its feathers). □□ **plume·less** *adj.* **plume·like** *adj.* **plum·er·y** *n.* [ME f. OF f. L *pluma* down]

plum·met /plúmit/ *n. & v.* ● *n.* **1** a plumb or plumb line. **2** a sounding line. **3** a weight attached to a fishing line to keep the float upright. ● *v.intr.* (**plum·met·ed, plum·met·ing**) fall or plunge rapidly. [ME f. OF *plommet* dimin. (as PLUMB¹)]

plum·my /plúmee/ *adj.* (**plum·mi·er, plum·mi·est**) **1** abounding or rich in plums. **2** *colloq.* **a** (of a voice) sounding affectedly rich or deep in tone. **b** snobbish. **3** *colloq.* good; desirable.

plu·mose /plóomōs/ *adj.* **1** feathered. **2** featherlike. [L *plumosus* f. PLUME)]

plump¹ /plump/ *adj. & v.* ● *adj.* (esp. of a person or animal or part of the body) having a full rounded shape; fleshy; filled out. ● *v.tr. & intr.* (often foll. by *up, out*) make or become plump; fatten. □□ **plump·ish** *adj.* **plump·ly** *adv.* **plump·ness** *n.* **plump·y** *adj.* [ME *plompe* f. MDu. *plomp* blunt, MLG *plump, plomp* shapeless, etc.]

plump² /plump/ *v., n., adv., & adj.* ● *v.* **1** *intr. & tr.* (often foll. by *down*) drop or fall abruptly (*plumped down on the chair; plumped it on the floor*). **2** *intr.* (foll. by *for*) decide definitely in favor of (one of two or more possibilities). **3** *tr.* (often foll. by *out*) utter abruptly; blurt out. ● *n.* an abrupt plunge; a heavy fall. ● *adv. colloq.* **1** with a sudden or heavy fall. **2** directly; bluntly (*I told him plump*). ● *adj. colloq.* direct; unqualified (*answered with a plump 'no'*). [ME f. MLG *plumpen*, MDu. *plompen*: orig. imit.]

plum pud·ding *n.* a rich boiled or steamed pudding with raisins, currants, spices, etc.

plu·mule /plóomyool/ *n.* **1** the rudimentary shoot or stem of an embryo plant. **2** a down feather on a young bird. □□ **plu·mu·la·ceous** /plóomyəláyshəs/ *adj.* (in sense 2). **plu·mu·lar** *adj.* (in sense 1). [F *plumule* or L *plumula*, dimin. (as PLUME)]

plum·y /plóomee/ *adj.* (**plum·i·er, plum·i·est**) **1** plumelike; feathery. **2** adorned with plumes.

plun·der /plúndər/ *n.* ● *v.tr.* **1** rob (a place or person) forcibly of goods, e.g., as in war. **2** rob systematically. **3** (also *absol.*) steal or embezzle (goods). ● *n.* **1** the violent or dishonest acquisition of property. **2** property acquired by plundering. **3** *colloq.* profit; gain. □□ **plun·der·er** *n.* [LG *plündern* lit. 'rob of household goods' f. MHG *plunder* clothing, etc.]

plunge /plunj/ *v. & n.* ● *v.* **1** (usu. foll. by *in, into*) **a** *tr.* thrust forcefully or abruptly. **b** *intr.* dive; propel oneself forcibly. **c** *intr. & tr.* enter or cause to enter a certain condition or embark on a certain course abruptly or impetuously (*they plunged into a lively discussion; the room was plunged into darkness*). **2** *tr.* immerse completely. **3** *intr.* **a** move suddenly and dramatically downward. **b** (foll. by *down, into*, etc.) move with a rush (*plunged down the stairs*). **c** diminish rapidly (*share prices have plunged*). **4** *intr.* (of a horse) start violently forward. **5** *intr.* (of a ship) pitch. **6** *intr. colloq.* gamble heavily; run into debt. ● *n.* a plunging action or movement; a dive. □ **take the plunge** *colloq.* commit oneself to a (usu. risky) course of action. [ME f. OF *plungier* ult. f. L *plumbum* plummet]

plung·er /plúnjər/ *n.* **1** a part of a mechanism that works with a plunging or thrusting movement. **2** a rubber cup on a handle for clearing blocked pipes by a plunging and sucking action. **3** *colloq.* a reckless gamble.

plung·ing neck·line *n.* a low-cut neckline.

plunk /plungk/ *n. & v.* ● *n.* **1** the sound made by the sharply plucked string of a stringed instrument. **2** a heavy blow or thud. ● *v.* **1** *intr.*

& tr. sound or cause to sound with a plunk. **2** *tr.* hit abruptly. **3** *tr.* set down hurriedly or clumsily. **4** *tr.* (usu. foll. by *down*) set down firmly. [imit.]

plu·per·fect /plóopárfikt/ *adj. & n. Gram.* ● *adj.* (of a tense) denoting an action completed prior to some past point of time specified or implied, formed in English by *had* and the past participle, as: *he had gone by then*. ● *n.* the pluperfect tense. [mod.L *plusperfectum* f. L *plus quam perfectum* more than perfect]

plu·ral /plóorəl/ *adj. & n.* ● *adj.* **1** more than one in number. **2** *Gram.* (of a word or form) denoting more than one, or (in languages with dual number) more than two. ● *n. Gram.* **1** a plural word or form. **2** the plural number. □□ **plu·ral·ly** *adv.* [ME f. OF *plurel* f. L *pluralis* f. *plus pluris* more]

▶**1.** The apostrophe is often, but not always, used to form the plural of letters (*r's*) and numbers (*7's*), as well as single words referred to themselves (*four the's in one sentence*). **2.** The regular plurals of abbreviations and acronyms may be spelled by simply adding an *-s*: *CDs, MiGs*. They may also, especially if periods are involved, employ an apostrophe: *D.D.S.'s*. **3.** The plurals of all proper names should end in *-s* or *-es*, with no apostrophe: *the Smiths, the Joneses, the Rosses*. Exceptions include a few names that would have an *-es* but that would not be pronounced that way: *all the Kings Louis of France*.

plu·ral·ism /plóorəlizəm/ *n.* **1** holding more than one office, esp. an ecclesiastical office or benefice, at a time. **2** a form of society in which the members of minority groups maintain their independent cultural traditions. **3** *Philos.* a system that recognizes more than one ultimate principle (cf. MONISM 2). □□ **plu·ral·ist** *n.* **plu·ral·is·tic** *adj.* **plu·ral·is·ti·cal·ly** *adv.*

plu·ral·i·ty /plóorálitee/ *n.* (*pl.* **·ties**) **1** the state of being plural. **2** = PLURALISM 1. **3** a large or the greater number. **4** a majority that is not absolute. [ME f. OF *pluralité* f. LL *pluralitas* (as PLURAL)]

▶See note at MAJORITY.

plu·ral·ize /plóorəliz/ *v.* **1** *tr. & intr.* make or become plural. **2** *tr.* express in the plural. **3** *intr.* hold more than one ecclesiastical office or benefice at a time.

pluri- /plóoree/ *comb. form* several. [L *plus pluris* more, *plures* several]

plus /plus/ *prep., adj., n., & conj.* ● *prep.* **1** *Math.* with the addition of (*3 plus 4 equals 7*). ¶ Symbol: +. **2** (of temperature) above zero (*plus 2° C*). **3** *colloq.* with; having gained; newly possessing (*returned plus a new car*). ● *adj.* **1** (after a number) and above (*fifty plus*). **2** (after a grade, etc.) somewhat better than (*C plus*). **3** *Math.* positive. **4** having a positive electrical charge. **5** (*attrib.*) additional; extra (*plus business*). ● *n.* **1** = PLUS SIGN. **2** *Math.* an additional or positive quantity. **3** an advantage (*experience is a definite plus*). ● *conj. colloq. disp.* also; and furthermore (*they arrived late, plus they were hungry*). [L, = more]

▶The use of **plus** as a conjunction meaning 'and furthermore' (*plus we will be pleased to give you personal financial advice*) is considered incorrect by many people.

plus fours *n.pl.* long wide men's knickers usu. worn for golf, etc.

plush /plush/ *n. & adj.* ● *n.* cloth of silk, cotton, etc., with a long soft nap. ● *adj.* **1** made of plush. **2** plushy. □□ **plush·ly** *adv.* **plush·ness** *n.* [obs. F *pluche* contr. f. *peluche* f. OF *peluchier* f. It. *peluzzo* dimin. of *pelo* f. L *pilus* hair]

plush·y /plúshee/ *adj.* (**plush·i·er, plush·i·est**) *colloq.* stylish; luxurious. □□ **plush·i·ness** *n.*

plus sign *n.* the symbol +, indicating addition or a positive value.

plu·tarch·y /plóotaarkee/ *n.* (*pl.* **·ies**) plutocracy. [Gk *ploutos* wealth + *–arkhia* –rule]

Plu·to /plóotō/ *n.* the outermost known planet of the solar system. [L f. Gk *Ploutōn* god of the underworld]

plu·toc·ra·cy /plootókrəsee/ *n.* (*pl.* **·cies**) **1 a** a government by the wealthy. **b** a nation governed in this way. **2** a wealthy elite or ruling class. □□ **plu·to·crat·ic** /plóotəkrátik/ *adj.* **plu·to·crat·i·cal·ly** *adv.* [Gk *ploutokratia* f. *ploutos* wealth + –CRACY]

▶See note at ARISTOCRACY.

plu·to·crat /plóotəkrat/ *n.* **1** a member of a plutocracy or wealthy elite. **2** a wealthy and influential person.

plu·ton /plóoton/ *n. Geol.* a body of plutonic rock. [back-form. f. PLUTONIC]

Plu·to·ni·an /plootōneeən/ *adj.* **1** infernal. **2** of the infernal regions. [L *Plutonius* f. Gk *Ploutōnios* (as PLUTO)]

plu·ton·ic /plootónik/ *adj.* **1** *Geol.* (of rock) formed as igneous rock by solidification below the surface of the earth. **2** (**Plutonic**) = PLUTONIAN. [formed as PLUTONIAN]

plu·to·ni·um /plootōneeəm/ *n. Chem.* a dense silvery radioactive metallic transuranic element of the actinide series, used in some nuclear reactors and weapons. ¶ Symb.: Pu. [PLUTO (as the next planet beyond Neptune) + –IUM]

plu·vi·al /plóoveeəl/ *adj. & n.* ● *adj.* **1** of rain; rainy. **2** *Geol.* caused by rain. ● *n.* a period of prolonged rainfall. □□ **plu·vi·ous** *adj.* (in sense 1). [L *pluvialis* f. *pluvia* rain]

plu·vi·om·e·ter /plóoveeómitər/ *n.* a rain gauge. □□ **plu·vi·o·met·ric** /–veeəmétrik/ *adj.* **plu·vi·o·met·ri·cal** *adj.* **plu·vi·o·met·ri·cal·ly** *adv.* [L *pluvia* rain + –METER]

ply[1] /plī/ n. (pl. **·ies**) **1** a thickness or layer of certain materials, esp. wood or cloth (*three-ply*). **2** a strand of yarn or rope, etc. [ME f. F *pli* f. *plier, pleier* f. L *plicare* fold]

ply[2] /plī/ v. (**·ies, ·ied**) **1** tr. use or wield vigorously (a tool, weapon, etc.). **2** tr. work steadily at (one's business or trade). **3** tr. (foll. by *with*) **a** supply (a person) continuously (with food, drink, etc.). **b** approach repeatedly (with questions, demands, etc.). **4 a** intr. (often foll. by *between*) (of a vehicle, etc.) travel regularly (to and fro between two points). **b** tr. work (a route) in this way. **5** intr. (of a taxi driver, boatman, etc.) attend regularly for custom (*ply for trade*). **6** intr. sail to windward. [ME *plye*, f. APPLY]

ply·wood /plíwʊd/ n. a strong thin board consisting of two or more layers glued and pressed together with the direction of the grain alternating.

PM abbr. **1** Postmaster. **2** postmortem. **3** Prime Minister.

Pm symb. Chem. the element promethium.

p.m. abbr. between noon and midnight. [L *post meridiem*]

PMS abbr. premenstrual syndrome.

pneu·mat·ic /nōōmátik, nyōō–/ adj. **1** of or relating to air or wind. **2** containing or operated by compressed air. **3** connected with or containing air cavities esp. in the bones of birds or in fish. □□ **pneu·mat·i·cal·ly** adv. **pneu·ma·tic·i·ty** /nōōmətísitee, nyōō–/ n. [F *pneumatique* or L *pneumaticus* f. Gk *pneumatikos* f. *pneuma* wind f. *pneō* breathe]

pneu·mat·ic drill n. a drill driven by compressed air, for breaking up a hard surface.

pneu·mat·ics /nōōmátiks, nyōō–/ n.pl. (treated as sing.) the science of the mechanical properties of gases.

pneu·mat·ic trough n. a shallow container used in laboratories to collect gases in jars over the surface of water or mercury.

pneumato- /nōōmətō, nyōō–/ comb. form denoting: **1** air. **2** breath. **3** spirit. [Gk f. *pneuma* (as PNEUMATIC)]

pneu·ma·tol·o·gy /nōōmətóləjee, nyōō–/ n. **1** the branch of theology concerned with the Holy Ghost and other spiritual concepts. **2** archaic psychology. □□ **pneu·ma·to·log·i·cal** /–təlójikəl/ adj.

pneu·mat·o·phore /nōōmátəfawr, nyōō–, nōōmə–, nyōō–/ n. **1** the gaseous cavity of various hydrozoa, such as the Portuguese man-of-war. **2** an aerial root specialized for gaseous exchange found in various plants growing in swampy areas.

pneumo- /nōōmō, nyōō–/ comb. form denoting the lungs. [abbr. of *pneumono-* f. Gk *pneumōn* lung]

pneu·mo·co·ni·o·sis /nōōmōkōneeósis, nyōō–/ n. a lung disease caused by inhalation of dust or small particles. [PNEUMO- + Gk *konis* dust]

pneu·mo·gas·tric /nōōmōgástrik, nyōō–/ adj. of or relating to the lungs and stomach.

pneu·mo·nec·to·my /nōōmənéktəmee, nyōō–/ n. (pl. **·mies**) Surgery the surgical removal of a lung or part of a lung.

pneu·mo·nia /nōōmónyə, nyōō–/ n. a bacterial inflammation of one lung (**single pneumonia**) or both lungs (**double pneumonia**) causing the air sacs to fill with pus and become solid. □□ **pneu·mon·ic** /–mónik/ adj. [L f. Gk f. *pneumōn* lung]

pneu·mo·ni·tis /nōōmənítis, nyōō–/ n. an inflammation of the lungs usu. caused by a virus.

pneu·mo·tho·rax /nōōmōtháwraks, nyōō–/ n. the presence of air or gas in the cavity between the lungs and the chest wall.

PNG abbr. Papua New Guinea.

PO abbr. **1** Post Office. **2** postal order. **3** Petty Officer.

Po symb. Chem. the element polonium.

po /pō/ n. (pl. **pos**) Brit. colloq. a chamber pot.

poach[1] /pōch/ v.tr. **1** cook (an egg) without its shell in or over boiling water. **2** cook (fish, etc.) by simmering in a small amount of liquid. □□ **poach·er** n. [ME f. OF *pochier* f. *poche* POKE[2]]

poach[2] /pōch/ v. **1** tr. (also absol.) catch (game or fish) illegally. **2** intr. (often foll. by *on*) trespass or encroach (on another's property, ideas, etc.). **3** tr. appropriate illicitly or unfairly (a person, thing, idea, etc.). **4** tr. Tennis, etc., take (a shot) in one's partner's portion of the court. **5 a** tr. trample or cut up (turf) with hoofs. **b** intr. (of land) become sodden by being trampled. □□ **poach·er** n. [earlier *poche*, perh. f. F *pocher* put in a pocket (as POACH[1])]

po·chard /póchərd/ n. any duck of the genus *Aythya*, esp. *A. ferina*, the male of which has a bright reddish-brown head and neck and a gray breast. [16th c.: orig. unkn.]

pock /pok/ n. (also **pock·mark**) **1** a small pus-filled spot on the skin, esp. caused by chickenpox or smallpox. **2** a mark or scar left by or resembling this. □□ **pock·y** adj. [OE *poc* f. Gmc]

pock·et /pókit/ n. & v. • n. **1** a small bag sewn into or on clothing, for carrying small articles. **2** a pouchlike compartment in a suitcase, car door, etc. **3** one's financial resources (*it is beyond my pocket*). **4** an isolated group or area (*a few pockets of resistance remain*). **5 a** a cavity in the earth containing ore, esp. gold. **b** a cavity in rock, esp. filled with foreign matter. **6** a pouch at the corner or on the side of a billiard table into which balls are driven. **7** = AIR POCKET. **8** (attrib.) **a** of a suitable size and shape for carrying in a pocket. **b** smaller than the usual size. **9** the area of a baseball mitt or glove around the center of the palm. • v.tr. (**pock·et·ed, pock·et·ing**) **1** put into one's pocket. **2** appropriate, esp. dishonestly. **3** confine as in a pocket. **4** submit to (an injury or affront). **5** conceal or suppress (one's feelings). **6** Billiards, etc., drive (a ball) into a pocket. □ **in pocket 1** having gained in a transaction. **2** (of money) available. **in a person's pocket 1** under a person's control. **2** close to or intimate with a person. **out of pocket** having lost in a transaction. **put one's hand in one's pocket** spend or provide money. □□ **pock·et·a·ble** adj. **pock·et·less** adj. **pock·et·y** adj. (in sense 5 of n.). [ME f. AF *poket(e)* dimin. of *poke* POKE[2]]

pock·et bat·tle·ship n. hist. a warship armored and equipped like, but smaller than, a battleship.

pock·et·book /pókitbʊk/ n. **1** a notebook. **2** a booklike case for papers or money carried in a pocket. **3** a purse or handbag. **4** a paperback or other small book. **5** economic resources.

pock·et bor·ough n. Brit. hist. a borough in which the election of political representatives was controlled by one person or family.

pock·et·ful /pókitfʊl/ n. (pl. **·fuls**) as much as a pocket will hold.

pock·et knife n. a knife with a folding blade or blades, for carrying in the pocket.

pock·et mon·ey n. money for minor expenses.

pock·et ve·to n. an executive veto of a legislative bill by allowing it to go unsigned.

pock·marked adj. bearing marks resembling or left by pocks.

po·co /pókō/ adv. Mus. a little; somewhat (*poco adagio*). [It.]

pod /pod/ n. & v. • n. **1** a long seed vessel esp. of a leguminous plant, e.g., a pea. **2** the cocoon of a silkworm. **3** the case surrounding grasshopper eggs. **4** a narrow-necked eel net. **5** a compartment suspended under an aircraft for equipment, etc. • v. (**pod·ded, pod·ding**) **1** intr. bear or form pods. **2** tr. remove (peas, etc.) from pods. □ **in pod** colloq. pregnant. [back-form. f. dial. *podware, podder* field crops, of unkn. orig.]

po·da·gra /pədágrə, pódəgrə/ n. Med. gout of the foot, esp. the big toe. □□ **po·dag·ral** adj. **po·dag·ric** adj. **po·dag·rous** adj. [L f. Gk *pous podos* foot + *agra* seizure]

pod·dy /pódee/ adj., n., & v. colloq. • adj. **1** Brit. corpulent; obese. **2** Austral. (of a calf, lamb, etc.) fed by hand. • n. (pl. **·dies**) Austral. **1** an unbranded calf. **2** a calf fed by hand. • v.tr. Austral. feed (a young animal) by hand. [E dial. word: f. POD + –Y[1]]

podg·y Brit. var. of PUDGY.

po·di·a·try /pədíətree/ n. Med. care and treatment of the foot. □□ **po·di·a·trist** n. [Gk *pous podos* foot + *iatros* physician]

po·di·um /pódeeəm/ n. (pl. **po·di·ums** or **po·di·a** /–deeə/) **1** a continuous projecting base or pedestal around a room or house, etc. **2** a raised platform around the arena of an amphitheater. **3** a platform or rostrum. [L f. Gk *podion* dimin. of *pous pod-* foot]

pod·zol /pódzol, –zawl/ n. (also **pod·sol** /–sol, –sawl/) a soil with minerals leached from its surface layers into a lower stratum. □□ **pod·zol·ize** v.tr. & intr. [Russ. f. *pod* under, *zola* ashes]

po·em /póəm/ n. **1** a metrical composition, usu. concerned with feeling or imaginative description. **2** an elevated composition in verse or prose. **3** something with poetic qualities (*a poem in stone*). [F *poème* or L *poema* f. Gk *poēma* = *poiēma* f. *poieō* make]

po·e·sy /póəzee, –see/ n. archaic **1** poetry. **2** the art or composition of poetry. [ME f. OF *poesie* ult. f. L *poesis* f. Gk *poēsis* = *poiēsis* making, poetry (as POEM)]

po·et /póit/ n. (fem. **po·et·ess** /póətis/) **1** a writer of poems. **2** a person possessing high powers of imagination or expression, etc. [ME f. OF *poete* f. L *poeta* f. Gk *poētēs* = *poiētēs* maker, poet (as POEM)]

po·et·as·ter /póətástər/ n. a paltry or inferior poet. [mod.L (as POET): see –ASTER]

po·et·ic /pō-étik/ adj. (also **po·et·i·cal** /–tikəl/) **1 a** of or like poetry or poets. **b** written in verse. **2** elevated or sublime in expression. □□ **po·et·i·cal·ly** adv. [F *poétique* f. L *poeticus* f. Gk *poētikos* (as POET)]

po·et·i·cize /pō-étisīz/ v.tr. make (a theme) poetic.

po·et·ic jus·tice n. a well-deserved unforeseen retribution or reward.

po·et·ic li·cense n. a writer's or artist's transgression of established rules for effect.

po·et·ics /pō-étiks/ n. **1** the art of writing poetry. **2** the study of poetry and its techniques.

po·et·ize /póətīz/ v.intr. **1** write or speak in verse or in a poetic style. **2** represent in poetic form. [F *poétiser* (as POET)]

po·et lau·re·ate n. a poet appointed to write poems for official state occasions.

po·et·ry /póətree/ n. **1** the art or work of a poet. **2** poems collectively. **3** a poetic or tenderly pleasing quality. **4** anything compared to poetry. [ME f. med.L *poetria* f. L *poeta* POET, prob. after *geometry*]

Po·ets' Cor·ner n. a part of Westminster Abbey in London where several poets are buried or commemorated.

po·faced /pō-fáyst/ adj. Brit. **1** solemn-faced; humorless. **2** smug. [20th c.: perh. f. PO, infl. by *poker-faced*]

po•go stick /pógō/ *n.* a toy consisting of a spring-loaded stick with rests for the feet, for jumping around on. [20th c.: orig. uncert.]

po•grom /pógrəm, pəgrúm, –gróm/ *n.* an organized massacre (orig. of Jews in Russia). [Russ., = devastation f. *gromit'* destroy]

poign•ant /póynyənt/ *adj.* **1** painfully sharp to the emotions or senses; deeply moving. **2** arousing sympathy. **3** sharp or pungent in taste or smell. **4** pleasantly piquant. **5** *archaic* (of words, etc.) sharp; severe. □□ **poign•ance** *n.* **poign•an•cy** *n.* **poign•ant•ly** *adv.* [ME f. OF, pres. part. of *poindre* prick f. L *pungere*]

poi•ki•lo•therm /póykiləthərm, póykilə–/ *n.* an organism that regulates its body temperature by behavioral means, such as basking or burrowing; a cold-blooded organism (cf. HOMEOTHERM). □□ **poi•ki•lo•ther•mal** *adj.* **poi•ki•lo•ther•mi•a** /–thə́rmeeə/ *n.* **poi•ki•lo•ther•mic** *adj.* **poi•ki•lo•ther•my** *n.* [Gk *poikilos* multicolored, changeable + *thermē* heat]

poi•lu /pwaalóo/ *n. hist.* a French private soldier, esp. as a nickname. [F, lit. hairy f. *poil* hair]

poin•ci•an•a /póynseeánə/ *n.* any tropical tree of the genus *Poinciana*, with bright showy red flowers. [mod.L f. M. de *Poinci*, 17th-c. governor in the West Indies + *-ana* fem. suffix]

poin•set•ti•a /poynséteeə, –sétə/ *n.* a shrub, *Euphorbia pulcherrima*, with large showy scarlet or cream-colored bracts surrounding small yellow flowers. [mod.L f. J. R. *Poinsett*, Amer. diplomat d. 1851]

point /poynt/ *n. & v.* ● *n.* **1** the sharp or tapered end of a tool, weapon, pencil, etc. **2** a tip or extreme end. **3** that which in geometry has position but not magnitude, e.g., the intersection of two lines. **4** a particular place or position (*Bombay and points east; point of contact*). **5 a** a precise or particular moment (*at the point of death*). **b** the critical or decisive moment (*when it came to the point, he refused*). **6** a very small mark on a surface. **7 a** a dot or other punctuation mark, esp. = PERIOD. **b** a dot or small stroke used in Semitic languages to indicate vowels or distinguish consonants. **8** = DECIMAL POINT. **9** a stage or degree in progress or increase (*abrupt to the point of rudeness; at that point we gave up*). **10** a level of temperature at which a change of state occurs (*freezing point*). **11** a single item; a detail or particular (*we differ on these points; it is a point of principle*). **12 a** a unit of scoring in games or of measuring value, etc. **b** an advantage or success in less quantifiable contexts such as an argument or discussion. **c** a unit of weight (2 mg) for diamonds. **d** a unit (of varying value) in quoting the price of stocks, etc. **e** a percentage point. **13 a** (usu. prec. by *the*) the significant or essential thing; what is actually intended or under discussion (*that was the point of the question*). **b** (usu. with *neg.* or *interrog.*; often foll. by *in*) sense or purpose; advantage or value (*saw no point in staying*). **c** (usu. prec. by *the*) a salient feature of a story, joke, remark, etc. (*don't see the point*). **14** a distinctive feature or characteristic (*it has its points; tact is not his good point*). **15** pungency; effectiveness (*their comments lacked point*). **16 a** each of 32 directions marked at equal distances round a compass. **b** the corresponding direction toward the horizon. **17** (usu. in *pl.*) *Brit.* a junction of two railroad lines, with a pair of linked tapering rails that can be moved laterally to allow a train to pass from one line to the other; = SWITCH *n.* 5. **18** *Brit.* = electrical outlet. **19** (usu. in *pl.*) each of a set of electrical contacts in the distributor of a motor vehicle. **20** *Cricket* **a** a fielder on the off side near the batsman. **b** this position. **21** the tip of the toe in ballet. **22** a promontory. **23** the prong of a deer's antler. **24** the extremities of a dog, horse, etc. **25** *Printing* a unit of measurement for type bodies (in the US and UK 0.351 mm, in Europe 0.376 mm). **26** *Heraldry* any of nine particular positions on a shield used for specifying the position of charges, etc. **27** *Mil.* a small leading party of an advanced guard, or the lead soldier's position in a patrol unit. **28** *Naut.* a short piece of cord at the lower edge of a sail for tying up a reef. **29** the act or position of a dog in pointing. ● *v.* **1** (usu. foll. by *to, at*) **a** tr. direct or aim (a finger, weapon, etc.). **b** *intr.* direct attention in a certain direction (*pointed to the house across the road*). **2** *intr.* (foll. by *at, toward*) **a** aim or be directed to. **b** tend toward. **3** *intr.* (foll. by *to*) indicate; be evidence of (*it all points to murder*). **4** *tr.* give point or force to (words or actions). **5** *tr.* fill in or repair the joints of (brickwork) with smoothly finished mortar or cement. **6** *tr.* **a** punctuate. **b** insert points in (written Hebrew, etc.). **c** mark (Psalms, etc.) with signs for chanting. **7** *tr.* sharpen (a pencil, tool, etc.). **8** *tr.* (also *absol.*) (of a dog) indicate the presence of (game) by acting as pointer. □ **at all points** in every part or respect. **at the point of** (often foll. by verbal noun) on the verge of; about to do (the action specified). **beside the point** irrelevant or irrelevantly. **have a point** be correct or effective in one's contention. **in point** apposite; relevant. **in point of fact** see FACT. **make** (or **prove**) **a** (or **one's**) **point** establish a proposition; prove one's contention. **make a point of** (often foll. by verbal noun) insist on; treat or regard as essential. **on** (or **upon**) **the point of** (foll. by verbal noun) about to do (the action specified). **point out** (often foll. by *that* + clause) indicate; show; draw attention to. **point up** emphasize; show as important. **score points off** get the better of in an argument, etc. **see** (or esp. *Brit.* **take**) **a per-**son's point concede that a person has made a valid contention. **to the point** relevant or relevantly. **up to a point** to some extent but not completely. **win on points** *Boxing* win by scoring more points, not by a knockout.

WORD HISTORY point

Middle English: the noun partly from Old French *point*, from Latin *punctum* 'something that is pricked,' giving rise to the senses 'unit, mark, point in space or time'; partly from Old French *pointe*, from Latin *puncta* 'pricking,' giving rise to the senses 'sharp tip, promontory.' The verb derives partly from Old French *pointer* 'sharpen,' but some senses derive from the English noun.

point-blank *adj.* **1 a** (of a shot) aimed or fired horizontally at a range very close to the target. **b** (of a distance or range) very close. **2** (of a remark, question, etc.) blunt; direct. ● *adv.* **1** at very close range. **2** directly, bluntly.

point du•ty *n. Brit.* the duties of a police officer or other official stationed at a junction to control traffic.

point•ed /póyntid/ *adj.* **1** sharpened or tapering to a point. **2** (of a remark, etc.) having point; penetrating; cutting. **3** emphasized; made evident. □□ **point•ed•ly** *adv.* **point•ed•ness** *n.*

point•er /póyntər/ *n.* **1** a thing that points, e.g., the index hand of a gauge, etc. **2** a rod for pointing to features on a map, chart, etc. **3** *colloq.* a hint, clue, or indication. **4 a** a dog of a breed that on scenting game stands rigid looking toward it. **b** this breed. **5** (in *pl.*) two stars in the Big Dipper in line with the pole star.

poin•til•lism /pwántilizəm, póyn–/ *n. Art* a technique of impressionist painting using tiny dots of various pure colors, which become blended in the viewer's eye. □□ **poin•til•list** *n. & adj.* **poin•til•lis•tic** /–lístik/ *adj.* [F *pointillisme* f. *pointiller* mark with dots]

point•ing /póynting/ *n.* **1** cement or mortar used to fill the joints of brickwork, esp. when added externally to a wall to improve its appearance and weatherproofing. **2** the process of producing this.

point lace *n.* thread lace made wholly with a needle.

point•less /póyntlis/ *adj.* **1** without a point. **2** lacking force, purpose, or meaning. **3** (in games) without a point scored. □□ **point•less•ly** *adv.* **point•less•ness** *n.*

point of hon•or *n.* an action or circumstance that affects one's reputation.

point of no re•turn *n.* a point in a journey or enterprise at which it becomes essential or more practical to continue to the end.

point of or•der *n.* a query in a debate, etc., as to whether correct procedure is being followed.

point-of-sale *n.* (usu. *attrib.*) denoting advertising, etc., at the actual location at which goods are retailed.

point of view *n.* **1** a position from which a thing is viewed. **2** a particular way of considering a matter.

points•man /póyntsmən/ *n.* (*pl.* **•men**) *Brit.* **1** a railroad switchman. **2** a police officer or traffic warden directing traffic.

point-to-point *n.* a steeplechase over a marked course for horses used regularly in hunting.

point•y /póyntee/ *adj.* (**point•i•er, point•i•est**) having a noticeably sharp end; pointed.

poise[1] /poyz/ *n. & v.* ● *n.* **1** composure or self-possession of manner. **2** equilibrium; a stable state. **3** carriage (of the head, etc.). ● *v.* **1** *tr.* balance; hold suspended or supported. **2** *tr.* carry (one's head, etc., in a specified way). **3** *intr.* be balanced; hover in the air, etc.

poise[2] /poyz/ *n. Physics* a unit of dynamic viscosity, such that a tangential force of one dyne per square centimeter causes a velocity change one centimeter per second between two parallel planes in a liquid separated by one centimeter. [J. L. M. *Poiseuille*, Fr. physician d. 1869]

WORD HISTORY poise

late Middle English (in the sense 'weight'): from Old French *pois* (noun), *peser* (verb), from an alteration of Latin *pensum* 'weight,' from the verb *pendere* 'weigh.' From the early senses of 'weight' and 'measure of weight' arose the notion of 'equal weight, balance,' leading to the extended senses 'composure' and 'elegant deportment.'

poised /poyzd/ *adj.* **1** composed; self-assured. **2** (often foll. by *for*, or *to* + infin.) ready for action.

poi•son /póyzən/ *n. & v.* ● *n.* **1** a substance that when introduced into or absorbed by a living organism causes death or injury, esp. one that kills by rapid action even in a small quantity. **2** *colloq.* a harmful influence or principle, etc. **3** *Physics & Chem.* a substance that interferes with the normal progress of a nuclear reaction, chain reaction, catalytic reaction, etc. ● *v. tr.* **1** administer poison to (a person or animal). **2** kill or injure or infect with poison. **3** infect (air, water, etc.) with poison. **4** (esp. as **poisoned** *adj.*) treat (a weapon) with poison. **5** corrupt or pervert (a person or mind). **6** spoil or destroy (a person's pleasure, etc.). **7** render (land, etc.) foul and unfit for its purpose by a noxious application, etc. □□ **poi•son•er** *n.*

poi·son·ous adj. **poi·son·ous·ly** adv. [ME f. OF poison, poisonner (as POTION)]

poi·son gas n. = GAS n. 4.

poi·son i·vy n. a N. American climbing plant, Rhus radicans, secreting an irritant oil from its leaves.

poi·son oak n. a bushy plant, Rhus toxicodendron, that secretes an irritant oil from its leaves.

poi·son-pen let·ter n. an anonymous libelous or abusive letter.

poi·son su·mac n. a swamp shrub, Rhus vernix, that secretes an irritant oil.

Pois·son dis·tri·bu·tion /pwaasón/ n. Statistics a discrete frequency distribution that gives the probability of events occurring in a fixed time. [S. D. Poisson, French mathematician d. 1840]

poke[1] /pōk/ v. & n. ●v. 1 (foll. by in, up, down, etc.) a tr. thrust or push with the hand, point of a stick, etc. b intr. be thrust forward. 2 intr. (foll. by at, etc.) make thrusts with a stick, etc. 3 tr. thrust the end of a finger, etc., against. 4 tr. (foll. by in) produce (a hole, etc., in a thing) by poking. 5 tr. thrust forward, esp. obtrusively. 6 tr. stir (a fire) with a poker. 7 intr. a (often foll. by about, along, around) move or act desultorily; putter. b (foll. by about, into) pry; search casually. 8 tr. coarse sl. have sexual intercourse with. 9 tr. (foll. by up) colloq. confine (esp. oneself) in a poky place. ●n. 1 the act or an instance of poking. 2 a thrust or nudge. 3 a punch; a jab. 4 a a projecting brim or front of a woman's bonnet or hat. b (in full poke bonnet) a bonnet having this. □ poke fun at ridicule; tease. poke (or stick) one's nose into colloq. pry or intrude into (esp. a person's affairs). [ME f. MDu. and MLG poken, of unkn. orig.]

poke[2] /pōk/ n. dial. a bag or sack. □ buy a pig in a poke see PIG. [ME f. ONF poke, poque = OF poche: cf. POUCH]

pok·er[1] /pókər/ n. a stiff metal rod with a handle for stirring an open fire.

pok·er[2] /pókər/ n. a card game in which bluff is used as players bet on the value of their hands. [19th c.: orig. unkn.: cf. G pochen to brag, Pochspiel bragging game]

pok·er face n. 1 the impassive countenance appropriate to a poker player. 2 a person with this. □□ **pok·er-faced** adj.

poke·weed /pókweed/ n. a tall hardy American plant, Phytolacca americana, with spikes of cream flowers and purple berries that yield emetics and purgatives. [poke, Algonquian word + WEED]

pok·ey /pókee/ n. sl. prison. [perh. f. POKY]

pok·y /pókee/ adj. (pok·i·er, pok·i·est) 1 (of a room, etc.) small and cramped. 2 slow. □□ **pok·i·ly** adv. **pok·i·ness** n. [POKE[1] (in colloq. sense 'confine')]

Po·lack /pólok, –lak/ n. sl. offens. a person of Polish origin. [F Polaque and G Polack f. Pol. Polak]

po·lar /pólər/ adj. 1 a of or near a pole of the earth or a celestial body, or of the celestial sphere. b (of a species or variety) living in the north polar region. 2 having magnetic polarity. 3 a (of a molecule) having a positive charge at one end and a negative charge at the other. b (of a compound) having electric charges. 4 Geom. of or relating to a pole. 5 directly opposite in character or tendency. 6 colloq. (esp. of weather) very cold. □□ **po·lar·ly** adv. [F polaire or mod.L polaris (as POLE[2])]

po·lar bear n. a white bear, Ursus maritimus, of the Arctic regions.

po·lar bod·y n. a small cell produced from an oocyte during the formation of an ovum, which does not develop further.

po·lar cir·cle n. each of the circles parallel to the equator at a distance of 23° 27′ from either pole.

polar bear

po·lar co·or·di·nates n.pl. a system by which a point can be located with reference to two angles.

po·lar dis·tance n. the angular distance of a point on a sphere from the nearest pole.

polari- /póləri/ comb. form polar. [mod.L polaris (as POLAR)]

po·lar·im·e·ter /pólərímitər/ n. an instrument used to measure the polarization of light or the effect of a substance on the rotation of the plane of polarized light. □□ **po·lar·i·met·ric** /–métrik/ adj. **po·lar·im·e·try** n.

po·lar·i·scope /póláriskōp/ n. = POLARIMETER. □□ **po·lar·i·scop·ic** /–skópik/ adj.

po·lar·i·ty /pəláritee/ n. (pl. ·ties) 1 the tendency of a lodestone, magnetized bar, etc., to point with its extremities to the magnetic poles of the earth. 2 the condition of having two poles with contrary qualities. 3 the state of having two opposite tendencies, opinions, etc. 4 the electrical condition of a body (positive or negative). 5 a magnetic attraction toward an object or person.

po·lar·ize /pólərīz/ v. 1 tr. restrict the vibrations of (a transverse wave, esp. light) to one direction. 2 tr. give magnetic or electric polarity to (a substance or body). 3 tr. reduce the voltage of (an electric cell) by the action of electrolysis products. 4 tr. & intr. divide into

two groups of opposing opinion, etc. □□ **po·lar·iz·a·ble** adj. **po·lar·i·za·tion** n. **po·lar·iz·er** n.

po·lar·og·ra·phy /pólərógrəfee/ n. Chem. the analysis by measurement of current-voltage relationships in electrolysis between mercury electrodes. □□ **po·lar·o·graph·ic** /–ərəgráfik/ adj.

Po·lar·oid /póləroyd/ n. Trademark 1 material in thin plastic sheets that produces a high degree of plane polarization in light passing through it. 2 a a type of camera with internal processing that produces a finished print rapidly after each exposure. b a print made with such a camera. 3 (in pl.) sunglasses with lenses made from Polaroid. [POLARI- + –OID]

po·lar star n. = POLESTAR.

pol·der /póldər/ n. a piece of low-lying land reclaimed from the sea or a river, esp. in the Netherlands. [MDu. polre, Du. polder]

Pole /pōl/ n. 1 a native or national of Poland. 2 a person of Polish descent. [G f. Pol. Polanie, lit. field dwellers f. pole field]

pole[1] /pōl/ n. & v. ●n. 1 a long slender rounded piece of wood or metal, esp. with the end placed in the ground as a support, etc. 2 a wooden shaft fitted to the front of a vehicle and attached to the yokes or collars of draft animals. 3 = PERCH[1] 3. ●v. tr. 1 provide with poles. 2 push or propel (a small boat) with a pole. □ under bare poles Naut. with no sail set. up the pole Brit. sl. 1 crazy; eccentric. 2 in difficulty. [OE pāl ult. f. L palus stake]

pole[2] /pōl/ n. 1 (in full north pole, south pole) a each of the two points in the celestial sphere about which the stars appear to revolve. b each of the extremities of the axis of rotation of the earth or another body. c see MAGNETIC POLE. 2 each of the two opposite points on the surface of a magnet at which magnetic forces are strongest. 3 each of two terminals (positive and negative) of an electric cell or battery, etc. 4 each of two opposed principles or ideas. 5 Geom. each of two points in which the axis of a circle cuts the surface of a sphere. 6 a fixed point to which others are referred. 7 Biol. an extremity of the main axis of any spherical or oval organ. □ be poles apart differ greatly, esp. in nature or opinion. □□ **pole·ward** adj. **pole·wards** adj. & adv. [ME f. L polus f. Gk polos pivot, axis, sky]

▶The spellings are North Pole and South Pole when used as geographical designations.

pole·ax /pólaks/ n. & v. ●n. 1 a battleax. 2 a butcher's ax. ●v.tr. hit or kill with or as if with a poleax. [ME pol(l)ax, –ex f. MDu. pol(l)aex, MLG pol(l)exe (as POLL, AX)]

pole·cat /pólkat/ n. 1 US a skunk. 2 Brit. a small European brownish black fetid flesh-eating mammal, Mustela putorius, of the weasel family. [pole (unexplained) + CAT]

po·lem·ic /pəlémik/ n. & adj. ●n. 1 a controversial discussion. 2 Polit. a verbal or written attack, esp. on a political opponent. ●adj. (also **po·lem·i·cal**) involving dispute; controversial. □□ **po·lem·i·cal·ly** adv. **po·lem·i·cist** /–misist/ n. **po·lem·i·cize** v.tr. **pol·e·mize** /pólimīz/ v.tr. [med.L polemicus f. Gk polemikos f. polemos war]

po·lem·ics /pəlémiks/ n.pl. the art or practice of controversial discussion.

po·len·ta /pəléntə, pō–/ n. mush made of cornmeal, etc. [It. f. L, = pearl barley]

pole po·si·tion n. the most favorable position at the start of a race (orig. next to the inside boundary fence).

pole·star /pólstar/ n. 1 Astron. a star in Ursa Minor now about 1° distant from the celestial north pole. 2 a a thing or principle serving as a guide. b a center of attraction.

pole vault n. (also Brit. pole jump) the sport of vaulting over a high bar with the aid of a long flexible pole held in the hands that gives extra spring. ●v.intr. take part in this sport. □□ **pole-vault·er** n.

po·lice /pəlées/ n. & v. ●n. 1 (usu. prec. by the) the civil force of a government, responsible for maintaining public order. 2 (as pl.) the members of a police force (several hundred police). 3 a force with similar functions of enforcing regulations (military police; transit police). ●v. tr. 1 control (a country or area) by means of police. 2 provide with police. 3 keep order in; control; monitor. [F f. med.L politia POLICY[1]]

po·lice con·sta·ble n. see CONSTABLE.

po·lice dog n. a dog, esp. a German shepherd, used in police work.

po·lice·man /pəléesmən/ n. (pl. ·men; fem. **po·lice·wom·an**, pl. ·wom·en) a member of a police force.

po·lice of·fi·cer n. a policeman or policewoman.

po·lice state n. a totalitarian country controlled by political police supervising the citizens' activities.

po·lice sta·tion n. the office of a local police force.

pol·i·cy[1] /pólisee/ n. (pl. ·cies) 1 a course or principle of action adopted or proposed by a government, party, business, or individual, etc. 2 prudent conduct; sagacity. [ME f. OF policie f. L politia f. Gk politeia citizenship f. politēs citizen f. polis city]

pol·i·cy[2] /pólisee/ n. (pl. ·cies) 1 a contract of insurance. 2 a document containing this. [F police bill of lading, contract of insurance,

f. Prov. *poliss*(*i*)*a* prob. f. med.L *apodissa, apodixa,* f. L *apodixis* f. Gk *apodeixis* evidence, proof (as APO-, *deiknumi* show)]

pol·i·cy·hold·er /póliseehóldər/ *n.* a person or body holding an insurance policy.

po·li·o /póleeō/ *n.* = POLIOMYELITIS. [abbr.]

po·li·o·my·e·li·tis /póleeōmí-ilítis/ *n. Med.* an infectious viral disease that affects the central nervous system and that can cause temporary or permanent paralysis. [mod.L f. Gk *polios* gray + *muelos* marrow]

Po·lish /pólish/ *adj. & n. ● adj.* 1 of or relating to Poland. 2 of the Poles or their language. *● n.* the language of Poland. [POLE + -ISH[1]]

pol·ish /pólish/ *v. & n. ● v.* 1 *tr. & intr.* make or become smooth or glossy esp. by rubbing. 2 (esp. as **polished** *adj.*) refine or improve; add finishing touches to. *● n.* 1 a substance used for polishing. 2 smoothness or glossiness produced by friction. 3 the act or an instance of polishing. 4 refinement or elegance of manner, conduct, etc. □ **polish off** 1 finish (esp. food) quickly. 2 *colloq.* kill; murder. **polish up** revise or improve (a skill, etc.). □□ **pol·ish·a·ble** *adj.* **pol·ish·er** *n.* [ME f. OF *polir* f. L *polire* *polit–*]

SYNONYM TIP polish

GLOSS, LUSTER, SHEEN. All of these words refer to a smooth, shining, or bright surface that reflects light. If this surface is produced by rubbing or friction, the correct word is **polish** (*the car's mirrorlike polish was the result of regular waxing and buffing*). **Gloss,** on the other hand, suggests the hard smoothness associated with lacquered, varnished, or enameled surfaces (*a high-gloss paint*). **Luster** is associated with the light reflected from the surfaces of certain materials, such as silk or pearl (*the moon on the breast of the new-fallen snow gave a luster of midday to objects below*). **Sheen** describes a glistening or radiant brightness that is also associated with specific materials (*her hair had a rich, velvety sheen*).

Pol·ish no·ta·tion *n. Math.* a system of formula notation without brackets and punctuation.

po·lit·bu·ro /pólitbyoʻorō, pəlít–/ *n.* (*pl.* **·ros**) the principal policy-making committee of a Communist party, esp. in the former USSR. [Rus. *politbyuro* f. *politícheskoe byuró* political bureau]

po·lite /pəlít/ *adj.* (**po·lit·er, po·lit·est**) 1 having good manners; courteous. 2 cultivated; cultured. 3 refined; elegant (*polite letters*). □□ **po·lite·ly** *adv.* **po·lite·ness** *n.* [L *politus* (as POLISH)]

po·li·tesse /pólités/ *n.* formal politeness. [F f. It. *politezza, pulitezza* f. *pulito* polite]

pol·i·tic /pólitik/ *adj. & v. ● adj.* 1 (of an action) judicious; expedient. 2 (of a person:) **a** prudent; sagacious. **b** scheming; sly. 3 political (now only in *body politic*). *● v.intr.* (**pol·i·ticked, pol·i·tick·ing**) engage in politics. □□ **pol·i·tic·ly** *adv.* [ME f. OF *politique* f. L *politicus* f. Gk *politikos* f. *politēs* citizen f. *polis* city]

po·lit·i·cal /pəlítikəl/ *adj.* 1 **a** of or concerning government, or public affairs generally. **b** of, relating to, or engaged in politics. **c** belonging to or forming part of a civil administration. 2 having an organized form of society or government. 3 taking or belonging to a side in politics or in controversial matters. 4 relating to or affecting interests of status or authority in an organization rather than matters of principle (*a political decision*). □□ **po·lit·i·cal·ly** *adv.* [L *politicus* (as POLITIC)]

po·lit·i·cal ac·tion com·mit·tee *n.* a permanent organization that collects and distributes funds for political purposes. ¶ Abbr.: PAC.

po·lit·i·cal a·sy·lum *n.* protection given by a government to a political refugee from another country.

po·lit·i·cal cor·rect·ness *n.* 1 avoidance of forms of expression and action that exclude or marginalize sexual, racial, and cultural minorities. 2 advocacy of this.

po·lit·i·cal e·con·o·mist *n.* a student of or expert in political economy.

po·lit·i·cal e·con·o·my *n.* the study of the economic aspects of government.

po·lit·i·cal ge·og·ra·phy *n.* the study of the boundaries and the possessions of nations.

po·lit·i·cal·ly cor·rect *adj.* (also **po·lit·i·cal·ly in·cor·rect**) in (or out of) conformance with political correctness.

po·lit·i·cal pris·on·er *n.* a person imprisoned for political beliefs or actions.

po·lit·i·cal sci·ence *n.* the study of systems of government. □□ **po·lit·i·cal sci·en·tist** *n.*

po·li·ti·cian /pólitíshən/ *n.* 1 a person engaged in or concerned with politics, esp. as a practitioner. 2 a person skilled in politics. 3 *derog.* a person with self-interested political concerns.

po·lit·i·cize /pəlítisīz/ *v.* 1 *tr.* **a** give a political character to. **b** make politically aware. 2 *intr.* engage in or talk politics. □□ **po·lit·i·ci·za·tion** *n.*

po·lit·i·co /pəlítikō/ *n.* (*pl.* **·cos**) *colloq.* a politician or political enthusiast. [Sp. or It. (as POLITIC)]

politico- /pəlítikō/ *comb. form* 1 politically. 2 political and (*politico-social*). [Gk *politikos*: see POLITIC]

pol·i·tics /pólitiks/ *n.pl.* 1 (treated as *sing.* or *pl.*) **a** the art and science of government. **b** public life and affairs as involving authority and government. 2 (usu. treated as *pl.*) **a** a particular set of ideas, principles, or commitments in politics (*what are their politics?*). **b** activities concerned with the acquisition or exercise of authority or government. **c** an organizational process or principle affecting authority, status, etc. (*the politics of the decision*).

pol·i·ty /pólitee/ *n.* (*pl.* **·ties**) 1 a form or process of civil government or constitution. 2 an organized society; a nation as a political entity. [L *politia* f. Gk *politeia* f. *politēs* citizen f. *polis* city]

pol·ka /pólkə, pólkə/ *n. & v. ● n.* 1 a lively dance of Bohemian origin in duple time. 2 the music for this. *● v.intr.* (**pol·kas, pol·kaed** /–kəd/ or **pol·ka'd, pol·ka·ing** /–kəing/) dance the polka. [F and G f. Czech *půlka* half-step f. *půl* half]

pol·ka dot *n.* a round dot as one of many forming a regular pattern on a textile fabric, etc.

poll /pōl/ *n. & v. ● n.* 1 **a** the process of voting at an election. **b** the counting of votes at an election. **c** the result of voting. **d** the number of votes recorded (*a heavy poll*). **e** (also **polls**) place for voting. 2 = GALLUP POLL, OPINION POLL. 3 **a** a human head. **b** the part of this on which hair grows (*flaxen poll*). 4 a hornless animal, esp. one of a breed of hornless cattle. *● v.* 1 *tr.* **a** take the vote or votes of. **b** (in *passive*) have one's vote taken. **c** (of a candidate) receive (so many votes). **d** give (a vote). 2 *tr.* record the opinion of (a person or group) in an opinion poll. 3 *intr.* give one's vote. 4 *tr.* cut off the top of (a tree or plant), esp. make a pollard of. 5 *tr.* (esp. as **polled** *adj.*) cut the horns off (cattle). 6 *tr. Computing* check the status of (a computer system) at intervals. □□ **poll·ee** /pōleé/ *n.* (in sense 2 of *n.*). **poll·ster** *n.* [ME, perh. f. LG or Du.]

pol·lack /pólək/ *n.* (also **pol·lock**) a European marine fish, *Pollachius pollachius,* with a characteristic protruding lower jaw, used for food. [earlier (Sc.) *podlock*: orig. unkn.]

pol·lan /pólən/ *n.* a freshwater fish, *Coregonus pollan,* found in Irish lakes. [perh. f. Ir. *poll* deep water]

pol·lard /pólərd/ *n. & v. ● n.* 1 **a** an animal that has lost or cast its horns. **b** an ox, sheep, or goat of a hornless breed. 2 a tree whose branches have been cut off to encourage the growth of new young branches, esp. a riverside willow. 3 **a** the bran sifted from flour. **b** a fine bran containing some flour. *● v.tr.* make (a tree) a pollard. [POLL + -ARD]

pol·len /pólən/ *n.* the fine dustlike grains discharged from the male part of a flower containing the gamete that fertilizes the female ovule. □□ **pol·len·less** *adj.* **pol·lin·ic** /pəlínik/ *adj.* [L *pollen pollinis* fine flour, dust]

pol·len a·nal·y·sis *n.* = PALYNOLOGY.

pol·len count *n.* an index of the amount of pollen in the air, published esp. for the benefit of those allergic to it.

pol·lex /póleks/ *n.* (*pl.* **pol·li·ces** /–liseez/) the innermost digit of a forelimb, usu. the thumb in primates. [L, = thumb or big toe]

pol·lie var. of POLLY.

pol·li·nate /pólinayt/ *v.tr.* (also *absol.*) sprinkle (a stigma) with pollen. □□ **pol·li·na·tion** /–náyshən/ *n.* **pol·li·na·tor** *n.*

pol·ling /póling/ *n.* the registering or casting of votes.

pol·ling booth *n.* a compartment in which a voter stands to mark a paper ballot or use a voting machine.

pol·ling day *n.* the day of a local or general election.

pol·ling place *n.* a building where voting takes place during an election.

pol·lin·ic see POLLEN.

pol·lin·if·er·ous /pólinífərəs/ *adj.* bearing or producing pollen.

pol·li·wog /póleewog/ *n.* (also **pol·ly·wog**) *dial.* a tadpole. [earlier *polwigge, polwygle* f. POLL + WIGGLE]

pol·lock var. of POLLACK.

poll tax *n. hist.* a tax levied on every adult.

pol·lute /pəloʻot/ *v.tr.* 1 contaminate or defile (the environment). 2 make foul or filthy. 3 destroy the purity or sanctity of. □□ **pol·lu·tant** *adj. & n.* **pol·lut·er** *n.* **pol·lu·tion** *n.* [ME f. L *polluere pollut–*]

pol·ly /pólee/ *n.* (also **pol·lie**) (*pl.* **·lies**) *Austral.* a politician. [abbr.]

Pol·ly·an·na /póleeánə/ *n.* a cheerful optimist; an excessively cheerful person. □□ **Pol·ly·an·na·ish** *adj.* **Pol·ly·an·na·ism** *n.* [character in a novel (1913) by E. Porter]

pol·ly·wog var. of POLLIWOG.

po·lo /pólō/ *n.* a game of Asian origin played on horseback with a long-handled mallet. [Balti, = ball]

pol·o·naise /pólənáyz, pó–/ *n. & adj. ● n.* 1 a dance of Polish origin in triple time. 2 the music for this. 3 *hist.* a woman's dress consisting of a bodice and a draped skirt open from the waist downward to show an underskirt. *● adj.* cooked in a Polish style. [F, fem. of *polonais* Polish f. med.L *Polonia* Poland]

po·lo-neck *n. Brit.* a high round turned-over collar; a turtleneck.

po·lo·ni·um /pəlóneeəm/ *n. Chem.* a rare radioactive metallic element, occurring naturally in uranium ores. ¶ Symb.: **Po**. [F & mod.L f. med.L *Polonia* Poland (the discoverer's native country) + -IUM]

po·lo shirt *n.* a pullover shirt, usu. of knit fabric, with a rounded neckband or a turnover collar.

po·lo stick *n.* a mallet for playing polo.

pol·ter·geist /póltərgīst/ *n.* a noisy mischievous ghost, esp. one manifesting itself by physical damage. [G f. *poltern* create a disturbance + *Geist* GHOST]

pol·troon /poltroˊoͤn/ *n.* a spiritless coward. □□ **pol·troon·er·y** *n.* [F *poltron* f. It. *poltrone* perh. f. *poltro* sluggard]

pol·y /pólee/ *n.* (*pl.* **pol·ys**) esp. *Brit. colloq.* polytechnic. [abbr.]

poly-¹ /pólee/ *comb. form* denoting many or much. [Gk *polu-* f. *polus* much, *polloi* many]

poly-² /pólee/ *comb. form Chem.* polymerized (*polyunsaturated*). [POLYMER]

pol·y·a·del·phous /póleeədélfəs/ *adj. Bot.* having numerous stamens grouped into three or more bundles.

pol·y·am·ide /póleeámīd/ *n. Chem.* any of a class of condensation polymers produced from the interaction of an amino group of one molecule and a carboxylic acid group of another, and which includes many synthetic fibers such as nylon.

pol·y·an·dry /póleeandree/ *n.* **1** polygamy in which a woman has more than one husband. **2** *Bot.* the state of having numerous stamens. □□ **pol·y·an·drous** /-ándrəs/ *adj.* [POLY-¹ + *andry* f. Gk *anēr andros* male]

▶See note at POLYGAMY.

pol·y·an·thus /póleeánthəs/ *n.* (*pl.* **pol·y·an·thus·es**) **1** a hybridized primrose, *Primula polyantha.* **2** a narcissus, *Narcissus tazetta,* with small white or yellow flowers. [mod.L, formed as POLY-¹ + Gk *anthos* flower]

pol·y·car·bon·ate /póleekaˊarbənayt/ *n.* any of a class of polymers in which the units are linked through a carbonate group, mainly used as molding materials.

pol·y·chaete /pólikeet/ *n.* any aquatic annelid worm of the class Polychaeta, including lugworms and ragworms, having numerous bristles on the fleshy lobes of each body segment. □□ **pol·y·chae·tan** /-keˊet'n/ *adj.* **pol·y·chae·tous** /-keˊetəs/ *adj.*

pol·y·chro·mat·ic /póleekrōmátik/ *adj.* **1** many-colored. **2** (of radiation) containing more than one wavelength. □□ **pol·y·chro·ma·tism** /-krōmətizəm/ *n.*

pol·y·chrome /póleekrōm/ *adj. & n.* ● *adj.* painted, printed, or decorated in many colors. ● *n.* **1** a work of art in several colors, esp. a colored statue. **2** varied coloring. □□ **pol·y·chro·mic** /-krómik/ *adj.* **pol·y·chro·mous** /-krómas/ *adj.* [F f. Gk *polukhrōmos* as POLY-¹, *khrōma* color]

pol·y·chro·my /póleekrómee/ *n.* the art of painting in several colors, esp. as applied to ancient pottery, architecture, etc. [F *polychromie* (as POLYCHROME)]

pol·y·clin·ic /póleeklinik/ *n.* a clinic devoted to various diseases; a general hospital.

pol·y·crys·tal·line /póleekríst'lin, –līn, –leen/ *adj.* (of a solid substance) consisting of many crystalline parts at various orientations, e.g., a metal casting.

pol·y·cy·clic /póleesíklik, –sík–/ *adj. Chem.* having more than one ring of atoms in the molecule.

pol·y·dac·tyl /póleedáktil/ *adj. & n.* ● *adj.* (of an animal) having more than five fingers or toes. ● *n.* a polydactyl animal.

pol·y·es·ter /pólee-éstər/ *n.* any of a group of condensation polymers used to form synthetic fibers or to make resins.

pol·y·eth·ene /pólee-étheen/ *n. Chem.* = POLYETHYLENE.

pol·y·eth·yl·ene /pólee-éthileen/ *n. Chem.* a tough light thermoplastic polymer of ethylene, usu. translucent and flexible or opaque and rigid, used for packaging and insulating materials. Also called **polyethene** or **polythene**.

po·lyg·a·mous /pəlígəməs/ *adj.* **1** having more than one wife or husband at the same time. **2** having more than one mate. **3** bearing

some flowers with stamens only, some with pistils only, some with both, on the same or different plants. □□ **pol·y·gam·ic** /póligá mik/ *adj.* **po·lyg·a·mist** /–gəmist/ *n.* **po·lyg·a·mous·ly** *adv.* [Gk *polugamos* (as POLY-¹, *–gamos* marrying)]

po·lyg·a·my /pəlígəmee/ *n.* the practice of having more than one spouse at a time.

▶**Polygamy,** meaning 'having more than one spouse,' may apply to men or women. **Polygyny** is specifically the practice of having more than one wife, and **polyandry** is the term for having more than one husband.

pol·y·gene /póleejeen/ *n. Biol.* each of a group of independent genes that collectively affect a characteristic.

pol·y·gen·e·sis /póleejénisis/ *n.* the (usu. postulated) origination of a race or species from several independent stocks. □□ **pol·y·gen·e·tic** /–jinétik/ *adj.*

po·lyg·e·ny /pəlíjənee/ *n.* the theory that the human species originated from several independent pairs of ancestors. □□ **po·lyg·e·nism** *n.* **po·lyg·e·nist** *n.*

pol·y·glot /póleeglot/ *adj. & n.* ● *adj.* **1** of many languages. **2** (of a person) speaking or writing several languages. **3** (of a book, esp. the Bible) with the text translated into several languages. ● *n.* **1** a polyglot person. **2** a polyglot book, esp. a Bible. □□ **pol·y·glot·tal** *adj.* **pol·y·glot·tic** *adj.* **pol·y·glot·ism** *n.* **pol·y·glot·tism** *n.* [F *polyglotte* f. Gk *poluglōttos* (as POLY-¹, *glōtta* tongue)]

pol·y·gon /póleegon/ *n.* a plane figure with many (usu. a minimum of three) sides and angles. □□ **po·lyg·o·nal** /pəlígənəl/ *adj.* [LL *polygonum* f. Gk *polugōnon* (neut. adj.) (as POLY-¹ + *–gōnos* angled)]

pol·y·gon of forc·es *n.* a polygon that represents by the length and direction of its sides all the forces acting on a body or point.

po·lyg·o·num /pəlígənəm/ *n.* any plant of the genus *Polygonum,* with small bell-shaped flowers. Also called **knotgrass** or **knotweed.** [mod.L f. Gk *polugonon*]

pol·y·graph /póleegraf/ *n.* a machine designed to detect and record changes in physiological characteristics (e.g., rates of pulse and breathing), used esp. as a lie-detector.

po·lyg·y·ny /pəlíjinee/ *n.* polygamy in which a man has more than one wife. □□ **po·lyg·y·nous** /pəlíjinəs/ *adj.* [POLY-¹ + *gyny* f. Gk *gunē* woman]

▶See note at polygamy.

pol·y·he·dron /póleeheˊedrən/ *n.* (*pl.* **pol·y·he·dra** /–drə/) a solid figure with many (usu. more than six) faces. □□ **pol·y·he·dral** *adj.* **pol·y·he·dric** *adj.* [Gk *poluedron* neut. of *poluedros* (as POLY-¹, *hedra* base)]

pol·y·his·tor /póleehístər/ *n.* = POLYMATH.

pol·y·math /póleemath/ *n.* **1** a person of much or varied learning. **2** a great scholar. □□ **pol·y·math·ic** /–máthik/ *adj.* **po·lym·a·thy** /pəlíməthee/ *n.* [Gk *polumathēs* (as POLY-¹, *math-* stem *manthanō* learn)]

pol·y·mer /pólimər/ *n.* a compound composed of one or more large molecules that are formed from repeated units of smaller molecules. □□ **pol·y·mer·ic** /–mérik/ *adj.* **po·lym·er·ism** *n.* **po·lym·er·ize** *v.intr. & tr.* **po·lym·er·i·za·tion** *n.* [G f. Gk *polumeros* having many parts (as POLY-¹, *meros* share)]

po·lym·er·ous /pəlíməros/ *adj. Biol.* having many parts.

pol·y·mor·phism /póleemáwrfizəm/ *n.* **1 a** *Biol.* the existence of various forms in the successive stages of the development of an organism. **b** = PLEOMORPHISM. **2** *Chem.* = ALLOTROPY. □□ **pol·y·mor·phic** *adj.* **pol·y·mor·phous** *adj.*

Pol·y·ne·sian /póleeneˊezhən/ *adj. & n.* ● *adj.* of or relating to Polynesia, a group of Pacific islands including New Zealand, Hawaii, Samoa, etc. ● *n.* **1 a** native of Polynesia. **b** a person of Polynesian descent. **2** the family of languages including Maori, Hawaiian, and Samoan. [as POLY-¹ + Gk *nēsos* island]

pol·y·neu·ri·tis /póleenooͤrítis, nyoͤoͤ–/ *n.* any disorder that affects many of the peripheral nerves. □□ **pol·y·neu·rit·ic** /–rítik/ *adj.*

pol·y·no·mi·al /pólinómeeəl/ *n. & adj. Math.* ● *n.* an expression of more than two algebraic terms, esp. the sum of several terms that contain different powers of the same variable(s). ● *adj.* of or being a polynomial. [POLY-¹ after *multinomial*]

po·lyn·ya /pəlínyə/ *n.* a stretch of open water surrounded by ice, esp. in the Arctic seas. [Russ. f. *pole* field]

pol·yp /pólip/ *n.* **1** *Zool.* an individual coelenterate. **2** *Med.* a small usu. benign growth protruding from a mucous membrane. [F *polype,* ult. f. Gk *pōlupos* cuttlefish, polyp (as POLY-¹, *pous podos* foot)]

pol·y·par·y /póliperee/ *n.* (*pl.* **·ies**) the common stem or support of a colony of polyps. [mod.L *polyparium* (as POLYP)]

pol·y·pep·tide /póleepéptīd/ *n. Biochem.* a peptide formed by the combination of about ten or more amino acids. [G *Polypeptid* (as POLY-², PEPTONE)]

po·lyph·a·gous /pəlífəgəs/ *adj. Zool.* able to feed on various kinds of food.

pol·y·phase /pólifayz/ *adj. Electr.* (of a device or circuit) designed to supply or use simultaneously several alternating currents of the same voltage but with different phases.

pol·y·phone /póleefōn/ n. Phonet. a symbol or letter that represents several different sounds.

pol·y·phon·ic /póleefónik/ adj. **1** Mus. (of vocal music, etc.) in two or more relatively independent parts; contrapuntal. **2** Phonet. (of a letter, etc.) representing more than one sound. □□ **pol·y·phon·i·cal·ly** adv. [Gk poluphōnos (as POLY-1, phōnē voice, sound)]

po·lyph·o·ny /pəlifənee/ n. (pl. **-nies**) **1** Mus. **a** polyphonic style in musical composition; counterpoint. **b** a composition written in this style. **2** Philol. the symbolization of different vocal sounds by the same letter or character. □□ **po·lyph·o·nous** adj.

pol·y·ploid /póleeployd/ n. & adj. Biol. ● n. a nucleus or organism that contains more than two sets of chromosomes. ● adj. of or being a polyploid. □□ **pol·y·ploi·dy** n. [G (as POLY-1, –PLOID)]

pol·y·pod /póleepod/ adj. & n. Zool. ● adj. having many feet. ● n. a polypod animal. [F polypode (adj.) f. Gk (as POLYP)]

pol·y·po·dy /póleepōdee/ n. (pl. **-dies**) any fern of the genus Polypodium, usu. found in woods growing on trees, walls, and stones. [ME f. L polypodium f. Gk polupodion (as POLYP)]

pol·yp·oid /póleepoyd/ adj. of or like a polyp. □□ **pol·yp·ous** /–pəs/ adj.

pol·y·pro·pene /póleeprópeen/ n. = POLYPROPYLENE.

pol·y·pro·pyl·ene /póleeprópileen/ n. Chem. any of various polymers of propylene including thermoplastic materials used for films, fibers, or molding materials. Also called **polypropene**.

pol·y·sac·cha·ride /póleesákərīd/ n. any of a group of carbohydrates whose molecules consist of long chains of monosaccharides.

pol·y·se·my /póleeséemee, pəlísəmee/ n. Philol. the existence of many meanings (of a word, etc.). □□ **pol·y·se·mic** /–séemik/ adj. **pol·y·se·mous** /–séeməs, –səməs/ adj. [POLY-1 + Gk sēma sign]

pol·y·sty·rene /póleestíreen/ n. a thermoplastic polymer of styrene, usu. hard and colorless or expanded with a gas to produce a lightweight rigid white substance, used for insulation and in packaging.

pol·y·syl·lab·ic /póleesilábik/ adj. **1** (of a word) having many syllables. **2** characterized by the use of words of many syllables. □□ **pol·y·syl·lab·i·cal·ly** adv.

pol·y·syl·la·ble /póleesíləbəl/ n. a polysyllabic word.

pol·y·tech·nic /póleetéknik/ n. & adj. ● n. an institution of higher education offering courses in many esp. vocational or technical subjects. ● adj. dealing with or devoted to various vocational or technical subjects. [F polytechnique f. Gk polutekhnos (as POLY-1 tekhnē art)]

pol·y·tet·ra·fluor·o·eth·y·lene /pólitétrəflóorō-éthileen, –fláwr–/ n. Chem. a tough translucent polymer resistant to chemicals and used to coat cooking utensils, etc. ¶ Abbr.: **PTFE**. [POLY-2 + TETRA- + FLUORO- + ETHYLENE]

pol·y·the·ism /póleetheéizm/ n. the belief in or worship of more than one god. □□ **pol·y·the·ist** n. **pol·y·the·is·tic** adj. [F polythéisme f. Gk polutheos of many gods (as POLY-1, theos god)]

pol·y·thene /póleetheen/ n. Brit. = POLYETHYLENE.

pol·y·to·nal·i·ty /póleetōnálitee/ n. Mus. the simultaneous use of two or more keys in a composition. □□ **pol·y·to·nal** /–tōnəl/ adj.

pol·y·un·sat·u·rat·ed /póleeunsáchərəytid/ adj. Chem. (of a compound, esp. a fat or oil molecule) containing several double or triple bonds and therefore capable of further reaction.

pol·y·u·re·thane /póleeyōorəthayn/ n. any polymer containing the urethane group, used in adhesives, paints, plastics, foams, etc.

pol·y·va·lent /póleeváylənt/ adj. Chem. having a valence of more than two, or several valencies. □□ **pol·y·va·lence** n.

pol·y·vi·nyl ac·e·tate /póleevínil/ n. Chem. a soft plastic polymer used in paints and adhesives. ¶ Abbr.: **PVA**.

pol·y·vi·nyl chlo·ride /póleevínil/ n. a tough transparent solid polymer of vinyl chloride, easily colored and used for a wide variety of products including pipes, flooring, etc. ¶ Abbr.: **PVC**.

pol·y·zo·an /póleezṓən/ n. = BRYOZOAN.

pom /pom/ n. Brit. a Pomeranian dog. [abbr.]

pom·ace /púmis, póm–/ n. **1** the mass of crushed apples in cider making before or after the juice is pressed out. **2** the refuse of fish, etc., after the oil has been extracted, generally used as a fertilizer. [ME f. med.L pomacium cider f. L pomum apple]

po·made /pōmáyd, –maád/ n. & v. ● n. scented dressing for the hair and the skin of the head. ● v.tr. anoint with pomade. [F pommade f. It. pomata f. med.L f. L pomum apple (from which it was orig. made)]

po·man·der /pómandər, pōmán–/ n. **1** a ball of mixed aromatic substances placed in a cupboard, etc., or hist. carried in a box, bag, etc., as a protection against infection. **2** a (usu. spherical) container for this. **3** a spiced orange, etc., similarly used. [earlier pom(e)amber f. AF f. OF pome d'embre f. med.L pomum de ambra apple of ambergris]

po·ma·tum /pōmáytəm, pəmaát–/ n. & v.tr. = POMADE. [mod.L f. L pomum apple]

pome /pōm/ n. a firm-fleshed fruit in which the carpels from the central core enclose the seeds, e.g., the apple, pear, and quince. □□ **po·mif·er·ous** /pəmífərəs/ adj. [ME f. OF ult. f. poma pl. of L pomum fruit, apple]

pome·gran·ate /pómigranit, pómgranit, púm–/ n. **1 a** an orange-sized fruit with a tough reddish outer skin and containing many seeds in a red pulp. **b** the tree bearing this fruit, Punica granatum, native to N. Africa and W. Asia. **2** an ornamental representation of a pomegranate. [ME f. OF pome grenate (as POME, L granatum having many seeds f. granum seed)]

pom·e·lo /pómələō/ n. (pl. **-los**) **1** = SHADDOCK. **2** = GRAPEFRUIT. [19th c.: orig. unkn.]

Pom·er·a·ni·an /póməráyneeən/ n. **1** a small dog with long silky hair, a pointed muzzle, and pricked ears. **2** this breed. [Pomerania in Germany and Poland]

pom·fret /pómfrit, púm–/ n. **1** any of various fish of the family Stromateidae of the Indian and Pacific Oceans. **2** a dark-colored deep-bodied marine fish, Brama brama, used as food. [app. f. Port. pampo]

po·mi·cul·ture /pómikulchər/ n. fruit-growing. [L pomum fruit + CULTURE]

pom·mel /pómǝl, púm–/ n. & v. ● n. **1** a knob, esp. at the end of a sword hilt. **2** the upward projecting front part of a saddle. ● v.tr. (**pom·meled, pom·mel·ing** or **pom·melled, pom·mel·ling**) = PUMMEL. [ME f. OF pomel f. Rmc pomellum (unrecorded), dimin. of L pomum fruit, apple]

pom·mel horse n. a vaulting horse fitted with a pair of curved handgrips.

po·mol·o·gy /pōmólǝjee/ n. the science of fruit-growing. □□ **po·mo·log·i·cal** /–məlójikəl/ adj. **po·mol·o·gist** n. [L pomum fruit + –LOGY]

pomp /pomp/ n. **1** a splendid display; splendor. **2** (often in pl.) vainglory (the pomps and vanities of this wicked world). [ME f. OF pompe f. L pompa f. Gk pompē procession, pomp f. pempō send]

pom·pa·dour /pómpədawr, –dōor/ n. **1** a man's hairstyle in which the hair is combed up from the forehead without a part. **2** a woman's hairstyle in which the hair in turned back off the forehead into a roll. [f. Marquise de Pompadour, the mistress of Louis XV of France d. 1764]

pom·pa·no /pómpǝnō/ n. (pl. **-nos**) any of various fish of the family Carangidae or Stromateidae of the Atlantic and Pacific Oceans, used as food. [Sp. pámpano]

pom·pom¹ /pómpom/ n. an automatic quick-firing gun esp. on a ship. [imit.]

pom·pom² /pómpom/ n. (also **pom·pon** /–pon/) **1** an ornamental ball or tuft of wool, silk, or ribbons, often worn on hats or clothing. **2** (often attrib.) (usu. **pompon**) a dahlia or chrysanthemum with small tightly-clustered petals. [F, of unkn. orig.]

pomp·ous /pómpəs/ adj. **1** self-important, affectedly grand or solemn. **2** (of language) pretentious; unduly grand in style. **3** archaic magnificent; splendid. □□ **pom·pos·i·ty** /pompósitee/ n. (pl. **-ties**) **pomp·ous·ly** adv. **pomp·ous·ness** n. [ME f. OF pompeux f. LL pomposus (as POMP)]

ponce /pons/ n. & v. Brit. sl. ● n. **1** a man who lives off a prostitute's earnings; a pimp. **2** offens. a homosexual; an effeminate man. ● v.intr. act as a ponce. □ **ponce about** move about effeminately or ineffectually. □□ **pon·cey** adj. (also **pon·cy**) (in sense 2 of n.). [perh. f. POUNCE¹]

pon·cho /pónchō/ n. (pl. **-chos**) **1** a S. American cloak made of a blanketlike piece of cloth with a slit in the middle for the head. **2** a garment in this style, esp. one waterproof and worn as a raincoat. [S.Amer. Sp., f. Araucan]

pond /pond/ n. & v. ● n. **1** a fairly small body of still water formed naturally or by hollowing or embanking. **2** joc. the sea, esp. the Atlantic Ocean. ● v. **1** tr. hold back; dam up (a stream, etc.). **2** intr. form a pond. [ME var. of POUND³]

pon·der /póndər/ v. **1** tr. weigh mentally; think over; consider. **2** intr. (usu. foll. by on, over) think; muse. [ME f. OF ponderer f. L ponderare f. pondus –eris weight]

pon·der·a·ble /póndərəbəl/ adj. having appreciable weight or significance. □□ **pon·der·a·bil·i·ty** /–bílitee/ n. [LL ponderabilis (as PONDER)]

pon·der·a·tion /póndəráyshən/ n. literary the act or an instance of weighing, balancing, or considering. [L ponderatio (as PONDER)]

pon·der·o·sa /póndərṓsə/ n. **1** a N. American pine tree, Pinus ponderosa. **2** the timber of this tree. [mod.L, fem. of L ponderosus: see PONDEROUS]

pon·der·ous /póndərəs/ adj. **1** heavy; unwieldy. **2** laborious. **3** (of style, etc.) dull; tedious. □□ **pon·der·os·i·ty** /–rósitee/ n. **pon·der·ous·ly** adv. **pon·der·ous·ness** n. [ME f. L ponderosus f. pondus –eris weight]

poncho

pond·weed /póndweed/ n. any of various aquatic plants, esp. of the genus *Potamogeton*, growing in still or running water.

pone[1] /pōn/ n. *US dial.* **1** unleavened cornbread, esp. as made by Native Americans. **2** a fine light bread made with milk, eggs, etc. **3** a cake or loaf of this. [Algonquian, = bread]

pone[2] /pōne, pōn/ n. the dealer's opponent in two-handed card games. [L, 2nd sing. imper. of *ponere* place]

pong /pong/ n. & v. *Brit. colloq.* ●n. an unpleasant smell. ●v.intr. stink. □□ **pon·gy** /póngee/ adj. (**pong·i·er, pong·i·est**). [20th c.: orig. unkn.]

pon·gee /ponjée, pun–, pónjee/ n. **1** a soft usu. unbleached type of Chinese silk fabric. **2** an imitation of this in cotton, etc. [perh. f. Chin. dial. *punchī* own loom, i.e., homemade]

pon·gid /pónjid/ n. & adj. ●n. any ape of the family Pongidae, including gorillas, chimpanzees, and orangutans. ● adj. of or relating to this family. [mod.L *Pongidae* f. *Pongo* the genus name: see PONGO 1]

pon·go /pónggō/ n. (pl. **·gos**) **1** an orangutan. **2** *Naut. sl.* a soldier. [Congolese *mpongo*, orig. of African apes]

pon·iard /pónyərd/ n. a small slim dagger. [F *poignard* f. OF *poignal* f. med.L *pugnale* f. L *pugnus* fist]

pons /ponz/ n. (pl. **pon·tes** /pónteez/) *Anat.* (in full **pons Varolii** /vərőleeī/ the part of the brain stem that links the medulla oblongata and the thalamus. [L, = bridge: *Varolii* f. C. *Varoli*, It. anatomist d. 1575]

pons as·i·no·rum n. /ásináwrəm/ any difficult proposition, orig. a rule of geometry from Euclid ('bridge of asses').

pont /pont/ n. *S.Afr.* a flat-bottomed ferryboat. [Du.]

pontes pl. of PONS.

pon·ti·fex /póntifeks/ n. (pl. **pon·tif·i·ces** /pontífiseez/) **1** = PONTIFF. **2** *Rom.Antiq.* a member of the principal college of priests in Rome. [L *pontifex –ficis* f. *pons pontis* bridge + *–fex* f. *facere* make]

Pon·ti·fex Max·i·mus n. **1** (in ancient Rome) the head of the principal college of priests. **2** (in the Roman Catholic Church) a title of the pope.

pon·tiff /póntif/ n. *RC Ch.* (in full **sovereign** or **supreme pontiff**) the pope. [F *pontife* (as PONTIFEX)]

pon·tif·i·cal /pontífikəl/ adj. & n. ●adj. **1** *RC Ch.* of or befitting a pontiff; papal. **2** pompously dogmatic; with an attitude of infallibility. ●n. **1** an office book containing rites to be performed by bishops. **2** (in pl.) the vestments and insignia of a bishop, cardinal, or abbot. □□ **pon·tif·i·cal·ly** adv. [ME f. F *pontifical* or L *pontificalis* (as PONTIFEX)]

Pon·tif·i·cal Mass n. a high Mass, usu. celebrated by a cardinal, bishop, etc.

pon·tif·i·cate v. & n. ●v.intr. /pontífikayt/ **1 a** play the pontiff; pretend to be infallible. **b** be pompously dogmatic. **2** *RC Ch.* officiate as bishop, esp. at mass. ●n. /pontífikat/ **1** the office of pontifex, bishop, or pope. **2** the period of this. [L *pontificatus* (as PONTIFEX)]

pon·tif·i·ces pl. of PONTIFEX.

pon·toon[1] /pontóon/ n. & v. ●n. **1** a flat-bottomed boat. **2** **a** each of several boats, hollow metal cylinders, etc., used to support a temporary bridge. **b** a bridge so formed; a floating platform. **3** = CAISSON 1, 2. **4** a float for a seaplane. ●v.tr. cross (a river) by means of pontoons. [F *ponton* f. L *ponto –onis* f. *pons pontis* bridge]

pontoon, 3

pon·toon[2] /pontóon/ n. *Brit.* = BLACKJACK[1] 1. [prob. corrupt.]

po·ny /pónee/ n. (pl. **·nies**) **1** a horse of any small breed. **2** a small drinking glass. **3** (in pl.) *sl.* racehorses. **4** a literal translation of a foreign-language text, used by students. **5** *Brit. sl.* £25. [perh. f. *poulney* (unrecorded) f. F *poulenet* dimin. of *poulain* foal]

po·ny ex·press n. (also **Po·ny Ex·press**) *US Hist.* an express delivery system of the early 1860s that carried mail, etc., by relays of pony riders.

po·ny·tail /póneetayl/ n. a person's hair drawn back, tied, and hanging down like a pony's tail.

pooch /pōōch/ n. *sl.* a dog. [20th c.: orig. unkn.]

poo·dle /pōōd'l/ n. **1 a** a dog of a breed with a curly coat that is usually clipped. **b** this breed. **2** *Brit.* a lackey or servile follower. [G *Pudel(hund)* f. LG *pud(d)eln* splash in water: cf. PUDDLE]

poof /pōōf, pŏōf/ n. (also **poove** /pōōv/) *Brit. sl. derog.* **1** an effeminate man. **2** a male homosexual. □□ **poof·y** /pōōfee/ adj. [19th c.: cf. PUFF in sense 'braggart']

pooh /pōō/ int. (also **poo**) ●int. expressing impatience or contempt. ●n. *sl.* **1** excrement. **2** an act of defecation. [imit.]

Pooh-Bah /pōōbaá/ n. (also **pooh-bah**) a holder of many offices at once. [a character in W. S. Gilbert's *The Mikado* (1885)]

pooh-pooh /pōōpōō/ v.tr. express contempt for; ridicule; dismiss (an idea, etc.) scornfully. [redupl. of POOH]

poo·ka /pōōkə/ n. *Ir.* a hobgoblin. [Ir. *púca*]

pool[1] /pōōl/ n. & v. ●n. **1** a small body of still water, usu. of natural formation. **2** a small shallow body of any liquid. **3** = SWIMMING POOL. **4** a deep place in a river. ●v. **1** tr. form into a pool. **2** intr. (of blood) become static. [OE *pōl*, MLG, MDu. *pōl*, OHG *pfuol* f. WG]

pool[2] /pōōl/ n. & v. ●n. **1 a** (often *attrib.*) a common supply of persons, vehicles, commodities, etc., for sharing by a group of people (*a car pool*). **b** a group of persons sharing duties, etc. (*a typing pool*). **2 a** the collective amount of players' stakes in gambling, etc. **b** a receptacle for this. **3 a** a joint commercial venture, esp. an arrangement between competing parties to fix prices and share business to eliminate competition. **b** the common funding for this. **4** any of several games similar to billiards played on a pool table with usu. 16 balls. **5** a group of contestants who compete against each other in a tournament for the right to advance to the next round. ●v.tr. **1** put (resources, etc.) into a common fund. **2** share (things) in common. **3** (of transport or organizations, etc.) share (traffic, receipts). **4** *Austral. sl.* **a** involve (a person) in a scheme, etc., often by deception. **b** implicate; inform on. [F *poule* (= hen) in same sense: assoc. with POOL[1]]

pool·room /pōōlrōōm, –rŏōm/ n. **1** a place for playing pool; pool hall. **2** a bookmaking establishment.

poon[1] /pōōn/ n. any E. Indian tree of the genus *Calophyllum*. [Sinh. *pūna*]

poon[2] /pōōn/ n. esp. *Austral. sl.* a simple or foolish person. [orig. unkn.]

poon oil n. an oil from the seeds of the poon tree, used in medicine and for lamps.

poop[1] /pōōp/ n. & v. ●n. the stern of a ship; the aftermost and highest deck. ●v.tr. **1** (of a wave) break over the stern of (a ship). **2** (of a ship) receive (a wave) over the stern. [ME f. OF *pupe, pope* ult. f. L *puppis*]

poop[2] /pōōp/ v.tr. (esp. as **pooped** adj.) *colloq.* exhaust; tire out. [20th c.: orig. unkn.]

poop[3] /pōōp/ n. *sl.* up to date or inside information; the lowdown. [20th c.: orig. unkn.]

poop[4] /pōōp/ n. & v. *sl.* ●n. excrement. ●v. intr. defecate. [f. earlier 'break wind,' prob. f. ME *powpen* sound a horn]

poor /pŏōr/ adj. & n. ●adj. **1** lacking adequate money or means to live comfortably. **2 a** (foll. by *in*) deficient in (a possession or quality) (*the poor in spirit*). **b** (of soil, ore, etc.) unproductive. **3 a** scanty; inadequate (*a poor crop*). **b** less good than is usual or expected (*poor visibility; is a poor driver; in poor health*). **c** paltry; inferior (*poor condition; came a poor third*). **4** a deserving pity or sympathy; unfortunate (*you poor thing*). **b** with reference to a dead person (*as my poor father used to say*). **5** spiritless; despicable (*is a poor creature*). **6** often *iron.* or *joc.* humble; insignificant (*in my poor opinion*). ●n. (the **poor**) poor people collectively. □ **poor man's** an inferior or cheaper substitute for. **poor white** (or **poor white trash**) *offens.* a member of a socially inferior group of white people. **take a poor view of** regard with disfavor or pessimism. [ME & OF *pov(e)re, poure* f. L *pauper*]

poor box n. a collection box, esp. in church, for the relief of the poor.

poor boy n. (also **poor-boy**) = SUBMARINE SANDWICH.

poor·house /pŏōrhows/ n. *hist.* = WORKHOUSE 2.

poor law n. *hist.* a law relating to the support of paupers.

poor·ly /pŏōrlee/ adv. & adj. ●adv. **1** scantily; defectively. **2** with no great success. **3** meanly; contemptibly. ●predic. adj. unwell.

poor·ness /pŏōrnis/ n. **1** defectiveness. **2** the lack of some good quality or constituent.

poor rate n. *Brit. hist.* a rate or assessment for relief or support of the poor.

poor re·la·tion n. an inferior or subordinate member of a family or any other group.

poor-spir·it·ed adj. timid; cowardly.

poove var. of POOF.

pop[1] /pop/ n., v., & adv. ●n. **1** a sudden sharp explosive sound as of a cork when drawn. **2** *colloq.* an effervescent soft drink. **3** = POP FLY. ●v. (**popped, pop·ping**) **1** intr. & tr. make or cause to make a pop. **2** intr. & tr. (foll. by *in, out, up, down,* etc.) go, move, come, or put unexpectedly or in a quick or hasty manner (*pop out to the store; pop in for a visit; pop it on your head*). **3 a** intr. & tr. burst, making a popping sound. **b** tr. heat (popcorn, etc.) until it pops. **4** intr. (often foll. by *at*) *colloq.* fire a gun (at birds, etc.). **5** tr. *Brit. sl.* pawn. **6** tr. *sl.* take or inject (a drug, etc.). **7** intr. (often foll. by *up*) (of a ball) rise up into the air. ●adv. with the sound of a pop (*heard it go pop*). □ **in pop** *Brit. sl.* in pawn. **pop off** *colloq.* **1** die. **2** quietly slip away (cf. sense 2 of v.). **pop one's clogs** *Brit. sl.* die. **pop the question** *colloq.* propose marriage. [ME: imit.]

pop[2] /pop/ adj. & n. *colloq.* ●adj. **1** in a popular or modern style. **2** performing popular music, etc. (*pop group; pop star*). ●n. **1** pop music. **2** a pop record or song (*top of the pops*). [abbr.]

pop[3] /pop/ n. esp. *colloq.* father. [abbr. of POPPA]

pop. *abbr.* population.

pop·a·dam var. of POPPADAM.

pop art *n.* art based on modern popular culture and the mass media, esp. as a critical comment on traditional fine art values.

pop·corn /pópkawrn/ *n.* **1** corn which bursts open when heated. **2** these kernels when popped.

pop cul·ture *n.* commercial culture based on popular taste.

pope[1] /pōp/ *n.* **1** (as title usu. **Pope**) the head of the Roman Catholic Church (also called the Bishop of Rome). **2** the head of the Coptic Church and Orthodox patriarch of Alexandria. **3** = RUFF[2]. □□ **pope·dom** *n.* **pope·less** *adj.* [OE f. eccl.L *pāpa* bishop, pope f. eccl.Gk *papas* = Gk *pappas* father: cf. PAPA]

pope[2] /pōp/ *n.* a parish priest of the Orthodox Church in Russia, etc. [Russ. *pop* f. OSlav. *popŭ* f. WG f. eccl.Gk (as POPE[1])]

pop·er·y /pópəree/ *n. derog.* the papal system; the Roman Catholic Church.

pope's nose *n. sl.* the tail of a cooked chicken, turkey, etc.

pop-eyed *adj. colloq.* **1** having bulging eyes. **2** wide-eyed (with surprise, etc.).

pop fes·ti·val *n.* a festival at which popular music, etc., is performed.

pop fly *n. Baseball* a high fly ball hit esp. to the infield.

pop·gun /pópgun/ *n.* **1** a child's toy gun which shoots a pellet, etc., by the compression of air with a piston. **2** *derog.* an inefficient firearm.

pop·in·jay /pópinjay/ *n.* **1** a fop; a conceited person; a coxcomb. **2 a** *archaic* a parrot. **b** *hist.* a figure of a parrot on a pole as a mark to shoot at. [ME f. AF *papeiaye*, OF *papingay*, etc., f. Sp. *papagayo* f. Arab. *babaġā*: assim. to JAY]

pop·ish /pópish/ *adj. derog.* Roman Catholic. □□ **pop·ish·ly** *adv.*

pop·lar /póplər/ *n.* **1** any tree of the genus *Populus*, with a usu. rapidly growing trunk and tremulous leaves. **2** = TULIP TREE. [ME f. AF *popler*, OF *poplier* f. *pople* f. L *populus*]

pop·lin /póplin/ *n.* a plain woven fabric usu. of cotton, with a corded surface. [obs. F *papeline* perh. f. It. *papalina* (fem.) PAPAL, f. the papal town Avignon where it was made]

pop·lit·e·al /poplíteeəl, –líteeəl/ *adj.* of the hollow at the back of the knee. [mod.L *popliteus* f. L *poples* –*itis* this hollow]

pop·o·ver /pópōvər/ *n.* a light puffy hollow muffin made from an egg-rich batter.

pop·pa /pópə/ *n. colloq.* father (esp. as a child's word). [var. of PAPA]

pop·pa·dam /pópədəm/ *n.* (also **pop·pa·dom, popadam**) *Ind.* a thin, crisp, spiced bread eaten with curry, etc. [Tamil *pappaḍam*]

pop·per /pópər/ *n.* **1 a** a person or thing that pops. **b** a device or machine for making popcorn. **2** *colloq.* a small vial of amyl nitrite used for inhalation. **3** *Brit. colloq.* a snap fastener.

pop·pet /pópit/ *n.* **1** (also **pop·pet valve**) *Engin.* a mushroom-shaped valve, lifted bodily from its seat rather than hinged. **2** (in full **poppet head**) the head of a lathe. **3** a small square piece of wood fitted inside the gunwale or washstrake of a boat. **4** *Brit. colloq.* (esp. as a term of endearment) a small or dainty person. [ME *popet(te)*, ult. f. L *pup(p)a*: cf. PUPPET]

pop·pet-head *n.* **1** *Brit.* the frame at the top of a mineshaft supporting pulleys for the ropes used in hoisting. **2** = POPPET 2.

pop·ple /pópəl/ *v. & n.* ● *v.intr.* (of water) tumble or bubble; toss to and fro. ● *n.* the act or an instance of rolling, tossing, or rippling of water. □□ **pop·ply** *adj.* [ME prob. f. MDu. *popelen* murmur, quiver, of imit. orig.]

pop·py /pópee/ *n.* (*pl.* **·pies**) any plant of the genus *Papaver*, with showy often red flowers and a milky sap with narcotic properties. □□ **pop·pied** *adj.* [OE *popig, papæg*, etc., f. med.L *papauum* f. L *papaver*]

pop·py·cock /pópeekok/ *n. sl.* nonsense. [Du. dial. *pappekak*]

pop-shop *n. Brit. sl.* a pawnbroker's shop.

Pop·si·cle /pópsikəl/ *n. Trademark* a flavored ice confection on a stick.

pop·u·lace /pópyələs/ *n.* **1** the common people. **2** *derog.* the rabble. [F f. It. *popolaccio* f. *popolo* people + –*accio* pejorative suffix]

pop·u·lar /pópyələr/ *adj.* **1** liked or admired by many people or by a specified group (*popular teachers; a popular hero*). **2 a** of or carried on by the general public (*popular meetings*). **b** prevalent among the general public (*popular discontent*). **3** adapted to the understanding, taste, or means of the people (*popular science; popular medicine*). □□ **pop·u·lar·ism** *n.* **pop·u·lar·i·ty** /–láritee/ *n.* **pop·u·lar·ly** *adv.* [ME f. AF *populer*, OF *populeir* or L *popularis* f. *populus* people]

pop·u·lar front *n.* a party or coalition representing left-wing elements.

pop·u·lar·ize /pópyələrīz/ *v.tr.* **1** make popular. **2** cause (a person, principle, etc.) to be generally known or liked. **3** present (a technical subject, specialized vocabulary, etc.) in a popular or readily understandable form. □□ **pop·u·lar·i·za·tion** /–rəzáyshən/ *n.* **pop·u·lar·iz·er** *n.*

pop·u·lar mu·sic *n.* songs, folk tunes, etc., appealing to popular tastes.

pop·u·late /pópyəlayt/ *v.tr.* **1** inhabit; form the population of (a town, country, etc.). **2** supply with inhabitants; people (*a densely populated district*). [med.L *populare populat*- (as PEOPLE)]

pop·u·la·tion /pópyəláyshən/ *n.* **1 a** the inhabitants of a place, country, etc., referred to collectively. **b** any specified group within this (*the Polish population of Chicago*). **2** the total number of any of these (*a population of eight million; the seal population*). **3** the act or process of supplying with inhabitants (*the population of forest areas*). **4** *Statistics* any finite or infinite collection of items under consideration. [LL *populatio* (as PEOPLE)]

pop·u·la·tion ex·plo·sion *n.* a sudden large increase of population.

pop·u·list /pópyəlist/ *n. & adj.* ● *n.* a member or adherent of a political party seeking support mainly from the ordinary people. ● *adj.* of or relating to such a political party. □□ **pop·u·lism** *n.* **pop·u·lis·tic** /–lístik/ *adj.* [L *populus* people]

Pop·u·list Par·ty *n. hist.* a US political party formed in 1891 that advocated the interests of labor and farmers, free coinage of silver, a graduated income tax, and government control of monopolies.

pop·u·lous /pópyələs/ *adj.* thickly inhabited. □□ **pop·u·lous·ly** *adv.* **pop·u·lous·ness** *n.* [ME f. LL *populosus* (as PEOPLE)]

pop-up *adj. & n.* ● *adj.* **1** (of a toaster, etc.) operating so as to move the object (toast when ready, etc.) quickly upward. **2** (of a book, greeting card, etc.) containing three-dimensional figures, illustrations, etc., that rise up when the page is turned. **3** *Computing* (of a menu or other utility) able to be superimposed on the screen being worked on and suppressed rapidly. ● *n.* **1** a pop-up picture in a book. **2 a** book containing such pictures. **3** *Baseball* = POP FLY. **4** *Computing* a pop-up menu or other utility.

por·bea·gle /páwrbeegəl/ *n.* a large shark, *Lamna nasus*, having a pointed snout. [18th-c. Corn. dial., of unkn. orig.]

por·ce·lain /páwrsəlin, páwrslin/ *n.* **1** a hard vitrified translucent ceramic. **2** objects made of this. □□ **por·cel·la·ne·ous** /páwrsəláyneeəs/ *adj.* **por·cel·la·nous** /porsélənəs/ *adj.* [F *porcelaine* cowrie, porcelain f. It. *porcellana* f. *porcella* dimin. of *porca* sow (a cowrie being perh. likened to a sow's vulva) f. L *porca* fem. of *porcus* pig]

por·ce·lain clay *n.* = KAOLIN.

por·ce·lain shell *n.* = COWRIE.

porch /pawrch/ *n.* **1** a covered shelter for the entrance of a building. **2** a veranda. **3** (**the Porch**) = *the Stoa* (see STOA 2). □□ **porched** *adj.* **porch·less** *adj.* [ME f. OF *porche* f. L *porticus* (transl. Gk *stoa*) f. *porta* passage]

por·cine /páwrsīn, –sin/ *adj.* of or like pigs. [F *porcin* or f. L *porcinus* f. *porcus* pig]

por·cu·pine /páwrkyəpīn/ *n.* **1** any rodent of the family Hystricidae native to Africa, Asia, and SE Europe, or the family Erethizontidae native to America, having defensive spines or quills. **2** (*attrib.*) denoting any of various animals or other organisms with spines. □□ **por·cu·pin·ish** *adj.* **por·cu·pin·y** *adj.* [ME f. OF *porc espin* f. Prov. *porc espi(n)* ult. f. L *porcus* pig + *spina* thorn]

porcupine 1

por·cu·pine fish *n.* a marine fish, *Diodon hystrix*, covered with sharp spines and often distending itself into a spherical shape.

pore[1] /pawr/ *n. esp. Biol.* a minute opening in a surface through which gases, liquids, or fine solids may pass. [ME f. OF f. L *porus* f. Gk *poros* passage, pore]

pore[2] /pawr/ *v.intr.* (foll. by *over*) **1** be absorbed in studying (a book, etc.). **2** meditate on, think intently about (a subject). [ME *pure*, etc. perh. f. OE *purian* (unrecorded): cf. PEER[1]]

por·gy /páwrgee/ *n.* (*pl.* **·gies**) any usu. marine fish of the family Sparidae, used as food. Also called **sea bream**. [18th c.: orig. uncert.: cf. Sp. & Port. *pargo*]

po·rif·er /páwrifər/ *n.* any aquatic invertebrate of the phylum Porifera, including sponges. [mod.L *Porifera* f. L *porus* PORE[1] + –*fer* bearing]

pork /pawrk/ *n.* **1** the (esp. unsalted) flesh of a pig, used as food. **2** = PORK BARREL [ME *porc* f. OF *porc* f. L *porcus* pig]

pork bar·rel *n. US colloq.* government funds as a source of political benefit.

pork·er /páwrkər/ *n.* **1** a pig raised for food. **2** a young fattened pig.

pork·ling /páwrkling/ *n.* a young or small pig.

pork pie *n.* a pie of ground pork, etc., eaten cold.

pork·pie hat /páwrkpī/ *n.* a hat with a flat crown and a brim turned up all around.

pork·y[1] /páwrkee/ *adj. & n.* ● *adj.* (**pork·i·er, pork·i·est**) **1** *colloq.* fleshy; fat. **2** of or like pork. ● *n. Brit. rhyming sl.* a lie (short for *porky pie*).

pork·y[2] /páwrkee/ *n.* (*pl.* **·ies**) *colloq.* a porcupine. [abbr.]

porn /pawrn/ *n. colloq.* pornography. [abbr.]

por·no /páwrnō/ *n. & adj. colloq.* ● *n.* pornography. ● *adj.* pornographic. [abbr.]

por·nog·ra·phy /pawrnógrəfee/ *n.* printed or visual material containing the explicit description or display of sexual organs or activity, intended to stimulate erotic rather than aesthetic or emotional feelings. □□ **por·nog·ra·pher** n. **por·no·graph·ic** /–nəgráfik/ adj. **por·no·graph·i·cal·ly** adv. [Gk *pornographos* writing of prostitutes f. *pornē* prostitute + *graphō* write]

po·rous /páwrəs/ adj. **1** full of pores. **2** letting through air, water, etc. **3** (of an argument, security system, etc.) leaky; admitting infiltration. □□ **po·ros·i·ty** /porósitee/ n. **po·rous·ly** adv. **po·rous·ness** n. [ME f. OF *poreux* f. med.L *porosus* f. L *porus* PORE¹]

por·phyr·i·a /pawrfíreeə/ n. any of a group of genetic disorders associated with abnormal metabolism of various pigments. [mod.L f. *porphyrin* purple substance excreted by porphyria patients f. Gk *porphura* purple]

por·phy·ry /páwrfiree/ n. (pl. **·ries**) **1** a hard rock quarried in ancient Egypt, composed of crystals of white or red feldspar in a red matrix. **2** Geol. an igneous rock with large crystals scattered in a matrix of much smaller crystals. □□ **por·phy·rit·ic** /–rítik/ adj. [ME ult. f. med.L *porphyreum* f. Gk *porphuritēs* f. *porphura* purple]

por·poise /páwrpəs/ n. any of various small toothed whales of the family Phocaenidae, esp. of the genus *Phocaena*, with a low triangular dorsal fin and a blunt rounded snout. [ME *porpays*, etc.; f. OF *po(u)rpois*, etc.; ult. f. L *porcus* pig + *piscis* fish]

por·ridge /páwrij, pór–/ n. **1** a dish consisting of oatmeal or another cereal boiled in water or milk. **2** Brit. sl. imprisonment. □□ **por·ridg·y** adj. [16th c.: alt. of POTTAGE]

por·rin·ger /páwrinjər, pór–/ n. a small bowl, often with a handle, for soup, stew, etc. [earlier *pottinger* f. OF *potager* f. *potage* (see POTTAGE): –n– as in *messenger*, etc.]

port¹ /pawrt/ n. **1** a harbor. **2** a place of refuge. **3** a town or place possessing a harbor, esp. one where customs officers are stationed. [OE f. L *portus* & ME prob. f. OF f. L *portus*]

port² /pawrt/ n. (in full **port wine**) a strong, sweet, dark red (occas. brown or white) fortified wine of Portugal. [shortened form of *Oporto*, city in Portugal from which port is shipped]

port³ /pawrt/ n. & v. ● n. the left side (looking forward) of a ship, boat, or aircraft (cf. STARBOARD). ● v.tr. (also absol.) turn (the helm) to port. [prob. orig. the side turned toward PORT¹]

port⁴ /pawrt/ n. **1 a** an opening in the side of a ship for entrance, loading, etc. **b** a porthole. **2** an aperture for the passage of steam, water, etc. **3** Electr. a socket or aperture in an electronic circuit, esp. in a computer network, where connections can be made with peripheral equipment. **4** an aperture in a wall, etc., for a gun to be fired through. **5** esp. Sc. a gate or gateway, esp. of a walled town. [ME & OF *porte* f. L *porta*]

port⁵ /pawrt/ v. & n. ● v.tr. Mil. carry (a rifle, or other weapon) diagonally across and close to the body with the barrel, etc., near the left shoulder (esp. *port arms!*). ● n. **1** Mil. this position. **2** external deportment; carriage; bearing. [ME f. OF *port* ult. f. L *portare* carry]

port·a·ble /páwrtəbəl/ adj. & n. ● adj. easily movable; convenient for carrying (*portable TV*; *portable computer*). ● n. a portable object, e.g., a radio, typewriter, etc. (*decided to buy a portable*). □□ **port·a·bil·i·ty** n. **port·a·ble·ness** n. **port·a·bly** adv. [ME f. OF *portable* or LL *portabilis* f. L *portare* carry]

port·age /páwrtij, –taázh/ n. & v. ● n. **1** the carrying of boats or goods between two navigable waters. **2** a place at which this is necessary. **3 a** the act or an instance of carrying or transporting. **b** the cost of this. ● v.tr. convey (a boat or goods) between navigable waters. [ME f. OF f. *porter*: see PORT⁵]

por·tal¹ /páwrt'l/ n. a doorway or gate, etc., esp. a large and elaborate one. [ME f. OF f. med.L *portale* (neut. adj.): see PORTAL²]

por·tal² /páwrt'l/ adj. **1** of or relating to an aperture in an organ through which its associated vessels pass. **2** of or relating to the portal vein. [mod.L *portalis* f. L *porta* gate]

por·tal vein n. a vein conveying blood to the liver from the spleen, stomach, pancreas, and intestines.

por·ta·men·to /páwrtəméntó/ n. (pl. **por·ta·men·ti** /–tee/) Mus. **1** the act or an instance of gliding from one note to another in singing, playing the violin, etc. **2** piano playing in a manner intermediate between legato and staccato. [It., = carrying]

por·ta·tive /páwrtətiv/ adj. **1** serving to carry or support. **2** Mus. hist. (esp. of a small pipe organ) portable. [ME f. OF *portatif*, app. alt. of *portatil* f. med.L *portatilis* f. L *portare* carry]

port·cul·lis /pawrtkúlis/ n. a strong heavy grating sliding up and down in vertical grooves, lowered to block a gateway in a fortress, etc. □□ **port·cul·lised** adj. [ME f. OF *porte coleice* sliding door f. *porte* door f. L *porta* + *col(e)ice* fem. of *couleïs* sliding ult. f. L *colare* filter]

Porte /pawrt/ n. (in full **the Sublime** or **Ottoman Porte**) hist. the Ottoman court at Constantinople. [F (*la Sublime Porte* = the exalted gate), transl. of Turk. title of the central office of the Ottoman government]

porte co·chère /páwrt kōsháir/ n. **1** a covered passage large enough for vehicles to pass through, usu. into a courtyard. **2** a roofed structure extending from the entrance of a building over a place where vehicles stop to discharge passengers. [F f. *porte* PORT⁴ + *cochère* (fem. adj.) f. *coche* COACH]

por·tend /pawrténd/ v.tr. **1** foreshadow as an omen. **2** give warning of. [ME f. L *portendere portent-* f. *por-* PRO-¹ + *tendere* stretch]

por·tent /páwrtent/ n. **1** an omen, a sign of something to come, esp. something of a momentous or calamitous nature. **2** a prodigy; a marvelous thing. [L *portentum* (as PORTEND)]

por·ten·tous /pawrténtəs/ adj. **1** like or serving as a portent. **2** pompously solemn. □□ **por·ten·tous·ly** adv.

PRONUNCIATION TIP | **portentous**

Perhaps because it resembles words like *pretentious* and *contentious*, this word is sometimes mispronounced as though it ended in *-tious*.

por·ter¹ /páwrtər/ n. **1 a** a person employed to carry luggage, etc., at an airport, hotel, etc. **b** (also **hospital porter**) a hospital employee who moves equipment or patients. **2** a dark brown bitter beer brewed from charred or browned malt (orig. made as a drink for porters). **3** a sleeping-car attendant. **4** a cleaning person or maintenance worker, as in a hospital, etc. □□ **por·ter·age** n. [ME f. OF *port(e)our* f. med.L *portator –oris* f. *portare* carry]

por·ter² /páwrtər/ n. Brit. a gatekeeper or doorkeeper, esp. of a large building. [ME & AF, OF *portier* f. LL *portarius* f. *porta* door]

por·ter·house /páwrtərhows/ n. **1** hist. a house at which porter and other drinks were sold. **2** a house where steaks, chops, etc., were served.

por·ter·house steak n. a thick steak cut from the thick end of a sirloin.

port·fire /páwrtfīr/ n. a device for firing rockets, igniting explosives in mining, etc. [after F *porte-feu* f. *porter* carry + *feu* fire]

port·fo·li·o /pawrtfőleeó/ n. (pl. **·os**) **1** a case for keeping loose sheets of paper, drawings, etc. **2** a range of investments held by a person, a company, etc. **3** the office of a minister of state. **4** samples of an artist's work. [It. *portafogli* f. *portare* carry + *foglio* leaf f. L *folium*]

port·hole /páwrt-hōl/ n. **1** an (esp. glassed-in) aperture in a ship's or aircraft's side for the admission of light. **2** hist. an aperture in a wall for pointing a cannon through.

por·ti·co /páwrtikó/ n. (pl. **·coes** or **·cos**) a colonnade; a roof supported by columns at regular intervals usu. attached as a porch to a building. [It. f. L *porticus* PORCH]

portico

por·tière /pawrtyáir, –téer/ n. a curtain hung over a door or doorway. [F f. *porte* door f. L *porta*]

por·tion /páwrshən/ n. & v. ● n. **1** a part or share. **2** the amount of food allotted to one person. **3** a specified or limited quantity. **4** one's destiny or lot. **5** a dowry. ● v.tr. **1** divide (a thing) into portions. **2** (foll. by *out*) distribute. **3** give a dowry to. **4** (foll. by *to*) assign (a thing) to (a person). □□ **por·tion·less** adj. (in sense 5 of n.). [ME f. OF *porcion* portion f. L *portio –onis*]

Port·land ce·ment /páwrtlənd/ n. a cement manufactured from chalk and clay that when hard resembles Portland stone in color.

Port·land stone /páwrtlənd/ n. a limestone from the Isle of Portland in Dorset, England, used in building.

port·ly /páwrtlee/ adj. (**port·li·er**, **port·li·est**) **1** corpulent; stout. **2** archaic of a stately appearance. □□ **port·li·ness** n. [PORT⁵ (in the sense 'bearing') + -LY¹]

port·man·teau /pawrtmántó, páwrtmantó/ n. (pl. **port·man·teaus** or **port·man·teaux** /–ō, –ő, –tōz, –tőz/) a leather trunk for clothes, etc., opening into two equal parts. [F *portmanteau* f. *porter* carry f. L *portare* + *manteau* MANTLE]

port·man·teau word n. a word blending the sounds and combining the meanings of two others, e.g., *motel* from *motor* and *hotel*.

port of call n. a place where a ship or a person stops on a journey.

por·to·la·no /páwrt'laánó/ n. (also **por·to·lan** /páwrt'laán/) (pl. **por·to·la·nos** or **por·to·lans**) hist. a book of sailing directions with charts, descriptions of harbors, etc. [It. *portolano* f. *porto* PORT¹]

por·trait /páwrtrit, –trayt/ n. **1** a representation of a person or animal, esp. of the face, made by drawing, painting, photography, etc. **2** a verbal picture; a graphic description. **3** (in graphic design, etc.) a format in which the height of an illustration, etc., is greater than the width (cf. LANDSCAPE). [F, past part. of OF *portraire* PORTRAY]

por·trait·ist /páwrtritist/ n. a person who takes or paints portraits.

por·trai·ture /páwrtritchor/ n. **1** the art of painting or taking portraits. **2** graphic description. **3** a portrait. [ME f. OF (as PORTRAIT)]

por·tray /pawrtráy/ v.tr. **1** represent (an object) by a painting, carving, etc; make a likeness of. **2** describe graphically. **3** represent dramatically. □□ **por·tray·a·ble** adj. **por·tray·al** n. **por·tray·er** n. [ME f. OF *portraire* f. *por-* = PRO-¹ + *traire* draw f. L *trahere*]

Port Sa·lut /páwr səlŏŏ/ n. a pale mild type of cheese. [after the Trappist monastery in France where it was first produced]

port tack n. see TACK[1] 4.

Por·tu·guese /páwrchəgeéz, –geés/ n. & adj. • n. (pl. same) **1 a** a native or national of Portugal. **b** a person of Portuguese descent. **2** the language of Portugal and Brazil. • adj. of or relating to Portugal or its people or language. [Port. portuguez f. med.L portugalensis]

Por·tu·guese man-of-war n. a dangerous tropical or subtropical marine hydrozoan of the genus Physalia with a large crest and a poisonous sting.

port watch n. see WATCH 3b.

POS abbr. point-of-sale.

pose[1] /pōz/ v. & n. • v. **1** intr. assume a certain attitude of body, esp. when being photographed or being painted for a portrait. **2** intr. (foll. by as) set oneself up as or pretend to be (another person, etc.) (posing as a celebrity). **3** intr. behave affectedly in order to impress others. **4** tr. put forward or present (a question, etc.). **5** tr. place (an artist's model, etc.) in a certain attitude or position. • n. **1** an attitude of body or mind. **2** an attitude or pretense, esp. one assumed for effect (his generosity is a mere pose). [F poser (v.), pose (n.) f. LL pausare PAUSE: some senses by confusion with L ponere place (cf. COMPOSE)]

pose[2] /pōz/ v.tr. puzzle (a person) with a question or problem. [obs. appose f. OF aposer var. of oposer OPPOSE]

pos·er /pōzər/ n. **1** a person who poses (see POSE[1] v. 3). **2** a puzzling question or problem.

po·seur /pōzŏr/ n. (fem. po·seuse /pōzŏz/) a person who poses for effect or behaves affectedly. [F f. poser POSE[1]]

posh /posh/ adj. & adv. colloq. • adj. **1** elegant; stylish. **2** esp. Brit. of or associated with the upper classes (spoke with a posh accent). • adv. esp. Brit. in a stylish or upper-class way (talk posh; act posh). □□ **posh·ly** adv. **posh·ness** n.

WORD HISTORY posh

early 20th century: perhaps from slang posh, denoting a dandy. There is no evidence to support the popular etymology that posh is formed from the initials of port out starboard home (referring to the more comfortable staterooms out of the heat of the sun, on ships between England and India).

---

pos·it /pózit/ v. & n. • v.tr. (**pos·it·ed, pos·it·ing**) **1** assume as a fact; postulate. **2** put in place or position. • n. Philos. a statement made on the assumption that it will prove valid. [L ponere posit- place]

po·si·tion /pəzíshən/ n. & v. • n. **1** a place occupied by a person or thing. **2** the way in which a thing or its parts are placed or arranged (sitting in an uncomfortable position). **3** the proper place (in position). **4** the state of being advantageously placed (jockeying for position). **5** a person's mental attitude; a way of looking at a question (changed their position on nuclear disarmament). **6** a person's situation in relation to others (puts one in an awkward position). **7** rank or status; high social standing. **8** paid employment. **9** a place where troops, etc., are posted for strategical purposes (the position was stormed). **10** the configuration of chessmen, etc., during a game. **11** a specific pose in ballet, etc. (hold first position). **12** Logic **a** a proposition. **b** a statement of a proposition. • v.tr. place in position. □ **in a position to** enabled by circumstances, resources, information, etc., to (do, state, etc.). □□ **po·si·tion·al** adj. **po·si·tion·al·ly** adv. **po·si·tion·er** n. [ME f. OF position or L positio –onis (as POSIT)]

po·si·tion pa·per n. (in government, business, etc.) a written report of attitudes or intentions.

pos·i·tive /pózitiv/ adj. & n. • adj. **1** formally or explicitly stated; definite; unquestionable (positive proof). **2** (of a person) convinced, confident, or overconfident in his or her opinion (positive that I was not there). **3** a absolute; not relative. **b** Gram. (of an adjective or adverb) expressing a simple quality without comparison (cf. COMPARATIVE, SUPERLATIVE). **4** colloq. downright; complete (it would be a positive miracle). **5 a** constructive; directional (positive criticism; positive thinking). **b** favorable; optimistic (positive reaction; positive outlook). **6** Med. marked by the presence rather than absence of qualities or symptoms (the test was positive). **7** esp. Philos. dealing only with matters of fact; practical (cf. POSITIVISM 1). **8** tending in a direction naturally or arbitrarily taken as that of increase or progress (clockwise rotation is positive). **9** greater than zero (positive and negative integers) (opp. NEGATIVE). **10** Electr. of, containing, producing, or denoting an electric charge opposite to that carried by electrons. **11** (of a photographic image) showing lights and shades or colors

---

WORD HISTORY positive

late Middle English: from Old French positif, -ive or Latin positivus, from posit- 'placed,' from the verb ponere. The original sense referred to laws as being formally 'laid down,' which gave rise to the sense 'explicitly laid down and admitting no question,' hence 'very sure, convinced.'

---

true to the original (opp. NEGATIVE). • n. a positive adjective, photograph, quantity, etc. □□ **pos·i·tive·ly** adv. **pos·i·tive·ness** n. **pos·i·tiv·i·ty** /pózitívitee/ n.

pos·i·tive feed·back n. **1** a constructive response to an experiment, questionnaire, etc. **2** Electronics the return of part of an output signal to the input, tending to increase the amplification, etc.

pos·i·tive ge·ot·ro·pism n. the tendency of roots to grow toward the center of the earth.

pos·i·tive pole n. the north-seeking pole.

pos·i·tive ray n. Physics a canal ray.

pos·i·tive sign n. = PLUS SIGN.

pos·i·tiv·ism /pózitivizəm/ n. **1** Philos. the philosophical system of Auguste Comte, recognizing only nonmetaphysical facts and observable phenomena, and rejecting metaphysics and theism. **2** a religious system founded on this. **3** = LOGICAL POSITIVISM. □□ **pos·i·tiv·ist** n. **pos·i·tiv·is·tic** adj. **pos·i·tiv·is·ti·cal·ly** /–vístiklee/ adv. [F positivisme (as POSITIVE)]

pos·i·tron /pózitron/ n. Physics an elementary particle with a positive charge equal to the negative charge of an electron and having the same mass as an electron. [POSITIVE + –TRON]

po·sol·o·gy /pəsóləjee, pō–/ n. the study of the dosage of medicines. □□ **pos·o·log·i·cal** /pósəlójikəl/ adj. [F posologie f. Gk posos how much]

poss. abbr. **1** possession. **2** possessive. **3** possible. **4** possibly.

pos·se /pósee/ n. **1** a strong force or company or assemblage. **2** (in full **posse comitatus** /kómitáytəs/) **a** a body of constables, enforcers of the law, etc. **b** a body of men summoned by a sheriff, etc., to enforce the law. [med.L, = power f. L posse be able: comitatus = of the county]

pos·sess /pəzés/ v.tr. **1** hold as property; own. **2** have a faculty, quality, etc. (they possess a special value for us). **3** (also refl.; foll. by in) maintain (oneself, one's soul, etc.) in a specified state (possess oneself in patience). **4 a** (of a demon, etc.) occupy; have power over (a person, etc.) (possessed by the devil). **b** (of an emotion, infatuation, etc.) dominate; be an obsession of (possessed by fear). **5** have sexual intercourse with (esp. a woman). □ **be possessed of** own; have. **possess oneself of** take or get for one's own. **what possessed you?** an expression of incredulity. □□ **pos·ses·sor** n. **pos·ses·so·ry** adj. [OF possesser f. L possidēre possess- f. potis able + sedēre sit]

pos·ses·sion /pəzéshən/ n. **1** the act or state of possessing or being possessed. **2 a** the thing possessed. **b** a foreign territory subject to a state or ruler. **3** the act or state of actual holding or occupancy. **4** Law power or control similar to lawful ownership but which may exist separately from it (prosecuted for possession of narcotic drugs). **5** (in pl.) property, wealth, subject territory, etc. **6** Sports temporary control, in team sports, of the ball, puck, etc., by a particular player. □ **in possession 1** (of a person) possessing. **2** (of a thing) possessed. **in possession of 1** having in one's possession. **2** maintaining control over (in possession of one's wits). **in the possession of** held or owned by. **take possession** (often foll. by of) become the owner or possessor of a thing). □□ **pos·ses·sion·less** adj. [ME f. OF possession or L possessio –onis (as POSSESS)]

pos·ses·sive /pəzésiv/ adj. & n. • adj. **1** showing a desire to possess or retain what one already owns. **2** showing jealous and domineering tendencies toward another person. **3** Gram. indicating possession. • n. (in full **possessive case**) Gram. the case of nouns and pronouns expressing possession. □□ **pos·ses·sive·ly** adv. **pos·ses·sive·ness** n. [L possessivus (as POSSESS), transl. Gk kt ētikē (ptōsis case)]

▶**1.** Form the possessive of all singulars by adding -'s: Ross's, Fox's, Reese's. A few classical and other foreign names are traditional exceptions to this rule, e.g., Jesus', Euripides', which take an apostrophe only. **2.** Form the possessive of plurals by adding an apostrophe to the plural form: the Rosses' house, the Perezes' car. See also note at ITS.

pos·ses·sive pro·noun n. each of the pronouns indicating possession (my, your, his, their, etc.) or the corresponding absolute forms (mine, yours, his, theirs, etc.).

pos·set /pósit/ n. hist. a drink made of hot milk curdled with ale, wine, etc., often flavored with spices, formerly used as a remedy for colds, etc. [ME poshote: orig. unkn.]

pos·si·bil·i·ty /pósibílitee/ n. (pl. **·ties**) **1** the state or fact of being possible, or an occurrence of this (outside the range of possibility; saw no possibility of going away). **2** a thing that may exist or happen (there are three possibilities). **3** (usu. in pl.) the capability of being used, improved, etc.; the potential of an object or situation (esp. have possibilities). [ME f. OF possibilité or LL possibilitas –tatis (as POSSIBLE)]

pos·si·ble /pósibəl/ adj. & n. • adj. **1** capable of existing or happening; that may be managed, achieved, etc. (came as early as possible; did as much as possible). **2** that is likely to happen, etc. (few thought their victory possible). **3** acceptable; potential (a possible way of doing it). • n. **1** a possible candidate, member of a team, etc. **2** (prec. by the) whatever is likely, manageable, etc. **3** the highest possible score, esp. in shooting, etc. [ME f. OF possible or L possibilis f. posse be able]

pos·si·bly /pósiblee/ *adv.* **1** perhaps. **2** in accordance with possibility (*cannot possibly refuse*).

pos·sum /pósəm/ *n.* **1** *colloq.* = OPOSSUM **1**. **2** *Austral. & NZ colloq.* a phalanger resembling an American opossum. □ **play possum 1** pretend to be asleep or unconscious when threatened. **2** feign ignorance. [abbr.]

post¹ /pōst/ *n. & v.* ● *n.* **1 a** a long stout piece of timber or metal set upright in the ground, etc.: **a** to support something, esp. in building. **b** to mark a position, boundary, etc. **c** to carry notices. **2** a pole, etc., marking the start or finish of a race. **3** a metal pin, as on a pierced earring. ● *v.tr.* **1** (often foll. by *up*) **a** attach (a paper, etc.) in a prominent place; stick up (*post no bills*). **b** announce or advertise by placard or in a published text. **2** publish the name of (a ship, etc.) as overdue or missing. **3** placard (a wall, etc.) with handbills, etc. **4** achieve (a score in a game, etc.). [OE f. L *postis*: in ME also f. OF, etc.]

post² /pōst/ *n., v., & adv.* ● *n.* **1** esp. *Brit.* the official conveyance of packages, letters, etc.; the mail (*send it by post*). **2** esp. *Brit.* a single collection, dispatch, or delivery of the mail; the letters, etc., dispatched (*has the post arrived yet?*). **3** esp. *Brit.* a place where letters, etc., are dealt with; a post office or mailbox (*take it to the post*). **4** *hist.* **a** one of a series of couriers who carried mail on horseback between fixed stages. **b** a letter carrier; a mail cart. ● *v.* **1** *tr.* esp. *Brit.* put (a letter, etc.) in the mail. **2** *tr.* (esp. as **posted** *adj.*) supply a person with information (*keep me posted*). **3** *tr.* **a** enter (an item) in a ledger (*post the transation in the second column*). **b** (often foll. by *up*) complete (a ledger) in this way. **c** carry (an entry) from an auxiliary book to a more formal one, or from one account to another. **4** *intr.* **a** travel with haste; hurry. **b** *hist.* travel with relays of horses. ● *adv.* express; with haste. [F *poste* (fem.) f. It. *posta* ult. f. L *ponere posit-* place]

post³ /pōst/ *n. & v.* ● *n.* **1** a place where a soldier is stationed or that he patrols. **2** a place of duty. **3 a** a position taken up by a body of soldiers. **b** a force occupying this. **c** a fort. **4** a situation; paid employment. **5** = TRADING POST. **6** *Naut. hist.* a commission as an officer in command of a vessel of 20 guns or more. ● *v.tr.* **1** place or station (soldiers, an employee, etc.). **2** esp. *Brit.* appoint to a post or command. [F *poste* (masc.) f. It. *posto* f. Rmc *postum* (unrecorded) f. L *ponere posit-* place]

post- /pōst/ *prefix* after in time or order. [from or after L *post* (adv. & prep.)]

post·age /póstij/ *n.* the amount charged for sending a letter, etc., by mail, usu. prepaid in the form of a stamp (*$5 for postage*).

post·age me·ter *n.* a machine for printing prepaid postage and a postmark.

post·age stamp *n.* an official stamp affixed to or imprinted on a letter, etc., indicating the amount of postage paid.

post·al /póstˈl/ *adj.* **1** of the post office or mail. **2** by mail.

post·al code *n. Brit. & Canadian* = POSTCODE. □□ **post·al·ly** *adv.* [F (*poste* POST²)]

post·al or·der *n. Brit.* a money order issued by the Post Office, payable to a specified person.

Post·al Un·ion *n.* a union of the governments of various countries for the regulation of international postage.

post·bag /póstbag/ *n. Brit.* = MAILBAG.

post·box /póstboks/ *n. Brit.* a mailbox.

post·card /póstkaard/ *n.* a card, often with a photograph on one side, for sending a short message by mail without an envelope.

post-chaise *n.* (*pl.* **post-chaises**) *hist.* a fast carriage drawn by horses that were changed at regular intervals.

post·clas·si·cal /póstklásikəl/ *adj.* (esp. of Greek and Roman literature) later than the classical period.

post·code /póstkōd/ *n. Brit., Austral., & NZ* a group of letters, or letters and figures, that are added to a mailing address to assist sorting.

post·co·i·tal /póstkóit'l, -kō-éet'l/ *adj.* occurring or existing after sexual intercourse. □□ **post·co·i·tal·ly** *adv.*

post·date *v. & n.* ● *v.tr.* /póstdáyt/ affix or assign a date later than the actual one to (a document, event, etc.). ● *n.* /póstdayt/ such a date.

post·doc·tor·al /póstdóktərəl/ *adj.* of or relating to research undertaken after the completion of doctoral research.

post en·try /póst/ *n.* (*pl.* **·tries**) a late or subsequent entry, esp. in a race or in bookkeeping.

post·er /póstər/ *n.* **1** a placard in a public place. **2** a large printed picture. **3** *Brit.* a billposter.

poste rest·ante /póst restóNT/ *n. Brit.* **1** a direction on a letter to indicate that it should be kept at a specified post office until collected by the addressee. **2** general delivery; the department in a post office where such letters are kept. [F, = letter(s) remaining]

pos·te·ri·or /posteéereeər, pō-/ *adj. & n.* ● *adj.* **1** later; coming after in series, order, or time. **2** situated at the back. ● *n.* (in *sing.* or *pl.*) the buttocks. □□ **pos·te·ri·or·i·ty** /-áwritee, -ór-/ *n.* **pos·te·ri·or·ly** *adv.* [L, compar. of *posterus* following f. *post* after]

pos·ter·i·ty /postéritee/ *n.* **1** all succeeding generations. **2** the descendants of a person. [ME f. OF *posterité* f. L *posteritas –tatis* f. *posterus*: see POSTERIOR]

pos·tern /póstərn, pó-/ *n.* **1** a back door. **2** a side way or entrance. [ME f. OF *posterne, posterle,* f. LL *posterula* dimin. of *posterus*: see POSTERIOR]

post·er paint *n.* a gummy opaque paint.

post ex·change *n. Mil.* a store at a military base, etc. ¶ Abbr.: **PX**.

post·fix *n. & v.* ● *n.* /póstfiks/ a suffix. ● *v.tr.* /póstfiks/ append (letters) at the end of a word.

post·gla·cial /póstgláyshəl/ *adj. & n.* ● *adj.* formed or occurring after a glacial period. ● *n.* a postglacial period or deposit.

post·grad·u·ate /pōstgrájōoət/ *adj. & n.* ● *adj.* **1** (of a course of study) carried on after taking a high school or college degree. **2** of or relating to students following this course of study (*postgraduate fees*). ● *n.* a postgraduate student.

posthaste *adv.* with great speed or immediacy.

post·hu·mous /póschəməs/ *adj.* **1** occurring after death. **2** (of a child) born after the death of its father. **3** (of a book, etc.) published after the author's death. □□ **post·hu·mous·ly** *adv.* [L *postumus* last (superl. f. *post* after): in LL *posth-* by assoc. with *humus* ground]

pos·tiche /posteésh/ *n.* a hairpiece, worn as an adornment. [F, = false, f. It. *posticcio*]

post·ie /póstee/ *n. Brit. colloq.* a postman or postwoman. [abbr.]

pos·til /póstil/ *n. hist.* **1** a marginal note or comment, esp. on a text of Scripture. **2** a commentary. [ME f. OF *postille* f. med.L *postilla,* of uncert. orig.]

pos·til·ion /postílyən, pō-/ *n.* (also **pos·til·lion**) the rider on the near (left-hand side) horse drawing a coach, etc., when there is no coachman. [F *postillon* f. It. *postiglione* post boy f. *posta* POST²]

Post·im·pres·sion·ism /póstimpréshənizəm/ *n.* artistic aims and methods developed as a reaction against impressionism and intending to express the individual artist's conception of the objects represented rather than the ordinary observer's view. □□ **Post·im·pres·sion·ist** *n. & adj.* **Post·im·pres·sion·is·tic** *adj.*

post·in·dus·tri·al /póstindústreeəl/ *adj.* relating to or characteristic of a society or economy that no longer relies on heavy industry.

post·lim·i·ny /pōstlíminee/ *n.* **1** (in international law) the restoration of persons and things taken in war to their former status. **2** (in Roman law) the right of a banished person or captive to resume civic privileges on return from exile. [L *postliminium* (as POST-, *limen liminis* threshold)]

post·lude /póstlōod/ *n. Mus.* a concluding voluntary. [POST-, after PRELUDE]

post·man /póstmən/ *n.* (*pl.* **·men**; *fem.* **post·wom·an,** *pl.* **·wom·en**) a person who is employed to deliver and collect letters, etc.

post·man's knock *n. Brit.* = POST OFFICE 2b.

post·mark /póstmaark/ *n. & v.* ● *n.* an official mark stamped on a letter, esp. one giving the place, date, etc., of sending or arrival, and serving to cancel the stamp. ● *v.tr.* mark (an envelope, etc.) with this.

post·mas·ter /póstmastər/ *n.* the person in charge of a post office.

post·mas·ter gen·er·al *n.* the head of a country's postal service.

post·mil·len·ni·al /póstmiléneeəl/ *adj.* following the millennium.

post·mil·len·ni·al·ism /póstmiléneeəlizəm/ *n.* the doctrine that a second Advent will follow the millennium. □□ **post·mil·len·ni·al·ist** *n.*

post·mis·tress /póstmistris/ *n.* a woman in charge of a post office.

post·mod·ern /póstmódərn/ *adj.* (in literature, architecture, the arts, etc.) denoting a movement reacting against modern tendencies, esp. by drawing attention to former conventions. □□ **post·mod·ern·ism** *n.* **post·mod·ern·ist** *n. & adj.*

post·mor·tem /pōstmáwrtəm/ *n., adv., & adj.* ● *n.* **1** (in full **postmortem examination**) an examination made after death, esp. to determine its cause. **2** *colloq.* a discussion analysing the course and result of a game, election, etc. ● *adv. & adj.* after death. [L]

post·na·tal /póstnáyt'l/ *adj.* characteristic of or relating to the period after childbirth.

post·nup·tial /póstnúpshəl/ *adj.* after marriage.

post-o·bit *n. & n.* ● *n.* /póstóbit/ esp. *Brit.* a bond given to a lender by a borrower to secure a sum for payment on the death of another person from whom the borrower expects to inherit. ● *adj.* /póstóbit/ taking effect after death. [L *post obitum* f. *post* after + *obitus* decease f. *obire* die]

Post Of·fice *n.* **1** the public department or corporation responsible for postal services and (in some countries) telecommunication. **2** (**post office**) **a** a room or building where postal business is carried on. **b** a kissing game played esp. by children in which kisses are given for the pretended delivery of a letter.

post of·fice box *n.* a numbered box in a post office where letters are kept until called for.

post·paid /póstpáyd/ *adj.* on which postage has been paid.

post·par·tum /póstpaártəm/ *adj.* following childbirth.

post·pone /pōstpón, pəspón/ *v.tr.* cause or arrange (an event, etc.)

to take place at a later time. □□ **post•pon•a•ble** *adj.* **post•pone•ment** *n.* **post•pon•er** *n.* [L *postponere* (as POST-, *ponere posit-* place)]

SYNONYM TIP postpone

ADJOURN, DEFER, DELAY, SUSPEND. All of these verbs have to do with putting things off. **Defer** is the broadest in meaning; it suggests putting something off until a later time (*to defer payment; to defer a discussion*). If you **postpone** an event or activity, you put it off intentionally, usually until a definite time in the future (*we postponed the party until the next weekend*). If you **adjourn** an activity, you postpone it until another day or place; *adjourn* is usually associated with meetings or other formal gatherings that are brought to an end and then resumed (*the judge adjourned the hearing until the following morning*). If you **delay** something, you postpone it because of obstacles (*delayed by severe thunderstorms and highway flooding*) or because you are reluctant to do it (*to delay going to the dentist*). **Suspend** suggests stopping an activity for a while, usually for a reason (*forced to suspend work on the bridge until the holiday weekend was over*).

---

post•po•si•tion /pṓstpəzíshən/ *n.* **1** a word or particle, esp. an enclitic, placed after the word it modifies, e.g., *–ward* in *homeward* and *at* in *the books we looked at*. **2** the use of a postposition. □□ **post•po•si•tion•al** *adj. & n.* **post•pos•i•tive** /pṓstpózitiv/ *adj. & n.* **post•pos•i•tive•ly** *adv.* [LL *postpositio* (as POSTPONE)]
post•pran•di•al /pṓstprándeeəl/ *adj.* formal or joc. after dinner or lunch. [POST- + L *prandium* a meal]
post•script /pṓstskript, pṓskript/ *n.* **1** an additional paragraph or remark, usu. at the end of a letter after the signature and introduced by 'PS.' **2** any additional information, action, etc. [L *postscriptum* neut. past part. of *postscribere* (as POST-, *scribere* write)]
post-tax /pṓst-táks/ *adj.* = AFTER-TAX.
pos•tu•lant /póschələnt/ *n.* a candidate, esp. for admission into a religious order. [F *postulant* or L *postulans –antis* (as POSTULATE)]
pos•tu•late *v. & n.* • *v.tr.* /póschəlayt/ **1** (often foll. by *that* + clause) assume as a necessary condition, esp. as a basis for reasoning; take for granted. **2** claim. **3** (in ecclesiastical law) nominate or elect to a higher rank. • *n.* /póschələt/ **1** a thing postulated. **2** a fundamental prerequisite or condition. **3** *Math.* an assumption used as a basis for mathematical reasoning. □□ **pos•tu•la•tion** /–láyshən/ *n.* [L *postulare postulat-* demand]
pos•tu•la•tor /póschəlaytər/ *n.* **1** a person who postulates. **2** *RC Ch.* a person who presents a case for canonization or beatification.
pos•ture /póschər/ *n. & v.* • *n.* **1** the relative position of parts, esp. of the body (*in a reclining posture*). **2** carriage or bearing (*improved by good posture and balance*). **3** a mental or spiritual attitude or condition. **4** the condition or state (of affairs, etc.) (*in more diplomatic postures*). • *v.* **1** *intr.* assume a mental or physical attitude, esp. for effect (*inclined to strut and posture*). **2** *tr.* pose (a person). □□ **pos•tur•al** *adj.* **pos•tur•er** *n.* [F f. It. *postura* f. L *positura* f. *ponere posit-* place]
post•war /pṓstwáwr/ *adj.* occurring or existing after a war (esp. the most recent major war).
po•sy /pṓzee/ *n.* (*pl.* **•sies**) **1** a small bunch of flowers. **2** *archaic* a short motto, line of verse, etc., inscribed within a ring. [alt. f. POESY]
po•sy ring *n.* a ring engraved with a motto, etc.
pot¹ /pot/ *n. & v.* • *n.* **1** a vessel, usu. rounded, of ceramic ware or metal or glass for holding liquids or solids or for cooking in. **2 a** a coffeepot, flowerpot, teapot, etc. **b** = CHIMNEY POT. **c** = LOBSTER POT. **3** a drinking vessel of pewter, etc. **4** the contents of a pot (*ate a whole pot of jam*). **5** the total amount of the bet in a game, etc. **6** *colloq.* a large sum (*pots of money*). **7** *Brit. sl.* a vessel given as a prize in an athletic contest, esp. a silver cup. **8** = POTBELLY. • *v.tr.* (**pot•ted, pot•ting**) **1** place in a pot. **2** (usu. as **potted** *adj.*) preserve in a sealed pot (*potted shrimps*). **3** *Brit.* sit (a young child) on a chamber pot. **4** *Brit.* pocket (a ball) in billiards, etc. **5** shoot at, hit, or kill (an animal) with a potshot. **6** seize or secure. **7** *Brit.* abridge or epitomize (*in a potted version; potted wisdom*). □ **go to pot** *colloq.* deteriorate; be ruined. **put a person's pot on** *Austral. & NZ sl.* inform on a person. □□ **pot•ful** *n.* (*pl.* **•fuls**). [OE *pott*, corresp. to OFris., MDu., MLG *pot*, f. pop.L]
pot² /pot/ *n. sl.* marijuana. [prob. f. Mex. Sp. *potiguaya*]
po•ta•ble /pṓtəbəl/ *adj.* drinkable. □□ **po•ta•bil•i•ty** /–bílitee/ *n.* [F *potable* or LL *potabilis* f. L *potare* drink]
po•tage /pōtaázh/ *n.* thick soup. [F (as POTTAGE)]
po•tam•ic /pətámik, pō–/ *adj.* of rivers. □□ **po•ta•mol•o•gy** /pṓtəmólijee/ *n.* [Gk *potamos* river]
pot•ash /pótash/ *n.* an alkaline potassium compound, usu. potassium carbonate or hydroxide. [17th-c. *pot-ashes* f. Du. *pot-asschen* (as POT¹, ASH¹): orig. obtained by leaching vegetable ashes and evaporating the solution in iron pots]
po•tas•si•um /pətáseeəm/ *n. Chem.* a soft silvery white metallic element occurring naturally in seawater and various minerals, an

essential element for living organisms, and forming many useful compounds used industrially. ¶ Symb.: K. □□ **po•tas•sic** *adj.* [POTASH + –IUM]
po•tas•si•um chlo•ride *n.* a white crystalline solid used as a fertilizer and in photographic processing.
po•tas•si•um cy•a•nide *n.* a highly toxic solid that can be hydrolyzed to give poisonous hydrogen cyanide gas. Also called **cyanide**.
po•tas•si•um i•o•dide *n.* a white crystalline solid used as an additive to table salt to prevent iodine deficiency.
po•tas•si•um per•man•ga•nate *n.* a purple crystalline solid that is used in solution as an oxidizing agent and disinfectant.
po•ta•tion /pōtáyshən/ *n.* **1** a drink. **2** the act or an instance of drinking. **3** (usu. in *pl.*) the act or an instance of tippling. □□ **po•ta•to•ry** /pṓtətawree/ *adj.* [ME f. OF *potation* or L *potatio* f. *potare* drink]
po•ta•to /pətáytō/ *n.* (*pl.* **•toes**) **1** a starchy plant tuber that is cooked and used for food. **2** the plant, *Solanum tuberosum*, bearing this. **3** = SWEET POTATO. **4** *Brit. colloq.* a hole in (esp. the heel of) a sock or stocking. [Sp. *patata* var. of Taino *batata*]

SPELLING TIP potatoes

To remember the *-oes* ending of the plural *potatoes*, use the mnemonic: "Pota*toes* grow with their *toes* in the dirt."

---

po•ta•to chip *n.* a thin slice of potato deep-fried, eaten as a snack food.
pot-au-feu /páwtōfő/ *n.* **1** the traditional French dish of boiled meat and vegetables. **2** the soup or broth from it. **3** a large cooking pot of the kind common in France. [F, = pot on the fire]
pot•bel•ly /pótbelee/ *n.* (*pl.* **–lies**) **1** a protruding stomach. **2** a person with this. **3** a small bulbous stove. □□ **pot•bel•lied** *adj.*
pot•boil•er /pótboylər/ *n.* **1** a work of literature or art done merely to make the writer or artist a living. **2** a writer or artist who does this.
pot-bound *adj.* (of a plant) having roots that fill the flowerpot, leaving no room to expand.
potch /poch/ *n.* an opal of inferior quality. [19th c.: orig. unkn.]
pot cheese *n.* a type of cottage cheese.
po•teen /pōtéen, pə–/ *n.* (also **po•theen** /–chéen/) *Ir.* alcohol made illicitly, usu. from potatoes. [Ir. *poitín* dimin. of *pota* POT¹]
po•tent¹ /pṓt'nt/ *adj.* **1** powerful; strong. **2** (of a reason) cogent; forceful. **3** (of a male) capable of sexual erection or orgasm. **4** *literary* mighty. □□ **po•tence** *n.* **po•ten•cy** *n.* **po•tent•ly** *adv.* [L *potens –entis* pres. part. of *posse* be able]
po•tent² /pṓt'nt/ *adj. & n. Heraldry* • *adj.* **1 a** formed of crutch-shaped pieces. **b** (esp. of a cross) having a straight br across the end of each extremity. **2** (of a fur) formed by a series of such shapes. • *n.* this fur. [ME f. OF *potence* crutch f. L *potentia* power (as POTENT¹)]
po•ten•tate /pṓt'ntayt/ *n.* a monarch or ruler. [ME f. OF *potentat* or L *potentatus* dominion (as POTENT²)]
po•ten•tial /pəténshəl/ *adj. & n.* • *adj.* capable of coming into being or action; latent. • *n.* **1** the capacity for use or development; possibility (*achieved its highest potential*). **2** usable resources. **3** *Physics* the quantity determining the energy of mass in a gravitational field or of charge in an electric field. □□ **po•ten•ti•al•i•ty** /–sheeálitee/ *n.* **po•ten•tial•ize** *v.tr.* **po•ten•tial•ly** *adv.* [ME f. OF *potencial* or LL *potentialis* f. *potentia* (as POTENT¹)]
po•ten•tial bar•ri•er *n.* a region of high potential impeding the movement of particles, etc.
po•ten•tial dif•fer•ence *n.* the difference of electric potential between two points.
po•ten•tial en•er•gy *n.* a body's ability to do work by virtue of its position relative to others, stresses within itself, electric charge, etc.
po•ten•ti•ate /pəténsheeayt/ *v.tr.* **1** make more powerful, esp. increase the effectiveness of (a drug). **2** make possible. [as POTENT¹ after SUBSTANTIATE]
po•ten•til•la /pṓt'ntílə/ *n.* any plant or shrub of the genus *Potentilla*; a cinquefoil. [med.L, dimin. of L *potens* POTENT¹]
po•ten•ti•om•e•ter /pəténsheeómitər/ *n.* an instrument for measuring or adjusting small electrical potentials. □□ **po•ten•ti•o•met•ric** /–sheeəmétrik/ *adj.* **po•ten•ti•om•e•try** /–sheeómitree/ *n.*
pot•head /póthed/ *n. sl.* a person who smokes marijuana frequently.
po•theen var. of POTEEN.
poth•er /póthər/ *n. & v.* • *n.* a noise; commotion; fuss. • *v.* **1** *tr.* fluster; worry. **2** *intr.* make a fuss. [16th c.: orig. unkn.]
pot•herb /pótərb, –hərb/ *n.* any herb grown in a kitchen garden or a pot.
pot•hole /pót-hōl/ *n. & v.* • *n.* **1** *Geol.* a deep hole or system of caves and underground riverbeds formed by the erosion of rock esp. by the action of water. **2** a deep hole in the ground or a riverbed. **3** a hole in a road surface caused by wear, weather, or subsidence. • *v.intr. Brit.* explore potholes. □□ **pot•holed** *adj.* **pot•hol•er** *n.* **pot•hol•ing** *n.*
po•tion /pṓshən/ *n.* a liquid medicine, drug, poison, etc. [ME f. OF f. L *potio –onis* f. *potus* having drunk]
pot•latch /pótlach/ *n.* (among Native Americans of the Pacific

Northwest) a ceremonial festival of gift giving or destruction of the owner's property to display wealth. [Chinook f. Nootka *patlatsh* gift]

pot·luck /pótlək/ *n.* **1** whatever (hospitality, food, etc.) is available. **2** a meal to which each guest brings a dish to share.

pot of gold *n.* an imaginary reward; an ideal; a jackpot.

po·to·roo /pótərōō/ *n. Austral.* any small marsupial of the genus *Potorus*, native to Australia and Tasmania; a rat kangaroo. [Aboriginal]

pot·pie /pótpī/ *n.* a pie of meat, vegetables, etc., with a crust baked in a pot or deep-dish pie plate.

pot plant *n.* **1** a marijuana plant. **2** *Brit.* a plant grown in a flowerpot.

pot·pour·ri /pópoōrée/ *n.* **1** a mixture of dried petals and spices used to perfume a room, etc. **2** a musical or literary medley. [F, = rotten pot]

pot roast *n. & v.* •*n.* a piece of meat cooked slowly in a covered dish. •*v.* (**pot-roast**) cook (a piece of meat) in this way.

pot·sherd /pótshərd/ *n.* a broken piece of pottery, esp. one found on an archaeological site.

pot·shot /pótshot/ *n.* **1** a shot aimed unexpectedly or at random at someone or something with no chance of self-defense. **2** a shot aimed at a game bird or other animal purely to kill it for food, without regard to the rules of the sport. **3** *fig.* a criticism, esp. a random or unfounded one.

pot·tage /pótij/ *n. archaic* soup; stew. [ME f. OF *potage* (as POT[1])]

pot·ter[1] /pótər/ *n.* a maker of ceramic vessels. [OE *pottere* (as POT[1])]

pot·ter[2] /pótər/ *Brit.* var. of PUTTER[3].

pot·ter's field *n.* a burial place for paupers, strangers, etc. (after Matt. 27:7).

pot·ter's wheel *n.* a horizontal revolving disk to carry clay for making pots.

pot·ter·y /pótəree/ *n.* (*pl.* **-ies**) **1** vessels, etc., made of fired clay. **2** a potter's work. **3** a potter's workshop. [ME f. OF *poterie* f. *potier* POTTER[2]]

pot·ting shed /póting/ *n.* a building in which plants are potted and tools, etc., are stored.

pot·tle /pót'l/ *n.* **1** *Brit.* a small carton for strawberries, etc. **2** *archaic* **a** a measure for liquids; a half gallon. **b** a pot, etc., containing this. [ME f. OF *potel* (as POT[1])]

pot·to /pótō/ *n.* (*pl.* **-tos**) **1** a W. African lemurlike mammal, *Perodicticus potto.* **2** a kinkajou. [perh. f. Guinea dial.]

potter's wheel

Pott's frac·ture /pots/ *n.* a fracture of the lower end of the fibula, usu. with dislocation of the ankle. [P. Pott, Engl. surgeon d. 1788]

pot·ty[1] /pótee/ *adj.* (**pot·ti·er, pot·ti·est**) *Brit. sl.* **1** foolish or crazy. **2** insignificant; trivial (esp. *potty little*). □□ **pot·ti·ness** *n.* [19th c.: orig. unkn.]

pot·ty[2] /pótee/ *n.* (*pl.* **-ties**) *colloq.* a small pot for toilet-training a child.

pouch /powch/ *n. & v.* •*n.* **1** a small bag or detachable outside pocket. **2** a baggy area of skin underneath the eyes, etc. **3 a** a pocketlike receptacle in which marsupials carry their young during lactation. **b** any of several similar structures in various animals, e.g., in the cheeks of rodents. **4** a soldier's ammunition bag. **5** a lockable bag for mail or dispatches. **6** *Bot.* a baglike cavity, esp. the seed vessel, in a plant. •*v.tr.* **1** put or make into a pouch. **2** take possession of; pocket. **3** make (part of a dress, etc.) hang like a pouch. □□ **pouched** *adj.* **pouch·y** *adj.* [ME f. ONF *pouche*: cf. POKE[2]]

pouffe /poof/ *n.* (also **pouf**) a large firm cushion used as a low seat or footstool. [F *pouf*; ult. imit.]

pou·larde /poōlaárd/ *n.* (also **pou·lard**) a domestic hen that has been spayed and fattened for eating. [F *poularde* f. *poule* hen]

poult[1] /pōlt/ *n.* a young domestic fowl, turkey, pheasant, etc. [ME, contr. f. PULLET]

poult[2] /poōlt/ *n.* (in full **poult-de-soie** /poōdəswaá/) a fine corded silk or taffeta, usu. colored. [F, of unkn. orig.]

poul·ter·er /póltərər/ *n. Brit.* a dealer in poultry and usu. game. [ME *poulter* f. OF *pouletier* (as PULLET)]

poul·tice /póltis/ *n. & v.* •*n.* a soft medicated and usu. heated mass applied to the body and kept in place with muslin, etc., for relieving soreness and inflammation. •*v.tr.* apply a poultice to. [orig. *pultes* (pl.) f. L *puls pultis* pottage, pap, etc.]

poul·try /póltree/ *n.* domestic fowls (ducks, geese, turkeys, chickens, etc.), esp. as a source of food. [ME f. OF *pouletrie* (as POULTERER)]

pounce[1] /powns/ *v. & n.* •*v.intr.* **1** spring or swoop, esp. as in capturing prey. **2** (often foll. by *on, upon*) **a** make a sudden attack. **b** seize eagerly upon an object, remark, etc. (*pounced on what we said*). •*n.* **1** the act or an instance of pouncing. **2** the claw or talon of a bird of prey. □□ **pounc·er** *n.* [perh. f. PUNCHEON[1]]

---

pounce[2] /powns/ *n. & v.* •*n.* **1** a fine powder formerly used to prevent ink from spreading on unglazed paper. **2** powdered charcoal, etc., dusted over a perforated pattern to transfer the design to the object beneath. •*v.tr.* **1** dust with pounce. **2** transfer (a design, etc.) by use of pounce. **3** smooth (paper, etc.) with pounce or pumice. □□ **pounc·er** *n.* [F *ponce, poncer* f. L *pumex* PUMICE]

poun·cet box /pównsit/ *n. archaic* a small box with a perforated lid for perfumes, etc. [16th c.: perh. orig. erron. f. *pounced* (= perforated) *box*]

pound[1] /pownd/ *n.* **1** a unit of weight equal to 16 oz. avoirdupois (0.4536 kg), or 12 oz. troy (0.3732 kg). **2** (in full **pound sterling**) (*pl.* same or **pounds**) the chief monetary unit of the UK and several other countries. [OE *pund* ult. f. L *pondo* Roman pound weight of 12 ounces]

pound[2] /pownd/ *v. & n.* •*v.* **1** *tr.* **a** crush or beat with repeated heavy blows. **b** pummel, esp. with the fists. **c** grind to a powder or pulp. **2** *intr.* (foll. by *at, on*) deliver heavy blows or gunfire. **3** *intr.* (foll. by *along*, etc.) make one's way heavily or clumsily. **4** *intr.* (of the heart) beat heavily. •*n.* a heavy blow or thump; the sound of this. □ **pound into** instill (an attitude, behavior, etc.) forcefully (*pounded into me*). **pound out 1** produce with or as if with heavy blows. **2** remove (an attitude, behavior, etc.) forcefully (*pounded out of him*). □□ **pound·er** *n.* [OE *pūnian*, rel. to Du. *puin*, LG *pün* rubbish]

pound[3] /pownd/ *n. & v.* •*n.* **1** an enclosure where stray animals or officially removed vehicles are kept until redeemed. **2** a place of confinement. •*v.tr.* enclose (cattle, etc.) in a pound. [ME f. OE *pund-* in *pundfald*: see PINFOLD]

pound·age /pówndij/ *n.* **1 a** weight in pounds. **b** a person's weight, esp. that which is regarded as excess. **2** *Brit.* a commission or fee of so much per pound sterling or weight. **3** *Brit.* a percentage of the total earnings of a business, paid as wages.

pound·al /pównd'l/ *n. Physics* a unit of force equal to the force required to give a mass of one pound an acceleration of one foot per second. [POUND[1] + *-al* perh. after *quintal*]

pound cake *n.* a rich cake orig. containing a pound (or equal weights) of each chief ingredient.

pound coin *n.* (also **pound note**) a coin or note worth one pound sterling.

pound·er /pówndər/ *n.* (usu. in *comb.*) **1** a thing or person weighing a specified number of pounds (*a five-pounder*). **2** a gun carrying a shell of a specified number of pounds. **3** a thing worth, or a person possessing, so many pounds sterling.

pound lock *n.* a lock with two gates to confine water and often a side reservoir to maintain the water level.

pound of flesh *n.* any legitimate but crippling demand.

pound sign *n.* **1** the sign #. **2** the sign £, representing a pound.

pour /pawr/ *v.* **1** *intr. & tr.* (usu. foll. by *down, out, over*, etc.) flow or cause to flow esp. downwards in a stream or shower. **2** *tr.* dispense (a drink) by pouring. **3** *intr.* (of rain, or with *it* as subject) fall heavily. **4** *intr.* (usu. foll. by *in, out*, etc.) come or go in profusion or rapid succession (*the crowd poured out; letters poured in; poems poured from her fertile mind*). **5** *tr.* discharge or send freely (*poured forth arrows*). **6** *tr.* (often foll. by *out*) utter at length or in a rush (*poured out their story; poured scorn on my attempts*). □ **pour cold water on** see COLD. **pour it on** progress or work quickly or with all one's energy. **pour oil on troubled waters** calm a disagreement or disturbance, esp. with conciliatory words. **when it rains, it pours** (or **it never rains but it pours**) misfortunes rarely come singly. □□ **pour·a·ble** *adj.* **pour·er** *n.* [ME: orig. unkn.]

pour·boire /poōrbwaár/ *n.* a gratuity or tip. [F, = *pour boire* (money) for drinking]

pout[1] /powt/ *v. & n.* •*v.* **1** *intr.* **a** push the lips forward as an expression of displeasure or sulking. **b** (of the lips) be pushed forward. **2** *tr.* push (the lips) forward in pouting. •*n.* **1** such an action or expression. **2** (**the pouts**) a fit of sulking. □□ **pout·er** *n.* **pout·ing·ly** *adv.* **pout·y** *adj.* [ME, perh. f. OE *putian* (unrecorded) be inflated: cf. POUT[2]]

pout[2] /powt/ *n.* **1** = BIB[1] 3. **2** = EELPOUT. **3** = BULLHEAD. [OE *-puta* in *ælepūta* eelpout, f. WG]

pout·er /pówtər/ *n.* **1** a person who pouts. **2** a kind of pigeon able to inflate its crop considerably.

pov·er·ty /póvərtee/ *n.* **1** the state of being poor; want of the necessities of life. **2** (often foll. by *of, in*) scarcity or lack. **3** inferiority; poorness; meanness. **4** *Eccl.* renunciation of the right to individual ownership of property esp. by a member of a religious order. [ME f. OF *poverte, poverté* f. L *paupertas –tatis* f. *pauper* poor]

pov·er·ty line *n.* (also **pov·er·ty lev·el**) the minimum income level, as defined by a government standard, needed to secure the necessities of life.

pov·er·ty-strick·en *adj.* extremely poor.

POW *abbr.* prisoner of war.

---

pow /pow/ *int.* expressing the sound of a blow or explosion. [imit.]

pow·der /pówdər/ *n. & v.* •*n.* 1 a substance in the form of fine dry particles. 2 a medicine or cosmetic in this form. 3 = GUNPOWDER. •*v.tr.* 1 a apply powder to. b sprinkle or decorate with or as with powder. 2 (esp. as powdered *adj.*) reduce to a fine powder (*powdered milk*). □ keep one's powder dry be cautious and alert. take a powder *sl.* depart quickly. □□ pow·der·y *adj.* [ME f. OF *poudre* f. L *pulvis pulveris* dust]

pow·der blue *n.* pale blue.

pow·der flask *n.* (also **pow·der horn**) *hist.* a small case for carrying gunpowder.

pow·der keg *n.* 1 a barrel of gunpowder. 2 a dangerous or volatile situation.

pow·der mon·key *n. hist.* a boy employed on board ship to carry powder to the guns.

pow·der puff *n.* a soft pad for applying powder to the skin, esp. the face.

pow·der-puff *adj.* 1 designating an activity intended for or restricted to women. 2 lightweight; frivolous.

pow·der room *n.* a women's toilet in a public building.

pow·er /pówər/ *n. & v.* •*n.* 1 the ability to do or act (*will do all in my power; has the power to change color*). 2 a particular faculty of body or mind (*lost the power of speech; powers of persuasion*). 3 a government, influence, or authority. b political or social ascendancy or control (*the party in power*). 4 authorization; delegated authority (*power of attorney; police powers*). 5 (often foll. by *over*) personal ascendancy. 6 an influential person, group, or organization (*the press is a power in the land*). 7 a military strength. b a nation having international influence, esp. based on military strength (*the leading powers*). 8 vigor; energy. 9 an active property or function (*has a high heating power*). 10 *colloq.* a large number or amount (*has done me a power of good*). 11 the capacity for exerting mechanical force or doing work (*horsepower*). 12 mechanical or electrical energy as distinct from hand labor (often *attrib.: power tools; power steering*). 13 a a public supply of (esp. electrical) energy. b a particular source or form of energy (*hydroelectric power*). 14 a mechanical force applied, e.g., by means of a lever. 15 *Physics* the rate of energy output. 16 the product obtained when a number is multiplied by itself a certain number of times (*2 to the power of 3 = 8*). 17 the magnifying capacity of a lens. 18 a a deity. b (in *pl.*) the sixth order of the ninefold celestial hierarchy. •*v.tr.* 1 supply with mechanical or electrical energy. 2 (foll. by *up, down*) increase or decrease the power supplied to (a device); switch on or off. □ in the power of under the control of. power behind the throne a person who asserts authority or influence without having formal status. the powers that be those in authority. □□ pow·ered *adj.* (also in *comb.*). [ME & AF *poer*, etc., OF *poeir* ult. f. L *posse* be able]

pow·er·boat /pówərbōt/ *n.* a powerful motorboat.

pow·er block *n.* a group of nations constituting an international political force.

pow·er brakes *n.pl.* automotive brakes in which engine power supplements that provided by the driver's pressure on the brake pedal.

pow·er cut *n.* esp. *Brit.* = POWER FAILURE.

pow·er dive *n. & v.* •*n.* a steep dive of an aircraft with the engines providing thrust. •*v.intr.* perform a power dive.

pow·er fail·ure *n.* a temporary withdrawal or failure of an electric power supply.

pow·er·ful /pówərfool/ *adj.* 1 having much power or strength. 2 politically or socially influential. □□ pow·er·ful·ly *adv.* pow·er·ful·ness *n.*

pow·er·house /pówərhows/ *n.* 1 = POWER PLANT. 2 a person or thing of great energy.

pow·er·less /pówərlis/ *adj.* 1 without power or strength. 2 (often foll. by *to* + infin.) wholly unable (*powerless to help*). □□ pow·er·less·ly *adv.* pow·er·less·ness *n.*

pow·er line *n.* a conductor supplying electrical power, esp. one supported by pylons or poles.

pow·er of at·tor·ney *n.* the authority to act for another person in legal or financial matters.

pow·er pack *n.* 1 a unit for supplying power. 2 the equipment for converting an alternating current (from an electrical outlet) to a direct current at a different (usu. lower) voltage.

pow·er plant *n.* (also **pow·er sta·tion**) 1 a facility producing esp. electrical power. 2 source of power, as an engine.

pow·er play *n.* 1 tactics involving the concentration of players at a particular point. 2 similar tactics in business, politics, etc., involving a concentration of resources, effort, etc. 3 *Ice Hockey* a situation in which one team has an extra skater owing to a penalty on the opposing team.

pow·er point *n. Brit.* an electrical outlet.

pow·er-shar·ing *n.* a policy agreed upon between parties or within a coalition to share responsibility for decision making and political action.

pow·er stroke *n.* the stroke of an internal-combustion engine, in which the piston is moved downward by the expansion of gases.

pow-wow /pów-wow/ *n. & v.* •*n.* a conference or meeting for discussion (orig. among Native Americans). •*v.tr.* hold a powwow. [Algonquian *powah, powwaw* magician (lit. 'he dreams')]

pox /poks/ *n.* 1 any virus disease producing a rash of pimples that become pus-filled and leave pockmarks on healing. 2 *colloq.* = SYPHILIS. 3 a plant disease that causes pocklike spots. □ a pox on *archaic* an exclamation of anger or impatience with (a person). [alt. spelling of *pocks* pl. of POCK]

poz·zo·la·na /pótsəláanə/ *n.* (also **puz·zo·la·na**) a volcanic ash used for mortar or hydraulic cement. [It., f. *pozz(u)olana* (adj.) of *Pozzuoli* near Naples]

pp *abbr.* pianissimo.

pp. *abbr.* pages.

p.p. *abbr.* (also **pp**) *per pro.*

p.p.b. *abbr.* parts per billion.

ppd. *abbr.* 1 postpaid. 2 prepaid.

p.p.m. *abbr.* parts per million.

PPO *abbr.* PREFERRED PROVIDER ORGANIZATION.

PPS *abbr.* 1 additional postscript. 2 *Brit.* Parliamentary Private Secretary.

PR *abbr.* 1 public relations. 2 Puerto Rico. 3 proportional representation.

Pr *symb. Chem.* the element praseodymium.

pr. *abbr.* pair.

prac·ti·ca·ble /práktikəbəl/ *adj.* 1 that can be done or used. 2 possible in practice. □□ prac·ti·ca·bil·i·ty /-bílitee/ *n.* prac·ti·ca·ble·ness *n.* prac·ti·ca·bly *adv.* [F *praticable* f. *pratiquer* put into practice (as PRACTICAL)]

►See note at PRACTICAL.

prac·ti·cal /prá ktikəl/ *adj. & n.* •*adj.* 1 of or concerned with practice or use rather than theory. 2 suited to use or action; designed mainly to fulfill a function (*practical shoes*). 3 (of a person) inclined to action rather than speculation; able to make things function well. 4 a that is such in effect though not nominally (*for all practical purposes*). b virtual (*in practical control*). 5 feasible; concerned with what is actually possible (*practical politics*). •*n. Brit.* a practical examination or lesson. □□ prac·ti·cal·i·ty /-kálitee/ *n.* (*pl.* ·ties) prac·ti·cal·ness *n.* [earlier *practic* f. obs. F *practique* or LL *practicus* f. Gk *praktikos* f. *prassō* do, act]

►**Practical** and **practicable** are sometimes confused. **Practical** means 'concerning practice,' that is, 'useful; functional.' **Practicable** comes from *practice able*, meaning 'able to be practiced,' or 'able to be done; possible.' Some things —especially ideas—can be both: Nuclear rockets may be both practical (that is, there is something to be gained from developing them) and practicable (that is, they may be possible).

prac·ti·cal joke *n.* a humorous trick played on a person.

prac·ti·cal·ly /práktiklee/ *adv.* 1 virtually; almost (*practically nothing*). 2 in a practical way.

prac·tice /práktis/ *n. & v.* •*n.* 1 habitual action or performance (*the practice of teaching; makes a practice of saving*). 2 a habit or custom (*has been my regular practice*). 3 a repeated exercise in an activity in order to acquire the development of a skill (*to sing well needs much practice*). b a session of this (*time for target practice*). 4 action or execution as opposed to theory. 5 the professional work or business of a doctor, lawyer, etc. (*has a practice in town*). 6 an established method of legal procedure. 7 procedure generally, esp. of a specified kind (*bad practice*). •*v.tr. & intr.* (also *Brit.* **practise**) 1 *tr.* perform habitually; carry out in action (*practice the same method; practice what you preach*). 2 *tr. & intr.* (foll. by *in, on*) do repeatedly, as an exercise, to improve a skill; exercise oneself in or on (an activity requiring skill) (*had to practice in the art of speaking; practice your reading*). 3 *tr.* (as **practiced** *adj.*) experienced, expert (*a practiced liar; with a practiced hand*). 4 *tr.* a pursue or be engaged in (a profession, religion, etc.). b (as **practicing** *adj.*) currently active or engaged in (a profession or activity) (*a practicing Christian; a practicing lawyer*). 5 *intr.* (foll. by *on, upon*) take advantage of; impose upon. 6 *intr. archaic* scheme; contrive (*when first we practice to deceive*). □ in practice 1 when actually applied; in reality. 2 skillful because of recent exercise in a particular pursuit. out of practice lacking a former skill from lack of recent practice. put into practice actually apply (an idea, method, etc.). □□ prac·tic·er *n.* [ME f. OF *pra(c)tiser* or med.L *practizare* alt. f. *practicare* (as PRACTICAL)]

prac·ti·cian /praktíshən/ *n.* a worker; a practitioner. [obs. F *practicien* f. *practique* f. med.L *practica* f. Gk *praktikē* fem. of *praktikos*: see PRACTICAL]

prac·tise *Brit.* var. of PRACTICE *v.*

prac·ti·tion·er /praktíshənər/ *n.* a person practicing a profession, esp. medicine (*general practitioner*). [obs. *practitian* = PRACTICIAN]

prad /prad/ *n.* esp. *Austral. sl.* a horse. [by metathesis f. Du. *paard* f. LL *paraveredus*: see PALFREY]

prae- /pree/ *prefix* = PRE- (esp. in words regarded as Latin or relating to Roman antiquity). [L: see PRE-]

prae·ci·pe /preésipee, prés-/ *n.* 1 a writ demanding action or an explanation of inaction. **2** an order requesting a writ. [L (the first word of the writ), imper. of *praecipere* enjoin: see PRECEPT]

prae·co·cial *Brit.* var. of PRECOCIAL.

prae·mu·ni·re /preemyŏŏníree/ *n. hist.* a writ charging a sheriff to summon a person accused of asserting or maintaining papal jurisdiction in England. [med.L, = forewarn, for L *praemonēre* (as PRAE-, *monēre* warn): the words *praemunire facias* that you warn (a person to appear) occur in the writ]

prae·no·men /preenṓmen/ *n.* an ancient Roman's first or personal name (e.g., *Marcus* Tullius Cicero). [L f. *prae* before + *nomen* name]

prae·sid·i·um var. of PRESIDIUM.

prae·tor /preétər/ *n.* (also **pre·tor**) *Rom. Hist.* each of two ancient Roman magistrates ranking below consul. □□ **prae·to·ri·al** /-tóreeəl/ *adj.* **prae·tor·ship** *n.* [ME f. F *préteur* or L *praetor* (perh. as PRAE-, *ire it-* go)]

prae·to·ri·an /preetáwreeən/ *adj. & n.* (also **pre·to·ri·an**) *Rom. Hist.* ● *adj.* of or having the powers of a praetor. ● *n.* a man of praetorian rank. [ME f. L *praetorianus* (as PRAETOR)]

prae·to·ri·an guard *n. Rom. Hist.* the bodyguard of the Roman emperor.

prag·mat·ic /pragmátik/ *adj.* **1** dealing with matters with regard to their practical requirements or consequences. **2** treating the facts of history with reference to their practical lessons. **3** *hist.* of or relating to the affairs of a state. **4** (also **prag·mat·i·cal**) **a** concerning pragmatism. **b** meddlesome. **c** dogmatic. □□ **prag·mat·i·cal·i·ty** /-tikálitee/ *n.* **prag·mat·i·cal·ly** *adv.* [LL *pragmaticus* f. Gk *pragmatikos* f. *pragma -matos* deed]

prag·mat·ics /pragmátiks/ *n.pl.* (usu. treated as *sing.*) the branch of linguistics dealing with language in use.

prag·mat·ic sanc·tion *n. hist.* an imperial or royal ordinance issued as a fundamental law, esp. regarding a question of royal succession.

prag·ma·tism /prágmətizəm/ *n.* **1** a pragmatic attitude or procedure. **2** a philosophy that evaluates assertions solely by their practical consequences and bearing on human interests. □□ **prag·ma·tist** *n.* **prag·ma·tis·tic** /-tístik/ *adj.* [Gk *pragma*: see PRAGMATIC]

prag·ma·tize /prágmətīz/ *v.tr.* **1** represent as real. **2** rationalize (a myth).

prah·u var. of PROA.

prai·rie /práiree/ *n.* a large area of usu. treeless grassland esp. in central N. America. [F f. OF *praerie* ult. f. L *pratum* meadow]

prai·rie chick·en *n.* a central N. American grouse, *Tympanuchus cupido.*

prai·rie dog *n.* any central or western N. American rodent of the genus *Cynomys*, living in burrows and making a barking sound.

prai·rie oys·ter *n.* **1** a seasoned raw egg or egg yolk, often served in a drink as a cure for a hangover. **2** the cooked testis of a calf served as food.

prai·rie schoon·er *n.* a covered wagon used by the 19th-c. pioneers in crossing the prairies.

prai·rie wolf *n.* = COYOTE.

praise /prayz/ *v. & n.* ● *v.tr.* **1** express warm approval or admiration of. **2** glorify (God) in words. ● *n.* the act or an instance of praising; commendation (*won high praise; were loud in their praises*). □ **praise be!** an exclamation of pious gratitude. **sing the praises of** commend (a person) highly. □□ **praise·ful** *adj.* **prais·er** *n.* [ME f. OF *preisier* price, prize, praise, f. LL *pretiare* f. L *pretium* price: cf. PRIZE[1]]

SYNONYM TIP praise

ACCLAIM, COMMEND, EULOGIZE, EXTOL, LAUD. If your dog sits when you tell him to sit, you'll want to **praise** him for his obedience. *Praise* is a general term for expressing approval, esteem, or commendation that usually suggests the judgment of a superior (*the teacher's praise for her students*). If a salesperson goes out of his way to help you, you may want to **commend** him to his superior, which is a more formal, public way of praising someone, either verbally or in writing. If you're watching a performance and want to express your approval verbally or with applause, **acclaim** is the verb you're looking for. **Laud** and **extol** suggest the highest of *praise*, although *laud* may imply that the praise is excessive (*the accomplishments for which she was lauded were really nothing out of the ordinary*). *Extol*, which comes from the Latin meaning to raise up, suggests that you're trying to magnify whatever or whomever you're praising (*to extol her virtues so that everyone would vote for her*). If you want to *praise* someone who has died recently, you will **eulogize** him or her, which means to speak or write your *praise* for a special occasion, such as a funeral.

---

praise·wor·thy /práyzwərthee/ *adj.* worthy of praise; commendable. □□ **praise·wor·thi·ly** *adv.* **praise·wor·thi·ness** *n.*

Pra·krit /práakrit/ *n.* any of the ancient or medieval vernacular dialects of north and central India that existed alongside or were derived from Sanskrit. [Skr. *prākṛta* unrefined: cf. SANSKRIT]

pra·line /práaleen, práy-/ *n.* any of several candies made with almonds, pecans, or other nuts and sugar. [F f. Marshal de Plessis-Praslin, Fr. soldier d. 1675, whose cook invented it]

prall·tril·ler /práaltrilər/ *n.* a musical ornament consisting of one rapid alternation of the written note with the note immediately above it. [G f. *prallen* rebound + *Triller* TRILL]

pram[1] /pram/ *n. Brit.* a baby carriage. [abbr. of PERAMBULATOR]

pram[2] /praam/ *n.* (also **praam**) **1** a flat-bottomed gunboat or Baltic Sea cargo boat. **2** a Scandinavian ship's dinghy. [MDu. *prame, praem*, MLG *prām(e)*, f. OSlav. *pramŭ*]

pra·na /práanə/ *n.* (in Hinduism) breath as a life-giving force. **2** the breath; breathing. [Skr.]

prance /prans/ *v. & n.* ● *v.intr.* **1** (of a horse) raise the forelegs and spring from the hind legs. **2** (often foll. by *about*) walk or behave in an arrogant manner. ● *n.* **1** the act of prancing. **2** a prancing movement. □□ **pranc·er** *n.* [ME: orig. unkn.]

pran·di·al /prándeeəl/ *adj.* of a meal, usu. dinner. [L *prandium* meal]

prang /prang/ *v. & n. Brit. sl.* ● *v.tr.* **1** crash or damage (an aircraft or vehicle). **2** bomb (a target) successfully. ● *n.* the act or an instance of pranging. [imit.]

prank /prangk/ *n.* a practical joke; a piece of mischief. □□ **prank·ful** *adj.* **prank·ish** *adj.* **prank·some** *adj.* [16th c.: orig. unkn.]

prank·ster /prángkstər/ *n.* a person fond of playing pranks.

prase /prayz/ *n.* a translucent leek-green type of quartz. [F f. L *prasius* f. Gk *prasios* (adj.) leek-green f. *prason* leek]

pra·se·o·dym·i·um /práyzeeōdímeeəm, práysee-/ *n. Chem.* a soft silvery metallic element of the lanthanide series, occurring naturally in various minerals and used in catalyst mixtures. ¶ Symb.: **Pr**. [G *Praseodym* f. Gk *prasios* (see PRASE) from its green salts, + G *Didym* DIDYMIUM]

prat /prat/ *n. Brit. sl.* **1** a silly or foolish person. **2** the buttocks. [16th-c. cant: orig. unkn.]

prate /prayt/ *v. & n.* ● *v.* **1** *intr.* chatter; talk too much. **2** *intr.* talk foolishly or irrelevantly. **3** *tr.* tell or say in a prating manner. ● *n.* prating; idle talk. □□ **prat·er** *n.* **prat·ing** *adj.* [ME f. MDu., MLG *praten*, prob. imit.]

prat·fall /prátfawl/ *n. sl.* **1** a fall on the buttocks. **2** a humiliating failure.

prat·in·cole /prátingkōl/ *n.* any of various birds of the subfamily Glareolinae, inhabiting sandy and stony areas and feeding on insects. [mod.L *pratincola* f. L *pratum* meadow + *incola* inhabitant]

pra·tique /prateék/ *n.* a license to have dealings with a port, granted to a ship after quarantine or on showing a clean bill of health. [F, = practice, intercourse, f. It. *pratica* f. med.L *practica*: see PRACTICIAN]

prat·tle /prát'l/ *v. & n.* ● *v.intr. & tr.* chatter or say in a childish or inconsequential way. ● *n.* **1** childish chatter. **2** inconsequential talk. □□ **prat·tler** *n.* **prat·tling** *adj.* [MLG *pratelen* (as PRATE)]

prau var. of PROA.

prawn /prawn/ *n. & v.* ● *n.* any of various marine crustaceans, resembling a shrimp but usu. larger. ● *v.intr.* fish for prawns. [ME *pra(y)ne*, of unkn. orig.]

prax·is /práksis/ *n.* **1** accepted practice or custom. **2** the practicing of an art or skill. [med.L f. Gk, = doing, f. *prassō* do]

pray /pray/ *v.* (often foll. by *for* or *to* + infin. or *that* + clause) **1** *intr.* (often foll. by *to*) say prayers (to God, etc.); make devout supplication. **2** *a tr.* entreat; beseech. **b** *tr. & intr.* ask earnestly (*prayed to be released*). **3** *tr.* (as *imper.*) *archaic* please (*pray tell me*). [ME f. OF *preier* f. LL *precare* f. L *precari* entreat]

prayer[1] /prair/ *n.* **1 a** solemn request or thanksgiving to God or an object of worship (*say a prayer*). **b** a formula or form of words used in praying (*the Lord's prayer*). **c** the act of praying (*be at prayer*). **d** a religious service consisting largely of prayers (*morning prayers*). **2 a** an entreaty to a person. **b** a thing entreated or prayed for. □ **not have a prayer** *colloq.* have no chance (of success, etc.). □□ **prayer·less** *adj.* [ME f. OF *preiere* ult. f. L *precarius* obtained by entreaty f. *prex precis* prayer]

pray·er[2] /práyər/ *n.* a person who prays.

prayer book *n.* a book containing the forms of prayer in regular use.

prayer·ful /práirfŏŏl/ *adj.* **1** (of a person) given to praying; devout. **2** (of speech, actions, etc.) characterized by or expressive of prayer. □□ **prayer·ful·ly** *adv.* **prayer·ful·ness** *n.*

prayer rug *n.* (also **prayer mat**) a small carpet knelt on by Muslims when praying.

prayer wheel *n.* a revolving cylindrical box inscribed with or containing prayers, used esp. by Tibetan Buddhists.

pray·ing man·tis *n.* a mantis, *Mantis religiosa*, that holds its forelegs in a position suggestive of hands folded in prayer, while waiting to pounce on its prey.

pre- /pree/ *prefix* before (in time, place, order, degree, or importance). [from or after L *prae-* f. *prae* (adv. & prep.)]

preach /preech/ *v.* **1 a** *intr.* deliver a sermon or religious address. **b** *tr.* deliver (a sermon); proclaim or expound. **2** *intr.* give moral advice in an obtrusive way. **3** *tr.* advocate or inculcate (a quality or

See page xx for the **Key to Pronunciation**.

practice, etc.). □□ **preach·a·ble** *adj.* [ME f. OF *prechier* f. L *praedicare* proclaim, in eccl.L preach (as PRAE-, *dicare* declare)]

preach·er /préechər/ *n.* a person who preaches, esp. a minister of religion. [ME f. AF *prech(o)ur*, OF *prech(e)or* f. eccl.L *praedicator* (as PREACH)]

preach·i·fy /préechifī/ *v.intr.* (·**fies**, ·**fied**) *colloq.* preach or moralize tediously.

preach·ment /préechmənt/ *n.* usu. *derog.* preaching; sermonizing.

preach·y /préechee/ *adj.* (**preach·i·er**, **preach·i·est**) *colloq.* inclined to preach or moralize. □□ **preach·i·ness** *n.*

pre·ad·o·les·cent /préead'lésənt/ *adj. & n.* ● *adj.* **1** (of a child) having nearly reached adolescence. **2** of or relating to the two or three years preceding adolescence. ● *n.* a preadolescent child. □□ **pre·ad·o·les·cence** *n.*

pre·am·ble /prée-ámbəl/ *n.* **1** a preliminary statement or introduction. **2** the introductory part of a constitution, statute, or deed, etc. □□ **pre·am·bu·lar** /–ámbyŏŏlər/ *adj.* [ME f. OF *preambule* f. med.L *praeambulum* f. LL *praeambulus* (adj.) going before (as PRE-, AMBLE)]

pre·amp /prée-ámp/ *n.* = PREAMPLIFIER. [abbr.]

pre·am·pli·fi·er /prée-ámplifīər/ *n.* an electronic device that amplifies a very weak signal (e.g., from a microphone or pickup) and transmits it to a main amplifier. □□ **pre·am·pli·fied** *adj.*

pre·ar·range /préeəráynj/ *v.tr.* arrange beforehand. □□ **pre·ar·range·ment** *n.*

pre·a·tom·ic /préeətómik/ *adj.* existing or occurring before the use of atomic weapons or energy.

preb·end /prébənd/ *n. Eccl.* **1** the stipend of a canon or member of a chapter. **2** a portion of land or tithe from which this is drawn. □□ **pre·ben·dal** /pribénd'l, prébən–/ *adj.* [ME f. OF *prebende* f. LL *praebenda* pension, neut.pl. gerundive of L *praebēre* grant f. *prae* forth + *habēre* hold]

preb·en·dar·y /prébəndəree/ *n.* (*pl.* ·**ies**) **1** the holder of a prebend. **2** an honorary canon. □□ **preb·en·dar·y·ship** *n.* [ME f. med.L *praebendarius* (as PREBEND)]

Pre·cam·bri·an /préekámbreeən/ *adj. & n. Geol.* ● *adj.* of or relating to the earliest era of geological time from the formation of the earth to the first forms of life. ● *n.* this era.

pre·can·cer /préekánsər, –kántsər/ *n.* a precancerous state or condition.

pre·can·cer·ous /préekánsrəs, –kántsər–/ *adj.* having the tendency to develop into a cancer. □□ **pre·can·cer·ous·ly** *adv.*

pre·car·i·ous /prikáireeəs/ *adj.* **1** uncertain; dependent on chance (*makes a precarious living*). **2** insecure; perilous (*precarious health*). □□ **pre·car·i·ous·ly** *adv.* **pre·car·i·ous·ness** *n.* [L *precarius*: see PRAYER[1]]

pre·cast /préekást/ *adj.* (of concrete) cast in its final shape before positioning.

prec·a·tive /prékətiv/ *adj.* (also **prec·a·to·ry** /–tawree/) (of a word or form) expressing a wish or request. [LL *precativus* f. *precari* pray]

pre·cau·tion /prikáwshən/ *n.* **1** an action taken beforehand to avoid risk or ensure a good result. **2** (in *pl.*) *colloq.* the use of contraceptives. **3** caution exercised beforehand; prudent foresight. □□ **pre·cau·tion·ar·y** *adj.* [F *précaution* f. LL *praecautio* *–onis* f. L *praecavēre* (as PRAE-, *cavēre caut-* beware of)]

pre·cede /priseéd/ *v.tr.* **1 a** (often as **preceding** *adj.*) come or go before in time, order, importance, etc. (*preceding generations*; *the preceding paragraph*). **b** walk, etc., in front of (*preceded by our guide*). **2** (foll. by *by*) cause to be preceded (*must precede this measure by milder ones*). [OF *preceder* f. L *praecedere* (as PRAE-, *cedere cess-* go)]

prec·e·dence /présidəns, priseéd'ns/ *n.* (also **prec·e·den·cy**) **1** priority in time, order, or importance, etc. **2** the right to precede others on formal occasions. □ **take precedence** (often foll. by *over, of*) have priority (over).

prec·e·dent *n. & adj.* ● *n.* /présidənt/ a previous case or legal decision, etc., taken as a guide for subsequent cases or as a justification. ● *adj.* /priseéd'nt, présidənt/ preceding in time, order, importance, etc. □□ **prec·e·dent·ly** /présidəntlee/ *adv.* [ME f. OF (n. & adj.) (as PRECEDE)]

prec·e·dent·ed /présidentid/ *adj.* having or supported by a precedent.

pre·cent /prisént/ *v.* **1** *intr.* act as a precentor. **2** *tr.* lead the singing of (a psalm, etc.). [back-form. f. PRECENTOR]

pre·cen·tor /priséntər/ *n.* **1** a person who leads the singing or (in a synagogue) the prayers of a congregation. **2** *Brit.* a minor canon who administers the musical life of a cathedral. □□ **pre·cen·tor·ship** *n.* [F *précenteur* or L *praecentor* f. *praecinere* (as PRAE-, *canere* sing)]

pre·cept /préesept/ *n.* **1** a command; a rule of conduct. **2 a** moral instruction (*example is better than precept*). **b** a general or proverbial maxim. **3** *Law* a writ, order, or warrant. □□ **pre·cep·tive** /–séptiv/ *adj.* [ME f. L *praeceptum* neut. past part. of *praecipere praecept-* warn, instruct (as PRAE-, *capere* take)]

pre·cep·tor /priséptər/ *n.* a teacher or instructor. □□ **pre·cep·to·ri·al**

pre·cep·tor·ship *n.* **pre·cep·tress** /–tris/ *n.* [L *praeceptor* (as PRECEPT)]

pre·cess /preesés, prééses/ *v.* to undergo or be subject to precession.

pre·ces·sion /priséshən/ *n.* the slow movement of the axis of a spinning body around another axis. □□ **pre·ces·sion·al** *adj.* [LL *praecessio* (as PRECEDE)]

pre·ces·sion of the e·qui·nox·es *n.* **1** the slow retrograde motion of equinoctial points along the ecliptic. **2** the resulting earlier occurrence of equinoxes in each successive sidereal year.

pre-Chris·tian /préekrischən/ *adj.* before Christ or the advent of Christianity.

pre·cinct /préesingkt/ *n.* **1** an enclosed or specially designated area. **2** (in *pl.*) **a** the surrounding area or environs. **b** the boundaries. **3 a** a subdivision of a county, city, etc., for police or electoral purposes. **b** a police station in such a subdivision. **c** (in *pl.*) a neighborhood. [ME f. med.L *praecinctum* neut. past part. of *praecingere* encircle (as PRAE-, *cingere* gird)]

pre·ci·os·i·ty /présheeósitee/ *n.* overrefinement in art or language, esp. in the choice of words. [OF *préciosité* f. L *pretiositas* f. *pretiosus* (as PRECIOUS)]

pre·cious /préshəs/ *adj. & adv.* ● *adj.* **1** of great value or worth. **2** beloved; much prized (*precious memories*). **3** affectedly refined, esp. in language or manner. **4** *colloq.* often *iron.* a considerable (*a precious lot you know about it*). **b** expressing contempt or disdain (*you can keep your precious flowers*). ● *adv. colloq.* extremely; very (*tried precious hard*; *had precious little left*). □□ **pre·cious·ly** *adv.* **pre·cious·ness** *n.* [ME f. OF *precios* f. L *pretiosus* f. *pretium* price]

pre·cious met·als *n.pl.* gold, silver, and platinum.

pre·cious stone *n.* a piece of mineral having great value esp. as used in jewelry.

prec·i·pice /présipis/ *n.* **1** a vertical or steep face of a rock, cliff, mountain, etc. **2** a dangerous situation. [F *précipice* or L *praecipitium* falling headlong, precipice (as PRECIPITOUS)]

pre·cip·i·tant /prisípit'nt/ *adj. & n.* ● *adj.* = PRECIPITATE *adj.* ● *n. Chem.* a substance that causes another substance to precipitate. □□ **pre·cip·i·tance** *n.* **pre·cip·i·tan·cy** *n.* [obs. F *précipitant* pres. part. of *précipiter* (as PRECIPITATE)]

pre·cip·i·tate *v., adj., & n.* ● *v.tr.* /prisípitayt/ **1** hasten the occurrence of; cause to occur prematurely. **2** (foll. by *into*) send rapidly into a certain state or condition (*were precipitated into war*). **3** throw down headlong. **4** *Chem.* cause (a substance) to be deposited in solid form from a solution. **5** *Physics* **a** cause (dust, etc.) to be deposited from the air on a surface. **b** condense (vapor) into drops and so deposit it. ● *adj.* /prisípitət/ **1** headlong; violently hurried (*precipitate departure*). **2** (of a person or act) hasty; rash; inconsiderate. ● *n.* /prisípitət/ **1** *Chem.* a substance precipitated from a solution. **2** *Physics* moisture condensed from vapor by cooling and depositing, e.g., rain or dew. □□ **pre·cip·i·ta·ble** /–sípitəbəl/ *adj.* **pre·cip·i·ta·bil·i·ty** *n.* **pre·cip·i·tate·ly** /–sípitətlee/ *adv.* **pre·cip·i·tate·ness** /–sípitətnəs/ *n.* **pre·cip·i·ta·tor** *n.*

▶The adjectives **precipitate** and **precipitous** are sometimes confused. **Precipitate** means 'sudden, hasty': *a precipitate decision*; *precipitate flight by the fugitive*. **Precipitous** means 'steep': *the precipitous slope of the moutain*; *a precipitous decline in stock prices*.

WORD HISTORY   precipitate

early 16th century: from Latin *praecipitat-* 'thrown headlong,' from the verb *praecipitare*, from *praeceps, praecip(it)-* ' headlong,' from *prae* 'before' + *caput* 'head.' The original sense of the verb was 'hurl down, send violently;' hence 'cause to move rapidly,' which gave rise to sense 1 (early 17th century).

pre·cip·i·ta·tion /prisípitáyshən/ *n.* **1** the act of precipitating or the process of being precipitated. **2** rash haste. **3 a** rain or snow, etc., falling to the ground. **b** a quantity of this. [F *précipitation* or L *praecipitatio* (as PRECIPITATE)]

pre·cip·i·tous /prisípitəs/ *adj.* **1 a** of or like a precipice. **b** dangerously steep. **2** = PRECIPITATE *adj.* □□ **pre·cip·i·tous·ly** *adv.* **pre·cip·i·tous·ness** *n.* [obs. F *pré cipiteux* f. L *praeceps* (as PRECIPITATE)]

▶See note at PRECIPITATE.

pré·cis /práysee/ *n. & v.* ● *n.* (*pl.* same or /–seez/) a summary or abstract, esp. of a text or speech. ● *v.tr.* (**pré·cis·es** /–seez/; **pré·cised** /–seed/; **pré·cis·ing** /–seeing/) make a précis of. [F, = PRECISE (as n.)]

pre·cise /prisís/ *adj.* **1 a** accurately expressed. **b** definite; exact. **2 a** punctilious; scrupulous in being exact, observing rules, etc. **b** often *derog.* rigid; fastidious. **3** identical; exact (*at that precise moment*). □□ **pre·cise·ness** *n.* [F *précis* *–ise* f. L *praecidere praecis-* cut short (as PRAE-, *caedere* cut)]

pre·cise·ly /prisíslee/ *adv.* **1** in a precise manner; exactly. **2** (as a reply) quite so; as you say.

pre·ci·sian /prisízhən/ *n.* a person who is rigidly precise or punctilious, esp. in religious observance. □□ **pre·ci·sian·ism** *n.*

pre·ci·sion /prisízhən/ *n.* **1** the condition of being precise; accuracy. **2** the degree of refinement in measurement, etc. **3** (*attrib.*) marked by or adapted for precision (*precision instruments*; *precision* timing). □□ **pre•ci•sion•ism** n. **pre•ci•sion•ist** n. [F précision or L praecisio (as PRECISE)]

pre•clas•si•cal /preeklásikəl/ adj. before a period regarded as classical, esp. in music and literature.

pre•clin•i•cal /preeklínikəl/ adj. **1** of or relating to the first, chiefly theoretical, stage of a medical or dental education. **2** (of a stage in a disease) before symptoms can be identified.

pre•clude /priklṓod/ v.tr. **1** (foll. by from) prevent; exclude (precluded from taking part). **2** make impossible; remove (so as to preclude all doubt). □□ **pre•clu•sion** /-klṓozhən/ n. **pre•clu•sive** /-klṓosiv/ adj. [L praecludere praeclus- (as PRAE-, claudere shut)]

pre•co•cial /prikṓshəl/ adj. & n. (Brit. **prae•co•cial**) • adj. (esp. of a bird) having young that can feed themselves as soon as they are hatched. • n. a precocial bird or animal. (cf. ALTRICIAL). [L praecox –cocis (as PRECOCIOUS)]

pre•co•cious /prikṓshəs/ adj. **1** (of a person, esp. a child) prematurely developed in some faculty or characteristic. **2** (of an action, etc.) indicating such development. **3** (of a plant) flowering or fruiting early. □□ **pre•co•cious•ly** adv. **pre•co•cious•ness** n. **pre•coc•i•ty** /-kósitee/ n. [L praecox –cocis f. praecoquere ripen fully (as PRAE-, coquere cook)]

pre•cog•ni•tion /preekognishən/ n. (supposed) foreknowledge, esp. of a supernatural kind. □□ **pre•cog•ni•tive** /-kógnitiv/ adj. [LL praecognitio (as PRE-, COGNITION)]

pre•co•i•tal /preekṓit'l, -kō-eet'l/ adj. preceding sexual intercourse. □□ **pre•co•i•tal•ly** adv.

pre•Co•lum•bi•an /preekəlúmbeeən/ adj. before the arrival in America of Columbus.

pre•con•ceive /preekənseev/ v.tr. (esp. as **preconceived** adj.) form (an idea or opinion, etc.) beforehand; anticipate in thought.

pre•con•cep•tion /preekənsépshən/ n. **1** a preconceived idea. **2** a prejudice.

pre•con•cert /preekənsért/ v.tr. arrange or organize beforehand.

pre•con•di•tion /preekəndíshən/ n. & v. • n. a prior condition, that must be fulfilled before other things can be done. • v.tr. bring into a required condition beforehand.

pre•co•nize /preekəníz/ v.tr. **1** proclaim or commend publicly. **2** summon by name. **3** RC Ch. (of the pope) approve publicly the appointment of (a bishop, etc.). □□ **pre•co•ni•za•tion** n. [ME f. med.L praeconizare f. L praeco –onis herald]

pre•con•scious /preekónshəs/ adj. & n. Psychol. • adj. /preekónshəs/ **1** preceding consciousness. **2** of or associated with a part of the mind below the level of immediate conscious awareness, from which memories and emotions can be recalled. • n. /preekónshəs/ this part of the mind. □□ **pre•con•scious•ness** n.

pre•cook /preekṓok/ v.tr. cook in advance.

pre•cool /preekṓol/ v.tr. cool in advance.

pre•cur•sor /prikórsər, preekér-/ n. **1 a** a forerunner. **b** a person who precedes in office, etc. **2** a harbinger. **3** a substance from which another is formed by decay or chemical reaction, etc. [L praecursor f. praecurrere praecurs- (as PRAE-, currere run)]

pre•cur•so•ry /prikórsəree/ adj. (also **pre•cur•sive** /-siv/) **1** preliminary; introductory. **2** (foll. by of) serving as a harbinger of. [L praecursorius (as PRECURSOR)]

pre•cut /preekút/ v.tr. (past and past part. •**cut**) cut in advance.

pred. abbr. predicate.

pre•da•cious /pridáyshəs/ adj. (also **pre•da•ceous**) **1** (of an animal) predatory. **2** relating to such animals (predacious instincts). □□ **pre•da•cious•ness** n. **pre•dac•i•ty** /-dásitee/ n. [L praeda booty: cf. audacious]

pre•date /preedáyt/ v.tr. exist or occur at a date earlier than.

pre•da•tion /pridáyshən/ n. **1** (usu. in pl.) = DEPREDATION. **2** Zool. the natural preying of one animal on others. [L praedatio –onis taking of booty f. L praeda booty]

pred•a•tor /prédətər/ n. **1** an animal naturally preying on others. **2** a predatory person, institution, etc. [L praedator plunderer f. praedari seize as plunder f. praeda booty (as PREDACIOUS)]

pred•a•to•ry /prédətawree/ adj. **1** (of an animal) preying naturally upon others. **2** (of a nation, state, or individual) plundering or exploiting others. □□ **pred•a•to•ri•ly** adv. **pred•a•to•ri•ness** n. [L praedatorius (as PREDATOR)]

pre•de•cease /preedisées/ v. & n. • v.tr. die earlier than (another person). • n. a death preceding that of another.

pred•e•ces•sor /prédisesər, preé-/ n. **1** a former holder of an office or position with respect to a later holder (my immediate predecessor). **2** an ancestor. **3** a thing to which another has succeeded (the new plan will share the fate of its predecessor). [ME f. OF predecesseur f. LL praedecessor (as PRAE-, decessor retiring officer, as DECEASE)]

pre•del•la /pridélə/ n. **1** an altar step, or raised shelf at the back of an altar. **2** a painting or sculpture on this, or any picture forming an appendage to a larger one, esp. beneath an altarpiece. [It., = stool]

pre•des•ti•nar•i•an /preedéstináireeən/ n. & adj. • n. a person who believes in predestination. • adj. of or relating to predestination.

pre•des•ti•nate v. & adj. • v.tr. /preedéstinayt/ = PREDESTINE. • adj.

/-déstinət/ predestined. [ME f. eccl.L praedestinare praedestinat- (as PRAE-, destinare establish)]

pre•des•ti•na•tion /preedestinayshən/ n. Theol. (as a belief or doctrine) the divine foreordaining of all that will happen, esp. with regard to the salvation of some and not others. [ME f. eccl.L praedestinatio (as PREDESTINATE)]

pre•des•tine /preedéstin/ v.tr. **1** determine beforehand. **2** ordain in advance by divine will or as if by fate. [ME f. OF predestiner or eccl.L praedestinare PREDESTINATE v.]

pre•de•ter•mine /preedítórmin/ v.tr. **1** determine or decree beforehand. **2** predestine. □□ **pre•de•ter•min•a•ble** adj. **pre•de•ter•mi•nate** /-nət/ adj. **pre•de•ter•mi•na•tion** /-LL praedeterminare (as PRAE-, DETERMINE)]

pre•di•al /preedeeəl/ adj. & n. hist. • adj. **1 a** of land or farms. **b** rural; agrarian. **c** (of a slave, tenant, etc.) attached to farms or the land. **2** (of a tithe) consisting of agricultural produce. • n. a predial slave. [med.L praedialis f. L praedium farm]

pred•i•ca•ble /prédikəbəl/ adj. & n. • adj. that may be predicated or affirmed. • n. **1** a predicable thing. **2** (in pl.) Logic the five classes to which predicates belong: genus, species, difference, property, and accident. □□ **pred•i•ca•bil•i•ty** n. [med.L praedicabilis that may be affirmed (as PREDICATE)]

pred•ic•a•ment /pridíkəmənt/ n. **1** a difficult, unpleasant, or embarrassing situation. **2** Philos. a category in (esp. Aristotelian) logic. [ME (in sense 2) f. LL praedicamentum thing predicated: see PREDICATE]

pred•i•cant /prédikənt/ adj. & n. hist. • adj. (of a religious order) engaged in preaching. • n. a predicant person, esp. a Dominican friar. [L praedicans part. of praedicare (as PREDICATE)]

pred•i•cate v. & n. • v.tr. /prédikayt/ **1** assert or affirm as true or existent. **2** (foll. by on) found or base (a statement, etc.) on. • n. /-kət/ **1** Gram. what is said about the subject of a sentence, etc. (e.g., went home in John went home). **2** Logic **a** what is predicated. **b** what is affirmed or denied of the subject by means of the copula (e.g., mortal in all men are mortal). □□ **pred•i•ca•tion** /-káyshən/ n. [L praedicare praedicat- proclaim (as PRAE-, dicare declare)]

pred•i•ca•tive /prédikaytiv/ adj. **1** Gram. (of an adjective or noun) forming or contained in the predicate, as old in the dog is old (but not in the old dog) and house in there is a large house (opp. ATTRIBUTIVE). **2** that predicates. □□ **pred•i•ca•tive•ly** adv. [L praedicativus (as PREDICATE)]

pre•dict /pridíkt/ v.tr. (often foll. by that + clause) make a statement about the future; foretell; prophesy. □□ **pre•dic•tive** adj. **pre•dic•tive•ly** adv. **pre•dic•tor** n. [L praedicere praedict- (as PRAE-, dicere say)]

pre•dict•a•ble /pridíktəbəl/ adj. that can be predicted or is to be expected. □□ **pre•dict•a•bil•i•ty** n. **pre•dict•a•bly** adv.

SYNONYM TIP predict

AUGUR, DIVINE, FORECAST, FORESHADOW, FORETELL, PROGNOSTICATE, PROPHESY. While all of these words refer to telling something before it happens, **predict** is the most commonly used and applies to the widest variety of situations. It can mean anything from hazarding a guess (to predict he'd never survive the year) to making an astute inference based on facts or statistical evidence (to predict that the Republicans would win the election). When a meteorologist tells us whether it will rain or snow tomorrow, he or she is said to **forecast** the weather, a word that means predict but is used particularly in the context of weather and other phenomena that cannot be predicted easily (to forecast an influx of women into the labor force). **Divine** and **foreshadow** mean to suggest the future rather than to predict it, especially by giving or evaluating subtle hints or clues. To divine something is to perceive it through intuition or insight (to divine in the current economic situation the disaster that lay ahead), while foreshadow can apply to anyone or anything that gives an indication of what is to come (her abrupt departure that night foreshadowed the breakdown in their relationship). **Foretell**, like foreshadow, can refer to the clue rather than the person who gives it and is often used in reference to the past (evidence that foretold the young girl's violent end). **Augur** means to divine or foreshadow something by interpreting signs and omens (the turnout on opening night augured well for the play's success). **Prophesy** connotes either inspired or mystical knowledge of the future and suggests more authoritative wisdom than augur (a baseball fan for decades, he prophesied the young batter's rise to stardom). Although anyone who has inside information or knowledge of signs and symptoms can **prognosticate**, it is usually a doctor who does so by looking at the symptoms of a disease to predict its future outcome.

---

pre•dic•tion /pridíkshən/ n. **1** the art of predicting or the process of being predicted. **2** a thing predicted; a forecast. [L praedictio –onis (as PREDICT)]

pre•di•gest /preedijést/ v.tr. **1** render (food) easily digestible before being eaten. **2** make (reading matter) easier to read or understand. □□ **pre·di·ges·tion** /–jéschən/ *n.*

pre·di·lec·tion /préd'lékshən, pree–/ *n.* (often foll. by *for*) a preference or special liking. [F *prédilection* ult. f. L *praediligere praedilect-* prefer (as PRAE-, *diligere* select): see DILIGENT]

pre·dis·pose /preedispóz/ *v.tr.* **1** influence favorably in advance. **2** (foll. by *to*, or *to* + infin.) render liable or inclined beforehand. □□ **pre·dis·po·si·tion** /–pəzishən/ *n.*

pred·ni·sone /prédnizōn, –sōn/ *n.* a synthetic drug similar to cortisone, used to relieve rheumatic and allergic conditions and to treat leukemia. [perh. f. pregnant + *diene* + cortisone]

pre·dom·i·nant /pridóminənt/ *adj.* **1** predominating. **2** being the strongest or main element. □□ **pre·dom·i·nance** *n.* **pre·dom·i·nant·ly** *adv.*

pre·dom·i·nate /pridóminayt/ *v.intr.* **1** (foll. by *over*) have or exert control. **2** be superior. **3** be the strongest or main element; preponderate (*a garden in which dahlias predominate*). [med.L *praedominari* (as PRAE-, DOMINATE)]

pre·dom·i·nate·ly /pridóminətlee/ *adv.* = *predominantly* (see PREDOMINANT). [rare *predominate* (adj.) = PREDOMINANT]

pre·dy·nas·tic /preedinástik/ *adj.* of or relating to a period before the normally recognized dynasties (esp. of ancient Egypt).

pre·ech·o /pree-ékō/ *n.* (pl. **-oes**) **1** a faint copy heard just before an actual sound in a recording, caused by the accidental transfer of signals. **2** a foreshadowing.

pre·e·clamp·si·a /preeiklámpseeə/ *n.* a condition of pregnancy characterized by high blood pressure and other symptoms associated with eclampsia. □□ **pre·e·clamp·tic** *adj. & n.*

pre·e·lect /preeilékt/ *v.tr.* elect beforehand.

pre·e·lec·tion /preeilékshən/ *n.* **1** an election held beforehand. **2** (*attrib.*) (esp. of an act or undertaking) done or given before an election.

pre·em·bry·o /pree-émbreeō/ *n. Med.* a human embryo in the first fourteen days after fertilization. □□ **pre·em·bry·on·ic** /–breeónik/ *adj.*

pree·mie /preemee/ *n. colloq.* an infant born prematurely.

pre·em·i·nent /pree-éminənt/ *adj.* **1** surpassing others. **2** outstanding; distinguished in some quality. **3** principal; leading; predominant. □□ **pre·em·i·nence** *n.* **pre·em·i·nent·ly** *adv.* [ME f. L *praeeminens* (as PRAE-, EMINENT)]

pre·empt /pree-émpt/ *v.* **1** *tr.* **a** forestall. **b** acquire or appropriate in advance. **2** *tr.* prevent (an attack) by disabling the enemy. **3** *tr.* obtain by preemption. **4** *tr.* take for oneself (esp. public land) so as to have the right of preemption. **5** *intr. Bridge* make a preemptive bid. □□ **pre·emp·tor** *n.* **pre·emp·to·ry** *adj.* [back-form. f. PREEMPTION]

pre·emp·tion /pree-émpshən/ *n.* **1 a** the purchase or appropriation by one person or party before the opportunity is offered to others. **b** the right to purchase (esp. public land) in this way. **2** prior appropriation or acquisition. [med.L *praeemptio* (as PRAE-, *emere* empt-buy)]

pre·emp·tive /pree-émptiv/ *adj.* **1** preempting; serving to preempt. **2** (of military action) intended to prevent attack by disabling the enemy (*a preemptive strike*). **3** *Bridge* (of a bid) intended to be high enough to discourage further bidding.

▶See note at PEREMPTORY.

preen /preen/ *v.tr. & refl.* **1** (of a bird) straighten (the feathers or itself) with its beak. **2** (of a person) primp or admire (oneself, one's hair, clothes, etc.). **3** (often foll. by *on*) congratulate or pride (oneself). □□ **preen·er** *n.* [ME, app. var. of earlier *prune* (perh. rel. to PRUNE²): assoc. with Sc. & dial. *preen* pierce, pin]

preen gland *n.* a gland situated at the base of a bird's tail and producing oil used in preening.

pre·es·tab·lish /preeistáblish/ *v.tr.* establish beforehand.

pre·ex·ist /preeigzíst/ *v.intr.* exist at an earlier time. □□ **pre·ex·ist·ence** *n.* **pre·ex·ist·ent** *adj.*

pref. *abbr.* **1** prefix. **2** preface. **3 a** preference. **b** preferred.

pre·fab /preefáb/ *n. colloq.* a prefabricated building, esp. a small house. [abbr.]

pre·fab·ri·cate /preefábrikayt/ *v.tr.* **1** manufacture sections of (a building, etc.) prior to their assembly on a site. **2** produce in an artificially standardized way. □□ **pre·fab·ri·ca·tion** /–brikáyshən/ *n.*

pref·ace /préfəs/ *n. & v.* ● *n.* **1** an introduction to a book stating its subject, scope, etc. **2** the preliminary part of a speech. **3** *Eccl.* the introduction to the central part of a Eucharistic service. ● *v.tr.* **1** (foll. by *with*) introduce or begin (a speech or event) (*prefaced my remarks with a warning*). **2** provide (a book, etc.) with a preface. **3** (of an event, etc.) lead up to (another). □□ **pref·a·to·ri·al** /–fətáwreeəl/ *adj.* **pref·a·to·ry** /–fətawree/ *adj.* [ME f. OF f. med.L *praefatia* for L *praefatio* f. *praefari* (as PRAE-, *fari* speak)]

pre·fect /preefekt/ *n.* **1** *Rom. Antiq.* a senior magistrate or military commander. **2** a student monitor, as in a private school. **3** the chief administrative officer of certain government departments, esp. in France. □□ **pre·fec·tor·al** /–féktərəl/ *adj.* **pre·fec·to·ri·al** /–táwreeəl/

adj. [ME f. OF f. L *praefectus* past part. of *praeficere* set in authority over (as PRAE-, *facere* make)]

pre·fec·ture /preefekchər/ *n.* **1** a district under the government of a prefect. **2** a prefect's office, tenure, or official residence. □□ **pre·fec·tur·al** /prifékchərəl/ *adj.* [F *préfecture* or L *praefectura* (as PREFECT)]

pre·fer /prifər/ *v.tr.* (**pre·ferred, pre·fer·ring**) **1** (often foll. by *to*, or *to* + infin.) choose; like better (*would prefer to stay; prefers coffee to tea*). **2** submit (information, an accusation, etc.) for consideration. **3** promote or advance (a person). [ME f. OF *preferer* f. L *praeferre* (as PRAE-, *ferre lat-* bear)]

pref·er·a·ble /préfərəbəl, *disp.* prifér–/ *adj.* **1** to be preferred. **2** more desirable. □□ **pref·er·a·bly** *adv.*

pref·er·ence /préfərəns, préfrəns/ *n.* **1** the act or an instance of preferring or being preferred. **2** a thing preferred. **3 a** the favoring of one person, etc., before others. **b** *Commerce* the favoring of one country by admitting its products at a lower import duty. **4** *Law* a prior right, esp. to the payment of debts. □ **in preference to** as a thing preferred over (another). [F *préférence* f. med.L *praeferentia* (as PREFER)]

pref·er·ence shares *n.pl.* (also **pref·er·ence stock**) *Brit.* = PREFERRED STOCK.

pref·er·en·tial /préfərénshəl/ *adj.* **1** of or involving preference (*preferential treatment*). **2** giving or receiving a favor. **3** *Commerce* (of a tariff, etc.) favoring particular countries. **4** (of voting) in which the voter puts candidates in order of preference. □□ **pref·er·en·tial·ly** *adv.* [as PREFERENCE, after *differential*]

pre·fer·ment /prifərmənt/ *n.* **1** act or state of being preferred. **2** promotion to office.

pre·ferred pro·vid·er or·gan·i·za·tion *n.* a health insurance plan that allows members to choose their own physicians, etc. ¶ Abbr.: PPO.

pre·ferred stock *n.* stock whose entitlement to dividend takes priority over that of common stock.

pre·fig·ure /preefígyər/ *v.tr.* **1** represent beforehand by a figure or type. **2** imagine beforehand. □□ **pre·fig·u·ra·tion** *n.* **pre·fig·ur·a·tive** /–rətiv/ *adj.* **pre·fig·ure·ment** *n.* [ME f. eccl.L *praefigurare* (as PRAE-, FIGURE)]

pre·fix /preefiks/ *n. & v.* ● *n.* **1** a verbal element placed at the beginning of a word to adjust or qualify its meaning (e.g., *ex-, non-, re-*) or (in some languages) as an inflectional formative. **2** a title placed before a name (e.g., *Mr.*). ● *v.tr.* (often foll. by *to*) **1** add as an introduction. **2** join (a word or element) as a prefix. □□ **pre·fix·a·tion** *n.* **pre·fix·ion** /–fíkshən/ *n.* [earlier as verb: ME f. OF *prefixer* (as PRAE-, FIX): (n.) f. L *praefixum*]

GRAMMAR TIP | **Prefixes**

Prefix	Meaning	Example
a-	on, in, into	afire, abed
	in the act of	aflutter
	not	apolitical
ab-; a-; ad-; a-; ac-	from, away, off	abdicate; avert
	to, toward	adverb; ascribe; accede
	at, near	adjacent
an-	not	anastigmatic
	without	anarchy
ana-	back, again	anachronism
	up, upward	anode
ante-	before	antebellum
anti-	against, opposed to	antiaircraft
	not, opposite of	antisocial
apo-	from, away, off	apocryphal
arch-	chief, principal	archbishop; architect
	extreme, ultra	archconservative
bi-	two	bisect
	twice, once every two	biannual
cata-	down, downward	cataract
	against	catapult
circum-	around, on all sides	circumlocution
cis-	on this side of	cislunar
co-	with, together	cooperate
	joint, fellow	coauthor
com-; col-; con-	with, together, altogether	combine; collaborate; congress
contra-	against	contradict
de-	to do the opposite of	decentralize
	down, lower	depress
	away, off	derail
	to remove, take away	defrost
demi-	half, partial	demigod
	smaller than ordinary	demitasse
di-	twice, double, two	diphthong; dissyllable

Prefix	Meaning	Example
dia-; di-	through, across	diameter; diocese
dis-	opposite, lack of	dishonest
	apart, away	dismiss
dys-	bad, defective	dysfunctional
en-; em-	to cause to be, make	enable; employ
	to put in, put on	enthrone; emblem
epi-; ep-	on, upon, above, in addition, toward	epidemic; epitaph; ephemeral
eu-	good, well, true	euphoria
ex-; e-	former, formerly	ex-president
	out of, from, out	exhale; emerge
	thoroughly, utterly	exterminate; evaporate
extra-	outside, beyond	extraordinary
fore-	front, in front	forepaw
	before, beforehand	foregoing
hemi-	half	hemisphere
hyper-	over, excessive, above, exceedingly	hypercritical, hypersensitive
hypo-	under, beneath	hypodermic
	to a lesser degree	hypothyroid
in-; il-; im-; ir-	not, lack of, opposite of	incorrect; illegal; impatient; irregular
	in, into, on, upon	inscribe; illuminate; imbibe; irrigate
infra-	below, beneath	infrastructure
inter-	one with the other	intercommunicate
	between, among	interpose
intra-	within, inside	intramural
intro-	inward, within, into	introduce
meta-	between, among	metacarpus
	change of state	metabolism
	behind, after	metathorax
mis-	bad, badly	misgovern
	wrong, wrongly	mispronounce
non-	not, opposite of, lack of, failure	nonbreakable, nonliving
ob-; op-; of-; o-	against, in the way, hindering	obstruct; oppose; offend; omit
	inversely, contrary	oblate
	toward, to	obvert; offer
	on, over	obtuse
para-	beside, near	parathyroid
	beyond	parapsychology
	related to, subordinate to	paramedical, paralegal
per-	throughout	perpetual
peri-	around, surrounding	perimeter
post-	after, in time	postwar
	after, in space	postnasal
pre-	before	prewar
pro-	forward	proceed
	forth, out	proclaim
	on the side of	pro-British
	in place of, acting as	proconsul
	before, preceding	prologue
	in front of	proscenium
quasi-	partly, as if	quasi-judicial
re-	again, anew	reappear
	back	repay
semi-	exactly half	semicircle
	about half, partly	semicivilized
sub-	under, below	subnormal
	down, further, again	subdivide
	near, nearly	subtropical
	lower, subordinate	subhead
super-	over, above	superimpose
	besides, further	superadd
	in high proportion	superabundant
	surpassing	supernatural
syn-; syl-; sym-	with, together, jointly	synagogue; syllogism; symbol
trans-	across, over, through	transcontinental
	beyond, on the other side of	transcend, transoceanic
	to or into a different condition	transform, transmigration

Prefix	Meaning	Example
ultra-	beyond	ultraviolet
	extremely	ultramodern
un-	not	unequal
	the opposite of	ungodly
uni-	one, a single	unicellular
up-	up	update
vice-	one who acts in place of another	vice president, viceroy

pre·flight /preˊflīt/ *attrib.adj.* occurring or provided before an aircraft flight.

pre·form /preˊfáwrm/ *v.tr.* form beforehand. □□ **pre·for·ma·tion** /-máyshən/ *n.*

pre·for·ma·tive /preˊfáwrmətiv/ *adj. & n.* ●*adj.* 1 forming beforehand. 2 prefixed as the formative element of a word. ●*n.* a preformative syllable or letter.

pre·fron·tal /preˊfrúnt'l/ *adj.* 1 in front of the frontal bone of the skull. 2 in the forepart of the frontal lobe of the brain.

pre·fron·tal lo·bot·o·my *n.* the surgical cutting of the nerve fibers that connect the frontal lobes with the rest of the brain, formerly used in psychosurgery.

pre·gla·cial /preˊgláyshəl/ *adj.* before a glacial period.

preg·na·ble /prégnəbəl/ *adj.* able to be captured, etc.; not impregnable. [ME f. OF *prenable* takable: see IMPREGNABLE¹]

preg·nan·cy /prégnənsee/ *n.* (*pl.* **·cies**) the condition or an instance of being pregnant.

preg·nant /prégnənt/ *adj.* 1 (of a woman or female animal) having a child or young developing in the uterus. 2 full of meaning; significant or suggestive (*a pregnant pause*). 3 (esp. of a person's mind) imaginative; inventive. 4 (foll. by *with*) full of; abundant in (*pregnant with danger*). □□ **preg·nant·ly** *adv.* (in sense 2). [ME f. F *prégnant* or L *praegnans –antis*, earlier *praegnas* (prob. as PRAE-, (g)*nasci* be born)]

preg·nant con·struc·tion *n. Gram.* one in which more is implied than the words express (e.g., *not have a chance* implying *of success*, etc.).

pre·heat /preˊheeet/ *v.tr.* heat beforehand.

pre·hen·sile /preˊhénsəl, –sīl/ *adj. Zool.* (of a tail or limb) capable of grasping. □□ **pre·hen·sil·i·ty** /–sílitee/ *n.* [F *préhensile* f. L *prehendere prehens-* (as PRE-, *hendere* grasp)]

pre·hen·sion /prihénshən/ *n.* 1 grasping; seizing. 2 mental apprehension. [L *prehensio* (as PREHENSILE)]

pre·his·tor·ic /preˊhistáwrik, –stór–/ *adj.* 1 of or relating to the period before written records. 2 *colloq.* utterly out of date. □□ **pre·his·to·ri·an** /–stáwreeən, –stór–/ *n.* **pre·his·tor·i·cal·ly** *adv.* **pre·his·to·ry** /–hístəree/ *n.* [F *préhistorique* (as PRE-, HISTORIC)]

pre·hu·man /preˊhyōōmən/ *adj.* existing before the time of humans.

pre·ig·ni·tion /preˊeigníshən/ *n.* the premature firing of the explosive mixture in an internal combustion engine.

pre·judge /preˊejúj/ *v.tr.* 1 form a premature judgment on (a person, issue, etc.). 2 pass judgment on (a person) before a trial or proper inquiry. □□ **pre·judg·ment** *n.* **pre·ju·di·ca·tion** /–jōōdikáyshən/ *n.*

prej·u·dice /préjədis/ *n. & v.* ●*n.* 1 a a preconceived opinion. b (usu. foll. by *against, in favor of*) bias or partiality. c intolerance of or discrimination against a person or group, esp. on account of race, religion, or gender (*racial prejudice*). 2 harm or injury that results or may result from some action or judgment (*to the prejudice of*). ●*v.tr.* 1 impair the validity or force of (a right, claim, statement, etc.). 2 (esp. as prejudiced *adj.*) cause (a person) to have a prejudice. □ **without prejudice** (often foll. by *to*) without detriment (to any existing right or claim). [ME f. OF *prejudice* f. L *praejudicium* (as PRAE-, *judicium* judgment)]

prej·u·di·cial /préjədíshəl/ *adj.* causing prejudice; detrimental. □□ **prej·u·di·cial·ly** *adv.* [ME f. OF *prejudiciel* (as PREJUDICE)]

prel·a·cy /préləsee/ *n.* (*pl.* **·cies**) 1 church government by prelates. 2 (prec. by *the*) prelates collectively. 3 the office or rank of prelate. [ME f. AF *prelacie* f. med.L *prelatia* (as PRELATE)]

pre·lap·sar·i·an /preˊlapsáireeən/ *adj. Theol.* before the Fall of Adam and Eve.

prel·ate /prélət/ *n.* a high ecclesiastical dignitary, e.g., a bishop, abbot, etc. □□ **pre·lat·ic** /prilátik/ *adj.* **pre·lat·i·cal** *adj.* [ME f. OF *prelat* f. med.L *praelatus* past part.: see PREFER]

prel·a·ture /préləchər, –choor/ *n.* 1 the office of prelate. 2 (prec. by *the*) prelates collectively. [F *prélature* f. med.L *praelatura* (as PRELATE)]

pre·lim /preˊelim, prilím/ *n. colloq.* preliminary. [abbr.]

pre·lim·i·nar·y /prilíminəree/ *adj., n., & adv.* ●*adj.* introductory; preparatory. ●*n.* (*pl.* **·ies**) (usu. in *pl.*) 1 a preliminary action or arrangement (*dispense with the preliminaries*). 2 a a preliminary trial or contest. b a preliminary examination. ●*adv.* (foll. by *to*) preparatory to; in advance of (*was completed preliminary to the main event*).

See page xx for the **Key to Pronunciation**.

□□ **pre·lim·i·nar·i·ly** adv. [mod.L praeliminaris or F préliminaire (as PRE-, L limen liminis threshold)]

pre·lit·er·ate /preélítərət/ adj. of or relating to a society or culture that has not developed the use of writing.

prel·ude /prélyōōd, práylōōd, preé–/ n. & v. ● n. (often foll. by to) 1 an action, event, or situation serving as an introduction. 2 the introductory part of a poem, etc. 3 a an introductory piece of music, often preceding a fugue or forming the first piece of a suite or beginning an act of an opera. b a short piece of music of a similar type, esp. for the piano. ● v.tr. 1 serve as a prelude to. 2 introduce with a prelude. □□ **pre·lu·di·al** /prilōōdeeəl/ adj. [F prélude or med.L praeludium f. L praeludere praelus- (as PRAE-, ludere play)]

pre·mar·i·tal /preémárít'l/ adj. existing or (esp. of sexual relations) occurring before marriage. □□ **pre·mar·i·tal·ly** adv.

pre·ma·ture /preemǝchŏŏr, –tyŏŏr, –tŏŏr/ adj. 1 a occurring or done before the usual or proper time; too early (a premature decision). b too hasty (must not be premature). 2 (of a baby, esp. a viable one) born (esp. three or more weeks) before the end of the full term of gestation. □□ **pre·ma·ture·ly** adv. **pre·ma·ture·ness** n. **pre·ma·tu·ri·ty** /–chŏŏrətee/ n. [L praematurus very early (as PRAE-, MATURE)]

pre·max·il·lar·y /preemáksileree/ adj. in front of the upper jaw.

pre·med /preeméd/ n. colloq. a premedical course of study or student. [abbr.]

pre·med·i·cal /preemédikəl/ adj. of or relating to preparation for a course of study in medicine.

pre·med·i·tate /preemédǝtayt/ v.tr. (often as **premeditated** adj.) think out or plan (an action) beforehand (premeditated murder). □□ **pre·med·i·ta·tion** n. [L praemeditari (as PRAE-, MEDITATE)]

pre·men·stru·al /preeménstrōōəl/ adj. of, occurring, or experienced before menstruation (premenstrual tension). □□ **pre·men·stru·al·ly** adv.

pre·men·stru·al syn·drome n. any of a complex of symptoms (including tension, fluid retention, etc.) experienced by some women in the days immediately preceding menstruation. ¶ Abbr.: **PMS**

pre·mier /prǝmeér, –myeér, preémeer/ n. & adj. ● n. a prime minister or other head of government in certain countries. ● adj. 1 first in importance, order, or time. 2 of earliest creation; oldest. □□ **pre·mier·ship** n. [ME f. OF = first, f. L (as PRIMARY)]

pre·miere /prǝmeér, –myáir/ n., adj., & v. (also **pre·mière**) ● n. the first performance or showing of a play or movie. ● adj. = PREMIER adj. 1. ● v.tr. give a premiere of. [F, fem. of premier (adj.) (as PREMIER)]

pre·mil·len·ni·al /preémileéneeəl/ adj. existing or occurring before the millennium, esp. with reference to the supposed second coming of Christ. □□ **pre·mil·len·ni·al·ism** n. **pre·mil·len·ni·al·ist** n.

prem·ise /prémis/ n. & v. ● n. 1 Logic (also esp. Brit. **prem·iss**) a previous statement from which another is inferred. 2 (in pl.) a a house or building with its grounds and appurtenances. b Law houses, land, etc., previously specified in a document, etc. ● v. 1 tr. say or write by way of introduction. 2 tr. & intr. assert or assume as a premise. □ **on the premises** in the building, etc., concerned. [ME f. OF premisse f. med.L praemissa (propositio) (proposition) set in front f. L praemittere praemiss- (as PRAE-, mittere send)]

prem·iss esp. Brit. var. of PREMISE n. 1

pre·mi·um /preémeeəm/ n. 1 an amount to be paid for a contract of insurance. 2 a a sum added to interest, wages, etc.; a bonus. b a sum added to ordinary charges. 3 a reward or prize. 4 (attrib.) (of a commodity) of best quality and therefore more expensive. 5 an item offered free or cheaply as an incentive to buy, sample, or subscribe to something. □ **at a premium** 1 highly valued; above the usual or nominal price. 2 scarce and in demand. **put a premium on** 1 provide or act as an incentive to. 2 attach special value to. [L praemium booty, reward (as PRAE-, emere buy, take)]

pre·mo·lar /preemólər/ adj. & n. ● adj. in front of a molar tooth. ● n. (in an adult human) each of eight teeth situated in pairs between each of the four canine teeth and each first molar.

pre·mo·ni·tion /preémǝníshǝn, preé–/ n. a forewarning; a presentiment. □□ **pre·mon·i·tor** /primónitǝr/ n. **pre·mon·i·to·ry** /primónitawree/ adj. [F prémonition or LL praemonitio f. L praemonēre praemonit- (as PRAE-, monēre warn)]

Pre·mon·stra·ten·sian /primónstrǝténseeǝn/ adj. & n. hist. ● adj. of or relating to an order of regular canons founded at Prémontré in France in 1120, or of the corresponding order of nuns. ● n. a member of either of these orders. [med.L Praemonstratensis f. Praemonstratus the abbey of Prémontré (lit. = foreshown)]

pre·morse /preémawrs/ adj. Bot. & Zool. with the end abruptly terminated. [L praemordēre praemors- bite off (as PRAE-, mordēre bite)]

pre·na·tal /preenáyt'l/ adj. of or concerning the period before birth. □□ **pre·na·tal·ly** adv.

pren·tice /préntis/ n. & v. archaic ● n. = APPRENTICE. ● v.tr. (as **prenticed** adj.) apprenticed. □□ **pren·tice·ship** n. [ME f. APPRENTICE]

pren·tice hand n. an inexperienced hand.

pre·nup·tial /preenúpshǝl/ adj. existing or occurring before marriage.

pre·nup·tial con·tract n. a contract between two persons intending to marry each other, setting out the terms and conditions of their marriage and usu. the division of property in the event of divorce.

pre·oc·cu·pa·tion /pree-ókyǝpáyshǝn/ n. 1 the state of being preoccupied. 2 a thing that engrosses or dominates the mind. [F préoccupation or L praeoccupatio (as PREOCCUPY)]

pre·oc·cu·py /pree-ókyǝpi/ v.tr. (·pies, ·pied) 1 (of a thought, etc.) dominate or engross the mind of (a person) to the exclusion of other thoughts. 2 (as **preoccupied** adj.) otherwise engrossed; mentally distracted. 3 occupy beforehand. [PRE- + OCCUPY, after L praeoccupare seize beforehand]

pre·oc·u·lar /pree-ókyǝlǝr/ adj. in front of the eye.

pre·or·dain /preeawrdáyn/ v.tr. ordain or determine beforehand.

prep /prep/ n. & v. colloq. ● n. 1 a a student in a preparatory school. b a preparatory school. 2 Brit. a the preparation of school work by a pupil. b the period when this is done. ● v. intr. attend a preparatory school. [abbr. of PREPARATION]

prep. abbr. preposition.

pre·pack·age /preépákij/ v.tr. (also **pre·pack** /–pák/) package (goods) on the site of production or before retail.

pre·paid past and past part. of PREPAY.

prep·a·ra·tion /prépǝráyshǝn/ n. 1 the act or an instance of preparing; the process of being prepared. 2 (often in pl.) something done to make ready. 3 a specially prepared substance, esp. a food or medicine. 4 work done by students to prepare for a lesson. 5 Mus. the sounding of the discordant note in a chord in the preceding chord where it is not discordant, lessening the effect of the discord. [ME f. OF f. L praeparatio –onis (as PREPARE)]

pre·par·a·tive /pripárǝtiv/ adj. & n. ● adj. preparatory. ● n. a preparatory act. □□ **pre·par·a·tive·ly** adv. [ME f. OF preparatif –ive f. med.L praeparativus (as PREPARE)]

pre·par·a·to·ry /pripárǝtawree, –páir–, prépǝrǝ–/ adj. & adv. ● adj. (often foll. by to) serving to prepare; introductory. ● adv. (often foll. by to) in a preparatory manner (was packing preparatory to departure). □□ **pre·par·a·to·ri·ly** adv. [ME f. LL praeparatorius (as PREPARE)]

pre·par·a·to·ry school n. a usu. private school preparing pupils for college.

pre·pare /pripáir/ v. 1 tr. make or get ready for use, consideration, etc. 2 tr. make ready or assemble (food, a meal, etc.) for eating. 3 a tr. make (a person or oneself) ready or disposed in some way (prepares students for university; prepared them for a shock). b intr. put oneself or things in readiness; get ready (prepare to jump). 4 tr. make (a chemical product, etc.) by a regular process; manufacture. 5 tr. Mus. lead up to (a discord). □ **be prepared** (often foll. by for, or to + infin.) be disposed or willing to. □□ **pre·par·er** n. [ME f. F préparer or L praeparare (as PRAE-, parare make ready)]

pre·par·ed·ness /pripáiridnis/ n. a state of readiness, esp. for war.

pre·pay /preépáy/ v.tr. (past and past part. **pre·paid**) 1 pay (a charge) in advance. 2 pay postage on (a letter or package, etc.) before mailing. □□ **pre·pay·a·ble** adj. **pre·pay·ment** n.

pre·pense /pripéns/ adj. (usu. placed after noun) esp. Law deliberate; intentional (malice prepense). □□ **pre·pense·ly** adv. [earlier prepensed past part. of obs. prepense v.) alt. f. earlier purpense f. AF & OF purpenser (as PUR-, penser): see PENSIVE]

pre·plan /preéplán/ v.tr. (**pre·planned**, **pre·plan·ning**) plan in advance.

pre·pon·der·ant /pripóndǝrǝnt/ adj. surpassing in influence, power, number, or importance; predominant; preponderating. □□ **pre·pon·der·ance** n. **pre·pon·der·ant·ly** adv.

pre·pon·der·ate /pripóndǝrayt/ v.intr. (often foll. by over) 1 a be greater in influence, quantity, or number. b predominate. 2 a be of greater importance. b weigh more. [L praeponderare (as PRAE-, PONDER)]

prep·o·si·tion / prépǝzíshǝn/ n. Gram. a word governing (and usu. preceding) a noun or pronoun and expressing a relation to another word or element, as in: "the man on the platform," "came after dinner," "what did you do it for?" □□ **prep·o·si·tion·al** adj. **prep·o·si·tion·al·ly** adv. [ME f. L praepositio f. praeponere praeposit- (as PRAE-, ponere place)]

GRAMMAR TIP preposition

Ending a Sentence with a Preposition. There is an old story that when criticized for ending a sentence with a preposition, Winston Churchill said, "That is the kind of English up with which I will not put." His point is clear: Don't mutilate a sentence just to avoid ending it with a preposition. Although it is usually more effective to end a sentence with a noun or other more forceful construction, this is not a rule to be followed slavishly. It is perfectly permissible, for example, to say, *I have no idea where he came from* or *They had a great deal to be thankful for.* It is also permissible to end a sentence with a preposition when the preposition is functioning as an adverb (*she's the most unusual person I've ever run across*).

pre·pos·i·tive /preepózitiv/ *adj. Gram.* (of a word, particle, etc.) that should be placed before or prefixed. [LL *praepositivus* (as PREPOSITION)]

pre·pos·sess /preepəzés/ *v.tr.* **1** (usu. in *passive*) (of an idea, feeling, etc.) take possession of (a person); imbue. **2 a** prejudice (usu. favorably and spontaneously). **b** (as **prepossessing** *adj.*) attractive; appealing. □□ **pre·pos·ses·sion** /-zéshən/ *n.*

pre·pos·ter·ous /pripóstərəs/ *adj.* **1** utterly absurd; outrageous. **2** contrary to nature, reason, or common sense. □□ **pre·pos·ter·ous·ly** *adv.* **pre·pos·ter·ous·ness** *n.* [L *praeposterus* reversed, absurd (as PRAE-, *posterus* coming after)]

pre·po·tent /pripót'nt/ *adj.* **1** greater than others in power, influence, etc. **2** dominant in transmitting hereditary qualities. □□ **pre·po·tence** *n.* **pre·po·ten·cy** *n.* [ME f. L *praepotens* –*entis,* part. of *praeposse* (as PRAE-, *posse* be able)]

prep·py /prépee/ *n. & adj.* (also **prep·pie**) *US colloq.* • *n.* (*pl.* **·pies**) a person attending an expensive private school or who strives to look like such a person. • *adj.* (**prep·pi·er, prep·pi·est**) **1** like a preppy. **2** neat and fashionable. [PREP (SCHOOL) + –Y²]

pre·pran·di·al /preeprándeeəl/ *adj. formal* or *joc.* before a meal, esp. dinner. [PRE- + L *prandium* a meal]

pre·pref·er·ence /preepréfərəns, –préfrəns/ *adj. Brit.* (of shares, claims, etc.) ranking before preference shares, etc.

pre·print /preeprint/ *n.* a printed document issued in advance of general publication.

pre·proc·es·sor /preeprósesər/ *n.* a computer program that modifies data to conform with the input requirements of another program.

prep school /prep/ *n.* = PREPARATORY SCHOOL. [abbr. of PREPARATORY]

pre·pu·bes·cence /preepyōōbésəns/ *n.* the time, esp. the last two or three years, before puberty. □□ **pre·pu·bes·cent** *adj.*

pre·pub·li·ca·tion /preepublikáyshən/ *adj. & n.* • *attrib.adj.* produced or occurring before publication. • *n.* publication in advance or beforehand.

pre·puce /preepyōōs/ *n.* **1** = FORESKIN. **2** the fold of skin surrounding the clitoris. □□ **pre·pu·tial** /preepyōōshəl/ *adj.* [ME f. L *praeputium*]

pre·quel /preekwəl/ *n.* a story, movie, etc., whose events or concerns precede those of an existing work. [PRE- + SEQUEL]

Pre-Raph·a·el·ite /preeráfeeəlit/ *n. & adj.* • *n.* a member of a group of English 19th-c. artists, including Holman Hunt, Millais, and D. G. Rossetti, emulating the work of Italian artists before the time of Raphael. • *adj.* **1** of or relating to the Pre-Raphaelites. **2** (**pre-Raphaelite**) (esp. of a woman) like a type painted by a Pre-Raphaelite (e.g., with long thick curly auburn hair). □□ **pre-Raph·a·el·it·ism** *n.*

Pre-Raph·a·el·ite Broth·er·hood *n.* the chosen name of the Pre-Raphaelites.

pre·re·cord /preerikáwrd/ *v.tr.* record (esp. material for broadcasting) in advance.

pre·req·ui·site /preerékwizit/ *adj. & n.* • *adj.* required as a precondition. • *n.* a prerequisite thing.

▶See note at PERQUISITE.

pre·rog·a·tive /prirógətiv/ *n.* **1** a right or privilege exclusive to an individual or class. **2** (in full **royal prerogative**) *Brit.* the right of the sovereign, theoretically subject to no restriction. [ME f. OF *prerogative* or L *praerogativa* privilege (orig. to vote first) f. *praerogativus* asked first (as PRAE-, *rogare* ask)]

PRONUNCIATION TIP prerogative

The formally correct pronunciation of this word is reflective of its spelling ("pri-ROG-a-tiv"). But in conversation many speakers say it as if the first *r* were dropped.

Pres. *abbr.* President.

pres·age /présij/ *n. & v.* • *n.* **1** an omen or portent. **2** a presentiment or foreboding. • *v.tr.* (also /prisáyj/) **1** portend; foreshadow. **2** give warning of (an event, etc.) by natural means. **3** (of a person) predict or have a presentiment of. □□ **pres·age·ful** *adj.* **pres·ag·er** *n.* [ME f. F *présage, présager* f. L *praesagium* f. *praesagire* forebode (as PRAE-, *sagire* perceive keenly)]

pres·by·o·pi·a /prézbeeōpeeə, prés–/ *n.* farsightedness caused by loss of elasticity of the eye lens, occurring esp. in middle and old age. □□ **pres·by·op·ic** /–beeópik/ *adj.* [mod.L f. Gk *presbus* old man + *ōps ōpos* eye]

pres·by·ter /prézbitər/ *n.* **1** an elder in the early Christian Church. **2** (in episcopal churches) a minister of the second order; a priest. **3** (in the Presbyterian Church) an elder. □□ **pres·byt·er·al** /–bítərəl/ *adj.* **pres·byt·er·ate** /–bítərət/ *n.* **pres·by·te·ri·al** /–téereeəl/ *adj.* **pres·byt·er·ship** *n.* [eccl.L f. Gk *presbuteros* elder, compar. of *presbus* old]

Pres·by·te·ri·an /prézbiteéreeən/ *adj. & n.* • *adj.* (of a church) governed by elders all of equal rank. • *n.* **1** a member of a Presbyterian Church. **2** an adherent of the Presbyterian system. □□ **Pres·by·te·ri·an·ism** *n.* [eccl.L *presbyterium* (as PRESBYTERY)]

pres·by·ter·y /prézbiteree/ *n.* (*pl.* **·ies**) **1** the eastern part of a chancel beyond the choir; the sanctuary. **2 a** a body of presbyters. **b** a

district represented by this. **3** the house of a Roman Catholic priest. [ME f. OF *presbiterie* f. eccl.L f. Gk *presbuterion* (as PRESBYTER)]

pre·school /preeskōōl/ *adj.* of or relating to the time before a child is old enough to go to school. □□ **pre·school·er** *n.*

pre·scient /préshənt, –eeənt, prē–/ *adj.* having foreknowledge or foresight. □□ **pre·science** *n.* **pre·scient·ly** *adv.* [L *praescire praescient-* know beforehand (as PRAE-, *scire* know)]

pre·scind /prisínd/ *v.* **1** *tr.* (foll. by *from*) cut off (a part from a whole), esp. prematurely or abruptly. **2** *intr.* (foll. by *from*) leave out of consideration. **3** withdraw or turn away in thought. [L *praescindere* (as PRAE-, *scindere* cut)]

pre·scribe /priskr íb/ *v.* **1** *tr.* **a** advise the use of (a medicine, etc.), esp. by an authorized prescription. **b** recommend, esp. as a benefit (*prescribed a change of scenery*). **2** *tr.* lay down or impose authoritatively. **3** *intr.* (foll. by *to, for*) assert a prescriptive right or claim. □□ **pre·scrib·er** *n.* [L *praescribere praescript-* direct in writing (as PRAE-, *scribere* write)]

▶**Prescribe** and **proscribe** are sometimes confused, but they are nearly opposite in meaning. **Prescribe** means 'advise the use of' or 'impose authoritatively,' whereas **proscribe** means 'denounce or ban.' Examples of each are as follows: *Our teacher prescribed topics to be covered; The doctor prescribed a painkiller; The principal proscribed tabloid newspapers from the school library; A totalitarian regime may prescribe some books and proscribe others.*

SPELLING TIP prescribe/proscribe

A doctor *pre*scribes medicine by writing a *pre*scription. To *pro*scribe means to *pro*hibit.

---

pre·script /preeskript/ *adj. & n.* • *adj.* prescribed. • *n.* an ordinance, law, or command. [L *praescriptum* neut. past part.: see PRESCRIBE]

pre·scrip·tion /priskrípshən/ *n.* **1** the act or an instance of prescribing. **2 a** a doctor's (usu. written) instruction for the preparation and use of a medicine. **b** a medicine prescribed. **3** (in full **positive prescription**) uninterrupted use or possession from time immemorial or for the period fixed by law as giving a title or right. **4 a** an ancient custom viewed as authoritative. **b** a claim founded on long use. [ME f. OF f. L *praescriptio –onis* (as PRESCRIBE)]

pre·scrip·tive /priskríptiv/ *adj.* **1** prescribing. **2** *Linguistics* concerned with or laying down rules of usage. **3** based on prescription (*prescriptive right*). **4** prescribed by custom. □□ **pre·scrip·tive·ly** *adv.* **pre·scrip·tive·ness** *n.* **pre·scrip·tiv·ism** *n.* **pre·scrip·tiv·ist** *n. & adj.* [LL *praescriptivus* (as PRESCRIBE)]

pre·se·lect /preeselékt/ *v.tr.* select in advance. □□ **pre·se·lec·tion** *n.*

pre·se·lec·tive /preeseléktiv/ *adj.* that can be selected or set in advance.

pre·se·lec·tor /preeseléktər/ *n.* any of various devices for selecting a mechanical or electrical operation in advance of its execution.

pres·ence /prézəns/ *n.* **1 a** the state or condition of being present (*your presence is requested*). **b** existence; location (*the presence of a hospital nearby*). **2** a place where a person is (*was admitted to their presence*). **3 a** a person's appearance or bearing, esp. when imposing (*an august presence*). **b** a person's force of personality (esp. *have presence*). **4** a person or thing that is present (*there was a presence in the room*). **5** representation for reasons of political influence (*maintained a presence*). □ **in the presence of** in front of; observed by. [ME f. OF f. L *praesentia* (as PRESENT¹)]

pres·ence of mind *n.* the ability to remain calm and take quick, sensible action in a sudden difficulty.

pres·ent¹ /prézənt/ *adj. & n.* • *adj.* **1** (usu. *predic.*) being in the place in question (*was present at the trial*). **2 a** now existing, occurring, or being such (*during the present season*). **b** now being considered or discussed, etc. (*in the present case*). **3** *Gram.* expressing an action, etc., now going on or habitually performed (*present participle*; *present tense*). • *n.* (prec. by *the*) **1** the time now passing (*no time like the present*). **2** *Gram.* the present tense. □ **at present** now. **by these presents** *Law* by this document (*know all men by these presents*). **for the present 1** just now. **2** as far as this present is concerned. **present company excepted** excluding those who are here now. [ME f. OF f. L *praesens –entis* part. of *praeesse* be at hand (as PRAE-, *esse* be)]

pre·sent² /prizént/ *v. & n.* • *v.tr.* **1** introduce, offer, or exhibit, esp. for public attention or consideration. **2 a** (with a thing as object, usu. foll. by *to*) offer, give, or award as a gift (to a person), esp. formally or ceremonially. **b** (with a person as object, foll. by *with*) make available to; cause to have (*presented them with a new car; that presents us with a problem*). **3 a** (of a company, producer, etc.) put (a form of entertainment) before the public. **b** (of a performer, etc.) introduce or put before an audience. **4** introduce (a person) formally (*may I present my fiancée?*). **5** offer; give (compliments, etc.) (*may I present my card; present my regards to your family*). **6 a** (of a circumstance) reveal (some quality, etc.) (*this presents some difficulty*). **b** exhibit (an appearance, etc.) (*presented a tough exterior*). **7** (of an idea, etc.) offer or suggest itself. **8** deliver (a check, bill, etc.) for acceptance or payment. **9 a** (usu. foll. by *at*) aim (a weapon). **b** hold out (a weapon) in a position for aiming. **10** (*refl.* or *absol.*) *Med.* (of a patient or illness, etc.) come forward for or undergo initial medical examination. **11** (*absol.*) *Med.* (of a part of a fetus) be directed toward the cervix at the time of delivery. **12** (foll. by *to*) *Law* bring formally under notice; submit (an offense, complaint, etc.). **13** (foll. by *to*) *Eccl.* recommend (a clergyman) to a bishop for institution to a benefice. • *n.* the position of presenting arms in salute. □ **present arms** hold a rifle, etc., vertically in front of the body as a salute. **present oneself 1** appear. **2** come forward for examination, etc. □□ **pre·sent·er** *n.* (in sense 3 of *v.*). [ME f. OF *presenter* f. L *praesentare* (as PRESENT¹)]

pre·sent³ /préznt/ *n.* a gift; a thing given or presented. □ **make a present of** give as a gift. [ME f. OF (as PRESENT¹), orig. in phr. *mettre une chose en present à quelqu'un* put a thing into the presence of a person]

SYNONYM TIP **present³**

BONUS, DONATION, GIFT, GRATUITY, LAGNIAPPE, LARGESS. What's the difference between a birthday **present** and a Christmas **gift**? Both words refer to something given as an expression of friendship, affection, esteem, etc. But *gift* is a more formal term, suggesting something of monetary value that is formally bestowed on an individual, group, or institution (*a gift to the university*). *Present*, on the other hand, implies something of less value that is an expression of goodwill (*a housewarming present, a present for the teacher*). **Largess** is a somewhat pompous term for a very generous *gift* that is conferred in an ostentatious or condescending way, often on many recipients (*the king's largess, the largess of our government*). A *gratuity* is associated with tipping and other forms of voluntary compensation for special attention or service above and beyond what is included in a charge (*known for her generous gratuities, the duchess enjoyed watching the waiters compete with each other to serve her*), while a **lagniappe** is a Southern word, used chiefly in Louisiana and southeast Texas, for either a *gratuity* or a small *gift* given to a customer along with a purchase. If you give money or anything else as a *gift* to a philanthropic, charitable, or religious organization, it is known as a **donation** (*donations for the poor*). But if your employer gives you money at the end of the year, it isn't a Christmas *gift*; it's a Christmas **bonus**.

---

pre·sent·a·ble /prizéntəbəl/ *adj.* **1** of good appearance; fit to be presented to other people. **2** fit for presentation. □□ **pre·sent·a·bil·i·ty** /–bílitee/ *n.* **pre·sent·a·ble·ness** *n.* **pre·sent·a·bly** *adv.*

pres·en·ta·tion /prézəntáyshən, prée zen–/ *n.* **1 a** the act or an instance of presenting; the process of being presented. **b** a thing presented. **2** the manner or quality of presenting. **3** a demonstration or display of materials, information, etc.; a lecture. **4** an exhibition or theatrical performance. **5** a formal introduction. **6** the position of the fetus in relation to the cervix at the time of delivery. □□ **pres·en·ta·tion·al** *adj.* **pres·en·ta·tion·al·ly** *adv.* [ME f. OF f. LL *praesentatio –onis* (as PRESENT²)]

pres·en·ta·tion·ism /prézəntáyshənizəm, prée zen–/ *n. Philos.* the doctrine that in perception the mind has immediate cognition of the object. □□ **pres·en·ta·tion·ist** *n.*

pres·en·ta·tive /prizéntətiv/ *adj.* **1** *Philos.* subject to direct cognition. **2** *hist.* (of a benefice) to which a patron has the right of presentation. [prob. f. med.L (as PRESENTATION)]

pres·ent-day *adj.* *adj.* of this time; modern.

pres·en·tee /prézəntée, prizén–/ *n.* **1** the recipient of a present. **2** a person presented. [ME f. AF (as PRESENT²)]

pre·sen·tient /preesénshənt, –sheeónt/ *adj.* (often foll. by *of*) having a presentiment. [L *praesentiens* (as PRAE-, SENTIENT)]

pre·sen·ti·ment /prizéntimənt, –séntimənt/ *n.* a vague expectation; a foreboding (esp. of misfortune). [obs. F *présentiment* (as PRE-, SENTIMENT)]

pres·ent·ly /prézəntlee/ *adv.* **1** soon; after a short time. **2** at the present time; now.

▶In *The pain will lessen presently*, the meaning of **presently** is 'soon'; in *Limited resources are presently available*, the meaning is 'at this moment.' Both senses are widely used.

pre·sent·ment /prizéntmənt/ *n.* **1** an act or a manner of presenting. **2** the presenting of a bill, note, etc., esp. for payment. **3** the act of presenting information, esp. a statement on oath by a jury of a fact known to them. [ME f. OF *presentement* (as PRESENT²)]

pres·er·va·tion /prézərváyshən/ *n.* **1** the act of preserving or process of being preserved. **2** a state of being well or badly preserved (*in an excellent state of preservation*). [ME f. OF f. med.L *praeservatio –onis* (as PRESERVE)]

pres·er·va·tion·ist /prézərváyshənist/ *n.* a supporter or advocate of preservation, esp. of wildlife or historic buildings.

pre·serv·a·tive /prizôrvətiv/ *n. & adj.* • *n.* a substance for preserv-

ing perishable foods, wood, etc. • *adj.* tending to preserve. [ME f. OF *preservatif –ive* f. med.L *praeservativus –um* (as PRESERVE)]

pre·serve /prizôrv/ *v. & n.* • *v.tr.* **1 a** keep safe or free from harm, decay, etc. **b** keep alive (a name, memory, etc.). **2** maintain (a thing) in its existing state. **3** retain (a quality or condition). **4 a** treat or refrigerate (food) to prevent decomposition or fermentation. **b** prepare (fruit or vegetables) by boiling with sugar, canning, etc., for long-term storage. **5** keep (wildlife, a river, etc.) undisturbed for private use. • *n.* (in *sing.* or *pl.*) **1** preserved fruit; jam. **2** a place where game or fish, etc., are preserved. **3** a sphere or area of activity regarded as a person's own. □□ **pre·serv·a·ble** *adj.* **pre·serv·er** *n.* [ME f. OF *preserver* f. LL *praeservare* (as PRAE-, *servare* keep)]

pre·set /préesét/ *v.tr.* (**·set·ting**; *past* and *past part.* **·set**) **1** set or fix (a device) in advance of its operation. **2** settle or decide beforehand.

pre·shrunk /préeshrúngk/ *adj.* (of a fabric or garment) treated so that it shrinks during manufacture and not in use.

pre·side /prizíd/ *v.intr.* **1** (often foll. by *at, over*) be in a position of authority, esp. as the chairperson or president. **2 a** exercise control or authority. **b** (foll. by *at*) play a featured instrument (*presided at the piano*). [F *présider* f. L *praesidere* (as PRAE-, *sedere* sit)]

pres·i·den·cy /prézidənsee/ *n.* (*pl.* **·cies**) **1** the office, term, or function of president. **2** the office of the President of the United States. **3** a Mormon administrative or governing body. [Sp. & Port. *presidencia*, It. *presidenza* f. med.L *praesidentia* (as PRESIDE)]

pres·i·dent /prézidənt/ *n.* **1** the elected head of a republican government. **2** the head of a college, university, company, society, etc. **3** a person in charge of a meeting, council, etc. □□ **pres·i·den·tial** /–dénshəl/ *adj.* **pres·i·den·tial·ly** *adv.* **pres·i·dent·ship** *n.* [ME f. OF f. L (as PRESIDE)]

pre·sid·i·um /prisídeeəm, –zídeeəm/ *n.* (also **prae·sid·i·um**) a standing executive committee in a Communist country, esp. *hist.* in the former USSR. [Russ. *prezidium* f. L *praesidium* protection, etc. (as PRESIDE)]

pre-So·crat·ic /préesəkrátik, –sō–/ *adj.* (of philosophy) of the time before Socrates.

press¹ /pres/ *v. & n.* • *v.* **1** *tr.* apply steady force to (a thing in contact) (*pressed the two surfaces together*). **2** *tr.* **a** compress or apply pressure to a thing to flatten, shape, or smooth it, as by ironing (*got the curtains pressed*). **b** squeeze (a fruit, etc.) to extract its juice. **c** manufacture (a record, etc.) by molding under pressure. **3** *tr.* (foll. by *out of, from*, etc.) squeeze (juice, etc.). **4** *tr.* embrace or caress by squeezing (*pressed my hand*). **5** *intr.* (foll. by *on, against*, etc.) exert pressure. **6** *intr.* be urgent; demand immediate action (*time was pressing*). **7** *intr.* (foll. by *for*) make an insistent demand. **8** *intr.* (foll. by *up, around*, etc.) form a crowd. **9** *intr.* (foll. by *on, forward*, etc.) hasten insistently. **10** *tr.* (often in *passive*) (of an enemy, etc.) bear heavily on. **11** *tr.* (often foll. by *for*, or *to* + infin.) urge or entreat (*pressed me to stay; pressed me for an answer*). **12** *tr.* (foll. by *on, upon*) **a** put forward or urge (an opinion, claim, or course of action). **b** insist on the acceptance of (an offer, a gift, etc.). **13** *tr.* insist on (*did not press the point*). **14** *intr.* (foll. by *on*) produce a strong mental or moral impression; oppress; weigh heavily. **15** *intr.* *Sports* try too hard and so perform inadequately. **16** (in weightlifting) raise weight in a press. • *n.* **1** the act or an instance of pressing (*give it a slight press*). **2 a** a device for compressing, flattening, shaping, extracting juice, etc. (*flower press; wine press*). **b** a machine that applies pressure to a workpiece by means of a tool, in order to punch shapes, bend it, etc. **3** = PRINTING PRESS. **4** (prec. by *the*) **a** the art or practice of printing. **b** newspapers, journalists, etc., generally or collectively (*read it in the press; pursued by the press*). **5** a notice or piece of publicity in newspapers, etc. (*got a good press*). **6** (**Press**) **a** a printing house or establishment. **b** a publishing company (*Yale University Press*). **7 a** crowding. **b** a crowd (of people, etc.). **8** the pressure of affairs. **9** a large usu. shelved cupboard for clothes, books, etc. **10** (in basketball) an aggressive close defense. **11** (in weightlifting) an exercise in which the weight is lifted so that the arms are fully extended, without moving the legs or feet. □ **at** (or **in**) **press** (or **the press**) being printed. **be pressed for** have barely enough (time, etc.). **go** (or **send**) **to press** go or send to be printed. **press the button 1** set machinery in motion. **2** *colloq.* take a decisive initial step. [ME f. OF *presser*, *presse* f. L *pressare* frequent. of *premere* press³]

press² /pres/ *v. & n.* • *v.tr.* **1** *hist.* force to serve in the army or navy; impress. **2** bring into use as a makeshift (*was pressed into service*). • *n. hist.* compulsory enlistment esp. in the navy; impressment. [alt. f. obs. *prest* (v. & n.) f. OF *prest* loan, advance pay f. *prester* f. L *praestare* furnish (as PRAE-, *stare* stand)]

press a·gent *n.* a person employed to attend to advertising and press publicity.

press box *n.* a reporters' enclosure esp. at a sports event.

press-but·ton *adj. Brit.* = PUSH BUTTON.

press con·fer·ence *n.* an interview given to journalists to make an announcement or answer questions.

pressed steel *n.* steel sheet that has been shaped by molding under pressure when solid.

press gal·ler·y *n.* a gallery for reporters esp. in a legislative assembly.

press-gang /présgang/ *n. & v.* ● *n.* **1** *hist.* a body of men employed to press men into service in the army or navy. **2** any group using similar coercive methods. ● *v.tr.* force into service.

press·ing /présing/ *adj. & n.* ● *adj.* **1** urgent (*pressing business*). **2 a** urging strongly (*a pressing invitation*). **b** persistent; importunate (*since you are so pressing*). ● *n.* **1** a thing made by pressing, esp. a record, compact disc, etc. **2** a series of these made at one time. **3** the act or an instance of pressing a thing, esp. a record or grapes, etc. (*all at one pressing*). □□ **press·ing·ly** *adv.*

press·man /présmən/ *n.* (*pl.* **·men**) **1** an operator of a printing press. **2** *Brit.* a journalist.

press·mark /présmaark/ *n.n. Brit.* an assigned number or mark showing the location of a book, etc., in a library.

press-on *adj.* (of a material) that can be pressed or ironed on.

press re·lease *n.* an official statement issued to newspapers for information.

press-stud *n. Brit.* = SNAP FASTENER.

press-up *n.* = PUSH-UP.

pres·sure /préshər/ *n. & v.* ● *n.* **1 a** the exertion of continuous force on or against a body by another in contact with it. **b** the force exerted. **c** the amount of this (expressed by the force on a unit area) (*atmospheric pressure*). **2** urgency; the need to meet a deadline, etc. (*work under pressure*). **3** affliction or difficulty (*under financial pressure*). **4** constraining influence (*if pressure is brought to bear*). ● *v.tr.* **1** apply pressure to. **2 a** coerce. **b** (often foll. by *into*) persuade (*was pressured into attending*). [ME f. L *pressura* (as PRESS¹)]

pres·sure cook·er *n.* an airtight pot for cooking quickly under steam pressure. □□ **pres·sure-cook** *v.tr.*

pres·sure gauge *n.* a gauge showing the pressure of steam, etc.

pres·sure group *n.* a group or association formed to promote a particular interest or cause by influencing public policy.

pres·sure point *n.* **1** a point where an artery can be pressed against a bone to inhibit bleeding. **2** a point on the skin sensitive to pressure. **3** a target for political pressure or influence.

pres·sure suit *n.* an inflatable suit for flying at a high altitude.

pres·sur·ize /préshəriz/ *v.tr.* **1** (esp. as **pressurized** *adj.*) maintain normal atmospheric pressure in (an aircraft cabin, etc.) at a high altitude. **2** raise to a high pressure. **3** pressure (a person). □□ **pres·sur·i·za·tion** *n.*

pres·sur·ized-wa·ter re·ac·tor *n. Brit.* a nuclear reactor in which the coolant is water at high pressure.

pres·ti·dig·i·ta·tor /préstidíjitaytər/ *n. formal* a magician. □□ **pres·ti·dig·i·ta·tion** /–táyshən/ *n.* [F *prestidigitateur* f. *preste* nimble (as PRES-TO) + L *digitus* finger]

pres·tige /prestéezh/ *n.* **1** respect, reputation, or influence derived from achievements, power, associations, etc. **2** (*attrib.*) having or conferring prestige. □□ **pres·tige·ful** *adj.*

WORD HISTORY prestige

mid-17th century (in the sense 'illusion, magic trick'): from French, literally 'illusion, glamor,' from late Latin *praestigium* 'illusion,' from Latin *praestigiae* (plural) 'magic tricks.' The transference of meaning occurred by way of the sense 'dazzling influence, glamor,' used with negative intent.

---

pres·tig·ious /prestéejəs, –stíj–/ *adj.* having or showing prestige. □□ **pres·tig·ious·ly** *adv.* **pres·tig·ious·ness** *n.* [orig. = deceptive, f. L *praestigiosus* f. *praestigiae* juggler's tricks]

pres·tis·si·mo /prestísimō/ *adv. & n. Mus.* ● *adv.* in a very quick tempo. ● *n.* (*pl.* **·mos**) a movement or passage played in this way. [It., superl. (as PRESTO)]

pres·to /préstō/ *adv. & n.* ● *adv.* **1** *Mus.* in quick tempo. **2** (in a magician's formula in performing a trick) quickly. ● *n.* (*pl.* **·tos**) *Mus.* a movement to be played in a quick tempo. [It. f. LL *praestus* f. L *praesto* ready]

pre·stressed /préestrést/ *adj.* strengthened by stressing in advance, esp. of concrete by means of stretched rods or wires put in during manufacture.

pre·sum·a·bly /prizoomablee/ *adv.* as may reasonably be presumed.

pre·sume /prizoom/ *v.* **1** *tr.* (often foll. by *that* + clause) suppose to be true; take for granted. **2** *tr.* (often foll. by *to* + infin.) **a** take the liberty; be impudent enough (*presumed to question their authority*). **b** dare; venture (*may I presume to ask?*). **3** *intr.* be presumptuous; take liberties. **4** *intr.* (foll. by *on, upon*) take advantage of or make unscrupulous use of (a person's good nature, etc.). □□ **pre·sum·a·ble** *adj.* **pre·sum·ed·ly** /–zoomidlee/ *adv.* [ME f. OF *presumer* f. L *praesumere praesumpt-* anticipate, venture (as PRAE-, *sumere* take)]

pre·sum·ing /prizooming/ *adj.* presumptuous. □□ **pre·sum·ing·ly** *adv.* **pre·sum·ing·ness** *n.*

pre·sump·tion /prizúmpshən/ *n.* **1** arrogance; presumptuous behavior. **2 a** the act of presuming a thing to be true. **b** a thing that is or may be presumed to be true; a belief based on reasonable evidence. **3** a ground for presuming (*a strong presumption against their being*

guilty). **4** *Law* an inference from known facts. [ME f. OF *presumpcion* f. L *praesumptio –onis* (as PRESUME)]

pre·sump·tive /prizúmptiv/ *adj.* **1** based on presumption or inference. **2** giving reasonable grounds for presumption (*presumptive evidence*). □□ **pre·sump·tive·ly** *adv.* [F *présomptif –ive* f. LL *praesumptivus* (as PRESUME)]

pre·sump·tu·ous /prizúmpchŏŏəs/ *adj.* unduly or overbearingly confident and presuming. □□ **pre·sump·tu·ous·ly** *adv.* **pre·sump·tu·ous·ness** *n.* [ME f. OF *presumptueus* f. LL *praesumptuosus, –tiosus* (as PRESUME)]

pre·sup·pose /preesəpóz/ *v.tr.* (often foll. by *that* + clause) **1** assume beforehand. **2** require as a precondition; imply. [ME f. OF *presupposer*, after med.L *praesupponere* (as PRE-, SUPPOSE)]

pre·sup·po·si·tion /preesúpəzíshən/ *n.* **1** the act or an instance of presupposing. **2** a thing assumed beforehand as the basis of argument, etc. [med.L *praesuppositio* (as PRAE-, *supponere* as SUPPOSE)]

pre·tax /préetáks/ *adj.* (of income or profits) before the deduction of taxes.

pre·teen /preetéen/ *adj.* of or relating to a child just under the age of thirteen.

pre·tence esp. *Brit.* var. of PRETENSE.

pre·tend /priténd/ *v. & adj.* ● *v.* **1** *tr.* claim or assert falsely so as to deceive (*pretend knowledge; pretended that they were foreigners*). **2 a** *tr.* imagine to oneself in play (*pretended to be monsters; pretended it was night*). **b** *absol.* make pretense, esp. in imagination or play; make believe (*they're just pretending*). **3** *tr.* **a** profess, esp. falsely or extravagantly (*does not pretend to be a scholar*). **b** (as **pretended** *adj.*) falsely claim to be such (*a pretended friend*). **4** *intr.* (foll. by *to*) **a** lay claim to (a right or title, etc.). **b** profess to have (a quality, etc.). **5** *tr.* (foll. by *to*) aspire or presume; venture (*I cannot pretend to guess*). ● *adj. colloq.* pretended; in pretense (*pretend money*). [ME f. F *prétendre* or f. L (as PRAE-, *tendere tent-*, later *tens-* stretch)]

pre·tend·er /priténdər/ *n.* **1** a person who claims a throne or title, etc. **2** a person who pretends.

pre·tense /preetens, priténs/ *n.* (also **pretence**) **1** pretending; make-believe. **2 a** a pretext or excuse (*on the slightest pretense*). **b** a false show of intentions or motives (*under the pretense of friendship; under false pretenses*). **3** (foll. by *to*) a claim, esp. a false or ambitious one (*has no pretense to any great talent*). **4 a** affectation; display. **b** pretentiousness; ostentation (*stripped of all pretense*). [ME f. AF *pretense* ult. f. med.L *pretensus* pretended (as PRETEND)]

pre·ten·sion /priténshən/ *n.* **1** (often foll. by *to*) **a** an assertion of a claim. **b** a justifiable claim (*has no pretensions to the name; has some pretensions to be included*). **2** pretentiousness. [med.L *praetensio, –tio* (as PRETEND)]

pre·ten·tious /priténshəs/ *adj.* **1** making an excessive claim to great merit or importance. **2** ostentatious. □□ **pre·ten·tious·ly** *adv.* **pre·ten·tious·ness** *n.* [F *prétentieux* (as PRETENSION)]

preter- /preetər/ *comb. form* more than. [L *praeter* (adv. & prep.), = past, beyond]

pret·er·it /prétərit/ *adj. & n.* (also **preter·ite**) *Gram.* ● *adj.* expressing a past action or state. ● *n.* a preterit tense or form. [ME f. OF *preterite* or L *praeteritus* past part. of *praeterire* pass (as PRETER-, *ire it-* go)]

pre·term *adj.* /préetərm/ born or occurring prematurely.

pre·ter·mit /preetərmít/ *v.tr.* (**pre·ter·mit·ted, pre·ter·mit·ting**) *formal* **1** omit to mention (a fact, etc.). **2** omit to do or perform; neglect. **3** leave off (a custom or continuous action) for a time. □□ **pre·ter·mis·sion** /–míshən/ *n.* [L *praetermittere* (as PRETER-, *mittere miss-* let go)]

pre·ter·nat·u·ral /preetərnáchərəl/ *adj.* outside the ordinary course of nature; supernatural. □□ **pre·ter·nat·u·ral·ism** *n.* **pre·ter·nat·u·ral·ly** *adv.*

pre·text /préetekst/ *n.* **1** an ostensible or alleged reason or intention. **2** an excuse offered. □ **on** (or **under**) **the pretext** (foll. by *of*, or *that* + clause) professing as one's object or intention. [L *praetextus* outward display f. *praetexere praetext-* (as PRAE-, *texere* weave)]

pre·tor var. of PRAETOR.

pre·to·ri·an var. of PRAETORIAN.

pret·ti·fy /pritifí/ *v.tr.* (**·fies, ·fied**) make (a thing or person) pretty esp. in an affected way. □□ **pret·ti·fi·ca·tion** *n.* **pret·ti·fi·er** *n.*

pret·ty /prítee/ *adj., n., v., & adv.* ● *adj.* (**pret·ti·er, pret·ti·est**) **1** attractive in a delicate way without being truly beautiful or handsome (*a pretty child; a pretty dress; a pretty tune*). **2** fine or good of

---

WORD HISTORY pretty

Old English *prættig*; related to Middle Dutch *pertich* 'brisk, clever,' obsolete Dutch *prettig* 'humorous, sporty,' from a West Germanic base meaning 'trick.' The sense development 'deceitful, cunning, clever, skillful, admirable, pleasing' has parallels in adjectives such as *fine, nice,* etc.

---

its kind (*a pretty wit*). **3** *iron.* considerable; fine (*a pretty penny; a pretty mess you have made*). ● *adv. colloq.* fairly; moderately; considerably (*am pretty well; find it pretty difficult*). ● *n.* (*pl.* **-ties**) a pretty person (esp. as a form of address to a child). ● *v.tr.* (**-ties, -tied**) (often foll. by *up*) make pretty or attractive. □ **pretty much** (or **nearly** or **well**) *colloq.* almost; very nearly. **sitting pretty** *colloq.* in a favorable or advantageous position. □□ **pret·ti·ly** *adv.* **pret·ti·ness** *n.* **pret·ty·ish** *adj.*

pret·ty-pret·ty *adj. Brit.* too pretty.

pret·zel /prétsəl/ *n.* a crisp or chewy knot-shaped or stick-shaped bread, usu. salted. [G]

pre·vail /priváyl/ *v.intr.* **1** (often foll. by *against, over*) be victorious or gain mastery. **2** be the more usual or predominant. **3** exist or occur in general use or experience; be current. **4** (foll. by *on, upon*) persuade. **5** (as **prevailing** *adj.*) predominant; generally current or accepted (*prevailing opinion*). □□ **pre·vail·ing·ly** *adv.* [ME f. L *praevalēre* (as PRAE-, *valēre* have power), infl. by AVAIL]

pre·vail·ing wind *n.* the wind that most frequently occurs at a place.

prev·a·lent /prévələnt/ *adj.* **1** generally existing or occurring. **2** predominant. □□ **prev·a·lence** *n.* **prev·a·lent·ly** *adv.* [as PREVAIL]

SYNONYM TIP prevalent

ABUNDANT, COMMON, COPIOUS, PLENTIFUL, PREVAILING, RIFE. Wildflowers might be **prevalent** in the mountains during the spring months, but a particular type of wildflower might be the **prevailing** one. *Prevalent*, in other words, implies widespread occurrence or acceptance in a particular place or time (*a prevalent belief in the nineteenth century*), while *prevailing* suggests that something exists in such quantity it surpasses all others or leads all others in acceptance, usage, or belief (*the prevailing theory about the evolution of man*). Wildflowers might also be **abundant** in the valleys—a word that, unlike *prevalent* and *prevailing*, is largely restricted to observations about a place and may suggest oversupply (*an abundant harvest*). **Plentiful**, on the other hand, refers to a large or full supply without the connotations of oversupply (*a country where jobs were plentiful*). If wildflowers are **rife**, it means that they are not only *prevalent* but spreading rapidly; if they're **copious**, it means they are being produced in such quantity that they constitute a rich or flowing abundance (*to weep copious tears*). What often happens, with wildflowers as well as with other beautiful things, is that they become so *abundant* they are regarded as **common**, a word meaning usual or ordinary (*the common cold*). Like *prevalent*, *common* can apply to a time as well as a place (*an expression common during the Depression*). But neither *abundant* nor *common* connotes dominance as clearly as *prevalent* does.

pre·var·i·cate /priváríkayt/ *v.intr.* **1** speak or act evasively or misleadingly. **2** quibble; equivocate. □□ **pre·var·i·ca·tion** /–rikáyshən/ *n.* **pre·var·i·ca·tor** *n.* [L *praevaricari* walk crookedly, practice collusion, in eccl.L transgress (as PRAE-, *varicari* straddle f. *varus* bent, knock-kneed)]

▶Prevaricate means 'act or speak evasively, ' e.g., *When the teacher asked what I was reading, I knew I would have to prevaricate or risk a detention.* It is sometimes confused with *procrastinate*, which means 'postpone or put off an action,' e.g., *He procrastinated until it was too late.*

pre·ven·ient /privéenyənt/ *adj. formal* preceding something else. [L *praeveniens* pres. part. of *praevenire* (as PREVENT)]

pre·vent /privént/ *v.tr.* **1** (often foll. by *from* + verbal noun) stop from happening or doing something; hinder; make impossible (*the weather prevented me from going*). **2** *archaic* go or arrive before; precede. □□ **pre·vent·a·ble** *adj.* (also **pre·vent·i·ble**). **pre·vent·a·bil·i·ty** *n.* **pre·vent·er** *n.* **pre·ven·tion** /–vénshən/ *n.* [ME = anticipate, f. L *praevenire praevent-* come before, hinder (as PRAE-, *venire* come)]

pre·vent·a·tive /privéntətiv/ *adj. & n.* = PREVENTIVE. □□ **pre·vent·a·tive·ly** *adv.*

pre·ven·tive /privéntiv/ *adj. & n.* ● *adj.* serving to prevent, esp. preventing disease, breakdown, etc. (*preventive medicine; preventive maintenance*). ● *n.* a preventive agent, measure, drug, etc. □□ **pre·ven·tive·ly** *adv.*

▶Avoid adding an unnecessary syllable to **preventive**. The variant "preventative" is best avoided.

pre·view /préevyoo/ *n. & v.* ● *n.* **1** the act of seeing in advance. **2 a** the showing of a movie, play, exhibition, etc., before it is seen by the general public. **b** (also **pre·vue**) an advance promotional sample of a movie; trailer. ● *v.tr.* see or show in advance.

pre·vi·ous /préeveeəs/ *adj. & adv.* ● *adj.* **1** (often foll. by *to*) coming before in time or order. **2** done or acting hastily. ● *adv.* (foll. by *to*) before (*had called previous to writing*). □□ **pre·vi·ous·ly** *adv.* **pre·vi·ous·ness** *n.* [L *praevius* (as PRAE-, *via* way)]

pre·vi·ous ques·tion *n.* *Parl.* a motion concerning the vote on a main question.

pre·vise /privíz/ *v.tr. literary* foresee or forecast (an event, etc.).

□□ **pre·vi·sion** /–vízhən/ *n.* **pre·vi·sion·al** *adj.* [L *praevidēre praevis-* (as PRAE-, *vidēre* see)]

pre·vue var. of PREVIEW *n.* 2b.

pre·war /préewáwr/ *adj.* existing or occurring before a war (esp. the most recent major war).

prex /preks/ *n.* (also **prex·y**) *sl.* a president (esp. of a college). [abbr.]

prey /pray/ *n. & v.* ● *n.* **1** an animal that is hunted or killed by another for food. **2** (often foll. by *to*) a person or thing that is influenced by or vulnerable to (something undesirable) (*became a prey to morbid fears*). **3** *Bibl.* or *archaic* plunder, booty, etc. ● *v.intr.* (foll. by *on, upon*) **1** seek or take as prey. **2** make a victim of. **3** (of a disease, emotion, etc.) exert a harmful influence (*fear preyed on his mind*). □□ **prey·er** *n.* [ME f. OF *preie* f. L *praeda* booty]

pri·ap·ic /príápik/ *adj.* phallic. [*Priapos* (as PRIAPISM) + –IC]

pri·a·pism /prípizəm/ *n.* **1** lewdness; licentiousness. **2** *Med.* persistent erection of the penis. [F *priapisme* f. LL *priapismus* f. Gk *priapismos* f. *priapizō* be lewd f. *Priapos* god of procreation]

price /pris/ *n. & v.* ● *n.* **1 a** the amount of money or goods for which a thing is bought or sold. **b** value or worth (*a pearl of great price; beyond price*). **2** what is or must be given, done, sacrificed, etc., to obtain or achieve something. **3** the odds in betting (*starting price*). **4** a sum of money offered or given as a reward, esp. for the capture or killing of a person. ● *v.tr.* **1** fix or find the price of (a thing for sale). **2** estimate the value of. □ **above** (or **beyond** or **without**) **price** so valuable that no price can be stated. **at any price** no matter what the cost, sacrifice, etc. (*peace at any price*). **at a price** at a high cost. **price on a person's head** a reward for a person's capture or death. **price oneself out of the market** lose to one's competitors by charging more than customers are willing to pay. **set a price on** declare the price of. **what price . . . ?** (often foll. by verbal noun) *colloq.* **1** *iron.* the expected or much boasted . . . proves disappointing (*what price your friendship now?*). **2** *Brit.* what is the chance of . . . ? (*what price your finishing the course?*). □□ **priced** *adj.* (also in *comb.*). **pric·er** *n.* [(n.) ME f. OF *pris* f. L *pretium*: (v.) var. of *prise* = PRIZE[1]]

price-fix·ing *n.* (also **price fix·ing**) the maintaining of prices at a certain level by agreement between competing sellers.

price·less /príslis/ *adj.* **1** invaluable; beyond price. **2** *colloq.* very amusing or absurd. □□ **price·less·ly** *adv.* **price·less·ness** *n.*

price tag *n.* **1** the label on an item showing its price. **2** the cost of an enterprise or undertaking.

price war *n.* fierce competition among traders cutting prices.

pric·ey /prísee/ *adj.* (also **pric·y**) (**pric·i·er, pric·i·est**) *colloq.* expensive. □□ **pric·i·ness** *n.*

prick /prik/ *v. & n.* ● *v.* **1** *tr.* pierce slightly; make a small hole in. **2** *tr.* (foll. by *off, out*) mark (esp. a pattern) with small holes or dots. **3** *tr.* trouble mentally (*my conscience is pricking me*). **4** *intr.* feel a pricking sensation. **5** *intr.* (foll. by *at, into*, etc.) make a thrust as if to prick. **6** *tr.* (foll. by *in, off, out*) plant (seedlings, etc.) in small holes pricked in the earth. **7** *tr. Brit. archaic* mark off (a name in a list, esp. to select a sheriff) by pricking. **8** *tr. archaic* spur or urge on (a horse, etc.). ● *n.* **1** the act or an instance of pricking. **2** a small hole or mark made by pricking. **3** a pain caused as by pricking. **4** a mental pain (*felt the pricks of conscience*). **5** *coarse sl.* **a** the penis. **b** *derog.* (as a term of contempt) a contemptible or mean-spirited person. **6** *archaic* a goad for oxen. □ **kick against the pricks** *Brit.* persist in futile resistance. **prick up one's ears 1** (of a dog, etc.) make the ears erect when on the alert. **2** (of a person) become suddenly attentive. [OE *prician* (v.), *pricca* (n.)]

prick·er /príkər/ *n.* **1** one that pricks, as an animal or plant. **2** a small thorn or other sharp pointed outgrowth.

prick·et /príkit/ *n.* **1** a male fallow deer in its second year, having straight unbranched horns. **2** a spike for holding a candle. [ME f. AL *prikettus –um*, dimin. of PRICK]

prick·le /príkəl/ *n. & v.* ● *n.* **1 a** a small thorn. **b** *Bot.* a thornlike process developed from the epidermis of a plant. **2** a hard pointed spine of a hedgehog, etc. **3** a prickling sensation. ● *v.tr. & intr.* affect or be affected with a sensation as of pricking. [OE *pricel* PRICK: (v.) also dimin. of PRICK]

prick·ly /príklee/ *adj.* (**prick·li·er, prick·li·est**) **1** (esp. in the names of plants and animals) having prickles. **2 a** (of a person) ready to take offense. **b** (of a topic, argument, etc.) full of contentious or complicated points; thorny. **3** tingling. □□ **prick·li·ness** *n.*

prick·ly heat *n.* an itchy inflammation of the skin, causing a tingling sensation and common in hot countries.

prick·ly pear *n.* **1** any cactus of the genus *Opuntia*, native to arid regions of America, bearing barbed bristles and large pear-shaped prickly fruits. **2** its fruit.

prick·ly pop·py *n.* a tropical poppylike plant, *Argemone mexicana*, with prickly leaves and yellow flowers.

pric·y var. of PRICEY.

pride /prid/ *n. & v.* ● *n.* **1 a** a feeling of elation or satisfaction at achievements, qualities, or possessions, etc., that do one credit. **b** an object of this feeling. **2** a high or overbearing opinion of one's worth or importance. **3** a proper sense of what befits one's position; self-respect. **4** a group or company (of animals, esp. lions).

5 the best condition; the prime. ● *v.refl.* (foll. by *on, upon*) be proud of. □ **my, his**, etc., **pride and joy** a thing of which one is very proud. **take pride** (or **a pride**) **in 1** be proud of. **2** maintain in good condition or appearance. □□ **pride·ful** *adj.* **pride·ful·ly** *adv.* **pride·less** *adj.* [OE *prȳtu, prȳte, prȳde* f. *prūd* PROUD]

pride of place *n.* the most important or prominent position.
pride of the morn·ing *n.* a mist or shower at sunrise, supposedly indicating a fine day to come.
prie-dieu /preedyố/ *n.* (*pl.* **prie-dieux** *pronunc.* same) a kneeling desk for prayer. [F, = pray God]
priest /preest/ *n.* **1** an ordained minister of the Roman Catholic or Orthodox Church, or of the Anglican Church (above a deacon and below a bishop), authorized to perform certain rites and administer certain sacraments. **2** an official minister of a non-Christian religion. □□ **priest·less** *adj.* **priest·like** *adj.* **priest·ling** *n.* [OE *prēost*, ult. f. eccl.L *presbyter*: see PRESBYTER]
priest·ess /prếestis/ *n.* a female priest of a non-Christian religion.
priest·hood /prếest-hood/ *n.* (usu. prec. by *the*) **1** the office or position of a priest. **2** priests in general.
priest·ly /prếestlee/ *adj.* of or associated with priests. □□ **priest·li·ness** *n.* [OE *prēostlic* (as PRIEST)]
prig /prig/ *n.* a self-righteously correct or moralistic person. □□ **prig·ger·y** *n.* **prig·gish** *adj.* **prig·gish·ly** *adv.* **prig·gish·ness** *n.* [16th-c. cant, = tinker: orig. unkn.]
prim /prim/ *adj. & v.* ● *adj.* (**prim·mer, prim·mest**) **1** (of a person or manner) stiffly formal and precise. **2** (of a woman or girl) demure. **3** prudish. ● *v.tr.* (**primmed, prim·ming**) **1** form (the face, lips, etc.) into a prim expression. **2** make prim. □□ **prim·ly** *adv.* **prim·ness** *n.* [17th-c.: prob. orig. cant f. OF *prin* prime excellent f. L *primus* first]
pri·ma bal·le·ri·na /préemə/ *n.* the chief female dancer in a ballet or ballet company. [It.]
pri·ma·cy /prímməsee/ *n.* (*pl.* **·cies**) **1** preeminence. **2** the office of an ecclesiastical primate. [ME f. OF *primatie* or med.L *primatia* (as PRIMATE)]
pri·ma don·na /préemə/ *n.* (*pl.* **pri·ma don·nas**) **1** the chief female singer in an opera or opera company. **2** a temperamentally self-important person. □□ **pri·ma don·na·ish** *adj.* [It.]
pri·ma fa·ci·e /prímməfáyshee, –shee-ee, shə, préemə/ *adv. & adj.* ● *adv.* at first sight; from a first impression (*seems prima facie to be guilty*). ● *adj.* (of evidence) based on the first impression (*can see a prima facie reason for it*). [ME f. L, fem. ablat. of *primus* first, *facies* FACE]
pri·mal /prímməl/ *adj.* **1** primitive; primeval. **2** chief; fundamental. □□ **pri·mal·ly** *adv.* [med.L *primalis* f. L *primus* first]
pri·ma·ry /prímeree, –mᵊree/ *adj. & n.* ● *adj.* **1 a** of the first importance; chief (*that is our primary concern*). **b** fundamental; basic. **2** earliest; original; first in a series. **3** of the first rank in a series; not derived (*the primary meaning of a word*). **4** designating any of the colors red, green, and blue, or for pigments red, blue, and yellow, from which all other colors can be obtained by mixing. **5** (of a battery or cell) generating electricity by irreversible chemical reaction. **6** (of education) for young children, esp. below the age of 11. **7** (**Primary**) *Geol.* of the lowest series of strata. **8** *Biol.* belonging to the first stage of development. **9** (of an industry or source of production) concerned with obtaining or using raw materials. ● *n.* (*pl.* **·ries**) **1** a thing that is primary. **2** (in full **primary election**) a preliminary election to appoint delegates to a party convention or to select the candidates for a principal election. **3** = PRIMARY PLANET. **4** (**Primary**) *Geol.* the Primary period. **5** = PRIMARY FEATHER. **6** = PRIMARY COIL. □□ **pri·ma·ri·ly** /prímérilee/ *adv.* [ME f. L *primarius* f. *primus* first]
pri·ma·ry coil *n.* a coil to which current is supplied in a transformer.
pri·ma·ry feath·er *n.* a large flight feather of a bird's wing.

pri·ma·ry in·dus·try *n.* industry (such as mining, forestry, agriculture, etc.) that provides raw materials for conversion into commodities and products for the consumer.
pri·ma·ry plan·et *n.* a planet that directly orbits the sun (cf. SECONDARY PLANET).
pri·ma·ry school *n.* a school where young children are taught, esp. the first three elementary grades and kindergarten.
pri·mate /prímayt/ *n.* **1** any animal of the order Primates, the highest order of mammals, including tarsiers, lemurs, apes, monkeys, and human beings. **2** an archbishop. □□ **pri·ma·tial** /-máyshəl/ *adj.* **pri·ma·tol·o·gy** /-mətóləjee/ *n.* (in sense 1). [ME f. OF *primat* f. L *primas -atis* (adj.) of the first rank f. *primus* first, in med.L = primate]
pri·ma·ve·ra¹ /préemavaírə/ *n.* **1** a Central American tree, *Cybistax donnellsmithii*, bearing yellow blooms. **2** the hard light-colored timber from this. [Sp., = spring (the season) f. L *primus* first + *ver* SPRING]
pri·ma·ve·ra² /préemavaírə/ *adj.* (of pasta, seafood, etc.) made with or containing an assortment of sliced vegetables. [It. *primavera* spring, springtime]
prime¹ /prim/ *adj. & n.* ● *adj.* **1** chief; most important (*the prime agent; the prime motive*). **2** (esp. of beef) first-rate; excellent. **3** primary; fundamental. **4** *Math.* **a** (of a number) divisible only by itself and 1 (e.g., 2, 3, 5, 7, 11). **b** (of numbers) having no common factor but 1. ● *n.* **1** the state of the highest perfection of something (*in the prime of life*). **2** (prec. by *the*; foll. by *of*) the best part. **3** the beginning or first age of anything. **4** *Eccl.* **a** the second canonical hour of prayer, appointed for the first hour of the day (i.e., 6 a.m.). **b** the office of this. **c** *archaic* this time. **5** a prime number. **6** *Printing* a symbol (') added to a letter, etc., as a distinguishing mark, or to a figure as a symbol for minutes or feet. **7** the first of eight parrying positions in fencing. **8** *Mus.* tonic. □□ **prime·ness** *n.* [(n.) OE *prīm* f. L *prima* (*hora*) first (hour), & MF f. OF *prime*: (adj.) ME f. OF f. L *primus* first]
prime² /prim/ *v.tr.* **1** prepare (a thing) for use or action. **2** prepare (a gun) for firing or (an explosive) for detonation. **3 a** pour (liquid) into a pump to prepare it for working. **b** inject fuel into (the cylinder or carburetor of an internal-combustion engine). **4** prepare (wood, etc.) for painting by applying a substance that prevents paint from being absorbed. **5** equip (a person) with information, etc. **6** ply (a person) with food or drink in preparation for something. [16th c.: orig. unkn.]
prime cost *n.* the direct cost of a commodity in terms of materials, labor, etc.
prime me·rid·i·an *n.* **1** the meridian from which longitude is reckoned, esp. that passing through Greenwich. **2** the corresponding line on a map.
prime min·is·ter *n.* the head of an elected parliamentary government; the principal minister of a nation or sovereign.
prime mov·er *n.* **1** an initial natural or mechanical source of motive power. **2** the author of a fruitful idea.
prim·er¹ /prímər/ *n.* **1** a substance used to prime wood, etc. **2** a cap, cylinder, etc., used to ignite the powder of a cartridge, etc.
prim·er² /prímər, prímər/ *n.* **1** an elementary textbook for teaching children to read. **2** an introductory book. [ME f. AF f. med.L *primarius -arium* f. L *primus* first]

prime rate *n.* the lowest rate at which money can be borrowed commercially.
prime time *n.* the time at which a radio or television audience is expected to consist of the greatest number of people.
pri·me·val /primếevəl/ *adj.* **1** of or relating to the earliest age of the world. **2** ancient; primitive. □□ **pri·me·val·ly** *adv.* [L *primaevus* f. *primus* first + *aevum* age]
prime ver·ti·cal *n.* the great circle of the heavens passing through the zenith and the E. and W. points of the horizon.
prim·ing¹ /príming/ *n.* **1** a mixture used by painters for a preparatory coat. **2** a preparation of sugar added to beer. **3 a** gunpowder placed in the pan of a firearm. **b** a train of powder connecting the fuse with the charge in blasting, etc.
prim·ing² /príming/ *n.* an acceleration of the tides taking place from the neap to the spring tides. [*prime* (v.) f. PRIME¹ + –ING¹]
pri·mip·a·ra /primípərə/ *n.* (*pl.* **pri·mip·a·rae** /–ree/) a woman who is bearing a child for the first time. □□ **pri·mip·a·rous** *adj.* [mod.L fem. f. *primus* first + –*parus* f. *parere* bring forth]
prim·i·tive /prímmitiv/ *adj. & n.* ● *adj.* **1** early; ancient; at an early stage

of civilization (*primitive humans*). **2** undeveloped; crude; simple (*primitive methods*). **3** original; primary. **4** *Gram. & Philol.* (of words or language) radical; not derivative. **5** *Math.* (of a line, figure, etc.) from which another is derived, from which some construction begins, etc. **6** (of a color) primary. **7** *Geol.* of the earliest period. **8** *Biol.* appearing in the earliest or a very early stage of growth or evolution. • *n.* **1 a** a painter of the period before the Renaissance. **b** a modern imitator of such. **c** an untutored painter with a direct naïve style. **d** a picture by such a painter. **2** a primitive word, line, etc. □□ **prim•i•tive•ly** *adv.* **prim•i•tive•ness** *n.* [ME f. OF *primitif –ive* or L *primitivus* first of its kind f. *primitus* in the first place f. *primus* first]

prim•i•tiv•ism /prímitivizəm/ *n.* **1** primitive behavior. **2** belief in the superiority of what is primitive. **3** the practice of primitive art. □□ **prim•i•tiv•ist** *n. & adj.*

pri•mo /préemō/ *n.* (*pl.* •mos) **1** *Mus.* the leading or upper part in a duet, etc. **2** *colloq.* first-rate; excellent.

pri•mo•gen•i•tor /prímōjénitər/ *n.* **1** the earliest ancestor of a people, etc. **2** an ancestor. [var. of *progenitor*, after PRIMOGENITURE]

pri•mo•gen•i•ture /prímōjénichər/ *n.* **1** the fact or condition of being the firstborn child. **2** (in full **right of primogeniture**) the right of succession belonging to the firstborn, esp. the feudal rule by which the whole real estate of an intestate passes to the eldest son. □□ **pri•mo•gen•i•tal** *adj.* **pri•mo•gen•i•tar•y** *adj.* [med.L *primogenitura* f. L *primo* first + *genitura* f. *gignere* genit– beget]

pri•mor•di•al /prímáwrdeeəl/ *adj.* **1** existing at or from the beginning; primeval. **2** original; fundamental. □□ **pri•mor•di•al•i•ty** /–mawrdeeálitee/ *n.* **pri•mor•di•al•ly** *adv.* [ME f. LL *primordialis* (as PRIMORDIUM)]

pri•mor•di•um /prímáwrdeeəm/ *n.* (*pl.* **pri•mor•di•a** /–deeə/) *Biol.* an organ or tissue in the early stages of development. [L, neut. of *primordius* original f. *primus* first + *ordiri* begin]

primp /primp/ *v.tr.* **1** make (the hair, one's clothes, etc.) neat or overly tidy. **2** *refl.* groom (oneself) painstakingly. [dial. var. of PRIM]

prim•rose /prímrōz/ *n.* **1 a** any plant of the genus *Primula*, esp. *P. vulgaris*, bearing pale yellow flowers. **b** the flower of this. **2 a** pale yellow color. [ME *primerose*, corresp. to OF *primerose* and med.L *prima rosa*, lit. first rose: reason for the name unkn.]

prim•rose path *n.* the pursuit of pleasure, esp. with disastrous consequences (with ref. to Shakesp. *Hamlet* I. iii. 50).

prim•u•la /prímyələ/ *n.* any plant of the genus *Primula*, bearing primroselike flowers in a wide variety of colors during the spring, including primroses, cowslips, and polyanthuses. [med.L, fem. of *primulus* dimin. of *primus* first]

pri•mum mo•bi•le /prímoom móbilee, preémoom móbilay/ *n.* **1** the central or most important source of motion or action. **2** *Astron.* in the medieval version of the Ptolemaic system, an outer sphere supposed to move around the earth in 24 hours carrying the inner spheres with it. [med.L, = first moving thing]

Pri•mus /príməs/ *n. Brit. Trademark* a brand of portable stove burning oil for cooking, etc. [L (as PRIMUS)]

pri•mus /príməs/ *n.* the presiding bishop of the Scottish Episcopal Church. [L, = first]

pri•mus in•ter pa•res /preémoosíntər paáres, prímǝsíntǝr páireez/ *n.* a first among equals; the senior or representative member of a group. [L]

prince /prins/ *n.* (as a title usu. **Prince**) **1** a male member of a royal family other than a reigning king. **2** (in full **prince of the blood**) a son or grandson of a British monarch. **3** a ruler of a small nation, actually or nominally subject to a king or emperor. **4** (as an English rendering of foreign titles) a noble usu. ranking next below a duke. **5** (as a courtesy title in some connections) a duke, marquess, or earl. **6** (often foll. by *of*) the chief or greatest (*the prince of novelists*). □□ **prince•dom** *n.* **prince•let** *n.* **prince•like** *adj.* **prince•ship** *n.* [ME f. OF f. L *princeps principis* first, chief, sovereign f. *primus* first + *capere* take]

Prince Charm•ing *n.* an idealized young hero or lover.

prince con•sort *n.* **1** the husband of a reigning female sovereign who is himself a prince. **2** the title conferred on him.

prince•ling /prínsling/ *n.* a young or insignificant prince.

prince•ly /prínslee/ *adj.* (**prince•li•er, prince•li•est**) **1 a** of or worthy of a prince. **b** held by a prince. **2 a** sumptuous; generous; splendid. **b** (of a sum of money) substantial. □□ **prince•li•ness** *n.*

Prince of Dark•ness *n.* Satan.

Prince of Peace *n.* Christ.

Prince of Wales *n.* the heir apparent to the British throne, as a title conferred by the monarch.

prince roy•al *n.* the eldest son of a reigning monarch.

prince's-feath•er *n.* a tall plant, *Amaranthus hypochondriacus*, with feathery spikes of small red flowers.

prin•cess /prínses/ *n.* (as a title usu. **Princess**) **1** the wife of a prince. **2** a female member of a royal family other than a reigning queen. **3** (in full **princess of the blood**) a daughter or granddaughter of a

British monarch. **4** a preeminent woman or thing personified as a woman. [ME f. OF *princesse* (as PRINCE)]

Prin•cess Re•gent *n.* **1** a princess who acts as regent. **2** the wife of a Prince Regent.

Prin•cess Roy•al *n.* a monarch's eldest daughter, as a title conferred by the monarch.

prin•ci•pal /prí nsipəl/ *adj. & n.* • *adj.* **1** (usu. *attrib.*) first in rank or importance; chief (*the principal town of the district*). **2** main; leading (*a principal cause of my success*). **3** (of money) constituting the original sum invested or lent. • *n.* **1** a head, ruler, or superior. **2** the head of an elementary, middle, or high school. **3** the leading performer in a concert, play, etc. **4** a capital sum as distinguished from interest or income. **5** a person for whom another acts as agent, etc. **6** (in the UK) a civil servant of the grade below Secretary. **7** the person actually responsible for a crime. **8** a person for whom another is surety. **9** each of the combatants in a duel. **10** a main rafter or girder providing support for other members in a framed structure. **11** an organ stop sounding an octave above the diapason. **12** *Mus.* the leading player in each section of an orchestra. □□ **prin•ci•pal•ship** *n.* [ME f. OF f. L *principalis* first, original (as PRINCE)]

▶**Principal** means 'most important' or 'person in charge': *my principal reason for coming tonight*; *the high school principal*. It also means 'a capital sum': *the principal would be repaid in five years.* **Principle** means 'rule, basis for conduct': *Her principles kept her from stealing despite her poverty.*

SPELLING TIP principal/principle

To keep the *-pal* and *-ple* endings of these words straight, use the mnemonic: "The princi*pal* is the students' *pal*, but a princi*ple* is just a ru*le*."

---

prin•ci•pal boy *n.* (also **prin•ci•pal girl**) *Brit.* an actress who takes the leading male (or female) part in a pantomime.

prin•ci•pal clause *n. Gram.* a clause to which another clause is subordinate.

prin•ci•pal•i•ty /prínsipálitee/ *n.* (*pl.* •ties) **1** a nation ruled by a prince. **2** the government of a prince. **3** (in *pl.*) the fifth order of the ninefold celestial hierarchy. **4** (**the Principality**) *Brit.* Wales. [ME f. OF *principalité* f. LL *principalitas –tatis* (as PRINCIPAL)]

prin•ci•pal•ly /prínsiplee/ *adv.* for the most part; chiefly.

prin•ci•pal parts *n.pl. Gram.* the parts of a verb from which all other parts can be deduced.

prin•ci•pate /prínsipayt/ *n.* **1** a nation ruled by a prince. **2** supreme office or authority. **3** *Rom.Hist.* the rule of the early emperors during which some republican forms were retained. [ME f. OF *principat* or L *principatus* first place]

prin•ci•ple /prínsipəl/ *n.* **1** a fundamental truth or law as the basis of reasoning or action (*arguing from first principles*; *moral principles*). **2 a** a personal code of conduct (*a person of high principle*). **b** (in *pl.*) such rules of conduct (*has no principles*). **3** a general law in physics, etc. (*the uncertainty principle*). **4** a law of nature forming the basis for the construction or working of a machine, etc. **5** a fundamental source; a primary element (*held water to be the first principle of all things*). **6** *Chem.* a constituent of a substance, esp. one giving rise to some quality, etc. □ **in principle** as regards fundamentals but not necessarily in detail. **on principle** on the basis of a moral attitude (*I refuse on principle*). [ME f. OF *principe* f. L *principium* source, (in *pl.*) foundations (as PRINCE)]

▶See note at PRINCIPAL.

SPELLING TIP principle

See note at PRINCIPAL.

---

prin•ci•pled /prínsipəld/ *adj.* based on or having (esp. praiseworthy) principles of behavior.

prink /pringk/ *v.* **1** *tr.* (usu. *refl.*) PRIMP. **2** (of a bird) preen. **3** *intr.* dress oneself up. [16th c.: prob. f. *prank* dress, adorn, rel. to MLG *prank* pomp, Du. *pronk* finery]

print /print/ *n., v., & adj.* • *n.* **1** an indentation or mark on a surface left by the pressure of a thing in contact with it (*fingerprint*; *footprint*). **2 a** printed lettering or writing (*large print*). **b** words in printed form. **c** a printed publication, esp. a newspaper. **d** the quantity of a book, etc., printed at one time. **e** the state of being printed. **3** a picture or design printed from a block or plate. **4 a** *Photog.* a picture produced on paper from a negative. **b** a copy of a motion picture suitable for showing. **5** a printed cotton fabric. • *v.tr.* **1 a** produce or reproduce (a book, picture, etc.) by applying inked types, blocks, or plates, to paper, vellum, etc. **b** (of an author, publisher, or editor) cause (a book or manuscript, etc.) to be produced or reproduced in this way. **2** express or publish in print. **3 a** (often foll. by *on, in*) impress or stamp (a mark or figure on a surface). **b** (often foll. by *with*) impress or stamp (a soft surface, e.g., of butter or wax, with a seal, die, etc.). **4** (often *absol.*) write (words or letters) without joining, in imitation of typography. **5** (often foll. by *off, out*) *Photog.* produce (a picture) by the transmission of light through a negative. **6** (usu. foll. by *out*) (of a computer, etc.) produce output in printed form. **7** mark (a textile fabric) with a decorative design in colors. **8** (foll. by *on*) impress (an idea, scene, etc., on the mind or memory). **9** transfer (a colored or plain design) from paper, etc., to the unglazed or glazed surface of ceramic ware. ● *adj.* of, for, or concerning printed publications. □ **appear in print** have one's work published. **in print 1** (of a book, etc.) available from the publisher. **2** in printed form. **out of print** no longer available from the publisher. □□ **print‧a‧ble** *adj.* **print‧a‧bil‧i‧ty** /príntəbílitee/ *n.* **print‧less** *adj.* (in sense 1 of *n.*). [ME f. OF *priente, preinte*, fem. past part. of *preindre* press f. L *premere*]

print‧ed cir‧cuit *n.* an electric circuit with thin strips of conductive material on a flat insulating sheet, usu. made by a process like printing.

print‧er /príntər/ *n.* **1** a person who prints books, magazines, advertising matter, etc. **2** the owner of a printing business. **3** a device that prints, esp. as part of a computer system.

print‧er's dev‧il *n. hist.* an errand boy in a printing office.

print‧er's mark *n.* a device used as a printer's trademark.

print‧er‧y /príntəree/ *n.* (*pl.* **‧ies**) a printer's office or works.

print‧head /prínt-hed/ *n.* the component in a printer (see PRINTER 3) that assembles and prints the characters on the paper.

print‧ing /prínting/ *n.* **1** the production of printed books, etc. **2** a single impression of a book. **3** printed letters or writing imitating them.

print‧ing press *n.* a machine for printing from types or plates, etc.

print‧mak‧er /príntmaykər/ *n.* a person who makes a print. □□ **print‧mak‧ing** *n.*

print‧out /príntowt/ *n.* computer output in printed form.

print‧works /príntwərks/ *n.* a factory where fabrics are printed.

pri‧or /príər/ *adj., adv., & n.* ● *adj.* **1** earlier. **2** (often foll. by *to*) coming before in time, order, or importance. ● *adv.* (foll. by *to*) before (*decided prior to their arrival*). ● *n.* **1** the superior officer of a religious house or order. **2** (in an abbey) the officer next under the abbot. □□ **pri‧o‧rate** /-rət/ *n.* **pri‧or‧ess** /príəris/ *n.* **pri‧or‧ship** *n.* [L, = former, elder, compar. of OL *pri* = L *prae* before]

pri‧or‧i‧tize /príáwritìz, -ór-/ *v. tr.* rank in order of priority.

pri‧or‧i‧ty /príáwritee, -ór-/ *n.* (*pl.* **-ties**) **1** the fact or condition of being earlier or antecedent. **2** precedence in rank, etc. **3** an interest having prior claim to consideration. □□ **pri‧or‧i‧ti‧za‧tion** *n.* [ME f. OF *priorité* f. med.L *prioritas -tatis* f. L prior (as PRIOR)]

pri‧o‧ry /príəree/ *n.* (*pl.* **-ries**) a monastery governed by a prior or a convent governed by a prioress. [ME f. AF *priorie*, med.L *prioria* (as PRIOR)]

prise esp. *Brit.* var. of PRIZE³.

prism /prízəm/ *n.* **1** a solid geometric figure whose two ends are similar, equal, and parallel rectilinear figures, and whose sides are parallelograms. **2** a transparent body in this form, usu. triangular with refracting surfaces at an acute angle with each other, which separates white light into a spectrum of colors. □□ **pris‧mal** /prízməl/ *adj.* [LL *prisma* f. Gk *prisma prismatos* thing sawn f. *prizō* to saw]

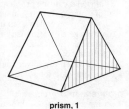

prism, 1

pris‧mat‧ic /prizmátik/ *adj.* **1** of, like, or using a prism. **2 a** (of colors) distributed by or as if by a transparent prism. **b** (of light) displayed in the form of a spectrum. □□ **pris‧mat‧i‧cal‧ly** *adv.* [F *prismatique* f. Gk *prisma* (as PRISM)]

pris‧moid /prízmoyd/ *n.* a body like a prism, with similar but unequal parallel polygonal ends. □□ **pris‧moi‧dal** *adj.*

pris‧on /prízən/ *n. & v.* ● *n.* **1** a place in which a person is kept in captivity, esp. a building to which persons are legally committed while awaiting trial or for punishment; a jail. **2** custody; confinement (*in prison*). ● *v. tr. poet.* (**pris‧oned, pris‧on‧ing**) put in prison. [ME f. OF *prisun, -on* f. L *prensio -onis* f. *prehensio* f. *prehendere prehens-* lay hold of]

pris‧on camp *n.* **1** a camp for prisoners of war or political prisoners. **2** a minimum-security prison.

pris‧on‧er /príznər/ *n.* **1** a person kept in prison. **2** *Brit.* (in full **pris‧oner at the bar**) a person in custody on a criminal charge and on trial. **3** a person or thing confined by illness, another's grasp, etc. **4** (in full **prisoner of war**) a person who has been captured in war. □ **take prisoner** seize and hold as a prisoner. [ME f. AF *prisoner*, OF *prisonier* (as PRISON)]

pris‧on‧er of con‧science *n.* a person imprisoned by a government for holding political or religious views it does not tolerate.

pris‧on‧er's base *n.* a game played by two teams of children, each occupying a distinct base or home.

pris‧sy /prísee/ *adj.* (**pris‧si‧er, pris‧si‧est**) prim; prudish. □□ **pris‧si‧ly** *adv.* **pris‧si‧ness** *n.* [perh. f. PRIM + SISSY]

pris‧tine /prísteen, pristeén/ *adj.* **1** in its original condition; unspoiled. **2** *disp.* spotless; fresh as if new. **3** ancient; primitive. [L *pristinus* former]

prith‧ee /príthee/ *int. archaic* pray; please. [= *I pray thee*]

pri‧va‧cy /prívəsee/ *n.* **1 a** the state of being private and undisturbed.

b a person's right to this. **2** freedom from intrusion or public attention. **3** avoidance of publicity.

pri‧vate /prívət/ *adj. & n.* ● *adj.* **1** belonging to an individual; one's own; personal (*private property*). **2** confidential; not to be disclosed to others (*private talks*). **3** kept or removed from public knowledge or observation. **4 a** not open to the public. **b** for an individual's exclusive use (*private room*). **5** (of a place) secluded; affording privacy. **6** (of a person) not holding public office or an official position. **7** (of education) conducted outside the government system. **8** (of a person) retiring; reserved; unsociable. **9** (of a company) not having publicly traded shares. ● *n.* **1** a soldier with a rank below corporal. **2** (in *pl.*) *colloq.* the genitals. □ **in private** privately; in private company or life. □□ **pri‧vate‧ly** *adv.* [ME f. L *privatus*, orig. past part. of *privare* deprive]

pri‧vate bill *n.* a legislative bill affecting an individual or corporation only.

pri‧vate de‧tec‧tive *n.* a usu. freelance detective carrying out investigations outside an official police force, for a private employer.

pri‧va‧teer /prívəteér/ *n.* **1** an armed vessel owned and officered by private individuals holding a government commission and authorized for war service. **2 a** a commander of such a vessel. **b** (in *pl.*) its crew. □□ **pri‧va‧teer‧ing** *n.* [PRIVATE, after *volunteer*]

pri‧va‧teers‧man /prívəteérzmən/ *n.* (*pl.* **‧men**) = PRIVATEER 2.

pri‧vate en‧ter‧prise *n.* **1** a business or businesses not under government control. **2** individual initiative.

pri‧vate eye *n. colloq.* a private detective.

pri‧vate first class *n.* a soldier ranking above an ordinary private but below a corporal.

pri‧vate house *n.* the dwelling house of a private person, as distinct from a shop, office, or public building.

pri‧vate in‧ves‧ti‧ga‧tor *n.* private detective.

pri‧vate law *n.* the body of laws relating to individual persons and private property.

pri‧vate life *n.* life as a private person, not as an official, public performer, etc.

pri‧vate parts *n. pl.* the genitals.

pri‧vate prac‧tice *n.* **1** *US* an independent practice, esp. of law, medicine, or counseling services. **2** *Brit.* medical practice that is not part of the National Health Service.

pri‧vate press *n.* a printing establishment operated by a private person or group not primarily for profit and usu. on a small scale.

pri‧vate school *n.* **1** *US* a school not supported mainly by the government. **2** *Brit.* a school supported wholly by the payment of fees.

pri‧vate sec‧re‧tar‧y *n.* a secretary dealing with the personal and confidential concerns of a business executive.

pri‧vate sec‧tor *n.* the part of the economy free of direct government control.

pri‧vate war *n.* **1** a feud between persons or families disregarding the law of murder, etc. **2** hostilities against members of another nation without the sanction of one's own government.

pri‧vate wrong *n.* an offense against an individual but not against society as a whole.

pri‧va‧tion /prívávshən/ *n.* **1** lack of the comforts or necessities of life (*suffered many privations*). **2** (often foll. by *of*) loss or absence (of a quality). [ME f. L *privatio* (as PRIVATE)]

priv‧a‧tive /prívətiv/ *adj.* **1** consisting in or marked by the loss or removal or absence of some quality or attribute. **2** (of a term) denoting the privation or absence of a quality, etc. **3** *Gram.* (of a particle, etc.) expressing privation, as Gk *a-* = 'not.' □□ **priv‧a‧tive‧ly** *adv.* [F *privatif –ive* or L *privativus* (as PRIVATION)]

pri‧va‧tize /prívətìz/ *v. tr.* make private, esp. transfer (a business, etc.) to private as distinct from government control or ownership. □□ **pri‧va‧ti‧za‧tion** *n.*

priv‧et /prívit/ *n.* any deciduous or evergreen shrub of the genus *Ligustrum*, esp. *L. vulgare* bearing small white flowers and black berries, and much used for hedges. [16th c.: orig. unkn.]

priv‧i‧lege /prívilij, prívlij/ *n. & v.* ● *n.* **1 a** a right, advantage, or immunity, belonging to a person, class, or office. **b** the freedom of members of a legislative assembly when speaking at its meetings. **2** a special benefit or honor (*it is a privilege to meet you*). **3** a monopoly or patent granted to an individual, corporation, etc. **4** *Stock Exch.* an option to buy or sell. ● *v. tr.* **1** invest with a privilege. **2** (foll. by *to* + infin.) allow (a person) as a privilege (to do something). **3** (often foll. by *from*) exempt (a person from a liability, etc.). [ME f. OF *privilege* f. L *privilegium* bill or law affecting an individual, f. *privus* private + *lex legis* law]

priv‧i‧leged /prívilijd, prívlijd/ *adj.* **1 a** invested with or enjoying a certain privilege or privileges; honored; favored. **b** exempt from standard regulations or procedures. **c** powerful; affluent. **2** (of information, etc.) confidential; restricted.

priv‧i‧ty /prívitee/ *n.* (*pl.* **-ties**) **1** *Law* a relation between two parties that is recognized by law, e.g., that of blood, lease, or service. **2** (often foll. by *to*) the state of being privy (to plans, etc.). [ME f. OF *priveté* f. med.L *privitas –tatis* f. L *privus* private]

priv•y /prívee/ *adj. & n.* ●*adj.* **1** (foll. by *to*) sharing in the secret of (a person's plans, etc.). **2** *archaic* hidden; secret. ●*n.* (*pl.* **•ies**) **1** a toilet, esp. an outhouse. **2** *Law* a person having a part or interest in any action, matter, or thing. □□ **priv•i•ly** *adv.* [ME f. OF *privé* f. L *privatus* PRIVATE]

Priv•y Coun•cil *n.* **1** (in the UK) a body of advisers appointed by the sovereign (now chiefly on an honorary basis and including present and former government ministers, etc.). **2** usu. *hist.* a sovereign's or governor-general's private counselors. □□ **priv•y coun•ci•lor** *n.*

priv•y purse *n. Brit.* **1** an allowance from the public revenue for the monarch's private expenses. **2** the keeper of this.

priv•y seal *n.* (in the UK) a seal formerly affixed to documents that are afterward to pass the Great Seal or that do not require it.

prix fixe /prée fíks/ *adj.* (of a meal) consisting of several courses served at a total fixed price.

prize[1] /prīz/ *n. & v.* ●*n.* **1** something that can be won in a competition, lottery, etc. **2** a reward given as a symbol of victory or superiority. **3** something striven for or worth striving for (*missed all the great prizes of life*). **4** (*attrib.*) **a** to which a prize is awarded (*a prize bull; a prize poem*). **b** supremely excellent or outstanding of its kind. ●*v.tr.* value highly (*a much prized possession*). [(n.) ME, var. of PRICE: (v.) ME f. OF *pris-* stem of *preisier* PRAISE]

prize[2] /prīz/ *n. & v.* ●*n.* **1** a ship or property captured in naval warfare. **2** a find or windfall. ●*v.tr.* make a prize of. [ME f. OF *prize* taking, booty, fem. past part. of *prendre* f. L *prehendere prehens-* seize: later identified with PRIZE[1]]

prize[3] /pr iz/ *v. & n.* (also **prise**) ●*v.tr.* force open or out by leverage (*prized up the lid; prized the box open*). ●*n.* leverage; purchase. [ME & OF *prise* levering instrument (as PRIZE[1])]

prize•fight /prízfīt/ *n.* a boxing match fought for prize money. □□ **prize•fight•er** *n.*

prize•man /prízmən/ *n. Brit.* (*pl.* **•men**) a winner of a prize, esp. a specified academic one.

prize mon•ey *n.* money offered as a prize.

prize ring *n.* **1** an enclosed area (now usu. a square) for prizefighting. **2** the practice of prizefighting.

prize•win•ner /prízwinər/ *n.* a winner of a prize. □□ **prize•win•ning** *adj.*

pro[1] /prō/ *n. & adj. colloq.* ●*n.* (*pl.* **pros**) a professional. ●*adj.* professional. □ **pro-am** involving professionals and amateurs. [abbr.]

pro[2] /prō/ *adj., n., & prep.* ●*adj.* (of an argument or reason) for; in favor. ●*n.* (*pl.* **pros**) a reason or argument for or in favor. ●*prep.* in favor of. [L, = for, on behalf of]

pro-[1] /prō/ *prefix* **1** favoring or supporting (*pro-government*). **2** acting as a substitute or deputy for (*proconsul*). **3** forward (*produce*). **4** forward and downward (*prostrate*). **5** onward (*proceed; progress*). **6** in front of (*protect*). [L *pro* in front (of), for, on behalf of, instead of, on account of]

pro-[2] /prō/ *prefix* before in time, place, order, etc. (*problem; proboscis; prophet*). [Gk]

pro•a /próə/ *n.* (also **prau, prah•u** /práà-oō/) a Malay boat, esp. with a large triangular sail and a canoelike outrigger. [Malay *prāu, prāhū*]

pro•ac•tive /prō-áktiv/ *adj.* **1** (of a person, policy, etc.) creating or controlling a situation by taking the initiative. **2** of or relating to mental conditioning or a habit, etc., which has been learned. □□ **pro•ac•tion** /-ákshən/ *n.* **pro•ac•tive•ly** *adv.* **pro•ac•tiv•i•ty** /-tívitee/ *n.* [PRO-[2], after REACTIVE]

prob. *abbr.* **1** probable. **2** probably. **3** problem.

prob•a•bi•lism /próbəbəlizəm/ *n.* **1** *Philos.* the doctrine that probability is the basis for belief and action since certainty is impossible. **2** *RC Ch.* an ethical theory that it is allowable to follow any one of many conflicting opinions even though an opposing one may be more probable.

prob•a•bi•lis•tic /próbəbəlístik/ *adj.* **1** relating to or established by probabilism. **2** based on or subject to probability.

prob•a•bil•i•ty /próbəbílitee/ *n.* (*pl.* **•ties**) **1** the state or condition of being probable. **2** the likelihood of something happening. **3** a probable or most probable event (*the probability is that they will come*). **4** *Math.* the extent to which an event is likely to occur, measured by the ratio of the favorable cases to the whole number of cases possible. □ **in all probability** most probably. [F *probabilité* or L *probabilitas* (as PROBABLE)]

prob•a•ble /próbəbəl/ *adj. & n.* ●*adj.* **1** (often foll. by *that* + clause) that may be expected or prove true; likely (*the probable explanation; it is probable that they forgot*). **2** statistically likely but not proven. ●*n.* a probable candidate, member of a team, etc. □□ **prob•a•bly** *adv.* [ME f. OF f. L *probabilis* f. *probare* prove]

prob•a•ble cause *n. Law* a reasonable ground for suspicion that a usu. criminal charge is justified; used esp. in cases in which a police search has been made without a search warrant.

pro•band /próband/ *n.* a person forming the starting point for the

genetic study of a family, etc. [L *probandus*, gerundive of *probare* test]

pro•bang /próbang/ *n. Surgery* a flexible rod with a sponge or ball, etc., at the end for introducing medications into or removing obstructions from the throat. [17th c. (named *provang* by its inventor): orig. unkn., perh. alt. after *probe*]

pro•bate /próbayt/ *n. & v.* ●*n.* **1** the official proving of a will. **2** a verified copy of a will. ●*v.tr.* **1** establish the validity of (a will). **2** to put (a criminal offender) on probation. [ME f. L *probatum* neut. past part. of *probare* PROVE]

pro•ba•tion /prəbáyshən/ *n.* **1** *Law* a system of suspending the sentence of a criminal offender subject to a period of good behavior under supervision. **2** a process or period of testing the character or abilities of a person in a certain role, esp. of a new employee. **3** a moral trial or discipline. □ **on probation** undergoing probation, esp. legal supervision. □□ **pro•ba•tion•al** *adj.* **pro•ba•tion•ar•y** *adj.* [ME f. OF *probation* or L *probatio* (as PROVE)]

pro•ba•tion•er /próbáyshənər/ *n.* **1** a person on probation, e.g., a newly appointed nurse, teacher, etc. **2** a criminal offender on probation. □□ **pro•ba•tion•er•ship** *n.*

pro•ba•tion of•fi•cer *n.* an official supervising offenders on probation.

pro•ba•tive /próbətiv/ *adj.* affording proof; evidential. [L *probativus* (as PROVE)]

probe /prōb/ *n. & v.* ●*n.* **1** a penetrating investigation. **2** any small device, esp. an electrode, for measuring, testing, etc. **3** a blunt surgical instrument usu. of metal for exploring a wound, etc. **4** (in full **space probe**) an unmanned exploratory spacecraft transmitting information about its environment. ●*v.* **1** *tr.* examine or inquire into closely. **2** *tr.* explore (a wound or part of the body) with a probe. **3** *tr.* penetrate with or as with a sharp instrument, esp. in order to explore. **4** *intr.* make an investigation with or as with a probe (*the detective probed into her past life*). □□ **probe•a•ble** *adj.* **prob•er** *n.* **prob•ing•ly** *adv.* [LL *proba* proof, in med.L = examination, f. L *probare* test]

prob•it /próbit/ *n. Statistics* a unit of probability based on deviation from the mean of a standard distribution. [*probability unit*]

pro•bi•ty /próbitee, prób–/ *n.* uprightness; honesty. [F *probité* or L *probitas* f. *probus* good]

prob•lem /próbləm/ *n.* **1** a doubtful or difficult matter requiring a solution (*how to prevent it is a problem; the problem of ventilation*). **2** something hard to understand, accomplish, or deal with. **3** (*attrib.*) **a** causing problems; difficult to deal with (*problem child*). **b** (of a play, novel, etc.) in which a social or other problem is treated. **4 a** *Physics & Math.* an inquiry starting from given conditions to investigate or demonstrate a fact, result, or law. **b** *Geom.* a proposition in which something has to be constructed (cf. THEOREM). **5 a** (in various games, esp. chess) an arrangement of men, cards, etc., in which the solver has to achieve a specified result. **b** a puzzle or question for solution. [ME f. OF *probleme* or L *problema* f. Gk *problēma –matos* f. *proballō* (as PRO-[2], *ballō* throw)]

prob•lem•at•ic /próbləmátik/ *adj.* (also **prob•lem•at•i•cal**) **1** difficult; posing a problem. **2** doubtful or questionable. **3** *Logic* enunciating or supporting what is possible but not necessarily true. □□ **prob•lem•at•i•cal•ly** *adv.* [F *problématique* or LL *problematicus* f. Gk *problēmatikos* (as PROBLEM)]

pro bo•no *adj.* pertaining to a service, esp. legal work, for which no fee is charged.

pro•bos•cid•e•an /próbəsídeeən, próbósídeéən/ *adj. & n.* (also **pro•bos•cid•i•an**) ●*adj.* **1** having a proboscis. **2** of or like a proboscis. **3** of the mammalian order Proboscidea, including elephants and their extinct relatives. ●*n.* a mammal of this order. [mod.L *Proboscidea* (as PROBOSCIS)]

pro•bos•cis /próbósis/ *n.* **1** the long flexible trunk or snout of some mammals, e.g., an elephant or tapir. **2** the elongated mouth parts of some insects. **3** the sucking organ in some worms. **4** *joc.* the human nose. □□ **pro•bos•cid•if•er•ous** /–sídifərəs/ *adj.* **pro•bos•cid•i•form** /–sídifawrm/ *adj.* [L *proboscis –cidis* f. Gk *proboskis* f. *proboskō* (as PRO-[2], *boskō* feed)]

pro•bos•cis mon•key *n.* a monkey, *Nasalis larvatus*, native to Borneo, the male of which has a large pendulous nose.

pro•caine /prókayn/ *n.* (also **pro•cain**) a synthetic compound used as a local anesthetic. [PRO-[1] + COCAINE]

pro•car•y•ote var. of PROKARYOTE.

pro•ce•dure /prəséejər/ *n.* **1** a way of proceeding, esp. a mode of conducting business or a legal action. **2** a mode of performing a task. **3** a series of actions conducted in a certain order or manner. **4** a proceeding. **5** *Computing* = SUBROUTINE. □□ **pro•ce•dur•al** *adj.* **pro•ce•dur•al•ly** *adv.* [F *procédure* (as PROCEED)]

pro•ceed /prəseéd, prō–/ *v.intr.* **1** (often foll. by *to*) go forward or on further; make one's way. **2** (often foll. by *with*, or *to* + infin.) continue; go on with an activity (*proceeded with their work; proceeded to tell the whole story*). **3** (of an action) be carried on or continue (*the case will now proceed*). **4** adopt a course of action (*how shall we proceed?*). **5** go on to say. **6** (foll. by *against*) start a lawsuit (against a person). **7** (often foll. by *from*) come forth or originate (*shouts pro-*

ceeded from the bedroom). [ME f. OF *proceder* f. L *procedere process-* (as PRO-¹, *cedere* go)]

pro•ceed•ing /prōséeding, prǝ–/ *n.* **1** an action or piece of conduct. **2** (in *pl.*) (in full **legal proceedings**) a legal action; a lawsuit. **3** (in *pl.*) a published report of discussions or a conference. **4** (in *pl.*) business, actions, or events in progress (*the proceedings were enlivened by a dog running onto the field*).

pro•ceeds /prōseedz/ *n.pl.* money produced by a transaction or other undertaking. [pl. of obs. *proceed* (n.) f. PROCEED]

proc•ess¹ /próses, pró–/ *n. & v. • n.* **1** a course of action or proceeding, esp. a series of stages in manufacture or some other operation. **2** the progress or course of something (*in process of construction*). **3** a natural or involuntary operation or series of changes (*the process of growing old*). **4** a legal action; a summons or writ. **5** *Anat., Zool., & Bot.* a natural appendage or outgrowth on an organism. • *v.tr.* **1** handle or deal with by a particular process. **2** treat (food, esp. to prevent decay) (*processed cheese*). **3** *Computing* operate on (data) by means of a program. □ **in process of time** as time goes on. □□ **proc•ess•a•ble** *adj.* [ME f. OF *proces* f. L *processus* (as PROCEED)]

pro•cess² /prōsés/ *v.intr.* walk in procession. [back-form. f. PROCESSION]

pro•ces•sion /prǝséshǝn/ *n.* **1** a number of people or vehicles, etc., moving forward in orderly succession, esp. at a ceremony, demonstration, or festivity. **2** the movement of such a group (*go in procession*). **3** a regular succession of things; a sequence. **4** *Theol.* the emanation of the Holy Spirit. □□ **pro•ces•sion•ist** *n.* [ME f. OF f. L *processio –onis* (as PROCEED)]

pro•ces•sion•al /prǝséshǝnǝl/ *adj. & n. • adj.* **1** of processions. **2** used, carried, or sung in processions. • *n. Eccl.* a book of processional hymns, etc. [med.L *processionalis* (adj.), *–ale* (n.) (as PROCESSION)]

proc•es•sor /prósesǝr, pró–/ *n.* a machine that processes things, esp.: **1** = CENTRAL PROCESSOR. **2** = FOOD PROCESSOR.

proc•ess serv•er *n.* a person who serves legal summonses or writs.

pro•cès-ver•bal /prōsáy-verbáal/ *n.* (*pl.* **pro•cès-ver•baux** /–bó/) a written report of proceedings; minutes. [F]

pro•choice *adj.* (also **pro•choice**) in favor of the right to legal abortion.

pro•chro•nism /prókrǝnizǝm/ *n.* the action of referring an event, etc., to an earlier date than the true one. [PRO-² + Gk *khronos* time]

pro•claim /prōkláym, prǝ–/ *v.tr.* **1** (often foll. by *that* + clause) announce or declare publicly or officially. **2** declare (a person) to be (a king, traitor, etc.). **3** reveal as being (*an accent that proclaims you a Southerner*). □□ **pro•claim•er** *n.* **proc•la•ma•tion** /próklǝmáyshǝn/ *n.* **pro•clam•a•to•ry** /–klámǝtawree/ *adj.* [ME *proclame* f. L *proclamare* cry out (as PRO-¹, CLAIM)]

pro•clit•ic /prōklítik/ *adj. & n. Gram. • adj.* (of a monosyllable) closely attached in pronunciation to a following word and having itself no accent. • *n.* such a word, e.g., *at* in *at home.* □□ **pro•clit•i•cal•ly** *adv.* [mod.L *procliticus* f. Gk *proklinō* lean forward, after LL *encliticus*: see ENCLITIC]

pro•cliv•i•ty /prōklívitee/ *n.* (*pl.* **•ties**) a tendency or inclination. [L *proclivitas* f. *proclivis* inclined (as PRO-¹, *clivus* slope)]

pro•con•sul /prōkónsǝl/ *n.* **1** *Rom.Hist.* a governor of a province, in the later republic usu. an ex-consul. **2** a governor of a modern colony, etc. **3** a deputy consul. □□ **pro•con•su•lar** /–kónsǝlǝr/ *adj.* **pro•con•su•late** /–kónsǝlǝt/ *n.* **pro•con•sul•ship** *n.* [ME f. L, earlier *pro consule* (one acting) for the consul]

pro•cras•ti•nate /prōkrástinayt/ *v.* **1** *intr.* defer action; delay, esp. intentionally. **2** *tr.* defer or delay, esp. intentionally or habitually. □□ **pro•cras•ti•na•tion** /–náyshǝn/ *n.* **pro•cras•ti•na•tive** /–nǝtiv/ *adj.* **pro•cras•ti•na•tor** *n.* **pro•cras•ti•na•to•ry** /–nǝtawree/ *adj.* [L *procrastinare procrastinat-* (as PRO-¹, *crastinus* of tomorrow f. *cras* tomorrow]

▶See note at PREVARICATE.

pro•cre•ate /prókreeayt/ *v.tr.* (often *absol.*) bring (offspring) into existence by the natural process of reproduction. □□ **pro•cre•ant** /prókreeǝnt/ *adj.* **pro•cre•a•tive** *adj.* **pro•cre•a•tion** *n.* **pro•cre•a•tor** *n.* [L *procreare procreat-* (as PRO-¹, *creare* create)]

Pro•crus•te•an /prōkrústeeǝn/ *adj.* seeking to enforce uniformity by forceful or ruthless methods. [Gk *Prokroustēs*, lit. stretcher, f. *prokrouō* beat out: the name of a legendary robber who fitted victims to a bed by stretching them or cutting off parts of them]

proc•tol•o•gy /proktólǝjee/ *n.* the branch of medicine concerned with the anus and rectum. □□ **proc•to•log•i•cal** /–tǝlójikǝl/ *adj.* **proc•tol•o•gist** *n.* [Gk *prōktos* anus + –LOGY]

proc•tor /próktǝr/ *n.* **1** a supervisor of students in an examination, etc. **2** *Brit.* an officer (usu. one of two) at certain universities, appointed annually and having mainly disciplinary functions. **3** *Brit. Law* a person managing causes in a court (now chiefly ecclesiastical) that administers civil or canon law. □□ **proc•to•ri•al** /–táwreeǝl/ *adj.* **proc•tor•ship** *n.* [ME, syncopation of PROCURATOR]

proc•to•scope /próktǝskōp/ *n.* a medical instrument for inspecting the rectum. [Gk *prōktos* anus + –SCOPE]

pro•cum•bent /prōkúmbǝnt/ *adj.* **1** lying on the face; prostrate.

2 *Bot.* growing along the ground. [L *procumbere* fall forward (as PRO-¹, *cumbere* lay oneself)]

proc•u•ra•tion /prókyŏŏráyshǝn/ *n.* **1** the action of procuring, obtaining, or bringing about. **2** the function or an authorized action of an attorney. [ME f. OF *procuration* or L *procuratio* (as PROCURE)]

proc•u•ra•tor /prókyŏŏraytǝr/ *n.* **1** an agent or proxy, esp. one who has power of attorney. **2** *Rom.Hist.* a treasury officer in an imperial province. □□ **proc•u•ra•to•ri•al** /–rǝtáwreeǝl/ *adj.* **proc•u•ra•tor•ship** *n.* [ME f. OF *procurateur* or L *procurator* administrator, finance agent (as PROCURE)]

pro•cure /prōkyŏŏr, prǝ–/ *v.tr.* **1** obtain, esp. by care or effort; acquire (*managed to procure a copy*). **2** bring about (*procured their dismissal*). **3** (also *absol.*) obtain (people) for prostitution. □□ **pro•cur•a•ble** *adj.* **pro•cur•al** *n.* **pro•cure•ment** *n.* [ME f. OF *procurer* f. L *procurare* take care of, manage (as PRO-¹, *curare* see to)]

pro•cur•er /prōkyŏŏrǝr, prǝ–/ *n.* a person who obtains people for prostitution. [ME f. AF *procurour*, OF *procureur* f. L *procurator*: see PROCURATOR]

prod /prod/ *v. & n. • v.* (**prod•ded, prod•ding**) **1** *tr.* poke with the finger or a pointed object. **2** *tr.* stimulate or goad to action. **3** *intr.* (foll. by *at*) make a prodding motion. • *n.* **1** a poke or thrust. **2** a stimulus to action. **3** a pointed instrument. □□ **prod•der** *n.* [16th c.: perh. imit.]

prod•i•gal /pródigǝl/ *adj. & n. • adj.* **1** recklessly wasteful. **2** (foll. by *of*) lavish. • *n.* **1** a prodigal person. **2** (in full **prodigal son**) a repentant wastrel, returned wanderer, etc. (Luke 15:11–32). □□ **prod•i•gal•i•ty** /–gálitee/ *n.* **prod•i•gal•ly** *adv.* [med.L *prodigalis* f. L *prodigus* lavish]

pro•di•gious /prǝdíjǝs/ *adj.* **1** marvelous or amazing. **2** enormous. **3** abnormal. □□ **pro•di•gious•ly** *adv.* **pro•di•gious•ness** *n.* [L *prodigiosus* (as PRODIGY)]

prod•i•gy /pródijee/ *n.* (*pl.* **•gies**) **1** a person endowed with exceptional qualities or abilities, esp. a precocious child. **2** a marvelous thing, esp. one out of the ordinary course of nature. **3** (foll. by *of*) a wonderful example (of a quality). [L *prodigium* portent]

pro•drome /pródrōm/ *n.* **1** a preliminary book or treatise. **2** *Med.* a premonitory symptom. □□ **prod•ro•mal** /–drómǝl/ *adj.* **pro•drom•ic** /prōdrómik/ *adj.* [F f. mod.L f. Gk *prodromos* precursor (as PRO-², *dromos* running)]

pro•duce *v. & n. • v.tr.* /prǝdóŏs, –dyóŏs/ **1** bring forward for consideration, inspection, or use (*will produce evidence*). **2** manufacture (goods) from raw materials, etc. **3** bear or yield (offspring, fruit, a harvest, etc.). **4** bring into existence. **5** cause or bring about (a reaction, sensation, etc.). **6** *Geom.* extend or continue (a line). **7 a** bring (a play, performer, book, etc.) before the public. **b** supervise the production of (a movie, broadcast, etc.). • *n.* /pródŏos, –dyŏos, pró–/ **1 a** what is produced, esp. agricultural products. **b** fruits and vegetables collectively. **2** (often foll. by *of*) a result (of labor, efforts, etc.). **3** a yield, esp. in the assay of ore. **4** offspring (esp. of a female animal). □□ **pro•duc•i•ble** /–sib'l/ *adj.* **pro•duc•i•bil•i•ty** *n.* [ME f. L *producere* (as PRO-¹, *ducere duct-* lead)]

pro•duc•er /prǝdóŏsǝr, –dyóŏ–/ *n.* **1 a** *Econ.* a person who produces goods or commodities. **b** a person who or thing which produces something or someone. **2 a** a person generally responsible for the production of a movie, play, or radio or television program (apart from the direction of the acting). **b** *Brit.* the director of a play or broadcast program. **3** an organism that produces its own food from inorganic compounds.

pro•duc•er gas *n.* a combustible gas formed by passing air, or air and steam, through red-hot carbon.

prod•uct /pródukt/ *n.* **1** a thing or substance produced by natural process or manufacture. **2** a result (*the product of their labors*). **3** *Math.* a quantity obtained by multiplying quantities together. [ME f. L *productum*, neut. past part. of *producere* PRODUCE]

pro•duc•tion /prǝdúkshǝn/ *n.* **1** the act or an instance of producing; the process of being produced. **2** the process of being manufactured, esp. in large quantities (*go into production*). **3** a total yield. **4** a thing produced, esp. a literary or artistic work, a movie, broadcast, play, etc. □□ **pro•duc•tion•al** *adj.* [ME f. OF f. L *productio –onis* (as PRODUCT)]

pro•duc•tion line *n.* a systematized sequence of mechanical or manual operations involved in producing a commodity.

pro•duc•tive /prǝdúktiv/ *adj.* **1** of or engaged in the production of goods. **2 a** producing much (*productive soil; a productive writer*). **b** (of the mind) inventive; creative. **3** *Econ.* producing commodities of exchangeable value (*productive labor*). **4** (foll. by *of*) producing or giving rise to (*productive of great annoyance*). □□ **pro•duc•tive•ly** *adv.* **pro•duc•tive•ness** *n.* [F *productif –ive* or LL *productivus* (as PRODUCT)]

pro•duc•tiv•i•ty /próduktívitee, pró–/ *n.* **1** the capacity to produce. **2** the quality or state of being productive. **3** the effectiveness of productive effort, esp. in industry. **4** production per unit of effort.

pro•em /próim/ *n.* **1** a preface or preamble to a book or speech. **2** a beginning or prelude. □□ **pro•e•mi•al** /prō-eémeeəl/ *adj.* [ME f. OF *proeme* or L *prooemium* f. Gk *prooimion* prelude (as PRO-², *oimē* song)]

Prof. *abbr.* Professor.

prof /prof/ *n. colloq.* a professor. [abbr.]

pro•fane /prōfáyn, prə–/ *adj. & v.* ● *adj.* **1** not belonging to what is sacred or biblical; secular. **2 a** irreverent; blasphemous. **b** vulgar; obscene. **3** (of a rite, etc.) heathen; pagan. **4** not initiated into religious rites or any esoteric knowledge. ● *v.tr.* **1** treat (a sacred thing) with irreverence or disregard. **2** violate or pollute (something entitled to respect). □□ **prof•a•na•tion** /prófənáyshən/ *n.* **pro•fane•ly** *adv.* **pro•fane•ness** *n.* **pro•fan•er** *n.* [ME *prophane* f. OF *prophane* or med.L *prophanus* f. L *profanus* before (i.e. outside) the temple, not sacred (as PRO-¹, *fanum* temple)]

pro•fan•i•ty /prōfánitee, prə–/ *n.* (*pl.* **-ties**) **1** a profane act. **2** profane language; blasphemy. [LL *profanitas* (as PROFANE)]

pro•fess /prəfés, prō–/ *v.* **1** *tr.* claim openly to have (a quality or feeling). **2** *tr.* (foll. by *to* + infin.) pretend. **3** *tr.* (often foll. by *that* + clause; also *refl.*) declare (*profess ignorance; professed herself satisfied*). **4** *tr.* affirm one's faith in or allegiance to. **5** *tr.* receive into a religious order under vows. **6** *tr.* have as one's profession or business. **7 a** *tr.* teach (a subject) as a professor. **b** *intr.* perform the duties of a professor. [ME f. L *profitēri profess-* declare publicly (as PRO-¹, *fatēri* confess)]

pro•fessed /prəfést, prō–/ *adj.* **1** self-acknowledged (*a professed Christian*). **2** alleged; ostensible. **3** claiming to be duly qualified. **4** (of a monk or nun) having taken the vows of a religious order. □□ **pro•fess•ed•ly** /–fésidlee/ *adv.* (in senses 1, 2).

pro•fes•sion /prəféshən/ *n.* **1** a vocation or calling, esp. one that involves some branch of advanced learning or science (*the medical profession*). **2** a body of people engaged in a profession. **3** a declaration or avowal. **4** a declaration of belief in a religion. **5 a** the declaration or vows made on entering a religious order. **b** the ceremony or fact of being professed in a religious order. □ **the oldest profession** prostitution. □□ **pro•fes•sion•less** *adj.*

WORD HISTORY profession

Middle English (denoting the vow made on entering a religious order): via Old French from Latin *professio(n-)*, from *profiteri* 'declare publicly' (source of *profess*). Senses 1 and 2 derive from the notion of an occupation that one 'professes' to be skilled in.

---

pro•fes•sion•al /prəféshənəl/ *adj. & n.* ● *adj.* **1** of or belonging to or connected with a profession. **2 a** having or showing the skill of a professional; competent. **b** worthy of a professional (*professional conduct*). **3** engaged in a specified activity as one's main paid occupation (cf. AMATEUR) (*a professional boxer*). **4** *derog.* engaged in a specified activity regarded with disfavor (*a professional agitator*). ● *n.* a professional person. □□ **pro•fes•sion•al•ly** *adv.*

pro•fes•sion•al•ism /prəféshənəlizəm/ *n.* the qualities or typical features of a profession or of professionals, esp. competence, skill, etc. □□ **pro•fes•sion•al•ize** *v.tr.*

pro•fes•sor /prəfésər/ *n.* **1 a** (often as a title) a university academic of the highest rank. **b** a university teacher. **c** a teacher of some specific art, sport, or skill. **2** a person who professes a religion. □□ **pro•fes•sor•ate** /–rət/ *n.* **pro•fes•so•ri•al** /prófisáwreeəl/ *adj.* **pro•fes•so•ri•al•ly** *adv.* **pro•fes•so•ri•ate** /–fisáwreeət/ *n.* **pro•fes•sor•ship** *n.* [ME f. OF *professeur* or L *professor* (as PROFESS)]

SPELLING TIP professor

To remember the single *f* in this word, think of the abbreviation for *professor*: *prof.*, with only one *f*.

---

prof•fer /prófər/ *v. & n.* ● *v.tr.* (esp. as **proffered** *adj.*) offer (a gift, services, a hand, etc.). ● *n.* an offer or proposal. [ME f. AF & OF *proffrir* (as PRO-¹, *offrir* OFFER)]

pro•fi•cient /prəfíshənt/ *adj. & n.* ● *adj.* (often foll. by *in, at*) adept; expert. ● *n.* a person who is proficient. □□ **pro•fi•cien•cy** /–shənsee/ *n.* **pro•fi•cient•ly** *adv.* [L *proficiens proficient-* (as PROFIT)]

pro•file /prófil/ *n. & v.* ● *n.* **1 a** an outline (esp. of a human face) as seen from one side. **b** a representation of this. **2 a** a short biographical or character sketch. **b** a report, esp. one written by a teacher on a pupil's academic and social progress. **3** *Statistics* a representation by a graph or chart of information (esp. on certain characteristics) recorded in a quantified form. **4** a characteristic personal manner or attitude. **5** a vertical cross section of a structure. **6** a flat outline piece of scenery on stage. ● *v.tr.* **1** represent in profile. **2** give a profile to. **3** write a profile about. □ **in profile** as seen from one side. **keep a low profile** remain inconspicuous. □□ **pro•fil•er** *n.* **pro•fil•ist** *n.* [obs. It. *profilo, profilare* (as PRO-¹, *filare* spin f. L *filare* f. *filum* thread)]

prof•it /prófit/ *n. & v.* ● *n.* **1** an advantage or benefit. **2** financial gain; excess of returns over expenditures. ● *v.* (**prof•it•ed, prof•it•**

---

ing) **1** *tr.* (also *absol.*) be beneficial to. **2** *intr.* obtain an advantage or benefit (*profited by the experience*). **3** *intr.* make a profit. □ **at a profit** with financial gain. □□ **prof•it•less** *adj.* [ME f. OF f. L *profectus* progress, profit f. *proficere profect-* advance (as PRO-¹, *facere* do)]

prof•it•a•ble /prófitəbəl/ *adj.* **1** yielding profit; lucrative. **2** beneficial; useful. □□ **prof•it•a•bil•i•ty** /–bílitee/ *n.* **prof•it•a•ble•ness** *n.* **prof•it•a•bly** *adv.* [ME f. OF (as PROFIT)]

prof•it and loss *n.* a statement on which gains are credited and losses debited so as to show the net profit or loss at any time.

prof•it•eer /prófiteér/ *v. & n.* ● *v.intr.* make or seek to make excessive profits, esp. illegally or in black market conditions. ● *n.* a person who profiteers.

pro•fit•er•ole /prəfítərōl/ *n.* a small hollow pastry usu. filled with cream and covered with chocolate sauce. [F, dimin. of *profit* PROFIT]

prof•it mar•gin *n.* the profit remaining in a business after costs have been deducted.

prof•it shar•ing *n.* the sharing of profits esp. between employer and employees.

prof•it tak•ing *n.* the sale of shares, etc., at a time when profit will accrue.

prof•li•gate /prófligət/ *adj. & n.* ● *adj.* **1** licentious; dissolute. **2** recklessly extravagant. ● *n.* a profligate person. □□ **prof•li•ga•cy** /–gəsee/ *n.* **prof•li•gate•ly** *adv.* [L *profligatus* dissolute, past part. of *profligare* overthrow, ruin (as PRO-¹, *fligere* strike down)]

pro for•ma /prō fáwrmə/ *adv., adj., & n.* ● *adv. & adj.* as or being a matter of form; for the sake of form. ● *n.* (in full **pro-forma invoice**) an invoice sent in advance of goods supplied. [L]

pro•found /prəfównd, prō–/ *adj. & n.* ● *adj.* (**pro•found•er, pro•found•est**) **1 a** having or showing great knowledge or insight (*a profound treatise*). **b** demanding deep study or thought (*profound doctrines*). **2** (of a state or quality) deep; intense; unqualified (*a profound sleep; profound indifference*). **3** at or extending to a great depth (*profound crevasses*). **4** coming from a great depth (*a profound sigh*). **5** (of a disease) deep-seated. ● *n.* (prec. by *the*) *poet.* the vast depth (of the ocean, soul, etc.). □□ **pro•found•ly** *adv.* **pro•found•ness** *n.* **pro•fun•di•ty** /–fúnditee/ *n.* (*pl.* **-ties**). [ME f. AF & OF *profund, profond* f. L *profundus* deep (as PRO-¹, *fundus* bottom)]

pro•fuse /prəfyóõs, prō–/ *adj.* **1** (often foll. by *in, of*) lavish; extravagant (*was profuse in her generosity*). **2** (of a thing) exuberantly plentiful; abundant (*profuse bleeding; a profuse variety*). □□ **pro•fuse•ly** *adv.* **pro•fuse•ness** *n.* **pro•fu•sion** /–fyóõzhən/ *n.* [ME f. L *profusus* past part. of *profundere profus-* (as PRO-¹, *fundere fus-* pour)]

SYNONYM TIP profuse

EXTRAVAGANT, LAVISH, LUSH, LUXURIANT, PRODIGAL. Something that is **profuse** is poured out or given freely, often to the point of exaggeration or excess (*profuse apologies*). **Extravagant** also suggests unreasonable excess, but with an emphasis on wasteful spending (*her gift was much too extravagant for the occasion*). Someone who is **prodigal** is so recklessly *extravagant* that his or her resources will ultimately be exhausted (*the prodigal heir to the family fortune*). Another way to end up impoverished is through **lavish** spending, a word that combines extravagance with generosity or a lack of moderation (*lavish praise, lavish furnishings*). While *lavish, extravagant* and *prodigal* are often used to describe human behavior, **lush** and **luxuriant** normally refer to things. What is *luxuriant* is produced in great quantity, suggesting that it is not only *profuse* but gorgeous (*luxuriant auburn hair*). Something described as *lush* is not only *luxuriant* but has reached a peak of perfection (*the lush summer grass*).

---

pro•gen•i•tive /prōjénitiv/ *adj.* capable of or connected with the production of offspring.

pro•gen•i•tor /prōjénitər/ *n.* **1** the ancestor of a person, animal, or plant. **2** a political or intellectual predecessor. **3** the origin of a copy. □□ **pro•gen•i•to•ri•al** /–táwreeəl/ *adj.* **pro•gen•i•tor•ship** *n.* [ME f. OF *progeniteur* f. L *progenitor –oris* f. *progignere progenit-* (as PRO-¹, *gignere* beget)]

prog•e•ny /prójinee/ *n.* **1** the offspring of a person or other organism. **2** a descendant or descendants. **3** an outcome or issue. [ME f. OF *progenie* f. L *progenies* f. *progignere* (as PROGENITOR)]

pro•ges•ter•one /prōjéstərōn/ *n.* a steroid hormone released by the corpus luteum which stimulates the preparation of the uterus for pregnancy (see also PROGESTOGEN). [*progest*in (as PRO-², GESTATION) + luteo*sterone* f. CORPUS LUTEUM + STEROL]

pro•ges•to•gen /prōjéstəjin/ *n.* **1** any of a group of steroid hormones (including progesterone) that maintain pregnancy and prevent further ovulation during it. **2** a similar hormone produced synthetically.

pro•glot•tid /prōglótid/ *n.* (also **pro•glot•tis**) (*pl.* **pro•glot•ti•des** /–glótideez/) each segment in the strobile of a tapeworm that contains a complete reproductive system. [mod.L f. Gk *proglōssis* (as PRO-², *glōssis* f. *glōssa, glōtta* tongue), from its shape]

prog•na•thous /prognáythəs, prógnəthəs/ *adj.* **1** having a projecting jaw. **2** (of a jaw) projecting. □□ **prog·nath·ic** /prognáthik/ *adj.* **prog· na·thism** *n.* [PRO-² + Gk *gnathos* jaw]

prog·no·sis /prognósis/ *n.* (*pl.* **prog·no·ses** /–seez/) **1** a forecast; a prognostication. **2** a forecast of the course of a disease. [LL f. Gk *prognōsis* (as PRO-², *gignōskō* know)]

prog·nos·tic /prognóstik/ *n. & adj.* ● *n.* **1** (often foll. by *of*) an advance indication or omen, esp. of the course of a disease, etc. **2** a prediction; a forecast. ● *adj.* foretelling; predictive (*prognostic of a good result*). □□ **prog·nos·ti·cal·ly** *adv.* [ME f. OF *pronostique* f. L *prognosticum* f. Gk *prognōstikon* neut. of *prognōstikos* (as PROGNOSIS)]

prog·nos·ti·cate /prognóstikayt/ *v.tr.* **1** (often foll. by *that* + clause) foretell; foresee; prophesy. **2** (of a thing) betoken; indicate (future events, etc.). □□ **prog·nos·ti·ca·ble** /–kəbəl/ *adj.* **prog·nos·ti·ca·tion** *n.* **prog·nos·ti·ca·tive** /–kətiv/ *adj.* **prog·nos·ti·ca·tor** *n.* **prog·nos· ti·ca·to·ry** /–kətawree/ *adj.* [med.L *prognosticare* (as PROGNOSTIC)]

pro·gram /prógram, –grəm/ *n. & v.* (*Brit.* **pro·gramme**) ● *n.* **1** a usu. printed list of a series of events, performers, etc., at a public function, etc. **2** a radio or television broadcast. **3** a plan of future events (*the program is dinner and an early night*). **4** a course or series of studies, lectures, etc.; a syllabus. **5** a series of coded instructions to control the operation of a computer or other machine. ● *v.tr.* (**pro· grammed, pro·gram·ming**; also **pro·gramed, pro·gram·ing**) **1** make a program or definite plan of. **2** express (a problem) or instruct (a computer) by means of a program. □□ **pro·gram·ma·ble** *adj.* **pro· gram·ma·bil·i·ty** /–gramǝbílitee/ *n.* **pro·gram·mat·ic** /–grǝmátik/ *adj.* **pro·gram·mat·i·cal·ly** /–grǝmátiklee/ *adv.* **pro·gram·mer** *n.* **pro· gram·er** *n.* [LL *programma* f. Gk *programma* –*atos* f. *prographō* write publicly (as PRO-², *graphō* write)]

pro·gram mu·sic *n.* a piece of music intended to tell a story, evoke images, etc.

prog·ress *n. & v.* ● *n.* /prógres/ **1** forward or onward movement toward a destination. **2** advance or development toward completion, betterment, etc.; improvement (*has made little progress this term; the progress of civilization*). **3** *Brit. archaic* a state journey or official tour, esp. by royalty. ● *v.* /prǝgrés/ **1** *intr.* move or be moved forward or onward; continue (*the argument is progressing*). **2** *intr.* /prǝgrés/ advance or develop toward completion, improvement, etc. (*science progresses*). **3** *tr.* cause (work, etc.) to make regular progress. □ **in progress** in the course of developing; going on. [ME f. L *progressus* f. *progredi* (as PRO-¹, *gradi* walk)]

pro·gres·sion /prǝgréshǝn/ *n.* **1** the act or an instance of progressing (*a mode of progression*). **2** a succession; a series. **3** *Math.* **a** = ARITHMETIC PROGRESSION. **b** = GEOMETRIC PROGRESSION. **c** = HARMONIC PROGRESSION. **4** *Mus.* passing from one note or chord to another. □□ **pro·gres·sion·al** *adj.* [ME f. OF *progression* or L *progressio* (as PROGRESS)]

pro·gres·sion·ist /prǝgréshǝnist/ *n.* **1** an advocate of or believer in esp. political or social progress. **2** a person who believes in the theory of gradual progression to higher forms of life.

pro·gres·sive /prǝgrésiv/ *adj. & n.* ● *adj.* **1** moving forward (*progressive motion*). **2** proceeding step-by-step; cumulative (*progressive drug use*). **3 a** (of a political party, government, etc.) favoring or implementing rapid progress or social reform. **b** modern; efficient (*this is a progressive company*). **4** (of disease, violence, etc.) increasing in severity or extent. **5** (of taxation) at rates increasing with the sum taxed. **6** (of a card game, dance, etc.) with periodic changes of partners. **7** *Gram.* (of an aspect) expressing an action in progress, e.g., *am writing, was writing*. **8** (of education) informal and without strict discipline, stressing individual needs. ● *n.* (also **Progressive**) an advocate of progressive political policies. □□ **pro· gres·sive·ly** *adv.* **pro·gres·sive·ness** *n.* **pro·gres·siv·ism** *n.* **pro· gres·siv·ist** *n. & adj.* [F *progressif* –*ive* or med.L *progressivus* (as PROGRESS)]

prog·ress re·port *n.* an account of progress made.

pro·hib·it /prōhíbit/ *v.tr.* (**pro·hib·it·ed, pro·hib·it·ing**) (often foll. by *from* + verbal noun) **1** formally forbid, esp. by authority. **2** prevent;

make impossible (*his accident prohibits him from playing football*). □□ **pro·hib·it·er** *n.* **pro·hib·i·tor** *n.* [ME f. L *prohibēre* (as PRO-¹, *habēre* hold)]

pro·hib·it·ed de·grees *n.pl.* degrees of blood relationship within which marriage is forbidden.

pro·hi·bi·tion /próhibíshǝn, prōíbíshǝn/ *n.* **1** the act or an instance of forbidding; a state of being forbidden. **2** *Law* an edict or order that forbids. **3** (usu. **Prohibition**) the period (1920–33) in the US when the manufacture and sale of alcoholic beverages was prohibited by law. □□ **pro·hi·bi·tion·ar·y** *adj.* **pro·hi·bi·tion·ist** *n.* [ME f. OF *prohibition* or L *prohibitio* (as PROHIBIT)]

pro·hib·i·tive /prōhíbitiv/ *adj.* **1** prohibiting. **2** (of prices, taxes, etc.) so high as to prevent purchase, use, abuse, etc. (*published at a prohibitive price*). □□ **pro·hib·i·tive·ly** *adv.* **pro·hib·i·tive·ness** *n.* **pro· hib·i·to·ry** *adj.* [F *prohibitif* –*ive* or L *prohibitivus* (as PROHIBIT)]

proj·ect *n. & v.* *n.* /prójekt/ **1** a plan; a scheme. **2** a planned undertaking. **3** a usu. long-term task undertaken by a student or group of students to be submitted for grading. **4** (often *pl.*) a housing development, esp. for low-income residents. ● *v.* /prǝjékt/ **1** *tr.* plan or contrive (a course of action, scheme, etc.). **2** *intr.* protrude; jut out. **3** *tr.* throw; cast; impel. **4** *tr.* extrapolate (results, etc.) to a future time; forecast (*I project that we will produce two million next year*). **5** *tr.* cause (light, shadow, images, etc.) to fall on a surface, screen, etc. **6** *tr.* cause (a sound, esp. the voice) to be heard at a distance. **7** *tr.* (often *refl.* or *absol.*) express or promote (oneself or an image) forcefully or effectively. **8** *tr. Geom.* **a** draw straight lines from a center or parallel lines through every point of (a given figure) to produce a corresponding figure on a surface or a line by intersecting it. **b** draw (such lines). **c** produce (such a corresponding figure). **9** *tr.* make a projection (of the earth, sky, etc.). **10** *tr. Psychol.* **a** (also *absol.*) attribute (an emotion, etc.) to an external object or person, esp. unconsciously. **b** (*refl.*) project (oneself) into another's feelings, the future, etc.

WORD HISTORY   **project**

late Middle English (in the sense 'preliminary design, tabulated statement'): from Latin *projectum* 'something prominent,' neuter past participle of *projicere* 'throw forth,' from *pro-* 'forth' + *jacere* 'to throw.' Early senses of the verb were 'plan, devise' and 'cause to move forward.'

pro·jec·tile /prǝjéktǝl, –tíl/ *n. & adj.* ● *n.* **1** a missile, esp. fired by a rocket. **2** a bullet, shell, etc., fired from a gun. **3** any object thrown as a weapon. ● *adj.* **1** capable of being projected by force, esp. from a gun. **2** projecting or impelling. [mod.L *projectilis* (adj.), –*ile* (n.) (as PROJECT)]

pro·jec·tion /prǝjékshǝn/ *n.* **1** the act or an instance of projecting; the process of being projected. **2** a thing that projects or obtrudes. **3** the presentation of an image, etc., on a surface or screen. **4 a** a forecast or estimate based on present trends (*a projection of next year's profits*). **b** this process. **5 a** a mental image or preoccupation viewed as an objective reality. **b** the unconscious transfer of one's own impressions or feelings to external objects or persons. **6** *Geom.* the act or an instance of projecting a figure. **7** the representation on a plane surface of any part of the surface of the earth or a celestial sphere (*Mercator projection*). □□ **pro·jec·tion·ist** *n.* (in sense 3). [L *projectio* (as PROJECT)]

pro·jec·tive /prǝjéktiv/ *adj.* **1** *Geom.* **a** relating to or derived by projection. **b** (of a property of a figure) unchanged by projection. **2** *Psychol.* mentally projecting or projected (*a projective imagination*). □□ **pro·jec·tive·ly** *adv.*

pro·jec·tive ge·om·e·try *n.* the study of the projective properties of geometric figures.

pro·jec·tor /prǝjéktǝr/ *n.* **1 a** an apparatus containing a source of light and a system of lenses for projecting slides or movies onto a screen. **b** an apparatus for projecting rays of light. **2** a person who forms or promotes a project. **3** *archaic* a promoter of speculative companies.

pro·kar·y·ote /prōkáreeōt/ *n.* (also **pro·car·y·ote**) an organism in which the chromosomes are not separated from the cytoplasm by a membrane; a bacterium (cf. EUKARYOTE). □□ **pro·kar·y·ot·ic** /–reeótik/ *adj.* [PRO-² + KARYO- + –*ote* as in ZYGOTE]

pro·lac·tin /prōláktin/ *n.* a hormone released from the anterior pituitary gland that stimulates milk production after childbirth. [PRO-¹ + LACTATION]

pro·lapse /prōlaps/ *n. & v.* ● *n.* (also **pro·lap·sus** /–lápsǝs/) **1** the forward or downward displacement of a part or organ. **2** the prolapsed part or organ, esp. the womb or rectum. ● *v.intr.* undergo prolapse. [L *prolabi prolaps-* (as PRO-¹, *labi* slip)]

pro·late /prōlayt/ *adj. Geom.* (of a spheroid) lengthened in the direction of a polar diameter (cf. OBLATE²). [L *prolatus* past part. of *proferre* prolong (as PRO-¹, *ferre* carry)]

pro·la·tive /prōláytiv/ *adj. Gram.* serving to continue or complete a predication, e.g., *go* (prolative infinitive) in *you may go*.

prole /prōl/ *adj. & n. derog. colloq.* ● *adj.* proletarian. ● *n.* a proletarian. [abbr.]

pro·leg /prōleg/ *n.* a fleshy abdominal limb of a caterpillar or other larva. [PRO-¹ + LEG]

pro·le·gom·e·non /prōligómĭnon, –nən/ *n.* (*pl.* **pro·le·gom·e·na**) (usu. in *pl.*) an introduction or preface to a book, etc., esp. when critical or discursive. □□ **pro·le·gom·e·nar·y** *adj.* **pro·le·gom·e·nous** *adj.* [L f. Gk, neut. passive pres. part. of *prolegō* (as PRO-², *legō* say)]

pro·lep·sis /prōlépsis/ *n.* (*pl.* **pro·lep·ses** /–seez/) **1** the anticipation and answering of possible objections in rhetorical speech. **2** anticipation. **3** the representation of a thing as existing before it actually does or did so, as in *he was a dead man when he entered.* **4** *Gram.* the anticipatory use of adjectives, as in *paint the town red.* □□ **pro·lep·tic** *adj.* [LL f. Gk *prolēpsis* f. *prolambanō* anticipate (as PRO-², *lambanō* take)]

pro·le·tar·i·an /prōlitáireeən/ *adj. & n.* ● *adj.* of or concerning the proletariat. ● *n.* a member of the proletariat. □□ **pro·le·tar·i·an·ism** *n.* **pro·le·tar·i·an·ize** *v.tr.* [L *proletarius* one who served the state not with property but with offspring (*proles*)]

pro·le·tar·i·at /prōlitáireeət/ *n.* (also **pro·le·tar·i·ate**) **1 a** *Econ.* wage earners collectively, esp. those without capital and dependent on selling their labor. **b** esp. *derog.* the lowest class of the community, esp. when considered as uncultured. **2** *Rom.Hist.* the lowest class of citizens. [F *prolétariat* (as PROLETARIAN)]

pro-life /prōlíf/ *adj.* in favor of preserving life, esp. in opposing abortion.

pro·lif·er·ate /prōlífərayt/ *v.* **1** *intr.* reproduce; increase rapidly in numbers; grow by multiplication. **2** *tr.* produce (cells, etc.) rapidly. □□ **pro·lif·er·a·tion** /–fəráyshən/ *n.* **pro·lif·er·a·tive** /–rətiv/ *adj.* [back-form. f. *proliferation* f. F *prolifération* f. *prolifère* (as PROLIFEROUS)]

pro·lif·er·ous /prōlífərəs/ *adj.* **1** (of a plant) producing many leaf or flower buds; growing luxuriantly. **2** growing or multiplying by budding. **3** spreading by proliferation. [L *proles* offspring + –FEROUS]

pro·lif·ic /prōlífik/ *adj.* **1** producing many offspring or much output. **2** (often foll. by *of*) abundantly productive. **3** (often foll. by *in*) abounding; copious. □□ **pro·lif·i·ca·cy** *n.* **pro·lif·i·cal·ly** *adv.* **pro·lif·ic·ness** *n.* [med.L *prolificus* (as PROLIFEROUS)]

pro·lix /prōlíks, prōliks/ *adj.* (of speech, writing, etc.) lengthy; tedious. □□ **pro·lix·i·ty** /–líksitee/ *n.* **pro·lix·ly** *adv.* [ME f. OF *prolixe* or L *prolixus* poured forth, extended (as PRO-¹, *liquēre* be liquid)]

pro·loc·u·tor /prōlókyətər/ *n.* **1** *Eccl.* the chairperson esp. of the lower house of convocation of either province of the Church of England. **2** a spokesperson. □□ **pro·loc·u·tor·ship** *n.* [ME f. L f. *proloqui prolocut-* (as PRO-¹, *loqui* speak)]

pro·log·ize /prōlawgīz, –logīz/ *v.intr.* (also **pro·logu·ize**) write or speak a prologue. [med.L *prologizare* f. Gk *prologizō* speak prologue (as PROLOGUE)]

pro·logue /prōlawg, –log/ *n. & v.* (also **pro·log**) ● *n.* **1 a** a preliminary speech, poem, etc., esp. introducing a play (cf. EPILOGUE). **b** the actor speaking the prologue. **2** (usu. foll. by *to*) any act or event serving as an introduction. ● *v.tr.* (**pro·logues, pro·logued, pro·logu·ing**) introduce with or provide with a prologue. [ME *prolog* f. OF *prologue* f. L *prologus* f. Gk *prologos* (as PRO-¹, *logos* speech)]

pro·long /prəláwng, –lóng/ *v.tr.* **1** extend (an action, condition, etc.) in time or space. **2** lengthen the pronunciation of (a syllable, etc.). **3** (as **prolonged** *adj.*) lengthy, esp. tediously so. □□ **pro·lon·ga·tion** *n.* **pro·longed·ly** /–idli/ *adv.* **pro·long·er** *n.* [ME f. OF *prolonger* f. LL *prolongare* (as PRO-¹, *longus* long)]

pro·lu·sion /prəlṓzhən/ *n. formal* **1** a preliminary essay or article. **2** a first attempt. □□ **pro·lu·so·ry** /–lṓsəree, –zə–/ *adj.* [L *prolusio* f. *proludere prolus-* practice beforehand (as PRO-¹, *ludere lus-* play)]

prom /prom/ *n. colloq.* **1** a school or college formal dance. **2** *Brit.* = PROMENADE *n.* 4a. **3** *Brit.* = PROMENADE CONCERT. [abbr.]

prom·e·nade /prómənáyd, –náad/ *n. & v.* ● *n.* **1** a walk, or sometimes a ride or drive, taken esp. for display, social intercourse, etc. **2** a school or university ball or dance. **3** a march of dancers in country dancing, etc. **4 a** *Brit.* a paved public walk along the sea front at a resort. **b** any paved public walk. ● *v.* **1** *intr.* make a promenade. **2** *tr.* lead (a person, etc.) about a place esp. for display. **3** *tr.* make a promenade through (a place). [F f. *se promener* walk, refl. of *promener* take for a walk]

prom·e·nade con·cert *n. Brit.* a concert at which the audience, or part of it, can stand, sit on the floor, or move about.

prom·e·nade deck *n.* an upper deck on a passenger ship where passengers may promenade.

prom·eth·a·zine /prōméthəzeen/ *n.* an antihistamine drug used to treat allergies, motion sickness, etc. [PROPYL + d*imethy*lamine + *phenothiaz*ine]

Pro·me·the·an /prəmeeetheeən/ *adj.* daring or inventive like Prometheus, who in Greek myth was punished for stealing fire from the gods and giving it to the human race along with other skills.

pro·me·thi·um /prəmeeetheeəm/ *n. Chem.* a radioactive metallic element of the lanthanide series occurring in nuclear waste material. ¶ Symb.: **Pm**. [*Prometheus*: see PROMETHEAN]

prom·i·nence /próminəns/ *n.* **1** the state of being prominent. **2** a prominent thing, esp. a jutting outcrop, mountain, etc. **3** *Astron.* a stream of incandescent gas projecting above the sun's chromosphere. [obs.F f. L *prominentia* jutting out (as PROMINENT)]

prom·i·nent /próminənt/ *adj.* **1** jutting out; projecting. **2** conspicuous. **3** distinguished; important. □□ **prom·i·nen·cy** *n.* **prom·i·nent·ly** *adv.* [L *prominēre* jut out: cf. EMINENT]

pro·mis·cu·ous /prəmiskyŏŏəs/ *adj.* **1 a** (of a person) having frequent and diverse sexual relationships, esp. transient ones. **b** (of sexual relationships) of this kind. **2** of mixed and indiscriminate composition or kinds; indiscriminate (*promiscuous hospitality*). **3** *colloq.* carelessly irregular; casual. □□ **prom·is·cu·i·ty** /prómiskyŏŏitee/ *n.* **pro·mis·cu·ous·ly** *adv.* **pro·mis·cu·ous·ness** *n.* [L *promiscuus* (as PRO-¹, *miscēre* mix)]

prom·ise /prómis/ *n. & v.* ● *n.* **1** an assurance that one will or will not undertake a certain action, behavior, etc. (*a promise of help*; *gave a promise to be generous*). **2** a sign or signs of future achievements, good results, etc. (*a writer of great promise*). ● *v.tr.* **1** (usu. foll. by *to* + infin., or *that* + clause; also *absol.*) make (a person) a promise, esp. to do, give, or procure (a thing) (*I promise you a fair hearing; they promise not to be late; promised that he would be there; cannot positively promise*). **2 a** afford expectations of (*the discussions promise future problems; promises to be a good cook*). **b** (foll. by *to* + infin.) seem likely to (*is promising to rain*). **3** *colloq.* assure; confirm (*I promise you, it will not be easy*). **4** (usu. in *passive*) esp. *archaic* betroth (*she is promised to another*). □ **promise oneself** look forward to (a pleasant time, etc.). **promise well** (or **ill**, etc.) hold out good (or bad, etc.) prospects. □□ **prom·is·ee** /–seé/ *n.* esp. *Law.* **prom·is·er** *n.* **prom·i·sor** *n.* esp. *Law.* [ME f. L *promissum* neut. past part. of *promittere* put forth, promise (as PRO-¹, *mittere* send)]

prom·ised land *n.* **1** *Bibl.* Canaan (Gen. 12:7, etc.). **2** any desired place, esp. heaven.

prom·is·ing /prómising/ *adj.* likely to turn out well; hopeful; full of promise (*a promising start*). □□ **prom·is·ing·ly** *adv.*

prom·is·so·ry /prómisawree/ *adj.* **1** conveying or implying a promise. **2** (often foll. by *of*) full of promise. [med.L *promissorius* f. *promissor* (as PROMISE)]

prom·is·so·ry note *n.* a signed document containing a written promise to pay a stated sum to a specified person or the bearer at a specified date or on demand.

pro·mo /prómō/ *n. & adj. colloq.* ● *n.* (*pl.* **·mos**) **1** publicity blurb or advertisement. **2** a trailer for a television program. ● *adj.* promotional. [abbr.]

prom·on·to·ry /próməntawree/ *n.* (*pl.* **·ries**) **1** a point of high land jutting out into the sea, etc.; a headland. **2** *Anat.* a prominence or protuberance in the body. [med.L *promontorium* alt. (after *mons montis* mountain) f. L *promunturium* (perh. f. PRO-¹, *mons*)]

pro·mote /prəmṓt/ *v.tr.* **1** (often foll. by *to*) advance or raise (a person) to a higher office, rank, grade, etc. (*was promoted to captain*). **2** help forward; encourage; support actively (a cause, process, desired result, etc.) (*promoted women's suffrage*). **3** publicize and sell (a product). **4** attempt to ensure the passing of (a legislative act). **5** *Chess* raise (a pawn) to the rank of queen, etc., when it reaches the opponent's side of the board. □□ **pro·mot·a·ble** *adj.* **pro·mot·a·bil·i·ty** *n.* **pro·mo·tion** /–mṓshən/ *n.* **pro·mo·tion·al** *adj.* **pro·mo·tive** *adj.* [ME f. L *promovēre promot-* (as PRO-¹, *movēre* move)]

pro·mot·er /prəmṓtər/ *n.* **1** a person who promotes. **2** a person who finances, organizes, etc., a sporting event, theatrical production, etc. **3** a person who promotes the formation of a company, project, etc. **4** *Chem.* an additive that increases the activity of a catalyst. [earlier *promotour* f. AF f. med.L *promotor* (as PROMOTE)]

prompt /prompt/ *adj., adv., v., & n.* ● *adj.* **1 a** acting with alacrity; ready. **b** made, done, etc., readily or at once (*a prompt reply*). **2 a** (of a payment) made quickly or immediately. **b** (of goods) for immediate delivery and payment. ● *adv.* punctually. ● *v.tr.* **1** (usu. foll. by *to*, or *to* + infin.) incite; urge (*prompted them to action*). **2 a** (also *absol.*) supply a forgotten word, sentence, etc., to (an actor, reciter, etc.). **b** assist (a hesitating speaker) with a suggestion. **3** give rise to; inspire (a feeling, thought, action, etc.). ● *n.* **1 a** an act of prompting. **b** a thing said to help the memory of an actor, etc. **c** = PROMPTER 2. **d** *Computing* an indication or sign on a computer screen to show that the system is waiting for input. **2** the time limit for the payment of an account, stated on a prompt note. □□ **prompt·ing** *n.* **promp·ti·tude** *n.* **prompt·ly** *adv.* **prompt·ness** *n.* [ME f. OF *prompt* or L *promptus* past part. of *promere prompt-* produce (as PRO-¹, *emere* take)]

prompt·er /prómptər/ *n.* **1** a person who prompts. **2** *Theatr.* a person seated out of sight of the audience who prompts the actors.

prompt side *n.* the side of the stage where the prompter sits, usu. to the actor's right in the US, or left in the UK.

prom·ul·gate /prómɔlgayt/ *v.tr.* **1** make known to the public; disseminate; promote (a cause, etc.). **2** proclaim (a decree, news, etc.).

□□ **prom•ul•ga•tion** /–gáyshən/ n. **prom•ul•ga•tor** n. [L promulgare (as PRO-¹, mulgēre milk, cause to come forth)]

pro•mulge /prōmúlj/ v.tr. archaic = PROMULGATE. [PROMULGATE]

pro•na•os /prōnáyos/ n. (pl. **pro•na•oi** /–náyoy/) Gk Antiq. the space in front of the body of a temple, enclosed by a portico and projecting side walls. [L f. Gk pronaos hall of a temple (as PRO-², NA-OS)]

pro•nate /prónayt/ v.tr. put (the hand, forearm, etc.) into a prone position (with the palm downwards) (cf. SUPINATE). □□ **pro•na•tion** /–náyshən/ n. [back-form. f. pronation (as PRONE)]

pro•na•tor /prōnáytər/ n. Anat. any muscle producing or assisting in pronation.

prone /prōn/ adj. **1 a** lying face downward (cf. SUPINE). **b** lying flat; prostrate. **c** having the front part downwards, esp. the palm of the hand. **2** (usu. foll. by to, or to + infin.) disposed or liable, esp. to a bad action, condition, etc. (is prone to bite his nails). **3** (usu. in comb.) more than usually likely to suffer (accident-prone). **4** archaic with a downward slope or direction. □□ **prone•ly** adv. **prone•ness** /prón--nis/ n. [ME f. L pronus f. pro forward]

prong /prong/ n. & v. ● n. each of two or more projecting pointed parts at the end of a fork, etc. ● v.tr. **1** pierce or stab with a fork. **2** turn up (soil) with a fork. □□ **pronged** adj. (also in comb.). [ME (also prang), perh. rel. to MLG prange pinching instrument]

pro•nom•i•nal /prōnóminəl/ adj. of, concerning, or being a pronoun. □□ **pro•nom•i•nal•ize** v.tr. **pro•nom•i•nal•ly** adv. [LL pronominalis f. L pronomen (as PRO-¹, nomen, nominis noun)]

pro•noun /pró nown/ n. a word used instead of and to indicate a noun already mentioned or known, esp. to avoid repetition (e.g., we, their, this, ourselves). [PRO-¹, + NOUN, after F pronom, L pronomen (as PRO-¹, nomen name)]

pro•nounce /prənówns/ v. **1** tr. (also absol.) utter or speak (words, sounds, etc.) in a certain way. **2** tr. **a** utter or deliver (a judgment, sentence, curse, etc.) formally or solemnly. **b** proclaim or announce officially (I pronounce you husband and wife). **3** tr. state or declare, as being one's opinion (the apples were pronounced excellent). **4** intr. (usu. foll. by on, for, against, in favor of) pass judgment; give one's opinion (pronounced for the defendant). □□ **pro•nounce•a•ble** /–nównsəbəl/ adj. **pro•nounce•ment** n. **pro•nounc•er** n. [ME f. OF pronuncier f. L pronuntiare (as PRO-¹, nuntiare announce f. nuntius messenger)]

pro•nounced /prənównst/ adj. **1** (of a word, sound, etc.) uttered. **2** strongly marked; decided (a pronounced flavor; a pronounced limp). □□ **pro•nounc•ed•ly** /–nównsidlee/ adv.

pron•to /próntō/ adv. colloq. promptly; quickly. [Sp. f. L (as PROMPT)]

pro•nun•ci•a•tion /prənúnseeáyshən/ n. **1** the way in which a word is pronounced, esp. with reference to a standard. **2** the act or an instance of pronouncing. **3** a person's way of pronouncing words, etc. [ME f. OF prononciation or L pronuntiatio (as PRONOUNCE)]

proof /proof/ n., adj., & v. ● n. **1** facts, evidence, argument, etc., establishing or helping to establish a fact (proof of their honesty; no proof that he was there). **2** Law the spoken or written evidence in a trial. **3** a demonstration or act of proving (not capable of proof; in proof of my assertion). **4** a test or trial (put them to the proof; the proof of the pudding is in the eating). **5** the standard of strength of distilled alcoholic spirits. **6** Printing a trial impression taken from type or film, used for making corrections before final printing. **7** the stages in the resolution of a mathematical or philosophical problem. **8** each of a limited number of impressions from an engraved plate before the ordinary issue is printed and usu. (in full **proof before letters**) before an inscription or signature is added. **9** a photographic print made for selection, etc. **10** a newly issued coin struck from a polished die esp. for collectors, etc. ● adj. **1** impervious to penetration, ill effects, etc. (proof against the harshest weather). **2** (in comb.) able to withstand damage or destruction by a specified agent (soundproof; childproof). **3** being of proof alcoholic strength. **4** (of armor) of tried strength. ● v.tr. **1** proofread **2** make (something) proof, esp. make (fabric) waterproof. **3** make a proof of (a printed work, engraving, etc.). □□ **proof•less** adj. [ME prōf prōve, earlier prēf, etc., f. OF proeve, prueve f. LL proba f. L probare (see PROVE): adj. and sometimes v. formed app. by ellipsis f. phr. of proof = proved to be impenetrable]

proof-of-pur•chase n. a sales receipt, product label, etc., that serves as proof that a product has been purchased.

proof pos•i•tive n. absolutely certain proof.

proof•read /proofreed/ v.tr. (past and past part. **•read** /–red/) read (esp. printer's proofs) and mark any errors. □□ **proof•read•er** n. **proof•read•ing** n.

proof sheet n. a sheet of printer's proof.

proof spir•it n. a mixture of alcohol and water having proof strength.

prop¹ /prop/ n. & v. ● n. **1** a rigid support, esp. one not an integral part of the thing supported. **2** a person who supplies support, assistance, comfort, etc. **3** Rugby a forward at either end of the front row of a scrum. ● v.tr. (**propped, prop•ping**) (often foll. by against, up, etc.) support with or as if with a prop (propped him against the wall; propped it up with a brick). [ME prob. f. MDu. proppe: cf. MLG, MDu. proppen (v.)]

A **pronoun** is a word that takes the place of a noun. Our language would be cumbersome without pronouns. You could say, "Mrs. Smith asked John to be careful with Mrs. Smith's car when John borrowed the car to take John's date home." But it is easier to say, "Mrs. Smith asked John to be careful with her car when he borrowed it to take his date home." The noun that is replaced or referred to by the pronoun is called the antecedent. Every pronoun must have an antecedent, either stated or understood. In our example, Mrs. Smith, John, and car are antecedents, and the pronouns her, he, his, and it relieve you of the necessity of repeating the nouns. There are five kinds of pronouns: personal, relative, interrogative, demonstrative (definite), and indefinite. **Personal pronouns** stand for the name of a person, a place, or a thing. English has seven personal pronouns: I, you, he, she, it, we, and they. All seven are nominative (they can be used as the subject in a sentence or clause); they "do" the action. Any one will take the place of a noun in the sentence: ...saw Mary. Each of the seven personal pronouns has a form in which it can be used as an object, whether direct or indirect: me, you, him, her, it, us, and them. They receive some kind of action—some action happens "to" them. Any one will take the place of a noun in the sentence: Mary saw.... In speaking and writing, people often misuse personal pronouns in sentences with forms of the verb to be (is, are, am, was, and were). After such verbs, the nominative of the personal pronoun should be used: It is I. Choosing the right pronoun to follow a preposition—such as to, for, at, or between—can be troublesome, too. Prepositions call for the object form of the pronoun: she talked to Mary and me (not Mary and I). If we add -self or -selves to a personal pronoun, it becomes a compound form: myself, yourself, herself, itself, ourselves, themselves. This form may be **intensive** (giving emphasis) or **reflexive** (expressing action turned back on the subject). Do not use the compound form when you should use a simple personal pronoun. It is wrong to say my brother and **myself** are going; say instead my brother and **I** are going. Instead of give the book to **myself**, say give the book to **me**. Use compound pronouns in constructions such as **I myself** am going (intensive) and he shaves **himself** (reflexive). **Relative pronouns** serve a double purpose. First, they connect two clauses (groups of words containing a subject and a verb): she did not buy the same book **that** he did. Second, they relate back to a noun or a pronoun in a preceding clause: she went with the boy **who** lives on Oak Street. Words frequently used as relative pronouns are that, what, which, who, whom, and whose. **Compound relative pronouns** in common use are whatever, whichever, and whoever. **Interrogative pronouns**—what, which, and who—are used to ask questions. They ask the identity, the nature, or the possessor of whatever is in question: **Who** was there? **Which** of the books is yours? **Demonstrative** (or **Definite**) **Pronouns.** That, these, this, and those answer the question "which?" by pointing out a particular person or thing: **that** is all wrong; **this** is the one I want; **those** are too expensive; **these** are just perfect. **Indefinite pronouns** also answer the question "which?" But in so doing, they do not refer to definite persons or things: **somebody** took my pencil; **neither** will do the job. Other indefinite pronouns include both, each, many, one, and other. Like demonstrative pronouns, many indefinite pronouns are adjectives: **both** boys were absent; **neither** book is mine.

---

prop² /prop/ n. Theatr. colloq. **1** = PROPERTY 3. **2** (in pl.) a property man or mistress. [abbr.]

prop³ /prop/ n. colloq. an aircraft propeller. [abbr.]

prop. abbr. **1** proper; properly. **2** property. **3** proprietary. **4** proprietor. **5** proposition.

pro•pae•deu•tic /própidōótik, –dyōó–/ adj. & n. ● adj. serving as an introduction to higher study; introductory. ● n. (esp. in pl.) preliminary learning; a propaedeutic subject, study, etc. □□ **pro•pae•deu•ti•cal** adj. [PRO-² + Gk paideutikos of teaching, after Gk propaideuō teach beforehand]

prop•a•gan•da /própəgándə/ n. **1 a** an organized program of publicity, selected information, etc., used to propagate a doctrine, practice, etc. **b** usu. derog. the information, doctrines, etc., propagated in this way. **2** (**Propaganda**) RC Ch. a committee of cardinals responsible for foreign missions. [It. f. mod.L congregatio de propaganda fide congregation for propagation of the faith]

prop•a•gan•dist /própəgándist/ n. a member or agent of a propaganda organization; a person who spreads propaganda. □□ **prop•a•gan•dism** n. **prop•a•gan•dis•tic** adj. **prop•a•gan•dis•ti•cal•ly** adv. **prop•a•gan•dize** v.intr. & tr.

prop•a•gate /própəgayt/ **1** tr. **a** breed specimens of (a plant, animal, etc.) by natural processes from the parent stock. **b** (refl. or absol.) (of a plant, animal, etc.) reproduce itself. **2 a** tr. disseminate; spread (a statement, belief, theory, etc.). **b** *intr.* grow more widespread or numerous; spread. **3** *tr.* hand down (a quality, etc.) from one generation to another. **4** *tr.* extend the operation of; transmit (a vibration, earthquake, etc.). □□ **prop•a•ga•tion** /–gáyshən/ *n.* **prop•a•ga•tive** *adj.* [L *propagare propagat-* multiply plants from layers, f. *propago* (as PRO-¹, *pangere* fix, layer)]

prop•a•ga•tor /própəgaytər/ *n.* **1** a person or thing that propagates. **2** a small box that can be heated, used for germinating seeds or raising seedlings.

pro•pane /própayn/ *n.* a gaseous hydrocarbon of the alkane series used as bottled fuel. ¶ Chem. formula: C_3H_8. [PROPIONIC (ACID) + –ANE¹]

pro•pa•no•ic ac•id /própənóik/ *n. Chem.* = PROPIONIC ACID. [PROPANE + –IC]

pro•pa•none /própənōn/ *n. Chem. Brit.* = ACETONE. [PROPANE + –ONE]

pro•pel /prəpél/ *v.tr.* (**pro•pelled, pro•pel•ling**) **1** drive or push forward. **2** urge on; encourage. [ME, = expel, f. L *propellere* (as PRO-¹, *pellere puls-* drive)]

pro•pel•lant /prəpélənt/ *n. & adj.* (also **pro•pel•lent**) ● *n.* **1** a thing that propels. **2** an explosive that fires bullets, etc., from a firearm. **3** a substance used as a reagent in a rocket engine, etc., to provide thrust. ● *adj.* propelling; capable of driving or pushing forward.

pro•pel•ler /prəpélər/ *n.* **1** a person or thing that propels. **2** a revolving shaft with blades, esp. for propelling a ship or aircraft (cf. *screw propeller,* see SCREW 6).

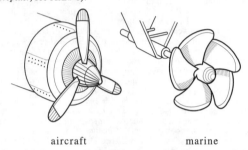

aircraft   marine

propeller 2

pro•pel•ler shaft *n.* a shaft transmitting power from an engine to a propeller or to the driven wheels of a motor vehicle.

pro•pel•ler tur•bine *n.* a turbo-propeller.

pro•pene /própeen/ *n. Chem.* = PROPYLENE. [PROPANE + ALKENE]

pro•pen•si•ty /prəpénsitee/ *n.* (*pl.* **•ties**) an inclination or tendency (*has a propensity for wandering*). [*propense* f. L *propensus* inclined, past part. of *propendēre* (as PRO-¹, *pendēre* hang)]

prop•er /própər/ *adj., adv., & n.* ● *adj.* **1 a** accurate; correct (*in the proper sense of the word; gave him the proper amount*). **b** fit; suitable; right (*at the proper time; do it the proper way*). **2** decent; respectable, esp. excessively so (*not quite proper*). **3** (usu. foll. by *to*) belonging or relating exclusively or distinctively; particular; special (*with the respect proper to them*). **4** (usu. placed after noun) strictly so called; real; genuine (*this is the crypt, not the cathedral proper*). **5** esp. *Brit. colloq.* thorough; complete (*had a proper row about it*). **6** (usu. placed after noun) *Heraldry* in the natural, not conventional, colors (*a peacock proper*). **7** *dial.* (of a person) handsome; comely. **8** (usu. with possessive pronoun) own (*with my proper eyes*). ● *adv. Brit. dial.* or *colloq.* **1** completely; very (*felt proper daft*). **2** (with reference to speech) in a genteel manner (*learn to talk proper*). ● *n. Eccl.* the part of a service that varies with the season or feast. □□ **prop•er•ness** *n.* [ME f. OF *propre* f. L *proprius* one's own, special]

prop•er frac•tion *n.* a fraction that is less than unity, with the numerator less than the denominator.

prop•er•ly /própərlee/ *adv.* **1** fittingly; suitably (*do it properly*). **2** accurately; correctly (*properly speaking*). **3** rightly (*he very properly refused*). **4** with decency; respectably (*behave properly*). **5** esp. *Brit. colloq.* thoroughly (*they were properly ashamed*).

prop•er mo•tion *n. Astron.* the part of the apparent motion of a fixed star, etc., that is due to its actual movement in space relative to the sun.

prop•er noun *n.* (also **prop•er name**) *Gram.* a name used for an individual person, place, animal, country, title, etc., and spelled with a capital letter, e.g., Jane, London, Everest.

prop•er psalms *n.pl.* (also **prop•er les•sons,** etc.) *Eccl.* psalms or lessons, etc., appointed for a particular day.

prop•er•tied /própərteed/ *adj.* having property, esp. land.

prop•er•ty /própərtee/ *n.* (*pl.* **•ties**) **1 a** something owned; a possession, esp. a house, land, etc. **b** *Law* the right to possession, use, etc. **c** possessions collectively, esp. real estate (*has money in property*). **2** an attribute, quality, or characteristic (*has the property of dissolving grease*). **3** a movable object used on a theater stage, in a mov-

ie, etc. **4** *Logic* a quality common to a whole class but not necessary to distinguish it from others. [ME through AF f. OF *propriété* f. L *proprietas –tatis* (as PROPER)]

prop•er•ty man *n.* (also **prop•er•ty mis•tress**) a man (or woman) in charge of theatrical properties.

prop•er•ty tax *n.* a tax levied directly on property.

pro•phase /prófayz/ *n. Biol.* the phase in cell division in which chromosomes contract and each becomes visible as two chromatids. [PRO-² + PHASE]

proph•e•cy /pró fisee/ *n.* (*pl.* **•cies**) **1 a** a prophetic utterance, esp. Biblical. **b** a prediction of future events (*a prophecy of massive inflation*). **2** the faculty, function, or practice of prophesying (*the gift of prophecy*). [ME f. OF *profecie* f. LL *prophetia* f. Gk *proph ēteia* (as PROPHET)]

▶Note that **prophesy** is the verb, **prophecy** the noun.

proph•e•sy /prófisī/ *v.* (**•sies, •sied**) **1** *tr.* (usu. foll. by *that, who,* etc.) foretell (an event, etc.). **2** *intr.* speak as a prophet; foretell future events. **3** *intr. archaic* expound the Scriptures. □□ **proph•e•si•er** /–sīər/ *n.* [ME f. OF *profecier* (as PROPHECY)]

proph•et /prófit/ *n.* (*fem.* **proph•et•ess** /–tis/) **1** a teacher or interpreter of the supposed will of God, esp. any of the Old Testament or Hebrew prophets. **2 a** a person who foretells events. **b** a person who advocates and speaks innovatively for a cause (*a prophet of the new order*). **3** (**the Prophet**) **a** muhammad. **b** Joseph Smith, founder of the Mormons, or one of his successors. **c** (in *pl.*) the prophetic writings of the Old Testament. **4** *Brit. colloq.* a tipster. □□ **proph•et•hood** *n.* **proph•et•ism** *n.* **proph•et•ship** *n.* [ME f. OF *prophete* f. L *propheta, prophetes* f. Gk *prophētēs* spokesman (as PRO-², *phētēs* speaker f. *phēmi* speak)]

pro•phet•ic /prəfétik/ *adj.* **1** (often foll. by *of*) containing a prediction; predicting. **2** of or concerning a prophet. □□ **pro•phet•i•cal** *adj.* **proph•et•i•cal•ly** *adv.* **pro•phet•i•cism** /–sizəm/ *n.* [F *prophétique* or LL *propheticus* f. Gk *prophētikos* (as PROPHET)]

pro•phy•lac•tic /prófiláktik, próf–/ *adj. & n.* ● *adj.* tending to prevent disease. ● *n.* **1** a preventive medicine or course of action. **2** a condom. [F *prophylactique* f. Gk *prophulaktikos* f. *prophulassō* (as PRO-², *phulassō* guard)]

pro•phy•lax•is /prófiláksis, próf–/ *n.* (*pl.* **pro•phy•lax•es** /–seez/) preventive treatment against disease. [mod.L f. PRO-² + Gk *phulaxis* act of guarding]

pro•pin•qui•ty /prəpíngkwitee/ *n.* **1** nearness in space; proximity. **2** close kinship. **3** similarity. [ME f. OF *propinquité* or L *propinquitas* f. *propinquus* near f. *prope* near to]

pro•pi•on•ic ac•id /própeeónik/ *n.* a colorless sharp-smelling liquid carboxylic acid used for inhibiting the growth of mold in bread. ¶ Chem. formula: C_2H_5COOH. Also called **propanoic acid.** □□ **pro•pi•o•nate** /própeeənayt/ *n.* [F *propionique,* formed as PRO-² + Gk *piōn* fat, as being the first in the series of 'true' fatty acids]

pro•pi•ti•ate /prōpísheeayt/ *v.tr.* appease (an offended person, etc.). □□ **pro•pi•ti•a•tor** *n.* [L *propitiare* (as PROPITIOUS)]

pro•pi•ti•a•tion /prōpísheeáyshən/ *n.* **1** appeasement. **2** *Bibl.* atonement, esp. Christ's. **3** *archaic* a gift, etc., meant to propitiate. [ME f. LL *propitiatio* (as PROPITIATE)]

pro•pi•ti•a•to•ry /prōpísheeətawree,–píshə–/ *adj.* serving or intended to propitiate (*a propitiatory smile*). □□ **pro•pi•ti•a•to•ri•ly** *adv.* [ME f. LL *propitiatorius* (as PROPITIATE)]

pro•pi•tious /prəpíshəs/ *adj.* **1** (of an omen, etc.) favorable. **2** (often foll. by *for, to*) (of the weather, an occasion, etc.) suitable. **3** well-disposed (*the fates were propitious*). □□ **pro•pi•tious•ly** *adv.* **pro•pi•tious•ness** *n.* [ME f. OF *propicieus* or L *propitius*]

prop•jet /própjet/ *n.* a jet airplane powered by turboprops.

prop•o•lis /própəlis/ *n.* a red or brown resinous substance collected by bees from buds for use in constructing hives. [L f. Gk *propolis* suburb, bee glue, f. PRO-² + *polis* city]

pro•po•nent /prəpōnənt/ *n. & adj.* ● *n.* a person advocating a motion, theory, or proposal. ● *adj.* proposing or advocating a theory, etc. [L *proponere* (as PROPOUND)]

pro•por•tion /prəpáwrshən/ *n. & v.* ● *n.* **1 a** a comparative part or share (*a large proportion of the profits*). **b** a comparative ratio (*the proportion of births to deaths*). **2** the correct or pleasing relation of things or parts of a thing (*the house has fine proportions; exaggerated out of all proportion*). **3** (in *pl.*) dimensions; size (*large proportions*). **4** *Math.* **a** an equality of ratios between two pairs of quantities, e.g., 3:5 and 9:15. **b** a set of such quantities. **c** *Math.* = RULE OF THREE; see also DIRECT PROPORTION, INVERSE PROPORTION. ● *v.tr.* (usu. foll. by *to*) make (a thing, etc.) proportionate (*must proportion the punishment to the crime*). □ **in proportion 1** by the same factor. **2** without exaggerating (importance, etc.) (*must get the facts in proportion*). □□ **pro•por•tioned** *adj.* (also in *comb.*). **pro•por•tion•less** *adj.* **pro•por•tion•ment** *n.* [ME f. OF *proportion* or L *proportio* (as PRO-¹, PORTION)]

▶Except in certain long-established phrases, such as *proportional* representation, the derivatives *proportional* and *proportionate* may be used interchangeably.

pro·por·tion·a·ble /prəpáwrshənəbəl/ *adj.* = PROPORTIONAL. □□ **pro·por·tion·a·bly** *adv.*

pro·por·tion·al /prəpáwrshənəl/ *adj. & n.* ● *adj.* in due proportion; comparable (*a proportional increase in the expense; resentment proportional to his injuries*). ● *n. Math.* each of the terms of a proportion. □□ **pro·por·tion·al·i·ty** /–nálitee/ *n.* **pro·por·tion·al·ly** *adv.*

pro·por·tion·al rep·re·sen·ta·tion *n.* an electoral system in which all parties gain seats in proportion to the number of votes cast for them.

pro·por·tion·ate /prəpáwrshənət/ *adj.* = PROPORTIONAL. □□ **pro·por·tion·ate·ly** *adv.*

pro·pos·al /prəpózəl/ *n.* **1 a** the act or an instance of proposing something. **b** a course of action, etc., so proposed (*the proposal was never carried out*). **2** an offer of marriage.

pro·pose /prəpóz/ *v.* **1** *tr.* (also *absol.*) put forward for consideration or as a plan. **2** *tr.* (usu. foll. by *to* + infin., or verbal noun) intend; purpose (*propose to open a restaurant*). **3** *intr.* (usu. foll. by *to*) make an offer of marriage. **4** *tr.* nominate (a person) as a member of a society, for an office, etc. **5** *tr.* offer (a person's health, a person, etc.) as a subject for a toast. □□ **pro·pos·er** *n.* [ME f. OF *proposer* f. L *proponere* (as PROPOUND)]

prop·o·si·tion /própəzíshən/ *n. & v.* ● *n.* **1** a statement or assertion. **2** a scheme proposed; a proposal. **3** *Logic* a statement consisting of subject and predicate that is subject to proof or disproof. **4** *colloq.* a problem, opponent, prospect, etc., that is to be dealt with (*a difficult proposition*). **5** *Math.* a formal statement of a theorem or problem, often including the demonstration. **6 a** an enterprise, etc., with regard to its likelihood of commercial, etc., success. **b** a person regarded similarly. **7** *colloq.* a sexual proposal. ● *v.tr. colloq.* make a proposal (esp. of sexual intercourse) to. □ **not a proposition** unlikely to succeed. □□ **prop·o·si·tion·al** *adj.* [ME f. OF *proposition* or L *propositio* (as PROPOUND)]

pro·pound /prəpównd/ *v.tr.* **1** offer for consideration; propose. **2** esp. *Brit. Law* produce (a will, etc.) before the proper authority so as to establish its legality. □□ **pro·pound·er** *n.* [earlier *propoune*, *propone* f. L *proponere* (as PRO-¹, *ponere posit-* place): cf. *compound*, *expound*]

pro·pri·e·tar·y /prəpríəteree/ *adj.* **1 a** of, holding, or concerning property (*the proprietary classes*). **b** of or relating to a proprietor (*proprietary rights*). **2** held in private ownership. [LL *proprietarius* (as PROPERTY)]

pro·pri·e·tar·y med·i·cine *n.* any of several drugs, medicines, etc., produced by private companies under brand names.

pro·pri·e·tar·y name *n.* (also **pro·pri·e·tar·y term**) a name of a product, etc., registered by its owner as a trademark and not usable by another without permission.

pro·pri·e·tor /prəpríətər/ *n.* (*fem.* **pro·pri·e·tress**) **1** a holder of property. **2** the owner of a business, etc., esp. of a hotel. □□ **pro·pri·e·to·ri·al** /–táwreeəl/ *adj.* **pro·pri·e·to·ri·al·ly** /–táwreeəlee/ *adv.* **pro·pri·e·tor·ship** *n.*

pro·pri·e·ty /prəprí-itee/ *n.* (*pl.* **·ties**) **1** fitness; rightness (*doubt the propriety of refusing him*). **2** correctness of behavior or morals (*highest standards of propriety*). **3** (in *pl.*) the details or rules of correct conduct (*must observe the proprieties*). [ME, = ownership, peculiarity f. OF *propriété* PROPERTY]

pro·pri·o·cep·tive /própreeəséptiv/ *adj.* relating to stimuli produced and perceived within an organism, esp. relating to the position and movement of the body. [L *proprius* own + RECEPTIVE]

prop·to·sis /proptósis/ *n. Med.* protrusion or displacement, esp. of an eye. [LL f. Gk *proptōsis* (as PRO-², *piptō* fall)]

pro·pul·sion /prəpúlshən/ *n.* **1** the act or an instance of driving or pushing forward. **2** an impelling influence. □□ **pro·pul·sive** /–púlsiv/ *adj.* [med.L *propulsio* f. L *propellere* (as PROPEL)]

pro·pyl /própil/ *n. Chem.* the univalent radical of propane. ¶ Chem. formula: C_3H_7. [PROPIONIC (ACID) + -YL]

prop·y·la *pl.* of PROPYLON.

prop·y·lae·um /própilee·əm, pró-/ *n.* (*pl.* **prop·y·lae·a** /–lee·ə/) **1** the entrance to a temple. **2 (the Propylaeum)** the entrance to the Acropolis at Athens. [L f. Gk *propulaion* (as PRO-², *pulē* gate)]

pro·pyl·ene /própəleen/ *n. Chem.* a gaseous hydrocarbon of the alkene series used in the manufacture of chemicals. ¶ Chem. formula: C_3H_6.

prop·y·lon /própəlon, pró-/ *n.* (*pl.* **prop·y·lons** or **prop·y·la** /–lə/) = PROPYLAEUM. [L f. Gk *propulon* (as PRO-², *pulē* gate)]

pro ra·ta /prō ráytə, raátə/ *adj. & adv.* ● *adj.* proportional. ● *adv.* proportionally. [L, = according to the rate]

pro·rate /próráyt/ *v.tr.* allocate or distribute pro rata. □□ **pro·ra·tion** *n.*

pro·rogue /prōróg/ *v.* (**pro·rogues**, **pro·rogued**, **pro·rogu·ing**) **1** *tr.* discontinue the meetings of (a parliament, etc.) without dissolving it. **2** *intr.* (of a parliament, etc.) be prorogued. □□ **pro·ro·ga·tion** /prórəgáyshən/ *n.* [ME *proroge* f. OF *proroger*, –*guer* f. L *prorogare* prolong (as PRO-¹, *rogare* ask)]

pros- /pros/ *prefix* **1** to; toward. **2** in addition. [Gk f. *pros* (prep.)]

---

pro·sa·ic /prōzáyik/ *adj.* **1** like prose; lacking poetic beauty. **2** unromantic; dull; commonplace (*took a prosaic view of life*). □□ **pro·sa·i·cal·ly** *adv.* **pro·sa·ic·ness** *n.* [F *prosaïque* or LL *prosaicus* (as PROSE)]

pro·sa·ist /prózayist/ *n.* **1** a prose writer. **2** a prosaic person. □□ **pro·sa·ism** *n.* [F *prosaïste* f. L *prosa* PROSE]

pros and cons *n.* reasons or considerations for and against a proposition, etc.

pro·sce·ni·um /prəseéneeəm/ *n.* (*pl.* **pro·sce·ni·ums** or **pro·sce·ni·a** /–neeə/) **1** the part of the stage in front of the drop or curtain, usu. with the enclosing arch. **2** the stage of an ancient theater. [L f. Gk *proskēnion* (as PRO-², *skēnē* stage)]

pro·sciut·to /prōshoótō/ *n.* (*pl.* **·tos**) specially cured ham, usu. sliced thin and used as an hors d'oeuvre. [It.]

pro·scribe /prəskríb/ *v.tr.* **1** banish; exile (*proscribed from the club*). **2** put (a person) outside the protection of the law. **3** reject or denounce (a practice, etc.) as dangerous, etc. □□ **pro·scrip·tion** /–skrípshən/ *n.* **pro·scrip·tive** /–skríptiv/ *adj.* [L *proscribere* (as PRO-¹, *scribere script-* write)]

▶See note at PRESCRIBE.

SPELLING TIP proscribe

See note at PRESCRIBE.

---

prose /prōz/ *n. & v.* ● *n.* **1** the ordinary form of the written or spoken language (opp. POETRY, VERSE) (*Milton's prose works*). **2** a passage of prose, esp. for translation into a foreign language. **3** a tedious speech or conversation. **4** a plain matter-of-fact quality (*the prose of existence*). **5** *Eccl.* = SEQUENCE 8. ● *v.* **1** *intr.* (usu. foll. by *about*, *away*, etc.) talk tediously (*was prosing away about his dog*). **2** *tr.* turn (a poem, etc.) into prose. **3** *tr.* write prose. □□ **pros·er** *n.* [ME f. OF f. L *prosa* (*oratio*) straightforward (discourse), fem. of *prosus*, earlier *prorsus* direct]

pro·sec·tor /prōséktər/ *n.* a person who dissects dead bodies in preparation for an anatomical lecture, etc. [LL = anatomist, f. *prosecare prosect-* (as PRO-¹, *secare* cut), perh. after F *prosecteur*]

pros·e·cute /prósikyoot/ *v.tr.* **1** (also *absol.*) **a** institute legal proceedings against (a person). **b** institute a prosecution with reference to (a claim, crime, etc.) (*decided not to prosecute*). **2** follow up; pursue (an inquiry, studies, etc.). **3** carry on (a trade, pursuit, etc.). □□ **pros·e·cut·a·ble** *adj.* [ME f. L *prosequi prosecut-* (as PRO-¹, *sequi* follow)]

pros·e·cu·tion /prósikyóoshən/ *n.* **1 a** the institution and carrying on of a criminal charge in a court. **b** the carrying on of legal proceedings against a person. **c** the prosecuting party in a court case (*the prosecution denied this*). **2** the act or an instance of prosecuting (*met her in the prosecution of his hobby*). [OF *prosecution* or LL *prosecutio* (as PROSECUTE)]

pros·e·cu·tor /prósikyóotər/ *n.* (also **pros·e·cut·ing at·tor·ney**) a person who prosecutes, esp. in a criminal court. □□ **pros·e·cu·to·ri·al** /–táwreeəl/ *adj.*

prose i·dyll *n.* a short description in prose of a picturesque, esp. rustic, incident, character, etc.

pros·e·lyte /prósilit/ *n. & v.* ● *n.* **1** a person converted, esp. recently, from one opinion, creed, party, etc., to another. **2** a convert to Judaism. ● *v.tr.* = PROSELYTIZE. □□ **pros·e·lyt·ism** /–səlitizəm/ *n.* [ME f. LL *proselytus* f. Gk *prosēluthos* stranger, convert (as PROS-, stem *ēluth-* of *erkhomai* come)]

pros·e·lyt·ize /prósilitiz/ *v.tr.* (also *absol.*) convert (a person or people) from one belief, etc., to another, esp. habitually. □□ **pros·e·lyt·iz·er** *n.*

pros·en·chy·ma /proséngkimə/ *n.* a plant tissue of elongated cells with interpenetrating tapering ends, occurring esp. in vascular tissue. □□ **pros·en·chy·mal** *adj.* **pros·en·chym·a·tous** /–kímətəs/ *adj.* [Gk *pros* toward + *egkhuma* infusion, after *parenchyma*]

prose po·em *n.* (also **prose po·et·ry**) a piece of imaginative poetic writing in prose.

pro·si·fy /prózifi/ *v.* (**·fies**, **·fied**) **1** *tr.* turn into prose. **2** *tr.* make prosaic. **3** *intr.* write prose.

pro·sit /prózit/ *int.* an expression used in drinking a person's health. [G f. L, = may it benefit]

pros·o·dy /prósədee/ *n.* **1** the theory and practice of versification; the laws of meter. **2** the study of speech rhythms. □□ **pro·sod·ic** /prəsódik/ *adj.* **pros·o·dist** *n.* [ME f. L *prosodia* accent f. Gk *prosōidia* (as PROS-, ODE)]

PRONUNCIATION TIP prosody

Although this word closely resembles *prose* (pronounced "PROZE"), its first syllable correctly rhymes with the first syllable of *prospect*.

---

pros·o·pog·ra·phy /prósəpógrəfee/ *n.* (*pl.* **·phies**) **1** a description of a person's appearance, personality, social and family connections, career, etc. **2** the study of such descriptions, esp. in Roman history. □□ **pros·o·pog·ra·pher** *n.* **pros·o·po·graph·ic** /–pəgráfik/ *adj.* **pros·o·po·graph·i·cal** *adj.* [mod.L *prosopographia* f. Gk *prosōpon* face, person]

pros·o·po·poe·ia /prósəpəpéeə/ *n.* the rhetorical introduction of a pretended speaker or the personification of an abstract thing. [L f. Gk *prosōpopoiia* f. *prosōpon* person + *poieō* make]

pros·pect /próspekt/ *n. & v.* ● *n.* **1 a** (often in *pl.*) an expectation, esp. of success in a career, etc. (*his prospects were brilliant; offers a gloomy prospect; no prospect of success*). **b** something one has to look forward to (*don't relish the prospect of meeting him*). **2** an extensive view of landscape, etc. (*a striking prospect*). **3** a mental picture (*a new prospect in his mind*). **4 a** a place likely to yield mineral deposits. **b** a sample of ore for testing. **c** the resulting yield. **5** a possible or probable customer, subscriber, etc. ● *v.* **1** *intr.* (usu. foll. by *for*) **a** explore a region for gold, etc. **b** look out for or search for something. **2** *tr.* **a** explore (a region) for gold, etc. **b** work (a mine) experimentally. **c** (of a mine) promise (a specified yield). □ **in prospect 1** in sight; within view. **2** within the range of expectation, likely. **prospect well** (or **ill**, etc.) (of a mine) promise well (or ill, etc.). □□ **pros·pect·less** *adj.* **pros·pec·tor** *n.*

WORD HISTORY prospect

late Middle English (as a noun denoting the action of looking toward a distant object): from Latin *prospectus* 'view,' from *prospicere* 'look forward,' from *pro-* 'forward' + *specere* 'to look.' Early use, referring to a view or landscape, gave rise to the meaning 'mental picture' (mid-16th century), whence 'anticipated event.'

pro·spec·tive /prəspéktiv/ *adj.* **1** concerned with or applying to the future (*implies a prospective obligation*) (cf. RETROSPECTIVE). **2** some day to be; expected; future (*prospective bridegroom*). □□ **pro·spec·tive·ly** *adv.* **pro·spec·tive·ness** *n.* [obs. F *prospectif –ive* or LL *prospectivus* (as PROSPECTUS)]

pro·spec·tus /prəspéktəs/ *n.* a printed document advertising or describing a school, commercial enterprise, forthcoming book, etc. [L, = prospect f. *prospicere* (as PRO-¹, *specere* look)]

pros·per /próspər/ *v.* **1** *intr.* succeed; thrive (*nothing he touches prospers*). **2** *tr.* make successful (*Heaven prosper him*). [ME f. OF *prosperer* or L *prosperare* (as PROSPEROUS)]

pros·per·i·ty /prospéritee/ *n.* a state of being prosperous; wealth or success.

pros·per·ous /próspərəs/ *adj.* **1** successful; rich (*a prosperous merchant*). **2** flourishing; thriving (*a prosperous enterprise*). **3** auspicious (*a prosperous wind*). □□ **pros·per·ous·ly** *adv.* **pros·per·ous·ness** *n.* [ME f. obs. F *prospereus* f. L *prosper(us)*]

pros·ta·glan·din /próstəglándin/ *n.* any of a group of hormonelike substances causing contraction of the muscles in mammalian (esp. uterine) tissues, etc. [G f. PROSTATE + GLAND¹ + –IN]

pros·tate /próstayt/ *n.* (in full **prostate gland**) a gland surrounding the neck of the bladder in male mammals and releasing a fluid forming part of the semen. □□ **pros·tat·ic** /–státik/ *adj.* [F f. mod.L *prosta·ta* f. Gk *prostatēs* the one that stands before (as PRO-², *statos* standing)]

pros·the·sis /prósthéesis/ *n.* (*pl.* **pros·the·ses** /–seez/) **1** an artificial part supplied to replace a missing body part, e.g., a false breast, leg, tooth, etc. **2** *Gram.* the addition of a letter or syllable at the beginning of a word, e.g., *be–* in *beloved.* □□ **pros·thet·ic** /–thétik/ *adj.* **pros·thet·i·cal·ly** *adv.* [LL f. Gk *prosthesis* f. *prostithēmi* (as PROS-, *tithēmi* place)]

pros·thet·ics /prosthétiks/ *n.pl.* (usu. treated as *sing.*) the branch of medicine or dentistry supplying and fitting prostheses.

pros·ti·tute /próstitoot, –tyoot/ *n. & v.* ● *n.* **1 a** a woman who engages in sexual activity for payment. **b** (usu. **male prostitute**) a man or boy who engages in sexual activity, esp. with homosexual men, for payment. **2** a person who debases himself or herself for personal gain. ● *v. tr.* **1** (esp. *refl.*) make a prostitute of (esp. oneself). **2 a** misuse (one's talents, skills, etc.) for money. **b** offer (oneself, one's honor, etc.) for unworthy ends, esp. for money. □□ **pros·ti·tu·tion** /–tóoshən/ *n.* **pros·ti·tu·tor** *n.* [L *prostituere prostitut-* offer for sale (as PRO-¹, *statuere* set up, place)]

pros·trate *adj. & v.* ● *adj.* **1 a** lying face downwards, esp. in submission. **b** lying horizontally. **2** overcome, esp. by grief, exhaustion, etc. (*prostrate with self-pity*). **3** *Bot.* growing along the ground. ● *v. tr.* **1** lay (a person, etc.) flat on the ground. **2** (*refl.*) throw (oneself) down in submission. **3** (of fatigue, illness, etc.) overcome; reduce to extreme physical weakness. □□ **pros·tra·tion** /prostráyshən/ *n.* [ME f. L *prostratus* past part. of *prosternere* (as PRO-¹, *sternere strat-* lay flat)]

pros·y /prózee/ *adj.* (**pros·i·er, pros·i·est**) tedious; commonplace; dull (*prosy talk*). □□ **pros·i·ly** *adv.* **pros·i·ness** *n.*

Prot. *abbr.* Protestant.

prot·ac·tin·i·um /prótaktíneeəm/ *n.* *Chem.* a radioactive metallic element whose chief isotope yields actinium by decay. ¶ Symb.: **Pa**. [G (as PROTO-, ACTINIUM)]

pro·tag·o·nist /prōtágənist/ *n.* **1** the chief person in a drama, story, etc. **2** the leading person in a contest, etc.; a principal performer. **3** (usu. foll. by *of, for*) *disp.* an advocate or champion of a cause, course of action, etc. (*a protagonist of women's rights*). [Gk *prōtagōnistēs* (as PROTO-, *agō nistēs* actor)]

▶The original meaning of this word is 'chief or leading person,' e.g., *The novelist's first challenge is to create a protagonist the reader can identify with.* However, it is also used, usually with *of* or *for*, to mean 'a supporter or champion of a cause, etc.,' e.g., *Protagonists of peace rallied at the Capitol.*

prot·a·mine /prótəmeen, protámin/ *n.* any of a group of proteins found in association with chromosomal DNA in the sperm of birds and fish. [PROTO- + AMINE]

prot·a·sis /prótəsis/ *n.* (*pl.* **prot·a·ses** /–seez/) the clause expressing the condition in a conditional sentence. □□ **pro·tat·ic** /prōtátik/ *adj.* [L, f. Gk *protasis* proposition (as PRO-², *teinō* stretch)]

pro·te·a /próteeə/ *n.* any shrub of the genus *Protea* native to S. Africa, with conelike flower heads. [mod.L f. PROTEUS, with ref. to the many species]

pro·te·an /próteeən, –teéən/ *adj.* **1** variable; taking many forms. **2** (of an artist, writer, etc.) versatile. [after *Proteus*: see PROTEUS]

pro·te·ase /próteeays/ *n.* any enzyme able to hydrolyze proteins and peptides by proteolysis. [PROTEIN + –ASE]

pro·tect /prətékt/ *v. tr.* **1** (often foll. by *from, against*) keep (a person, thing, etc.) safe; defend; guard (*goggles protected her eyes from dust; guards protected the military base*). **2** *Econ.* shield (domestic industry) from competition by imposing import duties on foreign goods. **3** cover; provide funds to meet (a bill, bank draft, etc.). [L *protegere protect-* (as PRO-¹, *tegere* cover)]

pro·tec·tion /prətékshən/ *n.* **1 a** the act or an instance of protecting. **b** the state of being protected; defense (*affords protection against the weather*). **c** a thing, person, or animal that provides protection (*bought a dog as protection*). **2** (also **pro·tec·tion·ism**) *Econ.* the theory or practice of protecting domestic industries. **3** *colloq.* **a** immunity from molestation obtained by payment to organized criminals, etc., under threat of violence. **b** (in full **protection money**) payment, as bribes, made to police, etc., for overlooking criminal activities. **c** (in full **protection money**) the money so paid, esp. on a regular basis. **4** = SAFE-CONDUCT. **5** *archaic* the keeping of a woman as a mistress. □□ **pro·tec·tion·ist** *n.* [ME f. OF *protection* or LL *protectio* (as PROTECT)]

pro·tec·tive /prətéktiv/ *adj. & n.* ● *adj.* **1** protecting; intended or intending to protect. **2** (of a person) tending to protect in a possessive way. ● *n. Brit.* something that protects, esp. a condom. □□ **pro·tec·tive·ly** *adv.* **pro·tec·tive·ness** *n.*

pro·tec·tive col·or·ing *n.* coloring disguising or camouflaging a plant or animal.

pro·tec·tive cus·to·dy *n.* the detention of a person for his or her own protection.

pro·tec·tor /prətéktər/ *n.* (*fem.* **pro·tec·tress** /–tris/) **1 a** a person who protects. **b** a guardian or patron. **2** *hist.* a regent in charge of a kingdom during the minority, absence, etc., of the sovereign. **3** (often in *comb.*) a thing or device that protects. **4** (**Protector**) (in full **Lord Protector of the Commonwealth**) *Brit. hist.* the title of Oliver Cromwell 1653–58 and his son Richard Cromwell 1658–59. □□ **pro·tec·tor·al** *adj.* **pro·tec·tor·ship** *n.* [ME f. OF *protecteur* f. LL *protector* (as PROTECT)]

pro·tec·tor·ate /prətéktərət/ *n.* **1 a** a nation that is controlled and protected by another. **b** such a relation of one nation to another. **2** *hist.* **a** the office of the protector of a kingdom or nation. **b** the period of this, esp. in England under the Cromwells 1653–59.

pro·té·gé /prótizhay, protizháy/ *n.* (**pro·té·gée** *pronunc.* same) a person under the protection, patronage, tutelage, etc., of another. [F, past part. of *protéger* f. L *protegere* PROTECT]

pro·tein /próteen/ *n.* any of a group of organic compounds composed of one or more chains of amino acids and forming an essential part of all living organisms. □□ **pro·tein·a·ceous** /–teenáyshəs/ *adj.* **pro·tein·ic** /–teenik/ *adj.* **pro·tei·nous** /–teenəs/ *adj.* [F *protéine,* G *Protein* f. Gk *prōteios* primary]

pro tem /prō tém/ *adj. & adv. colloq.* = PRO TEMPORE. [abbr.]

pro tem·po·re /prō témpəree/ *adj. & adv.* for the time being. [L]

pro·te·ol·y·sis /próteeólisis/ *n.* the splitting of proteins or peptides by the action of enzymes esp. during the process of digestion. □□ **pro·te·o·lyt·ic** /–teeəlítik/ *adj.* [mod.L f. PROTEIN + –LYSIS]

Prot·er·o·zo·ic /prótərəzóik, prō–/ *adj. & n. Geol.* ● *adj.* of or relating to the later part of the Precambrian era, characterized by the oldest forms of life. ● *n.* this time. [Gk *proteros* former + *zōē* life, *zōos* living]

pro·test *n. & v.* ● *n.* /prótest/ **1** a statement of dissent or disapproval; a remonstrance (*made a protest*). **2** (often *attrib.*) a usu. public demonstration of objection to government, etc., policy (*marched in protest; protest demonstration*). **3** a solemn declaration. **4** *Law* a written declaration, usu. by a notary public, that a bill has been presented and payment or acceptance refused. ● *v.* /prətést, prō–/ **1** *intr.* (usu. foll. by *against, at, about,* etc.) make a protest against an action, proposal, etc. **2** *tr.* (often foll. by *that* + clause; also *absol.*)

affirm (one's innocence, etc.) solemnly, esp. in reply to an accusation, etc. **3** *tr. Law* write or obtain a protest in regard to (a bill). 4 *tr.* object to (a decision, etc.). □ **under protest** unwillingly. □□ **pro·test·er** *n.* **pro·test·ing·ly** *adv.* **pro·tes·tor** *n.* [ME f. OF *protest* (n.), *protester* (v.), f. L *protestari* (as PRO-[1], *testari* assert f. *testis* witness)]

Prot·es·tant /prótistənt/ *n. & adj.* ●*n.* **1** a member or follower of any of the western Christian Churches that are separate from the Roman Catholic Church in accordance with the principles of the Reformation. **2** (**protestant**) (also /prətéstənt/) a protesting person. ●*adj.* **1** of or relating to any of the Protestant Churches or their members, etc. **2** (**protestant**) (also /prətéstənt/) protesting. □□ **Prot·es·tant·ism** *n.* **Prot·es·tant·ize** *v.tr. & intr.* [mod.L *protestans*, part. of L *protestari* (see PROTEST)]

prot·es·ta·tion /prótistáyshən, próte–/ *n.* **1** a strong affirmation. **2** a protest. [ME f. OF *protestation* or LL *protestatio* (as PROTESTANT)]

Pro·te·us /próteeəs, –tyoos/ *n.* **1** a changing or inconstant person or thing. **2** (**proteus**) any bacterium of the genus *Proteus*, usu. found in the intestines and feces of animals. [L f. Gk *Prōteus* a sea god able to take various forms at will]

pro·tha·la·mi·um /próthəláymeeəm/ *n.* (also **pro·tha·la·mi·on** /–meeən/) (*pl.* **pro·tha·la·mi·a** /–meeə/) a song or poem to celebrate a forthcoming wedding. [title of a poem by Spenser, after *epithalamium*]

pro·thal·li·um /prótháleeəm/ *n.* (*pl.* **pro·thal·li·a** /–eeə/) *Bot.* the gametophyte of certain plants, esp. a fern. [mod.L f. PRO-[2] + Gk *thallion* dimin. of *thallos*: see PROTHALLUS]

pro·thal·lus /próthálɔs/ *n.* (*pl.* **pro·thal·li** /–lī/) = PROTHALLIUM [mod.L f. PRO-[2] + Gk *thallos* green shoot]

proth·e·sis /próthisis/ *n.* (*pl.* **proth·e·ses** /–seez/) *Gram.* = PROSTHESIS 3. □□ **pro·thet·ic** /prəthétik/ *adj.* [Gk f. *protithēmi* (as PRO-[2], *tithēmi* place)]

pro·thon·o·tar·y /próthəánəteree, próthɔnótəree/ *n.* a chief clerk in some law courts, orig. in the Byzantine court.

pro·tist /prótist/ *n.* any usu. unicellular organism of the kingdom Protista, with both plant and animal characteristics, including bacteria, algae, and protozoa. □□ **pro·tis·tol·o·gy** /–tistólɔjee/ *n.* [mod.L *Protista* f. Gk *prōtista* neut. pl. superl. f. *prōtos* first]

pro·ti·um /próteeəm, –sheeəm/ *n.* the ordinary isotope of hydrogen as distinct from heavy hydrogen (cf. DEUTERIUM, TRITIUM). [mod.L f. PROTO- + –IUM]

proto- /prótō/ *comb. form* **1** original; primitive (*protoGermanic*; *protoSlavic*). **2** first; original (*protomartyr*; *protophyte*). [Gk *prōto-* f. *prōtos* first]

pro·to·col /prótɔkawl, –kol/ *n. & v.* ●*n.* **1 a** official, esp. diplomatic, formality and etiquette observed on governmental or military occasions, etc. **b** the rules, formalities, etc., of any procedure, group, etc. **2** the original draft of a diplomatic document, esp. of the terms of a treaty agreed to in conference and signed by the parties. **3** a formal statement of a transaction. **4** the official formulae at the beginning and end of a charter, papal bull, etc. **5** a plan or record of experimental observation, medical treatment, etc. **6** *Computing* a set of rules governing the electronic transmission of data between computers. ●*v.* (**pro·to·colled, pro·to·col·ling**) **1** *intr.* draw up a protocol or protocols. **2** *tr.* record in a protocol.

WORD HISTORY protocol

late Middle English (denoting the original notation of an agreement, forming the legal authority for future dealings relating to it): from Old French *prothocole*, via medieval Latin from Greek *prōtokollon* 'first page, flyleaf,' from *prōtos* 'first' + *kolla* 'glue.' Sense 1 derives from French *protocole*, the collection of set forms of etiquette to be observed by the French head of state, and the name of the government department responsible for this (in the 19th century).

pro·to·lan·guage /prótōlanggwij/ *n.* a language from which other languages are believed to have been derived.

pro·to·mar·tyr /prótōmaártər/ *n.* the first martyr in any cause, esp. the first Christian martyr, St. Stephen.

pro·ton /próton/ *n. Physics* a stable elementary particle with a positive electric charge, equal in magnitude to that of an electron, and occurring in all atomic nuclei. □□ **pro·ton·ic** /prətónik/ *adj.* [Gk, neut. of *prōtos* first]

pro·ton·o·tar·y /prɔtáánəteree, prótɔnótəree/ *n.* (*pl.* **·ies**) var. of PROTHONOTARY. [med.L *protonotarius* f. late Gk *protonotarios* (as PROTO-, NOTARY)]

Pro·ton·o·tar·y A·pos·tol·ic *n.* (also **Pro·ton·o·tar·y A·pos·tol·i·cal**) a member of the college of prelates who register papal acts, direct the canonization of saints, etc.

pro·to·phyte /prótɔfīt/ *n.* a unicellular plant bearing gametes.

pro·to·plasm /prótɔplazəm/ *n.* the material comprising the living part of a cell, consisting of a nucleus embedded in membrane-enclosed cytoplasm. □□ **pro·to·plas·mal** /–plazməl/ *adj.* **pro·to·plas·mat·ic** /–mátik/ *adj.* **pro·to·plas·mic** *adj.* [Gk *protoplasma* (as PROTO-, PLASMA)]

---

pro·to·plast /prótɔplast/ *n.* the protoplasm of one cell. □□ **pro·to·plas·tic** *adj.* [F *protoplaste* or LL *protoplastus* f. Gk *protoplastos* (as PROTO-, *plassō* mold)]

pro·to·the·ri·an /prótōtheéreeən/ *n. & adj.* ●*n.* any mammal of the subclass Prototheria, including monotremes. ●*adj.* of or relating to this subclass. [PROTO- + Gk *thēr* wild beast]

pro·to·type /prótɔtip/ *n.* **1** an original thing or person of which or whom copies, imitations, improved forms, representations, etc., are made. **2** a trial model or preliminary version of a vehicle, machine, etc. **3** a thing or person representative of a type; an exemplar. □□ **pro·to·typ·al** *adj.* **pro·to·typ·ic** /–típik/ *adj.* **pro·to·typ·i·cal** *adj.* **pro·to·typ·i·cal·ly** *adv.* [F *prototype* or LL *prototypus* f. Gk *prototupos* (as PROTO-, TYPE)]

pro·to·zo·an /prótɔzóɔn/ *n. & adj.* ●*n.* (also **pro·to·zo·on** /–zó-on/) (*pl.* **pro·to·zo·a** /–zó/ or **pro·to·zo·ans**) any usu. unicellular and microscopic organism of the subkingdom Protozoa, including amoebas and ciliates. ●*adj.* (also **pro·to·zo·ic** /–zó-ik/) of or relating to this phylum. □□ **pro·to·zo·al** *adj.* [mod.L (as PROTO-, Gk *zōion* animal)]

pro·tract /prótrákt, prɔ–/ *v.tr.* **1 a** prolong or lengthen in space or esp. time (*protracted their stay for some weeks*). **b** (as **protracted** *adj.*) of excessive length or duration (*a protracted illness*). **2** draw (a plan, etc.) to scale. □□ **pro·tract·ed·ly** *adv.* **pro·tract·ed·ness** *n.* [L *protrahere* *protract-* (as PRO-[1], *trahere* draw)]

pro·trac·tile /prótráktil, –til, prɔ–/ *adj.* (of a part of the body, etc.) capable of being protruded or extended.

pro·trac·tion /prótrákshɔn, prɔ–/ *n.* **1** the act or an instance of protracting; the state of being protracted. **2** a drawing to scale. **3** the action of a protractor muscle. [F *protraction* or LL *protractio* (as PRO-, TRACT)]

pro·trac·tor /prótráktɔr, prɔ–/ *n.* **1** an instrument for measuring angles, usu. in the form of a graduated semicircle. **2** a muscle serving to extend a limb, etc.

protractor

pro·trude /prótróod/ *v.* **1** *intr.* extend beyond or above a surface; project. **2** *tr.* thrust or cause to thrust forth. □□ **pro·trud·ent** *adj.* **pro·tru·si·ble** /–sɔbɔl, –zɔ–/ *adj.* **pro·tru·sion** /–tróozhɔn/ *n.* **pro·tru·sive** *adj.* [L *protrudere* (as PRO-[1], *trudere* trus- thrust)]

pro·tru·sile /prɔtróosil, –sil/ *adj.* (of a limb, etc.) capable of being thrust forward. [PRO-[1] + *extrusile*: see EXTRUDE]

pro·tu·ber·ant /prótóobɔrɔnt, –tyóo–, prɔ–/ *adj.* bulging out; prominent (*protuberant eyes*). □□ **pro·tu·ber·ance** *n.* [LL *protuberare* (as PRO-[1], *tuber* bump)]

proud /prowd/ *adj.* **1** feeling greatly honored or pleased (*am proud to know him; proud of his friendship*). **2 a** (often foll. by *of*) valuing oneself, one's possessions, etc., highly, or esp. too highly; haughty; arrogant (*proud of his ancient name*). **b** (often in *comb.*) having a proper pride; satisfied (*proud of a job well done*). **3 a** (of an occasion, etc.) justly arousing pride (*a proud day for us; a proud sight*). **b** (of an action, etc.) showing pride (*a proud wave of the hand*). **4** (of a thing) imposing; splendid. **5** *Brit.* slightly projecting from a surface, etc. (*the nail stood proud of the plank*). **6** (of flesh) overgrown around a healing wound. **7** *Brit.* (of water) swollen in flood. □ **do proud** *colloq.* **1** treat (a person) with lavish generosity or honor (*they did us proud on our anniversary*). **2** (*refl.*) act honorably or worthily. □□ **proud·ly** *adv.* **proud·ness** *n.* [OE *prūt, prūd* f. OF *prud, prod* oblique case of *pruz*, etc., valiant, ult. f. L *prode* f. L *prodesse* be of value (as PRO-[1], *esse* be)]

Prov. *abbr.* **1** Proverbs (Old Testament). **2** Province. **3** Provençal.

prove /proov/ *v.* (*past part.* **proved** or **prov·en**) **1** *tr.* (often foll. by *that* + clause) demonstrate the truth of by evidence or argument. **2** *intr.* **a** (usu. foll. by *to* + infin.) be found (*it proved to be untrue*). **b** emerge incontrovertibly as (*will prove the winner*). **3** *tr. Math.* test the accuracy of (a calculation). **4** *tr.* establish the genuineness and validity of (a will). **5** *intr.* (of dough) rise in breadmaking. **6** *tr.* = PROOF 3. **7** *tr.* subject (a gun, etc.) to a testing process. **8** *tr. archaic* test the qualities of; try. □ **prove oneself** show one's abilities, courage, etc. □□ **prov·a·ble** *adj.* **prov·a·bil·i·ty** /próovɔbílitee/ *n.* **prov·a·bly** *adv.* [ME f. OF *prover* f. L *probare* test, approve, demonstrate f. *probus* good]

prov·e·nance /próvinɔns/ *n.* **1** the place of origin or history, esp. of a work of art, etc. **2** origin. [F f. *provenir* f. L *provenire* (as PRO-[1], *venire* come)]

Pro·ven·çal /próvɔnsaál, próv–/ *adj. & n.* ●*adj.* **1** of or concerning the language, inhabitants, landscape, etc., of Provence, a former province of SE France. **2** (also **Pro·ven·çale**) cooked with garlic and tomato and usu. onions, olive oil, and herbs. ●*n.* **1** a native of

Provence. **2** the language of Provence. [F (as PROVINCIAL f. *provincia* as L colloq. name for southern Gaul under Roman rule)]

prov•en•der /próvindər/ *n.* **1** animal fodder. **2** *joc.* food for human beings. [ME f. OF *provendre, provende* ult. f. L *praebenda* (see PREBEND)]

pro•ve•ni•ence /prəveényəns, –veéneeəns/ *n.* = PROVENANCE. [L *provenire* f. *venire* come]

prov•erb /próvərb/ *n.* **1** a short pithy saying in general use, held to embody a general truth. **2** a person or thing that is notorious (*he is a proverb for inaccuracy*). **3** (**Proverbs** or **Book of Proverbs**) a didactic poetic Old Testament book of maxims attributed to Solomon and others. [ME f. OF *proverbe* or L *proverbium* (as PRO-¹, *verbum* word)]

pro•ver•bi•al /prəvórbeeəl/ *adj.* **1** (esp. of a specific characteristic, etc.) as well-known as a proverb; notorious (*his proverbial honesty*). **2** of or referred to in a proverb (*the proverbial ill wind*). □□ **pro•ver•bi•al•i•ty** /–beeálitee/ *n.* **pro•ver•bi•al•ly** *adv.* [ME f. L *proverbialis* (as PROVERB)]

pro•vide /prəvíd/ *v.* **1** *tr.* supply; furnish (*provided them with food; provided food for them; provided a chance for escape*). **2** *intr.* **a** (usu. foll. by *for, against*) make due preparation (*provided for any eventuality; provided against invasion*). **b** (usu. foll. by *for*) prepare for the maintenance of a person, etc. **3** *tr.* (also *refl.*) equip with necessities. **4** *tr.* (usu. foll. by *that*) stipulate in a will, statute, etc. [ME f. L *providēre* (as PRO-¹, *vidēre vis–* see)]

pro•vid•ed /prəvídid/ *adj. & conj.* ● *adj.* supplied; furnished. ● *conj.* (often foll. by *that*) on the condition or understanding (that).

prov•i•dence /próvidəns/ *n.* **1** the protective care of God or nature. **2** (**Providence**) God in this aspect. **3** timely care or preparation; foresight; thrift. [ME f. OF *providence* or L *providentia* (as PROVIDE)]

prov•i•dent /próvidənt, –dent/ *adj.* having or showing foresight; thrifty. □□ **prov•i•dent•ly** *adv.* [ME f. L (as PROVIDE)]

prov•i•den•tial /próvidénshəl/ *adj.* **1** of or by divine foresight or interposition. **2** opportune; lucky. □□ **prov•i•den•tial•ly** *adv.* [PROVIDENCE + –IAL, after *evidential*, etc.]

pro•vid•er /prəvídər/ *n.* **1** a person or thing that provides. **2** the breadwinner of a family, etc.

pro•vid•ing /prəvíding/ *conj.* = PROVIDED *conj.*

prov•ince /próvins/ *n.* **1** a principal administrative division of some countries. **2** (**the provinces**) the whole of a country outside major cities, esp. regarded as uncultured, unsophisticated, etc. **3** a sphere of action; business (*outside my province as a teacher*). **4** a branch of learning, etc. (*in the province of aesthetics*). **5** *Eccl.* a district under an archbishop or a metropolitan. **6** *Rom.Hist.* a territory outside Italy under a Roman governor. [ME f. OF f. L *provincia* charge, province]

pro•vin•cial /prəvínshəl/ *adj. & n.* ● *adj.* **1 a** of or concerning a province. **b** of or concerning the provinces. **2** unsophisticated or uncultured in manner, speech, opinion, etc. ● *n.* **1** an inhabitant of a province or the provinces. **2** an unsophisticated or uncultured person. **3** *Eccl.* the head or chief of a province or of a religious order in a province. □□ **pro•vin•ci•al•i•ty** /–sheeálitee/ *n.* **pro•vin•cial•ize** *v.tr.* **pro•vin•cial•ly** *adv.* [ME f. OF f. L *provincialis* (as PROVINCE)]

pro•vin•cial•ism /prəvínshəlizəm/ *n.* **1** provincial manners, fashion, mode of thought, etc., esp. regarded as restricting or narrow. **2** a word or phrase peculiar to a provincial region. **3** concern for one's local area rather than one's country. □□ **pro•vin•cial•ist** *n.*

pro•vi•sion /prəvízhən/ *n. & v.* ● *n.* **1 a** the act or an instance of providing (*made no provision for his future*). **b** something provided (*a provision of bread*). **2** (in *pl.*) food, drink, etc., esp. for an expedition. **3 a** a legal or formal statement providing for something. **b** a clause of this. ● *v.tr.* supply (an expedition, etc.) with provisions. □□ **pro•vi•sion•er** *n.* **pro•vi•sion•less** *adj.* **pro•vi•sion•ment** *n.* [ME f. OF f. L *provisio –onis* (as PROVIDE)]

pro•vi•sion•al /prəvízhənəl/ *adj. & n.* ● *adj.* **1** providing for immediate needs only; temporary. **2** (**Provisional**) designating the unofficial wing of the Irish Republican Army (IRA), advocating terrorism. ● *n.* (**Provisional**) a member of the Provisional wing of the IRA. □□ **pro•vi•sion•al•i•ty** /–álitee/ *n.* **pro•vi•sion•al•ly** *adv.* **pro•vi•sion•al•ness** *n.*

pro•vi•so /prəvízō/ *n.* (*pl.* **•sos**) **1** a stipulation. **2** a clause of stipulation or limitation in a document. [L, neut. ablat. past part. of *providēre* PROVIDE, in med.L phr. *proviso quod* it being provided that]

pro•vi•so•ry /prəvízəree/ *adj.* **1** conditional; having a proviso. **2** making provision (*provisory care*). □□ **pro•vi•so•ri•ly** *adv.* [F *provisoire* or med.L *provisorius* (as PROVIDE)]

Pro•vo /próvō/ *n.* (*pl.* **•vos**) *colloq.* a member of the Provisional IRA. [abbr.]

prov•o•ca•tion /próvəkáyshən/ *n.* **1** the act or an instance of provoking; a state of being provoked (*did it under severe provocation*). **2** a cause of annoyance. **3** *Law* an action, insult, etc., held to be likely to provoke physical retaliation. [ME f. OF *provocation* or L *provocatio* (as PROVOKE)]

pro•voc•a•tive /prəvókətiv/ *adj. & n.* ● *adj.* **1** (usu. foll. by *of*) tend-

ing to provoke, esp. anger or sexual desire. **2** intentionally annoying. ● *n.* a provocative thing. □□ **pro•voc•a•tive•ly** *adv.* **pro•voc•a•tive•ness** *n.* [ME f. obs. F *provocatif –ive* f. LL *provocativus* (as PROVOKE)]

pro•voke /prəvók/ *v.tr.* **1 a** (often foll. by *to*, or *to* + infin.) rouse or incite (*provoked him to fury*). **b** (often as **provoking** *adj.*) annoy; irritate; exasperate. **2** call forth; instigate (indignation, an inquiry, a storm, etc.). **3** (usu. foll. by *into* + verbal noun) irritate or stimulate (a person) (*the itch provoked him into scratching*). **4** tempt; allure. **5** cause; give rise to (*will provoke discussion*). □□ **pro•vok•a•ble** *adj.* **pro•vok•ing•ly** *adv.* [ME f. OF *provoquer* f. L *provocare* (as PRO-¹, *vocare* call)]

pro•vo•lo•ne /próvəlónee/ *n.* a medium hard Italian cheese, often with a mild smoked flavor.

pro•vost /próvōst, próvəst/ *n.* **1** a high administrative officer in a university. **2** *Brit.* the head of some colleges, esp. at Oxford or Cambridge. **3** *Eccl.* **a** the head of a chapter in a cathedral. **b** *hist.* the head of a religious community. **4** *Sc.* the head of a municipal corporation or burgh. **5** the Protestant minister of the principal church of a town, etc., in Germany, etc. **6** = PROVOST MARSHAL. □□ **pro•vost•ship** *n.* [ME f. OE *profost* & AF *provost, prevost* f. med.L *propositus* for *praepositus* past part. of *praeponere* set over]

pro•vost guard *n.* /próvō/ a body of soldiers under a provost marshal.

pro•vost mar•shal *n.* /próvō/ **1** the head of military police within a military command, as on a military base. **2** the master-at-arms of a ship in which a court-martial is to be held.

prow /prow/ *n.* **1** the bow of a ship adjoining the stem. **2** a pointed or projecting front part. [F *proue* f. Prov. *proa* or It. dial. *prua* f. L *prora* f. Gk *prōira*]

prow•ess /prówis/ *n.* **1** skill; expertise. **2** valor; gallantry. [ME f. OF *proesce* f. *prou* valiant]

prowl /prowl/ *v. & n.* ● *v.* **1** *tr.* roam (a place) in search or as if in search of prey, plunder, etc. **2** *intr.* (often foll. by *about, around*) move about like a hunter. ● *n.* the act or an instance of prowling. □ **on the prowl** in search of something, esp. sexual contact, etc. □□ **prowl•er** *n.* [ME *prolle*, of unkn. orig.]

prowl car *n.* a police squad car.

prox. *abbr.* proximo.

prox•e•mics /prokseémiks/ *n. Sociol.* the study of socially conditioned spatial factors in ordinary human relations. [PROXIMITY + –emics: cf. *phonemics*]

prox•i•mal /próksiməl/ *adj.* situated toward the center of the body or point of attachment. □□ **prox•i•mal•ly** *adv.* [L *proximus* nearest]

prox•i•mate /próksimət/ *adj.* **1** nearest or next before or after (in place, order, time, causation, thought process, etc.). **2** approximate. □□ **prox•i•mate•ly** *adv.* [L *proximatus* past part. of *proximare* draw near (as PROXIMAL)]

prox•im•i•ty /proksímitee/ *n.* nearness in space, time, etc. (*sat in close proximity to them*). [ME f. F *proximité* or L *proximitas* (as PROXIMAL)]

prox•im•i•ty fuse *n.* (also **prox•im•i•ty fuze**) an electronic device causing a projectile to explode when near its target.

prox•im•i•ty of blood *n.* kinship.

prox•i•mo /próksimō/ *adj. Commerce archaic* of next month (*the third proximo*). [L *proximo mense* in the next month]

prox•y /próksee/ *n.* (*pl.* **•ies**) (also *attrib.*) **1** the authorization given to a substitute or deputy (*a proxy vote; was married by proxy*). **2** a person authorized to act as a substitute, etc. **3 a** a document giving the power to act as a proxy, esp. in voting. **b** a vote given by this. [ME f. obs. *procuracy* f. med.L *procuratia* (as PROCURATION)]

prude /prood/ *n.* a person having or affecting an attitude of extreme propriety or modesty, esp. in sexual matters. □□ **prud•er•y** /proodəree/ *n.* (*pl.* **•ies**). **prud•ish** *adj.* **prud•ish•ly** *adv.* **prud•ish•ness** *n.* [F, back-form. f. *prudefemme* fem. of *prud'homme* good man and true f. *prou* worthy]

pru•dent /prood'nt/ *adj.* **1** (of a person or conduct) careful to avoid undesired consequences; circumspect. **2** discreet. □□ **pru•dence** *n.* **pru•dent•ly** *adv.* [ME f. OF *prudent* or L *prudens = providens* PROVIDENT]

pru•den•tial /proodénshəl/ *adj. & n.* ● *adj.* of, involving, or marked by prudence (*prudential motives*). ● *n.* (in *pl.*) **1** prudential considerations or matters. **2** minor administrative or financial matters. □□ **pru•den•tial•ism** *n.* **pru•den•tial•ist** *n.* **pru•den•tial•ly** *adv.* [PRUDENT + –IAL, after *evidential*, etc.]

pru•i•nose /prooinōs/ *adj.* esp. *Bot.* covered with white powdery granules; frosted in appearance. [L *pruinosus* f. *pruina* hoarfrost]

prune¹ /proon/ *n.* **1** a dried plum. **2** *colloq.* a stupid or disliked person. [ME f. OF ult. f. L *prunum* f. Gk *prou(m)non* plum]

prune² /proon/ *v.tr.* **1 a** (often foll. by *down*) trim (a tree, etc.) by cutting away dead or overgrown branches, etc. **b** (usu. foll. by *off, away*) lop (branches, etc.) from a tree. **2** reduce (costs, etc.) (*must try to prune expenses*). **3 a** (often foll. by *of*) clear (a book, etc.) of superfluous matter. **b** remove (superfluous matter). □□ **prun•er** *n.* [ME *prouyne* f. OF *pro(o)ignier* ult. f. L *rotundus* ROUND]

pru•nel•la¹ /proonélə/ *n.* any plant of the genus *Prunella*, esp. *P. vul-*

garis, bearing pink, purple, or white flower spikes, and formerly thought to cure quinsy. Also called **self-heal**. [mod.L, = quinsy: earlier *brunella* dimin. of med.L *brunus* brown]

pru·nel·la² /proōnélə/ *n.* a strong silk or worsted fabric used formerly for academic gowns, the uppers of women's shoes, etc. [perh. f. F *prunelle*, of uncert. orig.]

prun·ing hook *n.* a long-handled hooked cutting tool used for pruning.

pru·ri·ent /proōreeənt/ *adj.* **1** having an unhealthy obsession with sexual matters. **2** encouraging such an obsession. □□ **pru·ri·ence** *n.* **pru·ri·en·cy** *n.* **pru·ri·ent·ly** *adv.* [L *prurire* itch, be wanton]

pru·ri·go /proōrígō/ *n.* a skin disease marked by severe itching. □□ **pru·ri·i·nous** /proōríjinəs/ *adj.* [L *prurigo –ginis* f. *prurire* to itch]

pru·ri·tus /proōrítəs/ *n.* severe itching of the skin. □□ **pru·rit·ic** /–rítik/ *adj.* [L, = itching (as PRURIGO)]

Prus·sian /prúshən/ *adj. & n.* ● *adj.* of or relating to Prussia, a former German kingdom, or relating to its rigidly militaristic tradition. ● *n.* a native of Prussia.

Prus·sian blue *n.* a deep blue pigment, ferric ferrocyanide, used in painting and dyeing.

prus·sic /prúsik/ *adj.* of or obtained from Prussian blue. □ **prussic acid** hydrocyanic acid. [F *prussique* f. *Prusse* Prussia]

pry¹ /prī/ *v.intr.* (**pries, pried**) **1** (usu. foll. by *into*) inquire presumptuously (into a person's private affairs, etc.). **2** (usu. foll. by *into, about*, etc.) look or peer inquisitively. □□ **pry·ing** *adj.* **pry·ing·ly** *adv.* [ME *prie*, of unkn. orig.]

pry² /prī/ *v.tr.* (**pries, pried**) (often foll. by *out of, open*, etc.) = PRIZE³. [back-form. f. PRIZE]

PS *abbr.* **1** postscript. **2** *Brit.* Police Sergeant. **3** private secretary. **4** prompt side.

Ps. *abbr.* (*pl.* **Pss.**) Psalm, Psalms (Old Testament).

psalm /saam/ *n.* **1 a** (also **Psalm**) any of the sacred songs contained in the Book of Psalms. **b** (**the Psalms** or **the Book of Psalms**) the book of the Old Testament containing the Psalms. **2** a sacred song or hymn. □□ **psalm·ic** *adj.* [OE (*p*)*sealm* f. LL *psalmus* f. Gk *psalmos* song sung to a harp f. *psallō* pluck]

psalm·ist /saámist/ *n.* **1** the author or composer of a psalm. **2** (**the Psalmist**) David or the author of any of the Psalms. [LL *psalmista* (as PSALM)]

psal·mo·dy /saámədee, sál–/ *n.* **1** the practice or art of singing psalms, hymns, etc., esp. in public worship. **2 a** the arrangement of psalms for singing. **b** the psalms so arranged. □□ **psal·mod·ic** /salmódik/ *adj.* **psal·mo·dist** *n.* **psal·mo·dize** *v.intr.* [ME f. LL *psalmodia* f. Gk *psalmōidia* singing to a harp (as PSALM, *ōidē* song)]

psal·ter /sáwltər/ *n.* (**the psal·ter** or **the Psal·ter**) **1 a** the Book of Psalms. **b** a version of this (*the English Psalter*). **2** a copy of the Psalms, esp. for liturgical use. [ME f. AF *sauter*, OF *sautier*, & OE (*p*)*saltere* f. LL *psalterium* f. Gk *psaltērion* stringed instrument (*psallō* pluck), in eccl.L Book of Psalms]

psal·te·ri·um /sawlteéreeəm/ *n.* the third stomach of a ruminant, the omasum. [L (see PSALTER): named from its booklike form]

psal·ter·y /sáwltəree/ *n.* (*pl.* **·ies**) an ancient and medieval instrument like a dulcimer but played by plucking the strings with the fingers or a plectrum. [ME f. OF *sauterie*, etc., f. L (as PSALTER)]

p's and q's *n.* □ **mind one's p's and q's 1** attend to one's own conduct and manners. **2** attend to one's own accuracy in work.

PSAT *abbr.* Preliminary Scholastic Assessment Test.

pse·phol·o·gy /sefóləjee/ *n.* the statistical study of elections, voting, etc. □□ **pse·pho·log·i·cal** /–əlójikəl/ *adj.* **pse·pho·log·i·cal·ly** *adv.* **pse·phol·o·gist** *n.* [Gk *psēphos* pebble, vote + –LOGY]

pseud /soōd/ *adj. & n. Brit. colloq.* ● *adj.* intellectually or socially pretentious; not genuine. ● *n.* such a person; a poseur. [abbr. of PSEUDO]

pseud- var. of PSEUDO-.

pseud. *abbr.* pseudonym.

pseud·e·pig·ra·pha /soōdipígrəfə/ *n.pl.* **1** Jewish writings ascribed to various Old Testament prophets, etc., but written during or just before the early Christian period. **2** spurious writings. □□ **pseud·e·pig·ra·phal** *adj.* **pseud·ep·i·graph·ic** /–gráfik/ *adj.* **pseud·ep·i·graph·i·cal** *adj.* [neut. pl. of Gk *pseudepigraphos* with false title (as PSEUDO-, EPIGRAPH)]

pseu·do /soōdō/ *adj. & n.* ● *adj.* **1** sham; spurious. **2** insincere. ● *n. Brit.* (*pl.* **·dos**) a pretentious or insincere person. [see PSEUDO-]

pseudo- /soōdō/ *comb. form* (also **pseud-** before a vowel) **1** supposed or purporting to be but not really so; false; not genuine (*pseudointellectual; pseudepigrapha*). **2** resembling or imitating (often in technical applications) (*pseudomalaria*). [Gk f. *pseudēs* false, *pseudos* falsehood]

pseu·do·carp /soōdōkaarp/ *n.* a fruit formed from parts other than the ovary, e.g., the strawberry or fig. Also called **accessory fruit**. [PSEUDO- + Gk *karpos* fruit]

pseu·do·morph /soōdəmawrf/ *n.* **1** a crystal, etc., consisting of one mineral with the form characteristic of another. **2** a false form. □□ **pseu·do·mor·phic** /–máwrfik/ *adj.* **pseu·do·mor·phism** *n.* **pseu·do·mor·phous** /–máwrfəs/ *adj.* [PSEUDO- + Gk *morphē* form]

pseu·do·nym /soōdənim/ *n.* a fictitious name, esp. one assumed by

an author. [F *pseudonyme* f. Gk *pseudōnymos* (as PSEUDO-, –ōnumos f. *onoma* name)]

pseu·don·y·mous /soōdóniməs/ *adj.* writing or written under a false name. □□ **pseu·do·nym·i·ty** /soōdənímitee/ *n.* **pseu·don·y·mous·ly** *adv.*

pseu·do·pod /soōdōpod/ *n.* = PSEUDOPODIUM. [mod.L (as PSEUDOPODIUM)]

pseu·do·po·di·um /soōdōpṓdeeəm/ *n.* (*pl.* **pseu·do·po·di·a** /–deeə/) (in amoeboid cells) a temporary protrusion of protoplasm for movement, feeding, etc. [mod.L (as PSEUDO-, PODIUM)]

pseu·do·sci·ence /soōdōsīəns/ *n.* a pretended or spurious science. □□ **pseu·do·sci·en·tif·ic** /–sīəntifik/ *adj.*

psf. *abbr.* (also **p.s.f.**) pounds per square foot.

pshaw /shaw, pshaw/ *int. archaic* an expression of contempt or impatience. [imit.]

psi /sī, psī/ *n.* **1** the twenty-third letter of the Greek alphabet (Ψ, ψ). **2** supposed parapsychological faculties, phenomena, etc., regarded collectively. [Gk]

p.s.i. *abbr.* pounds per square inch.

psil·o·cy·bin /sīləsíbin/ *n.* a hallucinogenic alkaloid found in Mexican mushrooms of the genus *Psilocybe*. [*Psilocybe* f. Gk *psilos* bald + *kubē* head]

psi·lo·sis /sīlṓsis/ *n.* = SPRUE². [Gk *psilōsis* f. *psilos* bare]

psit·ta·cine /sítəsīn/ *adj.* of or relating to parrots; parrotlike. [L *psittacinus* f. *psittacus* f. Gk *psittakos* parrot]

psit·ta·co·sis /sítəkósis/ *n.* a contagious viral disease of birds transmissible (esp. from parrots) to human beings as a form of pneumonia. [mod.L f. L *psittacus* (as PSITTACINE) + –OSIS]

pso·as /sṓəs/ *n.* either of two muscles used in flexing the hip joint. [Gk, accus. pl. of *psoa*, taken as sing.]

pso·ri·a·sis /sərīəsis/ *n.* a skin disease marked by red scaly patches. □□ **pso·ri·at·ic** /sáwreeátik/ *adj.* [mod.L f. Gk *psōriasis* f. *psōriaō* have an itch f. *psōra* itch]

psst /pst/ *int.* (also **pst**) a whispered exclamation seeking to attract a person's attention surreptitiously. [imit.]

PST *abbr.* Pacific Standard Time.

psych /sīk/ *v.tr. colloq.* (also **psyche**) **1** (usu. foll. by *up*; often *refl.*) prepare (oneself or another person) mentally for an ordeal, etc. **2 a** (usu. foll. by *out*) analyze (a person's motivation, etc.) for one's own advantage (*can't psych him out*). **b** subject to psychoanalysis. **3** (often foll. by *out*) influence a person psychologically, esp. negatively; intimidate; frighten. [abbr.]

psych. /sīk/ (also **psychol.**) *abbr.* **1** psychological. **2** psychology.

psy·che /sīkee/ *n.* **1** the soul; the spirit. **2** the mind. **3** var. of PSYCH. [L f. Gk *psukhē* breath, life, soul]

psy·che·de·lia /sīkideéleeə, –deélyə/ *n.pl.* **1** psychedelic articles, esp. posters, paintings, etc. **2** psychedelic drugs.

psy·che·del·ic /sīkidélik/ *adj. & n.* ● *adj.* **1 a** expanding the mind's awareness, etc., esp. through the use of hallucinogenic drugs. **b** (of an experience) hallucinatory; bizarre. **c** (of a drug) producing hallucinations. **2** *colloq.* **a** producing an effect resembling that of a psychedelic drug; having vivid colors or designs, etc. **b** (of colors, patterns, etc.) bright, bold and often abstract. ● *n.* a hallucinogenic drug. □□ **psy·che·del·i·cal·ly** *adv.* [irreg. f. Gk (as PSYCHE, *dēlos* clear, manifest)]

psy·chi·a·try /sīkíətree/ *n.* the study and treatment of mental disease. □□ **psy·chi·at·ric** /–keeátrik/ *adj.* **psy·chi·at·ri·cal** *adj.* **psy·chi·at·ri·cal·ly** *adv.* **psy·chi·a·trist** /–kīətrist/ *n.* [as PSYCHE + *iatreia* healing f. *iatros* healer]

psy·chic /sīkik/ *adj. & n.* ● *adj.* **1 a** (of a person) considered to have occult powers, such as telepathy, clairvoyance, etc. **b** (of a faculty, phenomenon, etc.) inexplicable by natural laws. **2** of the soul or mind. **3** *Bridge* (of a bid) made on the basis of a hand not usually considered strong enough to support it. ● *n.* **1** a person considered to have psychic powers; a medium. **2** *Bridge* a psychic bid. **3** (in *pl.*) the study of psychic phenomena. [Gk *psukhikos* (as PSYCHE)]

psy·chi·cal /sīkikəl/ *adj.* **1** concerning psychic phenomena or faculties (*psychical research*). **2** of the soul or mind. □□ **psy·chi·cal·ly** *adv.* **psy·chi·cism** /–kisizəm/ *n.* **psy·chi·cist** /–kisist/ *n.*

psy·cho /sīkō/ *n. & adj. colloq.* ● *n.* (*pl.* **·chos**) a psychopath. ● *adj.* psychopathic. [abbr.]

psycho- /sīkō/ *comb. form* relating to the mind or psychology. [Gk *psukho-* (as PSYCHE)]

psy·cho·ac·tive /sīkō-áktiv/ *adj.* affecting the mind.

psy·cho·a·nal·y·sis /sīkōənálisis/ *n.* a therapeutic method of treating mental disorders by investigating the interaction of conscious and unconscious elements in the mind and bringing repressed fears and conflicts into the conscious mind. □□ **psy·cho·a·lyze** /–ánəlīz/ *v.tr.* **psy·cho·an·a·lyst** /–ánəlist/ *n.* **psy·cho·an·a·lyt·ic** /–ənəlítik/ *adj.* **psy·cho·an·a·lyt·i·cal** *adj.* **psy·cho·an·a·lyt·i·cal·ly** *adv.*

psy·cho·bab·ble /sīkōbábəl/ *n. colloq. derog.* jargon used in popular psychology. □□ **psy·cho·bab·bler** *n.*

psy·cho·dra·ma /síkōdraamə, –drámə/ n. 1 a form of psychotherapy in which patients act out events from their past. 2 a play or movie, etc., in which psychological elements are the main interest.

psy·cho·dy·nam·ics /síkōdīnámiks/ n.pl. (treated as sing.) the study of the activity of and the interrelation between the various parts of an individual's personality or psyche. □□ **psy·cho·dy·nam·ic** adj. **psy·cho·dy·nam·i·cal·ly** adv.

psy·cho·gen·e·sis /síkōjénisis/ n. the study of the origin of the mind's development.

psy·cho·ki·ne·sis /síkōkinéesis/ n. the movement of objects supposedly by mental effort without the action of natural forces.

psy·cho·lin·guis·tics /síkōlinggwístiks/ n.pl. (treated as sing.) the study of the psychological aspects of language and language acquisition. □□ **psy·cho·lin·guist** /–línggwist/ n. **psy·cho·lin·guis·tic** adj.

psy·cho·log·i·cal /síkəlójikəl/ adj. 1 of, relating to, or arising in the mind. 2 of or relating to psychology. 3 colloq. (of an ailment, etc.) having a basis in the mind; imaginary (her cold is psychological). □□ **psy·cho·log·i·cal·ly** adv.

psy·cho·log·i·cal block n. a mental inability or inhibition caused by emotional factors.

psy·cho·log·i·cal mo·ment n. the most appropriate time for achieving a particular effect or purpose.

psy·cho·log·i·cal war·fare n. a campaign directed at reducing an opponent's morale.

psy·chol·o·gy /síkólǝjee/ n. (pl. ·gies) 1 the scientific study of the human mind and its functions, esp. those affecting behavior in a given context. 2 a treatise on or theory of this. 3 a the mental characteristics or attitude of a person or group. b the mental factors governing a situation or activity (the psychology of crime). □□ **psy·chol·o·gist** n. **psy·chol·o·gize** v.tr. & intr. [mod.L psychologia (as PSYCHO-, –LOGY)]

psy·cho·met·rics /síkōmétriks/ n.pl. (treated as sing.) the science of measuring mental capacities and processes.

psy·chom·e·try /síkómitree/ n. 1 the supposed divination of facts about events, people, etc., from inanimate objects associated with them. 2 the measurement of mental abilities. □□ **psy·cho·met·ric** /–kǝmétrik/ adj. **psy·cho·met·ri·cal·ly** adv. **psy·chom·e·trist** n.

psy·cho·mo·tor /síkōmōtǝr/ adj. concerning the study of movement resulting from mental activity.

psy·cho·neu·ro·sis /síkōnoorōsis, –nyoo–/ n. neurosis, esp. with the indirect expression of emotions. □□ **psy·cho·neu·rot·ic** /–noorótik, –nyoo–/ adj.

psy·cho·path /síkǝpath/ n. 1 a person suffering from chronic mental disorder esp. with abnormal or violent social behavior. 2 a mentally or emotionally unstable person. □□ **psy·cho·path·ic** /–páthik/ adj. **psy·cho·path·i·cal·ly** adv.

psy·cho·pa·thol·o·gy /síkōpǝthólǝjee/ n. 1 the scientific study of mental disorders. 2 a mentally or behaviorally disordered state. □□ **psy·cho·path·o·log·i·cal** /–pathǝlójikǝl/ adj.

psy·chop·a·thy /síkópǝthee/ n. psychopathic or psychologically abnormal behavior.

psy·cho·phys·ics /síkōfíziks/ n. the science of the relation between the mind and the body. □□ **psy·cho·phys·i·cal** adj.

psy·cho·phys·i·ol·o·gy /síkōfizeeólǝjee/ n. the branch of physiology dealing with mental phenomena. □□ **psy·cho·phys·i·o·log·i·cal** /–zeeǝlójikǝl/ adj.

psy·cho·sex·u·al /síkōsékshooǝl/ adj. of or involving the psychological aspects of the sexual impulse. □□ **psy·cho·sex·u·al·ly** adv.

psy·cho·sis /síkósis/ n. (pl. **psy·cho·ses** /–seez/) a severe mental derangement, esp. when resulting in delusions and loss of or defective contact with external reality. [Gk psukhōsis f. psukhoō give life to (as PSYCHE)]

psy·cho·so·cial /síkósóshǝl/ adj. of or involving the influence of social factors or human interactive behavior. □□ **psy·cho·so·cial·ly** adv.

psy·cho·so·mat·ic /síkōsǝmátik/ adj. 1 (of an illness, etc.) caused or aggravated by mental conflict, stress, etc. 2 of the mind and body together. □□ **psy·cho·so·mat·i·cal·ly** adv.

psy·cho·sur·ger·y /síkōsúrjǝree/ n. brain surgery as a means of treating mental disorder. □□ **psy·cho·sur·gi·cal** adj.

psy·cho·ther·a·py /síkōthérǝpee/ n. the treatment of mental disorder by psychological means. □□ **psy·cho·ther·a·peu·tic** /–pyóotik/ adj. **psy·cho·ther·a·pist** n.

psy·chot·ic /síkótik/ adj. & n. ● adj. of or characterized by a psychosis. ● n. a person suffering from a psychosis. □□ **psy·chot·i·cal·ly** adv.

psy·cho·tro·pic /síkōtrópik, –tróp–/ n. (of a drug) acting on the mind. [PSYCHO- + Gk tropē turning: see TROPIC]

psy·chrom·e·ter /síkrómitǝr/ n. a thermometer consisting of a dry bulb and a wet bulb for measuring atmospheric humidity. [Gk psukhros cold + –METER]

PT abbr. 1 physical therapy. 2 physical training.

Pt symb. Chem. the element platinum.

pt. abbr. 1 part. 2 pint. 3 point. 4 port.

PTA abbr. Parent-Teacher Association.

ptar·mi·gan /taármigǝn/ n. any of various grouses of the genus Lagopus, esp. L. mutus, with black or gray plumage in the summer and white in the winter. [Gael. tàrmachan: p- after Gk words in pt-]

PT boat n. a military patrol boat armed with torpedoes, etc. [Patrol Torpedo]

pter·i·dol·o·gy /téridólǝjee/ n. the study of ferns. □□ **pter·i·do·log·i·cal** /–dǝlójikǝl/ adj. **pter·i·dol·o·gist** n. [Gk pteris –idos fern + –LOGY]

pte·rid·o·phyte /tǝrídǝfīt, térǝ'dō–/ n. any flowerless plant of the division Pteridophyta, including ferns, club mosses, and horsetails. [Gk pteris –idos fern + phuton plant]

ptero- /térō/ comb. form wing. [Gk pteron wing]

pter·o·dac·tyl /térǝdáktil/ n. a large extinct flying birdlike reptile with a long slender head and neck.

pter·o·pod /térǝpod/ n. a marine gastropod with the middle part of its foot expanded into a pair of winglike lobes. [PTERO- + Gk pous podos foot]

pter·o·saur /térǝsawr/ n. any of a group of extinct flying reptiles with large batlike wings, including pterodactyls. [PTERO- + Gk saura lizard]

pter·o·yl·glu·tam·ic ac·id /térō-ilglootámik/ n. = FOLIC ACID. [pteroic acid + –YL + GLUTAMIC (ACID)]

pter·y·goid proc·ess /térigoyd/ adj. each of a pair of processes from the sphenoid bone in the skull. [Gk pterux –ugos wing]

PTFE abbr. polytetrafluoroethylene.

ptis·an /tízǝn, tizán/ n. a nourishing drink, esp. barley water. [ME & OF tizanne, etc., f. L ptisana f. Gk ptisanē peeled barley]

PTO abbr. 1 Parent-Teacher Organization. 2 please turn over. 3 power takeoff.

Ptol·e·ma·ic /tólimáyik/ adj. hist. 1 of or relating to Ptolemy, a 2nd-c. Alexandrian astronomer, or his theories. 2 of or relating to the Ptolemies, Macedonian rulers of Egypt from the death of Alexander the Great (323 BC) to the death of Cleopatra (30 BC). [L Ptolemaeus f. Gk Ptolemaios]

Ptol·e·ma·ic sys·tem n. the theory that the earth is the stationary center of the universe (cf. COPERNICAN SYSTEM).

pto·maine /tómayn/ n. any of various amine compounds, some toxic, in putrefying animal and vegetable matter. [F ptomaïne f. It. ptomaina irreg. f. Gk ptōma corpse]

pto·maine poi·son·ing n. food poisoning.

pto·sis /tósis/ n. a drooping of the upper eyelid due to paralysis, etc. □□ **pto·tic** /tótik/ adj. [Gk ptōsis f. piptō fall]

Pty. abbr. Austral., NZ, & S.Afr. proprietary.

pty·a·lin /tíǝlin/ n. an enzyme that hydrolyzes certain carbohydrates and is found in the saliva of humans and some other animals. [Gk ptualon spittle]

Pu symb. Chem. the element plutonium.

pub /pub/ n. colloq. 1 a tavern or bar. 2 Brit. a public house. 3 Austral. a hotel.

pub. abbr. (also **publ.**) 1 public. 2 publication. 3 published. 4 publisher. 5 publishing.

pub-crawl n. esp. Brit. colloq. a drinking tour of several pubs.

pu·ber·ty /pyóobǝrtee/ n. the period during which adolescents reach sexual maturity and become capable of reproduction. □□ **pu·ber·tal** adj. [ME f. F puberté or L pubertas f. puber adult]

pu·bes[1] /pyóobeez/ n. (pl. **same**) 1 the lower part of the abdomen at the front of the pelvis, covered with hair from puberty. 2 the hair appearing on the pubic region.[L]

pu·bes[2] pl. of PUBIS.

pu·bes·cence /pyóobésǝns/ n. 1 the time when puberty begins. 2 Bot. soft down on the leaves and stems of plants. 3 Zool. soft down on various parts of animals, esp. insects. □□ **pu·bes·cent** adj. [F pubescence or med.L pubescentia f. L pubescere reach puberty]

pu·bic /pyóobik/ adj. of or relating to the pubes or pubis.

pu·bis /pyóobis/ n. (pl. **pu·bes** /–beez/) either of a pair of bones forming the two sides of the pelvis. [L os pubis bone of the PUBES[1]]

pub·lic /públik/ adj. & n. ● adj. 1 of or concerning the people as a whole (a public holiday; the public interest). 2 open to or shared by all the people (public library; public meeting). 3 done or existing openly (made his views public; a public protest). 4 a (of a service, funds, etc.) provided by or concerning local or central government (public money; public records; public expenditure). b (of a person) in government (had a distinguished public career). 5 well-known; famous (a public figure). 6 Brit. of, for, or acting for, a university (public examination). ● n. 1 (as sing. or pl.) the community in general, or members of the community. 2 a section of the community having a particular interest or some special connection (the reading public; my public demands my loyalty). 3 Brit. colloq. a = PUBLIC BAR. b = PUBLIC HOUSE. □ **go public** become a public company or corporation. **in public** openly; publicly. **in the public domain** belonging to the public as a whole, esp. not subject to copyright. **in the public eye** famous or notorious. **make public** publicize; make known; publish. □□ **pub·lic·ly** adv. [ME f. OF public or L publicus f. pubes adult]

pub•lic act *n.* an act of legislation affecting the public as a whole.

pub•lic-ad•dress sys•tem *n.* loudspeakers, microphones, amplifiers, etc., used in addressing large audiences.

pub•li•can /públikən/ *n.* **1 a** *Brit.* the keeper of a public house. **b** *Austral.* the keeper of a hotel. **2** *Rom.Hist.* & *Bibl.* a tax collector. [ME f. OF *publicani* f. L *publicanus* f. *publicum* public revenue (as PUBLIC)]

pub•li•ca•tion /públikáyshən/ *n.* **1 a** the preparation and issuing of a book, newspaper, engraving, music, etc., to the public. **b** a book, etc., so issued. **2** the act or an instance of making something publicly known. [ME f. OF f. L *publicatio –onis* (as PUBLISH)]

pub•lic bar *n.* *Brit.* the least expensive bar in a public house.

pub•lic bill *n.* a bill of legislation affecting the public as a whole.

pub•lic com•pa•ny *n.* *Brit.* a company that sells shares to all buyers on the open market.

pub•lic cor•po•ra•tion *n.* a large corporation whose shares are sold or traded publicly.

pub•lic de•fend•er *n.* an attorney who provides legal representation at public expense for defendants who cannot afford their own attorney.

pub•lic en•e•my *n.* a notorious wanted criminal.

pub•lic fig•ure *n.* a famous person.

pub•lic health *n.* the provision of adequate sanitation, drainage, etc., by government.

pub•lic house *n.* *Brit.* an inn providing alcoholic drinks for consumption on the premises.

pub•li•cist /públisist/ *n.* **1** a publicity agent or public relations manager. **2** a journalist, esp. concerned with current affairs. **3** *archaic* a writer or other person skilled in international law. □□ **pub•li•cism** *n.* **pub•li•cis•tic** /–sístik/ *adj.* [F *publiciste* f. L *(jus) publicum* public law]

pub•lic•i•ty /públisitee/ *n.* **1 a** the professional exploitation of a product, company, person, etc., by advertising or popularizing. **b** material or information used for this. **2** public exposure; notoriety. [F *publicité* (as PUBLIC)]

pub•lic•i•ty a•gent *n.* a person employed to produce or heighten public exposure.

pub•li•cize /públisīz/ *v.tr.* advertise; make publicly known.

pub•lic land *n.* land owned by the government and usu. open for use by the public.

pub•lic law *n.* **1** the law of relations between individuals and the government. **2** = PUBLIC ACT.

pub•lic lend•ing right *n.* (in the UK) the right of authors to payment when their books, etc., are lent by public libraries.

pub•lic li•bel *n.* a published libel.

pub•lic nui•sance *n.* **1** an illegal act against the public generally. **2** *colloq.* an obnoxious person.

pub•lic o•pin•ion *n.* views, esp. moral, prevalent among the general public.

pub•lic own•er•ship *n.* the government ownership of the means of production, distribution, and exchange.

pub•lic pros•e•cu•tor *n.* a law officer conducting criminal proceedings on behalf of the state or in the public interest.

pub•lic purse *n.* the national treasury.

Pub•lic Rec•ord Of•fice *n.* an institution keeping official archives, esp. birth, marriage, and death certificates, for public inspection.

pub•lic re•la•tions *n.* the professional maintenance of a favorable public image, esp. by a company, famous person, etc.

pub•lic school *n.* **1** *US, Austral.,* & *Sc.,* etc., a free, government-supported school. **2** *Brit.* a private tuition-paying secondary school, esp. for boarders.

pub•lic sec•tor *n.* that part of an economy, industry, etc., that is controlled by the government.

pub•lic serv•ant *n.* a government official.

pub•lic spir•it *n.* a willingness to engage in community action.

pub•lic tel•e•vi•sion *n.* television funded by government appropriation and private donations rather than by advertising.

pub•lic trans•por•ta•tion *n.* buses, trains, etc., charging set fares and running on fixed routes, esp. when government-owned.

pub•lic u•til•i•ty *n.* an organization supplying water, gas, etc., to the community.

pub•lic works *n.pl.* building operations, etc., done by or for the government on behalf of the community.

pub•lic wrong *n.* an offense against society as a whole.

pub•lish /públish/ *v.tr.* **1** (also *absol.*) (of an author, publisher, etc.) prepare and issue (a book, newspaper, etc.) for public sale. **2** make generally known. **3** announce (an edict, etc.) formally; read (marriage banns). **4** *Law* communicate (a libel, etc.) to a third party. □□ **pub•lish•a•ble** *adj.* [ME *puplise*, etc., f. OF *puplier, publier* f. L *publicare* (as PUBLIC)]

pub•lish•er /públishər/ *n.* **1** a person or esp. a company that produces and distributes copies of a book, newspaper, etc., for sale. **2** the owner or chief executive of a publishing company. **3** a person or thing that publishes.

puce /pyōōs/ *adj.* & *n.* dark red or purplish brown. [F, = flea(-color) f. L *pulex –icis*]

puck[1] /puk/ *n.* a rubber disk used in ice hockey. [19th c.: orig. unkn.]

puck[2] /puk/ *n.* **1** a mischievous or evil sprite. **2** a mischievous child. □□ **puck•ish** *adj.* **puck•ish•ly** *adv.* **puck•ish•ness** *n.* **puck•like** *adj.* [OE *pūca*: cf. Welsh *pwca,* Ir. *púca*]

puck•a var. of PUKKA.

puck•er /púkər/ *v.* & *n.* ● *v.tr.* & *intr.* (often foll. by *up*) gather or cause to gather into wrinkles, folds, or bulges (*puckered her eyebrows; this seam is puckered up*). ● *n.* such a wrinkle, bulge, fold, etc. □□ **puck•er•y** *adj.* [prob. frequent., formed as POKE[2], POCKET (cf. PURSE)]

pud /pŏŏd/ *n.* *Brit. colloq.* = PUDDING. [abbr.]

pud•ding /pŏŏding/ *n.* **1 a** any of various dessert dishes, usu. containing flavoring, sugar, milk, etc. (*chocolate pudding; rice pudding*). **b** *Brit.* a savory dish containing flour, suet, etc. (*steak and kidney pudding*). **c** *Brit.* the dessert course of a meal. **d** the intestines of a pig, etc., stuffed with oatmeal, spices, blood, etc. **2** *colloq.* a person or thing resembling a pudding. **3** *Naut.* (also **pud•den•ing** /pŏŏd'ning/) esp. *Brit.* a pad or fender to prevent chafing between vessels, etc., esp. while being towed. □ **in the pudding club** *Brit. sl.* pregnant. □□ **pud•ding•like** *adj.* [ME *poding* f. OF *boudin* black pudding ult. f. L *botellus* sausage: see BOWEL]

pud•ding face *n.* *Brit. colloq.* a large fat face.

pud•ding head *n.* *colloq.* a stupid person.

pud•ding stone *n.* a conglomerate rock consisting of rounded pebbles in a siliceous matrix.

pud•dle /púd'l/ *n.* & *v.* ● *n.* **1** a small pool, esp. of rainwater on a road, etc. **2** clay and sand mixed with water and used as a watertight covering for embankments, etc. **3** a circular patch of disturbed water made by the blade of an oar at each stroke. ● *v.* **1** *tr.* **a** knead (clay and sand) into puddle. **b** line (a canal, etc.) with puddle. **c** to coat the roots of (a plant) with mud to reduce water loss during transplantation. **2** *intr.* make puddle from clay, etc. **3** *tr.* stir (molten iron) to produce wrought iron by expelling carbon. **4** *intr.* **a** wade or wallow in mud or shallow water. **b** busy oneself in an untidy way. **5** *tr.* make (water, etc.) muddy. **6** *tr.* work (mixed water and clay) to separate gold or opal. **7** to be covered with puddles (*the field puddled*). □□ **pud•dler** *n.* **pud•dly** *adj.* [ME *podel, puddel,* dimin. of OE *pudd* ditch]

pud•dle jump•er *n.* *sl.* a small, light plane for short distances or commercial routes.

pu•den•cy /pyŏŏd'nsee/ *n.* *literary* modesty; shame. [LL *pudentia* (as PUDENDUM)]

pu•den•dum /pyŏŏdéndəm/ *n.* (*pl.* **pu•den•da** /–də/) (usu. in *pl.*) the genitals, esp. of a woman. □□ **pu•den•dal** *adj.* **pu•dic** /pyŏŏdik/ *adj.* [L *pudenda (membra* parts), neut. pl. of gerundive of *pudēre* be ashamed]

pudg•y /púeje/ *adj.* (**pudg•i•er, pudg•i•est**) *colloq.* (esp. of a person) plump; slightly overweight. □□ **pudge** *n.* **pudg•i•ly** *adv.* **pudg•i•ness** *n.* [f. *podge* a short fat person]

pueb•lo /pwéblō/ *n.* (*pl.* **-los**) **1** (**Pueblo**) a member of a Native American people of the southwestern US. **2** a Native American settlement of the southwestern US, esp. one consisting of multistoried adobe houses built by the Pueblo people. [Sp., = people, f. L *populus*]

pu•er•ile /pyŏŏəril, pyŏŏril, –rīl/ *adj.* **1** trivial; childish; immature. **2** of or like a child. □□ **pu•er•ile•ly** *adv.* **pu•er•il•i•ty** /–rílitee/ *n.* (*pl.* **-ties**). [F *puéril* or L *puerilis* f. *puer* boy]

pu•er•per•al /pyŏŏ-órpərəl/ *adj.* of or caused by childbirth. [L *puerperus* f. *puer* child + *–parus* bearing]

pu•er•per•al fe•ver *n.* fever following childbirth and caused by uterine infection.

Puer•to Ri•can /pwértō reékən, páwrtə/ *n.* & *adj.* ● *n.* **1** a native of Puerto Rico, an island of the West Indies. **2** a person of Puerto Rican descent. ● *adj.* of or relating to Puerto Rico or its inhabitants.

puff /puf/ *n.* & *v.* ● *n.* **1 a** a short quick blast of breath or wind. **b** the sound of this; a similar sound. **c** a small quantity of vapor, smoke, etc., emitted in one blast; an inhalation or exhalation from a cigarette, pipe, etc. (*went up in a puff of smoke; took a puff from his cigarette*). **2** a light pastry containing jam, cream, etc. **3** a gathered mass of material in a dress, etc. (*puff sleeve*). **4** a protuberant roll of hair. **5 a** an extravagantly enthusiastic review of a book, etc., esp. in a newspaper. **b** *Brit.* an advertisement for goods, etc., esp. in a newspaper. **6** = POWDER PUFF. **7** an eiderdown. **8** *Brit. colloq.* one's life (*in all my puff*). ● *v.* **1** *intr.* emit a puff of air or breath; blow with short blasts. **2** *intr.* (usu. foll. by *away, out,* etc.) (of a person smoking, a steam engine, etc.) emit or move with puffs (*puffing away at his cigar; a train puffed out of the station*). **3** *tr.* esp. *Brit.* (usu. in passive; often foll. by *out*) put out of breath (*arrived somewhat puffed; completely puffed him out*). **4** *intr.* breathe hard; pant. **5** *tr.* utter pantingly (*"No more," he puffed*). **6** *intr.* & *tr.* (usu. foll. by *up, out*) become or cause to become inflated; swell (*his eye was inflamed and puffed up*). **7** *tr.* (usu. foll. by *out, up, away*) blow or emit (dust, smoke, a light object, etc.) with a puff. **8** *tr.* smoke (a pipe, etc.) in puffs. **9** *tr.* (usu. as **puffed up** *adj.*) elate; make proud or boastful. **10** *tr.* advertise or promote (goods, a book, etc.) with exaggerated or false praise. **puff up** = sense 9 of *v.* [ME *puf*, *puffe*, perh. f. OE, imit. of the sound of breath]

puff ad·der *n.* a large venomous African viper, *Bitis arietans*, which inflates the upper part of its body and hisses when excited.

puff·ball /púfbawl/ *n.* any fungus of the genus *Lycoperdon* and related genera producing a ball-shaped spore-bearing structure that releases its contents in a powdery cloud when broken.

puff·er /púfər/ *n.* **1** a person or thing that puffs. **2** any tropical fish of the family *Tetraodontidae*, able to inflate itself into a spherical form. Also called **globe fish**. **3** = PUFF-PUFF. □□ **puff·er·y** *n.*

puf·fin /púfin/ *n.* any of various seabirds of the family Alcidae native to the N. Atlantic and N. Pacific, esp. *Fratercula arctica*, having a large head with a brightly colored triangular bill and black and white plumage. [ME *poffin*, *pophyn*, of unkn. orig.]

puff pas·try *n.* light flaky pastry.

puff-puff *n. Brit.* a childish word for a steam engine or train.

puff·y /púfee/ *adj.* (**puff·i·er**, **puff·i·est**) **1** swollen, esp. of the face, etc. **2** fat. **3** gusty. **4** short-winded. □□ **puff·i·ly** *adv.* **puff·i·ness** *n.*

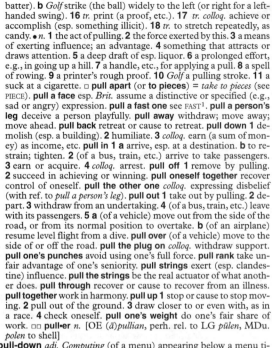

Atlantic puffin

pug[1] /pug/ *n.* **1** (in full **pugdog**) **a** a dwarf breed of dog like a bulldog with a broad flat nose and deeply wrinkled face. **b** a dog of this breed. **2** *Brit.* a small locomotive for shunting, etc. □□ **pug·gish** *adj.* **pug·gy** *adj.* [16th c.: perh. f. LG or Du.]

pug[2] /pug/ *n. & v.* ● *n.* loam or clay mixed and prepared for making bricks, pottery, etc. ● *v.tr.* (**pugged, pug·ging**) **1** prepare (clay) thus. **2** pack (esp. the space under the floor to deaden sound) with pug, sawdust, etc. □□ **pug·ging** *n.* [19th c.: orig. unkn.]

pug[3] /pug/ *n. sl.* a boxer. [abbr. of PUGILIST]

pug[4] /pug/ *n. & v.* ● *n.* the footprint of an animal. ● *v.tr.* (**pugged, pug·ging**) track by pugs. [Hindi *pag* footprint]

pug·ga·ree /púgəree/ *n.* **1** an E. Indian turban. **2** a thin muslin scarf tied around a sun helmet, etc., and shielding the neck. [Hindi *pagri* turban]

pu·gi·list /pyōojilist/ *n.* a boxer, esp. a professional. □□ **pu·gi·lism** *n.* **pu·gi·lis·tic** *adj.* [L *pugil* boxer]

pug mill *n.* a mill for preparing pug.

pug·na·cious /pugnáyshəs/ *adj.* quarrelsome; disposed to fight. □□ **pug·na·cious·ly** *adv.* **pug·na·cious·ness** *n.* **pug·nac·i·ty** /-násitee/ *n.* [L *pugnax –acis* f. *pugnare* fight f. *pugnus* fist]

pug nose *n.* a short squat or snub nose. □□ **pug-nosed** *adj.*

puis·ne /pyōonee/ *adj. Brit. Law* denoting a judge of a superior court inferior in rank to chief justices. [OF f. *puis* f. L *postea* afterwards + *né* born f. L *natus*: cf. PUNY]

puis·sance /pwísəns, pyōo-ís-, pyōó-is-/ *n. literary* great power, might, or influence. [ME (in sense 2) f. OF (as PUISSANT)]

puis·sant /pwísənt, pyōo-ís-, pyōó-is-/ *adj. literary* or *archaic* having great power or influence; mighty. □□ **puis·sant·ly** *adv.* [ME f. OF f. L *posse* be able: cf. POTENT[1]]

puke /pyōok/ *v. & n. sl.* ● *v.tr. & intr.* vomit. □□ **puk·ey** *adj.* [16th c.: prob. imit.]

puk·ka /púkə/ *adj.* (also **puk·kah, puck·a**) *Anglo-Ind.* **1** genuine. **2** of good quality; reliable (*did a pukka job*). **3** of full weight. [Hindi *pakkā* cooked, ripe, substantial]

pul·chri·tude /púlkritōod, –tyōod/ *n. literary* beauty. □□ **pul·chri·tu·di·nous** /–tōodinəs, –tyōod–/ *adj.* [ME f. L *pulchritudo –dinis* f. *pulcher –chri* beautiful]

pule /pyōol/ *v.intr.* cry querulously or weakly; whine; whimper. [16th c.: prob. imit.: cf. F *piauler*]

Pu·litz·er prize /pōólitsər, pyōo-/ *n.* each of a group of annual awards for achievements in American journalism, literature, and music. [J. *Pulitzer*, Amer. newspaper publisher d. 1911]

pull /pōol/ *v. & n.* ● *v.* **1** *tr.* exert force upon (a thing) tending to move it to oneself or the origin of the force (*stop pulling my hair*). **2** *tr.* cause to move in this way (*pulled it nearer*; *pulled me into the room*). **3** *intr.* exert a pulling force (*the horse pulls well*; *the engine will not pull*). **4** *tr.* extract (a cork or tooth) by pulling. **5** *tr.* damage (a muscle, etc.) by abnormal strain. **6 a** *tr.* move (a boat) by pulling on the oars. **b** *intr.* (of a boat, etc.) be caused to move, esp. in a specified direction. **7** *intr.* (often foll. by *up*) proceed with effort (up a hill, etc.). **8** *tr.* (foll. by *on*) bring out (a weapon) for use against (a person). **9 a** *tr.* check the speed of (a horse), esp. so as to make it lose the race. **b** *intr.* (of a horse) strain against the bit. **10** *tr.* attract or secure (custom or support). **11** *tr.* draw (liquor) from a barrel, etc. **12** *intr.* (foll. by *at*) tear or pluck at. **13** *intr.* (often foll. by *on, at*) inhale deeply; draw or suck (on a pipe, etc.). **14** *tr.* (often foll. by *up*) remove (a plant) by the root. **15** *tr.* **a** *Baseball* hit (a ball) to the left (for a right-handed batter) or to the right (for a left-handed

batter). **b** *Golf* strike (the ball) widely to the left (or right for a left-handed swing). **16** *tr.* print (a proof, etc.). **17** *tr. colloq.* achieve or accomplish (esp. something illicit). **18** *tr.* to stretch repeatedly, as candy. ● *n.* **1** the act of pulling. **2** the force exerted by this. **3** a means of exerting influence; an advantage. **4** something that attracts or draws attention. **5** a deep draft of esp. liquor. **6** a prolonged effort, e.g., in going up a hill. **7** a handle, etc., for applying a pull. **8** a spell of rowing. **9** a printer's rough proof. **10** *Golf* a pulling stroke. **11** a suck at a cigarette. □ **pull apart** (or **to pieces**) = *take to pieces* (see PIECE). **pull a face** esp. *Brit.* assume a distinctive or specified (e.g., sad or angry) expression. **pull a fast one** see FAST[1]. **pull a person's leg** deceive a person playfully. **pull away** withdraw; move away; move ahead. **pull back** retreat or cause to retreat. **pull down 1** demolish (e.g. a building). **2** humiliate. **3** *colloq.* earn (a sum of money) as income, etc. **pull in 1 a** arrive, esp. at a destination. **b** to restrain; tighten. **2** (of a bus, train, etc.) arrive to take passengers. **3** earn or acquire. **4** *colloq.* arrest. **pull off 1** remove by pulling. **2** succeed in achieving or winning. **pull oneself together** recover control of oneself. **pull the other one** *colloq.* expressing disbelief (with ref. to *pull a person's leg*). **pull out 1** take out by pulling. **2** depart. **3** withdraw from an undertaking. **4** (of a bus, train, etc.) leave with its passengers. **5 a** (of a vehicle) move out from the side of the road, or from its normal position to overtake. **b** (of an airplane) resume level flight from a dive. **pull over** (of a vehicle) move to the side of or off the road. **pull the plug on** *colloq.* withdraw support. **pull one's punches** avoid using one's full force. **pull rank** take unfair advantage of one's seniority. **pull strings** exert (esp. clandestine) influence. **pull the strings** be the real actuator of what another does. **pull through** recover or cause to recover from an illness. **pull together** work in harmony. **pull up 1** stop or cause to stop moving. **2** pull out of the ground. **3** draw closer to or even with, as in a race. **4** check oneself. **pull one's weight** do one's fair share of work. □□ **pull·er** *n.* [OE (*ā*)*pullian*, perh. rel. to LG *pūlen*, MDu. *polen* to shell]

pull-down *adj. Computing* (of a menu) appearing below a menu title when selected.

pul·let /pōolit/ *n.* a young hen, esp. one less than one year old. [ME f. OF *poulet* dimin. of *poule* ult. fem. of L *pullus* chicken]

pul·ley /pōolee/ *n. & v.* ● *n.* (*pl.* **·leys**) **1** a grooved wheel or set of wheels for a rope, etc., to pass over, set in a block and used for changing the direction of a force. **2** a wheel or drum fixed on a shaft and turned by a belt, used esp. to increase speed or power. ● *v.tr.* (**·leys, ·leyed**) **1** hoist or work with a pulley. **2** provide with a pulley. [ME f. OF *polie* prob. ult. f. med. Gk *polidion* (unrecorded) pivot, dimin. of *polos* POLE[2]]

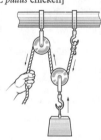

pulley 1

pull-in *n. n. Brit.* a roadside café or other stopping place.

Pull·man /pōolmən/ *n.* **1** a railroad car affording special comfort, esp. one with sleeping berths. **2** (in full **Pullman trunk** or **case**) a large suitcase. [G. M. *Pullman*, Amer. designer d. 1897]

pull·o·ver /pōolōvər/ *n.* a knitted garment put on over the head and covering the top half of the body.

pull-tab *n.* (of a can) a ring or tab that is pulled to open a can.

pul·lu·late /púlyəlayt/ *v.intr.* **1** (of a seed, shoot, etc.) bud, sprout; germinate. **2** (esp. of an animal) swarm; throng; breed prolifically. **3** develop; spring up; come to life. **4** (foll. by *with*) abound. □□ **pul·lu·lant** *adj.* **pul·lu·la·tion** /–láyshən/ *n.* [L *pullulare* sprout f. *pullulus* dimin. of *pullus* young of an animal]

pul·mo·nar·y /pōolməneree, púl–/ *adj.* **1** of or relating to the lungs. **2** having lungs or lunglike organs. **3** affected with or susceptible to lung disease. □□ **pul·mo·nate** /–nayt, –nət/ *adj.* [L *pulmonarius* f. *pulmo –onis* lung]

pul·mo·nar·y ar·ter·y *n.* the artery conveying blood from the heart to the lungs.

pul·mo·nar·y vein *n.* the vein carrying oxygenated blood from the lungs to the heart.

pul·mon·ic /pōolmónik, pul–/ *adj.* = PULMONARY 1. [F *pulmonique* or f. mod.L *pulmonicus* f. L *pulmo* (as PULMONARY)]

pulp /pulp/ *n. & v.* ● *n.* **1** the soft fleshy part of fruit, etc. **2** any soft thick wet mass. **3** a soft shapeless mass derived from rags, wood, etc., used in papermaking. **4** (often *attrib.*) poor quality (often sensational) writing orig. printed on rough paper (*pulp fiction*). **5** vascular tissue filling the interior cavity and root canals of a tooth. **6** *Mining* pulverized ore mixed with water. ● *v.* **1** *tr.* reduce to pulp. **2** *tr.* withdraw (a publication) from the market, usu. recycling the paper. **3** *tr.* remove pulp from. **4** *intr.* become pulp. □□ **pulp·er** *n.* **pulp·less** *adj.* **pulp·y** *adj.* **pulp·i·ness** *n.* [L *pulpa*]

pul·pit /pōolpit, púl–/ *n.* **1** a raised enclosed platform in a church, etc., from which the preacher delivers a sermon. **2** (prec. by *the*) preachers or preaching collectively. [ME f. L *pulpitum* scaffold, platform]

pulp·wood /púlpwŏŏd/ n. timber suitable for making pulp.

pul·que /pŏŏlkay, pŏŏlkee, pŏŏl–/ n. a Mexican fermented drink made from the sap of the maguey. [17th c.: Amer. Sp., of unkn. orig.]

pul·que bran·dy n. a strong intoxicant made from pulque.

pul·sar /púlsaar/ n. Astron. a cosmic source of regular and rapid pulses of radiation usu. at radio frequencies, e.g., a rotating neutron star. [*pulsating* st*ar*, after *quasar*]

pul·sate /púlsayt/ v.intr. 1 expand and contract rhythmically; throb. 2 vibrate; quiver; thrill. □□ **pul·sa·tion** /–sáyshən/ n. **pul·sa·tor** n. **pul·sa·to·ry** /púlsətawree/ adj. [L *pulsare* frequent. of *pellere* puls- drive, beat]

pul·sa·tile /púlsətil, –tīl/ adj. 1 of or having the property of pulsation. 2 (of a musical instrument) played by percussion. [med.L *pulsatilis* (as PULSATE)]

pulse[1] /puls/ n. & v. ● n. 1 a a rhythmical throbbing of the arteries as blood is propelled through them, esp. as felt in the wrists, temples, etc. b each successive beat of the arteries or heart. c (in full **pulse rate**) the number of such beats in a specified period of time, esp. one minute. 2 a throb or thrill of life or emotion. 3 a latent feeling. 4 a single vibration of sound, electric current, light, etc., esp. as a signal. 5 a musical beat. 6 any regular or recurrent rhythm, e.g., of the stroke of oars. ● v.intr. 1 pulsate. 2 (foll. by *out, in*, etc.) transmit, etc., by rhythmical beats. □ **pulse modulation** a type of modulation in which pulses are varied to represent a signal. □□ **pulse·less** adj. [ME f. OF *pous* f. L *pulsus* f. *pellere* puls- drive, beat]

pulse[2] /puls/ n. (as *sing*. or *pl*.) 1 the edible seeds of various leguminous plants, e.g., chickpeas, lentils, beans, etc. 2 the plant or plants producing this. [ME f. OF *pols* f. L *puls pultis* porridge of meal, etc.]

pul·sim·e·ter /pulsímitər/ n. an instrument for measuring the rate or force of a pulse.

pul·ver·ize /púlvərīz/ v. 1 tr. reduce to fine particles. 2 intr. be reduced to dust. 3 colloq. tr. a demolish. b defeat utterly. □□ **pul·ver·iz·a·ble** adj. **pul·ver·i·za·tion** n. **pul·ver·iz·er** n. [ME f. LL *pulverizare* f. *pulvis pulveris* dust]

pul·ver·u·lent /pulvéryələnt, –vérə–/ adj. 1 consisting of fine particles; powdery. 2 likely to crumble. [L *pulverulentus* (as PULVERIZE)]

pu·ma /pyŏŏmə, pŏŏ–/ n. a large American wild cat, *Felis concolor*, usu. with a plain tawny coat. Also called **cougar**, **panther**, or **mountain lion**. [Sp. f. Quechua]

pum·ice /púmis/ n. & v. ● n. (in full **pumice stone**) 1 a light porous volcanic rock often used as an abrasive in cleaning or polishing substances. 2 a piece of this used for removing callused skin, etc. ● v.tr. rub or clean with a pumice. □□ **pu·mi·ceous** /pyŏŏmíshəs/ adj. [ME f. OF *pomis* f. L *pumex pumicis* (dial. *pom*-): cf. POUNCE[2]]

pum·mel /púməl/ v.tr. (**pum·meled** or **pum·melled**, **pum·mel·ing** or **pum·mel·ling**) strike repeatedly, esp. with the fist. [alt. f. POMMEL]

pump[1] /pump/ n. & v. ● n. 1 a machine, usu. with rotary action or the reciprocal action of a piston, for raising or moving liquids, compressing gases, inflating tires, etc. 2 a physiological or electromagnetic process or mechanism having a similar purpose. 3 an instance of pumping; a stroke of a pump. ● v. 1 tr. (often foll.by *in, out, into, up*, etc.) raise or remove (liquid, gas, etc.) with a pump. 2 tr. (often foll. by *up*) fill (a tire, etc.) with air. 3 tr. a remove (water, etc.) with a pump. b (foll. by *out*) remove liquid from (a place, well, etc.) with a pump. 4 intr. work a pump. 5 tr. (often foll. by *out*) cause to move, pour forth, etc., as if by pumping. 6 tr. question (a person) persistently to obtain information. 7 tr. a move vigorously up and down. b shake (a person's hand) effusively. 8 tr. (usu. foll. by *up*) arouse; excite. □ **pump iron** (also **pump up**) colloq. exercise with weights. [ME *pumpe, pompe* (orig. Naut.): prob. imit.]

pump[2] /pump/ n. 1 a usu. medium-heeled slip-on women's dress shoe. 2 a slip-on men's patent leather shoe for formal wear. [16th c.: orig. unkn.]

pum·per·nick·el /púmpərnikəl/ n. German-style dark, coarse rye bread. [G, earlier = lout, bumpkin, of uncert. orig.]

pump·kin /púmpkin, púng–/ n. 1 the rounded orange edible gourd of a vine (*Cucurbita pepa*). 2 Brit. a any of various plants of the genus *Cucurbita*, esp. *C. maxima*, with large lobed leaves and tendrils. b the large rounded yellow fruit of this with a thick rind and edible flesh. [alt. f. earlier *pompon, pumpion* f. obs. F *po(m)pon* f. L *pepo* -*onis* f. Gk *pepōn* large melon: see PEPO]

pun[1] /pun/ n. & v. ● n. the humorous use of a word to suggest different meanings, or of words of the same sound and different meanings. ● v.intr. (**punned, pun·ning**) (foll. by *on*) make a pun or puns with (words). □□ **pun·ning·ly** adv. [17th c.: perh. f. obs. *pundigrion*, a fanciful formation]

pun[2] /pun/ v.tr. (**punned, pun·ning**) Brit. consolidate (earth or rubble) by pounding or ramming. □□ **pun·ner** n. [dial. var. of POUND[2]]

pu·na /pŏŏnə/ n. 1 a high plateau in the Peruvian Andes. 2 = MOUNTAIN SICKNESS. [Quechua, in sense 1]

pumpkin 1

punch[1] /punch/ v. & n. ● v.tr. 1 strike bluntly, esp. with a closed fist. 2 prod or poke with a blunt object. 3 a pierce a hole in (metal, paper, a ticket, etc.) as or with a punch. b pierce (a hole) by punching. 4 drive (cattle) by prodding with a stick, etc. ● n. 1 a blow with a fist. 2 the ability to deliver this. 3 colloq. vigor; momentum; effective force. □ **punch in** (or **out**) record the time of one's arrival at (or departure from) work by punching a time clock. □□ **punch·er** n. [ME, var. of POUNCE[1]]

punch[2] /punch/ n. 1 any of various devices or machines for punching holes in materials (e.g., paper, leather, metal, plaster). 2 a tool or machine for impressing a design or stamping a die on a material. [perh. an abbr. of PUNCHEON[1], or f. PUNCH[1]]

punch[3] /punch/ n. a drink of fruit juices, sometimes mixed with wine or liquor, served cold or hot. [17th c.: orig. unkn.]

punch[4] /punch/ n. 1 (**Punch**) a humpbacked, hook-nosed figure in a puppet show called *Punch and Judy*. 2 (in full **Suffolk punch**) a short-legged thickset draft horse. □ **as pleased as Punch** showing great pleasure. [abbr. of PUNCHINELLO]

punch bowl n. 1 a bowl in which punch is mixed and served. 2 esp. Brit. a deep round hollow in a hill.

punch card n. Also called **punched card** (or **tape**) a card or paper tape perforated according to a code, for conveying instructions or data to a data processor, etc.

punch-drunk adj. stupefied from or as though from a series of heavy blows.

pun·cheon[1] /púnchən/ n. 1 a short post, esp. one supporting a roof in a coal mine. 2 = PUNCH[2]. 3 a heavy timber finished on one side only, used in flooring, etc. [ME f. OF *poinson, po(i)nchon*, ult. f. L *pungere punct*- prick]

pun·cheon[2] /púnchən/ n. a large cask for liquids, etc., holding from 72 to 120 gallons. [ME f. OF *poinson, po(i)nchon*, of unkn. orig. (prob. not the same as in PUNCHEON[1])]

Pun·chi·nel·lo /púnchinélō/ n. (pl. -**los**) 1 the chief character in a traditional Italian puppet show. 2 a short stout person of comical appearance. [Neapolitan dial. *Polecenella*, It. *Pulcinella*, perh. dimin. of *pollecena*, young turkey-cock with a hooked beak f. *pulcino* chicken ult. f. L *pullus*]

punch·ing bag n. a usu. suspended stuffed or inflated bag used for punching as a form of exercise or training.

punch line n. words giving the point of a joke or story.

punch-up n. Brit. colloq. a fistfight; a brawl.

punch·y /púnchee/ adj. (**punch·i·er, punch·i·est**) 1 having punch or vigor; forceful. 2 = PUNCH-DRUNK. □□ **punch·i·ly** adv. **punch·i·ness** n.

punc·tate /púngktayt/ adj. Biol. marked or studded with points, dots, spots, etc. □□ **punc·ta·tion** /–táyshən/ n. [L *punctum* (as POINT)]

punc·til·i·o /pungktíleeō/ n. (pl. -**os**) 1 a delicate point of ceremony or honor. 2 the etiquette of such points. 3 petty formality. [It. *puntiglio* & Sp. *puntillo* dimin. of *punto* POINT]

punc·til·i·ous /pungktíleeəs/ adj. 1 attentive to formality or etiquette. 2 precise in behavior. □□ **punc·til·i·ous·ly** adv. **punc·til·i·ous·ness** n. [F *pointilleux* f. *pointille* f. It. (as PUNCTILIO)]

punc·tu·al /púngkchŏŏəl/ adj. 1 observant of the appointed time. 2 neither early nor late. 3 Geom. of a point. □□ **punc·tu·al·i·ty** /–áli-tee/ n. **punc·tu·al·ly** adv. [ME f. med.L *punctualis* f. L *punctum* POINT]

punc·tu·ate /púngkchŏŏ-ayt/ v.tr. 1 insert punctuation marks in. 2 interrupt at intervals (*punctuated his tale with heavy sighs*). 3 emphasize. [med.L *punctuare punctuat*- (as PUNCTUAL)]

punc·tu·a·tion /púngkchŏŏ-áyshən/ n. 1 the system or arrangement of marks used to punctuate a written passage. 2 the practice or skill of punctuating. [med.L *punctuatio* (as PUNCTUATE)]

punc·tu·a·tion mark n. any of the marks (e.g., period and comma) used in writing to separate sentences and phrases, etc., and to clarify meaning.

punc·ture /púngkchər/ n. & v. ● n. 1 a pierced hole, esp. the accidental piercing of a pneumatic tire. 2 a hole made in this way. ● v. 1 tr. make a puncture in. 2 intr. become punctured. 3 tr. prick or pierce. 4 tr. cause (hopes, confidence, etc.) to collapse; dash; deflate. [ME f. L *punctura* f. *pungere punct*- prick]

pun·dit /púndit/ n. 1 (also **pan·dit**) a Hindu learned in Sanskrit and in the philosophy, religion, and jurisprudence of India. 2 often iron. a a learned expert or teacher. b a critic. □□ **pun·dit·ry** n. [Hind. *paṇḍit* f. Skr. *paṇḍita* learned]

pun·gent /púnjənt/ adj. 1 having a sharp or strong taste or smell. 2 (of remarks) penetrating; biting; caustic. 3 Biol. having a sharp point. □□ **pun·gen·cy** n. **pun·gent·ly** adv. [L *pungere* pres. part. of *pungere* prick]

Pu·nic /pyŏŏnik/ adj. & n. ● adj. 1 of or relating to ancient Carthage in N. Africa. 2 treacherous. ● n. the language of Carthage, related to Phoenician. [L *Punicus, Poenicus* f. *Poenus* f. Gk *Phoinix* Phoenician]

Pu·nic faith n. treachery.

pun·ish /púnish/ *v.tr.* **1** cause (an offender) to suffer for an offense. **2** inflict a penalty for (an offense). **3** *colloq.* inflict severe blows on (an opponent). **4 a** tax severely; subject to severe treatment. **b** abuse or treat improperly. □□ **pun·ish·a·ble** *adj.* **pun·ish·er** *n.* **pun·ish·ing** *adj.* (in sense 4a). **pun·ish·ing·ly** *adv.* [ME f. OF *punir* f. L *punire* = *poenire* f. *poena* penalty]

pun·ish·ment /púnishmənt/ *n.* **1** the act or an instance of punishing; the condition of being punished. **2** the loss or suffering inflicted in this. **3** *colloq.* severe treatment or suffering. [ME f. AF & OF *punisse-ment* f. *punir*]

pu·ni·tive /pyoónitiv/ *adj.* (also **pu·ni·to·ry** /–tawree/) **1** inflicting or intended to inflict punishment. **2** (of taxation, etc. ● *n.* extremely severe. □□ **pu·ni·tive·ly** *adv.* [F *punitif –ive* or med.L *punitivus* (as PUNISHMENT)]

pu·ni·tive damages *n.pl. Law* additional compensation awarded by a court to a plaintiff in a suit as punishment to the defendant.

Pun·ja·bi /poonjaábee/ *n. & adj.* ● *n.* (*pl.* **Pun·ja·bis**) **1** a native of the Punjab in India. **2** the language of this people. ● *adj.* of or relating to the Punjab. [Hindi *panjābī*]

punk /pungk/ *n. & adj.* ● *n.* **1 a** a worthless person or thing (often as a general term of abuse). **b** nonsense. **2 a** (in full **punk rock**) a loud fast-moving form of rock music with crude and aggressive effects. **b** (in full **punk rocker**) a devotee of this. **3** a hoodlum or ruffian. **4** a young male homosexual partner. **5** an inexperienced person; a novice. **6** soft crumbly wood used as tinder. **7** a spongy fungal substance, esp. as used as a fuse. ● *adj.* **1** worthless; poor in quality. **2** denoting punk rock and its associations. **3** (of wood) rotten; decayed. □□ **punk·y** *adj.* [18th c.: orig. unkn.: cf. SPUNK]

pun·kah /púngkə/ *n.* **1** (in India) a fan usu. made from the leaf of the palmyra. **2** a large swinging cloth fan hung from the ceiling and worked by a cord or electrically. [Hindi *pankhā* fan f. Skr. *pakṣaka* f. *pakṣa* wing]

pun·net /púnit/ *n. Brit.* a small light basket or container for fruit or vegetables. [19th c.: perh. dimin. of dial. *pun* POUND[1]]

pun·ster /púnstər/ *n.* a person who makes puns, esp. habitually.

punt[1] /punt/ *n. & v.* ● *n.* a long narrow flat-bottomed boat, square at both ends, used mainly on rivers and propelled by a long pole. ● *v.* **1** *tr.* propel (a punt) with a pole. **2** *intr. & tr.* travel or convey in a punt. [ME f. MLG *punte, punto* & MDu. *ponte* ferryboat f. L *ponto* Gaulish transport vessel]

punt[2] /punt/ *v. & n.* ● *v.tr.* kick (a ball, as in football or rugby) after it has dropped from the hands and before it reaches the ground. ● *n.* such a kick. [prob. f. dial. *punt* push forcibly: cf. BUNT[3]]

punt[3] /punt/ *v. & n.* ● *v.intr.* **1** (in some card games) lay a stake against the bank. **2** *Brit. colloq.* **a** bet on a horse, etc. **b** speculate in shares, etc. ● *n.* **1** esp. *Brit.* a bet. **2** a point in faro. **3** a person who plays against the bank in faro. [F *ponter* f. *ponte* player against the bank f. Sp. *punto* POINT]

punt[4] /poont/ *n.* the chief monetary unit of the Republic of Ireland. [Ir., = pound]

punt·er /púntər/ *n.* **1** one who punts, esp. one who punts a ball. **2** *Brit.* a person who gambles or lays a bet. **3** *Brit.* **a** *colloq.* a customer or client; a member of an audience. **b** *colloq.* a participant in any activity; a person. **c** *sl.* a prostitute's client. **4** a point in faro.

pu·ny /pyoónee/ *adj.* (**pu·ni·er, pu·ni·est**) **1** undersized. **2** weak; feeble. **3** petty. □□ **pu·ni·ly** *adv.* **pu·ni·ness** *n.* [phonetic spelling of PUISNE]

pup /pup/ *n. & v.* ● *n.* **1** a young dog. **2** a young wolf, rat, seal, etc. **3** esp. *Brit.* an unpleasant or arrogant young man. ● *v.tr.* (**pupped, pup·ping**) (also *absol.*) bring forth (pups). ● **in pup** (of a dog, wolf, etc.) pregnant. **sell a person a pup** *Brit.* swindle a person, esp. by selling something worthless. [back-form. f. PUPPY as if a dimin. in –Y[2]]

pu·pa /pyoópə/ *n.* (*pl.* **pu·pae** /–pee/) an insect in the stage of development between larva and imago. □□ **pu·pal** *adj.* [mod.L f. L *pupa* girl, doll]

pu·pate /pyoópayt/ *v.intr.* become a pupa. □□ **pu·pa·tion** *n.*

pu·pil[1] /pyoópəl/ *n.* a person who is taught by another, esp. a student in relation to a teacher. □□ **pu·pil·age** *n.* (also **pu·pil·lage**). **pu·pil·lar·y** *adj.* [ME, orig. = orphan, ward f. OF *pupille* or L *pupillus*, *–illa*, dimin. of *pupus* boy, *pupa* girl]

pu·pil[2] /pyoópəl/ *n.* the dark circular opening in the center of the iris of the eye, varying in size to regulate the passage of light to the retina. □□ **pu·pil·lar** *adj.* (also **pu·pil·ar**). **pu·pil·lar·y** *adj.* (also **pu·pi·lar·y**). [OF *pupille* or L *pupilla*, dimin. of *pūpa* doll (as PUPIL[1]): so called from the tiny images visible in the eye]

pu·pip·a·rous /pyoopípərəs/ *adj. Entomol.* bringing forth young which are already in a pupal state. [mod.L *pupipara* neut. pl. of *pupiparus* (as PUPA, *parere* bring forth)]

pup·pet /púpit/ *n.* **1** a small figure representing a human being or animal and moved by various means as entertainment. **2** a person whose actions are controlled by another. □□ **pup·pet·ry** *n.* [later form of POPPET]

pup·pet·eer /púpiteér/ *n.* a person who works puppets.

pup·pet state *n.* a country that is nominally independent but actually under the control of another power.

pup·py /púpee/ *n.* (*pl.* **·pies**) **1** a young dog. **2** a conceited or arrogant young man. □□ **pup·py·hood** *n.* **pup·py·ish** *adj.* [ME perh. f. OF *po(u)pee* doll, plaything, toy f. Rmc (as POPPET)]

pup·py fat *n. Brit.* temporary fatness of a child or adolescent.

pup·py love *n.* romantic attachment or affection between adolescents.

pup tent *n.* a small two-person tent, usu. made of two pieces fastened together.

pur- /pər/ *prefix* = PRO-[1] (*purchase; pursue*). [AF f. OF *por-, pur-, pour-* f. L *por-, pro-*]

Pu·ra·na /poooraánə/ *n.* any of a class of Sanskrit sacred writings on Hindu mythology, folklore, etc. □□ **Pu·ra·nic** *adj.* [Skr. *purāṇa* ancient legend, ancient, f. *purā* formerly]

pur·blind /pórblind/ *adj.* **1** partly blind. **2** obtuse; dim-witted. □□ **pur·blind·ness** *n.* [ME *pur(e)* blind f. PURE orig. in sense 'utterly,' with assim. to PUR-]

pur·chase /pórchis/ *v. & n.* ● *v.tr.* **1** acquire by payment; buy. **2** obtain or achieve at some cost. **3** *Naut.* haul up (an anchor, etc.) by means of a pulley, lever, etc. ● *n.* **1** the act or an instance of buying. **2** something bought. **3** *Law* the acquisition of property by one's personal action and not by inheritance. **4 a** a firm hold on a thing to move it or to prevent it from slipping; leverage. **b** a device or tackle for moving heavy objects. **5** the annual rent or return from land. □□ **pur·chas·a·ble** *adj.* **pur·chas·er** *n.* [ME f. AF *purchacer*, OF *pourchacier* seek to obtain (as PUR-, CHASE[1])]

pur·dah /pórdə/ *n. Ind.* **1** a system in certain Muslim and Hindu societies of screening women from strangers by means of a veil or curtain. **2** a curtain in a house, used for this purpose. [Urdu & Pers. *pardah* veil, curtain]

pure /pyoor/ *adj.* **1** unmixed; unadulterated (*pure white; pure alcohol*). **2** of unmixed origin or descent (*pure-blooded*). **3** chaste. **4** morally or sexually undefiled; not corrupt. **5** conforming absolutely to a standard of quality; faultless. **6** guiltless. **7** sincere. **8** mere; simple; nothing but; sheer (*it was pure malice*). **9** (of a sound) not discordant; perfectly in tune. **10** (of a subject of study) dealing with abstract concepts and not practical application. **11 a** (of a vowel) not joined with another in a diphthong. **b** (of a consonant) not accompanied by another. □□ **pure·ness** *n.* [ME f. OF *pur* pure f. L *purus*]

pure·bred /pyoórbred/ *adj. & n.* ● *adj.* belonging to a recognized breed of unmixed lineage. ● *n.* a purebred animal.

pu·rée /pyooráy, pyoorée/ *n. & v.* ● *n.* a pulp of vegetables or fruit, etc., reduced to a smooth, creamy substance. ● *v.tr.* (**pu·rées, pu·réed**) make a purée of. [F]

pure·ly /pyoórlee/ *adv.* **1** in a pure manner. **2** merely; solely; exclusively.

pure sci·ence *n.* a science depending on deductions from demonstrated truths (e.g., mathematics or logic), or one studied without practical applications.

pur·fle /pórfəl/ *n. & v.* ● *n.* **1** an ornamental border, esp. on a violin, etc. **2** *archaic* the ornamental or embroidered edge of a garment. ● *v.tr.* **1** decorate with a purfle. **2** (often foll. by *with*) ornament (the edge of a building). **3** beautify. □□ **pur·fling** *n.* [ME f. OF *porfil, porfiler* ult. f. L *filum* thread]

pur·ga·tion /pərgáyshən/ *n.* **1** purification. **2** purging of the bowels. **3** spiritual cleansing, esp. (*RC Ch.*) of a soul in purgatory. **4** *hist.* the cleansing of oneself from accusation or suspicion by an oath or ordeal. [ME f. OF *purgation* or L *purgatio* (as PURGE)]

pur·ga·tive /pórgətiv/ *adj. & n.* ● *adj.* **1** serving to purify. **2** strongly laxative. ● *n.* **1** a purgative thing. **2** a laxative. [ME f. OF *purgatif –ive* or LL *purgativus* (as PURGE)]

pur·ga·to·ry /pórgətawree/ *n. & adj.* ● *n.* (*pl.* **·ries**) **1** the condition or supposed place of spiritual cleansing, esp. (*RC Ch.*) of those dying in the grace of God but having to expiate venial sins, etc. **2** a place or state of temporary suffering or expiation. ● *adj.* purifying. □□ **pur·ga·to·ri·al** /–táwreeəl/ *adj.* [ME f. AF *purgatorie*, OF *–oire* f. med.L *purgatorium*, neut. of LL *purgatorius* (as PURGE)]

purge /pərj/ *v. & n.* ● *v.tr.* **1** (often foll. by *of, from*) make physically or spiritually clean. **2** remove by a cleansing or erasing (as of computer files) process. **3 a** rid (an organization, party, etc.) of persons regarded as undesirable. **b** remove (a person regarded as undesirable) from an organization, party, etc., often violently or by force. **4 a** empty (the bowels). **b** empty the bowels of. **5** *Law* atone for or wipe out (an offense, esp. contempt of court). ● *n.* **1 a** the act or an instance of purging. **b** the removal, often in a forcible or violent manner, of people regarded as undesirable from an organization, party, etc. **2** a purgative. □□ **purg·er** *n.* [ME f. OF *purg(i)er* f. L *purgare* purify f. *purus* pure]

pu·ri·fy /pyoórifi/ *v.tr.* (**·fies, ·fied**) **1** (often foll. by *of, from*) cleanse or make pure. **2** make ceremonially clean. **3** clear of extraneous elements. □□ **pu·ri·fi·ca·tion** /–fikáshən/ *n.* **pu·ri·fi·ca·to·ry** /–rífəkətáwree/ *adj.* **pu·ri·fi·er** *n.* [ME f. OF *purifier* f. L *purificare* (as PURE)]

Pu·rim /poóorim, pooréėm/ *n.* a Jewish spring festival commemorating the defeat of Haman's plot to massacre the Jews (Esth. 9). [Heb., pl. of *pūr*, perh. = LOT *n*. 2]

pu•rine /pyŏŏreen/ *n*. **1** *Chem.* an organic nitrogenous base forming uric acid on oxidation. **2** any of a group of derivatives with purinelike structure, including the nucleotide constituents adenine and guanine. [G *Purin* L *purus* pure + *uricum* uric acid + *–in* –INE[4]]

pur•ist /pyŏŏrist/ *n*. a stickler for or advocate of scrupulous purity, esp. in language or art. □□ **pur•ism** *n*. **pu•ris•tic** *adj*. [F *puriste* f. *pur* PURE]

pu•ri•tan /pyŏŏrit'n/ *n*. & *adj*. • *n*. **1** (**Puritan**) *hist*. a member of a group of English Protestants who regarded the Reformation of the Church under Elizabeth as incomplete and sought to simplify and regulate forms of worship. **2** a purist member of any party. **3** a person practicing or affecting extreme strictness in religion or morals. • *adj*. **1** *hist*. of or relating to the Puritans. **2** scrupulous and austere in religion or morals. □□ **pu•ri•tan•ism** *n*. [LL *puritas* (as PURITY) after earlier *Catharan* (as CATHAR)]

pu•ri•tan•i•cal /pyŏŏritánikəl/ *adj*. often *derog*. practicing or affecting strict religious or moral behavior. □□ **pu•ri•tan•i•cal•ly** *adv*.

pu•ri•ty /pyŏŏritee/ *n*. **1** pureness; cleanness. **2** freedom from physical or moral pollution. [ME f. OF *pureté*, with assim. to LL *puritas –tatis* f. L *purus* pure]

purl[1] /pərl/ *n*. & *v*. • *n*. **1** a knitting stitch made by putting the needle through the front of the previous stitch and passing the yarn around the back of the needle. **2** a cord of twisted gold or silver wire for bordering. **3** a chain of minute loops; a picot. **4** the ornamental edges of lace, ribbon, etc. • *v.tr*. (also *absol*.) knit with a purl stitch. [orig. *pyrle*, *pirle* f. Sc. *pirl* twist: the knitting sense may be f. a different word]

purl[2] /pərl/ *v*. & *n*. • *v.intr*. (of a brook, etc.) flow with a swirling motion and babbling sound. • *n*. this motion or sound. [16th c.: prob. imit.: cf. Norw. *purla* bubble up]

purl•er /pərlər/ *n*. *Brit. colloq*. a headlong fall. [*purl* upset, rel. to PURL[1]]

pur•lieu /pərlyŏŏ/ *n*. (*pl*. **pur•lieus**) **1** a person's bounds or limits. **2** a person's usual haunts. **3** *Brit. hist*. a tract on the border of a forest, esp. one earlier included in it and still partly subject to forest laws. **4** (in *pl*.) the outskirts; an outlying region. [ME *purlew*, prob. alt. after F *lieu* place f. AF *purale(e)*, OF *pouralee* a going around to settle the boundaries f. *po(u)raler* traverse]

pur•lin /pərlin/ *n*. a horizontal beam along the length of a roof, resting on principals and supporting the common rafters or boards. [ME: orig. uncert.]

pur•loin /pərlóyn/ *v.tr*. literary steal; pilfer. □□ **pur•loin•er** *n*. [ME f. AF *purloigner* put away, do away with (as PUR-, *loign* far f. L *longe*)]

pur•ple /pərpəl/ *n*., *adj*., & *v*. • *n*. **1** a color intermediate between red and blue. **2** (in full **Tyrian purple**) a crimson dye obtained from some mollusks. **3** a purple robe, esp. as the dress of an emperor or senior magistrate. **4** the scarlet official dress of a cardinal. **5** (prec. by *the*) a position of rank, authority, or privilege. • *adj*. of a purple color. • *v.tr*. & *intr*. make or become purple. □ **born in** (or **to**) **the purple 1** born into a reigning family. **2** belonging to the most privileged class. □□ **pur•ple•ness** *n*. **pur•plish** *adj*. **pur•ply** *adj*. [OE alt. f. *purpure* *purpuran* f. L *purpura* (as PURPURA)]

Pur•ple Heart *n*. a US military decoration for those wounded in action.

pur•ple pas•sage *n*. (also **pur•ple prose** or **pur•ple patch**) an overly ornate or elaborate passage, esp. in a literary composition.

pur•port *v*. & *n*. • *v.tr*. /pərpáwrt/ **1** profess; be intended to seem (*purports to be the royal seal*). **2** (often foll. by *that* + clause) (of a document or speech) have as its meaning; state. • *n*. /pórpawrt/ **1** the ostensible meaning of something. **2** the sense or tenor (of a document or statement). □□ **pur•port•ed•ly** /–páwrtidlee/ *adv*. [ME f. AF & OF *purport*, *porport* f. *purporter* f. med.L *proportare* (as PRO-[1], *portare* carry)]

pur•pose /pərpəs/ *n*. & *v*. • *n*. **1** an object to be attained; a thing intended. **2** the intention to act. **3** resolution; determination. **4** the reason for which something is done or made. • *v.tr*. have as one's purpose; design; intend. □ **on purpose** intentionally. **to no purpose** with no result or effect. **to the purpose 1** relevant. **2** useful. [ME f. OF *porpos*, *purpos* f. L *proponere* (as PROPOUND)]

pur•pose-built *adj*. (also **pur•pose-made**) *esp. Brit*. built or made for a specific purpose.

pur•pose•ful /pərpəsfŏŏl/ *adj*. **1** having or indicating purpose. **2** intentional. **3** resolute. □□ **pur•pose•ful•ly** *adv*. **pur•pose•ful•ness** *n*.

pur•pose•less /pərpəslis/ *adj*. having no aim or plan. □□ **pur•pose•less•ly** *adv*. **pur•pose•less•ness** *n*.

pur•pose•ly /pərpəslee/ *adv*. on purpose; intentionally.

pur•pos•ive /pərpəsiv, pərpó–/ *adj*. **1** having or serving a purpose. **2** done with a purpose. **3** (of a person or conduct) having purpose or resolution; purposeful. □□ **pur•pos•ive•ly** *adv*. **pur•pos•ive•ness** *n*.

pur•pu•ra /pərpyŏŏrə/ *n*. **1** a disease characterized by purple or livid spots on the skin, due to internal bleeding from small blood vessels. **2** any mollusk of the genus *Purpura*, some of which yield a purple dye. □□ **pur•pu•ric** /–pyŏŏrik/ *adj*. [L f. Gk *porphura* purple]

pur•pure /pərpyŏŏr/ *n*. & *adj*. *Heraldry* purple. [OE *purpure* & OF *purpre* f. L *purpura* (as PURPURA)]

pur•pu•rin /pərpyŏŏrin/ *n*. a red dye occurring naturally in madder roots, or manufactured synthetically.

purr /pər/ *v*. & *n*. • *v*. **1** *intr*. (of a cat) make a low vibratory sound expressing contentment. **2** *intr*. (of machinery, etc.) make a similar sound. **3** *intr*. (of a person) express pleasure. **4** *tr*. utter or express (words or contentment) in this way. • *n*. a purring sound. [imit.]

purse /pərs/ *n*. & *v*. • *n*. **1** a small pouch of leather, etc., for carrying money on the person. **2** a small bag for carrying personal effects, esp. one carried by a woman. **3** a receptacle resembling a purse in form or purpose. **4** money; funds. **5** a sum collected as a present or given as a prize in a contest. • *v*. **1** *tr*. (often foll. by *up*) pucker or contract (the lips). **2** *intr*. become contracted and wrinkled. □ **hold the purse strings** have control of expenditure. [OE *purs* f. med.L *bursa*, *byrsa* purse f. Gk *bursa* hide, leather]

purs•er /pərsər/ *n*. an officer on a ship who keeps the accounts, esp. the head steward in a passenger vessel. □□ **purs•er•ship** *n*.

purs•lane /pərslin, –layn/ *n*. any of various plants of the genus *Portulaca*, esp. *P. oleracea*, with green or golden leaves, used as a salad vegetable and herb. [ME f. OF *porcelaine* (cf. PORCELAIN) alt. f. L *porcil(l)aca*, *portulaca*]

pur•su•ance /pərsŏŏəns/ *n*. (foll. by *of*) the carrying out or observance (of a plan, idea, etc.).

pur•su•ant /pərsŏŏənt/ *adj*. & *adv*. • *adj*. pursuing. • *adv*. (foll. by *to*) conforming to or in accordance with. □□ **pur•su•ant•ly** *adv*. [ME, = prosecuting, f. OF *po(u)rsuiant* part. of *po(u)rsu(iv)ir* (as PURSUE): assim. to AF *pursuer* and PURSUE]

pur•sue /pərsŏŏ/ *v*. (**pur•sues**, **pur•sued**, **pur•su•ing**) **1** *tr*. follow with intent to overtake or capture or do harm to. **2** *tr*. continue or proceed along (a route or course of action). **3** *tr*. follow or engage in (study or other activity). **4** *tr*. proceed in compliance with (a plan, etc.). **5** *tr*. seek after; aim at. **6** *tr*. continue to investigate or discuss (a topic). **7** *tr*. seek the attention or acquaintance of (a person) persistently. **8** *tr*. (of misfortune, etc.) persistently assail. **9** *tr*. persistently attend; stick to. **10** *intr*. go in pursuit. □□ **pur•su•a•ble** *adj*. **pur•su•er** *n*. [ME f. AF *pursiwer*, *–suer* = OF *porsivre*, etc. ult. f. L *prosequi* follow after]

pur•suit /pərsŏŏt/ *n*. **1** the act or an instance of pursuing. **2** an occupation or activity pursued. □ **in pursuit of** pursuing. [ME f. OF *poursuite* (as PUR-, SUIT)]

pur•sui•vant /pərswivənt/ *n*. **1** *Brit*. an officer of the College of Arms ranking below a herald. **2** a follower or attendant. [ME f. OF *pursivant* pres. part. of *pursivre* (as PURSUE)]

pur•sy /pərsee/ *adj*. **1** short-winded. **2** corpulent. □□ **pur•si•ness** *n*. [ME, earlier *pursive* f. AF *porsif* f. OF *polsif* f. *polser* breathe with difficulty f. L *pulsare* (as PULSATE)]

pu•ru•lent /pyŏŏrələnt, pyŏŏryə–/ *adj*. **1** consisting of or containing pus. **2** discharging pus. □□ **pu•ru•lence** *n*. **pu•ru•len•cy** *n*. **pu•ru•lent•ly** *adv*. [F *purulent* or L *purulentus* (as PUS)]

pur•vey /pərváy/ *v*. **1** *tr*. provide or supply (articles of food) as one's business. **2** *intr*. (often foll. by *for*) **a** make provision. **b** act as supplier. □□ **pur•vey•or** *n*. [ME f. AF *purveier*, OF *porveiir* f. L *providēre* PROVIDE]

pur•vey•ance /pərváyəns/ *n*. **1** the act of purveying. **2** *Brit. hist*. the right of the sovereign to provisions, etc., at a fixed price. [ME f. OF *porveance* f. L *providentia* PROVIDENCE]

pur•view /pərvyŏŏ/ *n*. **1** the scope or range of a document, scheme, etc. **2** the range of physical or mental vision. [ME f. AF *purveü*, OF *porveü* past part. of *porveiir* (as PURVEY)]

pus /pus/ *n*. a thick yellowish or greenish liquid produced from infected tissue. [L *pus puris*]

push /pŏŏsh/ *v*. & *n*. • *v*. **1** *tr*. exert a force on (a thing) to move it away from oneself or from the origin of the force. **2** *tr*. cause to move in this direction. **3** *intr*. exert such a force (*do not push against the door*). **4** *tr*. press; depress (*push the button for service*). **5** *intr*. & *tr*. **a** thrust forward or upward. **b** project or cause to project (*pushes out new roots; the cape pushes out into the sea*). **6** *intr*. move forward by force or persistence. **7** *tr*. make (one's way) by pushing. **8** *intr*. exert oneself, esp. to surpass others. **9** *tr*. (often foll. by *to, into,* or *to* + infin.) urge or impel. **10** *tr*. tax the abilities or tolerance of; press (a person) hard. **11** *tr*. pursue (a claim, etc.). **12** *tr*. promote the use or sale or adoption of, e.g., by advertising. **13** *intr*. (foll. by *for*) demand persistently (*pushed hard for reform*). **14** *tr*. *colloq*. sell (a drug) illegally. **15** *tr*. *colloq*. to approach, esp. in age (*pushing thirty*). • *n*. **1** the act or an instance of pushing; a shove or thrust. **2** the force exerted in this. **3** a vigorous effort. **4** a military attack in force. **5** enterprise; determination to succeed. **6** the use of influence to advance a person. **7** the pressure of affairs. **8** a crisis. **9** (prec. by *the*) *Brit. colloq*. dismissal, esp. from employment. **10** *Austral. sl*. a group of people with a common interest; a clique. □ **be pushed for**

colloq. have very little of (esp. time). **if** (or **when**) **push comes to shove** when a problem must be faced; in a crisis. **push along** (often in *imper.*) *Brit. colloq.* depart; leave. **push around** *colloq.* bully. **push one's luck 1** take undue risks. **2** act presumptuously. **push off 1 a** set off; depart. **b** push with an oar, etc., to get a boat out into a river, etc. **2** esp. *Brit.* (often in *imper.*) *colloq.* go away. **push through** get (a scheme, proposal, etc.) completed or accepted quickly. [ME f. OF *pousser, pou(l)ser* f. L *pulsare* (as PULSATE)]

push-bike *n. Brit. colloq.* a bicycle worked by pedals.

push but·ton *n.* **1** a button to be pushed esp. to operate an electrical device. **2** (*attrib.*) operated in this way.

push·cart /pooshkaart/ *n.* a handcart or barrow, esp. one used by a street vendor.

push·chair /pooshchair/ *n. Brit.* = STROLLER.

push·er /pooshər/ *n.* **1** *colloq.* an illegal seller of drugs. **2** *colloq.* a pushing or pushy person. **3** a child's utensil for pushing food onto a spoon, etc.

push·ful /pooshfool/ *adj.* esp. *Brit.* pushy; arrogantly self-assertive. □□ **push·ful·ly** *adv.*

push·ing /pooshing/ *adj.* **1** pushy; aggressively ambitious. **2** *colloq.* having nearly reached (a specified age). □□ **push·ing·ly** *adv.*

push·o·ver /pooshōvər/ *n. colloq.* **1** something that is easily done. **2** a person who can easily be overcome, persuaded, etc.

push-pull *n. Electr.* consisting of two valves, etc., operated alternately.

push·rod /pooshrod/ *n.* a rod operated by cams that opens and closes the valves in an internal combustion engine.

push start *n. & v.* • *n.* the starting of a motor vehicle by pushing it to turn the engine. • *v.tr.* start (a vehicle) in this way.

Push·tu /pushtoo/ *n. & adj.* = PASHTO. [Pers. *puštū*]

push-up *n.* an exercise in which the body, extended and prone, is raised upwards by pushing down with the hands until the arms are straight.

push·y /pooshee/ *adj.* (**push·i·er, push·i·est**) *colloq.* **1** excessively or unpleasantly self-assertive. **2** selfishly determined to succeed. □□ **push·i·ly** *adv.* **push·i·ness** *n.*

pu·sil·lan·i·mous /pyoosilánimas/ *adj.* lacking courage; timid. □□ **pu·sil·la·nim·i·ty** /-lánimitee/ *n.* **pu·sil·lan·i·mous·ly** *adv.* [eccl.L *pusillanimis* f. *pusillus* very small + *animus* mind]

puss /poos/ *n. colloq.* **1 a** cat (esp. as a form of address). **2** a girl. **3** *Brit.* a hare. [prob. f. MLG *pūs,* Du. *poes,* of unkn. orig.]

pus·sy /poosee/ *n.* (*pl.* **-sies**) **1** (also **pus·sy·cat**) *colloq.* a cat. **2** *coarse sl.* the vulva.

pus·sy·foot /pooseefoot/ *v.intr.* **1** move stealthily or warily. **2** act cautiously or noncommittally. □□ **pus·sy·foot·er** *n.*

pus·sy wil·low *n.* any of various willows, esp. *Salix discolor,* with furry catkins.

pus·tu·late *v. & adj.* • *v.tr. & intr.* /púschəlayt/ form into pustules. • *adj.* /-chələt/ of or relating to a pustule or pustules. □□ **pus·tu·la·tion** /-láyshən/ *n.* [LL *pustulare* f. *pustula:* see PUSTULE]

pus·tule /púschool/ *n.* a pimple containing pus. □□ **pus·tu·lar** *adj.* **pus·tu·lous** *adj.* [ME f. OF *pustule* or L *pustula*]

put¹ /poot/ *v., n., & adj.* • *v.* (**put·ting**; *past* and *past part.* **put**) **1** *tr.* move to or cause to be in a specified place or position (*put it in your pocket; put the children to bed; put your signature here*). **2** *tr.* bring into a specified condition, relation, or state (*puts me in great difficulty; an accident put the car out of action*). **3** *tr.* **a** (often foll. by *on*) impose or assign (*where do you put the blame?*). **b** (foll. by *on, to*) impose or enforce the existence of (*put a stop to it*). **4** *tr.* **a** cause (a person) to go or be, habitually or temporarily (*put them at their ease; put them on the right track*). **b** *refl.* imagine (oneself) in a specified situation (*put yourself in my shoes*). **5** *tr.* (foll. by *for*) substitute (one thing for another). **6** *tr.* express (a thought or idea) in a specified way (*to put it mildly*). **7** *tr.* (foll. by *at*) estimate (an amount, etc., at a specified amount) (*put the cost at $50*). **8** *tr.* (foll. by *into*) express or translate in (words, or another language). **9** *tr.* (foll. by *into*) invest (money in an asset, e.g., land). **10** *tr.* (foll. by *on*) stake (money) (*on a horse, etc.*). **11** *tr.* (foll. by *to*) apply or devote to a use or purpose (*put it to good use*). **12** *tr.* (foll. by *to*) submit for consideration or attention (*let me put it to you another way; shall now put it to a vote*). **13** *tr.* (foll. by *to*) subject (a person) to (death, suffering, etc.). **14** *tr.* throw (esp. a shot or weight) as an athletic sport or exercise. **15** *tr.* (foll. by *to*) couple (an animal) with (another of the opposite sex) for breeding. **16** *intr.* (foll. by *back, off, out,* etc.) (of a ship, etc.) proceed or follow a course in a specified direction. • *n.* **1** a throw of the shot or weight. **2** *Stock Exch.* the option of selling stock or a commodity at a fixed price at a given date. • *adj.* stationary; fixed (*stay put*). □ **put about 1** spread (information, rumor, etc.). **2** *Naut.* turn around; put (a ship) on the opposite tack. **3** *Brit.* trouble; distress. **put across 1** make acceptable or effective. **2** express in an understandable way. **3** (often in

pussy willow

put it (or **one**) **across** achieve by deceit. **put aside 1** = *put by.* **2** set aside; ignore. **put away 1** put (a thing) back in the place where it is normally kept. **2** set (money, etc.) aside for future use. **3 a** confine or imprison. **b** commit to a mental institution. **4** consume (food and drink), esp. in large quantities. **5** put (an old or sick animal) to death. **put back 1** restore to its proper or former place. **2** change (a planned event) to a later date or time. **put a bold,** etc., **face on it** see FACE. **put by** lay (money, etc.) aside for future use. **put down 1** suppress by force or authority. **2** *colloq.* snub or humiliate. **3** record or enter in writing. **4** enter the name of (a person) on a list, esp. as a member or subscriber. **5** (foll. by *as, for*) account, reckon, or categorize. **6** (foll. by *to*) attribute (*put it down to bad planning*). **7** put (an old or sick animal) to death. **8** preserve or store (eggs, etc.) for future use. **9** pay (a specified sum) as a deposit. **10** put (a baby) to bed. **11** land (an aircraft). **12** stop to let (passengers) get off. **put an end to** see END. **put one's finger on** identify, esp. a problem or difficulty. **put one's foot down** see FOOT. **put one's foot in it** see FOOT. **put forth 1** (of a plant) send out (buds or leaves). **2** *formal* submit or put into circulation. **put forward** suggest or propose. **put in 1** enter or submit (a claim, etc.). **b** (foll. by *for*) submit a claim for (a specified thing). **2** (foll. by *for*) be a candidate for (an appointment, election, etc.). **3** spend (time). **4** perform (a spell of work) as part of a whole. **5** interpose (a remark, blow, etc.). **6** insert as an addition. **put in an appearance** see APPEARANCE. **put a person in mind of** see MIND. **put it to a person** (often foll. by *that* + clause) challenge a person to deny. **put one's mind to** see MIND. **put off 1 a** postpone. **b** postpone an engagement with (a person). **2** (often foll. by *with*) evade (a person) with an excuse, etc. **3** hinder or dissuade. **put on 1** clothe oneself with. **2** cause (an electrical device, light, etc.) to function. **3** cause (esp. transport) to be available; provide. **4** stage (a play, show, etc.). **5 a** pretend to be affected by (an emotion). **b** assume; take on (a character or appearance). **c** (**put it on**) exaggerate one's feelings, etc. **6** increase one's weight by (a specified amount). **7** (foll. by *to*) make aware of or put in touch with (*put us on to their new accountant*). **8** *colloq.* tease; play a trick on. **put out 1 a** (often as **put out** *adj.*) disconcert or annoy. **b** (often *refl.*) inconvenience (*don't put yourself out*). **2** extinguish (a fire or light). **3** *Baseball* cause (a batter or runner) to be out. **4** dislocate (a joint). **5** exert (strength, etc.). **6** allocate (work) to be done off the premises. **7** blind (a person's eyes). **8** issue; publish. **9** *coarse sl.* engage in sexual intercourse. **put out of its,** etc., **misery** see MISERY. **put over 1** make acceptable or effective. **2** express in an understandable way. **3** postpone. **4** achieve by deceit. **put one over** (usu. foll. by *on*) get the better of; outsmart; trick. **put a sock in it** see SOCK¹. **put store by** see STORE. **put through 1** carry out or complete (a task or transaction). **2** (often foll. by *to*) connect (a person) by telephone to another. **put to flight** see FLIGHT². **put together 1** assemble (a whole) from parts. **2** combine (parts) to form a whole. **put under** render unconscious by anesthetic, etc. **put up 1** build or erect. **2** to can; preserve (food) for later use. **3** take or provide accommodation for (*friends put me up for the night*). **4** engage in (a fight, struggle, etc.) as a form of resistance. **5** present (a proposal). **6 a** present oneself for election. **b** propose for election. **7** provide (money) as a backer in an enterprise. **8** display (a notice). **9** publish (banns). **10** offer for sale or competition. **11** esp. *Brit.* raise (a price, etc.). **put upon** *colloq.* make unfair or excessive demands on; take advantage of (a person). **put a person up to** (usu. foll. by verbal noun) instigate a person in (*put them up to stealing the money*). **put up with** endure; tolerate; submit to. **put the wind up** see WIND¹. **put a person wise** see WISE¹. **put words into a person's mouth** see MOUTH. □□ **put·ter** *n.* [ME f. an unrecorded OE form *putian,* of unkn. orig.]

put² var. of PUTT.

pu·ta·tive /pyootativ/ *adj.* reputed; supposed (*his putative father*). □□ **pu·ta·tive·ly** *adv.* [ME f. OF *putatif -ive* or LL *putativus* f. L *putare* think]

put-down *n. colloq.* an act or instance of snubbing or humiliating (someone).

put·log /pútlawg, -log/ *n.* (also **put·lock** /-lok/) a short horizontal timber projecting from a wall, on which scaffold floorboards rest. [17th c.: orig. uncert.]

put-on *n. colloq.* a deception or hoax.

put out to ten·der *v.* seek tenders or bids for (work, etc.).

put-put /pútpút/ *n. & v.* • *n.* **1** the rapid intermittent sound of a small gasoline engine. **2** *colloq.* a small boat using such an engine. • *v.intr.* (**put-put·ted, put-put·ting**) make this sound. [imit.]

pu·tre·fy /pyootrifi/ *v.* (**-fies, -fied**) **1** *intr. & tr.* become or make putrid; go bad. **2** *intr.* fester; suppurate. **3** *intr.* become morally corrupt. □□ **pu·tre·fa·cient** /-fáyshənt/ *adj.* **pu·tre·fac·tion** /-fákshən/ *n.* **pu·tre·fac·tive** /-fáktiv/ *adj.* [ME f. L *putrefacere* f. *puter putris* rotten]

pu·tres·cent /pyootrésənt/ *adj.* **1** in the process of rotting. **2** of or accompanying this process. □□ **pu·tres·cence** *n.* [L *putrescere* incept. of *putrere* (as PUTRID)]

pu·trid /pyootrid/ *adj.* **1** decomposed; rotten. **2** foul; noxious. **3** corrupt. **4** *sl.* of poor quality; contemptible; very unpleasant. □□ **pu-**

trid·i·ty /–tríditee/n. **pu·trid·ly** adv. **pu·trid·ness** n. [L *putridus* f. *putrēre* to rot f. *puter putris* rotten]

putsch /pŏoch/ n. an attempt at political revolution; a violent uprising. [Swiss G, = thrust, blow]

putt /put/ v. & n. (also *Brit.* **put**) • v.tr. (**put·ted, put·ting**) strike (a golf ball) gently to get it into or nearer to a hole on a putting green. • n. a putting stroke. [differentiated f. PUT¹]

put·tee /pútee/ n. **1** a long strip of cloth wound spirally around the leg from ankle to knee for protection and support. **2** a leather legging. [Hindi *paṭṭī* band, bandage]

putt·er¹ /pútər/ n. **1** a golf club used in putting. **2** a golfer who putts.

putt·er² /pútər/ n. & v. = PUT-PUT. [imit.]

putt·er³ /pútər/ v. (also *Brit.* **pot·ter**) **1** intr. **a** (often foll. by *about, around*) work or occupy oneself in a desultory but pleasant manner (*likes puttering around in the garden*). **b** (often foll. by *at, in*) dabble in a subject or occupation. **2** intr. go slowly; dawdle; loiter. **3** tr. (foll. by *away*) fritter away (one's time, etc.). □□ **putt·er·er** n. [var. sp. of *potter*, a frequent. of dial. *pote* push f. OE *potian*]

put·ting green n. (in golf) the area of close-cropped grass around a hole.

put·to /pŏotō/ n. (pl. **put·ti** /–tee/) a representation of a naked child (esp. a cherub or a cupid) in (esp. Renaissance) art. [It., = boy, f. L *putus*]

put·ty /pútee/ n. & v. • n. (pl. **·ties**) **1** a cement made from whiting and raw linseed oil, used for fixing panes of glass, filling holes in woodwork, etc. **2** a fine white mortar of lime and water, used in pointing brickwork, etc. **3** a polishing powder usu. made from tin oxide, used in jewelry work. • v.tr. (**·ties, ·tied**) cover, fix, join, or fill up with putty. □ **putty in a person's hands** someone who is overcompliant, or easily influenced. [F *potée*, lit. potful]

put-up adj. fraudulently presented or devised.

putz /puts/ n. & v. • n. **1** *coarse sl.* the penis. **2** *sl.* a simple-minded foolish person. • v.intr. *sl.* (usu. foll. by *around*) move (about) or occupy oneself in an aimless or idle manner. [Yiddish *puts* ornament]

puz·zle /púzəl/ n. & v. • n. **1** a difficult or confusing problem; an enigma. **2** a problem or toy designed to test knowledge or ingenuity. • v. **1** tr. confound or disconcert mentally. **2** intr. (usu. foll. by *over*, etc.) be perplexed (about). **3** tr. (usu. as **puzzling** adj.) require much thought to comprehend (*a puzzling situation*). **4** tr. (foll. by *out*) solve or understand by hard thought. □□ **puz·zle·ment** n. **puz·zling·ly** adv. [16th c.: orig. unkn.]

puz·zler /púzlər/ n. a difficult question or problem.

puz·zo·la·na var. of POZZOLANA.

PVA abbr. polyvinyl acetate.

PVC abbr. polyvinyl chloride.

Pvt. abbr. private.

p.w. abbr. per week.

PWA abbr. person with AIDS.

PX abbr. post exchange.

py·ae·mi·a *Brit.* var. ofPYEMIA.

pyc·nic var. of PYKNIC.

pye-dog /pídawg, –dog/ n. (also **pie-dog, pi-dog**) a vagrant mongrel, esp. in Asia. [Anglo-Ind. *pye, paë*, Hindi *pāhī* outsider + DOG]

py·e·li·tis /píolítis/ n. inflammation of the renal pelvis. [Gk *puelos* trough, basin + –ITIS]

py·e·mi·a /pī-éemeeə/ n. blood poisoning caused by the spread of pus-forming bacteria in the bloodstream from a source of infection. □□ **py·e·mic** adj. [mod.L f. Gk *puon* pus + *haima* blood]

pyg·my /pígmee/ n. (also **pig·my**) (pl. **·mies**) **1** a member of a small people of equatorial Africa and parts of SE Asia. **2** a very small person, animal, or thing. **3** an insignificant person. **4** (*attrib.*) **a** of or relating to pygmies. **b** (of a person, animal, etc.) dwarf. □□ **pyg·mae·an** /pigméeən, pígmee–/ adj. (also **pyg·me·an**) [ME f. L *pygmaeus* f. Gk *pugmaios* dwarf f. *pugmē* the length from elbow to knuckles, fist]

py·jam·as esp. *Brit.* var. of PAJAMAS.

pyk·nic /píknik/ adj. & n. (also **pyc·nic**) *Anthropol.* • adj. characterized by a thick neck, large abdomen, and relatively short limbs. • n. a person of this body type. [Gk *puknos* thick]

py·lon /pílon/ n. **1** a tall structure erected as a support (esp. for electric power cables) or boundary or decoration. **2** a gateway, esp. of an ancient Egyptian temple. **3** a structure marking a path for aircraft. **4** a structure supporting an aircraft engine. [Gk *pulōn* f. *pulē* gate]

py·lo·rus /pīláwrəs, pi–/ n. (pl. **py·lo·ri** /–rī/) *Anat.* the opening from the stomach into the duodenum. □□ **py·lor·ic** /–láwrik/ adj. [LL f. Gk *pulōros, pulouros* gatekeeper f. *pulē* gate + *ouros* warder]

py·or·rhe·a /pīərée·ə/ n. **1** a disease of periodontal tissue causing shrinkage of the gums and loosening of the teeth. **2** any discharge of pus. [Gk *puo*- f. *puon* pus + *rhoia* flux f. *rheō* flow]

py·ra·can·tha /pírəkánthə/ n. any evergreen thorny shrub of the genus *Pyracantha*, having white flowers and bright red or yellow berries. [L f. Gk *purakantha*]

pyr·a·mid /pírəmid/ n. & v. • n. **1 a** a monumental structure, usu. of stone, with a square base and sloping sides meeting centrally at an apex, esp. an ancient Egyptian royal tomb. **b** a similar structure, esp. a Mayan temple of this type. **2** a solid of this type with a base of three or more sides. **3** a pyramid-shaped thing or pile of things. • v. **1** tr. to build or shape into a pyramid. **2** intr. to speculate, as in the stock market, using paper profits as a margin for further stock acquisitions. □□ **py·ram·i·dal** /–rámid'l/ adj. **py·ram·i·dal·ly** adv. **py·ra·mid·ic** /–mídik/ adj. (also **pyr·a·mid·i·cal**). **pyr·a·mid·i·cal·ly** adv. **pyr·a·mid·wise** adj. [ME f. L *pyramis* f. Gk *puramis –idos*]

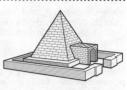

pyramid 1

pyr·a·mid sell·ing n. a system of selling goods in which rights are sold to an increasing number of distributors at successively lower levels.

pyre /pīr/ n. a heap of combustible material, esp. a funeral pile for burning a corpse. [L *pyra* f. Gk *pura* f. *pur* fire]

py·re·thrin /pīreéthrin, –réth–/ n. any of several active constituents of pyrethrum flowers used in the manufacture of insecticides.

py·re·thrum /pīreéthrəm, –réth–/ n. **1** any of several aromatic chrysanthemums of the genus *Chrysanthemum*. **2** an insecticide made from the dried flowers of these plants. [L f. Gk *purethron* feverfew]

py·ret·ic /pīrétik/ adj. of, for, or producing fever. [mod.L *pyreticus* f. Gk *puretos* fever]

Py·rex /píreks/ n. *Trademark* a hard heat-resistant type of glass, often used for cookware. [invented word]

py·rex·i·a /pīrékseeə/ n. *Med.* = FEVER. □□ **py·rex·i·al** adj. **py·rex·ic** adj. **py·rex·i·cal** adj. [mod.L f. Gk *purexis* f. *puressō* be feverish f. *pur* fire]

py·ri·dine /pírədeen/ n. *Chem.* a colorless volatile odorous liquid, formerly obtained from coal tar, used as a solvent and in chemical manufacture. ¶ *Chem.* formula: C_5H_5N. [Gk *pur* fire + –ID⁴ + –INE⁴]

pyr·i·dox·ine /píridókseen, –sin/ n. a vitamin of the B complex found in yeast, and important in the body's use of unsaturated fatty acids. Also called **vitamin B₆**. [PYRIDINE + OX- + –INE⁴]

py·rim·i·dine /pírimideen, pi–/ n. **1** *Chem.* an organic nitrogenous base. **2** any of a group of derivatives with similar structure, including the nucleotide constituents uracil, thymine, and cytosine. [G *Pyrimidin* f. *Pyridin* (as PYRIDINE, IMIDE)]

py·rite /pírīt/ n. = PYRITES. [F *pyrite* or L (as PYRITES)]

py·ri·tes /pīríteez, pírīts/ n. (in full **iron pyrites**) a yellow lustrous form of iron disulfide. □□ **py·rit·ic** /–rítik/ adj. **py·ri·tif·er·ous** /–ritifərəs/ adj. **py·ri·tize** /píritiz/ v.tr. **py·ri·tous** /pírítəs/ adj. [L f. Gk *purītēs* of fire (*pur*)]

py·ro /pírō/ n. *colloq.* a pyromaniac.

pyro- /pírō/ *comb. form* **1** denoting fire. **2** *Chem.* denoting a new substance formed from another by elimination of water (*pyrophosphate*). **3** *Mineral.* denoting a mineral, etc., showing some property or change under the action of heat, or having a fiery red or yellow color. [Gk *puro*- f. *pur* fire]

py·ro·clas·tic /pírōklástik/ adj. (of rocks, etc.) formed as the result of a volcanic eruption. □□ **py·ro·clast** n.

py·ro·e·lec·tric /pírōiléktrik/ adj. having the property of becoming electrically charged when heated. □□ **py·ro·e·lec·tric·i·ty** /–trísitee/ n.

py·ro·gal·lol /pírōgálawl, –ol, –gáwl/ n. a weak acid used as a developer in photography, etc.

py·ro·gen·ic /pírōjénik/ adj. (also **py·rog·e·nous** /pírójinəs/) **1 a** producing heat, esp. in the body. **b** producing fever. **2** produced by combustion or volcanic processes.

py·rog·ra·phy /pírógrəfee/ n. **1** a technique for forming designs on wood, etc., by burning. **2** a design made with this technique.

py·ro·lig·ne·ous /pírōlígneeəs/ adj. produced by the action of fire or heat on wood.

py·rol·y·sis /píróləsis/ n. chemical decomposition brought about by heat. □□ **py·ro·lyt·ic** /pírəlítik/ adj.

py·ro·lyze /pírəlíz/ v.tr. decompose by pyrolysis. [PYROLYSIS after *analyze*]

py·ro·ma·ni·a /pírōmáyneeə/ n. an obsessive desire to set fire to things. □□ **py·ro·ma·ni·ac** n.

py·rom·e·ter /pírómitər/ n. an instrument for measuring high temperatures, esp. in furnaces and kilns. □□ **py·ro·met·ric** /–rəmétrik/ adj. **py·ro·met·ri·cal·ly** adv. **py·rom·e·try** /–rómitree/ n.

py·rope /pírōp/ n. a deep red variety of garnet. [ME f. OF *pirope* f. L *pyropus* f. Gk *purōpos* gold-bronze, lit. fiery-eyed, f. *pur* fire + *ōps* eye]

py·ro·phor·ic /pírōfáwrik, –fór–/ adj. (of a substance) liable to ignite spontaneously on exposure to air. [mod.L *pyrophorus* f. Gk *purophoros* fire-bearing f. *pur* fire + *pherō* bear]

py·ro·sis /pīrṓsis/ *n. Med.* a burning sensation in the lower part of the chest, combined with the return of gastric acid to the mouth. Also called **heartburn**. [mod.L f. Gk *purōsis* f. *puroō* set on fire f. *pur* fire]

py·ro·tech·nic /pírōtéknik/ *adj.* **1** of or relating to fireworks. **2** (of wit, etc.) brilliant or sensational. □□ **py·ro·tech·ni·cal** *adj.* **py·ro·tech·nist** *n.* **py·ro·tech·ny** *n.* [PYRO- + Gk *tekhnē* art]

py·ro·tech·nics /pírōtékniks/ *n.pl.* **1** the art of making fireworks. **2** a display of fireworks. **3** any brilliant display.

py·rox·ene /pīrókseen/ *n.* any of a group of minerals commonly found as components of igneous rocks, composed of silicates of calcium, magnesium, and iron. [PYRO- + Gk *xenos* stranger (because supposed to be alien to igneous rocks)]

py·rox·y·lin /pīróksilin/ *n.* a form of nitrocellulose, soluble in ether and alcohol, used as a basis for lacquers, artificial leather, etc. [F *pyroxyline* (as PYRO-, Gk *xulon* wood)]

pyr·rhic[1] /pírik/ *adj.* (of a victory) won at too great a cost to be of use to the victor. [*Pyrrhus* of Epirus, who defeated the Romans at Asculum in 279 BC, but sustained heavy losses]

pyr·rhic[2] /pírik/ *n. & adj.* ● *n.* a metrical foot of two short or unaccented syllables. ● *adj.* written in or based on pyrrhics. [L *pyrrhichius* f. Gk *purrhikhios* (*pous*) pyrrhic (foot)]

Pyr·rho·nism /píronizəm/ *n.* **1** the philosophy of Pyrrho of Elis (*c.*300 BC), maintaining that certainty of knowledge is unattainable. **2** skepticism; philosophic doubt. □□ **Pyr·rho·nist** *n.* [Gk *Purrhōn* Pyrrho]

pyr·u·vate /pīrṓovayt/ *n. Biochem.* any salt or ester of pyruvic acid.

py·ru·vic ac·id /pīrṓovik/ *n.* an organic acid occurring as an intermediate in many stages of metabolism. [as PYRO- + L *uva* grape]

Py·thag·o·re·an /pīthágəreéən/ *adj. & n.* ● *adj.* of or relating to the Greek philosopher Pythagoras (6th c. BC) or his philosophy, esp. regarding the transmigration of souls. ● *n.* a follower of Pythagoras.

Py·thag·o·re·an the·o·rem /pīthágəreéən/ *n.* the theorem attributed to Pythagoras (see PYTHAGOREAN) that the square of the hypotenuse of a right triangle is equal to the sum of the squares of the other two sides.

Pyth·i·an /pítheeən/ *adj.* of or relating to Delphi (in central Greece) or its ancient oracle of Apollo. [L *Pythius* f. Gk *Puthios* f. *Puthō*, an older name of Delphi]

py·thon /píthon, –thən/ *n.* any constricting snake of the family Pythonidae, esp. of the genus *Python*, found throughout the tropics in the Old World. □□ **py·thon·ic** /–thónik/ *adj.* [L f. Gk *Puthōn* a huge serpent or monster killed by Apollo]

py·tho·ness /píthənis, píth–/ *n.* **1** the Pythian priestess. **2** a witch. [ME f. OF *phitonise* f. med.L *phitonissa* f. LL *pythonissa* fem. of *pytho* f. Gk *puthōn* soothsaying demon: cf. PYTHON]

py·u·ri·a /pīyoóreeə/ *n. Med.* the presence of pus in urine. [Gk *puon* pus + –URIA]

pyx /piks/ *n.* (also **pix**) **1** *Eccl.* the vessel in which the consecrated bread of the Eucharist is kept. **2** a box at a mint in which specimen coins are deposited to be tested by weight and assayed. [ME f. L (as PYXIS)]

pyx·id·i·um /piksídeeəm/ *n.* (*pl.* **pyx·id·i·a** /–deeə/) *Bot.* a seed-capsule with a top that comes off like the lid of a box. [mod.L f. Gk *puxidion*, dimin. of *puxis*: see PYXIS]

pyx·is /píksis/ *n.* (*pl.* **pyx·i·des** /–sideez/) **1** a small box or casket. **2** = PYXIDIUM. [ME f. L f. Gk *puxis* f. *puxos* BOX[3]]

Q

Q¹ /kyoo/ *n.* (also **q**) (*pl.* **Qs** or **Q's**) the seventeenth letter of the alphabet.

Q² *abbr.* (also **Q.**) **1** question. **2** esp. *Brit.* Queen, Queen's.

qa·di /kaádi, káydi/ *n.* (also **ka·di**) (*pl.* **·dis**) a judge in a Muslim country. [Arab. *ḳāḍī* f. *ḳaḍā* to judge]

qb *abbr.* quarterback.

QED *abbr.* QUOD ERAT DEMONSTRANDUM.

Q fever /kyoo/ *n.* a mild febrile disease caused by rickettsias. [*Q* = query]

qib·la var. of KIBLAH.

Qld. *abbr.* Queensland.

QM *abbr.* quartermaster.

qr. *abbr.* quarter(s).

Q-ship /kyooship/ *n.* an armed vessel disguised as a merchant ship used as a decoy to lure submarines into attack range. [*Q* = query]

QSO *abbr.* quasi-stellar object; quasar.

qt. *abbr.* quart(s).

q.t. *n. colloq.* quiet (esp. on the q.t.). [abbr.]

Q-tip /kyootip/ *n. Trademark* a swab consisting of a thin stick with cotton affixed to each end.

qty. *abbr.* quantity.

qu. *abbr.* **1** query. **2** question.

qua /kwaa/ *conj.* in the capacity of; as being (*Napoleon qua general*). [L, ablat. fem. sing. of *qui* who (rel. pron.)]

quack¹ /kwak/ *v. & n.* ● *n.* the harsh sound made by ducks. ● *v.intr.* **1** utter this sound. **2** *colloq.* talk loudly and foolishly. [imit.: cf. Du. *kwakken*, G *quacken* croak, quack]

quack² /kwak/ *n.* **1 a** an unqualified practitioner of medicine. **b** (*attrib.*) of or characteristic of unskilled medical practice (*quack cure*). **2 a** a charlatan. **b** (*attrib.*) of or characteristic of a charlatan; fraudulent; sham. **3** *sl.* any doctor or medical officer. □□ **quack·er·y** *n.* **quack·ish** *adj.* [abbr. of quacksalver f. Du. (prob. f. obs. *quacken* prattle + *salf* SALVE¹)]

quad¹ /kwod/ *n. colloq.* a quadrangle. [abbr.]

quad² /kwod/ *n. colloq.* = QUADRUPLET 1. [abbr.]

quad³ /kwod/ *n. Printing* a piece of blank metal type used in spacing. [abbr. of earlier QUADRAT]

quad⁴ /kwod/ *n. & adj.* ● *n.* quadraphony. ● *adj.* quadraphonic. [abbr.]

quad·ra·ge·nar·i·an /kwódrəjináireeən/ *n. & adj.* ● *n.* a person from 40 to 49 years old. ● *adj.* of this age. [LL *quadragenarius* f. *quadrageni* distrib. of *quadraginta* forty]

Quad·ra·ges·i·ma /kwódrəjésimə/ *n.* the first Sunday in Lent. [LL, fem. of L *quadragesimus* fortieth f. *quadraginta* forty, Lent having 40 days]

quad·ra·ges·i·mal /kwódrəjésiməl/ *adj.* **1** (of a fast, esp. in Lent) lasting forty days. **2** Lenten.

quad·ran·gle /kwódranggəl/ *n.* **1** a four-sided plane figure, esp. a square or rectangle. **2 a** a four-sided yard or courtyard, esp. enclosed by buildings, as in some colleges. **b** such a courtyard with the buildings around it. **3** the land area represented on one map sheet as published by the U.S. Geological Survey. □□ **quad·ran·gu·lar** /-ránggyələr/ *adj.* [ME f. OF f. LL *quadrangulum* square, neut. of *quadrangulus* (as QUADRI-, ANGLE¹)]

quad·rant /kwódrənt/ *n.* **1** a quarter of a circle's circumference. **2** a plane figure enclosed by two radii of a circle at right angles and the arc cut off by them. **3** a quarter of a sphere, etc. **4 a** a thing, esp. a graduated strip of metal, shaped like a quarter circle. **b** an instrument graduated (esp. through an arc of 90°) for taking angular measurements. □□ **quad·ran·tal** /-dránt'l/ *adj.* [ME f. L *quadrans -antis* quarter f. *quattuor* four]

quad·ra·phon·ic /kwódrəfónik/ *adj.* (also **quad·ro·phon·ic** or **quad·ri·phon·ic**) (of sound reproduction) using four transmission channels. □□ **quad·ra·phon·i·cal·ly** *adv.* **quad·ra·phon·ics** *n.pl.* **qua·draph·o·ny** /-rófənee/ *n.* [QUADRI- + STEREOPHONIC]

quad·rat /kwódrət/ *n.* **1** *Ecol.* a small area marked out for study. **2** = QUAD³. [var. of QUADRATE]

quad·rate *adj., n., & v.* ● *adj.* /kwódrət/ esp. *Anat. & Zool.* square or rectangular (*quadrate bone; quadrate muscle*). ● *n.* /kwódrət/ **1** a quadrate bone or muscle. **2** a rectangular object. ● *v.* /kwodráyt/ **1** *tr.* make square. **2** *intr. & tr.* (often foll. by *with*) conform or make conform. [ME f. L *quadrare quadrat-* make square f. *quattuor* four]

quad·rat·ic /kwodrátik/ *adj. & n. Math.* ● *adj.* **1** involving the second and no higher power of an unknown quantity or variable (*quadratic equation*). **2** square. ● *n.* **1** a quadratic equation. **2** (in *pl.*) the branch of algebra dealing with these. [F *quadratique* or mod.L *quadraticus* (as QUADRATE)]

quad·ra·ture /kwódrəchər/ *n.* **1** *Math.* the process of constructing a square with an area equal to that of a figure bounded by a curve, e.g., a circle. **2** *Astron.* **a** each of two points at which the moon is 90° from the sun as viewed from earth. **b** the position of a heavenly body in relation to another 90° away. [F *quadrature* or L *quadratura* (as QUADRATE)]

quad·ren·ni·al /kwodréneeəl/ *adj.* **1** lasting four years. **2** recurring every four years. □□ **quad·ren·ni·al·ly** *adv.* [as QUADRENNIUM]

quad·ren·ni·um /kwodréneeəm/ *n.* (*pl.* **quad·ren·ni·ums** or **quad·ren·ni·a** /-eeə/) a period of four years. [L *quadriennium* (as QUADRI-, *annus* year)]

quadri- /kwódree/ (also **quadr-** or **quadru-**) *comb. form* denoting four. [L f. *quattuor* four]

quad·ric /kwódrik/ *adj. & n. Geom.* ● *adj.* (of a surface) described by an equation of the second degree. ● *n.* a quadric surface. [L *quadra* square]

quad·ri·ceps /kwódriseps/ *n. Anat.* a four-part muscle at the front of the thigh. [mod.L (as QUADRI-, BICEPS)]

quad·ri·fid /kwódrifid/ *adj. Bot.* having four divisions or lobes. [L *quadrifidus* (as QUADRI-, *findere fid-* cleave)]

quad·ri·lat·er·al /kwódrilátərəl/ *adj. & n.* ● *adj.* having four sides. ● *n.* a four-sided figure. [LL *quadrilaterus* (as QUADRI-, *latus lateris* side)]

quad·rille¹ /kwodríl/ *n.* **1** a square dance containing usu. five figures. **2** the music for this. [F f. Sp. *cuadrilla* troop, company f. *cuadra* square or It. *quadriglia* f. *quadra* square]

quad·rille² /kwodríl/ *n.* a card game for four players with forty cards, fashionable in the 18th c. [F, perh. f. Sp. *cuartillo* f. *cuarto* fourth, assim. to QUADRILLE¹]

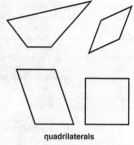

quadrilaterals

quad·ril·lion /kwodrílyən/ *n.* (*pl.* same or **quad·ril·lions**) a thousand raised to the fifth (or esp. *Brit.* the eighth) power (10^{15} and 10^{24} respectively). [F (as QUADRI-, MILLION)]

quad·ri·no·mi·al /kwódrinómeeəl/ *n. & adj. Math.* ● *n.* an expression of four algebraic terms. ● *adj.* of or being a quadrinomial. [QUADRI- + Gk *nomos* part, portion]

quad·ri·par·tite /kwódripaártīt/ *adj.* **1** consisting of four parts. **2** shared by or involving four parties.

quad·ri·ple·gi·a /kwódripléejeeə, -jə/ *n. Med.* paralysis of all four limbs. □□ **quad·ri·ple·gic** *adj. & n.* [mod.L (as QUADRI-, Gk *plēgē* blow, strike)]

quad·ri·va·lent /kwódriváylənt/ *adj. Chem.* having a valence of four.

quad·riv·i·um /kwodríveeəm/ *n. hist.* the medieval university studies of arithmetic, geometry, astronomy, and music. [L, = the place where four roads meet (as QUADRI-, *via* road)]

quad·roon /kwodro͞on/ *n.* a person of one-quarter black ancestry. [Sp. *cuarterón* f. *cuarto* fourth, assim. to QUADRI-]

quad·ro·phon·ic var. of QUADRAPHONIC.

quadru- var. of QUADRI-.

quad·ru·ma·nous /kwodro͞omənəs/ *adj.* (of primates other than humans) four-handed, i.e. with opposable digits on all four limbs. [mod.L *quadrumana* neut. pl. of *quadrumanus* (as QUADRI-, L *manus* hand)]

quad·ru·ped /kwódrəped/ *n. & adj.* • *n.* a four-footed animal, esp. a four-footed mammal. • *adj.* four-footed. □□ **quad·ru·pe·dal** /-ro͞o-pid'l/ *adj.* [F *quadrupède* or L *quadrupes –pedis* f. *quadru-* var. of QUADRI- + L *pes ped-* foot]

quad·ru·ple /kwodro͞opəl, –dru̇p–, kwódro͞opəl/ *adj., n., & v.* • *adj.* **1** fourfold. **2 a** having four parts. **b** involving four participants (*quadruple alliance*). **3** being four times as many or as much. **4** (of time in music) having four beats in a bar. • *n.* a fourfold number or amount. • *v.tr. & intr.* multiply by four; increase fourfold. □□ **quad·ru·ply** *adv.* [F f. L *quadruplus* (as QUADRI-, *–plus* as in *duplus* DUPLE)]

quad·ru·plet /kwodro͞oplit, –dru̇p–, kwódro͞oplit/ *n.* **1** each of four children born at one birth. **2** a set of four things working together. **3** *Mus.* a group of four notes to be performed in the time of three. [QUADRUPLE, after *triplet*]

quad·ru·pli·cate *adj. & v.* • *adj.* /kwodro͞oplikət/ **1** fourfold. **2** of which four copies are made. • *v.tr.* /-kayt/ **1** multiply by four. **2** make four identical copies of. □ **in quadruplicate** in four identical copies. □□ **quad·ru·pli·ca·tion** /-káyshən/ *n.* [L *quadruplicare* f. *quadruplex –plicis* fourfold: cf. QUADRUPED, DUPLEX]

quad·ru·plic·i·ty /kwódro͞oplísitee/ *n.* the state of being fourfold. [L *quadruplic –plicis* (see QUADRUPLICATE), after *duplicity*]

quaes·tor /kwéstər, kwée–/ *n.* either of two ancient Roman magistrates with mainly financial responsibilities. □□ **quaes·to·ri·al** /-stáwreeəl/ *adj.* **quaes·tor·ship** *n.* [ME f. L f. *quaerere quaesit-* seek]

quaff /kwof, kwaf, kwawf/ *v. literary* **1** *tr. & intr.* drink deeply. **2** *tr.* drain (a cup, etc.) in long drafts. □□ **quaff·a·ble** *adj.* **quaff·er** *n.* [16th c.: perh. imit.]

quag /kwag, kwog/ *n.* a marshy or boggy place. □□ **quag·gy** *adj.* [rel. to dial. *quag* (v.) = shake: prob. imit.]

quag·ga /kwágə/ *n.* an extinct zebralike mammal, *Equus quagga*, formerly native to S. Africa, with yellowish-brown stripes on the head, neck, and forebody. [Xhosa-Kaffir *iqwara*]

quag·mire /kwágmīr, kwóg–/ *n.* **1** a soft boggy or marshy area that gives way underfoot. **2** a hazardous or awkward situation. [QUAG + MIRE]

qua·hog /kwáwhawg, –hog, kwṓ–, kṓ–/ *n.* (also **qua·haug**) an edible clam, *Marcenaria* (formerly *Venus*) *mercinaria*, of the Atlantic coast of N. America. [Narragansett Indian]

quaich /kwaykh/ *n.* (also **quaigh**) *Sc.* a kind of drinking cup, usu. of wood and with two handles. [Gael. *cuach* cup, prob. f. L *caucus*]

quail[1] /kwayl/ *n.* (*pl.* same or **quails**) **1** any small migratory Old World bird of the genus *Coturnix*, with a short tail and related to the partridge. **2** any small migratory New World bird of the genus *Colinus*, esp. the bobwhite. [ME f. OF *quaille* f. med.L *coacula* (prob. imit.)]

quail[2] /kwayl/ *v.intr.* flinch; be apprehensive with fear. [ME, of unkn. orig.]

quaint /kwaynt/ *adj.* **1** piquantly or attractively unfamiliar or old-fashioned. **2** unusual; odd. □□ **quaint·ly** *adv.* **quaint·ness** *n.*

quail[1] (bobwhite)

Middle English: from Old French *cointe*, from Latin *cognitus* 'ascertained,' past participle of *cognoscere* 'to know, understand.' The original sense was 'wise, clever,' also 'marked by ingenuity or cunning; intricate,' hence 'out of the ordinary,' giving rise to the current sense (late 18th century)

quake /kwayk/ *v. & n.* • *v.intr.* **1** shake; tremble. **2** (of a person) shake or shudder (*was quaking with fear*). • *n.* **1** *colloq.* an earthquake. **2** an act of quaking. □□ **quak·y** *adj.* (**quak·i·er, quak·i·est**). [OE *cwacian*]

Quak·er /kwáykər/ *n.* a member of the Society of Friends, a Christian movement devoted to peaceful principles and eschewing formal doctrine, sacraments, and ordained ministers. □□ **Quak·er·ish** *adj.* **Quak·er·ism** *n.* [QUAKE + -ER[1]]

quak·ing grass *n.* any grass of the genus *Briza*, having slender stalks and trembling in the wind. Also called **dodder-grass**.

qual·i·fi·ca·tion /kwólifikáyshən/ *n.* **1** the act or an instance of qualifying. **2** (often in *pl.*) a quality, skill, or accomplishment fitting a

person for a position or purpose. **3 a** a circumstance, condition, etc., that modifies or limits (*the statement had many qualifications*). **b** a thing that detracts from completeness or absoluteness (*their relief had one qualification*). **4** a condition that must be fulfilled before a right can be acquired, etc. **5** an attribution of a quality (*the qualification of our policy as opportunist is unfair*). □□ **qual·i·fi·ca·to·ry** /–lífikətawree/ *adj.* [F *qualification* or med.L *qualificatio* (as QUALIFY)]

qual·i·fy /kwólifī/ *v.* (**·fies, ·fied**) **1** *tr.* make competent or fit for a position or purpose. **2** *tr.* make legally entitled. **3** *intr.* (foll. by *for* or *as*) (of a person) satisfy the conditions or requirements for (a position, award, competition, etc.). **4** *tr.* add reservations to; modify or make less absolute (a statement or assertion). **5** *tr. Gram.* (of a word, esp. an adjective) attribute a quality to another word, esp. a noun. **6** *tr.* moderate; mitigate; make less severe or extreme. **7** *tr.* alter the strength or flavor of. **8** *tr.* (foll. by *as*) attribute a specified quality to; describe as (*the idea was qualified as absurd*). **9** *tr.* (as **qualifying** *adj.*) serving to determine those that qualify (*qualifying examination*). **10** (as **qualified** *adj.*) **a** having the qualifications necessary for a particular office or function. **b** dependent on other factors; not definite (*a qualified "yes"*). □□ **qual·i·fi·a·ble** *adj.* **qual·i·fi·er** *n.* [F *qualifier* f. med.L *qualificare* f. L *qualis* such as]

qual·i·ta·tive /kwólitaytiv/ *adj.* concerned with or depending on quality (*led to a qualitative change in society*). □□ **qual·i·ta·tive·ly** *adv.* [LL *qualitativus* (as QUALITY)]

qual·i·ta·tive a·nal·y·sis *n. Chem.* detection of the constituents, as elements, functional groups, etc., present in a substance (opp. QUANTITATIVE ANALYSIS).

qual·i·ty /kwólitee/ *n.* (*pl.* **·ties**) **1** the degree of excellence of a thing (*of good quality; poor in quality*). **2 a** general excellence (*their work has quality*). **b** (*attrib.*) of high quality (*a quality product*). **3** a distinctive attribute or faculty; a characteristic trait. **4** the relative nature or kind or character of a thing. **5** the distinctive timbre of a voice or sound. **6** *archaic* high social standing (*people of quality*). **7** *Logic* the property of a proposition's being affirmative or negative. [ME f. OF *qualité* f. L *qualitas –tatis* f. *qualis* of what kind]

qual·i·ty con·trol *n.* a system of maintaining standards in manufactured products by testing a sample of the output against the specification.

qualm /kwaam, kwawm/ *n.* **1** a misgiving; an uneasy doubt esp. about one's own conduct. **2** a scruple of conscience. **3** a momentary faint or sick feeling. □□ **qualm·ish** *adj.* [16th c.: orig. uncert.]

COMPUNCTION, DEMUR, MISGIVING, SCRUPLE. To have **qualms** is to have an uneasy, often sickening, feeling that you have acted or are about to act against your better judgment (*She had qualms about leaving a nine-year-old in charge of an infant*). **Misgivings** are even stronger, implying a disturbed state of mind because you're no longer confident that what you're doing is right (*His misgivings about letting his 80-year-old mother drive herself home turned out to be justified*). **Compunction** implies a momentary pang of conscience because what you are doing or are about to do is unfair, improper, or wrong (*They showed no compunction in carrying out their devious plans*). **Scruples** suggest a more highly-developed conscience or sense of honor; it implies that you have principles, and that you would be deeply disturbed if you thought you were betraying them (*Her scruples would not allow her to participate in what she considered anti-feminist activities*). **Demur** connotes hesitation to the point of delay, but the delay is usually caused by objections or indecision rather than a sense of conscience (*They accepted his decision without demur*).

quan·da·ry /kwóndəree, –dree/ *n.* (*pl.* **·ries**) **1** a state of perplexity. **2** a difficult situation; a practical dilemma. [16th c.: orig. uncert.]

quant /kwont/ *n. & v. Brit.* • *n.* a punting pole with a prong at the bottom to prevent it sinking into the mud, as used by Norfolk (England) bargemen, etc. • *v.tr.* (also *absol.*) propel (a boat) with a quant. [15th c.: perh. f. L *contus* f. Gk *kontos* boat pole]

quan·ta *pl.* of QUANTUM.

quan·tal /kwónt'l/ *adj.* **1** composed of discrete units; varying in steps, not continuously. **2** of or relating to a quantum or quantum theory. □□ **quan·tal·ly** *adv.* [L *quantus* how much]

quan·tic /kwóntik/ *n. Math.* a rational integral homogeneous function of two or more variables.

quan·ti·fy /kwóntifī/ *v.tr.* (**·fies, ·fied**) **1** determine the quantity of. **2** measure or express as a quantity. **3** *Logic* define the application of (a term or proposition) by the use of *all, some*, etc., e.g., "for all *x* if *x* is A then *x* is B." □□ **quan·ti·fi·a·ble** *adj.* **quan·ti·fi·a·bil·i·ty** *n.* **quan·ti·fi·ca·tion** /–fikáyshən/ *n.* **quan·ti·fi·er** *n.* [med.L *quantificare* (as QUANTAL)]

quan·ti·ta·tive /kwóntitaytiv/ *adj.* **1 a** concerned with quantity. **b** measured or measurable by quantity. **2** of or based on the quantity of syllables. □□ **quan·ti·ta·tive·ly** *adv.* [med.L *quantitativus* (as QUANTITY)]

quan·ti·ta·tive a·nal·y·sis *n. Chem.* measurement of the amounts of the constituents of a substance (opp. QUALITATIVE ANALYSIS).

quan·ti·tive /kwóntitiv/ *adj.* = QUANTITATIVE. □□ **quan·ti·tive·ly** *adv.*

quan·ti·ty /kwóntitee/ *n.* (*pl.* **·ties**) **1** the property of things that is measurable. **2** the size or extent or weight or amount or number. **3** a specified or considerable portion or number or amount (*buys in quantity; the quantity of heat in a body*). **4** (in *pl.*) large amounts or numbers; an abundance (*quantities of food; is found in quantities on the shore*). **5** the length or shortness of vowel sounds or syllables. **6** *Math.* **a** a value, component, etc., that may be expressed in numbers. **b** the figure or symbol representing this. [ME f. OF *quantité* f. L *quantitas –tatis* f. *quantus* how much]

quan·ti·ty the·o·ry *n.* the hypothesis that prices correspond to changes in the monetary supply.

quan·tize /kwóntiz/ *v.tr.* **1** form into quanta. **2** apply quantum mechanics to. □□ **quan·ti·za·tion** *n.*

quan·tum /kwóntəm/ *n.* (*pl.* **quan·ta** /-tə/) **1** *Physics* **a** a discrete quantity of energy proportional in magnitude to the frequency of radiation it represents. **b** an analogous discrete amount of any other physical quantity. **2 a** a required or allowed amount. **b** a share or portion. [L, neut. of *quantus* how much]

quan·tum jump *n.* (also **quantum leap**) **1** a sudden large increase or advance. **2** *Physics* an abrupt transition in an atom or molecule from one quantum state to another.

quan·tum me·chan·ics *n.* (also **quantum theory**) *Physics* a system or theory using the assumption that energy exists in discrete units.

quan·tum num·ber *n. Physics* any integer or half odd integer that defines the magnitude of various discrete states of a particle or system.

qua·qua·ver·sal /kwáykwəvórsəl/ *adj. Geol.* pointing in every direction. [LL *quaquaversus* f. *quaqua* wheresoever + *versus* toward]

quar·an·tine /kwáwrənteen, kwór-/ *n. & v.* ● *n.* **1** isolation imposed on persons or animals that have arrived from elsewhere or been exposed to, and might spread, infectious or contagious disease. **2** the period of this isolation. ● *v.tr.* impose such isolation on; put in quarantine. [It. *quarantina* forty days f. *quaranta* forty]

quark[1] /kwawrk, kwaark/ *n. Physics* any of several postulated components of elementary particles. [invented word, assoc. with "Three quarks for Muster Mark" in Joyce's *Finnegans Wake* (1939)]

quark[2] /kwawrk, kwaark/ *n.* a type of European lowfat curd cheese. [G]

quar·rel[1] /kwáwrəl, kwór-/ *n. & v.* ● *n.* **1** a usu. verbal contention or altercation between individuals or with others. **2** a rupture of friendly relations. **3** an occasion of complaint against a person, a person's actions, etc. ● *v.intr.* (**quar·reled** or **quar·relled**, **quar·rel·ing** or **quar·rel·ling**) **1** (often foll. by *with*) take exception; find fault. **2** fall out; have a dispute; break off friendly relations. □□ **quar·rel·er** *n.* **quar·rel·ler** *n.* [ME f. OF *querele* f. L *querel(l)a* complaint f. *queri* complain]

SYNONYM TIP quarrel[1]

ALTERCATION, DISPUTE, FEUD, ROW, SPAT, SQUABBLE, WRANGLE. Family feuds come in a variety of shapes and sizes. A husband and his wife may have a **quarrel**, which suggests a heated verbal argument, with hostility that may persist even after it is over (*it took them almost a week to patch up their quarrel*). Siblings tend to have **squabbles**, which are childlike disputes over trivial matters, although they are by no means confined to childhood (*frequent squabbles over who would pick up the check*). A **spat** is also a petty *quarrel*, but unlike *squabble*, it suggests an angry outburst followed by a quick ending without hard feelings (*another spat in an otherwise loving relationship*). A **row** is more serious, involving noisy quarreling and the potential for physical violence (*a row that woke the neighbors*). Neighbors are more likely to have an **altercation**, which is usually confined to verbal blows but may involve or threaten physical ones (*an altercation over the location of the fence*). A **dispute** is also a verbal argument, but one that is carried on over an extended period of time (*an ongoing dispute over who was responsible for taking out the garbage*). Two families who have been enemies for a long time are probably involved in a **feud**, which suggests a bitter *quarrel* that lasts for years or even generations (*the feud between the Hatfields and the McCoys*). There is no dignity at all in being involved in a **wrangle**, which is an angry, noisy, and often futile *dispute* in which both parties are unwilling to listen to the other's point of view.

quar·rel[2] /kwáwrəl, kwór-/ *n.* **1** *hist.* a short heavy square-headed arrow or bolt used in a crossbow or arbalest. **2** = QUARRY[3]. [ME f. OF *quar(r)el* ult. f. LL *quadrus* square]

quar·rel·some /kwáwrəlsəm, kwór-/ *adj.* given to or characterized by quarreling. □□ **quar·rel·some·ly** *adv.* **quar·rel·some·ness** *n.*

quar·ry[1] /kwáwree, kwór-/ *n. & v.* ● *n.* (*pl.* **·ries**) **1** an excavation made by taking stone, etc., for building, etc. **2** a place from which stone, etc., may be extracted. **3** a source of information, knowledge, etc. ● *v.* (**·ries**, **·ried**) **1** *tr.* extract (stone) from a quarry. **2** *tr.* extract (facts, etc.) laboriously from books, etc. **3** *intr.* laboriously

search documents, etc. [ME f. med.L *quare(r)ia* f. OF *quarriere* f. L *quadrum* square]

quar·ry[2] /kwáwree, kwór-/ *n.* (*pl.* **·ries**) **1** the object of pursuit by a bird of prey, hounds, hunters, etc. **2** an intended victim or prey.

WORD HISTORY quarry[2]

Middle English: from Old French *cuiree*, an alteration, influenced by *cuir* 'leather' and *curer* 'clean, disembowel,' of *couree*, which is based on Latin *cor* 'heart.' Originally the term denoted the parts of a deer that, after a hunt, were placed on the hide and given as a reward to the hounds.

quar·ry[3] /kwáwree, kwór-/ *n.* (*pl.* **·ries**) **1** (also **quarrel**) a diamond-shaped pane of glass as used in lattice windows. **2** (in full **quarry tile**) an unglazed floor tile. [a later form of QUARREL[2] in the same sense]

quar·ry·man /kwáwreemən, kwór-/ *n.* a worker in a quarry.

quart /kwawrt/ *n.* **1** a liquid measure equal to a quarter of a gallon; two pints (.95 liter). **2** a vessel containing this amount. **3** a unit of dry measure, equivalent to one-thirty-second of a bushel (1.1 liter). **4** /kaart/ (also **quarte**) the fourth of eight parrying positions in fencing. [ME f. OF *quarte* f. L *quarta* fem. of *quartus* fourth f. *quattuor* four]

quar·tan /kwáwrt'n/ *adj.* (of a fever, etc.) recurring every fourth day. [ME f. OF *quartaine* f. L (*febris* fever) *quartana* f. *quartus* fourth]

quarte var. of QUART 4.

quar·ter /kwáwrtər/ *n. & v.* ● *n.* **1** each of four equal parts into which a thing is or might be divided. **2** a period of three months. **3** a point of time 15 minutes before or after any hour. **4** a school term, usu. 10–12 weeks. **5 a** 25 cents. **b** a coin of this denomination. **6** a part of a town, esp. as occupied by a particular class or group (*residential quarter*). **7 a** a point of the compass. **b** a region at such a point. **8** the direction, district, or source of supply, etc. (*help from any quarter; came from all quarters*). **9** (in *pl.*) **a** lodgings; an abode. **b** *Mil.* the living accommodation of troops, etc. **10 a** one fourth of a lunar month. **b** the moon's position between the first and second (**first quarter**) or third and fourth (**last quarter**) of these. **11 a** each of the four parts into which an animal's or bird's carcass is divided, each including a leg or wing. **b** (in *pl.*) *hist.* the four parts into which a traitor, etc., was cut after execution. **c** (in *pl.*) *Brit.* = HINDQUARTERS. **12** mercy offered or granted to an enemy in battle, etc., on condition of surrender. **13 a** *Brit.* a grain measure equivalent to 8 bushels. **b** one-fourth of a hundredweight (25 lb. or *Brit.* 28 lb.). **14** *Heraldry* **a** each of four divisions on a shield. **b** a charge occupying this, placed in chief. **15** either side of a ship abaft the beam. **16** *Sports* each of four equal periods into which a game is divided, as in football or basketball. ● *v.tr.* **1** divide into quarters. **2** *hist.* divide (the body of an executed person) in this way. **3 a** put (troops, etc.) into quarters. **b** station or lodge in a specified place. **4** (foll. by *on*) impose (a person) on another as a lodger. **5** cut (a log) into quarters, and these into planks so as to show the grain well. **6** range or traverse (the ground) in every direction. **7** *Heraldry* **a** place or bear (charges or coats of arms) on the four quarters of a shield's surface. **b** add (another's coat) to one's hereditary arms. **c** (foll. by *with*) place in alternate quarters with. **d** divide (a shield) into four or more parts by vertical and horizontal lines. [ME f. AF *quarter*, OF *quartier* f. L *quartarius* fourth part (of a measure) f. *quartus* fourth]

quar·ter·age /kwáwrtərij/ *n.* **1** a quarterly payment. **2** a quarter's wages, allowance, pension, etc.

quar·ter·back /kwáwrtərbak/ *n. & v. Football* ● *n.* a player who directs offensive play. ● *v.* **1** *intr.* to play at this position. **2** *tr.* to direct the action of, as a quarterback.

quar·ter bind·ing *n.* the type of bookbinding in which the spine is bound in one material (usu. leather) and the sides in another.

quar·ter day *n. Brit.* one of four days on which quarterly payments are due, tenancies begin and end, etc.

quar·ter·deck /kwáwrtərdek/ *n.* **1** part of a ship's upper deck near the stern, usu. reserved for officers. **2** the officers of a ship or the navy.

quar·ter·fi·nal /kwáwrtərfín'l/ *adj. & n. Sports* ● *adj.* relating to a match or round immediately preceding a semifinal. ● *n.* a quarter-final match, round, or contest.

quar·ter hour *n.* **1** a period of 15 minutes. **2** = sense 3 of *n.*

quar·ter·ing /kwáwrtəring/ *n. & adj.* ● *n.* **1** (in *pl.*) the coats of arms marshaled on a shield to denote the alliances of a family with others. **2** the provision of quarters for soldiers. **3** the act or an instance of dividing, esp. into four equal parts. **4** timber sawn into lengths, used for high-quality floorboards, etc. ● *adj.* (of the wind, waves, etc.) coming from abaft the beam of a ship.

quar·ter·ly /kwáwrtərlee/ *adj., adv., & n.* ● *adj.* **1** produced, payable, or occurring once every quarter of a year. **2** (of a shield) quartered.

• *adv.* **1** once every quarter of a year. **2** in the four, or in two diagonally opposite, quarters of a shield. • *n.* (*pl.* **·lies**) a quarterly review or magazine.

quar·ter·mas·ter /kwáwrtərmastər/ *n.* **1** an army officer in charge of quartering, rations, etc. **2** a naval petty officer in charge of steering, signals, etc.

Quar·ter·mas·ter Gen·er·al *n.* the head of the army branch in charge of quartering, etc.

quar·tern /kwáwrtərn/ *n. Brit. archaic* a quarter of a pint. □ **quartern loaf** a four-pound loaf. [ME, = quarter f. AF *quartrun*, OF *quart*(*e*)*ron* f. QUART fourth or *quartier* QUARTER]

quar·ter note *n. Mus.* a note with a duration of one quarter of a whole note.

quar·ter ses·sions *n. hist.* (in the UK) a court of limited criminal and civil jurisdiction and of appeal, usu. held quarterly.

quar·ter·staff /kwáwrtərstaf/ *n. hist.* a stout pole 6–8 feet long, formerly used as a weapon.

quar·ter tone *n. Mus.* half a semitone.

quar·tet /kwawrtét/ *n.* (also **quar·tette**) **1** *Mus.* **a** a composition for four voices or instruments. **b** the performers of such a piece. **2** any group of four. [It. *quartetto* f. *quarto* fourth f. L *quartus*]

quar·tic /kwáwrtik/ *adj. & n. Math.* • *adj.* involving the fourth and no higher power of an unknown quantity or variable. • *n.* a quartic equation. [L *quartus* fourth]

quar·tile /kwáwrtīl, –til/ *adj. & n.* • *adj. Astrol.* relating to the aspect of two celestial bodies 90° apart. • *n.* **1** a quartile aspect. **2** *Statistics* one of three values of a variable dividing a population into four equal groups as regards the value of that variable. [med.L *quartilis* f. L *quartus* fourth]

quar·to /kwáwrtō/ *n.* (*pl.* **·tos**) *Printing* **1** the size given by folding a (usu. specified) sheet of paper twice. **2** a book consisting of sheets folded in this way. ¶ Abbr.: **4to.** □ **quarto paper** paper folded in this way and cut into sheets. [L (*in*) *quarto* (in) the fourth (of a sheet), ablat. of *quartus* fourth]

quartz /kwawrts/ *n.* a mineral form of silica that crystallizes as hexagonal prisms. □ **quartz lamp** a quartz tube containing mercury vapor and used as a light source. [G *Quarz* f. WSlav. *kwardy*]

quartz clock *n.* a clock operated by vibrations of an electrically driven quartz crystal.

quartz·ite /kwáwrtsīt/ *n.* a metamorphic rock consisting mainly of quartz.

qua·sar /kwáyzaar, –zər, –saar, –sər/ *n. Astron.* any of a class of starlike celestial objects having a spectrum with a large red shift. [*quasi-stellar*]

quash /kwosh/ *v.tr.* **1** annul; reject as not valid, esp. by a legal procedure. **2** suppress; crush (a rebellion, etc.). [ME f. OF *quasser, casser* annul f. LL *cassare* f. *cassus* null, void or f. L *cassare* frequent. of *quatere* shake]

qua·si /kwáyzī, kwaázee/ *adj.* resembling; seemingly. [L, = as if, almost]

quasi- /kwáyzī, kwaázee/ *comb. form* **1** seemingly; apparently but not really (*quasi-scientific*). **2** being partly or almost (*quasi-independent*). [L *quasi* as if, almost]

quas·sia /kwósha/ *n.* **1** an evergreen tree, *Quassia amara*, native to S. America. **2** the wood, bark, or root of this tree, yielding a bitter medicinal tonic and insecticide. [G *Quassi*, 18th-c. Surinam slave, who discovered its medicinal properties]

quat·er·cen·ten·a·ry /kwótərsenténəree, –sént'neree/ *n. & adj.* • *n.* (*pl.* **·ies**) **1** a four-hundredth anniversary. **2** a festival marking this. • *adj.* of this anniversary. [L *quater* four times + CENTENARY]

quat·er·nar·y /kwótərneree, kwətórnəree/ *adj. & n.* • *adj.* **1** having four parts. **2** (**Quaternary**) *Geol.* of or relating to the most recent period in the Cenozoic era with evidence of many species of present-day plants and animals (cf. PLEISTOCENE, HOLOCENE). • *n.* (*pl.* **·ies**) **1** a set of four things. **2** (**Quaternary**) *Geol.* the Quaternary period or system. [ME f. L *quaternarius* f. *quaterni* distrib. of *quattuor* four]

qua·ter·ni·on /kwətórneeən/ *n.* **1** a set of four. **2** *Math.* a complex number of the form $w + xi + yj + zk$, where w, x, y, z are real numbers and i, j, k are imaginary units that satisfy certain conditions. [ME f. LL *quaternio –onis* (as QUATERNARY)]

qua·torze /kətáwrz/ *n.* a set of four aces, kings, queens, or jacks, in one hand at piquet, scoring fourteen. [F *quatorze* fourteen f. L *quattuordecim*]

quat·rain /kwótrayn/ *n.* a stanza of four lines, usu. with alternate rhymes. [F f. *quatre* four f. L *quattuor*]

quat·re·foil /kátərfoyl, kátrə–/ *n.* a four-pointed or four-leafed figure, esp. as an ornament in architectural tracery, resembling a flower or clover leaf. [ME f. AF f. *quatre* four: see FOIL[2]]

quat·tro·cen·to /kwátrōchéntō/ *n.* the style of Italian art of the 15th c. □□ **quat·tro·cen·tist** *n.* [It., = 400 used with reference to the years 1400–99]

qua·ver /kwáyvər/ *v. & n.* • *v.* **1** *intr.* **a** (esp. of a voice or musical sound) vibrate; shake; tremble. **b** use trills or shakes in singing. **2** *tr.*

a sing (a note or song) with quavering. **b** (often foll. by *out*) say in a trembling voice. • *n.* **1** *Mus.* = EIGHTH NOTE. **2** a trill in singing. **3** a tremble in speech. □□ **qua·ver·ing·ly** *adv.* [ME f. *quave*, perh. f. OE *cwafian* (unrecorded: cf. *cwacian* QUAKE)]

qua·ver·y /kwáyvəree/ *adj.* (of a voice, etc.) tremulous. □□ **qua·ver·i·ness** *n.*

quay /kee, kay/ *n.* a solid, stationary, artificial landing place lying alongside or projecting into water for loading and unloading ships. □□ **quay·age** *n.* [ME *key*(*e*), *kay* f. OF *kay* f. Gaulish *caio* f. OCelt.]

quay·side /kéesīd, káy–/ *n.* the land forming or near a quay.

Que. *abbr.* Quebec.

quean /kween/ *n. archaic* an impudent or ill-behaved girl or woman. [OE *cwene* woman: cf. QUEEN]

quea·sy /kwéezee/ *adj.* (**·si·er, ·si·est**) **1 a** (of a person) feeling nausea. **b** (of a person's stomach) easily upset; weak of digestion. **2** (of the conscience, etc.) overscrupulous; tender. **3** (of a feeling, thought, etc.) uncomfortable; uneasy. □□ **quea·si·ly** *adv.* **quea·si·ness** *n.* [ME *queysy, coisy* perh. f. AF & OF, rel. to OF *coisir* hurt]

Quech·ua /kéchwə, –waa/ *n.* **1** a member of a central Peruvian native people. **2** a S. American native language widely spoken in Peru and neighboring countries. □□ **Quech·uan** *adj.* [Sp. f. Quechua]

queen /kween/ *n. & v.* • *n.* **1** (as a title usu. **Queen**) a female sovereign, etc., esp. the hereditary ruler of an independent nation. **2** (in full **queen consort**) a king's wife. **3** a woman, country, or thing preeminent or supreme in a specified area or of its kind (*tennis queen*; *the queen of roses*). **4** the fertile female among ants, bees, etc. **5** the most powerful piece in chess. **6** a playing card with a picture of a queen. **7** *sl.* a male homosexual, esp. an effeminate one. **8 a** an honored female, e.g., the Virgin Mary (*Queen of Heaven*). **b** an ancient goddess (*Venus, queen of love*). **9** a mock sovereign on some occasion (*beauty queen; queen of the May*). **10** a person's sweetheart, wife, or mistress. **11** (**the Queen**) (in the UK) the national anthem when there is a female sovereign. • *v.* **1** *tr.* make (a woman) queen. **2** *tr. Chess* convert (a pawn) into a queen when it reaches the opponent's side of the board. **3** *intr.* to act like a queen, esp. to act imperiously or flamboyantly. □□ **queen·dom** *n.* **queen·hood** *n.* **queen·less** *adj.* **queen·like** *adj.* **queen·ship** *n.* [OE *cwēn* f. Gmc; cf. QUEAN]

Queen Anne's lace *n.* a widely cultivated orig. Eurasian herb, *Daucus carota*, with a whitish taproot; wild carrot.

queen bee *n.* **1** the fertile female in a hive. **2** the chief or controlling woman in an organization or social group.

queen dow·a·ger *n.* the widow of a king.

queen·ie /kwéenee/ *n. sl.* = QUEEN *n.* 7.

queen·ly /kwéenlee/ *adj.* (**queen·li·er, queen·li·est**) **1** fit for or appropriate to a queen. **2** majestic; queenlike. □□ **queen·li·ness** *n.*

queen moth·er *n.* the dowager who is mother of the sovereign.

queen post *n.* one of two upright timbers between the tie beam and principal rafters of a roof truss.

Queens·ber·ry Rules /kwéenzberee, –bəree/ *n.pl.* the standard rules, esp. of boxing. [the 8th Marquis of *Queensberry*, Engl. nobleman d. 1900, who supervised the preparation of boxing laws in 1867]

queen's bish·op *n.* (also **queen's knight**, etc.) *Chess* (of pieces which exist in pairs) the piece starting on the queen's side of the board.

queen's col·or *n.* (also **king's color** or **regimental color**) a flag carried by a regiment.

queen's coun·sel *n.* (also **king's counsel**) *Brit.* a counsel to the Crown, taking precedence over other barristers.

Queen's Eng·lish *n.* (also **King's English**) the English language as correctly written or spoken in Britain.

Queen's Guide *n.* (also **King's Guide**) *Brit.* a Guide (sense 10) who has reached the highest rank of proficiency.

queen-size *adj.* (also **queen-sized**) of an extra-large size, between full-size and king-size.

queen's pawn *n. Chess* the pawn in front of the queen at the beginning of a game.

Queen's Speech *n.* (also **King's Speech**) (in the UK) a statement including the Government's proposed measures read by the sovereign at the opening of Parliament.

queer /kweer/ *adj., n., & v.* • *adj.* **1** strange; odd; eccentric. **2** shady; suspect; of questionable character. **3 a** esp. *Brit.* slightly ill; giddy; faint. **b** *Brit. sl.* drunk. **4** *sl.* (often *derog.*) homosexual. **5** *colloq.* (of a person or behavior) crazy; unbalanced; slightly mad. **6** *sl.* counterfeit. • *n. sl.* (often *derog.*) a homosexual. • *v.tr. sl.* spoil; put out of order. □ **in Queer Street** *Brit. sl.* in a difficulty; in debt, trouble, or disrepute. **queer a person's pitch** *Brit.* spoil a person's chances, esp. secretly or maliciously. □□ **queer·ish** *adj.* **queer·ly** *adv.* **queer·ness** *n.* [perh. f. G *quer* oblique (as THWART)]

quell /kwel/ *v.tr.* **1 a** crush or put down (a rebellion, etc.). **b** reduce (rebels, etc.) to submission. **2** suppress or alleviate (fear, anger, etc.). □□ **quell·er** *n.* (also in *comb.*). [OE *cwellan* kill f. Gmc]

quench /kwench/ *v.tr.* **1** satisfy (thirst) by drinking. **2** extinguish (a fire or light, etc.). **3** cool, esp. with water (heat, a heated thing). **4** esp. *Metallurgy* cool (a hot substance) in cold water, air, oil, etc. **5 a** stifle or suppress (desire, etc.). **b** *Physics & Electronics* inhibit or prevent (oscillation, luminescence, etc.) by counteractive means.

□□ **quench·a·ble** *adj.* **quench·er** *n.* **quench·less** *adj.* [ME f. OE *-cwencan* causative f. *-cwincan* be extinguished]

que·nelle /kənél/ *n.* a poached seasoned dumpling of minced fish or meat. [F, of unkn. orig.]

que·rist /kwéerist/ *n.* *literary* a person who asks questions; a questioner. [L *quaerere* ask]

quern /kwərn/ *n.* **1** a hand mill for grinding grain. **2** a small hand mill for pepper, etc. [OE *cweorn(e)* f. Gmc]

quern stone *n.* a millstone.

quer·u·lous /kwérələs, kwéryə-/ *adj.* complaining; peevish. □□ **quer·u·lous·ly** *adv.* **quer·u·lous·ness** *n.* [LL *querulosus* or L *querulus* f. *queri* complain]

que·ry /kwéeree/ *n. & v.* • *n.* (*pl.* **·ries**) **1** a question, esp. expressing doubt or objection. **2** a question mark, or the word *query* spoken or written to question accuracy or as a mark of interrogation. • *v.* (**·ries**, **·ried**) **1** *tr.* (often foll. by *whether, if,* etc. + clause) ask or inquire. **2** *tr.* call (a thing) in question in speech or writing. **3** *tr.* dispute the accuracy of. [Anglicized form of *quaere* f. L *quaerere* ask, after INQUIRY]

quest /kwest/ *n. & v.* • *n.* **1** a search or the act of seeking. **2** the thing sought, esp. the object of a medieval knight's pursuit. • *v.* **1** *intr.* (often foll. by *about*) **a** (often foll. by *after, for*) go around in search of something. **b** (of a dog, etc.) search around for game. **2** *tr. poet.* search for; seek out. □ **in quest of** seeking. □□ **quest·er** *n.* **quest·ing·ly** *adv.* [ME f. OF *queste, quester* ult. f. L *quaerere quaest-* seek]

ques·tion /kwéschən/ *n. & v.* • *n.* **1** a sentence worded or expressed so as to seek information. **2 a** doubt about or objection to a thing's truth, credibility, advisability, etc. (*allowed it without question*). **b** the raising of such doubt, etc. **3** a matter to be discussed or decided or voted on. **4** a problem requiring an answer or solution. **5** (foll. by *of*) a matter or concern depending on conditions (*it's a question of money*). • *v.tr.* **1** ask questions of; interrogate. **2** subject (a person) to examination. **3** throw doubt upon; raise objections to. **4** seek information from the study of (phenomena, facts). □ **a question of time** be certain to happen sooner or later. **beyond all question** undoubtedly. **call in** (or **into**) **question** make a matter of dispute; query. **come into question** be discussed; become of practical importance. **in question 1** that is being discussed or referred to (*the person in question*). **2** in dispute (*that was never in question*). **is not the question** is irrelevant. **out of the question** too impracticable, etc., to be worth discussing; impossible. **put the question** require supporters and opponents of a proposal to record their votes. **without question** see *beyond all question* above. □□ **ques·tion·er** *n.* **ques·tion·ing·ly** *adv.* **ques·tion·less** *adj.* [ME f. AF *questiun*, OF *question, questiun* f. L *quaestio -onis* f. *quaerere quaest-* seek]

ques·tion·a·ble /kwéschənəbəl/ *adj.* **1** doubtful as regards truth or quality. **2** not clearly in accordance with honesty, honor, wisdom, etc. □□ **ques·tion·a·bil·i·ty** /-əbílitee/ *n.* **ques·tion·a·ble·ness** *n.* **ques·tion·a·bly** *adv.*

ques·tion·ar·y /kwéschəneree/ *n.* (*pl.* **·ies**) = QUESTIONNAIRE. [med.L *quaestionarium* or F (as QUESTIONNAIRE)]

ques·tion mark *n.* a punctuation mark (?) indicating a question.

ques·tion·naire /kwéschənáir/ *n.* **1** a formulated series of questions, esp. for statistical study. **2** a document containing these. [F f. *questionner* QUESTION + *-aire* -ARY[1]]

ques·tion time *n.* Brit. Parl. a period during parliamentary proceedings when members may question ministers.

quet·zal /ketsáal, -sál/ *n.* **1** any of various brightly colored birds of the family Trogonidae, esp. the Central and S. American *Pharomachrus mocinno*, the male of which has long green tail coverts. **2** the chief monetary unit of Guatemala. [Sp. f. Aztec f. *quetzalli* the bird's tail feather]

queue /kyōō/ *n. & v.* • *n.* **1** esp. Brit. a line or sequence of persons, vehicles, etc., awaiting their turn to be attended to or to proceed. **2** a pigtail or braid of hair. **3** *Computing* a sequence of jobs or processes waiting to be acted upon. • *v.intr.* (**queues, queued, queu·ing** or **queue·ing**) esp. Brit. (often foll. by *up*) (of persons, etc.) form a line; take one's place in a line. [F f. L *cauda* tail]

quib·ble /kwíbəl/ *n. & v.* • *n.* **1** a petty objection; a trivial point of criticism. **2** a play on words; a pun. **3** an evasion; an insubstantial argument which relies on an ambiguity, etc. • *v.intr.* use quibbles. □□ **quib·bler** *n.* **quib·bling** *adj.* **quib·bling·ly** *adv.* [dimin. of obs. *quib* prob. f. L *quibus* dative & ablat. pl. of *qui* who (familiar from use in legal documents)]

quiche /keesh/ *n.* an unsweetened custard pie with a savory filling. [F]

quiche Lor·raine *n.* a quiche made with ham or bacon and usu. Swiss or Gruyère cheese.

quick /kwik/ *adj., adv., & n.* • *adj.* **1** taking only a short time (*a quick worker; a quick visit*). **2 a** arriving after a short time; prompt (*quick action; quick results*). **b** (of an action, occurrence, etc.) sudden; hasty; abrupt. **3** with only a short interval (*in quick succession*). **4** lively; intelligent. **a** acute; alert (*has a quick ear*). **b** agile; nimble; energetic. **6** (of a temper) easily roused. **7** *archaic* living; alive (*the quick and the dead*). • *adv.* **1** quickly; at a rapid rate. **2** (as *int.*) come, go, etc., quickly. • *n.* **1** the soft flesh below the nails, or the

skin, or a sore. **2** the seat of feeling or emotion (*cut to the quick*). □ **be quick** act quickly. **quick with child** *archaic* at a stage of pregnancy when movements of the fetus have been felt. □□ **quick·ly** *adv.* **quick·ness** *n.*

WORD HISTORY quick

Old English *cwic, cwicu* 'alive, animated, alert' (hence the sense in the biblical phrase "the quick and the dead"), of Germanic origin; related to Dutch *kwiek* 'sprightly' and German *keck* 'saucy,' from an Indo-European root shared by Latin *vivus* 'alive' and Greek *bios* 'life.'

quick-and-dirt·y *adj.* hurriedly made or done.

quick·en /kwíkən/ *v.* **1** *tr. & intr.* make or become quicker; accelerate. **2** *tr.* give life or vigor to; rouse; animate; stimulate. **3** *intr.* **a** (of a woman) reach a stage in pregnancy when movements of the fetus can be felt. **b** (of a fetus) begin to show signs of life. **4** *tr. archaic* kindle; make (a fire) burn brighter. **5** *intr.* come to life.

SYNONYM TIP quicken

ANIMATE, ENLIVEN, INVIGORATE, STIMULATE, VITALIZE. While all of these verbs mean to make alive or lively, **quicken** suggests the rousing or renewal of life, especially life that has been inert or suspended (*She felt the baby quicken during her second trimester of pregnancy*). **Animate** means to impart life, motion, or activity to something that previously lacked such a quality (*a discussion animated by the presence of so many young people*). **Stimulate** means to goad into activity from a state of inertia, inactivity, or lethargy (*the professor's constant questions stimulated her students to do more research*), while **enliven** refers to a stimulating influence that brightens or makes lively what was previously dull, depressed, or torpid (*A sudden change in the weather enlivened the group's activities*). **Invigorate** and **vitalize** both mean to fill with vigor or energy, but the former refers to physical energy (*invigorated by the climb up the mountain*), while the latter implies that energy has been imparted in a nonphysical sense (*to vitalize an otherwise dull meeting*).

quick-fire *adj.* **1** (of repartee, etc.) rapid. **2** firing shots in quick succession.

quick fix *n.* an expedient but inadequate repair or solution.

quick·ie /kwíkee/ *n. colloq.* **1** a thing done or made quickly or hastily. **2** a drink taken quickly. **3** a hasty act of sexual intercourse.

quick·lime /kwíklīm/ *n.* = LIME[1] *n.* 1.

quick march *n. Mil.* **1** a march in quick time. **2** the command to begin this.

quick·sand /kwíksand/ *n.* **1** loose wet sand that sucks in anything placed or falling into it. **2** a bed of this.

quick·set /kwíkset/ *adj. & n. Brit.* • *adj.* (of a hedge) formed of cuttings of plants, esp. hawthorn set in the ground to grow. • *n.* **1** such cuttings. **2** a hedge formed in this way.

quick·sil·ver /kwíksilvər/ *n. & v.* • *n.* **1** mercury. **2** mobility of temperament or mood. • *v.tr.* coat (mirror glass) with an amalgam of tin.

quick·step /kwíkstep/ *n. & v.* • *n.* a fast foxtrot (cf. QUICK STEP). • *v.intr.* (**·stepped, ·step·ping**) dance the quickstep.

quick step *n. Mil.* a step used in quick time (cf. QUICKSTEP).

quick stud·y *n.* one who learns rapidly.

quick-tem·pered *adj.* quick to lose one's temper; irascible.

quick time *n. Mil.* marching at about 120 paces per minute.

quick-wit·ted /kwíkwítid/ *adj.* quick to grasp a situation, make repartee, etc. □□ **quick-wit·ted·ness** *n.*

quid[1] /kwid/ *n.* (*pl.* same) *Brit. sl.* one pound sterling. □ **not the full quid** *Austral. sl.* mentally deficient. **quids in** *sl.* in a position of profit. [prob. f. *quid* the nature of a thing f. L *quid* what, something]

quid[2] /kwid/ *n.* a lump of tobacco for chewing. [dial. var. of CUD]

quid·di·ty /kwíditee/ *n.* (*pl.* **·ties**) **1** *Philos.* the essence of a person or thing; what makes a thing what it is. **2** a quibble; a trivial objection. [med.L *quidditas* f. L *quid* what]

quid·nunc /kwídnungk/ *n. archaic* a newsmonger; a person given to gossip. [L *quid* what + *nunc* now]

quid pro quo /kwid prō kwó/ *n.* **1** a thing given as compensation. **2** return made (for a gift, favor, etc.). [L, = something for something]

qui·es·cent /kwiésənt, kwee-/ *adj.* **1** motionless; inert. **2** silent; dormant. □□ **qui·es·cence** *n.* **qui·es·cen·cy** *n.* **qui·es·cent·ly** *adv.* [L *quiescere* f. *quies* QUIET]

qui·et /kwíət/ *adj., n., & v.* • *adj.* (**qui·et·er, qui·et·est**) **1** with little or no sound or motion. **2 a** of gentle or peaceful disposition. **b** shy; reticent; reserved. **3** (of a color, piece of clothing, etc.) unobtrusive; not showy. **4** not overt; private; disguised (*quiet resentment*). **5** undisturbed; uninterrupted; free or far from vigorous action (*a quiet time for prayer*). **6** informal; simple (*just a quiet wedding*).

7 enjoyed in quiet (*a quiet smoke*). **8** tranquil; not anxious or remorseful. • *n.* **1** silence; stillness. **2** an undisturbed state; tranquillity. **3** a state of being free from urgent tasks or agitation (*a period of quiet*). **4** a peaceful state of affairs (*could do with some quiet*). • *v.* **1** *tr.* soothe; make quiet. **2** *intr.* (often foll. by *down*) become quiet or calm. □ **be quiet** (esp. in *imper.*) cease talking, etc. **keep quiet 1** refrain from making a noise. **2** (often foll. by *about*) suppress or refrain from disclosing information, etc. **on the quiet** unobtrusively; secretly. □□ **qui·et·ly** *adv.* **qui·et·ness** *n.* [ME f. AF *quiete* f. OF *quiet(e)*, *quieté* f. L *quietus* past part. of *quiescere*: see QUIESCENT]

qui·et·en /kwíət'n/ *v.tr. & intr. Brit.* (often foll. by *down*) make or become quiet.

qui·et·ism /kwíətizəm/ *n.* **1** a passive attitude toward life, with devotional contemplation and abandonment of the will, as a form of religious mysticism. **2** the principle of nonresistance. □□ **qui·et·ist** *n. & adj.* **qui·et·is·tic** *adj.* [It. *quietismo* (as QUIET)]

qui·e·tude /kwí-itōod, –tyōod/ *n.* a state of quiet.

qui·e·tus /kwī-eétəs/ *n.* **1** something which quiets or represses. **2** discharge or release from life; death; final riddance. [med.L *quietus est* he is quit (QUIET) used as a form of acquittal]

quiff /kwif/ *n. Brit.* **1** a man's tuft of hair, brushed upward over the forehead. **2** a curl plastered down on the forehead. [20th c.: orig. unkn.]

quill /kwil/ *n. & v.* • *n.* **1** a large feather in a wing or tail. **2** the hollow stem of this. **3** (in full **quill pen**) a pen made of a quill. **4** (usu. in *pl.*) the spines of a porcupine. **5** a musical pipe made of a hollow stem. • *v.tr.* form into cylindrical quill-like folds; goffer. [ME prob. f. (M)LG *quiele*]

quill co·verts *n.* the feathers covering the base of quill feathers.

quilt¹ /kwilt/ *n. & v.* • *n.* **1** a bedcovering made of padding enclosed between layers of cloth, etc., and kept in place by patterned stitching. **2** a bedspread of similar design (*patchwork quilt*). • *v.tr.* **1** cover or line with padded material. **2** make or join together (pieces of cloth with padding between) after the manner of a quilt. **3** sew up (a coin, letter, etc.) between two layers of a garment, etc. **4** compile (a literary work) out of extracts or borrowed ideas. □□ **quilt·er** *n.* **quilt·ing** *n.* [ME f. OF *coilte*, *cuilte* f. L *culcita* mattress, cushion]

quilt² /kwilt/ *v.tr. Austral. sl.* thrash; clout. [perh. f. QUILT¹]

quim /kwim/ *n. coarse sl.* the female genitals. [18th c.: orig. unkn.]

quin·a·crine /kwínəkreen, –krin/ *n.* an antimalarial drug derived from acridine. [*quinine* + *acridine*]

qui·na·ry /kwínəree/ *adj.* **1** of the number five. **2** having five parts. [L *quinarius* f. *quini* distrib. of *quinque* five]

qui·nate /kwínayt/ *adj. Bot.* (of a leaf) having five leaflets. [L *quini* (as QUINARY)]

quince /kwins/ *n.* **1** a hard acidic pear-shaped fruit used chiefly in preserves. **2** any shrub or small tree of the genus *Cydonia*, esp. *C. oblonga*, bearing this fruit. [ME, orig. collect. pl. of obs. *quoyn, coyn*, f. OF *cooin* f. L *cotoneum* var. of *cydoneum* (apple) of *Cydonia* in Crete]

quin·cen·ten·ar·y /kwínsenténəree, –sént'neree/ *n. & adj.* • *n.* (*pl.* **·ies**) **1** a five-hundredth anniversary. **2** a festival marking this. • *adj.* of this anniversary. □□ **quin·cen·ten·ni·al** /–téneeəl/ *adj. & n.* [irreg. f. L *quinque* five + CENTENARY]

quin·cunx /kwínkungks/ *n.* five objects set so that four are at the corners of a square or rectangle and the fifth is at its center, e.g., the five on dice or cards. **2** this arrangement, esp. in planting trees. □□ **quin·cun·cial** /–kúnshəl/ *adj.* **quin·cun·cial·ly** *adv.* [L, = fivetwelfths f. *quinque* five, *uncia* twelfth]

qui·nel·la /kwinélə/ *n.* a form of betting in which the bettor must select the first two place winners in a race, not necessarily in the correct order. [Amer. Sp. *quiniela*]

qui·nine /kwínīn, kwín–/ *n.* **1** an alkaloid found esp. in cinchona bark. **2** a bitter drug containing this, used as a tonic and to reduce fever. [*quina* cinchona bark f. Sp. *quina* f. Quechua *kina* bark]

qui·nine wa·ter *n.* a carbonated beverage flavored with quinine.

quin·ol /kwínol/ *n.* = HYDROQUINONE.

quin·o·line /kwínəleen, –lin/ *n. Chem.* an oily amine obtained from the distillation of coal tar or by synthesis and used in the preparation of drugs, etc.

qui·none /kwínōn, kwinón/ *n. Chem.* **1** a yellow crystalline derivative of benzene with the hydrogen atoms on opposite carbon atoms replaced by two of oxygen. **2** any in a class of similar compounds.

quin·qua·ge·nar·i·an /kwíngkwəjináireeən/ *n. & adj.* • *n.* a person from 50 to 59 years old. • *adj.* of or relating to this age. [L *quinquagenarius* f. *quinquageni* distrib. of *quinquaginta* fifty]

Quin·qua·ges·i·ma /kwíngkwəjésimə/ *n.* (in full **Quinquagesima Sunday**) the Sunday before the beginning of Lent. [med. L, fem. of L *quinquagesimus* fiftieth f. *quinquaginta* fifty, after QUADRAGESIMA]

quinque- /kwíngkwee/ *comb. form* five. [L f. *quinque* five]

quin·quen·ni·al /kwíngkwéneeəl/ *adj.* **1** lasting five years. **2** recurring every five years. □□ **quin·quen·ni·al·ly** *adv.* [L *quinquennis* (as QUIN-QUENNIUM)]

quin·quen·ni·um /kwinkwéneeəm/ *n.* (*pl.* **quin·quen·ni·ums** or **quin·**

quen·ni·a /–neeə/) a period of five years. [L f. *quinque* five + *annus* year]

quin·que·va·lent /kwíngkwəváylənt/ *adj.* having a valence of five.

quin·sy /kwínzee/ *n.* an inflammation of the throat, esp. an abscess in the region around the tonsils. □□ **quin·sied** *adj.* [ME f. OF *quinencie* f. med.L *quinancia* f. Gk *kunagkhē* f. *kun-* dog + *agkhō* throttle]

quint /kwint/ *n.* **1** a sequence of five cards in the same suit in piquet, etc. **2** *colloq.* a quintuplet. [F *quinte* f. L *quinta* fem. of *quintus* fifth f. *quinque* five]

quin·tain /kwint'n/ *n. hist.* **1** a post set up as a target in tilting, and often provided with a sandbag to swing around and strike an unsuccessful tilter. **2** the medieval military exercise of tilting at such a mark. [ME f. OF *quintaine* perh. ult. f. L *quintana* camp market f. *quintus* (*manipulus*) fifth (maniple)]

quin·tal /kwint'l/ *n.* **1** a weight of about 100 lb. **2** (in the UK) a weight of 112 lb. (a hundredweight). **3** a weight of 100 kg. [ME f. OF *quintal*, med.L *quintale* f. Arab. *kintār*]

quin·tan /kwint'n/ *adj.* (of a fever, etc.) recurring every fifth day. [L *quintana* f. *quintus* fifth]

quinte /kant/ *n.* the fifth of eight parrying positions in fencing. [F: see QUINT]

quin·tes·sence /kwintésəns/ *n.* **1** the most essential part of any substance; a refined extract. **2** (usu. foll. by *of*) the purest and most perfect, or most typical, form, manifestation, or embodiment of some quality or class. **3** (in ancient philosophy) a fifth substance (beside the four elements) forming heavenly bodies and pervading all things. □□ **quin·tes·sen·tial** /kwíntisénshəl/ *adj.* **quin·tes·sen·tial·ly** *adv.* [ME (in sense 3) f. F f. med.L *quinta essentia* fifth ESSENCE]

quin·tet /kwintét/ *n.* (also **quin·tette**) **1** *Mus.* **a** a composition for five voices or instruments. **b** the performers of such a piece. **2** any group of five. [F *quintette* f. It. *quintetto* f. *quinto* fifth f. L *quintus*]

quin·til·lion /kwintílyən/ *n.* (*pl.* same or **quin·til·lions**) a thousand raised to the sixth (or esp. *Brit.* the tenth) power (10^{18} and 10^{30} respectively). □□ **quin·til·lionth** *adj. & n.* [L *quintus* fifth + MILLION]

quint ma·jor *n.* a quint headed by an ace.

quin·tu·ple /kwintōopəl, –tyōo–, –túpəl, kwíntəpəl/ *adj., n., & v.* • *adj.* **1** fivefold; consisting of five parts. **2** involving five parties. **3** (of time in music) having five beats in a bar. • *n.* a fivefold number or amount. • *v.tr. & intr.* multiply by five; increase fivefold. □□ **quin·tu·ply** *adv.* [F *quintuple* f. L *quintus* fifth, after QUADRUPLE]

quin·tu·plet /kwintúplit, –tōo–, –tyōo–, kwíntə–/ *n.* **1** each of five children born at one birth. **2** a set of five things working together. **3** *Mus.* a group of five notes to be performed in the time of three or four. [QUINTUPLE, after QUADRUPLET, TRIPLET]

quin·tu·pli·cate *adj. & v.* • *adj.* /kwintōoplikət, –tyōo–/ **1** fivefold. **2** of which five copies are made. • *v.tr. & intr.* /–kayt/ multiply by five. □ **in quintuplicate** in five identical copies. **2** in groups of five. [F *quintuple* f. L *quintus* fifth, after QUADRUPLICATE]

quip /kwip/ *n. & v.* • *n.* **1** a clever saying; an epigram; a sarcastic remark, etc. **2** a quibble; an equivocation. • *v.intr.* (**quipped**, **quipping**) make quips. □□ **quip·ster** *n.* [abbr. of obs. *quippy* perh. f. L *quippe* forsooth]

qui·pu /keepōo, kwee–/ *n.* the ancient Peruvians' substitute for writing by variously knotting threads of various colors. [Quechua, = knot]

quire /kwīr/ *n.* **1** four sheets of paper, etc., folded to form eight leaves, as often in medieval manuscripts. **2** any collection of leaves one within another in a manuscript or book. **3** 25 (also 24) sheets of paper. □ **in quires** unbound; in sheets. [ME f. OF *qua(i)er* ult. f. L *quaterni* set of four (as QUATERNARY)]

quirk /kwork/ *n.* **1** a peculiarity of behavior. **2** a trick of fate; a freak. **3** a flourish in writing. **4** (often *attrib.*) *Archit.* a hollow in a molding. □□ **quirk·ish** *adj.* **quirk·y** *adj.* (**quirk·i·er, quirk·i·est**). **quirk·i·ly** *adv.* **quirk·i·ness** *n.* [16th c.: orig. unkn.]

quirt /kwort/ *n. & v.* • *n.* a short-handled riding whip with a braided leather lash. • *v.tr.* strike with this. [Sp. *cuerda* CORD]

quis·ling /kwízling/ *n.* **1** a person cooperating with an occupying enemy; a collaborator or fifth columnist. **2** a traitor. □□ **quis·ling·ite** *adj. & n.* [V. Quisling, renegade Norwegian Army officer d. 1945]

quit /kwit/ *v. & adj.* • *v.tr.* (**quit·ting**; *past* and *past part.* **quit** or **quitted**) **1** (also *absol.*) give up; let go; abandon (a task, etc.). **2** cease; stop (*quit grumbling*). **3** *a* leave or depart from (a place, person, employment, etc.). **b** (*absol.*) (of a tenant) leave occupied premises (esp. notice to quit). **4** (*refl.*) acquit; behave (*quit oneself well*). • *predic.adj.* (foll. by *of*) rid (*glad to be quit of the problem*). □ **quit hold of** loose. [ME f. OF *quitte, quitter* f. med.L *quittus* f. L *quietus* QUIET]

quitch /kwich/ *n.* (in full **quitch grass**) = COUCH². [OE *cwice*, perh. rel. to QUICK]

quite /kwit/ *adv.* **1** completely; entirely; wholly; to the utmost extent; in the fullest sense. **2** somewhat; rather; to some extent. **3** (often foll. by *so*) said to indicate agreement. **4** absolutely; definitely; very much. □ **quite another** (or **other**) very different (*that's quite another matter*). **quite a few** *colloq.* a fairly large number of. **quite something** a remarkable thing. [ME f. obs. *quite* (adj.) = QUIT]

quits /kwits/ *predic.adj.* on even terms by retaliation or repayment (*then we'll be quits*). □ **call it** (or *Brit.* **cry**) **quits** acknowledge that things are now even; agree not to proceed further in a quarrel, etc. [perh. colloq. abbr. of med.L *quittus*: see QUIT]

quit·tance /kwit'ns/ *n.* **1** (foll. by *from*) a release. **2** an acknowledgement of payment; a receipt. [ME f. OF *quitance* f. *quiter* QUIT]

quit·ter /kwitər/ *n.* **1** a person who gives up easily. **2** a shirker.

quiv·er[1] /kwivər/ *v. & n.* ● *v.* **1** *intr.* tremble or vibrate with a slight rapid motion, esp.: **a** (usu. foll. by *with*) as the result of emotion (*quiver with anger*). **b** (usu. foll. by *in*) as the result of air currents, etc. (*quiver in the breeze*). **2** *tr.* (of a bird) make (its wings) quiver. ● *n.* a quivering motion or sound. □□ **quiv·er·ing·ly** *adv.* **quiv·er·y** *adj.* [ME f. obs. *quiver* nimble: cf. QUAVER]

quiv·er[2] /kwivər/ *n.* a case for holding arrows. □ **have an arrow** (or **shaft**) **left in one's quiver** not be resourceless. [ME f. AF *quiver* f.WG (cf. OE *cocor*)]

quiver[2]

quiv·er·ful /kwivərfŏŏl/ *n.* (*pl.* **-fuls**) esp. *Brit.* **1** as much as a quiver can hold. **2** many children of one parent (Ps. 127:5). [QUIVER[2]]

qui vive /kee veev/ *n.* □ **on the qui vive** on the alert; watching for something to happen. [F, = lit. '(long) live who?', i.e., on whose side are you?, as a sentry's challenge]

quix·ot·ic /kwiksótik/ *adj.* **1** extravagantly and romantically chivalrous; having no regard for material interests in comparison with honor or devotion. **2** visionary; pursuing lofty but unattainable ideals. **3** *derog.* ridiculously impractical; preposterous; foolhardy. □□ **quix·ot·i·cal·ly** *adv.* **quix·o·tism** /kwiksətizəm/ *n.* **quix·o·try** /kwiksətree/ *n.* [Don *Quixote*, hero of Cervantes' romance f. Sp. *quixote* thigh armor]

quiz[1] /kwiz/ *n. & v.* ● *n.* (*pl.* **quiz·zes**) **1 a** a quick or informal test. **b** an interrogation, examination, or questionnaire. **2** (also **quiz show**) a test of knowledge, esp. between individuals or teams as a form of entertainment. ● *v.tr.* (**quizzed, quiz·zing**) examine by questioning. [19th-c. dial.: orig. unkn.]

quiz[2] /kwiz/ *v. & n. archaic Brit.* ● *v.tr.* (**quizzed, quiz·zing**) **1** look curiously at; observe the ways or oddities of; survey through an eyeglass. **2** make fun of; regard mockingly. ● *n.* (*pl.* **quiz·zes**) **1 a** hoax; a practical joke. **2 a** an odd or eccentric person; a person of ridiculous appearance. **b** a person given to quizzing. □□ **quiz·zer** *n.* [18th c.: orig. unkn.]

quiz·zi·cal /kwízikəl/ *adj.* **1** expressing or done with mild or amused perplexity. **2** strange; comical. □□ **quiz·zi·cal·i·ty** /-kálitee/ *n.* **quiz·zi·cal·ly** *adv.* **quiz·zi·cal·ness** *n.*

quod /kwod/ *n. Brit. sl.* prison. [17th c.: orig. unkn.]

quod erat demonstrandum /kwod érət démənstrándəm, éraat démónstraándŏŏm/ (esp. at the conclusion of a proof, etc.) which was the thing to be proved. ¶ Abbr.: **QED.** [L]

quod·li·bet /kwódlibet/ *n.* **1** *hist.* **a** a topic for philosophical or theological discussion. **b** an exercise on this. **2** a whimsical medley of well-known tunes. □□ **quod·li·betarian** /-bitáyreeən/ *n.* **quod·li·bet·i·cal** /-likétikol/ *adj.* **quod·li·bet·i·cal·ly** *adv.* [ME f. L f. *quod* what + *libet* it pleases one]

quod vi·de /kwod veéday, vídee/ which see (in cross references, etc.). ¶ Abbr.: **q.v.** [L]

quoin /koyn, kwoin/ *n. & v.* ● *n.* **1** an external angle of a building. **2** a stone or brick forming an angle; a cornerstone. **3** a wedge used for locking type in a chase. **4** a wedge for raising the level of a gun, keeping the barrel from rolling, etc. ● *v.tr.* secure or raise with quoins. □□ **quoin·ing** *n.* [var. of COIN]

quoit /koyt, kwoit/ *n. & v.* ● *n.* **1** a heavy flattish sharp-edged iron ring thrown to encircle an iron peg or to land as near as possible to the peg. **2** (in *pl.*) a game consisting of aiming and throwing these. **3** a ring of rope, rubber, etc., for use in a similar game. **4** *Brit.* **a** the flat stone of a dolmen. **b** the dolmen itself. ● *v.tr.* fling like a quoit. [ME: orig. unkn.]

quok·ka /kwókə/ *n.* a small Australian short-tailed wallaby, *Setonix brachyurus.* [Aboriginal name]

quon·dam /kwóndəm, –dam/ *predic.adj.* that once was; sometime; former. [L (adv.), = formerly]

Quon·set hut /kwónsit/ *n. Trademark* a prefabricated metal building with a semicylindrical corrugated roof. [*Quonset* Point, Rhode Island, where it was first made]

Quonset hut

quo·rate /kwáwrət, –rayt/ *adj. Brit.* (of a meeting) attended by a quorum. [QUORUM]

quo·rum /kwáwrəm/ *n.* the fixed minimum number of members that must be present to make the proceedings of an assembly or society legally valid. [L, = of whom (we wish that you be two, three, etc.), in the wording of commissions]

quo·ta /kwôtə/ *n.* **1** the share that an individual person, group, or company is bound to contribute to or entitled to receive from a total. **2** a quantity of goods, etc., which under official controls must be manufactured, exported, imported, etc. **3** the number of immigrants allowed to enter a country annually, or students allowed to enroll in a course, etc. [med.L *quota* (*pars*) how great (a part), fem. of *quotus* f. *quot* how many]

quot·a·ble /kwôtəbəl/ *adj.* worth, or suitable for, quoting. □□ **quot·a·bil·i·ty** *n.*

quo·ta·tion /kwōtáyshən/ *n.* **1** the act or an instance of quoting or being quoted. **2** a passage or remark quoted. **3** *Mus.* a short passage or tune taken from one piece of music to another. **4** *Stock Exch.* an amount stated as the current price of stocks or commodities. **5** a contractor's estimate. [med.L *quotatio* (as QUOTE)]

quo·ta·tion mark *n.* each of a set of punctuation marks, single (' ') or double (" "), used to mark the beginning and end of a quoted passage, a book title, etc., or words regarded as slang or jargon.

quote /kwōt/ *v. & n.* ● *v.tr.* **1** cite or appeal to (an author, book, etc.) in confirmation of some view. **2** repeat a statement by (another person) or copy out a passage from (*don't quote me*). **3** (often *absol.*) **a** repeat or copy out (a passage) usu. with an indication that it is borrowed. **b** (foll. by *from*) cite (an author, book, etc.). **4** (foll. by *as*) cite (an author, etc.) as proof, evidence, etc. **5 a** enclose (words) in quotation marks. **b** (as *int.*) (in dictation, reading aloud, etc.) indicate the presence of opening quotation marks (*he said, quote, "I shall stay"*). **6** (often foll. by *at*) state the price of (a commodity, bet, etc.) (*quoted at 200 to 1*). **7** *Stock Exch.* regularly list the price of. ● *n. colloq.* **1** a passage quoted. **2 a** a price quoted. **b** a contractor's estimate. **3** (usu. in *pl.*) quotation marks. [ME, earlier 'mark with numbers,' f. med.L *quotare* f. *quot* how many, or as QUOTA]

quoth /kwōth/ *v.tr.* (only in 1st and 3rd person) *archaic* said. [OE *cwæth* past of *cwethan* say f. Gmc]

quo·tid·i·an /kwotídeeən/ *adj. & n.* ● *adj.* **1** daily; of every day. **2** commonplace; trivial. ● *n.* (in full **quotidian fever**) a fever recurring every day. [ME f. OF *cotidien* & L *cotidianus* f. *cotidie* daily]

quo·tient /kwôshənt/ *n.* a result obtained by dividing one quantity by another. [ME f. L *quotiens* how many times f. *quot* how many, by confusion with –ENT]

Qu·r'an var. of KORAN.

q.v. *abbr.* quod vide.

qwer·ty /kwórtee/ *attrib.adj.* denoting the standard keyboard on English-language typewriters, word processors, etc., with *q, w, e, r, t,* and *y* as the first keys on the top row of letters.

qy. *abbr.* query.

R

R[1] /aar/ *n.* (also **r**) (*pl.* **Rs** or **R's**) the eighteenth letter of the alphabet.
R[2] *abbr.* (also **R.**) **1** river. **2** *Brit.* Regina (*Elizabeth R*). **3** *Brit.* Rex. **4** (also ®) registered as a trademark. **5** (in names of societies, etc.) Royal. **6** *Chess* rook. **7** ratio. **8** rand. **9** regiment. **10** *Electr.* resistance. **11** radius. **12** roentgen. **13** (of movies) classified as prohibited to people under a certain age (as 17) unless accompanied by a parent or guardian.
r. *abbr.* (also **r**) **1** right. **2** recto. **3** run(s). **4** radius.
RA *abbr.* **1** regular army. **2** rear admiral. **3 a** (in the UK) Royal Academy. **b** (in the UK) royal academician. **4** *Astron.* right ascension.
Ra *symb. Chem.* the element radium.
rab·bet /rábit/ *n. & v.* ● *n.* a step-shaped channel, etc., cut along the edge or face or projecting angle of a length of wood, etc., usu. to receive the edge or tongue of another piece. ● *v.tr.* **1** join or fix with a rabbet. **2** make a rabbet in. [ME f. OF *rab(b)at* abatement, recess f. *rabattre* REBATE]
rab·bet plane *n.* a plane for cutting a groove along an edge.
rab·bi /rábī/ *n.* (*pl.* **rab·bis**) **1** a Jewish scholar or teacher, esp. of the law. **2** a person appointed as a Jewish religious leader. □□ **rab·bin·ate** /rábinət/ *n.* [ME & OE f. eccl.L f. Gk *rhabbi* f. Heb. *rabbî* my master f. *rab* master + pronominal suffix]
rab·bin·i·cal /rəbínikəl/ *adj.* of or relating to rabbis, or to Jewish law or teaching. □□ **rab·bin·i·cal·ly** *adv.*
rab·bit /rábit/ *n. & v.* ● *n.* **1 a** any of various burrowing gregarious plant-eating mammals of the family Leporidae, esp. the eastern cottontail, *Sylvilagus floridanus*, with long ears and a short tail, varying in color from brown in the wild to black and white, and kept as a pet or for meat. **b** a hare. **c** the fur of the rabbit. **2** *Brit. colloq.* a poor performer in any sport or game. ● *v.intr.* **1** hunt rabbits. **2** (often foll. by *on, away*) *Brit. colloq.* talk excessively or pointlessly; chatter (*rabbiting on about his school*). □□ **rab·bit·y** *adj.* [ME perh. f. OF: cf. F dial. *rabotte*, Walloon *robète*, Flem. *robbe*]
rab·bit ears *n.* a television antenna consisting of two movable rods, usu. on top of the set.
rab·bit punch *n.* a short chop with the edge of the hand to the nape of the neck.
rab·bit's foot *n.* the foot of a rabbit, carried to bring luck.
rab·bit war·ren *n.* **1** an area in which rabbits have their burrows, or are kept for meat, etc. **2** a densely populated or labyrinthine office area, building, district, etc.
rab·ble[1] /rábəl/ *n.* **1** a disorderly crowd; a mob. **2** a contemptible or inferior set of people. **3** (prec. by *the*) the lower or disorderly classes of the populace. [ME: orig. uncert.]
rab·ble[2] /rábəl/ *n.* an iron bar with a bent end for stirring molten metal, etc. [F *râble* f. med.L *rotabulum*, L *rutabulum* fire shovel f. *ruere rut-* rake up]
rab·ble-rous·er *n.* a person who stirs up the rabble or a crowd of people in agitation for social or political change. □□ **rab·ble-rous·ing** *adj. & n.*
Rab·e·lai·si·an /rábəláyzeeən, –zhən/ *adj. & n.* ● *adj.* **1** of or like Rabelais or his writings. **2** marked by exuberant imagination and language, coarse humor, and satire. ● *n.* an admirer or student of Rabelais. [F. *Rabelais*, Fr. satirist d. 1553]
rab·id /rábid/ *adj.* **1** furious; violent (*rabid hatred*). **2** unreasoning; headstrong; fanatical (*a rabid anarchist*). **3** affected with rabies; mad. **4** of or connected with rabies. □□ **rab·id·i·ty** /rəbíditee/ *n.* **rab·id·ly** *adv.* **rab·id·ness** *n.* [L *rabidus* f. *rabere* rave]
ra·bies /ráybeez/ *n.* a contagious and fatal viral disease, esp. of dogs, cats, raccoons, etc., transmissible through the saliva to humans, etc., and causing madness and convulsions; hydrophobia. [L f. *rabere* rave]
rac·coon /rakoʻon/ *n.* (also **ra·coon**) **1** any grayish-brown furry N. American nocturnal flesh-eating mammal of the genus *Procyon*, with a bushy, ringed tail and masklike band across the eyes. **2** the fur of the raccoon. [Algonquian dial.]

raccoon

race[1] /rays/ *n. & v.* ● *n.* **1** a contest of speed between runners, horses, vehicles, ships, etc. **2** (in *pl.*) a series of these for horses, dogs, etc., at a fixed time on a regular course. **3** a contest between persons to be first to achieve something. **4 a** a strong or rapid current flowing through a narrow channel in the sea or a river (*a tide race*). **b** the channel of a stream, etc. (*a millrace*). **5** each of two grooved rings in a ball bearing or roller bearing. **6** *Austral.* a fenced passageway for drafting sheep, etc. **7** (in weaving) the channel along which the shuttle moves. **8** *archaic* **a** the course of the sun or moon. **b** the course of life (*has run his race*). ● *v.* **1** *intr.* take part in a race. **2** *tr.* have a race with. **3** *tr.* try to surpass in speed. **4** *intr.* (foll. by *with*) compete in speed with. **5** *tr.* cause (a horse, car, etc.) to race. **6 a** *intr.* move swiftly; go at full or (of an engine, propeller, the pulse, etc.) excessive speed. **b** *tr.* cause (a person or thing) to do this (*raced the bill through the House*). **7** *intr.* (usu. as **racing** *adj.*) follow or take part in horse racing (*a racing man*). □ **out of the race** (of a person, etc., in contention for something) having no chance. [ME, = running, f. ON *rás*]
race[2] /rays/ *n.* **1** each of the major divisions of humankind, having distinct physical characteristics. **2** a tribe, nation, etc., regarded as of a distinct ethnic stock. **3** the fact or concept of division into races (*discrimination based on race*). **4** a genus, species, breed, or variety of animals, plants, or microorganisms. **5** a group of persons, animals, or plants connected by common descent. **6** any great division of living creatures (*the feathered race; the four-footed race*). **7** descent; kindred (*of noble race; separate in language and race*). **8** a class of persons, etc., with some common feature (*the race of poets*). [F f. It. *razza*, of unkn. orig.]
race[3] /rays/ *n.* a ginger root. [OF *rais, raiz* f. L *radix radicis* root]
race car *n.* a car built for racing on a prepared track.
race·course /ráyskawrs/ *n.* a ground or track for esp. horse racing.
race·go·er /ráysgōər/ *n.* a person who frequents horse races.
race·horse /ráys-hors/ *n.* a horse bred or kept for racing.
race·mate /rayseʻemayt, rásə–/ *n. Chem.* a racemic mixture.
ra·ceme /rayseʻem, rə–/ *n. Bot.* a flower cluster with the separate flowers attached by short equal stalks at equal distances along a central stem (cf. CYME). [L *racemus* grape bunch]
ra·ce·mic /rayseʻemik, –sém–, rə–/ *adj. Chem.* composed of equal numbers of dextrorotatory and levorotatory molecules of a compound. □□ **rac·e·mize** /rásimīz/ *v.tr. & intr.* [RACEME + –IC, orig. of tartaric acid in grape juice]
rac·e·mose /rásimōs/ *adj.* **1** *Bot.* in the form of a raceme. **2** *Anat.* (of a gland, etc.) clustered. [L *racemosus* (as RACEME)]
rac·er /ráysər/ *n.* **1** a horse, yacht, bicycle, etc., of a kind used for racing. **2** a circular horizontal rail along which the traversing platform of a heavy gun moves. **3** a person or thing that races.
race re·la·tions *n.pl.* relations between members of different races usu. in the same country.
race ri·ot *n.* an outbreak of violence due to racial antagonism.
race·track /ráystrak/ *n.* **1** = RACECOURSE. **2** a track for automobile racing.
race·way /ráysway/ *n.* **1** a track or channel along which something runs, esp.: **a** esp. *Brit.* a channel for water. **b** a groove in which ball bearings run. **c** a pipe or tubing enclosing electrical wires. **2 a** a track for trotting, pacing, or harness racing. **b** = RACETRACK.
ra·chis /ráykis/ *n.* (*pl.* **ra·chis·es** or **rach·i·des** /rákideez, ráy–/) **1** *Bot.* **a** a stem of grass, etc., bearing flower stalks at short intervals. **b** the axis of a compound leaf or frond. **2** *Anat.* the vertebral column or the cord from which it develops. **3** *Zool.* a feather shaft, esp. the part bearing the barbs. □□ **ra·chid·i·al** /rəkideeəl/ *adj.* [mod.L f. Gk *rhakhis* spine: the E pl. *–ides* is erron.]
ra·chi·tis /rəkítis/ *n.* rickets. □□ **ra·chit·ic** /–kítik/ *adj.* [mod.L f. Gk *rhakhitis* (as RACHIS)]
ra·cial /ráyshəl/ *adj.* **1** of or concerning race (*racial diversities; racial minority*). **2** on the grounds of or connected with difference in race (*racial discrimination; racial tension*). □□ **ra·cial·ly** *adv.*
ra·cial·ism /ráyshəlizəm/ *n.* = RACISM 1. □□ **ra·cial·ist** *n. & adj.*
rac·ism /ráysizəm/ *n.* **1 a** a belief in the superiority of a particular race; prejudice based on this. **b** antagonism toward other races, esp. as a result of this. **2** the theory that human abilities, etc., are determined by race. □□ **rac·ist** *n. & adj.*
rack[1] /rak/ *n. & v.* ● *n.* **1 a** a framework usu. with rails, bars, hooks, etc., for holding or storing things. **b** a frame for holding animal fodder. **2** a cogged or toothed bar or rail engaging with a wheel or pinion, etc., or using pegs to adjust the position of something. **3 a** *hist.* an instrument of torture stretching the victim's joints by the turning of rollers to which the wrists and ankles were tied. **b** a cause of suffering or anguish. ● *v.tr.* **1** (of disease or pain) inflict suffering on. **2** *hist.* torture (a person) on the rack. **3** place in or on a rack. **4** shake violently. **5** injure by straining. **6** *Brit.* oppress

(tenants) by exacting excessive rent. **7** exhaust (the land) by excessive use. □ **on the rack** in distress or under strain. **rack one's brains** make a great mental effort (*racked my brains for something to say*). **rack up** accumulate or achieve (a score, etc.). [ME *rakke* f. MDu., MLG *rak, rek*, prob. f. *recken* stretch]

SPELLING TIP rack¹

The relationship between the forms **rack** and **wrack** is complicated. The most common noun sense of *rack* 'a framework for holding and storing things' is always spelled *rack*, never *wrack*. The figurative senses of the verb, deriving from the type of torture in which someone is stretched on a *rack*, can, however, be spelled either *rack* or *wrack*: thus *racked with guilt* or *wracked with guilt*; *rack your brains* or *wrack your brains*; *the bank was racked by internal division* or *the bank was wracked by internal division*. In addition, the phrase *rack and ruin* can also be spelled *wrack and ruin*. In the contexts mentioned here as having the variant *wrack*, *rack* is always the commoner spelling.

rack² /rak/ *n.* destruction (esp. rack and ruin). [var. of WRACK, WRECK]
rack³ /rak/ *n.* a joint of lamb, etc., including the front ribs. [perh. f. RACK¹]
rack⁴ /rak/ *v.tr.* (often foll. by *off*) draw off (wine, beer, etc.) from the lees. [ME f. Prov. *arracar* f. *raca* stems and husks of grapes, dregs]
rack⁵ /rak/ *n. & v.* ● *n.* driving clouds. ● *v.intr.* (of clouds) be driven before the wind. [ME, prob. of Scand. orig.: cf. Norw. and Sw. dial. *rak* wreckage, etc. f. *reka* drive]
rack⁶ /rak/ *n. & v.* ● *n.* a horse's gait between a trot and a canter. ● *v.intr.* progress in this way.
rack•et¹ /rákit/ *n.* (also **rac•quet**) **1** a hand-held implement with a round or oval frame strung with catgut, nylon, etc., used in tennis, squash, etc. **2** (in *pl.*) a ball game for two or four persons played with rackets in a plain four-walled court. **3** a snowshoe resembling a tennis racket. [F *racquette* f. It. *racchetta* f. Arab. *rāḥa* palm of the hand]

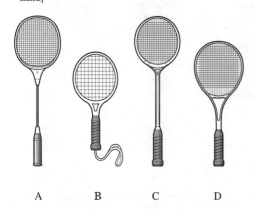

A. badminton racket   C. squash racket
B. racquetball racket   D. tennis racket

rackets¹

rack•et² /rákit/ *n.* **1 a** a disturbance; an uproar; a din. **b** social excitement; gaiety. **2** *sl.* **a** a scheme for obtaining money or attaining other ends by fraudulent and often violent means. **b** a dodge; a sly game. **3** *colloq.* an activity; a way of life; a line of business (*starting up a new racket*). □□ **rack•et•y** *adj.* [16th c.: perh. imit.]
rack•et•eer /rákitéer/ *n.* a person who operates a dishonest or illegal business, as gambling, extortion, etc. □□ **rack•et•eer•ing** *n.*
rack•et•tail *n.* a S. American hummingbird, *Loddigesia mirabilis*, with a racket-shaped tail.
rack rail•way = COG RAILWAY.
rack rent *n. & v.* ● *n.* **1** a high rent, annually equaling the full value of the property to which it relates. **2** an extortionate rent. ● *v.tr.* (**rack-rent**) exact this from (a tenant) or for (land).
rack-rent•er *n.* a tenant paying or a landlord exacting an extortionate rent.
rack wheel *n.* a cogwheel.
ra•con /ráykon/ *n.* a radar beacon that can be identified and located by its response to a radar signal from a ship, etc. [radar + beacon]
rac•on•teur /rákontőr/ *n.* (*fem.* **rac•on•teuse** /–tőz/) a teller of interesting anecdotes. [F f. *raconter* relate, RECOUNT]

ra•coon var. of RACCOON.
rac•quet var. of RACKET¹.
rac•quet•ball /rákətbawl/ *n.* a game played with rackets and a rubber ball on an enclosed, four-walled court.
rac•y /ráysee/ *adj.* (**rac•i•er, rac•i•est**) **1** lively and vigorous in style. **2** risqué, suggestive. **3** having characteristic qualities in a high degree (*a racy flavor*). □□ **rac•i•ly** *adv.* **rac•i•ness** *n.* [RACE² + –Y¹]
rad¹ /rad/ *n.* (*pl.* same) radian. [abbr.]
rad² /rad/ *n. & adj.* ● *n. sl.* a political radical. ● *adj. sl.* wonderful; terrific. [abbr.]
rad³ /rad/ *n. Physics* a unit of absorbed dose of ionizing radiation, corresponding to the absorption of 0.01 joule per kilogram of absorbing material. [radiation absorbed dose]
ra•dar /ráydaar/ *n.* **1** a system for detecting the direction, range, or presence of aircraft, ships, and other objects, by sending out pulses of high-frequency electromagnetic waves. **2** the apparatus used for this. [radio detecting and ranging]
ra•dar trap *n.* the use of radar to detect vehicles exceeding a speed limit.
rad•dle /rád'l/ *n. & v.* (also **rud•dle**) ● *n.* red ocher (often used to mark sheep). ● *v.tr.* **1** color with raddle or too much rouge. **2** (as **raddled** *adj.*) worn out; untidy, unkempt. [rel. to obs. *rud* red]
ra•di•al /ráydeeəl/ *adj. & n.* ● *adj.* **1** of, concerning, or in rays. **2** arranged like rays or radii; having the position or direction of a radius. **b** having spokes or radiating lines. **c** acting or moving along lines diverging from a center. **3** *Anat.* relating to the radius (*radial artery*). **4** (of a vehicle tire) having the core fabric layers arranged radially at right angles to the circumference and the tread strengthened. ● *n.* **1** *Anat.* the radial nerve or artery. **2** a radial tire. □□ **ra•di•al•ly** *adv.* [med.L *radialis* (as RADIUS)]
ra•di•al en•gine *n.* an engine having cylinders arranged along radii.
ra•di•al sym•me•try *n.* symmetry occurring about any number of lines or planes passing through the center of an organism, etc.
ra•di•al ve•loc•i•ty *n.* esp. *Astron.* the speed of motion along a radial line, esp. between a star, etc., and an observer.
ra•di•an /ráydeeən/ *n. Geom.* a unit of angle, equal to an angle at the center of a circle, the arc of which is equal in length to the radius. [RADIUS + –AN]
ra•di•ant /ráydeeənt/ *adj. & n.* ● *adj.* **1** emitting rays of light. **2** (of eyes or looks) beaming with joy or hope or love. **3** (of beauty) splendid or dazzling. **4** (of light) issuing in rays. **5** operating radially. **6** extending radially; radiating. ● *n.* **1** the point or object from which light or heat radiates, esp. in an electric or gas heater. **2** *Astron.* a radiant point. □□ **ra•di•ance** *n.* **ra•di•an•cy** *n.* **ra•di•ant•ly** *adv.* [ME f. L *radiare* (as RADIUS)]
ra•di•ant heat *n.* heat transmitted by radiation, not by conduction or convection.
ra•di•ant point *n.* **1** a point from which rays or radii proceed. **2** *Astron.* the apparent focal point of a meteor shower.
ra•di•ate *v. & adj.* ● *v.* /ráydeeayt/ **1** *intr.* **a** emit rays of light, heat, or other electromagnetic waves. **b** (of light or heat) be emitted in rays. **2** *tr.* emit (light, heat, or sound) from a center. **3** *tr.* transmit or demonstrate (life, love, joy, etc.) (*radiates happiness*). **4** *intr. & tr.* diverge or cause to diverge or spread from a center. **5** *tr.* (as **radiated** *adj.*) with parts arranged in rays. ● *adj.* /ráydeeət/ having divergent rays or parts radially arranged. □□ **ra•di•ate•ly** *adv.* **ra•di•a•tive** /–ətiv/ *adj.* [L *radiare radiat-* (as RADIUS)]
ra•di•a•tion /ráydeeáyshən/ *n.* **1** the act or an instance of radiating; the process of being radiated. **2** *Physics* **a** the emission of energy as electromagnetic waves or as moving particles. **b** the energy transmitted in this way, esp. invisibly. **3** (in full **radiation therapy**) treatment of cancer and other diseases using radiation, such as X rays or ultraviolet light. □□ **ra•di•a•tion•al** *adj.* **ra•di•a•tion•al•ly** *adv.* [L *radiatio* (as RADIATE)]
ra•di•a•tion chem•is•try *n.* the study of the chemical effects of radiation on matter.
ra•di•a•tion sick•ness *n.* sickness caused by exposure to radiation, such as X rays or gamma rays.
ra•di•a•tor /ráydeeaytər/ *n.* **1** a person or thing that radiates. **2 a** a device for heating a room, etc., consisting of a metal case through which hot water or steam circulates. **b** a usu. portable oil or electric heater resembling this. **3** an engine-cooling device in a motor vehicle or aircraft with a large surface for cooling circulating water.
ra•di•a•tor grille *n.* a grille at the front of a motor vehicle allowing air to circulate to the radiator.
rad•i•cal /rádikəl/ *adj. & n.* ● *adj.* **1** of the root or roots; fundamental (*a radical error*). **2** far-reaching; thorough; going to the root (*radical change*). **3 a** advocating thorough reform; holding extreme political views; left-wing; revolutionary. **b** (of a measure, etc.) advanced by or according to principles of this kind. **4** forming the basis; primary (*the radical idea*). **5** *Math.* of the root of a number or quantity. **6** (of surgery, etc.) seeking to ensure the removal of all diseased tissue. **7** of the roots of words. **8** *Mus.* belonging to the root of a chord. **9** *Bot.* of, or springing direct from, the root. **10** *Brit. hist.* belonging to an extreme section of the liberal party. **11** *US*

hist. seeking extreme anti-South action in the period leading to the Civil War. ● *n.* **1** a person holding radical views or belonging to a radical party. **2** *Chem.* **a** a free radical. **b** an element or atom or a group of these normally forming part of a compound and remaining unaltered during the compound's ordinary chemical changes. **3** the root of a word. **4** a fundamental principle; a basis. **5** *Math.* **a** a quantity forming or expressed as the root of another. **b** a radical sign. □□ **rad‧i‧cal‧ism** *n.* **rad‧i‧cal‧ize** *v.tr. & intr.* **rad‧i‧cal‧i‧za‧tion** *n.* **rad‧i‧cal‧ly** *adv.* **rad‧i‧cal‧ness** *n.* [ME f. LL *radicalis* f. L *radix radicis* root]

rad‧i‧cal sign *n.* √, ³√, etc., indicating the square, cube, etc., root of the number following.

ra‧dic‧chi‧o /rədeékeeō/ *n.* (*pl.* **·os**) a variety of chicory with dark red leaves. [It., = chicory]

rad‧i‧ces *pl.* of RADIX.

rad‧i‧cle /rádikəl/ *n.* **1** the part of a plant embryo that develops into the primary root; a rootlet. **2** a rootlike subdivision of a nerve or vein. □□ **ra‧dic‧u‧lar** /rədíkyŏolər/ *adj.* [L *radicula* (as RADIX)]

ra‧di‧i *pl.* of RADIUS.

ra‧di‧o /ráydeeō/ *n. & v.* ● *n.* (*pl.* **·os**) **1** (often *attrib.*) **a** the transmission and reception of sound messages, etc., by electromagnetic waves of radio frequency. **b** an apparatus for receiving, broadcasting, or transmitting radio signals. **c** a message sent or received by radio. **2 a** sound broadcasting in general (*prefers the radio*). **b** a broadcasting station, channel, or organization (*Armed Forces Radio*). ● *v.* (**·oed**) **1** *tr.* **a** send (a message) by radio. **b** send a message to (a person) by radio. **2** *intr.* communicate or broadcast by radio. [short for *radiotelegraphy*, etc.]

radio- /ráydeeō/ *comb. form* **1** denoting radio or broadcasting. **2 a** connected with radioactivity. **b** denoting artificially prepared radioisotopes of elements (*radiocesium*). **3** connected with rays or radiation. **4** *Anat.* belonging to the radius in conjunction with some other part (*radiocarpal*). [RADIUS + -O- or f. RADIO]

ra‧di‧o‧ac‧tive /ráydeeō-áktiv/ *adj.* of or exhibiting radioactivity. □□ **ra‧di‧o‧ac‧tive‧ly** *adv.*

ra‧di‧o‧ac‧tiv‧i‧ty /ráydeeō-aktívitee/ *n.* the spontaneous disintegration of atomic nucleii, with the emission of usu. penetrating radiation or particles.

ra‧di‧o as‧tron‧o‧my *n.* the branch of astronomy concerned with the radio-frequency range of the electromagnetic spectrum.

ra‧di‧o‧bi‧ol‧o‧gy /ráydeeōbīóləjee/ *n.* the biology concerned with the effects of radiation on organisms and the application in biology of radiological techniques. □□ **ra‧di‧o‧bi‧o‧log‧i‧cal** /-bīəlójikəl/ *adj.* **ra‧di‧o‧bi‧o‧log‧i‧cal‧ly** *adv.* **ra‧di‧o‧bi‧ol‧o‧gist** *n.*

ra‧di‧o car *n.* an automobile, esp. a taxicab or police vehicle, equipped with a two-way radio.

ra‧di‧o‧car‧bon /ráydeeōkáarbən/ *n.* a radioactive isotope of carbon.

ra‧di‧o‧car‧bon dat‧ing = CARBON DATING.

ra‧di‧o‧chem‧is‧try /ráydeeōkémistree/ *n.* the chemistry of radioactive materials. □□ **ra‧di‧o‧chem‧i‧cal** *adj.* **ra‧di‧o‧chem‧ist** *n.*

ra‧di‧o‧el‧e‧ment /ráydeeō-élimənt/ *n.* a natural or artificial radioactive element or isotope.

ra‧di‧o fix *n.* the position of an aircraft, ship, etc., found by radio.

ra‧di‧o fre‧quen‧cy *n.* the frequency band of telecommunication, ranging from 10^4 to 10^{11} or 10^{12} Hz.

ra‧di‧o gal‧ax‧y *n.* a galaxy emitting radiation in the radio-frequency range of the electromagnetic spectrum.

ra‧di‧o‧gen‧ic /ráydeeōjénik/ *adj.* **1** produced by radioactivity. **2** suitable for broadcasting by radio. □□ **ra‧di‧o‧gen‧i‧cal‧ly** *adv.*

ra‧di‧o‧go‧ni‧om‧e‧ter /ráydeeōgŏneeómitər/ *n.* an instrument for finding direction using radio waves.

ra‧di‧o‧gram /ráydeeōgram/ *n.* **1** a picture obtained by X rays, gamma rays, etc. **2** a radiotelegram. [RADIO- + -GRAM]

ra‧di‧o‧graph /ráydeeōgráf/ *n. & v.* ● *n.* **1** an instrument recording the intensity of radiation. **2** = RADIOGRAM 2. ● *v.tr.* obtain a picture of by X ray, gamma ray, etc. □□ **ra‧di‧og‧ra‧pher** /-deeógrəfər/ *n.* **ra‧di‧o‧graph‧ic** *adj.* **ra‧di‧o‧graph‧i‧cal‧ly** *adv.* **ra‧di‧og‧ra‧phy** /-deeógrəfee/ *n.*

ra‧di‧o ham *n.* see HAM.

ra‧di‧o‧im‧mu‧nol‧o‧gy /ráydeeō-ímyənóləjee/ *n.* the application of radiological techniques in immunology.

ra‧di‧o‧i‧so‧tope /ráydeeō-ísətōp/ *n.* a radioactive isotope. □□ **ra‧di‧o‧i‧so‧top‧ic** /-tópik/ *adj.* **ra‧di‧o‧i‧so‧top‧i‧cal‧ly** *adv.*

ra‧di‧o‧lar‧i‧an /ráydeeōláireeən/ *n.* any marine protozoan of the order Radiolaria, having a siliceous skeleton and radiating pseudopodia. [mod.L *radiolaria* f. L *radiolus* dimin. of RADIUS]

ra‧di‧ol‧o‧gy /ráydeeóləjee/ *n.* the scientific study of X rays and other high-energy radiation, esp. as used in medicine. □□ **ra‧di‧o‧log‧ic** /-deeəlójik/ *adj.* **ra‧di‧o‧log‧i‧cal** /-deeəlójikəl/ *adj.* **ra‧di‧ol‧o‧gist** *n.*

ra‧di‧om‧e‧ter /ráydeeómitər/ *n.* an instrument for measuring the intensity or force of radiation. □□ **ra‧di‧om‧e‧try** *n.*

radiometer

ra‧di‧o‧met‧ric /ráydeeōmétrik/ *adj.* of or relating to the measurement of radioactivity.

ra‧di‧o‧met‧ric dat‧ing *n.* a method of dating geological specimens by determining the relative proportions of the isotopes of a radioactive element present in a sample.

ra‧di‧on‧ics /ráydeeóniks/ *n.pl.* (usu. treated as *sing.*) the study and interpretation of radiation believed to be emitted from substances, esp. as a form of diagnosis. [RADIO- + -*onics*, after ELECTRONICS]

ra‧di‧o‧nu‧clide /ráydeeōnŏoklīd, -nyŏo-/ *n.* a radioactive nuclide.

ra‧di‧o‧paque /ráydeeōpáyk/ *adj.* opaque to X rays or similar radiation. □□ **ra‧di‧o‧pac‧i‧ty** /-pásitee/ *n.* [RADIO- + OPAQUE]

ra‧di‧o‧phon‧ic /ráydeeōfónik/ *adj.* of or relating to synthetic sound, esp. music, produced electronically.

ra‧di‧os‧co‧py /ráydeeóskəpee/ *n.* the examination by X rays, etc., of objects opaque to light. □□ **ra‧di‧o‧scop‧ic** /-deeəskópik/ *adj.*

ra‧di‧o‧sonde /ráydeeōsond/ *n.* a miniature radio transmitter broadcasting information about pressure, temperature, etc., from various levels of the atmosphere, carried esp. by balloon. [RADIO- + G *Sonde* probe]

ra‧di‧o star *n.* a small star, etc., emitting strong radio waves.

ra‧di‧o‧tel‧e‧gram /ráydeeōtéligram/ *n.* a telegram sent by radio, usu. from a ship to land.

ra‧di‧o‧te‧leg‧ra‧phy /ráydeeōtilégrəfee/ = WIRELESS TELEGRAPHY. □□ **ra‧di‧o‧tel‧e‧graph** /-téligraaf/ *n.*

ra‧di‧o‧te‧leph‧o‧ny /ráydeeōtiléfənee/ *n.* telephony using radio transmission. □□ **ra‧di‧o‧tel‧e‧phone** /-télifōn/ *n.* **ra‧di‧o‧tel‧e‧phon‧ic** /-telifónik/ *adj.*

ra‧di‧o tel‧e‧scope *n.* a directional aerial system for collecting and analyzing radiation in the radio-frequency range from stars, etc.

ra‧di‧o‧tel‧ex /ráydeeōtéleks/ *n.* a telex sent usu. from a ship to land.

ra‧di‧o‧ther‧a‧py /ráydeeōthérəpee/ *n.* radiation therapy (see RADIATION). □□ **ra‧di‧o‧ther‧a‧peu‧tic** /-pyŏotik/ *adj.* **ra‧di‧o‧ther‧a‧pist** *n.*

rad‧ish /rádish/ *n.* **1** a cruciferous plant, *Raphanus sativus*, with a fleshy pungent root. **2** this root, eaten esp. raw in salads, etc. [OE *rædic* f. L *radix radicis* root]

ra‧di‧um /ráydeeəm/ *n.* *Chem.* a radioactive metallic element orig. obtained from pitchblende, etc., used esp. in luminous materials and in radiotherapy. ¶ Symb.: **Ra**. [L *radius* ray]

ra‧di‧um ther‧a‧py *n.* the treatment of disease by the use of radium.

ra‧di‧us /ráydeeəs/ *n. & v.* ● *n.* (*pl.* **ra‧di‧i** /-dee-ī/ or **ra‧di‧us‧es**) **1** *Math.* **a** a straight line from the center to the circumference of a circle or sphere. **b** a radial line from the focus to any point of a curve. **c** the length of the radius of a circle, etc. **2 a** usu. specified distance from a center in all directions (*within a radius of 20 miles*; *has a large radius of action*). **3 a** the thicker and shorter of the two bones in the human forearm (cf. ULNA). **b** the corresponding bone in a vertebrate's foreleg or a bird's wing. **4** any of the five armlike structures of a starfish. **5 a** any of a set of lines diverging from a point like the radii of a circle. **b** an object of this kind, e.g., a spoke. **6 a** the outer rim of a composite flower head, e.g., a daisy. **b** a radiating branch of an umbel. ● *v.tr.* give a rounded form to (an edge, etc.). [L, = staff, spoke, ray]

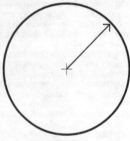

radius 1a

ra‧di‧us vec‧tor *n.* *Math.* a variable line drawn from a fixed point to an orbit or other curve, or to any point as an indication of the latter's position.

ra‧dix /ráydiks/ *n.* (*pl.* **ra‧di‧ces** /-díseez/ or **ra‧dix‧es**) **1** *Math.* a number or symbol used as the basis of a numeration scale (e.g., ten in the decimal system). **2** (usu. foll. by *of*) a source or origin. [L, = root]

ra‧dome /ráydōm/ *n.* a dome or other structure, transparent to radio waves, protecting radar equipment, esp. on the outer surface of an aircraft. [radar + *dome*]

ra‧don /ráydon/ *n.* *Chem.* a gaseous radioactive inert element arising from the disintegration of radium, and used in radiotherapy. ¶ Symb.: **Rn**. [RADIUM after *argon*, etc.]

rad‧u‧la /rájŏolə/ *n.* (*pl.* **rad‧u‧lae** /-lee/ or **rad‧u‧las**) a filelike structure in mollusks for scraping off food particles and drawing them into the mouth. □□ **rad‧u‧lar** *adj.* [L, = scraper f. *radere* scrape]

RAF *abbr.* (in the UK) Royal Air Force.

Raf‧fer‧ty's rules /ráfərteez/ *n.* *Austral. & NZ colloq.* no rules at all, esp. in boxing. [E dial. corrupt. of *refractory*]

raf‧fi‧a /ráfeeə/ *n.* (also **ra‧phi‧a**) **1** a palm tree, *Raphia ruffia*, native to Madagascar, having very long leaves. **2** the fiber from its leaves used for making hats, baskets, etc., and for tying plants, etc. [Malagasy]

raf·fi·nate /ráfinayt/ *n. Chem.* a refined liquid oil produced by solvent extraction of impurities. [F *raffiner* + –ATE¹]

raff·ish /ráfish/ *adj.* **1** disreputable; rakish. **2** tawdry. □□ **raff·ish·ly** *adv.* **raff·ish·ness** *n.* [as RAFT² + –ISH¹]

raf·fle¹ /ráfəl/ *n. & v. • n.* a fund-raising lottery with goods as prizes. *• v.tr.* (often foll. by *off*) dispose of by means of a raffle. [ME, a kind of dice game, f. OF *raf(f)le*, of unkn. orig.]

raf·fle² /ráfəl/ *n.* **1** rubbish; refuse. **2** debris. [ME, perh. f. OF *ne rifle, ne rafle* nothing at all]

raft¹ /raft/ *n. & v. • n.* **1** a flat floating structure of logs or other materials for conveying persons or things. **2** a lifeboat or small (often inflatable) boat, esp. for use in emergencies. **3** a floating accumulation of trees, ice, etc. *• v.* **1** *tr.* transport as or on a raft. **2** *tr.* cross (water) on a raft. **3** *tr.* form into a raft. **4** *intr.* (often foll. by *across*) work a raft (across water, etc.). [ME f. ON *raptr* RAFTER]

raft² /raft/ *n. colloq.* **1** a large collection. **2** (foll. by *of*) a crowd. [*raff* rubbish, perh. of Scand. orig.]

raf·ter¹ /ráftər/ *n.* each of the sloping beams forming the framework of a roof. □□ **raf·tered** *adj.* [OE *ræfter*, rel. to RAFT¹]

raft·er² /ráftər/ *n.* **1** a person who builds rafts. **2** a person who travels by raft.

rafts·man /ráftsmən/ *n.* (*pl.* **·men**) a worker on a raft.

rag¹ /rag/ *n.* **1 a** a torn, frayed, or worn piece of woven material. **b** one of the irregular scraps to which cloth, etc., is reduced by wear and tear. **2 a** (in *pl.*) old or worn clothes. **b** (usu. in *pl.*) *colloq.* a garment of any kind. **3** (*collect.*) scraps of cloth used as material for paper, stuffing, etc. **4** *derog.* **a** a flag, handkerchief, curtain, etc. **5** (usu. with *neg.*) the smallest scrap of cloth, etc. (*not a rag to cover him*). **6** an odd scrap; an irregular piece. **7** a jagged projection, esp. on metal. □ **in rags 1** much torn. **2** in old torn clothes. **rags to riches** poverty to affluence. [ME, prob. back-form. f. RAGGED]

rag² /rag/ *n. & v. • n. Brit.* **1** a fund-raising program of stunts, parades, and entertainment organized by students. **2** *colloq.* a prank. **3 a** a rowdy celebration. **b** a noisy disorderly scene. *• v.* (**ragged, rag·ging**) **1** *tr.* tease; torment; play rough jokes on. **2** *tr.* scold; reprove severely. **3** *intr. Brit.* engage in rough play; be noisy and riotous. [18th c.: orig. unkn.: cf. BULLYRAG]

rag³ /rag/ *n.* **1** a large, coarse roofing slate. **2** any of various kinds of hard, coarse, sedimentary stone that break into thick slabs. [ME: orig. unkn., but assoc. with RAG¹]

rag⁴ /rag/ *n. Mus.* a ragtime composition or tune. [perh. f. RAGGED: see RAGTIME]

ra·ga /ráagə/ *n.* (also **rag** /raag/) *Ind. Mus.* **1** a pattern of notes used as a basis for improvisation. **2** a piece using a particular raga. [Skr., = color, musical tone]

rag·a·muf·fin /rágəmufin/ *n.* a person in ragged dirty clothes, esp. a child. [prob. based on RAG¹: cf. 14th-c. *ragamoffyn* the name of a demon]

rag-and-bone man *n. Brit.* an itinerant dealer in old clothes, furniture, etc.

rag·bag /rágbag/ *n.* **1** a bag in which scraps of fabric, etc., are kept for use. **2** a miscellaneous collection.

rag book *n. Brit.* = CLOTH BOOK.

rag doll *n.* a stuffed doll made of cloth.

rage /rayj/ *n. & v. • n.* **1** fierce or violent anger. **2** a fit of this (*flew into a rage*). **3** the violent action of a natural force (*the rage of the storm*). **4** (foll. by *for*) **a** a vehement desire or passion. **b** a widespread temporary enthusiasm or fashion. **5** *poet.* poetic, prophetic, or martial enthusiasm or ardor. **6** *sl.* a lively frolic. *• v.intr.* **1** be full of anger. **2** (often foll. by *at, against*) speak furiously or madly; rave. **3** (of wind, battle, fever, etc.) be violent; be at its height; continue unchecked. **4** *Austral. sl.* seek enjoyment; go on a spree. □ **all the rage** popular; fashionable. [ME f. OF *rager* ult. f. L RABIES]

rag·ged /rágid/ *adj.* **1 a** (of clothes, etc.) torn; frayed. **b** (of a place) dilapidated. **2** rough; shaggy; hanging in tufts. **3** (of a person) in ragged clothes. **4** with a broken or jagged outline or surface. **5** faulty; imperfect. **6 a** lacking finish, smoothness, or uniformity (*ragged rhymes*). **b** (of a sound) harsh, discordant. **7** exhausted (*esp. be run ragged*). □□ **rag·ged·ly** *adv.* **rag·ged·ness** *n.* **rag·ged·y** *adj.* [ME f. ON *roggvathr* tufted]

rag·ged rob·in *n.* a pink-flowered campion, *Lychnis flos-cuculi*, with tattered petals.

rag·gle-tag·gle /rágəltagəl/ *adj.* untidy and scruffy. [app. fanciful var. of RAGTAG]

rag·lan /ráglən/ *n.* (often *attrib.*) an overcoat without shoulder seams, the sleeves running up to the neck. [Lord *Raglan*, Brit. commander d. 1855]

rag·lan sleeve *n.* a sleeve of the kind on a raglan coat.

raglan sleeves

rag·man /rágmən/ *n.* = RAGPICKER.

ra·gout /ragóo/ *n. & v. • n.* meat in small pieces stewed with vegetables and highly seasoned. *• v.tr.* cook (food) in this way. [F *ragoût* f. *ragoûter* revive the taste of]

rag pa·per *n.* paper made from cotton or linen pulp.

rag·pick·er /rágpikər/ *n.* a collector and seller of rags.

rag·stone /rágstōn/ *n.* = RAG³ 2.

rag·tag /rágtag/ *n. & adj. • n.* (in full **ragtag and bobtail**) *derog.* the rabble or common people. *• adj.* motley. [earlier *tag-rag, tag and rag*, f. RAG¹ + TAG¹]

rag·time /rágtim/ *n. & adj. • n.* music characterized by a syncopated melodic line and regularly accented accompaniment, evolved by African-American musicians in the 1890s and played esp. on the piano. *• adj. sl.* disorderly, disreputable, inferior (*a ragtime army*). [prob. f. RAG⁴]

rag trade *n. colloq.* the business of designing, making, and selling clothes.

rag·u·ly /rágyəlee/ *adj. Heraldry* like a row of sawn-off branches. [perh. f. RAGGED after *nebuly*]

rag·weed /rágweed/ *n.* any plant of the genus *Ambrosia*, esp. *A. trifida*, with allergenic pollen.

rag·wort /rágwort, –wawrt/ *n.* any yellow-flowered ragged-leaved plant of the genus *Senecio*.

rah /raa/ *int. colloq.* an expression of encouragement, approval, etc., esp. to a team or a player. [shortening of HURRAH]

raid /rayd/ *n. & v. • n.* **1** a rapid surprise attack, esp.: **a** by troops, aircraft, etc., in warfare. **b** to commit a crime or do harm. **2** a surprise attack by police, etc., to arrest suspected persons or seize illicit goods. **3** *Stock Exch.* an attempt to lower prices by the concerted selling of shares. **4** (foll. by *on, upon*) a forceful or insistent attempt to make a person or thing provide something. *• v.tr.* **1** make a raid on (a person, place, or thing). **2** plunder; deplete. □□ **raid·er** *n.* [ME, Sc. form of OE *rād* ROAD¹]

rail¹ /rayl/ *n. & v. • n.* **1** a level or sloping bar or series of bars: **a** used to hang things on. **b** running along the top of a set of banisters. **c** forming part of a fence or barrier as protection against contact, falling over, etc. **2** a steel bar or continuous line of bars laid on the ground, usu. as one of a pair forming a railroad track. **3** (often *attrib.*) a railroad (*send it by rail; rail fares*). **4** (in *pl.*) the inside boundary fence of a racecourse. **5** a horizontal piece in the frame of a paneled door, etc. (cf. STILE²). *• v.tr.* **1** furnish with a rail or rails. **2** (usu. foll. by *in, off*) enclose with rails (*a small space was railed off*). **3** convey (goods) by rail. □ **off the rails** disorganized; out of order; deranged. **over the rails** over the side of a ship. □□ **rail·age** *n.* **rail·less** *adj.* [ME f. OF *reille* iron rod f. L *regula* RULE]

rail² /rayl/ *v.intr.* (often foll. by *at, against*) complain using abusive language; rant. □□ **rail·er** *n.* **rail·ing** *n. & adj.* [ME f. F *railler* f. Prov. *ralhar* jest, ult. f. L *rugire* bellow]

rail³ /rayl/ *n.* any bird of the family Rallidae, often inhabiting marshes, esp. the Virginia rail and corn crake. [ME f. ONF *raille* f. Rmc, perh. imit.]

rail·car /ráylkaar/ *n.* **1** any railroad car. **2** a railroad vehicle consisting of a single powered car.

rail fence *n.* a fence made of posts and rails.

rail·head /ráylhed/ *n.* **1** the furthest point reached by a railroad under construction. **2** the point on a railroad at which road transport of goods begins.

rail·ing /ráyling/ *n.* **1** (usu. in *pl.*) a fence or barrier made of rails. **2** the material of this.

rail·ler·y /ráyləree/ *n.* (*pl.* **·ies**) **1** good-humored ridicule; rallying. **2** an instance of this. [F *raillerie* (as RAIL²)]

rail·road /ráylrōd/ *n. & v. • n.* **1** a track or set of tracks made of steel rails upon which goods trucks and passenger trains run. **2** such a system worked by a single company (*B & O Railroad*). **3** the organization and personnel required for its working. **4** a similar set of tracks for other vehicles, etc. *• v.tr.* **1** (often foll. by *to, into, through*, etc.) rush or coerce (a person or thing) (*railroaded me into going too*). **2** send (a person) to prison by means of false evidence. **3** transport by railroad.

rail·road yard *n.* the area where rolling stock is kept and made up into trains.

rail·way /ráylway/ *n. esp. Brit.* = RAILROAD

rail·way·man /ráylwaymən/ *n.* (*pl.* **·men**) *Brit.* a railroad employee.

rai·ment /ráymənt/ *n. archaic* clothing. [ME f. obs. *arrayment* (as ARRAY)]

rain /rayn/ *n. & v. • n.* **1 a** the condensed moisture of the atmosphere falling visibly in separate drops. **b** the fall of such drops. **2** (in *pl.*) **a** rainfalls. **b** (prec. by *the*) the rainy season in tropical countries. **3 a** falling liquid or solid particles or objects. **b** the rainlike descent of these. **c** a large or overwhelming quantity (*a rain of congratulations*). *• v.* **1** *intr.* (prec. by *it* as subject) rain falls (*it is raining; if it rains*). **2 a** *intr.* fall in showers or like rain (*tears rained down their cheeks; blows rain upon him*). **b** *tr.* (prec. by *it* as subject) send in large quantities (*it rained blood; it is raining invitations*). **3** *tr.* send down like rain; lavishly bestow (*rained benefits on us; rained blows upon him*). **4** *intr.* (of the sky, the clouds, etc.) send down rain. □ **rain**

cats and dogs see CAT. **rain out** (esp. in *passive*) cause (an event, etc.) to be terminated or canceled because of rain. **rain or shine** whether it rains or not. □□ **rain·less** *adj*. [OE *regn*, *rēn*, *regnian* f. Gmc]

rain·bird /ráynbərd/ *n*. any of several birds said to foretell rain by their cry, esp. the black-billed and yellow-billed cuckoos.

rain·bow /ráynbō/ *n. & adj.* ● *n*. **1** an arch of colors (conventionally red, orange, yellow, green, blue, indigo, violet) formed in the sky (or across a waterfall, etc.) opposite the sun by reflection, twofold refraction, and dispersion of the sun's rays in falling rain or in spray or mist. **2** a similar effect formed by the moon's rays. ● *adj.* many-colored. [OE *regnboga* (as RAIN, BOW¹)]

rain·bow trout *n*. a large trout, *Salmo gairdneri*, orig. of the Pacific coast of N. America.

rain check *n*. **1** a ticket given for later use when a sports or other outdoor event is interrupted or postponed by rain. **2** a promise that an offer will be maintained though deferred.

rain cloud *n*. a cloud bringing rain.

rain·coat /ráynkōt/ *n*. a waterproof or water-resistant coat.

rain date *n*. a date on which an event postponed by rain is held.

rain·drop /ráyndrop/ *n*. a single drop of rain. [OE *regndropa*]

rain·fall /ráynfawl/ *n*. **1** a fall of rain. **2** the quantity of rain falling within a given area in a given time.

rain for·est *n*. luxuriant tropical forest with heavy rainfall.

rain gauge *n*. an instrument measuring rainfall.

rain·mak·ing /ráynmayking/ *n*. the action of attempting to increase rainfall by artificial means.

rain·proof /ráynprŏof/ *adj*. (esp. of a building, garment, etc.) resistant to rainwater.

rain shad·ow *n*. a region shielded from rain by mountains, etc.

rain·storm /ráynstawrm/ *n*. a storm with heavy rain.

rain·wa·ter /ráynwawtər, –wotər/ *n*. water obtained from collected rain, as distinct from a well, etc.

rain·y /ráynee/ *adj*. (**rain·i·er**, **rain·i·est**) **1** (of weather, a climate, day, region, etc.) in or on which rain is falling or much rain usually falls. **2** (of cloud, wind, etc.) laden with or bringing rain. □□ **rain·i·ly** *adv*. **rain·i·ness** *n*. [OE *rēnig* (as RAIN)]

rain·y day *n*. a time of special need in the future.

raise /rayz/ *v. & n.* ● *v.tr.* **1** put or take into a higher position. **2** (often foll. by *up*) cause to rise or stand up or be vertical; set upright. **3** increase the amount or value or strength of (*raised their prices*). **4** (often foll. by *up*) construct or build up. **5** levy or collect or bring together (*raise money; raise an army*). **6** cause to be heard or considered (*raise a shout; raise an objection*). **7** set going or bring into being; arouse (*raise a protest; raise hopes*). **8** bring up; educate. **9** breed or grow (*raise one's own vegetables*). **10** promote to a higher rank. **11** (foll. by *to*) *Math*. multiply a quantity to a specified power. **12** cause (bread) to rise with yeast. **13** *Cards* **a** a bet more than (another player). **b** increase (a stake). **c** *Bridge* make a bid contracting for more tricks in the same suit as (one's partner); increase (a bid) in this way. **14** abandon or force an enemy to abandon (a siege or blockade). **15** remove (a barrier or embargo). **16** cause (a ghost, etc.) to appear (opp. LAY¹ 6b). **17** *colloq*. find (a person, etc., wanted). **18** establish contact with (a person, etc.) by radio or telephone. **19** (usu. as **raised** *adj*.) *Brit*. cause (pastry, etc.) to stand without support (*a raised pie*). **20** *Naut*. come in sight of (land, a ship, etc.). **21** make a nap on (cloth). **22** extract from the earth. ● *n*. **1** *Cards* an increase in a stake or bid (cf. sense 13 of *v*.). **2** an increase in salary. □ **raise Cain**, **raise the devil** *colloq*. make a disturbance. **raise a dust** *Brit*. **1** cause turmoil. **2** obscure the truth. **raise one's eyebrows** see EYEBROW. **raise one's eyes** see EYE. **raise from the dead** restore to life. **raise one's glass to** drink the health or good fortune of. **raise one's hand to** make as if to strike (a person). **raise one's hat** (often foll. by *to*) remove it momentarily as a gesture of courtesy or respect. **raise hell** *colloq*. make a disturbance. **raise a laugh** esp. *Brit*. cause others to laugh. **raise a person's spirits** give him or her new courage or cheerfulness. **raise one's voice** speak, esp. louder and in anger. **raise the wind** *Brit*. procure money for a purpose. □□ **rais·a·ble** *adj*. [ME f. ON *reisa*, rel. to REAR²]

raised beach *n*. *Geol*. a beach lying above water level owing to changes since its formation.

rai·sin /ráyzən/ *n*. a partially dried grape. □□ **rai·sin·y** *adj*. [ME f. OF ult. f. L *racemus* grape bunch]

rai·son d'ê·tre /ráyzon détrə/ *n*. (*pl*. **rai·sons d'ê·tre** *pronunc*. same) a purpose or reason that accounts for or justifies or originally caused a thing's existence. [F, = reason for being]

raj /raaj/ *n*. (prec. by *the*) *hist*. British sovereignty in India. [Hindi *rāj* reign]

ra·ja /ráajə/ *n*. (also **ra·jah**) *hist*. **1** an Indian king or prince. **2** a petty dignitary or noble in India. **3** a Malay or Javanese chief. □□ **ra·ja·ship** *n*. [Hindi *rājā* f. Skr. *rājan* king]

Raj·put /ráajpŏot/ *n*. (also **Raj·poot**) a member of a Hindu soldier caste claiming Kshatriya descent. [Hindi *rājpūt* f. Skr. *rājan* king + *putrá* son]

rake¹ /rayk/ *n. & v.* ● *n*. **1 a** an implement consisting of a pole with

a crossbar toothed like a comb at the end, or with several tines held together by a crosspiece, for drawing together hay, etc., or smoothing loose soil or gravel. **b** a wheeled implement for the same purpose. **2** a similar implement used for other purposes, e.g., by a croupier drawing in money at a gaming table. ● *v.* **1** *tr*. (usu. foll. by *out, together, up,* etc.) collect or gather or remove with or as with a rake. **2** *tr*. make tidy or smooth with a rake (*raked it level*). **3** *intr*. use a rake. **4** *tr. & intr*. search with or as with a rake; search thoroughly; ransack. **5** *tr.* **a** direct gunfire along (a line) from end to end. **b** sweep with the eyes. **c** (of a window, etc.) have a commanding view of. **6** *tr*. scratch or scrape. □ **rake in** *colloq*. amass (profits, etc.). **rake it in** *colloq*. make much money. **rake up** (or **over**) revive the memory of (past quarrels, grievances, etc.). □□ **rak·er** *n*. [OE *raca*, *racu* f. Gmc, partly f. ON *raka* scrape, rake]

rake² /rayk/ *n*. a dissolute man of fashion. [short for archaic *rakehell* in the same sense]

rake³ /rayk/ *v. & n.* ● *v.* **1** *tr. & intr*. set or be set at a sloping angle. **2** *intr.* **a** (of a mast or funnel) incline from the perpendicular toward the stern. **b** (of a ship or its bow or stern) project at the upper part of the bow or stern beyond the keel. ● *n*. **1** a raking position or build. **2** the amount by which a thing rakes. **3** the slope of the stage or the auditorium in a theater. **4** the slope of a seat back, etc. **5** the angle of the edge or face of a cutting tool. [17th c.: prob. rel. to G *ragen* project, of unkn. orig.]

rake-off *n*. *colloq*. a commission or share, esp. in a disreputable deal.

rake's prog·ress *n*. esp. *Brit*. a progressive deterioration, esp. through self-indulgence (the title of a series of engravings by Hogarth 1735).

ra·ki /raakeé, rákee, ráakee, –kə/ *n*. (*pl*. **ra·kis**) any of various liquors made in E. Europe and the Middle East. [Turk. *raqi*]

rak·ish¹ /ráykish/ *adj*. dashing; jaunty. □□ **rak·ish·ly** *adv*. **rak·ish·ness** *n*.

rak·ish² /ráykish/ *adj*. (of a ship) smart and fast looking, seemingly built for speed and therefore open to suspicion of piracy. [RAKE³, assoc. with RAKE²]

ra·ku /ráakŏo/ *n*. a kind of Japanese earthenware, usu. lead-glazed. [Jap., lit. enjoyment]

rale /raal/ *n*. an abnormal rattling sound heard in the auscultation of unhealthy lungs. [F f. *râler* to rattle]

rall. /ral/ *adv., adj. & n.* = RALLENTANDO. [abbr.]

ral·len·tan·do /ráləntándō, ráaləntaándō/ *adv., adj., & n. Mus.* ● *adv. & adj.* with a gradual decrease of speed. ● *n*. (*pl*. **-dos** or **ral·len·tan·di** /–dee/) a passage to be performed in this way. [It.]

ral·line /rálin, –in/ *adj*. of the bird-family Rallidae (see RAIL³). [mod.L *rallus* RAIL³]

ral·ly¹ /rálee/ *v. & n.* ● *v.* (**·lies**, **·lied**) **1** *tr. & intr*. (often foll. by *round, behind, to*) bring or come together as support or for concentrated action. **2** *tr. & intr*. bring or come together again after a rout or dispersion. **3 a** *intr*. renew a conflict. **b** *tr*. cause to do this. **4 a** *tr*. revive (courage, etc.) by an effort of will. **b** *tr*. rouse (a person or animal) to fresh energy. **c** *intr*. pull oneself together. **5** *intr*. recover after illness or prostration or fear; regain health or consciousness; revive. **6** *intr*. (of share prices, etc.) increase after a fall. ● *n*. (*pl*. **·lies**) **1** an act of reassembling forces or renewing conflict; a reunion for fresh effort. **2** a recovery of energy after or in the middle of exhaustion or illness. **3** a mass meeting of supporters or persons having a common interest. **4** a competition for motor vehicles, usu. over public roads. **5** (in tennis, etc.) an extended exchange of strokes between players. □□ **ral·li·er** *n*. [F *rallier* (as RE-, ALLY¹)]

ral·ly² /rálee/ *v.tr.* (**·lies**, **·lied**) subject to good-humored ridicule. [F *railler*: see RAIL²]

ral·ly-cross *n*. *Brit*. motor racing over roads and cross-country.

RAM /ram/ *abbr*. **1** *Computing* random-access memory; internally stored software or data that is directly accessible, not requiring sequential search or reading. **2** (in the UK) Royal Academy of Music.

ram /ram/ *n. & v.* ● *n*. **1** an uncastrated male sheep. **2** (**the Ram**) the zodiacal sign or constellation Aries. **3** *hist.* **a** = BATTERING RAM. **b** a beak projecting from the bow of a warship, for piercing the sides of other ships. **c** a warship with such a beak. **4** the falling weight of a pile-driving machine. **5 a** a hydraulic water-raising or lifting machine. **b** the piston of a hydrostatic press. **c** the plunger of a force pump. **6** *Austral. sl.* an accomplice in petty crime. ● *v.tr.* (**rammed**, **ram·ming**) **1** force or squeeze into place by pressure. **2** (usu. foll. by *down, in, into*) beat down or drive in by heavy blows. **3** (of a ship, vehicle,

ram 1 (bighorn sheep)

etc.) strike violently; crash against. **4** (foll. by *against, at, on, into*) dash or violently impel. □ **ram home** stress forcefully (an argument, lesson, etc.). □□ **ram•mer** *n.* [OE *ram(m)*, perh. rel. to ON *rammr* strong]

Ram•a•dan /rámədan, ramədaán/ *n.* (also **Ram•a•dhan**) the ninth month of the Muslim year, during which strict fasting is observed from sunrise to sunset. [Arab. *ramaḍān* f. *ramaḍa* be hot; reason for name uncert.]

ra•mal /ráymǝl/ *adj. Bot.* of or proceeding from a branch. [L *ramus* branch]

Ra•man effect /ráamǝn/ *n.* the change of frequency in the scattering of radiation in a medium, used in spectroscopic analysis. [Sir C. V. *Raman*, Ind. physicist d. 1970]

ram•ble /rámbǝl/ *v. & n.* • *v.intr.* **1** walk for pleasure, with or without a definite route. **2** wander in discourse; talk or write disconnectedly. • *n.* a walk taken for pleasure. [prob. f. MDu. *rammelen* (of an animal) wander about in sexual excitement, frequent. of *rammen* copulate with, rel. to RAM]

ram•bler /rámblǝr/ *n.* **1** a person who rambles. **2** a straggling or climbing rose (*crimson rambler*).

ram•bling /rámbling/ *adj.* **1** peripatetic; wandering. **2** disconnected; desultory; incoherent. **3** (of a house, street, etc.) irregularly arranged. **4** (of a plant) straggling; climbing. □□ **ram•bling•ly** *adv.*

ram•bunc•tious /rambúngkshǝs/ *adj. colloq.* **1** uncontrollably exuberant. **2** unruly. □□ **ram•bunc•tious•ly** *adv.* **ram•bunc•tious•ness** *n.* [19th c.: orig. unkn.]

ram•bu•tan /rambóot'n/ *n.* **1** a red, plum-sized prickly fruit. **2** an East Indian tree, *Nephelium lappaceum*, that bears this. [Malay *rambūtan* f. *rambut* hair, in allusion to its spines]

ram•e•kin /rámikin/ *n.* (also **ram•e•quin**) **1** a small dish for baking and serving an individual portion of food. **2** food served in such a dish, esp. a small quantity of cheese baked with bread crumbs, eggs, etc. [F *ramequin*, of LG or Du. orig.]

ram•ie /rámee, ráy–/ *n.* **1** any of various tall East Asian plants of the genus *Boehmeria*, esp. *B. nivea*. **2** a strong fiber obtained from this, woven into cloth. [Malay *rāmī*]

ram•i•fi•ca•tion /rámifikáyshǝn/ *n.* **1** the act or an instance of ramifying; the state of being ramified. **2** a subdivision of a complex structure or process comparable to a tree's branches. **3** a consequence, esp. when complex or unwelcome. [F f. *ramifier*: see RAM-IFY]

ram•i•fy /rámifī/ *v.* (•**fies**, •**fied**) **1** *intr.* form branches or subdivisions or offshoots; branch out. **2** *tr.* (usu. in *passive*) cause to branch out; arrange in a branching manner. [F *ramifier* f. med.L *ramificare* f. L *ramus* branch]

ram•jet /rámjet/ *n.* a type of jet engine in which air is drawn in and compressed by the forward motion of the engine.

ram•mer see RAM.

ra•mose /rámōs, ráy–/ *adj.* branched; branching. [L *ramosus* f. *ramus* branch]

ramp[1] /ramp/ *n. & v.* • *n.* **1** a slope or inclined plane, esp. for joining two levels of ground, floor, etc. **2** (in full **boarding ramp**) movable stairs for entering or leaving an aircraft. **3** an upward bend in a staircase railing. **4** *Brit.* a transverse ridge in a road to control the speed of vehicles. • *v.* **1** *tr.* furnish or build with a ramp. **2** *intr.* **a** assume or be in a threatening posture. **b** (often foll. by *about*) storm; rage; rush. **c** *Heraldry* be rampant. **3** *intr. Archit.* (of a wall) ascend or descend to a different level. [ME (as verb in heraldic sense) f. F *rampe* f. OF *ramper* creep, crawl]

ramp[2] /ramp/ *n. & v. Brit. sl.* • *n.* a swindle or racket, esp. one conducted by the levying of exorbitant prices. • *v.* **1** *intr.* engage in a ramp. **2** *tr.* subject (a person, etc.) to a ramp. [16th c.: orig. unkn.]

ram•page *v. & n.* • *v.intr.* /rámpáyj/ **1** (often foll. by *about*) rush wildly or violently about. **2** rage; storm. • *n.* /rámpayj/ wild or violent behavior. □ **on the rampage** rampaging. □□ **ram•pa•geous** *adj.* **ram•pag•er** *n.* [18th c., perh. f. RAMP[1]]

ramp•ant /rámpǝnt/ *adj.* **1** (placed after noun) *Heraldry* (of an animal) standing on its left hind foot with its forepaws in the air (*lion rampant*). **2** unchecked, flourishing excessively (*rampant violence*). **3** violent or extravagant in action or opinion (*rampant theorists*). **4** rank; luxuriant. □□ **ram•pan•cy** *n.* **ram•pant•ly** *adv.* [ME f. OF, part. of *ramper*: see RAMP[1]]

ram•part /rámpaart/ *n. & v.* • *n.* **1 a** a defensive wall with a broad top and usu. a stone parapet. **b** a walkway on top of such a wall. **2** a defense or protection. • *v.tr.* fortify or protect with or as with a rampart. [F *rempart, rempar* f. *remparer* fortify f. *emparer* take possession of, ult. f. L *ante* before + *parare* prepare]

ram•pi•on /rámpeeǝn/ *n.* **1** a bellflower, *Campanula rapunculus*, with white tuberous roots used as a salad. **2** any of various plants of the genus *Phyteuma*, with clusters of hornlike buds and flowers. [ult. f. med.L *rapuncium, rapontium*, prob. f. L *rapum* RAPE[2]]

ram•rod /rámrod/ *n.* **1** a rod for ramming down the charge of a muzzleloading firearm. **2** a thing that is very straight or rigid.

ram•shack•le /rámshakǝl/ *adj.* (usu. of a house or vehicle) tumble-

down; rickety. [earlier *ramshackled* past part. of obs. *ransackle* RAN-SACK]

ram•sons /rámzǝnz, –sǝnz/ *n.* (usu. treated as *sing.*) **1** a broad-leaved garlic, *Allium ursinum*, with elongate pungent-smelling bulbous roots. **2** the root of this, eaten as a relish. [OE *hramsan* pl. of *hram-sa* wild garlic, later taken as sing.]

ran *past* of RUN.

ranch /ranch/ *n. & v.* • *n.* **1 a** a cattle-breeding establishment, esp. in the western US and Canada. **b** a farm where other animals are bred (*mink ranch*). **2** (in full **ranch house**) a single-story or split-level house. • *v.intr.* farm on a ranch. [Sp. *rancho* group of persons eating together]

ranch•er /ránchǝr/ *n.* a person who farms on a ranch.

ran•che•ro /rancháirō/ *n.* (*pl.* •**ros**) a person who farms or works on a ranch, esp. in Mexico. [Sp. (as RANCH)]

ran•cid /ránsid/ *adj.* smelling or tasting like rank stale fat. □□ **ran•cid•i•ty** /–síditee/ *n.* **ran•cid•ness** *n.* [L *rancidus* stinking]

ran•cor /rángkǝr/ *n.* (*Brit.* **ran•cour**) inveterate bitterness; malignant hate; spitefulness. □□ **ran•cor•ous** *adj.* **ran•cor•ous•ly** *adv.* [ME f. OF f. LL *rancor –oris* (as RANCID)]

rand[1] /rand, raant/ *n.* **1** the chief monetary unit of South Africa. **2** *S.Afr.* a ridge of high ground on either side of a river. [Afrik., = edge, rel. to RAND[2]: sense 1 f. *the Rand*, gold-field district near Johannesburg]

rand[2] /rand/ *n.* a leveling strip of leather between the heel and sides of a shoe or boot. [OE f. Gmc]

R & B *abbr.* (also **R. & B.**) rhythm and blues.

R & D *abbr.* (also **R. & D.**) research and development.

ran•dom /rándǝm/ *adj.* **1** made, done, etc., without method or conscious choice (*random selection*). **2** *Statistics* **a** with equal chances for each item. **b** given by a random process. **3** (of masonry) with stones of irregular size and shape. □ **at random** without aim or purpose or principle. □□ **ran•dom•ize** *v.tr.* **ran•dom•i•za•tion** *n.* **ran•dom•ly** *adv.* **ran•dom•ness** *n.* [ME f. OF *randon* great speed f. *randir* gallop]

ran•dom-ac•cess *adj. Computing* (of a memory or file) having all parts directly accessible, so that it need not be read sequentially.

ran•dom er•ror *n. Statistics* an error in measurement caused by factors that vary from one measurement to another.

R and R *abbr.* (also **R. and R.**) **1** rescue and resuscitation. **2** rest and recreation (or recuperation or relaxation). **3** rock and roll.

rand•y /rándee/ *adj.* (**rand•i•er**, **rand•i•est**) **1** esp. *Brit.* lustful; eager for sexual gratification. **2** *Sc.* loud-tongued; boisterous; lusty. □□ **rand•i•ly** *adv.* **rand•i•ness** *n.* [perh. f. obs. *rand* f. obs. Du. *randen, ranten* RANT]

ra•nee var. of RANI.

rang *past* of RING[2].

range /raynj/ *n. & v.* • *n.* **1 a** the region between limits of variation, esp. as representing a scope of effective operation (*a voice of astonishing range; the whole range of politics*). **b** such limits. **c** a limited scale or series (*the range of the thermometer readings is about 10 degrees*). **d** a series representing variety or choice; a selection. **2** the area included in or concerned with something. **3 a** the distance attainable by a gun or projectile (*the enemy is out of range*). **b** the distance between a gun or projectile and its objective. **4** a row, series, line, or tier, esp. of mountains or buildings. **5 a** an open or enclosed area with targets for shooting. **b** a testing ground for military equipment. **6** a cooking stove with one or more ovens and a set of burners on the top surface. **7** the area over which a thing, esp. a plant or animal, is distributed (*gives the ranges of all species*). **8** the distance that can be covered by a vehicle or aircraft without refueling. **9** the distance between a camera and the subject to be photographed. **10** the extent of time covered by a forecast, etc. **11 a** a large area of open land for grazing or hunting. **b** a tract over which

---

SYNONYM TIP range

COMPASS, GAMUT, LATITUDE, REACH, SCOPE, SWEEP. To say that someone has a wide **range** of interests implies that these interests are not only extensive but varied. Another way of expressing the same idea would be to say that the person's interests run the **gamut** from t.v. quiz shows to nuclear physics, a word that suggests a graduated scale or series running from one extreme to another. **Compass** implies a *range* of knowledge or activity that falls within very definite limits reminiscent of a circumference (*within the compass of her abilities*), while **sweep** suggests more of an arc-shaped *range* of motion or activity (*the sweep of the searchlight*) or a continuous extent or stretch (*a broad sweep of lawn*). **Latitude** and **scope** both emphasize the idea of freedom, although *scope* implies great freedom within prescribed limits (*the scope of the investigation*), while *latitude* means freedom from such limits (*she was granted more latitude than usual in interviewing the disaster victims*). Even someone who has a wide *range* of interests and a broad *scope* of authority, however, will sooner or later come up against something that is beyond his or her **reach**, which suggests the furthest limit of effectiveness or influence.

one wanders. **12** lie; direction (*the range of the strata is east and west*). ● *v.* **1** *intr.* **a** reach; lie spread out; extend; be found or occur over a specified district; vary between limits (*ages ranging from twenty to sixty*). **b** run in a line (*ranges north and south*). **2** *tr.* (usu. in *passive* or *refl.*) place or arrange in a row or ranks or in a specified situation or order or company (*ranged their troops; ranged themselves with the majority party; trees ranged in ascending order of height*). **3** *intr.* rove; wander (*ranged through the woods; his thoughts range over past, present, and future*). **4** *tr.* traverse in all directions (*ranging the woods*). **5** *Brit.* *Printing* **a** *intr.* (of type) lie flush at the ends of successive lines. **b** *intr.* (of type) lie flush. **6** *intr.* **a** (often foll. by *with*) be level. **b** (foll. by *with, among*) rank; find one's right place (*ranges with the great writers*). **7** *intr.* **a** (of a gun) send a projectile over a specified distance (*ranges over a mile*). **b** (of a projectile) cover a specified distance. **c** obtain the range of a target by adjustment after firing past it or short of it. [ME f. OF *range* row, rank f. *ranger* f. *rang* RANK[1]]

range find·er *n.* an instrument for estimating the distance of an object, esp. one to be shot at or photographed.

range pole *n.* *Surveying* a pole or rod for setting a straight line.

rang·er /ráynjər/ *n.* **1** a keeper of a national or royal park or forest. **2** a member of a body of armed men, esp.: **a** a mounted soldier. **b** a commando. **3** a wanderer. □□ **rang·er·ship** *n.*

rang·y /ráynjee/ *adj.* (**rang·i·er, rang·i·est**) **1** (of a person) tall and slim. **2** hilly; mountainous.

ra·ni /ráanee/ *n.* (also **ra·nee**) *hist.* a raja's wife or widow; a Hindu queen. [Hindi *rānī* = Skr. *rājñī* fem. of *rājan* king]

rank[1] /rangk/ *n. & v.* ● *n.* **1 a** a position in a hierarchy; a grade of advancement. **b** a distinct social class; a grade of dignity or achievement (*people of all ranks; in the top rank of performers*). **c** high social position (*persons of rank*). **2** a row or line. **3 a** single line of soldiers drawn up abreast. **4** *Brit.* a place where taxis stand to await customers. **5** order; array. **6** *Chess* a row of squares across the board (cf. FILE[2]). ● *v.* **1** *intr.* have rank or place (*ranks next to the chief of staff*). **2** *tr.* classify; give a certain grade to. **3** *tr.* arrange (esp. soldiers) in a rank or ranks. **4 a** *tr.* take precedence of (a person) in respect to rank; outrank. **b** *intr.* have the senior position among the members of a hierarchy, etc. □ **break rank** fail to remain in line. **close ranks** maintain solidarity. **keep rank** remain in line. **pull rank** use one's superior rank to gain advantage, coerce another, etc. **rise from the ranks 1** (of a private or a noncommissioned officer) receive a commission. **2** (of a self-made man or woman) advance by one's own exertions. [OF *ranc, renc,* f. Gmc, rel. to RING[1]]

rank[2] /rangk/ *adj.* **1** too luxuriant; choked with or apt to produce weeds or excessive foliage. **2 a** foul-smelling; offensive. **b** loathsome; indecent; corrupt. **3** flagrant; virulent; gross; complete; unmistakable; strongly marked (*rank outsider*). □□ **rank·ly** *adv.* **rank·ness** *n.* [OE *ranc* f. Gmc]

rank and file *n.* ordinary undistinguished people.

rank·er /rángkər/ *n.* esp. *Brit.* **1** a soldier in the ranks. **2** a commissioned officer who has been in the ranks.

rank·ing /rángking/ *n. & adj.* ● *n.* ordering by rank; classification. ● *adj.* having a high rank or position.

ran·kle /rángkəl/ *v.intr.* **1** (of envy, disappointment, etc., or their cause) cause persistent annoyance or resentment. **2** *archaic* (of a wound, sore, etc.) fester; continue to be painful. [ME (in sense 2) f. OF *rancler* f. *rancle, draoncle* festering sore f. med.L *dranculus, dracunculus* dimin. of *draco* serpent]

ranks *n.pl.* the common soldiers, i.e., privates and corporals.

ran·sack /ránsak/ *v.tr.* **1** pillage or plunder (a house, country, etc.). **2** thoroughly search (a place, a receptacle, a person's pockets, one's conscience, etc.). □□ **ran·sack·er** *n.* [ME f. ON *rannsaka* f. *rann* house + *–saka* f. *sœkja* seek]

ran·som /ránsəm/ *n. & v.* ● *n.* **1** a sum of money or other payment demanded or paid for the release of a prisoner. **2** the liberation of a prisoner in return for this. ● *v.tr.* **1** buy the freedom or restoration of; redeem. **2** hold to ransom. **3** release for a ransom. □□ **ran·som·er** *n.* (in sense 1 of *v.*). [ME f. OF *ransoun(er)* f. L *redemptio –onis* REDEMPTION]

rant /rant/ *v. & n.* ● *v.* **1** *intr.* use bombastic language. **2** *tr. & intr.* declaim; recite theatrically. **3** *tr. & intr.* preach noisily. **4** *intr.* (often foll. by *about, on*) speak vehemently or intemperately. ● *n.* **1** a piece of ranting; a tirade. **2** empty turgid talk. □□ **rant·er** *n.* **rant·ing·ly** *adv.* [Du. *ranten* rave]

ra·nun·cu·la·ceous /rənúngkyəláyshəs/ *adj.* of or relating to the family Ranunculaceae of flowering plants, including clematis and delphiniums.

ra·nun·cu·lus /rənúngkyələs/ *n.* (*pl.* **ra·nun·cu·lus·es** or **ra·nun·cu·li** /–lī/) any plant of the genus *Ranunculus*, usu. having bowl-shaped flowers with many stamens and carpels, esp. buttercups. [L, orig. dimin. of *rana* frog]

rap[1] /rap/ *n. & v.* ● *n.* **1** a smart, slight blow. **2** a knock; a sharp tapping sound. **3** *sl.* blame; censure; punishment. **4** *sl.* a conversation. **5 a** a rhyming monologue recited rhythmically to prerecorded music. **b** (in full **rap music**) a style of pop music with a pronounced

beat and words recited rather than sung. ● *v.* (**rapped, rap·ping**) **1** *tr.* strike smartly. **2** *intr.* knock; make a sharp tapping sound (*rapped on the table*). **3** *tr.* criticize adversely. **4** *intr.* *sl.* talk. □ **beat the rap** escape punishment. **rap on** (or **over**) **the knuckles** ● *n.* a reprimand or reproof. ● *v.* reprimand; reprove. **rap out 1** *Brit.* utter (an oath, order, pun, etc.) abruptly or on or on the spur of the moment. **2** *Spiritualism* express (a message or word) by raps. **take the rap** suffer the consequences, esp. for a crime, etc., committed by another. □□ **rap·per** *n.* [ME, prob. imit.]

rap[2] /rap/ *n.* a small amount, the least bit (*don't care a rap*). [Ir. *ropaire* Irish counterfeit coin]

ra·pa·cious /rəpáyshəs/ *adj.* grasping; extortionate; predatory. □□ **ra·pa·cious·ly** *adv.* **ra·pa·cious·ness** *n.* **ra·pac·i·ty** /rəpásitee/ *n.* [L *rapax –acis* f. *rapere* snatch]

rape[1] /rayp/ *n. & v.* ● *n.* **1 a** the act of forcing another person to have sexual intercourse. **b** forcible sodomy. **2** (often foll. by *of*) violent assault; forcible interference; violation. **3** *esp. hist.* carrying off (esp. of a woman) by force. **4** an instance of rape. ● *v.tr.* **1** commit rape on (a person, usu. a woman). **2** violate; assault; pillage. **3** *esp. hist.* take by force. [ME f. AF *rap(er)* f. L *rapere* seize]

rape[2] /rayp/ *n.* a plant, *Brassica napus*, grown as food for livestock and for its seed, from which oil is made. Also called **colza** or **cole**. [ME f. L *rapum, rapa* turnip]

rape[3] /rayp/ *n. hist.* (in the UK) any of the six ancient divisions of Sussex. [OE, var. of *rāp* ROPE, with ref. to the fencing off of land]

rape[4] /rayp/ *n.* **1** the refuse of grapes after wine making, used in making vinegar. **2** a vessel used in vinegar making. [F *râpe*, med.L *raspa*]

rape·seed /ráypseed/ *n.* the seed of the rape plant.

rape·seed oil *n.* an oil made from rapeseed and used as a lubricant and in foodstuffs.

ra·phi·a var. of RAFFIA.

ra·phide /ráyfīd/ *n.* a needle-shaped crystal of an irritant substance such as oxalic acid formed in a plant. [back-form. f. *raphides* pl. of *raphis* f. Gk *rhaphis –idos* needle]

rap·id /rápid/ *adj. & n.* ● *adj.* **1** quick; swift. **2** acting or completed in a short time. **3** (of a slope) descending steeply. **4** *Photog.* fast. ● *n.* (usu. in *pl.*) a steep descent in a riverbed, with a swift current. □□ **ra·pid·i·ty** /rəpíditee/ *n.* **rap·id·ly** *adv.* **rap·id·ness** *n.* [L *rapidus* f. *rapere* seize]

rap·id eye move·ment *n.* a type of jerky movement of the eyes during periods of dreaming. ¶ Abbr.: **REM**.

rap·id-fire *adj.* (*attrib.*) fired, asked, etc., in quick succession.

ra·pi·er /ráypeeər, ráypyər/ *n.* a light slender sword used for thrusting. [prob. f. Du. *rapier* or LG *rappir*, f. F *rapière*, of unkn. orig.]

rap·ine /rápin, –īn/ *n. rhet.* plundering; robbery. [ME f. OF or f. L *rapina* f. *rapere* seize]

rap·ist /ráypist/ *n.* a person who commits rape.

rap·pa·ree /rápəree/ *n. hist.* a 17th-c. Irish irregular soldier or freebooter. [Ir. *rapaire* short pike]

rap·pee /rapée/ *n.* a coarse kind of snuff. [F (*tabac*) *râpé* rasped (tobacco)]

rap·pel /rapél/ *n. & v.* (**rap·pelled, rap·pel·ling**; or **rap·peled, rap·pel·ing**) *n.* technique or act of controlled descent from a height, as a steep rockface, by using a doubled rope coiled around the body and fixed at a higher point, with which one slides downward gradually. ● *v. intr.* make a descent in this way. [F, = recall, f. *rappeler* (as RE-, APPEAL)]

rap·port /rapáwr/ *n.* **1** relationship or communication, esp. when useful and harmonious (*in rapport with; establish a rapport*). **2** *Spiritualism* communication through a medium. [F f. *rapporter* (as RE-, AP-, *porter* f. L *portare* carry)]

rap·por·teur /rápawrtŏr/ *n.* a person who prepares an account of the proceedings of a committee, etc., for a higher body. [F (as RAPPORT)]

rap·proche·ment /raprōshmón/ *n.* the resumption of harmonious relations, esp. between nations. [F f. *rapprocher* (as RE-, APPROACH)]

rap·scal·lion /rapskályon/ *n. archaic or joc.* rascal; scamp; rogue. [earlier *rascallion*, perh. f. RASCAL]

rapt /rapt/ *adj.* **1** fully absorbed or intent; enraptured (*listen with rapt attention*). **2** carried away with joyous feeling or lofty thought. **3** carried away bodily. □□ **rapt·ly** *adv.* **rapt·ness** *n.* [ME f. L *raptus* past part. of *rapere* seize]

rap·tor /ráptər/ *n.* any bird of prey, e.g., an owl, falcon, or eagle. [L, = ravisher, plunderer f. *rapere rapt–* seize]

rap·to·ri·al /raptáwreeəl/ *adj. & n.* ● *adj.* (of a bird or animal) adapt-

rapier

ed for seizing prey; predatory. ● *n.* **1** = RAPTOR. **2** a predatory animal. [L *raptor*: see RAPTOR]

rap•ture /rápchər/ *n.* **1 a** ecstatic delight; mental transport. **b** (in *pl.*) great pleasure or enthusiasm or the expression of it. **2** a *archaic* the act of transporting a person from one place to another. **b** (**the Rapture**) the transporting of believers to heaven at the second coming of Christ. **3** a mystical experience in which the soul gains a knowledge of divine things. □ **go into** (or **be in**) **raptures** be enthusiastic; talk enthusiastically. □□ **rap•tur•ous** *adj.* **rap•tur•ous•ly** *adv.* **rap•tur•ous•ness** *n.* [obs. F *rapture* or med.L *raptura* (as RAPT)]

ra•ra a•vis /ráirə áyvis, ráarə áavis/ *n.* (*pl.* **ra•rae a•ves** /–ree –veez/) a rarity; a kind of person or thing rarely encountered. [L, = rare bird]

rare¹ /rair/ *adj.* (**rar•er**, **rar•est**) **1** seldom done or found or occurring; uncommon; unusual; few and far between. **2** esp. *Brit.* exceptionally good (*had a rare time*). **3** of less than the usual density, with only loosely packed substance (*the rare atmosphere of the mountaintops*). □□ **rare•ness** *n.* [ME f. L *rarus*]

rare² /rair/ *adj.* (**rar•er**, **rar•est**) (of meat) cooked lightly, so as to be still red inside. [var. of obs. *rear* half-cooked (of eggs), f. OE *hrēr*]

rare bird *n.* = RARA AVIS.

rare•bit /ráirbit/ *n.* = WELSH RABBIT. [RARE¹ + BIT¹]

rare earth *n.* **1** a lanthanide element. **2** an oxide of such an element.

rar•ee-show /ráireeshō/ *n.* **1** a show or spectacle. **2** a show carried about in a box; a peep show. [app. = *rare show* as pronounced by Savoyard showmen]

rar•e•fy /ráirifī/ *v.* (**·fies**, **·fied**) (esp. as **rarefied** *adj.*) **1** *tr.* & *intr.* make or become less dense or solid (*rarefied air*). **2** *tr.* purify or refine (a person's nature, etc.). **3** *tr.* make (an idea, etc.) subtle. **b** (as **rarefied** *adj.*) refined; subtle; elevated; exalted; select. □□ **rar•e•fac•tion** /–fákshən/ *n.* **rar•e•fac•tive** *adj.* **rar•e•fi•ca•tion** /–fikáyshən/ *n.* [ME f. OF *rarefier* or med.L *rarificare* f. L *rarefacere* f. *rarus* rare + *facere* make]

rare gas *Brit.* = NOBLE GAS.

rare•ly /ráirlee/ *adv.* **1** seldom; not often. **2** in an unusual degree; exceptionally. **3** exceptionally well.

rar•ing /ráiring/ *adj.* (foll. by *to* + infin.) *colloq.* enthusiastic, eager (*raring to go*). [part. of rare, dial. var. of ROAR or REAR²]

rar•i•ty /ráiritee/ *n.* (*pl.* **·ties**) **1** rareness. **2** an uncommon thing, esp. one valued for being rare. [F *rareté* or L *raritas* (as RARE¹)]

ras•cal /ráskəl/ *n.* often *joc.* a dishonest or mischievous person, esp. a child. □□ **ras•cal•dom** *n.* **ras•cal•ism** *n.* **ras•cal•i•ty** /–kálitee/ *n.* (*pl.* **·ties**). **ras•cal•ly** *adj.* [ME f. OF *rascaille* rabble, prob. ult. f. L *radere ras-* scrape]

rase var. of RAZE.

rash¹ /rash/ *adj.* reckless; impetuous; hasty; acting or done without due consideration. □□ **rash•ly** *adv.* **rash•ness** *n.* [ME, prob. f. OE *ræsc* (unrecorded) f. Gmc]

rash² /rash/ *n.* **1** an eruption of the skin in spots or patches. **2** (usu. foll. by *of*) a sudden widespread phenomenon, esp. of something unwelcome (*a rash of strikes*). [18th c.: prob. rel. to OF *ra(s)che* eruptive sores, = It. *raschia* itch]

rash•er /ráshər/ *n.* a thin slice of bacon or ham. [16th c.: orig. unkn.]

rasp /rasp/ *n.* & *v.* ● *n.* **1** a coarse kind of file having separate teeth. **2** a rough grating sound. ● *v.* **1** *tr.* **a** scrape with a rasp. **b** scrape roughly. **c** (foll. by *off, away*) remove by scraping. **2** *intr.* make a grating sound. **b** *tr.* say gratingly or hoarsely. **3** *tr.* grate upon (a person or a person's feelings); irritate. □□ **rasp•ing•ly** *adv.* **rasp•y** *adj.* [ME f. OF *raspe(r)* ult. f. WG]

rasp•ber•ry /rázberee/ *n.* (*pl.* **·ries**) **1 a** a bramble, *Rubus idaeus*, having usu. red berries consisting of numerous drupelets on a conical receptacle. **b** this berry. **2** any of various red colors. **3** *colloq.* **a** a

sound made with the lips expressing dislike, derision, or disapproval (orig. *raspberry tart*, rhyming sl. = *fart*). **b** a show of strong disapproval (*got a raspberry from the audience*). [16th-c. *rasp* (now dial.) f. obs. *raspis*, of unkn. orig., + BERRY]

rasp•er /ráspər/ *n.* **1** a person or thing that rasps. **2** *Hunting Brit.* a high difficult fence.

Ras•ta /raástə, rást–/ *n.* & *adj.* = RASTAFARIAN. [abbr.]

Ras•ta•far•i•an /raástəfaáreeən, rástəfáir–/ *n.* & *adj.* ● *n.* a member of a sect of Jamaican origin regarding blacks as a chosen people and the former Emperor Haile Selassie of Ethiopia (d. 1975, titled *Ras Tafari*) as God. ● *adj.* of or relating to this sect. □□ **Ras•ta•far•i•an•ism** *n.*

ras•ter /rástər/ *n.* a pattern of scanning lines for a cathode-ray tube picture. [G, = screen, f. L *rastrum* rake f. *radere ras-* scrape]

rat /rat/ *n.* & *v.* ● *n.* **1 a** any of several rodents of the genus *Rattus* (*brown rat*). **b** any similar rodent (*muskrat*; *water rat*). **2** a deserter from a party, cause, difficult situation, etc.; a turncoat (from the superstition that rats desert a sinking ship). **3** *colloq.* an unpleasant person. **4** a worker who refuses to join a strike, or a strikebreaker. **5** (in *pl.*) *sl.* an exclamation of contempt, annoyance, etc. ● *v.intr.* (**rat•ted**, **rat•ting**) **1** (of a person or dog) hunt or kill rats. **2** *colloq.* desert a cause, party, etc. **3** *colloq.* (foll. by *on*) **a** betray; let down. **b** inform on. [OE *ræt* & OF *rat*]

rat•a•ble /ráytəbəl/ *adj.* (also **rate•a•ble**) **1** *Brit.* liable to payment of rates. **2** able to be rated or estimated. □□ **rat•a•bil•i•ty** /–bílitee/ *n.* **rat•a•bly** *adv.*

rat•a•ble val•ue *n. Brit.* the value formerly ascribed to a building for the assessment of local rates.

rat•a•fi•a /rátəféeə/ *n.* **1** a liqueur flavored with almonds or kernels of peach, apricot, or cherry. **2** a kind of cookie similarly flavored. [F, perh. rel. to TAFIA]

ra•tan var. of RATTAN.

rat•a•plan /rátəplán/ *n.* & *v.* ● *n.* a drumming sound. ● *v.* (**rat•a•planned**, **rat•a•plan•ning**) **1** *tr.* play (a tune) on or as on a drum. **2** *intr.* make a rataplan. [F: imit.]

rat-a-tat /rátətát/ *n.* (also **rat-a-tat-tat**) a rapping or knocking sound. [imit.]

ra•ta•touille /rátətóŏ-ee, raátaa–/ *n.* a vegetable dish made of stewed eggplant, onions, tomatoes, zucchini, and peppers. [F dial.]

rat•bag /rátbag/ *n. Austral. sl.* an unpleasant or disgusting person.

ratch /rach/ *n.* **1** a ratchet. **2** a ratchet wheel. [perh. f. G *Ratsche*: cf. RATCHET]

ratch•et /ráchit/ *n.* & *v.* ● *n.* **1** a set of teeth on the edge of a bar or wheel in which a device engages to ensure motion in one direction only. **2** (in full **ratchet wheel**) a wheel with a rim so toothed. ● *v.* **1** *tr.* **a** provide with a ratchet. **b** make into a ratchet. **2** *tr.* & *intr.* move as under the control of a ratchet. □ **ratchet up** (or **down**) move steadily or by degrees (*health costs continue to ratchet up*). [F *rochet* blunt lance-head, bobbin, ratchet, etc., prob. ult. f. Gmc]

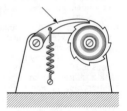

ratchet 1

rate¹ /rayt/ *n.* & *v.* ● *n.* **1** a stated numerical proportion between two sets of things (the second usu. expressed as unity), esp. as a measure of amount or degree (*moving at a rate of 50 miles per hour*) or as the basis of calculating an amount or value (*a rate of taxation*). **2** a fixed or appropriate charge or cost or value; a measure of this (*postal rates*; *the rate for the job*). **3** rapidity of movement or change (*traveling at a great rate*; *prices increasing at a dreadful rate*). **4** class or rank (*first-rate*). **5** *Brit.* **a** an assessment levied by local authorities on the assessed value of buildings and land owned or leased. **b** (in *pl.*) the amount payable by this. ● *v.* **1** *tr.* **a** estimate the worth or value of (*I do not rate him very highly*; *how do you rate your chances of winning the race?*). **b** assign a fixed value to (a coin or metal) in relation to a monetary standard. **c** assign a value to (work, the power of a machine, etc.). **2** *tr.* consider; regard as (*I rate them among my benefactors*). **3** *intr.* (foll. by *as*) rank or be rated. **4** *tr. Brit.* **a** subject to the payment of a local rate. **b** value for the purpose of assessing rates. **5** *tr.* be worthy of, deserve. **6** *tr. Naut.* place in a specified class (*see* RATING¹). □ **at any rate** in any case; whatever happens. **at this** (or **that**) **rate** if this example is typical or this assumption is true. [ME f. OF f. med.L *rata* f. L *pro rata parte* or *portione* according to the proportional share f. *ratus* past part. of *rēri* reckon]

rate² /rayt/ *v.tr.* scold angrily. [ME: orig. unkn.]

rate³ var. of RET.

rate•a•ble var. of RATABLE.

ra•tel /ráyt'l, raá–/ *n.* an African and Indian nocturnal flesh-eating burrowing mammal, *Mellivora capensis*. Also called **honey badger**. [Afrik., of unkn. orig.]

rate•pay•er /ráytpayər/ *n.* **1** a customer of a utility company, etc. **2** *Brit.* a person liable to local tax (see RATE¹ *n.* 5).

rat•fink /rátfingk/ *n. sl.* = FINK.

rathe /rayth/ *adj. poet.* coming, blooming, etc., early in the year or day. [OE *hræth, hræd* f. Gmc]

rath·er /ráthər/ *adv.* **1** (often foll. by *than*) by preference; for choice (*would rather not go; would rather stay than go*). **2** (usu. foll. by *than*) more truly; as a more likely alternative (*is stupid rather than honest*). **3** more precisely (*a book, or rather, a pamphlet*). **4** slightly; to some extent; somewhat (*became rather drunk; I rather think you know him*). **5** /raathér/ *Brit.* (as an emphatic response) indeed; assuredly (*Did you like it? —Rather!*). □ **had** (or **would**) **rather** prefer to. [ME f. OE *hrathor,* compar. of *hræthe* (adv.) f. *hræth* (adj.): see RATHE]

raths·kel·ler /ráatskelər, rát–, ráth–/ *n.* a beer hall or restaurant in a basement. [G, = (restaurant in) town-hall cellar]

rat·i·fy /rátifī/ *v.tr.* (·**fies,** ·**fied**) confirm or accept (an agreement made in one's name) by formal consent, signature, etc. □□ **rat·i·fi·a·ble** *adj.* **rat·i·fi·ca·tion** /–fikáyshən/ *n.* **rat·i·fi·er** *n.* [ME f. OF *ratifier* f. med.L *ratificare* (as RATE[1])]

rat·ing[1] /ráyting/ *n.* **1** the act or an instance of placing in a rank or class or assigning a value to. **2** the estimated standing of a person as regards credit, etc. **3** *Brit.* a noncommissioned sailor. **b** a person's position or class on a ship's books. **4** *Brit.* an amount fixed as a local tax rate. **5** the relative popularity of a broadcast program as determined by the estimated size of the audience. **6** *Naut.* any of the classes into which racing yachts are distributed by tonnage.

rat·ing[2] /ráyting/ *n.* an angry reprimand.

ra·tio /ráysheeō, ráyshō/ *n.* (*pl.* ·**tios**) the quantitative relation between two similar magnitudes determined by the number of times one contains the other integrally or fractionally (*in the ratio of three to two; the ratios 1:5 and 20:100 are the same*). [L (as RATE[1])]

ra·ti·oc·i·nate /rásheeósinayt/ *v.intr. literary* go through logical processes of reasoning, esp. using syllogisms. □□ **ra·ti·oc·i·na·tion** /–ōsináyshən, –ósináyshən/ *n.* **ra·ti·oc·i·na·tive** *adj.* **ra·ti·oc·i·na·tor** *n.* [L *ratiocinari* (as RATIO)]

ra·tion /ráshən, ráy–/ *n. & v.* ● *n.* **1** a fixed official allowance of food, clothing, etc., in a time of shortage. **2** (foll. by *of*) a single portion of provisions, fuel, clothing, etc. **3** (usu. in *pl.*) a fixed daily allowance of food, esp. in the armed forces (and formerly of forage for animals). **4** (in *pl.*) provisions. ● *v.tr.* **1** limit (persons or provisions) to a fixed ration. **2** (usu. foll. by *out*) distribute (food, etc.) in fixed quantities. [F f. It. *razione* or Sp. *ración* f. L *ratio –onis* reckoning, RATIO]

ra·tion·al /ráshənəl/ *adj.* **1** of or based on reasoning or reason. **2** sensible, sane, moderate; not foolish nor absurd nor extreme. **3** endowed with reason or reasoning. **4** rejecting what is unreasonable or cannot be tested by reason in religion or custom. **5** *Math.* (of a quantity or ratio) expressible as a ratio of whole numbers. □□ **ra·tion·al·i·ty** /–nálitee/ *n.* **ra·tion·al·ly** *adv.* [ME f. L *rationalis* (as RATION)]

ra·tion·ale /ráshənál/ *n.* **1** (often foll. by *for*) the fundamental reason or logical basis of anything. **2** a reasoned exposition; a statement of reasons. [mod.L, neut. of L *rationalis*: see RATIONAL]

ra·tion·al·ism /ráshənəlizəm/ *n.* **1** *Philos.* the theory that reason is the foundation of certainty in knowledge (opp. *empiricism* (see EMPIRIC), SENSATIONALISM). **2** *Theol.* the practice of treating reason as the ultimate authority in religion. **3** a belief in reason rather than religion as a guiding principle in life. □□ **ra·tion·al·ist** *n.* **ra·tion·al·is·tic** *adj.* **ra·tion·al·is·ti·cal·ly** *adv.*

ra·tion·al·ize /ráshənəlīz/ *v.* **1 a** *tr.* offer or subconsciously adopt a rational but specious explanation of (one's behavior or attitude). **b** *intr.* explain one's behavior or attitude in this way. **2** *tr.* make logical and consistent. **3** *tr.* make (a business, etc.) more efficient by reorganizing it to reduce or eliminate waste of labor, time, or materials. **4** *tr.* (often foll. by *away*) explain or explain away rationally. **5** *tr. Math.* eliminate irrational quantities from (an equation, etc.) **6** *intr.* be or act as a rationalist. □□ **ra·tion·al·i·za·tion** *n.* **ra·tion·al·iz·er** *n.*

rat·ite /rátīt/ *adj. & n.* ● *adj.* (of a bird) having a keelless breastbone, and unable to fly (opp. CARINATE). ● *n.* a flightless bird, e.g., an ostrich, emu, cassowary, or moa. [L *ratis* raft]

rat kan·ga·roo *n. Austral.* any of various small ratlike marsupials of the family Potoroidae, having kangaroolike hind limbs for jumping.

rat·line /rátlin/ *n.* (also **rat·lin**) (usu. in *pl.*) any of the small lines fastened across a sailing ship's shrouds like ladder rungs. [ME: orig. unkn.]

ra·toon /rətōōn/ *n. & v.* ● *n.* a new shoot springing from a root of sugarcane, etc., after cropping. ● *v.intr.* send up ratoons. [Sp. *retoño* sprout]

rat race *n.* a fiercely competitive struggle for position, power, etc.

rats·bane /rátsbayn/ *n.* anything poisonous to rats, esp. a plant.

rat-tail /rát-tayl/ *n.* **1** the grenadier fish. **2** a horse with a hairless tail. **3** such a tail.

rat-tail *adj.* shaped like a rat's tail (*rat-tail file*)

rat·tan /rətán/ *n. & adj.* (also **ra·tan**) ● *n.* **1** any East Indian climbing palm of the genus *Calamus*, etc., with long, thin, jointed pliable stems. **2** a piece of rattan stem used as a walking stick, etc. ● *adj.* made from (usu. woven) rattan (*a rattan armchair*). [earlier *rot(t)ang* f. Malay *rōtan* prob. f. *raut* pare]

rat·ter /rátər/ *n.* **1** a dog or other animal that hunts rats. **2** *Brit. sl.* a person who betrays a cause, party, friend, etc.

rat·tle /rát'l/ *v. & n.* ● *v.* **1 a** *intr.* give out a rapid succession of short, sharp, hard sounds. **b** *tr.* make (a cup and saucer, window, etc.) do this. **c** *intr.* cause such sounds by shaking something (*rattled at the door*). **2 a** *intr.* move with a rattling noise. **b** *intr.* drive a vehicle or ride or run briskly. **c** *tr.* esp. *Brit.* cause to move quickly (*the bill was rattled through Parliament*). **3 a** *tr.* (usu. foll. by *off*) say or recite rapidly. **b** *intr.* (usu. foll. by *on*) talk in a lively thoughtless way. **4** *tr. colloq.* disconcert; alarm; fluster; make nervous; frighten. ● *n.* **1** a rattling sound. **2** an instrument or plaything made to rattle, esp. in order to amuse babies or to give an alarm. **3** the set of horny rings in a rattlesnake's tail. **4** a plant with seeds that rattle in their cases when ripe (*red rattle; yellow rattle*). **5** uproar; bustle; noisy gaiety; racket. **6 a** a noisy flow of words. **b** empty chatter; trivial talk. **7** *archaic* a lively or thoughtless incessant talker. □ **rattle the saber** threaten war. □□ **rat·tly** *adj.* [ME, prob. f. MDu. & LG *ratelen* (imit.)]

rat·tler /rátlər/ *n.* **1** a thing that rattles, esp. an old or rickety vehicle. **2** *colloq.* a rattlesnake. **3** *Brit. sl.* a remarkably good specimen of anything. **4** *colloq.* a fast freight train.

rat·tle·snake /rát'lsnayk/ *n.* any of various poisonous American snakes of the family Viperidae, esp. of the genus *Crotalus* or *Sistrurus*, with a rattling structure of horny rings in its tail.

rat·tle·trap /rát'ltrap/ *n. & adj. colloq.* ● *n.* a rickety old vehicle, etc. ● *adj.* rickety.

rat·tling /rátling/ *adj. & adv.* ● *adj.* **1** that rattles. **2** brisk; vigorous (*a rattling pace*). ● *adv.* remarkably (*a rattling good story*).

rat·ty /rátee/ *adj.* (**rat·ti·er, rat·ti·est**) **1** relating to or infested with rats. **2** *Brit. colloq.* irritable or angry. **3** *colloq.* **a** shabby; wretched; nasty. **b** unkempt; seedy; dirty. □□ **rat·ti·ly** *adv.* **rat·ti·ness** *n.*

rau·cous /ráwkəs/ *adj.* harsh sounding; loud and hoarse. □□ **rau·cous·ly** *adv.* **rau·cous·ness** *n.* [L *raucus*]

raun·chy /ráwnchee/ *adj.* (**raun·chi·er, raun·chi·est**) *colloq.* **1** coarse; earthy; boisterous; sexually provocative. **2** slovenly; grubby. □□ **raun·chi·ly** *adv.* **raun·chi·ness** *n.* [20th c.: orig. unkn.]

rav·age /rávij/ *v. & n.* ● *v.tr.* devastate; plunder. ● *n.* **1** the act or an instance of ravaging; devastation; damage. **2** (usu. in *pl.*; foll. by *of*) destructive effect (*survived the ravages of winter*). □□ **rav·ag·er** *n.* [F *ravage(r)* alt. f. *ravine* rush of water]

rave[1] /rayv/ *v. & n.* ● *v.* **1** *intr.* talk wildly or furiously in or as in delirium. **2** *intr.* (usu. foll. by *about, of, over*) speak with rapturous admiration; go into raptures. **3** *tr.* bring into a specified state by raving (*raved himself hoarse*). **4** *tr.* utter with ravings (*raved their grief*). **5** *intr.* (of the sea, wind, etc.) howl; roar. **6** *tr. & intr. Brit. colloq.* enjoy oneself freely (esp. *rave it up*). ● *n.* **1** (usu. *attrib.*) *colloq.* a highly enthusiastic review of a film, play, etc. (*a rave review*). **2** *Brit. sl.* **a** an infatuation. **b** a temporary fashion or craze. **3** (also **rave-up**) *Brit. colloq.* a lively party. **4** *Brit.* the sound of the wind, etc., raving. **5** a dance party, often involving drug use. [ME, prob. f. ONF *raver,* rel. to (M)LG *reven* be senseless, rave]

rave[2] /rayv/ *n.* **1** a rail of a cart. **2** (in *pl.*) a permanent or removable framework added to the sides of a cart to increase its capacity. [var. of dial. *rathe* (15th c., of unkn. orig.)]

rav·el /rávəl/ *v. & n.* ● *v.* **1** *tr. & intr.* entangle or become entangled or knotted. **2** *tr.* confuse or complicate (a question or problem). **3** *intr.* fray out. **4** *tr.* (often foll. by *out*) disentangle; unravel; distinguish the separate threads or subdivisions of. ● *n.* **1** a tangle or knot. **2** a complication. **3** a frayed or loose end. [prob. f. Du. *ravelen* tangle, fray out, unweave]

rave•lin /rávlin/ *n. hist.* an outwork of fortifications, with two faces forming a salient angle. [F f. obs. It. *ravellino*, of unkn. orig.]

rav•el•ing /rávəling/ *n.* a thread from fabric that is frayed or unraveled.

ra•ven[1] /ráyvən/ *n. & adj.* ● *n.* a large glossy blue-black crow, *Corvus corax*, feeding chiefly on carrion, etc., having a hoarse cry. ● *adj.* glossy black (*raven tresses*). [OE *hræfn* f. Gmc]

rav•en[2] /rávən/ *v.* **1** *intr.* **a** plunder. **b** (foll. by *after*) seek prey or booty. **c** (foll. by *about*) go plundering. **d** prowl for prey (*ravening beast*). **2 a** *tr.* devour voraciously. **b** *intr.* (usu. foll. by *for*) have a ravenous appetite. **c** *intr.* (often foll. by *on*) feed voraciously. [OF *raviner* ravage ult. f. L *rapina* RAPINE]

rav•en•ous /rávənəs/ *adj.* **1** very hungry; famished. **2** (of hunger, eagerness, etc., or of an animal) voracious. **3** rapacious. □□ **rav•en•ous•ly** *adv.* **rav•en•ous•ness** *n.* [ME f. OF *ravineus* (as RAVEN[2])]

rav•in /rávin/ *n. poet.* or *rhet.* **1** robbery; plundering. **2** the seizing and devouring of prey. **3** prey. [ME f. OF *ravine* f. L *rapina* RAPINE]

ra•vine /rəvéen/ *n.* a deep narrow gorge or cleft. □□ **ra•vined** *adj.* [F (as RAVIN)]

rav•ing /ráyving/ *n., adj., & adv.* ● *n.* (usu. in *pl.*) wild or delirious talk. ● *adj.* **1** delirious; frenzied. **2** remarkable; intensive (*a raving beauty*). ● *adv.* intensively; wildly (*raving mad*). □□ **rav•ing•ly** *adv.*

ra•vi•o•li /ráveeólee/ *n.* small pasta envelopes containing cheese, ground meat, etc. [It.]

rav•ish /rávish/ *v.tr.* **1** commit rape on (a woman). **2** enrapture; fill with delight. **3** *archaic* **a** carry off (a person or thing) by force. **b** (of death, circumstances, etc.) take from life or from sight. □□ **rav•ish•er** *n.* **rav•ish•ment** *n.* [ME f. OF *ravir* ult. f. L *rapere* seize]

rav•ish•ing /rávishing/ *adj.* entrancing; delightful; very beautiful. □□ **rav•ish•ing•ly** *adv.*

raw /raw/ *adj. & n.* ● *adj.* **1** (of food) uncooked. **2** in the natural state; not processed or manufactured (*raw sewage*). **3** (of alcoholic spirit) undiluted. **4** (of statistics, etc.) not analyzed or processed. **5** (of a person) inexperienced; untrained; new to an activity (*raw recruits*). **6 a** stripped of skin; having the flesh exposed. **b** sensitive to the touch from having the flesh exposed. **c** sensitive to emotional pain, etc. **7** (of the atmosphere, day, etc.) chilly and damp. **8 a** crude in artistic quality; lacking finish. **b** unmitigated; brutal. **9** (of the edge of cloth) without hem or selvage. **10** (of silk) as reeled from cocoons. **11** (of grain) unmalted. ● *n.* a raw place on a person's or horse's body. □ **come the raw prawn** (foll. by *with*) *Austral. sl.* attempt to deceive (someone). **in the raw 1** in its natural state without mitigation (*life in the raw*). **2** naked. **touch on the raw** *Brit.* upset (a person) on a sensitive matter. □□ **raw•ish** *adj.* **raw•ly** *adv.* **raw•ness** *n.* [OE *hrēaw* f. Gmc]

raw•boned /ráwbōnd/ *adj.* gaunt and bony.

raw deal *n.* harsh or unfair treatment.

raw•hide /ráwhīd/ *n.* **1** untanned hide. **2** a rope or whip of this.

raw ma•te•ri•al *n.* that from which the process of manufacture makes products.

raw si•en•na *n.* a brownish-yellow ferruginous earth used as a pigment.

raw um•ber *n.* umber in its natural state, dark yellow in color.

ray[1] /ray/ *n. & v.* ● *n.* **1** a single line or narrow beam of light from a small or distant source. **2** a straight line in which radiation travels to a given point. **3** (in *pl.*) radiation of a specified type (*gamma rays*; *X rays*). **4** a trace or beginning of an enlightening or cheering influence (*a ray of hope*). **5 a** any of a set of radiating lines or parts or things. **b** any of a set of straight lines passing through one point. **6** the marginal portion of a composite flower, e.g., a daisy. **7 a** a radial division of a starfish. **b** each of a set of bones, etc., supporting a fish's fin. ● *v.* **1** *intr.* (foll. by *forth*, *out*) (of light, thought, emotion, etc.) issue in or as if in rays. **2** *intr. & tr.* radiate. □□ **rayed** *adj.* **ray•less** *adj.* **ray•let** *n.* [ME f. OF *rai* f. L *radius*: see RADIUS]

ray[2] /ray/ *n.* a large cartilaginous fish of the order Batoidea, with a broad flat body, winglike pectoral fins, and a long slender tail, used as food. [ME f. OF *raie* f. L *raia*]

ray gun *n.* (esp. in science fiction) a gun causing injury or damage by the emission of rays.

ray•on /ráyon/ *n.* any of various textile fibers or fabrics made from cellulose. [arbitrary f. RAY[1]]

raze /rayz/ *v.tr.* (also *Brit.* **rase**) **1** completely destroy; tear down (esp. *raze to the ground*). **2** erase; scratch out (esp. in abstract senses). [ME *rase* = wound slightly f. OF *raser* shave close ult. f. L *radere ras-* scrape]

ra•zor /ráyzər/ *n. & v.* ● *n.* an instrument with a sharp blade used in cutting hair, esp. from the skin. ● *v.tr.* **1** use a razor on. **2** shave; cut down close. [ME f. OF *rasor* (as RAZE)]

ra•zor•back /ráyzərbak/ *n.* an animal with a sharp ridged back, esp. a wild hog of the southern US.

ra•zor•bill /ráyzərbil/ *n.* a black and white auk, *Alca torda*, with a sharp-edged bill.

ra•zor clam *n.* any of various bivalve mollusks of the family Solenidae, with a thin, elongated shell.

ra•zor's edge *n.* **1** a keen edge. **2** a sharp mountain ridge. **3** a critical situation (*found themselves on the razor's edge*). **4** a sharp line of division.

ra•zor wire *n.* wire with sharpened projections, often coiled atop walls for security.

razz /raz/ *n. & v. sl.* ● *n.* = RASPBERRY 3. ● *v.tr.* tease; ridicule. [*razzberry*, corrupt. of RASPBERRY]

raz•zle-daz•zle /rázəldázəl/ *n.* (also **raz•zle**) *sl.* **1 a** glamorous excitement; bustle. **b** a spree. **2** extravagant publicity. [redupl. of DAZZLE]

razz•ma•tazz /rázmətáz/ *n.* (also **raz•za•ma•tazz** /rázəmə–/) *colloq.* **1** = RAZZLE-DAZZLE. **2** insincere actions; double-talk. [prob. alt. f. RAZZLE-DAZZLE]

Rb *symb. Chem.* the element rubidium.

RBI *abbr. Baseball* run(s) batted in (a run credited to the batter for enabling a runner to score during his turn at bat).

RC *abbr.* **1** Roman Catholic. **2** reinforced concrete.

RCAF *abbr.* Royal Canadian Air Force.

RCMP *abbr.* Royal Canadian Mounted Police.

RCN *abbr.* Royal Canadian Navy.

RD *abbr.* Rural Delivery.

Rd. *abbr.* Road (in names).

RDA *abbr.* **1** recommended daily allowance. **2** recommended dietary allowance.

RDF *abbr.* radio direction finder.

Re *symb. Chem.* the element rhenium.

re[1] /ray, ree/ *prep.* **1** in the matter of (as the first word in a heading, esp. of a legal document). **2** *colloq.* about; concerning. [L, ablat. of *res* thing]

re[2] /ray/ *n. Mus.* **1** (in tonic sol-fa) the second note of a major scale. **2** the note D in the fixed-do system. [ME *re* f. L *resonare*: see GAMUT]

re- /ree, ri, re/ *prefix* **1** attachable to almost any verb or its derivative; meaning: **a** once more; afresh; anew (*readjust*; *renumber*). **b** back; with return to a previous state (*reassemble*; *reverse*). **2** (also **red-** before a vowel, as in *redolent*) in verbs and verbal derivatives denoting: **a** in return; mutually (*react*; *resemble*). **b** opposition (*repel*; *resist*). **c** behind or after (*relic*; *remain*). **d** retirement or secrecy (*recluse*; *reticence*). **e** off; away; down (*recede*; *relegate*; *repress*). **f** frequentative or intensive force (*redouble*; *refine*; *resplendent*). **g** negative force (*recant*; *reveal*). [L *re-*, *red-*, again, back, etc.]

▶A hyphen is sometimes used to distinguish the compound from a more familiar one-word form (*re-form* = 'form again'; *re-sign* = 'sign again:').

re•ab•sorb /reeəbsáwrb, –záwrb/ *v.tr.* absorb again. □□ **re•ab•sorp•tion** /–ábsáwrpshən, –zawrp–/ *n.*

re•ac•cept /reeəksépt/ *v.tr.* accept again. □□ **re•ac•cep•tance** *n.*

re•ac•cus•tom /reeəkústəm/ *v.tr.* accustom again.

reach /reech/ *v. & n.* ● *v.* **1** *intr. & tr.* (often foll. by *out*) stretch out; extend. **2** *intr.* stretch out a limb, the hand, etc.; make a reaching motion or effort. **3** *intr.* (often foll. by *for*) make a motion or effort to touch or get hold of, or to attain (*reached for his pipe*). **4** *tr.* get as far as; arrive at (*reached Lincoln at lunchtime*; *your letter reached me today*). **5** *tr.* get to or attain (a specified point) on a scale (*the temperature reached 90°*; *the number of applications reached 100*). **6** *intr.* (foll. by *to*) attain to; be adequate for (*my income will not reach to it*). **7** *tr.* succeed in achieving; attain (*have reached an agreement*). **8** *tr.* make contact with the hand, etc., or by telephone, etc. (*was out all day and could not be reached*). **9** *tr.* succeed in influencing or having the required effect on (*could not manage to reach their audience*). **10** *tr.* hand; pass (*reach that book for me*). **11** *tr.* take with an outstretched hand. **12** *intr. Naut.* sail with the wind abeam or abaft the beam. ● *n.* **1** the extent to which a hand, etc., can be reached out, influence exerted, motion carried out, or mental powers used (*it is beyond my reach*). **2** an act of reaching out. **3** a continuous extent, esp. a stretch of river between two bends, or the part of a canal between locks. **4** *Naut.* a distance traversed in reaching. **5** a pole connecting the rear axle, or a wagon, to the bolster or bar at the front. □ **out of reach** not able to be reached or attained. □□ **reach•a•ble** *adj.* **reach•er** *n.* [OE *rēcan* f. WG]

reach-me-down *Brit.* = HAND-ME-DOWN.

re•ac•quaint /reeəkwáynt/ *v.tr. & refl.* (usu. foll. by *with*) make (a person or oneself) acquainted again. □□ **re•ac•quaint•ance** *n.*

re•ac•quire /reeəkwír/ *v.tr.* acquire anew. □□ **re•ac•qui•si•tion** /reē-akwizíshən/ *n.*

re•act /reeákt/ *v.* **1** *intr.* (foll. by *to*) respond to a stimulus; undergo a change or show behavior due to some influence (*how did they react to the news?*). **2** *intr.* (often foll. by *against*) be actuated by repulsion to; tend in a reverse or contrary direction. **3** *intr.* (often foll. by *upon*) produce a reciprocal or responsive effect; act upon the agent (*they react upon each other*). **4** *intr.* (foll. by *with*) *Chem.* &

Physics (of a substance or particle) be the cause of activity or interaction with another (*nitrous oxide reacts with the metal*). **5** *tr.* (foll. by *with*) *Chem.* cause (a substance) to react with another. **6** *intr. Mil.* make a counterattack. **7** *intr. Stock Exch.* (of shares) fall after rising. [RE- + ACT or med.L *reagere react-* (as RE-, L *agere* do, act)]

re‑act /rēe‑ákt/ *v.tr.* act (a part) again.

re‑act‑ance /reeáktəns/ *n. Electr.* a component of impedance in an AC circuit, due to capacitance or inductance or both.

re‑act‑ant /reeáktənt/ *n. Chem.* a substance that takes part in, and undergoes change during, a reaction.

re‑ac‑tion /reeákshən/ *n.* **1** the act or an instance of reacting; a responsive or reciprocal action. **2 a** a responsive feeling (*what was your reaction to the news?*). **b** an immediate or first impression. **3** the occurrence of a (physical or emotional) condition after a period of its opposite. **4** a bodily response to an external stimulus, e.g., a drug. **5** a tendency to oppose change or to advocate return to a former system, esp. in politics. **6** the interaction of substances undergoing chemical change. **7** propulsion by emitting a jet of particles, etc., in the direction opposite to that of the intended motion. □□ **re‑ac‑tion‑ist** *n. & adj.* [REACT + –ION or med.L *reactio* (as RE-, ACTION)]

re‑ac‑tion‑ar‑y /reeákshəneree/ *adj. & n.* ● *adj.* tending to oppose (esp. political) change and advocate return to a former system. ● *n.* (*pl.* **‑ies**) a reactionary person.

re‑ac‑ti‑vate /reeáktivayt/ *v.tr.* restore to a state of activity; bring into action again. □□ **re‑ac‑ti‑va‑tion** /–váyshən/ *n.*

re‑ac‑tive /reeáktiv/ *adj.* **1** showing reaction. **2** of or relating to reactance. □□ **re‑ac‑tiv‑i‑ty** /–tívitee/ *n.*

re‑ac‑tor /reeáktər/ *n.* **1** a person or thing that reacts. **2** (in full **nuclear reactor**) an apparatus or structure in which a controlled nuclear chain reaction releases energy. **3** *Electr.* a component used to provide reactance, esp. an inductor. **4** an apparatus for the chemical reaction of substances. **5** *Med.* a person who has a reaction to a drug, etc.

read /reed/ *v. & n.* ● *v.* (*past* and *past part.* **read** /red/) **1** *tr.* (also *absol.*) reproduce mentally or (often foll. by *aloud, out, off*, etc.) vocally the written or printed words of (a book, author, etc.) by following the symbols with the eyes or fingers. **2** *tr.* convert or be able to convert into the intended words or meaning (written or other symbols or the things expressed in this way). **3** *tr.* interpret mentally. **4** *tr.* deduce or declare an (esp. accurate) interpretation of (*read the expression on my face*). **5** *tr.* (often foll. by *that* + clause) find (a thing) recorded or stated in print, etc. (*I read somewhere that you are leaving*). **6** *tr.* interpret (a statement or action) in a certain sense (*my silence is not to be read as consent*). **7** *tr.* (often foll. by *into*) assume as intended or deducible from a writer's words; find (implications) (*you read too much into my letter*). **8** *tr.* bring into a specified state by reading (*read myself to sleep*). **9** *tr.* (of a meter or other recording instrument) show (a specified figure, etc.) (*the thermometer reads 20°*). **10** *intr.* convey meaning in a specified manner when read (*it reads persuasively*). **11** *intr.* sound or affect a hearer or reader as specified when read (*the book reads like a parody*). **12 a** *tr. esp. Brit.* study by reading (esp. a subject at university). **b** *intr.* carry out a course of study by reading (*is reading for the bar*). **13** *tr.* (as **read** /red/) versed in a subject (esp. literature) by reading (*a well-read person; was widely read in law*). **14** *tr.* **a** (of a computer) copy or transfer (data). **b** (foll. by *in, out*) enter or extract (data) in an electronic storage device. **15** *tr.* **a** understand or interpret (a person) by hearing words or seeing signs, gestures, etc. **b** interpret (cards, a person's hand, etc.) as a fortune teller. **c** interpret (the sky) as an astrologer or meteorologist. **16** *tr. Printing* check the correctness of and emend (a proof). **17** *tr.* (of an editor or text) give as the word or words probably used or intended by an author. ● *n.* **1** *esp. Brit.* a period of reading. **2** *colloq.* a book, etc., as regards its readability (*is a really good read*). □ **read a book like a book** understand a person's motives, etc. **read between the lines** look for or find hidden meaning (in a document, etc.). **read lips** determine what is being said by a person who cannot be heard by studying the movements of the speaker's lips. **read out 1** read aloud. **2** expel from a political party, etc. **read up** make a special study of (a subject). [OE *rǣdan* advise, consider, discern f. Gmc]

read‑a‑ble /réedəbəl/ *adj.* **1** able to be read; legible. **2** interesting or pleasant to read. □□ **read‑a‑bil‑i‑ty** /–bílitee/ *n.* **read‑a‑ble‑ness** *n.* **read‑a‑bly** *adv.*

re‑a‑dapt /réeədápt/ *v.intr. & tr.* become or cause to become adapted anew. □□ **re‑a‑dap‑ta‑tion** /rée‑adaptáyshən/ *n.*

re‑ad‑dress /réeədrés/ *v.tr.* **1** change the address of (a letter or parcel). **2** address (a problem, etc.) anew. **3** speak or write to anew.

read‑er /réedər/ *n.* **1** a person who reads or is reading. **2** a book of extracts for learning, esp. a language. **3** a device for producing an image that can be read from microfilm, etc. **4** *Brit.* a university lecturer of the highest grade below professor. **5** a publisher's employee who reports on submitted manuscripts. **6** a printer's proof-corrector. **7** a person appointed to read aloud, esp. parts of a service in a church. [OE (as READ)]

read‑er‑ship /réedərship/ *n.* **1** the readers of a newspaper, etc. **2** the number or extent of these.

read‑i‑ly /rédlee/ *adv.* **1** without showing reluctance; willingly. **2 a** without difficulty. **b** without delay.

read‑ing /réeding/ *n.* **1 a** the act or an instance of reading or perusing (*the reading of the will*). **b** matter to be read (*have plenty of reading with me*). **c** the specified quality of this (*it made exciting reading*). **2** (in *comb.*) used for reading (*reading lamp; reading room*). **3** literary knowledge (*a person of wide reading*). **4** an entertainment at which a play, poems, etc., are read (*poetry reading*). **5** a figure, etc., shown by a meter or other recording instrument. **6** an interpretation or view taken (*what is your reading of the facts?*). **7** an interpretation made (of drama, music, etc.). **8** each of the successive occasions on which a bill must be presented to a legislature for acceptance (see also FIRST READING, SECOND READING, THIRD READING). **9** the version of a text, or the particular wording, conjectured or given by an editor, etc. □ [OE (as READ)]

re‑ad‑just /réeəjúst/ *v.tr.* adjust again or to a former state. □□ **re‑ad‑just‑ment** *n.*

re‑ad‑mit /réeədmít/ *v.tr.* (**re‑ad‑mit‑ted, re‑ad‑mit‑ting**) admit again. □□ **re‑ad‑mis‑sion** /–admíshən/ *n.*

read‑only *adj. Computing* (of a memory) able to be read at high speed but not capable of being changed by program instructions.

re‑a‑dopt /réeədópt/ *v.tr.* adopt again. □□ **re‑a‑dop‑tion** *n.*

read‑out /réedowt/ *n.* **1** display of information, as on a gauge, etc. **2** the information displayed.

read‑write *adj. Computing* capable of reading existing data and accepting alterations or further input (cf. READ-ONLY).

read‑y /rédee/ *adj., adv., n., & v.* ● *adj.* (**read‑i‑er, read‑i‑est**) (usu. *predic.*) **1** with preparations complete (*dinner is ready*). **2** in a fit state (*are you ready to go?*). **3** willing, inclined, or resolved (*he is always ready to complain; I am ready for anything; a ready accomplice*). **4** within reach; easily secured (*a ready source of income*). **5** fit for immediate use (*was ready to hand*). **6** immediate; unqualified (*found ready acceptance*). **7** prompt; quick; facile (*is always ready with excuses; has a ready wit*). **8** (foll. by *to* + infin.) about to do something (*a bud just ready to burst*). **9** provided beforehand. ● *adv. esp. Brit.* **1** beforehand. **2** so as not to require doing when the time comes for use (*the boxes are ready packed*). ● *n.* (*pl.* **‑ies**) *Brit. sl.* **1** (*prec. by the*) = READY MONEY. **2** (in *pl.*) paper currency. ● *v.tr.* (**‑ies, ‑ied**) make ready; prepare. □ **at the ready** ready for action. **make ready** prepare. **ready, steady** (or **get set**), **go** the usual formula for starting a race. □□ **read‑i‑ness** *n.* [ME *rædi(g), re(a)di,* f. OE *rǣde* f. Gmc]

read‑y‑made *adj.* (also **read‑y‑to‑wear**) **1** (esp. of clothes) made in a standard size, not to measure. **2** already available; convenient (*a ready-made excuse*).

read‑y‑mix *adj.* (also **read‑y‑mixed**) (of concrete, paint, food, etc.) having some or all of the constituents already mixed together.

read‑y mon‑ey *n.* **1** available cash. **2** payment on the spot.

read‑y reck‑on‑er *n.* a book or table listing standard numerical calculations as used esp. in commerce.

re‑af‑firm /réeəfərm/ *v.tr.* affirm again. □□ **re‑af‑fir‑ma‑tion** /–afərmáyshən/ *n.*

re‑af‑for‑est /réeəfáwrist, –fór–/ *v.tr. Brit.* = REFOREST. □□ **re‑af‑for‑es‑ta‑tion** /–stáyshən/ *n.*

re‑a‑gent /ree‑áyjənt/ *n. Chem.* **1** a substance used to cause a reaction, esp. to detect another substance. **2** a reactive substance or force. [RE- + AGENT: cf. REACT]

re‑al¹ /reel/ *adj. & adv.* ● *adj.* **1** actually existing as a thing or occurring in fact. **2** genuine; rightly so called; not artificial or merely apparent. **3** *Law* consisting of or relating to immovable property such as land or houses (*real estate*) (cf. PERSONAL PROPERTY). **4** appraised by purchasing power; adjusted for changes in the value of money (*real value; income in real terms*). **5** *Philos.* having an absolute and necessary and not merely contingent existence. **6** *Math.* (of a quantity) having no imaginary part (see IMAGINARY 2). **7** *Optics* (of an image, etc.) such that light actually passes through it. ● *adv. colloq.* really, very. □ **for real** *colloq.* as a serious or actual concern; in earnest. **real live** (*attrib.*) often *joc.* actual; not pretended or simulated (*a real live burglar*). □□ **re‑al‑ness** *n.* [AF = OF *reel*, LL *realis* f. L *res* thing]

▶**Real** is an adjective that should be used only to describe a noun (*these shoes are made out of real leather*). Although *real* is often used as an adverb in spoken American English (*she's real good with children*), this is formally incorrect. In writing, use *really* in this context.

re‑al² /rayaá l/ *n. hist.* a former coin and monetary unit of various Spanish-speaking countries. [Sp., noun use of *real* (adj.) (as ROYAL)]

re‑al ale *n. Brit.* beer regarded as brewed in a traditional way, with secondary fermentation in the cask.

re‑al es‑tate *n.* property, esp. land and buildings.

re·al es·tate a·gent *n.* a person whose business is the sale or lease of buildings and land on behalf of others.

re·al·gar /reeálgər/ *n.* a mineral of arsenic sulfide used as a pigment and in fireworks. [ME f. med.L f. Arab. *rahj al-ğār* dust of the cave]

re·a·lign /réeəlín/ *v.tr.* **1** align again. **2** regroup in politics, etc. □□ **re·a·lign·ment** *n.*

re·al·ism /réeəlizəm/ *n.* **1** the practice of regarding things in their true nature and dealing with them as they are. **2** fidelity to nature in representation; the showing of life, etc., as it is in fact. **3** *Philos.* **a** the doctrine that universals or abstract concepts have an objective existence (opp. NOMINALISM). **b** the belief that matter as an object of perception has real existence. □□ **re·al·ist** *n.*

re·al·is·tic /réeəlístik/ *adj.* **1** regarding things as they are; following a policy of realism. **2** based on facts rather than ideals. □□ **re·al·is·ti·cal·ly** *adv.*

re·al·i·ty /reeálitee/ *n.* (*pl.* **·ties**) **1** what is real or existent or underlies appearances. **2** (foll. by *of*) the real nature of (a thing). **3** real existence; the state of being real. **4** resemblance to an original (*the model was impressive in its reality*). □ **in reality** in fact. [med.L *realitas* or F *réalité* (as REAL[1])]

re·al·ize /réeəliz/ *v.tr.* **1** (often foll. by *that* + clause) (also *absol.*) be fully aware of; conceive as real. **2** (also *absol.*) understand clearly. **3** present as real; make realistic; give apparent reality to (*the story was powerfully realized on stage*). **4** convert into actuality; achieve (*realized a childhood dream*). **5 a** convert into money. **b** acquire (profit). **c** be sold for (a specified price). **6** *Mus.* reconstruct (a part) in full from a figured bass. □□ **re·al·i·za·ble** *adj.* **re·al·iz·a·bil·i·ty** /-əbílitee/ *n.* **re·al·i·za·tion** *n.* **re·al·iz·er** *n.*

re·al life *n.* life lived by actual people, as distinct from fiction, drama, etc.

re·al·lo·cate /rée-áləkayt/ *v.tr.* allocate again or differently. □□ **re·al·lo·ca·tion** /-káyshən/ *n.*

re·al·lot /réeəlót/ *v.tr.* (**re·al·lot·ted**, **re·al·lot·ting**) allot again or differently. □□ **re·al·lot·ment** *n.*

re·al·ly /rée'ə lee, réelee/ *adv.* **1** in reality; in fact. **2** positively; assuredly (*really useful*). **3** (as a strong affirmative) indeed; I assure you. **4** an expression of mild protest or surprise. **5** (in *interrog.*) (expressing disbelief) is that so? (*They're musicians.—Really?*).

▶See note at REAL.

realm /relm/ *n.* **1** *formal* esp. *Law* a kingdom. **2** a sphere or domain (*the realm of imagination*). [ME f. OF *realme*, *reaume*, f. L *regimen* –*minis* (see REGIMEN): infl. by OF *reiel* ROYAL]

re·al Mc·Coy see McCOY.

re·al mon·ey *n.* **1** current coin or notes; cash. **2** large amount of money.

re·al·po·li·tik /rayaálpōliteek/ *n.* politics based on realities and material needs, rather than on morals or ideals. [G]

re·al ten·nis *n. Brit.* the original form of tennis played on an indoor court.

re·al thing *n.* (usu. **the real thing**) (of an object or emotion) genuine; not inferior.

re·al time *n. & adj.* ● *n.* the actual time during which a process or event occurs. ● *adj.* (**real-time**) *Computing* (of a system) in which the response time is of the order of milliseconds, e.g., in an airline booking system.

re·al·tor /réeəltər/ *n.* a real estate agent, esp. (**Realtor**) a member of the National Association of Realtors.

PRONUNCIATION TIP realtor

Careful speakers avoid the (quite common) pronunciation of this word as "REE-lah-ter."

---

re·al·ty /réeəltee/ *n. Law* real estate (opp. PERSONALTY).

ream[1] /reem/ *n.* **1** twenty quires or 500 (formerly 480) sheets of paper (or a larger number, to allow for waste). **2** (in *pl.*) a large quantity of paper or writing (*wrote reams about it*). [ME *rēm*, *rīm* f. OF *raime*, etc., ult. f. Arab. *rīzma* bundle]

ream[2] /reem/ *v.tr.* **1** widen (a hole in metal, etc.) with a borer. **2** turn over the edge of (a cartridge case, etc.). **3** *Naut.* open (a seam) for caulking. **4** squeeze the juice from (fruit). □□ **ream·er** *n.* [19th c.: orig. uncert.]

re·an·i·mate /rée-ánimayt/ *v.tr.* **1** restore to life. **2** restore to activity or liveliness. □□ **re·an·i·ma·tion** /-máyshən/ *n.*

reap /reep/ *v.tr.* **1** cut or gather (a crop, esp. grain) as a harvest. **2** harvest the crop of (a field, etc.). **3** receive as the consequence of one's own or others' actions. [OE *ripan*, *reopan*, of unkn. orig.]

reap·er /réepər/ *n.* **1** a person who reaps. **2** a machine for reaping. □ **the reaper** (or **grim reaper**) death personified.

re·ap·pear /réeəpeer/ *v.intr.* appear again or as previously. □□ **re·ap·pear·ance** *n.*

re·ap·ply /réeəplí/ *v.tr. & intr.* (**·plies**, **·plied**) apply again, esp. submit a further application (for a position, etc.). □□ **re·ap·pli·ca·tion** /rée-aplikáyshən/ *n.*

re·ap·point /réeəpóynt/ *v.tr.* appoint again to a position previously held. □□ **re·ap·point·ment** *n.*

re·ap·por·tion /réeəpáwrshən/ *v.tr.* apportion again or differently. □□ **re·ap·por·tion·ment** *n.*

re·ap·praise /réeəprayz/ *v.tr.* appraise or assess again. □□ **re·ap·prais·al** *n.*

rear[1] /reer/ *n. & adj.* ● *n.* **1** the back part of anything. **2** the space behind, or position at the back of, anything (*a large house with a terrace at the rear*). **3** the hindmost part of an army or fleet. **4** *colloq.* the buttocks. ● *adj.* at the back. □ **bring up the rear** come last. **in the rear** behind; at the back. [prob. f. (*in the*) REARWARD or REAR GUARD]

rear[2] /reer/ *v.* **1** *tr.* **a** bring up and educate (children). **b** breed and care for (animals). **c** cultivate (crops). **2** *intr.* (of a horse, etc.) raise itself on its hind legs. **3** *tr.* **a** set upright. **b** build. **c** hold upward (*rear one's head*). **4** *intr.* extend to a great height. □□ **rear·er** *n.* [OE *rēran* f. Gmc]

rear ad·mir·al *n.* a naval officer ranking below vice admiral.

rear guard *n.* **1** a body of troops detached to protect the rear, esp. in retreats. **2** a defensive or conservative element in an organization, etc.

rear·guard ac·tion *n.* **1** *Mil.* an engagement undertaken by a rear guard. **2** a defensive stand in argument, etc., esp. when losing.

re·arm /rée-aárm/ *v.tr.* (also *absol.*) arm again, esp. with improved weapons. □□ **re·ar·ma·ment** *n.*

rear·most /réermōst/ *adj.* farthest back.

re·ar·range /réeəráynj/ *v.tr.* arrange again in a different way. □□ **re·ar·range·ment** *n.*

re·ar·rest /réeərést/ *v. & n.* ● *v.tr.* arrest again. ● *n.* an instance of rearresting or being rearrested.

rear·view mir·ror *n.* a mirror fixed inside the windshield of a motor vehicle enabling the driver to see traffic, etc., behind.

rear·ward /réerwərd/ *n., adj., & adv.* ● *n.* rear, esp. in prepositional phrases (*to the rearward of; in the rearward*). ● *adj.* to the rear. ● *adv.* (also **rear·wards**) toward the rear. [AF *rerewarde* = REAR GUARD]

re·as·cend /réeəsénd/ *v.tr. & intr.* ascend again or to a former position. □□ **re·as·cen·sion** /-sénshən/ *n.*

rea·son /réezon/ *n. & v.* ● *n.* **1** a motive, cause, or justification (*has good reasons for doing this; there is no reason to be angry*). **2** a fact adduced or serving as this (*I can give you my reasons*). **3** the intellectual faculty by which conclusions are drawn from premises. **4** sanity (*has lost his reason*). **5** *Logic* a premise of a syllogism, esp. a minor premise when given after the conclusion. **6** a faculty transcending the understanding and providing a priori principles; intuition. **7** sense; sensible conduct; what is right or practical or practicable; moderation. ● *v.* **1** *intr.* form or try to reach conclusions by connected thought. **2** *intr.* (foll. by *with*) use an argument (with a person) by way of persuasion. **3** *tr.* (foll. by *that* + clause) conclude or assert in argument. **4** *tr.* (foll. by *why, whether, what* + clause) discuss; ask oneself. **5** *tr.* (foll. by *into, out of*) persuade or move by argument (*I reasoned them out of their fears*). **6** *tr.* (foll. by *out*) think or work out (consequences, etc.). **7** *tr.* (often as **reasoned** *adj.*) express in logical or argumentative form. **8** *tr.* embody reason in (an amendment, etc.). □ **by reason of** owing to. **in** (or **within**) **reason** within the bounds of sense or moderation. **it stands to reason** (often foll. by *that* + clause) it is evident or logical. **listen to reason** be persuaded to act sensibly. **see reason** acknowledge the force of an argument. **with reason** justifiably. □□ **rea·son·er** *n.* **rea·son·ing** *n.* **rea·son·less** *adj.* [ME f. OF *reisun, res(o)un, raisoner*, ult. f. L *ratio* –*onis* f. *rēri rat-* consider]

▶**Reason** means 'cause or basis,' so it is redundant to say "the reason is because"; the preferred usage is *the reason is that*: *The reason the car won't start is that* (not *because*) *the battery cable came loose.*

rea·son·a·ble /réezənəbəl/ *adj.* **1** having sound judgment; moderate; ready to listen to reason. **2** in accordance with reason; not absurd. **3 a** within the limits of reason; not greatly less or more than might be expected. **b** inexpensive; not extortionate. **c** tolerable; fair. **4** *archaic* endowed with the faculty of reason. □□ **rea·son·a·ble·ness** *n.* **rea·son·a·bly** *adv.* [ME f. OF *raisonable* (as REASON) after L *rationabilis*]

re·as·sem·ble /réeəsémbəl/ *v.intr. & tr.* assemble again or into a former state. □□ **re·as·sem·bly** *n.*

re·as·sert /réeəsért/ *v.tr.* assert again. □□ **re·as·ser·tion** /-sérshən/ *n.*

re·as·sess /réeəsés/ *v.tr.* assess again, esp. differently. □□ **re·as·sess·ment** *n.*

re·as·sign /réeəsín/ *v.tr.* assign again or differently. □□ **re·as·sign·ment** *n.*

re·as·sume /réeəsoóm/ *v.tr.* take on oneself or undertake again. □□ **re·as·sump·tion** /-súmpshən/ *n.*

re·as·sure /réeəshoór/ *v.tr.* **1** restore confidence to; dispel the apprehensions of. **2** confirm in an opinion or impression. □□ **re·as·sur·ance** *n.* **re·as·sur·er** *n.* **re·as·sur·ing** *adj.* **re·as·sur·ing·ly** *adv.*

re·at·tach /réeətách/ *v.tr.* attach again or in a former position. □□ **re·at·tach·ment** *n.*

re·at·tain /réeətáyn/ *v.tr.* attain again. □□ **re·at·tain·ment** *n.*

re·at·tempt /réeətémpt/ *v.tr.* attempt again, esp. after failure.

Ré·au·mur scale /ráyōmyŏŏr/ *n.* the obsolete scale of temperature at which water freezes at 0° and boils at 80° under standard conditions. [R. de *Réaumur*, Fr. physicist d. 1757]

reave /reev/ *v.* (*past* and *past part.* **reaved** or **reft** /reft/) *archaic* **1** *tr.* **a** (foll. by *of*) forcibly deprive of. **b** (foll. by *away, from*) take by force or carry off. **2** *intr.* make raids; plunder; = REIVE. [OE *rēafian* f. Gmc: cf. ROB]

re·a·wak·en /reeəwáykən/ *v.tr. & intr.* awaken again.

re·bar·ba·tive /reebaárbətiv/ *adj. literary* repellent; unattractive. [F *rébarbatif* –*ive* f. *barbe* beard]

re·bate[1] /reébayt/ *n. & v.* ● *n.* **1** a partial refund of money paid. **2** a deduction from a sum to be paid; a discount. ● *v.tr.* pay back as a rebate. □□ **re·bat·a·ble** *adj.* **re·bat·er** *n.* [earlier = diminish: ME f. OF *rabattre* (as RE-, ABATE)]

re·bate[2] /reébayt/ *n. & v.tr.* = RABBET. [respelling of RABBET, after RE-BATE[1]]

re·bec /reébek/ *n.* (also **re·beck**) *Mus.* a medieval usu. three-stringed instrument played with a bow. [F *rebec* var. of OF *rebebe rubebe* f. Arab. *rabāb*]

reb·el *n., adj., & v.* ● *n.* /rébəl/ **1** a person who fights against, resists, or refuses allegiance to, the established government. **2** a person or thing that resists authority or control. ● *adj.* /rébəl/ (*attrib.*) **1** rebellious. **2** of or concerning rebels. **3** in rebellion. ● *v.intr.* /ribél/ (**rebelled, rebelling**) (usu. foll. by *against*) **1** act as a rebel; revolt. **2** feel or display repugnance. [ME f. OF *rebelle, rebeller* f. L *rebellis* (as RE-, *bellum* war)]

re·bel·lion /ribélyən/ *n.* open resistance to authority, esp. (an) organized armed resistance to an established government. [ME f. OF f. L *rebellio –onis* (as REBEL)]

re·bel·lious /ribélyəs/ *adj.* **1** tending to rebel; insubordinate. **2** in rebellion. **3** defying lawful authority. **4** (of a thing) unmanageable; refractory. □□ **re·bel·lious·ly** *adv.* **re·bel·lious·ness** *n.* [ME f. REBELLION + -OUS or f. earlier *rebellous* + -IOUS]

re·bid /reébíd/ *v. & n.* ● *v.* (**rebidding**; *past* and *past part.* **rebid**) *Cards* **1** *intr.* bid again. **2** *tr.* bid (a suit) again at a higher level. ● *n.* **1** the act of rebidding. **2** a bid made in this way.

re·bind /reébínd/ *v.tr.* (*past* and *past part.* **rebound**) bind (esp. a book) again or differently.

re·birth /reébárth/ *n.* **1** a new incarnation. **2** spiritual enlightenment. **3** a revival (*the rebirth of learning*). □□ **re·born** /reébáwrn/ *adj.*

re·boot /reébŏŏt/ *v.tr.* (often *absol.*) *Computing* start (a system) again.

re·bore *v. & n.* ● *v.tr.* /reébáwr/ make a new boring in, esp. widen the bore of (the cylinder in an internal-combustion engine). ● *n.* /reébawr/ **1** the process of doing this. **2** a rebored engine.

re·bound[1] *v. & n.* ● *v.intr.* /ribównd/ **1** spring back after action or impact. **2** (foll. by *upon*) (of an action) have an adverse effect upon (the doer). ● *n.* /reébownd/ **1** the act or an instance of rebounding; recoil. **2** a reaction after a strong emotion. □ **on the rebound** while still recovering from an emotional shock, esp. rejection by a lover. □□ **re·bound·er** *n.* [ME f. OF *rebonder, rebondir* (as RE-, BOUND[1])]

re·bound[2] /reébównd/ *past* and *past part.* of REBIND.

re·broad·cast /reébráwdkast/ *v. & n.* ● *v.tr.* (*past* **rebroadcast** or **rebroadcasted**; *past part.* **rebroadcast**) broadcast again. ● *n.* a repeat broadcast.

re·buff /ribúf/ *n. & v.* ● *n.* **1** a rejection of one who makes advances, proffers help or sympathy, shows interest or curiosity, makes a request, etc. **2** a repulse; a snub. ● *v.tr.* give a rebuff to. [obs. F *rebuffe(r)* f. It. *ribuffo, ribuffare, rabbuffo, rabbuffare* (as RE-, *buffo* puff)]

re·build /reébíld/ *v.tr.* (*past* and *past part.* **rebuilt**) build again or differently.

re·buke /ribyŏ́ŏk/ *v. & n.* ● *v.tr.* reprove sharply; subject to protest or censure. ● *n.* **1** the act of rebuking. **2** the process of being rebuked. **3** a reproof. □□ **re·buk·er** *n.* **re·buk·ing·ly** *adv.* [ME f. AF & ONF *rebuker* (as RE-, OF *buchier* beat, orig. cut down wood f. *busche* log)]

re·bur·y /reébéree/ *v.tr.* (**·ies, ·ied**) bury again. □□ **re·bur·i·al** *n.*

re·bus /reébəs/ *n.* **1** an enigmatic representation of a word (esp. a name), by pictures, etc., suggesting its parts. **2** *Heraldry* a device suggesting the name of its bearer. [F *rébus* f. L *rebus*, ablat. pl. of *res* thing]

rebus for "To be or not to be"

re·but /ribút/ *v.tr.* (**rebutted, rebutting**) **1** refute or disprove (evidence or a charge). **2** force or turn back; check. □□ **re·but·ment** *n.* **re·but·ta·ble** *adj.* **re·but·tal** *n.* [ME f. AF *rebuter*, OF *rebo(u)ter* (as RE-, BUTT[1])]

re·but·ter /ribútər/ *n.* **1** a refutation. **2** *Law* a defendant's reply to the plaintiff's surrejoinder. [AF *rebuter* (as REBUT)]

833 **Réaumur scale ~ recede**

rec. *abbr.* **1** receipt. **2** record. **3** recreation.

re·cal·ci·trant /rikálsitrənt/ *adj. & n.* ● *adj.* **1** obstinately disobedient. **2** objecting to restraint. ● *n.* a recalcitrant person. □□ **re·cal·ci·trance** *n.* **re·cal·ci·trant·ly** *adv.* [L *recalcitrare* (as RE-, *calcitrare* kick out with the heels f. *calx calcis* heel)]

re·cal·cu·late /reékálkyəlayt/ *v.tr.* calculate again. □□ **re·cal·cu·la·tion** /–láyshən/ *n.*

re·ca·lesce /reékəlés/ *v.intr.* grow hot again (esp. of iron allowed to cool from white heat, whose temperature rises at a certain point for a short time). □□ **re·ca·les·cence** *n.* [L *recalescere* (as RE-, *calescere* grow hot)]

re·call /rikáwl/ *v. & n.* ● *v.tr.* **1** summon to return from a place or from a different occupation, inattention, a digression, etc. **2** recollect; remember. **3** bring back to memory; serve as a reminder of. **4** revoke or annul (an action or decision). **5** cancel or suspend the appointment of (an official sent overseas, etc.). **6** revive; resuscitate. **7** take back (a gift). ● *n.* (also /reékawl/) **1** the act or an instance of recalling, esp. a summons to come back. **2** the act of remembering. **3** the ability to remember. **4** the possibility of recalling, esp. in the sense of revoking (*beyond recall*). **5** removal of an elected official from office. **6** a request from a manufacturer that consumers return a product for repair, replacement, etc. □□ **re·call·a·ble** *adj.*

re·cant /rikánt/ *v.* **1** *tr.* withdraw and renounce (a former belief or statement) as erroneous or heretical. **2** *intr.* disavow a former opinion, esp. with a public confession of error. □□ **re·can·ta·tion** /reékantáyshən/ *n.* **re·cant·er** *n.* [L *recantare* revoke (as RE-, *cantare* sing, chant)]

re·cap /reékap/ *v. & n. colloq.* ● *v.tr. & intr.* (**recapped, recapping**) recapitulate. ● *n.* recapitulation. [abbr.]

re·cap·i·tal·ize /reékápitəliz/ *v.tr.* capitalize (shares, etc.) again. □□ **re·cap·i·tal·i·za·tion** *n.*

re·ca·pit·u·late /reékəpíchəlayt/ *v.tr.* **1** go briefly through again; summarize. **2** go over the main points or headings of. □□ **re·ca·pit·u·la·tive** /–ələtiv/ *adj.* **re·ca·pit·u·la·to·ry** /–lətáwree/ *adj.* [L *recapitulare* (as RE-, *capitulum* CHAPTER)]

re·ca·pit·u·la·tion /reékəpíchəláyshən/ *n.* **1** the act or an instance of recapitulating. **2** *Biol.* the reappearance in embryos of successive type-forms in the evolutionary line of development. **3** *Mus.* part of a movement, esp. in sonata form, in which themes from the exposition are restated. [ME f. OF *recapitulation* or LL *recapitulatio* (as RECAPITULATE)]

re·cap·ture /reékápchər/ *v. & n.* ● *v.tr.* **1** capture again; recover by capture. **2** reexperience (a past emotion, etc.). ● *n.* the act or an instance of recapturing.

re·cast /reékást/ *v. & n.* ● *v.tr.* (*past* and *past part.* **recast**) **1** put into a new form. **2** improve the arrangement of. **3** change the cast of (a play, etc.). ● *n.* **1** the act or an instance of recasting. **2** a recast form.

rec·ce /rékee/ *n. & v.* esp. *Brit. colloq.* ● *n.* a reconnaissance. ● *v.tr. & intr.* (**recced, recceing**) reconnoiter. [abbr.]

recd. *abbr.* received.

re·cede[1] /riseéd/ *v.intr.* **1** go or shrink back or farther off. **2** be left at an increasing distance by an observer's motion. **3** slope back-

SYNONYM TIP rebuke

ADMONISH, CENSURE, CHIDE, REPRIMAND, REPROACH, REPROVE, SCOLD. All of these verbs mean to criticize or express disapproval, but which one you use depends on how upset you are. If you want to go easy on someone, you can **admonish** or **reprove**, both of which indicate mild and sometimes kindly disapproval. To *admonish* is to warn or counsel someone, usually because a duty has been forgotten or might be forgotten in the future (*to admonish her about leaving the key in the lock*), while *reprove* also suggests mild criticism aimed at correcting a fault or pattern of misbehavior (*he was reproved for his lack of attention in class*). To **chide** someone is also to express mild disapproval, but often in a nagging way (*he chided her into apologizing*). If you want to express your disapproval formally or in public, use **censure** or **reprimand**. You can *censure* someone either directly or indirectly (*the judge censured the lawyer for violating courtroom procedures; a newspaper article that censured "deadbeat dads"*), while *reprimand* suggests a direct confrontation (*reprimanded by his parole officer for leaving town without reporting his whereabouts*). If you're irritated enough to want to express your disapproval quite harshly and at some length, you can **scold** (*to scold a child for jaywalking*), although for one adult to *scold* another is often seen as inappropriate, as we associate scolding with the behavior of adults (especially parents) to children. **Rebuke** is the harshest word of this group, meaning to criticize sharply or sternly, often in the midst of some action (*they left the party after she had rebuked him for drinking too much*).

See page xx for the **Key to Pronunciation.**

ward (*a receding chin*). **4** decline in force or value. **5** (foll. by *from*) withdraw from (an engagement, opinion, etc.). **6** (of a man's hair) cease to grow at the front, sides, etc. [ME f. L *recedere* (as RE-, *cedere cess-* go)]

re·cede² /réeséed/ *v.tr.* cede back to a former owner.

re·ceipt /riseét/ *n. & v.* • *n.* **1** the act or an instance of receiving or being received into one's possession (*will pay on receipt of the goods*). **2** a written acknowledgment of this, esp. of the payment of money. **3** (usu. in *pl.*) an amount of money, etc., received. **4** *archaic* a recipe. • *v.tr.* place a written or printed receipt on (a bill). [ME *receit(e)* f. AF & ONF *receite*, OF *reçoite*, *recete* f. med.L *recepta* fem. past part. of L *recipere* RECEIVE: −*p*- inserted after L]

re·ceive /riseév/ *v.tr.* **1** take or accept (something offered or given) into one's hands or possession. **2** acquire; be provided with or given (*have received no news; will receive a small fee*). **3** accept delivery of (something sent). **4** have conferred or inflicted on one (*received many honors; received a heavy blow to the head*). **5 a** stand the force or weight of. **b** bear up against; encounter with opposition. **6** consent to hear (a confession or oath) or consider (a petition). **7** (also *absol.*) accept or have dealings with (stolen property knowing of the theft). **8** admit; consent or prove able to hold; provide accommodation for (*received many visitors*). **9** (of a receptacle) be able to hold (a specified amount or contents). **10** greet or welcome, esp. in a specified manner (*how did they receive your offer?*). **11** entertain as a guest, etc. **12** admit to membership of a society, organization, etc. **13** be marked more or less permanently with (an impression, etc.). **14** convert (broadcast signals) into sound or pictures. **15 a** *Tennis* be the player to whom the server serves (the ball). **b** *Football* be the player or team to whom the ball is kicked or thrown. **16** (often as **received** *adj.*) give credit to; accept as authoritative or true (*received opinion*). **17** eat or drink (the Eucharistic bread and wine). □ **be at** (or **on**) **the receiving end** *colloq.* bear the brunt of something unpleasant. □□ **re·ceiv·a·ble** *adj.* [ME f. OF *receivre*, *reçoivre* f. L *recipere recept-* (as RE-, *capere* take)]

Re·ceived Pro·nun·ci·a·tion *n.* (also **Re·ceived Stand·ard**) the form of spoken English based on educated speech in southern England.

re·ceiv·er /riseévər/ *n.* **1** a person or thing that receives. **2** the part of a machine or instrument that receives sound, signals, etc. (esp. the part of a telephone that contains the earpiece). **3** esp. *Brit.* (in full **official receiver**) a person appointed by a court to administer the property of a bankrupt or insane person, or property under litigation. **4** a radio or television receiving apparatus. **5** a person who receives stolen goods. **6** *Chem.* a vessel for collecting the products of distillation, chromatography, etc. **7 a** *Baseball* = CATCHER 2. **b** *Football* an offensive player eligible to catch a forward pass.

re·ceiv·er·ship /riseévərship/ *n.* **1** the office of official receiver. **2** the state of being dealt with by a receiver (esp. *in receivership*).

re·cen·sion /risénshən/ *n.* **1** the revision of a text. **2** a particular form or version of a text resulting from such revision. [L *recensio* f. *recensēre* revise (as RE-, *censēre* review)]

re·cent /réesənt/ *adj. & n.* • *adj.* **1** not long past; that happened, appeared, began to exist, or existed lately. **2** not long established; lately begun; modern. **3** (**Recent**) *Geol.* = HOLOCENE. • *n.* *Geol.* = HOLOCENE. □□ **re·cen·cy** *n.* **re·cent·ly** *adv.* **re·cent·ness** *n.* [L *recens recentis* or F *récent*]

re·cep·ta·cle /riséptəkəl/ *n.* **1** a containing vessel, place, or space. **2** *Bot.* **a** the common base of floral organs. **b** the part of a leaf or thallus in some algae where the reproductive organs are situated. [ME f. OF *receptacle* or L *receptaculum* (as RECEPTION)]

re·cep·tion /risépshən/ *n.* **1** the act or an instance of receiving or the process of being received, esp. of a person into a place or group. **2** the manner in which a person or thing is received (*got a cool reception*). **3** a social occasion for receiving guests, esp. after a wedding. **4** a formal or ceremonious welcome. **5** (also **re·cep·tion desk**) a place where guests or clients, etc., report on arrival at a hotel, office, etc. **6 a** the receiving of broadcast signals. **b** the quality of this (*we have excellent reception*). [ME f. OF *reception* or L *receptio* (as RECEIVE)]

re·cep·tion·ist /risépshənist/ *n.* a person employed in a hotel, office, etc., to receive guests, clients, etc.

re·cep·tion room *n.* a room available or suitable for receiving company or visitors.

re·cep·tive /riséptiv/ *adj.* **1** able or quick to receive impressions or ideas. **2** concerned with receiving stimuli, etc. □□ **re·cep·tive·ly** *adv.* **re·cep·tive·ness** *n.* **re·cep·tiv·i·ty** /réeseptívitee/ *n.* [F *réceptif* –*ive* or med.L *receptivus* (as RECEPTION)]

re·cep·tor /riséptər/ *n.* (often *attrib.*) *Biol.* **1** an organ able to respond to an external stimulus such as light, heat, or a drug, and to transmit a signal to a sensory nerve. **2** a region of a cell, tissue, etc., that responds to a molecule or other substance. [OF *receptour* or L *receptor* (as RECEPTIVE)]

re·cess /réeses, risés/ *n. & v.* • *n.* **1** a space set back in a wall; a niche. **2** (often in *pl.*) a remote or secret place (*the innermost recesses*). **3** a temporary cessation from work, esp. of Congress, a court of law,

or during a school day. **4** *Anat.* a fold or indentation in an organ. **5** *Geog.* a receding part of a mountain chain, etc. • *v.* **1** *tr.* make a recess in. **2** *tr.* place in a recess; set back. **3 a** *intr.* take a recess; adjourn. **b** *tr.* order a temporary cessation from the work of (a court, etc.). [L *recessus* (as RECEDE)]

re·ces·sion /riséshən/ *n.* **1** a temporary decline in economic activity or prosperity. **2** a receding or withdrawal from a place or point. **3** a receding part of an object; a recess. □□ **re·ces·sion·ar·y** *adj.* [L *recessio* (as RECESS)]

re·ces·sion·al /riséshənəl/ *adj. & n.* • *adj.* sung while the clergy and choir withdraw after a service. • *n.* a recessional hymn.

re·ces·sive /risésiv/ *adj.* **1** tending to recede. **2** *Phonet.* (of an accent) falling near the beginning of a word. **3** *Genetics* (of an inherited characteristic) appearing in offspring only when not masked by a dominant characteristic inherited from one parent. □□ **re·ces·sive·ly** *adv.* **re·ces·sive·ness** *n.* [RECESS after *excessive*]

re·charge *v. & n.* • *v.tr.* /réechaarj/ **1** charge again. **2** reload. • *n.* /réechaarj/ **1** a renewed charge. **2** material, etc., used for this. □□ **re·charge·a·ble** *adj.*

ré·chauf·fé /ráyshōfáy/ *n.* **1** a warmed-up dish. **2** a rehash. [F past part. of *réchauffer* (as RE-, CHAFE)]

re·check *v. & n.* • *v.tr. & intr.* /réechék/ check again. • *n.* /réechek/ a second or further check or inspection.

re·cher·ché /rəsháirsháy/ *adj.* **1** carefully sought out; rare or exotic. **2** far-fetched; obscure. [F, past part. of *rechercher* (as RE-, *chercher* seek)]

re·chris·ten /réekrísən/ *v.tr.* **1** christen again. **2** give a new name to.

re·cid·i·vist /risídivist/ *n.* a person who relapses into crime. □□ **re·cid·i·vism** *n.* **re·cid·i·vis·tic** *adj.* [F *récidiviste* f. *récidiver* f. med.L *recidivare* f. L *recidivus* f. *recidere* (as RE-, *cadere* fall)]

rec·i·pe /résipee/ *n.* **1** a statement of the ingredients and procedure required for preparing cooked food. **2** an expedient; a device for achieving something. **3** a medical prescription. [2nd sing. imper. (as used in prescriptions) of L *recipere* take, RECEIVE]

re·cip·i·ent /risípeeənt/ *n. & adj.* • *n.* a person who receives something. • *adj.* **1** receiving. **2** receptive. □□ **re·cip·i·en·cy** *n.* [F *récipient* f. It. *recipiente* or L *recipiens* f. *recipere* RECEIVE]

re·cip·ro·cal /risíprəkəl/ *adj. & n.* • *adj.* **1** in return (*offered a reciprocal greeting*). **2** mutual (*their feelings are reciprocal*). **3** *Gram.* (of a pronoun) expressing mutual action or relation (as in *each other*). **4** inversely correspondent; complementary (*natural kindness matched by a reciprocal severity*). • *n.* *Math.* an expression or function so related to another that their product is one ($^1/_2$ is the reciprocal of 2). □□ **re·cip·ro·cal·i·ty** /–kálitee/ *n.* **re·cip·ro·cal·ly** *adv.* [L *reciprocus* ult. f. re- back + pro forward]

re·cip·ro·cate /risíprəkayt/ *v.* **1** *tr.* return or requite (affection, etc.). **2** *intr.* (foll. by *with*) offer or give something in return (*reciprocated with an invitation to lunch*). **3** *tr.* give and receive mutually; interchange. **4 a** *intr.* (of a part of a machine) move backward and forward. **b** *tr.* cause to do this. □□ **re·cip·ro·ca·tion** /–káyshən/ *n.* **re·cip·ro·ca·tor** *n.* [L *reciprocare reciprocat-* (as RECIPROCAL)]

re·cip·ro·cat·ing en·gine *n.* an engine using a piston or pistons moving up and down in cylinders.

rec·i·proc·i·ty /résiprósitee/ *n.* **1** the condition of being reciprocal. **2** mutual action. **3** give and take, esp. the interchange of privileges between countries and organizations. [F *réciprocité* f. *réciproque* f. L *reciprocus* (as RECIPROCATE)]

re·cir·cu·late /réesórkyəlayt/ *v.tr. & intr.* circulate again, esp. make available for reuse. □□ **re·cir·cu·la·tion** /–láyshən/ *n.*

re·cit·al /risít'l/ *n.* **1** the act or an instance of reciting or being recited. **2** the performance of a program of music by a solo instrumentalist or singer or by a small group. **3** (foll. by *of*) a detailed account of (connected things or facts); a narrative. **4** *Law* the part of a legal document that states the facts. □□ **re·cit·al·ist** *n.*

rec·i·ta·tion /résitáyshən/ *n.* **1** the act or an instance of reciting. **2** a thing recited. [OF *recitation* or L *recitatio* (as RECITE)]

rec·i·ta·tive /résitəteév/ *n.* **1** musical declamation of the kind usual in the narrative and dialogue parts of opera and oratorio. **2** the words or part given in this form. [It. *recitativo* (as RECITE)]

re·cite /risít/ *v.* **1** *tr.* repeat aloud or declaim (a poem or passage) from memory, esp. before an audience. **2** *intr.* give a recitation. **3** *tr.* mention in order; enumerate. □□ **re·cit·er** *n.* [ME f. OF *reciter* or L *recitare* (as RE-, CITE)]

reck /rek/ *v. archaic* or *poet.* (only in *neg.* or *interrog.*) **1** *tr.* (foll. by *of*) pay heed to; take account of; care about. **2** *tr.* pay heed to. **3** *intr.* (usu. with *it* as subject) be of importance (*it recks little*). [OE *reccan*, rel. to OHG *ruohhen*]

reck·less /réklis/ *adj.* disregarding the consequences or danger, etc.; lacking caution; rash. □□ **reck·less·ly** *adv.* **reck·less·ness** *n.* [OE *reccelēas* (as RECK)]

reck·on /rékən/ *v.* **1** *tr.* count or compute by calculation. **2** *tr.* (foll. by *in*) count in or include in computation. **3** *tr.* (often foll. by *as* or *to be*) consider or regard (*reckon him wise; reckon them to be beyond hope*). **4** *tr.* **a** (foll. by *that* + clause) consider or be of the considered opinion. **b** *colloq.* (foll. by *to* + infin.) expect (*reckons to finish by Friday*). **5** *intr.* make calculations; add up an account or sum. **6** *intr.* (foll. by *on, upon*) rely on, count on, or base plans on. **7** *intr.* (foll. by *with*) **a** take into account. **b** settle accounts with. **8** *US dial.* think; suppose (*I reckon I'll just stay home tonight*). □ **reckon up 1** count up; find the total of. **2** settle accounts. **to be reckoned with** of considerable importance; not to be ignored.

WORD HISTORY reckon

Old English *(ge)recenian* 'recount, relate,' of West Germanic origin; related to Dutch *rekenen* and German *rechnen* 'to count (up).' Early senses included 'give an account of items received' and 'mention things in order,' which gave rise to the notion of 'calculation' and hence of 'coming to a conclusion.'

reck·on·er /rékənər/ *n.* = READY RECKONER.

reck·on·ing /rékəning/ *n.* **1** the act or an instance of counting or calculating. **2** a consideration or opinion. **3 a** the settlement of an account. **b** an account.

re·claim /rikláym/ *v. & n.* • *v.tr.* **1** seek the return of (one's property). **2** claim in return or as a rebate, etc. **3** bring under cultivation, esp. from a state of being under water. **4 a** win back or away from vice or error or a waste condition; reform. **b** tame; civilize. • *n.* the act or an instance of reclaiming; the process of being reclaimed. □□ **re·claim·a·ble** *adj.* **re·claim·er** *n.* **rec·la·ma·tion** /réklǝmáyshǝn/ *n.* [ME f. OF *reclamer reclaim-* f. L *reclamare* cry out against (as RE-, *clamare* shout)]

re·clas·si·fy /reeklásifi/ *v.tr.* (·**fies**, ·**fied**) classify again or differently. □□ **re·clas·si·fi·ca·tion** /–fikáyshǝn/ *n.*

rec·li·nate /réklinayt/ *adj. Bot.* bending downward. [L *reclinatus*, past part. of *reclinare* (as RECLINE)]

re·cline /riklín/ *v.* **1** *intr.* assume or be in a horizontal or leaning position, esp. in resting. **2** *tr.* cause to recline or move from the vertical. □□ **re·clin·a·ble** *adj.* [ME f. OE *recliner* or L *reclinare* bend back, recline (as RE-, *clinare* bend)]

re·clin·er /riklínǝr/ *n.* **1** a comfortable chair for reclining in. **2** a person who reclines.

re·clothe /reeklṓth/ *v.tr.* clothe again or differently.

rec·luse /réklōōs, riklṓōs/ *n. & adj.* • *n.* a person given to or living in seclusion or isolation, esp. as a religious discipline; a hermit. • *adj.* favoring seclusion; solitary. □□ **re·clu·sion** /riklōōzhǝn/ *n.* **re·clu·sive** *adj.* [ME f. OF *reclus recluse* past part. of *reclure* f. L *recludere reclus-* (as RE-, *claudere* shut)]

rec·og·ni·tion /rékǝgníshǝn/ *n.* the act or an instance of recognizing or being recognized. □□ **re·cog·ni·to·ry** /rikógnitáwree, –tree/ *adj.* [L *recognitio* (as RECOGNIZE)]

re·cog·ni·zance /rikógnizǝns, –kónǝ–/ *n.* **1** a bond by which a person undertakes before a court, etc., to observe some condition, e.g., to appear when summoned. **2** a sum pledged as surety for this. [ME f. OF *recon(n)issance* (as RE-, COGNIZANCE)]

re·cog·ni·zant /rikógnizǝnt/ *adj.* (usu. foll. by *of*) **1** showing recognition (of a favor, etc.). **2** conscious or showing consciousness (of something).

rec·og·nize /rékǝgniz/ *v.tr.* **1** identify (a person or thing) as already known; know again. **2** realize or discover the nature of. **3** (foll. by *that*) realize or admit. **4** acknowledge the existence, validity, character, or claims of. **5** show appreciation of; reward. **6** (foll. by *as, for*) treat or acknowledge. **7** (of a chairperson, etc.) allow (a person) to speak in a debate, etc. □□ **rec·og·niz·a·ble** *adj.* **rec·og·niz·a·bil·i·ty** /–ǝbílitee/ *n.* **rec·og·niz·a·bly** *adv.* **re·cog·niz·er** *n.* [OF *recon(n)iss-* stem of *reconnaistre* f. L *recognoscere recognit-* (as RE-, *cognoscere* learn)]

PRONUNCIATION TIP recognize

Be careful not to ignore the *g* sound in this word; it should be pronounced "REK-og-nize."

re·coil /rikóyl/ *v. & n.* • *v.intr.* **1** suddenly move or spring back in fear, horror, or disgust. **2** shrink mentally in this way. **3** rebound after an impact. **4** (foll. by *on, upon*) have an adverse reactive effect on (the originator). **5** (of a gun) be driven backward by its discharge. **6** retreat under an enemy's attack. **7** *Physics* (of an atom, etc.) move backward by the conservation of momentum on emission of a particle. • *n.* (also /réekoyl/) **1** the act or an instance of recoiling. **2** the sensation of recoiling. [ME f. OF *reculer* (as RE-, L *culus* buttocks)]

rec·ol·lect /rékǝlékt/ *v.tr.* **1** remember. **2** succeed in remembering; call to mind. [L *recolligere recollect-* (as RE-, COLLECT[1])]

re·col·lect /reekǝlékt/ *v.tr.* **1** collect again. **2** (*refl.*) recover control of (oneself).

rec·ol·lec·tion /rékǝlékshǝn/ *n.* **1** the act or power of recollecting. **2** a thing recollected. **3 a** a person's memory (*to the best of my recollection*). **b** the time over which memory extends (*happened within my recollection*). □□ **rec·ol·lec·tive** *adj.* [F *recollection* or med.L *recollectio* (as RECOLLECT)]

re·col·o·nize /reekólǝniz/ *v.tr.* colonize again. □□ **re·co·lo·ni·za·tion** *n.*

re·col·or /reekúlǝr/ *v.tr.* color again or differently.

re·com·bi·nant /reekómbinǝnt/ *adj. & n. Biol.* • *adj.* (of a gene, etc.) formed by recombination. • *n.* a recombinant organism or cell.

re·com·bi·nant DNA *n.* DNA that has been recombined using constituents from different sources.

re·com·bi·na·tion /réekombináyshǝn/ *n. Biol.* the rearrangement, esp. by crossing over in chromosomes, of nucleic acid molecules forming a new sequence of the constituent nucleotides.

re·com·bine /reekǝmbín/ *v.tr. & intr.* combine again or differently.

re·com·mence /reekǝméns/ *v.tr. & intr.* begin again. □□ **re·com·mence·ment** *n.*

rec·om·mend /rékǝménd/ *v.tr.* **1 a** suggest as fit for some purpose or use. **b** suggest (a person) as suitable for a particular position. **2** (often foll. by *that* + clause or *to* + infin.) advise as a course of action, etc. (*I recommend that you stay where you are*). **3** (of qualities, conduct, etc.) make acceptable or desirable. **4** *Brit.* (foll. by *to*) commend or entrust (to a person or a person's care). □□ **rec·om·mend·a·ble** *adj.* **rec·om·men·da·tion** *n.* **rec·om·mend·a·to·ry** /–dǝtawree/ *adj.* **rec·om·mend·er** *n.* [ME (in sense 4) f. med.L *recommendare* (as RE-, COMMEND)]

re·com·mit /reekǝmít/ *v.tr.* (**re·com·mit·ted, re·com·mit·ting**) **1** commit again. **2** return (a bill, etc.) to a committee for further consideration. □□ **re·com·mit·ment** *n.* **re·com·mit·tal** *n.*

rec·om·pense /rékǝmpens/ *v. & n.* • *v.tr.* **1** make amends to (a person) or for (a loss, etc.). **2** requite; reward or punish (a person or action). • *n.* **1** a reward; requital. **2** retribution; satisfaction given for an injury. [ME f. OF *recompense(r)* f. LL *recompensare* (as RE-, COMPENSATE)]

re·com·pose /reekǝmpṓz/ *v.tr.* compose again or differently.

rec·on·cile /rékǝnsil/ *v.tr.* **1** make friendly again after an estrangement. **2** (usu. in *refl.* or *passive*; foll. by *to*) make acquiescent or contentedly submissive to (something disagreeable or unwelcome) (*was reconciled to failure*). **3** settle (a quarrel, etc.). **4 a** harmonize; make compatible. **b** show the compatibility of by argument or in practice (*cannot reconcile your views with the facts*). □□ **rec·on·cil·a·ble** *adj.* **rec·on·cil·a·bil·i·ty** /–sílǝbilitee/ *n.* **rec·on·cile·ment** *n.* **rec·on·cil·er** *n.* **rec·on·cil·i·a·tion** /–sileeáyshǝn/ *n.* **rec·on·cil·i·a·to·ry** /–sileeǝtáwree/ *adj.* [ME f. OF *reconcilier* or L *reconciliare* (as RE-, *conciliare* CONCILIATE)]

SPELLING TIP reconcile

To re*concile* is to bring *con*flict to a *c*lose.

rec·on·dite /rékǝndit, rikón–/ *adj.* **1** (of a subject or knowledge) abstruse; out of the way; little known. **2** (of an author or style) dealing in abstruse knowledge or allusions; obscure. □□ **rec·on·dite·ly** *adv.* **rec·on·dite·ness** *n.* [L *reconditus* (as RE-, *conditus* past part. of *condere* hide)]

PRONUNCIATION TIP recondite

The argument over whether the stress in this word should be on the first syllable or the second goes back to the 18th century. Although either pronunciation may be encountered, placing the stress on the first syllable is preferred.

re·con·di·tion /reekǝndíshǝn/ *v.tr.* **1** overhaul; refit; renovate. **2** make usable again. □□ **re·con·di·tion·er** *n.*

re·con·fig·ure /reekǝnfígyǝr/ *v.tr.* configure again or differently. □□ **re·con·fig·u·ra·tion** *n.*

re·con·firm /reekǝnfórm/ *v.tr.* confirm, establish, or ratify anew. □□ **re·con·fir·ma·tion** /–konformáyshǝn/ *n.*

re·con·nais·sance /rikónisǝns/ *n.* **1** a survey of a region, esp. a military examination to locate an enemy or ascertain strategic features. **2** a preliminary survey or inspection. [F (earlier *–oissance*) f. stem of *reconnaître* (as RECONNOITER)]

re·con·nect /reekǝnékt/ *v.tr.* connect again. □□ **re·con·nec·tion** /–nékshǝn/ *n.*

re·con·noi·ter /reekǝnóytǝr, rékǝ–/ *v. & n.* • *v.* **1** *tr.* make a reconnaissance of (an area, enemy position, etc.). **2** *intr.* make a reconnaissance. • *n.* a reconnaissance. [obs. F *reconnoître* f. L *recognoscere* RECOGNIZE]

re·con·quer /reekóngkǝr/ *v.tr.* conquer again. □□ **re·con·quest** *n.*

re·con·sid·er /reekǝnsídǝr/ *v.tr. & intr.* consider again, esp. for a possible change of decision. □□ **re·con·sid·er·a·tion** *n.*

re·con·sign /reekǝnsín/ *v.tr.* consign again or differently. □□ **re·con·sign·ment** *n.*

re·con·sol·i·date /reekǝnsólidayt/ *v.tr. & intr.* consolidate again. □□ **re·con·sol·i·da·tion** /–dáyshǝn/ *n.*

re·con·sti·tute /reekónstitoot, –tyoot/ *v.tr.* **1** build up again from parts; reconstruct. **2** reorganize. **3** restore the previous constitution of (dried food, etc.) by adding water. □□ **re·con·sti·tu·tion** /–tṓōshǝn/ *n.*

re·con·struct /reekǝnstrúkt/ *v.tr.* **1** build or form again. **2 a** form a mental or visual impression of (past events) by assembling the evidence for them. **b** reenact (a crime). **3** reorganize. □□ **re•con•struct•a•ble** adj. (also **re•con•struct•i•ble**). **re•con•struc•tion** /–strúkshən/ n. **re•con•struc•tive** adj. **re•con•struc•tor** n.

re•con•vene /re̅ekənve̅en/ v.tr. & intr. convene again, esp. (of a meeting, etc.) after a pause in proceedings.

re•con•vert /re̅ekənvórt/ v.tr. convert back to a former state. □□ **re•con•ver•sion** /–vórzhən/ n.

re•cord n. & v. ● n. /rékərd/ **1 a** a piece of evidence or information constituting an (esp. official) account of something that has occurred, been said, etc. **b** a document preserving this. **2** the state of being set down or preserved in writing or some other permanent form (is a matter of record). **3 a** (in full **phonograph record**) a thin plastic disk carrying recorded sound in grooves on each surface, for reproduction by a record player. **b** a trace made on this or some other medium, e.g., magnetic tape. **4 a** an official report of the proceedings and judgment in a court of justice. **b** a copy of the pleadings, etc., constituting a case to be decided by a court (see also COURT OF RECORD). **5 a** the facts known about a person's past (has an honorable record of service). **b** a list of a person's previous criminal convictions. **6** the best performance (esp. in sport) or most remarkable event of its kind on record (often attrib.: a record attempt). **7** an object serving as a memorial of a person or thing; a portrait. **8** Computing a number of related items of information that are handled as a unit. ● v.tr. /rikáwrd/ **1** set down in writing or some other permanent form for later reference, esp. as an official record. **2** convert (sound, a broadcast, etc.) into permanent form for later reproduction. **3** establish or constitute a historical or other record of. □ **break** (or **beat**) **the record** outdo all previous performances, etc. **for the record** as an official statement, etc. **go on record** state one's opinion or judgment openly or officially, so that it is recorded. **have a record** be known as a criminal. **a matter of record** a thing established as a fact by being recorded. **off the record** as an unofficial or confidential statement, etc. **on record** officially recorded; publicly known. **put** (or **get** or **set**, etc.) **the record straight** correct a misapprehension. □□ **re•cord•a•ble** adj.

WORD HISTORY record

Middle English: from Old French record 'remembrance,' from recorder 'bring to remembrance,' from Latin recordari 'remember,' based on cor, cord- 'heart.' The noun was earliest used in law to denote the fact of something being written down as evidence. The verb originally meant 'narrate orally or in writing,' also 'repeat so as to commit to memory.'

re•cord•er /rikáwrdər/ n. **1** an apparatus for recording, esp. a tape recorder. **2 a** a keeper of records. **b** a person who makes an official record. **3** Brit. **a** a barrister or solicitor of at least ten years' standing, appointed to serve as a part-time judge. **b** hist. a judge in certain courts. **4** Mus. a woodwind instrument like a flute but blown through the end and having a more hollow tone. □□ **re•cord•er•ship** n. (in sense 3). [ME f. AF recordour, OF recordeur & f. RECORD (in obs. sense 'practice a tune')]

re•cord•ing /rikáwrding/ n. **1** the process by which audio or video signals are recorded for later reproduction. **2** material or a program recorded.

re•cord•ing en•gi•neer n. a specialist who controls the recording of a record album, television show, etc.

re•cord•ist /rikáwrdist/ n. **1** a person who records sound, esp. for a motion picture. **2** = RECORDING ENGINEER.

rec•ord play•er n. an apparatus for reproducing sound from phonograph records.

re•count¹ /rikáwnt/ v.tr. **1** narrate. **2** tell in detail. [ONF & AF reconter (as RE-, COUNT¹)]

re•count² v. & n. ● v. /re̅ekáwnt/ tr. count again. ● n. /re̅ekáwnt/ a recounting, esp. of votes in an election.

re•coup /rikáo̅o̅p/ v.tr. **1** recover or regain (a loss). **2** compensate or reimburse for a loss. **3** Law deduct or keep back (part of a sum due). □ **recoup oneself** recover a loss. □□ **re•coup•a•ble** adj. **re•coup•ment** n. [F recouper (as RE-, couper cut)]

re•course /re̅ekawrs, rikáwrs/ n. **1** resorting to a possible source of help. **2** a person or thing resorted to. □ **have recourse to** turn to (a person or thing) for help. **without recourse** a formula used by the endorser of a bill, etc., to disclaim responsibility for payment. [ME f. OF recours f. L recursus (as RE-, COURSE)]

re•cov•er /rikávər/ v. & n. ● v. **1** tr. regain possession or use or control of; reclaim. **2** intr. return to health or consciousness or to a normal state or position (have recovered from my illness; the country never recovered from the war). **3** tr. obtain or secure (compensation, etc.) by legal process. **4** tr. retrieve or make up for (a loss, setback, etc.). **5** refl. regain composure or consciousness or control of one's limbs. **6** tr. retrieve (reusable substances) from industrial waste. ● n. the recovery of a normal position in fencing, etc. □□ **re•cov•er•**

a•ble adj. **re•cov•er•a•bil•i•ty** /–vərəbílitee/ n. **re•cov•er•er** n. [ME f. AF recoverer, OF recovrer f. L recuperare RECUPERATE]

SYNONYM TIP recover

RECLAIM, RECOUP, REGAIN, RESTORE, RETRIEVE. If you lose or let go of something and find it either by chance or with effort, you **recover** it (to recover the stolen artwork). Although it is often used interchangeably with recover, **regain** puts more emphasis on getting back something of which you have been deprived, usually after a laborious search or effort (to regain one's position as chairperson, to regain one's eyesight). **Recoup** refers to the recovery of something similar or equivalent to what has been lost, usually in the form of compensation (He tried to recoup his gambling losses). **Reclaim** and **restore** both involve bringing something back to its original condition or to a better or more useful state. Reclaim is usually associated with land (to reclaim neglected farmlands), while restore is linked to buildings or objects of art (to restore an 18th-century house). **Retrieve** implies that something has slipped beyond reach, and that a concerted effort or search is required to recover it (her desperate efforts to retrieve the family dog from the flooded house).

re•cov•er /re̅ekúvər/ v.tr. **1** cover again. **2** provide (a chair, etc.) with a new cover.

re•cov•er•y /rikúvəree/ n. (pl. **•ies**) **1** the act or an instance of recovering; the process of being recovered. **2** Golf a stroke bringing the ball out of a bunker, etc. [ME f. AF recoverie, OF reco(u)vree (as RECOVER)]

rec•re•ant /rékreeənt/ adj. & n. literary ● adj. **1** craven; cowardly. **2** apostate. ● n. **1** a coward. **2** an apostate. □□ **rec•re•an•cy** n. **rec•re•ant•ly** adv. [ME f. OF, part. of recroire f. med.L (se) recredere yield in trial by combat (as RE-, credere entrust)]

re-cre•ate /re̅ekree-áyt/ v.tr. create over again. □□ **re-cre•a•tion** n.

rec•re•a•tion /rékree-áyshən/ n. **1** the process or means of refreshing or entertaining oneself. **2** a pleasurable activity. □□ **rec•re•a•tion•al** adj. **rec•re•a•tion•al•ly** adv. **rec•re•a•tive** /rékreeáytiv/ adj. [ME f. OF f. L recreatio –onis f. recreare create again, renew]

re•crim•i•nate /rikríminayt/ v.intr. make mutual or counter accusations. □□ **re•crim•i•na•tion** /–náyshən/ n. **re•crim•i•na•tive** /–nətiv/ adj. **re•crim•i•na•to•ry** /–nətawree/ adj. [med.L recriminare (as RE-, criminare accuse f. crimen CRIME)]

re•cross /re̅ekráws, –krós/ v.tr. & intr. cross or pass over again.

re•cru•desce /re̅ekro̅o̅dés/ v.intr. (of a disease or difficulty, etc.) break out again, esp. after a dormant period. □□ **re•cru•des•cence** n. **re•cru•des•cent** adj. [back-form. f. recrudescent, –ence f. L recrudescere (as RE-, crudus raw)]

re•cruit /rikro̅o̅t/ n. & v. ● n. **1** a serviceman or servicewoman newly enlisted and not yet fully trained. **2** a new member of a society or organization. **3** a beginner. ● v. **1** tr. enlist (a person) as a recruit. **2** tr. form (an army, etc.) by enlisting recruits. **3** intr. get or seek recruits. **4** tr. replenish or reinvigorate (numbers, strength, etc.). □□ **re•cruit•a•ble** adj. **re•cruit•er** n. **re•cruit•ment** n. [earlier = reinforcement, f. obs. F dial. recrute ult. f. F recroître increase again f. L recrescere]

re•crys•tal•ize /re̅ekrístəliz/ v.tr. & intr. crystallize again. □□ **re•crys•tal•i•za•tion** n.

rec•ta pl. of RECTUM.

rec•tal /réktəl/ adj. of or by means of the rectum. □□ **rec•tal•ly** adv.

rec•tan•gle /réktanggəl/ n. a plane figure with four straight sides and four right angles, esp. one with the adjacent sides unequal. [F rectangle or med.L rectangulum f. LL rectiangulum f. L rectus straight + angulus ANGLE¹]

rec•tan•gu•lar /rektánggyələr/ adj. **1 a** shaped like a rectangle. **b** having the base or sides or section shaped like a rectangle. **2 a** placed at right angles. **b** having parts or lines placed at right angles. □□ **rec•tan•gu•lar•i•ty** /–láritee/ n. **rec•tan•gu•lar•ly** adv.

rec•tan•gu•lar co•or•di•nates n.pl. coordinates measured along axes at right angles.

rec•tan•gu•lar hy•per•bo•la n. a hyperbola with rectangular asymptotes.

rec•ti pl. of RECTUS.

rec•ti•fi•er /réktifiər/ n. **1** a person or thing that rectifies. **2** Electr. an electrical device that allows a current to flow preferentially in one direction by converting an alternating current into a direct one.

rec•ti•fy /réktifi/ v.tr. (**•fies**, **•fied**) **1** adjust or make right; correct; amend. **2** purify or refine, esp. by repeated distillation. **3** find a straight line equal in length to (a curve). **4** convert (alternating current) to direct current. □□ **rec•ti•fi•a•ble** adj. **rec•ti•fi•ca•tion** /–fikáyshən/ n. [ME f. OF rectifier f. med.L rectificare f. L rectus right]

rec•ti•lin•e•ar /réktilíneeər/ adj. (also **rec•ti•lin•e•al** /–eeəl/) **1** bounded or characterized by straight lines. **2** in or forming a straight line. □□ **rec•ti•lin•e•ar•i•ty** /–neeáritee/ n. **rec•ti•lin•e•ar•ly** adv. [LL rectilineus f. L rectus straight + linea LINE¹]

rec•ti•tude /réktito̅o̅d, –tyo̅o̅d/ n. **1** moral uprightness. **2** righteousness. **3** correctness. [ME f. OF rectitude or LL rectitudo f. L rectus right]

rec•to /réktō/ n. (pl. **•tos**) **1** the right-hand page of an open book. **2** the front of a printed leaf of paper or manuscript (opp. VERSO). [L recto (folio) on the right (leaf)]

rec•tor /réktər/ n. **1** (in the Church of England) the incumbent of a parish where all tithes formerly passed to the incumbent (cf. VIC-AR). **2** RC Ch., Episcopal Ch. a priest in charge of a church or religious institution. **3 a** the head of some schools, universities, and colleges. **b** (in Scotland) an elected representative of students on a university's governing body. □□ **rec•tor•ate** /-rət/ n. **rec•to•ri•al** /-táwreeəl/ adj. **rec•tor•ship** n. [ME f. OF rectour or L rector ruler f. regere rect- rule]

rec•to•ry /réktəree/ n. (pl. **•ries**) **1** a rector's house. **2** (in the Church of England) a rector's benefice. [AF & OF rectorie or med.L rectoria (as RECTOR)]

rec•trix /réktriks/ n. (pl. **rec•tri•ces** /-triseez/) a bird's strong tail feather that directs flight. [L, fem. of rector ruler: see RECTOR]

rec•tum /réktəm/ n. (pl. **rec•tums** or **rec•ta** /-tə/) the final section of the large intestine, terminating at the anus. [L rectum (intestinum) straight (intestine)]

rec•tus /réktəs/ n. (pl. **rec•ti** /-tī/) Anat. a straight muscle. [L, = straight]

re•cum•bent /rikúmbənt/ adj. lying down; reclining. □□ **re•cum•ben•cy** n. **re•cum•bent•ly** adv. [L recumbere recline (as RE-, cumbere lie)]

re•cu•per•ate /rikóoʊpərayt/ v. **1** intr. recover from illness, exhaustion, loss, etc. **2** tr. regain (health, something lost, etc.). □□ **re•cu•per•a•ble** adj. **re•cu•per•a•tion** /-ráyshən/ n. **re•cu•per•a•tive** /-rətiv/ adj. **re•cu•per•a•tor** n. [L recuperare recuperat- recover]

re•cur /rikór/ v.intr. (**re•curred**, **re•cur•ring**) **1** occur again; be repeated. **2** (of a thought, idea, etc.) come back to one's mind. (foll. by to) go back in thought or speech. □□ **re•cur•rence** n. [L recurrere recurs- (as RE-, currere run)]

▶Recur and recurrence are generally regarded as better style than reoccur and reoccurrence.

re•cur•rent /rikórənt, -kúr-/ adj. **1** recurring; happening repeatedly. **2** (of a nerve, vein, branch, etc.) turning back so as to reverse direction. □□ **re•cur•rent•ly** adv.

re•cur•ring dec•i•mal = REPEATING DECIMAL.

re•cur•sion /rikórzhən/ n. **1** the act or an instance of returning. **2** Math. the repeated application of a procedure or definition to a previous result to obtain a series of values. □□ **re•cur•sive** adj. [LL recursio (as RECUR)]

re•cur•sion for•mu•la n. Math. an expression giving successive terms of a series, etc.

re•curve /rikórv/ v.tr. & intr. bend backward. □□ **re•cur•vate** /-vayt, -vət/ adj. **re•cur•va•ture** n. [L recurvare recurvat- (as RE-, curvare bend)]

rec•u•sant /rékyəzənt, rikyóo-/ n. & adj. ● n. a person who refuses submission to an authority or compliance with a regulation, esp. Brit. hist. a Roman Catholic who refused to attend services of the Church of England. ● adj. of or being a recusant. □□ **rec•u•sance** n. **rec•u•san•cy** n. [L recusare refuse]

re•cy•cle /réesíkəl/ v.tr. return (material) to a previous stage of a cyclic process, esp. convert (waste) to reusable material. □□ **re•cy•cla•ble** adj.

red /red/ adj. & n. ● adj. **1** of or near the color seen at the least-refracted end of the visible spectrum, of shades ranging from that of blood to pink or deep orange. **2** flushed in the face with shame, anger, etc. **3** (of the eyes) bloodshot or red-rimmed with weeping. **4** (of the hair) reddish-brown; orange; tawny. **5** involving or having to do with bloodshed, burning, violence, or revolution. **6** colloq. communist or socialist. **7** (Red) (formerly) Soviet or Russian (the Red Army). **8** (of wine) made from dark grapes and colored by their skins. ● n. **1** a red color or pigment. **2** red clothes or material (dressed in red). **3** colloq. a communist or socialist. **4 a** a red ball, piece, etc., in a game or sport. **b** the player using such pieces. **5** the debit side of an account (in the red). **6** a red light. □□ **red•dish** adj. **red•dy** adj. **red•ly** adv. **red•ness** n.

> **WORD HISTORY** red
>
> Old English rēad, of Germanic origin; related to Dutch rood and German rot, from an Indo-European root shared by Latin rufus, ruber, Greek eruthros, and Sanskrit rudhira 'red.'

re•dact /ridákt/ v.tr. put into literary form; edit for publication. □□ **re•dac•tor** n. [L redigere redact- (as RE-, agere bring)]

re•dac•tion /ridákshən/ n. **1** preparation for publication. **2** revision; editing; rearrangement. **3** a new edition. □□ **re•dac•tion•al** adj. [F rédaction f. LL redactio (as REDACT)]

red ad•mi•ral n. a butterfly, Vanessa atalanta, with red bands on each pair of wings.

red a•lert n. **1** Mil. an alert sounded or given when an enemy attack appears imminent. **2** the signal for this.

re•dan /ridán/ n. a fieldwork with two faces forming a salient angle. [F f. redent notching (as RE-, dent tooth)]

red ar•se•nic = REALGAR.

red-blood•ed adj. virile; vigorous.

red-blood•ed•ness n. vigor; spirit.

red•breast /rédbrest/ n. colloq. a robin, esp. the N. American robin, Turdus migratorius.

red-brick /rédbrik/ adj. Brit. (of a university) founded relatively recently.

red•bud /rédbud/ n. any American tree of the genus Cercis, with pale pink flowers.

red•cap /rédkap/ n. **1** a baggage porter. **2** Brit. a member of the military police.

red car•pet n. privileged treatment of an eminent visitor.

red ce•dar n. an American juniper, Juniperus virginiana.

red cell n. (also **red cor•pus•cle**) an erythrocyte.

red cent n. the lowest-value (orig. copper) coin; a trivial sum (not worth a red cent).

red•coat /rédkōt/ n. hist. a British soldier (so called from the scarlet uniform of most regiments).

Red Cres•cent n. an organization like the Red Cross in Muslim countries.

red cross n. **1** St. George's cross, the national emblem of England. **2** the Christian side in the crusades.

Red Cross n. **1** an international organization (originally medical) bringing relief to victims of war or natural disaster. **2** the emblem of this organization.

redd /red/ v.tr. (past and past part. **redd**) dial. **1** clear up. **2** arrange; tidy; compose; settle. [ME: cf. MLG, MDu. redden]

red deer n. a deer, Cervus elaphus, of Europe and Asia, with a rich red-brown summer coat turning dull brown in winter.

red•den /réd'n/ v.tr. & intr. make or become red.

red•dle /réd'l/ n. red ocher; ruddle. [var. of RUDDLE]

red dust•er Brit. colloq. = RED ENSIGN.

red dwarf n. an old, relatively cool star.

rede /reed/ n. & v. esp. Brit. archaic ● n. advice, counsel. ● v.tr. **1** advise. **2** read (a riddle or dream). [OE rēd f. Gmc, rel. to READ (of which the verb is a ME var. retained for archaic senses)]

re•dec•o•rate /réedékərayt/ v.tr. decorate again or differently. □□ **re•dec•o•ra•tion** /-ráyshən/ n.

re•deem /rideem/ v.tr. **1** buy back; recover by expenditure of effort or by a stipulated payment. **2** make a single payment to discharge (a regular charge or obligation). **3** convert (tokens or bonds, etc.) into goods or cash. **4** (of God or Christ) deliver from sin and damnation. **5** make up for; be a compensating factor in (has one redeeming feature). **6** (foll. by from) save from (a defect). **7** refl. save (oneself) from blame. **8** purchase the freedom of (a person). **9** save (a person's life) by ransom. **10** save or rescue or reclaim. **11** fulfill (a promise). □□ **re•deem•a•ble** adj. [ME f. OF redimer or L redimere redempt- (as RE-, emere buy)]

re•deem•er /rideemər/ n. a person who redeems. □ the Redeemer Christ.

re•de•fine /réedifín/ v.tr. define again or differently. □□ **re•def•i•ni•tion** /-definíshən/ n.

re•demp•tion /ridémpshən/ n. **1** the act or an instance of redeeming; the process of being redeemed. **2** man's deliverance from sin and damnation. **3** a thing that redeems. □□ **re•demp•tive** adj. [ME f. OF f. L redemptio (as REDEEM)]

red en•sign see ENSIGN.

re•de•ploy /réediplóy/ v.tr. send (troops, workers, etc.) to a new place or task. □□ **re•de•ploy•ment** n.

re•de•sign /réedizín/ v.tr. design again or differently.

re•de•ter•mine /réeditórmin/ v.tr. determine again or differently. □□ **re•de•ter•mi•na•tion** n.

re•de•vel•op /réedivéləp/ v.tr. develop anew (esp. an urban area, with new buildings). □□ **re•de•vel•op•er** n. **re•de•vel•op•ment** n.

red-eye n. **1** = RUDD. **2** a late-night or overnight flight. **3** sl. cheap whiskey.

red-faced adj. embarrassed; ashamed.

red•fish /rédfish/ n. **1** a bright red food fish, Sebastes marinus, of the N. Atlantic; a rosefish. **2** Brit. a male salmon in the spawning season.

red flag n. **1** the symbol of socialist revolution. **2** a warning of danger.

red fox n. a fox, Vulpes vulpes, having a characteristic deep red or fawn coat.

red gi•ant n. a relatively cool giant star.

red grouse n. a subspecies of the willow ptarmigan, native to Britain and noted for its lack of white winter plumage.

Red Guard n. hist. a member of a militant youth movement in China (1966–76).

red gum n. **1** a teething rash in children. **2 a** a reddish resin. **b** any of various kinds of eucalyptus yielding this.

red-hand•ed adj. in or just after the act of committing a crime, doing wrong, etc. (caught them red-handed).

red hat n. **1** a cardinal's hat. **2** the symbol of a cardinal's office.

red·head /rédhed/ *n.* a person with red hair.

red-head·ed *adj.* **1** (of a person) having red hair. **2** (of birds, etc.) having a red head (*red-headed woodpecker*).

red heat *n.* **1** the temperature or state of something so hot as to emit red light. **2** great excitement.

red her·ring *n.* **1** dried smoked herring. **2** a misleading clue or distraction (so called from the practice of using the scent of red herring in training hounds).

red hot *n.* **1** *colloq.* a hot dog. **2** a small, red candy with a strong cinnamon flavor.

red-hot *adj.* **1** heated until red. **2** highly exciting. **3** (of news) fresh; completely new. **4** intensely excited. **5** enraged.

red-hot pok·er *n.* any plant of the genus *Kniphofia*, with spikes of usually red or yellow flowers.

re·di·al /réedíol, –díl/ *v.tr. & intr.* dial again.

re·did *past* of REDO.

Red In·di·an *offens. esp. Brit.* = REDSKIN.

red·in·gote /rédinggōt/ *n.* a woman's long coat with a cutaway front or a contrasting piece on the front. [F f. E *riding coat*]

red·in·te·grate /ridíntigrayt/ *v.tr.* **1** restore to wholeness or unity. **2** renew or reestablish in a united or perfect state. □□ **red·in·te·gra·tion** /–gráyshən/ *n.* **red·in·te·gra·tive** /–grətiv/ *adj.* [ME f. L *redintegrare* (as RE-, INTEGRATE)]

re·di·rect /réedirékt, –dī–/ *v.tr.* direct again, esp. change the address of (a letter). □□ **re·di·rec·tion** *n.*

re·dis·cov·er /réediskúvər/ *v.tr.* discover again. □□ **re·dis·cov·er·y** *n.* (*pl.* **·ies**)

re·dis·solve /réedizólv/ *v.tr. & intr.* dissolve again. □□ **re·dis·so·lu·tion** /–disəlóóshən/ *n.*

re·dis·tri·bute /réedistríbyŏŏt/ *v.tr.* distribute again or differently. □□ **re·dis·tri·bu·tion** /–byŏŏshən/ *n.* **re·dis·tri·bu·tive** /–tríbyŏŏtiv/ *adj.*

re·di·vide /réedivíd/ *v.tr.* divide again or differently. □□ **re·di·vi·sion** /–vízhən/ *n.*

red·i·vi·vus /rédivívos, –véevəs/ *adj.* (placed after noun) come back to life. [L (as RE-, *vivus* living)]

red lead *n.* a red form of lead oxide used as a pigment.

red-let·ter day *n.* a day that is pleasantly noteworthy or memorable (orig. a festival marked in red on the calendar).

red light *n.* **1** a signal to stop on a road, railroad, etc. **2** a warning or refusal.

red-light dis·trict *n.* a district containing many brothels.

red man *offens.* = REDSKIN.

red ma·ple *n.* a tree, *Acer rubram*, of eastern and central N. America, with reddish flowers and red leaves in the autumn.

red meat *n.* meat that is red when raw (e.g., beef or lamb).

red mul·let *n.* a marine fish, *Mullus surmuletus*, valued as food.

red·neck /rédnek/ *n.* usually *derog.* a working-class, politically conservative or reactionary white person, esp. in the rural southern US.

re·do /réedŏŏ/ *v.tr.* (*3rd sing. present* **re·does**; *past* **re·did**; *past part.* **re·done**) **1** do again or differently. **2** redecorate.

red oak *n.* any of several oak trees, as *Quercus rubra* or *Q. borealis*, of eastern N. America.

red·o·lent /rédələnt/ *adj.* **1** (foll. by *of, with*) strongly reminiscent or suggestive or mentally associated. **2** fragrant. **3** having a strong smell; odorous. □□ **red·o·lence** *n.* **red·o·lent·ly** *adv.* [ME f. OF *redolent* or L *redolēre* (as RE-, *olēre* smell)]

re·dou·ble /réedúbəl/ *v. & n.* • *v.* **1** *tr. & intr.* make or grow greater or more intense or numerous; intensify; increase. **2** *intr. Bridge* double again a bid already doubled by an opponent. • *n. Bridge* the redoubling of a bid. [F *redoubler* (as RE-, DOUBLE)]

re·doubt /ridówt/ *n. Mil.* an outwork or fieldwork usu. square or polygonal and without flanking defenses. [F *redoute* f. obs. It. *ridotta* f. med.L *reductus* refuge f. past part. of L *reducere* withdraw (see REDUCE): –*b*– after DOUBT (cf. REDOUBTABLE)]

re·doubt·a·ble /ridówtəbəl/ *adj.* formidable, esp. as an opponent. □□ **re·doubt·a·bly** *adv.* [ME f. OF *redoutable* f. *redouter* fear (as RE-, DOUBT)]

re·dound /ridównd/ *v.intr.* **1** (foll. by *to*) (of an action, etc.) make a great contribution to (one's credit or advantage, etc.). **2** (foll. by *upon, on*) come as the final result to; come back or recoil upon. [ME, orig. = overflow, f. OF *redonder* f. L *redundare* surge (as RE-, *unda* wave)]

re·dox /réedoks/ *n. Chem.* (often *attrib.*) oxidation and reduction. [*reduction* + *oxidation*]

red pep·per *n.* **1** cayenne pepper. **2** the ripe fruit of the capsicum plant, *Capsicum annuum*.

red pine *n.* a pine tree, *Pinus resinosa*, of eastern N. America.

red·poll /rédpōl/ *n.* any of several small finches with a red patch on the forehead.

re·draft /réedráft/ *v.tr.* draft (a writing or document) again.

re·draw /réedráw/ *v.tr.* (*past* **re·drew**; *past part.* **re·drawn**) draw again or differently.

re·dress /ridrés/ *v. & n.* • *v.tr.* **1** remedy or rectify (a wrong or grievance, etc.). **2** readjust; set straight again. • *n.* (also /réedres/) **1** reparation for a wrong. **2** (foll. by *of*) the act or process of redressing (a grievance, etc.). □ **redress the balance** restore equality. □□ **re·dress·a·ble** *adj.* **re·dress·al** *n.* **re·dress·er** *n.* (also **re·dres·sor**). [ME f. OF *redresse(r)*, *redrecier* (as RE-, DRESS)]

re·dress /réedrés/ *v.tr. & intr.* dress again or differently.

red roan see ROAN[1].

red roan *adj. & n.* • *adj.* bay mixed with white or gray. • *n.* a red roan animal.

red rose *n. Brit. Hist.* the emblem of Lancashire or the Lancastrians.

red san·dal·wood *n.* the red wood from either of two SE Asian trees, *Adenanthera pavonina* and *Pterocarpus santalinus*, used as lumber and to produce a red dye.

red·shank /rédshangk/ *n.* either of two Old World sandpipers, *Tringa totanus* and *T. erythropus*, with bright red legs.

red·shift /rédshift/ *n. Astron.* the displacement of the spectrum to longer wavelengths in the light coming from distant galaxies, etc., in recession.

red·skin /rédskin/ *n. colloq. offens.* a Native American.

red spi·der = SPIDER MITE.

red squir·rel *n.* a N. American squirrel, *Tamiasciurus hudsonicus*, with reddish fur.

red·start /rédstaart/ *n.* **1** any European red-tailed songbird of the genus *Phoenicurus*. **2** any of various similar American warblers of the family Parulidae. [RED + OE *steort* tail]

red tape *n.* excessive bureaucracy or adherence to formalities, esp. in public business.

re·duce /ridŏŏs, –dyŏŏs/ *v.* **1** *tr. & intr.* make or become smaller or less. **2** *tr.* (foll. by *to*) bring by force or necessity (to some undesirable state or action) (*reduced them to tears*; *were reduced to begging*). **3** *tr.* convert to another (esp. simpler) form (*reduced it to a powder*). **4** *tr.* convert (a fraction) to the form with the lowest terms. **5** *tr.* (foll. by *to*) bring or simplify or adapt by classification or analysis (*the dispute may be reduced to three issues*). **6** *tr.* make lower in status or rank. **7** *tr.* lower the price of. **8** *intr.* lessen one's weight or size. **9** *tr.* weaken (*is in a very reduced state*). **10** *tr.* impoverish. **11** *tr.* subdue; bring back to obedience. **12** *Chem. intr. & tr.* **a** combine or cause to combine with hydrogen. **b** undergo or cause to undergo addition of electrons. **13** *tr. Chem.* convert (oxide, etc.) to metal. **14** *tr.* **a** (in surgery) restore (a dislocated, etc.) part to its proper position. **b** remedy (a dislocation, etc.) in this way. **15** *tr. Photog.* make (a negative or print) less dense. **16** *tr. Cookery* boil off excess liquid from. □ **reduce to the ranks** demote (an NCO) to the rank of private. □□ **re·duc·er** *n.* **re·duc·i·ble** *adj.* **re·duc·i·bil·i·ty** *n.*

Late Middle English: from Latin *reducere*, from *re-* 'back, again' + *ducere* 'bring, lead.' The original sense was 'bring back' (hence 'restore,' now surviving in sense 14); from this developed the senses 'bring to a different state' and then 'bring to a simpler or lower state' (hence sense 3); and finally 'diminish in size or amount' (sense 1, dating from the late 18th century).

re·duced cir·cum·stanc·es *n.pl.* poverty after relative prosperity.

re·duc·ing a·gent *n. Chem.* a substance that brings about reduction by oxidation and losing electrons.

re·duc·ti·o ad ab·sur·dum /ridúkteeō ad absórdəm/ *n.* a method of proving the falsity of a premise by showing that the logical consequence is absurd; an instance of this. [L, = reduction to the absurd]

re·duc·tion /ridúkshən/ *n.* **1** the act or an instance of reducing; the process of being reduced. **2** an amount by which prices, etc., are reduced. **3** a reduced copy of a picture, etc. **4** an arrangement of an orchestral score for piano, etc. □□ **re·duc·tive** *adj.* [ME f. OF *reduction* or L *reductio* (as REDUCE)]

re·duc·tion·ism /ridúkshənizəm/ *n.* **1** the tendency to or principle of analyzing complex things into simple constituents. **2** often *derog.* the doctrine that a system can be fully understood in terms of its isolated parts, or an idea in terms of simple concepts. □□ **re·duc·tion·ist** *n.* **re·duc·tion·is·tic** /–nístik/ *adj.*

re·dun·dant /ridúndənt/ *adj.* **1** superfluous; not needed. **2** that can be omitted without any loss of significance. **3** *Brit.* (of a person) no longer needed for work and therefore unemployed. **4** *Engin. & Computing* (of a component) not needed but included in case of failure in another component. □□ **re·dun·dan·cy** *n.* (*pl.* **·cies**). **re·dun·dant·ly** *adv.* [L *redundare* redundant- (as REDOUND)]

re·du·pli·cate /ridŏŏplikayt, –dyŏŏ–/ *v.tr.* **1** make double. **2** repeat. **3** repeat (a letter or syllable or word) exactly or with a slight change (e.g., hurly-burly, go-go). □□ **re·du·pli·ca·tion** /–káyshən/ *n.* **re·du·pli·ca·tive** /–kətiv/ *adj.* [LL *reduplicare* (as RE-, DUPLICATE)]

red wa·ter *n.* **1** a bacterial disease of calves, a symptom of which is the passing of reddish urine. **2** a mass of water made red by pigmented plankton, esp. *Gonyanlax tamarensis*.

red·wing /rédwing/ *n.* a thrush, *Turdus iliacus*, with red underwings showing in flight.

red•wing black•bird *n.* (also **red-winged black•bird**) a N. American blackbird, *Agelaius phoeniceus*, the male of which is marked with scarlet wing patches.

red•wood /rédwŏŏd/ *n.* **1** an exceptionally large Californian conifer, *Sequoia sempervirens*, yielding red wood. **2** any tree yielding red wood.

ree•bok var of RHEBOK.

re•ech•o /rée-ékō/ *v.intr. & tr.* (**·oes, ·oed**) **1** echo. **2** echo repeatedly; resound.

reed[1] /reed/ *n. & v. • n.* **1 a** any of various water or marsh plants with a firm stem, esp. of the genus *Phragmites*. **b** a tall straight stalk of this. **2** (*collect.*) reeds growing in a mass or used as material esp. for thatching. **3** *Brit.* wheat straw prepared for thatching. **4** a pipe of reed or straw. **5 a** the vibrating part of the mouthpiece of some wind instruments, e.g., the oboe and clarinet, made of reed or other material and producing the sound. **b** (esp. in *pl.*) a reed instrument. **6** a weaver's comblike implement for separating the threads of the warp and correctly positioning the weft. **7** (in *pl.*) a set of semicylindrical adjacent moldings like reeds laid together. **• v.tr. 1** thatch with reed. **2** make (straw) into reed. **3** fit (a musical instrument) with a reed. **4** decorate with a molding of reeds. [OE *hrēod* f. WG]

reed[2] /reed/ *n. Brit.* the abomasum. [OE *rēada*]

reed•buck /reédbuk/ *n.* an antelope, *Redunca redunca*, native to W. Africa.

reed•ed /reédid/ *adj. Mus.* (of an instrument) having a vibrating reed.

reed•ing /reéding/ *n. Archit.* a small semicylindrical molding or ornamentation (cf. REED[1] *n.* 7).

re•ed•it /rée-édit/ *v.tr.* edit again or differently. □□ **re•e•di•tion** /rééidíshǝn/ *n.*

reed or•gan *n.* a harmonium, etc., with the sound produced by metal reeds.

reed pipe *n.* **1** a wind instrument with sound produced by a reed. **2** a pipe-organ pipe with a reed.

reed stop *n.* a reeded organ stop.

re•ed•u•cate /rée-édjǝkayt/ *v.tr.* educate again, esp. to change a person's views or beliefs. □□ **re•ed•u•ca•tion** /–káyshǝn/ *n.*

reed•y /reédee/ *adj.* (**reed•i•er, reed•i•est**) **1** full of reeds. **2** like a reed, esp. in weakness or slenderness. **3** (of a voice) like a reed instrument in tone; not full. □□ **reed•i•ness** *n.*

reef[1] /reef/ *n.* **1** a ridge of rock or coral, etc., at or near the surface of the sea. **2 a** a lode of ore. **b** the bedrock surrounding this. [earlier *riff(e)* f. MDu., MLG *rif, ref,* f. ON *rif* RIB]

reef[2] /reef/ *n. & v. Naut.* **• n.** each of several strips across a sail, for taking it in or rolling it up to reduce the surface area in a high wind. **• v.tr. 1** take in a reef or reefs of (a sail). **2** shorten (a topmast or a bowsprit). [ME *riff, refe* f. Du. *reef, rif* f. ON *rif* RIB, in the same sense: cf. REEF[1]]

reef•er /reéfǝr/ *n.* **1** *sl.* a marijuana cigarette. **2** a thick close-fitting double-breasted jacket. [REEF[2] (in sense 1, = a thing rolled) + –ER[1]]

reef knot *n.* a double knot made symmetrically to hold securely and cast off easily.

reek /reek/ *v. & n. • v.intr.* (often foll. by *of*) **1** smell strongly and unpleasantly. **2** have unpleasant or suspicious associations (*this reeks of corruption*). **3** give off smoke or fumes. **• n. 1** a foul or stale smell. **2** esp. *Sc.* smoke. **3** vapor; a visible exhalation (esp. from a chimney). □□ **reek•y** *adj.* [OE *rēocan* (v.), *rēc* (n.), f. Gmc]

reel /reel/ *n. & v. • n.* **1** a cylindrical device on which thread, silk, yarn, paper, film, wire, etc., are wound. **2** a quantity of thread, etc., wound on a reel. **3** a device for winding and unwinding a line as required, esp. in fishing. **4** a revolving part in various machines. **5 a** a lively folk or Scottish dance, of two or more couples facing each other. **b** a piece of music for this. **• v. 1** *tr.* wind (thread, a fishing line, etc.) on a reel. **2** *tr.* (foll. by *in, up*) draw (fish, etc.) in or up by the use of a reel. **3** *intr.* stand or walk or run unsteadily. **4** *intr.* be shaken mentally or physically. **5** *intr.* rock from side to side, or swing violently. **6** *intr.* dance a reel. □ **reel off** say or recite very rapidly and without apparent effort. □□ **reel•er** *n.* [OE *hrēol*, of unkn. orig.]

re•e•lect /rée-ilékt/ *v.tr.* elect again, esp. to a further term of office. □□ **re•e•lec•tion** /–ilékshǝn/ *n.*

re•em•bark /rée-imbaárk/ *v.intr. & tr.* go or put on board ship again. □□ **re•em•bar•ka•tion** *n.*

re•e•merge /rée-imǝrj/ *v.intr.* emerge again; come back out. □□ **re•e•mer•gence** *n.* **re•e•mer•gent** *adj.*

re•em•pha•size /rée-émfǝsīz/ *v.tr.* place renewed emphasis on. □□ **re•em•pha•sis** /–émfǝsis/ *n.*

re•em•ploy /rée-implóy/ *v.tr.* employ again. □□ **re•em•ploy•ment** *n.*

re•en•act /rée-inákt/ *v.tr.* act out (a past event). □□ **re•en•act•ment** *n.*

re•en•list /rée-inlíst/ *v.intr.* enlist again, esp. in the armed services. □□ **re•en•list•er** *n.*

re•en•ter /rée-éntǝr/ *v.tr. & intr.* enter again; go back in. □□ **re•en•trance** /–éntrǝns/ *n.*

re•en•trant /rée-éntrǝnt/ *adj. & n. • adj.* **1** esp. *Fortification* (of an angle) pointing inward (opp. SALIENT). **2** *Geom.* reflex. **• n.** a reentrant angle.

re•en•try /rée-éntree/ *n.* (*pl.* **·tries**) **1** the act of entering again, esp. (of a spacecraft, missile, etc.) reentering the earth's atmosphere. **2** *Law* an act of retaking or repossession.

re•e•quip /rée-ikwíp/ *v.tr. & intr.* (**·e•quipped, ·e•quip•ping**) provide or be provided with new equipment.

re•e•rect /rée-irékt/ *v.tr.* erect again.

re•es•tab•lish /rée-istáblish/ *v.tr.* establish again or anew. □□ **re•es•tab•lish•ment** *n.*

re•e•val•u•ate /rée-ivályŏŏ-ayt/ *v.tr.* evaluate again or differently. □□ **re•e•val•u•a•tion** /–áyshǝn/ *n.*

reeve[1] /reev/ *n.* **1** *hist.* **a** the chief administrator of a town or district. **b** *Brit.* an official supervising a landowner's estate. **c** any of various minor local officials. **2** *Can.* the president of a village or town council. [OE (*ge*)*rēfa, girēfa*]

reeve[2] /reev/ *v.tr.* (*past* **rove** /rōv/ or **reeved**) *Naut.* **1** (usu. foll. by *through*) thread (a rope or rod, etc.) through a ring or other aperture. **2** pass a rope through (a block, etc.). **3** fasten (a rope or block) in this way. [prob. f. Du. *rēven* REEF[2]]

reeve[3] /reev/ *n.* a female ruff (see RUFF[1]). [17th c.: orig. unkn.]

re•ex•am•ine /rée-igzámin/ *v.tr.* examine again or further (esp. a witness after cross-examination). □□ **re•ex•am•i•na•tion** /–náyshǝn/ *n.*

re•ex•port *v. & n. • v.tr.* /rée-ikspáwrt/ export again (esp. imported goods after further processing or manufacture). **• n.** /rée-ékspawrt/ **1** the process of reexporting. **2** something reexported. □□ **re•ex•por•ta•tion** *n.* **re•ex•port•er** *n.*

ref /ref/ *n. colloq.* a referee in sports. [abbr.]

ref. *abbr.* **1** reference. **2** refer to.

re•face /rée-fáys/ *v.tr.* put a new facing on (a building).

re•fash•ion /rée-fáshǝn/ *v.tr.* fashion again or differently.

re•fec•tion /rifékshǝn/ *n. literary* **1** refreshment by food or drink (*we took refection*). **2** a light meal. [ME f. OF f. L *refectio –onis* f. *reficere* (as REFECTORY)]

re•fec•to•ry /riféktǝree/ *n.* (*pl.* **·ries**) a room used for communal meals, esp. in a monastery or college. [LL *refectorium* f. L *reficere* refresh (as RE-, *facere* make)]

re•fec•to•ry ta•ble *n.* a long narrow table.

re•fer /rifǝr/ *v.* (**re•ferred, re•fer•ring**) (usu. foll. by *to*) **1** *tr.* trace or ascribe (to a person or thing as a cause or source) (*referred their success to their popularity*). **2** *tr.* consider as belonging (to a certain date or place or class). **3** *tr.* send on or direct (a person, or a question for decision) (*the matter was referred to arbitration; referred him to her previous answer*). **4** *intr.* make an appeal or have recourse to (some authority or source of information) (*referred to his notes*). **5** *tr.* send (a person) to a medical specialist, etc. **6** *tr.* (foll. by *back to*) send (a proposal, etc.) back to (a lower body, court, etc.). **7** *intr.* (foll. by *to*) (of a person speaking) make an allusion or direct the hearer's attention (*decided not to refer to our other problems*). **8** *intr.* (foll. by *to*) (of a statement, etc.) have a particular relation; be directed (*this paragraph refers to the events of last year*). **9** *tr.* (foll. by *to*) interpret (a statement) as being directed to (a particular context, etc.). **10** *tr.* fail (a candidate in an examination). □□ **re•fer•a•ble** /riférǝbǝl, réfǝr–/ *adj.* **re•fer•rer** *n.* [ME f. OF *referer* f. L *referre* carry back (as RE–, *ferre* bring)]

ref•er•ee /réfǝree/ *n. & v. • n.* **1** an umpire, esp. in sports, such as football, boxing, etc. **2** a person whose opinion or judgment is sought in some connection, or who is referred to for a decision in a dispute, etc. **3** *Brit.* a person willing to testify to the character of an applicant for employment, etc. **• v.** (**ref•er•ees, ref•er•eed**) **1** *intr.* act as referee. **2** *tr.* be the referee of (a game, etc.).

ref•er•ence /réfǝrǝns, réfrǝns/ *n. & v.* **• n. 1** the referring of a matter for decision or settlement or consideration to some authority. **2** the scope given to this authority. **3** (foll. by *to*) **a** a relation or respect or correspondence (*success seems to have little reference to merit*). **b** an allusion (*made no reference to our problems*). **c** a direction to a book, etc., (or a passage in it) where information may be found. **d** a book or passage so cited. **4 a** the act of looking up a passage, etc., or looking in a book for information. **b** the act of referring to a person, etc., for information. **5 a** a written testimonial supporting an applicant for employment, etc. **b** a person giving this. **• v.tr.** provide (a book, etc.) with references to authorities. □ **with** (or **in**) **reference to** regarding; as regards; about. **without reference to** not taking account of. □□ **ref•er•en•tial** /réfǝrénshǝl/ *adj.*

ref•er•ence book *n.* a book intended to be consulted for information on individual matters rather than read continuously.

ref•er•ence li•brar•y *n.* a library in which the books are for consultation, not loan.

ref•er•en•dum /réfǝréndǝm/ *n.* (*pl.* **ref•er•en•dums** or **ref•er•en•da** /–dǝ/) **1** the process of referring a political question to the electorate for a direct decision by general vote. **2** a vote taken by referendum. [L, gerund or neut. gerundive of *referre*: see REFER]

ref•er•ent /réfǝrǝnt/ *n.* the idea or thing that a word, etc., symbolizes. [L *referens* (as REFERENDUM)]

See page xx for the **Key to Pronunciation**.

re·fer·ral /rifə́rəl/ *n.* the referring of an individual to an expert or specialist for advice, esp. the directing of a patient by a general practitioner to a medical specialist.

re·fill *v. & n.* ● *v.tr.* /reefíl/ **1** fill again. **2** provide a new filling for. ● *n.* /reefil/ **1** a new filling. **2** the material for this. □□ **re·fill·a·ble** *adj.*

re·fine /rifín/ *v.* **1** *tr.* free from impurities or defects; purify; clarify. **2** *tr. & intr.* make or become more polished or elegant or cultured. **3** *tr. & intr.* make or become more subtle or delicate in thought, feelings, etc. □□ **re·fin·a·ble** *adj.* [RE- + FINE[1] *v.*]

re·fined /rifínd/ *adj.* **1** characterized by polish or elegance or subtlety. **2** purified; clarified.

re·fine·ment /rifínmənt/ *n.* **1** the act of refining or the process of being refined. **2** fineness of feeling or taste. **3** polish or elegance in behavior or manner. **4** an added development or improvement (*a car with several refinements*). **5** a piece of subtle reasoning. **6** a fine distinction. **7** a subtle or ingenious example or display (*all the refinements of reasoning*). [REFINE + −MENT, after F *raffinement*]

re·fin·er /rifínər/ *n.* a person or firm whose business is to refine crude oil, metal, sugar, etc.

re·fin·er·y /rifínəree/ *n.* (*pl.* **·ies**) a place where oil, etc., is refined.

re·fit *v. & n.* ● *v.tr. & intr.* /reefít/ (**re·fit·ted, re·fit·ting**) make or become fit or serviceable again (esp. of a ship undergoing renewal and repairs). ● *n.* /reefit/ the act or an instance of refitting; the process of being refitted. □□ **re·fit·ment** *n.*

refl. *abbr.* **1** reflex. **2** reflexive.

re·flate /reefláyt/ *v.tr.* cause reflation of (a currency or economy, etc.). [RE- after *inflate, deflate*]

re·fla·tion /reefláyshən/ *n.* the inflation of a financial system to restore its previous condition after deflation. □□ **re·fla·tion·ar·y** *adj.* [RE- after *inflation, deflation*]

re·flect /riflékt/ *v.* **1** *tr.* **a** (of a surface or body) throw back (heat, light, sound, etc.). **b** cause to rebound (*reflected light*). **2** *tr.* (of a mirror) show an image of; reproduce to the eye or mind. **3** *tr.* correspond in appearance or effect to; have as a cause or source (*their behavior reflects a wish to succeed*). **4** *tr.* **a** (of an action, result, etc.) show or bring (credit, discredit, etc.). **b** (*absol.*; usu. foll. by *on, upon*) bring discredit on. **5 a** *intr.* (often foll. by *on, upon*) meditate on; think about. **b** *tr.* (foll. by *that, how*, etc., + clause) consider; remind oneself. **6** *intr. Brit.* (usu. foll. by *upon, on*) make disparaging remarks. [ME f. OF *reflecter* or L *reflectere* (as RE-, *flectere flex-* bend)]

re·flect·ing tel·e·scope = REFLECTOR.

re·flec·tion /riflékshən/ *n.* (also *Brit.* **re·flex·ion**) **1** the act or an instance of reflecting; the process of being reflected. **2 a** reflected light, heat, or color. **b** a reflected image. **3** meditation; reconsideration (*on reflection*). **4** (often foll. by *on*) discredit or a thing bringing discredit. **5** (often foll. by *on, upon*) an idea arising in the mind; a comment or apothegm. **6** (usu. foll. by *of*) a consequence; evidence (*a reflection of how she feels*). □□ **re·flec·tion·al** *adj.* [ME f. OF *reflexion* or LL *reflexio* (as REFLECT), with assim. to *reflect*]

re·flec·tive /rifléktiv/ *adj.* **1** (of a surface, etc.) giving a reflection or image. **2** (of mental faculties) concerned in reflection or thought. **3** (of a person or mood, etc.) thoughtful; given to meditation. □□ **re·flec·tive·ly** *adv.* **re·flec·tive·ness** *n.*

re·flec·tor /rifléktər/ *n.* **1** a piece of glass or metal, etc., for reflecting light in a required direction, e.g., a red one on the back of a motor vehicle or bicycle. **2 a** a telescope, etc., using a mirror to produce images. **b** the mirror itself.

re·flet /rəfláy/ *n.* luster or iridescence, esp. on pottery. [F f. It. *riflesso* reflection, REFLEX]

re·flex /reefleks/ *adj. & n.* ● *adj.* **1** (of an action) independent of the will, as an automatic response to the stimulation of a nerve (e.g., a sneeze). **2** (of an angle) exceeding 180°. **3** bent backward. **4** (of light) reflected. **5** (of a thought, etc.) introspective; directed back upon itself or its own operations. **6** (of an effect or influence) reactive; coming back upon its author or source. ● *n.* **1** a reflex action. **2** a sign or secondary manifestation (*law is a reflex of public opinion*). **3** reflected light or a reflected image. **4** a word formed by development from an earlier stage of a language. □□ **re·flex·ly** *adv.* [L *reflexus* (as REFLECT)]

re·flex arc *n. Anat.* the sequence of nerves involved in a reflex action.

re·flex cam·er·a *n.* a camera with a ground-glass focusing screen on which the image is formed by a combination of lens and mirror, enabling the scene to be correctly composed and focused.

re·flex·i·ble /rifléksibəl/ *adj.* capable of being reflected. □□ **re·flex·i·bil·i·ty** /−bílitee/ *n.*

re·flex·ion var. of REFLECTION.

re·flex·ive /rifléksiv/ *adj. & n. Gram.* ● *adj.* **1** (of a word or form) referring back to the subject of a sentence (esp. of a pronoun, e.g.,

myself). **2** (of a verb) having a reflexive pronoun as its object (as in *to wash oneself*). ● *n.* a reflexive word or form, esp. a pronoun. □□ **re·flex·ive·ly** *adv.* **re·flex·ive·ness** *n.* **re·flex·iv·i·ty** /−sí vitee/ *n.*

re·flex·ol·o·gy /reefleksóləjee/ *n.* **1** a system of massage through reflex points on the feet, hands, and head, used to relieve tension and treat illness. **2** *Psychol.* the scientific study of reflexes. □□ **re·flex·ol·o·gist** *n.*

ref·lu·ent /réfloоənt/ *adj.* flowing back (*refluent tide*). □□ **ref·lu·ence** *n.* [ME f. L *refluere* (as RE-, *fluere* flow)]

re·flux /reefluks/ *n. & v.* ● *n.* **1** a backward flow. **2** *Chem.* a method of boiling a liquid so that any vapor is liquefied and returned to the boiler. ● *v.tr. & intr. Chem.* boil or be boiled under reflux.

re·fo·cus /reefókəs/ *v.tr.* (**re·fo·cused, re·fo·cus·ing** or **re·fo·cussed, re·fo·cus·sing**) adjust the focus of (esp. a lens).

re·for·est /reefáwrist, fór−/ *v.tr.* replant former forest land with trees. □□ **re·for·est·a·tion** /−stáyshən/ *n.*

re·forge /reefáwrj/ *v.tr.* forge again or differently.

re·form /rifáwrm/ *v., n., & adj.* ● *v.* **1** *tr. & intr.* make or become better by the removal of faults and errors. **2** *tr.* abolish or cure (an abuse or malpractice). **3** *tr.* correct (a legal document). **4** *tr. Chem.* convert (a straight-chain hydrocarbon) by catalytic reaction to a branched-chain form for use as gasoline. ● *n.* **1** the removal of faults or abuses, esp. of a moral or political or social kind. **2** an improvement made or suggested. ● *adj.* of or relating to reform. □□ **re·form·a·ble** *adj.* [ME f. OF *reformer* or L *reformare* (as RE-, FORM)]

re·form /reefáwrm/ *v.tr. & intr.* form again.

re·for·mat /reefáwrmat/ *v.tr.* (**re·for·mat·ted, re·for·mat·ting**) format anew.

ref·or·ma·tion /réfərmáyshən/ *n.* the act of reforming or process of being reformed, esp. a radical change for the better in political or religious or social affairs. □ **the Reformation** *hist.* a 16th-c. movement for the reform of abuses in the Roman Church ending in the establishment of the Reformed and Protestant churches. □□ **Ref·or·ma·tion·al** *adj.* [ME f. OF *reformation* or L *reformatio* (as REFORM)]

re·for·ma·tion /reefawrmáyshən/ *n.* the process or an instance of forming or being formed again.

re·form·a·tive /rifáwrmətiv/ *adj.* tending or intended to produce reform. [OF *reformatif −ive* or med.L *reformativus* (as REFORM)]

re·form·a·to·ry /rifáwrmətawree/ *n. & adj.* ● *n.* (*pl.* **·ries**) = REFORM SCHOOL. ● *adj.* reformative.

Re·formed Church *n.* a church that has accepted the principles of the Reformation, esp. a Calvinist church (as distinct from Lutheran).

re·form·er /rifáwrmər/ *n.* a person who advocates or brings about (esp. political or social) reform.

re·form·ism /rifáwrmizəm/ *n.* a policy of reform rather than abolition or revolution. □□ **re·form·ist** *n.*

Re·form Ju·da·ism *n.* a simplified and rationalized form of Judaism.

re·form school *n.* an institution to which young offenders are sent to be reformed.

re·for·mu·late /reefáwrmyəlayt/ *v.tr.* formulate again or differently. □□ **re·for·mu·la·tion** /−láyshən/ *n.*

re·fract /rifrákt/ *v.tr.* **1** (of water, air, glass, etc.) deflect (a ray of light, etc.) at a certain angle when it enters obliquely from another medium. **2** determine the refractive condition of (the eye). [L *refringere refract-* (as RE-, *frangere* break)]

re·frac·tion /rifrákshən/ *n.* the process by which or the extent to which light is refracted. [F *réfraction* or LL *refractio* (as REFRACT)]

re·frac·tive /rifráktiv/ *adj.* of or involving refraction.

re·frac·tom·e·ter /reefraktómitər/ *n.* an instrument for measuring an index of refraction. □□ **re·frac·to·met·ric** /−təmétrik/ *adj.* **re·frac·tom·e·try** *n.*

re·frac·tor /rifráktər/ *n.* **1** a refracting medium or lens. **2** a telescope using a lens to produce an image.

re·frac·to·ry /rifráktəree/ *adj. & n.* ● *adj.* **1** stubborn; unmanageable, rebellious. **2 a** (of a wound, disease, etc.) not yielding to treatment. **b** (of a person, etc.) resistant to infection. **3** (of a substance) hard to fuse or work. ● *n.* (*pl.* **·ries**) a substance especially resistant to heat, corrosion, etc. □□ **re·frac·to·ri·ly** *adv.* **re·frac·to·ri·ness** *n.* [alt. of obs. *refractary* f. L *refractarius* (as REFRACT)]

re·frain[1] /rifráyn/ *v.intr.* (foll. by *from*) avoid doing (an action); forbear; desist (*refrain from smoking*). □□ **re·frain·ment** *n.* [ME f. OF *refrener* f. L *refrenare* (as RE-, *frenum* bridle)]

re·frain[2] /rifráyn/ *n.* **1** a recurring phrase or number of lines, esp. at the ends of stanzas. **2** the music accompanying this. [ME f. OF *refrain* (earlier *refrait*) ult. f. L *refringere* (as RE-, *frangere* break), because the refrain 'broke' the sequence]

re·fran·gi·ble /rifránjibəl/ *adj.* that can be refracted. □□ **re·fran·gi·bil·i·ty** *n.* [mod.L *refrangibilis* f. *refrangere* = L *refringere*: see REFRACT]

re·freeze /reefreez/ *v.tr. & intr.* (*past* **re·froze**; *past part.* **re·fro·zen**) freeze again.

re·fresh /rifrésh/ *v.tr.* **1 a** (of food, rest, amusement, etc.) give fresh spirit or vigor to. **b** (esp. *refl.*) revive with food, rest, etc. (*refreshed myself with a short sleep*). **2** revive or stimulate (the memory), esp. by consulting the source of one's information. **3** make cool. **4** restore to a certain condition, esp. by provision of fresh supplies, equipment, etc.; replenish. **5** *Computing* **a** restore an image to the screen. **b** replace an image with one that displays more recent information. [ME f. OF *refreschi(e)r* f. *fres fresche* FRESH]

re·fresh·er /rifréshər/ n. **1** something that refreshes, esp. a drink. **2** *Brit. Law* an extra fee payable to counsel in a prolonged case.

re·fresh·er course n. a course reviewing or updating previous studies.

re·fresh·ing /rifréshing/ adj. **1** serving to refresh. **2** welcome or stimulating because sincere or untypical (*refreshing innocence*). □□ **re·fresh·ing·ly** adv.

re·fresh·ment /rifréshmənt/ n. **1** the act of refreshing or the process of being refreshed in mind or body. **2** (usu. in *pl.*) food or drink that refreshes. **3** something that refreshes or stimulates the mind. [ME f. OF *refreschement* (as REFRESH)]

re·frig·er·ant /rifríjərənt/ n. & adj. ● n. **1** a substance used for refrigeration. **2** *Med.* a substance that cools or allays fever. ● adj. cooling. [F *réfrigérant* or L *refrigerant-* (as REFRIGERATE)]

re·frig·er·ate /rifríjərayt/ v. **1** tr. & intr. make or become cool or cold. **2** tr. subject (food, etc.) to cold in order to freeze or preserve it. □□ **re·frig·er·a·tion** /-ráyshən/ n. **re·frig·er·a·tive** /-rətiv/ adj. [L *refrigerare* (as RE-, *frigus frigoris* cold)]

re·frig·er·a·tor /rifríjəraytər/ n. a cabinet or room in which food, etc., is kept cold.

re·frig·er·a·to·ry /rifríjərətawree/ adj. & n. ● adj. serving to cool. ● n. (pl. ·ries) *hist.* a cold-water vessel attached to a still for condensing vapor. [mod.L *refrigeratorium* (n.), L *refrigeratorius* (adj.) (as REFRIGERATE)]

re·frin·gent /rifrínjənt/ adj. *Physics* refracting. □□ **re·frin·gence** n. **re·frin·gen·cy** n. [L *refringere*: see REFRACT]

re·froze past of REFREEZE.

re·fro·zen past part. of REFREEZE.

reft past part. of REAVE.

re·fu·el /reefyóoəl/ v. **1** intr. replenish a fuel supply. **2** tr. supply with more fuel.

ref·uge /réfyooj/ n. **1** a shelter from pursuit or danger or trouble. **2** a person or place, etc., offering this. **3 a** a person, thing, or course resorted to in difficulties. **b** a pretext; an excuse. **4** *Brit.* a traffic island. [ME f. OF f. L *refugium* (as RE-, *fugere* flee)]

ref·u·gee /réfyoojeé/ n. a person taking refuge, esp. in a foreign country from war or persecution or natural disaster. [F *réfugié* past part. of (*se*) *réfugier* (as REFUGE)]

re·ful·gent /rifúljənt/ adj. *literary* shining; gloriously bright. □□ **re·ful·gence** n. **re·ful·gent·ly** adv. [L *refulgēre* (as RE-, *fulgēre* shine)]

re·fund[1] v. & n. ● v. /rifúnd/ tr. (also *absol.*) **1** pay back (money or expenses). **2** reimburse (a person). ● n. /reéfund/ **1** an act of refunding. **2** a sum refunded; a repayment. □□ **re·fund·a·ble** adj. **re·fund·er** n. [ME in sense 'pour back,' f. OF *refonder* or L *refundere* (as RE-, *fundere* pour), later assoc. with FUND]

re·fund[2] /reéfúnd/ v.tr. fund (a debt, etc.) again.

re·fur·bish /rifórbish/ v.tr. **1** brighten up. **2** restore and redecorate. □□ **re·fur·bish·ment** n.

re·fur·nish /reéfórnish/ v.tr. furnish again or differently.

re·fus·al /rifyóozəl/ n. **1** the act or an instance of refusing; the state of being refused. **2** (in full **first refusal**) the right or privilege of deciding to take or leave a thing before it is offered to others.

re·fuse[1] /rifyóoz/ v. **1** tr. withhold acceptance of or consent to (*refuse an offer, refuse orders*). **2** tr. (often foll. by *to* + infin.) decline unwillingness (*I refuse to go; the car refuses to start; I refuse!*). **3** tr. (often with double object) not grant (a request) made by (a person) (*refused me a day off; I could not refuse them*). **4** tr. (also *absol.*) (of a horse) be unwilling to jump (a fence, etc.). □□ **re·fus·a·ble** adj. **re·fus·er** n. [ME f. OF *refuser* prob. ult. f. L *recusare* (see RECUSANT) after *refutare* REFUTE]

ref·use[2] /réfyoos/ n. items rejected as worthless; waste. [ME, perh. f. OF *refusé* past part. (as REFUSE[1])]

re·fuse·nik /rifyóoznik/ n. *hist.* a Jew refused permission to emigrate to Israel from the former Soviet Union. [REFUSE[1] + -NIK]

re·fute /rifyóot/ v.tr. **1** prove the falsity or error of (a statement, etc., or the person advancing it). **2** rebut or repel by argument. **3** *disp.* deny or contradict (without argument). □□ **re·fut·a·ble** adj. **re·fut·al** n. **ref·u·ta·tion** /réfyootáyshən/ n. **re·fut·er** n. [L *refutare* (as RE-; cf. CONFUTE]

▶ Strictly speaking, **refute** means 'prove (a person or statement) to be wrong,' e.g., *No amount of research can either confirm or refute the story*. However, it is sometimes used to mean simply 'deny or repudiate.' This usage is considered incorrect by some.

reg /reg/ n. *colloq.* regulation. [abbr.]

re·gain /rigáyn/ v.tr. obtain possession or use of after loss (*regain consciousness*). [F *regagner* (as RE-, GAIN)]

re·gal /reégəl/ adj. **1** royal; of or by a monarch or monarchs. **2** fit for a monarch; magnificent. □□ **re·gal·ly** adv. [ME f. OF *regal* or L *regalis* f. *rex regis* king]

re·gale /rigáyl/ v.tr. **1** entertain lavishly with feasting. **2** (foll. by *with*) entertain or divert with (talk, etc.). **3** (of beauty, flowers, etc.) give delight to. □□ **re·gale·ment** n. [F *régaler* f. OF *gale* pleasure]

re·ga·li·a /rigáylyə/ n.pl. **1** the insignia of royalty used at coronations. **2** the insignia of an order or of civic dignity. **3** any distinctive or elaborate clothes, accoutrements, etc.; trappings; finery. [med.L, = royal privileges, f. L neut. pl. of *regalis* REGAL]

re·gal·ism /reégəlizəm/ n. the doctrine of a sovereign's ecclesiastical supremacy.

re·gal·i·ty /rigálitee/ n. (pl. ·ties) **1** the state of being a king or queen. **2** an attribute of sovereign power. **3** a royal privilege. [ME f. OF *regalité* or med.L *regalitas* (as REGAL)]

re·gard /rigáard/ v. & n. ● v.tr. **1** gaze on steadily (usu. in a specified way) (*regarded them suspiciously*). **2** give heed to; take into account; let one's course be affected by. **3** look upon or contemplate mentally in a specified way (*I regard them kindly; I regard it as an insult*). **4** (of a thing) have relation to; have some connection with. ● n. **1** a gaze; a steady or significant look. **2** (foll. by *to, for*) attention or care. **3** (foll. by *for*) esteem; kindly feeling; respectful opinion. **4 a** a respect; a point attended to (*in this regard*). **b** (usu. foll. by *to*) reference; connection, relevance. **5** (in *pl.*) an expression of friendliness in a letter, etc.; compliments (*sent my best regards*). □ **as regards** about; concerning; in respect of. **in** (or **with**) **regard to** as concerns; in respect of. [ME f. OF *regard* f. *regarder* (as RE-, *garder* GUARD)]

re·gard·ant /rigáard'nt/ adj. *Heraldry* (of a beast, etc.) looking backward. [AF & OF (as REGARD)]

re·gard·ful /rigáardfŏŏl/ adj. (foll. by *of*) mindful of; paying attention to.

re·gard·ing /rigáarding/ prep. about; concerning; in respect of.

re·gard·less /rigáardlis/ adj. & adv. ● adj. (foll. by *of*) without regard or consideration for (*regardless of the expense*). ● adv. without paying attention (*carried on regardless*). □□ **re·gard·less·ly** adv. **re·gard·less·ness** n.

▶See note at IRREGARDLESS.

re·gath·er /reégáthər/ v.tr. & intr. **1** gather or collect again. **2** meet again.

re·gat·ta /rigáatə, -gátə/ n. a sporting event consisting of a series of boat or yacht races. [It. (Venetian)]

regd. abbr. registered.

re·gen·cy /reéjənsee/ n. (pl. ·cies) **1** the office of regent. **2** a commission acting as regent. **3 a** the period of office of a regent or regency commission. **b** (**Regency**) a particular period of a regency, esp. (in Britain) from 1811 to 1820, and (in France) from 1715 to 1723 (often *attrib.: Regency costume*). [ME f. med.L *regentia* (as REGENT)]

re·gen·er·ate v. & adj. ● v. /rijénərayt/ **1** tr. & intr. bring or come into renewed existence; generate again. **2** tr. improve the moral condition of. **3** tr. impart new, more vigorous, and spiritually greater life to (a person or institution, etc.). **4** intr. reform oneself. **5** tr. invest with a new and higher spiritual nature. **6** intr. & tr. *Biol.* regrow or cause (new tissue) to regrow to replace lost or injured tissue. **7** tr. & intr. *Chem.* restore or be restored to an initial state of reaction or process. ● adj. /rijénərət/ **1** spiritually born again. **2** reformed. □□ **re·gen·er·a·tion** /-jenəráyshən/ n. **re·gen·er·a·tive** /-rətiv/ adj. **re·gen·er·a·tive·ly** adv. **re·gen·er·a·tor** n. [L *regenerare* (as RE-, GENERATE)]

re·gent /reéjənt/ n. & adj. ● n. **1** a person appointed to administer a kingdom because the monarch is a minor or is absent or incapacitated. **2** a member of the governing body of a state university. ● adj. (placed after noun) acting as regent (*prince regent*). [ME f. OF *regent* or L *regere* rule]

re·gent bird n. an Australian bower bird, *Sericulus chrysocephalus*.

re·ger·mi·nate /reéjórminayt/ v.tr. & intr. germinate again. □□ **re·ger·mi·na·tion** /-jərmináyshən/ n.

reg·gae /régay/ n. a W. Indian style of music with a strongly accented subsidiary beat. [W.Ind.]

reg·i·cide /réjisid/ n. **1** a person who kills or takes part in killing a king. **2** the act of killing a king. □□ **reg·i·cid·al** adj. [L *rex regis* king + -CIDE]

re·gild /reégíld/ v.tr. gild again, esp. to renew faded or worn gilding.

re·gime /rayzheém/ n. (also **ré·gime**) **1** a method or system of government. **b** *derog.* a particular government. **2** a prevailing order or system of things. **3** the conditions under which a scientific or industrial process occurs. **4** = REGIMEN 1. [F *régime* (as REGIMEN)]

reg·i·men /réjimen/ n. **1** esp. *Med.* a prescribed course of exercise, way of life, and diet. **2** *archaic* a system of government. [L f. *regere* rule]

reg·i·ment n. & v. ● n. /réjimənt/ **1 a** a permanent unit of an army usu. commanded by a colonel and divided into several companies or troops or batteries and often into two battalions. **b** an operational unit of artillery, etc. **2** (usu. foll. by *of*) a large array or number. **3** *archaic* rule; government. ● v.tr. /réjiment/ **1** organize (esp. oppressively) in groups or according to a system. **2** form into a regiment or regiments. □□ **reg·i·ment·ed** adj. **reg·i·men·ta·tion** n. [ME (in sense 3) f. OF f. LL *regimentum* (as REGIMEN)]

reg·i·men·tal /réjimént'l/ adj. & n. ● adj. of or relating to a regiment.

● *n.* (in *pl.*) military uniform, esp. of a particular regiment. □□ **reg·i·men·tal·ly** *adv.*

Re·gi·na /rijínə/ *n. Brit. Law* the reigning queen (following a name or in the titles of lawsuits, e.g., *Regina v. Jones*, the Crown versus Jones). [L, = queen f. *rex regis* king]

re·gion /reéjən/ *n.* **1** an area of land, or division of the earth's surface, having definable boundaries or characteristics (*a mountainous region; the region between the river and the sea*). **2** an administrative district, esp. in Scotland. **3** a part of the body around or near some organ, etc. (*the lumbar region*). **4** a sphere or realm (*the region of metaphysics*). **5 a** a separate part of the world or universe. **b** a layer of the atmosphere or the sea according to its height or depth. □ **in the region of** approximately. □□ **re·gion·al** *adj.* **re·gion·al·ism** *n.* **re·gion·al·ist** *n. & adj.* **re·gion·al·ize** *v. tr.* **re·gion·al·ly** *adv.* [ME f. OF f. L *regio –onis* direction, district f. *regere* direct]

re·gis·seur /ráyzheesór/ *n.* the director of a theatrical production, esp. a ballet. [F *régisseur* stage manager]

reg·is·ter /réjistər/ *n. & v.* ● *n.* **1** an official list, e.g., of births, marriages, and deaths; of shipping; of professionally qualified persons; or of qualified voters in a constituency. **2** a book in which items are recorded for reference. **3** a device recording speed, force, etc. **4** (in electronic devices) a location in a store of data, used for a specific purpose and with quick access time. **5 a** the range of a voice or instrument. **b** a part of this range (*lower register*). **6** an adjustable plate for widening or narrowing an opening and regulating a draft, esp. in a fire grate. **7 a** a set of organ pipes. **b** a sliding device controlling this. **8** = CASH REGISTER. **9** *Linguistics* each of several forms of a language (colloquial, formal, literary, etc.) usually used in particular circumstances. **10** *Printing* the exact correspondence of the position of printed matter on the two sides of a leaf. **11** *Printing & Photog.* the correspondence of the position of color components in a printed positive. ● *v.* **1** *tr.* set down (a name, fact, etc.) formally; record in writing. **2** *tr.* make a mental note of; notice. **3** *tr.* enter or cause to be entered in a particular register. **4** *tr.* entrust (a letter, etc.) to a post office for transmission by registered mail. **5** *intr. & refl.* put one's name on a register, esp. as an eligible voter or as a guest in a register kept by a hotel, etc. **6** *tr.* (of an instrument) record automatically; indicate. **7 a** *tr.* express (an emotion) facially or by gesture (*registered surprise*). **b** *intr.* (of an emotion) show in a person's face or gestures. **8** *intr.* make an impression on a person's mind (*did not register at all*). **9** *intr. & tr. Printing* correspond or cause to correspond exactly in position. **10** *tr.* make known formally or publicly; cause (an opinion, grievance, etc.) to be recorded or noted (*I wish to register my disapproval*). □□ **reg·is·tra·ble** *adj.* [ME & OF *registre, registre* or med.L *regestrum, registrum,* alt. of *regestum* f. LL *regesta* things recorded (as RE-, L *gerere gest-* carry)]

reg·is·tered mail *n.* mail recorded at the post office and guaranteed against loss, damage, etc., during transmission.

reg·is·tered nurse *n.* a nurse with graduate training who has passed a state certification exam and is licensed to practice nursing.

reg·is·trar /réjistraár/ *n.* **1** an official responsible for keeping a register or official records. **2** the chief administrative officer in a university. **3** *Brit.* a middle-ranking hospital doctor undergoing training as a specialist; resident. **4** (in the UK) the judicial and administrative officer of the High Court, etc. □□ **reg·is·trar·ship** *n.* [med.L *registrarius* f. *registrum* REGISTER]

reg·is·tra·tion /réjistráyshən/ *n.* **1** the act or an instance of registering; the process of being registered. **2** a certificate, etc., that attests to the registering (of a person, vehicle, etc.). [obs. F *régistration* or med.L *registratio* (as REGISTRAR)]

reg·is·try /réjistree/ *n.* (*pl.* **·tries**) **1** a place or office where registers or records are kept. **2** registration. [obs. *registery* f. med.L *registerium* (as REGISTER)]

re·gi·us pro·fes·sor /reéjeeəs/ *n. Brit.* the holder of a chair founded by a sovereign (esp. one at Oxford or Cambridge instituted by Henry VIII) or filled by Crown appointment. [L, = royal, f. *rex regis* king]

re·glaze /reéglayz/ *v. tr.* glaze (a window, etc.) again.

reg·let /réglit/ *n.* **1** *Archit.* a narrow strip separating moldings. **2** *Printing* a thin strip of wood or metal separating type. [F *réglet* dimin. of *règle* (as RULE)]

reg·nal /régnəl/ *adj.* of a reign. [AL *regnalis* (as REIGN)]

reg·nal year *n.* a year reckoned from the date or anniversary of a sovereign's accession.

reg·nant /régnənt/ *adj.* **1** reigning (*queen regnant*). **2** (of things, qualities, etc.) predominant, prevalent. [L *regnare* REIGN]

reg·o·lith /régolith/ *n. Geol.* unconsolidated solid material covering the bedrock of a planet. [erron. f. Gk *rhēgos* rug, blanket + –LITH]

re·gorge /rigáwrj/ *v.* **1** *tr.* bring up or expel again after swallowing. **2** *intr.* gush or flow back from a pit, channel, etc. [F *regorger* or RE- + GORGE]

re·grade /reégráyd/ *v. tr.* grade again or differently.

re·gress *v. & n.* ● *v.* /rigrés/ **1** *intr.* move backward, esp. (in abstract

senses) return to a former state. **2** *intr. & tr. Psychol.* return or cause to return mentally to a former stage of life, esp. through hypnosis or mental illness. ● *n.* /reégres/ **1** the act or an instance of going back. **2** reasoning from effect to cause. [ME (as n.) f. L *regressus* f. *regredi regress-* (as RE-, *gradi* step)]

re·gres·sion /rigréshən/ *n.* **1** a backward movement, esp. a return to a former state. **2** a relapse or reversion. **3** *Psychol.* a return to an earlier stage of development, esp. through hypnosis or mental illness. **4** *Statistics* a measure of the relation between the mean value of one variable (e.g., output) and corresponding values of other variables (e.g., time and cost). [L *regressio* (as REGRESS)]

re·gres·sive /rigrésiv/ *adj.* **1** regressing; characterized by regression. **2** (of a tax) proportionally greater on lower incomes. □□ **re·gres·sive·ly** *adv.* **re·gres·sive·ness** *n.*

re·gret /rigrét/ *v. & n.* ● *v. tr.* (**re·gret·ted, re·gret·ting**) **1** (often foll. by *that* + clause) feel or express sorrow or repentance or distress over (an action or loss, etc.) (*I regret that I forgot; regretted your absence*). **2** (often foll. by *to* + infin. or *that* + clause) acknowledge with sorrow or remorse (*I regret to say that you are wrong; regretted he would not be attending*). ● *n.* **1** a feeling of sorrow, repentance, disappointment, etc., over an action or loss, etc. **2** (often in *pl.*) an (esp. polite or formal) expression of disappointment or sorrow at an occurrence, inability to comply, etc. (*refused with many regrets*). □ **give** (or **send**) **one's regrets** formally decline an invitation. [ME f. OF *regreter* bewail]

re·gret·ful /rigrétfool/ *adj.* feeling or showing regret. □□ **re·gret·ful·ly** *adv.* **re·gret·ful·ness** *n.*

re·gret·ta·ble /rigrétəbəl/ *adj.* (of events or conduct) undesirable; unwelcome; deserving censure. □□ **re·gret·ta·bly** *adv.*

re·group /reégroóp/ *v. tr. & intr.* group or arrange again or differently. □□ **re·group·ment** *n.*

re·grow /reégró/ *v. intr. & tr.* grow again, esp. after an interval. □□ **re·growth** *n.*

Regt. *abbr.* Regiment.

reg·u·la·ble /régyələbəl/ *adj.* able to be regulated.

reg·u·lar /régyələr/ *adj. & n.* ● *adj.* **1** conforming to a rule or principle; systematic. **2 a** (of a structure or arrangement) harmonious; symmetrical (*regular features*). **b** (of a surface, line, etc.) smooth; level; uniform. **3** acting or done or recurring uniformly or calculably in time or manner; habitual; constant; orderly. **4** conforming to a standard of etiquette or procedure; correct; according to convention. **5** properly constituted or qualified; not defective or amateur; pursuing an occupation as one's main pursuit (*cooks as well as a regular cook; has no regular profession*). **6** *Gram.* (of a noun, verb, etc.) following the normal type of inflection. **7** *colloq.* complete; thorough; absolute (*a regular hero*). **8** *Geom.* **a** (of a figure) having all sides and all angles equal. **b** (of a solid) bounded by a number of equal figures. **9** *Eccl.* (placed before or after noun) **a** bound by religious rule. **b** belonging to a religious or monastic order (*canon regular*). **10** (of forces or troops, etc.) relating to or constituting a permanent professional body (*regular soldiers; regular police force*). **11** (of a person) defecating or menstruating at predictable times. **12** *Bot.* (of a flower) having radial symmetry. **13** *colloq.* likable; normal; reliable (esp. as *regular guy*). ● *n.* **1** a regular soldier. **2** *colloq.* a regular customer, visitor, etc. **3** *Eccl.* one of the regular clergy. **4** *colloq.* a person permanently employed. □ **keep regular hours** do the same thing, esp. going to bed and getting up, at the same time each day. □□ **reg·u·lar·i·ty** /–láritee/ *n.* **reg·u·lar·ize** *v. tr.* **reg·u·lar·i·za·tion** *n.* **reg·u·lar·ly** *adv.* [ME *reguler, regular* f. OF *reguler* f. L *regularis* f. *regula* RULE]

reg·u·lar oc·ta·he·dron *n.* an octahedron contained by equal and equilateral triangles.

reg·u·late /régyəlayt/ *v. tr.* **1** control by rule. **2** subject to restrictions. **3** adapt to requirements. **4** alter the speed of (a machine or clock) so that it may work accurately. □□ **reg·u·la·tive** /–lətiv/ *adj.* **reg·u·la·tor** *n.* **reg·u·la·to·ry** /–lətáwree/ *adj.* [LL *regulare regulat-* f. L *regula* RULE]

reg·u·la·tion /régyəláyshən/ *n.* **1** the act or an instance of regulating; the process of being regulated. **2** a prescribed rule; an authoritative direction. **3** (*attrib.*) **a** in accordance with regulations; of the correct type, etc. (*the regulation speed; a regulation tie*). **b** *colloq.* usual (*the regulation soup*).

reg·u·lus /régyələs/ *n.* (*pl.* **reg·u·lus·es** or **reg·u·li** /–lī/) *Chem.* **1** the purer or metallic part of a mineral that separates by sinking on reduction. **2** an impure metallic product formed during the smelting of various ores. □□ **reg·u·line** /–līn/ *adj.* [L, dimin. of *rex regis* king: orig. of a metallic form of antimony, so called because of its readiness to combine with gold]

re·gur·gi·tate /rigórjitayt/ *v.* **1** *tr.* bring (swallowed food) up again to the mouth. **2** *tr.* cast or pour out again (*required by the exam to regurgitate facts*). **3** *intr.* be brought up again; gush back. □□ **re·gur·gi·ta·tion** /–táyshən/ *n.* [med.L *regurgitare* (as RE-, L *gurges gurgitis* whirlpool)]

re·hab /reéhab/ *n. colloq.* rehabilitation. [abbr.]

re·ha·bil·i·tate /reéhəbílitayt/ *v. tr.* **1** restore to effectiveness or normal life by training, etc., esp. after imprisonment or illness. **2** re-

re·ha·bil·i·ta·tion /–táyshən/ *n.* **re·ha·bil·i·ta·tive** *adj.* [med.L *rehabilitare* (as RE-, HABILITATE)]

re·han·dle /re͞ehánd'l/ *v.tr.* **1** handle again. **2** give a new form or arrangement to.

re·hang /re͞eháng/ *v.tr.* (*past* and *past part.* **re·hung**) hang (esp. a picture or a curtain) again or differently.

re·hash *v. & n.* ● *v.tr.* /re͞ehásh/ put (old material) into a new form without significant change or improvement. ● *n.* /re͞ehash/ **1** material rehashed. **2** the act or an instance of rehashing.

re·hear /re͞ehe͞er/ *v.tr.* (*past* and *past part.* **re·heard** /re͞ehérd/) hear again.

re·hears·al /rihə́rsəl/ *n.* **1** the act or an instance of rehearsing. **2** a trial performance or practice of a play, recital, etc.

re·hearse /rihə́rs/ *v.* **1** *tr.* practice (a play, recital, etc.) for later public performance. **2** *intr.* hold a rehearsal. **3** *tr.* train (a person) by rehearsal. **4** *tr.* recite or say over. **5** *tr.* give a list of; enumerate. □□ **re·hears·er** *n.* [ME f. AF *rehearser*, OF *reherc(i)er*, perh. formed as RE- + *hercer* to harrow f. *herse* harrow: see HEARSE]

re·heat *v. & n.* ● *v.tr.* /re͞ehe͞et/ heat again. ● *n.* /re͞ehe͞et/ the process of using the hot exhaust to burn extra fuel in a jet engine and produce extra power. □□ **re·heat·er** *n.*

re·heel /re͞ehe͞el/ *v.tr.* fit (a shoe, etc.) with a new heel.

re·ho·bo·am /re͞ehəbóəm/ *n.* a wine bottle of about six times the standard size. [*Rehoboam* King of Israel (1 Kings 11–14)]

re·house /re͞ehówz/ *v.tr.* provide with new housing.

re·hung *past* and *past part.* of REHANG.

re·hy·drate /re͞ehīdráyt/ *v.* **1** *intr.* absorb water again after dehydration. **2** *tr.* add water to (esp. food) again to restore to a palatable state. □□ **re·hy·drat·a·ble** *adj.* **re·hy·dra·tion** /–dráyshən/ *n.*

Reich /rīkh/ *n.* the former German state, esp. the Third Reich. [G, = empire]

Reichs·tag /rīkhstaag/ *n. hist.* **1** the main legislature of the German state under the Second and Third Reichs. **2** the building in which this met. [G]

re·i·fy /re͞eifī/ *v.tr.* (·**fies**, ·**fied**) convert (a person, abstraction, etc.) into a thing; materialize. □□ **re·i·fi·ca·tion** /–fikáyshən/ *n.* [L *res* thing + –FY]

reign /rayn/ *v. & n.* ● *v.intr.* **1** hold royal office; be king or queen. **2** have power or predominance; prevail; hold sway (*confusion reigns*). **3** (as **reigning** *adj.*) (of a winner, champion, etc.) currently holding the title, etc. ● *n.* **1** sovereignty, rule. **2** the period during which a sovereign rules. [ME f. OF *reigne* kingdom f. L *regnare* f. *rex regis* king]

re·ig·nite /re͞eignít/ *v.tr. & intr.* ignite again.

reign of ter·ror *n.* a period of remorseless repression or bloodshed, esp. a period of the French Revolution 1793–94.

re·im·burse /re͞eimbə́rs/ *v.tr.* **1** repay (a person who has expended money). **2** repay (a person's expenses). □□ **re·im·burs·a·ble** *adj.* **re·im·burse·ment** *n.* **re·im·burs·er** *n.* [RE- + obs. *imburse* put in a purse f. med.L *imbursare* (as IM-, PURSE)]

re·im·port *v. & n.* ● *v.tr.* /re͞eimpáwrt/ import (goods processed from exported materials). ● *n.* /re͞e-ímpawrt/ **1** the act or an instance of reimporting. **2** a reimported item. □□ **re·im·por·ta·tion** *n.*

re·im·pose /re͞eimpóz/ *v.tr.* impose again, esp. after a lapse. □□ **re·im·po·si·tion** /–pəzíshən/ *n.*

rein /rayn/ *n. & v.* ● *n.* (in *sing.* or *pl.*) **1** a long narrow strap with each end attached to the bit, used to guide or check a horse, etc., in riding or driving. **2** a similar device used to restrain a young child. **3** (a means of) control or guidance; a curb; a restraint. ● *v.tr.* **1** check or manage with reins. **2** (foll. by *up, back*) pull up or back with reins. **3** (foll. by *in*) hold in as with reins; restrain. **4** govern; restrain; control. □ **draw rein 1** stop one's horse. **2** pull up. **3** abandon an effort. **give free rein to** remove constraints from; allow full scope to. **keep a tight rein on** allow little freedom to. □□ **rein·less** *adj.* [ME f. OF *rene, reigne*, earlier *resne*, ult. f. L *retinēre* RETAIN]

re·in·car·na·tion /re͞einkaarnáyshən/ *n.* (in some beliefs) the rebirth of a soul in a new body. □□ **re·in·car·nate** /–káarnayt/ *v.tr.* **re·in·car·nate** /–káarnət/ *adj.*

re·in·cor·po·rate /re͞einkáwrpərayt/ *v.tr.* incorporate afresh. □□ **re·in·cor·po·ra·tion** /–ráyshən/ *n.*

rein·deer /ráyndeer/ *n.* (*pl.* same or **rein·deers**) a subarctic deer, *Rangifer tarandus*, of which both sexes have large antlers, used domestically for drawing sleds and as a source of milk, flesh, and hide. [ME f. ON *hreindȳri* f. *hreinn* reindeer + *dȳr* DEER]

rein·deer moss *n.* an arctic lichen, *Cladonia rangiferina*, with short branched stems growing in clumps.

re·in·fect /re͞einfékt/ *v.tr.* infect again. □□ **re·in·fec·tion** /re͞einfékshən/ *n.*

re·in·force /re͞einfáwrs/ *v.tr.* strengthen or support, esp. with additional personnel or material or by an increase of numbers or quantity or size, etc. [earlier *renforce* f. F *renforcer*]

re·in·forced con·crete *n.* concrete with metal bars or wire, etc., embedded to increase its tensile strength.

re·in·force·ment /re͞einfáwrsmənt/ *n.* **1** the act or an instance of reinforcing; the process of being reinforced. **2** a thing that reinforces. **3** (in *pl.*) reinforcing personnel or equipment, etc.

re·in·sert /re͞einsə́rt/ *v.tr.* insert again. □□ **re·in·ser·tion** /–sérshən/ *n.*

re·in·state /re͞einstáyt/ *v.tr.* **1** replace in a former position. **2** restore (a person, etc.) to former privileges. □□ **re·in·state·ment** *n.*

re·in·sure /re͞einsho͞or/ *v.tr. & intr.* insure again (esp. of an insurer securing the risk by transferring some or all of it to another insurer). □□ **re·in·sur·ance** *n.* **re·in·sur·er** *n.*

re·in·te·grate /re͞e-íntigrayt/ *v.tr.* **1** esp. *Brit.* = REDINTEGRATE. **2** integrate back into society. □□ **re·in·te·gra·tion** /–gráyshən/ *n.*

re·in·ter /re͞eintə́r/ *v.tr.* inter (a corpse) again. □□ **re·in·ter·ment** *n.*

re·in·ter·pret /re͞eintə́rprit/ *v.tr.* interpret again or differently. □□ **re·in·ter·pre·ta·tion** *n.*

re·in·tro·duce /re͞eintrado͞os, –dyo͞os/ *v.tr.* introduce again. □□ **re·in·tro·duc·tion** /–dúkshən/ *n.*

re·in·vest /re͞einvést/ *v.tr.* invest again (esp. money in other property, etc.). □□ **re·in·vest·ment** *n.*

re·in·vig·or·ate /re͞einvígərayt/ *v.tr.* impart fresh vigor to. □□ **re·in·vig·or·a·tion** /–ráyshən/ *n.*

re·is·sue *v. & n.* ● *v.tr.* /re͞e-ísho͞o/ (**re·is·sues, re·is·sued, re·is·su·ing**) issue again or in a different form. ● *n.* /re͞e-ísho͞o/ a new issue, esp. of a previously published book.

REIT /re͞et/ *abbr.* real estate investment trust.

re·it·er·ate /re͞e-ítərayt/ *v.tr.* say or do again or repeatedly. □□ **re·it·er·a·tion** /–ráyshən/ *n.* **re·it·er·a·tive** /–raytiv, –rətiv/ *adj.* [L *reiterare* (as RE-, ITERATE)]

reive /re͞ev/ *v.intr.* esp. *Sc.* make raids; plunder. □□ **reiv·er** *n.* [var. of REAVE]

re·ject *v. & n.* ● *v.tr.* /rijékt/ **1** put aside or send back as not to be used or done or complied with, etc. **2** refuse to accept or believe in. **3** rebuff or snub (a person). **4** (of a body or digestive system) cast up again; vomit; evacuate. **5** *Med.* show an immune response to (a transplanted organ or tissue) so that it fails to survive. ● *n.* /re͞ejekt/ a thing or person rejected as unfit or below standard. □□ **re·ject·a·ble** /rijéktəbəl/ *adj.* **re·ject·er** /rijéktər/ *n.* (also **re·jec·tor**) **re·jec·tion** /–jékshən/ *n.* **re·jec·tive** *adj.* [ME f. L *rejicere* reject- (as RE-, *jacere* throw)]

re·jig·ger /re͞ejígər/ *v.tr.* rearrange or alter, esp. in an unethical way.

re·joice /rijóys/ *v.* **1** *intr.* feel great joy. **2** *intr.* (foll. by *that* + clause or *to* + infin.) be glad. **3** *intr.* (foll. by *in, at*) take delight. **4** *intr.* celebrate some event. **5** *tr.* cause joy to. □□ **re·joic·er** *n.* **re·joic·ing·ly** *adv.* [ME f. OF *rejoir rejoiss-* (as RE-, JOY)]

re·join[1] /re͞ejóyn/ *v.* **1** *tr. & intr.* join together again; reunite. **2** *tr.* join (a companion, etc.) again.

re·join[2] /rijóyn/ *v.* **1** *tr.* say in answer; retort. **2** *intr. Law* reply to a charge or pleading in a lawsuit. [ME f. OF *rejoindre rejoign-* (as RE-, JOIN)]

re·join·der /rijóyndər/ *n.* **1** what is said in reply. **2** a retort. **3** *Law* a reply by rejoining. [AF *rejoinder* (unrecorded: as REJOIN[2])]

re·ju·ve·nate /rijo͞ovinayt/ *v.tr.* make young or as if young again. □□ **re·ju·ve·na·tion** /–náyshən/ *n.* **re·ju·ve·na·tor** *n.* [RE- + L *juvenis* young]

re·ju·ve·nesce /rijo͞ovinés/ *v.* **1** *intr.* become young again. **2** *Biol.* **a** *intr.* (of cells) gain fresh vitality. **b** *tr.* impart fresh vitality to (cells). □□ **re·ju·ve·nes·cent** *adj.* **re·ju·ve·nes·cence** *n.* [LL *rejuvenescere* (as RE-, L *juvenis* young)]

re·kin·dle /re͞ekínd'l/ *v.tr. & intr.* kindle again.

-rel /rəl/ *suffix* with diminutive or derogatory force (*cockerel; scoundrel*). [from or after OF –*erel(le*)]

rel. *abbr.* **1** relating. **2** relative. **3** released. **4** religion. **5** religious.

re·la·bel /re͞eláybəl/ *v.tr.* (**re·la·beled, re·la·bel·ing;** esp. *Brit.* **re·la·belled, re·la·bel·ling**) label (esp. a commodity) again or differently.

re·lapse /riláps/ *v. & n.* ● *v.intr.* (usu. foll. by *into*) fall back or sink again (into a worse state after an improvement). ● *n.* (also /re͞elaps/) the act or an instance of relapsing, esp. a deterioration in a patient's condition after a partial recovery. □□ **re·laps·er** *n.* [L *relabi relaps-* (as RE-, *labi* slip)]

re·laps·ing fe·ver *n.* a bacterial infectious disease with recurrent periods of fever.

re·late /riláyt/ *v.* **1** *tr.* narrate or recount (incidents, a story, etc.). **2** *tr.* (in *passive;* often foll. by *to*) be connected by blood or marriage. **3** *tr.* (usu. foll. by *to, with*) bring into relation (with one another); establish a connection between (*cannot relate your opinion to my own experience*). **4** *intr.* (foll. by *to*) have reference to; concern (*see only what relates to themselves*). **5** *intr.* (foll. by *to*) **a** bring oneself into relation to; associate with. **b** feel emotionally or sympathetically involved or connected; respond (*they relate well to one another*). □□ **re·lat·a·ble** *adj.* [L *referre relat-* bring back: see REFER]

re·lat·ed /riláytid/ *adj.* **1** connected by blood or marriage. **2** having (mutual) relation; associated; connected. □□ **re·lat·ed·ness** *n.*

re·la·ter /riláytər/ *n.* (also **re·la·tor**) a person who relates something, esp. a story; a narrator.

re•la•tion /riláyshən/ n. **1 a** what one person or thing has to do with another. **b** the way in which one person stands or is related to another. **c** the existence or effect of a connection, correspondence, contrast, or feeling prevailing between persons or things, esp. when qualified in some way (*bears no relation to the facts; enjoyed good relations for many years*). **2** a relative; a kinsman or kinswoman. **3** (in *pl.*) **a** (foll. by *with*) dealings (with others). **b** sexual intercourse. **4** = RELATIONSHIP. **5 a** narration (*his relation of the events*). **b** a narrative. □ **in relation to** as regards. [ME f. OF *relation* or L *relatio* (as RELATE)]

re•la•tion•al /riláyshənəl/ adj. **1** of, belonging to, or characterized by relation. **2** having relation.

re•la•tion•al da•ta•base n. *Computing* a database structured to recognize the relation of stored items of information.

re•la•tion•ship /riláyshənship/ n. **1** the fact or state of being related. **2** *colloq.* **a** a connection or association (*enjoyed a good working relationship*). **b** an emotional (esp. sexual) association between two people. **3** a condition or character due to being related. **4** kinship.

rel•a•tive /rélətiv/ adj. & n. ● adj. **1** considered or having significance in relation to something else (*relative velocity*). **2** (also foll. by *to*) existing or quantifiable only in terms of individual perception or consideration; not absolute nor independent (*truth is relative to your perspective; it's all relative, though, isn't it?*). **3** (foll. by *to*) proportioned to (something else) (*growth is relative to input*). **4** implying comparison or contextual relation (*"heat" is a relative word*). **5** comparative; compared one with another (*their relative advantages*). **6** having mutual relations; corresponding in some way; related to each other. **7** (foll. by *to*) having reference or relating (*the facts relative to the issue*). **8** involving a different but corresponding idea (*the concepts of husband and wife are relative to each other*). **9** *Gram.* **a** (of a word, esp. a pronoun) referring to an expressed or implied antecedent and attaching a subordinate clause to it, e.g., *which, who*. **b** (of a clause) attached to an antecedent by a relative word. **10** *Mus.* (of major and minor keys) having the same key signature. **11** (of a service rank) corresponding in grade to another in a different service. **12** pertinent; relevant; related to the subject (*need more relative proof*). ● n. **1** a person connected by blood or marriage. **2** a species related to another by common origin (*the apes, the human species' closest relatives*). **3** *Gram.* a relative word, esp. a pronoun. **4** *Philos.* a relative thing or term. □□ **rel•a•tiv•al** /–tívəl/ adj. (in sense 3 of n.). **rel•a•tive•ly** adv. **rel•a•tive•ness** n. [ME f. OF *relatif –ive* or LL *relativus* having reference or relation (as RELATE)]

SPELLING TIP relative

To remember the *a* in the middle of *relative*, use the mnemonic: "*A relative* is someone to whom you can *relate*."

---

rel•a•tive a•tom•ic mass esp. *Brit.* = ATOMIC WEIGHT.

rel•a•tive den•si•ty = SPECIFIC GRAVITY.

rel•a•tive hu•mid•i•ty n. the proportion of moisture to the value for saturation at the same temperature.

rel•a•tive mo•lec•u•lar mass esp. *Brit.* = MOLECULAR WEIGHT.

rel•a•tiv•ism /rélətivizəm/ n. the doctrine that knowledge is relative, not absolute. □□ **rel•a•tiv•ist** n.

rel•a•tiv•is•tic /rélətivístik/ adj. *Physics* (of phenomena, etc.) accurately described only by the theory of relativity. □□ **rel•a•tiv•is•ti•cal•ly** adv.

rel•a•tiv•i•ty /rélətívitee/ n. **1** the fact or state of being relative. **2** *Physics* **a** (**special theory of relativity** or **special relativity**) a theory based on the principle that all motion is relative and that light has its constant velocity, regarding space-time as a four-dimensional continuum, and modifying previous conceptions of geometry. **b** (**general theory of relativity** or **general relativity**) a theory extending this to gravitation and accelerated motion.

re•la•tor /riláytər/ n. **1** var. of RELATER. **2** *Law* a person who brings a public lawsuit, esp. regarding the abuse of an office or franchise. [L (as RELATE)]

re•lax /riláks/ v. **1 a** tr. & intr. (of the body, a muscle, etc.) make or become less stiff or rigid (*his frown relaxed into a smile*). **b** tr. & intr. make or become loose or slack; diminish in force or tension (*relaxed my grip*). **c** tr. & intr. (also as int.) make or become less tense or anxious. **2** tr. & intr. make or become less formal or strict (*rules were relaxed*). **3** tr. reduce or abate (one's attention, efforts, etc.). **4** intr. cease work or effort. **5** tr. (as **relaxed** adj.) at ease; unperturbed. □□ **re•lax•ed•ly** adv. **re•lax•ed•ness** n. **re•lax•er** n. [ME f. L *relaxare* (as RE-, LAX)]

re•lax•ant /ríláksənt/ n. & adj. ● n. a drug, etc., that relaxes and reduces tension. ● adj. causing relaxation.

re•lax•a•tion /réeláksáyshən/ n. **1** the act of relaxing or state of being relaxed. **2** recreation or rest, esp. after a period of work. **3** a partial remission or relaxing of a penalty, duty, etc. **4** a lessening of severity, precision, etc. **5** *Physics* the restoration of equilibrium following disturbance. [L *relaxatio* (as RELAX)]

re•lay[1] /réelay/ n. & v. ● n. **1** a fresh set of people or horses substi-

tuted for tired ones. **2** a gang of workers, supply of material, etc., deployed on the same basis (*operated in relays*). **3** = RELAY RACE. **4 a** device activating changes in an electric circuit, etc., in response to other changes affecting itself. **5 a** a device to receive, reinforce, and transmit a telegraph message, a broadcast program, etc. **b** a relayed message or transmission. ● v.tr. (also /rilay/) **1** receive (a message, broadcast, etc.) and transmit it to others. **2 a** arrange in relays. **b** provide with or replace by relays. [ME f. OF *relai* (n.), *relayer* (v.) (as RE-, *laier* ult. f. L *laxare*): cf. RELAX]

re•lay[2] /réeláy/ v.tr. (*past* and *past part.* **re•laid**) lay again or differently.

re•lay race n. a race between teams of which each member in turn covers part of the distance.

re•learn /réelórn/ v.tr. learn again.

re•lease /rilées/ v. & n. ● v.tr. **1** (often foll. by *from*) set free; liberate; unfasten. **2** allow to move from a fixed position. **3 a** make (information, a recording, etc.) publicly or generally available. **b** issue (a film, etc.) for general exhibition. **4** *Law* **a** remit (a debt). **b** surrender (a right). **c** make over (property or money) to another. ● n. **1** deliverance or liberation from a restriction, duty, or difficulty. **2** a handle or catch that releases part of a mechanism. **3** a document or item of information made available for publication (*press release*). **4 a** a film or record, etc., that is released. **b** the act or an instance of releasing or the process of being released in this way. **5** *Law* **a** the act of releasing (property, money, or a right) to another. **b** a document effecting this. □□ **re•leas•a•ble** adj. **re•leas•ee** /–seé/ n. (in sense 4 of v.). **re•leas•er** n. **re•leas•or** n. (in sense 4 of v.). [ME f. OF *reles* (n.), *relesser* (v.), *relaiss(i)er* f. L *relaxare*: see RELAX]

rel•e•gate /réligayt/ v.tr. **1** consign or dismiss to an inferior or less important position; demote. **2** transfer (a sports team) to a lower division of a league, etc. **3** banish or send into exile. **4** (foll. by *to*) **a** transfer (a matter) for decision or implementation. **b** refer (a person) for information. □□ **rel•e•ga•ble** /–ligəbəl/ adj. **rel•e•ga•tion** /–gáyshən/ n. [L *relegare relegat-* (as RE-, *legare* send)]

re•lent /rilént/ v.intr. **1** abandon a harsh intention. **2** yield to compassion. **3** relax one's severity; become less stern. [ME f. med.L *relentare* (unrecorded), formed as RE- + L *lentāre* bend f. *lentus* flexible]

re•lent•less /riléntlis/ adj. **1** unrelenting; insistent and uncompromising. **2** continuous; oppressively constant (*the pressure was relentless*). □□ **re•lent•less•ly** adv. **re•lent•less•ness** n.

re•let /réelét/ v.tr. (•let•ting; *past* and *past part.* •let) esp. *Brit.* let (a property) for a further period or to a new tenant.

rel•e•vant /rélivənt/ adj. (often foll. by *to*) bearing on or having reference to the matter in hand. □□ **rel•e•vance** n. **rel•e•van•cy** n. **rel•e•vant•ly** adv. [med.L *relevans*, part. of L *relevare* RELIEVE]

re•li•a•ble /rilíəbəl/ adj. **1** that may be relied on. **2** of sound and consistent character or quality. □□ **re•li•a•bil•i•ty** /–bílitee/ n. **re•li•a•ble•ness** n. **re•li•a•bly** adv.

re•li•ance /rilíəns/ n. **1** (foll. by *in, on*) trust, confidence (*put full reliance in you*). **2** a thing relied upon. □□ **re•li•ant** adj.

rel•ic /rélik/ n. **1** an object interesting because of its age or association. **2** a part of a deceased holy person's body or belongings kept as an object of reverence. **3** a surviving custom or belief, etc., from a past age. **4** a memento or souvenir. **5** (in *pl.*) what has survived destruction or wasting or use. **6** (in *pl.*) the dead body or remains of a person. [ME *relike, relique*, etc. f. OF *relique* f. L *reliquiae*: see RELIQUIAE]

rel•ict /rélikt/ n. **1 a** a geological or other object surviving in its primitive form. **b** an animal or plant known to have existed in the same form in previous geological ages. **2** (foll. by *of*) *archaic* a widow. [L *relinquere relict-* leave behind (as RE-, *linquere* leave): sense 2 f. OF *relicte* f. L *relicta*]

re•lief /rilééf/ n. **1 a** the alleviation of or deliverance from pain, distress, anxiety, etc. **b** the feeling accompanying such deliverance. **2** a feature, etc., that diversifies monotony or relaxes tension. **3** assistance (esp. financial) given to those in special need or difficulty (*rent relief*). **4 a** the replacing of a person or persons on duty by another or others. **b** a person or persons replacing others in this way. **5** *Brit.* (usu. *attrib.*) a thing supplementing another in some service, esp. an extra vehicle providing public transport at peak times. **6 a** a method of molding or carving or stamping in which the design stands out from the surface, with projections proportioned and more (**high relief**) or less (**low** or **bas-relief**) closely approximating those of the objects depicted. **b** a piece of sculpture, etc., in relief. **c** a representation of relief given by an arrangement of line or color or shading. **7** vividness; distinctness (*brings the facts out in sharp relief*). **8** (foll. by *of*) the reinforcement (esp. the raising of a siege) of a place. **9** esp. *Law* the redress of a hardship or grievance. [ME f AF *relef*, OF *relief* (in sense 6 F *relief* f. It. *rilievo*) f. *relever*: see RELIEVE]

re•lief map n. **1** a map indicating hills and valleys by shading, etc., rather than by contour lines alone. **2** a map model showing elevations and depressions, usu. on an exaggerated relative scale.

re•lief print•ing = LETTERPRESS 1.

re•lieve /riléév/ v.tr. **1** bring or provide aid or assistance to. **2** alleviate or reduce (pain, suffering, etc.). **3** mitigate the tedium or monotony of. **4** bring military support for (a besieged place). **5** release (a person) from a duty by acting as or providing a substitute. **6** (foll. by *of*) take (a burden or responsibility) away from (a person). **7** bring into relief; cause to appear solid or detached. □ **relieve one's feelings** *Brit.* use strong language or vigorous behavior when annoyed. **relieve oneself** urinate or defecate. □□ **re·liev·a·ble** *adj.* **re·liev·er** *n.* [ME f. OF relever f. L relevare (as RE-, *levis* light)]

re·lieved /rileevd/ *predic.adj.* freed from anxiety or distress (*am very relieved to hear it*). □□ **re·liev·ed·ly** *adv.*

re·lie·vo /rileevō/ *n.* (*pl.* **·vos**) (also **ri·lie·vo** /reelyáyvō/ *pl.* **-vi** /–vee/) = RELIEF 6. [It. *rilievo* RELIEF 6]

re·light /reelít/ *v.tr.* light (a fire, etc.) again.

religio- /rilijeeō/ *comb. form* **1** religion. **2** religious.

re·li·gion /rilíjən/ *n.* **1** the belief in a superhuman controlling power, esp. in a personal God or gods entitled to obedience and worship. **2** the expression of this in worship. **3** a particular system of faith and worship. **4** life under monastic vows (*the way of religion*). **5** a thing that one is devoted to (*football is their religion*). □□ **re·li·gion·less** *adj.* [ME f. AF *religiun*, OF *religion* f. L *religio –onis* obligation, bond, reverence]

re·li·gion·ism /rilíjənizəm/ *n.* excessive religious zeal. □□ **re·li·gion·ist** *n.*

re·li·gi·ose /rilíjeeōs/ *adj.* excessively religious. [L *religiosus* (as RELIGIOUS)]

re·li·gi·os·i·ty /rilíjeeósitee/ *n.* the condition of being religious or religiose. [ME f. L *religiositas* (as RELIGIOUS)]

re·li·gious /rilíjəs/ *adj. & n.* ● *adj.* **1** devoted to religion; pious; devout. **2** of or concerned with religion. **3** of or belonging to a monastic order. **4** scrupulous; conscientious (*a religious attention to detail*). ● *n.* (*pl.* same) a person bound by monastic vows. □□ **re·li·gious·ly** *adv.* **re·li·gious·ness** *n.* [ME f. AF *religius*, OF *religious* f. L *religiosus* (as RELIGION)]

re·line /reelín/ *v.tr.* renew the lining of (a garment, etc.).

re·lin·quish /rilíngkwish/ *v.tr.* **1** surrender or resign (a right or possession). **2** give up or cease from (a habit, plan, belief, etc.). **3** relax hold of (an object held). □□ **re·lin·quish·ment** *n.* [ME f. OF *relinquir* f. L *relinquere* (as RE-, *linquere* leave)]

SYNONYM TIP relinquish

ABANDON, CEDE, SURRENDER, WAIVE, YIELD Of all these verbs meaning to let go or give up, **relinquish** is the most general. It can imply anything from simply releasing one's grasp (*she relinquished the wheel*) to giving up control or possession reluctantly (*after the defeat, he was forced to relinquish his command*). **Surrender** also implies giving up, but usually after a struggle or show of resistance (*the villagers were forced to surrender to the guerrillas*). **Yield** is a milder synonym for *surrender*, implying some concession, respect, or even affection on the part of the person who is surrendering (*she yielded to her mother's wishes and stayed home*). **Waive** also suggests a concession, but it seldom implies force or necessity. It means to give up voluntarily a right or claim to something (*she waived her right to have a lawyer present*). To **cede** is to give up by legal transfer or according to the terms of a treaty (*the French ceded the territory that is now Louisiana*). If one *relinquishes* something finally and completely, often because of weariness or discouragement, the correct word is **abandon** (*they finally abandoned all hope of being rescued*).

---

rel·i·quar·y /rélikweree/ *n.* (*pl.* **·ies**) esp. *Relig.* a receptacle for relics. [F *reliquaire* (as RELIC)]

re·liq·ui·ae /rilíkweeï, -ee/ *n.pl.* **1** remains. **2** *Geol.* fossil remains of animals or plants. [L f. *reliquus* remaining, formed as RE- + *linquere* liq- leave]

rel·ish /rélish/ *n. & v.* ● *n.* **1** (often foll. by *for*) **a** great liking or enjoyment. **b** keen or pleasurable longing (*had no relish for traveling*). **2 a** an appetizing flavor. **b** an attractive quality (*fishing loses its relish in winter*). **3** a condiment eaten with plainer food to add flavor, as chopped sweet pickle, etc. **4** (foll. by *of*) a distinctive taste or tinge. ● *v.tr.* **1 a** get pleasure out of; enjoy greatly. **b** look forward to; anticipate with pleasure (*did not relish what lay before her*). **2** add relish to. □□ **rel·ish·a·ble** *adj.*

WORD HISTORY relish

Middle English: alteration of obsolete *reles*, from Old French *reles* 'remainder,' from *relaisser* 'to release.' The early noun sense was 'odor, taste' giving rise to 'appetizing flavor, piquant taste' (mid-17th century), and hence sense 3 (late 18th century).

---

re·live /reelív/ *v.tr.* live (an experience, etc.) over again, esp. in the imagination.

re·load /reelṓd/ *v.tr.* (also *absol.*) load (esp. a gun or a camera, etc.) again.

re·lo·cate /reelṓkayt/ *v.* **1** *tr.* locate in a new place. **2** *tr. & intr.* move to a new place (esp. to live or work). □□ **re·lo·ca·tion** /–káyshən/ *n.*

re·luc·tant /rilúktənt/ *adj.* (often foll. by *to* + infin.) unwilling or dis-

inclined (*most reluctant to agree*). □□ **re·luc·tance** *n.* **re·luc·tant·ly** *adv.* [L *reluctari* (as RE-, *luctari* struggle)]

re·ly /rilí/ *v.intr.* (**·lies, ·lied**) (foll. by *on, upon*) **1** depend on with confidence or assurance (*am relying on your judgment*). **2** be dependent on (*relies on her for everything*). [ME (earlier senses 'rally, be a vassal of') f. OF *relier* bind together f. L *religare* (as RE-, *ligare* bind)]

REM /rem/ *abbr.* rapid eye movement.

rem /rem/ *n.* (*pl.* same) a unit of effective absorbed dose of ionizing radiation in human tissue, equivalent to one roentgen of X rays. [roentgen equivalent *man*]

re·made *past* and *past part.* of REMAKE.

re·main /rimáyn/ *v.intr.* **1 a** be left over after others or other parts have been removed or used or dealt with. **b** (of a period of time) be still to elapse. **2** be in the same place or condition during further time; continue to exist or stay; be left behind (*remained at home; it will remain cold*). **3** (foll. by *compl.*) continue to be (*remained calm; remains president*). **4** (as **remaining** *adj.*) left behind; not having been used or dealt with. [ME f. OF *remain-* stressed stem of *remanoir* or f. OF *remaindre* ult. f. L *remanēre* (as RE-, *manēre* stay)]

re·main·der /rimáyndər/ *n. & v.* ● *n.* **1** a part remaining or left over. **2** remaining persons or things. **3** a number left after division or subtraction. **4** the copies of a book left unsold when demand has fallen. **5** *Law* an interest in an estate that becomes effective in possession only when a prior interest (devised at the same time) ends. ● *v.tr.* dispose of (a remainder of books) at a reduced price. [ME (in sense 5) f. AF, = OF *remaindre*: see REMAIN]

re·mains /rimáynz/ *n.pl.* **1** what remains after other parts have been removed or used, etc. **2 a** traces of former animal or plant life (*fossil remains*). **b** relics of antiquity, esp. of buildings (*Roman remains*). **3** a person's body after death. **4** an author's (esp. unpublished) works left after death.

re·make *v. & n.* ● *v.tr.* /reemáyk/ (*past* and *past part.* **re·made**) make again or differently. ● *n.* /reemayk/ a thing that has been remade, esp. a movie.

re·man /reemán/ *v.tr.* (**re·manned, re·man·ning**) **1** equip (troops, etc.) with new personnel. **2** make courageous again.

re·mand /rimánd/ *v. & n.* ● *v.tr.* **1** return (a prisoner) to custody, esp. to allow further inquiries to be made. **2** return (a case) to a lower court for reconsideration. ● *n.* a recommittal to custody. □ **on remand** in custody pending trial. [ME f. LL *remandare* (as RE-, *mandare* commit)]

rem·a·nent /rémənənt/ *adj.* **1** remaining; residual. **2** (of magnetism) remaining after the magnetizing field has been removed. □□ **rem·a·nence** *n.* [ME f. L *remanēre* REMAIN]

re·mark /rimaárk/ *v. & n.* ● *v.* **1** *tr.* (often foll. by *that* + clause) **a** say by way of comment. **b** take notice of; regard with attention. **2** *intr.* (usu. foll. by *on, upon*) make a comment. ● *n.* **1** a written or spoken comment; anything said. **2 a** the act of noticing or observing (*worthy of remark*). **b** the act of commenting (*let it pass without remark*). [F *remarque, remarquer* (as RE-, MARK[1])]

re·mark·a·ble /rimaárkəbəl/ *adj.* **1** worth notice; exceptional; extraordinary. **2** striking; conspicuous. □□ **re·mark·a·ble·ness** *n.* **re·mark·a·bly** *adv.* [F *remarquable* (as REMARK)]

re·mar·ry /reemáree/ *v.intr. & tr.* (**·ries, ·ried**) marry again. □□ **re·mar·riage** *n.*

re·mas·ter /reemástər/ *v.tr.* make a new master of (a recording), esp. to improve the sound quality.

re·match /reemach/ *n.* a return match or game.

re·meas·ure /reeméezhər/ *v.tr.* measure again. □□ **re·meas·ure·ment** *n.*

re·me·di·al /rimeédeeəl/ *adj.* **1** affording or intended as a remedy (*remedial therapy*). **2** (of teaching) for those in need of improvement in a particular discipline (*remedial math; remedial reading*). □□ **re·me·di·al·ly** *adv.* [LL *remedialis* f. L *remedium* (as REMEDY)]

rem·e·dy /rémidee/ *n. & v.* ● *n.* (*pl.* **·dies**) (often foll. by *for, against*) **1** a medicine or treatment (for a disease, etc.). **2** a means of counteracting or removing anything undesirable. **3** redress; legal or other reparation. **4** the margin within which coins as minted may differ from the standard fineness and weight. ● *v.tr.* (**·dies, ·died**) **1** rectify; make good. **2** heal; cure (a person, diseased part, etc.) □□ **re·me·di·a·ble** /rimeédeeəbəl/ *adj.* [ME f. AF *remedie*, OF *remede* or L *remedium* (as RE-, *medēri* heal)]

re·mem·ber /rimémbər/ *v.tr.* **1** keep in the memory; not forget. **2 a** (also *absol.*) bring back into one's thoughts, call to mind (knowledge or experience, etc.). **b** (often foll. by *to* + infin. or *that* + clause) have in mind (a duty, commitment, etc.) (*will you remember to lock the door?*). **3** think of or acknowledge (a person) in some connection, esp. in making a gift, etc. **4** (foll. by *to*) convey greetings from (one person) to (another) (*remember me to your mother*). **5** mention (in prayer). □ **remember oneself** recover one's manners or intentions after a lapse. □□ **re·mem·ber·er** *n.* [ME f. OF *remembrer* f. LL *rememorari* (as RE-, L *memor* mindful)]

re·mem·brance /rimémbrəns/ n. **1** the act of remembering or process of being remembered. **2** a memory or recollection. **3** a keepsake or souvenir. **4** (in pl.) greetings conveyed through a third person. [ME f. OF (as REMEMBER)]

Re·mem·brance Day n. **1** Brit. = REMEMBRANCE SUNDAY. **2** (in Canada) Nov. 11, observed in memory of those who died in World Wars I and II; Armistice Day.

Re·mem·brance Sun·day n. (in the UK) the Remembrance Day holiday, observed on the Sunday nearest Nov. 11.

re·mex /réemeks/ n. (pl. **rem·i·ges** /rémijeez/) a primary or secondary feather in a bird's wing. [L, = rower, f. remus oar]

re·mind /rimínd/ v.tr. **1** (foll. by of) cause (a person) to remember or think of. **2** (foll. by to + infin. or that + clause) cause (a person) to remember (a commitment, etc.) (remind them to pay their bills).

re·mind·er /rimíndər/ n. **1 a** a thing that reminds, esp. a letter or bill. **b** a means of reminding; an aide-mémoire. **2** (often foll. by of) a memento or souvenir.

re·mind·ful /rimíndfŏŏl/ adj. (often foll. by of) acting as a reminder; reviving the memory.

rem·i·nisce /réminís/ v.intr. (often foll. by about) indulge in reminiscence. □□ **rem·i·nis·cer** n. [back-form. f. REMINISCENCE]

rem·i·nis·cence /réminísəns/ n. **1** the act of remembering things past; the recovery of knowledge by mental effort. **2 a** a past fact or experience that is remembered. **b** the process of narrating this. **3** (in pl.) a collection in literary form of incidents and experiences that a person remembers. **4** Philos. (esp. in Platonism) the theory of the recovery of things known to the soul in previous existences. **5** a characteristic of one thing reminding or suggestive of another. □□ **rem·i·nis·cen·tial** /–nisénshəl/ adj. [LL reminiscentia f. L reminisci remember]

rem·i·nis·cent /réminísənt/ adj. **1** (foll. by of) tending to remind one of or suggest. **2** concerned with reminiscence. **3** (of a person) given to reminiscing. □□ **rem·i·nis·cent·ly** adv.

re·mise /rimeéz/ v. & n. ● v.intr. **1** Law surrender or make over (a right or property). **2** Fencing make a remise. ● n. Fencing a second thrust made after the first has failed. [F f. remis, remise past part. of remettre put back: cf. REMIT]

re·miss /rimís/ adj. careless of duty; lax; negligent. □□ **re·miss·ly** adv. **re·miss·ness** n. [ME f. L remissus past part. of remittere slacken: see REMIT]

re·mis·si·ble /rimísibəl/ adj. that may be remitted. [F rémissible or LL remissibilis (as REMIT)]

re·mis·sion /rimíshən/ n. **1** (often foll. by of) forgiveness (of sins, etc.). **2** the remitting of a debt or penalty, etc. **3** a diminution of force, effect, or degree (esp. of disease or pain). **4** Brit. the reduction of a prison sentence on account of good behavior. □□ **re·mis·sive** /–mísiv/ adj. [ME f. OF remission or L remissio (as REMIT)]

re·mit v. & n. ● v. /rimít/ (**re·mit·ted**, **re·mit·ting**) **1** tr. cancel or refrain from exacting or inflicting (a debt or punishment, etc.). **2** intr. & tr. abate or slacken; cease or cease from partly or entirely. **3** tr. send (money, etc.) in payment. **4** tr. cause to be conveyed by mail. **5** tr. **a** (foll. by to) refer (a matter for decision, etc.) to some authority. **b** Law send back (a case) to a lower court. **6** tr. **a** (often foll. by to) postpone or defer. **b** (foll. by in, into) send or put back into a previous state. **7** tr. Theol. (usu. of God) pardon (sins, etc.). ● n. /réemit, rimít/ **1** the terms of reference of a committee, etc. **2** an item remitted for consideration. □□ **re·mit·ta·ble** /–mítəbəl/ adj. **re·mit·tal** n. **re·mit·tee** /reemiteé/ n. **re·mit·ter** n. [ME f. L remittere remiss- (as RE-, mittere send)]

re·mit·tance /rimít'ns/ n. **1** money sent, esp. by mail, for goods or services or as an allowance. **2** the act of sending money.

re·mit·tance man n. hist. an emigrant subsisting on remittances from home.

re·mit·tent /rimít'nt/ adj. (of a fever) that abates at intervals. [L remittere (as REMIT)]

re·mix v. & n. ● v.tr. /reémíks/ mix again. ● n. /réemiks/ a sound recording that has been remixed.

rem·nant /rémnənt/ n. **1** a small remaining quantity. **2** a piece of cloth, etc., left when the greater part has been used or sold. **3** (foll. by of) a surviving trace (a remnant of the empire). [ME (earlier remenant) f. OF remenant f. remenoir REMAIN]

re·mod·el /reémódl/ v.tr. (**·eled**, **·el·ing**; esp. Brit. **re·mod·elled**, **re·mod·el·ling**) **1** model again or differently. **2** reconstruct.

re·mod·i·fy /reémódifi/ v.tr. (**·fies**, **·fied**) modify again. □□ **re·mod·i·fi·ca·tion** /–fikáyshən/ n.

re·mold v. & n. (Brit. **re·mould**) ● v.tr. /reémóld/ **1** mold again; refashion. **2** reform the tread of (a tire). ● n. Brit. /réemóld/ a remolded tire.

re·mon·e·tize /reémónitiz, –mún–/ v.tr. restore (a metal, etc.) to its former position as legal tender. □□ **re·mon·e·ti·za·tion** n.

re·mon·strance /rimónstrəns/ n. **1** the act or an instance of remonstrating. **2** an expostulation or protest. [ME f. obs. F remonstrance or med.L remonstrantia (as REMONSTRATE)]

re·mon·strate /rémonstráyt, rimón–/ v. **1** intr. (foll. by with) make a protest; argue forcibly (remonstrated with them over the delays). **2** tr. (often foll. by that + clause) urge protestingly. □□ **re·mon·strant** /–mónstrənt/ adj. **re·mon·stra·tion** /rémənstráyshən/ n. **re·mon·stra·tive** /rimónstrətiv/ adj. **re·mon·stra·tor** n. [med.L remonstrare (as RE-, monstrare show)]

re·mon·tant /rimóntənt/ adj. & n. ● adj. blooming more than once a year. ● n. a remontant rose. [F f. remonter REMOUNT]

rem·o·ra /rémərə, rimáwrə/ n. Zool. any of various marine fish of the family Echeneidae, which attach themselves by modified suckerlike fins to other fish and to ships. [L, = hindrance (as RE-, mora delay, from the former belief that the fish slowed ships down)]

re·morse /rimáwrs/ n. **1** deep regret for a wrong committed. **2** compunction; a compassionate reluctance to inflict pain (esp. in without remorse). [ME f. OF remors f. med.L remorsus f. L remordēre remors- vex (as RE-, mordēre bite)]

re·morse·ful /rimáwrsfŏŏl/ adj. filled with repentance. □□ **re·morse·ful·ly** adv.

re·morse·less /rimáwrslis/ adj. **1** without compassion or compunction. **2** relentless; unabating. □□ **re·morse·less·ly** adv. **re·morse·less·ness** n.

remora

re·mort·gage /reémáwrgij/ v. & n. ● v.tr. (also absol.) mortgage again; revise the terms of an existing mortgage on (a property). ● n. a different or altered mortgage.

re·mote /rimót/ adj. & n. ● adj. (**re·mot·er**, **re·mot·est**) **1** far away in place or time. **2** out of the way; situated away from the main centers of population, society, etc. **3** distantly related (a remote ancestor). **4** slight; faint (esp. in not the remotest chance, idea, etc.). **5** (of a person) aloof; not friendly. **6** (foll. by from) widely different; separate by nature (ideas remote from the subject). ● n. = REMOTE CONTROL. □□ **re·mote·ly** adv. **re·mote·ness** n. [ME f. L remotus (as RE-MOVE)]

re·mote con·trol n. **1** control of a machine or apparatus from a distance by means of signals transmitted from a radio or electronic device. **2** the device used to control a machine remotely. □□ **re·mote-con·trolled** adj.

re·mould Brit. var. of REMOLD.

re·mount v. & n. ● v. /reémównt/ **1 a** tr. mount (a horse, etc.) again. **b** intr. get on horseback again. **2** tr. get on to or ascend (a ladder, hill, etc.) again. **3** tr. provide (a person) with a fresh horse, etc. **4** tr. put (a picture) on a fresh mount. ● n. /reémownt/ **1** a fresh horse for a rider. **2** a supply of fresh horses for a regiment.

re·mov·al /rimŏŏvəl/ n. **1** the act or an instance of removing; the process of being removed. **2** Brit. the transfer of furniture and other contents on moving to another house. **3** a dismissal from an office or post; deposition. **b** (an act of) murder.

re·move /rimŏŏv/ v. & n. ● v. **1** tr. take off or away from the place or position occupied; detach (remove the top carefully). **2** tr. a move or take to another place; change the situation of (will you remove the dishes?). **b** get rid of; eliminate (will remove all doubts). **3** tr. cause to be no longer present or available; take away (all privileges were removed). **4** tr. (often foll. by from) dismiss (from office). **5** tr. colloq. kill; assassinate. **6** tr. (in passive; foll. by from) distant or remote in condition (the country is not far removed from anarchy). **7** tr. (as **removed** adj.) (esp. of cousins) separated by a specified number of steps of descent (a first cousin twice removed = a grandchild of a first cousin). **8** formal **a** intr. (usu. foll. by from, to) change one's home or place of residence. **b** tr. conduct the removal of. ● n. **1** esp. Brit. a degree of remoteness; a distance. **2** a stage in a gradation; a degree (is several removes from what I expected). **3** Brit. a form or division in some schools. □□ **re·mov·a·ble** adj. **re·mov·a·bil·i·ty** /–mŏŏvəbílitee/ n. **re·mov·er** n. (esp. in sense 8b of v.). [ME f. OF removeir f. L removēre remot- (as RE-, movēre move)]

re·mu·ner·ate /rimyŏŏnərayt/ v.tr. **1** reward; pay for services rendered. **2** serve as or provide recompense for (toil, etc.) or to (a person). □□ **re·mu·ner·a·tion** /–ráyshən/ n. **re·mu·ner·a·tive** /–rətiv, –raytiv/ adj. **re·mu·ner·a·to·ry** /–rətawree/ adj. [L remunerari (as RE-, munus muneris gift)]

Ren·ais·sance /rénəsáans, –záans, esp. Brit. rináysəns/ n. **1** the revival of art and literature under the influence of classical models in the 14th–16th c. **2** the period of this. **3** the culture and style of art, architecture, etc., developed during this era. **4** (**renaissance**) any similar revival. [F renaissance (as RE-, F naissance birth f. L nascentia or F naître naiss- be born f. Rmc: cf. NASCENT)]

re·nal /reénəl/ adj. of or concerning the kidneys. [F rénal f. LL renalis f. L renes kidneys]

re·name /reénáym/ v.tr. name again; give a new name to.

re·nas·cence /rinásəns, rináy–/ n. **1** rebirth; renewal. **2** = RENAISSANCE. [RENASCENT]

re·nas·cent /rinásənt, rináy–/ adj. springing up anew; being reborn. [L renasci (as RE-, nasci be born)]

ren·con·tre /renkóntər/ *n. archaic* = RENCOUNTER. [F (as RENCOUNTER)]

ren·coun·ter /renkównter/ *n. & v.* ● *n.* **1** an encounter; a chance meeting. **2** a battle, skirmish, or duel. ● *v.tr.* encounter; meet by chance. [F *rencontre(r)* (as RE-, ENCOUNTER)]

rend /rend/ *v.* (*past* and *past part.* **rent** /rent/) *archaic* or *rhet.* **1** *tr.* (foll. by *off, from, away,* etc.; also *absol.*) tear or wrench forcibly. **2** *tr. & intr.* split or divide in pieces or into factions (*a country rent by civil war*). **3** *tr.* cause emotional pain to (the heart, etc.). □ **rend the air** sound piercingly. **rend one's garments** (or **hair**) display extreme grief or rage. [OE *rendan,* rel. to MLG *rende*]

ren·der /réndər/ *v.tr.* **1** cause to be or become; make (*rendered us helpless*). **2** give or pay (money, service, etc.), esp. in return or as a thing due (*render thanks; rendered good for evil*). **3** (often foll. by *to*) **a** give (assistance) (*rendered aid to the injured man*). **b** show (obedience, etc.). **c** do (a service, etc.). **4 a** submit; send in; present (an account, reason, etc.). **b** *Law* (of a judge or jury) deliver formally (a judgment or verdict). **5 a** represent or portray artistically, musically, etc. **b** act (a role); represent (a character, idea, etc.) (*the dramatist's conception was well rendered*). **c** *Mus.* perform; execute. **6** translate (*rendered the poem into French*). **7** (often foll. by *down*) melt down (fat, etc.) esp. to clarify; extract by melting. **8** cover (stone or brick) with a coat of plaster. **9** *archaic* **a** give back; hand over; deliver; give up; surrender (*render unto Caesar the things that are Caesar's*). **b** show (obedience). □□ **ren·der·er** *n.* [ME f. OF *rendre* ult. f. L *reddere reddit-* (as RE-, *dare* give)]

ren·der·ing /réndəring/ *n.* **1 a** the act or an instance of performing music, drama, etc.; an interpretation or performance (*an excellent rendering of the part*). **b** a translation. **2 a** the act or an instance of plastering stone, brick, etc. **b** this coating. **3** the act or an instance of giving, yielding, or surrendering.

ren·dez·vous /róndəyvōō, –dō–/ *n. & v.* ● *n.* (*pl.* same /–vōōz/) **1** an agreed or regular meeting place. **2** a meeting by arrangement. **3** a place appointed for assembling troops, ships, etc. ● *v.intr.* (**ren·dez·vouses** /–vōōz/; **ren·dez·voused** /–vōōd/; **ren·dez·vous·ing** /–vōōing/) meet at a rendezvous. [F *rendez-vous* present yourselves f. *rendre:* see RENDER]

ren·di·tion /rendíshən/ *n.* (often foll. by *of*) **1** an interpretation or rendering of a dramatic role, piece of music, etc. **2** a visual representation. [obs. F f. *rendre* RENDER]

ren·e·gade /rénigayd/ *n., adj., & v.* ● *n.* **1** a person who deserts a party or principles. **2** an apostate; a person who abandons one religion for another. ● *adj.* traitorous, heretical. ● *v.intr.* become a renegade. [Sp. *renegado* f. med.L *renegatus* (as RE-, L *negare* deny)]

ren·e·ga·do /rénigáydō, –gáa–/ *n.* (*pl.* **·dos**) *archaic* = RENEGADE. [Sp. (as RENEGADE)]

re·nege /riníg, –nég, –néeg/ *v.* **1** *intr.* **a** go back on one's word; change one's mind; recant. **b** (foll. by *on*) go back on (a promise or undertaking or contract). **2** *tr.* deny; renounce; abandon (a person, faith, etc.). **3** *intr. Cards* revoke. □□ **re·neg·er** *n.* [med.L *renegare* (as RE-, L *negare* deny)]

re·ne·go·ti·ate /réenigósheeayt/ *v.tr.* (also *absol.*) negotiate again or on different terms. □□ **re·ne·go·ti·a·ble** /–sheeəbəl, –shəbəl/ *adj.* **re·ne·go·ti·a·tion** /–sheeáyshən/ *n.*

re·new /rinōō, –nyōō/ *v.tr.* **1** revive; regenerate; make new again; restore to the original state. **2** reinforce; resupply; replace. **3** repeat or reestablish; resume after an interruption (*renewed our acquaintance; a renewed attack*). **4** get, begin, make, say, give, etc., anew. **5** (also *absol.*) grant or be granted a continuation of or continued validity of (a license, subscription, lease, etc.). **6** recover (one's youth, strength, etc.). □□ **re·new·a·ble** *adj.* **re·new·a·bil·i·ty** /–nyōō-bílitee/ *n.* **re·new·al** *n.* **re·new·er** *n.*

ren·i·form /rénifawrm, rée–/ *adj.* esp. *Med.* kidney-shaped. [L *ren* kidney + –FORM]

ren·net /rénit/ *n.* **1** curdled milk found in the stomach of an unweaned calf, used in curdling milk for cheese, junket, etc. **2** a preparation made from the stomach membrane of a calf or from certain fungi, used for the same purpose. [ME, prob. f. an OE form *rynet* (unrecorded), rel. to RUN]

ren·nin /rénin/ *n. Biochem.* an enzyme secreted into the stomach of unweaned mammals causing the clotting of milk. [RENNET + –IN]

re·nom·i·nate /réenóminayt/ *v.tr.* nominate for a further term of office. □□ **re·nom·i·na·tion** /–náyshən/ *n.*

re·nounce /rinówns/ *v.* **1** consent formally to abandon; surrender; give up (a claim, right, possession, etc.). **2** *tr.* repudiate; refuse to recognize any longer (*renouncing their father's authority*). **3** *tr.* **a** decline further association or disclaim relationship with (*renounced my former friends*). **b** withdraw from; discontinue; forsake. **4** *intr. Law* refuse or resign a right or position esp. as an heir or trustee. **5** *intr. Cards* follow with a card of another suit when having no card of the suit led (cf. REVOKE). □ **renounce the world** abandon society or material affairs. □□ **re·nounce·a·ble** *adj.* **re·nounce·ment** *n.* **re·nounc·er** *n.* [ME f. OF *renoncer* f. L *renuntiare* (as RE-, *nuntiare* announce)]

ren·o·vate /rénəvayt/ *v.tr.* **1** restore to good condition; repair. **2** make new again. □□ **ren·o·va·tion** /–váyshən/ *n.* **ren·o·va·tive** *adj.* **ren·o·va·tor** *n.* [L *renovare* (as RE-, *novus* new)]

re·nown /rinówn/ *n.* fame; high distinction; celebrity (*a city of great renown*). [ME f. AF *ren(o)un,* OF *renon, renom* f. *renomer* make famous (as RE-, L *nominare* NOMINATE)]

re·nowned /rinównd/ *adj.* famous; celebrated.

rent¹ /rent/ *n. & v.* ● *n.* **1** a tenant's periodical payment to an owner or landlord for the use of land or premises. **2** payment for the use of a service, equipment, etc. ● *v.* **1** *tr.* (often foll. by *from*) take, occupy, or use at a rent (*rented a boat from the marina*). **2** *tr.* (often foll. by *out*) let or hire (a thing) for rent. **3** *intr.* (foll. by *for, at*) be let or hired out at a specified rate (*the room rents for $300 per month*). □ **for rent** available to be rented. [ME f. OF *rente* f. Rmc (as RENDER)]

rent² /rent/ *n.* **1** a large tear in a garment, etc. **2** an opening in clouds, etc. **3** a cleft, fissure, or gorge. [obs. *rent* var. of REND]

rent³ *past* and *past part.* of REND.

rent-a- (in *comb.*) denoting availability for hire (*rent-a-car*).

rent·a·ble /réntəbəl/ *adj.* **1** available or suitable for renting. **2** giving an adequate ratio of profit to capital. □□ **rent·a·bil·i·ty** /–bílitee/ *n.*

ren·tal /rént'l/ *n.* **1** the amount paid or received as rent. **2** the act of renting. **3** an income from rents. **4** a rented house, etc. [ME f. AF *rental* or AL *rentale* (as RENT¹)]

rent·er /réntər/ *n.* **1** a person who rents. **2** *Cinematog.* (in the UK) a person who distributes motion pictures. **3** *Brit. sl.* a male prostitute.

rent-free *adj. & adv.* with exemption from rent.

ren·tier /ró*n*tyay/ *n.* a person living on dividends from property, investments, etc. [F f. *rente* dividend]

rent-roll *n.* the register of a landlord's properties, with the rents due from them; the sum of one's income from rent.

re·num·ber /réenúmbər/ *v.tr.* change the number or numbers given or allocated to.

re·nun·ci·a·tion /rinúnseeáyshən/ *n.* **1** the act or an instance of renouncing or giving up. **2** self-denial. **3** a document expressing renunciation. □□ **re·nun·ci·ant** /rinúnseeənt/ *n. & adj.* **re·nun·ci·a·tive** /–seeátiv/ *adj.* **re·nun·ci·a·to·ry** /–seeətáwree, –shətáwree/ *adj.* [ME f. OF *renonciation* or LL *renuntiatio* (as RENOUNCE)]

ren·voi /renvóy/ *n. Law* the act or an instance of referring a case, dispute, etc., to a different jurisdiction. [F f. *renvoyer* send back]

re·oc·cu·py /ree-ókyəpī/ *v.tr.* (**·pies, ·pied**) occupy again. □□ **re·oc·cu·pa·tion** /–páyshən/ *n.*

re·oc·cur /ree·ókŕr/ *v.intr.* (**re·oc·curred, re·oc·cur·ring**) occur again or habitually. □□ **re·oc·cur·rence** /–kúrəns/ *n.*

▶See note at RECUR.

re·o·pen /ree-ópən/ *v.tr. & intr.* open again.

re·or·der /ree-áwrdər/ *v. & n.* ● *v.tr.* order again. ● *n.* a renewed or repeated order for goods.

re·or·gan·ize /ree-áwrgənīz/ *v.tr.* organize differently. □□ **re·or·gan·i·za·tion** /–záyshən/ *n.* **re·or·gan·iz·er** *n.*

re·or·i·ent /ree-áwree-ent, –óree-ent/ *v.tr.* **1** give a new direction to (ideas, etc.); redirect (a thing). **2** help (a person) find his or her bearings again. **3** change the outlook of (a person). **4** (*refl.,* often foll. by *to*) adjust oneself to or come to terms with something.

re·or·i·en·tate /ree-áwreeəntayt, –óreeən–/ *v.tr.* = REORIENT. □□ **re·or·i·en·ta·tion** /–táyshən/ *n.*

Rep. *abbr.* **1** Representative (in Congress, state legislature, etc.). **2** Republican. **3** Republic.

rep¹ /rep/ *n. colloq.* a representative, esp. a salesperson. [abbr.]

rep² /rep/ *n. colloq.* **1** repertory. **2** a repertory theater or company. [abbr.]

rep³ /rep/ *n.* (also **repp**) a textile fabric with a corded surface, used in curtains and upholstery. [F *reps,* of unkn. orig.]

rep⁴ /rep/ *n. sl.* reputation. [abbr.]

re·pack /réepák/ *v.tr.* pack again.

re·pack·age /réepákij/ *v.tr.* **1** package again or differently. **2** present in a new form. □□ **re·pack·ag·ing** *n.*

re·pag·i·nate /réepájinayt/ *v.tr.* paginate again; renumber the pages of. □□ **re·pag·i·na·tion** /–náyshən/ *n.*

re·paid *past* and *past part.* of REPAY.

re·paint *v. & n.* ● *v.tr.* /réepáynt/ **1** paint again or differently. **2** restore the paint or coloring of. ● *n.* /réepaynt/ the act of repainting.

re·pair¹ /ripáir/ *v. & n.* ● *v.tr.* **1** restore to good condition after damage or wear. **2** renovate or mend by replacing or fixing parts or by compensating for loss or exhaustion. **3** set right or make amends for (loss, wrong, error, etc.). ● *n.* **1** the act or an instance of restoring to sound condition (*in need of repair; closed during repair*). **2** the result of this (*the repair is hardly visible*). **3** good or relative condition for working or using (*must be kept in repair; in good repair*). □□ **re·pair·a·ble** *adj.* **re·pair·er** *n.* [ME f. OF *reparer* f. L *reparare* (as RE-, *parare* make ready)]

re·pair² /ripáir/ *v. & n.* ● *v.intr.* (foll. by *to*) resort; have recourse; go often or in great numbers or for a specific purpose (*repaired to Spain*). ● *n. archaic* **1** resort (*have repair to*). **2** a place of frequent resort. **3** popularity (*a place of great repair*). [ME f. OF *repaire(r)* f. LL *repatriare* REPATRIATE]

re·pair·man /ripáirmən/ *n.* (*pl.* **·men**) a person who repairs machinery, etc.

re·pand /ripánd/ *adj. Bot.* with an undulating margin; wavy. [L *repandus* (as RE-, *pandus* bent)]

re·pap·er /reépáypər/ *v.tr.* paper (a wall, etc.) again.

rep·a·ra·ble /répərəbəl, ripáirəbəl/ *adj.* (of a loss, etc.) that can be made good. □□ **rep·a·ra·bil·i·ty** *n.* **rep·a·ra·bly** *adv.* [F f. L *reparabilis* (as REPAIR¹)]

rep·a·ra·tion /répəráyshən/ *n.* **1** the act or an instance of making amends. **2 a** compensation. **b** (esp. in *pl.*) compensation for war damage paid by the defeated nation, etc. **3** the act or an instance of repairing or being repaired. □□ **re·par·a·tive** /ripáirətiv/ *adj.* [ME f. OF f. LL *reparatio –onis* (as REPAIR)]

rep·ar·tee /répaartee´, –táy/ *n.* **1** the practice or faculty of making witty retorts; sharpness or wit in quick reply. **2 a** a witty retort. **b** witty retorts collectively. [F *repartie* fem. past part. of *repartir* start again, reply promptly (as RE-, *partir* PART)]

re·par·ti·tion /reépaartíshən/ *v.tr.* partition again.

re·pass /reépás/ *v.tr. & intr.* pass again, esp. on the way back. [ME f. OF *repasser*]

re·past /ripást/ *n.* **1** a meal, esp. of a specified kind (*a light repast*). **2** food and drink supplied for or eaten at a meal. [ME f. OF *repaistre* f. LL *repascere repast-* feed]

re·pa·tri·ate *v. & n.* ● *v.tr.* **1** *tr.* restore (a person) to his or her native land. **2** *intr.* return to one's own native land. ● *n.* a person who has been repatriated. □□ **re·pa·tri·a·tion** /–áyshən/ *n.* [LL *repatriare* (as RE-, L *patria* native land)]

re·pay /reépáy/ *v.* (*past* and *past part.* **re·paid**) **1** *tr.* pay back (money). **2** *tr.* return (a blow, visit, etc.). **3** *tr.* make repayment to (a person). **4** *tr.* make return for; requite (a service, action, etc.) (*must repay their kindness; the book repays close study*). **5** *tr.* (often foll. by *for*) give in recompense. **6** *intr.* make repayment. □□ **re·pay·a·ble** *adj.* **re·pay·ment** *n.* [OF *repaier* (as RE-, PAY¹)]

re·peal /ripeel/ *v. & n.* ● *v.tr.* revoke, rescind, or annul (a law, act of Congress, etc.). ● *n.* the act or an instance of repealing. □□ **re·peal·a·ble** *adj.* [ME f. AF *repeler*, OF *rapeler* (as RE-, APPEAL)]

re·peat /ripeet/ *v. & n.* ● *v.tr.* **1** *tr.* say or do over again. **2** *tr.* recite, rehearse, report, or reproduce (something from memory) (*repeated a poem*). **3** *tr.* imitate (an action, etc.). **4 a** *intr.* recur; appear again, perhaps several times (*a repeating pattern*). **b** *refl.* recur in the same or a similar form (*history repeats itself*). **5** *tr.* used for emphasis (*am not, repeat not, going*). **6** *intr.* (of food) be tasted intermittently for some time after being swallowed as a result of belching or indigestion. **7** *intr.* (of a watch, etc.) strike the last quarter, etc., over again when required. **8** *intr.* (of a firearm) fire several shots without reloading. **9** *intr.* illegally vote more than once in an election. ● *n.* **1 a** the act or an instance of repeating. **b** a thing repeated (often *attrib.: repeat performance*). **2** a repeated broadcast. **3** *Mus.* **a** a passage intended to be repeated. **b** a mark indicating this. **4** a pattern repeated in wallpaper, etc. **5** *Commerce* **a** a consignment similar to a previous one. **b** an order given for this; a reorder. □ **repeat oneself** say or do the same thing over again. □□ **re·peat·a·ble** *adj.* **re·peat·a·bil·i·ty** /–peétəbílitee/ *n.* **re·peat·ed·ly** *adv.* [ME f. OF *repeter* f. L *repetere* (as RE-, *petere* seek)]

re·peat·er /ripeétər/ *n.* **1** a person or thing that repeats. **2** a firearm that fires several shots without reloading. **3** a watch or clock that repeats its last strike when required. **4** a device for the automatic retransmission or amplification of an electrically transmitted message. **5** a signal lamp indicating the state of another that is invisible.

re·peat·ing dec·i·mal *n.* a decimal fraction in which the same figures repeat indefinitely.

re·pê·chage /répisha´azh/ *n.* (in rowing, etc.) an extra contest in which the runners-up in the eliminating heats compete for a place in the final. [F *repêcher* fish out, rescue]

re·pel /ripél/ *v.tr.* (**re·pelled**, **re·pel·ling**) **1** drive back; ward off; repulse. **2** refuse admission or approach or acceptance to (*repel an assailant*). **3** be repulsive or distasteful to. □□ **re·pel·ler** *n.* [ME f. L *repellere* (as RE-, *pellere puls-* drive)]

re·pel·lent /ripélənt/ *adj. & n.* ● *adj.* **1** that repels. **2** disgusting; repulsive. ● *n.* a substance that repels esp. insects, etc. □□ **re·pel·lence** *n.* **re·pel·len·cy** *n.* **re·pel·lent·ly** *adv.* [L *repellere* (as REPEL)]

▶ **Repellent** and **repulsive** are very close in meaning, but the latter, perhaps because of its sound, is felt to express stronger feeling.

re·pent¹ /ripént/ *v.* **1** *intr.* (often foll. by *of*) feel deep sorrow about one's actions, etc. **2** *tr.* (also *absol.*) wish one had not done; regret (one's wrong, omission, etc.); resolve not to continue (a wrongdoing, etc.). **3** *refl.* (often foll. by *of*) archaic feel regret or penitence about (*now I repent me*). □□ **re·pent·ance** *n.* **re·pent·ant** *adj.* **re·pent·er** *n.* [ME f. OF *repentir* (as RE-, *pentir* ult. f. L *paenitēre*)]

re·pent² /reépənt/ *adj. Bot.* creeping, esp. growing along the ground or just under the surface. [L *repere* creep]

re·peo·ple /reépeépəl/ *v.tr.* people again; increase the population of.

re·per·cus·sion /reépərkúshən, répər–/ *n.* **1** (often foll. by *of*) an indirect effect or reaction following an event or action (*consider the repercussions of moving*). **2** the recoil after impact. **3** an echo or reverberation. □□ **re·per·cus·sive** /–kúsiv/ *adj.* [ME f. OF *repercussion* or L *repercussio* (as RE-, PERCUSSION)]

rep·er·toire /répərtwaar/ *n.* **1** a stock of pieces, etc., that a company or a performer knows or is prepared to give. **2** a stock of regularly performed pieces, regularly used techniques, etc. (*went through his repertoire of excuses*). [F *répertoire* f. LL (as REPERTORY)]

rep·er·to·ry /répərtawree/ *n.* (*pl.* **·ries**) **1** = REPERTOIRE. **2** the theatrical performance of various plays for short periods by one company. **3 a** a repertory company. **b** repertory theaters regarded collectively. **4** a store or collection, esp. of information, instances, etc. [LL *repertorium* f. L *reperire repert-* find]

rep·er·to·ry com·pa·ny *n.* a theatrical company that performs plays from a repertoire.

rep·e·tend /répitend/ *n.* **1** the recurring figures of a decimal. **2** the recurring word or phrase; a refrain. [L *repetendum* (as REPEAT)]

ré·pé·ti·teur /repétitőr/ *n.* **1** a tutor or coach of musicians, esp. opera singers. **2** a person who supervises ballet rehearsals, etc. [F]

rep·e·ti·tion /répitíshən/ *n.* **1 a** the act or an instance of repeating or being repeated. **b** the thing repeated. **2** a copy or replica. **3** a piece to be learned by heart. **4** the recurrence of a musical instrument to repeat a note quickly. □□ **rep·e·ti·tion·al** *adj.* **rep·e·ti·tion·ar·y** *adj.* [F *répétition* or L *repetitio* (as REPEAT)]

SPELLING TIP repetition

In the word *repetition*, there is a repetition of the letter *e*.

---

rep·e·ti·tious /répitíshəs/ *adj.* characterized by repetition, esp. when unnecessary or tiresome. □□ **rep·e·ti·tious·ly** *adv.* **rep·e·ti·tious·ness** *n.*

re·pet·i·tive /ripétitiv/ *adj.* characterized by, or consisting of, repetition; monotonous. □□ **re·pet·i·tive·ly** *adv.* **re·pet·i·tive·ness** *n.*

re·pet·i·tive strain in·ju·ry *n.* injury arising from the continued repeated use of particular muscles, esp. during keyboarding, etc.

re·phrase /reéfráyz/ *v.tr.* express in an alternative way.

re·pine /ripín/ *v.intr.* (often foll. by *at*, *against*, *for*) fret; be discontented. [RE- + PINE², after *repent*]

re·pique /ripeek/ *n. & v.* ● *n.* (in piquet) the winning of 30 points on cards alone before beginning to play. ● *v.* (**re·piques**, **re·piqued**, **re·piqu·ing**) **1** *intr.* score repique. **2** *tr.* score repique against (another person). [F *repic* (as RE-, PIQUE²)]

re·place /ripláys/ *v.tr.* **1** put back in place. **2** take the place of; succeed; be substituted for. **3** find or provide a substitute for; renew. **4** (often foll. by *with*, *by*) fill up the place of. **5** (in *passive*, often foll. by *by*) be succeeded or have one's place filled by another; be superseded. □□ **re·place·a·ble** *adj.* **re·plac·er** *n.*

SYNONYM TIP replace

DISPLACE, SUPERSEDE, SUPPLANT. When a light bulb burns out, you **replace** it, meaning that you substitute something new or functioning for what is lost, destroyed, or worn out. If something *replaces* what is obsolete or ineffective with something that is superior, more up-to-date, or more authoritative, the correct verb is **supersede** (*The computer superseded the electric typewriter*). In contrast, **displace** suggests that something or someone has been ousted or dislodged forcibly, without necessarily implying that it was inferior or ineffective (*A growing number of workers were being displaced by machines*). **Supplant** is more restricted in meaning; it suggests that someone or something has been *displaced* by force, fraud, or innovation (*The democratic government had been supplanted by a power-hungry tyrant*). It can also mean something is uprooted or wiped out (*The English immigrants gradually supplanted the island's native inhabitants*).

---

re·place·ment /ripláysmənt/ *n.* **1** the act or an instance of replacing or being replaced. **2** a person or thing that takes the place of another.

re·plan /reéplán/ *v.tr.* (**re·planned**, **re·plan·ning**) plan again or differently.

re·plant /reéplánt/ *v.tr.* **1** transfer (a plant, etc.) to a larger pot, a new site, etc. **2** plant (ground) again; provide with new plants.

re·play *v. & n.* ● *v.tr.* /reépláy/ play (a match, recording, etc.) again. ● *n.* /reéplay/ the act or an instance of replaying a match, a recording, or a recorded incident in a game, etc.

re·plen·ish /riplénish/ *v.tr.* **1** (often foll. by *with*) fill up again. **2** renew (a supply, etc.). **3** (as **replenished** *adj.*) filled; fully stored or stocked; full. □□ **re·plen·ish·er** *n.* **re·plen·ish·ment** *n.* [ME f. OF *replenir* (as RE-, *plenir* f. *plein* full f. L *plenus*)]

re·plete /ripleet/ *adj.* (often foll. by *with*) **1** filled or well-supplied with. **2** stuffed; gorged; sated. □□ **re·plete·ness** *n.* **re·ple·tion** *n.* [ME f. OF *replet replete* or L *repletus* past part. of *replēre* (as RE-, *plēre* plet- fill)]

re·plev·in /riplévən/ *n. Law* **1** the provisional restoration or recovery of distrained goods pending the outcome of trial and judgment. **2** a writ granting this. **3** the action arising from this process. [ME f. AF f. OF *replevir* (as REPLEVY)]

re‑plev‑y /riplévee/ *v.tr.* (**·ies, ·ied**) *Law* recover by replevin. [OF *replevir* recover f. Gmc]

rep‑li‑ca /réplikə/ *n.* **1** a duplicate of a work made by the original artist. **2 a** a facsimile; an exact copy. **b** (of a person) an exact likeness; a double. **3** a copy or model, esp. on a smaller scale. [It. f. *replicare* REPLY]

rep‑li‑cate *v., adj., & ● v.tr.* /réplikayt/ **1** repeat (an experiment, etc.). **2** make a replica of. **3** fold back. ● *adj.* /‑kət/ *Bot.* folded back on itself. ● *n.* /‑kət/ *Mus.* a tone one or more octaves above or below the given tone. □□ **rep‑li‑ca‑ble** /‑kəbəl/ *adj.* (in sense 1 of *v.*). **rep‑li‑ca‑bil‑i‑ty** /‑bílitee/ *n.* (in sense 1 of *v.*). **rep‑li‑ca‑tive** /‑kətiv/ *adj.* [L *replicare* (as RE‑, *plicare* fold)]

rep‑li‑ca‑tion /réplikáyshən/ *n.* **1** a reply or response, esp. a reply to an answer. **2** *Law* the plaintiff's reply to the defendant's plea. **3 a** the act or an instance of copying. **b** a copy. **c** the process by which genetic material or a living organism gives rise to a copy of itself. [ME f. OF *replicacion* f. L *replicatio –onis* (as REPLICATE)]

re‑ply /riplí/ *v. & n.* ● *v.* (**·plies, ·plied**) **1** *intr.* (often foll. by *to*) make an answer; respond in word or action. **2** *tr.* say in answer (*he replied, "Suit yourself"*). ● *n.* (*pl.* **·plies**) **1** the act of replying (*what did they say in reply?*). **2** what is replied; a response. **3** *Law* = REPLICATION. □ **reply paid** *Brit.* **1** *hist.* (of a telegram) with the cost of a reply prepaid by the sender. **2** (of an envelope, etc.) for which the addressee undertakes to pay postage; postpaid. □□ **re‑pli‑er** *n.* [ME f. OF *replier* f. L (as REPLICATE)]

re‑pol‑ish /reépólish/ *v.tr.* polish again.

re‑pop‑u‑late /reépópyəlayt/ *v.tr.* populate again or increase the population of. □□ **re‑pop‑u‑la‑tion** /‑láyshən/ *n.*

re‑port /ripáwrt/ *v. & n.* ● *v.* **1** *tr.* **a** bring back or give an account of. **b** state as fact or news; narrate or describe or repeat, esp. as an eyewitness or hearer, etc. **c** relate as spoken by another. **2** *tr.* make an official or formal statement about. **3** *tr.* (often foll. by *to*) name or specify (an offender or offense) (*will report you for insubordination; reported them to the police*). **4** *intr.* (often foll. by *to*) present oneself as having returned or arrived (*report to the manager on arrival*). **5** *tr.* (also *absol.*) take down word for word or summarize or write a description of for publication. **6** *intr.* make or draw up or send in a report. **7** *intr.* (often foll. by *to*) be responsible (to a superior, supervisor, etc.) (*reports directly to the managing director*). **8** *tr.* (often foll. by *out*) (of a committee, etc.) send back (a bill, etc.), with comments and recommendations, to a legislature, etc. **9** *intr.* (often foll. by *of*) give a report to convey that one is well, badly, etc., impressed (*reports well of the prospects*). **10** *intr.* (usu. foll. by *on*) investigate or scrutinize for a journalistic report; act as a reporter. ● *n.* **1** an account given or opinion formally expressed after investigation or consideration. **2** a description, summary, or reproduction of an event or speech or legal case, esp. for newspaper publication or broadcast. **3** common talk; rumor. **4** the way a person or thing is spoken of (*I hear a good report of you*). **5** a periodical statement on (esp. a student's) work, conduct, etc. **6** the sound of an explosion. □ **report back** deliver a report to the person, organization, etc., for whom one acts, etc. □□ **re‑port‑a‑ble** *adj.* **re‑port‑ed‑ly** *adv.*

WORD HISTORY	report

Late Middle English: from Old French *reporter* (verb), *report* (noun), from Latin *reportare* 'bring back,' from *re‑* 'back' + *portare* 'carry.' The sense 'give an account' gave rise to 'submit a formal report' and hence 'inform an authority of one's presence' (sense 4, mid‑19th century) and 'be accountable for one's activities (to a superior)' (sense 7, late 19th century).

re‑port‑age /ripáwrtij, répawrtaázh/ *n.* **1** the describing of events, esp. the reporting of news, etc., for the press and for broadcasting. **2** the typical style of this. **3** factual presentation in a book, etc. [REPORT, after F]

re‑port card *n.* an official report issued by a school showing a student's grades, progress, etc.

re‑port‑ed speech *n. Brit.* the speaker's words with the changes of person, tense, etc., usual in reports, e.g., *he said that he would go* (opp. DIRECT SPEECH).

re‑port‑er /ripáwrtər/ *n.* **1** a person employed to report news, etc., for newspapers or broadcasts. **2** a person who reports.

rep‑or‑to‑ri‑al /rípawrtáwreeəl/ *adj.* **1** of newspaper reporters. **2** relating to or characteristic of a report. □□ **rep‑or‑to‑ri‑al‑ly** *adv.* [REPORTER, after *editorial*]

re‑pose¹ /ripóz/ *n. & v.* ● *n.* **1** the cessation of activity or excitement or toil. **2** sleep. **3** a peaceful or quiescent state; stillness; tranquillity. **4** *Art* a restful effect; harmonious combination. **5** composure or ease of manner. ● *v.* **1** *intr. & refl.* lie down in rest (*reposed on a sofa*). **2** *tr.* (often foll. by *on*) lay (one's head, etc.) to rest (on a pillow, etc.). **3** *intr.* (often foll. by *in, on*) lie, be lying or laid, esp. in sleep or death. **4** *tr.* give rest to; refresh with rest. **5** *intr.* esp. *Brit.* (foll. by *on, upon*) be supported or based on. **6** *intr.* (foll. by *on*) (of

memory, etc.) dwell on. □□ **re‑pos‑al** *n.* **re‑pose‑ful** *adj.* **re‑pose‑ful‑ly** *adv.* **re‑pose‑ful‑ness** *n.* [ME f. OF *repos(er)* f. LL *repausare* (as RE‑, *pausare* PAUSE)]

re‑pose² /ripóz/ *v.tr.* (foll. by *in*) place (trust, etc.) in. □□ **re‑pos‑al** *n.* [RE‑ + POSE¹ after L *reponere reposit–*]

re‑po‑si‑tion /reépəzíshən/ *v.* **1** *tr.* move or place in a different position. **2** *intr.* adjust or alter one's position.

re‑pos‑i‑to‑ry /ripózitawree/ *n.* (*pl.* **·ries**) **1** a place where things are stored or may be found, esp. a warehouse or museum. **2** a receptacle. **3** (often foll. by *of*) **a** a book, person, etc., regarded as a store of information, etc. **b** the recipient of confidences or secrets. [obs. F *repositoire* or L *repositorium* (as REPOSE²)]

re‑pos‑sess /reépəzés/ *v.tr.* regain possession of (esp. property or goods on which repayment of a debt is in arrears). □□ **re‑pos‑ses‑sion** *n.* **re‑pos‑ses‑sor** *n.*

re‑pot /reépót/ *v.tr.* (**re‑pot‑ted, re‑pot‑ting**) put (a plant) in another, esp. larger, pot.

re‑pous‑sé /rəpōosáy/ *adj. & n.* ● *adj.* hammered into relief from the reverse side. ● *n.* ornamental metalwork fashioned in this way. [F, past part. of *repousser* (as RE‑, *pousser* PUSH)]

repp var. of REP³.

repped /rept/ *adj.* having a surface like rep.

repr. *abbr.* **1** represent, represented, etc. **2** reprint, reprinted, etc.

rep‑re‑hend /réprihénd/ *v.tr.* rebuke; blame; find fault with. □□ **rep‑re‑hen‑sion** *n.* [ME f. L *reprehendere* (as RE‑, *prehendere* seize)]

rep‑re‑hen‑si‑ble /réprihénsibəl/ *adj.* deserving censure or rebuke; blameworthy. □□ **rep‑re‑hen‑si‑bil‑i‑ty** *n.* **rep‑re‑hen‑si‑bly** *adv.* [LL *reprehensibilis* (as REPREHEND)]

rep‑re‑sent /réprizént/ *v.tr.* **1** stand for or correspond to (*the comment does not represent all our views*). **2** (often in *passive*) be a specimen or example of; exemplify (*all types of people were represented in the audience*). **3** act as an embodiment of; symbolize (*the eagle represents the United States; numbers are represented by letters*). **4** call up in the mind by description or portrayal or imagination; place a likeness of before the mind or senses. **5** serve or be meant as a likeness of. **6 a** state by way of expostulation or persuasion (*represented the rashness of it*). **b** (foll. by *to*) try to bring (the facts influencing conduct) home to (*represented the risks to his client*). **7 a** (often foll. by *as, to be*) describe or depict as; declare or make out (*represented them as martyrs; not what you represent it to be*). **b** (often *refl.*; usu. foll by *as*) portray; assume the guise of; pose as (*represents himself as an honest broker*). **8** (foll. by *that* + clause) allege. **9** show, or play the part of, on stage. **10** fill the place of; be a substitute or deputy for; be entitled to act or speak for (*the president was represented by the secretary of state*). **11** be elected as a member of Congress, a legislature, etc., by (*represents a rural constituency*). □□ **rep‑re‑sent‑a‑ble** *adj.* **rep‑re‑sent‑a‑bil‑i‑ty** /‑əbílitee/ *n.* [ME f. OF *representer* or f. L *repraesentare* (as RE‑, PRESENT²)]

rep‑re‑sen‑ta‑tion /réprizentáyshən/ *n.* **1** the act or an instance of representing or being represented. **2** a thing (esp. a painting, etc.) that represents another. **3** (esp. in *pl.*) a statement made by way of allegation or to convey opinion. [ME f. OF *representation* or L *repraesentatio* (as REPRESENT)]

rep‑re‑sen‑ta‑tion‑al /réprizentáyshənəl/ *adj.* of representation. □□ **rep‑re‑sen‑ta‑tion‑al‑ism** *n.* **rep‑re‑sen‑ta‑tion‑al‑ist** *adj. & n.*

rep‑re‑sen‑ta‑tion‑al art *n.* art seeking to portray the physical appearance of a subject.

rep‑re‑sen‑ta‑tion‑ism /réprizentáyshənizəm/ *n.* the doctrine that perceived objects are only a representation of real external objects. □□ **rep‑re‑sen‑ta‑tion‑ist** *n.*

rep‑re‑sen‑ta‑tive /réprizéntətiv/ *adj. & n.* ● *adj.* **1** typical of a class or category. **2** containing typical specimens of all or many classes (*a representative sample*). **3 a** consisting of elected deputies, etc. **b** based on the representation of a nation, etc., by such deputies (*representative government*). **4** (foll. by *of*) serving as a portrayal or symbol of (*representative of their attitude to work*). **5** that presents or can present ideas to the mind (*imagination is a representative faculty*). **6** (of art) representational. ● *n.* **1** (foll. by *of*) a sample, specimen, or typical embodiment or analog of. **2 a** the agent of a person or society. **b** a salesperson. **3** a delegate; a substitute. **4** a deputy in a representative assembly. □□ **rep‑re‑sen‑ta‑tive‑ly** *adv.* **rep‑re‑sen‑ta‑tive‑ness** *n.* [ME f. OF *representatif –ive* or med.L *repraesentativus* (as REPRESENT)]

re‑press /riprés/ *v.tr.* **1 a** check; restrain; keep under; quell. **b** suppress; prevent from sounding, rioting, or bursting out. **2** *Psychol.* actively exclude (an unwelcome thought) from conscious awareness. **3** (usu. as **repressed** *adj.*) subject (a person) to the suppression of his or her thoughts or impulses. □□ **re‑press‑er** *n.* **re‑press‑i‑ble** *adj.* **re‑pres‑sion** /‑préshən/ *n.* **re‑pres‑sive** *adj.* **re‑pres‑sive‑ly** *adv.* **re‑pres‑sive‑ness** *n.* **re‑pres‑sor** *n.* [ME f. L *reprimere* (as RE‑, *premere* PRESS¹)]

re‑price /reéprís/ *v.tr.* price again or differently.

re•prieve /ripreev/ *v. & n.* ●*v.tr.* **1** remit, commute, or postpone the execution of (a condemned person). **2** give respite to. ●*n.* **1 a** the act or an instance of reprieving or being reprieved. **b** a warrant for this. **2** respite; a respite or temporary escape.

WORD HISTORY reprieve

Late 15th century (as the past participle *repryed*): from Anglo-Norman French *repris* (source of *reprise*), past participle of *reprendre*, from Latin *re*- 'back' + *prehendere* 'seize.' The insertion of -*v*- (16th century) remains unexplained. Sense development has undergone a reversal, from the early meaning 'send back to prison,' via 'postpone (a legal process),' to the current sense 'rescue from impending punishment.'

---

rep•ri•mand /réprimand/ *n. & v.* ●*n.* (often foll. by *for*) an official or sharp rebuke (for a fault, etc.). ●*v.tr.* administer this to. [F *réprimande*(*r*) f. Sp. *reprimenda* f. L *reprimenda* neut. pl. gerundive of *reprimere* REPRESS]

re•print *v. & n.* ●*v.tr.* /reeprínt/ print again. ●*n.* /reeprint/ **1** the act or an instance of reprinting a book, etc. **2** the book, etc., reprinted. **3** the quantity reprinted. □□ **re•print•er** *n.*

re•pris•al /ripprízəl/ *n.* **1** (an act of) retaliation. **2** *hist.* the forcible seizure of a foreign subject or his or her goods as an act of retaliation. [ME (in sense 2) f. AF *reprisaille* f. med.L *reprisalia* f. *repraehensalia* (as REPREHEND)]

re•prise /ripréez/ *n.* **1** a repeated passage in music. **2** a repeated item in a musical program. [F, fem. past part. of *reprendre* (see REPRIEVE)]

re•pro /reeprō/ *n.* (*pl.* •pros) (often *attrib.*) **1** a reproduction or copy. **2** (also **reproduction proof**) a proof, usu. on glossy paper, that can be used as photographic copy for a printing plate. [abbr.]

re•proach /riprōch/ *v. & n.* ●*v.tr.* **1** express disapproval to (a person) for a fault, etc. **2** scold; rebuke; censure. **3** *archaic* rebuke (an offense). ●*n.* **1** a rebuke or censure (*heaped reproaches on them*). **2** (often foll. by *to*) a thing that brings disgrace or discredit (*their behavior is a reproach to us all*). **3** a disgraced or discredited state (*live in reproach and ignominy*). **4** (in *pl.*) *RC Ch.* a set of antiphons and responses for Good Friday representing the reproaches of Christ to his people. □ **above** (or **beyond**) **reproach** perfect. □□ **re•proach•a•ble** *adj.* **re•proach•er** *n.* **re•proach•ing•ly** *adv.* [ME f. OF *reproche*(*r*) f. Rmc (as RE-, L *prope* near)]

re•proach•ful /riprōchfŏŏl/ *adj.* full of or expressing reproach. □□ **re•proach•ful•ly** *adv.* **re•proach•ful•ness** *n.*

rep•ro•bate /réprəbayt/ *n., adj., & v.* ●*n.* **1** an unprincipled person; a person of highly immoral character. **2** a person who is condemned by God. ●*adj.* **1** immoral. **2** hardened in sin. ●*v.tr.* **1** express or feel disapproval of; censure. **2** (of God) condemn; exclude from salvation. □□ **rep•ro•ba•tion** /-báyshən/ *n.* [ME f. L *reprobare* *reprobat*-disapprove (as RE-, *probare* approve)]

re•proc•ess /reepróses, -prō-/ *v.tr.* process again or differently.

re•pro•duce /reeprədŏŏs, -dyŏŏs/ *v.* **1** *tr.* produce a copy or representation of. **2** *tr.* cause to be seen or heard, etc., again (*tried to reproduce the sound exactly*). **3** *intr.* produce further members of the same species by natural means. **4** *refl.* produce offspring (*reproduced itself several times*). **5** *intr.* give a specified quality or result when copied (*reproduces badly in black and white*). **6** *tr.* *Biol.* form afresh (a lost part, etc., of the body). □□ **re•pro•duc•er** *n.* **re•pro•duc•i•ble** *adj.* **re•pro•duc•i•bil•i•ty** /-əbílitee/ *n.* **re•pro•duc•i•bly** *adv.*

re•pro•duc•tion /reeprədúkshən/ *n.* **1** the act or an instance of reproducing. **2** a copy of a work of art, esp. a print or photograph of a painting. **3** (*attrib.*) (of furniture, etc.) made in imitation of a certain style or of an earlier period. □□ **re•pro•duc•tive** *adj.* **re•pro•duc•tive•ly** *adv.* **re•pro•duc•tive•ness** *n.*

re•pro•gram /reeprógram/ *v.tr.* (**re•pro•grammed**, **re•pro•gram•ming**) program (esp. a computer) again or differently. □□ **re•pro•gram•ma•ble** /-prógraməbəl, -prōgrám-/ *adj.*

re•prog•ra•phy /riprógrəfee/ *n.* the science and practice of copying documents by photography, xerography, etc. □□ **re•prog•ra•pher** *n.* **re•pro•graph•ic** /reeprəgráfik/ *adj.* **re•pro•graph•i•cal•ly** *adv.* [REPRODUCE + -GRAPHY]

re•proof¹ /riprŏŏf/ *n.* **1** blame (*a glance of reproof*). **2** a rebuke; words expressing blame. [ME f. OF *reprove* f. *reprover* REPROVE]

re•proof² /reeprŏŏf/ *v.tr.* **1** esp. *Brit.* render (a coat, etc.) waterproof again. **2** make a fresh proof of (printed matter, etc.).

re•prove /riprŏŏv/ *v.tr.* rebuke (a person, a person's conduct, etc.). □□ **re•prov•a•ble** *adj.* **re•prov•er** *n.* **re•prov•ing•ly** *adv.* [ME f. OF *reprover* f. LL *reprobare* disapprove: see REPROBATE]

rep•tant /réptənt/ *adj.* (of a plant or animal) creeping. [L *reptare* *reptant*- frequent. of *repere* crawl]

rep•tile /réptil/ *n. & adj.* ●*n.* **1** any cold-blooded scaly animal of the class Reptilia, including snakes, lizards, crocodiles, turtles, tortoises, etc. **2** a mean, groveling, or repulsive person. ●*adj.* **1** (of an animal) creeping. **2** mean; groveling. □□ **rep•til•i•an** /-tíleeən, -tílyən/ *adj. & n.* [ME f. LL *reptilis* f. L *repere* *rept*- crawl]

re•pub•lic /ripú blik/ *n.* **1** a nation in which supreme power is held by the people or their elected representatives or by an elected or nominated president, not by a monarch, etc. **2** a society with equality among its members (*the literary republic*). [F *république* f. L *respublica* f. *res* concern + *publicus* PUBLIC]

re•pub•li•can /ripúblikən/ *adj. & n.* ●*adj.* **1** of or constituted as a republic. **2** characteristic of a republic. **3** advocating or supporting republican government. ●*n.* **1** a person advocating or supporting republican government. **2** (**Republican**) a member or supporter of the Republican party. **3** an advocate of a united Ireland. □□ **re•pub•li•can•ism** *n.*

Re•pub•li•can par•ty *n.* one of the two main US political parties, favoring a lesser degree of central power (cf. DEMOCRATIC PARTY).

re•pub•lish /reepúblish/ *v.tr.* (also *absol.*) publish again or in a new edition, etc. □□ **re•pub•li•ca•tion** /-likáyshən/ *n.*

re•pu•di•ate /ripyŏŏdeeayt/ *v.tr.* **1 a** disown; disavow; reject. **b** refuse dealings with. **c** deny. **2** refuse to recognize or obey (authority or a treaty). **3** refuse to discharge (an obligation or debt). **4** (in some cultures) divorce (one's spouse). □□ **re•pu•di•a•ble** *adj.* **re•pu•di•a•tion** /-áyshən/ *n.* **re•pu•di•a•tor** *n.* [L *repudiare* f. *repudium* divorce]

re•pug•nance /ripúgnəns/ *n.* (also **re•pug•nan•cy**) **1** (usu. foll. by *to*, *against*) antipathy; aversion. **2** (usu. foll. by *of*, *between*, *to*, *with*) inconsistency or incompatibility of ideas, statements, etc. [ME (in sense 2) f. F *répugnance* or L *repugnantia* f. *repugnare* oppose (as RE-, *pugnare* fight)]

re•pug•nant /ripúgnənt/ *adj.* **1** (often foll. by *to*) extremely distasteful. **2** (often foll. by *to*) contradictory. **3** (often foll. by *with*) incompatible. **4** *poet.* refractory; resisting. □□ **re•pug•nant•ly** *adv.* [ME f. F *répugnant* or L (as REPUGNANCE)]

re•pulse /ripúls/ *v. & n.* ●*v.tr.* **1** drive back (an attack or attacking enemy) by force of arms. **2 a** rebuff (friendly advances or their maker). **b** refuse (a request or offer or its maker). **3** be repulsive to; repel. **4** foil in controversy. ●*n.* **1** the act or an instance of repulsing or being repulsed. **2** a rebuff. [L *repellere* *repuls*- drive back (as RE-PEL)]

re•pul•sion /ripúlshən/ *n.* **1** aversion; disgust. **2** esp. *Physics* the force by which bodies tend to repel each other or increase their mutual distance (opp. ATTRACTION). [LL *repulsio* (as REPEL)]

re•pul•sive /ripú lsiv/ *adj.* **1** causing aversion or loathing; loathsome; disgusting. **2** *Physics* exerting repulsion. **3** *archaic* (of behavior, etc.) cold; unsympathetic. □□ **re•pul•sive•ly** *adv.* **re•pul•sive•ness** *n.* [F *répulsif* -*ive* or f. REPULSE]

▶See note at REPELLENT.

re•pur•chase /reepórchis/ *v. & n.* ●*v.tr.* purchase again. ●*n.* the act or an instance of purchasing again.

re•pu•ri•fy /reepyŏŏrifī/ *v.tr.* (•**fies**, •**fied**) purify again. □□ **re•pu•ri•fi•ca•tion** /-fikáyshən/ *n.*

rep•u•ta•ble /répyətəbəl/ *adj.* of good repute; respectable. □□ **rep•u•ta•bly** *adv.* [obs. F or f. med.L *reputabilis* (as REPUTE)]

rep•u•ta•tion /répyətáyshən/ *n.* **1** what is generally said or believed about a person's or thing's character or standing (*has a reputation for dishonesty*). **2** the state of being well thought of; distinction; respectability (*have my reputation to think of*). **3** (foll. by *of*, *for* + verbal noun) credit or discredit for a particular habit or characteristic (*has the reputation of driving hard bargains*). [ME f. L *reputatio* (as REPUTE)]

re•pute /ripyŏŏt/ *n. & v.* ●*n.* reputation (*known by repute*). ●*v.tr.* **1** (as **reputed** *adj.*) (often foll. by *to* + infin.) be generally considered or reckoned (*is reputed to be the best*). **2** (as **reputed** *adj.*) passing as being, but probably not being (*his reputed father*). □□ **re•put•ed•ly** *adv.* [ME f. OF *reputer* or L *reputare* (as RE-, *putare* think)]

re•quest /rikwést/ *n. & v.* ●*n.* **1** the act or an instance of asking for something; a petition (*came at his request*). **2** a thing asked for. **3** the state of being sought after; demand (*in great request*). **4** a letter, etc., asking for a particular recording, etc., to be played, as on a radio program, often with a personal message. ●*v.tr.* **1** ask to be given or allowed or favored with (*request a hearing*; *requests your presence*). **2** (foll. by *to* + infin.) ask a person to do something (*requested her to answer*). **3** (foll. by *that* + clause) ask that. □ **by** (or **on**) **request** in response to an expressed wish. □□ **re•quest•er** *n.* [ME f. OF *requeste*(*r*) ult. f. L *requaerere* (as REQUIRE)]

req•ui•em /rékweeəm, reékwee-/ *n.* **1** (**Requiem**) (also *attrib.*) *RC Ch.*, *Anglican Ch.* a Mass for the repose of the souls of the dead. **2** *Mus.* the musical setting for this. [ME f. accus. of L *requies* rest, the initial word of the mass]

re•qui•es•cat /rékwee-éskat, -kaat/ *n.* a wish or prayer for the repose of a dead person. [L, = may he or she rest (in peace)]

re•quire /rikwīr/ *v.tr.* **1** need; depend on for success or fulfillment (*the work requires much patience*). **2** lay down as an imperative (*did all that was required by law*). **3** command; instruct (a person, etc.). **4** order; insist on (an action or measure). **5** (often foll. by *of*, *from*, or *that* + clause) demand (of or from a person) as a right. **6** wish to have (*is there anything else you require*). □□ **re•quir•er** *n.* **re•quire•ment** *n.* [ME f. OF *requere* ult. f. L *requirere* (as RE-, *quaerere* seek)]

req•ui•site /rékwizit/ *adj. & n.* ●*adj.* required by circumstances; necessary to success, etc. ●*n.* (often foll. by *for*) a thing needed (for some purpose). □□ **req•ui•site•ly** adv. [ME f. L requisitus past part. (as REQUIRE)]

req•ui•si•tion /rékwizíshən/ n. & v. •n. **1** an official order laying claim to the use of property or materials. **2** a formal written demand that some duty should be performed. **3** being called or put into service. •v.tr. demand the use or supply of, esp. by requisition order. □□ **req•ui•si•tion•er** n. **req•ui•si•tion•ist** n. [F réquisition or L requisitio (as REQUIRE)]

re•quite /rikwít/ v.tr. **1** make return for (a service). **2** (often foll. by with) reward or avenge (a favor or injury). **3** (often foll. by for) make return to (a person). **4** (often foll. by for, with) repay with good or evil (requite like for like; requite hate with love). □□ **re•quit•al** n. [RE- + quite var. of QUIT]

re•ran past of RERUN.

re•read /rée-réed/ v. & n. •v.tr. (past and past part. **re•read** /–réd/) read again. •n. an instance of reading again. □□ **re•read•a•ble** adj.

rere•dos /rérədos, rírə–/ n. Eccl. an ornamental screen covering the wall at the back of an altar. [ME f. AF f. OF areredos f. arere behind + dos back: cf. ARREARS]

re•re•lease /rée-rilées/ v. & n. •v.tr. release (a recording, motion picture, etc.) again. •n. a rereleased recording, motion picture, etc.

re•route /rée-róot, –rówt/ v.tr. send or carry by a different route.

re•run v. & n. •v.tr. /rée-rún/(**re•run•ning**; past **re•ran**; past part. **re•run**) run (a race, television program, etc.) again. •n. /rée-run/ **1** the act or an instance of rerunning. **2** a television program, etc., shown again.

Res. abbr. Reservation.

re•sale /réesáyl/ n. the sale of a thing previously bought. □□ **re•sal•a•ble** adj.

re•sched•ule /réeskéjool/ v.tr. alter the schedule of; replan.

re•scind /risínd/ v.tr. abrogate; revoke; cancel. □□ **re•scind•a•ble** adj. **re•scind•ment** n. **re•scis•sion** /–sízhən/ n. [L rescindere resciss- (as RE-, scindere cut)]

re•script /réeskrípt/ n. **1** a Roman emperor's written reply to an appeal for guidance, esp. on a legal point. **2** RC Ch. the Pope's decision on a question of doctrine or papal law. **3** an official edict or announcement. **4 a** the act or an instance of rewriting. **b** the thing rewritten. [L rescriptum, neut. past part. of rescribere rescript- (as RE-, scribere write)]

res•cue /réskyoo/ v. & n. •v.tr. (**res•cues, res•cued, res•cu•ing**) **1** (often foll. by from) save or set free or bring away from attack, custody, danger, or harm. **2** Law a unlawfully liberate (a person). **b** forcibly recover (property). •n. the act or an instance of rescuing or being rescued; deliverance. □□ **res•cu•a•ble** adj. **res•cu•er** n. [ME rescowe f. OF rescoure f. Rmc, formed as RE- + L excutere (as EX-¹, quatere shake)]

re•seal /réeséel/ v.tr. seal again. □□ **re•seal•a•ble** adj.

re•search /risórch, réesorch/ n. & v. •n. **1 a** the systematic investigation into and study of materials, sources, etc., in order to establish facts and reach new conclusions. **b** (usu. in pl.) an endeavor to discover new or collate old facts, etc., by the scientific study of a subject or by a course of critical investigation. **2** (attrib.) engaged in or intended for research (research assistant). •v. **1** do research into or for. **2** intr. make researches. □□ **re•search•a•ble** adj. **re•search•er** n. [obs. F recerche (as RE-, SEARCH)]

re•search and de•vel•op•ment n. (often attrib.) (in industry, etc.) work directed toward the innovation, introduction, and improvement of products and processes.

re•seat /réeséet/ v.tr. **1** (also refl.) seat (oneself, a person, etc.) again. **2** provide with a fresh seat or seats.

re•sect /risékt/ v.tr. Surgery **1** cut out part of (a lung, etc.). **2** pare down (bone, cartilage, etc.). □□ **re•sec•tion** n. **re•sec•tion•al** adj. **re•sec•tion•ist** n. [L resecare resect- (as RE-, secare cut)]

re•se•da /riséedə/ n. **1** any plant of the genus Reseda, with sweet-scented flowers, e.g., a mignonette. **2** (also /réz–/) the pale green color of mignonette flowers. [L, perh. f. imper. of resedare assuage, with ref. to its supposed curative powers]

re•se•lect /réesilékt/ v.tr. select again or differently. □□ **re•se•lec•tion** n.

re•sell /réesél/ v.tr. (past and past part. **re•sold**) sell (an object, etc.) after buying it.

re•sem•blance /rizémbləns/ n. (often foll. by to, between, of) a likeness or similarity. □□ **re•sem•blant** adj. [ME f. AF (as RESEMBLE)]

re•sem•ble /rizémbəl/ v.tr. be like; have a similarity to, or features in common with, or the same appearance as. □□ **re•sem•bler** n. [ME f. OF resembler (as RE-, sembler f. L similare f. similis like)]

re•sent /rizént/ v.tr. show or feel indignation at; be aggrieved by (a circumstance, action, or person) (we resent being patronized). [obs. F resentir (as RE-, L sentire feel)]

re•sent•ful /rizéntfool/ adj. feeling resentment. □□ **re•sent•ful•ly** adv. **re•sent•ful•ness** n.

re•sent•ment n. (often foll. by at, of) indignant or bitter feelings; anger. [It. risentimento or F ressentiment (as RESENT)]

res•er•pine /risórpeen, –pin, résorpeen, –pin/ n. an alkaloid obtained from plants of the genus Rauwolfia, used as a tranquilizer and in

the treatment of hypertension. [G Reserpin f. mod.L Rauwolfia (f. L. Rauwolf, Ger. botanist d. 1596) serpentina]

res•er•va•tion /rézərváyshən/ n. **1** the act or an instance of reserving or being reserved. **2** a booking (of a room, berth, seat, etc.). **3** the thing booked, e.g., a room in a hotel. **4** an express or tacit limitation or exception to an agreement, etc. (had reservations about the plan). **5** an area of land reserved for a particular group, as a tract designated by the federal government for use by Native Americans. **6** Brit. a strip of land between the lanes of a divided highway. **7 a** a right or interest retained in an estate being conveyed. **b** the clause reserving this. **8** Eccl. **a** the practice of retaining for some purpose a portion of the Eucharistic elements (esp. the bread) after celebration. **b** RC Ch. the power of absolution reserved to a superior. **c** RC Ch. the right reserved to the pope of nomination to a vacant benefice. [ME f. OF reservation or LL reservatio (as RESERVE)]

re•serve /rizórv/ v. & n. •v.tr. **1** postpone; put aside; keep back for a later occasion or special use. **2** order to be specially retained or allocated for a particular person or at a particular time. **3** retain or secure, esp. by formal or legal stipulation (reserve the right to). **4** postpone delivery of (judgment, etc.) (reserved my comments until the end). •n. **1** a thing reserved for future use; an extra stock or amount (a great reserve of strength; huge energy reserves). **2** a limitation, qualification, or exception attached to something (accept your offer without reserve). **3 a** self-restraint; reticence; lack of cordiality (difficult to overcome his reserve). **b** (in artistic or literary expression) absence from exaggeration or ill-proportioned effects. **4** a company's profit added to capital. **5** (in sing. or pl.) assets kept readily available as cash or at a central bank, or as gold or foreign exchange (reserve currency). **6** (in sing. or pl.) **a** troops withheld from action to reinforce or protect others. **b** forces in addition to the regular army, navy, air force, etc., but available in an emergency. **7** a member of the military reserve. **8** an extra player chosen to be a possible substitute on a team. **9** a place reserved for special use, esp. as a habitat for a native tribe or for wildlife (game reserve; nature reserve). **10** the intentional suppression of the truth (exercised a certain amount of reserve). **11** (in the decoration of ceramics or textiles) an area that still has the original color of the material or the color of the background. □ **in reserve** unused and available if required. **with all** (or **all proper**) **reserve** esp. Brit. without endorsing. **without reserve** without limits or restraints; freely. □□ **re•serv•a•ble** adj. **re•serv•er** n. [ME f. OF reserver f. L reservare (as RE-, servare keep)]

re•serve /réesórv/ v.tr. & intr. serve again.

re•served /rizórvd/ adj. **1** reticent; slow to reveal emotion or opinions; uncommunicative. **2 a** set apart; destined for some use or fate. **b** (often foll. by for, to) left by fate for; falling first or only to. □□ **re•serv•ed•ly** /–vidlee/ adv. **re•serv•ed•ness** n.

re•serve price n. the lowest acceptable price stipulated for an item sold at an auction.

re•serv•ist /rizórvist/ n. a member of the reserve forces.

res•er•voir /rézorvwaar/ n. **1** a large natural or artificial lake used as a source of water supply. **2 a** any natural or artificial receptacle esp. for or of fluid. **b** a place where fluid, etc., collects. **3** a part of a machine, etc., holding fluid. **4** (usu. foll. by of) a reserve or supply esp. of information. [F réservoir f. réserver RESERVE]

re•set /réesét/ v.tr. (**re•set•ting**; past and past part. **re•set**) set (a broken bone, gems, a mechanical device, etc.) again or differently. □□ **re•set•ta•ble** adj. **re•set•ta•bil•i•ty** /–sétəbílitee/ n.

re•set•tle /réesét'l/ v.tr. & intr. settle again. □□ **re•set•tle•ment** n.

re•shape /réeshayp/ v.tr. shape or form again or differently.

re•shuf•fle /réeshúfəl/ v. & n. •v.tr. **1** shuffle (cards) again. **2** interchange the posts of (government ministers, etc.). •n. the act or an instance of reshuffling.

re•side /rizíd/ v.intr. **1** (often foll. by at, in, abroad, etc.) (of a person) have one's home; dwell permanently. **2** (of power, a right, etc.) rest or be vested in. **3** (of an incumbent official) be in residence. **4** (foll. by in) (of a quality) be present or inherent in. [ME, prob. back-form. f. RESIDENT infl. by F résider or L residēre (as RE-, sedēre sit)]

res•i•dence /rézidəns/ n. **1** the act or an instance of residing. **2 a** the place where a person resides; an abode. **b** a mansion; the official house of a government minister, etc. **c** a house, esp. one of considerable pretension (returned to their Beverly Hills residence). □ **in residence** dwelling at a specified place, esp. for the performance of duties or work. [ME f. OF residence or med.L residentia f. L residēre: see RESIDE]

res•i•den•cy /rézidənsee/ n. (pl. **•cies**) **1** = RESIDENCE 1, 2a. **2** a period of specialized medical training; the position of a resident. **3** Brit. hist. the official residence of the governor-general's representative or other government agent at an Indian native court; the territory supervised by this official. **4** Brit. a musician's regular en-

See page xx for the **Key to Pronunciation.**

gagement at a club, etc. **5** esp. *Brit.* a group or organization of intelligence agents in a foreign country. **6** *attrib.* based on or related to residence (*residency requirement for in-state tuition*).

res·i·dent /rézidənt/ *n. & adj.* ● *n.* **1** (often foll. by *of*) **a** a permanent inhabitant (of a town or neighborhood). **b** a bird belonging to a species that does not migrate. **2** *Brit.* a guest in a hotel, etc., staying overnight. **3** *hist.* a British government agent in any semi-independent nation, esp. the governor-general's agent at an Indian native court. **4** a medical graduate engaged in specialized practice under supervision in a hospital. **5** *Brit.* an intelligence agent in a foreign country. ● *adj.* **1** residing; in residence. **2 a** having quarters on the premises of one's work, etc. (*resident housekeeper, resident doctor*). **b** working regularly in a particular place. **3** located in; inherent (*powers of feeling are resident in the nerves*). **4** (of birds, etc.) nonmigratory. □□ **res·i·dent·ship** *n.* (in sense 3 of *n.*). [ME f. OF *resident* or L: see RESIDE]

res·i·den·tial /rézidénshəl/ *adj.* **1** suitable for or occupied by private houses (*residential area*). **2** used as a residence (*residential hotel*). **3** based on or connected with residence (*the residential qualification for voters; a residential course of study*). □□ **res·i·den·tial·ly** *adv.*

res·i·den·ti·ar·y /rézidénshee-eree, –shəree/ *adj. & n.* ● *adj.* of, subject to, or requiring, official residence. ● *n.* (*pl.* **-ies**) an ecclesiastic who must officially reside in a place. [med.L *residentiarius* (as RESIDENCE)]

re·sid·u·a *pl.* of RESIDUUM.

re·sid·u·al /rizíjōōəl/ *adj. & n.* ● *adj.* **1** remaining; left as a residue or residuum. **2** *Math.* resulting from subtraction. **3** (in calculation) still unaccounted for or not eliminated. ● *n.* **1** a quantity left over or *Math.* resulting from subtraction. **2** an error in calculation not accounted for or eliminated. □□ **re·sid·u·al·ly** *adv.*

re·sid·u·ar·y /rizíjōōeree/ *adj.* **1** of the residue of an estate (*residuary bequest*). **2** of or being a residuum; residual; still remaining.

res·i·due /rézidōō, –dyōō/ *n.* **1** what is left over or remains; a remainder; the rest. **2** *Law* what remains of an estate after the payment of charges, debts, and bequests. **3** esp. *Chem.* a residuum. [ME f. OF *residu* f. L *residuum*: see RESIDUUM]

re·sid·u·um /rizíjōōəm/ *n.* (*pl.* **re·sid·u·a** /–jōōə/) **1** *Chem.* a substance left after combustion or evaporation. **2** a remainder or residue. [L, neut. of *residuus* remaining f. *residēre*: see RESIDE]

re·sign /rizín/ *v.* **1** *intr.* **a** (often foll. by *from*) give up office, one's employment, etc. (*resigned from the faculty*). **b** (often foll. by *as*) retire (*resigned as chief executive*). **2** *tr.* give up (office, one's employment, etc.); surrender; hand over (a right, charge, task, etc.). **3** *tr.* give up (hope, etc.). **4** *refl.* (usu. foll. by *to*) **a** reconcile (oneself, one's mind, etc.) to the inevitable (*have resigned myself to the idea*). **b** surrender (oneself to another's guidance). **5** *intr. Chess*, etc., discontinue play and admit defeat. □□ **re·sign·er** *n.* [ME f. OF *resigner* f. L *resignare* unseal, cancel (as RE-, *signare* sign, seal)]

re-sign /réesín/ *v.tr. & intr.* sign again.

res·ig·na·tion /rézignáyshən/ *n.* **1** the act or an instance of resigning, esp. from one's job or office. **2** the document, etc., conveying this intention. **3** the state of being resigned; the uncomplaining endurance of a sorrow or difficulty. [ME f. OF f. med.L *resignatio* (as RESIGN)]

re·signed /rizínd/ *adj.* (often foll. by *to*) having resigned oneself; submissive, acquiescent. □□ **re·sign·ed·ly** /–zínidlee/ *adv.* **re·sign·ed·ness** *n.*

re·sile /rizíl/ *v.intr.* **1** (of something stretched or compressed) recoil to resume a former size and shape; spring back. **2** have or show resilience or recuperative power. **3** (usu. foll. by *from*) withdraw from a course of action. [obs. F *resilir* or L *resilire* (as RE-, *salire* jump)]

re·sil·ient /rizílyənt/ *adj.* **1** (of a substance, etc.) recoiling; springing back; resuming its original shape after bending, stretching, compression, etc. **2** (of a person) readily recovering from shock, depression, etc.; buoyant. □□ **re·sil·ience** *n.* **re·sil·ien·cy** *n.* **re·sil·ient·ly** *adv.* [L *resiliens resilient-* (as RESILE)]

res·in /rézin/ *n. & v.* ● *n.* **1** an adhesive flammable substance insoluble in water, secreted by some plants, and often extracted by incision, esp. from fir and pine (cf. GUM[1]). **2** (in full **synthetic resin**) a solid or liquid organic compound made by polymerization, etc., and used in plastics, etc. ● *v.tr.* rub or treat with resin. □□ **res·in·ate** /–nət/ *n.* **res·in·ate** /–nayt/ *v.tr.* **res·in·oid** *adj. & n.* **res·in·ous** *adj.* [ME *resyn, rosyn* f. L *resina* & med.L *rosina, rosinum*]

re·sist /rizíst/ *v.tr. & n.* ● *v.* **1** *tr.* withstand the action or effect of; repel. **2** *tr.* stop the course or progress of; prevent from reaching, penetrating, etc. **3** *tr.* abstain from (pleasure, temptation, etc.). **4** *tr.* strive against; try to impede; refuse to comply with (*resist arrest*). **5** *intr.* offer opposition; refuse to comply. ● *n.* a protective coating of a resistant substance, applied esp. to parts of a fabric that are not to take dye or to parts of pottery that are not to take glaze or luster. ● **cannot** (or **could not**, etc.) **resist 1** (foll. by verbal noun) feel obliged or strongly inclined to (*cannot resist teasing me about it*). **2** is certain to be amused, attracted, etc., by (*can't resist children's clothes*). □□ **re·sist·ant** *adj.* **re·sist·er** *n.* **re·sist·i·ble** *adj.* **re·**

sist·i·bil·i·ty *n.* [ME f. OF *resister* or L *resistere* (as RE-, *sistere* stop, redupl. of *stare* stand)]

re·sist·ance /rizí stəns/ *n.* **1** the act or an instance of resisting; refusal to comply. **2** the power of resisting (*showed resistance to wear and tear*). **3** *Biol.* the ability to withstand adverse conditions. **4** the impeding, slowing, or stopping effect exerted by one material thing on another. **5** *Physics* **a** the property of hindering the conduction of electricity, heat, etc. **b** the measure of this in a body. ¶ Symb.: R. **6** a resistor. **7** (in full **resistance movement**) a secret organization resisting authority, esp. in an occupied country. [ME f. F *résistance, résistence* f. LL *resistentia* (as RESIST)]

To remember the *-ance* ending of *resistance*, use the mnemonic: "You can increase your resis*tan*ce to the sun with a *tan* ."

---

re·sis·tive /rizístiv/ *adj.* **1** able to resist. **2** *Electr.* of or concerning resistance.

re·sis·tiv·i·ty /réezistívitee/ *n. Electr.* a measure of the resisting power of a specified material to the flow of an electric current.

re·sist·less /rizístlis/ *adj. archaic poet.* **1** irresistible; relentless. **2** unresisting. □□ **re·sist·less·ly** *adv.*

re·sis·tor /rizístər/ *n. Electr.* a device having resistance to the passage of an electrical current.

re·sold *past* and *past part.* of RESELL.

re·sol·u·ble /rizólyəbəl/ *adj.* **1** that can be resolved. **2** (foll. by *into*) analyzable. [F *résoluble* or L *resolubilis* (as RESOLVE, after *soluble*)]

res·o·lute /rézəlōōt/ *adj.* (of a person or a person's mind or action) determined; decided; firm of purpose; not vacillating. □□ **res·o·lute·ly** *adv.* **res·o·lute·ness** *n.* [L *resolutus* past part. of *resolvere* (see RESOLVE)]

SYNONYM TIP   resolute

CONSTANT, DECISIVE, DETERMINED, FAITHFUL, STAUNCH. Any of the above adjectives might apply to you if you take a stand on something and stick to it, or show your loyalty to a person, country, or cause. If you show unswerving loyalty to someone or something to which you are tied (as in marriage, friendship, etc.), you would be described as **faithful** (*a faithful wife, a faithful Republican*). **Constant** also implies a firm or steady attachment to someone or something, but with less emphasis on vows, pledges, and obligations; it is the opposite of fickleness rather than of unfaithfulness (*a constant if not a faithful husband*). To be described as **staunch** carries loyalty one step further, implying an unwillingness to be dissuaded or turned aside (*a staunch friend who refused to believe the rumors that were circulating*). To be called **resolute** means that you are both *staunch* and steadfast, but the emphasis here is on character and a firm adherence to your own goals and purposes rather than to those of others (*resolute in insisting upon her right to be heard*). **Determined** and **decisive** are less forceful words. You can be *decisive* in almost any situation, as long as you have a choice among alternatives and don't hesitate in taking a stand (*decisive as always, she barely glanced at the menu before ordering*). *Determined*, unlike *resolute*, suggests a stubborn will rather than a conscious adherence to goals or principles (*he was determined to be home before the holidays*).

---

res·o·lu·tion /rézəlōōshən/ *n.* **1** a resolute temper or character; boldness and firmness of purpose. **2** a thing resolved on; an intention (*New Year's resolutions*). **3 a** a formal expression of opinion or intention by a legislative body or public meeting. **b** the formulation of this (*passed a resolution*). **4** (usu. foll. by *of*) the act or an instance of solving doubt or a problem or question (*toward a resolution of the difficulty*). **5 a** separation into components; decomposition. **b** the replacing of a single force, etc., by two or more jointly equivalent to it. **6** (foll. by *into*) analysis; conversion into another form. **7** *Mus.* the act or an instance of causing discord to pass into concord. **8** *Physics*, etc., the smallest interval measurable by a scientific instrument; the resolving power. **9** *Med.* the disappearance of inflammation, etc., without suppuration. **10** *Prosody* the substitution of two short syllables for one long. [ME f. L *resolutio* (as RESOLVE)]

re·sol·u·tive /rézəlōōtiv/ *adj. Med.* having the power or ability to dissolve. [med.L *resolutivus* (as RESOLVE)]

re·solve /rizólv/ *v. & n.* ● *v.* **1** *intr.* make up one's mind; decide firmly (*resolve to do better*). **2** *tr.* (of circumstances, etc.) cause (a person) to do this (*events resolved him to leave*). **3** *tr.* (foll. by *that* + clause) (of an assembly or meeting) pass a resolution by vote (*the committee resolved that immediate action should be taken*). **4** *intr. & tr.* (often foll. by *into*) separate or cause to separate into constituent parts; disintegrate; analyze; dissolve. **5** *tr.* (of optical or photographic equipment) separate or distinguish between closely adjacent objects. **6** *tr. & intr.* (foll. by *into*) convert or be converted. **7** *tr. & intr.* (foll. by *into*) reduce by mental analysis into. **8** *tr.* solve; explain; clear up; settle (doubt, argument, etc.). **9** *tr. & intr. Mus.* convert or be converted into concord. **10** *tr. Med.* remove (inflammation, etc.) without suppuration. **11** *tr. Prosody* replace (a long syllable) by two short syllables. **12** *tr. Mech.* replace (a force, etc.) by two or more jointly equivalent to it. ● *n.* **1 a** a firm mental decision or intention; a resolution (*made a resolve not to go*). **b** a formal resolution by a legislative body or public meeting. **2** resoluteness; steadfastness. □□ **re·solv·a·ble** *adj.* **re·solv·a·bil·i·ty** /–zólvəbílitee/ *n.* **re·solv·er** *n.* [ME f. L *resolvere resolut-* (as RE-, SOLVE)]

re·solved /rizólvd/ *adj.* resolute; determined. □□ **re·solv·ed·ly** /–zólvidlee/ *adv.* **re·solv·ed·ness** *n.*

re·sol·vent /rizólvənt/ *adj. & n.* esp. *Med.* ● *adj.* (of a drug, application, substance, etc.) effecting the resolution of a tumor, etc. ● *n.* such a drug, etc.

re·solv·ing pow·er an instrument's ability to distinguish very small or very close objects.

res·o·nance /rézənəns/ *n.* **1** the reinforcement or prolongation of sound by reflection or synchronous vibration. **2** *Mech.* a condition in which an object or system is subjected to an oscillating force having a frequency close to its own natural frequency. **3** *Chem.* the property of a molecule having a structure best represented by two or more forms rather than a single structural formula. **4** *Physics* a short-lived elementary particle that is an excited state of a more stable particle. [OF f. L *resonantia* echo (as RESONANT)]

res·o·nant /rézənənt/ *adj.* **1** (of sound) echoing; resounding; continuing to sound; reinforced or prolonged by reflection or synchronous vibration. **2** (of a body, room, etc.) tending to reinforce or prolong sounds esp. by synchronous vibration. **3** (often foll. by *with*) (of a place) resounding. **4** of or relating to resonance. □□ **res·o·nant·ly** *adv.* [F *résonnant* or L *resonare resonant-* (as RE-, *sonare* sound)]

res·o·nate /rézənayt/ *v.intr.* produce or show resonance; resound. [L *resonare resonat-* (as RESONANT)]

res·o·na·tor /rézənaytər/ *n. Mus.* **1** an instrument responding to a single note and used for detecting it in combinations. **2** an appliance for giving resonance to sound or other vibrations.

re·sorb /risáwrb, –záwrb/ *v.tr.* absorb again. □□ **re·sorb·ence** *n.* **re·sorb·ent** *adj.* [L *resorbēre resorpt-* (as RE-, *sorbēre* absorb)]

re·sor·cin /rizáwrsin/ *n.* = RESORCINOL.

re·sor·cin·ol /rizáwrsinawl, –nol/ *n. Chem.* a crystalline organic compound usu. made by synthesis and used in the production of dyes, drugs, resins, etc. [RESIN + ORCINOL]

re·sorp·tion /rizáwrpshən/ *n.* **1** the act or an instance of resorbing; the state of being resorbed. **2** the absorption of tissue within the body. □□ **re·sorp·tive** /–zórptiv/ *adj.* [RESORB after *absorption*]

re·sort /rizáwrt/ *n. & v.* ● *n.* **1** a place frequented esp. for vacations or for a specified purpose or quality (*seaside resort; health resort*). **2 a** a thing to which one has recourse; an expedient or measure (*a taxi was our best resort*). **b** (foll. by *to*) recourse to; use of (*to resort to violence*). **3** a tendency to frequent or be frequented (*places of great resort*). ● *v.intr.* **1** (foll. by *to*) turn to as an expedient (*resorted to threats*). **2** (foll. by *to*) go often or in large numbers to. □ **in the** (or **as a**) **last resort** when all else has failed. □□ **re·sort·er** *n.* [ME f. OF *resortir* (as RE-, *sortir* come or go out)]

re·sort /rée-sáwrt/ *v.tr.* sort again or differently.

re·sound /rizównd/ *v.* **1** *intr.* (often foll. by *with*) (of a place) ring or echo (*the hall resounded with laughter*). **2** *intr.* (of a voice, instrument, sound, etc.) produce echoes; go on sounding; fill the place with sound. **3** *intr.* **a** (of fame, a reputation, etc.) be much talked of. **b** (foll. by *through*) produce a sensation (*the call resounded through Europe*). **4** *tr.* (often foll. by *of*) proclaim or repeat loudly (the praises) of a person or thing (*resounded the praises of Greece*). **5** *tr.* (of a place) reecho (a sound). [ME f. RE- + SOUND[1] *v.*, after OF *resoner* or L *resonare*: see RESONANT]

re·sound·ing /rizównding/ *adj.* **1** in senses of RESOUND. **2** unmistakable; emphatic (*was a resounding success*). □□ **re·sound·ing·ly** *adv.*

re·source /réesawrs, –zawrs, risáwrs, –záwrs/ *n.* **1** an expedient or device (*escape was their only resource*). **2** (usu. in *pl.*) **a** the means available to achieve an end, fulfill a function, etc. **b** a stock or supply that can be drawn on. **c** available assets. **3** (in *pl.*) a country's collective wealth or means of defense. **4** *Brit.* a leisure occupation (*reading is a pleasant resource*). **5 a** (often in *pl.*) skill in devising expedients (*a person of great resource*). **b** practical ingenuity; quick wit (*full of resource*). **6** *archaic* the possibility of aid (*lost without resource*). □ **one's own resources** one's own abilities, ingenuity, etc. □□ **re·source·ful** *adj.* **re·source·ful·ly** *adv.* **re·source·ful·ness** *n.* **re·source·less** *adj.* **re·source·less·ness** *n.* [F *ressource, ressourse,* fem. past part. of OF dial. *resourdre* (as RE-, L *surgere* rise)]

re·spect /rispékt/ *n. & v.* ● *n.* **1** deferential esteem felt or shown toward a person or quality. **2 a** (foll. by *of, for*) heed or regard. **b** (foll. by *to*) attention to or consideration of (*without respect to the results*). **3** an aspect, detail, particular, etc. (*correct except in this one respect*). **4** reference; relation (*a morality that has no respect to religion*). **5** (in *pl.*) a person's polite messages or attentions (*give my respects to your mother*). ● *v.tr.* **1** regard with deference, esteem, or honor. **2 a** avoid interfering with, harming, degrading, insulting, injuring, or interrupting. **b** treat with consideration. **c** refrain from offending, corrupting, or tempting (a person, a person's feelings, etc.). □ **in respect of** *Brit.* = *with respect to.* **in respect that** because. **with all due respect** a mollifying formula preceding an expression of one's disagreement with another's views. **with respect to** regarding; in reference to; as concerns. □□ **re·spect·er** *n.* [ME f. OF *respect* or L *respectus* f. *respicere* (as RE-, *specere* look at) or f. *respectare* frequent. of *respicere*]

re·spect·a·bil·i·ty /rispéktəbílitee/ *n.* **1** the state of being respectable. **2** those who are respectable.

re·spect·a·ble /rispéktəbəl/ *adj.* **1** deserving or enjoying respect (*an intellectually respectable hypothesis; a respectable elder statesman*). **2 a** (of people) of good social standing or reputation (*comes from a respectable middle-class family*). **b** characteristic of or associated with people of such status or character (*a respectable neighborhood; a respectable profession*). **3 a** honest and decent in character or conduct. **b** characterized by (a sense of) convention or propriety; socially acceptable (*respectable behavior; a respectable publication*). **c** *derog.* highly conventional; prim. **4 a** commendable; meritorious (*an entirely respectable ambition*). **b** comparatively good or competent; passable; tolerable (*a respectable effort; speaks respectable French*). **5** reasonably good in condition or appearance; presentable. **6** appreciable in number, size, amount, etc. (*earns a very respectable salary*). **7** accepted or tolerated on account of prevalence (*materialism has become respectable again*). □□ **re·spect·a·bly** *adv.*

re·spect·ful /rispéktfool/ *adj.* showing deference (*stood at a respectful distance*). □□ **re·spect·ful·ly** *adv.* **re·spect·ful·ness** *n.*

re·spect·ing /rispékting/ *prep.* with reference or regard to; concerning.

re·spec·tive /rispéktiv/ *adj.* concerning or appropriate to each of several individually; proper to each (*go to your respective places*). [F *respectif –ive* f. med.L *respectivus* (as RESPECT)]

re·spec·tive·ly /rispéktivlee/ *adv.* for each separately or in turn, and in the order mentioned (*she and I gave $10 and $1, respectively*).

re·spell /réespél/ *v.tr.* spell again or differently, esp. phonetically.

res·pi·ra·ble /réspərəbəl, rispírə–/ *adj.* (of air, gas, etc.) able or fit to be breathed. [F *respirable* or LL *respirabilis* (as RESPIRE)]

res·pi·rate /réspirayt/ *v.tr.* subject to artificial respiration. [backform. f. RESPIRATION]

res·pi·ra·tion /réspiráyshən/ *n.* **1 a** the act or an instance of breathing. **b** a single inspiration or expiration; a breath. **2** *Biol.* in living organisms, the process involving the release of energy and carbon dioxide from the oxidation of complex organic substances. [ME f. F *respiration* or L *respiratio* (as RESPIRE)]

res·pi·ra·tor /réspiraytər/ *n.* **1** an apparatus worn over the face to prevent poison gas, cold air, dust particles, etc., from being inhaled. **2** *Med.* an apparatus for maintaining artificial respiration.

re·spire /rispír/ *v.* **1** *intr.* breathe air. **2** *intr.* inhale and exhale air. **3** *intr.* (of a plant) carry out respiration. **4** *tr.* breathe (air, etc.). **5** *intr.* breathe again; take a breath. **6** *intr.* get rest or respite; recover hope or spirit. □□ **res·pi·ra·to·ry** /réspərətawree, rispírə–/ *adj.* [ME f. OF *respirer* or f. L *respirare* (as RE-, *spirare* breathe)]

res·pite /réspit/ *n. & v.* ● *n.* **1** an interval of rest or relief. **2** a delay permitted before the discharge of an obligation or the suffering of a penalty. ● *v.tr.* **1** grant respite to; reprieve (a condemned person). **2** postpone the execution or exaction of (a sentence, obligation, etc.). **3** give temporary relief from (pain or care) or to (a sufferer). [ME f. OF *respit* f. L *respectus* RESPECT]

re·splend·ent /rispléndənt/ *adj.* brilliant; dazzlingly or gloriously bright. □□ **re·splend·ence** *n.* **re·splend·en·cy** *n.* **re·splend·ent·ly** *adv.* [ME f. L *resplendēre* (as RE-, *splendēre* glitter)]

re·spond /rispónd/ *v. & n.* ● *v.* **1** *intr.* answer; give a reply. **2** *intr.* act or behave in an answering or corresponding manner. **3** *intr.* (usu. foll. by *to*) show sensitiveness to by behavior or change (*does not respond to kindness*). **4** *intr.* (of a congregation) make answers to a priest, etc. **5** *intr. Bridge* make a bid on the basis of a partner's preceding bid. **6** *tr.* say (something) in answer. ● *n.* **1** *Archit.* a half pillar or half pier attached to a wall to support an arch, esp. at the end of an arcade. **2** *Eccl.* a responsory; a response to a versicle. □□ **re·spond·ence** *n.* **re·spond·en·cy** *n.* **re·spond·er** *n.* [ME f. OF *respondre* answer ult. f. L *respondēre respons-* answer (as RE-, *spondēre* pledge)]

re·spond·ent /rispóndənt/ *n. & adj.* ● *n.* **1** a defendant, esp. in an appeal or divorce case. **2** a person who makes an answer or defends an argument, etc. ● *adj.* **1** giving answers. **2** (foll. by *to*) responsive. **3** in the position of defendant.

re·sponse /rispóns/ *n.* **1** an answer given in word or act; a reply. **2** a feeling, movement, change, etc., caused by a stimulus or influence. **3** (often in *pl.*) *Eccl.* any part of the liturgy said or sung in answer to the priest; a responsory. **4** *Bridge* a bid made in responding. [ME f. OF *respons(e)* or L *responsum* neut. past part. of *respondēre* RESPOND]

re·spon·si·bil·i·ty /rispónsibílitee/ *n.* (*pl.* **·ties**) **1 a** (often foll. by *for, of*) the state or fact of being responsible (*refuses all responsibility for it; will take the responsibility of doing it*). **b** authority; the ability to act independently and make decisions (*a job with more responsibility*). **2** the person or thing for which one is responsible (*the food is my responsibility*). □ **on one's own responsibility** without authorization.

re•spon•si•ble /rispónsibəl/ *adj.* **1** (often foll. by *to, for*) liable to be called to account (to a person or for a thing). **2** morally accountable for one's actions; capable of rational conduct. **3** of good credit, position, or repute; respectable; evidently trustworthy. **4** (often foll. by *for*) being the primary cause (*a short circuit was responsible for the power failure*). **5** (of a ruler or government) not autocratic. **6** involving responsibility (*a responsible job*). □□ **re•spon•si•ble•ness** *n.* **re•spon•si•bly** *adv.* [obs. F f. L *respondēre*: see RESPOND]

re•spon•sive /rispónsiv/ *adj.* **1** (often foll. by *to*) responding readily (to some influence). **2** sympathetic; impressionable. **3 a** answering. **b** by way of answer. **4** (of a liturgy, etc.) using responses. □□ **re•spon•sive•ly** *adv.* **re•spon•sive•ness** *n.* [F *responsif –ive* or LL *responsivus* (as RESPOND)]

re•spon•so•ry /rispónsəree/ *n.* (*pl.* **-ries**) an anthem said or sung by a soloist and choir after a lesson. [ME f. LL *responsorium* (as RESPOND)]

re•spray *v. & n.* •*v.tr.* /reespráy/ spray again (esp. to change the color or of the paint on a vehicle, etc.). •*n.* /reespray/ the act or an instance of respraying.

rest[1] /rest/ *v. & n.* •*v.* **1** *intr.* cease, abstain, or be relieved from exertion, action, movement, or employment; be tranquil. **2** *intr.* be still or asleep, esp. to refresh oneself or recover strength. **3** *tr.* give relief or repose to; allow to rest (*a chair to rest my legs*). **4** *intr.* (foll. by *on, upon, against*) lie on; be supported by; be spread out on; be propped against. **5** *intr.* (foll. by *on, upon*) depend; be based; rely. **6** *intr.* (foll. by *on, upon*) (of a look) light upon or be steadily directed on. **7** *tr.* (foll. by *on, upon*) place for support or foundation. **8** *intr.* (of a problem or subject) be left without further investigation or discussion (*let the matter rest*). **9** *intr.* **a** lie in death. **b** (foll. by *in*) lie buried in (a churchyard, etc.). **10** *tr.* (as **rested** *adj.*) refreshed or reinvigorated by resting. **11** *intr.* conclude the calling of witnesses in a court case (*the prosecution rests*). **12** *intr.* (of land) lie fallow. **13** *intr.* (foll. by *in*) repose trust in (*am content to rest in God*). •*n.* **1** repose or sleep, esp. in bed at night (*get a good night's rest*). **2** freedom from or the cessation of exertion, worry, activity, etc. (*we had a brief rest during the eye of the hurricane, but then the wind began howling again*). **3** a period of resting (*take a 15-minute rest*). **4** a support or prop for holding or steadying something. **5** *Mus.* **a** an interval of silence of a specified duration. **b** the sign denoting this. **6** a place of resting or abiding, esp. a lodging place or shelter for travelers. **7** a pause in elocution. **8** a caesura in verse. □ **at rest** not moving; not agitated or troubled; dead. **lay to rest** inter (a corpse). **rest one's case** conclude one's argument, etc. **rest** (or **God rest**) **his** (or **her**) **soul** may God grant his (or her) soul repose. **rest on one's laurels** see LAUREL. **rest on one's oars** see OAR. **rest up** rest oneself thoroughly. **set** (or **put**) **to** (or **at**) **rest** settle or relieve (a question, a person's mind, etc.). □□ **rest•er** *n.* [OE *ræst, rest* (n.), *ræstan, restan* (v.)]

rest[2] /rest/ *n. & v.* •*n.* (prec. by *the*) **1** the remaining part or parts; the others; the remainder of some quantity or number (*finish what you can and leave the rest*). **2** *Brit. Econ.* the reserve fund, esp. of the Bank of England. **3** *hist.* a rally in tennis. •*v.intr.* **1** remain in a specified state (*rest assured*). **2** (foll. by *with*) be left in the hands or charge of (*the final arrangements rest with you*). □ **and all the rest** (or **the rest of it**) and all else that might be mentioned; et cetera. **for the rest** as regards anything else. [ME f. OF *reste rester* f. L *restare* (as RE-, *stare* stand)]

rest ar•e•a = REST STOP.

re•start *v. & n.* •*v.tr. & intr.* /reestáart/ begin again. •*n.* /reestaart/ a new beginning.

re•state /reestáyt/ *v.tr.* express again or differently, esp. more clearly or convincingly. □□ **re•state•ment** *n.*

res•tau•rant /réstərənt, –raant, ré straant/ *n.* public premises where meals or refreshments may be had. [F f. *restaurer* RESTORE]

res•tau•rant car *n. Brit.* a dining car on a train.

res•tau•ra•teur /réstərətór/ *n.* a restaurant owner or manager. [F (as RESTAURANT)]

rest•ful /réstfool/ *adj.* **1** favorable to quiet or repose. **2** free from disturbing influences. **3** soothing. □□ **rest•ful•ly** *adv.* **rest•ful•ness** *n.*

rest•har•row /rést-haró/ *n.* any tough-rooted plant of the genus *Ononis*, native to Europe and the Mediterranean. [obs. *rest* (v.) = ARREST (in sense 'stop') + HARROW]

rest home *n.* a place where old or frail people can be cared for.

res•ti•tu•tion /réstitōōshən, –tyōō–/ *n.* **1** (often foll. by *of*) the act or an instance of restoring a thing to its proper owner. **2** reparation for an injury (esp. *make restitution*). **3** esp. *Theol.* the restoration of a thing to its original state. **4** the resumption of an original shape or position because of elasticity. □□ **res•ti•tu•tive** /réstitōōtiv, –tyōō–/ *adj.* [ME f. OF *restitution* or L *restitutio* f. *restituere restitut-* restore (as RE-, *statuere* establish)]

res•tive /réstiv/ *adj.* **1** fidgety; restless. **2** (of a horse) refusing to advance; stubbornly standing still or moving backward or sideways; refractory. **3** (of a person) unmanageable; rejecting control. □□ **res•tive•ly** *adv.* **res•tive•ness** *n.* [ME f. OF *restif –ive* f. Rmc (as REST[2])]

rest•less /réstlis/ *adj.* **1** finding or affording no rest. **2** uneasy; agitated. **3** constantly in motion, fidgeting, etc. □□ **rest•less•ly** *adv.* **rest•less•ness** *n.* [OE *restlēas* (as REST, –LESS)]

rest mass *n. Physics* the mass of a body when at rest.

re•stock /reestók/ *v.tr.* (also *absol.*) stock again or differently.

res•to•ra•tion /réstəráyshən/ *n.* **1 a** the act or an instance of restoring (a building, etc.) or of being restored. **b** = RESTITUTION 1. **2** a model or drawing representing the supposed original form of an extinct animal, ruined building, etc. **3 a** the reestablishment of a monarch, etc. **b** the period of this. **4** (**Restoration**) *hist.* **a** (prec. by *the*) the reestablishment of Charles II as king of England in 1660. **b** (often *attrib.*) the literary period following this (*Restoration comedy*). [17th-c. alt. (after RESTORE) of *restauration*, ME f. OF *restauration* or LL *restauratio* (as RESTORE)]

re•stor•a•tive /ristáwrətiv, –stór–/ *adj. & n.* •*adj.* tending to restore health or strength. •*n.* a restorative medicine, food, etc. (*needs a restorative*). □□ **re•stor•a•tive•ly** *adv.* [ME var. of obs. *restaurative* f. OF *restauratif –ive* (as RESTORE)]

re•store /ristáwr/ *v.tr.* **1** bring back or attempt to bring back to the original state by rebuilding, repairing, repainting, emending, etc. **2** bring back to health, etc.; cure. **3** give back to the original owner, etc.; make restitution of. **4** reinstate; bring back to dignity or right. **5** replace; put back; bring back to a former condition. **6** make a representation of the supposed original state of (a ruin, extinct animal, etc.). **7** reinstate by conjecture (missing words in a text, missing pieces, etc.). □□ **re•stor•a•ble** *adj.* **re•stor•er** *n.* [ME f. OF *restorer* f. L *restaurare*]

re•strain /ristráyn/ *v.tr.* **1** (often *refl.*, usu. foll. by *from*) check or hold in; keep in check or under control or within bounds. **2** repress; keep down. **3** confine; imprison. □□ **re•strain•a•ble** *adj.* **re•strain•er** *n.* [ME f. OF *restrei(g)n-* stem of *restreindre* f. L *restringere restrict-* (as RE-, *stringere* tie)]

re-strain /reestráyn/ *v.tr.* strain again.

re•strain•ed•ly /ristráynidlee/ *adv.* with self-restraint.

re•straint /ristráynt/ *n.* **1** the act or an instance of restraining or being restrained. **2** a stoppage; a check; a controlling agency or influence. **3 a** self-control; avoidance of excess or exaggeration. **b** austerity of literary expression. **4** reserve of manner. **5** confinement, esp. because of insanity. **6** something that restrains or holds in check; bondage; shackles. □ **in restraint of** in order to restrain. [ME f. OF *restreinte* fem. past part. of *restreindre*: see RESTRAIN]

re•straint of trade *n.* action seeking to interfere with free-market conditions.

re•strict /ristríkt/ *v.tr.* (often foll. by *to, within*) **1** confine; bound; limit (*restricted parking; restricted them to five days a week*). **2** subject to limitation. **3** withhold from general circulation or disclosure. □□ **re•strict•ed•ly** *adv.* **re•strict•ed•ness** *n.* [L *restringere*: see RESTRAIN]

re•stric•tion /ristríkshən/ *n.* **1** the act or an instance of restricting; the state of being restricted. **2** a thing that restricts. **3** a limitation placed on action. □□ **re•stric•tion•ist** *adj. & n.* [ME f. OF *restriction* or L *restrictio* (as RESTRICT)]

re·stric·tive /ristríktiv/ *adj.* imposing restrictions. □□ **re·stric·tive·ly** *adv.* **re·stric·tive·ness** *n.* [ME f. OF *restrictif* –*ive* or med.L *restrictivus* (as RESTRICT)]

re·stric·tive clause *n. Gram.* a relative clause, usu. without surrounding commas.

re·string /réestríng/ *v.tr.* (*past* and *past part.* **re·strung**) **1** fit (esp. a musical instrument) with new strings. **2** thread (beads, etc.) on a new string.

rest room *n.* a public toilet in a restaurant, store, office building, etc.

re·struc·ture /réestrúkchər/ *v.tr.* give a new structure to; rebuild; rearrange.

rest stop *n.* an area along a highway for travelers to stop for rest, refreshment, etc.

re·stud·y /réestúdee/ *v.tr.* (·**ies**, ·**ied**) study again.

re·style /réestíl/ *v.tr.* **1** reshape; remake in a new style. **2** give a new designation to (a person or thing).

re·sult /rizúlt/ *n. & v.* ● *n.* **1** a consequence, issue, or outcome of something. **2** a satisfactory outcome; a favorable result (*gets results*). **3** a quantity, formula, etc., obtained by calculation. **4** (in *pl.*) a list of scores or winners, etc., in an examination or sporting event. ● *v.intr.* **1** (often foll. by *from*) arise as the actual consequence or follow as a logical consequence (from conditions, causes, etc.). **2** (often foll. by *in*) have a specified end or outcome (*resulted in a large profit*). □ **without result** in vain; fruitless. □□ **re·sult·ful** *adj.* **re·sult·less** *adj.* [ME f. med.L *resultare* f. L (as RE-, *saltare* frequent. of *salire* jump)]

re·sult·ant /rizúlt'nt/ *adj. & n.* ● *adj.* resulting, esp. as the total outcome of more or less opposed forces. ● *n. Math.* a vector equivalent to two or more acting in different directions at the same point.

re·sume /rizóom/ *v. & n.* ● *v.* **1** *tr. & intr.* begin again or continue after an interruption. **2** *tr. & intr.* begin to speak, work, or use again; recommence. **3** *tr.* get back; take back; recover; reoccupy (*resume one's seat*). ● *n.* = RÉSUMÉ. □□ **re·sum·a·ble** *adj.* [ME f. OF *resumer* or L *resumere resumpt-* (as RE-, *sumere* take)]

ré·su·mé /rézŏomay/ *n.* (also **re·su·mé**, **re·su·me**) **1** a summary, esp. of a person's employment history. **2** a curriculum vitae. [F past part. of *résumer* (as RESUME)]

re·sump·tion /rizúmpshən/ *n.* the act or an instance of resuming (*ready for the resumption of negotiations*). □□ **re·sump·tive** *adj.* [ME f. OF *resumption* or LL *resumptio* (as RESUME)]

re·su·pi·nate /risŏopinayt, –nət/ *adj.* (of a leaf, etc.) upside down. [L *resupinatus* past part. of *resupinare* bend back: see SUPINE]

re·sur·face /réesúrfis/ *v.* **1** *tr.* lay a new surface on (a road, etc.). **2** *intr.* rise or arise again; turn up again.

re·sur·gent /risúrjənt/ *adj.* **1** rising or arising again. **2** tending to rise again. □□ **re·sur·gence** *n.* [L *resurgere resurrect-* (as RE-, *surgere* rise)]

res·ur·rect /rézərékt/ *v.* **1** *tr. colloq.* revive the practice, use, or memory of. **2** *tr.* take from the grave; exhume. **3** *tr.* dig up. **4** *tr. & intr.* raise or rise from the dead. [back-form. f. RESURRECTION]

res·ur·rec·tion /rézərékshən/ *n.* **1** the act or an instance of rising from the dead. **2** (**Resurrection**) **a** Christ's rising from the dead. **b** the rising of the dead at the Last Judgment. **3** a revival after disuse, inactivity, or decay. **4** exhumation. **5** the unearthing of a lost or forgotten thing; restoration to vogue or memory. □□ **res·ur·rec·tion·al** *adj.* [ME f. OF f. LL *resurrectio* –*onis* (as RESURGENT)]

res·ur·rec·tion plant *n.* any of various plants, including club mosses of the genus *Selaginella* and the Rose of Jericho, unfolding when moistened after being dried.

re·sur·vey *v. & n.* ● *v.tr.* /réesərváy/ survey again; reconsider. ● *n.* /réesərvay/ the act or an instance of resurveying.

re·sus·ci·tate /risúsitayt/ *v.tr. & intr.* **1** revive from unconsciousness or apparent death. **2** return or restore to vogue, vigor, or vividness. □□ **re·sus·ci·ta·tion** /–táyshən/ *n.* **re·sus·ci·ta·tive** *adj.* **re·sus·ci·ta·tor** *n.* [L *resuscitare* (as RE-, *suscitare* raise)]

ret /ret/ *v.* (also **rate** /rayt/) (**ret·ted**, **ret·ting**) **1** *tr.* soften (flax, hemp, etc.) by soaking or by exposure to moisture. **2** *intr.* (often as **retted** *adj.*) (of hay, etc.) be spoiled by wet or rot. [ME, rel. to ROT]

ret. *abbr.* **1** retired. **2** returned.

re·ta·ble /ritáybəl, réetay–, rétə–/ *n.* **1** a frame enclosing decorated panels above the back of an altar. **2** a shelf. [F *rétable, retable* f. Sp. *retablo* f. med.L *retrotabulum* rear table (as RETRO-, TABLE)]

re·tail /réetayl/ *n., adj., adv., & v.* ● *n.* the sale of goods in relatively small quantities to the public, and usu. not for resale (cf. WHOLESALE). ● *adj. & adv.* by retail; at a retail price (*do you buy wholesale or retail?*). ● *v.* (also /ritáyl/) **1** *tr.* sell (goods) in retail trade. **2** *intr.* (often foll. by *at, for*) (of goods) be sold in this way (esp. for a specified price) (*retails at $4.95*). **3** *tr.* recount; relate details of. □□ **re·tail·er** *n.* [ME f. OF *retaille* a piece cut off f. *retaillier* (as RE-, TAIL²)]

re·tail price in·dex *n.* an index of the variation in the prices of retail goods.

re·tain /ritáyn/ *v.tr.* **1 a** keep possession of; not lose; continue to have, practice, or recognize. **b** not abolish, discard, or alter. **2** keep in one's memory. **3 a** keep in place; hold fixed. **b** hold (water, etc.). **4** secure the services of (a person, esp. an attorney) with a preliminary payment. □□ **re·tain·a·ble** *adj.* **re·tain·a·bil·i·ty** /–taynəbílitee/

n. **re·tain·ment** *n.* [ME f. AF *retei(g)n-* f. stem of OF *retenir* ult. f. L *retinēre retent-* (as RE-, *tenēre* hold)]

re·tain·er /ritáynər/ *n.* **1** a person or thing that retains. **2** *Law* a fee for retaining an attorney, etc. **3 a** *hist.* a dependent or follower of a person of rank. **b** *joc.* an old and faithful friend or servant (esp. *old retainer*). **4** *Brit.* a reduced rent paid to retain accommodation during a period of nonoccupancy.

re·tain·ing fee *n.* a fee paid to secure a person, service, etc.

re·tain·ing wall *n.* a wall supporting and confining a mass of earth or water.

re·take *v. & n.* ● *v.tr.* /réetáyk/ (*past* **re·took**; *past part.* **re·tak·en**) **1** take again. **2** recapture. ● *n.* /réetayk/ **1 a** the act or an instance of retaking. **b** a thing retaken, e.g., an examination. **2 a** the act or an instance of filming a scene or recording music, etc., again. **b** the scene or recording obtained in this way.

re·tal·i·ate /ritáleeayt/ *v.* **1** *intr.* repay an injury, insult, etc., in kind; attack in return; make reprisals. **2** *tr.* **a** (usu. foll. by *upon*) cast (an accusation) back upon a person. **b** repay (an injury or insult) in kind. □□ **re·tal·i·a·tion** /–áyshən/ *n.* **re·tal·i·a·tive** /–táleeətiv/ *adj.* **re·tal·i·a·tor** *n.* **re·tal·i·a·to·ry** /–táleeətáwree/ *adj.* [L *retaliare* (as RE-, *talis* such)]

re·tard /ritaárd/ *v. & n.* ● *v.tr.* **1** make slow or late. **2** delay the progress, development, arrival, or accomplishment of. ● *n.* **1** retardation. **2** /réetard/ *sl. derog.* a person with a mental handicap. □□ **re·tar·dant** *adj. & n.* /réetaardáyshən/ *n.* **re·tar·da·tive** /–ətiv/ *adj.* **re·tar·da·to·ry** /–ətáwree/ *adj.* **re·tard·er** *n.* **re·tard·ment** *n.* [F *retarder* f. L *retardare* (as RE-, *tardus* slow)]

re·tar·date /ritaárdayt/ *adj. & n.* ● *adj.* mentally retarded. ● *n.* a mentally retarded person. [L *retardare*: see RETARD]

re·tard·ed /ritaárdid/ *adj.* backward in mental or physical development.

retch /rech/ *v. & n.* ● *v.intr.* make a motion of vomiting esp. involuntarily and without effect. ● *n.* such a motion or the sound of it. [var. of (now dial.) *reach* f. OE *hrǣcan* spit, ON *hrækja* f. Gmc, of imit. orig.]

retd. *abbr.* **1** retired. **2** returned.

re·te /réetee/ *n.* (*pl.* **re·ti·a** /–teeə, –sheeə, –shə/) *Anat.* an elaborate network or plexus of blood vessels and nerve cells. [L *rete* net]

re·teach /réeteéch/ *v.tr.* (*past* and *past part.* **re·taught**) teach again or differently.

re·tell /réetél/ *v.tr.* (*past* and *past part.* **re·told**) tell again or in a different version.

re·ten·tion /riténshən/ *n.* **1 a** the act or an instance of retaining; the state of being retained. **b** the ability to retain things experienced or learned; memory. **2** *Med.* the failure to evacuate urine or another secretion. [ME f. OF *retention* or L *retentio* (as RETAIN)]

re·ten·tive /riténtiv/ *adj.* **1** (often foll. by *of*) tending to retain (moisture, etc.). **2** (of memory or a person) not forgetful. **3** *Surgery* (of a ligature, etc.) serving to keep something in place. □□ **re·ten·tive·ly** *adv.* **re·ten·tive·ness** *n.* [ME f. OF *retentif* –*ive* or med.L *retentivus* (as RETAIN)]

re·tex·ture /réetékschər/ *v.tr.* treat (material, a garment, etc.) so as to restore its original texture.

re·think *v. & n.* ● *v.tr.* /réethíngk/ (*past* and *past part.* **re·thought**) think about (something) again, esp. with a view to making changes. ● *n.* /réethingk/ a reassessment; a period of rethinking.

re·ti·a *pl.* of RETE.

re·ti·ar·i·us /réeshee-áireeəs/ *n.* (*pl.* **re·ti·ar·i·i** /–áireei, –áiree-ee/) a Roman gladiator using a net to trap his opponent. [L f. *rete* net]

ret·i·cence /rétisəns/ *n.* **1** the avoidance of saying all one knows or feels, or of saying more than is necessary; reserve in speech. **2** a disposition to silence; taciturnity. **3** the act or an instance of holding back some fact. **4** abstinence from overemphasis in art. □□ **ret·i·cent** *adj.* **ret·i·cent·ly** *adv.* [L *reticentia* f. *reticēre* (as RE-, *tacēre* be silent)]

ret·i·cle /rétikəl/ *n.* a network of fine threads or lines in the focal plane of an optical instrument to help accurate observation. [L *reticulum*: see RETICULUM]

re·tic·u·la *pl.* of RETICULUM.

re·tic·u·late *v. & adj.* ● *v.tr. & intr.* /ritíkyəlayt/ **1** divide or be divided in fact or appearance into a network. **2** arrange or be arranged in small squares or with intersecting lines. ● *adj.* /–yələt, –layt/ reticulated. □□ **re·tic·u·late·ly** *adv.* **re·tic·u·la·tion** /–láyshən/ *n.* [L *reticulatus* reticulated (as RETICULUM)]

ret·i·cule /rétikyŏol/ *n.* **1** = RETICLE. **2** usu. *hist.* a woman's netted or other bag, esp. with a drawstring, carried or worn to serve the purpose of a pocket. [F *réticule* f. L (as RETICULUM)]

re·tic·u·lum /ritíkyələm/ *n.* (*pl.* **re·tic·u·la** /–lə/) **1** a netlike structure; a fine network, esp. of membranes, etc., in living organisms. **2** a ruminant's second stomach. □□ **re·tic·u·lar** *adj.* **re·tic·u·lose** *adj.* [L, dimin. of *rete* net]

re·tie /réetí/ *v.tr.* (**re·ty·ing**) tie again.

re·ti·form /réetifawrm, réti–/ adj. netlike; reticulated. [L rete net + –FORM]

ret·i·na /rétʹnə/ n. (pl. **ret·i·nas**, **ret·i·nae** /–nee/) a layer at the back of the eyeball sensitive to light, and triggering nerve impulses via the optic nerve to the brain where the visual image is formed. □□ **ret·i·nal** adj. [ME f. med.L f. L rete net]

ret·i·ni·tis /rétʹnítis/ n. inflammation of the retina.

ret·i·nol /rétʹnawl, –nol/ n. a vitamin found in green and yellow vegetables, egg yolk, and fish-liver oil, essential for growth and vision in dim light. Also called **vitamin A**. [RETINA + –OL[1]]

ret·i·nue /rétʹnoo, –yoo/ n. a body of attendants accompanying an important person. [ME f. OF retenue fem. past part. of retenir RETAIN]

re·tire /ritír/ v. **1** a intr. leave office or employment, esp. because of age (retire from the army; retire on a pension). **b** tr. cause (a person) to retire from work. **2** intr. withdraw; go away; retreat. **3** intr. seek seclusion or shelter. **4** intr. go to bed. **5** tr. withdraw (troops). **6** tr. Baseball (of a batter or side) put out. **7** tr. Econ. withdraw (a bill or note) from circulation or currency. □ **retire from the world** become a recluse. **retire into oneself** become uncommunicative or unsociable. □□ **re·tir·ee** n. **re·tir·er** n. [F retirer (as RE–, tirer draw)]

re·tired /ritírd/ adj. **1** a having retired from employment (a retired teacher). **b** Brit. relating to a retired person (received retired pay). **2** withdrawn from society or observation; secluded (lives a retired life). □□ **re·tired·ness** n.

re·tire·ment /ritírmənt/ n. **1** a the act or an instance of retiring. **b** the condition of having retired. **2** a seclusion or privacy. **b** a secluded place. **3** income, esp. pension, on which a retired person lives.

re·tir·ing /ritíring/ adj. shy; fond of seclusion. □□ **re·tir·ing·ly** adv.

re·told past and past part. of RETELL.

re·took past of RETAKE.

re·tool /réetóol/ v.tr. equip (a factory, etc.) with new tools.

re·tor·sion /ritáwrshən/ n. (also **re·tor·tion**) retaliation by one nation on another, as for unfair trade, etc.

re·tort[1] /ritáwrt/ n. & v. • n. **1** an incisive or witty or angry reply. **2** the turning of a charge or argument against its originator. **3** a retaliation. • v. **1** a tr. say by way of a retort. **b** intr. make a retort. **2** tr. repay (an insult or attack) in kind. **3** tr. (often foll. by on, upon) return (mischief, a charge, sarcasm, etc.) to its originator. **4** tr. (often foll. by against) make (an argument) tell against its user. **5** tr. (as **retorted** adj.) recurved; twisted or bent backward. [L retorquēre retort– (as RE–, torquēre twist)]

re·tort[2] /ritáwrt, réetawrt/ n. & v. • n. **1** a vessel usu. of glass with a long recurved neck used in distilling liquids. **2** a vessel for heating mercury for purification, coal to generate gas, or iron and carbon to make steel. • v.tr. purify (mercury) in a retort. [F retorte f. med.L retorta fem. past part. of retorquēre: see RETORT[1]]

re·tor·tion /ritáwrshən/ n. **1** the act or an instance of bending back; the condition of being bent back. **2** = RETORSION. [RETORT[1], perh. after contortion]

retort[2]

re·touch /réetúch/ v. & n. • v.tr. improve or repair (a composition, picture, photographic negative or print, etc.) by fresh touches or alterations. • n. the act or an instance of retouching. □□ **re·touch·er** n. [prob. f. F retoucher (as RE–, TOUCH)]

re·trace /réetráys/ v.tr. **1** go back over (one's steps, etc.). **2** trace back to a source or beginning. **3** recall the course of in one's memory. [F retracer (as RE–, TRACE[1])]

re·tract /ritrákt/ v. **1** tr. (also absol.) withdraw or revoke (a statement or undertaking). **2** a tr. & intr. (esp. with ref. to part of the body) draw or be drawn back or in. **b** tr. draw (an undercarriage, etc.) into the body of an aircraft. □□ **re·tract·a·ble** adj. **re·trac·tion** n. **re·trac·tive** adj. [L retrahere or (in sense 1) retractare (as RE–, trahere tract– draw)]

re·trac·tile /ritráktil, –tíl/ adj. capable of being retracted. □□ **re·trac·til·i·ty** /–tílitee/ n. [RETRACT, after contractile]

re·trac·tor /ritráktər/ n. **1** a muscle used for retracting. **2** a device for retracting.

re·train /réetráyn/ v.tr. & intr. train again or further, esp. for new work.

re·tral /réetrəl, rét–/ adj. Biol. posterior; at the back. [RETRO– + –AL]

re·trans·late /réetranzláyt, –trans–, reetránzláyt, –tráns–/ v.tr. translate again, esp. back into the original language. □□ **re·trans·la·tion** n.

re·trans·mit /réetranzmít, –trans–/ v.tr. (**re·trans·mit·ted**, **re·trans·mit·ting**) transmit (esp. radio signals or broadcast programs) back again or to a greater distance. □□ **re·trans·mis·sion** /–míshən/ n.

re·tread v. & n. • v.tr. /réetréd/ (past **re·trod**; past part. **re·trod·den**) **1** tread (a path, etc.) again. **2** put a fresh tread on (a tire). • n. /réetred/ a retreaded tire.

re·treat /ritréet/ v. & n. • v. **1** a intr. (esp. of military forces) go back, retire; relinquish a position. **b** tr. cause to retreat; move back. **2** intr. (esp. of features) recede; slope back. • n. **1** a the act or an instance of retreating. **b** Mil. a signal for this. **2** withdrawal into privacy or security. **3** a place of shelter or seclusion. **4** a period of seclusion for prayer and meditation. **5** Mil. a bugle call at sunset, signaling the lowering of the flag. **6** a place for the reception of the elderly or others in need of care. [ME f. OF retret (n.), retraiter (v.) f. L retrahere: see RETRACT]

re·trench /ritrénch/ v. **1** a tr. reduce the amount of (costs). **b** intr. cut down expenses; introduce economies. **2** tr. shorten or abridge. □□ **re·trench·ment** n. [obs. F retrencher (as RE–, TRENCH)]

re·tri·al /réetríəl/ n. a second or further (judicial) trial.

ret·ri·bu·tion /rétribyóoshən/ n. requital usu. for evil done; vengeance. □□ **re·trib·u·tive** /ritríbyətiv/ adj. **re·trib·u·to·ry** /ritríbyətawree/ adj. [ME f. LL retributio (as RE–, tribuere tribut– assign)]

re·trieve /ritréev/ v. & n. • v.tr. **1** a regain possession of. **b** recover by investigation or effort of memory. **2** a restore to knowledge or recall to mind. **b** obtain (information stored in a computer, etc.). **3** (of a dog) find and bring in (killed or wounded game, etc.). **4** (foll. by from) recover or rescue (esp. from a bad state). **5** restore to a flourishing state; revive. **6** repair or set right (a loss or error, etc.) (managed to retrieve the situation). • n. the possibility of recovery (beyond retrieve). □□ **re·triev·a·ble** adj. **re·triev·al** n. [ME f. OF retroeve- stressed stem of retrover (as RE–, trover find)]

re·triev·er /ritréevər/ n. **1** a a dog of a breed used for retrieving game. **b** this breed. **2** a person who retrieves something.

ret·ro /rétrō/ adj. & n. sl. • adj. **1** reviving or harking back to the past. **2** retroactive. • n. retro fashion or style.

retro- /rétrō/ comb. form **1** denoting action back or in return (retroact; retroflex). **2** Anat. & Med. denoting location behind. [L retro backward]

ret·ro·act /rétrō-ákt/ v.intr. **1** operate in a backward direction. **2** have a retrospective effect. **3** react. □□ **ret·ro·ac·tion** n.

ret·ro·ac·tive /rétrō-áktiv/ adj. (esp. of legislation) having retrospective effect. □□ **ret·ro·ac·tive·ly** adv. **ret·ro·ac·tiv·i·ty** /–tivitee/ n.

ret·ro·cede /rétrōséed/ v. **1** intr. move back; recede. **2** tr. cede back again. □□ **ret·ro·ced·ence** n. **ret·ro·ced·ent** adj. **ret·ro·ces·sion** /–séshən/ n. **ret·ro·ces·sive** /–sésiv/ adj. [L retrocedere (as RETRO–, cedere cess– go)]

ret·ro·choir /rétrōkwir/ n. the part of a cathedral or large church behind the high altar. [med.L retrochorus (as RETRO–, CHOIR)]

re·trod past of RETREAD.

re·trod·den past part. of RETREAD.

ret·ro·fit /rétrōfit/ v.tr. (**-fit·ted**, **·fit·ting**) modify (machinery, vehicles, etc.) to incorporate changes and developments introduced after manufacture. [RETROACTIVE + REFIT]

ret·ro·flex /rétrəfleks/ adj. (also **ret·ro·flexed**) **1** Anat., Med., & Bot. turned backward. **2** Phonet. pronounced with the tip of the tongue curled up toward the hard palate. □□ **ret·ro·flex·ion** /–flékshən/ n. [L retroflectere retroflex– (as RETRO–, flectere bend)]

ret·ro·gra·da·tion /rétrōgrədáyshən/ n. Astron. **1** the apparent backward motion of a planet in the zodiac. **2** the apparent motion of a celestial body from east to west. **3** backward movement of the lunar nodes on the ecliptic. [LL retrogradatio (as RETRO–, GRADATION)]

ret·ro·grade /rétrəgrayd/ adj., n., & v. • adj. **1** directed backward; retreating. **2** reverting esp. to an inferior state; declining. **3** inverse; reversed (in retrograde order). **4** Astron. in or showing retrogradation. • n. a degenerate person. • v.intr. **1** move backward; recede; retire. **2** decline; revert. **3** Astron. show retrogradation. □□ **ret·ro·grade·ly** adv. [ME f. L retrogradus (as RETRO–, gradus step, gradi walk)]

ret·ro·gress /rétrəgrés/ v.intr. **1** go back; move backward. **2** deteriorate. □□ **ret·ro·gres·sive** adj. [RETRO–, after PROGRESS v.]

ret·ro·gres·sion /rétrəgréshən/ n. **1** backward or reversed movement. **2** a return to a less advanced state; a reversal of development; a decline or deterioration. **3** Astron. = RETROGRADATION. □□ **ret·ro·gres·sive** /–grésiv/ adj. **ret·ro·gres·sive·ly** adv. [RETRO–, after progression]

ret·ro·ject /rétrōjekt/ v.tr. throw back (usu. opp. PROJECT). [RETRO–, after PROJECT v.]

ret·ro·rock·et /rétrō-rokit/ n. an auxiliary rocket for slowing down a spacecraft, etc., e.g., when reentering the earth's atmosphere.

re·trorse /ritráwrs/ adj. Biol. turned back or down. □□ **re·trorse·ly** adv. [L retrorsus = retroversus (as RETRO–, versus past part. of vertere turn)]

ret·ro·spect /rétrəspekt/ n. **1** (foll. by to) regard or reference to precedent or authority, or to previous conditions. **2** a survey of past time or events. □ **in retrospect** when looked back on. [RETRO–, after PROSPECT n.]

ret·ro·spec·tion /rétrəspékshən/ n. **1** the action of looking back esp. into the past. **2** an indulgence or engagement in retrospect. [prob. f. retrospect (v.) (as RETROSPECT)]

ret·ro·spec·tive /rétrəspéktiv/ adj. & n. • adj. **1** looking back on or dealing with the past. **2** (of an exhibition, recital, etc.) showing an artist's development over his or her lifetime. **3** esp. *Brit.* (of a statute, etc.) applying to the past as well as the future; retroactive. **4** (of a view) lying to the rear. •*n.* a retrospective exhibition, recital, etc. □□ **ret•ro•spec•tive•ly** *adv.*

ret•ro•ster•nal /rétrōstə́rnəl/ *adj. Anat.* & *Med.* behind the breastbone.

ret•rous•sé /retrōōsáy/ *adj.* (of the nose) turned up at the tip. [F, past part. of *retrousser* tuck up (as RE-, TRUSS)]

ret•ro•vert /rétrōvərt/ *v.tr.* **1** turn backward. **2** *Med.* (as **retroverted** *adj.*) (of the womb) having a backward inclination. □□ **ret•ro•ver•sion** /-və́rzhən, -shən/ *n.* [LL *retrovertere* (as RETRO-, *vertere* versturn)]

ret•ro•vi•rus /rétrōvīrəs/ *n. Biol.* any of a group of RNA viruses that form DNA during the replication of their RNA. [mod.L f. initial letters of *reverse transcriptase* + VIRUS]

re•try /reetrí/ *v.tr.* (•**tries**, •**tried**) try (a defendant or lawsuit) a second or further time. □□ **re•tri•al** *n.*

ret•si•na /retseénə/ *n.* a Greek wine flavored with resin. [mod. Gk]

re•tune /reetōōn, -tyōōn/ *v.tr.* **1** tune (a musical instrument) again or differently. **2** tune (a radio, etc.) to a different frequency.

re•turf /reétərf/ *v.tr.* provide with new turf.

re•turn /ritə́rn/ *v.* & *n.* •*v.* **1** *intr.* come or go back. **2** *tr.* bring or put or send back to the person or place, etc., where originally belonging or obtained (*returned the fish to the river; have you returned my scissors?*). **3** *tr.* pay back or reciprocate; give in response (*decided not to return the compliment*). **4** *tr.* yield (a profit). **5** *tr.* say in reply; retort. **6** *tr.* (in tennis, etc.) hit or send (the ball) back after receiving it. **7** *tr.* state or mention or describe officially, esp. in answer to a writ or formal demand. **8** *tr.* elect, esp. reelect, to political office, etc. **9** *tr. Cards* lead (a suit) previously led or bid by a partner. **b** lead (a suit or card) after taking a trick. **10** *tr. Archit.* continue (a wall, etc.) in a changed direction, esp. at right angles. •*n.* **1** the act or an instance of coming or going back. **2 a** the act or an instance of giving or sending or putting or paying back. **b** a thing given or sent back. **3** a key on a computer or typewriter to start a new line. **4** (in *sing.* or *pl.*) **a** the proceeds or profit of an undertaking. **b** the acquisition of these. **5** a formal report or statement compiled or submitted by order (*an income-tax return*). **6** (in full **return match** or game) a second match, etc., between the same opponents. **7** esp. *Brit. Electr.* a conductor bringing a current back to its source. **8** a response or reply. **9** (in *pl.*) a report on votes counted in an election (*early returns from the third district*). **10** *Archit.* a part receding from the line of the front, e.g., the side of a house or of a window opening. □ **in return** as an exchange or reciprocal action. **many happy returns (of the day)** a greeting on a birthday, etc. □□ **re•turn•a•ble** *adj.* **re•turn•er** *n.* **re•turn•less** *adj.* [ME f. OF *returner* (as RE-, TURN)]

re•turn•a•ble /ritə́rnəbəl/ *adj.* & *n.* •*adj.* **1** intended to be returned, as an empty beverage container. **2** required by law to be returned, as a court writ. •*n.* an empty beverage container, especially a bottle or can, that can be returned for a refund of the deposit paid at purchase.

re•turn•ee /rítərneé/ *n.* a person who returns home from abroad, esp. after war service.

re•turn tick•et *n.* **1** a ticket for the returning portion of a trip. **2** *Brit.* a round-trip ticket.

re•tuse /ritōōs, -tyōōs/ *adj.* esp. *Bot.* having a broad end with a central depression. [L *retundere retus-* (as RE-, *tundere* beat)]

re•ty•ing *pres. part.* of RETIE.

re•type /reetíp/ *v.tr.* type again, esp. to correct errors.

re•u•ni•fy /reéyōōnifī/ *v.tr.* (•**fies**, •**fied**) restore (esp. separated territories) to a political unity. □□ **re•u•ni•fi•ca•tion** /-fikáyshən/ *n.*

re•un•ion /reeyōōnyən/ *n.* **1 a** the act or an instance of reuniting. **b** the condition of being reunited. **2** a social gathering esp. of people formerly associated. [F *réunion* or AL *reunio* f. L *reunire* unite (as RE-, UNION)]

re•u•nite /reéyōōnít/ *v.tr.* & *intr.* bring or come back together.

re•up•hol•ster /reéəphólstər, -əpól-/ *v.tr.* upholster anew. □□ **re•up•hol•ster•y** *n.*

re•use *v.* & *n.* •*v.tr.* /reéyōōz/ use again or more than once. •*n.* /reéyōōs/ a second or further use. □□ **re•us•a•ble** /-yōōzəbəl/ *adj.*

re•u•ti•lize /reéyōōt'līz/ *v.tr.* utilize again or for a different purpose. □□ **re•u•ti•li•za•tion** /-záyshən/ *n.*

Rev. *abbr.* **1** Reverend. **2** Revelation (New Testament).

rev /rev/ *n.* & *v. colloq.* •*n.* (in *pl.*) the number of revolutions of an engine per minute; RPMs (*running at 3,000 revs*). •*v.* (**revved, revving**) **1** *intr.* (of an engine) revolve; turn over. **2** *tr.* (also *absol.*; often foll. by *up*) cause (an engine) to run quickly. [abbr.]

re•vac•ci•nate /reéváksinayt/ *v.tr.* vaccinate again. □□ **re•vac•ci•na•tion** /-náyshən/ *n.*

re•val•ue /reéványōō/ *v.tr.* (**re•val•ues, re•val•ued, re•val•u•ing**) *Econ.* give a different value to, esp. give a higher value to, (a currency) in relation to other currencies or gold (opp. DEVALUE). □□ **re•val•u•a•tion** /-vályōōáyshən/ *n.*

re•vamp /reévámp/ *v.tr.* **1** renovate; revise; improve. **2** patch up. [RE- + VAMP[1]]

re•vanch•ism /rivánchizəm/ *n. Polit.* a policy of seeking to retaliate, esp. to recover lost territory. □□ **re•vanch•ist** *n.* & *adj.* [F *revanche* (as REVENGE)]

re•var•nish /reévaárnish/ *v.tr.* varnish again.

re•veal[1] /riveél/ *v.tr.* **1** display or show; allow to appear. **2** (often as **revealing** *adj.*) disclose; divulge; betray (*revealed his plans; a revealing remark*). **3** *tr.* (in *refl.* or *passive*) come to sight or knowledge. **4** *Relig.* (esp. of God) make known by inspiration or supernatural means. □□ **re•veal•a•ble** *adj.* **re•veal•er** *n.* **re•veal•ing•ly** *adv.* [ME f. OF *reveler* or L *revelare* (as RE-, *velum* veil)]

re•veal[2] /riveél/ *n.* an internal side surface of an opening or recess, esp. of a doorway or a window aperture. [obs. *revale* (v.) lower f. OF *revaler* f. *avaler* (as RE-, VAIL)]

re•veal•ed re•li•gion *n.* a religion based on divine revelation (opp. NATURAL RELIGION).

rev•eil•le /révəlee/ *n.* a military wake-up signal sounded in the morning on a bugle or drums, etc. [F *réveillez* imper. pl. of *réveiller* awaken (as RE-, *veiller* f. L *vigilare* keep watch)]

rev•el /révəl/ *v.* & *n.* •*v.* (**rev•eled, rev•el•ing** or **rev•elled, rev•el•ling**) **1** *intr.* have a good time; be extravagantly festive. **2** *intr.* (foll. by *in*) take keen delight in. **3** *tr.* (foll. by *away*) throw away (money or time) in revelry. •*n.* (in *sing.* or *pl.*) the act or an instance of reveling. □□ **rev•el•er** *n.* **rev•el•ry** *n.* (*pl.* •**ies**). [ME f. OF *reveler* riot f. L *rebellare* REBEL *v.*]

rev•e•la•tion /révəláyshən/ *n.* **1 a** the act or an instance of revealing, esp. the supposed disclosure of knowledge to humankind by a divine or supernatural agency. **b** knowledge disclosed in this way. **2** a striking disclosure (*it was a revelation to me*). **3** (**Revelation** or *colloq.* **Revelations**) (in full **the Revelation of St. John the Divine**) the last book of the New Testament, describing visions of heaven. □□ **rev•e•la•tion•al** *adj.* [ME f. OF *revelation* or LL *revelatio* (as REVEAL[1])]

rev•e•la•tion•ist /révəláyshənist/ *n.* a believer in divine revelation.

re•vel•a•to•ry /révəlatawree, rəvélə-/ *adj.* serving to reveal, esp. something significant. [L *revelare*: see REVEAL[1]]

re•ve•nant /révənənt/ *n.* a person who has returned, esp. supposedly from the dead. [F, pres. part. of *revenir*: see REVENUE]

re•venge /rivénj/ *n.* & *v.* •*n.* **1** retaliation for an offense or injury. **2** an act of retaliation. **3** the desire for this; a vindictive feeling. **4** (in games) a chance to win after an earlier defeat. •*v.* **1** *tr.* (in *refl.* or *passive*; often foll. by *on, upon*) inflict retaliation for an offense. **2** *tr.* take revenge for (an offense). **3** *tr.* avenge (a person). **4** *intr.* take vengeance. □□ **re•veng•er** *n.* [ME f. OF *revenger, revencher* f. LL *revindicare* (as RE-, *vindicare* lay claim to)]

re•venge•ful /rivénjfōōl/ *adj.* eager for revenge. □□ **re•venge•ful•ly** *adv.* **re•venge•ful•ness** *n.*

rev•e•nue /révənōō, -nyōō/ *n.* **1 a** income, esp. of a large amount, from any source. **b** (in *pl.*) items constituting this. **2** a government's annual income from which public expenses are met. **3** the department of the civil service collecting this. [ME f. OF *revenu(e)* past part. of *revenir* f. L *revenire* return (as RE-, *venire* come)]

rev•e•nue tar•iff *n.* a tax imposed to raise revenue, rather than to affect trade.

re•verb /rivə́rb, reévərb/ *v.* & *n.* •*v.* reverberate. •*n. Mus. colloq.* **1** reverberation. **2** a device to produce this. [abbr.]

re•ver•ber•ate /rivə́rbərayt/ *v.* **1 a** *intr.* (of sound, light, or heat) be returned or echoed or reflected repeatedly. **b** *tr.* return (a sound, etc.) in this way. **2** *intr.* (of a story, rumor, etc.) be heard much or repeatedly. □□ **re•ver•ber•ant** *adj.* **re•ver•ber•ant•ly** *adv.* **re•ver•ber•a•tion** /-ráyshən/ *n.* **re•ver•ber•a•tive** /-rətiv/ *adj.* **re•ver•ber•a•tor** *n.* **re•ver•ber•a•to•ry** /-rətawree/ *adj.* [L *reverberare* (as RE-, *verberare* lash f. *verbera* (pl.) scourge)]

re•ver•ber•a•to•ry fur•nace *n.* a furnace constructed to throw heat back on to the substance exposed to it.

re•vere /riveér/ *v.tr.* hold in deep and usu. affectionate or religious respect; venerate. [F *révérer* or L *reverēri* (as RE-, *verēri* fear)]

SYNONYM TIP **revere**

ADMIRE, ADORE, IDOLIZE, VENERATE, WORSHIP. We might **admire** someone who walks a tightrope between two skyscrapers, **idolize** a rock star, **adore** our mothers, and **revere** a person like Martin Luther King, Jr. Each of these verbs conveys the idea of regarding someone or something with respect and honor, but they differ considerably in terms of the feelings they connote. *Admire* suggests a feeling of delight and enthusiastic appreciation (*to admire the courage of the mountain climber*), while *adore* implies the tenderness and warmth of unquestioning love (*he adored babies*). *Idolize* is an extreme form of adoration, suggesting a slavish, helpless love, although it is not always meant in a negative sense (*she had idolized the work of Tolstoy since she was a schoolgirl*). We *revere* individuals and institutions who command our respect for their accomplishments or attributes (*he revered his old English professor*). **Ven-erate** and **worship** are usually found in a religious context (*we venerate saints and worship God*) but both words may be used in other contexts as well. *Venerate* is usually associated with dignity and advanced age (*to venerate the old man who had founded the company more than 50 years ago*), while *worship* connotes an excessive and uncritical respect (*the young girls who waited outside the stage door worshiped the ground he walked on*).

rev•er•ence /révərəns, révrəns/ *n. & v.* • *n.* **1 a** the act of revering or the state of being revered (*hold in reverence; feel reverence for*). **b** the capacity for revering (*lacks reverence*). **2** (also /révəráəns/) *archaic* a gesture showing that one reveres; a bow or curtsy. **3** (**Reverence**) a title used of or to some members of the clergy. • *v.tr.* regard or treat with reverence. [ME f. OF f. L *reverentia* (as REVERE)]

rev•er•end /révərənd, révrənd/ *adj. & n.* • *adj.* (esp. as the title of a clergyman) deserving reverence. • *n. colloq.* a clergyman. [ME f. OF *reverend* or L *reverendus* gerundive of *reverēri*: see REVERE]

Rev•er•end Moth•er *n.* the title of the Mother Superior of a convent.

rev•er•ent /révərənt, révrənt/ *adj.* feeling or showing reverence. □□ **rev•er•ent•ly** *adv.* [ME f. L *reverens* (as REVERE)]

rev•er•en•tial /révərénshəl/ *n.* of the nature of, due to, or characterized by reverence. □□ **rev•er•en•tial•ly** *adv.* [med.L *reverentialis* (as REVERE)]

rev•er•ie /révəree/ *n.* **1** a fit of abstracted musing (*was lost in a reverie*). **2** *archaic* a fantastic notion or theory; a delusion. **3** *Mus.* an instrumental piece suggesting a dreamy or musing state. [obs. F *resverie* f. OF *reverie* rejoicing, revelry f. *rever* be delirious, of unkn. orig.]

re•vers /rivéer/ *n.* (*pl.* same /–véerz/) **1** the turned-back edge of a garment revealing the undersurface. **2** the material on this surface. [F, = REVERSE]

re•verse /rivárs/ *v., adj., & n.* • *v.* **1** *tr.* turn the other way around or up or inside out. **2** *tr.* change to the opposite character or effect (*reversed the decision*). **3** *intr. & tr.* travel or cause to travel backward. **4** *tr.* make (an engine, etc.) work in a contrary direction. **5** *tr.* revoke or annul (a decree, act, etc.). **6** *intr.* (of a dancer, esp. in a waltz) revolve in the opposite direction. • *adj.* **1** placed or turned in an opposite direction or position. **2** opposite or contrary in character or order; inverted. • *n.* **1** the opposite or contrary (*the reverse is the case; is the reverse of the truth*). **2** the contrary of the usual manner. **3** an occurrence of misfortune; a disaster, esp. a defeat in battle (*suffered a reverse*). **4** reverse gear or motion. **5** the reverse side of something. **6 a** the side of a coin or medal, etc., bearing the secondary design. **b** this design (cf. OBVERSE). **7** the verso of a book leaf. □ **reverse arms** hold a rifle with the butt upward. **reverse the charges** make the recipient of a telephone call responsible for payment. □□ **re•ver•sal** *n.* **re•verse•ly** *adv.* **re•vers•er** *n.* **re•vers•i•ble** *adj.* **re•vers•i•bil•i•ty** *n.* **re•vers•i•bly** *adv.* [ME f. OF *revers* (n.), *reverser* (v.), f. L *revertere* *revers-* (as RE-, *vertere* turn)]

re•verse fault *n. Geol.* a fault in which the overlying side of a mass of rock is displaced upward in relation to the underlying side.

re•verse gear *n.* a gear used to make a vehicle, etc., travel backward.

re•vers•ing light *Brit.* = BACKUP LIGHT.

re•ver•sion /rivárzhən/ *n.* **1 a** the legal right (esp. of the original owner, or his or her heirs) to possess or succeed to property on the death of the present possessor. **b** property to which a person has such a right. **2** *Biol.* a return to ancestral type. **3** a return to a previous state, habit, etc. **4** a sum payable on a person's death, esp. by way of life insurance. □□ **re•ver•sion•al** *adj.* **re•ver•sion•ar•y** *adj.* [ME f. OF *reversion* or L *reversio* (as REVERSE)]

re•vert /rivárt/ *v.* **1** *intr.* (foll. by *to*) return to a former state, practice, opinion, etc. **2** *intr.* (of property, an office, etc.) return by reversion. **3** *intr.* fall back into a wild state. **4** *tr.* turn (one's eyes or steps) back. □□ **re•vert•er** *n.* (in sense 2). [ME f. OF *revertir* or L *revertere* (as REVERSE)]

re•vert•i•ble /rivártibəl/ *adj.* (of property) subject to reversion.

re•vet /rivét/ *v.tr.* (**re•vet•ted, re•vet•ting**) face (a rampart, wall, etc.) with masonry, esp. in fortification. [F *revêtir* f. OF *revestir* f. LL *revestire* (as RE-, *vestire* clothe f. *vestis*)]

re•vet•ment /rivétmənt/ *n.* a retaining wall or facing. [F *revêtement* (as REVET)]

re•view /rivyōo/ *n. & v.* • *n.* **1** a general survey or assessment of a subject or thing. **2** a retrospect or survey of the past. **3** revision or reconsideration (*is under review*). **4** a display and formal inspection of troops, etc. **5** a published account or criticism of a book, play, etc. **6** a periodical publication with critical articles on current events, the arts, etc. **7** a second view. • *v.tr.* **1** survey or look back on. **2** reconsider or revise. **3** hold a review of (troops, etc.). **4** write a review of (a book, play, etc.). **5** view again. □□ **re•view•a•ble** *adj.* **re•view•al** *n.* **re•view•er** *n.* [obs. F *reveue* f. *revoir* (as RE-, *voir* see)]

re•vile /rivíl/ *v.* **1** *tr.* abuse; criticize abusively. **2** *intr.* talk abusively;

rail. □□ **re•vile•ment** *n.* **re•vil•er** *n.* **re•vil•ing** *n.* [ME f. OF *reviler* (as RE-, VILE)]

re•vise /rivíz/ *v. & n.* • *v.tr.* **1** examine or reexamine and improve or amend (esp. written or printed matter). **2** consider and alter (an opinion, etc.). **3** (also *absol.*) *Brit.* read again (work learned or done) to improve one's knowledge, esp. for an examination. • *n. Printing* a proof sheet including corrections made in an earlier proof. □□ **re•vis•a•ble** *adj.* **re•vis•al** *n.* **re•vis•er** *n.* **re•vi•so•ry** *adj.* [F *réviser* look at, or L *revisere* f. *revidēre* f. *videre vis-* see]

Re•vised Stand•ard Ver•sion *n.* a revision in 1946–52 of the King James Version of the Bible.

Re•vised Ver•sion *n.* a revision in 1881–85 of the King James Version of the Bible.

re•vi•sion /rivízhən/ *n.* **1** the act or an instance of revising; the process of being revised. **2** a revised edition or form. □□ **re•vi•sion•ar•y** *adj.* [OF *revision* or LL *revisio* (as REVISE)]

re•vi•sion•ism /rivízhənizəm/ *n.* often *derog.* **1** a policy of revision or modification, esp. of Marxism on evolutionary socialist (rather than revolutionary) or pluralist principles. **2** any departure from or modification of accepted doctrine, theory, view of history, etc. □□ **re•vi•sion•ist** *n. & adj.*

re•vis•it /réevízit/ *v.tr.* visit again.

re•vi•tal•ize /réevít'līz/ *v.tr.* imbue with new life and vitality. □□ **re•vi•tal•i•za•tion** /–záyshən/ *n.*

re•viv•al /rivívəl/ *n.* **1** the act or an instance of reviving; the process of being revived. **2** a new production of an old play, etc. **3** a revived use of an old practice, custom, etc. **4 a** a reawakening of religious fervor. **b** one or a series of evangelistic meetings to promote this. **5** restoration to bodily or mental vigor or to life or consciousness.

re•viv•al•ism /rivívəlizəm/ *n.* belief in or the promotion of a revival, esp. of religious fervor. □□ **re•viv•al•ist** *n.* **re•viv•al•is•tic** /–lístik/ *adj.*

re•vive /rivív/ *v.intr. & tr.* **1** come or bring back to consciousness or life or strength. **2** come or bring back to existence, use, notice, etc. □□ **re•viv•a•ble** *adj.* [ME f. OF *revivre* or LL *revivere* (as RE-, L *vivere* live)]

re•viv•er /rivívər/ *n.* **1** a person or thing that revives. **2** *Brit. colloq.* a stimulating drink. **3** *Brit.* a preparation used for restoring faded colors, etc.

re•viv•i•fy /rivívifi/ *v.tr.* (**•fies, •fied**) restore to animation, activity, vigor, or life. □□ **re•viv•i•fi•ca•tion** /–fikáyshən/ *n.* [F *revivifier* or LL *revivificare* (as RE-, VIVIFY)]

re•voke /rivók/ *v. & n.* • *v.* **1** *tr.* rescind, withdraw, or cancel (a decree or promise, etc.). **2** *intr. Cards* fail to follow suit when able to do so; renege. • *n. Cards* the act of revoking. □□ **re•vo•ca•ble** /révəkəbəl/ *adj.* **rev•o•ca•bil•i•ty** /révəkəbílitee/ *n.* **rev•o•ca•tion** /révəkáyshən/ *n.* **rev•o•ca•to•ry** /révəkətawree/ *adj.* **re•vok•er** *n.* [ME f. OF *revoquer* or L *revocare* (as RE-, *vocare* call)]

re•volt /rivólt/ *v. & n.* • *v.* **1** *intr.* a rise in rebellion against authority. **b** (as **revolted** *adj.*) having revolted. **2 a** *tr.* (often in *passive*) affect with strong disgust; nauseate (*was revolted by the thought of it*). **b** (often foll. by *at, against*) feel strong disgust. • *n.* **1** an act of rebelling. **2** a state of insurrection (*in revolt*). **3** a sense of loathing. **4** a mood of protest or defiance. [F *révolter* f. It. *rivoltare* ult. f. L *revolvere* (as REVOLVE)]

re•volt•ing /rivólting/ *adj.* disgusting; horrible. □□ **re•volt•ing•ly** *adv.*

rev•o•lute /révəlōot/ *adj. Bot.*, etc. having a rolled-back edge. [L *revolutus* past part. of *revolvere*: see REVOLVE]

rev•o•lu•tion /révəlōoshən/ *n.* **1 a** the forcible overthrow of a government or social order, in favor of a new system. **b** (in Marxism) the replacement of one ruling class by another; the class struggle that is expected to lead to political change and the triumph of communism. **2** any fundamental change or reversal of conditions. **3** the act or an instance of revolving. **4 a** motion in orbit or a circular course or around an axis or center; rotation. **b** the single completion of an orbit or rotation. **c** the time taken for this. **5** a cyclic recurrence. □□ **rev•o•lu•tion•ism** *n.* **rev•o•lu•tion•ist** *n.* [ME f. OF *revolution* or LL *revolutio* (as REVOLVE)]

rev•o•lu•tion•ar•y /révəlōoshəneree/ *adj. & n.* • *adj.* **1** involving great and often violent change or innovation. **2** of or causing political revolution. **3** (**Revolutionary**) of or relating to a particular revolution, esp. the American Revolution. • *n.* (*pl.* **•ies**) an instigator or supporter of political revolution.

rev•o•lu•tion•ize /révəlōoshəníz/ *v.tr.* introduce fundamental change to.

rev•o•lu•tion count•er *Brit.* = TACHOMETER 2.

re•volve /rivólv/ *v.* **1** *intr. & tr.* turn or cause to turn around, esp. on an axis; rotate. **2** *intr.* move in a circular orbit. **3** *tr.* ponder (a problem, etc.) in the mind. □ **revolve on** esp. *Brit.* depend on. □□ **re•volv•a•ble** *adj.* [ME f. L *revolvere* (as RE-, *volvere* roll)]

re•volv•er /rivólvər/ *n.* a pistol with revolving chambers enabling several shots to be fired without reloading.

re•volv•ing cred•it *n.* credit that is automatically renewed as debts are paid off.

revolver

re·volv·ing door *n.* **1** a door with usu. four partitions turning around a central axis. **2** a situation in which the same events or problems recur in a continuous cycle (*many patients are trapped in a revolving door of admission, discharge, and readmission*). **3** a place or organization that people tend to enter and leave very quickly. **4** a situation in which someone moves from an influential government position to a position in a private company, or vice versa (*the revolving door between the administration and private lobbying firms*).

re·vue /rivyóō/ *n.* a theatrical entertainment of a series of short usu. satirical sketches and songs. [F, = REVIEW *n.*]

re·vul·sion /rivúlshən/ *n.* **1** abhorrence; a sense of loathing. **2** a sudden violent change of feeling. **3** a sudden reaction in taste, fortune, trade, etc. **4** *Med.* counterirritation; the treatment of one disordered organ, etc., by acting upon another. [F *revulsion* or L *revulsio* (as RE-, *vellere vuls-* pull)]

re·vul·sive /rivúlsiv/ *adj. & n. Med.* • *adj.* producing revulsion. • *n.* a revulsive substance.

re·ward /riwáwrd/ *n. & v.* • *n.* **1 a** a return or recompense for service or merit. **b** requital for good or evil; retribution. **2** a sum offered for the detection of a criminal, the restoration of lost property, etc. • *v.tr.* give a reward to (a person) or for (a service, etc.). □□ **re·ward·less** *adj.* [ME f. AF, ONF *reward* = OF *reguard* REGARD]

re·ward·ing /riwáwrding/ *adj.* (of an activity, etc.) well worth doing; providing satisfaction. □□ **re·ward·ing·ly** *adv.*

re·wash /rée̲wáwsh, –wósh/ *v.tr.* wash again.

re·weigh /réeway̲/ *v.tr.* weigh again.

re·wind /réewínd/ *v. & n.* • *v.tr.* (*past* and *past part.* **re·wound**) wind (a film or tape, etc.) back to the beginning. • *n.* **1** function on a tape deck, camera, etc., to rewind (tape, film, etc.). **2** the control that activates this function. □□ **re·wind·er** *n.*

re·wire /réewír/ *v.tr.* provide (a building, etc.) with new wiring. □□ **re·wir·a·ble** *adj.*

re·word /réewórd/ *v.tr.* change the wording of.

re·work /réewórk/ *v.tr.* revise; refashion; remake.

re·wound *past* and *past part.* of REWIND.

re·wrap /réeráp/ *v.tr.* (**re·wrapped, re·wrap·ping**) wrap again or differently.

re·write *v. & n.* • *v.tr.* /réerít/ (*past* **re·wrote**; *past part.* **re·writ·ten**) write again or differently. • *n.* /réerít/ **1** the act or an instance of rewriting. **2** a thing rewritten.

Rex /reks/ *n.* the reigning king (following a name or in the titles of lawsuits, e.g., *Rex v. Jones*, the Crown versus Jones). [L]

Reye's syn·drome /ríz, ráz/ *n. Med.* an acute, often fatal brain disease of children that usually follows a viral infection such as influenza or chicken pox and that is associated with the use of aspirin. [for Australian pediatrician Ralph D.K. *Reye*]

Reyn·ard /ráynərd, –naard, rénərd/ *n.* a fox (esp. as a proper name in stories). [ME f. OF *Renart* name of a fox in the *Roman de Renart*]

Reyn·olds num·ber /rénəldz/ *n. Physics* a quantity indicating the degree of turbulence of flow past an obstacle, etc. [O. *Reynolds*, Engl. physicist d. 1912]

Rf *symb. Chem.* the element rutherfordium.

r.f. *abbr.* (also **RF**) radio frequency.

RFC *abbr.* Reconstruction Finance Corporation.

RFD *abbr.* rural free delivery.

Rh¹ *symb. Chem.* the element rhodium.

Rh² see RH FACTOR.

r.h. *abbr.* right hand.

rhab·do·man·cy /rábdəmansee/ *n.* the use of a divining rod, esp. for discovering subterranean water or mineral ore. [Gk *rhabdomanteia* f. *rhabdos* rod: see –MANCY]

Rhad·a·man·thine /rádəmánthin, –thīn/ *adj.* stern and incorruptible in judgment. [*Rhadamanthus* f. L f. Gk *Rhadamanthos*, name of a judge in the underworld]

Rhae·to·Ro·mance /réetōrómáns/ *adj. & n.* (also **Rhae·to·ro·man·ic** /–mánik/ • *adj.* of or in any of the Romance dialects of SE Switzerland and Tyrol, esp. Romansh and Ladin. • *n.* any of these dialects. [L *Rhaetus* of Rhaetia in the Alps + ROMANIC]

rhap·sode /rápsōd/ *n.* a reciter of epic poems, esp. of Homer in ancient Greece. [Gk *rhapsōidos* f. *rhaptō* stitch + *ōidē* song, ODE]

rhap·so·dist /rápsədist/ *n.* a person who rhapsodizes.

rhap·so·dize /rápsədīz/ *v.intr.* talk or write rhapsodies.

rhap·so·dy /rápsədee/ *n.* (*pl.* **·dies**) **1** an enthusiastic, ecstatic, or extravagant utterance or composition. **2** *Mus.* a piece of music in one extended movement, usu. emotional in character. **3** *Gk Antiq.* an epic poem, or part of it, of a length for one recitation. □□ **rhap·sod·ic** /rapsódik/ *adj.* **rhap·sod·i·cal** *adj.* (in senses 1, 2). [L *rhapsodia* f. Gk *rhapsōidia* (as RHAPSODE)]

rhat·a·ny /rát'nee/ *n.* (*pl.* **·nies**) **1** either of two American shrubs, *Krameria trianda* and *K. argentea*, having an astringent root when dried. **2** the root of either of these. [mod.L *rhatania* f. Port. *ratanha*, Sp. *ratania*, f. Quechua *rataña*]

rhe·a /rée̲ə/ *n.* any of several S. American flightless birds of the family Rheidae, like but smaller than an ostrich. [mod.L genus name f. L f. Gk *Rhea* mother of Zeus]

rhe·bok /rée̲bok/ *n.* (also esp. *Brit.* **ree·bok**) a small S. African antelope, *Pelea capreolus*, with sharp horns. [Du., = roebuck]

Rhen·ish /rénish/ *adj. & n.* • *adj.* of the Rhine River and the regions adjoining it. • *n.* wine from this area. [ME *rynis, rynisch*, etc., f. AF *reneis*, OF *r(a)inois* f. L *Rhenanus* f. *Rhenus* Rhine]

rhe·ni·um /ré̲eneeəm/ *n. Chem.* a rare metallic element of the manganese group, occurring naturally in molybdenum ores and used in the manufacture of superconducting alloys. ¶ Symb.: **Re**. [mod.L f. L *Rhenus* Rhine]

rhe·ol·o·gy /reeóləjee/ *n.* the science dealing with the flow and deformation of matter. □□ **rhe·o·log·i·cal** /–əlójikəl/ *adj.* **rhe·ol·o·gist** *n.* [Gk *rheos* stream + –LOGY]

rhe·o·stat /ré̲eəstat/ *n. Electr.* an instrument used to control a current by varying the resistance. □□ **rhe·o·stat·ic** /–státik/ *adj.* [Gk *rheos* stream + –STAT]

rhe·sus /ré̲esəs/ *n.* (in full **rhesus monkey**) a small catarrhine monkey, *Macaca mulatta*, common in N. India. [mod.L, arbitrary use of L *Rhesus* f. Gk *Rhēsos*, mythical King of Thrace]

rhe·sus ba·by *n.* an infant with a hemolytic disorder caused by the incompatibility of its own Rh-positive blood with its mother's Rh-negative blood.

rhe·sus fac·tor = RH FACTOR.

rhe·tor /ré̲etər/ *n.* **1** an ancient Greek or Roman teacher or professor of rhetoric. **2** usu. *derog.* an orator. [ME f. LL *rethor* f. L *rhetor* f. Gk *rhētōr*]

rhet·o·ric /rétərik/ *n.* **1** the art of effective or persuasive speaking or writing. **2** language designed to persuade or impress (often with an implication of insincerity or exaggeration, etc.). [ME f. OF *rethorique* f. L *rhetorica, –ice* f. Gk *rhētorikē (tekhnē)* (art) of rhetoric (as RHETOR)]

rhe·tor·i·cal /ritáwrikəl, –tór–/ *adj.* **1 a** expressed in terms intended to persuade or impress **b** (of a question) asked in order to produce an effect or to make a statement rather than to elicit information. **2** of the nature of rhetoric. **3 a** of or relating to the art of rhetoric. **b** given to rhetoric; oratorical. □□ **rhe·tor·i·cal·ly** *adv.* [ME f. L *rhetoricus* f. Gk *rhētorikos* (as RHETOR)]

rhe·tor·i·cal ques·tion *n.* a question asked not for information but to produce an effect, e.g., *who cares?* for *nobody cares.*

rhet·o·ri·cian /rétəríshən/ *n.* **1** an orator. **2** a teacher of or expert in rhetoric. **3** a rhetorical speaker or writer. [ME f. OF *rethoricien* (as RHETORICAL)]

rheum /rōōm/ *n.* a watery discharge from a mucous membrane, esp. of the eyes or nose. □□ **rheum·y** *adj.* [ME f. OF *reume* ult. f. Gk *rheuma –atos* stream f. *rheō* flow]

rheu·mat·ic /rōōmátik/ *adj. & n.* • *adj.* **1** of, relating to, or suffering from rheumatism. **2** producing or produced by rheumatism. • *n.* a person suffering from rheumatism. □□ **rheu·mat·i·cal·ly** *adv.* **rheu·ma·tick·y** *adj. colloq.* [ME f. OF *reumatique* or L *rheumaticus* f. Gk *rheumatikos* (as RHEUM)]

rheu·mat·ic fe·ver *n.* a noninfectious fever with inflammation and pain in the joints.

rheu·ma·tism /rōōmətizəm/ *n.* any disease marked by inflammation and pain in the joints, muscles, or fibrous tissue, esp. rheumatoid arthritis. [F *rhumatisme* or L *rheumatismus* f. Gk *rheumatismos* f. *rheumatizō* f. *rheuma* stream]

rheu·ma·toid /rōōmətoyd/ *adj.* having the character of rheumatism.

rheu·ma·toid ar·thri·tis *n.* a chronic progressive disease causing inflammation and stiffening of the joints.

rheu·ma·tol·o·gy /rōōmətóləjee/ *n.* the study of rheumatic diseases. □□ **rheu·ma·to·log·i·cal** /–təlójikəl/ *adj.* **rheu·ma·tol·o·gist** *n.*

Rh fac·tor *n. Physiol.* an antigen occurring on the red blood cells of most humans and some other primates (as in the rhesus monkey, in which it was first observed).

rhi·nal /rínəl/ *adj. Anat.* of a nostril or nose. [Gk *rhis rhin-*: see RHINO–]

rhine·stone /rínstōn/ *n.* an imitation diamond or other precious stone. [*Rhine*, river and region in Germany + STONE]

rhi·ni·tis /rīnítis/ *n.* inflammation of the mucous membrane of the nose. [Gk *rhis rhinos* nose]

rhi·no¹ /rínō/ *n.* (*pl.* same or **·nos**) *colloq.* a rhinoceros. [abbr.]

rhi·no² /rínō/ *n. Brit. sl.* money. [17th c.: orig. unkn.]

rhino- /rínō/ *comb. form Anat.* the nose. [Gk *rhis rhinos* nostril, nose]

rhi·noc·er·os /rīnósərəs/ *n.* (*pl.* same or **rhi·noc·er·os·es**) any of various large thick-skinned plant-eating ungulates of the family Rhinocerotidae of Africa and S. Asia, with one horn or in some cases two horns on the nose and plated or folded skin. □□ **rhi·noc·er·ot·ic** /rīnósərótik/ *adj.* [ME f. L f. Gk *rhinokerōs* (as RHINO-, *keras* horn)]

black rhinoceros

See page xx for the **Key to Pronunciation**.

rhi·noc·er·os bird = OXPECKER.

rhi·noc·er·os horn n. a mass of keratinized fibers, reputed to have medicinal or aphrodisiac powers.

rhi·no·phar·yn·ge·al /rínōfarínjeeəl, -jəl, -fərínjeeəl/ adj. of or relating to the nose and pharynx.

rhi·no·plas·ty /rínōplastee/ n. plastic surgery of the nose. □□ **rhi·no·plas·tic** adj.

rhizo- /rízō/ comb. form Bot. a root. [Gk rhiza root]

rhi·zo·carp /rízōkaarp/ n. a plant with a perennial root but stems that wither. [RHIZO- + Gk karpos fruit]

rhi·zoid /rízoyd/ adj. & n. Bot. ● adj. rootlike. ● n. a root hair or filament in mosses, ferns, etc.

rhi·zome /rízōm/ n. an underground rootlike stem bearing both roots and shoots. [Gk rhizōma f. rhizoō take root (as RHIZO-)]

rhi·zo·pod /rízōpod, -zə-/ n. any protozoa of the class Rhizopodea, forming rootlike pseudopodia.

rho /rō/ n. the seventeenth letter of the Greek alphabet (Ρ, ρ). [Gk]

rho·da·mine /ródəmeen, -min/ n. Chem. any of various red synthetic dyes used to color textiles. [RHODO- + AMINE]

Rhode Is·land Red /rōd/ n. an orig. American breed of domestic fowl with brownish-red plumage.

Rhodes schol·ar·ship /rōdz/ n. any of several scholarships awarded annually and tenable at Oxford University by students from certain Commonwealth countries, South Africa, the United States, and Germany. □□ **Rhodes schol·ar** n. [Cecil Rhodes, Brit. statesman d. 1902, who founded them]

rho·di·um /ródeeəm/ n. Chem. a hard white metallic element of the platinum group, occurring naturally in platinum ores and used in making alloys and plating jewelry. ¶ Symb.: **Rh**. [Gk rhodon rose (from the color of the solution of its salts)]

rhodo- /ródō/ comb. form esp. Mineral. & Chem. rose-colored. [Gk rhodon rose]

rho·do·chro·site /ródōkrósīt/ n. a mineral form of manganese carbonate occurring in rose-red crystals. [Gk rhodokhrous rose-colored]

rho·do·den·dron /ródədéndrən/ n. any evergreen shrub of the genus Rhododendron, with large clusters of trumpet-shaped flowers. [L, = oleander, f. Gk (as RHODO-, dendron tree)]

rho·dop·sin /ródópsin/ n. a light-sensitive pigment in the retina. Also called **visual purple**. [Gk rhodon rose + opsis sight]

rho·do·ra /rədáwrə/ n. a N. American pink-flowered shrub, Rhodora canadense. [mod.L f. L plant-name f. Gk rhodon rose]

rhomb /rom/ n. = RHOMBUS. □□ **rhom·bic** adj. [F rhombe or L rhombus]

rhom·bi pl. of RHOMBUS.

rhom·bo·he·dron /rómbəheedrən/ n. (pl. **·he·drons** or **·he·dra** /-drə/) **1** a solid bounded by six equal rhombuses. **2** a crystal in this form. □□ **rhom·bo·he·dral** adj. [RHOMBUS, after polyhedron, etc.]

rhom·boid /rómboyd/ adj. & n. ● adj. (also **rhom·boi·dal** /-bóyd'l/) having or nearly having the shape of a rhombus. ● n. a quadrilateral of which only the opposite sides and angles are equal. [F rhomboïde or LL rhomboides f. Gk rhomboeidēs (as RHOMB)]

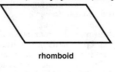

rhomboid

rhom·boi·de·us /rombóydeeəs/ n. (pl. **rhom·boi·de·i** /-dee-ī/) Anat. a muscle connecting the scapula to the vertebrae. [mod.L rhomboideus RHOMBOID]

rhom·bus /rómbəs/ n. (pl. **rhom·bus·es** or **rhom·bi** /-bī/) Geom. a parallelogram with oblique angles and equal sides. [L f. Gk rhombos]

rhu·barb /róobaarb/ n. **1 a** any of various plants of the genus Rheum, esp. R. rhaponticum, producing long fleshy dark-red leafstalks cooked as food. **b** the leafstalks of this. **2 a** a root of a Chinese and Tibetan plant of the genus Rheum. **b** a purgative made from this. **3 a** Brit. colloq. a murmurous conversation or noise, esp. the

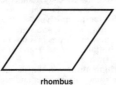

rhombus

rhubarb 1

repetition of the word "rhubarb" by crowd actors. **b** sl. nonsense; worthless stuff. **4** sl. a heated dispute.

rhumb /rum/ n. Naut. **1** any of the 32 points of the compass. **2** the angle between two successive compass points. **3** (in full **rhumb line**) **a** a line cutting all meridians at the same angle. **b** the line followed by a ship sailing in a fixed direction. [F rumb prob. f. Du. ruim room, assoc. with L rhombus: see RHOMBUS]

rhum·ba var. of RUMBA.

rhyme /rīm/ n. & v. ● n. **1** identity of sound between words or the endings of words, esp. in verse. **2** (in sing. or pl.) verse having rhymes. **3 a** the use of rhyme. **b** a poem having rhymes. **4** a word providing a rhyme. ● v. **1** intr. **a** (of words or lines) produce a rhyme. **b** (foll. by with) act as a rhyme (with another). **2** intr. make or write rhymes; versify. **3** tr. put or make (a story, etc.) into rhyme. **4** tr. (foll. by with) treat (a word) as rhyming with another. □ **rhyme or reason** sense; logic. □□ **rhyme·less** adj. **rhym·er** n. **rhym·ist** n. [ME rime f. OF rime f. med.L rithmus, rythmus f. L f. Gk rhuthmos RHYTHM]

rhyme·ster /rímstər/ n. a writer of (esp. simple or inferior) rhymes.

rhym·ing slang n. slang that replaces words by rhyming words or phrases, e.g., stairs by apples and pears, often with the rhyming element omitted (as in butcher's, short for butcher's hook, meaning 'look' in Cockney rhyming slang).

rhy·o·lite /ríəlīt/ n. a fine-grained volcanic rock of granitic composition. [G Rhyolit f. Gk rhuax lava stream + lithos stone]

rhythm /ríthəm/ n. **1** a measured flow of words and phrases in verse or prose determined by various relations of long and short or accented and unaccented syllables. **2** the aspect of musical composition concerned with periodical accent and the duration of notes. **3** Physiol. movement with a regular succession of strong and weak elements. **4** a regularly recurring sequence of events. **5** Art a harmonious correlation of parts. □□ **rhythm·less** adj. [F rhythme or L rhythmus f. Gk rhuthmos, rel. to rhēo flow]

rhythm and blues n. popular music with a blues theme and a strong rhythm.

rhyth·mic /ríthmik/ adj. (also **rhyth·mi·cal**) **1** relating to or characterized by rhythm. **2** regularly occurring. □□ **rhyth·mi·cal·ly** adv. [F rhythmique or L rhythmicus (as RHYTHM)]

rhyth·mic·i·ty /rithmísitee/ n. **1** rhythmical quality or character. **2** the capacity for maintaining a rhythm.

rhythm meth·od n. birth control by avoiding sexual intercourse when ovulation is likely to occur.

rhythm sec·tion n. the part of a dance band or jazz band mainly supplying rhythm, usu. consisting of piano, bass, and drums.

RI abbr. Rhode Island (also in official postal use).

ri·a /reeə/ n. Geog. a long narrow inlet formed by the partial submergence of a river valley. [Sp. ría estuary]

ri·al /reeáwl, -áal/ n. (also **ri·yal**) the monetary unit of several Middle Eastern countries. [Pers. f. Arab. riyal f. Sp. real ROYAL]

rib /rib/ n. & v. ● n. **1** each of the curved bones articulated in pairs to the spine and protecting the thoracic cavity and its organs. **2** a joint of meat from this part of an animal. **3** a ridge or long, raised piece often of stronger or thicker material across a surface or through a structure serving to support or strengthen it. **4** any of a ship's transverse curved timbers forming the framework of the hull. **5** Knitting a combination of plain and purl stitches producing a ribbed somewhat elastic fabric. **6** each of the hinged rods supporting the fabric of an umbrella. **7** a vein of a leaf or an insect's wing. **8** Aeron. a structural member in an airfoil. ● v.tr. (**ribbed, ribbing**) **1** provide with ribs; act as the ribs of. **2** colloq. make fun of; tease. **3** mark with or form into ridges. □□ **rib·less** adj.

rib·ald /ríbəld/ adj. & n. ● adj. (of language or its user) coarsely or disrespectfully humorous; scurrilous. ● n. a user of ribald language. [ME (earlier sense 'low-born retainer') f. OF ribau(l)d f. riber pursue licentious pleasures f. Gmc]

rib·ald·ry /ríbəldree/ n. ribald talk or behavior.

rib·and /ríbənd/ n. a ribbon. [ME f. OF riban, prob. f. a Gmc compound of BAND[1]]

ribbed /ribd/ adj. having ribs or riblike markings.

rib·bing /ríbing/ n. **1** ribs or a riblike structure. **2** colloq. the act or an instance of teasing.

rib·bon /ríbən/ n. **1 a** a narrow strip or band of fabric, used esp. for trimming or decoration. **b** material in this form. **2** a ribbon of a special color, etc., worn to indicate some honor or membership of a sports team, etc. **3** a long, narrow strip of anything, e.g., impregnated material forming the inking agent in a typewriter. **4** (in pl.) ragged strips (torn to ribbons). □□ **rib·boned** adj. [var. of RIBAND]

rib·bon·fish /ríbənfish/ n. any of various long slender flat fishes of the family Trachypteridae.

rib·bon worm *n.* a nemertean.

rib cage *n.* the wall of bones formed by the ribs around the chest.

ri·bo·fla·vin /ríbōfláyvin/ *n.* a vitamin of the B complex, found in liver, milk, and eggs, essential for energy production. Also called **vitamin B₂**. [RIBOSE + L *flavus* yellow]

ri·bo·nu·cle·ic ac·id /ríbənōōkleéik, –kláyik, –nyōō–/ *n.* a nucleic acid yielding ribose on hydrolysis, present in living cells, esp. in ribosomes where it is involved in protein synthesis. ¶ Abbr.: **RNA**. [RIBOSE + NUCLEIC ACID]

ri·bose /ríbōs/ *n.* a sugar found in many nucleosides and in several vitamins and enzymes. [G, alt. f. *Arabinose* a related sugar]

ri·bo·some /ríbəsōm/ *n. Biochem.* each of the minute particles consisting of RNA and associated proteins found in the cytoplasm of living cells, concerned with the synthesis of proteins. □□ **ri·bo·so·mal** *adj.* [RIBONUCLEIC (ACID) + –SOME³]

rib·wort /ríbwərt, –wawrt/ *n.* a kind of plantain with long, narrow ribbed leaves (see PLANTAIN¹).

rice /rīs/ *n. & v.* ● *n.* **1** a swamp grass, *Oryza sativa*, cultivated in marshes, esp. in Asia. **2** the grains of this, used as cereal food. ● *v.tr.* sieve (cooked potatoes, etc.) into thin strings. □□ **ric·er** *n.* [ME *rys* f. OF *ris* f. It. *riso*, ult. f. Gk *oruza*, of oriental orig.]

rice pa·per *n.* edible paper made from the pith of an Asian tree and used for painting and in cookery.

ri·cer·car /reécharkaár/ *n.* (also **ri·cer·ca·re** /–kaáre/) an elaborate contrapuntal instrumental composition in fugal or canonic style, esp. of the 16th–18th c. [It., = seek out]

rich /rich/ *adj. & n.* ● *adj.* **1** having much wealth. **2** (often foll. by *in*, *with*) splendid; costly; elaborate (*rich tapestries*; *rich with lace*). **3** valuable (*rich offerings*). **4** copious; abundant; ample (*a rich harvest*; *a rich supply of ideas*). **5** (often foll. by *in*, *with*) (of soil or a region, etc.) abounding in natural resources or means of production; fertile (*rich in nutrients*; *rich with vines*). **6** (of food or diet) containing much fat or spice, etc. **7** (of the fuel-air mixture in an internal-combustion engine) containing a high proportion of fuel. **8** (of color or sound or smell) mellow and deep; strong and full. **9 a** (of an incident or assertion, etc.) highly amusing or ludicrous; outrageous. **b** (of humor) earthy. ● *n.* (**the rich**) (used with a *pl. v.*) wealthy persons, collectively (*the rich get richer*). □□ **rich·en** *v.intr. & tr.* **rich·ness** *n.* [OE *rīce* f. Gmc f. Celt., rel. to L *rex* king: reinforced in ME f. OF *riche* rich, powerful, of Gmc orig.]

rich·es /ríchiz/ *n.pl.* abundant means; valuable possessions. [ME *richesse* f. OF *richeise* f. *riche* RICH, taken as pl.]

rich·ly /ríchlee/ *adv.* **1** in a rich way. **2** fully; thoroughly (*richly deserves success*).

Rich·ter scale /ríktər/ *n.* a scale of 0 to 10 for representing the strength of an earthquake. [C. F. *Richter*, Amer. seismologist d. 1985]

ri·cin /rísin, rís–/ *n.* a toxic substance obtained from castor beans and causing gastroenteritis, jaundice, and heart failure. [mod.L *ricinus communis* castor oil]

rick¹ /rik/ *n. & v.* ● *n.* (also **hay·rick**) a stack of hay, wheat, etc., built into a regular shape and usu. thatched. ● *v.tr.* form into a rick or ricks. [OE *hrēac*, of unkn. orig.]

rick² /rik/ *n. & v. Brit.* (also **wrick**) ● *n.* a slight sprain or strain. ● *v.tr.* sprain or strain slightly. [ME *wricke* f. MLG *wricken* move about, sprain]

rick·ets /ríkits/ *n.* (treated as *sing.* or *pl.*) a disease of children with softening of the bones (esp. the spine) and bowlegs, caused by a deficiency of vitamin D. [17th c.: orig. uncert., but assoc. by medical writers with Gk *rhakhitis* RACHITIS]

rick·ett·si·a /rikétseeə/ *n.* a parasitic microorganism of the genus *Rickettsia* causing typhus and other febrile diseases. □□ **rick·ett·si·al** *adj.* [mod.L f. H. T. *Ricketts*, Amer. pathologist d. 1910]

rick·et·y /ríkitee/ *adj.* **1 a** insecure or shaky in construction; likely to collapse. **b** feeble. **2 a** suffering from rickets. **b** resembling or of the nature of rickets. □□ **rick·et·i·ness** *n.* [RICKETS + –Y¹]

rick·ey /ríkee/ *n.* (*pl.* **·eys**) a drink made with liquor (esp. gin), lime juice, etc. [20th c.: prob. f. the surname *Rickey*]

rick·rack /ríkrak/ *n.* (also esp. *Brit.* **ric·rac**) a zigzag braided trimming, esp. for garments. [redupl. of RACK¹]

rick·sha /ríkshaw/ *n.* (also **rick·shaw**) a light two-wheeled hooded vehicle drawn by one or more persons. [abbr. of *jinricksha*, *jinrikshaw* f. Jap. *jinrikisha* f. *jin* person + *riki* power + *sha* vehicle]

ric·o·chet /ríkəshay, rikəsháy/ *n. & v.* ● *n.* **1** the action of a projectile, esp. a shell or bullet, in rebounding off a surface. **2** a hit made after this. ● *v.intr.* (**ric·o·cheted** /–shayd/; **ric·o·chet·ing** /–shaying/) (of a projectile) rebound one or more times from a surface. [F, of unkn. orig.]

ricksha

ri·cot·ta /rikótə, –káwtaa/ *n.* a soft Italian cheese resembling cottage cheese. [It., = recooked, f. L *recoquere* (as RE-, *coquere* cook)]

ric·rac esp. *Brit.* var. of RICKRACK.

ric·tus /ríktəs/ *n. Anat. & Zool.* the expanse or gape of a mouth or beak. □□ **ric·tal** *adj.* [L, = open mouth f. *ringi rict-* to gape]

rid /rid/ *v.tr.* (**rid·ding**; *past* and *past part.* **rid** or *archaic* **rid·ded**) (foll. by *of*) make (a person or place) free of something unwanted. □ **be** (or **get**) **rid of** be freed or relieved of (something unwanted); dispose of. [ME, earlier = 'clear (land, etc.)' f. ON *rythja*]

rid·dance /rídəns/ *n.* the act of getting rid of something. □ **good riddance** welcome relief from an unwanted person or thing.

rid·den *past part.* of RIDE.

rid·dle¹ /ríd'l/ *n. & v.* ● *n.* **1** a question or statement testing ingenuity in divining its answer or meaning. **2** a puzzling fact or thing or person. ● *v.* **1** *intr.* speak in or propound riddles. **2** *tr.* solve or explain (a riddle). □□ **rid·dler** *n.* [OE *rǣdels*, *rǣdelse* opinion, riddle, rel. to READ]

rid·dle² /ríd'l/ *v. & n.* ● *v.tr.* (usu. foll. by *with*) **1** make many holes in, esp. with gunshot. **2** (in *passive*) fill; spread through; permeate (*was riddled with errors*). **3** pass through a riddle. ● *n.* a coarse sieve. [OE *hriddel*, earlier *hrīder*: cf. *hrīdrian* sift]

rid·dling /rídling/ *adj.* expressed in riddles; puzzling. □□ **rid·dling·ly** *adv.*

ride /rīd/ *v. & n.* ● *v.* (*past* **rode** /rōd/; *past part.* **rid·den** /ríd'n/) **1** *tr.* travel or be carried on (a bicycle, etc.) or in (a vehicle). **2** *intr.* (often foll. by *on*, *in*) travel or be conveyed (on a bicycle or in a vehicle). **3** *tr.* sit on and control or be carried by (a horse, etc.). **4** *intr.* (often foll. by *on*) be carried (on a horse, etc.). **5** *tr.* be carried or supported by (*the ship rides the waves*). **6** *tr.* **a** traverse on horseback, etc., going over or through (*ride 50 miles*; *rode the prairie*). **b** compete or take part in on horseback, etc. (*rode a good race*). **7** *intr.* **a** lie at anchor; float buoyantly. **b** (of the moon) seem to float. **8** *intr.* (foll. by *in*, *on*) rest in or on while moving. **9** *tr.* yield to (a blow) so as to reduce its impact. **10** *tr.* give a ride to; cause to ride (*rode the child on his back*). **11** *tr.* (of a rider) cause (a horse, etc.) to move forward (*rode their horses at the fence*). **12** *tr.* **a** (in *passive*; foll. by *by*, *with*) be oppressed or dominated by; be infested with (*was ridden with guilt*). **b** (as **ridden** *adj.*) infested or afflicted (usu. in *comb.*: *a rat-ridden cellar*). **13** *intr.* (of a thing normally level or even) project or overlap. **14** *tr. colloq.* mount (a sexual partner) in copulation. **15** *tr.* annoy or seek to annoy. ● *n.* **1** an act or period of travel in a vehicle. **2** a spell of riding on a horse, bicycle, person's back, etc. **3** esp. *Brit.* a path (esp. through woods) for riding on. **4** the quality of sensations when riding (*gives a bumpy ride*). □ **let a thing ride** leave it alone; let it take its natural course. **ride again** reappear, esp. unexpectedly and reinvigorated. **ride down** overtake or trample on horseback. **ride herd on** see HERD. **ride high** be elated or successful. **ride out** come safely through (a storm, etc., or a danger or difficulty). **ride roughshod over** see ROUGHSHOD. **ride shotgun** **1** *hist.* carry a shotgun while riding on top of a stage coach as a guard. **2** guard or keep watch (over someone or something), esp. in transit. **3** ride in the front passenger seat of a vehicle. **ride up** (of a garment, carpet, etc.) work or move out of its proper position. **take for a ride** *colloq.* hoax or deceive. **2** *sl.* abduct in order to murder. □□ **rid·a·ble** *adj.* [OE *rīdan*]

rid·er /rídər/ *n.* **1** a person who rides (esp. a horse). **2 a** an additional clause amending or supplementing a document. **b** an addition or amendment to a legislative bill. **c** a corollary. **d** *Brit.* a recommendation, etc., added to a judicial verdict. **3** *Math.* a problem arising as a corollary of a theorem, etc. **4** a piece in a machine, etc., that surmounts or bridges or works on or over others. **5** (in *pl.*) an additional set of timbers or iron plates strengthening a ship's frame. □□ **rid•er•less** *adj.* [OE *rīdere* (as RIDE)]

ridge /rij/ *n. & v.* • *n.* **1** the line of the junction of two surfaces sloping upward toward each other (*the ridge of a roof*). **2** a long, narrow hilltop, mountain range, or watershed. **3** any narrow elevation across a surface. **4** *Meteorol.* an elongated region of high barometric pressure. **5** *Agriculture* a raised strip of arable land, usu. one of a set separated by furrows. **6** *Hort.* a raised hotbed for melons, etc. • *v.* **1** *tr.* mark with ridges. **2** *tr. Agriculture* break up (land) into ridges. **3** *tr. Hort.* plant (cucumbers, etc.) in ridges. **4** *tr. & intr.* gather into ridges. □□ **ridg•y** *adj.* [OE *hrycg* f. Gmc]

ridge•pole /rij'pōl/ *n.* **1** the horizontal pole of a long tent. **2** a beam along the ridge of a roof.

ridge•way /rij'way/ *n. Brit.* a road or track along a ridge.

rid•i•cule /ridikyōōl/ *n. & v.* • *n.* subjection to derision or mockery. • *v.tr.* make fun of; subject to ridicule; laugh at. [F or f. L *ridiculum* neut. of *ridiculus* laughable f. *ridēre* laugh]

ri•dic•u•lous /ridíkyələs/ *adj.* **1** deserving or inviting ridicule. **2** unreasonable; absurd. □□ **ri•dic•u•lous•ly** *adv.* **ri•dic•u•lous•ness** *n.* [L *ridiculosus* (as RIDICULE)]

rid•ing[1] /rīding/ *n.* **1** in senses of RIDE *v.* **2** the practice or skill of riders of horses. **3** = RIDE *n.* 3.

rid•ing[2] /rīding/ *n.* **1** each of three former administrative divisions (**East Riding, North Riding, West Riding**) of Yorkshire, England. **2** an electoral division of Canada. [OE *thriding* (unrecorded) f. ON *thrithjungr* third part f. *thrithi* THIRD: *th-* was lost owing to the preceding *-t* or *-th* of *north*, etc.]

rid•ing light esp. *Brit.* = ANCHOR LIGHT.

rid•ing school *n.* an establishment teaching skills in horsemanship.

Ries•ling /reezling, reés-/ *n.* **1** a kind of dry white wine produced in Europe, California, etc. **2** the variety of grape from which this is produced. [G]

rife /rīf/ *predic.adj.* **1** of common occurrence; widespread. **2** (foll. by *with*) abounding in; teeming with. □□ **rife•ness** *n.* [OE *rȳfe* prob. f. ON *rifr* acceptable f. *reifa* enrich, *reifr* cheerful]

riff /rif/ *n. & v.* • *n.* a short repeated phrase in jazz, etc. • *v.intr.* play riffs. [20th c.: abbr. of RIFFLE *n.*]

rif•fle /rifəl/ *v. & n.* • *v.* **1** *tr.* **a** turn (pages) in quick succession. **b** shuffle (playing cards), esp. by flexing and combining the two halves of a pack. **2** *intr.* (often foll. by *through*) leaf quickly (through pages). • *n.* **1** the act or an instance of riffling. **2** (in gold panning) a groove or slat set in a trough or sluice to catch gold particles. **3 a** a shallow part of a stream where the water flows brokenly. **b** a patch of waves or ripples on water. [perh. var. of RUFFLE]

riff-raff /rifraf/ *n.* (often prec. by *the*) rabble; disreputable or undesirable persons. [ME *riff and raff* f. OF *rif et raf*]

ri•fle[1] /rīfəl/ *v. & n.* • *n.* **1** a gun with a long, rifled barrel, esp. one fired from shoulder level. **2** (in *pl.*) riflemen. • *v.tr.* make spiral grooves in (a gun or its barrel or bore) to make a bullet spin. [OF *rifler* graze, scratch f. Gmc]

ri•fle[2] /rīfəl/ *v.tr. & (foll. by through) intr.* **1** search and rob, esp. of all that can be found. **2** carry off as booty. [ME f. OF *rifler* graze, scratch, plunder f. ODu. *riffelen*]

rifle[1]

ri•fle•bird /rīfəlbərd/ *n.* any dark green Australian bird of paradise of the genus *Ptiloris*.

ri•fle•man /rīfəlmən/ *n.* (*pl.* **-men**) **1** a soldier armed with a rifle. **2** a person skilled in shooting a rifle.

ri•fle range *n.* a place for rifle practice.

ri•fling /rīfling/ *n.* the arrangement of grooves on the inside of a gun's barrel.

rift /rift/ *n. & v.* • *n.* **1 a** a crack or split in an object. **b** an opening in a cloud, etc. **2** a cleft or fissure in earth or rock. **3** a disagreement; a breach in friendly relations. • *v.tr.* tear or burst apart. □□ **rift•less** *adj.* **rift•y** *adj.* [ME, of Scand. orig.]

rift val•ley *n.* a steep-sided valley formed by subsidence of the earth's crust between nearly parallel faults.

rig[1] /rig/ *n. & v.* • *v.* (**rigged, rig•ging**) **1 a** provide (a sailing ship) with sails, rigging, etc. **b** prepare ready for sailing. **2** (often foll. by *out, up*) fit with clothes or other equipment. **3** (foll. by *up*) set up hastily or as a makeshift. **4** assemble and adjust the parts of (an aircraft). • *n.* **1** the arrangement of masts, sails, rigging, etc. of a sailing ship. **2** equipment for a special purpose, e.g., a radio transmitter. **3** a truck, esp. a tractor-trailer. **4** esp. *Brit.* a person's or thing's look as determined by clothing, equipment, etc., esp. uniform. □ **in full rig** esp. *Brit. colloq.* smartly or ceremonially dressed. □□ **rigged** *adj.* (also in *comb.*). [ME, perh. f. Scand. orig.: cf. Norw. *rigga* bind or wrap up]

rig[2] /rig/ *v. & n.* • *v.tr.* (**rigged, rig•ging**) manage or conduct fraudulently (*they rigged the election*). • *n.* **1** a trick or dodge. **2** a way of swindling. □ **rig the market** cause an artificial rise or fall in prices. □□ **rig•ger** *n.* [19th c.: orig. unkn.]

rig•a•doon /rigədōōn/ *n.* **1** a lively dance in duple or quadruple time for two persons. **2** the music for this. [F *rigodon, rigaudon,* perh. f. its inventor *Rigaud*]

rig•ger /rigər/ *n.* **1** a person who rigs or who arranges rigging. **2** (of a rowboat) = OUTRIGGER 5a. **3** a ship rigged in a specified way. **4** a worker on an oil rig.

rig•ging /riging/ *n.* **1** a ship's spars, ropes, etc., supporting and controlling the sails. **2** the ropes and wires supporting the structure of an airship or biplane.

right /rīt/ *adj., n., v., adv., & int.* • *adj.* **1** (of conduct, etc.) just; morally or socially correct (*it is only right to tell you; I want to do the right thing*). **2** true; correct; not mistaken (*you were right about the weather*). **3** less wrong or not wrong (*which is the right way to town?*). **4** more or most suitable or preferable (*the right person for the job; along the right lines*). **5** in a sound or normal condition; physically or mentally healthy; satisfactory (*the engine doesn't sound right*). **6 a** on or toward the side of the human body that corresponds to the position of east if one regards oneself as facing north. **b** on or toward that part of an object that is analogous to a person's right side or (with opposite sense) that is nearer to a spectator's right hand. **7** (of a side of fabric, etc.) meant for display or use (*turn it right side up*). **8** esp. *Brit. colloq.* or *archaic* real; properly so called (*made a right mess of it; a right royal welcome*). • *n.* **1** that which is morally or socially correct or just; fair treatment (often in *pl.*: *the rights and wrongs of the case*). **2** (often foll. by *to,* or *to* + infin.) a justification or fair claim (*has no right to speak like that*). **3** a thing one may legally or morally claim; the state of being entitled to a privilege or immunity or authority to act (*a right of reply; human rights*). **4** the right-hand part or region or direction. **5** *Boxing* **a** the right hand. **b** a blow with this. **6** (often **Right**) *Polit.* **a** a group or section favoring conservatism (orig. the more conservative section of a European legislature, seated on the president's right). **b** such conservatives collectively. **7** the side of a stage that is to the right of a person facing the audience. **8** (esp. in marching) the right foot. **9** the right wing of an army. • *v.tr.* **1** (often *refl.*) restore to a proper or straight or vertical position. **2 a** correct (mistakes, etc.); set in order. **b** avenge (a wrong or a wronged person); make reparation for or to. **c** vindicate; justify; rehabilitate. • *adv.* **1** straight (*right on*). **2** *colloq.* immediately; without delay (*I'll be right back; do it right now*). **3** (foll. by *to, around, through,* etc.) all the way (*sank right to the bottom; ran right around the block*). **b** (foll. by *off, out,* etc.) completely (*came right off its hinges; am right out of butter*). **4** exactly; quite (*right in the middle*). **5** justly; properly; correctly; truly; satisfactorily (*did not act right; not holding it right; if I remember right*). **6** on or to the right side. **7** *archaic* very; to the full (*am right glad to hear it; dined right royally*). • *int. colloq.* expressing agreement or assent. □ **as right as rain** perfectly sound and healthy. **by right** (or **rights**) if rights were done. **do right by** act dutifully toward (a person). **in one's own right** through one's own position or effort, etc. **in the right** having justice or truth on one's side. **in one's right mind** sane; competent to think and act. **of** (or **as of**) **right** having legal or moral, etc., entitlement. **on the right side of 1** in the favor of (a person, etc.). **2** somewhat less than (a specified age). **put** (or **set**) **right 1** restore to order, health, etc. **2** correct the mistaken impression, etc., of (a person). **put** (or **set**) **to rights** make correct or well ordered. **right and left** (or **right, left, and center**) on all sides. **right away** (or **off**) immediately. **right on!** *colloq.* an expression of strong approval or encouragement. **right you are!** *colloq.* an exclamation of assent. **she's** (or **she'll be**) **right** *Austral. colloq.* that will be all right. **too right** esp. *Brit. sl.* an expression of agreement. **within one's rights** not exceeding one's authority or entitlement. □□ **right•a•ble** *adj.* **right•er** *n.* **right•ish** *adj.* **right•less** *adj.* **right•less•ness** *n.* **right•ness** *n.* [OE *riht* (adj.), *rihtan* (v.), *rihte* (adv.)]

right•a•bout face *n.* **1** a right turn continued to face the rear. **2** a reversal of policy. **3** a hasty retreat.

right an•gle *n.* an angle of 90°, made by lines meeting with equal angles on either side. □ **at right angles** placed to form a right angle. □□ **right-an•gled** *adj.*

right arm *n.* one's most reliable helper.

right as•cen•sion *n. Astron.* longitude measured along the celestial equator.

right bank *n.* the bank of a river on the right facing downstream.

right•en /rīt'n/ *v.tr.* esp. *Brit.* make right or correct.

right•eous /ríchəs/ *adj.* **1** (of a person or conduct) morally right; virtuous; law-abiding. **2** *sl.* perfectly wonderful; fine and genuine (*she executed some righteous ski jumps*). □□ **right•eous•ly** *adv.* **right•eous•ness** *n.* [OE *rihtwīs* (as RIGHT *n.* + −WISE or RIGHT *adj.* + WISE[2]), assim. to *bounteous,* etc.]

right field *n. Baseball* the part of the outfield to the right of center field from the perspective of home plate.

right•ful /rítfōōl/ *adj.* **1 a** (of a person) legitimately entitled to (a position, etc.) (*the rightful heir*). **b** (of status or property, etc.) that one is entitled to. **2** (of an action, etc.) equitable; fair. □□ **right‑ful‑ly** *adv.* **right‑ful‑ness** *n.* [OE *rihtful* (as RIGHT *n.*)]

right hand *n.* **1** = RIGHT‑HAND MAN. **2** the most important position next to a person (*stand at God's right hand*).

right‑hand *adj.* **1** on or toward the right side of a person or thing (*right-hand drive*). **2** done with the right hand (*right-hand blow*). **3** (of a screw) = RIGHT‑HANDED 4b.

right‑hand‑ed **1** using the right hand by preference as more serviceable than the left. **2** (of a tool, etc.) made to be used with the right hand. **3** (of a blow) struck with the right hand. **4 a** turning to the right; toward the right. **b** (of a screw) advanced by turning to the right (clockwise).

right‑hand‑er *n.* **1** a right-handed person. **2** a right-handed blow.

right‑hand man *n.* an indispensable or chief assistant.

right‑ism /rítizəm/ *n. Polit.* the principles or policy of the right. □□ **right‑ist** *n. & adj.*

right‑ly /rítlee/ *adv.* justly; properly; correctly; justifiably.

right‑mind‑ed *adj.* (also **right-thinking**) having sound views and principles.

right‑most /rítmōst/ *adj.* farthest to the right.

right‑o /rítṓ/ *int. Brit. colloq.* expressing agreement or assent.

right of search *n. Naut.* see SEARCH.

right of us‑er *n. Law* **1** a right to use. **2** a presumptive right arising from the user.

right of vis‑it‑a‑tion *n.* the right to conduct a visitation of a vessel, not including the right of search.

right of way *n.* **1** a right established by usage to pass over another's ground. **2** a path subject to such a right. **3** the right of one vehicle to proceed before another.

Right Rev‑er‑end *n.* the title of a bishop.

right sphere *n. Astron.* see SPHERE.

right‑to‑die *adj.* pertaining to the avoidance of using artificial life support in case of severe illness or injury.

right‑to‑know *adj.* pertaining to laws that make government or company records available to individuals.

right‑to‑life *adj.* pertaining to the movement opposing abortion.

right‑to‑work *adj.* pertaining to legislation outlawing obligatory union membership.

right turn *n.* a turn that brings one's front to face as one's right side did before.

right‑ward /rítwərd/ *adv. & adj.* ● *adv.* (also **right‑wards** /–wərdz/) toward the right. ● *adj.* going toward or facing the right.

right whale *n.* any large-headed whale of the family Balaenidae, rich in whalebone and easily captured.

right wing *n.* **1** an offensive position on the right side of a team in sports such as hockey and soccer. **2** the conservative section of a political party or system. □□ **right‑wing** *adj.* **right‑wing‑er** *n.*

rig‑id /ríjid/ *adj.* **1** not flexible; that cannot be bent (*a rigid frame*). **2** (of a person, conduct, etc.) **a** inflexible; unbending; harsh (*a rigid disciplinarian; rigid economy*). **b** strict; precise; punctilious. □□ **ri‑gid‑i‑ty** /rəjíditee/ *n.* **rig‑id‑ly** *adv.* **rig‑id‑ness** *n.* [F *rigide* or L *rigidus* f. *rigēre* be stiff]

ri‑gid‑i‑fy /ríjidifī/ *v.tr. & intr.* (**‑fies**, **‑fied**) make or become rigid.

rig‑ma‑role /rígmərōl/ (also **rig‑a‑ma‑role** /rígə–/) *n.* **1** a lengthy and complicated procedure. **2 a** a rambling or meaningless account or tale. **b** such talk. [orig. *ragman roll* = a catalog, of unkn. orig.]

rig‑or¹ /rígər/ *n. Med.* **1** a sudden feeling of cold with shivering accompanied by a rise in temperature, preceding a fever, etc. **2** rigidity of the body caused by shock or poisoning, etc. [ME f. L f. *rigēre* be stiff]

rig‑or² /rígər/ *n.* (*Brit.* **rig‑our**) **1 a** severity; strictness; harshness. **b** (often in *pl.*) severity of weather or climate; extremity of cold. **c** (in *pl.*) harsh measures or conditions. **2** logical exactitude. **3** strict enforcement of rules, etc. (*the utmost rigor of the law*). **4** austerity of life; puritanical discipline. [ME f. OF *rigor* f. L *rigor* (as RIGOR¹)]

rig‑or mor‑tis /rígər máwrtis/ *n.* stiffening of the body after death. [L, = stiffness of death]

rig‑or‑ous /rígərəs/ *adj.* **1** characterized by or showing rigor; strict, severe. **2** strictly exact or accurate. **3** (of the weather) cold, severe. □□ **rig‑or‑ous‑ly** *adv.* **rig‑or‑ous‑ness** *n.* [OF *rigorous* or LL *rigorosus* (as RIGOR¹)]

rig‑our *Brit.* var. of RIGOR².

rig‑out *Brit. colloq.* an outfit of clothes.

Rig‑Ve‑da /rigváydə, –véedə/ *n.* the oldest and principal of the Hindu Vedas (see VEDA). [Skr. *rigvéda* f. *ric* praise + *véda* VEDA]

rile /rīl/ *v.tr.* **1** *colloq.* anger; irritate. **2** make (water) turbulent or muddy. [var. of ROIL]

Ri‑ley /rílee/ *n.* □ **the life of Riley** *colloq.* a carefree existence. [20th c.: orig. unkn.]

ri‑lie‑vo var. of RELIEVO.

rill /ril/ *n.* **1** a small stream. **2** a shallow channel cut in the surface of soil or rocks by running water. **3** (also **rille**) *Astron.* a cleft or narrow valley on the moon's surface. [LG *ril, rille*]

rim /rim/ *n. & v.* ● *n.* **1 a** a raised edge or border. **b** a margin or verge, esp. of something circular. **2** the part of a pair of spectacles surrounding the lenses. **3** the outer edge of a wheel, on which the tire

is fitted. **4** a boundary line (*the rim of the horizon*). ● *v.tr.* (**rimmed**, **rim‑ming**) **1 a** provide with a rim. **b** be a rim for or to. **2** edge; border. □□ **rim‑less** *adj.* **rimmed** *adj.* (also in *comb.*). [OE *rima* edge: cf. ON *rimi* ridge (the only known cognate)]

rime¹ /rīm/ *n. & v.* ● *n.* **1** frost, esp. formed from cloud or fog. **2** *poet.* hoarfrost. ● *v.tr.* cover with rime. [OE *hrīm*]

rime² *archaic* var. of RHYME.

ri‑mose /rímōs, rímṓs/ *adj.* (also **ri‑mous** /–məs/) esp. *Bot.* full of chinks or fissures. [L *rimosus* f. *rima* chink]

rim‑y /rímee/ *adj.* (**rim‑i‑er**, **rim‑i‑est**) frosty; covered with frost.

rind /rīnd/ *n. & v.* ● *n.* **1** the tough outer layer or covering of fruit and vegetables, cheese, bacon, etc. **2** the bark of a tree or plant. ● *v.tr.* strip the bark from. □□ **rind‑ed** *adj.* (also in *comb.*). **rind‑less** *adj.* [OE *rind(e)*]

rin‑der‑pest /ríndərpest/ *n.* a virulent infectious disease of ruminants (esp. cattle). [G f. *Rinder* cattle + *Pest* PEST]

ring¹ /ring/ *n. & v.* ● *n.* **1** a circular band, usu. of precious metal, worn on a finger as an ornament or a token of marriage or betrothal. **2** a circular band of any material. **3** the rim of a cylindrical or circular object, or a line or band around it. **4** a mark or part having the form of a circular band (*had rings around his eyes; smoke rings*). **5** = ANNUAL RING. **6 a** an enclosure for a circus performance, betting at races, the showing of cattle, etc. **b** (prec. by *the*) bookmakers collectively. **c** a roped enclosure for boxing or wrestling. **7 a** a group of people or things arranged in a circle. **b** such an arrangement. **8** a combination of traders, bookmakers, spies, politicians, etc., acting together usu. illicitly for the control of operations or profit. **9** a circular or spiral course. **10** *Brit.* = GAS RING. **11** *Astron.* **a** a thin band or disk of particles, etc., around a planet. **b** a halo around the moon. **12** *Archaeol.* a circular prehistoric earthwork usu. of a bank and ditch. **13** *Chem.* a group of atoms each bonded to two others in a closed sequence. **14** *Math.* a set of elements with two binary operations, addition and multiplication, the second being distributive over the first and associative. ● *v.tr.* **1** make or draw a circle around. **2** (often foll. by *around, about, in*) encircle or hem in (game or cattle). **3** put a ring through the nose of (a pig, bull, etc.). **4** cut (fruit, vegetables, etc.) into rings. **n** **run** (or **make**) **rings around** *colloq.* outclass or outwit (another person). □□ **ringed** *adj.* (also in *comb.*). **ring‑less** *adj.* [OE *hring* f. Gmc]

ring² /ring/ *v. & n.* ● *v.* (*past* **rang** /rang/; *past part.* **rung** /rung/) **1** *intr.* (often foll. by *out*, etc.) give a clear resonant or vibrating sound of or as of a bell (*a shot rang out; a ringing laugh; the telephone rang*). **2** *tr.* **a** make (esp. a bell) ring. **b** (*absol.*) call for service or attention by ringing a bell (*you rang, madam?*). **3** *tr.* (also *absol.*; often foll. by *up*) esp. *Brit.* call by telephone (*will ring you on Monday; did you ring?*). **4** *intr.* (usu. foll. by *with, to*) (of a place) resound or be permeated with a sound, or an attribute, e.g., fame (*the theater rang with applause*). **5** *intr.* (of the ears) be filled with a sensation of ringing. **6** *tr.* **a** sound (a peal, etc.) on bells. **b** (of a bell) sound (the hour, etc.). **7** *tr.* (foll. by *in, out*) usher in or out with bell-ringing (*ring in the month of May; rang out the Old Year*). **8** *intr.* (of sentiments, etc.) convey a specified impression (*words rang hollow*). ● *n.* **1** a ringing sound or tone. **2 a** the act of ringing a bell. **b** the sound caused by this. **3** *colloq.* a telephone call (*give me a ring*). **4** a specified feeling conveyed by an utterance (*had a melancholy ring*). **5** a set of, esp. church, bells. □ **ring back** esp. *Brit.* make a return telephone call to (a person who has telephoned earlier). **ring a bell** see BELL¹. **ring down** (or **up**) **the curtain 1** cause the curtain to be lowered or raised. **2** (foll. by *on*) mark the end or the beginning of (an enterprise, etc.). **ring in one's ears** (or **heart**, etc.) linger in the memory. **ring off** *Brit.* end a telephone call by replacing the receiver. **ring true** (or **false**) convey an impression of truth or falsehood. **ring up 1** record (an amount, etc.) on a cash register. **2** *Brit.* call by telephone. □□ **ringed** *adj.* (also in *comb.*). **ring‑er** *n.* **ring‑ing** *adj.* **ring‑ing‑ly** *adv.* [OE *hringan*]

ring‑bark /ríngbaark/ *v.tr.* cut a ring in the bark of (a tree) to kill it or retard its growth and thereby improve fruit production; girdle.

ring bind‑er *n.* a loose-leaf binder with ring-shaped clasps that can be opened to pass through holes in the paper.

ring cir‑cuit *n. Brit.* an electrical circuit serving a number of power points with one fuse in the supply to the circuit.

ring‑dove /ríngduv/ *n.* **1** = WOOD PIGEON. **2** the collared dove.

ringed plov‑er *n.* either of two small plovers, *Charadrius hiaticula* and *C. dubius.*

ring‑er /ríngər/ *n. sl.* **1 a** an athlete or horse entered in a competition by fraudulent means, esp. as a substitute. **b** a person's double, esp. an impostor. **2** *Austral.* the fastest shearer in a sheep-shearing shed. **3** a person who rings, e.g., a bell ringer. □ **be a ringer** (or **dead ringer**) **for** resemble (a person) exactly. [RING² + –ER¹]

ring fin·ger *n.* the finger next to the little finger, esp. of the left hand, on which the wedding ring is usu. worn.

ring·hals /ríŋhals/ *n.* a large venomous snake, *Hemachatus hemachatus*, of Southern Africa, with a white ring or two across the neck. [Afrik. *rinkhals* f. *ring* RING¹ + *hals* neck]

ring·lead·er /ríŋleedər/ *n.* a leading instigator, esp. in an illicit or illegal activity.

ring·let /ríŋlit/ *n.* **1** a curly lock of hair, esp. a long one. **2** a butterfly, *Aphantopus hyperantus*, with spots on its wings. **3** *Astron.* one of the thin rings within the major rings of Saturn. □□ **ring·let·ed** *adj.* **ring·let·y** *adj.*

ring·mas·ter /ríŋmastər/ *n.* the person directing a circus performance.

ring-necked *adj. Zool.* having a band or bands of color around the neck.

ring ou·zel *n.* a European thrush, *Turdus torquatus*, with a white crescent across its breast.

ring-pull *n. Brit.* = PULL-TAB.

ring road *n.* esp. *Brit.* a bypass encircling a town.

ring·side /ríŋsīd/ *n.* (often *attrib.*) **1** the area immediately beside a boxing ring or circus ring, etc. **2** an advantageous position from which to observe or monitor something. □□ **ring·sid·er** *n.*

ring·ster /ríŋstər/ *n.* a person who participates in a political or commercial ring (see RING¹ *n.* 8).

ring·tail /ríŋtayl/ *n.* **1** a ring-tailed opossum, lemur, or phalanger. **2** a golden eagle up to its third year. **3** a female northern harrier.

ring-tailed *adj.* **1** (of monkeys, lemurs, raccoons, etc.) having a tail ringed in alternate colors. **2** with the tail curled at the end.

ring·worm /ríŋwərm/ *n.* any of various fungous infections of the skin causing circular inflamed patches, esp. on a child's scalp.

rink /riŋk/ *n.* **1** an area of natural or artificial ice for skating or playing ice hockey, etc. **2** an enclosed area for roller-skating. **3** a building containing either of these. **4** a strip of the green used for playing a match of lawn bowling. **5** a team in lawn bowling or curling. [ME (orig. Sc.), = jousting ground: perh. orig. f. OF *renc* RANK¹]

rinse /rins/ *v. & n.* ● *v.tr.* (often foll. by *through, out*) **1** wash with clean water. **2** apply liquid to. **3** wash lightly. **4** put (clothes, etc.) through clean water to remove soap or detergent. **5** (foll. by *out, away*) clear (impurities) by rinsing. **6** treat (hair) with a rinse. ● *n.* **1** the act or an instance of rinsing (*give it a rinse*). **2** a solution for cleansing the mouth. **3** a dye for the temporary tinting of hair (*a blue rinse*). □□ **rins·er** *n.* [ME f. OF *rincer, raincier*, of unkn. orig.]

ri·ot /ríət/ *n. & v.* ● *n.* **1 a** a disturbance of the peace by a crowd; an occurrence of public disorder. **b** (*attrib.*) involved in suppressing riots (*riot police; riot shield*). **2** uncontrolled revelry; noisy behavior. **3** (foll. by *of*) a lavish display or enjoyment (*a riot of emotion; a riot of color and sound*). **4** *colloq.* a very amusing thing or person (*everyone thought she was a riot*). ● *v.intr.* **1** make or engage in a riot. **2** behave in an unrestrained way. □ **read the Riot Act** put a firm stop to insubordination, etc.; give a severe warning (from the name of a former act partly read out to disperse rioters). **run riot 1** throw off all restraint. **2** (of plants) grow or spread uncontrolled. □□ **ri·ot·er** *n.* **ri·ot·less** *adj.* [ME f. OF *riote, rioter, rihoter*, of unkn. orig.]

ri·ot·ous /ríətəs/ *adj.* **1** marked by or involving rioting. **2** characterized by wanton conduct. **3** wildly profuse. □□ **ri·ot·ous·ly** *adv.* **ri·ot·ous·ness** *n.* [ME f. OF (as RIOT)]

RIP *abbr.* rest in peace (used on graves). [L *requiescat* (pl. *requiescant*) *in pace*]

rip¹ /rip/ *v. & n.* ● *v.tr. & intr.* (**ripped, rip·ping**) **1** *tr.* tear or cut (a thing) quickly or forcibly away or apart (*ripped out the lining; ripped the book up*). **2** *tr.* **a** make (a hole, etc.) by ripping. **b** make a long tear or cut in. **3** *intr.* come violently apart; split. **4** *intr.* rush along. ● *n.* **1** a long tear or cut. **2** an act of ripping. □ **let rip** *colloq.* **1** act or proceed without restraint. **2** speak violently. **3** not check the speed of or interfere with (a person or thing). **rip into** attack (a person) verbally. **rip off** *colloq.* defraud; steal. [ME: orig. unkn.]

rip² /rip/ *n.* a stretch of rough water in the sea or in a river, caused by the meeting of currents. [18th c.: perh. rel. to RIP¹]

rip³ /rip/ *n.* **1** a dissolute person. **2** a rascal. **3** a worthless horse. [perh. f. *rep*, abbr. of REPROBATE]

ri·par·i·an /ripáireeən/ *adj. & n.* esp. *Law* ● *adj.* of or on a riverbank (*riparian rights*). ● *n.* an owner of property on a riverbank. [L *riparius* f. *ripa* bank]

rip cord *n.* a cord for releasing a parachute from its pack.

rip cur·rent *n.* **1** a strong surface current from the shore. **2** a state of conflicting psychological forces.

ripe /rīp/ *adj.* **1** (of grain, fruit, cheese, etc.) ready to be reaped or picked or eaten. **2** mature; fully developed (*ripe in judgment; a ripe beauty*). **3** (of a person's age) advanced. **4** (often foll. by *for*) fit or ready (*when the time is ripe; land ripe for development*). **5** (of the complexion, etc.) red and full like ripe fruit. □□ **ripe·ly** *adv.* **ripe·ness** *n.* [OE *rīpe* f. WG]

rip·en /rípən/ *v.tr. & intr.* make or become ripe.

ri·pie·no /ripyáynō/ *n.* (pl. **·nos** or **ri·pie·ni** /-nee/) *Mus.* a body of accompanying instruments in baroque concerto music. [It. (as RE-, *pieno* full)]

rip-off *n. colloq.* **1** a fraud or swindle. **2** financial exploitation.

ri·poste /ripóst/ *n. & v.* ● *n.* **1** a quick sharp reply or retort. **2** a quick return thrust in fencing. ● *v.intr.* deliver a riposte. [F *ri(s)poste*, *ri(s)poster* f. It. *risposta* RESPONSE]

rip·per /rípər/ *n.* **1** a person or thing that rips. **2** a murderer who rips the victims' bodies.

rip·ping /rípiŋ/ *adj. Brit. archaic sl.* very enjoyable (*a ripping good yarn*). □□ **rip·ping·ly** *adv.*

rip·ple¹ /rípəl/ *n. & v.* ● *n.* **1** a ruffling of the water's surface; a small wave or series of waves. **2 a** a gentle lively sound that rises and falls, e.g., of laughter or applause. **b** a brief wave of emotion, excitement, etc. (*the new recruit caused a ripple of interest in the company*). **3** a wavy appearance in hair, material, etc. **4** *Electr.* a slight variation in the strength of a current, etc. **5** ice cream with added syrup giving a colored ripple effect (*raspberry ripple*). **6** a riffle in a stream. ● *v.* **1 a** *intr.* form ripples; flow in ripples. **b** *tr.* cause to do this. **2** *intr.* show or sound like ripples. □□ **rip·plet** *n.* **rip·ply** *adj.* [17th c.: orig. unkn.]

rip·ple² /rípəl/ *n. & v.* ● *n.* a toothed implement used to remove seeds from flax. ● *v.tr.* treat with a ripple. [corresp. to MDu. & MLG *repel(en)*, OHG *riffila, rifilōn*]

rip·rap /ríprap/ *n.* a collection of loose stone as a foundation for a structure. [redupl. of RAP¹]

rip-roar·ing /ríprawriŋ/ *adj.* **1** wildly noisy or boisterous. **2** excellent, first-rate. □□ **rip-roar·ing·ly** *adv.*

rip·saw /rípsaw/ *n.* a coarse saw for sawing wood along the grain.

rip·snort·er /rípsnawrtər/ *n. colloq.* an energetic, remarkable, or excellent person or thing. □□ **rip·snort·ing** *adj.* **rip·snort·ing·ly** *adv.*

rip·tide /ríptīd/ *n.* = RIP CURRENT.

rise /rīz/ *v. & n.* ● *v.intr.* (*past* **rose** /rōz/; *past part.* **ris·en** /rízən/) **1** move from a lower position to a higher one; come or go up. **2** grow, project, expand, or incline upward; become higher. **3** (of the sun, moon, or stars) appear above the horizon. **4 a** get up from lying or sitting or kneeling (*rose to their feet; rose from the table*). **b** get out of bed, esp. in the morning (*do you rise early?*). **5** recover a standing or vertical position; become erect (*rose to my full height*). **6** *Brit.* (of a meeting, etc.) cease to sit for business; adjourn (*Parliament rises next week; the court will rise*). **7** reach a higher position or level or amount (*the flood has risen; prices are rising*). **8** develop greater intensity, strength, volume, or pitch (*the color rose in her cheeks; the wind is rising; their voices rose with excitement*). **9** make progress; reach a higher social position (*rose from the ranks*). **10 a** come to the surface of liquid (*bubbles rose from the bottom; waited for the fish to rise*). **b** (of a person) react to provocation (*rise to the bait*). **11** become or be visible above the surroundings, etc., stand prominently (*mountains rose to our right*). **12 a** (of buildings, etc.) undergo construction from the foundations (*office buildings were rising all around*). **b** (of a tree, etc.) grow to a (usu. specified) height. **13** come to life again (*rise from the ashes; risen from the dead*). **14** (of dough) swell by the action of yeast, etc. **15** (often foll. by *up*) cease to be quiet or submissive; rebel (*rise in arms*). **16** originate; have as its source (*the river rises in the mountains*). **17** (of wind) start to blow. **18** (of a person's spirits) become cheerful. **19** (of a barometer) show a higher atmospheric pressure. **20** (of a horse) rear (*rose on its hind legs*). **21** (of a bump, blister, etc.) form. ● *n.* **1** an act or manner or amount of rising. **2** an upward slope or hill or movement (*a rise in the road; the house stood on a rise; the rise and fall of the waves*). **3** an increase in sound or pitch. **4 a** an increase in amount, extent, etc. (*a rise in unemployment*). **b** *Brit.* an increase in salary, wages, etc. **5** an increase in status or power. **6** social, commercial, or political advancement; upward progress. **7** the movement of fish to the surface. **8** origin. **9 a** the vertical height of a step, arch, incline, etc. **b** = RISER 2. □ **get a rise out of** *colloq.* provoke an emotional reaction from (a person), esp. by teasing. **on the rise** on the increase. **rise above 1** be superior to (petty feelings, etc.). **2** show dignity or strength in the face of (difficulty, poor conditions, etc.). **rise and shine** (usu. as *imper.*) *colloq.* get out of bed; wake up. **rise in the world** attain a higher social position. **rise to** develop powers equal to (an occasion). [OE *rīsan* f. Gmc]

ris·er /rízər/ *n.* **1** a person who rises, esp. from bed (*an early riser*). **2** a vertical section between the treads of a staircase. **3** a vertical pipe for the flow of liquid or gas.

rish·i /ríshee/ *n.* (pl. **rish·is**) a Hindu sage or saint. [Skr. *ṛiṣi*]

ris·i·ble /rízibəl/ *adj.* **1** laughable; ludicrous. **2** inclined to laugh. **3** *Anat.* relating to laughter (*risible nerves*). □□ **ris·i·bil·i·ty** *n.* **ris·i·bly** *adv.* [LL *risibilis* f. L *ridēre ris-* laugh]

ris·ing /ríziŋ/ *adj. & n.* ● *adj.* **1** going up; getting higher. **2** increasing (*rising costs*). **3** advancing to maturity or high standing (*the rising generation; a rising young lawyer*). **4** approaching a higher level, grade, etc. (*rising seniors*) or a specified age (*the rising fives*). **5** (of ground) sloping upward. ● *n.* a revolt or insurrection; uprising.

risk /risk/ *n. & v.* ● *n.* **1** a chance or possibility of danger, loss, injury, or other adverse consequences (*a health risk; a risk of fire*). **2** a person or thing causing a risk or regarded in relation to risk (*is a poor* *risk*). • *v.tr.* **1** expose to risk. **2** accept the chance of (*could not risk getting wet*). **3** venture on. □ **at risk** exposed to danger. **at one's (own) risk** accepting responsibility or liability. **at the risk of** with the possibility of (an adverse consequence). **put at risk** expose to danger. **risk one's neck** put one's own life in danger. **run a** (or **the**) **risk** (often foll. by *of*) expose oneself to danger or loss, etc. **take** (or **run**) **a risk** chance the possibility of danger, etc. [F *risque*, *risquer* f. It. *risco* danger, *riscare* run into danger]

risk cap•i•tal = VENTURE CAPITAL.

risk•y /rískee/ *adj.* (**risk•i•er**, **risk•i•est**) **1** involving risk. **2** *Brit.* = RISQUÉ. □□ **risk•i•ly** *adv.* **risk•i•ness** *n.*

Ri•sor•gi•men•to /risáwrjiméntō/ *n. hist.* a movement for the unification and independence of Italy (achieved in 1870). [It., = resurrection]

ri•sot•to /risáwtō, –sótō, –záwtō/ *n.* (*pl.* **•tos**) an Italian dish of rice cooked in stock with meat, onions, etc. [It.]

ris•qué /riskáy/ *adj.* (of a story, etc.) slightly indecent or liable to shock. [F, past part. of *risquer* RISK]

ris•sole /risól, rísol/ *n.* a pastry filled with a mixture of meat or fish and spices, usu. deep-fried. [F f. OF *ruissole*, *roussole* ult. f. LL *russeolus* reddish f. L *russus* red]

rit. /rit/ *abbr. Mus.* ritardando.

ri•tar•dan•do /réetardándō/ *adv. & n. Mus.* (*pl.* **•dos** or **ri•tar•dan•di** /–dee/) = RALLENTANDO. [It.]

rite /rīt/ *n.* **1** a religious or solemn observance or act (*burial rites*). **2** an action or procedure required or usual in this. **3** a body of customary observances characteristic of a church or a part of it (*the Latin rite*). □□ **rite•less** *adj.* [ME f. OF *rit*, *rite* or L *ritus* (esp. religious) usage]

ri•te•nu•to /réetǝnóotō/ *adv. & n. Mus.* • *adv.* with immediate reduction of speed. • *n.* (*pl.* **•tos** or **ri•te•nu•ti** /–tee/) a passage played in this way. [It.]

rite of pas•sage *n.* (often in *pl.*) a ritual or event marking a stage of a person's advance through life, e.g., marriage.

ri•tor•nel•lo /réetawrnéllō/ *n. Mus.* (*pl.* **•los** or **ri•tor•nel•li** /–lee/) a short instrumental refrain, interlude, etc., in a vocal work. [It., dimin. of *ritorno* RETURN]

rit•u•al /ríchooǝl/ *n. & adj.* • *n.* **1** a prescribed order of performing rites. **2** a procedure regularly followed. • *adj.* of or done as a ritual or rites (*ritual murder*). □□ **rit•u•al•ize** *v.tr. & intr.* **rit•u•al•i•za•tion** *n.* **rit•u•al•ly** *adv.* [L *ritualis* (as RITE)]

rit•u•al•ism /ríchooǝlizǝm/ *n.* the regular or excessive practice of ritual. □□ **rit•u•al•ist** *n.* **rit•u•al•is•tic** *adj.* **rit•u•al•is•ti•cal•ly** *adv.*

ritz•y /rítsee/ *adj.* (**ritz•i•er**, **ritz•i•est**) *colloq.* **1** high-class; luxurious. **2** ostentatiously smart. □□ **ritz•i•ly** *adv.* **ritz•i•ness** *n.* [*Ritz*, the name of luxury hotels f. C. *Ritz*, Swiss hotel owner d. 1918]

riv. *abbr.* river.

ri•val /rívǝl/ *n. & v.* • *n.* **1** a person competing with another for the same objective. **2** a person or thing that equals another in quality. **3** (*attrib.*) being a rival or rivals (*a rival firm*). • *v.tr.* **1** be the rival of or comparable to. **2** seem or claim to be as good as. [L *rivalis*, orig. = using the same stream, f. *rivus* stream]

ri•val•ry /rívǝlree/ *n.* (*pl.* **•ries**) the state or an instance of being rivals; competition.

rive /rīv/ *v.* (*past* **rived**; *past part.* **riv•en** /rívǝn/) *archaic* or *poet.* **1** *tr.* split or tear apart violently. **2 a** *tr.* split (wood or stone). **b** *intr.* be split. [ME f. ON *rífa*]

riv•er /rívǝr/ *n.* **1** a copious natural stream of water flowing in a channel to the sea or a lake, etc. **2** a copious flow (*a river of lava*; *rivers of blood*). **3** (*attrib.*) (in the names of animals, plants, etc.) living in or associated with the river. □ **sell down the river** *colloq.* betray or let down. □□ **riv•ered** *adj.* (also in *comb.*). **riv•er•less** *adj.* [ME f. AF *river*, *rivere*, OF *riviere* river or riverbank ult. f. L *riparius* f. *ripa* bank]

riv•er blind•ness = ONCHOCERCIASIS.

riv•er•ine /rívǝrīn, –reen/ *adj.* of or on a river or riverbank; riparian.

riv•er•side /rívǝrsīd/ *n.* the ground along a riverbank.

riv•et /rívit/ *n. & v.* • *n.* a nail or bolt for holding together metal plates, etc., its headless end being beaten out or pressed down when in place. • *v.tr.* **1 a** join or fasten with rivets. **b** beat out or press down the end of (a nail or bolt). **c** fix; make immovable. **2 a** (foll. by *on*, *upon*) direct intently (one's eyes or attention, etc.). **b** (esp. as **riveting** *adj.*) engross (a person or the attention). □□ **riv•et•er** *n.* [ME f. OF f. *river* clench, of unkn. orig.]

rivet

riv•i•er•a /ríveeáirǝ/ *n.* (often **Riv•i•er•a**) a coastal region with a subtropical climate, vegetation, etc., esp. that of SE France and NW Italy. [It., = seashore]

riv•ière /reevyáir/ *n.* a gem necklace, esp. of more than one string. [F, = RIVER]

riv•u•let /rívyǝlit/ *n.* a small stream. [obs. *riveret* f. F, dimin. of *rivière* RIVER, perh. after It. *rivoletto* dimin. of *rivolo* dimin. of *rivo* f. L *rivus* stream]

ri•yal var. of RIAL.

rm. *abbr.* room.

r months *n.pl.* the months with *r* in their names (September to April) as the season for oysters.

r.m.s. *abbr. Math.* root-mean-square.

RN *abbr.* **1** registered nurse. **2** (in the UK) Royal Navy.

Rn *symb. Chem.* the element radon.

RNA *abbr.* ribonucleic acid.

roach[1] /rōch/ *n.* (*pl.* same) a small freshwater fish, esp. *Rutilus rutilus*, allied to the carp. [ME f. OF *roc(h)e*, of unkn. orig.]

roach[2] /rōch/ *n.* **1** *colloq.* a cockroach. **2** *sl.* the butt of a marijuana cigarette. [abbr.]

roach[3] /rōch/ *n. Naut.* an upward curve in the foot of a sail. [18th c.: orig. unkn.]

road[1] /rōd/ *n.* **1 a** a path or way with a specially prepared surface, used by vehicles, pedestrians, etc. **b** the part of this used by vehicles (*don't step in the road*). **2 a** one's way or route (*our road took us through unexplored territory*). **b** a method or means of accomplishing something. **3** an underground passage in a mine. **4** a railroad. **5** (usu. in *pl.*) a partly sheltered piece of water near the shore in which ships can ride at anchor. □ **by road** using transport along roads. **get out of the** (or **my**, etc.) **road** esp. *Brit. colloq.* cease to obstruct a person. **in the** (or **my**, etc.) **road** esp. *Brit. colloq.* obstructing a person or thing. **one for the road** *colloq.* a final (esp. alcoholic) drink before departure. **on the road** traveling, esp. as a firm's representative, itinerant performer, or vagrant. **the road to** the way of getting to or achieving (*the road to Miami*; *the road to ruin*). **take the road** set out. □□ **road•less** *adj.* [OE *rād* f. *rīdan* RIDE]

road[2] /rōd/ *v.tr.* (also *absol.*) (of a dog) follow and pursue (a game bird) by the scent of its trail. [19th c.: orig. unkn.]

road•bed /rōdbed/ *n* **1** the foundation structure of a railroad. **2** the material laid down to form a road. **3** the part of a road on which vehicles travel.

road•block /ródblok/ *n.* a barrier or barricade on a road, esp. one set up by the authorities to stop and examine traffic.

road hog *n. colloq.* a reckless or inconsiderate motorist.

road•house /ródhows/ *n.* an inn or club on a country road.

road•ie /ródee/ *n. sl.* an assistant employed by a touring band of musicians to erect and maintain equipment.

road man•ag•er *n.* the organizer and supervisor of a musicians' tour.

road map *n.* a map showing the roads of a country or area.

road met•al *n. Brit.* broken stone used in road making or for railroad ballast.

road•run•ner /ródrunǝr/ *n.* a bird of Mexican and US deserts, *Geococcyx californianus*, related to the cuckoo, known as a poor flier but a fast runner.

road show *n.* **1 a** a performance given by a touring company, esp. a group of pop musicians. **b** a company giving such performances. **2** a radio or television program done on location.

roadrunner

road•side /ródsīd/ *n.* the strip of land beside a road.

road sign *n.* a sign giving information or instructions to road users.

road•stead /ródsted/ *n.* = ROAD[1] 5. [ROAD[1] + *stead* in obs. sense 'place']

road•ster /ródstǝr/ *n.* **1** an open car without rear seats. **2** a horse or bicycle for use on the road.

road test *n.* a test of the performance of a vehicle on the road.

road•way /ródway/ *n.* **1** a road. **2** = ROAD[1] 1b. **3** the part of a bridge or railroad used for traffic.

road•work /ródwǝrk/ *n.* **1** the construction or repair of roads, or other work involving digging up a road surface. **2** athletic exercise or training involving running on roads.

road•wor•thy /ródwǝrthee/ *adj.* **1** fit to be used on the road. **2** (of a person) fit to travel. □□ **road•wor•thi•ness** *n.*

roam /rōm/ *v. & n.* • *v.* **1** *intr.* ramble; wander. **2** *tr.* travel unsystematically over, through, or about. • *n.* an act of roaming; a ramble. □□ **roam•er** *n.* [ME: orig. unkn.]

roan[1] /rōn/ *adj. & n.* • *adj.* (of an animal, esp. a horse or cow) having a coat of which the prevailing color is thickly interspersed with hairs of another color, esp. bay or sorrel or chestnut mixed with white or gray. • *n.* a roan animal. [OF, of unkn. orig.]

roan[2] /rōn/ *n.* soft sheepskin leather used in bookbinding as a substitute for morocco. [ME, perh. f. *Roan*, old name of *Rouen* in N. France]

roar /rawr/ *n. & v.* • *n.* **1** a loud, deep, hoarse sound, as made by a lion, thunder, a loud engine, or a person in pain, rage, or excitement. **2** a loud laugh. • *v.* **1** *intr.* **a** utter or make a roar. **b** utter loud laughter. **c** (of a horse) make a loud noise in breathing as a symptom of disease. **2** *intr.* travel in a vehicle at high speed, esp. with the engine roaring. **3** *tr.* (often foll. by *out*) say, sing, or utter (words, an oath, etc.) in a loud tone. □□ **roar•er** *n*. [OE *rārian*, of imit. orig.]

roar•ing /ráwring/ *adj*. in senses of ROAR *v*. □ **roaring drunk** very drunk and noisy. **roaring trade** (or **business**) esp. *Brit*. very brisk trade or business. □□ **roar•ing•ly** *adv*.

roar•ing for•ties *n.pl*. stormy ocean tracts between lat. 40° and 50° S.

roar•ing twen•ties *n.pl*. the decade of the 1920s (with ref. to its postwar buoyancy).

roast /rōst/ *v*., *adj*., & *n*. • *v*. 1 *tr*. **a** cook (food, esp. meat) in an oven or by exposure to open heat. **b** heat (coffee beans) before grinding. 2 *tr*. heat (the ore of metal) in a furnace. 3 *tr*. **a** expose (a torture victim) to fire or great heat. **b** *tr. & refl*. expose (oneself or part of oneself) to warmth. 4 *tr*. criticize severely; denounce. 5 *intr*. undergo roasting. • *attrib.adj*. (of meat or a potato, chestnut, etc.) roasted. • *n*. 1 **a** roast meat. **b** a dish of this. **c** a piece of meat for roasting. 2 the process of roasting. 3 a party where roasted food is eaten. 4 a banquet to honor a person at which the honoree is subjected to good-natured ridicule. [ME f. OF *rost*, *rostir*, f. Gmc]

roast•er /rōstər/ *n*. 1 a person or thing that roasts. 2 **a** an oven or dish for roasting food in. **b** an ore-roasting furnace. **c** a coffee-roasting apparatus. 3 something fit for roasting, e.g., a fowl, a potato, etc.

roast•ing /rōsting/ *adj. & n*. • *adj*. very hot. • *n*. 1 in senses of ROAST *v*. 2 a severe criticism or denunciation.

rob /rob/ *v.tr*. (**robbed, rob•bing**) (often foll. by *of*) 1 take unlawfully from, esp. by force or threat of force (*robbed the safe; robbed her of her jewels*). 2 deprive of what is due or normal (*was robbed of my sleep*). 3 (*absol*.) commit robbery. 4 *colloq*. cheat; swindle. □ **rob Peter to pay Paul** take away from one to give to another; discharge one debt by incurring another. [ME f. OF *rob(b)er* f. Gmc: cf. REAVE] ▶In law, to **rob** is to take something from someone by causing fear of harm, whether or not actual harm occurs. The term is widely, but incorrectly, used to mean simple *theft*, e.g.: *Our house was robbed while we were away.*

rob•ber /róbər/ *n*. a person who commits robbery. [ME f. AF & OF (as ROB)]

rob•ber bar•on *n*. 1 a plundering feudal lord. 2 an unscrupulous plutocrat.

rob•ber•y /róbəree/ *n*. (*pl*. **-ies**) 1 **a** the act or process of robbing, esp. with force or threat of force. **b** an instance of this. 2 excessive financial demand or cost; overcharging or swindling (*set us back $50—it was sheer robbery*). [ME f. OF *roberie* (as ROB)]

robe /rōb/ *n. & v*. • *n*. 1 a long, loose outer garment. 2 a loose, usu. belted garment worn over nightwear, while resting, or after bathing. 3 a baby's outer garment, esp. at a christening. 4 (often in *pl*.) a long outer garment worn as an indication of the wearer's rank, office, profession, etc.; a gown or vestment. 5 a blanket or wrap of fur. • *v*. 1 *tr*. clothe (a person) in a robe; dress. 2 *intr*. put on one's robes or vestments. [ME f. OF f. Gmc (as ROB, orig. sense 'booty')]

rob•in /róbin/ *n*. 1 a red-breasted thrush, *Turdus migratorius*. 2 (also **rob•in red•breast**) a small brown European bird, *Erithacus rubecula*, the adult of which has a red throat and breast. 3 a bird similar in appearance, etc., to either of these. [ME f. OF, familiar var. of the name *Robert*]

Rob•in Hood *n*. (with ref. to the legend of the medieval forest outlaw) a person who acts illegally or unfavorably toward the rich for the benefit of the poor.

ro•bin•i•a /rəbíneeə/ *n*. any N. American tree or shrub of the genus *Robinia*, e.g., a locust tree or false acacia. [mod.L, f. J. *Robin*, 17th-c. French gardener]

rob•o•rant /róbərənt/ *adj. & n*. *Med*. • *adj*. strengthening. • *n*. a strengthening drug. [L *roborare* f. *robur* –*oris* strength]

ro•bot /róbot/ *n*. 1 a machine capable of carrying out a complex series of actions automatically, esp. one programmable by a computer. 2 (esp. in science fiction) a machine resembling a human being and able to replicate certain human functions automatically. 3 a person who behaves in a mechanical or unemotional manner. □□ **ro•bot•ic** /–bótik/ *adj*. **ro•bot•ize** *v.tr*. [Czech (in K. Čapek's play *R.U.R.* (*Rossum's Universal Robots*) 1920), f. *robota* forced labor]

ro•bot bomb *n*. a pilotless aircraft with an explosive warhead.

ro•bot•ics /róbótiks/ *n.pl*. the study of robots; the art or science of their design and operation.

ro•bust /rōbúst/ *adj*. (**ro•bust•er, ro•bust•est**) 1 (of a person, animal, or thing) strong and sturdy, esp. in physique or construction. 2 (of exercise, discipline, etc.) vigorous; requiring strength. 3 (of intellect or mental attitude) straightforward, not given to nor confused by subtleties. 4 (of a statement, etc.) bold; firm; unyielding. 5 (of wine, etc.) full-bodied. □□ **ro•bust•ly** *adv*. **ro•bust•ness** *n*. [F *robuste* or L *robustus* firm and hard f. *robus*, *robur* oak, strength]

roc /rok/ *n*. a gigantic bird of Eastern legend. [Sp. *rocho* ult. f. Arab *ru<u>k</u>*]

ro•caille /rōkí/ *n*. 1 an 18th-c. style of ornamentation based on rock and shell motifs. 2 a rococo style. [F f. *roc* (as ROCK[1])]

roc•am•bole /rókəmbōl/ *n*. an alliaceous European plant, *Allium scorodoprasum*, with a garliclike bulb used for seasoning. [F f. G *Rockenbolle*]

roche mou•ton•née /ráwsh m⊙⊙tawnáy/ *n*. *Geol*. a small, bare outcrop of rock shaped by glacial erosion. [F, = fleecy rock]

roch•et /róchit/ *n*. a vestment resembling a surplice, used chiefly by bishops and abbots. [ME f. OF, dimin. f. Gmc]

rock[1] /rok/ *n*. 1 **a** the hard material of the earth's crust, exposed on the surface or underlying the soil. **b** a similar material on other planets. 2 *Geol*. any natural material, hard or soft (e.g., clay), consisting of one or more minerals. 3 **a** a mass of rock projecting and forming a hill, cliff, reef, etc. **b** (**the Rock**) Gibraltar. 4 a large detached stone. 5 a stone of any size. 6 a firm and dependable support or protection. 7 esp. *Brit*. a source of danger or destruction. 8 *Brit*. a hard usu. cylindrical stick of candy made from sugar with flavoring, esp. of peppermint. 9 (in *pl*.) *sl*. money. 10 *sl*. a precious stone, esp. a diamond. 11 *sl*. a solid form of cocaine. 12 (in *pl*.) *coarse sl*. the testicles. □ **between a rock and a hard place** forced to choose between two unpleasant or difficult alternatives. **get one's rocks off** *coarse sl*. 1 achieve sexual satisfaction. 2 obtain enjoyment. **on the rocks** *colloq*. 1 short of money. 2 broken down. 3 (of a drink) served over ice cubes. □□ **rock•less** *adj*. **rock•let** *n*. **rock•like** *adj*. [ME f. OF *ro(c)que*, *roche*, med.L *rocca*, of unkn. orig.]

rock[2] /rok/ *v. & n*. • *v*. 1 *tr*. move gently back and forth in or as if in a cradle; set or maintain such motion (*rock him to sleep; the ship was rocked by the waves*). 2 *intr*. be or continue in such motion (*sat rocking in his chair; the ship was rocking on the waves*). 3 **a** *intr*. sway from side to side; shake; oscillate; reel (*the house rocks*). **b** *tr*. cause to do this (*an earthquake rocked the house*). 4 *tr*. distress; perturb. 5 *intr*. dance to or play rock music. • *n*. 1 a rocking movement (*gave the chair a rock*). 2 a spell of rocking (*had a rock in his chair*). 3 **a** = ROCK AND ROLL. **b** any of a variety of types of modern popular music with a rocking or swinging beat, derived from rock and roll. □ **rock the boat** *colloq*. disturb the equilibrium of a situation. [OE *roccian*, prob. f. Gmc]

rock•a•bil•ly /rókəbilee/ *n*. a type of popular music combining elements of rock and roll and hillbilly music. [blend of *rock and roll* and *hillbilly*]

rock and roll *n*. (also **rock 'n' roll**) a type of popular dance music originating in the 1950s, characterized by a heavy beat and simple melodies, often with a blues element. □□ **rock and roll•er** *n*.

rock bed *n*. a base of rock or a rocky bottom.

rock-bot•tom *adj*. (of prices, etc.) the very lowest. □□ **rock bot•tom** *n*.

rock•bound /rókbównd/ *adj*. (of a coast) rocky and inaccessible.

rock can•dy *n*. sugar crystallized in large masses onto a string or stick, eaten as candy.

rock crys•tal *n*. transparent colorless quartz usu. in hexagonal prisms.

rock dove *n*. a wild dove, *Columba livia*, frequenting rocks, supposed ancestor of the domestic pigeon.

rock•er /rókər/ *n*. 1 a person or thing that rocks. 2 a curved bar or similar support, on which something can rock. 3 a rocking chair. 4 **a** a young devotee of rock music, characteristically associated with leather clothing and motorcycles. **b** a performer of rock music. 5 an ice skate with a highly curved blade. 6 a switch constructed on a pivot mechanism operating between the "on" and "off" positions. 7 any rocking device forming part of a mechanism. □ **off one's rocker** *sl*. crazy.

rock•er•y /rókəree/ *n*. (*pl*. **-ies**) a rock garden.

rock•et[1] /rókit/ *n. & v*. • *n*. 1 a cylindrical projectile that can be propelled to a great height or distance by combustion of its contents, used esp. as a firework or signal. 2 an engine using a similar principle but not dependent on air intake for its operation. 3 a rocket-propelled missile, spacecraft, etc. 4 *Brit. sl*. a severe reprimand. • *v*. 1 *tr*. bombard with rockets. 2 *intr*. **a** move rapidly upward or away. **b** increase rapidly (*prices rocketed*). [F *roquette* f. It. *rochetto* dimin. of *rocca* ROCK[2], with ref. to its cylindrical shape]

rock•et[2] /rókit/ *n*. 1 (also **sweet rock•et**) any of various fast-growing plants, esp. of the genus *Hesperis* or *Sisymbrium*. 2 a cruciferous annual plant, *Eruca sativa*, grown for salad. Also called **arugula**. [F *roquette* f. It. *rochetta*, *ruchetta* dimin. of *ruca* f. L *eruca* downy-stemmed plant]

rock•e•teer /rókiteer/ *n*. 1 a discharger of rockets. 2 a rocket expert or enthusiast.

rock•et•ry /rókitree/ *n*. the science or practice of rocket propulsion.

rock face *n*. a vertical surface of natural rock.

rock•fall /rókfawl/ *n*. 1 a descent of loose rocks. 2 a mass of fallen rock.

rock•fish /rókfish/ *n*. 1 any of various fishes that live among rocks. 2 = STRIPED BASS.

rock gar•den *n*. a garden in which interesting stones and rocks are a chief feature.

rock•hop•per /rók-hopər/ *n*. a small penguin, *Eudyptes crestatus*, of the Antarctic and New Zealand, with a crest of feathers on the forehead.

rock·ing chair *n.* a chair mounted on rockers or springs for gently rocking in.

rock·ing horse *n.* a model of a horse on rockers or springs for a child to rock on.

rock·ing stone *n.* a poised boulder easily rocked.

rock·ling /rókling/ *n.* any of various small marine fish of the cod family, esp. of the genus *Ciliata* and *Rhinomenus,* found in pools among rocks.

rocking horse

rock pi·geon = ROCK DOVE.

rock plant *n.* any plant growing on or among rocks.

rock rab·bit *n.* any of several species of hyrax; pika.

rock·rose /rókrōz/ *n.* any plant of the genus *Cistus, Helianthum,* etc., with roselike flowers.

rock salt *n.* common salt as a solid mineral.

rock·shaft /rókshaft/ *n.* a shaft that oscillates about an axis without making complete revolutions.

rock wool *n.* inorganic material made into matted fiber, esp. for insulation or soundproofing.

rock·y[1] /rókee/ *adj. & n.* • *adj.* **1** of or like rock. **2** full of or abounding in rock or rocks (*a rocky shore*). **3 a** firm as a rock; determined; steadfast. **b** unfeeling; cold; hard. • *n.* (**the Rockies**) the Rocky Mountains in western N. America. □□ **rock·i·ness** *n.*

rock·y[2] /rókee/ *adj.* (**rock·i·er, rock·i·est**) *colloq.* unsteady; tottering. □□ **rock·i·ly** *adv.* **rock·i·ness** *n.* [ROCK[2]]

ro·co·co /rəkókō/ *adj. & n.* • *adj.* **1** of a late baroque style of decoration prevalent in 18th-c. continental Europe, with asymmetrical patterns involving scrollwork, shell motifs, etc. **2** (of literature, music, architecture, and the decorative arts) highly ornamented; florid. • *n.* the rococo style. [F, joc. alt. f. ROCAILLE]

rod /rod/ *n.* **1** a slender straight bar, esp. of wood or metal. **2** this as a symbol of office. **3 a** a stick or bundle of twigs used in caning or flogging. **b** (prec. by *the*) the use of this; punishment; chastisement. **4 a** = FISHING ROD. **b** an angler using a rod. **5 a** a slender straight round stick growing as a shoot on a tree. **b** this when cut. **6** (as a measure) a perch or square perch (see PERCH[1]). **7** *sl.* = HOT ROD. **8** *sl.* a pistol or revolver. **9** *Anat.* any of numerous rod-shaped structures in the eye, detecting dim light. □□ **rod·less** *adj.* **rod·let** *n.* **rod·like** *adj.* [OE *rodd,* prob. rel. to ON *rudda* club]

rode[1] *past of* RIDE.

rode[2] /rōd/ *v.intr.* **1** (of wildfowl) fly landward in the evening. **2** (of woodcock) fly in the evening during the breeding season. [18th c.: orig. unkn.]

ro·dent /rōd'nt/ *n. & adj.* • *n.* any mammal of the order Rodentia with strong incisors and no canine teeth, e.g., rat, mouse, squirrel, beaver, porcupine. • *adj.* **1** of the order Rodentia. **2** gnawing (esp. *Med.* of slow-growing ulcers). □□ **ro·den·tial** /-dénshəl/ *adj.* [L *rodere ros-* gnaw]

ro·den·ti·cide /rədéntisīd/ *n.* a poison used to kill rodents.

ro·de·o /ródiō, rōdáyō/ *n.* (*pl.* **·os**) **1** an exhibition or entertainment involving cowboys' skills in handling animals. **2** an exhibition of other skills, e.g., in motorcycling. **3 a** a roundup of cattle on a ranch for branding, etc. **b** an enclosure for this. [Sp. f. *rodear* go round ult. f. L *rotare* ROTATE[1]]

rod·o·mon·tade /ródəmontáyd, -táad, ródə-/ *n., adj., & v.* • *n.* **1** boastful or bragging talk or behavior. **2** an instance of this. • *adj.* boastful or bragging. • *v.intr.* brag; talk boastfully. [F f. obs. It. *rodomontada* f. F *rodomont* & It. *rodomonte* f. the name of a boastful character in the *Orlando* epics]

roe[1] /rō/ *n.* **1** (also **hard roe**) the mass of eggs in a female fish's ovary. **2** (also **soft roe**) the milt of a male fish. □□ **roed** *adj.* (also in *comb.*). [ME *row(e), rough,* f. MLG, MDu. *roge(n),* OHG *rogo, rogan,* ON *hrogn*]

roe[2] /rō/ *n.* (*pl.* same or **roes**) (also **roe deer**) a small European and Asian deer, *Capreolus capreolus.* [OE *rā(ha)*]

roe·buck /rōbuk/ *n.* (*pl.* same or **roe·bucks**) a male roe deer.

roent·gen /réntgən, -jən, rúnt-/ *n.* a unit of ionizing radiation, the amount producing one electrostatic unit of positive or negative ionic charge in one cubic centimeter of air under standard conditions. [W. C. *Röntgen,* Ger. physicist d. 1923, discoverer of X rays]

roent·gen·og·ra·phy /réntgənógrəfee, -jə-, rúnt-/ *n.* photography using X rays.

roent·gen·ol·o·gy /réntgənóləjee, -jə-, rúnt-/ *n.* = RADIOLOGY.

roent·gen rays *n.pl.* X rays.

ro·ga·tion /rōgáyshən/ *n.* (usu. in *pl.*) *Eccl.* a solemn supplication, esp. for the harvest, consisting of the litany of the saints chanted on the three days before Ascension Day. □□ **ro·ga·tion·al** *adj.* [ME f. L *rogatio* f. *rogare* ask]

Ro·ga·tion Days *n.pl.* the three days before Ascension Day.

Ro·ga·tion Sun·day *n.* the Sunday preceding the Rogation Days.

rog·er /rójər/ *int. & v.* • *int.* **1** your message has been received and understood (used in radio communication, etc.). **2** *sl.* I agree. • *v. Brit. coarse sl.* **1** *intr.* have sexual intercourse. **2** *tr.* have sexual intercourse with (a woman). [the name *Roger,* code for *R*]

rogue /rōg/ *n. & v.* • *n.* **1** a dishonest or unprincipled person. **2** *joc.* a mischievous person, esp. a child. **3** (usu. *attrib.*) **a** a wild animal driven away or living apart from the herd and of fierce temper (*rogue elephant*). **b** a stray, irresponsible, or undisciplined person or thing (*rogue trader*). **4** an inferior or defective specimen among many acceptable ones. • *v.tr.* remove rogues (sense 4 of *n.*) from. [16th-c. cant word: orig. unkn.]

ro·guer·y /rógəree/ *n.* (*pl.* **·ies**) conduct or an action characteristic of rogues.

rogues' gal·ler·y *n.* a collection of photographs of known criminals, etc., used for identification of suspects.

ro·guish /rógish/ *adj.* **1** playfully mischievous. **2** characteristic of rogues. □□ **ro·guish·ly** *adv.* **ro·guish·ness** *n.*

roil /royl/ *v.tr.* **1** make (a liquid) turbid by agitating it. **2** = RILE 1. [perh. f. OF *ruiler* mix mortar f. LL *regulare* regulate]

roist·er /róystər/ *v.intr.* (esp. as **roistering** *adj.*) revel noisily; be uproarious. □□ **roist·er·er** *n.* **roist·er·ing** *n.* **roist·er·ous** *adj.* [obs. *roister* roisterer f. F *rustre* ruffian var. of *ruste* f. L *rusticus* RUSTIC]

role /rōl/ *n.* (also **rôle**) **1** an actor's part in a play, motion picture, etc. **2** a person's or thing's characteristic or expected function (*the role of the tape recorder in language learning*). [F *rôle* and obs. F *roule, rolle,* = ROLL *n.*]

role mod·el *n.* a person looked to by others as an example in a particular role.

role-play·ing *n.* an exercise in which participants act the part of another character, used in psychotherapy, language teaching, etc.

roll /rōl/ *v. & n.* • *v.* **1** *intr.* move or go in some direction by turning over and over on an axis or by a rotary movement (*the ball rolled under the table; a barrel started rolling*). **b** *tr.* cause to do this (*rolled the barrel into the cellar*). **2** *tr.* make revolve between two surfaces (*rolled the clay between his palms*). **3 a** *intr.* (foll. by *along, by,* etc.) move or advance on or (of time, etc.) as if on wheels, etc. (*the bus rolled past; the years rolled by*). **b** *tr.* cause to do this (*rolled the dessert cart to our table*). **c** *intr.* (of a person) be conveyed in a vehicle (*the farmer rolled by on his tractor*). **4 a** *tr.* turn over and over on itself to form a more or less cylindrical or spherical shape (*rolled a newspaper*). **b** *tr.* make by forming material into a cylinder or ball (*rolled a cigarette; rolled a huge snowball*). **c** *tr.* accumulate into a mass (*rolled the dough into a ball*). **d** *intr.* (foll. by *into*) make a specified shape of itself (*the caterpillar rolled into a ball*). **5** *tr.* flatten or form by passing a roller, etc., over or by passing between rollers (*roll the lawn; roll pastry*) **6** *intr. & tr.* change or cause to change direction by rotatory movement (*his eyes rolled; he rolled his eyes*). **7** *intr.* **a** wallow; turn about in a fluid or a loose medium (*the dog rolled in the dust*). **b** (of a horse, etc.) lie on its back and kick about, esp. in an attempt to dislodge its rider. **8** *intr.* **a** (of a moving ship, aircraft, or vehicle) sway to and fro on an axis parallel to the direction of motion. **b** walk with an unsteady swaying gait (*they rolled out of the bar*). **9 a** *intr.* undulate; show or go with an undulating surface or motion (*rolling hills; rolling mist; the waves roll in*). **b** *tr.* carry or propel with such motion (*the river rolls its waters to the sea*). **10 a** *intr.* (of machinery) start functioning or moving (*the cameras rolled; the train began to roll*). **b** *tr.* cause (machinery) to do this. **11** *intr. & tr.* sound or utter with a vibratory or trilling effect (*words rolled off his tongue; thunder rolled in the distance; he rolls his r*s). **12** *sl.* **a** *tr.* overturn (a car, etc.). **b** *intr.* (of a car, etc.) overturn. **13** *tr.* throw (dice). **14** *tr. sl.* rob (esp. a helpless victim). • *n.* **1** a rolling motion or gait; rotation; spin; undulation (*the roll of the hills*). **2 a** a spell of rolling (*a roll in the mud*). **b** a gymnastic exercise in which the body is rolled into a tucked position and turned in a forward or backward circle. **c** (esp. **a roll in the hay**) *colloq.* an act of sexual intercourse or erotic fondling. **3** the continuous rhythmic sound of thunder or a drum. **4** *Aeron.* a complete revolution of an aircraft about its longitudinal axis. **5 a** a cylinder formed by turning flexible material over and over on itself without folding (*a roll of carpet; a roll of wallpaper*). **b** esp. *Brit.* a filled cake or pastry of similar form (*fig roll; sausage roll*). **6 a** a small portion of bread individually baked. **b** this with a specified filling (*ham roll*). **7** a more or less cylindrical or semicylindrical straight or curved mass of something (*rolls of fat; a roll of hair*). **8 a** an official list or register (*the electoral roll*). **b** the total numbers on this (*the schools' rolls have fallen*). **c** a document, esp. an official record, in scroll form. **9** a cylinder or roller, esp. to shape metal in a rolling mill. **10** *Archit.* **a** a molding of convex section. **b** a spiral scroll of an Ionic capital. **11** *colloq.* money, esp. as bills rolled together. □ **be rolling in** *colloq.* have plenty of (esp. money). **on a roll** *sl.* experiencing a bout of success or progress; engaged in a period of intense activity. **roll back** cause (esp. prices) to decrease.

rolled into one combined in one person or thing. **roll in 1** arrive in great numbers or quantity. **2** wallow; luxuriate in. **rolling drunk** swaying or staggering from drunkenness. **roll on** v. tr. **1** put on or apply by rolling. **2** (in *imper.*) *Brit. colloq.* (of a time, in eager expectation) come quickly (*roll on Friday!*). **roll out** unroll; spread out. **roll over 1** esp. *Brit.* send a (person) sprawling or rolling. **2 a** *Econ.* finance the repayment of (maturing stock, etc.) by an issue of new stock. **b** reinvest funds in a similar financial instrument (*we decided to roll over the CDs*). **roll up 1** *colloq.* arrive in a vehicle; appear on the scene. **2** make into or form a roll. **3** *Mil.* drive the flank of (an enemy line) back and around so that the line is shortened or surrounded. **roll with the punches** withstand adversity, difficulties, etc. **roll up one's sleeves** see SLEEVE. □□ **roll·a·ble** adj. [ME f. OF rol(l)er, rouler, ro(u)lle f. L rotulus dimin. of rota wheel]

roll·a·way /rólǝway/ adj. (of a bed, etc.) that can be removed on wheels or casters.

roll bar n. an overhead metal bar strengthening the frame of a vehicle (esp. in racing) and protecting the occupants if the vehicle overturns.

roll call n. a process of calling out a list of names to establish who is present.

rolled gold n. gold in the form of a thin coating applied to a baser metal by rolling.

rolled oats n. oats that have been husked and crushed.

roll·er /rólǝr/ n. **1 a** a hard revolving cylinder for smoothing the ground, spreading ink or paint, crushing or stamping, rolling up cloth on, etc., used alone or as a rotating part of a machine. **b** a cylinder for diminishing friction when moving a heavy object. **2** a small cylinder on which hair is rolled for setting. **3** a long, swelling wave. **4** (also **roll·er band·age**) a long surgical bandage rolled up for convenient application. **5** a kind of tumbler pigeon. **6 a** any brilliantly plumaged bird of the family Coraciidae, with characteristic tumbling display-flight. **b** a breed of canary with a trilling song.

roll·er bear·ing n. a bearing like a ball bearing but with small cylinders instead of balls.

Roll·er·blade /rólǝrblayd/ n. & v. • n. *Trademark* an in-line skate. v. intr. skate using Rollerblades.

roll·er coast·er n. an amusement ride consisting of an elevated track with open-car trains that rise and plunge steeply.

roll·er-coast·er adj. & v. • adj. that goes up and down, or changes, suddenly and repeatedly. • v. intr. (or **roll·er-coast**) go up and down or change in this way.

roller bearing

roll·er skate see SKATE[1].

roll·er tow·el n. a towel with the ends joined, hung on a roller.

rol·lick /rólik/ v. & n. • v. intr. (esp. as **rollicking** adj.) be jovial or exuberant; indulge in high spirits; revel. • n. **1** exuberant gaiety. **2** a spree or escapade. [19th-c., prob. dial.: perh. f. ROMP + FROLIC]

roll·ing mill n. a machine or factory for rolling metal into shape.

roll·ing pin n. a cylinder for rolling out pastry, dough, etc.

roll·ing stock n. **1** the locomotives, cars, or other vehicles, used on a railroad. **2** the road vehicles of a company.

roll·ing stone n. a person who is unwilling to settle for long in one place.

roll neck *Brit.* = TURTLENECK.

roll-on attrib. & n. • (attrib.) (of deodorant, etc.) applied by means of a rotating ball in the neck of the container. • n. *Brit.* a light elastic corset.

roll-on roll-off adj. (of a ship, a method of transport, etc.) in which vehicles are driven directly on at the start of the voyage and off at the end of it.

roll·o·ver /rólōvǝr/ n. **1** *Econ.* the extension or transfer of a debt or other financial relationship. **2** *colloq.* the overturning of a vehicle, etc.

roll-top desk n. a desk with a flexible cover sliding in curved grooves.

roll-your-own n. a hand-rolled cigarette.

ro·ly-po·ly /róleepólee/ n. & adj. • n. (pl. ·lies) *Brit.* (also **ro·ly-po·ly pud·ding**) a sweet pastry dough covered with jam, etc., formed into a roll, and boiled, steamed, or baked. • adj. (usu. of a child) pudgy; plump. [prob. formed on ROLL]

ROM /rom/ n. *Computing* a memory not capable of being changed by program instruction. [read-only memory]

Rom /rōm/ n. (pl. **Ro·ma** /rómǝ/) a male gypsy. [Romany, = man, husband]

Rom. abbr. Romans (New Testament).

rom. abbr. roman (type).

Ro·ma·ic /rōmáyik/ n. & adj. • n. the vernacular language of modern Greece. • adj. of or relating to this language. [Gk *Rhōmaikos* Roman (used esp. of the Eastern Empire)]

ro·maine /rōmáyn/ n. a cos lettuce. [F, fem. of *romain* (as ROMAN)]

ro·ma·ji /rómǝjee/ n. a system of romanized spelling used to transliterate Japanese. [Jap.]

Ro·man /rómǝn/ adj. & n. • adj. **1 a** of ancient Rome or its territory or people. **b** *archaic* of its language. **2** of medieval or modern Rome. **3** of papal Rome, esp. = ROMAN CATHOLIC. **4** of a kind ascribed to the early Romans (*Roman virtue*). **5** surviving from a period of Roman rule (*Roman road*). **6** (**roman**) (of type) of a plain upright kind used in ordinary print. **7** (of the alphabet, etc.) based on the ancient Roman system with letters A–Z. • n. **1 a** a citizen of the ancient Roman Republic or Empire. **b** a soldier of the Roman Empire. **2** a citizen of modern Rome. **3** = ROMAN CATHOLIC. **4** (**roman**) roman type. **5** (in *pl.*) the Christians of ancient Rome. [ME f. OF *Romain* (n. & adj.) f. L *Romanus* f. *Roma* Rome]

Ro·man à clef /rómáanaakláy/ n. (pl. **ro·mans à clef** pronunc. same) a novel in which real persons or events appear with invented names. [F, = novel with a key]

Ro·man can·dle n. a firework discharging a series of flaming colored balls and sparks.

Ro·man Cath·o·lic /rómǝn/ adj. & n. • adj. of the part of the Christian Church acknowledging the pope as its head. • n. a member of this Church. □□ **Ro·man Ca·thol·i·cism** n. [17th-c. transl. L (*Ecclesia*) *Romana Catholica* (*et Apostolica*), app. orig. as a conciliatory term: see ROMAN, CATHOLIC]

ro·mance /rōmáns/ n., adj., & v. • n. (also *disp.* /rómans/) **1** an atmosphere or tendency characterized by a sense of remoteness from or idealization of everyday life. **2 a** a prevailing sense of wonder or mystery surrounding the mutual attraction in a love affair. **b** sentimental or idealized love. **c** a love affair. **3 a** a literary genre with romantic love or highly imaginative unrealistic episodes forming the central theme. **b** a work of this genre. **4** a medieval tale, usu. in verse, of some hero of chivalry, of the kind common in the Romance languages. **5** a exaggeration or picturesque falsehood. **b** an instance of this. **6** (**Romance**) the languages descended from Latin regarded collectively. **7** *Mus.* a short informal piece. • adj. (**Romance**) of any of the languages descended from Latin (French, Italian, Spanish, etc.). • v. **1** intr. exaggerate or distort the truth, esp. fantastically. **2** tr. court; woo; court the favor of, esp. by flattery. [ME f. OF *romanz*, –*ans*, –*ance*, ult. f. L *Romanicus* ROMANIC]

ro·manc·er /rōmánsǝr/ n. **1** a writer of romances, esp. in the medieval period. **2** a liar who resorts to fantasy.

Ro·man Em·pire n. *hist.* that established by Augustus in 27 BC and divided by Theodosius in AD 395 into the Western or Latin and Eastern or Greek Empire.

Ro·man·esque /rómǝnésk/ n. & adj. • n. a style of architecture prevalent in Europe c. 900–1200, with massive vaulting and round arches (cf. NORMAN). • adj. of the Romanesque style of architecture. [F f. *roman* ROMANCE]

ro·man-fleuve /rómoNflóv/ n. (pl. **ro·mans-fleuves** pronunc. same) **1** a novel featuring the leisurely description of the lives of members of a family, etc. **2** a sequence of self-contained novels. [F, = river novel]

Ro·man hol·i·day n. enjoyment derived from others' discomfiture.

Ro·ma·ni·an /rōmáyneeǝn/ n. & adj. (also **Ru·ma·ni·an** /rōō–/) • n. **1 a** a native or national of Romania in E. Europe. **b** a person of Romanian descent. **2** the language of Romania. • adj. of or relating to Romania or its people or language.

Ro·man·ic /rōmánik/ n. & adj. • n. = ROMANCE n. 6. • adj. **1 a** of or relating to Romance. **b** Romance-speaking. **2** descended from the ancient Romans or inheriting aspects of their social or political life. [L *Romanicus* (as ROMAN)]

Ro·man·ism /rómǝnizǝm/ n. often *offens.* Roman Catholicism.

Ro·man·ist /rómǝnist/ n. **1** a student of Roman history or law or of the Romance languages. **2 a** a supporter of Roman Catholicism. **b** a Roman Catholic. [mod.L *Romanista* (as ROMAN)]

ro·man·ize /rómǝnīz/ v. tr. **1** make Roman or Roman Catholic in character. **2** put into the Roman alphabet or into roman type. □□ **ro·man·i·za·tion** n.

Ro·man law n. the law-code developed by the ancient Romans and forming the basis of many modern codes.

Ro·man nose n. one with a high bridge; an aquiline nose.

Ro·man nu·mer·al n. any of the Roman letters representing numbers: I = 1, V = 5, X = 10, L = 50, C = 100, D = 500, M = 1000.

Ro·man·o /rōmáanō/ n. a strong-tasting hard cheese, orig. made in Italy. [It.,= Roman]

Romano- /rōmáanō/ comb. form Roman; Roman and (*Romano-British*).

Ro·mansh /rōmánsh, –máansh/ n. & adj. (also **Ru·mansh** /rōō–/) • n. the Rhaeto-Romanic dialects, esp. as spoken in the Swiss canton of Grisons. • adj. of these dialects. [Romansh *Ruman(t)sch, Roman(t)sch* f. med.L *romanice* (adv.) (as ROMANCE)]

ro·man·tic /rōmántik/ adj. & n. • adj. **1** of, characterized by, or suggestive of an idealized, sentimental, or fantastic view of reality; remote from experience (*a romantic picture; a romantic setting*). **2** inclined toward or suggestive of romance in love (*a romantic woman; a romantic evening; romantic words*). **3** (of a person) imaginative; visionary; idealistic. **4 a** (of style in art, music, etc.) concerned more with feeling and emotion than with form and aesthetic qualities; preferring grandeur or picturesqueness to finish and proportion. **b** (also **Romantic**) of or relating to the 18th–19th-century romantic movement or style in the European arts. **5** (of a project, etc.) unpractical; fantastic. ● *n* **1** a romantic person. **2** a romanticist. □□ **ro·man·ti·cal·ly** *adv.* [*romant* tale of chivalry, etc., f. OF f. *romanz* ROMANCE]

ro·man·ti·cism /rōmántisizəm/ *n.* (also **Romanticism**) adherence to a romantic style in art, music, etc.

ro·man·ti·cist /rōmántisist/ *n.* (also **Romanticist**) a writer or artist of the romantic school.

ro·man·ti·cize /rōmántisīz/ *v.* **1** *tr.* **a** make or render romantic or unreal (*a romanticized account of war*). **b** describe or portray in a romantic fashion. **2** *intr.* indulge in romantic thoughts or actions □□ **ro·man·ti·ci·za·tion** *n.*

Rom·a·ny /rómənee, ró–/ *n. & adj.* ● *n.* (*pl.* **·nies**) **1** a Gypsy. **2** the Indo-European language of the Gypsies. ● *adj.* **1** of or concerning Gypsies. **2** of the Romany language. [Romany *Romani* fem. and pl. of *Romano* (adj.) (ROM)]

Ro·me·o /rómeeō/ *n.* (*pl.* **·os**) a passionate male lover or seducer. [the hero of Shakesp. *Romeo and Juliet*]

Rom·ish /rómish/ *adj.* usu. *derog.* Roman Catholic.

rom·ney·a /rómneeə/ *n.* any shrub of the genus *Romneya*, bearing poppylike flowers. [T. *Romney* Robinson, Brit. astronomer d. 1882]

romp /romp/ *v. & n.* ● *v.intr.* **1** play about roughly and energetically. **2** (foll. by *along*, *past*, etc.) *colloq.* proceed without effort. ● *n.* a spell of romping or boisterous play. □ **romp in** (or **home**) *Brit. colloq.* finish as the easy winner. □□ **romp·ing·ly** *adv.* **romp·y** *adj.* (**romp·i·er, romp·i·est**). [perh. var. of RAMP[1]]

romp·er /rómpər/ *n.* (usu. in *pl.*) (also esp. *Brit.* **romp·er suit**) a one-piece garment, esp. for a child, that covers the trunk and has short pants.

ronde /rond/ *n.* **1** a dance in which the dancers move in a circle. **2** a course of talk, activity, etc. [F, fem. of *rond* ROUND *adj.*]

ron·deau /róndō, róndō/ *n.* (*pl.* **ron·deaux** *pronunc.* same or /–dōz/) a poem of ten or thirteen lines with only two rhymes throughout and with the opening words used twice as a refrain. [F, earlier *rondel*: see RONDEL]

ron·del /rónd'l, rondél/ *n.* a rondeau, esp. one of special form. [ME f. OF f. *rond* ROUND: cf. ROUNDEL]

ron·do /róndō/ *n.* (*pl.* **·dos**) *Mus.* a form with a recurring leading theme, often found in the final movement of a sonata or concerto, etc. [It. f. F *rondeau*: see RONDEAU]

ro·nin /rónin/ *n. hist.* (in feudal Japan) a lordless wandering samurai; an outlaw. [Jap.]

rönt·gen /réntgən/, etc., var. of ROENTGEN, etc.

roo /roō/ *n.* (also **'roo**) *Austral. colloq.* a kangaroo. [abbr.]

rood /roōd/ *n.* **1** a crucifix, esp. one raised on a screen or beam at the entrance to the chancel. **2** a quarter of an acre. [OE *rōd*]

rood loft *n.* a gallery on top of a rood screen.

rood screen *n.* a wooden or stone carved screen separating nave and chancel.

roof /roōf/ *n. & v.* ● *n.* (*pl.* **roofs** or *disp.* **rooves** /roōvz, roōvz/) **1 a** the upper covering of a building, usu. supported by its walls. **b** the top of a covered vehicle. **c** the top inner surface of an oven, refrigerator, etc. **2** the overhead rock in a cave or mine, etc. **3** the branches or the sky, etc., overhead. **4** (of prices, etc.) the upper limit or ceiling. ● *v.tr.* **1** (often foll. by *in, over*) cover with or as with a roof. **2** be the roof of. □ **go through the roof** *colloq.* (of prices, etc.)

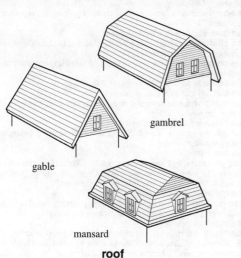

gambrel

gable

mansard

roof

reach extreme or unexpected heights. **hit** (or **go through** or **raise**) **the roof** *colloq.* become very angry. **raise the roof 1** create a noisy racket. **2** protest noisily. **a roof over one's head** somewhere to live. **under one roof** in the same building. **under a person's roof** in a person's house (esp. with ref. to hospitality). □□ **roofed** *adj.* (also in *comb.*). **roof·less** *adj.* [OE *hrōf*]

roof·age /roōfij, roōf–/ *n.* esp. *Brit.* the expanse of a roof or roofs.

roof·er /roōfər, roōf–/ *n.* a person who constructs or repairs roofs.

roof gar·den *n.* **1** a garden on the flat roof of a building. **2** a roof-top restaurant.

roof·ing /roōfing, roōf–/ *n.* **1** material for constructing a roof. **2** the process of constructing a roof or roofs.

roof of the mouth *n.* the palate.

roof rack *n.* a framework for carrying luggage, etc. on the roof of a vehicle.

roof·scape /roōfskayp, roōf–/ *n.* esp. *Brit.* a scene or view of roofs.

roof·top /roōftop, roōf–/ *n.* **1** the outer surface of a roof. **2** (esp. in *pl.*) the level of a roof.

roof·tree /roōftree, roōf–/ *n.* a roof's ridgepole.

roo·i·nek /róynek, roō-ee–/ *n. S.Afr. sl. offens.* a British or English-speaking South African. [Afrik., = red-neck]

rook[1] /roōk/ *n. & v.* ● *n.* **1** a black European and Asiatic bird, *Corvus frugilegus*, of the crow family, nesting in colonies in treetops. **2** a sharper, esp. at dice or cards; a person who lives off inexperienced gamblers, etc. ● *v.tr.* **1** charge (a customer) extortionately. **2** win money from (a person) at cards, etc., esp. by swindling. [OE *hrōc*]

rook[2] /roōk/ *n.* a chess piece with its top in the shape of a battlement; castle. [ME f. OF *roc*(*k*) ult. f. Arab. *rukk*, orig. sense uncert.]

rook·er·y /roōkəree/ *n.* (*pl.* **·ies**) **1 a** a colony of rooks. **b** a clump of trees having rooks' nests. **2** a colony of seabirds (esp. penguins) or seals.

rook·ie /roōkee/ *n. sl.* **1** a new recruit, esp. in the army or police. **2** member of a sports team in his or her first season. [corrupt. of *recruit*, after ROOK[1]]

room /roōm, roōm/ *n. & v.* ● *n.* **1 a** space that is or might be occupied by something; capaciousness or ability to accommodate contents (*it takes up too much room; there is plenty of room; we have no room here for idlers*). **b** space in or on (*schoolroom*). **2 a** a part of a building enclosed by walls or partitions, floor, and ceiling. **b** (in *pl.*) a set of these occupied by a person or family; apartments, etc. **c** persons present in a room (*the room fell silent*). **3** (in *comb.*) a room or area for a specified purpose (*reading room*). **4** (foll. by *for*, or *to* + infin.) opportunity or scope (*room to improve things; no room for dispute*). ● *v.intr.* have a room or rooms; lodge; board. □ **make room** (often foll. by *for*) clear a space (for a person or thing) by removal of others; make way; yield place. **not** (or **no**) **room to swing a cat** a very confined space. □□ **–roomed** *adj.* (in *comb.*). **room·ful** *n.* (*pl.* **·fuls**). [OE *rūm* f. Gmc]

room·er /roōmər, roōm–/ *n.* a renter of a room in another's house.

room·ette /roōmét, roōm–/ *n.* **1** a private single compartment in a railroad sleeping car. **2** a small bedroom, etc., for rent.

room·ie /roōmee, roōm–/ *n. colloq.* a roommate.

room·ing house *n.* a house with rented rooms for lodging.

room·mate /roōm-mayt, roōm–/ *n.* a person occupying the same room, apartment, etc., as another.

room serv·ice *n.* (in a hotel, etc.) service of food or drink taken to a guest's room.

room·y /roōmee, roō–/ *adj.* (**room·i·er, room·i·est**) having much room; spacious. □□ **room·i·ly** *adv.* **room·i·ness** *n.*

roost /roōst/ *n. & v.* ● *n.* **1** a branch or other support on which a bird perches, esp. a place where birds regularly settle to sleep. **2** a place offering temporary sleeping accommodation. ● *v.* **1** *intr.* **a** (of a bird) settle for rest or sleep. **b** (of a person) stay for the night. **2** *tr.* provide with a sleeping place. □ **come home to roost** (of a scheme, etc.) recoil unfavorably upon the originator. **rule the roost** hold a position of control; be in charge (esp. of others). [OE *hrōst*]

roost·er /roōstər/ *n.* esp. a male domestic fowl; cock.

rooster

root[1] /roōt, roōt/ *n. & v.* ● *n.* **1 a** the part of a plant normally below the ground, attaching it to the earth and conveying nourishment to it from the soil. **b** (in *pl.*) such a part divided into branches or fibers. **c** the corresponding organ of an epiphyte; the part attaching ivy to its support. **d** the permanent underground stock of a plant. **e** any small plant with a root for transplanting. **2 a** any plant, e.g., a turnip or carrot, with an edible root. **b** such a root. **3** (in *pl.*) the sources of or reasons for one's long-standing emotional attachment to a place, community, etc. **4 a** the embedded part of a bodily organ or structure, e.g., hair, tooth, nail, etc. **b** the part of a thing attaching it to a greater or more fundamental whole. **c** (in *pl.*) the base of a mountain, etc. **5 a** the basic cause, source, or origin (*love of money is the root of all evil; has its roots in the distant past*). **b** (*attrib.*) (of an idea, etc.) from which the rest originated. **6** the basis of something, its means of continuance or growth (*has its root(s) in selfishness; has no root in the nature of things*). **7** the essential substance or nature of something (*get to the root of things*). **8** *Math.* **a** a number or quantity that when multiplied by itself a usu. specified number of times gives a specified number or quantity (*the cube root of eight is two*). **b** a square root. **c** a value of an unknown quantity satisfying a given equation. **9** *Philol.* any ultimate unanalyzable element of language; a basis, not necessarily surviving as a word in itself, on which words are made by the addition of prefixes or suffixes or by other modification. **10** *Mus.* the fundamental note of a chord. **11** *Bibl.* a scion, an offshoot (*there shall be a root of Jesse*). • *v.* **1 a** *intr.* take root or grow roots. **b** *tr.* cause to do this (*take care to root them firmly*). **2** *tr.* **a** fix firmly; establish (*fear rooted him to the spot*). **b** (as **rooted** *adj.*) firmly established (*her affection was deeply rooted; rooted objection to*). **3** *tr.* (usu. foll. by *out, up*) drag or dig up by the roots. □ **pull up by the roots 1** uproot. **2** eradicate; destroy. **put down roots 1** begin to draw nourishment from the soil. **2** become settled or established. **root and branch** thorough(ly), radical(ly). **root out** find and get rid of. **strike at the root** (or **roots**) of set about destroying. **take root 1** begin to grow and draw nourishment from the soil. **2** become fixed or established. □□ **root·age** *n.* **root·ed·ness** *n.* **root·less** *adj.* **root·let** *n.* **root·like** *adj.* **root·y** *adj.* [OE *rōt* f. ON *rót*, rel. to WORT & L *radix*: see RADIX]

root² /rōot, rŏŏt/ *v.* **1 a** *intr.* (of an animal, esp. a pig) turn up the ground with the snout, beak, etc., in search of food. **b** *tr.* (foll. by *up*) turn up (the ground) by rooting. **2 a** *intr.* (foll. by *around, in*, etc.) rummage. **b** *tr.* (foll. by *out* or *up*) find or extract by rummaging. **3** *intr.* (foll. by *for*) *sl.* encourage by applause or support. □□ **root·er** *n.* (in sense 3). [earlier *wroot* f. OE *wrōtan* & ON *róta*: rel. to OE *wrōt* snout]

root beer *n.* a carbonated drink made from an extract of roots of certain plants.

root ca·nal *n.* *Dentistry* surgery to remove the diseased nerve of a tooth.

root-mean-square *n.* *Math.* the square root of the arithmetic mean of the squares of a set of values.

root sign *Math.* = RADICAL SIGN.

root·stock /rōotstok, rŏŏt-/ *n.* **1** a rhizome. **2** a plant into which a graft is inserted. **3** a primary form from which offshoots have arisen.

rooves see ROOF.

rope /rōp/ *n. & v.* • *n.* **1 a** stout cord made by twisting together strands of hemp, sisal, flax, cotton, nylon, wire, or similar material. **b** a piece of this. **c** a lasso. **2** (foll. by *of*) a quantity of onions, garlic bulbs, pearls, etc., strung together. **3** (in *pl.*, prec. by *the*) **a** the conditions in some sphere of action (*know the ropes; show a person the ropes*). **b** the ropes enclosing a boxing or wrestling ring, etc. **4** (prec. by *the*) **a** a noose or halter for hanging a person. **b** execution by hanging. • *v.* **1** *tr.* fasten, secure, or catch with rope. **2** *tr.* (usu. foll. by *off, in*) enclose (a space) with rope. **3** *Mountaineering* **a** *tr.* connect (a party) with a rope; attach (a person) to a rope. **b** (*absol.*) put on a rope. **c** *intr.* (foll. by *down, up*) climb down or up using a rope. □ **give a person plenty of rope** (or **enough rope to hang himself** or **herself**) give a person enough freedom of action to bring about his or her own downfall. **on the rope** *Mountaineering* roped together. **on the ropes 1** *Boxing* forced against the ropes by the opponent's attack. **2** near defeat. **rope in** persuade to take part. **rope into** persuade to take part in (*was roped into doing the laundry*). [OE *rāp* f. Gmc]

rope lad·der *n.* two long ropes connected by short crosspieces, used as a ladder.

rope·man·ship /rōpmənship/ *n.* skill in ropewalking or climbing with ropes.

rope mold·ing *n.* a molding cut spirally in imitation of rope strands.

rope of sand *n.* esp. *Brit.* delusive security.

rope's end *n.* *hist.* a short piece of rope used to flog (formerly, esp. a sailor) with.

rope·walk /rōpwawk/ *n.* a long stretch of ground or building where ropes are made.

rope·walk·er /rōpwawkər/ *n.* a performer on a tightrope. □ **rope·walking** the action of performing on a tightrope.

rope·way /rōpway/ *n.* a cable railroad; tramway.

rope yarn 1 material obtained by unpicking rope strands, or used for making them. **2** a piece of this. **3** *Brit.* a mere trifle.

rop·ing /rōping/ *n.* a set or arrangement of ropes.

rop·y /rōpee/ *adj.* (also **rop·ey**) (**rop·i·er**, **rop·i·est**) **1** (of wine, bread, etc.) forming viscous or stringy threads. **2** like a rope. **3** *Brit. colloq.* **a** poor in quality. **b** unwell. □□ **rop·i·ly** *adv.* **rop·i·ness** *n.*

roque /rōk/ *n.* croquet played on a hard court surrounded by a bank. [alt. form of ROQUET]

Roque·fort /rōkfərt/ *n.* *Trademark* **1** a soft blue cheese made from sheep's milk. **2** a salad dressing made of this. [*Roquefort* in S. France]

ro·quet /rōkáy/ *v. & n.* *Croquet* • *v.* (**ro·queted, ro·quet·ing**) **1** *tr.* **a** cause one's ball to strike (another ball). **b** (of a ball) strike (another). **2** *intr.* strike another ball thus. • *n.* an instance of roqueting. [app. arbitr. f. CROQUET *v.*, orig. used in the same sense]

ror·qual /ráwrkwəl/ *n.* any of various whales of the family Balaenopteridae, esp. *Balaenoptera musculus*, having a dorsal fin. Also called **finback** or **fin whale**. [F f. Norw. *røyrkval* f. OIcel. *reythr* the specific name + *hvalr* WHALE¹]

Ror·schach test /ráwrshaak/ *n.* *Psychol.* a type of personality test in which a standard set of inkblot designs is presented one by one to the subject, who is asked to describe what they suggest or resemble. [H. *Rorschach*, Swiss psychiatrist d. 1922]

rort /rawrt/ *n.* *Austral.* *sl.* **1** a trick; a fraud; a dishonest practice. **2** a wild party. [back-form. f. RORTY]

ror·ty /ráwrtee/ *adj.* (**ror·ti·er, ror·ti·est**) *Brit. sl.* **1** splendid; boisterous; rowdy (*had a rorty time*). **2** coarse; earthy. [19th c.: orig. unkn.]

ro·sace /rózays/ *n.* **1** esp. *Brit.* a rose window. **2** a rose-shaped ornament or design; rosette. [F f L *rosaceus*: see ROSACEOUS]

ro·sa·ceous /rōzáyshəs/ *adj.* *Bot.* of the large plant family Rosaceae, which includes the rose. [L *rosaceus* f. *rosa* rose]

ros·an·i·line /rōzánilin, -lin/ *n.* **1 a** an organic base derived from aniline. **b** a red dye obtained from this. **2** fuchsin. [ROSE¹ + ANILINE]

ro·sar·i·an /rəzáireeən/ *n.* a person who cultivates roses, esp. professionally. [L *rosarium* ROSARY]

ro·sar·i·um /rəzáireeəm/ *n.* a rose garden. [L (as ROSARY)]

ro·sa·ry /rózəree/ *n.* (*pl.* **-ries**) **1** *RC Ch.* **a** a form of devotion in which prayers are said while counting them on a special string of beads. **b** a string of 55 (or 165) beads for keeping count in this. **c** a book containing this devotion. **2** a similar string of beads used in other religions. **3** a rose garden or rose bed. [ME f. L *rosarium* rose garden, neut. of *rosarius* (as ROSE¹)]

ros·coe /róskō/ *n.* *sl.* a gun, esp. a pistol or revolver. [the name *Roscoe*]

rose¹ /rōz/ *n., adj., & v.* • *n.* **1** any prickly bush or shrub of the genus *Rosa*, bearing usu. fragrant flowers generally of a red, pink, yellow, or white color. **2** this flower. **3** any flowering plant resembling this (*rose of Sharon; rockrose*). **4** a light crimson color; pink. **b** (usu. in *pl.*) a rosy complexion (*roses in her cheeks*). **5 a** a representation of the flower in heraldry or decoration (esp. as the national emblem of England). **b** a rose-shaped design, e.g., on a compass card, etc. **6** the sprinkling nozzle of a watering can or hose. **7** an ornamental through which the shaft of a doorknob passes. **8 a** a rose diamond. **b** a rose window. **9** (in *pl.*) used in various phrases to express favorable circumstances, ease, success, etc. (*roses all the way; everything's roses*). **10** an excellent person or thing, esp. a beautiful woman (*English rose; rose between two thorns*). • *adj.* = ROSE-COLORED 1. • *v.tr.* (esp. as **rosed** *adj.*) make (one's face, cheeks, etc.) rosy. □ **see** (or **look**) **through rose-colored** (or **-tinted**) **glasses** regard (circumstances, etc.) with unfounded favor or optimism. **under the rose** = SUB ROSA. □□ **rose·less** *adj.* **rose·like** *adj.* [ME f. OE *rōse* f. L *rosa*]

rose² past of RISE.

ro·sé /rōzáy/ *n.* any light pink wine, colored by only brief contact with red grape skins. [F, = pink]

rose ap·ple *n.* **1** a tropical tree of the genus *Syzygium*, cultivated for its foliage and fragrant fruit. **2** this fruit.

ro·se·ate /rózeeət, -ayt/ *adj.* **1** = ROSE-COLORED. **2** having a partly pink plumage (*roseate spoonbill; roseate tern*). [L *roseus* rosy (as ROSE¹)]

rose·bay /rózbay/ *n.* an oleander, rhododendron, or, esp. *Brit.*, willow herb.

rose·bud /rózbud/ *n.* a bud of a rose.

rose chaf·er *n.* a destructive beetle, *Macrodactylus subspinosis*, frequenting roses, fruit trees, etc.

rose-colored *adj.* **1** of a rose color. **2** optimistic; sanguine; cheerful (*takes rose-colored views*).

rose comb *n.* a flat fleshy comb of a fowl.

rose-cut *adj.* cut as a rose diamond.

rose dia·mond *n.* a hemispherical diamond with the curved part cut in triangular facets.

rose·fish /rózfish/ *n.* = REDFISH 1.

rose ge·ra·ni·um *n.* a pink-flowered, sweet-scented pelargonium, *Pelargonium graveolus*.

rose hip = HIP².

ro·sel·la /rəzélə/ *n.* **1** any brightly colored Australian parakeet of the genus *Platycercus*. **2** *Austral.* an easily shorn sheep. [corrupt. of *Rosehill*, NSW, where the bird was first found]

rose mad·der *n.* a pale pink pigment.

ro·se·ma·ling /rózəmaaling/ *n.* the art of painting wooden furniture, etc., with flower motifs. [Norw., = rose painting]

rose mal·low = HIBISCUS.

rose·mar·y /rózmairee, -məree/ *n.* an evergreen fragrant shrub, *Rosmarinus officinalis*, with leaves used as a culinary herb, in perfumery, etc., and taken as an emblem of remembrance. [ME, earlier *rosmarine* ult. f. L *ros marinus* f. *ros* dew + *marinus* MARINE, with assim. to ROSE[1] and *Mary* name of the Virgin]

rose of Jer•i•cho *n.* a resurrection plant, *Anastatica hierochuntica.*

rose of Shar•on *n.* **1 a** a species of hypericum, *Hypericum calycinum,* with dense foliage and golden-yellow flowers. Also called **Aaron's beard. b** a shrub, *Hibiscus syriacus,* of the mallow family, with rose, lavender, or white flowers. **2** *Bibl.* a flowering plant of unknown identity.

ro•se•o•la /rōzeeólǝ, rōzéeǝlǝ/ *n.* **1** a rosy rash in measles and similar diseases. **2** a mild febrile disease of infants. □□ **ro•se•o•lar** *adj.* **ro•se•o•lous** *adj.* [mod. var. of RUBEOLA f. L *roseus* rose-colored]

rose-pink *adj.* pink like a rose; rose-colored.

rose-red *adj. & n.* • *adj.* red like a rose, rose-colored. • *n.* this color.

ros•er•y /rózǝree/ *n. (pl.* **-ies)** *Brit.* a rose garden.

rose-tint•ed = ROSE-COLORED.

Ro•set•ta stone /rōzétǝ/ *n.* a key to previously unattainable understanding. [a stone found near *Rosetta* in Egypt, with a trilingual inscription of the 2nd c. BC in Egyptian hieroglyphs, demotic, and Greek, important in the decipherment of hieroglyphs]

ro•sette /rōzét/ *n.* **1** a rose-shaped ornament made usu. of ribbon and worn esp. as the badge of a contest official, etc., or as an award or the symbol of an award in a competition. **2** *Archit.* **a** a carved or molded ornament resembling or representing a rose. **b** a rose window. **3** an object or symbol or arrangement of parts resembling a rose. **4** *Biol.* **a** a roselike cluster of parts. **b** markings resembling a rose. **5** esp. *Brit.* a rose diamond. □□ **ro•set•ted** *adj.* [F dimin. of *rose* ROSE[1]]

rose wa•ter *n.* perfume made from roses.

rose win•dow *n.* a circular window, usu. with roselike or spokelike tracery.

rose•wood /rózwŏŏd/ *n.* any of several fragrant close-grained woods used in making furniture.

Rosh Ha•sha•nah /ráwsh hǝsháwnǝ, –shaá–, haashaanaá, rósh/ *n.* (also **Rosh Ha•sha•na**) the Jewish New Year. [Heb., = beginning (lit. "head") of the year]

Ro•shi /róshee/ *n. (pl.* **Ro•shis**) the spiritual leader of a community of Zen Buddhist monks. [Jap.]

Ro•si•cru•cian /rōzikrŏŏshǝn, rózi–/ *n. & adj.* • *n.* **1** *hist.* a member of a 17th–18th-c. society devoted to the study of metaphysical and mystical lore (said to have been founded in 1484 by Christian Rosenkreuz). **2** a member of any of several later organizations deriving from this. • *adj.* of or relating to the Rosicrucians. □□ **Ro•si•cru•cian•ism** *n.* [mod.L *rosa crucis* (or *crux*), as Latinization of G *Rosenkreuz*]

ros•in /rózin/ *n. & v.* • *n.* resin, esp. the solid residue after distillation of oil of turpentine from crude turpentine. • *v.tr.* (**ros•ined, ros•in•ing**) **1** rub (esp. the bow of a violin, etc.) with rosin. **2** smear or seal up with rosin. □□ **ros•in•y** *adj.* [ME, alt. f. RESIN]

ro•so•li•o /rǝzólyō/ *n.* (also **ro•so•gli•o**) *(pl.* **-os**) a sweet cordial of liquor, sugar, and flavoring, esp. rose petals and cloves. [It., f. mod.L *ros solis* dew of the sun]

ros•ter /róstǝr/ *n. & v.* • *n.* **1** a list or plan showing turns of duty or leave for individuals or groups esp. of a military force. **2** *Sports* a list of players. • *v.tr.* place on a roster. [Du. *rooster* list, orig. gridiron f. *roosten* ROAST, with ref. to its parallel lines]

ros•tra *pl.* of ROSTRUM.

ros•tral /róstrǝl/ *adj.* **1** *Zool. & Bot.* of or on the rostrum. **2** *Anat.* **a** nearer the hypophysial area in the early embryo. **b** nearer the region of the nose and mouth in postembryonic life. **3** (of a column, etc.) adorned with the rams of ancient warships or with representations of these. □□ **ros•tral•ly** *adv.*

ros•trat•ed /róstraytid/ *adj.* **1** *Zool. & Bot.* having or ending in a rostrum. **2** = ROSTRAL 3. [L *rostratus* (as ROSTRUM)]

ros•trum /róstrǝm/ *n. (pl.* **ros•tra** /–strǝ/ or **ros•trums**) **1 a** a platform for public speaking. **b** a conductor's platform facing the orchestra. **c** a similar platform for other purposes, e.g., for supporting a movie or television camera. **2** *Zool. & Bot.* a beak, stiff snout, or beaklike part, esp. of an insect or arachnid. **3** *Rom.Antiq.* the beaklike projection of a warship. □□ (all in sense 2) **ros•trate** /–trayt/ *adj.* **ros•tri•form** *adj.*

WORD HISTORY | **rostrum**

Mid-16th century: from Latin, literally 'beak' (from *rodere* 'gnaw,' the source of *rodent*). The word was originally used (at first in the plural *rostra*) to denote a place in the Forum in ancient Rome that was decorated with the beaks or prows of captured warships and was used as a platform for public speakers.

---

ros•y /rózee/ *adj.* (**ros•i•er, ros•i•est**) **1** colored like a pink or red rose (esp. of the complexion as indicating good health, of a blush, wine, the sky, light, etc.). **2** optimistic; hopeful; cheerful (*a rosy future; a rosy attitude to life*). □□ **ros•i•ly** *adv.* **ros•i•ness** *n.*

rot /rot/ *v.,n., & intr. v.* • *v.* (**rot•ted, rot•ting**) **1** *intr.* **a** (of animal or vegetable matter) lose its original form by the chemical action of bacteria, fungi, etc.; decay. **b** (foll. by *off, away*) crumble or drop from a stem, etc., through decomposition. **2** *intr.* **a** (of society, institu-

---

tions, etc.) gradually perish from lack of activity, participation, or use. **b** (of a prisoner, etc.) waste away (*left me to rot in prison*); (of a person) languish. **3** *tr.* cause to rot; make rotten. **4** *tr. Brit. sl.* tease; abuse; denigrate. **5** *intr. Brit. sl.* joke. • *n.* **1** the process or state of rotting. **2** *sl.* nonsense; an absurd or foolish statement, argument, or proposal. **3** *Brit.* a sudden series of (usu. unaccountable) failures; a rapid decline in standards, etc. (*a rot set in; we must try to stop the rot*). **4** (often prec. by *the*) a virulent liver disease of sheep. • *int.* expressing incredulity or ridicule. [OE *rotian* (v.): (n.) ME, perh. f. Scand.: cf. Icel., Norw. *rot*]

ro•ta /rótǝ/ *n.* **1** esp. *Brit.* a list of persons acting, or duties to be done, in rotation; a roster. **2** (**Rota**) *RC Ch.* the supreme ecclesiastical and secular court. [L, = wheel]

Ro•tar•i•an /rōtáireeǝn/ *n. & adj.* • *n.* a member of a Rotary club. • *adj.* of Rotarians or Rotary club. [ROTARY + –AN]

ro•ta•ry /rótǝree/ *adj. & n.* • *adj.* acting by rotation (*rotary drill; rotary pump*). • *n. (pl.* **-ries) 1** a rotary machine. **2** a traffic circle. **3** (**Rotary**) (in full **Rotary International**) a worldwide charitable society of business people, orig. named from members entertaining in rotation. [med.L *rotarius* (as ROTA)]

Ro•ta•ry Club *n.* a local branch of Rotary.

ro•ta•ry wing *adj.* (of an aircraft) deriving lift from rotary airfoils.

ro•tate[1] /rótayt/ *v.* **1** *intr. & tr.* move around an axis or center, revolve. **2 a** *tr.* take or arrange in rotation. **b** *intr.* act or take place in rotation (*the chairmanship will rotate*). □□ **ro•tat•a•ble** *adj.* **ro•ta•tive** /rótǝtiv/ *adj.* **ro•ta•to•ry** /rótǝtawree/ *adj.* [L *rotare* f. *rota* wheel]

ro•tate[2] /rótayt/ *adj. Bot.* wheel-shaped. [formed as ROTA]

ro•ta•tion /rōtáyshǝn/ *n.* **1** the act or an instance of rotating or being rotated. **2** a recurrence; a recurrent series or period; a regular succession of various members of a group in office, etc. **3** a system of growing different crops in regular order to avoid exhausting the soil. □□ **ro•ta•tion•al** *adj.* **ro•ta•tion•al•ly** *adv.* [L *rotatio*]

ro•ta•tor /rótaytǝr/ *n.* **1** a machine or device for causing something to rotate. **2** *Anat.* a muscle that rotates a limb, etc. **3** a revolving apparatus or part. [L (as ROTATE[1])]

ROTC /rótsee/ *abbr.* Reserve Officers Training Corps.

rote /rōt/ *n.* (usu. prec. by *by*) mechanical or habitual repetition (with ref. to acquiring knowledge). [ME: orig. unkn.]

ro•te•none /rót'nōn/ *n.* a toxic crystalline substance obtained from the roots of derris and other plants, used as an insecticide. [Jap. *rotenon* f. *roten* derris]

rot•gut /rótgut/ *n.* inferior whiskey.

Roth IRA *n.* an individual retirement account allowing savings of after-tax earnings without additional tax on the interest earned.

ro•ti•fer /rótifǝr/ *n.* any minute aquatic animal of the phylum Rotifera, with rotatory organs used in swimming and feeding. [mod.L *rotiferus* f. L *rota* wheel + *–fer* bearing]

ro•tis•ser•ie /rōtisǝree/ *n.* **1** a cooking appliance with a rotating spit for roasting and barbecuing meat. **2** esp. *Brit.* a restaurant, etc., where meat is roasted or barbecued. [F *rôtisserie* (as ROAST)]

ro•to•gra•vure /rótǝgrǝvyŏŏr/ *n.* **1** a printing system using a rotary press with intaglio cylinders, usu. running at high speed. **2** a sheet, etc., printed with this system. [G *Rotogravur* (name of a company) assim. to PHOTOGRAVURE]

ro•tor /rótǝr/ *n.* **1** a rotary part of a machine, esp. in the distributor of an internal-combustion engine. **2** a set of radiating airfoils around a hub on a helicopter, providing lift when rotated. [irreg. for ROTATOR]

ro•to•till•er /rótǝtilǝr/ *n.* a machine with a rotating blade for breaking up or tilling the soil. □□ **ro•to•till** *v.tr.* [*Trademark,* ROTARY + TILL[3]]

rot•ten /rót'n/ *adj.* (**rot•ten•er, rot•ten•est**) **1** rotting or rotted; falling to pieces or liable to break or tear from age or use. **2 a** morally, socially, or politically corrupt. **b** despicable; contemptible. **3** *sl.* **a** disagreeable; unpleasant (*had a rotten time*). **b** (of a plan, etc.) illadvised, unsatisfactory (*a rotten idea*). **c** disagreeably ill (*feel rotten today*). □□ **rot•ten•ly** *adv.* **rot•ten•ness** *n.* [ME f. ON *rottinn,* rel. to ROT, RET]

rot•ten bor•ough *n. hist.* (before 1832) an English borough able to elect a member of Parliament though having very few voters.

rot•ten•stone /rot'nstōn/ *n.* decomposed siliceous limestone used as a powder for polishing metals.

rot•ter /rótǝr/ *n.* esp. *Brit. sl.* an objectionable, unpleasant, or reprehensible person. [ROT]

Rott•wei•ler /rótwīlǝr/ *n.* **1** a dog of a tall black-and-tan breed. **2** this breed. [G f. *Rottweil* in SW Germany]

ro•tund /rōtúnd/ *adj.* **1** a circular; round. **b** (of a person) large and plump, pudgy. **2** (of speech, literary style, etc.) sonorous, grandiloquent. □□ **ro•tun•di•ty** *n.* **ro•tund•ly** *adv.* [L *rotundus* f. *rotare* ROTATE[1]]

ro•tun•da /rōtúndǝ/ *n.* **1** a building with a circular ground plan, esp. one with a dome. **2** a circular hall or room. [earlier *rotonda* f. It.

See page xx for the **Key to Pronunciation.**

rotonda (*camera*) round (chamber), fem. of *rotondo* round (as RO-TUND)]

rou·ble var. of RUBLE.

rou·é /rŏō-áy/ *n.* a debauchee, esp. an elderly one; a rake. [F, past part. of *rouer* break on wheel, = one deserving this]

rouge /rŏōzh/ *n. & v.* •*n.* **1** a red powder or cream used for coloring the cheeks. **2** powdered ferric oxide, etc., as a polishing agent, esp. for metal. •*v.* **1** *tr.* color with rouge. **2** *intr.* **a** apply rouge to one's cheeks. **b** become red; blush. [F, = red, f. L *rubeus*, rel. to RED]

rouge et noir /rŏōzhaynwaár/ *n.* a gambling game using a table with red and black marks, on which players place stakes.

rough /ruf/ *adj., adv., n., & v.* •*adj.* **1 a** having an uneven or irregular surface, not smooth or level or polished. **b** *Tennis* applied to the side of a racket from which the twisted gut projects. **2** (of ground, country, etc.) having many bumps, obstacles, etc. **3 a** hairy; shaggy. **b** (of cloth) coarse in texture. **4 a** (of a person or behavior) not mild nor quiet nor gentle; boisterous; unrestrained (*rough manners*; *rough play*). **b** (of language, etc.) coarse; indelicate. **c** (of wine, etc.) sharp or harsh in taste. **d** (of a sound, the voice, etc.) harsh; discordant; gruff; hoarse. **5** (of the sea, weather, etc.) violent; stormy. **6** disorderly; riotous (*a rough part of town*). **7** harsh; insensitive; inconsiderate (*rough words*; *rough treatment*). **8 a** unpleasant; severe; demanding (*had a rough time*). **b** esp. *Brit.* unfortunate; unreasonable; undeserved (*had rough luck*). **c** (foll. by *on*) hard or unfair toward. **9** lacking finish, elaboration, comfort, etc. (*rough accommodations*; *a rough welcome*). **10** incomplete; rudimentary (*a rough attempt*). **11 a** inexact; approximate; preliminary (*a rough estimate*; *a rough sketch*). **b** (of stationery, etc.) esp. *Brit.* for use in writing rough notes, etc. **12** esp. *Brit. colloq.* **a** ill; unwell (*am feeling rough*). **b** depressed; dejected. •*adv.* in a rough manner (*the land should be plowed rough*; *play rough*). •*n.* **1** (usu. prec. by *the*) a hard part or aspect of life; hardship (*take the rough with the smooth*). **2** rough ground (*over rough and smooth*). **3** esp. *Brit.* a rough or violent person (*met a bunch of roughs*). **4** *Golf* rough ground off the fairway between tee and green. **5** an unfinished or provisional or natural state (*have written it in rough*; *shaped from the rough*); a rough draft or sketch. **6** esp. *Brit.* (prec. by *the*) the general way or tendency (*is true in the rough*). •*v.tr.* **1** (foll. by *up*) ruffle (feathers, hair, etc.) by rubbing against the grain. **2 a** (foll. by *out*) shape or plan roughly. **b** (foll. by *in*) sketch roughly. **3** give the first shaping to (a gun, lens, etc.). □ **the rough edge** (or **side**) **of one's tongue** severe or harsh words. **rough it** do without basic comforts. **rough up** *sl.* treat (a person) with violence; attack violently. **sleep rough** *Brit.* sleep outdoors, or not in a proper bed. □□ **rough·ness** *n.* [OE *rūh* f. WG]

rough·age /rúfij/ *n.* **1** coarse material with a high fiber content, the part of food that stimulates digestion. **2** coarse fodder. [ROUGH + ‑AGE 3]

rough-and-read·y *n.* rough or crude but effective; not elaborate or over-particular.

rough-and-tum·ble *adj. & n.* •*adj.* irregular; scrambling; disorderly. •*n.* a haphazard fight; a scuffle.

rough breath·ing see BREATHING.

rough·cast /rúfkast/ *n., adj., & v.* •*n.* plaster of lime and gravel, used on outside walls. •*adj.* **1** (of a wall, etc.) coated with roughcast. **2** (of a plan, etc.) roughly formed; preliminary. •*v.tr.* (*past* and *past part.* ·**cast**) **1** coat (a wall) with roughcast. **2** prepare (a plan, essay, etc.) in outline.

rough coat *n.* a first coat of plaster applied to a surface.

rough cop·y *n.* **1** esp. *Brit.* = ROUGH DRAFT. **2** a copy of a picture, etc. showing only the essential features.

rough deal *n.* hard or unfair treatment.

rough dia·mond *n.* **1** an uncut diamond. **2** (also **diamond in the rough**) a person of good nature but rough manners.

rough draft *n.* a first or original draft (of a story, report, document, etc.).

rough-dry *v.tr.* (·**dries**, ·**dried**) (of clothes) dry without ironing.

rough·en /rúfən/ *v.tr. & intr.* make or become rough.

rough-han·dle *v.tr.* treat or handle roughly.

rough-hew *v.tr.* (*past part.* ·**hewed** or ·**hewn**) shape out roughly; give crude form to.

rough-hewn *adj.* uncouth; unrefined.

rough·house /rúfhows/ *n. & v. sl.* •*n.* a disturbance or row; boisterous play. •*v.* **1** *tr.* handle (a person) roughly. **2** *intr.* make a disturbance; act violently.

rough·ish /rúfish/ *adj.* somewhat rough.

rough jus·tice *n. Brit.* **1** treatment that is approximately fair. **2** treatment that is not at all fair.

rough·ly /rúflee/ *adv.* **1** in a rough manner. **2** approximately (*roughly 20 people attended*). □ **roughly speaking** in an approximate sense (*it is, roughly speaking, a square*).

rough·neck /rúfnek/ *n. colloq.* **1** a rough or rowdy person. **2** a worker on a drill rig.

rough pas·sage *n.* **1** a crossing over rough sea. **2** a difficult time or experience.

rough ride *n.* a difficult time or experience.

rough·rid·er /rúfrídər/ *n.* **1** a person who breaks in or can ride unbroken horses. **2** (**Rough Rider**) a member of the cavalry unit in which Theodore Roosevelt fought during the Spanish-American War.

rough·shod /rúfshod/ *adj.* (of a horse) having shoes with nail heads projecting to prevent slipping. □ **ride roughshod over** treat inconsiderately or arrogantly.

rough stuff *n. colloq.* boisterous or violent behavior.

rough tongue *n. Brit.* a habit of rudeness in speaking.

rough trade *n. sl.* a tough or sadistic element among male homosexuals.

rough work *n.* esp. *Brit.* **1** preliminary or provisional work. **2** *colloq.* violence. **3** a task requiring the use of force.

rou·lade /rŏōlaád/ *n.* **1** a dish cooked or served in the shape of a roll, esp. a rolled piece of meat with a filling. **2** *Mus.* a florid passage of runs in classical music for a solo virtuoso, esp. one sung to one syllable. [F f. *rouler* to roll]

rou·leau /rŏōló/ *n.* (*pl.* **rou·leaux** or **rou·leaus** /‑lóz/) **1** a cylindrical packet of coins. **2** a coil or roll of ribbon, etc., esp. as trimming. [F f. *rôle* ROLL *n.*]

rou·lette /rŏōlét/ *n.* **1** a gambling game using a table in which a ball is dropped on to a revolving wheel with numbered compartments, players betting on the number at which the ball comes to rest. **2** *Math.* a curve generated by a point on a curve rolling on another. **3 a** a revolving toothed wheel used in engraving. **b** a similar wheel for making perforations between postage stamps in a sheet. □□ **rou·let·ted** *adj.* (in sense 3b). [F, dimin. of *rouelle* f. LL *rotella* dimin. of L *rota* wheel]

round /rownd/ *adj., n., adv., prep., & v.* •*adj.* **1** shaped like or approximately like a circle, sphere, or cylinder; having a convex or circular outline or surface; curved; not angular. **2** done with or involving circular motion. **3 a** entire; continuous; complete (*a round dozen*); fully expressed or developed; all together; not broken or defective or scanty. **b** (of a sum of money) considerable. **4** genuine; candid; outspoken; (of a statement, etc.) categorical; unmistakable. **5** (usu. *attrib.*) (of a number) expressed for convenience or as an estimate in fewer significant numerals or with a fraction removed (*spent $297.32, or in round figures $300*). **6 a** (of a style) flowing. **b** (of a voice) not harsh. **7** *Phonet.* (of a vowel) pronounced with rounded lips. •*n.* **1** a round object or form. **2 a** a revolving motion; a circular or recurring course (*the earth in its yearly round*). **b** a regular recurring series of activities or functions (*one's daily round*; *a continuous round of pleasure*). **c** a recurring succession or series of meetings for discussion, etc. (*a new round of talks on disarmament*). **3 a** esp. *Brit.* a fixed route on which things are regularly delivered (*milk round*). **b** a route or sequence by which people or things are regularly supervised or inspected (*a watchman's round*; *a doctor's rounds*). **4** an allowance of something distributed or measured out, esp.: **a** a single provision of drinks, etc., to each member of a group. **b** ammunition to fire one shot; the act of firing this. **5 a** esp. *Brit.* a slice across a loaf of bread. **b** esp. *Brit.* a sandwich made from whole slices of bread. **c** a thick disk of beef cut from the haunch as a joint. **6** each of a set or series, a sequence of actions by each member of a group in turn, esp. **a** one spell of play in a game, etc. **b** one stage in a competition. **7** *Golf* the playing of all the holes in a course once. **8** *Archery* a fixed number of arrows shot from a fixed distance. **9** (**the round**) a form of sculpture in which the figure stands clear of any ground (cf. RELIEF 6a). **10** *Mus.* a canon for three or more unaccompanied voices singing at the same pitch or in octaves. **11** (in *pl.*) *Brit. Mil.* **a** a watch that goes around inspecting sentries. **b** a circuit made by this. **12** a rung of a ladder. **13** (foll. by *of*) the circumference, bounds, or extent of (*in all the round of Nature*). •*adv.* = AROUND *adv.* 5–12. •*prep.* = AROUND *prep.* 5–12. •*v.* **1 a** *tr.* give a round shape to. **b** *intr.* assume a round shape. **2** *tr.* double or pass around (a corner, cape, etc.). **3** *tr.* express (a number) in a less exact but more convenient form (also foll. by *down* when the number is decreased and *up* when it is increased). **4** *tr.* pronounce (a vowel) with rounded lips. □ **in the round 1** with all features shown; all things considered. **2** *Theatr.* with the audience around at least three sides of the stage. **3** (of sculpture) with all sides shown; not in relief. **make the round of** go around. **make one's rounds** take a customary route for inspection, etc. **make the rounds** (of news, etc.) be passed on from person to person, etc. **round about 1** in a ring (about); all around; on all sides (of). **2** with a change to an opposite position. **3** approximately (*cost round about $50*). **round and round** several times around. **round down** see sense 3 of *v.* **round off** (or **out**) **1** bring to a complete or symmetrical or well-ordered state. **2** smooth out; blunt the corners or angles of. **round out** = *round off* 1. **round peg in a square hole** = *square peg in a round hole* (see PEG). **round up** collect or bring together, esp. by going around (see also sense 3 of *v.*). □□ **round•ish** *adj.* **round•ness** *n.* [ME f. OF *ro(u)nd-* stem of *ro(o)nt*, *reont* f. L *rotundus* ROTUND)]

round•a•bout /równd∂bowt/ *n. & adj.* • *n.* **1** *Brit.* = TRAFFIC CIRCLE. **2** *Brit.* = MERRY-GO-ROUND 1. • *adj.* circuitous; circumlocutory; indirect.

round brack•ets *Brit.* = *parentheses* (see PARENTHESIS).

round dance *n.* **1** a dance in which couples move in circles around the ballroom. **2** a dance in which the dancers form one large circle.

roun•del /równd'l/ *n.* **1** a small disk, esp. a decorative medallion. **2** *Brit.* a circular identifying mark painted on military aircraft, e.g., the red, white, and blue of the RAF. **3** a poem, esp. a modified rondeau, of eleven lines in three stanzas. [ME f. OF *rondel(le)* (as ROUND)]

roun•de•lay /równdilay/ *n.* a short simple song with a refrain. [F *rondelet* (as RONDEL), with assim. to LAY³ or *virelay*]

round•er /równdər/ *n. Brit.* **1** (in *pl.*; treated as *sing.*) a baseball-like game with a bat and ball in which players after hitting the ball run through a round of bases. **2** a complete run of a player through all the bases as a unit of scoring in rounders.

Round•head /równdhed/ *n. hist.* a member of the Parliamentary party in the English Civil War. [f. their custom of wearing the hair cut short]

round•house /równdhows/ *n.* **1** a circular repair shed for railroad locomotives, built around a turntable. **2** *sl.* **a** a blow given with a wide sweep of the arm. **b** *Baseball* (also *attrib.*) a pitch made with a sweeping sidearm motion (*his best pitch was a big roundhouse curve*). **3** *hist.* a prison; a place of detention. **4** *Naut.* a cabin or set of cabins on the after part of the quarterdeck, esp. on a sailing ship.

round•ly /równdlee/ *adv.* **1** bluntly; in plain language; severely (*was roundly criticized*; *told them roundly that he refused*). **2** in a thoroughgoing manner (*go roundly to work*). **3** in a circular way (*swells out roundly*).

round rob•in *n.* **1** a petition, esp. with signatures written in a circle to conceal the order of writing. **2** a tournament in which each competitor plays in turn against every other.

round-shoul•dered *adj.* with shoulders bent forward so that the back is rounded.

rounds•man /równdzmən/ *n.* (*pl.* **-men**) **1** *Brit.* a person on a regular route delivering and taking orders for milk, bread, etc. **2** a police officer in charge of a patrol. **3** *Austral.* a journalist covering a specified subject (*political roundsman*).

Round Ta•ble *n.* (in allusion to that at which King Arthur and his knights sat so that none should have precedence) **1** an international charitable association that holds discussions, debates, etc., and undertakes community service. **2** (**round table**) an assembly for discussion, esp. at a conference (often *attrib.*: *round-table talks*).

round trip *n.* a trip to one or more places and back again (esp. by a circular route).

round•up /równdup/ *n.* **1** a systematic rounding up of people or things. **2** a summary; a résumé of facts or events.

round•worm /równdwərm/ *n.* a nematode worm, esp. a parasitic one found in the intestines of mammals.

roup¹ /rowp/ *n. & v. Sc. & No. of Engl.* • *n.* an auction. • *v.tr.* sell by auction. [ME 'to shout,' f. Scand. orig.]

roup² /roop/ *n.* an infectious poultry disease, esp. of the respiratory tract. □□ **roup•y** *adj.* [16th c.: orig. unkn.]

rouse /rowz/ *v.* **1 a** *tr.* (often foll. by *from*, *out of*) bring out of sleep; wake. **b** *intr.* (often foll. by *up*) cease to sleep; wake up. **2** (often foll. by *up*) **a** *tr.* stir up; make active or excited; startle out of inactivity or confidence or carelessness (*roused them from their complacency*; *was roused to protest*). **b** *intr. & refl.* become active. **3** *tr.* provoke to anger (*is terrible when roused*). **4** *tr.* evoke (feelings). **5** *tr.* (usu. foll. by *in*, *out*, *up*) *Naut.* haul vigorously. **6** *tr.* startle (game) from a lair or cover. **7** *tr.* stir (liquid, esp. beer while brewing). □□ **rous•a•ble** *adj.* **rous•er** *n.* [orig. as a hawking and hunting term, so prob. f. AF: orig. unkn.]

rous•ing /rówzing/ *adj.* **1** exciting; stirring (*a rousing cheer*; *a rousing song*). **2** (of a fire) blazing strongly. □□ **rous•ing•ly** *adv.*

roust /rowst/ *v.tr.* **1** (often foll. by *up*, *out*) **a** rouse; stir up. **b** root out.

2 *sl.* jostle; harass; rough up. □ **roust around** esp. *Brit.* rummage. [perh. alt. of ROUSE]

roust•a•bout /rówstəbowt/ *n.* **1** a laborer on an oil rig. **2** an unskilled or casual laborer. **3** a dock laborer or deckhand. **4** a circus laborer.

rout¹ /rowt/ *n. & v.* • *n.* **1 a** a disorderly retreat of defeated troops. **b** a heavy defeat. **2 a** an assemblage or company, esp. of revelers or rioters. **b** *Law* an assemblage of three or more persons who have made a move toward committing an illegal act. **3** riot; tumult; disturbance; clamor; fuss. **4** *Brit. archaic* a large evening party or reception. • *v.tr.* put to rout. □ **put to rout** put to flight; defeat utterly. [ME f. AF *rute*, OF *route* ult. f. L *ruptus* broken]

rout² /rowt/ *v.* **1** *intr. & tr.* = ROOT². **2** *tr.* cut a groove, or any pattern not extending to the edges, in (a wooden or metal surface). □ **rout out** force or fetch out of bed or from a house or a hiding place. [var. of ROOT²]

route /root, rowt/ *n. & v.* • *n.* **1** a way or course taken (esp. regularly) in getting from a starting point to a destination. **2** a round traveled in delivering, selling, or collecting goods. **3** *Mil. archaic* marching orders. • *v.tr.* send or forward or direct to be sent by a particular route. [ME f. OF *r(o)ute* road ult. f. L *ruptus* broken]

route•man /rówtmən/ *n.* a delivery person working on an assigned route.

route march *n.* a training march for troops.

rout•er /rówtər/ *n.* any of various tools used in routing, including a two-handled plane used in carpentry, a power machine for routing, etc.

rou•tine /rooteen/ *n., adj., & v.* • *n.* **1** a regular course or procedure, an unvarying performance of certain acts. **2** a set sequence in a performance, esp. a dance, comedy act, etc. **3** *Computing* a sequence of instructions for performing a task. • *adj.* **1** performed as part of a routine; unvarying; mechanical (*routine duties*; *a routine job shelling peas*). **2** of a customary or standard kind. • *v.tr.* organize according to a routine. □□ **rou•tine•ly** *adv.* [F (as ROUTE)]

rou•tin•ism /rooteenizəm/ *n.* the prevalence of routine. □□ **rou•tin•ist** *n. & adj.*

rou•tin•ize /rooteeniz, rootniz/ *v.tr.* subject to a routine; make into a matter of routine. □□ **rou•tin•i•za•tion** *n.*

roux /roo/ *n.* (*pl.* same) a cooked mixture of fat (esp. butter) and flour used in making sauces, etc. [F, = browned (butter): see RUSSET]

rove¹ /rōv/ *v. & n.* • *v.* **1** *intr.* wander without a settled destination; roam; ramble. **2** *intr.* (of eyes) look in changing directions. **3** *tr.* wander over or through. • *n.* an act of roving (*on the rove*). [ME, orig. a term in archery = shoot at a casual mark with the range not determined, perh. f. dial. *rave* stray, prob. of Scand. orig.]

rove² *past* of REEVE².

rove³ /rōv/ *n. & v.* • *n.* a sliver of cotton, wool, etc., drawn out and slightly twisted. • *v.tr.* form into roves. [18th c.: orig. unkn.]

rove⁴ /rōv/ *n.* a small metal plate or ring for a rivet to pass through and be clenched over, esp. in boat building. [ON *ró*, with excrescent *v*]

rove bee•tle *n.* any long-bodied beetle of the family Staphylinidae, usu. found in decaying animal and vegetable matter.

rov•er¹ /rōvər/ *n.* **1** a roving person; a wanderer. **2** *Croquet* **a** a ball that has passed through all the wickets but has not yet struck the last peg. **b** a player whose ball is a rover. **3** *Archery* **a** a mark chosen at undetermined range. **b** a mark for long-distance shooting.

rov•er² /rōvər/ *n.* a sea robber, a pirate. [ME f. MLG, MDu. *rōver* f. *rōven* rob, rel. to REAVE]

rov•er³ /rōvər/ *n.* a person or machine that makes roves of fiber.

rov•ing com•mis•sion *n.* authority given to a person or persons conducting an inquiry to travel as may be necessary.

rov•ing eye *n.* a tendency to ogle or toward infidelity.

row¹ /rō/ *n.* **1** a number of persons or things in a more or less straight line. **2** a line of seats across a theater, etc. (*in the front row*). **3** a street with a continuous line of houses along one or each side. **4** a line of plants in a field or garden. **5** a horizontal line of entries in a table, etc. □ **a hard** (or **tough**) **row to hoe** a difficult task. **in a row 1** forming a row. **2** *colloq.* in succession (*two Sundays in a row*). [ME *raw*, *row*, f. OE f. Gmc]

row² /rō/ *v. & n.* • *v.* **1** *tr.* propel (a boat) with oars. **2** *tr.* convey (a passenger) in a boat in this way. **3** *intr.* propel a boat in this way. **4** *tr.* make (a stroke) or achieve (a rate of striking) in rowing. **5** *tr.* compete in (a race) by rowing. **6** *tr.* row a race with. • *n.* **1** a spell of rowing. **2** an excursion in a rowboat. □ **row down** esp. *Brit.* overtake in a rowing, esp. bumping, race. **row out** exhaust by rowing (*the crew were completely rowed out at the finish*). **row over** esp. *Brit.* complete the course of a boat race with little effort, owing to the absence or inferiority of competitors. □□ **row•er** *n.* [OE *rōwan* f. Gmc, rel. to RUDDER, L *remus* oar]

row³ /row/ *n. & v. colloq.* • *n.* **1** a loud noise or commotion. **2** a fierce quarrel or dispute. **3 a** a severe reprimand. **b** the condition of being reprimanded (*shall get into a row*). ● *v.* **1** *intr.* make or engage in a row. **2** *tr.* reprimand. □ **make** (or **kick up**) **a row 1** raise a noise. **2** make a vigorous protest. [18th-c. sl.: orig. unkn.]

row·an /róən, rów–/ *n.* **1** the European mountain ash. **2** a similar tree, *Sorbus americana*, native to N. America. **3** (also **row·an·ber·ry**) the scarlet berry of either of these trees. [Scand., corresp. to Norw. *rogn, raun*, Icel. *reynir*]

row·boat /róbōt/ *n.* a small boat propelled by oars.

row·dy /równdee/ *adj. & n.* ● *adj.* (**row·di·er, row·di·est**) noisy and disorderly. ● *n.* (*pl.* ·**dies**) a rowdy person. □□ **row·di·ly** *adv.* **row·di·ness** *n.* **row·dy·ism** *n.* [19th-c. US, orig. = lawless backwoodsman: orig. unkn.]

row·el /rówəl/ *n. & v.* ● *n.* **1** a spiked revolving disk at the end of a spur. **2** a circular piece of leather, etc., with a hole in the center inserted under a horse's skin to promote drainage of an infection. ● *v.tr.* **1** urge with a rowel. **2** insert a rowel in. [ME f. OF *roel(e)* f. LL *rotella* dimin. of L *rota* wheel]

row·en /rówən/ *n.* (in *sing.* or *pl.*) a season's second growth of hay or grass; an aftermath. [ME f. OF *regain* (as GAIN)]

row house *n.* any of a row of houses joined by common sidewalls.

row·ing boat *Brit.* = ROWBOAT.

row·ing ma·chine *n.* a device for exercising the muscles used in rowing.

row·lock /rólok, rólək, rúlək/ *n. Brit.* = OARLOCK.

roy·al /róyəl/ *adj. & n.* ● *adj.* **1** of or suited to or worthy of a king or queen. **2** in the service or under the patronage of a king or queen. **3** belonging to the king or queen (*the royal hands; the royal anger*). **4** of the family of a king or queen. **5** kingly; majestic; stately; splendid. **6** on a great scale; of exceptional size or quality; first-rate (*gave us royal entertainment; had a royal time*). ● *n.* **1** *colloq.* a member of the royal family. **2** a royal sail or mast. **3** a royal stag. **4** a size of paper, about 620 x 500 mm (25 x 20 in.). □□ **roy·al·ly** *adv.* [ME f. OF *roial* f. L *regalis* REGAL]

Roy·al Air Force *n.* the British air force.

roy·al as·sent *n.* see ASSENT.

roy·al blue *n.* a deep vivid blue.

roy·al duke *n. Brit.* a duke who is also a royal prince.

roy·al fam·i·ly *n.* the family to which a sovereign belongs.

roy·al fern *n.* a fern, *Osmunda regalis*, with huge spreading fronds.

roy·al flush *n.* see FLUSH[3].

roy·al·ist /róyəlist/ *n.* **1 a** a supporter of monarchy. **b** *hist.* a supporter of the royal side in the English Civil War. **2** *hist.* a loyalist in the American Revolution. □□ **roy·al·ism** *n.*

roy·al jel·ly *n.* a substance secreted by honeybee workers and fed by them to future queen bees.

Roy·al Ma·rine *n.* a British marine (see MARINE *n.* 2).

roy·al mast *n.* a mast above a topgallant mast.

Roy·al Na·vy *n.* the British navy.

roy·al plu·ral *n. Brit.* the first person plural "we" used by a single person.

roy·al sail *n.* a sail above a topgallant sail.

Roy·al So·ci·e·ty *n. Brit.* (in full **Royal Society of London**) a society founded in 1662 to promote scientific discussion.

roy·al stag *n.* esp. *Brit.* a stag with a head of 12 or more points.

roy·al stand·ard *n.* a banner bearing royal heraldic arms.

roy·al ten·nis *n.* = COURT TENNIS.

roy·al·ty /róyəltee/ *n.* (*pl.* ·**ties**) **1** the office or dignity or power of a king or queen; sovereignty. **2 a** royal persons. **b** a member of a royal family. **3** a sum paid to a patentee for the use of a patent or to an author, etc., for each copy of a book, etc., sold or for each public performance of a work. **4 a** a royal right (now esp. over minerals) granted by a sovereign to an individual or corporation. **b** a payment made by a producer of minerals, oil, or natural gas to the owner of the site or of the mineral rights over it.

Late Middle English: from Old French *roialte*, from *roial* (as in *royal*). The sense 'royal right (especially over minerals)' (late 15th century) developed into the sense 'payment made by a mining company to the site owner' (mid-19th century), which was then transferred to payments for the permission to hold patents and issue published materials; this permission was originally granted by a monarch.

roz·zer /rózər/ *n. Brit. sl.* a policeman. [19th c.: orig. unkn.]

RP *abbr. Brit.* Received Pronunciation.

r.p.m. *abbr.* revolutions per minute.

rps *abbr.* (also **r.p.s.**) revolutions per second.

RR *abbr.* **1** railroad. **2** rural route.

RS *abbr.* (in the UK) Royal Society.

Rs. *abbr.* rupee(s).

RSA *abbr.* Republic of South Africa.

RSFSR *abbr. hist.* Russian Soviet Federated Socialist Republic.

RSV *abbr.* Revised Standard Version (of the Bible).

RSVP *abbr.* (in an invitation, etc.) please answer. [F *répondez s'il vous plaît*]

RT *abbr.* **1** radio telegraphy. **2** radio telephony.

rt. *abbr.* right.

rte. *abbr.* route.

Rt. Hon. *abbr.* Right Honorable.

Rt. Revd. *abbr.* (also **Rt. Rev.**) Right Reverend.

Ru *symb. Chem.* the element ruthenium.

rub[1] /rub/ *v. & n.* ● *v.* (**rubbed, rub·bing**) **1** *tr.* move one's hand or another object with firm pressure over the surface of. **2** *tr.* (usu. foll. by *against, in, on, over*) apply (one's hand, etc.) in this way. **3** *tr.* clean or polish or make dry or bare by rubbing. **4** *tr.* (often foll. by *over*) apply (polish, ointment, etc.) by rubbing. **5** *tr.* (foll. by *in, into, through*) use rubbing to make (a substance) go into or through something. **6** *tr.* (often foll. by *together*) move or slide (objects) against each other. **7** *intr.* (foll. by *against, on*) move with contact or friction. **8** *tr.* chafe or make sore by rubbing. **9** *intr.* (of cloth, skin, etc.) become frayed or worn or sore or bare with friction. **10** *tr.* reproduce the design of (a sepulchral brass or stone, etc.) by rubbing paper laid on it with heelball or colored chalk, etc. **11** *tr.* (foll. by *to*) reduce to powder, etc., by rubbing. ● *n.* **1** a spell or an instance of rubbing (*give it a rub*). **2 a** an impediment or difficulty (*there's the rub*). **b** an inequality of the ground impeding or diverting a bowl in lawn bowling; the diversion or hindering of a bowl by this. □ **rub along** *Brit. colloq.* cope or manage without undue difficulty. **rub away** remove by rubbing. **rub elbows with** associate or come into contract with (another person), esp. socially. **rub one's hands** esp. *Brit.* rub one's hands together usu. in sign of keen satisfaction, or for warmth. **rub it in** (or **rub a person's nose in it**) emphasize or repeat an embarrassing fact, etc. **rub noses** rub one's nose against another's in greeting. **rub off 1** (usu. foll. by *on*) be transferred by contact; be transmitted (*some of his attitudes have rubbed off on me*). **2** remove by rubbing. **rub of** (or **on**) **the green** *Golf* an accidental interference with the course or position of a ball. **rub on** *Brit. colloq.* = **rub along**. **rub out 1** erase with an eraser. **2** *sl.* kill; eliminate. **rub shoulders with** = *rub elbows with*. **rub up** *Brit.* **1** polish (a tarnished object). **2** brush up (a subject or one's memory). **3** mix (pigment, etc.) into paste by rubbing. **rub the wrong way** irritate or repel as by stroking a cat against the lie of its fur. [ME *rubben*, perh. f. LG *rubben*, of unkn. orig.]

rub[2] /rub/ *n.* = RUBBER[2]. [abbr.]

rub-a-dub /rúbədub/ *n. & v.* ● *n.* **1** the rolling sound of a drum. **2** (also **rub-a-dub-dub**) *Austral. rhyming sl.* a pub. ● *v.intr.* (**rub-a-dubbed, rub-a-dub-bing**) make this sound. [imit.]

ru·ba·to /roobáatō/ *adj. & n. Mus.* ● *n.* (*pl.* ·**tos** or **ru·ba·ti** /–tee/) temporary disregarding of strict tempo. ● *adj.* performed with a flexible tempo. [It., = robbed]

rub·ber[1] /rúbər/ *n.* **1** a tough elastic polymeric substance made from the latex of plants or synthetically. **2** esp. *Brit.* a piece of this or another substance for erasing pencil or ink marks. **3** *colloq.* a condom. **4** (in *pl.*) galoshes. **5** a person who rubs; a masseur or masseuse. **6 a** an implement used for rubbing. **b** part of a machine operating by rubbing. □□ **rub·ber·y** *adj.* **rub·ber·i·ness** *n.*

Mid-16th century: from the verb RUB + -ER[1]. The original sense was 'an implement (such as a hard brush) used for rubbing and cleaning.' Because an early use of the elastic substance (previously known as *caoutchouc*) was to rub out pencil marks, *rubber* gained the sense 'eraser' in the late 18th century. The sense was subsequently (mid-19th century) generalized to refer to the substance in any form or use, at first often differentiated as *India rubber*.

rub·ber[2] /rúbər/ *n.* **1** a match of three or five successive games between the same sides or persons at whist, bridge, tennis, etc. **2** (prec. by *the*) **a** the act of winning two games in a rubber. **b** a third game when each side has won one. [orig. unkn.: used as a term in lawn bowling from *c.* 1600]

rub·ber band *n.* a loop of rubber for holding papers, etc., together.

rub·ber·ize /rúbəriz/ *v.tr.* treat or coat with rubber.

rub·ber·neck /rúbərnek/ *n. & v. colloq.* ● *n.* a person, esp. a tourist, who stares inquisitively or stupidly. ● *v.intr.* act in this way.

rub·ber plant *n.* **1** an evergreen plant, *Ficus elastica*, with dark-green shiny leaves, often cultivated as a houseplant. **2** (also **rubber tree**) any of various tropical trees yielding latex, esp. *Hevea brasiliensis*.

rub·ber stamp *n.* **1** a device for inking and imprinting on a surface. **2 a** a person who mechanically copies or agrees to others' actions. **b** an indication of such agreement. □□ **rub·ber-stamp** *v.tr.*

rub·bing /rúbing/ *n.* **1** in senses of RUB[1] *v.* **2** an impression or copy made by rubbing (see RUB[1] *v.* 10).

rub·bing al·co·hol *n.* an isopropyl alcohol solution for external application.

rub·bish /rúbish/ *n. & v.* ● *n.* esp. *Brit.* **1** waste material; debris; refuse; litter. **2** worthless material or articles; junk. **3** (often as *int.*) absurd ideas or suggestions; nonsense. ● *v.tr. Brit. colloq.* **1** criticize severely. **2** reject as worthless. □□ **rub·bish·y** adj. [ME f. AF *rub-bous*, etc., perh. f. RUBBLE]

rub·ble /rúbəl/ n. **1** waste or rough fragments of stone or brick, etc. **2** pieces of undressed stone used, esp. as fill, for walls. **3** water-worn stones. □□ **rub·bly** adj. [ME *robyl, rubel*, of uncert. orig.: cf. OF *robe* spoils]

rube /rōōb/ n. *colloq.* a country bumpkin. [abbr. of the name *Reuben*]

Rube Gold·berg /rōōb góldbərg/ adj. unnecessarily or comically complex in design. [for US cartoonist (1883–1970) noted for such drawings]

ru·bel·la /rōōbélə/ n. *Med.* an acute infectious viral disease with a red rash; German measles. [mod.L, neut. pl. of L *rubellus* reddish]

ru·bel·lite /rōōbəlīt/ n. a red variety of tourmaline. [L *rubellus* reddish]

ru·be·o·la /rōōbeeólə, –béeələ/ n. *Med.* measles. [med.L f. L *rubeus* red]

Ru·bi·con /rōōbikon/ n. a boundary that once crossed betokens irrevocable commitment; a point of no return. [the ancient name of a stream forming the boundary of Julius Caesar's province and crossed by him in 49 BC as the start of a war with Pompey]

ru·bi·cund /rōōbikund/ adj. (of a face, complexion, or person in these respects) ruddy; high-colored. □□ **ru·bi·cun·di·ty** /–kúnditee/ n. [F *rubicond* or L *rubicundus* f. *rubēre* be red]

ru·bid·i·um /rōōbídeeəm/ n. *Chem.* a soft silvery element occurring naturally in various minerals and as the radioactive isotope rubidium-87. ¶ Symb.: **Rb**. [L *rubidus* red (with ref. to its spectral lines)]

ru·bi·fy /rōōbifī/ v.tr. (·**fies**, ·**fied**) **1** make red. **2** *Med.* (of a counter-irritant) stimulate (the skin, etc.) to redness. □□ **ru·be·fa·cient** /–fáyshənt/ adj. & n. **ru·be·fac·tion** /–fákshən/ n. [ME f. OF *rubifier, rubefier* f. med.L *rubificare* f. L *rubefacere* f. *rubeus* red]

ru·big·i·nous /rōōbíjinəs/ adj. *formal* rust-colored. [L *rubigo- inis* rust]

ru·ble /rōōbəl/ n. (also **rou·ble**) the chief monetary unit of Russia, the USSR (*hist.*), and some other former republics of the USSR. [F f. Russ. *rubl'*]

ru·bric /rōōbrik/ n. **1** a direction for the conduct of divine service inserted in a liturgical book. **2** a heading or passage in red or special lettering. **3** explanatory words. **4** an established custom. □□ **ru·bri·cal** adj.

Late Middle English *rubrish* (originally referring to a heading, section of text, etc., written in red for distinctiveness), from Old French *rubriche*, from Latin *rubrica (terra)* 'red (earth or ocher as writing material),' from the base of *rubeus* 'red'; the later spelling is influenced by the Latin form.

ru·bri·cate /rōōbrikayt/ v.tr. **1** mark with red; print or write in red. **2** provide with rubrics. □□ **ru·bri·ca·tion** /–káyshən/ n. **ru·bri·ca·tor** n. [L *rubricare* f. *rubrica*: see RUBRIC]

rub-up n. *Brit.* an act of polishing something.

ru·by /rōōbee/ n., adj., & v. • n. (pl. ·**bies**) **1** a rare precious stone consisting of corundum with a color varying from deep crimson or purple to pale rose. **2** a glowing, purple-tinged red color. • adj. of this color. • v.tr. (·**bies**, ·**bied**) dye or tinge ruby color. [ME f. OF *rubi* f. med.L *rubinus* (*lapis*) red (stone), rel. to L *rubeus* red]

ru·by an·ni·ver·sa·ry n. the fortieth anniversary of a wedding.

ru·by glass n. glass colored with oxides of copper, iron, lead, tin, etc.

ru·by-throat·ed hum·ming·bird n. a hummingbird of eastern N. America, *Archilochus colubris*, the male of which has a bright red throat.

ruche /rōōsh/ n. a frill or gathering of lace, etc., as a trimming. □□ **ruched** adj. **ruch·ing** n. [F f. med.L *rusca* tree bark, of Celt. orig.]

ruck[1] /ruk/ n. **1** (prec. by *the*) the main body of competitors not likely to overtake the leaders. **2** an undistinguished crowd of persons or things. [ME, = stack of fuel, heap, rick: app. Scand., = Norw. *ruka* in the same senses]

ruck[2] /ruk/ v. & n. • v.tr. & intr. (often foll. by *up*) make or become creased or wrinkled. • n. a crease or wrinkle. [ON *hrukka*]

ruck·sack /rúksak, rōōk–/ n. = BACKPACK n. [G f. *rucken* dial. var. of *Rücken* back + *Sack* SACK[1]]

ruck·us /rúkəs/ n. a fracas or commotion. [cf. RUCTION, RUMPUS]

ruc·tion /rúkshən/ n. *colloq.* **1** a disturbance or tumult. **2** (in pl.) unpleasant arguments or reactions. [19th c.: orig. unkn.]

rud·beck·i·a /rudbékeeə/ n. a composite garden plant of the genus *Rudbeckia*, native to N. America. [mod.L f. O. *Rudbeck*, Sw. botanist d. 1740]

rudd /rud/ n. (pl. same) a red-finned freshwater fish, *Scardinius erythrophthalmus*, of the carp family. [app. rel. to *rud* red color f. OE *rudu*, rel. to RED]

rud·der /rúdər/ n. **1 a** a flat piece hinged vertically to the stern of a ship for steering. **b** a vertical airfoil pivoted from the horizontal stabilizer of an aircraft, for controlling its horizontal movement. **2** a

guiding principle, etc. □□ **rud·der·less** adj. [OE *rōther* f. WG *rōthra-* f. the stem of ROW[2]]

rud·dle var. of RADDLE.

rud·dock /rúdək/ n. *dial.* the robin redbreast. [OE *rudduc* (as RUDDLE)]

rud·dy /rúdee/ adj. & v. • adj. (**rud·di·er**, **rud·di·est**) **1 a** (of a person or complexion) freshly or healthily red. **b** (of health, youth, etc.) marked by this. **2** reddish. **3** *Brit. colloq.* bloody; damnable. • v.tr. & intr. (·**dies**, ·**died**) make or grow ruddy. □□ **rud·di·ly** adv. **rud·di·ness** n. [OE *rudig* (as RUDD)]

rudder 1b

rude /rōōd/ adj. **1** (of a person, remark, etc.) impolite or offensive. **2** roughly made or done; lacking subtlety or accuracy (*a rude shelter*). **3** primitive or uneducated (*rude simplicity*). **4** abrupt; sudden; startling; violent (*a rude awakening; a rude reminder*). **5** *colloq.* indecent; lewd (*a rude joke*). **6** esp. *Brit.* vigorous or hearty (*rude health*). □ **be rude to** speak impolitely to; insult. □□ **rude·ly** adv. **rude·ness** n. **rud·ish** adj. [ME f. OF f. L *rudis* unwrought]

CALLOW, CRUDE, ILL-MANNERED, ROUGH, UNCIVIL, UNCOUTH. Someone who lacks consideration for the feelings of others and who is deliberately insolent is **rude** (*It was rude of you not to introduce me to your friends*). **Ill-mannered** suggests that the person is ignorant of the rules of social behavior rather than deliberately rude (*an ill-mannered child*), while **uncivil** implies disregard for even the most basic rules of social behavior among civilized people (*His uncivil response resulted in his being kicked out of the classroom*). **Rough** is used to describe people who lack polish and refinement (*He was a rough but honest man*), while **crude** is a more negative term for individuals and behavior lacking culture, civility, and tact (*to make a crude gesture*). **Uncouth** describes what seems strange, awkward, or unmannerly rather than rude (*his uncouth behavior at the wedding*). Although individuals of any age may be rude, crude, ill-mannered, or uncouth, **callow** almost always applies to those who are young or immature; it suggests naïveté and lack of sophistication (*He was surprisingly callow for a man of almost 40*).

ru·der·al /rōōdərəl/ adj. & n. • adj. (of a plant) growing on or in rubbish or rubble. • n. a ruderal plant. [mod.L *ruderalis* f. L *rudera* pl. of *rudus* rubble]

ru·di·ment /rōōdimənt/ n. **1** (in pl.) the elements or first principles of a subject. **2** (in pl.) an imperfect beginning of something undeveloped or yet to develop. **3** a part or organ imperfectly developed as being vestigial or having no function (e.g., the breast in males). [F *rudiment* or L *rudimentum* (as RUDE, after *elementum* ELEMENT)]

ru·di·men·ta·ry /rōōdiméntəree/ adj. **1** involving basic principles; fundamental. **2** incompletely developed; vestigial. □□ **ru·di·men·ta·ri·ly** /–mentáirəlee, –méntərilee/ adv. **ru·di·men·ta·ri·ness** /–méntəreenis, –méntreenis/ n.

rue[1] /rōō/ v. & n. • v.tr. (**rues, rued, ru·ing**) repent of; bitterly feel the consequences of; wish to be undone or nonexistent (esp. *rue the day*). • n. *archaic* **1** repentance; dejection at some occurrence. **2** compassion or pity. [OE *hrēow, hrēowan*]

rue[2] /rōō/ n. a perennial evergreen shrub, *Ruta graveolens*, with bitter strong-scented leaves formerly used in medicine. [ME f. OF f. L *ruta* f. Gk *rhutē*]

rue·ful /rōōfŏōl/ adj. expressing sorrow, genuine or humorously affected. □□ **rue·ful·ly** adv. **rue·ful·ness** n. [ME, f. RUE[1]]

ru·fes·cent /rōōfésənt/ adj. reddish. □□ **ru·fes·cence** n. [L *rufescere* f. *rufus* reddish]

ruff[1] /ruf/ n. **1 a** a projecting starched frill worn around the neck, esp. in the 16th c. **2** a projecting or conspicuously colored ring of feathers or hair around a bird's or animal's neck. **3** a domestic pigeon like a jacobin. **4** (*fem.* **reeve** /reev/) a Eurasian wading bird, *Philomachus pugnax*, of which the male has a ruff and ear tufts in the breeding season. □□ **ruff·like** adj. [perh. f. *ruff* = ROUGH]

ruff[1] 1

ruff[2] /ruf/ n. (also **ruffe**) any of various fish, esp. a perchlike freshwater fish, *Gymnocephalus cernua*, found in European lakes and rivers. [ME, prob. f. ROUGH]

ruff[3] /ruf/ *v. & n.* ● *v.intr. & tr.* trump at cards. ● *n.* an act of ruffing. [orig. the name of a card game: f. OF *roffle, rouffle,* = It. *ronfa* (perh. alt. of *trionfo* TRUMP[1])]

ruf•fi•an /rúfeeən/ *n.* a violent, lawless person. □□ **ruf•fi•an•ism** *n.* **ruf•fi•an•ly** *adv.* [F *ruf(f)ian* f. It. *ruffiano,* perh. f. dial. *rofia* scurf]

ruf•fle /rúfəl/ *v. & n.* ● *v.* **1** *tr.* disturb the smoothness or tranquillity of. **2** *tr.* upset the calmness of (a person). **3** *tr.* gather (lace, etc.) into a ruffle. **4** *tr.* (often foll. by *up*) (of a bird) erect (its feathers) in anger, display, etc. **5** *intr.* undergo ruffling. **6** *intr.* lose smoothness or calmness. ● *n.* **1** an ornamental gathered or goffered frill of lace, etc., worn at the opening of a garment esp. around the wrist, breast, or neck. **2** perturbation; bustle. **3** a rippling effect on water. **4** the ruff of a bird, etc. (see RUFF[1] 2). **5** *Mil.* a vibrating drumbeat. [ME: orig. unkn.]

ru•fous /róőfəs/ *adj.* (esp. of animals) reddish-brown. [L *rufus* red, reddish]

rug /rug/ *n.* **1** a floor covering of shaggy material or thick pile. **2** esp. *Brit.* a thick woolen coverlet or wrap. □ **pull the rug (out) from under** deprive of support; weaken; unsettle. [prob. f. Scand.: cf. Norw. dial. *rugga* coverlet, Sw. *rugg* ruffled hair: rel. to RAG[1]]

rug•by /rúgbee/ *n.* (also **Rug•by foot•ball**) a team game played with an oval ball that may be kicked, carried, and passed from hand to hand. [*Rugby* School in central England, where it was first played]

rug•ged /rúgid/ *adj.* **1** (of ground or terrain) having a rough uneven surface. **2** (of features) strongly marked; irregular in outline. **3 a** unpolished; lacking gentleness or refinement (*rugged grandeur*). **b** harsh in sound. **c** austere; unbending (*rugged honesty*). **d** involving hardship (*a rugged life*). **4** (esp. of a machine) robust; sturdy. □□ **rug•ged•ly** *adv.* **rug•ged•ness** *n.* [ME, prob. f. Scand.: cf. RUG, and Sw. *rugga,* roughen]

rug•ger /rúgər/ *n. Brit. colloq.* rugby.

ru•gose /róőgōs/ *adj.* esp. *Biol.* wrinkled; corrugated. □□ **ru•gose•ly** *adv.* **ru•gos•i•ty** /-gósitee/ *n.* [L *rugosus* f. *ruga* wrinkle]

ru•in /róőin/ *n. & v.* ● *n.* **1** a destroyed or wrecked state (*after centuries of neglect, the palace fell to ruin*). **2 a** a person's or thing's downfall or elimination (*the ruin of my hopes*). **b** *archaic* a woman's loss of chastity by seduction or rape; dishonor resulting from this. **3 a** the complete loss of one's property or position (*bring to ruin*). **b** a person who has suffered ruin. **4** (in *sing.* or *pl.*) the remains of a building, etc., that has suffered ruin (*an old ruin; ancient ruins*). **5** a cause of ruin; a destructive thing or influence (*will be the ruin of us*). ● *v.* **1** *tr.* **a** bring to ruin (*your extravagance has ruined me*). **b** utterly impair or wreck (*the rain ruined my hat*). **c** *archaic* seduce and abandon (a woman). **2** *tr.* (esp. as **ruined** *adj.*) reduce to ruins. **3** *intr. poet.* fall headlong or with a crash. □ **in ruins 1** in a state of ruin. **2** completely wrecked (*their hopes were in ruins*). [ME f. OF *ruine* f. L *ruina* f. *ruere* fall]

ru•in•a•tion /róőináyshən/ *n.* **1** the act of bringing to ruin. **2** the act of ruining or the state of being ruined. [obs. *ruinate* (as RUIN)]

ru•in•ous /róőinəs/ *adj.* **1** bringing ruin; disastrous (*at ruinous expense*). **2** in ruins; dilapidated. □□ **ru•in•ous•ly** *adv.* **ru•in•ous•ness** *n.* [ME f. L *ruinosus* (as RUIN)]

rule /róől/ *n. & v.* ● *n.* **1** a principle to which an action conforms or is required to conform. **2** a prevailing custom or standard; the normal state of things. **3** government or dominion (*under British rule; the rule of law*). **4** a graduated straight measure used in carpentry, etc.; a ruler. **5** *Printing* **a** a thin strip of metal for separating headings, columns, etc. **b** a thin line or dash. **6** a code of discipline of a religious order. **7** *Law* an order made by a judge or court. ● *v.* **1** *tr.* exercise decisive influence over; keep under control. **2** *tr. &* (often foll. by *over*) *intr.* have sovereign control of (*rules over a vast kingdom*). **3** *tr.* (often foll. by *that* + clause) pronounce authoritatively (*was ruled out of order*). **4** *tr.* **a** make parallel lines across (paper). **b** make (a straight line) with a ruler, etc. **5** *intr.* (of prices or goods, etc., in regard to price or quality, etc.) have a specified general level; be for the most part (*the market ruled high*). **6** *tr.* (in *passive*; foll. by *by*) consent to follow (advice, etc.); be guided by. □ **as a rule** usually; more often than not. **by rule** in a regulation manner; mechanically. **rule out** exclude; pronounce irrelevant or ineligible. **rule the roost** (or *Brit.* **roast**) be in control. **run the rule over** *Brit.* examine cursorily for correctness or adequacy. □□ **rule•less** *adj.* [ME f. OF *reule, reuler* f. LL *regulare* f. L *regula* straight stick]

rule of the road *n.* the custom or law regulating which side of the road is to be taken by vehicles (also riders or ships) meeting or passing each other.

rule of three *n.* a method of finding a number in the same ratio to one given as exists between two others given.

rule of thumb *n.* a rule for general guidance, based on experience or practice rather than theory.

rul•er /róőlər/ *n.* **1** a person exercising government or dominion. **2** a straight usu. graduated strip or cylinder of wood, metal, etc., used to draw lines or measure distance. □□ **rul•er•ship** *n.*

rul•ing /róőling/ *n. & adj.* ● *n.* an authoritative decision or announcement. ● *adj.* dominant; prevailing; currently in force (*ruling prices*).

rul•ing pas•sion *n.* a motive that habitually directs one's actions.

rum[1] /rum/ *n.* **1** a spirit distilled from sugarcane residues or molasses. **2** *colloq.* intoxicating liquor in general (*the demon rum*). [17th c.: perh. abbr. of contemporary forms *rumbullion, rumbustion,* of unkn. orig.]

rum[2] /rum/ *adj. Brit. colloq.* **1** odd; strange; queer. **2** difficult; dangerous. □□ **rum•ly** *adv.* **rum•ness** *n.* [16th-c. cant, orig. = fine, spirited, perh. var. of ROM]

Ru•ma•ni•an var. of ROMANIAN.

Ru•mansh var. of ROMANSH.

rum•ba /rúmbə, rŏŏm–/ *n. & v.* (also **rhum•ba**) ● *n.* **1** a Cuban dance. **2 a** a ballroom dance imitative of this. **b** the music for it. ● *v.tr.* (**rum•bas, rum•baed** /–bəd/, **rum•ba•ing** /–bə-ing/) dance the rumba. [Amer. Sp.]

rum ba•ba see BABA.

rum•ble /rúmbəl/ *v. & n.* ● *v.* **1** *intr.* make a continuous deep resonant sound as of distant thunder. **2** *intr.* (foll. by *along, by, past,* etc.) (of a person or vehicle) move with a rumbling noise. **3** *intr.* engage in a street fight, esp. as part of a gang. **4** *tr.* (often foll. by *out*) utter or say with a rumbling sound. **5** *tr. Brit. sl.* find out about (esp. something illicit). ● *n.* **1** a rumbling sound. **2** *sl.* a street fight between gangs. □□ **rum•bler** *n.* [ME *romble,* prob. f. MDu. *rommelen, rummelen* (imit.)]

rum•ble seat *n.* an uncovered folding seat in the rear of an automobile.

rum•ble strip *n.* a closely-spaced series of ridges built into a roadway as a warning to drivers.

rum•bus•tious /rumbúschəs/ *adj.* esp. *Brit. colloq.* boisterous, noisy, uproarious. □□ **rum•bus•tious•ly** *adv.* **rum•bus•tious•ness** *n.* [prob. var. of *robustious* boisterous, ROBUST]

ru•men /róőmen/ *n.* (*pl.* **ru•mi•na** /–minə/ or **ru•mens**) the first stomach of a ruminant, in which food, esp. cellulose, is partly digested by bacteria. [L *rumen ruminis* throat]

rum go *n.* (also **rum do** or **rum start**) *colloq.* a surprising occurrence or unforeseen turn of affairs.

ru•mi•nant /róőminənt/ *n. & adj.* ● *n.* an animal that chews the cud regurgitated from its rumen. ● *adj.* **1** of or belonging to ruminants. **2** contemplative; given to or engaged in meditation. [L *ruminari ruminant–* (as RUMEN)]

ru•mi•nate /róőminayt/ *v.* **1** *tr. &* (foll. by *over, on,* etc.) *intr.* meditate, ponder. **2** *intr.* (of ruminants) chew the cud. □□ **ru•mi•na•tion** /–náyshən/ *n.* **ru•mi•na•tive** /–nətiv/ *adj.* **ru•mi•na•tive•ly** *adv.* **ru•mi•na•tor** *n.*

rum•mage /rúmij/ *v. & n.* ● *v.* **1** *tr. &* (foll. by *in, through, among*) *intr.* search, esp. untidily and unsystematically. **2** *tr.* (foll. by *out, up*) find among other things. **3** *tr.* (foll. by *about*) disarrange; make untidy in searching. ● *n.* **1** an instance of rummaging. **2** things found by rummaging; a miscellaneous accumulation. □□ **rum•mag•er** *n.*

WORD HISTORY rummage

Late 15th century: from Old French *arrumage,* from *arrumer* 'stow (in a hold),' from Middle Dutch *ruim* 'room.' In early use the word referred to the arranging of items such as casks in the hold of a ship, giving rise (early 17th century) to the verb sense 'make a search of (a vessel).'

rum•mage sale *n.* a sale of miscellaneous usu. secondhand articles, esp. for charity.

rum•mer /rúmər/ *n.* a large drinking glass. [rel. to Du. *roemer,* LG *römer* f. *roemen* praise, boast]

rum•my[1] /rúmee/ *n.* any of various card games in which the players try to form sets and sequences of cards. [20th c.: orig. unkn.]

rum•my[2] /rúmee/ *n. & adj.* ● *n. sl.* a drunkard or sot. ● *adj. Brit. colloq.* = RUM[2].

ru•mor /róőmər/ *n. & v.* (*Brit.* **ru•mour**) ● *n.* **1** general talk or hearsay of doubtful accuracy. **2** (often foll. by *of,* or *that* + clause) a current but unverified statement or assertion (*heard a rumor that you are leaving*). ● *v.tr.* (usu. in *passive*) report by way of rumor (*it is rumored that you are leaving; you are rumored to be leaving*). [ME f. OF *rumur, rumor* f. L *rumor –oris* noise]

rump /rump/ *n.* **1** the hind part of a mammal, esp. the buttocks. **2 a** a small or contemptible remnant of a parliament or similar body. **b** (**the Rump**) *hist.* the remnant of the English Long Parliament 1648–53 or after its restoration in 1659. □□ **rump•less** *adj.* [ME, prob. f. Scand.]

rum•ple /rúmpəl/ *v.tr. & intr.* make or become creased or ruffled. □□ **rum•ply** *adj.* [obs. *rumple* (n.) f. MDu. *rompel* f. *rompe* wrinkle]

rump roast *n.* a cut of beef from the rump.

rum•pus /rúmpəs/ *n. colloq.* a disturbance, brawl, row, or uproar. [18th c.: prob. fanciful]

rum•pus room *n.* a room, usu. in the basement of a house, for games and play.

run /run/ *v. & n.* ● *v.* (**run•ning**; *past* **ran** /ran/; *past part.* **run**) **1** *intr.* go with quick steps on alternate feet, never having both or all feet on the ground at the same time. **2** *intr.* flee; abscond. **3** *intr.* go or travel hurriedly, briefly, etc. **4** *intr.* **a** advance by or as by rolling or on wheels, or smoothly or easily. **b** be in action or operation (*left the engine running*). **5** *intr.* be current or operative; have duration (*the lease runs for 99 years*). **6** *intr.* (of a bus, train, etc.) travel or be traveling on its route (*the train is running late*). **7** *intr.* (of a play, exhibition, etc.) be staged or presented (*is now running at the Apollo*). **8** *intr.* extend; have a course or order or tendency (*the road runs by the coast*; *prices are running high*). **9 a** *intr.* compete in a race. **b** *intr.* finish a race in a specified position. **c** *tr.* compete in (a race). **10** *intr.* (often foll. by *for*) seek election (*ran for president*). **11 a** *intr.* (of a liquid, etc., or its container) flow or be wet; drip. **b** *tr.* flow with (a specified liquid) (*after the massacre, the rivers ran blood*). **12** *tr.* **a** cause (water, etc.) to flow. **b** fill (a bath) with water. **13** *intr.* spread rapidly or beyond the proper place (*ink ran over the table*; *a shiver ran down my spine*). **14** *intr. Cricket* (of a batsman) run from one wicket to the other in scoring a run. **15** *tr.* traverse or make one's way through or over (a course, race, or distance). **16** *tr.* perform (an errand). **17** *tr.* publish (an article, etc.) in a newspaper or magazine. **18 a** *tr.* cause (a machine or vehicle, etc.) to operate. **b** *intr.* (of a mechanism or component, etc.) move or work freely. **19** *tr.* direct or manage (a business, household, etc.). **20** *tr. Brit.* own and use (a vehicle) regularly. **21** *tr.* take (a person) for a journey in a vehicle (*shall I run you to the post office?*). **22** *tr.* cause to run or go in a specified way (*ran the car into a tree*). **23** *tr.* enter (a horse, etc.) for a race. **24** *tr.* smuggle (guns, etc.). **25** *tr.* chase or hunt. **26** *tr.* allow (an account) to accumulate for a time before paying. **27** *intr. Naut.* (of a ship, etc.) go straight and fast. **28** *intr.* (of salmon) go upriver from the sea. **29** *intr.* (of a color in a fabric) spread from the dyed parts. **30 a** *intr.* (of a thought, the eye, the memory, etc.) pass in a transitory or cursory way (*ideas ran through my mind*). **b** *tr.* cause (one's eye) to look cursorily (*ran my eye down the page*). **c** *tr.* pass (a hand, etc.) rapidly over (*ran his fingers down her spine*). **31** *intr.* (of hosiery) unravel along a line from the point of a snag. **32** *intr.* (of a candle) gutter. **33** *intr.* (of an orifice, esp. the eyes or nose) exude liquid matter. **34** *tr.* sew (fabric) loosely or hastily with running stitches; baste. **35** *tr.* turn (cattle, etc.) out to graze. • *n.* **1** an act or spell of running. **2** a short trip or excursion, esp. for pleasure. **3** a distance traveled. **4** a general tendency of development or movement. **5** a rapid motion. **6** a regular route. **7 a** a continuous or long stretch or spell or course (*a 50-foot run of wiring*; *had a run of bad luck*). **b** a series or sequence, esp. of cards in a specified suit. **8** (often foll. by *on*) **a** a high general demand (for a commodity, currency, etc.) (*a run on the dollar*). **b** a sudden demand for repayment by a large number of customers of (a bank). **9** a quantity produced in one period of production (*a print run*). **10** a general or average type or class (*not typical of the general run*). **11 a** *Baseball* a point scored by a base runner upon touching home plate safely. **b** *Cricket* a point scored by the batsmen each running to the other's wicket, or an equivalent point awarded for some other reason. **12** (foll. by *of*) free use of or access to (*had the run of the house*). **13 a** an animal's regular track. **b** an enclosure for domestic animals or fowls. **c** a range of pasture. **14** a line of unraveled stitches, esp. from the point of a snag (in hosiery). **15** *Mus.* a rapid scale passage. **16** a class or line of goods. **17** a batch or drove of animals born or reared together. **18** a shoal of fish in motion. **19** a trough for water to run in. **20** a small stream or brook. **21 a** a single journey, esp. by an aircraft. **b** (of an aircraft) a flight on a straight and even course at a constant speed before or while dropping bombs. **c** an offensive military operation. **22** a slope used for skiing or tobogganing, etc. **23** (**the runs**) *colloq.* an attack of diarrhea. □ **at a run** running. **on the run 1** escaping; running away. **2** hurrying about from place to place. **run about 1** bustle; hurry from one person or place to another. **2** (esp. of children) play or wander without restraint. **run across 1** happen to meet. **2** (foll. by *to*) make a brief journey or a flying visit (to a place). **run afoul of** collide or become entangled with (another vessel, etc.). **run after 1** pursue with attentions; seek the society of. **2** give much time to (a pursuit, etc.). **3** pursue at a run. **run against 1** oppose, as in an election. **2** esp. *Brit.* happen to meet. **run along** *colloq.* depart. **run around 1** *Brit.* take from place to place by car, etc. **2** deceive or evade repeatedly. **3** (often foll. by *with*) *sl.* engage in sexual relations (esp. casually or illicitly). **run at** attack by charging or rushing. **run away 1** get away by running; flee; abscond. **2** elope. **3** (of a horse) bolt. **run away with 1** carry off (a person, stolen property, etc.). **2** win (a prize) easily. **3** accept (a notion) hastily. **4** (of expense, etc.) consume (money, etc.). **5** (of a horse) bolt with (a rider, a carriage or its occupants). **run a blockade** see BLOCKADE. **run down 1** knock down or collide with. **2** reduce the strength or numbers of (resources). **3** (of an unwound clock, etc.) stop. **4** (of a person or a person's health) become feeble from overwork or underfeeding. **5** discover after a search. **6** disparage. **run dry** cease to flow; be exhausted. **run for it** seek safety by fleeing. **a run** (or **a good run**) **for one's money 1** vigorous competition. **2** pleasure or reward derived from an activity. **run the gauntlet** see GAUNTLET[2]. **run a person hard** (or **close**) press a person severely in a race or competition, or in comparative merit. **run high 1** (of the sea) have a strong current with a high tide. **2** (of feelings) be strong. **run in 1** *colloq.* arrest. **2** (of a combatant) rush to close quarters. **3** incur (a debt). **4** *Brit.* run (a new engine or vehicle) carefully in the early stages. **run in the family** (of a trait) be common in the members of a family. **run into 1** collide with. **2** encounter. **3** reach as many as (a specified figure). **4** fall into (a practice, absurdity, etc.). **5** be continuous or coalesce with. **run into the ground** *colloq.* bring (a person, vehicle, etc.) to exhaustion, disrepair, etc. **run its course** follow its natural progress; be left to itself. **run low** (or **short**) become depleted; have too little (*our money ran short*; *we ran short of gas*). **run off 1** flee. **2** produce (copies, etc.) on a machine. **3** decide (a race or other contest) after a series of heats or in the event of a tie. **4** flow or cause to flow away. **5** write or recite fluently. **6** digress suddenly. **run off at the mouth** *sl.* talk incessantly. **run off one's feet** very busy. **run on 1** (of written characters) be joined together. **2** continue in operation. **3** elapse. **4** speak volubly. **5** talk incessantly. **6** *Printing* continue on the same line as the preceding matter. **run** (or **pass**) **one's eye over** see EYE. **run out 1** come to an end; become used up. **2** (foll. by *of*) exhaust one's stock of. **3** escape from a containing vessel. **4** expel; drive out (*they ran him out of town*). **run out on** *colloq.* desert (a person). **run over 1** overflow; extend beyond. **2** study or repeat quickly. **3** (of a vehicle or its driver) pass over; knock down or crush. **4** touch (the notes of a piano, etc.) in quick succession. **5** (often foll. by *to*) go quickly by a brief journey or for a quick visit. **run ragged** exhaust (a person). **run rings around** see RING[1]. **run riot** see RIOT. **run a** (or **the**) **risk** see RISK. **run the show** *colloq.* dominate in an undertaking, etc. **run a temperature** be feverish. **run through 1** examine or rehearse briefly. **2** peruse. **3** deal successively with. **4** consume (an estate, etc.) by reckless or quick spending. **5** traverse. **6** pervade. **7** pierce with a sword, etc. **8** draw a line through (written words). **run to 1** have the money or ability for. **2** reach (an amount or number). **3** (of a person) show a tendency to (*runs to fat*). **4 a** be enough for (some expense or undertaking). **b** have the resources or capacity for. **5** fall into (ruin). **run to earth** (or **ground**) **1** *Hunting* chase to its lair. **2** discover after a long search. **run to meet** anticipate (one's troubles, etc.). **run to seed** see SEED. **run up 1** accumulate (a debt, etc.) quickly. **2** build or make hurriedly. **3** raise (a flag). **4** grow quickly. **5** rise in price. **6** (foll. by *to*) amount to. **7** force (a rival bidder) to bid higher. **8** add up (a column of figures). **9** (foll. by *to*) go quickly by a brief journey or for a quick visit. **run up against** meet with (a difficulty or difficulties). **run upon** (of a person's thoughts, etc.) be engrossed by; dwell upon. **run wild** grow or stray unchecked or undisciplined or untrained. □□ **run•na•ble** *adj.* [OE *rinnan*]

run•a•bout /rúnəbowt/ *n.* a light car, boat, or aircraft.

run•a•round /rúnərownd/ *n.* (esp. in phr. *give a person the runaround*) deceit or evasion.

run•a•way /rúnəway/ *n.* **1** a fugitive. **2** an animal or vehicle that is running out of control. **3** (*attrib.*) **a** that is running away or out of control (*runaway inflation*; *had a runaway success*). **b** done or performed after running away (*a runaway wedding*).

run•ci•ble spoon /rúnsibəl/ *n.* a fork curved like a spoon, with three broad prongs, one edged. [nonsense word used by E. Lear, Engl. humorist d. 1888, perh. after *rouncival* large pea]

run•ci•nate /rúnsinayt, –nət/ *adj. Bot.* (of a leaf) saw-toothed, with lobes pointing toward the base. [mod.L *runcinatus* f. L *runcina* PLANE[2] (formerly taken to mean saw)]

run•down /rúndown/ *n.* **1** *Baseball* a play in which a base runner is caught between two bases and is chased by fielders who try to tag the runner out. **2** a summary or brief analysis.

run-down *adj.* **1** decayed after prosperity. **2** enfeebled through overwork, etc.

rune /ro͞on/ *n.* **1** any of the letters of the earliest Germanic alphabet used by Scandinavians and Anglo-Saxons from about the 3rd c. and formed by modifying Roman or Greek characters to suit carving. **2** a similar mark of mysterious or magic significance. **3** a Finnish poem or a division of it. □□ **ru•nic** *adj.* [ON *rún* (only in pl. *rúnar*) magic sign, rel. to OE *rūn*]

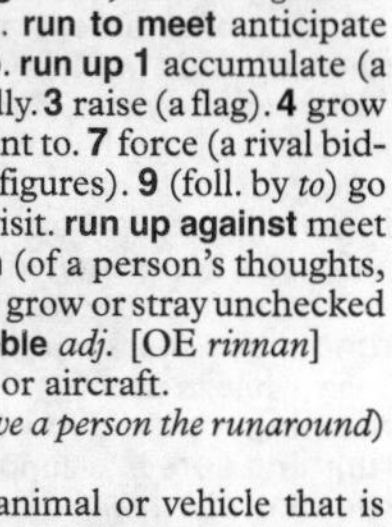

runes 2

rune-staff *n.* **1** a magic wand inscribed with runes. **2** a runic calendar.

rung[1] /rung/ *n.* **1** each of the horizontal supports of a ladder. **2** a strengthening crosspiece in the structure of a chair, etc. □□ **runged** *adj.* **rung•less** *adj.* [OE *hrung*]

rung[2] *past part.* of RING[2].

run-in *n.* **1** the approach to an action or event. **2** a quarrel.

run•let /rúnlit/ *n.* a small stream.

run•nel /rúnəl/ *n.* **1** a brook or rill. **2** a gutter. [later form (assim. to RUN) of *rinel* f. OE *rynel* (as RUN)]

run·ner /rúnər/ n. **1** a person, horse, etc. that runs, esp. in a race. **2 a** a creeping plant stem that can take root. **b** a twining plant. **3** a rod or groove or blade on which a thing slides. **4** a sliding ring on a rod, etc. **5** a messenger, scout, collector, or agent for a bank, etc.; a tout. **6** hist. a police officer. **7** a running bird. **8 a** a smuggler. **b** = blockade-runner. **9** a revolving millstone. **10** Naut. a rope in a single block with one end around a tackle block and the other having a hook. **11** (in full **runner bean**) esp. Brit. a twining bean plant, Phaseolus coccineus, with red flowers and long green seed pods. Also called **scarlet runner**. **12** each of the long pieces on the underside of a sled, etc., that forms the contact in sliding. **13** a roller for moving a heavy article. **14** a long, narrow ornamental cloth or rug. □ **do a runner** Brit. sl. leave hastily; flee.

run·ner-up n. (pl. **run·ners-up** or **run·ner-ups**) the competitor or team taking second place.

run·ning /rúning/ n. & adj. • n. **1** the action of runners in a race, etc. **2** the way a race, etc., proceeds. **3** management; control; operation • adj. **1** continuing on an essentially continuous basis though changing in detail (a running battle). **2** consecutive; one after another (three days running). **3** done with a run (a running jump). □ **in** (or **out of**) **the running** (of a competitor) with a good (or poor) chance of winning. **make** (or **take up**) **the running** take the lead; set the pace. **take a running jump** (esp. as int.) Brit. sl. go away.

run·ning ac·count n. esp. Brit. a current account.

run·ning board n. a footboard on either side of a vehicle.

run·ning com·men·ta·ry n. an oral description of events as they occur.

run·ning fire n. successive shots from a line of troops, etc.

run·ning gear n. the moving or running parts of a machine, esp. the wheels and suspension of a vehicle.

run·ning hand n. writing in which the pen, etc., is not lifted after each letter.

run·ning head n. (also **run·ning head·line**) a heading printed at the top of a number of consecutive pages of a book, etc.

run·ning knot n. a knot that slips along the rope, etc., and changes the size of a noose.

run·ning light n. **1** any of the navigational lights displayed by a ship, aircraft, etc., during hours of darkness. **2** Brit. lights on a motor vehicle that remain illuminated while the vehicle is running.

run·ning mate n. **1** a candidate for a secondary position in an election. **2** a horse entered in a race in order to set the pace for another horse from the same stable that is intended to win.

run·ning re·pairs n.pl. minor or temporary repairs, etc., to machinery while in use.

run·ning rope n. a rope that is freely movable through a pulley, etc.

run·ning sore n. a suppurating sore.

run·ning stitch n. **1** a line of small nonoverlapping stitches for gathering, etc. **2** one of these stitches.

run·ning wa·ter n. water flowing in a stream or from a tap, etc.

run·ny /rúnee/ adj. (**run·ni·er**, **run·ni·est**) **1** tending to run or flow. **2** excessively fluid.

run·off /rúnawf/ n. **1** an additional competition, election, race, etc., after a tie. **2** an amount of rainfall that is carried off an area by streams and rivers.

run-of-the-mill adj. ordinary; undistinguished.

run-on adj. designating something that is continued without a break.

GRAMMAR TIP run-on

Run-on Sentences. A **run-on sentence** is two or more complete sentences or independent clauses that are joined without the proper punctuation or a conjunction. Most run-on sentences are either *comma splices* or *fused sentences*. A **comma splice** joins two independent clauses with a comma (*I don't care if he can't read, I like him anyway*), when what is needed is a semicolon, dash, or period. A **fused sentence** is two independent clauses run together without any punctuation at all (*the trick is to get in line early then you're almost guaranteed to get a ticket*). Most run-on sentences can be corrected by: (1) inserting a period to form two separate sentences; (2) inserting a comma and a coordinating conjunction (*and*, *but*, or *or*) between the two independent clauses; (3) inserting a semicolon; or (4) subordinating one clause to the other (for example: *if you get in line early, you're almost guaranteed to get a ticket*).

---

runt /runt/ n. **1** a small piglet, puppy, etc., esp. the smallest in a litter. **2** a weakling; an undersized person. **3** esp. Brit. a large domestic pigeon. □□ **runt·y** adj. [16th c.: orig. unkn.]

run-through n. **1** a rehearsal. **2** a brief survey.

run-up n. **1** esp. Brit. (often foll. by to) the period preceding an important event. **2** Golf a low approach shot.

run·way /rúnway/ n. **1** a specially prepared surface along which aircraft take off and land. **2** a trail to an animal's watering place. **3** an incline down which logs are slid. **4** a narrow walkway extending

out from a stage into an auditorium. **5** a passageway along which football players, etc., run to enter the field.

ru·pee /roopee, roopee/ n. the chief monetary unit of India, Pakistan, Sri Lanka, Nepal, Mauritius, and the Seychelles. [Hind. rūpiyah f. Skr. rūpya wrought silver]

ru·pi·ah /roopeeə/ n. the chief monetary unit of Indonesia. [as RUPEE]

rup·ture /rúpchər/ n. & v. • n. **1** the act or an instance of breaking; a breach. **2** a breach of harmonious relations; a disagreement and parting. **3** Med. an abdominal hernia. • v. **1** tr. break or burst (a cell or membrane, etc.). **2** tr. sever (a connection). **3** intr. undergo a rupture. **4** tr. & intr. affect with or suffer a hernia. □□ **rup·tur·a·ble** adj. [ME f. OF rupture or L ruptura f. rumpere rupt- break]

ru·ral /roorəl/ adj. **1** in, of, or suggesting the country (opp. URBAN); pastoral or agricultural (in rural seclusion; a rural constituency). **2** often derog. characteristic of country people; rustic; plain; simple. □□ **ru·ral·ism** n. **ru·ral·ist** n. **ru·ral·i·ty** /-rálitee/ n. **ru·ral·ize** v. **ru·ral·i·za·tion** n. **ru·ral·ly** adv. [ME f. OF rural or LL ruralis f. rus ruris the country]

ru·ral dean see DEAN[1].

ru·ral free de·liv·er·y n. (also **ru·ral de·liv·er·y serv·ice**) postal delivery to mailboxes in rural areas. ¶ Abbr.: **RFD.**

Ru·ri·ta·ni·an /roorìtáyneeən/ adj. relating to or characteristic of romantic adventure or its setting. [Ruritania, an imaginary setting in SE Europe in the novels of Anthony Hope (d. 1933)]

ruse /rooz/ n. a stratagem or trick. [ME f. OF f. ruser drive back, perh. ult. f. L rursus backward: cf. RUSH[1]]

rush[1] /rush/ v. & n. • v. **1** intr. go, move, or act precipitately or with great speed. **2** tr. move or transport with great haste (was rushed to the hospital). **3** intr. (foll. by at) **a** move suddenly and quickly toward. **b** begin impetuously. **4** tr. perform or deal with hurriedly (don't rush your dinner; the bill was rushed through Congress). **5** tr. force (a person) to act hastily. **6** tr. attack or capture by sudden assault. **7** tr. Brit. sl. overcharge (a customer). **8** tr. pay attentions to (a person) with a view to securing acceptance of a proposal. **9** tr. pass (an obstacle) with a rapid dash. **10** intr. flow, fall, spread, or roll impetuously or fast (felt the blood rush to my face; the river rushes past). **11** tr. & intr. Football advance the ball in a running play or plays. • n. **1** an act of rushing; a violent advance or attack. **2** a period of great activity; a commotion. **3** (attrib.) done with great haste or speed (a rush job). **4** a sudden migration of large numbers. **5** a surge of emotion, excitement, etc. **6** (foll. by on, for) a sudden, strong demand for a commodity. **7** (in pl.) colloq. the first prints of a film after a period of shooting. **8** Football **a** the act of carrying the ball. **b** an attempt by a defensive player or players to reach the passer or kicker. □ **rush one's fences** Brit. act with undue haste. □□ **rush·er** n. **rush·ing·ly** adv. [ME f. AF russher, = OF ruser, russer: see RUSE]

rush[2] /rush/ n. **1 a** any marsh or waterside plant of the family Juncaceae, with naked slender tapering pith-filled stems (properly leaves) formerly used for strewing floors and still used for making chair bottoms and plaiting baskets, etc. **b** a stem of this. **c** (collect.) rushes as a material. **2** archaic a thing of no value (not worth a rush). □□ **rush·like** adv. **rush·y** adj. [OE rysc, rysce, corresp. to MLG, MHG rusch]

rush can·dle n. a candle made by dipping the pith of a rush in tallow.

rush hour n. a time each day when traffic is at its heaviest.

rush·light /rúshlìt/ n. Brit. a rush candle.

rusk /rusk/ n. a slice of bread rebaked usu. as a light biscuit, esp. as food for babies. [Sp. or Port. rosca twist, coil, roll of bread]

rus·set /rúsit/ adj. & n. • adj. **1** reddish-brown. **2** archaic rustic; homely; simple. • n. **1** a reddish-brown color. **2** a kind of roughskinned, russet-colored apple. **3** hist. a coarse, homespun reddishbrown or gray cloth used for simple clothing. **4** a baking potato, esp. one from Idaho. □□ **rus·set·y** adj. [ME f. AF f. OF rosset, rousset, dimin. of roux red f. Prov. ros, It. rosso f. L russus red]

Rus·sia leath·er /rúshə/ n. a durable bookbinding leather from skins impregnated with birch-bark oil. [Russia in E. Europe]

Rus·sian /rúshən/ n. & adj. • n. **1 a** a native or national of Russia or the former Soviet Union. **b** a person of Russian descent. **2** the language of Russia and the official language of the former Soviet Union. • adj. **1** of or relating to Russia. **2** of or in Russian. □□ **Rus·sian·ize** v.tr. **Rus·sian·i·za·tion** n. **Rus·sian·ness** n. [med.L Russianus]

Rus·sian boot n. a boot that loosely encloses the calf.

Rus·sian ol·ive = OLEASTER.

Rus·sian rou·lette n. **1** an act of daring in which one (usu. with others in turn) squeezes the trigger of a revolver held to one's head with one chamber loaded, having first spun the chamber. **2** a potentially dangerous enterprise.

Rus·si·fy /rúsifì/ v.tr. (**·fies**, **·fied**) make Russian in character. □□ **Rus·si·fi·ca·tion** n.

Rus·ki /rúskee, roos-, roos-/ n. (also **Russ·ky**) (pl. **Russ·kis** or **·kies**) often offens. a Russian or (formerly) a Soviet citizen. [RUSSIAN after Russ. surnames ending in –ski]

Russo- /rúsō/ comb. form Russian; Russian and.

Rus•so•phile /rúsəfīl/ *n.* a person who is fond of Russia or the Russians.

rust /rust/ *n. & v.* ● *n.* **1 a** a reddish or yellowish brown coating formed on iron or steel by oxidation, esp. as a result of moisture. **b** a similar coating on other metals. **2 a** any of various plant diseases with rust-colored spots caused by fungi of the order Uredinales. **b** the fungus causing this. **3** an impaired state due to disuse or inactivity. ● *v.* **1** *tr. & intr.* affect or be affected with rust; undergo oxidation. **2** *intr.* (of bracken, etc.) become rust-colored. **3** *intr.* (of a plant) be attacked by rust. **4** *intr.* lose quality or efficiency by disuse or inactivity. □□ **rust•less** *adj.* [OE *rūst* f. Gmc]

rus•tic /rústik/ *adj. & n.* ● *adj.* **1** having the characteristics of or associations with the country or country life. **2** unsophisticated; simple; unrefined. **3** of rude or country workmanship. **4** made of untrimmed branches or rough lumber (*a rustic bench*). **5** (of lettering) freely formed. **6** *Archit.* with rough-hewn or roughened surface or with sunk joints. ● *n.* a person from or living in the country, esp. a simple, unsophisticated one. □□ **rus•ti•cal•ly** *adv.* **rus•tic•i•ty** /–tísitee/ *n.* [ME f. L *rusticus* f. *rus* the country]

rus•ti•cate /rústikayt/ *v.* **1** *intr.* retire to or live in the country. **2** *tr.* make rural. **3** *tr. Brit.* dismiss (a student) temporarily from a university. □□ **rus•ti•ca•tion** /–káyshən/ *n.* [L *rusticari* live in the country (as RUSTIC)]

rus•tle /rúsəl/ *v. & n.* ● *v.* **1** *intr. & tr.* make or cause to make a gentle sound as of dry leaves blown in a breeze. **2** *intr.* (often foll. by *along*, etc.) move with a rustling sound. **3** *tr.* (also *absol.*) steal (cattle or horses). **4** *intr. colloq.* hustle. ● *n.* a rustling sound or movement. □ **rustle up** *colloq.* produce quickly when needed. □□ **rus•tler** *n.* (esp. in sense 3 of *v.*). [ME *rustel*, etc. (imit.): cf. obs. Flem. *ruysselen*, Du. *ritselen*]

rust•proof /rústproof/ *adj. & v.* ● *adj.* (of a metal) not susceptible to corrosion by rust. ● *v.tr.* make rustproof.

rust•y /rústee/ *adj.* (**rust•i•er, rust•i•est**) **1** rusted or affected by rust. **2** stiff with age or disuse. **3** (of knowledge, etc.) faded or impaired by neglect (*my French is a bit rusty*). **4** rust-colored. **5** (of black clothes) discolored by age. **6 a** of antiquated appearance. **b** anti-

quated or behind the times. **7** (of a voice) croaking or creaking. □□ **rust•i•ly** *adv.* **rust•i•ness** *n.* [OE *rūstig* (as RUST)]

rut¹ /rut/ *n. & v.* ● *n.* **1** a deep track made by the passage of wheels. **2** an established (esp. tedious) mode of practice or procedure. ● *v.tr.* (**rut•ted, rut•ting**) mark with ruts. □ **in a rut** following a fixed (esp. tedious or dreary) pattern of behavior that is difficult to change. □□ **rut•ty** *adj.* [prob. f. OF *rote* (as ROUTE)]

rut² /rut/ *n. & v.* ● *n.* the periodic sexual excitement of a male deer, goat, sheep, etc. ● *v.intr.* (**rut•ted, rut•ting**) be affected with rut. □□ **rut•tish** *adj.* [ME f. OF *rut, ruit* f. L *rugitus* f. *rugire* roar]

ru•ta•ba•ga /rootəbáygə/ *n.* a large yellow-fleshed turnip, *Brassica napus*, orig. from Sweden. Also called **swede**. [Sw. dial. *rotabagge*]

ru•the•ni•um /roothéeneeəm/ *n. Chem.* a rare hard white metallic transition element, occurring naturally in platinum ores, and used as a chemical catalyst and in certain alloys. ¶ Symb.: **Ru**. [med.L *Ruthenia* Russia (from its discovery in ores from the Urals)]

ruth•er•for•di•um /rúthərfáwrdeeəm/ *n. Chem.* an artificially made transuranic metallic element produced by bombarding an isotope of californium. ¶ Symb.: **Rf**. [E. *Rutherford*, Engl. physicist d. 1937]

ruth•less /roothlis/ *adj.* having no pity nor compassion. □□ **ruth•less•ly** *adv.* **ruth•less•ness** *n.* [ME, f. *ruth* compassion f. RUE¹]

ru•tile /rooteel/ –tīl/ *n.* a mineral form of titanium dioxide. [F *rutile* or G *Rutil* f. L *rutilus* reddish]

RV *abbr.* **1** Revised Version (of the Bible). **2** recreational vehicle.

-ry /ree/ *suffix* = –ERY (*infantry; rivalry*). [shortened f. –ERY, or by analogy]

rye /rī/ *n.* **1 a** a cereal plant, *Secale cereale*, with spikes bearing florets that yield wheatlike grains. **b** the grain of this used for bread and fodder. **2** (in full **rye whiskey**) whiskey distilled from fermented rye. [OE *ryge* f. Gmc]

rye•grass /rígras/ *n.* any forage or lawn grass of the genus *Lolium*, esp. *L. perenne* or *L. multiflorum*. [obs. *ray grass*, of unkn. orig.]

ry•o•kan /reéōkaán/ *n.* a traditional Japanese inn. [Jap.]

ry•ot /ríot/ *n.* (in India) a peasant. [Urdu *ra'īyat* f. Arab. *ra'īya* flock, subjects f. *ra'ā* to pasture]

S

S[1] /es/ n. (also **s**) (pl. **Ss** or **S's** /ésiz/) **1** the nineteenth letter of the alphabet. **2** an S-shaped object or curve.

S[2] abbr. (also **S.**) **1** Saint. **2** siemens. **3** society. **4** south, southern.

S[3] symb. Chem. the element sulfur.

s. abbr. **1** second(s). **2** shilling(s). **3** singular. **4** son. **5** succeeded. [sense 2 orig. f. L solidus: see SOLIDUS]

-s' /s; z after a vowel sound or voiced consonant/ suffix denoting the possessive case of plural nouns and sometimes of singular nouns ending in s (the boys' shoes; Charles' book). [as –'s[1]]

's- /s, z/ prefix archaic (esp. in oaths) God's ('sblood; 'struth). [abbr.]

's /s; z after a vowel sound or voiced consonant/ abbr. **1** is; has (he's; it's; John's; Charles's). **2** us (let's). **3** colloq. does (what's he say?).

-s[1] /s;z after a vowel sound or voiced consonant, e.g., ways, bags/ suffix denoting the plurals of nouns (cf. –ES[1]). [OE –as pl. ending]

-s[2] /s;z after a vowel sound or voiced consonant, e.g., ties, begs/ suffix forming the 3rd person sing. present of verbs (cf. –ES[2]). [OE dial., prob. f. OE 2nd person sing. present ending –es, –as]

-s[3] /s;z after a vowel sound or voiced consonant, e.g., besides/ suffix **1** forming adverbs (afterwards; besides; mornings). **2** forming possessive pronouns (hers; ours). [formed as–'s[1]]

-s[4] /s;z after a vowel sound or voiced consonant/ suffix forming nicknames or pet names (Fats; Cutes). [after –s[1]]

-'s[1] /s;z after a vowel sound or voiced consonant/ suffix denoting the possessive case of singular nouns and of plural nouns not ending in –s (John's book; the book's cover; the children's shoes). [OE genit. sing. ending]

-'s[2] /s; z after a vowel sound or voiced consonantz/ suffix denoting the plural of a letter or symbol (S's; 8's). [as –s[1]]

SA abbr. **1** Salvation Army. **2** sex appeal. **3 a** South Africa. **b** south America. **c** South Australia. **4** hist. Sturmabteilung (the paramilitary force of the Nazi party).

sa·a·dil·la /sábədílə, –déeə/ n. **1** a Mexican plant, Schoenocaulon officinale, with seeds yielding veratrine. **2** a preparation of these seeds, used in medicine and agriculture. [Sp. cebadilla dimin. of cebada barley]

Sab·a·oth /sábay-oth, sábee–, səbáy-ōth/ n.pl. Bibl. heavenly hosts (see HOST[1] 3) (Lord of Sabaoth). [ME f. LL f. Gk Sabaōth f. Heb. ṣᵉbāōt̲ pl. of ṣābā host (of heaven)]

Sab·ba·tar·i·an /sábətáireeən/ n. & adj. ● n. **1** a strict Sabbath-keeping Jew. **2** a Christian who favors observing Sunday strictly as the Sabbath. **3** a Christian who observes Saturday as the Sabbath. ● adj. relating to or holding the tenets of Sabbatarians. □□ **Sab·ba·tar·i·an·ism** n. [LL sabbatarius f. L sabbatum: see SABBATH]

Sab·bath /sábəth/ n. **1** (in full **Sabbath day**) a day of rest and religious observance kept by Christians on Sunday, Jews on Saturday, and Muslims on Friday. **2** a period of rest. [OE sabat, L sabbatum, & OF sabbat, f. Gk sabbaton f. Heb. šabbāt f. šāḇaṯ to rest]

sab·bat·i·cal /səbátikəl/ adj. & n. ● adj. **1** of or appropriate to the Sabbath. **2** (of leave) granted at intervals to a university teacher for study or travel, orig. every seventh year. ● n. a period of sabbatical leave. □□ **sab·bat·i·cal·ly** adv. [LL sabbaticus f. Gk sabbatikos of the sabbath]

sab·bat·i·cal year n. **1** Bibl. every seventh year, prescribed by the Mosaic law to be observed as a "sabbath," during which the land was allowed to rest. **2** a year's sabbatical leave.

sa·ber /sáybər/ n. & v. (Brit. **sa·bre**) ● n. **1** a cavalry sword with a curved blade. **2** a cavalry soldier with horse. **3** a light fencing sword with a tapering blade. ● v.tr. cut down or wound with a saber. [F, earlier sable f. G Sabel, Säbel, Schabel f. Pol. szabla or Magyar szablya]

sa·ber rat·tling n. a display or threat of military force.

sa·ber-toothed adj. designating any of various extinct mammals having long, saber-shaped upper canines.

Sa·bi·an /sáybeeən/ adj. & n. ● adj. of a sect classed in the Koran with Muslims, Jews, and Christians, as believers in the true God. ● n. a member of this sect. [Arab. ṣābi']

Sa·bine /sáybīn/ adj. & n. ● adj. of or relating to a people of the central Apennines in ancient Italy. ● n. a member of this people. [L Sabinus]

Sa·bin vac·cine /sáybin/ n. an oral vaccine giving immunity against poliomyelitis. [A. B. Sabin, US virologist b. 1906]

saber

sa·ble[1] /sáybəl/ n. **1 a** a small, brown-furred, flesh-eating mammal, Martes zibellina, of N. Europe and parts of N. Asia, related to the marten. **b** its skin or fur. **2** a fine paintbrush made of sable fur. [ME f. OF f. med.L sabelum f. Slav.]

sa·ble[2] /sáybəl/ n. & adj. ● n. **1** esp. poet. black. **2** (in pl.) mourning garments. **3** (in full **sable antelope**) a large stout-horned African antelope, Hippotragus niger, the males of which are mostly black in old age. ● adj. **1** (usu. placed after noun) Heraldry black. **2** esp. poet. dark, gloomy. □□ **sa·bled** adj. **sa·bly** adv. [ME f. OF (in Heraldry): gen. taken to be identical with SABLE[1], although sable fur is dark brown]

sab·ot /sabó, sábō/ n. **1** a kind of simple shoe hollowed out from a block of wood. **2** a wooden-soled shoe. □□ **sa·boted** /sábōd/ adj. [F, blend of savate shoe + botte boot]

sab·o·tage /sábətaazh/ n. & v. ● n. deliberate damage to productive capacity, esp. as a political act. ● v.tr. **1** commit sabotage on. **2** destroy; spoil; make useless (sabotaged my plans). [F f. saboter make a noise with sabots, bungle, willfully destroy: see SABOT]

sab·o·teur /sábətör/ n. a person who commits sabotage. [F]

sa·bra /saábrə/ n. a Jew born in Israel. [mod. Heb. sābrāh opuntia fruit]

sa·bre Brit. var. of SABER.

SAC /sak/ abbr. Strategic Air Command.

Sac /sak, sawk/ n. SAUK.

sac /sak/ n. **1** a baglike cavity, enclosed by a membrane, in an animal or plant. **2** the distended membrane surrounding a hernia, cyst, tumor, etc. [F sac or L saccus SACK[1]]

sac·cade /sakaád/ n. a brief rapid movement of the eye between fixation points. □□ **sac·cad·ic** /səkaádik/ adj. [F, = violent pull, f. OF saquer, sachier pull]

sac·cate /sákayt/ adj. Bot. **1** dilated into a bag. **2** contained in a sac.

sac·cha·ride /sákərīd/ n. Chem. = SUGAR n. 2. [mod.L saccharum sugar + –IDE]

sac·cha·rim·e·ter /sákərímitər/ n. any instrument, esp. a polarimeter, for measuring the sugar content of a solution. [F saccharimètre (as SACCHARIDE)]

sac·cha·rin /sákərin/ n. a very sweet substance used as a nonfattening substitute for sugar. [G (as SACCHARIDE) + –IN]

sac·cha·rine /sákərin, –reen, –rīn/ adj. **1** sugary. **2** of, containing, or like sugar. **3** unpleasantly overpolite, sentimental, etc.

saccharo- /sákərō/ comb. form sugar; sugar and. [Gk sakkharon sugar]

sac·cha·ro·gen·ic /sákərōjénik/ adj. producing sugar.

sac·cha·rom·e·ter /sákərómitər/ n. any instrument, esp. a hydrometer, for measuring the sugar content of a solution.

sac·cha·rose /sákərōs/ n. sucrose. [mod.L saccharum sugar + –OSE[2]]

sac·ci·form /sáksifawrm/ adj. sac-shaped. [L saccus sac + –FORM]

sac·cule /sákyōol/ n. a small sac or cyst. □□ **sac·cu·lar** adj. [L sacculus (as SAC)]

sac·er·do·tal /sásərdótəl, sák–/ adj. **1** of priests or the priestly office; priestly. **2** (of a doctrine, etc.) ascribing sacrificial functions and supernatural powers to ordained priests; claiming excessive authority for the priesthood. □□ **sac·er·do·tal·ism** n. **sac·er·do·tal·ist** n. **sac·er·do·tal·ly** adv. [ME f. OF sacerdotal or L sacerdotalis f. sacerdos –dotis priest]

sa·chem /sáychəm/ n. **1** the supreme leader of some Native American tribes. **2** sl. a political leader. [Narragansett, = SAGAMORE]

sa·chet /sasháy/ n. **1** a small bag or packet containing a small portion of a substance, esp. shampoo. **2 a** small perfumed bag. **3 a** dry perfume for laying among clothes, etc. **b** a packet of this. [F, dimin. of sac f. L saccus]

sack[1] /sak/ n. & v. ● n. **1 a** a large, strong bag, usu. made of burlap, paper, or plastic, for storing or conveying goods. **b** (usu. foll. by of) this with its contents (a sack of potatoes). **c** a quantity contained in a sack. **2** (prec. by the) colloq. dismissal from employment. **3** (prec. by the) sl. bed. **4 a** a woman's short, loose dress with a sacklike appearance. **b** archaic or hist. a woman's loose gown, or a silk train attached to the shoulders of this. **5** a man's or woman's loose-hanging coat not shaped to the back. ● v.tr. **1** put into a sack or sacks. **2** colloq. dismiss from employment. □□ **sack·ful** n. (pl. **·fuls**).

sack·like adj. [OE sacc f. L saccus f. Gk sakkos, of Semitic orig.]

sack[2] /sak/ v. & n. ● v.tr. **1** plunder and destroy (a captured town, etc.). **2** steal valuables from (a place). ● n. the sacking of a captured place. [orig. as noun, f. F sac in phr. mettre à sac put to sack, f. It. sacco SACK[1]]

sack³ /sak/ *n. hist.* a white wine formerly imported into Britain from Spain and the Canary Islands (*sherry sack*). [16th-c. *wyne seck*, f. F *vin sec* dry wine]

sack•but /sákbut/ *n.* an early form of trombone. [F *saquebute*, earlier *saqueboute* hook for pulling a man off a horse f. *saquer* pull, *boute* (as BUTT¹)]

sack•cloth /sák-klawth, -kloth/ *n.* **1** a coarse fabric of flax or hemp. **2** clothing made of this, formerly worn as a penance or in mourning (esp. sackcloth and ashes).

sack•ing /sáking/ *n.* material for making sacks; sackcloth.

sack race *n.* a race between competitors in sacks up to the waist or neck.

sa•cra *pl.* of SACRUM.

sa•cral /sáykrəl, sá–/ *adj.* **1** *Anat.* of or relating to the sacrum. **2** *Anthropol.* of or for sacred rites. [E or L *sacrum:* see SACRUM]

sac•ra•ment /sákrəmənt/ *n.* **1** a religious ceremony or act of the Christian churches regarded as an outward and visible sign of inward and spiritual grace: applied by the Eastern, pre-Reformation Western, and Roman Catholic churches to the seven rites of baptism, confirmation, the Eucharist, penance, extreme unction, ordination, and matrimony, but restricted by most Protestants to baptism and the Eucharist. **2** a thing of mysterious and sacred significance; a sacred influence, symbol, etc. **3** (also **Blessed** or Holy Sacrament) (prec. by *the*) **a** the Eucharist. **b** the consecrated elements, esp. the bread or Host. **4** an oath or solemn engagement taken.

sac•ra•men•tal /sákrəmént'l/ *adj. & n.* ● *adj.* **1** of or of the nature of a sacrament or the sacraments. **2** (of a doctrine, etc.) attaching great importance to the sacraments. ● *n.* an observance analogous to but not reckoned among the sacraments, e.g., the use of holy water or the sign of the cross. □□ **sac•ra•men•tal•ism** *n.* **sac•ra•men•tal•ist** *n.* **sac•ra•men•tal•i•ty** /–tálitee/ *n.* **sac•ra•men•tal•ly** *adv.* [ME f. F *sacramental* or LL *sacramentalis* (as SACRAMENT)]

sa•crar•i•um /səkráireeəm/ *n.* (*pl.* **sa•crar•i•a** /–reeə/) **1** the sanctuary of a church. **2** *RC Ch.* a piscina. **3** *Rom. Antiq.* a shrine; the room (in a house) containing the penates. [L f. *sacer sacri* holy]

sa•cred /sáykrid/ *adj.* **1 a** (often foll. by *to*) exclusively dedicated or appropriated (to a god or to some religious purpose). **b** made holy by religious association. **c** connected with religion; used for a religious purpose (*sacred music*). **2 a** safeguarded or required by religion, reverence, or tradition. **b** sacrosanct. **3** (of writings, etc.) embodying the laws or doctrines of a religion. □□ **sa•cred•ly** *adv.* **sa•cred•ness** *n.* [ME, past part. of obs. *sacre* consecrate f. OF *sacrer* f. L *sacrare* f. *sacer, sacr–* holy]

Sa•cred Col•lege *n. RC Ch.* the body of cardinals.

sa•cred cow *n. colloq.* an idea or institution unreasonably held to be above criticism (with ref. to the Hindus' respect for the cow as a holy animal).

Sa•cred Heart *n. RC Ch.* the heart of Christ as an object of devotion.

sa•cred i•bis *n.* an ibis, *Threskiornis aethiopica*, native to Africa and Madagascar, venerated by the ancient Egyptians.

sa•cred num•ber *n.* a number associated with religious symbolism, e.g., 7.

sac•ri•fice /sákrifīs/ *n. & v.* ● *n.* **1 a** the act of giving up something valued for the sake of something else more important or worthy. **b** a thing given up in this way. **c** the loss entailed in this. **2 a** the slaughter of an animal or person or the surrender of a possession as an offering to a deity. **b** an animal, person, or thing offered in this way. **3** an act of prayer, thanksgiving, or penitence as propitiation. **4** *Theol.* **a** Christ's offering of himself in the Crucifixion. **b** the Eucharist as either a propitiatory offering of the body and blood of Christ or an act of thanksgiving. **5** (in games) a loss incurred deliberately to avoid a greater loss or to obtain a compensating advantage. ● *v.* **1** *tr.* give up (a thing) as a sacrifice. **2** *tr.* (foll. by *to*) devote or give over to. **3** *tr.* (also *absol.*) kill or kill as a sacrifice. □□ **sac•ri•fi•cial** /–físhəl/ *adj.* **sac•ri•fi•cial•ly** /–físhəlee/ *adv.* [ME f. OF f. L *sacrificium* f. *sacrificus* (as SACRED)]

sac•ri•lege /sákrilij/ *n.* the violation or misuse of what is regarded as sacred. □□ **sac•ri•le•gious** /–líjəs/ *adj.* **sac•ri•le•gious•ly** *adv.* [ME f. OF f. L *sacrilegium* f. *sacrilegus* stealer of sacred things, f. *sacer sacri* sacred + *legere* take possession of]

sac•ris•tan /sákristən/ *n.* **1** a person in charge of a sacristy and its contents. **2** *archaic* the sexton of a parish church. [ME f. med.L *sacristanus* (as SACRED)]

sac•ris•ty /sákristee/ *n.* (*pl.* **•ties**) a room in a church where the vestments, sacred vessels, etc., are kept and the celebrant can prepare for a service. [F *sacristie* or It. *sacrestia* or med.L *sacristia* (as SACRED)]

sacro- /sákrō, sáy–/ *comb. form* denoting the sacrum (*sacroiliac*).

sac•ro•il•i•ac /sákrōíleeak, sákrō–/ *adj. & n.* ● *adj.* of or relating to the juncture of the sacrum and the ilium bones of the pelvis ● *n.* the sacroiliac region.

sac•ro•sanct /sákrōsangkt/ *adj.* (of a person, place, law, etc.) most sacred; inviolable. □□ **sac•ro•sanc•ti•ty** /–sángktitee/ *n.* [L *sacrosanctus* f. *sacro* ablat. of *sacrum* sacred rite (see SACRED) + *sanctus* (as SAINT)]

sac•rum /sáykrəm, sák–/ *n.* (*pl.* **sac•ra** /–krə/ or **sac•rums**) *Anat.* a triangular bone formed from fused vertebrae and situated between the two hipbones of the pelvis. [L *os sacrum* transl. Gk *hieron osteon* sacred bone (from its sacrificial use)]

SAD *abbr.* seasonal affective disorder.

sad /sad/ *adj.* (**sad•der**, **sad•dest**) **1** unhappy; feeling sorrow or regret. **2** causing or suggesting sorrow (*a sad story*). **3** regrettable. **4** shameful; deplorable (*is in a sad state*). **5** (of a color) dull; neutral-tinted. **6** (of dough, etc.) *Brit.* heavy, having failed to rise. □□ **sad•ly** *adv.* **sad•ness** *n.*

sad•den /sád'n/ *v.tr. & intr.* make or become sad.

sad•dle /sád'l/ *n. & v.* ● *n.* **1** a seat of leather, etc., usu. raised at the front and rear, fastened on a horse, etc., for riding. **2** a seat for the rider of a bicycle, etc. **3** a cut of meat consisting of the two loins. **4** a ridge rising to a summit at each end. **5** the part of a draft horse's harness to which the shafts are attached. **6** a part of an animal's back resembling a saddle in shape or marking. **7** the rear part of a male fowl's back. **8** a support for a cable or wire on top of a suspension bridge, pier, or telegraph pole. **9** a fireclay bar for supporting ceramic ware in a kiln. ● *v.tr.* **1** put a saddle on (a horse, etc.). **2 a** (foll. by *with*) burden (a person) with a task, responsibility, etc. **b** (foll. by *on, upon*) impose (a burden) on a person. □ **in the saddle 1** mounted. **2** in office or control. □□ **sad•dle•less** *adj.* [OE *sadol, sadul* f. Gmc]

saddle 1

sad•dle•back /sád'lbak/ *n.* **1** *Archit.* a tower-roof with two opposite gables. **2** a hill with a concave upper outline. **3** a black pig with a white stripe across the back. **4** any of various birds with a saddle-like marking esp. a New Zealand bird, *Philesturnus carunculatus.* □□ **sad•dle•backed** *adj.*

sad•dle•bag /sád'lbag/ *n.* **1** each of a pair of bags laid across a horse, etc., behind the saddle. **2** a bag attached behind the saddle of a bicycle or motorcycle.

sad•dle•bow /sád'lbō/ *n.* the arched front or rear of a saddle.

sad•dle•cloth /sád'lklawth/ *n.* a cloth laid on a horse's back under the saddle.

sad•dle horse *n.* a horse for riding.

sad•dler /sádlər/ *n.* a maker of or dealer in saddles and other equipment for horses.

sad•dler•y /sádləree/ *n.* (*pl.* **•ies**) **1** the saddles and other equipment of a saddler. **2** a saddler's business or premises.

sad•dle shoes *n.pl.* laced shoes with yokes that contrast in color with the rest of the upper.

sad•dle sore *n. & adj.* ● *n.* **1** a chafe from riding on a saddle. **2** a sore on a horse from the chafing of a saddle. ● *adj.* (**saddle-sore**) chafed from riding on a saddle.

sad•dle stitch *n.* a stitch of thread or a wire staple passed through the center of a magazine or booklet.

sad•dle•tree /sád'ltree/ *n.* the frame of a saddle.

Sad•du•cee /sájəsee, sádyə–/ *n.* a member of a Jewish sect or party of the time of Christ that denied the resurrection of the dead, the existence of spirits, and the obligation of the traditional oral law (cf. PHARISEE, ESSENE). □□ **Sad•du•ce•an** /–seéən/ *adj.* [OE *sadducēas* f. LL *Sadducaeus* f. Gk *Saddoukaios* f. Heb. *ṣ°dûḳî*, prob. = descendant of Zadok (2 Sam. 8:17)]

sa•dhu /saádoo/ *n.* (in India) a holy man, sage, or ascetic. [Skr., = holy man]

sa•dism /sáydizəm, sád–/ *n.* **1** a form of sexual perversion characterized by the enjoyment of inflicting pain or suffering on others (cf. MASOCHISM). **2** *colloq.* the enjoyment of cruelty to others. □□ **sa-**

dist *n.* **sa·dis·tic** /sədístik/ *adj.* **sa·dis·ti·cal·ly** *adv.* [F *sadisme* f. Count or Marquis de *Sade*, Fr. writer d. 1814]

sa·do·mas·o·chism /sáydōmásəkizəm, sádō–/ *n.* the combination of sadism and masochism in one person. □□ **sa·do·mas·o·chist** *n.* **sa·do·mas·o·chis·tic** /–kístik/ *adj.*

sad sack *n. colloq.* a very inept person, esp. a soldier.

sa·fa·ri /səfáaree/ *n.* (*pl.* **sa·fa·ris**) **1** a hunting or scientific expedition, esp. in E. Africa (*go on safari*). **2** a sightseeing trip to see African animals in their natural habitat. [Swahili f. Arab. *safara* travel]

sa·fa·ri park *n.* an enclosed area where lions, etc., are kept in the open and through which visitors may drive.

sa·fa·ri suit *n.* a lightweight suit usu. with short sleeves and four pleated pockets in the jacket.

safe /sayf/ *adj. & n.* ● *adj.* **1 a** free of danger or injury. **b** (often foll. by *from*) out of or not exposed to danger (*safe from their enemies*). **2** affording security or not involving danger or risk (*put it in a safe place*). **3** reliable; certain; that can be counted on (*a safe catch; a safe method; is safe to win*). **4** prevented from escaping or doing harm (*have got him safe behind bars*). **5** (also **safe and sound**) uninjured; with no harm done. **6** cautious and unenterprising; consistently moderate. ● *n.* a strong, lockable cabinet, etc., for valuables. □ **on the safe side** with a margin of security against risks. □□ **safe·ly** *adv.* **safe·ness** *n.* [ME f. AF *saf*, OF *sauf* f. L *salvus* uninjured: (n.) orig. *save* f. SAVE¹]

safe bet *n.* a bet that is certain to succeed.

safe-con·duct *n.* **1** a privilege of immunity from arrest or harm, esp. on a particular occasion. **2** a document securing this.

safe·crack·er /sáyfkrakər/ *n.* a person who breaks open and robs safes.

safe-de·pos·it box *n.* a secured box (esp. in a bank vault) for storing valuables.

safe·guard /sáyfgaard/ *n. & v.* ● *n.* **1** a proviso, stipulation, quality, or circumstance that tends to prevent something undesirable. **2** a safe conduct. ● *v.tr.* guard or protect (rights, etc.) by a precaution or stipulation. [ME f. AF *salve garde*, OF *sauve garde* (as SAFE, GUARD)]

safe house *n.* a place of refuge or rendezvous for spies, etc.

safe·keep·ing /sáyfkeeping/ *n.* preservation in a safe place.

safe·light /sáyflīt/ *n. Photog.* a filtered light for use in a darkroom.

safe pe·ri·od *n.* the time during and near the menstrual period when conception is least likely.

safe sex *n.* sexual activity in which precautions are taken to reduce the risk of spreading sexually transmitted diseases, esp. AIDS.

safe·ty /sáyftee/ *n.* (*pl.* **·ties**) **1** the condition of being safe; freedom from danger or risks. **2** (*attrib.*) **a** designating any of various devices for preventing injury from machinery (*safety bar, safety lock*). **b** designating items of protective clothing (*safety helmet*). [ME *sauvete* f. OF *sauveté* f. med.L *salvitas –tatis* f. L *salvus* (as SAFE)]

safe·ty belt *n.* **1** = SEAT BELT. **2** any belt or strap securing a person to prevent injury.

safe·ty catch *n.* a contrivance for locking a gun trigger or preventing the accidental operation of machinery.

safe·ty cur·tain *n.* a fireproof curtain that can be lowered to cut off the auditorium in a theater from the stage.

safe·ty-de·pos·it box *n.* = SAFE-DEPOSIT BOX.

safe·ty fac·tor *n.* (also **fac·tor of safe·ty**) **1** the ratio of a material's strength to an expected strain. **2** a margin of security against risks.

safe·ty film *n.* a cinematographic film on a slow-burning or nonflammable base.

safe·ty first *n.* a motto advising caution.

safe·ty fuse *n.* **1** a fuse (see FUSE²) containing a slow-burning composition for firing detonators from a distance. **2** *Electr.* a protective fuse (see FUSE¹).

safe·ty glass *n.* glass that will not splinter when broken.

safe·ty lamp *n.* a miner's lamp so protected as not to ignite firedamp.

safe·ty match *n.* a match igniting only on a specially prepared surface.

safe·ty net *n.* **1** a net placed to catch an acrobat, etc., in case of a fall. **2** a provision of security, etc.

safe·ty pin *n.* a pin with a point that is bent back to the head and is held in a guard when closed.

safe·ty ra·zor *n.* a razor with a guard to reduce the risk of cutting the skin.

safe·ty valve *n.* **1** (in a steam boiler) a valve opening automatically to relieve excessive pressure. **2** a means of giving harmless vent to excitement, etc.

saf·flow·er /sáflowr/ *n.* **1 a** a thistlelike plant, *Carthamus tinctorius*, yielding a red dye. **b** its dried petals. **2** a dye made from these, used in rouge, etc. [Du. *saffloer* or G *Safflor* f. OF *saffleur* f. obs. It. *saffiore*, of unkn. orig.]

saf·flow·er oil *n.* oil expressed from safflower seeds, used for food, paints, medicines, etc.

saf·fron /sáfrən/ *n. & adj.* ● *n.* **1** a bright yellow-orange food coloring and flavoring made from the dried stigmas of the crocus, *Cro-*

cus sativus. **2** the color of this. ● *adj.* saffron-colored. □□ **saf·fron·y** *adj.* [ME f. OF *safran* f. Arab. *za'farān*]

saf·ra·nine /sáfrəneen, –nin/ *n.* (also **saf·ra·nin** /–nin/) any of a large group of mainly red dyes used in biological staining, etc. [F *safranine* (as SAFFRON): orig. of dye from saffron]

sag /sag/ *v. & n.* ● *v.intr.* (**sagged, sag·ging**) **1** sink or subside under weight or pressure, esp. unevenly. **2** have a downward bulge or curve in the middle. **3 a** fall in price. **b** (of a price) fall. **4** (of a ship) drift from its course, esp. to leeward. ● *n.* **1 a** the amount that a rope, etc., sags. **b** the distance from the middle of such a curve to a straight line between the supports. **2** a sinking condition; subsidence. **3** a fall in price. **4** *Naut.* a tendency to leeward. □□ **sag·gy** *adj.* [ME f. MLG *sacken*, Du. *zakken* subside]

sa·ga /sáagə/ *n.* **1** a long story of heroic achievement, esp. a medieval Icelandic or Norwegian prose narrative. **2** a series of connected books giving the history of a family, etc. **3** a long, involved story. [ON, = narrative, rel. to SAW³]

sa·ga·cious /səgáyshəs/ *adj.* **1** mentally penetrating; gifted with discernment; having practical wisdom. **2** acute-minded; shrewd. **3** (of a saying, plan, etc.) showing wisdom. **4** (of an animal) exceptionally intelligent; seeming to reason or deliberate. □□ **sa·ga·cious·ly** *adv.* **sa·gac·i·ty** /səgásitee/ *n.* [L *sagax sagacis*]

sag·a·more /ságəmawr/ *n.* = SACHEM 1. [Penobscot *sagamo*]

sage¹ /sayj/ *n.* **1** an aromatic herb, *Salvia officinalis*, with dull grayish-green leaves. **2** its leaves used in cookery. **3** any plant of the genus *Salvia*. □□ **sag·y** *adj.* [ME f. OF *sauge* f. L *salvia* healing plant f. *salvus* safe]

sage² /sayj/ *n. & adj.* ● *n.* **1** often *iron.* a profoundly wise person. **2** any of the ancients traditionally regarded as the wisest of their time. ● *adj.* **1** profoundly wise, esp. from experience. **2** of or indicating profound wisdom. **3** often *iron.* wise-looking; solemn-faced. □□ **sage·ly** *adv.* **sage·ness** *n.* **sage·ship** *n.* [ME f. OF ult. f. L *sapere* be wise]

sage·brush /sáyjbrush/ *n.* **1** a growth of shrubby aromatic plants of the genus *Artemisia*, esp. *A. tridentata*, found in some semiarid regions of western N. America. **2** this plant.

sage green *n.* the color of sage leaves.

sag·ger /ságər/ *n.* (also **sag·gar**) a protective fireclay box enclosing ceramic ware while it is being fired. [prob. contr. of SAFEGUARD]

sag·it·tal /sájit'l/ *adj. Anat.* **1** of or relating to the suture between the parietal bones of the skull. **2** in the same plane as this, or in a parallel plane. [F f. med.L *sagittalis* f. *sagitta* arrow]

Sag·it·tar·i·us /sájitáireeəs/ *n.* **1** a constellation, traditionally regarded as contained in the figure of an archer. **2 a** the ninth sign of the zodiac (the Archer). **b** a person born when the sun is in this sign. □□ **Sag·it·tar·i·an** *adj. & n.* [ME f. L, = archer, f. *sagitta* arrow]

sag·it·tate /sájitayt/ *adj. Bot. & Zool.* shaped like an arrowhead.

sa·go /sáygō/ *n.* (*pl.* **·gos**) **1** a kind of starch, made from the powdered pith of the sago palm and used in puddings, etc. **2** (in full **sago palm**) any of several tropical palms and cycads, esp. *Cycas circinalis* and *Metroxylon sagu*, from which sago is made. [Malay *sāgū* (orig. through Port.)]

sa·gua·ro /səgwáarō, səwáarō/ *n.* (*pl.* **·ros**) a giant cactus, *Carnegiea gigantea*, of the SW United States and Mexico. [Mex. Sp.]

sa·hib /saab, saáhib/ *n.* **1** *hist.* (in India) a form of address, often placed after the name, to European men. **2** *colloq.* a gentleman (*pukka sahib*). [Urdu f. Arab. *ṣāḥib* friend, lord]

said *past* and *past part.* of SAY.

▶In colloquial American English there is a tendency to use *go* or *goes*, or *like*, as a quotation marker in place of *said* ("*So he goes, 'Well, what time do you want to leave?' and I'm like, 'How about noon?'*"). Avoid this highly informal practice in writing.

sai·ga /sígə, sáy–/ *n.* an antelope, *Saiga tatarica*, of the Asian steppes. [Russ.]

sail /sayl/ *n. & v.* ● *n.* **1** a piece of material (orig. canvas, now usu. nylon, etc.) extended on rigging to catch the wind and propel a boat or ship. **2** a ship's sails collectively. **3 a** a voyage or excursion on a sailing ship. **b** a voyage of specified duration. **4** a ship, esp. as discerned from its sails. **5** (*collect.*) ships in a squadron or company (*a fleet of twenty sail*). **6** (in *pl.*) *Naut.* esp. *Brit.* **a** *sl.* a maker or repairer of sails. **b** *hist.* a chief petty officer in charge of rigging. **7** a wind-catching apparatus, usu. a set of boards, attached to the arm of a windmill. **8 a** the dorsal fin of a sailfish. **b** the tentacle of a nautilus. **c** the float of a Portuguese man-of-war. ● *v.* **1** *intr.* travel on water by the use of sails or engine power. **2** *tr.* a navigate (a ship, etc.). **b** travel on (a sea). **3** *tr.* set (a toy boat) afloat. **4** *intr.* glide or move smoothly or in a

saguaro cactus

See page xx for the **Key to Pronunciation**.

stately manner. **5** *intr.* (often foll. by *through*) *colloq.* succeed easily (*sailed through the exams*). □ **sail close to** (or **near**) **the wind 1** sail as nearly against the wind as possible. **2** *colloq.* come close to indecency or dishonesty; risk overstepping the mark. **sail into** *colloq.* attack physically or verbally with force. **take in sail** (or **the sails**) **1** furl the sail or sails of a vessel. **2** esp. *Brit.* moderate one's ambitions. **trim sails** cut expenses, etc. **under sail** with sails set. □□ **sail•a•ble** *adj.* **sailed** *adj.* (also in *comb.*). **sail•less** *adj.* [OE *segel* f. Gmc]

sail arm *n.* the arm of a windmill.

sail•board /sáylbawrd/ *n.* a board with a mast and sail, used in windsurfing. □□ **sail•board•er** *n.* **sail•board•ing** *n.*

sail•boat /sáylbōt/ *n.* a boat driven by sails.

sail•cloth /sáylklawth, –klŏth/ *n.* **1** canvas for sails, upholstery, tents, etc. **2** a canvaslike dress material.

sail•er /sáylər/ *n.* a ship of specified sailing power (*a good sailer*).

sail•fish /sáylfish/ *n.* **1** any fish of the genus *Istiophorus*, with a large dorsal fin. **2** a basking shark.

sail•ing boat *n. Brit.* = SAILBOAT.

sail•ing or•ders *n.pl.* instructions to a captain regarding departure, destination, etc.

sail•or /sáylər/ *n.* **1** a seaman or mariner, esp. one below the rank of officer. **2** a person considered as liable or not liable to seasickness (*a good sailor*). □□ **sail•or•ing** *n.* **sail•or•less** *adj.* **sail•or•ly** *adj.* [var. of SAILER]

sail•or hat *n.* **1** a straw hat with a straight narrow brim and flat top. **2** a hat with a turned-up brim in imitation of a sailor's.

sail•plane /sáylplayn/ *n.* a glider designed for sustained flight.

sain•foin /sáynfoyn, sán–/ *n.* a leguminous plant, *Onobrychis viciifolia*, grown for fodder and having pink flowers. [obs. F *saintfoin* f. mod.L *sanum foenum* wholesome hay (because of its medicinal properties)]

saint /saynt/ *n. & v.* • *n.* (abbr. **St.** or **S.**; *pl.* **Sts.** or **SS.**) **1** a holy or (in some churches) a canonized person regarded as having a place in heaven. **2** (**Saint** or **St.**) the title of a saint or archangel, hence the name of a church, etc. (*St. Paul's*) or (often with the loss of the apostrophe) the name of a town, etc. (*St. Andrews*). **3** a very virtuous person; a person of great real or affected holiness (*would try the patience of a saint*). **4** a member of the company of heaven (*with all the angels and saints*). **5** (*Bibl.*, *archaic*, and used by Puritans, Mormons, etc.) one of God's chosen people; a member of the Christian Church or one's own branch of it. • *v.tr.* **1** canonize; admit to the calendar of saints. **2** call or regard as a saint. **3** (as **saint•ed** *adj.*) sacred; of a saintly life; worthy to be regarded as a saint. □□ **saint•dom** *n.* **saint•hood** *n.* **saint•like** *adj.* **saint•ship** *n.* [ME f. OF *seint*, *saint* f. L *sanctus* holy, past part. of *sancire* consecrate]

St. An•drew's cross /ándrōōz/ *n.* an X-shaped cross.

St. An•tho•ny cross /ánthənee/ *n.* (also **St. An•tho•ny's cross** /ánthəneez/) a T-shaped cross.

St. An•tho•ny's fire /ánthənee/ *n.* erysipelas or ergotism.

St. Ber•nard /bərnaárd/ *n.* (in full **St. Bernard dog**) **1** a very large dog of a breed orig. kept to rescue travelers by the monks of the Hospice on the Great St. Bernard pass in the Alps. **2** this breed.

St. Bernard

St. El•mo's fire /élmōz/ *n.* a luminous electrical discharge sometimes seen on a ship or aircraft during a storm.

St. George's cross /jáwrjiz/ *n.* a +-shaped cross, red on a white background.

St. John's-wort /jónzwərt/ *n.* any yellow-flowered plant of the genus *Hypericum*, esp. *H. androsaemum*.

St. Luke's sum•mer /lōōks/ *n. Brit.* a period of fine weather expected about Oct. 18.

saint•ly /sáyntlee/ *adj.* (**saint•li•er**, **saint•li•est**) very holy or virtuous. □□ **saint•li•ness** *n.*

St. Mar•tin's sum•mer /maárt'nz/ *n. Brit.* a period of fine weather expected about Nov. 11.

saint•pau•lia /səntpáwleeə/ *n.* any plant of the genus *Saintpaulia*, esp. the African violet. [Baron W. von *Saint Paul*, Ger. soldier d. 1910, its discoverer]

saint's day *n.* a church festival in memory of a saint.

St. Vi•tus's dance /vítəsiz, vítəs/ *n.* = SYDENHAM'S CHOREA.

saith /seth, sáyith/ *archaic 3rd sing. present* of SAY.

saithe /sayth/ *n. Sc.* a codlike fish, *Pollachius virens*, with skin that soils fingers like wet coal. Also called **coalfish**, **coley**, and **pollock**. [ON *seithr*]

sake[1] /sayk/ *n.* □ **for Christ's** (or **God's** or **goodness'** or **Heaven's** or **Pete's**, etc.) **sake** an expression of urgency, impatience, supplication, anger, etc. **for old times' sake** in memory of former times. **for the sake of** (or **for a person's sake**) **1** out of consideration for; in the interest of; because of; owing to (*for my own sake as well as yours*). **2** in order to please, honor, get, or keep (*for the sake of uniformity*). [OE *sacu* contention, charge, fault, sake f. Gmc]

sake[2] /sáakee, –ke/ *n.* a Japanese alcoholic drink made from rice. [Jap.]

sa•ker /sáykər/ *n.* **1** a large falcon, *Falco cherrug*, used in falconry, esp. the larger female bird. **2** *hist.* an old form of cannon. [ME f. OF *sacre* (in both senses), f. Arab. *ṣakr*]

sa•ki /sáakee/ *n.* (*pl.* **sa•kis**) any monkey of the genus *Pithecia* or *Chiropotes*, native to S. America, having coarse fur and a long nonprehensile tail. [F f. Tupi *çahy*]

Sak•ta var. of SHAKTA.

Sak•ti var. of SHAKTI.

sal /sál/ *n. Pharm.* salt.

sa•laam /səláam/ *n. & v.* • *n.* **1** the esp. Islamic salutation denoting 'peace.' **2** (in India) an obeisance, with or without the salutation, consisting of a low bow of the head and body with the right palm on the forehead. **3** (in *pl.*) respectful compliments. • *v.* **1** *tr.* make a salaam to (a person). **2** *intr.* make a salaam. [Arab. *salām*]

sal•a•ble /sáyləbəl/ *adj.* (also **sale•a•ble**) fit to be sold; finding purchasers. □□ **sal•a•bil•i•ty** /–bílitee/ *n.*

sa•la•cious /səláyshəs/ *adj.* **1** lustful; lecherous. **2** (of writings, pictures, talk, etc.) tending to cause sexual desire. □□ **sa•la•cious•ly** *adv.* **sa•la•cious•ness** *n.* **sa•lac•i•ty** /səlásitee/ *n.* [L *salax salacis* f. *salire* leap]

sal•ad /sáləd/ *n.* **1** a cold dish of various mixtures of raw or cooked vegetables or herbs, usu. seasoned with oil, vinegar, etc. **2** a vegetable or herb suitable for eating raw. [ME f. OF *salade* f. Prov. *salada* ult. f. L *sal* salt]

sal•ad cream *n. Brit.* creamy salad dressing.

sal•ad days *n.pl.* a period of youthful inexperience.

sal•ad dress•ing *n.* a mixture of oil, vinegar, etc., used in a salad.

sa•lade var. of SALLET.

sal•a•man•der /sáləmandər/ *n.* **1** *Zool.* any tailed newtlike amphibian of the order Urodela, esp. the genus *Salamandra*, once thought able to endure fire. **2** a mythical lizardlike creature credited with this property. **3** a portable cooking device, esp. one with burners. **4** an elemental spirit living in fire. **5** a red-hot iron used for lighting pipes, gunpowder, etc. **6** a metal plate heated and placed over food to brown it. □□ **sal•a•man•drian** /–mándreeən/ *adj.* **sal•a•man•drine** /–mándrin/ *adj.* **sal•a•man•droid** /–mándroyd/ *adj. & n.* (in sense 1). [ME f. OF *salamandre* f. L *salamandra* f. Gk *salamandra*]

sa•la•mi /səláamee/ *n.* (*pl.* **sa•la•mis**) a highly seasoned orig. Italian sausage often flavored with garlic. [It., *pl.* of *salame*, f. LL *salare* (unrecorded) to salt]

sal am•mo•ni•ac /sál əmóneeak/ *n.* ammonium chloride, a white crystalline salt. [L *sal ammoniacus* 'salt of Ammon,' associated with the Roman temple of Ammon in N. Africa]

sa•lar•i•at /səláireeət/ *n.* the salaried class. [F f. *salaire* (see SALARY), after *prolétariat*]

sal•a•ry /sáləree/ *n. & v.* • *n.* (*pl.* **•ries**) a fixed regular payment, usu. monthly or quarterly, made by an employer to an employee, esp. a professional or white-collar worker (cf. WAGE *n.* 1). • *v.tr.* (**•ries**, **•ried**) (usu. as **salaried** *adj.*) pay a salary to. [ME f. AF *salarie*, OF *salaire* f. L *salarium* orig. soldier's salt-money f. *sal* salt]

sale /sayl/ *n.* **1** the exchange of a commodity for money, etc.; an act or instance of selling. **2** the amount sold (*the sales were enormous*). **3** the rapid disposal of goods at reduced prices for a period, esp. at the end of a season, etc. **4 a** an event at which goods are sold. **b** a public auction. □ **for** (or **up for**) **sale** offered for purchase. **on sale** available for purchase, esp. at a reduced price. [OE *sala* f. ON]

sale•a•ble var. of SALABLE.

sal•ep /sáləp/ *n.* a starchy preparation of the dried tubers of various orchids, used in cookery and formerly medicinally. [F f. Turk. *sālep* f. Arab. (*kuṣa-'l-*) *ta'lab* fox, fox's testicles]

sal•e•ra•tus /sáləráytəs/ *n.* an ingredient of baking powder consisting mainly of potassium or sodium bicarbonate; baking soda. [mod.L *sal aeratus* aerated salt]

sale•room /sáylrōōm, –rŏŏm/ *n.* esp. *Brit.* a salesroom.

sales•clerk /sáylzklərk/ *n.* a salesperson in a retail store.

sales de•part•ment *n.* the section of a firm concerned with selling as opposed to manufacturing or dispatching goods.

sales•girl /sáylzgərl/ *n.* a saleswoman.

Sa•le•sian /səléezhən, –shən/ *n. & adj.* • *n.* a member of an educational religious order within the RC Church. • *adj.* of or relating to this order. [St. François de *Sales*, Fr. RC bishop d. 1622]

sales•la•dy /sáylzlaydee/ *n.* (*pl.* **•dies**) a saleswoman.

sales·man /sáylzmən/ n. (pl. **·men**; fem. **sales·wom·an**, pl. **·wom·en**) a person employed to sell goods or services in a store or on a route, etc., or as an agent between the producer and retailer.

sales·man·ship /sáylzmənship/ n. 1 skill in selling. 2 the techniques used in selling.

sales·per·son /sáylzpersən/ n. a salesman or saleswoman (used as a neutral alternative).

sales·room /sáylzroom, –room/ n. a room for the display and purchase of items, esp. at an auction.

sales talk n. persuasive talk to promote the sale of goods or the acceptance of an idea, etc.

sales tax n. a tax on sales or on the receipts from sales.

Sa·li·an /sáyleeən, –yən/ adj. & n. • adj. of or relating to the Salii, a 4th-c. Frankish people living near the Ijssel River, from which the Merovingians were descended. • n. a member of this people. [LL Salii]

Sal·ic /sálik, sáy–/ adj. = SALIAN. [F Salique or med.L Salicus f. Salii (as SALIAN)]

sal·i·cet /sálisit/ n. an organ stop like a salicional but one octave higher. [as SALICIONAL]

sal·i·cin /sálisin/ n. (also **sal·i·cine** /–seen/) a bitter crystalline glucoside with analgesic properties, obtained from poplar and willow bark. [F salicine f. L salix –icis willow]

sa·li·cion·al /səlíshənəl/ n. an organ stop with a soft reedy tone like that of a willow pipe. [G f. L salix as SALICIN]

Sal·ic law n. hist. 1 a law excluding females from dynastic succession, esp. as the alleged fundamental law of the French monarchy. 2 a Frankish law book extant in Merovingian and Carolingian times.

sal·i·cyl·ic ac·id /sálisílik/ n. a bitter chemical used as a fungicide and in the manufacture of aspirin and dyestuffs. □□ **sa·lic·y·late** /səlísilayt/ n. [salicyl its radical f. F salicyle (as SALICIN)]

sa·li·ent /sáylyənt/ adj. & n. • adj. 1 jutting out; prominent; conspicuous; most noticeable. 2 (of an angle, esp. in fortification) pointing outward (opp. REENTRANT). 3 Heraldry (of a lion, etc.) standing on its hind legs with the forepaws raised. 4 archaic a leaping or dancing. b (of water, etc.) jetting forth. • n. a salient angle or part of a work in fortification; an outward bulge in a line of military attack or defense. □□ **sa·li·ence** n. **sa·li·en·cy** n. **sa·li·ent·ly** adv. [L salire leap]

sa·li·en·tian /sáylee–énshən/ adj. & n. = ANURAN. [mod.L Salientia (as SALIENT)]

sa·li·ent point n. archaic the initial stage, origin, or first beginning.

sa·lif·er·ous /səlífərəs/ adj. Geol. (of rock, etc.) containing much salt. [L sal salt + –FEROUS]

sa·li·na /səlínə, –lee–/ n. a salt lake. [Sp. f. med.L, = salt pit (as SALINE)]

sa·line /sáyleen, –līn/ adj. & n. • adj. 1 (of natural waters, springs, etc.) impregnated with or containing salt or salts. 2 (of food or drink, etc.) tasting of salt. 3 of chemical salts. 4 of the nature of a salt. 5 (of medicine) containing a salt or salts of alkaline metals or magnesium. • n. 1 a salt lake, spring, marsh, etc. a salt pan or saltworks. 3 a saline substance, esp. a medicine. 4 a solution of salt in water. □□ **sa·lin·i·ty** /səlínitee/ n. **sal·i·ni·za·tion** /sálinizáyshən/ n. **sal·i·nom·e·ter** /sálinómitər/ n. [ME f. L sal salt]

sa·li·va /səlívə/ n. liquid secreted into the mouth by glands to provide moisture and facilitate chewing and swallowing. □□ **sal·i·var·y** /sáliveree/ adj. [ME f. L]

sal·i·vate /sálivayt/ v. 1 intr. secrete or discharge saliva esp. in excess or in greedy anticipation. 2 tr. produce an unusual secretion of saliva in (a person) usu. with mercury. □□ **sal·i·va·tion** /–váyshən/ n. [L salivare (as SALIVA)]

sa·li·va test n. a scientific test requiring a saliva sample.

Salk vac·cine /sawlk/ n. a vaccine developed against polio. [J. E. Salk, Amer. scientist b. 1914]

sal·let /sálit/ n. (also **sa·lade** /səláad/) hist. a light helmet with an outward-curving rear part. [F salade ult. f. L caelare engrave f. caelum chisel]

sal·low[1] /sáló/ adj. & v. • adj. (**sal·low·er**, **sal·low·est**) (of the skin or complexion, or of a person) of a sickly yellow or pale brown. • v.tr. & intr. make or become sallow. □□ **sal·low·ish** adj. **sal·low·ness** n. [OE salo dusky f. Gmc]

sal·low[2] /sáló/ n. Brit. 1 a willow tree, esp. one of a low-growing or shrubby kind. 2 the wood or a shoot of this. □□ **sal·low·y** adj. [OE salh salg– f. Gmc, rel. to OHG salaha, ON selja, L salix]

sal·ly[1] /sálee/ n. & v. (pl. **·lies**) • n. 1 a sudden charge from a fortification upon its besiegers; a sortie. 2 a going forth; an excursion. 3 a witticism; a piece of banter; a lively remark, esp. by way of attack upon a person or thing or of a diversion in argument. 4 a sudden start into activity; an outburst. 5 archaic an escapade. • v.intr. (**·lies**, **·lied**) 1 (usu. foll. by out, forth) go for a walk, set out on a journey, etc. 2 (usu. foll. by out) make a military sally. 3 archaic issue or come out suddenly. [F saillie fem. past part. of saillir issue f. OF salir f. L salire leap]

sal·ly[2] /sálee/ n. Brit. (pl. **·lies**) 1 the part of a bell rope prepared with inwoven wool for holding. 2 a the first movement of a bell when set for ringing. b the bell's position when set. [perh. f. SALLY[1] in sense 'leaping motion']

sal·ly hole n. the hole through which the bell rope passes.

Sal·ly Lunn /sálee lún/ n. a sweet, light teacake, usu. served hot. [perh. f. the name of a woman selling them at Bath c.1800]

sal·ly port n. an opening in a fortification for making a sally from.

sal·ma·gun·di /sálməgúndee/ n. (pl. **sal·ma·gun·dis**) 1 a dish of chopped meat, anchovies, eggs, onions, etc., and seasoning, usu. served as a salad. 2 a general mixture; a miscellaneous collection of articles, subjects, qualities, etc. [F salmigondis of unkn. orig.]

Sal·ma·naz·ar /sálmənázər/ n. a wine bottle of about 12 times the standard size. [Shalmaneser king of Assyria (2 Kings 17-18)]

sal·mi /sálmee/ n. (pl. **sal·mis**) a ragout or casserole esp. of partly roasted gamebirds. [F, abbr. formed as SALMAGUNDI]

salm·on /sámən/ n. & adj. • n. (pl. same or (esp. of types) **salm·ons**) 1 any anadromous fish of the family Salmonidae, esp. of the genus Salmo, much prized for its (often smoked) pink flesh. 2 Austral. & NZ the barramundi or a similar fish. • adj. salmon pink. □□ **sal·mo·noid** adj. & n. (in sense 1). **sal·mon·y** adj. [ME f. AF sa(u)moun, OF saumon f. L salmo –onis]

sal·mo·nel·la /sálmənélə/ n. (pl. **sal·mo·nel·lae** /–lee/) 1 any bacterium of the genus Salmonella, esp. any of various serotypes causing food poisoning. 2 food poisoning caused by infection with salmonellae. □□ **sal·mo·nel·lo·sis** /–lósis/ n. [mod.L f. D. E. Salmon, Amer. veterinary surgeon d. 1914]

salm·on pink n. the color of salmon flesh.

salm·on trout n. a large, silver-colored trout, Salmo trutta.

sa·lon /sólón, saláwn/ n. 1 the reception room of a large or fashionable house. 2 a room or establishment where a hairdresser, beautician, etc., conducts business. 3 hist. a meeting of eminent people in the reception room of a (esp. Parisian) lady of fashion. 4 (**Salon**) an annual exhibition in Paris of the work of living artists. [F: see SALOON]

sa·lon mu·sic n. light music often played by a small orchestra.

sa·loon /səlóón/ n. 1 a drinking establishment; bar; tavern. 2 (in full **saloon car**) Brit. an automobile with a closed body and no partition behind the driver; sedan. 3 a public room on a ship. 4 esp. Brit. a a large room or hall, esp. in a hotel or public building. b a public room or gallery for a specified purpose (billiard saloon; shooting saloon). 5 (in full **saloon bar**) Brit. the more comfortable room in a bar. 6 (in full **saloon car**) Brit. a luxurious railroad car serving as a lounge, etc. [F salon f. It. salone augment. of sala hall]

sa·loon deck n. a deck for passengers using the saloon.

sa·loon keep·er n. a bartender, manager, or owner of a bar.

sal·pi·glos·sis /sálpiglósis/ n. any solanaceous plant of the genus Salpiglossis, cultivated for its funnel-shaped flowers. [mod.L, irreg. f. Gk salpigx trumpet + glōssa tongue]

salping- /sálping/ comb. form Med. denoting the Fallopian tubes. [Gk salpigx salpiggos, lit. 'trumpet']

sal·pin·gec·to·my /sálpinjéktəmee/ n. (pl. **·mies**) Med. the surgical removal of the Fallopian tubes.

sal·pin·gi·tis /sálpinjítis/ n. Med. inflammation of the Fallopian tubes.

sal·sa /saalsə/ n. 1 a kind of dance music of Latin American origin, incorporating jazz and rock elements. 2 a dance performed to this music. 3 a spicy sauce made from tomatoes, chilies, onions, etc., often served as a dip or condiment. [Sp. (as SAUCE)]

sal·si·fy /sálsifee, –fī/ n. (pl. **·fies**) 1 a European plant, Tragopogon porrifolius, with long cylindrical fleshy roots. 2 this root used as a vegetable. [F salsifis f. obs. It. salsefica, of unkn. orig.]

SALT /sawlt/ abbr. Strategic Arms Limitation Talks (or Treaty).

salt /sawlt/ n., adj., & v. • n. 1 (also **com·mon salt**) sodium chloride; the substance that gives seawater its characteristic taste, gotten in crystalline form by mining from strata consisting of it or by the evaporation of seawater, and used for seasoning or preserving food, or for other purposes. 2 a chemical compound formed from the reaction of an acid with a base, with all or part of the hydrogen of the acid replaced by a metal or metallike radical. 3 sting; piquancy; pungency; wit (added salt to the conversation). 4 (in sing. or pl.) a a substance resembling salt in taste, form, etc. (bath salts; Epsom salts; smelling salts). b (esp. in pl.) this type of substance used as a laxative. 5 (also **old salt**) an experienced sailor. 6 (in pl.) an exceptional rush of seawater up river. • adj. 1 impregnated with, containing, or tasting of salt; cured or preserved or seasoned with salt. 2 (of a plant) growing in the sea or in salt marshes. 3 (of tears, etc.) bitter. 4 (of wit) pungent. • v.tr. 1 cure or preserve with salt or brine. 2 season with salt. 3 make (a narrative, etc.) piquant. 4 sprinkle (the ground, etc.) with salt, esp. in order to melt snow, etc. 5 treat with a solution of salt or mixture of salts. □ **eat salt with** Brit. be a guest of. **not made of salt** Brit. not disconcerted by wet weather. **put salt on the tail of** capture (with ref. to jocular directions given to children for catching a bird). **salt an account** Brit. sl. set an extremely high or low price for articles. **salt away** (or **down**) *sl.* lay away or stash money, etc.; save. **salt the books** *sl.* show receipts as larger than they really have been. **salt lake** a lake of salt water. **salt a mine** *sl.* introduce extraneous ore, material, etc., to make the source seem rich. **the salt of the earth** a person or people of great worthiness, reliability, honesty, etc.; those whose qualities are a model for the rest (Matt. 5: 13). **take with a grain of salt** regard as exaggerated; be incredulous about; believe only part of. **worth one's salt** efficient; capable. □□ **salt‧ish** *adj.* **salt‧less** *adj.* **salt‧ly** *adv.* **salt‧ness** *n.* [OE *s(e)alt s(e)altan*, OS, ON, Goth. *salt*, OHG *salz* f. Gmc]

salt-and-pep‧per *adj.* (of materials, etc., and esp. of hair) with light and dark colors mixed together.

sal‧ta‧rel‧lo /sáltərélō, sáwl–/ *n.* (*pl.* **‧los** or **sal‧ta‧rel‧li** /–lee/) an Italian and Spanish dance for one or two persons, with sudden skips. [It. *salterello*, Sp. *saltarelo*, rel. to It. *saltare* and Sp. *saltar* leap, dance f. L *saltare* (as SALTATION)]

sal‧ta‧tion /saltáyshən, sawl–/ *n.* **1** the act or an instance of leaping or dancing; a jump. **2** a sudden transition or movement. □□ **sal‧ta‧to‧ry** /sáltətawree, sáwl–/ *adj.* **sal‧ta‧to‧ri‧al** /–tətáwreeəl/ *adj.* [L *saltatio* f. *saltare* frequent. of *salire* *salt–* leap]

salt‧bush /sáwltbōōsh/ *n.* an edible plant, *Atriplex hortensis*, with red, yellow, or green leaves sometimes used as a substitute for spinach or sorrel. Also called **orache**.

salt‧cel‧lar /sáwltselər/ *n.* **1** a vessel holding salt for table use. **2** *Brit. colloq.* an unusually deep hollow above the collarbone, esp. found in women. [SALT + obs. *saler* f. AF f. OF *salier* salt-box f. L (as SALARY), assim. to CELLAR]

salt dome *n.* a mass of salt forced up into sedimentary rocks.

salt‧er /sáwltər/ *n.* **1** a manufacturer or dealer in salt. **2** a worker at a saltworks. **3** a person who salts fish, etc. **4** = DRYSALTER. [OE *sealtere* (as SALT)]

salt‧ern /sáwltərn/ *n.* **1** a saltworks. **2** a set of pools for the natural evaporation of seawater. [OE *sealtærn* (as SALT, *ærn* building)]

salt glaze *n.* a hard stoneware glaze produced by throwing salt into a hot kiln containing the ware.

salt grass *n.* grass growing in salt meadows or in alkaline regions.

salt horse *n. Naut. sl.* **1** salted beef. **2** a naval officer with general duties.

sal‧ti‧grade /sáltigrayd, sáwl–/ *adj. & n. Zool.* ● *adj.* (of arthropods) moving by leaping or jumping. ● *n.* a saltigrade arthropod, e.g., a jumping spider, beach flea, etc. [mod.L *Saltigradae* f. L *saltus* leap f. *salire* *salt–* + *–gradus* walking]

sal‧tine /sawltéen/ *n.* a lightly salted, square, flat cracker.

salt‧ing /sáwlting/ *n. Brit.* **1** in senses of SALT *v.* **2** (esp. in *pl.*) *Geol.* a salt marsh; a marsh overflowed by the sea.

sal‧tire /sáwlteer, –tīr, sál–/ *n. Heraldry* a design formed by a bend and a bend sinister crossing like a St. Andrew's cross. □ **in saltire** arranged in this way. □□ **sal‧tire‧wise** *adv.* [ME f. OF *sau(l)toir*, etc., stirrup cord, stile, saltire, f. med.L *saltatorium* (as SALTATION)]

salt lick *n.* **1** a place where animals go to lick salt from the ground. **2** this salt.

salt marsh *n.* a marsh, esp. one flooded by the tide, often used as a pasture for collecting water for salt making.

salt mead‧ow *n.* a meadow subject to flooding with salt water.

salt mine *n.* a mine yielding rock salt.

salt pan *n.* a vessel, or a depression near the sea, used for getting salt by evaporation.

salt‧pe‧ter /sáwltpeetər/ *n.* (*Brit.* **salt‧pe‧tre**) potassium nitrate, a white crystalline salty substance used in preserving meat and as a constituent of gunpowder. [ME f. OF *sal petre* f. med.L *salpetra* prob. for *salpetrae* (unrecorded) salt of rock (i.e. found as an incrustation): assim. to SALT]

salt‧shak‧er /sáwltshaykər/ *n.* a container of salt for sprinkling on food.

salt spoon *n.* a small spoon usu. with a short handle and a roundish deep bowl for serving table salt.

sal‧tus /sáltəs, sáw–/ *n. literary* a sudden transition; a breach of continuity. [L, = leap]

salt‧wa‧ter /sáwltwawtər/ *adj.* **1** of or living in the sea. **2** pertaining to or made with salt water.

salt wa‧ter *n.* **1** sea water. **2** *sl.* tears.

salt well *n.* a bored well yielding brine.

salt‧works /sáwltwərks/ *n.pl.* a place where salt is produced.

salt‧wort /sáwltwərt, –wawrt/ *n.* any plant of the genus *Salsola*; glasswort.

salt‧y /sáwltee/ *adj.* (**salt‧i‧er**, **salt‧i‧est**) **1** tasting of, containing, or preserved with salt. **2** racy; risqué. □□ **salt‧i‧ness** *n.*

sa‧lu‧bri‧ous /səlōōbreeəs/ *adj.* **1** health-giving; healthy. **2** (of surroundings, etc.) pleasant; agreeable. □□ **sa‧lu‧bri‧ous‧ly** *adv.* **sa‧lu‧bri‧ous‧ness** *n.* **sa‧lu‧bri‧ty** *n.* [L *salubris* f. *salus* health]

sa‧lu‧ki /səlōōkee/ *n.* (*pl.* **sa‧lu‧kis**) **1** a tall, swift, slender dog of a silky-coated breed with large ears and a fringed tail and feet. **2** this breed. [Arab. *salūkī*]

sal‧u‧tar‧y /sályətəree/ *adj.* **1** producing good effects; beneficial.

2 *archaic* health-giving. [ME f. F *salutaire* or L *salutaris* f. *salus –utis* health]

sal‧u‧ta‧tion /sályətáyshən/ *n.* **1** a sign or expression of greeting or recognition of another's arrival or departure. **2** (usu. in *pl.*) words spoken or written to inquire about another's health or well-being. □□ **sal‧u‧ta‧tion‧al** *adj.* [ME f. OF *salutation* or L *salutatio* (as SALUTE)]

sa‧lu‧ta‧to‧ry /səlōōtətawree/ *adj. & n.* ● *adj.* of salutation. ● *n.* (*pl.* **‧ries**) an oration, esp. as given by a member of a graduating class, often the second-ranking member. □□ **sa‧lu‧ta‧to‧ri‧an** /–táwreeən/ *n.* (in sense of n.). [L *salutatorius* (as SALUTE)]

sa‧lute /səlōōt/ *n. & v.* ● *n.* **1** a gesture of respect, homage, or courteous recognition, esp. made to or by a person when arriving or departing. **2 a** *Mil. & Naut.* a prescribed or specified movement of the hand or of weapons or flags as a sign of respect or recognition. **b** (prec. by *the*) the attitude taken by an individual soldier, sailor, policeman, etc., in saluting. **3** the discharge of a gun or guns as a formal or ceremonial sign of respect or celebration. **4** *Fencing* the formal performance of certain guards, etc., by fencers before engaging. ● *v.* **1 a** *tr.* make a salute to. **b** *intr.* (often foll. by *to*) perform a salute. **2** *tr.* greet; make a salutation to. **3** *tr.* (foll. by *with*) receive or greet with (a smile, etc.). **4** *tr. archaic* hail as (king, etc.). □ **take the salute 1** (of the highest officer present) acknowledge it by gesture as meant for him. **2** receive ceremonial salutes by members of a procession. □□ **sa‧lut‧er** *n.* [ME f. L *salutare* f. *salus –utis* health]

sal‧vage /sálvij/ *n. & v.* ● *n.* **1** the rescue of a ship, its cargo, or other property, from loss at sea, destruction by fire, etc. **2** the property, etc., saved in this way. **3 a** the saving and utilization of waste paper, scrap material, etc. **b** the materials salvaged. **4** payment made or due to a person who has saved a ship or its cargo. ● *v.tr.* **1** save from a wreck, fire, etc. **2** retrieve or preserve (something favorable) in adverse circumstances (*tried to salvage some dignity*). □□ **sal‧vage‧a‧ble** *adj.* **sal‧vag‧er** *n.* [F f. med.L *salvagium* f. L *salvare* SAVE¹]

sal‧va‧tion /salváyshən/ *n.* **1** the act of saving or being saved; preservation from loss, calamity, etc. **2** deliverance from sin and its consequences and admission to heaven, brought about by Christ. **3** a religious conversion. **4** a person or thing that saves (*was the salvation of*). □□ **sal‧va‧tion‧ism** *n.* **sal‧va‧tion‧ist** *n.* (both nouns esp. with ref. to the Salvation Army). [ME f. OF *sauvacion, salvacion*, f. eccl.L *salvatio –onis* f. *salvare* SAVE¹, transl. Gk *sōtēria*]

Sal‧va‧tion Ar‧my *n.* a worldwide evangelical group organized on quasi-military lines for the revival of Christianity and helping the poor.

salve¹ /sav, saav/ *n. & v.* ● *n.* **1** a healing ointment. **2** (often foll. by *for*) a thing that is soothing or consoling for wounded feelings, an uneasy conscience, etc. **3** *archaic* a thing that explains away a discrepancy or palliates a fault. ● *v.tr.* **1** soothe (pride, self-love, conscience, etc.). **2** *archaic* anoint (a wound, etc.). **3** *archaic* smooth over; make good; vindicate; harmonize. [OE *s(e)alf(e), s(e)alfian* f. Gmc; senses 1 and 3 of v. partly f. L *salvare* SAVE¹]

salve² /salv/ *v.tr.* **1** save (a ship or its cargo) from loss at sea. **2** save (property) from fire. □□ **salv‧a‧ble** *adj.* [back-form. f. SALVAGE]

sal‧ver /sálvər/ *n.* a tray usu. of gold, silver, brass, or electroplate, on which drinks, letters, etc., are offered. [F *salve* tray for presenting food to the king f. Sp. *salva* assaying of food f. *salvar* SAVE: assoc. with *platter*]

Sal‧ve Re‧gi‧na /sáalvay rəjeéna/ *n.* **1** a Roman Catholic hymn or prayer said or sung to the Virgin Mary. **2** the music for this. [f. the opening words *salve regina* hail (holy) queen]

sal‧vi‧a /sálveeə/ *n.* any plant of the genus *Salvia*, esp. *S. splendens* with red or blue flowers. [L, = SAGE¹]

sal‧vo¹ /sálvō/ *n.* (*pl.* **‧voes** or **‧vos**) **1** the simultaneous firing of artillery or other guns, esp. as a salute or in a seafight. **2** a number of bombs released from aircraft at the same moment. **3** a round or volley of applause. [earlier *salve* f. F f. It. *salva* salutation (as SAVE¹)]

sal‧vo² /sálvō/ *n.* (*pl.* **‧vos**) **1** a saving clause; a reservation (*with an express salvo of their rights*). **2** a tacit reservation. **3** a quibbling evasion; a bad excuse. **4** an expedient for saving reputation or soothing pride or conscience. [L, ablat. of *salvus* SAFE as used in *salvo jure* without prejudice to the rights of (a person)]

sal vo‧la‧ti‧le /sál vōlát'lee/ *n.* ammonium carbonate, esp. in the form of a flavored solution in alcohol used as smelling salts. [mod.L, = volatile salt]

sal‧vor /sálvər/ *n.* a person or ship making or assisting in salvage. [SALVE²]

SAM *abbr.* surface-to-air missile.

Sam. *abbr.* Samuel (Old Testament).

sa‧ma‧dhi /səmaádee/ *n. Buddhism & Hinduism* **1** a state of concentration induced by meditation. **2** a state into which a perfected holy man is said to pass at his apparent death. [Skr. *samādhi* contemplation]

sam‧a‧ra /sámərə, səmáirə, səmaá–/ *n. Bot.* a winged seed from the sycamore, ash, etc. [mod.L f. L, = elm-seed]

Sa‧mar‧i‧tan /səmárit'n/ *n. & adj.* ● *n.* **1** (in full **good Samaritan**) a charitable or helpful person (with ref. to Luke 10:33). **2** a native of Samaria in West Jordan. **3** the language of this people. ● *adj.* of Samaria or the Samaritans. □□ **Sa•mar•i•tan•ism** *n.* [LL *Samaritanus* f. Gk *Samareitēs* f. *Samareia* Samaria]

sa•mar•i•um /səmáireeəm/ *n. Chem.* a soft, silvery metallic element of the lanthanide series, occurring naturally in monazite, etc., and used in making ferromagnetic alloys. ¶ Symb.: **Sm**. [*samarskite* the mineral in which its spectrum was first observed, f. *Samarski* name of a 19th-c. Russ. official]

sam•ba /sámbə, saám–/ *n. & v.* ● *n.* **1** a Brazilian dance of African origin. **2** a ballroom dance imitative of this. **3** the music for this. ● *v.intr.* (**sam•bas, sam•baed** /–bəd/, **sam•ba•ing** /–bə-ing/) dance the samba. [Port., of Afr. orig.]

sam•bar /sámbər, saám–/ *n.* (also **sam•ba, sam•bhar**) either of two large deer, *Cervus unicolor* or *C. equinus*, native to S. Asia. [Hindi *sā(m)bar*]

Sam Browne /sam brówn/ *n.* (in full **Sam Browne belt**) an army officer's belt and the shoulder strap supporting it. [Sir *Samuel* J. *Browne*, Brit. military commander d. 1901]

same /saym/ *adj., pron., & adv.* ● *adj.* **1** (often prec. by *the*) identical; not different; unchanged (*everyone was looking in the same direction; the same car was used in another crime; saying the same thing over and over*). **2** unvarying; uniform; monotonous (*the same old story*). **3** (usu. prec. by *this, these, that, those*) (of a person or thing) previously alluded to; just mentioned; aforesaid (*this same man was later my husband*). ● *pron.* (prec. by *the*) **1** the same person or thing (*the others asked for the same*). **2** *Law* or *archaic* the person or thing just mentioned (*detected the youth breaking in and apprehended the same*). ● *adv.* (usu. prec. by *the*) similarly; in the same way (*we all feel the same; I want to go, the same as you do*). □ **all** (or **just**) **the same 1** emphatically the same. **2** in spite of changed conditions, adverse circumstances, etc. (*but you should offer, all the same*). **at the same time 1** simultaneously. **2** notwithstanding, in spite of circumstances, etc. **be all** (or **just**) **the same to** an expression of indifference or impartiality (*it's all the same to me what we do*). **by the same token** see TOKEN. **same here** *colloq.* the same applies to me. **the same to you!** may you do, have, find, etc., the same thing; likewise. **the very same** emphatically the same. □□ **same•ness** *n.* [ME f. ON *sami, sama*, with Gmc cognates]

▶Do not use **same** in place of *identical*. You and your friend may have bought *identical* sweaters, but if you bought the *same* sweater, you will be sharing one clothing item between the two of you.

EQUAL, EQUIVALENT, IDENTICAL, SELFSAME, TANTAMOUNT. All of these adjectives describe what is not significantly different from something else. **Same** may imply, and **selfsame** always implies, that what is referred to is one thing and not two or more distinct things (*They go to the same restaurant every Friday night; This is the selfsame house in which the family once lived*). In one sense, **identical** is synonymous with **selfsame** (*the identical place where we first met*); but it can also imply exact correspondence in quality, shape, and appearance (*wearing identical raincoats*). **Equivalent** describes things that are interchangeable or that amount to the same thing in value, force, or significance (*the equivalent of a free hotel room at a luxury resort*), while **equal** implies exact correspondence in quantity, value, or size (*equal portions of food*). **Tantamount** is used to describe one of a pair of things, usually intangible, that are in effect equivalent to each other (*Her tears were tantamount to a confession of guilt*).

Sa•mhain /saáwin/ *n. Brit.* Nov. 1, celebrated by the Celts as a festival marking the beginning of winter. [Ir. *Samhain*]

sam•i•sen /sámisen/ *n.* a long three-stringed Japanese guitar, played with a plectrum. [Jap. f. Chin. *san-hsien* f. *san* three + *hsien* string]

sam•ite /sámīt, sáy–/ *n. hist.* a rich medieval dress fabric of silk occas. interwoven with gold. [ME f. OF *samit* f. med.L *examitum* f. med. Gk *hexamiton* f. Gk *hexa-* six + *mitos* thread]

sam•iz•dat /sáamizdaát, səmyizdaát/ *n.* a system of clandestine publication of banned literature in the former USSR. [Russ., = self-publishing house]

Sam•nite /sámnīt/ *n. & adj.* ● *n.* **1** a member of a people of ancient Italy often at war with republican Rome. **2** the language of this people. ● *adj.* of this people or their language. [ME f L *Samnites* (pl.), rel. to *Sabinus* SABINE]

Sa•mo•an /səmṓən/ *n. & adj.* ● *n.* **1** a native of Samoa, a group of islands in the Pacific. **2** the language of this people. ● *adj.* of or relating to Samoa or its people or language. [*Samoa*]

sam•o•var /sámovaar/ *n.* a Russian urn for making tea, with an internal heating tube to keep water at boiling point. [Russ., = self-boiler]

Sam•o•yed /sámoyed, səmóyed/ *n.* **1** a member of a people of northern Siberia. **2** the language

samovar

of this people. **3** (also **samoyed**) **a** a dog of a white Arctic breed. **b** this breed. [Russ. *samoed*]

Sam•o•yed•ic /sámoyédik/ *n. & adj.* ● *n.* the language of the Samoyeds. ● *adj.* of or relating to the Samoyeds.

samp /samp/ *n.* **1** coarsely ground corn. **2** porridge made of this. [Algonquian *nasamp* softened by water]

sam•pan /sámpan/ *n.* a small boat usu. with a stern oar or stern oars, used in the Far East. [Chin. *san-ban* f. *san* three + *ban* board]

sam•phire /sámfīr/ *n.* **1** an umbelliferous maritime rock plant, *Crithmum maritimum*, with aromatic fleshy leaves used in pickles. **2** the glasswort. [earlier *samp(i)ere* f. F (*herbe de*) *Saint Pierre* St Peter('s herb)]

sampan

sam•ple /sámpəl/ *n. & v.* ● *n.* **1** (also *attrib.*) a small part or quantity intended to show what the whole is like. **2** a small amount of fabric, food, or other commodity, esp. given to a prospective customer. **3** a specimen, esp. one taken for scientific testing or analysis. **4** an illustrative or typical example. ● *v.tr.* **1** take or give samples of. **2** try the qualities of. **3** get a representative experience of. [ME f. AF *assample*, OF *essample* EXAMPLE]

sam•pler[1] /sámplər/ *n.* a piece of embroidery worked in various stitches as a specimen of proficiency (often displayed on a wall, etc.). [OF *essamplaire* (as EXEMPLAR)]

sam•pler[2] /sámplər/ *n.* **1** a person who samples. **2** a collection of representative items, etc.

sam•pling /sámpling/ *n.* a technique in electronic music involving digitally encoding a piece of sound and reusing it as part of a composition or recording.

sam•sa•ra /səmsaárə/ *n. Ind. Philos.* the endless cycle of death and rebirth to which life in the material world is bound. □□ **sam•sa•ric** *adj.* [Skr. *saṃsāra* a wandering through]

sam•ska•ra /səmskaárə/ *n. Ind. Philos.* **1** a purificatory ceremony or rite marking an event in one's life. **2** a mental impression, instinct, or memory. [Skr. *saṃskāra* a making perfect, preparation]

Sam•son /sámsən/ *n.* a person of great strength or resembling Samson in some respect. [LL f. Gk *Sampsōn* f. Heb. *šimšôn* (Judg. 13–16)]

sam•son post *n.* **1** a strong pillar passing through the hold of a ship or between decks. **2** a post in a whaler to which a harpoon rope is attached.

sam•u•rai /sámoorī, sáa–/ *n.* (*pl.* same) **1** a Japanese army officer. **2** *hist.* a military retainer; a member of a military caste in Japan. [Jap.]

san•a•tive /sánətiv/ *adj.* **1** healing; curative. **2** of or tending to physical or moral health. [ME f. OF *sanatif* or LL *sanativus* f. L *sanare* cure]

san•a•to•ri•um /sánətáwreeəm/ *n.* (*pl.* **san•a•to•ri•ums** or **san•a•to•ri•a** /–reeə/) **1** an establishment for the treatment of invalids, esp. of convalescents and the chronically sick. **2** *Brit.* a room or building for sick people in a school, etc. [mod.L (as SANATIVE)]

sanc•ti•fy /sángktifī/ *v.tr.* (**•fies, •fied**) **1** consecrate; set apart or observe as holy. **2** purify or free from sin. **3** make legitimate or binding by religious sanction; justify; give the color of morality or innocence to. **4** make productive of or conducive to holiness. □□ **sanc•ti•fi•ca•tion** /–fikáyshən/ *n.* **sanc•ti•fi•er** *n.* [ME f. OF *saintifier* f. eccl.L *sanctificare* f. L *sanctus* holy]

sanc•ti•mo•ni•ous /sángktimṓneeəs/ *adj.* making a show of sanctity or piety. □□ **sanc•ti•mo•ni•ous•ly** *adv.* **sanc•ti•mo•ni•ous•ness** *n.* **sanc•ti•mo•ny** /sángktimṓnee/ *n.* [L *sanctimonia* sanctity (as SAINT)]

sanc•tion /sángkshən/ *n. & v.* ● *n.* **1** approval or encouragement given to an action, etc., by custom or tradition; express permission. **2** confirmation or ratification of a law, etc. **3 a** a penalty for disobeying a law or rule, or a reward for obeying it. **b** a clause containing this. **4** *Ethics* a consideration operating to enforce obedience to any rule of conduct. **5** (esp. in *pl.*) military or esp. economic action by a nation to coerce another to conform to an international agreement or norms of conduct. **6** *Law hist.* a law or decree. ● *v.tr.* **1** authorize, countenance, or agree to (an action, etc.). **2** ratify; attach a penalty or reward to; make binding. □□ **sanc•tion•a•ble** *adj.* [F f. L *sanctio –onis* f. *sancire sanct-* make sacred]

▶**Sanction** is confusing because it has two meanings that are almost opposite. In most domestic contexts, **sanction** means 'approval; permission': *Voters gave the measure their sanction.* In foreign affairs, **sanction** means 'penalty; deterrent': *International sanctions against the republic go into effect in January.*

sanc•ti•tude /sángktitōod, –tyōod/ *n. archaic* saintliness. [ME f. L *sanctitudo* (as SAINT)]

sanc•ti•ty /sángktitee/ *n.* (*pl.* **•ties**) **1** holiness of life; saintliness.

2 sacredness; the state of being hallowed. **3** inviolability. **4** (in *pl.*) sacred obligations, feelings, etc. [ME f. OF *sain(c)tité* or L *sanctitas* (as SAINT)]

sanc•tu•ar•y /sángkchŏoeree/ *n.* (*pl.* **•ies**) **1** a holy place; a church, temple, etc. **2 a** the inmost recess or holiest part of a temple, etc. **b** the part of the chancel containing the high altar. **3** a place where birds, wild animals, etc., are bred and protected. **4** a place of refuge, esp. for political refugees. **5 a** immunity from arrest. **b** the right to offer this. **6** *hist.* a sacred place where a fugitive from the law or a debtor was secured by medieval church law against arrest or violence. □ **take sanctuary** resort to a place of refuge.

WORD HISTORY sanctuary

Middle English (in sense 1): from Old French *sanctuaire*, from Latin *sanctuarium*, from *sanctus* 'holy.' The early sense 'a church or other sacred place where a fugitive was immune, by the law of the medieval church, from arrest' gave rise to senses 3 and 4.

sanc•tum /sángktəm/ *n.* (*pl.* **sanc•tums**) **1** a holy place. **2** *colloq.* a person's private room, study, or den. [L, neut. of *sanctus* holy, past part. of *sancire* consecrate: *sanctorum* genit. pl. in transl. of Heb. *ḳŏdešhaḳḳ°ḏāšîm* holy of holies]

sanc•tum sanc•to•rum /sangktórəm/ *n.* **1** the holy of holies in the Jewish temple. **2** = sense 2 of n. **3** an inner retreat. **4** an esoteric doctrine, etc.

Sanc•tus /sángktəs, saángktŏos/ *n.* (also **sanctus**) **1** the prayer or hymn beginning "Holy, holy, holy" said or sung at the end of the Eucharistic preface. **2** the music for this. [ME f. L, = holy]

Sanc•tus bell *n.* a handbell or the bell in the turret at the junction of the nave and the chancel, rung at the Sanctus or at the elevation of the Eucharist.

sand /sand/ *n. & v.* ● *n.* **1** a loose granular substance resulting from the wearing down of esp. siliceous rocks and found on the seashore, riverbeds, deserts, etc. **2** (in *pl.*) grains of sand. **3** (in *pl.*) an expanse or tracts of sand. **4** a light yellow-brown color like that of sand. **5** (in *pl.*) a sandbank. **6** *colloq.* firmness of purpose; grit. ● *v.tr.* **1** smooth or polish with sandpaper or sand. **2** sprinkle or overlay with, or bury under, sand. **3** adulterate (sugar, etc.) with sand. □ **the sands are running out** the allotted time is nearly at an end. □□ **sand•er** *n.* **sand•like** *adj.* [OE *sand* f. Gmc]

san•dal[1] /sánd'l/ *n. & v.* ● *n.* **1** a light shoe with an openwork upper or no upper, attached to the foot usu. by straps. **2** a strap for fastening a low shoe, passing over the instep or around the ankle. ● *v.tr.* **1** (esp. as **sandaled** *adj.*) put sandals on (a person, a person's feet) **2** fasten or provide (a shoe) with a sandal. [ME f. L *sandalium* f. Gk *sandalion* dimin. of *sandalon* wooden shoe, prob. of Asiatic orig.]

san•dal[2] /sánd'l/ *n.* = SANDALWOOD. [ME f. med.L *sandalum*, ult. f. Skr. *candana*]

san•dal tree *n.* any tree yielding sandalwood, esp. the white sandalwood, *Santalum album*, of India.

san•dal•wood /sánd'lwŏod/ *n.* **1** the scented wood of a sandal tree. **2** a perfume derived from this. **3** any tree from which such is derived.

san•dal•wood oil *n.* a yellow aromatic oil made from the sandal tree.

san•da•rac /sándərak/ *n.* (also **san•da•rach**) **1** the gummy resin of a N. African conifer, *Tetraclinis articulata*, used in making varnish. **2** *Brit.* = REALGAR. [L *sandaraca* f. Gk *sandarakē*, of Asiatic orig.]

sand•bag /sándbag/ *n. & v.* ● *n.* a bag filled with sand for use: **1** (in fortification) for making temporary defenses or for the protection of a building, etc., against blast and splinters or floodwaters. **2** as ballast esp. for a boat or balloon. **3** as a weapon to inflict a heavy blow without leaving a mark. **4** to stop a draft from a window or door. ● *v.tr.* (**•bagged**, **•bag•ging**) **1** barricade or defend. **2** place sandbags against (a window, chink, etc.). **3** fell with a blow from a sandbag. **4** coerce by harsh means. □□ **sand•bag•ger** *n.*

sand•bank /sándbangk/ *n.* a deposit of sand forming a shallow place in the sea or a river.

sand•bar /sándbaar/ *n.* a sandbank at the mouth of a river or on the coast.

sand•blast /sándblast/ *v. & n.* ● *v.tr.* roughen, treat, or clean with a jet of sand driven by compressed air or steam. ● *n.* this jet. □□ **sand•blast•er** *n.*

sand•box /sándboks/ *n.* **1** a box of sand, esp. one for children to play in. **2** *hist.* a device for sprinkling sand to dry ink.

sand•cas•tle /sándkasəl/ *n.* a shape like a castle made in sand, usu. by a child on the seashore.

sand crack *n.* **1** a fissure in a horse's hoof. **2** a crack in the human foot from walking on hot sand. **3** esp. *Brit.* a crack in brick due to imperfect mixing.

sand dol•lar *n.* any of various round, flat sea urchins, esp. of the order Clypeasteroida.

sand dune *n.* (also **sand hill**) a mound or ridge of sand formed by the wind.

sand•er•ling /sándərling/ *n.* a small wading bird, *Calidris alba*, of the sandpiper family. [perh. f. an OE form *sandyrthling* (unrecorded), as SAND + *yrthling* plowman, also the name of a bird)]

sand fly *n.* **1** any small fly of the genus *Simulium*. **2** any biting fly of the genus *Phlebotomus* transmitting the viral disease leishmaniasis.

sand flea *n.* a chigoe or a beach flea.

sand-grop•er *n. Austral.* **1** a gold-rush pioneer. **2** *joc.* a Western Australian.

san•dhi /sándee, saán–/ *n. Gram.* the process whereby the form of a word changes as a result of its position in an utterance (e.g., the change from *a* to *an* before a vowel). [Skr. *saṃdhi* putting together]

sand hill *n.* a sand dune.

sand•hog /sándhawg, –hog/ *n.* a person who works underwater laying foundations, constructing tunnels, etc.

sand hop•per *n.* any of various small jumping crustaceans of the order Amphipoda, burrowing on the seashore; a beach flea.

san•di•ver /sándivər/ *n.* liquid scum formed in glass making. [ME app. f. F *suin de verre* exhalation of glass f. *suer* to sweat]

sand lance *n.* any eellike fish of the family Ammodytidae or Hypotychidae. Also called **launce**.

sand•lot /sándlot/ *n.* a vacant lot or a piece of unoccupied sandy land used for children's games.

sand•man /sándman/ *n.* the personification of tiredness causing children's eyes to smart toward bedtime.

sand mar•tin *n.* = BANK SWALLOW.

sand•pa•per /sándpaypər/ *n. & v.* ● *n.* paper with sand or another abrasive stuck to it for smoothing or polishing. ● *v.tr.* smooth with sandpaper.

sand•pi•per /sándpīpər/ *n.* any of various wading birds of the family Scolopacidae, frequenting coastal areas.

sand•pit /sándpit/ *n.* **1** a pit from which sand is excavated. **2** *Brit.* a children's sandbox.

sand•soap /sándsōp/ *n.* heavy-duty gritty soap.

sand•stone /sándstōn/ *n.* **1** any

Western sandpiper

clastic rock containing particles visible to the naked eye. **2** a sedimentary rock of consolidated sand commonly red, yellow, brown, gray, or white.

sand•storm /sándstawrm/ *n.* a desert storm of wind with clouds of sand.

sand•wich /sándwich, sán–/ *n. & v.* ● *n.* **1** two or more slices of bread with a filling of meat, cheese, etc., between them. **2** *Brit.* a cake of two or more layers with jam or cream between (*bake a sponge sandwich*). ● *v.tr.* **1** put (a thing, statement, etc.) between two of another character. **2** squeeze in between others (*sat sandwiched in the middle*). [4th Earl of *Sandwich*, Engl. nobleman d. 1792, said to have eaten food in this form so as not to leave the gaming table]

sand•wich board *n.* two hinged advertisement boards made to hang from the shoulders.

sand•wich man *n.* (*pl.* **men**) a person hired to walk the streets displaying sandwich boards.

sand•wort /sándwort, –wawrt/ *n.* any low-growing plant of the genus *Arenaria*, usu. bearing small white flowers.

sand•y /sándee/ *adj.* (**sand•i•er**, **sand•i•est**) **1** having the texture of sand. **2** having much sand. **3 a** (of hair) yellowish-red. **b** (of a person) having sandy hair. □□ **sand•i•ness** *n.* **sand•y•ish** *adj.* [OE *sandig* (as SAND)]

sand yacht *n.* esp. *Brit.* = LAND YACHT.

sand•y blight *n. Austral.* conjunctivitis with sandlike grains in the eye; trachoma.

sane /sayn/ *adj.* **1** of sound mind; not mad. **2** (of views, etc.) moderate; sensible. □□ **sane•ly** *adv.* **sane•ness** *n.* [L *sanus* healthy]

sang *past* of SING.

san•ga•ree /sánggəreé/ *n.* **1** a cold drink of wine diluted and spiced. **2** sangria. [Sp. *sangría* SANGRIA]

sang-froid /saaNfrwáa/ *n.* composure, coolness, etc., in danger or under agitating circumstances. [F, = cold blood]

sang•rail /sánggráyl/ *n.* = GRAIL. [ME f. OF *saint graal* (as SAINT, GRAIL)]

san•gri•a /sanggreéə/ *n.* a sweet Spanish drink of iced red wine with lemonade, fruit, spices, etc. [Sp., = bleeding:]

san•gui•nar•y /sánggwəneree/ *adj.* **1** accompanied by or delighting in bloodshed. **2** bloody; bloodthirsty. **3** (of laws) inflicting death freely. □□ **san•gui•nar•i•ly** /–nérəlee/ *adv.* **san•gui•nar•i•ness** *n.* [L *sanguinarius* f. *sanguis –inis* blood]

san•guine /sánggwin/ *adj.* ● *adj.* **1** optimistic; confident. **2** (of the complexion) florid; bright; ruddy. **3** *hist.* of a ruddy complexion with a courageous,

sand dollar

hopeful and amorous disposition. **4** *hist.* of the temperament in which blood predominates over the other humors. **5** *Heraldry* or *literary* blood red. **6** *archaic* bloody; bloodthirsty. ●*n.* **1** a blood-red color. **2** a crayon of chalk colored red or flesh with iron oxide. □□ **san·guine·ly** *adv.* **san·guine·ness** *n.* (both in sense 1 of *n.*). [ME f. OF *sanguin* –*ine* blood-red f. L *sanguineus* (as SANGUINARY)]

san·guin·e·ous /sanggwíneeəs/ *adj.* **1** sanguinary. **2** *Med.* of or relating to blood. **3** blood-red. **4** full-blooded; plethoric. [L *sanguineus* (as SANGUINE)]

San·hed·rin /sanhédrin, –hee–, saan–/ *n.* (also **San·hed·rim** /–drim/) the highest court of justice and the supreme council in ancient Jerusalem with 71 members. [late Heb. *sanhedrîn* f. Gk *sunedrion* (as SYN–, *hedra* seat)]

san·i·cle /sánikəl/ *n.* any umbelliferous plant of the genus *Sanicula*, esp. *S. europaea*, formerly believed to have healing properties. [ME ult. f. med.L *sanicula* perh. f. L *sanus* healthy]

san·i·tar·i·um /sánitáireeəm/ *n.* (*pl.* **san·i·tar·i·ums** or **san·i·tar·i·a** /–reeə/) **1** an establishment for the restoration of health; sanatorium. **2** a health resort. [pseudo-L f. L *sanitas* health]

san·i·tar·y /sániteree/ *adj.* **1** of the conditions that affect health, esp. with regard to dirt and infection. **2** hygienic; free from or designed to kill germs, infection, etc. □□ **san·i·tar·i·an** /–áireeən/ *n. & adj.* **san·i·tar·i·ly** *adv.* **san·i·tar·i·ness** *n.* [F *sanitaire* f. L *sanitas*: see SANITY]

█ **SYNONYM TIP** sanitary

ANTISEPTIC, HEALTHFUL, HYGIENIC, SALUBRIOUS, STERILE. Americans thrive on cleanliness and the eradication of germs. They try to keep their homes **sanitary**, a term that goes beyond cleanliness to imply that measures have been taken to guard against infections or disease. They demand that their communities provide schools and workplaces that are **hygienic**—in other words, that adhere to the rules or standards promoting public health. But it would be almost impossible to duplicate the conditions found in a hospital, where everything that comes in contact with patients must be **sterile** or free of germs entirely. Most Americans are not so much interested in making their environment **antiseptic**, a word that is similar in meaning to *sterile* but implies preventing infections by destroying germs that are already present (*an antiseptic solution*) as they are in keeping it **healthful**, which means conducive to the health or soundness of the body. Many Americans, as they grow older, choose to move to a more **salubrious** climate, a word that applies primarily to an air quality that is invigorating and that avoids harsh extremes.

san·i·tar·y en·gi·neer *n.* a person dealing with systems needed to maintain public health.

san·i·tar·y nap·kin *n.* (*Brit.* **san·i·tar·y tow·el**) an absorbent pad used during menstruation.

san·i·tar·y ware *n.* porcelain for bathrooms, etc.

san·i·ta·tion /sánitáyshən/ *n.* **1** sanitary conditions. **2** the maintenance or improving of these. **3** the disposal of sewage and refuse from houses, etc. □□ **san·i·tate** /sánitayt/ *v.tr. & intr.* **san·i·ta·tion·ist** *n.* [irreg. f. SANITARY]

san·i·tize /sánitīz/ *v.tr.* **1** make sanitary; disinfect. **2** render (information, etc.) more acceptable by removing improper or disturbing material. □□ **san·i·tiz·er** *n.*

san·i·ty /sánitee/ *n.* **1 a** the state of being sane. **b** mental health. **2** the tendency to avoid extreme views. [ME f. L *sanitas* (as SANE)]

sank past of SINK.

sann·ya·si /sunyáasee/ *n.* (also **san·ya·si**) (*pl.* same) a Hindu religious mendicant. [Hindi & Urdu *sannyāsī* f. Skr. *saṃnyāsin* laying aside f. *saṃ* together, *ni* down, *as* throw]

sans /sanz, soN/ *prep. archaic or joc.* without. [ME f. OF *san(z)*, *sen(s)* ult. f. L *sine*, infl. by L *absentia* in the absence of]

sans·cu·lotte /sánzkyŏolót, –kŏo–, saaNkylawt/ *n.* **1** *hist.* a lower-class Parisian republican in the French Revolution. **2** an extreme republican or revolutionary. □□ **sans·cu·lot·tism** *n.* [F, lit. = without knee breeches]

San·skrit /sánskrit/ *n. & adj.* ●*n.* the ancient and sacred language of the Hindus in India. ●*adj.* of or in this language. □□ **San·skrit·ic** /–skrítik/ *adj.* **San·skrit·ist** *n.* [Skr. *saṃskṛta* composed, elaborated, f. *saṃ* together, *kṛ* make, –*ta* past part. ending]

sans ser·if /sánsérif/ *n. & adj.* (also **san·ser·if**) *Printing* ●*n.* a form of type without serifs. ●*adj.* without serifs. [app. f. SANS + SERIF]

San·ta Claus /sántə klawz/ *n.* (also *colloq.* **San·ta**) a legendary person said to bring children presents on the night before Christmas. [orig. US f. Du. dial. *Sante Klaas* St. Nicholas]

san·to·li·na /sántəleéenə/ *n.* any aromatic shrub of the genus *Santolina*, with finely divided leaves and usu. yellow flowers. [mod.L, var. of SANTONICA]

san·ton·i·ca /santónikə/ *n.* **1** a shrubby wormwood plant, *Artemisia cina*, yielding santonin. **2** the dried flower heads of this used as an anthelmintic. [L f. *Santones* an Aquitanian tribe]

san·to·nin /sántənin/ *n.* a toxic drug extracted from santonica and

---

other plants of the genus *Artemisia*, used as an anthelmintic. [SANTONICA + –IN]

san·ya·si var. of SANNYASI.

sap[1] /sap/ *n. & v.* ●*n.* **1** the vital juice circulating in plants. **2** vigor; vitality. **3** = SAPWOOD. ●*v.tr.* (**sapped, sap·ping**) **1** drain or dry (wood) of sap. **2** exhaust the vigor of (*my energy had been sapped by disappointment*). **3** remove the sapwood from (a log). □□ **sap·ful** *adj.* **sap·less** *adj.* [OE *sæp* prob. f. Gmc]

sap[2] /sap/ *n. & v.* ●*n.* **1** a tunnel or trench to conceal an assailant's approach to a fortified place; a covered siege trench. **2** an insidious or slow undermining of a belief, resolution, etc. ●*v.* (**sapped, sap·ping**) **1** *intr.* **a** dig a sap or saps. **b** approach by a sap. **2** *tr.* undermine; make insecure by removing the foundations. **3** *tr.* weaken or destroy insidiously. [ult. f. It. *zappa* spade, spadework, in part through F *sappe sap(p)er*, prob. of Arab. orig.]

sap[3] /sap/ *n. sl.* a foolish person. [abbr. of *sapskull* f. SAP[1] = sapwood + SKULL]

sa·pan·wood var. of SAPPANWOOD.

sap green *n. & adj.* ●*n.* **1** the pigment made from buckthorn berries. **2** the color of this. ●*adj.* of this color.

sap·id /sápid/ *adj. literary* **1** having (esp. an agreeable) flavor; savory; palatable; not insipid. **2** (of talk, writing, etc.) not vapid or uninteresting. □□ **sa·pid·i·ty** /səpíditee/ *n.* [L *sapidus* f. *sapere* taste]

sa·pi·ent /sáypeeənt/ *adj. literary* **1** wise. **2** aping wisdom; of fancied sagacity. □□ **sa·pi·ence** *n.* **sa·pi·ent·ly** *adv.* [ME f. OF *sapient* or L part. stem of *sapere* be wise]

sa·pi·en·tial /sáypee-énshəl/ *adj. literary* of or relating to wisdom. [ME f. F *sapiential* or eccl.L *sapientialis* f. L *sapientia* wisdom]

sap·ling /sápling/ *n.* **1** a young tree. **2** a youth. **3** a greyhound in its first year.

sap·o·dil·la /sápədílə, –deéyə/ *n.* a large evergreen tropical American tree, *Manilkara zapota*, with edible fruit and durable wood, and sap from which chicle is obtained. [Sp. *zapotillo* dimin. of *zapote* f. Aztec *tzápotl*]

sap·o·dil·la plum *n.* the fruit of the sapodilla tree.

sap·o·na·ceous /sápənáyshəs/ *adj.* **1** of, like, or containing soap; soapy. **2** *joc.* unctuous; flattering. [mod.L *saponaceus* f. L *sapo* –*onis* soap]

sa·pon·i·fy /səpónifī/ *v.* (**·fies, ·fied**) **1** *tr.* turn (fat or oil) into soap by reaction with an alkali. **2** *tr.* convert (an ester) to an acid and alcohol. **3** *intr.* become saponified. □□ **sa·pon·i·fi·a·ble** *adj.* **sa·pon·i·fi·ca·tion** /–fikáyshən/ *n.* [F *saponifier* (as SAPONACEOUS)]

sap·o·nin /sápənin/ *n.* any of a group of plant glycosides, esp. those derived from the bark of the tree *Quillaja saponaria*, that foam when shaken with water and are used in detergents and fire extinguishers. [F *saponine* f. L *sapo* –*onis* soap]

sa·por /sáypər, –pawr/ *n.* **1** a quality perceptible by taste, e.g., sweetness. **2** the distinctive taste of a substance. **3** the sensation of taste. [ME f. L *sapere* taste]

sap·pan·wood /səpánwŏod, sápən–/ *n.* (also **sap·an·wood**) the heartwood of an E. Indian tree, *Caesalpinia sappan*, formerly used as a source of red dye. [Du. *sapan* f. Malay *sapang*, of S. Indian orig.]

sap·per /sápər/ *n.* **1** a person who digs saps. **2** a military demolitions expert.

Sap·phic /sáfik/ *adj. & n.* ●*adj.* **1** of or relating to Sappho, poetess of Lesbos *c*.600 BC, or her poetry. **2** lesbian. ●*n.* (in *pl.*) (**sapphics**) verse in a meter associated with Sappho. [F *sa(p)phique* f. L *Sapphicus* f. Gk *Sapphikos* f. *Sapphō*]

sap·phire /sáfīr/ *n. & adj.* ●*n.* **1** a transparent blue precious stone consisting of corundum. **2** precious transparent corundum of any color. **3** the bright blue of a sapphire. **4** a hummingbird with bright blue coloring. ●*adj.* of sapphire blue. □□ **sap·phir·ine** /sáfirin, –rín, –reen/ *adj.* [ME f. OF *safir* f. L *sapphirus* f. Gk *sappheiros* prob. = lapis lazuli]

sap·phire an·ni·ver·sa·ry *n.* a 45th wedding anniversary.

sap·py /sápee/ *adj.* (**sap·pi·er, sap·pi·est**) **1** full of sap. **2** young and vigorous. **3** overly emotional or sentimental. □□ **sap·pi·ly** *adv.* **sap·pi·ness** *n.*

sapro- /sápro/ *comb. form Biol.* rotten, putrefying. [Gk *sapros* putrid]

sap·ro·gen·ic /sáprəjénik/ *adj.* causing or produced by putrefaction.

sa·proph·a·gous /saprófəgəs/ *adj.* feeding on decaying matter.

sap·ro·phile /sáprəfīl/ *n.* a bacterium inhabiting putrid matter. □□ **sa·proph·i·lous** /–prófiləs/ *adj.*

sap·ro·phyte /sáprəfīt/ *n.* any plant or microorganism living on dead or decayed organic matter. □□ **sap·ro·phyt·ic** /–fitik/ *adj.*

sap·wood /sápwŏod/ *n.* the soft outer layers of recently formed wood between the heartwood and the bark.

sar·a·band /sárəband/ *n.* **1** a stately old Spanish dance. **2** music for this or in its rhythm, usu. in triple time often with a long note on the second beat of the bar. [F *sarabande* f. Sp. & It. *zarabanda*]

Sar·a·cen /sárəsən/ *n. & adj. hist.* ●*n.* **1** an Arab or Muslim at the time of the Crusades. **2** a nomad of the Syrian and Arabian desert. • *adj.* of the Saracens. □□ **Sar•a•cen•ic** /sárəsénik/ *adj.* [ME f. OF *sar(r)azin, sar(r)acin* f. LL *Saracenus* f. late Gk *Sarakēnos* perh. f. Arab. *šaṛḳī* eastern]

Sar•a•cen corn *n. Brit. archaic* buckwheat.

Sar•a•cen's head *n.* the head of a Saracen or Turk as a heraldic charge or inn sign.

sa•ran•gi /səránggee/ *n.* (*pl.* **sa•ran•gis**) an E. Indian stringed instrument played with a bow. [Hindi *sāraṅgī*]

sa•ra•pe var. of SERAPE.

sar•casm /saárkazəm/ *n.* **1** a bitter or wounding remark. **2** a taunt, esp. one ironically worded. **3** language consisting of such remarks. **4** the use of or the faculty of using this. □□ **sar•cas•tic** /–kástik/ *adj.* **sar•cas•ti•cal•ly** *adv.* [F *sarcasme* or f. LL *sarcasmus* f. late Gk *sarkasmos* f. Gk *sarkazō* tear flesh, in late Gk gnash the teeth, speak bitterly f. *sarx sarkos* flesh]

sarce•net /saársənit/ *n.* (also **sarse•net**) a fine, soft, silk material used esp. for linings. [ME f. AF *sarzinett* perh. dimin. of *sarzin* SARACEN after OF *drap sarrasinois* Saracen cloth]

sar•co•ma /saarkṓmə/ *n.* (*pl.* **sar•co•mas** or **sar•co•ma•ta** /–mətə/) a malignant tumor of connective or other nonepithelial tissue. □□ **sar•co•ma•to•sis** /–mətṓsis/ *n.* **sar•co•ma•tous** *adj.* [mod.L f. Gk *sarkōma* f. *sarkoō* become fleshy f. *sarx sarkos* flesh]

sar•coph•a•gus /saarkófəgəs/ *n.* (*pl.* **sar•coph•a•gi** /–gī, –jī/) a stone coffin, esp. one adorned with a sculpture or inscription. [L f. Gk *sarkophagos* flesh-consuming (as SARCOMA, *–phagos* –eating)]

sar•co•plasm /saárkəplazəm/ *n. Anat.* the cytoplasm in which muscle fibrils are embedded. [Gk *sarx sarkos* flesh + PLASMA]

sar•cous /saárkəs/ *adj.* consisting of flesh or muscle. [Gk *sarx sarkos* flesh]

sard /saard/ *n.* a yellow or orange-red cornelian. [ME f. F *sarde* or L *sarda* = LL *sardius* f. Gk *sardios* prob. f. *Sardō* Sardinia]

sar•delle /saardél/ *n.* any of several fish resembling the sardine. [It. *sardella* dimin. of *sarda* f. L (as SARDINE[1])]

sar•dine[1] /saardeén/ *n.* a young pilchard or similar young or small herringlike marine fish. □ **like sardines** crowded close together (as sardines are in tins). [ME f. OF *sardine* = It. *sardina* f. L f. *sarda* f. Gk, perh. f. *Sardō* Sardinia]

sar•dine[2] /saárdin/ *n.* a precious stone mentioned in Rev. 4:3. [ME f. LL *sardinus* f. Gk *sardinos* var. of *sardios* SARD]

sar•di•us /saárdeeəs/ *n. Bibl.*, etc., a precious stone. [ME f. LL f. Gk *sardios* sard]

sar•don•ic /saardónik/ *adj.* **1** grimly jocular. **2** (of laughter, etc.) bitterly mocking or cynical. □□ **sar•don•i•cal•ly** *adv.* **sar•don•i•cism** /–nisizəm/ *n.* [F *sardonique*, earlier *sardonien* f. L *sardonius* f. Gk *sardonios* of Sardinia, alt. of *sardanios* Homeric epithet of bitter or scornful laughter]

sar•don•yx /saardóniks, saárd'n–/ *n.* onyx in which white layers alternate with sard. [ME f. L f. Gk *sardonux* (prob. as SARD, ONYX)]

sa•ree var. of SARI.

sar•gas•so /saargásō/ *n.* (also **sar•gas•sum**) (*pl.* **•sos** or **•soes** or **sar•gas•sa**) any seaweed of the genus *Sargassum*, with berrylike air vessels, found floating in islandlike masses, esp. in the Sargasso Sea of the N. Atlantic. Also called **gulfweed**. [Port. *sargaço*, of unkn. orig.]

sarge /saarj/ *n. sl.* sergeant. [abbr.]

sa•ri /saáree/ *n.* (also **sa•ree**) (*pl.* **sa•ris** or **sa•rees**) a length of cotton or silk draped around the body, traditionally worn as a main garment by women of India. [Hindi *sāṛ(h)ī*]

sark /saark/ *n. Sc. & No. of Engl.* a shirt or chemise. [ME *serk* f. ON *serkr* f. Gmc]

sar•ky /saárkee/ *adj.* (**sar•ki•er, sar•ki•est**) *Brit. sl.* sarcastic. □□ **sar•ki•ly** *adv.* **sar•ki•ness** *n.* [abbr.]

sar•men•tose /saárməntōs/ *adj.* (also **sar•men•tous** /–méntəs/) *Bot.* having long, thin trailing shoots. [L *sarmentosus* f. *sarmenta* (pl.) twigs, brushwood, f. *sarpere* to prune]

sa•rong /səráwng, –róng/ *n.* **1** a Malay and Javanese garment consisting of a long strip of (often striped) cloth worn by both sexes tucked around the waist or under the armpits. **2** a woman's garment resembling this. [Malay, lit. 'sheath']

sa•ros /saáros, –aws/ *n. Astron.* a period of about 18 years between repetitions of eclipses. [Gk f. Babylonian *šār* (*u*) 3,600 (years)]

sar•ru•so•phone /sərŏŏsəfōn/ *n.* a metal wind instrument played with a double reed like an oboe. [*Sarrus*, 19th-c. Fr. inventor]

sar•sa•pa•ril•la /sáspərilə, saárs–/ *n.* **1** a preparation of the dried roots of various plants, esp. smilax, used to flavor some drinks and medicines and formerly as a tonic. **2** any of the plants yielding this. [Sp. *zarzaparilla* f. *zarza* bramble, prob. + dimin. of *parra* vine]

sar•sen /saársən/ *n. Geol.* a sandstone boulder carried by ice during a glacial period. [prob. var. of SARACEN]

sarse•net var. of SARCENET.

sar•to•ri•al /saartáwreeəl/ *adj.* **1** of a tailor or tailoring. **2** of men's clothes. □□ **sar•to•ri•al•ly** *adv.* [L *sartor* tailor f. *sarcire sart-* patch]

sar•to•ri•us /saartáwreeəs/ *n. Anat.* the long, narrow muscle running across the front of each thigh. [mod.L f. L *sartor* tailor (the muscle being used in adopting a tailor's cross-legged posture)]

Sar•um use /sáirəm/ *n. Eccl.* the order of divine service used in the diocese of Salisbury before the Reformation. [med.L *Sarum* Salisbury, perh. f. L *Sarisburia*]

s.a.s.e. *abbr.* self-addressed stamped envelope.

sash[1] /sash/ *n.* a long strip or loop of cloth, etc., worn over one shoulder usu. as part of a uniform or insignia, or worn around the waist, usu. by a woman or child. □□ **sashed** *adj.* [earlier *shash* f. Arab. *šāš* muslin, turban]

sash[2] /sash/ *n.* **1** a frame holding the glass in a window and usu. made to slide up and down in the grooves of a window aperture. **2** esp. *Brit.* the glazed sliding pane of a greenhouse, etc. □□ **sashed** *adj.* [*sashes* corrupt. of CHASSIS, mistaken for pl.]

sa•shay /sasháy/ *v.intr. colloq.* walk or move ostentatiously, casually, or diagonally. [corrupt. of CHASSÉ]

sash cord *n.* a strong cord attaching the sash weights to a sash.

sa•shi•mi /saasheémee/ *n.* a Japanese dish of garnished raw fish in thin slices. [Jap.]

sash weight *n.* a weight attached to each end of a sash to balance it at any height.

sash win•dow *n.* a window with one or two sashes of which one or each can be slid vertically over the other to make an opening.

sa•sin /sásin, sáy–/ *n.* = *black buck*. [Nepali]

Sask. *abbr.* Saskatchewan.

Sas•quatch /sáskwoch, –kwach/ *n.* a supposed yetilike animal of NW America. Also called **Bigfoot**. [Amer. Indian]

sass /sas/ *n. & v. colloq.* • *n.* impudence; disrespectful mannerism or speech. • *v.tr.* be impudent to. [var. of SAUCE]

sas•sa•by /sásəbee/ *n.* (*pl.* **•bies**) a S. African antelope, *Damaliscus lunatus*, similar to the hartebeest. [Setswana *tsessébe, –ábi*]

sas•sa•fras /sásəfras/ *n.* **1** a small tree, *Sassafras albidum*, native to N. America, with aromatic leaves and bark. **2** a preparation of oil extracted from the leaves or bark of this tree, used medicinally or in perfumery. [Sp. *sasafrás* or Port. *sassafraz*, of unkn. orig.]

Sas•sa•ni•an /sasáyneeən/ *n. & adj.* (also **Sas•sa•nid** /sásənid/) • *n.* a member of a Persian dynasty ruling 211-651. • *adj.* of or relating to this dynasty. [*Sasan*, founder of the dynasty]

Sas•se•nach /sásənakh, –nak/ *n. & adj. Sc. & Ir.* usu. *derog.* • *n.* an English person. • *adj.* English. [Gael. *Sasunnoch*, Ir. *Sasanach* f. L *Saxones* Saxons]

sas•sy /sásee/ *adj.* (**sas•si•er, sas•si•est**) *colloq.* = SAUCY. □□ **sas•si•ly** *adv.* **sas•si•ness** *n.* [var. of SAUCY]

sas•tru•gi /sastrŏŏgee/ *n.pl.* wavelike irregularities on the surface of hard polar snow, caused by winds. [Russ. *zastrugi* small ridges]

SAT *abbr. Trademark* **1** Scholastic Assessment Test. **2** (formerly) Scholastic Aptitude Test.

Sat. *abbr.* Saturday.

sat *past* and *past part.* of SIT.

Sa•tan /sáyt'n/ *n.* the Devil; Lucifer. [OE f. LL *Satan* f. Gk f. Heb. *śāṭān* lit. 'adversary' f. *śaṭan* oppose, plot against]

sa•tan•ic /sətánik, say–/ *adj.* **1** of, like, or befitting Satan. **2** diabolical; hellish. □□ **sa•tan•i•cal•ly** *adv.*

Sa•tan•ism /sáyt'nizəm/ *n.* **1** the worship of Satan, with a travesty of Christian forms. **2** the pursuit of evil for its own sake. **3** deliberate wickedness. □□ **Sa•tan•ist** *n.* **Sa•tan•ize** *v.tr.*

Sa•tan•ol•o•gy /sáyt'nóləjee/ *n.* **1** beliefs concerning the Devil. **2** a history or collection of these.

sa•tay /saátay/ *n.* (also **sa•tai, sa•té**) an Indonesian and Malaysian dish consisting of small pieces of meat grilled on a skewer and usu. served with spiced peanut sauce. [Malayan *satai sate*, Indonesian *sate*]

SATB *abbr. Mus.* soprano, alto, tenor, and bass (as a combination of voices).

satch•el /sáchəl/ *n.* a small bag usu. of leather and hung from the shoulder with a strap, for carrying books, etc., esp. to and from school. [ME f. OF *sachel* f. L *saccellus* (as SACK[1])]

sate /sayt/ *v.tr.* **1** gratify (desire, or a desirous person) to the full. **2** cloy; surfeit; weary with overabundance (*sated with pleasure*). □□ **sate•less** *adj. poet.* [prob. f. dial. *sade*, OE *sadian* (as SAD), assim. to SATIATE]

sa•teen /sateén/ *n.* cotton fabric woven like satin with a glossy surface. [*satin* after *velveteen*]

sat•el•lite /sát'lit/ *n. & adj.* • *n.* **1** a celestial body orbiting the earth or another planet. **2** an artificial body placed in orbit around the earth or another planet. **3** a follower; a hanger-on. **4** an underling; a member of an important person's staff or retinue. • *adj.* **1** transmitted by satellite (*satellite communications; satellite television*). **2** dependent; secondary (*networks of small satellite computers*). □□ **sat•el•lit•ic** /–lítik/ *adj.* **sat•el•lit•ism** *n.* [F *satellite* or L *satelles satellitis* attendant]

sat•el•lite dish *n.* a concave dish-shaped antenna for receiving broadcasting signals transmitted by satellite.

sa•ti var. of SUTTEE.

sa•ti•ate /sáysheeayt/ *adj. & v.* • *adj. archaic* satiated. • *v.tr.* = SATE.

□□ **sa·tia·ble** /-shəbəl/ *adj. archaic.* **sa·ti·a·tion** /-áyshən/ *n.* [L *satiatus* past part. of *satiare* f. *satis* enough]

sa·ti·e·ty /sətí-itee/ *n.* **1** the state of being glutted or satiated. **2** the feeling of having too much of something. **3** (foll. by *of*) a cloyed dislike of. □ **to satiety** to an extent beyond what is desired. [obs. F *societé* f. L *satietas –tatis* f. *satis* enough]

sat·in /sát'n/ *n., adj., & v.* ● *n.* a fabric of silk or various synthetic fibers, with a glossy surface on one side produced by a twill weave with the weft threads almost hidden. ● *adj.* smooth as satin. ● *v.tr.* give a glossy surface to (paper). □□ **sat·in·ized** *adj.* **sat·in·y** *adj.* [ME f. OF f. Arab. *zaytūnī* of *Tseutung* in China]

sat·i·net /sát'nét/ *n.* (also **sat·i·nette**) a satinlike fabric made partly or wholly of cotton or synthetic fiber.

sat·in fin·ish *n.* **1** a polish given to silver, etc., with a metallic brush. **2** any effect resembling satin in texture produced on materials in various ways.

sat·in·flow·er /sát'nflowr/ *n.* **1** any plant of the genus *Clarkia*, with pink or lavender flowers. **2** = HONESTY 3.

sat·in pa·per *n.* fine glossy writing paper.

sat·in spar *n.* a fibrous variety of gypsum.

sat·in stitch *n.* a long, straight embroidery stitch, giving the appearance of satin.

sat·in white *n.* a white pigment of calcium sulfate and alumina.

sat·in·wood /sát'nwŏod/ *n.* **1 a** (in full **Ceylon satinwood**) a tree, *Chloroxylon swietenia*, native to central and southern India and Ceylon (Sri Lanka). **b** (in full **West Indian satinwood**) a tree, *Fagara flava*, native to the West Indies, Bermuda, the Bahamas, and southern Florida. **2** the yellow, glossy wood of either of these trees.

sat·ire /sátīr/ *n.* **1** the use of ridicule, irony, sarcasm, etc., to expose folly or vice or to lampoon an individual. **2** a work or composition in prose or verse using satire. **3** this branch of literature. **4** a thing that brings ridicule upon something else. **5** *Rom. Antiq.* a poetic medley, esp. a poem ridiculing prevalent vices or follies. [F *satire* or L *satira* later form of *satura* medley]

sa·tir·ic /sətírik/ *adj.* **1** of satire or satires. **2** containing satire (*wrote a satiric review*). **3** writing satire (*a satiric poet*). [F *satirique* or LL *satiricus* (as SATIRE)]

sa·tir·i·cal /sətírikəl/ *adj.* **1** = SATIRIC. **2** given to the use of satire in speech or writing or to cynical observation of others; sarcastic; humorously critical. □□ **sa·tir·i·cal·ly** *adv.*

sat·i·rist /sátərist/ *n.* **1** a writer of satires. **2** a satirical person.

sat·i·rize /sátīrīz/ *v.tr.* **1** assail or ridicule with satire. **2** write a satire upon. **3** describe satirically. □□ **sat·i·ri·za·tion** *n.* [F *satiriser* (as SATIRE)]

sat·is·fac·tion /sátisfákshən/ *n.* **1** the act or an instance of satisfying; the state of being satisfied (*heard this with great satisfaction*). **2** a thing that satisfies desire or gratifies feeling (*is a great satisfaction to me*). **3** a thing that settles an obligation or pays a debt. **4 a** (foll. by *for*) atonement; compensation (*demanded satisfaction*). **b** *Theol.* Christ's atonement for the sins of mankind. □ **to one's satisfaction** so that one is satisfied. [ME f. OF f. L *satisfactio –onis* (as SATISFY)]

sat·is·fac·to·ry /sátisfáktəree/ *adj.* **1** adequate; causing or giving satisfaction (*was a satisfactory pupil*). **2** satisfying expectations or needs; leaving no room for complaint (*a satisfactory result*). □□ **sat·is·fac·to·ri·ly** *adv.* **sat·is·fac·to·ri·ness** *n.* [F *satisfactoire* or med.L *satisfactorius* (as SATISFY)]

sat·is·fy /sátisfī/ *v.* (**·fies, ·fied**) **1** *tr.* **a** meet the expectations or desires of; comply with (a demand). **b** be accepted by (a person, his or her taste) as adequate; be equal to (a preconception, etc.). **2** *tr.* put an end to (an appetite or want) by supplying what was required. **3** *tr.* rid (a person) of an appetite or want in a similar way. **4** *intr.* give satisfaction; leave nothing to be desired. **5** *tr.* pay (a debt or creditor). **6** *tr.* adequately meet, fulfill, or comply with (conditions, obligations, etc.) (*has satisfied all the legal conditions*). **7** *tr.* (often foll. by *of, that*) provide with adequate information or proof; convince (*satisfied the others that they were right; satisfy the court of their innocence*). **8** *tr.* Math. (of a quantity) make (an equation) true. **9** *tr.* (in *passive*) **a** (foll. by *with*) contented or pleased with. **b** (foll. by *to*) demand no more than or consider it enough to do. □ **satisfy oneself** (often foll. by *that* + clause) be certain in one's own mind. □□ **sat·is·fi·a·ble** *adj.* **sat·is·fi·a·bil·i·ty** /–fīəbílitee/ *n.* **sat·is·fied·ly** *adv.* **sat·is·fy·ing** *adj.* **sat·is·fy·ing·ly** *adv.* [ME f. OF *satisfier* f. L *satisfacere satisfact-* f. *satis* enough]

sa·to·ri /sətáwree/ *n. Buddhism* sudden enlightenment. [Jap.]

sa·trap /sátrap, sáy–/ *n.* **1** a provincial governor in the ancient Persian empire. **2** a subordinate ruler, colonial governor, etc. [ME f. OF *satrape* or L *satrapa* f. Gk *satrapēs* f. OPers. *xšathra-pāvan* country protector]

sa·trap·y /sátrəpee, sáy–/ *n.* (pl. **·ies**) a province ruled over by a satrap.

sat·su·ma /satsŏomə, sátsŏomə/ *n.* **1** a variety of tangerine orig. grown in Japan. **2** (**Satsuma**) (in full **Satsuma ware**) cream-colored Japanese pottery. [*Satsuma* a province in Japan]

sat·u·rate /sáchərayt/ *v.tr.* **1** fill with moisture; soak thoroughly. **2** (often foll. by *with*) fill to capacity. **3** cause (a substance, solution, vapor, metal, or air) to absorb, hold, or combine with the greatest possible amount of another substance, or of moisture, magnetism, electricity, etc. **4** cause (a substance) to combine with the maximum amount of another substance. **5** supply (a market) beyond the point at which the demand for a product is satisfied. **6** (foll. by *with, in*) imbue with or steep in (learning, tradition, prejudice, etc.). **7** overwhelm (enemy defenses, a target area, etc.) by concentrated bombing. **8** (as **saturated** *adj.*) **a** (of color) full; rich; free from an admixture of white. **b** (of fat molecules) containing the greatest number of hydrogen atoms. □□ **sat·u·rate** /–rət/ *adj. literary.* **sat·u·ra·ble** /–rəbəl/ *adj.* **sat·u·rant** /–rənt/ *n. & adj.* [L *saturare* f. *satur* full]

sat·u·ra·tion /sáchəráyshən/ *n.* the act or an instance of saturating; the state of being saturated.

sat·u·ra·tion point *n.* the stage beyond which no more can be absorbed or accepted.

Sat·ur·day /sátərday, –dee/ *n. & adv.* ● *n.* the seventh day of the week, following Friday. ● *adv. colloq.* **1** on Saturday. **2** (**Saturdays**) on Saturdays; each Saturday. [OE *Sætern(es) dæg* transl. of L *Saturni dies* day of Saturn]

Sat·ur·day-night spe·cial *n. sl.* any inexpensive handgun that is easy to obtain and conceal.

Sat·urn /sátərn/ *n.* **1 a** the sixth planet from the sun, with a system of broad flat rings circling it, and the most distant of the five planets known in the ancient world. **b** *Astrol.* Saturn as a supposed astrological influence on those born under its sign, characterized by coldness and gloominess. **2** *Alchemy* the metal lead. □□ **Sa·tur·ni·an** /sətárneeən/ *adj.* [L *Saturnus*, Roman god of agriculture, identified with Kronos, father of Zeus, perh. f. Etruscan]

sat·ur·na·li·a /sátərnáyleeə/ *n.* (pl. same or **sat·ur·na·li·as**) **1** (usu. **Saturnalia**) *Rom. Hist.* the festival of Saturn in December, characterized by unrestrained merrymaking for all, the predecessor of Christmas. **2** (as *sing.* or *pl.*) a scene of wild revelry or tumult; an orgy. □□ **sat·ur·na·li·an** *adj.* [L, neut. pl. of *Saturnalis* (as SATURN)]

sa·tur·nic /sətárnik/ *adj. Med.* affected with lead poisoning. □□ **sat·ur·nism** /sátərnizəm/ [SATURN 2]

sa·tur·ni·id /sətárneeid/ *n.* any large moth of the family Saturniidae, including emperor moths. [mod.L]

sat·ur·nine /sátərnin/ *adj.* **1 a** of a sluggish gloomy temperament. **b** (of looks, etc.) dark and brooding. **2** *archaic* **a** of the metal lead. **b** *Med.* of or affected by lead poisoning. □□ **sat·ur·nine·ly** *adv.* [ME f. OF *saturnin* f. med.L *Saturninus* (as SATURN)]

sat·ya·gra·ha /sutyáagrəhə/ *n. Ind.* **1** *hist.* a policy of passive resistance to British rule advocated by Gandhi. **2** passive resistance as a policy. [Skr. f. *satya* truth + *āgraha* obstinacy]

sa·tyr /sáytər, sát–/ *n.* **1** (in Greek mythology) one of a class of Greek woodland gods with a horse's ears and tail, or (in Roman representations) with a goat's ears, tail, legs, and budding horns. **2** a lustful or sensual man. **3** = SATYRID. [ME f. OF *satyre* or L *satyrus* f. Gk *saturos*]

sa·ty·ri·a·sis /sáytyríəsis, sát–/ *n. Med.* excessive sexual desire in men. [LL f. Gk *saturiasis* (as SATYR)]

sa·tyr·ic /sətírik/ *adj.* (in Greek mythology) of or relating to satyrs. [L *satyricus* f. Gk *saturikos* (as SATYR)]

sa·tyr·ic dra·ma *n.* a kind of ancient Greek comic play with a chorus of satyrs.

sa·tyr·id /sáytərid, sát–, sətírid/ *n.* any butterfly of the family Satyridae, with distinctive eyelike markings on the wings. [mod.L *Satyridae* f. the genus name *Satyrus* (as SATYR)]

sauce /saws/ *n. & v.* ● *n.* **1** any of various liquid or semisolid preparations taken as a relish with food; the liquid constituent of a dish (*mint sauce; tomato sauce; chicken in a lemon sauce*). **2** something adding piquancy or excitement. **3** esp. *Brit. colloq.* impudence; impertinence. **4** stewed fruit, etc., eaten as dessert or used as a garnish. ● *v.tr.* **1** *colloq.* be impudent to. **2** *archaic* **a** season with sauce or condiments. **b** add excitement to. □ **sauce for the goose** what is appropriate in one case (by implication is appropriate in others). □□ **sauce·less** *adj.* [ME f. OF ult. f. L *salsus* f. *salere sals–* to salt f. *sal* salt]

sauce·boat /sáwsbōt/ *n.* a kind of small pitcher or dish used for serving sauces, etc.

sauce·pan /sáwspan/ *n.* a usu. metal cooking pan, usu. round with a lid and a long handle at the side, used for boiling, stewing, etc., on top of a stove. □□ **sauce·pan·ful** *n.* (pl. **·fuls**).

sau·cer /sáwsər/ *n.* **1** a shallow circular dish used for standing a cup on and to catch drips. **2** any similar dish used to stand a plant pot, etc., on. □□ **sau·cer·ful** *n.* (pl. **·fuls**). **sau·cer·less** *adj.* [ME, = condiment dish, f. OF *saussier(e)* sauceboat, prob. f. LL *salsarium* (as SAUCE)]

sau·cy /sáwsee/ *adj.* (**sau·ci·er, sau·ci·est**) **1** impudent; flippant. **2** *colloq.* smart-looking (*a saucy hat*). **3** *colloq.* smutty; suggestive. □□ **sau·ci·ly** *adv.* **sau·ci·ness** *n.* [earlier sense 'savory,' f. SAUCE]

Sau·di /sówdee, sáw–/ n. & adj. (also **Sau·di A·ra·bi·an**) • n. (pl. **Sau·dis**) **1 a** a native or national of Saudi Arabia. **b** a person of Saudi descent. **2** a member of the dynasty founded by King Saud. • adj. of or relating to Saudi Arabia or the Saudi dynasty. [A. Ibn-*Saud*, Arab. king d. 1953]

sau·er·kraut /sówərkrowt/ n. a German dish of chopped pickled cabbage. [G f. *sauer* SOUR + *Kraut* vegetable]

sau·ger /sáwgər/ n. a small N. American pike perch. [19th c.: orig. unkn.]

Sauk /sawk/ n. (also **Sak**) **1 a** a N. American people native to Wisconsin. **b** a member of this people. **2** the language of this people.

sau·na /sáwnə, sow–/ n. **1** a Finnish-style steam bath. **2** a building used for this. [Finn.]

saun·ter /sáwntər/ v. & n. • v.intr. **1** walk slowly; amble; stroll. **2** proceed without hurry or effort. • n. **1** a leisurely ramble. **2** a slow gait. □□ **saun·ter·er** n. [ME, = muse: orig. unkn.]

sau·ri·an /sáwreeən/ adj. of or like a lizard. [mod.L *Sauria* f. Gk *saura* lizard]

sau·ro·pod /sáwrōpod/ n. any of a group of plant-eating dinosaurs with a long neck and tail, and four thick limbs. [Gk *saura* lizard + *pous pod*- foot]

sau·ry /sáwree/ n. (pl. **·ries**) a long-beaked marine fish, *Scomberesox saurus*, of temperate waters. [perh. f. LL f. Gk *sauros* horse mackerel]

sau·sage /sáwsij/ n. **1 a** ground pork, beef, or other meat seasoned and often mixed with other ingredients, encased in cylindrical form in a skin, for cooking and eating hot or cold. **b** a length of this. **2** a sausage-shaped object. □ **not a sausage** Brit. colloq. nothing at all. [ME f. ONF *saussiche* f. med.L *salsicia* f. L *salsus*: see SAUCE]

sausage dog n. Brit. colloq. a dachshund.

sausage ma·chine n. **1** a sausage-making machine. **2** Brit. a relentlessly uniform process.

sau·té /sōtáy, saw–/ adj., n., & v. • adj. quickly cooked or browned in a little hot fat. • n. food cooked in this way. • v.tr. (**sau·téed** or **sau·téd**) cook in this way. [F, past part. of *sauter* jump]

Sau·ternes /sōtɔ́rn, saw–/ n. **1** a sweet white wine from Sauternes in the Bordeaux region of France. **2** (usu. **sauterne**) a type of semisweet white wine.

sav·age /sávij/ adj., n., & v. • adj. **1** fierce; cruel (*savage persecution*; *a savage blow*). **2** wild; primitive (*savage tribes*; *a savage animal*). **3** archaic (of scenery, etc.) uncultivated (*a savage scene*). **4** colloq. angry; bad-tempered (*in a savage mood*). **5** Heraldry (of the human figure) naked. • n. **1** Anthropol. derog. a member of a primitive tribe. **2** a cruel or barbarous person. • v.tr. **1** (esp. of a dog, wolf, etc.) attack and bite or trample. **2** (of a critic, etc.) attack fiercely. □□ **sav·age·dom** n. **sav·age·ly** adv. **sav·age·ness** n. **sav·age·ry** n. (pl. **·ies**). [ME f. OF *sauvage* wild f. L *silvaticus* f. *silva* a wood]

sa·van·na /səvánə/ n. (also **sa·van·nah**) a grassy plain in tropical and subtropical regions, with few or no trees. [Sp. *zavana* perh. of Carib orig.]

sa·vant /savánt, sávənt/ n. (fem. **sa·vante**) a learned person, esp. a distinguished scientist, etc. [F, part. of *savoir* know (as SAPIENT)]

sa·vate /səváat/ n. a form of boxing in which feet and fists are used. [F, orig. a kind of shoe: cf. SABOT]

save[1] /sayv/ v. & n. • v. **1** tr. (often foll. by *from*) rescue, preserve, protect, or deliver from danger, harm, discredit, etc. (*saved my life*; *saved me from drowning*). **2** tr. (often foll. by *up*) keep for future use; reserve; refrain from spending (*saved up $150 for a new bike*; *likes to save plastic bags*). **3** tr. (often refl.) **a** relieve (another person or oneself) from spending (money, time, trouble, etc.); prevent exposure to (annoyance, etc.) (*saved myself $50*; *a word processor saves time*). **b** obviate the need or likelihood of (*soaking saves scrubbing*). **4** tr. preserve from damnation; convert (*saved her soul*). **5** tr. & refl. husband or preserve (one's strength, health, etc.) (*saving himself for the last lap*; *save your energy*). **6** intr. (often foll. by *up*) save money for future use. **7** tr. **a** avoid losing (a game, match, etc.). **b** prevent an opponent from scoring (a goal, etc.). **c** stop (a ball, etc.) from entering the goal. • n. **1** Ice hockey, soccer, etc. the act of preventing an opponent's scoring, etc. **2** Bridge a sacrifice bid to prevent unnecessary losses. □ **save appearances** present a prosperous, respectable, etc., appearance. **save face** see FACE. **save one's breath** not waste time speaking to no effect. **save the day** find or provide a solution to difficulty or disaster. **save one's skin** (or **neck** or **bacon**) avoid loss, injury, or death; escape from danger. **save the tide** get in or out (of port, etc.) while it lasts. **save the trouble** avoid useless or pointless effort. □□ **sav·a·ble** adj. (also **save·a·ble**). [ME f. AF *sa(u)ver*, OF *salver, sauver* f. LL *salvare* f. L *salvus* SAFE]

save[2] /sayv/ prep. & conj. archaic or poet. • prep. except; but (*all save him*). • conj. (often foll. by *for*) unless; but; except (*happy save for one want*; *is well save that he has a cold*). [ME f. OF *sauf sauve* f. L *salvo, salva*, ablat. sing. of *salvus* SAFE]

save-all n. **1** a device to prevent waste. **2** hist. a pan with a spike for burning up candle ends.

sav·e·loy /sávəloy/ n. Brit. a seasoned red pork sausage, dried and

smoked, and sold ready to eat. [corrupt. of F *cervelas*, –*at*, f. It. *cervellata* (*cervello* brain)]

sav·er /sáyvər/ n. **1** a person who saves, esp. money. **2** (often in *comb.*) a device for economical use (of time, etc.) (*found the short cut a time-saver*). **3** Racing sl. a hedging bet.

sav·in /sávin/ n. (also **sav·ine**) **1** a bushy juniper, *Juniperus sabina*, usu. spreading horizontally, and yielding oil formerly used in the treatment of amenorrhea. **2** = RED CEDAR. [OE f. OF *savine* f. L *sabina* (*herba*) Sabine (herb)]

sav·ing /sáyving/ adj., n., & prep. • adj. (often in *comb.*) making economical use of (*labor-saving*). • n. **1** anything that is saved. **2** an economy (*a saving in expenses*). **3** (usu. in *pl.*) money saved (*used our savings to buy the car*). • prep. **1** with the exception of; except (*all saving that one*). **2** without offense to (*saving your presence*). [ME f. SAVE[1]: prep. prob. f. SAVE[2]]

▶Use **savings** in the modifying position (*savings bank, savings bond*) and when referring to money saved in a bank: *Your savings are fully insured.* When speaking of an act of saving, as when one obtains a discount on a purchase, the preferred form is **saving**: *With this coupon you will receive a saving* (not *savings*) *of $3.*

sav·ing clause n. Law a clause containing a stipulation of exemption, etc.

sav·ing grace n. **1** the redeeming grace of God. **2** a redeeming quality or characteristic.

sav·ings ac·count n. a bank account that earns interest and from which withdrawals are usu. made in person.

sav·ings and loan as·so·ci·a·tion n. an institution, usu. owned by depositors and regulated by state or federal government, that accepts funds for savings accounts and lends funds for mortgages.

sav·ings bank n. a bank receiving deposits at interest and returning the profits to the depositors.

sav·ior /sáyvyər/ n. (esp. Brit. **sav·iour**) **1** a person who saves or delivers from danger, destruction, etc. (*the savior of the nation*). **2** (**Savior**) (prec. by *the, our*) Christ. [ME f. OF *sauvëour* f. eccl.L *salvator –oris* (transl. Gk *sōtēr*) f. LL *salvare* SAVE[1]]

sav·oir faire /sávwaar fáir/ n. the ability to act suitably in any situation; tact. [F, = know how to do]

sa·voir vi·vre /véevrə/ n. knowledge of the world and the ways of society; ability to conduct oneself well; sophistication. [F, = know how to live]

sa·vor /sáyvər/ n. & v. (Brit. **sa·vour**) • n. **1** a characteristic taste, flavor, relish, etc. **2** a quality suggestive of or containing a small amount of another. **3** archaic a characteristic smell. • v. **1** tr. **a** appreciate and enjoy the taste of (food). **b** enjoy or appreciate (an experience, etc.). **2** intr. (foll. by *of*) **a** suggest by taste, smell, etc. (*savors of mushrooms*). **b** imply or suggest a specified quality (*savors of impertinence*). □□ **sa·vor·less** adj. [ME f. OF f. L *sapor –oris* f. *sapere* to taste]

sa·vor·y[1] /sáyvoree/ n. (pl. **·ies**) any herb of the genus *Satureia*, esp. *S. hortensis* and *S. montana*, used esp. in cookery. [ME *saverey*, perh. f. OE *sætherie* f. L *satureia*]

sa·vor·y[2] /sáyvoree/ adj. & n. (Brit. **sa·voury**) • adj. **1** having an appetizing taste or smell. **2** (of food) salty or piquant, not sweet (*a savory omelette*). **3** pleasant; acceptable. • n. (pl. **·ies**) Brit. a savory dish served as an appetizer or at the end of dinner. □□ **sa·vor·i·ly** adv. **sa·vor·i·ness** n. [ME f. OF *savoré* past part. (as SAVOR)]

sa·voy /səvóy/ n. a hardy variety of cabbage with wrinkled leaves. [*Savoy* in SE France]

Sa·voy·ard[1] /səvóyaard, sávoyáard/ n. & adj. • n. a native of Savoy in SE France. • adj. of or relating to Savoy or its people, etc. [F f. *Savoie* Savoy]

Sa·voy·ard[2] /səvóyaard, sávoyáard/ n. a devotee or performer of Gilbert and Sullivan operas. [*Savoy* Theatre in London, built for their presentation]

sav·vy /sávee/ v., n., & adj. sl. • v.intr. & tr. (**·vies**, **·vied**) know. • n. knowingness; shrewdness; understanding. • adj. (**sav·vi·er**, **sav·vi·est**) knowing; wise. [orig. Creole & Pidgin E after Sp. *sabe usted* you know]

saw[1] /saw/ n. & v. • n. **1 a** a hand tool having a toothed blade used to cut esp. wood with a to-and-fro movement. **b** any of several mechanical power-driven devices with a toothed rotating disk or moving band, for cutting. **2** Zool. etc., a serrated organ or part. • v. (*past part.* **sawed** or **sawn** /sawn/) **1** tr. **a** cut (wood, etc.) with a saw. **b** make (boards, etc.) with a saw. **2** intr. use a saw. **3 a** intr. move to and fro with a motion as of a saw or person sawing (*sawing away on his violin*). **b** tr. divide (the air, etc.) with gesticulations. □□ **saw·like** adj. [OE *saga* f. Gmc]

saw[2] past of SEE[1].

saw[3] n. a proverb; a maxim (*that's just an old saw*). [OE *sagu* f. Gmc, rel. to SAY: cf. SAGA]

saw·bones /sáwbōnz/ n. sl. a doctor or surgeon.

saw·buck /sáwbuk/ n. **1** a sawhorse. **2** sl. a $10 bill.

saw·dust /sáwdust/ n. powdery particles of wood produced in sawing.

saw-edged adj. with a jagged edge like a saw.

sawed-off adj. (also **sawn-off**) **1** (of a gun) having part of the barrel sawed off to make it easier to handle and give a wider field of fire. **2** *colloq.* (of a person) short.

saw·fish /sáwfish/ *n.* any large marine fish of the family Pristidae, with a toothed flat snout used as a weapon.

saw·fly /sáwflī/ *n.* (*pl.* **·flies**) any insect of the superfamily Tenthredinoidea, with a serrated ovipositor, the larvae of which are injurious to plants.

saw·horse /sáwhawrs/ *n.* a rack supporting wood for sawing.

saw·mill /sáwmil/ *n.* a factory in which wood is sawed mechanically into planks or boards.

sawfish

sawn *past part.* of SAW[1].

saw pit *n.* a pit in which the lower of two men working a pit saw stands.

saw set *n.* a tool for wrenching saw teeth in alternate directions to allow the saw to work freely.

saw·tooth /sáwtōōth/ *adj.* **1** (also **saw·toothed** /–tōōtht/) (esp. of a roof, wave, etc.) shaped like the teeth of a saw with one steep and one slanting side. **2** (of a wave form) showing a slow linear rise and rapid linear fall.

saw-whet owl *n.* a small N. American owl, *Aegolius acadicus*, noted for its harsh cry.

saw·yer /sáwyər/ *n.* **1** a person who saws lumber professionally. **2** an uprooted tree held fast by one end in a river. **3** *NZ* a large wingless horned grasshopper whose grubs bore in wood. [ME, earlier *sawer*, f. SAW[1]]

sax[1] /saks/ *n. colloq.* **1** a saxophone. **2** esp. *Brit.* a saxophone player. □□ **sax·ist** *n.* [abbr.]

sax[2] /saks/ *n.* (also **zax** /zaks/) a slater's chopper, with a point for making nail holes. [OE *seax* knife f. Gmc]

sax·a·tile /sáksətil, –tīl/ *adj.* living or growing on or among rocks. [F *saxatile* or L *saxatilis* f. *saxum* rock]

sax·horn /sáks-hawrn/ *n.* any of a series of different-sized brass wind instruments with valves and a funnel-shaped mouthpiece, used mainly in military and brass bands. [*Sax*, name of its Belgian inventors, + HORN]

sax·ic·o·line /saksíkəlin/ *adj.* (also **sax·ic·o·lous**) *Biol.* = SAXATILE. [mod.L *saxicolus* f. *saxum* rock + *colere* inhabit]

sax·i·frage /sáksifrij, –frayj/ *n.* any plant of the genus *Saxifraga*, growing on rocky or stony ground and usu. bearing small white, yellow, or red flowers. [ME f. OF *saxifrage* or LL *saxifraga* (*herba*) f. L *saxum* rock + *frangere* break]

Sax·on /sáksən/ *n. & adj.* ●*n.* **1** *hist.* **a** a member of the Germanic people that conquered parts of England in 5th–6th c. **b** (usu. **Old Saxon**) the language of the Saxons. **2** = ANGLO-SAXON. **3** a native of modern Saxony in Germany. **4** the Germanic (as opposed to Latin or Romance) elements of English. ●*adj.* **1** *hist.* of or concerning the Saxons. **2** belonging to or originating from the Saxon language or Old English. **3** of or concerning modern Saxony or Saxons. □□ **Sax·on·dom** *n.* **Sax·on·ism** *n.* **Sax·on·ist** *n.* **Sax·on·ize** /–nīz/ *v.tr. & intr.* [ME f. OF f. LL *Saxo –onis* f. Gk *Saxones* (pl.) f. WG: cf. OE *Seaxan, Seaxe* (pl.)]

Sax·on ar·chi·tec·ture *n.* the form of Romanesque architecture preceding the Norman in England.

Sax·on blue *n.* a solution of indigo in sulfuric acid as a dye.

sax·o·ny /sáksənee/ *n.* **1** a fine kind of wool. **2** cloth made from this. [*Saxony* in Germany f. LL *Saxonia* (as SAXON)]

sax·o·phone /sáksəfōn/ *n.* **1** a keyed brass reed instrument in several sizes and registers, used esp. in jazz and dance music. **2** a saxophone player. □□ **sax·o·phon·ic** /–fónik/ *adj.* **sax·o·phon·ist** /–sófənist, –səfōnist/ *n.* [*Sax* (as SAXHORN) + –PHONE]

say /say/ *v. & n.* ●*v.* (*3rd sing. present* **says** /sez/; *past* and *past part.* **said** /sed /) **1** *tr.* (often foll. by *that* + clause) **a** utter (specified words) in a speaking voice; remark (*said "Damn!"*; *said that he was satisfied*). **b** put into words; express (*that was well said ; cannot say what I feel*). **2** *tr.* (often foll. by *that* + clause) **a** state; promise or prophesy (*says that there will be war*). **b** have specified wording; indicate (*says here that he was killed*; *the clock says ten to six*). **3** *tr.* (in *passive*; usu. foll. by *to* + infin.) be asserted or described (*is said to be 93 years old*). **4** *tr.* (foll. by *to* + infin.) *colloq.* tell a person to do something (*he said to bring the car*). **5** *tr.* convey (information) (*spoke for an hour but said little*). **6** *tr.* put forward as an argument or excuse (*much to be said in favor of it*; *what have you to say for yourself?*). **7** *tr.* (often *absol.*) form and give an opinion or decision as to (*who did it I cannot say*; *please say which you prefer*). **8** *tr.* select, assume, or take as an example or (a

saxophone

specified number, etc.) as near enough (*shall we say this one?*; *I'd pay, say, $10*). **9** *tr.* **a** speak the words of (prayers, Mass, a grace, etc.). **b** repeat (a lesson, etc.); recite (*can't say his tables*). **10** *tr. Art*,etc., convey (inner meaning or intention) (*what is the director saying in this film?*). **11** *intr.* **a** speak; talk. **b** (in *imper.*) *poet.* tell me (*what is your name, say!*). **12** *tr.* (**the said**) *Law* or *joc.* the previously mentioned (*the said witness*). **13** *intr.* (as *int.*) an exclamation of surprise, to attract attention, etc. ●*n.* **1 a** an opportunity for stating one's opinion, etc. (*let him have his say*). **b** a stated opinion. **2** a share in a decision (*had no say in the matter*). □ **how say you?** *Law* how do you find? (addressed to the jury requesting its verdict). **I ,etc., cannot** (or **could not**) **say** I, etc., do not know. **I'll say** *colloq.* yes indeed. **I say!** *Brit.* an exclamation expressing surprise, drawing attention, etc. **it is said** the rumor is that. **not to say** and indeed; or possibly even (*his language was rude, not to say offensive*). **said he** (or **I**, etc.) *colloq.* or *poet.* he, etc., said. **say for oneself** say by way of conversation, oratory, etc. **say much** (or **something**) for indicate the high quality of. **say no** refuse or disagree. **say out** esp. *Brit.* express fully or candidly. **says I** (or **he**, etc.) esp. *Brit. colloq.* I, he, etc., said (used in reporting conversation). **say something** make a short speech. **says you!** *colloq.* I disagree. **say when** *colloq.* indicate when enough drink or food has been given. **say the word 1** indicate that you agree or give permission. **2** give the order, etc. **say yes** agree. **that is to say 1** in other words, more explicitly. **2** or at least. **they say** it is rumored. **to say nothing of** = *not to mention* (see MENTION). **what do** (or **would**) **you say to?** would you like? **when all is said and done** after all; in the long run. **you can say that again!** (or **you said it!**) *colloq.* I agree emphatically. **you don't say so** *colloq.* an expression of amazement or disbelief. □□ **say·a·ble** *adj.* **say·er** *n.* [OE *secgan* f. Gmc]

▶ See note at SAID.

say·ing /sáying/ *n.* **1** the act or an instance of saying. **2** a maxim, proverb, adage, etc. □ **as the saying goes** (or **is**) an expression used in introducing a proverb, cliché, etc. **go without saying** be too well known or obvious to need mention. **there is no saying** it is impossible to know.

say-so *n.* **1** the power of decision. **2** mere assertion (*cannot proceed merely on his say-so*).

SBA *abbr.* Small Business Administration.

Sb *symb. Chem.* the element antimony. [L *stibium*]

SbE *abbr.* south by east.

SBN *abbr.* Standard Book Number (cf. ISBN).

SbW *abbr.* south by west.

SC *abbr.* **1** South Carolina (also in official postal use). **2** *Brit.* special constable.

Sc *symb. Chem.* the element scandium.

sc. *abbr.* scilicet.

s.c. *abbr.* small capitals.

scab /skab/ *n. & v.* ●*n.* **1** a dry rough crust formed over a cut, sore, etc., in healing. **2** (often *attrib.*) *colloq. derog.* a person who refuses to strike or join a trade union, or who tries to break a strike by working. **3** the mange or a similar skin disease, esp. in animals. **4** a fungus plant disease causing scablike roughness. **5** a dislikeable person. ●*v.intr.* (**scabbed, scab·bing**) **1** act as a scab. **2** (of a wound, etc.) form a scab; heal over. □□ **scabbed** *adj.* **scab·by** *adj.* (**scab·bi·er, scab·bi·est**) **scab·bi·ness** *n.* **scab·like** *adj.* [ME f. ON *skabbr* (unrecorded), corresp. to OE *sceabb*]

•••

scab·bard /skábərd/ *n.* **1** *hist.* a sheath for a sword, bayonet, etc. **2** a sheath for a revolver, etc. [ME *sca(u)berc*, etc., f. AF prob. f. Frank.]

scab·bard fish *n.* any of various silvery-white marine fish shaped like a sword scabbard, esp. *Lepidopus caudatus.*

sca·bies /skáybeez/ *n.* a contagious skin disease causing severe itching (cf. ITCH). [ME f. L f. *scabere* scratch]

sca·bi·ous /skáybeeəs/ *n. & adj.* ● *n.* any plant of the genus *Scabiosa, Knautia,* etc., with pink, white, or esp. blue pincushion-shaped flowers. ● *adj.* affected with mange; scabby. [ME f. med.L *scabiosa (herba)* formerly regarded as a cure for skin disease: see SCABIES]

scab·rous /skábrəs, skáy–/ *adj.* **1** having a rough surface; bearing short stiff hairs, scales, etc.; scurfy. **2** (of a subject, situation, etc.) requiring tactful treatment; hard to handle with decency. **3 a** indecent; salacious. **b** behaving licentiously. □□ **scab·rous·ly** *adv.* **scab·rous·ness** *n.* [F *scabreux* or LL *scabrosus* f. L *scaber* rough]

scad /skad/ *n.* any fish of the family Carangidae native to tropical and subtropical seas, usu. having an elongated body and very large spiky scales. [17th c.: orig. unkn.]

scads /skadz/ *n.pl. colloq.* large quantities. [19th c.: orig. unkn.]

scaf·fold /skáfəld, –fōld/ *n. & v.* ● *n.* **1 a** *hist.* a raised wooden platform used for the execution of criminals. **b** a similar platform used for drying tobacco, etc. **2** = SCAFFOLDING. **3** (prec. by *the*) death by execution. ● *v.tr.* attach scaffolding to (a building). □□ **scaf·fold·er** *n.* [ME f. AF f. OF *(e)schaffaut*, earlier *escadafaut*: cf. CATAFALQUE]

scaf·fold·ing /skáfəlding, –fōlding/ *n.* **1 a** temporary structure formed of poles, planks, etc., erected by workers and used by them while building or repairing a house, etc. **b** materials used for this. **2** a temporary conceptual framework used for constructing theories, etc.

scagl·io·la /skalyólə/ *n.* imitation stone or plaster mixed with glue. [It. *scagliuola* dimin. of *scaglia* SCALE¹]

scal·a·ble /skáyləbəl/ *adj.* **1** capable of being scaled or climbed. **2** *Computing* (of a font) capable of being used in a range of sizes. □□ **scal·a·bil·i·ty** /–bílitee/ *n.*

sca·lar /skáylər/ *adj. & n. Math. & Physics* ● *adj.* (of a quantity) having only magnitude, not direction. ● *n.* a scalar quantity (cf. VECTOR). [L *scalaris* f. *scala* ladder; see SCALE³]

scal·a·wag /skáləwag/ *n.* (also **scal·ly·wag**) **1** a scamp; a rascal. **2** *US hist.* a white Southerner who supported Reconstructionists usu. for personal profit. [19th-c. US sl.: orig unknown.]

scald¹ /skawld/ *v. & n.* ● *v.tr.* **1** burn (the skin, etc.) with hot liquid or steam. **2** heat (esp. milk) to near boiling point. **3** (usu. foll. by *out*) clean (a pan, etc.) by rinsing with boiling water. **4** treat (poultry, etc.) with boiling water to remove feathers, etc. ● *n.* **1** a burn, etc., caused by scalding. **2** a skin disease caused esp. by air pollution, etc., affecting the fruits of some plants. □□ **scald·er** *n.* [ME f. AF, ONF *escalder*, OF *eschalder* f. LL *excaldare* (as EX-¹, L *calidus* hot)]

scald² var. of SKALD.

scald·ed cream *n. Brit.* a dessert made from milk scalded and allowed to stand.

scald·ing tears *n.* hot bitter tears of grief, etc.

scale¹ /skayl/ *n. & v.* ● *n.* **1** each of the small, thin, bony or horny overlapping plates protecting the skin of fish and reptiles. **2** something resembling a fish scale, esp.: **a** a pod or husk. **b** a flake of skin; a scab. **c** a rudimentary leaf, feather, or bract. **d** each of the structures covering the wings of butterflies and moths. **e** *Bot.* a layer of a bulb. **3 a** a flake formed on the surface of rusty iron. **b** a thick, white deposit formed in a kettle, boiler, etc., by the action of heat on water. **4** plaque formed on teeth. ● *v.* **1** *tr.* remove scale or scales from (fish, nuts, iron, etc.). **2** *tr.* remove plaque from (teeth) by scraping. **3** *intr.* **a** (of skin, metal, etc.) form, come off in, or drop, scales. **b** (usu. foll. by *off*) (of scales) come off. □ **scale fall from a person's eyes** a person is no longer deceived (cf. Acts 9:18). □□ **scaled** *adj.* (also in *comb.*). **scale·less** *adj.* **scal·er** *n.* [(n.) ME (= ladder): (v.) ME f. OF *escaler* or med.L *scalare* f. L *scala* f. *scandere* climb]

scale² /skayl/ *n. & v.* ● *n.* **1 a** (often in *pl.*) a weighing machine or device (*bathroom scales*). **b** (also **scale·pan**) each of the dishes on a simple scale balance. **2** (**the Scales**) the zodiacal sign or constellation Libra. ● *v.tr.* (of something weighed) show (a specified weight) in the scales. □ **throw into the scale** cause to be a factor in a contest, debate, etc. **tip** (or **turn**) **the scales 1** (usu. foll. by *at*) outweigh the opposite scalepan (at a specified weight); weigh. **2** (of a motive, circumstance, etc.) be decisive. [ME f. ON *skál* bowl f. Gmc]

scale³ /skayl/ *n. & v.* ● *n.* **1** a series of degrees; a graded classification system (*pay fees according to a prescribed scale; high on the social scale; seven points on the Richter scale*). **2 a** (often *attrib.*) *Geog. & Archit.* a ratio of size in a map, model, picture, etc. (*on a scale of one inch to the mile; a scale model*). **b** relative dimensions or degree (*generosity on a grand scale*). **3** *Mus.* an arrangement of all the notes in any system of music in ascending or descending order (*chromatic scale; major scale*). **4 a** a set of marks on a line used in measuring,

reducing, enlarging, etc. **b** a rule determining the distances between these. **c** a piece of metal, apparatus, etc., on which these are marked. **5** (in full **scale of notation**) *Math.* the ratio between units in a numerical system (*decimal scale*). ● *v.* **1** *tr.* **a** (also *absol.*) climb (a wall, height, etc.) esp. with a ladder. **b** climb (the social scale, heights of ambition, etc.). **2** *tr.* represent in proportional dimensions; reduce to a common scale. **3** *intr.* (of quantities, etc.) have a common scale; be commensurable. □ **in scale** (of drawing, etc.) in proportion to the surroundings, etc. **play** (or **sing**) **scales** *Mus.* perform the notes of a scale as an exercise for the fingers or voice. **scale down** make smaller in proportion; reduce in size. **scale up** make larger in proportion; increase in size. **to scale** with a uniform reduction or enlargement. □□ **scal·er** *n.*

> **WORD HISTORY** **scale³**
>
> Late Middle English (in the senses 'ladder' and 'climb with a scaling ladder'): from Latin *scala* 'ladder' (the verb via Old French *escaler* or medieval Latin *scalare*), from the base of Latin *scandere* 'to climb.'

scale ar·mor *n. hist.* armor formed of metal scales attached to leather, etc.

scale bug *n.* = SCALE INSECT.

scale fern *n.* any of various spleenworts, esp. *Asplenium ceterach.*

scale in·sect *n.* any of various insects, esp. of the family Coccidae, clinging to plants and secreting a shieldlike scale as covering.

sca·lene /skáyleen/ *adj. & n.* ● *adj.* (esp. of a triangle) having sides unequal in length. ● *n.* **1** (in full **scalene muscle**) = SCALENUS. **2** a scalene triangle. [LL *scalenus* f. Gk *skalēnos* unequal, rel. to *skolios* bent]

sca·lene cone *n.* (also **sca·lene cyl·in·der**) a cone (or cylinder) with the axis not perpendicular to the base.

sca·le·nus /skəleenəs/ *n.* (*pl.* **sca·le·ni** /–nī/) any of several muscles extending from the neck to the first and second ribs. [mod.L: see SCALENE]

scale-winged *adj.* lepidopterous.

scal·lion /skályən/ *n.* a shallot or spring onion; any long-necked onion with a small bulb. [ME f. AF *scal(o)un* = OF *escalo(i)gne* ult. f. L *Ascalonia (caepa)* (onion) of *Ascalon* in anc. Palestine]

scal·lop /skáləp, skól–/ *n. & v.* (also **scol·lop** /skól–/) ● *n.* **1** any of various bivalve mollusks of the family Pectinidae, esp. of the genus *Chlamys* or *Pecten,* much prized as food. **2** (in full **scallop shell**) **a** a single valve from the shell of a scallop, with grooves and ridges radiating from the middle of the hinge and edged with small rounded lobes, often used for cooking or serving food. **b** *hist.* a representation of this shell worn as a pilgrim's badge. **3** (in *pl.*) an ornamental edging cut in material in imitation of a scallop edge. **4** a small pan or dish shaped like a scallop shell and used for baking or serving food. ● *v.tr.* (**scal·loped, scal·lop·ing**) **1** cook in a scallop. **2** ornament (an edge or material) with scallops or scalloping. □□ **scal·lop·er** *n.* **scal·lop·ing** *n.* (in sense 3 of *n.*). [ME f. OF *escalope* prob. f. Gmc]

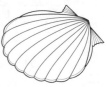

scallop 2

scal·ly·wag var. of SCALAWAG.

scalp /skalp/ *n. & v.* ● *n.* **1** the skin covering the top of the head, with the hair, etc., attached. **2 a** *hist.* the scalp of an enemy cut or torn away as a trophy by a Native American. **b** a trophy or symbol of triumph, conquest, etc. **3** *Sc.* a bare rock projecting above water, etc. ● *v.tr.* **1** *hist.* take the scalp of (an enemy). **2** criticize savagely. **3** defeat; humiliate. **4** *colloq.* resell (shares, tickets, etc.) at a high or quick profit. □□ **scalp·er** *n.* **scalp·less** *adj.* [ME, prob. of Scand. orig.]

scal·pel /skálpəl/ *n.* a small sharp surgical knife shaped for holding like a pen. [F *scalpel* or L *scalpellum* dimin. of *scalprum* chisel f. *scalpere* scratch]

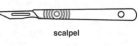

scalpel

scal·y /skáylee/ *adj.* (**scal·i·er, scal·i·est**) covered in or having many scales. □□ **scal·i·ness** *n.*

scam /skam/ *n. sl.* **1** a trick or swindle; a fraud. **2** esp. *Brit.* a story or rumor. [20th c.: orig. unkn.]

scam·mo·ny /skámənee/ *n.* (*pl.* **·nies**) an Asian plant, *Convolvulus scammonia,* bearing white or pink flowers, the dried roots of which are used as a purgative. [ME f. OF *scamonee, escamonie* or L *scammonia* f. Gk *skammōnia*]

scamp¹ /skamp/ *n. colloq.* a rascal; a rogue. □□ **scamp·ish** *adj.* [*scamp* rob on highway, prob. f. MDu. *schampen* decamp f. OF *esc(h)amper* (as EX-¹, L *campus* field)]

scamp² /skamp/ *v.tr.* do (work, etc.) in a perfunctory or inadequate way. [perh. formed as SCAMP¹: cf. SKIMP]

scamp·er /skámpər/ *v. & n.* ● *v.intr.* (usu. foll. by *about, through*) run and skip impulsively or playfully. •*n.* the act or an instance of scampering. [prob. formed as SCAMP[1]]

scam•pi /skámpee/ *n.pl.* **1** large shrimp. **2** (often treated as *sing.*) a dish of these sautéed in garlic butter. [It.]

scan /skan/ *v. & n.* •*v.* (**scanned, scan•ning**) **1** *tr.* look at intently or quickly (*scanned the horizon; rapidly scanned the speech for errors*). **2** *intr.* (of a verse, etc.) be metrically correct; be capable of being recited, etc., metrically (*this line doesn't scan*). **3** *tr.* **a** examine all parts of (a surface, etc.) to detect radioactivity, etc. **b** cause (a particular region) to be traversed by a radar, etc., beam. **4** *tr.* resolve (a picture) into its elements of light and shade in a prearranged pattern for the purposes, esp. of television transmission. **5** *tr.* test the meter of (a line of verse, etc.) by reading with the emphasis on its rhythm, or by examining the number of feet, etc. **6** *tr.* **a** make a scan of (the body or part of it). **b** examine (a patient, etc.) with a scanner. •*n.* **1** the act or an instance of scanning. **2** an image obtained by scanning or with a scanner. □□ **scan•na•ble** *adj.* [ME f. L *scandere* climb: in LL = scan verses (from the raising of one's foot in marking rhythm)]

scan•dal /skánd'l/ *n.* **1 a** a thing or a person causing general public outrage or indignation. **b** the outrage, etc., so caused, esp. as a subject of common talk. **c** malicious gossip or backbiting. **2** *Law* a public affront, esp. an irrelevant abusive statement in court. □□ **scan•dal•ous** *adj.* **scan•dal•ous•ly** *adv.* **scan•dal•ous•ness** *n.*

scan•dal•ize /skándəlīz/ *v.tr.* offend the moral feelings, sensibilities, etc., of; shock. [ME in sense 'make a scandal of' f. F *scandaliser* or eccl.L *scandaliso* f. Gk *skandalizō* (as SCANDAL)]

scan•dal•mon•ger /skánd'lmənggər, –monggər/ *n.* a person who spreads malicious scandal.

scan•dal sheet *n. derog.* a newspaper, etc., giving prominence to esp. malicious gossip.

Scan•di•na•vi•an /skándináyveeən/ *n. & adj.* •*n.* **1 a** a native or inhabitant of Scandinavia (Denmark, Norway, Sweden, and sometimes Finland and Iceland). **b** a person of Scandinavian descent. **2** the family of Germanic languages of Scandinavia. •*adj.* of or relating to Scandinavia or its people or languages. [L *Scandinavia*]

scan•di•um /skándeeəm/ *n. Chem.* a rare, soft, silver-white metallic element occurring naturally in lanthanide ores. ¶ Symb.: **Sc.** [mod. L f. *Scandia* Scandinavia (source of the minerals containing it)]

scan•na•ble see SCAN.

scan•ner /skánər/ *n.* **1 a** a device for scanning or systematically examining all the parts of something. **b** a device for monitoring several radio frequencies, esp. police or emergency frequencies. **2** a machine for measuring the intensity of radiation, ultrasound reflections, etc., from the body as a diagnostic aid. **3** a person who scans or examines critically. **4** a person who scans verse.

scan•sion /skánshən/ *n.* **1** the metrical scanning of verse. **2** the way a verse, etc., scans. [L *scansio* (LL of meter) f. *scandere* scans- climb]

scant /skant/ *adj. & v.* •*adj.* barely sufficient; deficient (*with scant regard for the truth; scant of breath*). •*v.tr. archaic* provide (a supply, material, a person, etc.) grudgingly; skimp; stint. □□ **scant•ly** *adv.* **scant•ness** *n.* [ME f. ON *skamt* neut. of *skammr* short]

scant•ling /skántling/ *n.* **1 a** a timber beam of small cross section. **b** a size to which a stone or timber is to be cut. **2** a set of standard dimensions for parts of a structure, esp. in shipbuilding. **3** (usu. foll. by *of*) *archaic* **a** a specimen or sample. **b** one's necessary supply; a modicum or small amount. [alt. after –LING[1] f. obs. *scantlon* f. OF *escantillon* sample]

scant•y /skántee/ *adj.* (**scant•i•er, scant•i•est**) **1** of small extent or amount. **2** barely sufficient. □□ **scant•i•ly** *adv.* **scant•i•ness** *n.* [obs. *scant* scanty supply f. ON *skamt* neut. adj.: see SCANT]

scape /skayp/ *n.* **1 a** long flower stalk coming directly from the root. **2** the base of an insect's antenna. [L *scapus* f. Gk *skapos*, rel. to SCEPTER]

-scape /skayp/ *comb. form* forming nouns denoting a view or a representation of a view (*moonscape; seascape*). [after LANDSCAPE]

scape•goat /skáypgōt/ *n. & v.* •*n.* **1** a person bearing the blame for the sins, shortcomings, etc., of others, esp. as an expedient. **2** *Bibl.* a goat sent into the wilderness after the Jewish chief priest had symbolically laid the sins of the people upon it (Lev. 16). •*v.tr.* make a scapegoat of. □□ **scape•goat•er** *n.* [*scape* (archaic, = escape) + GOAT, = the goat that escapes]

scape•grace /skáypgrays/ *n.* a rascal; a scamp, esp. a young person or child. [*scape* (as SCAPEGOAT) + GRACE = one who escapes the grace of God]

scaph•oid /skáfoyd/ *adj. & n. Anat.* = NAVICULAR. [mod.L *scaphoides* f. Gk *skaphoeidēs* f. *skaphos* boat]

scap•u•la /skápyələ/ *n.* (*pl.* **scap•u•lae** /–lee/ or **scap•u•las**) the shoulder blade. [LL, sing. of L *scapulae*]

scap•u•lar /skápyələr/ *adj. & n.* •*adj.* of or relating to the shoulder or shoulder blade. •*n.* **1 a** a monastic short cloak covering the shoulders. **b** a symbol of affiliation to an ecclesiastical order, consisting of two strips of cloth hanging down the breast and back and joined across the shoulders. **2** a bandage for or over the shoulders. **3** a scapular feather. [(adj.) f. SCAPULA: (n.) f. LL *scapulare* (as SCAPULA)]

scap•u•lar feath•er *n.* a feather growing near the insertion of the wing.

scap•u•lar•y /skápyələree/ *n.* (*pl.* **•ies**) **1** = SCAPULAR *n.* 1. **2** = SCAPULAR *n.* 3. [ME f. OF *eschapeloyre* f. med.L *scapelorium, scapularium* (as SCAPULA)]

scar[1] /skaar/ *n. & v.* •*n.* **1** a usu. permanent mark on the skin left after the healing of a wound, burn, or sore. **2** the lasting effect of grief, etc., on a person's character or disposition. **3** a mark left by damage, etc. (*the table bore many scars*). **4** a mark left on the stem, etc., of a plant by the fall of a leaf, etc. •*v.* (**scarred, scar•ring**) **1** *tr.* (esp. as **scarred** *adj.*) mark with a scar or scars (*was scarred for life*). **2** *intr.* heal over; form a scar. **3** *tr.* form a scar on. □□ **scar•less** *adj.* [ME f. OF *eschar(r)e* f. LL *eschara* f. Gk *eskhara* scab]

scar[2] /skaar/ *n.* (also *esp. Brit.* **scaur** /skawr/) a steep craggy outcrop of a mountain or cliff. [ME f. ON *sker* low reef in the sea]

scar•ab /skárəb/ *n.* **1 a** the sacred dung beetle of ancient Egypt. **b** = SCARABAEID. **2** an ancient Egyptian gem cut in the form of a beetle and engraved with symbols on its flat side, used as a signet, etc. [L *scarabaeus* f. Gk *skarabeios*]

scar•a•bae•id /skárəbeéid/ *n.* any beetle of the family Scarabaeidae, including the dung beetle, cockchafer, etc. [mod.L *Scarabaeidae* (as SCARAB)]

scarab

scar•a•mouch /skárəmoosh/ *n. archaic* a boastful coward; a braggart. [It. *Scaramuccia* stock character in Italian farce f. *scaramuccia* = SKIRMISH, infl. by F form *Scaramouche*]

scarce /skairs/ *adj. & adv.* •*adj.* **1** (usu. *predic.*) (esp. of food, money, etc.) insufficient for the demand; scanty. **2** hard to find; rare. •*adv. archaic* or *literary* scarcely. □ **make oneself scarce** *colloq.* keep out of the way; surreptitiously disappear. □□ **scarce•ness** *n.* [ME f. AF & ONF (*e*) *scars*, OF *eschars* f. L *excerpere*: see EXCERPT]

scarce•ly /skáirslee/ *adv.* **1** hardly; barely; only just (*I scarcely know her*). **2** surely not (*he can scarcely have said so*). **3** a mild or apologetic or ironical substitute for "not" (*I scarcely expected to be insulted*).

scar•ci•ty /skáirsitee/ *n.* (*pl.* **•ties**) (often foll. by *of*) a lack or inadequacy, esp. of food.

scare /skair/ *v. & n.* •*v.* **1** *tr.* frighten, esp. suddenly (*his expression scared us*). **2** *tr.* (as **scared** *adj.*) (usu. foll. by *of*, or *to* + infin.) frightened; terrified (*scared of his own shadow*). **3** *tr.* (usu. foll. by *away, off, up,* etc.) drive away by frightening. **4** *intr.* become scared (*they don't scare easily*). •*n.* **1** a sudden attack of fright (*gave me a scare*). **2** a general, esp. baseless, fear of war, invasion, epidemic, etc. (*a measles scare*). **3** a financial panic causing share selling, etc. □ **scare up** (or **out**) **1** frighten (game, etc.) out of cover. **2** *colloq.* manage to find; discover (*see if we can scare up a meal*). □□ **scar•er** *n.* [ME *skerre* f. ON *skirra* frighten f. *skjarr* timid]

scare•crow /skáirkrō/ *n.* **1** a human figure dressed in old clothes and set up in a field to scare birds away. **2** *colloq.* a badly dressed, grotesque-looking, or very thin person. **3** *archaic* an object of baseless fear.

scared•y-cat /skáirdeekat/ *n. colloq.* a timid person.

scare•head /skárhed/ *n.* a shockingly large or sensational newspaper headline.

scare•mon•ger /skáirmunggər, –monggər/ *n.* a person who spreads frightening reports or rumors. □□ **scare•mon•ger•ing** *n.*

scarf[1] /skaarf/ *n.* (*pl.* **scarfs** or **scarves** /skaarvz/) a square, triangular, or esp. long narrow strip of material worn around the neck, over the shoulders, or tied around the head for warmth or ornament. □□ **scarfed** *adj.* [prob. alt. of *scarp* (infl. by SCARF[2]) f. ONF *escarpe* = OF *escherpe* sash]

scarf[2] /skaarf/ *n. & v.* •*v.tr.* **1** join the ends of (pieces of esp. lumber, metal, or leather) by beveling or notching them to fit and then bolting, brazing, or sewing them together. **2** cut the blubber of (a whale). • *n.* **1** a joint made by scarfing. **2** a cut on a whale made by scarfing. [ME (earlier as noun) prob. f. OF *escarf* (unrecorded) perh. f. ON]

scarf³ /skaarf/ *v. tr. & intr.* (often foll. by *up* or *down*) eat, esp. quickly, voraciously, greedily, etc.

scarf•pin /skáarfpin/ *n.* = TIEPIN.

scarf•skin /skaarfskin/ *n.* the outermost layer of the skin constantly scaling off, esp. that at the base of the nails.

scar•i•fi•er /skárifiər, skáir-/ *n.* **1** a thing or person that scarifies. **2** a machine with prongs for loosening soil without turning it. **3** a spiked road-breaking machine.

scar•i•fy¹ /skárifí, skáir-/ *v. tr.* (•fies, •fied) **1 a** make superficial incisions in. **b** cut off skin from. **2** hurt by severe criticism, etc. **3** loosen (soil) with a scarifier. □□ **scar•i•fi•ca•tion** /–fikáyshən/ *n.* [ME f. F *scarifier* f. LL *scarificare* f. L *scarifare* f. Gk *skariphaomai* f. *skariphos* stylus]

scar•i•fy² /skáirifí/ *v. tr. & intr.* (•fies, •fied) *colloq.* scare; terrify.

PRONUNCIATION TIP scarify

Many people are tempted to pronounce this word as if it contained the word *scar.* But the correct pronunciation rhymes with *rarify.*

scar•i•ous /skáireeəs/ *adj.* (of a part of a plant, etc.) having a dry membranous appearance; thin and brittle. [F *scarieux* or mod.L *scariosus*]

scar•la•ti•na /skaárlətéenə/ *n.* = SCARLET FEVER. [mod.L f. It. *scarlattina* (*febbre scarlattina*) dimin. of *scarlatto* SCARLET]

scar•let /skáarlit/ *n. & adj.* • *n.* **1** a brilliant red color tinged with orange. **2** clothes or material of this color (*dressed in scarlet*). • *adj.* of a scarlet color. [ME f. OF *escarlate*: ult. orig. unkn.]

scar•let fe•ver *n.* an infectious bacterial fever, affecting esp. children, with a scarlet rash.

scar•let pim•per•nel *n.* a small annual wild plant, *Anagallis arvensis,* with small, esp. scarlet, flowers closing in rainy or cloudy weather. Also called **poor man's weather-glass.**

scar•let rash *n.* = ROSEOLA 1.

scar•let run•ner *n.* **1** a runner bean. **2** a scarlet-flowered climber bearing this bean.

scar•let wom•an *n. derog.* a notoriously promiscuous woman; a prostitute.

scar•oid /skároyd, skáir-/ *n. & adj.* • *n.* any colorful marine fish of the family Scaridae, native to tropical and temperate seas, including the scarus. • *adj.* of or relating to this family.

scarp /skaarp/ *n. & v.* • *n.* **1** the inner wall or slope of a ditch in a fortification (cf. COUNTERSCARP). **2** a steep slope. • *v. tr.* **1** make (a slope) perpendicular or steep. **2** provide (a ditch) with a steep scarp and counterscarp. **3** (as **scarped** *adj.*) (of a hillside, etc.) steep; precipitous. [It. *scarpa*]

scarp•er /skáarpər/ *v. intr. Brit. sl.* run away; escape. [prob. f. It. *scappare* escape, infl. by rhyming sl. *Scapa Flow* = go]

scar•us /skáirəs/ *n.* any fish of the genus *Scarus,* with brightly colored scales, and teeth fused to form a parrotlike beak used for eating coral. Also called **parrotfish.** [L f. Gk *skaros*]

scarves *pl.* of SCARF¹.

scar•y /skáiree/ *adj* (**scar•i•er, scar•i•est**) *colloq.* scaring; frightening. □□ **scar•i•ly** *adv.*

scat¹ /skat/ *v. & int. colloq.* • *v. intr.* (**scat•ted, scat•ting**) depart quickly. • *int.* go! [perh. abbr. of SCATTER]

scat² /skat/ *n. & v.* • *n.* improvised jazz singing using sounds imitating instruments, instead of words. • *v. intr.* (**scat•ted, scat•ting**) sing scat. [prob. imit.]

scathe /skayth/ *v. & n.* • *v. tr.* **1** *poet.* injure esp. by blasting or withering. **2** (as **scathing** *adj.*) witheringly scornful (*scathing sarcasm*). **3** (with *neg.*) do the least harm to (*shall not be scathed*) (cf. UNSCATHED). • *n.* (usu. with *neg.*) *archaic* harm; injury (*without scathe*). □□ **scathe•less** *predic.adj.* **scath•ing•ly** *adv.* [(v.) ME f. ON *skatha* = OE *sceathian*: (n.) OE f. ON *skathi* = OE *sceatha* malefactor, injury, f. Gmc]

sca•tol•o•gy /skatóləjee, skə-/ *n.* **1 a** a morbid interest in excrement. **b** a preoccupation with obscene literature, esp. that concerned with the excretory functions. **c** such literature. **2** the study of fossilized dung. **3** the study of excrement for esp. diagnosis. □□ **scat•o•log•i•cal** /–təlójikəl/ *adj.* [Gk *skōr skatos* dung + –LOGY]

sca•toph•a•gous /skatófogəs/ *adj.* feeding on dung. [as SCATOLOGY + Gk *–phagos* –eating]

scat•ter /skátər/ *v. & n.* • *v.* **1** *tr.* **a** throw here and there; strew (*scattered gravel on the road*). **b** cover by scattering (*scattered the road with gravel*). **2** *tr. & intr.* **a** move or cause to move in flight, etc.; disperse (*scattered to safety at the sound*). **b** disperse or cause (hopes, clouds, etc.) to disperse. **3** *tr.* (as **scattered** *adj.*) not clustered together; wide apart; sporadic (*scattered villages*). **4** *tr. Physics* deflect or diffuse (light, particles, etc.). **5 a** *intr.* (of esp. a shotgun) fire a charge

of shot diffusely. **b** *tr.* fire (a charge) in this way. • *n.* (also **scattering**) **1** the act or an instance of scattering. **2** a small amount scattered. **3** the extent of distribution of esp. shot. □□ **scat•ter•er** *n.* [ME, prob. var. of SHATTER]

SYNONYM TIP scatter

BROADCAST, DIFFUSE, DISPEL, DISPERSE, DISSEMINATE, DISSIPATE. If you **scatter** something, you throw it about in different directions, often using force (*the wind scattered leaves around the yard*). **Disperse** implies a scattering that completely breaks up a mass or assemblage and spreads the units far and wide (*the crowd dispersed as soon as the storm arrived; the ships were so widely dispersed that they couldn't see each other*). To **dispel** is to scatter or to drive away something that obscures, confuses, or bothers (*to dispel her fears*), while to **diffuse** is to lessen the intensity of something by spreading it out over a broader area (*the curtains diffused the bright sunlight pouring in the window*). **Dissipate** suggests that something has completely dissolved, disintegrated, or vanished (*early-morning mist dissipated by the sun*). **Broadcast** originally meant to *scatter* seed, but it is also used figuratively to mean make public (*the news of the President's defeat was broadcast the next morning*). **Disseminate** also means to publish or make public, but it implies a wider audience and usually a longer duration. You can spend a lifetime *disseminating* knowledge, in other words, but you would *broadcast* the news of the birth of your first grandchild.

scat•ter•brain /skátərbrayn/ *n.* a person given to silly or disorganized thought with lack of concentration. □□ **scat•ter•brained** *adj.*

scat•ter cush•ions *n.pl.* (also **scat•ter rugs,** etc.) cushions, rugs, etc., placed here and there for effect.

scat•ter•shot /skátərshot/ *n. & adj.* firing at random.

scat•ty /skátee/ *adj.* (**scat•ti•er, scat•ti•est**) *Brit. colloq.* scatterbrained; disorganized. □□ **scat•ti•ly** *adv.* **scat•ti•ness** *n.* [abbr.]

scaup /skawp/ *n.* any diving duck of the genus *Aythya.* [*scaup* Sc. var. of *scalp* mussel bed, which it frequents]

scaur var. of SCAR².

scav•enge /skávinj/ *v.* **1** *tr. & intr.* (usu. foll. by *for*) search for and collect (discarded items). **2** *tr.* remove unwanted products from (an internal-combustion engine cylinder, etc.). **3** feed on carrion, refuse, etc. [back-form. f. SCAVENGER]

scav•en•ger /skávinjər/ *n.* **1** a person who seeks and collects discarded items. **2** an animal, esp. a beetle, feeding on carrion, refuse, etc. □□ **scav•en•gery** *n.* [ME *scavager* f. AF *scawager* f. *scawage* f. ONF *escauwer* inspect f. Flem. *scauwen,* rel. to SHOW: for *–n–* cf. MESSENGER]

sca•zon /skáyzon, skáz-/ *n. Prosody* a Greek or Latin meter of limping character, esp. a trimeter of two iambuses and a spondee or trochee. [L f. Gk *skazōn* f. *skazō* limp]

Sc.D. *abbr.* Doctor of Science. [L *scientiae doctor*]

sce•na /sháynaa/ *n. Mus.* **1** an elaborate dramatic solo, usu. including recitative. **2** a scene or part of an opera. [It. f. L: see SCENE]

sce•nar•i•o /sináreeō, –náareeō/ *n.* (*pl.* •os) **1** an outline of the plot of a play, film, opera, etc., with details of the scenes, situations, etc. **2** a postulated sequence of future events. □□ **sce•nar•ist** *n.* (in sense 1). [It. (as SCENA)]

▶The proper meaning of this word is 'an outline of a plot' or 'a postulated sequence of events' (*the worst-case scenario*). It should not be used loosely to mean 'situation,' e.g., *a nightmare scenario.*

scend /send/ *n. & v. Naut.* • *n.* **1** the impulse given by a wave or waves (*scend of the sea*). **2** a plunge of a vessel. • *v. intr.* (of a vessel) plunge or pitch owing to the impulse of a wave. [alt. f. SEND or DESCEND]

scene /seen/ *n.* **1** a place in which events in real life, drama, or fiction occur; the locality of an event, etc. (*the scene was set in India; the scene of the disaster*). **2 a** an incident in real life, fiction, etc. (*distressing scenes occurred*) **b** a description or representation of an incident, etc. (*scenes of clerical life*). **3** a public incident displaying emotion, temper, etc., esp. when embarrassing to others (*made a scene in the restaurant*). **4 a** a continuous portion of a play in a fixed setting and usu. without a change of personnel; a subdivision of an act. **b** a similar section of a film, book, etc. **5 a** any of the pieces of scenery used in a play. **b** these collectively. **6** a landscape or a view (*a desolate scene*). **7** *colloq.* **a** an area of action or interest (*not my scene*). **b** a way of life; a milieu (*well known on the jazz scene*). **8** *archaic* the stage of a theater. □ **behind the scenes 1** *Theatr.* among the actors, scenery, etc., offstage. **2** unknown to the public; secret(ly). **come on the scene** arrive. **make the scene** participate or make an appearance in a particular activity or at a particular site (*make the theater scene in Greenwich Village*). **quit the scene** die; leave. **set the scene 1** describe the location of events. **2** give preliminary information. [L *scena* f. Gk *skēnē* tent; stage]

scene dock *n.* a space for storing scenery near the stage.

scen•er•y /séenəree/ *n.* **1** the general appearance of the natural features of a landscape, esp. when picturesque. **2** *Theatr.* the painted representations of landscape, rooms, etc., used as the background in a play, etc. [earlier *scenary* f. It. SCENARIO: assim. to –ERY]

scene·shift·er /séenshiftər/ *n.* a person who moves scenery in a theater. □□ **scene·shift·ing** *n.*

sce·nic /séenik/ *adj.* **1 a** picturesque; impressive or beautiful (*took the scenic route*). **b** of or concerning natural scenery (*flatness is the main scenic feature*). **2** (of a picture, etc.) representing an incident. **3** *Theatr.* of or on the stage (*scenic performances*). □□ **sce·ni·cal·ly** *adv.* [L *scenicus* f. Gk *skēnikos* of the stage (as SCENE)]

scent /sent/ *n. & v.* ●*n.* **1** a distinctive, esp. pleasant, smell (*the scent of hay*). **2 a** a scent trail left by an animal perceptible to hounds, etc. **b** clues, etc., that can be followed like a scent trail (*lost the scent in Paris*). **c** the power of detecting or distinguishing smells, etc., or of discovering things (*some dogs have little scent; the scent for talent*). **3** *Brit.* = PERFUME 2. **4** a trail laid in a paper chase. ●*v.* **1** *tr.* **a** discern by scent (*the dog scented game*). **b** sense the presence of (*scent treachery*). **2** *tr.* make fragrant or foul-smelling. **3** *tr.* (as **scented** *adj.*) having esp. a pleasant smell (*scented soap*). **4** *intr.* exercise the sense of smell (*goes scenting about*). **5** *tr.* apply the sense of smell to (*scented the air*). □ **on the scent** having a clue. **put** (or **throw**) **off the scent** deceive by false clues, etc. **scent out** discover by smelling or searching. □□ **scent·less** *adj.* [ME *sent* f. OF *sentir* perceive, smell, f. L *sentire*; –c– (17th c.) unexpl.]

scent gland *n.* (also **scent or·gan**) a gland in some animals secreting musk, civet, etc.

scep·sis *Brit.* var. of SKEPSIS.

scep·ter /séptər/ *n.* (*Brit.* **scep·tre**) **1** a staff borne esp. at a coronation as a symbol of sovereignty. **2** royal or imperial authority. □□ **scep·tered** *adj.* [ME f. OF (*s*)*ceptre* f. L *sceptrum* f. Gk *skēptron* f. *skēptō* lean on]

scep·tic *Brit.* var. of SKEPTIC.

scep·ti·cal *Brit.* var. of SKEPTICAL.

scep·tre *Brit.* var. of SCEPTER.

sch. *abbr.* **1** scholar. **2** school. **3** schooner.

scha·den·freu·de /sháad'nfroydə/ *n.* the malicious enjoyment of another's misfortunes. [G f. *Schaden* harm + *Freude* joy]

schap·pe /sháapə/ *n.* fabric or yarn made from waste silk. [G, = waste silk]

sched·ule /skéjōōl, –ōōəl/ *n. & v.* ●*n.* **1 a** a list or plan of intended events, times, etc. **b** a plan of work (*not on my schedule for next week*). **2** a list of rates or prices. **3** a timetable. **4** a tabulated inventory, etc., esp. as an appendix to a document. ●*v.tr.* **1** include in a schedule. **2** make a schedule of. **3** *Brit.* include (a building) in a list for preservation or protection. □□ **sched·ul·er** *n.*

WORD HISTORY schedule

Late Middle English (in the sense 'scroll, explanatory note, appendix'): from Old French *cedule*, from late Latin *schedula* 'slip of paper,' diminutive of *scheda*, from Greek *skhedē* 'papyrus leaf.' The verb dates from the mid-19th century.

schee·lite /sheelīt/ *n. Mineral.* calcium tungstate in its mineral crystalline form. [K. W. *Scheele*, Sw. chemist d. 1786]

sche·ma /skeemə/ *n.* (*pl.* **sche·ma·ta** /–mətə/ or **sche·mas**) **1** a synopsis, outline, or diagram. **2** a proposed arrangement. **3** *Logic* a syllogistic figure. **4** (in Kantian philosophy) a conception of what is common to all members of a class; a general type or essential form. [Gk *skhēma* –*atos* form, figure]

sche·mat·ic /skimátik, skee–/ *adj. & n.* ●*adj.* **1** of or concerning a scheme or schema. **2** representing objects by symbols, etc. ●*n.* a schematic diagram, esp. of an electronic circuit. □□ **sche·mat·i·cal·ly** *adv.*

sche·ma·tism /skeeəmətizəm/ *n.* a schematic arrangement or presentation. [mod.L *schematismus* f. Gk *skhēmatismos* (as SCHEMATIZE)]

sche·ma·tize /skeeəmətīz/ *v.tr.* **1** put in a schematic form; arrange. **2** represent by a scheme or schema. □□ **sche·ma·ti·za·tion** *n.*

scheme /skeem/ *n. & v.* ●*n.* **1 a** a systematic plan or arrangement for work, action, etc. **b** a proposed or operational systematic arrangement (*a color scheme*). **2** an artful or deceitful plot. **3** a timetable, outline, syllabus, etc. ●*v.* **1** *intr.* (often foll. by *for*, or to + infin.) plan esp. secretly or deceitfully; intrigue. **2** *tr.* plan to bring about, esp. artfully or deceitfully (*schemed their downfall*). □□ **schem·er** *n.*

WORD HISTORY scheme

Mid-16th century (denoting a figure of speech): from Latin *schema*, from Greek. An early sense included 'horoscope, representation of the position of celestial objects,' giving rise to 'diagram, design,' whence the current senses. The unfavorable notion 'plot' arose in the early 18th century.

schem·ing /skeeming/ *adj. & n.* ●*adj.* artful, cunning, or deceitful. ●*n.* plots; intrigues. □□ **schem·ing·ly** *adv.*

sche·moz·zle var. of SHEMOZZLE.

scher·zan·do /skairtsáandō/ *adv., adj., & n. Mus.* ●*adv. & adj.* in a playful manner. ●*n.* (*pl.* **scher·zan·dos** or **scher·zan·di** /–dee/) a

passage played in this way. [It., gerund of *scherzare* to jest (as SCHERZO)]

scher·zo /skáirtsō/ *n.* (*pl.* **·zos**) *Mus.* a vigorous, light, or playful composition, usu. as a movement in a symphony, sonata, etc. [It., lit. 'jest']

schil·ling /shíling/ *n.* **1** the chief monetary unit of Austria. **2** a coin equal to the value of one schilling. [G (as SHILLING)]

schip·per·ke /skípərkee, shíp–/ *n.* **1** a small, black, tailless dog of a breed with a ruff of fur around its neck. **2** this breed. [Du. dial., = little boatman, f. its use as a watchdog on barges]

schism /sízəm, skíz–/ *n.* **1 a** the division of a group into opposing sections or parties. **b** any of the sections so formed. **2 a** the separation of a church into two churches or the secession of a group owing to doctrinal, disciplinary, etc., differences. **b** the offense of causing or promoting such a separation. [ME f. OF *s*(*c*) *isme* f. eccl.L *schisma* f. Gk *skhisma* –*atos* cleft f. *skhizō* to split]

schis·mat·ic /sizmátik, skiz–/ *adj. & n.* (also **schis·mat·i·cal**) ●*adj.* inclining to, concerning, or guilty of, schism. ●*n.* **1** a holder of schismatic opinions. **2** a member of a schismatic faction or a seceded branch of a church. □□ **schis·mat·i·cal·ly** *adv.* [ME f. OF *scismatique* f. eccl.L *schismaticus* f. eccl.Gk *skhismatikos* (as SCHISM)]

schist /shist/ *n.* a foliated metamorphic rock composed of layers of different minerals and splitting into thin irregular plates. □□ **schis·tose** *adj.* [F *schiste* f. L *schistos* f. Gk *skhistos* split (as SCHISM)]

schis·to·some /shístəsōm/ *n.* = BILHARZIA 1. [Gk *skhistos* divided (as SCHISM) + *sōma* body]

schis·to·so·mi·a·sis /shístəsəmíəsis/ *n.* = BILHARZIASIS. [mod.L *Schistosoma* (the genus-name, as SCHISTOSOME)]

schi·zan·thus /skizánthəs/ *n.* any plant of the genus *Schizanthus*, with showy flowers in various colors, and finely divided leaves. [mod.L f. Gk *skhizō* to split + *anthos* flower]

schiz·o /skítsō/ *adj. & n. colloq.* ●*adj.* schizophrenic. ●*n.* (*pl.* **·os**) a schizophrenic. [abbr.]

schiz·o·carp /skízəkaarp, skítsə–/ *n. Bot.* any of a group of dry fruits that split into single-seeded parts when ripe. □□ **schiz·o·car·pic** /–kaárpik/ *adj.* **schiz·o·car·pous** /–kaárpəs/ *adj.* [Gk *skhizō* to split + *karpos* fruit]

schiz·oid /skítsoyd/ *adj. & n.* ●*adj.* (of a person or personality, etc.) tending to or resembling schizophrenia or a schizophrenic, but usu. without delusions. ●*n.* a schizoid person.

schiz·o·my·cete /skítsōmíseet, –míseet/ *n.* a former name for a bacterium. [Gk *skhizō* to split + *mukēs* –*ētos* mushroom]

schiz·o·phre·ni·a /skítsəfréeneeə, –fréneeə/ *n.* a mental disease marked by a breakdown in the relation between thoughts, feelings, and actions, frequently accompanied by delusions and retreat from social life. □□ **schiz·o·phren·ic** /–frénik/ *adj. & n.* [Mod.L f. Gk *skhizō* to split + *phrēn* mind]

schiz·o·thy·mi·a /skítsōthímeeə, skíz–/ *n. Psychol.* an introvert condition with a tendency to schizophrenia. □□ **schiz·o·thy·mic** *adj.* [mod.L (as SCHIZOPHRENIA + Gk *thumos* temper)]

schle·miel /shləméél/ *n. colloq.* a foolish or unlucky person. [Yiddish *shlumiel*]

schlep /shlep/ *v. & n.* (also **schlepp**) *colloq.* ●*v.* (**schlepped, schlepping**) **1** *tr.* carry; drag. **2** *intr.* go or work tediously or effortfully. ●*n.* (also **schlep·per**) a person or thing that is tedious, awkward, or slow. [Yiddish *shlepn* f. G *schleppen* drag]

schlie·ren /shléérən/ *n.* **1** a visually discernible area or stratum of different density in a transparent medium. **2** *Geol.* an irregular streak of mineral in igneous rock. [G, pl. of *Schliere* streak]

schlock /shlok/ *n. colloq.* inferior goods; trash. [Yiddish *shlak* a blow]

schmaltz /shmaalts/ *n. colloq.* sentimentality, esp. in music, drama, etc. □□ **schmaltz·y** *adj.* (**schmaltz·i·er, schmaltz·i·est**). [Yiddish f. G *Schmalz* dripping, lard]

schmuck /shmuk/ *n. sl.* a foolish or contemptible person. [Yiddish]

schnapps /shnaaps, shnaps/ *n.* any of various spirits drunk in N. Europe. [G, = dram of liquor f. LG & Du. *snaps* mouthful (as SNAP)]

schnau·zer /shnówzər, shnówtsər/ *n.* **1** a dog of a German breed with a close wiry coat and heavy whiskers around the muzzle. **2** this breed. [G f. *Schnauze* muzzle, SNOUT]

schnit·zel /shnítsəl/ *n.* a cutlet of veal. [G, = slice]

schnook /shnŏŏk/ *n. sl.* a dupe; a sucker; a simpleton. [Perh. f. G *Schnucke* a small sheep or Yiddish *shnuk* snout.]

schnor·kel var. of SNORKEL.

schnor·rer /shnawrər/ *n. sl.* a beggar or scrounger; a layabout. [Yiddish f. G *Schnurrer*]

schol·ar /skólər/ *n.* **1** a learned person, esp. in language, literature, etc.; an academic. **2** the holder of a scholarship. **3 a** a person with specified academic ability (*is a poor scholar*). **b** a person who learns (*am a scholar of life*). **4** *archaic colloq.* a person able to read and write. **5** *archaic* a schoolboy or schoolgirl. □□ **schol·ar·ly** *adj.* **schol·ar·li·ness** *n.* [ME f. OE *scol*(*i*)*ere* & OF *escol*(*i*)*er* f. LL *scholaris* f. L *schola* SCHOOL[1]]

schol·ar·ship /skólərship/ n. **1 a** academic achievement; learning of a high level. **b** the methods and standards characteristic of a good scholar (*shows great scholarship*). **2** payment from the funds of a school, university, local government, etc., to maintain a student in full-time education, awarded on the basis of scholarly achievement.

schol·ar's mate n. see MATE[2].

scho·las·tic /skəlástik/ adj. & n. ● adj. **1** of or concerning universities, schools, education, teachers, etc. **2** pedantic; formal (*shows scholastic precision*). **3** Philos. hist. of, resembling, or concerning the schoolmen, esp. in dealing with logical subtleties. ● n. **1** a student. **2** Philos. hist. a schoolman. **3** a theologian of scholastic tendencies. **4** RC Ch. a member of any of several religious orders, who is between the novitiate and the priesthood. □□ **scho·las·ti·cal·ly** adv. **scho·las·ti·cism** /–tisizəm/ n. [L *scholasticus* f. Gk *skholastikos* studious f. *skholazō* be at leisure, formed as SCHOOL[1]]

scho·li·ast /skóleeast/ n. hist. an ancient or medieval scholar, esp. a grammarian, who annotated ancient literary texts. □□ **scho·li·as·tic** adj. [Med.Gk *skholiastēs* f. *skholiazō* write scholia: see SCHOLIUM]

scho·li·um /skóleeəm/ n. (pl. **scho·li·a** /–leeə/) a marginal note or explanatory comment, esp. by an ancient grammarian on a classical text. [mod.L f. Gk *skholion* f. *skholē* disputation: see SCHOOL[1]]

school[1] /skool/ n. & v. ● n. **1 a** an institution for educating or giving instruction at any level including college or university, or esp. Brit. for children under 19 years. **b** (*attrib.*) associated with or for use in school (*a school bag; school dinners*). **2 a** the buildings used by such an institution. **b** the pupils, staff, etc., of a school. **c** the time during which teaching is done, or the teaching itself (*no school today*). **3 a** a branch of study with separate examinations at a university; a department or faculty (*the history school*). **b** Brit. the hall in which university examinations are held. **c** (in pl.) Brit. such examinations. **4 a** the disciples, imitators, or followers of a philosopher, artist, etc., (*the school of Epicurus*). **b** a group of artists, etc., whose works share distinctive characteristics. **c** a group of people sharing a cause, principle, method, etc. (*school of thought*). **5** Brit. a group of gamblers or of persons drinking together (*a poker school*). **6** colloq. instructive or disciplinary circumstances, occupation, etc. (*the school of adversity; learned in a hard school*). **7** hist. a medieval lecture room. **8** Mus. (usu. foll. by of) a handbook or book of instruction (*school of counterpoint*). **9** (in pl.; prec. by the) hist. medieval universities, their teachers, disputations, etc. ● v.tr. **1** send to school; provide for the education of. **2** (often foll. by to) discipline; train; control. **3** (as **schooled** adj.) (foll. by in) educated or trained (*schooled in humility*). □ **go to school 1** begin one's education. **2** attend lessons. **leave school 1** finish one's education. **2** terminate one's education before the completion of one's course of study, etc. **of the old school** according to former and esp. better tradition (*a gentleman of the old school*). [ME f. OE *scōl, scolu,* & f. OF *escole* ult. f. L *schola* school f. Gk *skholē* leisure, disputation, philosophy, lecture place]

school[2] /skool/ n. & v. ● n. (often foll. by of) a shoal of fish, porpoises, whales, etc. ● v.intr. form schools. [ME f. MLG, MDu. *schōle* f. WG]

school·a·ble /skoolǝbǝl/ adj. liable by age, etc., to compulsory education.

school age n. the age range in which children normally attend school. □□ **school-age** adj.

school board n. a board or authority for local education.

school·boy /skoolboy/ n. a boy attending school.

school·child /skoolchild/ n. a child attending school.

school days n.pl. the time of being at school, esp. in retrospect.

school·fel·low /skoolfelō/ n. esp. Brit. = SCHOOLMATE.

school·girl /skoolgǝrl/ n. a girl attending school.

school·house /skoolhows/ n. **1** a building used as a school. **2** Brit. a dwelling house adjoining a school.

school·ing /skooling/ n. **1** education, esp. at school. **2** training or discipline, esp. of an animal.

school·man /skoolmǝn/ n. (pl. **·men**) **1** hist. a teacher in a medieval European university. **2** RC Ch. hist. a theologian seeking to deal with religious doctrines by the rules of Aristotelian philosophy. **3** a person involved in academic pursuits.

school·marm /skoolmaarm/ n. colloq. (also **school·ma'am** /–maam/) a female schoolteacher, esp. in a rural school, characterized by priggishness and strict discipline. □□ **school·marm·ish** adj.

school·mas·ter /skoolmastǝr/ n. a head or assistant male teacher. □□ **school·mas·ter·ly** adj.

school·mas·ter·ing /skoolmastǝring/ n. teaching as a profession.

school·mate /skoolmayt/ n. a past or esp. present member of the same school.

school·mis·tress /skoolmistris/ n. a head or assistant female teacher.

school·mis·tress·y /skoolmistrisee/ adj. colloq. prim and fussy.

school of hard knocks n. experience gained from hard work, tough circumstances, etc.

school·room /skoolroom, –room/ n. a room used for lessons in a school.

school ship n. a training ship.

school·teach·er /skoolteechǝr/ n. a person who teaches in a school. □□ **school·teach·ing** n.

school·time /skooltim/ n. **1** lesson time at school or at home. **2** school days.

school year n. = ACADEMIC YEAR.

schoon·er /skoonǝr/ n. **1** a fore-and-aft rigged ship with two or more masts, the foremast being smaller than the other masts. **2 a** Brit. a measure or glass for esp. sherry. **b** US & Austral. a very tall beer glass. **3** US hist. = PRAIRIE SCHOONER. [18th c.: orig. uncert.]

schorl /shorl/ n. black tourmaline. [G *Schörl*]

schot·tische /shótish, shoteesh/ n. **1** a kind of slow polka. **2** the music for this. [G *der schottische Tanz* the Scottish dance]

Schott·ky ef·fect /shótkee/ n. Electronics the increase in thermionic emission from a solid surface due to the presence of an external electric field. [W. *Schottky*, Ger. physicist d. 1976]

Schrö·ding·er e·qua·tion /shróding ǝr, shráy–/ n. Physics a differential equation used in quantum mechanics for the wave function of a particle. [E. *Schrödinger*, Austrian physicist d. 1961]

schuss /shoos/ n. & v. ● n. a straight downhill run on skis. ● v.intr. make a schuss. [G, lit. 'shot']

schwa /shwaa/ n. (also **she·va** /shǝvaa/) Phonet. **1** the indistinct unstressed vowel sound as in *a* moment *ago*. **2** the symbol /ǝ/ representing this in the International Phonetic Alphabet. [G f. Heb. *šᵉwā*, app. f. *šaw'* emptiness]

sci·am·a·chy /síamǝkee/ n. formal **1** fighting with shadows. **2** imaginary or futile combat. [Gk *skiamakhia* (as SKIAGRAPHY, –*makhia* –fighting)]

sci·at·ic /síátik/ adj. **1** of the hip. **2** of or affecting the sciatic nerve. **3** suffering from or liable to sciatica. □□ **sci·at·i·cal·ly** adv. [F *sciatique* f. LL *sciaticus* f. L *ischiadicus* f. Gk *iskhiadikos* subject to sciatica f. *iskhion* hip joint]

sci·at·i·ca /síátikǝ/ n. neuralgia of the hip and thigh; a pain in the sciatic nerve. [ME f. LL *sciatica (passio)* fem. of *sciaticus*: see SCIATIC]

sci·at·ic nerve n. the largest nerve in the human body, running from the pelvis to the thigh.

sci·ence /síǝns/ n. **1** a branch of knowledge conducted on objective principles involving the systematized observation of and experiment with phenomena, esp. concerned with the material and functions of the physical universe (see also NATURAL SCIENCE). **2 a** systematic and formulated knowledge, esp. of a specified type or on a specified subject (*political science*). **b** the pursuit or principles of this. **3** an organized body of knowledge on a subject (*the science of philology*). **4** skillful technique rather than strength or natural ability. **5** archaic knowledge of any kind. [ME f. OF f. L *scientia* f. *scire* know]

sci·ence fic·tion n. fiction based on imagined future scientific discoveries or environmental changes, frequently dealing with space travel, life on other planets, etc.

sci·ence park n. an area devoted to scientific research or the development of science-based industries.

sci·en·ter /síéntǝr/ adv. Law intentionally; knowingly. [L f. *scire* know]

sci·en·tial /síénshǝl/ adj. concerning or having knowledge. [LL *scientialis* (as SCIENCE)]

sci·en·tif·ic /síǝntifik/ adj. **1 a** (of an investigation, etc.) according to rules laid down in exact science for performing observations and testing the soundness of conclusions. **b** systematic; accurate. **2** used in, engaged in, or relating to (esp. natural) science (*scientific discoveries; scientific terminology*). **3** assisted by expert knowledge. □□ **sci·en·tif·i·cal·ly** adv. [F *scientifique* or LL *scientificus* (as SCIENCE)]

sci·en·tism /síǝntizǝm/ n. **1 a** a method or doctrine regarded as characteristic of scientists. **b** the use or practice of this. **2** often derog. an excessive belief in or application of scientific method. □□ **sci·en·tis·tic** /–tístik/ adj.

sci·en·tist /síǝntist/ n. **1** a person with expert knowledge of a (usu. physical or natural) science. **2** a person using scientific methods.

Sci·en·tol·o·gy /síǝntólajee/ n. a religious system based on self-improvement and promotion through grades of esp. self-knowledge. □□ **Sci·en·tol·o·gist** n. [L *scientia* knowledge + –LOGY]

sci-fi /sífí/ n. (often attrib) colloq. science fiction. [abbr.: cf. HI-FI]

scil·i·cet /skéeliket, síliset/ adv. to wit; that is to say; namely (introducing a word to be supplied or an explanation of an ambiguity). [ME f. L, = *scire licet* one is permitted to know]

scil·la /sílǝ/ n. any liliaceous plant of the genus *Scilla*, related to the bluebell, usu. bearing small blue star-shaped or bell-shaped flowers and having long, glossy, straplike leaves. [L f. Gk *skilla*]

scim·i·tar /símitǝr, –taar/ n. an Oriental

scimitar

curved sword usu. broadening toward the point. [F *cimeterre*, It. *scimitarra*, etc., of unkn. orig.]

scin•ti•gram /síntigram/ *n.* an image of an internal part of the body, produced by scintigraphy.

scin•tig•ra•phy /sintígrəfee/ *n.* the use of a radioisotope and a scintillation counter to get an image or record of a bodily organ, etc. [SCINTILLATION + –GRAPHY]

scin•til•la /sintílə/ *n.* 1 a trace. 2 a spark. [L]

scin•til•late /síntilayt/ *v.intr.* 1 (esp. as **scintillating** *adj.*) talk cleverly or wittily; be brilliant. 2 sparkle; twinkle; emit sparks. 3 *Physics* fluoresce momentarily when struck by a charged particle, etc. □□ **scin•til•lant** *adj.* **scin•til•lat•ing•ly** *adv.* [L *scintillare* (as SCINTILLA)]

scin•til•la•tion /síntiláyshən/ *n.* 1 the process or state of scintillating. 2 the twinkling of a star. 3 a flash produced in a material by an ionizing particle, etc.

scin•til•la•tion count•er *n.* a device for detecting and recording scintillation.

scin•ti•scan /síntiskan/ *n.* an image or other record showing the distribution of radioactive traces in parts of the body, used in the detection and diagnosis of various diseases. [SCINTILLATION + SCAN]

sci•o•list /síəlist/ *n.* a superficial pretender to knowledge. □□ **sci•o•lism** *n.* **sci•o•lis•tic** *adj.* [LL *sciolus* smatterer f. L *scire* know]

sci•on /síən/ *n.* 1 (also **cion**) a shoot of a plant, etc., esp. one cut for grafting or planting. 2 a descendant; a younger member of (esp. a noble) family. [ME f. OF *ciun, cion, sion* shoot, twig, of unkn. orig.]

sci•re fa•ci•as /síree fáysheeas, skéere fáakee-aas/ *n. Law* a writ to enforce or annul a judgment, patent, etc. [L, = let (him) know]

sci•roc•co var. of SIROCCO.

scir•rhus /síras, skír–/ *n.* (*pl.* **scir•rhi** /–rī/) a carcinoma which is hard to the touch. □□ **scir•rhoid** *adj.* **scir•rhos•i•ty** /sirósitee/ *n.* **scir•rhous** *adj.* [mod.L f. Gk *skir(r)os* f. *skiros* hard]

scis•sel /skísəl/ *n.* waste clippings, etc., of metal produced during coin manufacture. [F *cisaille* f. *cisailler* clip with shears]

scis•sile /sísil, –īl/ *adj.* able to be cut or divided. [L *scissilis* f. *scindere sciss–* cut]

scis•sion /sízhən, sísh–/ *n.* 1 the act or an instance of cutting; the state of being cut. 2 a division or split. [ME f. OF *scission* or LL *scissio* (as SCISSILE)]

scis•sor /sízər/ *v.tr.* 1 (usu. foll. by *off, up, into*, etc.) cut with scissors. 2 (usu. foll. by *out*) clip out (a newspaper cutting, etc.).

scis•sorbill *n.* = SKIMMER 4.

scis•sors /sízərz/ *n.pl.* 1 (also **pair of scis•sors** *sing.*) an instrument for cutting fabric, paper, hair, etc., having two pivoted blades with finger and thumb holes in the handles, operating by closing on the material to be cut. 2 (treated as *sing.*) **a** a method of high jump with a forward and backward movement of the legs. **b** a hold in wrestling in which the opponent's body or esp. head is gripped between the legs. □□ **scis•sor•wise** *adv.* [ME *sisoures* f. OF *cisoires* f. LL *cisoria* pl. of *cisorium* cutting instrument (as CHISEL): assoc. with L *scindere sciss–* cut]

scis•sors and paste *n. & v.* a method of compiling a book, article, etc., from extracts from others or without independent research.

sci•u•rine /síyoorīn/ *adj.* 1 of or relating to the family Sciuridae, including squirrels and chipmunks. 2 squirrellike. □□ **sci•u•roid** *adj.* [L *sciurus* f. Gk *skiouros* squirrel f. *skia* shadow + *oura* tail]

scle•ra /skléerə/ *n.* the white of the eye; a white membrane coating the eyeball. □□ **scle•ral** *adj.* **scle•ri•tis** /skleerítis/ *n.* **scle•rot•o•my** /–rótəmee/ *n.* (*pl.* **•mies**). [mod.L f. fem. of Gk *sklēros* hard]

scle•ren•chy•ma /skleeréngkimə/ *n.* the woody tissue found in a plant, formed from lignified cells and usu. providing support. [mod.L f. Gk *sklēros* hard + *egkhuma* infusion, after *parenchyma*]

scle•roid /skléeroyd/ *adj. Bot. & Zool.* having a hard texture; hardened. [Gk *sklēros* hard]

scle•ro•ma /sklərómə/ *n.* (*pl.* **scle•ro•ma•ta** /–mətə/) an abnormal patch of hardened skin or mucous membrane. [Mod.L f. Gk *sklērōma* (as SCLEROSIS)]

scle•rom•e•ter /sklərómitər/ *n.* an instrument for determining the hardness of materials. [Gk *sklēros* hard + –METER]

scle•ro•phyll /skléerəfil/ *n.* any woody plant with leathery leaves retaining water. □□ **scle•ro•phyl•lous** /–rófiləs/ *adj.* [Gk *sklēros* hard + *phullon* leaf]

scle•ro•pro•tein /skléerōpróteen/ *n. Biochem.* any insoluble structural protein. [Gk *sklēros* hard + PROTEIN]

scle•rosed /skleeróst, –rōzd/ *adj.* affected by sclerosis.

scle•ro•sis /sklərósis/ *n.* 1 an abnormal hardening of body tissue (see also ARTERIOSCLEROSIS, ATHEROSCLEROSIS). 2 (in full **multiple** or disseminated **sclerosis**) a chronic and progressive disease of the nervous system resulting in symptoms including paralysis and speech defects. 3 *Bot.* the hardening of a cell wall with lignified matter. [ME f. med.L f. Gk *sklērōsis* f. *sklēroō* harden]

scle•rot•ic /sklərótik/ *adj. & n.* ● *adj.* 1 of or having sclerosis. 2 of or relating to the sclera. ● *n.* = SCLERA. □□ **scle•ro•ti•tis** /–rətítis/ *n.* [Med.L *sclerotica* (as SCLEROSIS)]

scle•rous /skléerəs/ *adj. Physiol.* hardened; bony. [Gk *sklēros* hard]

scoff[1] /skof/ *v. & n.* ● *v.intr.* (usu. foll. by *at*) speak derisively, esp. of

serious subjects; mock; be scornful. ● *n.* 1 mocking words; a taunt. 2 an object of ridicule. □□ **scoff•er** *n.* **scoff•ing•ly** *adv.* [Perh. f. Scand.: cf. early mod. Da. *skuf, skof* jest, mockery]

scoff[2] /skof/ *v. & n. colloq.* ● *v.tr. & intr.* eat greedily. ● *n.* food; a meal. [(n.) f. Afrik. *schoff* repr. Du. *schoft* quarter of a day (hence, meal): (v.) orig. var. of dial. *scaff*, assoc. with the noun]

scold /skōld/ *v. & n.* ● *v.* 1 *tr.* rebuke (esp. a child, employee, or inferior). 2 *intr.* find fault noisily; complain; rail. ● *n. archaic* a nagging or grumbling woman. □□ **scold•er** *n.* **scold•ing** *n.* [ME (earlier as noun), prob. f. ON *skáld* SKALD]

> **SYNONYM TIP** scold
>
> BERATE, CHIDE, REVILE, UPBRAID, VITUPERATE. A mother might **scold** a child who misbehaves, which means to rebuke in an angry, irritated, and often nagging way, whether or not such treatment is justified. **Chide** is more formal than scold, and it usually implies disapproval for specific failings (*She was chided by her teacher for using "less" instead of "fewer"*), while **berate** suggests a prolonged scolding, usually aimed at a pattern of behavior or way of life rather than a single misdeed and often combined with scorn or contempt for the person being criticized (*He berated his parents for being too protective and ruining his social life*). **Upbraid** also implies a lengthy expression of displeasure or criticism, but usually with more justification than scold and with an eye toward encouraging better behavior in the future (*The tennis coach upbraided her players for missing so many serves*). **Revile** and **vituperate** are reserved for very strong or even violent displays of anger. To *revile* is to use highly abusive and contemptuous language (*to revile one's opponent in the press*), while **vituperate** connotes even more violence in the attack (*The angry hockey players were held apart by their teammates, but they continued to vituperate each other with the foulest possible language*).

sco•lex /skóleks/ *n.* (*pl.* **sco•le•ces** /–léeseez/ or **scol•i•ces** /–liseez/) the head of a larval or adult tapeworm. [Mod.L f. Gk *skōlēx* worm]

sco•li•o•sis /skōleeósis, skól–/ *n.* an abnormal lateral curvature of the spine. □□ **sco•li•ot•ic** /–liótik/ *adj.* [Mod.L f. Gk f. *skolios* bent]

scol•lop var. of SCALLOP.

scol•o•pen•dri•um /skóləpéndreeəm/ *n.* any of various ferns, esp. hart's tongue. [Mod.L f. Gk *skolopendrion* f. *skolopendra* millipede (because of the supposed resemblance)]

scom•ber /skómbər/ *n.* any marine fish of the family Scombridae, including mackerels, tunas, and bonitos. □□ **scom•brid** *n.* **scom•broid** *adj. & n.* [L f. Gk *skombros*]

sconce[1] /skons/ *n.* 1 a flat candlestick with a handle. 2 a bracket candlestick to hang on a wall.

> **WORD HISTORY** sconce[1]
>
> Late Middle English (originally denoting a portable lantern with a screen to protect the flame): shortening of Old French *esconse* 'lantern,' or from medieval Latin *sconsa*, from Latin *absconsa (laterna)* 'dark (lantern),' from *abscondere* 'to hide.'

sconce[2] /skons/ *n.* 1 a small fort or earthwork usu. defending a ford, pass, etc. 2 *archaic* a shelter or screen. [Du. *schans* brushwood f. MHG *schanze*]

scone /skon, skōn/ *n.* a small sweet or savory cake of flour, shortening, and milk, baked quickly in an oven. [orig. Sc., perh. f. MDu. *schoon(broot)*, MLG *schon (brot)* fine (bread)]

scoop /skoop/ *n. & v.* ● *n.* 1 any of various objects resembling a spoon, esp.: **a** a short-handled deep shovel used for transferring grain, sugar, coal, coins, etc. **b** a large long-handled ladle used for transferring liquids. **c** the excavating part of a digging machine, etc. **d** *Med.* a long-handled spoonlike instrument used for scraping parts of the body, etc. **e** an instrument used for serving portions of mashed potato, ice cream, etc. 2 a quantity taken up by a scoop. 3 a movement of or resembling scooping. 4 a piece of news published by a newspaper, etc., in advance of its rivals. 5 a large profit made quickly or by anticipating one's competitors. 6 *Mus.* a singer's exaggerated portamento. 7 a scooped-out hollow, etc. ● *v.tr.* 1 (usu. foll. by *out*) hollow out with or as if with a scoop. 2 (usu. foll. by *up*) lift with or as if with a scoop. 3 forestall (a rival newspaper, reporter, etc.) with a scoop. 4 secure (a large profit, etc.), esp. suddenly. □□ **scoop•er** *n.* **scoop•ful** *n.* (*pl.* **•fuls**). [ME f. MDu., MLG *schōpe* bucket, etc., rel. to SHAPE]

scoop neck *n.* the rounded low-cut neck of a garment.

scoop net *n.* a net used for sweeping a river bottom, or for catching bait.

scoot /skoot/ *v. & n. colloq.* ● *v.intr.* run or dart away, esp. quickly. ● *n.* the act or an instance of scooting. [19th-c. US (earlier *scout*): orig. unkn.]

scoot•er /skóotər/ *n. & v.* ● *n.* 1 a child's toy consisting of a footboard mounted on two wheels and a long steering handle, propelled by resting one foot on the footboard and pushing the other against the ground. **2** (in full **motor scooter**) a light two-wheeled open motor vehicle with a shieldlike protective front. **3** a sailboat able to travel on either water or ice. • *v.intr.* travel or ride on a scooter. □□ **scoot·er·ist** *n.*

sco·pa /skópə/ *n.* (*pl.* **sco·pae** /–pee/) a small brushlike tuft of hairs, esp. on the leg of a bee for collecting pollen. [Sing. of L *scopae* = twigs, broom]

scope[1] /skōp/ *n.* **1 a** the extent to which it is possible to range; the opportunity for action, etc. (*this is beyond the scope of our research*). **b** the sweep or reach of mental activity, observation, or outlook (*an intellect limited in its scope*). **2** *Naut.* the length of cable extended when a ship rides at anchor. **3** *archaic* a purpose, end, or intention. [It. *scopo* aim f. Gk *skopos* target f. *skeptomai* look at]

scope[2] /skōp/ *n. colloq.* a telescope, microscope, or other device ending in *–scope*. [Abbr.]

-scope /skōp/ *comb. form* forming nouns denoting: **1** a device looked at or through (*kaleidoscope; telescope*). **2** an instrument for observing or showing (*gyroscope; oscilloscope*). □□ **–scopic** /skópik/ *comb. form* forming adjectives. [From or after mod.L *–scopium* f. Gk *skopeō* look at]

sco·pol·a·mine /skəpóləmeen, –min/ *n.* = HYOSCINE. [*Scopolia* genus name of the plants yielding it, f. G. A. *Scopoli*, It. naturalist d. 1788 + AMINE]

scop·u·la /skópyələ/ *n.* (*pl.* **scop·u·lae** /–lee/) any of various small brushlike structures, esp. on the legs of spiders. [LL, dimin. of L *scopa*: see SCOPA]

-scopy /skəpee/ *comb. form* indicating viewing or observation, usu. with an instrument ending in *–scope* (*microscopy*).

scor·bu·tic /skawrbyóotik/ *adj. & n.* • *adj.* relating to, resembling, or affected with scurvy. • *n.* a person affected with scurvy. □□ **scor·bu·ti·cal·ly** *adv.* [Mod.L *scorbuticus* f. med.L *scorbutus* scurvy, perh. f. MLG *schorbūk* f. *schoren* break + *būk* belly]

scorch /skawrch/ *v. & n.* • *v.* **1** *tr.* **a** burn the surface of with flame or heat so as to discolor, parch, injure, or hurt. **b** affect with the sensation of burning. **2** *intr.* become discolored, etc., with heat. **3** *tr.* (as **scorching** *adj.*) *colloq.* **a** (of the weather) very hot. **b** (of criticism, etc.) stringent; harsh. **4** *intr. colloq.* (of a motorist, etc.) go at excessive speed. • *n.* **1** a mark made by scorching. **2** *colloq.* a spell of fast driving, etc. □□ **scorch·ing·ly** *adv.* [ME, perh. rel. to *skorkle* in the same sense]

scorched earth pol·i·cy *n.* the burning of crops, etc., and the removing or destroying of anything that might be of use to an occupying enemy force.

scorch·er /skáwrchər/ *n.* **1** a person or thing that scorches. **2** *colloq.* **a** a very hot day. **b** *Brit.* a fine specimen.

score /skawr/ *n. & v.* • *n.* **1 a** the number of points, goals, runs, etc., made by a player, side, etc., in some games. **b** the total number of points, etc., at the end of a game (*the score was five to one*). **c** the act of gaining, esp. a goal (*an exciting score there!*). **2** (*pl.* same or **scores**) twenty or a set of twenty. **3** (in *pl.*) a great many (*scores of people arrived*). **4 a** a reason or motive (*rejected on the score of absurdity*). **b** topic; subject (*no worries on that score*). **5** *Mus.* **a** a usu. printed copy of a composition showing all the vocal and instrumental parts arranged one below the other. **b** the music composed for a film or play, esp. for a musical. **6** *colloq.* **a** a piece of good fortune. **b** the act or an instance of scoring off another person. **7** *colloq.* the state of affairs; the present situation (*asked what the score was*). **8** a notch, line, etc., cut or scratched into a surface. **9 a** an amount due for payment. **b** a running account kept by marks against a customer's name. **10** *Naut.* a groove in a block or deadeye to hold a rope. • *v.* **1** *tr.* **a** win or gain (a goal, run, points, etc., or success, etc.) (*scored six runs in the third inning*). **b** count for a score of (points in a game, etc.) (*a bull's-eye scores the most points*). **c** allot a score to (a competitor, etc.). **d** make a record of (a point, etc.). **2** *intr.* **a** make a score in a game (*failed to score*). **b** keep the tally of points, runs, etc., in a game. **3** *tr.* mark with notches, incisions, lines, etc.; slash; furrow (*scored his name on the desk*). **4** *intr.* secure an advantage by luck, cunning, etc. (*that is where he scores*). **5** *tr. Mus.* **a** orchestrate (a piece of music). **b** (usu. foll. by *for*) arrange for an instrument or instruments. **c** write the music for (a film, musical, etc.). **d** write out in a score. **6** *tr.* **a** (usu. foll. by *up*) mark (a total owed, etc.) in a score (see sense 9b of *n.*). **b** (usu. foll. by *against, to*) enter (an item of debt to a customer). **7** *intr. sl.* **a** obtain drugs illegally. **b** make a sexual conquest. **8** *tr.* (usu. foll. by *against, to*) mentally record (an offense, etc.). **9** *tr.* criticize (a person) severely. □ **keep score** (or **the score**) register the score as it is made. **know the score** *colloq.* be aware of the essential facts. **on the score of** *Brit.* for the reason that; because of. **on that score** so far as that is concerned. **score off** (or **score points off**) esp. *Brit. colloq.* humiliate, esp. verbally in repartee, etc. **score out** draw a line through (words, etc.). **score points with** make a favorable impression on. **settle a** (or **the**) **score** retaliate; commit an act of vengeance. □□ **scor·er** *n.* **scor·ing** *n. Mus.* [(n.) f. OE: sense 5 f. the line or bar drawn through all staves: (v.) partly f. ON *skora* f. ON *skor* notch, tally, twenty, f. Gmc: see SHEAR]

score·board /skáwrbawrd/ *n.* a large board for publicly displaying the score in a game or match.

score·card /skáwrkaard/ *n.* a card prepared for entering scores on and usu. for indicating players by name, number, etc.

sco·ri·a /skáwreeə/ *n.* (*pl.* **sco·ri·ae** /–ree-ee/) **1** cellular lava, or fragments of it. **2** the slag or dross of metals. □□ **sco·ri·a·ceous** /–reeáyshəs/ *adj.* [L f. Gk *skōria* refuse f. *skōr* dung]

sco·ri·fy /skáwrifī/ *v.tr.* (·**fies**, ·**fied**) **1** reduce to dross. **2** assay (precious metal) by treating a portion of its ore fused with lead and borax. □□ **sco·ri·fi·ca·tion** /–fikáyshən/ *n.* **sco·ri·fi·er** *n.*

scorn /skawrn/ *n. & v.* • *n.* **1** disdain; contempt; derision. **2** an object of contempt, etc. (*the scorn of all onlookers*). • *v.tr.* **1** hold in contempt or disdain. **2** (often foll. by *to* + infin.) abstain from or refuse to do as unworthy (*scorns lying; scorns to lie*). □ **think scorn of** *Brit.* despise. □□ **scorn·er** *n.* [ME f. OF *esc(h)arn(ir)* ult. f. Gmc: cf. OS *skern* MOCKERY]

scorn·ful /skáwrnfŏol/ *adj.* (often foll. by *of*) full of scorn; contemptuous. □□ **scorn·ful·ly** *adv.* **scorn·ful·ness** *n.*

Scor·pi·o /skáwrpeeō/ *n.* (*pl.* ·**os**) **1** a constellation, traditionally regarded as contained in the figure of a scorpion. **2 a** the eighth sign of the zodiac (the Scorpion). **b** a person born when the sun is in this sign. □□ **Scor·pi·an** *adj. & n.* [ME f. L (as SCORPION)]

scor·pi·oid /skáwrpeeoyd/ *adj. & n.* • *adj.* **1** *Zool.* of, relating to, or resembling a scorpion; of the scorpion order. **2** *Bot.* (of an inflorescence) curled up at the end, and uncurling as the flowers develop. • *n.* this type of inflorescence. [Gk *skorpioeidēs* (as SCORPIO)]

scorpion 1

scor·pi·on /skáwrpeeən/ *n.* **1** an arachnid of the order Scorpionida, with lobsterlike pincers and a jointed tail that can be bent over to inflict a poisoned sting on prey held in its pincers. **2** (in full **false scorpion**) a similar arachnid of the order Pseudoscorpionida, smaller and without a tail. **3** (**the Scorpion**) the zodiacal sign or constellation Scorpio. **4** *Bibl.* a whip with metal points (1 Kings 12:11). [ME f. OF f. L *scorpio –onis* f. *scorpius* f. Gk *skorpios*]

scor·pi·on fish *n.* any of various marine fish of the family Scorpaenidae, with venomous spines on the head and gills.

scor·pi·on fly *n.* any insect of the order Mecoptera, esp. of the family Panorpidae, the males of which have a swollen abdomen curved upward like a scorpion's sting.

scor·pi·on grass *n.* = FORGET-ME-NOT.

scor·zo·ne·ra /skáwrzəneérə/ *n.* **1** a composite plant, *Scorzonera hispanica*, with long, tapering purple-brown roots. **2** the root used as a vegetable. [It. f. *scorzone* venomous snake ult. f. med.L *curtio*]

Scot /skot/ *n.* **1 a** a native of Scotland. **b** a person of Scottish descent. **2** *hist.* a member of a Gaelic people that migrated from Ireland to Scotland around the 6th c. [OE *Scottas* (pl.) f. LL *Scottus*]

scot /skot/ *n. hist.* a payment corresponding to a modern tax, rate, etc. [ME f. ON *skot* & f. OF *escot*, of Gmc orig.: cf. SHOT[1]]

Scotch /skoch/ *adj. & n.* • *adj.* var. of SCOTTISH or SCOTS. • *n.* **1** var. of SCOTTISH or SCOTS. **2** Scotch whiskey. [Contr. of SCOTTISH]

▶See note at SCOTS.

scotch[1] /skoch/ *v. & n.* • *v.tr.* **1** put an end to; frustrate (*injury scotched his attempt*). **2** *archaic* **a** wound without killing; slightly disable. **b** make incisions in; score. • *n.* **1** *archaic* a slash. **2** a line drawn on the ground for hopscotch. [ME: orig. unkn.]

scotch[2] /skoch/ *n. & v.* • *n.* a wedge or block placed against a wheel, etc., to prevent its slipping. • *v.tr.* hold back (a wheel, barrel, etc.) with a scotch. [17th c.: perh. = *scatch* stilt f. OF *escache*]

Scotch broth *n.* a soup made from beef or mutton with pearl barley, etc.

Scotch egg *n.* a hard-boiled egg enclosed in sausage meat and fried.

Scotch·man /skóchmən/ *n.* (*pl.* ·**men**; *fem.* **Scotch·wom·an**, *pl.* ·**women**) = SCOTSMAN.

▶See note at SCOTS.

Scotch mist *n.* **1** a thick drizzly mist common in the Highlands of Scotland. **2** *Brit.* a retort made to a person implying that he or she has imagined or failed to understand something.

Scotch peb·ble *n.* agate, jasper, cairngorm, etc., found in Scotland.

Scotch pine *n.* a pine tree, *Pinus sylvestris*, native to Europe and Asia.

Scotch tape *n. & v. Trademark* • *n.* transparent adhesive tape. • *v.tr.* (**Scotch-tape**) stick with transparent adhesive tape (*I Scotch-taped my drawings to the walls*).

Scotch ter·ri·er *n.* = SCOTTISH TERRIER.

Scotch whis·key *n.* whiskey distilled in Scotland, esp. from malted barley.

sco·ter /skótər/ *n.* (*pl.* same or **sco·ters**) a large marine duck of the genus *Melanitta*. [17th c.: orig. unkn.]

scot-free *adj.* unharmed; unpunished; safe.

sco•tia /skōshə/ *n.* a concave molding, esp. at the base of a column. [L f. Gk *skotia* f. *skotos* darkness, with ref. to the shadow produced]

Scot•i•cism var. of SCOTTICISM.

Scot•i•cize var. of SCOTTICIZE.

Scot•land Yard /skótlənd/ *n.* **1** the headquarters of the London Metropolitan Police. **2** its Criminal Investigation Department. [Great and New *Scotland Yard*, streets where it was successively situated until 1967]

sco•to•ma /skətōmə/ *n.* (*pl.* **sco•to•ma•ta** /–mətə/) a partial loss of vision or blind spot in an otherwise normal visual field. [LL f. Gk *skotōma* f. *skotoō* darken f. *skotos* darkness]

Scots /skots/ *adj. & n.* esp. *Sc.* • *adj.* **1** = SCOTTISH *adj.* **2** in the dialect, accent, etc., of (esp. Lowlands) Scotland. • *n.* **1** = SCOTTISH *n.* **2** the form of English spoken in (esp. Lowlands) Scotland. [ME orig. *Scottis*, north. var. of SCOTTISH]

▶ In Scotland the terms **Scots** and **Scottish** are preferred to **Scotch**, and they mean the same (e.g., *a Scots/Scottish accent, miner, farmer*, etc.). **Scotch** is used in various compound nouns such as *Scotch broth, Scotch egg, Scotch whiskey*, etc. Similarly, **Scotsman** and **Scotswoman** are preferred to **Scotchman** and **Scotchwoman**.

Scots•man /skótsmən/ *n.* (*pl.* **•men**; *fem.* **Scots•wom•an**, *pl.* **•wom•en**) **1** a native of Scotland. **2** a person of Scottish descent.

Scot•ti•cism /skótisizəm/ *n.* (also **Scot•i•cism**) a Scottish phrase, word, or idiom. [LL *Scot(t)icus*]

Scot•ti•cize /skótisiz/ *v.* (also **Scot•i•cize**) **1** *tr.* imbue with or model on Scottish ways, etc. **2** *intr.* imitate the Scottish in idiom or habits.

Scot•tie /skótee/ *n. colloq.* **1** (also **Scot•tie dog**) a Scottish terrier. **2** a Scot.

Scot•tish /skótish/ *adj. & n.* • *adj.* of or relating to Scotland or its inhabitants. • *n.* (prec. by *the*; treated as *pl.*) the people of Scotland (see also SCOTS). □□ **Scot•tish•ness** *n.*

▶ See note at SCOTS.

Scot•tish ter•ri•er *n.* **1** a small terrier of a rough-haired short-legged breed. **2** this breed.

scoun•drel /skówndrəl/ *n.* an unscrupulous villain; a rogue. □□ **scoun•drel•dom** *n.* **scoun•drel•ism** *n.* **scoun•drel•ly** *adj.* [16th c.: orig. unkn.]

scour[1] /skowr/ *v. & n.* • *v.tr.* **1 a** cleanse or brighten by rubbing, esp. with soap, chemicals, sand, etc. **b** (usu. foll. by *away, off*, etc.) clear (rust, stains, reputation, etc.) by rubbing, hard work, etc. (*scoured the slur from his name*). **2** (of water, or a person with water) clear out (a pipe, channel, etc.) by flushing through. **3** *hist.* purge (the bowels) drastically. • *n.* **1** the act or an instance of scouring; the state of being scoured, esp. by a swift water current (*the scour of the tide*). **2** diarrhea in cattle. **3** a substance used for scouring. □□ **scour•er** *n.* [ME f. MDu., MLG *schüren* f. F *escurer* f. LL *excurare* clean (off) (as EX-[1], CURE)]

scour[2] /skowr/ *v.* **1** *tr.* hasten over (an area, etc.) searching thoroughly (*scoured the streets for him; scoured the pages of the newspaper*). **2** *intr.* range hastily, esp. in search or pursuit. [ME: orig. unkn.]

scourge /skərj/ *n. & v.* • *n.* **1** a whip used for punishment, esp. of people. **2** a person or thing seen as punishing, esp. on a large scale (*the scourge of famine; Genghis Khan, the scourge of Asia*). • *v.tr.* **1** whip. **2** punish; afflict; oppress. □□ **scourg•er** *n.* [ME f. OF *escorge* (n.), *escorgier* (v.) (ult. as EX-[1], L *corrigia* thong, whip)]

scour•ing rush *n.* any of various horsetail plants with a rough siliceous coating used for polishing wood, etc.

Scouse /skows/ *n. & adj. colloq.* • *n.* **1** the dialect of Liverpool. **2** (also **Scous•er** /skówsə/) a native of Liverpool. **3** (**scouse**) = LOBSCOUSE. • *adj.* of or relating to Liverpool. [Abbr. of LOBSCOUSE]

scout[1] /skowt/ *n. & v.* • *n.* **1** a person, esp. a soldier, sent out to get information about the enemy's position, strength, etc. **2** the act of seeking (esp. military) information (*on the scout*). **3** = TALENT SCOUT. **4** (**Scout**) a Boy Scout or Girl Scout. **5** esp. *Brit.* a domestic worker at a college, esp. at Oxford University. **6** esp. *Brit. colloq.* a person; a fellow. **7** a ship or aircraft designed for reconnoitering, esp. a small fast aircraft. • *v.* **1** *intr.* act as a scout. **2** *intr.* (foll. by *about, around*) make a search. **3** *tr.* (often foll. by *out*) *colloq.* explore to get information about (territory, etc.). □□ **scout•er** *n.* **scout•ing** *n.* [ME f. OF *escouter* listen, earlier *ascolter* ult. f. L *auscultare*]

scout[2] /skowt/ *v.tr.* reject (an idea, etc.) with scorn. [Scand.: cf. ON *skúta, skúti* taunt]

Scout•er /skówtər/ *n.* an adult member of the Boy Scouts.

scout•mas•ter /skówtmastər/ *n.* a person in charge of a group of Scouts.

scow /skow/ *n.* a flat-bottomed boat used as a lighter, etc. [Du. *schouw* ferry boat]

scowl /skowl/ *n. & v.* • *n.* a severe frown producing a sullen, bad-tempered, or threatening look on a person's face. • *v.intr.* make a scowl. □□ **scowl•er** *n.* [ME, prob. f. Scand.: cf. Da. *skule* look down or sidelong]

scr. *abbr.* scruple(s) (of weight).

scrab•ble /skrábəl/ *v. & n.* • *v.intr.* (often foll. by *about, at*) scratch or grope to find or collect or hold on to something. • *n.* **1** an act of

scrabbling. **2** (**Scrabble**) *Trademark* a game in which players build up words from letter blocks on a board. [MDu. *schrabbelen* frequent. of *schrabben* SCRAPE]

scrag /skrag/ *n. & v. Brit.* • *n.* **1** (also **scrag end**) the inferior end of a neck of mutton. **2** a skinny person or animal. **3** *colloq.* a person's neck. • *v.tr.* (**scragged, scrag•ging**) *sl.* **1** strangle, hang. **2** seize roughly by the neck. **3** handle roughly; beat up. [Perh. alt. f. dial. *crag* neck, rel. to MDu. *crāghe*, MLG *krage*]

scrag•gly /skráglee/ *adj.* sparse and irregular.

scrag•gy /skrágee/ *adj.* (**scrag•gi•er, scrag•gi•est**) thin and bony. □□ **scrag•gi•ly** *adv.* **scrag•gi•ness** *n.*

scram /skram/ *v.intr.* (**scrammed, scram•ming**) (esp. in *imper.*) *colloq.* go away. [20th c.: perh. f. SCRAMBLE]

scram•ble /skrámbəl/ *v. & n.* • *v.* **1** *intr.* make one's way over rough ground, rocks, etc., by clambering, crawling, etc. **2** *intr.* (foll. by *for, at*) struggle with competitors (for a thing or share of it). **3** *intr.* move with difficulty or awkwardly. **4** *tr.* **a** mix together indiscriminately. **b** jumble or muddle. **5** *tr.* cook (eggs) by heating them when broken and well mixed, often with butter, milk, etc. **6** *tr.* change the speech frequency of (a broadcast transmission or telephone conversation) so as to make it unintelligible without a corresponding decoding device. **7** *intr.* move hastily. **8** *tr. colloq.* execute (an action, etc.) awkwardly and inefficiently. **9** *intr.* (of fighter aircraft or their pilots) take off quickly in an emergency or for action. • *n.* **1** an act of scrambling. **2** a difficult climb or walk. **3** (foll. by *for*) an eager struggle or competition. **4** *Brit.* a motorcycle race over rough ground. **5** an emergency takeoff by fighter aircraft. [16th c. (imit.): cf. dial. synonyms *scamble, cramble*]

scram•bled eggs *n. colloq.* gold braid on a military officer's cap.

scram•bler /skrámblər/ *n.* a device for scrambling telephone conversations.

scran /skran/ *n. Brit. sl.* **1** food; eatables. **2** remains of food. □ **bad scran** *Ir.* bad luck. [18th c.: orig. unkn.]

scrap[1] /skrap/ *n. & v.* • *n.* **1** a small detached piece; a fragment or remnant. **2** rubbish or waste material. **3** an extract or cutting from something written or printed. **4** discarded metal for reprocessing (often *attrib.*: *scrap metal*). **5** (with *neg.*) the smallest piece or amount (*not a scrap of food left*). **6** (in *pl.*) **a** odds and ends. **b** bits of uneaten food. **7** (in *sing* or *pl.*) a residuum of melted fat or of fish with the oil expressed. • *v.tr.* (**scrapped, scrap•ping**) discard as useless. [ME f. ON *skrap*, rel. to *skrapa* SCRAPE]

scrap[2] /skrap/ *n. & v. colloq.* • *n.* a fight or rough quarrel, esp. a spontaneous one. • *v.intr.* (**scrapped, scrap•ping**) (often foll. by *with*) have a scrap. □□ **scrap•per** *n.* [Perh. f. SCRAPE]

scrap•book /skrápbook/ *n.* a book of blank pages for sticking cuttings, drawings, etc., in.

scrape /skrayp/ *v. & n.* • *v.* **1** *tr.* **a** move a hard or sharp edge across (a surface), esp. to make something smooth. **b** apply (a hard or sharp edge) in this way. **2** *tr.* (foll. by *away, off*, etc.) remove (a stain, projection, etc.) by scraping. **3** *tr.* **a** rub (a surface) harshly against another. **b** scratch or damage by scraping. **4** *tr.* make (a hollow) by scraping. **5 a** *tr.* draw or move with a sound of, or resembling, scraping. **b** *intr.* emit or produce such a sound. **c** *tr.* produce such a sound from. **6** *intr.* (often foll. by *along, by, through*, etc.) move or pass along while almost touching close or surrounding features, obstacles, etc. (*the car scraped through the narrow lane*). **7** *tr.* just manage to achieve (a living, an examination pass, etc.). **8** *intr.* (often foll. by *by, through*) **a** barely manage. **b** pass an examination, etc., with difficulty. **9** *tr.* (foll. by *together, up*) contrive to bring or provide; amass with difficulty. **10** *intr.* be economical. **11** *intr.* draw back a foot in making a clumsy bow. **12** *tr.* clear (a ship's bottom) of barnacles, etc. **13** *tr.* completely clear (a plate) of food. **14** *tr. Brit.* (foll. by *back*) draw (the hair) tightly back off the forehead. • *n.* **1** the act or sound of scraping. **2** a scraped place (on the skin, etc.). **3** *Brit.* a thinly applied layer of butter, etc., on bread. **4** the scraping of a foot in bowing. **5** *colloq.* an awkward predicament, esp. resulting from an escapade. □ **scrape acquaintance with** esp. *Brit.* contrive to get to know (a person). **scrape the barrel** *colloq.* be reduced to one's last resources. [ME f. ON *skrapa* or MDu. *schrapen*]

scrap•er /skráypər/ *n.* a device used for scraping, esp. for removing dirt, etc., from a surface.

scrap•er•board /skráypərbawrd/ *n.* = SCRATCHBOARD.

scrap heap *n.* **1** a pile of scrap materials. **2** a state of uselessness.

scrap•ie /skráypee, skráp–/ *n.* a viral disease of sheep involving the central nervous system and characterized by lack of coordination causing affected animals to rub against trees, etc., for support.

scrap•ing /skráyping/ *n.* **1** in senses of SCRAPE *v. & n.* **2** (esp. in *pl.*) a fragment produced by a scraper.

scrap mer•chant *n.* a dealer in scrap.

scrap•py /skrápee/ *adj.* (**scrap•pi•er, scrap•pi•est**) **1** consisting of scraps. **2** incomplete; carelessly arranged or put together. **3 a** quick to engage in fighting; argumentative. **b** (of a fighter) wiry and aggressive. □□ **scrap·pi·ly** adv. **scrap·pi·ness** n.

scrap·yard /skrápyaard/ n. a place where (esp. metal) scrap is collected.

scratch /skrach/ v., n., & adj. • v. **1** tr. score or mark the surface of with a sharp or pointed object. **2** tr. **a** make a long, narrow superficial wound in (the skin). **b** cause (a person or part of the body) to be scratched (scratched himself on the table). **3** tr. (also absol.) scrape without marking, esp. with the hand to relieve itching (stood there scratching). **4** tr. make or form by scratching. **5** tr. scribble; write hurriedly or awkwardly (scratched a quick reply; scratched a large A). **6** tr. (foll. by together, up, etc.) obtain (a thing) by scratching or with difficulty. **7** tr. (foll. by out, off, through) cancel or strike (out) with a pencil, etc. **8** tr. (also absol.) withdraw (a competitor, candidate, etc.) from a race or competition. **9** intr. (often foll. by about, around, etc.) **a** scratch the ground, etc., in search. **b** look around haphazardly (they were scratching about for evidence). • n. **1** a mark or wound made by scratching. **2** a sound of scratching. **3** a spell of scratching oneself. **4** colloq. a superficial wound. **5** a line from which competitors in a race (esp. those not receiving a handicap) start. **6** (in pl.) a disease of horses in which the pastern appears scratched. **7** sl. money. • attrib.adj. **1** collected by chance. **2** collected or made from whatever is available; heterogeneous (a scratch crew). **3** with no handicap given (a scratch race). □ **from scratch 1** from the beginning. **2** without help or advantage. **3** (of baked goods, etc.) without premixed ingredients. **scratch along** make a living, etc., with difficulty. **scratch one's head** be perplexed. **scratch my back and I will scratch yours 1** do me a favor and I will return it. **2** used in reference to mutual aid or flattery. **scratch the surface** deal with a matter only superficially. **up to scratch** up to the required standard. □□ **scratch·er** n. [ME, prob. f. synonymous ME scrat & cratch, both of uncert. orig.: cf. MLG kratsen, OHG krazzōn]

scratch·board /skráchbawrd/ n. cardboard or board with a blackened surface which can be scraped off for making white-line drawings.

scratch pad n. **1** a pad of paper for scribbling. **2** Computing a small fast memory for the temporary storage of data.

scratch·y /skráchee/ adj. (**scratch·i·er**, **scratch·i·est**) **1** tending to make scratches or a scratching noise. **2** (esp. of a garment) tending to cause itchiness. **3** (of a drawing, etc.) done in scratches or carelessly. □□ **scratch·i·ly** adv. **scratch·i·ness** n.

scrawl /skrawl/ v. & n. • v. **1** tr. & intr. write in a hurried untidy way. **2** tr. (foll. by out) cross out by scrawling over. • n. **1** a piece of hurried writing. **2** a scrawled note. □□ **scrawl·y** adj. [Perh. f. obs. scrawl sprawl, alt. of CRAWL]

scrawn·y /skráwnee/ adj. (**scrawn·i·er**, **scrawn·i·est**) lean; scraggy. □□ **scrawn·i·ness** n. [Var. of dial. scranny: cf. archaic scrannel (of sound) weak, feeble]

scream /skreem/ n. & v. • n. **1** a loud, high-pitched, piercing cry expressing fear, pain, extreme fright, etc. **2** the act of emitting a scream. **3** colloq. an irresistibly funny occurrence or person. • v. **1** intr. emit a scream. **2** tr. speak or sing (words, etc.) in a screaming tone. **3** intr. make or move with a shrill sound like a scream. **4** intr. laugh uncontrollably. **5** intr. be blatantly obvious or conspicuous. **6** intr. colloq. turn informer. [OE or MDu.]

scream·er /skréemər/ n. **1** a person or thing that screams. **2** any S. American gooselike bird of the family Anhimidae, frequenting marshland and having a characteristic shrill cry. **3** colloq. a tale that raises screams of laughter. **4** colloq. a sensational headline.

scree /skree/ n. (in sing. or pl.) **1** small loose stones. **2** a mountain slope covered with these. [prob. back-form. f. screes (pl.) ult. f. ON skritha landslip, rel. to skritha glide]

screech /skreech/ n. & v. • n. a harsh, high-pitched scream. • v.tr. & intr. utter with or make a screech. □□ **screech·er** n. **screech·y** adj. (**screech·i·er**, **screech·i·est**). [16th-c. var. of ME scritch (imit.)]

screech owl n. any owl that screeches instead of hooting, esp. a barn owl or a small American owl, Otus asio.

screed /skreed/ n. **1** a long usu. tiresome piece of writing or speech. **2 a** a strip of plaster or other material placed on a surface as a guide to thickness. **b** a leveled layer of material (e.g., concrete) applied to a floor or other surface. [ME, prob. var. of SHRED]

screen /skreen/ n. & v. • n. **1** a fixed or movable upright partition for separating, concealing, or sheltering from drafts or excessive heat or light. **2** a thing used as a shelter, esp. from observation. **3 a** a measure adopted for concealment. **b** the protection afforded by this (under the screen of night). **4 a** a blank usu. white or silver surface on which a photographic image is projected. **b** (prec. by the) movies or the motion-picture industry. **5** the surface of a cathode-ray tube or similar electronic device, esp. of a television, computer monitor, etc., on which images appear. **6** Brit. = WIND-SCREEN. **7** a frame with fine wire netting to keep out flies, mosquitoes, etc. **8** Physics a body intercepting light, heat, electric or magnetic induction, etc., in a physical apparatus. **9** Photog. a piece

of ground glass in a camera for focusing. **10** a large sieve or riddle, esp. for sorting grain, coal, etc., into sizes. **11** a system of checking for the presence or absence of a disease, ability, attribute, etc. **12** Printing a transparent, finely ruled plate or film used in halftone reproduction. **13** Mil. a body of troops, ships, etc., detached to warn of the presence of an enemy force. • v.tr. **1** (often foll. by from) **a** afford shelter to; hide partly or completely. **b** protect from detection, censure, etc. **2** (foll. by off) shut off or hide behind a screen. **3 a** show (a film, etc.) on a screen. **b** broadcast (a television program). **4** prevent from causing, or protect from, electrical interference. **5 a** test (a person or group) for the presence or absence of a disease. **b** check on (a person) for the presence or absence of a quality, esp. reliability or loyalty. **6** pass (grain, coal, etc.) through a screen. □□ **screen·a·ble** adj. **screen·er** n. [ME f. ONF escren, escran: cf. OHG skrank barrier]

screen·ing /skréening/ n. **1** the act of a person or thing that screens, as of applicants for employment. **2** the showing of a motion picture.

screen·ings /skréeningz/ n.pl. refuse separated by sifting.

screen·play /skréenplay/ n. the script of a motion picture or television show, etc., with acting instructions, scene directions, etc.

screen print·ing n. a process like stenciling with ink forced through a prepared sheet of fine material (orig. silk).

screen test n. an audition for a part in a motion picture.

screen·writ·er /skréenrītər/ n. a person who writes a screenplay.

screw /skrōō/ n. & v. • n. **1** a thin cylinder or cone with a spiral ridge or thread running around the outside (**male screw**) or the inside (**female screw**). **2** (in full **wood screw**) a metal male screw with a slotted head and a sharp point for fastening things, esp. in carpentry, by being rotated to form a thread in wood, etc. **3** (in full **screw bolt**) a metal male screw with a blunt end on which a nut is threaded to bolt things together. **4** a wooden or metal straight screw used to exert pressure. **5** (in sing. or pl.) an instrument of torture acting in this way. **6** (in full **screw propeller**) a form of propeller with twisted blades acting like a screw on the water or air. **7** one turn of a screw. **8** (foll. by of) Brit. a small twisted-up paper (filled with sugar, tobacco, etc.). **9** Brit. (in billiards, etc.) an oblique curling motion of the ball. **10** sl. a prison warden or guard. **11** Brit. sl. an amount of salary or wages. **12** coarse sl. **a** an act of sexual intercourse. **b** a partner in this. **13** Brit. sl. a mean or miserly person. **14** Brit. sl. a worn-out horse. • v. **1** tr. fasten or tighten with a screw or screws. **2** tr. turn (a screw). **3** intr. twist or turn around like a screw. **4** Brit. intr. (of a ball, etc.) swerve. **5** tr. **a** put psychological, etc., pressure on to achieve an end. **b** oppress. **6** tr. (foll. by

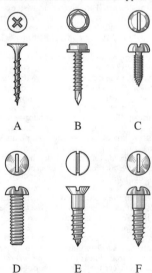

A   B   C

D   E   F

A   drywall screw

B   self-tapping hex head screw

C   sheet metal screw, pan head

D   machine screw, round head

E   wood screw, flat

F   wood screw, round head

screws

out of) extort (consent, money, etc.) from (a person). **7** *tr.* (also *absol.*) *coarse sl.* have sexual intercourse with. **8** *intr.* (of a rolling ball, or of a person, etc.) take a curling course; swerve. **9** *intr.* (often foll. by *up*) make tenser or more efficient. □ **have one's head screwed on the right way** *colloq.* have common sense. **have a screw loose** *colloq.* be slightly crazy. **put the screws on** *colloq.* exert pressure on, esp. to extort or intimidate. **screw up 1** contract or contort (one's face, etc.). **2** contract and crush into a tight mass (a piece of paper, etc.). **3** summon up (one's courage, etc.). **4** *sl.* **a** bungle or mismanage. **b** spoil or ruin (an event, opportunity, etc.). □□ **screw•a•ble** *adj.* **screw•er** *n.* [ME f. OF *escroue* female screw, nut, f. L *scrofa* sow]

screw•ball /skroōbawl/ *n. & adj. sl.* ● *n.* **1** *Baseball* a pitch thrown with spin opposite that of a curveball. **2** a crazy or eccentric person. ● *adj.* crazy.

screw cap *n.* = SCREW TOP.

screw cou•pling *n.* a female screw with threads at both ends for joining lengths of pipes or rods.

screw•driv•er /skroōdrivər/ *n.* a tool with a shaped tip to fit into the head of a screw to turn it.

screwed /skroōd/ *adj.* **1** twisted. **2** *sl.* **a** ruined; rendered ineffective. **b** esp. *Brit.* drunk.

screw eye *n.* a screw with a loop for passing cord, etc., through instead of a slotted head.

screw hook *n.* a hook to hang things on, with a screw point for fastening it.

screw jack *n.* a vehicle jack (see JACK[1]) worked by a screw device.

screw pine *n.* any plant of the genus *Pandanus*, with its leaves arranged spirally and resembling those of a pineapple.

screw plate *n.* a steel plate with threaded holes for making male screws.

screw tap *n.* a tool for making female screws.

screw top *n.* (also (with hyphen) *attrib.*) a cap or lid that can be screwed on to a bottle, jar, etc.

screw-up *n. sl.* a bungle, muddle, or mess.

screw valve *n.* a stopcock opened and shut by a screw.

screw•y /skroō-ee/ *adj.* (**screw•i•er**, **screw•i•est**) *sl.* **1** crazy or eccentric. **2** absurd. □□ **screw•i•ness** *n.*

scrib•ble[1] /skríbəl/ *v. & n.* ● *v.* **1** *tr. & intr.* write carelessly or hurriedly. **2** *intr.* often *derog.* be an author or writer. **3** *intr. & tr.* draw carelessly or meaninglessly. ● *n.* **1** a scrawl. **2** a hasty note, etc. **3** careless handwriting. □□ **scrib•bler** *n.* **scrib•bly** *adj.* [ME f. med.L *scribillare* dimin. of L *scribere* write]

scrib•ble[2] /skríbəl/ *v.tr.* card (wool, cotton, etc.) coarsely. [prob. f. LG: cf. G *schrubbeln* (in the same sense), frequent. f. LG *schrubben*: see SCRUB[1]]

scribe /skrīb/ *n. & v.* ● *n.* **1** a person who writes out documents, esp. an ancient or medieval copyist of manuscripts. **2** *Bibl.* an ancient Jewish record keeper or professional theologian and jurist. **3** (in full **scribe awl**) a pointed instrument for making marks on wood, bricks, etc., to guide a saw, or in sign writing. **4** *colloq.* a writer; a journalist. ● *v.tr.* mark (wood, etc.) with a scribe (see sense 3 of *n.*). □□ **scrib•al** *adj.* **scrib•er** *n.* [(n.) ME f. L *scriba* f. *scribere* write: (v.) perh. f. DESCRIBE]

scrim /skrim/ *n.* open-weave fabric for lining or upholstery, etc. [18th c.: orig. unkn.]

scrim•mage /skrímij/ *n. & v.* ● *n.* **1** a rough or confused struggle; a brawl. **2** *Football* a single play from the snap of the ball till the ball is dead. **3** *Sports* a practice game. ● *v.* **1** *intr.* engage in a scrimmage. **2** *tr. Sports* have a practice game (with). □□ **scrim•mag•er** *n.* [Var. of SKIRMISH]

scrimp /skrimp/ *v.* **1** *intr.* be sparing or parsimonious. **2** *tr.* use sparingly. □□ **scrimp•y** *adj.* [18th c., orig. Sc.: perh. rel. to SHRIMP]

scrim•shank /skrímshangk/ *v.intr. Brit. sl.* esp. *Mil.* shirk duty. □□ **scrim•shank•er** *n.* [19th c.: orig. unkn.]

scrim•shaw /skrímshaw/ *v. & n. v.tr.* (also *absol.*) adorn (shells, ivory, etc.) with carved or colored designs (as sailors' pastime at sea). ● *n.* work or a piece of work of this kind. [19th c.: perh. f. a surname]

scrip /skrip/ *n.* **1** a provisional certificate of money subscribed to a bank or company, etc., entitling the holder to a formal certificate and dividends. **2** (*collect.*) such certificates. **3** an extra share or shares instead of a dividend. [Abbr. of *subscription receipt*]

script /skript/ *n. & v.* ● *n.* **1** handwriting as distinct from print; written characters. **2** type imitating handwriting. **3** an alphabet or system of writing (*the Russian script*). **4** the text of a play, film, or broadcast. **5** an examinee's set of written answers. **6** *Law* an original document as distinct from a copy. ● *v.tr.* write a script for (a motion picture, etc.). [ME, = thing written, f. OF *escri(p)t* f. L *scriptum*, neut. past part. of *scribere* write]

scrip•to•ri•um /skriptáwreeəm/ *n.* (*pl.* **scrip•to•ri•a** /–reeə/ or **scrip•to•ri•ums**) a room set apart for writing, esp. in a monastery. □□ **scrip•to•ri•al** *adj.* [Med.L (as SCRIPT)]

scrip•tur•al /skrípchərəl/ *adj.* **1** of or relating to a scripture, esp. the Bible. **2** having the authority of a scripture. □□ **scrip•tur•al•ly** *adv.* [LL *scripturalis* f. L *scriptura*: see SCRIPTURE]

scrip•ture /skrípchər/ *n.* **1** sacred writings. **2** (**Scripture** or the Scriptures) **a** the Bible as a collection of sacred writings in Christianity. **b** the sacred writings of any other religion. [ME f. L *scriptura* (as SCRIPT)]

script•writ•er /skríptrītər/ *n.* a person who writes a script for a motion picture, broadcast, etc. □□ **script•writ•ing** *n.*

scrive•ner /skrívnər, skrívnər/ *n. hist.* **1** a copyist or drafter of documents. **2** a notary. **3** a broker. **4** a moneylender. [ME f. obs. *scrivein* f. OF *escrivein* ult. f. L (as SCRIBE)]

scro•bic•u•late /skrōbíkyələt, –layt/ *adj. Bot. & Zool.* pitted; furrowed. [L *scrobiculus* f. *scrobis* trench]

scrod /skrod/ *n.* a young cod or haddock, esp. as food. [19th c.: perh. rel. to SHRED]

scrof•u•la /skrófyələ/ *n. archaic* a disease with glandular swellings, prob. a form of tuberculosis. Also called **king's evil.** □□ **scrof•u•lous** *adj.* [ME f. med.L (sing.) f. LL *scrofulae* (pl.) scrofulous swelling, dimin. of L *scrofa* a sow]

scroll /skrōl/ *n. & v.* ● *n.* **1** a roll of parchment or paper esp. with writing on it. **2** a book in the ancient roll form. **3** an ornamental design or carving imitating a roll of parchment. ● *v.* **1** *tr.* (often foll. by *down, up*) move (a display on a computer screen) in order to view new material. **2** *tr.* inscribe in or like a scroll. **3** *intr.* curl up like paper. [ME *scrowle* alt. f. *rowle* ROLL, perh. after *scrow* (in the same sense), formed as ESCROW]

scrolled /skrōld/ *adj.* having a scroll ornament.

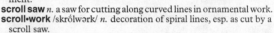

scroll 1

scroll saw *n.* a saw for cutting along curved lines in ornamental work.

scroll•work /skrōlwərk/ *n.* decoration of spiral lines, esp. as cut by a scroll saw.

Scrooge /skroōj/ *n.* a mean or miserly person. [a character in Dickens's *Christmas Carol*]

scro•tum /skrōtəm/ *n.* (*pl.* **scro•ta** /–tə/ or **scro•tums**) a pouch of skin containing the testicles. □□ **scro•tal** *adj.* [L]

scrounge /skrownj/ *v. & n. colloq.* ● *v.* **1** *tr.* (also *absol.*) obtain (things) illicitly or by cadging. **2** *intr.* search about to find something at no cost. ● *n.* an act of scrounging. □ **on the scrounge** engaged in scrounging. **scrounge around** forage or search haphazardly (*we scrounged around for loose change*). □□ **scroung•er** *n.* [var. of dial. *scrunge* steal]

scrub[1] /skrub/ *v. & n.* ● *v.* (**scrubbed, scrub•bing**) **1** *tr.* rub hard so as to clean, esp. with a hard brush. **2** *intr.* use a brush in this way. **3** *intr.* (often foll. by *up*) (of a surgeon, etc.) thoroughly clean the hands and arms by scrubbing, before operating. **4** *tr. colloq.* scrap or cancel (a plan, order, etc.). **5** *tr.* use water to remove impurities from (gas, etc.). ● *n.* the act or an instance of scrubbing; the process of being scrubbed. [ME prob. f. MLG, MDu. *schrobben, schrubben*]

scrub[2] /skrub/ *n.* **1 a** vegetation consisting mainly of brushwood or stunted forest growth. **b** an area of land covered with this. **2** (of livestock) of inferior breed or physique (often *attrib.*: *scrub horse*). **3** a small or dwarf variety (often *attrib.*: *scrub pine*). **4** *Sports colloq.* a team or player not of the first class. □□ **scrub•by** *adj.* [ME, var. of SHRUB[1]]

scrub•ber /skrúbər/ *n.* an apparatus using water or a solution for purifying gases, etc.

scrub brush *n.* (also **scrub•bing brush**) a hard brush for scrubbing floors.

scrub ty•phus *n.* a rickettsial disease of the W. Pacific transmitted by mites.

scruff[1] /skruf/ *n.* the back of the neck as used to grasp and lift or drag an animal or person by (esp. scruff of the neck). [alt. of *scuff*, perh. f. ON *skoft* hair]

scruff[2] /skruf/ *n. Brit.colloq.* an untidy or scruffy person. [Orig. = SCURF, later 'worthless thing,' or back-form. f. SCRUFFY]

scruff•y /skrúfee/ *adj.* (**scruff•i•er, scruff•i•est**) *colloq.* shabby; slovenly; untidy. □□ **scruff•i•ly** *adv.* **scruff•i•ness** *n.* [*Scruff* var. of SCURF + −Y[1]]

scrum /skrum/ *n.* **1** *Rugby* an arrangement of the forwards of each team in two opposing groups, each with arms interlocked and heads down, with the ball thrown in between to restart play. **2** *Brit. colloq.* a milling crowd. [abbr. of SCRUMMAGE]

scrum half *n.* a halfback who puts the ball into the scrum.

scrum•mage /skrúmij/ *n. Rugby* = SCRUM 1. [as SCRIMMAGE]

scrum•my /skrúmee/ *adj. Brit. colloq.* excellent; enjoyable; delicious. [SCRUMPTIOUS + −Y[1]]

scrump•tious /skrúmpshəs/ *adj. colloq.* **1** delicious. **2** pleasing; delightful. □□ **scrump•tious•ly** *adv.* **scrump•tious•ness** *n.* [19th c.: orig. unkn.]

scrunch /skrunch/ *v. & n.* ●*v.tr. & intr.* **1** (usu. foll. by *up*) make or become crushed or crumpled. **2** make or cause to make a crunching sound. ●*n.* the act or an instance of scrunching. [var. of CRUNCH]

scrunch·ie /skrúnchee/ *n.* a hair band of elastic enclosed by crumpled fabric, used for ponytails, etc.

scru·ple /skro͞opɔl/ *n. & v.* ●*n.* **1** (in *sing.* or *pl.*) **a** regard to the morality or propriety of an action. **b** a feeling of doubt or hesitation caused by this. **2** *Brit. hist.* an apothecaries' weight of 20 grains. **3** *archaic* a very small quantity. ●*v.intr.* **1** (foll. by *to* + infin.; usu. with *neg.*) be reluctant because of scruples (*did not scruple to stop their allowance*). **2** feel or be influenced by scruples. [F *scrupule* or L *scrupulus* f. *scrupus* rough pebble, anxiety]

scru·pu·lous /skro͞opyɔlɔs/ *adj.* **1** conscientious or thorough even in small matters. **2** careful to avoid doing wrong. **3** punctilious; over-attentive to details. □□ **scru·pu·los·i·ty** /–lósitee/ *n.* **scru·pu·lous·ly** *adv.* **scru·pu·lous·ness** *n.* [ME f. F *scrupuleux* or L *scrupulosus* (as SCRUPLE)]

scru·ti·neer /skro͞ot'néer/ *n. Brit.* a person who scrutinizes or examines something, esp. the conduct and result of a ballot.

scru·ti·nize /skro͞ot'nīz/ *v.tr.* look closely at; examine with close scrutiny. □□ **scru·ti·niz·er** *n.*

scru·ti·ny /skro͞ot'nee/ *n.* (*pl.* -**nies**) **1** a critical gaze. **2** a close investigation or examination of details. **3** an official examination of ballot papers to check their validity or accuracy of counting. [ME f. L *scrutinium* f. *scrutari* search f. *scruta* rubbish: orig. of ragcollectors]

scry /skrī/ *v.intr.* (-**ies**, -**ied**) divine by crystal gazing. □□ **scry·er** *n.* [shortening f. DESCRY]

scu·ba /sko͞obɔ/ *n.* (*pl.* **scu·bas**) an aqualung. □□ **scu·badive** *v.intr.* **scu·ba div·er** *n.* [Acronym f. *self-contained underwater breathing apparatus*]

scu·ba div·ing *n.* swimming underwater using a scuba, esp. as a sport.

scud /skud/ *v. & n.* ●*v.intr.* (**scud·ded**, **scud·ding**) **1** fly or run straight, fast, and lightly; skim along. **2** *Naut.* run before the wind. ●*n.* **1** a spell of scudding. **2** a scudding motion. **3** vapory driving clouds. **4** a driving shower; a gust. **5** wind-blown spray. **6** (**Scud**) a type of long-range surface-to-surface guided missile originally developed in the former Soviet Union. [Perh. alt. of SCUT, as if to race like a hare]

scuff /skuf/ *v. & n.* ●*v.* **1** *tr.* graze or brush against. **2** *tr.* mark or wear down (shoes) in this way. **3** *intr.* walk with dragging feet; shuffle. ●*n.* a mark of scuffing. [imit.]

scuf·fle /skúfɔl/ *n. & v.* ●*n.* a confused struggle or disorderly fight at close quarters. ●*v.intr.* engage in a scuffle. [prob. f. Scand.: cf. Sw. *skuffa* to push, rel. to SHOVE]

scul·dug·ger·y var. of SKULDUGGERY.

scull /skul/ *n. & v.* ●*n.* **1** either of a pair of small oars used by a single rower. **2** an oar placed over the stern of a boat to propel it, usu. by a twisting motion. **3** (in *pl.*) a race between boats with single pairs of oars. **4** a racing boat propelled by sculls. ●*v.tr.* propel (a boat) with sculls. [ME: orig. unkn.]

scul·ler /skúlɔr/ *n.* **1** a user of sculls. **2** a boat intended for sculling.

scul·ler·y /skúlɔree/ *n.* (*pl.* -**ies**) a small kitchen or room at the back of a house for washing dishes, etc. [ME f. AF *squillerie*, OF *escuelerie* f. *escuele* dish f. L *scutella* salver dimin. of *scutra* wooden platter]

scul·lion /skúlyɔn/ *n. archaic* **1** a cook's boy. **2** a person who washes dishes, etc. [ME: orig. unkn.]

scul·pin /skúlpin/ *n.* any of numerous fish of the family Cottidae, native to nontropical regions, having large spiny heads. [perh. f. obs. *scorpene* f. L *scorpaena* f. Gk *korpaina* a fish]

sculpt /skulpt/ *v.tr. & intr.* (also **sculp**) sculpture. [F *sculpter* f. *sculpteur* SCULPTOR: now regarded as an abbr.]

sculp·tor /skúlptɔr/ *n.* (*fem.* **sculp·tress** /–tris/) an artist who makes sculptures. [L (as SCULPTURE)]

sculp·ture /skúlpchɔr/ *n. & v.* ●*n.* **1** the art of making forms, often representational, in the round or in relief by chiseling stone, carving wood, modeling clay, casting metal, etc. **2** a work or works of sculpture. **3** *Zool. & Bot.* raised or sunken markings on a shell, etc. ●*v.* **1** *tr.* represent in or adorn with sculpture. **2** *intr.* practice sculpture. □□ **sculp·tur·al** *adj.* **sculp·tur·al·ly** *adv.* **sculp·tur·esque** *adj.* [ME f. L *sculptura* f. *sculpere sculpt-* carve]

scum /skum/ *n. & v.* ●*n.* **1** a layer of dirt, froth, or impurities, etc., forming at the top of liquid, esp. in boiling or fermentation. **2** (foll. by *of*) the most worthless part of something. **3** *colloq.* a worthless person or group. ●*v.* (**scummed**, **scum·ming**) **1** *tr.* remove scum from; skim. **2** *tr.* be or form a scum on. **3** *intr.* (of a liquid) develop scum. □□ **scum·my** *adj.* (**scum·mi·er**, **scum·mi·est**) *adj.* [ME f. MLG, MDu. *schūm*, OHG *scūm* f. Gmc]

scum·bag /skúmbag/ *n. sl.* **1** a condom. **2** a worthless despicable person.

scum·ble /skúmbɔl/ *v. & n.* ●*v.tr.* **1** modify (a painting) by applying a thin opaque coat of paint to give a softer or duller effect. **2** modify (a drawing) similarly with light penciling, etc. ●*n.* **1** material used in scumbling. **2** the effect produced by scumbling. [Perh. frequent. of SCUM *v.tr.*]

scun·ner /skúnɔr/ *v. & n. Sc.* ●*v.intr. & tr.* feel disgust; nauseate. ●*n.* **1** a strong dislike (esp. take a scunner at or against). **2** an object of loathing. [14th c.: orig. uncert.]

scup /skup/ *n.* an E. American fish, *Stenostomus chrysops*, a kind of porgy. [Narragansett *mishcup* thick-scaled f. *mishe* large + *cuppi* scale]

scup·per[1] /skúpɔr/ *n.* a hole at the edge of a boat's deck to allow water to run off. [ME (perh. f. AF) f. OF *escopir* f. Rmc *skuppire* (unrecorded) to spit: orig. imit.]

scup·per[2] /skúpɔr/ *v.tr. Brit. sl.* **1** sink (a ship or its crew). **2** defeat or ruin (a plan, etc.). **3** kill. [19th c.: orig. unkn.]

scurf /skɔrf/ *n.* **1** flakes on the surface of the skin, cast off as fresh skin develops below, esp. those of the head; dandruff. **2** any scaly matter on a surface. □□ **scurf·y** *adj.* [OE, prob. f. ON & earlier OE *sceorf*, rel. to *sceorfan* gnaw, *sceorfian* cut to shreds]

scur·ri·lous /skɔ́rilɔs, skúr–/ *adj.* **1** (of a person or language) grossly or indecently abusive. **2** given to or expressed with low humor. □□ **scur·ril·i·ty** /–rílitee/ *n.* (*pl.* -**ties**). **scur·ril·ous·ly** *adv.* **scur·ril·ous·ness** *n.* [F *scurrile* or L *scurrilus* f. *scurra* buffoon]

scur·ry /skɔ́ree, skúree/ *v. & n.* ●*v.intr.* (-**ries**, -**ried**) run or move hurriedly, esp. with short quick steps; scamper. ●*n.* (*pl.* -**ries**) **1** the act or sound of scurrying. **2** bustle; haste. **3** a flurry of rain or snow. [Abbr. of *hurry-scurry* redupl. of HURRY]

scur·vy /skúrvee/ *n. & adj.* ●*n.* a disease caused by a deficiency of vitamin C, characterized by swollen bleeding gums and the opening of previously healed wounds, esp. formerly affecting sailors. ●*adj.* (**scur·vi·er**, **scur·vi·est**) paltry; low; mean; dishonorable; contemptible. □□ **scur·vied** *adj.* **scur·vi·ly** *adv.* [SCURF +–Y[1]: noun sense by assoc. with F *scorbut* (cf. SCORBUTIC)]

scur·vy grass *n.* any cresslike seaside plant of the genus *Cochlearia*, orig. taken as a cure for scurvy.

scut /skut/ *n.* a short tail, esp. of a hare, rabbit, or deer. [ME: orig. unkn.: cf. obs. *scut* short, shorten]

scu·ta *pl.* of SCUTUM.

scu·tage /sky o͞otij/ *n. hist.* money paid by a feudal landowner instead of personal service. [ME f. med.L *scutagium* f. L *scutum* shield]

scutch /skuch/ *v.tr.* dress (fibrous material, esp. retted flax) by beating. □□ **scutch·er** *n.* [OF *escouche*, *escoucher* (dial.), *escousser*, ult. f. L *excutere excuss-* (as EX-[1], *quatere* shake)]

scutch·eon /skúchɔn/ *n.* **1** = ESCUTCHEON. **2** an ornamented brass, etc., plate around or over a keyhole. **3** a plate for a name or inscription. [ME f. ESCUTCHEON]

scute /sky o͞ot/ *n. Zool.* = SCUTUM. [L (as SCUTUM)]

scu·tel·lum /sky o͞otélɔm/ *n.* (*pl.* **scu·tel·la** /–lɔ/) *Bot. & Zool.* a scale, plate, or any shieldlike formation on a plant, insect, bird, etc., esp. one of the horny scales on a bird's foot. □□ **scu·tel·late** /sky o͞otélit, sky o͞otɔlayt/ *adj.* **scu·tel·la·tion** /sky o͞otɔláyshɔn/ *n.* [Mod.L dimin. of L *scutum* shield]

scut·ter /skútɔr/ *v. & n.* ●*v.intr. Brit. colloq.* scurry. ●*n.* the act or an instance of scuttering. [perh. alt. of SCUTTLE[2]]

scut·tle[1] /skút'l/ *n.* **1** a receptacle for carrying and holding a small supply of coal. **2** *Brit.* the part of an automobile between the windshield and the hood. [ME f. ON *skutill*, OHG *scuzzila* f. L *scutella* dish]

scut·tle[2] /skút'l/ *v. & n.* ●*v.intr.* **1** scurry; hurry along. **2** run away; flee from danger or difficulty. ●*n.* **1** a hurried gait. **2** a precipitate flight or departure. [cf. dial. *scuddle* frequent. of SCUD]

scut·tle[3] /skút'l/ *n. & v.* ●*n.* a hole with a lid in a ship's deck or side. ●*v.tr.* let water into (a ship) to sink it, esp. by opening the seacocks. [ME, perh. f. obs. F *escoutille* f. Sp. *escotilla* hatchway dimin. of *escota* cutting out cloth]

scut·tle·butt /skút'lbut/ *n.* **1** a water cask on the deck of a ship, for drinking from. **2** *colloq.* rumor; gossip.

scu·tum /sky o͞otɔm/ *n.* (*pl.* **scu·ta** /–tɔ/) each of the shieldlike plates or scales forming the bony covering of a crocodile, sturgeon, turtle, armadillo, etc. □□ **scu·tal** *adj.* **scu·tate** *adj.* [L, = oblong shield]

scuzz·y /skúzee/ *adj. sl.* abhorrent or disgusting. [Prob. f. DISGUSTING]

Scyl·la and Cha·ryb·dis /sílɔ ɔnd kɔríbdis/ *n.pl.* two dangers such that avoidance of one increases the risk from the other. [The names of a sea monster and whirlpool in Gk mythology]

scy·pho·zo·an /sífɔzóɔn/ *n. & adj.* ●*n.* any marine jellyfish of the class Scyphozoa, with tentacles bearing stinging cells. ●*adj.* of or relating to this class. [as SCYPHUS + Gk *zōion* animal]

scy·phus /sífɔs/ *n.* (*pl.* **scy·phi** /–fī/) **1** *GkAntiq.* a footless drinking cup with two handles below the level of the rim. **2** *Bot.* a cup-shaped part as in a narcissus flower or in lichens. □□ **scy·phose** *adj.* [mod.L f. Gk *skuphos*]

scythe /sīth/ *n. & v.* ●*n.* a mowing and reaping implement with a long curved blade swung

scythe

over the ground by a long pole with two short handles projecting from it. ● *v.tr.* cut with a scythe. [OE *sīthe* f. Gmc]

Scyth·i·an /sítheeən, –thee–/ *adj. & n.* ● *adj.* of or relating to ancient Scythia, a region north of the Black Sea. ●*n.* **1** an inhabitant of Scythia. **2** the language of this region. [L *Scythia* f. Gk *Skuthia* Scythia]

SD *abbr.* South Dakota (in official postal use).

S.Dak. *abbr.* South Dakota.

SDI *abbr.* strategic defense initiative.

SE *abbr.* **1** southeast. **2** southeastern. **3** Standard English.

Se *symb. Chem.* the element selenium.

se- /sə, see/ *prefix* apart, without (*seclude; secure*). [L f. OL *se* (prep. & adv.)]

sea /see/ *n.* **1** the expanse of salt water that covers most of the earth's surface and surrounds its landmasses. **2** any part of this as opposed to land or fresh water. **3** a particular (usu. named) tract of salt water partly or wholly enclosed by land (*the North Sea; the Dead Sea*). **4** a large inland lake (*the Sea of Galilee*). **5** the waves of the sea, esp. with reference to their local motion or state (*a choppy sea*). **6** (foll. by *of*) a vast quantity or expanse (*a sea of troubles; a sea of faces*). **7** (*attrib.*) living or used in, on, or near the sea (often prefixed to the name of a marine animal, plant, etc., having a superficial resemblance to what it is named after) (*see lettuce*). □ **at sea 1** in a ship on the sea. **2** (also **all at sea**) perplexed; confused. **by sea** in a ship or ships. **go to sea** become a sailor. **on the sea 1** in a ship at sea. **2** situated on the coast. **put** (or **put out**) **to sea** leave land or port. [OE *sǣ* f. Gmc]

sea an·chor *n.* a device such as a heavy bag dragged in the water to retard the drifting of a ship.

sea a·nem·o·ne *n.* any of various coelenterates of the order Actiniaria having a polypoid body bearing a ring of tentacles around the mouth.

sea an·gel *n.* an angelfish.

sea bass *n.* any of various marine fishes like the bass, esp. *Centropristis striatus.*

sea·bed /seébed/ *n.* the ground under the sea; the ocean floor.

sea·bird /seébərd/ *n.* a bird frequenting the sea or the land near the sea.

sea·board /seébawrd/ *n.* **1** the seashore or coastal region. **2** the line of a coast.

sea·borg·i·um /seebáwrgeeəm/ *n.* an artificially produced chemical element, atomic number 106. ¶ Symb.: **Sg**. [For US chemist Glenn T. Seaborg (b. 1912)]

sea·borne /seébawrn/ *adj.* transported by sea.

sea bream *n.* = PORGY.

sea breeze *n.* a breeze blowing toward the land from the sea, esp. during the day (cf. LAND BREEZE).

sea buck·thorn *n.* a maritime shrub, *Hippophaë rhamnoides* with orange berries.

sea change *n.* a notable or unexpected transformation (with ref. to Shakesp. *Tempest* I. ii. 403).

sea chest *n.* a sailor's storage chest.

sea coal *n. archaic* mineral coal, as distinct from charcoal, etc.

sea·coast /seékōst/ *n.* the land adjacent to the sea.

sea·cock /seékok/ *n.* a valve below a ship's waterline for letting water in or out.

sea cow *n.* **1** a sirenian. **2** a walrus.

sea cu·cum·ber *n.* a holothurian, esp. a bêche-de-mer.

sea dog *n.* an old or experienced sailor.

sea ea·gle *n.* any fish-eating eagle esp. of the genus *Haliaëtus.*

sea el·e·phant *n.* = ELEPHANT SEAL.

sea fan *n.* any colonial coral of the order Gorgonacea supported by a fanlike horny skeleton.

sea·far·er /seéfairər/ *n.* **1** a sailor. **2** a traveler by sea.

sea·far·ing /seéfairing/ *adj. & n.* traveling by sea, esp. regularly.

sea·food /seéfood/ *n.* edible sea fish or shellfish.

sea·front /seéfrənt/ *n.* the part of a coastal town directly facing the sea.

sea·girt /seégərt/ *adj. literary* surrounded by sea.

sea·go·ing /seégōing/ *adj.* **1** (of ships) fit for crossing the sea. **2** (of a person) seafaring.

sea goose·ber·ry *n.* any marine animal of the phylum Ctenophora, with an ovoid body bearing numerous cilia.

sea green *n.* bluish green (as of the sea).

sea·gull /seégul/ *n.* = GULL[1].

sea hare *n.* any of various marine mollusks of the order Anaspidea, having an internal shell and long extensions from its foot.

sea hol·ly *n.* a spiny-leaved blue-flowered evergreen plant, *Eryngium maritimum.*

sea horse *n.* **1** any of various small upright marine fish of the family Syngnathidae, esp. *Hip-*

sea horse

pocampus hippocampus, having a body suggestive of the head and neck of a horse. **2** a mythical creature with a horse's head and fish's tail.

sea is·land cot·ton *n.* a fine-quality long-stapled cotton grown on islands off the southern US.

sea kale *n.* a cruciferous maritime plant, *Crambe maritima*, having coarsely-toothed leaves and used as a vegetable.

seal[1] /seel/ *n. & v.* ●*n.* **1** a piece of wax, lead, paper, etc., with a stamped design, attached to a document as a guarantee of authenticity. **2** a similar material attached to a receptacle, envelope, etc., affording security by having to be broken to allow access to the contents. **3** an engraved piece of metal, gemstone, etc., for stamping a design on a seal. **4 a** a substance or device used to close an aperture or act as a fastening. **b** an amount of water standing in the trap of a drain to prevent foul air from rising. **5** an act or gesture or event regarded as a confirmation or guarantee (*gave her seal of approval to the venture*). **6** a significant or prophetic mark (*has the seal of death in his face*). **7** a decorative adhesive stamp. **8** esp. Eccl. a vow of secrecy; an obligation to silence. ●*v.tr.* **1** close securely or hermetically. **2** stamp or fasten with a seal. **3** fix a seal to. **4** certify as correct with a seal or stamp. **5** (often foll. by *up*) confine or fasten securely. **6** settle or decide (*their fate is sealed*). **7** (foll. by *off*) put barriers around (an area) to prevent entry and exit, esp. as a security measure. **8** apply a nonporous coating to (a surface) to make it impervious. □ **one's lips are sealed** one is obliged to keep a secret. **set one's seal to** (or **on**) authorize or confirm. □□ **seal·a·ble** *adj.* [ME f. AF *seal*, OF *seel* f. L *sigillum* dimin. of *signum* SIGN]

seal[2] /seel/ *n. & v.* ●*n.* any fish-eating amphibious sea mammal of the family Phocidae or Otariidae, with flippers and webbed feet. ●*v.intr.* hunt for seals. [OE *seolh seol-* f. Gmc]

seal·ant /seélənt/ *n.* material for sealing, esp. to make something airtight or watertight.

sea lav·en·der *n.* any maritime plant of the genus *Limonium*, with small brightly colored funnel-shaped flowers.

sealed-beam *adj.* designating a vehicle headlight with a sealed unit consisting of the light source, reflector, and lens.

sealed book *n.* see BOOK.

sealed or·ders *n.pl.* orders for procedure not to be opened before a specified time.

sea legs *n.pl.* the ability to keep one's balance and avoid seasickness when at sea.

seal·er /seélər/ *n.* a ship or person engaged in hunting seals.

seal·er·y /seéləree/ *n.* (*pl.* **·ies**) a place for hunting seals.

sea lev·el *n.* the mean level of the sea's surface, used in reckoning the height of hills, etc., and as a barometric standard.

sea lil·y *n.* any of various sessile echinoderms, esp. of the class Crinoidea, with long jointed stalks and featherlike arms for trapping food.

seal·ing wax *n.* a mixture of shellac and rosin with turpentine and pigment, softened by heating and used to make seals.

sea li·on *n.* any large, eared seal of the Pacific, esp. of the genus *Zalophus* or *Otaria.*

sea loch *n.* = LOCH 2.

seal ring *n.* a finger ring with a seal.

seal·skin /seélskin/ *n.* **1** the skin or prepared fur of a seal. **2** (often *attrib.*) a garment made from this.

Sea·ly·ham /seéleehəm, esp. *Brit.* –leeəm/ *n.* (in full **Sealyham terrier**) **1** a terrier of a wire-haired, short-legged breed. **2** this breed. [*Sealyham* in S. Wales]

seam /seem/ *n. & v.* ●*n.* **1** a line where two edges join, esp. of two pieces of cloth, etc., turned back and stitched together, or of boards fitted edge to edge. **2** a fissure between parallel edges. **3** a wrinkle or scar. **4** a stratum of coal, etc. ●*v.tr.* **1** join with a seam. **2** (esp. as **seamed** *adj.*) mark or score with or as with a seam. □ **bursting at the seams** full to overflowing. □□ **seam·er** *n.* **seam·less** *adj.* [OE *sēam* f. Gmc]

sea·man /seémən/ *n.* (*pl.* **·men**) **1** a sailor, esp. one below the rank of officer. **2** a person regarded in terms of skill in navigation (*a poor seaman*). □□ **sea·man·like** *adj.* **sea·man·ly** *adj.* [OE *sǣman* (as SEA, MAN)]

sea·man·ship /seémənship/ *n.* skill in managing a ship or boat.

sea mile *n.* = NAUTICAL MILE.

sea mouse *n.* any iridescent marine annelid of the genus *Aphrodite.*

seam·stress /seémstris/ *n.* (also **semp·stress** /semp–/) a woman who sews, esp. professionally. [OE *sēamestre* fem. f. *sēamere* tailor, formed as SEAM + –STER + –ESS[1]]

seam·y /seémee/ *adj.* (**seam·i·er, seam·i·est**) **1** marked with or showing seams. **2** unpleasant; disreputable (esp. the seamy side). □□ **seam·i·ness** *n.*

Sean·ad /shánəth/ *n.* the upper house of Parliament in the Republic of Ireland. [Ir., = senate]

se·ance /sáyons/ *n.* (also **sé·ance**) a meeting at which spiritualists attempt to make contact with the dead. [F *séance* f. OF *seoir* f. L *sedēre* sit]

sea on·ion *n.* = SQUILL 2.

sea ot·ter *n.* a Pacific otter, *Enhydra lutris*, using a stone balanced on its abdomen to crack bivalve mollusks.

sea pink *n.* a maritime plant, *Armeria maritima*, with bright pink flowers. Also called **thrift**.

sea·plane /séeplayn/ *n.* an aircraft designed to take off from and land and float on water.

sea·port /séepawrt/ *n.* a town with a harbor for seagoing ships.

sea purse *n.* the egg case of a skate or shark.

sea·quake /séekwayk/ *n.* an earthquake under the sea.

sear /seer/ *v. & adj.* ● *v.tr.* **1 a** scorch, esp. with a hot iron; cauterize; brand. **b** (as **searing** *adj.*) scorching; burning (*searing pain*). **2** cause pain or great anguish to. **3** brown (meat) quickly at a high temperature so that it will retain its juices in cooking. **4** make (one's conscience, feelings, etc.) callous. **5** *archaic* blast; wither. ● *adj.* var. of SERE². [OE *sēar* (adj.), *sēarian* (v.), f. Gmc]

search /sərch/ *v. & n.* ● *v.* **1** *tr.* look through or go over thoroughly to find something. **2** *tr.* examine or feel over (a person) to find anything concealed. **3** *tr.* a probe or penetrate into. **b** examine or question (one's mind, conscience, etc.) thoroughly. **4** *intr.* (often foll. by *for*) make a search or investigation. **5** *intr.* (as **searching** *adj.*) (of an examination) thorough; leaving no loopholes. **6** *tr.* (foll. by *out*) look probingly for; seek out. ● *n.* **1** an act of searching. **2** an investigation. □ **in search of** trying to find. **right of search** a belligerent's right to stop a neutral vessel and search it for prohibited goods. **search me!** *colloq.* I do not know. □□ **search·a·ble** *adj.* **search·er** *n.* **search·ing·ly** *adv.* [ME f. AF *sercher*, OF *cerchier* f. LL *circare* go round (as CIRCUS)]

search·light /sərchlīt/ *n.* **1** a powerful outdoor electric light with a concentrated beam that can be turned in any direction. **2** the light or beam from this.

search par·ty *n.* a group of people organized to look for a lost person or thing.

search war·rant *n.* an official authorization to enter and search a building.

sea room *n.* clear space at sea for a ship to turn or maneuver in.

sea salt *n.* salt produced by evaporating seawater.

sea·scape /séeskayp/ *n.* a picture or view of the sea.

Sea Scout *n.* a member of a maritime scouting association.

sea ser·pent *n.* (also **sea snake**) **1** a snake of the family Hydrophiidae, living in the sea. **2** an enormous legendary serpentlike sea monster.

sea·shell /séeshel/ *n.* the shell of a saltwater mollusk.

sea·shore /séeshawr/ *n.* **1** land close to or bordering on the sea. **2** *Law* the area between high and low water marks.

sea·sick /séesik/ *adj.* suffering from sickness or nausea from the motion of a ship at sea. □□ **sea·sick·ness** *n.*

sea·side /séesīd/ *n.* the seacoast, esp. as a holiday resort.

sea·son /séezən/ *n. & v.* ● *n.* **1** each of the four divisions of the year (spring, summer, autumn, and winter) associated with a type of weather and a stage of vegetation. **2** a time of year characterized by climatic or other features (*the dry season*). **3 a** the time of year when a plant is mature or flowering, etc. **b** the time of year when an animal breeds or is hunted. **4** a proper or suitable time. **5** a time when something is plentiful or active or in vogue. **6** (usu. prec. by *the*) = HIGH SEASON. **7** the time of year regularly devoted to an activity (*the football season*). **8** the time of year dedicated to social life generally (*went up to their cottage for the season*). **9** a period of indefinite or varying length. **10** *Brit. colloq.* = SEASON TICKET. ● *v.* **1** *tr.* flavor (food) with salt, herbs, etc. **2** *tr.* enhance with wit, excitement, etc. **3** *tr.* temper or moderate. **4** *tr. & intr.* **a** make or become suitable in the desired condition, esp. by exposure to the air or weather; mature. **b** (usu. as **seasoned** *adj.*) make or become experienced or accustomed (*seasoned soldiers*). □ **in season 1** (of foodstuff) available in plenty and in good condition. **2** (of an animal) in heat. **3** timely. □□ **sea·son·er** *n.* [ME f. OF *seson* f. L *satio -onis* (in Rmc sense 'seed time') f. *serere sat-* sow]

sea·son·a·ble /séezənəbəl/ *adj.* **1** suitable to or usual in the season. **2** opportune. **3** meeting the needs of the occasion. □□ **sea·son·a·ble·ness** *n.* **sea·son·a·bly** *adv.*

▶ **Seasonable** is sometimes confused with **seasonal**. *Seasonable* means 'usual or suitable for the season' or 'opportune, ' e.g., *Although seasonable, the weather was not warm enough for a picnic. Seasonal* means 'of, depending on, or varying with the season,' e.g., *Seasonal changes in labor requirements draw migrant workers to the area in spring and fall.*

sea·son·al /séezənəl/ *adj.* of, depending on, or varying with the season. □□ **sea·son·al·i·ty** /-nálitee/ *n.* **sea·son·al·ly** *adv.*

sea·son·al af·fec·tive dis·or·der *n.* a depressive state associated with late autumn and winter and thought to be caused by a lack of light.

sea·son·ing /séezəning/ *n.* condiments added to food.

sea squirt *n.* any marine tunicate of the class Ascidiacea, consisting of a baglike structure with apertures for the flow of water.

seat /seet/ *n. & v.* ● *n.* **1** a thing made or used for sitting on; a chair, stool, saddle, etc. **2** the buttocks. **3** the part of a garment covering the buttocks. **4** the part of a chair, etc., on which the sitter's weight directly rests. **5** a place for one person in a theater, vehicle, etc. **6** the occupation of a seat. **7** *Polit.* **a** the right to occupy a seat, esp. as a member of Congress, etc. **8** the part of a machine that supports or guides another part. **9** a site or location of something specified (*a seat of learning; the seat of the emotions*). **10** a country mansion, esp. with large grounds. **11** the manner of sitting on a horse, etc. ● *v.tr.* **1** cause to sit. **2 a** provide sitting accommodation for (*the theater seats 500*). **b** provide with seats. **3** (as **seated** *adj.*) sitting. **4** put or fit in position. □ **be seated** sit down. **by the seat of one's pants** *colloq.* by instinct rather than logic or knowledge. **take a** (or **one's**) **seat** sit down. □□ **seat·less** *adj.* [ME f. ON *sæti* (=OE *gesete* f. Gmc)]

seat belt *n.* a belt securing a person in the seat of a car, aircraft, etc.

-seater /séetər/ *n.* (in *comb.*) having a specified number of seats (*a 16-seater bus*).

seat·ing /séeting/ *n.* **1** seats collectively. **2** sitting accommodation.

SEATO /séetō/ *abbr.* Southeast Asia Treaty Organization.

sea trout *n.* = SALMON TROUT.

sea ur·chin *n.* a small marine echinoderm of the class Echinoidea, with a spherical or flattened spiny shell.

sea·wall /séewawl/ *n.* a wall or embankment erected to prevent encroachment by the sea.

sea·ward /séewərd/ *adv., adj., & n.* ● *adv.* (also **sea·wards** /-wərdz/) toward the sea. ● *adj.* going or facing toward the sea. ● *n.* such a direction or position.

sea·wa·ter /séewawtər/ *n.* water in or taken from the sea.

sea·way /séeway/ *n.* **1** an inland waterway open to seagoing ships. **2** a ship's progress. **3** a ship's path across the sea.

sea urchin

sea·weed /séeweed/ *n.* any of various algae growing in the sea or on the rocks on a shore.

sea·wor·thy /séewərthee/ *adj.* (esp. of a ship) fit to put to sea. □□ **sea·wor·thi·ness** *n.*

se·ba·ceous /sibáyshəs/ *adj.* fatty; of or relating to tallow or fat. [L *sebaceus* f. *sebum* tallow]

se·ba·ceous gland *n.* (also **se·ba·ceous fol·li·cle** or **se·ba·ceous duct**) a gland, etc., secreting or conveying oily matter to lubricate the skin and hair.

seb·or·rhe·a /sébəreeə/ *n.* excessive discharge of sebum from the sebaceous glands. □□ **seb·or·rhe·ic** *adj.* [SEBUM after *gonorrhea*, etc.]

se·bum /séebəm/ *n.* the oily secretion of the sebaceous glands. [mod.L f. L *sebum* grease]

SEC *abbr.* Securities and Exchange Commission.

Sec. *abbr.* secretary.

sec¹ *abbr.* secant.

sec² /sek/ *n. colloq.* (in phrases) a second (of time). [abbr.]

sec³ /sek/ *adj.* (of wine) dry. [F f. L *siccus*]

sec. *abbr.* second(s).

se·cant /séekant, -kənt/ *adj. & n. Math.* ● *adj.* cutting (*secant line*). ● *n.* **1** a line cutting a curve at one or more points. **2** the ratio of the hypotenuse to the shorter side adjacent to an acute angle (in a right triangle). ¶ Abbr.: **sec**. [F *sécant(e)* f. L *secare secant-* cut]

sec·a·teurs /sékətərz/ *n.pl.* esp. *Brit.* a pair of pruning shears for use with one hand. [F *sécateur* cutter, irreg. f. L *secare* cut]

sec·co /sékō/ *n.* the technique of painting on dry plaster with pigments mixed in water. [It., = dry, f. L *siccus*]

se·cede /siseéd/ *v.intr.* (usu. foll. by *from*) withdraw formally from membership of a political federation or a religious body. □□ **se·ced·er** *n.* [L *secedere secess-* (as SE-, *cedere* go)]

se·ces·sion /siséshən/ *n.* **1** the act or an instance of seceding. **2** (**Secession**) *hist.* the withdrawal of eleven southern states from the US Union in 1860–61, leading to the Civil War. □□ **se·ces·sion·al** *adj.* **se·ces·sion·ism** *n.* **se·ces·sion·ist** *n.* [F *sécession* or L *secessio* (as SECEDE)]

se·clude /siklood/ *v.tr.* (also *refl.*) **1** keep (a person or place) retired or away from company. **2** (esp. as **secluded** *adj.*) hide or screen from view. [ME f. L *secludere seclus-* (as SE-, *claudere* shut)]

se·clu·sion /sikloozhən/ *n.* **1** a secluded state; retirement; privacy. **2** a secluded place. □□ **se·clu·sion·ist** *n.* **se·clu·sive** /-kloosiv/ *adj.* [med.L *secusio* (as SECLUDE)]

sec·ond¹ /sékənd/ *n., adj., & v.* ● *n.* **1** the position in a sequence corresponding to that of the number 2 in the sequence 1–2. **2** something occupying this position. **3** the second person, etc., in a race or competition. **4** *Mus.* **a** an interval or chord spanning two consecutive notes in the diatonic scale (e.g., C to D). **b** a note sep-

arated from another by this interval. **5** = SECOND GEAR. **6** another person or thing in addition to one previously mentioned or considered (*the police officer was then joined by a second*). **7** (in *pl.*) **a** goods of a second or inferior quality. **b** coarse flour, or bread made from it. **8** (in *pl.*) *colloq.* **a** a second helping of food at a meal. **b** the second course of a meal. **9** an attendant assisting a combatant in a duel, boxing match, etc. **10** esp. *Brit.* **a** a place in the second class of an examination. **b** a person having this. ● *adj.* **1** that is the second; next after first. **2** additional; further; other besides one previously mentioned or considered (*ate a second cupcake*). **3** subordinate in position or importance, etc.; inferior. **4** *Mus.* performing a lower or subordinate part (*second violins*). **5** such as to be comparable to; closely reminiscent of (*a second Callas*). ● *v.tr.* **1** supplement; support; back up. **2** formally support or endorse (a nomination or resolution, etc., or its proposer). □ **at second hand** by hearsay, not direct observation, etc. **in the second place** as a second consideration, etc. **on second thought** after (brief) reconsideration. **second base 1** the second base (counterclockwise from home plate) in baseball. **2** the area around this base as defended by a fielder. **second to none** surpassed by no other. □□ **sec·ond·er** *n.* (esp. in sense 2 of *v.*). [ME f. OF f. L *secundus* f. *sequi* follow]
▶See notes at FIRST and FORMER.

sec·ond[2] /sékənd/ *n.* **1** a sixtieth of a minute of time or angular distance. ¶ Symb.: ("). **2** the SI unit of time, based on the natural periodicity of the cesium atom. ¶ Abbr.: **s**. **3** *colloq.* a very short time (*wait a second*). [F f. med.L *secunda* (*minuta*) secondary (minute)]

se·cond[3] /sikónd/ *v.tr. Brit.* transfer (a military officer or other official or worker) temporarily to other employment or to another position. □□ **se·cond·ment** *n.* [F *en second* in the second rank (of officers)]

Sec·ond Ad·vent *n.* = SECOND COMING.

sec·ond·ar·y /sékəndəree/ *adj. & n.* ● *adj.* **1** coming after or next below what is primary. **2** derived from or depending on or supplementing what is primary. **3** (of education, a school, etc.) for those who have had primary education, usu. from 11 to 18 years. **4** *Electr.* **a** (of a cell or battery) having a reversible chemical reaction and therefore able to store energy. **b** denoting a device using electromagnetic induction, esp. a transformer. ● *n.* (*pl.* **-ies**) **1** a secondary thing. **2** a secondary device or current. □□ **sec·ond·ar·i·ly** *adv.* **sec·ond·ar·i·ness** *n.* [ME f. L *secundarius* (as SECOND[1])]

sec·ond·ar·y col·or *n.* the result of mixing two primary colors.

sec·ond·ar·y feath·er *n.* a feather growing from the second joint of a bird's wing.

sec·ond·ar·y plan·et *n.* a satellite of a planet (cf. PRIMARY PLANET).

sec·ond·ar·y rain·bow *n.* an additional arch with the colors in reverse order formed inside or outside a rainbow by twofold reflection and twofold refraction.

sec·ond·ar·y sex·u·al char·ac·ter·is·tics *n.pl.* those distinctive of one sex but not directly related to reproduction.

sec·ond bal·lot *n.* a deciding ballot between candidates coming first (without an absolute majority) and second in a previous ballot.

sec·ond best *n.* a less adequate or desirable alternative. □□ **sec·ond-best** *adj.*

sec·ond cause *n. Logic* a cause that is itself caused.

sec·ond cham·ber *n.* the upper house of a bicameral parliament.

sec·ond child·hood *n.* a person's dotage.

sec·ond class *n.* the second-best group or category, esp. of hotel or train accommodation or of postal services. □□ **sec·ond-class** *adj. & adv.*

Sec·ond Com·ing *n. Theol.* the second advent of Christ on earth.

sec·ond cous·in *n.* a child of one's parent's first cousin.

sec·ond-de·gree *adj. Med.* denoting burns that cause blistering but not permanent scars.

se·conde /səkónd/ *n. Fencing* the second of eight parrying positions. [F, fem. of *second* SECOND[1]]

sec·ond fid·dle *n.* see FIDDLE.

sec·ond floor *n.* **1** the floor above the ground floor. **2** *Brit.*, etc., the floor two levels above the ground floor.

sec·ond gear *n.* the second (and next to lowest) in a sequence of gears.

sec·ond-gen·er·a·tion *n.* denoting the offspring of a first generation, esp. of immigrants.

sec·ond-guess *v. colloq.* **1** anticipate or predict by guesswork. **2** judge or criticize with hindsight.

sec·ond·hand /sékəndhánd/ *adj. & adv.* ● *adj.* **1 a** (of goods) having had a previous owner; not new. **b** (of a store, etc.) where such goods can be bought. **2** (of information, etc.) accepted on another's authority and not from original investigation. ● *adv.* **1** on a secondhand basis. **2** at second hand; not directly.

sec·ond hand *n.* a hand in some watches and clocks, recording seconds.

sec·ond hon·ey·moon *n.* a vacation like a honeymoon, taken by a couple after some years of marriage.

sec·ond in com·mand *n.* the officer next in rank to the commanding or chief officer.

sec·ond in·ten·tion *n.* **1** *Med.* the healing of a wound by granula-

tion. **2** *Logic* one's secondary conception (e.g., difference, identity, species).

sec·ond lieu·ten·ant *n.* in the US, the lowest-ranked commissioned officer of the army, air force, or marines.

sec·ond·ly /sékəndlee/ *adv.* **1** furthermore; in the second place. **2** as a second item.

sec·ond na·ture *n.* (often foll. by *to*) an acquired tendency that has become instinctive (*is second nature to him*).

se·con·do /sikóndō/ *n.* (*pl.* **se·con·di** /–dee/) *Mus.* the second or lower part in a duet, etc. [It.]

sec·ond of·fi·cer *n.* an assistant mate on a merchant ship.

sec·ond per·son *n. Gram.* see PERSON.

sec·ond-rate *adj.* of mediocre quality; inferior.

sec·ond-rat·er *n.* a person or thing that is second-rate.

sec·ond read·ing *n.* a second presentation of a bill to a legislative assembly, in the US to debate committee reports and in the UK to approve its general principles.

Sec·ond Reich *n.* the German Empire from 1871 to 1918.

sec·ond self *n.* a close friend or associate.

sec·ond sight *n.* the supposed power of being able to perceive future or distant events.

sec·ond string *n.* an alternative available in case of need.

sec·ond teeth *n.* the teeth that replace the baby teeth in a mammal.

sec·ond thoughts *n.* a new opinion or resolution reached after further consideration.

sec·ond wind *n.* **1** recovery of the power of normal breathing during exercise after initial breathlessness. **2** renewed energy to continue an effort.

se·cre·cy /seékrisee/ *n.* **1** the keeping of secrets as a fact, habit, or faculty. **2** a state in which all information is withheld (*was done in great secrecy*). □ **sworn to secrecy** having promised to keep a secret. [ME f. *secretie* f. obs. *secre* (adj.) or SECRET *adj.*]

se·cret /seékrit/ *adj. & n.* ● *adj.* **1** kept or meant to be kept private, unknown, or hidden from all or all but a few. **2** acting or operating secretly. **3** fond of, prone to, or able to preserve secrecy. **4** (of a place) hidden, completely secluded. ● *n.* **1** a thing kept or meant to be kept secret. **2** a thing known only to a few. **3** a mystery. **4** a valid but not commonly known or recognized method of achieving or maintaining something (*what's their secret?; correct breathing is the secret of good health*). **5** *RC Ch.* a prayer concluding the offertory of the mass. □ **in secret** secretly. **in** (or **in on**) **the secret** among the number of those who know it. **keep a secret** not reveal it. □□ **se·cret·ly** *adv.* [ME f. OF f. L *secretus* (adj.) separate, set apart f. *secernere secret-* (as SE-, *cernere* sift)]

se·cret a·gent *n.* a spy acting for a country.

sec·re·taire /sékritáir/ *n.* an escritoire. [F (as SECRETARY)]

sec·re·tar·i·at /sékritáireeət/ *n.* **1** a permanent administrative office or department, esp. a governmental one. **2** its members or premises. **3** the office of secretary. [F *secrétariat* f. med.L *secretariatus* (as SECRETARY)]

sec·re·tar·y /sékriteree/ *n.* (*pl.* **-ies**) **1** a person employed by an individual or in an office, etc., to assist with correspondence, keep records, make appointments, etc. **2** an official appointed by a society, etc., to conduct its correspondence, keep its records, etc. **3** an official in charge of a government department. □□ **sec·re·tar·i·al** /–táireeəl/ *adj.* **sec·re·tar·y·ship** *n.* [ME f. LL *secretarius* (as SECRET)]

sec·re·tar·y bird *n.* a long-legged, snake-eating African bird, *Sagitarius serpentarius*, with a crest likened to a quill pen stuck over a writer's ear.

sec•re•tar•y-gen•er•al *n.* the principal administrator of certain organizations, as the United Nations.

sec•re•tar•y of state *n.* **1** (in the US) the chief government official responsible for foreign affairs. **2** (in the UK) the head of a major government department.

se•cret bal•lot *n.* a ballot in which votes are cast in secret.

se•crete[1] /sikre̅et/ *v.tr. Biol.* (of a cell, organ, etc.) produce by secretion. □□ **se•cre•tor** *n.* **se•cre•to•ry** /se̅ekrətáwree/ *adj.* [back-form. f. SECRETION]

se•crete[2] /sikre̅et/ *v.tr.* conceal; put into hiding. [obs. *secret* (v.) f. SE-CRET]

se•cre•tion /sikre̅eshən/ *n.* **1** *Biol.* **a** a process by which substances are produced and discharged from a cell for a function in the organism or for excretion. **b** the secreted substance. **2** the act or an instance of concealing (*the secretion of stolen goods*). [F *sécrétion* or L *secretio* separation (as SECRET)]

se•cre•tive /se̅ekritiv, səkre̅e–/ *adj.* inclined to make or keep secrets; uncommunicative. □□ **se•cre•tive•ly** *adv.* **se•cre•tive•ness** *n.* [back-form. f. *secretiveness* after F *secrétivité* (as SECRET)]

se•cret po•lice *n.* a police force operating in secret for political purposes.

se•cret serv•ice *n.* **1** a government department concerned with espionage. **2** (**Secret Service**) a branch of the US Treasury Department charged with apprehending counterfeitors and with protecting the president and certain other officials and their families.

se•cret so•ci•e•ty *n.* a society whose members are sworn to secrecy about it.

sect /sekt/ *n.* **1 a** a body of people subscribing to religious doctrines usu. different from those of an established church from which they have separated. **b** usu. *derog.* a nonconformist or other church. **c** a party or faction in a religious body. **d** a religious denomination. **2** the followers of a particular philosopher or philosophy, or school of thought in politics, etc. [ME f. OF *secte* or L *secta* f. the stem of *sequi secut-* follow]

sect. *abbr.* section.

sec•tar•i•an /sektáiree̅ən/ *adj. & n.* • *adj.* **1** of or concerning a sect. **2** bigoted or narrow-minded in following the doctrines of one's sect. • *n.* **1** a member of a sect. **2** a bigot. □□ **sec•tar•i•an•ism** *n.* **sec•tar•i•an•ize** *v.tr.* [SECTARY]

sec•ta•ry /séktəree/ *n.* (*pl.* **-ries**) a member of a religious or political sect. [med.L *sectarius* adherent (as SECT)]

sec•tion /sékshən/ *n. & v.* • *n.* **1** a part cut off or separated from something. **2** each of the parts into which a thing is divided (actually or conceptually) or divisible or out of which a structure can be fitted together. **3** a distinct group or subdivision of a larger body of people (*the wind section of an orchestra*). **4** a subdivision of a book, document, statute, etc. **5 a** an area of land. **b** one square mile of land. **c** a particular district of a town (*residential section*). **6** a subdivision of an army platoon. **7** esp. *Surgery* a separation by cutting. **8** *Biol.* a thin slice of tissue, etc., cut off for microscopic examination. **9 a** the cutting of a solid by or along a plane. **b** the resulting figure or the area of this. **10** a representation of the internal structure of something as if cut across along a vertical or horizontal plane. **11** *Biol.* a group, esp. a subgenus. • *v.tr.* **1** arrange in or divide into sections. **2** *Brit.* cause (a person) to be compulsorily committed to a psychiatric hospital in accordance with a section of a mental health act. **3** *Biol.* cut into thin slices for microscopic examination. [F *section* or L *sectio* f. *secare sect-* cut]

sec•tion•al /sékshənəl/ *adj.* **1 a** relating to a section, esp. of a community. **b** partisan. **2** made in sections as, e.g., some furniture (*a sectional sofa*). **3** local rather than general. □□ **sec•tion•al•ism** *n.* **sec•tion•al•ist** *n. & adj.* **sec•tion•al•ize** *v.tr.* **sec•tion•al•ly** *adv.*

sec•tion mark *n.* the sign (§) used as a reference mark to indicate the start of a section of a book, etc.

sec•tor /séktər/ *n.* **1** a distinct part or branch of an enterprise, or of society, the economy, etc. **2** *Mil.* a subdivision of an area for military operations, controlled by one commander or headquarters. **3** the plane figure enclosed by two radii of a circle, ellipse, etc., and the arc between them. **4** a mathematical instrument consisting of two arms hinged at one end and marked with sines, tangents, etc., for making diagrams, etc. □□ **sec•tor•al** *adj.* [LL, techn. use of L *sector* cutter (as SECTION)]

sec•to•ri•al /sektáwree̅əl/ *adj.* **1** of or like a sector or sectors. **2** = CARNASSIAL.

sec•u•lar /sékyələr/ *adj. & n.* • *adj.* **1** concerned with the affairs of this world; not spiritual nor sacred. **2** (of education, etc.) not concerned with religion nor religious belief. **3 a** not ecclesiastical nor monastic. **b** (of clergy) not bound by a religious rule. **4** occurring once in an age or century. **5** lasting for or occurring over an indefinitely long time. • *n.* a secular priest. □□ **sec•u•lar•ism** *n.* **sec•u•lar•ist** *n.* **sec•u•lar•i•ty** /–láirətee/ *n.* **sec•u•lar•ize** *v.tr.* **sec•u•lar•i•za•tion** *n.* **sec•u•lar•ly** *adv.* [ME (in senses 1–3 f. OF *seculer*) f. L *saecularis* f. *saeculum* generation, age]

sec•u•lar var•i•a•tion *n. Astron.* variation compensated over a long period of time.

se•cund /se̅ekund, sikúnd/ *adj. Bot.* arranged on one side only (as the flowers of lily of the valley). □□ **se•cund•ly** *adv.* [L *secundus* (as SECOND[1])]

se•cure /sikyo̅or/ *adj. & v.* • *adj.* **1** untroubled by danger or fear. **2** safe against attack; impregnable. **3** reliable; certain not to fail (*the plan is secure*). **4** fixed or fastened so as not to give way or get loose or be lost (*made the door secure*). **5 a** (foll. by *of*) certain to achieve (*secure of victory*). **b** (foll. by *against, from*) safe; protected (*secure against attack*). • *v.tr.* **1** make secure or safe; fortify. **2** fasten, close, or confine securely. **3** succeed in obtaining or achieving (*have secured front seats*). **4** guarantee against loss (*a loan secured by property*). **5** compress (a blood vessel) to prevent bleeding. □□ **se•cur•a•ble** *adj.* **se•cure•ly** *adv.* **se•cure•ment** *n.* [L *securus* (as SE–, *cura* care)]

se•cu•ri•ty /sikyo̅oritee/ *n.* (*pl.* **-ties**) **1** a secure condition or feeling. **2** a thing that guards or guarantees. **3 a** the safety of a nation, company, etc., against espionage, theft, or other danger. **b** an organization for ensuring this. **4** a thing deposited or pledged as a guarantee of the fulfillment of an undertaking or the payment of a loan, to be forfeited in case of default. **5** (often in *pl.*) a certificate attesting credit or the ownership of stock, bonds, etc. □ **on security of** using as a guarantee. [ME f. OF *securité* or L *securitas* (as SECURE)]

se•cu•ri•ty blan•ket *n.* **1** an official sanction on information in the interest of security. **2** a blanket or other familiar object given as a comfort to a child.

Se•cu•ri•ty Coun•cil *n.* a permanent body of the United Nations seeking to maintain peace and security.

se•cu•ri•ty guard *n.* a person employed to protect the security of buildings, vehicles, etc.

se•cu•ri•ty risk *n.* a person whose presence may threaten security.

secy. *abbr.* secretary.

se•dan /sidán/ *n.* **1** (in full **sedan chair**) an enclosed chair for conveying one person, carried between horizontal poles by two porters, common in the 17th–18th c. **2** an enclosed automobile for four or more people. [perh. alt. f. It. dial., ult. f. L *sella* saddle f. *sedēre* sit]

se•date[1] /sidáyt/ *adj.* tranquil and dignified; equable; serious. □□ **se•date•ly** *adv.* **se•date•ness** *n.* [L *sedatus* past part. of *sedare* settle f. *sedēre* sit]

se•date[2] /sidáyt/ *v.tr.* put under sedation. [back-form. f. SEDATION]

se•da•tion /sidáyshən/ *n.* a state of rest or sleep, esp. produced by a sedative drug. [F *sédation* or L *sedatio* (as SEDATE[1])]

sed•a•tive /sédətiv/ *n. & adj.* • *n.* a drug, influence, etc., that tends to calm or soothe. • *adj.* calming; soothing; inducing sleep. [ME f. OF *sedatif* or med.L *sedativus* (as SEDATE[1])]

sed•en•tar•y /séd'nteree/ *adj.* **1** sitting (*a sedentary posture*). **2** (of work, etc.) characterized by much sitting and little physical exercise. **3** (of a person) spending much time seated. **4** *Zool.* not migratory, free-swimming, etc. □□ **sed•en•tar•i•ly** /–táirəlee/ *adv.* **sed•en•tar•i•ness** *n.* [F *sédentaire* or L *sedentarius* f. *sedēre* sit]

Se•der /sáydər/ *n.* the ritual for the first night or first two nights of the Passover. [Heb. *sēder* order]

sedge /sej/ *n.* **1** any grasslike plant of the genus *Carex* with triangular stems, usu. growing in wet areas. **2** an expanse of this plant. □□ **sedg•y** *adj.* [OE *secg* f. Gmc]

se•di•le /sidi̅lee/ *n.* (*pl.* **se•dil•i•a** /–di̅lee̅ə/) (usu. in *pl.*) *Eccl.* each of usu. three stone seats for priests in the south wall of a chancel, often canopied and decorated. [L, = seat f. *sedēre* sit]

sed•i•ment /sédimənt/ *n.* **1** matter that settles to the bottom of a liquid; dregs. **2** *Geol.* matter that is carried by water or wind and deposited on the surface of the land, and that may in time become consolidated into rock. □□ **sed•i•men•ta•ry** /–méntəree/ *adj.* **sed•i•men•ta•tion** /–táyshən/ *n.* [F *sédiment* or L *sedimentum* (as SEDILE)]

se•di•tion /sidíshən/ *n.* **1** conduct or speech inciting to rebellion or a breach of public order. **2** agitation against the authority of a government. □□ **se•di•tious** *adj.* **se•di•tious•ly** *adv.* [ME f. OF *sedition* or L *seditio* f. *sed–* = SE– + *ire it-* go]

se•duce /sido̅os, –dyo̅os/ *v.tr.* **1** tempt or entice into sexual activity or into wrongdoing. **2** coax or lead astray; tempt (*seduced by the smell of coffee*). □□ **se•duc•er** *n.* **se•duc•i•ble** *adj.* [L *seducere seduct-* (as SE–, *ducere* lead)]

se•duc•tion /sidúkshən/ *n.* **1** the act or an instance of seducing; the process of being seduced. **2** something that tempts or allures. [F *séduction* or L *seductio* (as SEDUCE)]

se•duc•tive /sidúktiv/ *adj.* tending to seduce; alluring; enticing. □□ **se•duc•tive•ly** *adv.* **se•duc•tive•ness** *n.* [SEDUCTION after *inductive*, etc.]

se•duc•tress /sidúktris/ *n.* a female seducer. [obs. *seductor* male seducer (as SEDUCE)]

sed•u•lous /séjələs/ *adj.* **1** persevering; diligent; assiduous. **2** (of an action, etc.) deliberately and consciously continued; painstaking. □□ **se•du•li•ty** /sido̅olitee, –dyo̅o–/ *n.* **sed•u•lous•ly** *adv.* **sed•u•lous•ness** *n.* [L *sedulus* zealous]

se•dum /séédəm/ *n.* any plant of the genus *Sedum*, with fleshy leaves and star-shaped yellow, pink, or white flowers, e.g., stonecrop. [L, = houseleek]

see[1] /see/ *v.* (*past* **saw** /saw/; *past part.* **seen** /seen/) **1** *tr.* discern by use of the eyes; observe; look at (*can you see that spider?; saw him fall over*). **2** *intr.* have or use the power of discerning objects with the eyes (*sees best at night*). **3** *tr.* discern mentally; understand (*I see what you mean; could not see the joke*). **4** *tr.* watch; be a spectator of (a motion picture, game, etc.). **5** *tr.* ascertain or establish by inquiry or research or reflection (*I will see if the door is open*). **6** *tr.* consider; deduce from observation (*I see that you are a brave man*). **7** *tr.* contemplate; foresee mentally (*we saw that no good would come of it; can see myself doing this job indefinitely*). **8** *tr.* look at for information (usu. in *imper.* as a direction in or to a book: *see page 15*). **9** *tr.* meet or be near and recognize (*I saw your mother in town*). **10** *tr.* **a** meet socially (*sees her sister most weeks*). **b** meet regularly as a boyfriend or girlfriend; court (*is still seeing that tall man*). **11** *tr.* give an interview to (*the doctor will see you now*). **12** *tr.* visit to consult (*went to see the doctor*). **13** *tr.* find out or learn, esp. from a visual source (*I see the match has been canceled*). **14 a** *intr.* reflect; consider further; wait until one knows more (*we shall have to see*). **b** *tr.* (foll. by *whether* or *if* + clause) consider; decide (on). **15** *tr.* interpret or have an opinion of (*I see things differently now*). **16** *tr.* experience; have presented to one's attention (*I never thought I would see this day*). **17** *tr.* recognize as acceptable; foresee (*do you see your daughter marrying this man?*). **18** *tr.* observe without interfering (*stood by and saw them squander my money*). **19** *tr.* (usu. foll. by *in*) find attractive or interesting (*can't think what she sees in him*). **20** *intr.* (usu. foll. by *to*, or *that* + infin.) make provision for; ensure; attend to (*shall see to your request immediately; see that he gets home safely*) (cf. *see to it*). **21** *tr.* escort or conduct (to a place, etc.) (*saw them home*). **22** *tr.* be a witness of (an event, etc.) (*see the New Year in*). **23** *tr.* supervise (an action, etc.) (*will stay and see the doors locked*). **24** *tr.* **a** (in gambling, esp. poker) equal (a bet). **b** equal the bet of (a player), esp. to see the player's cards. □ **as far as I can see** to the best of my understanding or belief. **as I see it** in my opinion. **do you see?** do you understand? **has seen better days** has declined from former prosperity, good condition, etc. **I'll be seeing you** *colloq.* an expression on parting. **I see** I understand (referring to an explanation, etc.). **let me see** an appeal for time to think before speaking, etc. **see about 1** attend to. **2** consider; look into. **see after 1** take care of. **2** = *see about*. **see the back of** esp. *Brit. colloq.* be rid of (an unwanted person or thing). **see a person damned first** esp. *Brit. colloq.* refuse categorically and with hostility to do what a person wants. **see eye to eye** see EYE. **see fit** see FIT[1]. **see here!** = *look here* (LOOK *int.*). **see into** investigate. **see life** gain experience of the world, often by enjoying oneself. **see the light 1** realize one's mistakes, etc. **2** suddenly see the way to proceed. **3** undergo religious conversion. **see the light of day** (usu. with *neg.*) come into existence. **see off 1** be present at the departure of (a person) (*saw them off at the airport*). **2** *Brit. colloq.* ward off; get the better of (*managed to see off an investigation into their working methods*). **see out 1** accompany out of a building, etc. **2** finish (a project, etc.) completely. **3** *Brit.* remain awake, alive, etc., until the end of (a period). **4** *Brit.* last longer than; outlive. **see over** *Brit.* inspect; tour and examine. **see reason** see REASON. **see red** become suddenly enraged. **see a person right** *Brit.* make sure that a person is rewarded, safe, etc. **see service** see SERVICE. **see stars** *colloq.* see lights before one's eyes as a result of a blow on the head. **see things** have hallucinations or false imaginings. **see through 1** not be deceived by; detect the true nature of. **2** penetrate visually. **see a person through** support a person during a difficult time; assist financially. **see a thing through** persist with it until it is completed. **see to** = *see about*. **see to it** (foll. by *that* + clause) ensure (*see to it that I am not disturbed*) (cf. sense 20 of *v.*). **see one's way clear** to feel able or entitled to. **see the world** see WORLD. **see you** (or **see you later**) *colloq.* an expression on parting. **we shall see 1** let us await the outcome. **2** a formula for declining to act at once. **will see about it** a formula for declining to act at once. **you see 1** you understand. **2** you will understand when I explain. □□ **see•a•ble** *adj.* [OE *seon* f. Gmc]

see[2] /see/ *n.* **1** the area under the authority of a bishop or archbishop, a diocese (*the see of Norwich*). **2** the office or jurisdiction of a bishop or archbishop (*fill a vacant see*). □ **See of Rome** the papacy, the Holy See. [ME f. AF *se(d)* ult. f. L *sedes* seat f. *sedēre* sit]

seed /seed/ *n. & v.* **1 a** a flowering plant's unit of reproduction (esp. in the form of grain) capable of developing into another such plant. **b** seeds collectively, esp. as collected for sowing (*is full of seed; to be kept for seed*). **2 a** semen. **b** milt. **3** (foll. by *of*) prime cause; beginning; germ (*seeds of doubt*). **4** *archaic* offspring; progeny; descendants (*the seed of Abraham*). **5** *Sports* a seeded player. **6** a small seedlike container for the application of radium, etc. **7** a seed crystal. • *v.* **1** *tr.* **a** place seeds in. **b** sprinkle with or as with seed. **2** *intr.* sow seeds. **3** *intr.* produce or drop seed. **4** *tr.* remove seeds from (fruit, etc.). **5** *tr.* place a crystal or crystalline substance in (a solution, etc.) to cause crystallization or condensation (esp. in a cloud to produce rain). **6** *tr. Sports* **a** assign to (a strong competitor in a

knockout competition) a position in an ordered list so that strong competitors do not meet each other in early rounds (*is seeded seventh*). **b** arrange (the order of play) in this way. **7** *intr.* go to seed. □ **go** (or **run**) **to seed 1** cease flowering as seed develops. **2** become degenerate; unkempt; ineffective, etc. **raise up seed** *archaic* beget children. □□ **seed•less** *adj.* [OE *sæd* f. Gmc, rel. to SOW[1]]

seed•bed /séédbed/ *n.* **1** a bed of fine soil in which to sow seeds. **2** a place of development.

seed•cake /séédkayk/ *n.* cake containing whole seeds esp. of sesame or caraway as flavoring.

seed coat *n.* the outer integument of a seed.

seed corn *n.* **1** good quality corn kept for seed. **2** *Brit.* assets reused for future profit or benefit.

seed crys•tal *n.* a crystal used to initiate crystallization.

seed•eat•er /séédeetər/ *n.* a bird (esp. a finch) living mainly on seeds.

seed•er /séédər/ *n.* **1** a person or thing that seeds. **2** a machine for sowing seed, esp. a drill. **3** an apparatus for seeding raisins, etc. **4** *Brit.* a spawning fish.

seed leaf *n.* a cotyledon.

seed•ling /séédling/ *n.* a young plant, esp. one raised from seed and not from a cutting, etc.

seed mon•ey *n.* money allocated to initiate a project.

seed pearl *n.* a very small pearl.

seed plot *n.* a place of development.

seed po•ta•to *n.* a potato kept for seed.

seeds•man /séédzmən/ *n.* (*pl.* **•men**) a dealer in seeds.

seed•time /séédtīm/ *n.* the sowing season.

seed ves•sel *n.* a pericarp.

seed•y /séédee/ *adj.* (**seed•i•er, seed•i•est**) **1** full of seed. **2** going to seed. **3** shabby looking; in worn clothes. **4** *colloq.* unwell. □□ **seed•i•ly** *adv.* **seed•i•ness** *n.*

see•ing /séé-ing/ *conj. & n.* • *conj.* (usu. foll. by *that* + clause) considering that; inasmuch as; because (*seeing that you do not know it yourself*). • *n. Astron.* the quality of observed images as determined by atmospheric conditions.

seek /seek/ *v.* (*past* and *past part.* **sought** /sawt/) **1 a** *tr.* make a search or inquiry for. **b** *intr.* (foll. by *for, after*) make a search or inquiry. **2** *tr.* **a** try or want to find or get. **b** ask for; request (*sought help from him; seeks my aid*). **3** *tr.* (foll. by *to* + infin.) endeavor or try. **4** *tr.* make for or resort to (a place or person, for advice, health, etc.) (*sought his bed; sought a fortune-teller; sought the shore*). **5** *tr. archaic* aim at; attempt. **6** *intr.* (foll. by *to*) *archaic* resort. □ **seek out 1** search for and find. **2** single out for companionship, etc. **to seek** (or **much to seek** or **far to seek**) esp. *Brit.* deficient, lacking, or not yet found (*the reason is not far to seek; an efficient leader is yet to seek*). □□ **seek•er** *n.* (also in *comb.*). [OE *sēcan* f. Gmc]

seel /seel/ *v.tr.* **1** *Falconry* sew shut a falcon's eyelids during its training. **2** *archaic* close (a person's eyes). [obs. *sile* f. F *ciller, siller,* or med.L *ciliare* f. L *cilium* eyelid]

seem /seem/ *v.intr.* **1** give the impression or sensation of being (*seems ridiculous; seems certain to win*). **2** (foll. by *to* + infin.) appear or be perceived or ascertained (*he seems to be breathing; they seem to have left*). □ **can't seem to** *colloq.* seem unable to. **do not seem to** *colloq.* somehow do not (*I do not seem to like him*). **it seems** (or **would seem**) (often foll.by *that* + clause) it appears to be true or the fact (in a hesitant, guarded, or ironical statement). [ME f. ON *sœma* honor f. *sœmr* fitting]

seem•ing[1] /séé-ming/ *adj.* **1** apparent but perhaps not real (*with seeming sincerity*). **2** apparent only; ostensible (*the seeming and the real; seeming virtuous*). □□ **seem•ing•ly** *adv.*

seem•ing[2] /séé-ming/ *n. literary* **1** appearance; aspect. **2** deceptive appearance.

seem•ly /séémlee/ *adj.* (**seem•li•er, seem•li•est**) conforming to propriety or good taste; decorous; suitable. □□ **seem•li•ness** *n.* [ME f. ON *sœmiligr* (as SEEM)]

seen *past part.* of SEE[1].

seep /seep/ *v. & n.* • *v.intr.* ooze out; percolate slowly. • *n.* a place where petroleum, etc. oozes slowly out of the ground. [perh. dial. form of OE *sipian* to soak]

seep•age /séépij/ *n.* **1** the act of seeping. **2** the quantity that seeps out.

seer[1] /séé-ər, seer/ *n.* **1** a person who sees. **2** a prophet; a person who sees visions; a person of supposed supernatural insight esp. as regards the future. [ME f. SEE[1]]

seer[2] /seer/ *n* an E. Indian (varying) measure of weight (about two pounds) or liquid measure (about one quart). [Hindi *ser*]

seer•suck•er /séérsukər/ *n.* material of linen, cotton, etc., with a puckered surface. [Pers. *šir o šakar,* lit. 'milk and sugar']

see•saw /séésaw/ *n., v., adj., & adv.* • *n.* **1 a** a device consisting of a long plank balanced on a central support for children to sit on at each end and move up and down by pushing the ground with their feet. **b** a game played on this. **2** an up-and-down or to-and-fro motion. **3** a contest in which the advantage repeatedly changes from one side to the other. • *v.intr.* **1** play on a seesaw. **2** move up and down as on a seesaw. **3** vacillate in policy, emotion, etc. • *adj. & adv.* with up-and-down or backward-and-forward motion (*seesaw motion*). □ **go seesaw** vacillate or alternate. [redupl. of SAW[1]]

seethe /seeth/ *v.* **1** *intr.* boil; bubble over. **2** *intr.* be very agitated, esp. with anger (*seething with discontent; I was seething inwardly*). **3** *tr. & intr. archaic* cook by boiling. □□ **seeth•ing•ly** *adv.* [OE *sēothan* f. Gmc]

see-through *adj.* (esp. of clothing) translucent.

seg•ment /ségmənt/ *n. & v.* • *n.* **1** each of several parts into which a thing is or can be divided or marked off. **2** *Geom.* a part of a figure cut off by a line or plane intersecting it, esp.: **a** the part of a circle enclosed between an arc and a chord. **b** the part of a line included between two points. **c** the part of a sphere cut off by any plane not passing through the center. **3** the smallest distinct part of a spoken utterance. **4** *Zool.* each of the longitudinal sections of the body of certain animals (e.g., worms). • *v.* (usu. /–mént/) **1** *intr. & tr.* divide into segments. **2** *intr. Biol.* (of a cell) undergo cleavage or divide into many cells. □□ **seg•men•tal** /–mént'l/ *adj.* **seg•men•tal•ize** /–mént'līz/ *v.tr.* **seg•men•tal•i•za•tion** *n.* **seg•men•tal•ly** /–mént'lee/ *adv.* **seg•men•ta•ry** /ségmǝntairee/ *adj.* **seg•men•ta•tion** /–táyshǝn/ *n.* [L *segmentum* f. *secare* cut]

se•go /séegó/ *n.* (*pl.* **-gos**) (in full **sego lily**) a N. American plant, *Calochortus nuttallii*, with green and white bell-shaped flowers. [Paiute]

seg•re•gate[1] /ségrigayt/ *v.* **1** *tr.* put apart from the rest; isolate. **2** *tr.* enforce racial segregation on (persons) or in (a community, etc.). **3** *intr.* separate from a mass and collect together. **4** *intr. Biol.* (of alleles) separate into dominant and recessive groups. □□ **seg•re•ga•ble** /–gǝbǝl/ *adj.* **seg•re•ga•tive** *adj.* [L *segregare* (as SE-, *grex gregis-* flock)]

seg•re•gate[2] /ségrigǝt, –gayt/ *adj.* **1** *Zool.* simple or solitary; not compound. **2** *archaic* set apart; separate. [L *segregatus* past part. (as SEGREGATE[1])]

seg•re•ga•tion /ségrigáyshǝn/ *n.* **1** enforced separation of racial groups in a community, etc. **2** the act or an instance of segregating; the state of being segregated. □□ **seg•re•ga•tion•al** *adj.* **seg•re•ga•tion•ist** *n. & adj.* [LL *segregatio* (as SEGREGATE[1])]

se•gue /ségway/ *v. & n.* esp. *Mus.* • *v.intr.* (**se•gues, se•gued, se•gue•ing**) (usu. foll. by *into*) go on without a pause. • *n.* an uninterrupted transition from one song or melody to another. [It., = follows]

se•gui•dil•la /ségidílyǝ, –déeyǝ/ *n.* **1** a Spanish dance in triple time. **2** the music for this. [Sp. f. *seguida* following f. *seguir* follow]

sei /say/ *n.* a small rorqual, *Balaenoptera borealis.* [Norw. *sejhval* sei whale]

sei•cen•to /saychéntó/ *n.* the style of Italian art and literature of the 17th c. [It., = 600, used with ref. to the years 1600–99]

seiche /saysh/ *n.* a fluctuation in the water level of a lake, etc., usu. caused by changes in barometric pressure. [Swiss F]

Seid•litz pow•ders /sédlits/ *n.* a laxative medicine of two powders mixed separately with water and then poured together to effervesce. [named with ref. to the mineral water of *Seidlitz* in Bohemia]

seif /seef, sayf/ *n.* (in full **seif dune**) a sand dune in the form of a long narrow ridge. [Arab. *saif* sword (from its shape)]

sei•gneur /saynyŏr/ *n.* (also **seign•ior** /sáynyáwr/) a feudal lord; the lord of a manor. □□ **sei•gneu•ri•al** *adj.* **seign•ior•i•al** /–nyáwreeǝl/ *adj.* [ME f. OF *seigneur, seignor* f. L SENIOR]

seign•ior•age /sáynyǝrij/ *n.* (also **seign•or•age**) **1 a** a profit made by issuing currency, esp. by issuing coins rated above their intrinsic value. **b** *hist.* a sovereign's right to a percentage on bullion brought to a mint for coining. **2** *hist.* something claimed by a sovereign or feudal superior as a prerogative. [ME f. OF *seignorage, seigneurage* (as SEIGNEUR)]

seign•ior•y /sáynyǝree/ *n.* (*pl.* **-ies**) **1** lordship; sovereign authority. **2** (also **sei•gneur•y**) a seigneur's domain. [ME f. OF *seignorie* (as SEIGNEUR)]

seine /sayn/ *n. & v.* • *n.* a fishing net for encircling fish, with floats at the top and weights at the bottom edge, and usu. hauled ashore. • *v.intr. & tr.* fish or catch with a seine. □□ **sein•er** *n.* [ME f. OF *saïne,* & OE *segne* f. WG f. L *sagena* f. Gk *sagēnē*]

seise var. of SEIZE 9.

sei•sin /séezin/ *n.* (also **sei•zin**) *Law* **1** possession of land by freehold. **2** the act of taking such possession. **3** what is so held. [ME f. AF *sesine,* OF *seisine, saisine* (as SEIZE)]

seis•mic /sízmik/ *adj.* of or relating to an earthquake or earthquakes. □□ **seis•mal** *adj.* **seis•mi•cal** *adj.* **seis•mi•cal•ly** *adv.* [Gk *seismos* earthquake f. *seiō* shake]

seismo- /sízmó/ *comb. form* earthquake. [Gk *seismos*]

seis•mo•gram /sízmǝgram/ *n.* a record given by a seismograph.

seis•mo•graph /sízmǝgraf/ *n.* an instrument that records the force, direction, etc., of earthquakes. □□ **seis•mo•graph•ic** *adj.* **seis•mo•graph•i•cal** *adj.*

seis•mol•o•gy /sīzmólǝjee/ *n.* the scientific study and recording of earthquakes and related phenomena. □□ **seis•mo•log•i•cal** /–mǝlóji-kǝl/ *adj.* **seis•mo•log•i•cal•ly** /–lójiklee/ *adv.* **seis•mol•o•gist** *n.*

seize /seez/ *v.* **1** *tr.* take hold of forcibly or suddenly. **2** *tr.* take possession of forcibly (*seized the fortress; seized power*). **3** *tr.* **a** take possession of (contraband goods, documents, etc.) by warrant or legal right; confiscate; impound. **b** arrest or apprehend (a person); take prisoner. **4** *tr.* affect suddenly (*panic seized us; was seized by apoplexy; was seized with remorse*). **5** *tr.* take advantage of (an opportunity). **6** *tr.* comprehend quickly or clearly. **7** *intr.* (usu. foll. by *on, upon*) **a** take hold of forcibly or suddenly. **b** take advantage eagerly (*seized on a pretext*). **8** *intr.* (usu. foll. by *up*) (of a moving part in a machine) become stuck or jammed from undue heat, friction, etc. **9** *tr.* (also **seise**) (usu. foll. by *of*) *Law* put in possession of. **10** *tr. Naut.* fasten or attach by binding with turns of yarn, etc. □ **seized** (or **seised**) **of 1** possessing legally. **2** aware or informed of. □□ **seiz•a•ble** *adj.* **seiz•er** *n.* [ME f. OF *seizir, saisir* give seisin f. Frank. f. L *sacire* f. Gmc]

SPELLING TIP **seize**

This word is an exception to the "*i* before *e* except after *c*" rule. Try the mnemonic: "You have to *see* something before you can *seize* it."

sei•zin var. of SEISIN.

seiz•ing /séezing/ *n. Naut.* a cord or cords used for seizing (see SEIZE 10).

sei•zure /séezhǝr/ *n.* **1** the act or an instance of seizing; the state of being seized. **2** a sudden attack of apoplexy, etc.; a stroke.

se•jant /séejǝnt/ *adj.* (placed after noun) *Heraldry* (of an animal) sitting upright on its haunches. [properly *seiant* f. OF var. of *seant* sitting f. *seoir* f. L *sedēre* sit]

Sekt /zekt/ *n.* a German sparkling white wine. [G]

se•la•chi•an /siláykeeǝn/ *n. & adj.* • *n.* any fish of the subclass Selachii, including sharks and dogfish. • *adj.* of or relating to this subclass. [mod.L *Selachii* f. Gk *selakhos* shark]

se•la•dang /sǝláǝdaang/ *n.* a Malayan gaur. [Malay]

se•lah /séelǝ, sélǝ/ *int.* often used at the end of a verse in Psalms and Habakkuk, supposed to be a musical direction. [Heb. *selāh*]

sel•dom /séldǝm/ *adv. & adj.* • *adv.* rarely; not often. • *adj.* rare; uncommon. [OE *seldan* f. Gmc]

se•lect /silékt/ *v. & adj.* • *v.tr.* choose, esp. as the best or most suitable. • *adj.* **1** chosen for excellence or suitability; choice. **2** (of a society, etc.) exclusive; cautious in admitting members. □□ **se•lect•a•ble** *adj.* **se•lect•ness** *n.* [L *seligere select-* (as SE-, *legere* choose)]

se•lect com•mit•tee *n.* a small committee appointed by a legislative body, etc., for a special purpose.

se•lect•ee /silektée/ *n.* one drafted for service in the armed forces.

se•lec•tion /silékshǝn/ *n.* **1** the act or an instance of selecting; the state of being selected. **2** a selected person or thing. **3** things from which a choice may be made. **4** *Biol.* the process in which environmental and genetic influences determine which types of organism thrive better than others, regarded as a factor in evolution. □□ **se•lec•tion•al** *adj.* **se•lec•tion•al•ly** *adv.* [L *selectio* (as SELECT)]

se•lec•tive /siléktiv/ *adj.* **1** using or characterized by selection. **2** able to select, esp. (of a radio receiver) able to respond to a chosen frequency without interference from others. □□ **se•lec•tive•ly** *adv.* **se•lec•tive•ness** *n.* **se•lec•tiv•i•ty** /sílektívitee, sél–, séel–/ *n.*

se•lec•tive serv•ice *n.* service in the armed forces under conscription.

se•lec•tor /siléktǝr/ *n.* **1** a person who selects, esp. one who selects a representative team in a sport. **2** a device that selects, esp. a device in a vehicle that selects the required gear.

sel•e•nite /sélinīt/ *n.* a form of gypsum occurring as transparent crystals or thin plates. □□ **sel•e•nit•ic** /–nítik/ *adj.* [L *selenites* f. Gk *selēnítēs lithos* moonstone f. *selēnē* moon]

se•le•ni•um /siléeneeǝm/ *n. Chem.* a nonmetallic element occurring naturally in various metallic sulfide ores and characterized by the variation of its electrical resistivity with intensity of illumination. ¶ Symb.: **Se.** □□ **sel•e•nate** /sélinayt/ *n.* **se•le•nic** /siléenik/ *adj.* **se•le•ni•ous** *adj.* [mod.L f. Gk *selēnē* moon + –IUM]

se•le•ni•um cell *n.* a piece of selenium used as a photoelectric device.

seleno- /siléenó/ *comb. form* moon. [Gk *selēnē* moon]

sel•e•nog•ra•phy /séelinógrǝfee/ *n.* the study or mapping of the moon. □□ **sel•e•nog•ra•pher** *n.* **se•le•no•graph•ic** /–nǝgráfik/ *adj.*

sel•e•nol•o•gy /séelinólǝjee/ *n.* the scientific study of the moon. □□ **sel•e•nol•o•gist** *n.*

self /self/ *n. & adj.* • *n.* (*pl.* **selves** /selvz/) **1** a person's or thing's own individuality or essence (*showed his true self*). **2** a person or thing as the object of introspection or reflexive action (*the consciousness of self*). **3 a** one's own interests or pleasure (*cares for nothing but self*). **b** concentration on these (*self is a bad guide to happiness*). **4** *Commerce or colloq.* myself, yourself, himself, etc. (*check drawn to self; ticket admitting self and friend*). **5** used in phrases equivalent to *myself, yourself, himself,* etc. (*his very self; your good selves*). **6** (*pl.* **selfs**) a flower of uniform color, or of the natural wild color. ● *adj.* **1** of the same color as the rest or throughout. **2** (of a flower) of the natural wild color. **3** (of color) uniform, the same throughout. □ **one's better self** one's nobler impulses. **one's former** (or **old**) **self** oneself as one formerly was. [OE f. Gmc]

self- /self/ *comb. form* expressing reflexive action: **1** of or directed toward oneself or itself (*self-respect; self-cleaning*). **2** by oneself or itself, esp. without external agency (*self-evident*). **3** on, in, for, or relating to oneself or itself (*self-absorbed; self-confident*).

self-a·ban·don /sélfəbándən/ *n.* (also **self-a·ban·don·ment**) the abandonment of oneself, esp. to passion or an impulse. □□ **self-a·ban·doned** *adj.*

self-a·base·ment /sélfəbáysmənt/ *n.* the abasement of oneself; self-humiliation; cringing.

self-ab·hor·rence /sélfəbháwrəns, –hór–/ *n.* the abhorrence of oneself; self-hatred.

self-ab·ne·ga·tion /sélfábnigáyshən/ *n.* the abnegation of oneself, one's interests, needs, etc.; self-sacrifice.

self-ab·sorp·tion /sélfəbsáwrpshən, –záwrp–/ *n.* **1** absorption in oneself. **2** *Physics* the absorption, by a body, of radiation emitted within it. □□ **self-ab·sorbed** /–sáwrbd, –záwrbd/ *adj.*

self-a·buse /sélfəbyóos/ *n.* **1** the reviling or abuse of oneself. **2** masturbation.

self-ac·cu·sa·tion /sélfákyoozáyshən/ *n.* the accusing of oneself. □□ **self-ac·cu·sa·to·ry** /–əkyóozətáwree/*adj.*

self-act·ing /sélfákting/ *adj.* acting without external influence or control; automatic. □□ **self-ac·tion** /–ákshən/ *n.* **self-ac·tiv·i·ty** /–aktívitee/ *n.*

self-ad·dressed /sélfədrést/ *adj.* (of an envelope, etc.) having one's own address on for return communication.

self-ad·he·sive /sélfədheésiv/ *adj.* (of an envelope, label, etc.) adhesive, esp. without being moistened.

self-ad·just·ing /sélfəjústing/ *adj.* (of machinery, etc.) adjusting itself. □□ **self-ad·just·ment** *n.*

self-ad·mi·ra·tion /sélfádməráyshən/ *n.* the admiration of oneself; pride; conceit.

self-ad·vance·ment /sélfədvánsmənt/ *n.* the advancement of oneself.

self-ad·ver·tise·ment /sélfádvərtízmənt, –ədvə́rtiz–/ *n.* the advertising or promotion of oneself. □□ **self-ad·ver·tis·er** /–ádvərtizər/ *n.*

self-af·fir·ma·tion /sélfáfərmáyshən/ *n. Psychol.* the recognition and assertion of the existence of the conscious self.

self-ag·gran·dize·ment /sélfəgrándizmənt/ *n.* the act or process of enriching oneself or making oneself powerful. □□ **self-ag·gran·diz·ing** /–grándizing/ *adj.*

self-a·nal·y·sis /sélfənálisis/ *n. Psychol.* the analysis of oneself, one's motives, character, etc. □□ **self-an·a·lyz·ing** /–ánəlizing/ *adj.*

self-ap·point·ed /sélfəpóyntid/ *adj.* designated so by oneself; not authorized by another (*a self-appointed guardian*).

self-ap·pre·ci·a·tion /sélfápreésheeáyshən/ *n.* a good opinion of oneself; conceit.

self-ap·pro·ba·tion /sélfáprəbáyshən/ *n.* = SELF-APPRECIATION.

self-ap·prov·al /sélfəpróovəl/ *n.* = SELF-APPRECIATION.

self-as·sem·bly /sélfəsémblee/ *n.* (often *attrib.*) construction (of furniture, etc.) from materials sold in kit form.

self-as·ser·tion /sélfəsórshən/ *n.* the aggressive promotion of oneself, one's views, etc. □□ **self-as·sert·ing** *adj.* **self-as·ser·tive** *adj.* **self-as·ser·tive·ness** *n.*

self-as·sur·ance /sélfəshóorəns/ *n.* confidence in one's own abilities, etc. □□ **self-as·sured** *adj.* **self-as·sur·ed·ly** *adv.*

self-a·ware /sélfəwáir/ *adj.* conscious of one's character, feelings, motives, etc. □□ **self-a·ware·ness** *n.*

self-be·got·ten /sélfbigót'n/ *adj.* produced by oneself or itself; not made externally.

self-be·tray·al /sélfbitráyəl/ *n.* **1** the betrayal of oneself. **2** the inadvertent revelation of one's true thoughts, etc.

self-bind·er /sélfbíndər/ *n.* a reaping machine with an automatic mechanism for binding the sheaves.

self-born /sélfbáwrn/ *adj.* produced by itself or oneself; not made externally.

self-ca·ter·ing /sélfkáytəring/ *adj. Brit.* (esp. of a vacation or vacation premises) providing rented accommodations with cooking facilities but without food.

self-cen·sor·ship /sélfsénsərship/ *n.* the censoring of oneself.

self-cen·tered /sélfséntərd/ *adj.* preoccupied with one's own personality or affairs. □□ **self-cen·tered·ly** *adv.* **self-cen·tered·ness** *n.*

self-clean·ing /sélfkleéning/ *adj.* (esp. of an oven) cleaning itself when heated, etc.

self-clos·ing /sélfklózing/ *adj.* (of a door, etc.) closing automatically.

self-cock·ing /sélfkóking/ *adj.* (of a gun) with the hammer raised by the trigger, not by hand.

self-col·lect·ed /sélfkəléktid/ *adj.* composed; serene; self-assured.

self-col·ored /sélfkúlərd/ *adj.* **1 a** having the same color throughout (*buttons and belt are self-colored*). **b** (of material) natural; undyed.

2 a (of a flower) of uniform color. **b** having its color unchanged by cultivation or hybridization.

self-com·mand /sélfkəmánd/ *n.* = SELF-CONTROL.

self-com·mun·ion /sélfkəmyóónyən/ *n.* meditation upon one's own character, conduct, etc.

self-con·ceit /sélfkənseét/ *n.* = SELF-SATISFACTION. □□ **self-con·ceit·ed** *adj.*

self-con·dem·na·tion /sélfkóndemnáyshən/ *n.* **1** the blaming of oneself. **2** the inadvertent revelation of one's own sin, crime, etc. □□ **self-con·demned** /–kəndémd/ *adj.*

self-con·fessed /sélfkənfést/ *adj.* openly admitting oneself to be (*a self-confessed thief*).

self-con·fi·dence /sélfkónfidəns/ *n.* = SELF-ASSURANCE. □□ **self-con·fi·dent** *adj.* **self-con·fi·dent·ly** *adv.*

self-con·grat·u·la·tion /sélfkəngráchəláyshən, –gráj–, –kəng–/ *n.* = SELF-SATISFACTION. □□ **self-con·grat·u·la·to·ry** /–kəngrátyoólətáwree/ *adj.*

self-con·quest /sélfkóngkwest/ *n.* the overcoming of one's worst characteristics, etc.

self-con·scious /sélfkónshəs/ *adj.* **1** socially inept through embarrassment or shyness. **2** *Philos.* having knowledge of one's own existence; self-contemplating. □□ **self-con·scious·ly** *adv.* **self-con·scious·ness** *n.*

self-con·sis·tent /sélfkənsístənt/ *adj.* (of parts of the same whole, etc.) consistent; not conflicting. □□ **self-con·sis·ten·cy** *n.*

self-con·sti·tut·ed /sélfkónstitóotid –tyóo–/ *adj.* (of a person, group, etc.) assuming a function without authorization or right; self-appointed.

self-con·tained /sélfkəntáynd/ *adj.* **1** (of a person) uncommunicative or reserved; independent, self-possessed. **2** *Brit.* (esp. of living accommodations) complete in itself. □□ **self-con·tain·ment** *n.*

self-con·tempt /sélfkəntémpt/ *n.* contempt for oneself. □□ **self-con·temp·tu·ous** *adj.*

self-con·tent /sélfkəntént/ *n.* satisfaction with oneself, one's life, achievements, etc. □□ **self-con·tent·ed** *adj.*

self-con·tra·dic·tion /sélfkóntrədíkshən/ *n.* internal inconsistency. □□ **self-con·tra·dic·to·ry** *adj.*

self-con·trol /sélfkəntról/ *n.* the power of controlling one's external reactions, emotions, etc.=uanimity. □□ **self-con·trolled** *adj.*

self-con·vict·ed /sélfkənvíktid/ *adj.* = *self-condemned* (see SELF-CONDEMNATION).

self-cor·rect·ing /sélfkərékting/ *adj.* correcting oneself or itself without external help.

self-cre·at·ed /sélfkreeáytid/ *adj.* created by oneself or itself. □□ **self-cre·a·tion** /–áyshən/ *n.*

self-crit·i·cal /sélfkrítikəl/ *adj.* critical of oneself, one's abilities, etc. □□ **self-crit·i·cism** /–tisizəm/ *n.*

self-de·cep·tion /sélfdisépshən/ *n.* deceiving oneself esp. concerning one's true feelings, etc. □□ **self-de·ceit** /–diseét/ *n.* **self-de·ceiv·er** /–diseévər/ *n.* **self-de·ceiv·ing** /–diseéving/ *adj.* **self-de·cep·tive** *adj.*

self-de·feat·ing /sélfdifeéting/ *adj.* (of an attempt, action, etc.) doomed to failure because of internal inconsistencies, etc.

self-de·fense /sélfdiféns/ *n.* **1** physical, speech, etc., intended as defense (*had to hit him in self-defense*). **2** (usu. **the noble art of self-defense**) boxing. □□ **self-de·fen·sive** *adj.*

self-de·light /sélfdilít/ *n.* delight in oneself or one's existence

self-de·lu·sion /sélfdilóózhən/ *n.* the act or an instance of deluding oneself.

self-de·ni·al /sélfdiníəl/ *n.* the negation of one's interests, needs, or wishes, esp. in favor of those of others; self-control; forbearance. □□ **self-de·ny·ing** *adj.*

self-de·ny·ing or·di·nance *n. hist.* a resolution of the Long Parliament 1645 depriving members of Parliament of civil and military office.

self-de·pend·ence /sélfdipéndəns/ *n.* dependence only on oneself or itself; independence. □□ **self-de·pend·ent** *adj.*

self-dep·re·ca·tion /sélfdéprikáyshən/ *n.* the act of disparaging or belittling oneself. □□ **self-dep·re·cat·ing** /–kayting/ *adj.* **self-dep·re·cat·ing·ly** *adv.*

self-de·spair /sélfdispáir/ *n.* despair with oneself.

self-de·stroy·ing /sélfdistróying/ *adj.* destroying oneself or itself.

self-de·struct /sélfdistrúkt/ *v. & adj.* ● *v.intr.* (of a spacecraft, bomb, etc.) explode or disintegrate automatically, esp. when preset to do so. ● *attrib.adj.* enabling a thing to self-destruct (*a self-destruct device*).

self-de·struc·tion /sélfdistrúkshən/ *n.* **1** the process or an act of destroying oneself or itself. **2** the process or an act of self-destructing. □□ **self-de·struc·tive** *adj.* **self-de·struc·tive·ly** *adv.*

self-de·ter·mi·na·tion /sélfditórmináyshən/ *n.* **1** a nation's right to determine its own allegiance, government, etc. **2** the ability to act with free will, as opposed to fatalism, etc. □□ **self-de·ter·mined** /–tórmind/ *adj.* **self-de·ter·min·ing** /–tórmining/ *adj.*

self-de·vel·op·ment /sélfdivéləpmənt/ n. the development of oneself, one's abilities, etc.

self-de·vo·tion /sélfdivóshən/ n. the devotion of oneself to a person or cause.

self-dis·ci·pline /sélfdísiplin/ n. the act of or ability to apply oneself, control one's feelings, etc.; self-control. □□ **self-dis·ci·plined** adj.

self-dis·cov·er·y /sélfdiskúvəree/ n. the process of acquiring insight into oneself, one's character, desires, etc.

self-dis·gust /sélfdisgúst/ n. disgust with oneself.

self-doubt /sélfdówt/ n. lack of confidence in oneself, one's abilities, etc.

self-drive /sélfdrív/ adj. Brit. (of a rented vehicle) driven by the renter.

self-ed·u·cat·ed /sélféjəkaytid/ adj. educated by oneself by reading, etc., without formal instruction. □□ **self-ed·u·ca·tion** /–káyshən/ n.

self-ef·fac·ing /sélfifáysing/ adj. retiring; modest; timid. □□ **self-ef·face·ment** n. **self-ef·fac·ing·ly** adv.

self-e·lec·tive /sélfiléktiv/ adj. Brit. (of a committee, etc.) proceeding esp. by coopting members, etc.

self-em·ployed /sélfimplóyd/ adj. working for oneself, as a freelance or owner of a business, etc.; not employed by an employer. □□ **self-em·ploy·ment** n.

self-es·teem /sélfistéem/ n. **1** a good opinion of oneself; self-confidence. **2** an unduly high regard for oneself; conceit.

self-ev·i·dent /sélfévidənt/ adj. obvious; without the need of evidence or further explanation. □□ **self-ev·i·dence** n. **self-ev·i·dent·ly** adv.

self-ex·am·i·na·tion /sélfigzámináyshən/ n. **1** the study of one's own conduct, reasons, etc. **2** the examining of one's body for signs of illness, etc.

self-ex·e·cut·ing /sélféksikyóoting/ adj. Law (of a law, legal clause, etc.) not needing legislation, etc., to be enforced; automatic.

self-ex·ist·ent /sélfigzístənt/ adj. existing without prior cause; independent.

self-ex·plan·a·to·ry /sélfiksplánətawree/ adj. easily understood; not needing explanation.

self-ex·pres·sion /sélfikspréshən/ n. the expression of one's feelings, thoughts, etc., esp. in writing, painting, music, etc. □□ **self-ex·pres·sive** adj.

self-faced /sélf-fáyst/ adj. (of stone) unhewn; undressed.

self-feed·er /sélf-féedər/ n. **1** a furnace, machine, etc., that renews its own fuel or material automatically. **2** a device for supplying food to farm animals automatically. □□ **self-feed·ing** adj.

self-fer·tile /sélf-fért'l/ adj. (of a plant, etc.) self-fertilizing. □□ **self-fer·til·i·ty** /–tílitee/ n.

self-fer·ti·li·za·tion /sélf-fért'lizáyshən/ n. the fertilization of plants by their own pollen, not from others. □□ **self-fer·ti·lized** /–fért'lizd/ adj. **self-fer·ti·liz·ing** /–fért'lizing/ adj.

self-fi·nanc·ing /sélf-fínansing, –fənán–/ adj. that finances itself, esp. (of a project or undertaking) that pays for its own implementation or continuation. □□ **self-fi·nance** v.tr.

self-flat·ter·y /sélf-flátəree/ n. = SELF-APPRECIATION. □□ **self-flat·ter·ing** adj.

self-for·get·ful /sélf-fərgétfŏol/ adj. unselfish. □□ **self-for·get·ful·ness** n.

self-ful·fill·ing /sélf-fŏolfíling/ adj. (of a prophecy, forecast, etc.) bound to come true as a result of actions brought about by its being made.

self-ful·fill·ment /sélf-fŏolfílmənt/ n. the fulfillment of one's own hopes and ambitions.

self-gen·er·at·ing /sélfjénərayting/ adj. generated by itself or oneself, not externally.

self-glo·ri·fi·ca·tion /sélfgláwrifikáyshən/ n. the proclamation of oneself, one's abilities, etc.; self-satisfaction.

self-gov·ern·ment /sélfgúvərnmənt/ n. **1** (esp. of a former colony, etc.) government by its own people. **2** = SELF-CONTROL. □□ **self-gov·erned** adj. **self-gov·ern·ing** adj.

self-grat·i·fi·ca·tion /sélfgrátifikáyshən/ n. **1** gratification or pleasing of oneself. **2** self-indulgence; dissipation. **3** masturbation. □□ **self-grat·i·fy·ing** adj.

self-hate /sélfháyt/ n. = SELF-HATRED.

self-ha·tred /sélfháytrid/ n. hatred of oneself, esp. of one's actual self when contrasted with one's imagined self.

self-heal /sélfhéel/ n. any of several plants, esp. Prunella vulgaris, believed to have healing properties.

self-help /sélfhélp/ n. **1** the theory that individuals should provide for their own support and improvement in society. **2** the act or faculty of providing for or improving oneself.

self-hood /sélfhŏod/ n. personality, separate and conscious existence.

self-im·age /sélfímij/ n. one's own idea or picture of oneself, esp. in relation to others.

self-im·por·tance /sélfimpáwrt'ns/ n. a high opinion of oneself; pompousness. □□ **self-im·por·tant** adj. **self-im·por·tant·ly** adv.

self-im·posed /sélfimpózd/ adj. (of a task or condition, etc.) imposed on and by oneself, not externally (self-imposed exile).

self-im·prove·ment /sélfimpróovmənt/ n. the improvement of one's own position or disposition by one's own efforts.

self-in·duced /sélfindóost, –dyóost/ adj. **1** induced by oneself or itself. **2** Electr. produced by self-induction.

self-in·duct·ance /sélfindúktəns/ n. Electr. the property of an electric circuit that causes an electromotive force to be generated in it by a change in the current flowing through it (cf. MUTUAL INDUCTANCE).

self-in·duc·tion /sélfindúkshən/ n. Electr. the production of an electromotive force in a circuit when the current in that circuit is varied. □□ **self-in·duc·tive** adj.

self-in·dul·gent /sélfindúljənt/ adj. indulging or tending to indulge oneself in pleasure, idleness, etc. □□ **self-in·dul·gence** n. **self-in·dul·gent·ly** adv.

self-in·flict·ed /sélfinflíktid/ adj. (esp. of a wound, damage, etc.) inflicted by and on oneself, not externally.

self-in·ter·est /sélfintrist, –tərist/ n. one's personal interest or advantage. □□ **self-in·ter·est·ed** adj.

self·ish /sélfish/ adj. **1** deficient in consideration for others; concerned chiefly with one's own personal profit or pleasure; actuated by self-interest. **2** (of a motive, etc.) appealing to self-interest. □□ **self·ish·ly** adv. **self·ish·ness** n.

self-jus·ti·fi·ca·tion /sélfjústifikáyshən/ n. the justification or excusing of oneself, one's actions, etc.

self-knowl·edge /sélfnólij/ n. the understanding of oneself, one's motives, etc.

self·less /sélflis/ adj. disregarding oneself or one's own interests; unselfish. □□ **self·less·ly** adv. **self·less·ness** n.

self-load·ing /sélflóding/ adj. (esp. of a gun) loading itself. □□ **self-load·er** n.

self-lock·ing /sélflóking/ adj. locking itself.

self-love /sélflúv/ n. **1** selfishness; self-indulgence. **2** Philos. regard for one's own well-being and happiness.

self-made /sélfmáyd/ adj. **1** successful or rich by one's own effort. **2** made by oneself.

self-mas·ter·y /sélfmástəree/ n. = SELF-CONTROL.

self·mate /sélfmayt/ n. Chess checkmate in which a player forces the opponent to achieve checkmate.

self-mock·ing /sélfmóking/ adj. mocking oneself or itself.

self-mo·tion /sélfmóshən/ n. motion caused by oneself or itself, not externally. □□ **self-mov·ing** /–móoving/ adj.

self-mo·ti·vat·ed /sélfmótivaytid/ adj. acting on one's own initiative without external pressure. □□ **self-mo·ti·va·tion** /–váyshən/ n.

self-mur·der /sélfmórdər/ n. = SUICIDE. □□ **self-mur·der·er** n.

self-ne·glect /sélfniglékt/ n. neglect of oneself.

self·ness /sélfnis/ n. **1** individuality; personality; essence. **2** selfishness or self-regard.

self-o·pin·ion·at·ed /sélfəpínyənaytid/ adj. **1** stubbornly adhering to one's own opinions. **2** arrogant. □□ **self-o·pin·ion** n.

self-per·pet·u·at·ing /sélfpərpéchŏo-ayting/ adj. perpetuating itself or oneself without external agency. □□ **self-per·pet·u·a·tion** /–áyshən/ n.

self-pit·y /sélfpítee/ n. extreme sorrow for one's own troubles, etc. □□ **self-pit·y·ing** adj. **self-pit·y·ing·ly** adv.

self-pol·li·na·tion /sélfpólináyshən/ n. the pollination of a flower by pollen from the same plant. □□ **self-pol·li·nat·ed** adj. **self-pol·li·nat·ing** adj. **self-pol·li·na·tor** n.

self-por·trait /sélfpáwrtrit/ n. a portrait or description of an artist, writer, etc., by himself or herself.

self-pos·sessed /sélfpəzést/ adj. habitually exercising self-control; composed. □□ **self-pos·ses·sion** /–zéshən/ n.

self-praise /sélfpráyz/ n. boasting; self-glorification.

self-pres·er·va·tion /sélfprézərváyshən/ n. **1** the preservation of one's own life, safety, etc. **2** this as a basic instinct of human beings and animals.

self-pro·claimed /sélfprəkláymd/ adj. proclaimed by oneself or itself to be such.

self-prop·a·gat·ing /sélfprópəgayting/ adj. (esp. of a plant) able to propagate itself.

self-pro·pelled /sélfprəpéld/ adj. (esp. of a motor vehicle, etc.) moving or able to move without external propulsion. □□ **self-pro·pel·ling** adj.

self-pro·tec·tion /sélfprətékshən/ n. protecting oneself or itself. □□ **self-pro·tec·tive** adj.

self-rais·ing /sélfráyzing/ adj. Brit. = SELF-RISING.

self-re·al·i·za·tion /sélfréeəlizáyshən/ n. **1** the development of one's faculties, abilities, etc. **2** this as an ethical principle.

self-re·cord·ing /sélfrikáwrding/ adj. (of a scientific instrument, etc.) automatically recording its measurements.

self-re·gard /sélfrigáard/ n. **1** a proper regard for oneself. **2 a** selfishness or conceit. **b** conceit.

self-reg·is·ter·ing /sélfréjistəring/ adj. (of a scientific instrument, etc.) automatically registering its measurements.

self-reg·u·lat·ing /sélfrégyəlayting/ adj. regulating oneself or itself without intervention. □□ **self-reg·u·la·tion** /–láyshən/ *n.* **self-reg·u·la·to·ry** /–lətawree/ *adj.*

self-re·li·ance /sélfrilíəns/ *n.* reliance on one's own resources, etc.; independence. □□ **self-re·li·ant** *adj.* **self-re·li·ant·ly** *adv.*

self-re·new·al /sélfrinóōəl, –nyóō–/ *n.* the act or process of renewing oneself or itself.

self-re·nun·ci·a·tion /sélfrinúnseeáyshən/ *n.* **1** = SELF-SACRIFICE. **2** unselfishness.

self-re·proach /sélfripróch/ *n.* reproach or blame directed at oneself. □□ **self-re·proach·ful** *adj.*

self-re·spect /sélfrispékt/ *n.* respect for oneself; a feeling that one is behaving with honor, dignity, etc. □□ **self-re·spect·ing** *adj.*

self-re·straint /sélfristráynt/ *n.* = SELF-CONTROL. □□ **self-re·strained** *adj.*

self-re·veal·ing /sélfrivéeling/ *adj.* revealing one's character, motives, etc., esp. inadvertently. □□ **self-rev·e·la·tion** /–révəláyshən/ *n.*

self-right·eous /sélfríchəs/ *adj.* excessively conscious of or insistent on one's rectitude, correctness, etc. □□ **self-right·eous·ly** *adv.* **self-right·eous·ness** *n.*

self-right·ing /sélfríting/ *adj.* (of a boat) righting itself when capsized.

self-ris·ing /sélfrízing/ *adj.* (of flour) having a raising agent already added.

self-rule /sélfróōl/ *n.* = SELF-GOVERNMENT 1.

self-sac·ri·fice /sélfsákrifis/ *n.* the negation of one's own interests, wishes, etc., in favor of those of others. □□ **self-sac·ri·fic·ing** *adj.*

self·same /sélfsaym/ *attrib.adj.* (prec. by *the*) the very same (*the self-same village*).

self-sat·is·fac·tion /sélfsátisfákshən/ *n.* excessive and unwarranted satisfaction with oneself, one's achievements, etc.; complacency. □□ **self-sat·is·fied** /–sátisfid/ *adj.* **self-sat·is·fied·ly** /–fidlee/ *adv.*

self-seal·ing /sélfséeling/ *adj.* **1** (of a pneumatic tire, fuel tank, etc.) automatically able to seal small punctures. **2** (of an envelope) self-adhesive.

self-seek·ing /sélfséeking/ *adj. & n.* seeking one's own welfare before that of others. □□ **self-seek·er** *n.*

self-se·lec·tion /sélfsilékshən/ *n.* the act of selecting oneself or itself. □□ **self-se·lect·ing** *adj.*

self-serv·ice /sélfsórvis/ *adj. & n.* ● *adj.* (often *attrib.*) **1** (of a store, restaurant, gas station, etc.) where customers serve themselves and pay at a checkout counter, etc. **2** (of a machine) serving goods after the insertion of coins. ● *n. colloq.* a self-service store, gas station, etc.

self-serv·ing /sélfsórving/ *adj.* = SELF-SEEKING.

self-slaugh·ter /sélfsláwtər/ *n.* = SUICIDE.

self-sown /sélfsón/ *adj.* grown from seed scattered naturally.

self-start·er /sélfstaártər/ *n.* **1** an electric appliance for starting a motor vehicle engine without the use of a crank. **2** an ambitious person who needs no external motivation.

self-ster·ile /sélfstéril, –íl/ *adj. Biol.* not being self-fertile. □□ **self-ste·ril·i·ty** /–stərílitee/ *n.*

self-styled /sélfstíld/ *adj.* called so by oneself; would-be; pretended (*a self-styled artist*).

self-suf·fi·cient /sélfsəfíshənt/ *adj.* **1 a** needing nothing; independent. **b** (of a person, nation, etc.) able to supply one's needs for a commodity, esp. food, from one's own resources. **2** content with one's own opinion; arrogant. □□ **self-suf·fi·cien·cy** *n.* **self-suf·fi·cient·ly** *adv.* **self-suf·fic·ing** /–səfísing/ *adj.*

self-sug·ges·tion /sélfsəgjés-chən, –səjés–/ *n.* = AUTOSUGGESTION.

self-sup·port·ing /sélfsəpáwrting/ *adj.* **1** capable of maintaining oneself or itself financially. **2** staying up or standing without external aid. □□ **self-sup·port** *n.*

self-sur·ren·der /sélfsəréndər/ *n.* the surrender of oneself or one's will, etc., to an influence, emotion, or other person.

self-sus·tain·ing /sélfsəstáyning/ *adj.* sustaining oneself or itself. □□ **self-sus·tained** *adj.*

self-taught /sélftáwt/ *adj.* educated or trained by oneself, not externally.

self-tor·ture /sélftáwrchər/ *n.* the inflicting of pain, esp. mental, on oneself.

self-willed /sélfwíld/ *adj.* obstinately pursuing one's own wishes. □□ **self-will** *n.*

self-wind·ing /sélfwínding/ *adj.* (of a watch, etc.) having an automatic winding apparatus.

self-worth /sélfwórth/ *n.* = SELF-ESTEEM 1.

Sel·juk /séljōōk/ *n. & adj.* ● *n.* a member of any of the Turkish dynasties (11th–13th c.) of central and western Asia preceding Ottoman rule. ● *adj.* of or relating to the Seljuks. □□ **Sel·juk·i·an** /–jōōkeeən/ *adj. & n.* [Turk. *seljūq* (name of their reputed ancestor)]

sell /sel/ *v. & n.* ● *v.* (*past* and *past part.* **sold** /sōld/) **1** *tr.* make over or dispose of in exchange for money. **2** *tr.* keep a stock of for sale or be a dealer in (*do you sell candles?*). **3** *intr.* (of goods) be purchased (*will never sell; these are selling well*). **4** *intr.* (foll. by *at, for*) have a specified price (*sells at $5*). **5** *tr.* betray for money or other reward (*sell one's country*). **6** *tr.* offer dishonorably for money or oth-

er consideration; make a matter of corrupt bargaining (*sell justice; sell oneself; sell one's honor*). **7** *tr.* **a** advertise or publish the merits of. **b** give (a person) information on the value of something; inspire (a person) with a desire to buy or acquire or agree to something. **8** *tr.* cause to be sold (*the author's name alone will sell many copies*). **9** *tr. Brit. sl.* disappoint by not keeping an engagement, etc., by failing in some way, or by trickery (*sold again!*). ● *n. colloq.* **1** a manner of selling (*soft sell*). **2** a deception or disappointment. □ **sell down the river** see RIVER. **sell the** (or **a**) **dummy** see DUMMY. **sell one's life dear** (or **dearly**) esp. *Brit.* do great injury before being killed. **sell off** sell the remainder of (goods) at reduced prices. **sell out 1 a** sell all one's stock-in-trade, one's shares in a company, etc. **b** sell (all or some of one's stock, shares, etc.). **2 a** betray. **b** be treacherous or disloyal. **sell the pass** see PASS[2]. **sell a pup** see PUP. **sell short** disparage; underestimate. **sell up** *Brit.* **1** sell one's business, house, etc. **2** sell the goods of (a debtor). **sold on** *colloq.* enthusiastic about. □□ **sell·a·ble** *adj.* [OE *sellan* f. Gmc]

sell-by date *n.* the latest recommended date of sale marked on the packaging of esp. perishable food.

sell·er /sélər/ *n.* **1** a person who sells. **2** a commodity that sells well or badly. □ **seller's** (or **sellers'**) **market** an economic position in which goods are scarce and expensive.

sell·ing point *n.* an advantageous feature.

sell·ing race *n.* a horse race after which the winning horse must be auctioned.

sell-out /sélowt/ *n.* **1** a commercial success, esp. the selling of all tickets for a show. **2** a betrayal.

selt·zer /séltsər/ *n.* (in full **seltzer water**) **1** medicinal mineral water from Nieder-Selters in Germany. **2** an artificial substitute for this; soda water. [G *Selterser* (adj.) f. *Selters*]

sel·vage /sélvij/ *n.* (also **sel·vedge**) **1 a** an edging that prevents cloth from unraveling (either an edge along the warp or a specially woven edging). **b** a border of different material or finish intended to be removed or hidden. **2** *Geol.* an alteration zone at the edge of a rock mass. **3** the edge plate of a lock with an opening for the bolt. [ME f. SELF + EDGE, after Du. *selfegghe*]

selves *pl.* of SELF.

se·man·teme /simánteem/ *n. Linguistics* a fundamental element expressing an image or idea. [F *sémantème* (as SEMANTIC)]

se·man·tic /simántik/ *adj.* relating to meaning in language; relating to the connotations of words. □□ **se·man·ti·cal·ly** *adv.* [F *sémantique* f. Gk *sēmantikos* significant f. *sēmainō* signify f. *sēma* sign]

se·man·tics /simántiks/ *n.pl.* (usu. treated as *sing.*) the branch of linguistics concerned with meaning. □□ **se·man·ti·cian** /–tíshən/ *n.* **se·man·ti·cist** /–tisist/ *n.*

sem·a·phore /séməfawr/ *n. & v.* ● *n.* **1** *Mil.*, etc., a system of sending messages by holding the arms or two flags in certain positions according to an alphabetic code. **2** a signaling apparatus consisting of a post with a movable arm or arms, lanterns, etc., for use (esp. on railroads) by day or night. ● *v.intr. & tr.* signal or send by semaphore. □□ **sem·a·phor·ic** *adj.* **sem·a·phor·i·cal·ly** /–fáwrikəl/ *adv.* [F *sémaphore*, irreg. f. Gk *sēma* sign + *–phoros* –PHORE]

se·ma·si·ol·o·gy /simáyseeóləjee/ *n.* semantics. □□ **se·ma·si·o·log·i·cal** /–seeəlójikəl/ *adj.* [G *Semasiologie* f. Gk *sēmasia* meaning f. *sēmainō* signify]

se·mat·ic /simátik/ *adj. Zool.* (of coloring, markings, etc.) significant; serving to warn off enemies or attract attention. [Gk *sēma sēmatos* sign]

sem·bla·ble /sémbləbəl/ *n. & adj.* ● *n.* a counterpart or equal. ● *adj. archaic* having the semblance of something; seeming. [ME f. OF (as SEMBLANCE)]

sem·blance /sémbləns/ *n.* **1** the outward or superficial appearance of something (*put on a semblance of anger*). **2** resemblance. [ME f. OF f. *sembler* f. L *similare, simulare* SIMULATE]

se·mé /səmáy/ *adj.* (also **se·mée**) *Heraldry* covered with small bearings of indefinite number (e.g., stars, fleurs-de-lis) arranged all over the field. [F, past part. of *semer* to sow]

sem·eme /sémeem, seé–/ *n. Linguistics* the unit of meaning carried by a morpheme. [as SEMANTIC]

se·men /séemən/ *n.* the reproductive fluid of male animals, containing spermatozoa in suspension. [ME f. L *semen seminis* seed f. *serere* to sow]

se·mes·ter /siméstər/ *n.* **1** half of the academic year in an educational institution, usu. an 18-week period. **2** a half-year course or term in (esp. German) universities. [G f. L *semestris* six-monthly f. *sex* six + *mensis* month]

sem·i /sémi, séemee/ *n.* (*pl.* **sem·is**) *colloq.* **1** a semitrailer; tractor-trailer. **2** *Brit.* a semidetached house. **3** a semifinal. [abbr.]

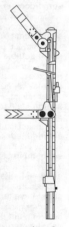

semaphore 2

semi- /sémee, sémī/ *prefix* **1** half (*semicircle*). **2** partly; in some degree or particular (*semiofficial; semidetached*). **3** almost (*a semismile*). **4** occurring or appearing twice in a specified period (*semiannual*). [F, It., etc., or L, corresp. to Gk HEMI-, Skr. *sāmi*]

sem·i·an·nu·al /sémeeányōōəl, sémī-/ *adj.* occurring, published, etc., twice a year. □□ **sem·i·an·nu·al·ly** *adv.*

sem·i·au·to·mat·ic /sémeeáwtəmátik, sémī-/ *adj.* **1** partially automatic. **2** (of a firearm) having a mechanism for continuous loading but not for continuous firing.

sem·i·base·ment /sémeebáysmənt, sémī-/ *n.* a story partly below ground level.

sem·i·bold /sémeebóld, sémī-/ *adj. Printing* printed in a type darker than normal but not as dark as bold.

sem·i·breve /sémeebrev, –breev, sémī-/ *n. esp. Brit. Mus.* = WHOLE NOTE.

sem·i·cir·cle /sémeesərkəl, sémī-/ *n.* **1** half of a circle or of its circumference. **2** a set of objects ranged in, or an object forming, a semicircle. [L *semicirculus* (as SEMI-, CIRCLE)]

sem·i·cir·cu·lar /sémeesə́rkyələr, sémī-/ *adj.* **1** forming or shaped like a semicircle. **2** arranged as or in a semicircle. [LL *semicircularis* (as SEMICIRCLE)]

sem·i·cir·cu·lar ca·nal *n.* one of three fluid-filled channels in the ear giving information to the brain to help maintain balance.

sem·i·civ·i·lized /sémeesívilīzd, sémī-/ *adj.* partially civilized.

sem·i·co·lon /sémikólən/ *n.* a punctuation mark (;) of intermediate value between a comma and a period.

sem·i·con·duct·ing /sémeekəndúkting, sémī-/ *adj.* having the properties of a semiconductor.

sem·i·con·duc·tor /sémeekəndúktər, sémī-/ *n.* a solid substance that is a nonconductor when pure or at a low temperature but has a conductivity between that of insulators and that of most metals when containing a suitable impurity or at a higher temperature and is used in integrated circuits, transistors, diodes, etc.

sem·i·con·scious /sémeekónshəs, sémī-/ *adj.* partly or imperfectly conscious.

sem·i·cyl·in·der /sémeesílindər, sémī-/ *n.* half of a cylinder cut longitudinally. □□ **sem·i·cy·lin·dri·cal** /–líndrikəl/ *adj.*

sem·i·de·po·nent /sémeedipónənt, sémī-/ *adj. Gram.* (of a Latin verb) having active forms in present tenses and passive forms with active sense in perfect tenses.

sem·i·de·tached /sémeeditácht, sémī-/ *adj. & n.* ● *adj.* (of a house) joined to another by a party wall on one side only. ● *n.* a semidetached house.

sem·i·di·am·e·ter /sémeedīámitər, sémī-/ *n.* half of a diameter; radius. [LL (as SEMI-, DIAMETER)]

sem·i·doc·u·men·ta·ry /sémeedókyəméntəree, sémī-/ *adj. & n.* ● *adj.* (of a motion picture) having a factual background and a fictitious story. ● *n.* (*pl.* **·ries**) a semidocumentary motion picture.

sem·i·dome /sémeedōm, sémī-/ *n.* **1** a halfdome formed by vertical section. **2** a part of a structure more or less resembling a dome.

sem·i·dou·ble /sémeedúbəl, sémī-/ *adj.* (of a flower) intermediate between single and double in having only the outer stamens converted to petals.

sem·i·fi·nal /sémeefínəl, sémī-/ *n.* a match or round immediately preceding the final.

sem·i·fi·nal·ist /sémeefínəlist, sémī-/ *n.* a competitor in a semifinal.

sem·i·fin·ished /sémeefinisht, sémī-/ *adj.* prepared for the final stage of manufacture.

sem·i·fit·ted /sémeefitid, sémī-/ *adj.* (of a garment) shaped to the body but not closely fitted.

sem·i·flu·id /sémeeflóoid, sémī-/ *adj. & n.* ● *adj.* of a consistency between solid and liquid. ● *n.* a semifluid substance.

sem·i·in·fi·nite /sémee-ínfinit, sémī-/ *adj. Math.* limited in one direction and stretching to infinity in the other.

sem·i·in·va·lid /sémee-ínvŏlid, sémī-/ *n.* a person somewhat enfeebled or partially disabled.

sem·i·liq·uid /sémeelíkwid, sémī-/ *adj. & n.* = SEMIFLUID.

sem·i·lu·nar /sémeelóōnər, sémī-/ *adj.* shaped like a half moon or crescent. [mod.L *semilunaris* (as SEMI-, LUNAR)]

sem·i·lu·nar bone *n.* a crescent-shaped bone in the carpus.

sem·i·lu·nar car·ti·lage *n.* a crescent-shaped cartilage in the knee.

sem·i·lu·nar valve *n.* a crescent-shaped valve in the heart.

sem·i·me·tal /sémeemét'l, sémī-/ *n.* a substance with some of the properties of metals. [mod.L *semimetallum* (as SEMI-, METAL)]

sem·i·month·ly /sémeemúnthlee, sémī-/ *adj. & adv.* ● *adj.* occurring, published, etc., twice a month. ● *adv.* twice a month.

sem·i·nal /séminəl/ *adj.* **1** of or relating to seed, semen, or reproduction. **2** germinal. **3** rudimentary; undeveloped. **4** (of ideas, etc.) providing the basis for future development. □□ **sem·i·nal·ly** *adv.* [ME f. OF *seminal* or L *seminalis* (as SEMEN)]

sem·i·nal flu·id *n.* semen.

sem·i·nar /séminaar/ *n.* **1** a small class at a university, etc., for discussion and research. **2** a short intensive course of study. **3** a conference of specialists. [G (as SEMINARY)]

sem·i·nar·y /séminaree/ *n.* (*pl.* **·ies**) **1** a training college for priests, rabbis, etc. **2** a place of education or development. □□ **sem·i·nar·i·an** /–náireeən/ *n.* **sem·i·na·rist** *n.* [ME f. L *seminarium* seed plot, neut. of *seminarius* (adj.) (as SEMEN)]

sem·i·nif·er·ous /sémeenífərəs, sémī-/ *adj.* **1** bearing seed. **2** conveying semen. [L *semin-* f. SEMEN + –FEROUS]

Sem·i·nole /séminōl/ *n.* **1 a** a N. American people native to Florida. **b** a member of this people. **2** the language of this people.

sem·i·of·fi·cial /sémeeófishəl, sémī-/ *adj.* **1** partly official; rather less than official. **2** (of communications to newspapers, etc.) made by an official with the stipulation that the source should not be revealed. □□ **sem·i·of·fi·cial·ly** *adv.*

se·mi·ol·o·gy /séemeeóləjee, sémee-/ *n.* (also **se·mei·ol·o·gy**) = SEMIOTICS. □□ **se·mi·o·log·i·cal** /–meeəlójikəl/ *adj.* **se·mi·ol·o·gist** *n.* [Gk *sēmeion* sign f. *sē ma* mark]

sem·i·o·paque /sémeeōpáyk, sémī-/ *adj.* not fully transparent.

se·mi·ot·ics /séemeeótiks, sém-/ *n.* (also **se·mei·ot·ics**) **1** the study of signs and symbols in various fields, esp. language. **2** *Med.* symptomatology. □□ **se·mi·ot·ic** *adj.* **se·mi·ot·i·cal** *adj.* **se·mi·ot·i·cal·ly** *adv.* **se·mi·o·ti·cian** /–tíshən/ *n.* [Gk *sēmeiōtikos* of signs (as SEMIOLOGY)]

sem·i·per·ma·nent /sémeepə́rmənənt, sémī-/ *adj.* rather less than permanent.

sem·i·per·me·a·ble /sémeepə́rmeeəbəl, sémī-/ *adj.* (of a membrane, etc.) allowing small molecules, but not large ones, to pass through.

sem·i·plume /sémeeplōōm, sémī-/ *n.* a feather with a firm stem and a downy web.

sem·i·pre·cious /sémeepréshəs, sémī-/ *adj.* (of a gem) less valuable than a precious stone.

sem·i·pro /sémeeprṓ, sémī-/ *adj. & n.* (*pl.* **·pros**) *colloq.* = SEMIPROFESSIONAL.

sem·i·pro·fes·sion·al /sémeeprəféshənəl, sémī-/ *adj. & n.* ● *adj.* **1** receiving payment for an activity but not relying on it for a living. **2** involving semiprofessionals. ● *n.* a semiprofessional musician, sportsman, etc.

sem·i·qua·ver /sémeekwayvər, sémī-/ *n. esp. Brit. Mus.* = *sixteenth note*.

sem·i·rig·id /sémeeríjid, sémī-/ *adj.* (of an airship) having a stiffened keel attached to a flexible gas container.

sem·i·skilled /sémeeskíld, sémī-/ *adj.* (of work or a worker) having or needing some training but less than for a skilled worker.

sem·i·skimmed /sémeeskímd, sémī-/ *adj.* (of milk) from which some cream has been skimmed.

sem·i·smile /sémeesmíl, sémī-/ *n.* an expression that is not quite a smile.

sem·i·sol·id /sémeesólid, sémī-/ *adj.* viscous; semifluid.

sem·i·sweet /sémeeswéet, sémī-/ *adj.* (of cookies, chocolate, etc.) slightly sweetened.

sem·i·syn·thet·ic /sémeesinthétik, sémī-/ *adj. Chem.* (of a substance) that is prepared synthetically but derives from a naturally occurring material.

Sem·ite /sémīt/ *n.* a member of any of the peoples supposed to be descended from Shem, son of Noah (Gen. 10:21 ff.), including esp. the Jews, Arabs, Assyrians, and Phoenicians. □□ **Sem·i·tism** /sémitizəm/ *n.* **Sem·i·tist** /sémítist/ *n.* **Sem·i·tize** /–tīz/ *v.tr.* **Sem·i·ti·za·tion** *n.* [mod.L *Semita* f. LL f. Gk *Sēm* Shem]

Se·mit·ic /simítik/ *adj.* **1** of or relating to the Semites, esp. the Jews. **2** of or relating to the languages of the family including Hebrew and Arabic. [mod.L *Semiticus* (as SEMITE)]

sem·i·tone /sémeetōn, sémī-/ *n. Mus.* the smallest interval used in classical European music; half a tone.

sem·i·trail·er /sémeetráylər, sémī-/ *n.* a trailer having wheels at the back but supported at the front by a towing vehicle.

sem·i·trans·par·ent /sémeetránzpárənt, sémī-, –páir/ *adj.* partially or imperfectly transparent.

sem·i·trop·ics /sémeetrópiks, sémī-/ *n.pl.* = SUBTROPICS. □□ **sem·i·trop·i·cal** *adj.*

sem·i·vow·el /sémeevowəl/ *n.* **1** a sound intermediate between a vowel and a consonant (e.g., *w*, *y*). **2** a letter representing this. [after L *semivocalis*]

sem·i·week·ly /sémeeweéklee, sémī-/ *adj. & adv.* ● *adj.* occurring; published, etc., twice a week. ● *adv.* twice a week.

sem·o·li·na /séməleénə/ *n.* **1** the hard grains left after the milling of flour, used in puddings, etc., and in pasta. **2** a pudding, etc., made of this. [It. *semolino* dimin. of *semola* bran f. L *simila* flour]

sem·pi·ter·nal /sémpitə́rnəl/ *adj. rhet.* eternal; everlasting. □□ **sem·pi·ter·nal·ly** *adv.* **sem·pi·ter·ni·ty** *n.* [ME f. OF *sempiternel* f. LL *sempiternalis* f. L *sempiternus* f. *semper* always + *aeternus* eternal]

sem·pli·ce /sémplichay/ *adv. Mus.* in a simple style of performance. [It., = SIMPLE]

sem·pre /sémpray/ *adv. Mus.* throughout; always (*sempre forte*). [It.]

semp·stress var. of SEAMSTRESS.

Sem·tex /sémteks/ *n. Trademark* a highly malleable, odorless plastic explosive. [prob. f. *Semtín*, a village in the Czech Republic near the place of production]

sen. *abbr.* **1 a** senator. **b** senate. **2** senior.

sen•ar•i•us /sináireeəs/ n. (pl. **sen•ar•i•i** /–ee–ī/) Prosody a verse of six feet, esp. an iambic trimeter. [L: see SENARY]

sen•a•ry /séenəree, sén–/ adj. of six, by sixes. [L senarius f. seni distrib. of sex six]

sen•ate /sénit/ n. 1 a legislative body, esp. the upper and smaller assembly in the US, France, and other countries, in the states of the US, etc. 2 the governing body of a university or college. 3 Rom.Hist. the state council of the republic and empire sharing legislative power with the popular assemblies, administration with the magistrates, and judicial power with the knights. [ME f. OF senat f. L senatus f. senex old man]

sen•a•tor /sénətər/ n. 1 a member of a senate. 2 (in Scotland) a Lord of Session. □□ **sen•a•to•ri•al** /–táwreeəl/ adj. **sen•a•tor•ship** n. [ME f. OF senateur f. L senator –oris (as SENATE)]

send /send/ v. (past and past part. **sent** /sent/) 1 tr. a order or cause to go or be conveyed (send a message to headquarters; sent me a book; sends goods all over the world). b propel; cause to move (send a bullet; sent him flying). c cause to go or become (send into raptures; send to sleep). d dismiss with or without force (sent her away; sent him about his business). 2 intr. send a message or letter (he sent to warn me). 3 tr. (of God, providence, etc.) grant or bestow or inflict; bring about; cause to be (send rain; send a judgment; send her victorious!). 4 tr. sl. affect emotionally; put into ecstasy. 5 tr. (freq. foll. by off or off) emit or give out (light, heat, odor, etc.); utter or produce (sound); cause (a voice, cry, etc.) to carry, or travel. □ **send away for** send an order to a dealer for (goods). **send down** Brit. 1 expel from a university. 2 sentence to imprisonment. **send for** 1 summon. 2 order by mail. **send in** 1 cause to go in. 2 submit (an entry, etc.) for a competition, etc. **send off** 1 get (a letter, parcel, etc.) dispatched. 2 attend the departure of (a person) as a sign of respect, etc. 3 Sports (of a referee) order (a player) to leave the field and take no further part in the game. **send off for** esp. Brit. = send away for. **send on** transmit to a further destination or in advance of one's own arrival. **send a person to Coventry** refuse to deal with a person. **send up** 1 cause to go up. 2 transmit to a higher authority. 3 colloq. satirize or ridicule, esp. by mimicking. 4 sentence to imprisonment. **send word** send information. □□ **send•a•ble** adj. **send•er** n. [OE sendan f. Gmc]

sen•dal /séndᵊl/ n. hist. 1 a thin, rich, silk material. 2 a garment of this. [ME f. OF cendal, ult. f. Gk sindōn]

send-off n. a demonstration of goodwill, etc., at the departure of a person, the start of a project, etc.

send-up n. colloq. a satire or parody.

Sen•e•ca /sénikə/ n. 1 a a N.American people native to western New York. b a member of this people. 2 the language of this people. □□ **Sen•e•can** adj.

se•ne•ci•o /sinéesheeō/ n. any composite plant of the genus Senecio, including many cultivated species as well as groundsel and ragwort. [L senecio old man, groundsel, with ref. to the hairy fruits]

se•nesce /sinés/ v.intr. grow old. □□ **se•nes•cence** n. **se•nes•cent** adj. [L senescere f. senex old]

sen•es•chal /sénishəl/ n. the steward or majordomo of a medieval estate [ME f. OF f. med.L seniscalus f. Gmc, = old servant]

se•nhor /saynáwr/ n. a title used of or to a Portuguese or Brazilian man. [Port. f. L senior: see SENIOR]

se•nho•ra /saynáwrə/ n. a title used of or to a Portuguese or a Brazilian married woman. [Port., fem. of SENHOR]

se•nho•ri•ta /sáynyəréetə/ n. a title used of or to a Portuguese or Brazilian unmarried woman. [Port., dimin. of SENHORA]

se•nile /séenil/ adj. & n. • adj. 1 of or characteristic of old age (senile apathy; senile decay). 2 having the weaknesses or diseases of old age. • n. a senile person. □□ **se•nil•i•ty** /siníleetee/ n. [F sénile or L senilis f. senex old man]

se•nile de•men•tia n. a severe form of mental deterioration in old age, characterized by loss of memory and disorientation, and most often due to Alzheimer's disease.

se•nior /séenyər/ adj. & n. • adj. 1 (often foll. by to) more or most advanced in age or standing. 2 of high or highest position. 3 (placed after a person's name) senior to another of the same name. 4 of the final year at a university, high school, etc. • n. 1 a person of advanced age or comparatively long service, etc. 2 one's elder, or one's superior in length of service, membership, etc. (is my senior). 3 a senior student. □□ **sen•ior•i•ty** /séenyáwritee, –yor–/ n. [ME f. L, = older, older man, compar. of senex senis old man, old]

sen•ior cit•i•zen n. an elderly person, esp. a retiree.

sen•ior col•lege n. a college in which the last two years' work is for a bachelor's degree is done.

sen•ior of•fi•cer n. an officer to whom a junior is responsible.

sen•na /sénə/ n. 1 a cassia tree. 2 a laxative prepared from the dried pod of this. [med.L sena f. Arab. sanā]

sen•net[1] /sénit/ n. hist. a signal call on a trumpet or cornet (in the stage directions of Elizabethan plays). [perh. var. of SIGNET]

sen•net[2] var. of SENNIT.

sen•night /sénīt/ n. archaic a week. [OE seofon nihta seven nights]

sen•nit /sénit/ n. 1 hist. plaited straw, palm leaves, etc., used for mak-

ing hats. 2 Naut. braided cordage made in flat or round or square form from 3 to 9 cords. [17th c.: orig. unkn.]

se•ñor /senyáwr/ n. (pl. **se•ño•res** /–rez/) a title used of or to a Spanish-speaking man. [Sp. f. L senior: see SENIOR]

señora /senyáwrə/ n. a title used of or to a Spanish-speaking married woman. [Sp., fem. of SE ÑOR]

se•ño•ri•ta /sényəréetə/ n. a title used of or to a Spanish-speaking unmarried woman. [Sp., dimin. of SEÑORA]

sen•sate /sénsayt/ adj. perceived by the senses. [LL sensatus having senses (as SENSE)]

sen•sa•tion /sensáyshən/ n. 1 the consciousness of perceiving or seeming to perceive some state or condition of one's body or its parts or senses or of one's mind or its emotions; an instance of such consciousness (lost all sensation in my left arm; had a sensation of giddiness; a sensation of pride; in search of a new sensation). 2 a a stirring of emotions or intense interest esp. among a large group of people (the news caused a sensation). b a person, event, etc., causing such interest. 3 the sensational use of literary, etc., material. [med.L sensatio f. L sensus SENSE]

sen•sa•tion•al /sensáyshənəl/ adj. 1 causing or intended to cause great public excitement, etc. 2 of or causing sensation. □□ **sen•sa•tion•al•ize** v.tr. **sen•sa•tion•al•ly** adv.

sen•sa•tion•al•ism /sensáyshənəlizəm/ n. 1 the use of or interest in the sensational in literature, political agitation, etc. 2 Philos. the theory that ideas are derived solely from sensation (opp. RATIONALISM). □□ **sen•sa•tion•al•ist** n. & adj. **sen•sa•tion•al•is•tic** /–lístik/ adj.

sense /sens/ n. & v. • n. 1 a any of the special bodily faculties by which sensation is roused (has keen senses; has a dull sense of smell). b sensitiveness of all or any of these. 2 the ability to perceive or feel or to be conscious of the presence or properties of things. 3 (foll. by of) consciousness; intuitive awareness (sense of having done well; sense of one's own importance). 4 (often foll. by of) a quick or accurate appreciation, understanding, or instinct regarding a specified matter (sense of the ridiculous; road sense; the moral sense). b the habit of basing one's conduct on such instinct. 5 practical wisdom or judgment; common sense; conformity to these (has plenty of sense; what is the sense of talking like that?; has more sense than to do that). 6 a a meaning; the way in which a word, etc., is to be understood (the sense of the word is clear; I mean that in the literal sense). b intelligibility or coherence or possession of a meaning. 7 the prevailing opinion among a number of people. 8 (in pl.) a person's sanity or normal state of mind (taken leave of his senses). 9 Math., etc., a a direction of movement. b that which distinguishes a pair of entities that differ only in that each is the reverse of the other. • v.tr. 1 perceive by a sense or senses. 2 be vaguely aware of. 3 realize. 4 (of a machine, etc.) detect. 5 understand. □ **bring a person to his** (or **her**) **senses** 1 cure a person of folly. 2 restore a person to consciousness. **come to one's senses** 1 regain consciousness. 2 become sensible after acting foolishly. **the five senses** sight, hearing, smell, taste, and touch. **in a** (or **one**) **sense** if the statement is understood in a particular way (what you say is true in a sense). **in one's senses** sane. **make sense** be intelligible or practicable. **make sense of** show or find the meaning of. **man** (or **woman**) **of sense** a sagacious man (or woman). **out of one's senses** in or into a state of madness (is out of her senses; frightened him out of his senses). **take leave of one's senses** go mad. **take the sense of the meeting** ascertain the prevailing opinion. **under a sense of wrong** feeling wronged. [ME f. L sensus faculty of feeling, thought, meaning, f. sentire sens- feel]

sense-da•tum n. (pl. **-da•ta**) Philos. an element of experience received through the senses.

sense•less /sénslis/ adj. 1 unconscious. 2 wildly foolish. 3 without meaning or purpose. 4 incapable of sensation. □□ **sense•less•ly** adv. **sense•less•ness** n.

sense of di•rec•tion n. the ability to know without guidance the direction in which one is or should be moving.

sense of hu•mor n. see HUMOR.

sense or•gan n. a bodily organ conveying external stimuli to the sensory system.

sen•si•bil•i•ty /sénsibílitee/ n. (pl. **•ties**) 1 capacity to feel (little finger lost its sensibility). 2 a openness to emotional impressions; susceptibility; sensitiveness (sensibility to kindness). b an exceptional or excessive degree of this (sense and sensibility). 3 (in pl.) emotional capacities or feelings. [ME f. LL sensibilitas (as SENSIBLE)]

sen•si•ble /sénsibəl/ adj. 1 having or showing wisdom or common sense; reasonable; judicious (a sensible person; a sensible compromise).

SYNONYM TIP sensible

LUCID, RATIONAL, SAGACIOUS, SANE. A **sensible** person brings an umbrella when rain is forecast. A **rational** one studies the weather map, observes the movement of the clouds across the sky, lis-

sky, listens to the forecast on the radio, and then decides whether or not an umbrella is necessary. *Sensible* implies the use of common sense and an appreciation of the value of experience (*a sensible decision not to travel until his injuries had healed*), while *rational* suggests the ability to reason logically and to draw conclusions from inferences (*a rational explanation for why she failed the exam*). **Lucid** and **sane**, like *rational*, are associated with coherent thinking. *Lucid* suggests a mind free of internal pressures or distortions (*lucid intervals during which he was able to recognize his wife and children*), while *sane* indicates freedom from psychosis or mental derangement (*judged to have been sane when she committed the crime*). *Sane* also has a meaning very close to that of *sensible* (*a sane approach to disciplining problem teenagers*). A **sagacious** person is an extremely shrewd one who is both discerning and practical. He or she can look out the window and tell whether it's going to rain just by studying the facial expressions of passersby as they glance nervously at the sky.

2 a perceptible by the senses (*sensible phenomena*). **b** great enough to be perceived; appreciable (*a sensible difference*). **3** (of clothing, etc.) practical and functional. **4** (foll. by *of*) aware; not unmindful (*was sensible of his peril*). □□ **sen·si·ble·ness** *n.* **sen·si·bly** *adv.* [ME f. OF *sensible* or L *sensibilis* (as SENSE)]

sen·si·ble ho·ri·zon *n.* see HORIZON 1b.

sen·si·tive /sénsitiv/ *adj. & n.* • *adj.* **1** (often foll. by *to*) very open to or acutely affected by external stimuli or mental impressions; having sensibility. **2** (of a person) easily offended or emotionally hurt. **3** (often foll. by *to*) (of an instrument, etc.) responsive to or recording slight changes. **4** (often foll. by *to*) **a** (of photographic materials) prepared so as to respond (esp. rapidly) to the action of light. **b** (of any material) readily affected by or responsive to external action. **5** (of a topic, etc.) subject to restriction of discussion to prevent embarrassment, ensure security, etc. **6** (of a market) liable to quick changes of price. • *n.* a person who is sensitive (esp. to supposed occult influences). □□ **sen·si·tive·ly** *adv.* **sen·si·tive·ness** *n.* [ME, = sensory, f. OF *sensitif –ive* or med.L *sensitivus*, irreg. f. L *sentire sens-* feel]

sen·si·tive plant *n.* **1** a plant whose leaves curve downward and leaflets fold together when touched, esp. mimosa. **2** a sensitive person.

sen·si·tiv·i·ty /sénsitívitee/ *n.* the quality or degree of being sensitive.

sen·si·tize /sénsitīz/ *v.tr.* **1** make sensitive. **2** *Photog.* make sensitive to light. **3** make (an organism, etc.) abnormally sensitive to a foreign substance. □□ **sen·si·ti·za·tion** *n.* **sen·si·tiz·er** *n.*

sen·si·tom·e·ter /sénsitómitər/ *n. Photog.* a device for measuring sensitivity to light.

sen·sor /sénsər/ *n.* a device giving a signal for the detection or measurement of a physical property to which it responds. [SENSORY, after MOTOR]

sen·so·ri·um /sensáwreeəm/ *n.* (*pl.* **sen·so·ri·a** /–reeə/ or **sen·so·ri·ums**) **1** the seat of sensation, the brain, brain and spinal cord, or gray matter of these. **2** *Biol.* the whole sensory apparatus including the nerve system. □□ **sen·so·ri·al** *adj.* **sen·so·ri·al·ly** *adv.* [LL f. L *sentire sens-* feel]

sen·so·ry /sénsəree/ *adj.* of sensation or the senses. □□ **sen·so·ri·ly** *adv.* [as SENSORIUM]

sen·su·al /sénshōōəl/ *adj.* **1 a** of or depending on the senses only and not on the intellect or spirit; carnal; fleshly (*sensual pleasures*). **b** given to the pursuit of sensual pleasures or the gratification of the appetites; self-indulgent sexually or in regard to food and drink; voluptuous; licentious. **c** indicative of a sensual nature (*sensual lips*). **2** of sense or sensation; sensory. **3** *Philos.* of, according to, or holding the doctrine of, sensationalism. □□ **sen·su·al·ism** *n.* **sen·su·al·ist** *n.* **sen·su·al·ize** *v.tr.* **sen·su·al·ly** *adv.* [ME f. LL *sensualis* (as SENSE)]

sen·su·al·i·ty /sénshōō-álitee/ *n.* gratification of the senses, self-indulgence. [ME f. F *sensualité* f. LL *sensualitas* (as SENSUAL)]

sen·sum /sénsəm/ *n.* (*pl.* **sen·sa** /–sə/) *Philos.* a sense-datum. [mod.L, neut. past part. of L *sentire* feel]

sen·su·ous /sénshōōəs/ *adj.* **1** of or derived from or affecting the senses, esp. aesthetically rather than sensually; aesthetically pleasing. **2** readily affected by the senses. □□ **sen·su·ous·ly** *adv.* **sen·su·ous·ness** *n.* [L *sensus* sense]

sent *past* and *past part.* of SEND.

sen·tence /s éntəns/ *n. & v.* • *n.* **1 a** a set of words complete in itself as the expression of a thought, containing or implying a subject and predicate, and conveying a statement, question, exclamation, or command. **b** a piece of writing or speech between two full stops or equivalent pauses, often including several grammatical sentences (*e.g., I went; he came*). **2 a** the decision of a court of law, esp. the punishment allotted to a person convicted in a criminal trial. **b** the declaration of this. **3** *Logic* a series of signs or symbols expressing a proposition in an artificial or logical language. • *v.tr.* **1** declare the sentence of (a convicted criminal, etc.). **2** (foll. by

to) declare (such a person) to be condemned to a specified punishment. □ **under sentence of** having been condemned to (*under sentence of death*). [ME f. OF f. L *sententia* opinion f. *sentire* be of opinion]

GRAMMAR TIP sentence

Parts of a Sentence. Every sentence has two basic parts: the **subject** and the **predicate**. The **subject** is a noun, a pronoun, or a phrase used as a noun. It tells who or what the sentence is about. In the sentence *The company president issued a formal apology for the defective product*, the **complete subject** is *the company president*; *president* is the **simple subject**. The **predicate** tells what the subject does or is. In the sentence above, the **complete predicate** is *issued a formal apology for the defective product*. The **simple predicate** is the verb *issued*.

GRAMMAR TIP sentence

Types of Sentences. Sentences are classified according to their function. **Declarative sentences** make a statement (*Monday is a holiday*) and end with a period. **Interrogative sentences** ask a question (*do we have to work on Monday?*) and end with a question mark. **Imperative sentences** make a request (*please arrive at work on time*) or give a command (*be at work on Monday or lose a day's pay*). **Exclamatory sentences** express strong feelings or emotions (*Hooray! A holiday for everyone!*) and end with an exclamation point. Many exclamatory sentences are simply declarative sentences that are stated with emphasis.

sen·ten·tial /sénténshəl/ *adj. Gram. & Logic* of a sentence. [L *sententialis* (as SENTENCE)]

sen·ten·tious /sénténshəs/ *adj.* **1** (of a person) fond of pompous moralizing. **2** (of a style) affectedly formal. **3** aphoristic; pithy; given to the use of maxims, affecting a concise impressive style. □□ **sen·ten·tious·ly** *adv.* **sen·ten·tious·ness** *n.* [L *sententiosus* (as SENTENCE)]

sen·tient /sénshənt/ *adj.* having the power of perception by the senses. □□ **sen·tience** *n.* **sen·tien·cy** *n.* **sen·tient·ly** *adv.* [L *sentire* feel]

sen·ti·ment /séntimənt/ *n.* **1** a mental feeling (*the sentiment of pity*). **2 a** the sum of what one feels on some subject. **b** a verbal expression of this. **3** the expression of a view or desire esp. as formulated for a toast (*concluded his speech with a sentiment*). **4** an opinion

---

SYNONYM TIP sentimental

EFFUSIVE, MAUDLIN, MAWKISH, MUSHY, ROMANTIC. If you are moved to tears by a situation that does not really warrant such a response, you're likely to be called **sentimental**, an adjective used to describe a willingness to get emotional at the slightest prompting and often refers to emotion that does not arise from genuine feeling (*a sentimental man who kept his dog's ashes in an urn on the mantel*). **Effusive** also applies to excessive or insincere displays of emotion, although it may be used in an approving sense (*effusive in her gratitude for the help she had received*). **Maudlin** derives from the name Mary Magdalene, who was often shown with her eyes swollen from weeping. It implies a lack of self-restraint, particularly in the form of excessive tearfulness. **Mawkish** carries sentimentality a step further, implying emotion so excessive that it provokes loathing or disgust (*mawkish attempts to win the audience over*). Although **romantic** at one time referred to an expression of deep feeling, nowadays it is often used disapprovingly to describe emotion that has little to do with the way things actually are and that is linked to an idealized vision of the way they should be (*she had a romantic notion of what it meant to be a "starving artist"*). **Mushy** suggests both excessive emotion or sentimentality and a contempt for romantic love (*a mushy love story*).

SYNONYM TIP sensuous

EPICUREAN, LUXURIOUS, SENSUAL, SYBARITIC, VOLUPTUOUS. **Sensuous** and **sensual** are often confused. *Sensuous* implies gratification of the senses for the sake of aesthetic pleasure or delight in the color, sound, or form of something (*a dress made from a soft, sensuous fabric*), while *sensual* implies gratification of the senses or indulgence of the appetites as an end in itself (*to lead a life of sensual excess*). **Luxurious** implies indulgence in sensuous or sensual pleasures, especially those that induce a feeling of physical comfort or satisfaction (*a luxurious satin coverlet*), while **epicurean** refers to taking delight in the pleasures of eating and drinking (*the epicurean life of a king and his courtiers*). To be **voluptuous** is to give oneself up to the pleasures of the senses, but it carries a suggestion of sensual rather than sensuous enjoyment (*the voluptuous sensation of having her back massaged*), while **sybaritic** means voluptuous to the point of being overrefined. *Sybaritic* also suggests indulgence in good food and drink, surrounded by things designed to soothe and charm the senses (*he lived alone, in sybaritic splendor*).

as distinguished from the words meant to convey it (*the sentiment is good though the words are injudicious*). **5** a view or tendency based on or colored with emotion (*animated by noble sentiments*). **6** such views collectively, esp. as an influence (*sentiment unchecked by reason is a bad guide*). **7** the tendency to be swayed by feeling rather than by reason. **8 a** mawkish tenderness. **b** the display of this. **9** an emotional feeling conveyed in literature or art. [ME f. OF *sentement* f. med.L *sentimentum* f. L *sentire* feel]

sen·ti·men·tal /séntimént'l/ *adj.* **1** of or characterized by sentiment. **2** showing or affected by emotion rather than reason. **3** appealing to sentiment. □□ **sen·ti·men·tal·ism** *n.* **sen·ti·men·tal·ist** *n.* **sen·ti·men·tal·i·ty** /–tálitee/ *n.* **sen·ti·men·tal·ize** *v.intr. & tr.* **sen·ti·men·tal·i·za·tion** *n.* **sen·ti·men·tal·ly** *adv.*

sen·ti·men·tal val·ue *n.* the value of a thing to a particular person because of its associations.

sen·ti·nel /séntinəl/ *n. & v. • n.* a sentry or lookout. *• v.tr.* (**sen·ti·neled, sen·ti·nel·ing**) **1** station sentinels at or in. **2** *poet.* keep guard over or in. [F *sentinelle* f. It. *sentinella*, of unkn. orig.]

sen·try /séntree/ *n.* (*pl.* **-tries**) a soldier, etc., stationed to keep guard. [perh. f. obs. *centrinel*, var. of SENTINEL]

sen·try box *n.* a wooden cabin intended to shelter a standing sentry.

se·pal /seepəl/ *n. Bot.* each of the divisions or leaves of the calyx. [F *sépale*, mod.L *sepalum*, perh. formed as SEPARATE + PETAL]

sep·a·ra·ble /sépərəbəl/ *adj.* **1** able to be separated. **2** *Gram.* (of a prefix, or a verb in respect of a prefix) written as a separate word in some collocations. □□ **sep·a·ra·bil·i·ty** *n.* **sep·a·ra·ble·ness** *n.* **sep·a·ra·bly** *adv.* [F *séparable* or L *separabilis* (as SEPARATE)]

sep·a·rate *adj., n., & v. • adj.* /sépərət, s éprət/ (often foll. by *from*) forming a unit that is or may be regarded as apart or by itself; physically disconnected, distinct, or individual (*living in separate rooms; the two questions are essentially separate*). *• n.* / sépərət, sépr ət/ **1** (in *pl.*) separate articles of clothing suitable for wearing together in various combinations. **2** an offprint. *• v.* /sép ərayt/ **1** *tr.* make separate; sever; disunite. **2** *tr.* prevent union or contact of. **3** *intr.* go different ways; disperse. **4** *intr.* cease to live together as a married couple. **5** *intr.* (foll. by *from*) secede. **6** *tr.* **a** divide or sort (milk, ore, fruit, light, etc.) into constituent parts or sizes. **b** (often foll. by *out*) extract or remove (an ingredient, waste product, etc.) by such a process for use or rejection. **7** *tr.* discharge or dismiss, esp. from an armed service, etc. □□ **sep·a·rate·ly** *adv.* **sep·a·rate·ness** *n.* **sep·a·ra·tive** /–rətiv/ *adj.* **sep·a·ra·to·ry** /–rətawree/ *adj.* [L *separare separat-* (as SE–, *parare* make ready)]

SPELLING TIP separate

To spell *separate* with the correct vowels, use the mnemonic: "There is *a rat* in sep*a*rate."

---

sep·a·ra·tion /sépəráyshən/ *n.* **1** the act or an instance of separating; the state of being separated. **2** (in full **judicial separation** or **legal separation**) an arrangement by which a husband and wife remain married but live apart. **3** any of three or more monochrome reproductions of a colored picture that can combine to reproduce the full color of the original. [ME f. OF f. L *separatio –onis* (as SEPARATE)]

sep·a·ra·tion or·der *n.* a court order for judicial separation.

sep·a·ra·tist /sépərətist, séprə–/ *n.* a person who favors separation, esp. for political or ecclesiastical independence (opp. UNIONIST 2). □□ **sep·a·ra·tism** *n.*

sep·a·ra·tor /sépəraytər/ *n.* a machine for separating, e.g., cream from milk.

Se·phar·di /sifaárdee/ *n.* (*pl.* **Se·phar·dim** /–dim/) a Jew of Spanish or Portuguese descent (cf. ASHKENAZI). □□ **Se·phar·dic** *adj.* [LHeb., f. s*ə*p*ā* ra*d*, a country mentioned in Obad. 20 and taken to be Spain]

se·pi·a /seepeeə/ *n.* **1** a dark reddish-brown color. **2 a** a brown pigment prepared from a black fluid secreted by cuttlefish, used in monochrome drawing and in watercolors. **b** a brown tint used in photography. **3** a drawing done in sepia. **4** the fluid secreted by cuttlefish. [L f. Gk *sēpia* cuttlefish]

se·poy /seepoy/ *n. hist.* a native Indian soldier under European, esp. British, discipline. [Urdu & Pers. *sipāhī* soldier f. *sipāh* army]

sep·pu·ku /sépŏokŏo, sepŏok–/ *n.* hara-kiri. [Jap.]

sep·sis /sépsis/ *n.* **1** the state of being septic. **2** blood poisoning. [mod.L f. Gk *sēpsis* f. *sēpō* make rotten]

Sept. *abbr.* **1** September. **2** Septuagint.

sept /sept/ *n.* a clan, esp. in Ireland. [prob. alt. of SECT]

sept- var. of SEPTI–.

sep·ta *pl.* of SEPTUM.

sep·tal[1] /séptəl/ *adj.* **1** of a septum or septa. **2** *Archaeol.* (of a stone or slab) separating compartments in a burial chamber. [SEPTUM]

sep·tal[2] /séptəl/ *adj.* of a sept or septs.

sep·tate /séptayt/ *adj. Bot., Zool., & Anat.* having a septum or septa; partitioned. □□ **sep·ta·tion** /–táyshən/ *n.*

sept·cen·ten·a·ry /séptsenténəree/ *n. & adj. • n.* (*pl.* **-ies**) **1** a seven-hundredth anniversary. **2** a festival marking this. *• adj.* of or concerning a septcentenary.

Sep·tem·ber /septémbər/ *n.* the ninth month of the year. [ME f. L *September* f. *septem* seven: orig. the seventh month of the Roman year]

sep·te·nar·i·us /séptináreeəs/ *n.* (*pl.* **sep·te·nar·i·i** /–ree-i/) *Prosody* a verse of seven feet, esp. a trochaic or iambic tetrameter catalectic. [L f. *septeni* distributive of *septem* seven]

sep·te·nar·y /séptəneree/ *adj. & n. • adj.* of seven, by sevens, on the basis of seven. *• n.* (*pl.* **-ies**) **1** a group or set of seven (esp. years). **2** a septenarius. [L *septenarius* (as SEPTENARIUS)]

sep·te·nate /séptinayt/ *adj. Bot.* **1** growing in sevens. **2** having seven divisions. [L *septeni* (as SEPTENARIUS)]

sep·ten·ni·al /septéneeəl/ *adj.* **1** lasting for seven years. **2** recurring every seven years. [LL *septennis* f. L *septem* seven + *annus* year]

sep·ten·ni·um /septéneeəm/ *n.* (*pl.* **sep·ten·ni·ums** or **sep·ten·ni·a** /–neeə/) a period of seven years.

sep·tet /séptét/ *n.* (also **sep·tette**) **1** *Mus.* **a** a composition for seven performers. **b** the performers of such a composition. **2** any group of seven. [G *Septett* f. L *septem* seven]

sept·foil /sétfoyl/ *n.* **1** a seven-lobed ornamental figure. **2** *archaic* tormentil. [LL *septifolium* after CINQUEFOIL, TREFOIL]

septi- /séptee/ *comb. form* (also **sept-** before a vowel) seven. [L f. *septem* seven]

sep·tic /séptik/ *adj.* contaminated with bacteria from a festering wound, etc.; putrefying. □□ **sep·ti·cal·ly** *adv.* **sep·tic·i·ty** /–tísitee/ *n.* [L *septicus* f. Gk *sēptikos* f. *sēpō* make rotten]

sep·ti·ce·mi·a /séptiseemeeə/ *n.* blood poisoning. □□ **sep·ti·ce·mic** *adj.* [mod.L f. Gk *sē ptikos* + *haima* blood]

sep·tic tank *n.* a tank in which the organic matter in sewage is disintegrated through bacterial activity.

sep·til·lion /septilyən/ *n.* (*pl.* same) a thousand raised to the eighth (or formerly, esp. *Brit.*, the fourteenth) power (10^{24} and 10^{42}, respectively). [F f. *sept* seven, after *billion*, etc.]

sep·ti·mal /séptiməl/ *adj.* of the number seven. [L *septimus* seventh f. *septem* seven]

sep·time /sépteem/ *n. Fencing* the seventh of the eight parrying positions. [L *septimus* (as SEPTIMAL)]

sep·ti·va·lent /septiváylənt/ *adj.* (also **sep·ta·va·lent**) *Chem.* having a valence of seven.

sep·tu·a·ge·nar·i·an /sépchŏoəjináireeən, –tŏo–, –tyŏo–/ *n. & adj. • n.* a person from 70 to 79 years old. *• adj.* of this age. [L *septuagenarius* f. *septuageni* distributive of *septuaginta* seventy]

Sep·tu·a·ges·i·ma /séptŏoəjésimə, –chŏo–, –tyŏo–/ *n.* (in full **Septuagesima Sunday**) the Sunday before Sexagesima. [ME f. L, = seventieth (day), formed as SEPTUAGINT, perh. after QUINQUAGESIMA or with ref. to the period of 70 days from Septuagesima to the Saturday after Easter]

Sep·tu·a·gint /séptŏoəjint, –tyŏo–/ *n.* a Greek version of the Old Testament including the Apocrypha, said to have been made about 270 BC by seventy-two translators. [L *septuaginta* seventy]

sep·tum /séptəm/ *n.* (*pl.* **sep·ta** /–tə/) *Anat., Bot., & Zool.* a partition such as that between the nostrils or the chambers of a poppy fruit or of a shell. [L *s(a)eptum* f. *saepire saept-* enclose f. *saepes* hedge]

sep·tu·ple /septŏoəpəl, –tyŏo–, –túpəl, séptŏoəpəl/ *adj., n., & v. • adj.* **1** sevenfold, having seven parts. **2** being seven times as many or as much. *• n.* a sevenfold number or amount. *• v.tr. & intr.* multiply by seven. [LL *septuplus* f. L *septem* seven]

sep·tup·let /septúplit, –tŏo–, –tyŏo–/ *n.* **1** one of seven children born at one birth. **2** *Mus.* a group of seven notes to be played in the time of four or six. [as SEPTUPLE, after TRIPLET, etc.]

se·pul·chral /sipúlkrəl/ *adj.* **1** of a tomb or interment (*sepulchral mound; sepulchral customs*). **2** suggestive of the tomb; funereal; gloomy; dismal (*sepulchral look*). □□ **se·pul·chral·ly** *adv.* [F *sépulchral* or L *sepulchralis* (as SEPULCHER)]

sep·ul·cher /sépəlkər/ *n. & v.* (also **sep·ul·chre**) *• n.* a tomb esp. cut in rock or built of stone or brick, a burial vault or cave. *• v.tr.* **1** lay in a sepulcher. **2** serve as a sepulcher for. [ME f. OF f. L *sepulc(h)rum* f. *sepelire sepult-* bury]

sep·ul·ture /sépəlchər/ *n. literary* the act or an instance of burying or putting in the grave. [ME f. OF f. L *sepultura* (as SEPULCHER)]

seq. *abbr.* (*pl.* **seqq.**) the following. [L *sequens*, etc.]

se·qua·cious /sikwáyshəs/ *adj.* **1** (of reasoning or a reasoner) not inconsequent; coherent. **2** *archaic* inclined to follow; lacking independence or originality; servile. □□ **se·qua·cious·ly** *adv.* **se·quac·i·ty** /sikwásitee/ *n.* [L *sequax* f. *sequi* follow]

se·quel /seekwəl/ *n.* **1** what follows (esp. as a result). **2** a novel, motion picture, etc., that continues the story of an earlier one. □ **in the sequel** *Brit.* as things developed afterward. [ME f. OF *sequelle* or L *sequel(l)a* f. *sequi* follow]

se·que·la /sikwéelə/ *n.* (*pl.* **se·que·lae** /–ee/) *Med.* (esp. in *pl.*) a morbid condition or symptom following a disease. [L f. *sequi* follow]

se·quence /seekwəns/ *n. & v. • n.* **1** succession; coming after or next.

2 order of succession (*shall follow the sequence of events; give the facts in historical sequence*). **3** a set of things belonging next to one another on some principle of order; a series without gaps. **4** a part of a motion picture, etc., dealing with one scene or topic. **5** a set of poems on one theme. **6** a set of three or more playing cards next to one another in value. **7** *Mus.* repetition of a phrase or melody at a higher or lower pitch. **8** *Eccl.* a hymn said or sung after the gradual or alleluia that precedes the gospel. **9** succession without implication of causality (opp. CONSEQUENCE). ● *v.tr.* **1** arrange in a definite order. **2** *Biochem.* ascertain the sequence of monomers in (esp. a polypeptide or nucleic acid). [ME f. LL *sequentia* f. L *sequens* pres. part. of *sequi* follow]

se•quence of tens•es *n. Gram.* the dependence of the tense of a subordinate verb on the tense of the principal verb, according to certain rules (e.g., *I think you* are, *thought you* were, *wrong*).

se•quenc•er /seékwɒnsər/ *n.* a programmable device for storing sequences of musical notes, chords, etc., and transmitting them when required to an electronic musical instrument.

se•quent /seékwənt/ *adj.* **1** following as a sequence or consequence. **2** consecutive. □□ **se•quent•ly** *adv.* [OF *sequent* or L *sequens* (as SEQUENCE)]

se•quen•tial /sikwénshəl/ *adj.* forming a sequence or consequence or sequela. □□ **se•quen•ti•al•i•ty** /–sheeálitee/ *n.* **se•quen•tial•ly** *adv.* [SEQUENCE, after CONSEQUENTIAL]

se•ques•ter /sikwéstər/ *v.tr.* **1** (esp. as **sequestered** *adj.*) seclude; isolate; set apart (*sequester oneself from the world; a sequestered life; a sequestered jury*). **2** = SEQUESTRATE. **3** *Chem.* bind (a metal ion) so that it cannot react. [ME f. OF *sequestrer* or LL *sequestrare* commit for safe keeping f. L *sequester* trustee]

se•ques•trate /sikwéstrayt/ *v.tr.* **1** confiscate; appropriate. **2** *Law* take temporary possession of (a debtor's estate, etc.). **3** *Eccl.* apply (the income of a benefice) to clearing the incumbent's debts or accumulating a fund for the next incumbent. □□ **se•ques•tra•ble** /–trəbəl/ *adj.* **se•ques•tra•tion** /seékwistráyshən/ *n.* **se•ques•tra•tor** /seékwistraytər/ *n.* [LL *sequestrare* (as SEQUESTER)]

se•ques•trum /sikwéstrəm/ *n.* (*pl.* **se•ques•tra** /–trə/) a piece of dead bone or other tissue detached from the surrounding parts. □□ **se•ques•tral** *adj.* [mod.L, neut. of L *sequester* standing apart]

se•quin /seékwin/ *n.* **1** a circular spangle for attaching to clothing as an ornament. **2** *hist.* a Venetian gold coin. □□ **se•quined** *adj.* (also **se•quinned**). [F f. It. *zecchino* f. *zecca* a mint f. Arab. *sikka* a die]

se•quoi•a /sikwóyə/ *n.* a Californian evergreen coniferous tree, *Sequoia sempervirens*, of very great height. [mod.L genus name, f. *Sequoiah*, the name of a Cherokee]

se•ra *pl.* of SERUM.

se•rac /serák/ *n.* one of the tower-shaped masses into which a glacier is divided at steep points by crevasses crossing it. [Swiss F *sérac*, orig. the name of a compact white cheese]

se•ragl•io /sərályō, raál–/ *n.* (*pl.* **•ios**) **1** a harem. **2** *hist.* a Turkish palace, esp. that of the sultan with government offices, etc., at Constantinople. [It. *serraglio* f. Turk. f. Pers. *sarāy* palace: cf. SERAI]

se•ra•i /serí/ *n.* a caravansary. [Turk. f. Pers. (as SERAGLIO)]

se•ra•pe /səráapee/ *n.* (also **sa•ra•pe** /sa–/, **za•ra•pe** /za–/) a shawl or blanket worn as a cloak by Spanish Americans. [Mexican Sp.]

ser•aph /sérəf/ *n.* (*pl.* **ser•a•phim** /–fim/ or **ser•aphs**) an angelic being, one of the highest order of the ninefold celestial hierarchy gifted esp. with love and associated with light, ardor, and purity. [back-form. f. *seraphim* (cf. CHERUB) (pl.) f. LL f. Gk *seraphim* f. Heb. *śᵉrāpīm*]

se•raph•ic /səráfik/ *adj.* **1** of or like the seraphim. **2** ecstatically adoring, fervent, or serene. □□ **se•raph•i•cal•ly** *adv.* [med.L *seraphicus* f. LL (as SERAPH)]

Serb /sərb/ *n. & adj.* ● *n.* **1** a native of Serbia in the former Yugoslavia. **2** a person of Serbian descent. ● *adj.* = SERBIAN. [Serbian *Srb*]

Ser•bi•an /sórbeeən/ *n. & adj.* ● *n.* **1** the dialect of the Serbs (cf. SERBO-CROAT). **2** = SERB. ● *adj.* of or relating to the Serbs or their dialect.

Serbo- /sórbō/ *comb. form* Serbian.

Ser•bo-Cro•at /sórbōkrṓat/ *n. & adj.* (also **Ser•bo-Cro•a•tian** /–krō-áyshən/) ● *n.* the main official language of the former Yugoslavia, combining Serbian and Croatian dialects. ● *adj.* of or relating to this language.

sere[1] /seer/ *n.* a catch of a gunlock holding the hammer at half or full cock. [prob. f. OF *serre* lock, bolt, grasp, f. *serrer* (see SERRIED)]

sere[2] /seer/ *adj.* (also **sear**) *literary* (esp. of a plant, etc.) withered; dried up. [see SEAR]

sere[3] /seer/ *n. Ecol.* a sequence of animal or plant communities. [L *serere* join in a SERIES]

se•rein /sərán/ *n.* a fine rain falling in tropical climates from a cloudless sky. [F f. OF *serain* ult. f. L *serum* evening f. *serus* late]

ser•e•nade /sérənáyd/ *n. & v.* ● *n.* **1** a piece of music sung or played at night, esp. by a lover under his lady's window, or suitable for this. **2** = SERENATA. ● *v.tr.* sing or play a serenade to. □□ **ser•e•nad•er** *n.* [F *sérénade* f. It. *serenata* f. *sereno* SERENE]

ser•e•na•ta /sérənáatə/ *n. Mus.* **1** a cantata with a pastoral subject. **2** a simple form of suite for orchestra or wind band. [It. (as SERENADE)]

ser•en•dip•i•ty /sérəndípitee/ *n.* the faculty of making happy and unexpected discoveries by accident. □□ **ser•en•dip•i•tous** *adj.* **ser•en•dip•i•tous•ly** *adv.* [coined by Horace Walpole (1754) after *The Three Princes of Serendip* (Sri Lanka), a fairy tale]

se•rene /sireén/ *adj. & n.* ● *adj.* (**se•ren•er**, **se•ren•est**) **1 a** (of the sky, the air, etc.) clear and calm. **b** (of the sea, etc.) unruffled. **2** placid; tranquil; unperturbed. ● *n. poet.* a serene expanse of sky, sea, etc. □ **all serene** *Brit. sl.* all right. □□ **se•rene•ly** *adv.* **se•rene•ness** *n.* [L *serenus*]

Se•rene High•ness *n.* a title used in addressing and referring to members of some European royal families (*His Serene Highness; Their Serene Highnesses; Your Serene Highness*).

se•ren•i•ty /sirénitee/ *n.* (*pl.* **•ties**) **1** tranquillity; being serene. **2** (**Se•renity**) a title used in addressing and referring to a reigning prince or similar dignitary (*your Serenity*). [F *sérénité* or L *serenitas* (as SERENE)]

serf /sərf/ *n.* **1** *hist.* a laborer not allowed to leave the land on which he worked; a villein. **2** an oppressed person; a drudge. □□ **serf•age** *n.* **serf•dom** *n.* **serf•hood** *n.* [OF f. L *servus* slave]

serge /sərj/ *n.* a durable twilled worsted, etc., fabric. [ME f. OF *sarge*, *serge* ult. f. L *serica* (*lana*): see SILK]

ser•geant /saárjənt/ *n.* **1** a noncommissioned army, marine, or air force officer next below warrant officer. **2** a police officer ranking below captain. □□ **ser•gean•cy** *n.* (*pl.* **•cies**). **ser•geant•ship** *n.* [ME f. OF *sergent* f. L *serviens –entis* servant f. *servire* SERVE]

ser•geant-at-arms *n.* (*pl.* **ser•geants-at-arms**) an official of a court or city or legislature, with ceremonial duties.

Ser•geant Ba•ker *n. Austral.* a large brightly colored marine fish, *Aulopus purpurissatus*.

ser•geant fish *n.* a marine fish, *Rachycentron canadum*, with lateral stripes suggesting a chevron.

ser•geant ma•jor *n.* **1** *Mil.* the highest-ranking noncommissioned officer. **2** a black-striped damselfish of the tropical western Atlantic.

sergt. *abbr.* sergeant.

se•ri•al /seéreeəl/ *n. & adj.* ● *n.* **1** a story, play, motion picture, etc., that is published, broadcast, or shown in regular installments. **2** a periodical. ● *adj.* **1** of or in or forming a series. **2** (of a story, etc.) in the form of a serial. **3** *Mus.* using transformations of a fixed series of notes (see SERIES). **4** (of a publication) appearing in successive parts published usu. at regular intervals; periodical. □□ **se•ri•al•i•ty** /–reeálitee/ *n.* **se•ri•al•ly** *adv.* [SERIES + –AL]

se•ri•al•ist /seéreeəlist/ *n.* a composer or advocate of serial music. □□ **se•ri•al•ism** *n.*

se•ri•al•ize /seéreeəlīz/ *v.tr.* **1** publish or produce in installments. **2** arrange in a series. **3** *Mus.* compose according to a serial technique. □□ **se•ri•al•i•za•tion** *n.*

se•ri•al kill•er *n.* a person who murders continually with no apparent motive.

se•ri•al num•ber *n.* a number showing the position of an item in a series.

se•ri•al rights *n.pl.* the right to publish a story or book as a serial.

se•ri•ate *adj. & v.* ● *adj.* /seéreeət/ in the form of a series; in orderly sequence. ● *v.tr.* /seéreeayt/ arrange in a seriate manner. □□ **se•ri•a•tion** /–reeáyshən/ *n.*

se•ri•a•tim /seéree-áytim, sér-/ *adv.* point by point; taking one subject, etc., after another in regular order (*consider seriatim*). [med.L f. L *series*, after LITERATIM, etc.]

Se•ric /seérik/ *adj. archaic* Chinese. [L *sericus*; see SILK]

se•ri•ceous /siríshəs/ *adj. Bot. & Zool.* covered with silky hairs. [LL *sericeus* silken]

ser•i•cul•ture /sérikulchər/ *n.* **1** silkworm breeding. **2** the production of raw silk. □□ **ser•i•cul•tur•al** *adj.* **ser•i•cul•tur•ist** *n.* [F *sériciculture* f. LL *sericum*: see SILK, CULTURE]

ser•i•e•ma /séree-eémə/ *n.* (also **car•i•am•a** /káreeáamə/) *Zool.* any S. American bird of the family Cariamidae, having a long neck and legs and a crest above the bill. [mod.L f. Tupi *siriema*, etc., crested]

se•ries /seéreez/ *n.* (*pl.* same) **1** a number of things of which each is similar to the preceding or in which each successive pair are similarly related; a sequence, succession, order, row, or set. **2** a set of successive games between the same teams. **3** a set of programs with the same actors, etc., or on related subjects but each complete in itself. **4** a set of lectures by the same speaker or on the same subject. **5 a** a set of successive issues of a periodical, of articles on one subject or by one writer, etc., esp. when numbered separately from a preceding or following set (*second series*). **b** a set of independent books in a common format or under a common title or supervised by a common general editor. **6** *Philately* a set of stamps, coins, etc., of different denominations but issued at one time, in one reign, etc. **7** *Geol.* **a** a set of strata with a common characteristic. **b** the rocks deposited during a specific epoch. **8** *Mus.* = TONE ROW. **9** *Electr.* **a** a set of circuits or components arranged so that the current passes through each successively. **b** a set of batteries, etc., having the positive electrode of each connected with the negative electrode of the next. **10** *Chem.* a set of elements with common properties or of compounds related in composition or structure. **11** *Math.* a set of quantities constituting a progression or having the several values determined by a common relation. □ **in series 1** in ordered succession. **2** *Electr.* (of a set of circuits or components) arranged so that the current passes through each successively. [L, = row, chain f. *serere* join, connect]

ser·if /sérif/ *n.* a slight projection finishing off a stroke of a letter as in T contrasted with T (cf. SANS SERIF). □□ **ser·iffed** *adj.* [perh. f. Du. *schreef* dash, line f. Gmc]

se·rig·ra·phy /sərígrəfee/ *n.* the art or process of printing designs by means of a silk screen. □□ **ser·i·graph** /sérigraf/ *n.* **se·rig·ra·pher** /sərígrəfər/ *n.* [irreg. f. L *sericum* SILK]

ser·in /sérin/ *n.* any small yellow Mediterranean finch of the genus *Serinus*, esp. the wild canary *S. serinus*. [F, of uncert. orig.]

se·rin·ga /sərínggə/ *n.* **1** = SYRINGA. **2** any of various rubber trees of the genus *Hevea*, native to Brazil. [F (as SYRINGA)]

se·ri·o·com·ic /séeree–ókómik/ *adj.* combining the serious and the comic; jocular in intention but simulating seriousness or vice versa. □□ **se·ri·o·com·i·cal·ly** *adv.*

se·ri·ous /séereeəs/ *adj.* **1** thoughtful; earnest; sober; sedate; responsible; not reckless nor given to trifling (*has a serious air, a serious young person*). **2** important, demanding consideration (*this is a serious matter*). **3** not slight or negligible (*a serious injury; a serious offense*). **4** sincere; in earnest; not ironic nor joking (*are you serious?*). **5** (of music and literature) not merely for amusement (opp. LIGHT² 5a). **6** not perfunctory (*serious thought*). **7** not to be trifled with (*a serious opponent*). **8** concerned with religion or ethics (*serious subjects*). □□ **se·ri·ous·ness** *n.* [ME f. OF *serieux* or LL *seriosus* f. L *serius*]

se·ri·ous·ly /séereeəslee/ *adv.* **1** in a serious manner (esp. introducing a sentence, implying that irony, etc., is now to cease). **2** to a serious extent. **3** *colloq.* (as an intensifier) very; really; substantially (*seriously rich*).

ser·jeant /sáarjənt/ *n.* *Brit.* (in full **serjeant-at-law,** *pl.* **ser·jeants-at-law**) *hist.* a barrister of the highest rank. [var. of SERGEANT]

ser·mon /sɔ́rmən/ *n.* **1** a spoken or written discourse on a religious or moral subject, esp. a discourse based on a text or passage of Scripture and delivered in a service by way of religious instruction or exhortation. **2** a piece of admonition or reproof; a lecture. **3** a moral reflection suggested by natural objects, etc. (*sermons in stones*). [ME f. AF *sermun*, OF *sermon* f. L *sermo –onis* discourse, talk]

ser·mon·ette /sɔ́rmənét/ *n.* a short sermon.

ser·mon·ize /sɔ́rmənīz/ *v.* **1** *tr.* deliver a moral lecture to. **2** *intr.* deliver a moral lecture. □□ **ser·mon·iz·er** *n.*

Ser·mon on the Mount *n.* the discourse of Christ recorded in Matt. 5–7.

se·rol·o·gy /seeróləjee/ *n.* the scientific study of blood sera and their effects. □□ **se·ro·log·i·cal** /–rəlójikəl/ *adj.* **se·rol·o·gist** *n.*

se·ro·sa /sərósə/ *n.* a serous membrane. [mod.L, fem. of med.L *serosus* SEROUS]

se·ro·tine /sérətin, –tīn/ *n.* a chestnut-colored European bat, *Eptesicus serotinus.* [F *sérotine* f. L *serotinus* late, of the evening, f. *serus* late]

ser·o·to·nin /sérətónin/ *n.* *Biol.* a compound present in blood serum, which constricts the blood vessels and acts as a neurotransmitter. [SERUM + TONIC + –IN]

se·rous /séerəs/ *adj.* of or like or producing serum; watery. □□ **se·ros·i·ty** /–rósitee/ *n.* [F *séreux* or med.L *serosus* (as SERUM)]

se·rous gland *n.* (also **se·rous mem·brane**) a gland or membrane with a serous secretion.

ser·pent /sɔ́rpənt/ *n.* **1** usu. *literary* **a** a snake, esp. of a large kind. **b** a scaly limbless reptile. **2** a sly or treacherous person, esp. one who exploits a position of trust to betray it. **3** *Mus.* an old bass wind instrument made from leather-covered wood, roughly in the form of an S. **4** (**the Serpent**) *Bibl.* Satan (see Gen. 3, Rev. 20). [ME f. OF f. L *serpens –entis* part. of *serpere* creep]

ser·pen·tine /sɔ́rpəntīn/ *adj., n.,* & *v.* ● *adj.* **1** of or like a serpent. **2** coiling; tortuous; sinuous; meandering; writhing (*the serpentine windings of the stream*). **3** cunning; subtle; treacherous. ● *n.* **1** a soft rock mainly of hydrated magnesium silicate, usu. dark green and sometimes mottled or spotted like a serpent's skin, taking a high polish and used as a decorative material. **2** *Skating* a figure of three circles in a line. ● *v.intr.* move sinuously; meander. [ME f. OF *serpentin* f. LL *serpentinus* (as SERPENT)]

ser·pen·tine verse *n.* a metrical line beginning and ending with the same word

ser·pig·i·nous /sərpíjinəs/ *adj.* (of a skin disease, etc.) creeping from one part to another. [med.L *serpigo –ginis* ringworm f. L *serpere* creep]

ser·pu·la /sɔ́rpyələ/ *n.* (*pl.* **ser·pu·lae** /–lee/) any of various marine worms of the family Serpulidae, living in intricately twisted shell-like tubes. [LL, = small serpent, f. L *serpere* creep]

ser·ra /sérə/ *n.* (*pl.* **ser·rae** /–ree/) a serrated organ, structure, or edge. [L, = saw]

ser·ra·dil·la /sérədílə/ *n.* (*pl.* **ser·ra·dil·lae** /–lee/) a clover, *Ornithopus sativus,* grown as fodder. [Port., dimin. of *serrado* serrated]

ser·ran /sérən/ *n.* any marine fish of the family Serranidae. [mod.L *serranus* f. L *serra* saw]

ser·rate *v.* & *adj.* ● *v.tr.* /seráyt/ (usu. as **serrated** *adj.*) provide with a sawlike edge. ● *adj.* /sérayt/ esp. Anat., *Bot.,* & *Zool.* notched like a saw. □□ **ser·ra·tion** /–ráyshən/ *n.* [LL *serrare serrat–* f. L *serra* saw]

ser·ried /séreed/ *adj.* (of ranks of soldiers, rows of trees, etc.) pressed together; without gaps; close. [past part. of *serry* press close prob. f. F *serré* past part. of *serrer* close ult. f. L *sera* lock, or past part. of obs. *serr* f. OF *serrer*]

ser·ru·late /séryələt, –layt, sérə–/ *adj.* esp. Anat., *Bot.,* & *Zool.* finely serrate; with a series of small notches. □□ **ser·ru·la·tion** /–láyshən/ *n.* [mod.L *serrulatus* f. L *serrula* dimin. of *serra* saw]

se·rum /séerəm/ *n.* (*pl.* **se·ra** /–rə/ or **se·rums**) **1 a** an amber-colored liquid that separates from a clot when blood coagulates. **b** whey. **2** *Med.* blood serum (usu. from a nonhuman mammal) as an antitoxin or therapeutic agent, esp. in inoculation. **3** a watery fluid in animal bodies. [L, = whey]

se·rum sick·ness *n.* a reaction to an injection of serum, characterized by skin eruption, fever, etc.

ser·val /sɔ́rvəl/ *n.* a tawny, black-spotted, long-legged African feline, *Felis serval.* [F f. Port. *cerval* deerlike f. *cervo* deer f. L *cervus*]

serv·ant /sɔ́rvənt/ *n.* **1** a person who has undertaken (usu. in return for stipulated pay) to carry out the orders of an individual or corporate employer, esp. a person employed in a house on domestic duties or as a personal attendant. **2** a devoted follower; a person willing to serve another (*a servant of Jesus Christ*). □ **your humble servant** *archaic* a formula preceding a signature or expressing ironical courtesy. **your obedient servant** a formula preceding a signature, now used only in certain (esp. *Brit.*) formal letters. [ME f. OF (as SERVE)]

serve /sɔrv/ *v.* & *n.* ● *v.* **1** *tr.* do a service for (a person, community, etc.). **2** *tr.* (also *absol.*) be a servant to. **3** *intr.* carry out duties (*served on six committees*). **4** *intr.* **a** (foll. by *in*) be employed in (an organization, esp. the armed forces, or a place, esp. a foreign country) (*served in the air force*). **b** be a member of the armed forces. **5 a** *tr.* be useful or serviceable for; meet the needs of; do what is required for (*serve a purpose; one packet serves him for a week*). **b** *intr.* meet requirements; perform a function (*a sofa serving as a bed*). **c** *intr.* (foll. by *to* + infin.) avail; suffice (*his attempt served only to postpone the inevitable; it serves to show the folly of such action*). **d** *tr.* (of the memory) to prove reliable; to assist or prompt (*if memory serves*). **6** *tr.* go through a due period of (office, apprenticeship, a prison sentence, etc.). **7** *tr.* set out or present (food) for those about to eat it (*asparagus served with butter; dinner was then served*). **8** *intr.* act as a waiter. **9** *tr.* **a** attend to (a customer in a store). **b** (foll. by *with*) supply with (goods) (*was serving a customer with apples; served the town with gas*). **10** *tr.* treat or act toward (a person) in a specified way (*has served me shamefully; you may serve me as you will*). **11** *tr.* **a** (often foll. by *on*) deliver (a writ, etc.) to the person concerned in a legally formal manner (*served a warrant on him*). **b** (foll. by *with*) deliver a writ, etc., to (a person) in this way (*served her with a summons*). **12** *tr.* *Tennis*, etc. **a** (also *absol.*) deliver (a ball, etc.) to begin or resume play. **b** produce (a fault, etc.) by doing this. **13** *tr.* *Mil.* keep (a gun, battery, etc.) firing. **14** *tr.* (of an animal, esp. a stallion, etc., hired for the purpose) copulate with (a female). **15** *tr.* distribute (*served out the ammunition; served the rations around*). **16** *tr.* render obedience to (a deity, etc.). **17** *Eccl.* **a** *intr.* act as a server. **b** *tr.* act as a server at (a service). **18** *intr.* (of a tide) be suitable for a ship to leave harbor, etc. **19** *tr.* *Naut.* bind (a rope, etc.) with thin cord to strengthen it. **20** *tr.* *Brit.* play (a trick, etc.) on. ● *n.* **1** *Tennis,* etc. **a** the act or an instance of serving. **b** a manner of serving. **c** a person's turn to serve. **2** *Austral. sl.* a reprimand. □ **it will serve** it will be adequate. **serve one's needs** (or **need**) be adequate. **serve out** *Brit.* retaliate on. **serve the purpose of** take the place of; be used as. **serve a person right** be a person's deserved punishment or misfortune. **serve one's time 1** esp. *Brit.* hold office for the normal period. **2** (also **serve time**) undergo imprisonment, apprenticeship, etc. **serve one's** (or **the**) **turn** be adequate. **serve up** offer for acceptance. [ME f. OF *servir* f. L *servire* f. *servus* slave]

▶Use **service** when you're talking about things (*I have to get my car serviced tomorrow*). Use **serve** when you're talking about people (*they serve their customers well*).

serv·er /sɔ́rvər/ *n.* **1** a person who serves. **2** *Eccl.* a person assisting the celebrant at a service, esp. the Eucharist.

serv·er·y /sɔ́rvəree/ *n.* *Brit.* (*pl.* **·ies**) a room from which meals, etc., are served and in which utensils are kept.

serv·ice¹ /sɔ́rvis/ *n.* & *v.* ● *n.* **1** the act of helping or doing work for another or for a community, etc. **2** work done in this way. **3** assistance or benefit given to someone. **4** the provision or system of supplying a public need, e.g., transport, or (*Brit.*) (often in *pl.*) the supply of water, gas, electricity, telephone, etc. **5 a** the fact or status of being a servant. **b** employment or a position as a servant. **6 a** state or period of employment doing work for an individual or organization (*resigned after 15 years' service*). **7 a** a public department or organization employing officials working for the government (*civil service; secret service*). **b** employment in this. **8** (in *pl.*) the armed forces. **9** (*attrib.*) of the kind issued to the armed forces (*a service revolver*). **10 a** a ceremony of worship according to prescribed forms. **b** a form of liturgy for this. **11 a** the provision of what is necessary for the installation and maintenance of a machine, etc., or operation. **b** a periodic routine maintenance of a motor vehicle, etc. **12** assistance or advice given to customers after the sale of goods. **13 a** the act or process of serving food, drinks, etc. **b** an extra charge nominally made for this. **14** a set of dishes, plates, etc., used for serving meals (*a dinner service*). **15** *Tennis*, etc. **a** the act or an instance of serving. **b** a person's turn to serve. **c** the manner or quality of serving. **d** (in full **service game**) a game in which a particular player serves. • *v.tr.* **1** provide service or services for, esp. maintain. **2** maintain or repair (a car, machine, etc.). **3** pay interest on (a debt). **4** supply with a service. □ **at a person's service** ready to serve or assist a person. **be of service** be available to assist. **in service 1** employed as a servant. **2** available for use. **on active service** serving in the armed forces in wartime. **out of service** not available for use. **see service 1** have experience of service, esp. in the armed forces. **2** (of a thing) be much used. **take service with** *Brit.* become a servant to. [ME f. OF *service* or L *servitium* f. *servus* slave]

▶See note at SERVE.

serv•ice² /sórvis/ *n.* (in full **service tree**) a European tree of the genus *Sorbus*, esp. *S. domestica* with toothed leaves, cream-colored flowers, and small round or pear-shaped fruit eaten when overripe. [earlier *serves*, pl. of obs. *serve* f. OE *syrfe* f. Gmc *surbhjōn* ult. f. L *sorbus*]

serv•ice•a•ble /sórvisəbəl/ *adj.* **1** useful or usable. **2** able to render service. **3** durable; capable of withstanding difficult conditions. **4** suited for ordinary use rather than ornamental. □□ **serv•ice•a•bil•i•ty** *n.* **serv•ice•a•ble•ness** *n.* **serv•ice•a•bly** *adv.* [ME f. OF *servisable* (as SERVICE¹)]

serv•ice ar•e•a *n.* **1** an area beside a major road for the supply of gasoline, refreshments, etc. **2** the area served by a broadcasting station.

serv•ice•ber•ry /sórvisberee/ *n.* **1** the fruit of the service tree. **2 a** any American shrub of the genus *Amelanchier*. **b** the edible fruit of this.

serv•ice book *n.* a book of authori̅z̅ed forms of worship of a church.

serv•ice charge *n.* an additional charge for service in a restaurant, hotel, etc.

serv•ice dress *n. Brit.* ordinary military, etc., uniform.

serv•ice in•dus•try *n.* one providing services not goods.

serv•ice line *n.* (in tennis, etc.) a line marking the limit of the area into which the ball must be served.

serv•ice•man /sórvisman/ *n.* (*pl.* **•men**) **1** a man serving in the armed forces. **2** a man providing service or maintenance.

serv•ice road *n.* a road parallel to a main road, serving houses, stores, etc.

serv•ice sta•tion *n.* an establishment beside a road selling gasoline and oil, etc., to motorists and often able to carry out maintenance.

serv•ice•wom•an /sórviswoomən/ *n.* (*pl.* **•wom•en**) a woman serving in the armed forces.

ser•vi•ette /sórvee-ét/ *n.* esp. *Brit.* a napkin for use at table. [ME f. OF f. *servir* SERVE]

ser•vile /sórvil/ *adj.* **1** of or being or like a slave or slaves. **2** slavish; fawning; completely dependent. □□ **ser•vile•ly** *adv.* **ser•vil•i•ty** /–vílitee/ *n.* [ME f. L *servilis* f. *servus* slave]

serv•ing /sórving/ *n.* a quantity of food served to one person.

ser•vi•tor /sórvitər/ *n.* **1** *archaic* **a** a servant. **b** an attendant. **2** *hist.* an Oxford undergraduate performing menial duties in exchange for assistance from college funds. □□ **ser•vi•tor•ship** *n.* [ME f. OF f. LL (as SERVE)]

ser•vi•tude /sórvitood, –tyood/ *n.* **1** slavery. **2** subjection (esp. involuntary); bondage. **3** *Law* the subjection of property to an easement. [ME f. OF f. L *servitudo –inis* f. *servus* slave]

ser•vo /sórvō/ *n.* (*pl.* **•vos**) **1** (in full **servomechanism**) a powered mechanism producing motion or forces at a higher level of energy than the input level, e.g., in the brakes and steering of large motor vehicles, esp. where feedback is employed to make the control automatic. **2** (in full **servomotor**) the motive element in a servomechanism. **3** (in *comb.*) of or involving a servomechanism (*servoassisted*). [L *servus* slave]

ses•a•me /sésəmee/ *n. Bot.* **1** an E. Indian herbaceous plant, *Sesamum indicum*, with seeds used as food and yielding an edible oil. **2** its seeds. □ **open sesame** a means of acquiring or achieving

what is normally unattainable (from the magic words used in the *Arabian Nights' Entertainments*). [L *sesamum* f. Gk *sēsamon, sēsamē*]

ses•a•moid /sésəmoyd/ *adj. & n.* • *adj.* shaped like a sesame seed; nodular (esp. of small independent bones developed in tendons passing over an angular structure such as the kneecap and the navicular bone). • *n.* a sesamoid bone.

sesqui- /séskwee/ *comb. form* **1** denoting one and a half. **2** *Chem.* (of a compound) in which there are three equivalents of a named element or radical to two others. [L (as SEMI-, –*que* and)]

ses•qui•cen•ten•ar•y /séskwisenténəree/ *n.* (*pl.* **•ies**) = SESQUICENTENNIAL.

ses•qui•cen•ten•n•ial /séskwisenténeeəl/ *n. & adj.* • *n.* a one-hundred-and-fiftieth anniversary. • *adj.* of or relating to a sesquicentennial.

ses•sile /sésil, –əl/ *adj.* **1** *Bot. & Zool.* (of a flower, leaf, eye, etc.) attached directly by its base without a stalk or peduncle. **2** fixed in one position; immobile. [L *sessilis* f. *sedēre sess-* sit]

ses•sile oak *n.* = DURMAST.

▶See note at EVERYBODY.

ses•sion /séshən/ *n.* **1** the process of assembly of a deliberative or judicial body to conduct its business. **2** a single meeting for this purpose. **3** a period during which such meetings are regularly held. **4** an academic year. **b** the period during which a school, etc., has classes. **5** a period devoted to an activity (*poker session; recording session*). **6** the governing body of a Presbyterian church. □ **in session** assembled for business; not on vacation. □□ **ses•sion•al** *adj.* [ME f. OF *session* or L *sessio –onis* (as SESSILE)]

ses•terce /séstərs/ *n.* (also **ses•ter•tius** /sestórshəs/) (*pl.* **ses•terc•es** /séstərseez/ or **ses•ter•ti•i** /–stórshee-ī/) an ancient Roman coin and monetary unit equal to one quarter of a denarius. [L *sestertius* (*nummus* coin) = 2¹/₂ f. *semis* half + *tertius* third]

ses•tet /sestét/ *n.* **1** the last six lines of a sonnet. **2** a sextet. [It. *sestetto* f. *sesto* f. L *sextus* a sixth]

ses•ti•na /sesteeənə/ *n.* a form of rhymed or unrhymed poem with six stanzas of six lines and a final triplet, all stanzas having the same six words at the line ends in six different sequences. [It. (as SESTET)]

set¹ /set / *v.* (**set• ting**; *past* and *past part.* **set**) **1** *tr.* put, lay, or stand (a thing) in a certain position or location (*set it on the table; set it upright*). **2** *tr.* (foll. by *to*) apply (one thing) to (another) (*set pen to paper*). **3** *tr.* **a** fix ready or in position. **b** dispose suitably for use, action, or display. **4** *tr.* **a** adjust the hands of (a clock or watch) to show the right time. **b** adjust (an alarm clock) to sound at the required time. **5** *tr.* **a** fix, arrange, or mount **b** insert (a jewel) in a ring, framework, etc. **6** *tr.* make (a device) ready to operate. **7** *tr.* lay (a table) for a meal. **8** *tr.* arrange (the hair) while damp so that it dries in the required style. **9** *tr.* (foll. by *with*) ornament or provide (a surface, esp. a precious item) (*gold set with gems*). **10** *tr.* bring by placing or arranging or other means into a specified state; cause to be (*set things in motion ; set it on fire*). **11** *intr. & tr.* harden or solidify (*the jelly is set; the cement has set*). **12** *intr.* (of the sun, moon, etc.) appear to move toward and below the earth's horizon (as the earth rotates). **13** *tr.* represent (a story, play, scene, etc.) as happening in a certain time or place. **14** *tr.* **a** (foll. by *to* + infin.) cause or instruct (a person) to perform a specified activity (*set them to work*). **b** (foll. by pres. part.) start (a person or thing) doing something (*set him chatting; set the ball rolling*). **15** *tr.* present or impose as work to be done or a matter to be dealt with (*set them an essay*). **16** *tr.* exhibit as a type or model (*set a good example*). **17** *tr.* initiate; take the lead in (*set the fashion; set the pace*). **18** *tr.* establish (a record, etc.). **19** *tr.* determine or decide (*the itinerary is set*). **20** *tr.* appoint or establish (*set them in authority*). **21** *tr.* join, attach, or fasten. **22** *tr.* **a** put parts of (a broken or dislocated bone, limb, etc.) into the correct position for healing. **b** deal with (a fracture or dislocation) in this way. **23** *tr.* (in full **set to music**) provide (words, etc.) with music for singing. **24** *tr.* (often foll. by *up*) *Printing* **a** arrange or produce (type or film, etc.) as required. **b** arrange the type or film, etc., for (a book, etc.). **25** *intr.* (of a tide, current, etc.) have a certain motion or direction. **26** *intr.* (of a face) assume a hard expression. **27** *tr.* **a** cause (a hen) to sit on eggs. **b** place (eggs) for a hen to sit on. **28** *tr.* put (a seed, plant, etc.) in the ground to grow. **29** *tr.* give the teeth of (a saw) an alternate outward inclination. **30** *tr.* esp. start (a fire). **31** *intr.* (of eyes, etc.) become motionless. **32** *intr.* feel or show a certain tendency (*opinion is setting against it*). **33** *intr.* **a** (of blossom) form into fruit. **b** (of fruit) develop from blossom. **c** (of a tree) develop fruit. **34** *intr.* (in full **set to partner**) (of a dancer) take a position facing one's partner. **35** *intr.* (of a hunting dog) take a rigid attitude indicating the presence of game. **36** *intr. dial.* or *sl.* **37** sink a nail head, esp. with a nail set. □ **set about 1** begin or take steps toward. **2** *Brit. colloq.* attack. **set a person (or thing) against (another) 1** consider or reckon (a person or thing) as a counterbalance or compensation for. **2** cause to oppose. **set apart** separate; reserve; differentiate. **set aside** see ASIDE. **set back 1** place further back in place or time. **2** impede or reverse the progress of. **3** *colloq.* cost (a person) a specified amount. **set by** save for future use. **set down 1** record in writing. **2** land an aircraft (*we were forced to set down just outside of Atlanta*). **3** (foll. by *to*) attribute to. **4** (foll. by *as*) explain or describe to oneself as. **set eyes on** see EYE. **set one's face against** see FACE. **set foot on** (or **in**) see FOOT. **set forth 1** begin a journey. **2** make known; expound. **set forward** begin to advance. **set free** release. **set one's hand to** see HAND. **set one's heart** (or **hopes**) **on** want or hope for eagerly. **set in 1** (of weather, a condition, etc.) begin (and seem likely to continue); become established. **2** insert (esp. a sleeve, etc., into a garment). **set in motion** put under way; implement the initial actions (of a plan, project, etc.) **set little by** consider to be of little value. **set a person's mind at rest** see MIND. **set much by** consider to be of much value. **set off 1** begin a journey. **2** detonate (a bomb, etc.). **3** initiate; stimulate. **4** cause (a person) to start laughing, talking, etc. **5** serve as an adornment or foil to; enhance. **6** (foll. by *against*) use as a compensating item. **set on** (or **upon**) **1** attack violently. **2** cause or urge to attack. **set out 1** begin a journey. **2** (foll. by *to* + infin.) aim or intend. **3** demonstrate, arrange, or exhibit. **4** mark out. **5** declare. **set the pace** determine the rate of speed, proficiency, etc. for others to follow. **set sail 1** hoist the sails. **2** begin a voyage. **set the scene** see SCENE. **set one's sights on** have an an object or goal. **set the stage** see STAGE. **set store by** (or **on**) see STORE. **set one's teeth 1** clench them. **2** summon one's resolve. **set to** begin doing something vigorously, esp. fighting, arguing, or eating. **set up 1** place in position or view. **2** organize or start (a business, etc.). **3** establish in some capacity. **4** supply the needs of. **5** begin making (a loud sound). **6** cause or make arrangements for (a condition or situation). **7** prepare (a task, etc., for another). **8** restore or enhance the health of (a person). **9** establish (a record). **10** propound (a theory). **11** *colloq.* put (a person) in a dangerous or vulnerable position. **set oneself up as** make pretensions to being. [OE *settan* f. Gmc]

▶**Set** and **sit** are sometimes confused. **Set** means 'place or put': *Set the flowers on top of the piano.* **Sit** means 'be seated': *Sit in this chair while I check the light meter.*

set[2] /set/ *n.* **1** a number of things or persons that belong together or resemble one another or are usually found together. **2** a collection or group. **3** a section of society consorting together or having similar interests, etc. **4** a collection of implements, vessels, etc., regarded collectively and needed for a specified purpose (*croquet set; tea set; a set of teeth*). **5** a piece of electric or electronic apparatus, esp. a radio or television receiver. **6** (in tennis, etc.) a group of games counting as a unit toward a match for the player or side that wins a defined number or proportion of the games. **7** *Math. & Logic* a collection of distinct entities, individually specified or satisfying specified conditions, forming a unit. **8** a group of pupils or students having the same average ability. **9 a** a slip, shoot, bulb, etc., for planting. **b** a young fruit just set. **10 a** a habitual posture or conformation; the way the head, etc., is carried or a dress, etc., flows. **b** (also **dead set**) a setter's pointing in the presence of game. **11** the way, drift, or tendency (of a current, public opinion, state of mind, etc.) (*the set of public feeling is against it*). **12** the way in which a machine, device, etc., is set or adjusted. **13** esp. *Austral. & NZ colloq.* a grudge. **14 a** the alternate outward deflection of the teeth of a saw. **b** the amount of this. **15** the last coat of plaster on a wall. **16** *Printing* **a** the amount of spacing in type controlling the distance between letters. **b** the width of a piece of type. **17** a warp or bend or displacement caused by continued pressure or a continued position. **18** a setting, including stage furniture, etc., for a play or motion picture, etc. **19** a sequence of songs or pieces performed in jazz or popular music. **20** the setting of the hair when damp. **21** (also **sett**) a badger's burrow. **22** (also **sett**) a granite paving block. **23** a predisposition or expectation influencing a response. **24** a number of people making up a square dance. □ **make a dead set at** *Brit.* **1** make a determined attack on. **2** seek to win the affections of. [sense 1 (and related senses) f. OF *sette* f. L *secta* SECT: other senses f. SET[1]]

set[3] /set/ *adj.* **1** in senses of SET[1]. **2** prescribed or determined in advance. **3** fixed; unchanging; unmoving. **4** (of a phrase or speech, etc.) having invariable or predetermined wording; not extempore. **5** prepared for action. **6** (foll. by *on, upon*) determined to acquire or achieve, etc. **7** (of a book, etc.) specified for reading in preparation for an examination. **8** (of a meal) served according to a fixed menu. [past part. of SET[1]]

se•ta /seetə/ *n.* (*pl.* **se•tae** /–tee/) *Bot. & Zool.* stiff hair; bristle. □□ **se•ta•ceous** /–táyshəs/ *adj.* [L, = bristle]

set•back /sétbak/ *n.* **1** a reversal or arrest of progress. **2** a relapse. **3** the recession of the upper part of a building from the lower part. **4** the automatic lowering of the temperature on a thermostat.

set fair *adj. Brit.* (of the weather) fine without a sign of breaking.

se•ti•fer•ous /sitífərəs/ *adj.* (also **se•tig•er•ous** /sitíjərəs/) *Biol.* having bristles. [L *seta* bristle, *setiger* bristly + –FEROUS, –GEROUS]

set•off /sétawf/ *n.* **1** a thing set off against another. **2** a thing of which the amount or effect may be deducted from that of another or an opposite tendency. **3** a counterbalance. **4** a counterclaim. **5** a thing that embellishes; an adornment to something. **6** *Printing* = OFFSET 7.

se•ton /seet'n/ *n. Surgery* a skein of cotton, etc., passed below the skin and left with the ends protruding to promote drainage, etc. [ME f. med.L *seto, seta* silk, app. f. L *seta* bristle]

se•tose /seetōs/ *adj. Biol.* bristly. [L *seta* bristle]

set piece *n.* **1** a formal or elaborate arrangement, esp. in art or literature. **2** fireworks arranged on scaffolding, etc.

set point *n. Tennis* **1** the state of a game when one side needs only one more point to win the set. **2** this point.

set screw *n.* a screw for adjusting or clamping parts of a machine.

set square *n.* a right-angled triangular plate for drawing lines, esp. at 90°, 45°, 60°, or 30°.

Set•swa•na var. of TSWANA (and the preferred form for the language).

sett var. of SET[2] 21, 22.

set•tee /seteé/ *n.* a seat (usu. upholstered), with a back and usu. arms, for more than one person. [18th c.: perh. a fanciful var. of SETTLE[2]]

set•ter /sétər/ *n.* **1 a** a dog of a large, long-haired breed trained to stand rigid when scenting game (see SET[1] 35). **b** this breed. **2** a person or thing that sets.

set the•o•ry *n.* the branch of mathematics concerned with the manipulation of sets.

set•ting /séting/ *n.* **1** the position or manner in which a thing is set. **2** the immediate surroundings (of a house, etc.). **3** the surroundings of any object regarded as its framework; the environment of a thing. **4** the place and time, scenery, etc., of a story, drama, etc. **5** a frame in which a jewel is set. **6** the music to which words of a poem, song, etc., are set. **7** a set of cutlery and other accessories for one person at a table. **8** the way in which or level at which a machine is set to operate.

set•tle[1] /sét'l/ *v.* **1** *tr. & intr.* (often foll. by *down*) establish or become established in a more or less permanent abode or way of life. **2** *intr. & tr.* (often foll. by *down*) **a** cease or cause to cease from wandering, disturbance, movement, etc. **b** adopt a regular or secure style of life. **c** (foll. by *to*) apply oneself (to work, an activity, a way of life, etc.) (*settled down to writing letters*). **3 a** *intr.* sit or come down to stay for some time. **b** *tr.* cause to do this. **4** *tr. & intr.* bring to or attain fixity, certainty, composure, or quietness. **5** *tr.* determine or decide or agree upon (*shall we settle a date?*). **6** *tr.* **a** resolve (a dispute, etc.). **b** deal with (a matter) finally. **7** *tr.* terminate (a lawsuit) by mutual agreement. **8** *intr.* **a** (foll. by *for*) accept or agree to (esp. an alternative not one's first choice). **b** (foll. by *on*) decide on. **9** *tr.* (also *absol.*) pay (a debt, an account, etc.). **10** *intr.* (as **settled** *adj.*) not likely to change for a time (*settled weather*). **11** *tr.* **a** aid the digestion of (food). **b** remedy the disordered state of (nerves, the stomach, etc.). **12** *tr.* **a** colonize. **b** establish colonists in. **13** *intr.* subside; fall to the bottom or on to a surface (*the foundations have settled; wait till the sediment settles; the dust will settle*). **14** *intr.* (of a ship) begin to sink. **15** *tr.* get rid of the obstruction of (a person) by argument or conflict or killing. □ **settle one's affairs** make any necessary arrangements (e.g., write a will) when death is near. **settle in** become established in a place. **settle up 1** (also *absol.*) pay (an account, debt, etc.). **2** finally arrange (a matter). **settle with 1** pay all or part of an amount due to (a creditor). **2** get revenge on. □□ **set•tle•a•ble** *adj.* [OE *setlan* (as SETTLE[2]) f. Gmc]

set•tle[2] /sét'l/ *n.* a bench with a high back and arms and often with a box fitted below the seat. [OE *setl* place to sit f. Gmc]

set•tle•ment /sét'lmənt/ *n.* **1** the act or an instance of settling; the process of being settled. **2 a** the colonization of a region. **b** a place or area occupied by settlers. **c** a small village. **3 a** a political or financial, etc., agreement. **b** an arrangement ending a dispute. **4 a** the terms on which property is given to a person. **b** a deed stating these. **c** the amount or property given. **5** the process of settling an account. **6** subsidence of a wall, house, soil, etc.

set•tler /sétlər/ *n.* a person who goes to settle in a new country or place; an early colonist.

set•tlor /sétlər/ *n. Law* a person who makes a settlement esp. of a property.

set-to *n.* (*pl.* **-tos**) *colloq.* a fight or argument.

set-up /setup/ *n.* **1** an arrangement or organization. **2** the manner or structure or position of this. **3** *colloq.* a trick or conspiracy, esp. to make an innocent person appear guilty. **4** the glass, ice, mixers, etc., for preparing alcoholic drinks.

sev•en /sévən/ *n. & adj.* ● *n.* **1** one more than six, or three less than ten; the sum of four units and three units. **2** a symbol for this (7, vii, VII). **3** a size, etc., denoted by seven. **4** a set or team of seven individuals. **5** the time of seven o'clock (*is it seven yet?*). **6** a card with seven pips. ● *adj.* that amount to seven. [OE *seofon* f. Gmc]

sev•en dead•ly sins *n.pl.* the sins of pride, covetousness, lust, anger, gluttony, envy, and sloth.

sev•en•fold /sévənfōld/ *adj. & adv.* **1** seven times as much or as many. **2** consisting of seven parts.

sev•en seas *n.pl.* (**the sev•en seas**) the oceans of the world: the

Arctic, Antarctic, N. Pacific, S. Pacific, N. Atlantic, S. Atlantic, and Indian Oceans.

sev·en·teen /sévəntéen/ *n. & adj.* ●*n.* **1** one more than sixteen, or seven more than ten. **2** a symbol for this (17, xvii, XVII). **3** a size, etc., denoted by seventeen. ● *adj.* that amount to seventeen. □□ **sev·en·teenth** *adj. & n.* [OE *seofontíene*]

sev·enth /sévənth/ *n. & adj.* ●*n.* **1** the position in a sequence corresponding to the number 7 in the sequence 1–7. **2** something occupying this position. **3** one of seven equal parts of a thing. **4** *Mus.* **a** an interval or chord spanning seven consecutive notes in the diatonic scale (e.g., C to B). **b** a note separated from another by this interval. ● *adj.* that is the seventh. □ **in seventh heaven** see HEAVEN. □□ **sev·enth·ly** *adv.*

Sev·enth-day Ad·vent·ists *n.pl.* a staunchly protestant branch of the Adventists with beliefs based rigidly on faith and the Scriptures and the imminent return of Christ to earth, and observing the sabbath on Saturday.

sev·en·ty /sévəntee/ *n. & adj.* ●*n.* (*pl.* **-ties**) **1** the product of seven and ten. **2** a symbol for this (70, lxx, LXX). **3** (in *pl.*) the numbers from 70 to 79, esp. the years of a century or of a person's life. ● *adj.* that amount to seventy. □□ **sev·en·ti·eth** *adj. & n.* **sev·en·ty·fold** *adj. & adv.* [OE *–seofontig*]

sev·en·ty-first *n.* (also **sev·en·ty-sec·ond**, etc.) the ordinal numbers between seventieth and eightieth.

sev·en·ty-one *n.* (also **sev·en·ty-two**, etc.) the cardinal numbers between seventy and eighty.

Sev·en Won·ders of the World *n.pl.* the seven buildings and monuments of the ancient world regarded as especially remarkable: the pyramids of Egypt; the Hanging Gardens of Babylon; the Mausoleum of Halicarnassus; the temple of Artemis at Ephesus in Asia Minor; the Colossus of Rhodes; the statue of Zeus at Olympia; and the Pharos of Alexandria.

sev·en-year itch *n.* a supposed tendency to infidelity after seven years of marriage.

sev·er /sévər/ *v.* **1** *tr. & intr.* (often foll. by *from*) divide, break, or make separate, esp. by cutting. **2** *tr. & intr.* break off or away; separate; part; divide (*severed our friendship*). **3** *tr.* end the employment contract of (a person). □□ **sev·er·a·ble** *adj.* [ME f. AF *severer*, OF *severer* ult. f. L *separare* SEPARATE *v.*]

sev·er·al /sévrəl/ *adj. & n.* ● *adj. & n.* more than two but not many. ● *adj.* **1** separate or respective; distinct (*all went their several ways*). **2** *Law* applied or regarded separately (opp. JOINT). □□ **sev·er·al·ly** *adv.* [ME f. AF f. AL *separalis* f. L *separ* SEPARATE *adj.*]

sev·er·al·ty /sévrəltee/ *n.* **1** separateness. **2** the individual or unshared tenure of an estate, etc. (esp. in severalty). [ME f. AF *severalte* (as SEVERAL)]

sev·er·ance /sévərəns, sévrəns/ *n.* **1** the act or an instance of severing. **2** a severed state.

sev·er·ance pay *n.* an amount paid to an employee on the early termination of a contract.

se·vere /sivéer/ *adj.* **1** rigorous, strict, and harsh in attitude or treatment (*a severe critic; severe discipline*). **2** serious; critical (*a severe shortage*). **3** vehement or forceful (*a severe storm*). **4** extreme (in an unpleasant quality) (*a severe winter; severe cold*). **5** arduous or exacting; making great demands on energy, skill, etc. (*severe competition*). **6** unadorned; plain in style (*severe dress*). □□ **se·vere·ly** *adv.* **se·ver·i·ty** /–véritee/ *n.* [F *sévère* or L *severus*]

sev·er·y /sévəree/ *n.* (*pl.* **-ies**) *Archit.* a space or compartment in a vaulted ceiling. [ME f. OF *civoire* (as CIBORIUM)]

Se·ville or·ange /səvíl/ *n.* a bitter orange used for marmalade. [*Seville* in Spain]

Sè·vres /sévrə/ *n.* fine porcelain, often with elaborate decoration, made at Sèvres in the suburbs of Paris.

sew /sō/ *v.tr.* (*past part.* **sewn** /sōn/ or **sewed**) **1** (also *absol.*) fasten, join, etc., by making stitches with a needle and thread or a sewing machine. **2** make (a garment, etc.) by sewing. **3** (often foll. by *on,*

in, etc.) attach by sewing (*shall I sew on your buttons?*). □ **sew up** **1** join or enclose by sewing. **2** *colloq.* (esp. in *passive*) satisfactorily arrange or finish dealing with (a project, etc.). **3** obtain exclusive use of. □□ **sew·er** *n.* [OE *si(o)wan*]

sew·age /sōó·ij/ (also **sew·er·age** /sōówərij/) *n.* waste matter, esp. excremental, conveyed in sewers.

sew·er /sōóər/ *n.* a conduit, usu. underground, for carrying off drainage water and sewage. [ME f. AF *sever(e)*, ONF *se(u)wiere* channel to carry off the overflow from a fishpond, ult. f. L *ex-* out of + *aqua* water]

sew·er·age /sōó·ərij/ *n.* **1** a system of or drainage by sewers. **2** = SEWAGE.

sew·er rat *n.* the common brown rat.

sew·ing /sō·ing/ *n.* a piece of material or work to be sewn.

sew·ing ma·chine /sō·ing/ *n.* a machine for sewing or stitching.

sewn *past part.* of SEW.

sex /seks/ *n., adj., & v.* ●*n.* **1** either of the main divisions (male and female) into which living things are placed on the basis of their reproductive functions. **2** the fact of belonging to one of these. **3** males or females collectively. **4** sexual instincts, desires, etc., or their manifestation. **5** *colloq.* sexual intercourse. ● *adj.* **1** of or relating to sex (*sex education*). **2** arising from a difference or consciousness of sex (*sex antagonism; sex urge*). ● *v.tr.* **1** determine the sex of. **2** (as **sexed** *adj.*) **a** having a sexual appetite (*highly sexed*). **b** having sexual characteristics. □□ **sex·er** *n.* [ME f. OF *sexe* or L *sexus*]

sex act *n.* (usu. prec. by *the*) (or an) act of sexual intercourse.

sex·a·ge·nar·i·an /séksəjináreeən/ *n. & adj.* ●*n.* a person from 60 to 69 years old. ● *adj.* of this age. [L *sexagenarius* f. *sexageni* distrib. of *sexaginta* sixty]

Sex·a·ges·i·ma /séksəjésimə/ *n.* the Sunday before Quinquagesima. [ME f. eccl.L, = sixtieth (day), prob. named loosely as preceding QUINQUAGESIMA]

sex·a·ges·i·mal /séksəjésiməl/ *adj. & n.* ● *adj.* **1** of sixtieths. **2** of sixty. **3** reckoning or reckoned by sixtieths. ●*n.* (in full **sexagesimal fraction**) a fraction with a denominator equal to a power of 60 as in the divisions of the degree and hour. □□ **sex·a·ges·i·mal·ly** *adv.* [L *sexagesimus* (as SEXAGESIMA)]

sex ap·peal *n.* sexual attractiveness.

sex·cen·ten·ar·y /séksenténəree/ *n. & adj.* ●*n.* (*pl.* **-ies**) **1** a six-hundredth anniversary. **2** a celebration of this. ● *adj.* **1** of or relating to a sexcentenary. **2** occurring every six hundred years.

sex change *n.* an apparent change of sex by surgical means and hormone treatment.

sex chro·mo·some *n.* a chromosome concerned in determining the sex of an organism, which in most animals are of two kinds, the X-chromosome and the Y-chromosome.

sex·en·ni·al /seksénee·əl/ *adj.* **1** lasting six years. **2** recurring every six years. [SEXI- + L *annus* year]

sex·foil /séksfoyl/ *n.* a six-lobed ornamental figure. [SEXI-, after CINQUEFOIL, TREFOIL]

sex hor·mone *n.* a hormone affecting sexual development or behavior.

sexi- /séksee/ *comb. form* (also **sex-** before a vowel) six. [L *sex* six]

sex·ism /séksizəm/ *n.* prejudice or discrimination, esp. against women, on the grounds of sex. □□ **sex·ist** *adj. & n.*

sex·i·va·lent /séksiváylənt/ *adj. Chem.* esp. *Brit.* = HEXAVALENT.

sex kit·ten *n. colloq.* a young woman who asserts her sex appeal.

sex·less /sékslis/ *adj.* **1** *Biol.* neither male nor female. **2** lacking in sexual desire or attractiveness. □□ **sex·less·ly** *adv.* **sex·less·ness** *n.*

sex life *n.* a person's activity related to sexual instincts.

sex-linked *adj. Genetics* carried on or by a sex chromosome.

sex ma·ni·ac *n. colloq.* a person needing or seeking excessive gratification of the sexual instincts.

sex ob·ject *n.* a person regarded mainly in terms of sexual attractiveness.

sex·ol·o·gy /seksóləjee/ *n.* the study of sexual life or relationships, esp. in human beings. □□ **sex·o·log·i·cal** /séksəlójikəl/ *adj.* **sex·ol·o·gist** *n.*

sex·par·tite /sekspaártīt/ *adj.* divided into six parts.

sex·ploi·ta·tion /séksploytáyshən/ *n. colloq.* the exploitation of sex, esp. commercially.

sex·pot /sékspot/ *n. colloq.* a sexy person (esp. a woman).

sex-starved *adj.* lacking sexual gratification.

sex sym·bol *n.* a person widely noted for sex appeal.

sext /sekst/ *n. Eccl.* **1** the canonical hour of prayer appointed for the sixth daytime hour (i.e., noon). **2** the office of sext. [ME f. L *sexta hora* sixth hour f. *sextus* sixth]

sex·tant /sékstənt/ *n.* an instrument with a graduated arc of 60° used in navigation and surveying for measuring the angular distance of objects by means of mirrors. [L *sextans –ntis* sixth part f. *sextus* sixth]

sex·tet /sekstét/ *n.* (also **sex·tette**)

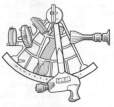

sextant

1 *Mus.* a composition for six voices or instruments. **2** the performers of such a piece. **3** any group of six. [alt. of SESTET after L *sex* six]

sex•til•lion /sekstílyən/ *n.* (*pl.* same or **sex•til•lions**) a thousand raised to the seventh (or formerly, esp. *Brit.*, the twelfth) power (10^{21} and 10^{36}, respectively) (cf. BILLION). □□ **sex•til•lionth** [F f. L *sex* six, after *septillion*, etc.]

sex•to /séksto͞o/ *n.* (*pl.* **·tos**) **1** a size of book or page in which each leaf is one-sixth that of a printing sheet. **2** a book or sheet of this size. [L *sextus* sixth, as QUARTO]

sex•to•dec•i•mo /sékstōdésimō/ *n.* (*pl.* **·mos**) **1** a size of book or page in which each leaf is one-sixteenth that of a printing sheet. **2** a book or sheet of this size. [L *sextus decimus* 16th (as QUARTO)]

sex•ton /sékstən/ *n.* a person who looks after a church and churchyard, often acting as bell ringer and gravedigger. [ME *segerstane*, etc., f. AF, OF *segerstein, secrestein* f. med.L *sacristanus* SACRISTAN]

sex•ton bee•tle *n.* any beetle of the genus *Necrophorus*, burying carrion to serve as a nidus for its eggs.

sex•tu•ple /sekstóo͞opəl, –tyóo͞o–, –túpəl, sékstóo͞opəl/ *adj., n., & v.* ● *adj.* **1** sixfold. **2** having six parts. **3** being six times as many or much. ● *n.* a sixfold number or amount. ● *v.tr. & intr.* multiply by six; increase sixfold. □□ **sex•tu•ply** *adv.* [med.L *sextuplus*, irreg. f. L *sex* six, after LL *quintuplus* QUINTUPLE]

sex•tu•plet /sekstúplit, –tóo͞o–, –tyóo͞o–, sékstóo͞o–, tyóo͞o–/ *n.* **1** each of six children born at one birth. **2** *Mus.* a group of six notes to be played in the time of four. [SEXTUPLE, after *triplet*, etc.]

sex•u•al /séksho͞oəl/ *adj.* **1** of or relating to sex, or to the sexes or the relations between them. **2** *Bot.* (of classification) based on the distinction of sexes in plants. **3** *Biol.* having a sex. □□ **sex•u•al•i•ty** /–áli-tee/ *n.* **sex•u•al•ly** *adv.* [LL *sexualis* (as SEX)]

sex•u•al in•ter•course *n.* the insertion of a man's erect penis into a woman's vagina, usu. followed by the ejaculation of semen.

sex•y /séksee/ *adj.* (**sex•i•er, sex•i•est**) **1** sexually attractive or stimulating. **2** sexually aroused. **3** concerned with or engrossed in sex. **4** *sl.* exciting great interest; appealing. □□ **sex•i•ly** *adv.* **sex•i•ness** *n.*

sez /sez/ *sl.* says (*sez you*). [phonetic repr.]

SF *abbr.* science fiction.

sf *abbr. Mus.* sforzando.

sfor•zan•do /sfawrtsaándō/ *adj., adv., & n.* (also **sfor•za•to** /–saáto/) ● *adj. & adv Mus.* with sudden emphasis. ● *n.* (*pl.* **·dos** or **sfor•zan•di** /–dee/) **1** a note or group of notes especially emphasized. **2** an increase in emphasis and loudness. [It., verbal noun and past part. of *sforzare* use force]

sfu•ma•to /sfo͞omaáto/ *adj. & n. Painting* ● *adj.* with indistinct outlines. ● *n.* the technique of allowing tones and colors to shade gradually into one another. [It., past part. of *sfumare* shade off f. s– = EX-1 + *fumare* smoke]

sfz *abbr. Mus.* sforzando.

SG *abbr.* **1** senior grade. **2** *Law* solicitor general. **3** specific gravity.

Sg *abbr.* SEABORGIUM.

sgd. *abbr.* signed.

sgraf•fi•to /sgraafeéto/ *n.* (*pl.* **sgraf•fi•ti** /–tee/) a form of decoration made by scratching through wet plaster on a wall or through slip on ceramic ware, showing a different-colored undersurface. [It., past part. of *sgraffire* scratch f. s– = EX-1 + *graffio* scratch]

Sgt. (also **SGT**) *abbr.* Sergeant.

sh *int.* calling for silence. [var. of HUSH]

sh. *abbr. Brit. hist.* shilling(s).

shab•by /shábee/ *adj.* (**shab•bi•er, shab•bi•est**) **1** in bad repair or condition; faded and worn; dingy; dilapidated. **2** dressed in old or worn clothes. **3** of poor quality. **4** contemptible; dishonorable (*a shabby trick*). □□ **shab•bi•ly** *adv.* **shab•bi•ness** *n.* **shab•by•ish** *adj.* [*shab* scab f. OE *sceabb* f. ON, rel. to SCAB]

shack /shak/ *n. & v.* ● *n.* a roughly built hut or cabin. ● *v.intr.* (foll. by *up*) *sl.* cohabit, esp. as lovers. [perh. f. Mex. *jacal*, Aztec *xacatli* wooden hut]

shack•le /shákəl/ *n. & v.* ● *n.* **1** a metal loop or link, closed by a bolt, to connect chains, etc. **2** a fetter enclosing the ankle or wrist. **3** (usu. in *pl.*) a restraint or impediment. ● *v.tr.* fetter; impede; restrain. [OE *sc(e)acul* fetter, corresp. to LG *shäkel* link, coupling, ON *skökull* wagon pole f. Gmc]

shack•le bolt *n.* **1** a bolt for closing a shackle. **2** a bolt with a shackle at its end.

shad /shad/ *n.* (*pl.* same or **shads**) *Zool.* any deep-bodied edible marine fish of the genus *Alosa*, spawning in fresh water. [OE *sceadd*, of unkn. orig.]

shad•dock /shádək/ *n. Bot.* **1** the largest citrus fruit, with a thick yellow skin and bitter pulp. Also called **pomelo.** **2** the tree, *Citrus grandis*, bearing these. [Capt. *Shaddock*, who introduced it to the W. Indies in the 17th c.]

shade /shayd/ *n. & v.* ● *n.* **1** comparative darkness (and usu. coolness) caused by shelter from direct light and heat. **2** a place or area sheltered from the sun. **3** a darker part of a picture, etc. **4** a color, esp. with regard to its depth or as distinguished from one nearly like it. **5** comparative obscurity. **6** a slight amount (*am a shade bet-*

ter today). **7** a translucent cover for a lamp, etc. **8** a screen excluding or moderating light. **9** an eye shield. **10** (in *pl.*) *colloq.* sunglasses. **11** a slightly differing variety (*all shades of opinion*). **12** *literary* **a** a ghost. **b** (in *pl.*) Hades. **13** (in *pl.*; foll. by *of*) suggesting reminiscence or unfavorable comparison (*shades of Dr Johnson!*). ● *v.* **1** *tr.* screen from light. **2** *tr.* cover, moderate, or exclude the light of. **3** *tr.* darken, esp. with parallel pencil lines to represent shadow, etc. **4** *intr. & tr.* (often foll. by *away, off, into*) (cause to) pass or change by degrees; border on. □ **in the shade** in comparative obscurity. **put in** (or **into**) **the shade** eclipse; surpass; appear superior. □□ **shade•less** *adj.* [OE *sc(e)adu* f. Gmc]

shad•ing /sháyding/ *n.* **1** the representation of light and shade, e.g., by penciled lines, on a map or drawing. **2** the graduation of tones from light to dark to create a sense of depth.

sha•doof /shədóof/ *n.* a pole with a bucket and counterbalance used esp. in Egypt for raising water. [Egypt. Arab. *šādūf*]

shad•ow /shádō/ *n. & v.* ● *n.* **1** shade or a patch of shade. **2** a dark figure projected by a body intercepting rays of light, often regarded as an appendage. **3** an inseparable attendant or companion. **4** a person secretly following another. **5** the slightest trace (*not the shadow of a doubt*). **6** a weak or insubstantial remnant or thing (*a shadow of his former self*). **7** (*attrib.*) *Brit.* denoting members of a political party in opposition holding responsibilities parallel to those of the government (*shadow minister; shadow cabinet*). **8** the shaded part of a picture. **9** a substance used to color the eyelids. **10** gloom or sadness. ● *v.tr.* **1** cast a shadow over. **2** secretly follow and watch the movements of. □□ **shad•ow•er** *n.* **shad•ow•less** *adj.* [repr. OE *scead(u)we*, oblique case of *sceadu* SHADE]

shadoof

shad•ow•box /shádōboks/ *v. intr.* box against an imaginary opponent as a form of training. □□ **shad•ow•box•ing** *n.*

shad•ow box *n.* a shallow case, usu. with a glass front panel or door, used to display and protect items.

shad•ow•graph /shádōgraf/ *n.* **1** an image or photograph made by means of X rays; = RADIOGRAM 1. **2** a picture formed by a shadow cast on a lighted surface. **3** an image formed by light refracted differently by different densities of a fluid.

shad•ow•y /shádōee/ *adj.* **1** like or having a shadow. **2** full of shadows. **3** vague; indistinct. **4 a** unreal; imaginary. **b** spectral; ghostly. □□ **shad•ow•i•ness** *n.*

shad•y /sháydee/ *adj.* (**shad•i•er, shad•i•est**) **1** giving shade. **2** situated in shade. **3** (of a person or behavior) disreputable; of doubtful honesty. □□ **shad•i•ly** *adv.* **shad•i•ness** *n.*

shaft /shaft/ *n. & v.* ● *n.* **1 a** an arrow or spear. **b** the long slender stem of these. **2** a remark intended to hurt or provoke (*a shaft of malice; shafts of wit*). **3** (foll. by *of*) **a** a ray (of light). **b** a bolt (of lightning). **4** the stem or handle of a tool, implement, etc. **5** a column, esp. between the base and capital. **6** a long narrow space, usu. vertical, for access to a mine, an elevator in a building, for ventilation, etc. **7** a long and narrow part supporting or connecting or driving a part or parts of greater thickness, etc. **8** each of the pair of poles between which a horse is harnessed to a vehicle. **9** the central stem of a feather. **10** *Mech.* a large axle or revolving bar transferring force by belts or cogs. **11** *colloq.* harsh or unfair treatment. ● *v.tr.* **1** *colloq.* treat unfairly. **2** *coarse sl.* (of a man) copulate with. [OE *scæ ft, sceaft* f. Gmc]

shaft•ing /sháfting/ *n. Mech.* **1** a system of connected shafts for transmitting motion. **2** material from which shafts are cut.

shag1 /shag/ *n.* **1** a rough growth or mass of hair, etc. **2** a coarse kind of cut tobacco. **3** a cormorant, esp. the crested cormorant, *Phalacrocorax aristotelis*. **4 a** a thick, shaggy carpet pile. **b** the carpet itself. [OE *sceacga*, rel. to ON *skegg* beard, OE *sceaga* coppice]

shag2 /shag/ *v. & tr. Brit. coarse sl.* ● *v.tr.* (**shagged, shag•ging**) **1** have sexual intercourse with. **2** (usu. in *passive*; often foll. by *out*) exhaust; tire out. ● *n.* (an act of) sexual intercourse. [18th c.: orig. unkn.]

shag3 /shag/ *v.tr.* (**shagged, shag•ging**) **1** pursue; chase after. **2** *Baseball* catch and return (fly balls) during practice.

shag•gy /shágee/ *adj.* (**shag•gi•er, shag•gi•est**) **1** hairy; rough-haired. **2** unkempt. **3** (of the hair) coarse and abundant. **4** *Biol.* having a hairlike covering. □□ **shag•gi•ly** *adv.* **shag•gi•ness** *n.*

shag•gy-dog sto•ry *n.* a long rambling story amusing only by its being inconsequential.

sha•green /shəgreén/ *n.* **1** a kind of untanned leather with a rough, granulated surface. **2** a sharkskin rough with natural denticles, used for rasping and polishing. [var. of CHAGRIN in the sense 'rough skin']

shah /shaa/ *n. hist.* a title of the former monarch of Iran. □□ **shah·dom** *n.* [Pers. *šāh* f. OPers. *k̠šāytiya* king]

shaikh var. of SHEIKH.

shake /shayk/ *v. & n.* ●*v.* (*past* **shook** /shŏŏk/; *past part.* **shak·en** /sháykən/) **1** *tr. & intr.* move forcefully or quickly up and down or to and fro. **2 a** *intr.* tremble or vibrate markedly. **b** *tr.* cause to do this. **3** *tr.* **a** agitate or shock. **b** *colloq.* upset the composure of. **4** *tr.* weaken or impair; make less convincing or firm or courageous (*shook his confidence*). **5** *intr.* (of a voice, note, etc.) make tremulous or rapidly alternating sounds; trill (*his voice shook with emotion*). **6** *tr.* brandish; make a threatening gesture with (one's fist, a stick, etc.). **7** *intr. colloq.* shake hands (*they shook on the deal*). **8** *tr. colloq.* = *shake off*. ●*n.* **1** the act or an instance of shaking; the process of being shaken. **2** a jerk or shock. **3** (in *pl.*; prec. by *the*) a fit of or tendency to trembling or shivering. **4** *Mus.* a trill. **5** = MILK SHAKE. **6** a shingle made by splitting sections from a log. □ **in two shakes** (**of a lamb's** or **dog's tail**) very quickly. **no great shakes** *colloq.* not very good or significant. **shake a person by the hand** = *shake hands*. **shake down 1** settle or cause to fall by shaking. **2** settle down. **3** become established; get into harmony with circumstances, surroundings, etc. **4** *sl.* extort money from. **shake the dust off one's feet** depart indignantly or disdainfully. **shake hands** (often foll. by *with*) clasp right hands at meeting or parting, in reconciliation or congratulation, or over a concluded bargain. **shake one's head** move one's head from side to side in refusal, denial, disapproval, or concern. **shake in one's shoes** (or **boots**) tremble with apprehension. **shake a leg 1** begin dancing. **2** make a start. **shake off 1** get rid of (something unwanted). **2** manage to evade (a person who is following or pestering one). **shake out 1** empty by shaking. **2** spread or open (a sail, flag, etc.) by shaking. **shake up 1** mix (ingredients) by shaking. **2** restore to shape by shaking. **3** disturb or make uncomfortable. **4** rouse from lethargy, apathy, conventionality, etc. □□ **shak·a·ble** *adj.* (also **shake·a·ble**). [OE *sc(e)acan* f. Gmc]

shake·down /sháykdown/ *n.* **1** a makeshift bed. **2** *sl.* a swindle; a piece of extortion. **3** (*attrib.*) *colloq.* denoting a voyage, flight, etc., to test a new ship or aircraft and its crew.

shak·en *past part.* of SHAKE.

shake·out /sháykowt/ *n.* **1** a rapid devaluation of securities, etc., sold in a stock exchange, etc. **2** a decline in the number of companies, services, products, etc., esp. as a result of competitive pressures.

shak·er /sháykər/ *n.* **1** a person or thing that shakes. **2** a container for shaking together the ingredients of cocktails, etc. **3** (**Shaker**) a member of an American religious sect living simply, in celibate mixed communities. □□ **Shak·er·ess** *n.* (in sense 3). **Shak·er·ism** *n.* (in sense 3). [ME, f. SHAKE: sense 3 from religious dances]

Shake·spear·e·an /shaykspeéreeən/ *adj. & n.* (also **Shake·spear·i·an**) ●*adj.* **1** of or relating to William Shakespeare, English dramatist d. 1616. **2** in the style of Shakespeare. ●*n.* a student of Shakespeare's works, etc.

shake-up *n.* an upheaval or drastic reorganization.

shak·o /sháykō/ *n.* (*pl.* **·os**) a cylindrical peaked

shako

military hat with a plume. [F *schako* f. Magyar *csákó* (*süveg*) peaked (cap) f. *csák* peak f. G *Zacken* spike]

Shak·ta /sháakta/ *n.* (also **Sak·ta**) a member of a Hindu sect worshiping the Shakti. [Skr. *śākta* relating to power or to the SHAKTI]

Shak·ti /shúkti/ *n.* (also **Sak·ti**) (in Hinduism) the female principle, esp. when personified as the wife of a god. [Skr. *śakti* power, divine energy]

sha·ku·ha·chi /sháakŏŏha͏chee/ *n.* (*pl.* **sha·ku·ha·chis**) a Japanese bamboo flute. [Jap. f. *shaku* a measure of length + *hachi* eight (tenths)]

shak·y /sháykee/ *adj.* (**shak·i·er, shak·i·est**) **1** unsteady; apt to shake; trembling. **2** unsound; infirm (*a shaky hand*). **3** unreliable; wavering (*a shaky promise; got off to a shaky start*). □□ **shak·i·ly** *adv.* **shak·i·ness** *n.*

shale /shayl/ *n.* soft, finely stratified rock that splits easily, consisting of consolidated mud or clay. □□ **shal·y** *adj.* [prob. f. G *Schale* f. OE *sc(e)alu* rel. to ON *skál* (see SCALE²)]

shale oil *n.* oil obtained from bituminous shale.

shall /shal, shəl/ *v.aux.* (*3rd sing. present* **shall**; archaic 2nd sing. present **shalt** as below; *past* **should** /shŏŏd, shəd/) (foll. by infin without *to*, or *absol.*; present and past only in use) **1** (in the 1st person) expressing the future tense (*I shall return soon*) or (with *shall* stressed) emphatic intention (*I shall have a party*). **2** (in the 2nd and 3rd persons) expressing a strong assertion or command rather than a wish (cf. WILL¹) (*you shall not catch me again; they shall go to the party*). **3** expressing a command or duty (*thou shalt not steal*; *they shall obey*). **4** (in 2nd-person questions) expressing an inquiry, esp. to avoid the form of a request (cf. WILL ¹) (*shall you go to France?*). □ **shall I?** do you want me to? [OE *sceal* f. Gmc]

▶**Shall** and **should** were traditionally used after *I* or *we*, and **will** and **would** after other pronouns, to express the ordinary future. **Shall** was sometimes also used to indicate an order: *You shall disperse or be arrested.* **Should** is still heard, especially in British English, in first-person conditional sentences: *I should like to visit Africa.* But these distinctions are all but lost in today's speech and writing.

shal·lot /shálət, shəlót/ *n.* an onionlike plant, *Allium ascalonicum,* with a cluster of small bulbs. [*eschalot* f. F *eschalotte* alt. of OF *eschaloigne*: see SCALLION]

shal·low /shálō/ *adj., n., & v.* ●*adj.* **1** of little depth. **2** superficial; trivial (*a shallow mind*). ●*n.* (often in *pl.*) a shallow place. ●*v.intr. & tr.* become or make shallow. □□ **shal·low·ly** *adv.* **shal·low·ness** *n.* [ME, prob. rel. to *schald*, OE *sceald* SHOAL²]

sha·lom /shaalóm/ *n. & int.* a Jewish salutation at meeting or parting. [Heb. *šālōm* peace]

shalt /shalt/ *archaic 2nd person sing.* of SHALL.

sham /sham/ *v., n., & adj.* ●*v.* (**shammed, sham·ming**) **1** *intr.* feign; pretend to be. **2** *tr.* **a** pretend to be. **b** simulate (*is shamming sleep*). ●*n.* **1** imposture; pretense. **2** a person or thing pretending or pretended to be what he or she or it is not. ●*adj.* pretended; counterfeit. □□ **sham·mer** *n.* [perh. north. dial. var. of SHAME]

sha·man /sháamən, sháy–/ *n.* a witch doctor or priest claiming to communicate with and receive healing powers from gods, etc. □□ **sha·man·ism** *n.* **sha·man·ist** *n. & adj.* **sha·man·is·tic** /–nístik/ *adj.* [G *Schamane* & Russ. *shaman* f. Tungusian *samán*]

sham·ble /shámbəl/ *v. & n.* ●*v.intr.* walk or run with a shuffling or awkward gait. ●*n.* a shambling gait. [prob. f. dial. *shamble* (adj.) ungainly, perh. f. *shamble legs* with ref. to straddling trestles: see SHAMBLES]

sham·bles /shámbəlz/ *n.pl.* (usu. treated as *sing.*) **1** *colloq.* a mess or muddle (*the room was a shambles*). **2** a butcher's slaughterhouse. **3** a scene of carnage. [pl. of *shamble* stool, stall f. OE *sc(e)amul* f. WG f. L *scamellum* dimin. of *scamnum* bench]

shame /shaym/ *n. & v.* ●*n.* **1** a feeling of distress or humiliation caused by consciousness of the guilt or folly of oneself or an associate. **2** a capacity for experiencing this feeling, esp. as imposing a restraint on behavior (*has no sense of shame*). **3** a state of disgrace, discredit, or intense regret. **4 a** a person or thing that brings disgrace, etc. **b** a thing or action that is wrong or regrettable. ●*v.tr.* **1** bring shame on; make ashamed; put to shame. **2** (foll. by *into, out of*) force by shame (*was shamed into confessing*). □ **for shame!** a reproof to a person for not showing shame. **put to shame** disgrace or humiliate by revealing superior qualities, etc. **shame on you!** you should be ashamed. **what a shame!** how unfortunate! [OE *sc(e)amu*]

shame·faced /sháymfáyst/ *adj.* **1** showing shame. **2** bashful; diffident. □□ **shame·fac·ed·ly** /–fáystlee, –fáysidlee/ *adv.* **shame·fac·ed·ness** *n.* [16th-c. alt. of *shamefast,* by assim. to FACE]

shame·ful /sháymfŏŏl/ *adj.* **1** that causes or is worthy of shame. **2** disgraceful; scandalous. □□ **shame·ful·ly** *adv.* **shame·ful·ness** *n.* [OE *sc (e)amful* (as SHAME, –FUL)]

shame·less /sháymlis/ *adj.* **1** having or showing no sense of shame. **2** impudent. □□ **shame·less·ly** *adv.* **shame·less·ness** *n.* [OE *sc(e)amlēas* (as SHAME, –LESS)]

sham·my /shámee/ *n.* (*pl.* **·mies**) (in full **shammy leather**) *colloq.* = CHAMOIS 2. [repr. corrupted pronunc.]

sham•poo /shampoo/ *n. & v.* • *n.* **1** liquid or cream used to lather and wash the hair. **2** a similar substance for washing a car or carpet, etc. **3** an act or instance of cleaning with shampoo. • *v.tr.* (**shampoos, sham•pooed**) wash with shampoo. [Hind. *chhāmpo*, imper. of *chhāmpnā* to press]

sham•rock /shámrok/ *n.* any of various plants with trifoliate leaves, esp. *Trifolium repens* or *Medicago lupulina*, used as the national emblem of Ireland. [Ir. *seamróg* trefoil, dimin. of *seamar* clover + *og* young]

sha•mus /sháymǝs/ *n. sl.* a detective. [20th c.: orig. uncert.]

shan•dy /shándee/ *n.* (*pl.* **•dies**) **1** a mixture of beer with lemonade. **2** (also **shandygaff**) a mixture of beer with ginger beer. [19th c.: orig. unkn.]

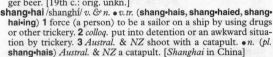

shamrock

shang•hai /shanghí/ *v. & n.* • *v.tr.* (**shang•hais, shang•haied, shang•hai•ing**) **1** force (a person) to be a sailor on a ship by using drugs or other trickery. **2** *colloq.* put into detention or an awkward situation by trickery. **3** *Austral. & NZ* shoot with a catapult. • *n.* (*pl.* **shang•hais**) *Austral. & NZ* a catapult. [*Shanghai* in China]

Shan•gri-la /shánggrilaá/ *n.* an imaginary paradise on earth. [the name of a hidden Tibetan valley in J. Hilton's *Lost Horizon* (1933)]

shank /shangk/ *n. & v.* • *n.* **1 a** the leg. **b** the lower part of the leg; the leg from knee to ankle. **c** the shinbone. **2** the lower part of an animal's foreleg, esp. as a cut of meat. **3** a shaft or stem. **4 a** the long narrow part of a tool, etc., joining the handle to the working end. **b** the stem of a key, spoon, anchor, etc. **c** the straight part of a nail or fishhook. **5** the narrow middle of the sole of a shoe. • *v.* *Golf* hit the golf ball with the shaft of the club. □□ **shanked** *adj.* (also in *comb.*). [OE *sceanca* f. WG]

shanks's mare *n.* (also **shanks's po•ny**) one's own legs as a means of conveyance.

shan•ny /shánee/ *n.* (*pl.* **•nies**) a long-bodied, olive-green European marine fish, *Blennius pholis.* [19th c.: orig. unkn.: cf. 18th-c. *shan*]

shan't /shant/ *contr.* shall not.

shan•tung /shantúng/ *n.* soft undressed Chinese silk, usu. undyed. [*Shantung*, Chinese province]

shan•ty[1] /shántee/ *n.* (*pl.* **•ties**) **1** a hut or cabin. **2** a crudely built shack. [19th c., orig. N.Amer.: perh. f. Can.F *chantier*]

shan•ty[2] /shántee/ *n.* (*pl.* **•ties**) var. of CHANTEY.

shan•ty town *n.* a poor or depressed area of a town, consisting of shanties.

SHAPE /shayp/ *abbr.* Supreme Headquarters Allied Powers Europe.

shape /shayp/ *n. & v.* • *n.* **1** the total effect produced by the outlines of a thing. **2** the external form or appearance of a person or thing. **3** a specific form or guise. **4** a description or sort or way (*not on offer in any shape or form*). **5** a definite or proper arrangement (*must get our ideas into shape*). **6 a** condition, as qualified in some way (*in good shape; in poor shape*). **b** (when unqualified) good condition (*back in shape*). **7** a person or thing as seen, esp. indistinctly or in the imagination (*a shape emerged from the mist*). **8** a mold or pattern. **9** *Brit.* a jelly, etc., shaped in a mold. **10** a piece of material, paper, etc., made or cut in a particular form. • *v.* **1** *tr.* give a certain shape or form to; fashion; create. **2** *tr.* (foll. by *to*) adapt or make conform. **3** *intr.* give signs of a future shape or development. **4** *tr.* frame mentally; imagine. **5** *intr.* assume or develop into a shape. **6** *tr.* direct (one's life, course, etc.). □ **lick** (or **knock** or **whip**) **into shape** make presentable or efficient. **shape up 1** take a (specified) form. **2** show promise; make good progress. **shape up well** be promising. □□ **shap•a•ble** *adj.* (also **shape•a•ble**). **shaped** *adj.* (also in *comb.*). **shap•er** *n.* [OE *gesceap* creation f. Gmc]

shape•less /sháyplis/ *adj.* lacking definite or attractive shape. □□ **shape•less•ly** *adv.* **shape•less•ness** *n.*

shape•ly /sháyplee/ *adj.* (**shape•li•er, shape•li•est**) **1** well formed or proportioned. **2** of elegant or pleasing shape or appearance. □□ **shape•li•ness** *n.*

shard /shaard/ *n.* **1** a broken piece of pottery or glass, etc. **2** = POTSHERD. **3** a fragment of volcanic rock. **4** the elytron of a beetle. [OE *sceard*: sense 3 f. *shard-borne* (Shakesp.) = born in a shard (dial., = cow-dung), wrongly taken as 'borne on shards']

share[1] /shair/ *n. & v.* • *n.* **1** a portion that a person receives from or gives to a common amount. **2 a** a part contributed by an individual to an enterprise or commitment. **b** a part received by an individual from this (*got a large share of the credit*). **3** part-proprietorship of property held by joint owners, esp. any of the equal parts into which a company's capital is divided entitling its owner to a proportion of the profits. • *v.* **1** *tr.* get or have or give a share of. **2** *tr.* use or benefit from jointly with others. **3** *intr.* have a share; be a sharer (*shall I share with you?*). **4** *intr.* (foll. by *in*) participate. **5** *tr. Brit.* (often foll. by *out*) **a** divide and distribute. **b** give away part of. □ **share and share alike** make an equal division. □□ **share•a•ble** *adj.* (also **shar•a•ble**). **shar•er** *n.* [ME f. OE *scearu* division, rel. to SHEAR]

share[2] /shair/ *n.* = PLOWSHARE. [OE *scear, scær* f. Gmc]

share•crop•per /sháirkropǝr/ *n.* a tenant farmer who gives a part of each crop as rent. □□ **share•crop** *v.tr. & intr.* (**•cropped, •crop•ping**).

share•hold•er /sháirhōldǝr/ *n.* an owner of shares in a company.

share•ware /sháirwair/ *n. Computing* software that is developed for sharing free of charge with other computer users rather than for sale.

sha•ri•ah /shaaree-aa/ *n.* the Muslim code of religious law. [Arab. *šarī'a*]

sha•rif /shǝreéf/ *n.* (also **she•reef, she•rif**) **1** a descendant of Muhammad through his daughter Fatima, entitled to wear a green turban or veil. **2** a Muslim leader. [Arab. *šarīf* noble f. *šarafa* be exalted]

shark[1] /shaark/ *n.* any of various large, usu. voracious marine fish with a long body and prominent dorsal fin. [16th c.: orig. unkn.]

shark[2] /shaark/ *n. colloq.* a person who unscrupulously exploits or swindles others. [16th c.: orig. perh. f. G *Schurke* worthless rogue: infl. by SHARK[1]]

bull shark

shark•skin /sháarkskin/ *n.* **1** the skin of a shark. **2** a smooth, dull-surfaced fabric.

sharp /shaarp/ *adj., n., adv., & v.* • *adj.* **1** having an edge or point able to cut or pierce. **2** tapering to a point or edge. **3** abrupt; steep; angular (*a sharp fall; a sharp turn*). **4** well-defined, clean-cut. **5 a** severe or intense (*has a sharp temper*). **b** (of food, etc.) pungent; keen (*a sharp appetite*). **c** (of a frost) severe; hard. **6** (of a voice or sound) shrill and piercing. **7** (of sand, etc.) composed of angular grains. **8** (of words, etc.) harsh or acrimonious (*had a sharp tongue*). **9** (of a person) acute; quick to perceive or comprehend. **10** quick to take advantage; artful; unscrupulous; dishonest. **11** vigorous or brisk. **12** *Mus.* **a** above the normal pitch. **b** (of a key) having a sharp or sharps in the signature. **c** (C, F, etc., **sharp**) a semitone higher than C, F, etc. **13** *colloq.* stylish or flashy with regard to dress. • *n.* **1** *Mus.* **a** a note raised a semitone above natural pitch. **b** the sign (♯) indicating this. **2** *colloq.* a swindler or cheat. **3** a fine sewing needle. • *adv.* **1** punctually (*at nine o'clock sharp*). **2** suddenly; abruptly; promptly (*pulled up sharp*). **3** at a sharp angle. **4** *Mus.* above the true pitch (*sings sharp*). • *v.* **1** *intr. archaic* cheat or swindle at cards, etc. **2** *tr. Mus.* make sharp. □□ **sharp•ly** *adv.* **sharp•ness** *n.* [OE *sc(e)arp* f. Gmc]

sharp•en /sháarpǝn/ *v.tr. & intr.* make or become sharp. □□ **sharp•en•er** *n.*

sharp end *n.* esp. *Brit. colloq.* **1** the bow of a ship. **2** the scene of direct action or decision.

sharp•er /sháarpǝr/ *n.* a swindler, esp. at cards.

sharp-eyed *adj.* having good sight; observant.

sharp•ish /sháarpish/ *adj. & adv. colloq.* • *adj.* fairly sharp. • *adv.* **1** fairly sharply. **2** quite quickly.

sharp prac•tice *n.* dishonest or barely honest dealings.

sharp-set *adj.* **1** set with a sharp edge. **2** hungry.

sharp•shoot•er /sháarpshootǝr/ *n.* a skilled marksman. □□ **sharp•shoot•ing** *n. & adj.*

sharp-wit•ted *adj.* keenly perceptive or intelligent.

shash•lik /sháashlik/ *n.* (in Asia and E. Europe) a kebab of mutton and garnishings. [Russ. *shashlyk*, ult. f. Turk. *šiš* spit, skewer: cf. SHISH KEBAB]

Shas•ta /shástǝ/ *n.* (in full **Shasta daisy**) a European plant, *Chrysanthemum maximum*, with large daisylike flowers. [*Shasta* in California]

Shas•tra /sháastrǝ/ *n.* Hindu sacred writings. [Hindi *śāstr*, Skr. *śāstra*]

shat•ter /shátǝr/ *v.* **1** *tr. & intr.* break suddenly in pieces. **2** *tr.* severely damage or utterly destroy (*shattered hopes*). **3** *tr.* greatly upset or discompose. **4** *tr.* (usu. as **shattered** *adj.*) exhaust. □□ **shat•ter•er** *n.* **shat•ter•ing** *adj.* **shat•ter•ing•ly** *adv.* **shat•ter-proof** *adj.* [ME, rel. to SCATTER]

shave /shayv/ *v. & n.* • *v.tr.* (*past part.* **shaved** or (as *adj.*) **shav•en**) **1** remove (bristles or hair) from the face, etc., with a razor. **2** (also *absol.*) remove bristles or hair with a razor from the face, etc., of (a person) or (a part of the body). **3 a** reduce by a small amount. **b** take (a small amount) away from. **4** cut thin slices from the surface of (wood, etc.) to shape it. **5** pass close to without touching; miss narrowly. • *n.* **1** an act of shaving or the process of being shaved. **2** a close approach without contact. **3** a narrow miss or escape; = CLOSE SHAVE. **4** a tool for shaving wood, etc. [OE *sc(e)afan* (sense 4 of noun f. OE *sceafa*) f. Gmc]

shave•ling /sháyvling/ *n.* **1** *archaic* a shaven person. **2** *often offens.* a head-shaven monk, friar, or priest. **3** *colloq.* a young boy.

shav•en see SHAVE.

shav•er /sháyvǝr/ *n.* **1** a person or thing that shaves. **2** an electric razor. **3** *colloq.* a young lad.

Sha·vi·an /sháyveeən/ *adj. & n.* ● *adj.* of or in the manner of G. B. Shaw, Irish-born dramatist d. 1950, or his ideas. ● *n.* an admirer of Shaw. [*Shavius*, Latinized form of *Shaw*]

shav·ing /sháyving/ *n.* **1** a thin strip cut off the surface of wood, etc. **2** (*attrib.*) used in shaving the face (*shaving cream*).

Sha·vu·oth /shəvőoəs, shäavőo-áwt/ *n.* (also **Sha·vu·ot**) the Jewish Pentecost. [Heb. *šābū'ôt* = weeks, with ref. to the weeks between Passover and Pentecost]

shaw /shaw/ *n.* **1** a small wooded area; thicket. **2** esp. *Brit.* the stalks and leaves of potatoes, turnips, etc. [perh. = SHOW *n.*]

shawl /shawl/ *n.* a piece of fabric, usu. rectangular and often folded into a triangle, worn over the shoulders or head or wrapped around a baby. □□ **shawled** *adj.* [Urdu, etc. f. Pers. *šāl*, prob. f. *Shāliāt* in India]

shawl col·lar *n.* a rolled collar extended down the front of a garment without lapel notches.

shawm /shawm/ *n. Mus.* a medieval double-reed wind instrument with a sharp penetrating tone. [ME f. OF *chalemie, chalemel, chalemeaus* (pl.), ult. f. L *calamus* f. Gk *kalamos* reed]

Shaw·nee /shawnée, shaa-/ *n.* **1 a** a N. American people native to the central Ohio valley. **b** a member of this people. **2** the language of this people.

she /shee/ *pron. & n.* ● *pron.* (*obj.* **her**; *poss.* **her**; *pl.* **they**) **1** the woman or girl or female animal previously named or in question. **2** a thing regarded as female, e.g., a vehicle or ship. **3** esp. *Austral. & NZ colloq.* it; the state of affairs (*she'll be right*). ● *n.* **1** a female; a woman. **2** (in *comb.*) female (*she-goat*). [ME *sc æ, sche*, etc., f. OE fem. demonstr. pron. & adj. *sīo, sēo*, acc. *sīe*]
▶ See note at EVERYBODY.

s/he *pron.* a written representation of "he or she" used to indicate both sexes.

shea /shee, shay/ *n.* a W. African tree, *Vitellaria paradoxa*, bearing nuts containing a large amount of fat. [Mandingo *si, se, sye*]

shea but·ter *n.* a butter made from this fat.

sheaf /sheef/ *n. & v.* ● *n.* (*pl.* **sheaves** /sheevz/) a group of things laid lengthways together and usu. tied, esp. a bundle of grain stalks tied after reaping, or a collection of papers. ● *v.tr.* make into sheaves. [OE *scēaf* f. Gmc (as SHOVE)]

sheal·ing var. of SHIELING.

shear /sheer/ *v. & n.* ● *v.* (*past* **sheared**, *archaic* **shore** /shor/; *past part.* **shorn** /shorn/ or **sheared**) **1** *tr.* cut with scissors or shears, etc. **2** *tr.* remove or take off by cutting. **3** *tr.* clip the wool off (a sheep, etc.). **4** *tr.* (foll. by *of*) a strip bare. **b** deprive. **5** *tr. & intr.* (often foll. by *off*) distort or be distorted, or break, from a structural strain. ● *n.* **1** *Mech. & Geol.* a strain produced by pressure in the structure of a substance, when its layers are laterally shifted in relation to each other. **2** (in *pl.*) (also **pair of shears** *sing.*) a large clipping or cutting instrument shaped like scissors for use in gardens, etc. □□ **shear·er** *n.* [OE *sceran* f. Gmc]

shear·ling /shéerling/ *n.* **1** a sheep that has been shorn once. **2** wool from a shearling.

shear·wa·ter /shéerwawtər, –wotər/ *n.* **1** any long-winged seabird of the genus *Puffinus*, usu. flying near the surface of the water. **2** = SKIMMER 4.

sheat·fish /shéetfish/ *n.* (*pl.* same or **sheat·fish·es**) a large freshwater catfish, *Silurus glanis*, native to European waters. [earlier *sheathfish*, prob. after G *Scheid*]

sheath /sheeth/ *n.* (*pl.* **sheaths** /sheethz, sheeths/) **1** a close-fitting cover, esp. for the blade of a knife or sword. **2** a condom. **3** *Bot., Anat., & Zool.* an enclosing case or tissue. **4** the protective covering around an electric cable. **5** a woman's close-fitting dress. □□ **sheath·less** *adj.* [OE *scǣth, scē ath*]

sheathe /sheeth/ *v.tr.* **1** put into a sheath. **2** encase; protect with a sheath. [ME f. SHEATH]

sheath·ing /shéething/ *n.* a protective casing or covering.

sheath knife *n.* a daggerlike knife carried in a sheath.

sheave[1] /sheev/ *v.tr.* make into sheaves.

sheave[2] /sheev/ *n.* a grooved wheel in a pulley block, etc., for a rope to run on. [ME f. OE *scife* (unrecorded) f. Gmc]

sheaves *pl.* of SHEAF.

she·bang /shibáng/ *n. sl.* **1** a matter or affair (esp. the whole shebang). **2** a shed or hut. [19th c.: orig. unkn.]

she·been /shibeén/ *n.* esp. *Ir.* an unlicensed house selling alcoholic liquor. [Anglo-Ir. *síbín* f. *séibe* mugful]

shed[1] /shed/ *n.* **1** a one-story structure usu. of wood for storage or shelter for animals, etc., or as a workshop. **2** a large roofed structure with one side open, for storing or maintaining machinery, etc. [app. var. of SHADE]

shed[2] /shed/ *v.tr.* (**shed·ding**; *past and past part.* **shed**) **1** let or cause to fall off (*trees shed their leaves*). **2** take off (clothes). **3** reduce (an electrical power load) by disconnection, etc. **4** cause to fall or flow (*shed blood; shed tears*). **5** disperse; diffuse; radiate (*shed light*). □ **shed light on** see LIGHT[1]. [OE *sc(e)adan* f. Gmc]

she'd /sheed/ *contr.* **1** she had. **2** she would.

shed·der /shédər/ *n.* **1** a person or thing that sheds. **2** a female salmon after spawning.

she-dev·il *n.* a malicious or spiteful woman.

sheen /sheen/ *n.* **1** a gloss or luster on a surface. **2** radiance; brightness. □□ **sheen·y** *adj.* [obs. *sheen* beautiful, resplendent f. OE *scēne*: sense assim. to SHINE]

sheep /sheep/ *n.* (*pl.* same) **1** any ruminant mammal of the genus *Ovis* with a thick woolly coat, esp. kept in flocks for its wool or meat, and noted for its timidity. **2** a bashful, timid, or silly person. **3** (usu. in *pl.*) **a** a member of a minister's congregation. **b** a parishioner. □ **separate the sheep from the goats** divide into superior and inferior groups (cf. Matt. 25:33). □□ **sheep·like** *adj.* [OE *scēp, scǣp, scēap*]

sheep

sheep-dip *n.* **1** a preparation for cleansing sheep of vermin or preserving their wool. **2** the place where sheep are dipped in this.

sheep·dog /shéepdawg, –dog/ *n.* **1** a dog trained to guard and herd sheep. **2 a** a dog of various breeds suitable for this. **b** any of these breeds.

sheep·fold /shéepfōld/ *n.* an enclosure for penning sheep.

sheep·ish /shéepish/ *adj.* **1** bashful; shy; reticent. **2** embarrassed through shame. □□ **sheep·ish·ly** *adv.* **sheep·ish·ness** *n.*

sheep·shank /shéepshangk/ *n.* a knot used to shorten a rope temporarily.

sheep·skin /shéepskin/ *n.* **1** a garment or rug of sheep's skin with the wool on. **2** leather from a sheep's skin used in bookbinding.

sheep·walk /shéepwawk/ *n. Brit.* a tract of land on which sheep are pastured.

sheer[1] /sheer/ *adj. & adv.* ● *adj.* **1** no more or less than; mere; unqualified; absolute (*sheer luck; sheer determination*). **2** (of a cliff or ascent, etc.) perpendicular; very steep. **3** (of a textile) very thin; diaphanous. ● *adv.* **1** directly; outright. **2** perpendicularly. □□ **sheer·ly** *adv.* **sheer·ness** *n.* [ME *schere* prob. f. dial. *shire* pure, clear f. OE *scīr* f. Gmc]

sheer[2] /sheer/ *v. & n.* ● *v.intr.* **1** esp. *Naut.* swerve or change course **2** (foll. by *away, off*) go away, esp. from a person or topic one dislikes or fears. ● *n. Naut.* a deviation from a course. [perh. f. MLG *scheren* = SHEAR *v.*]

sheer[3] /sheer/ *n.* the upward slope of a ship's lines toward the bow and stern. [prob. f. SHEAR *n.*]

sheer·legs /shéerlegz/ *n.pl.* (treated as *sing.*) a hoisting apparatus made from poles joined at or near the top and separated at the bottom for masting ships, installing engines, etc. [*sheer*, var. of SHEAR *n.* + LEG]

sheet[1] /sheet/ *n. & v.* ● *n.* **1** a large rectangular piece of cotton or other fabric, used esp. in pairs as inner bedclothes. **2 a** a broad usu. thin flat piece of material (e.g., paper or metal). **b** (*attrib.*) made in sheets (*sheet iron*). **3** a wide continuous surface or expanse of water, ice, flame, falling rain, etc. **4** a set of unseparated postage stamps. **5** *derog.* a newspaper, esp. a disreputable one. **6** a complete piece of paper of the size in which it was made, for printing and folding as part of a book. ● *v.* **1** *tr.* provide or cover with sheets. **2** *tr.* form into sheets. **3** *intr.* (of rain, etc.) fall in sheets. [OE *scēte, scīete* f. Gmc]

sheet[2] /sheet/ *n.* **1** a rope or chain attached to the lower corner of a sail for securing or controlling it. **2** (in *pl.*) the space at the bow or stern of an open boat. [ME f. OE *scēata*, ON *skaut* (as SHEET[1])]

sheet an·chor *n.* **1** a second anchor for use in emergencies. **2** a person or thing depended on in the last resort.

sheet bend *n.* a method of temporarily fastening one rope through the loop of another.

sheet·ing /shéeting/ *n.* fabric for making bed linen.

sheet light·ning *n.* a lightning flash with its brightness diffused by reflection.

sheet met·al *n.* metal formed into thin sheets by rolling, hammering, etc.

sheet mu·sic *n.* music published in cut or folded sheets, not bound.

sheikh /sheek, shayk/ *n.* (also **sheik, shaikh**) **1** a chief or head of an Arab tribe, family, or village. **2** a Muslim leader. □□ **sheikh·dom** *n.* [ult. f. Arab. *šayk* old man, sheikh, f. *šāk a* be or grow old]

shei·la /shéelə/ *n. Austral. & NZ sl.* a girl or young woman. [orig. *shaler* (of unkn. orig.): assim. to the name *Sheila*]

shek·el /shékəl/ *n.* **1** the chief monetary unit of modern Israel. **2** *hist.* a silver coin and unit of weight used in ancient Israel and the Middle East. **3** (in *pl.*) *colloq.* money; riches. [Heb. *šekel* f. *šākal* weigh]

shel·duck /shéldʌk/ *n.* (*pl.* same or **shel·ducks**; *masc.* **shel·drake**, *pl.* same or **shel·drakes**) any bright-plumaged coastal wild duck of the genus *Tadorna*, esp. *T. tadorna*. [ME prob. f. dial. *sheld* pied, rel. to MDu. *schillede* variegated, + DUCK[1], DRAKE]

shelf[1] /shelf/ *n.* (*pl.* **shelves** /shelvz/) **1 a** a thin flat piece of wood or metal, etc., projecting from a wall, or as part of a unit, used to support books, etc. **b** a flat-topped recess in a wall, etc., used for supporting objects. **2 a** a projecting horizontal ledge in a cliff face, etc. **b** a reef or sandbank under water. **c** = CONTINENTAL SHELF. □ **on the shelf 1** (of a woman) past the age when she might expect to be married. **2** (esp. of a retired person) no longer active or of use. **3** postponed, as a plan or project. □□ **shelved** /shelvd/ *adj.* **shelful** *n.* (*pl.* **·fuls**). **shelf·like** *adj.* [ME f. (M)LG *schelf*, rel. to OE *scylfe* partition, *scylf* crag]

shelf² /shelf/ *n. & v. Austral. sl.* ● *n.* an informer. ● *v.tr.* inform upon. [20th c.: orig. uncert.]

shelf life *n.* the amount of time for which a stored item of medicine, food, etc., remains usable.

shelf mark *n.* a notation on a book showing its place in a library.

shell /shel/ *n. & v.* ● *n.* **1 a** the hard outer case of many marine mollusks (*mussel shell*). **b** the esp. hard but fragile outer covering of a bird's, reptile's, etc., egg. **c** the usu. hard outer case of a nut kernel, seed, etc. **d** the carapace of a tortoise, turtle, etc. **e** the elytron or cocoon, etc., of many insects, etc. **2 a** an explosive projectile or bomb for use in a big gun or mortar. **b** a hollow metal or paper case used as a container for fireworks, explosives, cartridges, etc. **c** a cartridge. **3** a mere semblance or outer form without substance. **4** any of several things resembling a shell in being an outer case, esp.: **a** a light racing boat. **b** a hollow pastry case. **c** the metal framework of a vehicle body, etc. **d** the walls of an unfinished or gutted building, ship, etc. **e** an inner or roughly made coffin. **f** a building shaped like a conch. **g** the handguard of a sword. **5** a group of electrons with almost equal energy in an atom. ● *v.* **1** *tr.* remove the shell or pod from. **2** *tr.* bombard (a town, troops, etc.) with shells. **3** *tr.* provide or cover with a shell or shells. **4** *intr.* (usu. foll. by *off*) (of metal, etc.) come off in scales. **5** *intr.* (of a seed, etc.) be released from a shell. □ **come out of one's shell** cease to be shy; become communicative. **shell out** (also *absol.*) *colloq.* **1** pay (money). **2** hand over (a required sum). □□ **shelled** *adj.* **shell·less** *adj.* **shell·like** *adj.* **shell·proof** *adj.* (in sense 2a of *n.*). **shell·y** *adj.* [OE *sc(i)ell* f. Gmc: cf. SCALE¹]

she'll /sheel, shil/ *contr.* she will; she shall.

shel·lac /shəlák/ *n. & v.* ● *n.* lac resin melted into thin flakes and used for making varnish (cf. LAC¹). ● *v.tr.* (**shel·lacked, shel·lacking**) **1** varnish with shellac. **2** *sl.* defeat or thrash soundly. [SHELL + LAC, transl. F *laque en écailles* lac in thin plates]

shell·back /shélbak/ *n. sl.* an old sailor.

shell·fish /shélfish/ *n.* **1** an aquatic shelled mollusk, e.g., an oyster, mussel, etc. **2** a crustacean, e.g., a crab, shrimp, etc.

shell jack·et *n.* an army officer's tight-fitting jacket reaching to the waist.

shell mon·ey *n.* shells used as a medium of exchange, e.g., wampum.

shell pink *n.* a delicate pale pink.

shell shock *n.* a nervous breakdown resulting from exposure to battle. □□ **shell-shocked** *adj.*

shell·work /shélwərk/ *n.* ornamentation consisting of shells cemented onto wood, etc.

shel·ter /shéltər/ *n. & v.* ● *n.* **1** anything serving as a shield or protection from danger, bad weather, etc. **2 a** a place of refuge provided esp. for the homeless, etc. **b** an animal sanctuary. **3** a shielded condition; protection (*took shelter under a tree*). ● *v.* **1** *tr.* act or serve as shelter to; protect; conceal; defend (*sheltered them from the storm; had a sheltered upbringing*). **2** *intr. & refl.* find refuge; take cover (*sheltered under a tree; sheltered themselves behind the wall*). □□ **shel·ter·er** *n.* **shel·ter·less** *adj.* [16th c.: perh. f. obs. *sheltron* phalanx f. OE *scieldtruma* (as SHIELD, *truma* troop)]

shel·ter belt *n. Brit.* = WINDBREAK. a line of trees, etc., planted to protect crops, etc., from the wind.

shel·tie /shéltee/ *n.* (also **shel·ty**) (*pl.* **·ties**) a Shetland pony or sheepdog. [prob. repr. ON *Hjalti* Shetlander, as pronounced in Orkney]

shelve¹ /shelv/ *v.tr.* **1** put (books, etc.) on a shelf. **2 a** abandon or defer (a plan, etc.). **b** remove (a person) from active work, etc. **3** fit (a cupboard, etc.) with shelves. □□ **shelv·er** *n.* **shelv·ing** *n.* [*shelves* pl. of SHELF¹]

shelve² /shelv/ *v.intr.* (of ground, etc.) slope in a specified direction (*land shelved away to the horizon*). [perh. f. *shelvy* (adj.) having underwater reefs f. *shelve* (n.) ledge, f. SHELVE¹]

shelves *pl.* of SHELF.

she·moz·zle /shimózəl/ *n.* (also **sche·moz·zle**) *sl.* **1** a brawl or commotion. **2** a muddle. [Yiddish after LHeb. *šel-lōʾ-mazzāl* of no luck]

she·nan·i·gan /shinánigən/ *n.* (esp. in *pl.*) *colloq.* **1** high-spirited behavior; nonsense. **2** trickery; dubious maneuvers. [19th c.: orig. unkn.]

She·ol /shee-ōl/ *n.* the Hebrew underworld abode of the dead. [Heb. *šeʾōl*]

shep·herd /shépərd/ *n. & v.* ● *n.* **1** (*fem.* **shep·herd·ess** /shépərdis/) a person employed to tend sheep, esp. at pasture. **2** a member of the clergy, etc., who cares for and guides a congregation. ● *v.tr.* **1 a** tend (sheep, etc.) as a shepherd. **b** guide (followers, etc.). **2** marshal or drive (a crowd, etc.) like sheep. [OE *scēaphierde* (as SHEEP, HERD)]

shep·herd dog *n.* a sheepdog.

shep·herd's check *n.* (also **shep·herd's plaid**) **1** a small black and white check pattern. **2** woolen cloth with this pattern.

shep·herd's crook *n.* a staff with a hook at one end used by shepherds.

shep·herd's nee·dle *n.* a white-flowered common plant, *Scandix pecten-veneris*, with spiny fruit.

shep·herd's pie *n.* a dish of ground or diced meat under a layer of mashed potato.

shep·herd's purse *n.* a white-flowered, hairy weed, *Capsella bursa-pastoris*, with triangular or cordate pods.

sher·ard·ize /shérərdīz/ *v.tr.* coat (iron or steel) with zinc by heating in contact with zinc dust. [*Sherard* Cowper-Coles, Engl. inventor d. 1936]

Sher·a·ton /shérət'n/ *n.* (often *attrib.*) a style of furniture introduced in England *c.*1790, with delicate and graceful forms. [T. *Sheraton*, Engl. furniture maker d. 1806]

sher·bet /shárbət/ *n.* **1 a** a fruit-flavored ice confection. **b** *Brit.* a flavored sweet effervescent powder or drink. **2** a cooling drink of sweet, diluted fruit juices, used esp. in the Middle East. **3** *Austral. joc.* beer. [Turk. ş *erbet*, Pers. *šerbet* f. Arab. *šarba* drink f. *šariba* to drink: cf. SHRUB², SYRUP]

sherd /shərd/ *n.* = POTSHERD. [var. of SHARD]

she·reef (also **she·rif**) var. of SHARIF.

sher·iff /shérif/ *n.* **1** an elected officer in a county, responsible for keeping the peace. **2** *Brit.* **a** (also **High Sher·iff**) the chief executive officer of the Crown in a county, administering justice, etc. **b** an honorary officer elected annually in some towns. □□ **sher·iff·al·ty** *n.* (*pl.* **·ties**). **sher·iff·dom** *n.* **sher·iff·hood** *n.* **sher·iff·ship** *n.* [OE *scīr-gerēfa* (as SHIRE, REEVE¹)]

Sher·pa /shárpə/ *n.* (*pl.* same or **Sher·pas**) **1** a Himalayan people living on the borders of Nepal and Tibet, and skilled in mountaineering. **2** a member of this people. [native name]

sher·ry /shéree/ *n.* (*pl.* **·ries**) **1** a fortified wine orig. from S. Spain. **2** a glass of this. [earlier *sherris* f. Sp. (*vino de*) *Xeres* (now Jerez de la Frontera) in Andalusia]

sher·ry cob·bler *n.* see COBBLER 2.

sher·ry glass *n.* a small wineglass used for sherry.

she's /sheez/ *contr.* **1** she is. **2** she has.

Shet·land·er /shétləndər/ *n.* a native of the Shetland Islands, NNE of the mainland of Scotland.

Shet·land po·ny *n.* **1** a pony of a small, hardy, rough-coated breed. **2** this breed.

Shet·land sheep·dog *n.* **1** a small dog of a collielike breed. **2** this breed.

Shet·land wool *n.* a fine, loosely twisted wool from Shetland sheep.

shew *archaic* var. of SHOW.

shew·bread /shóbred/ *n.* twelve loaves that were displayed in a Jewish temple and renewed each sabbath.

Shi·a /sheeə/ *n.* one of the two main branches of Islam, esp. in Iran, that rejects the first three Sunni caliphs and regards Ali as Muhammad's first successor. [Arab. *šīʿa* party (of Ali, Muhammad's cousin and son-in-law)]

shi·at·su /shiátsoo/ *n.* a kind of therapy of Japanese origin, in which pressure is applied with the fingers to certain points of the body. [Jap., = finger pressure]

shib·bo·leth /shíbəleth/ *n.* a long-standing formula, doctrine, or phrase, etc., held to be true by a party or sect (*must abandon outdated shibboleths*). [ME f. Heb. *šibbōleṯ* ear of corn, used as a test of nationality for its difficult pronunciation (Judg. 12:6)]

shi·cer /shísər/ *n. Austral.* **1** *Mining* an unproductive claim or mine. **2** *sl.* a swindler, welsher, or cheat. **b** a worthless thing; a failure. [G *Scheisser* contemptible person]

shick·er /shíkər/ *adj.* (also **shick·ered** /shíkərd/) *Austral. & NZ sl.* drunk. [Yiddish *shiker* f. Heb. *šikkōr* f. *šākar* be drunk]

shield /sheeld/ *n. & v.* ● *n.* **1 a** esp. *hist.* a piece of armor of esp. metal, carried on the arm or in the hand to deflect blows from the head or body. **b** a thing serving to protect (*insurance is a shield against disaster*). **2** a thing resembling a shield, esp.: **a** a trophy in the form of a shield. **b** a protective plate or screen in machinery, etc. **c** a shieldlike part of an animal, esp. a shell. **d** a similar part of a plant. **e** *Geol.* a large rigid area of the earth's crust, usu. of Precambrian rock, which has been unaffected by later orogenic episodes. **f** a police officer's shield-shaped badge. **3** *Heraldry* a stylized representation of a shield used for displaying a coat of arms, etc. ● *v.tr.* protect or screen, esp. from blame or lawful punishment. □□ **shield·less** *adj.* [OE *sc(i)eld* f. Gmc: prob. orig. = board, rel. to SCALE¹]

shiel·ing /sheeling/ *n.* (also **sheal·ing**) *Sc.* **1** a roughly constructed hut orig. esp. for pastoral use. **2** pasture for cattle. [Sc. *shiel* hut: ME, of unkn. orig.]

shi·er *compar.* of SHY¹.

shi·est *superl.* of SHY¹.

shift /shift/ *v. & n.* ● *v.* **1** *intr. & tr.* change or move or cause to change or move from one position to another. **2** *tr. Brit.* remove, esp. with effort (*washing won't shift the stains*). **3** *Brit. sl.* **a** *intr.* hurry (*we'll have to shift!*). **b** *tr.* consume (food or drink) hastily or in bulk. **c** *tr.* sell (esp. dubious goods). **4** *intr.* contrive or manage as best one can **5 a** *tr.* change (gear) in a vehicle. **b** *intr.* change gear. **6** *intr.* (of cargo) get shaken out of place. **7** *intr. archaic* be evasive or indirect. • *n.* **1 a** the act or an instance of shifting. **b** the substitution of one thing for another; a rotation. **2 a** a relay of workers (*the night shift*). **b** the time for which they work (*an eight-hour shift*). **3 a** a device, stratagem, or expedient. **b** a dodge, trick, or evasion. **4 a** a woman's straight unwaisted dress. **b** *archaic* a loose-fitting undergarment. **5** a displacement of spectral lines, e.g., to the red end of the spectrum (see also RED SHIFT). **6** (also **sound shift**) a systematic change in pronunciation as a language evolves. **7** (in full **shift key**) a key on a keyboard used to switch between lowercase and uppercase, etc. **8** *Bridge* **a** a change of suit in bidding. **b** a change of suit in play. **9** the positioning of successive rows of bricks so that their ends do not coincide. **10 a** a gear lever in a motor vehicle. **b** a mechanism for this. □ **make shift** *Brit.* manage or contrive; get along somehow (*made shift without it*). **shift for oneself** rely on one's own efforts. **shift one's ground** take up a new position in an argument, etc. **shift off** esp. *Brit.* get rid of (responsibility, etc.) to another. □□ **shift•a•ble** *adj.* **shift•er** *n.* [OE *sciftan* arrange, divide, etc., f. Gmc]

shift•less /shíftlis/ *adj.* lacking resourcefulness; lazy; inefficient. □□ **shift•less•ly** *adv.* **shift•less•ness** *n.*

shift•y /shíftee/ *adj. colloq.* (**shift•i•er**, **shift•i•est**) not straightforward; evasive; deceitful. □□ **shift•i•ly** *adv.* **shift•i•ness** *n.*

shi•gel•la /shigélə/ *n.* (*pl.* **shi•gel•lae** /–lee/ or **shi•gel•las**) any airborne bacterium of the genus *Shigella*, some of which cause dysentery. [mod.L f. K. *Shiga*, Jap. bacteriologist d. 1957 + dimin. suffix]

shih tzu /shee dzóo, sheetsóo/ *n.* (*pl.* **shih tzus** or same) **1** a dog of a breed with long silky hair and short legs. **2** this breed. [Chin. *shizi* lion]

Shi•ite /shee-īt/ *n. & adj.* • *n.* an adherent of the Shia branch of Islam. • *adj.* of or relating to Shia. □□ **Shi•ism** /shee-izəm/ *n.*

shi•kar /shikaár/ *n. Ind.* hunting. [Urdu f. Pers. *šikār*]

shik•sa /shíksə/ *n. often offens.* (used by Jews) a gentile girl or woman. [Yiddish *shikse* f. Heb. *šiqsā* f. *sheqeṣ* detested thing + –*â* fem. suffix]

shill /shil/ *n.* a person employed to decoy or entice others into buying, gambling, etc. [prob. f. earlier *shillaber*, of unkn. orig.]

shil•le•lagh /shiláylee, –lə/ *n.* a thick stick of blackthorn or oak used in Ireland esp. as a weapon. [*Shillelagh* in County Wicklow, Ireland]

shil•ling /shíling/ *n.* **1** *hist.* a former British coin and monetary unit worth one-twentieth of a pound or twelve pence. **2** a monetary unit in Kenya, Tanzania, and Uganda. □ **take the King's** (or **Queen's**) **shilling** *Brit. hist.* enlist as a soldier (formerly a soldier was paid a shilling on enlisting). [OE *scilling*, f. Gmc]

shil•ling mark *n. hist.* = SOLIDUS.

shil•ly-shal•ly /shíleeshálee/ *v., adj., & n.* • *v.intr.* (**-lies**, **-lied**) hesitate to act or choose; be undecided; vacillate. • *adj.* vacillating. • *n.* indecision; vacillation. □□ **shil•ly-shal•ly•er** *n.* (also **–shal•li•er**). [orig. *shill I, shall I,* redupl. of *shall I?*]

shim /shim/ *n. & v.* • *n.* a thin strip of material used in machinery, etc., to make parts fit. • *v.tr.* (**shimmed**, **shim•ming**) fit or fill up with a shim. [18th c.: orig. unkn.]

shim•mer /shímər/ *v. & n.* • *v.intr.* shine with a tremulous or faint diffused light. • *n.* such a light. □□ **shim•mer•ing•ly** *adv.* **shim•mer•y** *adj.* [OE *scymrian* Gmc: cf. SHINE]

shim•my /shímee/ *n. & v.* • *n.* (*pl.* **-mies**) **1** *hist.* a kind of ragtime dance in which the whole body is shaken. **2** *archaic colloq.* = CHEMISE. **3** an abnormal vibration of esp. the front wheels of a motor vehicle. • *v.intr.* (**-mies**, **-mied**) **1 a** *hist.* dance a shimmy. **b** move in a similar manner. **2** shake or vibrate abnormally. [20th c.: orig. uncert.]

shin /shin/ *n. & v.* • *n.* **1** the front of the leg below the knee. **2** a cut of beef from the foreleg. • *v.tr. & (usu. foll. by up, down*) *intr.* (**shinned**, **shin•ning**) climb quickly by clinging with the arms and legs. [OE *sinu*]

shin•bone /shínbōn/ *n.* = TIBIA.

shin•dig /shíndig/ *n. colloq.* **1** a festive, esp. noisy, party. **2** = SHINDY 1. [prob. f. SHINDY]

shin•dy /shíndee/ *n.* (*pl.* **-dies**) *colloq.* **1** a brawl, disturbance, or noise (*kicked up a shindy*). **2** = SHINDIG 1. [perh. alt. of SHINTY]

shine /shīn/ *v. & n.* • *v.* (*past and past part.* **shone** /shon/ or **shined**) **1** *intr.* emit or reflect light; be bright; glow (*the lamp was shining; his face shone with gratitude*). **2** *intr.* (of the sun, a star, etc.) not be obscured by clouds; be visible. **3** *tr.* cause (a lamp, etc.) to shine. **4** *tr.* (*past and past part.* **shined**) make bright; polish (*shined his shoes*). **5** *intr.* be brilliant in some respect; excel (*does not shine in conversation; is a shining example*). • *n.* **1** light; brightness, esp. re-

flected. **2** a high polish; luster. **3** the act or an instance of shining esp. shoes. □ **shine up to** seek to ingratiate oneself with. **take the shine out of 1** spoil the brilliance or newness of. **2** throw into the shade by surpassing. **take a shine to** *colloq.* take a fancy to; like. □□ **shin•ing•ly** *adv.* [OE *scīnan* f. Gmc]

shin•er /shínər/ *n.* **1** a thing that shines. **2** *colloq.* a black eye. **3** any of various small silvery freshwater fish, esp. of the genus *Notropis*. **4** (usu. in *pl.*) *sl. archaic* money. **b** a jewel.

shin•gle¹ /shínggəl/ *n.* (in *sing.* or *pl.*) small rounded pebbles, esp. on a seashore. □□ **shin•gly** *adj.* [16th c.: orig. uncert.]

shin•gle² /shínggəl/ *n. & v.* • *n.* **1** a rectangular wooden tile used on roofs, spires, or esp. walls. **2** *archaic* **a** shingled hair. **b** the act of shingling hair. **3** a small signboard, esp. of a doctor, lawyer, etc. • *v.tr.* **1** roof or clad with shingles. **2** *archaic* **a** cut (a woman's hair) very short. **b** cut the hair of (a person or head) in this way. [ME app. f. L *scindula*, earlier *scandula*]

shin•gles /shínggəlz/ *n.pl.* (usu. treated as *sing.*) an acute painful viral inflammation of the nerve ganglia, with a skin eruption often forming a girdle around the middle of the body. [ME f. med.L *cingulus* f. L *cingulum* girdle f. *cingere* gird]

shin guard *n.* a protective pad for the shins, worn when playing football, etc.

shin•ny /shínee/ *v.intr.* (**-nies**, **-nied**) (usu. foll. by *up, down*) *colloq.* shin (up or down a tree, etc.).

Shin•to /shíntō/ *n.* the official religion of Japan incorporating the worship of ancestors and nature spirits. □□ **Shin•to•ism** *n.* **Shin•to•ist** *n.* [Jap. f. Chin. *shen dao* way of the gods]

shin•ty /shíntee/ *n.* (*pl.* **-ties**) *Brit.* **1** a game like hockey played with a ball and curved sticks, and taller goalposts. **2** a stick or ball used in shinty. [earlier *shinny*, app. f. the cry used in the game *shin ye, shin you, shin t' ye,* of unkn. orig.]

shin•y /shínee/ *adj.* (**shin•i•er**, **shin•i•est**) **1** having a shine; glistening; polished; bright. **2** (of clothing, esp. the seat of pants, etc.) having the nap worn off. □□ **shin•i•ly** *adv.* **shin•i•ness** *n.* [SHINE]

ship /ship/ *n. & v.* • *n.* **1 a** any large seagoing vessel (cf. BOAT). **b** a sailing vessel with a bowsprit and three, four, or five square-rigged masts. **2** an aircraft. **3** a spaceship. **4** *colloq.* a boat, esp. a racing boat. • *v.* (**shipped**, **ship•ping**) **1** *tr.* put, take or send away (goods, passengers, sailors, etc.) on board ship. **2** *tr.* **a** take in (water) over the side of a ship, boat, etc. **b** take (oars) from the rowlocks and lay them inside a boat. **c** fix (a rudder, etc.) in its place on a ship, etc. **d** step (a mast). **3** *intr.* **a** take ship; embark. **b** (of a sailor) take service on a ship (*shipped for Africa*). **4** *tr.* deliver (goods) to a forwarding agent for conveyance. □ **ship off 1** send or transport by ship. **2** *colloq.* send (a person) away. **take ship** embark. **when a person's ship comes in** when a person's fortune is made. □□ **ship•less** *adj.* **ship•pa•ble** *adj.* [OE *scip, scipian* f. Gmc]

-ship /ship/ *suffix* forming nouns denoting: **1** a quality or condition (*friendship; hardship*). **2** status, office, or honor (*authorship; lordship*). **3** a tenure of office (*chairmanship*). **4** a skill in a certain capacity (*workmanship*). **5** the collective individuals of a group (*membership*). [OE *-scipe*, etc., f. Gmc]

ship bis•cuit *n.* (also **ship bread**) *hist.* a hard, coarse kind of biscuit kept and eaten on board ship.

ship•board /shípbawrd/ *n.* (usu. *attrib.*) used or occurring on board a ship (*a shipboard romance*). □ **on shipboard** on board ship.

ship•build•er /shípbildər/ *n.* a person, company, etc., that constructs ships. □□ **ship•build•ing** *n.*

ship bur•i•al *n. Archaeol.* burial in a wooden ship under a mound.

ship-ca•nal *n.* a canal large enough for ships to pass inland.

ship•lap /shíplap/ *v. & n.* • *v.tr.* fit (boards) together for cladding, etc., so that each overlaps the one below. • *n.* such cladding.

ship•load /shíplōd/ *n.* a quantity of goods forming a cargo.

ship•mas•ter /shípmastər/ *n.* a ship's captain.

ship•mate /shípmayt/ *n.* a fellow member of a ship's crew.

ship•ment /shípmənt/ *n.* **1** an amount of goods shipped; a consignment. **2** the act or an instance of shipping goods, etc.

ship of the des•ert *n.* the camel.

ship of the line *n. hist.* a large battleship fighting in the front line of battle.

ship•own•er /shípōnər/ *n.* a person owning a ship or ships or shares in ships.

ship•per /shípər/ *n.* a person or company that sends or receives goods by ship, or by land or air. [OE *scipere* (as SHIP)]

ship•ping /shíping/ *n.* **1** the act or an instance of shipping goods, etc. **2** ships, esp. the ships of a country, port, etc.

ship•ping a•gent *n.* a person acting for a ship or ships at a port, etc.

ship-rigged *adj.* square-rigged.

ship's boat *n.* a small boat carried on board a ship.

ship's com•pa•ny *n.* a ship's entire crew.

ship•shape /shípshayp/ *adv. & predic.adj.* in good order; trim and neat.

ship's pa•pers *n.pl.* documents establishing the ownership, nationality, nature of the cargo, etc., of a ship.

ship•way /shípway/ *n.* a slope on which a ship is built and down which it slides to be launched.

ship•worm /shípwərm/ *n.* = TEREDO.

ship•wreck /shíprek/ *n. & v.* ●*n.* **1 a** the destruction of a ship by a storm, foundering, etc. **b** a ship so destroyed. **2** (often foll. by *of*) the destruction of hopes, dreams, etc. ●*v.* **1** *tr.* inflict shipwreck on (a ship, a person's hopes, etc.). **2** *intr.* suffer shipwreck.

ship•wright /shíprīt/ *n.* **1** a shipbuilder. **2** a ship's carpenter.

ship•yard /shípyaard/ *n.* a place where ships are built, repaired, etc.

shir•a•lee /shírəlee/ *n. Austral.* a tramp's swag or bundle. [20th c.: orig. unkn.]

shire /shīr/ *n. Brit.* **1** a county. **2** (**the Shires**) **a** a group of English counties with names ending or formerly ending in *–shire*, extending NE from Hampshire and Devon. **b** the midland counties of England. **c** the fox-hunting district of mainly Leicestershire and Northants. **3** *Austral.* a rural area with its own elected council. [OE *scīr*, OHG *scīra* care, official charge: orig. unkn.]

-shire /shər, sheer/ *suffix* forming the names of counties (*Derbyshire*; *Hampshire*).

shirk /shərk/ *v. & n.* ●*v.tr.* (also *absol.*) shrink from; avoid; get out of (duty, work, responsibility, fighting, etc.). ●*n.* a person who shirks. □□ **shirk•er** *n.* [obs. *shirk* (n.) sponger, perh. f. G *Schurke* scoundrel]

shirr /shər/ *n. & v.* ●*n.* **1** two or more rows of esp. elastic gathered threads in a garment, etc., forming smocking. **2** elastic webbing. ●*v.tr.* **1** gather (material) with parallel threads. **2** bake (eggs) without shells. □□ **shirr•ing** *n.* [19th c.: orig. unkn.]

shirt /shərt/ *n.* **1** an upper-body garment of cotton, etc., having a collar, sleeves, and esp. buttons down the front, and often worn under a jacket or sweater; a blouse. **2 a** an undershirt. **b** a T-shirt. **3** = NIGHTSHIRT . □ **keep one's shirt on** *colloq.* keep one's temper. **lose one's shirt** lose all that one has, as through gambling, etc. **the shirt off one's back** *colloq.* one's last remaining possessions. □□ **shirt•ed** *adj.* **shirt•ing** *n.* **shirt•less** *adj.*

WORD HISTORY **shirt**

Old English *scyrte*, of Germanic origin; related to Old Norse *skyrta* (source of *skirt*), Dutch *schort*, German *Schürze* 'apron,' also to *short*; probably from a base meaning 'short garment.'

---

shirt•dress /shərtdress/ *n.* = SHIRTWAIST sense 2. [SHIRT, DRESS]

shirt•front /shərtfrunt/ *n.* the breast of a shirt, esp. of a stiffened evening shirt.

shirt•sleeve /shərtsleev/ *n.* (usu. in *pl.*) the sleeve of a shirt. □ **in shirtsleeves** wearing a shirt with no jacket, etc., over it.

shirt•tail /shərttayl/ *n.* the lower curved part of a shirt below the waist.

shirt•waist /shərtwayst/ *n.* **1** a woman's dress with a bodice like a shirt. **2** a woman's blouse resembling a shirt. [SHIRT, WAIST]

shirt•y /shərtee/ *adj.* (**shirt•i•er**, **shirt•i•est**) *Brit. colloq.* angry; annoyed. □□ **shirt•i•ly** *adv.* **shirt•i•ness** *n.*

shish ke•bab /shísh kibób/ *n.* a dish of pieces of marinated meat and vegetables cooked and served on skewers. [Turk. *şiş kebabı* f. *şiş* skewer, KEBAB roast meat]

shit /shit/ *v., n., & int. coarse sl.* ●*v.* (**shit•ting**; *past* and *past part.* **shit** or **shat**) *intr. & tr.* expel feces from the body or cause (feces, etc.) to be expelled. ●*n.* **1** feces. **2** an act of defecating. **3** a contemptible or worthless person or thing. **4** nonsense. **5** an intoxicating drug, esp. cannabis. ●*int.* an exclamation of disgust, anger, etc. [OE *scītan* (unrecorded) f. Gmc]

▶This word is usually considered taboo.

shit•ty /shítee/ *adj.* (**shit•ti•er**, **shit•ti•est**) *coarse sl.* **1** disgusting; contemptible. **2** covered with excrement.

Shi•va var. of SIVA.

shiv•a•ree var. of CHARIVARI.

shiv•er[1] /shívər/ *v. & n.* ●*v.intr.* **1** tremble with cold, fear, etc. **2** suffer a quick trembling movement of the body; shudder. ●*n.* **1 a** momentary shivering movement. **2** (in *pl.*) an attack of shivering, esp. from fear or horror (*got the shivers in the dark*). □□ **shiv•er•er** *n.* **shiv•er•ing•ly** *adv.* **shiv•er•y** *adj.* [ME *chivere*, perh. f. *chavele* chatter (as JOWL[1])]

shiv•er[2] /shívər/ *n. & v.* ●*n.* (esp. in *pl.*) each of the small pieces into which esp. glass is shattered when broken; a splinter. ●*v.tr. & intr.* break into shivers. □ **shiver my** (or **me**) **timbers** a reputed piratical curse. [ME *scifre*, rel. to OHG *scivaro* splinter f. Gmc]

shi•voo /shivóo/ *n. Austral. colloq.* a party or celebration.

shoal[1] /shōl/ *n. & v.* ●*n.* **1** a great number of fish swimming together (cf. SCHOOL[2]). **2** a multitude; a crowd (*shoals of letters*). ●*v.intr.* (of fish) form shoals. [prob. readoption of MDu. *schōle* SCHOOL[2]]

shoal[2] /shōl/ *n., v., & adj.* ●*n.* **1 a** an area of shallow water. **b** a submerged sandbank visible at low water. **2** (esp. in *pl.*) hidden danger or difficulty. ●*v.* **1** *intr.* (of water) get shallower. **2** *tr.* (of a ship, etc.) move into a shallower part of (water). ●*adj. archaic* (of water) shallow. □□ **shoal•y** *adj.* [OE *sceald* f. Gmc, rel. to SHALLOW]

shoat /shōt/ *n.* a young pig, esp. newly weaned. [ME: cf. W.Flem. *schote*]

shock[1] /shok/ *n. & v.* ●*n.* **1** a violent collision, impact, tremor, etc. **2** a sudden and disturbing effect on the emotions, physical reac-

tions, etc. (*the news was a great shock*). **3** an acute state of prostration following a wound, pain, etc., esp. when much blood is lost (*died of shock*). **4** = ELECTRIC SHOCK. **5** a disturbance in stability causing fluctuations in an organization, monetary system, etc. ●*v.* **1** *tr.* **a** affect with shock; horrify; outrage; disgust; sadden. **b** (*absol.*) cause shock. **2** *tr.* (esp. in *passive*) affect with an electric or pathological shock. **3** *intr.* experience shock (*I don't shock easily*). **4** *intr. archaic* collide violently. □□ **shock•a•ble** *adj.* **shock•a•bil•i•ty** *n.* [F *choc, choquer*, of unkn. orig.]

shock[2] /shok/ *n. & v.* ●*n.* a group of usu. twelve sheaves of grain stood up with their heads together in a field. ●*v.tr.* arrange (grain) in shocks. [ME, perh. repr. OE *sc(e)oc* (unrecorded)]

shock[3] /shok/ *n.* an unkempt or shaggy mass of hair. [cf. obs. *shock(-dog)*, earlier *shough*, shaggy-haired poodle]

shock ab•sorb•er *n.* a device on a vehicle, etc., for absorbing shocks, vibrations, etc.

shock•er /shókər/ *n. colloq.* **1** a shocking, horrifying, unacceptable, etc., person or thing. **2** *hist.* a sordid or sensational novel, etc. **3** *Brit.* a shock absorber.

shock•ing /shóking/ *adj. & adv.* ●*adj.* **1** causing indignation or disgust. **2** *Brit. colloq.* very bad (*shocking weather*). ●*adv. colloq.* shockingly (*shocking bad manners*). □□ **shock•ing•ly** *adv.* **shock•ing•ness** *n.*

shock•ing pink *n.* a vibrant shade of pink.

shock•proof /shókproof/ *adj.* resistant to the effects of (esp. physical) shock.

shock tac•tics *n.pl.* **1** sudden and violent action. **2** *Mil.* a massed cavalry charge.

shock ther•a•py *n.* (also **shock treat•ment**) *Psychol.* a method of treating depressive patients by electric shock or drugs inducing coma and convulsions.

shock troops *n.pl.* troops specially trained for assault.

shock wave *n.* a sharp change of pressure in a narrow region traveling through air, etc., caused by explosion or by a body moving faster than sound.

shod *past* and *past part.* of SHOE.

shod•dy /shódee/ *adj. & n.* ●*adj.* (**shod•di•er**, **shod•di•est**) **1** trashy; shabby; poorly made. **2** counterfeit. ●*n.* (*pl.* **·dies**) **1 a** an inferior cloth made partly from the shredded fiber of old woolen cloth. **b** such fiber. **2** any thing of shoddy quality. □□ **shod•di•ly** *adv.* **shod•di•ness** *n.* [19th c.: orig. dial.]

shoe /shoo/ *n. & v.* ●*n.* **1** either of a pair of protective foot coverings of leather, plastic, etc., having a sturdy sole and not reaching above the ankle. **2** a metal rim nailed to the hoof of a horse, etc.; a horseshoe. **3** anything resembling a shoe in shape or use, esp.: **a** a drag for a wheel. **b** = BRAKE SHOE. **c** a socket. **d** a ferrule, esp. on a sled runner. **e** a mast step. **f** a box from which cards are dealt in casinos at baccarat, etc. ●*v.tr.* (**shoes**, **shoe•ing**; *past* and *past part.* **shod**) /shod/ **1** fit (esp. a horse, etc.) with a shoe or shoes. **2** protect (the end of a pole, etc.) with a metal shoe. **3** (as **shod** *adj.*) (in *comb.*) having shoes, etc., of a specified kind (*dry-shod; roughshod*). □ **be in a person's shoes** be in his or her situation, difficulty, etc. **if the shoe fits** (said of a generalized comment) it seems to be true (of a particular person). **where the shoe pinches** where one's difficulty or trouble is. □□ **shoe•less** *adj.* [OE *scōh, scōg(e)an* f. Gmc]

shoe•bill /shoobil/ *n.* an African storklike bird, *Balaeniceps rex*, with a large flattened bill for catching aquatic prey.

shoe•black /shooblak/ *n.* esp. *Brit.* = BOOTBLACK.

shoe•box /shooboks/ *n.* **1** a box for packing shoes. **2** a very small space or dwelling.

shoe buck•le *n.* a buckle worn as ornament or as a fastening on a shoe.

shoe•horn /shoohawrn/ *n.* a curved piece of horn, metal, etc., for easing the heel into a shoe.

shoe•lace /shoolays/ *n.* a cord for lacing up shoes.

shoe leath•er *n.* leather for shoes, esp. when worn through by walking.

shoe•mak•er /shoomaykər/ *n.* a maker of boots and shoes. □□ **shoe•mak•ing** *n.*

shoe•shine /shooshīn/ *n.* a polish given to shoes.

shoe•string /shoostring/ *n.* **1** a shoelace. **2** *colloq.* a small esp. inadequate amount of money (*living on a shoestring*). **3** (*attrib.*) barely adequate; precarious (*a shoestring majority*).

shoe tree *n.* a shaped block for keeping a shoe in shape when not worn.

sho•far /shófər, shawfaár/ *n.* (*pl.* **sho•froth** /shófrōt/) a ram's-horn trumpet used by Jews in religious ceremonies and as an ancient battle signal. [Heb. *šôfār*, pl. *šôfārô ṭ*]

sho•gun /shógən, –gun/ *n. hist.* any of a succession of Japanese hereditary commanders in chief and virtual rulers before 1868. □□ **sho•gun•ate** /–nət, –nayt/ *n.* [Jap., = general, f. Chin. *jiang jun*]

shone *past* and *past part.* of SHINE.

shoo /shŏŏ/ *int. & v.* ● *int.* an exclamation used to frighten away birds, children, etc. ● *v.* (**shoos, shooed**) **1** *intr.* utter the word "shoo!" **2** *tr.* (usu. foll. by *away*) drive (birds, etc.) away by shooing. [imit.]

shoo-in *n.* something easy or certain to succeed (*she's a shoo-in to win the election*).

shook[1] /shŏŏk/ *past* of SHAKE. ● *predic.adj. colloq.* **1** (foll. by *up*) emotionally or physically disturbed; upset. **2** (foll. by *on*) *Austral. & NZ* keen on; enthusiastic about (*not too shook on the English climate*).

shook[2] /shŏŏk/ *n.* a set of staves and headings for a cask, ready for fitting together. [18th c.: orig. unkn.]

shoot /shŏŏt/ *v., n., & int.* ● *v.* (*past* and *past part.* **shot** /shot/) **1** *tr.* **a** cause (a gun, bow, etc.) to fire. **b** discharge (a bullet, arrow, etc.) from a gun, bow, etc. **c** kill or wound (a person, animal, etc.) with a bullet, arrow, etc. from a gun, bow, etc. **2** *intr.* discharge a gun, etc., esp. in a specified way (*shoots well*). **3** *tr.* send out, discharge, propel, etc. (*shot out the contents; shot a glance at his neighbor*). **4** *intr.* (often foll. by *out, along, forth,* etc.) come or go swiftly or vigorously. **5** *intr.* **a** (of a plant, etc.) put forth buds, etc. **b** (of a bud, etc.) appear. **6** *intr.* **a** hunt game, etc., with a gun. **b** (usu. foll. by *over*) shoot game over an estate, etc. **7** *tr.* shoot game in or on (coverts, an estate, etc.). **8** *tr.* film or photograph (a scene, film, etc.). **9** *tr.* (also *absol.*) *Basketball,* etc. **a** score (a goal). **b** take a shot at (the goal). **10** *tr.* (of a boat) sweep swiftly down or under (a bridge, rapids, falls, etc.). **11** *tr.* move (a door bolt) to fasten or unfasten a door, etc. **12** *tr.* let (trash, a load, etc.) fall or slide from a container, truck, etc. **13** *intr.* **a** (usu. foll. by *through, up,* etc.) (of a pain) pass with a stabbing sensation. **b** (of part of the body) be intermittently painful. **14** *intr.* (often foll. by *out*) project abruptly (*the mountain shoots out against the sky*). **15** *tr.* (often foll. by *up*) *sl.* inject esp. oneself with (a drug). **16** *tr. colloq.* **a** play a game of (craps, pool, etc.). **b** throw (a die or dice). **17** *tr. Golf colloq.* make (a specified score) for a round or hole. **18** *tr. colloq.* pass (traffic lights at red). **19** *tr.* plane (the edge of a board) accurately. ● *n.* **1** the act or an instance of shooting. **2 a** a young branch or sucker. **b** the new growth of a plant. **3** *Brit.* **a** a hunting party, expedition, etc. **b** land shot over for game. **4** = CHUTE[1]. **5** a rapid in a stream. ● *int. colloq.* **1** a demand for a reply, information, etc. **2** *euphem.* an exclamation of disgust, anger, etc. (see SHIT). □ **shoot ahead** come quickly to the front of competitors, etc. **shoot one's bolt** see BOLT[1]. **shoot down 1** kill (a person) by shooting. **2** cause (an aircraft, its pilot, etc.) to crash by shooting. **3** argue effectively against (a person, argument, etc.). **shoot from the hip** speak or act in haste. **shoot it out** *sl.* engage in a decisive gun battle. **shoot one's mouth off** *sl.* talk too much or indiscreetly. **shoot up 1** grow rapidly, esp. (of a person) grow taller. **2** rise suddenly. **3** terrorize (a district) by indiscriminate shooting. **4** *sl.* = sense 15 of *v.* □□ **shoot·a·ble** *adj.* [OE *scē otan* f. Gmc: cf. SHEET[1], SHOT[1], SHUT]

shoot·er /shŏŏtər/ *n.* **1** a person or thing that shoots. **2 a** (in *comb.*) a gun or other device for shooting (*peashooter; six-shooter*). **b** *sl.* a pistol, etc. **3** a player who shoots or is able to shoot a goal in basketball, etc. **4** a person who throws a die or dice.

shoot·ing /shŏŏting/ *n. & adj.* ● *n.* **1** the act or an instance of shooting. **2 a** the right of shooting over an area of land. **b** an estate, etc., rented to shoot over. ● *adj.* moving, growing, etc., quickly (*a shooting pain in the arm*). □ **the whole shooting match** *colloq.* everything.

shoot·ing box *n.* (also **shoot·ing lodge**) *Brit.* a lodge used by hunters in the shooting season.

shoot·ing brake *n. Brit.* = STATION WAGON.

shoot·ing gal·ler·y *n.* a place used for shooting at targets with rifles, etc.

shoot·ing i·ron *n. colloq.* a firearm.

shoot·ing range *n.* a ground with butts for rifle practice.

shoot·ing star *n.* a small meteor moving rapidly and burning up on entering the earth's atmosphere.

shoot·ing stick *n.* a walking stick with a foldable seat.

shoot·ing war *n.* a war in which there is shooting (opp. COLD WAR, WAR OF NERVES, etc.).

shoot-out *n. colloq.* a decisive gun battle; showdown.

shop /shop/ *n. & v.* ● *n.* **1** a building, room, etc., for the retail sale of goods or services (*dress shop; beauty shop*); a store. **2** a place in which manufacture or repairing is done; a workshop (*metal shop*). **3** a profession, trade, business, etc., esp. as a subject of conversation (*talk shop*). **4** *colloq.* an institution, establishment, place of business, etc. ● *v.* (**shopped, shop·ping**) **1** *intr.* **a** go to a shop or shops to buy goods. **b** = WINDOW-SHOP. **2** *tr.* esp. *Brit. sl.* inform against (a criminal, etc.). □ **all over the shop** *Brit. colloq.* **1** in disorder (*scattered all over the shop*). **2** in every place (*looked for it all over the shop*). **3** wildly (*hitting out all over the shop*). **set up shop** establish oneself in business, etc. **shop around** look for the best bargain. □□ **shop·less** *adj.* **shop·py** *adj.* [ME f. AF & OF *eschoppe* booth f. MLG *schoppe*, OHG *scopf* porch]

shop as·sis·tant *n. Brit.* a person who serves customers in a shop.

shop boy *n.* (also **shop girl**) an assistant in a shop.

shop·keep·er /shópkeepər/ *n.* the owner and manager of a store. □□ **shop·keep·ing** *n.*

shop·lift·er /shópliftər/ *n.* a person who steals goods while appearing to shop. □□ **shop·lift** *v.tr. & intr.* **shop·lift·ing** *n.*

shop·per /shópər/ *n.* **1** a person who makes purchases in a store. **2** *Brit.* a shopping bag or carriage. **3** *Brit. sl.* an informer.

shop·ping /shóping/ *n.* **1** (often *attrib.*) the purchase of goods, etc. (*shopping expedition*). **2** goods purchased (*put the shopping on the table*).

shop·ping cen·ter *n.* an area or complex of stores, with associated facilities.

shop stew·ard *n.* a person elected by workers in a factory, etc., to represent them in dealings with management.

shop·worn /shópwawrn/ *adj.* **1** (of an article) soiled or faded by display in a shop. **2** (of a person, idea, etc.) grubby; tarnished; no longer fresh or new.

shor·an /sháwran/ *n.* a system of aircraft navigation using the return of two radar signals by two ground stations. [*short range* navigation]

shore[1] /shawr/ *n.* **1** the land that adjoins the sea or a large body of water. **2** (usu. in *pl.*) a country; a seacoast (*often visits these shores; on a distant shore*). **3** *Law* land between ordinary high and low water marks. □□ **shore·less** *adj.* **shore·ward** *adj. & adv.* **shore·wards** *adv.* [ME f. MDu., MLG *schōre,* perh. f. the root of SHEAR]

shore[2] /shawr/ *v. & n.* ● *v.tr.* (often foll. by *up*) support with or as if with a shore or shores; hold up. ● *n.* a prop or beam set obliquely against a ship, wall, tree, etc., as a support. □□ **shor·ing** *n.* [ME f. MDu., MLG *schōre* prop, of unkn. orig.]

shore[3] see SHEAR.

shore-based *adj.* operating from a base on shore.

shore leave *n. Naut.* **1** permission to go ashore. **2** a period of time ashore.

shore·line /sháwrlin/ *n.* the line along which a stretch of water, esp. a sea or lake, meets the shore.

shore·weed /sháwrweed/ *n.* a stoloniferous plant, *Littorella uniflora,* growing in shallow water.

shorn *past part.* of SHEAR.

short /shawrt/ *adj., adv., n., & v.* ● *adj.* **1 a** measuring little; not long from end to end (*a short distance*). **b** not long in duration; brief (*a short time ago; had a short life*). **c** seeming less than the stated amount (*a few short years of happiness*). **2** of small height; not tall (*a short square tower; was shorter than average*). **3 a** (usu. foll. by *of, on*) having a partial or total lack; deficient; scanty (*short of spoons; is rather short on sense*). **b** *colloq.* having little money. **c** not far-reaching; acting or being near at hand (*within short range*). **4 a** concise; brief (*kept his speech short*). **b** curt; uncivil (*was short with her*). **5** (of the memory) unable to remember distant events. **6** *Phonet. & Prosody* of a vowel or syllable: **a** having the lesser of the two recognized durations. **b** unstressed. **c** (of an English vowel) having a sound other than that called long (cf. LONG[1] *adj.* 8). **7 a** (of pastry) crumbling; not holding together. **b** (of clay) having poor plasticity. **8** esp. *Stock Exch.* **a** (of stocks, a stockbroker, crops, etc.) sold or selling when the amount is not in hand, with reliance on getting the deficit in time for delivery. **b** (of a bill of exchange) maturing at an early date. **9** *Brit.* (of a drink of liquor) undiluted. ● *adv.* **1** before the natural or expected time or place; abruptly (*pulled up short; cut short the celebrations*). **2** rudely; uncivilly (*spoke to him short*). ● *n.* **1 a** short circuit. **2** a short movie. **3** *Brit. colloq.* a short drink, esp. liquor. **4** *Stock Exch.* **a** a person who sells short. **b** (in *pl.*) short-dated stocks. **5** *Phonet.* **a** a short syllable or vowel. **b** a mark indicating that a vowel is short. **6** (in *pl.*) a mixture of bran and coarse flour. ● *v.tr. & intr.* short-circuit. □ **be caught** (or *Brit.* **taken**) **short 1** be put at a disadvantage. **2** be unprepared. **3** *Brit. colloq.* urgently need to urinate or defecate. **bring up** (or **pull up**) **short** check or pause abruptly. **come short** be inadequate or disappointing. **come short of** fail to reach or amount to. **for short** as a short name (*Tom for short*). **get** (or **have**) **by the short hairs** *colloq.* be in complete control of (a person). **go short** (often foll. by *of*) not have enough. **in short** to use few words; briefly. **in short order** immediately. **in the short run** over a short period of time. **in short supply** scarce. **in the short term** *in the short run.* **make short work of** accomplish, dispose of, destroy, consume, etc., quickly. **short end of the stick** an outcome in which one has less advantage than others (*his younger brother always got the short end of the stick*). **short and sweet** esp. *iron.* brief and pleasant. **short for** an abbreviation for (*"Bob" is short for "Robert"*). **short of 1** see sense 3a of *adj.* **2** less than (*nothing short of a miracle*). **3** distant from (*two miles short of home*). **4** without going so far as; except (*did everything short of destroying it*). **short of breath** panting; short-winded. **short on** *colloq.* see sense 3a of *adj.* □□ **short·ish** *adj.* **short·ness** *n.* [OE *sceort* f. Gmc: cf. SHIRT, SKIRT]

short·age /sháwrtij/ *n.* (often foll. by *of*) a deficiency; an amount lacking (*a shortage of 100 tons*).

short-arm *adj.* (of a blow, etc.) delivered with the arm not fully extended.

short·bread /sháwrtbred/ n. a crisp, rich, crumbly type of cookie made with butter, flour, and sugar.

short·cake /sháwrtkayk/ n. **1** = SHORTBREAD. **2** a cake made of short pastry and filled with fruit and cream.

short·change /sháwrtcháynj/ v.tr. rob or cheat by giving insufficient money as change.

short cir·cuit n. an electric circuit through small resistance, esp. instead of the resistance of a normal circuit. □□ **short-cir·cuit** v.

short·com·ing /sháwrtkuming/ n. failure to come up to a standard; a defect.

short com·mons n.pl. Brit. insufficient food.

short cut n. **1** a route shortening the distance traveled. **2** a quick way of accomplishing something.

short-day adj. (of a plant) needing the period of light each day to fall below some limit to cause flowering.

short di·vi·sion n. Math. division in which the quotient is written directly without being worked out in writing.

short drink n. a strong alcoholic drink served in small measures.

short-eared owl n. an owl, Asio flammeus, frequenting open country and hunting at dawn or dusk.

short·en /sháwrt'n/ v. **1** intr. & tr. become or make shorter or short; curtail. **2** tr. Naut. reduce the amount of (sail spread). **3** intr. & tr. (with reference to gambling odds, prices, etc.) become or make shorter; decrease.

short·en·ing /sháwrt'ning, sháwrtning/ n. fat used for making pastry, bread, etc.

short·fall /sháwrtfawl/ n. a deficit below what was expected.

short fuse n. colloq. a quick temper.

short game n. Golf the part of the game concerned with approach shots and putting.

short·hand /sháwrt-hand/ n. **1** (often attrib.) a method of rapid writing in abbreviations and symbols esp. for taking dictation. **2** an abbreviated or symbolic mode of expression.

short·hand·ed /sháwrt-hánded/ adj. undermanned or understaffed.

short haul n. **1** the transport of goods over a short distance. **2** a short-term effort.

short·horn /sháwrt-horn/ n. **1** an animal of a breed of cattle with short horns. **2** this breed.

short hun·dred·weight n. see HUNDREDWEIGHT.

short·ie var. of SHORTY.

short·list /sháwrtlist/ n. a selective list of candidates from which a final choice is made.

short-list v.tr. put on a shortlist.

short-lived adj. ephemeral; not long-lasting.

short·ly /sháwrtlee/ adv. **1** (often foll. by before, after) before long; soon (will arrive shortly; arrived shortly after him). **2** in a few words; briefly. **3** curtly. [OE scortlice (as SHORT, –LY²)]

short mark n. = BREVE 2.

short meas·ure n. less than the professed amount.

short me·ter n. Prosody a hymn stanza of four lines with 6, 6, 8, and 6 syllables.

short no·tice n. an insufficient length of warning time.

short odds n.pl. nearly equal stakes or chances in betting.

short-or·der adj. **1** prepared or provided quickly, esp. simple restaurant fare. **2** pertaining to one who provides this (a short-order cook).

short-range adj. **1** having a short range. **2** relating to a fairly immediate future time (short-range possibilities).

shorts /shawrts/ n.pl. **1** pants reaching only to the knees or higher. **2** underpants.

short score n. Mus. a score not giving all parts.

short shrift n. **1** rapid and unsympathetic dismissal; curt treatment. **2** archaic little time between condemnation and execution or punishment.

short sight n. the inability to focus except on comparatively near objects.

short·sight·ed /sháwrtsítid/ adj. **1** esp. Brit. = NEARSIGHTED. **2** lacking imagination or foresight. □□ **short·sight·ed·ly** adv. **short·sight·ed·ness** n.

short-sleeved adj. with sleeves not reaching below the elbow.

short-staffed adj. having insufficient staff.

short·stop /sháwrtstop/ n. a baseball fielder positioned between second and third base.

short sto·ry n. a story with a fully developed theme but shorter than a novel.

short tem·per n. self-control soon or easily lost. □□ **short-tem·pered** adj.

short-term adj. occurring in or relating to a short period of time.

short ti·tle n. an abbreviated form of a title of a book, etc.

short ton n. see TON¹.

short view n. (the short view) a consideration of the present and immediate future only.

short waist n. **1** a high or shallow waist of a dress. **2** a short upper body.

short·wave /sháwrtwáyv/ n. a radio wave of frequency greater than 3 MHz

short weight n. weight less than it is alleged to be.

short-wind·ed adj. **1** quickly exhausted of breath. **2** incapable of sustained effort.

short·y /sháwrtee/ n. (also **short·ie**) (pl. **·ies**) colloq. **1** a person shorter than average. **2** a short garment, esp. a nightgown or raincoat.

Sho·sho·ne /shəshón, –shónee/ n. (also **Sho·sho·ni**) **1 a** a N. American people native to the western US. **b** a member of this people. **2** the language of this people. □□ **Sho·sho·ne·an** adj.

shot¹ /shot/ n. **1** the act or an instance of firing a gun, cannon, etc. (several shots were heard). **2** an attempt to hit by shooting or throwing, etc. (took a shot at him). **3 a** a single nonexplosive missile for a cannon, gun, etc. **b** (pl. same or **shots**) a small lead pellet used in quantity in a single charge or cartridge in a shotgun. **c** (as pl.) these collectively. **4 a** a photograph. **b** a film sequence photographed continuously by one camera. **5 a** a stroke or a kick in a ball game. **b** colloq. an attempt to guess or do something (let her have a shot at it). **6** colloq. a person having a specified skill with a gun, etc. (is not a good shot). **7** a heavy ball thrown by a shot-putter. **8** the launch of a space rocket (a moonshot). **9** the range, reach, or distance to or at which a thing will carry or act (out of earshot). **10** a remark aimed at a person. **11** colloq. **a** a drink of esp. liquor. **b** an injection of a drug, vaccine, etc. (has had his shots). □ **like a shot** colloq. without hesitation; willingly; quickly. **shot in the arm** colloq. **1** stimulus or encouragement. **2** Brit. an alcoholic drink. **shot in the dark** a mere guess. □□ **shot·proof** adj. [OE sc(e)ot, gesc(e)ot f. Gmc: cf. SHOOT]

shot² /shot/ past and past part. of SHOOT.● adj. **1** (of colored material) woven so as to show different colors at different angles. **2** colloq. **a** exhausted; finished. **b** drunk. **3** (of a board edge) accurately planed. □ **be** (or **get**) **shot of** Brit. sl. be (or get) rid of. **shot through** permeated or suffused. [past part. of SHOOT]

shot³ /shot/ n. Brit. colloq. a reckoning, a bill, esp. at an inn, etc. (paid his shot). [ME, = SHOT¹: cf. OE scēotan shoot, pay, contribute, and SCOT]

shot·gun /shótgun/ n. a smoothbore gun for firing small shot at short range.

shot·gun mar·riage n. (also **shot·gun wed·ding**) colloq. an enforced or hurried wedding, esp. because of the bride's pregnancy.

shot put n. an athletic contest in which a shot is thrown a great distance. □□ **shot-put·ter** n.

shotgun

shot tow·er n. hist. a tower in which shot was made from molten lead poured through sieves at the top and falling into water at the bottom.

should /shood/ v.aux. (3rd sing. **should**) past of SHALL, used esp.: **1** in reported speech, esp. with the reported element in the 1st person (I said I should be home by evening). **2 a** to express a duty, obligation, or likelihood; = OUGHT¹ (I should tell you; you should have been more careful; they should have arrived by now). **b** (in the 1st person) to express a tentative suggestion (I should like to say something). **3 a** expressing the conditional mood in the 1st person (cf. WOULD) (I should have been killed if I had gone). **b** forming a conditional protasis or indefinite clause (if you should see him; should they arrive, tell them where to go). **4** expressing purpose = MAY, MIGHT¹ (in order that we should not worry).

▶**1.** For sense 1, cf. WILL¹ and WOULD, now more common, esp. to avoid implications of sense 2. **2.**See note at SHALL.

shoul·der /shóldər/ n. & v. ● n. **1 a** the part of the body at which the arm, foreleg, or wing is attached. **b** (in full **shoulder joint**) the end of the upper arm joining with the clavicle and scapula. **c** either of the two projections below the neck from which the arms hang. **2** the upper foreleg and shoulder blade of a pig, lamb, etc., when butchered. **3** (often in pl.) **a** the upper part of the back and arms. **b** this part of the body regarded as capable of bearing a burden or blame, providing comfort, etc. (needs a shoulder to cry on). **4** a strip of land next to a paved road (pulled over onto the shoulder). **5** a part of a garment covering the shoulder. **6** a part of anything resembling a shoulder in form or function, as in a bottle, mountain, tool, etc. ● v. **1 a** tr. push with the shoulder; jostle. **b** intr. make one's way by jostling (shouldered through the crowd). **2** tr. take (a burden, etc.) on one's shoulders (shouldered the family's problems). □ **put** (or **set**) **one's shoulder to the wheel** make an effort. **shoulder arms** hold a rifle with the barrel against the shoulder and the butt in the hand. **shoulder to shoulder 1** side by side. **2** with closed ranks or united effort. □□ **shoul·dered** adj. (also in comb.). [OE sculdor f. WG]

shoul·der bag n. a handbag that can be hung from the shoulder.

shoul·der belt n. a seat belt that passes over one shoulder and under the opposite arm.

shoul·der blade *n*. *Anat*. either of the large flat bones of the upper back; the scapula.

shoul·der board *n*. (also **shoul·der mark**) the stiffened shoulder strap of a naval officer bearing insignia of rank.

shoul·der-high *adj. &adv*. up to or as high as the shoulders.

shoul·der hol·ster *n*. a gun holster worn in the armpit.

shoul·der knot *n*. a knot of ribbon, metal, lace, etc., worn as part of a ceremonial dress.

shoul·der loop *n*. the shoulder strap of an army, air force, or marines officer.

shoul·der note *n*. *Printing* a marginal note at the top of a page.

shoul·der strap *n*. **1** a strip of fabric, leather, etc., suspending a bag or garment from the shoulder. **2** a strip of cloth from shoulder to collar on a military uniform bearing a symbol of rank, etc. **3** a similar strip on a raincoat.

shouldn't /shŏŏd'nt/ *contr*. should not.

shout /showt/ *v. & n*. •*v*. **1** *intr*. make a loud cry or vocal sound; speak loudly; speak loudly (*shouted for attention*). **2** *tr*. say or express loudly; call out (*shouted that the coast was clear*). **3** *tr*. (also *absol*.) *Austral. & NZ colloq*. treat (another person) to drinks, etc. •*n*. **1** a loud cry expressing joy, etc., or calling attention. **2** *Brit., Austral., & NZ colloq*. one's turn to order and pay for a round of drinks, etc. (*your shout, I think*). □ **all over but the shouting** *colloq*. the contest is virtually decided. **shout at** speak loudly to, etc. **shout down** reduce to silence by shouting. **shout for** call for by shouting. □□ **shout·er** *n*. [ME, perh. rel. to SHOOT: cf. ON *skúta* SCOUT]

shout-up *n*. *Brit. colloq*. a noisy argument.

shove /shuv/ *v. & n*. •*v*. **1** *tr*. (also *absol*.) push vigorously; move by hard or rough pushing (*shoved him out of the way*). **2** *intr*. (usu. foll. by *along, past, through*, etc.) make one's way by pushing (*shoved through the crowd*). **3** *tr. colloq*. put somewhere (*shoved it in the drawer*). •*n*. an act of shoving or of prompting a person into action. □ **shove off 1** start from the shore in a boat. **2** *sl*. depart; go away (*told him to shove off*). [OE *scúfan* f. Gmc]

shove-half·pen·ny *n*. (in the UK) a form of shuffleboard played with coins, etc., on a table, esp. in a bar or pub.

shov·el /shúvəl/ *n. & v*. •*n*. **1 a** a spadelike tool for shifting quantities of coal, earth, etc., esp. having the sides curved upward. **b** the amount contained in a shovel; a shovelful. **2** a machine or part of a machine having a similar form or function. •*v.tr*. **1** shift or clear (coal, etc.) with or as if with a shovel. **2** *colloq*. move (esp. food) in large quantities or roughly (*shoveled peas into his mouth*). □□ **shov·el·ful** *n*. (*pl*. **-fuls**) [OE *scofl* f. Gmc (see SHOVE)]

shov·el·board /shúvəlbawrd/ *n*. *Brit*. var. of SHUFFLEBOARD.

shov·el hat *n*. a broad-brimmed hat esp. worn by some English clergymen.

shov·el·head /shúvəlhed/ *n*. a shark, *Sphyrna tiburo*, like the hammerhead but smaller. Also called **bonnethead**.

shov·el·er /shúvələr, shúvlər/ *n*. (also esp. *Brit*. **shov·el·ler**) **1** a person or thing that shovels. **2** a duck, *Anas clypeata*, with a broad shovellike beak. [SHOVEL: sense 2 earlier *shovelard* f. –ARD, perh. after *mallard*]

show /shō/ *v. & n*. •*v*. (*past part*. **shown** /shōn/ or **showed**) **1** *intr. & tr*. be, or allow or cause to be, visible; manifest; appear (*the buds are beginning to show; white shows the dirt*). **2** *tr*. (often foll. by *to*) offer, exhibit, or produce (a thing) for scrutiny, etc. (*show your tickets please; showed him my poems*). **3** *tr*. **a** indicate (one's feelings) by one's behavior, etc. (*showed mercy to him*). **b** indicate (one's feelings to a person, etc.) (*showed him particular favor*). **4** *intr*. (of feelings, etc.) be manifest (*his dislike shows*). **5** *tr*. **a** demonstrate; point out; prove (*has shown it to be false; showed that he knew the answer*). **b** (usu. foll. by *how to* + infin.) cause (a person) to understand or be capable of doing (*showed them how to knit*). **6** *tr*. (*refl*.) exhibit oneself as being (*showed herself to be fair*). **7** *tr. & intr*. (with ref. to a movie) be presented or cause to be presented. **8** *tr*. exhibit (a picture, animal, flower, etc.) in a show. **9** *tr*. (often foll. by *in, out, up*, etc.) conduct or lead (*showed them to their rooms*). **10** *intr*. = *show up* 3 (*waited but he didn't show*). **11** *intr*. finish third or among the first three in a race. •*n*. **1** the act or an instance of showing; the state of being shown. **2 a** a spectacle, display, exhibition, etc. (*a fine show of blossom*). **b** a collection of things, etc., shown for public entertainment or in competition (*dog show; flower show*). **3 a** a play, etc., esp. a musical. **b** an entertainment program on television, etc. **c** any public entertainment or performance. **4 a** an outward appearance, semblance, or display (*made a show of agreeing; a show of strength*). **b** empty appearance; mere display (*did it for show; that's all show*). **5** *colloq*. an undertaking, business, etc. (*sold the whole show*). **6** esp. *Brit. colloq*. an opportunity of acting, defending oneself, etc. (*gave him a fair show; made a good show of it*). **7** *Med*. a discharge of blood, etc., from the vagina at the onset of childbirth. □ **get the show on the road** *colloq*. get started, begin an undertaking. **give the (whole) show away** demonstrate the inadequacies or reveal the truth. **good** (or **bad** or **poor**) **show!** esp. *Brit. colloq*. **1** that was well (or badly) done. **2** that was lucky (or unlucky). **nothing**

to **show for** no visible result of (effort, etc.). **on show** being exhibited. **show one's cards** = *show one's hand*. **show cause** *Law* allege with justification. **show a clean pair of heels** *colloq*. retreat speedily; run away. **show one's colors** make one's opinion clear. **show a person the door** dismiss or eject a person. **show one's face** make an appearance; let oneself be seen. **show fight** be persistent or belligerent. **show the flag** see FLAG¹. **show forth** *archaic* exhibit; expound. **show one's hand 1** disclose one's plans. **2** reveal one's cards. **show in** see sense 9 of *v*. **show a leg** *Brit. colloq*. get out of bed. **show off 1** display to advantage. **2** *colloq*. act pretentiously; display one's wealth, knowledge, etc. **show oneself 1** be seen in public. **2** see sense 6 of *v*. **show out** see sense 9 of *v*. **show around** take (a person) to places of interest; act as guide for (a person) in a building, etc. **show one's teeth** esp. *Brit*. reveal one's strength; be aggressive. **show through 1** be visible although supposedly concealed. **2** (of real feelings, etc.) be revealed inadvertently. **show up 1** make or be conspicuous or clearly visible. **2** expose (a fraud, impostor, inferiority, etc.). **3** *colloq*. appear; be present; arrive. **4** *colloq*. embarrass or humiliate (*don't show me up by wearing jeans*). **show the way 1** indicate what has to be done, etc., by attempting it first. **2** show others which way to go, etc. **show the white feather** *Brit*. appear cowardly (see also WHITE FEATHER). **show willing** esp. *Brit*. display a willingness to help, etc. [ME f. OE *scēawian* f. WG: cf. SHEEN]

show·biz /shóbiz/ *n*. *colloq*. = SHOW BUSINESS.

show·boat /shóbōt/ *n*. a river steamer on which theatrical performances are given.

show busi·ness *n*. *colloq*. the theatrical profession.

show·case /shókays/ *n. & v*. •*n*. **1** a glass case used for exhibiting goods, etc. **2** a place or medium for presenting (esp. attractively) to general attention. •*v.tr*. display in or as if in a showcase.

show·down /shódown/ *n*. **1** a final test or confrontation; a decisive situation. **2** the laying down face up of the players' cards in poker.

show·er /shówr/ *n. & v*. •*n*. **1** a brief fall of esp. rain, hail, sleet, or snow. **2 a** a brisk flurry of arrows, bullets, dust, stones, sparks, etc. **b** a similar flurry of gifts, letters, honors, praise, etc. **3** (in full **shower bath**) **a** a cubicle, bath, etc. in which one stands under a spray of water. **b** the apparatus, etc., used for this. **c** the act of bathing in a shower. **4** a group of particles initiated by a cosmic-ray particle in the earth's atmosphere. **5** a party for giving presents to a prospective bride, expectant mother, etc. **6** *Brit. sl*. a contemptible or unpleasant person or group of people. •*v*. **1** *tr*. **a** discharge (water, missiles, etc.) in a shower. **b** make wet with (or as if with) a shower. **2** *intr*. use a shower bath. **3** *tr*. (usu. foll. by *on, upon*) lavishly bestow (gifts, etc.). **4** *intr*. descend or come in a shower (*it showered on and off all day*). □□ **show·er·y** *adj*. [OE *scūr* f. Gmc]

show·er·proof /shówrprŏŏf/ *adj. & v*. •*adj*. resistant to light rain. •*v.tr*. render showerproof.

show·girl /shógərl/ *n*. an actress who sings and dances in musicals, variety shows, etc.

show·ing /shóing/ *n*. **1** the act or an instance of showing. **2** a usu. specified quality of performance (*made a poor showing*). **3** the presentation of a case; evidence (*on present showing it must be true*). [OE *scēawung* (as SHOW)]

show jump·ing *n*. the sport of riding horses over a course of fences and other obstacles, with penalty points for errors.

show·man /shómən/ *n*. (*pl*. **-men**) **1** the proprietor or manager of a circus, etc. **2** a person skilled in self-advertisement or publicity. □□ **show·man·ship** *n*.

shown *past part*. of SHOW.

show-off *n*. *colloq*. a person who shows off.

show of force *n*. proof that one is prepared to use force.

show of hands *n*. raised hands indicating a vote for or against, usu. without being counted.

show·piece /shópees/ *n*. **1** an item of work presented for exhibition or display. **2** an outstanding example or specimen.

show·place /shóplays/ *n*. a house, etc., that tourists go to see.

show·room /shóroom, –room/ *n*. a room in a factory, office building, etc., used to display goods for sale.

show·stop·per /shóstopər/ *n*. *colloq*. an act or performance receiving prolonged applause.

show tri·al *n*. esp. *hist*. a judicial trial designed by the government to terrorize or impress the public.

show win·dow *n*. a window for exhibiting goods, etc.

show·y /shóee/ *adj*. (**show·i·er**, **show·i·est**) **1** brilliant; gaudy; esp. vulgarly so. **2** striking. □□ **show·i·ly** *adv*. **show·i·ness** *n*.

s.h.p. *abbr*. shaft horsepower.

shrank *past* of SHRINK.

shrap·nel /shrápnəl/ *n*. **1** fragments of a bomb, etc., thrown out by an explosion. **2** a shell containing bullets or pieces of metal timed to burst short of impact. [Gen. H. *Shrapnel*, Brit. soldier d. 1842, inventor of the shell]

shred /shred/ *n. & v*. •*n*. **1** a scrap, fragment, or strip of esp. cloth, paper, etc. **2** the least amount; remnant (*not a shred of evidence*). •*v.tr*. (**shred·ded**, **shred·ding**) tear or cut into shreds. □ **tear to**

shreds completely refute (an argument, etc.). [OE *scrē ad* (unrecorded) piece cut off, *scrēadian* f. WG: see SHROUD]

shred·der /shrédər/ *n.* **1** a machine used to reduce documents to shreds. **2** any device used for shredding.

shrew /shrōō/ *n.* **1** any small, usu. insect-eating, mouselike mammal of the family Soricidae, with a long pointed snout. **2** a bad-tempered or scolding woman. □□ **shrew·ish** *adj.* (in sense 2). **shrew·ish·ly** *adv.* **shrew·ish·ness** *n.* [OE *scrēawa*, *scrǣwa* shrew-mouse: cf. OHG *scrawaz* dwarf, MHG *schrawaz*, etc. devil]

shrewd /shrōōd/ *adj.* **1** a showing astute powers of judgment; clever and judicious (*a shrewd observer*; *made a shrewd guess*). **b** (of a face, etc.) shrewd-looking. **2** *archaic* **a** (of pain, cold, etc.) sharp; biting. **b** (of a blow, thrust, etc.) severe; hard. **c** mischievous; malicious. □□ **shrewd·ly** *adv.* **shrewd·ness** *n.*

shriek /shreek/ *v. & n.* ● *v.* **1** *intr.* **a** utter a shrill screeching sound or words esp. in pain or terror. **b** (foll. by *of*) provide a clear or blatant indication of. **2** *tr.* **a** utter (sounds or words) by shrieking (*shrieked his name*). **b** indicate clearly or blatantly. ● *n.* a high-pitched piercing cry or sound; a scream. □ **shriek out** say in shrill tones. **shriek with laughter** laugh uncontrollably. □□ **shriek·er** *n.* [imit.: cf. dial. *screak*, ON *skr ækja*, and SCREECH]

shriev·al /shreévəl/ *adj.* of or relating to a sheriff. [*shrieve* obs. var. of SHERIFF]

shriev·al·ty /shreévəltee/ *n.* (*pl.* ·ties) **1** a sheriff's office or jurisdiction. **2** the tenure of this. [as SHRIEVAL + -*alty* as in mayoralty, etc.]

shrift /shrift/ *n. archaic* **1** confession to a priest. **2** confession and absolution. [OE *scrift* (verbal noun) f. SHRIVE]

shrike /shrīk/ *n.* any bird of the family Laniidae, with a strong hooked and toothed bill, that impales its prey of small birds and insects on thorns. Also called **butcher-bird**. [perh. rel. to OE *scric* thrush, MLG *schrīk* corncrake (imit.): cf. SHRIEK]

shrill /shril/ *adj. & v.* ● *adj.* **1** piercing and high-pitched in sound. **2** *derog.* (esp. of a protester) sharp; unrestrained; unreasoning. ● *v.* **1** *intr.* (of a cry, etc.) sound shrilly. **2** *tr.* (of a person, etc.) utter or send out (a song, complaint, etc.) shrilly. □□ **shrill·ly** *adv.* **shrill·ness** *n.* [ME, rel. to LG *schrell* sharp in tone or taste f. Gmc]

shrimp /shrimp/ *n. & v.* ● *n.* **1** (*pl.* same or **shrimps**) any of various small (esp. marine) edible crustaceans, with ten legs, gray-green when alive and pink when cooked. **2** *colloq.* a very small slight person. ● *v.intr.* go catching shrimps. □□ **shrimp·er** *n.* [ME, prob. rel. to MLG *schrempen* wrinkle, MHG *schrimpfen* contract, and SCRIMP]

shrimp

shrimp plant *n.* an evergreen shrub, *Justicia brandegeana*, bearing small white flowers in clusters of pinkish-brown bracts.

shrine /shrīn/ *n. & v.* ● *n.* **1** esp *RC Ch.* **a** a chapel, church, altar, etc., sacred to a saint, holy person, relic, etc. **b** the tomb of a saint, etc. **c** a casket, esp. containing sacred relics; a reliquary. **d** a niche containing a holy statue, etc. **2** a place associated with or containing memorabilia of a particular person, event, etc. **3** a Shinto place of worship. ● *v.tr. poet.* enshrine. [OE *scrī n* f. Gmc f. L *scrinium* case for books, etc.]

shrink /shringk/ *v. & n.* ● *v.* (*past* **shrank** /shrangk/; *past part.* **shrunk** /shrungk/ or (esp. as *adj.*) **shrunk·en** /shrúngkən/) **1** *tr. & intr.* make or become smaller; contract, esp. by the action of moisture, heat, or cold. **2** *intr.* (usu. foll. by *from*) **a** retire; recoil; flinch; cower (*shrank from her touch*). **b** be averse from doing (*shrinks from meeting them*). **3** (as **shrunken** *adj.*) (esp. of a face, person, etc.) having grown smaller esp. because of age, illness, etc. ● *n.* **1** the act or an instance of shrinking; shrinkage. **2** *sl.* a psychiatrist (from "head-shrinker"). □ **shrink into oneself** become withdrawn. □□ **shrink·a·ble** *adj.* **shrink·er** *n.* **shrink·ing·ly** *adv.* **shrink·proof** *adj.* [OE *scrincan*: cf. Sw. *skrynka* to shrink]

shrink·age /shríngkij/ *n.* **1 a** the process or fact of shrinking. **b** the degree or amount of shrinking. **2** an allowance made for the reduction in takings due to wastage, theft, etc.

shrink·ing vi·o·let *n.* an exaggeratedly shy person.

shrink-re·sist·ant *adj.* (of textiles, etc.) resistant to shrinkage when wet, etc.

shrink-wrap *v. & n.* ● *v.tr.* (·**wrapped**, ·**wrap·ping**) enclose (an article) in (esp. transparent) film that shrinks tightly on to it. ● *n.* plastic film used to shrink-wrap.

shrive /shrīv/ *v.tr.* (*past* **shrove** /shrōv/; *past part.* **shriv·en** /shrívən/) *Eccl. archaic* **1** (of a priest) hear the confession of, assign penance

to, and absolve. **2** (*refl.*) (of a penitent) submit oneself to a priest for confession, etc. [OE *scrīfan* impose as penance, WG f. L *scribere* write]

shriv·el /shrívəl/ *v.tr. & intr.* contract or wither into a wrinkled, folded, rolled-up, contorted, or dried-up state. [perh. f. ON: cf. Sw. dial. *skryvla* to wrinkle]

shriv·en *past part.* of SHRIVE.

shroud /shrowd/ *n. & v.* ● *n.* **1** a sheetlike garment for wrapping a corpse for burial. **2** anything that conceals like a shroud (*wrapped in a shroud of mystery*). **3** (in *pl.*) *Naut.* a set of ropes forming part of the standing rigging and supporting the mast or topmast. ● *v.tr.* **1** clothe (a body) for burial. **2** cover, conceal, or disguise (*hills shrouded in mist*). □□ **shroud·less** *adj.* [OE *scrūd* f. Gmc: see SHRED]

shroud-laid *adj.* (of a rope) having four strands laid right-handed on a core.

shrove *past* of SHRIVE.

Shrove·tide /shróvtīd/ *n.* Shrove Tuesday and the two days preceding it when it was formerly customary to be shriven. [ME *shrove* abnormally f. SHROVE]

Shrove Tues·day /shrōv/ *n.* the day before Ash Wednesday.

shrub[1] /shrub/ *n.* a woody plant smaller than a tree and having a very short stem with branches near the ground. □□ **shrub·by** *adj.* [ME f. OE *scrubb, scrybb* shrubbery: cf. NFris. *skrobb* brushwood, WFlem. *schrobbe* vetch, Norw. *skrubba* dwarf cornel, and SCRUB[2]]

shrub[2] /shrub/ *n.* a cordial made of sweetened fruit juice and spirits, esp. rum. [Arab. *šurb, šarāb* f. *šariba* to drink: cf. SHERBET, SYRUP]

shrub·ber·y /shrúbəree/ *n.* (*pl.* ·**ies**) an area planted with shrubs.

shrug /shrug/ *v. & n.* ● *v.* (**shrugged, shrug·ging**) **1** *intr.* slightly and momentarily raise the shoulders to express indifference, helplessness, contempt, etc. **2** *tr.* **a** raise (the shoulders) in this way. **b** shrug the shoulders to express (indifference, etc.) (*shrugged his consent*). ● *n.* the act or an instance of shrugging. □ **shrug off** dismiss as unimportant, etc., by or as if by shrugging. [ME: orig. unkn.]

shrunk (also **shrunk·en**) *past part.* of SHRINK.

shtick /shtik/ *n. sl.* a theatrical routine, gimmick, etc. [Yiddish f. G *Stück* piece]

shuck /shuk/ *n. & v.* ● *n.* **1** a husk or pod. **2** the shell of an oyster or clam. **3** (in *pl.*) *colloq.* an expression of contempt or regret or self-deprecation in response to praise. ● *v.tr.* **1** remove the shucks of; shell. **2** peel off or remove (*shucked his coat*). □□ **shuck·er** *n.* [17th c.: orig. unkn.]

shud·der /shúdər/ *v. & n.* ● *v.intr.* **1** shiver esp. convulsively from fear, cold, repugnance, etc. **2** feel strong repugnance, etc. (*shudder to think what might happen*). **3** (of a machine, etc.) vibrate or quiver. ● *n.* **1** the act or an instance of shuddering. **2** (in *pl.*; prec. by *the*) *colloq.* a state of shuddering. □□ **shud·der·ing·ly** *adv.* **shud·der·y** *adj.* [ME *shod (d)er* f. MDu. *schūderen*, MLG *schöderen* f. Gmc]

shuf·fle /shúfəl/ *v. & n.* ● *v.* **1** *tr. &intr.* move with a scraping, sliding, or dragging motion (*shuffles along; shuffling his feet*). **2** *tr.* **a** (also *absol.*) rearrange (a deck of cards) by sliding them over each other quickly. **b** rearrange; intermingle; confuse (*shuffled the documents*). **3** *tr.* (usu. foll. by *on, off, into*) assume or remove (clothes, a burden, etc.) esp. clumsily or evasively (*shuffled on his clothes; shuffled off responsibility*). **4** *intr.* **a** equivocate; prevaricate. **b** continually shift one's position; fidget. **5** *intr.* (foll. by *out of*) escape evasively (*shuffled out of the blame*). ● *n.* **1** a shuffling movement. **2** the act or an instance of shuffling cards. **3** a general change of relative positions. **4** a piece of equivocation; sharp practice. **5** a quick alternation of the position of the feet in dancing. □ **shuffle the cards** change policy, etc. □□ **shuf·fler** *n.* [perh. f. LG *schuffeln* walk clumsily f. Gmc: cf. SHOVE]

shuf·fle·board /shúfəlbawrd/ *n.* a game played by pushing disks with the hand or esp. with a long-handled cue over a marked surface. [earlier *shoveboard* f. SHOVE + BOARD]

shun /shun/ *v.tr.* (**shunned, shun·ning**) avoid; keep clear of (*shuns human company*). [OE *scunian*, of unkn. orig.]

shunt /shunt/ *v. & n.* ● *v.* **1** *intr. & tr.* diverge or cause (a train) to be diverted esp. onto a siding. **2** *tr. Electr.* provide (a current) with a shunt. **3** *tr.* **a** postpone or evade. **b** divert (a decision, etc.) on to another person, etc. ● *n.* **1** the act or an instance of shunting on to a siding. **2** *Electr.* a conductor joining two points of a circuit, through which more or less of a current may be diverted. **3** *Surgery* an alternative path for the circulation of the blood. **4** *Brit. sl.* a motor vehicle accident, esp. a collision of vehicles traveling close behind another. □□ **shunt·er** *n.* [ME, perh. f. SHUN]

shush /shŏŏsh, shush/ *int. & v.* ● *int.* = HUSH *int.* ● *v.* **1** *intr.* **a** a call for silence by saying *shush*. **b** be silent (*they shushed at once*). **2** *tr.* make or attempt to make silent. [imit.]

shut /shut/ *v.* (**shut·ting**; *past* and *past part.* **shut**) **1** *tr.* **a** move (a door, window, lid, lips, etc.) into position so as to block an aperture (*shut the lid*). **b** close or seal (a room, window, box, eye, mouth, etc.) by moving a door, etc. (*shut the box*). **2** *intr.* become or be capable of being closed or sealed (*the door shut with a bang; the lid shuts automatically*). **3** *intr. & tr.* esp. *Brit.* become or make (a store, business, etc.) closed for trade (*the shops shut at five; shuts his shop at five*). **4** *tr.* bring (a book, hand, telescope, etc.) into a folded-up or contracted state. **5** *tr.* (usu. foll. by *in, out*) keep (a person, sound, etc.) in or out of a room, etc., by shutting a door, etc. (*shut out the noise; shut them in*). **6** *tr.* (usu. foll. by *in*) catch (a finger, dress, etc.) by shutting something on it (*shut her finger in the door*). **7** *tr.* bar access to (a place, etc.) (*this entrance is shut*). □ **be** (or **get**) **shut of** *sl.* be (or get) rid of (*were glad to get shut of him*). **shut the door on** refuse to consider; make impossible. **shut down 1** stop (a factory, nuclear reactor, etc.) from operating. **2** (of a factory, etc.) stop operating. **3** push or pull (a window sash, etc.) down into a closed position. **shut one's eyes** (or **ears** or **heart** or **mind**) to pretend not, or refuse, to see (or hear or feel sympathy for or think about). **shut in** (of hills, houses, etc.) encircle, prevent access, etc., to or escape from (*were shut in by the sea on three sides*) (see also sense 5). **shut off 1** stop the flow of (water, gas, etc.) by shutting a valve. **2** separate from society, etc. **shut out 1** exclude (a person, light, etc.) from a place, situation, etc. **2** screen (landscape, etc.) from view. **3** prevent (a possibility, etc.). **4** block (a painful memory, etc.) from the mind. **5** prevent (an opponent) from scoring (see also sense 5). **shut up 1** close all doors and windows of (a house, etc.); bolt and bar. **2** imprison (a person). **3** close (a box, etc.) securely. **4** *colloq.* reduce to silence by rebuke, etc. **5** put (a thing) away in a box, etc. **6** (esp. in *imper.*) *colloq.* stop talking. **shut your face** (or **head** or **mouth** or **trap**)! *sl.* an impolite request to stop talking. [OE *scyttan* f. WG: cf. SHOOT]

shut•down /shútdown/ *n.* the closure of a factory, etc.

shut-eye *n. colloq.* sleep.

shut-in *n.* a person confined to home, bed, etc., due to infirmity, etc.

shut•off /shútawf/ *n.* **1** something used for stopping an operation. **2** a cessation of flow, supply, or activity.

shut•out /shútowt/ *n.* **1** a competition or game in which the losing side fails to score. **2** a preemptive bid in bridge.

shut•ter /shútər/ *n. & v.* ● *n.* **1** a person or thing that shuts. **2 a** each of a pair or set of panels fixed inside or outside a window for security or privacy or to keep the light in or out. **b** a structure of slats on rollers used for the same purpose. **3** a device that exposes the film in a photographic camera. **4** *Mus.* the blind of a swell box in an organ used for controlling the sound level. ● *v.tr.* **1** put up the shutters of. **2** provide with shutters. □ **put up the shutters 1** cease business for the day. **2** cease business, etc., permanently. □□ **shut•ter•less** *adj.*

shut•ter•bug /shútərbəg/ *n. colloq.* an amateur photographer who takes a great many pictures.

shut•ter•ing /shútəring/ *n.* esp. *Brit.* **1** = FORMWORK. **2** material for making shutters.

shut•tle /shút'l/ *n. & v.* ● *n.* **1 a** a bobbin with two pointed ends used for carrying the weft thread across between the warp threads in weaving. **b** a bobbin carrying the lower thread in a sewing machine. **2** a train, bus, etc., going to and fro over a short route continuously. **3** = SHUTTLECOCK. **4** = SPACE SHUTTLE. ● *v.* **1** *intr. & tr.* move or cause to move back and forth like a shuttle. **2** *intr.* travel in a shuttle. [OE *scytel* dart f. Gmc: cf. SHOOT]

shut•tle ar•ma•ture *n. Electr.* an armature with a single coil wound on an elongated iron bobbin.

shut•tle•cock /shút'lkok/ *n.* **1** a cork with a ring of feathers, or a similar device of plastic, used instead of a ball in badminton and in battledore. **2** a thing passed repeatedly back and forth. [SHUTTLE + COCK[1], prob. f. the flying motion]

shut•tle di•plo•ma•cy *n.* negotiations conducted by a mediator who travels successively to several countries.

shut•tle serv•ice *n.* a train or bus, etc., service operating back and forth over a short route.

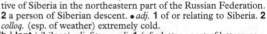
shuttlecock

shy[1] /shī/ *adj., v., & n.* ● *adj.* (**shy•er**, **shy•est** or **shi•er**, **shi•est**) **1 a** diffident or uneasy in company; timid. **b** (of an animal, bird, etc.) easily startled; timid. **2** (foll. by *of*) avoiding; wary of (*shy of his aunt; shy of going to meetings*). **3** (in *comb.*) showing fear of or distaste for (*gun-shy; work-shy*). **4** (often foll. by *of, on*) *colloq.* having lost; short of (*I'm shy three dollars; shy of the price of admission*). ● *v.intr.* (**shies, shied**) **1** (usu. foll. by *at*) (esp. of a horse) start suddenly aside (at an object, noise, etc.) in fright. **2** (usu. foll. by *away from, at*) avoid accepting or becoming involved in (a proposal, etc.) in alarm. ● *n.* a sudden startled movement. □□ **shy•er** *n.* **shy•ly** *adv.* (also **shy•ly**) **shy•ness** *n.* [OE *sceoh* f. Gmc]

shy[2] /shī/ *v. & n.* ● *v.tr.* (**shies, shied**) (also *absol.*) fling or throw (a

stone, etc.). ● *n.* (*pl.* **shies**) the act or an instance of shying. □ **have a shy at** *colloq.* **1** try to hit with a stone, etc. **2** make an attempt at. **3** jeer at. □□ **shy•er** *n.* [18th c.: orig. unkn.]

Shy•lock /shílok/ *n.* a hard-hearted moneylender; a miser. [character in Shakesp. *Merchant of Venice*]

shy•ster /shístər/ *n. colloq.* a person, esp. a lawyer, who uses unscrupulous methods. [19th c.: orig. uncert.]

SI *abbr.* **1** the international system of units of measurement (F *Système International*). **2** (Order of the) Star of India.

Si *symb. Chem.* the element silicon.

si /see/ *n. Mus.* = TE. [F f. It., perh. f. the initials of *Sancte Iohannis*: see GAMUT]

si•al•o•gogue /siáləgawg, –gog/ *n. & adj.* ● *n.* a medicine inducing the flow of saliva. ● *adj.* inducing such a flow. [F f. Gk *sialon* saliva + *agōgos* leading]

si•a•mang /seeəmang/ *n.* a large black gibbon, *Hylobates syndactylus*, native to Sumatra and the Malay peninsula. [Malay]

Si•a•mese /síəmeéz/ *n. & adj.* ● *n.* (*pl.* same) **1 a** a native of Siam (now Thailand) in SE Asia. **b** the language of Siam. **2** (in full **Si•amese cat**) **a** a cat of a cream-colored short-haired breed with a brown face and ears and blue eyes. **b** this breed. ● *adj.* of or concerning Siam, its people, or language.

Si•a•mese twins *n.* **1** twins joined at any part of the body and sometimes sharing organs, etc. **2** any closely associated pair.

sib /sib/ *n. & adj.* ● *n.* **1** a brother or sister (cf. SIBLING). **2** a blood relative. **3** a group of people recognized by an individual as his or her kindred. ● *adj.* (usu. foll. by *to*) esp. *Sc.* related; akin. [OE *sib* (b)]

Siamese cat

Si•be•ri•an /sībeéreeən/ *n. & adj.* ● *n.* **1** a native of Siberia in the northeastern part of the Russian Federation. **2** a person of Siberian descent. ● *adj.* **1** of or relating to Siberia. **2** *colloq.* (esp. of weather) extremely cold.

sib•i•lant /síbilənt/ *adj. & n.* ● *adj.* **1** (of a letter or set of letters, as *s, sh*) sounded with a hiss. **2** hissing (*a sibilant whisper*). ● *n.* a sibilant letter or letters. □□ **sib•i•lance** *n.* **sib•i•lan•cy** *n.* [L *sibilare* sibilant-hiss]

sib•i•late /síbilayt/ *v.tr. & intr.* pronounce with or utter a hissing sound. □□ **sib•i•la•tion** /–láyshən/ *n.*

sib•ling /síbling/ *n.* each of two or more children having one or both parents in common. [SIB + –LING[1]]

sib•ship /síbship/ *n.* **1** the state of belonging to a sib or the same sib. **2** a group of children having the same two parents.

sib•yl /síbil/ *n.* **1** any of certain women in ancient times supposed to utter the oracles and prophecies of a god. **2** a prophetess, fortune-teller, or witch. [ME f. OF *Sibile* or med.L *Sibilla* f. L *Sibylla* f. Gk *Sibulla*]

sib•yl•line /síbilin, –leen/ *adj.* **1** of or from a sibyl. **2** oracular; prophetic. [L *Sibyllinus* (as SIBYL)]

Sib•yl•line books *n.pl.* a collection of oracles belonging to the ancient Roman State and used for guidance by magistrates, etc.

sic[1] /sik/ *v.tr.* (**sicced, sic•cing**; also **sicked** /sikt/, **sick•ing**) (usu. in *imper.*) (esp. to a dog) set upon (a rat, etc.). [19th c., dial. var. of SEEK]

sic[2] /sik, seek/ *adv.* (usu. in brackets) used, spelled, etc., as written (confirming, or calling attention to, the form of quoted or copied words). [L, = thus]

sic•ca•tive /síkətiv/ *n. & adj.* ● *n.* a substance causing drying, esp. mixed with oil paint, etc., for quick drying. ● *adj.* having such properties. [LL *siccativus* f. *siccare* to dry]

sice[1] /sīs/ *n. Brit.* the six on dice. [ME f. OF *sis* f. L *sex* six]

sice[2] var. of SYCE.

Si•cil•ian /sisílyən/ *n. & adj.* ● *n.* **1** a native of Sicily, an island off the S. coast of Italy. **2** a person of Sicilian descent. **3** the Italian dialect of Sicily. ● *adj.* of or relating to Sicily. [L *Sicilia* Sicily]

sick[1] /sik/ *adj., n., & v.* ● *adj.* **1** (often in *comb.*) vomiting or tending to vomit (*I think I'm going to be sick; seasick*). **2** ill; affected by illness (*has been sick for a week; a sick man; sick with measles*). **3 a** (often foll. by *at*) esp mentally perturbed; disordered (*the product of a sick mind; sick at heart*). **b** (often foll. by *for*, or in *comb.*) pining; longing (*sick for a sight of home; lovesick*). **4** (often foll. by *of*) *colloq.* **a** disgusted; surfeited (*sick of chocolates*). **b** angry, esp. because of surfeit (*am sick of being teased*). **5** *colloq.* (of humor, etc.) jeering at misfortune, illness, death, etc.; morbid (*sick joke*). **6** (of a ship) needing repair (esp. of a specified kind) (*paint-sick*). ● *n. Brit. colloq.* vomit. ● *v.tr.* (usu. foll. by *up*) *Brit. colloq.* vomit (*sicked up his dinner*). □ **look sick** *colloq.* be unimpressive or embarrassed. **sick to one's stomach** vomiting or tending to vomit. **take sick** *colloq.* be taken ill. □□ **sick•ish** *adj.* [OE *sēoc* f. Gmc]

sick[2] var. of SIC[1].

sick•bay /síkbay/ *n.* **1** part of a ship used as a hospital. **2** any room, etc., for sick people.

sick·bed /síkbed/ *n.* **1** an invalid's bed. **2** the state of being an invalid.

sick build·ing syn·drome *n.* a high incidence of illness in office workers, attributed to the immediate working surroundings.

sick call *n.* **1** a visit by a doctor to a sick person, etc. **2** *Mil.* a summons for sick individuals to attend.

sick·en /síkən/ *v.* **1** *tr.* affect with loathing or disgust. **2** *intr.* **a** *Brit.* (often foll. by *for*) show symptoms of illness (*is sickening for measles*). **b** (often foll. by *at*, or *to* + infin.) feel nausea or disgust (*he sickened at the sight*). **3** (as **sickening** *adj.*) **a** loathsome; disgusting. **b** *colloq.* very annoying. □□ **sick·en·ing·ly** *adv.*

sick flag *n.* a yellow flag indicating disease at a quarantine station or on ship.

sick head·ache *n.* a migraine headache with vomiting.

sick·le /síkəl/ *n.* **1** a short-handled farming tool with a semicircular blade, used for cutting grain, lopping, or trimming. **2** anything sickle-shaped, esp. the crescent moon. [OE *sicol, sicel* f. L *secula* f. *secare* cut]

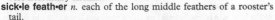

sick leave *n.* leave of absence granted because of illness.

sick·le cell *n.* a sickle-shaped blood cell, esp. as found in a type of severe hereditary anemia.

sickle

sick·le feath·er *n.* each of the long middle feathers of a rooster's tail.

sick list *n.* a list of the sick, esp. in a regiment, ship, etc.

sick·ly /síklee/ *adj.* (**sick·li·er, sick·li·est**) **1 a** of weak health; apt to be ill. **b** (of a person's complexion, look, etc.) languid, faint, or pale, suggesting sickness (*a sickly smile*). **c** (of light or color) faint; pale; feeble. **2** causing ill health (*a sickly climate*). **3** (of a book, etc.) sentimental or mawkish. **4** inducing or connected with nausea (*a sickly taste*). **5** (of a color, etc.) of an unpleasant shade inducing nausea (*a sickly green*). □□ **sick·li·ness** *n.* [ME, prob. after ON *sjukligr* (as SICK¹)]

sick·ness /síknis/ *n.* **1** the state of being ill; disease. **2** a specified disease (*sleeping sickness*). **3** vomiting or a tendency to vomit. [OE *sēocnesse* (as SICK¹, –NESS)]

sick·o /síkō/ *n.* (also **sick·ie** /síkee/) *sl.* a person who is mentally deranged or morally debased.

sick pay *n.* pay given to an employee, etc., on sick leave.

sick·room /síkrōōm, –rŏŏm/ *n.* **1** a room occupied by a sick person. **2** a room adapted for sick people.

si·dal·ce·a /sidálseeə/ *n.* any mallowlike plant of the genus *Sidalcea*, bearing racemes of white, pink, or purple flowers. [mod.L f. *Sida* + *Alcea*, names of related genera]

side /sid/ *n. & v.* ● *n.* **1 a** each of the more or less flat surfaces bounding an object (*a cube has six sides; this side up*). **b** a more or less vertical inner or outer plane or surface (*the side of a house; a mountainside*). **c** such a vertical lateral surface or plane as distinct from the top or bottom, front or back, or ends (*at the side of the house*). **2 a** the half of a person or animal that is on the right or the left, esp. of the torso (*has a pain in his right side*). **b** the left or right half of a specified part of a thing, area, building, etc. (*put the box on that side*). **c** (often in *comb.*) a position next to a person or thing (*graveside; seaside; stood at my side*). **d** a specified direction relating to a person or thing (*on the north side of; came from all sides*). **e** half of a butchered carcass (*a side of bacon*). **3 a** either surface of a thing regarded as having two surfaces. **b** the amount of writing needed to fill one side of a sheet of paper (*write three sides*). **4** any of several aspects of a question, character, etc. (*many sides to his character; look on the bright side*). **5 a** each of two sets of opponents in war, politics, games, etc. (*the side that bats first; much to be said on both sides*). **b** a cause or philosophical position, etc., regarded as being in conflict with another (*on the side of right*). **6 a** a part or region near the edge and remote from the center (*at the side of the room*). **b** (*attrib.*) a subordinate, peripheral, or detached part (*a side road; a side table*). **7 a** each of the bounding lines of a plane rectilinear figure (*a hexagon has six sides*). **b** each of two quantities stated to be equal in an equation. **8** a position nearer or farther than, or right or left of, a dividing line (*on this side of the Alps; on the other side of the road*). **9** a line of hereditary descent through the father or the mother. **10** (in full **side spin**) *Brit.* = ENGLISH *n.* 3. **11** *Brit. sl.* boastfulness; swagger (*has no side about him*). **12** *Brit. colloq.* a television channel (*shall we try another side?*). ● *v.intr.* (usu. foll. by *with*) take part or be on the same side as a disputant, etc. (*sided with his father*). □ **by the side of 1** close to. **2** compared with. **from side to side 1** right across. **2** alternately each way from a central line. **let the side down** *Brit.* fail one's colleagues, esp. by frustrating their efforts or embarrassing them. **on one side 1** not in the main or central position. **2** aside (*took him on one side to explain*). **on the ... side** fairly; somewhat (*qualifying an adjective: on the high side*). **on the side 1** as a sideline; in addition to one's regular work, etc. **2** secretly or illicitly. **3** as a side dish. **on this side of the grave** in life. **side by**

side standing close together, esp. for mutual support. **take sides** support one or other cause, etc. □□ **side·less** *adj.* [OE *sīde* f. Gmc]

side arms *n.pl.* swords, bayonets, or pistols.

side·band /sídband/ *n.* a range of frequencies near the carrier frequency of a radio wave, concerned in modulation.

side·bar /sídbaar/ *n.* **1** a short news article, printed alongside a major news story, that contains related incidental information. **2** *Law* discussion or consultation between a trial judge and counsel that the jury is not permitted to hear.

side bet *n.* a bet between opponents, esp. in card games, over and above the ordinary stakes.

side·board /sídbawrd/ *n.* a table or esp. a flat-topped cupboard at the side of a dining room for supporting and containing dishes, table linen, decanters, etc.

side·boards /sídbawrdz/ *n.pl. Brit. colloq.* = SIDEBURNS.

side·burns /sídbərnz/ *n.pl. colloq.* hair grown by a man down the sides of his face; side-whiskers. [*burnsides* pl. of *burnside* f. General *Burnside* d. 1881 who affected this style]

side·car /sídkaar/ *n.* **1** a small car for a passenger or passengers attached to the side of a motorcycle. **2** a cocktail of orange liqueur, lemon juice, and brandy.

side chap·el *n.* a chapel off the side aisle or at the side of a church.

sid·ed /sídid/ *adj.* **1** having sides. **2** (in *comb.*) having a specified side or sides (*one-sided*). □□ **–sid·ed·ly** *adv.* **sid·ed·ness** *n.* (also in *comb.*).

side dish *n.* an extra dish subsidiary to the main course.

side door *n.* **1** a door in or at the side of a building. **2** an indirect means of access.

side drum *n.* = SNARE DRUM.

side ef·fect *n.* a secondary, usu. undesirable, effect.

side-glance *n.* a sideways or brief glance.

side·hill /sídhil/ *n.* a hillside.

side is·sue *n.* a point that distracts attention from what is important.

side·kick /sídkik/ *n. colloq.* a close associate.

side·light /sídlit/ *n.* **1** a light from the side. **2** incidental information, etc. **3** esp. *Brit.* a light at the side of the front of a motor vehicle to warn of its presence. **4** *Naut.* the red port or green starboard light on a ship under way.

side·line /sídlin/ *n. & v.* ● *n.* **1** work, etc., done in addition to one's main activity. **2** (usu. in *pl.*) **a** a line bounding the side of a football field, tennis court, etc. **b** the space next to these where spectators, etc., sit. ● *v.tr.* remove (a player) from a team through injury, suspension, etc. □ **on** (or **from**) **the sidelines** in (or from) a position removed from the main action.

side·long /sídlawng, –long/ *adj. & adv.* ● *adj.* inclining to one side; oblique (*a sidelong glance*). ● *adv.* obliquely (*moved sidelong*). [*sideling* (as SIDE, –LING²): see –LONG]

side note *n.* a marginal note.

side-on *adv. & adj.* ● *adv.* from the side. ● *adj.* **1** from or toward one side. **2** (of a collision) involving the side of a vehicle.

si·de·re·al /sidéreeəl/ *adj.* of or concerning the constellations or fixed stars. [L *sidereus* f. *sidus sideris* star]

si·de·re·al clock *n.* a clock showing sidereal time.

si·de·re·al day *n.* the time between successive meridional transits of a star or esp. of the first point of Aries, about four minutes shorter than the solar day.

si·de·re·al time *n.* time measured by the apparent diurnal motion of the stars.

si·de·re·al year *n.* a year longer than the solar year by 20 minutes 23 seconds because of precession.

sid·er·ite /sídərit/ *n.* **1** a mineral form of ferrous carbonate. **2** a meteorite consisting mainly of nickel and iron. [Gk *sidēros* iron]

side road *n.* a minor or subsidiary road, esp. joining or diverging from a main road.

sid·er·o·stat /sídərəstat/ *n.* an instrument used for keeping the image of a celestial body in a fixed position. [L *sidus sideris* star, after *heliostat*]

side·sad·dle /sídsad'l/ *n. & adv.* ● *n.* a saddle for a woman rider having supports for both feet on the same side of the horse. ● *adv.* sitting in this position on a horse.

side sal·ad *n.* a salad served as a side dish.

side seat *n.* a seat in a vehicle, etc., in which the occupant has his back to the side of the vehicle.

side·show /sídshō/ *n.* **1** a minor show or attraction in an exhibition or entertainment. **2** a minor incident or issue.

side·slip /sídslip/ *n. & v.* ● *n.* **1** a skid. **2** *Aeron.* a sideways movement instead of forward. ● *v.intr.* **1** skid. **2** *Aeron.* move sideways instead of forward.

side·split·ting /sídspliting/ *adj.* causing violent laughter.

side·step /sídstep/ *n. & v.* ● *n.* a step taken sideways. ● *v.tr.* (**·stepped, ·step·ping**) **1** esp. *Football* avoid (esp. a tackle) by stepping sideways. **2** evade. □□ **side·step·per** *n.*

side street *n.* a minor or subsidiary street.

side·stroke /sídströk/ *n.* **1** a stroke toward or from a side. **2** an incidental action. **3** a swimming stroke in which the swimmer lies on his or her side.

side·swipe /sídswip/ *n. & v.* ●*n.* **1** a glancing blow along the side. **2** incidental criticism, etc. ●*v.tr.* hit with or as if with a sideswipe.

side ta·ble *n.* a table placed at the side of a room or apart from the main table.

side·track /sídtrak/ *n. & v.* ●*n.* a railroad siding. ●*v.tr.* **1** turn into a siding; shunt. **2 a** postpone, evade, or divert treatment or consideration of. **b** divert (a person) from considering, etc.

side trip *n.* a minor excursion during a voyage or trip; a detour.

side view *n.* **1** a view obtained sideways. **2** a profile.

side·walk /sídwawk/ *n.* a usu. paved pedestrian path at the side of a road.

side·wall /sídwawl/ *n.* **1** the part of a tire between the tread and the wheel rim. **2** a wall that forms the side of a structure.

side·ward /sídwərd/ *adj. & adv.* ●*adj.* = SIDEWAYS. ●*adv.* (also **side·wards** /–wərdz/) = SIDEWAYS.

side·ways /sídwayz/ *adv. & adj.* ●*adv.* **1** to or from a side (*moved sideways*). **2** with one side facing forward (*sat sideways on the bus*). ●*adj.* to or from a side (*a sideways movement*). □□ **side·wise** *adv. & adj.*

side·wheel·er *n.* a steamboat with paddle wheels.

side·whisk·ers *n.pl.* whiskers growing on the cheeks.

side wind *n.* **1** wind from the side. **2** an indirect agency or influence.

side·wind·er /sídwindər/ *n.* **1** a desert rattlesnake, *Crotalus cerastes*, native to N. America, moving with a lateral motion. **2** a sideways blow.

sid·ing /sídíng/ *n.* **1** a short track at the side of and opening on to a railroad line, used for switching trains. **2** material for the outside of a building, e.g., clapboards, shingles, etc.

si·dle /sídʼl/ *v. & n.* ●*v.intr.* (usu. foll. by *along, up*) walk in a timid, furtive, stealthy, or cringing manner. ●*n.* the act or an instance of sidling. [back-form. f. *sideling*, SIDELONG]

SIDS /sidz/ *abbr.* sudden infant death syndrome; crib death.

siege /seej/ *n.* **1 a** a military operation in which an attacking force seeks to compel the surrender of a fortified place by surrounding it and cutting off supplies, etc. **b** a similar operation by police, etc., to force the surrender of an armed person. **c** the period during which a siege lasts. **2** a persistent attack or campaign of persuasion. □ **lay siege to** esp. *Mil.* conduct the siege of. **raise the siege of** abandon or cause the abandonment of an attempt to take (a place) by siege. [ME f. OF *sege* seat f. *assegier* BESIEGE]

sie·mens /seémənz/ *n. Electr.* the SI unit of conductance, equal to one reciprocal ohm. ¶ Abbr.: **S**. [W. von *Siemens*, Ger. electrical engineer, d. 1892]

si·en·na /seénə/ *n.* **1** a kind of ferruginous earth used as a pigment in paint. **2** its color of yellowish-brown (**raw sienna**) or reddish-brown (**burnt sienna**). [It. (*terra di*) *Sienna* (earth of) Siena in Tuscany]

si·er·ra /seérə/ *n.* a long jagged mountain chain, esp. in Spain or Spanish America. [Sp. f. L *serra* saw]

si·es·ta /seéstə/ *n.* an afternoon sleep or rest esp. in hot countries. [Sp. f. L *sexta* (*hora*) sixth hour]

sieve /siv/ *n. & v.* ●*n.* a utensil having a perforated or meshed bottom for separating solids or coarse material from liquids or fine particles, or for reducing a soft solid to a fine pulp. ●*v.tr.* **1** put through or sift with a sieve. **2** examine (evidence, etc.) to select or separate. □ **head like a sieve** a memory that retains little. □□ **sieve·like** *adj.* [OE *sife* f. WG]

sift /sift/ *v.* **1** *tr.* sieve (material) into finer and coarser parts. **2** *tr.* (usu. foll. by *from, out*) separate (finer or coarser parts) from material. **3** *tr.* sprinkle (esp. sugar) from a perforated container. **4** *tr.* examine (evidence, facts, etc.) in order to assess authenticity, etc. **5** *intr.* (of snow, light, etc.) fall as if from a sieve. □ **sift through** examine by sifting. □□ **sift·er** *n.* (also in *comb.*). [OE *siftan* f. WG]

Sig. *abbr.* Signor.

sigh /sí/ *v. & n.* ●*v.* **1** *intr.* emit a long, deep, audible breath expressive of sadness, weariness, longing, relief, etc. **2** *intr.* (foll. by *for*) yearn for (a lost person or thing). **3** *tr.* utter or express with sighs (*"Never!" he sighed*). **4** *intr.* (of the wind, etc.) make a sound like sighing. ●*n.* **1** the act or an instance of sighing. **2** a sound made in sighing (*a sigh of relief*). [ME *sihen*, etc., prob. back-form. f. *sihte* past of *sihen* f. OE *sīcan*]

sight /sít/ *n. & v.* ●*n.* **1 a** the faculty of seeing with the eyes (*lost his sight*). **b** the act or an instance of seeing; the state of being seen. **2** a thing seen; a display, show, or spectacle (*not a pretty sight; a beautiful sight*). **3** a way of looking at or considering a thing (*in my sight he can do no wrong*). **4** a range of space within which a person, etc., can see or an object be seen (*he's out of sight; they are just coming into sight*). **5** (usu. in *pl.*) noteworthy features of a town, area, etc. (*went to see the sights*). **6 a** a device on a gun or optical instrument used for assisting the precise aim or observation. **b** the

aim or observation so gained (*got a sight of him*). **7** *colloq.* a person or thing having a ridiculous, repulsive, or disheveled appearance (*looked a perfect sight*). **8** *colloq.* a great quantity (*will cost a sight of money; is a sight better than he was*). ●*v.tr.* **1** get sight of, esp. by approaching (*they sighted land*). **2** observe the presence of (esp. aircraft, animals, etc.) (*sighted buffalo*). **3** take observations of (a star, etc.) with an instrument. **4 a** provide (a gun, quadrant, etc.) with sights. **b** adjust the sight of (a gun, etc.). **c** aim (a gun, etc.) with sights. □ **at first sight** on first glimpse or impression. **at** (or **on**) **sight** as soon as a person or a thing has been seen (*plays music at sight; liked him on sight*). **catch** (or **lose**) **sight of** begin (or cease) to see or be aware of. **get a sight of** manage to see; glimpse. **have lost sight of** no longer know the whereabouts of. **in sight 1** visible. **2** near at hand (*salvation is in sight*). **in** (or **within**) **sight of** so as to see or be seen from. **lower one's sights** become less ambitious. **out of my sight!** go at once! **out of sight 1** not visible. **2** *colloq.* excellent; delightful. **out of sight out of mind** we forget the absent. **put out of sight** hide; ignore. **set one's sights on** aim at (*set her sights on a directorship*). **sight for sore eyes** a welcome person or thing, esp. a visitor. **sight unseen** without previous inspection. □□ **sight·er** *n.* [OE (*ge*)*sihth*]

sight·ed /sítid/ *adj.* **1** capable of seeing; not blind. **2** (in *comb.*) having a specified kind of sight (*farsighted*).

sight·ing shot *n.* an experimental shot to guide riflemen in adjusting their sights.

sight·less /sítlis/ *adj.* **1** blind. **2** *poet.* invisible. □□ **sight·less·ly** *adv.* **sight·less·ness** *n.*

sight line *n.* a hypothetical line from a person's eye to what is seen.

sight·ly /sítlee/ *adj.* attractive to the sight; not unsightly. □□ **sight·li·ness** *n.*

sight-read *v.tr.* (*past* and *past part.* ·**read** /–red/) read and perform (music) at sight. □□ **sight read·er** *n.* **sight-read·ing** *n.*

sight·se·er /sítseeər/ *n.* a person who visits places of interest; a tourist. □□ **sight·see** *v.intr. & tr.* **sight·see·ing** *n.*

sight·worth·y /sítwurthee/ *adj.* worth seeing.

sig·il·late /sijilət/ *adj.* **1** (of pottery) having impressed patterns. **2** *Bot.* having seallike marks. [L *sigillatus* f. *sigillum* seal dimin. of *signum* sign]

sig·ma /sígmə/ *n.* the eighteenth letter of the Greek alphabet (Σ, σ, or, when final, ς). [L f. Gk]

sig·mate /sígmət, –mayt/ *adj.* **1** sigma-shaped. **2** S-shaped.

sig·moid /sígmoyd/ *adj. & n.* ●*adj.* **1** curved like the uncial sigma (⊂); crescent-shaped. **2** S-shaped. ●*n.* (in full **sigmoid flexure**) *Anat.* the curved part of the intestine between the colon and the rectum. [Gk *sigmoeidēs* (as SIGMA)]

sign /sín/ *n. & v.* ●*n.* **1 a** a thing indicating or suggesting a quality or state, etc.; a thing perceived as indicating a future state or occurrence (*violence is a sign of weakness; shows all the signs of decay*). **b** a miracle evidencing supernatural power; a portent (*did signs and wonders*). **2 a** a mark, symbol, or device used to represent something or to distinguish the thing on which it is put (*marked the jar with a sign*). **b** a technical symbol used in algebra, music, etc. (*a minus sign; a repeat sign*). **3** a gesture or action used to convey information, an order, request, etc. (*gave him a sign to leave; conversed by signs*). **4** a publicly displayed board, etc., giving information; a signboard or signpost. **5** any objective evidence of a disease, usu. specified (*Babinski's sign*). **6** a password (*advanced and gave the sign*). **7** any of the twelve divisions of the zodiac, named from the constellations formerly situated in them (*the sign of Cancer*). **8** the trail of a wild animal. **9** *Math.*, etc., the positiveness or negativeness of a quantity. **10** = SIGN LANGUAGE. ●*v.* **1** *tr.* **a** (also *absol.*) write (one's name, initials, etc.) on a document, etc., indicating that one has authorized it. **b** write one's name, etc., on (a document) as authorization. **2** *intr. & tr.* communicate by gesture, esp. using sign language (*signed to me to come; signed her speech to the hearing impaired in the audience*). **3** *tr. & intr.* engage or be engaged by signing a contract, etc. (see also **sign on, sign up**). **4** *tr.* mark with a sign (esp. with the sign of the cross in baptism). □ **make no sign** seem unconscious; not protest. **sign and countersign** secret words, etc., used as passwords. **sign away** convey (one's right, property, etc.) by signing a deed, etc. **sign for** acknowledge receipt of by signing. **sign off 1** end work, broadcasting, a letter, etc., esp. by writing or speaking one's name. **2** acknowledge by signature. **sign on 1** agree to a contract, employment, etc. **2** begin work, broadcasting, etc., esp. by writing or announcing one's name. **3** employ (a person). **sign up 1** engage or employ (a person). **2** enlist in the armed forces. **3 a** commit (another person or oneself) by signing, etc. (*signed you up for dinner*). **b** enroll (*signed up for evening classes*). □□ **sign·a·ble** *adj.* **sign·er** *n.* [ME f. OF *signe, signer* f. L *signum, signare*]

sig·nal[1] /sígnəl/ *n. & v.* ● *n.* **1 a** a usu. prearranged sign conveying information, guidance, etc., esp. at a distance (*waved as a signal to begin*). **b** a message made up of such signs (*signals made with flags*). **2** an immediate occasion for or cause of movement, action, etc. (*the uprising was a signal for repression*). **3** *Electr.* **a** an electrical impulse or impulses or radio waves transmitted as a signal. **b** a sequence of these. **4** a light, semaphore, etc., on a railroad giving instructions or warnings to train engineers, etc. **5** *Bridge* a prearranged mode of bidding or play to convey information to one's partner. ● *v.* **1** *intr.* make signals. **2** *tr.* **a** (often foll. by *to* + infin.) make signals to; direct. **b** transmit (an order, information, etc.) by signal; announce (*signaled her agreement; signaled that the town had been taken*). □□ **sig·nal·er** or **sig·nal·ler** *n.* [ME f. OF f. Rmc & med.L *signale* neut. of LL *signalis* f. L *signum* SIGN]

sig·nal[2] /sígnəl/ *adj.* remarkably good or bad; noteworthy (*a signal victory*). □□ **sig·nal·ly** *adv.* [F *signalé* f It. past part. *segnalato* distinguished f. *segnale* SIGNAL[1]]

sig·nal book *n.* a list of signals arranged for sending esp. naval and military messages.

sig·nal box *n. Brit.* = SIGNAL TOWER.

sig·nal·ize /sígnəlīz/ *v.tr.* **1** make noteworthy or remarkable. **2** lend distinction or luster to. **3** indicate.

sig·nal·man /sígnəlmən/ *n.* (*pl.* **-men**) **1** a railroad employee responsible for operating signals and switches. **2** a person who displays or receives naval, etc., signals.

sig·nal of dis·tress *n.* esp. *Naut.* an appeal for help, esp. from a ship, by firing flares.

sig·nal tow·er *n.* a building beside a railroad track from which signals are controlled.

sig·na·ry /sígnəree/ *n.* (*pl.* **-ries**) a list of signs constituting the syllabic or alphabetic symbols of a language. [L *signum* SIGN + -ARY[1], after *syllabary*]

sig·na·to·ry /sígnətawree/ *n. & adj.* ● *n.* (*pl.* **-ries**) a party or esp. a nation that has signed an agreement or esp. a treaty. ● *adj.* having signed such an agreement, etc. [L *signatorius* of sealing f. *signare signat-* mark]

sig·na·ture /sígnəchər/ *n.* **1 a** a person's name, initials, or mark used in signing a letter, document, etc. **b** the act of signing a document, etc. **2** *archaic* a distinctive action, characteristic, etc. **3** *Mus.* **a** = KEY SIGNATURE. **b** = TIME SIGNATURE. **4** *Printing* **a** a letter or figure placed at the foot of one or more pages of each sheet of a book as a guide for binding. **b** such a sheet after folding. **5** written directions given to a patient as part of a medical prescription. [med.L *signatura* (LL = marking of sheep), as SIGNATORY]

sig·na·ture tune *n.* **1** (also **signature song**) a song particularly identified with a musician or musical group. **2** esp. *Brit.* a distinctive tune used to introduce a particular program or performer on television or radio; theme song.

sign·board /sínbawrd/ *n.* a board with a name or symbol, etc., displayed outside a store or hotel, etc.

sig·net /sígnit/ *n.* **1** a seal used instead of or with a signature as authentication. **2** (prec. by *the*) the royal seal formerly used for special purposes in England and Scotland, and in Scotland later as the seal of the Court of Session. [ME f. OF *signet* or med.L *signetum* (as SIGN)]

sig·net ring *n.* a ring with a seal set in it.

sig·nif·i·cance /signífikəns/ *n.* **1** importance; noteworthiness (*his opinion is of no significance*). **2** a concealed or real meaning (*what is the significance of her statement?*). **3** the state of being significant. **4** *Statistics* the extent to which a result deviates from a hypothesis such that the difference is due to more than errors in sampling. [OF *significance* or L *significantia* (as SIGNIFY)]

sig·nif·i·cant /signífikənt/ *adj.* **1** having a meaning; indicative. **2** having an unstated or secret meaning; suggestive (*refused it with a signif-*

icant gesture). **3** noteworthy; important; consequential (*a significant figure in history*). **4** *Statistics* of or relating to the significance in the difference between an observed and calculated result. □□ **sig·nif·i·cant·ly** *adv.* [L *significare*: see SIGNIFY]

sig·nif·i·cant fig·ure *n.* (also **sig·nif·i·cant dig·it**) *Math.* a digit in a numerical expression that is given to show the precision of the expression, and not a zero used simply to fill vacant space at the beginning or end.

sig·nif·i·cant oth·er *n.* a person who is very important in one's life, esp. a spouse or lover.

sig·ni·fi·ca·tion /sígnifikáyshən/ *n.* **1** the act of signifying. **2** (usu. foll. by *of*) exact meaning or sense, esp. of a word or phrase. [ME f. OF f. L *significatio -onis* (as SIGNIFY)]

sig·nif·i·ca·tive /signífikaytiv/ *adj.* **1** (esp. of a symbol, etc.) signifying. **2** having a meaning. **3** (usu. foll. by *of*) serving as a sign or evidence. [ME f. OF *significatif -ive*, or LL *significativus* (as SIGNIFY)]

sig·ni·fy /sígnifī/ *v.* (**-fies, -fied**) **1** *tr.* be a sign or indication of (*a yawn signifies boredom*). **2** *tr.* mean; have as its meaning ("*Dr.*" *signifies "doctor"*). **3** *tr.* communicate; make known (*signified their agreement*). **4** *intr.* be of importance; matter (*it signifies little*). □□ **sig·ni·fi·er** *n.* [ME f. OF *signifier* f. L *significare* (as SIGN)]

sign lan·guage *n.* a system of communication by hand gestures, used esp. by the hearing impaired.

sign of the cross *n.* a Christian sign made in blessing or prayer, by tracing a cross from the forehead to the chest and to each shoulder, or in the air.

sign of the times *n.* a portent, etc., showing a likely trend.

si·gnor /seenyáwr/ *n.* (*pl.* **si·gno·ri** /-nyóree/) **1** a title or form of address used of or to an Italian-speaking man, corresponding to Mr. or sir. **2** an Italian man. [It. f. L *senior*: see SENIOR]

si·gno·ra /seenyáwrə/ *n.* **1** a title or form of address used of or to an Italian-speaking married woman, corresponding to Mrs. or madam. **2** a married Italian woman. [It., fem. of SIGNOR]

si·gno·ri·na /séenyəréenə/ *n.* **1** a title or form of address used of or to an Italian-speaking unmarried woman. **2** an Italian unmarried woman. [It., dimin. of SIGNORA]

sig·no·ry /séenyəree/ *n.* (*pl.* **-ries**) **1** = SEIGNIORY. **2** *hist.* the governing body of a medieval Italian republic. [ME f. OF *s(e)ignorie* (as SEIGNEUR)]

sign paint·er *n.* (also **sign writ·er**) a person who paints signboards, etc.

sign·post /sínpōst/ *n. & v.* ● *n.* **1** a post erected at a crossroads with arms indicating the direction to and sometimes also the distance from various places. **2** a means of guidance; an indication. ● *v.tr.* **1** provide with a signpost or signposts. **2** esp. *Brit.* indicate (a course of action, direction, etc.).

si·ka /seekə/ *n.* a small forest-dwelling deer, *Cervus nippon*, native to Japan. [Jap. *shika*]

Sikh /seek/ *n.* a member of an E. Indian monotheistic faith founded in the 16th c. [Hindi, = disciple, f. Skr. *sishya*]

Sikh·ism /seekizəm/ *n.* the religious tenets of the Sikhs.

si·lage /sílij/ *n. & v.* ● *n.* **1** storage in a silo. **2** green fodder that has been stored in a silo. ● *v.tr.* put into a silo. [alt. of ENSILAGE after *silo*]

sild /silt/ *n.* a small immature herring, esp. one caught in N. European seas. [Da. & Norw.]

si·lence /síləns/ *n. & v.* ● *n.* **1** absence of sound. **2** abstinence from speech or noise. **3** the avoidance of mentioning a thing, betraying a secret, etc. **4** oblivion; the state of not being mentioned. ● *v.tr.* make silent, esp. by coercion or superior argument. □ **in silence** without speech or other sound. **reduce** (or **put**) **to silence** refute in argument. [ME f. OF f. L *silentium* (as SILENT)]

si·lenc·er /sílənsər/ *n.* any of various devices for reducing the noise emitted by a gun, etc.

si·lent /sílənt/ *adj.* **1** not speaking; not uttering or making or accompanied by any sound. **2** (of a letter) written but not pronounced, e.g., *b* in *doubt*. **3** (of a movie) without a synchronized soundtrack. **4** (of a person) taciturn; speaking little. **5** (of an agreement) unspoken; unrecorded. **6** saying or recording nothing on some subject (*the records are silent on the incident*). **7** *Brit.* (of liquor) unflavored. □□ **si•lent•ly** *adv.* [L *silēre silent-* be silent]

si•lent ma•jor•i•ty *n.* those of moderate opinions who rarely assert them.

si•lent part•ner *n.* a partner not sharing in the actual work of a business.

si•le•nus /sīleenəs/ *n.* (*pl.* **si•le•ni** /–nī/) (in Greek mythology) a bearded old man like a satyr, sometimes with the tail and legs of a horse. [L f. Gk *seilēnos*]

si•lex /sīleks/ *n.* a kind of glass made of fused quartz. [L (as SILICA)]

sil•hou•ette /sílōō-ét/ *n. & v.* • *n.* **1 a** representation of a person or thing showing the outline only, usu. done in solid black on white or cut from paper. **2** the dark shadow or outline of a person or thing against a lighter background. • *v.tr.* represent or (usu. in *passive*) show in silhouette. □ **in silhouette** seen or placed in outline. [Étienne de *Silhouette*, Fr. author and politician d. 1767]

silhouette

sil•i•ca /sílikə/ *n.* silicon dioxide, occurring as quartz, etc., and as a principal constituent of sandstone and other rocks. □□ **si•li•ceous** /–líshəs/ *adj.* (also **si•li•cious**). **si•lic•ic** /–lísik/ *adj.* **si•lic•i•fy** /–lísifī/ *v.tr. & intr.* (**•fies**, **•fied**). **si•lic•i•fi•ca•tion** /–fikáyshən/ *n.* [L *silex –icis* flint, after *alumina*, etc.]

sil•i•ca gel *n.* hydrated silica in a hard granular form, used as a desiccant.

sil•i•cate /sílikayt, –kət/ *n.* any of the many insoluble compounds of a metal combined with silicon and oxygen, occurring widely in the rocks of the earth's crust.

sil•i•con /sílikən, –kon/ *n. Chem.* a nonmetallic element occurring widely in silica and silicates, and used in the manufacture of glass. ¶ Symb.: **Si**. [L *silex –icis* flint (after *carbon, boron*), alt. of earlier *silicium*]

sil•i•con car•bide *n.* = CARBORUNDUM.

sil•i•con chip *n.* a silicon microchip.

sil•i•cone /sílikōn/ *n.* any of the many polymeric organic compounds of silicon and oxygen with high resistance to cold, heat, water, and the passage of electricity.

Sil•i•con Val•ley *n.* an area southeast of San Francisco, CA, with a high concentration of electronics industries.

sil•i•co•sis /sílikósis/ *n.* lung fibrosis caused by the inhalation of dust containing silica. □□ **sil•i•cot•ic** /–kótik/ *adj.*

si•lique /sileék/ *the* long, narrow seedpod of a cruciferous plant. □□ **sil•i•quose** /síləkwōs/ *adj.* **sil•i•quous** /–kwəs/ *adj.* [L, = pod]

silk /silk/ *n.* **1** a fine, strong, soft lustrous fiber produced by silkworms in making cocoons. **2** a similar fiber spun by some spiders, etc. **3 a** a thread or cloth made from silk fiber. **b** a thread or fabric resembling silk. **4** (in *pl.*) kinds of silk cloth or garments made from it, esp. as worn by a jockey in a horse-owner's colors. **5** *Brit. colloq.* Queen's (or King's) Counsel, as having the right to wear a silk gown. **6** (*attrib.*) made of silk (*silk blouse*). **7** the silky styles of the female corn flower. □□ **silk•like** *adj.* [OE *sioloc, seolec* (cf. ON *silki*) f. LL *sericum* neut. of L *sericus* f. *seres* f. Gk *Sēres* an oriental people]

silk cot•ton *n.* kapok or a similar substance.

silk•en /sílkən/ *adj.* **1** made of silk. **2** wearing silk. **3** soft or lustrous as silk. **4** (of a person's manner, etc.) suave or insinuating. [OE *seolcen* (as SILK)]

silk gland *n.* a gland secreting the substance produced as silk.

silk hat *n.* a tall cylindrical hat covered with silk plush.

silk moth *n.* any of various large moths of the family Saturniidae, esp. *Hyalophora cecropia*.

silk-screen print•ing *n.* = SCREEN PRINTING.

silk•worm /sílkwərm/ *n.* the caterpillar of the moth *Bombyx mori*, which spins its cocoon of silk.

silk•y /sílkee/ *adj.* (**silk•i•er**, **silk•i•est**) **1** like silk in smoothness, softness, fineness, or luster. **2** (of a person's manner, etc.) suave; insinuating. □□ **silk•i•ly** *adv.* **silk•i•ness** *n.*

sill /sil/ *n.* (also *Brit.* **cill**) **1** a shelf or slab of stone, wood, or metal at the foot of a window or doorway. **2** a horizontal timber at the bottom of a dock or lock entrance, against which the gates close. **3** *Geol.* a tabular sheet of igneous rock intruded between other rocks and parallel with their planar structure. [OE *syll, sylle*]

sil•la•bub var. of SYLLABUB.

sil•li•man•ite /sílimənīt/ *n.* an aluminum silicate occurring in orthorhombic crystals or fibrous masses. [B. *Silliman*, Amer. chemist d. 1864]

sil•ly /sílee/ *adj. & n.* • *adj.* (**sil•li•er**, **sil•li•est**) **1** lacking sense; foolish; imprudent; unwise. **2** weak-minded. **3** *Cricket* (of a fielder or position) very close to the batsman (*silly mid off*). **4** *archaic* innocent; simple; helpless. **5** *colloq.* stunned (as) by a blow (*I was knocked silly*). • *n.* (*pl.* **•lies**) *colloq.* a foolish person. □□ **sil•li•ly** *adv.* **sil•li•ness** *n.* [later form of ME *sely* (dial. *seely*) happy, repr. OE *s ǣlig* (recorded in *unsǣlig* unhappy) f. Gmc]

sil•ly sea•son *n.* the time of year, usu. midsummer, when newspapers, etc., often publish trivial material for lack of important news.

si•lo /sílō/ *n. & v.* • *n.* (*pl.* **•los**) **1** a pit or airtight structure in which green crops are pressed and kept for fodder, undergoing fermentation. **2** a pit or tower for the storage of grain, cement, etc. **3** an underground chamber in which a guided missile is kept ready for firing. • *v.tr.* (**•loes**, **•loed**) make silage of. [Sp. f. L *sirus* f. Gk *siros* corn pit]

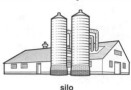

silo

silt /silt/ *n. & v.* • *n.* sediment deposited by water in a channel, harbor, etc. • *v.tr. & intr.* (often foll. by *up*) choke or be choked with silt. □□ **sil•ta•tion** /–táyshən/ *n.* **silt•y** *adj.* [ME, perh. rel. to Da., Norw. *sylt*, OLG *sulta*, OHG *sulza* salt marsh, formed as SALT]

silt•stone /síltstōn/ *n.* rock of consolidated silt.

Si•lu•ri•an /silóoreeən, sī–/ *adj. & n. Geol.* • *adj.* of or relating to the third period of the Paleozoic era with evidence of the first fish and land plants, and the formation of mountains and new land areas. • *n.* this period or system. [L *Silures*, a people of ancient SE Wales]

sil•va /sílvə/ *n.* (also **syl•va**) (*pl.* **syl•vae** /–vee/ or **syl•vas**) **1** the trees of a region, epoch, or environment. **2** a treatise on or a list of such trees. [L *silva* a wood]

sil•van var. of SYLVAN.

sil•ver /sílvər/ *n., adj., & v.* • *n. Chem.* **1** a grayish-white, lustrous, malleable, ductile, precious metallic element, occurring naturally as the element and in mineral form, and used chiefly with an admixture of harder metals for coin, plate, and ornaments, as a subordinate monetary medium, and in compounds for photography, etc. ¶ Symb.: **Ag**. **2** the color of silver. **3** silver or cupronickel coins. **4** esp. *Sc.* money. **5** silver vessels or implements, esp. cutlery. **6** household cutlery of any material. **7** = *silver medal*. • *adj.* **1** made wholly or chiefly of silver. **2** colored like silver. • *v.* **1** *tr.* coat or plate with silver. **2** *tr.* provide (a mirror glass) with a backing of tin amalgam, etc. **3** *tr.* (of the moon or a white light) give a silvery appearance to. **4 a** *tr.* turn (the hair) gray or white. **b** *intr.* (of the hair) turn gray or white. [OE *seolfor* f. Gmc]

sil•ver age *n.* a period regarded as inferior to a golden age, e.g., that of postclassical Latin literature in the early Imperial period.

sil•ver band *n. Brit.* a band playing silver-plated instruments.

sil•ver birch *n.* a common birch, *Betula alba*, with silver-colored bark.

sil•ver fir *n.* any fir of the genus *Abies*, with the undersides of its leaves colored silver.

sil•ver•fish /sílvərfish/ *n.* (*pl.* same or **•fish•es**) **1** any small silvery wingless insect of the order Thysanura, esp. *Lepisma saccharina* in houses and other buildings. **2** a silver-colored fish, esp. a colorless variety of goldfish.

sil•ver fox *n.* **1** an American red fox at a time when its fur is black with white tips. **2** its fur.

sil•ver gilt *n.* **1** gilded silver. **2** an imitation gilding of yellow lacquer over silver leaf.

sil•ver-gray *n.* a lustrous gray.

sil•ver ju•bi•lee *n.* a 25th anniversary.

sil•ver Lat•in *n.* literary Latin of the early Imperial period.

sil•ver leaf *n.* silver beaten into a very thin sheet.

sil•ver lin•ing *n.* a consolation or hopeful feature in misfortune.

sil•ver med•al *n.* a medal of silver, usu. awarded as second prize.

sil•vern /sílvərn/ *adj. archaic or poet.* = SILVER *adj.* [OE *seolfren, silfren* (as SILVER)]

sil•ver ni•trate *n.* a colorless solid that is soluble in water and formerly used in photography.

sil•ver pa•per *n. Brit.* **1** a fine, white tissue paper for wrapping silver. **2** aluminum or tin foil.

sil•ver plate *n.* vessels, spoons, etc., of copper, etc., plated with silver.

sil•ver salm•on *n.* a coho.

sil•ver screen *n.* (usu. prec. by *the*) motion pictures collectively.

sil•ver•side /sílvərsīd/ *n. Brit.* the upper side of a round of beef from the outside of the leg.

sil•ver•smith /sílvərsmith/ *n.* a worker in silver; a manufacturer of silver articles. □□ **sil•ver•smith•ing** *n.*

sil•ver sol•der *n.* solder containing silver.

sil•ver spoon *n.* a sign of future prosperity.

sil•ver stand•ard *n.* a system by which the value of a currency is defined in terms of silver, for which the currency may be exchanged.

Sil•ver Star *n. US Mil.* a decoration awarded for gallantry in action.

sil·ver tongue *n.* eloquence.

sil·ver·ware /sílvərwair/ *n.* **1** articles made of or coated with silver. **2** tableware of any metal.

sil·ver wed·ding *n.* the 25th anniversary of a wedding.

sil·ver·weed /sílvərweed/ *n.* a plant with silvery leaves, esp. a potentilla, *Potentilla anserina*, with silver-colored leaves.

sil·ver·y /sílvəree/ *adj.* **1** like silver in color or appearance. **2** having a clear, gentle, ringing sound. **3** (of the hair) white and lustrous. □□ **sil·ver·i·ness** *n.*

sil·vi·cul·ture /sílvikulchər/ *n.* (also **syl·vi·cul·ture**) the growing and tending of trees as a branch of forestry. □□ **sil·vi·cul·tur·al** /-kúlchərəl/ *adj.* **sil·vi·cul·tur·ist** /-kúlchərist/ [F f. L *silva* a wood + F *culture* CULTURE]

sim·i·an /símeeən/ *adj. & n.* ● *adj.* **1** of or concerning the anthropoid apes. **2** like an ape or monkey (*a simian walk*). ● *n.* an ape or monkey. [L *simia* ape, perh. f. L *simus* f. Gk *simos* flat-nosed]

sim·i·lar /símilər/ *adj.* **1** like; alike. **2** (often foll. by *to*) having a resemblance. **3** of the same kind, nature, or amount. **4** *Geom.* shaped alike. □□ **sim·i·lar·i·ty** /-láritee/ *n.* (*pl.* **·ties**). **sim·i·lar·ly** *adv.* [F *similaire* or med.L *similaris* f. L *similis* like]

sim·i·le /símilee/ *n.* **1** a figure of speech involving the comparison of one thing with another of a different kind, as an illustration or ornament (e.g., *as brave as a lion*). **2** the use of such comparison. [ME f. L, neut. of *similis* like]

si·mil·i·tude /simílitōōd, -tyōōd/ *n.* **1** the likeness, guise, or outward appearance of a thing or person. **2** a comparison or the expression of a comparison. **3** *archaic* a counterpart or facsimile. [ME f. OF *similitude* or L *similitudo* (as SIMILE)]

sim·mer /símər/ *v. & n.* ● *v.* **1** *intr. & tr.* be or keep bubbling or boiling gently. **2** *intr.* be in a state of suppressed anger or excitement. ● *n.* a simmering condition. □ **simmer down** become calm or less agitated. [alt. of ME (now dial.) *simper*, perh. imit.]

sim·nel cake /símnəl/ *n. Brit.* a rich fruit cake, usu. with a marzipan layer and decoration, eaten esp. at Easter or during Lent. [ME f. OF *simenel*, ult. f. L *simila* or Gk *semidalis* fine flour]

si·mon-pure /símənpyŏŏr/ *adj.* real; genuine. [(*the real*) *Simon Pure*, a character in Centlivre's *Bold Stroke for a Wife* (1717)]

si·mo·ny /símənee, sím-/ *n.* the buying or selling of ecclesiastical privileges, e.g., pardons or benefices. □□ **si·mo·ni·ac** /-móneeak/ *adj. & n.* **si·mo·ni·a·cal** /-níəkəl/ *adj.* [ME f. OF *simonie* f. LL *simonia* f. *Simon Magus* (Acts 8: 18)]

si·moom /simóōm/ *n.* (also **si·moon** /-móōn/) a hot, dry, dust-laden wind blowing at intervals esp. in the Arabian desert. [Arab. *samūm* f. *samma* to poison]

simp /simp/ *n. colloq.* a simpleton. [abbr.]

sim·pa·ti·co /simpátikō/ *adj.* congenial; likable. [It. & Sp. (as SYMPATHY)]

sim·per /símpər/ *v. & n.* ● *v.* **1** *intr.* smile in a silly or affected way. **2** *tr.* express by or with simpering. ● *n.* such a smile. □□ **sim·per·ing·ly** *adv.* [16th c.: cf. Du. and Scand. *semper*, *simper*, G *zimp(f)er* elegant, delicate]

sim·ple /símpəl/ *adj. & n.* ● *adj.* **1** easily understood or done; presenting no difficulty (*a simple explanation; a simple task*). **2** not complicated or elaborate; without luxury or sophistication. **3** not compound; consisting of or involving only one element or operation, etc. **4** absolute; unqualified; straightforward (*the simple truth; a simple majority*). **5** foolish or ignorant; gullible, feeble-minded (*am not so simple as to agree to that*). **6** plain in appearance or manner; unsophisticated; ingenuous; artless. **7** of low rank; humble; insignificant (*simple people*). **8** *Bot.* **a** consisting of one part. **b** (of fruit) formed from one pistil. ● *n. archaic* **1** an herb used medicinally. **2** a medicine made from it. □□ **sim·ple·ness** *n.* [ME f. OF f. L *simplus*]

sim·ple eye *n.* an eye of an insect, having only one lens.

sim·ple frac·ture *n.* a fracture of the bone only, without a skin wound.

sim·ple har·mon·ic mo·tion *n.* see HARMONIC.

sim·ple in·ter·est *n.* interest payable on a capital sum only (cf. *compound interest* (see COMPOUND)).

sim·ple in·ter·val *n. Mus.* an interval of one octave or less.

sim·ple ma·chine *n.* any of the basic mechanical devices for applying a force (e.g., an inclined plane, wedge, or lever).

sim·ple·mind·ed /símpəlmíndid/ *adj.* **1** natural; unsophisticated. **2** -feeble-minded. □□ **sim·ple·mind·ed·ly** *adv.* **sim·ple·mind·ed·ness** *n.*

sim·ple sen·tence *n.* a sentence with a single subject and predicate.

Sim·ple Si·mon *n.* a foolish person (from the nursery-rhyme character).

sim·ple time *n. Mus.* a time with two, three, or four beats in a bar.

sim·ple·ton /símpəltən/ *n.* a foolish, gullible, or half-witted person. [SIMPLE after surnames f. place-names in *-ton*]

sim·plex /símpleks/ *adj. & n.* ● *adj.* **1** simple; not compounded. **2** *Computing* (of a circuit) allowing transmission of signals in one direction only. ● *n.* a simple or uncompounded thing, esp. a word. [L, = single, var. of *simplus* simple]

sim·plic·i·ty /simplísitee/ *n.* the fact or condition of being simple. [OF *simplicité* or L *simplicitas* (as SIMPLEX)]

sim·pli·fy /símplifī/ *v. tr.* (**·fies, ·fied**) make simple; make easy or eas-

ier to do or understand. □□ **sim·pli·fi·ca·tion** /-fikáyshən/ *n.* [F *simplifier* f. med.L *simplificare* (as SIMPLE)]

sim·plism /símplizəm/ *n.* **1** affected simplicity. **2** the unjustifiable simplification of a problem, etc.

sim·plis·tic /simplístik/ *adj.* **1** excessively or affectedly simple. **2** oversimplified so as to conceal or distort difficulties. □□ **sim·plis·ti·cal·ly** *adv.*

sim·ply /símplee/ *adv.* **1** in a simple manner. **2** absolutely; without doubt (*simply astonishing*). **3** merely (*was simply trying to please*).

sim·u·la·crum /símyəláykrəm, -lák-/ *n.* (*pl.* **sim·u·la·cra** /-krə/) **1** an image of something. **2 a** a shadowy likeness; a deceptive substitute. **b** mere pretense. [L (as SIMULATE)]

sim·u·late /símyəlayt/ *v. tr.* **1 a** pretend to have or feel (an attribute or feeling). **b** pretend to be. **2** imitate or counterfeit. **3 a** imitate the conditions of (a situation, etc.), e.g., for training. **b** produce a computer model of (a process). **4** (as **simulated** *adj.*) made to resemble the real thing but not genuinely such (*simulated fur*). **5** (of a word) take or have an altered form suggested by (a word wrongly taken to be its source, e.g., *amuck*). □□ **sim·u·la·tion** /-láyshən/ *n.* **sim·u·la·tive** /-lətiv/ *adj.* [L *simulare* f. *similis* like]

sim·u·la·tor /símyəlaytər/ *n.* **1** a person or thing that simulates. **2** a device designed to simulate the operations of a complex system, used esp. in training.

si·mul·cast /síməlkast, sím–/ *n.* simultaneous transmission of the same program, as on radio and television. [SIMULTANEOUS + BROADCAST]

si·mul·ta·ne·ous /síməltáyneeəs, sím–/ *adj.* (often foll. by *with*) occurring or operating at the same time. □□ **si·mul·ta·ne·i·ty** /-tənáyitee/ *n.* **si·mul·ta·ne·ous·ly** *adv.* **si·mul·ta·ne·ous·ness** *n.* [med.L *simultaneus* f. L *simul* at the same time, prob. after *instantaneus*, etc.]

si·mul·ta·ne·ous e·qua·tions *n. pl.* equations involving two or more unknowns that are to have the same values in each equation.

sin[1] /sin/ *n. & v.* ● *n.* **1 a** the breaking of divine or moral law, esp. by a conscious act. **b** such an act. **2** an offense against good taste or propriety, etc. ● *v.* (**sinned, sin·ning**) **1** *intr.* commit a sin. **2** *intr.* (foll. by *against*) offend. **3** *tr. archaic* commit (a sin). □ **as sin** *colloq.* extremely (*ugly as sin*). **for one's sins** *joc.* as a judgment on one for something done. **like sin** *colloq.* vehemently or forcefully. **live in sin** *colloq.* live together without being married. □□ **sin·less** *adj.* **sin·less·ly** *adv.* **sin·less·ness** *n.* [OE *syn(n)*]

sin[2] /sī n/ *abbr.* sine.

Si·na·it·ic /sínayítik/ *adj.* of or relating to Mount Sinai or of the Sinai peninsula. [var. of *Sinaic* f. *Sinai* f. Heb. *sī nay*, with *t* added for euphony]

si·nan·thro·pus /sīnánthrəpəs, si–, sínanthrópəs, sín-/ *n.* an apelike human of the extinct genus *Sinanthropus*. [mod.L, as SINO- Chinese (remains having been found near Peking) + Gk *anthropos* man]

since /sins/ *prep., conj., & adv.* ● *prep.* throughout, or at a point in, the period between (a specified time, event, etc.) and the time present or being considered (*must have happened since yesterday; has been going on since June; the greatest composer since Beethoven*). ● *conj.* **1** during or in the time after (*what have you been doing since we met?; has not spoken since the dog died*). **2** for the reason that; because; inasmuch as (*since you are drunk I will drive you home*). **3** (*ellipt.*) as being (*a more useful, since better designed, tool*). ● *adv.* **1** from that time or event until now or the time being considered (*have not seen them since; had been healthy ever since; has since been cut down*). **2** ago (*happened many years since*). [ME, reduced form of obs. *sithence* or f. dial. *sin* (f. *sithen*) f. OE *siththon*]

sin·cere /sinseér/ *adj.* (**sin·cer·er, sin·cer·est**) **1** free from pretense or deceit; the same in reality as in appearance. **2** genuine; honest; frank. □□ **sin·cere·ness** *n.* **sin·cer·i·ty** /–séritee/ *n.* [L *sincerus* clean, pure]

sin·cere·ly /sinseérlee/ *adv.* in a sincere manner. □ **yours sincerely** a formula for ending an informal letter.

sin·ci·put /sínsipoot/ *n. Anat.* the front of the skull from the forehead to the crown. □□ **sin·cip·i·tal** /–sípitəl/ *adj.* [L f. *semi-* half + *caput* head]

sine /sin/ *n. Math.* **1** the trigonometric function that is equal to the ratio of the side opposite a given angle (in a right triangle) to the hypotenuse. **2** a function of the line drawn from one end of an arc perpendicularly to the radius through the other. [L *sinus* curve, fold of a toga, used in med.L as transl. of Arab. *jayb* bosom, sine]

si·ne·cure /sínikyoor, sín–/ *n.* a position that requires little or no work but usu. yields profit or honor. □□ **si·ne·cur·ism** *n.* **si·ne·cur·ist** *n.* [L *sine cura* without care]

sine curve *n.* (also **sine wave**) a curve representing periodic oscillations of constant amplitude as given by a sine function. Also called **sinusoid**.

si·ne di·e /sínee dí-ee, sínay deé-ay/ *adv.* (of business adjourned indefinitely) with no appointed date. [L, = without day]

si·ne qua non /sínay kwaa nón/ *n.* an indispensable condition or qualification. [L, = without which not]

sin·ew /sínyoo/ *n. & v.* ● *n.* **1** tough fibrous tissue uniting muscle to bone; a tendon. **2** (in *pl.*) muscles; bodily strength; wiriness. **3** (in *pl.*) that which forms the strength or framework of a plan, city, organization, etc. ● *v.tr. poet.* serve as the sinews of; sustain; hold together. □□ **sin·ew·less** *adj.* **sin·ew·y** *adj.* [OE *sin(e)we* f. Gmc]

sin·ews of war *n.pl.* money.

sin·fo·ni·a /sínfəneéə/ *n. Mus.* **1** a symphony. **2** (in Baroque music) an orchestral piece used as an introduction to an opera, cantata, or suite. **3** (**Sinfonia**; usu. in names) a symphony orchestra. [It., = SYMPHONY]

sin·fo·niet·ta /sínfənyétə/ *n. Mus.* **1** a short or simple symphony. **2** (**Sinfonietta**; usu. in names) a small symphony orchestra. [It., dimin. of *sinfonia*: see SINFONIA]

sin·ful /sínfool/ *adj.* **1** (of a person) committing sin, esp habitually. **2** (of an act) involving or characterized by sin. □□ **sin·ful·ly** *adv.* **sin·ful·ness** *n.* [OE *synfull* (as SIN, –FUL)]

sing /sing/ *v. & n.* ● *v.* (*past* **sang** /sang/; *past part.* **sung** /sung/) **1** *intr.* utter musical sounds with the voice, esp. words with a set tune. **2** *tr.* utter or produce by singing (*sing another song*). **3** *intr.* (of the wind, a kettle, etc.) make inarticulate melodious or humming, buzzing, or whistling sounds. **4** *intr.* (of the ears) be affected as with a buzzing sound. **5** *intr. sl.* turn informer; confess. **6** *intr. archaic* compose poetry. **7** *tr. & v.* (foll. by *of*) intr. celebrate in verse. **8** *tr.* (foll. by *in*, *out*) usher (esp. the new or old year) in or out with singing. **9** *tr.* bring to a specified state by singing (*sang the child to sleep*). ● *n.* **1** an act or spell of singing. **2** a meeting for amateur singing. □ **sing out** call out loudly; shout. **sing the praises of** see PRAISE. **sing up** sing more loudly. □□ **sing·a·ble** *adj.* **sing·er** *n.* **sing·ing·ly** *adv.* [OE *singan* f. Gmc]

sing. *abbr.* singular.

sing-a·long *n.* **1** a tune, etc., to which one can sing in accompaniment. **2** a gathering at which such tunes, etc., are sung.

singe /sinj/ *v. & n.* ● *v.* (**singe·ing**) **1** *tr. & intr.* burn superficially or lightly. **2** *tr.* burn the bristles or down off (the carcass of a pig or fowl) to prepare it for cooking. **3** *tr.* burn off the tips of (the hair) in hairdressing. ● *n.* a superficial burn. □ **singe one's wings** suffer some harm esp. in a risky attempt. [OE *sencgan* f. WG]

Singh /sing/ *n.* **1** a title adopted by the warrior castes of N. India. **2** a surname adopted by male Sikhs. [Hind. *singh* f. Skr. *sinhá* lion]

Sin·gha·lese var. of SINHALESE.

sin·gle /sínggəl/ *adj., n., & v.* ● *adj.* **1** one only; not double or multiple. **2** united or undivided. **3 a** designed or suitable for one person (*single room*). **b** used or done by one person, etc., or one set or pair. **4** one by itself; not one of several (*a single tree*). **5** regarded separately (*every single thing*). **6** not married. **7** *Brit.* (of a ticket) valid for a one-way trip only, not for the return. **8** (with *neg.* or *interrog.*) even one; not to speak of more (*did not see a single person*). **9** (of a flower) having only one circle of petals. **10** lonely; unaided. **11** *archaic* free from duplicity, sincere, consistent, guileless, ingenuous. ● *n.* **1** a single thing, or item in a series. **2** esp. *Brit.* a one-way ticket. **3 a** a recording with one piece of music, etc., on each side. **b** the piece of music, etc., on one side of a single. **4** *Baseball* a hit that allows the batter to reach first base safely. **5** *Cricket* a hit for one run. **6** (usu. in *pl.*) a game, esp. tennis, with one player on each side. **7** an unmarried person (*young singles*). **8** *sl.* a one-dollar note. ● *v.* **1** *tr.* (foll. by *out*) choose as an example or as distinguishable or to serve some purpose. **2** *intr. Baseball* hit a single.

---

sin·gle a·cros·tic *n.* an acrostic using the first letter only of each line.

sin·gle-act·ing *adj.* (of an engine, etc.) having pressure applied only to one side of the piston.

sin·gle-breast·ed *adj.* (of a coat, etc.) having only one set of buttons and buttonholes, not overlapping.

sin·gle com·bat *n.* a duel.

sin·gle cream *n. Brit.* thin cream with a relatively low fat content.

sin·gle-cut *adj.* (of a file) with grooves cut in one direction only, not crossing.

sin·gle-deck·er *adj.* esp. *Brit.* a bus having only one deck.

sin·gle en·try *adj.* denoting a system of bookkeeping in which each transaction is entered in one account only.

sin·gle file *n.* a line of people or things arranged one behind another.

sin·gle-hand·ed *adv. & adj.* ● *adv.* **1** without help from another. **2** with one hand. ● *adj.* **1** done, etc., single-handed. **2** for one hand. □□ **sin·gle-hand·ed·ly** *adv.*

sin·gle-lens re·flex *adj.* denoting a reflex camera in which a single lens serves the film and the viewfinder.

sin·gle-mind·ed *adj.* having or intent on only one purpose. □□ **sin·gle-mind·ed·ly** *adv.* **sin·gle-mind·ed·ness** *n.*

sin·gle par·ent *n.* a person bringing up a child or children without a partner.

sin·gles bar *n.* a bar for single people seeking company.

sin·gle seat·er *n.* a vehicle with one seat. □□ **sin·gle-seat·er** *adj.*

sin·gle·stick /sínggəlstik/ *n.* **1** a basket-hilted stick of about a sword's length. **2** one-handed fencing with this.

sin·glet /síngglit/ *n.* **1 a** a sleeveless athletic shirt. **b** *Brit.* a garment worn under or instead of a shirt; an undershirt. **2** a single unresolvable line in a spectrum. [SINGLE + –ET[1], after *doublet*, the garment being unlined]

sin·gle·ton /síngglətən/ *n.* **1** *Cards* one card only of a suit, esp. as dealt to a player. **2 a** a single person or thing. **b** an only child. **3** a single child or animal born, not a twin, etc. [SINGLE, after *simpleton*]

sin·gle·tree /síngglətree/ *n.* = WHIFFLETREE.

sing·song /síngsawng, –song/ *adj., n., & v.* ● *adj.* uttered with a monotonous rhythm or cadence. ● *n.* **1** a singsong manner. **2** *Brit.* an informal gathering for singing; a songfest. ● *v.intr. & tr.* (*past* and *past part.* **sing·songed**) speak or recite in a singsong manner.

sin·gu·lar /sínggyələr/ *adj. & n.* ● *adj.* **1** unique; much beyond the average; extraordinary. **2** eccentric or strange. **3** *Gram.* (of a word or form) denoting or referring to a single person or thing. **4** *Math.* possessing unique properties. **5** single; individual. ● *n. Gram.* **1** a singular word or form. **2** the singular number. □□ **sin·gu·lar·ly** *adv.* [ME f. OF *singuler* f. L *singularis* (as SINGLE)]

sin·gu·lar·i·ty /sínggyəláritee/ *n.* (*pl.* **·ties**) **1** the state or condition of being singular. **2** an odd trait or peculiarity. **3** *Physics & Math.* a point at which a function takes an infinite value, esp. in space-time when matter is infinitely dense. [ME f. OF *singularité* f. LL *singularitas* (as SINGULAR)]

sin·gu·lar·ize /sínggyələriz/ *v.tr.* **1** distinguish; individualize. **2** make singular. □□ **sin·gu·lar·i·za·tion** *n.*

sinh /sinch, sínaych/ *abbr. Math.* hyperbolic sine. [*sine* + hyperbolic]

Sin·ha·lese /sínhəleez, sína–/ *n. & adj.* (also **Sin·gha·lese** /sínggə–/) ● *n.* (*pl.* same) **1** a member of a people originally from N. India and now forming the majority of the population of Sri Lanka. **2** an Indic language spoken by this people. ● *adj.* of or relating to this people or language. [Skr. *si ṅhalam* Sri Lanka (Ceylon) + –ESE]

sin·is·ter /sínistər/ *adj.* **1** suggestive of evil; looking malignant or villainous. **2** wicked or criminal (*a sinister motive*). **3** of evil omen. **4** *Heraldry* of or on the left-hand side of a shield, etc. (i.e., to the observer's right). **5** *archaic* left-hand. □□ **sin·is·ter·ly** *adv.* **sin·is·ter·ness** *n.* [ME f. OF *sinistre* or L *sinister* left]

sin·is·tral /sínistrəl/ *adj. & n.* ● *adj.* **1** left-handed. **2** of or on the left. **3** (of a flatfish) with the left side uppermost. **4** (of a spiral shell) with whorls rising to the left and not (as usually) to the right. ● *n.* a left-handed person. □□ **sin·is·tral·i·ty** /–trálitee/ *n.* **sin·is·tral·ly** *adv.*

sin·is·trorse /sínistrawrs/ *adj.* rising toward the left, esp. of the spiral stem of a plant. [L *sinistrorsus* f. *sinister* left + *vorsus* past part. of *vertere* turn]

sink /singk/ *v. & n.* ● *v.* (*past* **sank** /sangk/ or **sunk** /sungk/; *past part.* **sunk** or **sunk·en**) **1** *intr.* fall or come slowly downward. **2** *intr.* disappear below the horizon (*the sun is sinking*). **3** *intr.* **a** go or come penetrate below the surface esp. of a liquid. **b** (of a ship) go to the bottom of the sea, etc. **4** *intr.* settle down comfortably (*sank into a chair*). **5** *intr.* **a** gradually lose strength or value or quality, etc.; decline (*my heart sank*). **b** (of the voice) descend in pitch or volume. **c** (of a sick person) approach death. **6** *tr.* send (a ship) to the bottom of the sea, etc. **7** *tr.* cause or allow to sink or penetrate (*sank its teeth into my leg*). **8** *tr.* cause the failure of (a plan, etc.) or the discomfiture of (a person). **9** *tr.* dig (a well) or bore (a shaft). **10** *tr.* engrave (a die) or inlay (a design). **11** *tr.* **a** invest (money) (*sunk a large sum into the business*). **b** lose (money) by investment. **12** *tr.* **a** cause (a ball) to enter a pocket in billiards, a hole at golf, etc. **b** achieve this by (a stroke). **13** *tr.* overlook or forget; keep in the background (*sank their differences*). **14** *intr.* (of a price, etc.) become lower. **15** *intr.* (of a storm or river) subside. **16** *intr.* (of ground) slope down, or reach a lower level by subsidence. **17** *intr.* (foll. by *on, upon*) (of darkness) descend (on a place). **18** *tr.* lower the level of. **19** *tr.* (usu. in *passive*; foll. by *in*) absorb; hold the attention of (*be sunk in thought*). •*n.* **1** a fixed basin with a water supply and outflow pipe. **2** a place where foul liquid collects. **3** a place of vice or corruption. **4** a pool or marsh in which a river's water disappears by evaporation or percolation. **5** *Physics* a body or process used to absorb or dissipate heat. **6** = SINKHOLE. □ **sink in 1** penetrate or make its way in. **2** become gradually comprehended (*paused to let the words sink in*). **sink or swim** even at the risk of complete failure (*determined to try, sink or swim*). □□ **sink•a•ble** *adj.* **sink•age** *n.* [OE *sincan* f. Gmc]

sink•er /síngkər/ *n.* **1** a weight used to sink a fishing line or sounding line. **2** *Baseball* (in full **sinkerball**) pitch thrown so that it curves sharply downward. **3** *colloq.* a doughnut.

sink•hole /síngkhōl/ *n. Geol.* a cavity in limestone, etc., into which a stream, etc., disappears.

sink•ing feel•ing *n.* a bodily sensation caused by hunger or apprehension.

sink•ing fund *n.* money set aside for the gradual repayment of a debt.

sin•ner /sínər/ *n.* a person who sins, esp. habitually.

sin•net var. of SENNIT.

Sinn Fein /shin fáyn/ *n.* a political movement and party seeking a united republican Ireland, often linked to the IRA. □□ **Sinn Fein•er** *n.* [Ir. *sinn féin* we ourselves]

Sino- /sínō/ *comb. form* Chinese; Chinese and (*Sino-American*). [Gk *Sinai* the Chinese]

si•no•logue /sínəlawg, –log, sín–/ *n.* an expert in sinology; sinologist. [F, formed as SINO- + Gk –*logos* speaking]

si•nol•o•gy /sīnóləjee, sin–/ *n.* the study of Chinese language, history, customs, etc. □□ **si•no•log•i•cal** /–nəlójikəl/ *adj.* **si•nol•o•gist** *n.*

sin•ter /síntər/ *n. & v.* •*n.* **1** a siliceous or calcareous rock formed by deposition from springs. **2** a substance formed by sintering. •*v.intr. & tr.* coalesce or cause to coalesce from powder into solid by heating. [G, = E *sinder* CINDER]

sin•u•ate /sínyōōət, –ayt/ *adj.* esp. *Bot.* wavy-edged; with distinct inward and outward bends along the edge. [L *sinuatus* past part. of *sinuare* bend]

sin•u•os•i•ty /sínyōō-ósitee/ *n.* (*pl.* **•ties**) **1** the state of being sinuous. **2** a bend, esp. in a stream or road. [F *sinuosité* or med.L *sinuositas* (as SINUOUS)]

sin•u•ous /sínyōōəs/ *adj.* with many curves; tortuous; undulating. □□ **sin•u•ous•ly** *adv.* **sin•u•ous•ness** *n.* [F *sinueux* or L *sinuosus* (as SINUS)]

si•nus /sínəs/ *n.* **1** a cavity of bone or tissue, esp. in the skull connecting with the nostrils. **2** *Med.* a fistula esp. to a deep abscess. **3** *Bot.* the curve between the lobes of a leaf. [L, = bosom, recess]

si•nus•i•tis /sínəsítis/ *n.* inflammation of a nasal sinus.

si•nus•oid /sínəsoyd/ *n.* **1** a curve having the form of a sine wave. **2** a small irregular-shaped blood vessel, esp. found in the liver. □□ **si•nus•oi•dal** /–sóyd'l/ *adj.* [F *sinusoïde* f. L *sinus*: see SINUS]

Si•on var. of ZION.

-sion /shən, zhən/ *suffix* forming nouns (see –ION) from Latin participial stems in –*s*– (*mansion; mission; persuasion*).

Sioux /sōō/ *n. & adj.* •*n.* (*pl.* same) **1** a member of a group of native N. American peoples. Also called **Dakota.** **2** the language of this group. • *adj.* of or relating to this people or language. □□ **Siou•an** /sōōən/ *adj. & n.* [F f. a native name]

sip /sip/ *v. & n.* •*v.tr. & intr.* (**sipped, sip•ping**) drink in one or more small amounts or by spoonfuls. •*n.* **1** a small mouthful of liquid (*a sip of brandy*). **2** the act of taking this. □□ **sip•per** *n.* [ME: perh. a modification of SUP[1]]

si•phon /sífən/ *n. & v.* (also **sy•phon**) •*n.* **1** a pipe or tube shaped like an inverted V or U with unequal legs to convey a liquid from a container to a lower level by atmospheric pressure. **2** (in full **si•phon bottle**) an aerated-water bottle from which liquid is forced out through a tube by the pressure of gas. **3** *Zool.* **a** a canal or conduit esp. in cephalopods. **b** the sucking tube of some insects, etc. •*v.tr. & intr.* (often foll. by *off*) **1** conduct or flow through a siphon. **2** divert or set aside (funds, etc.). □□ **si•phon•age** *n.* **si•phon•al** *adj.* **si•phon•ic** /–fónik/ *adj.* [F *siphon* or L *sipho –onis* f. Gk *siphōn* pipe]

si•pho•no•phore /sífónəfawr/ *n.* any usu. translucent marine hydrozoan of the order Siphonophora, e.g., the Portuguese man-of-war. [Gk *siphōno-* (as SIPHON, –PHORE)]

sip•pet /sípit/ *n.* **1** a small piece of bread, etc., soaked in liquid. **2** a piece of toast or fried bread as a garnish. **3** a fragment. [app. dimin. of SOP]

sir /sər/ *n.* **1** a polite or respectful form of address or mode of reference to a man. **2** (**Sir**) a titular prefix to the forename of a knight or baronet. [ME, reduced form of SIRE]

sir•dar /sərdaar/ *n. Ind.*, etc. **1** a person of high political or military rank. **2** a Sikh. [Urdu *sardār* f. Pers. *sar* head + *dār* possessor]

sire /sīr/ *n. & v.* •*n.* **1** the male parent of an animal, esp. a stallion kept for breeding. **2** *archaic* a respectful form of address, now esp. to a king. **3** *archaic poet.* a father or male ancestor. •*v.tr.* (esp. of a stallion) beget. [ME f. OF ult. f. L *senior*: see SENIOR]

si•ren /sírən/ *n.* **1 a** a device for making a loud prolonged signal or warning sound, esp. by revolving a perforated disk over a jet of compressed air or steam. **b** the sound made by this. **2** (in Greek mythology) each of a number of women or winged creatures whose singing lured unwary sailors onto rocks. **3** a sweet singer. **4** **a** a dangerously fascinating woman; a temptress. **b** a tempting pursuit, etc. **5** (*attrib.*) irresistibly tempting. **6** an eel-shaped tailed amphibian of the family Sirenidae. [ME f. OF *sereine, sirene* f. LL *Sirena* fem. f. L f. Gk *Seirēn*]

si•re•ni•an /sīréeneeən/ *adj. & n.* •*adj.* of the order Sirenia of large aquatic plant-eating mammals, e.g., the manatee and dugong. •*n.* any mammal of this order. [mod.L *Sirenia* (as SIREN)]

sir•loin /sərloyn/ *n.* the upper and choicer part of a loin of beef. [OF (as SUR-[1], LOIN)]

si•roc•co /sirókō/ *n.* (also **sci•roc•co**) (*pl.* **•cos**) **1** a Saharan simoom reaching the northern shores of the Mediterranean. **2** a warm sultry rainy wind in S. Europe. [F f. It. *scirocco*, ult. f. Arab. *Šarūk* east wind]

sir•rah /sírə/ *n. archaic* = SIR (as a form of address). [prob. f. ME *sĭrĕ* SIR]

sir•ree /sirée/ *int. colloq.* as an emphatic, esp. after *yes* or *no*. [SIR + emphatic suffix]

sir•up var. of SYRUP.

sis /sis/ *n. colloq.* a sister. [abbr.]

si•sal /sísəl/ *n.* **1** a Mexican plant, *Agave sisalana*, with large fleshy leaves. **2** the fiber made from this plant, used for cordage, ropes, etc. [*Sisal*, the port of Yucatan, Mexico]

sis•kin /sískin/ *n.* a dark-streaked, yellowish-green songbird, *Carduelis spinus*, allied to the goldfinch. [MDu. *siseken* dimin., rel. to MLG *sīsek*, MHG *zīse, zīsec*, of Slav. origin]

sis•sy /sísee/ *n. & adj.* (also **cis•sy**) *colloq.* •*n.* (*pl.* **•sies**) an effeminate or cowardly person. •*adj.* (**sis•si•er, sis•si•est**) effeminate; cowardly. □□ **sis•si•fied** *adj.* **sis•si•ness** *n.* **sis•sy•ish** *adj.* [SIS + –Y[2]]

sis•ter /sístər/ *n.* **1** a woman or girl in relation to sons and other daughters of her parents. **2 a** (often as a form of address) a close female friend or associate. **b** a female fellow member of a trade union, class, sect, or the human race. **3** a member of a female religious order. **4** (*attrib.*) of the same type or design or origin, etc. (*sister ship; prose, the younger sister of verse*). **5** *Brit.* a senior female nurse. □□ **sis•ter•less** *adj.* **sis•ter•ly** *adj.* **sis•ter•li•ness** *n.* [ME *sister* (f. ON), *suster*, etc. (repr. OE *sweoster* f. Gmc)]

sis•ter ger•man *n.* see GERMAN.

sis•ter•hood /sístərhŏŏd/ *n.* **1 a** the relationship between sisters. **b** sisterly friendliness; companionship; mutual support. **2 a** a society or association of women, esp. when bound by monastic vows or devoting themselves to religious or charitable work or the feminist cause. **b** its members collectively.

sis•ter-in-law *n.* (*pl.* **sis•ters-in-law**) **1** the sister of one's wife or husband. **2** the wife of one's brother. **3** the wife of one's brother-in-law.

Sis•ter of Mer•cy *n.* a member of an educational or charitable order of women, esp. that founded in Dublin in 1827.

sis•ter u•ter•ine *n.* see UTERINE.

Sis•tine /sísteen, sisteen/ *adj.* of any of the Popes called Sixtus, esp. Sixtus IV. [It. *Sistino* f. *Sisto* Sixtus]

Sis•tine Chap•el *n.* a chapel in the Vatican, with frescoes by Michelangelo and other painters.

sis•trum /sístrəm/ *n.* (*pl.* **sis•tra** /–trə/) a jingling metal instrument used by the ancient Egyptians esp. in the worship of Isis. [ME f. L f. Gk *seistron* f. *seiō* shake]

Sis•y•phe•an /sísifeeən/ *adj.* (of toil) endless and fruitless like that of Sisyphus in Greek mythology (whose task in Hades was to push uphill a stone that at once rolled down again).

sit /sit/ *v. & n.* •*v.* (**sit•ting**; *past* and *past part.* **sat** /sat/) **1** *intr.* adopt or be in a position in which the body is supported more or less upright by the buttocks resting on the ground or a raised seat, etc., with the thighs usu. horizontal. **2** *tr.* cause to sit; place in a sitting position. **3** *intr.* **a** (of a bird) perch. **b** (of an animal) rest with the hind legs bent and the body close to the ground. **4** *intr.* (of a bird) remain on its nest to hatch its eggs. **5** *intr.* **a** be engaged in an occupation in which the sitting position is usual. **b** (of a committee, legislative body, etc.) be engaged in business. **c** (of an individual)

be entitled to hold some office or position (*sat as a magistrate*). **6** *intr.* (usu. foll. by *for*) pose in a sitting position (for a portrait). **7** *intr.* (foll. by *for*) *Brit.* be a member of Parliament for (a constituency). **8** *tr. & (*foll. by *for*) *intr. Brit.* be a candidate for (an examination). **9** *intr.* be in a more or less permanent position or condition (esp. of inactivity or being out of use or out of place). **10** *intr.* (of clothes, etc.) fit or hang in a certain way. **11** *tr.* keep or have one's seat on (a horse, etc.). **12** *intr.* act as a babysitter. **13** *intr.* (often foll. by *before*) (of an army) take a position outside a city, etc., to besiege it. **14** *tr.* = SEAT *v.* 2a. • *n.* the way a dress, etc., sits on a person. □ **be sitting pretty** be comfortably or advantageously placed. **make a person sit up** *colloq.* surprise or interest a person. **sit at a person's feet** be a person's pupil. **sit at home** be inactive. **sit back** relax one's efforts. **sit by** look on without interfering. **sit down 1** sit after standing. **2** cause to sit. **3** *Brit.* (foll. by *under*) submit tamely to (an insult, etc.). **sit in 1** occupy a place as a protest. **2** (foll. by *for*) take the place of. **3** (foll. by *on*) be present as a guest or observer at (a meeting, etc.). **sit in judgment** assume the right of judging others; be censorious. **sit loosely on** not be very binding. **sit on 1** be a member of (a committee, etc.). **2** hold a session or inquiry concerning. **3** *colloq.* delay action about (*the government has been sitting on the report*). **4** *colloq.* repress or rebuke or snub (*felt rather sat on*). **sit on the fence** see FENCE. **sit on one's hands 1** take no action. **2** refuse to applaud. **sit out 1** take no part in (a dance, etc.). **2** stay till the end of (esp. an ordeal). **3** esp. *Brit.* sit outdoors. **4** *Brit.* outstay (other visitors). **sit tight** *colloq.* **1** remain firmly in one's place. **2** not be shaken off or move away or yield to distractions. **sit up 1** rise from a lying to a sitting position. **2** sit firmly upright. **3** go to bed later than the usual time. **4** *colloq.* become interested or aroused, etc. **sit up and take notice** *colloq.* have one's interest aroused, esp. suddenly. **sit well** esp. *Brit.* have a good seat in riding. **sit well on** esp. *Brit.* suit or fit. [OE *sittan* f. Gmc]
▶See note at SET.

si•tar /sitaár, sítaar/ *n.* a long-necked E. Indian lute with movable frets. □□ **si•tar•ist** /sitaárist/ *n.* [Hindi *sitār*]

sit•com /sítkom/ *n. colloq.* a situation comedy. [abbr.]

sit-down *adj.* (of a meal) eaten sitting at a table.

sit-down strike *n.* a strike in which workers refuse to leave their place of work.

site /sīt/ *n. & v.* • *n.* **1** the ground chosen or used for a town or building. **2** a place where some activity is or has been conducted (*camping site; launching site*). • *v.tr.* **1** locate or place. **2** provide with a site. [ME f. AF *site* or L *situs* local position]

sitar

sit-in *n.* a protest involving sitting in.

Sit•ka /sítkə/ *n.* (in full **Sitka spruce**) a fast-growing spruce, *Picea sitchensis*, native to N. America and yielding timber. [*Sitka* in Alaska]

sit•rep /sítrep/ *n. Brit.* a report on the current military situation in an area. [*situation report*]

sits vac /sits vák/ *abbr. Brit.* situations vacant, i.e., work available.

sit•ter /sítər/ *n.* **1** = *baby-sitter* (see BABY-SIT). **2** a person who sits, esp. for a portrait. **3** *Brit. colloq.* **a** an easy catch or shot. **b** an easy task. **4** a sitting hen. **5** *colloq.* the buttocks.

sit•ting /síting/ *n. & adj.* • *n.* **1** a continuous period of being seated, esp. engaged in an activity (*finished the book in one sitting*). **2** a time during which an assembly is engaged in business. **3** a session in which a meal is served (*dinner will be served in two sittings*). **4** *Brit. Law* = TERM 5c. **5** a clutch of eggs. • *adj.* **1** having sat down. **2** (of an animal or bird) not running or flying. **3** (of a hen) engaged in hatching. □ **sitting pretty** see PRETTY.

sit•ting duck *n.* (also **sit•ting tar•get**) *colloq.* a vulnerable person or thing.

sit•ting room *n.* **1** esp. *Brit.* a room in a house for relaxed sitting in; living room. **2** space enough to accommodate seated persons.

sit•u•ate *v. & adj.* • *v.tr.* /síchoo-ayt/ (usu. in *passive*) **1** put in a certain position or circumstances (*is situated at the top of a hill; how are you situated at the moment?*). **2** establish or indicate the place of; put in a context. • *adj.* /síchooət/ *Law* or *archaic* situated. [med.L *situare situat-* f. L *situs* site]
▶See note at LOCATE.

sit•u•a•tion /síchoo-áyshən/ *n.* **1** a place and its surroundings (*the house stands in a fine situation*). **2** a set of circumstances; a position in which one finds oneself; a state of affairs (*came out of a difficult situation with credit*). **3** an employee's position or job. **4** a critical point or complication in a drama. □□ **sit•u•a•tion•al** *adj.* [ME f. F *situation* or med.L *situatio* (as SITUATE)]

sit•u•a•tion com•e•dy *n.* **1** a comedy in which the humor derives from the situations the characters are placed in. **2** a television series featuring such humor.

sit•u•a•tions va•cant *n.pl.* (also **sit•u•a•tions want•ed**) esp. *Brit.* lists of employment offered and sought.

sit-up *n.* a physical exercise in which a person sits up without raising the legs from the ground.

sit-up•on *n. Brit. colloq.* the buttocks.

sitz bath /sítsbath, zits–/ *n.* **1** a usu. portable bath in which a person sits. **2** the bath taken by such means. [partial transl. of G *Sitzbad* f. *sitzen* sit + *Bad* bath]

Si•va /seevə, sheevə/ *n.* (also **Shi•va** /sheevə/) a Hindu deity associated with the powers of reproduction and dissolution, regarded by some as the supreme being and by others as a member of the triad. □□ **Si•va•ism** *n.* **Si•va•ite** *n. & adj.* [Skr. *Siva*, lit. the auspicious one]

six /siks/ *n. & adj.* • *n.* **1** one more than five, or four less than ten; the product of two units and three units. **2** a symbol for this (6, vi, VI). **3** a size, etc., denoted by six. **4** a set or team of six individuals. **5** *Cricket* a hit scoring six runs by clearing the boundary without bouncing. **6** the time of six o'clock (*is it six yet?*). **7** a card, etc., with six pips. • *adj.* that amount to six. □ **at sixes and sevens** in confusion or disagreement. **knock for six** *Brit. colloq.* utterly surprise or overcome (a person). **six of one and half a dozen of the other** a situation of little real difference between the alternatives. [OE *siex*, etc. f. Gmc]

Siva (Shiva)

six•ain /síksayn/ *n.* a six-line stanza. [F f. *six* six]

six•fold /síksfōld/ *adj. & adv.* **1** six times as much or as many. **2** consisting of six parts.

six-gun *n.* = SIX-SHOOTER.

six-pack *n.* six cans or bottles, as of beer, a soft drink, etc., packaged and sold as a unit.

six•pence /síkspəns/ *n. Brit.* **1** the sum of six pence, esp. before decimalization. **2** *hist.* a coin worth six old pence. □ **turn on a sixpence** *colloq.* make a sharp turn in a motor vehicle.

six•pen•ny /síkspənee, –penee/ *adj. Brit.* costing or worth six pence, esp. before decimalization.

six-shoot•er *n.* a revolver with six chambers.

sixte /sikst/ *n. Fencing* the sixth of the eight parrying positions. [F f. L *sextus* sixth]

six•teen /síksteén/ *n. & adj.* • *n.* **1** one more than fifteen, or six more than ten. **2** a symbol for this (16, xvi, XVI). **3** a size, etc., denoted by sixteen. **4** that amount to sixteen. □□ **six•teenth** *adj. & n.* [OE *siextiene* (as SIX, –TEEN)]

six•teen•mo /síksteénmō/ *n.* (*pl.* **•mos**) sextodecimo. [English reading of the symbol 16mo]

six•teenth note *n. Mus.* a note having the time value of one-sixteenth of a whole note and represented by a large dot with a two-hooked stem.

sixth /siksth/ *n. & adj.* • *n.* **1** the position in a sequence corresponding to that of the number 6 in the sequence 1–6. **2** something occupying this position. **3** any of six equal parts of a thing. **4** *Mus.* **a** an interval or chord spanning six consecutive notes in the diatonic scale (e.g., C to A). **b** a note separated from another by this interval. • *adj.* that is the sixth. □□ **sixth•ly** *adv.* [SIX]

sixth sense *n.* **1** a supposed faculty giving intuitive or extrasensory knowledge. **2** such knowledge.

Six•tine /síksteen, –tīn/ *adj.* = SISTINE. [mod.L *Sixtinus* f. *Sixtus*]

six•ty /síkstee/ *n. & adj.* • *n.* (*pl.* **•ties**) **1** the product of six and ten. **2** a symbol for this (60, lx, LX). **3** (in *pl.*) the numbers from 60 to 69, esp. the years of a century or of a person's life. **4** a set of sixty persons or things. • *adj.* that amount to sixty. □□ **six•ti•eth** *adj. & n.* **six•ty•fold** *adj. & adv.* [OE *siextig* (as SIX, –TY²)]

six•ty-first *n.* (also **six•ty-sec•ond**, etc.) the ordinal numbers between sixtieth and seventieth.

six•ty-four•mo /síksteefáwrmō/ *n.* (*pl.* **•mos**) **1** a size of book in which each leaf is one-sixty-fourth of a printing-sheet. **2** a book of this size (*after* DUODECIMO, etc.).

six•ty-fourth note *n. Mus.* a note having the time value of one-sixty-fourth of a whole note and represented by a large dot with a four-hooked stem.

six•ty-four thou•sand dol•lar ques•tion *n.* (or **six•ty-four dol•lar question**) a difficult and crucial question (from the top prize in a broadcast quiz show).

six•ty-nine *n.* sexual activity between two people involving mutual oral stimulation of the genitals.

six•ty-one *n.* (also **six•ty-two**, etc.) the cardinal numbers between sixty and seventy.

siz·a·ble /sízəbəl/ *adj.* (also **size·a·ble**) large or fairly large. □□ **siz·a·bly** *adv.*

siz·ar /sízər/ *n.* a student at Cambridge or at Trinity College, Dublin, paying reduced fees and formerly having certain menial duties. □□ **siz·ar·ship** *n.* [SIZE¹ = ration]

size¹ /síz/ *n. & v.* • *n.* 1 the relative bigness or extent of a thing; dimensions; magnitude (*is of vast size*; *size matters less than quality*). 2 each of the classes, usu. numbered, into which things otherwise similar, esp. garments, are divided according to size (*is made in several sizes*; *takes size 7 in gloves*; *is three sizes too big*). • *v.tr.* sort or group in sizes or according to size. □ **of a size** having the same size. **of some size** fairly large. **the size of** as big as. **the size of it** *colloq.* a true account of the matter (*that is the size of it*). **size up** 1 estimate the size of. 2 *colloq.* form a judgment of. **what size?** how big? □□ **sized** *adj.* (also in *comb.*). **siz·er** *n.* [ME f. OF *sise* f. *assise* ASSIZE, or f. ASSIZE]

size² /síz/ *n. & v.* • *n.* a gelatinous solution used in glazing paper, stiffening textiles, preparing plastered walls for decoration, etc. • *v.tr.* glaze or stiffen or treat with size. [ME, perh. = SIZE¹]

size·a·ble var. of SIZABLE.

siz·zle /sízl/ *v. & n.* • *v.intr.* 1 make a sputtering or hissing sound as of frying. 2 *colloq.* be in a state of great heat or excitement or marked effectiveness. • *n.* 1 a sizzling sound. 2 *colloq.* a state of great heat or excitement. □□ **siz·zler** *n.* **siz·zling** *adj. & adv.* (*sizzling hot*). [imit.]

SJ *abbr.* Society of Jesus.

sjam·bok /shámbok/ *n. & v.* • *n.* (in S. Africa) a rhinoceros-hide whip. • *v.tr.* flog with a sjambok. [Afrik. f. Malay *samboq, chambok* f. Urdu *ch ābuk*]

skald /skawld/ *n.* (also **scald**) (in ancient Scandinavia) a composer and reciter of poems honoring heroes and their deeds. □□ **skald·ic** *adj.* [ON *skáld*, of unkn. orig.]

skat /skat/ *n.* a three-handed card game with bidding. [G f. It. *scarto* a discard f. *scartare* discard]

skate¹ /skayt/ *n. & v.* • *n.* 1 each of a pair of steel blades (or of boots with blades attached) for gliding on ice. 2 (in full **roller skate**) each of a pair of metal frames with small wheels, fitted to shoes for riding on a hard surface. 3 a device on which a heavy object moves. • *v.* 1 a *intr.* move on skates. b *tr.* perform (a specified figure) on skates. 2 *intr.* (foll. by *over*) refer fleetingly to; disregard. □ **get one's skates on** *Brit. sl.* make haste. **skate on thin ice** *colloq.* behave rashly; risk danger, esp. by dealing with a subject needing tactful treatment. □□ **skat·er** *n.* [orig. *scates* (pl.) f. Du. *schaats* (sing.) f. ONF *escace*, OF *eschasse* stilt]

skate² /skayt/ *n.* (*pl.* same or **skates**) any ray of the family Rajidae, esp. *Raja batis*, a large, flat, rhomboidal fish used as food. [ME f. ON *skata*]

skate³ /skayt/ *n. sl.* a contemptible, mean, or dishonest person (esp. in *comb.*, as *cheapskate*). [19th c.: orig. uncert.]

skate·board /skáytbawrd/ *n. & v.* • *n.* a short narrow board on roller-skate wheels for riding on while standing. • *v.intr.* ride on a skateboard. □□ **skate·board·er** *n.*

skat·ing rink *n.* a piece of ice artificially made, or a floor used, for skating.

skean /skeen, ské·ən/ *n. hist.* a Gaelic dagger formerly used in Ireland and Scotland. [Gael. *sgian* knife, *dubh* black]

skean-dhu /-dŏō/ *n.* a dagger worn in the stocking as part of Highland costume.

sked /sked/ *n. & v.* esp. *Brit. colloq.* • *n.* = SCHEDULE *n.* • *v.tr.* (**sked·ded, sked·ding**) = SCHEDULE *v.* [abbr.]

ske·dad·dle /skidád'l/ *v. & n. colloq.* • *v.intr.* run away; depart quickly; flee. • *n.* a hurried departure or flight. [19th c.: orig. unkn.]

skeet /skeet/ *n.* a shooting sport in which a clay target is thrown from a trap to simulate the flight of a bird. [ON *skjóta* SHOOT]

skee·ter¹ /skée·tər/ *n. US dial., Austral. sl.* a mosquito. [abbr.]

skee·ter² var. of SKITTER.

skeg /skeg/ *n.* 1 a fin underneath the rear of a surfboard. 2 the after part of a vessel's keel or a projection from it. [ON *skeg* beard, perh. via Du. *scheg(ge)*]

skein /skayn/ *n.* 1 a loosely coiled bundle of yarn or thread. 2 a flock of wild geese, etc., in flight. 3 a tangle or confusion. [ME f. OF *escaigne*, of unkn. orig.]

skel·e·ton /skélit'n/ *n.* 1 a a hard internal or external framework of bones, cartilage, shell, woody fiber, etc., supporting or containing the body of an animal or plant. b the dried bones of a human being or other animal fastened together in the same relative positions as in life. 2 the supporting framework or structure or essential part of a thing. 3 a very thin or emaciated person or animal. 4 the remaining part of anything after its life or usefulness is gone. 5 an outline sketch; an epitome or abstract. 6 (*attrib.*) having only the essential or minimum number of persons, parts, etc. (*skeleton plan*; *skeleton staff*). □□ **skel·e·tal** *adj.* **skel·e·tal·ly** *adv.* **skel·e·ton·ize** *v.tr.* [mod.L f. Gk, neut. of *skeletos* dried-up f. *skellō* dry up]

skel·e·ton at the feast *n.* something that spoils one's pleasure; an intrusive worry.

skel·e·ton in the clos·et *n.* (also esp. *Brit.* **skel·e·ton in the cupboard**) a discreditable or embarrassing fact kept secret.

skel·e·ton key *n.* a key designed to fit many locks by having the interior of the bit hollowed.

skep /skep/ *n.* 1 a a wooden or wicker basket of any of various forms. b the quantity contained in this. 2 a straw or wicker beehive. [ME f. ON *skeppa*]

skep·sis /sképsis/ *n.* (*Brit.* **scep·sis**) 1 philosophic doubt. 2 skeptical philosophy. [Gk *skepsis* inquiry, doubt f. *skeptomai* consider]

skep·tic /sképtik/ *n. & adj.* (*Brit.* **scep·tic**) • *n.* 1 a person inclined to doubt all accepted opinions; a cynic. 2 a person who doubts the truth of Christianity and other religions. 3 *hist.* a person who accepts the philosophy of Pyrrhonism. • *adj.* = SKEPTICAL. □□ **skep·ti·cism** /-tisizəm/ *n.* [F *sceptique* or L *scepticus* f. Gk *skeptikos* (as SCEPSIS)]

skep·ti·cal /sképtikəl/ *adj.* (*Brit.* **scep·ti·cal**) 1 inclined to question the truth or soundness of accepted ideas, facts, etc.; critical; incredulous. 2 *Philos.* of or accepting the philosophy of Pyrrhonism, denying the possibility of knowledge. □□ **skep·ti·cal·ly** *adv.*

sker·rick /skérik/ *n.* (usu. with *neg.*) *Austral. colloq.* the smallest bit (*not a skerrick left*). [No. of Engl. dial.; orig. uncert.]

sker·ry /skéree/ *n.* (*pl.* **-ries**) *Sc.* a reef or rocky island. [Orkney dial. f. ON *sker*: cf. SCAR²]

sketch /skech/ *n. & v.* • *n.* 1 a rough, slight, merely outlined, or unfinished drawing or painting, often made to assist in making a more finished picture. 2 a brief account without many details conveying a general idea of something; a rough draft or general outline. 3 a very short play, usu. humorous and limited to one scene. 4 a short descriptive piece of writing. 5 a musical composition of a single movement. 6 *colloq.* a comical person or thing. • *v.* 1 *tr.* make or give a sketch of. 2 *intr.* draw sketches esp. of landscape (*went out sketching*). 3 *tr.* (often foll. by *in, out*) indicate briefly or in outline. □□ **sketch·er** *n.* [Du. *schets* or G *Skizze* f. It. *schizzo* f. *schizzare* make a sketch ult. f. Gk *skhēdios* extempore]

sketch·book /skéchbŏŏk/ *n.* a book or pad of drawing paper for doing sketches on.

sketch map *n.* a roughly-drawn map with few details.

sketch pad *n.* = SKETCHBOOK.

sketch·y /skéchee/ *adj.* (**sketch·i·er, sketch·i·est**) 1 giving only a slight or rough outline, like a sketch. 2 *colloq.* unsubstantial or imperfect esp. through haste. □□ **sketch·i·ly** *adv.* **sketch·i·ness** *n.*

skeu·o·morph /skyŏŏəmawrf/ *n.* 1 an object or feature copying the design of a similar artifact in another material. 2 an ornamental design resulting from the nature of the material used or the method of working it. □□ **skeu·o·mor·phic** /-máwrfik/ *adj.* [Gk *skeuos* vessel, implement + *morphē* form]

skew /skyŏō/ *adj., n., & v.* • *adj.* 1 oblique; slanting; set askew. 2 *Math.* a lying in three dimensions (*skew curve*). b (of lines) not coplanar. c (of a statistical distribution) not symmetrical. • *n.* 1 a slant. 2 *Statistics* skewness. • *v.* 1 *tr.* make skew. 2 *tr.* distort. 3 *intr.* move obliquely. 4 *intr.* twist. □ **on the skew** askew. □□ **skew·ness** *n.* [ONF *eskiu(w)er* (v.) = OF *eschuer*: see ESCHEW]

skew arch *n.* (also **skew bridge**) an arch (or bridge) with the line of the arch not at right angles to the abutment.

skew·back /skyŏŏbak/ *n.* the sloping face of the abutment on which an extremity of an arch rests.

skew·bald /skyŏŏbawld/ *adj. & n.* • *adj.* (of an animal) with irregular patches of white and another color (properly not black) (cf. PIEBALD). • *n.* a skewbald animal, esp. a horse. [ME *skued* (orig. uncert.), after PIEBALD]

skew chis·el *n.* a chisel with an oblique edge.

skew·er /skyŏŏər/ *n. & v.* • *n.* a long pin designed for holding meat compactly together while cooking. • *v.tr.* 1 fasten together or pierce with or as with a skewer. 2 criticize sharply. [17th c., var. of dial. *skiver*: orig. unkn.]

skew-eyed *adj. Brit.* squinting.

skew gear *n.* a gear consisting of two cogwheels having nonparallel, nonintersecting axes.

skew-whiff /skyŏŏwíf/ *adv. & adj. Brit. colloq.* askew.

ski /skee/ *n. & v.* • *n.* (*pl.* **skis** or **ski**) 1 each of a pair of long narrow pieces of wood, etc., usu. pointed and turned up at the front, fastened under the feet for traveling over snow. 2 a similar device under a vehicle or aircraft. 3 = WATER SKI. 4 (*attrib.*) for wear when skiing (*ski boots*). • *v.* (**skis, skied** /skeed/; **ski·ing**) 1 *intr.* travel on skis. 2 *tr.* ski at (a place). □□ **ski·a·ble** *adj.* [Norw. f. ON *skith* billet, snow shoe]

ski·ag·ra·phy /skíágrəfee/ *n.* (also *Brit.* **sci·ag·ra·phy**) the art of shading in drawing, etc. □□ **ski·a·gram** /skíəgram/ *n.* **ski·a·graph** /skíəgraf/ *n.* **ski·a·graph·ic** /-gráfik/ *adj.* [F *sciagraphie* f. L *sciagraphia* f. Gk *skiagraphia* f. *skia* shadow]

ski·bob /skéebob/ *n. & v.* • *n.* a machine like a bicycle with skis instead of wheels. • *v.intr.* (**·bobbed, ·bob·bing**) ride a skibob. □□ **ski·bob·ber** *n.*

skid /skid/ *v. & n.* • *v.* (**skid·ded, skid·ding**) 1 *intr.* (of a vehicle, a wheel, or a driver) slide on slippery ground, esp. sideways or obliquely. **2** *tr.* cause (a vehicle, etc.) to skid. **3** *intr.* slip; slide. **4** *intr. colloq.* fail or decline or err. **5** *tr.* support or move or protect or check with a skid. ● *n.* **1** the act or an instance of skidding. **2 a** a supporting plank, low platform, pallet, etc., usu. made of wood. **b** a piece of wood, etc., serving as a support, ship's fender, inclined plane, etc. **3** a braking device, esp. a wooden or metal shoe preventing a wheel from revolving or used as a drag. **4** a runner beneath an aircraft for use when landing. □ **hit the skids** *colloq.* enter a rapid decline or deterioration. **on the skids** *colloq.* **1** about to be discarded or defeated. **2** esp. *Brit.* ready for launching. **put the skids under** *colloq.* **1** hasten the downfall or failure of. **2** cause to hasten. [17th c.: orig. unkn.]

skid•doo /skidōo′/ *v.intr.* (also **skid•oo**) (**•oos**, **•ooed**) *sl.* go away; depart. [perh. f. SKEDADDLE]

skid road *n.* **1** a road for hauling logs along. **2** = SKID ROW.

skid row *n. colloq.* a part of a town frequented by vagrants, alcoholics, etc.

ski•er /skē′ər/ *n.* a person who skis.

skiff /skif/ *n.* a light rowboat or scull. [F *esquif* f. It. *schifo*, rel. to SHIP]

skif•fle /skif′əl/ *n.* a kind of folk music played by a small group, mainly with a rhythmic accompaniment to a singing guitarist, etc. [perh. imit.]

ski•jor•ing /skē′ejāwring/ *n.* a winter sport in which a skier is towed by a horse or vehicle. □□ **ski•jor•er** *n.* [Norw. *skikjøring* (as SKI, *kjøre* drive)]

ski jump *n.* **1** a steep slope leveling off before a sharp drop to allow a skier to leap through the air. **2** a jump made from this. □□ **ski jump•er** *n.* **ski jumping** *n.*

ski lift *n.* a device for carrying skiers up a slope, usu. on seats hung from an overhead cable.

skill /skil/ *n.* (often foll. by *in*) expertness; practiced ability; facility in an action; dexterity or tact. □□ **skill•less** *adj.* (*archaic* **skilless**). [ME f. ON *skil* distinction]

skilled /skild/ *adj.* **1** (often foll. by *in*) having or showing skill; skillful. **2** (of a worker) highly trained or experienced. **3** (of work) requiring skill or special training.

skil•let /skil′it/ *n.* **1** a frying pan. **2** *Brit.* a small metal kettle or saucepan with a long handle and usu. legs. [ME, perh. f. OF *escuelete* dimin. of *escuele* platter f. LL *scutella*]

skill•ful /skil′fŏŏl/ *adj.* (*Brit.* **skil•ful**) (often foll. by *at, in*) having or showing skill; practiced, expert, adroit, ingenious. □□ **skill•ful•ly** *adv.* **skill•ful•ness** *n.*

skim /skim/ *v. & n.* ● *v.* (**skimmed, skim•ming**) **1** *tr.* **a** take scum or cream or a floating layer from the surface of (a liquid). **b** take (cream, etc.) from the surface of a liquid. **2** *tr.* **a** keep touching lightly or nearly touching (a surface) in passing over. **b** deal with or treat (a subject) superficially. **3** *intr.* **a** (often foll. by *over, along*) go lightly over a surface, glide along in the air. **b** (foll. by *over*) = sense 2b of *v.* **4 a** *tr.* read superficially; look over cursorily; gather the salient facts contained in. **b** *intr.* (usu. foll. by *through*) read or look over cursorily. **5** *tr. sl.* conceal or divert (income) to avoid paying tax. ● *n.* **1** the act or an instance of skimming. **2** a thin covering on a liquid (*skim of ice*). □ **skim the cream off** take the best part of. [ME, back-form. f. SKIMMER]

skim•mer /skim′ər/ *n.* **1** a device for skimming liquids. **2** a person who skims. **3** a flat hat, esp. a broad-brimmed straw hat. **4** any long-winged marine bird of the genus *Rynchops* that feeds by skimming over water with its knifelike lower mandible immersed. **5** a hydroplane, hydrofoil, hovercraft, or other vessel that has little or no displacement at speed. **6** a sheathlike dress. [ME f. OF *escumoir* f. *escumer* f. *escume* SCUM]

skim•mi•a /skim′ēə/ *n.* any evergreen shrub of the genus *Skimmia*, native to E. Asia, with red berries. [mod.L f. Jap.]

skim milk *n.* (or **skimmed milk**) milk from which the cream has been skimmed.

ski•mo•bile /skē′əmōbēl/ *n.* = SNOWMOBILE.

skimp /skimp/ *v., adj., & n.* ● *v.* **1** *tr.* (often foll. by *in*) supply (a person, etc.) meagerly with food, money, etc. **2** *tr.* use a meager or insufficient amount of; stint (material, expenses, etc.). **3** *intr.* be parsimonious. ● *adj.* scanty. ● *n. colloq.* a small or scanty thing, esp. a skimpy garment. [18th c.: orig. unkn.: cf. SCRIMP]

skimp•y /skim′pē/ *adj.* (**skimp•i•er, skimp•i•est**) meager; not ample or sufficient. □□ **skimp•i•ly** *adv.* **skimp•i•ness** *n.*

skin /skin/ *n. & v.* ● *n.* **1** the flexible continuous covering of a human or other animal body. **2 a** the skin of a flayed animal with or without the hair. **b** a material prepared from skins, esp. of smaller animals (opp. HIDE²). **3** a person's skin with reference to its color or complexion (*has a fair skin*). **4** an outer layer or covering, esp. the coating of a plant, fruit, or sausage. **5** a film like skin on the surface of a liquid, etc. **6** a container for liquid, made of an animal's skin. **7 a** the planking or plating of a ship or boat, inside or outside the ribs. **b** the outer covering of any craft or vehicle, esp. an aircraft or spacecraft. **8** *Brit. sl.* a skinhead. **9** *Cards* a game in

which each player has one card which he bets will not be the first to be matched by a card dealt from the pack. **10** = GOLDBEATER'S SKIN. **11** *sl.* a condom. ● *v.* (**skinned, skin•ning**) **1** *tr.* remove the skin from. **2** (often foll. by *over*) **a** *tr.* cover (a sore, etc.) with or as with skin. **b** *intr.* (of a wound, etc.) become covered with new skin. **3** *tr. sl.* fleece or swindle. □ **be skin and bone** be very thin. **by** (or **with**) **the skin of one's teeth** by a very narrow margin. **change one's skin** undergo an impossible change of character, etc. **get under a person's skin** *colloq.* interest or annoy a person intensely. **have a thick** (or **thin**) **skin** be insensitive (or sensitive) to criticism, etc. **no skin off one's nose** *colloq.* a matter of indifference or even benefit to one. **to the skin** through all one's clothing (*soaked to the skin*). **with a whole skin** unwounded. □□ **skin•less** *adj.* **skin•like** *adj.* **skinned** *adj.* (also in *comb.*). [OE *scin(n)* f. ON *skinn*]

skin-deep *adj.* (of a wound, or of an emotion, an impression, beauty, etc.) superficial; not deep or lasting.

skin div•er *n.* a person who swims underwater without a diving suit, usu. with a mask, snorkel, flippers, etc. □□ **skin div•ing** *n.*

skin ef•fect *n. Electr.* the tendency of a high-frequency alternating current to flow through the outer layer only of a conductor.

skin flick *n. sl.* an explicitly pornographic film.

skin•flint /skin′flint/ *n.* a miserly person.

skin fric•tion *n.* friction at the surface of a solid and a fluid in relative motion.

skin•ful /skin′fŏŏl/ *n.* (*pl.* **•fuls**) *colloq.* enough liquor to make one drunk.

skin game *n. sl.* a swindling game; a swindle.

skin graft *n.* **1** the surgical transplanting of skin. **2** a piece of skin transferred in this way.

skin•head /skin′hed/ *n.* **1** a youth with close-cropped hair, esp. one of an aggressive gang. **2** a U.S. Marine recruit.

skink /skingk/ *n.* any small lizard of the family Scincidae. [F *scinc* or L *scincus* f. Gk *skigkos*]

skin•ner /skin′ər/ *n.* **1** a person who skins animals or prepares skins. **2** a dealer in skins; a furrier. **3** *Austral. Racing sl.* a result very profitable to bookmakers.

skin•ny /skin′ē/ *adj. & n.* ● *adj.* (**skin•ni•er, skin•ni•est**) **1** thin or emaciated. **2** (of clothing) tight-fitting. **3** made of or like skin. ● *n.* (**the skin•ny**) confidential information on a particular person or topic. □□ **skin•ni•ness** *n.*

skin•ny-dip *v.intr. colloq.* swim in the nude.

skint /skint/ *adj. Brit. sl.* having no money left. [= *skinned*, past part. of SKIN]

skin test *n.* a test to determine whether an immune reaction is elicited when a substance is applied to or injected into the skin.

skin•tight /skin′tīt/ *adj.* (of a garment) very close-fitting.

skip¹ /skip/ *v. & n.* ● *v.* (**skipped, skip•ping**) **1** *intr.* **a** move along lightly, esp. by taking two steps with each foot in turn. **b** jump lightly from the ground, esp. so as to clear a jump rope. **c** jump about; gambol; caper; frisk. **2** *intr.* (often foll. by *from, off, to*) move quickly from one point, subject, or occupation to another; be desultory. **3** *tr.* (also *absol.*) omit in dealing with a series or in reading (*skip every tenth row; always skips the small print*). **4** *tr. colloq.* not participate in. **5** *tr. colloq.* depart· quickly from; leave hurriedly. **6** *intr.* (often foll. by *out, off*) *colloq.* make off; disappear. **7** *tr.* make (a stone) ricochet on the surface of water. ● *n.* **1** a skipping movement or action. **2** *Computing* the action of passing over part of a sequence of data or instructions. **3** *colloq.* a person who defaults or absconds. □ **skip it** *sl.* **1** abandon a topic, etc. **2** make off; disappear. [ME, prob. f. Scand.]

skip² /skip/ *n.* **1** a cage, bucket, etc., in which workers or materials are lowered and raised in mines and quarries. **2** *Brit.* a large container for builders' refuse, etc. **3** = SKEP. [var. of SKEP]

skip³ /skip/ *n. & v.* ● *n.* the captain or director of a side at bowling or curling. ● *v.tr.* (**skipped, skip•ping**) be the skip of. [abbr. of SKIPPER¹]

skip•jack /skip′jak/ *n.* **1** (in full **skipjack tuna**) a small striped Pacific tuna, *Katsuwonus pelamus*, used as food. **2** a click beetle. **3** a kind of sailboat used off the east coast of the US. [SKIP¹ + JACK¹]

skip•lane /skē′plān/ *n.* an airplane having its undercarriage fitted with skis for landing on snow or ice.

skip•per¹ /skip′ər/ *n. & v.* ● *n.* **1** a sea captain, esp. the master of a small trading or fishing vessel **2** the captain of an aircraft. **3** the captain of a side in games. ● *v.tr.* act as captain of. [ME f. MDu., MLG *schipper* f. *schip* SHIP]

skip•per² /skip′ər/ *n.* **1** a person who skips. **2** any brown, thick-bodied butterfly of the family Hesperiidae.

skip•pet /skip′it/ *n.* a small, round wooden box to enclose and protect a seal attached to a document. [ME: orig. unkn.]

skip zone *n.* the annular region around a broadcasting station where neither direct nor reflected waves are received.

skirl /skərl/ *n. & v.* ● *n.* the shrill sound characteristic of bagpipes. ● *v.intr.* make a skirl. [prob. Scand.: ult. imit.]

skir•mish /skər′mish/ *n. & v.* ● *n.* **1** a piece of irregular or unpremeditated fighting, esp. between small or outlying parts of armies or fleets; a slight engagement. **2** a short argument or contest of wit, etc. •*v.intr.* engage in a skirmish. ▫▫ **skir•mish•er** *n.* [ME f. OF *eskirmir, escremir* f. Frank.]

skirr /skər/ *v.intr.* move rapidly, esp. with a whirring sound. [perh. rel. to SCOUR[1] or SCOUR[2]]

skir•ret /skírit/ *n.* a perennial umbelliferous plant, *Sium sisarum*, formerly cultivated in Europe for its edible root. [ME *skirwhit(e)*, perh. formed as SHEER[1], WHITE]

skirt /skərt/ *n. & v.* •*n.* **1** a woman's outer garment hanging from the waist. **2** the part of a coat, etc., that hangs below the waist. **3** a hanging part around the base of a hovercraft. **4** (in *sing.* or *pl.*) an edge, border, or extreme part. **5** (also esp. *Brit.* **bit of skirt**) *sl. offens.* a woman regarded as an object of sexual desire. **6** (in full **skirt of beef**, etc.) a the diaphragm and other membranes as food. **b** *Brit.* a cut of meat from the lower flank. **7** a flap of a saddle. **8** a surface that conceals or protects the wheels or underside of a vehicle or aircraft. •*v.* **1** *tr.* go along or around or past the edge of. **2** *tr.* be situated along. **3** *tr.* avoid dealing with (an issue, etc.). **4** *intr.* (foll. by *along*) go along the coast, a wall, etc. ▫▫ **skirt•ed** *adj.* (also in *comb.*). **skirt•less** *adj.* [ME f. ON *skyrta* shirt, corresp. to OE *scyrte*: see SHIRT]

skirt dance *n.* a dance with graceful manipulation of a full skirt.

skirt•ing /skórting/ *n.* **1** fabric suitable for skirt making. **2** a border or edge. **3** *Brit.* = BASEBOARD.

ski run *n.* a slope prepared for skiing.

skit /skit/ *n.* (often foll. by *on*) a light, usu. short, piece of satire or burlesque. [rel. to *skit* move lightly and rapidly, perh. f. ON (cf. *skjóta* SHOOT)]

skite /skīt/ *v. & n.* •*v.intr. Austral. & NZ colloq.* boast, brag. •*n.* **1** *Austral. & NZ colloq.* **a** a boaster. **b** boasting; boastfulness. **2** *Sc.* a drinking bout; a spree (*on the skite*) [Sc. & No. of Engl. dial., = a person regarded with contempt: cf. SKIT]

skit•ter /skítər/ *v.intr.* (also **skee•ter** /skéetər/) **1 a** (usu. foll. by *along, across*) move lightly or hastily. **b** (usu. foll. by *about, off*) hurry about; dart off. **2** fish by drawing bait jerkily across the surface of the water. [app. frequent. of dial. *skite*, perh. formed as SKIT]

skit•ter•y /skítəree/ *adj.* skittish; restless.

skit•tish /skítish/ *adj.* **1** lively; playful. **2** (of a horse, etc.) nervous; inclined to shy; fidgety. ▫▫ **skit•tish•ly** *adv.* **skit•tish•ness** *n.* [ME, perh. formed as SKIT]

skit•tle /skít'l/ *n. & v.* •*n.* **1** a pin used in the game of skittles. **2** (in *pl.*; usu. treated as *sing.*) (esp in the UK) **a** a game like ninepins played with usu. nine wooden pins set up at the end of an alley to be knocked down, usu. with wooden balls or a wooden disk. **b** (in full **table skittles**) a game played with similar pins set up on a board to be knocked down by swinging a suspended ball. **c** *Brit. colloq.* chess not played seriously. •*v.tr.* (often foll. by *out*) *Cricket* get (batsmen) out in rapid succession. [17th c. (also *kittle-pins*): orig. unkn.]

skive /skīv/ *v. & n.* •*v.* **1** *tr.* split or pare (hides, leather, etc.). **2** *intr. Brit. sl.* evade a duty; shirk. **b** (often foll. by *off*) avoid work by absenting oneself; play truant. •*n. sl.* **1** an instance of shirking. **2** an easy option. ▫▫ **skiv•er** *n.* [ON *skífa*, rel. to ME *schīve* slice]

skiv•vy /skívee/ *n.* (*pl.* **-vies**) **1 a** (in *pl.*) underwear of T-shirt and shorts. **b** a thin high-necked long-sleeved garment. **2** *Brit. colloq. derog.* a female domestic servant. [20th c.: orig. unkn.]

skoal /skōl/ *n.* used as a toast in drinking. [Da. *skaal*, Sw. *skål*, f. ON *skál* bowl]

sku•a /skyóõə/ *n.* **1** any of several predatory seabirds of the genus *Catharacta*, esp. the great skua *C. skua*. **2** *Brit.* = JAEGER 2. [mod.L f. Faroese *skúgvur*, ON *skúfr*]

skul•dug•ger•y /skuldúgəree/ *n.* (also **scul•dug•ger•y**, **skull•dug•ger•y**) trickery; unscrupulous behavior. [earlier *sculduddery*, orig. Sc. = unchastity (18th c.: orig. unkn.)]

skulk /skulk/ *v. & n.* •*v.intr.* **1** move stealthily, lurk, or keep oneself concealed, esp. in a cowardly or sinister way. **2** stay or sneak away in time of danger. **3** *Brit.* shirk duty. •*n.* **1** a person who skulks. **2** a group of foxes. ▫▫ **skulk•er** *n.* [ME f. Scand.: cf. Norw. *skulka* lurk, Da. *skulke*, Sw. *skolka* shirk]

skull /skul/ *n.* **1** the bony case of the brain of a vertebrate. **2 a** the part of the skeleton corresponding to the head. **b** this with the skin and soft internal parts removed. **c** a representation of this. **3** the head as the seat of intelligence. ▫ **out of one's skull** *sl.* out of one's mind; crazy. ▫▫ **skulled** *adj.* (also in *comb.*). [ME *scolle*: orig. unkn.]

skull and cross•bones *n.pl.* (also **skulls and cross•bones**) a representation of a skull with two thighbones crossed below it as an emblem of piracy or death.

skull•cap /skúlkap/ *n.* **1** a small, close-fitting, peakless cap. **2** the top part of the skull. **3** any plant of the genus *Scutellaria*, with helmet-shaped bilabiate flowers.

skull ses•sion *n. sl.* a discussion or conference.

skunk /skungk/ *n. & v.* •*n.* **1** any of various cat-sized flesh-eating mammals of the family Mustelidae, esp. *Mephitis mephitis* having a distinctive black and white striped fur and able to emit a powerful stench from a liquid secreted by its anal glands as a defense. **b** its fur. **2** *colloq.* a thoroughly contemptible person. •*v.tr.* **1** *sl.* defeat soundly. **2** fail to pay (a bill, etc.). [Algonquian *segankw, segongw*]

skunk bear *n. colloq.* a wolverine.

skunk cab•bage *n.* one of two N. American herbaceous plants, esp. *Symplocarpus foetidus*, with an offensive-smelling spathe.

sky /skī/ *n. & v.* •*n.* (*pl.* **skies**) (in *sing.* or *pl.*) **1** the region of the atmosphere and outer space seen from the earth. **2** the weather or climate evidenced by this. •*v.tr.* (**skies**, **skied**) **1** *Baseball*, etc., hit (a ball) high into the air. **2** hang (a picture) high on a wall. ▫ **the sky is the limit** there is practically no limit. **to the skies** very highly; without reserve (*praised to the skies*). **under the open sky** out of doors. ▫▫ **sky•ey** *adj.* **sky•less** *adj.* [ME *ski(es)* cloud(s) f. ON *ský*]

sky blue *n.* a bright, clear blue.

sky-blue pink *n.* an imaginary color.

sky•box /skíboks/ *n.* an elevated enclosure in a sports stadium containing plush seating, food services, and other amenities.

sky•cap /skíkap/ *n.* a person who carries baggage for passengers at airports.

sky-clad *adj. sl. esp. Brit.* naked (esp. in witchcraft).

sky cloth *n. Theatr.* a backcloth painted or colored to represent the sky.

sky•div•ing /skídīving/ *n.* the sport of performing acrobatic maneuvers under free fall with a parachute. ▫▫ **sky•dive** *v.intr.* **sky•div•er** *n.*

Skye ter•ri•er /skī/ *n.* a small, long-bodied, short-legged, long-haired, slate- or fawn-colored variety of Scottish terrier. [*Skye*, an island of the Inner Hebrides]

sky-high *adv. & adj.* as if reaching the sky; very high.

sky•jack /skíjak/ *v. & n. sl.* •*v.tr.* hijack (an aircraft). •*n.* an act of skyjacking. ▫▫ **sky•jack•er** *n.* [SKY + HIJACK]

sky•lark /skílaark/ *n. & v.* •*n.* a lark, *Alauda arvensis*, of Eurasia and N. Africa, that sings while hovering in flight. •*v.intr.* play tricks or practical jokes; indulge in horseplay; frolic. [SKY + LARK[1]: (v.) with pun on LARK[2]]

sky•light /skílīt/ *n.* a window set in the plane of a roof or ceiling.

sky•line /skílīn/ *n.* the outline of hills, buildings, etc., defined against the sky; the visible horizon.

sky pi•lot *n. sl.* a clergyman.

sky•rock•et /skírokkit/ *n. & v.* •*n.* a rocket exploding high in the air. •*v.intr.* (esp. of prices, etc.) rise very steeply or rapidly.

sky•sail /skísayl, –səl/ *n.* a light sail above the royal in a square-rigged ship.

sky•scape /skískayp/ *n.* **1** a picture chiefly representing the sky. **2** a view of the sky.

sky•scrap•er /skískraypər/ *n.* a very tall building of many stories. See illustration pages 946–947.

sky•ward /skíwərd/ *adv. & adj.* •*adv.* (also **sky•wards** /–wərdz/) toward the sky. •*adj.* moving skyward.

sky•watch /skíwoch/ *n.* the activity of watching the sky for aircraft, etc.

sky wave *n.* a radio wave reflected from the ionosphere.

sky•way /skíway/ *n.* **1** a route used by aircraft. **2** the sky as a medium of transport.

sky•writ•ing /skíriting/ *n.* legible smoke trails made by an airplane, esp. for advertising.

slab /slab/ *n. & v.* •*n.* **1** a flat, broad, fairly thick, usu. square or rectangular piece of solid material, esp. stone. **2** a large flat piece of cake, chocolate, etc. **3** (of lumber) an outer piece sawn from a log. **4** esp. *Brit.* a mortuary table. •*v.tr.* (**slabbed**, **slab•bing**) remove slabs from (a log or tree) to prepare it for sawing into planks. [ME: orig. unkn.]

slack[1] /slak/ *adj., n., v., & adv.* •*adj.* **1** (of rope, etc.) not taut. **2** inactive or sluggish. **3** negligent or remiss. **4** (of tide, etc.) neither ebbing nor flowing. **5** (of trade or business or a market) with little happening. **6** loose. **7** *Phonet.* lax. **8** relaxed; languid. •*n.* **1** the slack part of a rope (*haul in the slack*). **2** a slack time in trade, etc. **3** *colloq.* a spell of inactivity or laziness. **4** (in *pl.*) full-length loosely cut trousers for informal wear. •*v.* **1 a** *tr. & intr.* slacken. **b** *tr.* loosen (rope, etc.). **2** *intr. Brit. colloq.* take a rest; be lazy. **3** *tr.* slake (lime). •*adv.* **1** slackly. **2** slowly or insufficiently (*dry slack*; *bake slack*). ▫ **slack off 1** loosen. **2** lose or cause to lose vigor. **slack up** reduce the speed of a train, etc., before stopping. **take up the slack** use up a surplus or make up a deficiency; avoid an undesirable lull. ▫▫ **slack•ly** *adv.* **slack•ness** *n.* [OE *slæc* f. Gmc.]

slack[2] /slak/ *n.* coal dust or small pieces of coal. [ME prob. f. LG or Du.]

slack•en /slákən/ *v.tr. & intr.* make or become slack. ▫ **slacken off** = *slack off* (see SLACK[1]).

slack•er /slákər/ *n.* a shirker; an indolent person.

slack hand *n.* lack of full control in riding or governing.

slack lime *n.* slaked lime.

slack rein *n.* = slack hand.

slack suit *n.* casual clothes of slacks and a matching jacket or shirt.

slack wa•ter *n.* a time near the turn of the tide, esp. at low tide.

See page xx for the **Key to Pronunciation**.

slag /slag/ *n. & v.* ● *n.* **1** vitreous refuse left after ore has been smelted; dross separated in a fused state in the reduction of ore; clinkers. **2** volcanic scoria. **3** *Brit. sl. derog.* **a** a prostitute or promiscuous woman. **b** a worthless or insignificant person. ● *v.* (**slagged, slag·ging**) **1** *intr.* **a** form slag. **b** cohere into a mass like slag. **2** *tr.* (often foll. by *off*) *Brit. sl.* criticize; insult. □□ **slag·gy** *adj.* (**slag·gi·er, slag·gi·est**). [MLG *slagge*, perh. f. *slagen* strike, with ref. to fragments formed by hammering]

slag heap *n.* a hill of refuse from a mine, etc.

slag wool *n.* = MINERAL WOOL.

slain *past part.* of SLAY[1].

slain·te /sláːnchə/ *int.* a Gaelic toast: good health! [Gael. *sláinte*, lit. 'health']

slake /slayk/ *v.tr.* **1** assuage or satisfy (thirst, revenge, etc.). **2** disintegrate (quicklime) by chemical combination with water. [OE *slacian* f. *slæc* SLACK[1]]

sla·lom /sláːləm/ *n.* **1** a ski race down a zigzag course defined by artificial obstacles. **2** an obstacle race in canoes or cars or on skateboards or water skis. [Norw., lit. 'sloping track']

slam[1] /slam/ *v. & n.* ● *v.* (**slammed, slam·ming**) **1** *tr. & intr.* shut forcefully and loudly. **2** *tr.* put down (an object) with a similar sound. **3** *intr.* move violently (*he slammed out of the room*). **4** *tr. & intr.* put or come into sudden action (*slam the brakes on*). **5** *tr. sl.* criticize severely. **6** *tr. sl.* hit. **7** *tr. sl.* gain an easy victory over. ● *n.* **1** a sound of or as of a slammed door. **2** the shutting of a door, etc., with a loud bang. **3** (usu. prec. by *the*) *sl.* prison. [prob. f. Scand.: cf. ON *slam(b)ra*]

slam[2] /slam/ *n. Cards* the winning of every trick in a game. [orig. name of a card game: perh. f. obs. *slampant* trickery]

slam-bang *adv. & adj.* ● *adv.* with the sound of a slam. ● *adj. colloq.* impressive, exciting, or energetic.

slam·mer /slámər/ *n.* (usu. prec. by *the*) *sl.* prison.

slan·der /slándər/ *n. & v.* ● *n.* **1** a malicious, false, and injurious statement spoken about a person. **2** the uttering of such statements; calumny. **3** *Law* false oral defamation (cf. LIBEL). ● *v.tr.* utter slander about; defame falsely. □□ **slan·der·er** *n.* **slan·der·ous** *adj.* **slan·der·ous·ly** *adv.* [ME *sclaundre* f. AF *esclaundre*, OF *esclandre* alt. f. *escandle* f. LL *scandalum*: see SCANDAL]

slang /slang/ *n. & v.* ● *n.* words, phrases, and uses that are regarded as very informal and are often restricted to special contexts or are peculiar to a specified profession, class, etc. (*racing slang; schoolboy slang*). ● *v.* **1** *tr.* use abusive language to. **2** *intr.* use such language. [18th-c. cant: orig. unkn.]

slang·ing match *n. Brit.* a prolonged exchange of insults.

slang·y /slángee/ *adj.* (**slang·i·er, slang·i·est**) **1** of the character of slang. **2** fond of using slang. □□ **slang·i·ly** *adv.* **slang·i·ness** *n.*

slant /slant/ *v., n., & adj.* ● *v.* **1** *intr.* slope; diverge from a line; lie or go obliquely to a vertical or horizontal line. **2** *tr.* cause to do this. **3** *tr.* (often as **slanted** *adj.*) present (information) from a particular angle, esp. in a biased or unfair way. ● *n.* **1** a slope; an oblique position. **2** a way of regarding a thing; a point of view, esp. a biased one. ● *adj.* sloping; oblique. □ **on a** (or **the**) **slant** aslant. [aphetic form of ASLANT: (v.) rel. to ME *slent* f. ON *sletta* dash, throw]

slant-eyed *adj.* having slanting eyes.

slant height *n.* the height of a cone from the vertex to the periphery of the base.

slant·wise /slántwīz/ (also **slantways** /slántwayz/) *adv.* aslant.

slap /slap/ *v., n., & adv.* ● *v.* (**slapped, slap·ping**) **1** *tr. & intr.* strike with the palm of the hand or a flat object, or so as to make a similar noise. **2** *tr.* lay forcefully (*slapped the money on the table; slapped a writ on the offender*). **3** *tr.* put hastily or carelessly (*slap some paint on the walls*). **4** *tr.* (often foll. by *down*) *colloq.* reprimand or snub. ● *n.* **1** a blow with the palm of the hand or a flat object. **2** a slapping sound. ● *adv.* **1** with the suddenness or effectiveness or true aim of a blow; suddenly; fully; directly (*ran slap into him; hit me slap in the eye*). **2** = SLAP-BANG. □ **slap on the back** *n.* congratulations. ● *v.tr.* congratulate. [LG *slapp* (imit.)]

slap and tick·le *n. Brit. colloq.* lighthearted amorous amusement.

slap bang *adv.* **1** exactly; right. **2** violently; noisily; headlong.

slap·dash /slápdash/ *adj. & adv.* ● *adj.* hasty and careless. ● *adv.* in a slapdash manner.

slap·hap·py /sláp-hápee/ *adj. colloq.* **1** cheerfully casual or flippant. **2** punch-drunk.

slap in the face *n.* a rebuff or affront.

slap·jack /slápjak/ *n.* **1** a card game in which face-up jacks are slapped by the players' open hands. **2** a kind of pancake cooked on a griddle. [SLAP + JACK[1]]

slap on the wrist *n. & v.* ● *n. colloq.* a mild reprimand or rebuke. ● *v.tr. colloq.* reprimand.

slap shot *n. Ice Hockey* a powerful shot made with a full swing of the stick.

slap·stick /slápstik/ *n.* **1** boisterous knockabout comedy. **2** a flexible divided lath used by a clown. [SLAP + STICK[1]]

slap-up *adj. esp. Brit. colloq.* excellent; lavish; done regardless of expense (*slap-up meal*).

slash /slash/ *v. & n.* ● *v.* **1** *intr.* make a sweeping or random cut or cuts with a knife, sword, whip, etc. **2** *tr.* make such a cut or cuts at. **3** *tr.* make a long narrow gash or gashes in. **4** *tr.* reduce (prices, etc.) drastically. **5** *tr.* censure vigorously. **6** *tr.* make (one's way) by slashing. **7** *tr.* **a** lash (a person, etc.) with a whip. **b** crack (a whip). ● *n.* **1 a** a slashing cut or stroke. **b** a wound or slit made by this. **2** an oblique stroke; a virgule. **3** *Brit. sl.* an act of urinating. **4** debris resulting from the felling or destruction of trees. □□ **slash·er** *n.* [ME perh. f. OF *esclachier* break in pieces]

PUNCTUATION TIP | **slash**

The **slash** (/), also called **virgule**, or **solidus**, is used to show alternatives (*each student must have a permission slip signed by his/her parents*) and to separate lines of verse when a poem is written out as prose (*Some say the world will end in fire,/ Some say in ice*). While the use of slashes can be handy, sometimes they make writing more difficult to comprehend. If possible, rewrite the sentence so that a slash is not necessary (*all students must have signed permission slips from their parents*).

---

slash-and-burn *adj.* (of cultivation) in which vegetation is cut down, allowed to dry, and then burned off before seeds are planted.

slashed /slasht/ *adj.* (of a sleeve, etc.) having slits to show a lining or puffing of other material.

slash·ing /sláshing/ *adj.* vigorously incisive or effective.

slat /slat/ *n.* a thin narrow piece of wood or plastic or metal, esp. used in an overlapping series as in a fence or Venetian blind. [ME *s(c)lat* f. OF *esclat* splinter, etc. f. *esclater* split f. Rmc]

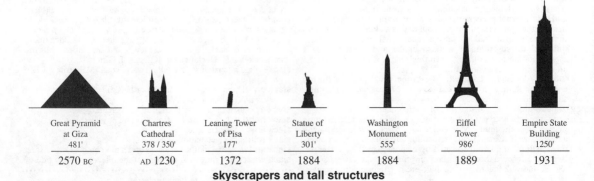

Great Pyramid at Giza	Chartres Cathedral	Leaning Tower of Pisa	Statue of Liberty	Washington Monument	Eiffel Tower	Empire State Building
481'	378 / 350'	177'	301'	555'	986'	1250'
2570 BC	AD 1230	1372	1884	1884	1889	1931

skyscrapers and tall structures

slate /slayt/ *n., v., & adj.* ● *n.* **1** a fine-grained, gray, green, or bluish-purple metamorphic rock easily split into flat smooth plates. **2** a piece of such a plate used as roofing material. **3** a piece of such a plate used for writing on, usu. framed in wood. **4** the color of slate. **5** a list of nominees for office, etc. ● *v.tr.* **1** cover with slates esp. as roofing. **2** *Brit. colloq.* criticize severely; scold. **3** make arrangements for (an event, etc.). **4** propose or nominate for office, etc. ● *adj.* made of slate. □ **on the slate** *Brit.* recorded as a debt to be paid. **wipe the slate clean** forgive or cancel the record of past offenses. □□ **slat·ing** *n.* **slat·y** *adj.* [ME *s(c)late* f. OF *esclate*, fem. form of *esclat* SLAT]

slate blue *n.* (also **slate black**) a shade of blue (or black) occurring in slate.

slate-col·ored *n.* a dark bluish or greenish gray.

slate gray *n.* a shade of gray occurring in slate.

slate pen·cil *n.* a small rod of soft slate used for writing on slate.

slat·er /sláytər/ *n.* **1** a person who slates roofs, etc. **2** a woodlouse or similar crustacean.

slath·er /sláthər/ *n. & v.* ● *n.* **1** (usu. in *pl.*) *colloq.* a large amount. **2** (often **open slather**) *Austral. & NZ sl.* unrestricted scope for action. ● *v.tr. colloq.* **1** spread thickly. **2** squander. [19th c.: orig. unkn.]

slat·ted /slátid/ *adj.* having slats.

slat·tern /slátərn/ *n.* a slovenly woman. □□ **slat·tern·ly** *adj.* **slat·tern·li·ness** *n.* [17th c.: rel. to *slattering* slovenly, f. dial. *slatter* to spill, slop, waste, frequent. of *slat* strike]

slaugh·ter /sláwtər/ *n. & v.* ● *n.* **1** the killing of an animal or animals for food. **2** the killing of many persons or animals at once or continuously; carnage; massacre. ● *v.tr.* **1** kill (people) in a ruthless manner or on a great scale. **2** kill for food; butcher. **3** *colloq.* defeat utterly. □□ **slaugh·ter·er** *n.* **slaugh·ter·ous** *adj.* [ME *slahter* ult. f. ON *slátr* butcher's meat, rel. to SLAY[1]]

slaugh·ter·house /sláwtərhows/ *n.* **1** a place for the slaughter of animals as food. **2** a place of carnage.

Slav /slaav/ *n. & adj.* ● *n.* a member of a group of peoples in Central and Eastern Europe speaking Slavic languages. ● *adj.* **1** of or relating to the Slavs. **2** Slavic. □□ **Slav·ism** *n.* [ME *Sclave* f. med.L *Sclavus*, late Gk *Sklabos*, & f. med.L *Slavus*]

slave /slayv/ *n. & v.* ● *n.* **1** a person who is the legal property of another or others and is bound to absolute obedience, a human chattel. **2** a drudge; a person working very hard. **3** (foll. by *of, to*) a helpless victim of some dominating influence (*slave of fashion*; *slave to duty*). **4** a machine, or part of one, directly controlled by another. ● *v.* **1** *intr.* (often foll. by *at, over*) work very hard. **2** *tr.* (foll. by *to*) subject (a device) to control by another. [ME f. OF *esclave* = med.L *sclavus, sclava* Slav (captive): see SLAV]

slave brace·let *n.* a bangle or chain of gold, etc., worn around the ankle.

slave driv·er *n.* **1** an overseer of slaves at work. **2** a person who works others hard. □□ **slave-drive** *v.tr.* (*past* **·drove**; *past part.* **·driv·en**)

slave la·bor *n.* forced labor.

slav·er[1] /sláyvər/ *n. hist.* a ship or person engaged in the slave trade.

slav·er[2] /slávər/ *n. & v.* ● *n.* **1** saliva running from the mouth. **2 a** fulsome or servile flattery. **b** drivel; nonsense. ● *v.intr.* **1** let saliva run from the mouth; dribble. **2** (foll. by *over*) show excessive sentimentality over, or desire for. [ME prob. f. LG or Du.: cf. SLOBBER]

slav·er·y /sláyvəree, sláyvree/ *n.* **1** the condition of a slave. **2** exhausting labor; drudgery. **3** the custom of having slaves.

slave ship *n. hist.* a ship transporting slaves, esp. from Africa.

Slave State *n.* (also **slave state**) *hist.* any of the Southern states of the US in which slavery was legal before the Civil War.

slave trade *n. hist.* the procuring, transporting, and selling of human beings, esp. African blacks, as slaves. □□ **slave trad·er** *n.*

slav·ey /sláyvee/ *n.* (*pl.* **·eys**) *Brit. colloq.* a maidservant, esp. a hard-worked one.

Slav·ic /slaávik/ *adj. & n.* ● *adj.* **1** of or relating to the group of Indo-European languages including Russian, Polish, and Czech. **2** of or relating to the Slavs. ● *n.* the Slavic language group.

slav·ish /sláyvish/ *adj.* **1** of, like, or as of slaves. **2** showing no attempt at originality or development. **3** abject; servile; base. □□ **slav·ish·ly** *adv.* **slav·ish·ness** *n.*

Sla·von·ic /sləvónik/ *adj. & n.* = SLAVIC.

slaw /slaw/ *n.* coleslaw. [Du. *sla*, shortened f. *salade* SALAD]

slay[1] /slay/ *v.tr.* (*past* **slew** /slōō/; *past part.* **slain** /slayn/) **1** *literary or joc.* kill. **2** *sl.* overwhelm with delight; convulse with laughter. □□ **slay·er** *n.* [OE *slēan* f. Gmc]

slay[2] var. of SLEY.

SLBM *abbr.* **1** submarine-launched ballistic missile. **2** sea-launched ballistic missile.

sleaze /sleez/ *n. & v. colloq.* ● *n.* **1** sleaziness. **2** a person of low moral standards. ● *v.intr.* move in a sleazy fashion. [back-form. f. SLEAZY]

slea·zy /sleezee/ *adj.* (**slea·zi·er**, **slea·zi·est**) **1** squalid; tawdry. **2** slatternly. **3** (of textiles, etc.) flimsy. □□ **slea·zi·ly** *adv.* **slea·zi·ness** *n.* [17th c.: orig. unkn.]

sled /sled/ *n. & v.* ● *n.* **1** a vehicle on runners for conveying loads or passengers esp. over snow, drawn by horses, dogs, or reindeer or pushed or pulled by one or more persons. **2** a toboggan. ● *v.intr.* (**sled·ded**, **sled·ding**) ride on a sled. [MLG *sledde*, rel. to SLIDE]

sledge[1] /slej/ *n. & v.* ● *n.* a heavy sled, esp. one drawn by draft animals. ● *v.intr. & tr.* travel or convey by sledge. [MDu. *sleedse*, rel. to SLED]

sledge[2] /slej/ *n.* = SLEDGEHAMMER.

sledge·ham·mer /sléjhamər/ *n.* **1** a large heavy hammer used to break stone, etc. **2** (*attrib.*) heavy or powerful (*a sledgehammer blow*). [OE *slecg*, rel. to SLAY[1]]

sleek /sleek/ *adj. & v.* ● *adj.* **1** (of hair, fur, or skin, or an animal or person with such hair, etc.) smooth and glossy. **2** looking well-fed and comfortable. **3** ingratiating. **4** (of a thing) smooth and polished. ● *v.tr.* make sleek, esp. by stroking or pressing down. □□ **sleek·ly** *adv.* **sleek·ness** *n.* **sleek·y** *adj.* [later var. of SLICK]

sleep /sleep/ *n. & v.* ● *n.* **1** a condition of body and mind such as that which normally recurs for several hours every night, in which the nervous system is inactive, the eyes closed, the postural muscles relaxed, and consciousness practically suspended. **2** a period of sleep (*shall try to get a sleep*). **3** a state like sleep, such as rest, quiet, negligence, or death. **4** the prolonged inert condition of hibernating animals. **5** a substance found in the corners of the eyes after sleep. ● *v.* (*past and past part.* **slept** /slept/) **1** *intr.* **a** be in a state of sleep. **b** fall asleep. **2** *intr.* (foll. by *at, in,* etc.) spend the night. **3** *tr.* provide sleeping accommodation for (*the*

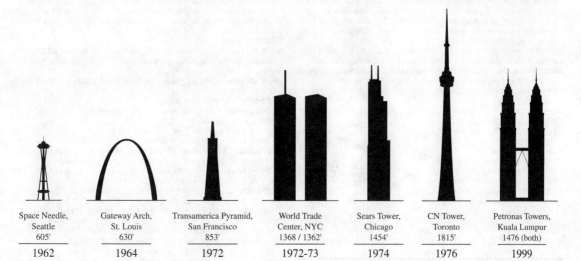

Space Needle, Seattle	Gateway Arch, St. Louis	Transamerica Pyramid, San Francisco	World Trade Center, NYC	Sears Tower, Chicago	CN Tower, Toronto	Petronas Towers, Kuala Lumpur
605'	630'	853'	1368 / 1362'	1454'	1815'	1476 (both)
1962	1964	1972	1972-73	1974	1976	1999

house sleeps six). **4** *intr.* (foll. by *with*, *together*) have sexual intercourse, esp. in bed. **5** *intr.* (foll. by *on*, *over*) not decide (a question) until the next day. **6** *intr.* (foll. by *through*) fail to be woken by. **7** *intr.* be inactive or dormant. **8** *intr.* be dead; lie in the grave. **9** *tr.* **a** (foll. by *off*) remedy by sleeping (*slept off his hangover*). **b** (foll. by *away*) spend in sleeping (*sleep the hours away*). **10** *intr.* (of a top) spin so steadily as to seem motionless. □ **get to sleep** manage to fall asleep. **go to sleep 1** enter a state of sleep. **2** (of a limb) become numbed by pressure. **in one's sleep** while asleep. **let sleeping dogs lie** avoid stirring up trouble. **put to sleep 1** anesthetize. **2** kill (an animal) painlessly. **sleep around** *colloq.* be sexually promiscuous. **sleep in 1** remain asleep later than usual in the morning. **2** sleep by night at one's place of work, as a domestic. **sleep like a log** (or **top**) sleep soundly. **sleep out** sleep by night out of doors, or not at one's place of work. [OE *slēp*, *slæp* (n.), *slē pan*, *slǣpan* (v.) f. Gmc]

sleep·er /slḗpər/ *n.* **1** a person or animal that sleeps. **2** a wooden or concrete beam laid horizontally as a support, esp. for railroad track. **3 a** a sleeping car. **b** a berth in this. **4 a** a ring worn on an earlobe to pierce it gradually. **b** a ring worn in a pierced ear to keep the hole from closing. **5** a thing that is suddenly successful after being undistinguished. **6** a child's one-piece night garment. **7** a spy or saboteur, etc., who remains inactive while establishing a secure position.

sleep·ing bag *n.* a lined or padded bag to sleep in esp. when camping, etc.

Sleep·ing Beau·ty *n.* a fairy-tale heroine who slept for 100 years.

sleep·ing car *n.* a railroad car provided with beds or berths; a Pullman.

sleep·ing part·ner *n. Brit.* = SILENT PARTNER.

sleep·ing pill *n.* a pill to induce sleep.

sleep·ing po·lice·man *n. Brit.* a ramp, etc., in the road intended to cause traffic to reduce speed.

sleep·ing sick·ness *n.* **1** any of several tropical diseases with extreme lethargy caused by a trypanosome transmitted by a tsetse fly bite. **2** *encephalitis lethargica*, a viral infection of the brain, with drowsiness and sometimes a coma.

sleep·less /slḗplis/ *adj.* **1** characterized by lack of sleep (*a sleepless night*). **2** unable to sleep. **3** continually active or moving. □□ **sleep·less·ly** *adv.* **sleep·less·ness** *n.*

sleep of the just *n.* sound sleep.

sleep·walk /slḗpwawk/ *v.intr.* walk or perform other actions while asleep. □□ **sleep·walk·er** *n.* **sleep·walk·ing** *n.*

sleep·y /slḗpee/ *adj.* (**sleep·i·er**, **sleep·i·est**) **1** drowsy; ready for sleep; about to fall asleep. **2** lacking activity or bustle (*a sleepy little town*). **3** habitually indolent; unobservant; etc. □□ **sleep·i·ly** *adv.* **sleep·i·ness** *n.*

sleep·y·head /slḗpeehed/ *n.* (esp. as a form of address) a sleepy or inattentive person.

sleep·y sick·ness *n. Brit.* = SLEEPING SICKNESS, 2.

sleet /sleet/ *n. & v.* ● *n.* **1** a mixture of snow and rain falling together. **2** hail or snow melting as it falls. **3** a thin coating of ice. ● *v.intr.* (prec. by *it* as subject) sleet falls (*it is sleeting*; *if it sleets*). □□ **sleet·y** *adj.* [ME prob. f. OE: rel. to MLG *slōten* (pl.) hail, MHG *slōz(e)* f. Gmc]

sleeve /sleev/ *n.* **1** the part of a garment that wholly or partly covers an arm. **2** the cover of a phonograph record. **3** a tube enclosing a rod or smaller tube. **4 a** a wind sock. **b** a drogue towed by an aircraft. □ **roll up one's sleeves** prepare to fight or work. **up one's sleeve** concealed but ready for use, in reserve. □□ **sleeved** *adj.* (also in *comb.*). **sleeve·less** *adj.* [OE *slēfe*, *slīefe*, *slȳf*]

sleeve cou·pling *n.* a tube for connecting shafts or pipes.

sleeve note *n.* a descriptive note on a record sleeve; liner note.

sleeve nut *n.* a long nut with right-hand and left-hand screw threads for drawing together pipes or shafts conversely threaded.

sleeve valve *n.* a valve in the form of a cylinder with a sliding movement.

sleev·ing /slḗving/ *n.* tubular covering for electric cable, etc.

sleigh /slay/ *n. & v.* ● *n.* a sled, esp. one for riding on. ● *v.intr.* travel on a sleigh. [orig. US, f. Du. *slee*, rel. to SLED]

sleigh bell *n.* any of a number of tinkling bells attached to the harness of a sleigh-horse, etc.

sleigh

sleight /slīt/ *n. archaic* **1** a deceptive trick or device or movement. **2** dexterity. **3** cunning. [ME *sleghth* f. ON *slœgth* f. *slœgr* SLY]

sleight of hand *n.* **1** dexterity, esp. in conjuring or fencing. **2** a display of dexterity, esp. a conjuring trick.

slen·der /sléndər/ *adj.* (**slen·der·er**, **slen·der·est**) **1 a** of small girth or breadth (*a slender pillar*). **b** gracefully thin (*a slender waist*). **2** rel-

atively small or scanty; slight; meager; inadequate (*slender hopes*; *slender resources*). □□ **slen·der·ly** *adv.* **slen·der·ness** *n.* [ME: orig. unkn.]

slen·der·ize /sléndərīz/ *v.* **1** *tr.* **a** make (a thing) slender. **b** make (one's figure) appear slender. **2** *intr.* make oneself slender; slim.

slen·der lo·ris *n.* see LORIS.

slept *past* and *past part.* of SLEEP.

sleuth /slooth/ *n. & v. colloq.* ● *n.* a detective. ● *v.* **1** *intr.* act as a detective. **2** *tr.* investigate. [orig. in *sleuthhound*: ME f. *sleuth* f. ON *slóth* track, trail: cf. SLOT[2]]

sleuth·hound /slóothhownd/ *n.* **1** a bloodhound. **2** *colloq.* a detective; an investigator.

slew[1] /sloo/ *v. & n.* (also **slue**) ● *v.tr. & intr.* (often foll. by *around*) turn or swing forcibly or with effort out of the forward or ordinary position. ● *n.* such a change of position. [18th-c. Naut.: orig. unkn.]

slew[2] *past* of SLAY[1].

slew[3] /sloo/ *n. colloq.* a large number or quantity. [Ir. *sluagh*]

sley /slay/ *n.* (also **slay**) a weaver's reed. [OE *slege*, rel. to SLAY[1]]

slice /slīs/ *n. & v.* ● *n.* **1** a thin, broad piece or wedge cut off or out esp. from meat or bread or a cake, pie, or large fruit. **2** a share; a part taken or allotted or gained (*a slice of territory*; *a slice of the profits*). **3** an implement with a broad flat blade for serving fish, etc., or for scraping or chipping; spatula. **4** *Golf & Tennis* a slicing stroke. ● *v.* **1** *tr.* (often foll. by *up*) cut into slices. **2** (foll. by *off*) cut (a piece) off. **3** *intr.* (foll. by *into*, *through*) cut with or like a knife. **4** *tr.* (also *absol.*) **a** *Golf* strike (the ball) so that it deviates away from the striker. **b** (in other sports) propel (the ball) forward at an angle. **5** *tr.* go through (air, etc.) with a cutting motion. □□ **slice·a·ble** *adj.* **slic·er** *n.* (also in *comb.*). [ME f. OF *esclice*, *esclicier* splinter f. Frank. *slītjan*, rel. to SLIT]

slice of life *n.* a realistic representation of everyday experience.

slick /slik/ *adj.*, *n.*, *& v.* ● *adj. colloq* **1 a** (of a person or action) skillful or efficient; dexterous (*gave a slick performance*). **b** superficially or pretentiously smooth and dexterous. **c** glib. **2 a** sleek; smooth. **b** slippery. ● *n.* **1** a smooth patch of oil, etc., esp. on the sea. **2** *Motor Racing* a smooth tire. **3** *colloq.* a glossy magazine. **4** *sl.* a slick person. ● *v.tr. colloq.* **1** make sleek or smart. **2** (usu. foll. by *down*) flatten (one's hair, etc.). □□ **slick·ly** *adv.* **slick·ness** *n.* [ME *slike(n)*, prob. f. OE: cf. SLEEK]

slick·er /slíkər/ *n.* **1** *colloq.* **a** a plausible rogue. **b** a smart and sophisticated city dweller (cf. CITY SLICKER). **2** a raincoat of smooth material.

slide /slīd/ *v. & n.* ● *v.* (*past* and *past part.* **slid** /slid/) **1 a** *intr.* move along a smooth surface with continuous contact on the same part of the thing moving (cf. ROLL). **b** *tr.* cause to do this (*slide the drawer into place*). **2** *intr.* move quietly; glide; go smoothly along. **3** *intr.* pass gradually or imperceptibly. **4** *intr.* glide over ice on one or both feet without skates (under gravity or with momentum got by running). **5** *intr.* (foll. by *over*) barely touch upon (a delicate subject, etc.). **6** *intr. & tr.* (often foll. by *into*) move or cause to move quietly or unobtrusively (*slid his hand into mine*). **7** *intr.* take its own course (*let it slide*). **8** *intr.* decline (*shares slid to a new low*). ● *n.* **1 a** the act or an instance of sliding. **b** a rapid decline. **2** an inclined plane down which children, goods, etc., slide; a chute. **3 a** a track made by or for sliding, esp. on ice. **b** a slope prepared with snow or ice for tobogganing. **4** a part of a machine or instrument that slides, esp. a slide valve. **5 a** a thing slid into place, esp. a piece of glass holding an object for a microscope. **b** a mounted transparency usu. placed in a projector for viewing on a screen. **6** = SLIDING SEAT. **7** a part or parts of a machine on or between which a sliding part works. □ **let things slide** be negligent; allow deterioration. □□ **slid·a·ble** *adj.* **slid·a·bly** *adv.* **slid·er** *n.* [OE *slīdan*]

slide fas·ten·er *n. Brit.* = ZIPPER.

slide rule *n.* a ruler with a sliding central strip, graduated logarithmically for making rapid calculations, esp. multiplication and division.

slide valve *n.* a sliding piece that opens and closes an aperture by sliding across it.

slide·way /slídway/ *n.* = SLIDE *n.* 7.

slid·ing door *n.* a door drawn across an aperture on a slide, not turning on hinges.

slid·ing keel *n. Naut. Brit.* a centerboard.

slid·ing roof *n. esp. Brit.* = SUNROOF.

slid·ing scale *n.* a scale of fees, taxes, wages, etc., that varies as a whole in accordance with variation of some standard.

slid·ing seat *n.* a seat able to slide to and fro on runners, etc., esp. in a racing scull to adjust the length of a stroke.

slight /slīt/ *adj.*, *v.*, *& n.* ● *adj.* **1 a** inconsiderable; of little significance (*has a slight cold*; *the damage is very slight*). **b** barely perceptible (*a slight smell of gas*). **c** not much or great or thorough; inadequate; scanty (*a conclusion based on very slight observation*; *paid him slight attention*). **2** slender; frail-looking (*saw a slight figure approaching*; *supported by a slight framework*). **3** (in *superl.*, with *neg.* or *interrog.*) any whatever (*paid not the slightest attention*). ● *v.tr.* **1** treat or speak of (a person, etc.) as not worth attention, fail in courtesy or respect toward; markedly neglect. **2** *hist.* make militarily useless;

raze (a fortification, etc.). • *n.* a marked piece of neglect; a failure to show due respect. □ **not in the slightest** not at all. **put a slight upon** = sense 1 of *v.* □□ **slight·ing·ly** *adv.* **slight·ish** *adj.* **slight·ly** *adv.* **slight·ness** *n.* [ME *slyght*, *sleght* f. ON *sléttr* level, smooth f. Gmc]

sli·ly var. of *slyly* (see SLY).

slim /slim/ *adj.*, *v.*, & *n.* • *adj.* (**slim·mer**, **slim·mest**) **1 a** of small girth or thickness; of long, narrow shape. **b** gracefully thin; slenderly built. **c** not fat nor overweight. **2** small, insufficient (*a slim chance of success*). **3** clever; artful; crafty; unscrupulous. • *v.* (**slimmed**, **slim·ming**) **1** *intr.* esp. *Brit.* make oneself slimmer by dieting, exercise, etc. **2** *tr.* make slim or slimmer. • *n.* esp. *Brit.* a course of slimming. □□ **slim·ly** *adv.* **slim·mer** *n.* **slim·ming** *n.* & *adj.* **slim·mish** *adj.* **slim·ness** *n.* [LG or Du. f. Gmc]

slime /slīm/ *n.* & *v.* • *n.* thick slippery mud or a substance of similar consistency, e.g., liquid bitumen or a mucus exuded by fish, etc. • *v.tr.* cover with slime. [OE *slīm* f. Gmc, rel. to L *līmus* mud, Gk *limnē* marsh]

slime mold *n.* a spore-bearing microorganism secreting slime.

slim·line /slīmlīn/ *adj.* of slender design.

slim·y /slīmee/ *adj.* (**slim·i·er**, **slim·i·est**) **1** of the consistency of slime. **2** covered, smeared with, or full of slime. **3** disgustingly dishonest, meek, or flattering. **4** slippery; hard to hold. □□ **slim·i·ly** *adv.* **slim·i·ness** *n.*

sling[1] /sling/ *n.* & *v.* • *n.* **1** a strap, belt, etc., used to support or raise a hanging weight, e.g., a rifle, a ship's boat, or goods being transferred. **2** a bandage looped around the neck to support an injured arm. **3** a strap or string used with the hand to give impetus to a small missile, esp. a stone. **4** *Austral. sl.* a tip or bribe. • *v.tr.* (*past* and *past part.* **slung** /slung/) **1** (also *absol.*) hurl (a stone, etc.) from a sling. **2** *colloq.* throw. **3** suspend with a sling; allow to swing suspended; arrange so as to be supported from above; hoist or transfer with a sling. □ **sling off at** *Austral. & NZ sl.* disparage; mock; make fun of. [ME, prob. f. ON *slyngva* (v.)]

sling[2] /sling/ *n.* a sweetened drink of liquor (esp. gin) and water. [18th c.: orig. unkn.]

sling-back *n.* an open-backed shoe held in place by a strap above the heel.

sling·er /slíngər/ *n.* a person who slings, esp. the user of a sling.

sling·shot /slíngshot/ *n.* a forked stick, etc., with elastic for shooting stones, etc.

slink[1] /slingk/ *v.intr.* (*past* and *past part.* **slunk** /slungk/) (often foll. by *off*, *away*, *by*) move in a stealthy or guilty or sneaking manner. [OE *slincan* crawl]

slink[2] /slingk/ *v.* & *n.* • *v.tr.* (also *absol.*) (of an animal) produce (young) prematurely. • *n.* **1** an animal, esp. a calf, so born. **2** its flesh. [app. f. SLINK[1]]

slink·y /slíngkee/ *adj.* (**slink·i·er**, **slink·i·est**) **1** stealthy. **2** (of a garment) close-fitting and flowing; sinuous. **3** gracefully slender. □□ **slink·i·ly** *adv.* **slink·i·ness** *n.*

slip[1] /slip/ *v.* & *n.* • *v.* (**slipped**, **slip·ping**) **1** *intr.* slide unintentionally esp. for a short distance; lose one's footing or balance or place by unintended sliding. **2** *intr.* go or move with a sliding motion (*as the door closes the catch slips into place*; *slipped into her nightgown*). **3** *intr.* escape restraint or capture by being slippery or hard to hold or by not being grasped (*the eel slipped through his fingers*). **4** *intr.* **a** make one's or its way unobserved or quietly or quickly (*just slip across to the baker's*; *errors will slip in*). **b** (foll. by *by*) (of time) go by rapidly or unnoticed. **5** *intr.* **a** make a careless or casual mistake. **b** fall below the normal standard; deteriorate; lapse. **6** *tr.* insert or transfer stealthily or casually or with a sliding motion (*slipped a coin into his hand*; *slipped the papers into his pocket*). **7** *tr.* **a** release from restraint (*slipped the greyhounds from the leash*). **b** detach (an anchor) from a ship. **c** *Brit.* detach (a railroad car) from a moving train. **d** release (the clutch of a motor vehicle) for a moment. **e** (of an animal) produce (young) prematurely. **8** *tr.* move (a stitch) to the other needle without knitting it. **9** *tr.* (foll. by *on*, *off*) pull (a garment) hastily on or off. **10** *tr.* escape from; give the slip to (*the dog slipped its collar*; *point slipped my mind*). • *n.* **1** the act or an instance of slipping. **2** an accidental or slight error. **3** a loose covering or garment, esp. a petticoat or pillowcase. **4 a** a reduction in the movement of a pulley, etc., due to slipping of the belt. **b** a reduction in the distance traveled by a ship or aircraft arising from the nature of the medium in which its propeller revolves. **5** (in *sing.* or *pl.*) **a** an artificial slope of stone, etc., on which boats are landed. **b** an inclined structure on which ships are built or repaired. **6** *Cricket* **a** a fielder stationed for balls glancing off the bat to the off side. **b** (in *sing.* or *pl.*) the position of such a fielder (*caught in the slips*; *caught at slip*). **7** *Brit.* a leash to slip dogs. □ **give a person the slip** escape from or evade him or her. **let slip 1** release accidentally or

slingshot

deliberately, esp. from a leash. **2** miss (an opportunity). **3** utter inadvertently. **let slip the dogs of war** *poet.* open hostilities. **let slip through one's fingers 1** lose hold of. **2** miss the opportunity of having. **slip away** depart without leave-taking, etc. **slip off** depart without leave-taking, etc. **slip something over on** *colloq.* outwit. **slip up** *colloq.* make a mistake. **there's many a slip 'twixt cup and lip** nothing is certain till it has happened. [ME prob. f. MLG *slippen*: cf. SLIPPERY]

slip[2] /slip/ *n.* **1 a** a small piece of paper esp. for writing on. **b** a long, narrow strip of thin wood, paper, etc. **c** esp. *Brit.* a printer's proof on such paper; a galley proof. **2** a cutting taken from a plant for grafting or planting; a scion. □ **slip of a** small and slim (*a slip of a girl*). [ME, prob. f. MDu., MLG *slippe* cut, strip, etc.]

slip[3] /slip/ *n.* clay in a creamy mixture with water, used mainly for decorating earthenware. [OE *slipa*, *slyppe* slime: cf. COWSLIP]

slip car·riage *n. Brit.* a railroad car on an express for detaching at a station where the rest of the train does not stop.

slip·case /slípcays/ *n.* a close-fitting case for a book.

slip cast·ing *n.* the manufacture of ceramic ware by allowing slip to solidify in a mold. □□ **slip-cast** *adj.*

slip coach *n. Brit.* = SLIP CARRIAGE.

slip·cov·er /slípkəvər/ *n.* & *v.* • *n.* **1** a removable covering for usu. upholstered furniture. **2** a jacket or slipcase for a book. • *v.tr* cover with a slipcover.

slip form *n.* a mold in which a structure of uniform cross section is cast by filling it with concrete and continually moving and refilling it.

slip hook *n.* a hook with a contrivance for releasing it readily when necessary; pelican hook.

slip·knot /slípnot/ *n.* **1** a knot that can be undone by a pull. **2** a running knot.

slip of the tongue *n.* a small mistake in which something is written (or said) unintentionally.

slip-on *adj.* & *n.* • *adj.* (of shoes or clothes) that can be easily slipped on and off. • *n.* a slip-on shoe or garment.

slip·o·ver /slípōvər/ *adj.* & *n.* • *adj.* (of a garment) to be slipped on over the head. • *n.* a garment thus put on.

slip·page /slípij/ *n.* **1** the act or an instance of slipping. **2 a** a decline, esp. in popularity or value. **b** failure to meet a deadline or fulfill a promise; delay.

slipped disk *n.* a disk between vertebrae that has become displaced and causes lumbar pain.

slip·per /slípər/ *n.* & *v.* • *n.* **1** a light, loose, comfortable indoor shoe. **2** a light slip-on shoe for dancing, etc. • *v.tr.* *Brit.* beat or strike with a slipper. □□ **slip·pered** *adj.*

slip·per·wort /slípərwort, –wawrt/ *n.* calceolaria.

slip·per·y /slípəree/ *adj.* **1** difficult to hold firmly because of smoothness, wetness, sliminess, or elusive motion. **2** (of a surface) difficult to stand on, causing slips by its smoothness or muddiness. **3** unreliable; unscrupulous; shifty. **4** (of a subject) requiring tactful handling. □□ **slip·per·i·ly** *adv.* **slip·per·i·ness** *n* [prob. coined by Coverdale (1535) after Luther's *schlipfferig*, MHG *slipferig* f. *slipfern*, *slipfen* f. Gmc: partly f. *slipper* slippery (now dial.) f. OE *slipor* f. Gmc]

slip·per·y elm *n.* **1** the N. American red elm, *Ulmus rubra.* **2** the medicinal inner bark of this.

slip·per·y slope *n.* a course leading to disaster.

slip·py /slípee/ *adj.* (**slip·pi·er**, **slip·pi·est**) *colloq.* slippery. □ **look (or be) slippy** *Brit.* look sharp; make haste. □□ **slip·pi·ness** *n.*

slip ring *n.* a ring for sliding contact in a dynamo or electric motor.

slip rope *n. Naut.* a rope with both ends on board so that casting loose either end frees the ship from its moorings.

slip sheet *n. Printing* a sheet of paper placed between newly printed sheets to prevent offset or smudging.

slip·shod /slípshod/ *adj.* **1** (of speech or writing, a speaker or writer, a method of work, etc.) careless; unsystematic; loose in arrangement. **2** slovenly. **3** having shoes down at the heel.

slip stitch *n.* **1** a loose stitch joining layers of fabric and not visible externally. **2** a stitch moved to the other needle without being knitted. □□ **slip-stitch** *v.*

slip·stream /slípstreem/ *n.* & *v.* • *n.* **1** a current of air or water driven back by a revolving propeller or a moving vehicle. **2** an assisting force regarded as drawing something along with or behind something else. • *v.tr.* **1** follow closely behind (another vehicle). **2** pass after traveling in another's slipstream.

slip·up /slípəp/ *n.* a mistake; a blunder.

slip·ware *n.* pottery decorated with slip.

slip·way /slípway/ *n.* a slip for building ships or landing boats.

slit /slit/ *n.* & *v.* • *n.* **1** a long, straight, narrow incision. **2** a long, narrow opening comparable to a cut. • *v.tr.* (**slit·ting**; *past* and *past part.* **slit**) **1** make a slit in; cut or tear lengthwise. **2** cut into strips. □□ **slit·ter** *n.* [ME *slitte*, rel. to OE *slītan*, f. Gmc]

slit-eyed adj. having long, narrow eyes.

slith·er /slíthər/ v. & n. • v.intr. slide unsteadily; go with an irregular slipping motion. • n. an instance of slithering. □□ **slith·er·y** adj. [ME var. of slidder (now dial.) f. OE slid(e)rian frequent. f. slid-, weak grade of slídan SLIDE]

slit-pock·et n. a pocket with a vertical opening giving access to the pocket or to a garment beneath.

slit trench n. a narrow trench for a soldier or a weapon.

slit·ty /slítee/ adj. (**slit·ti·er, slit·ti·est**) (of the eyes) long and narrow.

sliv·er /slívər/ n. & v. • n. 1 a long, thin piece cut or split off. 2 a piece of wood torn from a tree or from lumber. 3 a splinter, esp. from an exploded shell. 4 a strip of loose textile fibers after carding. • v.tr. & intr. 1 break off as a sliver. 2 break up into slivers. 3 form into slivers. [ME, rel. to slive cleave (now dial.) f. OE]

sliv·o·vitz /slívəvits/ n. a plum brandy made esp. in Romania and the former Yugoslavia. [Serbo-Croat šljivovica f. šljiva plum]

slob /slob/ n. 1 colloq. a stupid, careless, coarse, or fat person. 2 Ir. muddy land. □□ **slob·bish** adj. [Ir. slab mud f. E slab ooze, sludge, prob. f. Scand.]

slob·ber /slóbər/ v. & n. • v.intr. 1 slaver. 2 (foll. by over) show excessive sentiment. • n. saliva running from the mouth; slaver. □□ **slob·ber·y** adj. [ME, = Du. slobberen, of imit. orig.]

sloe /slō/ n. 1 = BLACKTHORN. 2 its small bluish-black fruit with a sharp sour taste. [OE slā(h) f. Gmc]

sloe-eyed adj. 1 having eyes of this color. 2 slant-eyed.

sloe gin n. a liqueur of sloes steeped in gin.

slog /slog/ v. & n. • v. (**slogged, slog·ging**) 1 intr. & tr. hit hard and usu. wildly, esp. in boxing or at cricket. 2 intr. (often foll. by away, on) walk or work doggedly. • n. 1 a hard random hit. 2 a hard steady work or walking. b a spell of this. □□ **slog·ger** n. [19th c.: orig. unkn.: cf. SLUG²]

slo·gan /slógən/ n. 1 a short catchy phrase used in advertising, etc. 2 a party cry; a watchword or motto. 3 hist. a Scottish Highland war cry. [Gael. sluagh-ghairm f. sluagh army + gairm shout]

sloop /slōp/ n. 1 a small, one-masted, fore-and-aft-rigged vessel with mainsail and jib. 2 (in full sloop of war) hist. a small warship with guns on the upper deck only. [Du. sloep(e), of unkn. orig.]

sloop-rigged adj. rigged like a sloop.

slop¹ /slop/ v. & n. • v. (**slopped, slop·ping**) 1 (often foll. by over) a intr. spill or flow over the edge of a vessel. b tr. allow to do this. 2 tr. make (the floor, clothes, etc.) wet or messy by slopping; spill or splash liquid on. 3 intr. (usu. foll. by over) gush; be effusive or maudlin. • n. 1 a quantity of liquid spilled or splashed. 2 weakly sentimental language. 3 (in pl.) waste liquid, esp. dirty water or the waste contents of kitchen, bedroom, or prison vessels. 4 (in sing. or pl.) unappetizing weak liquid food. 5 Naut. a choppy sea. □ slop about Brit. move about in a slovenly manner. slop out Brit. carry slops out (in prison, etc.). [earlier sense 'slush,' prob. rel. to slyppe: cf. COWSLIP]

slop² /slop/ n. 1 a worker's loose outer garment. 2 (in pl.) esp. Brit. ready-made or cheap clothing. 3 (in pl.) clothes and bedding supplied to sailors in the navy. 4 (in pl.) archaic wide baggy trousers esp. as worn by sailors. [ME: cf. OE oferslop surplice f. Gmc]

slop ba·sin n. (also slop bowl) Brit. a basin for the dregs of cups at the table.

slope /slōp/ n. & v. • n. 1 an inclined position or direction; a state in which one end or side is at a higher level than another; a position in a line neither parallel nor perpendicular to level ground nor to a line serving as a standard. 2 a piece of rising or falling ground. 3 a a difference in level between the two ends or sides of a thing (a slope of 5 yards). b the rate at which this increases with distance, etc. 4 a place for skiing on the side of a hill or mountain. 5 (prec. by the) the position of a rifle when sloped. • v. 1 intr. have or take a slope; slant esp. up or down; lie or tend obliquely, esp. to ground level. 2 tr. place or arrange or make in or at a slope. □ slope arms place one's rifle in a sloping position against one's shoulder. slope off esp. Brit. sl. go away, esp. to evade work, etc. [shortening of ASLOPE]

slop jar n. a jar or pail for removing household slops.

slop pail n. 1 a pail for carrying slops to feed livestock, esp. pigs. 2 a slop jar.

slop·py /slópee/ adj. (**slop·pi·er, slop·pi·est**) 1 a (of the ground) wet with rain; full of puddles. b (of food, etc.) watery and disagreeable. c (of a floor, table, etc.) wet with slops, having water, etc., spilled on it. 2 unsystematic; careless; not thorough. 3 (of a garment) ill-fitting or untidy; (of a person) wearing such garments. 4 (of sentiment or talk) weakly emotional; maudlin. 5 colloq. (of the sea) choppy. □□ **slop·pi·ly** adv. **slop·pi·ness** n.

slosh /slosh/ v. & n. • v. 1 intr. (often foll. by about) splash or flounder about; move with a splashing sound. 2 tr. Brit. sl. hit esp. heavily. 3 tr. colloq. a pour (liquid) clumsily. b pour liquid on. • n. 1 slush. 2 a an instance of splashing. b the sound of this. 3 Brit. sl. a heavy blow. 4 a quantity of liquid. [var. of SLUSH]

sloshed /slosht/ adj. sl. drunk.

---

slosh·y /slóshee/ adj. (**slosh·i·er, slosh·i·est**) 1 slushy. 2 sloppy; sentimental.

slot¹ /slot/ n. & v. • n. 1 a slit or other aperture in a machine, etc., for something (esp. a coin) to be inserted. 2 a slit, groove, channel, or long aperture into which something fits or in which something works. 3 an allotted place in an arrangement or scheme, esp. in a broadcasting schedule. • v. (**slot·ted, slot·ting**) 1 tr. & intr. place or be placed into or as if into a slot. 2 tr. provide with a slot or slots. [ME, = hollow of the breast, f. OF esclot, of unkn. orig.]

slot² /slot/ n. 1 the track of a deer, etc., esp. as shown by footprints. 2 a deer's foot. [OF esclot hoofprint of a horse, prob. f. ON slóth trail: cf. SLEUTH]

sloth /slawth, slōth/ n. 1 laziness or indolence; reluctance to make an effort. 2 any slow-moving nocturnal mammal of the family Bradypodidae or Megalonychidae of S. America, having long limbs and hooked claws for hanging upside down from branches of trees. [ME f. SLOW f. -TH²]

sloth bear n. a large-lipped black shaggy bear, Melursus ursinus, of India.

sloth·ful /sláwthfŏŏl, slóth-/ adj. lazy; characterized by sloth. □□ **sloth·ful·ly** adv. **sloth·ful·ness** n.

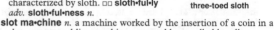
three-toed sloth

slot ma·chine n. a machine worked by the insertion of a coin in a slot, esp. a gambling machine operated by a pulled handle.

slouch /slowch/ v. & n. • v. 1 intr. stand or move or sit in a drooping, ungainly fashion. 2 tr. bend one side of the brim of (a hat) downward (opp. COCK¹). 3 intr. droop; hang down loosely. • n. 1 a slouching posture or movement, a stoop. 2 a downward bend of a hat brim (opp. COCK¹). 3 sl. an incompetent or slovenly worker or operator or performance (he's no slouch). □□ **slouch·y** adj. (**slouch·i·er, slouch·i·est**). [16th c.: orig. unkn.]

slouch hat n. a hat with a wide flexible brim.

slough¹ /slow, slōō (for 2)/ n. 1 a swamp; a miry place; a quagmire. 2 a marshy pond, backwater, etc. □□ **slough·y** adj. [OE slōh, slō(g)]

PRONUNCIATION TIP   slough

When referring to a bog or swamp, the usual pronunciation of this word rhymes with plow. But in some parts of North America, the noun is pronounced "SLOO." The verb slough is always pronounced to rhyme with rough.

slough² /sluf/ n. & v. • n. 1 a part that an animal casts or molts, esp. a snake's cast skin. 2 dead tissue that drops off from living flesh, etc. 3 a habit, etc., that has been abandoned. • v. 1 tr. cast off as a slough. 2 intr. (often foll. by off) drop off as a slough. 3 intr. cast off a slough. 4 intr. (often foll. by away, down) (of soil, rock, etc.) collapse or slide into a hole or depression. □□ **slough·y** adj. [ME, perh. rel. to LG slu(we) husk]

Slough of De·spond n. a state of hopeless depression (with ref. to Bunyan's Pilgrim's Progress).

Slo·vak /slóvaak, –vak/ n. & adj. • n. 1 a member of a Slavic people inhabiting Slovakia in central Europe, formerly part of Czechoslovakia and now an independent republic. 2 the West Slavic language of this people. • adj. of or relating to this people or language. [Slovak, etc., Slovák, rel. to SLOVENE]

slov·en /slúvən/ n. a person who is habitually untidy or careless. [ME perh. f. Flem. sloef dirty or Du. slof careless]

Slo·vene /slóveen, sləvéen/ (also **Slo·ve·ni·an** /–véeneeən/) n. & adj. • n. 1 a member of a Slavic people in Slovenia in the former Yugoslavia. 2 the language of this people. • adj. of or relating to Slovenia or its people or language. [G Slowene f. Styrian, etc., Slovenec f. OSlav. Slovĕ-, perh. rel. to slovo word]

slov·en·ly /slúvənlee/ adj. & adv. • adj. careless and untidy; unmethodical. • adv. in a slovenly manner. □□ **slov·en·li·ness** n.

slow /slō/ adj., adv., & v. • adj. 1 a taking a relatively long time to do a thing or cover a distance (also foll. by of: slow of speech). b not quick; acting or moving or done without speed. 2 gradual; obtained over a length of time (slow growth). 3 not producing, allowing, or conducive to speed (in the slow lane). 4 (of a clock, etc.) showing a time earlier than is the case. 5 (of a person) not understanding readily; not learning easily. 6 dull; uninteresting; tedious. 7 slack or sluggish (business is slow). 8 (of a fire or oven) giving little heat. 9 Photog. a (of a film) needing long exposure. b (of a lens) having a small aperture. 10 a reluctant; tardy (not slow to defend himself). b not hasty or easily moved (slow to take offense). 11 (of a tennis court, putting green, etc.) on which the ball bounces or runs slowly. • adv. 1 at a slow pace; slowly. 2 (in comb.) (slow-moving traffic). • v. (usu. foll. by down, up) 1 intr. & tr. reduce one's speed or the speed of (a vehicle, etc.). 2 intr. reduce one's pace of life; live or work less intensely. □ slow and sure of the attitude that haste is risky. slow but sure achieving the required result eventually. □□ **slow·ish** adj. **slow·ly** adv. **slow·ness** n. [OE sl áw f. Gmc]

slow·coach /slókōch/ n. Brit. = SLOWPOKE.

slow•down /slṓdown/ *n.* the action of slowing down, as in productivity.

slow hand•clap *n. Brit.* slow clapping by an audience as a sign of displeasure or boredom.

slow lo•ris *n.* see LORIS.

slow march *n.* the marching time adopted by troops in a funeral procession, etc.

slow match *n.* a slow-burning match for lighting explosives, etc.

slow mo•tion *n.* **1** the operation or speed of a film using slower projection or more rapid exposure so that actions, etc., appear much slower than usual. **2** the simulation of this in real action.

slow neu•tron *n.* a neutron with low kinetic energy esp. after moderation (cf. FAST NEUTRON (see FAST [1])).

slow poi•son *n.* a poison eventually causing death by repeated doses.

slow•poke /slṓpōk/ *n.* **1** a slow or lazy person. **2** a dull-witted person. **3** a person behind the times in opinions, etc.

slow re•ac•tor *n. Physics* a nuclear reactor using mainly slow neutrons (cf. FAST REACTOR (see FAST [1])).

slow vi•rus *n.* a progressive disease caused by a virus or viruslike organism that multiplies slowly in the host organism and has a long incubation period, such as scrapie.

slow-wit•ted *adj.* stupid.

slow•worm /slṓwǝrm/ *n.* a small European legless lizard, *Anguis fragilis*, giving birth to live young. Also called **blindworm**. [OE *slā-wyrm*: first element of uncert. orig., assim. to SLOW]

SLR *abbr.* **1** *Photog.* single-lens reflex. **2** self-loading rifle.

slub[1] /slub/ *n. & adj.* ● *n.* **1** a lump or thick place in yarn or thread. **2** fabric woven from thread, etc., with slubs. ● *adj.* (of material, etc.) with an irregular appearance caused by uneven thickness of the warp. [19th c.: orig. unkn.]

slub[2] /slub/ *n. & v.* wool slightly twisted in preparation for spinning. ● *v.tr.* (**slubbed, slub•bing**) twist (wool) in this way. [18th c.: orig. unkn.]

sludge /sluj/ *n.* **1** thick, greasy mud. **2** muddy or slushy sediment. **3** sewage. **4** *Mech.* an accumulation of dirty oil, esp. in the sump of an internal-combustion engine. **5** *Geol.* sea ice that is newly formed in small pieces. **6** (usu. *attrib.*) a muddy color (*sludge green*). □□ **sludg•y** *adj.* [cf. SLUSH]

slue var. of SLEW[1].

slug[1] /slug/ *n.* **1** a small shell-less mollusk of the class Gastropoda, usu. destructive to plants. **2** a bullet esp. of irregular shape. **b** a missile for an airgun. **3** *Printing* **a** a metal bar used in spacing. **b** a line of type in Linotype printing. **4** a shot of liquor. **5** a unit of mass, given an acceleration of 1 foot per second per second by a force of 1 lb. **6** a roundish lump of metal. **7** a disk-shaped metal piece, often used fraudulently as a coin or token. [ME *slugg(e)* sluggard, prob. f. Scand.]

slug[2] /slug/ *n. & v.* ● *v.tr.* (**slugged, slug•ging**) strike with a hard blow. ● *n.* a hard blow. □ **slug it out 1** fight it out. **2** endure; stick it out. □□ **slug•ger** *n.* [19th c.: orig. unkn.]

slug•a•bed /slúgǝbed/ *n. archaic* a lazy person who lies late in bed. [*slug* (v.) (see SLUGGARD) + ABED]

slug•gard /slúgǝrd/ *n.* a lazy, sluggish person. □□ **slug•gard•ly** *adj.* **slug•gard•li•ness** *n.* [ME f. *slug* (v.) be slothful (prob. f. Scand.: cf. SLUG[1]) + –ARD]

slug•gish /slúgish/ *adj.* inert; inactive; slow-moving; torpid; indolent (*a sluggish circulation; a sluggish stream*). □□ **slug•gish•ly** *adv.* **slug•gish•ness** *n.* [ME f. SLUG[1] or *slug* (v.): see SLUGGARD]

sluice /slōōs/ *n. & v.* ● *n.* **1** (also **sluice gate, sluice valve**) a sliding gate or other contrivance for controlling the volume or flow of water. **2** a sluiceway, esp. one for washing ore. **3** a place for rinsing. **4** the act or an instance of rinsing. **5** the water above or below or issuing through a floodgate. ● *v.* **1** *tr.* provide or wash with a sluice or sluices. **2** *tr.* rinse, pour or throw water freely upon. **3** *tr.* (foll. by *out, away*) wash out or away with a flow of water. **4** *tr.* flood with water from a sluice. **5** *intr.* (of water) rush out from a sluice, or as if from a sluice. [ME f. OF *escluse* ult. f. L *excludere* EXCLUDE]

sluice•way /slōōsway/ *n.* an artificial channel in which the flow of water is controlled by a sluice.

slum /slum/ *n. & v.* ● *n.* **1** an overcrowded and squalid back street, district, etc., usu. in a city and inhabited by very poor people. **2** a house or building unfit for human habitation. ● *v.intr.* (**slummed, slum•ming**) **1** live in slumlike conditions. **2** go about the slums through curiosity, to examine the condition of the inhabitants, or for charitable purposes. □ **slum it** *colloq.* put up with conditions less comfortable than usual. □□ **slum•my** *adj.* (**slum•mi•er, slum•mi•est**). **slum•mi•ness** *n.* [19th c.: orig. cant]

slum•ber /slúmbǝr/ *v. & n. poet. rhet.* ● *v.intr.* **1** sleep, esp. in a specified manner. **2** be idle, drowsy, or inactive. ● *n.* a sleep, esp. of a specified kind (*fell into a fitful slumber*). □ **slumber away** spend (time) in slumber. □□ **slum•ber•er** *n.* **slum•ber•ous** *adj.* **slum•brous** *adj.* [ME *slūmere*, etc. f. *slūmen* (v.) or *slū me* (n.) f. OE *slūma*: *–b–* as in *number*]

slum clear•ance *n.* the demolition of slums and rehousing of their inhabitants.

slum•lord /slúmlawrd/ *n.* the landlord of substandard housing, esp. one who fails to maintain the property while charging high rents.

slump /slump/ *n. & v.* ● *n.* **1** a sudden severe or prolonged fall in prices or values of commodities or securities. **2** a sharp or sudden decline in trade or business usu. bringing widespread unemployment. **3** a lessening of interest or commitment in a subject or undertaking. ● *v.intr.* **1** undergo a slump; fail; fall in price. **2** sit or fall heavily or limply (*slumped into a chair*). **3** lean or subside. [17th c., orig. 'sink in a bog': imit.]

slung *past* and *past part.* of SLING[1].

slunk *past* and *past part.* of SLINK[1].

slur /slǝr/ *v. & n.* ● *v.* (**slurred, slur•ring**) **1** *tr. & intr.* pronounce or write indistinctly so that the sounds or letters run into one another. **2** *tr. Mus.* **a** perform (a group of two or more notes) legato. **b** mark (notes) with a slur. **3** *tr.* put a slur on (a person or a person's character); make insinuations against. **4** *tr.* (usu. foll. by *over*) pass over (a fact, fault, etc.) lightly; conceal or minimize. ● *n.* **1** an imputation of wrongdoing; blame; stigma (*a slur on my reputation*). **2** the act or an instance of slurring in pronunciation, singing, or writing. **3** *Mus.* a curved line to show that two or more notes are to be sung to one syllable or played or sung legato. [17th c.: orig. unkn.]

slurp /slǝrp/ *v. & n.* ● *v.tr.* eat or drink noisily. ● *n.* the sound of this; a slurping gulp. [Du. *slurpen, slorpen*]

slur•ry /slúree/ *n.* (*pl.* **-ries**) **1** a semiliquid mixture of fine particles and water; thin mud. **2** thin liquid cement. **3** a fluid form of manure. **4** a residue of water and particles of coal left at coal-mine washing plants. [ME, rel. to dial. *slur* thin mud]

slush /slush/ *n.* **1** watery mud or thawing snow. **2** silly sentiment. [17th c., also *sludge* and *slutch*: orig. unkn.]

slush fund *n.* a reserve of money used for illicit purposes, esp. political bribery.

slush•y /slúshee/ *adj.* (**slush•i•er, slush•i•est**) **1** like slush; watery. **2** *colloq.* weakly sentimental; insipid. □□ **slush•i•ness** *n.*

slut /slut/ *n. derog.* a slovenly woman; a slattern; a hussy. □□ **slut•tish** *adj.* **slut•tish•ness** *n.* [ME: orig. unkn.]

sly /slī/ *adj.* (**sli•er, sli•est** or **sly•er, sly•est**) **1** cunning; crafty; wily. **2 a** (of a person) practicing secrecy or stealth. **b** (of an action, etc.) done, etc., in secret. **3** hypocritical; ironic. **4** knowing; arch; bantering; insinuating. **5** *Austral. & NZ sl.* (esp. of liquor) illicit. □ **on the sly** privately; covertly; without publicity (*smuggled some through on the sly*). □□ **sly•ly** *adv.* (also **sli•ly**). **sly•ness** *n.* [ME *sleh*, etc., f. ON *slœgr* cunning, orig. 'able to strike' f. *slóg-* past stem of *slá* strike: cf. SLEIGHT]

sly•boots /slī́bōōts/ *n. colloq.* a sly person.

sly dog *n. colloq.* a person who is discreet about mistakes or pleasures.

slype /slīp/ *n.* a covered way or passage between a cathedral, etc., transept and the chapter house or deanery. [perh. = *slipe* a long narrow piece of ground]

SM *abbr.* **1** sadomasochism. **2** sergeant major.

Sm *symb. Chem.* the element samarium.

smack[1] /smak/ *n., v., & adv.* ● *n.* **1** a sharp slap or blow esp. with the palm of the hand or a flat object. **2** a hard hit in baseball, etc. **3** a loud kiss (*gave her a hearty smack*). **4** a loud, sharp sound (*heard the smack as it hit the floor*). ● *v.* **1** *tr.* strike with the open hand, etc. **2** *tr.* part (one's lips) noisily in eager anticipation or enjoyment of food or another delight. **3** *tr.* crack (a whip). **4** *tr. & intr.* move, hit, etc., with a smack. ● *adv. colloq.* **1** with a smack. **2** suddenly; directly; violently (*landed smack on my desk*). **3** exactly (*hit it smack in the center*). □ **have a smack at** *colloq.* make an attempt, attack, etc., at. **a smack in the eye** (or **face**) *colloq.* a rebuff; a setback. [MDu. *smack(en)* of imit. orig.]

smack[2] /smak/ *v. & n.* (foll. by *of*) ● *v.intr.* **1** have a flavor of; taste of (*smacked of garlic*) **2** suggest the presence or effects of (*it smacks of nepotism*). ● *n.* **1** a flavor; a taste that suggests the presence of something. **2** (in a person's character, etc.) a barely discernible quality (*just a smack of superciliousness*). **3** (in food, etc.) a very small amount (*add a smack of ginger*). [OE *smæc*]

smack[3] /smak/ *n.* a single-masted sailboat for coasting or fishing. [Du. *smak* f. earlier *smacke*; orig. unkn.]

smack[4] /smak/ *n. sl.* a hard drug, esp. heroin, sold or used illegally. [prob. alt. of Yiddish *schmeck* sniff]

smack•er /smákǝr/ *n. sl.* **1** a loud kiss. **2** a resounding blow. **3** (usu. in *pl.*) *sl.* a dollar.

small /smawl/ *adj., n., & adv.* ● *adj.* **1** not large or big. **2** slender; thin. **3** not great in importance, amount, number, strength, or power. **4** not much; trifling (*a small token; paid small attention*). **5** insignificant; unimportant (*a small matter; from small beginnings*). **6** consisting of small particles (*small gravel; small shot*). **7** doing something on a small scale (*a small farmer*). **8** socially undistinguished; poor or humble. **9** petty; mean; ungenerous; paltry (*a small spite-*

ful nature). **10** lacking in imagination (*they have such small minds*). **11** young; not fully grown nor developed (*a small child*). • *n.* **1** the slenderest part of something (esp. small of the back). **2** (in *pl.*) *Brit. colloq.* small items of laundry, esp. underwear. • *adv.* into small pieces (*chop it small*). □ **feel** (or **look**) **small** be humiliated; appear mean or humiliated. **in a small way** unambitiously; on a small scale. **no small** considerable; a good deal of (*no small excitement about it*). **small potatoes** an insignificant person or thing. **small wonder** not very surprising; it is to be expected. □□ **small•ish** *adj.* **small•ness** *n.* [OE *smæl* f. Gmc]

small arms *n.pl.* portable firearms, esp. rifles, pistols, light machine guns, submachine guns, etc.
small beer *n.* **1** esp. *Brit.* a trifling matter; something unimportant. **2** weak beer.
small-bore *adj.* **1** denoting a firearm with a narrow bore, in international and Olympic shooting usu..22-inch caliber (5.6-millimeter bore). **2** trivial; unimportant.
small bow•er *n.* the port bower.
small cap•i•tal *n.* a capital letter which is of the same dimensions as the lowercase letters in the same typeface minus ascenders and descenders, as THIS.
small change *n.* **1** coins of low value. **2** something that is considered trivial.
small cir•cle *n.* see CIRCLE.
small-claims court *n.* a local court in which claims for small amounts can be heard and decided quickly and cheaply without legal representation.
small craft *n.* a general term for small boats and fishing vessels.
small fry *n.* **1** young children or the young of various species. **2** small or insignificant things or people.
small•hold•er /smáwlhōldər/ *n. Brit.* a person who farms a smallholding.
small•hold•ing /smáwlhōlding/ *n. Brit.* an agricultural holding smaller than a farm.
small hours *n.pl.* the early hours of the morning after midnight.
small in•tes•tine *n.* the part of the intestine that runs between the stomach and the large intestine.; the duodenum, jejunum, and ileum collectively.
small-mind•ed /smáwlmíndid/ *adj.* petty; of rigid opinions or narrow outlook. □□ **small-mind•ed•ly** *adv.* **small-mind•ed•ness** *n.*
small•pox /smáwlpoks/ *n. hist.* an acute contagious viral disease, with fever and pustules, usu. leaving permanent scars.
small print *n.* **1** printed matter in small type. **2** inconspicuous and usu. unfavorable limitations, etc., in a contract.
small prof•its and quick re•turns *n.pl.* the policy of an inexpensive store, etc., relying on large trade.
small-scale *adj.* made or occurring in small amounts or to a lesser degree.
small screen *n.* television.
small slam *n. Bridge* the bidding and winning of twelve of the thirteen tricks.
small-sword /smáwlsáwrd/ *n.* a light, tapering thrusting sword, esp. *hist.* for dueling.
small talk *n.* light social conversation about unimportant or uncontroversial matters.
small-time *adj. colloq.* unimportant or petty. □□ **small-tim•er** *n.*
small-town *adj.* relating to or characteristic of a small town; unsophisticated; provincial.
smalt /smawlt/ *n.* **1** glass colored blue with cobalt. **2** a pigment made by pulverizing this. [F f. It. *smalto* f. Gmc, rel. to SMELT[1]]

smarm /smaarm/ *v.tr. Brit. colloq.* **1** (often foll. by *down*) smooth or plaster down (hair, etc.) usu. with cream or oil. **2** flatter fulsomely. [orig. dial. (also *smalm*), of uncert. orig.]
smarm•y /smáarmee/ *adj.* (**smarm•i•er, smarm•i•est**) ingratiating; flattering; obsequious. □□ **smarm•i•ly** *adv.* **smarm•i•ness** *n.*
smart /smaart/ *adj., v., n., & adv.* • *adj.* **1 a** clever; ingenious; quick-witted (*a smart talker; gave a smart answer*). **b** keen in bargaining; quick to take advantage. **c** (of transactions, etc.) unscrupulous to the point of dishonesty. **2** well-groomed; neat; bright and fresh in appearance (*a smart suit*). **3** in good repair; showing bright colors, new paint, etc. (*a smart red bicycle*). **4** stylish; fashionable; prominent in society (*in all the smart restaurants; the smart set*). **5** quick; brisk (*set a smart pace*). **6** painfully severe; sharp; vigorous (*a smart blow*). • *v.intr.* **1** (of a person or a part of the body) feel or give acute pain or distress (*my eye smarts; smarting from the insult*). **2** (of an insult, grievance, etc.) rankle. **3** (foll. by *for*) suffer the consequences of (*you will smart for this*). • *n.* a bodily or mental sharp pain; a stinging sensation. • *adv.* smartly; in a smart manner. □ **look smart** esp. *Brit.* make haste. □□ **smart•ing•ly** *adv.* **smart•ish** *Brit. adj. & adv.* **smart•ly** *adv.* **smart•ness** *n.* [OE *smeart, smeortan*]
smart al•eck /álik/ *n.* (also **al•ec**) *colloq.* a person displaying ostentatious or smug cleverness. □□ **smart-al•eck•y** *adj.* [SMART + *Alec,* dimin. of the name *Alexander*]
smart-ass *n. sl.* = SMART ALECK.
smart bomb *n.* a bomb that can be guided directly to its target by use of radio waves, television, or lasers.
smart•en /smáart'n/ *v.tr. & intr.* (usu. foll. by *up*) make or become smart or smarter.
smart mon•ey *n.* **1** money paid or exacted as a penalty or compensation. **2** money invested by persons with expert knowledge.
smart•y /smáartee/ *n.* (*pl.* **-ies**) *colloq.* **1** a know-it-all; a smart aleck. **2** esp. *Brit.* a smartly dressed person; a member of a smart set. [SMART]
smart•y-pants *n.* = SMARTY 1.
smash /smash/ *v., n., & adv.* • *v.* **1** *tr. & intr.* (often foll. by *up*) **a** break into pieces; shatter. **b** bring or come to sudden or complete destruction, defeat, or disaster. **2** *tr.* (foll. by *into, through*) (of a vehicle, etc.) move with great force and impact. **3** *tr. & intr.* (foll. by *in*) break in with a crushing blow (*smashed in the window*). **4** *tr.* (in tennis, squash, etc.) hit (a ball, etc.) with great force, esp. downward (*smashed it back over the net*). **5** *intr.* esp. *Brit.* (of a business, etc.) go bankrupt; come to grief. **6** *tr.* (as **smashed** *adj.*) *sl.* intoxicated. • *n.* **1** the act or an instance of smashing; a violent fall, collision, or disaster. **2** the sound of this. **3** (in full **smash hit**) a very successful play, song, performer, etc. **4** a stroke in tennis, squash, etc., in which the ball is hit, esp. downward with great force. **5** a violent blow with a fist, etc. **6** esp. *Brit.* bankruptcy; a series of commercial failures. **7** a mixture of liquor (usu. brandy) with flavored water and ice. • *adv.* with a smash (*fell smash on the floor*). □ **go to smash** *Brit.* be ruined, etc. [18th c., prob. imit. after *smack, smite* and *bash, mash,* etc.]
smash•er /smáshər/ *n.* **1** a person or thing that smashes. **2** *Brit. colloq.* a very beautiful or pleasing person or thing.
smash•ing /smáshing/ *adj. colloq.* superlative; excellent; wonderful; beautiful. □□ **smash•ing•ly** *adv.*
smash-up /smáshəp/ *n. colloq.* a violent collision, esp. of motor vehicles; a complete smash.
smat•ter /smátər/ *n.* (also **smat•ter•ing**) **1** a slight superficial knowledge of a language or subject. **2** *colloq.* a small quantity. □□ **smat•ter•er** *n.* [ME *smatter* talk ignorantly, prate: orig. unkn.]
smear /smeer/ *v. & n.* • *v.tr.* **1** daub or mark with a greasy or sticky substance or with something that stains. **2** blot; smudge; obscure the outline of (writing, artwork, etc.). **3** defame the character of; slander; attempt to or succeed in discrediting (a person or his or her name) publicly. • *n.* **1** the act or an instance of smearing. **2** *Med.* **a** material smeared on a microscopic slide, etc., for examination. **b** a specimen of this. □□ **smear•er** *n.* **smear•y** *adj.* [OE *smierwan* f. Gmc]
smear test *n.* = CERVICAL SMEAR.
smeg•ma /smégmə/ *n.* a sebaceous secretion in the folds of the skin, esp. of the foreskin. □□ **smeg•mat•ic** /-mátik/ *adj.* [L f. Gk *smēgma -atos* detergent f. *smēkhō* cleanse]
smell /smel/ *n. & v.* • *n.* **1** the faculty of perceiving odors or scents (*has a fine sense of smell*). **2** the quality in substances that is perceived by this (*the smell of thyme; this rose has no smell*). **3** an unpleasant odor. **4** the act of inhaling to ascertain smell. • *v.* (*past* and *past part.* **smelled** or **smelt** /smelt/) **1** *tr.* perceive the smell of; examine by smell (*thought I could smell gas*). **2** *intr.* emit odor. **3** *intr.* seem by smell to be (*this milk smells sour*). **4** *intr.* (foll. by *of*) **a** be redolent of (*smells of fish*). **b** be suggestive of (*smells of dishonesty*). **5** *intr.* stink; be rank. **6** *tr.* perceive as if by smell; detect; discern; suspect (*smell a bargain; smell blood*). **7** *intr.* have or use a sense of smell. **8** *intr.* (foll. by *about*) sniff or search about. **9** *intr.* (foll. by *at*) inhale the smell of. □ **smell out 1** detect by smell; find out by investigation. **2** (of a dog, etc.) hunt out by smell. **smell a rat** be-

gin to suspect trickery, etc. □□ **smell·a·ble** *adj.* **smell·er** *n.* **smell·less** *adj.* [ME *smel(le)*, prob. f. OE]

smell·ing salts *n.pl.* ammonium carbonate mixed with scent to be sniffed as a restorative in faintness, etc.

smell·y /smélee/ *adj.* (**smell·i·er**, **smell·i·est**) having a strong or unpleasant smell. □□ **smell·i·ness** *n.*

smelt[1] /smelt/ *v.tr.* **1** separate metal from (ore) by melting. **2** extract or refine (metal) in this way. □□ **smelt·er** *n.* **smelt·er·y** *n.* (*pl.* ·**ies**) [MDu., MLG *smelten*, rel. to MELT]

smelt[2] *past* and *past part.* of SMELL.

smelt[3] /smelt/ *n.* (*pl.* same or **smelts**) any small green and silver fish of the genus *Osmerus*, etc., allied to salmon and used as food. [OE, of uncert. orig.: cf. SMOLT]

smew /smyoo/ *n.* a small merganser, *Mergus albellus*. [17th c., rel. to *smeath*, *smee* = smew, widgeon, etc.]

smid·gen /smíjən/ *n.* (also **smid·gin**) *colloq.* a small bit or amount. [perh. f. *smitch* in the same sense: cf. dial. *smitch* wood smoke]

smi·lax /smílaks/ *n.* **1** any climbing shrub of the genus *Smilax*, the roots of some species of which yield sarsaparilla. **2** a climbing kind of asparagus, *Asparagus medeoloides*, used decoratively by florists. [L f. Gk, = bindweed]

smile /smīl/ *v. & n.* ● *v.* **1** *intr.* relax the features into a pleased or kind or gently skeptical expression or a forced imitation of these, usu. with the lips parted and the corners of the mouth turned up. **2** *tr.* express by smiling (*smiled their consent*). **3** *tr.* give (a smile) of a specified kind (*smiled a sardonic smile*). **4** *intr.* (foll. by *on*, *upon*) adopt a favorable attitude toward; encourage (*fortune smiled on me*). **5** *intr.* have a bright or favorable aspect (*the smiling countryside*). **6** *tr.* (foll. by *away*) drive (a person's anger, etc.) away (*smiled their tears away*). **7** *intr.* (foll. by *at*) **a** ridicule or show indifference to (*smiled at my feeble attempts*). **b** favor; smile on. **8** *tr.* (foll. by *into*, *out of*) bring (a person) into or out of a specified mood, etc., by smiling (*smiled them into agreement*). ● *n.* **1** the act or an instance of smiling. **2** a smiling expression or aspect. □ **come up smiling** *colloq.* recover from adversity and cheerfully face what is to come. □□ **smile·less** *adj.* **smil·er** *n.* **smil·ey** *adj.* **smil·ing·ly** *adv.* [ME perh. f. Scand., rel. to SMIRK: cf. OHG *smîlenter*]

smirch /smərch/ *v. & n.* ● *v.tr.* mark, soil, or smear (a thing, a person's reputation, etc.). ● *n.* **1** a spot or stain. **2** a blot (on one's character, etc.). [ME: orig. unkn.]

smirk /smərk/ *n. & v.* ● *n.* an affected, conceited, or silly smile. ● *v.intr.* put on or wear a smirk. □□ **smirk·er** *n.* **smirk·ing·ly** *adv.* **smirk·y** *adj.* **smirk·i·ly** *adv.* [OE *sme(a)rcian*]

smit /smit/ *archaic past part.* of SMITE.

---

smite /smīt/ *v. & n.* ● *v.* (*past* **smote** /smōt/; *past part.* **smit·ten** /smít'n/) *archaic* or *literary* **1** *tr.* strike or hit. **2** *tr.* chastise; defeat. **3** *tr.* (in *passive*) **a** have a sudden strong effect on (*was smitten by his conscience*). **b** infatuate; fascinate (*was smitten by her beauty*). **4** *intr.* (foll. by *on*, *upon*) come forcibly or abruptly upon. ● *n.* a blow or stroke. □□ **smit·er** *n.* [OE *smītan* smear f. Gmc]

smith /smith/ *n. & v.* ● *n.* **1** (esp. in *comb.*) a worker in metal (*goldsmith*; *tinsmith*). **2** a person who forges iron; a blacksmith. **3** a craftsman (*wordsmith*). ● *v.tr.* make or treat by forging. [OE f. Gmc]

smith·er·eens /smíthəréenz/ *n.pl.* (also **smith·ers** /smíthərz/) small fragments (*smash into smithereens*). [19th c.: orig. unkn.]

smith·er·y /smíthəree/ *n.* (*pl.* ·**ies**) **1** a smith's work. **2** (esp. in naval dockyards) a smithy.

smith·y /smíthee/ *n.* (*pl.* ·**ies**) a blacksmith's workshop; a forge. [ME f. ON *smithja*]

smit·ten *past part.* of SMITE.

smock /smok/ *n. & v.* ● *n.* **1** a loose shirtlike garment with the upper part closely gathered in smocking. **2** a loose overall. ● *v.tr.* adorn with smocking. [OE *smoc*, prob. rel. to OE *smūgan* creep, ON *smjúga* put on a garment]

smock·ing /smóking/ *n.* an ornamental effect on cloth made by gathering the material tightly into pleats, often with embroidered stitches in a decorative pattern.

smog /smog, smawg/ *n.* fog intensified by smoke. □□ **smog·gy** *adj.* (**smog·gi·er**, **smog·gi·est**) [portmanteau word]

smoke /smōk/ *n. & v.* ● *n.* **1** a visible suspension of carbon, etc., in air, emitted from a burning substance. **2** an act or period of smoking tobacco (*had a quiet smoke*). **3** *colloq.* a cigarette or cigar (*got a smoke?*). **4** (**the Smoke**) *Brit. & Austral. colloq.* a big city, esp. London. ● *v.* **1** *intr.* **a** emit smoke or visible vapor (*smoking ruins*). **b** (of a lamp, etc.) burn badly with the emission of smoke. **c** (of a chimney or fire) discharge smoke into the room. **2** *a intr.* inhale and exhale the smoke of a cigarette or cigar or pipe. **b** *intr.* do this habitually. **c** *tr.* use (a cigarette, etc.) in this way. **3** *tr.* darken or preserve by the action of smoke (*smoked salmon*). **4** *tr.* spoil the taste of in cooking **5** *tr.* **a** rid of insects, etc., by the action of smoke. **b** subdue (insects, esp. bees) in this way. **6** *tr. archaic* make fun of. **7** *tr.* bring (oneself) into a specified state by smoking. □ **go up in smoke** *colloq.* **1** be destroyed by fire. **2** (of a plan, etc.) come to nothing. **smoke out 1** drive out by means of smoke. **2** drive out of hiding or secrecy, etc. □□ **smok·a·ble** *adj.* (also **smoke·a·ble**) [OE *smoca* f. weak grade of the stem of *smēocan* emit smoke]

smoke bomb *n.* a bomb that emits dense smoke on exploding.

smoke bush *n.* = SMOKE TREE.

smoked glass *n.* glass darkened with smoke.

smoke-dried *adj.* cured in smoke.

smoke·less /smōklis/ *adj.* having or producing little or no smoke.

smok·er /smōkər/ *n.* **1** a person or thing that smokes, esp. a person who habitually smokes tobacco. **2** a compartment on a train, in which smoking is allowed. **3** an informal social gathering of men.

smoke ring *n.* smoke from a cigarette, etc., exhaled in the shape of a ring.

smoke room *n. Brit.* = SMOKING ROOM.

smok·er's cough *n.* an ailment caused by excessive smoking.

smoke screen *n.* **1** a cloud of smoke diffused to conceal (esp. military) operations. **2** a device or ruse for disguising one's activities.

smoke·stack /smōkstak/ *n.* **1** a chimney or funnel for discharging the smoke of a locomotive or steamer. **2** a tall chimney.

smoke tree *n.* any ornamental shrub of the genus *Cotinus*, with feathery smokelike fruit stalks.

smok·ing /smōking/ *n. & adj.* ● *n.* the act of inhaling and exhaling from a cigarette, cigar, etc. ● *adj.* giving off smoke. [pres. part. of SMOKE]

smok·ing gun *n.* something that serves as indisputable proof, esp. of a crime.

smok·ing jack·et *n.* an ornamental jacket formerly worn by men while smoking.

smok·ing room *n.* a room in a hotel, club, house, etc., kept for smoking in.

smok·y /smōkee/ *adj.* (also **smok·ey**) (**smok·i·er**, **smok·i·est**) **1** emitting, veiled or filled with, or obscured by, smoke (*smoky fire*; *smoky room*). **2** stained with or colored like smoke (*smoky glass*). **3** having the taste or flavor of smoked food (*smoky bacon*). □□ **smok·i·ly** *adv.* **smok·i·ness** *n.*

smok·y quartz *n.* a semiprecious variety of quartz ranging in color from light grayish-brown to nearly black.

smol·der /smōldər/ *v. & n.* (*Brit.* **smoul·der**) ● *v.intr.* **1** burn slowly with smoke but without a flame; slowly burn internally or invisibly. **2** (of emotions, etc.) exist in a suppressed or concealed state. **3** (of a person) show silent or suppressed anger, hatred, etc. ● *n.* a smoldering or slow-burning fire. [ME, rel. to LG *smöln*, MDu. *smö len*]

· ·

smolt /smōlt/ *n.* a young salmon migrating to the sea for the first time. [ME (orig. Sc. & N.Engl.): orig. unkn.]

smooch /smōoch/ *n. & v. colloq.* ● *n.* **1** a spell of kissing and caressing. **2** *Brit.* a period of slow dancing close together. ● *v.intr.* engage in a smooch. □□ **smooch·er** *n.* **smooch·y** *adj.* (**smooch·i·er, smooch·i·est**). [dial. *smouch* imit.]

smoodge /smōoj/ *v.intr.* (also **smooge**) *Austral.* & *NZ* **1** behave in a fawning or ingratiating manner. **2** behave amorously. [prob. var. of dial. *smudge* kiss, sidle up to, beg in a sneaking way]

smooth /smōoth/ *adj., v., n., & adv.* ● *adj.* **1** having a relatively even and regular surface; free from perceptible projections, lumps, indentations, and roughness. **2** not wrinkled, pitted, scored, or hairy (*smooth skin*) **3** that can be traversed without check. **4** (of liquids) of even consistency; without lumps (*mix to a smooth paste*). **5** (of the sea, etc.) without waves or undulations. **6** (of a journey, passage, progress, etc.) untroubled by difficulties or adverse conditions. **7** having an easy flow or correct rhythm (*smooth breathing*; *a smooth meter*). **8 a** not harsh in sound or taste. **b** (of wine, etc.) not astringent. **9** (of a person, his or her manner, etc.) suave, conciliatory, flattering, unruffled, or polite (*a smooth talker; he's very smooth*). **10** (of movement, etc.) not suddenly varying; not jerky. ● *v.* **1** *tr. & intr.* (often foll. by *out, down*) make or become smooth. **2** (often foll. by *out, down, over, away*) **a** *tr.* reduce or get rid of (differences, faults, difficulties, etc.) in fact or appearance. **b** *intr.* (of difficulties, etc.) diminish; become less obtrusive (*it will all smooth over*). **3** *tr.* modify (a graph, curve, etc.) so as to lessen irregularities. **4** *tr.* free from impediments or discomfort (*smooth the way; smooth the declining years*). ● *n.* **1** a smoothing touch or stroke (*gave his hair a smooth*). **2** the easy part of life (*take the rough with the smooth*). ● *adv.* smoothly (*the course of true love never did run smooth*). □□ **smooth·a·ble** *adj.* **smooth·er** *n.* **smooth·ish** *adj.* **smooth·ly** *adv.* **smooth·ness** *n.* [OE *smōth*]

smooth·bore /smōothbawr/ *adj. & n.* ● *adj.* (of a gun) having an unrifled barrel. ● *n.* a gun with an unrifled barrel.

smooth-faced *adj.* **1** beardless. **2** hypocritically friendly.

smooth·ie /smōoṯhee/ *n. colloq.* **1** a person with a smooth, suave manner (see SMOOTH *adj.* 9). **2** a thick, smooth drink of fresh fruit puréed with milk, yogurt, or ice cream. [SMOOTH]

smooth·ing i·ron *n. hist.* a flatiron.

smooth mus·cle *n.* a muscle without striations, usu. occurring in hollow organs and performing involuntary functions.

smooth talk *n. colloq.* bland specious language. □□ **smooth-talk** *v.*

smooth-tongued *adj.* insincerely flattering.

smor·gas·bord /smáwrgəsbawrd/ *n.* a buffet offering a variety of hot and cold meats, salads, hors d'oeuvres, etc. [Sw. f. *smör* butter + *gås* goose, lump of butter + *bord* table]

smor·zan·do /smawrtsaándō/ *adj., adv., & n. Mus.* ● *adj. & adv.* dying away. ● *n.* (*pl.* **·dos** or **smor·zan·di** /–dee/) a smorzando passage. [It., gerund of *smorzare* extinguish]

smote *past of* SMITE.

smoth·er /smúthər/ *v. & n.* ● *v.* **1** *tr.* suffocate; stifle; kill by stopping the breath of or excluding air from. **2** *tr.* (foll. by *with*) overwhelm with (kisses, gifts, kindness, etc.) (*smothered with affection*). **3** *tr.* (foll. by *in, with*) cover entirely in or with (*chicken smothered in mayonnaise*). **4** *tr.* extinguish or deaden (a fire or flame) by covering it or heaping it with ashes, etc. **5** *intr.* **a** die of suffocation. **b** have difficulty breathing. **6** *tr.* (often foll. by *up*) suppress or conceal; keep from notice or publicity. **7** *tr.* defeat rapidly or utterly. ● *n.* **1** a cloud of dust or smoke. **2** obscurity caused by this. [ME *smorther* f. the stem of OE *smorian* suffocate]

smoth·ered mate *n. Chess* checkmate in which the king, having no vacant square to move to, is checkmated by a knight.

smoth·er·y /smúthəree/ *adj.* tending to smother; stifling.

smoul·der *Brit.* var. of SMOLDER.

Smrit·i /smríteee/ *n.* Hindu traditional teachings on religion, etc. [Skr. *smr̥ti* remembrance]

smudge¹ /smuj/ *n. & v.* ● *n.* **1** a blurred or smeared line or mark; a blot; a smear of dirt. **2** a stain or blot on a person's character, etc. ● *v.* **1** *tr.* make a smudge on. **2** *intr.* become smeared or blurred (*smudges easily*). **3** *tr.* smear or blur the lines of (writing, drawing, etc.) (*smudge the outline*). **4** *tr.* defile, sully, stain, or disgrace (a person's name, character, etc.). □□ **smudge·less** *adj.* [ME: orig. unkn.]

smudge² /smuj/ *n.* an outdoor fire with dense smoke made to keep off insects, protect plants against frost, etc. [*smudge* (v.) cure (herring) by smoking (16th c.: orig. unkn.)]

smudge pot *n.* a container holding burning material that produces a smudge.

smudg·y /smújee/ *adj.* (**smudg·i·er, smudg·i·est**) **1** smudged. **2** likely to produce smudges. □□ **smudg·i·ly** *adv.* **smudg·i·ness** *n.*

smug /smug/ *adj.* (**smug·ger, smug·gest**) self-satisfied; complacent. □□ **smug·ly** *adv.* **smug·ness** *n.* [16th c., orig. 'neat' f. LG *smuk* pretty]

smug·gle /smúgəl/ *v.tr.* **1** (also *absol.*) import or export (goods) illegally, esp. without payment of customs duties. **2** (foll. by *in, out*)

convey secretly. **3** (foll. by *away*) put into concealment. □□ **smug·gler** *n.* **smug·gling** *n.* [17th c. (also *smuckle*) f. LG *smukkeln smuggelen*]

smut /smut/ *n. & v.* ● *n.* **1** a small flake of soot, etc. **2** a spot or smudge made by this. **3** obscene or lascivious talk, pictures, or stories. **4 a** fungal disease of cereals in which the affected parts change to black powder. **b** any fungus of the order Ustilaginales causing this. ● *v.* (**smut·ted, smut·ting**) **1** *tr.* mark with smuts. **2** *tr.* infect (a plant) with smut. **3** *intr.* (of a plant) contract smut. □□ **smut·ty** *adj.* (**smut·ti·er, smut·ti·est**) (esp. in sense 3 of *n.*). **smut·ti·ly** *adv.* **smut·ti·ness** *n.* [rel. to LG *smutt*, MHG *smutz(en)*, etc.: cf. OE *smitt(ian)* smear, and SMUDGE¹]

Sn *symb. Chem.* the element tin.

snack /snak/ *n. & v.* ● *n.* **1** a light, casual, or hurried meal. **2** a small amount of food eaten between meals. **3** *Austral. sl.* something easy to accomplish. ● *v.intr.* eat a snack. [ME, orig. a snap or bite, f. MDu. *snac(k)* f. *snacken* (v.), var. of *snappen*]

snack bar *n.* a place where snacks are sold.

snaf·fle /snáfəl/ *n. & v.* ● *n.* (in full **snaffle bit**) a simple bridle bit without a curb and usu. with a single rein. ● *v.tr.* **1** put a snaffle on. **2** *Brit. colloq.* steal; seize; appropriate. [prob. f. LG or Du.: cf. MLG, MDu. *snavel* beak, mouth]

sna·fu /snafōo/ *adj. & n. sl.* ● *adj.* in utter confusion or chaos. ● *n.* this state. [acronym for "situation normal: *all* fouled (or fucked) *up*"]

snag¹ /snag/ *n. & v.* ● *n.* **1** an unexpected or hidden obstacle or drawback. **2** a jagged or projecting point or broken stump. **3** a tear in material, etc. **4** a short tine of an antler. ● *v.tr.* (**snagged, snag·ging**) **1** catch or tear on a snag. **2** clear (land, a waterway, a tree trunk, etc.) of snags. **3** catch or obtain by quick action. □□ **snagged** *adj.* **snag·gy** *adj.* [prob. f. Scand.: cf. Norw. dial. *snag (e)* sharp point]

snag² /snag/ *n.* (usu. in *pl.*) *Austral. sl.* a sausage. [20th c.: orig. unkn.]

snag·gle·tooth /snágəl/ *n.* (*pl.* **snag·gle·teeth**) an irregular or projecting tooth. □□ **snag·gle·toothed** *adj.* [SNAG¹ + –LE²]

snail /snayl/ *n.* **1** any slow-moving gastropod mollusk with a spiral shell to enclose the whole body. **2** a slow or lazy person; a dawdler. □□ **snail·like** *adj.* [OE *snæg(e)l* f. Gmc]

snail

snail's pace *n.* a very slow movement. □□ **snail-paced** *adj.*

snake /snayk/ *n. & v.* ● *n.* **1 a** any long, limbless reptile of the suborder Ophidia, including boas, pythons, and poisonous forms such as cobras and vipers. **b** a limbless lizard or amphibian. **2** (also **snake in the grass**) a treacherous person or secret enemy. **3 a** a plumber's snakelike device for clearing obstructed pipes. **b** an electrician's wirepuller. ● *v.intr.* move or twist like a snake. □□ **snake·like** *adj.* [OE *snaca*]

snake·bird /snáykbərd/ *n.* a fish-eating bird, *Anhinga anhinga*, with a long slender neck.

snake charm·er *n.* a person appearing to make snakes move by music, etc.

snake oil *n.* **1** any of various concoctions sold as medicine but without medicinal value. **2** speech, writing, or actions intended to deceive; bunkum.

snake pit *n.* **1** a pit containing snakes. **2** a scene of vicious behavior. **3** a mental hospital in which inhumane treatment is known or suspect.

snake·root /snáykrōot, –rŏŏt/ *n.* any of various N. American plants, esp. *Cimicifuga racemosa*, with roots reputed to contain an antidote to snake's poison.

snake's-head *n.* a bulbous plant, *Fritillaria meleagris*, with bell-shaped pendent flowers.

snak·y /snáykee/ *adj.* **1** of or like a snake. **2** winding; sinuous. **3** showing coldness, ingratitude, venom, or guile. **4 a** infested with snakes. **b** (esp. of the hair of the Furies) composed of snakes. **5** *Austral. sl.* angry; irritable. □□ **snak·i·ly** *adv.* **snak·i·ness** *n.*

snap /snap/ *v., n., adv., & adj.* ● *v.* (**snapped, snap·ping**) **1** *intr. & tr.* break suddenly or with a snap. **2** *intr. & tr.* emit or cause to emit a sudden sharp sound or crack. **3** *intr. & tr.* open or close with a snapping sound (*the bag snapped shut*). **4** *intr.* (often foll. by *at*) speak irritably or spitefully to (a person) (*did not mean to snap at you*). **b** *tr.* say irritably or spitefully. **5** *intr.* (often foll. by *at*) (esp. of a dog, etc.) make a sudden audible bite. **6** *tr. & intr.* move quickly (*snap into action*). **7** *tr.* take a snapshot of. **8** *tr. Football* put (the ball) into play on the ground by a quick backward movement. ● *n.* **1** an act or sound of snapping. **2** (often in *comb.*) a crisp cookie (*gingersnap*). **3** a snapshot. **4** (in full **cold snap**) a sudden brief spell of cold weather. **5** esp. *Brit.* **a** a card game in which players call "snap" when two similar cards are exposed. **b** (as *int.*) on noticing the (often unexpected) similarity of two things. **6** crispness of style; fresh vigor or liveliness in action; zest; dash; spring. **7** *sl.* an easy task (*it was a snap*). **8** *Football* the beginning of a play, when the ball is passed quickly back. ● *adv.* with the sound of a snap (*heard it go snap*). ● *adj.*

done or taken on the spur of the moment, unexpectedly, or without notice (*snap decision*). □ **snap at 1** accept (bait, a chance, etc.) eagerly **2** see senses 4a and 5 of *v*. **snap one's fingers 1** make an audible fillip, esp. in rhythm to music, etc. **2** (often foll. by *at*) defy; show contempt for. **snap off** break off or bite off. **snap out** say irritably. **snap out of** *sl*. get rid of (a mood, habit, etc.) by a sudden effort. **snap up 1** accept (an offer, a bargain) quickly or eagerly. **2** pick up or catch hastily or smartly. **3** interrupt (another person) before he or she has finished speaking. □□ **snap•pa•ble** *adj*. **snap•ping•ly** *adv*. [prob. f. MDu. or MLG *snappen*, partly imit.]

snap bean *n*. a bean grown for its pods, which are broken into pieces and eaten as a vegetable.

snap bolt *n*. (also **snap lock**) a bolt, etc., which locks automatically when a door or window closes.

snap-brim *adj*. (of a hat) with a brim that can be turned up and down at opposite sides.

snap•drag•on /snápdragən/ *n*. a plant, *Antirrhinum majus*, with a bag-shaped flower like a dragon's mouth.

snap fas•ten•er *n*. a two-piece device that snaps together, used esp. on garments, etc. (e.g., instead of buttons).

snap hook *n*. a hook with a spring allowing the entrance but barring the escape of a cord, link, etc.

snap•per /snápər/ *n*. **1** a person or thing that snaps. **2** any of several fish of the family Lutjanidae, used as food. **3** a snapping turtle. **4** a party cracker (as a toy).

snap•ping tur•tle *n*. any large American freshwater turtle of the family Chelydridae which seizes prey with a snap of its jaws.

snap•pish /snápish/ *adj*. **1** (of a person's manner or a remark) curt; ill-tempered; sharp. **2** (of a dog, etc.) inclined to snap. □□ **snap•pish•ly** *adv*. **snap•pish•ness** *n*.

snap•py /snápee/ *adj*. (**snap•pi•er, snap•pi•est**) *colloq*. **1** brisk; full of zest. **2** neat and elegant (*a snappy dresser*). **3** snappish. □ **make it snappy** be quick about it. □□ **snap•pi•ly** *adv*. **snap•pi•ness** *n*.

snap•shot /snápshot/ *n*. a casual photograph taken quickly with a hand-held camera.

snare /snair/ *n. & v*. • *n*. **1** a trap for catching birds or animals, esp. with a noose of wire or cord. **2** a thing that acts as a temptation. **3** a device for tempting an enemy, etc., to expose himself or herself to danger, failure, loss, capture, defeat, etc. **4** (in *sing*. or *pl*.) *Mus*. twisted strings of gut, hide, or wire stretched across the lower head of a snare drum to produce a rattling sound. **5** (in full **snare drum**) a small, double-headed drum fitted with snares, usu. played in a jazz or military band. **6** *Surgery* a wire loop for extracting polyps, etc. • *v.tr*. **1** catch (a bird, etc.) in a snare. **2** ensnare; lure or trap (a person) with a snare. □□ **snar•er** *n*. (also in *comb*.). [OE *sneare* f. ON *snara*: senses 4 & 5 prob. f. MLG or MDu.]

snark /snaark/ *n*. a fabulous animal, orig. the subject of a nonsense poem. [*The Hunting of the Snark* (1876) by Lewis Carroll]

snarl[1] /snaarl/ *v. & n*. • *v*. **1** *intr*. (of a dog) make an angry growl with bared teeth. **2** *intr*. (of a person) speak cynically; make bad-tempered complaints or criticisms. **3** *tr*. (often foll. by *out*) **a** utter in a snarling tone. **b** express (discontent, etc.) by snarling. • *n*. the act or sound of snarling. □□ **snarl•er** *n*. **snarl•ing•ly** *adv*. **snarl•y** *adj*. (**snarl•i•er, snarl•i•est**). [earlier *snar* f. (M)LG, MHG *snarren*]

snarl[2] /snaarl/ *v. & n*. • *v*. **1** *tr*. (often foll. by *up*) twist; entangle; confuse and hamper the movement of (traffic, etc.). **2** *intr*. (often foll. by *up*) become entangled, congested, or confused. **3** *tr*. adorn the exterior of (a narrow metal vessel) with raised work. • *n*. a knot or tangle. [ME f. *snare* (n. & v.): sense 3 perh. f. noun in dial. sense 'knot in wood']

snarl-up *n*. *colloq*. a traffic jam; a muddle; a mistake.

snatch /snach/ *v. & n*. • *v.tr*. **1** seize quickly, eagerly, or unexpectedly, esp. with outstretched hands. **2** steal (a wallet, handbag, etc.); kidnap. **3** secure with difficulty (*snatched an hour's rest*). **4** (foll. by *away, from*) take away or from, esp. suddenly (*snatched away my hand*). **5** (foll. by *from*) rescue narrowly (*snatched from the jaws of death*). **6** (foll. by *at*) a try to seize by stretching or grasping suddenly. **b** take (an offer, etc.) eagerly. • *n*. **1** an act of snatching (*made a snatch at it*). **2** a fragment of a song or talk, etc. (*caught a snatch of their conversation*). **3** *sl*. a kidnapping. **4** (in weight lifting) the rapid raising of a weight from the floor to above the head. **5** a short spell of activity, etc. □ **in** (or **by**) **snatches** in fits and starts. □□ **snatch•er** *n*. (esp. in sense 3 of *n*.). **snatch•y** *adj*. [ME *snecchen, sna(c)che*, perh. rel. to SNACK]

snaz•zy /snázee/ *adj*. (**snaz•zi•er, snaz•zi•est**) *sl*. smart or attractive, esp. in an ostentatious way. □□ **snaz•zi•ly** *adv*. **snaz•zi•ness** *n*. [20th c.: orig. unkn.]

sneak /sneek/ *v., n., & adj*. • *v*. **1** *intr. & tr*. (foll. by *in, out, past, away*, etc.) go or convey furtively; slink. **2** *tr. sl*. steal unobserved; make off with. **3** *intr. Brit. school sl*. tell tales; turn informer. **4** *intr*. (as **sneaking** *adj*.) a furtive; undisclosed (*have a sneaking affection for him*). **b** persistent in one's mind; nagging (*a sneaking feeling that it is not right*). • *n*. **1** a mean-spirited, cowardly, underhanded person. **2** *Brit. school sl*. a tattletale. • *adj*. acting or done without warning; secret (*a sneak attack*). □□ **sneak•ing•ly** *adv*. [16th c., prob. dial.: perh. rel. to ME *snike*, OE *snīcan* creep]

sneak•er /sneekər/ *n*. each of a pair of rubber-soled canvas, etc., shoes.

sneak thief *n*. a thief who steals without breaking in; a pickpocket.

sneak•y /sneekee/ *adj*. (**sneak•i•er, sneak•i•est**) given to or characterized by sneaking; furtive; mean. □□ **sneak•i•ly** *adv*. **sneak•i•ness** *n*.

sneck /snek/ *n. & v*. *Sc. & No. of Engl*. • *n*. a latch. • *v.tr*. latch (a door, etc); close or fasten with a sneck. [ME, rel. to SNATCH]

sneer /sneer/ *n. & v*. • *n*. a derisive smile or remark. • *v*. **1** *intr*. (often foll. by *at*) smile derisively. **2** *tr*. say sneeringly. **3** *intr*. (often foll. by *at*) speak covertly or ironically (*sneered at his attempts*). □□ **sneer•er** *n*. **sneer•ing•ly** *adv*. [16th c.: orig. unkn.]

sneeze /sneez/ *n. & v*. • *n*. **1** a sudden involuntary expulsion of air from the nose and mouth caused by irritation of the nostrils. **2** the sound of this. • *v.intr*. make a sneeze. □ **not to be sneezed at** *colloq*. not contemptible; considerable; notable. □□ **sneez•er** *n*. **sneez•y** *adj*. [ME *snese*, app. alt. of obs. *fnese* f. OE *-fnēsan*, ON *fnýsa* & replacing earlier and less expressive *nese*]

sneeze•wort /sneezwort, -wawrt/ *n*. a kind of yarrow, *Achillea ptarmica*, whose dried leaves are used to induce sneezing.

Snell's law /snelz/ *n*. *Physics* the law that the ratio of the sines of the angles of incidence and refraction of a wave are constant when it passes between two given media. [W. *Snell*, Du. mathematician d. 1626]

snib /snib/ *v. & n*. *Sc. & Ir*. • *v.tr*. (**snibbed, snib•bing**) bolt, fasten, or lock (a door, etc.). • *n*. a lock, catch, or fastening for a door or window. [19th c.: orig. uncert.]

snick /snik/ *v. & n*. • *v.tr*. **1** cut a small notch in. **2** make a small incision in. **3** *Cricket* deflect (the ball) slightly with the bat. • *n*. **1** a small notch or cut. **2** *Cricket* a slight deflection of the ball by the bat. [18th c.: prob. f *snick-a-snee* fight with knives]

snick•er /sníkər/ *v. & n. • v.intr*. **1** = SNIGGER *v*. **2** whinny; neigh. • *n*. **1** = SNIGGER *n*. **2** a whinny, a neigh. □□ **snick•er•ing•ly** *adv*. [imit.]

snick•et /sníkit/ *n Brit. dial*. a narrow passage between houses; an alleyway. [orig. unkn.]

snide /snid/ *adj. & n. • adj*. **1** sneering; slyly derogatory; insinuating. **2** counterfeit; bogus. **3** mean; underhanded. • *n*. a snide person or remark. □□ **snide•ly** *adv*. **snide•ness** *n*. [19th-c. colloq.: orig. unkn.]

sniff /snif/ *v. & n. • v*. **1** *intr*. draw up air audibly through the nose to stop it running or to detect a smell or as an expression of contempt. **2** *tr*. (often foll. by *up*) draw in (a scent, drug, liquid, or air) through the nose. **3** *tr*. draw in the scent of (food, drink, flowers, etc.) through the nose. • *n*. **1** an act or sound of sniffing. **2** the amount of air, etc., sniffed up. □ **sniff at 1** try the smell of; show interest in. **2** show contempt for or discontent with. **sniff out** detect; discover by investigation. □□ **sniff•ing•ly** *adv*. [ME, imit.]

snif•fer /snífər/ *n*. **1** a person who sniffs, esp. one who sniffs a drug or toxic substances (often in *comb.*: *glue-sniffer*). **2** *sl*. the nose. **3** *colloq*. any device for detecting gas, radiation, etc.

sniff•er dog *n*. *colloq*. a dog trained to sniff out drugs or explosives.

snif•fle /snífəl/ *v. & n. • v.intr*. sniff slightly or repeatedly. • *n*. **1** the act of sniffling. **2** (in *sing*. or *pl*.) a cold in the head causing a running nose and sniffling. □□ **snif•fler** *n*. **snif•fly** *adj*. [imit.: cf. SNIVEL]

snif•fy /snífee/ *adj*. *colloq*. **1** inclined to sniff. **2** disdainful; contemptuous. □□ **snif•fi•ly** *adv*. **snif•fi•ness** *n*.

snif•ter /sníftər/ *n*. **1** *sl*. a small drink of alcohol. **2** a balloon glass for brandy. [dial. *snift* sniff, perh. f. Scand.: imit.]

snif•ter valve *n*. a valve in a steam engine to allow air in or out.

snig•ger /snígər/ *n. & v*. • *n*. a half-suppressed secretive laugh. • *v.intr*. utter such a laugh. □□ **snig•ger•er** *n*. **snig•ger•ing•ly** *adv*. [var. of SNICKER]

snig•gle /snígəl/ *v.intr*. fish (for eels) by pushing bait into a hole. [ME *snig* small eel, of unkn. orig.]

snip /snip/ *v. & n*. • *v.tr*. (**snipped, snip•ping**) (also *absol*.) cut (cloth, a hole, etc.) with scissors or shears, esp. in small, quick strokes. • *n*. **1** an act of snipping. **2** a piece of material, etc., snipped off. **3** *sl*. a something easily achieved. **b** *Brit*. a bargain; something cheaply acquired. **4** (in *pl*.) hand shears for metal cutting (*tin snips*). □ **snip at 1** make snipping strokes at. **2** be curt and nasty toward. □□ **snip•ping** *n*. [LG & Du. *snippen* imit.]

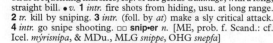

snifter 2

snipe /snip/ *n. & v*. • *n*. (*pl*. same or **snipes**) any of various wading birds frequenting marshes, etc., of the genus *Gallinago*, with a long, straight bill. • *v*. **1** *intr*. fire shots from hiding, usu. at long range. **2** *tr*. kill by sniping. **3** *intr*. (foll. by *at*) make a sly critical attack. **4** *intr*. go snipe shooting. □□ **snip•er** *n*. [ME, prob. f. Scand.: cf. Icel. *mýrisnípa*, & MDu., MLG *snippe*, OHG *snepfa*]

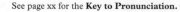

snipe eel *n.* any eel of the family Nemichthyidae, having a long, slender snout.

snipe fish *n.* any marine fish of the family Macrorhamphosidae, with a long, slender snout.

snip·pet /snípit/ *n.* **1** a small piece cut off. **2** (usu. in *pl.*; often foll. by *of*) **a** a scrap or fragment of information, knowledge, etc. **b** a short extract from a book, newspaper, etc. □□ **snip·pet·y** *adj.*

snip·py /snípee/ *adj.* (**snip·pi·er, snip·pi·est**) *colloq.* faultfinding, snappish, sharp. □□ **snip·pi·ly** *adv.* **snip·pi·ness** *n.*

snit /snit/ *n.* a rage; a sulk (esp. in a snit). [20th c.: orig. unkn.]

snitch /snich/ *v. & n.* **1** *tr.* steal. **2** *intr.* (often foll. by *on*) inform on a person. ● *n.* an informer. [17th c.: orig. unkn.]

sniv·el /snívəl/ *v. & n.* ● *v.intr.* **1** weep with sniffling. **2** run at the nose; make a repeated sniffing sound. **3** show weak or tearful sentiment. ● *n.* **1** running mucus. **2** hypocritical talk; cant. □□ **sniv·el·er** *n.* **sniv·el·ing** *adj.* **sniv·el·ing·ly** *adv.* [ME f. OE *snyflan* (unrecorded) f. *snofl* mucus: cf. SNUFFLE]

snob /snob/ *n.* **1 a** a person with an exaggerated respect for social position or wealth and who despises socially inferior connections. **b** (*attrib.*) related to or characteristic of this attitude. **2** a person who behaves with servility to social superiors. **3** a person who despises others whose (usu. specified) tastes or attainments are considered inferior (*an intellectual snob; a wine snob*). □□ **snob·ber·y** *n.* (*pl.* **·ies**). **snob·bish** *adj.* **snob·bish·ly** *adv.* **snob·bish·ness** *n.* **snob·by** *adj.* (**snob·bi·er, snob·bi·est**). [18th c. (now dial.) 'cobbler': orig. unkn.]

snood /snood/ *n.* **1** an ornamental hairnet usu. worn at the back of the head. **2** a ring of woolen, etc., material worn as a hood. **3** a short line attaching a hook to a main line in sea fishing. **4** *hist.* a ribbon or band worn by unmarried women in Scotland to confine their hair. [OE *snōd*]

snook[1] /snook, snook/ *n. sl.* a contemptuous gesture with the thumb to the nose and the fingers spread out. □ **cock a snook** = *thumb one's nose.* [19th c.: orig. unkn.]

snook[2] /snook, snook/ *n.* a marine fish, *Centropomus undecimalis*, used as food. [Du. *snoek* = PIKE[1], f. MLG *snôk*, prob. rel. to SNACK]

snook·er /snookər, snook–/ *n. & v.* ● *n.* **1** a game similar to pool in which the players use a cue ball (white) to pocket the other balls (15 red and 6 colored) in a set order. **2** a position in this game in which a direct shot at a permitted ball is impossible. ● *v.tr.* **1** (also *refl.*) subject (oneself or another player) to a snooker. **2** (esp. as **snookered** *adj.*) *sl.* defeat; thwart. [19th c.: orig. unkn.]

snoop /snoop/ *v. & n. colloq.* ● *v.intr.* **1** pry into matters one need not be concerned with. **2** (often foll. by *about, around*) investigate in order to find out transgressions of the law, etc. ● *n.* **1** an act of snooping. **2** a person who snoops; a detective. □□ **snoop·er** *n.* **snoop·y** *adj.* [Du. *snoepen* eat on the sly]

snoop·er·scope /snoopərskōp/ *n.* a device which converts infrared radiation into a visible image, esp. used for seeing in the dark.

snoot /snoot/ *n. sl.* the nose. [var. of SNOUT]

snoot·y /snootee/ *adj.* (**snoot·i·er, snoot·i·est**) *colloq.* supercilious; conceited. □□ **snoot·i·ly** *adv.* **snoot·i·ness** *n.* [20th c.: orig. unkn.]

snooze /snooz/ *n. & v. colloq.* ● *n.* a short sleep, esp. in the daytime. ● *v.intr.* take a snooze. □□ **snooz·er** *n.* **snooz·y** *adj.* (**snooz·i·er, snooz·i·est**). [18th-c. *sl.*: orig. unkn.]

snore /snawr/ *n. & v.* ● *n.* a snorting or grunting sound in breathing during sleep. ● *v.intr.* make this sound. □ **snore away** pass (time) sleeping or snoring. □□ **snor·er** *n.* **snor·ing·ly** *adv.* [ME, prob. imit.: cf. SNORT]

snor·kel /snáwrkəl/ *n. & v.* ● *n.* **1** a breathing tube for an underwater swimmer. **2** a device for supplying air to a submerged submarine. ● *v.intr.* use a snorkel. □□ **snor·kel·er** *n.* [G *Schnorchel*]

snorkel 1

snort /snawrt/ *n. & v.* ● *n.* **1** an explosive sound made by the sudden forcing of breath through the nose, esp. expressing indignation or incredulity. **2** a similar sound made by an engine, etc. **3** *colloq.* a small drink of liquor. **4** *sl.* an inhaled dose of a (usu. illegal) powdered drug. ● *v.* **1** *intr.* make a snort. **2** *intr.* (of an engine, etc.) make a sound resembling this. **3** *tr.* (also *absol.*) *sl.* inhale (a usu. illegal narcotic drug, esp. cocaine or heroin). **4** *tr.* express (defiance, etc.) by snorting. □ **snort out** express (words, emotions, etc.) by snorting. [ME, prob. imit.: cf. SNORE]

snort·er /snáwrtər/ *n.* esp. *Brit. colloq.* **1** something very impressive or difficult. **2** something vigorous or violent.

snot /snot/ *n. sl.* **1** nasal mucus. **2** a term of contempt for a person. [prob. f. MDu., MLG *snotte*, MHG *snuz*, rel. to SNOUT]

snot-rag *n. coarse* a handkerchief.

snot·ty /snótee/ *adj.* (**snot·ti·er, snot·ti·est**) *sl.* **1** running or foul with nasal mucus. **2** *colloq.* contemptible. **3** *colloq.* supercilious; conceited. □□ **snot·ti·ly** *adv.* **snot·ti·ness** *n.*

snout /snowt/ *n.* **1** the projecting nose and mouth of an animal. **2** *derog.* a person's nose. **3** the pointed front of a thing; a nozzle. **4** *Brit. sl.* tobacco or a cigarette. □□ **snout·ed** *adj.* (also in *comb.*). **snout·like** *adj.* **snout·y** *adj.* [ME f. MDu., MLG *snūt*]

snout bee·tle *n.* a weevil.

snow /snō/ *n. & v.* ● *n.* **1** atmospheric vapor frozen into ice crystals and falling to earth in light white flakes. **2** a fall of this, or a layer of it on the ground. **3** a thing resembling snow in whiteness or texture, etc. **4** a mass of flickering white spots on a television or radar screen, caused by interference or a poor signal. **5** *sl.* cocaine. **6** a dessert or other dish resembling snow. **7** frozen carbon dioxide. ● *v.* **1** *intr.* (prec. by *it* as subject) snow falls (*it is snowing; if it snows*). **2** *tr.* (foll. by *in, over, up*, etc.) confine or block with large quantities of snow. **3** *tr. & intr.* sprinkle or scatter or fall as or like snow. **4** *intr.* come in large numbers or quantities. **5** *tr. sl.* deceive or charm with plausible words. □ **be snowed under** be overwhelmed, esp. with work. □□ **snow·less** *adj.* **snow·like** *adj.* [OE *snāw* f. Gmc]

snow·ball /snōbawl/ *n. & v.* ● *n.* **1** snow pressed together into a ball, esp. for throwing in play. **2** anything that grows or increases rapidly like a snowball rolled on snow. ● *v.* **1** *intr. & tr.* throw or pelt with snowballs. **2** *intr.* increase rapidly.

snow·ball bush *n.* **1** any of several shrubs of the genus *Viburnum*. **2** a guelder rose.

snow·ber·ry /snōberee/ *n.* (*pl.* **·ries**) any shrub of the genus *Symphoricarpos*, with white berries.

snow·bird /snōbərd/ *n.* **1** a bird, such as the junco, commonly seen in snowy regions. **2** *colloq.* a person who moves from a cold climate to a warmer climate during the winter.

snow-blind *adj.* temporarily blinded by the glare of light reflected by large expanses of snow. □□ **snow blind·ness** *n.*

snow-blink /snōblingk/ *n.* the reflection in the sky of snow or ice fields.

snow-blow·er /snōblōər/ *n.* a machine that clears snow by blowing it to the side of the road, etc.

snow·board /snōbawrd/ *n.* a board similar to a wide ski, ridden over snow in an upright or surfing position. □□ **snow·board·er** *n.*

snow boot *n. Brit.* an overboot of rubber and cloth.

snow·bound /snōbownd/ *adj.* prevented by snow from going out or traveling.

snow-broth *n.* melted or melting snow.

snow·cap /snōkap/ *n.* **1** the tip of a mountain when covered with snow. **2** a white-crowned hummingbird, *Microchera albocoronata*, native to Central America. □□ **snow·capped** *adj.*

snow·drift /snōdrift/ *n.* a bank of snow heaped up by the action of the wind.

snow·drop /snōdrop/ *n.* a bulbous plant, *Galanthus nivalis*, with white drooping flowers in the early spring.

snow·fall /snōfawl/ *n.* **1** a fall of snow. **2** *Meteorol.* the amount of snow that falls on one occasion or on a given area within a given time.

snow·field /snōfeeld/ *n.* a permanent wide expanse of snow in mountainous or polar regions.

snow·flake /snōflayk/ *n.* **1** each of the small collections of crystals in which snow falls. **2 a** any bulbous plant of the genus *Leucojum*, with snowdroplike flowers. **b** the white flower of this plant.

snow goose *n.* a white Arctic goose, *Anser caerulescens*, with black-tipped wings.

snow job *n. sl.* an attempt at flattery or deception. □□ **snow-job** *v.tr.*

snow leop·ard *n.* = OUNCE[2].

snow line *n.* the level above which snow never melts entirely.

snow·man /snōman/ *n.* (*pl.* **·men**) a figure resembling a man, made of compressed snow.

snow·mo·bile /snōməbeel, –mō–/ *n.* a motor vehicle, esp. with runners or revolving treads, for traveling over snow.

snowmobile

snow owl *n.* = SNOWY OWL.

snow par·tridge *n.* a mainly white partridge, *Lerwa lerwa*.

snow·plow /snōplow/ *n.* a device, or a vehicle equipped with one, for clearing roads of thick snow.

snow·shoe /snōshoo/ *n. & v.* ● *n.* a flat device having a racket attached to a boot for walking on snow without sinking in. ● *v.intr.* travel on snowshoes. □□ **snow·sho·er** *n.*

snowshoes

snow•slide /snṓslīd/ n. an avalanche of snow.

snow•slip /snṓslip/ n. Brit. = SNOWSLIDE.

snow•storm /snṓstawrm/ n. a heavy fall of snow, esp. with a high wind.

snow-white adj. pure white.

snow•y /snṓee/ adj. (**snow•i•er, snow•i•est**) **1** of or like snow. **2** (of the weather, etc.) with much snow. □□ **snow•i•ly** adv. **snow•i•ness** n.

snowy owl n. a large white owl, Nyctea scandiaca, native to the Arctic.

Snr. abbr. esp. Brit. senior.

snub /snub/ v., n., & adj. • v.tr. (**snubbed, snub•bing**) **1** rebuff or humiliate with sharp words or a marked lack of cordiality. **2** check the movement of (a boat, horse, etc.) esp. by a rope wound around a post, etc. • n. an act of snubbing; a rebuff. • adj. short and blunt in shape. □□ **snub•ber** n. **snub•bing•ly** adv. [ME f. ON snubba chide, check the growth of]

snub nose n. a short turned-up nose.

snub-nosed adj. **1** having a snub nose. **2** (of a gun) having a very short barrel.

snuff[1] /snuf/ n. & v. • n. the charred part of a candlewick. • v.tr. trim the snuff from (a candle). □ **snuff it** Brit. sl. die. **snuff out 1** extinguish by snuffing. **2** kill; put an end to. [ME snoffe, snuffe: orig. unkn.]

snuff[2] /snuf/ n. & v. • n. powdered tobacco or medicine taken by sniffing it up the nostrils. • v.intr. take snuff. □ **up to snuff** colloq. **1** up to standard. **2** Brit. knowing; not easily deceived. [Du. snuf (tabak tobacco) f. MDu. snuffen snuffle]

snuff•box /snúfboks/ n. a small usu. ornamental box for holding snuff.

snuff-col•ored adj. dark yellowish-brown.

snuff•er /snúfər/ n. **1** a small hollow cone with a handle used to extinguish a candle. **2** (in pl.) an implement like scissors used to extinguish a candle or trim its wick.

snuf•fle /snúfəl/ v. & n. • v. **1** intr. make sniffing sounds. **2 a** intr. speak nasally, whiningly, or like one with a cold. **b** tr. (often foll. by out) say in this way. **3** intr. breathe noisily as through a partially blocked nose. **4** intr. sniff. • n. **1** a snuffling sound or tone. **2** (in pl.) a partial blockage of the nose causing snuffling. **3** a sniff. □□ **snuf•fler** n. **snuf•fly** adj. [prob. f. LG & Du. snuffelen (as SNUFF²): cf. SNIVEL]

snuff•y[1] /snúfee/ adj. (**snuff•i•er, snuff•i•est**) **1** annoyed. **2** irritable. **3** supercilious or contemptuous. [SNUFF¹ + -Y¹]

snuff•y[2] /snúfee/ adj. like snuff in color or substance. [SNUFF² + -Y²]

snug /snug/ adj. & n. • adj. (**snug•ger, snug•gest**) **1 a** cozy, comfortable; sheltered; well enclosed or placed or arranged. **b** cozily protected from the weather or cold. **c** close-fitting. **2** (of an income, etc.) allowing comfort and comparative ease. • n. Brit. a small room in a pub or inn. □□ **snug•ly** adv. **snug•ness** n. [16th c. (orig. Naut.): prob. f. LG or Du. orig.]

snug•ger•y /snúgəree/ n. Brit. (pl. **-ies**) **1** a snug place, esp. a person's private room or den. **2** = SNUG n.

snug•gle /snúgəl/ v.intr. (usu. foll. by down, up, together) settle or draw into a warm comfortable position. [SNUG + -LE⁴]

So. abbr. South.

so[1] /sō/ adv. & conj. • adv. **1** (often foll. by that + clause) to such an extent, or to the extent implied (why are you so angry?; stop complaining so; they were so pleased that they gave us a bonus). **2** (with neg.; often foll. by as + clause) to the extent to which ... is or does, etc., or to the extent implied (was not so late as I expected; am not so eager as you). **3** (foll. by that or as + clause) to the degree or in the manner implied (so expensive that few can afford it; so small as to be invisible; am not so foolish as to agree to that). **4** (adding emphasis) to that extent; in that or a similar manner (I want to leave and so does she; you said it was good, and so it is). **5** to a great or notable degree (I am so glad). **6** (with verbs of state) in the way described (am not very fond of it but may become so). **7** (with verb of saying or thinking, etc.) as previously mentioned or described (I think so; so he said; so I should hope). • conj. (often foll. by that + clause) **1** with the result that (there was none left, so we had to go without). **2** in order that (came home early so that I could see you). **3** and then; as the next step (so then the car broke down; and so to bed). **4 a** (introducing a question) then; after that (so what did you tell them?). **b** (absol.) = so what? □ **and so on** (or **forth**) **1** and others of the same kind. **2** and in other similar ways. **so as** (foll. by to + infin.) in order to (did it so as to get it finished). **so be it** an expression of acceptance or resignation. **so far** see FAR. **so far as** see FAR. **so far so good** see FAR. **so long!** colloq. good-bye until we meet again. **so long as** see LONG¹. **so much 1** a certain amount (of). **2** a great deal of (is so much nonsense). **3** (with neg.) **a** less than; to a lesser extent (not so much forgotten as ignored). **b** not even (didn't give me so much as a penny). **so much for** that is all that need be done or said about. **so to say** (or **speak**) an expression of reserve or apology for an exaggeration or neologism, etc. **so what?** colloq. why should that be considered significant? [OE swā, etc.]

▶In positive constructions the adverb sense 2, as. . . as . . . is used: see AS¹.

so[2] var. of SOL¹.

-so /sō/ comb. form = -SOEVER.

soak /sōk/ v. & n. • v. **1** tr. & intr. make or become thoroughly wet through saturation with or in liquid. **2** tr. (of rain, etc.) drench. **3** tr. (foll. by in, up) **a** absorb (liquid). **b** acquire (knowledge, etc.) copiously. **4** refl. (often foll. by in) steep (oneself) in a subject of study, etc. **5** intr. (foll. by in, into, through) (of liquid) make its way or penetrate by saturation. **6** tr. colloq. extract money from by an extortionate charge, taxation, etc. (soak the rich). **7** intr. colloq. drink persistently; booze. **8** tr. (as **soaked** adj.) very drunk. • n. **1** the act of soaking or the state of being soaked. **2** a drinking bout. **3** colloq. a hard drinker. □□ **soak•age** n. **soak•er** n. **soak•ing** n. & adj. [OE socian rel. to soc sucking at the breast, sūcan SUCK]

so-and-so /sṓəndsō/ n. (pl. **so-and-sos**) **1** a particular person or thing not needing to be specified (told me to do so-and-so). **2** colloq. a person disliked or regarded with disfavor (the so-and-so left me behind).

soap /sōp/ n. & v. • n. **1** a cleansing agent that is a compound of fatty acid with soda or potash or (**insoluble soap**) with another metallic oxide, of which the soluble kinds when rubbed in water yield a lather used in washing. **2** colloq. = SOAP OPERA. • v.tr. **1** apply soap to. **2** scrub or rub with soap. □□ **soap•less** adj. **soap•like** adj. [OE sāpe f. WG]

soap•bark /sṓpbaark/ n. an American tree, Quillaja saponaria, with bark yielding saponin.

soap•ber•ry /sṓpberee/ n. (pl. **-ries**) any of various tropical American shrubs, esp. of the genus Sapindus, with fruits yielding saponin.

soap•box /sṓpboks/ n. **1** a box for holding soap. **2** a makeshift stand for a public speaker.

soap op•er•a n. a broadcast drama, usu. serialized in many episodes, dealing with sentimental or melodramatic domestic themes (so called because orig. sponsored in the US by soap manufacturers).

soap•stone /sṓpstōn/ n. steatite.

soap•suds /sṓpsudz/ n.pl. = SUDS 1.

soap•wort /sṓpwort, -wawrt/ n. a European plant, Saponaria officinalis, with pink or white flowers and leaves yielding a soapy substance.

soap•y /sṓpee/ adj. (**soap•i•er, soap•i•est**) **1** of or like soap. **2** containing or smeared with soap. **3** (of a person or manner) unctuous or flattering. □□ **soap•i•ly** adv. **soap•i•ness** n.

soar /sawr/ v.intr. **1** fly or rise high. **2** reach a high level or standard (prices soared). **3** maintain height in the air without flapping the wings or using power. □□ **soar•er** n. **soar•ing•ly** adv. [ME f. OF essorer ult. f. L (as EX-¹, aura breeze)]

S.O.B. abbr. sl. (also **SOB**) = SON OF A BITCH.

sob /sob/ v. & n. • v. (**sobbed, sob•bing**) **1** intr. draw breath in convulsive gasps usu. with weeping under mental distress or physical exhaustion. **2** tr. (usu. foll. by out) utter with sobs. **3** tr. bring (oneself) to a specified state by sobbing (sobbed themselves to sleep). • n. a convulsive drawing of breath, esp. in weeping. □□ **sob•ber** n. **sob•bing•ly** adv. [ME sobbe (prob. imit.)]

so•ber /sṓbər/ adj. & v. • adj. (**so•ber•er, so•ber•est**) **1** not affected by alcohol. **2** not given to excessive drinking of alcohol. **3** moderate; well-balanced; tranquil; sedate. **4** not fanciful or exaggerated (the sober truth). **5** (of a color, etc.) quiet and inconspicuous. • v.tr. & intr. (often foll. by down, up) make or become sober or less wild, reckless, enthusiastic, visionary, etc. (a sobering thought). □ **as sober as a judge** completely sober. □□ **so•ber•ing•ly** adv. **so•ber•ly** adv. [ME f. OF sobre f. L sobrius]

so•bri•e•ty /səbrí-itee/ n. the state of being sober. [ME f. OF sobrieté or L sobrietas (as SOBER)]

so•bri•quet /sṓbrikay, -ket/ n. (also **sou•bri•quet** /sōō-/) **1** a nickname. **2** an assumed name. [F, orig. = 'tap under the chin']

sob sis•ter n. a journalist who writes or edits sentimental stories.

sob sto•ry n. a story or explanation appealing mainly to the emotions.

Soc. abbr. **1** Socialist. **2** Society.

soc•age /sókij/ n. (also **soc•cage**) a feudal tenure of land involving payment of rent or other non-military service. [ME f. AF socage f. soc f. OE sōcn SOKE]

so-called adj. commonly designated or known as, often incorrectly.

soc•cer /sókər/ n. a game played by two teams of eleven players with a round ball that cannot be touched with the hands during play except by the goalkeepers. [shortening of Association football + -ER³]

so•cia•ble /sṓshəbəl/ adj. & n. • adj. **1** fitted for or liking the society of other people; ready and willing to talk and act with others. **2** (of a person's manner or behavior, etc.) friendly. **3** (of a meeting, etc.) marked by friendliness; not stiff or formal. • n. **1** an open carriage with facing side seats. **2** esp. Brit. an S-shaped couch for two occupants partly facing each other. **3** a social. □□ **so•cia•bil•i•ty** /–bílitee/ n. **so•cia•ble•ness** n. **so•cia•bly** adv. [F sociable or L sociabilis f. sociare to unite f. socius companion]

so•cial /sóshəl/ adj. & n. ● adj. **1** of or relating to society or its organization. **2** concerned with the mutual relations of human beings or of classes of human beings. **3** living in organized communities; unfitted for a solitary life (a human is a social animal). **4 a** needing companionship; gregarious; interdependent. **b** cooperative; practicing the division of labor. **5** existing only as a member of a compound organism. **6 a** (of insects) living together in organized communities. **b** (of birds) nesting near each other in communities. **7** (of plants) growing thickly together and monopolizing the ground they grow on. ● n. a social gathering, esp. one organized by a club, congregation, etc. □□ **so•cial•i•ty** /sósheeálitee/ n. **so•cial•ly** adv. [F social or L socialis allied f. socius friend]

so•cial an•thro•pol•o•gy n. the comparative study of peoples through their culture and kinship systems.

so•cial climb•er n. derog. a person anxious to gain a higher social status.

so•cial con•tract n. (also **so•cial com•pact**) an agreement to cooperate for social benefits, e.g., by sacrificing some individual freedom for government protection.

so•cial de•moc•ra•cy n. a socialist system achieved by democratic means. □□ **so•cial dem•o•crat** n.

so•cial dis•ease n. a venereal disease.

so•cial•ism /sóshəlizəm/ n. **1** a political and economic theory of social organization which advocates that the community as a whole should own and control the means of production, distribution, and exchange. **2** policy or practice based on this theory. □□ **so•cial•ist** n. & adj. **so•cial•is•tic** adj. **so•cial•is•ti•cal•ly** adv. [F socialisme (as SOCIAL)]

so•cial•ite /sóshəlīt/ n. a person prominent in fashionable society.

so•cial•ize /sóshəlīz/ v. **1** intr. act in a sociable manner. **2** tr. make social. **3** tr. organize on socialistic principles. □□ **so•cial•i•za•tion** n.

so•cial•ized med•i•cine n. the provision of medical services for all from public funds.

so•cial or•der n. the network of human relationships in society.

so•cial re•al•ism n. the expression of social or political views in art.

so•cial sci•ence n. **1** the scientific study of human society and social relationships. **2** a branch of this (e.g., politics or economics). **so•cial sci•en•tist** n.

so•cial sec•re•tar•y n. a person who makes arrangements for the social activities of a person or organization.

so•cial se•cu•ri•ty n. (usu. **So•cial Se•cu•ri•ty**) a US government program of assistance to the elderly, disabled, etc., funded by mandatory contributions from employers and employees.

so•cial serv•ice n. philanthropic activity.

so•cial serv•ices n. services provided by the government for the community, esp. education, health, and housing.

so•cial war n. hist. a war fought between allies.

so•cial work n. work of benefit to those in need of help or welfare, esp. done by specially trained personnel. □□ **so•cial work•er** n.

so•ci•e•ty /səsíetee/ n. (pl. **-ties**) **1** the sum of human conditions and activity regarded as a whole functioning interdependently. **2** a social community (all societies must have firm laws). **3 a** a social mode of life. **b** the customs and organization of an ordered community. **4** Ecol. a plant community. **5 a** the socially advantaged or prominent members of a community (society would not approve). **b** this, or a part of it, qualified in some way (is not done in polite society). **6** participation in hospitality; other people's homes or company (avoids society). **7** companionship; company (avoids the society of such people). **8** an association of persons united by a common aim or interest or principle (formed a music society). □□ **so•ci•e•tal** adj. (esp. in sense 1). **so•ci•e•tal•ly** adv. [F société f. L societas –tatis f. socius companion]

So•ci•e•ty of Friends n. see QUAKER.

So•ci•e•ty of Je•sus n. see JESUIT.

socio- /sóseeō, sósheeō/ comb. form **1** of society (and). **2** of or relating to sociology (and). [L socius companion]

so•ci•o•bi•ol•o•gy /sóseeōbīólajee, sósheeō–/ n. the scientific study of the biological aspects of social behavior. □□ **so•ci•o•bi•o•log•i•cal** /–bīólójikəl/ adj. **so•ci•o•bi•o•log•i•cal•ly** adv. **so•ci•o•bi•ol•o•gist** n.

so•ci•o•cul•tur•al /sóseeōkúlchərəl, sósheeō–/ adj. combining social and cultural factors. □□ **so•ci•o•cul•tur•al•ly** adv.

so•ci•o•ec•o•nom•ic /sóseeōékənómik, –éekə–, sósheeō–/ adj. relating to or concerned with the interaction of social and economic factors. □□ **so•ci•o•ec•o•nom•i•cal•ly** adv.

so•ci•o•lin•guis•tic /sóseeōlíngwístik, sósheeō–/ adj. relating to or concerned with language in its social aspects. □□ **so•ci•o•lin•guist** n. **so•ci•o•lin•guis•ti•cal•ly** adv.

so•ci•o•lin•guis•tics /sóseeōlíngwístiks, sósheeō–/ n. the study of language in relation to social factors.

so•ci•ol•o•gy /sóseeólajee, sóshee–/ n. **1** the study of the development, structure, and functioning of human society. **2** the study

of social problems. □□ **so•ci•o•log•i•cal** /–əlójikəl/ adj. **so•ci•o•log•i•cal•ly** adv. **so•ci•ol•o•gist** n. [F sociologie (as SOCIO-, –LOGY)]

so•ci•om•e•try /sóseeómitree, sóshee–/ n. the study of relationships within a group of people. □□ **so•ci•o•met•ric** /–əmétrik/ adj. **so•ci•o•met•ri•cal•ly** adv. **so•ci•om•e•trist** n.

so•ci•o•path /sóseeōpath, sóshee–/ n. Psychol. a person who is asocial or antisocial and who lacks a social conscience, as a psychopath. □□ **so•ci•o•path•ic** adj.

sock¹ /sok/ n. (pl. **socks** or colloq. **sox** /soks/) **1** a short knitted covering for the foot, usu. not reaching the knee. **2** a removable inner sole put into a shoe for warmth, etc. **3** an ancient Greek or Roman comic actor's light shoe. **4** comic drama. □ **pull one's socks up** Brit. colloq. make an effort to improve. **put a sock in it** sl. be quiet. **sock away** put away money as savings. [OE socc f. L soccus comic actor's shoe, light low-heeled slipper, f. Gk sukkhos]

sock² /sok/ v. & n. colloq. ● v.tr. hit (esp. a person) forcefully. ● n. **1** a hard blow. **2** the power to deliver a blow. □ **sock it to** sl. attack or address (a person) vigorously. [c. 1700 (cant): orig. unkn.]

sock•et /sókit/ n. & v. ● n. **1** a natural or artificial hollow for something to fit into or stand firm or revolve in. **2** Electr. a device receiving a plug, lightbulb, etc., to make a connection. **3** Golf the part of an iron club into which the shaft is fitted. ● v.tr. (**sock•et•ed, sock•et•ing**) **1** place in or fit with a socket. **2** Golf hit (a ball) with the socket of a club. [ME f. AF, dimin. of OF soc plowshare, prob. of Celt. orig.]

sock•eye /sókī/ n. a blue-backed salmon of Alaska, etc., Oncorhynchus nerka. [Salish sukai fish of fishes]

sock•ing /sóking/ adv. & adj. Brit. ● adv. colloq. exceedingly; very (a socking great diamond ring). ● adj. sl. confounded.

so•cle /sókəl/ n. Archit. a plain low block or plinth serving as a support for a column, urn, statue, etc., or as the foundation of a wall. [F f. It. zoccolo orig. 'wooden shoe' f. L socculus f. soccus SOCK¹]

So•crat•ic /səkrátik, sō–/ adj. & n. ● adj. of or relating to the Greek philosopher Socrates (d. 399 BC) or his philosophy, esp. the method associated with him of seeking the truth by a series of questions and answers. ● n. a follower of Socrates. □□ **So•crat•i•cal•ly** adv. [L Socraticus f Gk Sōkratikos f. Sōkratēs]

So•crat•ic e•len•chus n. the Socratic method of eliciting truth by question and answer, esp. as used to refute an argument.

So•crat•ic i•ro•ny n. a pose of ignorance assumed in order to entice others into making statements that can then be challenged.

sod¹ /sod/ n. & v. ● n. **1** turf or a piece of turf. **2** the surface of the ground. ● v.tr. (**sod•ded, sod•ding**) cover (the ground) with sods. □ **under the sod** in the grave. [ME f. MDu., MLG sode, of unkn. orig.]

sod² /sod/ n. & v. esp. Brit. coarse sl. ● n. **1** an unpleasant or awkward person or thing. **2** a person of a specified kind; a fellow (the lucky sod). ● v.tr. (**sod•ded, sod•ding**) **1** (often absol. or as int.) as an exclamation of annoyance (sod them, I don't care!). **2** (as **sodding** adj.) a general term of contempt. □ **sod off** go away. **Sod's Law** = MURPHY's LAW. [abbr. of SODOMITE]

so•da /sódə/ n. **1** any of various compounds of sodium in common use, e.g., washing soda, baking soda. **2** (in full **soda water**) water made effervescent by impregnation with carbon dioxide under pressure and used alone or with alcohol as a drink (orig. made with sodium bicarbonate). **3** (also **so•da pop**) esp. US regional a sweet effervescent soft drink. [med.L, perh. f. sodanum glasswort (used as a remedy for headaches) f. soda headache f. Arab. ṣudā' f. ṣada'a split]

so•da bis•cuit n. **1** a biscuit made with baking soda and either sour milk or buttermilk. **2** (also **so•da crack•er**) a cracker made with baking soda.

so•da bread n. bread leavened with baking soda.

so•da foun•tain n. **1** a device supplying soda water. **2** a store or counter equipped with this. **3** a store or counter for preparing and serving sodas, sundaes, and ice cream.

so•da lime n. a mixture of calcium oxide and sodium hydroxide.

so•dal•i•ty /sódálitee/ n. (pl. **-ties**) a confraternity or association, esp. a Roman Catholic devotional or charitable group. [F sodalité or L sodalitas f. sodalis comrade]

sod•den /sódən/ adj. & v. ● adj. **1** saturated with liquid; soaked through. **2** rendered stupid or dull, etc., with drunkenness. **3** (of bread, etc.) doughy; heavy and moist. ● v.intr. & tr. become or make sodden. □□ **sod•den•ly** adv. **sod•den•ness** n. [archaic past part. of SEETHE]

so•di•um /sódeeəm/ n. Chem. a soft silver white reactive metallic element, occurring naturally in soda, salt, etc., that is important in industry and is an essential element in living organisms. ¶ Symb.: Na. □□ **so•dic** adj. [SODA + –IUM]

so•di•um bi•car•bon•ate n. a white soluble powder used in the manufacture of fire extinguishers and effervescent drinks.

so•di•um car•bon•ate n. a white powder with many commercial applications including the manufacture of soap and glass.

so•di•um chlo•ride n. a colorless crystalline compound occurring naturally in sea water and halite; common salt.

so•di•um hy•drox•ide n. a deliquescent compound which is strongly alkaline and used in the manufacture of soap and paper. Also called **caustic soda.**

so•di•um ni•trate n. a white powdery compound used mainly in the manufacture of fertilizers.

so•di•um-va•por lamp n. (also **so•di•um lamp**) a lamp using an electrical discharge in sodium vapor and giving a yellow light.

Sod•om /sódəm/ n. a wicked or depraved place. [*Sodom* in ancient Palestine, destroyed for its wickedness (Gen. 18– 19)]

sod•om•ite /sódəmīt/ n. a person who practices sodomy. [ME f. OF f. LL *Sodomita* f. Gk *Sodomitēs* inhabitant of Sodom f. *Sodoma* Sodom]

sod•om•y /sódəmee/ n. sexual intercourse involving anal or oral copulation. □□ **sod•om•ize** v.tr. [ME f. med.L *sodomia* f. LL *peccatum Sodomiticum* sin of Sodom: see SODOM]

so•ev•er /sō-évər/ adv. *literary* of any kind; to any extent (*how great soever it may be*).

-soever /sō-évər/ comb. form (added to relative pronouns, adverbs, and adjectives) of any kind; to any extent (*whatsoever; howsoever*).

so•fa /sófə/ n. a long upholstered seat with a back and arms, for two or more people. [F, ult. f. Arab. *ṣuffa*]

so•fa bed n. a sofa that can be converted into a temporary bed.

sof•fit /sófit/ n. the underside of an architrave, arch, balcony, etc. [F *soffite* or It. *soffitta, –itto* ult. f. L *suffixus* (as SUFFIX)]

S. of S. abbr. Song of Songs (Old Testament).

soft /sawft, soft/ adj., adv., & v. ● adj. 1 (of a substance, material, etc.) lacking hardness or firmness; yielding to pressure; easily cut. 2 (of cloth, etc.) having a smooth surface or texture; not rough or coarse. 3 (of air, etc.) mellow; mild; balmy; not noticeably cold or hot. 4 (of water) free from mineral salts and therefore good for lathering. 5 (of a light or color, etc.) not brilliant or glaring. 6 (of a voice or sounds) gentle and pleasing. 7 *Phonet* **a** (of a consonant) sibilant or palatal (as *c* in *ice*, *g* in *age*). **b** voiced or unaspirated. 8 (of an outline, etc.) not sharply defined. 9 (of an action or manner, etc.) gentle; conciliatory; complimentary; amorous. 10 (of the heart or feelings, etc.) compassionate; sympathetic. 11 (of a person) **a** feeble; lenient; silly; sentimental. **b** weak; not robust. 12 *colloq.* (of a job, etc.) easy. 13 (of drugs) mild; not likely to cause addiction. 14 (of radiation) having little penetrating power. 15 (also **soft-core**) (of pornography) suggestive or erotic but not explicit. 16 *Stock Exch.* (of currency, prices, etc.) likely to fall in value. 17 *Polit.* moderate; willing to compromise (*the soft left*). 18 peaceful (*soft slumbers*). 19 *Brit.* (of the weather, etc.) rainy or moist or thawing. ● adv. softly (*play soft*). ● n. a silly weak person. □ **be soft on** *colloq.* 1 be lenient toward. 2 be infatuated with. **have a soft spot for** be fond of or affectionate toward (a person). **soft in the head** feebleminded. □□ **soft•ish** adj. **soft•ness** n. [OE *sōfte* agreeable, earlier *sēfte* f. WG]

soft•ball /sáwftbawl, sóft–/ n. 1 a ball like a baseball but larger and pitched underhand. 2 a modified form of baseball using this.

soft-boiled adj. (of an egg) lightly boiled with the yolk soft or liquid.

soft-cen•tered adj. (of a person) softhearted; sentimental.

soft coal n. bituminous coal.

soft-cov•er /sáwftcəvər/ adj. & n. ● adj. (of a book) bound in flexible covers. ● n. a softcover book.

soft drink n. a nonalcoholic usu. effervescent drink.

soft•en /sáwfən, sófən/ v. 1 tr. & intr. make or become soft or softer. 2 tr. (often foll. by *up*) **a** reduce the strength of (defenses) by bombing or some other preliminary attack. **b** reduce the resistance of (a person). □□ **soft•en•er** n.

soft•en•ing of the brain n. a morbid degeneration of the brain, esp. in old age.

soft fo•cus n. *Photog.* the slight deliberate blurring of a picture.

soft fruit n. *Brit.* small stoneless fruit (strawberry, currant, etc.).

soft fur•nish•ings n. *Brit.* curtains, rugs, etc.

soft goods n. textiles.

soft-head•ed adj. feebleminded. □□ **soft-head•ed•ness** n.

soft-heart•ed /sáwft-haártid, sóft–/ adj. tender; compassionate; easily moved. □□ **soft-heart•ed•ness** n.

soft•ie var. of SOFTY.

soft land•ing n. a landing by a spacecraft without its suffering major damage.

soft•ly /sáwftlee, sóft–/ adv. in a soft, gentle, or quiet manner. □ **softly softly** (of an approach or strategy) cautious; discreet and cunning.

soft op•tion n. the easier alternative.

soft pal•ate n. the rear part of the palate.

soft paste n. denoting an 'artificial' porcelain containing glassy materials and fired at a comparatively low temperature.

soft ped•al n. a pedal on a piano that makes the tone softer. □□ **soft-ped•al** v.

soft roe see ROE[1].

soft sell n. restrained or subtly persuasive salesmanship. □□ **soft-sell** v.tr.

soft soap n. 1 a semifluid soap made with potash. 2 *colloq.* persuasive flattery. □□ **soft-soap** v.tr.

soft-spo•ken adj. speaking with a gentle voice.

soft tis•sues n. tissues of the body that are not bony or cartilaginous.

soft touch n. *colloq.* a gullible person, esp. over money.

soft•ware /sáwftwair, sóft–/ n. the programs and other operating information used by a computer (opp. HARDWARE 3).

soft•wood /sáwftwood, sóft–/ n. the wood of pine, spruce, or other conifers, easily sawn.

soft•y /sáwftee, sóftee/ n. (also **soft•y**) *colloq.* a weak or silly or softhearted person.

sog•gy /sógee/ adj. (**sog•gi•er, sog•gi•est**) sodden; saturated; dank. □□ **sog•gi•ly** adv. **sog•gi•ness** n. [dial. *sog* a swamp]

soi-di•sant /swaádeezón/ adj self-styled or pretended. [F f. *soi* oneself + *disant* saying]

soi•gné /swaanyáy/ adj. (*fem.* **soi•gnée** *pronunc.* same) carefully finished or arranged; well-groomed. [past part. of F *soigner* take care of f. *soin* care]

soil[1] /soyl/ n. 1 the upper layer of earth in which plants grow, consisting of disintegrated rock usu. with an admixture of organic remains (*alluvial soil; rich soil*). 2 ground belonging to a nation; territory (*on British soil*). □□ **soil•less** adj. **soil•y** adj. [ME f. AF, perh. f. L *solium* seat, taken in sense of L *solum* ground]

soil[2] /soyl/ v. & n. ● v.tr. 1 make dirty; smear or stain with dirt (*soiled linen*). 2 tarnish; defile; bring discredit to (*would not soil my hands with it*). ● n. 1 a dirty mark; a stain, smear, or defilement. 2 filth; refuse matter. [ME f. OF *suiller, soiller*, etc., ult. f. L *sucula* dimin. of *sus* pig]

soil[3] /soyl/ v.tr. feed (cattle) on fresh green fodder (orig. for purging). [perh. f. SOIL[2]]

soil me•chan•ics n. the study of the properties of soil as affecting its use in civil engineering.

soil pipe n. the discharge pipe of a toilet.

soil sci•ence n. pedology.

soi•rée /swaaráy/ n. an evening party, usu. in a private house, for conversation or music. [F f. *soir* evening]

so•journ /sójərn/ n. & v. ● n. a temporary stay. ● v.intr. stay temporarily. □□ **so•journ•er** n. [ME f. OF *sojorn*, etc. f. LL SUB- + *diurnum* day]

soke /sōk/ n. *Brit. hist.* 1 a right of local jurisdiction. 2 a district under a particular jurisdiction and administration. [ME f. AL *sōca* f. OE *sōcn* prosecution f. Gmc]

Sol /sol/ n. (in Roman mythology) the sun, esp. as a personification. [ME f. L]

sol[1] /sōl/ n. (also **so** /sō/) *Mus.* 1 (in tonic sol-fa) the fifth note of a major scale. 2 the note G in the fixed do system. [*sol* f. ME *sol* f. L *solve*: see GAMUT]

sol[2] /sol/ n. *Chem.* a liquid suspension of a colloid. [abbr. of SOLUTION]

so•la[1] /sólə/ n. a pithy E. Indian swamp plant, *Aeschynomene indica*. [Urdu & Bengali *solā*, Hindi *sholā*]

so•la[2] *fem.* of SOLUS.

sol•ace /sóləs/ n. & v. ● n. comfort in distress, disappointment, or tedium. ● v.tr. give solace to. □ **solace oneself with** find compensation or relief in. [ME f. OF *solas* f. L *solatium* f. *solari* CONSOLE[1]]

so•lan /sólən/ n. (in full **solan goose**) a gannet, *Sula bassana*. [prob. f. ON *súla* gannet + *önd, and-* duck]

sol•a•na•ceous /sólənáyshəs/ adj. of or relating to the plant family Solanaceae, including potatoes, nightshades, and tobacco. [mod.L *solanaceae* f. L *sōl ānum* nightshade]

so•lar /sólər/ adj. & n. ● adj. of, relating to, or reckoned by the sun (*solar eclipse; solar time*). ● n. *Brit.* 1 a solarium. 2 an upper chamber in a medieval house. [ME f. L *solaris* f. *sol* sun]

so•lar bat•ter•y n. (also **so•lar cell**) a device converting solar radiation into electricity.

so•lar con•stant n. the quantity of heat reaching the earth from the sun.

so•lar day n. the interval between successive meridian transits of the sun at a place.

so•lar•i•um /səláireeəm/ n. (*pl.* **so•lar•i•a** /–reeə/) a room equipped with sunlamps at intervals and with extensive areas of glass for exposure to the sun. [L, = sundial, sunning place (as SOLAR)]

so•lar•ize /sólərīz/ v.intr. & tr. *Photog.* undergo or cause to undergo change in the relative darkness of parts of an image by long exposure. □□ **so•lar•i•za•tion** n.

so•lar month n. one twelfth of the solar year.

so•lar pan•el n. a panel designed to absorb the sun's rays as a source of energy for operating electricity or heating.

so•lar plex•us n. a complex of radiating nerves at the pit of the stomach.

so•lar sys•tem n. the sun and the celestial bodies whose motion it governs.

so•lar wind *n.* the continuous flow of charged particles from the sun.

so•lar year *n.* the time taken for the earth to travel once around the sun, equal to 365 days, 5 hours, 48 minutes, and 46 seconds.

so•la•ti•um /səláysheeəm/ *n.* (*pl.* **so•la•ti•a** /–sheeə/) a thing given as a compensation or consolation. [L, = SOLACE]

so•la to•pi *n.* an Indian sun helmet made from the pith of the sola plant.

sold *past* and *past part.* of SELL.

sol•der /sódər/ *n. & v.* ● *n.* **1** a fusible alloy used to join less fusible metals or wires, etc. **2** a cementing or joining agency. ● *v.tr.* join with solder. □□ **sol•der•a•ble** *adj.* **sol•der•er** *n.* [ME f. OF *soudure* f. *souder* f. L *solidare* fasten f. *solidus* SOLID]

sol•der•ing i•ron *n.* a tool used for applying solder.

sol•dier /sóljər/ *n. & v.* ● *n.* **1** a person serving in or having served in an army. **2** (in full **common soldier**) an enlisted person in an army. **3** a military commander of specified ability (*a great soldier*). **4** (in full **soldier ant**) a wingless ant or termite with a large head and jaws for fighting in defense of its colony. **5** (in full **soldier beet•le**) a reddish colored beetle, *Rhagonycha fulva*, with flesh-eating larvae. ● *v.intr.* serve as a soldier (*was off soldiering*). □ **soldier on** *colloq.* persevere doggedly. □□ **sol•dier•ly** *adj.* **sol•dier•ship** *n.* [ME *souder*, etc. f. OF *soudier, soldier* f. *soulde* (soldier's) pay f. L *solidus*: see SOLIDUS]

sol•dier of Christ *n.* an active or proselytizing Christian.

sol•dier of for•tune *n.* an adventurous person ready to take service under any government or person; a mercenary.

sol•dier•y /sóljəree/ *n.* (*pl.* **•ies**) **1** soldiers, esp. of a specified character. **2** a group of soldiers.

sole[1] /sōl/ *n. & v.* ● *n.* **1** the undersurface of the foot. **2** the part of a shoe, sock, etc., corresponding to this (esp. excluding the heel). **3** the lower surface or base of an implement, e.g., a plow, golf club head, etc. **4** the floor of a ship's cabin. ● *v.tr.* provide (a shoe, etc.) with a sole. □□ **–soled** *adj.* (in *comb.*). [OF ult. f. L *solea* sandal, sill: cf. OE unrecorded *solu* or *sola* f. *solum* bottom, pavement, sole]

sole[2] /sōl/ *n.* any flatfish of the family Soleidae, esp. *Solea solea*, used as food. [ME f. OF f. Prov. *sola* ult. f. L *solea* (as SOLE[1], named from its shape)]

sole[3] /sōl/ *adj.* **1** (*attrib.*) one and only; single; exclusive (*the sole reason; has the sole right*). **2** *archaic* or *Law* (esp. of a woman) unmarried. **3** *archaic* alone; unaccompanied. □□ **sole•ly** *adv.* [ME f. OF *soule* f. L *sola* fem. of *solus* alone]

sol•e•cism /sólisizəm/ *n.* **1** a mistake of grammar or idiom; a blunder in speaking or writing. **2** a piece of bad manners or incorrect behavior. □□ **sol•e•cist** *n.* **sol•e•cis•tic** *adj.* [F *solécisme* or L *soloecismus* f. Gk *soloikismos* f. *soloikos* speaking incorrectly]

sol•emn /sóləm/ *adj.* **1** serious and dignified (*a solemn occasion*). **2** formal; accompanied by ceremony (*a solemn oath*). **3** mysteriously impressive. **4** (of a person) serious or cheerless in manner (*looks rather solemn*). **5** full of importance; weighty (*a solemn warning*). **6** grave; sober; deliberate; slow in movement or action (*a solemn promise; solemn music*). □□ **sol•emn•ly** *adv.* **sol•emn•ness** *n.* [ME f. OF *solemne* f. L *sol(l)emnis* customary, celebrated at a fixed date f. *sollus* entire]

so•lem•ni•ty /səlémnitee/ *n.* (*pl.* **•ties**) **1** the state of being solemn; a solemn character or feeling; solemn behavior. **2** a rite or celebration; a piece of ceremony. [ME f. OF *solem(p)nité* f. L *sollemnitas –tatis* (as SOLEMN)]

sol•em•nize /sóləmnīz/ *v.tr.* **1** duly perform (a ceremony, esp. of marriage). **2** celebrate (a festival, etc.). **3** make solemn. □□ **sol•em•ni•za•tion** *n.* [ME f. OF *solem(p)niser* f. med.L *solemnizare* (as SOLEMN)]

Sol•emn Mass *n.* = HIGH MASS.

so•le•noid /sólənoyd, sól–/ *n.* a cylindrical coil of wire acting as a magnet when carrying electric current. □□ **so•le•noi•dal** /–nóyd'l/ *adj.* [F *solénoïde*, f. Gk *sōlēn* channel, pipe]

sol-fa /sólfaa/ *n. & v.* ● *n.* = SOLMIZATION; (cf. TONIC SOL-FA). ● *v.tr.* (**• fas, •faed**) sing (a tune) with sol-fa syllables. [SOL[1] + FA]

sol•fa•ta•ra /sólfətaarə/ *n.* a volcanic vent emitting only sulfurous and other vapors. [name of a volcano near Naples, f. It. *solfo* sulfur]

sol•feg•gio /solféjeeō/ *n.* (*pl.* **sol•feg•gi** /–jee/) (also **sol•fège**) *Mus.* **1** an exercise in singing using sol-fa syllables. **2** solmization. [It. (as SOL-FA)]

so•li *pl.* of SOLO.

so•lic•it /səlísit/ *v.* (**so•lic•it•ed, so•lic•it•ing**) **1** *tr. &* (foll. by *for*) *intr.* ask repeatedly or earnestly for or seek or invite (business, etc.). **2** *tr.* (often foll. by *for*) make a request or petition to (a person). **3** *tr.* accost (a person) and offer one's services as a prostitute. □□ **so•lic•i•ta•tion** *n.* [ME f. OF *solliciter* f. L *sollicitare* agitate f. *sollicitus* anxious f. *sollus* entire + *citus* past part., = set in motion]

so•lic•i•tor /səlísitər/ *n.* **1** a person who solicits. **2** a canvasser. **3** the chief law officer of a city, county, etc. **4** *Brit.* a member of the legal profession qualified to deal with conveyancing, draw up wills,

etc., and to advise clients and instruct barristers. [ME f. OF *solliciteur* (as SOLICIT)]

So•lic•i•tor Gen•er•al *n.* **1** (in the US) the law officer below the Attorney General. **2** (in the UK) the Crown law officer below the Attorney General or (in Scotland) below the Lord Advocate.

so•lic•i•tous /səlísitəs/ *adj.* **1** (often foll. by *of, about,* etc.) showing interest or concern. **2** (foll. by *to* + infin.) eager; anxious. □□ **so•lic•i•tous•ly** *adv.* **so•lic•i•tous•ness** *n.* [L *sollicitus* (as SOLICIT)]

so•lic•i•tude /səlísitōōd, –tyōōd/ *n.* **1** the state of being solicitous; solicitous behavior. **2** anxiety or concern. [ME f. OF *sollicitude* f. L *sollicitudo* (as SOLICITOUS)]

sol•id /sólid/ *adj. & n.* ● *adj.* (**sol•id•er, sol•id•est**) **1** firm and stable in shape; not liquid or fluid (*solid food; water becomes solid at 32°F*). **2** of one material throughout, not hollow or containing cavities (*a solid sphere*). **3** of the same substance throughout (*solid silver*). **4** of strong material or construction or build; not flimsy or slender, etc. **5 a** having three dimensions. **b** concerned with solids (*solid geometry*). **6 a** sound and reliable; genuine (*solid arguments*). **b** staunch and dependable (*a solid Republican*). **7** sound but without any special flair, etc. (*a solid piece of work*). **8** financially sound. **9** (of time) uninterrupted; continuous (*spend four solid hours on it*). **10 a** unanimous; undivided (*support has been pretty solid so far*). **b** (foll. by *for*) united in favor of. **11** (of printing) without spaces between the lines, etc. **12** (of a tire) without a central air space. **13** (foll. by *with*) *colloq.* on good terms. **14** *Austral. & NZ colloq.* severe; unreasonable. ● *n.* **1** a solid substance or body. **2** (in *pl.*) solid food. **3** *Geom.* a body or magnitude having three dimensions. □□ **sol•id•ly** *adv.* **sol•id•ness** *n.* [ME f. OF *solide* f. L *solidus*, rel. to *salvus* safe, *sollus* entire]

sol•id an•gle *n.* an angle formed by planes, etc., meeting at a point.

sol•i•dar•i•ty /sólidáritee/ *n.* **1** unity or agreement of feeling or action, esp. among individuals with a common interest. **2** mutual dependence. [F *solidarité* f. *solidaire* f. *solide* SOLID]

sol•id col•or *n.* color covering the whole of an object, without a pattern, etc.

sol•id-drawn *adj.* (of a tube, etc.) pressed or drawn out from a solid bar of metal.

sol•i•di *pl.* of SOLIDUS.

so•lid•i•fy /səlídifī/ *v.tr. & intr.* (**•fies, •fied**) make or become solid. □□ **so•lid•i•fi•ca•tion** /–fikáyshən/ *n.* **so•lid•i•fi•er** *n.*

so•lid•i•ty /səlíditee/ *n.* the state of being solid; firmness.

sol•id so•lu•tion *n.* solid material containing one substance uniformly distributed in another.

sol•id state *n.* the state of matter that retains its boundaries without support.

sol•id-state *adj.* using the electronic properties of solids (e.g., a semiconductor) to replace those of vacuum tubes, etc.

sol•i•dus /s ólidəs/ *n.* (*pl.* **sol•i•di** /–dī/) **1** an oblique stroke (/) used in writing fractions (3/4), to separate other figures and letters, or to denote alternatives (*and/or*) and ratios (*miles/day*). **2** (in full **solidus curve**) a curve in a graph of the temperature and composition of a mixture, below which the substance is entirely solid. **3** *hist.* a gold coin of the later Roman Empire. [ME (in sense 3) f. L: see SOLID]

PUNCTUATION TIP solidus

See note at SLASH.

---

so•li•fluc•tion /sóliflúkshən, sól–/ *n.* the gradual movement of wet soil, etc., down a slope. [L *solum* soil + L *fluctio* flowing f. *fluere fluct-* flow]

so•lil•o•quy /səlíləkwee/ *n.* (*pl.* **•quies**) **1** the act of talking when alone or regardless of any hearers, esp. in drama. **2** part of a play involving this. □□ **so•lil•o•quist** *n.* **so•lil•o•quize** *v.intr.* [LL *soliloquium* f. L *solus* alone + *loqui* speak]

sol•i•ped /sóliped/ *adj. & n.* ● *adj.* (of an animal) solid hoofed. ● *n.* a solid hoofed animal. [F *solipède* or mod.L *solipes –pedis* f. L *solidipes* f. *solidus* solid + *pes* foot]

sol•ip•sism /sólipsizəm/ *n.* *Philos.* the view that the self is all that exists or can be known. □□ **sol•ip•sist** *n.* **sol•ip•sis•tic** *adj.* **sol•ip•sis•ti•cal•ly** *adv.* [L *solus* alone + *ipse* self]

sol•i•taire /sólitáir/ *n.* **1** a diamond or other gem set by itself. **2** a ring having a single gem. **3** any of several card games for one player. **4** any of various extinct dodolike flightless birds of the family Raphidae. **5** any American thrush of the genus *Myadestes*. [F f. L *solitarius* (as SOLITARY)]

sol•i•tar•y /sóliteree/ *adj. & n.* ● *adj.* **1** living alone; not gregarious; without companions; lonely (*a solitary existence*). **2** (of a place) secluded or unfrequented. **3** single or sole (*a solitary instance*). **4** (of an insect) not living in communities. **5** *Bot.* growing singly; not in a cluster. ● *n.* (*pl.* **•ies**) **1** a recluse or anchorite. **2** *colloq.* = SOLITARY CONFINEMENT. □□ **sol•i•tar•i•ly** *adv.* **sol•i•tar•i•ness** *n.* [ME f. L *solitarius* f. *solus* alone]

sol•i•tar•y con•fine•ment *n.* isolation of a prisoner in a separate cell as a punishment.

sol•i•tude /sólitōōd, –tyōōd/ *n.* **1** the state of being solitary. **2** a lonely place. [ME f. OF *solitude* or L *solitudo* f. *solus* alone]

sol•mi•za•tion /sólmizáyshən/ n. Mus. a system of associating each note of a scale with a particular syllable, now usu. *do re mi fa sol la ti*, with do as C in the fixed-do system and as the keynote in the movable-do or tonic sol-fa system. □□ **sol•mi•zate** /sólmizayt/ v.intr. & tr. [F *solmisation* (as SOL[1], MI)]

so•lo /sólō/ n., v., & adv. •n. (pl. •los) **1** (pl. •los or so•li /–lee/) **a** a vocal or instrumental piece or passage, or a dance, performed by one person with or without accompaniment. **b** (attrib.) performed or performing a solo (*solo passage; solo violin*). **2 a** an unaccompanied flight by a pilot in an aircraft. **b** anything done by one person unaccompanied. **c** (attrib.) unaccompanied; alone. **3** (in full **solo whist**) **a** a card game like whist in which one player may oppose the others. **b** a declaration or the act of playing to win five tricks at this. •v. (•loes, •loed) **1** intr. perform a solo, esp. a solo flight. **2** tr. perform or achieve as a solo. •adv. unaccompanied; alone (*flew solo for the first time*). [It. f. L *solus* alone]

so•lo•ist /sóloist/ n. a performer of a solo, esp. in music.

Sol•o•mon /sóləmən/ n. a very wise person. □□ **Sol•o•mon•ic** /sóləmónik/ adj. [*Solomon*, king of Israel in the 10th c. BC, famed for his wisdom]

Sol•o•mon's seal n. **1** a figure like the Star of David. **2** any liliaceous plant of the genus *Polygonatum*, with arching stems and drooping green and white flowers.

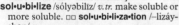
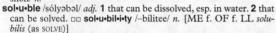

Solomon's seal 1

sol•stice /sólstis, sól–, sáwl–/ n. **1** either of the times when the sun is farthest from the equator. **2** the point in its ecliptic reached by the sun at a solstice. □□ **sol•sti•tial** /–stíshəl/ adj. [ME f. OF f. L *solstitium* f. *sol* sun + *sistere stit*- make stand]

sol•u•bi•lize /sólyəbiliz/ v.tr. make soluble or more soluble. □□ **sol•u•bi•li•za•tion** /–lizáyshən/ n.

sol•u•ble /sólyəbəl/ adj. **1** that can be dissolved, esp. in water. **2** that can be solved. □□ **sol•u•bil•i•ty** /–bílitee/ n. [ME f. OF f. LL *solubilis* (as SOLVE)]

sol•u•ble glass n. = WATER GLASS.

so•lus /sóləs/ predic.adj. (fem. **so•la** /–lə/) (esp. in a stage direction) alone; unaccompanied. [L]

sol•ute /sólyoot, sólyoot/ n. a dissolved substance. [L *solutum*, neut. of *solutus*: see SOLVE]

so•lu•tion /səloóshən/ n. **1 a** the act or a means of solving a problem or difficulty. **b** an explanation, answer, or decision. **2 a** the conversion of a solid or gas into a liquid by mixture with a liquid solvent. **b** a liquid mixture produced by this. **c** the state resulting from this (*held in solution*). **3** the act of dissolving or the state of being dissolved. **4** the act of separating or breaking. [ME f. OF f. L *solutio –onis* (as SOLVE)]

so•lu•tion set n. Math. the set of all the solutions of an equation or condition.

So•lu•tre•an /səloótreeən/ adj. & n. (also **So•lu•tri•an**) •adj. of the Paleolithic period in Europe following the Aurignacian and preceding the Magdalenian. •n. the culture of this period. [*Solutré* in E. France, where remains of it were found]

sol•vate /sólvayt/ v.intr. & tr. enter or cause to enter combination with a solvent. □□ **sol•va•tion** /–váyshən/ n.

solve /solv/ v.tr. find an answer to, or an action or course that removes or effectively deals with (a problem or difficulty). □□ **solv•a•ble** adj. **solv•er** n. [ME, = loosen, f. L *solvere solut*- unfasten, release]

sol•vent /sólvənt/ adj. & n. •adj. **1** able to dissolve or form a solution with something. **2** having enough money to meet one's liabilities. •n. **1** a solvent liquid, etc. **2** a dissolving or weakening agent. □□ **sol•ven•cy** n. (in sense 2).

so•ma[1] /sómə/ n. **1** the body as distinct from the soul. **2** the body of an organism as distinct from its reproductive cells. [Gk *sōma –atos* body]

so•ma[2] /sómə/ n. **1** an intoxicating drink used in Vedic ritual. **2** a plant yielding this. [Skr. *sōma*]

So•ma•li /sōmáalee, sə–/ n. & adj. •n. **1** (pl. same or **So•ma•lis**) a member of a Hamitic Muslim people of Somalia in NE Africa. **2** the Cushitic language of this people. •adj. of or relating to this people or language. □□ **So•ma•li•an** adj. [native name]

so•mat•ic /sōmátik, sə–/ adj. of or relating to the body, esp. as distinct from the mind. □□ **so•mat•i•cal•ly** adv. [Gk *sōmatikos* (as SOMA[1])]

so•mat•ic cell n. any cell of a living organism except the reproductive cells.

somato- /sómátō, sómətō/ comb. form the human body. [Gk *sōma –atos* body]

so•mat•o•gen•ic /sómátōjénik, sómə–/ adj. originating in the body.

so•ma•tol•o•gy /sómətóləjee/ n. the study of the physical characteristics of living bodies.

so•ma•to•ton•ic /sómátōtónik, sómə–/ adj. like a mesomorph in temperament, with predominantly physical interests.

so•mat•o•tro•phin /sómátətrófin, sómə–/ (also **so•mat•o•tro•pin**) n.

a growth hormone secreted by the pituitary gland. [as SOMATO-, TROPHIC]

so•mat•o•type /sómátətip, sómətə–/ n. physique expressed in relation to various extreme types.

som•ber /sómbər/ adj. (also **som•bre**) **1** dark; gloomy (*a somber sky*). **2** oppressively solemn or sober. **3** dismal, foreboding (*a somber prospect*). □□ **som•ber•ly** adv. **som•ber•ness** n. [F *sombre* f. OF *sombre* (n.) ult. f. L SUB- + *umbra* shade]

som•bre•ro /sombráirō/ n. (pl. •ros) a broad-brimmed felt or straw hat worn esp. in Mexico and the southwest US. [Sp. f. *sombra* shade (as SOMBER)]

some /sum/ adj., pron., & adv. •adj. **1** an unspecified amount or number of (*some water; some apples; some of them*). **2** that is unknown or unnamed (*will return some day; some fool has locked the door; to some extent*). **3** denoting an approximate number (*waited some twenty minutes*). **4** a considerable amount or number of (*went to some trouble*). **5** (usu. stressed) **a** at least a small amount of (*do have some consideration*). **b** such to a certain extent (*that is some help*). **c** colloq. notably such (*I call that some story*). •pron. some people or things; some number or amount (*I have some already; would you like some more?*). •adv. colloq. to some extent (*we talked some; do it some more*). □ **and then some** sl. and plenty more than that. **some few** see FEW. [OE *sum* f. Gmc]

-some[1] /səm/ suffix forming adjectives meaning: **1** adapted to; productive of (*cuddlesome; fearsome*). **2** characterized by being (*fulsome; lithesome*). **3** apt to (*tiresome; meddlesome*). [OE –*sum*]

-some[2] /səm/ suffix forming nouns from numerals, meaning 'a group of (so many)' (*foursome*). [OE *sum* SOME, used after numerals in genit. pl.]

-some[3] /sōm/ comb. form denoting a portion of a body, esp. of a cell (*chromosome; ribosome*). [Gk *sōma* body]

some•bod•y /súmbodee, –budee, –bud2e/ pron. & n. •pron. some person. •n. (pl. •ies) a person of importance (*is really somebody now*).

some•day /súmday/ adv. at some time in the future.

some day adv. at some point in the future.

some•how /súmhow/ adv. **1** for some reason or other (*somehow I never liked them*). **2** in some unspecified or unknown way (*he somehow dropped behind*). **3** no matter how (*must get it finished somehow*).

some•one /súmwun/ n. & pron. = SOMEBODY.

some•place /súmplays/ adv. colloq. = SOMEWHERE.

som•er•sault /súmərsawlt/ n. & v. (also **sum•mer•sault**) •n. an acrobatic movement in which a person turns head over heels in the air or on the ground and lands on the feet. •v.intr. perform a somersault. [OF *sombresault* alt. f. *sobresault* ult. f. L *supra* above + *saltus* leap f. *salire* to leap]

some•thing /súmthing/ n., pron., & adv. •n. & pron. **1 a** some unspecified or unknown thing (*have something to tell you; something has happened*). **b** (in full **something or other**) as a substitute for an unknown or forgotten description (*a student of something or other*). **2** a known or understood but unexpressed quantity, quality, or extent (*there is something about it I do not like; is something of a fool*). **3** colloq. an important or notable person or thing (*the party was quite something*). •adv. archaic in some degree. □ **or something** or some unspecified alternative possibility (*must have run away or something*). **see something of** encounter (a person) briefly or occasionally. **something else 1** something different. **2** colloq. something exceptional. **something like 1** an amount in the region of (*left something like a million dollars*). **2** somewhat like (*shaped something like a cigar*). **3** colloq. impressive; a fine specimen of. **something of** to some extent; in some sense (*is something of an expert*). [OE *sum thing* (as SOME, THING)]

some•time /súmtim/ adv. & adj. •adv. **1** at some unspecified time. **2** formerly. •attrib.adj. **1** former (*the sometime mayor*). **2** occasional.

some•times /súmtimz/ adv. at some times; occasionally.

some•what /súmhwut, –hwot, –hwət, –wut, –wot, –wət/ adv., n., & pron. •adv. to some extent (*behavior that was somewhat strange; answered somewhat hastily*). •n. & pron. archaic something (*loses somewhat of its force*). □ **more than somewhat** colloq. very (*was more than somewhat perplexed*).

some•when /súmhwen, –wen/ adv. colloq. at some time.

some•where /súmhwair, –wair/ adv. & pron. •adv. in or to some place. •pron. some unspecified place. □ **get somewhere** colloq. achieve success. **somewhere about** approximately.

so•mite /sómit/ n. each body division of a metamerically segmented animal. □□ **so•mit•ic** /sómítik/ adj. [Gk *sōma* body + –ITE[1]]

som•me•lier /suməlyáy, saw–/ n. a wine steward. [F, = butler, f. *somme* pack (as SUMPTER)]

som•nam•bu•lism /somnámbyəlizəm/ n. **1** sleepwalking. **2** a condition of the brain inducing this. □□ **som•nam•bu•lant** adj. **som•nam•bu•lar•ly** adv. **som•nam•bu•list** n. **som•nam•bu•lis•tic** adj. **som•nam•bu•lis•ti•cal•ly** adv. [L *somnus* sleep + *ambulare* walk]

som·nif·er·ous /somnífərəs/ adj. inducing sleep; soporific. [L somnifer f. somnium dream]

som·no·lent /sómnələnt/ adj. **1** sleepy; drowsy. **2** inducing drowsiness. **3** Med. in a state between sleeping and waking. □□ **som·no·lence** n. **som·no·len·cy** n. **som·no·lent·ly** adv. [ME f. OF sompnolent or L somnolentus f. somnus sleep]

son /sun/ n. **1** a boy or man in relation to either or both of his parents. **2 a** a male descendant. **b** (foll. by of) a male member of a family, nation, etc. **3** a person regarded as inheriting an occupation, quality, etc., or associated with a particular attribute (sons of freedom; sons of the soil). **4** (in full **my son**) a form of address, esp. to a boy. **5** (**the Son**) (in Christian belief) the second person of the Trinity. □□ **son·less** adj. **son·ship** n. [OE sunu f. Gmc]

so·nant /sónənt/ adj. & n. Phonet. ● adj. (of a sound) voiced and syllabic. ● n. a voiced sound, esp. other than a vowel and capable of forming a syllable, e.g., l, m, n, ng, r. □□ **so·nan·cy** n. [L sonare sonant- sound]

so·nar /sónaar/ n. **1** a system for the underwater detection of objects by reflected or emitted sound. **2** an apparatus for this. [sound navigation and ranging, after radar]

so·na·ta /sənáatə/ n. a composition for one instrument or two (one usu. being a piano accompaniment), usu. in several movements with one (esp. the first) or more in sonata form. [It., = sounded (orig. as distinct from sung): fem. past part. of sonare sound]

so·na·ta form n. a type of composition in three sections (exposition, development, and recapitulation) in which two themes (or subjects) are explored according to set key relationships.

son·a·ti·na /sónəteénə/ n. a simple or short sonata. [It., dimin. of SONATA]

sonde /sond/ n. a device sent up to obtain information about atmospheric conditions, esp. = RADIOSONDE. [F, = sounding(-line)]

sone /sōn/ n. a unit of subjective loudness, equal to 40 phons. [L sonus sound]

son et lu·mière /sáwn ay loōmyair/ n. an entertainment by night at a historic monument, building, etc., using lighting effects and recorded sound to give a dramatic narrative of its history. [F, = sound and light]

song /sawng, song/ n. **1** a short poem or other set of words set to music or meant to be sung. **2** singing or vocal music (burst into song). **3** a musical composition suggestive of a song. **4** the musical cry of some birds. **5** a short poem in rhymed stanzas. **6** archaic poetry or verse. □ **for a song** colloq. very cheaply. **on song** Brit. colloq. performing exceptionally well. □□ **song·less** adj. [OE sang f. Gmc (as SING)]

song and dance n. colloq. **1** a fuss or commotion. **2** an elaborate or complicated story, esp. one intended to distract or confuse.

song·bird /sáwngbərd, sóng–/ n. a bird with a musical call.

song·book /sáwngbook, sóng–/ n. a collection of songs with music.

song cy·cle n. a set of musically linked songs with a unifying theme.

Song of Songs n. (also **Song of Sol·o·mon**) a poetic Old Testament book traditionally attributed to Solomon.

song·smith /sáwngsmith, sóng–/ n. a writer of songs.

song spar·row n. a N. American sparrow, Melospiza melodia, with a characteristic musical song.

song·ster /sáwngstər, sóng–/ n. (fem. **song·stress** /–stris/) **1** a singer, esp. a fluent and skillful one. **2** a songbird. **3** a poet. **4** a songbook. [OE sangestre (as SONG, –STER)]

song thrush n. a thrush, Turdus philomelos, of Europe and W. Asia, with a song partly mimicked from other birds.

song·writ·er /sáwng–rītər, sóng–/ n. a writer of songs or the music for them.

son·ic /sónik/ adj. of or relating to or using sound or sound waves. □□ **son·i·cal·ly** adv. [L sonus sound]

son·ic bar·ri·er n. = SOUND BARRIER (see SOUND¹).

son·ic boom n. a loud explosive noise caused by the shock wave from an aircraft when it passes the speed of sound.

son·ic mine n. a mine exploded by the sound of a passing ship.

son-in-law n. (pl. **sons-in-law**) the husband of one's daughter.

son·net /sónit/ n. & v. ● n. a poem of 14 lines (usu. pentameters) using any of a number of formal rhyme schemes, in English usu. having ten syllables per line. ● v. (**son·net·ed**, **son·net·ing**) **1** intr. write sonnets. **2** tr. address sonnets to. [F sonnet or It. sonetto dimin. of suono SOUND¹]

son·net·eer /sónitéer/ n. a writer of sonnets.

son·ny /súnee/ n. colloq. a familiar form of address to a young boy.

son·o·bu·oy /sónəboō-ee, –boy/ n. a buoy for detecting underwater sounds and transmitting them by radio. [L sonus sound + BUOY]

son of a bitch n. coarse sl. a general term of contempt.

son of a gun n. colloq. a jocular or affectionate form of address or reference.

son·o·gram /sónəgram/ n. Med. an image of internal organs or structures produced by ultrasound waves, used for diagnostic purposes.

so·nom·e·ter /sənómitər/ n. **1** an instrument for measuring the vibration frequency of a string, etc. **2** an audiometer. [L sonus sound + –METER]

so·no·rous /sónərəs, sənáwrəs/ adj. **1** having a loud, full, or deep sound; resonant. **2** (of a speech, style, etc.) imposing; grand. □□ **so·nor·i·ty** /sən áwritee/ n. **so·no·rous·ly** adv. **so·no·rous·ness** n. [L sonorus f. sonor sound]

PRONUNCIATION TIP sonorous

The older pronunciation of this word placed the stress on the second syllable ("suh-NOR-us"), but "SAHN-or-us," with the stress on the first syllable, is now much more common in American English.

son·sy /sónsee/ adj. (also **son·sie**) (**son·si·er**, **son·si·est**) Sc. **1** plump; buxom. **2** of a cheerful disposition. **3** bringing good fortune. [ult. f. Ir. & Gael. sonas good fortune f. sona fortunate]

sook /soōk/ n. Austral. & NZ sl. **1** derog. a timid bashful person; a coward or sissy. **2** a hand-reared calf. [E dial. suck, call word for a calf]

soon /soōn/ adv. **1** after no long interval of time (shall soon know the result). **2** relatively early (must you go so soon?). **3** (prec. by how) early (with relative rather than distinctive sense) (how soon will it be ready?). **4** readily or willingly (in expressing choice or preference: which would you sooner do?; would as soon stay behind). □ **as** (or **so**) **soon as** (implying a causal or temporal connection) at the moment that; not later than; as early as (came as soon as I heard about it; disappears as soon as it's time to pay). **no sooner ... than** at the very moment that (we no sooner arrived than the rain stopped). **sooner or later** at some future time; eventually. □□ **soon·ish** adv. [OE sōna f. WG]

soot /soot/ n. & v. ● n. a black carbonaceous substance rising in fine flakes in the smoke of wood, coal, oil, etc., and deposited on the sides of a chimney, etc. ● v.tr. cover with soot. [OE sōt f. Gmc]

sooth /soōth/ n. archaic truth; fact. □ **in sooth** really; truly. [OE sōth (orig. adj., = true) f. Gmc]

soothe /soōth/ v.tr. **1** calm (a person or feelings). **2** soften or mitigate (pain). **3** archaic flatter or humor. □□ **sooth·er** n. **sooth·ing** adj. **sooth·ing·ly** adv. [OE sōthian verify f. sōth true: see SOOTH]

sooth·say·er /soōthsayər/ n. a diviner or seer. [ME, = one who says the truth: see SOOTH]

soot·y /soōtee/ adj. (**soot·i·er**, **soot·i·est**) **1** covered with or full of soot. **2** (esp. of an animal or bird) black or brownish black. □□ **soot·i·ly** adv. **soot·i·ness** n.

SOP abbr. (also **S.O.P.**) standard operating procedure.

sop /sop/ n. & v. ● n. **1** a piece of bread, etc., dipped in gravy, etc. **2** a thing given or done to pacify or bribe. ● v. (**sopped**, **sop·ping**) **1** intr. be drenched (came home sopping). **2** tr. (foll. by up) absorb (liquid) in a towel, etc. **3** tr. wet thoroughly; soak. [OE sopp, corresp. to MLG soppe, OHG sopfa bread and milk, prob. f. a weak grade of the base of OE sūpan: see SUP¹]

soph. /sof/ abbr. sophomore.

soph·ism /sófizəm/ n. a false argument, esp. one intended to deceive. [ME f. OF sophime f. L f. Gk sophisma clever device f. sophizomai become wise f. sophos wise]

soph·ist /sófist/ n. **1** one who reasons with clever but fallacious arguments. **2** Gk Antiq. a paid teacher of philosophy and rhetoric, esp. one associated with moral skepticism and specious reasoning. □□ **so·phis·tic** /–fístik/ adj. **so·phis·ti·cal** adj. **soph·is·ti·cal·ly** adv. [L sophistes f. Gk sophistēs f. sophizomai: see SOPHISM]

so·phis·ti·cate v., adj., & n. ● v. /səfístikayt/ **1** tr. make (a person, etc.) educated, cultured, or refined. **2** tr. make (equipment or techniques, etc.) highly developed or complex. **3** tr. **a** involve (a subject) in sophistry. **b** mislead (a person) by sophistry. **4** tr. deprive (a person or thing) of its natural simplicity, make artificial by worldly experience, etc. **5** tr. tamper with (a text, etc.) for purposes of argument, etc. **6** tr. adulterate (wine, etc.). **7** intr. use sophistry. ● adj. /səfístikət/ sophisticated. ● n. /səfístikət/ a sophisticated person. □□ **so·phis·ti·ca·tion** /–káyshən/ n. [med.L sophisticare tamper with f. sophisticus (as SOPHISM)]

so·phis·ti·cat·ed /səfístikaytid/ adj. **1** (of a person) educated and refined; discriminating in taste and judgment. **2** (of a thing, idea, etc.) highly developed and complex. □□ **so·phis·ti·cat·ed·ly** adv.

soph·ist·ry /sófistree/ n. (pl. **·ries**) **1** the use of sophisms. **2** a sophism.

soph·o·more /sófəmawr, sófmawr/ n. a second-year college or high school student. [earlier sophumer f. sophum, obs. var. of SOPHISM]

SPELLING TIP sophomore

Although it is acceptable to pronounce this word as if it had only two syllables ("SOF-mawr"), when spelling it, don't ignore the -o- following the -ph-.

soph·o·mor·ic /sofəmáwrik, –mór–/ adj. **1** of or relating to a sophomore. **2** overconfident and intellectually pretentious but immature and lacking judgment.

So•phy /sṓfee/ n. (pl. **•phies**) hist. a ruler of Persia in the 16th – 17th c. [Pers. ṣafī surname of the dynasty, f. Arab. ṣafī-ud-dīn pure of religion, title of the founder's ancestor]

sop•o•rif•ic /sópərífik/ adj. & n. • adj. tending to produce sleep. • n. a soporific drug or influence. □□ **sop•o•rif•er•ous** adj. **sop•o•rif•i•cal•ly** adv. [L sopor sleep + -FIC]

sop•ping /sóping/ adj. (also **sop•ping wet**) soaked with liquid; wet through. [pres. part. of SOP v.]

sop•py /sópee/ adj. (**sop•pi•er**, **sop•pi•est**) 1 colloq. **a** silly or foolish in a feeble or self-indulgent way. **b** mawkishly sentimental. 2 Brit. colloq. (foll. by on) foolishly infatuated with. 3 soaked with water. □□ **sop•pi•ly** adv. **sop•pi•ness** n. [SOP + -Y 1]

so•pra•ni•no /sóprəneénō/ n. (pl. **•nos**) Mus. an instrument higher than soprano, esp. a recorder or saxophone. [It., dimin. of SOPRANO]

so•pran•o /səprắnō, –praä–/ n. (pl. **•os** or **so•pran•i** /–nee/) 1 **a** the highest singing voice. **b** a female or boy singer with this voice. **c** a part written for it. 2 **a** an instrument of a high or the highest pitch in its family. **b** its player. [It. f. sopra above f. L supra]

so•pran•o clef n. an obsolete clef placing middle C on the lowest line of the staff.

so•ra /sáwrə/ n. (in full **sora rail**) a bird, Porzana carolina, frequenting N. American marshes. [prob. a native name]

sorb /sawrb/ n. 1 = service tree (see SERVICE2). 2 (in full **sorb apple**) its fruit. [F sorbe or L sorbus service tree, sorbum service berry]

sor•be•fa•cient /sáwrbifáyshənt/ adj. & n. Med. • adj. causing absorption. • n. a sorbefacient drug, etc. [L sorbēre suck in + -FACIENT]

sor•bet /sawrbáy, sáwrbit/ n. 1 a frozen confection of water, sugar, and usu. fruit flavoring. 2 = SHERBET. [F f. It. sorbetto f. Turk. şerbet f. Arab. šarba to drink: cf. SHERBET]

Sorb•i•an /sáwrbeeən/ n. & adj. (pertaining to) a west Slavic people or their language. Also called **Lusatian** or **Wendish**.

sor•cer•er /sáwrsərər/ n. (fem. **sor•cer•ess** /–ris/) a person who claims to use magic powers; a magician or wizard. □□ **sor•cer•ous** adj. **sor•cer•y** n. (pl. **•ies**). [obs. sorcer f. OF sorcier ult. f. L sors sortis lot]

sor•did /sáwrdid/ adj. 1 dirty or squalid. 2 ignoble, mean, or mercenary. 3 avaricious or niggardly. 4 dull colored. □□ **sor•did•ly** adv. **sor•did•ness** n. [F sordide or L sordidus f. sordēre be dirty]

sor•di•no /sawrdeénō/ n. (pl. **sor•di•ni** /–nee/) Mus. a mute for a bowed or wind instrument. [It. f. sordo mute f. L surdus]

sore /sawr/ adj., n., & adv. • adj. 1 (of a part of the body) painful from injury or disease (has a sore arm). 2 (of a person) suffering pain. 3 (often foll. by about, at) angry or vexed. 4 archaic grievous or severe (in sore need). • n. 1 a sore place on the body. 2 a source of distress or annoyance (reopen old sores). • adv. archaic grievously; severely. □□ **sore•ness** n. [OE sār (n. & adj.), sāre (adv.), f. Gmc]

sore•head /sáwrhed/ n. a touchy or disgruntled person.

so•rel /sáwrəl/ n. Brit. a male fallow deer in its third year. [var. of SORREL]

sore•ly /sáwrlee/ adv. 1 extremely; badly (am sorely tempted; sorely in need of repair). 2 severely (am sorely vexed). [OE sārlīce (as SORE, -LY2)]

sore point n. a subject causing distress or annoyance.

sore throat n. an inflammation of the membrane lining the back of the mouth, etc.

sor•ghum /sáwrgəm/ n. any tropical cereal grass of the genus Sorghum, e.g., durra. [mod.L f. It. sorgo, perh. f. unrecorded Rmc syricum (gramen) Syrian (grass)]

so•ri pl. of SORUS.

So•rop•ti•mist /sóróptimist/ n. a member of an international association of clubs for professional and business women. [L soror sister + optimist (as OPTIMISM)]

so•ror•i•ty /səráwritee, –rór–/ n. (pl. **•ties**) a female students' society in a university or college, usu. for social purposes. [med.L sororitas or L soror sister, after fraternity]

so•ro•sis /sərṓsis/ n. (pl. **so•ro•ses** /–seez/) Bot. a fleshy compound fruit, e.g., a pineapple or mulberry. [mod.L f. Gk sōros heap]

sorp•tion /sáwrpshən/ n. absorption or adsorption happening jointly or separately. [back-form. f. absorption, adsorption]

sor•rel¹ /sáwrəl, sór–/ n. any acid leaved herb of the genus Rumex, used in salads and for flavoring. [ME f. OF surele, sorele f. Gmc]

sor•rel² /sáwrəl, sór–/ n. & adj. • adj. of a light reddish-brown color. • n. 1 this color. 2 a sorrel animal, esp. a horse. 3 Brit. a sorel. [ME f. OF sorel f. sor yellowish f. Frank.]

sor•row /sáwrō, sór–/ n. & v. • n. 1 mental distress caused by loss or disappointment, etc. 2 a cause of sorrow. 3 lamentation. • v.intr. 1 feel sorrow. 2 mourn. □□ **sor•row•er** n. **sor•row•ing** adj. [OE sorh, sorg]

sor•row•ful /sáwrōfŏol, sór–/ adj. 1 feeling or showing sorrow. 2 distressing; lamentable. □□ **sor•row•ful•ly** adv. **sor•row•ful•ness** n. [OE sorhful (as SORROW, -FUL)]

sor•ry /sáwree, sór–/ adj. (**sor•ri•er**, **sor•ri•est**) 1 (predic.) pained or regretful or penitent (were sorry for what they had done; am sorry that you have to go). 2 (predic.; foll. by for) feeling pity or sympathy for (a person). 3 as an expression of apology. 4 wretched; in a poor state (a sorry sight). □ **sorry for oneself** dejected. □□ **sor•ri•ly** adv. **sor•ri•ness** n. [OE s ārig f. WG (as SORE, -Y2)]

sort /sawrt/ n. & v. • n. 1 a group of things, etc., with common attributes; a class or kind. 2 (foll. by of) roughly of the kind specified (is some sort of doctor). 3 colloq. a person of a specified character or kind (a good sort). 4 Printing a letter or piece in a font of type. 5 Computing the arrangement of data in a prescribed sequence. 6 archaic a manner or way. • v.tr. (often foll. by out, over) arrange systematically or according to type, class, etc. □ **after a sort** after a fashion. **in some sort** to a certain extent. **of a sort** (or **of sorts**) colloq. not fully deserving the name (a holiday of sorts). **out of sorts** 1 slightly unwell. 2 in low spirits; irritable. **sort of** colloq. as it were; to some extent (I sort of expected it). **sort out** 1 separate into sorts. 2 select (things of one or more sorts) from a miscellaneous group. 3 disentangle or put into order. 4 resolve (a problem or difficulty). 5 colloq. deal with or reprimand (a person). □□ **sort•a•ble** adj. **sort•er** n. **sort•ing** n. [ME f. OF sorte ult. f. L sors sortis lot, condition]

►See note at KIND.

sor•tie /sáwrtee, sawrtée/ n. & v. • n. 1 a sally, esp. from a besieged garrison. 2 an operational flight by a single military aircraft. • v.intr. (**sor•ties**, **sor•tied**, **sor•tie•ing**) make a sortie; sally. [F, fem. past part. of sortir go out]

sor•ti•lege /sáwrt'lij/ n. divination by lots. [ME f. OF f. med.L sortilegium sorcery f. L sortilegus sorcerer (as SORT, legere choose)]

so•rus /sáwrəs/ n. (pl. **so•ri** /–rī/) Bot. a heap or cluster, esp. of spore cases on the underside of a fern leaf, or in a fungus or lichen. [mod.L f. Gk sōros heap]

SOS /ésṓ-és/ n. (pl. **SOSs**) 1 an international code signal of extreme distress, used esp. by ships at sea. 2 an urgent appeal for help. 3 Brit. a message broadcast to an untraceable person in an emergency. [chosen as being easily transmitted and recognized in Morse code]

so-so adj. & adv. • adj. (usu. predic.) indifferent; not very good. • adv. indifferently; only moderately well.

sos•te•nu•to /sóstənṓtō/ adv., adj., & n. Mus. • adv. & adj. in a sustained or prolonged manner. • n. (pl. **•tos**) a passage to be played in this way. [It., past part. of sostenere SUSTAIN]

sot /sot/ n. & v. • n. a habitual drunkard. • v.intr. (**sot•ted**, **sot•ting**) Brit. drink alcohol habitually. □□ **sot•tish** adj. [OE sott & OF sot foolish, f. med.L sottus, of unkn. orig.]

so•te•ri•ol•o•gy /sətéereeóləjee/ n. Theol. the doctrine of salvation. [Gk sōtēria salvation + -LOGY]

So•thic /sṓthik, sóth–/ adj. of or relating to the Dog Star, esp. with ref. to the ancient Egyptian year fixed by its heliacal rising. [Gk Sōthis f. the Egypt. name of the Dog Star]

sot•to vo•ce /sótō vṓchee, sáwt-tō váwche/ adv. in an undertone or aside. [It. sotto under + voce voice]

sou /sṓo/ n. 1 hist. a former French coin of low value. 2 (usu. with neg.) colloq. a very small amount of money (hasn't a sou). [F, orig. pl. sous f. OF sout f. L SOLIDUS]

sou•brette /sṓobrét/ n. 1 a coquettish maidservant or similar female character in a comedy. 2 an actress taking this part. [F f. Prov. soubreto fem. of soubret coy f. sobrar f. L superare be above]

sou•bri•quet var. of SOBRIQUET.

sou•chong /sṓochóng, –shóng/ n. a fine variety of black tea. [Chin. xiao small + zhong sort]

souf•fle /sṓofəl/ n. Med. a low murmur heard in the auscultation of various organs, etc. [F f. souffler blow f. L sufflare]

souf•flé /sṓofláy/ n. & adj. • n. 1 a light dish usu. made with flavored egg yolks added to stiffly beaten egg whites and baked (cheese soufflé). 2 any of various light dishes made with beaten egg whites. • adj. 1 light and frothy (omelette soufflé). 2 (of ceramics) decorated with small spots. [F past part. (as SOUFFLE)]

sough /sow, suf/ v. & n. • v.intr. make a moaning, whistling, or rushing sound as of the wind in trees, etc. • n. this sound. [OE swōgan resound]

sought past and past part. of SEEK.

sought-af•ter adj. much in demand; generally desired or courted.

souk /sṓok/ n. (also **suk, sukh, suq**) a marketplace in Arab countries. [Arab. sūk]

soul /sōl/ n. 1 the spiritual or immaterial part of a human being, often regarded as immortal. 2 the moral or emotional or intellectual nature of a person or animal. 3 the personification or pattern of something (the very soul of discretion). 4 an individual (not a soul in sight). 5 **a** a person regarded with familiarity or pity, etc. (the poor soul was utterly confused). **b** a person regarded as embodying moral or intellectual qualities (left that to meaner souls). 6 a person regarded as the animating or essential part of something (the life and soul of the party). 7 emotional or intellectual energy or intensity, esp. as revealed in a work of art (pictures that lack soul). 8 African-American culture, music, ethnic pride, etc. □ **upon my soul** an exclamation of surprise. □□ **–souled** adj. (in comb.). [OE sāwol, sāwel, sāwl, f. Gmc]

soul-des·troy·ing adj. (of an activity, etc.) deadeningly monotonous.

soul food n. traditional southern African-American foods.

soul·ful /sólfool/ adj. **1** having or expressing or evoking deep feeling. **2** colloq. overly emotional. □□ **soul·ful·ly** adv. **soul·ful·ness** n.

soul·less /sól-lis/ adj. **1** lacking sensitivity or noble qualities. **2** having no soul. **3** undistinguished or uninteresting. □□ **soul·less·ly** adv. **soul·less·ness** n.

soul mate n. a person ideally suited to another.

soul mu·sic n. a kind of music incorporating elements of rhythm and blues and gospel music, popularized by African Americans

soul of hon·or n. a person incapable of dishonorable conduct.

soul-search·ing n. & adj. ● n. the examination of one's emotions and motives. ● adj. characterized by this.

sound[1] /sownd/ n. & v. ● n. **1 a** a sensation caused in the ear by the vibration of the surrounding air or other medium. **2 a** vibrations causing this sensation. **b** similar vibrations whether audible or not. **3** what is or may be heard. **4** an idea or impression conveyed by words (don't like the sound of that). **5** mere words (sound and fury). **6** (in full **musical sound**) sound produced by continuous and regular vibrations (opp. NOISE n. 3). **7** any of a series of articulate utterances (vowel and consonant sounds). **8** music, speech, etc., accompanying a movie or other visual presentation. **9** (often attrib.) broadcasting by radio as distinct from television. **10** a distinctive musical style or set of characteristics (pop music with a classical sound). ● v. **1** intr. & tr. emit or cause to emit sound. **2** tr. utter or pronounce (sound a note of alarm). **3** intr. convey an impression when heard (you sound worried). **4** tr. give an audible signal for (an alarm, etc.). **5** tr. test (the lungs, etc.) by noting the sound produced. **6** tr. cause to resound; make known (sound their praises). □ **sound off** talk loudly or express one's opinions forcefully. □□ **sound·less** adj. **sound·less·ly** adv. **sound·less·ness** n. [ME f. AF soun, OF son (n.), AF suner, OF soner (v.) f. L sonus]

sound[2] /sownd/ adj. & adv. ● adj. **1** healthy; not diseased or injured. **2** undamaged; in good condition. **3** (of an opinion or policy, etc.) correct; orthodox; well-founded; judicious; legally valid. **4** financially secure (a sound investment). **5** undisturbed (a sound sleep). **6** severe; hard (a sound blow). ● adv. soundly (sound asleep). □□ **sound·ly** adv. **sound·ness** n. [ME sund, isund f. OE gesund f. WG]

sound[3] /sownd/ v. & n. ● v. tr. & intr. **1** tr. test the depth or quality of the bottom of (the sea or a river, etc.). **2** tr. (often foll. by out) inquire (esp. cautiously or discreetly) into the opinions or feelings of (a person). **3** tr. find the depth of water in (a ship's hold). **4** tr. get records of temperature, humidity, pressure, etc., from (the upper atmosphere). **5** tr. examine (a person's bladder, etc.) with a probe. **6** intr. (of a whale or fish) dive to the bottom. ● n. a surgeon's probe. □□ **sound·er** n. [ME f. OF sonder ult. f. L SUB- + unda wave]

sound[4] /sownd/ n. **1 a** a narrow passage of water connecting two seas or a sea with a lake, etc. **b** an arm of the sea. **2** a fish's air bladder. [OE sund, = ON sund swimming, strait, f. Gmc (as SWIM)]

sound bar·ri·er n. the high resistance of air to objects moving at speeds near that of sound.

sound bite n. a short extract from a recorded interview, chosen for its pungency or appropriateness.

sound·board /sówndbawrd/ n. a thin sheet of wood over which the strings of a piano, etc., pass to increase the sound produced.

sound box n. the hollow chamber providing resonance and forming the body of a stringed musical instrument.

sound ef·fect n. a sound other than speech or music made artificially for use in a play, movie, etc.

sound en·gi·neer n. an engineer dealing with acoustics, etc.

sound hole n. an aperture in the belly of some stringed instruments.

sound·ing[1] /sównding/ n. **1 a** the action or process of measuring the depth of water, now usu. by means of echo. **b** an instance of this (took a sounding). **2** (in pl.) **a** a region close to the shore of the right depth for sounding. **b** Naut. measurements taken by sounding. **c** cautious investigation (made soundings as to his suitability). **3 a** the determination of any physical property at a depth in the sea or at a height in the atmosphere. **b** an instance of this.

sound·ing[2] /sównding/ adj. **1** giving forth (esp. loud or resonant) sound (sounding brass). **2** emptily boastful, resonant, or imposing (sounding promises).

sound·ing bal·loon n. a balloon used to obtain information about the upper atmosphere.

sound·ing board n. **1** a canopy over a pulpit, etc., to direct sound toward the congregation. **2** = SOUNDBOARD. **3 a** a means of causing opinions, etc., to be more widely known (used his students as a sounding board). **b** a person, etc., used as a trial audience.

sound·ing line n. a line used in sounding the depth of water.

sound·ing rod n. a rod used in finding the depth of water in a ship's hold (see SOUND[3]).

sound post n. a small prop between the belly and back of some stringed instruments.

sound·proof /sówndproof/ adj. & v. ● adj. impervious to sound. ● v. tr. make soundproof.

sound shift n. see SHIFT n. 6.

sound spec·tro·graph n. an instrument for analyzing sound into its frequency components.

sound·track /sówndtrak/ n. **1** the recorded sound element of a movie, television broadcast, etc. **2** this recorded on the edge of a film, videotype, etc., in optical or magnetic form.

sound wave n. a wave of compression and rarefaction, by which sound is propagated in an elastic medium, e.g., air.

soup /soop/ n. & v. ● n. **1 a** a liquid dish made by boiling meat, fish, or vegetables, etc., in stock or water. **2** sl. nitroglycerine or gelignite, esp. for safe-cracking. **3** sl. the chemicals in which film is developed. **4** colloq. fog; thick cloud. ● v. tr. (usu. foll. by up) colloq. **1** increase the power and efficiency of (an engine). **2** increase the power or impact of (writing, music, etc.). □ **in the soup** colloq. in difficulties. [F soupe sop, broth, f. LL suppa f. Gmc: cf. SOP, SUP[1]]

soup and fish n. Brit. colloq. evening dress.

soup·çon /soopsáwn, soopsón/ n. a very small quantity; a dash. [F f. OF sou(s)peçon f. med.L suspectio –onis: see SUSPICION]

soup kitch·en n. a place dispensing soup, etc., to the poor.

soup plate n. a deep wide-rimmed plate for serving soup.

soup·spoon /soopspoon/ n. a spoon, usu. with a large rounded bowl, for eating soup.

soup·y /soopee/ adj. (**soup·i·er**, **soup·i·est**) **1** of or resembling soup. **2** colloq. sentimental; mawkish. □□ **soup·i·ly** adv. **soup·i·ness** n.

sour /sowr/ adj., n., & v. ● adj. **1** having an acid taste like lemon or vinegar, esp. because of unripeness (sour apples). **2 a** (of food, esp. milk or bread) bad because of fermentation. **b** smelling or tasting rancid or unpleasant. **3** (of a person, temper, etc.) harsh; morose; bitter. **4** (of a thing) unpleasant; distasteful. **5** (of the soil) deficient in lime and usually dank. ● n. **1** a drink with lemon or lime juice (whiskey sour). **2** an acid solution used in bleaching, etc. ● v. tr & intr. make or become sour (soured the cream; soured by misfortune). □ **go** (or **turn**) **sour 1** (of food, etc.) become sour. **2** turn out badly (the job went sour on him). **3** lose one's enthusiasm. □□ **sour·ish** adj. **sour·ly** adv. **sour·ness** n. [OE sūr f. Gmc]

source /sawrs/ n. & v. ● n. **1** a spring or fountainhead from which a stream issues (the sources of the Nile). **2** a place, person, or thing from which something originates (the source of all our troubles). **3** a person or document, etc., providing evidence (reliable sources of information; historical source material). **4 a** a body emitting radiation, etc. **b** Physics a place from which a fluid or current flows. **c** Electronics a part of a transistor from which carriers flow into the interelectrode channel. ● v. tr. obtain (esp. components) from a specified source. □ **at source** at the point of origin or issue. [ME f. OF sors, sourse, past part. of sourdre rise f. L surgere]

source·book /sáwrsbook/ n. a collection of documentary sources for the study of a subject.

source crit·i·cism n. the evaluation of different, esp. successive, literary or historical sources.

sour cream n. cream deliberately fermented by adding bacteria.

sour·dough /sówrdō/ n. **1** fermenting dough, esp. that left over from a previous baking, used as leaven. **2** an old-timer in Alaska, etc. [dial., = leaven, in allusion to piece of sour dough for raising bread baked in winter]

sour grapes n. resentful disparagement of something one cannot personally acquire.

sour mash n. a brewing or distilling mash made acid to promote fermentation.

sour·puss /sówrpoos/ n. colloq. an ill-tempered person. [SOUR + PUSS = face]

sour·sop /sówrsop/ n. **1** a W. Indian evergreen tree, Annona muricata. **2** the large succulent fruit of this tree.

sous- /soo/ prefix (in words adopted from French) subordinate; under (sous-chef). [F]

sou·sa·phone /soozəfōn/ n. a large brass bass wind instrument encircling the player's body. □□ **sou·sa·phon·ist** n. [J. P. Sousa, Amer. bandmaster d. 1932, after saxophone]

souse /sows/ v. & n. ● v. tr. **1** put (pickles, fish, etc.) in brine. **2** tr. & intr. plunge into liquid. **3** tr. (as **soused** adj.) colloq. drunk. **4** tr. (usu. foll. by in) soak (a thing) in liquid. **5** tr. (usu. foll. by over) throw (liquid) over a thing. ● n. **1 a** a pickling brine made with salt. **b** food, esp. a pig's head, etc., in pickle. **2 a** a dip, plunge, or drenching in water. **3** colloq. **a** a drinking bout. **b** a drunkard. [ME f. OF sous, souz pickle f. OS sultia, OHG sulza brine f. Gmc: cf. SALT]

sou·tache /sootásh/ n. a narrow flat ornamental braid used to trim garments. [F f. Magyar sujtás]

sou·tane /sootáan/ n. RC Ch., Anglican Ch. a cassock worn by a priest. [F f. It. sottana f. sotto under f. L subtus]

sou·ter /sootər/ n. Sc. & No. of Engl. a shoemaker; a cobbler. [OE sū tere f. L sutor f. suere sut- sew]

sou·ter·rain /sootərayn/ n. esp. Archaeol. an underground chamber or passage. [F f. sous under + terre earth]

south /sowth/ *n., adj., adv., & v.* ● *n.* **1** the point of the horizon 90° clockwise from east. **2** the compass point corresponding to this. **3** the direction in which this lies. **4** (usu. **the South**) **a** the part of the world or a country or a town lying to the south. **b** the southern states of the US. **5** *Bridge* a player occupying the position designated 'south'. ● *adj.* **1** toward, at, near, or facing the south (*a south wall; south country*). **2** coming from the south (*south wind*). ● *adv.* **1** toward, at, or near the south (*they traveled south*). **2** (foll. by *of*) further south than. ● *v.intr.* **1** move toward the south. **2** (of a celestial body) cross the meridian. □ **south by east** (or **west**) between south and south-southeast (or south-southwest). **to the south** (often foll. by *of*) in a southerly direction. [OE *s ūth*]

South Af·ri·can *adj. & n.* ● *adj.* of or relating to the republic of South Africa. ● *n.* **1** a native or inhabitant of South Africa. **2** a person of South African descent.

South A·mer·i·can *adj. & n.* ● *adj.* of or relating to South America. ● *n.* a native or inhabitant of South America.

south·bound /sówthbownd/ *adj.* traveling or leading southward.

South·down /sówthdown/ *n.* **1** a sheep of a breed raised esp. for mutton, orig. in England. **2** this breed.

south·east *n., adj., & adv.* ● *n.* **1** the point of the horizon midway between south and east. **2** the compass point corresponding to this. **3** the direction in which this lies. **4** (**Southeast**) the part of a country or town lying to the southeast. ● *adj.* of, toward, or coming from the southeast. ● *adv.* toward, at, or near the southeast. □□ **south·east·er·ly** *adj. & adv.* **south·east·ern** *adj.*

south·east·er /sówtheéstər, sou·éestər/ *n.* a southeast wind

south·er /sówthər/ *n.* a south wind.

south·er·ly /súthərlee/ *adj., adv., & n.* ● *adj. & adv.* **1** in a southern position or direction. **2** (of a wind) blowing from the south. ● *n.* (*pl.* **·lies**) a southerly wind.

south·ern /súthərn/ *adj.* esp. Geog. **1** of or in the south; inhabiting the south. **2** lying or directed toward the south (*at the southern end*). □□ **south·ern·most** *adj.* [OE *sútherne* (as SOUTH, −ERN)]

Southern Cross *n.* a southern constellation in the shape of a cross.

south·ern·er /súthərnər/ *n.* a native or inhabitant of the south.

southern hem·i·sphere *n.* the half of the earth below the equator.

southern lights *n.* the aurora australis.

southern states *n.* the states in the south, esp. the southeast, of the US, esp. those identified with the Confederacy.

south·ern·wood /súthərnwŏod/ *n.* a bushy kind of wormwood, *Artemisia abrotanum*.

south·ing /sówthing/ *n.* **1** a southern movement. **2** *Naut.* the distance traveled or measured southward. **3** *Astron.* the angular distance of a star, etc., south of the celestial equator.

south·paw /sówthpaw/ *n. & adj. colloq.* ● *n.* a left-handed person, esp. a left-handed pitcher in baseball. ● *adj.* left-handed.

south pole *n.* see POLE[2].

South Sea *n.* the southern Pacific Ocean.

south-south·east *n.* the point or direction midway between south and southeast.

south-south·west *n.* the point or direction midway between south and southwest.

south·ward /sówthwərd/ *adj., adv., & n.* ● *adj. & adv.* (also **south·wards**) toward the south. ● *n.* a southward direction or region.

south·west *n., adj., & adv.* ● *n.* **1** the point of the horizon midway between south and west. **2** the compass point corresponding to this. **3** the direction in which this lies. **4** (**Southwest**) the part of a country or town lying to the southwest. ● *adj.* of, toward, or coming from the southwest. ● *adv.* toward, at, or near the southwest. □□ **south·west·er·ly** *adj. & adv.* **south·west·ern** *adj.*

south·west·er /sówthwéstər, sow·wéstər/ *n.* a southwest wind.

south wind *n.* a wind blowing from the south.

sou·ve·nir /sóovəneér/ *n. & v.* ● *n.* (often foll. by *of*) a memento of an occasion, place, etc. ● *v.tr. Brit. sl.* take as a "souvenir"; pilfer; steal. [F f. *souvenir* remember f. L *subvenire* occur to the mind (as SUB-, *venire* come)]

souv·la·ki /sóovlaakee/ *n.* (*pl.* **souv·la·kia** /−keeə/) a Greek dish of pieces of meat (usu. lamb) grilled on a skewer. [mod. Gk]

sou'·wes·ter /sow·wéstər/ *n.* **1** = SOUTH-WESTER. **2** a waterproof hat with a broad flap covering the neck.

sov. /sov/ *abbr. Brit.* sovereign.

sov·er·eign /sóvrin/ *n. & adj.* ● *n.* **1** a supreme ruler, esp. a monarch. **2** *Brit. hist.* a gold coin nominally worth £1. ● *adj.* **1 a** supreme (*sovereign power*). **b** unmitigated (*sovereign contempt*). **2** excellent; effective (*a sovereign remedy*). **3** possessing independent national power (*a sovereign state*). **4** royal (*our sovereign lord*). □□ **sov·er·eign·ly** *adv.*

sov·er·eign·ty *n.* (*pl.* **·ties**). [ME f. OF *so(u)verain* f. L: −*g*− by assoc. with *reign*]

so·vi·et /sóveeət, sóv−/ *n. & adj. hist.* ● *n.* **1** an elected local, district, or national council in the former USSR. **2** (**Soviet**) a citizen of the

sou'wester 2

former USSR. **3** a revolutionary council of workers, peasants, etc., before 1917. ● *adj.* (usu. **Soviet**) of or concerning the former Soviet Union. □□ **So·vi·et·ize** *v.tr.* **So·vi·et·i·za·tion** *n.* [Russ. *sovet* council]

so·vi·et·ol·o·gist /sóveeətóləjist, sóv−/ *n.* a person who studies the former Soviet Union.

sow[1] /sō/ *v.tr.* (*past* **sowed** /sōd/; *past part.* **sown** /sōn/ or **sowed**) **1** (also *absol.*) **a** scatter or put (seed) on or in the earth. **b** (often foll. by *with*) plant (a field, etc.) with seed. **2** initiate; arouse (*sowed doubt in her mind*). **3** (foll. by *with*) cover thickly with. □ **sow the seed** (or **seeds**) of first give rise to; implant (an idea, etc.). □□ **sow·er** *n.* **sow·ing** *n.* [OE *sāwan* f. Gmc]

sow[2] /sow/ *n.* **1 a** a female adult pig, esp. after farrowing. **b** a female guinea pig. **c** the female of some other species. **2 a** the main trough through which molten iron runs into side channels to form pigs. **b** a large block of iron so formed. **3** (in full **sow bug**) a woodlouse. [OE *sugu*]

sow·bread /sówbred/ *n.* a tuberous plant, *Cyclamen hederifolium*, with solitary nodding flowers.

sown *past part.* of SOW[1].

sow this·tle /sów thisəl/ *n.* any plant of the genus *Sonchus* with thistle-like leaves and milky juice.

sox *colloq. pl.* of SOCK[1].

soy /soy/ *n.* (also **soy·a** /sóyə/) **1** (also **soy sauce**) a sauce made esp. in Asia from pickled soybeans. **2** = SOYBEAN. [Jap. *shō-yu* f. Chin. *shi-you* f. *shi* salted beans + *you* oil]

soy·bean /sóybeen/ *n.* a leguminous plant, *Glycine soja*, orig. of SE Asia, cultivated for the edible oil and flour it yields, and used as a replacement for animal protein in certain foods. **b** the seed of this. [Du. *soja* f. Malay *soi* (as SOY)]

soz·zled /sózəld/ *adj. colloq.* very drunk. [past part. of dial. *sozzle* mix sloppily (prob. imit.)]

SP *abbr.* starting price.

spa /spaa/ *n.* **1** a curative mineral spring. **2** a place or resort with this. **3** a fashionable resort or hotel. **4** a hot tub, esp. one with a whirlpool device. **5** = HEALTH SPA. [*Spa* in Belgium]

space /spays/ *n. & v.* ● *n.* **1 a** a continuous unlimited area or expanse which may or may not contain objects, etc. **b** an interval between one, two, or three dimensional points or objects (*a space of 10 feet*). **c** an empty area; room (*clear a space in the corner; occupies too much space*). **2** a large unoccupied region (*the wide open spaces*). **3** = OUTER SPACE. **4** a place, seat, berth, etc., made available (*no space on the bus*). **5** an interval of time (*in the space of an hour*). **6** the amount of paper used in writing, etc. (*hadn't the space to discuss it*). **7 a** a blank between printed, typed, or written words, etc. **b** a piece of metal providing this. **8** *Mus.* each of the blanks between the lines of a staff. ● *v.tr.* **1** set or arrange at intervals. **2** put spaces between (esp. words, letters, lines, etc,. in printing, typing, or writing). **3** (as **spaced** *adj.*) (often foll. by *out*) *sl.* in a state of euphoria, esp. from taking drugs. □□ **spac·er** *n.* **spac·ing** *n.* (esp. in sense 2 of *v.*). [ME f. OF *espace* f. L *spatium*]

space age *n.* the era when space travel has become possible.

space bar *n.* a long key on a keyboard for making a space between words, etc.

space ca·det *n. sl.* a person who appears absentminded or removed from reality.

space·craft /spáyskraft/ *n.* a vehicle used for traveling in space.

space flight *n.* **1** a journey through space. **2** = SPACE TRAVEL.

space heat·er *n.* a heater, usu. electric, that warms a limited space, as a room.

space·man /spáysman/ *n.* (*pl.* **·men**; *fem.* **space·wom·an**, *pl.* **·wom·en**) a person who travels through outer space; space traveler.

space probe *n.* = PROBE *n.* 4.

space-sav·ing *adj.* occupying little space.

space·ship /spáys-ship/ *n.* a spacecraft, esp. one controlled by its crew.

space shut·tle *n.* a rocket for repeated use carrying people and cargo between the earth and space.

space sta·tion *n.* an artificial satellite used as a base for operations in space.

space·suit /spáys-sŏot, −syŏot/ *n.* a garment designed to allow an astronaut to survive in space.

space-time *n.* (also **space-time con·tin·u·um**) the fusion of the concepts of space and time, esp. as a four-dimensional continuum.

space trav·el *n.* travel through outer space. □□ **space trav·el·er** *n.*

space walk *n.* any physical activity by an astronaut in space outside a spacecraft.

spac·ey /spáysee/ *adj.* (also **spac·y**) *sl.* **1** seemingly out of touch with reality; disoriented. **2** being in a confused or dazed state because of the influence of mind-altering drugs.

spa·cial var. of SPATIAL.

spa·cious /spáyshəs/ *adj.* having ample space; covering a large area; roomy. □□ **spa·cious·ly** adv. **spa·cious·ness** n. [ME f. OF spacios or L spatiosus (as SPACE)]

Spack·le /spákəl/ n. Trademark a pastelike compound used for filling holes and cracks in plasterboard.

spade[1] /spayd/ n. & v. ●n. **1** a tool used for digging or cutting the ground, etc., with a sharp-edged metal blade and a long handle. **2** a tool of a similar shape for various purposes, e.g., for removing the blubber from a whale. **3** anything resembling a spade. ●v.tr. dig over (ground) with a spade. □ **call a spade a spade** speak plainly or bluntly. □□ **spade·ful** n. (pl. **·fuls**). [OE spadu, spada]

spade[2] /spayd/ n. **1** a a playing card of a suit denoted by black inverted heart-shaped figures with small stalks. **b** (in pl.) this suit. **2** sl. offens. an African-American. □ **in spades** sl. to a high degree; with great force. [It. spade pl. of spada sword f. L spatha f. Gk spathē, rel. to SPADE[1]: assoc. with the shape of a pointed spade]

spade beard n. an oblong-shaped beard.

spade foot n. a square spadelike enlargement at the end of a chair leg.

spade·work /spáydwərk/ n. hard or routine preparatory work.

spa·dille /spədíl/ n. **1** the ace of spades in ombre and quadrille. **2** the highest trump, esp. the ace of spades. [F f. Sp. espadilla dimin. of espada sword (as SPADE[2])]

spa·dix /spáydiks/ n. (pl. **spa·di·ces** /-seez/) Bot. a spike of flowers closely arranged round a fleshy axis and usu. enclosed in a spathe. □□ **spa·di·ceous** /-díshəs/ adj. [L f. Gk, = palm branch]

spae /spay/ v.intr. & tr. Sc. foretell; prophesy. [ME f. ON spá]

spa·ghet·ti /spəgétee/ n. pasta made in solid strings, between macaroni and vermicelli in thickness. [It., pl. of dimin. of spago string: Bolognese It., = of Bologna]

spa·ghet·ti squash n. a type of squash whose flesh forms spaghettilike strands when cooked.

spa·ghet·ti west·ern n. a movie about the American West made cheaply in Italy.

spa·hi /spáahee/ n. hist. **1** a member of the Turkish irregular cavalry. **2** a member of the Algerian cavalry in French service. [Turk. sipāhī formed as SEPOY]

spake /spayk/ archaic past of SPEAK.

spall /spawl/ n. & v. ●n. a splinter or chip, esp. of rock. ●v.intr. & tr. break up or cause (ore) to break up in preparation for sorting. [ME (also spale): orig. unkn.]

spall·a·tion /spawláyshən/ n. Physics the breakup of a bombarded nucleus into several parts.

spal·peen /spalpéen/ n. Ir. **1** a rascal; a villain. **2** a youngster. [Ir. spailpín, of unkn. orig.]

Spam /spam/ n. Trademark a canned meat product made mainly from ham. [spiced ham]

span[1] /span/ n. & v. ●n. **1** the full extent from end to end in space or time (the span of a bridge; the whole span of history). **2** each arch or part of a bridge between piers or supports. **3** the maximum lateral extent of an airplane, its wing, a bird's wing, etc. **4 a** the maximum distance between the tips of the thumb and little finger. **b** this as a measurement, equal to 9 inches. **5** a short distance or time (our life is but a span). ●v. (**spanned**, **span·ning**) **1** tr. **a** (of a bridge, arch, etc.) stretch from side to side; extend across (the bridge spanned the river). **b** (of a builder, etc.) bridge (a river, etc.). **2** tr. extend across (space or a period of time, etc.). **3** tr. measure or cover the extent of (a thing) with one's hand with the fingers stretched (spanned a tenth on the piano). [OE span(n) or OF espan]

span[2] /span/ n. **1** Naut. a rope with both ends fastened to take purchase in a loop. **2** a matched pair of horses, mules, etc. **3** S.Afr. a team of two or more pairs of oxen. [LG & Du. span f. spannen unite]

span[3] see SPICK-AND-SPAN.

span[4] /span/ archaic past of SPIN.

span·drel /spándril/ n. Archit. **1** the almost triangular space between one side of the outer curve of an arch, a wall, and the ceiling or framework. **2** the space between the shoulders of adjoining arches and the ceiling or molding above. [perh. f. AF spaund(e)re, or f. espaundre EXPAND]

span·drel wall n. a wall built on the curve of an arch, filling in the spandrel.

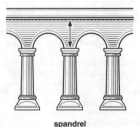

spandrel

spang /spang/ adv. colloq. exactly; completely (spang in the middle). [20th c.: orig. unkn.]

span·gle /spánggəl/ n. & v. ●n. **1** a small thin piece of glittering material esp. used in quantity to ornament a dress, etc.; a sequin. **2** a small sparkling object. **3** (in full **spangle gall**) a spongy excrescence on oak-leaves. ●v.tr. (esp. as **spangled** adj.) cover with or as with spangles (spangled costume). □□ **span·gly** /spángglee/ adj. [ME f. spang f. MDu. spange, OHG spanga, ON spöng brooch f. Gmc]

Span·iard /spányərd/ n. **1 a** a native or inhabitant of Spain in southern Europe. **b** a person of Spanish descent. **2** NZ a spear grass. [ME f. OF Espaignart f. Espaigne Spain]

span·iel /spányəl/ n. **1 a** a dog of any of various breeds with a long silky coat and drooping ears. **b** any of these breeds. **2** an obsequious or fawning person. [ME f. OF espaigneul Spanish (dog) f. Rmc Hispaniolus (unrecorded) f. Hispania Spain]

Span·ish /spánish/ adj. & n. ●adj. of or relating to Spain or its people or language. ●n. **1** the language of Spain and Spanish America. **2** (prec. by the; treated as pl.) the people of Spain. [ME f. Spain, with shortening of the first element]

Span·ish A·mer·i·ca n. those parts of America orig. settled by Spaniards, including Central and South America and part of the West Indies.

Span·ish Ar·ma·da n. hist. the Spanish war fleet sent against England in 1588.

Span·ish bay·o·net n. a yucca, Yucca aloifolia, with stiff sharp-pointed leaves.

Span·ish chest·nut n. = CHESTNUT n. 1b.

Span·ish fly n. a bright green beetle, Lytta vesicatoria, formerly dried and used for raising blisters, as a supposed aphrodisiac, etc.

Span·ish gui·tar n. the standard six-stringed acoustic guitar, used esp. for classical and folk music.

Span·ish mack·er·el n. any of various large mackerels, esp. Scomberomorus colias or S. maculatus.

Span·ish Main n. hist. the NE coast of South America between the Orinoco River and Panama, and adjoining parts of the Caribbean Sea.

Span·ish moss n. an epiphytic plant, Tillandsia usneoides, common in the southern US, with grayish-green fronds that hang from the branches of trees.

Span·ish om·e·let n. an omelet served with a sauce of tomatoes, onions, and green peppers.

Span·ish on·ion n. a large mild-flavored onion.

Span·ish rice n. rice cooked with chopped onions, peppers, tomatoes, spices, etc.

spank /spangk/ v. & n. ●v. **1** tr. slap, esp. on the buttocks, with the open hand. **2** intr. (of a horse, etc.) move briskly, esp. between a trot and a gallop. ●n. a slap, esp. with the open hand on the buttocks. [perh. imit.]

spank·er /spángkər/ n. **1** a person or thing that spanks. **2** Naut. a fore-and-aft sail set on the after side of the mizzenmast. **3** a fast horse. **4** colloq. a person or thing of notable size or quality.

spank·ing /spángking/ adj., adv., & n. ●adj. **1** (esp. of a horse) moving quickly; lively; brisk (at a spanking trot). **2** colloq. striking; excellent. ●adv. colloq. very; exceedingly (spanking clean). ●n. the act or an instance of slapping, esp. on the buttocks as a punishment for children.

span·ner /spánər/ n. **1** the crossbar of a bridge, etc. **2** Brit. an instrument for turning or gripping a nut on a screw, etc. (cf. WRENCH). □ **a spanner in the works** Brit. colloq. a drawback or impediment. [G spannen draw tight: see SPAN[2]]

span roof n. a roof with two inclined sides (cf. PENTHOUSE 2, LEAN-TO).

spar[1] /spaar/ n. **1** a stout pole esp. used for the mast, yard, etc., of a ship. **2** the main longitudinal beam of an airplane wing. [ME sparre, sperre f. OF esparre or ON sperra or direct f. Gmc: cf. MDu., MLG sparre, OS, OHG sparro]

spar[2] /spaar/ v. & n. ●v.intr. (**sparred**, **spar·ring**) **1** (often foll. by at) make the motions of boxing without landing heavy blows. **2** engage in argument (they are always sparring). **3** (of a gamecock) fight with the feet or spurs. ●n. **1 a** a sparring motion. **b** a boxing match. **2** a cockfight. **3** an argument or dispute. [ME f. OE sperran, spyrran, of unkn. orig.: cf. ON sperrask kick out]

spar[3] /spaar/ n. any crystalline, easily cleavable, and non-lustrous mineral, e.g., calcite or fluorspar. □□ **spar·ry** adj. [MLG, rel. to OE sp æren of plaster, sp ærstān gypsum]

spar bu·oy n. a buoy made of a spar with one end moored so that the other stands up.

spar deck n. the light upper deck of a vessel.

spare /spair/ adj., n., & v. ●adj. **1 a** not required for ordinary use; extra (have no spare cash; spare time). **b** reserved for emergency or occasional use (slept in the spare room). **2** lean; thin. **3** scanty; frugal; not copious (a spare diet; a spare prose style). **4** colloq. not wanted or used by others (a spare seat in the front row). ●n. **1** a spare part; a duplicate. **2** Bowling the knocking down of all the pins with the first two balls. ●v. **1** tr. afford to give up or do without; dispense with (cannot spare him just now; can spare you a couple). **2** tr. **a** abstain from killing, hurting, wounding, etc. (*spared his feelings; spared her life*). **b** abstain from inflicting or causing; relieve from (*spare me this talk; spare my blushes*). **3** *tr.* be frugal or grudging of (*no expense spared*). **4** *intr. archaic* be frugal. □ **go spare** *Brit. colloq.* **1** become extremely angry or distraught. **2** be unwanted by others. **not spare oneself** exert one's utmost efforts. **to spare** left over; additional (*an hour to spare*). □□ **spare·ly** *adv.* **spare·ness** *n.* **spar·er** *n.* [OE *spær, sparian* f. Gmc]

spare part *n.* a duplicate part to replace a lost or damaged part of a machine, etc.

spare·ribs /spáir-ríbs/ *n.* closely trimmed ribs of esp. pork. [prob. f. MLG *ribbesper*, by transposition and assoc. with SPARE]

spare tire *n.* **1** an extra tire carried in a motor vehicle for emergencies. **2** *colloq.* a roll of fat round the waist.

sparge /spaarj/ *v.tr.* moisten by sprinkling, esp. in brewing. □□ **sparg·er** *n.* [app. f. L *spargere* sprinkle]

spar·ing /spáiring/ *adj.* **1** inclined to save; economical. **2** restrained; limited. □□ **spar·ing·ly** *adv.* **spar·ing·ness** *n.*

spark¹ /spaark/ *n. & v.* ● *n.* **1** a fiery particle thrown off from a fire, or remaining lit in ashes, or produced by a flint, match, etc. **2** (often foll. by *of*) a particle of a quality, etc. (*not a spark of life; a spark of interest*). **3** *Electr.* **a** a light produced by a sudden disruptive discharge through the air, etc. **b** such a discharge serving to ignite the explosive mixture in an internal combustion engine. **4 a** a flash of wit, etc. **b** anything causing interest, excitement, etc. **c** a witty or lively person. **5** a small bright object or point, e.g., in a gem. **6** (**Sparks**) a nickname for a radio operator or an electrician. ● *v.* **1** *intr.* emit sparks of fire or electricity. **2** *tr.* (often foll. by *off*) stir into activity; initiate (a process) suddenly. **3** *intr. Electr.* produce sparks at the point where a circuit is interrupted. □□ **spark·less** *adj.* **spark·y** *adj.* [ME f. OE *sp ǣrca, spearca*]

spark² /spaark/ *n. & v.* ● *n.* **1** a lively young fellow. **2** a gallant; a beau. ● *v.intr.* play the gallant. □□ **spark·ish** *adj.* [prob. a fig. use of SPARK¹]

spark cham·ber *n.* an apparatus designed to show ionizing particles.

spark gap *n.* the space between electric terminals where sparks occur.

spark·ing plug *n. Brit.* = SPARK PLUG.

spar·kle /spaárkəl/ *v. & n.* ● *v.intr.* **1 a** emit or seem to emit sparks; glitter; glisten (*her eyes sparkled*). **b** be witty; scintillate (*sparkling repartee*). **2** (of wine, etc.) effervesce (cf. STILL¹ *adj.* 4). ● *n.* **1** a gleam or spark. **2** vivacity; liveliness. □□ **spark·ly** *adj.* [ME f. SPARK¹ + -LE⁴]

spar·kler /spaárklər/ *n.* **1** a person or thing that sparkles. **2** a hand-held sparkling firework. **3** *colloq.* a diamond or other gem.

spark plug *n.* a device for firing the explosive mixture in an internal combustion engine.

spar·ling /spaárling/ *n.* a European smelt, *Osmerus eperlanus*. [ME f. OF *esperlinge*, of Gmc orig.]

spar·oid /spároyd/ *n. & adj.* ● *n.* any marine fish of the family Sparidae, e.g., a porgy. ● *adj.* of or concerning the Sparidae. [mod.L *Sparoides* f. L *sparus* f. Gk *sparos* sea bream]

spar·ring part·ner *n.* **1** a boxer employed to engage in sparring with another as training. **2** a person with whom one enjoys arguing.

spar·row /spáró/ *n.* **1** any small brownish gray bird of the genus *Passer*, esp. the house sparrow and tree sparrow. **2** any of various birds of similar appearance such as the hedge sparrow. [OE *spearwa* f. Gmc]

spar·row·grass /spárógras/ *n. dial.* or *colloq.* asparagus.

spar·row·hawk /spáróhawk/ *n.* a small hawk, *Accipiter nisus*, that preys on small birds.

sparse /spaars/ *adj.* thinly dispersed or scattered; not dense (*sparse population; sparse graying hair*). □□ **sparse·ly** *adv.* **sparse·ness** *n.* **spar·si·ty** *n.* [L *sparsus* past part. of *spargere* scatter]

Spar·tan /spaárt'n/ *adj. & n.* ● *adj.* **1** of or relating to Sparta in ancient Greece. **2 a** possessing the qualities of courage, endurance, stern frugality, etc., associated with Sparta. **b** (of a regime, conditions, etc.) lacking comfort; austere. ● *n.* a citizen of Sparta. [ME f. L *Spartanus* f. *Sparta* f. Gk *Sparta, -tē*]

spar·ti·na /spaarteénə/ *n.* any grass of the genus *Spartina*, with rhizomatous roots and growing in wet or marshy ground. [Gk *spartinē* rope]

spasm /spázəm/ *n.* **1** a sudden involuntary muscular contraction. **2** a sudden convulsive movement or emotion, etc. (*a spasm of coughing*). **3** (usu. foll. by *of*) *colloq.* a brief spell of an activity. [ME f. OF *spasme* or L *spasmus* f. Gk *spasmos, spasma* f. *spaō* pull]

spas·mod·ic /spazmódik/ *adj.* **1** of, caused by, or subject to, a spasm or spasms (*a spasmodic asthma*). **2** occurring or done by fits and starts (*spasmodic efforts*). □□ **spas·mod·i·cal·ly** *adv.* [mod.L *spasmodicus* f. Gk *spasmōdēs* (as SPASM)]

spas·tic /spástik/ *adj. & n.* ● *adj.* **1** *Med.* suffering from a spasm or spasms of the muscles. **2** *sl. offens.* weak; feeble; incompetent. **3** spasmodic. ● *n. Med. offens.* a person suffering from cerebral palsy. □□ **spas·ti·cal·ly** *adv.* **spas·tic·i·ty** /-tísitee/ *n.* [L *spasticus* f. Gk *spastikos* pulling f. *spaō* pull]

spat¹ *past* and *past part.* of SPIT¹.

spat² /spat/ *n.* **1** (usu. in *pl.*) *hist.* a short cloth gaiter protecting the

shoe from mud, etc. **2** a cover for an aircraft wheel. [abbr. of SPATTERDASH]

spat³ /spat/ *n. & v. colloq.* ● *n.* **1** a petty quarrel. **2** a slight amount. ● *v.intr.* (**spat·ted, spat·ting**) quarrel pettily. [prob. imit.]

spat⁴ /spat/ *n. & v.* ● *n.* the spawn of shellfish, esp. the oyster. ● *v.* (**spat·ted, spat·ting**) **1** *intr.* (of an oyster) spawn. **2** *tr.* shed (spawn). [AF, of unkn. orig.]

spatch·cock /spáchkok/ *n. & v.* ● *n.* a chicken or esp. game bird split open and grilled. ● *v.tr.* **1** treat (poultry) in this way. **2** esp. *Brit. colloq.* insert or interpolate (a phrase, sentence, story, etc.) esp. incongruously. [orig. in Ir. use, expl. by Grose (1785) as f. *dispatch-cock*, but cf. SPITCHCOCK]

spate /spayt/ *n.* **1** a river flood (*the river is in spate*). **2** a large or excessive amount (*a spate of inquiries*). [ME, Sc. & North Engl.: orig. unkn.]

spathe /spayth/ *n. Bot.* a large bract or pair of bracts enveloping a spadix or flower cluster. □□ **spa·tha·ceous** /spətháyshəs/ *adj.* [L f. Gk *spathē* broad blade, etc.]

spath·ic /spáthik/ *adj.* (of a mineral) like spar (see SPAR³), esp. in cleavage. □□ **spa·those** *adj.* [*spath* spar f. G *Spath*]

spath·ic i·ron ore *n.* = SIDERITE.

spa·tial /spáyshəl/ *adj.* (also **spa·cial**) of or concerning space (*spatial extent*). □□ **spa·ti·al·i·ty** /-sheeálitee/ *n.* **spa·tial·ize** *v.tr.* **spa·tial·ly** *adv.* [L *spatium* space]

spa·ti·o·tem·po·ral /spáysheeōtémpərəl/ *adj. Physics & Philos.* belonging to both space and time or to space-time. □□ **spa·ti·o·tem·po·ral·ly** *adv.* [formed as SPATIAL + TEMPORAL]

spat·ter /spátər/ *v. & n.* ● *v.* **1** *tr.* **a** (often foll. by *with*) splash (a person, etc.) (*spattered him with mud*). **b** scatter or splash (liquid, mud, etc.) here and there. **2** *intr.* (of rain, etc.) fall here and there (*glass spattered down*). **3** *tr.* slander (a person's honor, etc.). ● *n.* **1** (usu. foll. by *of*) a splash (*a spatter of mud*). **2** a quick pattering sound. [frequent. f. base as in Du., LG *spatten* burst, spout]

spat·ter·dash /spátərdash/ *n.* **1** (usu. in *pl.*) *hist.* a cloth or other legging to protect the stockings, etc., from mud, etc. **2** = ROUGHCAST.

spat·u·la /spáchələ/ *n.* **1** a broad-bladed flat implement used for spreading, lifting, stirring, mixing (food), etc. **2** *Brit.* = TONGUE DEPRESSOR. [L, var. of *spathula*, dimin. of *spatha* SPATHE]

spat·u·late /spáchələt/ *adj.* **1** spatula shaped. **2** (esp. of a leaf) having a broad rounded end. [SPATULA]

spav·in /spávin/ *n. Vet.* a disease of a horse's hock with a hard bony tumor or excrescence. □□ **spav·ined** *adj.* [ME f. OF *espavin*, var. of *esparvain* f. Gmc]

spawn /spawn/ *v. & n.* ● *v.* **1 a** *tr.* (also *absol.*) (of a fish, frog, mollusk, or crustacean) produce (eggs). **b** *intr.* be produced as eggs or young. **2** *tr. derog.* or *colloq.* (of people) produce (offspring). **3** *tr.* produce or generate, esp. in large numbers. ● *n.* **1** the eggs of fish, frogs, etc. **2** *derog.* human or other offspring. **3** a white fibrous matter from which fungi are produced; mycelium. □□ **spawn·er** *n.* [ME f. AF *espaundre* shed roe, OF *espandre* EXPAND]

spay /spay/ *v.tr.* sterilize (a female animal) by removing the ovaries. [ME f. AF *espeier*, OF *espeer* cut with a sword f. *espee* sword f. L *spatha*: see SPATHE]

SPCA *abbr.* Society for the Prevention of Cruelty to Animals.

speak /speek/ *v.* (*past* **spoke** /spōk/; *past part.* **spo·ken** /spṓkən/) **1** *intr.* make articulate verbal utterances in an ordinary (not singing) voice. **2** *tr.* **a** utter (words). **b** make known or communicate (one's opinion, the truth, etc.) in this way (*never speaks sense*). **3** *intr.* **a** (foll. by *to, with*) hold a conversation (*spoke to him for an hour; spoke with them about their work*). **b** (foll. by *of*) mention in writing, etc. (*speaks of it in her novel*). **c** (foll. by *for*) articulate the feelings of (another person, etc.) in speech or writing (*speaks for our generation*). **4** *intr.* (foll. by *to*) **a** address; converse with (a person, etc.). **b** speak in confirmation of or with reference to (*spoke to the resolution; can speak to his innocence*). **c** *colloq.* reprove (*spoke to them about their lateness*). **5** *intr.* make a speech before an audience, etc. (*spoke for an hour on the topic; has a good speaking voice*). **6** *tr.* use or be able to use (a specified language) (*cannot speak French*). **7** *intr.* (of a gun, a musical instrument, etc.) make a sound. **8** *intr.* (usu. foll. by *to*) *poet.* communicate feeling, etc.; affect; touch (*the sunset spoke to her*). **9** *intr.* (of a hound) bark. **10** *tr.* hail and hold communication with (a ship). **11** *tr. archaic* (of conduct, etc.) show (a person) to be (*his conduct speaks him generous*). **b** be evidence of (*the loud laugh speaks the vacant mind*). □ **not** (or **nothing**) **to speak of** not (or nothing) worth mentioning; practically not (or nothing). **speak for it·self** need no supporting evidence. **speak for oneself 1** give one's own opinions. **2** not presume to speak for others. **speak one's mind** speak bluntly or frankly. **speak out** speak loudly or freely; give one's opinion. **speak up** = *speak out*. **speak volumes** (of a fact, etc.) be very significant. **speak volumes** (or **well**, etc.) **for 1** be abundant evidence of. **2** place in a favorable light. □□ **speak·a·ble** *adj.* [OE *sprecan*, later *specan*]

speak·eas·y /spéekeezee/ n. (pl. **·ies**) an illicit liquor store or drinking club during Prohibition in the US.

speak·er /spéekər/ n. **1** a person who speaks, esp. in public. **2** a person who speaks a specified language (esp. in comb.: a French speaker). **3** (**Speaker**) the presiding officer in a legislative assembly, esp. the House of Representatives (in the US) or the House of Commons (in the UK). **4** = LOUDSPEAKER. □□ **speak·er·ship** n.

speak·er·phone /spéekərfōn/ n. a telephone equipped with a microphone and loudspeaker, allowing it to be used without picking up the handset.

speak·ing /spéeking/ n. & adj. ● n. the act or an instance of uttering words, etc. ● adj. **1** that speaks; capable of articulate speech. **2** (of a portrait) lifelike; true to its subject (a speaking likeness). **3** (in comb.) speaking or capable of speaking a specified foreign language (French-speaking). **4** with a reference or from a point of view specified (roughly speaking; professionally speaking). □ **on speaking terms** (foll. by with) **1** slightly acquainted. **2** on friendly terms.

speak·ing ac·quaint·ance n. **1** a person one knows slightly. **2** this degree of familiarity.

speak·ing tube n. a tube for conveying the voice from one room, building, etc., to another.

spear /speer/ n. & v. ● n. **1** a thrusting or throwing weapon with a pointed usu. steel tip and a long shaft. **2** a similar barbed instrument used for catching fish, etc. **3** archaic a spearman. **4** a pointed stem of asparagus, etc. ● v.tr. **1** pierce or strike with or as if with a spear (speared an olive). **2** catch (a baseball, etc.) with a thrusting motion. [OE spere]

spear gun n. a gun used to propel a spear in underwater fishing.

spear·head /spéerhed/ n. & v. ● n. **1** the point of a spear. **2** an individual or group chosen to lead a thrust or attack. ● v.tr. act as the spearhead of (an attack, etc.).

spear·man /spéermən/ n. (pl. **·men**) archaic a person, esp. a soldier, who uses a spear.

spear·mint /spéermint/ n. a common garden mint, Mentha spicata, used in cooking and to flavor chewing gum.

spear side n. the male side of a family.

spear·wort /spéerwərt, –wawrt/ n. an aquatic plant, Ranunculus lingua, with thick hollow stems, long narrow spear-shaped leaves, and yellow flowers.

spec¹ /spek/ n. colloq. a commercial speculation or venture. □ **on spec** in the hope of success; as a gamble; on the off chance. [abbr. of SPECULATION]

spec² /spek/ n. colloq. a detailed working description; a specification. [abbr. of SPECIFICATION]

spe·cial /spéshəl/ adj. & n. ● adj. **1 a** particularly good; exceptional; out of the ordinary (bought them a special present; today is a special day; took special trouble). **b** peculiar; specific; not general (lacks the special qualities required; the word has a special sense). **2** for a particular purpose (sent on a special assignment). **3** in which a person specializes (statistics is his special field). **4** denoting education for children with particular needs, e.g., the handicapped. ● n. a special person or thing, e.g., a special train, radio or televisions broadcast, examination, edition of a newspaper, dish on a menu, etc. □□ **spe·cial·ly** adv. **spe·cial·ness** n. [ME f. OF especial ESPECIAL or L specialis (as SPECIES)]

Spe·cial Branch n. (in the UK) a police department dealing with political security.

spe·cial case n. **1** a written statement of fact presented by litigants to a court. **2** an exceptional or unusual case.

spe·cial cor·re·spond·ent n. a journalist writing for a newspaper on special events or a special area of interest.

spe·cial de·liv·er·y n. a delivery of mail in advance of the regular delivery.

spe·cial draw·ing rights n. the right to purchase extra foreign currency from the International Monetary Fund.

spe·cial e·di·tion n. an extra edition of a newspaper including later news than the ordinary edition.

spe·cial ef·fects n. movie or television illusions created by props, or camera work, or generated by computer.

Spe·cial Forc·es n. U.S. Army personnel specially trained in guerrilla warfare.

spe·cial in·ten·tion n. (also **par·tic·u·lar in·ten·tion**) RC Ch. a special aim or purpose for which a Mass is celebrated, prayers are said, etc.

spe·cial in·ter·est n. (also **spe·cial in·ter·est group**) an organization, corporation, etc., that seeks advantage, usu. by lobbying for favorable legislation.

spe·cial·ist /spéshəlist/ n. (usu. foll. by in) **1** a person who is trained in a particular branch of a profession, esp. medicine (a specialist in dermatology). **2** a person who especially or exclusively studies a subject or a particular branch of a subject. □□ **spe·cial·ism** n. **spe·cial·is·tic** /–lístik/ adj.

spe·ci·al·i·ty /spésheeálitee/ n. (pl. **·ties**) Brit. = SPECIALTY 1. [ME f. OF especialité or LL specialitas (as SPECIAL)]

spe·cial·ize /spéshəliz/ v. **1** intr. (often foll. by in) **a** be or become a specialist (specializes in optics). **b** devote oneself to an area of interest, skill, etc. (specializes in insulting people). **2** Biol. **a** tr. (esp. in passive) adapt or set apart (an organ, etc.) for a particular purpose. **b** intr. (of an organ, etc.) become adapted, etc., in this way. **3** tr. make specific or individual. **4** tr. modify or limit (an idea, statement, etc.). □□ **spe·cial·i·za·tion** n. [F spécialiser (as SPECIAL)]

spe·cial ju·ry n. = BLUE-RIBBON JURY.

Spe·cial O·lym·pics n. a program modeled on the Olympics that features sports competitions for physically and mentally handicapped persons.

spe·cial plead·ing n. **1** Law pleading with reference to new facts in a case. **2** (in general use) a specious or unfair argument favoring the speaker's point of view.

spe·cial prov·i·dence n. a particular instance of God's providence.

spe·cial·ty /spéshəltee/ n. (pl. **·ties**) **1** a special pursuit, product, operation, etc., to which a company or a person gives special attention. **2** Law an instrument under seal; a sealed contract. [ME f. OF (e)specialté (as SPECIAL)]

spe·cial ver·dict n. Law a verdict stating the facts as proved but leaving the court to draw conclusions from them.

spe·ci·a·tion /spéesheeáyshən, spées–/ n. Biol. the formation of a new species in the course of evolution.

spe·cie /spéeshee, –see/ n. coin money as opposed to paper money. [L, ablat. of SPECIES in phrase in specie]

spe·cies /spéesheez, –seez/ n. (pl. same) **1** a class of things having some characteristics in common. **2** Biol. a category in the system of classification of living organisms consisting of similar individuals capable of exchanging genes or interbreeding. **3** a kind or sort. **4** Logic a group subordinate to a genus and containing individuals agreeing in some common attribute(s) and called by a common name. **5** Law a form or shape given to materials. **6** Eccl. the visible form of each of the elements of consecrated bread and wine in the Eucharist. [L, = appearance, kind, beauty, f. specere look]

spe·cif·ic /spisifik/ adj. & n. ● adj. **1** clearly defined; definite (has no specific name; told me so in specific terms). **2** relating to a particular subject; peculiar (a style specific to that). **3 a** of or concerning a species (the specific name for a plant). **b** possessing, or concerned with, the properties that characterize a species (the specific forms of animals). **4** (of a duty or a tax) assessed by quantity or amount, not by the value of goods. ● n. **1** archaic a specific medicine or remedy. **2** a specific aspect or factor (shall we discuss specifics?). □□ **spe·cif·i·cal·ly** adv. **spe·cif·ic·i·ty** /spésifisitee/ n. **spe·cif·ic·ness** n. [LL specificus (as SPECIES)]

spec·i·fi·ca·tion /spésifikáyshən/ n. **1** the act or an instance of specifying; the state of being specified. **2** (esp. in pl.) a detailed description of the construction, workmanship, materials, etc., of work done or to be done, prepared by an architect, engineer, etc. **3** a description by an applicant for a patent of the construction and use of his invention. **4** Law the conversion of materials into a new product not held to be the property of the owner of the materials. [med.L specificatio (as SPECIFY)]

spec·i·fic cause n. the cause of a particular form of a disease.

spec·i·fic dif·fer·ence n. a factor that differentiates a species.

spec·i·fic dis·ease n. a disease caused by one identifiable agent.

spec·i·fic grav·i·ty n. the ratio of the density of a substance to the density of a standard, as water for a liquid and air for a gas.

spec·i·fic heat ca·pac·i·ty n. the heat required to raise the temperature of the unit mass of a given substance by a given amount (usu. one degree).

spec·i·fic per·for·mance n. Law the performance of a contractual duty, as ordered in cases where damages would not be adequate remedy.

spec·i·fy /spésifi/ v.tr. (**·fies**, **·fied**) **1** (also absol.) name or mention expressly (specified the type he needed). **2** (usu. foll. by that + clause) name as a condition (specified that he must be paid at once). **3** include in specifications (a French window was not specified). □□ **spec·i·fi·a·ble** /–fíəbəl/ adj. **spec·i·fi·er** n. [ME f. OF specifier or LL specificare (as SPECIFIC)]

spec·i·men /spésimən/ n. **1** an individual or part taken as an example of a class or whole, esp. when used for investigation or scientific examination (specimens of copper ore; a specimen of your handwriting). **2** Med. a sample of urine for testing. **3** colloq. a person of a specified sort. [L f. specere look]

spe·ci·ol·o·gy /spéeseeóləjee/ n. the scientific study of species or of their origin, etc. □□ **spe·ci·o·log·i·cal** /–seeəlójikəl/ adj.

spe·cious /spéeshəs/ adj. **1** superficially plausible but actually wrong (a specious argument). **2** misleadingly attractive in appearance. □□ **spe·ci·os·i·ty** /–sheeósitee/ n. **spe·cious·ly** adv. **spe·cious·ness** n. [ME, = beautiful, f. L speciosus (as SPECIES)]

speck /spek/ n. & v. ● n. **1** a small spot, dot, or stain. **2** (foll. by of) a particle (speck of dirt). **3** a rotten spot in fruit. ● v.tr. (esp. as **specked** adj.) marked with specks. □□ **speck·less** adj. [OE specca: cf. SPECKLE]

speck·le /spékəl/ n. & v. ● n. a small spot, mark, or stain, esp. in quantity on the skin, a bird's egg, etc. ● *v.tr.* (esp. as **speckled** *adj.*) mark with speckles or patches. [ME f. MDu. *spekkel*]

specs /speks/ *n.pl. colloq.* a pair of eyeglasses. [abbr.]

spec•ta•cle /spéktəkəl/ *n.* 1 a public show, ceremony, etc. 2 anything attracting public attention (*a charming spectacle; a disgusting spectacle*). □ **make a spectacle of oneself** make oneself an object of ridicule. [ME f. OF f. L *spectaculum* f. *spectare* frequent. of *specere* look]

spec•ta•cled /spéktəkəld/ *adj.* 1 wearing spectacles. 2 (of an animal) having facial markings resembling spectacles.

spec•ta•cled bear *n.* a S. American bear, *Tremarctos ornatus*.

spec•ta•cled co•bra *n.* the Indian cobra.

spec•ta•cles /spéktəkəlz/ *n.pl. old-fashioned* or jocular eyeglasses.

spec•tac•u•lar /spektákyələr/ *adj. & n.* ● *adj.* 1 of or like a public show; striking; amazing; lavish. 2 strikingly large or obvious (*a spectacular increase in output*). ● *n.* an event intended to be spectacular, esp. a musical movie or play. □□ **spec•tac•u•lar•ly** *adv.* [SPECTACLE, after *oracular*, etc.]

spec•tate /spéktayt/ *v.intr.* be a spectator, esp. at a sporting event. [-back-form. f. SPECTATOR]

spec•ta•tor /spéktáytər/ *n.* a person who looks on at a show, game, incident, etc. □□ **spec•ta•to•ri•al** /–tətáwreeəl/ *adj.* [F *spectateur* or L *spectator* f. *spectare*: see SPECTACLE]

spec•ta•tor sport *n.* a sport attracting spectators rather than participants.

spec•ter /spéktər/ *n.* (*Brit.* **spec•tre**) 1 a ghost. 2 a haunting presentiment or preoccupation (*the specter of war*). 3 (in *comb.*) used in the names of some animals because of their thinness, transparency, etc. (*specter bat; specter crab*). [F *spectre* or L *spectrum*: see SPECTRUM]

Spec•ter of the Brock•en *n.* a huge shadowy image of the observer projected on mists about a mountaintop (observed on the Brocken in Germany).

spec•tra *pl.* of SPECTRUM.

spec•tral /spéktrəl/ *adj.* 1 a of or relating to specters or ghosts. b ghostlike. 2 of or concerning spectra or the spectrum (*spectral colors; spectral analysis*). □□ **spec•tral•ly** *adv.*

spectro- /spéktrō/ *comb. form* a spectrum.

spec•tro•chem•is•try /spéktrōkémistree/ *n.* chemistry based on the study of the spectra of substances.

spec•tro•gram /spéktrəgram/ *n.* a record obtained with a spectrograph.

spec•tro•graph /spéktrəgraf/ *n.* an apparatus for photographing or otherwise recording spectra. □□ **spec•tro•graph•ic** *adj.* **spec•tro•graph•i•cal•ly** *adv.* **spec•trog•ra•phy** /spektrógrəfee/ *n.*

spec•tro•he•li•o•graph /spéktrōheéleeəgraf/ *n.* an instrument for taking photographs of the sun in the light of one wavelength only.

spec•tro•he•li•o•scope /spéktrōheéleeəskōp/ *n.* a device similar to a spectroheliograph, for visual observation.

spec•trom•e•ter /spektrómitər/ *n.* an instrument used for the measurement of observed spectra. □□ **spec•tro•met•ric** /spéktrəmétrik/ *adj.* **spec•trom•e•try** *n.* [G *Spektrometer* or F *spectromètre* (as SPECTRO-, –METER)]

spec•tro•pho•tom•e•ter /spéktrōfōtómitər/ *n.* an instrument for measuring and recording the intensity of light in various parts of the spectrum. □□ **spec•tro•pho•to•met•ric** /–təmétrik/ *adj.* **spec•tro•pho•tom•e•try** *n.*

spec•tro•scope /spéktrəskōp/ *n.* an instrument for producing and recording spectra for examination. □□ **spec•tro•scop•ic** /–skópik/ *adj.* **spec•tro•scop•i•cal** *adj.* **spec•tro•scop•ist** /–tróskəpist/ *n.* **spec•tros•co•py** /–tróskəpee/ *n.* [G *Spektroskop* or F *spectroscope* (as SPECTRO-, –SCOPE)]

spec•trum /spéktrəm/ *n.* (*pl.* **spec•tra** /–trə/) 1 the band of colors, as seen in a rainbow, etc., arranged in a progressive series according to their refrangibility or wavelength. 2 the entire range of wavelengths of electromagnetic radiation. 3 a an image or distribution of parts of electromagnetic radiation arranged in a progressive series according to wavelength. b this as characteristic of a body or substance when emitting or absorbing radiation. 4 a similar image or distribution of energy, mass, etc., arranged according to frequency, charge, etc. 5 the entire range or a wide range of anything arranged by degree or quality, etc. 6 (in full **ocular spectrum**) an afterimage. [L, = image, apparition f. *specere* look]

spec•trum a•nal•y•sis *n.* (also **spec•tral a•nal•y•sis**) chemical analysis by means of a spectroscope.

spec•u•la *pl.* of SPECULUM.

spec•u•lar /spékyələr/ *adj.* 1 of or having the nature of a speculum. 2 reflecting. [L *specularis* (as SPECULUM)]

spec•u•lar i•ron ore *n.* lustrous hematite.

spec•u•late /spékyəlayt/ *v.* 1 *intr.* (usu. foll. by *on, upon, about*) form a theory or conjecture, esp. without a firm factual basis; meditate (*speculated on their prospects*). 2 *tr.* (foll. by *that, how*, etc., + clause) conjecture; consider (*speculated how he might achieve it*). 3 *intr.* a invest in stocks, etc., in the hope of gain but with the possibility of loss. b gamble recklessly. □□ **spec•u•la•tor** *n.* [L *speculari* spy out, observe f. *specula* watchtower f. *specere* look]

spec•u•la•tion /spékyəláyshən/ *n.* 1 the act or an instance of speculating; a theory or conjecture (*made no speculation as to her age; is given to speculation*). 2 a a speculative investment or enterprise (*bought it as a speculation*). b the practice of business speculating. [ME f. OF *speculation* or LL *speculatio* (as SPECULATE)]

spec•u•la•tive /spékyələtiv, –lay–/ *adj.* 1 of, based on, engaged in, or inclined to speculation. 2 (of a business investment) involving the risk of loss (*a speculative builder*). □□ **spec•u•la•tive•ly** *adv.* **spec•u•la•tive•ness** *n.* [ME f. OF *speculatif –ive* or LL *speculativus* (as SPECULATE)]

spec•u•lum /spékyələm/ *n.* (*pl.* **spec•u•la** /–lə/) 1 *Surgery* an instrument for dilating the cavities of the human body for inspection. 2 a mirror, usu. of polished metal, esp. in a reflecting telescope. 3 *Ornithol.* a lustrous colored area on the wing of some birds, esp. ducks. [L, = mirror, f. *specere* look]

spec•u•lum met•al *n.* an alloy of copper and tin used as a mirror, esp. in a telescope.

sped *past* and *past part.* of SPEED.

speech /speech/ *n.* 1 the faculty or act of speaking. 2 a usu. formal address or discourse delivered to an audience or assembly. 3 a manner of speaking (*a man of blunt speech*). 4 a remark (*after this speech he was silent*). 5 the language of a nation, region, group, etc. 6 *Mus.* the act of sounding in an organ pipe, etc. □□ **speech•ful** *adj.* [OE *sprēc*, later *spēc* f. WG, rel. to SPEAK]

speech day *n. Brit.* an annual prize-giving day in many schools, usu. marked by speeches, etc.

speech•i•fy /speéchifī/ *v.intr.* (**•fies, •fied**) *joc.* or *derog.* make esp. boring or long speeches. □□ **speech•i•fi•ca•tion** /–fikáyshən/ *n.* **speech•i•fi•er** *n.*

speech•less /speéchlis/ *adj.* 1 temporarily unable to speak because of emotion, etc. (*speechless with rage*). 2 mute. □□ **speech•less•ly** *adv.* **speech•less•ness** *n.* [OE *spēclē as* (as SPEECH, –LESS)]

speech ther•a•py *n.* treatment to improve defective speech. □□ **speech ther•a•pist** *n.*

speed /speed/ *n. & v.* ● *n.* 1 rapidity of movement (*with all speed; at full speed*). 2 a rate of progress or motion over a distance in time (*attains a high speed*). 3 an arrangement of gears yielding a specific ratio in a bicycle or automobile transmission. 4 *Photog.* a the sensitivity of film to light. b the light-gathering power of a lens. c the duration of an exposure. 5 *sl.* an amphetamine drug, esp. methamphetamine. 6 *archaic* success; prosperity (*send me good speed*). ● *v.* (*past* and *past part.* **sped** /sped/) 1 *intr.* go fast (*sped down the street*). 2 (*past* and *past part.* **speed•ed**) a *intr.* (of a motorist, etc.) travel at an illegal or dangerous speed. b *tr.* regulate the speed of (an engine, etc.). c *tr.* cause (an engine, etc.) to go at a fixed speed. 3 *tr.* send fast or on its way (*speed an arrow from the bow*). 4 *intr. & tr. archaic* be or make prosperous or successful (*God speed you!*). □ **at speed** esp. *Brit.* moving quickly. **speed up** move or work at greater speed. □□ **speed•er** *n.* [OE *spēd, spēdan* f. Gmc]

speed•ball /speédbawl/ *n. sl.* a mixture of cocaine with heroin or morphine.

speed•boat /speédbōt/ *n.* a motor boat designed for high speed.

speed bump *n.* (also *Brit.* **speed hump**) a transverse ridge in the road to control the speed of vehicles.

speed lim•it *n.* the maximum speed at which a road vehicle may legally be driven in a particular area, etc.

speed mer•chant *n. Brit. colloq.* a motorist who enjoys driving fast.

speed•o /speédō/ *n.* (*pl.* **•os**) *Brit. colloq.* = SPEEDOMETER. [abbr.]

speed•om•e•ter /spidómitər/ *n.* an instrument on a motor vehicle, etc., indicating its speed to the driver. [SPEED + METER¹]

speed•way /speédway/ *n.* 1 a a road or track used for automobile racing. b a highway for high-speed travel. 2 a motorcycle racing. b a stadium or track used for this.

speed•well /speédwel/ *n.* any small herb of the genus *Veronica*, with a creeping or ascending stem and tiny blue or pink flowers. [app. f. SPEED + WELL¹]

speed•y /speédee/ *adj.* (**speed•i•er, speed•i•est**) 1 moving quickly; rapid. 2 done without delay; prompt (*a speedy answer*). □□ **speed•i•ly** *adv.* **speed•i•ness** *n.*

speiss /spīs/ *n.* a compound of arsenic, iron, etc., formed in smelting certain lead ores. [G *Speise* food, amalgam]

spe•le•ol•o•gy /speéleeóləjee/ *n.* 1 the scientific study of caves. 2 the exploration of caves. □□ **spe•le•o•log•i•cal** /–leeəlójikəl/ *adj.* **spe•le•ol•o•gist** *n.* [F *spéléologie* f. L *spelaeum* f. Gk *spēlaion* cave]

spell¹ /spel/ *v.tr.* (*past* and *past part.* **spelled** or esp. *Brit.* **spelt**) 1 (also *absol.*) write or name the letters that form (a word, etc.) in correct sequence (*spell 'exaggerate'; cannot spell properly*). 2 a (of letters) make up or form (a word, etc.). b (of circumstances, a scheme, etc.) result in; involve (*spell ruin*). □ **spell out** 1 make out (words, writing, etc.) letter by letter. 2 explain in detail (*spelled out what the change would mean*). □□ **spell•a•ble** *adj.* [ME f. OF *espel(l)er,* f. Frank. (as SPELL²)]

spell² /spel/ *n.* 1 a form of words used as a magical charm or incantation. **2** an attraction or fascination exercised by a person, activity, quality, etc. □ **under a spell** mastered by or as if by a spell. [OE *spel(l)* f. Gmc]

spell[3] /spel/ *n. & v.* •*n.* **1** a short or fairly short period (*a cold spell in April*). **2** a turn of work (*did a spell of woodwork*). **3** *Austral.* a period of rest from work. •*v.* **1** *tr.* **a** relieve or take the place of (a person) in work, etc. **b** allow to rest briefly. **2** *intr. Austral.* take a brief rest. [earlier as verb: later form of dial. *spele* take place of f. OE *spelian*, of unkn. orig.]

spell·bind /spélbīnd/ *v.tr.* (*past* and *past part.* **spell·bound**) **1** bind with or as if with a spell; entrance. **2** (as **spellbound** *adj.*) entranced or fascinated, esp. by a speaker, activity, quality, etc. □□ **spell·bind·er** *n.* **spell·bind·ing·ly** *adv.*

spell·er /spélər/ *n.* **1** a person who spells, esp. in a specified way (*is a poor speller*). **2** a book on spelling.

spel·li·can var. of SPILLIKIN.

spell·ing /spéling/ *n.* **1** the process or activity of writing or naming the letters of a word, etc. **2** the way a word is spelled. **3** the ability to spell (*his spelling is weak*).

spell·ing bee *n.* a spelling competition.

spelt[1] esp. *Brit. past* and *past part.* of SPELL[1].

spelt[2] /spelt/ *n.* a species of wheat, *Triticum aestivum*. [OE f. OS *spelta* (OHG *spelza*), ME f. MLG, MDu. *spelte*]

spel·ter /spéltər/ *n.* impure zinc, esp. for commercial purposes. [corresp. to OF *espeautre*, MDu. *speauter*, G *Spialter*, rel. to PEWTER]

spe·lunk·er /spilúngkər, speélung–/ *n.* a person who explores caves, esp. as a hobby. □□ **spe·lunk·ing** *n.* [obs. *spelunk* cave f. L *spelunca*]

spence /spens/ *n.* esp. *Brit. archaic* a pantry or larder. [ME f. OF *despense* f. L *dispensa* fem. past part. of *dispendere*: see DISPENSE]

spen·cer[1] /spénsər/ *n.* **1** a short close-fitting jacket. **2** esp. *Brit.* a woman's thin usu. woolen undershirt worn for extra warmth in winter. [prob. f. the 2nd Earl *Spencer*, Engl. politician d. 1834]

spen·cer[2] /spénsər/ *n. Naut.* a trysail. [perh. f. K. *Spencer* (early 19th c.)]

spend /spend/ *v.tr.* (*past* and *past part.* **spent** /spent/) **1** (usu. foll. by *on*) **a** (also *absol.*) pay out (money) in making a purchase, etc. (*spent $5 on a new pen*). **b** pay out (money) for a particular person's benefit or for the improvement of a thing (*had to spend $200 on the car*). **2 a** use or consume (time or energy) (*shall spend no more effort; how do you spend your Sundays?*). **b** (also *refl.*) use up; exhaust; wear out (*their ammunition was all spent; his anger was soon spent; spent herself campaigning for justice*). **3** *tr.* (as **spent** *adj.*) having lost its original force or strength; exhausted (*the storm is spent; spent bullets*). □ **spend a penny** *Brit. colloq.* urinate or defecate (from the coin-operated locks of public toilets). □□ **spend·a·ble** *adj.* **spend·er** *n.* [OE *spendan* f. L *expendere* (see EXPEND): in ME perh. also f. obs. *dispend* f. OF *despendre* expend f. L *dispendere*: see DISPENSE]

spend·ing mon·ey *n.* pocket money.

spend·thrift /spéndthrift/ *n. & adj.* •*n.* an extravagant person; a prodigal. •*adj.* extravagant; prodigal.

Spen·se·ri·an /spenseéreeən/ *adj.* of, relating to, or in the style of Edmund Spenser, Engl. poet d. 1599. [E. *Spenser*]

Spen·se·ri·an stan·za *n.* the stanza used by Spenser in the *Faerie Queene*, with eight iambic pentameters and an alexandrine, rhyming ababbcbcc.

spent *past* and *past part.* of SPEND.

sperm /spərm/ *n.* (*pl.* same or **sperms**) **1** = SPERMATOZOON. **2** the male reproductive fluid containing spermatozoa; semen. **3** = SPERM WHALE. **4** = SPERMACETI. **5** = SPERM OIL. [ME f. LL *sperma* f. Gk *sperma -atos* seed f. *speirō* sow: in *sperm whale* an abbr. of SPERMACETI]

sper·ma·cet·i /spərməsétee/ *n.* a white waxy substance produced by the sperm whale to aid buoyancy, and used in the manufacture of candles, ointments, etc. □□ **sper·ma·cet·ic** *adj.* [ME f. med.L f. LL *sperma* sperm + *ceti* genit. of *cetus* f. Gk *kētos* whale, from the belief that it was whale spawn]

sper·ma·ry /spérmaree/ *n.* (*pl.* **-ries**) an organ in which human or animal sperm are generated. [mod.L *spermarium* (as SPERM)]

sper·mat·ic /spərmátik/ *adj.* of or relating to a sperm or spermary. [LL *spermaticus* f. Gk *spermatikos* (as SPERM)]

sper·mat·ic cord *n.* a bundle of nerves, ducts, and blood vessels passing to the testicles.

sper·ma·tid /spérmətid/ *n. Biol.* an immature male sex cell formed from a spermatocyte, which may develop into a spermatozoon.

spermato- /spərmátō/ *comb. form Biol.* a sperm or seed.

sper·mat·o·cyte /spərmátəsīt, spórmətō–/ *n.* a cell produced from a spermatogonium and which may divide by meiosis into spermatids.

sper·mat·o·gen·e·sis /spərmátəjénisis, spórmətə–/ *n.* the production or development of mature spermatozoa. □□ **sper·ma·to·ge·net·ic** /–jinétik/ *adj.*

sper·mat·o·go·ni·um /spərmátəgōneeəm, spórmə–/ *n.* (*pl.* **sper·mat·o·go·ni·a** /–neeə/) a cell produced at an early stage in the formation of spermatozoa, from which spermatocytes develop. [SPERM + mod.L *gonium* f. Gk *gonos* offspring, seed]

sper·mat·o·phore /spərmátəfawr, spórmə–/ *n.* an albuminous capsule containing spermatozoa found in various invertebrates. □□ **sper·mat·o·phor·ic** /–fáwrik, –fór–/ *adj.*

sper·mat·o·phyte /spərmátəfīt, spórmə–/ *n.* any seed-bearing plant.

sper·ma·to·zo·id /spərmátəzóid, spórmə–/ *n.* the mature motile male sex cell of some plants.

sper·ma·to·zo·on /spərmátəzṓ-on, –ən, spórmə–/ *n.* (*pl.* **sper·ma·to·zo·a** /–zṓə/) the mature motile sex cell in animals. □□ **sper·ma·to·zo·al** *adj.* **sper·ma·to·zo·an** *adj.* **sper·ma·to·zo·ic** *adj.* [SPERM + Gk *zōion* animal]

sperm bank *n.* a supply of semen stored for use in artificial insemination.

sperm count *n.* the number of spermatozoa in one ejaculation or a measured amount of semen.

sper·mi·cide /spə́rmisīd/ *n.* a substance able to kill spermatozoa. □□ **sper·mi·cid·al** /–síd'l/ *adj.*

spermo- /spórmō/ *comb. form* = SPERMATO-.

sperm oil *n.* an oil obtained from the head of a sperm whale, and used as a lubricant.

sperm whale *n.* a large whale, *Physeter macrocephalus*, hunted for the spermaceti and sperm oil contained in its bulbous head, and for the ambergris found in its intestines. Also called **cachalot**.

spew /spyoō/ *v.* (also **spue**) **1** *tr. & intr.* vomit. **2** (often foll. by *out*) **a** *tr.* expel (contents) rapidly and forcibly. **b** *intr.* (of contents) be expelled in this way. □□ **spew·er** *n.* [OE *spīwan, spēowan* f. Gmc]

SPF *abbr.* sun protection factor.

sp. gr. *abbr.* specific gravity.

sphag·num /sfágnəm/ *n.* (*pl.* **sphag·na** /–nə/) (in full **sphagnum moss**) any moss of the genus *Sphagnum*, growing in bogs and peat, and used as packing for plants, as fertilizer, etc. [mod.L f. Gk *sphagnos* a moss]

sphal·er·ite /sfálərīt/ *n.* a common zinc ore principally composed of zinc sulfide. [Gk *sphaleros* deceptive: cf. BLENDE]

spheno- /sfeénō/ *comb. form Anat.* the sphenoid bone. [Gk f. *sphēn* wedge]

sphe·noid /sfeénoyd/ *adj. & n.* •*adj.* **1** wedge shaped. **2** of or relating to the sphenoid bone. •*n.* (in full **sphenoid bone**) a large compound bone forming the base of the cranium behind the eyes. □□ **sphe·noi·dal** /–nóyd'l/ *adj.* [mod.L *sphenoides* f. Gk *sphē noeidēs* f. *sphēn* wedge]

sphere /sfeer/ *n. & v.* •*n.* **1** a solid figure, or its surface, with every point on its surface equidistant from its center. **2** an object having this shape; a ball or globe. **3 a** any celestial body. **b** a globe representing the earth. **c** *poet.* the heavens; the sky. **d** the sky perceived as a vault upon or in which celestial bodies are represented as lying. **e** *hist.* each of a series of revolving concentrically arranged spherical shells in which celestial bodies were formerly thought to be set in a fixed relationship. **4 a** a field of action, influence, or existence (*have done much within their own sphere*). **b** a (usu. specified) stratum of society or social class (*moves in quite another sphere*). •*v.tr. archaic* or *poet.* **1** enclose in or as in a sphere. **2** form into a sphere. □ **music** (or **harmony**) **of the spheres** the natural harmonic tones supposedly produced by the movement of the celestial spheres (see sense 3e of *n.*) or the bodies fixed in them. **oblique** (or **parallel** or **right**) **sphere** the sphere of the apparent heavens at a place where there is an oblique, zero, or right angle between the equator and the horizon. □□ **spher·al** *adj.* [ME *sper(e)* f. OF *espere* f. LL *sphera*, L f. Gk *sphaira* ball]

-sphere /sfeer/ *comb. form* **1** having the form of a sphere (*bathysphere*). **2** a region around the earth (*atmosphere*).

sphere of in·flu·ence *n.* the claimed or recognized area of a nation's interests, an individual's control, etc.

spher·ic /sfeérik, sfér–/ *adj.* = SPHERICAL. □□ **sphe·ric·i·ty** /–rísitee/ *n.*

spher·i·cal /sfeérikəl, sfér–/ *adj.* **1** shaped like a sphere; globular. **2 a** of or relating to the properties of spheres (*spherical geometry*). **b** formed inside or on the surface of a sphere (*spherical triangle*). □□ **spher·i·cal·ly** *adv.* [LL *sphaericus* f. Gk *sphairikos* (as SPHERE)]

spher·i·cal ab·er·ra·tion *n.* a loss of definition in the image produced by a spherically curved mirror or lens.

spher·i·cal an·gle *n.* an angle formed by the intersection of two great circles of a sphere.

sphe·roid /sfeéroyd/ *n.* **1** a spherelike but not perfectly spherical body. **2** a solid generated by a half-revolution of an ellipse about its major axis (**prolate spheroid**) or minor axis (**oblate spheroid**). □□ **sphe·roi·dal** /–óyd'l/ *adj.* **sphe·roi·dic·i·ty** /–dísitee/ *n.*

sphe·rom·e·ter /sfeerómitər/ *n.* an instrument for finding the radius of a sphere and for the exact measurement of the thickness of small bodies. [F *sphéromètre* (as SPHERE, –METER)]

spher·ule /sfeérool, –yool, sfér–/ *n.* a small sphere. □□ **spher·u·lar** *adj.* [LL *sphaerula* dimin. of L *sphaera* (as SPHERE)]

spher·u·lite /sfeéryəlīt, sfeérə–, sfér–/ *n.* a vitreous globule as a constituent of volcanic rocks. □□ **spher·u·lit·ic** /–lítik/ *adj.*

sphinc·ter /sfíngktər/ *n. Anat.* a ring of muscle surrounding and serving to guard or close an opening or tube, esp. the anus. □□ **sphinc·ter·al** *adj.* **sphinc·tered** *adj.* **sphinc·te·ri·al** /–teéreeəl/ *adj.* **sphinc·ter·ic** /–térik/ *adj.* [L f. Gk *sphigktēr* f. *sphiggō* bind tight]

sphin·gid /sfínggid/ *n.* any hawk moth of the family Sphingidae. [as SPHINX + -ID³]

sphinx /sfíngks/ *n.* **1** (Sphinx) (in Greek mythology) the winged monster of Thebes, having a woman's head and a lion's body, whose riddle Oedipus guessed and who consequently killed herself. **2** *Antiq.* **a** any of several ancient Egyptian stone figures having a lion's body and a human or animal head. **b** (the Sphinx) the huge stone figure of a sphinx near the Pyramids at Giza. **3** an enigmatic or inscrutable person. **4 a** a hawk moth. **b** a species of baboon, *Papio sphinx*. [L f. Gk *Sphigx*, app. f. *sphiggō* draw tight]

sphra·gis·tics /sfrəjístiks/ *n.pl.* (also treated as *sing.*) the study of engraved seals. [F *sphragistique* (n. & adj.) f. Gk *sphragistikos* f. *sphragis* seal]

sphygmo- /sfigmṓ/ *comb. form Physiol.* a pulse or pulsation. [Gk *sphugmo-* f. *sphugmos* pulse f. *sphuzō* to throb]

sphyg·mo·gram /sfígməgram/ *n.* a record produced by a sphygmograph.

sphyg·mo·graph /sfígməgraf/ *n.* an instrument for showing the character of a pulse in a series of curves. □□ **sphyg·mo·graph·ic** *adj.* **sphyg·mo·graph·i·cal·ly** *adv.* **sphyg·mog·ra·phy** /-mógrəfee/ *n.*

sphyg·mol·o·gy /sfigmóləjee/ *n.* the scientific study of the pulse. □□ **sphyg·mo·log·i·cal** /-məlójikəl/ *adj.*

sphyg·mo·ma·nom·e·ter /sfígmōmənómitər/ *n.* an instrument for measuring blood pressure. □□ **sphyg·mo·man·o·met·ric** /-nəmétrik/ *adj.*

spi·ca /spíkə/ *n.* **1** *Bot.* a spike or spikelike form. **2** *Surgery* a spiral bandage with reversed turns, suggesting an ear of corn. □□ **spi·cate** /-kayt/ *adj.* **spi·cat·ed** /-káytid/ *adj.* [L, = spike, ear of corn, rel. to *spina* SPINE: in sense 2 after Gk *stakhus*]

spic·ca·to /spikáatō/ *n., adj., & adv. Mus.* • *n.* (*pl.* ·**tos**) **1** a style of staccato playing on stringed instruments involving bouncing the bow on the strings. **2** a passage in this style. • *adj.* performed or to be performed in this style. • *adv.* in this style. [It., = detailed, distinct]

spice /spīs/ *n. & v.* • *n.* **1** an aromatic or pungent vegetable substance used to flavor food, e.g., cloves, pepper, or mace. **2** spices collectively (*a dealer in spice*). **3 a** an interesting or piquant quality. **b** (foll. by *of*) a slight flavor or suggestion (*a spice of malice*). • *v.tr.* **1** flavor with spice. **2** add an interesting or piquant quality to (*a book spiced with humor*). [ME f. OF *espice(r)* f. L *species* specific kind: in LL pl. = merchandise]

spice·bush /spísbŏosh/ *n.* any aromatic shrub of the genus *Lindera* or *Calycanthus*, native to America.

spick-and-span /spík ən spán/ (also **spic-and-span**) *adj.* **1** fresh and new. **2** neat and clean. [16th-c. *spick and span new*, emphatic extension of ME *span new* f. ON *spán-nýr* f. *spánn* chip + *nýr* new]

spic·ule /spíkyōōl/ *n.* **1** any small sharply pointed body. **2** *Zool.* a small hard calcareous or siliceous body, esp. in the framework of a sponge. **3** *Bot.* a small or secondary spike. **4** *Astron.* a spikelike prominence, esp. one appearing as a jet of gas in the sun's corona. □□ **spic·u·lar** *adj.* **spic·u·late** /-lət/ *adj.* [mod.L *spicula*, *spiculum*, dimins. of SPICA]

spic·y /spísee/ *adj.* (**spic·i·er, spic·i·est**) **1** of, flavored with, or fragrant with spice. **2** piquant; pungent; sensational or improper (*a spicy story*). □□ **spic·i·ly** *adv.* **spic·i·ness** *n.*

spi·der /spídər/ *n. & v.* • *n.* **1 a** any eight-legged arthropod of the order Araneae with a round unsegmented body, many of which spin webs for the capture of insects as food. **b** any of various similar or related arachnids, e.g., a red spider. **2** any object comparable to a spider, esp. as having numerous or prominent legs or radiating spokes. **3** a frying pan, esp. one with legs or feet. **4** *Brit.* a radiating series of elastic ties used to hold a load in place on a vehicle, etc. • *v.intr.* **1** move in a scuttling manner suggestive of a spider (*fingers spidered across the map*). **2** cause to move or appear in this way. **3** (as **spidering** *adj.*) spiderlike in form, manner, or movement (*spidering streets*). □□ **spi·der·ish** *adj.* [OE *spīthra* (as SPIN)]

spi·der crab *n.* any of various crabs of the family Majidae with a pear-shaped body and long thin legs.

spi·der·man /spídərman/ *n.* (*pl.* ·**men**) *Brit. colloq.* a person who works at great heights in building construction.

spi·der mite *n.* any of various mites of the family Tetranychidae infesting hothouse plants, esp. vines.

spi·der mon·key *n.* any S. American monkey of the genus *Ateles*, with long limbs and a prehensile tail.

spi·der plant *n.* any of various house plants with long narrow striped leaves.

spi·der·wort /spídərwərt, -wawrt/ *n.* any plant of the genus *Tradescantia*, esp. *T. virginiana*, having flowers with long hairy stamens.

spi·der·y /spídəree/ *adj.* elongated and thin (*spidery handwriting*).

spie·gel·ei·sen /spéegəlīzən/ *n.* an alloy of iron and manganese, used in steel making. [G f. *Spiegel* mirror + *Eisen* iron]

spiel /speel, shpeel/ *n. & v. sl.* • *n.* **1** a glib speech or story, esp. a salesman's patter. • *v.* **1** *intr.* speak glibly; hold forth. **2** *tr.* reel off (patter, etc.). □□ **spiel·er** *n.* [G, = play, game]

spiff /spif/ *v. tr. colloq.* (usu. foll. by *up*) remodel; refurnish; make neat or clean.

spiff·ing /spífing/ *adj. Brit. archaic sl.* **1** excellent. **2** smart; handsome. [19th c.: orig. unkn.]

spiff·y /spífee/ *adj.* (**spiff·i·er, spiff·i·est**) *sl.* stylish; smart. □□ **spiff·i·ly** *adv.*

spif·li·cate /spíflikayt/ *v.tr.* (also **spif·fli·cate**) *esp. Brit. joc.* **1** destroy. **2** beat (in a fight, etc.). [18th c.: fanciful]

spig·ot /spígət/ *n.* **1** a small peg or plug, esp. for insertion into the vent hole of a cask. **2 a** a faucet. **b** a device for controlling the flow of liquid in a faucet. **3** the plain end of a pipe section fitting into the socket of the next one. [ME, perh. f. Prov. *espigou(n)* f. L *spiculum* dimin. of *spicum* = SPICA]

spike¹ /spīk/ *n. & v.* • *n.* **1 a** a sharp point. **b** a pointed piece of metal, esp. the top of an iron railing, etc. **2 a** any of several metal points set into the sole of a running shoe to prevent slipping. **b** (in *pl.*) a pair of running shoes with spikes. **3** = SPINDLE *n.* 7. **4** a large stout nail esp. as used for railways. **5** *sl.* a hypodermic needle. **6** *Brit. sl.* a doss house. **7** *Electronics* a pulse of very short duration in which a rapid increase in voltage is followed by a rapid decrease. **8** the act of propelling a volleyball, football, etc., rapidly downward. • *v.tr.* **1** a fasten or provide with spikes. **b** fix on or pierce with spikes. **2** (of a newspaper editor, etc.) reject (a story), esp. by filing it on a spike. **3** *colloq.* **a** lace (a drink) with alcohol, a drug, etc. **b** contaminate (a substance) with something added. **4** make useless; put an end to; thwart (an idea, etc.). **5** propel (a volleyball, football, etc.) rapidly downward. **6** *hist.* plug up the vent of (a gun) with a spike. [ME perh. f. MLG, MDu. *spiker*, rel. to SPOKE¹]

spike² /spīk/ *n.* **1** a flower cluster formed of many flower heads attached closely on a long stem. **2** a separate sprig of any plant in which flowers form a spikelike cluster. □□ **spike·let** *n.* [ME, = ear of corn, f. L SPICA]

spike heel *n.* a high tapering heel of a woman's shoe.

spike·nard /spíknaard/ *n.* **1** *Bot.* an E. Indian plant, *Nardostachys grandiflora*. **2** *hist.* a costly perfumed ointment made from this. [ME ult. f. med.L *spica nardi* (as SPIKE², NARD) after Gk *nardostakhus*]

spik·y¹ /spíkee/ *adj.* (**spik·i·er, spik·i·est**) **1** like a spike; having many spikes. **2** *colloq.* easily offended; prickly. □□ **spik·i·ly** *adv.* **spik·i·ness** *n.*

spik·y² /spíkee/ *adj. Bot.* having spikes or ears.

spile /spīl/ *n. & v.* • *n.* **1** a wooden peg or spigot. **2** a large timber or pile for driving into the ground. **3** a small spout for tapping the sap from a sugar maple, etc. • *v.tr.* tap (a cask, etc.) with a spile in order to draw off liquid. [MDu., MLG, = wooden peg, etc.: in sense 'pile' app. alt. of PILE²]

spill¹ /spil/ *v. & n.* • *v.* (*past and past part.* **spilled** or **spilt**) **1** *intr. & tr.* fall or run or cause (a liquid, powder, etc.) to fall or run out of a vessel, esp. unintentionally. **2 a** *tr. & intr.* throw (a person, etc.) from a vehicle, saddle, etc. **b** *intr.* (esp. of a crowd) tumble out quickly from a place, etc. (*the fans spilled into the street*). **3** *tr. sl.* disclose (information, etc.). **4** *tr. Naut.* **a** empty (a sail) of wind. **b** lose (wind) from a sail. • *n.* **1 a** the act or an instance of spilling or being spilled. **b** a quantity spilled. **2** a tumble or fall, esp. from a horse, etc. (*had a nasty spill*). **3** *Austral.* the vacating of all or several posts of a parliamentary party to allow reorganization. □ **spill the beans** *colloq.* divulge information, etc., esp. unintentionally or indiscreetly. **spill blood** be guilty of bloodshed. **spill the blood of** kill or injure (a person). **spill over 1** overflow. **2** (of a surplus population) be forced to move (cf. OVERSPILL). □□ **spill·age** /spílij/ *n.* **spill·er** *n.* [OE *spillan* kill, rel. to OE *spildan* destroy: orig. unkn.]

spill² /spil/ *n.* a thin strip of wood, folded or twisted paper, etc., used for lighting a fire, candles, a pipe, etc. [ME, rel. to SPILE]

spil·li·kin /spílikin/ *n.* (also **spel·li·can** /spélikən/) **1** a jackstraw. **2** (in *pl.*) a game of jackstraws. [SPILL² + -KIN]

spill·o·ver /spílōvər/ *n.* **1 a** the process or an instance of spilling over. **b** a thing that spills over. **2** a consequence, repercussion, or byproduct.

spill·way /spílway/ *n.* a passage for surplus water from a dam.

spilt *past and past part.* of SPILL¹.

spilth /spilth/ *n.* **1** material that is spilled. **2** the act or an instance of spilling. **3** an excess or surplus.

spin /spin/ *v. & n.* • *v.* (**spin·ning**; *past and past part.* **spun** /spun/) **1** *intr. & tr.* turn or cause (a person or thing) to turn or whirl around quickly. **2** *tr.* (also *absol.*) **a** draw out and twist (wool, cotton, etc.) into threads. **b** make (yarn) in this way. **c** make a similar type of thread from (a synthetic substance, etc.). **3** *tr.* (of a spider, silkworm, etc.) make (a web, gossamer, a cocoon, etc.) by extruding a fine viscous thread. **4** *tr.* tell or write (a story, essay, article, etc.) (*spins a good tale*). **5** *tr.* impart spin to (a ball). **6** *intr.* (of a person's head, etc.) be dizzy through excitement, astonishment, etc. **7** *tr.* attempt to interpret or slant (a media report) a certain way. **8** *tr.* shape (metal) on a mold in a lathe, etc. **9** *intr.* (of a ball) move through the air with spin. **10** *tr.* (as **spun** *adj.*) converted into threads (*spun glass*; *spun gold*; *spun sugar*). **11** *tr.* fish in (a stream, pool, etc.) with a spinner. **12** *tr.* toss (a coin). **13** *tr.* = *spin-dry* (see SPIN-DRYER). **14** *intr.* (of an airplane) to descend in a spin. •*n.* **1** a spinning motion; a whirl. **2** an aircraft's diving descent combined with rotation. **3 a** a revolving motion through the air, esp. in a rifle bullet or in a billiard, tennis, or table tennis ball struck aslant. **b** *Baseball* a twisting motion given to the ball in pitching. **4** *colloq.* a brief drive in a motor vehicle, airplane, etc., esp. for pleasure. **5** *Physics* the intrinsic angular momentum of an elementary particle. **6** emphasis; interpretation. **7** *Austral.* & *NZ sl.* a piece of good or bad luck. □ **spin off 1** throw off by centrifugal force in spinning. **2** create or establish as a by-product or derivative endeavor. **spin out 1** prolong (a discussion, etc.). **2** make (a story, money, etc.) last as long as possible. **3** spend or consume (time, one's life, etc., by discussion or in an occupation, etc.). **spin a yarn** *orig. Naut.* tell a story. [OE *spinnan*]

spi•na bif•i•da /spínə bífidə/ *n.* a congenital defect of the spine, in which part of the spinal cord and its meninges are exposed through a gap in the backbone. [mod.L (as SPINE, BIFID)]

spin•ach /spínich, –nij/ *n.* **1** a green garden vegetable, *Spinacia oleracea*, with succulent leaves. **2** the leaves of this plant used as food. □□ **spi•na•ceous** /–náyshəs/ *adj.* **spin•ach•y** *adj.* [prob. MDu. *spinaetse*, *spinag(i)e*, f. OF *espinage*, *espinache* f. med.L *spinac(h)ia*, etc. f. Arab. 'isfān āḵ f. Pers. ispān āḵ: perh. assim. to L *spina* SPINE, with ref. to its prickly seeds]

spin•ach beet *n.* a variety of beet cultivated for its edible leaves.

spi•nal /spín'l/ *adj.* of or relating to the spine (*spinal curvature*; *spinal disease*). □□ **spi•nal•ly** *adv.* [LL *spinalis* (as SPINE)]

spi•nal ca•nal *n.* a cavity through the vertebrae containing the spinal cord.

spi•nal col•umn *n.* the spine.

spi•nal cord *n.* a cylindrical structure of the central nervous system enclosed in the spine, connecting all parts of the body with the brain.

spin•dle /spínd'l/ *n. & v.* •*n.* **1 a** a pin in a spinning wheel used for twisting and winding the thread. **b** a small bar with tapered ends used for the same purpose in hand spinning. **c** a pin bearing the bobbin of a spinning machine. **2** a pin or axis that revolves or on which something revolves. **3** a turned piece of wood used as a banister, chair leg, etc. **4** *Biol.* a spindle-shaped mass of microtubules formed when a cell divides. **5** a varying measure of length for yarn. **6** a slender person or thing. **7 a** a pointed metal rod standing on a base and used for filing news items, etc., esp. when rejected for publication. **b** a similar spike used for bills, etc. •*v.intr.* have, or grow into, a long slender form. [OE *spinel* (as SPIN)]

spin•dle ber•ry *n.* the fruit of the spindle tree.

spin•dle-shanks *n.* a person with long thin legs. □□ **spin•dle-shanked** *adj.*

spin•dle-shaped *adj.* having a circular cross section and tapering toward each end.

spin•dle side *n.* = DISTAFF SIDE.

spin•dle tree *n.* any shrub or small tree of the genus *Euonymus*, esp. *E. europaeus* with greenish white flowers, pink or red berries, and hard wood used for spindles.

spin•dly /spíndlee/ *adj.* (**spin•dli•er**, **spin•dli•est**) long or tall and thin; thin and weak.

spin doc•tor *n.* a political pundit who is employed to promote a favorable interpretation of political developments to the media.

spin•drift /spíndrift/ *n.* spray blown along the surface of the sea. [Sc. var. of *spoondrift* f. *spoon* run before wind or sea + DRIFT]

spin-dry•er *n.* (also **spin-dri•er**) a machine for drying wet clothes, etc., centrifugally in a revolving drum. □□ **spin-dry** (**•dries**, **•dried**) *v.*

spine /spīn/ *n.* **1** a series of vertebrae extending from the skull to the small of the back, enclosing the spinal cord and providing support for the thorax and abdomen; the backbone. **2** *Zool.* & *Bot.* any hard pointed process or structure. **3** a sharp ridge or projection, esp. of a mountain range or slope. **4** a central feature, main support, or source of strength. **5** the part of a book's jacket or cover that encloses the fastened edges of the pages and usu. faces outwards on a shelf. □□ **spined** *adj.* [ME f. OF *espine* f. L *spina* thorn, backbone]

spine chill•er *n.* a frightening story, movie, etc. □□ **spine-chill•ing** *adj.*

spi•nel /spínél/ *n.* **1** any of a group of hard crystalline minerals of various colors, consisting chiefly of oxides of magnesium and aluminum. **2** any substance of similar composition or properties. [F *spinelle* f. It. *spinella*, dimin. of *spina*: see SPINE]

spine•less /spínlis/ *adj.* **1 a** having no spine; invertebrate. **b** (of a fish) having no spines on the fins. **2** (of a person) lacking energy or resolution; weak and purposeless. □□ **spine•less•ly** *adv.* **spine•less•ness** *n.*

spi•nel ru•by *n.* a deep red variety of spinel used as a gem.

spin•et /spínit, spinét/ *n. Mus.* **1** *hist.* a small harpsichord with oblique strings. **2** a small upright piano. [obs. F *espinette* f. It. *spinet-*

ta virginal, spinet, dimin. of *spina* thorn, etc. (as SPINE), with ref. to the plucked strings]

spine-tin•gling *adj.* thrilling; pleasurably exciting.

spin•i•fex /spínifeks/ *n.* any Australian grass of the genus *Spinifex*, with coarse, spiny leaves. [mod.L f. L *spina* SPINE + *-fex* maker f. *facere* make]

spin•na•ker /spínəkər/ *n.* a large triangular sail carried opposite the mainsail of a racing yacht running before the wind. [fanciful f. *Sphinx*, name of yacht first using it, perh. after *spanker*]

spin•ner /spínər/ *n.* **1** a person or thing that spins. **2** *Cricket* **a** a spin bowler. **b** a spun ball. **3** a spin-dryer. **4 a** a real or artificial fly for esp. trout fishing. **b** revolving bait. **5** a manufacturer or merchant engaged in (esp. cotton) spinning. **6** a fairing attached to and moving with an airplane propeller. **7** = SPINNERET. **8** *archaic* a spider.

spin•ner•et /spínəret/ *n.* **1** the spinning organ in a spider, silkworm, etc. **2** a device for forming filaments of synthetic fiber.

spin•ney /spínee/ *n.* (*pl.* **•neys**) *Brit.* a small wood; a thicket. [OF *espinei* f. L *spinetum* thicket f. *spina* thorn]

spin•ning jen•ny *n. hist.* a machine for spinning with more than one spindle at a time.

spin•ning ma•chine *n.* a machine that spins fibers continuously.

spin•ning top *n.* = TOP[2].

spin•ning wheel *n.* a household machine for spinning yarn or thread with a spindle driven by a wheel attached to a crank or treadle.

spin-off *n.* an incidental result or results, esp. as a side benefit from industrial technology.

spi•nose /spínōs/ *adj.* (also **spi•nous** /–nəs/) *Bot.* (of a plant) having many spines.

Spi•no•zism /spinōzizəm/ *n. Philos.* the doctrine of Spinoza that there is one infinite substance of which extension and thought are attributes and human beings are changing forms. □□ **Spi•no•zist** *n.* **Spi•no•zis•tic** *adj.* [B. de *Spinoza*, Du. philosopher d. 1677]

spin•ster /spínstər/ *n.* **1** an unmarried woman. **2** a woman, esp. elderly, thought unlikely to marry. □□ **spin•ster•hood** *n.* **spin•ster•ish** *adj.* **spin•ster•ish•ness** *n.* [ME, orig. = woman who spins]

spin•thar•i•scope /spinthárəskōp/ *n.* an instrument with a fluorescent screen showing the incidence of alpha particles by flashes. [irreg. f. Gk *spintharis* spark + –SCOPE]

spi•nule /spínyool/ *n. Bot.* & *Zool.* a small spine. □□ **spin•u•lose** *adj.* **spin•u•lous** *adj.* [L *spinula* dimin. of *spina* SPINE]

spin•y /spínee/ *adj.* (**spin•i•er**, **spin•i•est**) **1** full of spines; prickly. **2** perplexing; troublesome; thorny. □□ **spin•i•ness** *n.*

spin•y ant•eat•er *n.* = ECHIDNA.

spin•y lob•ster *n.* any of various large edible crustaceans of the family Palinuridae, esp. *Palinuris vulgaris*, with a spiny shell and no large anterior claws.

spi•ra•cle /spírəkəl/ *n.* (also **spi•rac•u•lum** /spírákyələm/) (*pl.* **spi•ra•cles** or **spi•rac•u•la** /–rákyələ/) an external respiratory opening in insects, whales, and some fish. □□ **spi•rac•u•lar** /–rákyələr/ *adj.* [L *spiraculum* f. *spirare* breathe]

spi•rae•a var. of SPIREA.

spi•ral /spírəl/ *adj., n., & v.* •*adj.* **1** winding about a center in an enlarging or decreasing continuous circular motion, either on a flat plane or rising in a cone; coiled. **2** winding continuously along or as if along a cylinder, like the thread of a screw. •*n.* **1** a plane or three-dimensional spiral curve. **2** a spiral spring. **3** a spiral formation in a shell, etc. **4** a spiral galaxy. **5** a progressive rise or fall of prices, wages, etc., each responding to an upward or downward stimulus provided by the other (*a spiral of rising prices and wages*). **6** *Football.* a kick or pass in which the ball rotates on its long axis while in the air. •*v.* (**spi•raled** or **spi•ralled**, **spi•ral•ing** or **spi•ral•ling**) **1** *intr.* move in a spiral course, esp. upwards or downwards. **2** *tr.* make spiral. **3** *intr.* esp. Econ. (of prices, wages, etc.) rise or fall, esp. rapidly (cf. sense 5 of *n.*). □□ **spi•ral•i•ty** /–rálitee/ *n.* **spi•ral•ly** *adv.* [F *spiral* or med.L *spiralis* (as SPIRE[2])]

spi•ral bal•ance *n.* a device for measuring weight by the torsion of a spiral spring.

spi•ral gal•ax•y *n.* a galaxy in which the matter is concentrated mainly in one or more spiral arms.

spi•ral stair•case *n.* a staircase rising in a spiral round a central axis.

spi•rant /spírənt/ *adj.* & *n. Phonet.* •*adj.* (of a consonant) uttered with a continuous expulsion of breath, esp. fricative. •*n.* such a consonant. [L *spirare spirant-* breathe]

spire[1] /spīr/ *n. & v.* •*n.* **1** a tapering cone- or pyramid-shaped structure built esp. on a church tower (cf. STEEPLE). **2** the continuation of a tree trunk above the point where branching begins. **3** any tapering thing, e.g., the spike of a flower. •*v.tr.* **1** extend upward like a spire. **2** provide with a spire. □□ **spir•y** /spíree/ *adj.* [OE *spīr*]

spire[1]

spire² /spír/ *n.* **1 a** a spiral; a coil. **b** a single twist of this. **2** the upper part of a spiral shell. [F f. L *spira* f. Gk *speira* coil]

spi•re•a /spíréeə/ *n.* (also **spi•rae•a**) any rosaceous shrub of the genus *Spiraea*, with clusters of small white or pink flowers. [L f. Gk *speiraia* f. *speira* coil]

spi•ril•lum /spírílom/ *n.* (*pl.* **spi•ril•la** /-lə/) **1** any bacterium of the genus *Spirillum*, characterized by a rigid spiral structure. **2** any bacterium with a similar shape. [mod.L, irreg. dimin. of L *spira* SPIRE²]

spir•it /spírit/ *n. & v.* ●*n.* **1 a** the vital animating essence of a person or animal (*was sadly broken in spirit*). **b** the intelligent nonphysical part of a person; the soul. **2 a** a rational or intelligent being without a material body. **b** a supernatural being such as a ghost, fairy, etc. (*haunted by spirits*). **3** a prevailing mental or moral condition or attitude; a mood; a tendency (*public spirit*; *took it in the wrong spirit*). **4 a** (in *pl.*) strong distilled liquor, e.g., brandy, whiskey, gin, rum. **b** a distilled volatile liquid (*wood spirits*). **c** purified alcohol (*methylated spirits*). **d** a solution of a volatile principle in alcohol; a tincture (*spirits of ammonia*). **5 a** a person's mental or moral nature or qualities, usu. specified (*has an unbending spirit*). **b** a person viewed as possessing these (*is an ardent spirit*). **c** (in full **high spirit**) courage; energy; vivacity; dash (*played with spirit*; *infused him with spirit*). **6** the real meaning as opposed to lip service or verbal expression (*the spirit of the law*). **7** *archaic* an immaterial principle thought to govern vital phenomena (*animal spirits*). ●*v.tr.* (**spirited**, **spiriting**) **1** (usu. foll. by *away*, *off*, etc.) convey rapidly and secretly by or as if by spirits. **2** animate or cheer up a person. □ **in (or in the) spirit** inwardly (*shall be with you in spirit*). **the spirit moves a person** he or she feels inclined to (do something) (orig. in Quaker use). [ME f. AF (*e*)*spirit*, OF *esp(e)rit*, f. L *spiritus* breath, spirit f. *spirare* breathe]

spir•it•ed /spíritid/ *adj.* **1** full of spirit; animated, lively, brisk, or courageous (*a spirited attack*; *a spirited translation*). **2** having a spirit or spirits of a specified kind (*high spirited*; *mean spirited*). □□ **spir•it•ed•ly** *adv.* **spir•it•ed•ness** *n.*

spir•it gum *n.* a quick-drying solution of gum used esp. for attaching false hair.

spir•it lamp *n.* a lamp burning methylated alcohol or other liquid fuel instead of oil.

spir•it•less /spíritlis/ *adj.* lacking courage, vigor, or vivacity. □□ **spir•it•less•ly** *adv.* **spir•it•less•ness** *n.*

spir•it lev•el *n.* a bent glass tube nearly filled with alcohol used to test horizontality by the position of an air bubble.

spir•it of wine *n.* (also **spir•its of wine**) *archaic* purified alcohol.

spir•its of salt *n. archaic* hydrochloric acid.

spir•it•u•al /spírichōoəl/ *adj. & n.* ●*adj.* **1** of or concerning the spirit as opposed to matter. **2** concerned with sacred or religious things; holy; divine; inspired (*the spiritual life*; *spiritual songs*). **3** (of the mind, etc.) refined; sensitive; not concerned with the material. **4** (of a relationship, etc.) concerned with the soul or spirit, etc., not with external reality (*his spiritual home*). ●*n.* a religious song derived from the musical traditions of African-American people in the southern US. □□ **spir•it•u•al•i•ty** /-chōo-álitee/ *n.* **spir•it•u•al•ly** *adv.* **spir•it•u•al•ness** *n.* [ME f. OF *spirituel* f. L *spiritualis* (as SPIRIT)]

spir•it•u•al•ism /spírichōoəlizəm/ *n.* **1 a** the belief that the spirits of the dead can communicate with the living, esp. through mediums. **b** the practice of this. **2** *Philos.* the doctrine that the spirit exists as distinct from matter, or that spirit is the only reality (cf. MATERIALISM). □□ **spir•it•u•al•ist** *n.* **spir•it•u•al•is•tic** *adj.*

spir•it•u•al•ize /spírichōoəlīz/ *v.tr.* **1** make (a person or a person's character, thoughts, etc.) spiritual; elevate. **2** attach a spiritual as opposed to a literal meaning to. □□ **spir•it•u•al•i•za•tion** *n.*

spir•it•u•el /spírichōo-él/ *adj.* (also **spir•it•u•elle**) (of the mind) refined and yet spirited; witty. [F *spirituel*, fem. *-elle* (as SPIRITUAL)]

spir•it•u•ous /spírichōoəs/ *adj.* **1** containing much alcohol. **2** distilled, as whiskey, rum, etc. (*spirituous liquor*). □□ **spir•it•u•ous•ness** *n.* [L *spiritus* spirit, or F *spiritueux*]

spiro-¹ /spíró/ *comb. form* a coil. [L *spira*, Gk *speira* coil]

spiro-² /spíró/ *comb. form* breath. [irreg. f. L *spirare* breathe]

spi•ro•chete /spírōkeet/ *n.* (also **spi•ro•chaete**) any of various flexible spiral-shaped bacteria. [SPIRO-¹ + Gk *khaitē* long hair]

spi•ro•graph /spírəgraf/ *n.* an instrument for recording breathing movements. □□ **spi•ro•graph•ic** *adj.* **spi•ro•graph•i•cal•ly** *adv.*

spi•ro•gy•ra /spírójírə/ *n.* any freshwater alga of the genus *Spirogyra*, with cells containing spiral bands of chlorophyll. [mod.L f. SPIRO-¹ + Gk *guros* gura round]

spi•rom•e•ter /spírómitər/ *n.* an instrument for measuring the air capacity of the lungs.

spirt var. of SPURT.

spit¹ /spit/ *v. & n.* ●*v.* (**spitting**; *past and past part.* **spat** /spat/ or **spit**) **1** *intr.* **a** eject saliva from the mouth. **b** do this as a sign of hatred or contempt (*spat at him*). **2** *tr.* (usu. foll. by *out*) **a** eject (saliva, blood, food, etc.) from the mouth (*spat the meat out*). **b** utter (oaths, threats, etc.) vehemently (*"Damn you!" he spat*). **3** *intr.* (of a fire, pen, pan, etc.) send out sparks, ink, hot fat, etc. **4** *intr.* (of rain) fall lightly (*it's only spitting*). **5** *intr.* (esp. of a cat) make a spitting or hissing noise in anger or hostility. ●*n.* **1** spittle. **2** the act or

an instance of spitting. **3** the foamy liquid secretion of some insects used to protect their young. □ **the spit of** *colloq.* the exact double of (cf. SPITTING IMAGE). **spit chips** *Austral. sl.* **1** feel extreme thirst. **2** be angry or frustrated. **spit it out** *colloq.* say what is on one's mind. **spit up** regurgitate; vomit. □□ **spit•ter** *n.* [OE *spittan*, of imit. orig.: cf. SPEW]

spit² /spit/ *n. & v.* ●*n.* **1** a slender rod on which meat is skewered before being roasted on a fire, etc.; a skewer. **2 a** a small point of land projecting into the sea. **b** a long narrow underwater bank. ●*v.tr.* (**spit•ted**, **spit•ting**) **1** thrust a spit through (meat, etc.). **2** pierce or transfix with a sword, etc. □□ **spit•ty** *adj.* [OE *spitu* f. WG]

spit³ /spit/ *n.* esp. *Brit.* (*pl.* same or **spits**) a spade-depth of earth (*dig it two spit deep*). [MDu. & MLG, = OE *spittan* dig with spade, prob. rel. to SPIT²]

spit and pol•ish *n.* **1** the cleaning and polishing duties of a soldier, etc. **2** exaggerated neatness and smartness.

spit•ball /spítbawl/ *n. & v.* ●*n.* **1** a ball of chewed paper, etc., used as a missile. **2** a baseball moistened by the pitcher to affect its flight. ●*v.intr.* throw out suggestions for discussion. □□ **spit•ball•er** *n.*

spitch•cock /spíchkok/ *n. & v.* ●*n.* an eel split and grilled or fried. ●*v.tr.* prepare (an eel, fish, bird, etc.) in this way. [16th c.: orig. unkn.: cf. SPATCHCOCK]

spit curl *n.* a tight curl usu. pressed against the forehead, cheek, or temple.

spite /spīt/ *n. & v.* ●*n.* **1** ill will; malice toward a person (*did it from spite*). **2** a grudge. ●*v.tr.* thwart; mortify; annoy (*does it to spite me*). □ **in spite of** notwithstanding. **in spite of oneself**, etc., though one would rather have done otherwise. [ME f. *despit* DESPITE]

spite•ful /spítfool/ *adj.* motivated by spite; malevolent. □□ **spite•ful•ly** *adv.* **spite•ful•ness** *n.*

spit•fire /spítfīr/ *n.* a person with a fiery temper.

spit roast *n.* cook on a spit.

spit•ting co•bra *n.* the African black-necked cobra, *Naja nigricollis*, that ejects venom by spitting, not striking.

spit•ting dis•tance *n.* a very short distance.

spit•ting im•age *n.* (foll. by *of*) *colloq.* the exact double of (another person or thing).

spit•tle /spít'l/ *n.* saliva, esp. as ejected from the mouth. □□ **spit•tly** *adj.* [alt. of ME (now dial.) *spattle* = OE *spātl* f. *spǣtan* to spit, after SPIT¹]

spit•toon /spitóon/ *n.* a metal or earthenware pot with esp. a funnel shaped top, used for spitting into.

spitz /spits/ *n.* **1** any of a stocky type of dog with a pointed muzzle and a tail curved over the back, as a Pomeranian, Samoyed, etc. **2** this breed. [G *Spitz(hund)* f. *spitz* pointed + *Hund* dog]

spiv /spiv/ *n. Brit. colloq.* a man, often characterized by flashy dress, who makes a living by illicit or unscrupulous dealings. □□ **spiv•vish** *adj.* **spiv•vy** *adj.* [20th c.: orig. unkn.]

splanch•nic /splángknik/ *adj.* of or relating to the viscera; intestinal. [mod.L *splanchnicus* f. Gk *splagkhnikos* f. *splagkhna* entrails]

splash /splash/ *v. & n.* ●*v.* **1** *intr. & tr.* spatter or cause (liquid) to spatter in small drops. **2** *tr.* cause (a person) to be spattered with liquid, etc. (*splashed them with mud*) **3** *intr.* **a** (of a person) cause liquid to spatter (*was splashing about in the bath*). **b** (usu. foll. by *across*, *along*, etc.) move while spattering liquid, etc. (*splashed across the carpet in his boots*). **c** step, fall, or plunge, etc., into a liquid, etc., so as to cause a splash (*splashed into the sea*). **d** (foll. by *down*) (of a spacecraft) land in the sea after flight. **4** *tr.* display (news) prominently. **5** *tr.* decorate with scattered color. **6** *tr. Brit.* spend (money) ostentatiously. ●*n.* **1** the act or an instance of splashing. **2 a** a quantity of liquid splashed. **b** the resulting noise (*heard a splash*). **3** a spot or patch of dirt, etc., splashed on to a thing. **4** a prominent news feature, etc. **5** a daub or patch of color, esp. on an animal's coat. **6** *colloq.* a small quantity of liquid, esp. of soda water, etc., to dilute liquor. □ **make a splash** attract much attention, esp. by extravagance. **splash out** *Brit. colloq.* spend money freely. □□ **splash•y** *adj.* **splash•i•er**, **splash•i•est**. [alt. of PLASH¹]

splash•board /spláshbawrd/ (*Brit.* **splash•back**) *n.* a panel behind a sink, etc., to protect the wall from splashes.

splash•down /spláshdown/ *n.* the landing of a spacecraft in the sea.

splat¹ /splat/ *n.* a flat piece of thin wood in the center of a chair back. [*splat* (v.) split up, rel. to SPLIT]

splat² /splat/ *n., adv., & v. colloq.* ●*n.* a sharp cracking or slapping sound (*hit the wall with a splat*). ●*adv.* with a splat (*fell splat into the puddle*). ●*v.intr. & tr.* (**splat•ted**, **splat•ting**) fall or hit with a splat. [abbr. of SPLATTER]

splat•ter /splátər/ *v. & n.* ●*v.* **1** *tr. & intr.* splash esp. with a continuous noisy action. **2** *tr.* (often foll. by *with*) make wet or dirty by splashing. ●*n.* a noisy splashing sound. [imit.]

splay /splay/ *v., n., & adj.* ●*v.* **1** *tr.* (usu. foll. by *out*) spread (the elbows, feet, etc.) out. **2** *intr.* (of an aperture or its sides) diverge in shape or position. **3** *tr.* construct (a window, doorway, aperture, etc.) so that it diverges or is wider at one side of the wall than the other. ● *n.* a surface making an oblique angle with another, e.g., the splayed side of a window or embrasure. ● *adj.* **1** wide and flat. **2** turned outward. [ME f. DISPLAY]

splay·foot /spláyfŏŏt/ *n.* a broad flat foot turned outward. □□ **splay·foot·ed** *adj.*

spleen /spleen/ *n.* **1** an abdominal organ involved in maintaining the proper condition of blood in most vertebrates. **2** lowness of spirits; moroseness, ill temper, spite (from the earlier belief that the spleen was the seat of such feelings) (*a fit of spleen; vented their spleen*). □□ **spleen·ful** *adj.* **spleen·y** *adj.* [ME f. OF *esplen* f. L *splen* f. Gk *splēn*]

spleen·wort /spleenwərt, –wawrt/ *n.* any fern of the genus *Asplenium*, formerly used as a remedy for disorders of the spleen.

splen- /spleen/ *comb. form Anat.* the spleen. [Gk (as SPLEEN)]

splen·dent /spléndənt/ *adj. formal* **1** shining; lustrous. **2** illustrious. [ME f. L *splendēre* to shine]

splen·did /spléndid/ *adj.* **1** magnificent; gorgeous; brilliant; sumptuous (*a splendid palace; a splendid achievement*). **2** dignified; impressive (*splendid isolation*). **3** excellent; fine (*a splendid chance*). □□ **splen·did·ly** *adv.* **splen·did·ness** *n.* [F *splendide* or L *splendidus* (as SPLENDENT)]

splen·dif·er·ous /splendífərəs/ *adj. colloq.* or *joc.* splendid. □□ **splen·dif·er·ous·ly** *adv.* **splen·dif·er·ous·ness** *n.* [irreg. f. SPLENDOR]

splen·dor /spléndər/ *n.* (*Brit.* **splen·dour**) **1** great or dazzling brightness. **2** magnificence; grandeur. [ME f. AF *splendeur* or L *splendor* (as SPLENDENT)]

splen·ec·to·my /splinéktəmee/ *n.* (*pl.* **·mies**) the surgical excision of the spleen.

sple·net·ic /splinétik/ *adj. & n.* ● *adj.* **1** ill·tempered; peevish. **2** of or concerning the spleen. ● *n.* a splenetic person. □□ **sple·net·i·cal·ly** *adv* [LL *spleneticus* (as SPLEEN)]

splen·ic /splénik/ *adj.* of or in the spleen. □□ **splen·oid** /spleenoyd/ *adj.* [F *splénique* or L *splenicus* f. Gk *splēnikos* (as SPLEEN)]

splen·ic fe·ver *n.* anthrax.

sple·ni·tis /spleenítis/ *n.* inflammation of the spleen.

sple·ni·us /spleeneeəs/ *n.* (*pl.* **sple·ni·i** /–nee-ī/) *Anat.* either section of muscle on each side of the neck and back serving to draw back the head. □□ **sple·ni·al** *adj.* [mod.L f. Gk *splēnion* bandage]

sple·nol·o·gy /spleenóləjee/ *n.* the scientific study of the spleen.

sple·no·meg·a·ly /spleenəmégəlee/ *n.* a pathological enlargement of the spleen. [SPLEN- f *megaly* (as MEGALO-)]

sple·not·o·my /spleenótəmee/ *n.* (*pl.* **·mies**) a surgical incision into or dissection of the spleen.

splice /splis/ *v. & n.* ● *v.tr.* **1** join the ends of (ropes) by interweaving strands. **2** join (pieces of timber, magnetic tape, film, etc.) in an overlapping position. **3** artificially combine genetic materials. **4** (esp. as **spliced** *adj.*) *colloq.* join in marriage. ● *n.* a joint consisting of two ropes, pieces of wood, film, etc., made by splicing. □ **splice the main brace** *Naut. hist.* issue an extra tot of rum. □□ **splic·er** *n.* [prob. f. MDu. *splissen*, of uncert. orig.]

spliff /splif/ *n.* (also **splif**) *sl.* a marijuana cigarette. [20th c.: orig. unkn.]

spline /splin/ *n. & v.* ● *n.* **1** a rectangular key fitting into grooves in the hub and shaft of a wheel and allowing longitudinal play. **2** a slat. **3** a flexible wood or rubber strip used esp. in drawing large curves. ● *v.tr.* fit with a spline (sense 1). [orig. E. Anglian dial., perh. rel. to SPLINTER]

splint /splint/ *n. & v.* ● *n.* **1 a** a strip of rigid material used for holding a broken bone, etc., when set. **b** a rigid or flexible strip of esp. wood used in basketwork, etc. **2** a tumor or bony excrescence on the inside of a horse's leg. **3** a thin strip of wood, etc., used to light a fire, pipe, etc. **4** = SPLINT BONE. ● *v.tr.* secure (a broken limb, etc.) with a splint or splints. [ME *splent(e)* f. MDu. *splinte* or MLG *splinte*, *splente* metal plate or pin, rel. to SPLINTER]

splint bone *n.* **1** either of two small bones in a horse's foreleg lying behind and close to the cannon bone. **2** the human fibula.

splint coal *n.* hard bituminous laminated coal burning with great heat.

splin·ter /splíntər/ *v. & n.* ● *v.tr. & intr.* break into fragments. ● *n.* a small thin sharp-edged piece broken off from wood, stone, etc. □□ **splin·ter·y** *adj.* [ME f. MDu. (= LG) *splinter*, *splenter*, rel. to SPLINT]

splin·ter group *n.* (also **splin·ter par·ty**) a group or party that has broken away from a larger one.

split /split/ *v. & n.* ● *v.* (**split·ting**; *past* and *past part.* **split**) **1** *intr. & tr.* break or cause to break forcibly into parts, esp. with the grain or into halves. **b** (often foll. by *up*) divide into parts (*split into groups; split up the money equally*). **c** *intr. Stock Exch.* divide into two or more shares for each share owned. **2** *tr. & intr.* (often foll. by *off, away*) remove or be removed by breaking, separating, or dividing (*split away from the main group*). **3** *intr. & tr.* **a** (usu. foll. by *up, on, over*, etc.) separate esp. through discord (*split up after ten years; they*

were *split on the question of picketing*). **b** (foll. by *with*) quarrel or cease association with (another person, etc.). **4** *tr.* cause the fission of (an atom). **5** *intr. & tr. sl.* leave, esp. suddenly. **6** *intr.* usu. foll. by *on*) *Brit. colloq.* betray secrets; inform (*split on them to the police*). **7** *intr.* **a** (as **splitting** *adj.*) (esp. of a headache) very painful; acute. **b** (of the head) suffer great pain from a headache, noise, etc. **8** *intr.* (of a ship) be wrecked. **9** *tr. colloq.* dilute (whiskey, etc.) with water. ● *n.* **1** the act or an instance of splitting; the state of being split. **2** a fissure, vent, crack, cleft, etc. **3** a separation into parties; a schism. **4** (in *pl.*) the athletic feat of leaping in the air or sitting down with the legs at right angles to the body in front and behind, or at the sides with the trunk facing forward. **5** a split willow shoot, etc., used for parts of basketwork. **6** each strip of steel, cane, etc., of the reed in a loom. **7** a single thickness of split hide. **8** the turning up of two cards of equal value in faro, so that the stakes are divided. **9 a** half a bottle of mineral water. **b** half a glass of liquor. **10** *colloq.* a division of money, esp. the proceeds of crime. **11** = BANANA SPLIT. □ **split the difference** take the average of two proposed amounts. **split hairs** make small and insignificant distinctions. **split one's sides** be convulsed with laughter. **split the ticket** (or one's **vote**) vote for candidates of more than one party in one election. **split the vote** (of a candidate or minority party) attract votes from another so that both are defeated by a third. □□ **split·ter** *n.* [orig. Naut. f. MDu. *splitten*, rel. to *spletten*, *splīten*, MHG *splīzen*]

split gear *n.* (also **split pul·ley** or **split wheel**) a gear, etc., made in halves for removal from a shaft.

split in·fin·i·tive *n.* a phrase consisting of an infinitive with an adverb, etc., inserted between *to* and the verb, e.g., *seems to really like it.*

split-lev·el *adj.* (of a building) having a room or rooms a fraction of a story higher than other parts.

split pea *n.* a dried pea split in half for cooking.

split per·son·al·i·ty *n.* the alteration or dissociation of personality occurring in some mental illnesses, esp. schizophrenia and hysteria.

split pin *n.* a metal cotter pin passed through a hole and held in place by its gaping split end.

split ring *n.* a small steel ring with two spiral turns, such as a key ring.

split screen *n.* a screen on which two or more separate images are displayed.

split sec·ond *n.* a very brief moment of time.

split shift *n.* a shift comprising two or more separate periods of duty.

splosh /splosh/ *v. & n. colloq.* ● *v.tr. & intr.* move with a splashing sound. ● *n.* **1** a splashing sound. **2** a splash of water, etc. **3** *Brit. sl.* money. [imit.]

splotch /sploch/ *n. & v.tr. colloq.* ● *n.* a daub, blot, or smear. ● *v.tr.* make a large, esp. irregular, spot or patch on. □□ **splotch·y** *adj.* [perh. f. SPOT + obs. *plotch* BLOTCH]

splurge /splərj/ *n. & v. colloq.* ● *n.* **1** an ostentatious display or effort. **2** an instance of sudden great extravagance. ● *v.intr.* (usu. foll. by *on*) spend effort or esp. large sums of money (*splurged on new furniture*). [19th-c. US: prob. imit.]

splut·ter /splútər/ *v. & n.* ● *v.* **1** *intr.* **a** speak in a hurried, vehement, or choking manner. **b** emit particles from the mouth, sparks, hot oil, etc., with spitting sounds. **2** *tr.* **a** speak or utter (words, threats, a language, etc.) rapidly or incoherently. **b** emit (food, sparks, hot oil, etc.) with a spitting sound. ● *n.* spluttering speech. □□ **splut·ter·er** *n.* **splut·ter·ing·ly** *adv.* [SPUTTER by assoc. with *splash*]

Spode /spōd/ *n.* a type of fine pottery or porcelain. [J. *Spode*, Engl. maker of china d. 1827]

spoil /spoyl/ *v. & n.* ● *v.* (*past* and *past part.* **spoiled** or esp. *Brit.* **spoilt**) **1** *tr.* **a** damage; diminish the value of (*was spoiled by the rain; will spoil all the fun*). **b** reduce a person's enjoyment, etc., of (*the news spoiled his dinner*). **2** *tr.* injure the character of (esp. a child, pet, etc.) by excessive indulgence. **3** *intr.* **a** (of food) go bad; decay; become unfit for eating. **b** (usu. in *neg.*) (of a joke, secret, etc.) become stale through long keeping. **4** *tr.* render (a ballot) invalid by improper marking. **5** *tr.* (foll. by *of*) *archaic* or *literary* plunder or deprive (a person of a thing) by force or stealth (*spoiled him of all his possessions*). ● *n.* **1** (usu. in *pl.*) **a** plunder taken from an enemy in war, or seized by force. **b** esp. *joc.* profit or advantages gained by succeeding to public office, high position, etc. **2** earth, etc., thrown up in excavating, dredging, etc. □ **be spoiling for** aggressively seek (a fight, etc.). **spoilt for choice** esp. *Brit.* having so many choices that it is difficult to choose. [ME f. OF *espoillier*, *espoille* f. L *spoliare* f. *spolium* spoil, plunder, or f. DESPOIL]

spoil·age /spóylij/ *n.* **1** paper spoiled in printing. **2** the spoiling of food, etc., by decay.

spoil·er /spóylər/ *n.* **1** a person or thing that spoils. **2 a** a device on an aircraft to retard its speed or reduce lift by interrupting the air flow. **b** a similar device on a vehicle to improve its road-holding at speed.

spoils·man /spóylzmən/ *n.* (*pl.* **·men**) esp. *Polit.* **1** an advocate of the spoils system. **2** a person who seeks to profit by it.

spoil·sport /spóylspawrt/ *n.* a person who spoils others' pleasure or enjoyment.

spoils sys·tem *n.* the practice of giving public office to the adherents of a successful party.

spoilt *esp. Brit. past* and *past part.* of SPOIL.

spoke[1] /spōk/ *n. & v.* • *n.* **1** each of the bars running from the hub to the rim of a wheel. **2** a rung of a ladder. **3** each radial handle of the wheel of a ship, etc. • *v.tr.* **1** provide with spokes. **2** obstruct (a wheel, etc.) by thrusting a spoke in. □ **put a spoke in a person's wheel** *Brit.* thwart or hinder a person. □□ **spoke·wise** *adv.* [OE *spāca* f. WG]

spoke[2] *past* of SPEAK.

spo·ken /spốkən/ *past part.* of SPEAK. • *adj.* (in *comb.*) speaking in a specified way (*smooth-spoken*; *well-spoken*). □ **spoken for** claimed; requisitioned (*this seat is spoken for*).

spoke·shave /spōkshayv/ *n.* a blade set between two handles, used for shaping spokes and other esp. curved work where an ordinary plane is not suitable.

spokes·man /spốksmən/ *n.* (*pl.* •men; *fem.* **spokes·wom·an**, *pl.* • wom·en) **1** a person who speaks on behalf of others, esp. in the course of public relations. **2** a person deputed to express the views of a group, etc. [irreg. f. SPOKE[2] after *craftsman*, etc.]

spokes·per·son /spốkspərsən/ *n.* (*pl.* •per·sons or •peo·ple) a spokesman or spokeswoman.

spo·li·a·tion /spốleeáyshən/ *n.* **1 a** plunder or pillage, esp. of neutral vessels in war. **b** extortion. **2** *Eccl.* the taking of the fruits of a benefice under a pretended title, etc. **3** *Law* the destruction, mutilation, or alteration of a document to prevent its being used as evidence. □□ **spo·li·a·tor** /–leeáytər/ *n.* **spo·li·a·to·ry** /–leeətáwree/ *adj.* [ME f. L *spoliatio* (as SPOIL)]

spon·da·ic /spondáyik/ *adj.* **1** of or concerning spondees. **2** (of a hexameter) having a spondee as a fifth foot. [F *spondaï* que or LL *spondaicus* = LL *spondiacus* f. Gk *spondeiakos* (as SPONDEE)]

spon·dee /spóndee/ *n. Prosody* a foot consisting of two long (or stressed) syllables. [ME f. OF *spondee* or L *spondeus* f. Gk *spondeios* (*pous* foot) f. *spondē* libation, as being characteristic of music accompanying libations]

spon·dy·li·tis /spóndəlítis/ *n.* inflammation of the vertebrae. [L *spondylus* vertebra f. Gk *spondulos* + –ITIS]

sponge /spunj/ *n. & v.* • *n.* **1** any aquatic animal of the phylum Porifera, with pores in its body wall and a rigid internal skeleton. **2 a** the skeleton of a sponge, esp. the soft light elastic absorbent kind used in bathing, cleaning surfaces, etc. **b** a piece of porous rubber or plastic, etc., used similarly. **3** a thing of spongelike absorbency or consistency, e.g., a sponge cake, porous metal, etc. (*lemon sponge*). **4** = SPONGER. **5** *colloq.* a person who drinks heavily. **6** cleaning with or as with a sponge (*gave the stove a quick sponge*). • *v.* **1** *tr.* wipe or clean with a sponge. **2** *tr.* (also *absol.*; often foll. by *down, over*) sluice water over (the body, a car, etc.). **3** *tr.* (often foll. by *out, away*, etc.) wipe off or efface (writing, a memory, etc.) with or as with a sponge. **4** *tr.* (often foll. by *up*) absorb with or as with a sponge. **5** *intr.* (often foll. by *on, upon*) live as a parasite; be dependent upon (another person). **6** *tr* obtain (drink, etc.) by sponging. **7** *intr.* gather sponges. **8** *tr.* apply paint with a sponge to (walls, furniture, etc.). □□ **sponge·a·ble** *adj.* **sponge·like** *adj.* **spon·gi·form** *adj.* (esp. in senses 1, 2). [OE f. L *spongia* f. Gk *spoggia, spoggos*]

sponge cake *n.* a very light cake with a spongelike consistency.

sponge cloth *n.* **1** soft, lightly woven cloth with a slightly wrinkled surface. **2** a thin spongy material used for cleaning.

sponge pud·ding *n. Brit.* a steamed or baked dessert dish of shortening, flour, and eggs with a usu. specified flavor.

spong·er /spúnjər/ *n.* a person who contrives to live at another's expense.

sponge rub·ber *n.* liquid rubber latex processed into a spongelike substance.

sponge tree *n.* a spiny tropical acacia, *Acacia farnesiana*, with globose heads of fragrant yellow flowers yielding a perfume. Also called **opopanax**.

spon·gy /spúnjee/ *adj.* (**spon·gi·er**, **spon·gi·est**) **1** like a sponge, esp. in being porous, compressible, elastic, or absorbent. **2** (of metal) finely divided and loosely coherent. □□ **spon·gi·ly** *adv.* **spon·gi·ness** *n.*

spon·sion /spónshən/ *n.* **1** being a surety for another. **2** a pledge or promise made on behalf of the government by an agent not authorized to do so. [L *sponsio* f. *spondēre spons-* promise solemnly]

spon·son /spónsən/ *n.* **1** a projection from the side of a warship or tank to enable a gun to be trained forward and aft. **2** a short subsidiary wing to stabilize a seaplane. **3** a triangular platform supporting the wheel on a paddle-steamer. **4** a flotation chamber along the gunwale of a canoe. [19th c.: orig. unkn.]

spon·sor /spónsər/ *n. & v.* • *n.* **1** a person who supports an activity done for charity by pledging money in advance. **2 a** a person or organization that promotes or supports an artistic or sporting activity, etc. **b** a business organization that promotes a broadcast program in return for advertising time. **3** an organization lending sup-

port to an election candidate. **4** a person who introduces a proposal for legislation. **5** *Eccles.* a godparent at baptism or esp. a person who presents a candidate for confirmation. **6** a person who makes himself or herself responsible for another. • *v.tr.* be a sponsor for. □□ **spon·so·ri·al** /sponsáwreeəl/ *adj.* **spon·sor·ship** *n.* [L (as SPONSION)]

spon·ta·ne·ous /spontáyneeəs/ *adj.* **1** acting or done or occurring without external cause. **2** voluntary; without external incitement (*made a spontaneous offer of his services*). **3** *Biol.* (of structural changes in plants and muscular activity esp. in young animals) instinctive; automatic; prompted by no motive. **4** (of bodily movement, literary style, etc.) gracefully natural and unconstrained. **5** (of sudden movement, etc.) involuntary; not due to conscious volition. **6** growing naturally without cultivation. □□ **spon·ta·ne·i·ty** /spóntənéeitee, –náyitee/ *n.* **spon·ta·ne·ous·ly** *adv.* **spon·ta·ne·ous·ness** *n.* [LL *spontaneus* f. *sponte* of one's own accord]

spon·ta·ne·ous com·bus·tion *n.* the ignition of a mineral or vegetable substance (e.g., a heap of rags soaked with oil, a mass of wet coal) from heat engendered within itself, usu. by rapid oxidation.

spon·ta·ne·ous gen·er·a·tion *n.* the supposed production of living from nonliving matter as inferred from the appearance of life (due in fact to bacteria, etc.) in some infusions; abiogenesis.

spoof /spoof/ *n. & v. colloq.* • *n.* **1** a parody. **2** a hoax or swindle. • *v.tr.* **1** parody. **2** hoax; swindle. □□ **spoof·er** *n.* **spoof·er·y** *n.* [invented by A. Roberts, English comedian d. 1933]

spook /spook/ *n. & v.* • *n.* **1** *colloq.* a ghost. **2** *sl.* a spy. • *v.* *sl.* **1** *tr.* frighten; unnerve; alarm. **2** *intr.* take fright; become alarmed. [Du., = MLG *spōk*, of unkn. orig.]

spook·y /spookee/ *adj.* (**spook·i·er**, **spook·i·est**) **1** *colloq.* ghostly; eerie. **2** *sl* nervous; easily frightened. **3** *sl.* of spies or espionage. □□ **spook·i·ly** *adv.* **spook·i·ness** *n.*

spool /spool/ *n. & v.* • *n.* **1 a** a reel for winding magnetic tape, photographic film, etc., on. **b** a reel for winding yarn, thread, or wire on. **c** a quantity of tape, yarn, etc., wound on a spool. **2** the revolving cylinder of an angler's reel. • *v.tr.* wind on a spool. [ME f. OF *espole* or f. MLG *spōle*, MDu. *spoele*, OHG *spuolo*, of unkn. orig.]

spoon /spoon/ *n. & v.* • *n.* **1 a** a utensil consisting of an oval or round bowl and a handle for conveying food (esp. liquid) to the mouth, for stirring, etc. **b** a spoonful, esp. of sugar. **c** (in *pl.*) *Mus.* a pair of spoons held in the hand and beaten together rhythmically. **2 a** spoon shaped thing, esp.: **a** (in full **spoon-bait**) a bright revolving piece of metal used as a lure in fishing. **b** an oar with a broad curved blade. **c** a wooden-headed golf club. **3** *colloq.* **a** a silly or demonstratively fond lover. **b** a simpleton. • *v.* **1** *tr.* (often foll. by *up, out*) take (liquid, etc.) with a spoon. **2** *colloq.* **a** *intr.* behave in an amorous way, esp. foolishly. **b** *tr. archaic* woo in a silly or sentimental way. □ **born with a silver spoon in one's mouth** born into affluence. □□ **spoon·er** *n.* **spoon·ful** *n.* (*pl.* •fuls). [OE *spōn* chip of wood f. Gmc]

spoon·bill /spoonbil/ *n.* **1** any large wading bird of the subfamily Plataleidae, having a bill with a very broad flat tip. **2** a shoveler duck.

spoon bread *n.* soft corn bread.

spoon·er·ism /spoonərizəm/ *n.* a transposition, usu. accidental, of the initial letters, etc., of two or more words, e.g., *you have hissed the mystery lectures.* [Rev. W. A. *Spooner*, English scholar d. 1930, reputed to make such errors in speaking]

spoon·feed /spoonfeed/ *v.tr.* (*past* and *past part.* **·fed**) **1** feed (a baby, etc.) with a spoon. **2** provide help, information, etc., to (a person) without requiring any effort on the recipient's part. **3** artificially encourage (an industry) by subsidies or import duties.

spoon·y /spoonee/ *adj. & n. colloq. archaic* • *adj.* (**spoon·i·er**, **spoon·i·est**) **1** (often foll. by *on*) sentimental; amorous. **2** foolish; silly. • *n.* (*pl.* •ies) a simpleton. □□ **spoon·i·ly** *adv.* **spoon·i·ness** *n.*

spoor /spoor/ *n. & v.* • *n.* the track, droppings, or scent of an animal. • *v.tr. & intr.* follow by the spoor. □□ **spoor·er** *n.* [Afrik. f. MDu. *spo(o)r* f. Gmc]

spo·rad·ic /spərádik, spaw–/ *adj.* occurring only here and there or occasionally; separate; scattered. □□ **spo·rad·i·cal·ly** *adv.* [med.L *sporadicus* f. Gk *sporadikos* f. *sporas* –*ados* scattered: cf. *speirō* to sow]

spo·ran·gi·um /spəránjeeəm/ *n.* (*pl.* **spo·ran·gi·a** /–jeeə/) *Bot.* a receptacle in which spores are found. □□ **spo·ran·gi·al** *adj.* [mod.L f. Gk *spora* SPORE + *aggeion* vessel]

spore /spawr/ *n.* **1** a specialized reproductive cell of many plants and microorganisms. **2** these collectively. [mod.L *spora* f. Gk *spora* sowing, seed f. *speirō* sow]

sporo- /spáwrō/ *comb. form Biol.* a spore. [Gk *spora* (as SPORE)]

spo·ro·gen·e·sis /spáwrōjénisis/ *n.* the process of spore formation.

spo·rog·e·nous /spərójinəs/ *adj.* producing spores.

spo·ro·phyte /spáwrōfīt/ *n.* a spore-producing form of plant with alternating sexual and asexual generations. □□ **spo·ro·phyt·ic** /–fítik/ *adj.* **spo·ro·phyt·i·cal·ly** *adv.*

spor·ran /spáwrən, spór–/ n. a pouch, usu. of leather or sealskin covered with fur, etc., worn by a Highland Scot in front of the kilt. [Gael. *sporan* f. med.L *bursa* PURSE]

sport /spawrt/ n. & v. • n. **1 a** a game or competitive activity, esp. an outdoor one involving physical exertion, e.g., baseball, football, racing, hunting. **b** (usu. in *pl*.) such activities collectively (*the world of sports*). **2** (in *pl*.) *Brit.* **a** a meeting for competing in sports, esp. track and field (*school sports*). **b** athletics. **3** amusement; diversion; fun. **4** *colloq.* **a** a fair or generous person. **b** a person behaving in a specified way, esp. regarding games, rules, etc. (*a bad sport at tennis*). **c** a form of address, esp. between males. **5** *Biol.* an animal or plant deviating suddenly or strikingly from the normal type. **6** a plaything or laughingstock (*was the sport of Fortune*). • v. **1** *intr.* **a** divert oneself; take part in a pastime. **b** frolic; gambol. **2** *tr.* wear, exhibit, or produce, esp. ostentatiously (*sported a gold tiepin*). **3** *intr. Biol.* become or produce a sport. □ **in sport** jestingly. **make sport of** make fun of; ridicule. □□ **sport·er** n. [ME f. DISPORT]

sport·ing /spáwrting/ adj. **1** interested in sports (*a sporting man*). **2** sportsmanlike; generous (*a sporting offer*). **3** concerned about or involved in sports (*a sporting dog; sporting news*). □ **a sporting chance** some possibility of success. □□ **sport·ing·ly** adv.

spor·tive /spáwrtiv/ adj. playful. □□ **spor·tive·ly** adv. **spor·tive·ness** n.

sport of kings n. horseracing (less often war, hunting, or surfing).

sports car n. a usu. open, low-built fast car.

sports·cast /spáwrtskast/ n. a broadcast of a sports event or information about sports. □□ **sports·cast·er** n.

sports coat n. (also **sports jack·et**) a man's jacket for informal wear.

sports·man /spáwrtsmən/ n. (pl. **-men**; *fem.* **sports·wom·an**, pl. **-wom·en**) **1** a person who takes part in sports, esp. professionally. **2** a person who behaves fairly and generously. □□ **sports·man·like** adj. **sports·man·ly** adj. **sports·man·ship** n.

sports·wear /spáwrtswair/ n. clothes worn for sports or for casual use.

sports writ·er n. a person who writes (esp. as a journalist) on sports.

sport·y /spáwrtee/ adj. (**sport·i·er**, **sport·i·est**) *colloq.* **1** fond of sports. **2** rakish; showy. □□ **sport·i·ly** adv. **sport·i·ness** n.

spor·ule /spáwryool/ n. a small spore or a single spore. □□ **spor·u·lar** adj. [F *sporule* or mod.L *sporula* (as SPORE)]

spot /spot/ n. & v. • n. **1 a** a small part of the surface of a thing distinguished by color, texture, etc., usu. round or less elongated than a streak or stripe (*a blue tie with pink spots*). **b** a small mark or stain. **c** a pimple. **d** a small circle or other shape used in various numbers to distinguish faces of dice, playing cards in a suit, etc. **e** a moral blemish or stain (*without a spot on his reputation*). **2 a** a particular place; a definite locality (*dropped it on this precise spot; the spot where Columbus landed*). **b** a place used for a particular activity (often in *comb.*: *nightspot*). **c** (prec. by *the*) *Soccer* the place from which a penalty kick is taken. **3** a particular part of one's body or aspect of one's character. **4 a** *colloq.* one's esp. regular position in an organization, program of events, etc. **b** a place or position in a performance or show (*did the spot before intermission*). **5** *Brit.* **a** *colloq.* a small quantity of anything (*a spot of lunch; a spot of trouble*). **b** a drop (*a spot of rain*). **c** *colloq.* a drink. **6** = SPOTLIGHT. **7** *colloq.* an awkward or difficult situation (esp. in *in a* (tight, etc.) spot). **8** (usu. *attrib.*) money paid or goods delivered immediately after a sale (*spot cash; spot silver*). **9** *Billiards*, etc. **a** a small round black patch to mark the position where a ball is placed at certain times. **b** (in full **spot ball**) the white ball distinguished from the other by two black spots. • v. (**spot·ted**, **spot·ting**) **1** *tr.* **a** *colloq.* single out beforehand (the winner of a race, etc.). **b** *colloq.* recognize the identity, nationality, etc., of (*spotted him at once as the murderer*). **c** watch for and take note of (trains, talent, etc.). **d** *colloq.* catch sight of. **e** *Mil.* locate (an enemy's position), esp. from the air. **2 a** *tr. & intr.* mark or become marked with spots. **b** *tr.* stain; soil (a person's character, etc.). **3** *intr.* rain slightly (*it was spotting with rain*). **4** *tr. Billiards* place (a ball) on a spot. □ **on the spot 1** at the scene of an action or event. **2** *colloq.* in a position such that response or action is required. **3** without delay or change of place; then and there. **4** (of a person) wide awake, equal to the situation, in good form at a game, etc. **put on the spot** *sl.* make to feel uncomfortable, awkward, etc. **spot on** *Brit. colloq.* adj. precise; on target. • adv. precisely. [ME, perh. f. MDu. *spotte*, LG *spot*, ON *spotti* small piece]

spot check n. a test made on the spot or on a randomly selected subject. □□ **spot-check** v.

spot height n. **1** the altitude of a point. **2** a figure on a map showing this.

spot·less /spótlis/ adj. immaculate; absolutely clean or pure. □□ **spot·less·ly** adv. **spot·less·ness** n.

spot·light /spótlit/ n. & v. • n. **1** a beam of light directed on a small area, esp. on a particular part of a theater stage or of the road in front of a vehicle. **2** a lamp projecting this. **3** full attention or publicity. • v.tr. (*past* and *past part.* **·light·ed** or **·lit**) **1** direct a spotlight on. **2** make conspicuous; draw attention to.

spot·ted /spótid/ adj. marked or decorated with spots. □□ **spot·ted·ness** n.

spot·ted dick n. (also **spot·ted dog**) *Brit.* **1** a suet pudding containing currants. **2** a Dalmatian dog.

spot·ted fe·ver n. **1** cerebrospinal meningitis. **2** typhus.

spot·ted hy·e·na n. a southern African hyena, *Crocuta crocuta*, that has a grayish-yellow to reddish coat with irregular dark spots, and a loud laughing call. Also called **laughing hyena**.

spot·ter /spótər/ n. **1** a person who watches over a gymnast, weightlifter, etc., during practice to avoid or prevent injuries. **2** (often in *comb.*) a person who spots people or things (*train spotter*). **3** an aviator or aircraft employed in locating enemy positions, etc.

spot·ty /spótee/ adj. (**spot·ti·er**, **spot·ti·est**) **1** marked with spots. **2** patchy; irregular. □□ **spot·ti·ly** adv. **spot·ti·ness** n.

spot-weld v.tr. welding two surfaces together in a series of discrete points. □□ **spot weld** n. **spot weld·ing** n.

spouse /spows, spowz/ n. a husband or wife. [ME *spūs(e)* f. OF *sp(o)us* (masc.), *sp(o)use* (fem.), vars. of *espous(e)* f. L *sponsus sponsa* past part. of *spondēre* betroth]

spout /spowt/ n. & v. • n. **1 a** a projecting tube or lip through which a liquid, etc., is poured from a teapot, kettle, pitcher, etc., or issues from a fountain, pump, etc. **b** a sloping trough down which a thing may be shot into a receptacle. **c** *hist.* a lift serving a pawnbroker's storeroom. **2** a jet or column of liquid, grain, etc. **3** (in full **spout hole**) a whale's blowhole. • v.tr. & intr. **1** discharge or issue forcibly in a jet. **2** utter (verses, etc.) or speak in a declamatory manner; speechify. □ **up the spout** *Brit. sl.* **1** useless; ruined; hopeless. **2** pawned. **3** pregnant. □□ **spout·er** n. **spout·less** adj. [ME f. MDu. *spouten*, orig. imit.]

SPQR abbr. hist. the Senate and people of Rome. [L *Senatus Populusque Romanus*]

sprag /sprag/ n. **1** a thick piece of wood or similar device used as a brake. **2** a support prop in a coal mine. [19th c.: orig. unkn.]

sprain /sprayn/ v. & n. • v.tr. wrench (an ankle, wrist, etc.) violently so as to cause pain and swelling but not dislocation. • n. **1** such a wrench. **2** the resulting inflammation and swelling. [17th c.: orig. unkn.]

sprang past of SPRING.

sprat /sprat/ n. & v. • n. **1** a small European herringlike fish, *Sprattus sprattus*, much used as food. **2** a similar fish, e.g., a sand eel or a young herring. • v.intr. (**sprat·ted**, **sprat·ting**) fish for sprats. □ **a sprat to catch a mackerel** a small risk to gain much. □□ **sprat·ter** n. **sprat·ting** n. [OE *sprot*]

sprawl /sprawl/ v. & n. • v. **1** *intr.* sit or lie or fall with limbs flung out or in an ungainly way. **b** *tr.* spread (one's limbs) in this way. **2** *intr.* (of handwriting, a plant, a town, etc.) be of irregular or straggling form. • n. **1** a sprawling movement or attitude. **2** a straggling group or mass. **3** the straggling expansion of an urban or industrial area. □□ **sprawl·ing·ly** adv. [OE *spreawlian*]

spray[1] /spray/ n & v. • n. **1** water or other liquid flying in small drops from the force of the wind, the dashing of waves, or the action of an atomizer, etc. **2** a liquid preparation to be applied in this form with an atomizer, etc., esp. for medical purposes. **3** an instrument or apparatus for such application. • v.tr. (also *absol.*) **1** throw (liquid) in the form of spray. **2** sprinkle (an object) with small drops or particles, esp. (a plant) with an insecticide. **3** (*absol.*) (of a tomcat) mark its environment with the smell of its urine, as an attraction to females. □□ **spray·a·ble** adj. **spray·er** n. [earlier *spry*, perh. rel. to MDu. *spra(e)yen*, MHG *sprӕ jen* sprinkle]

spray[2] /spray/ n. **1** a sprig of flowers or leaves, or a branch of a tree with branchlets or flowers, esp. a slender or graceful one. **2** an ornament in a similar form (*a spray of diamonds*). □□ **spray·ey** adj. [ME f. OE *spr ӕg* (unrecorded)]

spray gun n. a gunlike device for spraying paint, etc.

spray paint n. paint (a surface) by means of a spray.

spread /spred/ v. & n. • v. (*past* and *past part.* **spread**) **1** *tr.* (often foll. by *out*) **a** open or extend the surface of. **b** cause to cover a larger surface (*spread butter on bread*). **c** display to the eye or the mind (*the view was spread out before us*). **2** *intr.* (often foll. by *out*) have a wide or specified or increasing extent (*on every side spread a vast desert; spreading trees*). **3** *intr. & tr.* become or make widely known, felt, etc. (*rumors are spreading; spread a little happiness*). **4** *tr.* **a** cover the surface of (*spread the wall with paint; a meadow spread with daisies*). **b** lay (a table). • n. **1** the act or an instance of spreading. **2** capability of expanding (*has a large spread*). **3** diffusion (*spread of learning*). **4** breadth; compass (*arches of equal spread*). **5** an aircraft's wingspan. **6** increased bodily girth (*middle-aged spread*). **7** the difference between two rates, prices, scores, etc. **8** *colloq.* an elaborate meal. **9** a food paste for spreading on bread, etc. **10** a bedspread. **11** printed matter spread across two facing pages or across more than one column. **12** a ranch with extensive land. □ **spread oneself** be lavish or discursive. **spread one's wings** see WING. □□ **spread·a·ble** adj. **spread·er** n. [OE *–sprēdan* f. WG]

spread-ea·gle v., n. & adj. • v.tr. (usu. as **spread-eagled** adj.) **1** place (a person) with the arms and legs extended. **2** defeat utterly. **3** spread out. **4** lying prone with outstretched limbs. • n. (**spread**

eagle) an emblematic representation of an eagle with legs and wings extended. • *adj.* bombastic, esp. noisily patriotic.

spread•sheet /sprédsheet/ *n.* a computer program allowing manipulation and flexible retrieval of esp. tabulated numerical data.

spree /spree/ *n. & v. colloq.* • *n.* **1** a lively extravagant outing (*shopping spree*). **2** a bout of fun or drinking, etc. • *v. intr.* (**sprees, spreed**) have a spree. □ **on a spree** engaged in a spree. [19th c.: orig. unkn.]

sprig[1] /sprig/ *n. & v.* • *n.* **1** a small branch or shoot. **2** an ornament resembling this, esp. on fabric. **3** usu. *derog.* a youth or young man (*a sprig of the nobility*). • *v. tr.* (**sprigged, sprig•ging**) **1** ornament with sprigs (*a dress of sprigged muslin*). **2** (usu. as **sprigging** *n.*) decorate (ceramic ware) with ornaments in applied relief. □□ **sprig•gy** *adj.* [ME f. or rel. to LG *sprick*]

sprig[2] /sprig/ *n.* a small tapering headless tack; a brad. [ME: orig. unkn.]

spright•ly /sprítlee/ *adj.* (**spright•li•er, spright•li•est**) vivacious, lively; brisk. □□ **spright•li•ness** *n.* [*spright* var. of SPRITE + -LY[1]]

spring /spring/ *v. & n.* • *v.* (*past* **sprang** /sprang/ also **sprung** /sprung/; *past part.* **sprung**) **1** *intr.* jump; move rapidly or suddenly (*sprang from his seat; sprang through the gap; sprang to their assistance*). **2** *intr.* move rapidly as from a constrained position or by the action of a spring (*the branch sprang back; the door sprang to*). **3** *intr.* (usu. foll. by *from*) originate or arise (*springs from an old family; their actions spring from a false conviction*). **4** *intr.* (usu. foll. by *up*) come into being; appear, esp. suddenly (*a breeze sprang up; the belief has sprung up*). **5** *tr.* cause to act suddenly, esp. by means of a spring (*spring a trap*). **6** *tr.* (often foll. by *on*) produce or develop or make known suddenly or unexpectedly (*has sprung a new theory; loves to spring surprises*). **7** *tr. sl.* contrive the escape or release of. **8** *tr.* rouse (game) from earth or covert. **9 a** *intr.* become warped or split. **b** *tr.* split; crack (wood or a wooden implement). **10** *tr.* (usu. as **sprung** *adj.*) provide (a motor vehicle, etc.) with springs. **11 a** *tr. colloq.* spend (money). **b** *intr.* (usu. foll. by *for*) *sl.* pay for a meal, drink, etc. **12** *tr.* cause (a mine) to explode. • *n.* **1** a jump (*took a spring; rose with a spring*). **2** a backward movement from a constrained position; a recoil, e.g., of a bow. **3** elasticity; ability to spring back strongly (*a mattress with plenty of spring*). **4** a resilient device usu. of bent or coiled metal used esp. to drive clockwork or for cushioning in furniture or vehicles. **5 a** the season in which vegetation begins to appear, the first season of the year, in the N. hemisphere from March to May and in the S. hemisphere from September to November. **b** *Astron.* the period from the vernal equinox to the summer solstice. **c** (often foll. by *of*) the early stage of life, etc. **d** = SPRING TIDE. **6** a place where water, oil, etc., wells up from the earth; the basin or flow so formed (*hot springs; mineral springs*). **7** the motive for or origin of an action, custom, etc. (*the springs of human action*). **8** *sl.* an escape or release from prison. **9** the upward curve of a beam, etc., from a horizontal line. **10** the splitting or yielding of a plank, etc., under strain. □ **spring a leak** develop a leak (orig. *Naut.*, from timbers springing out of position). □□ **spring•less** *adj.* **spring•let** *n.* **spring•like** *adj.* [OE *springan* f. Gmc]

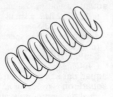

spring 4

spring bal•ance *n.* a balance that measures weight by the tension of a spring.

spring bed *n.* a bed with a spring mattress.

spring•board /sprand;springbawrd/ *n.* **1** a springy board giving impetus in leaping, diving, etc. **2** a source of impetus in any activity. **3** a platform inserted in the side of a tree, on which a lumberjack stands to chop at some height from the ground.

spring•bok /springbok/ *n.* **1** a southern African gazelle, *Antidorcas marsupialis*, with the ability to run with high springing jumps. **2** (**Springbok**) a South African, esp. one who has played for South Africa in international sporting competitions. [Afrik. f. Du. *springen* SPRING + *bok* antelope]

spring chick•en *n.* **1** a young fowl for eating (orig. available only in spring). **2** (esp. with *neg.*) a young person (*she's no spring chicken*).

spring clean•ing *n.* a thorough cleaning of a house or room, esp. in spring. □□ **spring-clean** *v.*

springe /sprinj/ *n.* a noose or snare for catching small game. [ME, rel. to obs. *sprenge*, and SPRING]

spring•er /springər/ *n.* **1** a person or thing that springs. **2 a** a small spaniel of a breed used to spring game. **b** this breed. **3** *Archit.* **a** the part of an arch where the curve begins. **b** the lowest stone of this. **c** the bottom stone of the coping of a gable. **d** a rib of a groined roof or vault. **4** a springbok.

spring fe•ver *n.* a restless or lethargic feeling sometimes associated with spring.

spring-load•ed *adj.* containing a compressed or stretched spring pressing one part against another.

spring mat•tress *n.* a mattress containing or consisting of springs.

spring on•ion *n.* esp. *Brit.* an onion taken from the ground before the bulb has formed, and eaten raw in salad.

spring roll *n.* an Asian snack consisting of a pancake filled with vegetables, etc., and fried.

spring•tail /springtayl/ *n.* any wingless insect of the order Collembola, leaping by means of a springlike caudal part.

spring•tide /springtid/ *n. poet.* = SPRINGTIME.

spring tide *n.* a tide just after new and full moon when there is the greatest difference between high and low water.

spring•time /springtim/ *n.* **1** the season of spring. **2** a time compared to this.

spring wa•ter *n.* water from a spring, as opposed to river or rain water.

spring•y /springee/ *adj.* (**spring•i•er, spring•i•est**) **1** springing back quickly when squeezed or stretched; elastic. **2** (of movements) as of a springy substance. □□ **spring•i•ly** *adv.* **spring•i•ness** *n.*

sprin•kle /springkəl/ *v. & n.* • *v. tr.* **1** scatter (liquid, ashes, crumbs, etc.) in small drops or particles. **2** (often foll. by *with*) subject (the ground or an object) to sprinkling with liquid, etc. **3** (of liquid, etc.) fall on in this way. **4** distribute in small amounts. • *n.* (usu. foll. by *of*) **1** a light shower. **2** = SPRINKLING. **3** (in *pl.*) candy particles used as a dessert topping, as on ice cream. [ME, perh. f. MDu. *sprenkelen*]

sprin•kler /springklər/ *n.* a person or thing that sprinkles, esp. a device for sprinkling water on a lawn or to extinguish fires.

sprin•kling /springkling/ *n.* (usu. foll. by *of*) a small thinly distributed number or amount.

sprint /sprint/ *v. & n.* • *v.* **1** *intr.* run a short distance at full speed. **2** *tr.* run (a specified distance) in this way. • *n.* **1** such a run. **2** a similar short spell of maximum effort in cycling, swimming, auto racing, etc. □□ **sprint•er** *n.* [ON *sprinta* (unrecorded), of unkn. orig.]

sprit /sprit/ *n.* a small spar reaching diagonally from the mast to the upper outer corner of the sail. [OE *sprē ot* pole, rel. to SPROUT]

sprite /sprit/ *n.* an elf, fairy, or goblin. [ME f. *sprit* var. of SPIRIT]

sprit•sail /spritsəl, –sayl/ *n.* **1** a sail extended by a sprit. **2** *hist.* a sail extended by a yard set under the bowsprit.

spritz /sprits/ *v. & n.* • *v. tr.* sprinkle, squirt, or spray. • *n.* the act or an instance of spritzing. [G *spritzen* to squirt]

spritz•er /spritsər/ *n.* a mixture of wine and soda water. [G *Spritzer* a splash]

sprock•et /sprókit/ *n.* **1** each of several teeth on a wheel engaging with links of a chain, e.g., on a bicycle, or with holes in film or tape or paper. **2** (also **sprock•et wheel**) a wheel with sprockets. [16th c.: orig. unkn.]

sprog /sprog/ *n. Brit. sl.* a child; a baby. [orig. services' sl., = new recruit: perh. f. obs. *sprag* lively young man]

sprocket

sprout /sprowt/ *v. & n.* • *v.* **1** *tr.* put forth; produce (shoots, hair, etc.) (*has sprouted a mustache*). **2** *intr.* begin to grow; put forth shoots. **3** *intr.* spring up, grow to a height. • *n.* **1** a shoot of a plant. **2** = BRUSSELS SPROUT. [OE *sprūtan* (unrecorded) f. WG]

spruce[1] /sprōōs/ *adj. & v.* • *adj.* neat in dress and appearance; trim; neat and fashionable. • *v. tr. & intr.* (also *refl.*; usu. foll. by *up*) make or become neat and fashionable. □□ **spruce•ly** *adv.* **spruce•ness** *n.* [perh. f. SPRUCE[2] in obs. sense 'Prussian,' in the collocation *spruce (leather) jerkin*]

spruce[2] /sprōōs/ *n.* **1** any coniferous tree of the genus *Picea*, with dense foliage growing in a distinctive conical shape. **2** the wood of this tree used as timber. [alt. of obs. *Pruce* Prussia: cf. PRUSSIAN]

spruce[3] /sprōōs/ *v. Brit. sl.* **1** *tr.* deceive. **2** *intr.* lie; practice deception. **3** *intr.* evade a duty; malinger. □□ **spruc•er** *n.* [20th c.: orig. unkn.]

spruce beer *n.* a fermented beverage using spruce twigs and needles as flavoring.

sprue[1] /sprōō/ *n.* **1** a channel through which metal or plastic is poured into a mold. **2** a piece of metal or plastic which has filled a sprue and solidified there. [19th c.: orig. unkn.]

sprue[2] /sprōō/ *n.* **1** = CELIAC DISEASE. **2** a tropical disease with ulceration of the mucous membrane of the mouth and chronic enteritis. [Du. *spruw* THRUSH[2]; cf. Flem. *spruwen* sprinkle]

sprung see SPRING.

sprung rhythm /sprung ríthəm/ *n.* a poetic meter approximating to speech, each foot having one stressed syllable followed by a varying number of unstressed.

spry /sprī/ *adj.* (**spry•er, spry•est**) active; lively. □□ **spry•ly** *adv.* **spry•ness** *n.* [18th c., dial. & US: orig. unkn.]

spud /spud/ *n. & v.* • *n.* **1** *sl.* a potato. **2** a small narrow spade for cutting the roots of weeds, etc. • *v. tr.* (**spud•ded, spud•ding**) **1** (foll.

by *up*, *out*) remove (weeds) with a spud. **2** (also *absol.*; often foll. by *in*) make the initial drilling for (an oil well). [ME: orig. unkn.]

spue var. of SPEW.

spu·man·te /spoomáantee, –tay/ *n.* a sparkling wine, esp. a sweet white Italian sparkling wine (cf. ASTI). [It., = 'sparkling']

spume /spyoom/ *n. & v.intr.* froth; foam. □□ **spu·mous** *adj.* **spum·y** *adj.* (**spum·i·er**, **spum·i·est**). [ME f. OF (*e*)*spume* or L *spuma*]

spu·mo·ni /spoomónee/ *n.* an ice-cream dessert of different colors and flavors, usu. layered, with nuts and candied fruits. [It. *spumone* f. *spuma* SPUME]

spun *past* and *past part.* of SPIN.

spunk /spungk/ *n.* **1** touchwood. **2** *colloq.* courage; mettle; spirit. **3** *Brit. coarse sl.* semen. [16th c.: orig. unkn.: cf. PUNK]

spunk·y /spúngkee/ *adj.* (**spunk·i·er**, **spunk·i·est**) *colloq.* brave; spirited. □□ **spunk·i·ly** *adv.*

spun silk *n.* a cheap material made of short-fibered and waste silk.

spun yarn *n. Naut.* a line formed of rope yarns twisted together.

spur /spər/ *n. & v.* • *n.* **1 a** a device with a small spike or a spiked wheel worn on a rider's heel for urging a horse forward. **2** a stimulus or incentive. **3** a spur-shaped thing, esp.: **a** a projection from a mountain or mountain range. **b** a branch road or railway. **c** a hard projection on a cock's leg. **d** a steel point fastened to the leg of a gamecock. **e** a climbing iron. **f** a small support for ceramic ware in a kiln. **4** *Bot.* **a** a slender hollow projection from part of a flower. **b** a short fruit-bearing shoot. • *v.*

spur 1 (on boot)

(**spurred**, **spur·ring**) **1** *tr.* prick (a horse) with spurs. **2** *tr.* **a** (often foll. by *on*) incite (a person) (*spurred him on to greater efforts*; *spurred her to try again*). **b** stimulate (interest, etc.). **3** *intr.* (often foll. by *on*, *forward*) ride a horse hard. **4** *tr.* (esp. as **spurred** *adj.*) provide (a person, boots, a gamecock) with spurs. □ **on the spur of the moment** on a momentary impulse; impromptu. **put** (or **set**) **spurs to 1** spur (a horse). **2** stimulate (resolution, etc.). □□ **spur·less** *adj.* [OE *spora*, *spura* f. Gmc, rel. to SPURN]

spurge /spərj/ *n.* any plant of the genus *Euphorbia*, exuding an acrid milky juice once used medicinally as a purgative. [ME f. OF *espurge* f. *espurgier* f. L *expurgare* (as EX-[1], PURGE)]

spur gear *n.* = SPUR WHEEL.

spurge lau·rel *n.* any shrub of the genus *Daphne*, esp. *D. laureola*, with small yellow flowers.

spu·ri·ous /spyŏoreeəs/ *adj.* **1** not genuine; not being what it purports to be; not proceeding from the pretended source (*a spurious excuse*). **2** having an outward similarity of form or function only. **3** (of offspring) illegitimate. □□ **spu·ri·ous·ly** *adv.* **spu·ri·ous·ness** *n.* [L *spurius* false]

SYNONYM TIP spurious

APOCRYPHAL, ARTIFICIAL, COUNTERFEIT, ERSATZ, SYNTHETIC. These adjectives pertain to what is false or not what it appears to be, although not all have negative connotations. **Artificial** implies manmade, especially in imitation of something natural (*artificial flowers*, *artificial turf*). A **synthetic** substance or material is one produced by a chemical process and used as a substitute for the natural substance it resembles (*boots made from synthetic rubber*). Something that is **counterfeit** is an imitation of something else—usually something rarer, finer, or more valuable—and is intended to deceive or defraud (*counterfeit bills*). **Spurious** also means false rather than true or genuine, but it carries no strong implication of being an imitation (*spurious letters falsely attributed to Winston Churchill*). **Ersatz** refers to an *artificial* substitute that is usually inferior (*ersatz tea made from birch bark and herbs*). The meaning of **apocryphal**, however, is much more restricted. It applies to accounts of the past whose truth or accuracy cannot be ascertained (*an apocryphal story about George Washington as a boy*).

spurn /spərn/ *v. & n.* • *v.* **1** reject with disdain; treat with contempt. **2** repel or thrust back with one's foot. • *n.* an act of spurning. □□ **spurn·er** *n.* [OE *spurnan*, *spornan*, rel. to SPUR]

spur-of-the-mo·ment *adj.* unpremeditated; impromptu.

spur·ry /spóree/ *n.* (also **spur·rey**) (*pl.* **·ries** or **·reys**) a slender plant of the genus *Spergula*, esp. the corn spurry, a white-flowered weed in fields, etc. [Du. *spurrie*, prob. rel. to med.L *spergula*]

spurt /spərt/ *v & n.* • *v.* **1** (also **spirt**) **a** *intr.* gush out in a jet or stream. **b** *tr.* cause (liquid, etc.) to do this. **2** *intr.* make a sudden effort. • *n.* **1** (also **spirt**) a sudden gushing out; a jet. **2** a short sudden effort or increase of pace, esp. in racing. [16th c.: orig. unkn.]

spur wheel *n.* a cog wheel with radial teeth.

sput·nik /spŏotnik, spút–/ *n.* each of a series of Russian artificial satellites launched from 1957. [Russ., = fellow traveler]

sput·ter /spútər/ *v. & n.* • *v.* **1** *intr.* emit spitting sounds, esp. when being heated. **2** *intr.* (often foll. by *at*) speak in a hurried or vehement fashion. **3** *tr.* emit with a spitting sound. **4** *tr.* speak or utter (words, threats, a language, etc.) rapidly or incoherently. **5** *tr. Physics* deposit (metal) by using fast ions, etc., to eject particles of it from a target. • *n.* a sputtering sound, esp. sputtering speech. □□ **sput·ter·er** *n.* [Du. *sputteren* (imit.)]

spu·tum /spyŏotəm/ *n.* (*pl.* **spu·ta** /–tə/) **1** saliva; spittle. **2** a mixture of saliva and mucus expectorated from the respiratory tract, usu. a sign of disease. [L, neut. past part. of *spuere* spit]

spy /spī/ *n. & v.* • *n.* (*pl.* **spies**) **1** a person who secretly collects and reports information on the activities, movements, etc., of an enemy, competitor, etc. **2** a person who keeps watch on others, esp. furtively. • *v.* (**spies**, **spied**) **1** *tr.* discern or make out, esp. by careful observation (*spied a house in the distance*). **2** *intr.* (often foll. by *on*) act as a spy; keep a close and secret watch. **3** *intr.* (often foll. by *into*) pry. □ **spy out** explore or discover, esp. secretly. □□ **spy·ing** *n.* [ME f. OF *espie* espying, *espier* espy f. Gmc]

spy·glass /spíglas/ *n.* a small telescope.

spy·hole /spíhōl/ *n.* a peephole.

sq. *abbr.* square.

squab /skwob/ *n. & adj.* • *n.* **1** a short fat person. **2** a young, esp. unfledged, pigeon or other bird. **3 a** a stuffed cushion. **b** *Brit.* the padded back or side of a car seat. **4** a sofa or couch. • *adj.* short and fat; squat. [17th c.: orig. unkn.: cf. obs. *quab* shapeless thing, Sw. dial. *sqvabba* fat woman]

squab·ble /skwóbəl/ *n. & v.* • *n.* a petty or noisy quarrel. • *v.intr.* engage in a squabble. □□ **squab·bler** *n.* [prob. imit.: cf. Sw. dial. *sqvabbel* a dispute]

squab·by /skwóbee/ *adj.* (**squab·bi·er**, **squab·bi·est**) short and fat; squat.

squab chick *n.* an unfledged bird.

squad /skwod/ *n.* **1** a small group of people sharing a task, etc. **2** *Mil.* a small number of soldiers assembled for drill, etc. **3** *Sports* a group of players forming a team. **4** (often in *comb.*) a specialized unit within a police force (*drug squad*). **5** a group or class of people of a specified kind (*the awkward squad*). [F *escouade* var. of *escadre* f. It. *squadra* SQUARE]

squad car *n.* a police car having a radio link with headquarters.

squad·ron /skwódrən/ *n.* **1** an organized body of persons. **2** a principal division of a cavalry regiment or armored formation, consisting of two troops. **3** a detachment of warships employed on a particular duty. **4 a** (in the US) a unit of the US Air Force with two or more flights. **b** (in the UK) a unit of the Royal Air Force with 10 to 18 aircraft. [It. *squadrone* (as SQUAD)]

squal·id /skwólid/ *adj.* **1** filthy; repulsively dirty. **2** degraded or poor in appearance. **3** wretched; sordid. □□ **squa·lid·i·ty** *n.* /–líditee/ **squal·id·ly** *adv.* **squal·id·ness** *n.* [L *squalidus* f. *squalēre* be rough or dirty]

squall /skwawl/ *n. & v.* • *n.* **1** a sudden or violent gust or storm of wind, esp. with rain or snow or sleet. **2** a discordant cry; a scream (esp. of a baby). **3** (esp. in *pl.*) trouble; difficulty. • *v.* **1** *intr.* utter a squall; scream; cry out violently as in fear or pain. **2** *tr.* utter in a screaming or discordant voice. □□ **squal·ly** *adj.* [prob. f. SQUEAL after BAWL]

squal·or /skwólər/ *n.* the state of being filthy or squalid. [L, as SQUALID]

squa·ma /skwáymə/ *n.* (*pl.* **squa·mae** /–mee/) **1** a scale on an animal or plant. **2** a thin scalelike plate of bone. **3** a scalelike feather. □□ **squa·mate** /–mayt/ *adj.* **squa·mose** *adj.* **squa·mous** *adj.* **squa·mule** *n.* [L *squama*]

squan·der /skwóndər/ *v.tr.* **1** spend (money, time, etc.) wastefully. **2** dissipate (a fortune, etc.) wastefully. □□ **squan·der·er** *n.* [16th c.: orig. unkn.]

square /skwair/ *n., adj., adv., & v.* • *n.* **1** an equilateral rectangle. **2 a** an object of this shape or approximately this shape. **b** a small square area on a game board. **c** a square scarf. **d** *Brit.* an academic cap with a stiff square top; a mortarboard. **3 a** an open (usu. four-sided) area surrounded by buildings, esp. one planted with trees, etc., and surrounded by houses. **b** an open area at the meeting of streets. **c** an area within barracks, etc., for drill. **d** a block of buildings bounded by four streets. **4** the product of a number multiplied by itself (*81 is the square of 9*). **5** an L-shaped or T-shaped instrument for obtaining or testing right angles. **6** *sl.* a conventional or old-fashioned person, one ignorant of or opposed to current trends. **7** a square arrangement of letters, figures, etc. **8** a body of infantry drawn up in rectangular form. **9** a unit of 100 sq. ft. as a measure of flooring, etc. **10** a square meal (*three squares a day*). • *adj.* **1** having the shape of a square. **2** having or in the form of a right angle (*table with square corners*). **3** angular and not round; of square section (*has a square jaw*). **4** designating a unit of measure equal to the area of a square whose side is one of the unit speci–

spyglass

fied (*square meter*). **5** (often foll. by *with*) **a** level; parallel. **b** on a proper footing; even; quits. **6 a** (usu. foll. by *to*) at right angles. **b** *Cricket* on a line through the stumps at right angles to the wicket. **7** having the breadth more nearly equal to the length or height than is usual (*a man of square frame*). **8** properly arranged; in good order; settled (*get things square*). **9** (also **all square**) **a** not in debt; with no money owed. **b** having equal scores, esp. *Golf* having won the same number of holes as one's opponent. **c** (of scores) equal. **10** fair and honest (*his dealings are not always quite square*). **11** uncompromising; direct; thorough (*was met with a square refusal*). **12** *sl.* conventional or old-fashioned; unsophisticated; conservative (cf. sense 6 of *n.*). **13** *Mus.* (of rhythm) simple; straightforward. • *adv.* **1** squarely (*sat square on her seat*). **2** fairly; honestly (*play square*). • *v.* **1** *tr.* make square or rectangular; give a rectangular cross-section to (timber, etc.). **2** *tr.* multiply (a number) by itself (*3 squared is 9*). **3** *tr. & intr.* (usu. foll. by *to, with*) adjust; make or be suitable or consistent; reconcile (*the results do not square with your conclusions*). **4** *tr.* mark out in squares. **5** *tr.* settle or pay (a bill, etc.). **6** *tr.* place (one's shoulders, etc.) squarely facing forward. **7** *tr. colloq.* **a** pay or bribe. **b** secure the acquiescence, etc., of (a person) in this way. **8** *tr.* (also *absol.*) make the scores of (a match, etc.) all square. **9** *intr.* assume the attitude of a boxer. **10** *tr. Naut.* **a** lay (yards) at right angles with the keel making them at the same time horizontal. **b** get (deadeyes) horizontal. **c** get (ratlines) horizontal and parallel to one another. □ **back to square one** *colloq.* back to the starting point with no progress made. **get square with** pay or compound with (a creditor). **on the square** *adj. colloq.* honest; fair. • *adv. colloq.* honestly; fairly (*can be trusted to act on the square*). **out of square** not at right angles. **square accounts with** see ACCOUNT. **square away** neaten up. **square the circle 1** construct a square equal in area to a given circle (a problem incapable of a purely geometrical solution). **2** do what is impossible. **square off 1** assume the attitude of a boxer. **2** *Austral.* placate or conciliate. **3** mark out in squares. **square peg in a round hole** see PEG. **square up** settle an account, etc. **square up to 1** move toward (a person) in a fighting attitude. **2** face and tackle (a difficulty, etc.) resolutely. □□ **square•ly** *adv.* **square•ness** *n.* **squar•er** *n.* **squar•ish** *adj.* [ME f. OF *esquare, esquarré, esquarrer*, ult. f. EX-[1] + L *quadra* square]

square brack•ets *n.* brackets of the form [ ].

square-built *adj.* of comparatively broad shape.

square dance *n.* a dance with usu. four couples facing inwards from four sides.

square deal *n.* a fair bargain; fair treatment.

squared pa•per *n.* esp. *Brit.* paper marked out in squares, esp. for plotting graphs.

square-eyed *adj. joc. Brit.* affected by or given to excessive viewing of television.

square meal *n.* a substantial and satisfying meal.

square meas•ure *n.* measure expressed in square units.

square num•ber *n.* the square of an integer e.g., 1, 4, 9, 16.

square pi•an•o *n.* an early type of piano, small and oblong in shape.

square-rigged *adj.* with the principal sails at right angles to the length of the ship and extended by horizontal yards slung to the mast by the middle (opp. *fore-and-aft rigged*).

square root *n.* the number that multiplied by itself gives a specified number (*3 is the square root of 9*).

square sail *n.* a four-cornered sail extended on a yard slung to the mast by the middle.

square shoot•er *n.* a person who is honest, fair, and straightforward.

square-should•ered *adj.* with broad and not sloping shoulders (cf. ROUND-SHOULDERED).

square-toed *adj.* **1** (of shoes or boots) having square toes. **2** wearing such shoes or boots. **3** formal; prim.

square wave *n. Physics* a wave with periodic sudden alternations between only two values of quantity.

squar•rose /skwáirōs, skwór-/ *adj. Bot. & Zool.* rough with scalelike projections. [L *squarrosus* scurfy, scabby]

squash[1] /skwosh/ *v. & n.* • *v.* **1** *tr.* crush or squeeze flat or into pulp. **2** *intr.* (often foll. by *into*) make one's way by squeezing. **3** *tr.* pack tight; crowd. **4** *tr.* **a** silence (a person) with a crushing retort, etc. **b** dismiss (a proposal, etc.). **c** quash (a rebellion). • *n.* **1** a crowd; a crowded assembly. **2 a** a sound of or as of something being squashed, or of a soft body falling. **3** *Brit.* a concentrated drink made of crushed fruit, etc., diluted with water. **4** a game played with rackets and a small ball against the walls of a closed court. **5** a squashed thing or mass. □□ **squash•y** *adj.* (**squash•i•er, squash•i•est**). **squash•i•ly** *adv.* **squash•i•ness** *n.* [alt. of QUASH]

squash[2] /skwosh/ *n.* (*pl.* same or **squash•es**) **1** any of various gourdlike trailing plants of the genus *Cucurbita*, esp. *C. maxima, C. moschata*, and *C. melopepo*, whose fruits may be used as a vegetable. **2** the fruit of these cooked and eaten. [obs. (*i*)*squoutersquash* f. Narragansett *asquutasquash* f. *asq* uncooked + *squash* green]

squash ten•nis *n.* a game similar to squash, played with a tennis ball.

squat /skwot/ *v., adj., & n.* • *v.* (**squat•ted, squat•ting**) **1** *intr.* **a** crouch

with the buttocks resting on the backs of the heels. **b** sit on the ground, etc., with the knees drawn up and the heels close to or touching the hams. **2** *tr.* put (a person) into a squatting position. **3** *intr. colloq.* sit down. **4 a** *intr.* act as a squatter. **b** *tr.* occupy (a building) as a squatter. **5** *intr.* (of an animal) crouch close to the ground. • *adj.* (**squat•ter, squat•test**) **1** (of a person, etc.) short and thick; dumpy. **2** in a squatting posture. • *n.* **1** a squatting posture. **2 a** a place occupied by a squatter or squatters. **b** being a squatter. □□ **squat•ly** *adv.* **squat•ness** *n.* [ME f. OF *esquatir* flatten f. *es-* EX-[1] + *quatir* press down, crouch ult. f. L *coactus* past part. of *cogere* compel: see COGENT]

squat•ter /skwótər/ *n.* **1** a person who takes unauthorized possession of unoccupied premises. **2** *Austral.* **a** a sheepfarmer, esp. on a large scale. **b** *hist.* a person who gets the right of pasturage from the government on easy terms. **3** a person who settles on new, esp. public, land without title. **4** a person who squats.

squaw /skwaw/ *n.* often *offens.* a Native American woman or wife. [Narragansett *squaws*, Massachusetts *squaw* woman]

squawk /skwawk/ *n. & v.* • *n.* **1** a loud harsh cry, esp. of a bird. **2** a complaint. • *v.tr. & intr.* utter with or make a squawk. □□ **squawk•er** *n.* [imit.]

squawk box *n. colloq.* a loudspeaker or intercom.

squaw man *n. offens.* a non–Native American man married to a Native American woman.

squaw win•ter *n.* (in N. America) a brief wintry spell before an Indian summer.

squeak /skweek/ *n. & v.* • *n.* **1 a** a short shrill cry as of a mouse. **b** a slight high-pitched sound as of an unoiled hinge. **2** (also **squeak•er** or **nar•row squeak**) a narrow escape; a success barely attained; a game or election won by a narrow margin. • *v.* **1** *intr.* make a squeak. **2** *tr.* utter (words) shrilly. **3** *intr.* (foll. by *by, through*) *colloq.* pass narrowly. **4** *intr. sl.* turn informer. [ME, imit.: cf. SQUEAL, SHRIEK, and Sw. *skv äka* croak]

squeak•er /skweékər/ *n.* **1** a person or thing that squeaks. **2** a young bird, esp. a pigeon. **3** *colloq.* a close contest.

squeak•y /skweékee/ *adj.* (**squeak•i•er, squeak•i•est**) making a squeaking sound. □□ **squeak•i•ly** *adv.* **squeak•i•ness** *n.*

squeak•y clean *adj.* **1** completely clean. **2** above criticism; beyond reproach.

squeal /skweel/ *n. & v.* • *n.* a prolonged shrill sound, esp. a cry of a child or a pig. • *v.* **1** *intr.* make a squeal. **2** *tr.* utter (words) with a squeal. **3** *intr. sl.* turn informer. **4** *intr. sl.* protest loudly or excitedly. □□ **squeal•er** *n.* [ME, imit.]

squeam•ish /skweémish/ *adj.* **1** easily nauseated or disgusted. **2** fastidious or overscrupulous in questions of propriety, honesty, etc. □□ **squeam•ish•ly** *adv.* **squeam•ish•ness** *n.* [ME var. of *squeamous* (now dial.), f. AF *escoymos*, of unkn. orig.]

squee•gee /skweéjee/ *n. & v.* • *n.* **1** a rubber-edged implement often set on a long handle and used for cleaning windows, etc. **2** a small similar instrument or roller used in photography. • *v.tr.* (**squee•gees, squee•geed**) treat with a squeegee. [*squeegee*, strengthened form of SQUEEZE]

squeeze /skweez/ *v. & n.* • *v.* **1** *tr.* **a** exert pressure on from opposite or all sides, esp. in order to extract moisture or reduce size. **b** compress with one's hand or between two bodies. **c** reduce the size of or alter the shape of by squeezing. **2** *tr.* (often foll. by *out*) extract (moisture) by squeezing. **3 a** *tr.* force (a person or thing) into or through a small or narrow space. **b** *intr.* make one's way by squeezing. **c** *tr.* make (one's way) by squeezing. **4** *tr.* **a** harass by exactions; extort money, etc., from. **b** constrain; bring pressure to bear on. **c** (usu. foll. by *out of*) obtain (money, etc.) by extortion, entreaty, etc. **d** *Bridge* subject (a player) to a squeeze. **5** *tr.* press or hold closely as a sign of sympathy, affection, etc. **6** *tr.* (often foll. by *out*) produce with effort (*squeezed out a tear*). • *n.* **1** an instance of squeezing; the state of being squeezed. **2 a** a close embrace. **b** *sl.* a close friend of the opposite sex, esp. a girlfriend or boyfriend. **3** a crowd or crowded state; a crush. **4** a small quantity produced by squeezing (*a squeeze of lemon*). **5** a sum of money extorted or exacted, esp. an illicit commission. **6** *Econ.* a restriction on borrowing, investment, etc., in a financial crisis. **7** an impression of a coin, etc., taken by pressing damp paper, wax, etc., against it. **8** (in full **squeeze play**) a *Bridge* leading winning cards until an opponent is

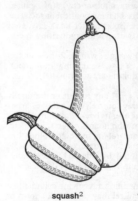

squash[2]

forced to discard an important card. **b** *Baseball* bunting a ball to the infield to enable a runner on third base to start for home as soon as the ball is pitched. **9** *colloq.* a difficult situation; an emergency. □ **put the squeeze on** *colloq.* coerce or pressure (a person). □□ **squeez•a•ble** *adj.* **squeez•er** *n.* [earlier *squise*, intensive of obs. *queise*, of unkn. orig.]

squeeze bot•tle *n.* a flexible container whose contents are extracted by squeezing it.

squeeze•box *n. colloq.* an accordion or concertina.

squelch /skwelch/ *v. & n.* ● *v.* **1** *intr.* **a** make a sucking sound as of treading in thick mud. **b** move with a squelching sound. **2** *tr.* **a** disconcert; silence. **b** stamp on; crush flat; put an end to. ● *n.* **1** an instance of squelching. **2** *Electronics.* a circuit in a radio receiver that eliminates output noise when the receiver is tuned to a frequency at which there is no signal or a very low signal. □□ **squelch•er** *n.* **squelch•y** *adj.* [imit.]

squib /skwib/ *n. & v.* ● *n.* **1** a small firework burning with a hissing sound and usu. with a final explosion. **2** a short satirical composition; a lampoon. ● *v.* (**squibbed, squib•bing**) **1** *tr. Football* kick (the ball) a comparatively short distance on a kickoff; execute (a kick) in this way. **2** *archaic* **a** *intr.* write lampoons. **b** *tr.* lampoon. [16th c.: orig. unkn.: perh. imit.]

squid /skwid/ *n. & v.* ● *n.* **1** any of various ten-armed cephalopods, esp. of the genus *Loligo*, used as bait or food. **2** artificial bait for fish imitating a squid in form. ● *v.intr.* (**squid•ded, squid•ding**) fish with squid as bait. [17th c.: orig. unkn.]

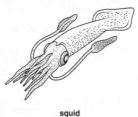

squid

squiffed /skwift/ *adj. sl.* = SQUIFFY.

squiff•y /skwifee/ *adj.* (**squiff•i•er, squiff•i•est**) esp. *Brit. sl.* slightly drunk. [19th c.: orig. unkn.]

squig•gle /skwigəl/ *n. & v.* ● *n.* a short curly line, esp. in handwriting or doodling. ● *v.* **1** *tr.* write in a squiggly manner; scrawl. **2** *intr.* wriggle; squirm. □□ **squig•gly** *adj.* [imit.]

squill /skwil/ *n.* **1** any bulbous plant of the genus *Scilla*, esp. *S. autumnalis*, **2** a seashore plant, *Urginea maritima*, having bulbs used in diuretic and purgative preparations. Also called **sea onion**. **3** any crustacean of the genus *Squilla*. [ME f. L *squilla, scilla* f. Gk *skilla*]

squinch /skwinch/ *v.* **1** *tr.* tense up the muscles of (one's eyes or face). **2** *intr.* crouch down in order to make oneself seem smaller or to occupy less space.

squint /skwint/ *v., n., & adj.* ● *v.* **1** *intr.* have the eyes turned in different directions; have a squint. **2** *intr.* (often foll. by *at*) look obliquely or with half closed eyes. **3** *tr.* close (one's eyes) quickly, hold (one's eyes) half shut. ● *n.* **1** = STRABISMUS. **2** a stealthy or sidelong glance. **3** *colloq.* a glance or look (*had a squint at it*). **4** an oblique opening through the wall of a church affording a view of the altar. **5** a leaning or inclination toward a particular object or aim. ● *adj.* **1** squinting. **2** looking different ways. □□ **squint•er** *n.* **squint•y** *adj.* [ASQUINT: (adj.) perh. f. *squint-eyed* f. obs. *squint* (adv.) f. ASQUINT]

squint-eyed *adj.* **1** squinting. **2** malignant; ill-willed.

squire /skwīr/ *n. & v.* ● *n.* **1** a country gentleman, esp. the chief landowner in a country district. **2** *hist.* a knight's attendant. **3** *Brit. colloq.* a jocular form of address to a man. **4** a local magistrate or judge in some rural districts. **5** *Austral.* a young snapper fish. ● *v.tr.* (of a man) attend upon or escort (a woman). □□ **squire•dom** *n.* **squire•hood** *n.* **squire•let** *n.* **squire•ling** *n.* **squire•ly** *adj.* **squire•ship** *n.* [ME f. OF *esquier* ESQUIRE]

squir•ar•chy /skwíraarkee/ *n.* (also **squir•ar•chy**) (*pl.* **•chies**) landowners collectively, esp. as a class having political or social influence; a class or body of squires. [SQUIRE, after HIERARCHY, etc.]

squirl /skwərl/ *n. colloq.* a flourish or twirl, esp. in handwriting. [perh. f. SQUIGGLE + TWIRL or WHIRL]

squirm /skwərm/ *v. & n.* ● *v.intr.* **1** wriggle; writhe. **2** show or feel embarrassment or discomfiture. ● *n.* a squirming movement. □□ **squirm•er** *n.* **squirm•y** *adj.* (**squirm•i•er, squirm•i•est**). [imit., prob. assoc. with WORM]

squir•rel /skwórəl, skwúr–/ *n. & v.* ● *n.* **1** any rodent of the family Sciuridae, e.g., the red squirrel, gray squirrel, etc., often of arboreal habits, with a bushy tail arching over its back, and pointed ears. **2** the fur of this animal. **3** a person who hoards objects, food, etc. ● *v.* (**squir•reled** or **squir•relled, squir•rel•ing** or **squir•rel•ing**) **1** (often foll. by *away*) hoard (objects, food, time, etc.) (*squirreled it away in the cupboard*). **2** *intr.* (often foll. by *around*) bustle around. [ME f. AF *esquirel*, OF *esquireul*, ult. f. L *sciurus* f. Gk *skiouros* f. *skia* shade + *oura* tail]

squir•rel cage *n.* **1** a small cage containing a revolving cylinder like a treadmill, on which a captive squirrel may exercise. **2** a form of rotor used in small electric motors, resembling the cylinder of a squirrel cage. **3** a monotonous or repetitive way of life.

squir•rel grass *n.* (also **squir•rel tail grass**) a grass, *Hordeum jubatum*, with bushy spikelets.

squir•rel•ly /skwórəlee, skwúr–/ *adj.* **1** like a squirrel. **2 a** inclined to bustle around. **b** (of a person) unpredictable; nervous; demented.

squir•rel mon•key *n.* a small yellow-haired monkey, *Saimiri sciureus*, native to S. America.

squirt /skwərt/ *v. & n.* ● *v.* **1** *tr.* eject (liquid or powder) in a jet as from a syringe. **2** *intr.* (of liquid or powder) be discharged in this way. **3** *tr.* splash with liquid or powder ejected by squirting. ● *n.* **1 a** a jet of water, etc. **b** a small quantity produced by squirting. **2 a** a syringe. **b** (in full **squirt gun**) a kind of toy gun using water as ammunition. **3** *colloq.* an insignificant but presumptuous person. □□ **squirt•er** *n.* [ME, imit.]

squish /skwish/ *n. & v.* ● *n.* a slight squelching sound. ● *v.* **1** *intr.* move with a squish. **2** *tr. colloq.* squash; squeeze. □□ **squish•y** *adj.* (**squish•i•er, squish•i•est**). [imit.]

squitch /skwich/ *n.* couch grass. [alt. f. QUITCH]

squiz /skwiz/ *n. Austral. & NZ sl.* a look or glance. [prob. f. QUIZ²]

Sr *symb. Chem.* the element strontium.

Sr. *abbr.* **1** Senior. **2** Señor. **3** Signor. **4** *Eccl.* Sister.

sr *abbr.* steradian(s).

Sri Lan•kan /shree lángkən, sree/ *n. & adj.* ● *n.* **1** a native or inhabitant of Sri Lanka (formerly Ceylon), an island in the Indian Ocean. **2** a person of Sri Lankan descent. ● *adj.* of or relating to Sri Lanka or its people.

SRO *abbr.* standing room only.

SS *abbr.* **1** steamship. **2** Saints. **3** *hist.* Nazi special police force. [sense 3 f. G *Schutz-Staffel*]

SSA *abbr.* Social Security Administration.

SSE *abbr.* south-southeast.

SSS *abbr.* Selective Service System.

SST *abbr.* supersonic transport.

SSW *abbr.* south-southwest.

St. *abbr.* **1** Street. **2** Saint.

st. *abbr.* stone (in weight).

-st var. of –EST².

sta. *abbr.* station.

stab /stab/ *v. & n.* ● *v.* (**stabbed, stab•bing**) **1** *tr.* pierce or wound with a (usu. short) pointed tool or weapon, e.g., a knife or dagger. **2** *intr.* (often foll. by *at*) aim a blow with such a weapon. **3** *intr.* cause a sensation like being stabbed (*stabbing pain*). **4** *tr.* hurt or distress (a person, feelings, conscience, etc.). **5** *intr.* (foll. by *at*) aim a blow at a person's reputation, etc. ● *n.* **1 a** an instance of stabbing. **b** a blow or thrust with a knife, etc. **2** a wound made in this way. **3** a sharply painful (physical or mental) sensation; a blow inflicted on a person's feelings. **4** *colloq.* an attempt; a try. □ **stab in the back** *n.* a treacherous or slanderous attack. ● *v.tr.* slander or betray. □□ **stab•ber** *n.* [ME: cf. dial. *stob* in sense 1 of *v.*]

sta•bile /stáybeel, –bil/ *n.* a rigid, freestanding abstract sculpture or structure of wire, sheet metal, etc. [L *stabilis* STABLE¹, after MOBILE]

sta•bil•i•ty /stəbílitee/ *n.* the quality or state of being stable. [ME f. OF *stableté* f. L *stabilitas* f. *stabilis* STABLE¹]

sta•bi•lize /stáybilīz/ *v.tr. & intr.* make or become stable. □□ **sta•bi•li•za•tion** *n.*

sta•bi•liz•er /stáybilīzər/ *n.* a device or substance used to keep something stable, esp.: **1** a gyroscope device to prevent rolling of a ship. **2** the horizontal airfoil in the tail assembly of an aircraft. **3** (in *pl.*) *Brit.* a pair of small wheels fitted to the rear wheel of a child's bicycle.

sta•ble¹ /stáybəl/ *adj.* (**sta•bler, sta•blest**) **1** firmly fixed or established; not easily adjusted, destroyed, or altered (*a stable structure; a stable government*). **2 a** firm; resolute; not wavering or fickle (*a stable and steadfast friend*). **b** (of a person) well-adjusted; sane; sensible. **3** *Chem.* (of a compound) not readily decomposing. **4** *Physics* (of an isotope) not subject to radioactive decay. □□ **sta•ble•ness** *n.* **sta•bly** *adv.* [ME f. AF *stable*, OF *estable* f. L *stabilis* f. *stare* stand]

sta•ble² /stáybəl/ *n. & v.* ● *n.* **1** a building set apart and adapted for keeping horses. **2** an establishment where racehorses are kept and trained. **3** the racehorses of a particular stable. **4** persons, products, etc., having a common origin or affiliation. **5** such an origin or affiliation. ● *v.tr.* put or keep (a horse) in a stable. □□ **sta•ble•ful** *n.* (*pl.* **•fuls**). [ME f. OF *estable* f. L *stabulum* f. *stare* stand]

sta•ble e•qui•lib•ri•um *n.* a state in which a body when disturbed tends to return to equilibrium.

sta•ble•man /stáybəlmən/ *n.* (*pl.* **•men**; *fem.* **sta•ble•wom•an**, *pl.* **•wom•en**) a person employed in a stable.

sta•bling /stáybling/ *n.* accommodation for horses.

sta•blish /stáblish/ *v.tr. archaic* fix firmly; establish; set up. [var. of ESTABLISH]

stac•ca•to /stəkáatō/ *adv., adj., & n.* esp. *Mus.* ● *adv. & adj.* with each sound or note sharply detached or separated from the others (cf. LEGATO, TENUTO). ● *n.* (*pl.* **•tos**) **1** a staccato passage in music, etc. **2** staccato delivery or presentation. [It., past part. of *staccare* = *distaccare* DETACH]

stac•ca•to mark *n.* a dot or stroke above or below a note, indicating that it is to be played staccato.

stack /stak/ n. & v. ● n. **1** a pile or heap, esp. in orderly arrangement. **2** a circular or rectangular pile of hay, straw, etc., or of grain in sheaf, often with a sloping thatched top; a rick. **3** colloq. a large quantity (a stack of work; has stacks of money). **4 a** a number of chimneys in a group. **b** = SMOKESTACK. **c** a tall factory chimney. **5** a stacked group of aircraft. **6** (also **stacks** or Brit. **stack-room**) a part of a library where books are compactly stored, esp. one to which the public does not have direct access. **7** Brit. a high detached rock, esp. off the coast of Scotland and the Orkneys. **8** a pyramidal group of rifles, a pile. **9** Computing a set of storage locations which store data in such a way that the most recently stored item is the first to be retrieved. **10** Brit. a measure for a pile of wood of 108 cu. ft. (30.1 cubic meters). ● v.tr. **1** pile in a stack or stacks. **2 a** arrange (cards) secretly for cheating. **b** manipulate (circumstances, etc.) to one's advantage. **3** cause (aircraft) to fly round the same point at different levels while waiting to land at an airport. □ **stack up** colloq. present oneself; measure up. □□ **stack‧a‧ble** adj. **stack‧er** n. [ME f. ON stakkr haystack f. Gmc]

stac‧te /stáktee/ n. a sweet spice used by the ancient Jews in making incense. [ME f. L f. Gk staktē f. stazō drip]

stad‧dle /stádəl/ n. a platform or framework supporting a rick, etc. [OE stathol base f. Gmc, rel. to STAND]

staddle-stone n. a stone supporting a staddle or rick, etc.

sta‧di‧um /stáydeeəm/ n. (pl. **sta‧di‧ums**) **1** an athletic or sports arena with tiers of seats for spectators. **2** (pl. **sta‧di‧ums** or **sta‧di‧a** /‑deeə/) Antiq. **a** a course for a footrace or chariot race. **b** a measure of length, about 607 feet or 185 meters. **3** a stage or period of development, etc. [ME f. L f. Gk stadion]

stadt‧hold‧er /staádhōldər, staát‑/ n. (also **stad‧hold‧er**) hist. **1** the chief magistrate of the United Provinces of the Netherlands. **2** the viceroy or governor of a province or town in the Netherlands. □□ **stadt‧hold‧er‧ship** n. [Du. stadhouder deputy f. stad STEAD + houder HOLDER, after med.L LOCUM TENENS]

staff[1] /staf/ n. & v. ● n. **1 a** a stick or pole for use in walking or climbing or as a weapon. **b** a stick or pole as a sign of office or authority. **c** a person or thing that supports or sustains. **d** a flagstaff. **e** Surveying a rod for measuring distances, heights, etc. **f** Brit. a token given to a driver on a single-track railroad as authority to proceed over a given section of line. **g** Brit. a spindle in a watch. **2 a** a body of persons employed in a business, etc. (editorial staff of a newspaper). **b** those in authority within an organization, esp. the teachers in a school. **c** Mil., etc., a body of officers assisting an officer in high command and concerned with an army, regiment, fleet, or air force as a whole (general staff). **3** (pl. **staffs** or **staves** /stayvz/) Mus. a set of usu. five parallel lines on any one or between any adjacent two of which a note is placed to indicate its pitch. ● v.tr. provide (an institution, etc.) with staff. □□ **staffed** adj. (also in comb.). [OE stæ f f. Gmc]

staff[2] /staf/ n. a mixture with a base of plaster of Paris used as a temporary building material. [19th c.: orig. unkn.]

staff‧age /stofaázh/ n. accessory items in a painting, esp. figures or animals in a landscape picture. [G f. staffieren decorate, perh. f. OF estoffer: see STUFF]

staff‧er /stáfər/ n. a member of a staff, esp. of a newspaper.

staff no‧ta‧tion n. Mus. notation by means of a staff, esp. as distinct from tonic sol-fa.

staff nurse n. Brit. a nurse ranking just below a sister.

Staffs. abbr. Staffordshire.

staff ser‧geant n. a noncommissioned officer ranking just above sergeant.

stag /stag/ n., adj., & v. ● n. **1** an adult male deer, esp. one with a set of antlers. **2** a man who attends a social gathering unaccompanied by a woman. **3** Brit. Stock Exch. a person who applies for shares of a new issue with a view to selling at once for a profit. ● adj. **1** for men only, as a party. **2** intended for men only, esp. pornographic material (stag films). **3** unaccompanied by a date. ● v.tr. (**stagged**, **stag‧ging**) **1** to attend a gathering unaccompanied. **2** Brit. Stock Exch. deal in (shares) as a stag. [ME f. OE stacga, stagga (unrecorded): cf. docga dog, frogga frog, etc., and ON steggr, steggi male bird]

stag bee‧tle n. any beetle of the family Lucanidae, the male of which has large branched mandibles resembling a stag's antlers.

stage /stayj/ n. & v. ● n. **1** a point or period in a process or development (reached a critical stage; is in the larval stage). **2 a** a raised floor or platform, esp. one on which plays, etc., are performed before an audience. **b** (prec. by the) the acting or theatrical profession, dramatic art or literature. **c** the scene of action (the stage of politics). **d** = LANDING STAGE. **3 a** a regular stopping place on a route. **b** the distance between two stopping places. **4** Astronaut. a section of a rocket with a separate engine, jettisoned when its propellant is exhausted. **5** Geol. a range of strata forming a subdivision of a series. **6** Electronics a single amplifying transistor or valve with the associated equipment. **7** the surface on which an object is placed for inspection through a microscope. ● v.tr. **1** present (a play, etc.) on stage. **2** arrange the occurrence of (staged a demonstration; staged a comeback). □ **go on the stage** become an actor. **hold the stage**

dominate a conversation, etc. **set the stage for** prepare the way for; provide the basis for. □□ **stage‧a‧ble** adj. **stage‧a‧bil‧i‧tee/** n. **stag‧er** n. [ME f. OF estage dwelling ult. f. L stare stand]

stage‧coach /stáyjkōch/ n. hist. a large enclosed horse-drawn coach running regularly by stages between two places.

stagecoach

stage‧craft /stáyjkraft/ n. skill or experience in writing or staging plays.

stage di‧rec‧tion n. an instruction in the text of a play as to the movement, position, tone, etc., of an actor, or sound effects, etc.

stage door n. an actors' and workers' entrance from the street to a theater behind the stage.

stage ef‧fect n. **1** an effect produced in acting or on the stage. **2** an artificial or theatrical effect produced in real life.

stage fright n. nervousness on facing an audience, esp. for the first time.

stage‧hand /stáyjhand/ n. a person handling scenery, etc., during a performance on stage.

stage left n. (also **stage right**) on the left (or right) side of the stage, facing the audience.

stage man‧ag‧er n. the person responsible for lighting, scenery, and other mechanical arrangements for a play, etc.

stage name n. a name assumed for professional purposes by an actor.

stage play n. a play performed on stage rather than broadcast, etc.

stage rights n. exclusive rights to perform a particular play.

stage-struck adj. filled with an inordinate desire to go on the stage.

stage whis‧per n. **1** an aside. **2** a loud whisper meant to be heard by others than the person addressed.

stag‧ey var. of STAGY.

stag‧fla‧tion /stagfláyshən/ n. Econ. a state of inflation without a corresponding increase of demand and employment. [stagnation (as STAGNATE) + INFLATION]

stag‧ger /stágər/ v. & n. ● v. **1 a** intr. walk unsteadily; totter. **b** tr. cause to totter (was staggered by the blow). **2 a** tr. shock; confuse; cause to hesitate or waver (the question staggered them; they were staggered at the suggestion). **b** intr. hesitate; waver in purpose. **3** tr. arrange (events, hours of work, etc.) so that they do not coincide. **4** tr. arrange (objects) so that they are not in line, esp.: **a** arrange (a road intersection) so that the side roads are not in line. **b** set (the spokes of a wheel) to incline alternately to right and left. ● n. **1** a tottering movement. **2** (in pl.) **a** a disease of the brain and spinal cord, esp. in horses and cattle, causing staggering. **b** giddiness. **3** an overhanging or slantwise or zigzag arrangement of like parts in a structure, etc. □□ **stag‧ger‧er** n. [alt. of ME stacker (now dial.) f. ON stakra frequent. of staka push, stagger]

stag‧ger‧ing /stágəring/ adj. **1** astonishing; bewildering. **2** that staggers. □□ **stag‧ger‧ing‧ly** adv.

stag‧hound /stághownd/ n. **1** any large dog of a breed used for hunting deer by sight or scent. **2** this breed.

stag‧ing /stáyjing/ n. **1** the presentation of a play, etc. **2 a** a platform or support or scaffolding, esp. temporary. **b** Brit. shelves for plants in a greenhouse.

stag‧ing ar‧e‧a n. an intermediate assembly point for troops, etc., in transit.

stag‧ing post n. a regular stopping place, esp. on an air route.

stag‧nant /stágnənt/ adj. **1** (of liquid) motionless, having no current; stale or foul due to this. **2** (of life, action, the mind, business, a person) showing no activity, dull, sluggish. □□ **stag‧nan‧cy** n. **stag‧nant‧ly** adv. [L stagnare stagnant- f. stagnum pool]

stag‧nate /stágnayt/ v.intr. be or become stagnant. □□ **stag‧na‧tion** /‑náyshən/ n.

stag night n. (also **stag par‧ty**) an all-male celebration, esp. in honor of a man about to marry.

stag‧y /stáyjee/ adj. (also **stag‧ey**) (**stag‧i‧er**, **stag‧i‧est**) theatrical; artificial; exaggerated. □□ **stag‧i‧ly** adv. **stag‧i‧ness** n.

staid /stayd/ adj. of quiet and steady character; sedate. □□ **staid‧ly** adv. **staid‧ness** n. [= stayed, past part. of STAY[1]]

stain /stayn/ v. & n. ● v. **1** tr. & intr. discolor or be discolored by the action of liquid sinking in. **2** tr. sully; blemish; spoil; damage (a reputation, character, etc.). **3** tr. color (wood, glass, etc.) by a process other than painting or covering the surface. **4** tr. impregnate (a specimen) for microscopic examination with coloring matter that makes the structure visible by being deposited in some parts more than in others. **5** tr. print colors on (wallpaper). ● n. **1** a discoloration, a spot or mark caused esp. by contact with foreign matter and not easily removed (a cloth covered with tea stains). **2 a** a blot or blemish. **b** damage to a reputation, etc. (*a stain on one's character*). **3** a substance used in staining. □□ **stain·a·ble** *adj.* **stain·er** *n.* [ME f. *distain* f. OF *desteindre desteign-* (as DIS-, TINGE)]

stained glass *n.* dyed or colored glass, esp. in a lead framework in a window (also (with hyphen) *attrib.*: *stained-glass window*).

stain·less /stáynlis/ *adj.* **1** (esp. of a reputation) without stains. **2** not liable to stain.

stain·less steel *n.* chrome steel not liable to rust or tarnish under ordinary conditions.

stair /stair/ *n.* **1** each of a set of fixed indoor steps (*on the top stair but one*). **2** (usu. in *pl.*) a set of esp. indoor steps (*passed him on the stairs*; *down a winding stair*). **3** (in *pl.*) a landing stage. □ **stair rod** a rod for securing a carpet against the base of the riser. [OE *st ǣger* f. Gmc]

stair·case /stáirkays/ *n.* **1** a flight of stairs and the supporting structure. **2** a part of a building containing a staircase.

stair·head /stáirhed/ *n.* a level space at the top of stairs.

stair·way /stáirway/ *n.* **1** a flight of stairs; a staircase. **2** the way up this.

stair·well /stáirwel/ *n.* the shaft in which a staircase is built.

stake[1] /stayk/ *n. & v.* ● *n.* **1** a stout stick or post sharpened at one end and driven into the ground as a support, boundary mark, etc. **2** *hist.* **a** the post to which a person was tied to be burned alive. **b** (prec. by *the*) death by burning as a punishment (*was condemned to the stake*). **3** a long vertical rod in basket-making. **4** a metalworker's small anvil fixed on a bench by a pointed prop. ● *v.tr.* **1** fasten, secure, or support with a stake or stakes. **2** (foll. by *off*, *out*) mark off (an area) with stakes. **3** state or establish (a claim). □ **pull** (or **pull up**) **stakes** depart; go to live elsewhere. **stake out** *colloq.* **1** place under surveillance. **2** place (a person) to maintain surveillance. [OE *staca* f. WG, rel. to STICK[2]]

stake[2] /stayk/ *n. & v.* ● *n.* **1** a sum of money, etc., wagered on an event, esp. deposited with a stakeholder. **2** (often foll. by *in*) an interest or concern, esp. financial. **3** (in *pl.*) **a** money offered as a prize, esp. in a horse race. **b** such a race (*maiden stakes*; *trial stakes*). ● *v.tr.* **1** a wager (*staked $5 on the next race*). **b** risk (*staked everything on convincing him*). **2** *colloq.* give financial or other support to. □ **at stake 1** risked; to be won or lost (*life itself is at stake*). **2** at issue; in question. □□ **stak·er** *n.* [16th c.: perh. f. STAKE[1]]

stake boat *n.* a boat anchored to mark the course for a boat race, etc.

stake bod·y *n.* (*pl.* **·ies**) a body for a truck, etc., having a flat open platform with removable posts along the sides.

stake·hold·er /stáyk-hōldər/ *n.* an independent party with whom each of those who make a wager deposits the money, etc., wagered.

stake net *n.* a fishing net hung on stakes.

stake·out /stáykowt/ *n. colloq.* a period of surveillance.

Sta·kha·nov·ite /stəkáanəvīt/ *n.* a worker (esp. in the former USSR) who increases his or her output to an exceptional extent, and so gains special awards. □□ **Sta·kha·nov·ism** *n. & adj.* [A. G. Stakhanov, Russian coal miner d. 1977]

sta·lac·tite /stɔláktīt, stálək-/ *n.* a deposit of calcium carbonate having the shape of a large icicle, formed by the trickling of water from the roof of a cave, cliff overhang, etc. □□ **sta·lac·tic** /-láktik/ *adj.* **sta·lac·ti·form** /-láktifawrm/ *adj.* **stal·ac·tit·ic** /-títik/ *adj.* [mod.L *stalactites* f. Gk *stalaktos* dripping f. *stalassō* drip]

sta·lag /stáalaag, stálag/ *n. hist.* a German prison camp, esp. for noncommissioned officers and privates. [G f. *Stamm* base, main stock, *Lager* camp]

sta·lag·mite /stɔlágmīt, stálag-/ *n.* a deposit of calcium carbonate formed by the dripping of water into the shape of a large inverted icicle rising from the floor of a cave, etc., often uniting with a stalactite. □□ **stal·ag·mit·ic** /-mítik/ *adj.* [mod.L *stalagmites* f. Gk *stalagma* a drop f. *stalassō* (as STALACTITE)]

stale[1] /stayl/ *adj. & v.* ● *adj.* (**stal·er**, **stal·est**) **1 a** not fresh; not quite new (*stale bread is best for toast*). **b** musty, insipid, or otherwise the worse for age or use. **2** trite or unoriginal (*a stale joke*; *stale news*). **3** (of an athlete or other performer) having ability impaired by excessive exertion or practice. **4** *Law* (esp. of a claim) having been left dormant for an unreasonably long time. ● *v.tr. & intr.* make or become stale. □□ **stale·ly** *adv.* **stale·ness** *n.* [ME, prob. f. AF & OF f. *estaler* halt: cf. STALL[1]]

stale[2] /stayl/ *n. & v.* ● *n.* the urine of horses and cattle. ● *v.intr.* (esp. of horses and cattle) urinate. [ME, perh. f. OF *estaler* adopt a position (cf. STALE[1])]

stale·mate /stáylmayt/ *n. & v.* ● *n.* **1** *Chess* a position counting as a draw, in which a player is not in check but cannot move except into check. **2** a deadlock or drawn contest. ● *v.tr.* **1** *Chess* bring (a player) to a stalemate. **2** bring to a standstill. [obs. *stale* (f. AF *estale* f. *estaler* be placed: cf. STALE[1]) + MATE[2]]

Sta·lin·ism /stáalinizəm/ *n.* **1** the policies followed by Stalin in the government of the former USSR, esp. centralization, totalitarianism, and the pursuit of socialism. **2** any rigid centralized authoritarian form of socialism. □□ **Sta·lin·ist** *n.* [J.V. *Stalin* (Dzhugashvili), Soviet statesman d. 1953]

stalk[1] /stawk/ *n.* **1** the main stem of a herbaceous plant. **2** the slender attachment or support of a leaf, flower, fruit, etc. **3** a similar support for an organ, etc., in an animal. **4** a slender support or linking shaft in a machine, object, etc., e.g., the stem of a wineglass. **5** the tall chimney of a factory, etc. □□ **stalked** *adj.* (also in *comb.*). **stalk·less** *adj.* **stalk·let** *n.* **stalk·like** *adj.* **stalk·y** *adj.* [ME *stalke*, prob. dimin. of (now dial.) *stale* rung of a ladder, long handle, f. OE *stalu*]

stalk[2] /stawk/ *v. & n.* ● *v.* **1 a** *tr.* pursue or approach (game or an enemy) stealthily. **b** *intr.* steal up to game under cover. **2** *intr.* stride, walk in a stately or haughty manner. ● *n.* **1** the stalking of game. **2** an imposing gait. □□ **stalk·er** *n.* (also in *comb.*). [OE f. Gmc, rel. to STEAL]

stalk-eyed *adj.* (of crabs, snails, etc.) having the eyes mounted on stalks.

stalk·ing-horse *n.* **1** a horse behind which a hunter is concealed. **2** a pretext concealing one's real intentions or actions.

stall[1] /stawl/ *n. & v.* ● *n.* **1 a** a trader's stand or booth in a market, etc., or outdoors. **b** a compartment in a building for the sale of goods. **c** a table in this on which goods are exposed. **2 a** a stable or cowhouse. **b** a compartment for one animal in this. **3 a** a fixed seat in the choir or chancel of a church, more or less enclosed at the back and sides and often canopied, esp. one appropriated to a clergyman (*canon's stall*; *dean's stall*). **b** the office or dignity of a canon, etc. **4** (usu. in *pl.*) *Brit.* each of a set of seats in a theater, usu. on the ground floor. **5 a** a compartment for one person in a shower, toilet, etc. **b** a compartment for one horse at the start of a race. **6 a** the stalling of an engine or aircraft. **b** the condition resulting from this. **7** a receptacle for one object. ● *v.* **1 a** *intr.* (of a motor vehicle or its engine) stop because of an overload on the engine or an inadequate supply of fuel to it. **b** *intr.* (of an aircraft or its pilot) reach a condition where the speed is too low to allow effective operation of the controls. **c** *tr.* cause (an engine or vehicle or aircraft) to stall. **2** *tr.* **a** put or keep (cattle, etc.) in a stall or stalls esp. for fattening (*a stalled ox*). **b** furnish (a stable, etc.) with stalls. **3** *intr.* **a** (of a horse or cart) stick fast as in mud or snow. **b** (of a car) be stuck in mud or snow. [OE *steall* f. Gmc, rel. to STAND: partly f. OF *estal* f. Frank.]

stall[2] /stawl/ *v. & n.* ● *v.* **1** *intr.* play for time when being questioned, etc. **2** *tr.* delay; obstruct; block. ● *n.* the act or an instance of stalling. □ **stall off** evade or deceive. [*stall* pickpocket's confederate, orig. 'decoy' f. AF *estal(e)*, prob. rel. to STALL[1]]

stall·age /stáwlij/ *n. Brit.* **1** space for a stall or stalls in a market, etc. **2** the rent for such a stall. **3** the right to erect such a stall. [ME f. OF *estalage* f. *estal* STALL[1]]

stall-feed *v.tr.* fatten (cattle) in a stall.

stall·hold·er /stáwlhōldər/ *n. Brit.* a person in charge of a stall at a market, etc.

stal·lion /stályən/ *n.* an uncastrated adult male horse, esp. one kept for breeding. [ME f. OF *estalon* ult. f. a Gmc root rel. to STALL[1]]

stal·wart /stáwlwərt/ *adj. & n.* ● *adj.* **1** strongly built; sturdy. **2** courageous; resolute; determined (*stalwart supporters*). ● *n.* a stalwart person, esp. a loyal uncompromising partisan. □□ **stal·wart·ly** *adv.* **stal·wart·ness** *n.* [Sc. var. of obs. *stalworth* f. OE *stǣlwierthe* f. *stǣl* place, WORTH]

sta·men /stáymən/ *n.* the male fertilizing organ of a flowering plant, including the anther containing pollen. □□ **stam·i·nif·er·ous** /stáminífərəs/ *adj.* [L *stamen staminis* warp in an upright loom, thread]

stam·i·na /stáminə/ *n.* the ability to endure prolonged physical or mental strain; staying power; power of endurance. [L, pl. of STA-MEN in sense 'warp, threads spun by the Fates']

stam·i·nate /stáminət, –nayt/ *adj.* (of a plant) having stamens, esp. stamens but not pistils.

stam·mer /stámər/ *v. & n.* ● *v.* **1** *intr.* speak (habitually, or on occasion from embarrassment, etc.) with halting articulation, esp. with pauses or rapid repetitions of the same syllable. **2** *tr.* (often foll. by *out*) utter (words) in this way (*stammered out an excuse*). ● *n.* **1** a tendency to stammer. **2** an instance of stammering. □□ **stam·mer·er** *n.* **stam·mer·ing·ly** *adv.* [OE *stamerian* f.WG]

stamp /stamp/ *v. & n.* ● *v.* **1 a** *tr.* bring down (one's foot) heavily on the ground, etc. **b** *tr.* crush, flatten, or bring into a specified state in this way (*stamped down the earth around the plant*). **c** *intr.* bring down one's foot heavily; walk with heavy steps. **2** *tr.* **a** impress (a pattern, mark, etc.) on metal, paper, butter, etc., with a die or similar instrument of metal, wood, rubber, etc. **b** impress (a surface) with a pattern, etc., in this way. **3** *tr.* affix a postage or other stamp to (an envelope or document). **4** *tr.* assign a specific character to; characterize; mark out (*stamps the story an invention*). **5** *tr.* crush or pulverize (ore, etc.). ● *n.* **1** an instrument for stamping a pattern or mark. **2 a** a mark or pattern made by this. **b** the impression of an official mark required to be made for revenue purposes on deeds, bills of exchange, etc., as evidence of payment of tax. **3** a small adhesive piece of paper indicating that a price, fee, or tax has been paid, esp. a postage stamp. **4** a mark impressed on or label, etc., affixed to a commodity as evidence of quality, etc. **5 a** a heavy downward blow with the foot. **b** the sound of this. **6 a** a characteristic mark or impression (*bears the stamp of genius*). **b** character; kind (*avoid people of that stamp*). **7** the block that crushes ore in a stamp mill. □ **stamp on 1** impress (an idea, etc.) on (the memory, etc.). **2** suppress. **stamp out 1** produce by cutting out with a die, etc. **2** put an end to; crush; destroy. □□ **stamp·er** *n.* [prob. f. OE *stampian* (v.) (unrecorded) f. Gmc: infl. by OF *estamper* (v.) and F *estampe* (n.) also f. Gmc]

Stamp Act *n.* an act concerned with stamp duty, esp. that imposing the duty on the American colonies in 1765 and repealed in 1766.

stamp col·lect·ing *n.* the collecting of postage stamps as objects of interest or value.

stamp col·lec·tor *n.* a person engaged in stamp collecting.

stamp du·ty *n.* (also **stamp tax**) a duty imposed on certain kinds of legal document.

stam·pede /stampḗd/ *n. & v.* ● *n.* **1** a sudden flight and scattering of a number of horses, cattle, etc. **2** a sudden flight or hurried movement of people due to interest or panic. **3** the spontaneous response of many persons to a common impulse. **4** *W. US* and *Canada* a festival combining a rodeo and other events and competitions. ● *v.* **1** *intr.* take part in a stampede. **2** *tr.* cause to do this. **3** *tr.* cause to act hurriedly or unreasonably. □□ **stam·ped·er** *n.* [Sp. *estampida* crash, uproar, ult. f. Gmc, rel. to STAMP]

stamp hinge *n.* a small piece of gummed transparent paper used for fixing postage stamps in an album, etc.

stamp·ing ground *n.* a favorite haunt or place of action.

stamp mill *n.* a mill for crushing ore, etc.

stance /stans/ *n.* **1** an attitude or position of the body, esp. when hitting a ball, etc. **2** a standpoint; an attitude of mind. **3** *Sc.* a site for a market, taxi stand, etc. [F f. It. *stanza*: see STANZA]

stanch[1] /stawnch, stanch, staanch/ *v.tr.* (also **staunch**) **1** restrain the flow of (esp. blood). **2** restrain the flow from (esp. a wound). [ME f. OF *estanchier* f. Rmc]

▶When you mean 'stop the flow of blood or some other liquid,' use **stanch** (rhymes with *ranch*). When you mean 'trustworthy' or 'loyal,' use **staunch** (rhymes with *launch*). These two words are often confused because *stanch* may also be pronounced to rhyme with *launch*.

stanch[2] var. of STAUNCH[1].

stan·chion /stánshən, –chən/ *n. & v.* ● *n.* **1** a post or pillar; an upright support; a vertical strut. **2** an upright bar, pair of bars, or frame for confining cattle in a stall. ● *v.tr.* **1** supply with a stanchion. **2** fasten (cattle) to a stanchion. [ME f. AF *stanchon*, OF *estanchon* f. *estance* prob. ult. f. L *stare* stand]

stand /stand/ *v. & n.* ● *v.* (*past* and *past part.* **stood** /stood/) **1** *intr.* have or take or maintain an upright position, esp. on the feet or a base. **2** *intr.* be situated or located (*there once stood a village*). **3** *intr.* be of a specified height (*stands six foot three*). **4** *intr.* be in a specified condition (*stands accused; the thermometer stood at 90°; the matter stands as follows; stood in awe of them*). **5** *tr.* place or set in an upright or specified position (*stood it against the wall*). **6** *intr.* **a** move to and remain in a specified position (*stand aside*). **b** take a specified attitude (*stand aloof*). **7** *intr.* maintain a position; avoid falling or moving or being moved (*the house will stand for another century; stood for hours arguing*). **8** *intr.* assume a stationary position; cease to move (*now stand still*). **9** *intr.* remain valid or unaltered; hold good (*the former conditions must stand*). **10** *intr. Naut.* hold a specified course (*stand in for the shore*). **11** *tr.* endure without yielding or complaining; tolerate (*cannot stand the pain; how can you stand him?*). **12** *tr.* provide for another or others at one's own expense (*stood him a drink*). **13** *intr.* (often foll. by *for*) esp. *Brit.* be a candidate (for an office, legislature, or constituency) (*stood for Parliament*). **14** *intr.* act in a specified capacity (*stood proxy*). **15** *tr.* undergo (trial). **16** *intr. Cricket* act as umpire. **17** *intr.* (of a dog) point; set. **18** *intr.* (in full **stand at stud**) (of a stallion) be available for breeding. ● *n.* **1** a cessation from motion or progress; a stoppage. **2 a** a halt made, or a stationary condition assumed, for the purpose of resistance. **b** resistance to attack or compulsion (esp. make a stand). **3 a** a position taken up (*took his stand near the door*). **b** an attitude adopted. **4** a rack, set of shelves, table, etc., on or in which things may be placed (*music stand; hatstand*). **5 a** a small open-fronted structure for a trader outdoors or in a market, etc. **b** esp. *Brit.* a structure occupied by a participating organization at an exhibition. **6** a standing place for vehicles (*cab stand*). **7 a** (*usu. in pl.*) a raised structure for persons to sit or stand on. **b** a witness box (*take the stand*). **8 a** *Theatr.*, etc., each halt made on a tour to give one or more performances. **b** *Sports* each place in which a traveling team plays one or more games (*5-game stand in Boston*). **9** a group of growing plants (*stand of trees; stand of clover*). □ **as it stands 1** in its present condition; unaltered. **2** in the present circumstances. **it stands to reason** see REASON. **stand alone** be unequaled. **stand and deliver!** *hist.* a highwayman's order to hand over valuables, etc. **stand at bay** see BAY[5]. **stand back 1** withdraw; take up a position further from the front. **2** withdraw psychologically in order to take an objective view. **stand by 1** stand nearby; look on without interfering (*will not stand by and see him ill-treated*). **2** uphold; support;

side with (a person). **3** adhere to; abide by (terms or promises). **4** *Naut.* stand ready to take hold of or operate (an anchor, etc.). **5** (often foll. by *for*) wait; stand ready for. **stand a chance** see CHANCE. **stand corrected** accept correction. **stand down 1** withdraw (a person) or retire from a team, witness box, or similar position. **2** *Brit.* cease to be a candidate, etc. **3** *Brit. Mil.* go off duty. **stand easy!** see EASY. **stand for 1** represent; signify; imply (*"US" stands for "United States"; democracy stands for a great deal more than that*). **2** (often with *neg.*) *colloq.* endure tolerate; acquiesce in. **3** espouse the cause of. **stand one's ground** maintain one's position, not yield. **stand high** be high in status, price, etc. **stand in** (usu. foll. by *for*) deputize; act in place of another. **stand in the breach** see BREACH. **stand in good stead** see STEAD. **stand in with** be in league with. **stand off 1** move or keep away; keep one's distance. **2** *Brit.* temporarily dispense with the services of (an employee). **stand on 1** insist on; observe scrupulously (*stand on ceremony; stand on one's dignity*). **2** *Naut.* continue on the same course. **stand on me** esp. *Brit. sl.* rely on me; believe me. **stand on one's own (two) feet** (or **legs**) be self-reliant or independent. **stand out 1** be prominent or conspicuous or outstanding. **2** (usu. foll. by *against, for*) hold out; persist in opposition or support or endurance. **stand over 1** stand close to (a person) to watch, control, threaten, etc. **2** be postponed, be left for later settlement, etc. **stand pat** see PAT[2]. **stand to 1** *Mil.* stand ready for an attack (esp. before dawn or after dark). **2** abide by; adhere to (terms or promises). **3** be likely or certain to (*stands to lose everything*). **4** uphold, support, or side with (a person). **stand treat** esp. *Brit.* bear the expense of entertainment, etc. **stand up 1 a** rise to one's feet from a sitting or other position. **b** come to or remain in or place in a standing position. **2** (of an argument, etc.) be valid. **3** *colloq.* fail to keep an appointment with. **stand up for 1** support; side with; maintain (a person or cause). **2** serve as best man, maid of honor, or other attendant in a wedding. **stand upon** = *stand on*. **stand up to 1** meet or face (an opponent) courageously. **2** be resistant to the harmful effects of (wear, use, etc.). **stand well** (usu. foll. by *with*) be on good terms or in good repute. **take one's stand on** base one's argument, etc., on; rely on. □□ **stand·er** *n.* [OE *standan* f. Gmc]

stand-a·lone *adj.* (of a computer) operating independently of a network or other system.

stand·ard /stándərd/ *n. & adj.* ● *n.* **1** an object or quality or measure serving as a basis or example or principle to which others conform or should conform or by which the accuracy or quality of others is judged (*by present-day standards*). **2 a** the degree of excellence, etc., required for a particular purpose (*not up to standard*). **b** average quality (*of a low standard*). **3** the ordinary procedure, or quality or design of a product, without added or novel features. **4** a distinctive flag, esp. the flag of a cavalry regiment as distinct from the *colors* of an infantry regiment. **5 a** an upright support. **b** an upright water or gas pipe. **6 a** a tree or shrub that grows on an erect stem of full height and stands alone without support. **b** a shrub grafted on an upright stem and trained in tree form (*standard rose*). **7** a thing recognized as a model for imitation, etc. **8** a tune or song of established popularity. **9 a** a system by which the value of a currency is defined in terms of gold or silver or both. **b** the prescribed proportion of the weight of fine metal in gold or silver coins. **10** a measure for lumber, equivalent to 165 cu. ft. (4.7 cubic meters). ● *adj.* **1** serving or used as a standard (*a standard size*). **2** of a normal or prescribed but not exceptional quality or size, etc. **3** having recognized and permanent value; authoritative (*the standard book on the subject*). **4** (of language) conforming to established educated usage (*Standard English*). [ME f. AF *estaundart*, OF *estendart* f. *estendre*, as EXTEND: in senses 5 and 6 of *n.* affected by association with STAND]

stand·ard-bear·er *n.* **1** a soldier who carries a standard. **2** a prominent leader in a cause.

Stand·ard·bred /stándərdbred/ *n.* **1** a horse of an American breed able to attain a specified speed, developed esp. for harness racing. **2** this breed.

stand·ard de·vi·a·tion *n. Statistics* a quantity calculated to indicate the extent of deviation for a group as a whole.

stand·ard·ize /stándərdīz/ *v.tr.* **1** cause to conform to a standard. **2** determine the properties of by comparison with a standard. □□ **stand·ard·iz·a·ble** *adj.* **stand·ard·i·za·tion** *n.* **stand·ard·iz·er** *n.*

stand·ard lamp *n. Brit.* = FLOOR LAMP.

stand·ard of liv·ing *n.* the degree of material comfort available to a person or class or community.

stand·ard time *n.* a uniform time for places in approximately the same longitude, established in a country or region by law or custom.

stand·by /stándbī/ *n. & adj.* ● *n.* (*pl.* **stand·bys**) **1** a person or thing ready if needed in an emergency, etc. **2** readiness for duty (*on standby*). ● *adj.* **1** ready for immediate use. **2** (of air travel) not booked in advance but allocated on the basis of earliest availability.

stand·ee /standeé/ n. colloq. a person who stands, esp. when all seats are occupied.

stand-in n. a deputy or substitute, esp. for an actor when the latter's acting ability is not needed.

stand·ing /stánding/ n. & adj. ● n. **1** esteem or repute, esp. high; status; position (people of high standing; is of no standing). **2** duration (a dispute of long standing). **3** length of service, membership, etc. ● adj. **1** that stands; upright. **2 a** established; permanent (a standing rule). **b** not made, raised, etc., for the occasion (a standing army). **3** (of a jump, start, race, etc.) performed from rest or from a standing position. **4** (of water) stagnant. **5** (of grain) unreaped. **6** (of a stallion) that stands at stud. **7** Printing (formerly, of type) not yet distributed after use. □ **all standing 1** Naut. without time to lower the sails. **2** taken by surprise. **in good standing** fully paid-up as a member, etc. **leave a person standing** make far more rapid progress than he or she.

stand·ing com·mit·tee n. a committee that is permanent during the existence of the appointing body.

stand·ing joke n. an object of permanent ridicule.

stand·ing or·der n. an instruction to follow a prescribed procedure in certain circumstances, as to a publisher, etc., for a regular supply of a periodical, etc.

stand·ing or·ders n. the rules governing the manner in which all business shall be conducted in a parliament, council, society, etc.

stand·ing o·va·tion n. prolonged applause during which the crowd or audience rise to their feet.

stand·ing rig·ging n. rigging which is fixed in position.

stand·ing room n. space to stand in.

stand·ing wave n. Physics the vibration of a system in which some particular points remain fixed while others between them vibrate with the maximum amplitude (cf. TRAVELING WAVE).

stand of arms n. Brit. Mil. a complete set of weapons for one individual.

stand of col·ors n. Brit. Mil. a regiment's flags.

stand-off n. a deadlock.

stand-off·ish /stándáwfish, -óf-/ adj. cold or distant in manner. □□ **stand·off·ish·ly** adv. **stand·off·ish·ness** n.

stand-out /stándowt/ n. a remarkable person or thing.

stand-pipe /stándpīp/ n. a vertical pipe extending from a water supply, esp. one connecting a temporary faucet to the main water supply.

stand-point /stándpoynt/ n. **1** the position from which a thing is viewed. **2** a mental attitude.

stand-still /stándstil/ n. a stoppage; an inability to proceed.

stand-up attrib. adj. **1** (of a meal) eaten standing. **2** (of a fight) violent, thorough, or fair and square. **3** (of a collar) upright, not turned down. **4** (of a comedian) performing by standing before an audience and telling jokes.

stan·hope /stánhōp/ n. a light open carriage for one with two or four wheels. [Fitzroy Stanhope, Engl. clergyman d. 1864, for whom the first one was made]

stank past of STINK.

stan·na·ry /stánəree/ n. (pl. ·ries) Brit. **1** a tin mine. **2** (usu. in pl.) a tin-mining district in Cornwall and Devon. [med.L stannaria (pl.) f. LL stannum tin]

stan·na·ry court n. a legal body for the regulation of tin miners in the stannaries.

stan·nic /stánik/ adj. Chem. of or relating to tetravalent tin (stannic acid; stannic chloride). [LL stannum tin]

stan·nous /stánəs/ adj. Chem. of or relating to bivalent tin (stannous salts; stannous chloride).

stan·za /stánzə/ n. **1** the basic metrical unit in a poem or verse consisting of a recurring group of lines (often four lines and usu. not more than twelve) which may or may not rhyme. **2** a group of four lines in some Greek and Latin meters. □□ **stan·za'd** adj. (also **stan·zaed**) (also in comb.). **stan·za·ic** /-záyik/ adj. [It., = standing place, chamber, stanza, ult. f. L stare stand]

sta·pe·li·a /stəpéeleeə/ n. any S. African plant of the genus Stapelia, with flowers having an unpleasant smell. [mod.L f. J. B. von Stapel, Du. botanist d. 1636]

sta·pes /stáypeez/ n. (pl. same) a small stirrup-shaped bone in the ear of a mammal. [mod.L f. med.L stapes stirrup]

staph·y·lo·coc·cus /stáfiləkókəs/ n. (pl. **staph·y·lo·coc·ci** /-kóksī, kókī/) any bacterium of the genus Staphylococcus, occurring in grapelike clusters, and sometimes causing pus formation usu. in the skin and mucous membranes of animals. □□ **staph·y·lo·coc·cal** adj. [mod.L f. Gk staphulē bunch of grapes + kokkos berry]

sta·ple¹ /stáypəl/ n. & v. ● n. a U-shaped metal bar or piece of wire with pointed ends for driving into, securing, or fastening together various materials or for driving through and clinching papers, netting, electric wire, etc. ● v.tr. provide or fasten with a staple. □□ **sta·pler** n. [OE stapol f. Gmc]

sta·ple² /stáypəl/ n., adj., & v. ● n. **1** the principal or an important article of commerce (the staples of local industry). **2** the chief element or a main component, e.g., of a diet. **3** a raw material. **4** the fiber of cotton or wool, etc., as determining its quality (cotton of fine staple). ● adj. **1** main or principal (staple commodities). **2** important as a product or an export. ● v.tr. sort or classify (wool, etc) according to fiber. [ME f. OF estaple market f. MLG, MDu. stapel market (as STAPLE¹)]

sta·ple gun n. a handheld device for driving in staples.

star /staar/ n. & v. ● n. **1** a celestial body appearing as a luminous point in the night sky. **2** (in full **fixed star**) such a body so far from the earth as to appear motionless (cf. PLANET, COMET). **3** a large naturally luminous gaseous body such as the sun is. **4** a celestial body regarded as influencing a person's fortunes, etc. (born under a lucky star). **5** a thing resembling a star in shape or appearance. **6** a star-shaped mark, esp. a white mark on a horse's forehead. **7** a figure or object with radiating points esp. as the insignia of an order, as a decoration or mark of rank, or showing a category of excellence (a five-star hotel; was awarded a gold star). **8 a** a famous or brilliant person; the principal or most prominent performer in a play, movie, etc. (the star of the show). **b** (attrib.) outstanding; particularly brilliant (star pupil). **9** (in full **star connection**) esp. Brit. Electr a Y--shaped arrangement of three-phase windings. ● v. (**starred, starring**) **1 a** tr. (of a movie, etc.) feature as a principal performer. **b** intr. (of a performer) be featured in a movie, etc. **2** (esp. as **starred** adj.) a mark, set, or adorn with a star or stars. **b** put an asterisk or star beside (a name, an item in a list, etc.). □ **my stars!** Old-fashioned colloq. an expression of surprise. □□ **star·dom** n. **star·less** adj. **star·like** adj. [OE steorra f. Gmc]

star ap·ple n. an edible, purple, applelike fruit (with a starlike cross section) of a tropical evergreen tree, Chrysophyllum cainito.

star·board /stáarbərd/ n. & v. Naut. & Aeron. ● n. the right-hand side (looking forward) of a ship, boat, or aircraft (cf. PORT³). ● v.tr. (also absol.) turn (the helm) to starboard. [OE stēorbord = rudder side (see STEER¹, BOARD), early Teutonic ships being steered with a paddle over the right side]

star·board tack n. see TACK ¹ 4.

star·board watch n. see WATCH n. 3b.

starch /staarch/ n. & v. ● n. **1** an odorless tasteless polysaccharide occurring widely in plants and obtained chiefly from cereals and potatoes, forming an important constituent of the human diet. **2** a preparation of this for stiffening fabric before ironing. **3** stiffness of manner; formality. ● v.tr. stiffen (clothing) with starch. □□ **starch·er** n. [earlier as verb: ME sterche f. OE stercan (unrecorded) stiffen f. Gmc: cf. STARK]

Star Cham·ber n. Brit. Law **1** hist. a court of civil and criminal jurisdiction noted for its arbitrary procedure, and abolished in 1640. **2** any arbitrary or oppressive tribunal.

starch·y /stáarchee/ adj. (**starch·i·er, starch·i·est**) **1 a** of or like starch. **b** containing much starch. **2** (of a person) precise; overly formal. □□ **starch·i·ly** adv. **starch·i·ness** n.

star-crossed adj. archaic ill-fated.

star·dust /stáardust/ n. **1** a twinkling mass. **2** a romantic mystical look or sensation. **3** a multitude of stars looking like dust.

stare /stair/ v. & n. ● v. **1** intr. (usu. foll. by at) look fixedly with eyes open, esp. as the result of curiosity, surprise, bewilderment, admiration, horror, etc. (sat staring at the door; stared in amazement). **2** intr. (of eyes) be wide open and fixed. **3** intr. be unpleasantly prominent or striking. **4** tr. (foll. by into) reduce (a person) to a specified condition by staring (stared me into silence). ● n. a staring gaze. □ **stare down** (or **out**) outstare. **stare a person in the face** be evident or imminent. □□ **star·er** n. [OE starian f. Gmc]

star·fish /stáarfish/ n. an echinoderm of the class Asteroidea with five or more radiating arms.

star fruit n. = CARAMBOLA.

star·gaze /stáargayz/ v.intr. **1** gaze at or study the stars. **2** gaze intently.

star·gaz·er /stáargayzər/ n. **1** colloq. usu. derog. or joc. an astronomer or astrologer. **2** Austral. sl. a horse that turns its head when galloping.

stark /staark/ adj. & adv. ● adj. **1** desolate; bare (a stark landscape). **2** sharply evident; brutally simple. (in stark contrast; the stark reality). **3** downright; sheer (stark madness). **4** completely naked. **5** archaic strong; stiff; rigid. ● adv. completely; wholly (stark mad; stark naked). □□ **stark·ly** adv. **stark·ness** n. [OE stearc f. Gmc: stark naked f. earlier start-naked f. obs. start tail: cf. REDSTART]

Stark ef·fect /staark/ n. Physics the splitting of a spectrum line into several components by the application of an electric field. [J. Stark, Ger. physicist d. 1957]

stark·ers /stáarkərz/ adj. Brit. sl stark naked.

star·let /stáarlit/ n. **1** a promising young performer, esp. a woman. **2** a little star.

star·light /stáarlīt/ n. **1** the light of the stars (walked home by starlight). **2** (attrib.) = STARLIT (a starlight night).

star·ling¹ /stáarling/ n. **1** a small gregarious partly migratory bird, Sturnus vulgaris, with blackish-brown speckled iridescent plumage, chiefly inhabiting cultivated areas. **2** any similar bird of the family Sturnidae. [OE *stærlinc* f. *stær* starling f. Gmc: cf. –LING¹]

star•ling² /staárling/ *n.* piles built around or upstream of a bridge or pier to protect it from floating debris, etc. [perh. corrupt. of (now dial.) *staddling* STADDLE]

star•lit /staárlit/ *adj.* **1** lighted by stars. **2** with stars visible.

star of Beth•le•hem *n.* any of various plants with starlike flowers esp. *Ornithogalum umbellatum* with white star-shaped flowers striped with green on the outside (see Matt. 2:9).

Star of Da•vid *n.* a figure consisting of two interlaced equilateral triangles used as a Jewish and Israeli symbol.

star of David

star route *n.* a rural mail delivery route served by private contractors.

star•ry /staáree/ *adj.* (**star•ri•er, star•ri•est**) **1** covered with stars. **2** resembling a star. □□ **star•ri•ly** *adv.* **star•ri•ness** *n.*

star•ry-eyed *adj. colloq.* **1** visionary; enthusiastic but impractical. **2** euphoric.

Stars and Bars *n.* the flag of the Confederate States of the US.

Stars and Stripes *n.* the national flag of the US.

star sap•phire *n.* a cabochon sapphire reflecting a starlike image due to its regular internal structure.

star shell *n.* an explosive projectile designed to burst in the air and light up the enemy's position.

star-span•gled *adj.* (esp. of the US national flag) covered or glittering with stars.

star stream *n.* a systematic drift of stars.

star-stud•ded *adj.* **1** (of the night sky) filled with stars. **2** featuring a number of famous people, especially performers.

START /staart/ *abbr.* Strategic Arms Reduction Treaty (or Talks).

start /staart/ *v. & n.* ● *v.* **1** *tr. & intr.* begin; commence (*started work; started crying; started to shout; the play starts at eight*). **2** *tr.* set (proceedings, an event, etc.) in motion (*start the meeting; started a fire*). **3** *intr.* (often foll. by *on*) make a beginning (*started on a new project*). **4** *intr.* (often foll. by *after, for*) set oneself in motion or action (*"wait!" he shouted, and started after her*). **5** *intr.* set out; begin a journey, etc. (*we start at 6 a.m.*). **6** (often foll. by *up*) **a** *intr.* (of a machine) begin operating (*the car wouldn't start*). **b** *tr.* cause (a machine, etc.) to begin operating (*tried to start the engine*). **7** *tr.* **a** cause or enable (a person) to make a beginning (with something) (*started me in business with $10,000*). **b** (foll. by pres. part.) cause (a person) to begin (doing something) (*the smoke started me coughing*). **c** *colloq.* complain or be critical (*don't you start*). **8** *tr.* (often foll. by *up*) found or establish; originate. **9** *intr.* (foll. by *at, with*) have as the first of a series of items, e.g., in a meal (*we started with soup*). **10** *tr.* give a signal to (competitors) to start in a race. **11** *intr.* (often foll. by *up, from*, etc.) make a sudden movement from surprise, pain, etc. (*started at the sound of my voice*). **12** *intr.* (foll. by *out, up, from*, etc.) spring out, up, etc. (*started up from the chair*). **13** *tr.* conceive (a baby). **14** *tr.* rouse (game, etc.) from its lair. **15** **a** *intr.* (of boards, etc.) spring from their proper position; give way. **b** *tr.* cause or experience (boards, etc.) to do this. **16** *intr.* (foll. by *out, to*, etc.) (of a thing) move or appear suddenly (*tears started to his eyes*). **17** *intr.* (foll. by *from*) (of eyes, usu. with exaggeration) burst forward (from their sockets, etc.). **18** *tr.* pour out (alcoholic beverages) from a cask. ● *n.* **1** a beginning of an event, action, journey, etc. (*missed the start; an early start tomorrow; made a fresh start*). **2** the place from which a race, etc., begins. **3** an advantage given at the beginning of a race, etc. (*a 15-second start*). **4** an advantageous initial position in life, business, etc. (*a good start in life*). **5** a sudden movement of surprise, pain, etc. (*you gave me a start*). **6** an intermittent or spasmodic effort or movement (esp. in or by fits and starts). **7** *colloq.* a surprising occurrence (*an odd start*). □ **for a start** *colloq.* as a beginning; in the first place. **get the start of** gain an advantage over. **start a hare** see HARE. **to start** *colloq.* **1** begin. **2** (foll. by *on*) make a beginning on. **start off 1** begin; commence (*started off on a lengthy monologue*). **2** begin to move (*it's time we started off*). **start out 1** begin a journey. **2** *colloq.* (foll. by *to* + infin) proceed as intending (to do something). **start over** begin again. **start something** *colloq.* cause trouble. **start up** arise; occur. **to start with 1** in the first place; before anything else is considered (*should never have been there to start with*). **2** at the beginning (*had six members to start with*). [OE (orig. in sense 11) f. Gmc]

start•er /staártər/ *n.* **1** a person or thing that starts. **2** an esp. automatic device for starting the engine of a motor vehicle, etc. **3** a person giving the signal for the start of a race. **4** a horse or competitor starting in a race, game, etc. (*a list of probable starters*). **5** *Baseball* **a** the pitcher who pitches first in a game. **b** a pitcher who normally starts games. **6** *Brit.* the first course of a meal. **7** the initial action, etc. □ **for starters** *sl.* to start with. **under starter's orders** (of racehorses, etc.) in a position to start a race and awaiting the starting signal.

start•ing block *n.* a shaped rigid block for bracing the feet of a runner at the start of a race.

start•ing gate *n.* a movable barrier for securing a fair start in horse races.

start•ing pis•tol *n.* a pistol used to give the signal for the start of a race.

start•ing point *n.* the point from which a journey, process, argument, etc., begins.

start•ing post *n.* the post from which competitors start in a race.

start•ing price *n.* the odds ruling at the start of a horse race.

start•ing stall *n.* a compartment for one horse at the start of a race.

star•tle /staárt'l/ *v.tr.* give a shock or surprise to; cause (a person, etc.) to start with surprise or sudden alarm. □□ **star•tler** *n.* [OE *steartlian* (as START, –LE⁴)]

star•tling /staártling/ *adj.* **1** surprising. **2** alarming (*startling news*). □□ **star•tling•ly** *adv.*

star turn *n.* the person or act that gives the most heralded or impressive performance in a movie, play, etc.

starve /staarv/ *v.* **1** *intr.* die of hunger; suffer from malnourishment. **2** *tr.* cause to die of hunger or suffer from lack of food. **3** *intr.* suffer from extreme poverty. **4** *intr. colloq.* (esp. as **starved** or **starving** *adjs.*) feel very hungry (*I'm starving*). **5** *intr.* **a** suffer from mental or spiritual want. **b** (foll. by *for*) feel a strong craving for (sympathy, amusement, knowledge, etc.). **6** *tr.* **a** (foll. by *for, of*) deprive of; keep scantily supplied with (*starved for affection*). **b** cause to suffer from mental or spiritual want. **7** *tr.* **a** (foll. by *into*) compel by starving (*starved into submission*). **b** (foll. by *out*) compel to surrender, etc., by starving (*starved them out*). **8** *intr. archaic* or *dial.* perish with or suffer from cold. □□ **star•va•tion** /–váyshən/ *n.* [OE *steorfan* die]

starve•ling /staárvling/ *n. & adj. archaic* ● *n.* a starving or ill-fed person or animal. ● *adj.* **1** starving. **2** meager.

Star Wars *n. colloq.* the strategic defense initiative of the U.S., begun in 1984.

star•wort /staárwərt, –wawrt/ *n.* a plant of the genus *Stellaria* with starlike flowers.

stash /stash/ *v. & n. colloq.* ● *v.tr.* (often foll. by *away*) **1** conceal; put in a safe or hidden place. **2** hoard; stow; store. ● *n.* **1** a hiding place or hideout. **2** a thing hidden; a cache. [18th c.: orig. unkn.]

sta•sis /stáysis, stásis/ *n.* (*pl.* **sta•ses** /–seez/) **1** inactivity; stagnation; a state of equilibrium. **2** a stoppage of circulation of any of the body fluids. [mod.L f. Gk f. *sta–* STAND]

-stasis /stásis, stáysis/ *comb. form* (*pl.* **•stases** /–seez/) *Physiol.* forming nouns denoting a slowing or stopping (*hemostasis*). □□ **–static** *comb. form* forming adjectives.

-stat /stat/ *comb. form* forming nouns with ref. to keeping fixed or stationary (*rheostat*). [Gk *statos* stationary]

stat. *abbr.* **1** at once. [L *statim*] **2** statistics. **3** statute.

state /stayt/ *n. & v.* ● *n.* **1** the existing condition or position of a person or thing (*in a bad state of repair; in a precarious state of health*). **2** *colloq.* **a** an excited, anxious, or agitated mental condition (esp. in a state). **b** an untidy condition. **3 a** an organized political community under one government; a commonwealth; a nation. **b** such a community forming part of a federal republic, esp. the United States of America. **c** (**the States**) the US. **4** (*attrib.*) **a** of, for, or concerned with the state (*state documents*). **b** reserved for or done on occasions of ceremony (*state apartments; state visit*). **5** (also **State**) civil government (*church and state; Secretary of State*). **6 a** pomp; rank; dignity (*as befits their state*). **b** imposing display; ceremony; splendor (*arrive in state*). **7** (**the States**) the legislative body in the UK islands of Jersey, Guernsey, and Alderney. **8** *Bibliog.* one of two or more variant forms of a single edition of a book. **9 a** an etched or engraved plate at a particular stage of its progress. **b** an impression taken from this. ● *v.tr.* **1** express, esp. fully or clearly, in speech or writing (*have stated my opinion; must state full particulars*). **2** fix; specify (*at stated intervals*). **3** *Law* specify the facts of (a case) for consideration. **4** *Mus.* play (a theme, etc.) so as to make it known to the listener. □ **in state** with all due ceremony. **of state** concerning politics or government. □□ **stat•a•ble** *adj.* **stat•ed•ly** *adv.* **state•hood** *n.* [ME: partly f. ESTATE, partly f. L STATUS]

state cap•i•tal•ism *n.* a system of state control and use of capital.

state•craft /stáytkraft/ *n.* the art of conducting affairs of state.

State De•part•ment *n.* the federal government department concerned with foreign affairs.

state•hood /stáythood/ *n.* the condition or status being a state, esp. a state of the United States.

state house *n.* the building where the legislature of a state meets.

state•less /stáytlis/ *adj.* **1** (of a person) having no nationality or citizenship. **2** without a state. □□ **state•less•ness** *n.*

state•ly /stáytlee/ *adj.* (**state•li•er, state•li•est**) dignified; imposing; grand. □□ **state•li•ness** *n.*

state·ly home n. *Brit.* a large magnificent house, esp. one open to the public.

state·ment /stáytmənt/ n. **1** the act or an instance of stating or being stated; expression in words. **2** a thing stated; a declaration (*that statement is unfounded*). **3** a formal account of facts, esp. to the police or in a court of law (*make a statement*). **4** a record of transactions in a bank account, etc. **5** a formal notification of an amount due.

state of e·mer·gen·cy n. a condition of danger or disaster affecting a country, esp. with normal constitutional procedures suspended.

state of grace n. the condition of being free from grave sin.

state of life n. rank and occupation.

state of the art n. **1** the current stage of development of a practical or technological subject. **2** (usu. **state-of-the-art**) (*attrib.*) using the latest equipment or techniques (*state-of-the-art weaponry*).

state of things n. (also **state of af·fairs** or esp. *Brit.* **state of play**) the circumstances; the current situation.

state of war n. the situation when war has been declared or is in progress.

stat·er /stáytər/ n. an ancient Greek gold or silver coin. [ME f. LL f. Gk *statēr*]

state·room /stáytrⁱm, -rⁱm/ n. **1** a private compartment in a passenger ship or train. **2** a state apartment in a palace, hotel, etc.

state's ev·i·dence n. *Law* evidence for the prosecution given by a participant in or accomplice to the crime at issue.

States Gen·er·al n. *hist.* the legislative body in the Netherlands, and in France before 1789.

state·side /stáytsíd/ adj. *colloq.* of, in, or toward the United States.

states·man /stáytsmən/ n. (pl. **·men**; *fem.* **states·wom·an**, pl. **·wom·en**) **1** a person skilled in affairs of state, esp. one taking an active part in politics. **2** a distinguished and capable politician. □□ **states·man·like** adj. **states·man·ly** adj. **states·man·ship** n. [= *state's man* after F *homme d'état*]

state so·cial·ism n. a system of state control of industries and services.

states' rights n. the rights and powers not assumed by the federal government of the United States but reserved to its individual states.

state tri·al n. prosecution by the government.

state u·ni·ver·si·ty n. a university managed by the public authorities of a state.

state·wide /stáytwíd/ adj. so as to include or cover a whole state.

stat·ic /státik/ adj. & n. ● adj. **1** stationary; not acting or changing; passive. **2** *Physics* a concerned with bodies at rest or forces in equilibrium (opp. DYNAMIC). **b** acting as weight but not moving (*static pressure*). **c** of statics. ● n. **1** static electricity. **2** electrical disturbances in the atmosphere or the interference with telecommunications caused by this. **3** *sl.* aggravation; fuss; criticism. [mod.L *staticus* f. Gk *statikos* f. *sta-* stand]

stat·i·cal /státikəl/ adj. = STATIC. □□ **stat·i·cal·ly** adv.

stat·ice /státisee, státis/ n. **1** sea lavender. **2** sea pink. [L f. Gk, fem. of *statikos* STATIC (with ref. to stanching of blood)]

stat·ic e·lec·tric·i·ty n. electricity not flowing as a current as that produced by friction.

stat·ic line n. a length of cord attached to an aircraft, etc., which releases a parachute without the use of a ripcord.

stat·ics /státiks/ n.pl. (usu. treated as *sing.*) **1** the science of bodies at rest or of forces in equilibrium (opp. DYNAMICS). **2** = STATIC. [STAT·IC n. in the same senses + -ICS]

sta·tion /stáyshən/ n. & v. ● n. **1 a** a regular stopping place on a public transportation route, esp. one on a railroad line with a platform and often one or more buildings. **b** these buildings (see also BUS STATION). **2** a place or building, etc., where a person or thing stands or is placed, esp. habitually or for a definite purpose. **3 a** a designated point or establishment where a particular service or activity is based or organized (*police station; polling station; research station*). **b** a branch post office. **4** an establishment involved in radio or television broadcasting. **5 a** a military or naval base esp. *hist.* in India. **b** the inhabitants of this. **6** position in life; rank or status (*ideas above your station*). **7** *Austral. & NZ* a large sheep or cattle farm. **8** *Bot.* a particular place where an unusual species, etc., grows. ● v.tr. **1** assign a station to. **2** put in position. [ME, = standing, f. OF f. L *statio -onis* f. *stare* stand]

sta·tion·ar·y /stáyshəneree/ adj. **1** remaining in one place; not moving (*hit a stationary car*). **2** not meant to be moved; not portable (*stationary troops; stationary engine*). **3** not changing in magnitude, number, quality, efficiency, etc. (*stationary temperature*). **4** (of a

SPELLING TIP stationary/stationery

To remember the *-ary* and *-ery* endings of these words, you can use the mnemonic: "Stationary means 'standing,' but letters are written on stationery."

planet) having no apparent motion in longitude. □□ **sta·tion·ar·i·ness** n. [ME f. L *stationarius* (as STATION)]

▶Be careful to distinguish **stationary** ('not moving, fixed') from **stationery** ('writing paper and other supplies').

sta·tion·ar·y bi·cy·cle n. a fixed exercise apparatus resembling a bicycle.

sta·tion·ar·y point n. *Math.* a point on a curve where the gradient is zero.

sta·tion·ar·y wave n. = STANDING WAVE.

sta·tion-bill n. *Naut.* a list showing the prescribed stations of a ship's crew for various drills or in an emergency.

sta·tion break n. a pause between or within broadcast programs for an announcement of the identity of the station transmitting them.

sta·tion·er /stáyshənər/ n. a person who sells writing materials, etc. [ME, = bookseller (as STATIONARY in med.L sense 'shopkeeper,' esp. bookseller, as opposed to peddler)]

Sta·tion·ers' Hall n. *Brit.* the hall of the Stationers' Company in London, at which a book was formerly registered for purposes of copyright.

sta·tion·er·y /stáyshəneree/ n. **1** writing materials such as pens, paper, etc. **2** writing paper, esp. with matching envelopes.

▶See note at STATIONARY.

SPELLING TIP stationary/stationery

See note at STATIONARY.

sta·tion hand n. *Austral.* a worker on a large sheep or cattle farm.

sta·tion house n. a police or fire station.

sta·tion·mas·ter /stáyshənmastər/ n. the official in charge of a railroad station.

sta·tion of the cross n. *RC Ch., Anglican Ch.* **1** each of a series of usu. 14 images or pictures, representing the events in Christ's passion, before which devotions are performed. **2** each of these devotions.

sta·tion wag·on n. a car with passenger seating and storage or extra seating area in the rear, accessible by a rear door.

stat·ism /stáytizəm/ n. centralized government administration and control of social and economic affairs.

stat·ist /státist, stáytist/ n. **1** a statistician. **2** a supporter of statism. [orig. 'politician' f. It. *statista* (as STATE)]

sta·tis·tic /stətístik/ n. & adj. ● n. a statistical fact or item. ● adj. = STATISTICAL. [G *statistisch, Statistik* f. *Statist* (as STATIST)]

sta·tis·ti·cal /stətístikəl/ adj. of or relating to statistics. □□ **sta·tis·ti·cal·ly** adv.

sta·tis·ti·cal phys·ics n. physics as it is concerned with large numbers of particles to which statistics can be applied.

sta·tis·ti·cal sig·nif·i·cance n. = SIGNIFICANCE 4.

sta·tis·tics /stətístiks/ n.pl. (usu. treated as *sing.*) the science of collecting and analyzing numerical data, esp. in or for large quantities, and usu. inferring proportions in a whole from proportions in a representative sample. **2** any systematic collection or presentation of such facts. □□ **stat·is·ti·cian** /státistíshən/ n.

sta·tor /stáytər/ n. *Electr.* the stationary part of a machine, esp. of an electric motor or generator. [STATIONARY, after ROTOR]

stat·o·scope /státəskōp/ n. an aneroid barometer used to show minute variations of pressure, esp. to indicate the altitude of an aircraft. [Gk *statos* fixed f. *sta-* stand + -SCOPE]

stat·u·ar·y /stáchōōeree/ adj. & n. ● adj. of or for statues (*statuary art*). ● n. (pl. **·ies**) **1** statues collectively. **2** the art of making statues. **3** a sculptor. [L *statuarius* (as STATUE)]

stat·u·ar·y mar·ble n. fine-grained white marble.

stat·ue /stáchōō/ n. a sculptured, cast, carved, or molded figure of a person or animal, esp. life-size or larger (cf. STATUETTE). □□ **stat·ued** adj. [ME f. OF f. L *statua* f. *stare* stand]

stat·u·esque /stáchōō-ésk/ adj. like, or having the dignity or beauty of, a statue. □□ **stat·u·esque·ly** adv. **stat·u·esque·ness** n. [STATUE + -ESQUE, after *picturesque*]

stat·u·ette /stáchōō-ét/ n. a small statue; a statue less than life-size. [F, dimin. of *statue*]

stat·ure /stáchər/ n. **1** the height of a (esp. human) body. **2** a degree of eminence, social standing, or advancement (*recruit someone of his stature*). □□ **stat·ured** adj. (also in *comb.*). [ME f. OF f. L *statura* f. *stare stat-* stand]

sta·tus /stáytəs, stát-/ n. **1** rank; social position; relation to others; relative importance (*not sure of their status in the hierarchy*). **2** a superior social, etc., position (*considering your status in the business*). **3** *Law* a person's legal standing which determines his or her rights and duties, e.g., citizen, alien, civilian, etc. **4** the state of affairs (*let me know if the status changes*). [L, = standing f. *stare* stand]

PRONUNCIATION TIP status

The pronunciation "STAY-tus" is more common in British English. In American English, both "STAY-tus" and "STAT-us" are considered acceptable.

sta·tus quo /st áytəs kwṓ, stá təs/ *n.* the existing state of affairs. [L, = the state in which]

sta·tus sym·bol *n.* a possession, etc., taken to indicate a person's high status.

stat·u·ta·ble /stáchŏŏtəbəl/ *adj.* = STATUTORY, esp. in amount or value. □□ **stat·u·ta·bly** *adv.*

stat·ute /stáchŏŏt/ *n.* **1** a written law passed by a legislative body. **2** a rule of a corporation, founder, etc., intended to be permanent (*against the university statutes*). **3** divine law (*kept thy statutes*). [ME f. OF *statut* f. LL *statutum* neut. past part. of L *statuere* set up f. *status*: see STATUS]

stat·ute book *n.* **1** a book or books containing the statute law. **2** the body of a country's statutes.

stat·ute law *n.* **1** (*collect.*) the body of principles and rules of law laid down in statutes as distinct from rules formulated in practical application (cf. COMMON LAW, CASE LAW). **2** a statute.

stat·ute mile *n.* see MILE 1.

stat·ute of lim·i·ta·tions *n.* a statute that sets a time limit during which legal action can be taken.

stat·ute roll *n.* **1** (in the UK) the rolls in the Public Records Office containing the statutes of the Parliament of England. **2** = STATUTE BOOK.

stat·utes at large *n.* the statutes as originally enacted, regardless of later modifications.

stat·u·to·ry /stáchətawree/ *adj.* **1** required, permitted, or enacted by statute (*statutory minimum; statutory provisions*). **2** (of a criminal offense) carrying a penalty prescribed by statute. □□ **stat·u·to·ri·ly** *adv.*

stat·u·to·ry rape *n.* the offense of sexual intercourse with a minor.

staunch[1] /stawnch, staanch/ *adj.* (also **stanch**) **1** trustworthy, loyal (*my staunch friend and supporter*). **2** (of a ship, joint, etc.) strong, watertight, airtight, etc. □□ **staunch·ly** *adv.* **staunch·ness** *n.* [ME f. OF *estanche* fem. of *estanc* f. Rmc: see STANCH[1]]

▶See note at STANCH[1].

staunch[2] var. of STANCH[1].

stave /stayv/ *n. & v.* ● *n.* **1** each of the curved pieces of wood forming the sides of a cask, barrel, etc. **2** = STAFF[1] *n.* 3. **3** a stanza or verse. **4** the rung of a ladder. ● *v.tr.* (*past* and *past part.* **stove** /stōv/ or **staved**) **1** break a hole in. **2** crush or knock out of shape. **3** fit or furnish (a cask, etc.) with staves. □ **stave in** crush by forcing inwards. **stave off** avert or defer (danger or misfortune). [ME, back-form. f. *staves*, pl. of STAFF[1]]

stave 1

stave rhyme *n.* alliteration, esp. in old Germanic poetry.

staves pl. of STAFF[1] *n.* 3.

staves·a·cre /stáyvzaykər/ *n.* a larkspur, *Delphinium staphisagria*, yielding seeds used as poison for vermin. [ME f. L *staphisagria* f. Gk *staphis agria* wild raisin]

stay[1] /stay/ *v. & v.* ● *v.* **1** *intr.* continue to be in the same place or condition; not depart or change (*stay here until I come back*). **2** *intr.* **a** (often foll. by *at, in, with*) have temporary residence as a visitor, etc. (*stayed with them for Christmas*). **b** *Sc. & S.Afr.* dwell permanently. **3** *archaic* or *literary* **a** *tr.* stop or check (progress, the inroads of a disease, etc.). **b** *intr.* (esp. in *imper.*) pause in movement, action, speech, etc. (*Stay! You forget one thing*). **4** *tr.* postpone (judgment, decision, execution, etc.). **5** *tr.* assuage (hunger, etc.) esp. for a short time. **6** *a intr.* show endurance. **b** *tr.* show endurance to the end of (a race, etc.). **7** *tr.* (often foll. by *up*) *literary* support; prop up (as or with a buttress, etc.). **8** *intr.* (foll. by *for, to*) wait long enough to share or join in an activity, etc. (*stay to supper; stay for the video*). **9** call a poker bet without a raise. ● *n.* **1 a** the act or an instance of staying or dwelling in one place. **b** the duration of this (*just a ten minute stay; a long stay in London*). **2** a suspension or postponement of a sentence, judgment, etc. (*was granted a stay of execution*). **3** *archaic* or *literary* a check or restraint (*will endure no stay; a stay upon his activity*). **4** endurance; staying power. **5** a prop or support. **6** (in *pl.*) *hist.* a corset esp. with whalebone, etc., stiffening, and laced. □ **has come** (or **is here**) **to stay** *colloq.* must be regarded as permanent. **stay the course** pursue a course of action or endure a struggle, etc., to the end. **stay one's hand** see HAND. **stay in** remain indoors or at home, esp. in school after hours as a punishment. **stay the night** remain until the next day. **stay put** *colloq.* remain where it is placed or where one is. **stay up** not go to bed (until late at night). □□ **stay·er** *n.* [AF *estai-* stem of OF *ester* f. L *stare* stand: sense 5 f. OF *estaye(r)* prop, formed as STAY[2]]

stay[2] /stay/ *n. & v.* ● *n.* **1** *Naut.* a rope or guy supporting a mast, spar, flagstaff, etc. **2** a tie-piece in an aircraft, etc. ● *v.tr.* **1** support (a mast, etc.) by stays. **2** put (a ship) on another tack. □ **be in stays** (of a sailing ship) be head to the wind with sails shaking while tacking. **miss stays** fail to be in stays. [OE *stæg* be firm, f. Gmc]

stay-at-home *adj. & n.* ● *adj.* remaining habitually at home. ● *n.* a person who does this.

stay·ing pow·er *n.* endurance; stamina.

stay·sail /stáysayl, stáysəl/ *n.* a triangular fore-and-aft sail extended on a stay.

STD *abbr.* **1** Doctor of Sacred Theology. **2** sexually transmitted disease. [sense 1 f. L *Sanctae Theologiae Doctor*]

std. *abbr.* standard.

stead /sted/ *n.* □ **in a person's** (or **thing's**) **stead** as a substitute; instead of him or her or it. **stand a person in good stead** be advantageous or serviceable to him or her. [OE *stede* f. Gmc]

stead·fast /stédfast/ *adj.* constant; firm; unwavering. □□ **stead·fast·ly** *adv.* **stead·fast·ness** *n.* [OE *stedefæst* (as STEAD, FAST[1])]

stead·ing /stéding/ *n.* esp. *Brit.* a farmstead.

stead·y /stédee/ *adj., v., adv., int., & n.* ● *adj.* (**stead·i·er**, **stead·i·est**) **1** firmly fixed or supported or standing or balanced; not tottering, rocking, or wavering. **2** done or operating or happening in a uniform and regular manner (*a steady pace; a steady increase*). **3 a** constant in mind or conduct; not changeable. **b** persistent. **4** (of a person) serious and dependable in behavior; of industrious and temperate habits; safe; cautious. **5** regular; established (*a steady girlfriend*). **6** accurately directed; not faltering; controlled (*a steady hand; a steady eye; steady nerves*). **7** (of a ship) on course and upright. ● *v.tr. & intr.* (**·ies**, **·ied**) make or become steady (*steady the boat*). ● *adv.* steadily (*hold it steady*). ● *int.* as a command or warning to take care. ● *n.* (*pl.* **·ies**) *colloq.* a regular boyfriend or girlfriend. □ **go steady** (often foll. by *with*) *colloq.* have as a regular boyfriend or girlfriend. **steady down** become steady. **steady on!** *Brit.* a call to take care. □□ **stead·i·er** *n.* **stead·i·ly** *adv.* **stead·i·ness** *n.* [STEAD = place, + -Y[1]]

stead·y-go·ing *adj.* staid; sober.

stead·y state *n.* an unvarying condition, esp. in a physical process, e.g., of the universe having no beginning and no end.

steak /stayk/ *n.* **1** a thick slice of meat (esp. beef) or fish, often cut for grilling, frying, etc. **2** beef cut for stewing or braising. [ME f. ON *steik* rel. to *steikja* roast on spit, *stikna* be roasted]

steak house *n.* a restaurant specializing in serving beefsteaks.

steak knife *n.* a table knife with a serrated steel blade for cutting steak.

steal /steel/ *v. & n.* ● *v.* (*past* **stole** /stōl/; *past part.* **sto·len** /stólən/) **1** *tr.* (also *absol.*) **a** take (another person's property) illegally. **b** take (property, etc.) without right or permission, esp. in secret with the intention of not returning it. **2** *tr.* obtain surreptitiously or by surprise (*stole a kiss*). **3** *tr.* **a** gain insidiously or artfully. **b** (often foll. by *away*) win or get possession of (a person's affections, etc.), esp. insidiously (*stole her heart away*). **4** *intr.* (foll. by *in, out, away, up,* etc.) **a** move, esp. silently or stealthily (*stole out of the room*). **b** (of a sound, etc.) become gradually perceptible. **5** *tr.* **a** (in various sports) gain (a run, the ball, etc.) surreptitiously or by luck. **b** *Baseball* run to (a base) while the pitcher is in the act of delivery. ● *n.* **1** *colloq.* the act or an instance of stealing or theft. **2** *colloq.* an unexpectedly easy task or good bargain. □ **steal a march on** get an advantage over by surreptitious means; anticipate. **steal the show** outshine other performers, esp. unexpectedly. **steal a person's thunder** use another person's words, ideas, etc., without permission and without giving credit. □□ **steal·er** *n.* (also in *comb.*). **steal·ing** *n.* [OE *stelan* f. Gmc]

stealth /stelth/ *n. & adj.* ● *n.* secrecy; a secret procedure. ● *adj. Mil. Aeron.* of an aircraft design intended to avoid detection by radar. □ **by stealth** surreptitiously. [ME f. OE (as STEAL, -TH[2])]

stealth·y /stélthee/ *adj.* (**stealth·i·er**, **stealth·i·est**) **1** (of an action) done with stealth; proceeding imperceptibly. **2** (of a person or thing) acting or moving with stealth. □□ **stealth·i·ly** *adv.* **stealth·i·ness** *n.*

steam /steem/ *n. & v.* ● *n.* **1 a** the gas into which water is changed by boiling, used as a source of power by virtue of its expansion of volume. **b** a mist of liquid particles of water produced by the condensation of this gas. **2** any similar vapor. **3 a** energy or power provided by a steam engine or other machine. **b** *colloq.* power or energy generally. **4** repressed or pent up feelings, etc. ● *v.* **1** *tr.* **a** cook (food) in steam. **b** soften or make pliable (lumber, etc.) or otherwise treat with steam. **2** *intr.* give off steam or other vapor, esp. visibly. **3** *intr.* **a** move under steam power (*the ship steamed down the river*). **b** (foll. by *ahead, away,* etc.) *colloq.* proceed or travel fast or with vigor. **4** *tr. & intr.* (usu. foll. by *up*) **a** cover or become covered with condensed steam. **b** (as **steamed up** *adj.*) *colloq.* angry or excited. **5** *tr.* (foll. by *open*, etc.) apply steam to the adhesive of (a sealed envelope) to get it open. □ **get up steam 1** generate enough power to work a steam engine. **2** work oneself into an energetic or angry state. **let** (or **blow**) **off steam** relieve one's pent up feelings or energy. **run out of steam** lose one's impetus or energy. **under one's own steam** without assistance; unaided. [OE *stēam* f. Gmc]

steam age *n.* the era when trains were drawn by steam locomotives.

steam bath *n.* a room, etc., filled with steam for bathing in.

steam·boat /steembōt/ *n.* a boat propelled by a steam engine.

steam boil·er *n.* a vessel (in a steam engine, etc.) in which water is boiled to generate steam.

steam en·gine *n.* **1** an engine which uses the expansion or rapid condensation of steam to generate power. **2** a locomotive powered by this.

steam·er /steemər/ *n.* **1** a person or thing that steams. **2** a vessel propelled by steam, esp. a ship. **3** a vessel in which things are steamed, esp. cooked by steam.

steam·er rug *n.* a small blanket used as a covering by passengers seated in deck chairs on a ship, etc.

steam gauge *n.* a pressure gauge attached to a steam boiler.

steam heat *n.* the warmth given out by steam-heated radiators, etc.

steam i·ron *n.* an electric iron that emits steam from holes in its flat surface, to improve its ironing ability.

steam or·gan *n.* a pipe organ driven by a steam engine and played by means of a keyboard or a system of punched cards.

steam pow·er *n.* the force of steam applied to machinery, etc.

steam·roll·er /steemrōlər/ *n. & v.* **•** *n.* **1** a heavy slow-moving vehicle with a roller, used to flatten new-made roads. **2** a crushing power or force. **•** *v.tr.* **1** crush forcibly or indiscriminately. **2** (foll. by *through*) force (a measure, etc.) through a legislature by overriding opposition.

steam·ship /steemship/ *n.* a ship propelled by a steam engine.

steam shov·el *n.* an excavator powered by steam.

steam train *n.* a train driven by a steam engine.

steam tur·bine *n.* a turbine in which a high-velocity jet of steam rotates a bladed disk or drum.

steam·y /steemee/ *adj.* (**steam·i·er, steam·i·est**) **1** like or full of steam. **2** *colloq.* erotic; salacious. □□ **steam·i·ly** *adv.* **steam·i·ness** *n.*

ste·ar·ic /steerik, steeárik/ *adj.* derived from stearin. □ **stearic acid** a solid saturated fatty acid obtained from animal or vegetable fats. □□ **ste·a·rate** /–rayt/ *n.* [F *stéarique* f. Gk *stear steatos* tallow]

ste·a·rin /steerin/ *n.* **1** a glyceryl ester of stearic acid, esp. in the form of a white crystalline constituent of tallow, etc. **2** a mixture of fatty acids used in candle making. [F *stéarine* f. Gk *stear steatos* tallow]

ste·a·tite /steeətīt/ *n.* a soapstone or other impure form of talc. □□ **ste·a·tit·ic** /–titik/ *adj.* [L *steatitis* f. Gk *steatītēs* f. *stear steatos* tallow]

ste·at·o·py·gi·a /steeátəpíjeeə, steeátə–/ *n.* an excess of fat on the buttocks. □□ **ste·at·o·py·gous** /–pígəs, –tópigəs/ *adj.* [mod.L (as STEATITE + Gk *pugē* rump)]

steed /steed/ *n. archaic* or *poet.* a horse, esp. a fast powerful one. [OE *stēda* stallion, rel. to STUD[2]]

steel /steel/ *n., adj., & v.* **•** *n.* **1** any of various alloys of iron and carbon with other elements increasing strength and malleability, much used for making tools, weapons, etc., and capable of being tempered to many different degrees of hardness. **2** hardness of character; strength; firmness (*nerves of steel*). **3 a** a rod of steel, usu. roughened and tapering, on which knives are sharpened. **b** a strip of steel for expanding a skirt or stiffening a corset. **c** a piece of steel used with flint for starting fires. **4** (not in *pl.*) *literary* a sword, lance, etc. (*foemen worthy of their steel*). **•** *adj.* **1** made of steel. **2** like or having the characteristics of steel. **•** *v.tr. & refl.* harden or make resolute (*steeled myself for a shock*). [OE *stȳle, stēli* f. Gmc, rel. to STAY[2]]

steel band *n.* a group of usu. W. Indian musicians with percussion instruments made from oil drums.

steel-clad *adj.* wearing armor.

steel en·grav·ing *n.* the process of engraving on or an impression taken from a steel-coated copper plate.

steel·head /steelhed/ *n.* a large N. American rainbow trout.

steel wool *n.* an abrasive substance consisting of a mass of fine steel shavings.

steel·work /steelwərk/ *n.* articles of steel.

steel·works /steelwərks/ *n.pl.* (usu. treated as *sing.*) a place where steel is manufactured. □□ **steel·work·er** *n.*

steel·y /steelee/ *adj.* (**steel·i·er, steel·i·est**) **1** of, or hard as, steel. **2** inflexibly severe; cold; ruthless (*steely composure; steely-eyed glance*). □□ **steel·i·ness** *n.*

steel·yard /steelyaard/ *n.* a kind of balance with a short arm to take the item to be weighed and a long graduated arm along which a weight is moved until it balances.

steen·bok /steenbok, stáyn–/ *n.* an African dwarf antelope, *Raphicerus campestris*. [Du. f. *steen* STONE + *bok* BUCK[1]]

steep[1] /steep/ *adj. & n.* **•** *adj.* **1** sloping sharply; almost perpendicular (*a steep hill; steep stairs*). **2** (of a rise or fall) rapid (*a steep drop in stock prices*). **3** (*predic.*) *colloq.* **a** (of a demand, price, etc.) exorbitant; unreasonable (esp. *a bit steep*). **b** (of a story, etc.) exaggerated; incredible. **•** *n.* a steep slope; a precipice. □□ **steep·en** *v.intr. & tr.* **steep·ish** *adj.* **steep·ly** *adv.* **steep·ness** *n.* [OE *stēap* f. WG, rel. to STOOP[1]]

steep[2] /steep/ *v. & n.* **•** *v.tr.* soak or bathe in liquid. **•** *n.* **1** the act or process of steeping. **2** the liquid for steeping. □ **steep in 1** pervade or imbue with (*steeped in misery*). **2** make deeply acquainted with (a subject, etc.) (*steeped in the classics*). [ME f. OE f. Gmc (as STOUP)]

stee·ple /steepəl/ *n.* a tall tower, esp. one surmounted by a spire, above the roof of a church. □□ **stee·pled** *adj.* [OE *stēpel stȳpel* f. Gmc (as STEEP[1])]

stee·ple·chase /steepəlchays/ *n.* **1** a horse race (orig. with a steeple as the goal) across the countryside or on a racetrack with ditches, hedges, etc., to jump. **2** a cross-country foot race. □□ **stee·ple·chas·er** *n.* **stee·ple·chas·ing** *n.*

stee·ple-crowned *adj.* (of a hat) with a tall pointed crown.

stee·ple·jack /steepəljak/ *n.* a person who climbs tall chimneys, steeples, etc., to do repairs, etc.

steer[1] /steer/ *v. & n.* **•** *v.* **1 a** guide (a vehicle, aircraft, etc.) by a wheel, etc. **b** guide (a vessel) by a rudder or helm. **2** *intr.* guide a vessel or vehicle in a specified direction (*tried to steer left*). **3** *tr.* direct (one's course). **4** *intr.* direct one's course in a specified direction (*steered for the railroad station*). **5** *tr.* guide the movement or trend of (*steered them into the garden; steered the conversation away from that subject*). **•** *n.* steering; guidance. □ **steer clear of** take care to avoid. □□ **steer·a·ble** *adj.* **steer·er** *n.* **steer·ing** *n.* (esp. in senses 1, 2 of *v.*). [OE *stieran* f. Gmc]

steer[2] /steer/ *n.* a young male bovine animal castrated before sexual maturity, esp. one raised for beef. [OE *stēor* f. Gmc]

steer·age /steerij/ *n.* **1** the act of steering. **2** the effect of the helm on a ship. **3** the part of a ship allotted to passengers traveling at the cheapest rate. **4** *hist.* (in a warship) quarters assigned to midshipmen, etc., just forward of the wardroom.

steer·ing col·umn *n.* the shaft or column which connects the steering wheel, handlebars, etc., of a vehicle to the rest of the steering mechanism.

steer·ing com·mit·tee *n.* a committee deciding the order of dealing with business, or priorities and the general course of operations.

steer·ing wheel *n.* a wheel by which a vehicle, etc., is steered.

steers·man /steerzmən/ *n.* (*pl.* **·men**) a helmsman.

steeve[1] /steev/ *n. & v. Naut.* **•** *n.* the angle of the bowsprit in relation to the horizontal. **•** *v.* **1** *intr.* (of a bowsprit) make an angle with the horizontal. **2** *tr.* cause (the bowsprit) to do this. [17th c.: orig. unkn.]

steeve[2] /steev/ *n. & v. Naut.* **•** *n.* a long spar used in stowing cargo. **•** *v.tr.* stow with a steeve. [ME f. OF *estiver* or Sp. *estivar* f. L *stipare* pack tight]

steg·o·sau·rus /stégəsáwrəs/ *n.* any of a group of plant-eating dinosaurs with a double row of large bony plates along the spine. [mod. L f. Gk *stegē* covering + *sauros* lizard]

stein /stīn/ *n.* a large earthenware, pewter, etc., mug, esp. for beer. [G, lit. 'stone']

stein·bock /stínbok/ *n.* **1** an ibex native to the Alps. **2** = STEENBOK. [G f. *Stein* STONE + *Bock* BUCK[1]]

ste·la /steelə/ *n.* (*pl.* **ste·lae** /–lee/) *Archaeol.* an upright slab or pillar usu. with an inscription and sculpture, esp. as a gravestone. [L f. Gk (as STELE)]

ste·le /steel, steelee/ *n.* **1** *Bot.* the axial cylinder of vascular tissue in the stem and roots of most plants. **2** *Archaeol.* = STELA. □□ **ste·lar** *adj.* [Gk *stēlē* standing block]

stel·lar /stélər/ *adj.* **1** of or relating to a star or stars. **2** having the quality of a star entertainer or performer; leading; outstanding. □□ **stel·li·form** *adj.* [LL *stellaris* f. L *stella* star]

stel·late /stélayt/ *adj.* (also **stel·lat·ed** /stélaytid/) **1** arranged like a star; radiating. **2** *Bot.* (of leaves) surrounding the stem in a whorl. [L *stellatus* f. *stella* star]

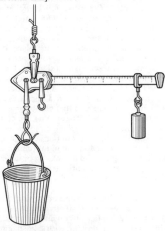

steelyard

stel•lu•lar /stélyələr/ *adj.* shaped like, or set with, small stars. [LL *stellula* dimin. of L *stella* star]

stem[1] /stem/ *n. & v.* • *n.* **1** the main body or stalk of a plant or shrub, usu. rising into light, but occasionally subterranean. **2** the stalk supporting a fruit, flower, or leaf, and attaching it to a larger branch, twig, or stalk. **3** a stem-shaped part of an object: **a** the slender part of a wineglass between the body and the foot. **b** the tube of a tobacco pipe. **c** a vertical stroke in a letter or musical note. **d** the winding shaft of a watch. **4** *Gram.* the root or main part of a noun, verb, etc., to which inflections are added; the part that appears unchanged throughout the cases and derivatives of a noun, persons of a tense, etc. **5** *Naut.* the main upright timber or metal piece at the bow of a ship to which the ship's sides are joined at the fore end (*from stem to stern*). **6** a line of ancestry, branch of a family, etc. (*descended from an ancient stem*). **7** (in full **drill stem**) a rotating rod, cylinder, etc., used in drilling. • *v.* **1** *intr.* (foll. by *from*) spring or originate from (*stems from a desire to win*). **2** *tr.* remove the stem or stems from (fruit, tobacco, etc.). **3** *tr.* (of a vessel, etc.) hold its own or make headway against (the tide, etc.). □□ **stem•less** *adj.* **stem•let** *n.* **stem•like** *adj.* **stemmed** *adj.* (also in *comb.*). [OE *stemn, stefn* f. Gmc, rel. to STAND]

stem[2] /stem/ *v. & n.* • *v.* (**stemmed, stem•ming**) **1** *tr.* check or stop. **2** *tr.* dam up (a stream, etc.). **3** *intr.* slide the tail of one ski or both skis outwards usu. in order to turn or slow down. • *n.* an act of stemming on skis. [ON *stemma* f. Gmc: cf. STAMMER]

stem cell *n. Biol.* an undifferentiated cell from which specialized cells develop.

stem•ma /stémə/ *n.* (*pl.* **stem•ma•ta** /stémətə/) **1** a family tree; a pedigree. **2** the line of descent, e.g., of variant texts of a work. **3** *Zool.* a simple eye; a facet of a compound eye. [L f. Gk *stemma* wreath f. *stephō* wreathe]

stem stitch *n.* an embroidery stitch used for narrow stems, etc.

stem turn *n.* a turn on skis made by stemming with one ski.

stem•ware /stémwair/ *n.* glasses with stems.

stem-wind•er /stémwíndər/ *n.* **1** a watch wound by turning a head on the end of a stem rather than by a key. **2** a rousing political speech.

stench /stench/ *n.* an offensive or foul smell. [OE *stenc* smell f. Gmc, rel. to STINK]

stench trap *n.* a trap in a sewer, etc., to prevent the upward passage of gas.

sten•cil /sténsil/ *n. & v.* • *n.* **1** a thin sheet of plastic, metal, card, etc., in which a pattern or lettering is cut, used to produce a corresponding pattern on the surface beneath it by applying ink, paint, etc. **2** the pattern, lettering, etc., produced by a stencil. **3** a waxed sheet, etc., from which a stencil is made by means of a typewriter. • *v.tr.* (**sten•ciled** or **sten•cilled, sten•cil•ing** or **sten•cil•ling**) **1** (often foll. by *on*) produce (a pattern) with a stencil. **2** decorate or mark (a surface) in this way. [ME f. OF *estanceler* sparkle, cover with stars, f. *estencele* spark ult. f. L *scintilla*]

Sten gun /sten/ *n.* a type of lightweight submachine gun. [*S* and *T* (the initials of the inventors' surnames, Shepherd and Turpin) + *–en* after BREN]

sten•o /sténō/ *n.* (*pl.* **•os**) *colloq.* a stenographer. [abbr.]

ste•nog•ra•phy /stənógrəfee/ *n.* shorthand or the art of writing this. □□ **ste•nog•ra•pher** *n.* **sten•o•graph•ic** /sténəgráfik/ *adj.* [Gk *stenos* narrow + –GRAPHY]

ste•no•sis /stinōsis/ *n. Med.* the abnormal narrowing of a passage in the body. □□ **ste•not•ic** /–nótik/ *adj.* [mod.L f. Gk *stenōsis* narrowing f. *stenoō* make narrow f. *stenos* narrow]

sten•o•type /sténətīp/ *n.* **1** a machine like a typewriter for recording speech in syllables or phonemes. **2** a symbol or the symbols used in this process. □□ **sten•o•typ•ist** *n.* [STENOGRAPHY + TYPE]

Sten•tor /sténtər/ *n.* (also **stentor**) a person with a powerful voice. □□ **sten•to•ri•an** /–táwreeən/ *adj.* [Gk *Stentōr*, herald in the Trojan War (Homer, *Iliad* v. 785)]

step /step/ *n. & v.* • *n.* **1 a** the complete movement of one leg in walking or running (*took a step forward*). **b** the distance covered by this. **c** (in *pl.*) the course followed by a person in walking, etc. **2** a unit of movement in dancing. **3** a measure taken, esp. one of several in a course of action (*took steps to prevent it; considered it a wise step*). **4 a** a surface on which a foot is placed on ascending or descending a stair or tread. **b** a block of stone or other platform before a door, altar, etc. **c** the rung of a ladder. **d** a notch cut for a foot in climbing ice. **e** a platform, etc., in a vehicle provided for ease in stepping up or down. **5** a short distance (*only a step from my door*). **6** the sound or mark made by a foot in walking, etc. (*heard a step on the stairs*). **7** the manner of walking, etc., as seen or heard (*know her by her step*). **8 a** a degree in the scale of promotion, advancement, or precedence. **b** one of a series of fixed points on a payscale, etc. **9 a** stepping (or not stepping) in time with others or music (esp. in or out of step). **b** the state of conforming to what others are doing (*refuses to keep step with the team*). **10** (in *pl.*) (also **pair of steps** *sing.*) *Brit.* = STEPLADDER. **11** *Mus.* a melodic interval of one degree of the scale, i.e. a tone or semitone. **12** *Naut.* a block, socket, or platform supporting a mast. • *v.* (**stepped, step•ping**) **1** *intr.* lift and set down one's foot or alternate feet in walking. **2** *intr.* come

or go in a specified direction by stepping. **3** *intr.* make progress in a specified way (*stepped into a new job*). **4** *tr.* (foll. by *off, out*) measure (distance) by stepping. **5** *tr.* perform (a dance). **6** *tr. Naut.* set up (a mast) in a step. □ **in a person's (foot)steps** following a person's example. **step down 1** resign from a position, etc. **2** *Electr.* decrease (voltage) by using a transformer. **step in 1** enter a room, house, etc. **2 a** intervene to help or hinder. **b** act as a substitute. **step on it** (or **on the gas**) *colloq.* **1** accelerate a motor vehicle. **2** hurry up. **step out 1** leave a room, house, etc. **2** be active socially. **3** take large steps. **step this way** a deferential formula meaning ' follow me.' **step up 1** increase; intensify (*must step up production*). **2** *Electr.* increase (voltage) using a transformer. **take a step** (or **steps**) implement a course of action leading to a specific result; proceed. **turn one's steps** go in a specified direction. **watch one's step** be careful. □□ **step•like** *adj.* **stepped** *adj.* **step•wise** *adv. & adj.* [OE *stæpe, stepe* (n.), *stæppan, steppan* (v.), f. Gmc]

step- /step/ *comb. form* denoting a relationship like the one specified but resulting from a parent's remarriage. [OE *stēop-* orphan-]

step aer•o•bics *n.* an exercise regimen using a step-climbing motion.

step-broth•er /stépbruthər/ *n.* a son of a stepparent by a marriage other than with one's father or mother.

step-by-step *adv.* gradually; cautiously; by stages or degrees.

step-child /stépchīld/ *n.* a child of one's husband or wife by a previous marriage. [OE *stēopcild* (as STEP-, CHILD)]

step cut *adj.* (of a gem) cut in straight facets around the center.

step-daugh•ter /stépdawtər/ *n.* a female stepchild. [OE *stēopdohtor* (as STEP-, DAUGHTER)]

step-fa•ther /stépfaathər/ *n.* a male stepparent. [OE *stēopfæder* (as STEP-, FATHER)]

steph•a•no•tis /stéfənótis/ *n.* any climbing tropical plant of the genus *Stephanotis*, cultivated for its fragrant waxy usu. white flowers. [mod.L f. Gk, = fit for a wreath f. *stephanos* wreath]

step-in *adj. & n. attrib.adj.* (of a garment or shoe) put on by being stepped into without unfastening. • *n.* such a garment or shoe.

step-lad•der /stépladər/ *n.* a short ladder with flat steps and a folding support, used without being leaned against a surface.

step-moth•er /stépmuthər/ *n.* a female stepparent. [OE *stēopmōdor* (as STEP-, MOTHER)]

step-par•ent /stép-pairənt/ *n.* a mother's or father's later husband or wife.

steppe /step/ *n.* a level grassy unforested plain, esp. in SE Europe and Siberia. [Russ *step'*]

step•ping-stone *n.* **1** a raised stone, usu. one of a set in a stream, muddy place, etc., to help in crossing. **2** a means or stage of progress to an end.

step-sis•ter /stépsistər/ *n.* a daughter of a stepparent by a marriage other than with one's father or mother.

step-son /stépsun/ *n.* a male stepchild. [OE *stēopsunu* (as STEP-, SON)]

step stool *n.* a stool with usu. folding steps used to reach high kitchen shelves, etc.

-ster /stər/ *suffix* denoting a person engaged in or associated with a particular activity or thing (*gangster; youngster*). [OE *–estre*, etc. f. Gmc]

ste•ra•di•an /stəráydeeən/ *n.* a solid angle equal to the angle at the center of a sphere subtended by a part of the surface equal in area to the square of the radius. ¶ Abbr.: **sr.** [Gk *stereos* solid + RADIAN]

ster•co•ra•ceous /stórkəráyshəs/ *adj.* **1** consisting of or resembling dung or feces. **2** living in dung. [L *stercus –oris* dung]

stere /steer/ *n.* a unit of volume equal to one cubic meter. [F *stère* f. Gk *stereos* solid]

ster•e•o /stéreeō, stéereeō/ *n. & adj.* • *n.* (*pl.* **•os**) **1 a** a stereophonic record player, tape recorder, etc. **b** = *stereophony* (see STEREOPHONIC). **2** = STEREOSCOPE. • *adj.* **1** = STEREOPHONIC. **2** = *stereoscopic* (see STEREOSCOPE) [abbr.]

stereo- /stéreeō, stéereeō/ *comb. form* solid; having three dimensions. [Gk *stereos* solid]

ster•e•o•bate /stéreeəbayt, stéereeə–/ *n. Archit.* a solid mass of masonry as a foundation for a building. [F *stéréobate* f. L *stereobata* f. Gk *stereobatēs* (as STEREO-, *bainō* walk)]

ster•e•o•chem•is•try /stéreeōkémistree, stéereeō–/ *n.* the branch of chemistry dealing with the three-dimensional arrangement of atoms in molecules.

ster•e•og•ra•phy /stéreeógrəfee, stéeree–/ *n.* the art of depicting solid bodies in a plane.

ster•e•o•i•so•mer /stéreeō-ísəmər, stéereeō–/ *n. Chem.* any of two or more compounds differing only in their spatial arrangement of atoms.

ster•e•om•e•try /stéreeómitree, stéeree–/ *n.* the measurement of solid bodies.

ster•e•o•phon•ic /stéreeōfónik, stéereeō–/ *adj.* (of sound reproduction) using two or more channels so that the sound has the effect of being distributed and of coming from more than one source. □□ **ster·e·o·phon·i·cal·ly** *adv.* **ster·e·oph·o·ny** /–reeófənee/ *n.*

ster·e·o·scope /stéreeəskōp, steéreeə–/ *n.* a device by which two photographs of the same object taken at slightly different angles are viewed together, giving an impression of depth and solidity as in ordinary human vision. □□ **ster·e·o·scop·ic** /–skópik/ *adj.* **ster·e·o·scop·i·cal·ly** *adv.* **ster·e·os·co·py** /–reeóskəpee/ *n.*

ster·e·o·type /stéreeətīp, steéree–/ *n. & v.* ● *n.* **1 a** a person or thing that conforms to an unjustifiably fixed, usu. standardized, mental picture. **b** such an impression or attitude. **2** a printing plate cast from a mold of composed type. ● *v.tr.* **1** (esp. as **stereotyped** *adj.*) standardize; cause to conform to a type. **2 a** print from a stereotype. **b** make a stereotype of. □□ **ster·e·o·typ·ic** /–típik/ *adj.* **ster·e·o·typ·i·cal** *adj.* **ster·e·o·typ·i·cal·ly** *adv.* **ster·e·o·typ·y** *n.* [F *stéréotype* (adj.) (as STEREO-, TYPE)]

ster·ic /stérik, steér–/ *adj.* *Chem.* relating to the spatial arrangement of atoms in a molecule, esp. as it affects chemical reactions. [irreg. f. Gk *stereos* solid]

ster·ic hin·drance *n.* the inhibiting of a chemical reaction by the obstruction of reacting atoms.

ster·ile /st érəl, –īl/ *adj.* **1** not able to produce seeds or fruit or (of an animal) young; barren. **2** unfruitful; unproductive (*sterile discussions*). **3** free from living microorganisms, etc. **4** lacking originality or emotive force; mentally barren. □□ **ster·ile·ly** *adv.* **ste·ril·i·ty** /stərílitee/ *n.* [F *stérile* or L *sterilis*]

ster·i·lize /stérilīz/ *v.tr.* **1** make sterile. **2** deprive of the power of reproduction. □□ **ster·i·liz·a·ble** *adj.* **ster·i·li·za·tion** *n.* **ster·i·liz·er** *n.*

ster·let /stárlit/ *n.* a small sturgeon, *Acipenser ruthenus*, found in the Caspian Sea area and yielding fine caviar. [Russ. *sterlyad '*]

ster·ling /stárling/ *adj. & n.* ● *adj.* **1** of or in British money (*pound sterling*). **2** (of a coin or precious metal) genuine; of standard value or purity. **3** (of a person or qualities, etc.) of solid worth; genuine; reliable (*sterling work*). ● *n.* **1** = British silver. **2** British money (*paid in sterling*). □□ **ster·ling·ness** *n.* [prob. f. late OE *steorling* (unrecorded) f. *steorra* star + –LING[1] (because some early Norman pennies bore a small star): recorded earlier in OF *esterlin*]

ster·ling ar·e·a *n.* a group of countries with currencies tied to British sterling and holding reserves mainly in sterling.

ster·ling sil·ver *n.* silver of 92$\frac{1}{2}$% purity.

stern[1] /stərn/ *adj.* severe; grim; strict; enforcing discipline or submission (*a stern expression; stern treatment*). □□ **stern·ly** *adv.* **stern·ness** *n.* [OE *styrne*, prob. f. a Gmc root = be rigid]

stern[2] /stərn/ *n.* **1** the rear part of a ship or boat. **2** any rear part. □□ **sterned** *adj.* (in *comb.*). **stern·most** *adj.* **stern·ward** *adj. & adv.* **stern·wards** *adv.* [ME prob. f. ON *stjórn* steering f. *stýra* STEER[1]]

ster·nal rib /stárnəl rib/ *n.* = TRUE RIB.

stern fore·most *adj.* moving backward.

stern on *adv.* with the stern presented.

ster·num /stárnəm/ *n.* (*pl.* **ster·nums** or **sterna** /–nə/) the breastbone. □□ **ster·nal** *adj.* [mod.L f. Gk *sternon* chest]

ster·nu·ta·tion /stárnyŭtáyshən/ *n.* *Med.* or *joc.* a sneeze or attack of sneezing. [L *sternutatio* f. *sternutare* frequent. of *sternuere* sneeze]

ster·nu·ta·tor /stárnyətaytər/ *n.* a substance, esp. poison gas, that causes nasal irritation, violent coughing, etc. □□ **ster·nu·ta·to·ry** /–nyŏŏtətawree/ *adj. & n.* (*pl.* **·ries**)

stern·way /stárnway/ *n.* *Naut.* a backward motion or impetus of a ship.

ste·roid /steéroyd, stér–/ *n.* *Biochem.* any of a group of organic compounds with a characteristic structure of four rings of carbon atoms, including many hormones, alkaloids, and vitamins. □□ **ste·roi·dal** /–róyd'l/ *adj.* [STEROL + –OID]

ste·rol /steérawl, –ol, stér–/ *n.* *Chem.* any of a group of naturally occurring steroid alcohols. [CHOLESTEROL, ERGOSTEROL, etc.]

ster·to·rous /stártərəs/ *adj.* (of breathing, etc.) labored and noisy; sounding like snoring. □□ **ster·to·rous·ly** *adv.* **ster·to·rous·ness** *n.* [*stertor*, mod.L f. L *stertere* snore]

stet /stet/ *v.* (**stet·ted**, **stet·ting**) **1** *intr.* (usu. as an instruction written on a proof, etc.) ignore or cancel the correction or alteration; let the original form stand. **2** *tr.* write 'stet' against; cancel the correction of (*printed word stand*) [L, = let it stand, f. *stare* stand]

steth·o·scope /stéthəskōp/ *n.* an instrument used in listening to the action of the heart, lungs, etc., usu. consisting

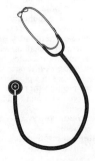

Stethoscope

of a circular piece placed against the chest, with tubes leading to earpieces. □□ **steth·o·scop·ic** /–skópik/ *adj.* **steth·o·scop·i·cal·ly** *adv.* **ste·thos·co·pist** /stethóskəpist/ *n.* **ste·thos·co·py** /stethóskəpee/ *n.* [F *stéthoscope* f. Gk *stēthos* breast: see –SCOPE]

Stet·son /stétsən/ *n.* *Trademark* a felt hat with a very wide brim and a high crown. [J. B. *Stetson*, Amer. hat maker d. 1906]

ste·ve·dore /steévədawr/ *n.* a person employed in loading and unloading ships. [Sp. *estivador* f. *estivar* stow a cargo f. L *stipare*: see STEEVE[2]]

Ste·ven·graph /steévəngraf/ *n.* a colorful woven silk picture. [T. *Stevens*, Engl. weaver d. 1888, whose firm made them]

stew[1] /stoo, styoo/ *v. & n.* ● *v.* **1** *tr. & intr.* cook by long simmering in a closed pot with liquid. **2** *intr.* *colloq.* be oppressed by heat or humidity, esp. in a confined space. **3** *intr.* *colloq.* **a** suffer prolonged embarrassment, anxiety, etc. **b** (foll. by *over*) fret or be anxious. **4** *tr.* *Brit.* make (tea) bitter or strong with prolonged brewing. **5** *tr.* (as **stewed** *adj.*) *colloq.* drunk. **6** *intr.* (often foll. by *over*) *colloq.* study hard. ● *n.* **1** a dish of stewed meat, etc. **2** *colloq.* an agitated or angry state (*be in a stew*). **3** *archaic* **a** a hot bath. **b** (in *pl.*) a brothel. □ **stew in one's own juice** be left to suffer the consequences of one's own actions. [ME f. OF *estuve, estuver* prob. ult. f. EX-[1] + Gk *tuphos* smoke, steam]

stew[2] /stoo, styoo/ *n.* *Brit.* **1** an artificial oyster bed. **2** a pond or large tank for keeping fish for eating. [ME f. F *estui* f. *estoier* confine ult. f. L *studium*: see STUDY]

stew·ard /stoóərd, styoó–/ *n. & v.* ● *n.* **1** a passengers' attendant on a ship or aircraft or train. **2** an official appointed to keep order or supervise arrangements at a meeting or show or demonstration, etc. **3** = SHOP STEWARD. **4** a person responsible for supplies of food, etc., for a college or club, etc. **5** a person employed to manage another's property. **6** *Brit.* the title of several officers of the government or the royal household (*Lord High Steward*). ● *v.tr.* act as a steward of (*will steward the meeting*). □□ **stew·ard·ship** *n.* [OE *stīweard* f. *stig* prob. = house, hall + *weard* WARD]

stew·ard·ess /stoóərdis, styoó–/ *n.* a female steward, esp. on a ship or aircraft.

stg. *abbr.* sterling.

stick[1] /stik/ *n.* **1 a** a short slender branch or length of wood broken or cut from a tree. **b** this trimmed for use as a support or weapon. **2** a thin rod or spike of wood, etc., for a particular purpose. **3 a** an implement used to propel the ball in hockey or polo, etc. **b** (in *pl.*) the raising of the stick above the shoulder in field hockey. **4** a gear lever, esp. in a motor vehicle. **5** the lever controlling the ailerons and elevators in an airplane. **6** a conductor's baton. **7 a** a slender piece of a thing, e.g., celery, dynamite, deodorant, etc. **b** a number of bombs or paratroops released rapidly from aircraft. **8** (often prec. by *the*) punishment, esp. by beating. **9** *esp. Brit.* *colloq.* adverse criticism; censure; reproof (*took a lot of stick*). **10** *colloq.* a piece of wood as part of a house or furniture (*a few sticks of furniture*). **11** *colloq.* a person, esp. one who is dull or unsociable (*a funny old stick*). **12** (in *pl.*; prec. by *the*) *colloq.* remote rural areas. **13** (in *pl.*) *Austral. sl.* goalposts. **14** *Naut. sl.* a mast or spar. □ **up sticks** *Brit. colloq.* go to live elsewhere. □□ **stick·less** *adj.* **stick·like** *adj.* [OE *sticca* f. WG]

stick[2] /stik/ *v.* (*past* and *past part.* **stuck** /stuk/) **1** *tr.* (foll. by *in, into, through*) insert or thrust (a thing or its point) (*stuck a finger in my eye; stick a pin through it*). **2** *tr.* insert a pointed thing into; stab. **3** *tr. & intr.* (foll. by *in, into, on*, etc.) **a** fix or be fixed on a pointed thing. **b** fix or be fixed by or as by a pointed end. **4** *tr. & intr.* fix or become or remain fixed by or as by adhesive, etc. (*stick a label on it; the label won't stick*). **5** *intr.* endure; remain a continued impression (*the scene stuck in my mind; the name stuck*). **6** *intr.* lose or be deprived of the power of motion or action through adhesion or jamming or other impediment. **7** *colloq.* **a** *tr.* put in a specified position or place, esp. quickly or haphazardly (*stick them down anywhere*). **b** *intr.* remain in a place (*stuck indoors*). **8** *colloq.* **a** *intr.* (of an accusation, etc.) be convincing or regarded as valid (*could not make the charges stick*). **b** *tr.* (foll. by *on*) place the blame for (a thing) on (a person). **9** *tr. Brit. colloq.* endure; tolerate (*could not stick it any longer*). **10** *tr.* (foll. by *at*) *colloq.* persevere with. □ **be stuck for** be at a loss for or in need of. **be stuck on** *colloq.* be infatuated with. **be stuck with** *colloq.* be unable to get rid of or escape from; be permanently involved with. **get stuck in** (or **into**) *sl.* begin in earnest. **stick around** *colloq.* linger; remain at the same place. **stick at it** *colloq.* persevere. **stick at nothing** allow nothing, esp. no scruples, to deter one. **stick by** (or **with**) stay loyal or close to. **stick 'em up!** *colloq.* hands up! **stick fast** adhere or become firmly fixed or trapped in a position or place. **stick in one's gizzard** see GIZZARD. **stick in one's throat** be against one's principles. **stick it on** *Brit. sl.* **1** make high charges. **2** tell an exaggerated story. **stick it out** *colloq.* put up with or persevere with a burden, etc., to the end. **stick one's neck** (or **chin**) **out** expose oneself to censure, etc., by acting or speaking boldly. **stick out** protrude or cause to protrude or project (*stuck his tongue out; stick out your chest*). **stick out for** persist in demanding. **stick out a mile** (or **like a sore thumb**) *colloq.* be very obvious or incongruous. **stick pigs** engage in pigsticking. **stick shift** a manual automotive transmission with a shift lever on the vehicle's floor or steering column. **stick to 1** remain close to or fixed on or to. **2** remain faithful to. **3** keep to (a subject, etc.) (*stick to the point*). **stick to a person's fingers** *colloq.* (of money) be embezzled by a person. **stick together** *colloq.* become or remain united or mutually loyal. **stick to one's guns** see GUN. **stick to it** persevere. **stick to one's last** see LAST³. **stick up 1** be or make erect or protruding upwards. **2** fasten to an upright surface. **3** *colloq.* rob or threaten with a gun. **stick up for** support or defend or champion (a person or cause). **stick up to** be assertive in the face of; offer resistance to. **stick with** *colloq.* remain in touch with or faithful to; persevere with. □□ **stick·a·bil·i·ty** /stíkəbílitee/ *n.* [OE *stician* f. Gmc]

stick·ball /stíkbawl/ *n.* a form of baseball played with a stick or broom handle and a rubber ball.

stick·er /stíkər/ *n.* **1** an adhesive label or notice, etc. **2** a person or thing that sticks. **3** a persistent person.

stick·er price *n.* the full price of a new item, esp. the price listed on a sticker attached to a new automobile.

stick·er shock *n.* *colloq.* surprise at a higher-than-expected retail price.

stick·ing plas·ter *n.* *Brit.* an adhesive bandage for wounds, etc.

stick·ing point *n.* the limit of progress, agreement, etc.

stick in·sect *n.* any usu. wingless female insect of the family Phasmidae with a twiglike body.

stick-in-the-mud *n.* *colloq.* an unprogressive or old-fashioned person.

stick·le·back /stíkəlbak/ *n.* any small fish of the family Gasterosteidae with sharp spines along the back. [ME f. OE *sticel* thorn, sting + *bæc* BACK]

stickleback

stick·ler /stíklər/ *n.* (foll. by *for*) a person who insists on something (*a stickler for accuracy*). [obs. *stickle* be umpire, ME *stightle* control, frequent. of *stight* f. OE *stiht(i)an* set in order]

stick·pin /stíkpin/ *n.* an ornamental tiepin.

stick-up *n.* *colloq.* an armed robbery.

stick·y /stíkee/ *adj. & n.* ● *adj.* (**stick·i·er, stick·i·est**) **1** tending or intended to stick or adhere. **2** glutinous; viscous. **3** (of the weather) humid. **4** *colloq.* awkward or uncooperative; intransigent (*was very sticky about giving me leave*). **5** *colloq.* difficult; awkward (*a sticky problem*). **6** *Brit. colloq.* very unpleasant or painful (*came to a sticky end*). ● *n. colloq.* glue. □□ **stick·i·ly** *adv.* **stick·i·ness** *n.*

stick·y·beak /stíkeebeek/ *n. & v. Austral. & NZ sl.* ● *n.* an inquisitive person. ● *v.intr.* pry.

stick·y wick·et *n.* **1** *Cricket* a playing field that has been drying after rain and is difficult for the batsman. **2** *colloq.* difficult or awkward circumstances.

stiff /stif/ *adj. & n.* ● *adj.* **1** rigid; not flexible. **2** hard to bend or move or turn, etc.; not working freely. **3** hard to cope with; needing strength or effort (*a stiff test; a stiff climb*). **4** severe or strong (*a stiff breeze; a stiff penalty; stiff opposition*). **5** (of a person or manner) formal; constrained; lacking spontaneity. **6** (of a muscle or limb, etc., or a person affected by these) aching when used, owing to previous exertion, injury, etc. **7** (of an alcoholic or medicinal drink) strong. **8** (*predic.*) *colloq.* to an extreme degree (*bored stiff; scared stiff*). **9** (foll. by *with*) *colloq.* abounding in (*a place stiff with tourists*). **10** *colloq.* (of a price, demand, etc.) unusually high; excessive. ● *n. sl.* **1** a corpse. **2 a** a foolish or useless person (*you big stiff*). **b** any person (*lucky stiff*). □□ **stiff·ish** *adj.* **stiff·ly** *adv.* **stiff·ness** *n.* [OE *stif* f. Gmc]

stiff·en /stífən/ *v.tr. & intr.* make or become stiff. □□ **stiff·en·er** *n.* **stiff·en·ing** *n.*

stiff neck *n.* a rheumatic condition in which the head cannot be turned without pain.

stiff-necked *adj.* obstinate or haughty.

stiff up·per lip *n.* determination; fortitude.

sti·fle¹ /stífəl/ *v.* **1** *tr.* smother; suppress (*stifled a yawn*). **2** *intr. & tr.* experience or cause to experience constraint of breathing (*stifling heat*). **3** *tr.* kill by suffocating. □□ **sti·fler** /stíflər/ *n.* **sti·fling·ly** *adv.* [perh. alt. of ME *stuffe, stuffle* f. OF *estouffer*]

sti·fle² /stífəl/ *n.* (in full **stifle joint**) a joint in the legs of horses, dogs, etc., equivalent to the knee in humans. [ME: orig. unkn.]

sti·fle bone *n.* the bone in front of the stifle joint in the legs of horses, dogs, etc.

stig·ma /stígmə/ *n.* (*pl.* **stig·mas** or esp. in sense 4 **stig·ma·ta** /-mətə, -maatə/) **1** a mark or sign of disgrace or discredit. **2** (foll. by *of*) a distinguishing mark or characteristic. **3** the part of a pistil that receives the pollen in pollination. **4** (in *pl.*) *Eccl.* (in Christian belief) marks corresponding to those left on Christ's body by the Crucifixion, said to have appeared on the bodies of St. Francis of Assisi and others. **5** a mark or spot on the skin or on a butterfly wing. **6** *Med.* a visible sign or characteristic of a disease. **7** an insect's spiracle. [L f. Gk *stigma –atos* a mark made by a pointed instrument, a brand, a dot: rel. to STICK¹]

stig·mat·ic /stigmátik/ *adj. & n.* ● *adj.* **1** of or relating to a stigma or

stigmas. **2** = ANASTIGMATIC. ● *n. Eccl.* a person bearing stigmata. □□ **stig·mat·i·cal·ly** *adv.*

stig·ma·tist /stígmətist/ *n. Eccl.* = STIGMATIC *n.*

stig·ma·tize /stígmətīz/ *v.tr.* **1** (often foll. by *as*) describe as unworthy or disgraceful. **2** *Eccl.* produce stigmata on. □□ **stig·ma·ti·za·tion** *n.* [F *stigmatiser* or med.L *stigmatizo* f. Gk *stigmatizō* (as STIGMA)]

stilb /stilb/ *n.* a unit of luminance equal to one candela per square centimeter. [F f. Gk *stilbō* glitter]

stil·bene /stílbeen/ *n. Chem.* an aromatic hydrocarbon forming phosphorescent crystals. [as STILB + –ENE]

stil·bes·trol /stilbéstrawl,–rol/ *n.* (*Brit.* **stil·boes·trol**) a powerful synthetic estrogen derived from stilbene. [STILBENE + ESTRUS]

stile¹ /stīl/ *n.* an arrangement of steps allowing people but not animals to climb over a fence or wall. [OE *stigel* f. a Gmc root *stig-* (unrecorded) climb]

stile² /stīl/ *n.* a vertical piece in the frame of a paneled door, wainscot, etc. (cf. RAIL¹ *n.* 5). [prob. f. Du. *stijl* pillar, doorpost]

sti·let·to /stilétō/ *n.* (*pl.* **·tos**) **1** a short dagger with a thick blade. **2** a pointed instrument for making eyelets, etc. **3** (in full **stiletto heel**) **a** a long tapering heel of a woman's shoe. **b** a shoe with such a heel. [It., dimin. of *stilo* dagger (as STYLUS)]

still¹ /stil/ *adj., n., adv., & v.* ● *adj.* **1** not or hardly moving. **2** with little or no sound; calm and tranquil (*a still evening*). **3** (of sounds) hushed; stilled. **4** (of a drink) not effervescent. **5** designed for or concerned with static photographs (*a still camera*). ● *n.* **1** deep silence (*in the still of the night*). **2** an ordinary static photograph (as opposed to a motion picture), esp. a single shot from a movie or videotape. ● *adv.* **1** without moving (*stand still*). **2** even now or at a particular time (*they still did not understand; why are you still here?*). **3** nevertheless; all the same. **4** (with *compar.*, etc.) even; yet; increasingly (*still greater efforts; still another explanation*). ● *v.tr. & intr.* make or become still. □ **still and all** *colloq.* nevertheless. **still waters run deep** a quiet manner conceals depths of feeling or knowledge or cunning. □□ **still·ness** *n.* [OE *stille* (adj. & adv.), *stillan* (v.), f. WG]

still² /stil/ *n.* an apparatus for distilling alcohol, etc. [obs. *still* (v.), ME f. DISTILL]

stil·lage /stílij/ *n.* a bench, frame, etc., for keeping articles off the floor while draining, drying, waiting to be packed, etc. [app. f. Du. *stellagie* scaffold f. *stellen* to place + F *–age*]

still·birth /stílbərth/ *n.* the birth of a dead child.

still·born /stílbawrn/ *adj.* **1** (of a child) born dead. **2** (of an idea, plan, etc.) abortive; not able to succeed.

still life *n.* (*pl.* **still lifes**) **1** a painting or drawing of inanimate objects such as fruit or flowers. **2** this genre of painting.

Still·son /stílsən/ *n.* (in full **Stillson wrench**) a large wrench with jaws that tighten as pressure is increased. [D. C. *Stillson*, its inventor d. 1899]

stil·ly /stílee/ *adv. & adj.* ● *adv.* in a still manner. ● *adj. poet.* still; quiet. [(adv.) OE *stillīce*: (adj.) f. STILL¹]

stilt /stilt/ *n.* **1** either of a pair of poles with supports for the feet enabling the user to walk at a distance above the ground. **2** each of a set of piles or posts supporting a building, etc. **3 a** any wading bird of the genus *Himantopus* with long legs. **b** (in *comb.*) denoting a long-legged kind of bird (*stilt-petrel*). **4** a three-legged support for ceramic ware in a kiln. □ **on stilts 1** supported by stilts. **2** bombastic; stilted. □□ **stilt·less** *adj.* [ME & LG *stilte* f. Gmc]

stilt·ed /stíltid/ *adj.* **1** (of a literary style, etc.) stiff and unnatural; bombastic. **2** standing on stilts. **3** *Archit.* (of an arch) with pieces of upright masonry between the imposts and the springers. □□ **stilt·ed·ly** *adv.* **stilt·ed·ness** *n.*

Stil·ton /stílt'n/ *n. Trademark* a kind of strong rich cheese, often with blue veins, orig. sold in Stilton in East Anglia.

stim·u·lant /stímyələnt/ *adj. & n.* ● *adj.* that stimulates, esp. bodily or mental activity. ● *n.* **1** a stimulant substance, esp. a drug or alcoholic drink. **2** a stimulating influence. [L *stimulare stimulant-* urge, goad]

stim·u·late /stímyəlayt/ *v.tr.* **1** apply or act as a stimulus to. **2** animate; excite; arouse. **3** be a stimulant to. □□ **stim·u·lat·ing** *adj.* **stim·u·lat·ing·ly** *adv.* **stim·u·la·tion** /–láyshən/ *n.* **stim·u·la·tive** *adj.* **stim·u·la·tor** *n.*

stim·u·lus /stímyələs/ *n.* (*pl.* **stim·u·li** /–lī/) **1** a thing that rouses to activity or energy. **2** a stimulating or rousing effect. **3** a thing that evokes a specific functional reaction in an organ or tissue. [L, = goad, spur, incentive]

sti·my var. of STYMIE.

sting /sting/ *n. & v.* ● *n.* **1** a sharp often poisonous wounding organ of an insect, snake, nettle, etc. **2 a** the act of inflicting a wound with this. **b** the wound itself or the pain caused by it. **3** a wounding or painful quality or effect (*the sting of hunger; stings of remorse*). **4** pungency; sharpness; vigor (*a sting in the voice*). **5** *sl.* a swindle or robbery. ● *v.* (*past* and *past part.* **stung** /stung/) **1 a** *tr.* wound or pierce with a sting. **b** *intr.* be able to sting; have a sting. **2** *intr. & tr.* feel or cause to feel a tingling physical or sharp mental pain. **3** *tr.* (foll. by *into*) incite by a strong or painful mental effect (*was stung into replying*). **4** *tr. sl.* swindle or charge exorbitantly. □ **sting in the tail** unexpected pain or difficulty at the end. □□ **sting·ing·ly** *adv.* **sting·less** *adj.* **sting·like** *adj.* [OE *sting* (n.), *stingan* (v.), f. Gmc]

sting·a·ree /stíngəree/ *n. US & Austral.* = STINGRAY.

sting·er /stíngər/ *n.* **1 a** = STING *n.* 1. **b** a stinging insect, snake, nettle, etc. **2** a sharp painful blow.

sting·ing net·tle *n.* a nettle, *Urtica dioica*, having stinging hairs.

sting·ray /stíng-ray/ *n.* any of various broad flatfish, esp. of the family Dasyatidae, having a long poisonous serrated spine at the base of its tail.

stin·gy /stínjee/ *adj.* (**stin·gi·er, stin·gi·est**) ungenerous; mean. □□ **stin·gi·ly** *adv.* **stin·gi·ness** *n.* [perh. f. dial. *stinge* STING]

ray (stingray)

stink /stingk/ *v. & n.* ● *v.* (*past* **stank** /stangk/ or **stunk** /stungk/; *past part.* **stunk**) **1** *intr.* emit a strong offensive smell. **2** *tr.* (often foll. by *out*) fill (a place) with a stink. **3** *tr.* (foll. by *out*, etc.) drive (a person) out, etc., by a stink. **4** *intr. colloq.* be or seem very unpleasant, contemptible, or scandalous. **5** *intr.* (foll. by *of*) *colloq.* have plenty of (esp. money). ● *n.* **1** a strong or offensive smell; a stench. **2** *colloq.* an outcry or fuss (*the affair caused quite a stink*). □ **like stink** *Brit. colloq.* intensely; extremely hard or fast, etc. (*working like stink*). [OE *stincan* ult. f. WG: cf. STENCH]

stink bomb *n.* a device emitting a stink when exploded.

stink·er /stíngkər/ *n.* **1** a person or thing that stinks. **2** *sl.* an objectionable person or thing. **3** *sl.* **a** a difficult task. **b** *Brit.* a letter, etc., conveying strong disapproval.

stink·horn /stíngk-hawrn/ *n.* any foul-smelling fungus of the order Phallales.

stink·ing /stíngking/ *adj. & adv.* ● *adj.* **1** that stinks. **2** *sl.* very objectionable. ● *adv. sl.* extremely and usu. objectionably (*stinking rich*). □□ **stink·ing·ly** *adv.*

stink·ing badg·er *n.* a teledu.

stink·o /stíngkō/ *adj. sl.* drunk.

stink·pot /stíngkpot/ *n. sl.* **1** a term of contempt for a person. **2** a vehicle or boat that emits foul exhaust fumes.

stink·weed /stíngkweed/ *n.* any of several foul-smelling plants.

stink·wood /stíngkwŏŏd/ *n.* an African tree, *Ocotea bullata*, with foul-smelling timber.

stint /stint/ *v. & n.* ● *v.* **1 a** *tr.* supply (food or aid, etc.) in an ungenerous amount or grudgingly. **b** *intr.* (foll. by *on*) be grudging or mean about. **2** (often *refl.*) supply (a person, etc.) in this way. ● *n.* **1** a limitation of supply or effort (*without stint*). **2** a fixed or allotted time or amount of work (*do one's stint*). **3** a small sandpiper, esp. a dunlin. **4** = STINTER. □□ **stint·er** *n.* **stint·less** *adj.* [OE *styntan* to blunt, dull, f. Gmc, rel. to STUNT[1]]

stipe /stip/ *n. Bot. & Zool.* a stalk or stem, esp. the support of a carpel, the stalk of a frond, the stem of a fungus, or an eyestalk. □□ **stip·i·form** *adj.* **stip·i·tate** /stípitayt/ *adj.* **stip·i·ti·form** /stipítiform/ *adj.* [F f. L *stipes*: see STIPES]

sti·pel /stípəl/ *n. Bot.* a secondary stipule at the base of the leaflets of a compound leaf. □□ **sti·pel·late** /stípélayt/ *adj.* [F *stipelle* f. mod.L *stipella* dimin. (as STIPULE)]

sti·pend /stípend/ *n.* a fixed regular allowance or salary. [ME f. OF *stipend(i)e* or L *stipendium* f. *stips* wages + *pendere* to pay]

sti·pen·di·ar·y /stipéndee-eree/ *adj. & n.* ● *adj.* **1** receiving a stipend. **2** working for pay, not voluntarily. ● *n.* (*pl.* **·ies**) a person receiving a stipend. [L *stipendiarius* (as STIPEND)]

sti·pes /stípeez/ *n.* (*pl.* **stip·i·tes** /stípiteez/) = STIPE. [L, = log, tree trunk]

stip·ple /stípəl/ *v. & n.* ● *v.* **1** *tr. & intr.* draw or paint or engrave, etc., with dots instead of lines. **2** *tr.* roughen the surface of (paint, cement, etc.). ● *n.* **1** the process or technique of stippling. **2** the effect of stippling. □□ **stip·pler** *n.* **stip·pling** *n.* [Du. *stippelen* frequent. of *stippen* to prick f. *stip* point]

stip·u·late[1] /stípyŏŏlayt/ *v.tr.* **1** demand or specify as part of a bargain or agreement. **2** (foll. by *for*) mention or insist upon as an essential condition. **3** (as **stipulated** *adj.*) laid down in the terms of an agreement. □□ **stip·u·la·tion** /–láyshən/ *n.* **stip·u·la·tor** *n.* [L *stipulari*]

stip·u·late[2] /stípyələt, –layt/ *adj. Bot.* having stipules. [L *stipula* (as STIPULE)]

stip·ule /stípyōōl/ *n.* a small leaflike appendage to a leaf, usu. at the base of a leaf stem. □□ **stip·u·lar** *adj.* [F *stipule* or L *stipula* straw]

stir[1] /stər/ *v. & n.* ● *v.* (**stirred, stir·ring**) **1** *tr.* move a spoon or other implement around and around in (a liquid, etc) to mix the ingredients or constituents. **2 a** *tr.* cause to move or be disturbed, esp.

slightly (*a breeze stirred the lake*). **b** *intr.* be or begin to be in motion (*not a creature was stirring*). **c** *refl.* rouse (oneself), esp. from a lethargic state. **3** *intr.* rise from sleep (*is still not stirring*). **4** *intr.* (foll. by *out of*) leave; go out of (esp. one's house). **5** *tr.* arouse or inspire or excite (the emotions, etc., or a person as regards these) (*was stirred to anger*; *it stirred the imagination*). **6** esp. *Austral. colloq.* **a** *tr.* annoy; tease. **b** *intr.* cause trouble. ● *n.* **1** an act of stirring (*give it a good stir*). **2** commotion or excitement; public attention (*caused quite a stir*). **3** the slightest movement (*not a stir*). □ **not stir a finger** make no effort to help. **stir the blood** inspire enthusiasm, etc. **stir in** mix (an added ingredient) with a substance by stirring. **stir one's stumps** *Brit. colloq.* **1** begin to move. **2** become active. **stir up 1** mix thoroughly by stirring. **2** incite (trouble, etc.) (*loved stirring things up*). **3** stimulate; excite; arouse (*stirred up their curiosity*). □□ **stir·less** *adj.* [OE *styrian* f. Gmc]

stir[2] /stər/ *n. sl.* a prison (esp. in stir). [19th c.: orig. unkn.]

stir-cra·zy *adj.* deranged from long imprisonment or confinement.

stir-fry /stárfrī/ *v. & n.* ● *v.tr.* (**-fries, -fried**) fry rapidly while stirring and tossing. ● *n.* a dish consisting of stir-fried meat, vegetables, etc.

stirk /stərk/ *n. Brit. dial.* a yearling bullock or heifer. [OE *stirc*, perh. dimin. of *stēor* STEER[2]: see –OCK]

stirps /stərps/ *n.* (*pl.* **stir·pes** /–peez/) **1** *Biol.* a classificatory group. **2** *Law* **a** a branch of a family. **b** its progenitor. [L, = stock]

stir·rer /stárər/ *n.* **1** a thing or a person that stirs. **2** *Brit. colloq.* a troublemaker; an agitator.

stir·ring /stáring/ *adj.* **1** stimulating; exciting; arousing. **2** actively occupied (*lead a stirring life*). □□ **stir·ring·ly** *adv.* [OE *styrende* (as STIR[1])]

stir·rup /stárəp, stír–/ *n.* **1** each of a pair of devices attached to each side of a horse's saddle, in the form of a loop with a flat base to support the rider's foot. **2** (*attrib.*) having the shape of a stirrup. **3** (in full **stirrup bone**) = STAPES. [OE *stigrāp* f. *stigan* climb (as STILE[1]) + ROPE]

stir·rup cup *n.* a cup of wine, etc., offered to a person about to depart, orig. on horseback.

stir·rup i·ron *n.* the metal loop of a stirrup.

stir·rup leath·er *n.* (also **stir·rup strap**) the strap attaching a stirrup to a saddle.

stirrup 1

stir·rup pump *n.* a hand-operated water pump with a foot rest, used to extinguish small fires.

stitch /stich/ *n. & v.* ● *n.* **1 a** (in sewing or knitting or crocheting, etc.) a single pass of a needle or the thread or loop, etc., resulting from this. **b** a particular method of sewing or knitting, etc. (*am learning a new stitch*). **2** (usu. in *pl.*) *Surgery* each of the loops of material used in sewing up a wound. **3** the least bit of clothing (*hadn't a stitch on*). **4** an acute pain in the side of the body induced by running, etc. ● *v.tr.* **1** sew; make stitches (in). **2** join or close with stitches. □ **in stitches** *colloq.* laughing uncontrollably. **stitch up 1** join or mend by sewing or stitching. **2** *Brit. sl.* betray or cheat. □□ **stitch·er** *n.* **stitch·er·y** *n.* **stitch·less** *adj.* [OE *stice* f. Gmc, rel. to STICK[2]]

stitch in time *n.* a timely remedy.

stitch·wort /stíchwort, –wawrt/ *n.* any plant of the genus *Stellaria*, esp. *S. media* with an erect stem and white starry flowers, once thought to cure a stitch in the side.

sti·ver /stívər/ *n.* the smallest quantity or amount (*don't care a stiver*). [Du. *stuiver* a small coin, prob. rel. to STUB]

sto·a /stóə/ *n.* (*pl.* **sto·as**) **1** a portico or roofed colonnade in ancient Greek architecture. **2** (**the Stoa**) the Stoic school of philosophy. [Gk: cf. STOIC]

stoat /stōt/ *n.* a carnivorous mammal, *Mustela erminea*, of the weasel family, having brown fur in the summer turning mainly white in the winter. Also called **ermine**. [ME: orig. unkn.]

sto·chas·tic /stōkástik/ *adj.* **1** determined by a random distribution of probabilities. **2** (of a process) characterized by a sequence of random variables. **3** governed by the laws of probability. □□ **sto·chas·ti·cal·ly** *adv.* [Gk *stokhastikos* f. *stokhazomai* aim at, guess f. *stokhos* aim]

stock /stok/ *n., adj., & v.* ● *n.* **1** a store of goods, etc., ready for sale or distribution, etc. **2** a supply or quantity of anything for use (*lay in winter stocks of fuel; a great stock of information*). **3** equipment or raw material for manufacture or trade, etc. (*rolling stock; paper stock*). **4 a** farm animals or equipment. **b** = FATSTOCK. **5 a** the capital of a business company. **b** shares in this. **6 a** one's reputation or popularity (*his stock is rising*). **b** an estimate or assessment. **c** confidence, esp. in reliability. **7 a** money lent to a government at fixed interest. **b** the right to receive such interest. **8** a line of ancestry; family origins (*comes from German stock*). **9** liquid made by stewing bones, vegetables, fish, etc., as a basis for soup, gravy, sauce, etc. **10** any of various fragrant-flowered cruciferous plants of the genus *Matthiola* or *Malcolmia* (orig. *stock-gillyflower*, so-called because it had a stronger stem than the clove gillyflower). **11** a plant into which a graft is inserted. **12** the main trunk of a tree, stem of a plant, etc. **13** (in *pl.*) *hist.* a wooden frame with holes for the feet and occas. the hands and head, in which offenders were locked as a public punishment. **14 a** = STOCK COMPANY. **b** the repertory of this. **15 a** a base or support or handle for an implement or machine. **b** the crossbar of an anchor. **16** the butt of a rifle, etc. **17 a** = HEAD-STOCK. **b** = TAILSTOCK. **18** (in *pl.*) the supports for a ship during building. **19** a band of material worn round the neck esp. in horse-back riding or below a clerical collar. **20** hard solid brick pressed in a mold. ● *adj.* **1** kept in stock and so regularly available (*stock sizes*). **2** perpetually repeated; hackneyed; conventional (*a stock answer*). ● *v.tr.* **1** have or keep (goods) in stock. **2 a** provide (a store or a farm, etc.) with goods, equipment, or livestock. **b** fill with items needed (*shelves well-stocked with books*). **3** fit (a gun, etc.) with a stock. □ **in stock** available immediately for sale, etc. **on the stocks** in construction or preparation. **out of stock** not immediately available for sale. **stock up 1** provide with or get stocks or supplies. **2** (foll. by *with*, *on*) get in or gather a stock of (food, fuel, etc.). **take stock 1** make an inventory of one's stock. **2** (often foll. by *of*) make a review or estimate of (a situation, etc.). **3** (foll. by *in*) concern oneself with. □□ **stock•er** *n.* **stock•less** *adj.* [OE *stoc*, *stocc* f. Gmc]

stock•ade /stókáyd/ *n. & v.* ● *n.* **1** a line or enclosure of upright stakes. **2** a military prison. ● *v.tr.* fortify with a stockade. [obs. F *estocade*, alt. of *estacade* f. Sp. *estacada*: rel. to STAKE[1]]

stock book *n.* a book or ledger showing amounts of goods, stocks or stores, etc., acquired and disposed of.

stock•breed•er /stókbreedər/ *n.* a farmer who raises livestock. □□ **stock•breed•ing** *n.*

stock•brok•er /stókbrōkər/ *n.* = BROKER 2. □□ **stock•brok•er•age** *n.* **stock•brok•ing** *n.*

stock•brok•er belt *n. Brit.* an affluent residential area, esp. near a business center such as London.

stock car *n.* **1** a specially modified production car for use in racing. **2** a railroad boxcar for transporting livestock.

stock com•pa•ny *n.* a repertory company performing mainly at a particular theater.

stock dove *n.* a European wild pigeon, *Columba oenas*, with a shorter tail and squarer head than a wood pigeon and breeding in tree trunks.

stock ex•change *n.* **1** a place where stocks and shares are bought and sold. **2** the dealers working there.

stock•fish /stókfish/ *n.* cod or a similar fish split and dried in the open air without salt.

stock•hold•er /stók-hōldər/ *n.* an owner of stocks or shares. □□ **stock•hold•ing** *n.*

stock•i•nette /stókinét/ *n.* (also **stock•i•net**) an elastic, knitted, usu. cotton material. [prob. f. *stocking net*]

stock•ing /stóking/ *n.* **1 a** either of a pair of long separate coverings for the legs and feet, usu. closely woven in wool or nylon and worn esp. by women and girls. **b** = SOCK[1]. **2** any close-fitting garment resembling a stocking (*bodystocking*). **3** a differently colored, usu. white, lower part of the leg of a horse, etc. □ **in one's stocking** (or **stock•inged**) **feet** without shoes (esp. while being measured). □□ **stock•inged** *adj.* (also in *comb.*). **stock•ing•less** *adj.* [STOCK in (now dial.) sense 'stocking' + −ING[1]]

stock•ing cap *n.* a knitted usu. conical cap.

stock•ing stuff•er *n.* a small present suitable for a Christmas stocking.

stock-in-trade *n.* **1** goods kept on sale by a retailer, dealer, etc. **2** all the requisites of a trade or profession. **3** a ready supply of characteristic phrases, attitudes, etc.

stock•job•ber /stókjobər/ *n.* **1** *US* = JOBBER 1b. **2** *Brit.* = JOBBER 2. □□ **stock•job•bing** *n.*

stock•list /stóklist/ *n. Brit.* a regular publication stating a dealer's stock of goods with current prices, etc.

stock•man /stókmən/ *n.* (*pl.* **-men**) **1 a** an owner of livestock. **b** *Austral.* a man in charge of livestock. **2** a person in charge of a stock of goods in a warehouse, etc.

stock mar•ket *n.* **1** = STOCK EXCHANGE. **2** transactions on this.

stock•pile /stókpīl/ *n. & v.* ● *n.* an accumulated stock of goods, materials, weapons, etc., held in reserve. ● *v.tr.* accumulate a stockpile of. □□ **stock•pil•er** *n.*

stock•pot /stókpot/ *n.* a pot for cooking stock for soup, etc.

stock•room /stókrōōm, −rŏŏm/ *n.* a room for storing goods in stock.

stock-still *adj.* without moving.

stock•tak•ing /stóktayking/ *n.* **1** the process of making an inventory of stock in a store, warehouse, etc. **2** a review of one's position and resources.

stock•y /stókee/ *adj.* (**stock•i•er**, **stock•i•est**) (of a person, plant, or animal) short and strongly built; thickset. □□ **stock•i•ly** *adv.* **stock•i•ness** *n.*

stock•yard /stókyaard/ *n.* an enclosure with pens, etc., for the sorting or temporary keeping of cattle.

stodge /stoj/ *n. & v.* esp. *Brit. colloq.* ● *n.* **1** food, esp. of a thick heavy kind. **2** an unimaginative person or idea. ● *v.tr.* stuff with food, etc. [earlier as verb: imit., after *stuff* and *podge*]

stodg•y /stójee/ *adj.* (**stodg•i•er**, **stodg•i•est**) **1** dull and uninterest-

ing. **2** (of a literary style, etc.) turgid and dull. **3** esp. *Brit.* (of food) heavy and indigestible. □□ **stodg•i•ly** *adv.* **stodg•i•ness** *n.*

stoep /stōōp/ *n. S.Afr.* a terraced veranda in front of a house. [Du., rel. to STEP]

sto•gy /stógee/ *n.* (also **sto•gie**) (*pl.* **-gies**) **1** a long narrow roughly-made cigar. **2** a rough heavy boot. [orig. *stoga*, short for *Conestoga* in Pennsylvania]

Sto•ic /stóik/ *n. & adj.* ● *n.* **1** a member of the ancient Greek school of philosophy founded at Athens by Zeno *c.* 308 BC, which sought virtue as the greatest good and taught control of one's feelings and passions. **2** (**stoic**) a stoical person. ● *adj.* **1** of or like the Stoics. **2** (**stoic**) = STOICAL. [ME f. L *stoicus* f. Gk *stōikos* f. STOA (with ref. to Zeno's teaching in the *Stoa Poikilē* or Painted Porch at Athens)]

sto•i•cal /stóikəl/ *adj.* having or showing great self-control in adversity. □□ **sto•i•cal•ly** *adv.*

stoi•chi•om•e•try /stóykeeómitree/ *n. Chem.* **1** the fixed, usu. rational numerical relationship between the relative quantities of substances in a reaction or compound. **2** the determination or measurement of these quantities. □□ **stoi•chi•o•met•ric** /−keeəmétrik/ *adj.* [Gk *stoikheion* element + −METRY]

Sto•i•cism /stóisizəm/ *n.* **1** the philosophy of the Stoics. **2** (**stoicism**) a stoical attitude.

stoke /stōk/ *v.* (often foll. by *up*) **1 a** *tr.* feed and tend (a fire or furnace, etc.). **b** *intr.* act as a stoker. **2** *intr. colloq.* consume food, esp. steadily and in large quantities. [back-form. f. STOKER]

stoke•hold /stók-hōld/ *n.* a compartment in a steamship, containing its boilers and furnace.

stoke•hole /stók-hōl/ *n.* a space for stokers in front of a furnace.

stok•er /stókər/ *n.* a person who tends to the furnace on a steamship. [Du. f. *stoken* stoke f. MDu. *stoken* push, rel. to STICK[1]]

stokes /stōks/ *n.* (*pl.* same) the cgs unit of kinematic viscosity, corresponding to a dynamic viscosity of 1 poise and a density of 1 gram per cubic centimeter, equivalent to 10^{-4} square meters per second. [Sir G. G. *Stokes*, Brit. physicist d. 1903]

STOL *abbr. Aeron.* short take-off and landing.

stole[1] /stōl/ *n.* **1** a woman's long garment like a scarf, worn around the shoulders. **2** a strip of silk, etc., worn over the shoulders as a vestment by a priest. [OE *stol*, *stole* (orig. a long robe) f. L *stola* f. Gk *stolē* equipment, clothing]

stole[2] *past* of STEAL.

sto•len *past part.* of STEAL.

stol•id /stólid/ *adj.* **1** lacking or concealing emotion or animation. **2** not easily excited or moved. □□ **sto•lid•i•ty** /−líditee/ *n.* **stol•id•ly** *adv.* **stol•id•ness** *n.* [obs. F *stolide* or L *stolidus*]

sto•lon /stólon/ *n.* **1** *Bot.* a horizontal stem or branch that takes root at points along its length, forming new plants. **2** *Zool.* a branched stemlike structure in some invertebrates such as corals. □□ **sto•lon•ate** /−nayt/ *adj.* **sto•lo•nif•er•ous** /−nífərəs/ *adj.* [L *stolo −onis*]

sto•ma /stómə/ *n.* (*pl.* **sto•mas** or **sto•ma•ta** /−mətə/) **1** *Bot.* a minute pore in the epidermis of a leaf. **2 a** *Zool.* a small mouthlike opening in some lower animals. **b** *Surgery* a similar artificial orifice made in the stomach. □□ **sto•mal** *adj.* [mod.L f. Gk *stoma −atos* mouth]

stom•ach /stúmək/ *n. & v.* ● *n.* **1 a** the internal organ in which the first part of digestion occurs, being in humans a pear-shaped enlargement of the alimentary canal linking the esophagus to the small intestine. **b** any of several such organs in animals, esp. ruminants, in which there are four (cf. RUMEN, RETICULUM, OMASUM, ABOMASUM). **2 a** the belly, abdomen, or lower front of the body (*pit of the stomach*). **b** a protuberant belly (*what a stomach he has got!*). **3** (usu. foll. by *for*) **a** an appetite (for food). **b** liking, readiness, or inclination (for controversy, conflict, danger, or an undertaking) (*had no stomach for the fight*). ● *v.tr.* **1** find sufficiently palatable to swallow or keep down. **2** submit to or endure (an affront, etc.) (usu. with *neg.*: *cannot stomach it*). □ **on an empty stomach** not having eaten recently. **on a full stomach** soon after a large meal. □□ **stom•ach•ful** *n.* (*pl.* **-fuls**). **stom•ach•less** *adj.* [ME *stomak* f. OF *stomaque*, *estomac* f. L *stomachus* f. Gk *stomakhos* gullet f. *stoma* mouth]

stom•ach ache *n.* a pain in the abdomen or bowels.

stom•ach•er /stúmakər/ *n. hist.* **1** a front piece of a woman's dress covering the breast and pit of the stomach, often jeweled or embroidered. **2** an ornament worn on the front of a bodice. [ME, prob. f. OF *estomachier* (as STOMACH)]

sto•mach•ic /stəmákik/ *adj. & n.* ● *adj.* **1** of or relating to the stomach. **2** promoting the appetite or assisting digestion. ● *n.* a medicine or stimulant for the stomach. [F *stomachique* or L *stomachicus* f. Gk *stomakhikos* (as STOMACH)]

stom•ach pump *n.* a syringe for forcing liquid, etc., into or esp. out of the stomach.

stom•ach tube *n.* a tube introduced into the stomach via the gullet for emptying it.

sto•ma•ta *pl.* of STOMA.

See page xx for the **Key to Pronunciation**.

sto·ma·ti·tis /stómətítis/ *n. Med.* inflammation of the mucous membrane of the mouth.

sto·ma·tol·o·gy /stómətóləjee/ *n.* the scientific study of the mouth or its diseases. □□ **sto·mat·o·log·i·cal** /–tələjikəl/ *adj.* **sto·ma·tol·o·gist** *n.*

stomp /stomp/ *v. & n.* ● *v.intr.* tread or stamp heavily. ● *n.* a lively jazz dance with heavy stamping. □□ **stomp·er** *n.* [US dial. var. of STAMP]

stone /stōn/ *n. & v.* ● *n.* **1 a** a solid nonmetallic mineral matter, of which rock is made. **b** a piece of this, esp. a small piece. **2** *Building* **a** = LIMESTONE (*Portland stone*). **b** = SANDSTONE (*Bath stone*). **3** *Mineral.* = PRECIOUS STONE. **4** a stony meteorite; an aerolite. **5** (often in *comb.*) a piece of stone of a definite shape or for a particular purpose (*tombstone; stepping-stone*). **6 a** a thing resembling stone in hardness or form, e.g., the hard case of the kernel in some fruits. **b** *Med.* (often in *pl.*) a hard morbid concretion in the body esp. in the kidney or gallbladder (*gallstones*). **7** (*pl.* same) *Brit.* a unit of weight equal to 14 lb. (6.35 kg). **8** (*attrib.*) **a** made of stone. **b** of the color of stone. ● *v.tr.* **1** pelt with stones. **2** remove the stones from (fruit). **3** face or pave, etc., with stone. **4** sharpen, polish, etc., by rubbing with or against a stone. □ **cast** (or **throw**) **stones** (or **the first stone**) make aspersions on a person's character, etc. **leave no stone unturned** try all possible means. **stone cold** completely cold. **stone cold sober** completely sober. **stone the crows** *Brit. sl.* an exclamation of surprise or disgust. **a stone's throw** a short distance. □□ **stoned** *adj.* (also in *comb.*). **stone·less** *adj.* **ston·er** *n.* [OE *stān* f. Gmc]

Stone Age *n.* a prehistoric period when weapons and tools were made of stone.

stone·chat /stónchat/ *n.* any small brown bird of the thrush family with black and white markings, esp. *Saxicola torquata* with a call like stones being knocked together.

stone coal *n.* anthracite.

stone·crop /stónkrop/ *n.* any succulent plant of the genus *Sedum*, usu. having yellow or white flowers and growing among rocks or in walls.

stone·cut·ter /stónkutər/ *n.* a person or machine that cuts or carves stone.

stoned /stōnd/ *adj. sl.* under the influence of alcohol or drugs.

stone-dead *adj.* completely dead.

stone-deaf *adj.* completely deaf.

stone·fish /stónfish/ *n.* (*pl.* same) a venomous tropical fish, *Synanceia verrucosa*, with poison glands underlying its erect dorsal spines. Also called **devilfish**.

stone·fly /stónflī/ *n.* (*pl.* **·flies**) any insect of the order Plecoptera, with aquatic larvae found under stones.

stone fruit *n.* a fruit with flesh or pulp enclosing a stone.

stone-ground /stón-grownd/ *adj.* (of grain) ground with millstones.

stone·hatch /stónhach/ *n.* a ringed plover.

stone·ma·son /stónmaysən/ *n.* a person who cuts, prepares, and builds with stone. □□ **stone·ma·son·ry** *n.*

stone pars·ley *n.* an umbelliferous hedge plant, *Sison amomum*, with aromatic seeds.

stone pine *n.* a S. European pine tree, *Pinus pinea*, with branches at the top spreading like an umbrella.

stone pit *n.* a quarry.

stone·wall /stónwawl/ *v. tr. & intr.* obstruct (discussion or investigation) or be obstructive with evasive answers or denials, etc. □□ **stone·wall·er** *n.* **stone·wall·ing** *n.*

stoneware /stónwair/ *n.* ceramic ware that is impermeable and partly vitrified but opaque.

stone·washed /stónwawsht, –wosht/ *adj.* (of a garment or fabric, esp. denim) washed with abrasives to produce a worn or faded appearance.

stone·work /stónwərk/ *n.* **1** masonry. **2** the parts of a building made of stone. □□ **stone·work·er** *n.*

stone·wort /stónwərt, –wawrt/ *n.* **1** = STONE PARSLEY. **2** any plant of the genus *Chara*, with a calcareous deposit on the stem.

ston·y /stónee/ *adj.* (**ston·i·er, ston·i·est**) **1** full of or covered with stones (*stony soil; a stony road*). **2** hard; rigid. **b** cold; unfeeling; uncompromising (*a stony stare; a stony silence*). □□ **ston·i·ly** *adv.* **ston·i·ness** *n.* [OE *stānig* (as STONE)]

ston·y-broke *adj. Brit. sl.* entirely without money.

ston·y-heart·ed *adj.* unfeeling; obdurate.

stood *past* and *past part.* of STAND.

stooge /stooj/ *n. & v. colloq.* ● *n.* **1** a butt or foil, esp. for a comedian; straight man. **2** an assistant or subordinate, esp. for routine or unpleasant work. **3** a compliant person; a puppet. ● *v.intr.* **1** (foll. by *for*) act as a stooge for. **2** *Brit.* (foll. by *about, around*, etc.) move about aimlessly. [20th c.: orig. unkn.]

stook /stook, stook/ *n. & v. Brit.* ● *n.* a group of sheaves of grain stood on end in a field. ● *v.tr.* arrange in stooks. [ME *stouk*, from or rel. to MLG *stūke*]

stool /stool/ *n. & v.* ● *n.* **1** a seat without a back or arms, usu. for one

person and consisting of a wooden slab on three or four short legs. **2 a** = FOOTSTOOL. **b** a low bench for kneeling on. **3** (usu. in *pl.*) = FECES. **4** the root or stump of a tree or plant from which the shoots spring. **5** a decoy bird in hunting. ● *v.intr.* (of a plant) throw up shoots from the root. □ **fall between two stools** fail from vacillation between two courses, etc. [OE *stōl* f. Gmc, rel. to STAND]

stool·ie /stóolee/ *n. sl.* a person acting as a stool pigeon.

stool pi·geon *n.* **1** a person acting as a decoy (orig. a decoy of a pigeon fixed to a stool). **2** a police informer.

stoop¹ /stoop/ *v. & n.* ● *v.* **1** *tr.* bend (one's head or body) forward and downward. **2** *intr.* carry one's head and shoulders bowed forward. **3** *intr.* (often foll. by *down*) lower the body by bending forward, sometimes also bending at the knee. **4** *intr.* (foll. by *to* + infin.) deign or condescend. **5** *intr.* (foll. by *to*) descend or lower oneself to (some conduct) (*has stooped to crime*). **6** *intr.* (of a hawk, etc.) swoop on its prey. ● *n.* **1** a stooping posture. **2** the downward swoop of a hawk, etc. [OE *st ūpian* f. Gmc, rel. to STEEP¹]

stoop² /stoop/ *n.* a porch or small veranda or set of steps in front of a house. [Du. *stoep*: see STOEP]

stoop³ var. of STOUP.

stop /stop/ *v. & n.* ● *v.* (**stopped, stop·ping**) **1** *tr.* **a** put an end to (motion, etc.); completely check the progress or motion or operation of. **b** effectively hinder or prevent (*stopped them playing so loudly*). **c** discontinue (an action or sequence of actions) (*stopped playing; stopped my visits*). **2** *intr.* come to an end; cease (*supplies suddenly stopped*). **3** *intr.* cease from motion or speaking or action; make a halt or pause (*the car stopped at the lights; he stopped in the middle of a sentence; my watch has stopped*). **4** *tr.* cause to cease action; defeat. **5** *tr. sl.* receive (a blow, etc.). **6** *intr. esp. Brit.* remain; stay for a short time. **7** *tr.* (often foll. by *up*) block or close up (a hole or leak, etc.). **8** *tr.* not permit or supply as usual; discontinue or withhold (*shall stop their wages*). **9** *tr.* (in full **stop payment of** or **on**) instruct a bank to withhold payment on (a check). **10** *tr. Brit.* put a filling in (a tooth). **11** *tr.* obtain the required pitch from (the string of a violin, etc.) by pressing at the appropriate point with the finger. **12** *tr.* plug the upper end of (an organ pipe), giving a note an octave lower. **13** *tr. Bridge* be able to prevent opponents from taking all the tricks in (a suit). **14** *tr.* make (a sound) inaudible. **15** *tr. Boxing* **a** parry (a blow). **b** knock out (an opponent). **16** *tr. Hort.* pinch back (a plant). **17** *tr.* make (a clock, factory, etc.) cease working. **18** *tr. Naut.* make fast; stopper (a cable, etc.). ● *n.* **1** the act or an instance of stopping; the state of being stopped (*put a stop to; the vehicle was brought to a stop*). **2** a place designated for a bus or train, etc., to stop. **3** *Brit.* a punctuation mark, esp. a sentence-ending period. **4** a device for stopping motion at a particular point. **5** a change of pitch effected by stopping a string. **6 a** (in an organ) a row of pipes of one character. **b** a knob, etc., operating these. **7** a manner of speech adopted to produce a particular effect. **8** *Optics & Photog.* = DIAPHRAGM 3. **9 a** the effective diameter of a lens. **b** a device for reducing this. **c** a unit of change of relative aperture or exposure (with a reduction of one stop equivalent to halving it). **10** (of sound) = PLOSIVE. **11** (in telegrams, etc.) a period. **12** *Bridge* a card or cards stopping a suit. **13** *Naut.* a small line used as a lashing. □ **put a stop to** cause to end, esp. abruptly. **stop at nothing** be ruthless. **stop by** (also *absol.*) call at (a place). **stop dead** (or **short**) cease abruptly. **stop down** *Photog.* reduce the aperture of (a lens) with a diaphragm. **stop one's ears 1** put one's fingers in one's ears to avoid hearing. **2** refuse to listen. **stop in** pay a brief visit. **stop off** (or **over**) break one's journey. **stop out 1** stay out. **2** cover (part of an area) to prevent printing, etching, etc. **stop press** *Brit.* **1** (often *attrib.*) late news inserted in a newspaper after printing has begun. **2** a column in a newspaper reserved for this. **with all the stops out** exerting extreme effort. □□ **stop·less** *adj.* **stop·pa·ble** *adj.* [ME f. OE *–stoppian* f. LL *stuppare* STUFF: see ESTOP]

stop-and-go *n.* alternate stopping and restarting, esp. in traffic.

stop·bank /stópbangk/ *n. Austral. & NZ* an embankment built to prevent river flooding.

stop·cock /stópkok/ *n.* an externally operated valve regulating the flow of a liquid or gas through a pipe, etc.

stop drill *n.* a drill with a shoulder limiting the depth of penetration.

stope /stōp/ *n.* a steplike part of a mine where ore, etc., is being extracted. [app. rel. to STEP *n.*]

stop·gap /stópgap/ *n.* (often *attrib.*) a temporary substitute.

stop-go *n.* **1** = STOP-AND-GO. **2** *Brit.* the alternate restriction and stimulation of economic demand.

stop knob *n.* a knob controlling an organ stop.

stop light *n.* a red traffic light.

stop-off /stópawf, –of/ *n.* = STOPOVER.

stop·o·ver /stópōvər/ *n.* a break in one's journey.

stop·page /stópij/ *n.* **1** the condition of being blocked or stopped. **2** a stopping (of pay). **3** a stopping or interruption of work in a factory, etc.

stop·per /stópər/ *n. & v.* ● *n.* **1** a plug for closing a bottle, etc. **2** a person or thing that stops something. **3** *Naut.* a rope or clamp, etc., for checking and holding a rope cable or chain cable. ●*v.tr.* close or secure with a stopper. □ **put a stopper on 1** put an end to (a thing). **2** keep (a person) quiet.

stop·ping /stóping/ *n. Brit.* a filling for a tooth.

stop·ple /stópəl/ *n. & v.* ●*n.* a stopper or plug. ●*v.tr.* close with a stopple. [ME: partly f. STOP + –LE[1], partly f. ESTOPPEL]

stop valve *n.* a valve closing a pipe against the passage of liquid.

stop vol·ley *n.* (esp. in tennis) a checked volley close to the net, dropping the ball dead on the other side.

stop·watch /stópwoch/ *n.* a watch with a mechanism for recording elapsed time, used to time races, etc.

stor·age /stáwrij/ *n.* **1 a** the storing of goods, etc. **b** a particular method of storing or the space available for it. **2** the cost of storing. **3** the electronic retention of data in a computer, etc.

stor·age bat·ter·y *n.* (also **stor·age cell**) a battery (or cell) for storing electricity.

sto·rax /stáwraks/ *n.* **1 a** a fragrant resin, obtained from the tree *Styrax officinalis* and formerly used in perfume. **b** this tree. **2** (in full **Levant** or liquid storax) a balsam obtained from the tree *Liquidambar orientalis*. [L f. Gk, var. of STYRAX]

store /stawr/ *n. & v.* ●*n.* **1** a quantity of something kept available for use (*a store of wine; a store of wit*). **2** (in *pl.*) **a** articles for a particular purpose accumulated for use (*naval stores*). **b** a supply of these or the place where they are kept. **3 a** = DEPARTMENT STORE. **b** a retail outlet or shop. **c** a shop selling basic necessities (*general store*). **4** *Brit.* a warehouse for the temporary keeping of furniture, etc. **5** *Brit.* a device in a computer for storing retrievable data; a memory. ●*v.tr.* **1** put (furniture, etc.) in storage. **2** (often foll. by *up*, *away*) accumulate (provisions, energy, electricity, etc.) for future use. **3** stock or provide with something useful (*a mind stored with facts*). **4** (of a receptacle) have storage capacity for. **5** enter or retain (data) for retrieval. □ **in store 1** kept in readiness. **2** coming in the future. **3** (foll. by *for*) destined or intended. **set** (or **lay** or **put**) **store by** (or **on**) consider important or valuable. □□ **stor·a·ble** *adj.* **stor·er** *n.* [ME f. obs. *astore* (*n. & v.*) f. OF *estore, estorer* f. L *instaurare* renew: cf. RESTORE]

store·front /stáwrfrunt/ *n.* **1** the side of a store facing the street. **2** a room at the front of a store.

store·house /stáwrhows/ *n.* a place where things are stored.

store·keep·er /stáwrkeepər/ *n.* the owner or manager of a store.

store·man /stáwrmən/ *n.* (*pl.* **-men**) *Brit.* a person responsible for stored goods.

store·room /stáwr-room, –room/ *n.* a room in which items are stored.

sto·rey *Brit.* var. of STORY[2].

sto·ri·at·ed /stáwreeaytid/ *adj.* decorated with historical, legendary, or emblematic designs. □□ **sto·ri·a·tion** /–áyshən/ *n.* [shortening of HISTORIATED]

sto·ried /stáwreed/ *adj. literary* celebrated in or associated with stories or legends.

stork /stawrk/ *n.* **1** any long-legged large wading bird of the family Ciconiidae, esp. *Ciconia ciconia* with white plumage, black wingtips, a long reddish beak, and red feet, nesting esp. on tall buildings. **2** this bird as the pretended bringer of babies. [OE *storc*, prob. rel. to STARK (from its rigid posture)]

stork's-bill *n.* a plant of the genus *Pelargonium* or *Erodium*.

storm /stawrm/ *n. & v.* ●*n.* **1** a violent disturbance of the atmosphere with strong winds and usu. with thunder and rain or snow, etc. **2** *Meteorol.* a wind intermediate between gale and hurricane, esp. (on the Beaufort scale) of 55–72 m.p.h. **3** a violent disturbance of the established order in human affairs. **4** (foll. by *of*) **a** a violent shower of missiles or blows. **b** an outbreak of applause, indignation, hisses, etc. (*they were greeted by a storm of abuse*). **5 a** a direct assault by troops on a fortified place. **b** the capture of a place by such an assault. ●*v.* **1** *intr.* (often foll. by *at*, *away*) talk violently; rage; bluster. **2** *intr.* (usu. foll. by *in*, *out of*, etc.) move violently or angrily (*stormed out of the meeting*). **3** *tr.* attack or capture by storm. **4** *intr.* (of wind, rain, etc.) rage; be violent. □ **take by storm 1** capture by direct assault. **2** rapidly captivate (a person, audience, etc.). □□ **storm·less** *adj.* **storm·proof** *adj.* [OE f. Gmc]

storm bird *n.* = STORM PETREL.

storm·bound /stáwrmbownd/ *adj.* prevented by storms from leaving port or continuing a voyage.

storm cel·lar *n.* an underground shelter for refuge from severe storms.

storm cen·ter *n.* **1** the point to which the wind blows spirally inward in a cyclonic storm. **2** a subject, etc., upon which agitation or disturbance is concentrated.

storm cloud *n.* **1** a heavy rain cloud. **2** a threatening state of affairs.

storm col·lar *n.* a high coat collar that can be turned up and fastened.

white stork

storm door *n.* an additional outer door for protection in bad weather or winter.

storm glass *n.* a sealed tube containing a solution of which the clarity is thought to change when storms approach.

storm·ing par·ty *n.* a detachment of troops ordered to begin an assault.

storm in a tea·cup *n. Brit.* great excitement over a trivial matter.

storm pet·rel *n.* any of various birds of the family Hydrobatidae, especially Wilson's storm petrel (*Oceanites oceanicus*), a small sea bird with dark plumage.

storm sail *n.* a sail of smaller size and stouter canvas than the corresponding one used in ordinary weather.

storm sig·nal *n.* a device warning of an approaching storm.

storm troop·er *n. hist.* a member of the Nazi political militia. **2** a member of the shock troops.

storm troops *n.* **1** = SHOCK TROOPS (see SHOCK[1]). **2** *hist.* the Nazi political militia.

storm win·dow *n.* an additional outer window used like a storm door.

storm·y /stáwrmee/ *adj.* (**storm·i·er**, **storm·i·est**) **1** of or affected by storms. **2** (of a wind, etc.) violent; raging; vehement. **3** full of angry feeling or outbursts; lively; boisterous (*a stormy meeting*). □□ **storm·i·ly** *adv.* **storm·i·ness** *n.*

storm·y pet·rel *n.* **1** = STORM PETREL. **2** a person causing unrest.

sto·ry[1] /stáwree/ *n.* (*pl.* **-ries**) **1** an account of imaginary or past events; a narrative, tale, or anecdote. **2** the past course of the life of a person or institution, etc. (*my story is a strange one*). **3** (in full **story line**) the narrative or plot of a novel or play, etc. **4** facts or experiences that deserve narration. **5** *colloq.* a fib or lie. **6** a narrative or descriptive item of news. □ **the old** (or **same old**) **story** the familiar or predictable course of events. **the story goes** it is said. **to cut** (or **make**) **a long story short** a formula excusing the omission of details. [ME *storie* f. AF *estorie* (OF *estoire*) f. L *historia* (as HISTORY)]

sto·ry[2] /stáwree/ *n.* (also *Brit.* **sto·rey**) (*pl.* **-ries**) **1** any of the parts into which a building is divided horizontally; the whole of the rooms, etc., having a continuous floor (*a third-story window; a house of five stories*). **2** a thing forming a horizontal division. □□ **–sto·ried** (in *comb.*). [ME f. AL *historia* HISTORY (perh. orig. meaning a tier of painted windows or sculpture)]

sto·ry·board /stáwreebawrd/ *n.* a displayed sequence of pictures, etc., outlining the plan of a movie, television advertisement, etc.

sto·ry·book /stáwreebook/ *n.* **1** a book of stories for children. **2** (*attrib.*) unreal; romantic (*a storybook ending*).

sto·ry·tell·er /stáwreetelər/ *n.* **1** a person who tells stories. **2** *colloq.* a liar. □□ **sto·ry·tell·ing** *n. & adj.*

stoup /stoop/ *n.* (also **stoop**) **1** a basin for holy water. **2** *archaic* a flagon, beaker, or drinking vessel. [ME f. ON *staup* (= OE *stēap*) f. Gmc, rel. to STEEP[2]]

stout /stowt/ *adj. & n.* ●*adj.* **1** somewhat fat; corpulent; bulky. **2** of considerable thickness or strength (*a stout stick*). **3** brave; resolute; vigorous (*a stout fellow; put up stout resistance*). ●*n.* a strong dark beer brewed with roasted malt or barley. □□ **stout·ish** *adj.* **stout·ly** *adv.* **stout·ness** *n.* [ME f. AF & dial. OF *stout* f. WG, perh. rel. to STILT]

stout heart *n.* courage; resolve.

stout·heart·ed /stówt-hártəd/ *adj.* courageous. □□ **stout·heart·ed·ly** *adj.* **stout·heart·ed·ness** *n.*

stove[1] /stōv/ *n. & v.* ●*n.* **1** a closed apparatus burning fuel or electricity for heating or cooking. **2** *Brit. Hort.* a hothouse with artificial heat. ●*v.tr. Brit.* force or raise (plants) in a stove. □ **stove-enamel** a heatproof enamel produced by the treatment of enameled objects in a stove. [ME = sweating room, f. MDu., MLG *stove*, OHG *stuba* f. Gmc, perh. rel. to STEW[1]]

stove[2] *past* and *past part.* of STAVE *v.*

stove·pipe /stóvpīp/ *n.* a pipe conducting smoke and gases from a stove to a chimney.

stove·pipe hat *n. colloq.* a tall silk hat.

stow /stō/ *v.tr.* **1** pack (goods, etc.) tidily and compactly. **2** *Naut.* place (a cargo or provisions) in its proper place and order. **3** fill (a receptacle) with articles compactly arranged. **4** (usu. in *imper.*) *sl.* abstain or cease from (*stow the noise!*). □ **stow away 1** place (a thing) where it will not cause an obstruction. **2** be a stowaway on a ship, etc. **3** eat; consume (*he stowed away three servings of pie*). [ME, f. BESTOW: in Naut. use perh. infl. by Du. *stouwen*]

stow·age /stóij/ *n.* **1** the act or an instance of stowing. **2** a place for this.

stow·a·way /stóəway/ *n.* a person who hides on board a ship or aircraft, etc., to get free passage.

STP *abbr.* **1** standard temperature and pressure. **2** a hallucinogen related to amphetamine.

str. *abbr.* **1** strait. **2** stroke (of an oar).

stra·bis·mus /strəbízməs/ n. Med. the abnormal condition of one or both eyes not correctly aligned in direction; a squint. □□ **stra·bis·mal** adj. **stra·bis·mic** adj. [mod.L f. Gk *strabismos* f. *strabizō* squint f. *strabos* squinting]

Strad /strad/ n. colloq. a Stradivarius. [abbr.]

strad·dle /strád'l/ v. & n. • v. 1 tr. a sit or stand across (a thing) with the legs wide apart. b be situated across or on both sides of (*the town straddles the border*). 2 intr. a sit or stand in this way. b (of the legs) be wide apart. 3 tr. part (one's legs) widely. 4 tr. drop shots or bombs short of and beyond (a target). 5 tr. vacillate between two policies, etc., regarding (an issue). • n. 1 the act or an instance of straddling. 2 Stock Exch. an option giving the holder the right of either calling for or delivering stock at a fixed price. □□ **strad·dler** n. [alt. of *striddle*, back-form. f. *striddlings* astride f. *strid-* = STRIDE]

Strad·i·var·i·us /strádiváireeəs/ n. a violin or other stringed instrument made by Antonio Stradivari of Cremona (d. 1737) or his followers. [Latinized f. *Stradivari*]

strafe /strayf/ v. & n. • v.tr. 1 bombard; harass with gunfire. 2 reprimand. 3 abuse. 4 beat soundly. • n. an act of strafing. [joc. adaptation of G catchword (1914) *Gott strafe England* may God punish England]

strag·gle /strágəl/ v. & n. • v.intr. 1 lack or lose compactness or tidiness. 2 be or become dispersed or sporadic. 3 trail behind others in a march or race, etc. 4 (of a plant, beard, etc.) grow long and loose. • n. a body or group of straggling or scattered persons or things. □□ **strag·gler** n. **strag·gly** adj. (**strag·gli·er, strag·gli·est**). [ME, perh. rel. to dial. *strake* go, rel. to STRETCH]

straight /strayt/ adj., n., & adv. • adj. 1 a extending uniformly in the same direction; without a curve or bend, etc. b Geom. (of a line) lying on the shortest path between any two of its points. 2 successive; uninterrupted (*three straight wins*). 3 in proper order or place or condition; duly arranged; level; symmetrical (*is the picture straight?; put things straight*). 4 honest; candid; not evasive (*a straight answer*). 5 (of thinking, etc.) logical; unemotional. 6 (of drama, etc.) serious as opposed to popular or comic; employing the conventional techniques of its art form. 7 a unmodified. b (of a drink) undiluted. 8 Brit. colloq. (of music) classical. 9 colloq. a (of a person, etc.) conventional or respectable. b heterosexual. 10 (of an arch) flat-topped. 11 (of a person's back) not bowed. 12 (of the hair) not curly or wavy. 13 (of a knee) not bent. 14 (of the legs) not bowed or knock-kneed. 15 (of a garment) not flared. 16 coming direct from its source. 17 (of an aim, look, blow, or course) going direct to the mark. • n. 1 the straight part of something, esp. the concluding stretch of a racetrack. 2 a straight condition. 3 a sequence of five cards in poker. 4 colloq. a a conventional person. b a heterosexual. • adv. 1 in a straight line; direct; without deviation or hesitation or circumlocution (*came straight from Paris; I told them straight*). 2 in the right direction; with a good aim (*shoot straight*). 3 correctly (*can't see straight*). 4 archaic at once or immediately. □ **go straight** live an honest life after being a criminal. **the straight and narrow** morally correct behavior. **straight away** at once; immediately. **straight from the shoulder 1** (of a blow) well delivered. **2** (of a verbal attack) delivered in a frank or direct manner. **straight off** colloq. without hesitation, deliberation, etc. (*cannot tell you straight off*). **straight up** colloq. **1** truthfully; honestly. **2 a** (of food, drink, etc.) without admixture or dilution. **b** (of liquor) without ice. □□ **straight·ish** adj. **straight·ly** adv. **straight·ness** n. [ME, past part. of STRETCH]

straight an·gle n. an angle of 180°.

straight·a·way /stráytəway/ adj. & n. • adj. 1 (of a course, etc.) straight. 2 straightforward. • n. a straight course, track, road, etc.

straight cut adj. (of tobacco) cut lengthwise into long silky fibers.

straight·edge /stráytej/ n. a bar with one edge accurately straight, used for testing.

straight eight n. 1 an internal combustion engine with eight cylinders in line. 2 a vehicle having this.

straight·en /stráyt'n/ v.tr. & intr. 1 (often foll. by out) make or become straight. 2 (foll. by up) stand erect after bending. □□ **straight·en·er** n.

straight eye n. the ability to detect deviation from the straight.

straight face n. an intentionally expressionless face, esp. avoiding a show of amusement. □□ **straight-faced** adj.

straight fight n. Brit. Polit. a direct contest between two candidates.

straight flush n. see FLUSH³.

straight·for·ward /stráytfáwrwərd/ adj. 1 honest or frank. 2 (of a task, etc.) uncomplicated. □□ **straight·for·ward·ly** adv. **straight·for·ward·ness** n.

straight man n. a comedian's stooge.

straight-out adj. 1 uncompromising. 2 straightforward; genuine.

straight ra·zor n. a razor with a straight blade that is hinged to a handle into which it can be folded.

straight·way /stráytway/ adv. archaic = straight away.

strain¹ /strayn/ v. & n. • v. 1 tr. & intr. stretch tightly; make or become taut or tense. 2 tr. exercise (oneself, one's senses, a thing, etc.) intensely or excessively; press to extremes. 3 a intr. make an intensive effort. b intr. (foll. by *after*) strive intensely for (*straining after perfection*). 4 intr. (foll. by *at*) tug; pull (*the dog strained at the leash*). 5 intr. hold out with difficulty under pressure (*straining under the load*). 6 tr. a distort from the true intention or meaning. b apply (authority, laws, etc.) beyond their province or in violation of their true intention. 7 tr. overtask or injure by overuse or excessive demands (*strain a muscle; strained their loyalty*). 8 a tr. clear (a liquid) of solid matter by passing it through a sieve, etc. b tr. (foll. by *out*) filter (solids) out from a liquid. c intr. (of a liquid) percolate. 9 tr. hug or squeeze tightly. 10 tr. use (one's ears, eyes, voice, etc.) to the best of one's power. • n. 1 a the act or an instance of straining. b the force exerted in this. 2 an injury caused by straining a muscle, etc. 3 a a severe demand on physical strength or resources. b the exertion needed to meet this (*is suffering from strain*). 4 (in sing. or pl.) a snatch or spell of music or poetry. 5 a tone or tendency in speech or writing (*more in the same strain*). 6 Physics a the condition of a body subjected to stress; molecular displacement. b a quantity measuring this, equal to the amount of deformation usu. divided by the original dimension. □ **strain every nerve** make every possible effort. **strain oneself 1** injure oneself by effort. **2** make undue efforts. □□ **strain·able** adj. [ME f. OF *estreindre estreign-* f. L *stringere strict-* draw tight]

strain² /strayn/ n. 1 a breed or stock of animals, plants, etc. 2 a moral tendency as part of a person's character (*a strain of aggression*). [ME, = progeny, f. OE *strēon* (recorded in *ġestrēonan* beget), rel. to L *struere* build]

strained /straynd/ adj. 1 constrained; forced; artificial. 2 (of a relationship) mutually distrustful or tense. 3 (of an interpretation) involving an unreasonable assumption; far-fetched; labored.

strain·er /stráynər/ n. a device for straining liquids, vegetables, etc.

strait /strayt/ n. & adj. • n. 1 (in sing. or pl.) a narrow passage of water connecting two seas or large bodies of water. 2 (usu. in pl.) difficulty, trouble, or distress (usu. *in dire* or *desperate straits*). • adj. archaic 1 narrow; limited; confined or confining. 2 strict or rigorous. □□ **strait·ly** adv. **strait·ness** n. [ME *streit* f. OF *estreit* tight, narrow f. L *strictus* STRICT]

strait·en /stráyt'n/ v. 1 tr. restrict in range or scope. 2 tr. (as **straitened** adj.) (esp. of circumstances) characterized by poverty. 3 tr. & intr. archaic make or become narrow.

strait·jack·et /stráytjakit/ n. & v. (also **straight·jack·et**) • n. 1 a strong garment with long arms for confining the arms of a violent prisoner, mental patient, etc. 2 restrictive measures. • v.tr. (·**jack·et·ed, ·jack·et·ing**) 1 restrain with a straitjacket. 2 severely restrict.

strait·laced /stráytláyst/ adj. (also **straight·laced**) severely virtuous; morally scrupulous; puritanical.

strake /strayk/ n. 1 a continuous line of planking or plates from the stem to the stern of a ship. 2 a section of the iron rim of a wheel. [ME: prob. rel. to OE *streccan* STRETCH]

stra·mo·ni·um /strəmóneeəm/ n. 1 datura. 2 the dried leaves of this plant used in the treatment of asthma. [mod.L, perh. f. Tartar *turman* horse medicine]

strand¹ /strand/ n. & v. • v. 1 tr. & intr. run aground. 2 tr. (as **stranded** adj.) in difficulties, esp. without money or means of transport. 3 tr. Baseball leave a runner on base at the end of an inning. • n. rhet. or poet. the margin of a sea, lake, or river, esp. the foreshore. [OE]

strand² /strand/ n. & v. • n. 1 each of the threads or wires twisted around each other to make a rope or cable. 2 a a single thread or strip of fiber. b a constituent filament. 3 something representing a strand or rope (*strand of pearls*). 4 a lock of hair. 5 an element or strain in any composite whole. • v.tr. 1 break a strand in (a rope). 2 arrange in strands. [ME: orig. unkn.]

strange /straynj/ adj. 1 unusual; peculiar; surprising; eccentric; novel. 2 a (often foll. by *to*) unfamiliar; alien; foreign (*lost in a strange land*). b not one's own (*strange gods*). 3 (foll. by *to*) unaccustomed. 4 not at ease; out of one's element (*felt strange in such company*). □ **feel strange** be unwell. **strange to say** it is surprising or unusual (that). □□ **strange·ly** adv. [ME f. OF *estrange* f. L *extraneus* EXTRANEOUS]

strange·ness /stráynjnis/ n. 1 the state or fact of being strange or unfamiliar, etc. 2 Physics a property of certain elementary particles that is conserved in strong interactions.

strange par·ti·cle n. Physics an elementary particle classified as having a nonzero value for strangeness.

stran·ger /stráynjər/ n. 1 a person who does not know or is not known in a particular place or company. 2 (often foll. by *to*) a person one does not know (*was a complete stranger to me*). 3 (foll. by *to*) a person entirely unaccustomed to (a feeling, experience, etc.) (*no stranger to controversy*). 4 a floating tea leaf, etc., held to foretell the arrival of a visitor. 5 Parl. (in the UK) a person who is not a member or official of the House of Commons. [ME f. OF *estrangier* ult. f. L (as STRANGE)]

stran·gle /stránggəl/ v.tr. 1 squeeze the windpipe or neck of, esp. so as to kill. 2 hamper or suppress (a movement, impulse, cry, etc.).

□□ **stran·gler** *n.* [ME f. OF *estrangler* f. L *strangulare* f. Gk *straggalaō* f. *straggalē* halter: cf. *straggos* twisted]

997

stranglehold ~ stream

stran·gle·hold /stránggəlhōld/ *n.* **1** an illegal wrestling hold that throttles an opponent. **2** a deadly grip. **3** complete and exclusive control.

stran·gles /stránggəlz/ *n.pl.* (usu. treated as *sing.*) an infectious streptococcal fever, esp. affecting the respiratory tract, in a horse, donkey, etc. [pl. of *strangle* (n.) f. STRANGLE]

stran·gu·late /strángyəlayt/ *v.tr. Surgery* **1** prevent circulation through (a vein, intestine, etc.) by compression. **2** remove (a tumor, etc.) by binding with a cord. [L *strangulare strangulat-* (as STRANGLE)]

stran·gu·lat·ed her·ni·a *n. Med.* a hernia in which the protruding part is constricted, preventing circulation.

stran·gu·la·tion /strángyəláyshən/ *n.* **1** the act of strangling or the state of being strangled. **2** the act of strangulating. [L *strangulatio* (as STRANGULATE)]

stran·gu·ry /stránggyəree/ *n.* a condition in which urine is passed painfully and in drops. □□ **stran·gu·ri·ous** /-gyŏŏreeəs/ *adj.* [ME f. L *stranguria* f. Gk *straggouria* f. *stragx –ggos* drop squeezed out + *ouron* urine]

strap /strap/ *n. & v.* ● *n.* **1** a strip of leather or other flexible material, often with a buckle or other fastening for holding things together, etc. **2** a thing like this for keeping a garment in place. **3** a loop for grasping to steady oneself in a moving vehicle. **4 a** a strip of metal used to secure or connect. **b** a leaf of a hinge. **5** *Bot.* a tongue-shaped part in a floret. **6** (prec. by *the*) punishment by beating with a strap. ● *v.tr.* (**strapped, strap·ping**) **1** (often foll. by *down, up,* etc.) secure or bind with a strap. **2** beat with a strap. **3** (esp. as **strapped** *adj.*) *colloq.* subject to a shortage. **4** *Brit.* (often foll. by *up*) close (a wound) or bind (a part) with an adhesive bandage. □□ **strap·per** *n.* **strap·py** *adj.* [dial. form of STROP]

strap·hang·er /stráp-hangər/ *n. sl.* a standing passenger in a bus or subway, esp. a regular commuter. □□ **strap·hang** *v.intr.*

strap·less /stráplis/ *adj.* (of a garment) without straps, esp. shoulder straps.

strap·pa·do /strəpáydō, -paá–/ *n.* (*pl.* **·dos**) *hist.* **1** a form of torture in which the victim is raised from the ground by a rope and made to fall from a height almost to the ground then stopped with a jerk. **2** an application of this. **3** the instrument used. [F *(e)strapade* f. It. *strappata* f. *strappare* snatch]

strap·ping /stráping/ *adj.* (esp. of a person) large and sturdy.

strap-work *n.* ornamentation imitating braided straps.

stra·ta *pl.* of STRATUM.

▶See note at STRATUM.

strat·a·gem /strátəjəm/ *n.* **1** a cunning plan or scheme, esp. for deceiving an enemy. **2** trickery. [ME f. F *stratagème* f. L *stratagema* f. Gk *stratēgēma* f. *stratēgeō* be a general (*stratēgos*) f. *stratos* army + *agō* lead]

stra·tal see STRATUM.

stra·te·gic /strətéejik/ *adj.* **1** of or serving the ends of strategy; useful or important with regard to strategy (*strategic considerations; strategic move*). **2** (of materials) essential in fighting a war. **3** (of bombing or weapons) done or for use against an enemy's home territory as a longer-term military objective (opp. TACTICAL). □□ **stra·te·gi·cal** *adj.* **stra·te·gi·cal·ly** *adv.* **stra·te·gics** *n.pl.* (usu. treated as *sing.*). [F *stratégique* f. Gk *stratēgikos* (as STRATAGEM)]

stra·te·gic de·fense in·i·ti·a·tive *n.* a proposed US system of defense against nuclear weapons using satellites. ¶ Abbr.: **SDI**.

strat·e·gy /strátijee/ *n.* (*pl.* **·gies**) **1** the art of war. **2 a** the management of an army or armies in a campaign. **b** the art of moving troops, ships, aircraft, etc., into favorable positions (cf. TACTICS). **c** an instance of this or a plan formed according to it. **3** a plan of action or policy in business or politics, etc. (*economic strategy*). □□ **strat·e·gist** *n.* [F *stratégie* f. Gk *stratēgia* generalship f. *stratēgos*: see STRATAGEM]

strath /strath/ *n. Sc.* a broad mountain valley. [Gael. *srath*]

strath·spey /strathspáy/ *n.* **1** a slow Scottish dance. **2** the music for this. [*Strathspey,* valley of the river Spey]

stra·ti *pl.* of STRATUS.

stra·ti·cu·late /strətíkyələt/ *adj. Geol.* (of rock formations) arranged in thin strata. [STRATUM, after *vermiculate,* etc.]

strat·i·fy /strátifí/ *v.tr.* (**·fies, ·fied**) **1** (esp. as **stratified** *adj.*) arrange in strata. **2** construct in layers, social grades, etc. □□ **strat·i·fi·ca·tion** /-fikáyshən/ *n.* [F *stratifier* (as STRATUM)]

stra·tig·ra·phy /strətígrəfee/ *n. Geol. & Archaeol.* **1** the order and relative position of strata. **2** the study of this as a means of historical interpretation. □□ **strat·i·graph·ic** /strátigráfik/ *adj.* **strat·i·graph·i·cal** *adj.* [STRATUM + -GRAPHY]

strato- /strátō/ *comb. form* status.

stra·to·cir·rus /strátōsírəs/ *n.* clouds combining stratus and cirrus features.

stra·toc·ra·cy /strətókrəsee/ *n.* (*pl.* **·cies**) **1** a military government. **2** domination by soldiers. [Gk *stratos* army + -CRACY]

stra·to·cu·mu·lus /strátōkyŏŏmyələs/ *n.* clouds combining cumulus and stratus features.

strat·o·pause /strátōpawz/ *n.* the interface between the stratosphere and the ionosphere.

strat·o·sphere /strátəsfeer/ *n.* **1** a layer of atmospheric air above the troposphere extending to about 50 km above the earth's surface, in which the lower part changes little in temperature and the upper part increases in temperature with height (cf. IONOSPHERE). **2** a very high or the highest place, degree, etc. □□ **strat·o·spher·ic** /-féerik, –férik/ *adj.* [STRATUM + SPHERE after *atmosphere*]

stra·tum /stráytəm, strát–/ *n.* (*pl.* **stra·ta** /-tə/) **1** esp. Geol. or *Archaeol.* a layer or set of successive layers of any deposited substance. **2** an atmospheric layer. **3** a layer of tissue, etc. **4 a** a social grade, class, etc. (*the various strata of society*). **b** *Statistics* each of the groups into which a population is divided in stratified sampling. □□ **stra·tal** *adj.* [L, = something spread or laid down, neut. past part. of *sternere* strew]

▶The singular is **stratum**, 'a layer.' The plural, **strata**, is sometimes mistaken for singular.

stra·tus /stráytəs, strát–/ *n.* (*pl.* **stra·ti** /-tī/) a continuous horizontal sheet of cloud. [L, past part. of *sternere*: see STRATUM]

straw /straw/ *n.* **1** dry cut stalks of grain for use as fodder or as material for thatching, packing, making hats, etc. **2 a** single stalk or piece of straw. **3** a thin hollow paper or plastic tube for sucking a drink from a glass, etc. **4** an insignificant thing (*not worth a straw*). **5** the pale yellow color of straw. **6** a straw hat. □ **catch** (or **grasp**) **at straws** resort to an utterly inadequate expedient in desperation, like a person drowning. □□ **straw·y** *adj.* [OE *strēaw* f. Gmc, rel. to STREW]

straw·ber·ry /stráwberee/ *n.* (*pl.* **·ries**) **1 a** any plant of the genus *Fragaria,* esp. any of various cultivated varieties, with white flowers, trifoliate leaves, and runners. **b** the pulpy red edible fruit of this, having a seed-studded surface. **2** a deep pinkish-red color. [OE *strēa(w)berige, strēowberige* (as STRAW, BERRY): reason for the name unkn.]

straw·ber·ry blond *n.* **1** reddish blond hair. **2** a person with such hair.

straw·ber·ry mark *n.* a soft reddish birthmark

straw·ber·ry pear *n.* **1** a W. Indian cactaceous plant, *Hylocereus undatus.* **2** the fruit of this.

straw·ber·ry roan *adj. & n.* ● *adj.* (of an animal, esp. a horse or cow) chestnut mixed with white or gray. ● *n.* a strawberry roan animal.

straw·ber·ry tree *n.* an evergreen tree, *Arbutus unedo,* bearing strawberrylike fruit.

straw boss *n.* an assistant foreman.

straw-col·ored *adj.* of pale yellow.

straw in the wind *n.* a slight hint of future developments.

straw man *n.* **1** an insubstantial person; an imaginary person set up as an opponent. **2** a stuffed effigy. **3** a person undertaking a financial commitment without adequate means.

straw vote *n.* (also **straw poll**) an unofficial ballot as a test of opinion.

straw-worm *n.* a caddis-worm.

stray /stray/ *v., n., & adj.* ● *v.intr.* **1 a** wander from the right place; become separated from one's companions, etc.; go astray. **b** (often foll. by *from, off*) digress. **2** deviate morally. **3** (as **strayed** *adj.*) that has gone astray. ● *n.* **1** a person or thing that has strayed, esp. a domestic animal. **2** (esp. in *pl.*) electrical phenomena interfering with radio reception; static. ● *adj.* **1** strayed or lost. **2** isolated; found or occurring occasionally (*a stray customer or two; hit by a stray bullet*). **3** *Physics* wasted or unwanted (*eliminate stray magnetic fields*). □□ **stray·er** *n.* [ME f. AF & OF *estrayer* (v.), AF *strey* (n. & adj.) f. OF *estraié* (as ASTRAY)]

streak /streek/ *n. & v.* ● *n.* **1** a long thin usu. irregular line or band, esp. distinguished by color (*black with red streaks; a streak of light above the horizon*). **2** a strain or element in a person's character (*has a streak of mischief*). **3** a spell or series (*a winning streak*). **4** a line of bacteria, etc., placed on a culture medium. ● *v.* **1** *tr.* **a** mark with streaks. **b** lighten (strands of hair) chemically for a streaked effect. **2** *intr.* move very rapidly. **3** *intr. colloq.* run naked in a public place as a stunt. □□ **streak·er** *n.* **streak·ing** *n.* [OE *strica* pen stroke f. Gmc: rel. to STRIKE]

streak of light·ning *n.* a sudden prominent flash of lightning.

streak·y /stréekee/ *adj.* (**streak·i·er, streak·i·est**) **1** full of streaks. **2** *Brit.* (of bacon) with alternate streaks of fat and lean. □□ **streak·i·ly** *adv.* **streak·i·ness** *n.*

stream /streem/ *n. & v.* ● *n.* **1** a flowing body of water, esp. a small river. **2 a** the flow of a fluid or of a mass of people (*a stream of lava*). **b** (in *sing.* or *pl.*) a large quantity of something that flows or moves along. **3** a current or direction in which things are moving or tending (*against the stream*). **4** *Brit.* a group of schoolchildren taught together as being of similar ability for a given age. ● *v.* **1** *intr.* flow or move as a stream. **2** *intr.* run with liquid (*my eyes were streaming*). **3** *intr.* (of a banner or hair, etc.) float or wave in the wind. **4** *tr.*

emit a stream of (blood, etc.). **5** *tr. Brit.* arrange (schoolchildren) in streams. □ **go with the stream** *Brit.* do as others do. **on stream** (of a factory, etc.) in operation. □□ **stream·less** *adj.* **stream·let** *n.* [OE *strēam* f. Gmc]

stream an·chor *n.* an anchor intermediate in size between a bower and a kedge, esp. for use in warping.

stream·er /stréemər/ *n.* **1** a long narrow flag. **2** a long narrow strip of ribbon or paper, esp. in a coil that unrolls when thrown. **3** a banner headline. **4** (in *pl.*) the aurora borealis or australis.

stream·line /stréemlīn/ *v. & n.* ● *v.tr.* **1** give (a vehicle, etc.) the form which presents the least resistance to motion. **2** make (an organization, process, etc.) simple or more efficient or better organized. **3** (as **streamlined** *adj.*) **a** having a smooth, slender, or elongated form; aerodynamic. **b** having a simplified and more efficient structure or organization. ● *n.* **1** the natural course of water or air currents. **2** (often *attrib.*) the shape of an aircraft, car, etc., calculated to cause the least air resistance.

stream of con·scious·ness *n.* **1** *Psychol.* a person's thoughts and conscious reactions to events perceived as a continuous flow. **2** a literary style depicting events in such a flow in the mind of a character.

street /street/ *n.* **1 a** a public road in a city, town, or village. **b** this with the houses or other buildings on each side. **2** the persons who live or work on a particular street. □ **in the street 1** in the area outside the houses. **2** (of Stock Exchange business) done after closing time. **on the streets 1** living by prostitution. **2** homeless. **streets ahead** (often foll. by *of*) *Brit. colloq.* much superior (to). **take to the streets** gather outdoors in order to protest, etc. **up** (or **right up**) **a person's street** esp. *Brit.* see ALLEY. □□ **street·ed** *adj.* (also in *comb.*). **street·ward** *adj. & adv.* [OE *strēt* f. LL *strāta* (*via*) paved (way), fem. past part. of *sternere* lay down]

street Ar·ab *n.* often *offens.* **1** a homeless child. **2** an urchin.

street·car /stréetkaar/ *n.* a commuter vehicle that operates on rails in city streets.

street smarts *n.* social savvy gained from hard experience.

street val·ue *n.* the value of drugs sold illicitly.

street·walk·er /stréetwawkər/ *n.* a prostitute seeking customers in the street. □□ **street·walk·ing** *n. & adj.*

street·wise /stréetwīz/ *n.* familiar with the ways of modern urban life.

strength /strengkth, strength, strenth/ *n.* **1** the state of being strong; the degree or respect in which a person or thing is strong. **2 a** a person or thing affording strength or support. **b** an attribute making for strength of character (*patience is your great strength*). **3** the number of persons present or available. **4** a full complement (*below strength*). □ **from strength** from a strong position. **from strength to strength** with ever-increasing success. **in strength** in large numbers. **on the strength of** relying on; on the basis of. **the strength of** the essence or main features of. □□ **strength·less** *adj.* [OE *strengthu* f. Gmc (as STRONG)]

strength·en /stréngkthən, strén–/ *v.tr. & intr.* make or become stronger. □ **strengthen a person's hand** (or **hands**) encourage a person to vigorous action. □□ **strength·en·er** *n.*

stren·u·ous /strényōōəs/ *adj.* **1** requiring or using great effort. **2** energetic or unrelaxing. □□ **stren·u·ous·ly** *adv.* **stren·u·ous·ness** *n.* [L *strenuus* brisk]

strep /strep/ *n. colloq.* = STREPTOCOCCUS. □ **strep throat** an acute sore throat caused by hemolytic streptococci and characterized by fever and inflammation.

strep·to·coc·cus /stréptəkókəs/ *n.* (*pl.* **strep·to·coc·ci** /–kóksī, –kókī/) any bacterium of the genus *Streptococcus*, usu. occurring in chains, some of which cause infectious diseases. □□ **strep·to·coc·cal** *adj.* [Gk *streptos* twisted f. *strephō* turn + COCCUS]

strep·to·my·cin /stréptəmísin/ *n.* an antibiotic produced by the bacterium *Streptomyces griseus*, effective against many disease-producing bacteria. [Gk *streptos* (as STREPTOCOCCUS) + *mukēs* fungus]

stress /stres/ *n. & v.* ● *n.* **1 a** pressure or tension exerted on a material object. **b** a quantity measuring this. **2 a** a demand on physical or mental energy. **b** distress caused by this (*suffering from stress*). **3 a** emphasis (*the stress was on the need for success*). **b** accentuation; emphasis laid on a syllable or word. **c** an accent, esp. the principal one in a word (*the stress is on the first syllable*). **4** *Mech.* force per unit area exerted between contiguous bodies or parts of a body. ● *v.tr.* **1** lay stress on; emphasize. **2** subject to mechanical or physical or mental stress. □ **lay stress on** indicate as important. □□ **stress·less** *adj.* [ME f. DISTRESS, or partly f. OF *estresse* narrowness, oppression, ult. f. L *strictus* STRICT]

stress·ful /strésfŏŏl/ *adj.* causing stress; mentally tiring (*had a stressful day*). □□ **stress·ful·ly** *adv.* **stress·ful·ness** *n.*

stretch /strech/ *v. & n.* ● *v.* **1** *tr. & intr.* draw or be drawn or admit of being drawn out into greater length or size. **2** *tr. & intr.* make or become taut. **3** *tr. & intr.* place or lie at full length or spread out (*with a canopy stretched over them*). **4** *tr.* (also *absol.*) **a** extend (an

arm, leg, etc.). **b** (often *refl.*) thrust out one's limbs and tighten one's muscles after being relaxed. **5** *intr.* have a specified length or extension; extend (*farmland stretches for many miles*). **6** *tr.* strain or exert extremely or excessively; exaggerate (*stretch the truth*). **7** *intr.* (as **stretched** *adj.*) elongated or extended. ● *n.* **1** a continuous extent or expanse or period (*a stretch of open road*). **2** the act or an instance of stretching; the state of being stretched. **3** (*attrib.*) able to stretch; elastic (*stretch fabric*). **4 a** *colloq.* a period of imprisonment. **b** a period of service. **5** the straight side of a racetrack. **6** *Naut.* the distance covered on one tack. □ **at full stretch** working to capacity. **at a stretch 1** in one continuous period (*slept for two hours at a stretch*). **2** with much effort. **stretch one's legs** exercise oneself by walking. **stretch out 1** *tr.* extend (a hand or foot, etc.). **2** *intr. & tr.* last for a longer period; prolong. **3** *tr.* make (money, etc.) last for a sufficient time. **stretch a point** agree to something not normally allowed. **stretch one's wings** see WING. □□ **stretch·a·ble** *adj.* **stretch·a·bil·i·ty** /stréchəbílitee/ *n.* **stretch·y** *adj.* **stretch·i·ness** *n.* [OE *streccan* f. WG: cf. STRAIGHT]

stretch·er /stréchər/ *n. & v.* ● *n.* **1** a framework of two poles with canvas, etc., between, for carrying sick, injured, or dead persons in a lying position. **2** a brick or stone laid with its long side along the face of a wall (cf. HEADER). **3** a board in a boat against which a rower presses the feet. **4** a rod or bar as a tie between chair legs, etc. **5** a wooden frame over which a canvas is stretched ready for painting. **6** *archaic sl.* an exaggeration or lie. ● *v.tr.* (often foll. by *off*) convey (a sick or injured person) on a stretcher.

stretch marks *n.* marks on the skin resulting from a gain of weight, or on the abdomen after pregnancy.

stret·to /strétō/ *adv. Mus.* in quicker time. [It., = narrow]

strew /strōō/ *v.tr.* (*past part.* **strewn** or **strewed**) **1** scatter or spread about over a surface. **2** (usu. foll. by *with*) spread (a surface) with scattered things. □□ **strew·er** *n.* [OE *stre(o)wian*]

stri·a /strīə/ *n.* (*pl.* **·ae** /stríee/) **1** *Anat., Zool., Bot., & Geol.* **a** a linear mark on a surface. **b** a slight ridge, furrow, or score. **2** *Archit.* a fillet between the flutes of a column. [L]

stri·ate *adj. & v. Anat., Zool., Bot., & Geol.* ● *adj.* /stríət/ (also **stri·at·ed** /stríaytid/) marked with striae. ● *v.tr.* /stríayt/ mark with striae. □□ **stri·a·tion** /stríáyshən/ *n.*

strick·en /stríkən/ *adj.* **1** affected or overcome with illness or misfortune, etc. (*stricken with measles; grief-stricken*). **2** leveled with a strickle. **3** (often foll. by *from*, etc.) *Law* deleted. □ **stricken in years** *archaic* enfeebled by age. [archaic past part. of STRIKE]

strick·le /stríkəl/ *n.* **1** a rod used in strike measure. **2** a whetting tool. [OE *stricel*, rel. to STRIKE]

strict /strikt/ *adj.* **1** precisely limited or defined; without exception or deviation (*lives in strict seclusion*). **2 a** (of a person) severe; rigorous in upholding standards of conscience or morality. **b** requiring complete compliance or exact performance; enforced rigidly (*gave strict orders*). □□ **strict·ness** *n.* [L *strictus* past part. of *stringere* tighten]

strict coun·ter·point *n.* an academic exercise in writing counterpoint, not necessarily intended as a composition.

strict·ly /stríktlee/ *adv.* **1** in a strict manner. **2** (also **strict·ly speak·ing**) applying words in their strict sense (*he is, strictly, an absconder*). **3** *colloq.* definitely.

stric·ture /stríkchər/ *n.* **1** (usu. in *pl.*; often foll. by *on*, *upon*) a critical or censorious remark. **2** *Med.* a morbid narrowing of a canal or duct in the body. □□ **stric·tured** *adj.* [ME f. L *strictura* (as STRICT)]

stride /strīd/ *v. & n.* ● *v.* (*past* **strode** /strōd/; *past part.* **strid·den** /strídn/) **1** *intr. & tr.* walk with long firm steps. **2** *tr.* cross with one step. **3** *tr.* bestride; straddle. ● *n.* **1 a** a single long step. **b** the length of this. **2** a person's gait as determined by the length of stride. **3** (usu. in *pl.*) progress (*has made great strides*). **4** a settled rate of progress (*get into one's stride; be thrown out of one's stride*). **5** (in *pl.*) *sl. Brit.* trousers. **6** the distance between the feet parted either laterally or as in walking. □ **take in one's stride 1** clear (an obstacle) without changing one's gait to jump. **2** manage without difficulty. □□ **strid·er** *n.* [OE *strīdan*]

stri·dent /stríd'nt/ *adj.* loud and harsh. □□ **stri·den·cy** *n.* **stri·dent·ly** *adv.* [L *stridere* strident- creak]

strid·u·late /stríjəlayt/ *v.intr.* (of insects, esp. the cicada and grasshopper) make a shrill sound by rubbing esp. the legs or wing cases together. □□ **strid·u·lant** *adj.* **strid·u·la·tion** /–láyshən/ *n.* [F *striduler* f. L *stridulus* creaking (as STRIDENT)]

strife /strīf/ *n.* **1** conflict; struggle between opposed persons or things. **2** *Austral. colloq.* trouble of any kind. [ME f. OF *estrif*: cf. OF *estriver* STRIVE]

strig·il /stríjil/ *n.* Gk & Rom. Antiq. a skin scraper used by bathers after exercise. **2** a structure on the leg of an insect used to clean its antennae, etc. [L *strigilis* f. *stringere* graze]

stri·gose /strígōs/ *adj.* **1** (of leaves, etc.) having short stiff hairs or scales. **2** (of an insect, etc.) streaked, striped, or ridged. [L *striga* swath, furrow]

strike /strīk/ *v. & n.* ● *v.* (*past* **struck** /struk/; *past part.* **struck** or *archaic* **strick·en** /stríkən/) **1 a** *tr.* subject to an impact. **b** *tr.* deliver (a blow) or inflict a blow on. **2** *tr.* come or bring sharply into contact with (*the ship struck a rock*). **3** *tr.* propel or divert with a blow (*struck the ball into the pond*). **4** *intr.* (foll. by *at*) try to hit. **5** *tr.* cause to penetrate (*struck terror into him*). **6** *tr.* ignite (a match) or produce (sparks, etc.) by rubbing. **7** *tr.* make (a coin) by stamping. **8** *tr.* produce (a musical note) by striking. **9 a** *tr.* (also *absol.*) (of a clock) indicate (the time) by the sounding of a chime, etc. **b** *intr.* (of time) be indicated in this way. **10** *tr.* **a** attack or affect suddenly (*was struck with sudden terror*). **b** (of a disease) afflict. **11** *tr.* cause to become suddenly (*was struck dumb*). **12** *tr.* reach or achieve (*strike a balance*). **13** *tr.* agree on (a bargain). **14** *tr.* assume (an attitude) suddenly and dramatically. **15** *tr.* **a** discover or come across. **b** find (oil, etc.) by drilling. **c** encounter (an unusual thing, etc.). **16** come to the attention of or appear to (*it strikes me as silly; an idea suddenly struck me*). **17 a** *intr.* (of employees) engage in a strike; cease work as a protest. **b** *tr.* act in this way against (an employer). **18 a** *tr.* lower or take down (a flag, tent, stage set, etc.). **b** *intr.* signify surrender by striking a flag; surrender. **19** *intr.* take a specified direction (*struck east*). **20** *tr.* **a** (also *absol.*) secure a hook in the mouth of (a fish) by jerking the tackle. **b** (of a fish) snatch at (bait, the hook, etc.) **21** *tr.* (of a snake) wound with its fangs. **22** *intr.* (of oysters) attach themselves to a bed. **23 a** *tr.* insert (the cutting of a plant) in soil to take root. **b** *tr.* (also *absol.*) (of a plant or cutting, etc.) put forth (roots). **24** *tr.* level (grain, etc., or the measure) in strike measure. **25** *tr.* **a** ascertain (a balance) by deducting credit or debit from the other. **b** arrive at (an average, state of balance) by equalizing all items. **26** compose (a jury) esp. by allowing both sides to reject the same number. **27** cancel; cross out. • *n.* **1** the act or an instance of striking. **2 a** the organized refusal by employees to work until some grievance is remedied. **b** a similar refusal to participate in some other expected activity. **3** a sudden find or success (*a lucky strike*). **4** an attack, esp. from the air. **5** *Baseball* a pitched ball counted against a batter, either for failure to hit it into fair territory or because it passes through the strike zone. **6** the act of knocking down all the pins with the first ball in bowling. **7** horizontal direction in a geological structure. **8** a strickle. □ **on strike** taking part in an industrial, etc., strike. **strike at the root** (or **roots**) **of** see ROOT[1]. **strike back 1** strike or attack in return. **2** (of a gas burner) burn from an internal point before the gas has become mixed with air. **strike down 1** knock down. **2** bring low; afflict (*struck down by a virus*). **strike home 1** deal an effective blow. **2** have an intended effect (*my words struck home*). **strike in 1** intervene in a conversation, etc. **2** (of a disease) attack the interior of the body from the surface. **strike it rich** *colloq.* find a source of abundance or success. **strike a light 1** produce a light by striking a match. **2** *Brit. sl.* an expression of surprise, disgust, etc. **strike lucky** esp. *Brit.* have a lucky success. **strike measure** measurement by passing a rod across the top of a heaped measure to ensure that it is exactly full. **strike off 1** remove with a stroke. **2** delete (a name, etc.) from a list. **3** produce (copies of a document). **strike oil 1** find oil by sinking a shaft. **2** attain prosperity or success. **strike out 1** hit out. **2** act vigorously. **3** delete (an item or name, etc.). **4** set off or begin (*struck out eastwards*). **5** use the arms and legs in swimming. **6** forge or devise (a plan, etc.). **7** *Baseball* **a** dismiss (a batter) by means of three strikes. **b** be dismissed in this way. **c** sl. fail. **strike through** delete (a word, etc.) with a stroke of one's pen. **strike up 1** start (an acquaintance, conversation, etc.) esp. casually. **2** (also *absol.*) begin playing (a tune, etc.). **strike upon 1** have (an idea, etc.) luckily occur to one. **2** (of light) illuminate. **strike while the iron is hot** act promptly at a good opportunity. **struck on** *Brit. colloq.* infatuated with. □□ **strik•a•ble** *adj.* [OE *strīcan* go, stroke f. WG]

strike•bound /stríkbownd/ *adj.* immobilized or closed by a strike.

strike•break•er /stríkbraykər/ *n.* a person working or employed in place of others who are on strike. □□ **strike•break** *v.intr.*

strike•out /stríkowt/ *n. Baseball* an out charged against a batter who has three strikes and credited to the pitcher.

strike pay *n.* an allowance paid to strikers by their trade union.

strik•er /stríkər/ *n.* **1** a person or thing that strikes. **2** an employee on strike. **3** *Sports* the player who is to strike, or who is to be the next to strike, the ball. **4** *Soccer* an attacking dplayer positioned well forward in order to score goals. **5** *Brit.* a device striking the primer in a gun.

strike zone *n. Baseball* an area between a batter's knees and armpits and over home plate through which a pitch must pass in order to be called a strike.

strik•ing /stríking/ *adj. & n.* • *adj.* **1** impressive; attracting attention. **2** (of a clock) making a chime to indicate the hours, etc. • *n.* the act or an instance of striking. □ **within striking distance** near enough to hit or achieve. □□ **strik•ing•ly** *adv.* **strik•ing•ness** *n.*

strik•ing force *n.* (also **strike force**) a military body ready to attack at short notice.

Strine /strīn/ *n.* **1** a comic transliteration of Australian speech, e.g., *Emma Chissitt* = "How much is it?". **2** (esp. uneducated) Australian English. [= *Australian* in Strine]

string /string/ *n. & v.* • *n.* **1** twine or narrow cord. **2** a piece of this or of similar material used for tying or holding together, pulling, etc. **3** a length of catgut or wire, etc., on a musical instrument, producing a note by vibration. **4 a** (in *pl.*) the stringed instruments in an orchestra, etc. **b** (*attrib.*) relating to or consisting of stringed instruments (*string quartet*). **5** (in *pl.*) an awkward condition or complication (*the offer has no strings*). **6** a set of things strung together; a series or line of persons or things (*a string of beads; a string of oaths*). **7** a group of racehorses trained at one stable. **8** a tough piece connecting the two halves of a peapod, etc. **9** a piece of catgut, etc., interwoven with others to form the head of a tennis, etc., racket. **10** = STRINGBOARD. **11** *Sports* a group of players that normally play together as a team. • *v.* (*past* and *past part.* **strung** /strung/) **1** *tr.* supply with a string or strings. **2** *tr.* tie with string. **3** *tr.* thread (beads, etc.) on a string. **4** *tr.* arrange in or as a string. **5** *tr.* remove the strings from (a bean, etc.). **6** *tr.* place a string ready for use on (a bow). **7** *tr. colloq.* hoax. **8** *intr.* (of glue, etc.) become stringy. **9** *intr. Billiards* make the preliminary strokes that decide which player begins. □ **on a string** under one's control or influence. **string along** *colloq.* **1** deceive, esp. by appearing to comply with (a person). **2** (often foll. by *with*) keep company (with). **string out** extend; prolong (esp. unduly). **string up 1** hang up on strings, etc. **2** kill by hanging. **3** *Brit.* make tense. □□ **string•less** *adj.* **string•like** *adj.* [OE *streng* f. Gmc: cf. STRONG]

string bass *n. Mus.* a double bass.

string bean *n.* **1** any of various beans eaten in their fibrous pods, esp. runner beans or snap beans. **2** *colloq.* a tall thin person.

string•board /stríngbawrd/ *n.* a supporting timber or skirting in which the ends of a staircase steps are set.

stringed /stringd/ *adj.* (of musical instruments) having strings (also in *comb.*: *twelve-stringed guitar*).

strin•gen•do /strinjéndō/ *adj. & adv. Mus.* with increasing speed. [It. f. *stringere* press: see STRINGENT]

strin•gent /strínjənt/ *adj.* **1** (of rules, etc.) strict; precise; requiring exact performance; leaving no loophole or discretion. **2** (of a money market, etc.) tight; hampered by scarcity; unaccommodating; hard to operate in. □□ **strin•gen•cy** *n.* **strin•gent•ly** *adv.* [L *stringere* draw tight]

string•er /stríngər/ *n.* **1** a longitudinal structural member in a framework, esp. of a ship or aircraft. **2** *colloq.* a newspaper correspondent not on the regular staff. **3** = STRINGBOARD.

string•halt /strínghawlt/ *n.* spasmodic movement of a horse's hind leg.

string the•o•ry *n. Physics* a proposed structure for the mathematical representation of elementary particles.

string tie *n.* a very narrow necktie.

string vest *n.* a loosely-woven mesh vest.

string•y /stríngee/ *adj.* (**string•i•er, string•i•est**) **1** (of food, etc.) fibrous; tough. **2** of or like string. **3** (of a person) tall, wiry, and thin. **4** (of a liquid) viscous; forming strings. □□ **string•i•ly** *adv.* **string•i•ness** *n.*

strip[1] /strip/ *v. & n.* • *v.* (**stripped, strip•ping**) **1** *tr.* (often foll. by *of*) remove the clothes or covering from (a person or thing). **2** *intr.* (often foll. by *off*) undress oneself. **3** *tr.* (often foll. by *of*) deprive (a person) of property or titles. **4** *tr.* leave bare of accessories or fittings. **5** *tr.* remove bark and branches from (a tree). **6** *tr.* (often foll. by *down*) remove the accessory fittings of or take apart (a machine, etc.) to inspect or adjust it. **7** *tr.* milk (a cow) to the last drop. **8** *tr.* remove the old hair from (a dog). **9** *tr.* remove the stems from (tobacco). **10** *tr.* tear the thread from (a screw). **11** *tr.* tear the teeth from (a gearwheel). **12** *tr.* remove (paint) or remove paint from (a surface) with solvent. **13** *tr.* (often foll. by *from*) pull or tear (a covering or property, etc.) off (*stripped the masks from their faces*). **14** *intr.* (of a screw) lose its thread. **15** *intr.* (of a bullet) issue from a rifled gun without spin owing to a loss of surface. • *n.* **1** an act of stripping, esp. of undressing in striptease. **2** *Brit colloq.* the identifying outfit worn by the members of a sports team while playing. [ME f. OE *bestrīepan* plunder f. Gmc]

strip[2] /strip/ *n.* **1** a long narrow piece (*a strip of land*). **2** a narrow flat bar of iron or steel. **3** (in full **strip cartoon**) = COMIC STRIP. [ME, from or rel. to MLG *strippe* strap, thong, prob. rel. to STRIPE]

strip club *n.* a club at which striptease performances are given.

stripe /strīp/ *n.* **1** a long narrow band or strip differing in color or texture from the surface on either side of it (*black with a red stripe*). **2** *Mil.* a chevron, etc., denoting military rank. **3** a category of character, opinion, etc. (*a man of that stripe*). **4** (usu. in *pl.*) *archaic* a blow with a scourge or lash. **5** (in *pl.*, treated as *sing.*) *colloq.* a tiger. [perh. back-form. f. *striped*: cf. MDu., MLG *strīpe*, MHG *strīfe*]

striped /strīpt/ *adj.* marked with stripes (also in *comb.*: *red-striped*).

striped bass *n.* a fish, *Morone saxatilis*, with dark stripes along its sides, used for food and game along the N. American coasts.

strip light *n.* a tubular fluorescent lamp.

strip•ling /strípling/ *n.* a youth not yet fully grown. [ME, prob. f. STRIP[2] + -LING[1], in the sense of having a figure not yet filled out]

strip mill *n.* a mill in which steel slabs are rolled into strips.

strip mine *n.* a mine worked by removing the material that overlies the ore, etc. □□ **strip-mine** *v.*

strip•per /strípər/ *n.* **1** a person or thing that strips something. **2** a device or solvent for removing paint, etc. **3** a striptease performer.

strip search *n. & v.* ● *n.* a search of a person involving the removal of all clothes. ● *v.tr.* search in this way. □□ **strip-search** *v.*

strip•tease /stríptéez/ *n. & v.* ● *n.* an entertainment in which the performer gradually undresses before the audience. ● *v.intr.* perform a striptease. □□ **strip•teas•er** *n.*

strip•y /strípee/ *adj.* (**strip•i•er, strip•i•est**) striped; having many stripes.

strive /strív/ *v.intr.* (*past* **strove** /stróv/; *past part.* **striv•en** /strívən/) **1** (often foll. by *for*, or *to* + infin.) try hard; make efforts (*strive to succeed*). **2** (often foll. by *with*, *against*) struggle or contend. □□ **striv•er** *n.* [ME f. OF *estriver*, rel. to *estrif* STRIFE]

strobe /strób/ *n. colloq.* **1** a stroboscope. **2** a stroboscopic lamp. [abbr.]

stro•bi•la /stróbílə/ *n.* (*pl.* **stro•bi•lae** /-lee/) **1** a chain of proglottids in a tapeworm. **2** a sessile polyplike form which divides horizontally to produce jellyfish larvae. [mod.L f. Gk *strobílē* twisted lint plug f. *strephō* twist]

stro•bile /stróbil, -bəl/ *n.* **1** the cone of a pine, etc. **2** the layered flower of the hop. [F *strobile* or LL *strobilus* f. Gk *strobilos* f. *strephō* twist]

stro•bi•lus /stróbíləs/ *n.* (*pl.* **stro•bi•li** /-lī/) *Bot.* = STROBILE 1. [LL (as STROBILE)]

stro•bo•scope /stróbəskōp/ *n.* **1** *Physics* an instrument for determining speeds of rotation, etc., by shining a bright light at intervals so that a rotating object appears stationary. **2** a lamp made to flash intermittently, esp. for this purpose. □□ **stro•bo•scop•ic** /-skópik/ *adj.* **stro•bo•scop•i•cal** *adj.* **stro•bo•scop•i•cal•ly** *adv.* [Gk *strobos* whirling + -SCOPE]

strode *past* of STRIDE.

stro•ga•noff /stráwgənawf, stró-/ *adj.* (of meat) cut into strips and cooked in a sour cream sauce (*beef stroganoff*). [P. *stroganoff*, 19th-c. Russ. diplomat]

stroke /strók/ *n. & v.* ● *n.* **1** the act or an instance of striking; a blow or hit (*with a single stroke; a stroke of lightning*). **2** a sudden disabling attack or loss of consciousness caused by an interruption in the flow of blood to the brain, esp. through thrombosis; apoplexy. **3 a** an action or movement esp. as one of a series. **b** the time or way in which such movements are done. **c** the slightest such action (*has not done a stroke of work*). **4** the whole of the motion (of a wing, oar, etc.) until the starting position is regained. **5** (in rowing) the mode or action of moving the oar (*row a fast stroke*). **6** the whole motion (of a piston) in either direction. **7** *Golf* the action of hitting (or hitting at) a ball with a club, as a unit of scoring. **8** a mode of moving the arms and legs in swimming. **9** a method of striking with the bat, etc., in games, etc. (*hits with an unorthodox stroke*). **10** a specially successful or skillful effort (*a stroke of diplomacy*). **11 a** a mark made by the movement in one direction of a pen or pencil or paintbrush. **b** a similar mark printed. **12** a detail contributing to the general effect in a description. **13** the sound made by a striking clock. **14** (in full **stroke oar**) the oar or oarsman nearest the stern, setting the time of the stroke. **15** the act or a spell of stroking. ● *v.tr.* **1** pass one's hand gently along the surface (of hair or fur, etc.); caress lightly. **2** act as the stroke of (a boat or crew). **3** hit (a ball), esp. smoothly or well. **4** *colloq.* flatter; seek to influence by flattery. □ **at a stroke** by a single action. **off one's stroke** not performing as well as usual. **on the stroke** punctually. **stroke a person the wrong way** irritate a person. [OE *strācian* f. Gmc, rel. to STRIKE]

stroke of gen•ius *n.* an original or strikingly successful idea.

stroke of luck *n.* (also **stroke of good luck**) an unforeseen opportune occurrence.

stroke play *n. Golf* play in which the score is reckoned by counting the number of strokes taken for the round (cf. MATCH PLAY (see MATCH¹)).

stroll /stról/ *v. & n.* ● *v.intr.* saunter or walk in a leisurely way. ● *n.* a short leisurely walk (*go for a stroll*). [orig. of a vagrant, prob. f. G *strollen, strolchen* f. *Strolch* vagabond, of unkn. orig.]

stroll•er /strólər/ *n.* **1** a person who strolls. **2** a folding chair on wheels, for pushing a child in.

stro•ma /strómə/ *n.* (*pl.* **stro•ma•ta** /-mətə/) *Biol.* **1** the framework of an organ or cell. **2** a fungous tissue containing spore-producing bodies. □□ **stro•mat•ic** /-mátik/ *adj.* [mod.L f. LL f. Gk *strōma* coverlet]

strong /strawng, strong/ *adj. & adv.* ● *adj.* (**strong•er** /stráwnggər, stróng-/; **strong•est** /stráwnggist, stróng-/) **1** having the power of resistance; able to withstand great force or opposition; not easily damaged or overcome (*strong material; strong faith; a strong character*). **2** (of a person's constitution) able to overcome, or not liable to, disease. **3** (of a person's nerves) proof against fright, irritation, etc. **4** (of a patient) restored to health. **5** (of an economy) stable and prosperous; (of a market) having steadily high or rising prices. **6** capable of exerting great force or of doing much; muscular; powerful. **7** forceful or powerful in effect (*a strong wind; a strong protest*). **8** decided or firmly held (*a strong suspicion; strong views*). **9** (of an argument, etc.) convincing or striking. **10** powerfully affecting the senses or emotions (*a strong light; strong acting*). **11** powerful in terms of size or numbers or quality (*a strong army*). **12** capable of doing much when united (*a strong combination*). **13 a** formidable; likely to succeed (*a strong candidate*). **b** tending to assert or dominate (*a strong personality*). **14** (of a solution or drink, etc.) containing a large proportion of a substance in water or another solvent (*strong tea*). **15** *Chem.* (of an acid or base) fully ionized into cations and anions in aqueous solution. **16** (of a group) having a specified number (*200 strong*). **17** (of a voice) loud or penetrating. **18** (of food or its flavor) pungent. **19** (esp. of a person's breath) bad smelling. **20** (of a literary style) vivid and terse. **21** (of a measure) drastic. **22** *Gram.* in Germanic languages: **a** (of a verb) forming inflections by change of vowel within the stem rather than by the addition of a suffix (e.g., *swim, swam*). **b** (of a noun or adjective) belonging to a declension in which the stem originally ended otherwise than in *-n* (opp. WEAK 9). **23** having validity or credence (*a stong possibility; a strong chance*). **24** unmistakable; noticeable (*a strong resemblance; a strong accent*). ● *adv.* strongly (*the tide is running strong*). □ **come it strong** *Brit. colloq.* go to great lengths; use exaggeration. **come on strong** act aggressively, flamboyantly, etc. **going strong** *colloq.* continuing action vigorously; in good health. □□ **strong•ish** *adj.* **strong•ly** *adv.* [OE f. Gmc: cf. STRING]

strong-arm *adj.* using force (*strong-arm tactics*).

strong•box /stráwngboks, stróng-/ *n.* a strongly made small chest for valuables.

strong drink *n.* alcohol, esp. liquor.

strong•hold /stráwnghōld, stróng-/ *n.* **1** a fortified place. **2** a secure refuge. **3** a center of support for a cause, etc.

strong in•ter•ac•tion *n.* (also **strong force**) *Physics* interaction between certain elementary particles that is very strong but is effective only at short distances.

strong lan•guage *n.* forceful language; swearing.

strong-mind•ed *adj.* having determination. □□ **strong-mind•ed•ness** *n.*

strong point *n.* **1** a thing at which one excels. **2** a specially fortified defensive position.

strong•room /stráwngroom, -room, stróng-/ *n.* a room designed to protect valuables against fire and theft.

strong stom•ach *n.* a stomach not easily affected by nausea.

strong suit *n.* **1** a suit at cards in which one can take tricks. **2** a thing at which one excels.

stron•ti•a /strónshə/ *n. Chem.* strontium oxide. [*strontian* native strontium carbonate f. Strontian in the Highland region of Scotland, where it was discovered]

stron•ti•um /strónteeəm/ *n. Chem.* a soft silver white metallic element occurring naturally in various minerals. ¶ Symb.: **Sr**. [STRONTIA + -IUM]

stron•ti•um 90 *n.* a radioactive isotope of strontium concentrated selectively in bones and teeth when taken into the body.

stron•ti•um ox•ide *n.* a white compound used in the manufacture of fireworks.

strop /strop/ *n. & v.* ● *n.* **1** a device, esp. a strip of leather, for sharpening razors. **2** *Naut.* a collar of leather or spliced rope or iron used for handling cargo. ● *v.tr.* (**stropped, strop•ping**) sharpen on or with a strop. [ME f. MDu., MLG *strop*, OHG *strupf*, WG f. L *stroppus*]

stro•phan•thin /strəfánthin/ *n.* a white crystalline poisonous glucoside extracted from various tropical plants of the genus *Strophanthus* and used as a heart medication. [mod.L *strophanthin* f. Gk *strophos* twisted cord + *anthos* flower]

stro•phe /strófee/ *n.* **1 a** a turn in dancing made by an ancient Greek chorus. **b** lines recited during this. **c** the first section of an ancient Greek choral ode or of one division of it. **2** a group of lines forming a section of a lyric poem. □□ **stroph•ic** *adj.* [Gk *strophē*, lit. turning, f. *strephō* turn]

strop•py /strópee/ *adj.* (**strop•pi•er, strop•pi•est**) *Brit. colloq.* bad-tempered; awkward to deal with. □□ **strop•pi•ly** *adv.* **strop•pi•ness** *n.* [20th c.: perh. abbr. of OBSTREPEROUS]

strove *past* of STRIVE.

strow /stró/ *v.tr.* (*past part.* **strown** /strón/ or **strowed**) *archaic* = STREW. [var. of STREW]

struck *past* and *past part.* of STRIKE.

struc•tur•al /strúkchərəl/ *adj.* of, concerning, or having a structure. □□ **struc•tur•al•ly** *adv.*

struc•tur•al en•gi•neer•ing *n.* the branch of civil engineering concerned with the structures of esp. large buildings, etc.

struc•tur•al for•mu•la *n. Chem.* a formula showing the arrangement of atoms in the molecule of a compound.

struc•tur•al•ism /strúkchərəlizəm/ *n.* **1** the doctrine that structure rather than function is important. **2** structural linguistics. **3** structural psychology. □□ **struc•tur•al•ist** *n. & adj.*

struc•tur•al lin•guis•tics *n.* the study of language as a system of interrelated elements.

struc·tur·al psy·chol·o·gy *n.* the study of the arrangement and composition of mental states and conscious experiences.

struc·tur·al steel *n.* strong mild steel in shapes suited to construction work.

struc·ture /strúkchər/ *n. & v.* • *n.* **1 a** a whole constructed unit, esp. a building. **b** the way in which a building, etc., is constructed (*has a flimsy structure*). **2** a set of interconnecting parts of any complex thing; a framework (*the structure of a sentence; a new wages structure*). • *v.tr.* give structure to; organize; frame. □□ **struc·tured** *adj.* (also in *comb.*). **struc·ture·less** *adj.* [ME f. OF *structure* or L *structura* f. *struere struct-* build]

stru·del /stróŏd'l/ *n.* a confection of thin pastry rolled up around a filling and baked (*apple strudel*). [G]

strug·gle /strúgəl/ *v. & n.* • *v.intr.* **1** make forceful or violent efforts to get free of restraint or constriction. **2** (often foll. by *for*, or *to* + infin.) make violent or determined efforts under difficulties; strive hard (*struggled for supremacy; struggled to get the words out*). **3** (foll. by *with, against*) contend; fight strenuously (*struggled with the disease; struggled against superior numbers*). **4** (foll. by *along, up,* etc.) make one's way with difficulty (*struggled to my feet*). **5** (esp. as **struggling** *adj.*) have difficulty in gaining recognition or a living (*a struggling artist*). • *n.* **1** the act or a spell of struggling. **2** a hard or confused contest. **3** a determined effort under difficulties. □□ **strug·gler** *n.* [ME *strugle* frequent. of uncert. orig. (perh. imit.)]

strug·gle for ex·ist·ence *n.* (also **strug·gle for life**) the competition between organisms esp. as an element in natural selection, or between persons seeking a livelihood.

strum /strum/ *v. & n.* • *v.tr.* (**strummed, strum·ming**) **1** play on (a stringed or keyboard instrument), esp. carelessly or unskillfully. **2** play (a tune, etc.) in this way. • *n.* the sound made by strumming. □□ **strum·mer** *n.* [imit.: cf. THRUM¹]

stru·ma /stróōmə/ *n.* (*pl.* **stru·mae** /-mee/) **1** *Med.* **a** = SCROFULA. **b** = GOITER. **2** *Bot.* a cushionlike swelling of an organ. □□ **stru·mose** *adj.* **stru·mous** *adj.* [L, = scrofulous tumor]

strum·pet /strúmpit/ *n. archaic* or *rhet.* a prostitute. [ME: orig. unkn.]

strung *past* and *past part.* of STRING. □ **strung out** sl. **1** a debilitated from long drug use. **b** addicted to a drug. **c** stupefied or agitated or incoherent from using drugs. **2** exhausted physically or emotionally.

strut /strut/ *n. & v.* • *n.* **1** a bar forming part of a framework and designed to resist compression. **2** a strutting gait. • *v.* (**strut·ted, strut·ting**) **1** *intr.* walk with a pompous or affected stiff erect gait. **2** *tr.* brace with a strut or struts. □□ **strut·ter** *n.* **strut·ting·ly** *adv.* [ME 'bulge, swell, strive,' earlier *stroute* f. OE *strūtian* be rigid (?)]

stru·thi·ous /stróōtheeəs/ *adj.* of or like an ostrich. [L *struthio* ostrich]

strych·nine /stríknin, -nin, -neen/ *n.* a vegetable alkaloid obtained from plants of the genus *Strychnos* (esp. nux vomica), bitter and highly poisonous, formerly used as a stimulant and (in small amounts) a medication. □□ **strych·nic** *adj.* [F f. L *strychnos* f. Gk *strukhnos* a kind of nightshade]

Sts. *abbr.* Saints.

Stu·art /stóōərt, styóō-/ *adj. & n.* • *adj.* of or relating to the royal family ruling Scotland 1371–1714 and England 1603– 1649 and 1660–1714. • *n.* a member of this family.

stub /stub/ *n. & v.* • *n.* **1** the remnant of a pencil, cigarette, etc., after use. **2** part of a check, receipt, etc., retained as a record. **3** a stunted tail, etc. **4** the stump of a tree, tooth, etc. **5** (*attrib.*) going only part of the way through (*stub mortise; stub tenon*). • *v.tr.* (**stubbed, stub·bing**) **1** strike (one's toe) against something. **2** (usu. foll. by *out*) extinguish (a lighted cigarette) by pressing the lighted end against something. **3** (foll. by *up*) grub up by the roots. **4** clear (land) of stubs. □ **stub-axle** an axle supporting only one wheel of a pair. [OE *stub, stubb* f. Gmc]

stub·ble /stúbəl/ *n.* **1** the cut stalks of cereal plants left sticking up after the harvest. **2 a** cropped hair or a cropped beard. **b** a short growth of unshaven hair. □□ **stub·bled** *adj.* **stub·bly** *adj.* [ME f. AF *stuble,* OF *estuble* f. L *stupla, stupula* var. of *stipula* straw]

stub·born /stúbərn/ *adj.* **1** unreasonably obstinate. **2** unyielding; obdurate; inflexible. **3** refractory; intractable. □□ **stub·born·ly** *adv.* **stub·born·ness** *n.* [ME *stiborn, stoburn,* etc., of unkn. orig.]

stub·by /stúbee/ *adj. & n.* • *adj.* (**stub·bi·er, stub·bi·est**) short and thick. • *n.* (*pl* **-bies**) *Austral. colloq.* a small squat bottle of beer. □□ **stub·bi·ly** *adv.* **stub·bi·ness** *n.*

stuc·co /stúkō/ *n. & v.* • *n.* (*pl.* **-coes**) plaster or cement used for coating wall surfaces or molding into architectural decorations. • *v.tr.* (**-coes, -coed**) coat with stucco. [It., of Gmc orig.]

stuck *past* and *past part.* of STICK².

stuck-up *adj. colloq.* affectedly superior and aloof; snobbish.

stud¹ /stud/ *n. & v.* • *n.* **1** a large-headed nail, boss, or knob, projecting from a surface esp. for ornament. **2** a double button esp. for use with two buttonholes in a shirt front. **3** a small object projecting slightly from a road surface as a marker, etc. **4** a rivet or crosspiece in each link of a chain cable. **5 a** a post to which laths, plasterboard, etc., are nailed. **b** the height of a room as indicated by the length of this. **6** a metal or rubber projection on an auto-

mobile tire providing greater traction. • *v.tr.* (**stud·ded, stud·ding**) **1** set with or as with studs. **2** (as **studded** *adj.*) (foll. by *with*) thickly set or strewn (*studded with diamonds*). **3** be scattered over or about (a surface). [OE *studu, stuthu* post, prop, rel. to G *stü tzen* to prop]

stud² /stud/ *n.* **1 a** a number of horses kept for breeding, etc. **b** a place where these are kept. **2** (in full **stud horse**) a stallion. **3** *colloq.* a young man (esp. one noted for sexual prowess). **4** (in full **stud poker**) a form of poker with betting after the dealing of successive rounds of cards face up. □ **at stud** (of a male horse) publicly available for breeding on payment of a fee. [OE *stōd* f. Gmc: rel. to STAND]

stud·book /stúdbŏok/ *n.* a book containing the pedigrees of horses.

stud·ding /stúding/ *n.* the woodwork of a lath-and-plaster or plasterboard wall.

stud·ding sail /stúdingsayl, stúnsəl/ *n.* a sail set on a small extra yard and boom beyond the leech of a square sail in light winds. [16th c.: orig. uncert.: perh. f. MLG, MDu. *stōtinge* a thrusting]

stu·dent /stóōd'nt, styóōd–/ *n.* **1** a person who is studying, esp. at university or another place of higher education. **2** (*attrib.*) studying in order to become (*a student nurse*). **3** a person of studious habits. **4** *Brit.* a graduate recipient of a stipend from the foundation of a college, esp. a fellow of Christ Church, Oxford. [ME f. L *studēre* f. *studium* STUDY]

stu·dent driv·er *n.* a person who is learning to drive a motor vehicle and has not yet passed a driving test.

stud farm *n.* a place where horses are bred.

stu·di·o /stóōdeeō, styóō–/ *n.* (*pl.* **-os**) **1** the workroom of a painter or photographer, etc. **2 a** place where movies or recordings are made or where television or radio programs are made or produced. **3** = studio apartment. [It. f. L (as STUDY)]

stu·di·o a·part·ment *n.* an apartment having only one main room, a kitchenette, and bath.

stu·di·o couch *n.* a couch that can be converted into a bed.

stu·di·ous /stóōdeeəs, styóō–/ *adj.* **1** devoted to or assiduous in study or reading. **2** studied; deliberate; painstaking (*with studious care*). **3** (foll by *to* + infin. or *in* + verbal noun) showing care or attention. **4** (foll. by *of* + verbal noun) anxiously desirous. □□ **stu·di·ous·ly** *adv.* **stu·di·ous·ness** *n.* [ME f. L *studiosus* (as STUDY)]

stud·y /stúdee/ *n. & v.* • *n.* (*pl.* **-ies**) **1** the devotion of time and attention to acquiring information or knowledge, esp. from books. **2** (in *pl.*) the pursuit of academic knowledge (*continued their studies abroad*). **3** a room used for reading, writing, etc. **4** a piece of work, esp. a drawing, done for practice or as an experiment (*a study of a head*). **5** the portrayal in literature or another art form of an aspect of behavior or character, etc. **6** a musical composition designed to develop a player's skill. **7** a thing worth observing closely (*your face was a study*). **8** a thing that has been or deserves to be investigated. **9** *Theatr.* **a** the act of memorizing a role. **b** a person who memorizes a role. **10** *archaic* a thing to be secured by pains or attention. • *v.* (**-ies, -ied**) **1** *tr.* make a study of; investigate or examine (a subject) (*study law*). **2** *intr.* (often foll. by *for*) apply oneself to study. **3** *tr.* scrutinize or earnestly contemplate (*studied their faces; studying the problem*). **4** *tr.* try to learn (the words of one's role, etc.). **5** *tr.* take pains to achieve (a result) or pay regard to (a subject or principle, etc.). **6** *tr.* (as **studied** *adj.*) deliberate; intentional; affected (*with studied politeness*). **7** *tr.* read (a book) attentively. **8** *tr.* (foll. by *to* + infin.) *archaic* **a** be on the watch. **b** try constantly to manage. □ **in a brown study** in a reverie; absorbed in one's thoughts. **make**

SYNONYM TIP **stubborn**

DOGGED, INTRACTABLE, OBDURATE, OBSTINATE, PERTINACIOUS. If you're the kind of person who takes a stand and then refuses to back down, your friends might say you have a **stubborn** disposition, a word that implies an innate resistance to any attempt to change one's purpose, course, or opinion. People who are *stubborn* by nature exhibit this kind of behavior in most situations, but they might be **obstinate** in a particular instance (*a stubborn child, he was obstinate in his refusal to eat vegetables*). *Obstinate* implies sticking persistently, especially in the face of persuasion or attack, to an opinion, purpose, or course of action. While *obstinate* is usually a negative term, **dogged** can be either positive or negative, implying both tenacious, often sullen, persistence (*dogged pursuit of a college degree, even though he knew he would end up in the family business*) and great determination (*dogged loyalty to a cause*). **Obdurate** usually connotes a *stubborn* resistance marked by harshness and lack of feeling (*to be obdurate in ignoring their pleas*), while **intractable** means *stubborn* in a headstrong sense and difficult for others to control or manage (*intractable pain*). No matter how *stubborn* you are, you probably don't want to be called **pertinacious**, which implies persistence to the point of being annoying or unreasonable (*a pertinacious panhandler*).

a **study of** investigate carefully. □□ **stud·ied·ly** *adv.* **stud·ied·ness** *n.* [ME f. OF *estudie* f. L *studium* zeal, study]

stud·y group *n.* a group of people meeting from time to time to study a particular subject or topic.

stuff /stuf/ *n. & v.* ● *n.* **1** the material that a thing is made of; material that may be used for some purpose. **2** a substance or things or belongings of an indeterminate kind or a quality not needing to be specified (*there's a lot of stuff about it in the newspapers*). **3** a particular knowledge or activity (*know one's stuff*). **4** *Brit.* woolen fabric (esp. as distinct from silk, cotton, and linen). **5** valueless matter; trash; refuse; nonsense (*take that stuff away*). **6** (prec. by *the*) a *colloq.* an available supply of something, esp. alcohol or drugs. **b** *sl.* money. ● *v.* **1** *tr.* pack (a receptacle) tightly (*stuff a cushion with feathers; a head stuffed with weird notions*). **2** *tr.* (foll. by *in, into*) force or cram (a head) (*stuffed the socks in the drawer*). **3** *tr.* fill out the skin of (an animal or bird, etc.) with material to restore the original shape (*a stuffed owl*). **4** *tr.* fill (poultry, vegetables, etc.) with a mixture, as of rice or seasoned bread crumbs, esp. before cooking. **5 a** *tr. & refl.* fill (a person or oneself) with food. **b** *tr. & intr.* eat greedily. **6** *tr.* push, esp. hastily or clumsily (*stuffed the note behind the cushion*). **7** *tr.* (usu. in *passive*; foll. by *up*) block up (a person's nose, etc.). **8** *tr. sl.* (esp. as an expression of contemptuous dismissal) dispose of as unwanted (*you can stuff the job*). **9** *tr.* place bogus votes in (a ballot box). **10** *tr. Brit. coarse sl. offens.* have sexual intercourse with (a woman). □ **bit of stuff** *Brit. sl. offens.* a woman regarded as an object of sexual desire. **do one's stuff** *colloq.* do what one has to. **get stuffed** *Brit. sl.* an exclamation of dismissal, contempt, etc. **stuff and nonsense** *Brit.* an exclamation of incredulity or ridicule. **stuff it** *sl.* an expression of rejection or disdain. **that's the stuff** *colloq.* that is what is wanted. □□ **stuff·er** *n.* (also in *comb.*). [ME *stoffe* f. OF *estoffe* (n.), *estoffer* (v.) equip, furnish f. Gk *stupho* draw together]

stuffed shirt *n. colloq.* a pompous person.

stuff·ing /stúfing/ *n.* **1** padding used to stuff cushions, etc. **2** a mixture used to stuff poultry, vegetables, etc., esp. before cooking. □ **knock** (or **take**) **the stuffing out of** *colloq.* beat soundly; defeat.

stuff·ing box *n.* a box packed with material, to allow the working of an axle while remaining airtight.

stuff·y /stúfee/ *adj.* (**stuff·i·er, stuff·i·est**) **1** (of a room or the atmosphere in it) lacking fresh air or ventilation; close. **2** dull or uninteresting. **3** (of a person's nose, etc.) stuffed up. **4** (of a person) dull and conventional. □□ **stuff·i·ly** *adv.* **stuff·i·ness** *n.*

stul·ti·fy /stúltifí/ *v.tr.* (**·fies, ·fied**) **1** make ineffective, useless, or futile, esp. as a result of tedious routine (*stultifying boredom*). **2** cause to appear foolish or absurd. **3** negate or neutralize. □□ **stul·ti·fi·ca·tion** /-fikáyshən/ *n.* **stul·ti·fi·er** *n.* [LL *stultificare* f. L *stultus* foolish]

stum /stum/ *n. & v.* ● *n.* unfermented grape juice; must. ● *v.tr.* (**stummed, stum·ming**) **1** prevent from fermenting, or secure (wine) against further fermentation in a cask, by the use of sulfur, etc. **2** renew the fermentation of (wine) by adding stum. [Du. *stommen* (v.), *stom* (n.) f. *stom* (adj.) dumb]

stum·ble /stúmbəl/ *v. & n.* ● *v.* **1** *intr.* lurch forward or have a partial fall from catching or striking or misplacing one's foot. **2** *intr.* (often foll. by *along*) walk with repeated stumbles. **3** *intr.* make a mistake or repeated mistakes in speaking, etc. **4** *intr.* (foll. by *on, upon, across*) find or encounter by chance (*stumbled on a disused well*). ● *n.* an act of stumbling. □□ **stum·bler** *n.* **stum·bling·ly** *adv.* [ME *stumble* (with euphonic *b*) corresp. to Norw. *stumla*: rel. to STAMMER]

stum·ble·bum /stúmbəlbum/ *n. colloq.* a clumsy or inept person.

stum·bling block *n.* an obstacle or circumstance causing difficulty or hesitation.

stump /stump/ *n. & v.* ● *n* **1** the projecting remnant of a cut or fallen tree. **2** the similar remnant of anything else (e.g., a branch or limb) cut off or worn down. **3** *Cricket* each of the three uprights of a wicket. **4** (in *pl.*) *joc.* the legs. **5** the stump of a tree, or other place, used by an orator to address a meeting. **6** a cylinder of rolled paper or other material with conical ends for shading, blending, softening pencil marks and other uses in drawing. ● *v.* **1** *tr.* (of a question, etc.) be too hard for; puzzle. **2** *tr.* (as **stumped** *adj.*) at a loss; baffled. **3** *tr. Cricket* (esp. of a wicket-keeper) put (a batsman) out by touching the stumps with the ball while the batsman is out of the crease. **4** *intr.* walk stiffly or noisily as on a wooden leg. **5** *tr.* (also *absol.*) traverse (a district) making political speeches. **6** *tr.* use a stump on (a drawing, line, etc.). □ **on the stump** *colloq.* engaged in political speechmaking or agitation. **stump up** *Brit. colloq.* pay or produce (the money required). **up a stump** in difficulties. [ME *stompe* f. MDu. *stomp*, OHG *stumpf*]

stump·er /stúmpər/ *n. colloq.* **1** a puzzling question. **2** *Cricket* a wicket-keeper.

stump·y /stúmpee/ *adj.* (**stump·i·er, stump·i·est**) short and thick. □□ **stump·i·ly** *adv.* **stump·i·ness** *n.*

stun /stun/ *v.tr.* (**stunned, stun·ning**) **1** knock senseless; stupefy. **2** bewilder or shock. **3** (of a sound) deafen temporarily. [ME f. OF *estoner* ASTONISH]

stung *past* and *past part.* of STING.

stunk *past* and *past part.* of STINK.

stun·ner /stúnər/ *n. colloq.* a stunning person or thing.

stun·ning /stúning/ *adj. colloq.* extremely impressive or attractive. □□ **stun·ning·ly** *adv.*

stunt¹ /stunt/ *v.tr.* **1** retard the growth or development of. **2** dwarf; cramp. □□ **stunt·ed·ness** *n.* [*stunt* foolish (now dial.), MHG *stunz*, ON *stuttr* short f. Gmc, perh. rel. to STUMP]

stunt² /stunt/ *n.* **1** something unusual done to attract attention. **2** a trick or daring maneuver. **3** a display of concentrated energy. ● *v.intr.* perform stunts. [orig. unkn.: first used in 19th-c. US college sports]

stunt man *n.* (also **stunt wom·an**) a man (or woman) employed to take an actor's place in performing dangerous stunts.

stu·pa /stoopə/ *n.* a round usu. domed building erected as a Buddhist shrine. [Skr. *stūpa*]

stupe¹ /stoop, styoop/ *n. & v.* ● *n.* a soft cloth, etc., soaked in hot water, wrung out, and applied as a poultice. ● *v.tr.* treat with this. [ME f. L f. Gk *stupē* tow]

stupe² /stoop, styoop/ *n. sl.* a foolish or stupid person.

stu·pe·fy /stoopifi, styoo-/ *v.tr.* (**·fies, ·fied**) **1** make stupid or insensible (*stupefied with drink*). **2** stun with astonishment (*the news was stupefying*). □□ **stu·pe·fa·cient** /-fáyshənt/ *adj. & n.* **stu·pe·fac·tion** /-fákshən/ *n.* **stu·pe·fac·tive** *adj.* **stu·pe·fi·er** *n.* **stu·pe·fy·ing** *adj.* **stu·pe·fy·ing·ly** *adv.* [F *stupéfier* f. L *stupefacere* f. *stupēre* be amazed]

stu·pen·dous /stoopéndəs, styoo-/ *adj.* amazing or prodigious, esp. in terms of size or degree (*a stupendous achievement*). □□ **stu·pen·dous·ly** *adv.* **stu·pen·dous·ness** *n.* [L *stupendus* gerundive of *stupēre* be amazed at]

stu·pid /stoopid, styoo-/ *adj. & n.* (**stu·pid·er, stu·pid·est**) ● *adj.* **1** unintelligent; slow-witted; foolish (*a stupid fellow*). **2** typical of stupid persons (*put it in a stupid place*). **3** uninteresting or boring. **4** in a state of stupor or lethargy. **5** obtuse; lacking in sensibility. ● *n. colloq.* a stupid person. □□ **stu·pid·i·ty** /-píditee/ *n.* (*pl.* **·ties**). **stu·pid·ly** *adv.* [F *stupide* or L *stupidus* (as STUPENDOUS)]

SYNONYM TIP **stupid**

ASININE, DENSE, DULL, DUMB, OBTUSE, SLOW, UNINTELLIGENT. If you want to impugn someone's intelligence, the options are almost limitless. You can call the person **stupid**, a term that implies a sluggish, slow-witted lack of intelligence. **Asinine** is a harsher word, implying asslike or foolish behavior rather than slow-wittedness (*a woman her age looked asinine in a miniskirt*). Calling someone **dumb** is risky, because it is not only a very informal word (*you dumb bunny!*), but because it also means mute and is associated with the offensive expression "deaf and *dumb*," used to describe people who cannot hear or speak. **Dense** implies an inability to understand even simple facts or instructions (*too dense to get the joke*), while **dull** suggests a sluggishness of mind unrelieved by any hint of quickness, brightness, or liveliness (*a dull stare*). **Slow** also implies a lack of quickness in comprehension or reaction and is often used as a euphemistic substitute for *stupid* (*a special class for students who were slow*). **Obtuse** is a more formal word for slow-wittedness, but with a strong undercurrent of scorn (*it almost seemed as though he were being deliberately obtuse*). You can't go wrong with a word like **unintelligent**, which is probably the most objective term for low mental ability and the least likely to provoke an angry response (*unintelligent answers to the teacher's questions*).

stu·por /stoopər, styoo-/ *n.* a dazed, torpid, or helplessly amazed state. □□ **stu·por·ous** *adj.* [ME f. L (as STUPENDOUS)]

stur·dy /stúrdee/ *adj. & n.* ● *adj.* (**stur·di·er, stur·di·est**) **1** robust; strongly built. **2** vigorous and determined (*sturdy resistance*). ● *n.* vertigo in sheep caused by a tapeworm larva encysted in the brain. □□ **stur·died** *adj.* (in sense of *n.*). **stur·di·ly** *adv.* **stur·di·ness** *n.* [ME 'reckless, violent,' f. OF *esturdi, estourdi* past part. of *estourdir* stun, daze ult. f. L *ex* EX-¹ + *turdus* thrush (taken as a type of drunkenness)]

stur·geon /stúrjən/ *n.* any large sharklike fish of the family Acipenseridae, etc., swimming up river to spawn, used as food and a source of caviar and isinglass. [ME f. AF *sturgeon*, OF *esturgeon* ult. f. Gmc]

Sturm und Drang /shtoorm oont dráng/ *n.* a literary and artistic movement in Germany in the late 18th c., characterized by the expression of emotional unrest and strong feeling. [G, = storm and stress]

stut·ter /stútər/ *v. & n.* ● *v.* **1** *intr.* stammer, esp. by involuntarily repeating the first consonants of words. **2** *tr.* (often foll. by *out*) utter (words) in this way. ● *n.* **1** the act or habit of stuttering. **2** an instance of stuttering. □□ **stut·ter·er** *n.* **stut·ter·ing·ly** *adv.* [frequent. of ME (now dial.) *stut* f. Gmc]

sty¹ /stí/ *n. & v.* ● *n.* (*pl.* **sties**) **1** a pen or enclosure for pigs. **2** a filthy room or dwelling. **3** a place of debauchery. ● *v.tr. & intr.* (**sties, stied**) lodge in a sty. [OE *stī*, prob. = *stig* hall (cf. STEWARD), f. Gmc]

sty[2] /stī/ *n.* (also **stye**) (*pl.* **sties** or **styes**) an inflamed swelling on the edge of an eyelid. [*styany* (now dial.) = *styan eye* f. OE *stīgend* sty, lit. 'riser' f. *stīgan* rise + EYE, shortened as if = *sty on eye*]

Styg·i·an /stíjeeən/ *adj.* **1** (in Greek mythology) of or relating to the Styx, a river in Hades. **2** *literary* dark; gloomy; indistinct. [L *stygius* f. Gk *stugios* f. *Stux –ugos* Styx f. *stugnos* hateful, gloomy]

style /stīl/ *n. & v.* ● *n.* **1** a kind or sort, esp. in regard to appearance and form (*an elegant style of house*). **2** a manner of writing or speaking or performing (*written in a florid style; started off in fine style*). **3** the distinctive manner of a person or school or period, esp. in relation to painting, architecture, furniture, dress, etc. **4** the correct way of designating a person or thing. **5 a** a superior quality or manner (*do it in style*). **b** = FORM *n.* 9 (*bad style*). **c** state of popularity; fashion. **6** a particular make, shape, or pattern (*in all sizes and styles*). **7** a method of reckoning dates (*old style; new style*). **8** = STYLUS 2. **9** the gnomon of a sundial. **10** *Bot.* the narrow extension of the ovary supporting the stigma. **11** (in *comb.*) = –WISE. ● *v.tr.* **1** design or make, etc., in a particular (esp. fashionable) style. **2** designate in a specified way. □□ **style·less** *adj.* **style·less·ness** *n.* **styl·er** *n.* [ME f. OF *stile, style* f. L *stilus*: spelling *style* due to assoc. with Gk *stulos* column]

sty·let /stílit/ *n.* **1** a slender pointed instrument; a stiletto. **2** *Med.* the stiffening wire of a catheter; a probe. [F *stilet* f. It. STILETTO]

sty·li *pl.* of STYLUS.

styl·ish /stílish/ *adj.* **1** fashionable; elegant. **2** having a superior quality, manner, etc. □□ **styl·ish·ly** *adv.* **styl·ish·ness** *n.*

styl·ist /stílist/ *n.* **1 a** a designer of fashionable styles, etc. **b** a hairdresser. **2 a** a writer noted for or aspiring to good literary style. **b** (in sports or music) a person who performs with style.

sty·lis·tic /stílístik/ *adj.* of or concerning esp. literary style. □□ **sty·lis·ti·cal·ly** *adv.* [STYLIST + –IC, after G *stilistisch*]

sty·lis·tics /stílístiks/ *n.* the study of literary style.

sty·lite /stílīt/ *n. Eccl. hist.* an ancient or medieval ascetic living on top of a pillar. [eccl.Gk *stulitēs* f. *stulos* pillar]

styl·ize /stílīz/ *v.tr.* (esp. as **stylized** *adj.*) paint, draw, etc., (a subject) in a conventional nonrealistic style. □□ **styl·i·za·tion** *n.* [STYLE + –IZE, after G *stilisieren*]

sty·lo /stílō/ *n.* (*pl.* **·los**) *colloq.* = STYLOGRAPH. [abbr.]

sty·lo·bate /stíləbayt/ *n. Archit.* a continuous base supporting a row of columns. [L *stylobata* f. Gk *stulobatēs* f. *stulos* pillar, *bainō* walk]

sty·lo·graph /stíləgraf/ *n.* a kind of fountain pen having a point instead of a split nib. □□ **sty·lo·graph·ic** *adj.* [STYLUS + –GRAPH]

sty·loid /stíloyd/ *adj. & n.* ● *adj.* resembling a stylus or pen. ● *n.* (in full **styloid process**) a spine of bone, esp. that projecting from the base of the temporal bone. [mod.L *styloides* f. Gk *stuloeidēs* f. *stulos* pillar]

sty·lus /stíləs/ *n.* (*pl.* **·li** /–lī/ or **·lus·es**) **1 a** a hard, esp. diamond or sapphire, point following a groove in a phonograph record and transmitting the recorded sound for reproduction. **b** a similar point producing such a groove when recording sound. **2 a** an ancient writing implement, a small rod with a pointed end for scratching letters on wax-covered tablets and a blunt end for obliterating them. **b** a thing of a similar shape esp. for engraving, tracing, etc. **3** *Computing* a pointing device used esp. with a graphics tablet. [erron. spelling of L *stilus*: cf. STYLE]

sty·mie /stímee/ *n. & v.* (also **sti·my**) ● *n.* (*pl.* **·mies**) **1** *Golf* a situation where an opponent's ball lies between the player and the hole, forming a possible obstruction to play (*lay a stymie*). **2** a difficult situation. ● *v.tr.* (**sty·mies, sty·mied, sty·my·ing** or **sty·mie·ing**) **1** obstruct; thwart. **2** *Golf* block (an opponent, a ball, or oneself) with a stymie. [19th c.: orig. unkn.]

styp·tic /stíptik/ *adj. & n.* ● *adj.* (of a drug, etc.) that checks bleeding. ● *n.* a styptic drug or substance. [ME f. L *stypticus* f. Gk *stuptikos* f. *stuphō* contract]

styp·tic pen·cil *n.* a pencil-shaped wand containing a styptic substance used to check bleeding from minor cuts, as from shaving.

sty·rax /stíraks/ *n.* **1** storax resin. **2** any tree or shrub of the genus *Styrax*, e.g., the storax tree. [L f. Gk *sturax*: cf. STORAX]

sty·rene /stíreen/ *n. Chem.* a liquid hydrocarbon easily polymerized and used in making plastics, etc. [STYRAX + –ENE]

Sty·ro·foam /stírəfōm/ *n. Trademark* a brand of expanded rigid lightweight polystyrene plastic.

su·a·ble /sóōəbəl/ *adj.* capable of being sued. □□ **su·a·bil·i·ty** /–bílitee/ *n.*

sua·sion /swáyzhən/ *n. formal* persuasion as opposed to force (*moral suasion*). □□ **sua·sive** /swáysiv/ *adj.* [ME f. OF *suasion* or L *suasio* f. *suadēre suas-* urge]

suave /swaav/ *adj.* **1** (of a person) smooth; polite; sophisticated. **2** (of a wine, etc.) bland; smooth. □□ **suave·ly** *adv.* **suave·ness** *n.* **suav·i·ty** /–vitee/ *n.* (*pl.* **·ties**). [F *suave* or L *suavis* agreeable: cf. SWEET]

sub /sub/ *n. & v. colloq.* ● *n.* **1** a submarine. **2** a subscription. **3** a substitute. **4** *Brit.* a subeditor. **5** *Brit. Mil.* a subaltern. **6** *Brit.* an advance or loan against expected income. ● *v.* (**subbed, sub·bing**) **1** *intr.* (usu. foll. by *for*) act as a substitute for a person. **2** *tr. Brit. colloq.* lend or advance (a sum) to (a person) against expected income. **3** *tr. Brit.* subedit. [abbr.]

sub- /sub, səb/ *prefix* (also **suc-** before *c*, **suf-** before *f*, **sug-** before *g*, **sup-** before *p*, **sur-** before *r*, **sus-** before *c, p, t*) **1** at or to or from a lower position (*subordinate; submerge; subtract; subsoil*). **2** secondary or inferior in rank or position (*subclass; subcommittee; sub-lieutenant; subtotal*). **3** somewhat; nearly; more or less (*subacid; subarctic; subaquatic*). **4** (forming verbs) denoting secondary action (*subdivide; sublet*). **5** denoting support (*subvention*). **6** (of a salt) basic (*subacetate*). [from or after L *sub-* f. *sub* under, close to, toward]

sub·ab·dom·i·nal /súbabdóminəl/ *adj.* below the abdomen.

sub·ac·id /súbásid/ *adj.* moderately acid or tart (*subacid fruit; a subacid remark*). □□ **sub·a·cid·i·ty** /súbəsíditee/ *n.* [L *subacidus* (as SUB-, ACID)]

sub·a·cute /súbəkyóōt/ *adj. Med.* (of a condition) between acute and chronic.

sub·a·gen·cy /súbáyjənsee/ *n.* (*pl.* **·cies**) a secondary or subordinate agency. □□ **sub·a·gent** *n.*

sub·al·pine /súbálpīn/ *adj.* of or situated in the higher slopes of mountains just below the timberline.

sub·al·tern /subáwltərn/ *n. & adj.* ● *n. Brit. Mil.* an officer below the rank of captain, esp. a second lieutenant. ● *adj.* **1** of inferior rank. **2** /súbaltərn/ *Logic* (of a proposition) particular; not universal. [LL *subalternus* f. *alternus* ALTERNATE *adj.*]

sub·ant·arc·tic /súbantaárktik, –aártik/ *adj.* of or like regions immediately north of the Antarctic Circle.

sub·a·quat·ic /súbəkwátik, –əkwótik/ *adj.* **1** of more or less aquatic habits or kind. **2** underwater.

sub·a·que·ous /súbáykweeəs, –ák–/ *adj.* **1** existing, formed, or taking place under water. **2** lacking in substance or strength; wishy-washy.

sub·arc·tic /súbaárktik, –aártik/ *adj.* of or like regions immediately south of the Arctic Circle.

sub·as·tral /súbástrəl/ *adj.* terrestrial.

sub·a·tom·ic /súbətómik/ *adj.* occurring in or smaller than an atom.

sub·au·di·tion /súbawdíshən/ *n.* **1** the act of mentally supplying an omitted word or words in speech. **2** the act or process of understanding the unexpressed; reading between the lines. [LL *subauditio* f. *subaudire* understand (as SUB-, AUDITION)]

sub·ax·il·la·ry /súbáksileree/ *adj.* **1** *Bot.* in or growing beneath the axil. **2** beneath the armpit.

sub·base·ment /súbbaysmənt/ *n.* a story below a basement.

sub·branch /súbbranch/ *n.* a secondary or subordinate branch.

sub·breed /súbbreed/ *n.* a secondary or inferior breed.

sub·cat·e·go·ry /súbkátigawree/ *n.* (*pl.* **·ries**) a secondary or subordinate category. □□ **sub·cat·e·gor·ize** *v.tr.* **sub·cat·e·gor·i·za·tion** *n.*

sub·cau·dal /súbkáwdəl/ *adj.* of or concerning the region under the tail or the back part of the body.

sub·class /súbklas/ *n.* **1** a secondary or subordinate class. **2** *Biol.* a taxonomic category below a class.

sub·clause /súbklawz/ *n.* **1** esp. *Law* a subsidiary section of a clause. **2** *Gram.* a subordinate clause.

sub·cla·vi·an /súbkláyveeən/ *adj. & n.* ● *adj.* (of an artery, etc.) lying or extending under the collar bone. ● *n.* such an artery. [mod.L *subclavius* (as SUB-, *clavis* key): cf. CLAVICLE]

sub·clin·i·cal /súbklínikəl/ *adj. Med.* (of a disease) not yet presenting definite symptoms.

sub·com·mis·sion·er /súbkəmíshənər/ *n.* a deputy commissioner.

sub·com·mit·tee /súbkəmitee/ *n.* a secondary committee.

sub·com·pact /səbkómpakt/ *n. & adj.* a car that is smaller than a compact.

sub·con·i·cal /súbkónikəl/ *adj.* approximately conical.

sub·con·scious /súbkónshəs/ *adj. & n.* ● *adj.* of or concerning the part of the mind which is not fully conscious but influences actions, etc. ● *n.* this part of the mind. □□ **sub·con·scious·ly** *adv.* **sub·con·scious·ness** *n.*

sub·con·ti·nent /súbkóntinənt/ *n.* **1** a large land mass, smaller than a continent. **2** a large geographically or politically independent part of a continent. □□ **sub·con·ti·nen·tal** /–nént'l/ *adj.*

sub·con·tract *v. & n.* ● *v.* /súbkəntrákt/ **1** *tr.* employ a firm, etc., to do (work) as part of a larger project. **2** *intr.* make or carry out a subcontract. ● *n.* /súbkóntrakt/ a secondary contract, esp. to supply materials, labor, etc. □□ **sub·con·trac·tor** /–kóntraktər/ *n.*

sub·con·tra·ry /súbkóntreeree/ *adj. & n. Logic* ● *adj.* (of a proposition) incapable of being false at the same time as another. ● *n.* (*pl.* **·ries**) such a proposition. [LL *subcontrarius* (as SUB-, CONTRARY), transl. Gk *hupenantios*]

sub·cor·date /súbkáwrdayt/ *adj.* approximately heart-shaped.

sub·cor·ti·cal /súbkáwrtikəl/ *adj. Anat.* below the cortex.

sub·cos·tal /súbkóstəl/ *adj. Anat.* below the ribs.

sub·cra·ni·al /súbkráyneeəl/ *adj. Anat.* below the cranium.

sub·crit·i·cal /súbkrítikəl/ *adj. Physics* of less than critical mass, etc.

sub·cul·ture /súbkulchər/ *n.* a cultural group within a larger culture, often having beliefs or interests at variance with those of the larger culture. □□ **sub•cul•tur•al** /–kúlchərəl/ *adj.*

sub•cu•ta•ne•ous /súbkyŏŏtáyneeəs/ *adj.* under the skin. □□ **sub•cu•ta•ne•ous•ly** *adv.*

sub•dea•con /súbdeékən/ *n. Eccl.* a minister of the order immediately below a deacon. □□ **sub•di•ac•o•nate** /–diákənayt,–nət/ *n.* **sub•deaconate** /–deékənit/ *n.*

sub•dean /súbdeén/ *n.* an official ranking immediately below, or acting as a deputy for, a dean. □□ **sub•dean•er•y** *n. (pl. •ies).* **sub•dec•a•nal** /–dikáyn'l/ *adj.*

sub•de•lir•i•ous /súbdileereeəs/ *adj.* capable of becoming delirious; mildly delirious. □□ **sub•de•lir•i•um** *n.*

sub•di•vide /súbdivíd/ *v.tr. & intr.* divide again after a first division. [ME f. L *subdividere* (as SUB-, DIVIDE)]

sub•di•vi•sion /súbdivízhən/ *n.* **1** the act or an instance of subdividing. **2** a secondary or subordinate division. **3 a** an area of land divided into plots for sale. **b** a housing development in such an area.

sub•dom•i•nant /súbdóminənt/ *n. Mus.* the fourth note of the diatonic scale of any key.

sub•due /səbdóō, –dyóō/ *v.tr.* (**sub•dues, sub•dued, sub•du•ing**) **1** conquer, subjugate, or tame (an enemy, nature, one's emotions, etc.). **2** (as **subdued** *adj.*) softened; lacking in intensity; toned down (*subdued light; in a subdued mood*). □□ **sub•du•a•ble** *adj.* **sub•du•al** *n.* [ME *sodewe* f. OF *so(u)duire* f. L *subducere* (as SUB-, *ducere* lead, bring) used with the sense of *subdere* conquer (as SUB-, –*dere* put)]

sub•ed•i•tor /súbéditər/ *n. Brit.* **1** an assistant editor. **2** a person who edits material for printing in a book, newspaper, etc. □□ **sub•ed•it** *v.tr.* (•**ed•it•ed, ed•it•ing**). **sub•ed•i•to•ri•al** /–táwreeəl/ *adj.*

sub•e•rect /súbirékt/ *adj.* (of an animal, plant, etc.) almost erect.

su•be•re•ous /sŏōbeéreeəs/ *adj.* (also **su•ber•ic** /sŏōbérik/, **su•ber•ose** /sŏōbərōs/) **1** of or concerning cork. **2** corky. [L *suber* cork, cork oak]

sub•fam•i•ly /súbfamilee/ *n. (pl. •lies)* **1** *Biol.* a taxonomic category below a family. **2** any subdivision of a group.

sub•floor /súbflawr/ (also **sub•floor•ing**) *n.* a foundation for a floor in a building.

sub•form /súbfawrm/ *n.* a subordinate or secondary form.

sub•fusc /súbfusk/ *adj. & n.* ● *adj. formal* dull; dusky; gloomy. ● *n. Brit.* formal clothing at some universities. [L *subfuscus* f. *fuscus* dark brown]

sub•ge•nus /súbjeénəs/ *n.* (*pl.* **sub•gen•er•a** /–jénərə/) *Biol.* a taxonomic category below a genus. □□ **sub•ge•ner•ic** /–jinérik/ *adj.*

sub•gla•cial /súbgláyshəl/ *adj.* next to or at the bottom of a glacier.

sub•group /súbgrŏōp/ *n. Math.,* etc., a subset of a group.

sub•head /súbhed/ *n.* (also **sub•head•ing**) **1** a subordinate heading or title in a chapter, article, etc. **2** a subordinate division in a classification.

sub•hu•man /súbhyŏōmən/ *adj.* **1** (of an animal) closely related to humans. **2** (of behavior, intelligence, etc.) less than human.

subj. *abbr.* **1** subject. **2** subjective. **3** subjunctive.

sub•ja•cent /súbjáysənt/ *adj.* underlying; situated below. [L *subjacēre* (as SUB-, *jacēre* lie)]

sub•ject *n., adj., adv., & v.* ● *n.* /súbjikt/ **1 a** a matter, theme, etc., to be discussed, described, represented, dealt with, etc. **b** (foll. by *for*) a person, circumstance, etc., giving rise to specified feeling, action, etc. (*a subject for congratulation*). **2** a department or field of study (*his best subject is geography*). **3** *Gram.* a noun or its equivalent about which a sentence is predicated and with which the verb agrees. **4 a** any person except a monarch living under a monarchy or any other form of government (*the ruler and his subjects*). **b** any person owing obedience to another. **5** *Philos.* **a** a thinking or feeling entity; the conscious mind; the ego, esp. as opposed to anything external to the mind. **b** the central substance or core of a thing as opposed to its attributes. **6** *Mus.* a theme of a fugue or sonata; a leading phrase or motif. **7** a person of specified mental or physical tendencies (*a hysterical subject*). **8** *Logic* the part of a proposition about which a statement is made. **9 a** a person or animal undergoing treatment, examination, or experimentation. **b** a dead body for dissection. ● *adj.* /súbjikt/ **1** (often foll. by *to*) owing obedience to a government, colonizing power, force, etc.; in subjection. **2** (foll. by *to*) liable, exposed, or prone to (*is subject to infection*). **3** (foll. by *to*) conditional upon; on the assumption of (*the arrangement is subject to your approval*). ● *adv.* /súbjikt/ (foll. by *to*) conditionally upon (*subject to your consent, I propose to try again*). ● *v.tr.* /səbjékt/ **1** (foll. by *to*) make liable; expose; treat (*subjected us to hours of waiting*). **2** (usu. foll. by *to*) subdue (a nation, person, etc.) to one's control, etc. □□ **sub•jec•tion** /səbjékshən/ *n.* **sub•ject•less** /súbjiktlis/ *adj.* [ME *soget*, etc. f. OF *suget*, etc. f. L *subjectus* past part. of *subjicere* (as SUB-, *jacere* throw)]

sub•ject and ob•ject *n. Psychol.* the ego or self and the non-ego; consciousness and that of which it is or may be conscious.

sub•ject cat•a•log *n.* a catalog, esp. in a library, arranged according to the subjects treated.

sub•ject head•ing *n.* a heading in an index collecting references to a subject.

sub•jec•tive /səbjéktiv/ *adj. & n.* ● *adj.* **1** (of art, literature, written history, a person's views, etc.) proceeding from personal idiosyncrasy or individuality; not impartial or literal. **2** esp. *Philos.* proceeding from or belonging to the individual consciousness or perception; imaginary, partial, or distorted. **3** *Gram.* of or concerning the subject. ● *n. Gram.* the nominative. □□ **sub•jec•tive•ly** *adv.* **sub•jec•tive•ness** *n.* **sub•jec•tiv•i•ty** /subjektívitee/ *n.* [ME f. L *subjectivus* (as SUBJECT)]

sub•jec•tive case *n. Gram.* the nominative.

sub•jec•tiv•ism /səbjéktivizəm/ *n. Philos.* the doctrine that knowledge is merely subjective and that there is no external or objective truth. □□ **sub•jec•tiv•ist** *n.*

sub•ject mat•ter *n.* the matter treated of in a book, lawsuit, etc.

sub•join /súbjóyn/ *v.tr.* add or append (an illustration, anecdote, etc.) at the end. [obs. F *subjoindre* f. L *subjungere* (as SUB-, *jungere* junct- join)]

sub•joint /súbjoynt/ *n.* a secondary joint (in an insect's leg, etc.).

sub ju•di•ce /sub jóōdisee, sŏōb yóōdikay/ *adj. Law* under judicial consideration and therefore prohibited from public discussion elsewhere. [L, = under a judge]

sub•ju•gate /súbjəgayt/ *v.tr.* bring into subjection; subdue; vanquish. □□ **sub•ju•ga•ble** /–gəbəl/ *adj.* **sub•ju•ga•tion** /–gáyshən/ *n.* **sub•ju•ga•tor** *n.* [ME f. LL *subjugare* bring under the yoke (as SUB-, *jugum* yoke)]

sub•junc•tive /səbjúngktiv/ *adj. & n. Gram.* ● *adj.* (of a mood) denoting what is imagined or wished or possible (e.g., *if I were you; God help you; be that as it may*). ● *n.* **1** the subjunctive mood. **2** a verb in this mood. □□ **sub•junc•tive•ly** *adv.* [F *subjonctif –ive* or LL *subjunctivus* f. L (as SUBJOIN), transl. Gk *hupotaktikos*, as being used in subjoined clauses]

sub•king•dom /súbkingdəm/ *n. Biol.* a taxonomic category below a kingdom.

sub•lease *n. & v.* ● *n.* /súblees/ a lease of a property by a tenant to a subtenant. ● *v.tr.* /súbleés/ lease (a property) to a subtenant.

sub•les•see /súblesee/ *n.* a person who holds a sublease.

sub•les•sor /súblesáwr/ *n.* a person who grants a sublease.

sub•let *n. & v.* ● *n.* /súblet/ = SUBLEASE *n.* ● *v.tr.* /súblét/ (•**let•ting**; *past* and *past part.* •**let**) = SUBLEASE *v.*

sub•lieu•ten•ant /súblŏōténənt/ *n. Brit.* a naval officer ranking immediately below lieutenant.

sub•li•mate *v., adj., & n.* ● *v.* /súblimayt/ **1** *tr. & intr.* divert (the energy of a primitive impulse, esp. sexual) into a culturally more acceptable activity. **2** *tr. & intr. Chem.* convert (a substance) from the solid state directly to its vapor by heat, and usu. allow it to solidify again. **3** *tr.* refine; purify; idealize. ● *adj.* /súblimət, –mayt/ **1** *Chem.* (of a substance) sublimated. **2** purified; refined. ● *n.* /súblimət/ *Chem.* **1** a sublimated substance. **2** = CORROSIVE SUBLIMATE. □□ **sub•li•ma•tion** /–máyshən/ *n.* [L *sublimare sublimat-* SUBLIME *v.*]

sub•lime /səblím/ *adj. & v.* ● *adj.* (**sub•lim•er, sub•lim•est**) **1** of the most exalted, grand, or noble kind; awe inspiring (*sublime genius*). **2** (of indifference, impudence, etc.) arrogantly unruffled; extreme (*sublime ignorance*). ● *v.* **1** *tr. & intr. Chem.* = SUBLIMATE *v.* **2. 2** *tr.* purify or elevate by or as if by sublimation; make sublime. **3** *intr.* become pure by or as if by sublimation. □□ **sub•lime•ly** *adv.* **sub•lim•i•ty** /–límitee/ *n.* [L *sublimis* (as SUB-, second element perh. rel. to *limen* threshold, *limus* oblique)]

Sub•lime Porte *n.* see PORTE.

sub•lim•i•nal /səblíminəl/ *adj. Psychol.* (of a stimulus, etc.) below the threshold of sensation or consciousness. □□ **sub•lim•i•nal•ly** *adv.* [SUB- + L *limen –inis* threshold]

sub•lim•i•nal ad•ver•tis•ing *n.* the use of subliminal images in advertising on television, etc., to influence the viewer at an unconscious level.

sub•lim•i•nal self *n.* the part of one's personality outside conscious awareness.

sub•lin•gual /súblínggwəl/ *adj.* under the tongue. [SUB- + L *lingua* tongue]

sub•lit•to•ral /súblítərəl/ *adj.* **1** (of plants, animals, deposits, etc.) living or found on the seashore just below the low tide line. **2** of or concerning the seashore.

sub•lu•nar•y /súblŏōnéree, sublŏōnəree/ *adj.* **1** beneath the moon. **2** *Astron.* **a** within the moon's orbit. **b** subject to the moon's influence. **3** of this world; earthly. [LL *sublunaris* (as SUB-, LUNAR)]

sub•ma•chine gun /súbməsheén/ *n.* a hand-held lightweight machine gun.

sub•mar•gin•al /súbmaárjinəl/ *adj.* **1** esp. Econ. not reaching minimum requirements. **2** (of land) that cannot be farmed profitably.

sub•ma•rine /súbməreén/ *n. & adj.* ● *n.* **1** a vessel, esp. a warship, capable of operating under water and usu. equipped with torpedoes, missiles, and a periscope. **2** = SUBMARINE SANDWICH. ● *adj.* existing, occurring, done, or used under the surface of the sea (*submarine cable*). □□ **sub•ma•rin•er** /–mareénər, səbmárinər/ *n.*

sub·ma·rine sand·wich *n.* a large sandwich usu. consisting of a halved roll, meat, cheese, lettuce, tomato, etc.

sub·max·il·lar·y /submáksileree/ *adj.* beneath the lower jaw.

sub·me·di·ant /súbmeédeeənt/ *n. Mus.* the sixth note of the diatonic scale of any key.

sub·men·tal /súbmént'l/ *adj.* under the chin.

sub·merge /səbmérj/ *v.* **1** *tr.* **a** place under water; flood; inundate. **b** flood or inundate with work, problems, etc. **2** *intr.* (of a submarine, its crew, a diver, etc.) dive below the surface of water. □□ **sub·mer·gence** *n.* **sub·mer·gi·ble** *adj.* **sub·mer·sion** /–mórzhən, –shən/ *n.* [L *submergere* (as SUB-, *mergere* mers- dip)]

sub·mers·i·ble /səbmérsibəl/ *n. & adj.* ● *n.* a submarine operating under water for short periods, esp. one used for deep-sea diving. ● *adj.* capable of being submerged. [*submerse* (v.) = SUBMERGE]

sub·mi·cro·scop·ic /súbmíkrəskópik/ *adj.* too small to be seen by an ordinary microscope.

sub·min·i·a·ture /súbmíneeəchər, –chōōr/ *adj.* **1** of greatly reduced size. **2** (of a camera) very small and using 16-mm film.

sub·mis·sion /səbmíshən/ *n.* **1 a** the act or an instance of submitting; the state of being submitted. **b** anything that is submitted. **2** humility; meekness; obedience; submissiveness (*showed great submission of spirit*). **3** *Law* a theory, etc., submitted by a lawyer to a judge or jury. **4** (in wrestling) the surrender of a participant yielding to the pain of a hold. [ME f. OF *submission* or L *submissio* (as SUBMIT)]

sub·mis·sive /səbmísiv/ *adj.* **1** humble; obedient. **2** yielding to power or authority; willing to submit. □□ **sub·mis·sive·ly** *adv.* **sub·mis·sive·ness** *n.* [SUBMISSION after *remissive*, etc.]

sub·mit /səbmít/ *v.* (**sub·mit·ted, sub·mit·ting**) **1** (usu. foll. by *to*) **a** *intr.* cease resistance; give way; yield (*had to submit to defeat; will never submit*). **b** *refl.* surrender (oneself) to the control of another, etc. **2** *tr.* present for consideration or decision. **3** *tr.* (usu. foll. by *to*) subject (a person or thing) to an operation, process, treatment, etc. (*submitted it to the flames*). **4** *tr.* esp. Law urge or represent esp. deferentially (*that, I submit, is a misrepresentation*). □□ **sub·mit·ter** *n.* [ME f. L *submittere* (as SUB-, *mittere* miss- send)]

sub·mul·ti·ple /súbmúltipəl/ *n. & adj.* ● *n.* a number that can be divided exactly into a specified number. ● *adj.* being such a number.

sub·nor·mal /súbnáwrməl/ *adj.* **1** (esp. as regards intelligence) below normal. **2** less than normal. □□ **sub·nor·mal·i·ty** /–málitee/ *n.*

sub·nu·cle·ar /súbnōōkleeər, –nyōō–/ *adj. Physics* occurring in or smaller than an atomic nucleus.

sub·oc·u·lar /súbókyələr/ *adj.* situated below or under the eyes.

sub·or·bit·al /súbáwrbit'l/ *adj.* **1** situated below the orbit of the eye. **2** (of a spaceship, etc.) not completing a full orbit of the earth.

sub·or·der /súbawrdər/ *n.* a taxonomic category between an order and a family. □□ **sub·or·di·nal** /–órdin'l/ *adj.*

sub·or·di·nar·y /súbáwrd'neree/ *n.* (*pl.* **-ies**) *Heraldry* a device or bearing that is common but less so than ordinaries.

sub·or·di·nate *adj., n., & v.* ● *adj.* /səbáwrd'nət/ (usu. foll. by *to*) of inferior importance or rank; secondary; subservient. ● *n.* /səbáwrd'nət/ a person working under another's control or orders. ● *v.tr.* /səbáwrd'nayt/ (usu. foll. by *to*) **1** make subordinate; treat or regard as of minor importance. **2** make subservient. □□ **sub·or·di·nate·ly** *adv.* **sub·or·di·na·tion** /–náyshən/ *n.* **sub·or·di·na·tive** /səbáwrd'nətiv/ *adj.* [med.L *subordinare, subordinat-* (as SUB-, L *ordinare* ordain)]

sub·or·di·nate clause *n.* a clause serving as an adjective, adverb, or noun in a main sentence because of its position or a preceding conjunction.

sub·orn /səbáwrn/ *v.tr.* induce by bribery, etc., to commit perjury or any other unlawful act. □□ **sub·or·na·tion** *n.* **sub·orn·er** *n.* [L *subornare* incite secretly (as SUB-, *ornare* equip)]

sub·ox·ide /súbóksīd/ *n. Chem.* an oxide containing the smallest proportion of oxygen.

sub·phy·lum /súbfíləm/ *n.* (*pl.* **sub·phy·la** /–lə/) *Biol.* a taxonomic category below a phylum.

sub·plot /súbplot/ *n.* a subordinate plot in a play, etc.

sub·poe·na /səpeénə/ *n. & v.* ● *n.* a writ ordering a person to appear in court. ● *v.tr.* (*past and past part.* **sub·poe·naed** or **sub·poe·na'd**) serve a subpoena on. [ME f. L *sub poena* under penalty (the first words of the writ)]

sub·re·gion /súbreéjən/ *n.* a division of a region, esp. with regard to natural life. □□ **sub·re·gion·al** /–reéjənəl/ *adj.*

sub·rep·tion /səbrépshən/ *n. formal* the obtaining of a thing by surprise or misrepresentation. [L *subreptio* purloining f. *subripere* (as SUB-, *rapere* snatch)]

sub·ro·ga·tion /súbrəgáyshən/ *n. Law* the substitution of one party for another as creditor, with the transfer of rights and duties. □□ **sub·ro·gate** /súbrəgayt/ *v.tr.* [LL *subrogatio* f. *subrogare* choose as substitute (as SUB-, *rogare* ask)]

sub ro·sa /sub rózə/ *adj. & adv.* (of communication, consultation, etc.) in secrecy or confidence. [L, lit. 'under the rose,' as emblem of secrecy]

sub·rou·tine /súbrōōteen/ *n. Computing* a routine designed to perform a frequently used operation within a program.

sub·scribe /səbskríb/ *v.* **1** (usu. foll. by *to, for*) **a** *tr. & intr.* contribute (a specified sum) or make or promise a contribution to a fund, project, charity, etc., esp. regularly. **b** *intr.* enter one's name in a list of contributors to a charity, etc. **c** *tr.* raise or guarantee raising (a sum) by so subscribing. **2** *intr.* (usu. foll. by *to*) express one's agreement with an opinion, resolution, etc. (*cannot subscribe to that*). **3** *tr.* **a** write (esp. one's name) at the foot of a document, etc. (*subscribed a motto*). **b** write one's name at the foot of; sign (a document, picture, etc.). **4** *tr. & intr.* arrange to receive a periodical; cable television service, etc., regularly. [ME f. L *subscribere* (as SUB-, *scribere* script- write)]

sub·scrib·er /səbskríbər/ *n.* **1** a person who subscribes. **2** a person paying for the renting of a telephone line, television cable connection, etc.

sub·script /súbskript/ *adj. & n.* ● *adj.* written or printed below the line, esp. *Math.* (of a symbol) written below and to the right of another symbol. ● *n.* a subscript number or symbol. [L *subscriptus* (as SUBSCRIBE)]

sub·scrip·tion /səbskrípshən/ *n.* **1 a** the act or an instance of subscribing. **b** money subscribed. **2 a** an agreement to take and pay for usu. a specified number of issues of a newspaper, magazine, etc. **b** the money paid by this. **3** a signature on a document, etc. **4** *Brit.* a fee for the membership of a society, etc., esp. paid regularly. [ME f. L *subscriptio* (as SUBSCRIBE)]

sub·scrip·tion con·cert *n.* each of a series of concerts, etc., for which tickets are sold in advance.

sub·sec·tion /súbsekshən/ *n.* a division of a section.

sub·sel·li·um /səbséleeəm/ *n.* (*pl.* **sub·sel·li·a** /–leeə/) = MISERICORD 1. [L f. *sella* seat]

sub·se·quence[1] /súbsikwəns/ *n.* a subsequent incident; a consequence.

sub·se·quence[2] /súbseékwəns/ *n.* a sequence forming part of a larger one.

sub·se·quent /súbsikwənt/ *adj.* (usu. foll. by *to*) following a specified event, etc., in time, esp. as a consequence. □□ **sub·se·quent·ly** *adv.* [ME f. OF *subsequent* or L *subsequi* (as SUB-, *sequi* follow)]

sub·serve /səbsórv/ *v.tr.* serve as a means of furthering (a purpose, action, etc.). [L *subservire* (as SUB-, SERVE)]

sub·ser·vi·ent /səbsórveeənt/ *adj.* **1** cringing; obsequious. **2** (usu. foll. by *to*) serving as a means; instrumental. **3** (usu. foll. by *to*) subordinate. □□ **sub·ser·vi·ence** *n.* **sub·ser·vi·en·cy** *n.* **sub·ser·vi·ent·ly** *adv.* [L *subserviens subservient-* (as SUBSERVE)]

sub·set /súbset/ *n.* **1** a secondary part of a set. **2** *Math.* a set all the elements of which are contained in another set.

sub·shrub /súbshrub/ *n.* a low-growing or small shrub.

sub·side /səbsíd/ *v.intr.* **1** cease from agitation; become tranquil; abate (*excitement subsided*). **2** (of water, suspended matter, etc.) sink. **3** (of the ground) cave in; sink. **4** (of a building, ship, etc.) sink lower in the ground or water. **5** (of a swelling, etc.) become less. **6** usu. *joc.* (of a person) sink into a sitting, kneeling, or lying posture. □□ **sub·sid·ence** /–síd'ns, súbsíd'ns/ *n.* [L *subsidere* (as SUB-, *sidere* settle rel. to *sedēre* sit)]

sub·sid·i·ar·i·ty /səbsídeeáritee/ *n.* (*pl.* **-ties**) **1** the quality of being subsidiary. **2** the principle that a central authority should perform only tasks which cannot be performed effectively at a local level.

sub·sid·i·ar·y /səbsídee–airee/ *adj. & n.* ● *adj.* **1** serving to assist or supplement; auxiliary. **2** (of a company) controlled by another. **3** (of troops): **a** paid for by subsidy. **b** hired by another nation. ● *n.* (*pl.* **-ies**) **1** a subsidiary thing or person; an accessory. **2** a subsidiary company. □□ **sub·sid·i·ar·i·ly** *adv.* [L *subsidiarius* (as SUBSIDY)]

sub·si·dize /súbsidīz/ *v.tr.* **1** pay a subsidy to. **2** reduce the cost of by subsidy (*subsidized lunches*). □□ **sub·si·di·za·tion** *n.* **sub·si·diz·er** *n.*

sub·si·dy /súbsidee/ *n.* (*pl.* **-dies**) **1 a** money granted by the government or a public body, etc., to keep down the price of commodities, etc. (*housing subsidy*). **b** money granted to a charity or other undertaking held to be in the public interest. **c** any grant or contribution of money. **2** money paid by one nation to another in return for military, naval, or other aid. **3** *hist.* **a** a parliamentary grant to the sovereign for government needs. **b** a tax levied on a particular occasion. [ME f. AF *subsidie*, OF *subside* f. L *subsidium* assistance]

sub·sist /səbsíst/ *v.* **1** *intr.* (often foll. by *on*) keep oneself alive; be kept alive (*subsists on vegetables*). **2** *intr.* remain in being; exist. **3** *intr.* (foll. by *in*) be attributable to (*its excellence subsists in its freshness*). **4** *tr. archaic* provide sustenance for. □□ **sub·sist·ent** *adj.* [L *subsistere* stand firm (as SUB-, *sistere* set, stand)]

sub·sist·ence /səbsístəns/ *n.* **1** the state or an instance of subsisting. **2 a** the means of supporting life; a livelihood. **b** a minimal level of existence or the income providing this (*a bare subsistence*).

sub·sist·ence al·low·ance *n.* (also **sub·sist·ence mon·ey**) an allowance or advance on pay granted esp. as traveling expenses.

See page xx for the **Key to Pronunciation.**

sub·sist·ence farm·ing *n.* farming which directly supports the farmer's household without producing a significant surplus for trade.

sub·soil /súbsoyl/ *n.* soil lying immediately under the surface soil (opp. TOPSOIL).

sub·son·ic /súbsónik/ *adj.* relating to speeds less than that of sound. □□ **sub·son·i·cal·ly** *adv.*

sub·spe·cies /súbspeesheez, –seez/ *n.* (*pl.* same) *Biol.* a taxonomic category below a species, usu. a fairly permanent geographically isolated variety. □□ **sub·spe·cif·ic** /–spəsífik/ *adj.*

subst. *abbr.* 1 substantive. 2 substitute.

sub·stance /súbstəns/ *n.* 1 a the essential material, esp. solid, forming a thing (*the substance was transparent*). b a particular kind of material having uniform properties (*this substance is salt*). 2 a reality; solidity (*ghosts have no substance*). b seriousness or steadiness of character (*there is no substance in him*). 3 additive drugs or alcohol, etc. (*problems of substance abuse*). 4 the theme or subject of esp. a work of art, argument, etc. (*prefer the substance to the style*). 5 the real meaning or essence of a thing. 6 wealth and possessions (*a woman of substance*). 7 *Philos.* the essential nature underlying phenomena, which is subject to changes and accidents. □ **in substance** generally; apart from details. [ME f. OF f. L *substantia* (as SUB-, *stare* stand)]

sub·stand·ard /súbstándərd/ *adj.* 1 of less than the required or normal quality or size; inferior. 2 (of language) not conforming to standard usage.

sub·stan·tial /səbstánshəl/ *adj.* 1 a of real importance, value, or validity (*made a substantial contribution*). b of large size or amount (*awarded substantial damages*). 2 of solid material or structure; stout (*a man of substantial build; a substantial house*). 3 commercially successful; wealthy. 4 essential; true in large part (*substantial truth*). 5 having substance; real. □□ **sub·stan·ti·al·i·ty** /–sheeálitee/ *n.* **sub·stan·tial·ly** *adv.* [ME f. OF *substantiel* or LL *substantialis* (as SUBSTANCE)]

sub·stan·tial·ism /səbstánshəlizəm/ *n. Philos.* the doctrine that behind phenomena there are substantial realities. □□ **sub·stan·tial·ist** *n.*

sub·stan·tial·ize /səbstánshəliz/ *v.tr. & intr.* invest with or acquire substance or actual existence.

sub·stan·ti·ate /səbstánsheeayt/ *v.tr.* prove the truth of (a charge, statement, claim, etc.); give good grounds for. □□ **sub·stan·ti·a·tion** /–áyshən/ *n.* [med.L *substantiare* give substance to (as SUBSTANCE)]

sub·stan·tive /súbstəntiv/ *adj. & n.* ● *adj.* (also /səbstántiv/) 1 having separate and independent existence. 2 *Law* relating to rights and duties. 3 (of an enactment, motion, resolution, etc.) made in due form as such; not amendable. 4 *Gram.* expressing existence. 5 (of a dye) not needing a mordant. 6 *Mil.* (of a rank, etc.) permanent, not acting or temporary. 7 *archaic* denoting a substance. ● *n. Gram.* = NOUN. □□ **sub·stan·ti·val** /–tívəl/ *adj.* **sub·stan·tive·ly** *adv.* esp. Gram. [ME f. OF *substantif –ive*, or LL *substantivus* (as SUBSTANCE)]

sub·stan·tive verb *n.* the verb 'to be.'

sub·sta·tion /súbstayshən/ *n.* a subordinate station, esp. one reducing the high voltage of electric power transmission to that suitable for supply to consumers.

sub·stit·u·ent /səbstíchōōənt/ *adj. & n. Chem.* ● *adj.* (of a group of atoms) replacing another atom or group in a compound. ● *n.* such a group. [L *substituere substituent-* (as SUBSTITUTE)]

sub·sti·tute /súbstitōōt, –tyōōt/ *n. & v.* ● *n.* 1 a (also *attrib.*) a person or thing acting or serving in place of another. b an artificial alternative to a natural substance (*butter substitute*). 2 *Sc. Law* a deputy. ● *v.* 1 *intr. & tr.* (often foll. by *for*) act or cause to act as a substitute; put or serve in exchange (*substituted for her mother; substituted it for the broken one*). 2 *tr.* (usu. foll. by *by, with*) colloq. replace (a person or thing) with another. 3 *tr. Chem.* replace (an atom or group in a molecule) with another. □□ **sub·sti·tut·a·ble** *adj.* **sub·sti·tut·a·bil·i·ty** *n.* **sub·sti·tu·tion** /–tōōshən, –tyōō–/ *n.* **sub·sti·tu·tion·al** *adj.* **sub·sti·tu·tion·ar·y** /–tōōshənəree, –tyōō–/ *adj.* **sub·sti·tu·tive** *adj.* [ME f. L *substitutus* past part. of *substituere* (as SUB-, *statuere* set up)]

sub·strate /súbstrayt/ *n.* 1 = SUBSTRATUM. 2 a surface to be painted, printed, etc., on. 3 *Biol.* a the substance upon which an enzyme acts. b the surface or material on which any particular organism grows. [Anglicized f. SUBSTRATUM]

sub·stra·tum /súbstraytəm, –strát–/ *n.* (*pl.* **sub·stra·ta** /–tə/) 1 an underlying layer or substance. 2 a layer of rock or soil beneath the surface. 3 a foundation or basis (*there is a substratum of truth in it*). [mod.L, past part. of L *substernere* (as SUB-, *sternere* strew): cf. STRATUM]

sub·struc·ture /súbstrukchər/ *n.* an underlying or supporting structure. □□ **sub·struc·tur·al** *adj.*

sub·sume /səbsōōm, –syōōm/ *v.tr.* (usu. foll. by *under*) include (an instance, idea, category, etc.) in a rule, class, category, etc. □□ **sub·sum·a·ble** *adj.* **sub·sump·tion** /–súmpshən/ *n.* [med.L *subsumere* (as SUB-, *sumere sumpt-* take)]

sub·ten·ant /súbténənt/ *n.* a person who leases a property from a tenant. □□ **sub·ten·an·cy** *n.*

sub·tend /səbténd/ *v.tr.* 1 a (usu. foll. by *at*) (of a line, arc, figure, etc.) form (an angle) at a particular point when its extremities are joined at that point. b (of an angle or chord) have bounding lines or points that meet or coincide with those of (a line or arc). 2 *Bot.* (of a bract, etc.) extend under so as to embrace or enfold. [L *subtendere* (as SUB-, *tendere* stretch)]

sub·ter·fuge /súbtərfyōōj/ *n.* 1 a an attempt to avoid blame or defeat, esp. by lying or deceit. b a statement, etc., resorted to for such a purpose. 2 this as a practice or policy. [F *subterfuge* or LL *subterfugium* f. L *subterfugere* escape secretly f. *subter* beneath + *fugere* flee]

sub·ter·mi·nal /súbtárminəl/ *adj.* nearly at the end.

sub·ter·ra·ne·an /súbtəráyneeən/ *adj.* 1 existing, occurring, or done under the earth's surface. 2 secret; underground; concealed. □□ **sub·ter·ra·ne·ous·ly** *adv.* [L *subterraneus* (as SUB-, *terra* earth)]

sub·text /súbtekst/ *n.* an underlying often distinct theme in a piece of writing or conversation.

sub·til·ize /sút'liz/ *v.* 1 *tr.* a make subtle. b elevate; refine. 2 *intr.* (usu. foll. by *upon*) argue or reason subtly. □□ **sub·til·i·za·tion** *n.* [F *subtiliser* or med.L *subtilizare* (as SUBTLE)]

sub·ti·tle /súbtit'l/ *n. & v.* ● *n.* 1 a secondary or additional title of a book, etc. 2 a printed caption at the bottom of a movie, etc., esp. translating dialogue. ● *v.tr.* provide with a subtitle or subtitles.

sub·tle /sút'l/ *adj.* (**sub·tler**, **sub·tlest**) 1 evasive or mysterious; hard to grasp (*subtle charm; a subtle distinction*). 2 (of scent, color, etc.) faint; delicate; elusive (*subtle perfume*). 3 a capable of making fine distinctions; perceptive; acute (*subtle intellect; subtle senses*). b ingenious; elaborate; clever (*a subtle device*). 4 *archaic* crafty; cunning. □□ **sub·tle·ness** *n.* **sub·tly** *adv.* [ME f. OF *sotil* f. L *subtilis*]

sub·tle·ty /sút'ltee/ *n.* (*pl.* **·ties**) 1 something subtle; the quality of being subtle. 2 a fine distinction; an instance of hair-splitting. [ME f. OF *s(o)utilté* f. L *subtilitas –tatis* (as SUBTLE)]

sub·ton·ic /súbtónik/ *n. Mus.* the note below the tonic, the seventh note of the diatonic scale of any key.

sub·to·tal /súbtōt'l/ *n.* the total of one part of a group of figures to be added.

sub·tract /səbtrákt/ *v.tr.* (often foll. by *from*) deduct (a part, quantity, or number) from another. □□ **sub·tract·er** *n.* (cf. SUBTRACTOR). **sub·trac·tion** /–trákshən/ *n.* **sub·trac·tive** *adj.* [L *subtrahere subtract-* (as SUB-, *trahere* draw)]

sub·tract·or /səbtráktər/ *n. Electronics* a circuit or device that produces an output dependent on the difference of two inputs.

sub·tra·hend /súbtrəhend/ *n. Math.* a quantity or number to be subtracted. [L *subtrahendus* gerundive of *subtrahere*: see SUBTRACT]

sub·trop·ics /súbtrópiks/ *n.pl.* the regions adjacent to or bordering on the tropics. □□ **sub·trop·i·cal** *adj.*

su·bu·late /súbyəlat/ *adj. Bot. & Zool.* slender and tapering. [L *subula* awl]

sub·urb /súbərb/ *n.* an outlying district of a city, esp. residential. [ME f. OF *suburbe* or L *suburbium* (as SUB-, *urbs urbis* city)]

sub·ur·ban /səbárbən/ *adj.* 1 of or characteristic of suburbs. 2 *derog.* provincial, uncultured, or naïve. □□ **sub·ur·ban·ite** *n.* **sub·ur·ban·ize** *v.tr.* **sub·ur·ban·i·za·tion** *n.* [L *suburbanus* (as SUBURB)]

sub·ur·bi·a /səbárbeeə/ *n.* often *derog.* the suburbs, their inhabitants, and their way of life.

sub·ven·tion /səbvénshən/ *n.* a grant of money from a government, etc.; a subsidy. [ME f. OF f. LL *subventio –onis* f. L *subvenire subvent-* assist (as SUB-, *venire* come)]

sub·ver·sive /səbvársiv/ *adj. & n.* ● *adj.* (of a person, group, organization, activity, etc.) seeking to subvert (esp. a government). ● *n.* a subversive person; a revolutionary. □□ **sub·ver·sion** /–várzhən, –shən/ *n.* **sub·ver·sive·ly** *adv.* **sub·ver·sive·ness** *n.* [med.L *subversivus* (as SUBVERT)]

sub·vert /səbvárt/ *v.tr.* esp. Polit. overturn, overthrow, or upset (religion, government, morality, etc.). □□ **sub·vert·er** *n.* [ME f. OF *subvertir* or L *subvertere* (as SUB-, *vertere vers-* turn)]

sub·way /súbway/ *n.* 1 an underground, usu. electrically powered, railroad. 2 a a tunnel beneath a road, etc., for pedestrians. b an underground passage for pipes, cables, etc.

sub·ze·ro /súbzeérō/ *adj.* (esp. of temperature) lower than zero.

suc- /suk, sək/ *prefix* assim. form of SUB- before *c*.

suc·ce·da·ne·um /súksidáyneeəm/ *n.* (*pl.* **suc·ce·da·ne·a** /–neeə/) a substitute, esp. for a medicine or drug. □□ **suc·ce·da·ne·ous** *adj.* [mod.L, neut. of L *succedaneus* (as SUCCEED)]

suc·ceed /səkseéd/ *v.* 1 *intr.* a (often foll. by *in*) accomplish one's purpose; have success; prosper (*succeeded in his ambition*). b (of a plan, etc.) be successful. 2 a *tr.* follow in order; come immediately after (*night succeeded day*). b *intr.* (foll. by *to*) come next; be subsequent. 3 *intr.* (often foll. by *to*) come by an inheritance, office, title, or property (*succeeded to the throne*). 4 *tr.* take over an office, property, inheritance, etc., from (*succeeded his father; succeeded the manager*). □ **nothing succeeds like success** one success leads to others. □□ **suc·ceed·er** *n.* [ME f. OF *succeder* or L *succedere* (as SUB-, *cedere cess-* go)]

suc·cen·tor /səkséntər/ *n. Eccl.* a precentor's deputy in some cathedrals. □□ **suc·cen·tor·ship** *n.* [LL f. L *succinere* (as SUB-, *canere* sing)]

suc·cès de scan·dale /sooksáy də sko Ndáál/ *n.* a book, play, etc., having great success because of its scandalous nature or associations. [F]

suc·cess /səksés/ *n.* **1** the accomplishment of an aim; a favorable outcome (*their efforts met with success*). **2** the attainment of wealth, fame, or position (*spoiled by success*). **3** a thing or person that turns out well. **4** *archaic* a usu. specified outcome of an undertaking (*ill success*). [L *successus* (as SUCCEED)]

suc·cess·ful /səksésfool/ *adj.* having success; prosperous. □□ **suc·cess·ful·ly** *adv.* **suc·cess·ful·ness** *n.*

suc·ces·sion /səkséshən/ *n.* **1 a** the process of following in order; succeeding. **b** a series of things or people in succession. **2 a** the right of succeeding to a throne, an office, inheritance, etc. **b** the act or process of so succeeding. **c** those having such a right. **3** *Biol.* the order of development of a species or community; = SERE[3]. □ **in quick succession** following one another at short intervals. **in succession** one after another, without intervention. **in succession to** as the successor of. **settle the succession** determine who shall succeed. □□ **suc·ces·sion·al** *adj.* [ME f. OF *succession* or L *successio* (as SUCCEED)]

suc·ces·sion state *n.* a nation resulting from the partition of a previously existing country.

suc·ces·sive /səksésiv/ *adj.* following one after another; running; consecutive. □□ **suc·ces·sive·ly** *adv.* **suc·ces·sive·ness** *n.* [ME f. med.L *successivus* (as SUCCEED)]

suc·ces·sor /səksésər/ *n.* (often foll. by *to*) a person or thing that succeeds another. [ME f. OF *successour* f. L *successor* (as SUCCEED)]

suc·cinct /səksíngkt/ *adj.* briefly expressed; terse; concise. □□ **suc·cinct·ly** *adv.* **suc·cinct·ness** *n.* [ME f. L *succinctus* past part. of *succingere* tuck up (as SUB-, *cingere* gird)]

suc·cin·ic acid /suksínik/ *n. Chem.* a crystalline dibasic acid derived from amber, etc. □□ **suc·ci·nate** /súksinayt/ *n.* [F *succinique* f. L *succinum* amber]

suc·cor /súkər/ *n. & v.* ● *n.* **1** aid; assistance, esp. in time of need. **2** (in *pl.*) *archaic* reinforcements of troops. ● *v.tr.* assist or aid (esp. a person in danger or distress). □□ **suc·cor·less** *adj.* [ME f. OF *socours* f. med.L *succursus* f. L *succurrere* (as SUB-, *currere curs-* run)]

suc·co·ry /súkəree/ *n.* = CHICORY 1. [alt. f. *cicoree*, etc., early forms of CHICORY]

suc·co·tash /súkətash/ *n.* a dish of green corn and beans boiled together. [Narragansett *msiquatash*]

Suc·coth /sóókəs, sóókót/ *n.* (also **Suk·koth**) the Jewish autumn thanksgiving festival commemorating the sheltering in the wilderness. [Heb. *sukkôt* pl. of *sukkāh* thicket, hut]

suc·cour *Brit.* var. of SUCCOR.

suc·cu·bus /súkyəbəs/ *n.* (*pl.* **suc·cu·bi** /-bī/) a female demon believed to have sexual intercourse with sleeping men. [LL *succuba* prostitute, med.L *succubus* f. *succubare* (as SUB-, *cubare* lie)]

suc·cu·lent /súkyələnt/ *adj. & n.* ● *adj.* **1** juicy; palatable. **2** *colloq.* desirable. **3** *Bot.* (of a plant, its leaves, or stems) thick and fleshy. ● *n. Bot.* a succulent plant, esp. a cactus. □□ **suc·cu·lence** *n.* **suc·cu·lent·ly** *adv.* [L *succulentus* f. *succus* juice]

suc·cumb /səkúm/ *v.intr.* (usu. foll. by *to*) **1** be forced to give way; be overcome (*succumbed to temptation*). **2** be overcome by death (*succumbed to his injuries*). [ME f. OF *succomber* or L *succumbere* (as SUB-, *cumbere* lie)]

such /such/ *adj. & pron.* ● *adj.* **1** (often foll. by *as*) of the kind or degree in question or under consideration (*such a person; such people; people such as these*). **2** (usu. foll. by *as to* + infin. or *that* + clause) so great; in such high degree (*not such a fool as to believe them; had such a fright that he fainted*). **3** of a more than normal kind or degree (*we had such an enjoyable evening; such crude language*). **4** of the kind or degree already indicated, or implied by the context (*there are no such things; such is life*). **5** *Law* or *formal* the aforesaid; of the aforesaid kind. ● *pron.* **1** the thing or action in question or referred to (*such were his words; such was not my intention*). **2 a** *Commerce* or *colloq.* the aforesaid thing or things; it, they, or them (*those without tickets should purchase such*). **b** similar things; suchlike (*brought sandwiches and such*). □ **as such** as being what has been indicated or named (*a stranger is welcomed as such; there is no theater as such*). **such and such** ● *adj.* of a particular kind but not needing to be specified. ● *n.* a person or thing of this kind. **such and such a person** someone; so-and-so. **such as 1** of a kind that; like (*a person such as we all admire*). **2** for example (*insects, such as moths and bees*). **3** those who (*such as don't need help*). **such as it is** despite its shortcomings (*you are welcome to it, such as it is*). **such a one** (usu. foll. by *as*) such a person or such a thing. **2** *archaic* some person or thing unspecified. [OE *swilc, swylc* f. Gmc: cf. LIKE[1]]

such·like /súchlīk/ *adj. & n. colloq.* ● *adj.* of such a kind. ● *n.* things, people, etc., of such a kind.

suck /suk/ *v. & n.* ● *v.* **1** *tr.* draw (a fluid) into the mouth by making a partial vacuum. **2** *tr.* (also *absol.*) **a** draw milk or other fluid from or through (the breast, etc., or a container). **b** extract juice from (a fruit) by sucking. **3** *tr.* **a** draw sustenance, knowledge, or advan-

tage from (a book, etc.). **b** imbibe or gain (knowledge, advantage, etc.) as if by sucking. **4** *tr.* roll the tongue around (a candy, teeth, one's thumb, etc.). **5** *intr.* make a sucking action or sound (*sucking at his pipe*) **6** *intr.* (of a pump, etc.) make a gurgling or drawing sound. **7** *tr.* (usu. foll. by *down, in*) engulf, smother, or drown in a sucking movement. **8** *intr. sl.* be or seem very unpleasant, contemptible, or unfair. ● *n.* **1** the act or an instance of sucking, esp. at the breast. **2** the drawing action or sound of a whirlpool, etc. **3** (often foll. by *of*) a small drink of alcohol. **4** (in *pl.*; esp. as *int.*) *Brit. colloq.* **a** an expression of disappointment. **b** an expression of derision or amusement at another's discomfiture. □ **give suck** *archaic* (of a mother, dam, etc.) suckle. **suck dry 1** exhaust the contents of (a bottle, the breast, etc.) by sucking. **2** exhaust (a person's sympathy, resources, etc.) as if by sucking. **suck in 1** absorb. **2** = sense 7 of *v.* **3** involve (a person) in an activity, etc., esp. against his or her will. **suck up 1** (often foll. by *to*) *colloq.* behave obsequiously, esp. for one's own advantage. **2** absorb. [OE *sūcan*, = L *sugere*]

suck·er /súkər/ *n. & v.* ● *n.* **1 a** a person or thing that sucks. **b** a sucking pig, newborn whale, etc. **2** *sl.* **a** a gullible or easily deceived person. **b** (foll. by *for*) a person especially susceptible to. **3 a** a rubber cup, etc., that adheres to a surface by suction. **b** an organ enabling an organism to cling to a surface by suction. **4** *Bot.* a shoot springing from the rooted part of a stem, from the root at a distance from the main stem, from an axil, or occasionally from a branch. **5** any of various fish that has a mouth capable of or seeming to be capable of adhering by suction. **6 a** the piston of a suction pump. **b** a pipe through which liquid is drawn by suction. **7** *colloq.* a lollipop. ● *v. Bot.* **1** *tr.* remove suckers from. **2** *intr.* produce suckers. **3** *tr. sl.* cheat; fool.

suck·ing /súking/ *adj.* **1** (of a child, animal, etc.) not yet weaned. **2** *Zool.* unfledged (*sucking dove*).

suck·ing fish *n.* = REMORA.

suck·le /súkəl/ *v.* **1** *tr.* **a** feed (young) from the breast or udder. **b** nourish (*suckled his talent*). **2** *intr.* feed by sucking the breast, etc. □□ **suck·ler** *n.* [ME, prob. back-form. f. SUCKLING]

suck·ling /súkling/ *n.* an unweaned child or animal.

su·crose /sóokrōs/ *n. Chem.* sugar; a disaccharide obtained from sugar cane, sugar beet, etc. [F *sucre* SUGAR]

suc·tion /súkshən/ *n.* **1** the act or an instance of sucking. **2 a** the production of a partial vacuum by the removal of air, etc., in order to force in liquid, etc., or procure adhesion. **b** the force produced by this process (*suction keeps the lid on*). [LL *suctio* f. L *sugere suct-* SUCK]

suc·tion pump *n.* a pump for drawing liquid through a pipe into a chamber emptied by a piston.

suc·to·ri·al /suktáwreeəl/ *adj. Zool.* **1** adapted for or capable of sucking. **2** having a sucker for feeding or adhering. □□ **suc·to·ri·an** *n.* [mod.L *suctorius* (as SUCTION)]

Su·da·nese /sóodənéez/ *adj. & n.* ● *adj.* of or relating to Sudan, a republic in NE Africa, or the Sudan region south of the Sahara. ● *n.* (*pl.* same) **1** a native, national, or inhabitant of Sudan. **2** a person of Sudanese descent.

su·da·to·ri·um /sóodətáwreeəm/ *n.* (*pl.* **su·da·to·ri·a** /-reeə/) esp. Rom. Antiq. **1** a hot air or steam bath. **2** a room where such a bath is taken. [L, neut. of *sudatorius*: see SUDATORY]

su·da·to·ry /sóodətawree/ *adj. & n.* ● *adj.* promoting perspiration. ● *n.* (*pl.* **-ries**) **1** a sudatory drug. **2** = SUDATORIUM. [L *sudatorius* f. *sudare* sweat]

sudd /sud/ *n.* floating vegetation impeding the navigation of the White Nile. [Arab., = obstruction]

sud·den /súd'n/ *adj. & n.* ● *adj.* occurring or done unexpectedly or without warning; abrupt; hurried; hasty (*a sudden storm; a sudden departure*). ● *n. archaic* a hasty or abrupt occurrence. □ **all of a sudden** unexpectedly; hurriedly; suddenly. □□ **sud·den·ly** *adv.* **sud·den·ness** *n.* [ME f. AF *sodein, sudein*, OF *soudain* f. LL *subitanus* f. L *subitaneus* f. *subitus* sudden]

sud·den death *n. colloq.* a decision in a tied game, etc., dependent on one move, card, toss of a coin, etc.

sud·den in·fant death syn·drome *n. Med.* the death of a seemingly healthy infant from an unknown cause; crib death. ¶ Abbr.: SIDS.

su·dor·if·er·ous /sóodərífərəs/ *adj.* (of a gland, etc.) secreting sweat. [LL *sudorifer* f. L *sudor* sweat]

su·dor·if·ic /sóodərífik/ *adj. & n.* ● *adj.* (of a drug) causing sweating. ● *n.* a sudorific drug. [mod.L *sudorificus* f. L *sudor* sweat]

Su·dra /sóodrə/ *n.* a member of the lowest of the four great Hindu castes. [Skr. *śūdra*]

suds /sudz/ *n. & v.* ● *n.pl.* **1** froth of soap and water. **2** *colloq.* beer. ● *v.* **1** *intr.* form suds. **2** *tr.* lather, cover, or wash in soapy water. □□ **suds·y** *adj.* [orig. = fen waters, etc., of uncert. orig.: cf. MDu., MLG *sudde*, MDu. *sudse* marsh, bog, prob. rel. to SEETHE]

sue /soo/ *v.* (**sues, sued, su·ing**) **1** *tr.* (also *absol.*) *Law* institute legal proceedings against (a person). **2** *tr.* (also *absol.*) entreat (a person). **3** *intr.* (often foll. by *to, for*) *Law* make application to a court of law for redress. **4** *intr.* (often foll. by *to, for*) make entreaty to a person for a favor. **5** *tr.* (often foll. by *out*) make a petition in a court of law for and obtain (a writ, pardon, etc.). □□ **su·er** *n.* [ME f. AF *suer, siwer,* etc., f. OF *siu-,* etc., stem of *sivre* f. L *sequi* follow]

suede /swayd/ *n.* (often *attrib.*) **1** leather, esp. kidskin, with the flesh side rubbed to make a velvety nap. **2** (also **suede cloth**) a woven fabric resembling suede. [F (*gants de*) *Suède* (gloves of) Sweden]

su·et /sóo-it/ *n.* the hard white fat on the kidneys or loins of oxen, sheep, etc., used in cooking, etc. □□ **su·et·y** *adj.* [ME f. AF f. OF *seu* f. L *sebum* tallow]

su·et pud·ding *n.* a pudding of chopped suet, flour, spices, etc., usu. boiled or steamed.

suf- /suf, səf/ *prefix* assim. form of SUB- before *f*.

suf·fer /súfər/ *v.* **1** *intr.* **a** undergo pain, grief, etc. (*suffers acutely; suffers from neglect*). **b** be damaged; decline (*your reputation will suffer*). **2** *tr.* undergo, experience, or be subjected to (pain, loss, grief, defeat, change, etc.) (*suffered banishment*). **3** *tr.* put up with; tolerate (*does not suffer fools gladly*). **4** *intr.* undergo martyrdom. **5** *tr.* (foll. by *to* + infin.) *archaic* allow. □□ **suf·fer·a·ble** *adj.* **suf·fer·er** *n.* **suf·fer·ing** *n.* [ME f. AF *suffrir, soeffrir,* OF *sof(f)rir* f. L *sufferre* (as SUB-, *ferre* bear)]

suf·fer·ance /súfərəns, súfrəns/ *n.* **1** tacit consent; abstinence from objection. **2** *archaic* submissiveness. □ **on sufferance** with toleration implied by lack of consent or objection. [ME f. AF, OF *suffraunce* f. LL *sufferentia* (as SUFFER)]

suf·fice /səfís/ *v.* **1** *intr.* (often foll. by *for,* or *to* + infin.) be enough or adequate (*that will suffice for our purpose; suffices to prove it*). **2** *tr.* meet the needs of; satisfy (*six sufficed him*). □ **suffice it to say** I shall content myself with saying. [ME f. OF *suffire* (*suffis-*) f. L *sufficere* (as SUB-, *facere* make)]

suf·fi·cien·cy /səfishənsee/ *n.* (*pl.* **·cies**) **1** (often foll. by *of*) an adequate amount or adequate resources. **2** *archaic* being sufficient; ability; efficiency. [LL *sufficientia* (as SUFFICIENT)]

suf·fi·cient /səfishənt/ *adj.* **1** sufficing; adequate; enough (*is sufficient for a family; didn't have sufficient funds*). **2** = SELF-SUFFICIENT. **3** *archaic* competent; of adequate ability, resources, etc. □□ **suf·fi·cient·ly** *adv.* [ME f. OF *sufficient* or L *sufficiens* (as SUFFICE)]

suf·fix /súfiks/ *n. & v.* ● *n.* **1** a verbal element added at the end of a word to form a derivative (e.g., *–ation, –fy, –ing, –itis*). **2** *Math.* = SUBSCRIPT. ● *v.tr.* (also /səfíks/) append, esp. as a suffix. □□ **suf·fix·a·tion** *n.* [*suffixum, suffixus* past part. of L *suffigere* (as SUB-, *figere* fix-fasten)]

GRAMMAR TIP Suffixes

Suffix	Meaning	Example
-able	that can be	obtainable
	suitable for; giving	comfortable
	inclined to	peaceable
	fit to; deserving of	wearable, lovable
-age	action; process	breakage
	group; collection of	baggage
	state or rank of	peerage
	cost of; fee for	postage
	house or place of	orphanage, anchorage
-al, -ial	having the nature of	ornamental; facial
	act of	arrival
-an; -ean; -ian	native of	American; European
	having to do with	Shakespearean
-ana; -iana	collection of; about	Americana; Burnsiana
-ance; -ancy	act of	resistance
	thing that	conveyance
	quality or state of	buoyancy
-ant	state or condition of	defiant
	one who	assistant
-ary	place for	infirmary
	collection of	statuary
	having to do with	legendary
-ate	having to do with	collegiate
	make or cause to be	alienate
	produce	ulcerate
	supply or treat with	aerate
	combine with	oxygenate
-ation	act or process of	computation
-cle, -cule	little, small	particle; molecule
-cy	state of being	bankruptcy
	position or rank	captaincy
-dom	rank or realm of	kingdom
	condition of	freedom
-ed	having, or having characteristics of	long-legged, bigoted, honeyed

Suffix	Meaning	Example
-en	cause to be; make	blacken
	cause to have	strengthen
	to become	sicken
	made of; have look of	silken
	plural	oxen
-ence	state of being	indifference
-ent	one who	president
-er, -ier, -yer	one who does or is concerned with	reporter, cashier; lawyer
	person living in	New Yorker
	more (comparative)	smarter
	action or process of	waiver
-ery	the art of	cookery
	the condition of	slavery
	quality or action of	knavery
	a place where	bindery
-ese	having to do with	Chinese
-esque	in the style of	Romanesque
	like a	statuesque
-ess	female	heiress
-est	most (superlative)	smartest
-et	little, small	owlet
-ette	little, small	dinette
-ful	full of	cupful, playful
-fy	make or cause to be	electrify, simplify
-hood	state of being	childhood
-ible	can be, able to be	divisible
-ic	having to do with	atmospheric
	having the nature of	heroic
	containing	alcoholic
	made or caused by	volcanic
	like; similar to	meteoric
-ical	of the nature of	critical, political
-ing	act of person or thing	acting, running
-ion	act or process of	admission
	state or condition of	subjection
-ish	somewhat	sweetish
	like a	childish
	having to do with	English
	tending to	bookish
-ism	act or practice of	baptism
	quality or condition	heroism
	doctrine or theory	Darwinism
-ist	expert in	botanist
	one who believes in	socialist
-ite	native of	Denverite
	descendant of	Israelite
	follower of	Jacobite
-itis	inflammation of	tonsillitis
-ity	state of	acidity
-ive	having to do with	sportive
-ize	become or resemble	Americanize
	treat or combine with	oxidize
-less	without	meatless
	that does not	tireless
	that cannot be	countless
-let	little, small	booklet
-like	like; similar to	homelike
-ling	little, small	duckling
-ly	in a manner	cheerfully
	like a	ghostly
-ment	act or state of	enjoyment
	condition of being	amazement
	product or result of	pavement
-most	most (superlative)	uppermost
-ness	state or quality of	greatness
-oid	like, similar to	adenoid, spheroid
-or	person or thing that does something	auditor, actor, elevator
	act, state, quality, or condition	error, horror, labor, terror
-ory	place for	conservatory
	tending or inclined to	conciliatory
-osis	abnormal condition	psychosis
-ous	full of	poisonous
-ry	occupation or work of	dentistry
	collection of	citizenry
-ship	condition of being	partnership
	office or occupation	authorship
	act, power, or skill	horsemanship
-some	tending to	meddlesome
-ster	person who	trickster
-tion	act or state of	locomotion
-ule	little, small	capsule, globule
-ure	act or process of	closure
-ward	toward; leading to	homeward

suf·fo·cate /súfəkayt/ v. **1** tr. choke or kill by stopping breathing, esp. by pressure, fumes, etc. **2** tr. (often foll. by by, with) produce a choking or breathless sensation in, esp. by excitement, terror, etc. **3** intr. be or feel suffocated or breathless. □□ **suf·fo·cat·ing** adj. **suf·fo·cat·ing·ly** adv. **suf·fo·ca·tion** /-káyshən/ n. [L suffocare (as SUB-, fauces throat)]

Suf·folk /súfək/ n. **1** a sheep of a black-faced breed raised for food. **2** this breed. [Suffolk in S. England]

suf·fra·gan /súfrəgən/ n. (in full **suffragan bishop** or **bishop suffragan**) **1** a bishop appointed to help a diocesan bishop in the administration of a diocese. **2** a bishop in relation to his archbishop or metropolitan. □□ **suf·fra·gan·ship** n. [ME f. AF & OF, repr. med.L suffraganeus assistant (bishop) f. L suffragium (see SUFFRAGE): orig. of a bishop summoned to vote in synod]

suf·fra·gan see n. the see of a suffragan bishop.

suf·frage /súfrij/ n. **1 a** the right to vote in political elections (full adult suffrage). **b** a view expressed by voting; a vote (gave their suffrages for and against). **c** opinion in support of a proposal, etc. **2** (esp. in pl.) Eccl. **a** a prayer made by a priest in the liturgy. **b** a short prayer made by a congregation, esp. in response to a priest. **c** archaic an intercessory prayer. [ME f. L suffragium, partly through F suffrage]

suf·fra·gette /súfrəjét/ n. hist. a woman seeking the right to vote through organized protest. [SUFFRAGE + -ETTE]

suf·fra·gist /súfrəjist/ n. esp. hist. a person who advocates the extension of suffrage, esp. to women. □□ **suf·fra·gism** n.

suf·fuse /səfyóoz/ v.tr. **1** (of color, moisture, etc.) spread from within to color or moisten (a blush suffused her cheeks). **2** cover with color, etc. □□ **suf·fu·sion** /-fyóozhən/ n. [L suffundere suffus- (as SUB-, fundere pour)]

Su·fi /sóofee/ n. (pl. **Su·fis**) a Muslim ascetic and mystic. □□ **Su·fic** adj. **Su·fism** n. [Arab. ṣūfī, perh. f. ṣūf wool (from the woolen garment worn)]

sug- /sug, səg/ prefix assim. form of SUB- before g.

sug·ar /shŏŏgər/ n., v., & int. • n. **1** a sweet crystalline substance obtained from various plants, esp. the sugar cane and sugar beet, used in cooking, confectionery, brewing, etc.; sucrose. **2** Chem. any of a group of soluble usu. sweet-tasting crystalline carbohydrates found esp. in plants, e.g., glucose. **3** colloq. darling; dear (used as a term of address). **4** sweet words; flattery. **5** anything comparable to sugar encasing a pill in reconciling a person to what is unpalatable. **6** sl. a narcotic drug, esp. heroin or LSD (taken on a lump of sugar). • v.tr. **1** sweeten with sugar. **2** make (one's words, meaning, etc.) more pleasant or welcome. **3** coat with sugar (sugared almond). **4** spread a sugar mixture on (a tree) to catch moths. **5** make maple syrup or maple sugar by sugaring off. • int. euphem. = SHIT int. □ **sugar off** boil down maple sap into maple syrup and sugar. **sugar the pill** see PILL. □□ **sug·ar·less** adj. [ME f. OF çukre, sukere f. It. zucchero prob. f. med.L succarum f. Arab. sukkar]

sug·ar beet n. a beet, Beta vulgaris, from which sugar is extracted.

sug·ar cane n. Bot. any perennial tropical grass of the genus Saccharum, esp. S. officinarum, with tall stout jointed stems from which sugar is made.

sug·ar-coat v. to enclose in sugar. □□ **sug·ar-coat·ed** adj.

sug·ar dad·dy n. (pl. **-dies**) sl. an older man who lavishes gifts on a younger partner.

sug·ar-gum n. Bot. an Australian eucalyptus, Eucalyptus cladocalyx, with sweet foliage eaten by cattle.

sug·ar loaf n. a conical molded mass of sugar.

sug·ar ma·ple n. any of various trees, esp. Acer saccharum, from the sap of which sugar is made.

sug·ar of lead n. Chem. = LEAD ACETATE (see LEAD²).

sug·ar pea n. a variety of pea eaten whole including the pod.

sug·ar·plum /shŏŏgərplum/ n. archaic a small round candy of flavored boiled sugar.

sug·ar soap n. Brit. an alkaline compound for cleaning or removing paint.

sug·ar·y /shŏŏgəree/ adj. **1** containing or resembling sugar. **2** excessively sweet or esp. sentimental. **3** falsely sweet or pleasant (sugary compliments). □□ **sug·ar·i·ness** n.

sug·gest /səgjést, səjést/ v.tr. **1** (often foll. by that + clause) propose (a theory, plan, or hypothesis) (suggested to them that they should wait; suggested a different plan). **2 a** cause (an idea, memory, association, etc.) to present itself; evoke (this poem suggests peace). **b** hint at (his behavior suggests guilt). □ **suggest itself** (of an idea, etc.) come into the mind. □□ **sug·gest·er** n. [L suggerere suggest- (as SUB-, gerere bring)]

sug·gest·i·ble /səgjéstəbəl, səjés-/ adj. **1** capable of being suggested. **2** open to suggestion; easily swayed. □□ **sug·gest·i·bil·i·ty** n.

sug·ges·tion /səgjéschən, səjés-/ n. **1** the act or an instance of suggesting; the state of being suggested. **2** a theory, plan, etc., suggested (made a helpful suggestion). **3** a slight trace; a hint (a suggestion of garlic). **4** Psychol. **a** the insinuation of a belief, etc., into the mind. **b** such a belief, etc. [ME f. OF f. L suggestio -onis (as SUGGEST)]

sug·ges·tive /səgjéstiv, səjés-/ adj. **1** (usu. foll. by of) conveying a suggestion; evocative. **2** (esp. of a remark, joke, etc.) indecent; improper; racy. □□ **sug·ges·tive·ly** adv. **sug·ges·tive·ness** n.

su·i·cid·al /sóoisíd'l/ adj. **1** inclined to commit suicide. **2** of or concerning suicide. **3** self-destructive; fatally or disastrously rash. □□ **su·i·cid·al·ly** adv.

su·i·cide /sóoisīd/ n. & v. • n. **1 a** the intentional killing of oneself. **b** a person who commits suicide. **2** a self-destructive action or course (political suicide). **3** (attrib.) Mil. designating a highly dangerous or deliberately suicidal operation, etc. (a suicide mission). • v.intr. commit suicide. [mod.L suicida, suicidium f. L sui of oneself]

su·i·cide pact n. an agreement between two or more people to commit suicide together.

su·i ge·ne·ris /sóo-ī jénəris, sóo-ee, sóo-ee gén-/ adj. of its own kind; unique. [L]

su·i ju·ris /sóo-ī jŏŏris, sóo-ee, sóo-ee yŏŏris/ adj. Law of age; independent. [L]

su·int /swint/ n. the natural grease in sheep's wool. [F f. suer sweat]

suit /sóot/ n. & v. • n. **1 a** a set of outer clothes of matching material for men, consisting usu. of a jacket, trousers, and sometimes a vest. **b** a similar set of clothes for women usu. having a skirt instead of trousers. **c** (esp. in comb.) a set of clothes for a special occasion, occupation, etc. (playsuit; swimsuit). **2 a** any of the four sets (spades, hearts, diamonds, clubs) into which a pack of cards is divided. **b** a player's holding in a suit (his strong suit was clubs). **c** Bridge one of the suits as proposed trumps in bidding, frequently as opposed to no trumps. **3** (in full **suit at law**) a lawsuit (criminal suit). **4 a** a petition, esp. to a person in authority. **b** the process of courting a woman (paid suit to her). **5** (usu. foll. by of) a set of sails, armor, etc. • v. **1** tr. go well with (a person's figure, features, character, etc.); become. **2** tr. (also absol.) meet the demands or requirements of; satisfy; agree with (does not suit all tastes; that date will suit). **3** tr. make fitting or appropriate; accommodate; adapt (suited his style to his audience). **4** tr. (as **suited** adj.) appropriate; well-fitted (not suited to be an engineer). **5** intr. (usu. foll. by with) go well with the appearance, etc., of a person (red hair suits with her complexion). □ **suit the action to the word** carry out a promise or threat at once. **suit oneself 1** do as one chooses. **2** find something that satisfies one.

WORD HISTORY suit

Middle English: from sieute, from a feminine past participle of an alteration of Latin sequi 'follow.' Early senses included 'attendance at a court' and 'legal process.' The notion of 'make agreeable or appropriate' dates from the late 16th century.

---

suit·a·ble /sóotəbəl/ adj. (usu. foll. by to, for) well fitted for the purpose; appropriate. □□ **suit·a·bil·i·ty** n. **suit·a·ble·ness** n. **suit·a·bly** adv. [SUIT + -ABLE, after agreeable]

suit·case /sóotkays/ n. a usu. oblong case for carrying clothes, etc., having a handle and often a flat hinged lid. □□ **suit·case·ful** n. (pl. **·fuls**)

suite /sweet/ n. **1** a set of things belonging together, esp.: **a** a set of rooms in a hotel, etc. **b** furniture intended for the same room and of the same design. **2** Mus. **a** a set of instrumental compositions, orig. in dance style, to be played in succession. **b** a set of selected pieces from an opera, musical, etc., arranged to be played as one instrumental work. **3** a set of people in attendance; a retinue. [F (as SUIT)]

suit·ing /sóoting/ n. cloth used for making suits.

suit·or /sóotər/ n. **1** a man seeking to marry a specified woman; a wooer. **2** a plaintiff or petitioner in a lawsuit. [ME f. AF seutor, suitour, etc., f. L secutor -oris f. sequi secut- follow]

suk (also **sukh**) var. of SOUK.

su·ki·ya·ki /sóokeeyaákee, skeeyaá-/ n. a Japanese dish of sliced meat simmered with vegetables and sauce. [Jap.]

Suk·koth var. of SUCCOTH.

sul·cate /súlkayt/ adj. grooved; fluted; channeled. [L sulcatus, past part. of sulcare furrow (as SULCUS)]

sul·cus /súlkəs/ n. (pl. **sul·ci** /-sī/) Anat. a groove or furrow, esp. on the surface of the brain. [L]

sul·fa /súlfə/ n. any drug derived from sulfanilamide (often attrib.: sulfa drug). [abbr.]

sul·fam·ic acid /sulfámik/ n. a strong acid used in weedkiller, an amide of sulfuric acid. □□ **sul·fa·mate** /súlfəmayt/ n. [SULFUR + AMIDE]

sul·fa·nil·a·mide /súlfənīləmīd/ n. a colorless sulfonamide drug with anti-bacterial properties. [sulfanilic (SULFUR, ANILINE) + AMIDE]

sul·fate /súlfayt/ n. a salt or ester of sulfuric acid. [F sulfate f. L sulfur]

sul·fide /súlfīd/ n. Chem. a binary compound of sulfur.

sul·fite /súlfīt/ n. Chem. a salt or ester of sulfurous acid. [F sulfite alt. of sulfate SULFATE)]

sul·fon·a·mide /sulfónəmīd/ n. a substance derived from an amide of a sulfonic acid, able to prevent the multiplication of some pathogenic bacteria. [SULFONE + AMIDE]

sul·fo·nate /súlfənayt/ n. & v. Chem. ● n. a salt or ester of sulfonic acid. ● v.tr. convert into a sulfonate by reaction with sulfuric acid.

sul·fone /súlfōn/ n. an organic compound containing the SO_2 group united directly to two carbon atoms. □□ **sul·fon·ic** /–fónik/ adj. [G Sulfon (as SULFUR)]

sul·fur /súlfər/ n. & v. ● n. **1 a** a pale yellow nonmetallic element having crystalline and amorphous forms, burning with a blue flame and a suffocating smell, and used in making gunpowder, matches, and sulfuric acid, in the vulcanizing of rubber, and in the treatment of skin diseases. ¶ Symb.: **S. b** (attrib.) like or containing sulfur. **2** the material of which hellfire and lightning were believed to consist. **3** any yellow butterfly of the family Pieridae. **4** a pale greenish yellow color. ● v.tr. **1** treat with sulfur. **2** fumigate with sulfur. □□ **sul·fur·y** adj. [ME f. AF sulf (e)re, OF soufre f. L sulfur, sulp(h)ur]

sul·fu·rate /súlfyərayt/, –fə–/ v.tr. impregnate, fumigate, or treat with sulfur, esp. in bleaching. □□ **sul·fu·ra·tion** /–ráyshən/ n. **sul·fu·ra·tor** n.

sul·fur can·dle n. a candle burned to produce sulfur dioxide for fumigating.

sul·fur di·ox·ide n. a colorless pungent gas formed by burning sulfur in air and used as a food preservative.

sul·fu·re·ous /sulfyóoreeəs/ adj. **1** of, like, or suggesting sulfur. **2** sulfur-colored; yellow. [L sulphureus f. SULFUR]

sul·fu·ret·ed /súlfyŏorétid/ adj. archaic containing sulfur in combination. [sulphuret sulfide f. mod.L sulphuretum]

sul·fu·ret·ed hy·dro·gen n. hydrogen sulfide.

sul·fu·ric /sulfyŏorik/ adj. Chem. containing sexivalent sulfur. [F sulfurique (as SULFUR)]

sul·fu·ric ac·id n. a dense, oily, colorless, highly acid and corrosive fluid much used in the chemical industry. ¶ Chem. formula: H_2SO_4.

sul·fu·rize /súlfyəriz/, –fə–/ v.tr. = SULFURATE. □□ **sul·fu·ri·za·tion** n. [F sulfuriser (as SULFUR)]

sul·fur·ous /súlfərəs, –fyŏo r–/ adj. **1** relating to or suggestive of sulfur, esp. in color. **2** Chem. containing quadrivalent sulfur. [L sulphurosus f. SULFUR]

sul·fur·ous ac·id n. an unstable weak acid used as a reducing and bleaching acid.

sul·fur spring n. a spring impregnated with sulfur or its compounds.

sulk /sulk/ v. & n. ● v.intr. indulge in a sulk; be sulky. ● n. (also in pl., prec. by the) a period of sullen, esp. resentful, silence (having a sulk; got the sulks). □□ **sulk·er** n. [perh. back-form. f. SULKY]

sulk·y /súlkee/ adj. & n. (**sulk·i·er**, **sulk·i·est**) **1** sullen, morose, or silent, esp. from resentment or ill temper. **2** sluggish. ● n. (pl. ·**ies**) a light two-wheeled horse-drawn vehicle for one, esp. used in harness racing. □□ **sulk·i·ly** adv. **sulk·i·ness** n. [perh. f. obs. sulke hard to dispose of]

sulky

sul·lage /súlij/ n. filth; refuse; sewage. [perh. f. AF suillage f. souiller SOIL²]

sul·len /súlən/ adj. & n. ● adj. **1** morose; resentful; sulky; unforgiving; unsociable. **2 a** (of a thing) slow moving. **b** dismal; melancholy (a sullen sky). ● n. (in pl., usu. prec. by the) archaic a sullen frame of mind; depression. □□ **sul·len·ly** adv. **sul·len·ness** n. [16th-c. alt. of ME solein f. AF f. sol SOLE³]

sul·ly /súlee/ v.tr. (·**lies**, ·**lied**) **1** disgrace or tarnish (a person's reputation or character, a victory, etc.). **2** poet. dirty; soil. [perh. f. F souiller (as SOIL²)]

sul·tan /súlt'n/ n. **1 a** a Muslim sovereign. **b** (**the Sultan**) hist. the sultan of Turkey. **2** a variety of white domestic fowl from Turkey. □□ **sul·tan·ate** /–nayt/ n. [F sultan or med.L sultanus f. Arab. sulṭān power, ruler f. saluṭa rule]

sul·tan·a /sultánə, –táanə/ n. **1 a** a seedless raisin used in cakes, etc. **b** the small, pale yellow grape producing this. **2** the mother, wife, concubine, or daughter of a sultan. [It., fem. of sultano = SULTAN]

sul·try /súltree/ adj. (**sul·tri·er**, **sul·tri·est**) **1** (of the atmosphere or the weather) hot or oppressive; close. **2** (of a person, character, etc.) attractive in a way that suggests a passionate nature (she exuded a sultry charm). □□ **sul·tri·ly** adv. **sul·tri·ness** n. [obs. sulter SWELTER]

sum /sum/ n. & v. ● n. **1** the total amount resulting from the addition of two or more items, facts, ideas, feelings, etc. (the sum of two and three is five; the sum of their objections is this). **2** a particular amount of money (paid a large sum for it). **3 a** an arithmetical problem (could not work out the sum). **b** (esp. pl.) esp. Brit. colloq. arithmetic work, esp. at an elementary level (was good at sums). ● v.tr. (**summed**, **sum·ming**) find the sum of. □ **in sum** in brief. **sum up 1** (esp. of a judge) recapitulate or review the evidence in a case,

etc. **2** form or express an idea of the character of (a person, situation, etc.). **3** collect into or express as a total or whole. [ME f. OF summe, somme f. L summa main part, fem. of summus highest]

su·mac /sóomak, shóo–/ n. (also **su·mach**) **1** any shrub or tree of the genus Rhus, having reddish cone-shaped fruits used as a spice in cooking. **2** the dried and ground leaves of this used in tanning and dyeing. [ME f. OF sumac or med.L sumac(h) f. Arab. summāk]

Su·me·ri·an /sŏoméereeən, –mér–/ adj. & n. ● adj. of or relating to the early and non-Semitic element in the civilization of ancient Babylonia. ● n. **1** a member of the early non-Semitic people of ancient Babylonia. **2** the Sumerian language. [F sumérien f. Sumer in Babylonia]

sum·ma /sóomə, súmə/ n. (pl. **sum·mae** /–mee/) a summary of what is known of a subject. [ME f. L: see SUM]

sum·ma cum lau·de /sóomə koom lówday, –də, –dee/ adv. & adj. (of a degree, diploma, etc.) of the highest standard; with the highest distinction. [L, = with highest praise]

sum·ma·rize /súmərīz/ v.tr. make or be a summary of; sum up. □□ **sum·ma·rist** n. **sum·ma·riz·a·ble** adj. **sum·ma·ri·za·tion** n. **sum·ma·riz·er** n.

sum·ma·ry /súməree/ n. & adj. ● n. (pl. ·**ries**) a brief account; an abridgment. ● adj. **1** dispensing with needless details or formalities; brief (a summary account). **2** Law (of a trial, etc.) without the customary legal formalities (summary justice). □□ **sum·mar·i·ly** /səmáirilee/ adv. **sum·mar·i·ness** n. [ME f. L summarium f. L summa SUM]

sum·ma·ry con·vic·tion n. a conviction made by a judge or magistrates without a jury.

sum·ma·ry ju·ris·dic·tion n. the authority of a court to use summary proceedings and arrive at a judgment.

sum·ma·ry of·fense n. an offense within the scope of a summary court.

sum·ma·tion /səmáyshən/ n. **1** the finding of a total or sum; an addition. **2** a summing-up. □□ **sum·ma·tion·al** adj.

sum·mer¹ /súmər/ n. & v. ● n. **1** the warmest season of the year, in the N. hemisphere from June to August and in the S. hemisphere from December to February. **2** Astron. the period from the summer solstice to the autumnal equinox. **3** the hot weather typical of summer. **4** (often foll. by of) the mature stage of life; the height of achievement, powers, etc. **5** (esp. in pl.) poet. a year (esp. of a person's age) (a child of ten summers). **6** (attrib.) characteristic of or suitable for summer (summer clothes). ● v. **1** intr. (usu. foll. by at, in) pass the summer. **2** tr. (often foll. by at, in) pasture (cattle). □□ **sum·mer·less** adj. **sum·mer·ly** adv. **sum·mer·y** adj. [OE sumor]

sum·mer² /súmər/ n. (in full **summertree**) a horizontal bearing beam, esp. one supporting joists or rafters. [ME f. AF sumer, somer packhorse, beam, OF somier f. LL sagmarius f. sagma f. Gk sagma packsaddle]

sum·mer light·ning n. sheet lightning without thunder, resulting from a distant storm.

sum·mer·sault var. of SOMERSAULT.

sum·mer school n. **1** a course of lectures, etc., held during the summer vacation, esp. at a university. **2** a course or series of courses held during the summer vacation allowing students to make up work missed or failed, or to accelerate toward their degrees.

sum·mer sol·stice n. the time at which the sun is farthest north from the equator, about June 21 in the northern hemisphere.

sum·mer squash n. any of various cultivated squashes whose fruit is used as a vegetable.

sum·mer·time /súmərtīm/ n. the season or period of summer.

sum·mer·weight adj. (of clothes) suitable for use in summer, esp. because of their light weight.

sum·ming-up n. **1** a review of evidence and a direction given by a judge to a jury. **2** a recapitulation of the main points of an argument, case, etc.

sum·mit /súmit/ n. **1** the highest point, esp. of a mountain; the apex. **2** the highest degree of power, ambition, etc. **3** (in full **summit meeting, talks**, etc.) a discussion, esp. on disarmament, etc., between heads of government. □□ **sum·mit·less** adj. [ME f. OF somet, somm (m)ete f. som top f. L summum neut. of summus]

sum·mon /súmən/ v.tr. **1** call upon to appear, esp. as a defendant or witness in a court of law. **2** (usu. foll. by to + infin.) call upon (summoned her to assist). **3** call together for a meeting or some other purpose (summoned the members to attend). □ **summon up** (often foll. by to, for) gather (courage, spirits, resources, etc.) (summoned up *her strength for the task*). □□ **sum·mon·a·ble** *adj.* **sum·mon·er** *n.* [ME f. OF *somondre* f. L *summonēre* (as SUB-, *monēre* warn)]

sum·mons /súmənz/ *n. & v.* ● *n.* (*pl.* **sum·mons·es**) **1** an authoritative or urgent call to attend on some occasion or do something. **2 a** a call to appear before a judge or magistrate. **b** the writ containing such a summons. *v.tr.* *esp.* Law serve with a summons. [ME f. OF *somonce, sumunse* f. L *summonita* fem. past part. of *summonēre*: see SUMMON]

sum·mum bo·num /sóᴓməm bónəm/ *n.* the highest good, esp. as the end or determining principle in an ethical system. [L]

su·mo /sóᴓmō/ *n.* (*pl.* **·mos**) **1** a style of Japanese wrestling in which a participant is defeated by touching the ground with any part of the body except the soles of the feet or by moving outside the marked area. **2** a sumo wrestler. [Jap.]

sump /sump/ *n.* **1** a pit, well, hole, etc., in which superfluous liquid collects in mines, machines, etc. **2** a cesspool. [ME, = marsh f. MDu., MLG *sump*, or (mining) G *Sumpf*, rel. to SWAMP]

sump·ter /súmptər/ *n.* *archaic* **1** a packhorse. **2** any pack animal (*sumpter-mule*). [ME f. OF *som(m)etier* f. LL f. Gk *sagma –atos* packsaddle: cf. SUMMER²]

sump·tu·ary /súmpchᴓᴓeree/ *adj.* **1** regulating expenditure. **2** (of a law or edict, etc.) limiting private expenditure in the interests of the government. [L *sumptuarius* f. *sumptus* cost f. *sumere* sumpt-take]

sump·tu·ous /súmpchᴓᴓəs/ *adj.* rich; lavish; costly (*a sumptuous setting*). □□ **sump·tu·os·i·ty** /–ósitee/ *n.* **sump·tu·ous·ly** *adv.* **sump·tu·ous·ness** *n.* [ME f. OF *somptueux* f. L *sumptuosus* (as SUMPTUARY)]

sum to·tal *n.* = SUM sense 1 of *n.*

Sun. *abbr.* Sunday.

sun /sun/ *n. & v.* ● *n.* **1 a** the star around which the earth orbits and from which it receives light and warmth. **b** any similar star in the universe with or without planets. **2** the light or warmth received from the sun (*pull down the blinds and keep out the sun*). **3** *poet.* a day or a year. **4** *poet.* a person or thing regarded as a source of glory, radiance, etc. ● *v.* (**sunned, sun·ning**) **1** *refl.* bask in the sun. **2** *tr.* expose to the sun. **3** *intr.* sun oneself. □ **against the sun** counterclockwise. **beneath** (or **under**) **the sun** anywhere in the world. **in the sun** exposed to the sun's rays. **one's sun is set** the time of one's prosperity is over. **take** (or **shoot**) **the sun** *Naut.* ascertain the altitude of the sun with a sextant in order to fix the latitude. **with the sun** clockwise. □□ **sun·less** *adj.* **sun·less·ness** *n.* **sun·like** *adj.* **sun·proof** *adj.* **sun·ward** *adj. & adv.* **sun·wards** *adv.* [OE *sunne, sunna*]

sun and plan·et *n.* a system of gearing cog wheels.

sun·bath /súnbath/ *n.* a period of exposing the body to the sun.

sun·bathe /súnbayth/ *v.intr.* bask in the sun, esp. to tan the body. □□ **sun·bath·er** *n.*

sun·beam /súnbeem/ *n.* a ray of sunlight.

sun bear *n.* a small black bear, *Helarctos malayanus*, of SE Asia, with a light-colored mark on its chest.

sun·bed /súnbed/ *n.* **1** *Brit.* a lightweight, usu. folding, chair with a seat long enough to support the legs, used for sunbathing. **2** a bed for lying on under a sun lamp.

sun·belt /súnbelt/ *n.* a strip of territory receiving a high amount of sunshine, esp. the region in the southern US stretching from California to Florida.

sun·bird /súnbərd/ *n.* any small brightly plumaged Old World bird of the family Nectariniidae, resembling a hummingbird.

sun-blind *n.* *Brit.* a window awning.

sun·block /súnblok/ *n.* a cream or lotion for protecting the skin from the sun.

sun·burn /súnbərn/ *n. & v.* ● *n.* reddening and inflammation of the skin caused by overexposure to the sun. ● *v.intr.* **1** suffer from sunburn. **2** (as **sunburned** or **sunburnt** *adj.*) suffering from sunburn; brown or tanned.

sun·burst /súnbərst/ *n.* **1** something resembling the sun and its rays, esp.: **a** an ornament, brooch, etc. **b** a firework. **2** the sun shining suddenly from behind clouds.

sun·dae /súnday, –dee/ *n.* a dish of ice cream with fruit, nuts, syrup, etc. [perh. f. SUNDAY]

sun dance *n.* a dance of some Native American tribes in honor of the sun.

Sun·day /súnday, –dee/ *n. & adv.* ● *n.* **1** the first day of the week, a Christian holiday and day of worship. **2** a newspaper published on a Sunday. ● *adv.* *colloq.* **1** on Sunday. **2** (**Sundays**) on Sundays; each Sunday. [OE *sunnandæg*, transl. of L *dies solis*, Gk *hēmera hēliou* day of the sun]

Sun·day best *n.* a person's best clothes, kept for Sunday use.

Sun·day let·ter *n.* = DOMINICAL LETTER.

Sun·day paint·er *n.* an amateur painter, esp. one with little training.

Sun·day school *n.* a school for the religious instruction of children on Sundays.

sun deck *n.* the upper deck of a cruise ship, etc.

sun·der /súndər/ *v.tr. & intr.* *archaic* or *literary* separate; sever. □ in

sunder apart. [OE *sundrian*, f. *āsundrian*, etc.: *in sunder* f. ME f. *o(n)sunder* ASUNDER]

sun·dew /súndᴓᴓ, –dyᴓᴓ/ *n.* any small insect-consuming bog plant of the family Droseraceae, esp. of the genus *Drosera* with hairs secreting drops of moisture.

sun·di·al /súndiəl/ *n.* an instrument showing the time by the shadow of a pointer cast by the sun onto a graduated disk.

sun disk *n.* a winged disk, emblematic of the sun god.

sun dog *n.* = PARHELION.

sun·down /súndown/ *n.* sunset.

sun·down·er /súndownər/ *n.* **1** *Austral.* a tramp who arrives at a sheep station, etc., in the evening for food and shelter too late to do any work. **2** *Brit. colloq.* an alcoholic drink taken at sunset.

sundial

sun·dress /súndres/ *n.* a dress without sleeves and with a low neck and back, designed for warm weather.

sun-dried *adj.* dried by the sun, not by artificial heat.

sun·dry /súndree/ *adj. & n.* ● *adj.* various; several (*sundry items*). ● *n.* (*pl.* **·dries**) (in *pl.*) items or oddments not mentioned individually. [OE *syndrig* separate, rel. to SUNDER]

sun·fast /súnfast/ *adj.* (of dye) not subject to fading by sunlight.

sun·fish /súnfish/ *n.* any of various almost spherical fish, esp. a large ocean fish, *Mola mola*.

sun·flow·er /súnflowr/ *n.* any very tall plant of the genus *Helianthus*, esp. *H. annus* with very large, showy, golden-rayed flowers, grown also for its seeds, which yield an edible oil.

sung *past part.* of SING.

sun·glass·es /súnglasiz/ *n.* glasses tinted to protect the eyes from sunlight or glare.

sun god *n.* the sun worshiped as a deity.

sun hat *n.* a hat designed to protect the head from the sun.

sun hel·met *n.* a helmet of cork, etc., formerly worn in the tropics.

sunflower

sun in splen·dor *n.* *Heraldry* the sun with rays and a human face.

sunk *past* and *past part.* of SINK.

sunk·en /súngkən/ *adj.* **1** that has been sunk. **2** beneath the surface; submerged. **3** (of the eyes, cheeks, etc.) hollow; depressed. [past part. of SINK]

sunk·en gar·den *n.* a garden placed below the general level of its surroundings.

sun-kissed *adj.* warmed or affected by the sun.

sun lamp *n.* **1** a lamp giving ultraviolet rays for an artificial suntan, therapy, etc. **2** *Cinematog.* a large lamp with a parabolic reflector used in film-making.

sun·light /súnlit/ *n.* light from the sun.

sun·lit /súnlit/ *adj.* illuminated by sunlight.

sun lounge *n.* *Brit.* = SUN PARLOR.

sunn /sun/ *n.* (in full **sunn hemp**) an E. Indian hemplike fiber. [Urdu & Hindi *san* f. Skr. *śáṇā* hempen]

Sun·na /sóᴓnə/ *n.* a traditional portion of Muslim law based on Muhammad's words or acts, accepted by Muslims as authoritative. [Arab., = form, way, course, rule]

Sun·ni /sóᴓnee/ *n. & adj.* ● *n.* (*pl.* same or **Sun·nis**) **1** one of the two main branches of Islam, regarding the Sunna as equal in authority to the Koran (cf. SHIA). **2** an adherent of this branch of Islam. ● *adj.* (also **Sun·nite**) of or relating to Sunni.

sun·ny /súnee/ *adj.* (**sun·ni·er, sun·ni·est**) **1 a** bright with sunlight. **b** exposed to or warmed by the sun. **2** cheery and bright in temperament. □ **the sunny side 1** the side of a house, street, etc., that gets most sun. **2** the more cheerful aspect of circumstances, etc. (*always looks on the sunny side*). □□ **sun·ni·ly** *adv.* **sun·ni·ness** *n.*

sun·ny·side up /súneesíd/ *adj.* (of an egg) fried on one side and served.

sun par·lor *n.* a room with large windows, designed to receive sunlight.

sun rays *n.* **1** sunbeams. **2** ultraviolet rays used therapeutically.

sun·rise /súnriz/ *n.* **1** the sun's rising at dawn. **2** the colored sky associated with this. **3** the time at which sunrise occurs.

sun·rise in·dus·try *n.* any newly established industry, esp. in electronics and telecommunications, regarded as signaling prosperity.

sun·roof /súnrᴓᴓf/ *n.* a section of an automobile roof that can be slid open.

sun·set /súnset/ *n. & adj.* ● *n.* **1** the sun's setting in the evening. **2** the colored sky associated with this. **3** the time at which sunset occurs. **4** the declining period of life. ● *adj.* pertaining to a law or government program subject to review for its continuation.

sun·shade /súnshayd/ *n.* **1** a parasol. **2** an awning.

sun·shine /súnshīn/ *n.* **1 a** the light of the sun. **b** an area lit by the sun. **2** good weather. **3** cheerfulness; joy (*brought sunshine into her life*). **4** *Brit. colloq.* a form of address. □□ **sun·shin·y** *adj.*

sun·spot /súnspot/ *n.* one of the dark patches, changing in shape and size and lasting for varying periods, observed on the sun's surface.

sun·star /súnstaar/ *n.* any starfish of the genus *Solaster*, with many rays.

sun stone *n.* a cat's eye gem, esp. feldspar with embedded flecks of hematite, etc.

sun·stroke /súnstrōk/ *n.* acute prostration or collapse from the excessive heat of the sun.

sun·tan /súntan/ *n. & v.* ● *n.* the brownish coloring of skin caused by exposure to the sun. ● *v.intr.* (·**tanned**, ·**tan·ning**) color the skin with a suntan.

sun·trap /súntrap/ *n. Brit.* a place sheltered from the wind and suitable for catching the sunshine.

sun·up /súnup/ *n.* sunrise.

sun vi·sor *n.* a fixed or movable shield at the top of a vehicle windshield to shield the eyes from the sun.

sup[1] /sup/ *v. & n.* ● *v.tr.* (**supped**, **sup·ping**) **1** take (soup, tea, etc.) by sips or spoonfuls. **2** esp. *No. of Engl. colloq.* drink (alcohol). ● *n.* a sip of liquid. [OE *sūpan*]

sup[2] /sup/ *v.intr.* (**supped**, **sup·ping**) (usu. foll. by *off, on*) archaic take supper. [OF *super, soper*]

sup- /sup, səp/ *prefix* assim. form of SUB- before *p*.

su·per /sóopər/ *n. & adj.* ● *adj.* **1** (also **su·per-du·per** /–dóopər/) *colloq.* (also as *int.*) exceptional; splendid. **2** esp. *Brit. Commerce* superfine. **3** esp. *Brit. Commerce* (of a measure) superficial, in square (not lineal or solid) measure (*120 super ft.; 120 ft. super*). ● *n. colloq.* **1** *Theatr.* a supernumerary actor. **2** a superintendent. **3** superphosphate. **4** an extra, unwanted, or unimportant person; a supernumerary. **5** *Commerce* superfine cloth or manufacture. [abbr.]

super- /sóopər/ *comb. form* forming nouns, adjectives, and verbs, meaning: **1** above, beyond, or over in place or time or conceptually (*superstructure; supernormal; superimpose*). **2** to a great or extreme degree (*superabundant; superhuman*). **3** extra good or large of its kind (*supertanker*). **4** of a higher kind, esp. in names of classificatory divisions (*superclass*). [from or after L *super-* f. *super* above, beyond]

su·per·a·ble /sóopərəbəl/ *adj.* able to be overcome. [L *superabilis* f. *superare* overcome]

su·per·a·bound /sóopərəbównd/ *v.intr.* be very or too abundant. [LL *superabundare* (as SUPER-, ABOUND)]

su·per·a·bun·dant /sóopərəbúndənt/ *adj.* abounding beyond what is normal or right. □□ **su·per·a·bun·dance** *n.* **su·per·a·bun·dant·ly** *adv.* [ME f. LL *superabundare*: see SUPERABOUND]

su·per·add /sóopərád/ *v.tr.* add over and above. □□ **su·per·ad·di·tion** /–ədíshən/ *n.* [ME f. L *superaddere* (as SUPER-, ADD)]

su·per·al·tar /sóopərawltər/ *n. Eccl.* a portable slab of stone consecrated for use on an unconsecrated altar, etc. [ME f. med.L *superaltare* (as SUPER-, ALTAR)]

su·per·an·nu·ate /sóopərányooayt/ *v.tr.* **1** retire (a person) with a pension **2** dismiss or discard as too old for use, work, etc. **3** (as **su·perannuated** *adj.*) too old for work or use; obsolete. □□ **su·per·an·nu·a·ble** *adj.* back-form. f. *superannuated* f. med.L *superannuatus* f. L SUPER- + *annus* year]

su·per·an·nu·a·tion /sóopərányoo-áyshən/ *n.* **1** a pension paid to a retired person. **2** *Brit.* a regular payment made toward this by an employed person. **3** the process or an instance of superannuating.

su·per·a·que·ous /sóopəráykweeəs, –ák–/ *adj.* above water.

su·perb /sóopórb/ *adj.* **1** of the most impressive, splendid, grand, or majestic kind (*superb courage; a superb specimen*). **2** *colloq.* excellent; fine. □□ **su·perb·ly** *adv.* **su·perb·ness** *n.* [F *superbe* or L *superbus* proud]

su·per·cal·en·der /sóopərkálindər/ *v.tr.* give a highly glazed finish to (paper) by extra calendering.

su·per·car·go /sóopərkaargō/ *n.* (*pl.* ·**goes**) an officer in a merchant ship managing sales, etc., of cargo. [earlier *supracargo* f. Sp. *sobrecargo* f. *sobre* over + *cargo* CARGO]

su·per·ce·les·tial /sóopərsiléschəl/ *adj.* **1** above the heavens. **2** more than heavenly. [LL *supercaelestis* (as SUPER-, CELESTIAL)]

su·per·charge /sóopərchaarj/ *v.tr.* **1** (usu. foll. by *with*) charge (the atmosphere, etc.) with energy, emotion, etc. **2** use a supercharger on (an internal combustion engine).

su·per·charg·er /sóopərchaarjər/ *n.* a device supplying air or fuel to an internal combustion engine at above normal pressure to increase efficiency.

su·per·cil·i·ar·y /sóopərsilee-eree/ *adj. Anat.* of or concerning the eyebrow; over the eye. [*supercilium* eyebrow (as SUPER-, *cilium* eyelid)]

su·per·cil·i·ous /sóopərsíleeəs/ *adj.* assuming an air of contemptuous indifference or superiority. □□ **su·per·cil·i·ous·ly** *adv.* **su·per·cil·i·ous·ness** *n.* [L *superciliosus* (as SUPERCILIARY)]

su·per·class /sóopərklas/ *n.* a taxonomic category between class and phylum.

su·per·co·lum·nar /sóopərkəlúmnər/ *adj. Archit.* having one order or set of columns above another. □□ **su·per·co·lum·ni·a·tion** /–neeáyshən/ *n.*

su·per·com·put·er /sóopərkəmpyóotər/ *n.* a powerful computer capable of dealing with complex problems. □□ **su·per·com·put·ing** *n.*

su·per·con·duc·tiv·i·ty /sóopərkónduktívitee/ *n. Physics* the property of zero electrical resistance in some substances at very low absolute temperatures. □□ **su·per·con·duct·ing** /–kəndúkting/ *adj.* **su·per·con·duc·tive** *adj.*

su·per·con·duc·tor /sóopərkəndúktər/ *n. Physics* a substance having superconductivity.

su·per·con·scious /sóopərkónshəs/ *adj.* transcending human consciousness. □□ **su·per·con·scious·ly** *adv.* **su·per·con·scious·ness** *n.*

su·per·cool /sóopərkóol/ *v. & adj.* ● *v. Chem.* **1** *tr.* cool (a liquid) below its freezing point without solidification or crystallization. **2** *intr.* (of a liquid) be cooled in this way. ● *adj. sl.* very cool, relaxed, etc.

su·per·crit·i·cal /sóopərkrítikəl/ *adj. Physics* of more than critical mass, etc.

su·per·du·per var. of SUPER *adj.* 1.

su·per·e·go /sóopəreégō, –égō/ *n.* (*pl.* ·**gos**) *Psychol.* the part of the mind that acts as a conscience and responds to social rules.

su·per·el·e·va·tion /sóopəréliváyshən/ *n.* the amount by which the outer edge of a curve on a road or railroad is above the inner edge.

su·per·em·i·nent /sóopəréminənt/ *adj.* supremely eminent, exalted, or remarkable. □□ **su·per·em·i·nence** *n.* **su·per·em·i·nent·ly** *adv.* [L *supereminēre* rise above (as SUPER-, EMINENT)]

su·per·er·o·ga·tion /sóopərérəgáyshən/ *n.* the performance of more than duty requires. □□ **su·per·er·og·a·to·ry** /–írógətawree/ *adj.* [LL *supererogatio* f. *supererogare* pay in addition (as SUPER-, *erogare* pay out)]

su·per·ex·cel·lent /sóopéréksələnt/ *adj.* very or supremely excellent. □□ **su·per·ex·cel·lence** *n.* **su·per·ex·cel·lent·ly** *adv.* [LL *superexcellens* (as SUPER-, EXCELLENT)]

su·per·fam·i·ly /sóopərfamilee/ *n.* (*pl.* ·**lies**) a taxonomic category between family and order.

su·per·fat·ted /sóopərfátid/ *adj.* (of soap) containing extra fat.

su·per·fe·cun·da·tion /sóopərfeékəndáyshən, –fékən–/ *n.* = SUPERFETATION 1.

su·per·fe·ta·tion /sóopərfeetáyshən/ *n.* **1** *Med. & Zool.* a second conception during pregnancy giving rise to embryos of different ages in the uterus. **2** *Bot.* the fertilization of the same ovule by different kinds of pollen. **3** the accretion of one thing on another. [F *superfétation* or f. mod.L *superfetatio* f. L *superfetare* (as SUPER-, *fetus* FETUS)]

su·per·fi·cial /sóopərfíshəl/ *adj.* **1** of or on the surface; lacking depth (*a superficial knowledge; superficial wounds*). **2** swift or cursory (*a superficial examination*). **3** apparent but not real (*a superficial resemblance*). **4** (esp. of a person) having no depth of character or knowledge; trivial; shallow. **5** esp. *Brit. Commerce* (of a measure) square (cf. SUPER *adj.* 3). □□ **su·per·fi·ci·al·i·ty** /–sheeálitee/ *n.* (*pl.* ·**ties**) **su·per·fi·cial·ly** *adv.* **su·per·fi·cial·ness** *n.* [LL *superficialis* f. L (as SUPERFICIES)]

SYNONYM TIP superficial

CURSORY, HASTY, SLAPDASH, SHALLOW. No one wants to be accused of being **superficial** or **shallow**, two adjectives that literally indicate a lack of depth (*a superficial wound, a shallow grave*). *Superficial* suggests too much concern with the surface or obvious aspects of something, and it is considered a derogatory term because it connotes a personality that is not genuine or sincere. *Shallow* is even more derogatory because it implies not only a refusal to explore something deeply but an inability to feel, sympathize, or understand. It is unlikely that a *shallow* person, in other words, will ever have more than *superficial* relationships with his or her peers. **Cursory**, which may or may not be a derogatory term, suggests a lack of thoroughness or attention to details rather than a concentration on *superficial* aspects (*a cursory glance at the newspaper*), while **hasty** emphasizes a refusal or inability to spend the necessary time on something (*a hasty review of the facts*). If you are **slapdash** in your approach, it means that you are both careless and *hasty* (*a slapdash job of cleaning up*).

---

su·per·fi·ci·es /sóopərfísheez, –fishee–eez/ *n.* (*pl.* same) *Geom.* a surface. [L (as SUPER-, *facies* face)]

su·per·fine /sóopərfin/ *adj.* **1** *Commerce* of high quality. **2** pretending great refinement. [med.L *superfinus* (as SUPER-, FINE[1])]

su·per·flu·i·ty /sóopərflóoitee/ *n.* (*pl.* ·**ties**) **1** the state of being superfluous. **2** a superfluous amount or thing. [ME f. OF *superfluité* f. LL *superfluitas –tatis* f. L *superfluus*: see SUPERFLUOUS]

su·per·flu·ous /sóopórflóoəs/ *adj.* more than enough; redundant;

needless. □□ **su·per·flu·ous·ly** *adv.* **su·per·flu·ous·ness** *n.* [ME f. L *superfluus* (as SUPER-, *fluere* to flow)]

su·per·gi·ant /sŏŏpərjīənt/ *n.* a star of very great luminosity and size.

su·per·glue /sŏŏpərglōō/ *n.* any of various adhesives with an exceptional bonding capability.

su·per·grass /sŏŏpərgras/ *n. Brit. colloq.* a police informer who implicates a large number of people.

su·per·heat /sŏŏpərhēet/ *v.tr. Physics* **1** heat (a liquid) above its boiling point without vaporization. **2** heat (a vapor) above its boiling point (*superheated steam*). □□ **su·per·heat·er** *n.*

su·per·het /sŏŏpərhet/ *n. colloq.* = SUPERHETERODYNE.

su·per·het·er·o·dyne /sŏŏpərhétərōdīn/ *adj. & n.* ● *adj.* denoting or characteristic of a system of radio reception in which a local variable oscillator is tuned to beat at a constant ultrasonic frequency with carrier wave frequencies, making it unnecessary to vary the amplifier tuning and securing greater selectivity. ● *n.* a superheterodyne receiver. [SUPERSONIC + HETERODYNE]

su·per·high·way /sŏŏpərhīway/ *n.* a multilane main road for fast traffic.

su·per·hu·man /sŏŏpərhyōōmən/ *adj.* **1** beyond normal human capability. **2** higher than man. □□ **su·per·hu·man·ly** *adv.* [LL *superhumanus* (as SUPER-, HUMAN)]

su·per·hu·mer·al /sŏŏpərhyōōmərəl/ *n. Eccl.* a vestment worn over the shoulders, e.g., an amice, ephod, or pallium. [LL *superhumerale* (as SUPER-, HUMERAL)]

su·per·im·pose /sŏŏpərimpóz/ *v.tr.* (usu. foll. by *on*) lay (a thing) on something else. □□ **su·per·im·po·si·tion** /–pəzíshən/ *n.*

su·per·in·cum·bent /sŏŏpərinkúmbənt/ *adj.* lying on something else.

su·per·in·duce /sŏŏpərindōōs, –dyōōs/ *v.tr.* introduce or induce in addition. [L *superinducere* cover over, bring from outside (as SUPER-, INDUCE)]

su·per·in·tend /sŏŏpərinténd/ *v.tr. & intr.* be responsible for the management or arrangement of (an activity, etc.); supervise and inspect. □□ **su·per·in·tend·ence** *n.* **su·per·in·tend·en·cy** *n.* [eccl.L *superintendere* (as SUPER-, INTEND), transl. Gk *episkopō*]

su·per·in·tend·ent /sŏŏpərinténdənt/ *n. & adj.* ● *n.* **1 a** a person who superintends. **b** a director of an institution, etc. **2 a** *US* a high-ranking official, often the chief of a police department. **b** *Brit.* a police officer above the rank of inspector. **3** the caretaker of a building. ● *adj.* superintending. [eccl.L *superintendent-* part. stem of *superintendere:* see SUPERINTEND]

SPELLING TIP superintendent

To remember the *-ent* ending of this word, you can use the mnemonic: "The building superintend*ent* collects the r*ent*."

su·pe·ri·or /sŏŏpéereeər/ *adj. & n.* ● *adj.* **1** in a higher position; of higher rank (*a superior officer; a superior court*). **2 a** above the average in quality, etc. (*made of superior leather*). **b** having or showing a high opinion of oneself; supercilious (*had a superior air*). **3** (often foll. by *to*) **a** better or greater in some respect (*superior to its rivals in speed*). **b** above yielding, making concessions, paying attention, etc. (*is superior to bribery; superior to temptation*). **4** further above or out; higher, esp.: **a** *Astron.* (of a planet) having an orbit further from the sun than the earth's **b** *Zool.* (of an insect's wings) folding over others. **c** *Printing* (of figures or letters) placed above the line. **d** *Bot.* (of the calyx) above the ovary. **e** *Bot.* (of the ovary) above the calyx. ● *n.* **1** a person superior to another in rank, character, etc. (*is deferential to his superiors; is her superior in courage*). **2** (*fem.* **su·pe·ri·or·ess** /–ris/) *Eccl.* the head of a monastery or other religious institution (*Mother Superior, Father Superior*). **3** *Printing* a superior letter or figure. □□ **su·pe·ri·or·ly** *adv.* [ME f. OF *superiour* f. L *superior –oris*, compar. of *superus* that is above f. *super* above]

su·pe·ri·or·i·ty /sŏŏpéereeáwritee, –ór–/ *n.* the state of being superior.

su·pe·ri·or·i·ty com·plex *n. Psychol.* an undue conviction of one's own superiority to others.

su·per·ja·cent /sŏŏpərjáysənt/ *adj.* overlying; superincumbent. [L *superjacēre* (as SUPER-, *jacēre* lie)]

su·per·la·tive /sŏŏpərlətiv/ *adj. & n.* ● *adj.* **1** of the highest quality or degree (*superlative wisdom*). **2** *Gram.* (of an adjective or adverb) expressing the highest or a very high degree of a quality (e.g., *bravest, most fiercely*) (cf. POSITIVE, COMPARATIVE). **3** exaggerated; excessive. ● *n.* **1** *Gram.* **a** the superlative expression or form of an adjective or adverb. **b** a word in the superlative. **2** something embodying excellence; the highest form of a thing. **3** an exaggerated or excessive statement, comment, expression, etc. □□ **su·per·la·tive·ly** *adv.* **su·per·la·tive·ness** *n.* [ME f. OF *superlatif –ive* f. LL *superlativus* f. L *superlatus* (as SUPER-, *latus* past part. of *ferre* take)]

su·per·lu·na·ry /sŏŏpərlōōnəree/ *adj.* **1** situated beyond the moon. **2** belonging to a higher world; celestial. [med.L *superlunaris* (as SUPER-, LUNAR)]

su·per·man /sŏŏpərman/ *n.* (*pl.* **·men**) **1** esp. Philos. the ideal superior man of the future. **2** *colloq.* a man of exceptional strength or

ability. [SUPER- + MAN, formed by G. B. Shaw after Nietzsche's G *Übermensch*]

su·per·mar·ket /sŏŏpərmaarkit/ *n.* a large self-service store selling foods, household goods, etc.

su·per·mun·dane /sŏŏpərmundáyn/ *adj.* superior to earthly things.

su·per·nal /sŏŏpэrnəl/ *adj. esp. poet.* **1** heavenly; divine. **2** of or concerning the sky. **3** lofty. □□ **su·per·nal·ly** *adv.* [ME f. OF *supernal* or med.L *supernalis* f. L *supernus* f. *super* above]

su·per·na·tant /sŏŏpэrnáyt'nt/ *adj. & n.* esp. Chem. ● *adj.* floating on the surface of a liquid. ● *n.* a supernatant substance. [SUPER- + *natant* swimming (as NATATION)]

su·per·nat·u·ral /sŏŏpэrnáchərəl/ *adj. & n.* ● *adj.* attributed to or thought to reveal some force above the laws of nature; magical; mystical. ● *n.* (prec. by *the*) supernatural, occult, or magical forces, effects, etc. □□ **su·per·nat·u·ral·ism** *n.* **su·per·nat·u·ral·ist** *n.* **su·per·nat·u·ral·ize** *v.tr.* **su·per·nat·u·ral·ly** *adv.* **su·per·nat·u·ral·ness** *n.*

su·per·nor·mal /sŏŏpэrnáwrmэl/ *adj.* beyond what is normal or natural. □□ **su·per·nor·mal·i·ty** /–málitee/ *n.*

su·per·no·va /sŏŏpэrnóvə/ *n.* (*pl.* **·no·vae** /–vee/ or **·no·vas**) *Astron.* a star that suddenly increases very greatly in brightness because of an explosion ejecting most of its mass.

su·per·nu·mer·ar·y /sŏŏpэrnŏŏmэreree, –nyŏŏ–/ *adj. & n.* ● *adj.* **1** in excess of the normal number; extra. **2** (of a person) engaged for extra work. **3** (of an actor) appearing on stage but not speaking. ● *n.* (*pl.* **·ies**) **1** an extra or unwanted person or thing. **2** a supernumerary actor; extra. **3** a person engaged for extra work. [LL *supernumerarius* (soldier) added to a legion already complete, f. L *super numerum* beyond the number]

su·per·or·der /sŏŏpэrawrdər/ *n. Biol.* a taxonomic category between order and class. □□ **su·per·or·di·nal** /–órdin'l/ *adj.*

su·per·or·di·nate /sŏŏpэráwrd'nэt/ *adj.* (usu. foll. by *to*) of superior importance or rank. [SUPER-, after *subordinate*]

su·per·phos·phate /sŏŏpэrfósfayt/ *n.* a fertilizer made by treating phosphate rock with sulfuric or phosphoric acid.

su·per·phys·i·cal /sŏŏpэrfizikэl/ *adj.* **1** unexplainable by physical causes; supernatural. **2** beyond what is physical.

su·per·pose /sŏŏpэrpóz/ *v.tr.* (usu. foll. by *on*) esp. Geom. place (a thing or a geometric figure) on or above something else, esp. so as to coincide. □□ **su·per·po·si·tion** /–pэzíshэn/ *n.* [F *superposer* (as SUPER-, POSE¹)]

su·per·pow·er /sŏŏpэrpowr/ *n.* a nation of supreme power and influence, esp. the US and the former USSR.

su·per·sat·u·rate /sŏŏpэsáchэrayt/ *v.tr.* add to (esp. a solution) beyond saturation point. □□ **su·per·sat·u·ra·tion** /–ráyshэn/ *n.*

su·per·scribe /sŏŏpэrskríb/ *v.tr.* **1** write (an inscription) at the top of or on the outside of a document, etc. **2** write an inscription over or on (a thing). □□ **su·per·scrip·tion** /–skrípshэn/ *n.* [L *superscribere* (as SUPER-, *scribere* script- write)]

su·per·script /sŏŏpэrskript/ *adj. & n.* ● *adj.* written or printed above the line, esp. Math. (of a symbol) written above and to the right of another. ● *n.* a superscript number or symbol. [L *superscriptus* past part. of *superscribere:* see SUPERSCRIBE]

su·per·sede /sŏŏpэrseed/ *v.tr.* **1 a** adopt or appoint another person or thing in place of. **b** set aside; cease to employ. **2** (of a person or thing) take the place of. □□ **su·per·sed·ence** *n.* **su·per·se·dure** /–séejэr/ *n.* **su·per·ses·sion** /–séshэn/ *n.* [OF *superseder* f. L *supersedēre* be superior to (as SUPER-, *sedēre sess-* sit)]

SPELLING TIP supersede

This is the only common word in English that ends in *-sede.* But there are others ending in *-cede* and *-ceed* that cause persistent spelling problems. Since there are so few, the best way to master their spelling is to memorize them:

  -cede words: accede, antecede, cede, concede, intercede, precede, recede, secede.

  -ceed words: exceed, proceed, succeed.

su·per·son·ic /sŏŏpэrsónik/ *adj.* designating or having a speed greater than that of sound. □□ **su·per·son·i·cal·ly** *adv.*

su·per·son·ics /sŏŏpэrsóniks/ *n.pl.* (treated as *sing.*) = ULTRASONICS.

su·per·star /sŏŏpэrstaar/ *n.* an extremely famous or renowned actor, movie star, athlete, etc. □□ **su·per·star·dom** *n.*

su·per·sti·tion /sŏŏpэrstíshэn/ *n.* **1** credulity regarding the supernatural. **2** an irrational fear of the unknown or mysterious. **3** misdirected reverence. **4** a practice, opinion, or religion based on these tendencies. **5** a widely held but unjustified idea of the effects or nature of a thing. □□ **su·per·sti·tious** *adj.* **su·per·sti·tious·ly** *adv.* **su·per·sti·tious·ness** *n.* [ME f. OF *superstition* or L *superstitio* (as SUPER-, *stare stat-* stand)]

su·per·store /sŏŏpэrstawr/ *n.* a very large store selling a wide range of goods.

See page xx for the **Key to Pronunciation.**

su·per·stra·tum /sóōpərstraytəm, –strat–/ *n.* (*pl.* **·stra·ta** /–tə/) an overlying stratum.

su·per·struc·ture /sóōpərstrukchər/ *n.* **1** the part of a building above its foundations. **2** a structure built on top of something else. **3** a concept or idea based on others. ▫▫ **su·per·struc·tur·al** *adj.*

su·per·sub·tle /sóōpərsút'l/ *adj.* extremely or excessively subtle. ▫▫ **su·per·sub·tle·ty** *n.*

su·per·tank·er /sóōpərtangkər/ *n.* a very large tanker ship.

su·per·tax /sóōpərtaks/ *n.* esp. *Brit.* a tax on incomes above a certain level, esp. a surtax.

su·per·ter·res·tri·al /sóōpərtəréstreeəl/ *adj.* **1** in or belonging to a region above the earth. **2** celestial.

su·per·ti·tle var. of SURTITLE.

su·per·ton·ic /sóōpərtónik/ *n. Mus.* the note above the tonic, the second note of the diatonic scale of any key.

su·per·vene /sóōpərveén/ *v.intr.* occur as an interruption in or a change from some state. ▫▫ **su·per·ven·ient** *adj.* **su·per·ven·tion** /–vénshən/ *n.* [L *supervenire* *supervent*- (as SUPER-, *venire* come)]

su·per·vise /sóōpərvīz/ *v.tr.* **1** superintend; oversee the execution of (a task, etc.). **2** oversee the actions or work of (a person). ▫▫ **su·per·vi·sion** /–vízhən/ *n.* **su·per·vi·sor** *n.* **su·per·vi·so·ry** *adj.* [med.L *supervidēre supervis*-, *super*-, *vidēre* see)]

su·per·wom·an /sóōpərwoŏmən/ *n.* (*pl.* **·wom·en**) *colloq.* a woman of exceptional strength or ability.

su·pi·nate /sóōpinayt/ *v.tr.* put (a hand or foreleg, etc.) into a supine position (cf. PRONATE). ▫▫ **su·pi·na·tion** /–náyshən/ *n.* [backform. f. *supination* f. L *supinatio* f. *supinare* f. *supinus*: see SUPINE]

su·pi·na·tor /sóōpinaytər/ *n. Anat.* a muscle in the forearm effecting supination.

su·pine *adj. & n.* ● *adj.* /sóōpín/ **1** lying face upwards (cf. PRONE). **2** having the front or ventral part upwards; (of the hand) with the palm upwards. **3** inert; indolent; morally or mentally inactive. ● *n.* /sóōpín/ a Latin verbal noun used only in the accusative and ablative cases, esp. to denote purpose (e.g., *mirabile dictu* wonderful to relate). ▫▫ **su·pine·ly** /–pínlee/ *adv.* **su·pine·ness** *n.* [L *supinus*, rel. to *super*: (n.) f. LL *supinum* neut. (reason only.)]

sup·per /súpər/ *n.* a light evening meal. ● **sing for one's supper** do something in return for a benefit. ▫▫ **sup·per·less** *adj.* [ME f. OF *soper, super*]

sup·plant /səplánt/ *v.tr.* dispossess and take the place of, esp. by underhand means. ▫▫ **sup·plant·er** *n.* [ME f. OF *supplanter* or L *supplantare* trip up (as SUB-, *planta* sole)]

sup·ple /súpəl/ *adj. & v.* ● *adj.* (**sup·pler, sup·plest**) **1** flexible; pliant; easily bent. **2** compliant; avoiding overt resistance; artfully or servilely submissive. ● *v.tr. & intr.* make or become supple. ▫▫ **sup·ple·ness** *n.* [ME f. OF *souple* ult. f. L *supplex supplicis* submissive]

sup·ple·jack /súpəljak/ *n.* any of various strong twining tropical shrubs, esp. *Berchemia scandens*. [SUPPLE + JACK[1]]

sup·ple·ly var. of SUPPLY[2].

sup·ple·ment *n. & v.* ● *n.* /súpləmənt/ **1** a thing or part added to remedy deficiencies (*dietary supplement*). **2** a part added to a book, etc., to provide further information. **3** a separate section, esp. a color magazine, added to a newspaper or periodical. **4** *Geom.* the amount by which an angle is less than 180° (cf. COMPLEMENT). ● *v.tr.* also /súplimént/ provide a supplement for. ▫▫ **sup·ple·men·tal** /–mént'l/ *adj.* **sup·ple·men·tal·ly** *adv.* **sup·ple·men·ta·tion** /–mentáyshən/ *n.* [ME f. L *supplementum* (as SUB-, *plēre* fill)]

sup·ple·men·ta·ry /súpliméntəree/ *adj.* forming or serving as a supplement; additional. ▫▫ **sup·ple·men·tar·i·ly** *adv.*

sup·ple·tion /səpleéshən/ *n.* the act or an instance of supplementing, esp. *Linguistics* the occurrence of unrelated forms to supply gaps in conjugation (e.g., *went* as the past of *go*). ▫▫ **sup·ple·tive** *adj.* [ME f. OF f. med.L *suppletio* *-onis* (as SUPPLY[1])]

sup·pli·ant /súpleeənt/ *adj. & n.* ● *adj.* **1** supplicating. **2** expressing supplication. ● *n.* a supplicating person. ▫▫ **sup·pli·ant·ly** *adv.* [ME f. F *supplier* beseech f. L (as SUPPLICATE)]

sup·pli·cate /súplikayt/ *v.* **1** *tr.* petition humbly to (a person) or for (a thing). **2** *intr.* (foll. by *to, for*) make a petition. ▫▫ **sup·pli·cant** *adj. & n.* **sup·pli·ca·tion** /–áyshən/ *n.* **sup·pli·ca·to·ry** *adj.* [ME f. L *supplicare* (as SUB-, *plicare* bend)]

sup·ply[1] /səplī/ *v. & n.* ● *v.tr.* (**·plies, ·plied**) **1** provide or furnish (a thing needed). **2** (often foll. by *with*) provide (a person, etc., with a thing needed). **3** meet or make up for (a deficiency or need, etc.). **4** fill (a vacancy, place, etc.) as a substitute. ● *n.* (*pl.* **·plies**) **1** the act or an instance of providing what is needed. **2** a stock, store, amount, etc., of something provided or obtainable (*a large supply of water; the gas supply*). **3** (in *pl.*) **a** the collected provisions and equipment for an army, expedition, etc. **b** *Brit.* a grant of money by Parliament for the costs of government. **c** *Brit.* a money allowance to a person. **4** (often *attrib.*) a person, esp. a schoolteacher or clergyman, acting as a temporary substitute for another. **5** (*attrib.*) providing supplies or a supply (*supply officer*). ● **in short supply** available in limited quantity. ▫▫ **sup·pli·er** *n.* [ME f. OF *so(u)pleer,* etc., f. L *supplēre* (as SUB-, *plēre* fill)]

sup·ply[2] /súplee/ *adv.* (also **sup·ple·ly** /súpəlee/) in a supple manner.

sup·ply and de·mand *n. Econ.* quantities available and required as factors regulating the price of commodities.

sup·ply-side *adj. Econ.* denoting a policy of low taxation and other incentives to produce goods and invest.

sup·port /səpáwrt/ *v. & n.* ● *v.tr.* **1** carry all or part of the weight of. **2** keep from falling or sinking or failing. **3** provide with a home and the necessities of life (*has a family to support*). **4** enable to last out; give strength to; encourage. **5** bear out; tend to substantiate or corroborate (a statement, charge, theory, etc.). **6** give help or countenance to; back up; second; further. **7** speak in favor of (a resolution, etc.). **8** be actively interested in (a particular team or sport). **9** take a part that is secondary to (a principal actor, etc.). **10** assist (a lecturer, etc.) by one's presence. **11** endure; tolerate (*can no longer support the noise*). **12** maintain or represent (a part or character) adequately. **13** back (an institution, etc.) financially. ● *n.* **1** the act or an instance of supporting; the process of being supported. **2** a person or thing that supports. ● **in support of** in order to support. ▫▫ **sup·port·a·ble** *adj.* **sup·port·a·bil·i·ty** *n.* **sup·port·a·bly** *adv.* **sup·port·ing·ly** *adv.* **sup·port·less** *adj.* [ME f. OF *supporter* f. L *supportare* (as SUB-, *portare* carry)]

sup·port·er /səpáwrtər/ *n.* **1** a person or thing that supports, esp. a person supporting a team, sport, political candidate, etc. **2** *Heraldry* the representation of an animal, etc., usu. one of a pair, holding up or standing beside an escutcheon. **3** = JOCKSTRAP.

sup·port·ive /səpáwrtiv/ *adj.* providing support or encouragement. ▫▫ **sup·port·ive·ly** *adv.* **sup·port·ive·ness** *n.*

sup·port price *n.* a minimum price guaranteed to a farmer for agricultural produce and maintained by subsidy, etc.

sup·pose /səpóz/ *v.tr.* (often foll. by *that* + clause) **1** assume, esp. in default of knowledge; be inclined to think (*I suppose they will return; what do you suppose he meant?*). **2** take as a possibility or hypothesis (*let us suppose you are right*). **3** (in *imper.*) as a formula of proposal (*suppose we go to the party*). **4** (of a theory or result, etc.) require as a condition (*design in creation supposes a creator*). **5** (in *imper.* or *pres. part.* forming a question) in the circumstances that; if (*suppose he won't let you; supposing we stay*). **6** (as **supposed** *adj.*) generally accepted as being so; believed (*his supposed brother; generally supposed to be wealthy*). **7** (in *passive*; foll. by *to* + infin.) **a** be expected or required (*was supposed to write to you*). **b** (with *neg.*) not have to; not be allowed to (*you are not supposed to go in there*). ● **I suppose so** an expression of hesitant agreement. ▫▫ **sup·pos·a·ble** *adj.* [ME f. OF *supposer* (as SUB-, POSE[1])]

sup·pos·ed·ly /səpózidlee/ *adv.* as is generally supposed.

sup·po·si·tion /súpəzíshən/ *n.* **1** a fact or idea, etc., supposed. **2** the act or an instance of supposing. ▫▫ **sup·po·si·tion·al** *adj.*

sup·po·si·tious /súpəzíshəs/ *adj.* hypothetical; assumed. ▫▫ **sup·po·si·tious·ly** *adv.* **sup·po·si·tious·ness** *n.* [partly f. SUPPOSITITIOUS, partly f. SUPPOSITION + –OUS]

sup·pos·i·ti·tious /səpózitíshəs/ *adj.* spurious; substituted for the real. ▫▫ **sup·pos·i·ti·tious·ly** *adv.* **sup·pos·i·ti·tious·ness** *n.* [L *supposititius, -icius* f. *supponere supposit*-substitute (as SUB- *ponere* place)]

sup·pos·i·to·ry /səpózitawree/ *n.* (*pl.* **·ries**) a medical preparation in the form of a cone, cylinder, etc., to be inserted into the rectum or vagina to melt. [ME f. med.L *suppositorium*, neut. of LL *suppositorius* placed underneath (as SUPPOSITITIOUS)]

sup·press /səprés/ *v.tr.* **1** end the activity or existence of, esp. forcibly. **2** prevent (information, feelings, a reaction, etc.) from being seen, heard, or known (*tried to suppress the report; suppressed a yawn*). **3 a** partly or wholly eliminate (electrical interference, etc.). **b** equip (a device) to reduce such interference due to it. **4** *Psychol.* keep out of one's consciousness. ▫▫ **sup·press·i·ble** *adj.* **sup·pres·sion** *n.* **sup·pres·sive** *adj.* **sup·pres·sor** *n.* [ME f. L *supprimere suppress*- (as SUB-, *premere* press)]

sup·pres·sant /səprésənt/ *n.* a suppressing or restraining agent, esp. a drug that suppresses the appetite.

sup·pu·rate /súpyərayt/ *v.intr.* **1** form pus. **2** fester. ▫▫ **sup·pu·ra·tion** /–ráyshən/ *n.* **sup·pu·ra·tive** /–rətiv/ *adj.* [L *suppurare* (as SUB-, *purare* as PUS)]

su·pra /sóōprə/ *adv.* above or earlier on (in a book, etc.). [L, = above]

supra- /sóōprə/ *prefix* **1** above. **2** beyond; transcending (*supranational*). [from or after L *supra*- f. *supra* above, beyond, before in time]

su·pra·max·il·lar·y /sóōprəmáksileree/ *adj.* of or relating to the upper jaw.

su·pra·mun·dane /sóōprəmundáyn/ *adj.* above or superior to the world.

su·pra·na·tion·al /sóōprənáshənəl/ *adj.* transcending national limits. ▫▫ **su·pra·na·tion·al·ism** *n.* **su·pra·na·tion·al·i·ty** /–nálitee/ *n.*

su·pra·or·bit·al /sóōprəáwrbit'l/ *adj.* situated above the orbit of the eye.

su·pra·re·nal /sóōprəreénəl/ *adj.* situated above the kidneys.

su·prem·a·cist /sooprémisist/ *n. & adj.* ● *n.* an advocate of the supremacy of a particular group, esp. determined by race or sex. ● *adj.* relating to or advocating such supremacy. ▫▫ **su·prem·a·cism** *n.*

su·prem·a·cy /sŏoprémɔsee/ n. (pl. **·cies**) **1** the state of being supreme. **2** supreme authority.

su·preme /sŏopreem/ adj. & n. ● adj. **1** highest in authority or rank. **2** greatest; most important. **3** (of a penalty or sacrifice, etc.) involving death. ● n. **1** a rich cream sauce. **2** a dish served in this. □□ **su·preme·ly** adv. **su·preme·ness** n. [L supremus, superl. of superus that is above f. super above]

su·prême /sŏoprém/ n. = SUPREME n. [F]

Su·preme Be·ing n. a name for God.

Su·preme Court n. the highest judicial court in a nation, etc.

su·preme pon·tiff n. see PONTIFF.

su·pre·mo /sŏopreemō/ n. Brit. (pl. **·mos**) **1** a supreme leader or ruler. **2** a person in overall charge. [Sp., = SUPREME]

suprv. abbr. supervisor.

Supt. abbr. Superintendent.

sur-[1] /sɔr/ prefix = SUPER- (surcharge; surrealism). [OF]

sur-[2] /sɔr/ prefix assim. form of SUB- before r.

su·ra /sŏorɔ/ n. (also **su·rah**) a chapter or section of the Koran. [Arab. s ūra]

su·rah /sŏorɔ/ n. a soft twilled silk for scarves, etc. [F pronunc. of Surat in India, where it was orig. made]

su·ral /sŏorɔl/ adj. of or relating to the calf of the leg (sural artery). [mod.L suralis f. L sura calf]

sur·cease /sɔrsees, sɔrseés/ n. & v. literary ● n. a cessation. ● v.intr. & tr. cease. [ME f. OF sursis, -ise (cf. AF sursise omission), past part. of OF surseoir refrain, delay f. L (as SUPERSEDE), with assim. to CEASE]

sur·charge n. & v. ● n. /sɔ́rchaarj/ **1** an additional charge or payment. **2** a charge made by assessors as a penalty for false returns of taxable property. **3** a mark printed on a postage stamp changing its value. **4** an additional or excessive load. **5** Brit. an amount in an official account not passed by the auditor and having to be refunded by the person responsible. **6** the showing of an omission in an account for which credit should have been given. ● v.tr. /sɔ́rchaarj, –chaárj/ **1** exact a surcharge from. **2** exact (a sum) as a surcharge. **3** mark (a postage stamp) with a surcharge. **4** overload. **5** fill or saturate to excess. [ME f. OF surcharger (as SUR-[1], CHARGE)]

sur·cin·gle /sɔ́rsinggɔl/ n. a band round a horse's body usu. to keep a pack, etc., in place. [ME f. OF surcengle (as SUR-[1], cengle girth f. L cingula f. cingere gird]

sur·coat /sɔ́rkōt/ n. **1** hist. a loose robe worn over armor. **2** a similar sleeveless garment worn as part of the insignia of an order of knighthood. **3** hist. an outer coat of rich material. [ME f. OF surcot (as SUR-[1], cot coat)]

sur·cu·lose /sɔ́rkyɔlōs/ adj. Bot. producing suckers. [L surculosus f. surculus twig]

surd /sɔrd/ adj. & n. ● adj. **1** Math. (of a number) irrational. **2** Phonet. (of a sound) uttered with the breath and not the voice (e.g., f, k, p, s, t). ● n. **1** Math. a surd number, esp. the root of an integer. **2** Phonet. a surd sound. [L surdus deaf, mute: sense 1 by mistransl. into L of Gk alogos irrational, speechless, through Arab. jaḏr aṣamm deaf root]

sure /shŏor/ adj. & adv. ● adj. **1** having or seeming to have adequate reason for a belief or assertion. **2** (often foll. by of, or that + clause) convinced. **3** (foll. by of) having a certain prospect or confident anticipation or satisfactory knowledge of. **4** reliable or unfailing (there is one sure way to find out). **5** (foll. by to + infin.) certain. **6** undoubtedly true or truthful. ● adv. colloq. certainly. □ **be sure** (in imper. or infin.; foll. by that + clause or to + infin.) take care to; not fail to (be sure to turn the lights out). **for sure** colloq. without doubt. **make sure 1** make or become certain; ensure. **2** (foll. by of) establish the truth or ensure the existence or happening of. **sure enough** colloq. **1** in fact; certainly. **2** with near certainty (they will come sure enough). **sure thing** n. a certainty. ● int. colloq. certainly. **to be sure 1** it is undeniable or admitted. **2** it must be admitted. □□ **sure·ness** n. [ME f. OF sur (earlier seür) f. L securus SECURE]

▶ Unless intending an informal effect, do not use **sure** when the adverb **surely** is meant: It surely was foolhardy to take on all these problems yourself; I surely was happy to see them again.

sure-fire adj. colloq. certain to succeed.

sure-foot·ed adj. never stumbling or making a mistake. □□ **sure-foot·ed·ly** adv. **sure-foot·ed·ness** n.

sure·ly /shŏo rlee/ adv. **1** with certainty (the time approaches slowly but surely). **2** as an appeal to likelihood or reason (surely that can't be right). **3** with safety; securely (the goat plants its feet surely).

sure·ty /shŏoritee/ n. (pl. **·ties**) **1** a person who takes responsibility for another's performance of an undertaking, e.g., to appear in court, or payment of a debt. **2** archaic a certainty. □ **of** (or **for**) **a surety** archaic certainly. **stand surety** become a surety; stand bail. □□ **sure·ty·ship** n. [ME f. OF surté, seürté f. L securitas –tatis SECURITY]

surf /sɔrf/ n. & v. ● n. **1** the swell of the sea breaking on the shore or reefs. **2** the foam produced by this. ● v.intr. ride the surf, with or as with a surfboard. □□ **surf·er** n. **surf·y** adj. [app. f. obs. suff, perh. assim. to surge: orig. applied to the Indian coast]

sur·face /sɔ́rfis/ n. & v. ● n. **1 a** the outside of a material body. **b** the

area of this. **2** any of the limits terminating a solid. **3** the upper boundary of a liquid or of the ground, etc. **4** the outward aspect of anything; what is apparent on a casual view or consideration (presents a large surface to view; all is quiet on the surface). **5** Geom. a set of points that has length and breadth but no thickness. **6** (attrib.) **a** of or on the surface (surface area). **b** superficial (surface politeness). ● v. **1** tr. give the required surface to (a road, paper, etc.). **2** intr. & tr. rise or bring to the surface. **3** intr. become visible or known. **4** intr. colloq. become conscious; wake up. □ **come to the surface** become perceptible after having been hidden. □□ **sur·faced** adj. (usu. in comb.). **sur·fac·er** n. [F (as SUR-[1], FACE)]

sur·face-ac·tive adj. (of a substance, e.g., a detergent) able to affect the wetting properties of a liquid.

sur·face mail n. mail carried over land and by sea, and not by air.

sur·face noise n. extraneous noise in playing a phonograph record, caused by imperfections in the grooves.

sur·face ten·sion n. the tension of the surface film of a liquid, tending to minimize its surface area.

sur·fac·tant /surfáktɔnt/ n. a substance which reduces surface tension. [surface-active]

surf·board /sɔ́rfbawrd/ n. a long narrow board used in surfing.

surf cast·ing n. fishing by casting a line into the sea from the shore.

sur·feit /sɔ́rfit/ n. & v. ● n. **1** an excess, esp. in eating or drinking. **2** a feeling of satiety or disgust resulting from this. ● v. (**sur·feit·ed, sur·feit·ing**) **1** tr. overfeed. **2** intr. overeat. **3** intr. & tr. (foll. by with) be or cause to be wearied through excess. [ME f. OF sorfe(i)t, surfe(i)t (as SUPER-, L facere fact- do)]

sur·fi·cial /surfishɔl/ adj. Geol. of or relating to the earth's surface. □□ **sur·fi·cial·ly** adv. [SURFACE after superficial]

surg. abbr. **1** surgeon. **2** surgery. **3** surgical.

surge /surj/ n. & v. ● n. **1** a sudden or impetuous onset (a surge of anger). **2** the swell of the waves at sea. **3** a heavy forward or upward motion. **4** a rapid increase in price, activity, etc. over a short period. **5** a sudden marked increase in voltage of an electric current. ● v.intr. **1** (of waves, the sea, etc.) rise and fall or move heavily forward. **2** (of a crowd, etc.) move suddenly and powerfully forward in large numbers. **3** (of an electric current, etc.) increase suddenly. **4** Naut. (of a rope, chain, or windlass) slip back with a jerk. [OF sourdre sourge-, or sorgir f. Cat., f. L surgere rise]

sur·geon /sɔ́rjɔn/ n. **1** a medical practitioner qualified to practice surgery. **2** a medical officer in a navy or army or military hospital. [ME f. AF surgien f. OF serurgien (as SURGERY)]

sur·geon fish n. any tropical marine fish of the genus Acanthurus with movable lancet-shaped spines on each side of the tail.

sur·geon gen·er·al n. (pl. **sur·geons gen·er·al**) the head of a public health service or of an army, etc., medical service.

sur·geon's knot n. a reef-knot with a double twist.

sur·ger·y /sɔ́rjɔree/ n. (pl. **·ies**) **1** the branch of medicine concerned with treatment of injuries or disorders of the body by incision, manipulation or alteration of organs, etc., with the hands or with instruments. **2** Brit. **a** a place where a doctor, dentist, etc., treats patients. **b** the occasion of this (the doctor will see you after surgery). **3** Brit. **a** a place where a member of Parliament, lawyer, or other professional person gives advice. **b** the occasion of this. [ME f. OF surgerie f. L chirurgia f. Gk kheirourgia handiwork, surgery f. kheir hand + erg- work]

sur·gi·cal /sɔ́rjikɔl/ adj. **1** of or relating to or done by surgeons or surgery. **2** resulting from surgery (surgical fever). **3 a** used in surgery. **b** (of a special garment, etc.) worn to correct a deformity, etc. **4** extremely precise. □□ **sur·gi·cal·ly** adv. [earlier chirurgical f. chirurgy f. OF sirurgie: see SURGEON]

sur·gi·cal spir·it n. methylated alcohol used in surgery for cleansing, disinfecting, etc.

su·ri·cate /sŏorikayt/ n. a South African burrowing mongoose, Suricata suricatta, with gray and black stripes. [F f. S.Afr. native name]

Su·ri·nam toad /sŏorinám, –naám/ n. = PIPA. [Surinam in S. America]

sur·ly /sɔ́rlee/ adj. (**sur·li·er, sur·li·est**) bad-tempered and unfriendly; churlish. □□ **sur·li·ly** adv. **sur·li·ness** n. [alt. spelling of obs. sirly haughty f. SIR + -LY[1]]

sur·mise /sɔrmíz/ n. & v. ● n. a conjecture or suspicion about the existence or truth of something. ● v. **1** tr. (often foll. by that + clause) infer doubtfully; make a surmise about. **2** tr. suspect the existence of. **3** intr. make a guess.

WORD HISTORY surmise

Late Middle English (denoting a formal legal allegation): from Anglo-Norman French and Old French surmise, feminine past participle of surmettre 'accuse,' from late Latin supermittere 'throw upon, put in afterwards,' from super- 'over' + mittere 'send.'

sur·mount /sərmównt/ v.tr. **1** overcome or get over (a difficulty or obstacle). **2** (usu. in *passive*) cap or crown (*peaks surmounted with snow*). □□ **sur·mount·a·ble** adj. [ME f. OF *surmonter* (as SUR-[1], MOUNT[1])]

sur·mul·let /sərmúlit, sórmul–/ n. the red mullet. [F *surmulet* f. OF *sor* red + *mulet* MULLET]

sur·name /sórnaym/ n. & v. • n. **1** a hereditary name common to members of a family, as distinct from a Christian or first name. **2** *archaic* an additional descriptive or allusive name attached to a person, sometimes becoming hereditary. • v.tr. **1** give a surname to. **2** give (a person a surname). **3** (as surnamed adj.) having as a family name. [ME, alt. of *surnoun* f. AF (as SUR-[1], NOUN name)]

sur·pass /sərpás/ v.tr. **1** outdo; be greater or better than. **2** (as surpassing adj.) preeminent; matchless (*of surpassing intelligence*). □□ **sur·pass·ing·ly** adv. [F *surpasser* (as SUR-[1], PASS[1])]

sur·plice /sórplis/ n. a loose white linen vestment reaching the knees, worn over a cassock by clergy and choristers at services. □□ **sur·pliced** adj. [ME f. AF *surplis*, OF *sourpelis*, f. med.L *superpellicium* (as SUPER-, *pellicia* PELISSE)]

sur·plus /sórpləs, –plus/ n. & adj. • n. **1** an amount left over when requirements have been met. **2 a** an excess of revenue over expenditure in a given period, esp. a financial year (opp. DEFICIT). **b** the excess value of a company's assets over the face value of its stock. • adj. exceeding what is needed or used. [ME f. AF *surplus*, OF *s(o)urplus* f. med.L *superplus* (as SUPER-, + *plus* more)]

sur·plus val·ue n. Econ. the difference between the value of work done and wages paid.

sur·prise /sərpríz/ n. & v. • n. **1** an unexpected or astonishing event or circumstance. **2** the emotion caused by this. **3** the act of catching a person, etc., unawares, or the process of being caught unawares. **4** (*attrib.*) unexpected; made or done, etc., without warning (*a surprise visit*). • v.tr. **1** affect with surprise; turn out contrary to the expectations of (*your answer surprised me; I surprised her by arriving early*). **2** (usu. in *passive*; foll. by *at*) shock; scandalize (*I am surprised at you*). **3** capture or attack by surprise. **4** come upon (a person) unawares (*surprised him taking a cookie*). **5** (foll. by *into*) startle (a person) by surprise into an action, etc. (*surprised them into consenting*). □ **take by surprise** affect with surprise, esp. by an unexpected encounter or statement. □□ **sur·pris·ed·ly** /–prízidlee/ adv. **sur·pris·ing** adj. **sur·pris·ing·ly** adv. **sur·pris·ing·ness** n. [OF, fem. past part. of *surprendre* (as SUR-[1], *prendre* f. L *praehendere* seize)]

SPELLING TIP surprise

To remember the *sur-* at the beginning of this word, use the mnemonic: "Anything that catches you off guard is *sur*ely a *sur*prise."

---

sur·ra /sŏŏrə/ n. a febrile disease transmitted by bites of flies and affecting horses and cattle in the tropics. [Marathi]

sur·re·al /səréeəl/ adj. **1** having the qualities of surrealism. **2** strange; bizarre. □□ **sur·re·al·i·ty** /–ree-álitee/ n. **sur·re·al·ly** adv. [back-form. f. SURREALISM, etc.]

sur·re·al·ism /səréeəlizəm/ n. a 20th-c. movement in art and literature aiming at expressing the subconscious mind, e.g., by the irrational juxtaposition of images. □□ **sur·re·al·ist** n. & adj. **sur·re·al·is·tic** adj. **sur·re·al·is·ti·cal·ly** adv. [F *surréalisme* (as SUR-[1], REALISM)]

sur·re·but·ter /sórribútər/ n. Law the plaintiff's reply to the defendant's rebutter. [SUR-[1] + REBUTTER, after SURREJOINDER]

sur·re·join·der /sórrijóyndər/ n. Law the plaintiff's reply to the defendant's rejoinder. [SUR-[1] + REJOINDER]

sur·ren·der /səréndər/ v. & n. • v. **1** tr. hand over; relinquish possession of, esp. on compulsion or demand; give into another's power or control. **2** intr. **a** accept an enemy's demand for submission. **b** give oneself up; cease from resistance; submit. **3** intr. & refl. (foll. by *to*) give oneself over to a habit, emotion, influence, etc. **4** tr. give up rights under (a life-insurance policy) in return for a smaller sum received immediately. **5** tr. give up (a lease) before its expiration. **6** tr. abandon (hope, etc.). • n. the act or an instance of surrendering. □ **surrender by bail** duly appear in a court of law after release on bail. [ME f. AF f. OF *surrendre* (as SUR-[1], RENDER)]

sur·ren·der val·ue n. the amount payable to one who surrenders a life-insurance policy.

sur·rep·ti·tious /sórəptíshəs/ adj. **1** covert; kept secret. **2** done by stealth; clandestine. □□ **sur·rep·ti·tious·ly** adv. **sur·rep·ti·tious·ness** n. [ME f. L *surrepticius –itius* f. *surripere surrept-* (as SUR-[1], *rapere* seize)]

sur·rey /sóree, súree/ n. (pl. **sur·reys**) a light four-wheeled carriage with two seats facing forward. [orig. of an adaptation of the *Surrey cart*, orig. made in *Surrey* in England]

sur·ro·gate /sórəgət, –gayt, súr–/ n. **1** a substitute, esp. for a person in a specific role or office. **2** Brit. a deputy, esp. of a bishop in granting marriage licenses. **3** a judge in charge of probate, inheritance, and guardianship. □□ **sur·ro·ga·cy** n. **sur·ro·gate·ship** n. [L *surrogatus* past part. of *surrogare* elect as a substitute (as SUR-[1], *rogare* ask)]

sur·ro·gate moth·er n. **1** a person acting the role of mother. **2** a woman who bears a child on behalf of another woman, usu. from her own egg fertilized by the other woman's partner.

sur·round /sərównd/ v. & n. • v.tr. **1** come or be all around; encircle; enclose. **2** (in *passive*; foll. by *by, with*) have on all sides (*the house is surrounded by trees*). • n. **1** an area or substance surrounding something. **2** Brit. **a** a border or edging, esp. an area between the walls and carpet of a room. **b** a floor-covering for this. □□ **sur·round·ing** adj. [ME = overflow, f. AF *sur(o)under*, OF *s (o)uronder* f. LL *superundare* (as SUPER-, *undare* flow f. *unda* wave)]

sur·round·ings /sərówndingz/ n.pl. the things in the neighborhood of, or the conditions affecting, a person or thing.

sur·tax /sórtaks/ n. & v. • n. an additional tax, esp. levied on incomes above a certain level. • v.tr. impose a surtax on. [F *surtaxe* (as SUR-[1], TAX)]

sur·ti·tle /sórtīt'l/ n. (also **su·per·ti·tle** /sŏŏpərtīt'l/) (esp. in opera) each of a sequence of captions projected above the stage, translating the text being sung.

sur·tout /sərtŏŏ, –tŏŏt/ n. hist. a man's heavy overcoat or frock coat. [F f. *sur* over + *tout* everything]

sur·veil·lance /sərváyləns/ n. close observation, esp. of a suspected person. [F f. *surveiller* (as SUR-[1], *veiller* f. L *vigilare* keep watch)]

sur·vey v. & n. • v.tr. /sərváy/ **1** take or present a general view of. **2** examine the condition of (a building, etc.). **3** determine the boundaries, extent, ownership, etc., of (a district, etc.). **4** poll the opinions of a group of people, esp. by a statistical sample. • n. /sórvay/ **1** a general view or consideration of something. **2 a** the act of surveying opinions, etc. **b** the result or findings of this, esp. in a written report. **3** an inspection or investigation. **4** a map or plan made by surveying an area. **5** a department carrying out the surveying of land. [ME f. AF *survei(e)r*, OF *so(u)rveeir* pres. stem *survey-*) f. med.L *supervidēre* (as SUPER-, *vidēre* see)]

sur·vey·or /sərváyər/ n. **1** a person who surveys land and buildings, esp. professionally. **2** Brit. an official inspector, esp. for measurement and valuation. **3** a person who carries out surveys. □□ **sur·vey·or·ship** n. (esp. in sense 2). [ME f. AF & OF *surve(i) our* (as SURVEY)]

sur·viv·al /sərvívəl/ n. **1** the process or an instance of surviving. **2** a person, thing, or practice that has remained from a former time.

sur·viv·al·ism /sərvívəlizəm/ n. the practicing of outdoor survival skills as a sport or hobby, esp. in the belief that these skills will be necessary at the collapse of civilization. □□ **sur·viv·al·ist** adj. & n.

sur·viv·al kit n. emergency rations, etc., esp. carried by military personnel, hikers, etc.

sur·viv·al of the fit·test n. the process or result of natural selection.

sur·vive /sərvív/ v. **1** intr. continue to live or exist; be still alive or existent. **2** tr. live or exist longer than. **3** tr. remain alive after going through, or continue to exist in spite of (a danger, accident, etc.). [ME f. AF *survivre*, OF *sourvivre* f. L *supervivere* (as SUPER-, *vivere* live)]

sur·vi·vor /sərvívər/ n. **1** a person who survives or has survived. **2** *Law* a joint tenant who has the right to the whole estate on the other's death.

sus- /sus, səs/ prefix assim. form of SUB- before *c, p, t*.

sus·cep·ti·bil·i·ty /səséptibílitee/ n. (pl. **·ties**) **1** the state of being susceptible. **2** (in *pl.*) a person's sensitive feelings. **3** *Physics* the ratio of magnetization to a magnetizing force.

sus·cep·ti·ble /səséptibəl/ adj. **1** impressionable; sensitive; easily moved by emotion. **2** (*predic.*) **a** (foll. by *to*) likely to be affected by; liable or vulnerable to (*susceptible to pain*). **b** (foll. by *of*) allowing; admitting of (*facts not susceptible of proof*). □□ **sus·cep·ti·bly** adv. [LL *susceptibilis* f. L *suscipere suscept-* (as SUB-, *capere* take)]

sus·cep·tive /səséptiv/ adj. **1** concerned with the receiving of emotional impressions or ideas. **2** receptive. **3** = SUSCEPTIBLE. [LL *susceptivus* (as SUSCEPTIBLE)]

su·shi /sŏŏshee/ n. a Japanese dish of balls of cold rice flavored and garnished, esp. with raw fish or shellfish. [Jap.]

sus·lik /súslik/ n. an E. European and Asian ground squirrel, *Citellus citellus*. [Russ.]

sus·pect v., n., & adj. • v.tr. /səspékt/ **1** have an impression of the existence or presence of (*suspects poisoning*). **2** (foll. by *to be*) believe tentatively, without clear ground. **3** (foll. by *that* + clause) be inclined to think. **4** (often foll. by *of*) be inclined to mentally accuse; doubt the innocence of (*suspect him of complicity*). **5** doubt the genuineness or truth of. • n. /súspekt/ a suspected person. • adj. /súspekt/ subject to or deserving suspicion or distrust; not sound or trustworthy. [ME f. L *suspicere suspect-* (as SUB-, *specere* look)]

sus·pend /səspénd/ v.tr. **1** hang up. **2** keep inoperative or undecided for a time; defer. **3** bar temporarily from a school, function, office, privilege, etc. **4** (as **suspended** adj.) (of solid particles or a body in a fluid medium) sustained somewhere between top and bottom. □ **suspend payment** (of a company) fail to meet its financial obligations; admit insolvency. □□ **sus·pen·si·ble** /səspénsibəl/ adj. [ME f. OF *suspendre* or L *suspendere suspens-* (as SUB-, *pendere* hang)]

sus·pend·ed an·i·ma·tion n. a temporary cessation of the vital functions without death.

sus·pend·ed sen·tence n. a judicial sentence left unenforced subject to good behavior during a specified period.

sus·pend·er /səspéndər/ n. 1 (in pl.) straps worn across the shoulders and supporting trousers, a skirt, etc. 2 Brit. an attachment to hold up a stocking or sock by its top.

sus·pense /səspéns/ n. 1 a state of anxious uncertainty or expectation. 2 Law a suspension; the temporary cessation of a right, etc. □ **keep in suspense** delay informing (a person) of urgent information. □□ **sus·pense·ful** adj. [ME f. AF & OF suspens f. past part. of L suspendere SUSPEND]

sus·pense ac·count n. an account in which items are entered temporarily before allocation to the right account.

sus·pen·sion /səspénshən/ n. 1 the act of suspending or the condition of being suspended. 2 the means by which a vehicle is supported on its axles. 3 a substance consisting of particles suspended in a medium. 4 Mus. the prolongation of a note of a chord to form a discord with the following chord. [F suspension or L suspensio (as SUSPEND)]

sus·pen·sion bridge n. a bridge with a roadway suspended from cables supported by structures at each end.

sus·pen·sive /səspénsiv/ adj. 1 having the power or tendency to suspend or postpone. 2 causing suspense. □□ **sus·pen·sive·ly** adv. **sus·pen·sive·ness** n. [F suspensif –ive or med.L suspensivus (as SUSPEND)]

sus·pen·so·ry /səspénsəree/ adj. (of a ligament, muscle, bandage, etc.) holding an organ, etc., suspended. [F suspensoire (as SUSPENSION)]

suspension bridge

sus·pi·cion /səspíshən/ n. 1 the feeling or thought of a person who suspects. 2 the act or an instance of suspecting; the state of being suspected. 3 (foll. by of) a slight trace of. **above suspicion** too obviously good, etc., to be suspected. **under suspicion** suspected. [ME f. AF suspeciun (OF sospeçon) f. med.L suspectio –onis f. L suspicere (as SUSPECT): assim. to F suspicion & L suspicio]

sus·pi·cious /səspíshəs/ adj. 1 prone to or feeling suspicion. 2 indicating suspicion (a suspicious glance). 3 inviting or justifying suspicion (a suspicious lack of surprise). □□ **sus·pi·cious·ly** adv. **sus·pi·cious·ness** n. [ME f. AF & OF f. L suspiciosus (as SUSPICION)]

suss /sus/ v. & n. (also **sus**) esp. Brit. sl. ●v.tr. (**sussed, sus·sing**) 1 suspect of a crime. 2 (usu. foll. by out) a investigate; inspect (go and suss out the restaurants). b work out; grasp; understand; realize (he had the market sussed). ●n. 1 a suspect. 2 a suspicion; suspicious behavior. □ **on suss** on suspicion (of having committed a crime). [abbr. of SUSPECT, SUSPICION]

Sus·sex /súsiks/ n. 1 a speckled or red domestic chicken of an English breed. 2 this breed. [Sussex in S. England]

sus·tain /səstáyn/ v.tr. 1 support, bear the weight of, esp. for a long period. 2 give strength to; encourage; support. 3 (of food) give nourishment to. 4 endure; stand; bear up against. 5 undergo or suffer (defeat or injury, etc.). 6 (of a court, etc.) uphold or decide in favor of (an objection, etc.). 7 substantiate or corroborate (a statement or charge). 8 a maintain or keep (a sound, effort, etc.) going continuously. b (as **sustained** adj.) maintained continuously over a long period. 9 continue to represent (a part, character, etc.) adequately. □□ **sus·tain·a·ble** adj. **sus·tain·ed·ly** /-stáynidlee/ adv. **sus·tain·er** n. **sus·tain·ment** n. [ME f. AF sustein-, OF so(u)stein-stressed stem of so(u)stenir f. L sustinēre sustent- (as SUB-, tenēre hold)]

sus·te·nance /sústinəns/ n. 1 a nourishment; food. b the process of nourishing. 2 a means of support; a livelihood. [ME f. AF sustenaunce, OF so(u)stenance (as SUSTAIN)]

sus·ten·ta·tion /sústəntáyshən/ n. formal 1 the support of life. 2 maintenance. [ME f. OF sustentation or L sustentatio f. sustentare frequent. of sustinēre SUSTAIN]

su·sur·ra·tion /sōōsəráyshən/ n. (also **su·sur·rus** /sōōsórəs/) literary a sound of whispering or rustling. [ME f. LL susurratio f. L susurrare]

sut·ler /sútlər/ n. hist. a person following an army and selling provisions, etc., to the soldiers. [obs. Du. soeteler f. soetelen befoul, perform mean duties, f. Gmc]

Su·tra /sōōtrə/ n. 1 an aphorism or set of aphorisms in Hindu literature. 2 a narrative part of Buddhist literature. 3 Jainist scripture. [Skr. sūtra thread, rule, f. siv SEW]

sut·tee /sutée, sútee/ n. (also **sa·ti**) (pl. **sut·tees** or **sa·tis**) esp. hist. 1 the Hindu practice of a widow immolating herself on her husband's funeral pyre. 2 a widow who undergoes or has undergone this. [Hindi & Urdu f. Skr. satī faithful wife f. sat good]

su·ture /sōōchər/ n. & v. ●n. 1 Surgery a the joining of the edges of a wound or incision by stitching. b the thread or wire used for this. 2 the seamlike junction of two bones, esp. in the skull. 3 Bot. &

Zool. a similar junction of parts. ●v.tr. Surgery stitch up (a wound or incision) with a suture. □□ **su·tur·al** adj. **su·tured** adj. [F suture or L sutura f. suere sut- sew]

su·ze·rain /sōōzərən,–rayn/ n. 1 a feudal overlord. 2 a sovereign state having some control over another state that is internally autonomous. □□ **su·ze·rain·ty** n. [F, app. f. sus above f. L su(r)sum upward, after souverain SOVEREIGN]

s.v. abbr. (in a reference) under the word or heading given. [f. L sub voce (or verbo)]

svelte /svelt/ adj. slender; graceful. [F f. It. svelto]

sw abbr. (also **SW**) 1 southwest. 2 southwestern. 3 switch. 4 short wave.

swab /swob/ n. & v. (also **swob**) ●n. 1 a mop or other absorbent device for cleaning or mopping up. 2 a an absorbent pad used in surgery, esp. one with a long stick handle. b a specimen of a possibly morbid secretion taken with a swab for examination. 3 sl. a sailor. 4 sl. a term of contempt for a person. ●v.tr. (**swab·bed, swab·bing**) 1 clean with a swab. 2 (foll. by up) absorb (moisture) with a swab. [back-form. f. swabber f. early modDu. zwabber f. a Gmc base = 'splash, sway']

swad·dle /swód'l/ v.tr. swathe (esp. an infant) in garments or bandages, etc. [ME f. SWATHE + -LE⁴]

swad·dling clothes n. narrow bandages formerly wrapped round a newborn child to restrain its movements and quieten it.

swag /swag/ n. & v. ●n. 1 sl. a the booty carried off by burglars, etc. b illicit gains. 2 a an ornamental festoon of flowers, etc. b a carved, etc., representation of this. c drapery of similar appearance. 3 Austral. & NZ a traveler's or miner's bundle of personal belongings. ●v. (**swagged, swag·ging**) 1 tr. arrange (a curtain, etc.) in swags. 2 intr. a hang heavily. b sway from side to side. 3 tr. cause to sway or sag. [16th c.: prob. f. Scand.]

swage /swayj/ n. & v. ●n. 1 a die or stamp for shaping wrought iron, etc., by hammering or pressure. 2 a tool for bending metal, etc. ●v.tr. shape with a swage. [F s(o)uage decorative groove, of unkn. orig.]

swage block n. a block with various perforations, grooves, etc., for shaping metal.

swag·ger /swágər/ v., n., & adj. ●v.intr. 1 walk arrogantly or self-importantly. 2 behave arrogantly; be domineering. ●n. 1 a swaggering gait or manner. 2 swaggering behavior. 3 a dashing or confident air or way of doing something. 4 Brit. stylishness. ●adj. 1 Brit. colloq. stylish or fashionable. 2 (of a coat) cut with a loose flare from the shoulders. □□ **swag·ger·er** n. **swag·ger·ing·ly** adv. [app. f. SWAG v. + -ER⁴]

swag·ger stick n. a short cane carried by a military officer.

swag·man /swágman/ n. (pl. **-men**) Austral. & NZ a tramp carrying a swag (see SWAG n. 3).

Swa·hi·li /swaaheélee/ n. (pl. same) 1 a member of a Bantu people of Zanzibar and adjacent coasts. 2 their language, used widely as a lingua franca in E. Africa. [Arab. sawāhil pl. of sāhil coast]

swain /swayn/ n. 1 archaic a country youth. 2 poet. a young male lover or suitor. [ME swein f. ON sveinn lad = OE swān swineherd, f. Gmc]

swal·low¹ /swólō/ v. & n. ●v. 1 tr. cause or allow (food, etc.) to pass down the throat. 2 intr. perform the muscular movement of the esophagus required to do this. 3 tr. a accept meekly; put up with (an affront, etc.). b accept credulously (an unlikely assertion, etc.). 4 tr. repress; resist the expression of (a feeling, etc.) (swallow one's pride). 5 tr. articulate (words, etc.) indistinctly. 6 tr. (often foll. by up) engulf or absorb; exhaust; cause to disappear. ●n. 1 the act of swallowing. 2 an amount swallowed in one action. □□ **swal·low·a·ble** adj. **swal·low·er** n. [OE swelg (n.), swelgan (v.) f. Gmc]

swal·low² /swólō/ n. any of various migratory swift-flying insect-eating birds of the family Hirundinidae, esp. Hirundo rustica, with a forked tail and long pointed wings. □ **one swallow does not make a summer** a warning against a hasty inference from one instance. [OE swealwe f. Gmc]

swal·low dive n. Brit. = SWAN DIVE.

swal·low·tail /swólōtayl/ n. 1 a deeply forked tail. 2 anything resembling this shape. 3 any butterfly of this family Papilionidae with wings extended at the back to this shape.

swallow²

swal·low-tailed adj. having a swallowtail.

swam past of SWIM.

swa·mi /swaámee/ n. (pl. **swa·mis**) a Hindu male religious teacher. [Hindi swāmī master, prince, f. Skr. svāmin]

swamp /swaamp/ n. & v. ●n. a piece of waterlogged ground; a bog or marsh. ●v. 1 a tr. overwhelm, flood, or soak with water. b intr. become swamped. 2 tr. overwhelm or make invisible, etc., with an excess or large amount of something. □□ **swamp•y** adj. (**swamp•i•er, swamp•i•est**). [17th c., = dial. *swamp* sunk (14th c.), prob. of Gmc orig.]

swan /swon/ n. & v. • n. **1** a large water bird of the genus *Cygnus*, etc., having a long flexible neck, webbed feet, and in most species snow-white plumage. **2** *literary* a poet. • v.intr. (**swanned, swan•ning**) (usu. foll. by *about, off*, etc.) *Brit. colloq.* move or go aimlessly or casually or with a superior air. □□ **swan•like** adj. & adv. [OE f. Gmc]

swan dive n. a dive with the arms outspread until close to the water.

swank /swangk/ n., v., & adj. *colloq.* • n. ostentation; swagger; bluff. • v.intr. behave with swank; show off. • adj. = SWANKY. [19th c.: orig. uncert.]

swank•pot /swángkpot/ n. *Brit. colloq.* a person behaving with swank.

swank•y /swángkee/ adj. (**swank•i•er, swank•i•est**) **1** marked by swank; ostentatiously smart or showy. **2** (of a person) inclined to swank; boastful. □□ **swank•i•ly** adv. **swank•i•ness** n.

swan-neck n. a curved structure shaped like a swan's neck.

swan•ner•y /swónoree/ n. (pl. **-ies**) a place where swans are bred.

Swan of A•von n. *Brit. literary* Shakespeare.

swans•down /swónzdown/ n. **1** the fine down of a swan, used in trimming clothing, etc. **2** a kind of thick cotton cloth with a soft nap on one side.

swan song n. **1** a person's last work or act before death or retirement, etc. **2** a song like that fabled to be sung by a dying swan.

swap /swop/ v. & n. (also **swop**) • v.tr. & intr. (**swapped, swap•ping**) exchange or barter (one thing for another). • n. **1** an act of swapping. **2** a thing suitable for swapping. **3** a thing swapped. □□ **swap•per** n. [ME, orig. = 'hit': prob. imit.]

swa•raj /swəráaj/ n. *hist.* self-government or independence for India. □□ **swa•raj•ist** n. [Skr., = self-ruling: cf. RAJ]

sward /swawrd/ n. *literary* **1** an expanse of short grass. **2** turf. □□ **sward•ed** adj. [OE *sweard* skin]

sware /swair/ *archaic past* of SWEAR.

swarf /swawrf/ n. **1** fine chips or filings of stone, metal, etc. **2** wax, etc., removed in cutting a phonograph record. [ON *svarf* file dust]

swarm¹ /swawrm/ n. & v. • n. **1** a cluster of bees leaving the hive with the queen to establish a new colony. **2** a large number of insects or birds moving in a cluster. **3** a large group of people, esp. moving over or filling a large area. **4** (in pl.; foll. by *of*) great numbers. **5** a group of zoospores. • v.intr. **1** move in or form a swarm. **2** gather or move in large numbers. **3** (foll. by *with*) (of a place) be overrun, crowded, or infested (*was swarming with tourists*). [OE *swearm* f. Gmc]

swarm² /swawrm/ v.intr. (foll. by *up*) & tr. climb (a rope or tree, etc.), esp. in a rush, by clasping or clinging with the hands and knees, etc. [16th c.: orig. unkn.]

swart /swawrt/ adj. *archaic* swarthy; dark-hued. [OE *sweart* f. Gmc]

swarth•y /swáwrthee/ adj. (**swarth•i•er, swarth•i•est**) dark; dark-complexioned. □□ **swarth•i•ly** adv. **swarth•i•ness** n. [var. of obs. *swarty* (as SWART)]

swash¹ /swosh/ v. • v. **1** intr. (of water, etc.) wash about; make the sound of washing or rising and falling. **2** tr. *archaic* strike violently. **3** intr. *archaic* swagger. • n. the motion or sound of swashing water. [imit.]

swash² /swosh/ adj. **1** inclined obliquely. **2** (of a letter) having a flourished stroke or strokes. [17th c.: orig. unkn.]

swash•buck•ler /swóshbuklər/ n. **1** a swaggering bully or ruffian. **2** a dashing or daring adventurer, esp. in a novel, movie, etc. □□ **swash•buck•ling** adj. & n. [SWASH¹ + BUCKLER]

swash plate n. an inclined disk revolving on an axle and giving reciprocating motion to a part in contact with it.

swas•ti•ka /swóstikə/ n. **1** an ancient symbol formed by an equal-armed cross with each arm continued at a right angle. **2** this with clockwise continuations as the symbol of Nazi Germany. [Skr. *svastika* f. *svastí* well-being f. *sú* good + *astí* being]

swat /swot/ v. & n. • v.tr. (**swat•ted, swat•ting**) **1** crush (a fly, etc.) with a sharp blow. **2** hit hard and abruptly. • n. **1** a swatting blow. **2** a homerun in baseball. [17th c. in the sense 'sit down': No. of Engl. dial. & US var. of SQUAT]

swatch /swoch/ n. **1** a sample, esp. of cloth or fabric. **2** a collection of samples. [17th c.: orig. unkn.]

swath /swoth, swawth/ n. (also **swathe** /swoth, swayth/) (pl. **swaths** /swoths, swawths/ or **swathes** /swothz, swaythz/) **1** a ridge of grass or grain, etc., lying after being cut. **2** a space left clear after the passage of a mower, etc. **3** a broad strip. □ **cut a wide swath** be effective in destruction. [OE *swæth, swathu*]

swathe /swoth, swayth/ v. & n. • v.tr. bind or enclose in bandages or garments, etc. • n. a bandage or wrapping. [OE *swathian*]

swat•ter /swótər/ n. an implement for swatting flies.

sway /sway/ v. & n. • v. **1** intr. & tr. lean or cause to lean unsteadily in different directions alternately. **2** intr. oscillate irregularly; waver. **3** tr. **a** control the motion or direction of. **b** have influence or rule over. • n. **1** rule, influence, or government (*hold sway*). **2** a swaying motion or position. [ME: cf. LG *swäjen* be blown to and fro, Du. *zwaaien* swing, wave]

swear /swair/ v. & n. • v. (past **swore** /swor/; past part. **sworn** /sworn/) **1** tr. **a** (often foll. by *to* + infin. or *that* + clause) state or promise solemnly or on oath. **b** take (an oath). **2** tr. *colloq.* say emphatically; insist (*swore he had not seen it*). **3** tr. cause to take an oath (*swore them to secrecy*). **4** intr. (often foll. by *at*) use profane or indecent language, esp. as an expletive or from anger. **5** tr. (often foll. by *against*) make a sworn affirmation of (an offense) (*swear treason against*). **6** intr. (foll. by *by*) **a** appeal to as a witness in taking an oath (*swear by Almighty God*). **b** *colloq.* have or express great confidence in (*swears by yoga*). **7** intr. (foll. by *to*; usu. in *neg.*) admit the certainty of (*could not swear to it*). **8** intr. (foll. by *at*) *Brit. colloq.* (of colors, etc.) fail to harmonize with. • n. a spell of swearing. □ **swear blind** *Brit. colloq.* affirm emphatically. **swear in** induct into office, etc., by administering an oath. **swear off** *colloq.* promise to abstain from (drink, etc.). **swear out** obtain an arrest warrant by making an accusation under oath. □□ **swear•er** n. [OE *swerian* f. Gmc, rel. to ANSWER]

sweat /swet/ n. & v. • n. **1** moisture exuded through the pores of the skin, esp. from heat or nervousness. **2** a state or period of sweating. **3** *colloq.* a state of anxiety (*was in a sweat about it*). **4** *colloq.* **a** drudgery; effort. **b** a laborious task or undertaking. **5** condensed moisture on a surface. • v. (past and past part. **sweat** or **sweat•ed**) **1** intr. exude sweat; perspire. **2** intr. be terrified, suffering, etc. **3** intr. (of a wall, etc.) exhibit surface moisture. **4** intr. drudge; toil. **5** tr. heat (meat or vegetables) slowly in fat or water to extract the juices. **6** tr. emit (blood, gum, etc.) like sweat. **7** tr. make (a horse, athlete, etc.) sweat by exercise. **8** tr. **a** cause to drudge or toil. **b** (as **sweat** adj.) (of goods, workers, or labor) produced by or subjected to long hours under poor conditions. **9** tr. subject (hides or tobacco) to fermentation in manufacturing. **10** join (metal pipes, tubing, etc.) by heating and use. soldering. □ **by the sweat of one's brow** by one's own hard work. **no sweat** *colloq.* there is no need to worry. **sweat blood** *colloq.* **1** work strenuously. **2** be extremely anxious. **sweat bullets** = *sweat blood*. **sweat it out** *colloq.* endure a difficult experience to the end. [ME *swet(e)*, alt. (after *swete* v. f. OE *swætan* OHG *sweizzen* roast) of *swote* f. OE *swāt* f. Gmc]

sweat•band /swétband/ n. a band of absorbent material inside a hat or around a wrist, etc., to soak up sweat.

sweat•er /swétər/ n. **1** a knitted jersey, pullover, or cardigan. **2** an employer who works employees hard in poor conditions for low pay.

sweat gland n. *Anat.* a spiral tubular gland below the skin secreting sweat.

sweat•ing sick•ness n. an epidemic fever with sweating prevalent in England in the 15th–16th c.

sweat•pants /swétpants/ n.pl. loose pants of absorbent cotton material worn for exercise, etc.

sweat•shirt /swétshərt/ n. a sleeved cotton pullover of absorbent material, as worn by athletes before and after exercise.

sweat•shop /swétshop/ n. a workshop where sweat labor is used.

sweat•suit /swétsoot/ n. a suit of a jacket or sweatshirt and pants intended for exercise, etc.

sweat•y /swétee/ adj. (**sweat•i•er, sweat•i•est**) **1** sweating; covered with sweat. **2** causing sweat. □□ **sweat•i•ly** adv. **sweat•i•ness** n.

Swede /sweed/ n. **1 a** a native or national of Sweden. **b** a person of Swedish descent. **2** (**swede**) (in full **swede turnip**) *Brit.* = RUTABAGA. [MLG & MDu. *Swēde*, prob. f. ON *Svíthjóth* f. *Svíar* Swedes + *thjóth* people]

Swed•ish /sweedish/ adj. & n. • adj. of or relating to Sweden or its people or language. • n. the language of Sweden.

sweep /sweep/ v. & n. • v. (past and past part. **swept** /swept/) **1** tr. clean or clear (a room or area, etc.) with or as with a broom. **2** intr. (often foll. by *up*) clean a room, etc., in this way. **3** tr. (often foll. by *up*) collect or remove (dirt or litter, etc.) by sweeping. **4** tr. (foll. by *aside, away*, etc.) **a** push with or as with a broom. **b** dismiss or reject abruptly (*their objections were swept aside*). **5** tr. (foll. by *along, down*, etc.) carry or drive along with force. **6** tr. (foll. by *off, away*, etc.) remove or clear forcefully. **7** tr. traverse swiftly or lightly (*the wind swept the hillside*). **8** tr. impart a sweeping motion to (*swept his hand across*). **9** tr. swiftly cover or affect (*a new fashion swept the country*). **10** intr. **a** glide swiftly; speed along with unchecked motion. **b** go majestically. **11** intr. (of geographical features, etc.) have continuous extent. **12** tr. drag (a river bottom, etc.) to search for something. **13** tr. (of artillery, etc.) include in the line of fire; cover the whole of. **14** tr. propel (a barge, etc.) with sweeps. **15** tr. win every game, etc., in (a series) (*the team swept their latest home game*). • n. **1** the act or motion or an instance of sweeping. **2** a curve in the road, a sweeping line of a hill, etc. **3** range or scope (*beyond the sweep of the human mind*). **4** = CHIMNEY SWEEP. **5** a sortie by aircraft. **6** *colloq.* = SWEEPSTAKE. **7** a long oar worked from a barge, etc. **8** the sail of a windmill. **9** a long pole mounted as a lever for raising buckets from a well. **10** *Electronics* the movement of a beam across the screen of a cathode-ray tube. **11** (in *pl.*) a period during which television ratings are monitored and advertising rates are set. □ **make a clean sweep of 1** completely abolish or expel. **2** win all the prizes, etc., in (a competition, etc.). **sweep away 1** abolish swiftly. **2** (usu. in *passive*) powerfully affect, esp. emotionally. **sweep under the carpet** see CARPET. [ME *swepe* (earlier *swōpe*) f. OE *swāpan*]

sweep·back /sweepbak/ *n.* the angle at which an aircraft's wing is set back from a position at right angles to the body.

sweep·er /sweepər/ *n.* **1** a person who cleans by sweeping. **2** a device for sweeping carpets, etc. **3** *Soccer* a defensive player positioned close to the goalkeeper.

sweep·ing /sweeping/ *adj. & n.* • *adj.* **1** wide in range or effect (*sweeping changes*). **2** taking no account of particular cases or exceptions (*a sweeping statement*). • *n.* (in *pl.*) dirt, etc., collected by sweeping. □□ **sweep·ing·ly** *adv.* **sweep·ing·ness** *n.*

sweep-sec·ond-hand *n.* a second hand on a clock or watch, moving on the same dial as the other hands.

sweep·stake /sweepstayk/ *n.* **1** a form of gambling on horse races or other contests in which all competitors' stakes are paid to the winners. **2** a race with betting of this kind. **3** a prize or prizes won in a sweepstake.

sweet /sweet/ *adj. & n.* • *adj.* **1** having the pleasant taste characteristic of sugar. **2** smelling pleasant like roses or perfume, esp. fragrant. **3** (of sound, etc.) melodious or harmonious. **4 a** not salt, sour, or bitter. **b** fresh, with flavor unimpaired by rottenness. **c** (of water) fresh and readily drinkable. **5** (of wine) having a sweet taste (opp. DRY). **6** highly gratifying or attractive. **7** amiable; pleasant (*has a sweet nature*). **8** *colloq.* (of a person or thing) pretty; charming; endearing. **9** (foll. by *on*) *colloq.* fond of; in love with. • *n.* **1** a sweet part of something; sweetness. **2** *Brit.* candy. **3** *Brit.* a dessert. **4** (in *pl.*) delights; gratification. **5** (esp. as a form of address) sweetheart, etc. □ **she's sweet** *Austral. sl.* all is well. □□ **sweet·ish** *adj.* **sweet·ly** *adv.* **sweet·ness** *n.* [OE *swēte* f. Gmc]

sweet-and-sour *adj.* cooked in a sauce containing sugar and vinegar or lemon, etc.

sweet bas·il *n.* see BASIL.

sweet bay *n.* = BAY².

sweet·bread /sweetbred/ *n.* the pancreas or thymus of an animal, esp. as food.

sweet·bri·er /sweetbriər/ *n.* a wild rose, *Rosa eglanteria* of Europe and central Asia; with hooked thorns and small fragrant pink flowers.

sweet chest·nut *n.* see CHESTNUT.

sweet cic·e·ly *n.* a white-flowered aromatic plant, *Myrrhis odorata.*

sweet corn *n.* **1** a kind of corn with kernels having a high sugar content. **2** these kernels, eaten as a vegetable when young.

sweet·en /sweet'n/ *v. tr. & intr.* **1** make or become sweet or sweeter. **2** make agreeable or less painful. □ **sweeten the pill** see PILL. □□ **sweet·en·ing** *n.*

sweet·en·er /sweet'nər/ *n.* **1** a substance used to sweeten food or drink. **2** *colloq.* a bribe or inducement.

sweet flag *n.* a marsh herb, *Acorus calamus,* of the arum family with an aromatic rootstock.

sweet gale *n.* see GALE².

sweet·heart /sweet-haart/ *n.* **1** a lover or darling. **2** a term of endearment (esp. as a form of address).

sweet·heart a·gree·ment *n.* (also **sweet·heart con·tract** or **sweet·heart deal**) *colloq.* an industrial agreement reached privately by employers and labor union representatives that is beneficial to them but not to the workers.

sweet·ie /sweetee/ *n. colloq.* **1** a sweetheart. **2** *Brit.* a candy. **3** (also **sweet·ie-pie**) a term of endearment (esp. as a form of address).

sweet·ing /sweeting/ *n.* **1** a sweet-flavored variety of apple. **2** *archaic* darling.

sweet·meal /sweetmeel/ *n. Brit.* **1** sweetened wholemeal. **2** a sweetmeal biscuit.

sweet·meat /sweetmeet/ *n.* **1** a candy. **2** a small fancy cake.

sweet·ness and light *n.* a display of (esp. uncharacteristic) mildness and reason.

sweet pea *n.* any dwarf or climbing plant of the genus *Lathyrus,* esp. *L. odoratus* with fragrant flowers in many colors.

sweet pepper *n.* a small *Capsicum* pepper with a relatively mild taste.

sweet po·ta·to *n.* **1** a tropical climbing plant, *Ipomoea batatas,* with sweet tuberous roots used for food. **2** the root of this.

sweet rock·et *n.* see ROCKET².

sweet rush *n.* (also **sweet sedge**) a kind of sedge with a thick creeping aromatic rootstock used in medicine and confectionery.

sweet·shop /sweetshop/ *n. Brit.* a store selling candy as its main item.

sweet·sop /sweetsop/ *n.* **1** a tropical American evergreen shrub, *Annona squamosa.* **2** the fruit of this, having a green rind and a sweet pulp.

sweet sul·tan *n.* a sweet-scented plant, *Centaurea moschata* or *C. suaveoleus.*

sweet talk *n. colloq.* flattery; blandishment. □□ **sweet-talk** *v.tr.*

sweet-tem·pered *adj.* amiable.

sweet tooth *n.* a liking for sweet-tasting foods.

sweet vi·o·let *n.* a sweet-scented violet, *Viola odorata.*

sweet wil·liam *n.* a plant, *Dianthus barbatus,* with clusters of vivid fragrant flowers.

sweet wil·liam catch·fly *n.* a pink-flowered European pink, *Silene armeria.*

swell /swel/ *v., n., & adj.* • *v.* (*past part.* **swol·len** /swōlən/ or **swelled**) **1** *intr. & tr.* grow or cause to grow bigger or louder or more intense; expand; increase in force or intensity. **2** *intr.* (often foll. by *up*) *& tr.* rise or raise up from the surrounding surface. **3** *intr.* (foll. by *out*) bulge. **4** *intr.* (of the heart as the seat of emotion) feel full of joy, pride, relief, etc. **5** *intr.* (foll. by *with*) be hardly able to restrain (pride, etc.). **6** (as **swollen** *adj.*) distended or bulging. • *n.* **1** an act or the state of swelling. **2** the heaving of the sea with waves that do not break, e.g., after a storm. **3 a** a crescendo. **b** a mechanism in an organ, etc., for obtaining a crescendo or diminuendo. **4** *colloq.* a person of distinction or of dashing or fashionable appearance. **5** a protuberant part. • *adj.* **1** *colloq.* fine; splendid; excellent. **2** *colloq.* smart, fashionable. □□ **swell·ish** *adj.* [OE *swellan* f. Gmc]

swell box *n. Mus.* a box in which organ pipes are enclosed, with a shutter for controlling the sound level.

swelled head *n.* (also **swol·len head**) *colloq.* conceit.

swell·ing /sweling/ *n.* an abnormal protuberance on or in the body.

swell or·gan *n. Mus.* a section of an organ with pipes in a swell box.

swel·ter /sweltər/ *v. & n.* • *v.intr.* (usu. as **sweltering** *adj.*) be uncomfortably hot. • *n.* a sweltering atmosphere or condition. □□ **swel·ter·ing·ly** *adv.* [base of (now dial.) *swelt* f. OE *sweltan* perish f. Gmc]

swept *past and past part.* of SWEEP.

swept-back *adj.* (of an aircraft wing) fixed at an acute angle to the fuselage, inclining outwards toward the rear.

swept-up *adj.* (of hair) = UPSWEPT.

swept-wing *adj.* (of an aircraft) having swept-back wings.

swerve /swurv/ *v. & n.* • *v.intr. & tr.* change or cause to change direction, esp. abruptly. • *n.* **1** a swerving movement. **2** divergence from a course. □□ **swerve·less** *adj.* **swerv·er** *n.* [ME, repr. OE *sweorfan* SCOUR¹]

SWG *abbr.* standard wire gauge.

swift /swift/ *adj., adv., & n.* • *adj.* **1** quick; rapid; soon coming or passing. **2** speedy; prompt (*a swift response; was swift to act*). • *adv.* (*archaic* except in *comb.*) swiftly (*swift-moving*). • *n.* **1** any swift-flying insect-eating bird of the family Apodidae, with long wings and a superficial resemblance to a swallow. **2** a revolving frame for winding yarn, etc., from. □□ **swift·ly** *adv.* **swift·ness** *n.* [OE, rel. to *swīfan* move in a course]

swift·ie /swiftee/ *n. Austral. sl.* **1** a deceptive trick. **2** a person who acts or thinks quickly.

swift·let /swiftlit/ *n.* a small swift of the genus *Collocalia.*

swig /swig/ *v. & n. colloq.* • *v.tr. & intr.* (**swigged**, **swig·ging**) drink in large swallows. • *n.* a swallow of drink, esp. a large amount. □□ **swig·ger** *n.* [16th c., orig. as noun in obs. sense 'liquor': orig. unkn.]

swill /swil/ *v. & n.* • *v.* **1** *tr. & intr.* drink greedily. **2** *tr.* (often foll. by *out*) *Brit.* rinse or flush; pour water over or through. • *n.* **1** mainly liquid refuse as pig food. **2** inferior liquor. **3** worthless matter, trash. **4** *Brit.* an act of rinsing. □□ **swill·er** *n.* [OE *swillan, swilian,* of unkn. orig.]

swim /swim/ *v. & n.* • *v.* (**swim·ming**; *past* **swam** /swam/; *past part.* **swum** /swum/) **1** *intr.* propel the body through water by working the arms and legs, or (of a fish) the fins and tail. **2** *tr.* **a** traverse (a stretch of water or its distance) by swimming. **b** compete in (a race) by swimming. **c** use (a particular stroke) in swimming. **3** *intr.* float on or at the surface of a liquid (*bubbles swimming on the surface*). **4** *intr.* appear to undulate or reel or whirl. **5** *intr.* have a dizzy effect or sensation (*my head swam*). **6** *intr.* (foll. by *in, with*) be flooded. • *n.* **1** a spell or the act of swimming. **2** a deep pool frequented by fish in a river. □ **in the swim** involved in or acquainted with what is going on. □□ **swim·ma·ble** *adj.* **swim·mer** *n.* [OE *swimman* f. Gmc]

swim blad·der *n.* a gas-filled sac in fishes used to maintain buoyancy.

swim·mer·et /swiməret/ *n.* a swimming foot in crustaceans.

swim·ming-cos·tume *n. Brit.* = SWIMSUIT.

swim·ming·ly /swiminglee/ *adv.* with easy and unobstructed progress.

swim·ming pool *n.* an indoor or outdoor pool for swimming.

swim·suit /swimsōōt/ *n.* garment worn for swimming. □□ **swim·suit·ed** *adj.*

swim·wear /swimwair/ *n.* clothing worn for swimming.

swin·dle /swind'l/ *v. & n.* • *v.tr.* (often foll. by *out of*) **1** cheat (a person) of money, possessions, etc. (*was swindled out of all his savings*). **2** cheat a person of (money, etc.) (*swindled all his savings out of him*).

• *n.* **1** an act of swindling. **2** a person or thing represented as what it is not. **3** a fraudulent scheme. □□ **swin·dler** *n.* [back-form. f. *swindler* f. G *Schwindler* extravagant maker of schemes, swindler, f. *schwindeln* be dizzy]

swine /swīn/ *n.* (*pl.* same) **1** a pig. **2** *colloq.* (*pl.* **swine** or **swines**) **a** a term of contempt or disgust for a person. **b** a very unpleasant or difficult thing. □□ **swin·ish** *adj.* (esp. in sense 2). **swin·ish·ly** *adv.* **swin·ish·ness** *n.* [OE *swīn* f. Gmc]

swine fe·ver *n.* an intestinal viral disease of pigs.

swine·herd /swínhərd/ *n.* a person who tends pigs.

swing /swing/ *v.* & *n.* • *v.* (*past* and *past part.* **swung** /swung/) **1** *intr.* & *tr.* move or cause to move with a to-and-fro or curving motion, as of an object attached at one end and hanging free at the other. **2** *intr.* & *tr.* **a** sway. **b** hang so as to be free to sway. **c** oscillate or cause to oscillate. **3** *intr.* & *tr.* revolve or cause to revolve. **4** *intr.* move by gripping something and leaping, etc. (*swung from tree to tree*). **5** *intr.* go with a swinging gait (*swung out of the room*). **6** *intr.* (foll. by *around*) move around to the opposite direction. **7** *intr.* change from one opinion or mood to another. **8** *intr.* (foll. by *at*) attempt to hit or punch. **9** **a** *intr.* (also **swing it**) play music with a swing rhythm. **b** *tr.* play (a tune) with swing. **10** *intr. colloq.* **a** be lively or up to date; enjoy oneself. **b** be promiscuous. **11** *intr. colloq.* (of a party, etc.) be lively, successful, etc. **12** *tr.* have a decisive influence on (esp. voting, etc.). **13** *tr. colloq.* deal with or achieve; manage. **14** *intr. colloq.* be executed by hanging. • *n.* **1** the act or an instance of swinging. **2** the motion of swinging. **3** the extent of swinging. **4** a swinging or smooth gait or rhythm or action. **5 a** a seat slung by ropes or chains, etc., for swinging on or in. **b** a spell of swinging on this. **6** an easy but vigorous continued action. **7 a** jazz or dance music with an easy flowing rhythm. **b** the rhythmic feeling or drive of this music. **8** a discernible change in opinion, esp. the amount by which votes or points scored, etc., change from one side to another. **9** *colloq.* the regular procedure or course of events (*get into the swing of things*). □ **swing the lead** *Brit. colloq.* malinger; shirk one's duty. **swings and roundabouts** *Brit.* a situation affording no eventual gain or loss (from the phr. *lose on the swings what you make on the roundabouts*). □□ **swing·er** *n.* (esp. in sense 10 of *v.*). [OE *swingan* to beat f. Gmc]

swing bridge *n.* a bridge that can be swung to one side to allow the passage of ships.

swinge /swinj/ *v.tr.* (**swinge·ing**) *archaic* strike hard; beat. [alt. f. ME *swenge* f. OE *swengan* shake, shatter, f. Gmc]

swinge·ing /swínjing/ *adj.* esp. *Brit.* **1** (of a blow) forcible. **2** huge or far-reaching, esp. in severity (*swingeing economies*). □□ **swinge·ing·ly** *adv.*

swing·ing /swínging/ *adj.* **1** (of gait, melody, etc.) vigorously rhythmical. **2** *colloq.* **a** lively; up to date; excellent. **b** promiscuous. □□ **swing·ing·ly** *adv.*

swing·ing door *n.* a door able to open in either direction and close itself when released.

swin·gle /swínggəl/ *n.* & *v.* • *n.* **1** a wooden instrument for beating flax and removing the woody parts from it. **2** the swinging part of a flail. • *v.tr.* clean (flax) with a swingle. [ME f. MDu. *swinghel* (as SWING, –LE¹)]

swin·gle·tree /swínggəltree/ *n.* esp. *Brit.* = WHIFFLETREE.

swing shift *n.* a work shift from afternoon to late evening.

swing·y /swíngee/ *adj.* (**swing·i·er**, **swing·i·est**) **1** (of music) characterized by swing (see SWING *n.* 7). **2** (of a skirt or dress) designed to swing with body movement.

swipe /swīp/ *v.* & *n. colloq.* • *v.* **1** *tr.* & (often foll. by *at*) *intr.* hit hard and recklessly. **2** *tr.* steal. **3** run (a credit card, etc.) through an electronic card reader. • *n.* a reckless hard hit or attempted hit. □□ **swip·er** *n.* [perh. var. of SWEEP]

swip·ple /swípəl/ *n.* the swingle of a flail. [ME, prob. formed as SWEEP + –LE¹]

swirl /swərl/ *v.* & *n.* • *v.intr.* & *tr.* move or flow or carry along with a whirling motion. • *n.* **1** a swirling motion of or in water, air, etc. **2** the act of swirling. **3** a twist or curl, esp. as part of a pattern or design. □□ **swirl·y** *adj.* [ME (orig. as noun): orig. Sc., perh. of LG or Du. orig.]

swish /swish/ *v.*, *n.*, & *adj.* • *v.* **1** *tr.* swing (a scythe or stick, etc.) audibly through the air, grass, etc. **2** *intr.* move with or make a swishing sound. **3** *tr.* (foll. by *off*) cut (a flower, etc.) in this way. • *n.* a swishing action or sound. • *adj. colloq.* smart, fashionable. □□ **swish·y** *adj.* [imit.]

Swiss /swis/ *adj.* & *n.* • *adj.* of or relating to Switzerland in Western Europe or its people. • *n.* (*pl.* same) **1** a native or inhabitant of Switzerland. **2** a person of Swiss descent. [F *Suisse* f. MHG *Swīz*]

Swiss chard *n.* = CHARD.

Swiss cheese *n.* a type of hard cheese with large holes that form during ripening.

Swiss steak *n.* a slice of beef that is flattened, floured, and braised with vegetables, etc.

switch /swich/ *n.* & *v.* • *n.* **1** a device for making and breaking the connection in an electric circuit. **2 a** a transfer, change-over, or deviation. **b** an exchange. **3** a slender flexible shoot cut from a tree. **4** a light tapering rod. **5** a device at the junction of railroad tracks for transferring a train from one track to another. **6** a tress of false or detached hair tied at one end used in hairdressing. • *v.* **1** *tr.* (foll. by *on*, *off*) turn (an electrical device) on or off. **2** *intr.* change or transfer position, subject, etc. **3** *tr.* change or transfer. **4** *tr.* reverse the positions of; exchange (*switched chairs*). **5** *tr.* esp. *Brit.* swing or snatch (a thing) suddenly (*switched it out of my hand*). **6** *tr.* beat or flick with a switch. □ **switch off** *colloq.* cease to pay attention. **switch over** change or exchange. □□ **switch·er** *n.* [earlier *swits*, *switz*, prob. f. LG]

switch·back /swíchbak/ *n.* **1** (often *attrib.*) a railroad or road with alternate sharp ascents and descents. **2** *Brit.* = ROLLER COASTER.

switch·blade /swíchblayd/ *n.* a pocket knife with the blade released by a spring.

switch·board /swíchbawrd/ *n.* an apparatus for varying connections between electric circuits, esp. for completing telephone calls.

switched-on *adj. colloq.* **1** up to date; aware of what is going on. **2** excited; turned on.

switch hit·ter *n. Baseball* batter able to hit right-handed or left-handed.

swith·er /swíthər/ *v.* & *n. Sc.* • *v.intr.* hesitate; be uncertain. • *n.* doubt or uncertainty. [16th c.: orig. unkn.]

swiv·el /swívəl/ *n.* & *v.* • *n.* a coupling between two parts enabling one to revolve without turning the other. • *v.* & *intr.* (**swiv·eled**, **swiv·el·ing** or **swiv·elled**, **swiv·el·ling**) turn on or as on a swivel. [ME f. weak grade *swif-* of OE *swīfan* sweep + –LE¹: cf. SWIFT]

swiv·el chair *n.* a chair with a seat able to be turned horizontally.

swizz /swiz/ *n.* (also **swiz**) (*pl.* **swizz·es**) *Brit. colloq.* **1** something unfair or disappointing. **2** a swindle. [abbr. of SWIZZLE²]

swiz·zle¹ /swízəl/ *n.* & *v. colloq.* • *n.* a mixed alcoholic drink, esp. of rum, made frothy by stirring. • *v.tr.* stir with a swizzle stick. [19th c.: orig. unkn.]

swiz·zle² /swízəl/ *n. Brit. colloq.* = SWIZZ. [20th c.: prob. alt. of SWINDLE]

swiz·zle stick *n.* a stick used for stirring drinks.

swob var. of SWAB.

swol·len *past part.* of SWELL.

swoon /swoon/ *v.* & *n. literary* • *v.intr.* faint; fall into a fainting fit. • *n.* an occurrence of fainting. [ME *swoune* perh. back-form. f. *swogning* (n.) f. *iswogen* f. OE *geswogen* overcome]

swoop /swoop/ *v.* & *n.* • *v.* **1** *intr.* (often foll. by *down*) descend rapidly like a bird of prey. **2** *intr.* (often foll. by *on*) make a sudden attack from a distance. **3** *tr.* (often foll. by *up*) *colloq.* snatch the whole of at one swoop. • *n.* a swooping or snatching movement or action. □ **at** (or **in**) **one fell swoop** see FELL⁴. [perh. dial. var. of obs. *swōpe* f. OE *swāpan*: see SWEEP]

swoosh /swoosh/ *n.* & *v.* • *n.* the noise of a sudden rush of liquid, air, etc. • *v.intr.* move with this noise. [imit.]

swop var. of SWAP.

sword /sawrd/ *n.* **1** a weapon usu. of metal with a long blade and hilt with a handguard, used esp. for thrusting or striking, and often worn as part of ceremonial dress. **2** (prec. by *the*) **a** war. **b** military power. □ **put to the sword** kill, esp. in war. □□ **sword·like** *adj.* [OE *sw(e)ord* f. Gmc]

sword-bear·er *n. Brit.* an official carrying the sovereign's, etc., sword on a formal occasion.

sword·bill /sáwrdbil/ *n.* a long-billed humming bird, *Ensifera ensifera*.

sword dance *n.* a dance in which the performers brandish swords or step about swords laid on the ground.

sword·fish /sáwrdfish/ *n.* a large marine fish, *Xiphias gladius*, with an extended swordlike upper jaw.

swordfish

sword grass *n.* a grass, *Scirpus americanus*, with swordlike leaves.

sword knot *n.* a ribbon or tassel attached to a sword hilt orig. for securing it to the wrist.

sword lil·y *n.* = GLADIOLUS.

sword of Dam·o·cles /dáməkleez/ *n.* an imminent danger (from *Damokles*, flatterer of Dionysius of Syracuse (4th c. BC) made to feast while a sword hung by a hair over him).

sword of jus·tice *n.* judicial authority.

Sword of State *n. Brit.* a sword borne before the sovereign on state occasions.

sword·play /sáwrdplay/ *n.* **1** fencing. **2** repartee; cut-and-thrust argument.

swords·man /sáwrdzmən/ *n.* (*pl.* **-men**) a person of (usu. specified) skill with a sword. □□ **swords·man·ship** *n.*

sword·stick /sáwrdstik/ *n.* a hollow walking stick containing a blade that can be used as a sword.

sword swal·low·er *n.* a person ostensibly or actually swallowing sword blades as entertainment.

sword•tail /sáwrdtayl/ n. **1** a tropical fish, *Xiphophorus helleri*, with a long tail. **2** = HORSESHOE CRAB.

swore *past* of SWEAR.

sworn /swawrn/ **1** *past part.* of SWEAR. **2** *adj.* bound by or as by an oath (*sworn enemies*).

swot /swot/ v. & n. Brit. colloq. • v. (**swot•ted, swot•ting**) **1** *intr.* study assiduously. **2** *tr.* (often foll. by *up*) study (a subject) hard or hurriedly. • n. **1** a person who swots. **2 a** hard study. **b** a thing that requires this. [dial. var. of SWEAT]

swum *past part.* of SWIM.

swung *past* and *past part.* of SWING.

swung dash n. a dash (~) with alternate curves used in printing to represent a word or part of a word previously spelled out.

syb•a•rite /síbərīt/ n. & adj. • n. a person who is self-indulgent or devoted to sensuous luxury. • adj. fond of luxury or sensuousness. □□ **syb•a•rit•ic** /–rítik/ adj. **syb•a•rit•i•cal** adj. **syb•a•rit•i•cal•ly** adv. **syb•a•rit•ism** n. [orig. an inhabitant of Sybaris in S. Italy, noted for luxury, f. L *sybarita* f. Gk *subaritēs*]

syc•a•mine /síkəmin, –min/ n. Bibl. the black mulberry tree, *Morus nigra* (see Luke 17:6; in modern versions translated as 'mulberry tree'). [L *sycaminus* f. Gk *sukaminos* mulberry tree f. Heb. *šikmāh* sycamore, assim. to Gk *sukon* fig]

syc•a•more /síkəmawr/ n. **1** any of several plane trees, esp. *Platanus occidentalis* of N. America, or its wood. **2** (in full **sycamore maple**) **a** a large maple, *Acer pseudoplatanus*, with winged seeds, grown for its shade and timber. **b** its wood. **3** Bibl. a fig tree, *Ficus sycomorus*, growing in Egypt, Syria, etc. [var. of SYCOMORE]

syce /sīs/ n. (also **sice**) Anglo-Ind. a groom. [Hind. f. Arab. *sā'is*, *sāyis*]

syc•o•more /síkəmawr/ n. Bot. = SYCAMORE 3. [ME f. OF *sic(h)amor* f. L *sycomorus* f. Gk *sukomoros* f. *sukon* fig + *moron* mulberry]

sy•co•ni•um /sīkóneeəm/ n. (pl. **sy•co•ni•a**) Bot. a fleshy hollow receptacle developing into a multiple fruit as in the fig. [mod.L f. Gk *sukon* fig]

syc•o•phant /síkəfant, síkə–/ n. a servile flatterer; a toady. □□ **syc•o•phan•cy** n. **syc•o•phan•tic** /–fántik/ adj. **syc•o•phan•ti•cal•ly** adv. [F *sycophante* or L *sycophanta* f. Gk *sukophantēs* informer f. *sukon* fig + *phainō* show: the reason for the name is uncert., and association with informing against the illegal exportation of figs from ancient Athens (recorded by Plutarch) cannot be substantiated]

sy•co•sis /sīkósis/ n. a skin disease of the bearded part of the face with inflammation of the hair follicles. [mod.L f. Gk *sukōsis* f. *sukon* fig: orig. of a figlike ulcer]

Syden•ham's cho•re•a n. chorea esp. in children as one of the manifestations of rheumatic fever. Also called **St. Vitus's dance**.

sy•e•nite /síənīt/ n. a gray crystalline rock of feldspar and hornblende with or without quartz. □□ **sy•e•nit•ic** /–nítik/ adj. [F *syénite* f. L *Syenites* (*lapis*) (stone) of *Syene* in Egypt]

syl- /sil/ prefix assim. form of SYN- before *l*.

syl•la•bar•y /síləberee/ n. (pl. **-ies**) a list of characters representing syllables and (in some languages or stages of writing) serving the purpose of an alphabet. [mod.L *syllabarium* (as SYLLABLE)]

syl•la•bi pl. of SYLLABUS.

syl•lab•ic /silábik/ adj. **1** of, relating to, or based on syllables. **2** *Prosody* based on the number of syllables. **3** (of a symbol) representing a whole syllable. **4** articulated in syllables. □□ **syl•lab•i•cal•ly** adv. **syl•la•bic•i•ty** /–ləbísitee/ n. [F *syllabique* or LL *syllabicus* f. Gk *sullabikos* (as SYLLABLE)]

syl•lab•i•ca•tion /silabikáyshən/ n. (also **syl•lab•i•fi•ca•tion**) (/–bifi-káyshən/) division into or articulation by syllables. □□ **syl•lab•i•fy** v.tr. (**-fies, -fied**) [med.L *syllabicatio* f. *syllabicare* f. L *syllaba*: see SYLLABLE]

syl•la•bize /síləbīz/ v.tr. divide into or articulate by syllables. [med.L *syllabizare* f. Gk *sullabizō* (as SYLLABLE)]

syl•la•ble /síləbəl/ n. & v. • n. **1** a unit of pronunciation uttered without interruption, forming the whole or a part of a word and usu. having one vowel sound often with a consonant or consonants before or after: there are two syllables in *water* and three in *inferno*. **2** a character or characters representing a syllable. **3** (usu. with *neg.*) the least amount of speech or writing (*did not utter a syllable*). • v.tr. pronounce by syllables; articulate distinctly. □□ **syl•la•bled** adj. (also in *comb.*). [ME f. AF *sillable* f. OF *sillabe* f. L *syllaba* f. Gk *sullabē* (as SYN-, *lambanō* take)]

syl•la•bub /síləbub/ n. (also **sil•la•bub**) **1** a drink of milk or cream mixed with wine or cider. **2** a dessert of cream or milk flavored with wine or liquor, sweetened, and whipped to thicken it. [16th c.: orig. unkn.]

syl•la•bus /síləbəs/ n. (pl. **syl•la•bus•es** or **syl•la•bi** /–bī/) **1 a** the program or outline of a course of study, teaching, etc. **b** a statement of the requirements for a particular examination. **2** *RC Ch.* a summary of points decided by papal decree regarding heretical doctrines or practices. [mod.L, orig. a misreading of L *sittybas* accus. pl. of *sittyba* f. Gk *sittuba* title or label]

syl•lep•sis /silépsis/ n. (pl. **syl•lep•ses** /–seez/) a figure of speech in which a word is applied to two others in different senses (e.g., *caught the train and a bad cold*) or to two others of which it gram-matically suits one only (e.g., *neither they nor it is working*) (cf. ZEUGMA). □□ **syl•lep•tic** adj. **syl•lep•ti•cal•ly** adv. [LL f. Gk *sullēpsis* taking together f. *sullambanō*: see SYLLABLE]

syl•lo•gism /síləjizəm/ n. **1** a form of reasoning in which a conclusion is drawn from two given or assumed propositions (premises): a common or middle term is present in the two premises but not in the conclusion, which may be invalid (e.g., *all trains are long*; *some buses are long*; *therefore some buses are trains*: the common term is *long*). **2** deductive reasoning as distinct from induction. □□ **syl•lo•gis•tic** adj. **syl•lo•gis•ti•cal•ly** adv. [ME f. OF *silogisme* or L *syllogismus* f. Gk *sullogismos* f. *sullogizomai* (as SYN-, *logizomai* to reason f. *logos* reason)]

syl•lo•gize /síləjīz/ v. **1** *intr.* use syllogisms. **2** *tr.* put (facts or an argument) in the form of syllogism. [ME f. OF *syllogiser* or LL *syllogizare* f. Gk *sullogizomai* (as SYLLOGISM)]

sylph /silf/ n. **1** an elemental spirit of the air. **2** a slender graceful woman or girl. **3** any hummingbird of the genus *Aglaiocercus* with a long forked tail. □□ **sylph•like** adj. [mod.L *sylphes*, G *Sylphen* (pl.), perh. based on L *sylvestris* of the woods + *nympha* nymph]

syl•va var. of SILVA.

syl•van /sílvən/ adj. (also **sil•van**) **1 a** of the woods. **b** having woods; wooded. **2** rural. [F *sylvain* (obs. *silvain*) or L *Silvanus* woodland deity f. *silva* a wood]

syl•vi•cul•ture var. of SILVICULTURE.

sym. abbr. **1** symbol. **2** symphony.

sym- /sim/ prefix assim. form of SYN- before *b, m, p*.

sym•bi•ont /símbeeont, –ənt/ n. an organism living in symbiosis. [Gk *sumbiōn –ountos* part. of *sumbioō* live together (as SYMBIOSIS)]

sym•bi•o•sis /símbee-ósis, –bī–/ n. (pl. **sym•bi•o•ses** /–seez/) **1 a** an interaction between two different organisms living in close physical association, usu. to the advantage of both (cf. ANTIBIOSIS). **b** an instance of this. **2 a** a mutually advantageous association or relationship between persons. **b** an instance of this. □□ **sym•bi•ot•ic** /–biótik/ adj. **sym•bi•ot•i•cal•ly** /–biótikəlee/ adv. [mod.L f. Gk *sumbiōsis* a living together f. *sumbioō* live together, *sumbios* companion (as SYN-, *bios* life)]

sym•bol /símbəl/ n. & v. • n. **1** a thing conventionally regarded as typifying, representing, or recalling something, esp. an idea or quality (*white is a symbol of purity*). **2** a mark or character taken as the conventional sign of some object, idea, function, or process, e.g., the letters standing for the chemical elements or the characters in musical notation. • v.tr. (**sym•boled, sym•bol•ing** or **sym•bolled, sym•bol•ling**) symbolize. □□ **sym•bol•o•gy** /–bóləjee/ n. [ME f. L *symbolum* f. Gk *sumbolon* mark, token (as SYN-, *ballō* throw)]

sym•bol•ic /simbólik/ adj. (also **sym•bol•i•cal** /–bólikəl/) **1** of or serving as a symbol. **2** involving the use of symbols or symbolism. □□ **sym•bol•i•cal•ly** adv. [F *symbolique* or LL *symbolicus* f. Gk *sumbolikos*]

sym•bol•ic log•ic n. the use of symbols to denote propositions, etc., in order to assist reasoning.

sym•bol•ism /símbəlizəm/ n. **1 a** the use of symbols to represent ideas. **b** symbols collectively. **2** an artistic and poetic movement or style using symbols and indirect suggestion to express ideas, emotions, etc. □□ **sym•bol•ist** n. **sym•bol•is•tic** adj.

sym•bol•ize /símbəlīz/ v.tr. **1** be a symbol of. **2** represent by means of symbols. □□ **sym•bol•i•za•tion** n. [F *symboliser* f. *symbole* SYMBOL]

sym•me•try /símitree/ n. (pl. **-tries**) **1 a** correct proportion of the parts of a thing; balance; harmony. **b** beauty resulting from this. **2 a** a structure that allows an object to be divided into parts of an equal shape and size and similar position to the point or line or plane of division. **b** the possession of such a structure. **c** approximation to such a structure. **3** the repetition of exactly similar parts facing each other or a center. **4** Bot. the possession by a flower of sepals and petals and stamens and pistils in the same number or multiples of the same number. □□ **sym•met•ric** /simétrik/ adj. **sym•met•ri•cal** adj. **sym•met•ri•cal•ly** adv. **sym•me•trize** v.tr. [obs. F *symmétrie* or L *summetria* f. Gk (as SYN-, *metron* measure)]

sym•pa•thec•to•my /símpəthéktəmee/ n. (pl. **-mies**) the surgical removal of a sympathetic ganglion, etc.

sym•pa•thet•ic /símpəthétik/ adj. & n. • adj. **1** of, showing, or expressing sympathy. **2** due to sympathy. **3** likable or capable of evoking sympathy. **4** (of a person) friendly and cooperative. **5** (foll. by *to*) inclined to favor (a proposal, etc.) (*was most sympathetic to the idea*). **6** (of a landscape, etc.) that touches the feelings by association, etc. **7** (of a pain, etc.) caused by a pain or injury to someone else or in another part of the body. **8** (of a sound, resonance, or string) sounding by a vibration communicated from another vibrating object. **9 a** designating the part of the nervous system consisting of nerves leaving the thoracic and lumbar regions of the spinal cord and connecting with the nerve cells in or near the viscera (see PARASYMPATHETIC). **b** (of a nerve or ganglion) belonging to this system. • n. **1** a sympathetic nerve. **2** the

sympathetic system. □□ **sym·pa·thet·i·cal·ly** adv. [SYMPATHY, after *pathetic*]

sym·pa·thet·ic mag·ic n. a type of magic that seeks to achieve an effect by performing an associated action or using an associated thing.

sym·pa·thize /símpəthīz/ v.intr. (often foll. by *with*) **1** feel or express sympathy; share a feeling or opinion. **2** agree with a sentiment or opinion. □□ **sym·pa·thiz·er** n. [F *sympathiser* (as SYMPATHY)]

sym·pa·thy /símpəthee/ n. (pl. **·thies**) **1 a** the state of being simultaneously affected with the same feeling as another. **b** the capacity for this. **2** (often foll. by *with*) **a** the act of sharing or tendency to share (with a person, etc.) in an emotion or sensation or condition of another person or thing. **b** (in *sing.* or *pl.*) compassion or commiseration; condolences. **3** (often foll. by *for*) a favorable attitude; approval. **4** (in *sing.* or *pl.*; often foll. by *with*) agreement (with a person, etc.) in opinion or desire. **5** (*attrib.*) in support of another cause (*sympathy strike*). □ **in sympathy** (often foll. by *with*) **1** having or showing or resulting from sympathy (with another). **2** by way of sympathetic action (*working to rule in sympathy*). [L *sympathia* f. Gk *sumpatheia* (as SYN-, *pathēs* f. *pathos* feeling)]

sym·pet·al·ous /simpét'ləs/ adj. Bot. having the petals united.

sym·phon·ic /simfónik/ adj. (of music) relating to or having the form or character of a symphony. □□ **sym·phon·i·cal·ly** adv.

sym·phon·ic po·em n. an extended orchestral piece, usu. in one movement, on a descriptive or rhapsodic theme.

sym·pho·nist /símfənist/ n. a composer of symphonies.

sym·pho·ny /símfənee/ n. (pl. **·nies**) **1** an elaborate composition usu. for full orchestra, and in several movements with one or more in sonata form. **2** an interlude for orchestra alone in a large-scale vocal work. **3** = SYMPHONY ORCHESTRA. [ME, = harmony of sound, f. OF *symphonie* f. L *symphonia* f. Gk *sumphōnia* (as SYN-, *–phōnos* f. *phōnē* sound)]

sym·pho·ny or·ches·tra n. a large orchestra suitable for playing symphonies, etc.

sym·phyl·lous /símfiləs/ adj. Bot. having the leaves united. [SYN- + Gk *phullon* leaf]

sym·phy·sis /símfisis/ n. (pl. **sym·phy·ses** /–seez/) **1** the process of growing together. **2 a** a union between two bones, esp. in the median plane of the body. **b** the place or line of this. □□ **sym·phys·e·al** /–físéeəl, –fízeeəl/ adj. **sym·phys·i·al** /–fízeeəl/ adj. [mod.L f. Gk *sumphusis* (as SYN-, *phusis* growth)]

sym·po·di·um /simpódeeəm/ n. (pl. **sym·po·di·a** /–deeə/) Bot. the apparent main axis or stem of a vine, etc., made up of successive secondary axes. □□ **sym·po·di·al** adj. [mod.L (as SYN-, Gk *pous podos* foot)]

sym·po·si·um /simpózeeəm/ n. (pl. **sym·po·si·a** /–zeeə/) **1 a** a conference or meeting to discuss a particular subject. **b** a collection of essays or papers for this purpose. **2** a philosophical or other friendly discussion. **3** a drinking party, esp. of the ancient Greeks with conversation, etc., after a banquet. [L f. Gk *sumposion* in sense 3 (as SYN-, *–potēs* drinker)]

symp·tom /símptəm/ n. **1** Med. a change in the physical or mental condition of a person, regarded as evidence of a disorder (cf. SIGN 5). **2** a sign of the existence of something. [ME *synthoma* f. med.L *sinthoma*, & f. LL *symptoma* f. Gk *sumptōma –atos* chance, symptom, f. *sumpiptō* happen (as SYN-, *piptō* fall)]

symp·to·mat·ic /símptəmátik/ adj. serving as a symptom. □□ **symp·to·mat·i·cal·ly** adv.

symp·tom·a·tol·o·gy /símptəmətóləjee/ n. the branch of medicine concerned with the study and interpretation of symptoms.

syn. abbr. **1** synonym. **2** synonymous. **3** synonymy.

syn- /sin/ prefix with, together, alike. [from or after Gk *sun*-f. *sun* with]

syn·aer·e·sis Brit. var. of SYNERESIS.

syn·aes·the·sia Brit. var. of SYNESTHESIA.

syn·a·gogue /sínəgog/ n. **1** the house of worship where a Jewish assembly or congregation meets for religious observance and instruction. **2** the assembly itself. □□ **syn·a·gog·al** /–gógəl/ adj. **syn·a·gog·i·cal** /–gójikəl/ adj. [ME f. OF *sinagoge* f. LL *synagoga* f. Gk *sunagōgē* meeting (as SYN-, *agō* bring)]

syn·apse /sínaps, sináps/ n. Anat. a junction of two nerve cells. [Gk *synapsis* (as SYN-, *hapsis* f. *haptō* join)]

syn·ap·sis /sínápsis/ n. (pl. **syn·ap·ses** /–seez/) **1** Anat. = SYNAPSE. **2** Biol. the fusion of chromosome pairs at the start of meiosis. □□ **syn·ap·tic** /–náptik/ adj. **syn·ap·ti·cal·ly** adv.

syn·ar·thro·sis /sínaarthrósis/ n. (pl. **syn·ar·thro·ses** /–seez/) Anat. an immovably fixed bone joint, e.g., the sutures of the skull. [SYN- + Gk *arthrōsis* jointing f. *arthron* joint]

sync /singk/ n. & v. (also **synch**) colloq. •n. synchronization. •v.tr. & intr. synchronize. □ **in** (or **out of**) **sync** (often foll. by *with*) harmonizing or agreeing well (or badly). [abbr.]

syn·carp /sínkaarp/ n. a compound fruit from a flower with several carpels, e.g., a blackberry. [SYN- + Gk *karpos* fruit]

syn·car·pous /sínkáarpəs/ adj. (of a flower or fruit) having the carpels united (opp. APOCARPOUS). [SYN- + Gk *karpos* fruit]

synch var. of SYNC.

syn·chon·dro·sis /síngkondrósis/ n. (pl. **syn·chon·dro·ses** /–seez/) Anat. an almost immovable bone joint bound by a layer of cartilage, as in the spinal vertebrae. [SYN- + Gk *khondros* cartilage]

synchro- /síngkrō/ comb. form synchronized; synchronous.

syn·chro·cy·clo·tron /síngkrōsíklotron/ n. a cyclotron able to achieve higher energies by decreasing the frequency of the accelerating electric field as the particles increase in energy and mass.

syn·chro·mesh /síngkrōmesh/ n. & adj. •n. a system of changing gears, esp. in motor vehicles, in which the driving and driven gearwheels are made to revolve at the same speed during engagement by means of a set of friction clutches, thereby easing the change. •adj. relating to or using this system. [abbr. of *synchronized mesh*]

syn·chron·ic /singkrónik/ adj. describing a subject (esp. a language) as it exists at one point in time (opp. DIACHRONIC). □□ **syn·chron·i·cal·ly** adv. [LL *synchronus*: see SYNCHRONOUS]

syn·chro·nism /síngkrənizəm/ n. **1** = SYNCHRONY. **2** the process of synchronizing sound and picture in cinematography, television, etc. □□ **syn·chro·nis·tic** adj. **syn·chro·nis·ti·cal·ly** adv. [Gk *sugkhronismos* (as SYNCHRONOUS)]

syn·chro·nize /síngkrəniz/ v. **1** intr. (often foll. by *with*) occur at the same time; be simultaneous. **2** tr. cause to occur at the same time. **3** tr. carry out the synchronism of (a movie, etc.). **4** tr. ascertain or set forth the correspondence in the date of (events). **5 a** tr. cause (clocks, etc.) to show a standard or uniform time. **b** intr. (of clocks, etc.) be synchronized. □□ **syn·chro·ni·za·tion** n. **syn·chro·niz·er** n.

syn·chro·nized swim·ming n. a form of swimming in which participants make coordinated leg and arm movements in time to music.

syn·chro·nous /síngkrənəs/ adj. (often foll. by *with*) existing or occurring at the same time. □□ **syn·chro·nous·ly** adv. [LL *synchronus* f. Gk *sugkhronos* (as SYN-, *khronos* time)]

syn·chro·nous mo·tor n. Electr. a motor having a speed exactly proportional to the current frequency.

syn·chro·ny /síngkrənee/ n. **1** the state of being synchronic or synchronous. **2** the treatment of events, etc., as being synchronous. [Gk *sugkhronos*: see SYNCHRONOUS]

syn·chro·tron /síngkrətron/ n. Physics a cyclotron in which the magnetic field strength increases with the energy of the particles to keep their orbital radius constant.

syn·cline /síngklin/ n. a rock bed forming a trough. □□ **syn·cli·nal** adj. [*synclinal* (as SYN-, Gk *klinō* lean)]

syn·co·pate /síngkəpayt/ v.tr. **1** Mus. displace the beats or accents in (a passage) so that strong beats become weak and vice versa. **2** shorten (a word) by dropping interior sounds or letters, as *symbology* for *symbolology*, *Gloster* for *Gloucester*. □□ **syn·co·pa·tion** /–páyshən/ n. **syn·co·pa·tor** n. [LL *syncopare* swoon (as SYNCOPE)]

syn·co·pe /síngkəpee/ n. **1** Gram. the omission of interior sounds or letters in a word (see SYNCOPATE 2). **2** Med. a temporary loss of consciousness caused by a fall in blood pressure. □□ **syn·co·pal** adj. [ME f. LL *syncopē* f. Gk *sugkopē* (as SYN-, *koptō* strike, cut off)]

syn·cre·tism /síngkrətizəm/ n. **1** Philos. & Theol. the process or an instance of syncretizing (see SYNCRETIZE). **2** Philol. the merging of different inflectional varieties in the development of a language. □□ **syn·cret·ic** /–krétik/ adj. **syn·cre·tist** n. **syn·cre·tis·tic** /–krətístik/ adj. [mod.L *syncretismus* f. Gk *sugkrētismos* f. *sugkrētizō* (of two parties) combine against a third f. *krēs* Cretan (orig. of ancient Cretan communities)]

syn·cre·tize /síngkrətiz/ v.tr. Philos. & Theol. attempt, esp. inconsistently, to unify or reconcile differing schools of thought.

syn·cy·tium /sinsísheeəm/ n. (pl. **syn·cy·tia** /–sheeə/) Biol. a mass of cytoplasm with several nuclei, not divided into separate cells. □□ **syn·cy·tial** /–síshəl/ adj. [formed as SYN- + –CYTE + –IUM]

synd. abbr. **1** syndicate. **2** syndicated.

syn·dac·tyl /sindáktil/ adj. (of an animal) having digits united as in webbed feet, etc. □□ **syn·dac·tyl·ism** n. **syn·dac·ty·lous** adj.

syn·de·sis /síndisis/ n. (pl. **syn·de·ses** /–seez/) Biol. = SYNAPSIS 2. [mod.L f. Gk *syndesis* binding together f. *sundeō* bind together]

syn·des·mo·sis /síndezmósis/ n. the union and articulation of bones by means of ligaments. [mod.L f. Gk *sundesmos* binding, fastening + –OSIS]

syn·det·ic /sindétik/ adj. Gram. of or using conjunctions. [Gk *sundetikos* (as SYNDESIS)]

syn·dic /síndik/ n. **1** a government official in various countries. **2** Brit. a business agent of certain universities and corporations. □□ **syn·di·cal** adj. [F f. LL *syndicus* f. Gk *sundikos* (as SYN-, – *dikos* f. *dikē* justice)]

syn·di·cal·ism /síndikəlizəm/ n. hist. a movement for transferring the ownership and control of the means of production and distribution to workers' unions. □□ **syn·di·cal·ist** n. [F *syndicalisme* f. *syndical* (as SYNDIC)]

syn·di·cate n. & v. •n. /síndikət/ **1** a combination of individuals or commercial firms to promote some common interest. **2** an association or agency supplying material simultaneously to a number of newspapers or periodicals. **3** a group of people who combine to buy or rent property, gamble, organize crime, etc. **4** a committee of syndics. ● *v.tr.* /síndikayt/ **1** form into a syndicate. **2** publish (material) through a syndicate. □□ **syn·di·ca·tion** /-káyshən/ *n.* [F *syndicat* f. med.L *syndicatus* f. LL *syndicus*: see SYNDIC]

syn·drome /síndrōm/ *n.* **1** a group of concurrent symptoms of a disease. **2** a characteristic combination of opinions, emotions, behavior, etc. □□ **syn·drom·ic** /-drómik/ *adj.* [mod.L f. Gk *sundromē* (as SYN-, *dromē* f. *dramein* to run)]

syne /sin/ *adv., conj., & prep. Sc.* since. [contr. f. ME *sithen* SINCE]

syn·ec·do·che /sinékdəkee/ *n.* a figure of speech in which a part is made to represent the whole or vice versa (e.g., *new faces at the meeting*). □□ **syn·ec·doch·ic** /-dókik/ *adj.* [ME f. L f. Gk *sunekdokhē* (as SYN-, *ekdokhē* f. *ekdekhomai* take up)]

syn·e·col·o·gy /sínikóləjee/ *n.* the ecological study of plant or animal communities. □□ **syn·e·co·log·i·cal** /-kəlójikəl/ *adj.* **syn·e·col·o·gist** *n.*

syn·er·e·sis /sináirisis/ *n.* (*pl.* **syn·er·e·ses** /-seez/) the contraction of two vowels into a diphthong or single vowel. [LL f. Gk *sunairesis* (as SYN-, *hairesis* f. *haireō* take)]

syn·er·gism /sínərjizəm/ *n.* (also **syn·er·gy** /sínərjee/) the combined effect of drugs, organs, etc., that exceeds the sum of their individual effects. □□ **syn·er·get·ic** /-jétik/ *adj.* **syn·er·gic** /-nórjik/ *adj.* **syn·er·gis·tic** *adj.* **syn·er·gis·ti·cal·ly** *adv.* [Gk *sunergos* working together (as SYN-, *ergon* work)]

syn·er·gist /sínərjist/ *n.* a medicine or a bodily organ (e.g., a muscle) that cooperates with another or others.

syn·es·the·sia /sínis-theézhə, -zeeə/ *n.* **1** *Psychol.* the production of a mental sense impression relating to one sense by the stimulation of another sense. **2** a sensation produced in a part of the body by stimulation of another part. □□ **syn·es·thet·ic** /-thétik/ *adj.* [mod.L f. SYN- after *anesthesia*]

syn·ga·my /sínggəmee/ *n. Biol.* the fusion of gametes or nuclei in reproduction. □□ **syn·ga·mous** *adj.* [SYN- + Gk *gamos* marriage]

syn·gen·e·sis /sinjénisis/ *n.* sexual reproduction from combined male and female elements.

syn·od /sínəd/ *n.* **1** an Episcopal council attended by delegated clergy and sometimes laity (see also *General Synod*). **2** a Presbyterian ecclesiastical court above the presbyteries and subject to the General Assembly. **3** any meeting for debate. [ME f. LL *synodus* f. Gk *sunodos* meeting (as SYN-, *hodos* way)]

syn·od·ic /sinódik/ *adj. Astron.* relating to or involving the conjunction of stars, planets, etc. [LL *synodicus* f. Gk *sunodikos* (as SYNOD)]

syn·od·i·cal /sinódikəl/ *adj.* **1** (also **syn·od·al** /sínəd'l/) of, relating to, or constituted as a synod. **2** = SYNODIC.

syn·od·ic pe·ri·od *n.* the time between the successive conjunctions of a planet with the sun.

syn·o·nym /sínənim/ *n.* **1** a word or phrase that means exactly or nearly the same as another in the same language (e.g., *shut* and *close*). **2** a word denoting the same thing as another but suitable to a different context (e.g., *serpent* for *snake*). **3** a word equivalent to another in some but not all senses (e.g., *ship* and *vessel*). □□ **syn·o·nym·ic** /-nímik/ *adj.* **syn·o·nym·i·ty** /-nímitee/ *n.* [ME f. L *synonymum* f. Gk *sunōnumon* neut. of *sunōnumos* (as SYN-, *onoma* name): cf. ANONYMOUS]

syn·on·y·mous /sinóniməs/ *adj.* (often foll. by *with*) **1** having the same meaning; being a synonym (of). **2** (of a name, idea, etc.) suggestive of or associated with another (*excessive drinking regarded as synonymous with violence*). □□ **syn·on·y·mous·ly** *adv.* **syn·on·y·mous·ness** *n.*

syn·on·y·my /sinónimee/ *n.* (*pl.* **·mies**) **1** the state of being synonymous. **2** the collocation of synonyms for emphasis (e.g., *in any shape or form*). **3 a** a system or collection of synonyms. **b** a treatise on synonyms. [LL *synonymia* f. Gk *sunōnumia* (as SYNONYM)]

syn·op·sis /sinópsis/ *n.* (*pl.* **syn·op·ses** /-seez/) **1** a summary or outline. **2** a brief general survey. □□ **syn·op·size** *v.tr.* [LL f. Gk (as SYN-, *opsis* seeing)]

syn·op·tic /sinóptik/ *adj. & n.* ● *adj.* **1** of, forming, or giving a synopsis. **2** taking or affording a comprehensive mental view. **3** of the Synoptic Gospels. **4** giving a general view of weather conditions. ● *n.* **1** a Synoptic Gospel. **2** the writer of a Synoptic Gospel. □□ **syn·op·ti·cal** *adj.* **syn·op·ti·cal·ly** *adv.* [Gk *sunoptikos* (as SYNOPSIS)]

Syn·op·tic Gos·pels *n.* the Gospels of Matthew, Mark, and Luke, describing events from a similar point of view.

syn·op·tist /sinóptist/ *n.* the writer of a Synoptic Gospel.

syn·os·to·sis /sínostósis/ *n.* the joining of bones by ankylosis, etc. [SYN- + Gk *osteon* bone + -OSIS]

syn·o·vi·a /sinóveeə, sī-/ *n. Physiol.* a viscous fluid lubricating joints and tendon sheaths. □□ **syn·o·vi·al** *adj.* [mod.L, formed prob. arbitrarily by Paracelsus]

syn·o·vi·al mem·brane *n.* a dense membrane of connective tissue secreting synovia.

syn·o·vi·tis /sínovítis, sī-/ *n.* inflammation of the synovial membrane.

syn·tac·tic /sintáktik/ *adj.* of or according to syntax. □□ **syn·tac·ti·cal** *adj.* **syn·tac·ti·cal·ly** *adv.* [Gk *suntaktikos* (as SYNTAX)]

syn·tag·ma /sintágmə/ *n.* (*pl.* **syn·tag·mas** or **syn·tag·ma·ta** /-mətə/) **1** a word or phrase forming a syntactic unit. **2** a systematic collec-

tion of statements. □□ **syn·tag·mat·ic** /-mátik/ *adj.* **syn·tag·mic** /-mik/ *adj.* [LL f. Gk *suntagma* (as SYNTAX)]

syn·tax /síntaks/ *n.* **1** the grammatical arrangement of words, showing their connection and relation. **2** a set of rules for or an analysis of this. [F *syntaxe* or LL *syntaxis* f Gk *suntaxis* (as SYN-, *taxis* f. *tassō* arrange)]

synth /sinth/ *n. colloq.* = SYNTHESIZER.

syn·the·sis /sínthisis/ *n.* (*pl.* **syn·the·ses** /-seez/) **1** the process or result of building up separate elements, esp. ideas, into a connected whole, esp. into a theory or system. **2** a combination or composition. **3** *Chem.* the artificial production of compounds from their constituents as distinct from extraction from plants, etc. **4** *Gram.* **a** the process of making compound and derivative words. **b** the tendency in a language to use inflected forms rather than groups of words, prepositions, etc. **5** the joining of divided parts in surgery. □□ **syn·the·sist** *n.* [L f. Gk *synthesis* (as SYN-, THESIS)]

syn·the·size /sínthisīz/ *v.tr.* (also **syn·the·tize** /-tīz/) **1** make a synthesis of. **2** combine into a coherent whole.

syn·the·siz·er /sínthisīzər/ *n.* an electronic musical instrument, esp. operated by a keyboard, producing a wide variety of sounds by generating and combining signals of different frequencies.

syn·thet·ic /sinthétik/ *adj. & n.* ● *adj.* **1** made by chemical synthesis, esp. to imitate a natural product (*synthetic rubber*). **2** (of emotions, etc.) affected; insincere. **3** *Logic* (of a proposition) having truth or falsity determinable by recourse to experience (cf. ANALYTIC 3). **4** *Philol.* using combinations of simple words or elements in compounded or complex words (cf. ANALYTICAL). ● *n. Chem.* a synthetic substance. □□ **syn·thet·i·cal** *adj.* **syn·thet·i·cal·ly** *adv.* [F *synthétique* or mod.L *syntheticus* f. Gk *sunthetikos* f. *sunthetos* f. *suntithēmi* (as SYN-, *tithēmi* put)]

syn·thet·ic res·in *n. Chem.* see RESIN *n.* 2.

syph·i·lis /sífilis/ *n.* a contagious venereal disease progressing from infection of the genitals via the skin and mucous membranes to the bones, muscles, and brain. □□ **syph·i·lit·ic** /-lítik/ *adj.* **syph·i·lize** /-līz/ *v.tr.* **syph·i·loid** /-loyd/ *adj.* [mod.L f. title (*Syphilis, sive Morbus Gallicus*) of a Latin poem (1530), f. *Syphilus*, a character in it, the supposed first sufferer from the disease]

sy·phon var. of SIPHON.

Syr·i·ac /séereeak/ *n. & adj.* ● *n.* the language of ancient Syria; western Aramaic. ● *adj.* in or relating to this language. [L *Syriacus* f. Gk *Suriakos* f. *Suria* Syria]

Syr·i·an /séereeən/ *n. & adj.* ● *n.* **1** a native or inhabitant of the modern nation of Syria in the Middle East; a person of Syrian descent. **2** a native or inhabitant of the region of Syria in antiquity or later. ● *adj.* of or relating to the region or state of Syria.

sy·rin·ga /siringgə/ *n. Bot.* **1** = MOCK ORANGE. **2** any plant of the genus *Syringa*, esp. the lilac. [mod.L, formed as SYRINX (with ref. to the use of its stems as pipe stems)]

sy·ringe /sirínj/ *n. & v.* ● *n.* **1** *Med.* **a** a tube with a nozzle and piston or bulb for sucking in and ejecting liquid in a fine stream, used in surgery. **b** (in full **hypodermic syringe**) a similar device with a hollow needle for insertion under the skin. **2** any similar device used in gardening, cooking, etc. ● *v.tr.* sluice or spray (the ear, a plant, etc.) with a syringe. [ME f. med.L *syringa* (as SYRINX)]

syr·inx /síringks/ *n.* (*pl.* **syr·inx·es** or **sy·rin·ges** /sirínjeez/) **1** a set of panpipes. **2** *Archaeol.* a narrow gallery cut in rock in an ancient Egyptian tomb. **3** the lower larynx or song organ of birds. □□ **sy·rin·ge·al** /sirínjeeəl/ *adj.* [L *syrinx -ngis* f. Gk *surigx suriggos* pipe, channel]

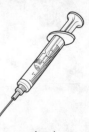

syringe 1

Syro- /síro/ *comb. form* Syrian; Syrian and (*Syro-Phoenician*). [Gk *Suro-* f. *Suros* a Syrian]

syr·up /sírəp, sór-/ *n.* (also **sir·up**) **1 a** a sweet sauce made by dissolving sugar in boiling water, often used for preserving fruit, etc. **b** a similar sauce of a specified flavor as a drink, medicine, etc. (*rose hip syrup*). **2** the condensed juice of various plants, such as sugarcane or the sugar maple; part of this remaining uncrystallized at various stages of refining; molasses. **3** excessive sweetness of style or manner. □□ **syr·up·y** *adj.* [ME f. OF *sirop* or med.L *siropus* f. Arab. *šarāb* beverage: cf. SHERBET, SHRUB[2]]

sys·sar·co·sis /sísaarkósis/ *n.* (*pl.* **sys·sar·co·ses** /-seez/) *Anat.* a connection between bones formed by intervening muscle. [mod.L f. Gk *sussarkōsis* (as SYN-, *sarx, sarkos* flesh)]

sys·tal·tic /sistáltik, sistáwl-/ *adj.* (esp. of the heart) contracting and dilating rhythmically; pulsatory (cf. SYSTOLE, DIASTOLE). [LL *systalticus* f. Gk *sustaltikos* (as SYN-, *staltos* f. *stellō* put)]

sys·tem /sístəm/ *n.* **1 a** a complex whole; a set of connected things or parts; an organized body of material or immaterial things. **b** the composition of such a body; arrangement; setup. **2** a set of devices (e.g., pulleys) functioning together. **3** *Physiol.* **a** a set of organs in the body with a common structure or function (*the digestive system*). **b** the human or animal body as a whole. **4 a** method; considered principles of procedure or classification. **b** classification. **5** orderliness. **6 a** a body of theory or practice relating to or prescribing a particular form of government, religion, etc. **b** (prec. by *the*) the prevailing political or social order, esp. regarded as oppressive and intransigent. **7** a method of choosing one's procedure in gambling, etc. **8** *Computing* a group of related hardware units or programs or both, esp. when dedicated to a single application. **9** one of seven general types of crystal structure. **10** a major group of geological strata (*the Devonian system*). **11** *Physics* a group of associated bodies moving under mutual gravitation, etc. **12** *Mus.* the braced staves of a score. □ **get a thing out of one's system** *colloq.* be rid of a preoccupation or anxiety. □□ **sys•tem•less** *adj.* [F *système* or LL *systema* f. Gk *sustēma* –*atos* (as SYN-, *histēmi* set up)]

sys•tem•at•ic /sístəmátik/ *adj.* **1** methodical; done or conceived according to a plan or system. **2** regular; deliberate (*a systematic liar*). □□ **sys•tem•at•i•cal•ly** *adv.* **sys•tem•a•tism** /sístəmətizəm/ *n.* **sys•tem•a•tist** /sístəmətist/ *n.* [F *systématique* f. LL *systematicus* f. late Gk *sustēmatikos* (as SYSTEM)]

sys•tem•at•ics /sístəmátiks/ *n.pl.* (usu. treated as *sing.*) the study or a system of classification; taxonomy.

sys•tem•at•ic the•ol•o•gy *n.* a form of theology in which the aim is to arrange religious truths in a self-consistent whole.

sys•tem•a•tize /sístəmətiz/ *v.tr.* **1** make systematic. **2** devise a system for. □□ **sys•tem•a•ti•za•tion** *n.* **sys•tem•a•tiz•er** *n.*

sys•tem•ic /sistémik/ *adj.* **1** *Physiol.* **a** of or concerning the whole body; not confined to a particular part (*systemic infection*). **b** (of blood circulation) other than pulmonary. **2** *Hort.* (of an insecticide, fungicide, etc.) entering the plant via the roots or shoots and passing through the tissues. □□ **sys•tem•i•cal•ly** *adv.* [irreg. f. SYSTEM]

sys•tem•ize /sístəmīz/ *v.tr.* = SYSTEMATIZE. □□ **sys•tem•i•za•tion** *n.* **sys•tem•iz•er** *n.*

sys•tems a•nal•y•sis *n.* the analysis of a complex process or operation in order to improve its efficiency, esp. by applying a computer system.

sys•to•le /sístəlee/ *n.* *Physiol.* the contraction of the heart, when blood is pumped into the arteries (cf. DIASTOLE). □□ **sys•tol•ic** /sistólik/ *adj.* [LL f. Gk *sustolē* f. *sustellō* contract (as SYSTALTIC)]

syz•y•gy /sízijee/ *n.* (*pl.* **•gies**) **1** *Astron.* conjunction or opposition, esp. of the moon with the sun. **2** a pair of connected or correlated things. [LL *syzygia* f. Gk *suzugia* f. *suzugos* yoked, paired (as SYN-, *zugon* yoke)]

T

T¹ /tee/ *n.* (also **t**) (*pl.* **Ts** or **T's**) **1** the twentieth letter of the alphabet. **2** a T-shaped thing (esp. *attrib.*: *T-joint*). □ **to a T** exactly; to perfection.

T² *abbr.* **1** tera–. **2** tesla. **3** tablespoon. **4** temperature.

T³ *symb. Chem.* the isotope tritium.

t. *abbr.* **1** ton(s). **2** teaspoon. **3** temperature.

't *pron. contr.* of IT¹ (*'tis*).

-t¹ /t/ *suffix* = –ED¹ (*crept; sent*).

-t² /t/ *suffix* = –EST² (*shalt*).

Ta *symb. Chem.* the element tantalum.

ta /taa/ *int. Brit. colloq.* thank you. [infantile form]

Ta·al /taal/ *n.* (prec. by *the*) *hist.* an early form of Afrikaans. [Du., = language, rel. to TALE]

tab¹ /tab/ *n. & v.* ● *n.* **1 a** a small flap or strip of material attached for grasping, fastening, or hanging up, or for identification. **b** a similar object as part of a garment, etc. **2** *colloq.* a bill or check (*picked up the tab*). **3** *Brit. Mil.* a marking on the collar distinguishing a staff officer. **4** a small or drawn-aside stage curtain. ● *v.tr.* (**tabbed, tab·bing**) provide with a tab or tabs. □ **keep tabs** (or **a tab**) **on** *colloq.* **1** keep account of. **2** have under observation. [prob. f. dial.: cf. TAG¹]

tab² /tab/ *n.* **1 a** a device on a typewriter for advancing to a sequence of set positions in tabular work. **b** a programmable key on a computer keyboard that moves the cursor forward a designated number of spaces. **2** = TABULATOR 3. [abbr.]

tab·ard /tábərd/ *n.* **1** a herald's official coat emblazoned with the arms of his master. **2** a woman's or girl's sleeveless jerkin. **3** *hist.* a knight's short emblazoned garment worn over armor. [ME f. OF *tabart*, of unkn. orig.]

tab·a·ret /tábərit/ *n.* an upholstery fabric of alternate satin and plain stripes. [prob. f. TABBY]

Ta·bas·co /təbáskó/ *n. Trademark* a pungent pepper sauce made from the fruit of *Capsicum frutescens*. [*Tabasco* in Mexico]

tab·bou·leh /təbóólə, –lee/ *n.* an Arabic vegetable salad made with cracked wheat. [Arab. *tabbūla*]

tab·by /tábee/ *n.* (*pl.* **-bies**) **1** (in full **tabby cat**) **a** a gray orange, or brownish cat mottled or streaked with dark stripes. **b** any domestic cat, esp. female. **2** a kind of watered silk. **3** a plain weave. [F *tabis* (in sense 2) f. Arab. *al-'attabiya* the quarter of Baghdad where tabby was manufactured: connection of other senses uncert.]

tab·er·nac·le /tábərnakəl/ *n.* **1** *hist.* a tent used as a sanctuary for the Ark of the Covenant by the Israelites during the Exodus. **2** *Eccl.* a canopied niche or receptacle esp. for the Eucharistic elements. **3** a place of worship, esp. in some Christian denominations. **4** *Bibl.* a fixed or movable habitation usu. of light construction. **5** *Naut.* a socket or double post for a hinged mast that can be lowered to pass under low bridges. □□ **tab·er·nac·led** *adj.* [ME f. OF *tabernacle* or L *tabernaculum* tent, dimin. of *taberna* hut]

ta·bes /táybeez/ *n. Med.* **1** emaciation. **2** (in full **tabes dorsalis**) locomotor ataxia; a form of neurosyphilis. □□ **ta·bet·ic** /təbétik/ *adj.* [L, = wasting away]

ta·bla /taáblə, túb–/ *n. Ind. Mus.* a pair of small drums played with the hands. [Hind. f. Arab. *ṭabla* drum]

tab·la·ture /táblɔchɔr/ *n. Mus.* an early form of notation indicating fingering (esp. in playing the lute), rhythm, and features other than notes. [F f. It. *tavolatura* f. *tavolare* set to music]

ta·ble /táybəl/ *n. & v.* ● *n.* **1** a piece of furniture with a flat top and one or more legs, providing a level surface for eating, writing, or working at, playing games on, etc. **2** a flat surface serving a specified purpose (*altar table; bird table*). **3 a** food provided in a household (*keeps a good table*). **b** a group seated at a table for dinner, etc. **4 a** a set of facts or figures systematically displayed, esp. in columns (*a table of contents*). **b** matter contained in this. **c** = MULTIPLICATION TABLE. **5** a flat surface for working on or for machinery to operate on. **6 a** a slab of wood or stone, etc., for bearing an inscription. **b** matter inscribed on this. **7** = TABLELAND. **8** *Archit.* **a** a flat usu. rectangular vertical surface. **b** a horizontal molding, esp. a cornice. **9 a** a flat surface of a gem. **b** a cut gem with two flat faces. **10** each half or quarter of a folding board for backgammon. **11** (prec. by *the*) *Bridge* the dummy hand. ● *v.tr.* **1** postpone consideration of (a matter). **2** *Brit.* bring forward for discussion or consideration at a meeting. **3** *Naut.* strengthen (a sail) with a wide hem. □ **at table** esp. *Brit.* taking a meal at a table. **lay on the table 1** submit for discussion. **2** postpone indefinitely. **on the table** offered for discussion. **turn the tables** (often foll. by *on*) reverse one's relations (with),

esp. by turning an inferior into a superior position (orig. in backgammon). **under the table** *colloq.* **1** drunk. **2** (esp. of a payment) covertly; secretly. □□ **ta·ble·ful** *n.* (*pl.* **-fuls**). **ta·bling** *n.* [ME f. OF f. L *tabula* plank, tablet, list]

tab·leau /tabló, táblō/ *n.* (*pl.* **tab·leaux** /–lōz/) **1** a picturesque presentation. **2** = TABLEAU VIVANT. **3** a dramatic or effective situation suddenly brought about. [F, = picture, dimin. of *table*: see TABLE]

tab·leau cur·tains *n.pl. Theatr.* a pair of curtains drawn open by a diagonal cord.

tab·leau vi·vant /veevaáN/ *n.* (*pl.* **tab·leaux vi·vants** *pronunc.* same) *Theatr.* a silent and motionless group of people arranged to represent a scene. [F, lit. 'living picture']

ta·ble·cloth /táybəlklawth, –kloth/ *n.* a cloth spread over the top of a table, esp. for meals.

ta·ble d'hôte /taábəl dót, taáblə/ *n.* a meal consisting of a set menu at a fixed price, esp. in a hotel (cf. À LA CARTE). [F, = host's table]

ta·ble knife *n.* a knife for use at meals, esp. in eating a main course.

ta·ble·land /táybəl-land/ *n.* an extensive elevated region with a level surface; a plateau.

ta·ble lin·en *n.* tablecloths, napkins, etc.

ta·ble man·ners *n.pl.* decorum or correct behavior while eating.

ta·ble salt *n.* salt for use at meals.

ta·ble·spoon /táybəlspoon/ *n.* **1** a large spoon for serving food. **2** an amount held by this. **3** a unit of measure equal to 15 ml or ¹/₂ fl. oz. □□ **ta·ble·spoon·ful** *n.* (*pl.* **-fuls**).

tab·let /táblit/ *n.* **1** a small measured and compressed amount of a substance, esp. of a medicine or drug. **2** a small flat piece of soap, etc. **3** a flat slab of stone or wood, esp. for display or an inscription. **4** *Archit.* = TABLE 8. **5** a writing pad. [ME f. OF *tablete* f. Rmc, dimin. of L *tabula* TABLE]

ta·ble talk *n.* miscellaneous informal talk at table.

ta·ble ten·nis *n.* an indoor game based on tennis, played with paddles and a ball bounced on a table divided by a net.

ta·ble·top /táybəltop/ *n.* **1** the top or surface of a table. **2** (*attrib.*) that can be placed or used on a tabletop.

ta·ble·ware /táybəlwair/ *n.* dishes, plates, utensils, etc., for use at meals.

ta·ble wine *n.* ordinary wine for drinking with a meal.

tab·loid /tábloyd/ *n. & adj.* ● *n.* **1** a newspaper, usu. popular in style with bold headlines and large photographs, having pages of half size. **2** anything in a compressed or concentrated form. ● *adj.* printed on newsprint and folded once lengthwise so as to be read like a magazine. [orig. the Trademark name of a medicine sold in tablets]

ta·boo /təbóō, ta–/ *n., adj., & v.* (also **tabu**) ● *n.* (*pl.* **ta·boos** or **ta·bus**) **1** a system or the act of setting a person or thing apart as sacred or accursed. **2** a prohibition or restriction imposed by social custom. ● *adj.* **1** avoided or prohibited, esp. by social custom (*taboo words*). **2** designated as sacred and prohibited. ● *v.tr.* (**ta·boos, ta·booed** or **ta·bus, ta·bued**) **1** put (a thing, practice, etc.) under taboo. **2** exclude or prohibit by authority or social influence. [Tongan *tabu*]

ta·bor /táybər/ *n. hist.* a small drum, esp. one used to accompany a pipe. [ME f. OF *tabor, tabur*: cf. TABLA, Pers. *tabīra* drum]

tab·o·ret /tábərit, tabərét, –ráy/ *n.* (*Brit.* **tab·ou·ret**) a low seat usu. without arms or a back. [F, = stool, dimin. as TABOR]

ta·bu var. of TABOO.

tab·u·lar /tábyələr/ *adj.* **1** of or arranged in tables or lists. **2** broad and flat like a table. **3** (of a crystal) having two broad flat faces. **4** formed in thin plates. □□ **tab·u·lar·ly** *adv.* [L *tabularis* (as TABLE)]

tab·u·la ra·sa /tábyələ raásə, –zə/ *n.* **1** an erased tablet. **2** the human mind (esp. at birth) viewed as having no innate ideas. [L, = scraped tablet]

tab·u·late /tábyəlayt/ *v.tr.* arrange (figures or facts) in tabular form. □□ **tab·u·la·tion** /–láyshən/ *n.* [LL *tabulare tabulat-* f. *tabula* table]

tab·u·la·tor /tábyəlaytər/ *n.* **1** a person or thing that tabulates. **2** = TAB² 1. **3** *Computing* a machine that produces lists or tables from a data storage medium such as punched cards.

tac·a·ma·hac /tákəməhak/ *n.* **1** a resinous gum obtained from certain tropical trees esp. of the genus *Calophyllum*. **2 a** the balsam poplar. **b** the resin of this. [obs. Sp. *tacamahaca* f. Aztec *tecomahiyac*]

ta·cet /tásit, táy–, taáket/ *v.intr. Mus.* an instruction for a particular voice or instrument to be silent. [L, = is silent]

tach·ism /táshizəm/ *n.* (also **ta·chisme**) a form of action painting with dabs of color arranged randomly to evoke a subconscious feeling. [F *tachisme* f. *tache* stain]

ta·chis·to·scope /təkístəskōp/ *n.* an instrument for very brief measured exposure of objects to the eye. □□ **ta·chis·to·scop·ic** /–skópik/ *adj.* [Gk *takhistos* swiftest + –SCOPE]

tach·o /tákō/ *n.* (*pl.* **–hos**) *Brit. colloq.* = TACHOMETER. [abbr.]

tacho– /tákō/ *comb. form* speed. [Gk *takhos* speed]

tach·o·graph /tákəgraf/ *n.* a device used esp. in heavy trucks and buses, etc., for automatically recording speed and travel time.

ta·chom·e·ter /təkómitər, ta–/ *n.* **1** an instrument for measuring the rate of rotation of a shaft and hence the speed of an engine or the speed or velocity of a vehicle. **2** a device for indicating the number or rate of revolutions of an engine, etc.

tachy– /tákee/ *comb. form* speed. [Gk *takhus* swift]

tach·y·car·di·a /tákikaárdeeə/ *n. Med.* an abnormally rapid heart rate. [TACHY– + Gk *kardia* heart]

ta·chyg·ra·phy /təkígrəfee/ *n.* **1** stenography, esp. that of the ancient Greeks and Romans. **2** the abbreviated medieval writing of Greek and Latin. □□ **ta·chyg·ra·pher** *n.* **tach·y·graph·ic** /tákigráfik/ *adj.* **tach·y·graph·i·cal** *adj.*

ta·chym·e·ter /təkímitər, ta–/ *n.* **1** *Surveying* an instrument used to locate points rapidly. **2** a speed indicator.

tac·it /tásit/ *adj.* understood or implied without being stated (*tacit consent*). □□ **tac·it·ly** *adv.* [L *tacitus* silent f. *tacēre* be silent]

tac·i·turn /tásitərn/ *adj.* reserved in speech; saying little; uncommunicative. □□ **tac·i·tur·ni·ty** /–tórnitee/ *n.* **tac·i·turn·ly** *adv.* [F *taciturne* or L *taciturnus* (as TACIT)]

tack[1] /tak/ *n. & v.* • *n.* **1** a small sharp broad-headed nail. **2** a pin used to attach papers, etc., to a bulletin board or other surface. **3** a long stitch used in fastening fabrics, etc., lightly or temporarily together. **4 a** the direction in which a ship moves as determined by the position of its sails and regarded in terms of the direction of the wind (*starboard tack*). **b** a temporary change of direction in sailing to take advantage of a side wind, etc. **5** a course of action or policy (*try another tack*). **6** *Naut.* **a** a rope for securing the corner of some sails. **b** the corner to which this is fastened. **7** a sticky condition of varnish, etc. **8** *Brit.* an extraneous clause appended to a bill in Parliament. • *v.* **1** *tr.* (often foll. by *down*, etc.) fasten with tacks. **2** *tr.* stitch (pieces of cloth, etc.) lightly together. **3** *tr.* (foll. by *to*, *on*) annex (a thing). **4** *intr.* **a** change a ship's course by turning its head to the wind (cf. WEAR[2]). **b** make a series of tacks. **5** *intr.* change one's conduct or policy, etc. **6** *tr. Brit.* append (a clause) to a bill. □□ **tack·er** *n.* [ME *tak*, etc., of uncert. orig.: cf. Bibl. *tache* clasp, link f. OF *tache*]

tack[2] /tak/ *n.* the saddle, bridle, etc., of a horse. [shortened f. TACKLE]

tack[3] /tak/ *n. colloq.* cheap or shoddy material; kitsch. [back-form. f. TACKY[2]]

tack·le /tákəl/ *n. & v.* • *n.* **1** equipment for a task or sport (*fishing tackle*). **2** a mechanism, esp. of ropes, pulley blocks, hooks, etc., for lifting weights, managing sails, etc. (*block and tackle*). **3** a windlass with its ropes and hooks. **4** an act of tackling in football, etc. **5** *Football* **a** the position next to the end of the forward line. **b** the player in this position. • *v.tr.* **1** try to deal with (a problem or difficulty). **2** grapple with or try to overcome (an opponent). **3** enter into discussion with. **4** obstruct, intercept, or seize and stop (a player running with the ball). **5** secure by means of tackle. □□ **tack·ler** *n.* **tack·ling** *n.* [ME, prob. f. MLG *takel* f. *taken* lay hold of]

tack·le block *n.* a pulley over which a rope runs.

tack·le fall *n.* a rope for applying force to the blocks of a tackle.

tack·y[1] /tákee/ *adj.* (**tack·i·er**, **tack·i·est**) (of glue or paint, etc.) still slightly sticky after application. □□ **tack·i·ness** *n.* [TACK[1] + –Y[1]]

tack·y[2] /tákee/ *adj.* (**tack·i·er**, **tack·i·est**) *colloq.* **1** showing poor taste or style. **2** shoddy or seedy. □□ **tack·i·ly** *adv.* **tack·i·ness** *n.* [19th c.: orig. unkn.]

ta·co /tákō/ *n.* (*pl.* **–cos**) a Mexican-style dish of usu. meat, cheese, lettuce, tomatoes, etc., in a folded or rolled fried tortilla. [Mex. Sp.]

tact /takt/ *n.* **1** adroitness in dealing with others or with difficulties arising from personal feeling. **2** intuitive perception of the right thing to do or say. [F f. L *tactus* touch, sense of touch f. *tangere tact–* touch]

tact·ful /táktfŏŏl/ *adj.* having or showing tact. □□ **tact·ful·ly** *adv.* **tact·ful·ness** *n.*

tac·tic /táktik/ *n.* **1** a tactical maneuver. **2** = TACTICS. [mod.L *tactica* f. Gk *taktikē* (*tekhnē* art): see TACTICS]

tac·ti·cal /táktikəl/ *adj.* **1** of, relating to, or constituting tactics (*a tactical retreat*). **2** (of bombing or weapons) done or for use in immediate support of military or naval operations (opp. STRATEGIC). **3** adroitly planning or planned. **4** *Brit.* (of voting) aimed at preventing the strongest candidate from winning by supporting the next strongest. □□ **tac·ti·cal·ly** *adv.* [Gk *taktikos* (as TACTICS)]

tac·tics /táktiks/ *n.pl.* **1** (also treated as *sing.*) the art of disposing armed forces esp. in contact with an enemy (cf. STRATEGY). **2 a** the

plans and means adopted in carrying out a scheme or achieving some end. **b** a skillful device or devices. □□ **tac·ti·cian** /taktíshən/ *n.* [mod.L *tactica* f. Gk *taktika* neut.pl. f. *taktos* ordered f. *tassō* arrange]

tac·tile /táktəl, –tīl/ *adj.* **1** of or connected with the sense of touch. **2** perceived by touch. **3** tangible. **4** *Art* (in painting) producing or concerning the effect of three-dimensional solidity. □□ **tac·tu·al** /tákchŏŏəl/ *adj.* (in senses 1, 2). **tac·til·i·ty** /–tílitee/ *n.* [L *tactilis* f. *tangere* touch]

tact·less /táktlis/ *adj.* having or showing no tact. □□ **tact·less·ly** *adv.* **tact·less·ness** *n.*

tad /tad/ *n. colloq.* a small amount (often used adverbially: *a tad salty*). [19th c.: orig. unkn.]

tad·pole /tádpōl/ *n.* a larva of an amphibian, esp. a frog, toad, or newt in its aquatic stage and breathing through gills. [ME *taddepolle* (as TOAD, POLL from the size of its head)]

tae·di·um vi·tae /teédeeəm veétī, vítee/ *n.* weariness of life (often as a pathological state, with a tendency to suicide). [L]

tae kwon do /tí kwón dó/ *n.* a Korean martial art similar to karate. [Korean *t'ae* trample + *kwn* fist + –*do* way]

tae·ni·a /teéneeə/ *n.* (also **te·ni·a**) (*pl.* **tae·ni·ae** /–nee-ee/ or **tae·ni·as**) **1** *Archit.* a fillet between a Doric architrave and frieze. **2** *Anat.* any flat ribbonlike structure, esp. the muscles of the colon. **3** any large tapeworm of the genus *Taenia*, esp. *T. saginata* and *T. soleum*, parasitic on humans. **4** *Gk Antiq.* a fillet or headband. □□ **tae·ni·oid** *adj.* [L f. Gk *tainia* ribbon]

taf·fe·ta /táfitə/ *n.* a fine lustrous silk or silklike fabric. [ME f. OF *taffetas* or med.L *taffata*, ult. f. Pers. *tāfta* past part. of *tāftan* twist]

taff·rail /táfrayl, –rəl/ *n. Naut.* a rail around a ship's stern. [earlier *tafferel* f. Du. *taffereel* panel, dimin. of *tafel* (as TABLE): assim. to RAIL[1]]

Taf·fy /táfee/ *n.* (*pl.* **–fies**) *Brit. colloq.* often *offens.* a Welshman. [supposed Welsh pronunc. of *Davy = David* (Welsh *Dafydd*)]

taf·fy /táfee/ *n.* (*pl.* **–fies**) **1** a chewy boiled sugar or molasses candy. **2** insincere flattery. [19th c.: orig. unkn.]

taf·i·a /táfeeə/ *n. W.Ind.* rum distilled from molasses, etc. [18th c.: orig. uncert.]

tag[1] /tag/ *n. & v.* • *n.* **1 a** a label, esp. one for tying on an object to show its address, price, etc. **b** *colloq.* an epithet or popular name serving to identify a person or thing. **c** *sl.* the signature or identifying mark of a graffiti artist. **2** a metal or plastic point at the end of a lace, etc., to assist insertion. **3** a loop at the back of a boot used in pulling it on. **4** a license plate of a motor vehicle. **5** a loose or ragged end of anything. **6** a ragged lock of wool on a sheep. **7** *Theatr.* a closing speech addressed to the audience. **8** a trite quotation or stock phrase. **9 a** the refrain of a song. **b** a musical phrase added to the end of a piece. **10** an animal's tail, or its tip. • *v.tr.* (**tagged**, **tag·ging**) **1** provide with a tag or tags. **2** (often foll. by *on*, *on to*) join or attach. **3** esp. *Brit. colloq.* follow closely or trail behind. **4** *Computing* identify (an item of data) by its type for later retrieval. **5** label radioactively (see LABEL *v.* 3). **6 a** find rhymes for (verses). **b** string (rhymes) together. **7** shear away tags from (sheep). **8** to give a ticket to, as for a traffic or parking violation. □ **tag along** (often foll. by *with*) go along or accompany passively. [ME: orig. unkn.]

tag[2] /tag/ *n. & v.* • *n.* **1** a children's game in which one chases the rest, and anyone who is caught then becomes the pursuer. **2** *Baseball* the act of tagging a runner. • *v.tr.* (**tagged**, **tag·ging**) **1** touch in a game of tag. **2** (often foll. by *out*) put (a runner) out by touching with the ball or with the hand holding the ball. [18th c.: orig. unkn.]

Ta·ga·log /təgaáləg, –lawg/ *n. & adj.* • *n.* **1** a member of the principal people of the Philippine Islands. **2** the language of this people. • *adj.* of or relating to this people or language. [Tagalog f. *taga* native + *ilog* river]

tag end *n.* the last remnant of something.

ta·glia·tel·le /táglyətélee/ *n.* a form of pasta in narrow ribbons. [It.]

Ta·hi·tian /təheéshən/ *n. & adj.* • *n.* **1** a native or inhabitant of Tahiti in the S. Pacific. **2** the language of Tahiti. • *adj.* of or relating to Tahiti or its people or language.

tahr /taar/ *n.* any goatlike mammal of the genus *Hemitragus*, esp. *H. jemlahicus* of the Himalayas. [native name in Nepal]

tah·sil /taaseél/ *n.* an administrative area in parts of India. [Urdu *taḥsīl* f. Arab., = collection]

t'ai chi ch'uan /tí chee chwaán/ *n.* (also **t'ai chi**) a Chinese martial art and system of calisthenics consisting of sequences of very slow controlled movements.

WORD HISTORY   **t'ai chi ch'uan**

Chinese, literally 'great ultimate boxing', from *tái* 'extreme' + *ji* 'limit' + *quán* 'fist, boxing.' In Taoism *t'ai chi* denoted the ultimate point, both source and limit, of the life force; t'ai chi ch'uan, believed to have been developed by a Taoist priest, is intended as a spiritual as well as physical exercise.

Taig /tayg/ *n.* esp. *Brit. & Ir. sl. offens.* (in Northern Ireland) a Protestant name for a Catholic. [var. of *Teague*, Anglicized spelling of the Irish name *Tadhg*, a nickname for an Irishman]

tai·ga /tígə/ *n.* coniferous forest lying between tundra and steppe, esp. in Siberia. [Russ.]

tail¹ /tayl/ *n. & v.* ● *n.* **1** the hindmost part of an animal, esp. when prolonged beyond the rest of the body. **2 a** a thing like a tail in form or position, esp. something extending downwards or outwards at an extremity. **b** the rear end of anything, e.g., of a procession. **c** a long train or line of people, vehicles, etc. **3 a** the rear part of an airplane, with the horizontal stabilizer and rudder, or of a rocket. **b** the rear part of a motor vehicle. **4** the luminous trail of particles following a comet. **5** the inferior or weaker part of anything, esp. in a sequence. **6 a** the part of a shirt below the waist. **b** the hanging part of the back of a coat. **7** (in *pl.*) *colloq.* **a** a tailcoat. **b** evening dress including this. **8** (in *pl.*) the reverse of a coin as a choice when tossing. **9** *colloq.* a person following or shadowing another. **10** an extra strip attached to the lower end of a kite. **11** the stem of a note in music. **12** the part of a letter (e.g., *y*) below the line. **13 a** the exposed end of a slate or tile in a wall. **b** the unexposed end of a brick or stone in a wall. **14** the slender backward prolongation of a butterfly's wing. **15** a comparative calm at the end of a gale. **16** a calm stretch following rough water in a stream. **17 a** the buttocks. **b** *sl. offens.* a (usu. female) sexual partner. ● *v.* **1** *tr.* remove the stalks of (fruit). **2** *tr. &* (foll. by *after*) *intr. colloq.* shadow or follow closely. **3** *tr.* provide with a tail. **4** *tr.* dock the tail of (a lamb, etc.). **5** *tr.* (often foll. by *onto*) join (one thing to another). □ **on a person's tail** closely following a person. **tail back** *Brit.* (of traffic) form a tailback. **tail in** fasten (timber) by one end into a wall, etc. **tail off** (or **away**) **1** become fewer, smaller, or fainter. **2** fall behind or away in a scattered line. **with one's tail between one's legs** in a state of dejection or humiliation. **with one's tail up** in good spirits; cheerful. □□ **tailed** *adj.* (also in *comb.*). **tail·less** *adj.* [OE *tægl, tægel* f. Gmc]

tail² /tayl/ *n. & adj. Law* ● *n.* limitation of ownership, esp. of an estate limited to a person and that person's heirs. ● *adj.* so limited (*estate tail; fee tail*). [ME f. OF *taille* notch, cut, tax, f. *taillier* cut ult. f. L *talea* twig]

tail·back /táylbak/ *n.* **1** *Football* on offense, a player positioned behind the quarterback. **2** *Brit.* a long line of traffic extending back from an obstruction.

tail·board /táylbawrd/ *n. Brit.* = TAILGATE 1.

tail·coat /táylkōt/ *n.* a man's morning or evening coat with a long skirt divided at the back into tails and cut away in front, worn as part of formal dress.

tail cov·ert *n.* any of the feathers covering the base of a bird's tail feathers.

tail end *n.* **1** the hindmost or lowest or last part. **2** (sense 5 of the *n.*).

tail·gate /táylgayt/ *n. & v.* ● *n.* **1 a** a hinged or removable flap at the rear of a station wagon, truck, etc. **b** the tail door of a station wagon or hatchback. **2** the lower end of a canal lock. ● *v. colloq.* **1** *intr.* drive too closely behind another vehicle. **2** *tr.* follow (a vehicle) too closely. □□ **tail·gat·er** *n.*

tail·ing /táyling/ *n.* **1** (in *pl.*) the refuse or inferior part of grain or ore, etc. **2** the part of a beam or projecting brick, etc, embedded in a wall.

tail·light /táyllīt/ *n.* a usu. red light at the rear of a train, motor vehicle, or bicycle.

tai·lor /táylər/ *n. & v.* ● *n.* a maker of clothes, esp. one who makes men's outer garments to measure. ● *v.* **1** *tr.* make (clothes) as a tailor. **2** *tr.* make or adapt for a special purpose. **3** *intr.* work as or be a tailor. **4** *tr.* (esp. as **tailored** *adj.*) make clothes for. **5** *tr.* (as **tailored** *adj.*) = TAILOR-MADE. □□ **tai·lor·ing** *n.* [ME & AF *taillour*, OF *tailleur* cutter, formed as TAIL²]

tai·lored /táylərd/ *adj.* (of clothing) well or closely fitted.

tai·lor-made *adj. & n.* ● *adj.* **1** (of clothing) made to order by a tailor. **2** made or suited for a particular purpose (*a job tailor-made for me*). ● *n.* a tailor-made garment.

tai·lor's chair *n.* a chair without legs for sitting cross-legged like a tailor at work.

tai·lor's twist *n.* a fine strong silk thread used by tailors.

tail·piece /táylpees/ *n.* **1** an appendage at the rear of anything. **2** the final part of a thing. **3** a decoration in a blank space at the end of a chapter, etc., in a book. **4** a piece of wood to which the strings of some musical instruments are attached at their lower ends.

tail·pipe /táylpīp/ *n.* the rear section of the exhaust pipe of a motor vehicle.

tail·plane /táylplayn/ *n. Brit.* = HORIZONTAL STABILIZER.

tail·spin /táylspin/ *n. & v.* ● *n.* **1** a spin (see SPIN *n.* 2) by an aircraft with the tail spiraling. **2** a state of chaos or panic. ● *v.intr.* (**-spin·ning**; *past* and *past part.* **-spun**) perform a tailspin.

tail·stock /táylstok/ *n.* the adjustable part of a lathe holding the fixed spindle.

tail off *n.* a decline or gradual reduction, esp. in demand.

tail skid *n.* a support for the tail of an aircraft when on the ground.

tail wind *n.* a wind blowing in the direction of travel of a vehicle or aircraft, etc.

taint /taynt/ *n. & v.* ● *n.* **1** a spot or trace of decay, infection, or some

bad quality. **2** a corrupt condition or infection. ● *v.* **1** *tr.* affect with a taint. **2** *tr.* (foll. by *with*) affect slightly. **3** *intr.* become tainted. □□ **taint·less** *adj.* [ME, partly f. OF *teint(e)* f. L *tinctus* f. *tingere* dye, partly f. ATTAINT]

tai·pan¹ /típán/ *n.* the head of a foreign business in China. [Chin.]

tai·pan² /típan/ *n.* a large venomous Australian snake, *Oxyuranus scutellatus*. [Aboriginal]

ta·ka·he /taákəhee/ *n.* = NOTORNIS. [Maori]

take /tayk/ *v. & n.* ● *v.* (**took** /tŏŏk/; **tak·en** /táykən/) **1** *tr.* lay hold of; get into one's hands. **2** *tr.* acquire; get possession of; capture, earn, or win. **3** *tr.* get the use of by purchase or formal agreement (*take an apartment*). **4** *tr.* (in a recipe) avail oneself of; use. **5** *tr.* use as a means of transport (*took a taxi*). **6** *tr.* regularly buy or subscribe to (a particular newspaper or periodical, etc.). **7** *tr.* obtain after fulfilling the required conditions (*take a degree*). **8** *tr.* occupy (*take a chair*). **9** *tr.* make use of (*take precautions*). **10** *tr.* consume as food or medicine (*took the pills*). **11** *intr.* **a** be successful or effective (*the inoculation did not take*). **b** (of a plant, seed, etc.) begin to grow. **12** *tr.* **a** require or use up (*will only take a minute; these things take time*). **b** accommodate; have room for (*the elevator takes three people*). **13** *tr.* cause to come or go with one; convey (*take the book home; the bus will take you all the way*). **14** *tr.* **a** remove; dispossess a person of (*someone has taken my pen*). **b** destroy; annihilate (*took her own life*). **c** (often foll. by *for*) *sl.* defraud; swindle. **15** *tr.* catch or be infected with (fire or fever, etc.). **16** *tr.* **a** experience or be affected by (*take fright; take pleasure*). **b** give play to (*take comfort*). **c** exert (*take courage; take no notice*). **d** exact; get (*take revenge*). **17** *tr.* find out and note (a name and address; a person's temperature, etc.) by inquiry or measurement. **18** *tr.* grasp mentally; understand (*I take your point; I took you to mean yes*). **19** *tr.* treat or regard in a specified way (*took the news calmly; took it badly*). **20** *tr* (foll. by *for* or *to be*) regard as being (*do you take me for an idiot?*). **21** *tr.* **a** accept (*take the offer*). **b** submit to (*take a joke; take no nonsense; took a risk*). **22** *tr.* choose or assume (*took a different view; took a job; took the initiative; took responsibility*). **23** *tr.* derive (*takes its name from the inventor*). **24** *tr.* (foll. by *from*) subtract (*take 3 from 9*). **25** *tr.* execute, make, or undertake; perform or effect (*take notes; take an oath; take a decision; take a look*). **26** *tr.* occupy or engage oneself in; indulge in; enjoy (*take a rest; take exercise; take a vacation*). **27** *tr.* conduct (*took the early class*). **28** *tr.* deal with in a certain way (*took the corner too fast*). **29** *tr.* **a** teach or be taught (a subject). **b** be examined in (a subject). **30** *tr.* make (a photograph) with a camera; photograph (a person or thing). **31** *tr.* use as an instance (*let us take Napoleon*). **32** *tr. Gram.* have or require as part of the appropriate construction (*this verb takes an object*). **33** *tr.* have sexual intercourse with (a woman). **34** *tr.* (in *passive*; foll. by *by*, *with*) be attracted or charmed by. **35** *tr. Baseball* to refrain from swinging at (a pitch). ● *n.* **1** an amount taken or caught in one session or attempt, etc. **2** a scene or sequence of film or videotape photographed continuously at one time. **3** money received by a business, esp. money received at a theater for seats. **4** *Printing* the amount of copy set up at one time. **5** a visible or emotional reaction, as to a surprise, etc. □ **be taken ill** become ill, esp. suddenly. **have what it takes** *colloq.* have the necessary qualities, etc., for success. **on the take** *sl.* accepting bribes. **take account of** see ACCOUNT. **take action** see ACTION. **take advantage of** see ADVANTAGE. **take advice** see ADVICE. **take after** resemble (esp. a parent or ancestor). **take against** *Brit.* begin to dislike, esp. impulsively. **take aim** see AIM. **take apart 1** dismantle. **2** *colloq.* beat or defeat. **take aside** see ASIDE. **take as read** esp. *Brit.* accept without reading or discussing. **take away 1** remove or carry elsewhere. **2** subtract. **3** *Brit.* buy (food, etc.) at a store or restaurant for eating elsewhere. **take back 1** retract (a statement). **2** convey (a person or thing) to his or her or its original position. **3** carry (a person) in thought to a past time. **4** *Printing* transfer to the previous line. **take a bath** *sl.* lose money. **take a bow** see BOW². **take the cake** *colloq.* be the most remarkable. **take care of** see CARE. **take a chance**, etc., see CHANCE. **take down 1** write down (spoken words). **2** remove (a structure) by separating it into pieces. **3** humiliate. **take effect** see EFFECT. **take five** (or **ten**) take a break, esp. from work. **take for granted** see GRANT. **take fright** see FRIGHT. **take from** diminish; weaken; detract from. **take heart** be encouraged. **take the heat** endure criticism, punishment, etc. **take hold** see HOLD¹. **take home** earn. **take ill** (or **sick**) *colloq.* be taken ill. **take in 1** accept as a boarder, etc. **2** undertake (work) at home. **3** make (a garment, etc.) smaller. **4** understand (*did you take that in?*). **5** cheat (*managed to take them all in*). **6** include or comprise. **7** *colloq.* visit (a place) on the way to another (*shall we take in the White House*). **8** furl (a sail). **9** regularly buy (a newspaper, etc.). **10** attend; watch (*take in a show*). **11** arrest. **take in hand 1** undertake; start doing or dealing with. **2** undertake the control or reform of (a person). **take into account** see ACCOUNT. **take it 1** (often foll. by *that* + clause) assume (*I take it that you have finished*). **2** see TAKE *v.* 19. **take it**

easy see EASY. **take it from me** (or **take my word for it**) I can assure you. **take it ill** resent it. **take it into one's head** see HEAD. **take it on one** (or **oneself**) (foll. by *to* + infin.) venture or presume. **take it or leave it** (esp. in *imper.*) an expression of indifference or impatience about another's decision after making an offer. **take it out of 1** exhaust the strength of. **2** penalize. **take it out on** relieve one's frustration by attacking or treating harshly. **take one's leave of** see LEAVE². **take a lot of** (or **some**) **doing** be hard to do. **take a person's name in vain** see VAIN. **take off 1 a** remove (clothing) from one's or another's body. **b** remove or lead away. **2** deduct (part of an amount). **3** depart, esp. hastily (*took off in a fast car*). **4** *colloq.* mimic humorously. **5** jump from the ground. **6** become airborne. **7** (of a scheme, enterprise, etc.) become successful or popular. **8** have (a period) away from work. **take oneself off** go away. **take on 1** undertake (work, a responsibility, etc.). **2** engage (an employee). **3** be willing or ready to meet (an adversary in a sport, an argument, etc., esp. a stronger one). **4** acquire (a new meaning, etc.). **5** esp. *Brit. colloq.* show strong emotion. **take orders** see ORDER. **take out 1** remove from within a place; extract. **2** escort on an outing. **3** get (a license or summons, etc.) issued. **4** buy (food) at a store, restaurant, etc., for eating elsewhere. **5** *Bridge* remove (a partner or a partner's call) from a suit by bidding a different one or no trumps. **6** murder or destroy. **take a person out of himself** (or **herself**) make a person forget his (or her) worries. **take over 1** succeed to the management or ownership of. **2** take control. **3** *Printing* transfer to the next line. **take part** see PART. **take place** see PLACE. **take a person's point** see POINT. **take shape** assume a distinct form; develop into something definite. **take sides** see SIDE. **take stock** see STOCK. **take the sun** see SUN. **take that!** an exclamation accompanying a blow, etc. **take one's time** not hurry. **take to 1** begin or fall into the habit of (*took to drink*). **2** have recourse to. **3** adapt oneself to. **4** form a liking for. **5** make for (*took to the hills*). **take to heart** see HEART. **take to one's heels** see HEEL¹. **take to pieces** see PIECE. **take the trouble** see TROUBLE. **take up 1** become interested or engaged in (a pursuit, a cause, etc.). **2** adopt as a protégé. **3** occupy (time or space). **4** begin (residence, etc.). **5** resume after an interruption. **6** interrupt or question (a speaker). **7** accept (an offer, etc.). **8** shorten (a garment). **9** lift up. **10** absorb (*sponges take up water*). **11** take (a person) into a vehicle. **12** pursue (a matter, etc.) further. **take a person up on** accept (a person's offer, etc.). **take up with** begin to associate with. □□ **tak‧a‧ble** *adj.* (also **take‧a‧ble**). [OE *tacan* f. ON *taka*]

▶See note at BRING.

take-a‧way *adj. & n. Brit. attrib.adj.* = TAKE-OUT. ●*n. Brit.* **1** an establishment selling take-out food. **2** the food itself.

take-home pay *n.* the pay received by an employee after the deduction of taxes, etc.

take-in *n.* a deception.

take‧off /táykawf/ *n.* **1** the act of becoming airborne. **2** *colloq.* an act of mimicking. **3** a place from which one jumps.

take-out *adj. & n.* ●*adj.* (of food) bought at a shop or restaurant for eating elsewhere. ●*n.* food sold for consumption elsewhere.

take‧o‧ver /táykōvər/ *n.* the assumption of control (esp. of a business); the buying out of one company by another.

tak‧er /táykər/ *n.* **1** a person who takes a bet. **2** a person who accepts an offer.

ta‧kin /táakin/ *n.* a large Tibetan horned ruminant, *Budorcas taxicolor.* [Mishmi]

tak‧ing /táyking/ *adj. & n.* ●*adj.* **1** attractive or captivating. **2** *archaic* catching or infectious. ●*n.* (in *pl.*) esp. *Brit.* an amount of money taken in business. □□ **tak‧ing‧ly** *adv.* **tak‧ing‧ness** *n.*

ta‧la /táalə/ *n.* any of the traditional rhythmic patterns of Indian music. [Skr.]

ta‧lar‧i‧a /təláireeə/ *n.pl.* (in Roman mythology) winged sandals as an attribute of Mercury, Iris, and others. [L, neut. pl. of *talaris* f. *talus* ankle]

talc /talk/ *n. & v.* ●*n.* **1** talcum powder. **2** any crystalline form of magnesium silicate that occurs in soft flat plates, usu. white or pale green in color and used as a lubricant, etc. ●*v.tr.* (**talcked, talck‧ing**) treat (a surface) with talc to lubricate or dry it. □□ **talc‧ose** *adj.* **talc‧ous** *adj.* **talc‧y** *adj.* (in sense 1). [F *talc* or med.L *talcum*, f. Arab. *ṭalk* f. Pers. *ṭalk*]

tal‧cum /tálkəm/ *n.* **1** = TALC. **2** (in full **talcum powder**) powdered talc for toilet and cosmetic use, usu. perfumed. [med.L: see TALC]

tale /tayl/ *n.* **1** a narrative or story, esp. fictitious and imaginatively treated. **2** a report of an alleged fact, often malicious or in breach of confidence (*all sorts of tales will get about*). **3** a lie; a falsehood. **4** *archaic* or *literary* a number or total (*the tale is complete*). [OE *talu* f. Gmc: cf. TELL¹]

tale‧bear‧er /táylbairər/ *n.* a person who maliciously gossips or reveals secrets. □□ **tale‧bear‧ing** *n. & adj.*

tal‧ent /tálənt/ *n.* **1** a special aptitude or faculty (*a talent for music; has real talent*). **2** high mental ability. **3** a person or persons of talent (*is a real talent; plenty of local talent*). **4** an ancient weight and

unit of currency, esp. among the Greeks. □□ **tal‧ent‧ed** *adj.* **tal‧ent‧less** *adj.* [OE *talente* & OF *talent* f. L *talentum* inclination of mind f. Gk *talanton* balance, weight, sum of money]

tal‧ent scout *n.* (also *Brit.* **tal‧ent spot‧ter**) a person looking for talented performers, esp. in sports and entertainment.

tale of a tub *n.* an idle fiction.

tales /taylz, táyleez/ *n. Law* **1** a writ for summoning jurors when a panel is deficient. **2** a list of persons who may be summoned. [ME f. L *tales* (*de circumstantibus*) such (of the bystanders), the first words of the writ]

tales‧man /taylzmən, táyleez-/ *n.* (*pl.* **−men**) *Law* a person summoned by a tales.

tale‧tell‧er /táyltelər/ *n.* **1** a person who tells stories. **2** a person who spreads malicious reports.

ta‧li *pl.* of TALUS¹.

tal‧i‧on /táleeən/ *n.* = LEX TALIONIS. [ME f. OF f. L *talio −onis* f. *talis* such]

tal‧i‧pes /tálipeez/ *n. Med.* = CLUBFOOT. [mod.L f. L *talus* ankle + *pes* foot]

tal‧i‧pot /tálipot/ *n.* a tall S. Indian palm, *Corypha umbraculifera*, with very large fan-shaped leaves that are used as sunshades, etc. [Malayalam *tālipat*, Hindi *tālpāt* f. Skr. *tālapattra* f. *tāla* palm + *pattra* leaf]

tal‧is‧man /tálizmən/ *n.* (*pl.* **tal‧is‧mans**) **1** an object, esp. an inscribed ring or stone, supposed to be endowed with magic powers esp. of averting evil from or bringing good luck to its holder. **2** a charm or amulet; a thing supposed to be capable of working wonders. □□ **tal‧is‧man‧ic** /−mánik/ *adj.* [F & Sp., = It. *talismano*, f. med.Gk *telesmon*, Gk *telesma* completion, religious rite f. *teleō* complete f. *telos* end]

talk /tawk/ *v. & n.* ●*v.* **1** *intr.* (often foll. by *to, with*) converse or communicate ideas by spoken words. **2** *intr.* have the power of speech. **3** *intr.* (foll. by *about*) **a** have as the subject of discussion. **b** (in *imper.*) *colloq.* as an emphatic statement (*talk about expense! It cost me $50*). **4** *tr.* express or utter in words; discuss (*you are talking nonsense; talked football all day*). **5** *tr.* use (a language) in speech (*is talking Spanish*). **6** *intr.* (foll. by *at*) address pompously. **7** *tr.* (usu. foll. by *into, out of*) bring into a specified condition, etc., by talking (*talked himself hoarse; how did you talk them into it?; talked them out of the difficulty*). **8** *intr.* reveal (esp. secret) information; betray secrets. **9** *intr.* gossip (*people are beginning to talk*). **10** *intr.* have influence (*money talks*). **11** *intr.* communicate by radio. ●*n.* **1** conversation or talking. **2** a particular mode of speech (*baby talk*). **3** an informal address or lecture. **4** a rumor or gossip (*there is talk of a merger*). **b** its theme (*their success was the talk of the town*). **c** empty words; verbiage (*mere talk*). **5** (often in *pl.*) extended discussions or negotiations. □ **know what one is talking about** be expert or authoritative. **now you're talking** *colloq.* I like what you say, suggest, etc. **talk away 1** consume (time) in talking. **2** carry on talking (*talk away! I'm listening*). **talk back 1** reply defiantly. **2** respond on a two-way radio transmission. **talk big** *colloq.* talk boastfully. **talk down** denigrate; belittle. **talk down to** speak patronizingly or condescendingly to. **talk a person down 1** silence a person by greater loudness or persistence. **2** bring (a pilot or aircraft) to landing by radio instructions from the ground. **talk of 1** discuss or mention. **2** (often foll. by verbal noun) express some intention of (*talked of moving to Dallas*). **talk of the town** what is being talked about generally. **talk out** *Brit.* block the course of (a bill in Parliament) by prolonging discussion to the time of adjournment. **talk over** discuss at length. **talk a person over** (or **around**) gain agreement or compliance from a person by talking. **talk shop** talk, esp. tediously or inopportunely, about one's occupation, business, etc. **talk tall** boast. **talk through one's hat** (or *Brit.* **neck**) *colloq.* **1** exaggerate. **2** bluff. **3** talk wildly or nonsensically. **talk to** reprove or scold (a person). **talk to oneself** soliloquize. **talk turkey** see TURKEY. **talk up** discuss (a subject) in order to arouse interest in it. **you can't** (or **can** or **should**) **talk** *colloq.* a reproof that the person addressed is just as culpable, etc., in the matter at issue. □□ **talk‧er** *n.* [ME *talken* frequent. verb f. TALE or TELL¹]

talk‧a‧thon /táwkəthon/ *n. colloq.* a prolonged session of talking or discussion. [TALK + MARATHON]

talk‧a‧tive /táwkətiv/ *adj.* fond of or given to talking. □□ **talk‧a‧tive‧ly** *adv.* **talk‧a‧tive‧ness** *n.*

talk‧back /táwkbak/ *n.* (often *attrib.*) a system of two-way communication by loudspeaker.

talk‧ie /táwkee/ *n.* esp. *hist.* a movie with a soundtrack, as distinct from a silent movie. [TALK + −IE, after *movie*]

talk‧ing /táwking/ *adj. & n.* ●*adj.* **1** that talks. **2** having the power of speech (*a talking parrot*). **3** expressive (*talking eyes*). ●*n.* in senses of TALK *v.*

talk‧ing book *n.* a recorded reading of a book, esp. for the blind.

talk‧ing head *n. colloq.* a commentator, etc., on television, speaking to the camera and viewed in close-up.

talk‧ing point *n.* a topic for discussion or argument.

talk‧ing-to *n. colloq.* a reproof or reprimand (*gave them a good talking-to*).

talk show *n.* a television or radio program featuring discussion of topical issues.

tall /tawl/ *adj. & adv.* • *adj.* **1** of more than average height. **2** of a specified height (*looks about six feet tall*). **3** higher than the surrounding objects (*a tall building*). **4** *colloq.* extravagant or excessive (*a tall story; tall talk*). • *adv.* as if tall; proudly; in a tall or extravagant way (*sit tall*). □□ **tall·ish** *adj.* **tall·ness** *n.* [ME, repr. OE *getæl* swift, prompt]

tal·lage /tálij/ *n. hist.* **1** a form of taxation on towns, etc., abolished in the 14th c. **2** a tax on feudal dependants, etc. [ME f. OF *taillage* f. *tailler* cut: see TAIL[2]]

tall·boy /táwlboy/ *n.* a tall chest of drawers sometimes in lower and upper sections or mounted on legs.

tall drink *n.* a drink served in a tall glass.

tall hat *n.* = TOP HAT.

tal·lith /táalis, taaleét/ *n.* a scarf worn by Jewish men esp. at prayer. [Rabbinical Heb. *ṭallīt* f. *ṭ illel* to cover]

tall or·der *n.* an exorbitant or unreasonable demand.

tall ship *n.* a sailing ship with more than one high mast.

tal·low /tálō/ *n. & v.* • *n.* the harder kinds of (esp. animal) fat melted down for use in making candles, soap, etc. • *v.tr.* grease with tallow. □□ **tal·low·ish** *adj.* **tal·low·y** *adj.* [ME *talg, talug*, f. MLG *talg, talch*, of unkn. orig.]

tal·low tree *n.* any of various trees, esp. *Sapium sebiferum* of China, yielding vegetable tallow.

tal·ly /tálee/ *n. & v.* • *n.* (*pl.* **-lies**) **1** the reckoning of a debt or score. **2** a total score or amount. **3 a** a mark registering a fixed number of objects delivered or received. **b** such a number as a unit. **4** *hist.* **a** a piece of wood scored across with notches for the items of an account and then split into halves, each party keeping one. **b** an account kept in this way. **5** a ticket or label for identification. **6** a corresponding thing, counterpart, or duplicate. • *v.* (**-lies, -lied**) (often foll. by *with*) **1** *intr.* agree or correspond. **2** *tr.* record or reckon by tally. □□ **tal·li·er** *n.* [ME f. AF *tallie*, AL *tallia, talia* f. L *talea*: cf. TAIL[2]]

tal·ly·ho /táleehó/ *int., n., & v.* • *int.* a huntsman's cry to the hounds on sighting a fox. • *n.* (*pl.* **-hos**) an utterance of this. • *v.* (**-hoes, -hoed**) **1** *intr.* utter a cry of "tallyho." **2** *tr.* indicate (a fox) or urge (hounds) with this cry. [cf. F *taïaut*]

tal·ly·man /táleemən/ *n.* (*pl.* **-men**) **1** a person who keeps a tally. **2** *Brit.* a person who sells goods on credit, esp. from door to door.

Tal·mud /táalmŏod, -məd, tál-/ *n.* the body of Jewish civil and ceremonial law and legend comprising the Mishnah and the Gemara. □□ **Tal·mud·ic** /-mŏodik, myŏo-/ *adj.* **Tal·mud·ist** *n.* [late Heb. *talmûd* instruction f. Heb. *lāma d* learn]

tal·on /tálən/ *n.* **1** a claw, esp. of a bird of prey. **2** the cards left after the deal in a card game. **3** the shoulder of a bolt against which the key presses in shooting it in a lock. **4** an ogee molding. □□ **tal·oned** *adj.* (also in *comb.*). [ME f. OF, = heel, ult. f. L *talus*: see TALUS[1]]

ta·lus[1] /táyləs, tál-/ *n.* (*pl.* **ta·li** /-lī/) *Anat.* the ankle bone supporting the tibia. Also called **astragalus**. [L, = ankle, heel]

ta·lus[2] /táyləs/ *n.* (*pl.* **ta·lus·es**) **1** the slope of a wall that tapers to the top or rests against a bank. **2** *Geol.* a sloping mass of fragments at the foot of a cliff. [F: orig. unkn.]

tam /tam/ *n.* a tam-o'-shanter. [abbr.]

tam·a·ble /táyməbəl/ *adj.* capable of being tamed. □□ **tam·a·bil·i·ty** /-bílitee/ *n.* **tam·a·ble·ness** *n.*

ta·ma·le /təmáalee/ *n.* a Mexican food of seasoned meat and corn flour steamed or baked in corn husks. [Mex. Sp. *tamal*, pl. *tamales*]

ta·man·du·a /təmándyŏoə/ *n.* any small Central and S. American arboreal anteater of the genus *Tamandua*, with a prehensile tail used in climbing. [Port. f. Tupi *tamanduà*]

tam·a·rack /támərak/ *n.* **1** an American larch, *Larix laricina*. **2** the wood from this. [f. Native Amer. lang.]

ta·ma·ril·lo /támərílo, -réeyō/ *n.* (*pl.* **-los**) a South American shrub, *Cyphomandra betacea*, with egg-shaped red fruit. [arbitrary marketing name: cf. Sp. *tomatillo* dimin. of *tomate* TOMATO]

tam·a·rin /támərin/ *n.* any S. American usu. insectivorous monkey of the genus *Saguinus*, having hairy crests and mustaches. [F f. Carib]

tam·a·rind /támərind/ *n.* **1** a tropical evergreen tree, *Tamarindus indica*. **2** the fruit of this, containing an acid pulp used as food and in making drinks. [med.L *tamarindus* f. Arab. *tamr-hindī* Indian date]

tam·a·risk /támərisk/ *n.* any shrub of the genus *Tamarix*, usu. with long slender branches and small pink or white flowers, that thrives by the sea. [ME f. LL *tamariscus*, L *tamarix*]

tam·bour /támbŏor/ *n. & v.* • *n.* **1** a drum. **2 a** a circular frame for holding fabric taut while it is being embroidered. **b** material embroidered in this way. **3** *Archit.* each of a sequence of cylindrical stones forming the shaft of a column. **4** *Archit.* the circular part of various structures. **5** *Archit.* a lobby with a ceiling and folding doors in a church porch, etc., to obviate drafts. **6** a sloping buttress or projection in some court games. **7** a rolling top or front for a desk, etc., made of strips of wood glued to a canvas backing. • *v.tr.* (also *absol.*) decorate or embroider on a tambour. [F f. *tabor* TABOR]

tam·bou·ra /tambŏorə/ *n. Mus.* an E. Indian stringed instrument used as a drone. [Arab. *ṭanbūra*]

tam·bou·rin /támbərin/ *n.* **1** a long narrow drum used in the Provence region of France. **2 a** a dance accompanied by a tambourin. **b** the music for this. [F, dimin. of TAMBOUR]

tam·bou·rine /támbəréen/ *n.* a percussion instrument consisting of a hoop with a parchment stretched over one side and jingling disks in slots around the hoop. □□ **tam·bou·rin·ist** *n.* [F, dimin. of TAMBOUR]

tame /taym/ *adj. & v.* • *adj.* **1** (of an animal) domesticated; not wild or shy. **2** insipid; lacking spirit or interest; dull (*tame acquiescence*). **3** (of a person) amenable and available. **4 a** (of land) cultivated. **b** (of a plant) produced by cultivation. • *v.tr.* **1** make tame; domesticate; break in. **2** subdue; curb; humble; break the spirit of. □□ **tame·ly** *adv.* **tame·ness** *n.* **tam·er** *n.* (also in *comb.*). [OE *tam* f. Gmc]

tambourine

tame·a·ble var. of TAMABLE.

Tam·il /támil, túm-, taá-/ *n. & adj.* • *n.* **1** a member of a Dravidian people inhabiting South India and Sri Lanka. **2** the language of this people. • *adj.* of this people or their language. □□ **Ta·mil·ian** /-míleeən/ *adj.* [native name *Tamiḷ*, rel. to DRAVIDIAN]

Tam·ma·ny /támənee/ *n.* (also **Tam·ma·ny Hall**) **1** a corrupt political organization or group. **2** corrupt political activities. □□ **Tam·ma·ny·ism** *n.* [orig. the name of a benevolent society in New York with headquarters at Tammany Hall, which later became the headquarters of the Democratic Party in New York]

tam·my /támee/ *n.* (*pl.* **-mies**) = TAM-O'-SHANTER.

tam-o'-shan·ter /táməshántər/ *n.* a round woolen or cloth cap of Scottish origin fitting closely round the brows but large and full above. [the hero of Burns's *Tam o' Shanter*]

tamp /tamp/ *v.tr.* **1** ram down (concrete, pipe tobacco, etc.). **2** pack (a detonation hole) full of clay, etc., to get the full force of an explosion. □□ **tam·per** *n.* **tamp·ing** *n.* (in sense 1). [perh. back-form. f. F *tampin* (var. of TAMPION, taken as = *tamping*]

tam·per /támpər/ *v.intr.* (foll. by *with*) **1** meddle with or make unauthorized changes in. **2** exert a secret or corrupt influence upon; bribe. □□ **tam·per·er** *n.*

tam o'shanter

tam·per·proof *adj.* (var. of TEMPER.)

tam·pi·on /támpeeən/ *n.* (also **tom·pi·on** /tóm-/) **1** a wooden stopper for the muzzle of a gun. **2** a plug, e.g., for the top of an organ pipe. [ME f. F *tampon*, nasalized var. of *tapon*, rel. to TAP[1]]

tam·pon /támpon/ *n. & v.* • *n.* a plug of soft material used to absorb fluid, esp. one inserted into the vagina during menstruation. • *v.tr.* (**tam·poned, tam·pon·ing**) plug with a tampon. [F: see TAMPION]

tam-tam /támtam/ *n.* a large metal gong. [Hindi: see TOM-TOM]

tan[1] /tan/ *n., adj., & v.* • *n.* **1** a brown skin color resulting from exposure to ultraviolet light. **2** a yellowish-brown color. **3** = TANBARK. **4** (in full **spent tan**) tan from which the tannic acid has been extracted, used for covering roads, etc. • *adj.* yellowish-brown. • *v.* (**tanned, tan·ning**) **1** *tr. & intr.* make or become brown by exposure to ultraviolet light. **2** *tr.* convert (raw hide) into leather by soaking in a liquid containing tannic acid or by the use of mineral salts, etc. **3** *tr. sl.* beat; whip. □□ **tan·na·ble** *adj.* **tan·ning** *n.* **tan·nish** *adj.* [OE *tannian*, prob. f. med.L *tanare, tannare*, perh. f. Celtic]

tan[2] /tan/ *abbr.* tangent.

tan·a·ger /tánəjər/ *n.* any small American bird of the subfamily Thraupidae, the male usu. having brightly-colored plumage. [mod.L *tanagra* f. Tupi *tangara*]

tan·bark /tánbaark/ n. 1 the bark of oak and other trees, used to obtain tannin. 2 bark, esp. of oak, bruised and used to tan hides.

tan·dem /tándəm/ n. & adv. • n. 1 a bicycle or tricycle with two or more seats one behind another. 2 a a group of two persons or machines, etc., with one behind or following the other. b (in full **tandem trailer**) a truck hauling two or more trailers. 3 a carriage driven tandem. • adv. with two or more horses harnessed one behind another (*drive tandem*). □ **in tandem** one behind another. [L, = at length (of time), used punningly]

tan·door /tándoor/ n. a clay oven. [Hind.]

tan·door·i /tandóoree/ n. food cooked over charcoal in a tandoor (often *attrib.*: *tandoori chicken*). [Hind.]

Tang /tang/ n. 1 a dynasty ruling China 618–c. 906. (*attrib.*) designating art and artifacts of this period. [Chin. *táng*]

tang[1] /tang/ n. 1 a strong taste or flavor or smell. 2 a a characteristic quality. b a trace; a slight hint of some quality, ingredient, etc. 3 the projection on the blade of a tool, esp. a knife, by which the blade is held firm in the handle. [ME f. ON *tange* point, tang of a knife]

tang[2] /tang/ v. & n. • v.tr. & intr. ring, clang; sound loudly. • n. a tanging sound. [imit.]

tan·ge·lo /tánjəlō/ n. (*pl.* **-los**) a hybrid of the tangerine and grapefruit. [TANGERINE + POMELO]

tan·gent /tánjənt/ n. & adj. • n. 1 a straight line, curve, or surface that meets another curve or curved surface at a point, but if extended does not intersect it at that point. 2 the ratio of the sides opposite and adjacent to an angle in a right-angled triangle. • adj. 1 (of a line or surface) that is a tangent. 2 touching. □ **on a tangent** diverging from a previous course of action or thought, etc. (*go off on a tangent*). □□ **tan·gen·cy** n. [L *tangere tangent-* touch]

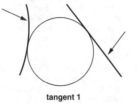

tangent 1

tan·gent gal·va·nom·e·ter n. a galvanometer with a coil through which the current to be measured is passed, its strength being proportional to the tangent of the angle of deflection.

tan·gen·tial /tanjénshəl/ adj. 1 of or along a tangent. 2 divergent. 3 peripheral. □□ **tan·gen·tial·ly** adv.

tan·ge·rine /tánjəreen/ n. 1 a small sweet orange-colored citrus fruit with a thin skin; a mandarin. 2 a deep orange-yellow color. [*Tangier* in Morocco]

tan·gi·ble /tánjəbəl/ adj. 1 perceptible by touch. 2 definite; clearly intelligible; not elusive or visionary (*tangible proof*). □□ **tan·gi·bil·i·ty** n. **tan·gi·ble·ness** n. **tan·gi·bly** adv. [F *tangible* or LL *tangibilis* f. *tangere* touch]

SYNONYM TIP tangible

APPRECIABLE, CORPOREAL, PALPABLE, PERCEPTIBLE, SENSIBLE. Anything that can be grasped, either with the hand or the mind, is **tangible** (*tangible assets, tangible objects*). **Palpable**, like *tangible*, means capable of being touched or felt (*a palpable mist*), but it is often applied to whatever evokes a tactile response from the body (*a palpable chill in the room*). **Perceptible** is used to describe something that just crosses the border between invisibility and visibility or some other sense barrier (*a perceptible change in her tone of voice, a perceptible odor of garlic*). **Sensible** means that which can clearly be perceived through the senses or which makes a strong impression on the mind through the medium of sensations. In contrast to *perceptible*, something that is *sensible* is more obvious or immediately recognized (*a sensible shift in the tenor of the conversation*). **Corporeal** means *tangible* or *material*, in contrast to things that are immaterial or spiritual (*corporeal goods*). Something that is **appreciable** is large enough to be measured, weighed, valued, estimated, or considered significant. An *appreciable* change in temperature, for example, can be determined by looking at a thermometer; a *palpable* change in temperature may be slight, but still great enough to be felt; and a *perceptible* change in temperature might be so slight that it almost—but not quite—escapes notice.

---

tan·gle[1] /tánggəl/ v. & n. • v. 1 a tr. intertwine (threads or hairs, etc.) in a confused mass; entangle. b intr. become tangled. 2 intr. (foll. by *with*) colloq. become involved (esp. in conflict or argument) with (*don't tangle with me*). 3 tr. complicate (*a tangled affair*). • n. 1 a confused mass of intertwined threads, etc. 2 a confused or complicated state (*be in a tangle; a love tangle*). [ME var. of obs. *tagle* of uncert. orig.]

tan·gle[2] /tánggəl/ n. any of various seaweeds, esp. of the genus *Laminaria* or *Fucus*. [prob. f. Norw. *taangel* f. ON *thöngull*]

tan·gly /tángglee/ adj. (**tan·gli·er, tan·gli·est**) tangled.

tan·go /tánggō/ n. & v. • n. (*pl.* **-gos**) 1 a slow S. American ballroom

---

dance. 2 the music for this. • v.intr. (**-goes, -goed**) dance the tango. [Amer. Sp.]

tan·gram /tánggram/ n. a Chinese puzzle square cut into seven pieces to be combined into various figures. [19th c.: orig. unkn.]

tang·y /tángee/ adj. (**tang·i·er, tang·i·est**) having a strong usu. spicy tang. □□ **tang·i·ness** n.

tanh /tansh, tanáych/ abbr. hyperbolic tangent.

tan·ist /tánist/ n. hist. the heir apparent to a Celtic chief, usu. his most vigorous adult relation, chosen by election. □□ **tan·ist·ry** n. [Ir. & Gael. *tánaiste* heir]

tank /tangk/ n. & v. • n. 1 a large receptacle or storage chamber usu. for liquid or gas. 2 a heavy armored fighting vehicle carrying guns and moving on a tracked carriage. 3 a container for the fuel supply in a motor vehicle. 4 the part of a locomotive tender containing water for the boiler. 5 a reservoir. 6 colloq. a prison cell or holding cell. 7 = TANK TOP. • v. (usu. foll. by *up*) 1 tr. store or place in a tank. 2 tr. fill the tank of (a vehicle, etc.) with fuel. 3 intr. & colloq. tr. (in *passive*) drink heavily; become drunk. □□ **tank·ful** n. (*pl.* **-fuls**). **tank·less** adj. [Gujurati *tānkh*, etc., perh. f. Skr. *tadāga* pond]

tank 2

tan·ka /tángkə/ n. a Japanese poem in five lines and thirty-one syllables giving a complete picture of an event or mood. [Jap.]

tank·age /tángkij/ n. 1 a storage in tanks. b a charge made for this. 2 the cubic content of a tank. 3 a kind of fertilizer obtained from animal bones, offal, etc.

tan·kard /tángkərd/ n. 1 a tall mug with a handle and sometimes a hinged lid, esp. of silver or pewter for beer. 2 the contents of or an amount held by a tankard (*drank a tankard of ale*). [ME: orig. unkn.: cf. MDu. *tanckaert*]

tank en·gine n. a train engine carrying fuel and water receptacles in its own frame, not in a tender.

tank·er /tángkər/ n. a ship, aircraft, or truck for carrying liquids or gases in bulk.

tank farm n. a tract of land with several large storage tanks.

tank farm·ing n. = HYDROPONICS.

tank top n. a sleeveless, close-fitting, collarless upper garment.

tan·ner[1] /tánər/ n. a person who tans hides.

tan·ner[2] /tánər/ n. Brit. hist. sl. a sixpence. [19th c.: orig. unkn.]

tan·ner·y /tánəree/ n. (*pl.* **-ies**) a place where hides are tanned.

tan·nic /tánik/ adj. 1 of or produced from tan. 2 (of wine) astringent; tasting of tannin. □□ **tan·nate** /-nayt/ n. [F *tannique* (as TANNIN)]

tan·nic ac·id n. a complex natural organic compound of a yellowish color used as a mordant and astringent.

tan·nin /tánin/ n. any of a group of complex organic compounds found in certain tree barks and oak galls, used in leather production and ink manufacture. [F *tanin* (as TAN[1], -IN)]

tan·nish see TAN[1].

tan·rec var. of TENREC.

tan·sy /tánzee/ n. (*pl.* **-sies**) any plant of the genus *Tanacetum*, esp. *T. vulgare* with yellow buttonlike flowers and aromatic leaves, formerly used in medicines and cooking. [ME f. OF *tanesie* f. med.L *athanasia* immortality f. Gk]

tan·ta·lite /tántəlīt/ n. a rare dense black mineral, the principal source of the element tantalum. [G & Sw. *tantalit* (as TANTALUM)]

tan·ta·lize /tántəlīz/ v.tr. 1 torment or tease by the sight or promise of what is unobtainable. 2 raise and then dash the hopes of; torment with disappointment. □□ **tan·ta·li·za·tion** n. **tan·ta·liz·er** n. **tan·ta·liz·ing·ly** adv. [Gk *Tantalos* mythical king of Phrygia condemned to stand in water that receded when he tried to drink it and under branches that drew back when he tried to pick the fruit]

tan·ta·lum /tántələm/ n. Chem. a rare hard white metallic element occurring naturally in tantalite, resistant to heat and the action of acids, and used in surgery and for electronic components. ¶ Symb.: **Ta**. □□ **tan·tal·ic** /-tálik/ adj. [formed as TANTALUS with ref. to its non-absorbent quality]

tan·ta·lus /tántələs/ n. 1 Brit. a stand in which liquor decanters may be locked up but visible. 2 a wood ibis, *Mycteria americana*. [see TANTALIZE]

tan·ta·mount /tántəmownt/ predic. adj. (foll. by *to*) equivalent to (*was tantamount to a denial*). [f. obs. verb f. It. *tanto montare* amount to so much]

tan·tiv·y /tantívee/ n. & adj. archaic • n. (*pl.* **-ies**) 1 a hunting cry. 2 a swift movement; a gallop or rush. • adj. swift. [17th c.: perh. an imit. of hoofbeats]

tant mieux /taaN myö/ int. so much the better. [F]

tant pis /taaN pee/ int. so much the worse. [F]

tan·tra /tántrə, tún-/ n. any of a class of Hindu or Buddhist mystical and magical writings. □□ **tan•tric** *adj.* **tan•trism** *n.* **tan•trist** *n.* [Skr., = loom, groundwork, doctrine f. *tan* stretch]

tan•trum /tántrəm/ *n.* an outburst of bad temper or petulance (*threw a tantrum*). [18th c.: orig. unkn.]

Taoi•seach /téeshəkh/ *n.* the Prime Minister of the Irish Republic. [Ir., = chief, leader]

Tao•ism /tówizəm, dów–/ *n.* a Chinese philosophy based on the writings of Lao-tzu (*c.*500 BC), advocating humility and religious piety. □□ **Tao•ist** /–ist/ *n.* **Tao•is•tic** /–ístik/ *adj.* [Chin. *dao* (right) way]

Taos /tows/ *n.* **1 a** a N. American people native to New Mexico. **b** a member of this people. **2** the language of this people.

tap¹ /tap/ *n. & v.* ●*n.* **1** = FAUCET. **2** an act of tapping a telephone, etc.; also, the device used for this. **3** *Brit.* a taproom. **4** an instrument for cutting the thread of a female screw. ●*v.tr.* (**tapped, tap•ping**) **1 a** provide (a cask) with a tap. **b** let out (a liquid) by means of, or as if by means of, a tap. **2** draw sap from (a tree) by cutting into it. **3 a** obtain information or supplies or resources from. **b** establish communication or trade with. **4** connect a listening device to (a telephone or telegraph line, etc.) to listen to a call or transmission. **5** cut a female screw thread in. □ **on tap 1** ready to be drawn off by tap. **2** *colloq.* ready for immediate use; freely available. □□ **tap•less** *adj.* **tap•pa•ble** *adj.* [OE *tæppian* (v.), *tæ ppa* (n.) f. Gmc]

tap² /tap/ *v. & n.* ●*v.* (**tapped, tap•ping**) **1** *intr.* (foll. by *at, on*) strike a gentle but audible blow. **2** *tr.* strike lightly (*tapped me on the shoulder*). **3** *tr.* (foll. by *against*, etc.) cause (a thing) to strike lightly (*tapped a stick against the window*). **4** select as if by tapping (*tapped for membership*). **5** *intr.* = tap-dance (see TAP DANCE). ●*n.* **1 a** a light blow; a rap. **b** the sound of this (*heard a tap at the door*). **2 a** = TAP DANCE (*goes to tap classes*). **b** a piece of metal attached to the toe and heel of a tap dancer's shoe to make the tapping sound. **3** (in *pl.*, usu. treated as *sing.*) **a** a bugle call for lights to be put out in army quarters. **b** a similar call played at a military funeral. □□ **tap danc•er** *n.* **tap danc•ing** *n.* **tap•per** *n.* [ME *tappe* (imit.), perh. through F *taper*]

ta•pa¹ /táapə/ *n.* **1** the bark of a paper mulberry tree. **2** cloth made from this, used in the Pacific islands. [Polynesian]

ta•pa² /táapə/ *n.* (usu. *pl.*) a Spanish-style appetizer typically served with wine or beer. [Sp., = cover, lid, perh. f. Gmc]

tap dance *n.* a form of display dance performed wearing shoes fitted with metal taps, with rhythmical tapping of the toes and heels. □□ **tap-dance** *v.intr.*

tape /tayp/ *n. & v.* ●*n.* **1** a narrow strip of woven material for tying up, fastening, etc. **2 a** a strip of material stretched across the finishing line of a race. **b** a similar strip for marking off an area or forming a notional barrier. **3** (in full **adhesive tape**) a strip of opaque or transparent paper or plastic, etc., esp. coated with adhesive for fastening, sticking, masking, insulating, etc. **4 a** = MAGNETIC TAPE. **b** a tape recording or tape cassette. **5** = TAPE MEASURE. ●*v.tr.* **1 a** tie up or join, etc., with tape. **b** apply tape to. **2** (foll. by *off*) seal or mark off an area or thing with tape. **3** record on magnetic tape. **4** measure with tape. □ **break the tape** win a race. **have** (or **get**) **a person or thing taped** *Brit. colloq.* understand a person or thing fully. **on tape** recorded on magnetic tape. □□ **tape•a•ble** *adj.* (esp. in sense 3 of *v.*). **tape•less** *adj.* **tape•like** *adj.* [OE *tæppa, tæ ppe*, of unkn. orig.]

tape deck *n.* an audio device for playing and usu. recording magnetic tape.

tape meas•ure *n.* a strip of tape or thin flexible metal marked for measuring lengths.

tap•er /táypər/ *n. & v.* ●*n.* **1** a wick coated with wax, etc., for lighting fires, candles, etc. **2** a slender candle. ●*v.* (often foll. by *off*) **1** *intr. & tr.* diminish or reduce in thickness toward one end. **2** *tr. & intr.* make or become gradually less. [OE *tapur, –or, –er* wax candle, f. L PAPYRUS, whose pith was used for candle wicks]

tape re•cord•er *n.* an apparatus for recording sounds on magnetic tape and afterwards reproducing them. □□ **tape-re•cord** *v.* **tape re•cord•ing** *n.*

tap•es•try /tápistree/ *n.* (*pl.* **–ies**) **1 a** a thick textile fabric in which colored weft threads are woven to form pictures or designs. **b** embroidery imitating this, usu. in wools on canvas. **c** a piece of such embroidery. **2** events or circumstances, etc., compared with a tapestry in being intricate, interwoven, etc. (*life's rich tapestry*). □□ **tap•es•tried** *adj.* [ME, alt. f. *tapissery* f. OF *tapisserie* f. *tapissier* tapestry worker or *tapisser* to carpet, f. *tapis*: see TAPIS]

ta•pe•tum /təpéetəm/ *n.* a membranous layer of the choroid membrane in the eyes of certain mammals, e.g., cats. [LL f. L *tapete* carpet]

tape•worm /táypwərm/ *n.* any flatworm of the class Cestoda, with a body like segmented tape, living as a parasite in the intestines.

tap•i•o•ca /tápeeókə/ *n.* a starchy substance in hard white grains obtained from cassava and used for puddings, etc. [Tupi-Guarani *tipioca* f. *tipi* dregs + *og, ok* squeeze out]

ta•pir /táypər, təpéer/ *n.* any nocturnal hoofed mammal of the genus *Tapirus*, native to Central and S. America and Malaysia, hav-

tapir

ing a short flexible protruding snout used for feeding on vegetation. □□ **ta•pir•oid** *adj. & n.* [Tupi *tapira*]

tap•is /tápee/ *n.* a covering or tapestry. □ **on the tapis** (of a subject) under consideration or discussion. [ME, a kind of cloth, f. OF *tapiz* f. LL *tapetium* f. Gk *tapētion* dimin. of *tapēs tapētos* tapestry]

ta•pote•ment /təpótmənt/ *n. Med.* rapid and repeated striking of the body as massage treatment. [F f. *tapoter* tap]

tap•per see TAP².

tap•pet /tápit/ *n.* a lever or projecting part used in machinery to give intermittent motion, often in conjunction with a cam. [app. f. TAP² + –ET¹]

tap•room /táprŏŏm, –rŏŏm/ *n.* a room in which alcoholic drinks are available on tap; a barroom.

tap root *n.* a tapering root growing vertically downwards.

tap•ster /tápstər/ *n.* a bartender. [OE *tæppestre* orig. fem. (as TAP¹, –STER)]

tap-tap *n.* a repeated tap; a series of taps.

ta•pu /táapŏŏ/ *n. & adj. NZ* = TABOO. [Maori]

tap wa•ter *n.* water from a piped supply.

tar¹ /taar/ *n. & v.* ●*n.* **1 a** a dark, thick, flammable liquid distilled from wood or coal, etc., and used as a preservative of wood and iron, in making roads, as an antiseptic, etc. **2** a similar substance formed in the combustion of tobacco, etc. ●*v.tr.* (**tarred, tar•ring**) cover with tar. □ **tar and feather** smear with tar and then cover with feathers as a punishment. **tarred with the same brush** having the same faults. [OE *te(o)ru* f. Gmc, rel. to TREE]

tar² /taar/ *n. colloq.* a sailor. [abbr. of TARPAULIN]

tar•a•did•dle /tárədid'l/ *n.* (also **tar•ra•did•dle**) *colloq.* **1** a petty lie. **2** pretentious nonsense. [18th c.: cf. DIDDLE]

tar•an•tel•la /tárəntélə/ *n.* (also **tar•an•telle** /–tél/) **1** a rapid whirling S. Italian dance. **2** the music for this. [It., f. *Taranto* in Italy (because the dance was once thought to be a cure for a tarantula bite): cf. TARANTISM]

tar•ant•ism /tárəntizəm/ *n. hist.* dancing mania, esp. that originating in S. Italy among those who had (actually or supposedly) been bitten by a tarantula. [mod.L *tarantismus*, It. *tarantismo* f. *Taranto* in S. Italy f. L *Tarentum*]

ta•ran•tu•la /təránchələ/ *n.* **1** any large, hairy, tropical spider of the family Theraphosidae. **2 a** a large black S. European spider, *Lycosa tarentula*, whose bite was formerly held to cause tarantism. [med.L f. It. *tarantola* (as TARANTISM)]

ta•rax•a•cum /təráksəkəm/ *n.* **1** any composite plant of the genus *Taraxacum*, including the dandelion. **2** a tonic, etc., prepared from the dried roots of this. [med.L f. Arab. *ṭarak šakūk* f. Pers. *tal k* bitter + *chakūk* purslane]

tarantula

tar•boosh /taarbŏŏsh/ *n.* a cap like a fez, sometimes worn as part of a turban. [Egypt. Arab. *ṭarbūš*, ult. f. Pers. *sar-būš* head cover]

Tar•de•noi•sian /taard'nóyzeeən/ *n. & adj. Archaeol.* ●*n.* a Mesolithic culture using small flint implements. ●*adj.* of or relating to this culture. [*Tardenois* in NE France, where remains of it were found]

tar•di•grade /taardigrayd/ *n. & adj.* ●*n.* any minute freshwater animal of the phylum Tardigrada, having a short plump body and four pairs of short legs. Also called **water bear**. ●*adj.* of or relating to this phylum. [F *tardigrade* f. L *tardigradus* f. *tardus* slow + *gradi* walk]

tar•dy /taardee/ *adj.* (**tar•di•er, tar•di•est**) **1** slow to act or come or happen. **2** delaying or delayed beyond the right or expected time. □□ **tar•di•ly** *adv.* **tar•di•ness** *n.* [F *tardif, tardive* ult. f. L *tardus* slow]

tare¹ /tair/ *n.* **1** vetch, esp. as a weed or fodder. **2** (in *pl.*) *Bibl.* an injurious grain weed (Matt. 13: 24-30). [ME: orig. unkn.]

tare² /tair/ *n.* **1** an allowance made for the weight of the packing or wrapping around goods. **2** the weight of a motor vehicle without its fuel or load. [ME f. F, = deficiency, tare, f. med.L *tara* f. Arab. *ṭarha* what is rejected f. *ṭaraḥa* reject]

tare and tret *n.* the arithmetical rule for computing a tare.

targe /taarj/ *n. archaic* = TARGET *n.* 5. [ME f. OF]

tar•get /taargit/ *n. & v.* ●*n.* **1** a mark or point fired or aimed at, esp. a round or rectangular object marked with concentric circles. **2** a person or thing aimed at, or exposed to gunfire, etc. (*they were an easy target*). **3** (also *attrib.*) an objective or result aimed at (*our export targets; target date*). **4** a person or thing against whom criticism, abuse, etc., is or may be directed. **5** *archaic* a shield or buckler, esp.

a small round one. • *v.tr.* (**tar•get•ed, tar•get•ing**) **1** identify or single out (a person or thing) as an object of attention or attack. **2** aim or direct (*missiles targeted on major cities; should target our efforts where needed*). □□ **tar•get•a•ble** *adj.* [ME, dimin. of ME and OF *targe* shield]

tar•iff /tárif/ *n. & v.* • *n.* **1** a table of fixed charges. **2 a** a duty on a particular class of imports or exports. **b** a list of duties or customs to be paid. **3** esp. *Brit.* standard charges agreed between insurers, etc. • *v.tr.* subject (goods) to a tariff. [F *tarif* f. It. *tariffa* f. Turk. *tarife* f. Arab. *ta'rīf(a)* f. '*arrafa* notify]

tar•la•tan /táarlət'n/ *n.* a thin, stiff, open-weave muslin. [F *tarlatane*, prob. of Ind. orig.]

Tar•mac /táarmak/ *n. & v.* • *n.* Trademark **1** = TARMACADAM. **2** a surface made of this, e.g., a runway. • *v.tr.* (**tarmac**) (**tar•macked, tar•mack•ing**) apply tarmacadam to. [abbr.]

tar•mac•ad•am /táarməkádəm/ *n.* a material of stone or slag bound with tar, used in paving roads, etc. [TAR[1] + MACADAM]

tarn /taarn/ *n.* a small mountain lake. [ME *terne, tarne* f. ON]

tar•na•tion /taarnáyshən/ *int.* esp. *dial. sl.* damn; blast. [alt. of DAMNATION, *darnation*]

tar•nish /táarnish/ *v. & n.* • *v.* **1** *tr.* lessen or destroy the luster of (metal, etc.). **2** *tr.* impair (one's reputation, etc.). **3** *intr.* (of metal, etc.) lose luster. • *n.* **1 a** a loss of luster. **b** a film of color formed on an exposed surface of a mineral or metal. **2** a blemish; a stain. □□ **tar•nish•a•ble** *adj.* [F *ternir* f. *terne* dark]

ta•ro /táarō, tárō/ *n.* (*pl.* –**ros**) a tropical plant of the arum family, *Colocasia esculenta*, with tuberous roots used as food. Also called eddo. [Polynesian]

ta•rot /tárō, tərō/ *n.* **1** (in *sing.* or *pl.*) **a** any of several games played with a pack of cards having five suits, the last of which is a set of permanent trumps. **b** a similar pack used in fortune-telling. **2 a** any of the trump cards. **b** any of the cards from a fortune-telling pack. [F *tarot*, It. *tarocchi*, of unkn. orig.]

tarp /taarp/ *n. colloq.* tarpaulin. [abbr.]

tar•pan /táarpan/ *n.* an extinct N. European primitive wild horse. [Kirghiz Tartar]

tar•pau•lin /taarpáwlin, táarpə–/ *n.* **1** heavy-duty waterproof cloth, esp. of tarred canvas or heavy plastic. **2** a sheet or covering of this. **3 a** a sailor's tarred or oilskin hat. **b** *archaic* a sailor. [prob. f. TAR[1] + PALL[1] + –ING[1]]

tar•pon /táarpon/ *n.* **1** a large silvery fish, *Tarpon atlanticus*, common in the tropical Atlantic. **2** a similar fish, *Megalops cyprinoides*, of the Pacific ocean. [Du. *tarpoen*, of unkn. orig.]

tar•ra•did•dle var. of TARADIDDLE.

tar•ra•gon /tárəgən/ *n.* a bushy herb, *Artemisia dracunculus*, with leaves used to flavor salads, stuffings, vinegar, etc. [= med.L *tarchon* f. med. Gk *tarkhōn*, perh. through Arab. f. Gk *drakōn* dragon]

tar•ry[1] /táaree/ *adj.* (**tar•ri•er, tar•ri•est**) of or like or smeared with tar. □□ **tar•ri•ness** *n.*

tar•ry[2] /táree/ *v.intr.* (–**ries, –ried**) *archaic* or *literary* **1** defer coming or going. **2** linger; stay; wait. **3** be tardy. □□ **tar•ri•er** *n.* [ME: orig. uncert.]

tar•sal /táarsəl/ *adj. & n.* • *adj.* of or relating to the bones in the ankle. • *n.* a tarsal bone. [TARSUS + –AL]

tar•si *pl.* of TARSUS.

tarsi– /táarsee/ *comb. form* (also **tarso–** /táarsō/) tarsus.

tar•si•a /táarseeə/ *n.* = INTARSIA. [It.]

tar•si•er /táarseeər/ *n.* any small, large-eyed, arboreal, nocturnal primate of the genus *Tarsius*, native to Borneo, the Philippines, etc., with a long tail and long hind legs used for leaping from tree to tree. [F (as TARSUS), from the structure of its foot]

tarso– *comb. form* var. of TARSI–.

tar•sus /táarsəs/ *n.* (*pl.* **tarsi** /–sī, –see/) **1 a** the group of bones forming the ankle and upper foot. **b** the shank of a bird's leg. **c** the terminal segment of a limb in insects. **2** the fibrous connective tissue of the eyelid. [mod.L f. Gk *tarsos* flat of the foot, rim of the eyelid]

tart[1] /taart/ *n.* **1** a small pie containing jam, fruit, etc., having no upper crust. **2** a pie with a fruit or sweet filling. □□ **tart•let** *n.* [ME f. OF *tarte* = med.L *tarta*, of unkn. orig.]

tart[2] /taart/ *n. & v.* • *n. sl.* **1** a prostitute; a promiscuous woman. **2** *offens.* a girl or woman. • *v.* (foll. by *up*) *colloq.* **1** *tr.* (usu. *refl.*) dress (oneself or a thing) up, esp. flashily or gaudily. **2** *intr.* dress up gaudily. [prob. abbr. of SWEETHEART]

tart[3] /taart/ *adj.* **1** sharp or acid in taste. **2** (of a remark, etc.) cutting; bitter. □□ **tart•ly** *adv.* **tart•ness** *n.* [OE *teart*, of unkn. orig.]

tar•tan[1] /táart'n/ *n.* **1** a pattern of colored stripes crossing at right angles, esp. the distinctive plaid worn by the Scottish Highlanders to denote their clan. **2** woolen fabric woven in this pattern (often *attrib.: a tartan scarf*). [perh. f. OF *tertaine, tiretaine*]

tar•tan[2] /táart'n/ *n.* a lateen-sailed single-masted ship used in the Mediterranean. [F *tartane* f. It. *tartana*, perh. f. Arab. *ṭarīda*]

Tar•tar /táartər/ *n. & adj.* (also **Ta•tar** /táatər/ except in sense 2 of *n.*) • *n.* **1 a** a member of a group of Central Asian peoples including Mongols and Turks. **b** the Turkic language of these peoples. **2** (**tar-**

tar**) a violent-tempered or intractable person. • *adj.* **1** of or relating to the Tartars. **2** of or relating to Central Asia E. of the Caspian Sea. □□ **Tar•tar•i•an** /–táireeən/ *adj.* [ME *tartre* f. OF *Tartare* or med.L *Tartarus*]

tar•tar /táartər/ *n.* **1** a hard deposit of saliva, calcium phosphate, etc., that forms on the teeth. **2** a deposit of acid potassium tartrate that forms a hard crust on the inside of a cask during the fermentation of wine. □□ **tar•tar•ize** /–tr. [ME f. med.L f. med.Gk *tartaron*]

tar•tare /taartáar/ *adj.* (in full **sauce tartare**) = TARTAR SAUCE. [F, = tartar]

tar•tar e•met•ic *n.* potassium antimony tartrate used as a mordant and in medicine (formerly as an emetic).

tar•tar•ic /taartárik/ *adj. Chem.* of or produced from tartar. [F *tartarique* f. med.L *tartarum*: see TARTAR]

tar•tar•ic ac•id *n.* a natural carboxylic acid found esp. in unripe grapes, used in baking-powders and as a food additive.

tar•tar sauce *n.* a sauce of mayonnaise and chopped pickles, capers, etc.

Tar•ta•rus /táartərəs/ *n.* (in Greek mythology): **1** an abyss below Hades where the Titans were confined. **2** a place of punishment in Hades. □□ **Tar•ta•re•an** /–táireeən/ *adj.* [L f. Gk *Tartaros*]

tar•trate /táartrayt/ *n. Chem.* any salt or ester of tartaric acid. [F (as TARTAR, –ATE[1])]

tar•tra•zine /táartrəzeen/ *n. Chem.* a brilliant yellow dye derived from tartaric acid and used to color food, drugs, and cosmetics. [as TARTAR + AZO– + –INE[4]]

tart•y /táartee/ *adj. colloq.* (**tart•i•er, tart•i•est**) (esp. of a woman) vulgar; gaudy; promiscuous. □□ **tart•i•ly** *adv.* **tart•i•ness** *n.* [TART[2] + –Y[1]]

Tar•zan /táarzən, –zan/ *n.* a man of great agility and powerful physique. [name of the hero of stories by E. R. Burroughs, Amer. writer d. 1950]

Tas. *abbr.* Tasmania.

Ta•shi la•ma /táashee láamə/ *n.* = PANCHEN LAMA.

task /task/ *n. & v.* • *n.* a piece of work to be done or undertaken. • *v.tr.* **1** make great demands on (a person's powers, etc.). **2** assign a task to. □ **take to task** rebuke; scold. [ME f. ONF *tasque* = OF *tasche* f. med.L *tasca*, perh. f. *taxa* f. L *taxare* TAX]

task force *n.* (also **task group**) **1** *Mil.* an armed force organized for a special operation. **2** a unit specially organized for a task.

task•mas•ter /táskmastər/ *n.* (*fem.* **task•mis•tress** /–mistris/) a person who imposes a task or burden, esp. regularly or severely.

Tas•ma•ni•an /tazmáyneeən/ *n. & adj.* • *n.* **1** a native of Tasmania, an island state of Australia. **2** a person of Tasmanian descent. • *adj.* of or relating to Tasmania. [*Tasmania* f. A. J. *Tasman*, Du. navigator d. 1659, who discovered the island]

Tas•ma•ni•an dev•il *n.* a nocturnal carnivorous marsupial similar to a badger, *Sarcophilus harrisii*, now found only in Tasmania.

Tass /tas, taas/ *n. hist.* the official news agency of the former Soviet Union. [the initials of Russ. *Telegrafnoe agentstvo Sovetskogo Soyuza* Telegraphic Agency of the Soviet Union]

tass /tas/ *n. Sc.* **1** a cup or small goblet. **2** a small draft of brandy, etc. [ME f. OF *tasse* cup f. Arab. *ṭāsa* basin f. Pers. *tast*]

tas•sel[1] /tásəl/ *n. & v.* • *n.* **1** a tuft of loosely hanging threads or cords, etc., attached for decoration to a cushion, scarf, cap, etc. **2** a tassellike head of some plants, esp. a flowerhead with prominent stamens at the top of a corn stalk. • *v* (**tas•seled, tas•sel•ing** or **tas•selled, tas•sel•ling**) **1** *tr.* provide with a tassel or tassels. **2** *intr.* (of corn, etc.) form tassels. **3** *tr.* remove the tassels from (corn, etc.). [ME f. OF *tas(s)el* clasp, of unkn. orig.]

tas•sel[2] /tásəl/ *n.* (also **tor•sel** /tór–/) a small piece of stone, wood, etc., supporting the end of a beam or joist. [OF ult. f. L *taxillus* small die, and *tessella*: see TESSELLATE]

tass•ie /tásee/ *n. Sc.* a small cup.

taste /tayst/ *n. & v.* • *n.* **1 a** the sensation characteristic of a soluble substance caused in the mouth and throat by contact with that substance (*disliked the taste of garlic*). **b** the faculty of perceiving this sensation (*was bitter to the taste*). **2 a** a small portion of food or drink taken as a sample. **b** a hint or touch of some ingredient or quality. **3** a slight experience (*a taste of success*). **4** (often foll. by *for*) a liking or predilection (*has expensive tastes; is not to my taste*). **5 a** aesthetic discernment in art, literature, conduct, etc., esp. of a specified kind (*a person of taste; dresses in poor taste*). **b** a style or manner based on this (*a novel of Victorian taste*). • *v.* **1** *tr.* sample or test the flavor of (food, etc.) by taking it into the mouth. **2** *tr.* (also *absol.*) perceive the flavor of (*could taste the lemon; cannot taste with a cold*). **3** *tr.* (esp. with *neg.*) eat or drink a small portion of (*had not tasted food for days*). **4** *tr.* have experience of (*had never tasted failure*). **5** *intr.* (often foll. by *of*) have a specified flavor (*tastes bitter; tastes of onions*). □ **a bad** (or **bitter**, etc.) **taste** *colloq.* a strong feeling of regret or unease. **taste blood** see BLOOD. **to taste** in the amount needed for a pleasing result (*add salt and pepper to taste*). □□ **taste•a•ble** *adj.* [ME, = touch, taste, f. OF *tast, taster* touch, try, taste, ult. perh. f. L *tangere* touch + *gustare* taste]

taste bud *n.* any of the cells or nerve endings on the surface of the tongue by which things are tasted.

taste•ful /táystfǒol/ *adj.* having, or done in, good taste. □□ **taste•ful•ly** *adv.* **taste•ful•ness** *n.*

taste•less /táystlis/ *adj.* **1** lacking flavor. **2** having, or done in, bad taste. □□ **taste•less•ly** *adv.* **taste•less•ness** *n.*

tast•er /táystər/ *n.* **1** a person employed to test food or drink by tasting it, esp. for quality or *hist.* to detect poisoning. **2** a small cup used by a wine taster. **3** an instrument for extracting a small sample from within a cheese. **4** a sample of food, etc. [ME f. AF *tastour*, OF *tasteur* f. *taster*: see TASTE]

tast•ing /táysting/ *n.* a gathering at which food or drink (esp. wine) is tasted and evaluated.

tast•y /táystee/ *adj.* (**tast•i•er**, **tast•i•est**) (of food) pleasing in flavor; appetizing. □□ **tast•i•ly** *adv.* **tast•i•ness** *n.*

tat[1] /tat/ *n. Brit. colloq.* **1 a** tatty or tasteless clothes; worthless goods. **b** rubbish; junk. **2** a shabby person. [back-form. f. TATTY]

tat[2] /tat/ *v.* (**tat•ted, tat•ting**) **1** *intr.* do tatting. **2** *tr.* make by tatting. [19th c.: orig. unkn.]

tat[3] see TIT[2].

ta-ta /taatáa/ *int. joc.* good-bye. [19th c.: orig. unkn.]

Ta•tar var. of TARTAR.

ta•ter /táytər/ *n.* (also *Brit.* **ta•tie** /–tee/, **ta•to** /–tō/) *sl.* = POTATO. [abbr.]

tat•ler *archaic* var. of TATTLER.

tat•ter /tátər/ *n.* (usu. in *pl.*) a rag; an irregularly torn piece of cloth or paper, etc. □ **in tatters** *colloq.* (of a negotiation, argument, etc.) ruined; demolished. □□ **tat•ter•y** *adj.* [ME f. ON *tötrar* rags: cf. Icel. *tö turr*]

tat•tered /tátərd/ *adj.* in tatters; ragged.

tat•ter•sall /tátərsawl/ *n* (in full **tattersall check**) a fabric with a pattern of colored lines forming squares like a tartan. [R. *Tattersall*, Engl. horseman d. 1795: from the traditional design of horse blankets]

tat•ting /táting/ *n.* **1** a kind of knotted lace made by hand with a small shuttle and used as trim, etc. **2** the process of making this. [19th c.: orig. unkn.]

tat•tle /tát'l/ *v. & n.* • *v.* **1** *intr.* prattle; chatter; gossip idly; speak indiscreetly. **2** *tr.* utter (words) idly; reveal (secrets). • *n.* gossip; idle or trivial talk. [ME f. MFlem. *tatelen, tateren* (imit.)]

tat•tler /tátlər/ *n.* a prattler; a gossip.

tat•tle•tale /tát'ltayl/ *n.* one who tells tales or informs, esp. a child.

tat•too[1] /tatōo/ *n.* (*pl* **tat•toos**) **1** an evening drum or bugle signal recalling soldiers to their quarters. **2** an elaboration of this with music and marching, presented as an entertainment. **3** a rhythmic tapping or drumming. [17th-c. *tap-too* f. Du. *taptoe*, lit. 'close the tap' (of the cask)]

tat•too[2] /tatōo/ *v. & n.* • *v.tr.* (**tat•toos, tat•tooed**) **1** mark (the skin) with an indelible design by puncturing it and inserting pigment. **2** make (a design) in this way. • *n.* (*pl.* **tat•toos**) a design made by tattooing. □□ **tat•too•er** *n.* **tat•too•ist** *n.* [Polynesian]

tat•ty /tátee/ *adj.* (**tat•ti•er, tat•ti•est**) esp. *Brit colloq.* **1** tattered; worn and shabby. **2** inferior. **3** tawdry. □□ **tat•ti•ly** *adv.* **tat•ti•ness** *n.* [orig. Sc., = shaggy, app. rel. to OE *tættec* rag, TATTER]

tau /tow, taw/ *n.* the nineteenth letter of the Greek alphabet (T, τ). [ME f. Gk]

tau cross *n.* a T-shaped cross.

taught *past* and *past part.* of TEACH.

taunt /tawnt/ *n. & v.* • *n.* a thing said in order to anger or wound a person. • *v.tr.* **1** assail with taunts. **2** reproach (a person) contemptuously. □□ **taunt•er** *n.* **taunt•ing•ly** *adv.* [16th c., in phr. *taunt for taunt* f. F *tant pour tant* tit for tat, hence a clever rejoinder]

tau par•ti•cle *n. Physics* an unstable, heavy, charged elementary particle of the lepton class.

taupe /tōp/ *n.* a gray with a tinge of another color, usu. brown. [F, = MOLE[1]]

tau•rine /táwreen, –rīn/ *adj.* of or like a bull; bullish. [L *taurinus* f. *taurus* bull]

Tau•rus /táwrəs/ *n.* **1** a constellation. **2 a** the second sign of the zodiac (the Bull). **b** a person born under this sign. □□ **Tau•re•an** *adj. & n.* [ME f. L, = bull]

taut /tawt/ *adj.* **1** (of a rope, muscles, etc.) tight; not slack. **2** (of nerves) tense. **3** (of a ship, etc.) in good order or condition. □□ **taut•en** *v.tr. & intr.* **taut•ly** *adv.* **taut•ness** *n.* [ME *touht, togt,* perh. = TOUGH, infl. by *tog-* past part. stem of obs. *tee* (OE *tēon*) pull]

tauto- /táwtō/ *comb. form* the same. [Gk, f. *tauto,* f. *auto* the same]

tau•tog /tawtóg/ *n.* a fish, *Tautoga onitis,* found off the Atlantic coast of N. America, used as food. [Narragansett *tautauog* (pl.)]

tau•tol•o•gy /tawtóləjee/ *n.* (*pl.* **–gies**) **1** the saying of the same thing twice over in different words, esp. as a fault of style (e.g., *arrived one after the other in succession*). **2** a statement that is necessarily true. □□ **tau•to•log•ic** /–t'lójik/ *adj.* **tau•to•log•i•cal** *adj.* **tau•to•log•i•cal•ly** *adv.* **tau•tol•o•gist** *n.* **tau•tol•o•gize** *v.intr.* **tau•tol•o•gous** /–ləgəs/ *adj.* [LL *tautologia* f. Gk (as TAUTO-, –LOGY)]

tau•to•mer /táwtəmər/ *n. Chem.* a substance that exists as two mutually convertible isomers in equilibrium. □□ **tau•to•mer•ic** /–mérik/ *adj.* **tau•tom•er•ism** /–tómərizəm/ *n.* [TAUTO- + –MER]

tau•toph•o•ny /tawtófənee/ *n.* repetition of the same sound. [TAUTO- + Gk *phōnē* sound]

tav•ern /távərn/ *n.* an inn or bar. [ME f. OF *taverne* f. L *taberna* hut, tavern]

ta•ver•na /təvə́rnə/ *n.* a Greek eating house. [mod. Gk (as TAVERN)]

taw[1] /taw/ *v.tr.* make (hide) into leather without the use of tannin, esp. by soaking in a solution of alum and salt. □□ **taw•er** *n.* [OE *tawian* f. Gmc]

taw[2] /taw/ *n.* **1** a large marble. **2** a game of marbles. **3** a line from which players throw marbles. [18th c.: orig. unkn.]

taw•dry /táwdree/ *adj. & n.* • *adj.* (**taw•dri•er, taw•dri•est**) **1** showy but worthless. **2** overly ornamented; gaudy; vulgar. • *n.* cheap or gaudy finery. □□ **taw•dri•ly** *adv.* **taw•dri•ness** *n.*

WORD HISTORY **tawdry**

Early 17th century: short for *tawdry lace,* a fine silk lace or ribbon worn as a necklace in the 16th–17th centuries, a contraction of *St. Audrey's lace:* Audrey was a later form of Etheldrida (died 679), patron saint of the English city of Ely, where tawdry laces, along with cheap imitations and other cheap finery, were traditionally sold at a fair.

---

taw•ny /táwnee/ *adj.* (**taw•ni•er, taw•ni•est**) of an orangish or yellowish brown color. □□ **taw•ni•ness** *n.* [ME f. AF *tauné,* OF *tané* f. *tan* TAN[1]]

taw•ny ea•gle *n.* a brownish African or Asian eagle, *Aquila rapax.*

taw•ny owl *n.* a reddish brown European owl, *Strix aluco.*

taws /tawz/ *n.* (also **tawse**) *Sc. hist. & Ir. hist.* a leather strap with a slit end formerly used in schools for punishing children. [app. pl. of obs. *taw* tawed leather, f. TAW[1]]

tax /taks/ *n. & v.* • *n.* **1** a contribution to government revenue compulsorily levied on individuals, property, or businesses (often foll. by *on: a tax on luxury goods*). **2** (usu. foll. by *on, upon*) a strain or heavy demand; an oppressive or burdensome obligation. • *v.tr.* **1** impose a tax on (persons or goods, etc.). **2** deduct tax from (income, etc.). **3** make heavy demands on (a person's powers or resources, etc.) (*you really tax my patience*). **4** (foll. by *with*) confront (a person) with a wrongdoing, etc. **5** call to account. **6** *Law* examine and assess (costs, etc.). □□ **tax•a•ble** *adj.* **tax•er** *n.* **tax•less** *adj.* [ME f. OF *taxer* f. L *taxare* censure, charge, compute, perh. f. Gk *tassō* fix]

tax•a *pl.* of TAXON.

tax•a•tion /taksáyshən/ *n.* the imposition or payment of tax. [ME f. AF *taxacioun,* OF *taxation* f. L *taxatio –onis* f. *taxare:* see TAX]

tax-de•duct•i•ble *adj.* (of expenditure) that may be paid out of income before the deduction of income tax.

tax e•va•sion *n.* the illegal nonpayment or underpayment of income tax.

tax-ex•empt *adj.* **1** exempt from taxes. **2** bearing tax-exempt interest.

tax-free *adj.* = TAX-EXEMPT.

tax ha•ven *n.* a country, etc., where income tax is low.

tax•i /táksee/ *n. & v.* • *n.* (*pl.* **tax•is**) **1** (in full **taxicab**) an automobile licensed to carry passengers for a fee and usu. fitted with a taximeter. **2** a boat, airplane, etc., similarly used. • *v.* (**tax•is, tax•ied, tax•i•ing** or **tax•y•ing**) **1 a** *intr.* (of an aircraft or pilot) move along the ground under the machine's own power before takeoff or after landing. **b** *tr.* cause (an aircraft) to taxi. **2** *intr. & tr.* go or convey in a taxi. [abbr. of *taximeter cab*]

tax•i danc•er *n.* a dancing partner available for a fee.

tax•i•der•my /táksidərmee/ *n.* the art of preparing, stuffing, and mounting the skins of animals with lifelike effect. □□ **tax•i•der•mal** /–dərməl/ *adj.* **tax•i•der•mic** /–dərmik/ *adj.* **tax•i•der•mist** *n.* [Gk *taxis* arrangement + *derma* skin]

tax•i driv•er *n.* a driver of a taxi.

tax•i•me•ter /tákseemeetər/ *n.* an automatic device fitted to a taxi, recording the distance traveled and the fare payable. [F *taximè tre* f. *taxe* tariff, TAX + –METER]

tax•is /táksis/ *n.* **1** *Surgery* the restoration of displaced bones or organs by manual pressure. **2** *Biol.* the movement of a cell or organism in response to an external stimulus. **3** *Gram.* order or arrangement of words. [Gk f. *tassō* arrange]

tax•i stand *n.* (*Brit.* **rank**) a place where taxis wait to be hired.

tax•man /táksman/ *n. colloq.* (*pl.* **–men**) an inspector or collector of taxes.

tax•on /táksən/ *n.* (*pl.* **tax•a** /táksə/) any taxonomic group. [back-form. f. TAXONOMY]

tax•on•o•my /taksónəmee/ *n.* **1** the science of the classification of living and extinct organisms. **2** the practice of this. □□ **tax•o•nom•ic** /–sənómik/ *adj.* **tax•o•nom•i•cal** /–sənómikəl/ *adj.* **tax•o•nom•i•cal•ly** /–sənómiklee/ *adv.* **tax•on•o•mist** *n.* [F *taxonomie* (as TAXIS, Gk *–nomia* distribution)]

tax•pay•er /tákspayər/ *n.* a person who pays taxes.

tax re•turn *n.* a declaration of income for taxation purposes.

tax shel·ter *n.* a means of organizing business affairs, etc., to minimize payment of tax.

tax year *n.* see fiscal year.

taz·za /táatsə/ *n.* a saucer-shaped cup, esp. one mounted on a pedestal. [It.]

TB *abbr.* **1** tubercle bacillus. **2** tuberculosis.

Tb *symb. Chem.* the element terbium.

T-bone /téebōn/ *n.* a T-shaped bone, esp. in steak from the thin end of a loin.

tbs. *abbr.* (also **tbsp.**) tablespoon.

Tc *symb. Chem.* the element technetium.

TD *abbr.* **1** touchdown. **2** Treasury Department.

Te *symb. Chem.* the element tellurium.

te var. of TI[2].

tea /tee/ *n. & v.* ● *n.* **1 a** (in full **tea plant**) an evergreen shrub or small tree, *Camellia sinensis*, of India, China, etc. **b** its dried leaves. **2** a drink made by infusing tea leaves in boiling water. **3** a similar drink made from the leaves of other plants or from another substance (*chamomile tea; beef tea*). **4 a** *Brit.* a light afternoon meal consisting of tea, bread, cakes, etc. **b** a cooked evening meal. **5** an afternoon party or reception at which tea is served. ● *v. Brit.* (**teaed** or **tea'd** /teed/) **1** *intr.* take tea. **2** *tr.* give tea to (a person). [17th-c. *tay, tey,* prob. f. Du. *tee* f. Chin. (Amoy dial.) *te,* = Mandarin dial. *cha*]

tea and sym·pa·thy *n. colloq.* hospitable behavior toward a troubled person.

tea bag *n.* a small porous bag of tea leaves for infusion.

tea ball *n.* a ball of perforated metal to hold tea leaves for infusion.

tea bread *n.* light or sweet bread for eating at tea.

tea break *n. Brit.* a pause in work, etc., to drink tea.

tea cad·dy *n.* a container for tea.

tea·cake /téekayk/ *n.* a light, usu. sweet cake, cookie, etc., eaten at tea.

tea cer·e·mo·ny *n.* an elaborate Japanese ritual of serving and drinking tea, as an expression of Zen Buddhist philosophy.

teach /teech/ *v. tr.* (*past* and *past part.* **taught** /tawt/) **1 a** give systematic information to (a person) or about (a subject or skill). **b** (*absol.*) practice this professionally. **c** enable (a person) to do something by instruction and training (*taught me to swim; taught me how to dance*). **2** advocate as a moral, etc., principle (*my parents taught me tolerance*). **3** (foll. by *to* + infin.) **a** induce (a person) by example or punishment to do or not to do a thing (*that will teach you to sit still; that will teach you not to laugh*). **b** *colloq.* make (a person) disinclined to do a thing (*I will teach you to interfere*). □ **teach a person a lesson** see LESSON. **teach school** be a teacher in a school. [OE *tǣcan* f. a Gmc root = 'show']

teach·a·ble /téechəbəl/ *adj.* **1** apt at learning. **2** (of a subject) that can be taught. □□ **teach·a·bil·i·ty** /–bílitee/ *n.* **teach·a·ble·ness** *n.*

teach·er /téechər/ *n.* a person who teaches, esp. in a school. □□ **teach·er·ly** *adj.*

tea chest *n.* a light metal-lined wooden box in which tea is transported.

teach-in *n.* **1** an informal lecture and discussion on a subject of public interest. **2** a series of these.

teach·ing /téeching/ *n.* **1** the profession of a teacher. **2** (often in *pl.*) what is taught; a doctrine.

teach·ing hos·pi·tal *n.* a hospital where medical students are taught.

teach·ing ma·chine *n.* any of various devices for giving instruction according to a program measuring pupils' responses.

tea co·zy *n.* a cover to keep a teapot warm.

tea·cup /téekup/ *n.* **1** a cup from which tea or other hot beverages are drunk. **2** an amount held by this, about 4 fluid ounces. □□ **tea·cup·ful** *n.* (*pl.* **–fuls**).

tea dance *n.* an afternoon tea with dancing.

tea gar·den *n.* a garden in which afternoon tea is served to the public.

teak /teek/ *n.* **1** a large deciduous tree, *Tectona grandis*, native to India and SE Asia. **2** its hard durable wood, used in shipbuilding and for furniture. [Port. *teca* f. Malayalam *tēkka*]

teal /teel/ *n.* (*pl.* same) **1** any of various small freshwater ducks of the genus *Anas*, esp. *A. crecca*. **2** a dark greenish blue color. [rel. to MDu. *tēling*, of unkn. orig.]

tea leaf *n.* **1** a dried leaf of tea, used to make a drink of tea. **2** (esp. in *pl.*) these after infusion or as dregs.

team /teem/ *n. & v.* ● *n.* **1** a set of players forming one side in a game, debate, etc. (*a hockey team*). **2** two or more persons working together. **3 a** a set of draft animals. **b** one animal or more in harness with a vehicle. ● *v.* **1** *intr. & tr.* (usu. foll. by *up*) join in a team or in common action (*decided to team up with them*). **2** *tr.* harness (horses, etc.) in a team. **3** *tr.* (foll. by *with*) match or coordinate (clothes). [OE *tēam* offspring f. a Gmc root = 'pull,' rel. to TOW[1]]

team·mate /téemmayt/ *n.* a member of the same team or group.

team spir·it *n.* willingness to act as a member of a group rather than as an individual.

team·ster /téemstər/ *n.* **1 a** a truck driver. **b** a member of the Teamsters Union. **2** a driver of a team of animals.

Team·sters Un·ion *n.* a shortened name referring to the International Brotherhood of Teamsters, Chauffeurs, Warehousemen, and Helpers of America.

team teach·ing *n.* teaching by a team of teachers working together.

team·work /téemwərk/ *n.* the combined action of a team, group, etc., esp. when effective and efficient.

tea·pot /téepot/ *n.* a pot with a handle, spout, and lid, in which tea is brewed and from which it is poured.

tea·poy /téepoy/ *n.* a small three- or four-legged table esp. for tea. [Hindi *tīn, tir*- three + Pers. *pāī* foot: sense and spelling infl. by TEA]

tear[1] /tair/ *v. & n.* ● *v.* (*past* **tore** /tor/; *past part.* **torn** /torn/) **1** *tr.* (often foll. by *up*) pull apart or to pieces with some force (*tear it in half; tore up the letter*). **2** *tr.* make a hole or rent in by tearing (*have torn my coat*). **b** make (a hole or rent). **3** *tr.* (foll. by *away, off,* etc.) pull violently or with some force (*tore the book away from me; tore off the cover; tore a page out; tore down the notice*). **4** *tr.* violently disrupt or divide (*the country was torn by civil war; torn by conflicting emotions*). **5** *intr. colloq.* go or travel hurriedly or impetuously (*tore across the road*). **6** *intr.* undergo tearing (*the curtain tore down the middle*). **7** *intr.* (foll. by *at*, etc.) pull violently or with some force. ● *n.* **1** a hole or other damage caused by tearing. **2** the torn part of a piece of cloth, etc. **3** *sl.* a spree; a drinking bout. □ **be torn between** have difficulty in choosing between. **tear apart 1** search (a place) exhaustively. **2** criticize forcefully. **tear into 1** attack verbally; reprimand. **2** make a vigorous start on (an activity). **tear oneself away** leave despite a strong desire to stay. **tear one's hair out** behave with extreme desperation or anger. **tear to shreds** *colloq.* refute or criticize thoroughly. **that's torn it** *Brit. colloq.* that has spoiled things, caused a problem, etc. □□ **tear·a·ble** *adj.* **tear·er** *n.* [OE *teran* f. Gmc]

tear[2] /teer/ *n.* **1** a drop of clear salty liquid secreted by glands that serves to moisten and wash the eye and is shed from it in grief or other strong emotions. **2** a tearlike thing; a drop. □ **in tears** crying; shedding tears. **without tears** presented so as to be learned or done easily. □□ **tear·like** *adj.* [OE *tēar*]

tear·a·way /táirəway/ *n. Brit.* **1** an impetuous or reckless young person. **2** a hooligan.

tear duct *n.* a drain for carrying tears to the eye or from the eye to the nose.

tear·ful /téerfool/ *adj.* **1** crying or inclined to cry. **2** causing or accompanied with tears; sad (*a tearful event*). □□ **tear·ful·ly** *adv.* **tear·ful·ness** *n.*

tear gas *n.* gas that disables by causing severe irritation to the eyes.

tear·ing /táiring/ *adj.* extreme; overwhelming; violent (*in a tearing hurry*).

tear·jerk·er /téerjərkər/ *n. colloq.* a story, film, etc., calculated to evoke sadness or sympathy.

tear·less /téerlis/ *adj.* not shedding tears. □□ **tear·less·ly** *adv.* **tear·less·ness** *n.*

tea·room /téeroom, –room/ *n.* a small restaurant or café where tea is served.

tea rose *n.* a hybrid shrub, *Rosa odorata*, with a scent resembling that of tea.

tease /teez/ *v. & n.* ● *v. tr.* (also *absol.*) **1 a** make fun of (a person or animal) playfully or unkindly or annoyingly. **b** tempt or allure esp. sexually, while refusing to satisfy the desire aroused. **2** pick (wool, hair, etc.) into separate fibers. **3** dress (cloth) esp. with teasels. ● *n.* **1** *colloq.* a person fond of teasing (*it was only a tease*). **2** an instance of teasing. **3** = TEASER 3. □ **tease out 1** separate (strands, etc.) by disentangling. **2** search out; elicit (information, etc.). □□ **teas·ing·ly** *adv.* [OE *tǣsan* f. WG]

tea·sel /téezəl/ *n. & v.* (also **tea·zel, tea·zle**) ● *n.* **1** any plant of the genus *Dipsacus*, with large prickly heads that are dried and used to raise the nap on woven cloth. **2** a device used as a substitute for teasels. ● *v. tr.* dress (cloth) with teasels. □□ **tea·sel·er** *n.* [OE *tǣs(e)l, = OHG *zeisala* (as TEASE)]

teas·er /téezər/ *n.* **1** *colloq.* a hard question or task. **2** a teasing person. **3** (also **tease**) a short introductory advertisement, etc.

tea set *n.* a set of china or silver, etc., for serving tea.

tear sheet *n.* a page that can be removed from a newspaper or magazine, etc., for use separately.

tea shop *n.* esp. *Brit.* = TEAROOM.

tea·spoon /téespoon/ *n.* **1** a small spoon for stirring tea. **2** an amount held by this. **3** a unit of measure equal to $^{1}/_{3}$ tablespoon, approx. 5 ml or $^{1}/_{6}$ fl. oz. □□ **tea·spoon·ful** *n.* (*pl.* **–fuls**).

teat /teet/ *n.* **1** a mammary nipple, esp. of an animal. **2** *Brit.* a thing resembling this, esp. a device of rubber, etc., for sucking milk from a bottle; a nipple. [ME f. OF *tete*, prob. of Gmc orig., replacing TIT[3]]

tea·time /téetim/ esp. *Brit. n.* the time in the afternoon when tea is served.

tea tow·el *n.* esp. *Brit.* a towel for drying washed dishes, etc.

tea tree *n. Austral. & NZ* an aromatic evergreen flowering shrub, *Leptospermum scoparium*; the manuka.

tea wag·on *n.* (*Brit.* **tea trol·ley**) a small wheeled cart from which tea is served.

tea·zel (also **tea·zle**) var. of TEASEL.

tec /tek/ *n. colloq.* a detective. [abbr.]

tech /tek/ *n. colloq.* **1** a technician. **2** a technical college. [abbr.]

tech·ne·ti·um /teknee'shəm, –sheeəm/ *n. Chem.* an artificially produced radioactive metallic element occurring in the fission products of uranium. ¶ Symb.: **Tc**. [mod.L f. Gk *tekhnētos* artificial f. *tekhnē* art]

tech·nic /téknik/ *n.* (usu. in *pl.*) **a** technology. **b** technical terms, details, methods, etc. **2** technique. □□ **tech ·ni·cist** /–nisist/ *n.* [L *technicus* f. Gk *tekhnikos* f. *tekhnē* art]

tech·ni·cal /téknikəl/ *adj.* **1** of or involving or concerned with the mechanical arts and applied sciences (*technical college; a technical education*). **2** of or relating to a particular subject or craft, etc., or its techniques (*technical terms; technical merit*). **3** (of a book or discourse, etc.) using technical language; requiring special knowledge to be understood. **4** due to mechanical failure (*a technical hitch*). **5** legally such; such in strict interpretation (*technical assault; lost on a technical point*). □□ **tech·ni·cal·ly** *adv.* **tech·ni·cal·ness** *n.*

tech·ni·cal hitch *n.* a temporary breakdown or problem in machinery, etc.

tech·ni·cal knock·out *n. Boxing* a termination of a fight by the referee on the grounds of a contestant's inability to continue, the opponent being declared the winner.

tech·ni·cal·i·ty /téknikálitee/ *n.* (*pl.* **–ties**) **1** the state of being technical. **2** a technical expression. **3** a technical point or detail (*was acquitted on a technicality*).

tech·ni·cian /tekníshən/ *n.* **1** an expert in the practical application of a science. **2** a person skilled in the technique of an art or craft. **3** a person employed to look after technical equipment and do practical work in a laboratory, etc.

Tech·ni·col·or /téknikulər/ *n.* (often *attrib.*) **1** *Trademark* a process of color cinematography using synchronized monochrome films, each of a different color, to produce a color print. **2** (usu. **technicolor**) *colloq.* **a** vivid color. **b** artificial brilliance. □□ **tech·ni·col·ored** *adj.* [TECHNICAL + COLOR]

tech·nique /teknéek/ *n.* **1** mechanical skill in an art. **2** a means of achieving one's purpose, esp. skillfully. **3** a manner of artistic execution in music, painting, etc. [F (as TECHNIC)]

tech·no·bab·ble /téknōbábəl/ *n. colloq.* incomprehensible technical jargon.

tech·noc·ra·cy /teknókrəsee/ *n.* (*pl.* **–cies**) **1** the government or control of society or industry by technical experts. **2** an instance or application of this. [Gk *tekhnē* art + –CRACY]

tech·no·crat /téknəkrat/ *n.* an exponent or advocate of technocracy. □□ **tech·no·crat·ic** /–krátik/ *adj.* **tech·no·crat·i·cal·ly** *adv.*

tech·no·log·i·cal /téknəlójikəl/ *adj.* of, using, or ascribable to technology. □□ **tech·no·log·i·cal·ly** *adv.*

tech·nol·o·gy /teknóləjee/ *n.* (*pl.* **–gies**) **1** the study or use of the mechanical arts and applied sciences. **2** these subjects collectively. □□ **tech·nol·o·gist** *n.* [Gk *tekhnologia* systematic treatment f. *tekhnē* art]

tech·y var. of TETCHY.

tec·ton·ic /tektónik/ *adj.* **1** *Geol.* relating to the deformation of the earth's crust or to the structural changes caused by this (see PLATE TECTONICS). **2** of or relating to building or construction. □□ **tec·ton·i·cal·ly** *adv.* [LL *tectonicus* f. Gk *tektonikos* f. *tektōn –onos* carpenter]

tec·ton·ics /tektóniks/ *n.pl.* (usu. treated as *sing.*) **1** *Geol.* the study of large-scale structural features (cf. PLATE TECTONICS). **2** *Archit.* the art and process of producing practical and aesthetically pleasing buildings.

tec·to·ri·al /tektáwreeəl/ *adj. Anat.* **1** forming a covering. **2** (in full **tectorial membrane**) the membrane covering the organ of Corti in the inner ear. [L *tectorium* a cover (as TECTRIX)]

tec·trix /téktriks/ *n.* (*pl.* **tec·tri·ces** /–triseez, –tríseez/) = COVERT *n.* 2. [mod.L f. L *tegere tect-* cover]

ted /ted/ *v.tr.* (**ted·ded, ted·ding**) turn over and spread out (grass, hay, or straw) to dry or for a bedding, etc. □□ **ted·der** *n.* [ME f. ON *tethja* spread manure f. *tad* dung, *toddi* small piece]

ted·dy /tédee/ *n.* (also **Ted·dy**) (*pl.* **–dies**) (in full **teddy bear**) a stuffed toy bear. [*Teddy*, nickname of *Theodore* Roosevelt, US president d. 1919, famous as a bear hunter]

Ted·dy boy /tédee/ *n. Brit. colloq.* **1** a youth, esp. of the 1950s, affecting an Edwardian style of dress and appearance. **2** a young rowdy male. [*Teddy*, nickname for *Edward*]

Te De·um /tee dée'əm, tay dáyəm/ **1 a** a hymn beginning *Te Deum laudamus*, 'We praise Thee, O God'. **b** the music for this. **2** an expression of thanksgiving or exultation. [L]

te·di·ous /teédeeəs/ *adj.* tiresomely long; wearisome. □□ **te·di·ous·ly** *adv.* **te·di·ous·ness** *n.* [ME f. OF *tedieus* or LL *taediosus* (as TEDIUM)]

te·di·um /teédeeəm/ *n.* the state of being tedious; boredom. [L *taedium* f. *taedēre* to weary]

tee[1] /tee/ *n.* = T[1]. [phonet. spelling]

tee[2] /tee/ *n. & v.* ● *n.* **1** *Golf* **a** a cleared space from which a golf ball is struck at the beginning of play for each hole. **b** a small support of wood or plastic from which a ball is struck at a tee. **2** a mark aimed at in bowls, quoits, curling, etc. ● *v.tr.* (**tees, teed**) (often foll. by *up*) *Golf* place (a ball) on a tee ready to strike it. □ **tee off 1** *Golf* play a ball from a tee. **2** *colloq.* start; begin. [earlier (17th-c.) *teaz*, of unkn. orig.: in sense 2 perh. = TEE[1]]

tee-hee /teehee'/ *n. & v.* (also **te-hee**) ● *n.* **1** a titter. **2** a restrained or contemptuous laugh. ● *v.intr.* (**tee-hees, tee-heed**) titter or laugh in this way. [imit.]

teem[1] /teem/ *v.intr.* **1** be abundant (*fish teem in these waters*). **2** (foll. by *with*) be full of or swarming with (*teeming with fish; teeming with ideas*). [OE *tēman*, etc., give birth to f. Gmc, rel. to TEAM]

teem[2] /teem/ *v.intr.* (often foll. by *down*) (of water, etc.) flow copiously; pour (*it was teeming with rain*). [ME *tēmen* f. ON *tœma* f. *tómr* (adj.) empty]

teen /teen/ *adj. & n.* ● *adj.* = TEENAGE. ● *n.* = TEENAGER. [abbr. of TEENAGE, TEENAGER]

-teen /teen/ *suffix* forming the names of numerals from 13 to 19. [OE inflected form of TEN]

teen·age /teénayj/ *adj.* relating to or characteristic of teenagers. □□ **teen·aged** *adj.*

teen·ag·er /teénayjər/ *n.* a person from 13 to 19 years of age.

teens /teenz/ *n.pl.* the years of one's age from 13 to 19 (*in one's teens*).

teen·sy /teénsee/ *adj.* (**teen·si·er, teen·si·est**) *colloq.* = TEENY. □□ **teensy-weensy** = TEENY-WEENY.

tee·ny /teénee/ *adj.* (**tee·ni·er, tee·ni·est**) *colloq.* tiny. [var. of TINY]

tee·ny·bop·per /teéneebopər/ *n. colloq.* a young teenager, usu. a girl, who follows the latest fashions in clothes, pop music, etc.

tee·ny-wee·ny *adj.* very tiny.

tee·pee var. of TEPEE.

tee-shirt var. of T-SHIRT.

tee·ter /teétər/ *v.intr.* **1** totter; stand or move unsteadily. **2** hesitate; be indecisive. □ **teeter on the brink** (or **edge**) be in imminent danger (of disaster, etc.). [var. of dial. *titter*]

teeth *pl.* of TOOTH.

teethe /teeth/ *v.intr.* grow or cut teeth, esp. baby teeth. □□ **teeth·ing** *n.*

teeth·ing ring *n.* a small ring for an infant to bite on while teething.

teeth·ing trou·bles *n.pl.* (also **teeth·ing prob·lems**) initial difficulties in an enterprise, etc., regarded as temporary.

tee·to·tal /teétót'l/ *adj.* advocating or characterized by total abstinence from alcohol. □□ **tee·to·tal·ism** *n.* [redupl. of TOTAL]

tee·to·tal·er /teétót'lər/ *n.* (also **tee·to·tal·ler**) a person advocating or practicing abstinence from alcoholic beverages.

tee·to·tum /teetótəm/ *n.* **1** a top with four sides lettered to determine whether the spinner has won or lost. **2** any top spun with the fingers. [*T* (the letter on one side) + L *totum* the whole (stakes), for which *T* stood]

teff /tef/ *n.* an African cereal, *Eragrostis tef.* [Amharic *ṭéf*]

TEFL *abbr.* teaching of English as a foreign language.

Tef·lon /téflon/ *n. Trademark* polytetrafluoroethylene, esp. used as a nonstick coating for kitchen utensils, etc. [*tetra*- + *fluor*- + *–on*]

teg·u·lar /tégyələr/ *adj.* **1** of or like tiles. **2** arranged like tiles. □□ **teg·u·lar·ly** *adv.* [L *tegula* tile f. *tegere* cover]

teg·u·ment /tégyəmənt/ *n.* the natural covering of an animal's body or part of it. □□ **teg·u·men·tal** /–mént'l/ *adj.* **teg·u·men·ta·ry** /–méntəreé/ *adj.* [L *tegumentum* f. *tegere* cover]

te-hee var. of TEE-HEE.

tek·tite /téktit/ *n. Geol.* a small roundish glassy body of unknown origin occurring in various parts of the earth. [G *Tektit* f. Gk *tēktos* molten f. *tēkō* melt]

Tel. *abbr.* **1** Telephone. **2 a** Telegraph. **b** Telegraphic.

tel·aes·the·sia *Brit.* var. of TELESTHESIA.

tel·a·mon /télamon/ *n.* (*pl.* **tel·a·mo·nes** /–móneez/) *Archit.* a male figure used as a pillar to support an entablature. [L *telamones* f. Gk *telamōnes* pl. of *Telamōn*, name of a mythical hero]

tele- /télee/ *comb. form* **1** at or to a distance (*telepathy*). **2** forming names of instruments for operating over long distances (*telescope*). **3** television (*telecast*). **4** done by means of the telephone (*teleconference*). [Gk *tēle-* f. *tēle* far off: sense 3 f. TELEVISION: sense 4 f. TELEPHONE]

tel·e·cam·er·a /télikamrə, –mərə/ *n.* **1** a television camera. **2** a telephotographic camera.

tel·e·cast /télikast/ *n. & v.* ● *n.* a television broadcast. ● *v.tr.* transmit by television. □□ **tel·e·cast·er** *n.* [TELE- + BROADCAST]

tel·e·cine /télisinee/ *n.* **1** the broadcasting of a movie or film on television. **2** equipment for doing this. [TELE- + CINE-]

tel·e·com·mu·ni·ca·tion /télikə myóōnikáyshən/ *n.* **1** communication over a distance by cable, telegraph, telephone, or broadcasting. **2** (usu. in *pl.*) the branch of technology concerned with this. [F *télécommunication* (as TELE-, COMMUNICATION)]

tel·e·com·mute /télikəmyóōt/ *v.intr.* (**tel·e·com·mut·ed, telecom-**

muting) work, esp. at home, communicating electronically with one's employer, etc., by computer, fax, and telephone.

tel·e·con·fer·ence /télikónfərəns, –frəns/ n. a conference with participants in different locations linked by telecommunication devices. □□ **tel·e·con·fer·enc·ing** n.

tel·e·fac·sim·i·le /télifaksímilee/ n. facsimile transmission (see FACSIMILE n. 2).

tel·e·fax /télifaks/ n. Trademark = TELEFACSIMILE. [abbr.]

tel·e·film /télifilm/ n. = TELECINE.

tel·e·gen·ic /télijénik/ adj. having an appearance or manner that looks attractive on television. [TELEVISION + –genic in PHOTOGENIC]

te·leg·o·ny /tilégənee/ n. Biol. the formerly supposed influence of a previous sire on the offspring of a dam with other sires. □□ **tel·e·gon·ic** /téligónik/ adj. [TELE- + Gk –gonia begetting]

tel·e·gram /téligram/ n. a message sent by telegraph. [TELE- + –GRAM, after TELEGRAPH]

tel·e·graph /téligraf/ n. & v. ●n. 1 a a system of or device for transmitting messages or signals over a distance esp. by making and breaking an electrical connection. b (attrib.) used in this system (telegraph pole; telegraph wire). 2 (in full **telegraph board**) Brit. = SCOREBOARD. ●v. 1 tr. send a message to by telegraph. 2 tr. send by telegraph. 3 tr. give an advance indication of. 4 intr. make signals (telegraphed to me to come up). □□ **te·leg·ra·pher** /tilégrəfər, téligrafər/ n. [F télégraphe (as TELE-, –GRAPH)]

tel·e·graph·ese /téligrəfeez/ n. colloq. or joc. an abbreviated style usual in telegrams.

tel·e·graph·ic /téligráfik/ adj. 1 of or by telegraphs or telegrams. 2 economically worded. □□ **tel·e·graph·i·cal·ly** adv.

tel·e·graph·ic ad·dress n. an abbreviated or other registered address for use in telegrams.

te·leg·ra·phist /tilégrəfist/ n. a person skilled or employed in telegraphy.

tel·e·graph key n. a device for making and breaking the electric circuit of a telegraph system.

tel·e·graph plant n. an E. Indian plant, Desmodium motorium, whose leaves have a spontaneous jerking motion.

tel·e·ki·ne·sis /télikineésis, –ki/ n. Psychol. movement of objects at a distance supposedly by paranormal means. □□ **tel·e·ki·net·ic** /–nétik/ adj. [mod.L (as TELE-, Gk kinēsis motion f. kineō move)]

tel·e·mark /télimaark/ n. & v. Skiing ●n. a swing turn with one ski advanced and the knee bent, used to change direction or stop short. ●v.intr. perform this turn. [Telemark in Norway]

tel·e·mar·ket·ing /télimaárkiting/ n. the marketing of goods, etc., by means of usu. unsolicited telephone calls. □□ **tel·e·mar·ket·er** n.

tel·e·mes·sage /télimesij/ n. Brit. a message sent by telephone or telex and delivered in written form.

te·lem·e·ter /tilémitər, télimeetər/ n. & v. ●n. an apparatus for recording the readings of an instrument and transmitting them by radio. ●v. 1 intr. record readings in this way. 2 tr. transmit (readings, etc.) to a distant receiving set or station. □□ **tel·e·met·ric** /teləmétrik/ adj. **te·lem·e·try** /tilémitree/ n.

tel·e·ol·o·gy /téleeóləjee, tee–/ n. (pl. –gies) Philos. 1 the explanation of phenomena by the purpose they serve rather than by postulated causes. 2 Theol. the doctrine of design and purpose in the material world. □□ **tel·e·o·log·ic** /–leeəlójik/ adj. **tel·e·o·log·i·cal** adj. **tel·e·o·log·i·cal·ly** adv. **tel·e·ol·o·gism** n. **tel·e·ol·o·gist** n. [mod.L teleologia f. Gk telos teleos end + –LOGY]

tel·e·ost /téleeost, tee–/ n. any fish of the subclass Teleostei of bony fish, including eels, plaice, salmon, etc. [Gk teleo- complete + osteon bone]

tel·e·path /télipath/ n. a telepathic person. [back-form. f. TELEPATHY]

te·lep·a·thy /tǝlépǝthee/ n. the supposed communication of thoughts or ideas otherwise than by the known senses. □□ **tel·e·path·ic** /télipáthik/ adj. **tel·e·path·i·cal·ly** adv. **te·lep·a·thist** n. **te·lep·a·thize** v.tr. & intr.

tel·e·phone /télifon/ n. & v. ●n. 1 an apparatus for transmitting sound (esp. speech) over a distance by wire or cord or radio, esp. by converting acoustic vibrations to electrical signals. 2 a transmitting and receiving instrument used in this. 3 a system of communication using a network of telephones. ●v. 1 tr. speak to (a person) by telephone. 2 tr. send (a message) by telephone. 3 intr. make a telephone call. □ **on the telephone** by use of or using the telephone. **over the telephone** by use of or using the telephone. □□ **tel·e·phon·er** n. **tel·e·phon·ic** /–fónik/ adj. **tel·e·phon·i·cal·ly** /–fóniklee/ adv.

tel·e·phone book n. a book listing telephone subscribers and numbers in a particular area.

tel·e·phone booth n. (Brit. also **tel·e·phone box**) a public booth or enclosure from which telephone calls can be made.

tel·e·phone call n. = CALL n. 4.

tel·e·phone di·rec·to·ry n. = TELEPHONE BOOK.

tel·e·phone ex·change n. = EXCHANGE n. 3.

tel·e·phone num·ber n. a number assigned to a particular telephone and used in making connections to it.

tel·e·phone op·er·a·tor n. an operator in a telephone exchange or at a switchboard.

te·leph·o·nist /tiléfənist/ n. Brit. an operator in a telephone exchange or at a switchboard.

te·leph·o·ny /tǝléfǝnee/ n. the use or a system of telephones.

tel·e·pho·to /télifótō/ n. (pl. –tos) (in full **telephoto lens**) a lens used in telephotography.

tel·e·pho·to·graph·ic /télifótəgráfik/ adj. of or for or using telephotography. □□ **tel·e·pho·to·graph·i·cal·ly** adv.

tel·e·pho·tog·ra·phy /télifótógrəfee/ n. the photographing of distant objects with a system of lenses giving a large image.

tel·e·port /télipawrt/ v.tr. Psychol. move by telekinesis. □□ **tel·e·por·ta·tion** n. [TELE- + PORT⁴ 3]

tel·e·print·er /téliprintər/ n. esp. Brit. = TELETYPEWRITER.

Tel·e·Promp·Ter /télipromptər/ n. Trademark a device used in television and filmmaking to project a speaker's script out of sight of the audience (cf. AUTOCUE).

tel·e·sales /télisaylz/ n.pl. selling by means of the telephone.

tel·e·scope /téliskōp/ n. & v. ●n. 1 an optical instrument using lenses or mirrors or both to make distant objects appear nearer and larger. 2 = RADIO TELESCOPE. ●v. 1 tr. press or drive (sections of a tube, colliding vehicles, etc.) together so that one slides into another like the sections of a folding telescope. 2 intr. close or be driven or be capable of closing in this way. 3 tr. compress so as to occupy less space or time. [It. telescopio or mod.L telescopium (as TELE-, –SCOPE)]

telescope 1

tel·e·scop·ic /téliskópik/ adj. 1 a of, relating to, or made with a telescope (telescopic observations). b visible only through a telescope (telescopic stars). 2 (esp. of a lens) able to focus on and magnify distant objects. 3 consisting of sections that telescope. □□ **tel·e·scop·i·cal·ly** adv.

tel·e·scop·ic sight n. a telescope used for sighting on a rifle, etc.

tel·e·soft·ware /télisawftwair, –sóft–/ n. software transmitted or broadcast to receiving terminals.

tel·es·the·sia /télis-theézhǝ/ n. (Brit. **tel·aes·the·sia**) Psychol. the supposed perception of distant occurrences or objects otherwise than by the recognized senses. □□ **tel·es·thet·ic** /–thétik/ adj. [mod.L, formed as TELE- + Gk aisthēsis perception]

tel·e·text /télitekst/ n. a news and information service, in the form of text and graphics, from a computer source transmitted to televisions with appropriate receivers.

tel·e·thon /télithon/ n. an exceptionally long television program, esp. to raise money for a charity. [TELE- + –thon in MARATHON]

Tel·e·type /télitīp/ n. & v. ●n. Trademark a kind of teletypewriter. ●v. (teletype) 1 intr. operate a teletypewriter. 2 tr. send by means of a teletypewriter.

tel·e·type·writ·er /télitípritər/ n. a device for transmitting telegraph messages as they are keyed, and for printing messages received.

tel·e·van·ge·list /télivánjǝlist/ n. an evangelical preacher who appears regularly on television to promote beliefs and appeal for funds.

tel·e·view·er /télivyōōǝr/ v.tr. a person who watches television. □□ **tel·e·view·ing** adj.

tel·e·vise /télivīz/ v.tr. transmit by television. □□ **tel·e·vis·a·ble** adj. [back-form. f. TELEVISION]

tel·e·vi·sion /télivízhǝn/ n. 1 a system for reproducing on a screen visual images transmitted (usu. with sound) by radio waves. 2 (in full **television set**) a device with a screen for receiving these signals. 3 the medium, art form, or occupation of broadcasting on television; the content of television programs.

tel·e·vis·u·al /télivízhooǝl/ adj. esp. Brit. relating to or suitable for television. □□ **tel·e·vis·u·al·ly** adv.

tel·ex /téleks/ n. & v. (also **Telex**) ●n. an international system of telegraphy with printed messages transmitted and received by teletypewriters using the public telecommunications network. ●v.tr. send or communicate with by telex. [TELEPRINTER + EXCHANGE]

tell¹ /tel/ v. (past and past part. **told** /tōld/) 1 tr. relate or narrate in speech or writing; give an account of (tell me a story). 2 tr. make known; express in words; divulge (tell me your name; tell me what you want). 3 tr. reveal or signify to (a person) (your face tells me everything). 4 tr. a utter (don't tell lies). b warn (I told you so). 5 intr. a (often foll. by of, about) divulge information or a description; reveal a secret (I told of the plan; promise you won't tell). b (foll. by on) colloq. inform against (a person). 6 tr. (foll. by to + infin.) give (a person) a direction or order (tell them to wait; do as you are told). 7 tr. assure (it's true, I tell you). 8 tr. explain in writing; instruct (this book tells you how to cook). 9 tr. decide; predict; determine; distinguish (cannot tell what might happen; how do you tell one from the other?). 10 intr. a (often foll. by on) produce a noticeable effect (every disappointment tells; the strain was beginning to tell on me). **b** reveal the truth (time will tell). **c** have an influence (the evidence tells against you). **11** tr. (often absol.) count (votes) at a meeting, election, etc. □ **tell apart** distinguish between (usu. with neg. or interrog.: could not tell them apart). **tell off 1** colloq. reprimand; scold **2** count off or detach for duty. **tell a tale** (or **its own tale**) be significant or revealing. **tell tales** report a discreditable fact about another. **tell (the) time** determine the time from the face of a clock or watch. **there is no telling** it is impossible to know (there's no telling what may happen). **you're telling me** colloq. I agree wholeheartedly. □□ **tell·a·ble** adj. [OE tellan f. Gmc, rel. to TALE]

tell² /tel/ n. Archaeol. an artificial mound in the Middle East, etc., formed by the accumulated remains of ancient settlements. [Arab. tall hillock]

tell·er /télər/ n. **1** a person employed to receive and pay out money in a bank, etc. **2** a person who counts (votes). **3** a person who tells esp. stories (a teller of tales). □□ **tell·er·ship** n.

tell·ing /téling/ adj. **1** having a marked effect; striking. **2** significant. □ **telling off** esp. Brit. colloq. a reproof or reprimand. □□ **tell·ing·ly** adv.

tell·tale /téltayl/ n. **1** a person who reveals (esp. discreditable) information about another's private affairs or behavior. **2** (attrib.) that reveals or betrays (a telltale smile). **3** a device for automatic indicating, monitoring, or registering of a process, etc.

tel·lu·ri·an /teloôreeən/ adj. & n. ● adj. of or inhabiting the earth. ● n. an inhabitant of the earth. [L tellus –uris earth]

tel·lu·ric /teloôrik/ adj. **1** of the earth as a planet. **2** of the soil. **3** Chem. of tellurium, esp. with valence 6. □□ **tel·lu·rate** /télyoôrət/ n. [L tellus –uris earth: sense 3 f. TELLURIUM]

tel·lu·ri·um /teloôreeəm/ n. Chem. a rare brittle lustrous silver-white element occurring naturally in ores of gold and silver, used in semiconductors. ¶ Symb.: **Te.** □□ **tel·lu·ride** /télyoôrīd/ n. **tel·lu·rite** /télyoôrīt/ n. **tel·lu·rous** adj. [L tellus –uris earth, prob. named in contrast to uranium]

tel·ly /télee/ n. (pl. **–lies**) esp. Brit. colloq. **1** television. **2** a television set. [abbr.]

tel·pher /télfər/ n. a system for transporting goods, etc., by electrically driven trucks or cable cars. □□ **tel·pher·age** n. [TELE- + –PHORE]

tel·son /télsən/ n. the last segment in the abdomen of crustaceans, etc. [Gk, = limit]

Tel·u·gu /télləgoô/ n. (also **Tel·e·gu**) (pl. same or **Tel·e·gus**) **1** a member of a Dravidian people in SE India. **2** the language of this people. [Telugu]

tem·er·ar·i·ous /téməráireeəs/ adj. reckless; rash. [L temerarius f. temere rashly]

te·mer·i·ty /timéritee/ n. **1** rashness. **2** audacity; impudence. [L temeritas f. temere rashly]

SYNONYM TIP temerity

AUDACITY, EFFRONTERY, FOOLHARDINESS, GALL, IMPETUOSITY, RASHNESS. The line that divides boldness from foolishness or stupidity is often a fine one. Someone who rushes boldly into a situation without thinking about the consequences might be accused of **rashness**, while **temerity** implies exposing oneself needlessly to danger while failing to estimate one's chances of success. Rashness, which applies primarily to bodily acts, may be considered a positive trait; but temerity, which usually applies to mental or social acts, is always negative (She had the temerity to criticize her teacher in front of the class). **Audacity** describes a different kind of boldness, one that disregards moral standards or social conventions (He had the audacity to ask her if she would mind paying for the trip). Someone who behaves with **foolhardiness** is reckless or downright foolish (Climbing the mountain after dark was foolhardiness and everyone knew it), while **impetuosity** describes an eager impulsiveness or behavior that is sudden, rash, and sometimes violent (His impetuosity had landed him in trouble before). **Gall** and **effrontery** are always derogatory terms. Effrontery is a more formal word for the flagrant disregard of the rules of propriety, courtesy, etc. (She had the effrontery to call the President by his first name), while gall is more colloquial and suggests outright insolence (He was the only one who had the gall to tell the boss off).

temp /temp/ n. & v. colloq. ● n. a temporary employee. ● v.intr. work as a temp. [abbr.]

temp.¹ /temp/ abbr. temperature.

temp.² /temp/ abbr. in the time of (temp. Henry I). [L tempore ablat. of tempus time]

tem·per /témpər/ n. & v. ● n. **1** habitual or temporary disposition of mind esp. as regards composure (a person of calm temper). **2 a** irritation or anger (in a fit of temper). **b** an instance of this (flew into a temper). **3** a tendency to have fits of anger (has a temper). **4** composure or calmness (keep one's temper; lose one's temper). **5** the condition of metal as regards hardness and elasticity. ● v.tr. **1** bring (metal or clay) to a proper hardness or consistency. **2** (often foll. by with) moderate or mitigate (temper justice with mercy). **3** tune or

modulate (a piano, etc.) so as to distance intervals correctly. □ **in a bad temper** angry; peevish. **in a good temper** in an amiable mood. **out of temper** angry; peevish. **show temper** be petulant. □□ **tem·per·a·ble** adj. **tem·per·a·tive** /-pərətiv/ adj. **tem·pered** adj. **tem·pered·ly** adv. **tem·per·er** n.

WORD HISTORY temper

Old English temprian ' bring something into the required condition by mixing it with something else,' from Latin temperare 'mingle, restrain oneself.' Sense development was probably influenced by Old French temprer 'to temper, moderate.' The noun originally denoted a correct or proportionate mixture of elements or qualities, also the combination of the four bodily humors, believed in medieval times to be the basis of temperament, hence sense 1 (late Middle English).

tem·per·a /témpərə/ n. a method of painting using an emulsion, e.g., of pigment with egg, esp. on canvas. [It.: cf. DISTEMPER¹]

tem·per·a·ment /témprəmənt/ n. **1** a person's distinct nature and character, esp. as determined by physical constitution and permanently affecting behavior (a nervous temperament; the artistic temperament). **2** a creative or spirited personality (was full of temperament). **3 a** an adjustment of intervals in tuning a piano, etc., so as to fit the scale for use in all keys. **b** (**equal temperament**) an adjustment in which the 12 semitones are at equal intervals. [ME f. L temperamentum (as TEMPER)]

tem·per·a·men·tal /témprəmént'l/ adj. **1** of or having temperament. **2 a** (of a thing) liable to erratic or moody behavior. **b** (of a thing, e.g., a machine) working unpredictably; unreliable. □□ **tem·per·a·men·tal·ly** adv.

tem·per·ance /témpərəns, témprəns/ n. **1** moderation or self-restraint esp. in eating and drinking. **2 a** total or partial abstinence from alcohol. **b** (attrib.) advocating or concerned with abstinence. [ME f. AF temperaunce f. L temperantia (as TEMPER)]

tem·per·ate /témpərət, témprət/ adj. **1** avoiding excess; self-restrained. **2** moderate. **3** (of a region or climate) characterized by mild temperatures. **4** abstemious. □□ **tem·per·ate·ly** adv. **tem·per·ate·ness** n. [ME f. L temperatus past part. of temperare: see TEMPER]

tem·per·ate zone n. the belt of the earth between the frigid and the torrid zones.

tem·per·a·ture /témprichər/ n. **1** the degree or intensity of heat of a body, air mass, etc., in relation to others, esp. as shown by a thermometer or perceived by touch, etc. **2** Med. the degree of internal heat of the body. **3** colloq. a body temperature above the normal (have a temperature). **4** the degree of excitement in a discussion, etc. □ **take a person's temperature** ascertain a person's body temperature, esp. as a diagnostic aid. [F température or L temperatura (as TEMPER)]

SPELLING TIP temperature

To remember the correct spelling of temperature, use the mnemonic: "We often lose our temper at high temperatures."

tem·per·a·ture-hu·mid·i·ty in·dex n. a quantity giving the measure of discomfort due to the combined effects of the temperature and humidity of the air.

-tempered /témpərd/ comb. form having a specified temper or disposition (bad-tempered; hot-tempered). □□ **–temperedly** adv. **–temperedness** n.

tem·pest /témpist/ n. **1** a violent windy storm. **2** violent agitation or tumult. [ME f. OF tempest(e) ult. f. L tempestas season, storm, f. tempus time]

tem·pes·tu·ous /tempéschoôəs/ adj. **1** stormy. **2** (of a person, emotion, etc.) turbulent; violent; passionate. □□ **tem·pes·tu·ous·ly** adv. **tem·pes·tu·ous·ness** n. [LL tempestuosus (as TEMPEST)]

tem·pi pl. of TEMPO.

Tem·plar /témplər/ n. **1** a lawyer or law student in London. **2** (in full **Knight Templar**) hist. a member of a religious and military order for the protection of pilgrims to the Holy Land, suppressed in 1312. [ME f. AF templer, OF templier, med.L templarius (as TEMPLE¹)]

tem·plate /témplit, –playt/ n. (also **tem·plet**) **1 a** a pattern or gauge, usu. a piece of thin board or metal plate, used as a guide in cutting or drilling metal, stone, wood, etc. **b** a flat card or plastic pattern esp. for cutting cloth for patchwork, etc. **2** a timber or plate used to distribute the weight in a wall or under a beam, etc. **3** Biochem. the molecular pattern governing the assembly of a protein, etc. [orig. templet: prob. f. TEMPLE³ + –ET¹, alt. after plate]

tem·ple¹ /témpəl/ n. **1** a building devoted to the worship, or regarded as the dwelling place, of a god or gods or other objects of religious reverence. **2** hist. any of three successive religious buildings of the Jews in Jerusalem. **3** a Reform or Conservative synagogue. **4** a place of Christian public worship, esp. a Protestant church in France. **5** any place in which God is regarded as residing, as the body of a Christian (I Cor. 6: 19). [OE *temp(e)l*, reinforced in ME by OF *temple*, f. L *templum* open or consecrated space]

tem·ple[2] /témpəl/ *n.* the flat part of either side of the head between the forehead and the ear. [ME f. OF ult. f. L *tempora* pl. of *tempus*]

tem·ple[3] /témpəl/ *n.* a device in a loom for keeping the cloth stretched. [ME f. OF, orig. the same word as TEMPLE[2]]

tem·ple block *n.* a percussion instrument consisting of a hollow block of wood that is struck with a stick.

tem·plet var. of TEMPLATE.

tem·po /témpō/ *n.* (*pl.* **–pos** or **tem·pi** /–pee/) **1** *Mus.* the speed at which music is or should be played, esp. as characteristic (*waltz tempo*). **2** the rate of motion or activity (*the tempo of the war is quickening*). [It. f. L *tempus* time]

tem·po·ral /témpərəl, témprəl/ *adj.* **1** of worldly as opposed to spiritual affairs; of this life; secular. **2** of or relating to time. **3** *Gram.* relating to or denoting time or tense (*temporal conjunction*). **4** of the temples of the head (*temporal artery; temporal bone*). □□ **tem·po·ral·ly** *adv.* [ME f. OF *temporel* or f. L *temporalis* f. *tempus –oris* time]

tem·po·ral·i·ty /témpərálitee/ *n.* (*pl.* **–ties**) **1** temporariness. **2** (usu. in *pl.*) a secular possession, esp. the properties and revenues of a religious corporation or an ecclesiastic. [ME f. LL *temporalitas* (as TEMPORAL)]

tem·po·ral pow·er *n.* the power of an ecclesiastic, esp. the Pope, in temporal matters.

tem·po·rar·y /témpəreree/ *adj. & n.* ● *adj.* lasting or meant to last only for a limited time (*temporary buildings; temporary relief*). ● *n.* (*pl.* **–ies**) a person employed temporarily (cf. TEMP). □□ **tem·po·rar·i·ly** /–pəráirilee/*adv.* **tem·po·rar·i·ness** *n.* [L *temporarius* f. *tempus –oris* time]

tem·po·rize /témpərīz/ *v.intr.* **1** avoid committing oneself so as to gain time; employ delaying tactics. **2** comply temporarily with the requirements of the occasion; adopt a time-serving policy. □□ **tem·po·ri·za·tion** *n.* **tem·po·riz·er** *n.* [F *temporiser* bide one's time f. med. L *temporizare* delay f. *tempus –oris* time]

tempt /tempt/ *v.tr.* **1** entice or incite (a person) to do a wrong or forbidden thing (*tempted him to steal it*). **2** allure; attract. **3** risk provoking (esp. an abstract force or power) (*would be tempting fate to try it*). **4** *archaic* make trial of; try the resolution of (*God did tempt Abraham*). □ **be tempted to** be strongly disposed to (*I am tempted to question this*). □□ **tempt·a·ble** *adj.* **tempt·a·bil·i·ty** /témptəbílitee/ *n.* [ME f. OF *tenter, tempter* test f. L *temptare* handle, test, try]

temp·ta·tion /temptáyshən/ *n.* **1 a** the act or an instance of tempting; the state of being tempted; incitement esp. to wrongdoing. **b** (**the Temptation**) the tempting of Christ by the Devil (see Matt. 4). **2** an attractive thing or course of action. **3** *archaic* putting to the test. [ME f. OF *tentacion, temptacion* f. L *temptatio –onis* (as TEMPT)]

tempt·er /témptər/ *n.* (*fem.* **tempt·ress** /–tris/) **1** a person who tempts. **2** (**the Tempter**) the Devil. [ME f. OF *tempteur* f. eccl.L *temptator –oris* (as TEMPT)]

tempt·ing /témpting/ *adj.* **1** attractive; inviting. **2** enticing to evil. □□ **tempt·ing·ly** *adv.*

tem·pu·ra /tempóórə/ *n.* a Japanese dish of fish, shellfish, or vegetables, dipped in batter and deep-fried. [Jap.]

ten /ten/ *n. & adj.* ● *n.* **1** one more than nine. **2** a symbol for this (10, x, X). **3** a size, etc., denoted by ten. **4** the time of ten o'clock (*is it ten yet?*). **5** a playing card with ten pips. **6** a ten-dollar bill. **7** a set of ten. ● *adj.* **1** that amount to ten. **2** (as a round number) several (*ten times as easy*).

ten. *abbr.* **1** tenor. **2** tenuto.

ten·a·ble /ténəbəl/ *adj.* **1** that can be maintained or defended against attack or objection (*a tenable position; a tenable theory*). **2** (foll. by *for, by*) (of an office, etc.) that can be held for (a specified period)

or by (a specified class of person). □□ **ten·a·bil·i·ty** *n.* **ten·a·ble·ness** *n.* [F f. *tenir* hold f. L *tenēre*]

ten·ace /ténays/ *n.* **1** two cards, one ranking immediately above, and the other immediately below, a card held by an opponent. **2** the holding of such cards. [F f. Sp. *tenaza*, lit. 'pincers']

te·na·cious /tináyshəs/ *adj.* **1** (often foll. by *of*) keeping a firm hold of property, principles, life, etc.; not readily relinquishing. **2** (of memory) retentive. **3** holding fast. **4** strongly cohesive. **5** persistent; resolute. **6** adhesive; sticky. □□ **te·na·cious·ly** *adv.* **te·na·cious·ness** *n.* **te·nac·i·ty** /tinásitee/ *n.* [L *tenax –acis* f. *tenēre* hold]

te·nac·u·lum /tənákyələm/ *n.* (*pl.* **te·nac·u·la** /–lə/) a surgeon's sharp hook for picking up arteries, etc. [L, = holding instrument, f. *tenēre* hold]

ten·an·cy /ténənsee/ *n.* (*pl.* **–cies**) **1** the status of a tenant; possession as a tenant. **2** the duration or period of this.

ten·ant /ténənt/ *n. & v.* ● *n.* **1** a person who rents land or property from a landlord. **2** (often foll. by *of*) the occupant of a place **3** *Law* a person holding real property by private ownership. ● *v.tr.* occupy as a tenant. □□ **ten·ant·a·ble** *adj.* **ten·ant·less** *adj.* [ME f. OF, pres. part. of *tenir* hold f. L *tenēre*]

ten·ant farm·er *n.* a person who farms rented land.

ten·ant·ry /ténəntree/ *n.* the tenants of an estate, etc.

tench /tench/ *n.* (*pl.* same) a European freshwater fish, *Tinca tinca*, of the carp family. [ME f. OF *tenche* f. LL *tinca*]

Ten Com·mand·ments see COMMANDMENT.

tend[1] /tend/ *v.intr.* **1** (usu. foll. by *to*) be apt or inclined (*tends to lose his temper*). **2** serve; conduce. **3** be moving; be directed; hold a course (*tends in our direction; tends downwards; tends to the same conclusion*). [ME f. OF *tendre* stretch f. L *tendere* tens- or *tent-*]

tend[2] /tend/ *v.* **1** *tr.* take care of; look after (a person, esp. an invalid; animals, esp. sheep; a machine). **2** *intr.* (foll. by *on, upon*) wait on. **3** *intr.* (foll. by *to*) give attention to. □□ **tend·ance** *n.* archaic. [ME f. ATTEND]

ten·den·cy /téndənsee/ *n.* (*pl.* **–cies**) **1** (often foll. by *to, toward*) a leaning or inclination; a way of tending. **2** a group within a larger political party or movement. [med.L *tendentia* (as TEND[1])]

ten·den·tious /tendénshəs/ *adj.* derog. (of writing, etc.) calculated to promote a particular cause or viewpoint; having an underlying purpose. □□ **ten·den·tious·ly** *adv.* **ten·den·tious·ness** *n.* [as TENDENCY + *-OUS*]

ten·der[1] /téndər/ *adj.* (**ten·der·er, ten·der·est**) **1** easily cut or chewed; not tough (*tender steak*). **2** easily touched or wounded; susceptible to pain or grief (*a tender heart; a tender conscience*). **3** easily hurt; sensitive (*tender skin; a tender place*). **4** delicate; fragile (*a tender plant*). **b** gentle; soft (*a tender touch*). **5** loving; affectionate; fond (*tender parents; wrote tender verses*). **6** requiring tact or careful handling; ticklish (*a tender subject*). **7** (of age) early; immature (*of tender years*). **8** (usu. foll. by *of*) solicitous; concerned (*tender of his honor*). □□ **ten·der·ly** *adv.* **ten·der·ness** *n.* [ME f. OF *tendre* f. L *tener*]

ten·der[2] /téndər/ *v. & n.* ● *v.* **1** *tr.* **a** offer; present (one's services, apologies, resignation, etc.). **b** offer (money, etc.) as payment. **2** *intr.* (often foll. by *for*) make a tender for the supply of a thing or the execution of work. ● *n.* an offer, esp. an offer in writing to execute work or supply goods at a fixed price. □ **put out to tender** seek tenders or bids for (work, etc.). □□ **ten·der·er** *n.* [OF *tendre*: see TEND[1]]

ten·der[3] /téndər/ *n.* **1** a person who looks after people or things. **2** a vessel attending a larger one to supply stores, convey passengers or orders, etc. **3** a special car closely coupled to a steam locomotive to carry fuel, water, etc. [ME f. TEND² or f. *attender* (as ATTEND)]

ten·der·foot /téndərfŏot/ *n.* a newcomer or novice, esp. to the outdoor life or to the Scouts.

ten·der-heart·ed *adj.* having a tender heart; easily moved by pity, etc. □□ **ten·der-heart·ed·ness** *n.*

ten·der·ize /téndəriz/ *v.tr.* make tender, esp. make (meat) tender by beating, etc. □□ **ten·der·iz·er** *n.*

ten·der·loin /téndərloyn/ *n.* **1** a long tender cut of beef or pork from the loin, along the vertebrae. **2** *sl.* a district of a city where vice and corruption are prominent.

ten·der mer·cies *n.pl.iron.* attention or treatment which is not in the best interests of its recipient.

ten·der spot *n.* a subject on which a person is touchy.

ten·don /téndən/ *n.* **1** a cord or strand of strong tissue attaching a muscle to a bone, etc. **2** (in a quadruped) = HAMSTRING. □□ **ten·di·ni·tis** /téndinítis/ *n.* **ten·di·nous** /–dinəs/ *adj.* [F *tendon* or med.L *tendo –dinis* f. Gk *tenōn* sinew f. *teinō* stretch]

ten·dril /téndril/ *n.* **1** each of the slender leafless shoots by which some climbing plants cling for support. **2** a slender curl of hair, etc. [prob. f. obs. F *tendrillon* dimin. of obs. *tendron* young shoot ult. f. L *tener* TENDER¹]

Ten·e·brae /ténəbray, –bree/ *n.pl.* **1** *RC Ch. hist.* church services for the last three days of Holy Week, at which candles are successively extinguished. **2** this office set to music. [L, = darkness]

ten·e·brous /ténibrəs/ *adj. literary* dark; gloomy [ME f. OF *tenebrus* f. L *tenebrosus* (as TENEBRAE)]

ten·e·ment /ténimənt/ *n.* **1** a room or a set of rooms forming a separate residence within a house or apartment building. **2** a house divided into and rented in tenements, esp. one that is overcrowded, in poor condition, etc. **3** a dwelling place. **4 a** a piece of land held by an owner. **b** *Law* any kind of permanent property, e.g., lands or rents, held from another. □□ **ten·e·men·tal** /–mént'l/ *adj.* **ten·e·men·ta·ry** /–méntəree/ *adj.* [ME f. OF f. med.L *tenementum* f. *tenēre* hold]

ten·e·ment house *n.* = sense 2.

te·nes·mus /tinézməs/ *n. Med.* a continual inclination to evacuate the bowels or bladder accompanied by painful straining. [med.L f. Gk *teinesmos* straining f. *teinō* stretch]

ten·et /ténit/ *n.* a doctrine, dogma, or principle held by a group or person. [L, = he, etc., holds f. *tenēre* hold]

ten·fold /ténfōld/ *adj. & adv.* **1** ten times as much or as many. **2** consisting of ten parts.

ten-gal·lon hat *n.* a cowboy's large wide-brimmed hat.

te·ni·a var. of TAENIA.

Tenn. *abbr.* Tennessee.

ten·né /ténee/ *n. &* (usu. placed after noun) adj. (also **ten·ny**) *Heraldry* orange-brown. [obs. F, var. of *tanné* TAWNY]

ten·ner /ténər/ *n. colloq.* a ten-dollar bill or ten-pound note. [TEN]

ten·nis /ténis/ *n.* a game in which two or four players strike a ball with rackets over a net stretched across a court. [ME *tenetz*, *tenes*, etc., app. f. OF *tenez* 'take, receive,' called by the server to an opponent, imper. of *tenir* take]

ten·nis ball *n.* a ball used in playing tennis.

ten·nis court *n.* a court used in playing tennis.

ten·nis el·bow *n.* chronic inflammation caused by or as by playing tennis.

ten·nis rack·et *n.* a racket used in playing tennis.

ten·nis shoe *n.* a light canvas or leather rubbersoled shoe suitable for tennis or general casual wear.

ten·ny var. of TENNÉ.

Ten·ny·so·ni·an /ténisóneeən/ *adj.* relating to or in the style of Alfred (Lord) Tennyson, Engl. poet d. 1892.

ten·on /ténən/ *n. & v.* ● *n.* a projecting piece of wood made for insertion into a corresponding cavity (esp. a mortise) in another piece. ● *v.tr.* **1** cut as a tenon. **2** join by means of a tenon. □□ **ten·on·er** *n.* [ME f. F f. *tenir* hold f. L *tenēre* hold]

ten·on saw *n.* a small saw with a strong brass or steel back for fine work.

ten·or /ténər/ *n.* **1 a** a singing voice between baritone and alto or countertenor, the highest of the ordinary adult male range. **b** a singer with this voice. **c** a part written for it. **2 a** an instrument, esp. a viola, recorder, or saxophone, of which the range is roughly that of a tenor voice. **b** (in full **tenor bell**) the largest bell of a peal or set. **3** (usu. foll. by *of*) the general purport or drift of a document or speech. **4** (usu. foll. by *of*) a settled or prevailing course or direction, esp. the course of a person's life or habits. **5** *Law* **a** the actual wording of a document. **b** an exact copy. **6** the subject to which a metaphor refers (opp. VEHICLE 4). [ME f. AF *tenur*, OF *tenour* f. L *tenor –oris* f. *tenēre* hold]

ten·or clef *n. Mus.* a clef placing middle C on the second highest line of the staff.

ten·o·syn·o·vi·tis /ténōsínəvítis/ *n.* inflammation and swelling of a tendon, usu. in the wrist, often caused by repetitive movements such as typing. [Gk *tenōn* tendon + SYNOVITIS]

te·not·o·my /tənótəmee/ *n.* (*pl.* **–mies**) the surgical cutting of a ten-

---

don, esp. as a remedy for a clubfoot. [F *ténotomie*, irreg. f. Gk *tenōn –ontos* tendon]

ten·pin /ténpin/ *n.* **1** a pin used in tenpin bowling. **2** (in *pl.*) = TENPIN BOWLING.

ten·pin bowl·ing *n.* a game developed from ninepins in which ten pins are set up at the end of an alley and bowled at to be knocked down.

ten·rec /ténrek/ *n.* (also **tan·rec** /tán–/) any hedgehoglike, tailless, insectivorous mammal of the family Tenrecidae, esp. *Tenrec ecaudatus* native to Madagascar. [F *tanrec*, f. Malagasy *tàndraka*]

tense¹ /tens/ *adj. & v.* ● *adj.* **1** stretched tight; strained (*tense cord*; *tense muscle*; *tense nerves*; *tense emotion*). **2** causing tenseness (*a tense moment*). **3** *Phonet.* pronounced with the vocal muscles tense. ● *v.tr. & intr.* make or become tense □ **tense up** become tense. □□ **tense·ly** *adv.* **tense·ness** *n.* **ten·si·ty** *n.* [L *tensus* past part. of *tendere* stretch]

tense² /tens/ *n. Gram.* **1** a form taken by a verb to indicate the time (also the continuance or completeness) of the action, etc. (*present tense*; *imperfect tense*). **2** a set of such forms for the various persons and numbers. □□ **tense·less** *adj.* [ME f. OF *tens* f. L *tempus* time]

GRAMMAR TIP tense

Verb Tenses. In the context of verbs and grammar, **tense** means 'time.' The *tense* of a verb tells when the action expressed by the verb takes place. English verbs have three main tenses: present, past, and future. The **present tense** describes a current state or action (*I drop the phone*), a habitual or repeated action (*I jog every day*), and sometimes, with an adverb, a future state or action (*the tax collector arrives tomorrow*). The **past tense** describes a past condition or completed action (*I dropped the phone the minute I heard*), or a recurring action in the past that does not extend to the present (*the tax collector reviewed all of our records*). The **future tense** describes a future condition or action (*I will jog again as soon as my injury heals*), an intention (*I will contact the tax collector tomorrow*), or a probability (*he will be in for a shock if he's audited*). The future tense always requires the use of the **auxiliary** (or **helping**) **verb** *will* or *shall*.

---

ten·sile /ténsəl, –sīl/ *adj.* **1** of or relating to tension. **2** capable of being drawn out or stretched. □□ **ten·sil·i·ty** /tensílitee/ *n.* [med.L *tensilis* (as TENSE¹)]

ten·sile strength *n.* resistance to breaking under tension.

ten·sim·e·ter /tensímitər/ *n.* **1** an instrument for measuring vapor pressure. **2** a manometer. [TENSION +METER]

ten·sion /ténshən/ *n. & v.* ● *n.* **1** the act or an instance of stretching; the state of being stretched; tenseness. **2** mental strain or excitement. **3** a strained (political, social, etc.) state or relationship. **4** *Mech.* the stress by which a bar, cord, etc., is pulled when it is part of a system in equilibrium or motion. **5** electromagnetic force (*high tension; low tension*). ● *v.tr.* subject to tension. □□ **ten·sion·al** *adj.* **ten·sion·al·ly** *adv.* **ten·sion·less** *adj.* [F *tension* or L *tensio* (as TEND¹)]

ten·son /ténsən, tensón/ *n.* (also **ten·zon** /téenzən, tenzón/) **1** a contest in versifying between troubadours. **2** a piece of verse composed for this. [F *tenson*, = Prov. *tenso* (as TENSION)]

ten·sor /ténsər/ *n.* **1** *Anat.* a muscle that tightens or stretches a part. **2** *Math.* a generalized form of vector involving an arbitrary number of indices. □□ **ten·so·ri·al** /–sáwreeəl/ *adj.* [mod.L (as TEND¹)]

tent¹ /tent/ *n. & v.* ● *n.* **1** a portable shelter or dwelling of canvas, cloth, etc., supported by a pole or poles and stretched by cords attached to pegs driven into the ground. **2** *Med.* a tentlike enclosure for control of the air supply to a patient. ● *v.* **1** *tr.* cover with or as with a tent. **2** *intr.* **a** encamp in a tent. **b** dwell temporarily. [ME f. OF *tente* ult. f. L *tendere* stretch: *tent stitch* may be f. another word]

tent² /tent/ *n.* a deep red sweet wine chiefly from Spain, used esp. as sacramental wine. [Sp. *tinto* deep-colored f. L *tinctus* past part.: see TINGE]

tent³ /tent/ *n. Surgery* a piece (esp. a roll) of lint, linen, etc., inserted into a wound or natural opening to keep it open. [ME f. OF *tente* f. *tenter* probe (as TEMPT)]

ten·ta·cle /téntəkəl/ *n.* **1** a long slender flexible appendage of an (esp. invertebrate) animal, used for feeling, grasping, or moving. **2** a thing used like a tentacle as a feeler, etc. **3** *Bot.* a sensitive hair or filament. □□ **ten·ta·cled** *adj.* (also in *comb.*). **ten·tac·u·lar** /–tákyələr/ *adj.* **ten·tac·u·late** /–tákyələt, –layt/ *adj.* [mod.L *tentaculum* f. L *tentare = temptare* (see TEMPT) + –*culum* –CULE]

ten·ta·tive /téntətiv/ *adj. & n.* ● *adj.* **1** done by way of trial; experimental. **2** hesitant; not definite (*tentative suggestion; tentative acceptance*). ● *n.* an experimental proposal or theory. □□ **ten·ta·tive·ly** *adv.* **ten·ta·tive·ness** *n.* [med.L *tentativus* (as TENTACLE)]

ten·ter¹ /téntər/ *n.* **1** a machine for stretching cloth to dry in shape. **2** = TENTERHOOK. [ME ult. f. med.L *tentorium* (as TEND¹)]

tent bed *n.* a bed with a tentlike canopy, or for a patient in a tent.

See page xx for the **Key to Pronunciation.**

tent cat·er·pil·lar *n.* any of several caterpillars of the genus *Malacosoma*, including *M. americanum* and *M. disstria* (forest tent caterpillar), that construct and live in large tentlike webs in trees.

tent coat *n.* (also **tent dress**) a coat (or dress) cut very full with no waistline.

ten·ter² /téntər/ *n. Brit.* **1** a person in charge of something, esp. of machinery in a factory. **2** a worker's unskilled assistant. [*tent* (now Sc.) pay attention, perh f. *tent* attention f. INTENT or obs. *attent* (as ATTEND)]

ten·ter·hook /téntərhŏŏk/ *n.* any of the hooks to which cloth is fastened on a tenter. □ **on tenterhooks** in a state of suspense or mental agitation due to uncertainty.

tent fly *n.* (*pl.* **flies**) **1** a flap at the entrance to a tent. **2** a piece of canvas stretched over the ridgepole of a tent leaving an open space but keeping off sun and rain.

tent peg *n.* any of the pegs to which the cords of a tent are attached.

tent peg·ging *n.* a sport in which a rider tries at full gallop to carry off on the point of a lance a tent peg fixed in the ground.

tenth /tenth/ *n. & adj.* ● *n.* **1** the position in a sequence corresponding to the number 10 in the sequence 1-10. **2** something occupying this position. **3** one of ten equal parts of a thing. **4** *Mus.* **a** an interval or chord spanning an octave and a third in the diatonic scale. **b** a note separated from another by this interval. ● *adj.* that is the tenth. □□ **tenth·ly** *adv.* [ME *tenthe*, alt. of OE *teogotha*]

tenth-rate *adj.* of extremely poor quality.

tent stitch *n.* **1** a series of parallel diagonal embroidery stitches. **2** such a stitch.

ten·u·is /tényŏŏis/ *n.* (*pl.* **ten·u·es** /-yoo-eez/) *Phonet.* a voiceless stop, e.g., *k, p, t.* [L, = thin, transl. Gk *psilos* smooth]

te·nu·i·ty /tinŏŏitee, -nyŏŏ-/ *n.* **1** slenderness. **2** (of a fluid, esp. air) rarity; thinness. [L *tenuitas* (as TENUIS)]

ten·u·ous /tényŏŏəs/ *adj.* **1** slight; of little substance (*tenuous connection*). **2** (of a distinction, etc.) oversubtle. **3** thin; slender; small. **4** rarefied. □□ **ten·u·ous·ly** *adv.* **ten·u·ous·ness** *n.* [L *tenuis*]

ten·ure /tényər/ *n.* **1** a condition, or form of right or title, under which (esp. real) property is held. **2** (often foll. by *of*) **a** the holding or possession of an office or property. **b** the period of this (*during his tenure of office*). **3** guaranteed permanent employment, esp. as a teacher or professor after a probationary period. [ME f. OF f. *tenir* hold f. L *tenēre*]

ten·ured /tényərd/ *adj.* **1** (of an official position) carrying a guarantee of permanent employment. **2** (of a teacher, professor, etc.) having guaranteed tenure of office.

ten·u·ri·al /tenyŏŏreeəl/ *adj.* of the tenure of land. □□ **ten·u·ri·al·ly** *adv.* [med.L *tenūra* TENURE]

te·nu·to /tənŏŏtó/ *adv., adj., & n. Mus.* ● *adv. & adj.* (of a note, etc.) sustained; given its full time value (cf. LEGATO, STACCATO). ● *n.* (*pl.* **-tos**) a note or chord played tenuto. [It., = held]

ten·zon var. of TENSON.

te·o·cal·li /téeəkálee/ *n.* (*pl.* **te·o·cal·lis**) a temple of the Aztecs or other Mexican peoples, usu. on a truncated pyramid. [Nahuatl f. *teotl* god + *calli* house]

te·pee /téepee/ *n.* (also **tee·pee**) a conical tent, made of skins, cloth, or canvas on a frame of poles, orig. used by Native Americans. [Sioux or Dakota *tīpī*]

teph·ra /téfrə/ *n.* fragmented rock, etc., ejected by a volcanic eruption. [Gk, = ash]

tep·id /tépid/ *adj.* **1** slightly warm. **2** unenthusiastic. □□ **tep·id·i·ty** /tipíditee/ *n.* **tep·id·ly** *adv.* **tep·id·ness** *n.* [L *tepidus* f. *tepēre* be lukewarm]

te·qui·la /tekéelə/ *n.* a Mexican liquor made from an agave. [*Tequila* in Mexico]

ter- /ter/ *comb. form* three; threefold (*tercentenary; tervalent*). [L *ter* thrice]

tera- /térə/ *comb. form* denoting a factor of 10^{12}. [Gk *teras* monster]

te·rai /tərí/ *n.* (in full **terai hat**) a wide-brimmed felt hat, often with a double crown, worn by travelers, etc., in subtropical regions. [*Terai*, belt of marshy jungle between Himalayan foothills and plains, f. Hindi *tarāī* moist (land)]

ter·aph /térəf/ *n.* (*pl.* **ter·a·phim**, also used as *sing.*) a small image as a domestic deity or oracle of the ancient Hebrews. [ME f. LL *theraphim*, Gk *theraphin* f. Heb. ṛrāpīm]

terato- /térətō/ *comb. form* monster. [Gk *teras -atos* monster]

te·rat·o·gen /tərátəjən/ *n. Med.* an agent or factor causing malformation of an embryo. □□ **te·rat·o·gen·ic** /térətōjénik/ *adj.* **ter·a·tog·e·ny** /térətójenee/ *n.*

ter·a·tol·o·gy /térətóləjee/ *n.* **1** *Biol.* the scientific study of animal or vegetable monstrosities. **2** mythology relating to fantastic crea-

tures, monsters, etc. □□ **ter·a·to·log·i·cal** /-təlójikəl/ *adj.* **ter·a·tol·o·gist** *n.*

ter·a·to·ma /térətómə/ *n. Med.* a tumor of heterogeneous tissues.

ter·bi·um /tórbeeəm/ *n. Chem.* a silvery metallic element of the lanthanide series. ¶ Symb.: **Tb**. [mod.L f. *Ytterby* in Sweden]

terce /tərs/ *n. Eccl.* **1** the office of the canonical hour of prayer appointed for the third daytime hour (i.e., 9 a.m.). **2** this hour. [var. of TIERCE]

ter·cel /tórsəl/ *n.* (also **tier·cel** /téersəl/) *Falconry* the male of the hawk, esp. a peregrine or goshawk. [ME f. OF *tercel*, ult. a dimin. of L *tertius* third, perh. from a belief that the third egg of a clutch produced a male bird, or that the male was one-third smaller than the female]

ter·cen·ten·ar·y /tórsenténəree, tərséntineree/ *n. & adj.* ● *n.* (*pl.* **-ies**) **1** a three-hundredth anniversary. **2** a celebration of this. ● *adj.* of this anniversary.

ter·cen·ten·ni·al /tórsenténeeəl/ *adj. & n.* ● *adj.* **1** occurring every three hundred years. **2** lasting three hundred years. ● *n.* a tercentenary.

ter·cet /tórsit/ *n.* (also **tier·cet** /téer-/) *Prosody* a set or group of three lines rhyming together or connected by rhyme with an adjacent triplet. [F f. It. *terzetto* dimin. of *terzo* third f. L *tertius*]

ter·e·bene /téribeen/ *n.* a mixture of terpenes prepared by treating oil of turpentine with sulfuric acid, used as an expectorant, etc. [TEREBINTH + -ENE]

ter·e·binth /téribinth/ *n.* a small Southern European tree, *Pistacia terebinthus*, yielding turpentine. [ME f. OF *terebinte* or L *terebinthus* f. Gk *terebinthos*]

ter·e·bin·thine /téribínthin, -thīn/ *adj.* **1** of the terebinth. **2** of turpentine. [L *terebinthinus* f. Gk *terebinthinos* (as TEREBINTH)]

te·re·do /təreedō/ *n.* (*pl.* **-dos**) any bivalve mollusk of the genus *Teredo*, esp. *T. navalis*, that bores into submerged wood, damaging ships, etc. Also called **shipworm**. [L f. Gk *terēdōn* f. *teirō* rub hard, wear away, bore]

te·rete /təreet/ *adj. Biol.* smooth and rounded; cylindrical. [L *teres -etis*]

ter·gal /tórgəl/ *adj.* of or relating to the back; dorsal. [L *tergum* back]

ter·gi·ver·sate /tórjiversáyt/ *v.intr.* **1** be apostate; change one's party or principles. **2** equivocate; make conflicting or evasive statements. **3** turn one's back on something. □□ **ter·gi·ver·sa·tion** /-sáyshən/ *n.* **ter·gi·ver·sa·tor** *n.* [L *tergiversari* turn one's back f. *tergum* back + *vertere* vers- turn]

ter·i·ya·ki /tereeyókee/ *n.* a dish consisting of meat, poultry, or fish that is marinated in seasoned soy sauce and grilled, sautéed, or broiled. [Jap. *teri* glaze + *yaki* broil]

term /tərm/ *n. & v.* ● *n.* **1** a word used to express a definite concept, esp. in a particular branch of study, etc. (*a technical term*). **2** (in *pl.*) language used; mode of expression (*answered in no uncertain terms*). **3** (in *pl.*) a relation or footing (*we are on familiar terms*). **4** (in *pl.*) **a** conditions or stipulations (*cannot accept your terms; do it on your own terms*). **b** charge or price (*his terms are $20 a lesson*). **5 a** a limited period of some state or activity (*for a term of five years*). **b** a period over which operations are conducted or results contemplated (*in the short term*). **c** a period of some weeks, alternating with holidays or vacation, during which instruction is given in a school, college, or university, or during which a court of law holds sessions. **d** a period of imprisonment. **e** a period of tenure. **6** *Logic* a word or words that may be the subject or predicate of a proposition. **7** *Math.* **a** each of the two quantities in a ratio. **b** each quantity in a series. **c** a part of an expression joined to the rest by + or − (e.g., *a, b, c* in *a + b − c*). **8** the completion of a normal length of pregnancy. **9** an appointed day, time, etc. **10** (in full **US** term for **years** or *Brit.* **term of years**) *Law* an interest in land for a fixed period. **11** = TERMINUS 6. **12** *archaic* a boundary or limit, esp. of time. ● *v.tr.* denominate; call; assign a term to (*the music termed classical*). □ **bring to terms** cause to accept conditions. **come to terms** yield; give way. **come to terms with 1** reconcile oneself to (a difficulty, etc.). **2** conclude an agreement with. **in set terms** in definite terms. **in terms** explicitly. **in terms of 1** in the language peculiar to; using as a basis of expression or thought. **2** by way of. **make terms** conclude an agreement. **on terms** on terms of friendship or equality. □□ **term·less** *adj.* **term·ly** *adj. & adv.* [ME f. OF *terme* f. L TERMINUS]

ter·ma·gant /tórməgənt/ *n. & adj.* ● *n.* **1** an overbearing or brawling woman; a virago or shrew. **2** (**Termagant**) *hist* an imaginary deity of violent and turbulent character, often appearing in morality plays. ● *adj.* violent; turbulent; shrewish. [ME *Tervagant* f. OF *Tervagan* f. It. *Trivigante*]

ter·mi·na·ble /tórminəbəl/ *adj.* **1** that may be terminated. **2** coming to an end after a certain time (*terminable annuity*). □□ **ter·mi·na·ble·ness** *n.*

ter·mi·nal /tórminəl/ *adj. & n.* ● *adj.* **1 a** (of a disease) ending in death; fatal. **b** (of a patient) in the last stage of a fatal disease. **c** (of a morbid condition) forming the last stage of fatal disease. **d** *colloq.* ruinous; disastrous; very great (*terminal laziness*). **2** of or forming a limit or terminus (*terminal station*). **3 a** *Zool.*, etc., ending a series (*terminal joints*). **b** *Bot.* growing at the end of a stem, etc. **4** of or done, etc., each term (*terminal accounts*; *terminal examinations*). • **n. 1** a terminating thing; an extremity. **2** a terminus for trains or long-distance buses. **3** a departure and arrival building for air passengers. **4** a point of connection for closing an electric circuit. **5** an apparatus for transmission of messages between a user and a computer, communications system, etc. **6** (in full **terminal figure**) = TERMINUS 6. **7** an installation where oil is stored at the end of a pipeline or at a port. □□ **ter·mi·nal·ly** *adv.* [L *terminalis* (as TERMINUS)]

ter·mi·nal ve·loc·i·ty *n.* a velocity of a falling body such that the resistance of the air, etc., prevents further increase of speed under gravity.

ter·mi·nate /tə́rminayt/ *v.* **1** *tr. & intr.* bring or come to an end. **2** *intr.* (foll. by *in*) (of a word) end in (a specified letter or syllable, etc.). **3** *tr.* end (a pregnancy) before term by artificial means. **4** *tr.* bound; limit. [L *terminare* (as TERMINUS)]

ter·mi·na·tion /tə̀rmináyshən/ *n.* **1** the act or an instance of terminating; the state of being terminated. **2** *Med.* an induced abortion. **3** an ending or result of a specified kind (*a happy termination*). **4** a word's final syllable or letters or letter esp. as an element in inflection or derivation. □ **put a termination to** (or **bring to a termination**) make an end of. □□ **ter·mi·na·tion·al** *adj.* [ME f. OF *termination* or L *terminatio* (as TERMINATE)]

ter·mi·na·tor /tə́rminaytər/ *n.* **1** a person or thing that terminates. **2** the dividing line between the light and dark part of a planetary body.

ter·min·er see OYER AND TERMINER.

ter·mi·ni *pl.* of TERMINUS.

ter·mi·no·log·i·cal /tə̀rminəlójikəl/ *adj.* of terminology. □□ **ter·mi·no·log·i·cal·ly** *adv.*

ter·mi·no·log·i·cal in·ex·act·i·tude *n. joc.* a lie.

ter·mi·nol·o·gy /tə̀rminóləjee/ *n.* (*pl.* **-gies**) **1** the system of terms used in a particular subject. **2** the science of the proper use of terms. □□ **ter·mi·nol·o·gist** *n.* [G *Terminologie* f. med.L TERMINUS term]

ter·mi·nus /tə́rminəs/ *n.* (*pl.* **ter·mi·ni** /-nī/ or **ter·mi·nus·es**) **1** a station or destination at the end of a railroad or bus route. **2** a point at the end of a pipeline, etc. **3** a final point; a goal. **4** a starting point. **5** *Math.* the end point of a vector, etc. **6** *Archit.* a figure of a human bust or an animal ending in a square pillar from which it appears to spring, orig. as a boundary marker. [L, = end, limit, boundary]

ter·mi·nus ad quem *n.* /ad kwém/ the finishing point of an argument, policy, period, etc.

ter·mi·nus an·te quem *n.* /ántee kwém/ the finishing point of a period.

ter·mi·nus a quo *n.* /aa kwó/ the starting point of an argument, policy, period, etc.

ter·mi·nus post quem *n.* /pōst kwém/ the starting point of a period.

ter·mi·ta·ry /tə́rmiteree/ *n.* (*pl.* **-ries**) a nest of termites, usu. a large mound of earth.

ter·mite /tə́rmīt/ *n.* a small antlike social insect of the order Isoptera, chiefly tropical and destructive to wood. [LL *termes* *-mitis*, alt. of L *tarmes* after *terere* rub]

ter·mor /tə́rmər/ *n. Law* a person who holds lands, etc., for a term of years, or for life. [ME f. AF *termer* (as TERM)]

term pa·per *n.* an essay or dissertation representative of the work done during a term.

terms of ref·er·ence *n.pl. Brit.* points referred to an individual or body of persons for decision or report; the scope of an inquiry, etc.; a definition of this.

tern[1] /tərn/ *n.* any marine bird of the subfamily Sterninae, like a gull but usu. smaller and with a long forked tail. [of Scand. orig.: cf. Da. *terne*, Sw. *tärna* f. ON *therna*]

tern[2] /tərn/ *n.* **1** a set of three, esp. three lottery numbers that when drawn together win a large prize. **2** such a prize. [F *terne* f. L *terni* three each]

ter·na·ry /tə́rnəree/ *adj.* **1** composed of three parts. **2** *Math.* using three as a base (*ternary scale*). [ME f. L *ternarius* f. *terni* three each]

ter·na·ry form *n. Mus.* the form of a movement in which the first subject is repeated after an interposed second subject in a related key.

ter·nate /tə́rnayt/ *adj.* **1** arranged in threes. **2** *Bot.* (of a leaf): **a** having three leaflets. **b** whorled in threes. □□ **ter·nate·ly** *adv.* [mod.L *ternatus* (as TERNARY)]

terne /tərn/ *n.* (in full **terneplate**) inferior tin plate alloyed with four parts lead. [prob. f. F *terne* dull: cf. TARNISH]

te·ro·tech·nol·o·gy /tə̀rōteknóləjee, teèr-/ *n.* esp. *Brit.* the branch of technology and engineering concerned with the installation and maintenance of equipment. [Gk *tēreō* take care of + TECHNOLOGY]

ter·pene /tə́rpeen/ *n. Chem.* any of a large group of unsaturated cyclic hydrocarbons found in the essential oils of plants, esp. conifers and oranges. [*terpentin* obs. var. of TURPENTINE]

terp·si·cho·re·an /tə̀rpsikəreéən, -káwreeən// *adj.* of or relating to dancing. [*Terpsichore* Muse of dancing]

terr. *abbr.* **1** terrace. **2** territory.

ter·ra al·ba /tə́rə álbə/ *n.* a white mineral, esp. pipe clay or pulverized gypsum. [L, = white earth]

ter·race /tə́rəs/ *n. & v.* • *n.* **1** each of a series of flat areas formed on a slope and used for cultivation. **2** a level paved area next to a house. **3 a** a row of houses on a raised level or along the top or face of a slope. **b** *Brit.* a row of houses built in one block of uniform style; a set of row houses. **4** *Brit.* a flight of wide shallow steps as for spectators at a sports ground. **5** *Geol.* a raised beach, or a similar formation beside a river, etc. • *v.tr.* form into or provide with a terrace or terraces. [OF ult. f. L *terra* earth]

ter·raced roof *n.* a flat roof.

ter·race house *n. Brit.* = row house.

ter·ra-cot·ta /térəkótə/ *n.* **1 a** unglazed usu. brownish red earthenware used chiefly as an ornamental building material and in modeling. **b** a statuette of this. **2** its color. [It. *terra cotta* baked earth]

ter·ra fir·ma /térə fə́rmə/ *n.* dry land; firm ground. [L, = firm land]

ter·rain /teráyn/ *n.* a tract of land as regarded by the physical geographer or the military tactician. [F, ult. f. L *terrenum* neut. of *terrenus* TERRENE]

ter·ra in·cog·ni·ta /térə inkógneetə, ínkogneétə/ *n.* an unknown or unexplored region. [L, = unknown land]

ter·ra·ma·ra /térəmaárə/ *n.* (*pl.* **ter·ra·ma·re** /-ray/) = TERRAMARE. [It. dial.: see TERRAMARE]

ter·ra·ma·re /térəmaáree/ *n.* **1** an ammoniacal earthy deposit found in mounds in prehistoric lake dwellings or settlements esp. in Italy. **2** such a dwelling or settlement. [F f. It. dial. *terra mara* f. *marna* marl]

ter·ra·pin /térəpin/ *n.* any of various N. American edible freshwater turtles of the family Emydidae. [Algonquian]

ter·rar·i·um /teráireeəm/ *n.* (*pl.* **ter·rar·i·ums** or **ter·rar·i·a** /-reeə/) **1** a vivarium for small land animals. **2** a sealed transparent globe, etc., containing growing plants. [mod.L f. L *terra* earth, after AQUARIUM]

ter·ra sig·il·la·ta /térə sígilaàtə, síjiláytə/ *n.* **1** astringent clay from Lemnos or Samos. **2** Samian ware. [med.L, = sealed earth]

ter·raz·zo /təráazō, -ráatsō/ *n.* (*pl.* **-zos**) a flooring material of stone chips set in concrete and given a smooth surface. [It., = terrace]

ter·rene /tereén/ *adj.* **1** of the earth; earthy; worldly. **2** of earth; earthly. **3** of dry land; terrestrial. [ME f. AF f. L *terrenus* f. *terra* earth]

terre-plein /táirplayn, térə-/ *n.* a level space where a battery of guns is mounted. [orig. a sloping bank behind a rampart f. F *terre-plein* f. It. *terrapieno* f. *terrapienare* fill with earth f. *terra* earth + *pieno* f. L *plenus* full]

ter·res·tri·al /təréstreeəl/ *adj. & n.* • *adj.* **1** of or on or relating to the earth; earthly. **2 a** of or on dry land. **b** *Zool.* living on or in the ground (opp. AQUATIC, ARBOREAL, AERIAL). **c** *Bot.* growing in the soil (opp. AQUATIC, EPIPHYTIC). **3** *Astron.* (of a planet) similar in size or composition to the earth. **4** of this world; worldly (*terrestrial sins*; *terrestrial interests*). • *n.* an inhabitant of the earth. □□ **ter·res·tri·al·ly** *adv.* [ME f. L *terrestris* f. *terra* earth]

ter·res·tri·al globe *n.* the earth.

ter·res·tri·al mag·net·ism *n.* the magnetic properties of the earth as a whole.

ter·res·tri·al tel·e·scope *n.* a telescope giving an erect image for observation of terrestrial objects.

ter·ret /térit/ *n.* (also **ter·rit**) each of the loops or rings on a harness pad for the driving reins to pass through. [ME, var. of *toret* (now dial.) f. OF *to(u)ret* dimin. of TOUR]

terre verte /táir váirt/ *n.* a soft green earth used as a pigment. [F, = green earth]

ter·ri·ble /téribəl/ *adj.* **1** *colloq.* very great or bad (*a terrible bore*). **2** *colloq.* very incompetent (*terrible at tennis*). **3** causing terror; fit to cause terror; awful; dreadful; formidable. **4** (*predic.*; usu. foll. by *about*) *colloq.* full of remorse; sorry (*I felt terrible about it*). □□ **ter·ri·ble·ness** *n.* [ME f. F f. L *terribilis* f. *terrēre* frighten]

ter·ri·bly /tériblee/ *adv.* **1** *colloq.* very; extremely (*he was terribly nice about it*). **2** in a terrible manner.

ter·ric·o·lous /teríkələs/ *adj.* living on or in the ground. [L *terricola* earth dweller f. *terra* earth + *colere* inhabit]

ter·ri·er[1] /téreeər/ *n.* **1 a** a small dog of various breeds originally used for driving out foxes, etc., from their holes. **b** any of these breeds. **2** an eager or tenacious person or animal. [ME f. OF (*chien*) *terrier* f. med.L *terrarius* f. L *terra* earth]

ter·ri·er[2] /téreeər/ *n. hist.* **1** a book recording the site, boundaries, etc., of the land of private persons or corporations. **2** a rent roll. **3** a collection of acknowledgments of vassals or tenants of a lordship. [ME f. OF *terrier* (adj.) = med.L *terrarius liber* (as TERRIER[1])]

ter·rif·ic /tərifik/ *adj.* **1** *colloq.* **a** of great size or intensity. **b** excellent (*did a terrific job*). **c** excessive (*making a terrific noise*). **2** causing terror. □□ **ter·rif·i·cal·ly** *adv.* [L *terrificus* f. *terrēre* frighten]

ter·ri·fy /térifī/ *v.tr.* (**-fies**, **-fied**) fill with terror; frighten severely (*terrified them into submission; is terrified of dogs*). □□ **ter·ri·fi·er** *n.* **ter·ri·fy·ing** *adj.* **ter·ri·fy·ing·ly** *adv.* [L *terrificare* (as TERRIFIC)]

See page xx for the **Key to Pronunciation**.

ter·rig·e·nous /teríjinəs/ *adj.* produced by the earth or the land (*terrigenous deposits*). [L *terrigenus* earthborn]

ter·rine /təreén/ *n.* **1** an earthenware vessel, esp. one in which pâté, etc., is cooked or sold. **2** pâté or similar food. [orig. form of TUREEN]

ter·rit var. of TERRET.

ter·ri·to·ri·al /téritáwreeəl/ *adj.* **1** of territory (*territorial possessions*). **2** limited to a district (*the right was strictly territorial*). **3** (of a person or animal, etc.) tending to defend an area of territory. **4** of any of the territories of the US or Canada. □□ **ter·ri·to·ri·al·i·ty** /–reeálitee/ *n.* **ter·ri·to·ri·al·ize** *v.tr.* **ter·ri·to·ri·al·i·za·tion** *n.* **ter·ri·to·ri·al·ly** *adv.* [LL *territorialis* (as TERRITORY)]

ter·ri·to·ri·al wa·ters *n.pl.* the waters under the jurisdiction of a nation, esp. the part of the sea within a stated distance of the shore (traditionally three miles from the low water mark).

ter·ri·to·ry /téritawree/ *n.* (*pl.* **–ries**) **1** the extent of the land under the jurisdiction of a ruler, nation, city, etc. **2** (**Territory**) an organized division of a country, esp. one not yet admitted to the full rights of a state. **3** a sphere of action or thought; a province. **4** the area over which a sales representative or distributor operates. **5** *Zool.* an area defended by an animal or animals against others of the same species. **6** an area defended by a team or player in a game. **7** a large tract of land. [ME f. L *territorium* f. *terra* land]

ter·ror /térər/ *n.* **1** extreme fear. **2 a** a person or thing that causes terror. **b** (also **ho·ly ter·ror**) *colloq.* a formidable person; a troublesome person or thing (*the twins are little terrors*). **3** the use of organized intimidation; terrorism. [ME f. OF *terrour* f. L *terror –oris* f. *terrēre* frighten]

ter·ror·ist /térərist/ *n.* (also *attrib.*) a person who uses or favors violent and intimidating methods of coercing a government or community. □□ **ter·ror·ism** *n.* **ter·ror·is·tic** *adj.* **ter·ror·is·ti·cal·ly** *adv.*

WORD HISTORY terrorist

Late 18th century: from French *terroriste*, from Latin *terror* (source of *terror*). The word was originally applied to supporters of the Jacobins in the French Revolution, who advocated repression and violence in pursuit of the principles of democracy and equality.

---

ter·ror·ize /térərīz/ *v.tr* **1** fill with terror. **2** use terrorism against. □□ **ter·ror·i·za·tion** *n.* **ter·ror·iz·er** *n.*

ter·ror-strick·en *adj.* (also **ter·ror-struck**) affected with terror.

ter·ry /téree/ *n. & adj.* ● *n.* (*pl.* **–ries**) a pile fabric with the loops uncut, used esp. for towels. ● *adj.* of this fabric. [18th c.: orig. unkn.]

terse /ters/ *adj.* (**ters·er**, **ters·est**) **1** (of language) brief; concise; to the point. **2** curt; abrupt. □□ **terse·ly** *adv.* **terse·ness** *n.* [L *tersus* past part. of *tergēre* wipe, polish]

SYNONYM TIP terse

CONCISE, LACONIC, PITHY, SENTENTIOUS, SUCCINCT. If you don't like to mince words, you'll make every effort to be **concise** in both your writing and speaking, which means to remove all superfluous details (*a concise summary of everything that happened*). **Succinct** is very close in meaning to *concise*, although it emphasizes compression and compactness in addition to brevity (*succinct instructions for what to do in an emergency*). If you're **laconic**, you are brief to the point of being curt, brusque, or even uncommunicative (*his laconic reply left many questions unanswered*). **Terse** can also mean clipped or abrupt (*a terse command*), but it usually connotes something that is both *concise* and polished (*a terse style of writing that was much admired*). A **pithy** statement is not only *succinct* but full of substance and meaning (*a pithy argument that no one could counter*). **Sententious** comes from a Latin word meaning *opinion*. Although it describes a condensed and *pithy* style or approach, it also connotes a pompous or moralizing attitude or tone (*the speaker was so sententious that half the audience slipped out before he was finished*).

---

ter·tian /tórshən/ *adj.* (of a fever) recurring every third day by inclusive counting. [ME (*fever*) *tersiane* f. L (*febris*) *tertiana* (as TERTIARY)]

ter·ti·ar·y /tórshee-eree, –shə ri/ *adj. & n.* ● *adj.* **1** third in order or rank, etc. **2** (**Tertiary**) *Geol.* of or relating to the first period in the Cenozoic era with evidence of the development of mammals and flowering plants (cf. PALEOCENE, EOCENE, OLIGOCENE, MIOCENE, PLIOCENE). ● *n.* **1** *Geol.* this period or system. **2** a member of the third order of a monastic body. [L *tertiarius* f. *tertius* third]

ter·ti·um quid /tórsheeəm kwíd, tértee-ŏŏm/ *n.* a third something, esp. intermediate between mind and matter or between opposite things. [L, app. transl. Gk *triton ti*]

ter·va·lent /tórváylənt/ *adj. Chem.* having a valence of three; trivalent. [TER– + *valent–* part. stem (as VALENCE[1])]

ter·za ri·ma /táirtsə reémə/ *n. Prosody* an arrangement of (esp. iambic pentameter) triplets rhyming *aba bcb cdc*, etc., as in Dante's *Divina Commedia*. [It., = third rhyme]

ter·zet·to /tairtséttō/ *n.* (*pl.* **–tos** or **ter·zet·ti** /–tee/) *Mus.* a vocal or instrumental trio. [It.: see TERCET]

TESL *abbr.* teaching of English as a second language.

tes·la /téslə/ *n.* a unit of magnetic flux density. [N. *Tèsla*, Croatian-born Amer. scientist d. 1943]

Tes·la coil *n.* a form of induction coil for producing high-frequency alternating currents.

TESOL /tésawl, –ol/ *abbr.* teaching of English to speakers of other languages.

tes·sel·late /tésəlayt/ *v.tr.* **1** make from tesserae. **2** *Math.* cover (a plane surface) by repeated use of a single shape. [L *tessellare* f. *tessella* dimin. of TESSERA]

tes·sel·lat·ed /tésəlaytid/ *adj.* **1** of or resembling mosaic. **2** *Bot. & Zool.* regularly checkered. [L *tessellatus* or It. *tessellato* (as TESSELLATE)]

tes·sel·la·tion /tésəláyshən/ *n.* **1** the act or an instance of tessellating; the state of being tessellated. **2** an arrangement of polygons without gaps or overlapping, esp. in a repeated pattern.

tes·ser·a /tésərə/ *n.* (*pl.* **tes·ser·ae** /–ree/) **1** a small square block used in mosaic. **2** *Gk & Rom. Antiq.* a small square of bone, etc., used as a token, ticket, etc. □□ **tes·ser·al** *adj.* [L f. Gk, neut. of *tesseres, tessares* four]

tes·si·tu·ra /tésitŏŏrə/ *n. Mus.* the range within which most tones of a voice part fall. [It., = TEXTURE]

test[1] /test/ *n. & v.* ● *n.* **1** a critical examination or trial of a person's or thing's qualities. **2** the means of so examining; a standard for comparison or trial; circumstances suitable for this (*success is not a fair test*). **3** a minor examination, esp. in school (*spelling test*). **4** *Brit. colloq.* a test match in cricket or rugby. **5** a ground for admission or rejection (*is excluded by our test*). **6** *Chem.* a reagent or a procedure employed to reveal the presence of another in a compound. **7** *Brit.* a movable hearth in a reverberating furnace with a cupel used in separating gold or silver from lead. **8** (*attrib.*) done or performed in order to test (*a test run*). ● *v.tr.* **1** put to the test; make trial of (a person or thing or quality). **2** try severely; tax a person's powers of endurance, etc. **3** *Chem.* examine by means of a reagent. **4** *Brit.* refine or assay (metal). □ **put to the test** cause to undergo a test. **test out** put (a theory, etc.) to a practical test. □□ **test·a·ble** *adj.* **test·a·bil·i·ty** /téstəbilitee/ *n.* **test·ee** /testeé/ *n.* [ME f. OF f. L *testu(m)* earthen pot, collateral form of *testa* TEST[2]]

test[2] /test/ *n.* the shell of some invertebrates, esp. foraminiferans and tunicates. [L *testa* tile, jug, shell, etc.: cf. TEST[1]]

Test. *abbr.* Testament.

tes·ta /téstə/ *n.* (*pl.* **tes·tae** /–tee/) *Bot.* a seed coat. [L (as TEST[2])]

tes·ta·ceous /testáyshəs/ *adj.* **1** *Biol.* having a hard continuous outer covering. **2** *Bot. & Zool.* of a brick red color. [L *testaceus* (as TEST[2])]

Test Act *n. Brit. hist.* **1** an act in force 1672–1828, requiring all persons before holding office in Britain to take oaths of supremacy and allegiance or an equivalent test. **2** an act of 1871 relaxing conditions for university degrees.

tes·ta·ment /téstəmənt/ *n.* **1** a will (esp. last will and testament). **2** (usu. foll. by *to*) evidence; proof (*is testament to his loyalty*). **3** *Bibl.* **a** a covenant or dispensation. **b** (**Testament**) a division of the Christian Bible (see OLD TESTAMENT, NEW TESTAMENT). **c** (**Testament**) a copy of the New Testament. [ME f. L *testamentum* will (as TESTATE): in early Christian L rendering Gk *diathēkē* covenant]

tes·ta·men·ta·ry /téstəméntəree/ *adj.* of or by or in a will. [L *testamentarius* (as TESTAMENT)]

tes·tate /téstayt/ *adj. & n.* ● *adj.* having left a valid will at death. ● *n.* a testate person. □□ **tes·ta·cy** *n.* (*pl.* **–cies**). [L *testatus* past part. of *testari* testify, make a will, f. *testis* witness]

tes·ta·tor /téstaytər, testáytə r/ *n.* (*fem.* **tes·ta·trix** /testáytriks/) a person who has made a will, esp. one who dies testate. [ME f. AF *testatour* f. L *testator* (as TESTATE)]

test bed *n.* equipment for testing aircraft engines before acceptance for general use.

test card *n. Brit.* = TEST PATTERN.

test case *n. Law* a case setting a precedent for other cases involving the same question of law.

test drive *n.* a drive taken to determine the qualities of a motor vehicle with a view to its regular use. **test-drive** *v.tr.* (*past* **–drove**; *past part.* **–driv·en**) drive (a vehicle) for this purpose.

test·er[1] /téstər/ *n.* **1** a person or thing that tests. **2** a sample of a cosmetic, etc., allowing customers to try it before purchase.

tes·ter[2] /téstər/ *n.* a canopy, esp. over a four-poster bed. [ME f. med.L *testerium, testrum, testura,* ult. f. L *testa* tile]

tes·tes *pl.* of TESTIS.

test flight *n.* a flight during which the performance of an aircraft is tested. □□ **test-fly** *v.tr.* (**–flies**; *past* **–flew**; *past part.* **–flown**) fly (an aircraft) for this purpose.

tes·ti·cle /téstikəl/ *n.* a male organ that produces spermatozoa, etc., esp. one of a pair enclosed in the scrotum behind the penis of a man and most mammals. □□ **tes·tic·u·lar** /–stíkyələr/ *adj.* [ME f. L *testiculus* dimin. of *testis* witness (of virility)]

tes·tic·u·late /testíkyələt/ *adj.* **1** having or shaped like testicles. **2** *Bot.*

(esp. of an orchid) having pairs of tubers so shaped. [LL *testiculatus* (as TESTICLE)]

tes·ti·fy /téstifī/ *v.* (**–fies, –fied**) **1** *intr.* (of a person or thing) bear witness (*testified to the facts*). **2** *intr. Law* give evidence. **3** *tr.* affirm or declare (*testified his regret; testified that she had been present*). **4** *tr.* (of a thing) be evidence of; evince. □□ **tes·ti·fi·er** *n.* [ME f. L *testificari* f. *testis* witness]

tes·ti·mo·ni·al /téstimôneeəl/ *n.* **1** a certificate of character, conduct, or qualifications. **2** a gift presented to a person (esp. in public) as a mark of esteem, in acknowledgment of services, etc. [ME f. OF *testimoignal* (adj.) f. *tesmoin* or LL *testimonialis* (as TESTIMONY)]

tes·ti·mo·ny /téstimônee/ *n.* (*pl.* **–nies**) **1** *Law* an oral or written statement under oath or affirmation. **2** declaration or statement of fact. **3** evidence; demonstration (*called him in testimony; produce testimony*). **4** *Bibl.* the Ten Commandments. **5** *archaic* a solemn protest or confession. [ME f. L *testimonium* f. *testis* witness]

tes·tis /téstis/ *n.* (*pl.* **tes·tes** /–teez/) *Anat. & Zool.* a testicle. [L, = witness: cf. TESTICLE]

test match *n.* a cricket or rugby match between teams of certain countries, usu. each of a series in a tour.

tes·tos·ter·one /testóstərōn/ *n.* a steroid androgen formed in the testicles. [TESTIS + STEROL + –ONE]

test pa·per *n.* **1** a minor examination paper. **2** *Chem.* a paper impregnated with a substance changing color under known conditions.

test pat·tern *n.* a still television picture transmitted outside normal program hours and designed for use in judging the quality and position of the image.

test pi·lot *n.* a pilot who test-flies aircraft.

test tube *n.* a thin glass tube closed at one end used for chemical tests, etc.

test-tube ba·by *n. colloq.* a baby conceived by *in vitro* fertilization.

tes·tu·di·nal /testŏod'nəl, –tyŏod–/ *adj.* of or shaped like a tortoise. [as TESTUDO]

tes·tu·do /testŏodō, testyŏo–/ *n.* (*pl.* **–dos** or **tes·tu·di·nes** /–dineez/) *Rom.Hist.* **1** a screen formed by a body of troops in close array with overlapping shields. **2** a movable screen to protect besieging troops. [L *testudo –dinis*, lit. 'tortoise' (as TEST²)]

tes·ty /téstee/ *adj.* (**tes·ti·er, tes·ti·est**) irritable; touchy. □□ **tes·ti·ly** *adv.* **tes·ti·ness** *n.* [ME f. AF *testif* f. OF *teste* head (as TEST²)]

te·tan·ic /titánik/ *adj.* of or such as occurs in tetanus. □□ **te·tan·i·cal·ly** *adv.* [L *tetanicus* f. Gk *tetanikos* (as TETANUS)]

tet·a·nus /tét'nəs/ *n.* **1** a bacterial disease affecting the nervous system and marked by tonic spasm of the voluntary muscles. **2** *Physiol.* the prolonged contraction of a muscle caused by rapidly repeated stimuli. □□ **tet·a·nize** *v.tr.* **tet·a·noid** *adj.* [ME f. L f. Gk *tetanos* muscular spasm f. *teinō* stretch]

tet·a·ny /tét'nee/ *n.* a disease with intermittent muscular spasms caused by malfunction of the parathyroid glands and a consequent deficiency of calcium. [F *tétanie* (as TETANUS)]

tetch·y /téchee/ *adj.* (also **tech·y**) (**–i·er, –i·est**) peevish; irritable. □□ **tetch·i·ly** *adv.* **tetch·i·ness** *n.* [prob. f. *tecche, tache* blemish, fault f. OF *teche, tache*]

tête-à-tête /táytaatáyt, tétaatét/ *n., adv., & adj.* ● *n.* **1** a private conversation or interview usu. between two persons. **2** an S-shaped sofa for two people to sit face to face. ● *adv.* together in private (*dined tête-à-tête*). ● *adj.* **1** private; confidential. **2** concerning only two persons. [F, lit. 'head-to-head']

tête-bêche /taytbésh, tét–/ *adj.* (of a postage stamp) printed upside down or sideways relative to another. [F f. *tête* head + *bêchevet* double bedhead]

teth·er /téthər/ *n. & v.* ● *n.* **1** a rope, etc., by which an animal is tied to confine it to the spot. **2** the extent of one's knowledge, authority, etc.; scope; limit. ● *v.tr.* tie (an animal) with a tether. □ **at the end of one's tether** having reached the limit of one's patience, resources, abilities, etc. [ME f. ON *tjóthr* f. Gmc]

tetra- /tétrə/ *comb. form* (also **tetr-** before a vowel) **1** four (*tetrapod*). **2** *Chem.* (forming names of compounds) containing four atoms or groups of a specified kind (*tetroxide*). [Gk f. *tettares* four]

tet·ra·chord /tétrəkawrd/ *n. Mus.* **1** a scale pattern of four notes, the interval between the first and last being a perfect fourth. **2** a musical instrument with four strings.

tet·ra·cy·clic /tétrəsíklik, –sí–/ *adj.* **1** *Bot.* having four circles or whorls. **2** *Chem.* (of a compound) having a molecular structure of four fused hydrocarbon rings.

tet·ra·cy·cline /tétrəsíkleen, –klin/ *n.* an antibiotic with a molecule of four rings. [TETRACYCLIC + –INE⁴]

tet·rad /tétrad/ *n.* **1** a group of four. **2** the number four. [Gk *tetras –ados* (as TETRA-)]

tet·ra·dac·tyl /tétrədáktil/ *n. Zool.* an animal with four toes on each foot. □□ **tet·ra·dac·tyl·ous** *adj.*

tet·ra·eth·yl lead /tétréthəl/ *n.* a liquid formerly added to gasoline as an antiknock agent.

tet·ra·gon /tétrəgon/ *n.* a plane figure with four angles and four sides. [Gk *tetragōnon* quadrangle (as TETRA-, –GON)]

te·trag·o·nal /tetrágənəl/ *adj.* **1** of or like a tetragon. **2** *Crystallog.* (of

a crystal) having three axes at right angles, two of them equal. □□ **te·trag·o·nal·ly** *adv.*

tet·ra·gram /tétrəgram/ *n.* a word of four letters.

Tet·ra·gram·ma·ton /tétrəgrámə ton/ *n.* the Hebrew name of God written in four letters, articulated as *Yahweh*, etc. [Gk (as TETRA-, *gramma, –atos* letter)]

tet·ra·gy·nous /titrájinəs/ *adj. Bot.* having four pistils.

tet·ra·he·dron /tétrəheedrən/ *n.* (*pl.* **tet·ra·he·dra** /–drə/ or **tet·ra·he·drons**) a four-sided solid; a triangular pyramid. □□ **tet·ra·he·dral** *adj.* [late Gk *tetraedron* neut. of *tetraedros* four-sided (as TETRA-, –HEDRON)]

te·tral·o·gy /tetráləjee, –tról–/ *n.* (*pl.* **–gies**) **1** a group of four related literary or operatic works. **2** *Gk Antiq.* a trilogy of tragedies with a satyric drama.

tet·ram·er·ous /tetrámərəs/ *adj.* having four parts.

te·tram·e·ter /tetrámitər/ *n. Prosody* a verse of four measures. [LL *tetrametrus* f. Gk *tetrametros* (as TETRA-, *metron* measure)]

te·tran·drous /tetrándrəs/ *adj. Bot.* having four stamens.

tet·ra·ple·gi·a /tétrəpleéjeeə, –jə/ *n. Med.* = QUADRIPLEGIA. □□ **tet·ra·ple·gic** *adj. & n.* [mod.L (as TETRA-, Gk *plēgē* blow, strike)]

tet·ra·ploid /tétrəployd/ *adj. & n. Biol.* ● *adj.* (of an organism or cell) having four times the haploid set of chromosomes. ● *n.* a tetraploid organism or cell.

tet·ra·pod /tétrəpod/ *n.* **1** *Zool.* an animal with four feet. **2** a structure supported by four feet radiating from a center. □□ **te·trap·o·dous** /titrápədəs/ *adj.* [mod.L *tetrapodus* f. Gk *tetrapous* (as TETRA-, *pous podos* foot)]

te·trap·ter·ous /tetráptərəs/ *adj. Zool.* having four wings. [mod.L *tetrapterus* f. Gk *tetrapteros* (as TETRA-, *pteron* wing)]

te·trarch /tétraark/ *n.* **1** *Rom.Hist.* **a** the governor of a fourth part of a country or province. **b** a subordinate ruler. **2** one of four joint rulers. □□ **te·trarch·ate** /–kayt/ *n.* **te·trar·chi·cal** /–raárkikəl/ *adj.* **te·trar·chy** *n.* (*pl.* **–chies**). [ME f. LL *tetrarcha* f. L *tetrarches* f. Gk *tetrarkhēs* (as TETRA-, *arkhō* rule)]

tet·ra·stich /tétrəstik/ *n. Prosody* a group of four lines of verse. [L *tetrastichon* f. Gk (as TETRA-, *stikhon* line)]

tet·ra·style /tétrəstīl/ *n. & adj.* ● *n.* a building with four pillars, esp. forming a portico in front or supporting a ceiling. ● *adj.* (of a building) built in this way. [L *tetrastylos* f. Gk *tetrastulos* (as TETRA-, STYLE)]

tet·ra·syl·la·ble /tétrəsíləbəl/ *n.* a word of four syllables. □□ **tet·ra·syl·lab·ic** /–lábik/ *adj.*

te·trath·lon /tetráthlon/ *n.* a contest comprising four events, esp. riding, shooting, swimming, and running. [TETRA- + Gk *athlon* contest, after PENTATHLON]

tet·ra·tom·ic /tétrətómik/ *adj. Chem.* having four atoms (of a specified kind) in the molecule.

tet·ra·va·lent /tétrəváylənt/ *adj. Chem.* having a valence of four; quadrivalent.

tet·rode /tétrōd/ *n.* a thermionic valve having four electrodes. [TETRA- + Gk *hodos* way]

tet·ter /tétər/ *n. archaic* or *dial.* a pustular skin eruption, e.g., eczema. [OE *teter*: cf. OHG *zittaroh*, G dial. *Zitteroch*, Skr. *dadru*]

Teut. *abbr.* Teutonic.

Teuto- /tóotō, tōó–/ *comb. form* = TEUTON.

Teu·ton /tóot'n, tyóótən/ *n.* **1** a member of a Teutonic nation, esp. a German. **2** *hist.* a member of a N. European tribe which attacked the Roman republic *c.* 110 BC. [L *Teutones, Teutoni*, f. an IE base meaning 'people' or 'country']

Teu·ton·ic /tōotónik, tyōó–/ *adj. & n.* ● *adj.* **1** relating to or characteristic of the Germanic peoples or their languages. **2** German. ● *n.* the early language usu. called Germanic. □□ **Teu·ton·i·cism** /–isizəm/ *n.* [F *teutonique* f. L *Teutonicus* (as TEUTON)]

Tex. *abbr.* Texas.

Tex·an /téksən/ *n. & adj.* ● *n.* a native or inhabitant of Texas. ● *adj.* of or relating to Texas.

Tex-Mex /téksméks/ *adj.* combining cultural elements from Texas and Mexico, as in cooking, music, etc.

text /tekst/ *n.* **1** the main body of a book as distinct from notes, appendices, pictures, etc. **2** the original words of an author or document, esp. as distinct from a paraphrase of or commentary on them. **3** a passage quoted from Scripture, esp. as the subject of a sermon. **4** a subject or theme. **5** (in *pl.*) books prescribed for study. **6** a textbook. **7** (in full **text hand**) a large kind of handwriting esp. for manuscripts. **8** lyrics, as to a song or poem. □□ **text·less** *adj.* [ME f. ONF *tixte, texte* f. L *textus* tissue, literary style (in med.L = Gospel) f. *texere* text- weave]

text·book /tékstbʊ̄ok/ *n. & adj.* ● *n.* a book for use in studying, esp. a standard account of a subject. ● *attrib.adj.* **1** exemplary; accurate (cf. COPYBOOK). **2** instructively typical. □□ **text·book·ish** *adj.*

text ed·i·tor *n. Computing* a system or program allowing the user to enter and edit text.

text proc·ess·ing *n. Computing* the manipulation of text, esp. transforming it from one format to another.

tex·tile /tékstil/ *n. & adj.* ● *n.* **1** any woven material. **2** any cloth. ● *adj.* **1** of weaving or cloth (*textile industry*). **2** woven (*textile fabrics*). **3** suitable for weaving (*textile materials*). [L *textilis* (as TEXT)]

tex·tu·al /tékschōōəl/ *adj.* of, in, or concerning a text (*textual errors*). □□ **tex·tu·al·ly** *adv.* [ME f. med.L *textualis* (as TEXT)]

tex·tu·al crit·i·cism *n.* the process of attempting to ascertain the correct reading of a text.

tex·tu·al·ist /tékschōōəlist/ *n.* a person who adheres strictly to the letter of the text. □□ **tex·tu·al·ism** *n.*

tex·ture /tékschər/ *n. & v.* ● *n.* **1** the feel or appearance of a surface or substance. **2** the arrangement of threads, etc., in textile fabric. **3** the arrangement of small constituent parts. **4** *Art* the representation of the structure and detail of objects. **5** *Mus.* the quality of sound formed by combining parts. **6** the quality of a piece of writing, esp. with reference to imagery, alliteration, etc. **7** quality of style resulting from composition (*the texture of her life*). ● *v.tr.* (usu. as **textured** *adj.*) provide with a texture. □□ **tex·tur·al** *adj.* **tex·tur·al·ly** *adv.* **tex·ture·less** *adj.* [ME f. L *textura* weaving (as TEXT)]

tex·tur·ize /tékschəriz/ *v.tr.* (usu. as **texturized** *adj.*) impart a particular texture to (fabrics or food).

Th *symb. Chem.* the element thorium.

Th. *abbr.* Thursday.

-th[1] /th/ *suffix* (also **–eth** /ith/) forming ordinal and fractional numbers from *four* onwards (*fourth; thirtieth*). [OE *–tha, –the, –otha, –othe*]

-th[2] /th/ *suffix* forming nouns denoting an action or process: **1** from verbs (*birth; growth*). **2** from adjectives (*breadth; filth; length*). [OE *–thu, –tho, –th*]

-th[3] *var.* of –ETH[2].

Thai /tí/ *n. & adj.* ● *n.* (*pl.* same or **Thais**) **1 a** a native or inhabitant of Thailand in SE Asia; a member of the largest ethnic group in Thailand. **b** a person of Thai descent. **2** the language of Thailand. ● *adj.* of or relating to Thailand or its people or language. [Thai, = free]

thal·a·mus /tháləməs/ *n.* (*pl.* **thal·a·mi** /–mī/) **1** *Anat.* either of two masses of gray matter in the forebrain, serving as relay stations for sensory tracts. **2** *Bot.* the receptacle of a flower. **3** *Gk Antiq.* an inner room or women's apartment. □□ **tha·lam·ic** /thəlámik, tháləmik/ *adj.* (in senses 1 and 2). [L f. Gk *thalamos*]

tha·las·sic /thəlásik/ *adj.* of the sea or seas, esp. small or inland seas. [F *thalassique* f. Gk *thalassa* sea]

tha·ler /táalər/ *n. hist.* a German silver coin. [G *T(h)aler*: see DOLLAR]

tha·lid·o·mide /thəlídəmīd/ *n.* a drug formerly used as a sedative but found in 1961 to cause fetal malformation when taken by a mother early in pregnancy. [ph*thali*mido glutar*imide*]

tha·lid·o·mide ba·by *n.* (also **tha·lid·o·mide child**) a baby or child born deformed from the effects of thalidomide.

thal·li *pl.* of THALLUS.

thal·li·um /tháleeəm/ *n. Chem.* a rare soft white metallic element, occurring naturally in zinc blende and some iron ores. ¶ Symb.: **Tl**. □□ **thal·lic** *adj.* **thal·lous** *adj.* [formed as THALLUS, from the green line in its spectrum]

thal·lo·phyte /tháləfit/ *n. Bot.* a plant having a thallus, e.g., algae, fungus, or lichen. [mod.L *Thallophyta* (as THALLUS) + –PHYTE]

thal·lus /tháləs/ *n.* (*pl.* **thal·li** /–lī/) a plant body without vascular tissue and not differentiated into root, stem, and leaves. □□ **thal·loid** *adj.* [L f. Gk *thallos* green shoot f. *thallō* bloom]

thal·weg /táalveg/ *n.* **1** *Geog.* a line where opposite slopes meet at the bottom of a valley, river, or lake. **2** *Law* a boundary between states along the center of a river, etc. [G f. *Thal* valley + *Weg* way]

than /than, thən/ *conj.* **1** introducing the second element in a comparison (*you are older than he is; you are older than he*). **2** introducing the second element in a statement of difference (*anyone other than me*). [OE *thanne*, etc., orig. the same word as THEN]
▶In less formal contexts, it is also possible to say *you are older than him*, with *than* treated as a preposition.

than·age /tháynij/ *n. hist.* **1** the rank of thane. **2** the land granted to a thane. [ME f. AF *thanage* (as THANE)]

than·a·tol·o·gy /thánətóləjee/ *n.* the scientific study of death and its associated phenomena and practices. [Gk *thanatos* death + –LOGY]

thane /thayn/ *n. hist.* **1** a man who held land from an English king or other superior by military service, ranking between ordinary freemen and hereditary nobles. **2** a man who held land from a Scottish king and ranked with an earl's son; the chief of a clan. □□ **thane·dom** *n.* [OE *theg(e)n* servant, soldier f. Gmc]

thank /thangk/ *v. & n.* ● *v.tr.* **1** express gratitude to (*thanked him for*

the present). **2** hold responsible (*you can thank yourself for that*). ● *n.* (in *pl.*) **1** gratitude (*expressed his heartfelt thanks*). **2** an expression of gratitude (*give thanks to all who helped*). **3** (as a formula) thank you (*thanks for your help; thanks very much*). □ **give thanks** say grace at a meal. **I will thank you** esp. *Brit.* a polite formula, now usu. *iron.* implying reproach (*I will thank you to go away*). **no** (or **small**) **thanks to** despite. **thank goodness** (or **God** or **heavens**, etc.) **1** *colloq.* an expression of relief or pleasure. **2** an expression of pious gratitude. **thanks to** as the (good or bad) result of (*thanks to my foresight; thanks to your obstinacy*). **thank you** a polite formula acknowledging a gift or service or an offer accepted or refused. [OE *thancian, thanc* f. Gmc, rel. to THINK]

thank·ful /thángkfōol/ *adj.* **1** grateful; pleased. **2** (of words or acts) expressive of thanks. □□ **thank·ful·ness** *n.* [OE *thancful* (as THANK, –FUL)]

thank·ful·ly /thángkfōolee/ *adv.* **1** in a thankful manner. **2** *disp.* let us be thankful; fortunately (*thankfully, nobody was hurt*). [OE *thancfullice* (as THANKFUL, –LY[2])]

thank·less /thángklis/ *adj.* **1** not expressing or feeling gratitude. **2** (of a task, etc.) giving no pleasure or profit. **3** not deserving thanks. □□ **thank·less·ly** *adv.* **thank·less·ness** *n.*

thanks·giv·ing /thángksgíving/ *n.* **1 a** the expression of gratitude, esp. as a prayer. **b** a form of words for this. **2** (**Thanksgiving** or Thanksgiving Day) a national holiday for giving thanks, the fourth Thursday in November in the US, usu. the second Monday in October in Canada.

thank you *n. colloq.* an instance of expressing thanks.

thar *var.* of TAHR.

that /that/ *pron., adj., adv., & conj.* ● *demons.pron.* (*pl.* **those** /thōz/) **1** the person or thing indicated, named, or understood, esp. when observed by the speaker or when familiar to the person addressed (*I heard that; who is that in the yard?; I knew all that before; that is not fair*). **2** (contrasted with *this*) the further or less immediate or obvious, etc., of two (*this bag is much heavier than that*). **3** the action, behavior, or circumstances just observed or mentioned (*don't do that again*). **4** *Brit.* (on the telephone, etc.) the person spoken to (*who is that?*). **5** esp. *Brit. colloq.* referring to a strong feeling just mentioned (*'Are you glad?' 'I am that'*). **6** (esp. in relative constructions) the one, the person, etc., described or specified in some way (*those who have cars can take the luggage; those unfit for use; a table like that described above*). **7** *that* (*pl.* **that**) used instead of *which* or *whom* to introduce a defining clause, esp. one essential to identification (*the book that you sent me; there is nothing here that matters*). ● *demons.adj.* (*pl.* **those** /thōz/) **1** designating the person or thing indicated, named, understood, etc. (cf. sense 1 of *pron.*) (*look at that dog; what was that noise?; things were easier in those days*). **2** contrasted with *this* (cf. sense 2 of *pron.*) (*this bag is heavier than that one*). **3** expressing strong feeling (*shall not easily forget that day*). ● *adv.* **1** to such a degree; so (*have done that much; will go that far*). **2** *colloq.* very (*not that good*). **3** /thət/ at which, on which, etc. (*at the speed that he was going he could not stop; the day that I first met her*). ● *conj.* /thət/ except when stressed/ introducing a subordinate clause indicating: **1** a statement or hypothesis (*they say that he is better; there is no doubt that he meant it; the result was that the handle fell off*). **2** a purpose (*we live that we may eat*). **3** a result (*am so sleepy that I cannot keep my eyes open*). **4** a reason or cause (*it is rather that he lacks the time*). **5** a wish (*Oh, that summer were here!*). □ **all that** very (*not all that good*). **and all that** (or **and that** *colloq.*) and all or various things associated with or similar to what has been mentioned; and so forth. **like that 1** of that kind (*is fond of books like that*). **2** in that manner; as you are doing; as he has been doing; etc. (*wish they would not talk like that*). **3** *colloq.* without effort (*did the job like that*). **4** of that character (*he would not accept any payment — he is like that*). **that is** (or **that is to say**) a formula introducing or following an explanation of a preceding word or words. **that's** *colloq.* you are (by virtue of present or future obedience, etc.) (*that's a good boy*). **that's more like it** an acknowledgment of improvement. **that's right** an expression of approval or *colloq.* assent. **that's that** a formula concluding a narrative or discussion or indicating completion of a task. **that there** *sl.* = sense 1 of *adj.* **that will do** no more is needed or desirable. [OE *thæt*, nom. & acc. sing. neut. of demons. pron. & adj. *se, sēo, th æt* f. Gmc; *those* f. OE *thās* pl. of *thes* THIS]
▶See note at WHICH.

thatch /thach/ *n. & v.* ● *n.* **1** a roofing material of straw, reeds, palm leaves, or similar material. **2** *colloq.* the hair of the head esp. when extremely thick. ● *v.tr.* (also *absol.*) cover (a roof or a building) with thatch. □□ **thatch·er** *n.* [n. late collateral form of *thack* (now dial.) f. OE *thæc*, after v. f. OE *theccan* f. Gmc, assim. to *thack*]

thau·ma·trope /tháwmətrōp/ *n. hist.* a disk or card with two different pictures on its two sides, which combine into one by the persistence of visual impressions when the disk is rapidly rotated. **2** a zoetrope. [irreg. f. Gk *thauma* marvel + *–tropos* –turning]

thau·ma·turge /tháwmətərj/ *n.* a worker of miracles; a wonder-worker. □□ **thau·ma·tur·gic** /–túrjik/ *adj.* **thau·ma·tur·gi·cal** /–túrjikəl/ *adj.* **thau·ma·tur·gist** *n.* **thau·ma·tur·gy** *n.* [med.L *thau-*

maturgus f. Gk *thaumatourgos* (adj.) f. *thauma –matos* marvel + *–ergos* –working]

thaw /thaw/ *v. & n.* ● *v.* **1** *intr.* (often foll. by *out*) (of ice or snow or a frozen thing) pass into a liquid or unfrozen state. **2** *intr.* (usu. prec. by *it* as subject) (of the weather) become warm enough to melt ice, etc. (*it began to thaw*). **3** *intr.* become warm enough to lose numbness, etc. **4** *intr.* become less cold or stiff in manner; become genial. **5** *tr.* (often foll. by *out*) cause to thaw. **6** *tr.* make cordial or animated. ● *n.* **1** the act or an instance of thawing. **2** the warmth of weather that thaws (*a thaw has set in*). **3** *Polit.* a relaxation of control or restriction. □□ **thaw·less** *adj.* [OE *thawian* f.WG; orig. unkn.]

the /before a vowel thee, before a consonant thə, when stressed thee/ *adj. & adv.* ● *adj.* (called the definite article) **1** denoting one or more persons or things already mentioned, under discussion, implied, or familiar (*gave the man a wave; shall let the matter drop; hurt myself in the arm; went to the theater*). **2** serving to describe as unique (*the President; the Mississippi*). **3 a** (foll. by defining adj.) which is, who are, etc. (*ignored the embarrassed Mr. Smith; Edward the Seventh*). **b** (foll. by adj. used *absol.*) denoting a class described (*from the sublime to the ridiculous*). **4** best known or best entitled to the name (with *the* stressed: *no relation to the Hemingway; this is the book on this subject*). **5** used to indicate a following defining clause or phrase (*the book that you borrowed; the best I can do for you; the bottom of a well*). **6 a** used to indicate that a singular noun represents a species, class, etc. (*the cat loves comfort; has the novel a future?; plays the harp well*). **b** used with a noun which figuratively represents an occupation, pursuit, etc. (*went on the stage; too fond of the bottle*). **c** (foll. by the name of a unit) a; per (*$5 the square yard; allow 8 minutes to the mile*). **d** *colloq.* designating a disease, affliction, etc. (*the measles; the toothache; the blues*). **7** (foll. by a unit of time) the present; the current (*man of the moment; questions of the day; book of the month*). **8** *colloq.* my; our (*the dog; the car*). **9** used before the surname of the chief of a Scottish or Irish clan (*the Macnab*). ● *adv.* (preceding comparatives in expressions of proportional variation) in or by that (or such a) degree; on that account (*the more the merrier; the more he gets the more he wants*). □ **all the** in the full degree to be expected (*that makes it all the worse*). **so much the** (tautologically) so much; in that degree (*so much the worse for him*). [((adj.) OE, replacing *se, sēo, thæt* (= THAT), f. Gmc: (adv.) f. OE *th ȳ, thē*, instrumental case]

the·an·dric /theeándrik/ *adj.* of the union, or by the joint agency, of the divine and human natures in Christ. [eccl.Gk *theandrikos* f. *theos* god + *anēr andros* man]

the·an·throp·ic /theeánthrópik/ *adj.* **1** both divine and human. **2** tending to embody deity in human form. [eccl.Gk *theanthrōpos* god man f. *theos* god + *anthrōpos* human being]

the·ar·chy /theé-aarkee/ *n.* (*pl.* **–chies**) **1** government by a god or gods. **2** a system or order of gods (*the Olympian thearchy*). [eccl.Gk *thearkhia* godhead f. *theos* god + *–arkhia* f. *arkhō* rule]

theat. *abbr.* **1** theater. **2** theatrical.

the·a·ter /theéətər/ *n.* (*Brit.* **the·a·tre**) **1 a** a building or outdoor area for dramatic performances. **b** (in full **mov·ie the·a·ter**) a building used for showing movies. **2 a** the writing and production of plays. **b** effective material for the stage (*makes good theater*). **c** action with a dramatic quality; dramatic character or effect. **3** a room or hall for lectures, etc., with seats in tiers. **4** (in full **operating theater**) **a** a room or lecture hall with rising tiers of seats to accommodate students' viewing of surgical procedures **b** *Brit.* = OPERATING ROOM. **5 a** a scene or field of action (*the theater of war*). **b** (*attrib.*) designating weapons intermediate between tactical and strategic (*theater nuclear missiles*). **6** a natural land formation in a gradually rising part-circle like ancient Greek and Roman theaters. [ME f. OF *t(h)eatre* or f. L *theatrum* f. Gk *theatron* f. *theaomai* behold]

the·a·ter·go·ing *adj.* frequenting theaters. □□ **the·a·ter·go·er** *n.*

the·a·ter-in-the-round *n.* a dramatic performance on a stage surrounded by spectators.

the·a·ter sis·ter *n. Brit.* a nurse supervising the nursing team in an operating theater.

the·at·ric /theeátrik/ *adj. & n.* ● *adj.* = THEATRICAL. ● *n.* (in *pl.*) theatrical actions.

the·at·ri·cal /theeátrikəl/ *adj. & n.* ● *adj.* **1** of or for the theater; of acting or actors. **2** (of a manner, speech, gesture, or person) calculated for effect; showy; artificial; affected. ● *n.* (in *pl.*) **1** dramatic performances (*amateur theatricals*). **2** theatrical actions. □□ **the·at·ri·cal·ism** *n.* **the·at·ri·cal·i·ty** /–kálitee/ *n.* **the·at·ri·cal·ize** *v.tr.* **the·at·ri·cal·i·za·tion** *n.* **the·at·ri·cal·ly** *adv.* [LL *theatricus* f. Gk *theatrikos* f. *theatron* THEATER]

The·ban /theébən/ *adj. & n.* ● *adj.* of or relating to Thebes in ancient Egypt or ancient Greece. ● *n.* a native or inhabitant of Thebes. [ME f. L *Thebanus* f. *Thebae* Thebes f. Gk *Thēbai*]

the·ca /theékə/ *n.* (*pl.* **the·cae** /theésee/) **1** *Bot.* a part of a plant serving as a receptacle. **2** *Zool.* a case or sheath enclosing an organ or organism. □□ **the·cate** *adj.* [L f. Gk *thēkē* case]

thé dan·sant /táy donsón/ *n.* = TEA DANCE. [F]

thee /thee/ *pron. objective case of* THOU[1]. [OE]

theft /theft/ *n.* **1** the act or an instance of stealing. **2** *Law* dishonest

appropriation of another's property with intent to deprive him or her of it permanently. [OE *thīefth, thēofth*, later *thēoft*, f. Gmc (as THIEF)]

thegn /thayn/ *n. hist.* an English thane. [OE: see THANE]

the·ine /theéin, theé-een/ *n.* = CAFFEINE. [mod.L *thea* tea + *–INE*[4]]

their /thair/ *poss.pron.* (*attrib.*) **1** of or belonging to them or themselves (*their house; their own business*). **2** (**Their**) (in the UK) (in titles) that they are (*Their Majesties*). **3** *disp.* as a third person sing. indefinite meaning 'his or her ' (*has anyone lost their purse?*). [ME f. ON *their(r)a* of them, genit. pl. of *sá* THE, THAT

▶**Their** is a possessive pronoun; **there** is an adverb meaning 'at that place'; and **they're** is a contraction of 'they are': *They're having a party at **their** camp next week; why don't we drive **there**?*

theirs /thairz/ *poss.pron.* the one or ones belonging to or associated with them (*it is theirs; theirs are over here*). □ **of theirs** of or belonging to them (*a friend of theirs*). [ME f. THEIR]

the·ism /theé-izəm/ *n.* belief in the existence of gods or a god, esp. a God supernaturally revealed to man (cf. DEISM) and sustaining a personal relation to his creatures. □□ **the·ist** *n.* **the·is·tic** *adj.* **the·is·ti·cal** *adj.* **the·is·ti·cal·ly** *adv.* [Gk *theos* god + *–ISM*]

them /them, thəm/ *pron. & adj.* ● *pron.* **1** objective case of THEY (*I saw them*). **2** *colloq.* they (*it's them again; is older than them*). **3** *archaic* themselves (*they fell and hurt them*). ● *adj. sl.* or *dial.* those (*them bones*). [ME *theim* f. ON: see THEY]

the·mat·ic /theemátik/ *adj.* **1** of or relating to subjects or topics (*thematic philately; the arrangement of the anthology is thematic*). **2** *Mus.* of melodic subjects (*thematic treatment*). **3** *Gram.* **a** of or belonging to a theme (*thematic vowel; thematic form*). **b** (of a form of a verb) having a thematic vowel. □□ **the·mat·i·cal·ly** *adv.* [Gk *thematikos* (as THEME)]

the·mat·ic cat·a·log *n. Mus.* a catalog giving the opening themes of works as well as their names, and other details.

theme /theem/ *n.* **1** a subject or topic on which a person speaks, writes, or thinks. **2** *Mus.* a prominent or frequently recurring melody or group of notes in a composition. **3** a school exercise, esp. an essay, on a given subject. **4** *Gram.* the stem of a noun or verb; the part to which inflections are added, esp. composed of the root and an added vowel. **5** *hist.* any of the 29 provinces in the Byzantine empire. [ME *teme* ult. f. Gk *thema –matos* f. *tithēmi* set, place]

theme park *n.* an amusement park organized around a unifying idea.

theme song *n.* **1** a recurrent melody in a musical play or movie. **2** a signature tune.

them·selves /themsélvz, –thə m–/ *pron.* **1 a** *emphat.* form of THEY or THEM. **b** *refl.* form of THEM; (cf. HERSELF). **2** in their normal state of body or mind (*are quite themselves again*). □ **be themselves** act in their normal, unconstrained manner.

then /then/ *adv., adj., & n.* ● *adv.* **1** at that time; at the time in question (*was then too busy; then comes the trouble; the then existing laws*). **2 a** next; afterwards; after that (*then he told me to come in*). **b** and also (*then, there are the children to consider*) **c** after all (*it is a problem, but then that is what we are here for*). **3 a** in that case; therefore; it follows that (*then you should have said so*). **b** if what you say is true (*but then why did you take it?*). **c** (implying grudging or impatient concession) if you must have it so (*all right then, have it your own way*). **d** used parenthetically to resume a narrative, etc. (*the policeman, then, knocked on the door*). ● *adj.* that or who was such at the time in question (*the then Senator*). ● *n.* that time (*until then*). □ **then and there** immediately and on the spot. [OE *thanne, thonne*, etc. f. Gmc, rel. to THAT, THE]

the·nar /theénər/ *n. Anat.* the ball of muscle at the base of the thumb. [earlier = palm of the hand: mod.L f. Gk]

thence /thens/ *adv.* (also **from thence**) *archaic* or *literary* **1** from that place or source. **2** for that reason. [ME *thannes, thennes* f. *thanne, thenne* f. OE *thanon(e)*, etc. f. WG]

thence·forth /thénsfáwrth/ *adv.* (also **from thence·forth**) *formal* from that time onward.

thence·for·ward /thénsfáwrwərd/ *adv. formal* thenceforth.

theo- /theé-ō/ *comb. form* God or gods. [Gk f. *theos* god]

the·o·bro·mine /theéəbrómin, –meen/ *n.* a bitter white alkaloid obtained from cacao seeds, related to caffeine. [*Theobroma* cacao genus: mod.L f. Gk *theos* god + *brōma* food, + *–INE*[4]]

the·o·cen·tric /theéəséntrik/ *adj.* having God or a god as its center.

the·oc·ra·cy /theeókrəsee/ *n.* (*pl.* **–cies**) **1** a form of government by God or a god directly or through a priestly order, etc. **2** (**the Theocracy**) the Jewish commonwealth from Moses to the monarchy. □□ **the·o·crat** /theéəkrat/ *n.* **the·o·crat·ic** /theeəkrátik/ *adj.* **the·o·crat·i·cal·ly** *adv.*

the·oc·ra·sy /theeókrəsee/ *n.* **1** the mingling of deities into one personality. **2** the union of the soul with God through contemplation (among Neoplatonists, etc.). [THEO- + Gk *krasis* mingling]

the·od·i·cy /theeódisee/ *n.* (*pl.* **–cies**) **1** the vindication of divine providence in view of the existence of evil. **2** an instance of this. □□ **the·od·i·ce·an** /–seeən/ adj. [THEO– + Gk dikē justice]

the·od·o·lite /theeód'lit/ n. a surveying instrument for measuring horizontal and vertical angles with a rotating telescope. □□ **the·od·o·lit·ic** /–lítik/ adj. [16th c. theodelitus, of unkn. orig.]

the·og·o·ny /theeógənee/ n. (pl. **–nies**) **1** the genealogy of the gods. **2** an account of this. [THEO– + Gk –gonia begetting]

theol. abbr. **1** theological. **2** theology.

the·o·lo·gian /theeəlójən/ n. a person trained in theology. [ME f. OF theologien (as THEOLOGY)]

the·o·log·i·cal /theeəlójikəl/ adj. of theology. □□ **the·o·log·i·cal·ly** adv. [med.L theologicalis f. L theologicus f. Gk theologikos (as THEOLOGY)]

the·o·log·i·cal vir·tues n. faith, hope, and charity.

the·ol·o·gy /theeólajee/ n. (pl. **–gies**) **1 a** the study of theistic (esp. Christian) religion. **b** a system of theistic (esp. Christian) religion. **c** the rational analysis of a religious faith. **2** a system of theoretical principles, esp. an impractical or rigid ideology. □□ **the·ol·o·gist** n. **the·ol·o·gize** v.tr. & intr. [ME f. OF theologie f. L theologia f. Gk (as THEO–, –LOGY)]

the·om·a·chy /theeóməkee/ n. (pl. **–chies**) strife among or against the gods. [THEO– + Gk makhē fight]

the·oph·a·ny /theeófənee/ n. (pl. **–nies**) a visible manifestation of God or a god to man.

the·o·phor·ic /theeəfórik/ adj. bearing the name of a god.

the·o·phyl·line /theeəfíleen, –lin/ n. an alkaloid similar to theobromine, found in tea leaves. [irreg. f. modL thea tea + Gk phullon leaf + –INE⁴]

the·or·bo /thee-áwrbō/ n. (pl. **–bos**) a two-necked musical instrument of the lute class much used in the seventeenth century. □□ **the·or·bist** n. [It. tiorba, of unkn. orig.]

the·o·rem /theeərəm, theerə m/ n. esp. Math. **1** a general proposition not self-evident but proved by a chain of reasoning; a truth established by means of accepted truths (cf. PROBLEM). **2** a rule in algebra, etc., esp. one expressed by symbols or formulae (binomial theorem). □□ **the·o·re·mat·ic** /–mátik/ adj. [F théorème or LL theorema f. Gk theōrēma speculation, proposition f. theōreō look at]

the·o·ret·ic /theeərétik/ adj. & n. ● adj. = THEORETICAL. ● n. (in sing. or pl.) the theoretical part of a science, etc. [LL theoreticus f. Gk theōrētikos (as THEORY)]

the·o·ret·i·cal /theeərétikəl/ adj. **1** concerned with knowledge but not with its practical application. **2** based on theory rather than experience or practice. □□ **the·o·ret·i·cal·ly** adv.

the·o·re·ti·cian /theeəritíshən, –theérit/ n. a person concerned with the theoretical aspects of a subject.

the·o·rist /theeərist, theérist/ n. a holder or inventor of a theory or theories.

the·o·rize /theeəríz, theéríz/ v.intr. evolve or indulge in theories. □□ **the·o·riz·er** n.

the·o·ry /theeəree, theéree/ n. (pl. **–ries**) **1** a supposition or system of ideas explaining something, esp. one based on general principles independent of the particular things to be explained (cf. HYPOTHESIS) (atomic theory; theory of evolution). **2** a speculative (esp. fanciful) view (one of my pet theories). **3** the sphere of abstract knowledge or speculative thought (this is all very well in theory, but how will it work in practice?). **4** the exposition of the principles of a science, etc. (the theory of music). **5** Math. a collection of propositions to illustrate the principles of a subject (probability theory; theory of equations). [LL theoria f. Gk theōria f. theōros spectator f. theōreō look at]

the·os·o·phy /theeósəfee/ n. (pl. **–phies**) any of various philosophies professing to achieve a knowledge of God by spiritual ecstasy, direct intuition, or special individual relations, esp. a modern movement following Hindu and Buddhist teachings and seeking universal brotherhood. □□ **the·os·o·pher** n. **the·o·soph·ic** /theeəsófik/ adj. **the·o·soph·i·cal** adj. **the·o·soph·i·cal·ly** adv. **the·os·o·phist** n. [med.L theosophia f. late Gk theosophia f. theosophos wise concerning God (as THEO–, sophos wise)]

ther·a·peu·tic /thérəpyóotik/ adj. **1** of, for, or contributing to the cure of disease. **2** contributing to general, esp. mental, well-being (finds walking therapeutic). □□ **ther·a·peu·ti·cal** adj. **ther·a·peu·ti·cal·ly** adv. **ther·a·peu·tist** n. [attrib. use of therapeutic, orig. form of THERAPEUTICS]

ther·a·peu·tics /thérəpyóotiks/ n.pl. (usu. treated as sing.) the branch of medicine concerned with the treatment of disease and the action of remedial agents. [F thérapeutique or LL therapeutica (pl.) f. Gk therapeutika neut. pl. of therapeutikos f. therapeuō wait on, cure]

ther·a·py /thérəpee/ n. (pl. **–pies**) **1** the treatment of physical or mental disorders, other than by surgery. **2 a** a particular type of such treatment. **b** psychotherapy. □□ **ther·a·pist** n. [mod.L therapia f. Gk therapeia healing]

Ther·a·va·da /thérəváadə/ n. a more conservative form of Buddhism, practiced in Burma (now Myanmar), Thailand, etc. [Pali theravāda f. thera elder, old + vāda speech, doctrine]

there /thair/ adv., n., & int. ● adv. **1** in, at, or to that place or position (lived there for some years; goes there every day). **2** at that point (in speech, performance, writing, etc.) (there he stopped). **3** in that respect (I agree with you there). **4** used for emphasis in calling attention (you there!; there goes the bell). **5** used to indicate the fact or existence of something (there is a house on the corner). ● n. that place (lives somewhere near there). ● int. **1** expressing confirmation, triumph, dismay, etc. (there! what did I tell you?). **2** used to soothe a child, etc. (there, there, never mind). □ **have been there before** sl. know all about it. **so there** colloq. that is my final decision (whether you like it or not). **there and then** immediately and on the spot. **there it is 1** that is the trouble. **2** nothing can be done about it. **there's** Brit. colloq. you are (by virtue of present or future obedience, etc.) (there's a dear). **there you are** (or **go**) colloq. **1** this is what you wanted, etc. **2** expressing confirmation, triumph, resignation, etc. [OE thær, thēr f. Gmc, rel. to THAT, THE]
▶See note at THEIR.

there·a·bouts /tháirəbówts/ adv. (also **there·a·bout**) **1** near that place (ought to be somewhere thereabouts). **2** near that number, quantity, etc. (two acres or thereabouts).

there·af·ter /tháiráftər/ adv. after that.

there·an·ent /tháirənént/ adv. Sc. about that matter.

there·at /tháirát/ adv. archaic **1** at that place. **2** on that account. **3** after that.

there·by /tháirbí/ adv. by that means; as a result of that. □ **thereby hangs a tale** much could be said about that.

there·for /tháirfáwr/ adv. archaic for that object or purpose.

there·fore /tháirfawr/ adv. for that reason; accordingly; consequently.

there·from /tháirfrúm, –fróm/ adv. formal from that or it.

there·in /tháirín/ adv. formal **1** in that place, etc. **2** in that respect.

there·in·af·ter /tháirináftər/ adv. formal later in the same document, etc.

there·in·be·fore /tháirinbifáwr/ adv. formal earlier in the same document, etc.

there·in·to /tháiríntoo/ adv. archaic into that place.

there·of /tháirúv, –óv/ adv. formal of that or it.

there·on /tháirón, –áwn/ adv. archaic on that or it (of motion or position).

there·out /tháirówt/ adv. archaic out of that; from that source.

there·to /tháirtóo/ adv. formal **1** to that or it. **2** in addition; to boot.

there·to·fore /tháirtoofáwr/ adv. formal before that time.

there·un·to /tháirúntoo/ adv. archaic to that or it.

there·up·on /tháirəpón, –páwn/ adv. **1** in consequence of that. **2** soon or immediately after that. **3** archaic upon that (of motion or position).

there·with /tháirwíth, –wíth/ adv. archaic **1** with that. **2** soon or immediately after that.

there·with·al /tháirwitháwl, –with–/ adv. archaic in addition; besides.

the·ri·ac /theéreeak/ n. archaic an antidote to the bites of poisonous animals, esp. snakes. [L theriaca f. Gk thēriakē antidote, fem. of thēriakos f. thēr wild beast]

the·ri·an·throp·ic /theéreeanthrópik/ adj. of or worshiping beings represented in combined human and animal forms. [Gk thērion dimin. of thēr wild beast + anthrōpos human being]

the·ri·o·mor·phic /theéreeəmáwrfik/ adj. (esp. of a deity) having an animal form. [as THERIANTHROPIC + Gk morphē form]

therm /thərm/ n. a unit of heat, equivalent to 100,000 British thermal units or 1.055 x 10⁸ joules. [Gk thermē heat]

ther·mae /thɔrmee/ n.pl. Gk & Rom. Antiq. public baths. [L f. Gk thermai (pl.) (as THERM)]

ther·mal /thɔrməl/ adj. & n. ● adj. **1** of, for, or producing heat. **2** promoting the retention of heat (thermal underwear). ● n. a rising current of heated air (used by gliders, balloons, and birds to gain height). □□ **ther·mal·ize** v.tr. & intr. **ther·mal·i·za·tion** n. **ther·mal·ly** adv. [F (as THERM)]

ther·mal print·er n. Comp. a printer that makes a text image by application of heat to thermally sensitive paper.

ther·mic /thɔrmik/ adj. of or relating to heat.

ther·mi·dor see LOBSTER.

therm·i·on /thɔrmíon/ n. an ion or electron emitted by a substance at high temperature. [THERMO– + ION]

therm·i·on·ic /thɔrmíonik/ adj. of or relating to electrons emitted from a substance at very high temperature.

therm·i·on·ic e·mis·sion n. the emission of electrons from a heated source.

therm·i·on·ic valve n. Brit. = VACUUM TUBE.

therm·i·on·ics /thɔrmíoniks/ n.pl. (treated as sing.) the branch of science and technology concerned with thermionic emission.

therm·is·tor /thɔrmístər/ n. Electr. a resistor whose resistance is greatly reduced by heating, used for measurement and control. [thermal resistor]

therm·ite /thɔrmīt/ n. (also **ther·mit** /–mit/) a mixture of finely powdered aluminum and iron oxide that produces a very high temperature on combustion (used in welding and for incendiary bombs). [G Thermit (as THERMO–, –ITE¹)]

thermo- /thə́rmō/ *comb. form* denoting heat. [Gk f. *thermos* hot, *thermē* heat]

ther·mo·chem·is·try /thərmōkémistree/ *n.* the branch of chemistry dealing with the quantities of heat evolved or absorbed during chemical reactions. □□ **ther·mo·chem·i·cal** *adj.*

ther·mo·cou·ple /thərmōkupəl/ *n.* a pair of different metals in contact at a point, generating a thermoelectric voltage that can serve as a measure of temperature at this point relative to their other parts.

ther·mo·dy·nam·ics /thərmōdīnámiks/ *n.pl.* (usu. treated as *sing.*) the science of the relations between heat and other (mechanical, electrical, etc.) forms of energy. □□ **ther·mo·dy·nam·ic** *adj.* **ther·mo·dy·nam·i·cal** *adj.* **ther·mo·dy·nam·i·cal·ly** *adv.* **ther·mo·dy·nam·i·cist** /–misist/ *n.*

ther·mo·e·lec·tric /thərmōiléktrik/ *adj.* producing electricity by a difference of temperatures. □□ **ther·mo·e·lec·tri·cal·ly** *adv.* **ther·mo·e·lec·tric·i·ty** /–ilektrísitee/ *n.*

ther·mo·gen·e·sis /thərmōjénisis/ *n.* the production of heat, esp. in a human or animal body.

ther·mo·gram /thə́rməgram/ *n.* a record made by a thermograph.

ther·mo·graph /thə́rməgraf/ *n.* 1 an instrument that gives a continuous record of temperature. 2 an apparatus used to obtain an image produced by infrared radiation from a human or animal body. □□ **ther·mo·graph·ic** /–gráfik/ *adj.*

ther·mog·ra·phy /thərmógrəfee/ *n.* *Med.* the taking or use of infrared thermograms, esp. to detect tumors.

ther·mo·la·bile /thərmōláybīl, –bil/ *adj.* (of a substance) unstable when heated.

ther·mo·lu·mi·nes·cence /thərmōlōōminésəns/ *n.* the property of becoming luminescent when pretreated and subjected to high temperatures, used as a means of dating ancient artifacts. □□ **ther·mo·lu·mi·nes·cent** *adj.*

ther·mol·y·sis /thərmólisis/ *n.* decomposition by the action of heat. □□ **ther·mo·lyt·ic** /–məlítik/ *adj.*

ther·mom·e·ter /thərmómitər/ *n.* an instrument for measuring temperature, esp. a graduated glass tube with a small bore containing mercury or alcohol which expands when heated. □□ **ther·mo·met·ric** /thərməmétrik/ *adj.* **ther·mo·met·ri·cal** *adj.* **ther·mom·e·try** *n.* [F *thermomètre* or mod.L *thermometrum* (as THERMO-, –METER)]

ther·mo·nu·cle·ar /thərmōnōōkleeər, –nyōō–/ *adj.* 1 relating to or using nuclear reactions that occur only at very high temperatures. 2 relating to or characterized by weapons using thermonuclear reactions.

ther·mo·phile /thə́rmōfīl/ *n. & adj.* (also **ther·mo·phil** /–l/) • *n.* a bacterium, etc., growing optimally at high temperatures. • *adj.* of or being a thermophile. □□ **ther·mo·phil·ic** /–fílik/ *adj.*

ther·mo·pile /thə́rmōpīl/ *n.* a set of thermocouples, esp. arranged for measuring small quantities of radiant heat.

ther·mo·plas·tic /thərmōplástik/ *adj. & n.* • *adj.* (of a substance) that becomes plastic on heating and hardens on cooling, and is able to repeat these processes. • *n.* a thermoplastic substance.

ther·mos /thə́rmos/ *n.* (in full **thermos bottle** or **flask**) *Trademark* a bottle, etc., with a double wall enclosing a vacuum so that the liquid in the inner receptacle retains its temperature. [Gk (as THERMO-)]

ther·mo·set·ting /thə́rmōséting/ *adj.* (of plastics) setting permanently when heated. □□ **ther·mo·set** *adj.*

ther·mo·sphere /thə́rməsfeer/ *n.* the region of the atmosphere beyond the mesosphere.

ther·mo·sta·ble /thərmōstáybəl/ *adj.* (of a substance) stable when heated.

ther·mo·stat /thə́rməstat/ *n.* a device that automatically regulates temperature, or that activates a device when the temperature reaches a certain point. □□ **ther·mo·stat·ic** *adj.* **ther·mo·stat·i·cal·ly** *adv.* [THERMO- + Gk *statos* standing]

ther·mo·tax·is /thə́rmōtáksis/ *n.* 1 the regulation of heat or temperature, esp. in warm-blooded animals. 2 movement or stimulation in a living organism caused by heat. □□ **ther·mo·tac·tic** *adj.* **ther·mo·tax·ic** *adj.*

ther·mo·tro·pism /thərmótrəpizəm/ *n.* the growing or bending of a plant toward or away from a source of heat. □□ **ther·mo·trop·ic** /thərmōtrópik/ *adj.*

the·sau·rus /thisáwrəs/ *n.* (*pl.* **the·sau·ri** /–rī/ or **the·sau·rus·es**) 1 a a collection of concepts or words arranged according to sense. b a book of synonyms and antonyms. 2 a dictionary or encyclopedia. [L f. Gk *thēsauros* treasure]

these *pl.* of THIS.

the·sis /theésis/ *n.* (*pl.* **the·ses** /–seez/) 1 a proposition to be maintained or proved. 2 a dissertation, esp. by a candidate for a degree. 3 (also *Brit.* /thésis/) an unstressed syllable or part of a metrical foot in Greek or Latin verse (opp. ARSIS). [ME f. LL f. Gk, = putting, placing, a proposition, etc., f. *the-* root of *tithēmi* place]

thes·pi·an /théspeeən/ *adj. & n.* • *adj.* of or relating to tragedy or drama. • *n.* an actor or actress. [Gk *Thespis* the traditional originator of Greek tragedy]

Thess. *abbr.* Thessalonians (New Testament).

the·ta /tháytə, theé–/ *n.* the eighth letter of the Greek alphabet (Θ, ϑ). [Gk]

the·ur·gy /theé-ərjee/ *n.* 1 a supernatural or divine agency, esp. in human affairs. b the art of securing this. 2 the magical science of the Neoplatonists. □□ **the·ur·gic** /–ə́rjik/ *adj.* **the·ur·gi·cal** *adj.* **the·ur·gist** *n.* [LL *theurgia* f. Gk *theourgia* f. *theos* god + *–ergos* working]

thew /thyōō/ *n.* (often in *pl.*) *literary* 1 muscular strength. 2 mental or moral vigor. [OE *thēaw* usage, conduct, of unkn. orig.]

they /thay/ *pron.* (*obj.* **them**; *poss.* **their**, **theirs**) 1 the people, animals, or things previously named or in question (*pl.* of HE, SHE, IT[1]). 2 people in general (*they say we are wrong*). 3 those in authority (*they have raised the fees*). 4 *disp.* as a third person sing. indefinite pronoun meaning 'he or she' (*anyone can come if they want to*). [ME *thei*, obj. *theim*, f. ON *their* nom. pl. masc., *theim* dat. pl. of *sá* THE that]
▶See note at EVERYBODY.

they'd /thayd/ *contr.* 1 they had. 2 they would.

they'll /thayl/ *contr.* 1 they will. 2 they shall.

they're /thair/ *contr.* they are.
▶See note at THEIR.

they've /thayv/ *contr.* they have.

THI *abbr.* temperature-humidity index.

thi·a·mine /thíəmin, –meen/ *n.* (also **thi·a·min**) a vitamin of the B complex, found in unrefined cereals, beans, and liver, a deficiency of which causes beriberi. Also called **vitamin B$_1$** or **aneurin**. [THIO- + *amin* from VITAMIN]

thick /thik/ *adj., n., & adv.* • *adj.* 1 a of great or specified extent between opposite surfaces (*a thick wall*; *a wall two meters thick*). b of large diameter (*a thick rope*). 2 a (of a line, etc.) broad; not fine. b (of script or type, etc.) consisting of thick lines. 3 a arranged closely; crowded together; dense. b numerous (*fell thick as peas*). c bushy; luxuriant (*thick hair*; *thick growth*). 4 (usu. foll. by *with*) densely covered or filled (*air thick with snow*). 5 a firm in consistency; containing much solid matter; viscous (*a thick paste*; *thick soup*). b made of thick material (*a thick coat*). 6 muddy; cloudy; impenetrable by sight (*thick darkness*). 7 *colloq.* (of a person) stupid; dull. 8 a (of a voice) indistinct. b (of an accent) pronounced; exaggerated. 9 *colloq.* intimate or very friendly (esp. thick as thieves). • *n.* a. thick part of anything. • *adv.* thickly (*snow was falling thick*; *blows rained down thick and fast*). □ **a bit thick** *colloq.* unreasonable or intolerable. **in the thick of** 1 at the busiest part of. 2 heavily occupied with. **through thick and thin** under all conditions; in spite of all difficulties. □□ **thick·ish** *adj.* **thick·ly** *adv.* [OE *thicce* (adj. & adv.) f. Gmc]

thick ear *n.* *Brit. sl.* the external ear swollen as a result of a blow (esp. give a person a thick ear).

thick·en /thíkən/ *v.* 1 *tr. & intr.* make or become thick or thicker. 2 *intr.* become more complicated (*the plot thickens*). □□ **thick·en·er** *n.*

thick·en·ing /thíkəning/ *n.* 1 the process of becoming thick or thicker. 2 a substance used to thicken liquid. 3 a thickened part.

thick·et /thíkit/ *n.* a tangle of shrubs or trees. [OE *thiccet* (as THICK, –ET[1])]

thick·head /thík-hed/ *n.* 1 *colloq.* a stupid person; a blockhead. 2 *Austral.* any bird of the genus *Pachycephala*; a whistler. □□ **thick·head·ed** *adj.* **thick·head·ed·ness** *n.*

thick·ness /thíknis/ *n.* 1 the state of being thick. 2 the extent to which a thing is thick. 3 a layer of material of a certain thickness (*three thicknesses of cardboard*). 4 a part that is thick or lies between opposite surfaces (*steps cut in the thickness of the wall*). [OE *thicnes* (as THICK, –NESS)]

thick·set /thíksét/ *adj. & n.* • *adj.* 1 heavily or solidly built. 2 set or growing close together. • *n.* a thicket.

thick-skinned *adj.* not sensitive to reproach or criticism.

thick-skulled *adj.* (also **thick-wit·ted**) stupid; dull; slow to learn.

thief /theef/ *n.* (*pl.* **thieves** /theevz/) a person who steals, esp. secretly and without violence. [OE *thēof* f. Gmc]

thieve /theev/ *v.* 1 *intr.* be a thief. 2 *tr.* steal (a thing). [OE *thēofian* (as THIEF)]

thiev·er·y /theévəree/ *n.* the act or practice of stealing.

thieves *pl.* of THIEF.

thiev·ish /theévish/ *adj.* given to stealing. □□ **thiev·ish·ly** *adv.* **thiev·ish·ness** *n.*

thigh /thī/ *n.* 1 the part of the human leg between the hip and the knee. 2 a corresponding part in other animals. □□ **–thighed** *adj.* (in *comb.*). [OE *thēh*, *thēoh*, *thīoh*, OHG *dioh*, ON *thjó* f. Gmc]

thigh-slap·per *n.* *colloq.* an exceptionally funny joke, etc.

thill /thil/ *n.* a shaft of a cart or carriage, esp. one of a pair. [ME: orig. unkn.]

thill-horse /thílhawrs/ *n.* (also **thill·er** /thílər/) a horse put between thills.

thim·ble /thímbəl/ *n.* 1 a metal or plastic cap, usu. with a closed end, worn to protect the finger and push the needle in sewing. **2** *Mech.* a short metal tube or ferrule, etc. **3** *Naut.* a metal ring concave on the outside and fitting in a loop of spliced rope to prevent chafing. [OE *thȳmel* (as THUMB, –LE¹)]

thim·ble·ful /thímbəlfŏŏl/ *n.* (*pl.* **–fuls**) a small quantity, esp. of liquid to drink.

thim·ble·rig /thímbəlrig/ *n.* a game often involving sleight of hand, in which three inverted thimbles or cups are moved about, contestants having to spot which is the one with a pea or other object beneath. □□ **thim·ble·rig·ger** *n.* [THIMBLE + RIG² in sense 'trick, dodge']

thin /thin/ *adj., adv., & v.* ● *adj.* (**thin·ner, thin·nest**) **1** having the opposite surfaces close together; of small thickness or diameter. **2 a** (of a line) narrow or fine. **b** (of a script or type, etc.) consisting of thin lines. **3** made of thin material (*a thin dress*). **4** lean; not plump. **5 a** not dense or copious (*thin hair; a thin haze*). **b** not full or closely packed (*a thin audience*). **6** of slight consistency (*a thin paste*). **7** weak; lacking an important ingredient (*thin blood; a thin voice*). **8** (of an excuse, argument, disguise, etc.) flimsy or transparent. ● *adv.* thinly (*cut the bread very thin*). ● *v.* (**thinned, thin·ning**) **1** *tr. & intr.* make or become thin or thinner. **2** *tr. & intr.* (often foll. by *out*) reduce; make or become less dense or crowded or numerous. **3** *tr.* (often foll. by *out*) remove some of a crop of (seedlings, saplings, etc.) or some young fruit from (a vine or tree) to improve the growth of the rest. □ **on thin ice** see ICE. **thin end of the wedge** see WEDGE¹. **thin on the ground** see GROUND¹. **thin on top** balding. □□ **thin·ly** *adv.* **thin·ness** *n.* **thin·nish** *adj.* [OE *thynne* f. Gmc]

SYNONYM TIP *thin*

GAUNT, LEAN, SKINNY, SLENDER, SPARE, SVELTE. You can't be too rich or too **thin**, but you can be too **skinny**. *Thin* describes someone whose weight is naturally low in proportion to his or her height, although it may also imply that the person is underweight (*She looked pale and thin after her operation*). *Skinny* is a more blunt and derogatory term for someone who is too *thin*, and it often implies underdevelopment (*a skinny little boy; a tall, skinny fashion model*). Most women would rather be called **slender**, which combines thinness with gracefulness and good proportions (*the slender legs of a Queen Anne table*), or better yet, **svelte**, a complimentary term that implies a slim, elegant figure (*After six months of dieting, she looked so svelte I hardly recognized her*). **Lean** and **spare** are used to describe people who are naturally *thin*, although *spare* suggests a more muscular leanness (*a tall, spare man who looked like Abraham Lincoln*). **Gaunt**, on the other hand, means so *thin* that the angularity of the bones can be seen beneath the skin (*looking gaunt after her latest bout with cancer*).

---

thin air *n.* a state of invisibility or nonexistence (*vanished into thin air*).

thine /thin/ *poss.pron. archaic* or *dial.* **1** (*predic.* or *absol.*) of or belonging to thee. **2** (*attrib.* before a vowel) = THY. [OE *thīn* f. Gmc]

thing /thing/ *n.* **1** a material or nonmaterial entity, idea, action, etc., that is or may be thought about or perceived. **2** an inanimate material object (*take that thing away*). **3** an unspecified object or item (*have a few things to buy*). **4** an act, idea, or utterance (*a silly thing to do*). **5** an event (*an unfortunate thing to happen*). **6** a quality (*patience is a useful thing*). **7** (with ref. to a person) expressing pity, contempt, or affection (*poor thing!; a dear old thing*). **8** a specimen or type of something (*quarks are an important thing in physics*). **9** *colloq.* **a** one's special interest or concern (*not my thing at all*). **b** an obsession, fear, or prejudice (*spiders are a thing of mine*). **10** esp. *Brit. colloq.* something remarkable (*now there's a thing!*). **11** (prec. by the) *colloq.* **a** what is conventionally proper or fashionable. **b** what is needed or required (*your suggestion was just the thing*). **c** what is to be considered (*the thing is, shall we go or not?*). **d** what is important (*the thing about them is their reliability*). **12** (in *pl.*) personal belongings or clothing (*where have I left my things?*). **13** (in *pl.*) equipment (*painting things*). **14** (in *pl.*) affairs in general (*not in the nature of things*). **15** (in *pl.*) circumstances or conditions (*things look good*). **16** (in *pl.* with a following adjective) all that is so describable (*all things Greek*). **17** (in *pl.*) *Law* property. □ **do one's own thing** *colloq.* pursue one's own interests or inclinations. **do things to** *colloq.* affect remarkably. **have a thing about** *colloq.* be obsessed, fearful, or prejudiced about. **make a thing of** *colloq.* **1** regard as essential. **2** cause a fuss about. **one** (or **just one**) **of those things** *colloq.* something unavoidable or to be accepted. [OE f. Gmc]

thing·a·ma·bob /thíngəməbŏb/ *n.* (also **thing·a·ma·jig** /thíngəmə-jig/) *colloq.* a person or thing whose name one has forgotten or does not know or does not wish to mention. [THING + meaningless suffix]

thing·y /thíngee/ *n.* (*pl.* **–ies**) = THINGAMABOB.

think /thingk/ *v. & n.* ● *v.* (*past* and *past part.* **thought** /thawt/) **1** *tr.*

(foll. by *that* + clause) be of the opinion (*we think that they will come*). **2** *tr.* (foll. by *that* + clause or *to* + infin.) judge or consider (*is thought to be a fraud*). **3** *intr.* exercise the mind positively with one's ideas, etc. (*let me think for a moment*). **4** *tr.* (foll. by *of* or *about*) **a** consider; be or become mentally aware of (*think of you constantly*). **b** form or entertain the idea of; imagine to oneself (*couldn't think of such a thing*). **c** choose mentally; hit upon (*think of a number*). **d** form or have an opinion of (*what do you think of them?*). **5** *tr.* have a half-formed intention (*I think I'll stay*). **6** *tr.* form a conception of (*cannot think how you do it*). **7** *tr.* reduce to a specified condition by thinking (*cannot think away a toothache*). **8** *tr.* recognize the presence or existence of (*the child thought no harm*). **9** *tr.* (foll. by *to* + infin.) intend or expect (*thinks to deceive us*). **10** *tr.* (foll. by *to* + infin.) remember (*did not think to lock the door*). ● *n. colloq.* an act of thinking (*must have a think about that*). □ **think again** revise one's plans or opinions. **think out loud** (or **aloud**) utter one's thoughts as soon as they occur. **think back** to recall (a past event or time). **think better of** change one's mind about (an intention) after reconsideration. **think big** see BIG. **think fit** see FIT¹. **think for oneself** have an independent mind or attitude. **think little** (or **nothing**) **of** consider to be insignificant or unremarkable. **think much** (or **highly**) **of** have a high opinion of. **think on** (or **upon**) *archaic* think of or about. **think out 1** consider carefully. **2** produce (an idea, etc.) by thinking. **think over** reflect upon in order to reach a decision. **think through** reflect fully upon (a problem, etc.). **think twice** use careful consideration, avoid hasty action, etc. **think up** *colloq.* devise; produce by thought. □□ **think·a·ble** *adj.* [OE *thencan thôhte gethôht* f. Gmc]

think·er /thíngkər/ *n.* **1** a person who thinks, esp. in a specified way (*an original thinker*). **2** a person with a skilled or powerful mind.

think·ing /thíngking/ *adj. & n.* ● *adj.* using thought or rational judgment. ● *n.* **1** opinion or judgment. **2** thought; train of thought. □ **put on one's thinking cap** *colloq.* meditate on a problem.

think tank *n.* a body of experts providing advice and ideas on specific national or commercial problems.

thin·ner /thínər/ *n.* a volatile liquid used to dilute paint, etc.

thin-skinned *adj.* sensitive to reproach or criticism; easily upset.

thio- /thí-ō/ *comb. form* sulfur, esp. replacing oxygen in compounds (*thio acid*). [Gk *theion* sulfur]

thi·ol /thíawl, –ol/ *n. Chem.* any organic compound containing an alcohol-like group but with sulfur in place of oxygen. [THIO- + –OL¹]

thi·o·sul·fate /thí-ōsúlfayt/ *n.* a sulfate in which one oxygen atom is replaced by sulfur.

thi·o·u·re·a /thí-ōyŏŏreeə/ *n.* a crystalline compound used in photography and the manufacture of synthetic resins.

third /thərd/ *n. & adj.* ● *n.* **1** the position in a sequence corresponding to that of the number 3 in the sequence 1–3. **2** something occupying this position. **3** each of three equal parts of a thing. **4** = THIRD GEAR. **5** *Mus.* **a** an interval or chord spanning three consecutive notes in the diatonic scale (e.g., C to E). **b** a note separated from another by this interval. **6** = THIRD BASE. **7** *Brit.* **a** a place in the third class in an examination. **b** a person having this. ● *adj.* that is the third. □□ **third·ly** *adv.* [OE *third(d)a*, thridda f. Gmc]
▶See note at FIRST.

third base *n.* **1** the third base (counterclockwise from home plate) in baseball. **2** the area around this base as defended by a fielder.

third-best *adj.* of third quality. ● *n.* a thing in this category.

third class *n., adj. & adv.* ● *n.* the third-best group or category, esp. of hotel and train accommodation. ● *adj.* **1** (**third-class**) belonging to or traveling by third class. **2** of lower quality; inferior. ● *adv.* by the third class (*travels third-class*).

third-de·gree *adj. & n.* ● *adj. Med.* denoting burns of the most severe kind, affecting tissue below the skin. ● *n.* (**the third degree**) long and harsh questioning, esp. by police, to obtain information or a confession.

third eye *n.* **1** *Hinduism & Buddhism* the 'eye of insight' in the forehead of an image of a deity, esp. the god Siva. **2** the faculty of intuitive insight.

third force *n.* a political group or party acting as a check on conflict between two opposing parties.

third gear *n.* the third in a sequence of gears.

third man *n. Cricket* **1** a fielder positioned near the boundary behind the slips. **2** this position.

third part *n.* each of three equal parts into which a thing is or might be divided.

third par·ty *n.* **1** another party besides the two principals. **2** a bystander, etc.

third per·son *n.* **1** = THIRD PARTY. **2** *Gram.* see PERSON.

third rail *n.* a metal rail that provides power to the trains of an electric railroad.

third-rate *adj.* inferior; very poor in quality.

third read·ing *n.* a third presentation of a bill to a legislative assembly, in the US to consider it for the last time, in the UK to debate committee reports.

Third Reich *n.* the Nazi regime, 1933–45.

Third World *n.* (usu. prec. by *the*) the developing countries of Asia, Africa, and Latin America.

thirst /thərst/ *n. & v.* ● *n.* **1** a physical need to drink liquid, or the feeling of discomfort caused by this. **2** a strong desire or craving (*a thirst for power*). ● *v.intr.* (often foll. by *for* or *after*) **1** feel thirst. **2** have a strong desire. [OE *thurst, thyrstan* f. WG]

thirst·y /thə́rstee/ *adj.* (**thirst·i·er, thirst·i·est**) **1** feeling thirst. **2** (of land, a season, etc.) dry or parched. **3** (often foll. by *for* or *after*) eager. **4** *colloq.* causing thirst (*thirsty work*). □□ **thirst·i·ly** *adv.* **thirst·i·ness** *n.* [OE *thurstig, thyrstig* (as THIRST, -Y¹)]

thir·teen /thərteé́n/ *n. & adj.* ● *n.* **1** one more than twelve, or three more than ten. **2** a symbol for this (13, xiii, XIII). **3** a size, etc., denoted by thirteen. ● *adj.* that amount to thirteen. □□ **thir·teenth** *adj. & n.* [OE *thrēotīene* (as THREE, -TEEN)]

thir·ty /thə́rtee/ *n. & adj.* ● *n.* (*pl.* **-ties**) **1** the product of three and ten. **2** a symbol for this (30, xxx, XXX). **3** (in *pl.*) the numbers from 30 to 39, esp. the years of a century or of a person's life. ● *adj.* that amount to thirty. □□ **thir·ti·eth** *adj. & n.* **thir·ty·fold** *adj. & adv.* [OE *thrītig* (as THREE, -TY²)]

thir·ty-first *n.* (**thir·ty-second**, etc.) the ordinal numbers between thirtieth and fortieth.

thir·ty-one *n.* (**thir·ty-two**, etc.) the cardinal numbers between thirty and forty.

thir·ty-sec·ond note *n. Mus.* a note having the time value of half a semiquaver and represented by a large dot with a three-hooked stem. Also called **demisemiquaver**.

this /this/ *pron., adj., & adv.* ● *demons.pron.* (*pl.* **these** /theez/) **1** the person or thing close at hand or indicated or already named or understood (*can you see this?; this is my cousin*). **2** (contrasted with *that*) the person or thing nearer to hand or more immediately in mind. **3** the action, behavior, or circumstances under consideration (*this won't do at all; what do you think of this?*). **4** (on the telephone): **a** the person spoken to. **b** the person speaking. ● *demons.adj.* (*pl.* **these** /theez/) **1** designating the person or thing close at hand, etc. (cf. senses 1, 2 of *pron.*). **2** (of time): **a** the present or current (*am busy all this week*). **b** relating to today (*this morning*). **c** just past or to come (*have been asking for it these three weeks*). **3** *colloq.* (in narrative) designating a person or thing previously unspecified (*then up came this policeman*). ● *adv.* to this degree or extent (*knew him when he was this high; did not reach this far*). □ **this and that** *colloq.* various unspecified examples of things (esp. trivial). **this here** *sl.* this particular (person or thing). **this much** the amount or extent about to be stated (*I know this much, that he was not there*). **this world** mortal life. [OE, neut. of *thes*]

this·tle /thísəl/ *n.* **1** any of various prickly composite herbaceous plants of the genus *Cirsium, Carlina,* or *Carduus,* etc., usu. with globular heads of purple flowers. **2** this as the Scottish national emblem. [OE *thistel* f. Gmc]

this·tle·down /thísəldown/ *n.* a light fluffy stuff attached to thistle seeds and blown about in the wind.

this·tly /thíslee/ *adj.* overgrown with thistles.

thith·er /thíthər, thi-/ *adv. archaic* or *formal* to or toward that place. [OE *thider,* alt. (after HITHER) of *thæder*]

thistle

thix·ot·ro·py /thiksótrəpee/ *n.* the property of becoming temporarily liquid when shaken or stirred, etc., and returning to a gel on standing. □□ **thix·o·trop·ic** /thíksətrópik/ *adj.* [Gk *thixis* touching + *tropē* turning]

tho' var. of THOUGH.

thole¹ /thōl/ *n.* **1** a pin in the gunwale of a boat as the fulcrum for an oar. **2** each of two such pins forming an oarlock. [OE *thol* fir tree, peg]

thole² /thōl/ *v.tr. Sc.* or *archaic* undergo or suffer (pain, grief, etc.). [OE *tholian* f. Gmc]

thole·pin /thólpin/ *n.* = THOLE¹.

tho·los /thólos/ *n.* (*pl.* **tho·loi** /-loy/) *Gk Antiq.* a dome-shaped tomb, esp. of the Mycenaean period. [Gk]

Tho·mism /tṓmizəm/ *n.* the doctrine of Thomas Aquinas, Italian scholastic philosopher and theologian d. 1274, or of his followers. □□ **Tho·mist** *n.* **Tho·mis·tic** /-místik/ *adj.* **Tho·mis·ti·cal** /-místikəl/ *adj.*

thong /thong/ *n. & v.* ● *n.* **1** a narrow strip of hide or leather used as the lash of a whip, as a halter or rein, etc. **2** = FLIP-FLOP 1. ● *v.tr.* **1** provide with a thong. **2** strike with a thong. [OE *thwang, thwong* f. Gmc]

tho·rax /tháwraks, thór-/ *n.* (*pl.* **tho·rax·es** or **tho·ra·ces** /tháwrəseez/) **1** *Anat. & Zool.* the part of the trunk between the neck and the abdomen. **2** *Gk Antiq.* a breastplate or cuirass. □□ **tho·ra·cal** /thórəkəl/ *adj.* **tho·rac·ic** /thawrásik/ *adj.* [L f. Gk *thōrax -akos*]

tho·ri·a /tháwreeə, thór-/ *n.* the oxide of thorium, used esp. in incandescent mantles.

tho·ri·um /tháwreeəm, thór-/ *n. Chem.* a radioactive metallic element

occurring naturally in monazite and used in alloys and for nuclear power. ¶ Symb.: **Th**. [*Thor,* Scand. god of thunder]

thorn /thawrn/ *n.* **1** a stiff sharp-pointed projection on a plant. **2** a thorn-bearing shrub or tree. **3** the name of an Old English and Icelandic runic letter, = th. □ **a thorn in one's side** (or **flesh**) a constant annoyance. □□ **thorn·less** *adj.* **thorn·proof** *adj.* [OE f. Gmc]

thorn ap·ple *n.* **1** a poisonous plant of the nightshade family, *Datura stramonium;* jimsonweed. **2** the prickly fruit of this.

thorn·back /tháwrnbak/ *n.* a ray, *Raja clavata,* with spines on the back and tail.

thorn·y /tháwrnee/ *adj.* (**thorn·i·er, thorn·i·est**) **1** having many thorns. **2** (of a subject) hard to handle without offense; problematic. □□ **thorn·i·ly** *adv.* **thorn·i·ness** *n.*

thor·ough /thúrō/ *adj.* **1** complete and unqualified; not superficial (*needs a thorough change*). **2** acting or done with great care and completeness (*the report is most thorough*). **3** absolute (*a thorough nuisance*). □□ **thor·ough·ly** *adv.* **thor·ough·ness** *n.* [orig. as adv. and prep. in the senses of *through,* f. OE *thuruh* var. of *thurh* THROUGH]

thor·ough·bass /thúrəbays/ *n.* = CONTINUO.

thor·ough·bred /thə́rōbred, thórə-, thúr-/ *adj. & n.* ● *adj.* **1** of pure breeding. **2** high-spirited. ● *n.* **1** a thoroughbred animal, esp. a horse. **2** (**Thoroughbred**) **a** a breed of racehorses originating from English mares and Arab stallions. **b** a horse of this breed.

thor·ough·fare /thórōfair, thórə-, thúr-/ *n.* a road or path open at both ends, esp. for traffic.

thor·ough·go·ing /thórōgṓing, thórə-, thúr-/ *adj.* **1** uncompromising; not superficial. **2** (usu. *attrib.*) extreme; out-and-out.

thor·ough-paced *adj.* **1** (of a horse) trained in all paces. **2** complete or unqualified.

thorp /thawrp/ *n.* (also **thorpe**) *archaic* a village or hamlet (now usually only in place-names). [OE *thorp, throp,* f. Gmc]

Thos. *abbr.* Thomas.

those *pl.* of THAT.

thou¹ /thow/ *pron.* (*obj.* **thee** /thee/; *poss.* **thy** or **thine;** *pl.* **ye** or **you**) second person singular pronoun, now replaced by *you* except in some formal, liturgical, dialect, and poetic uses. [OE *thu* f. Gmc]

thou² /thow/ *n.* (*pl.* same or **thous**) *colloq.* **1** a thousand. **2** one thousandth. [abbr.]

though /thō/ *conj. & adv.* ● *conj.* **1** despite the fact that (*though it was early we went to bed; though annoyed, I agreed*). **2** (introducing a possibility) even if (*ask him though he may refuse; would not attend though the Queen herself were there*). **3** and yet; nevertheless (*she read on, though not to the very end*). **4** in spite of being (*ready though unwilling*). ● *adv. colloq.* however; all the same (*I wish you had told me, though*). [ME *thoh,* etc., f. ON *thó,* etc., corresp. to OE *thēah,* f. Gmc]

thought¹ /thawt/ *n.* **1** the process or power of thinking; the faculty of reason. **2** a way of thinking characteristic of or associated with a particular time, people, group, etc. (*medieval European thought*). **3 a** sober reflection or consideration (*gave it much thought*). **b** care; regard; concern (*had no thought for others*). **4** an idea or piece of reasoning produced by thinking (*many good thoughts came out of the discussion*). **5** (foll. by *of* + verbal noun or *to* + infin.) a partly formed intention or hope (*gave up all thoughts of winning; had no thought to go*). **6** (usu. in *pl.*) what one is thinking; one's opinion (*have you any thoughts on this?*). **7** the subject of one's thinking (*my one thought was to get away*). **8** (prec. by *a*) *Brit.* somewhat (*seems to me a thought arrogant*). □ **give thought to** consider; think about. **in thought** thinking; meditating. **take thought** consider matters. □□ **-thought·ed** *adj.* (in *comb.*). [OE *thōht* (as THINK)]

thought² past and past part. of THINK.

thought·ful /tháwtfŏŏl/ *adj.* **1** engaged in or given to meditation. **2** (of a book, writer, remark, etc.) giving signs of serious thought. **3** (often foll. by *of*) (of a person or conduct) considerate; not haphazard or unfeeling. □□ **thought·ful·ly** *adv.* **thought·ful·ness** *n.*

thought·less /tháwtlis/ *adj.* **1** careless of consequences or of others' feelings. **2** due to lack of thought. □□ **thought·less·ly** *adv.* **thought·less·ness** *n.*

thought-pro·vok·ing *adj.* stimulating serious thought.

thou·sand /thówzənd/ *n. & adj.* ● *n.* (*pl.* **thou·sands** or (in sense 1) **thousand**) (in *sing.* prec. by *a* or *one*) **1** the product of a hundred and ten. **2** a symbol for this (1,000, m, M). **3** a set of a thousand things. **4** (in *sing.* or *pl.*) *colloq.* a large number. ● *adj.* that amount to a thousand. □□ **thou·sand·fold** *adj. & adv.* **thou·sandth** *adj. & n.* [OE *thūsend* f. Gmc]

thrall /thrawl/ *n. literary* **1** (often foll. by *of, to*) a slave (of a person, power, or influence). **2** bondage; a state of slavery or servitude (*in thrall*). □□ **thrall·dom** *n.* (also **thral·dom**). [OE *thrǣl* f. ON *thrǽll,* perh. f. a Gmc root = run]

thrash /thrash/ *v. & n.* ● *v.* **1** *tr.* beat severely, esp. with a stick or whip. **2** *tr.* defeat thoroughly in a contest. **3** *intr.* (of a paddle wheel, branch, etc.) act like a flail; deliver repeated blows. **4** *intr.* (foll. by *about, around*) move or fling the limbs about violently or in panic. **5** *intr.* (of a ship) keep striking the waves; make way against the wind or tide (*thrash to windward*). **6** *tr.* = THRESH 1. ● *n.* **1** an act of thrashing. **2** *Brit. colloq.* a party, esp. a lavish one. □ **thrash out** discuss to a conclusion. □□ **thrash•ing** *n.* [OE *therscan*, later *threscan*, f. Gmc]

thrash•er[1] /thráshər/ *n.* **1** a person or thing that thrashes. **2** = THRESHER.

thrash•er[2] /thráshər/ *n.* any of various long-tailed N. American thrushlike birds of the family Mimidae. [perh. f. E dial. *thrusher* = THRUSH[1]]

thrawn /thrawn/ *adj.* *Sc.* **1** perverse or ill-tempered. **2** misshapen; crooked. [Sc. form of *thrown* in obs. senses]

thread /thred/ *n. & v.* ● *n.* **1 a** a spun filament of cotton, silk, or glass, etc.; yarn. **b** a length of this. **2** a thin cord of twisted yarns used esp. in sewing and weaving. **3** anything regarded as threadlike with reference to its continuity or connectedness (*the thread of life; lost the thread of his argument*). **4** the spiral ridge of a screw. **5** (in *pl.*) *sl.* clothes. **6** a thin seam or vein of ore. ● *v.tr.* **1** pass a thread through the eye of (a needle). **2** put (beads) on a thread. **3** arrange (material in a strip form, e.g., film or magnetic tape) in the proper position on equipment. **4** make (one's way) carefully through a crowded place, over a difficult route, etc. **5** streak (hair, etc.) as with threads. **6** form a screw thread on. □ **hang by a thread** be in a precarious state, position, etc. □□ **thread•er** *n.* **thread•like** *adj.* [OE *thrēd* f. Gmc]

thread•bare /thrédbair/ *adj.* **1** (of cloth) so worn that the nap is lost and the thread visible. **2** (of a person) wearing such clothes. **3 a** hackneyed. **b** feeble or insubstantial (*a threadbare excuse*).

thread•fin /thrédfin/ *n.* any small tropical fish of the family Polynemidae, with long streamers from its pectoral fins.

thread mark *n.* a mark in the form of a thin line made in paper money with highly colored silk fibers to prevent photographic counterfeiting.

thread•worm /thrédwərm/ *n.* any of various, esp. parasitic, threadlike nematode worms, e.g., the pinworm.

thread•y /thrédee/ *adj.* (**thread•i•er, thread•i•est**) **1** of or like a thread. **2** (of a person's pulse) scarcely perceptible.

threat /thret/ *n.* **1 a** a declaration of an intention to punish or hurt. **b** *Law* a menace of bodily hurt or injury, such as may restrain a person's freedom of action. **2** an indication of something undesirable coming (*the threat of war*). **3** a person or thing as a likely cause of harm, etc. [OE *thrēat* affliction, etc., f. Gmc]

threat•en /thrét'n/ *v.tr.* **1 a** make a threat or threats against. **b** constitute a threat to; be likely to harm; put into danger. **2** be a sign or indication of (something undesirable). **3** (foll. by *to* + infin.) announce one's intention to do an undesirable or unexpected thing (*threatened to resign*). **4** (also *absol.*) give warning of the infliction of (harm, etc.) (*the clouds were threatening rain*). □□ **threat•en•er** *n.* **threat•en•ing** *adj.* **threat•en•ing•ly** *adv.* [OE *thrēatnian* (as THREAT)]

three /three/ *n. & adj.* ● *n.* **1 a** one more than two, or seven less than ten. **b** a symbol for this (3, iii, III). **2** a size, etc., denoted by three. **3** the time of three o'clock. **4** a set of three. **5** a card with three pips. ● *adj.* that amount to three. [OE *thrī* f. Gmc]

three-card mon•te *n.* (also **three-card trick**) a game in which bets are made on which is the queen (or other identified card) among three cards lying face downwards.

three cheers *n.* see CHEER.

three-col•or proc•ess *n.* a process of reproducing natural colors by combining photographic images in the three primary colors.

three-cor•nered *adj.* **1** triangular. **2** (of a contest, etc.) between three parties as individuals.

three-deck•er *n.* **1** a warship with three gun decks. **2** a novel in three volumes. **3** a sandwich with three slices of bread.

three-di•men•sion•al *adj.* having or appearing to have length, breadth, and depth.

three•fold /threefold/ *adj. & adv.* **1** three times as much or as many. **2** consisting of three parts.

three-hand•ed *adj.* **1** having or using three hands. **2** involving three players.

three-leg•ged race *n.* a running race between pairs, one member of each pair having the left leg tied to the right leg of the other.

three parts *n.* three quarters.

three•pence /thrépəns, thróopəns/ *n.* *Brit.* the sum of three pence, esp. before decimalization.

three•pen•ny /thrípnee, thróopənee/ *adj.* *Brit.* costing three pence, esp. before decimalization.

three•pen•ny bit *n.* *hist.* a former coin worth three old pence.

three-phase *adj.* (of an electric generator, motor, etc.) designed to supply or use simultaneously three separate alternating currents of the same voltage, but with phases differing by a third of a period.

three-piece *adj.* consisting of three items (esp. of a suit of clothes or a suite of furniture).

three-ply *adj. & n.* ● *adj.* of three strands, webs, or thicknesses. ● *n.* **1** three-ply wool. **2** three-ply wood made by gluing together three layers with the grain in different directions.

three-point land•ing *n.* *Aeron.* the landing of an aircraft on the two main wheels and the tail wheel or skid or front wheel simultaneously.

three-point turn *n.* a method of turning a vehicle around in a narrow space by moving forward, backward, and forward again in a sequence of arcs.

three-quar•ter *adj.* **1** consisting of three-fourths of something. **2** (of a portrait) going down to the hips or showing three-fourths of the face (between full face and profile).

three-quar•ters *n.pl.* three parts out of four.

three-ring cir•cus *n.* **1** a circus with three rings for simultaneous performances. **2** an extravagant display.

three Rs *n.* reading, writing (*joc.* 'riting), and arithmetic (*joc.* 'rithmetic), regarded as the fundamentals of learning.

three•score /threeskáwr/ *n.* *archaic* sixty.

three•some /threesəm/ *n.* **1** a group of three persons. **2** a game, etc., for three.

three-way *adj.* involving three ways or participants.

three-wheel•er *n.* a vehicle with three wheels.

threm•ma•tol•o•gy /thrémmətóləjee/ *n.* the science of breeding animals and plants. [Gk *thremma* –*matos* nursling + –LOGY]

thren•o•dy /thrénədee/ *n.* (also **thre•node** /thrénōd/) (*pl.* –**dies** or **thren•o•des**) **1** a lamentation, esp. on a person's death. **2** a song of lamentation. □□ **thre•no•di•al** /–nódeeəl/ *adj.* **thre•nod•ic** /–nódik/ *adj.* **thren•o•dist** /thrénədist/ *n.* [Gk *thrēnōidia* f. *thrēnos* wailing + *ōidē* ODE]

thre•o•nine /threeəneen, –nin/ *n.* *Biochem.* an amino acid, considered essential for growth. [*threose* (name of a tetrose sugar) ult. f. Gk *eruthros* red + –INE[4]]

thresh /thresh/ *v.* **1** *tr.* beat out or separate grain from (wheat, etc.). **2** *intr.* = THRASH 4. **3** *tr.* (foll. by *over*) analyze (a problem, etc.) in search of a solution. [var. of THRASH]

thresh•er /thréshər/ *n.* **1** a person or machine that threshes. **2** a shark, *Alopias vulpinus*, with a long upper lobe to its tail, that it can lash about.

thresh•ing floor *n.* a hard level floor for threshing, esp. with flails.

thresh•ing ma•chine *n.* a power-driven machine for separating the grain from the straw or husk. **thresh out** = *thrash out.*

thresh•old /thréshōld, thrésh-hōld/ *n.* **1** a strip of wood or stone forming the bottom of a doorway and crossed in entering a house or room, etc. **2** a point of entry or beginning (*on the threshold of a new century*). **3** *Physiol. & Psychol.* a limit below which a stimulus causes no reaction (*pain threshold*). **4** *Physics* a limit below which no reaction occurs, esp. a minimum dose of radiation producing a specified effect. **5** esp. *Brit.* (often *attrib.*) a step in a scale of wages or taxation, usu. operative in specified conditions. [OE *therscold, threscold*, etc., rel. to THRASH in the sense 'tread ']

threw *past of* THROW.

thrice /thrīs/ *adv. archaic* or *literary* **1** three times. **2** (esp. in *comb.*) highly (*thrice-blessed*). [ME *thries* f. *thrie* (adv.) f. OE *thrīwa, thrīga* (as THREE, –S[3])]

thrift /thrift/ *n.* **1** frugality; economical management. **2** a plant of the genus *Armeria*, esp. the sea pink. **3** a savings and loan association or savings bank. [ME f. ON (as THRIVE)]

thrift•less /thriftlis/ *adj.* wasteful; improvident. □□ **thrift•less•ly** *adv.* **thrift•less•ness** *n.*

thrift shop *n.* (also **thrift store**) a shop selling secondhand items usu. for charity.

thrift•y /thriftee/ *adj.* (**thrift•i•er, thrift•i•est**) **1** economical; frugal. **2** thriving; prosperous. □□ **thrift•i•ly** *adv.* **thrift•i•ness** *n.*

thrill /thril/ *n. & v.* ● *n.* **1 a** a wave or nervous tremor of emotion or sensation (*a thrill of joy; a thrill of recognition*). **b** a thrilling experience (*seeking new thrills*). **2** a throb or pulsation. **3** *Med.* a vibratory movement or resonance heard in auscultation. ● *v.* **1** *intr. & tr.* feel or cause to feel a thrill (*thrilled to the sound; a voice that thrilled millions*). **2** *intr.* quiver or throb with or as with emotion. **3** *intr.* (foll. by *through, over, along*) (of an emotion, etc.) pass with a thrill through, etc. (*fear thrilled through my veins*). □□ **thrill•ing** *adj.* **thrill•ing•ly** *adv.* [*thirl* (now dial.) f. OE *thyrlian* pierce f. *thȳrel* hole f. *thurh* THROUGH]

thrills and spills *n.* the excitement of potentially dangerous activities.

thrill•er /thrílər/ *n.* an exciting or sensational story or play, etc., esp. one involving crime or espionage.

thrips /thrips/ *n.* (*pl.* same) any insect of the order Thysanoptera, esp. a pest injurious to plants. [L f. Gk, = woodworm]

thrive /thrīv/ *v.intr.* (*past* **throve** /thrōv/ or **thrived**; *past part.* **thriv•en** /thrívən/ or **thrived**) **1** prosper or flourish. **2** grow rich. **3** (of a child, animal, or plant) grow vigorously. [ME f. ON *thrífask* refl. of *thrífa* grasp]

throat /thrōt/ *n.* **1 a** the windpipe or gullet. **b** the front part of the neck containing this. **2** *literary* **a** a voice, esp. of a songbird. **b** a thing compared to a throat, esp. a narrow passage, entrance, or exit. **3** *Naut.* the forward upper corner of a fore-and-aft sail. □ **cut one's own throat** bring about one's own downfall. **ram** (or **thrust**) **down a person's throat** force (a thing) on a person's attention. □□ **–throat•ed** adj. (in *comb.*). [OE *throte, throtu* f. Gmc]

throat•y /thrṓtee/ adj. (**throat•i•er, throat•i•est**) **1** (of a voice) deficient in clarity; hoarsely resonant. **2** guttural; uttered in the throat. **3** having a prominent or capacious throat. □□ **throat•i•ly** adv. **throat•i•ness** n.

throb /throb/ v. & n. •v.intr. (**throbbed, throb•bing**) **1** palpitate or pulsate, esp. with more than the usual force or rapidity. **2** vibrate or quiver with a persistent rhythm or with emotion. •n. a throbbing. **2** a palpitation or (esp. violent) pulsation. [ME, app. imit.]

throe /thrō/ n. (usu. in *pl.*) **1** a violent pang, esp. of childbirth or death. **2** anguish. □ **in the throes of** struggling with the task of. [ME *throwe* perh. f. OE *thrēa, thrawu* calamity, alt. perh. by assoc. with *woe*]

throm•bi pl. of THROMBUS.

throm•bin /thrómbin/ n. an enzyme promoting the clotting of blood. [as THROMBUS + –IN]

throm•bo•cyte /thrómbəsīt/ n. a blood platelet, a small plate of protoplasm concerned in the coagulation of blood. [as THROMBUS + –CYTE]

throm•bose /thrombṓz/ v.tr. & intr. affect with or undergo thrombosis. [back-form. f. THROMBOSIS]

throm•bo•sis /thrombṓsis/ n. (pl. **throm•bo•ses** /–seez/) the coagulation of the blood in a blood vessel or organ. □□ **throm•bot•ic** /–bótik/ adj. [mod.L f. Gk *thrombōsis* curdling (as THROMBUS)]

throm•bus /thrómbəs/ n. (pl. **throm•bi** /–bī/) a bloodclot formed in the vascular system and impeding blood flow. [mod.L f. Gk *thrombos* lump, bloodclot]

throne /thrōn/ n. & v. •n. **1** a chair of state for a sovereign or bishop, etc. **2** sovereign power (*came to the throne*). **3** (in *pl.*) the third order of the ninefold celestial hierarchy. **4** *colloq.* a toilet seat and bowl. •v.tr. place on a throne. □□ **throne•less** adj. [ME f. OF *trone* f. L *thronus* f. Gk *thronos* high seat]

throng /thrawng, throng/ n. & v. •n. **1** a crowd of people. **2** (often foll. by *of*) a multitude, esp. in a small space. •v. **1** intr. come in great numbers (*crowds thronged to the stadium*). **2** tr. flock into or crowd around; fill with or as with a crowd (*crowds thronged the streets*). [ME *thrang, throng*, OE *gethrang*, f. verbal stem *thring-thrang-*]

thros•tle /thrósəl/ n. **1** *Brit.* a song thrush. **2** (in full **throstle frame**) a machine for continuously spinning wool or cotton, etc. [OE f. Gmc: rel. to THRUSH[1]]

throt•tle /thrót'l/ n. & v. •n. **1 a** (in full **throttle valve**) a valve controlling the flow of fuel or steam, etc., in an engine. **b** (in full **throttle lever**) a lever or pedal operating this valve. **2** the throat, gullet, or windpipe. •v.tr. **1** choke or strangle. **2** prevent the utterance, etc., of. **3** control (an engine or steam, etc.) with a throttle. □ **throttle back** (or **down**) reduce the speed of (an engine or vehicle) by throttling. □□ **throt•tler** n. [ME *throtel* (v.), perh. f. THROAT + –LE[4] : (n.) perh. a dimin. of THROAT]

through /throo/ prep., adv., & adj. (also **thru**) •prep. **1 a** from end to end or from side to side of. **b** going in one side or end and out the other of. **2** between or among (*swam through the waves*). **3** from beginning to end of (*read through the letter; went through many difficulties; through the years*). **4** because of; by the agency, means, or fault of (*lost it through carelessness*). **5** up to and including (*Monday through Friday*). •adv. **1** through a thing; from side to side, end to end, or beginning to end; completely; thoroughly (*went through to the garden; would not let us through*). **2** having completed (esp. successfully) (*are through their exams*). **3** so as to be connected by telephone (*will put you through*). •attrib.adj. **1** (of a journey, route, etc.) done without a change of line or vehicle, etc., or with one ticket. **2** (of traffic) going through a place to its destination. □ **be through** *colloq.* **1** (often foll. by *with*) have finished. **2** (often foll. by *with*) cease to have dealings. **3** have no further prospects (*is through as a politician*). **through and through 1** thoroughly; completely. **2** through again and again. [OE *thurh* f. WG]

through•out /throo-ówt/ prep. & adv. •prep. right through; from end to end of (*throughout the town; throughout the 18th century*). •adv. in every part or respect (*the timber was rotten throughout*).

through•put /throopoot/ n. the amount of material put through a process, esp. in manufacturing or computing.

through•way /throo-way/ n. (also **thru•way**) a thoroughfare, esp. a highway.

throve past of THRIVE.

throw /thrō/ v. & n. •v.tr. (past **threw** /throo/; past part. **thrown** /thrōn/) **1** propel with some force through the air or in a particular direction. **2** force violently into a specified position or state (*the ship was thrown on the rocks; threw themselves down*). **3** compel suddenly to be in a specified condition (*was thrown out of work*). **4** turn or move (part of the body) quickly or suddenly (*threw an arm out*). **5** project or cast (light, a shadow, a spell, etc.). **6 a** bring to the ground in wrestling. **b** (of a horse) unseat (its rider). **7** *colloq.* disconcert (*the question threw me for a moment*). **8** (foll. by *on, off*, etc.)

1051   **throaty ~ thrust**

put (clothes, etc.) hastily on or off, etc. **9 a** cause (dice) to fall on a table. **b** obtain (a specified number) by throwing dice. **10** cause to pass or extend suddenly to another state or position (*threw in the army; threw a bridge across the river*). **11** move (a switch or lever) so as to operate it. **12 a** form (pottery) on a potter's wheel. **b** turn (wood, etc.) on a lathe. **13** have (a fit or tantrum, etc.). **14** give (a party). **15** *colloq.* lose (a contest or race, etc.) intentionally. **16** *Cricket* bowl (a ball) with an illegitimate sudden straightening of the elbow. **17** (of a snake) cast (its skin). **18** (of an animal) give birth to (young). **19** twist (silk, etc.) into thread or yarn. **20** (often foll. by *into*) put into another form or language, etc. •n. **1** an act of throwing. **2** the distance a thing is or may be thrown (*a record throw with the hammer*). **3** the act of being thrown in wrestling. **4** *Geol. & Mining* **a** a fault in strata. **b** the amount of vertical displacement caused by this. **5** a machine or device giving rapid rotary motion. **6 a** the movement of a crank or cam, etc. **b** the extent of this. **7** the distance moved by the pointer of an instrument, etc. **8 a** a light cover for furniture. **b** (in full **throw rug**) a light rug. **c** a shawl or scarf. **9** (prec. by *a*) *sl.* each; per item (*sold at $10 a throw*). □ **throw around** (or **about**) **1** throw in various directions. **2** spend (one's money) ostentatiously. **throw away 1** discard as useless or unwanted. **2** waste or fail to make use of (an opportunity, etc.). **3** discard (a card). **4** *Theatr.* speak (lines) with deliberate underemphasis. **5** (in *passive*; often foll. by *on*) be wasted (*the advice was thrown away on him*). **throw back 1** revert to ancestral character. **2** (usu. in *passive*; foll. by *on*) compel to rely on (*was thrown back on his savings*). **throw cold water on** see COLD. **throw down** cause to fall. **throw down the gauntlet** (or **glove**) issue a challenge. **throw good money after bad** incur further loss in a hopeless attempt to recoup a previous loss. **throw one's hand in 1** abandon one's chances in a card game, esp. poker. **2** give up; withdraw from a contest. **throw in 1** interpose (a word or remark). **2** include at no extra cost. **3** throw (a soccer ball) from the edge of the field where it has gone out of play. **4** *Baseball & Cricket* return (the ball) from the outfield. **5** *Cards* give (a player) the lead, to the player's disadvantage. **throw in one's lot with** see LOT. **throw in the towel** (or **the sponge**) admit defeat. **throw light on** see LIGHT[1]. **throw off 1** discard; contrive to get rid of. **2** write or utter in an offhand manner. **3** confuse or distract (a person speaking, thinking, or acting) from the matter in hand. **4** (of hounds or a hunt) begin hunting; make a start. **throw-off** the start in a hunt or race. **throw oneself at** seek blatantly as a spouse or sexual partner. **throw oneself into** engage vigorously in. **throw oneself on** (or **upon**) **1** rely completely on. **2** attack. **throw open** (often foll. by *to*) **1** cause to be suddenly or widely open. **2** make accessible. **throw out 1** put out forcibly or suddenly. **2** discard as unwanted. **3** expel (a troublemaker, etc.). **4** *Brit.* build (a wing of a house, a pier, or a projecting or prominent thing). **5** put forward tentatively. **6** reject (a proposal, etc.) **7** *Brit.* = throw off 3. **8** dislocate; strain (*threw out her shoulder*). **9** *Baseball & Cricket* put out (an opponent) by throwing the ball to the base or wicket. **throw over** desert or abandon. **throw stones** cast aspersions. **throw together 1** assemble hastily. **2** bring into casual contact. **throw up 1** abandon. **2** resign from. **3** *colloq.* vomit. **4** erect hastily. **5** bring to notice. **6** lift (a window) quickly. **throw one's weight around** (or **about**) *colloq.* act with unpleasant self-assertiveness. □□ **throw•a•ble** adj. **throw•er** n. (also in *comb.*). [OE *thrāwan* twist, turn f. WG]

throw•a•way /thrṓəway/ adj. **1** meant to be thrown away after (one) use. **2** (of lines, etc.) deliberately underemphasized. •n. a thing to be thrown away after (one) use.

throw•back /thrṓbak/ n. **1** reversion to ancestral character. **2** an instance of this.

throw•in n. the throwing in of a soccer ball during play.

throw•ster /thrṓstər/ n. a person who throws silk.

thru var. of THROUGH.

thrum[1] /thrum/ v. & n. •v. (**thrummed, thrum•ming**) **1** tr. play (a stringed instrument) monotonously or unskillfully. **2** intr. (often foll. by *on*) beat or drum idly or monotonously. •n. **1** such playing. **2** the resulting sound. [imit.]

thrum[2] /thrum/ n. & v. •n. **1** the unwoven end of a warp thread, or the whole of such ends, left when the finished web is cut away. **2** any short loose thread. •v.tr. (**thrummed, thrum•ming**) make of or cover with thrums. □□ **thrum•mer** n. **thrum•my** adj. [OE f. Gmc]

thrush[1] /thrush/ n. any small or medium-sized songbird of the family Turdidae, esp. a song thrush or mistle thrush (see SONG THRUSH). [OE *thrysce* f. Gmc: cf. THROSTLE]

thrush[2] /thrush/ n. **1 a** a fungal disease, esp. of children, marked by whitish vesicles in the mouth and throat. **b** a similar disease of the vagina. **2** inflammation affecting the frog of a horse's foot. [17th c.: orig. unkn.]

thrust /thrust/ v. & n. •v. (past and past part. **thrust**) **1** tr. push with a sudden impulse or with force (*thrust the letter into my pocket*). **2** tr.

(foll. by *on*) impose (a thing) forcibly; enforce acceptance of (a thing) (*had it thrust on me*). **3** *intr.* (foll. by *at*, *through*) pierce or stab; make a sudden lunge. **4** *tr.* make (one's way) forcibly. **5** *intr.* (foll. by *through*, *past*, etc.) force oneself (*thrust past me abruptly*). ● *n.* **1** a sudden or forcible push or lunge. **2** the propulsive force developed by a jet or rocket engine. **3** a strong attempt to penetrate an enemy's line or territory. **4** a remark aimed at a person. **5** the stress between the parts of an arch, etc. (often foll. by *of*) the chief theme or gist of remarks, etc. **7** an attack with the point of a weapon. **8** (in full **thrust fault**) *Geol.* a low-angle reverse fault, with older strata displaced horizontally over newer. □ **thrust oneself** (or **one's nose**) **in** obtrude; interfere. [ME *thruste*, etc. f. ON *þrýsta*]

thrust·er /thrústər/ *n.* **1** a person or thing that thrusts. **2** a small rocket engine used to provide extra or correcting thrust on a spacecraft.

thrust stage *n.* a stage extending into the audience.

thru·way var. of THROUGHWAY.

thud /thud/ *n. & v.* ● *n.* a low dull sound as of a blow on a nonresonant surface. ● *v.intr.* (**thud·ded**, **thud·ding**) make or fall with a thud. □□ **thud·ding·ly** *adv.*

WORD HISTORY thud

Late Middle English (originally Scots): probably from Old English *thyddan* 'to thrust, push'; related to *thoden* 'violent wind.' The noun is recorded earlier, denoting a sudden blast or gust of wind, later the sound of a thunderclap, whence a dull heavy sound. The verb dates from the early 16th century.

---

thug /thug/ *n.* **1** a vicious or brutal gangster or ruffian. **2** (**Thug**) *hist.* a member of a religious organization of robbers and assassins in India. □□ **thug·ger·y** *n.* **thug·gish** *adj.* **thug·gish·ly** *adv.* **thug·gish·ness** *n.* [Hindi & Marathi *ṭhag* swindler]

thug·gee /thugéé/ *n. hist.* murder practiced by the Thugs. □□ **thug·gism** *n.* [Hindi *ṭhagī* (as THUG)]

thu·ja /thóōyə/ *n.* (also **thu·ya**) any evergreen coniferous tree of the genus *Thuja*, with small leaves closely pressed to the branches; arborvitae. [mod.L f. Gk *thuia*, an Afr. tree]

thu·li·um /thóōleeəm, thyóō–/ *n. Chem.* a soft metallic element of the lanthanide series, occurring naturally in apatite. ¶ Symb.: **Tm**. [mod.L f. L *Thule* name of a region in the remote north]

thumb /thum/ *n. & v.* ● *n.* **1 a** a short thick terminal projection on the human hand, set lower and apart from the other four and opposable to them. **b** a digit of other animals corresponding to this. **2** part of a glove, etc., for a thumb. ● *v.* **1** *tr.* wear or soil (pages, etc.) with a thumb (*a well-thumbed book*). **2** *intr.* turn over pages with or as with a thumb (*thumbed through the directory*). **3** *tr.* request or obtain (a lift in a passing vehicle) by signaling with a raised thumb. **4** *tr.* gesture at (a person) with the thumb. □ **be all thumbs** be clumsy with one's hands. **thumb one's nose 1** put one's thumb up to one's nose with fingers extended up, a gesture of contempt. **2** display contempt or disdain. **under a person's thumb** completely dominated by a person. □□ **thumbed** *adj.* (also in *comb.*). **thumb·less** *adj.* [OE *þūma* f. a WG root = swell]

thumb in·dex *n. & v.* ● *n.* a set of lettered grooves cut down the side of a diary, dictionary, etc., for easy reference. ● *v.tr.* provide (a book, etc.) with these.

thumb·nail /thúmnayl/ *n.* **1** the nail of a thumb. **2** (*attrib.*) denoting conciseness (*a thumbnail sketch*).

thumb·print /thúmprint/ *n.* an impression of a thumb, esp. as used for identification.

thumb·screw /thúmskroō/ *n.* **1** an instrument of torture for crushing the thumbs. **2** a screw with a flattened head for turning with the thumb and forefinger.

thumbs-down *n.* an indication of rejection or failure.

thumbs-up *n.* an indication of satisfaction or approval.

thumb·tack /thúmtak/ *n.* a tack with a flat head pressing in with the thumb.

thump /thump/ *v. & n.* ● *v.* **1** *tr.* beat or strike heavily, esp. with the fist (*thumped the table for attention*). **2** *intr.* throb or pulsate strongly (*my heart was thumping*). **3** *intr.* (foll. by *at*, *on*, etc.) deliver blows, esp. to attract attention (*thumped on the door*). **4** *tr.* (often foll. by *out*) play (a tune on a piano, etc.) with a heavy touch. **5** *intr.* tread heavily. ● *n.* **1** a heavy blow. **2** the sound of this. □□ **thump·er** *n.* [imit.]

thump·ing /thúmping/ *adj. colloq.* big; prominent (*a thumping majority; a thumping lie*).

thun·der /thúndər/ *n. & v.* ● *n.* **1** a loud rumbling or crashing noise heard after a lightning flash and due to the expansion of rapidly heated air. **2** a resounding loud deep noise (*the thunder of an explosion*). **3** strong censure or denunciation. ● *v.* **1** *intr.* (prec. by *it* as subject) thunder sounds (*it is thundering; if it thunders*). **2** *intr.* make or proceed with a noise suggestive of thunder (*the applause thundered in my ears; the crowd thundered past*). **3** *tr.* utter or communicate (approval, disapproval, etc.) loudly or impressively. **4** *intr.* (foll.

by *against*, etc.) **a** make violent threats, etc., against. **b** criticize violently. □ **steal a person's thunder** spoil the effect of another's idea, action, etc., by expressing or doing it first. □□ **thun·der·er** *n.* **thun·der·less** *adj.* **thun·der·y** *adj.* [OE *thunor* f. Gmc]

thun·der·bolt /thúndərbōlt/ *n.* **1 a** a flash of lightning with a simultaneous crash of thunder. **b** a stone, etc., imagined to be a destructive bolt. **2** a sudden or unexpected occurrence or item of news. **3** a supposed bolt or shaft as a destructive agent, esp. as an attribute of a god.

thun·der·box *n. Brit. colloq.* a primitive toilet.

thun·der·clap /thúndərklap/ *n.* **1** a crash of thunder. **2** something startling or unexpected.

thun·der·cloud /thúndərklowd/ *n.* a cumulus cloud with a tall diffuse top, charged with electricity and producing thunder and lightning.

thun·der·head /thúndərhed/ *n.* a rounded cumulus cloud projecting upwards and heralding a thunderstorm.

thun·der·ing /thúndəring/ *adj. colloq.* very big or great (*a thundering nuisance*). □□ **thun·der·ing·ly** *adv.*

thun·der·ous /thúndərəs/ *adj.* **1** like thunder. **2** very loud. □□ **thun·der·ous·ly** *adv.* **thun·der·ous·ness** *n.*

thun·der·show·er /thóndərshowər/ *n.* a brief rain shower accompanied by thunder and sometimes lightning.

thun·der·storm /thúndərstawrm/ *n.* a storm with thunder and lightning and usu. heavy rain or hail.

thun·der·struck /thúndərstruk/ *adj.* amazed; overwhelmingly surprised or startled.

Thur. *abbr.* Thursday.

thu·ri·ble /thóōribəl, thyóō–/ *n.* a censer. [ME f. OF *thurible* or L *t(h)uribulum* f. *thus thur-* incense (as THURIFER)]

thu·ri·fer /thóōrifər, thyóō–/ *n.* an acolyte carrying a censer. [LL f. *thus thuris* incense f. Gk *thuos* sacrifice + *–fer* –bearing]

Thurs. *abbr.* Thursday.

Thurs·day /thórzday, –dee/ *n. & adv.* ● *n.* the fifth day of the week, following Wednesday. ● *adv. colloq.* **1** on Thursday. **2** (**Thursdays**) on Thursdays; each Thursday. [OE *thunresdæg, thur(e) sdæg*, day of thunder, representing LL *Jovis dies* day of Jupiter]

thus /thus/ *adv. formal* **1 a** in this way. **b** as indicated. **2 a** accordingly. **b** as a result or inference. **3** to this extent; so (*thus far; thus much*). □□ **thus·ly** *adv. colloq.* [OE (= OS *thus*), of unkn. orig.]

▶ There is never a need to expand the adverb **thus** to "thusly."

thu·ya var. of THUJA.

thwack /thwak/ *v. & n. colloq.* ● *v.tr.* hit with a heavy blow; whack. ● *n.* a heavy blow. [imit.]

thwaite /thwayt/ *n. Brit. dial.* a piece of wild land made arable (now usually only in place-names). [ON *thveit(i)* paddock, rel. to OE *thwītan* to cut]

thwart /thwawrt/ *v., n., prep., & adv.* ● *v.tr.* frustrate or foil (a person or purpose, etc.). ● *n.* a rower's seat placed across a boat. ● *prep. & adv. archaic* across; athwart. [ME *thwert* (adv.) f. ON *thvert* neut. of *thverr* transverse = OE *thwe(o)rh* f. Gmc]

SYNONYM TIP thwart

BAFFLE, BALK, FOIL, FRUSTRATE, INHIBIT. These verbs refer to the various ways in which we can outwit or overcome opposing forces. **Thwart** suggests using cleverness rather than force to bring about the defeat of an enemy or to block progress toward an objective (*to thwart a rebellion, to have one's goals thwarted by lack of education*). **Balk** also emphasizes setting up barriers (*a sudden reversal that balked their hopes for a speedy resolution*), but it is used more often as an intransitive verb meaning to stop at an obstacle and refuse to proceed (*he balked at appearing in front of the angry crowd*). To **baffle** is to cause defeat by bewildering or confusing (*the police were baffled by the lack of evidence*), while **foil** means to throw off course so as to discourage further effort (*her plan to arrive early was foiled by heavy traffic*). **Frustrate** implies rendering all attempts or efforts useless, so that nothing ever comes of them (*frustrated by the increasingly bad weather, they decided to work indoors*), while **inhibit** suggests forcing something into inaction (*to inhibit wage increases by raising corporate taxes*). Both *frustrate* and *inhibit* are used in a psychological context to suggest barriers that impede normal development or prevent the realization of natural desires (*he was both frustrated by her refusal to acknowledge his presence and inhibited by his own shyness*).

---

thy /thī/ *poss.pron.* (*attrib.*) (also **thine** /thīn/ before a vowel) of or belonging to thee: now replaced by *your* except in some formal, liturgical, dialect, and poetic uses. [ME *thī*, reduced f. *thīn* THINE]

thyme /tīm/ *n.* any herb or shrub of the genus *Thymus* with aromatic leaves, esp. *T. vulgaris* grown for culinary use. □□ **thym·y** *adj.* [ME f. OF *thym* f. L *thymum* f. Gk *thumon* f. *thuō* burn a sacrifice]

thy·mi *pl.* of THYMUS.

thy·mine /thímeen/ *n. Biochem.* a pyrimidine derivative found in all living tissue as a component base of DNA. [*thymic* (as THYMUS) + *–INE*[4]]

thy·mol /thímawl, –ōl/ *n.* *Chem.* a white crystalline phenol obtained from oil of thyme and used as an antiseptic. [as THYME f. –OL[1]]

thy·mus /thíməs/ *n.* (*pl.* **-mus·es** or **-mi** /–mī/) (in full **thymus gland**) *Anat.* a lymphoid organ situated in the neck of vertebrates (in humans becoming much smaller at the approach of puberty) producing lymphocytes for the immune response. [mod.L f. Gk *thumos*]

thy·ris·tor /thírīstər/ *n.* *Electronics* a semiconductor rectifier in which the current between two electrodes is controlled by a signal applied to a third electrode. [Gk *thura* gate + TRANSISTOR]

thyro- /thíró/ *comb. form* (also **thyreo-** /–reeó/) thyroid.

thy·roid /thíroyd/ *n. & adj.* ● *n.* (in full **thyroid gland**) **1** a large ductless gland in the neck of vertebrates secreting a hormone which regulates growth and development through the rate of metabolism. **2** an extract prepared from the thyroid gland of animals and used in treating goiter, etc. ● *adj. Anat. & Zool.* **1** connected with the thyroid cartilage (*thyroid artery*). **2** shield shaped. [obs.F *thyroide* or mod.L *thyroides*, irreg. f. Gk *thureoeidēs* f. *thureos* oblong shield]

thy·roid car·ti·lage *n.* a large cartilage of the larynx, the projection of which in humans forms the Adam's apple.

thy·rox·ine /thíróksin, –seen/ *n.* the main hormone produced by the thyroid gland, involved in controlling the rate of metabolic processes. [THYROID + OX- + –INE[4]]

thyr·sus /thórsəs/ *n.* (*pl.* **thyr·si** /–sī/) **1** *Gk & Rom. Antiq.* a staff tipped with an ornament like a pinecone, an attribute of Bacchus. **2** *Bot.* (also **thyr·se**) an inflorescence as in lilac, with the primary axis racemose and the secondary axis cymose. [L f. Gk *thursos*]

thy·self /thísélf/ *pron. archaic* emphat. & refl. form of THOU[1], THEE.

Ti *symb. Chem.* the element titanium.

ti[1] /tee/ *n.* any woody liliaceous plant of the genus *Cordyline*, esp. *C. terminalis* with edible roots. [Tahitian, Maori, etc.]

ti[2] /tee/ *n.* (also **te**) **1** (in tonic sol-fa) the seventh note of a major scale. **2** the note B in the fixed-do system. [earlier *si*: F f. It., perh. f. *Sancte Iohannes*: see GAMUT]

ti·ar·a /teeárə, –áarə, –áirə/ *n.* **1** a jeweled ornamental band worn on the front of a woman's hair. **2** a three-crowned diadem worn by a pope. **3** *hist.* a turban worn by ancient Persian kings. □□ **ti·ar·aed** *adj.* (also **ti·ar·a'd**). [L f. Gk, of unkn. orig.]

Ti·bet·an /tibét'n/ *n. & adj.* ● *n.* **1 a** a native of Tibet. **b** a person of Tibetan descent. **2** the language of Tibet. ● *adj.* of or relating to Tibet or its language.

tib·i·a /tíbeeə/ *n.* (*pl.* **tib·i·ae** /–bee-ee/) **1** *Anat.* the inner and usu. larger of two bones extending from the knee to the ankle. **2** the tibiotarsus of a bird. **3** the fourth segment of the leg in insects. □□ **tib·i·al** *adj.* [L, = shinbone]

tib·i·o·tar·sus /tíbeeōtáarsəs/ *n.* (*pl.* **tib·i·o·tar·si** /–sī/) the bone in a bird corresponding to the tibia fused at the lower end with some bones of the tarsus. [TIBIA + TARSUS]

tic /tik/ *n.* **1** a habitual spasmodic contraction of the muscles, esp. of the face. **2** a personality or behavioral quirk. [F f. It. *ticchio*: *douloureux* F, = painful]

tic dou·lou·reux *n.* /dōōlərōṓ, –rố/ trigeminal neuralgia.

tice /tīs/ *n. Brit.* **1** *Cricket* a ball bowled so that it pitches immediately under the bat. Also called **yorker.** **2** *Croquet* a stroke tempting an opponent to aim at one's ball. [*tice* (now dial.), = ENTICE]

tick[1] /tik/ *n. & v.* ● *n.* **1** a slight recurring click, esp. that of a watch or clock. **2** esp. *Brit. colloq.* a moment; an instant. **3** *Brit.* a mark (√) to denote correctness, check items in a list, etc. ● *v.* **1** *intr.* **a** (of a clock, etc.) make ticks. **b** (foll. by *away*) (of time, etc.) pass. **2** *intr.* (of a mechanism) work; function (*take it apart to see how it ticks*). **3** *tr. Brit.* **a** mark (a written answer, etc.) with a tick. **b** (often foll. by *off*) mark (an item in a list, etc.) with a tick in checking. □ **in two ticks** *Brit. colloq.* in a very short time. **tick off 1** *sl.* annoy, anger; dispirit. **2** *Brit. colloq.* reprimand. **tick over** *Brit.* **1** (of an engine, etc.) idle. **2** (of a person, project, etc.) be working or functioning at a basic or minimum level. **what makes a person tick** *colloq.* a person's motivation. □□ **tick·less** *adj.* [ME: cf. Du. *tik*, LG *tikk* touch, tick]

tick[2] /tik/ *n.* **1** any of various arachnids of the order Acarina, parasitic on the skin of warm-blooded vertebrates. **2** any of various insects of the family Hippoboscidae, parasitic on sheep and birds, etc. **3** *colloq.* an unpleasant or despicable person. [OE *ticca* (recorded as *ticia*); ME *teke, tyke*: cf. MDu., MLG *tēke*, OHG *zēcho*]

tick[3] /tik/ *n. Brit. colloq.* credit (*buy goods on tick*). [app. an abbr. of TICKET in phr. *on the ticket*]

tick[4] /tik/ *n.* **1** the cover of a mattress or pillow. **2** = TICKING. [ME *tikke, tēke* f. WG f. L *theca* f. Gk *thēkē* case]

tick·er /tíkər/ *n. colloq.* **1** the heart. **2** a watch. **3** a machine that receives and prints telegraphed messages onto paper tape.

tick·er tape *n.* **1** a paper strip from a ticker. **2** this or similar material thrown from windows, etc., along the route of a parade honoring a hero, etc.

tick·et /tíkit/ *n. & v.* ● *n.* **1** a written or printed piece of paper or card entitling the holder to enter a place, participate in an event, travel by public transport, use a public amenity, etc. **2** an official notification of a traffic offense, etc. (*parking ticket*). **3** *Brit.* a certif-

icate of discharge from the army. **4** a certificate of qualification as a ship's master, ship or airplane pilot, etc. **5** a label attached to a thing and giving its price or other details. **6** a list of candidates put forward by one group, esp. a political party. **7** (prec. by *the*) *colloq.* what is correct or needed. ● *v.tr.* (**tick·et·ed, tick·et·ing**) attach or serve a ticket to. □ **have tickets on oneself** *Austral. colloq.* be conceited. □□ **tick·et·ed** *adj.* **tick·et·less** *adj.* [obs.F *étiquet* f. OF *estiquet(te)* f. *estiquier, estechier* fix f. MDu. *steken*]

tick·et of·fice *n.* an office or kiosk where tickets are sold for transport, entertainment, etc.

tick·et-of-leave man *n. Brit. hist.* a prisoner or convict who had served part of his time and was granted certain concessions, esp. leave.

tick·et·y-boo /tíkəteebōō/ *adj. Brit. colloq.* all right; in order. [20th c.: orig. uncert.]

tick fe·ver *n.* a bacterial or rickettsial fever transmitted by the bite of a tick.

tick·ing /tíking/ *n.* a stout usu. striped material used to cover mattresses, etc. [TICK[4] + –ING[1]]

tick·le /tíkəl/ *v. & n.* ● *v.* **1 a** *tr.* apply light touches or strokes to (a person or part of a person's body) so as to excite the nerves and usu. produce laughter and spasmodic movement. **b** *intr.* feel this sensation (*my foot tickles*). **2** *tr.* excite agreeably; amuse or divert (a person, a sense of humor, vanity, etc.) (*was tickled at the idea; this will tickle your fancy*). **3** *tr.* catch (a trout, etc.) by rubbing it so that it moves backward into the hand. ● *n.* **1** an act of tickling. **2** a tickling sensation. □□ **tick·ler** *n.* **tick·ly** *adj.*

WORD HISTORY | tickle

Middle English (in the sense 'be delighted or thrilled,' surviving in *tickled pink*): perhaps a frequentative of TICK[1], or an alteration of Scots and dialect *kittle* 'to tickle,' of Germanic origin and related to Dutch *kittelen* and German *kizzeln.*

---

tick·led pink *adj.* (also **tick·led to death**) *colloq.* extremely amused or pleased.

tick·lish /tíklish/ *adj.* **1** sensitive to tickling. **2** (of a matter or person to be dealt with) difficult; requiring careful handling. □□ **tick·lish·ly** *adv.* **tick·lish·ness** *n.*

tic-tac var. of TICK-TACK.

tick-tack *n.* (also **tic-tac**) *Brit.* a kind of manual semaphore signaling used by bookmakers to exchange information.

tick-tack-toe *n.* (also **tic-tac-toe**) a game in which players alternate turns, seeking to complete a series of three Xs or Os marked in a nine-square grid.

tid·al /tíd'l/ *adj.* relating to, like, or affected by tides (*tidal basin; tidal river*). □□ **tid·al·ly** *adv.*

tid·al bore *n.* a large wave or bore caused by constriction of the spring tide as it enters a long narrow shallow inlet.

tid·al wave *n.* **1** = TSUNAMI. **2** a widespread manifestation of feeling, etc.

tid·bit /tídbit/ *n.* (*Brit.* **tit·bit** /tít–/) **1** a small morsel. **2** a choice item of news, etc. [perh. f. dial. *tid* tender + BIT[1]]

tid·dle·dy-winks var. of TIDDLY-WINKS.

tid·dler /tídlər/ *n. Brit. colloq.* **1** a small fish, esp. a stickleback or minnow. **2** an unusually small thing or person. [perh rel. to TIDDLY[2] and *tittlebat,* a childish form of *stickleback*]

tid·dly[1] /tídlee/ *adj.* (**tid·dli·er, tid·dli·est**) esp. *Brit. colloq.* slightly drunk. [19th c., earlier = a drink: orig. unkn.]

tid·dly[2] /tídlee/ *adj.* (**tid·dli·er, tid·dli·est**) *Brit. colloq.* little.

tid·dly-winks /tídleewingks/ *n.* (also **tid·dle·dy-** /tíd'ldee–/) a game played by flicking counters into a cup, etc. [19th c.: perh. rel. to TIDDLY[1]]

tide /tīd/ *n. & v.* ● *n.* **1 a** the periodic rise and fall of the sea due to the attraction of the moon and sun (see EBB *n.* 1, FLOOD *n.* 3). **b** the water as affected by this. **2** a time or season (usu. in *comb.*: *Whitsuntide*). **3** a marked trend of opinion, fortune, or events. ● *v.intr.* drift with the tide, esp. move in or out of a harbor with the help of the tide. □ **tide over** enable or help (a person) to deal with an awkward situation, difficult period, etc. (*the money will tide me over until Friday*). **work double tides** *Brit.* work twice the normal time, or extra hard. □□ **tide·less** *adj.* [OE *tīd* f. Gmc, rel. to TIME]

tide·land /tídland/ *n.* **1** land that is submerged at high tide. **2** land below the low-water mark but within a nation's territorial waters.

tide·mark /tídmaark/ *n.* **1** a mark made by the tide at esp. high water. **2** esp. *Brit.* **a** a mark left round a bathtub at the level of the water in it. **b** a line on a person's body, garment, etc., marking the extent to which it has been washed.

tide mill *n.* a mill with a waterwheel driven by the tide.

tide·ta·ble /tídtaybəl/ *n.* a table indicating the times of high and low tides at a place.

tide•wait•er /tídwaytər/ *n. hist.* a customs officer who boarded ships on their arrival to enforce the customs regulations.

tide•wa•ter /tídwawtər, –wotər/ *n.* **1** water brought up by or affected by tides. **2** (*attrib.*) affected by tides (*tidewater region*).

tide•wave /tídwayv/ *n.* an undulation of water passing round the earth and causing high and low tides.

tide•way /tídway/ *n.* **1** a channel in which a tide runs, esp. the tidal part of a river. **2** the ebb or flow in a tidal channel.

ti•dings /tídingz/ *n.* (as *sing.* or *pl.*) news; information. [OE *tídung*, prob. f. ON *títhindi* events f. *títhr* occurring]

ti•dy /tídee/ *adj., n., & v.* • *adj.* (**ti•di•er, ti•di•est**) **1** neat; orderly; methodically arranged. **2** (of a person) methodically inclined. **3** *colloq.* considerable (*it cost a tidy sum*). • *n.* (*pl.* **–dies**) **1** a receptacle for holding small objects. **2** esp. *Brit.* an act or spell of tidying. **3** a detachable ornamental cover for a chair back, arms, etc. • *v.tr.* (**–dies, –died**) (also *absol.*; often foll. by *up*) put in good order; make (oneself, a room, etc.) tidy. □□ **ti•di•ly** *adv.* **ti •di•ness** *n.* [ME, = timely, etc., f. TIDE + –Y¹]

tie /tí/ *v. & n.* • *v.* (**ty•ing**) **1** *tr.* **a** attach or fasten with string or cord, etc. (*tie the dog to the gate; tie his hands together; tied on a label*). **b** link conceptually. **2** *tr.* **a** form (a string, ribbon, shoelace, necktie, etc.) into a knot or bow. **b** form (a knot or bow) in this way. **3** *tr.* restrict or limit (a person) as to conditions, occupation, place, etc. (*is tied to his family*). **4** *intr.* (often foll. by *with*) achieve the same score or place as another competitor (*they tied at ten games each; tied with her for first place*). **5** *tr.* hold (rafters, etc.) together by a crosspiece, etc. **6** *tr. Mus.* **a** unite (written notes) by a tie. **b** perform (two notes) as one unbroken note. • *n.* **1** a cord, line, or chain, etc., used for fastening. **2** a strip of material worn round the collar and tied in a knot at the front with the ends hanging down. **3** a thing that unites or restricts persons; a bond or obligation (*family ties; ties of friendship*). **4** a draw, dead heat, or equality of score among competitors. **5** *Brit.* a match between any pair from a group of competing players or teams. **6** (also **tie beam**, etc.) a rod or beam holding parts of a structure together. **7** *Mus.* a curved line above or below two notes of the same pitch indicating that are to be played for the combined duration of their time values. **8** a beam laid horizontally as a support for railroad rails. **9** a shoe tied with a lace. □ **fit to be tied** *colloq.* very angry. **tie down** = TIE *v.* 3 above. **tie in** (foll. by *with*) bring into or have a close association or agreement. **tie the knot** *colloq.* get married. **tie up 1** bind or fasten securely with cord, etc. **2** invest or reserve (capital, etc.) so that it is not immediately available for use. **3** moor (a boat). **4** secure (an animal). **5** obstruct; prevent from acting freely. **6** secure or complete (an undertaking, etc.). **7** (often foll. by *with*) = *tie in. * **8** (usu. in *passive*) fully occupy (a person). □□ **tie•less** *adj.* [OE *tígan, tégan* (v.), *téah, tég* (n.) f. Gmc]

tied /tíd/ *adj. Brit.* **1** (of a house) occupied subject to the tenant's working for its owner. **2** (of a bar, etc.) bound to supply the products of a particular brewery only.

tie-dye *n.* (also **tie and dye**) a method of producing dyed patterns by tying string, etc., to protect parts of the fabric from the dye.

tie-in *n.* **1** a connection or association. **2** (often *attrib.*) a form of sale or advertising that offers or requires more than a single purchase. **3** the joint promotion of related commodities, etc. (e.g., a book and a movie).

tie-line *n.* a transmission line connecting parts of a system, esp. a telephone line connecting two private branch exchanges.

tie•pin /típin/ *n.* an ornamental pin or clip for holding a tie in place.

tier /teer/ *n.* **1** a row or rank or unit of a structure, as one of several placed one above another (*tiers of seats*). **2** a layer or rank. **3** *Naut.* **a** a circle of coiled cable. **b** a place for a coiled cable. □□ **tiered** *adj.* (also in *comb.*). [earlier *tire* f. F f. *tirer* draw, elongate f. Rmc]

tierce /teers/ *n.* **1** *Eccl.* = TERCE. **2** *Mus.* an interval of a major or minor third. **3** a sequence of three cards. **4** *Fencing* **a** the third of eight parrying positions. **b** the corresponding thrust. **5** *archaic* **a** a former wine measure of one-third of a pipe. **b** a cask containing a certain quantity (varying with the contents), esp. of provisions. [ME f. OF *t(i)erce* f. L *tertia* fem. of *tertius* third]

tierced /teerst/ *adj. Heraldry* divided into three parts of different tinctures.

tier•cel var. of TERCEL.

tier•cet var. of TERCET.

tiff /tif/ *n. & v.* • *n.* **1** a slight or petty quarrel. **2** a fit of peevishness. • *v.intr.* have a petty quarrel; bicker. [18th c.: orig. unkn.]

tif•fa•ny /tífanee/ *n.* (*pl.* **–nies**) thin gauze muslin. [orig. dress worn on Twelfth Night, f. OF *tifanie* f. eccl.L *theophania* f. Gk *theophaneia* Epiphany]

tif•fin /tífin/ *n. & v. Brit. & Ind.* • *n.* a light meal, esp. lunch. • *v.intr.* (**tif•fined, tif•fin•ing**) take lunch, etc. [app. f. *tiffing* sipping]

ti•ger /tígər/ *n.* **1 a** a large Asian feline, *Panthera tigris*, having a yellowish brown coat with black stripes. **b** a similar feline, as the jaguar or ocelot. **2** a domestic cat with similar stripping. **3** a fierce, energetic, or formidable person. □□ **ti•ger•ish** *adj.* **ti•ger•ish•ly** *adv.* [ME f. OF *tigre* f. L *tigris* f. Gk *tigris*]

ti•ger bee•tle *n.* any carnivorous beetle of the family Cicindelidae, with spotted or striped wing covers.

ti•ger cat *n.* **1** any moderate-sized feline resembling the tiger, e.g., the ocelot, serval, or margay. **2** *Austral.* any of various carnivorous marsupials of the genus *Dasyurus*, including the Tasmanian devil. **3** = sense 2.

ti•ger-eye *n.* (also **ti•ger's-eye**) **1** a yellowish brown striped gem of brilliant luster. **2** a pottery glaze of similar appearance.

ti•ger lil•y *n.* a tall garden lily, *Lilium tigrinum*, with flowers of dull orange spotted with black or purple.

ti•ger moth *n.* any moth of the family Arctiidae, esp. *Arctia caja*, having richly spotted and streaked wings suggesting a tiger's skin.

ti•ger wood *n.* a striped or streaked wood used for cabinet-making.

tight /tít/ *adj., n., & adv.* • *adj.* **1** closely held, drawn, fastened, fitting, etc. (*a tight hold; a tight skirt*). **2 a** closely and firmly put together (*a tight joint*). **b** close; evenly matched (*a tight finish*). **3** (of clothes, etc.) too closely fitting (*my shoes are rather tight*). **4** impermeable, impervious, esp. (in *comb.*) to a specified thing (*watertight*). **5** tense; stretched so as to leave no slack (*a tight bowstring*). **6** *colloq.* drunk. **7** *colloq.* (of a person) mean; stingy. **8 a** (of money or materials) not easily obtainable. **b** (of a money market) in which money is tight. **9** (of precautions, a program, a schedule, etc.) stringent; demanding. **b** presenting difficulties (*a tight situation*). **c** (of an organization, group, or member) strict; disciplined. **10** produced by or requiring great exertion or pressure (*a tight squeeze*). **11** (of control, etc.) strictly imposed. **12** *colloq.* friendly; close (*the two girls quickly became tight*). • *adv.* tightly (*hold tight!*). □□ **tight•ly** *adv.* **tight•ness** *n.* [prob. alt. of *thight* f. ON *théttr* watertight, of close texture]

tight cor•ner *n.* (also **tight place** or **tight spot**) a difficult situation.

tight•en /tít'n/ *v.tr. & intr.* (also foll. by *up*) make or become tight or tighter. □ **tighten one's belt** see BELT.

tight-fist•ed *adj.* stingy.

tight-fit•ting *adj.* **1** (of a garment) fitting close to and showing the contours of the body. **2** (of a lid or cover) forming a tight seal when placed on a container.

tight-lipped *adj.* with or as with the lips compressed to restrain emotion or speech.

tight•rope /títrōp/ *n.* a rope stretched tightly high above the ground, on which acrobats perform.

tights /títs/ *n.pl.* **1** a thin but not sheer close-fitting wool or nylon, etc., garment covering the legs and the lower part of the torso. **2** a similar garment worn by a dancer, acrobat, etc.

tight•wad /títwod/ *n. colloq.* a person who is miserly or stingy.

ti•glon /tíglən/ (also **ti•gon** /tígən/) *n.* the offspring of a tiger and a lioness (cf. LIGER). [portmanteau word f. TIGER + LION]

ti•gress /tígris/ *n.* **1** a female tiger. **2** a fierce or passionate woman.

tike var. of TYKE.

ti•ki /teekee/ *n.* (*pl.* **ti•kis**) esp. *NZ* a large wooden or small ornamental greenstone image representing a human figure. [Maori]

'til /til/ *prep. & conj. colloq.* = TILL¹.

▶ See note at UNTIL. **tilbury**

til•de /tíldə/ *n.* a mark (˜), put over a letter, e.g., over a Spanish *n* when pronounced *ny* (as in *señor*) or a Portuguese *a* or *o* when nasalized (as in *São Paulo*). [Sp., ult. f. L *titulus* TITLE]

tile /tíl/ *n. & v.* • *n.* **1** a thin slab of concrete or baked clay, etc., used in series for covering a roof or pavement, etc. **2** a similar slab of glazed pottery, cork, linoleum, etc., for covering a floor, wall, etc. **3** a thin flat piece used in a game (esp. mah-jongg). • *v.tr.* cover with tiles. □ **on the tiles** *Brit. colloq.* having a spree. [OE *tigule, –ele*, f. L *tegula*]

til•er /tílər/ *n.* **1** a person who makes or lays tiles. **2** the doorkeeper of a Freemasons' lodge.

til•ing /tíling/ *n.* **1** the process of fixing tiles. **2** an area of tiles.

till¹ /til/ *prep. & conj.* • *prep.* **1** up to or as late as (*wait till six o'clock; did not return till night*). **2** up to the time of (*faithful till death; waited till the end*). • *conj.* **1** up to the time when (*wait till I return*). **2** so long that (*laughed till I cried*). [OE & ON *til* to, rel. to TILL³]

▶ See note at UNTIL.

till² /til/ *n.* **1** a drawer for money in a store or bank, etc., esp. with a device recording the amount of each purchase. **2** a supply of money. [ME: orig. unkn.]

till³ /til/ *v.tr.* prepare and cultivate (land) for crops. □□ **till•a•ble** *adj.* **till•er** *n.* [OE *tilian* strive for, cultivate, f. Gmc]

till⁴ /til/ *n.* stiff clay containing boulders, sand, etc., deposited by melting glaciers and ice sheets. [17th c. (Sc.): orig. unkn.]

till•age /tílij/ *n.* **1** the preparation of land for bearing crops. **2** tilled land.

tiger 1a

till·er[1] /tílər/ *n.* a horizontal bar fitted to the head of a boat's rudder to turn it in steering. [ME f. AF *telier* weaver's beam f. med.L *telarium* f. L *tela* web]

till·er[2] /tílər/ *n. & v.* ● *n.* **1** a shoot of a plant springing from the bottom of the original stalk. **2** a sapling. **3** a sucker. ● *v.intr.* put forth tillers. [app. repr. OE *telgor* extended f. *telga* bough]

tilt /tilt/ *v. & n.* ● *v.* **1 a** *intr. & tr.* assume or cause to assume a sloping position; heel over. **b** incline or lean or cause to lean toward one side of an opinion, action, controversy, etc. **2** *intr.* (foll. by *at*) strike, thrust, or run at with a weapon, esp. in jousting. **3** *intr.* (foll. by *with*) engage in a contest. **4** *tr.* forge or work (steel, etc.) with a tilt hammer. ● *n.* **1** the act or an instance of tilting. **2** a sloping position. **3** an inclination or bias. **4** (of medieval knights, etc.) the act of charging with a lance against an opponent or at a mark, done for exercise or as a sport. **5** an encounter between opponents; an attack, esp. with argument or satire (*have a tilt at*). **6** = TILT HAMMER. □ **full** (or **at full**) **tilt 1** at full speed. **2** with full force. □□ **tilt·er** *n.* [ME *tilte* perh. f. an OE form rel. to *tealt* unsteady f. Gmc: weapon senses of unkn. orig.]

tilth /tilth/ *n.* **1** tillage; cultivation. **2** the condition of tilled soil (*in good tilth*). [OE *tilth(e)* (as TILL[3])]

tilt ham·mer *n.* a heavy pivoted hammer used in forging.

Tim. *abbr.* Timothy (New Testament).

tim·bal /tímbəl/ *n.* a kettledrum. [F *timbale*, earlier *tamballe* f. Sp. *atabal* f. Arab. *aṭ-ṭabl* the drum]

tim·bale /tímbəl, taNbaál/ *n.* a drum-shaped dish of ground meat or fish baked in a mold or pastry shell. [F: see TIMBAL]

tim·ber /tímbər/ *n.* **1** large standing trees suitable for lumber; woods or forest. **2** (esp. as *int.*) a warning cry that a tree is about to fall. **3** a prepaid piece of wood or beam, esp. as the rib of a vessel. **4** *Brit.* wood prepared for building, carpentry, etc. □□ **tim·ber·ing** *n.* [OE, = building, f. Gmc]

tim·bered /tímbərd/ *adj.* **1** (esp. of a building) made wholly or partly of lumber, esp. with partly exposed beams. **2** (of country) wooded.

tim·ber hitch *n.* a knot used in attaching a rope to a log or spar.

tim·ber·land /tímbərland/ *n.* land covered with forest yielding timber.

tim·ber·line /tímbərlin/ *n.* (on a mountain) the line or level above which no trees grow.

tim·ber wolf *n.* a type of large N. American gray wolf.

tim·bre /támbər, taNbrə/ (also **tim·ber**) *n.* the distinctive character of a musical sound or voice apart from its pitch and intensity. [F f. Rmc f. med.Gk *timbanon* f. Gk *tumpanon* drum]

tim·brel /tímbrəl/ *n. archaic* a tambourine or similar instrument. [dimin. of ME *timbre* f. OF (as TIMBRE, –LE[2])]

Tim·buk·tu /tímbuktoŏ/ *n.* any distant or remote place. [*Timbuktu* in W. Africa]

time /tim/ *n. & v.* ● *n.* **1** the indefinite continued progress of existence, events, etc., in past, present, and future regarded as a whole. **2 a** the progress of this as affecting persons or things (*stood the test of time*). **b** (**Time**) (in full **Father Time**) the personification of time, esp. as an old man with a scythe and hourglass. **3** a more or less definite portion of time belonging to particular events or circumstances (*the time of the Plague; prehistoric times; the scientists of the time*). **4** an allotted, available, or measurable portion of time; the period of time at one's disposal (*am wasting my time; had no time to visit; how much time do you need?*). **5** a point of time, esp. in hours and minutes (*the time is 7:30; what time is it?*). **6** (prec. by *a*) an indefinite period (*waited for a time*). **7** time or an amount of time as reckoned by a conventional standard (*the time allowed is one hour; ran the mile in record time; eight o'clock Eastern Standard time*). **8 a** an occasion (*last time I saw you*). **b** an event or occasion qualified in some way (*had a good time*). **9** a moment or definite portion of time destined or suitable for a purpose, etc. (*now is the time to act; shall we set a time?*). **10** (in *pl.*) expressing multiplication (*is four times as old; five times six is thirty*). **11** a lifetime (*will last my time*). **12** (in *sing.* or *pl.*) **a** the conditions of life of or of a period (*hard times; times have changed*). **b** (prec. by *the*) the present age, or that being considered. **13** *colloq.* a prison sentence (*is doing time*). **14 a** an apprenticeship (*served his time*). **b** a period of military service. **15** a period of gestation. **16** the date or expected date of childbirth (*is near her time*) or of death (*my time is drawing near*). **17** measured time spent in work (*put them on short time*). **18 a** any of several rhythmic patterns of music (*in waltz time*). **b** the duration of a note as indicated by a quarter note, whole note, etc. **19** *Brit.* the moment at which a bar closes. **20** = TIME OUT. ● *v.tr.* **1** choose the time or occasion for (*time your remarks carefully*). **2** do at a chosen or correct time. **3** arrange the time of arrival of. **4** ascertain the time taken by (a process or activity, or a person doing it). **5** regulate the time or duration of; set times for (*trains are timed to arrive every hour*). □ **against time** with utmost speed; so as to finish by a specified time (*working against time*). **ahead of time** earlier than expected. **ahead of one's time** having ideas too enlightened or advanced to be accepted by one's contemporaries. **all the time 1** during the whole of the time referred to (often despite

some contrary expectation, etc.) (*we never noticed, but he was there all the time*). **2** constantly (*nags all the time*). **3** at all times (*leaves a light on all the time*). **at one time 1** in or during a known but unspecified past period. **2** simultaneously (*ran three businesses at one time*). **at the same time 1** simultaneously; at a time that is the same for all. **2** nevertheless (*at the same time, I do not want to offend you*). **at a time** separately in the specified groups or numbers (*came three at a time*). **at times** occasionally; intermittently. **before time** (usu. prec. by *not*) before the due or expected time. **before one's time** prematurely (*old before his time*). **for the time being** for the present; until some other arrangement is made. **half the time** *colloq.* as often as not. **have no time for 1** be unable or unwilling to spend time on. **2** dislike. **have the time 1** be able to spend the time needed. **2** know from a watch, etc., what time it is. **have a time of it** undergo trouble or difficulty. **in no** (or **less than no**) **time 1** very soon. **2** very quickly. **in one's own good time** at a time and a rate decided by oneself. **in time 1** not late; punctual (*was in time to catch the bus*). **2** eventually (*in time you may agree*). **3** in accordance with a given rhythm or tempo, esp. of music. **in one's time** at or during some previous period of one's life (*in his time he was a great hurdler*). **keep good** (or **bad**) **time 1** (of a clock, etc.) record time accurately (or inaccurately). **2** be habitually punctual (or not punctual). **keep time** move or sing, etc., in time. **know the time of day** be well informed. **lose no time** (often foll. by *in* + verbal noun) act immediately (*lost no time in cashing the check*). **not before time** not too soon; timely. **on** (also **in**) **one's own time** outside working hours. **on time** see ON. **no time** *colloq.* a very short interval (*it was no time before they came*). **out of time 1** unseasonable; unseasonably. **2** not in rhythm. **pass the time of day** *colloq.* exchange a greeting or casual remarks. **time after time 1** repeatedly; on many occasions. **2** in many instances. **time and** (or **time and time**) **again** on many occasions. **the time of one's life** a period or occasion of exceptional enjoyment. **the time of day** the hour by the clock. **time-served** having completed a period of apprenticeship or training. **time was** there was a time (*time was when I could do that*). [OE *tīma* f. Gmc]

time and a half *n.* a rate of payment for (usu. overtime) work at one and a half times the normal rate.

time and mo·tion *n.* (usu. *attrib.*) concerned with measuring the efficiency of industrial and other operations.

time bomb *n.* a bomb designed to explode at a preset time.

time cap·sule *n.* a box, etc., containing objects typical of the present time, buried for discovery in the future.

time clock *n.* **1** a clock with a device for recording workers' hours of work. **2** a switch mechanism activated at preset times by a built-in clock.

time-con·sum·ing *adj.* using much or too much time.

time ex·po·sure *n.* the exposure of photographic film for longer than the maximum normal shutter setting.

time fac·tor *n.* the passage of time as a limitation on what can be achieved.

time frame *n.* period of time during which an action occurs or will occur.

time fuse *n.* a fuse calculated to burn for or explode at a given time.

time-hon·ored *adj.* esteemed by tradition or through custom.

time im·me·mo·ri·al *n.* a longer time than anyone can remember or trace.

time·keep·er /tímkeepər/ *n.* **1** a person who records time, esp. of workers or in a game. **2 a** a watch or clock as regards accuracy (*a good timekeeper*). **b** a person as regards punctuality. □□ **time·keep·ing** *n.*

time lag *n.* an interval of time between an event, a cause, etc., and its effect.

time-lapse *adj.* (of photography) using frames taken at long intervals to photograph a slow process, and shown continuously as if at normal speed.

time·less /tímlis/ *adj.* not affected by the passage of time; eternal. □□ **time·less·ly** *adv.* **time·less·ness** *n.*

time lim·it *n.* the limit of time within which a task must be done.

time·ly /tímlee/ *adj.* (**time·li·er**, **time·li·est**) opportune; coming at the right time. □□ **time·li·ness** *n.*

SYNONYM TIP timely

OPPORTUNE, PROPITIOUS, SEASONABLE. Some people seem to have a knack for doing or saying the right thing at the right time. A **timely** act or remark is one that comes at a moment when it is of genuine value or service (*a timely interruption*), while an **opportune** one comes in the nick of time, as if by accident, and exactly meets the needs of the occasion (*the taxi pulled up at an opportune moment, saving her the embarrassment of a prolonged farewell*). **Seasonable** applies to whatever is suited to the season of the year or fits

••

See page xx for the **Key to Pronunciation.**

in perfectly with the needs of the moment or the character of the occasion (*seasonable weather; a seasonable menu for a cold winter day*). **Propitious** means 'presenting favorable conditions.' While a warm day in December might not be *seasonable*, in other words, it might very well be *propitious* for the sailor setting off on a round-the-world cruise.

time off *n.* time for rest or recreation, etc.

time out *n.* **1** a brief intermission in a game, etc. **2** = TIME OFF.

time·piece /tímpees/ *n.* an instrument, such as a clock or watch, for measuring time.

tim·er /tímər/ *n.* **1** a person or device that measures or records time taken. **2** an automatic mechanism for activating a device, etc., at a preset time.

time·serv·er *n.* a person who changes his or her view to suit the prevailing circumstances, fashion, etc. □□ **time·serv·ing** *adj.* self-seeking or obsequious.

time-share *n.* a share in a property under a time-sharing arrangement.

time-shar·ing *n.* **1** the operation of a computer system by several users for different operations at one time. **2** the use of a vacation home at agreed different times by several joint owners.

time sheet *n.* a sheet of paper for recording hours of work, etc. **time signal** an audible (esp. broadcast) signal or announcement of the exact time of day.

time sig·na·ture *n. Mus.* an indication of tempo following a clef, expressed as a fraction with the numerator giving the number of beats in each bar and the denominator giving the kind of note getting one beat.

time switch *n.* a switch acting automatically at a preset time.

time·ta·ble /tímtaybəl/ *n. & v.* ● *n.* a list of times at which events are scheduled to take place, esp. the arrival and departure of buses or trains, etc., or *Brit.* a lesson plan in a school or college. ● *v.tr.* include in or arrange to a timetable; schedule.

time warp *n.* an imaginary distortion of space in relation to time, whereby persons or objects of one age can be moved to another.

time·work /tímwərk/ *n.* work paid for by the time it takes.

time·worn /tímwawrn/ *n.* impaired by age.

time zone *n.* a range of longitudes where a common standard time is used.

tim·id /tímid/ *adj.* (**tim·id·er, tim·id·est**) easily frightened; apprehensive; shy. □□ **ti·mid·i·ty** /–míditee/ *n.* **tim·id·ly** *adv.* **tim·id·ness** *n.* [F *timide* or L *timidus* f. *timēre* fear]

tim·ing /tíming/ *n.* **1** the way an action or process is timed, esp. in relation to others. **2** the regulation of the opening and closing of valves in an internal combustion engine.

ti·moc·ra·cy /tímókrəsee/ *n.* (*pl.* **–cies**) **1** a form of government in which possession of property is required in order to hold office. **2** a form of government in which rulers are motivated by love of honor. □□ **ti·mo·crat·ic** /tíməkrátik/ *adj.* [OF *timocracie* f. med.L *timocratia* f. Gk *timokratia* f. *timē* honor, worth + *kratia* –CRACY]

tim·or·ous /tímərəs/ *adj.* **1** timid; easily alarmed. **2** frightened. □□ **tim·or·ous·ly** *adv.* **tim·or·ous·ness** *n.* [ME f. OF *temoreus* f. med.L *timorosus* f. L *timor* f. *timēre* fear]

tim·o·thy /tíməthee/ *n.* (in full **timothy grass**) a fodder grass, *Phleum pratense.* [*Timothy* Hanson, who introduced it in Carolina *c.*1720]

tim·o·thy² /tíməthee/ *n. Austral. sl.* a brothel. [20th c.: orig. unkn.]

tim·pa·ni /tímpənee/ *n.pl.* (also **tym·pa·ni**) kettledrums. □□ **tim·pa·nist** *n.* [It., pl. of *timpano* = TYMPANUM]

tin /tin/ *n. & v.* ● *n.* **1** *Chem.* a silvery white malleable metallic element resisting corrosion, occurring naturally in cassiterite and other ores, and used esp. in alloys and for plating thin iron or steel sheets to form tin plate. ¶ Symb.: **Sn. 2 a** a vessel or container made of tin or tin-plated iron. **b** esp. *Brit.* an airtight sealed container made of tin plate or aluminum for preserving food. **3** = TINPLATE. **4** *Brit. sl.* money. ● *v.tr.* (**tinned, tin·ning**) **1** esp. *Brit.* seal (food) in an airtight can for preservation. **2** cover or coat with tin. [OE f. Gmc]

tin·a·mou /tínəmoo/ *n.* any South American bird of the family Tinamidae, resembling a grouse but related to the rhea. [F f. Galibi *tinamu*]

tin can *n.* a tin or aluminum container for preserving food, esp. an empty one.

tinc·ture /tíngkchər/ *n. & v.* ● *n.* (often foll. by *of*) **1** a slight flavor or trace. **2** a tinge (of a color). **3** a medicinal solution (of a drug) in alcohol (*tincture of quinine*). **4** *Heraldry* an inclusive term for the metals, colors, and furs used in coats of arms. **5** *Brit. colloq.* an alcoholic drink. ● *v.tr.* **1** color slightly; tinge, flavor. **2** (often foll. by *with*) affect slightly (with a quality). [ME f. L *tinctura* dyeing (as TINGE)]

tinc·to·ri·al /tíngktáwreeəl/ *adj.* **1** of or relating to color or dyeing. **2** producing color. [L *tinctorius* f. *tinctor* dyer: see TINGE]

tin·der /tíndər/ *n.* a dry substance such as wood that readily catches fire from a spark. □□ **tin·der·y** *adj.* [OE *tynder, tyndre* f. Gmc]

tin·der·box /tíndərboks/ *n.* **1** *hist.* a box containing tinder, flint, and steel, formerly used for kindling fires. **2** a potentially explosive or violent person, place, situation, etc.

tine /tin/ *n.* a prong or tooth or point of a fork, comb, antler, etc. □□ **tined** *adj.* (also in *comb.*). [OE *tind*]

tin·e·a /tíneeə/ *n. Med.* ringworm. [L, = moth, worm]

tin foil *n.* foil made of tin, aluminum, or tin alloy, used for wrapping food for cooking or storing.

ting /ting/ *n. & v.* ● *n.* a tinkling sound as of a bell. ● *v.intr. & tr.* emit or cause to emit this sound. [imit.]

tinge /tinj/ *v. & n.* ● *v.tr.* (also **tinge·ing**) (often foll. by *with*; often in *passive*) **1** color slightly (*is tinged with red*). **2** affect slightly (*regret tinged with satisfaction*). ● *n.* **1** a tendency toward or trace of some color. **2** a slight admixture of a feeling or quality. [ME f. L *tingere tinct-* dye, stain]

tin·gle /tínggəl/ *v. & n.* ● *v.* **1** *intr.* **a** feel a slight prickling, stinging, or throbbing sensation. **b** cause this (*the reply tingled in my ears*). **2** *tr.* make (the ear, etc.) tingle. ● *n.* a tingling sensation. [ME, perh. var. of TINKLE]

tin·gly /tínglee/ *adj.* (**tin·gli·er, tin·gli·est**) causing or characterized by tingling.

tin god *n.* **1** an object of unjustified veneration. **2** a self-important person.

tin hat *n. colloq.* a military steel helmet.

tin·horn /tínhawrn/ *n. & adj. sl.* ● *n.* a pretentious but unimpressive person. ● *adj.* cheap; pretentious.

tin·ker /tíngkər/ *n. & v.* ● *n.* **1** an itinerant mender of kettles and pans, etc. **2** *Sc. & Ir.* a gypsy. **3** *Brit. colloq.* a mischievous person or animal. **4** a spell of tinkering. **5** a rough-and-ready worker. ● *v.* **1** *intr.* (foll. by *at, with*) work in an amateurish or desultory way, esp. to adjust or mend machinery, etc. **2 a** *intr.* work as a tinker. **b** *tr.* repair (pots and pans). □□ **tin·ker·er** *n.* [ME: orig. unkn.]

tin·kle /tíngkəl/ *v. & n.* ● *v.* **1** *intr. & tr.* make or cause to make a succession of short light ringing sounds. **2** *intr. colloq.* urinate. ● *n.* **1** a tinkling sound. **2** *Brit. colloq.* a telephone call (*will give you a tinkle on Monday*). **3** *colloq.* an act of urinating. [ME f. obs. *tink* to chink (imit.)]

tin Liz·zie *n. colloq.* an old or decrepit car.

tin·ner /tínər/ *n.* **1** a tin miner. **2** a tinsmith.

tin·ni·tus /tínítəs, tíni–/ *n. Med.* a ringing in the ears. [L f. *tinnire tinnit–* ring, tinkle, of imit. orig.]

tin·ny /tínee/ *adj. & n.* ● *adj.* (**tin·ni·er, tin·ni·est**) **1** of or like tin. **2** (of a metal object) flimsy; insubstantial; of poor quality. **3 a** sounding like struck tin. **b** (of reproduced sound) thin and metallic, lacking low frequencies. **4** *Austral. sl.* lucky. ● *n.* (also **tin·nie**) (*pl.* **–nies**) *Austral. sl.* a can of beer. □□ **tin·ni·ly** *adv.* **tin·ni·ness** *n.*

Tin Pan Al·ley *n.* the world of composers and publishers of popular music.

tinplate *n.* (also **tin plate**) sheet iron or steel coated with tin. □□ **tin·plate** *v.tr.*

tin·pot /tínpot/ *adj.* cheap; inferior.

tin·sel /tínsəl/ *n. & v.* ● *n.* **1** glittering metallic strips, threads, etc., used as decoration to give a sparkling effect. **2** a fabric adorned with tinsel. **3** superficial brilliance or splendor. **4** (*attrib.*) showy; gaudy; flashy. ● *v.tr.* (**tin·seled, tin·sel·ing** or **tin·selled, tin·sel·ling**) adorn with or as with tinsel. □□ **tin·seled** *adj.* **tin·sel·ly** *adj.* [OF *estincele* spark f. L *scintilla*]

tin·smith /tínsmith/ *n.* a worker in tin and tin plate.

tin·snips /tínsnips/ *n.* a pair of clippers for cutting sheet metal.

tin sol·dier *n.* a toy soldier made of metal.

tin·stone /tínstōn/ *n. Geol.* = CASSITERITE.

tint /tint/ *n. & v.* ● *n.* **1** a variety of a color, esp. one made lighter by adding white. **2** a tendency toward or admixture of a different color (*red with a blue tint*). **3** a faint color spread over a surface, esp. as a background for printing on. **4** a set of parallel engraved lines to give uniform shading. **5** a dye for the hair. ● *v.tr.* apply a tint to; color. □□ **tint·er** *n.* [alt. of earlier *tinct* f. L *tinctus* dyeing (as TINGE), perh. infl. by It. *tinto*]

tin·tin·nab·u·la·tion /tíntinábyəláyshən/ *n.* a ringing or tinkling of bells. [as L *tintinnabulum* tinkling bell f. *tintinnare* redupl. form of *tinnire* ring]

tin·ware /tínwair/ *n.* articles made of tin or tin plate.

tin whis·tle *n.* = PENNY WHISTLE.

ti·ny /tínee/ *adj.* (**ti·ni·er, ti·ni·est**) very small or slight. □□ **ti·ni·ly** *adv.* **ti·ni·ness** *n.* [obs. *tine, tyne* (adj. & n.) small, a little: ME, of unkn. orig.]

-tion /shən/ *suffix* forming nouns of action, condition, etc. (see —ION, –ATION, –ITION, –UTION). [from or after F *–tion* or L *–tio –tionis*]

tip¹ /tip/ *n. & v.* ● *n.* **1** an extremity or end, esp. of a small or tapering thing (*tips of the fingers*). **2** a small piece or part attached to the end of a thing, e.g., a ferrule on a stick. **3** a leaf bud of tea. ● *v.tr.* (**tipped, tip·ping**) **1** provide with a tip. **2** (foll. by *in*) attach (a loose sheet) to a page at the inside edge. □ **on the tip of one's tongue** about to be said, esp. after difficulty in recalling to mind. **the tip of the iceberg** a small evident part of something much larger and more significant. □□ **tip·less** *adj.* **tip·py** *adj.* (in sense 3). [ME f. ON *typpi* (n.), *typpa* (v.), *typptr* tipped f. Gmc (rel. to TOP[1]): prob. reinforced by MDu. & MLG *tip*]

tip[2] /tip/ v. & n. ● v. (**tipped, tip·ping**) **1 a** *intr.* lean or slant. **b** *tr.* cause to do this. **2** *tr.* (foll. by *into*, etc.) **a** overturn or cause to over-balance (*was tipped into the pond*). **b** discharge the contents of (a container, etc.) in this way. ● n. **1 a** a slight push or tilt. **b** a glancing stroke, esp. in baseball. **2** *Brit.* a place where material (esp. trash) is dumped. □ **tip the balance** make the critical difference. **tip the scales** see SCALE[2]. [17th c.: orig. uncert.]

tip[3] /tip/ v. & n. ● v. (**tipped, tip·ping**) **1** *tr.* make a small present of money to, esp. for a service given (*have you tipped the waiter?*). **2** *tr.* name as the likely winner of a race or contest, etc. **3** *tr.* strike or touch lightly. **4** *tr. sl.* give; hand; pass (esp. in tip the wink below). ● n. **1** a small gift of money, esp. for a service given. **2** a piece of private or special information, esp. regarding betting or investment. **3** a small or casual piece of advice. □ **tip off** **1** give (a person) a hint or piece of special information or warning, discreetly or confidentially. **2** *Basketball* start play by throwing the ball up between two opponents. **tip a person the wink** *Brit.* give a person private information. □□ **tip·per** n. [ME: orig. uncert.]

tip·cat /típkat/ n. **1** a game with a short piece of wood tapering at the ends and struck with a stick. **2** this piece of wood.

tip·per /típər/ n. a person or thing that tips.

tip·pet /típit/ n. **1** a covering of fur, etc., for the shoulders formerly worn by women. **2** a similar garment worn as part of some official costumes, esp. by the clergy. **3** *hist.* a long narrow strip of cloth as part of or an attachment to a hood, etc. [ME, prob. f. TIP[1]]

tip·ple /típəl/ v. & n. ● v. **1** *intr.* drink intoxicating liquor habitually. **2** *tr.* drink (liquor) repeatedly in small amounts. ● n. *colloq.* a drink, esp. a strong one. □□ **tip·pler** n. [ME, back-form. f. *tippler*, of unkn. orig.]

tip-off n. (also **tip·off**) **1** a hint or warning, etc., given discreetly or confidentially. **2** *Basketball* the act of starting play with a tip off.

tip·staff /típstaf/ n. **1** a sheriff's officer. **2** a metal-tipped staff carried as a symbol of office. [contr. of *tipped staff*, i.e., tipped with metal]

tip·ster /típstər/ n. a person who gives tips, esp. about betting at horse races.

tip·sy /típsee/ adj. (**tip·si·er, tip·si·est**) **1** slightly intoxicated. **2** caused by or showing intoxication (*a tipsy leer*). □□ **tip·si·ly** adv. **tip·si·ness** n. [prob. f. TIP[2] = inclined to lean, unsteady: for *–sy* cf. FLIMSY, TRICKSY]

tip·sy cake n. *Brit.* a sponge cake soaked in wine or liquor and served with custard.

tip·toe /típtō/ n., v., & adv. ● n. the tips of the toes. ● v.intr. (**tip·toes, tip·toed, tip·toe·ing**) walk on tiptoe, or very stealthily. ● adv. (also **on tip·toe**) with the heels off the ground and the weight on the balls of the feet.

tip-top /típtóp/ adj., adv., & n. *colloq.* ● adj. & adv. highest in excellence; very best. ● n. the highest point of excellence.

ti·rade /tírayd, tiráyd/ n. a long vehement denunciation or declamation. [F, = long speech, f. It. *tirata* volley f. *tirare* pull f. Rmc]

ti·rail·leur /téeraayór, tírə lór/ n. **1** a sharpshooter. **2** a skirmisher. [F f. *tirailler* shoot independently f. *tirer* shoot, draw, f. Rmc]

tire[1] /tīr/ v. **1** *tr. & intr.* make or grow weary. **2** *tr.* exhaust the patience or interest of; bore. **3** *tr.* (in *passive*; foll. by *of*) have had enough of; be fed up with (*was tired of arguing*). [OE *tēorian*, of unkn. orig.]

tire[2] /tīr/ n. **1** a rubber covering, usu. inflatable, that fits around a wheel rim. **2** a band of metal placed around the rim of a wheel to strengthen it. [ME, perh. = archaic *tire* headdress]

tired /tīrd/ adj. **1** weary; exhausted; ready for sleep. **2** (of an idea, etc.) hackneyed. □□ **tired·ly** adv. **tired·ness** n.

SYNONYM TIP tired

EXHAUSTED, FATIGUED, TUCKERED, WEARY. **Tired** is what you are after you've cleaned the house, spent two hours reading a dull report, or trained for a marathon; it means that you are drained of your strength and energy, without any indication of degree. **Weary**, on the other hand, is how you feel after you've had to interrupt your dinner five or six times to answer the phone. It implies not only a depletion of energy but also the vexation that accompanies having to put up with something that is, or has become, disagreeable. **Exhausted** means that you are totally drained of strength and energy, a condition that may even be irreversible (*exhausted by battling a terminal disease*). **Fatigued** is a more precise word than either *tired* or *weary*; it implies a loss of energy through strain, illness, or overwork to the point where rest or sleep is essential (*fatigued after working a 24-hour shift*). **Tuckered** comes close in meaning to *fatigued* or *exhausted*, but often carries the suggestion of loss of breath (*tuckered out after running up six flights of stairs*).

tire·less /tírlis/ adj. having inexhaustible energy. □□ **tire·less·ly** adv. **tire·less·ness** n.

tire·some /tírsəm/ adj. **1** wearisome; tedious. **2** *Brit. colloq.* annoying (*how tiresome of you!*). □□ **tire·some·ly** adv. **tire·some·ness** n.

ti·ro *Brit.* var. of TYRO.

'tis /tiz/ *archaic* it is. [contr.]

ti·sane /tizán, –zaán/ n. an infusion of dried herbs, etc. [F: see PTISAN]

tis·sue /tíshoō/ n. **1** any of the coherent collections of specialized cells of which animals or plants are made (*muscular tissue; nervous tissue*). **2** = TISSUE PAPER. **3** a disposable piece of thin soft absorbent paper for wiping, drying, etc. **4** fine woven esp. gauzy fabric. **5** (foll. by *of*) a connected series; a web (*a tissue of lies*). [ME f. OF *tissu* rich material, past part. of *tistre* f. L *texere* weave]

tis·sue pa·per n. thin soft paper for wrapping or protecting fragile or delicate articles.

Tit. abbr. Titus (New Testament).

tit[1] /tit/ n. any of various small birds, esp. of the family Paridae. [prob. f. Scand.]

tit[2] /tit/ n. □ **tit for tat** /tat/ blow for blow; retaliation. [= earlier *tip for tap* (see TIP[2])]

tit[3] /tit/ n. **1** *colloq.* a nipple. **2** *coarse sl.* a woman's breast. □ **get on a person's tits** *Brit. coarse sl.* annoy; irritate. [OE: cf. MLG *titte*]

tit[4] /tit/ n. *Brit. coarse sl.* a term of contempt for a person. [20th c.: perh. f. TIT[3]]

Ti·tan /tít'n/ n. **1** (often **titan**) a person of very great strength, intellect, or importance. **2** (in Greek mythology) a member of a family of early gigantic gods, the offspring of Heaven and Earth. [ME f. L f. Gk]

ti·tan·ic[1] /titánik/ adj. **1** of or like the Titans. **2** gigantic; colossal. □□ **ti·tan·i·cal·ly** adv. [Gk *titanikos* (as TITAN)]

ti·tan·ic[2] /titánik, tee–/ adj. *Chem.* of titanium, esp. in quadrivalent form. □□ **ti·tan·ate** /tít'nayt, tít–/ n.

ti·ta·ni·um /titáyneeəm, tee–/ n. *Chem.* a gray metallic element occurring naturally in many clays, etc., and used to make strong light alloys that are resistant to corrosion. ¶ Symb.: **Ti**. [Gk (as TITAN) + –IUM, after *uranium*]

ti·ta·ni·um di·ox·ide n. (also **ti·ta·ni·um ox·ide**) a white oxide occurring naturally and used as a white pigment.

titch /tich/ n. (also **tich**) *Brit. colloq.* a small person. [*Tich*, stage name of Harry Relph (d. 1928), Engl. music hall comedian]

titch·y /tíchee/ adj. (**titch·i·er, titch·i·est**) *Brit. colloq.* very small.

ti·ter /títər/ n. *Chem.* the strength of a solution or the quantity of a constituent as determined by titration. [F, = TITLE]

tit·fer /títfər/ n. *Brit. sl.* a hat. [abbr. of *tit for tat*, rhyming sl.]

tithe /tīth/ n. & v. ● n. **1** one tenth of the annual product of land or labor, formerly taken as a tax for the support of the church and clergy. **2** a tenth part. ● v. **1** *tr.* subject to tithes. **2** *intr.* pay tithes. □□ **tith·a·ble** adj. [OE *teogotha* tenth]

tithe barn n. a barn built to hold tithes paid in kind.

tith·ing /títhing/ n. **1** the practice of taking or paying a tithe. **2** *Brit. hist.* a ten householders living near each other and collectively responsible for each other's behavior. **b** the area occupied by them. [OE *tīgething* (as TITHE, –ING[1])]

ti·ti /téetee/ n. (pl. **ti·tis**) any South American monkey of the genus *Callicebus*. [Tupi]

Ti·tian /tíshən/ adj. (in full **Titian red**) (of hair) reddish brown. [name of *Tiziano* Vecelli, It. painter d. 1576]

tit·il·late /tít'layt/ v.tr. **1** excite pleasantly. **2** tickle. □□ **tit·il·lat·ing·ly** adv. **tit·il·la·tion** /–láyshən/ n. [L *titillare titillat*–]

tit·i·vate /títivayt/ v.tr. (also **tit·ti·vate**) *colloq.* **1** adorn; smarten; spruce up. **2** (often *refl.*) put the finishing touches to. □□ **ti·ti·va·tion** /–váyshən/ n. [earlier *tidivate*, perh. f. TIDY after *cultivate*]

tit·lark /títlaark/ n. a pipit; the meadow pipit.

ti·tle /tít'l/ n. & v. ● n. **1** the name of a book, work of art, piece of music, etc. **2** the heading of a chapter, poem, document, etc. **3 a** the contents of the title page of a book. **b** a book regarded in terms of its title (*published 20 new titles*). **4** a caption or credit in a movie, broadcast, etc. **5** a form of nomenclature indicating a person's status (e.g., *professor, queen*) or used as a form of address or reference (e.g., *Lord, Mr.*). **6** a sports championship. **7** *Law* **a** the right to ownership of property with or without possession. **b** the facts constituting this. **c** (foll. by *to*) a just or recognized claim. **8** *Eccl.* **a** a fixed sphere of work and source of income as a condition for ordination. **b** a parish church in Rome under a cardinal. ● v.tr. **1** give a title to. **2** call by a title; term. [ME f. OF f. L *titulus* placard, title]

ti·tled /tít'ld/ adj. having a title of nobility or rank.

ti·tle deed n. a legal instrument as evidence of a right, esp. to property.

tit·ling[1] /títling/ n. the impressing of a title in gold leaf, etc., on the cover of a book.

ti·tling[2] /títling/ n. **1** a titlark. **2** a titmouse.

tit·mouse /títmows/ n. (pl. **tit·mice** /–mīs/) any of various small tits, esp. of the genus *Parus*. [ME *titmōse* f. TIT[1] + OE *māse* titmouse, assim. to MOUSE]

ti·tle page *n.* a page at the beginning of a book giving the title and particulars of authorship, etc.

ti·trate /títrayt/ *v.tr. Chem.* ascertain the amount of a constituent in (a solution) by measuring the volume of a known concentration of reagent required to complete the reaction. □□ **ti·trat·a·ble** *adj.* **ti·tra·tion** /–tráyshən/ *n.*

ti·tre *Brit.* var. of TITER.

ti·tle role *n.* the part in a play, etc., that gives it its name (e.g., Othello).

tit·ter /títər/ *v. & n.* ● *v.intr.* laugh in a furtive or restrained way; giggle. ● *n.* a furtive or restrained laugh. □□ **tit·ter·er** *n.* **tit·ter·ing·ly** *adv.* [imit.]

tit·ti·vate var. of TITIVATE.

tit·tle /tít'l/ *n.* **1** a small written or printed stroke or dot. **2** a particle; a whit (esp. in *not one jot or tittle*). [ME f. L (as TITLE)]

tit·tle·bat /tít'lbat/ *n. Brit.* a stickleback. [fanciful var.]

tit·tle-tat·tle /tít'ltat'l/ *n. & v.* ● *n.* petty gossip. ● *v.intr.* gossip; chatter. [redupl. of TATTLE]

tit·tup /títəp/ *v. & n.* ● *v.intr.* (**tit·tupped, tit·tup·ping** or **tit·tuped, tit·tup·ing**) go about friskily or jerkily; bob up and down; canter. ● *n.* such a gait or movement. [perh. imit. of hoofbeats]

tit·ty /títee/ *n.* (*pl.* **–ties**) *sl.* = TIT³.

tit·u·ba·tion /tichoobáyshən/ *n. Med.* unsteadiness, esp. as caused by nervous disorder. [L *titubatio* f. *titubare* totter]

tit·u·lar /tíchələr/ *adj. & n.* ● *adj.* **1** of or relating to a title (*the book's titular hero*). **2** existing, or being what is specified, in name or title only (*titular ruler; titular sovereignty*). ● *n.* **1** the holder of an office, etc., esp. a benefice, without the corresponding functions or obligations. **2** a titular saint. □□ **tit·u·lar·ly** *adv.* [F *titulaire* or mod.L *titularis* f. *titulus* TITLE]

tit·u·lar bish·op *n.* a bishop with a no longer existent see.

tit·u·lar saint *n.* the patron saint of a particular church.

tiz·zy /tízee/ *n.* (*pl.* **–zies**) (also **tizz, tiz**) *colloq.* a state of nervous agitation (*in a tizzy*). [20th c.: orig. unkn.]

TKO *abbr. Boxing* technical knockout.

Tl *symb. Chem.* the element thallium.

TLC *abbr. colloq.* tender loving care.

Tlin·git /tlíngkət, –gət, klíng–/ *n. & adj.* ● *n.* **1 a** a N. American people native to southern Alaska. **b** a member of this people. **2** the language of this people. ● *adj.* of or relating to this people or their language.

TM *abbr.* Transcendental Meditation.

Tm *symb. Chem.* the element thulium.

tme·sis /tméesis/ *n.* (*pl.* **tme·ses** /–seez/) *Gram.* the separation of parts of a compound word by an intervening word or words (esp. in colloq. speech, e.g., *can't find it any-damnedwhere*). [Gk *tmēsis* cutting f. *temnō* cut]

TN *abbr.* Tennessee (in official postal use).

tn *abbr.* **1** ton(s). **2** town.

tnpk. *abbr.* turnpike.

TNT *abbr.* trinitrotoluene, a high explosive formed from toluene by substitution of three hydrogen atoms with nitro groups.

to /tōō; tə (when unstressed)/ *prep. & adv.* ● *prep.* **1** introducing a noun: **a** expressing what is reached, approached, or touched (*fell to the ground; went to Paris; put her face to the window; five minutes to six*). **b** expressing what is aimed at: often introducing the indirect object of a verb (*throw it to me; explained the problem to them*). **c** as far as; up to (*went on to the end; have to stay from Tuesday to Friday*). **d** to the extent of (*were all drunk to a man; was starved to death*). **e** expressing what is followed (*according to instructions; made to order*). **f** expressing what is considered or affected (*am used to that; that is nothing to me*). **g** expressing what is caused or produced (*turn to stone; tear to shreds*). **h** expressing what is compared (*nothing to what it once was; comparable to any other; equal to the occasion; won by three to two*). **i** expressing what is increased (*add it to mine*). **j** expressing what is involved or composed as specified (*there is nothing to it; more to him than meets the eye*). **k** archaic for; by way of (*took her to wife*). **2** introducing the infinitive: **a** as a verbal noun (*to get there is the priority*). **b** expressing purpose, consequence, or cause (*we eat to live; left him to starve; am sorry to hear that*). **c** as a substitute for *to* + infinitive (*wanted to come but was unable to*). ● *adv.* **1** in the normal or required position or condition (*come to; heave to*). **2** (of a door) in a nearly closed position. □ **to and fro 1** backward and forward. **2** repeatedly between the same points. [OE *tō* (adv. & prep.) f. WG]

toad /tōd/ *n.* **1** any froglike amphibian of the family Bufonidae, esp. of the genus *Bufo*, breeding in water but living chiefly on land. **2** any of various similar amphibians including the Surinam toad. **3** a repulsive or detestable person. □□ **toad·ish** *adj.* [OE *tādige*, *tādde*, *tāda*, of unkn. orig.]

toad·fish /tódfish/ *n.* any marine fish of the family Batrachoididae, with a large head and wide mouth, making grunting noises by vibrating the walls of its swim bladder.

toad·flax /tódflaks/ *n.* **1** any plant of the genus *Linaria* or

Chaenorrhinum, with flaxlike leaves and spurred yellow or purple flowers. **2** a related plant, *Cymbalaria muralis*, with lilac flowers and ivy-shaped leaves.

toad-in-the-hole *n. Brit.* sausages or other meat baked in batter.

toad·stone /tódstōn/ *n.* a stone, sometimes precious, supposed to resemble or to have been formed in the body of a toad, formerly used as an amulet, etc.

toad·stool /tódstōōl/ *n.* the spore-bearing structure of various fungi, usu. poisonous, with a round top and slender stalk.

toad·y /tódee/ *n. & v.* ● *n.* (*pl.* **–ies**) a sycophant; an obsequious hanger-on. ● *v.tr. &* (foll. by *to*) intr. (**–ies, –ied**) behave servilely to; fawn upon. □□ **toad·y·ish** *adj.* **toad·y·ism** *n.* [contr. of *toadeater*, a charlatan's attendant who ate toads (regarded as poisonous)]

toast /tōst/ *n. & v.* ● *n.* **1** bread in slices browned on both sides by radiant heat. **2 a** a person (orig. esp. a woman) or thing in whose honor a company is requested to drink. **b** a call to drink or an instance of drinking in this way. ● *v.* **1** *tr.* cook or brown (bread, etc.) by radiant heat. **2** *intr.* (of bread, etc.) become brown in this way. **3** *tr.* warm (one's feet, oneself, etc.) at a fire, etc. **4** *tr.* drink to the health or in honor of (a person or thing). □ **have a person on toast** *Brit. colloq.* be in a position to deal with a person as one wishes.

> **WORD HISTORY**   **toast**
>
> Late Middle English (as a verb in the sense 'burn as the sun does, parch'): from Old French *toster* 'roast,' from Latin *torrere* 'parch.' Sense 2 derives from the practice of placing a small piece of toasted bread flavored with spices into a drink such as wine, later associated with the practice of toasting a woman in whose honor a company was requested to drink.

toast·er /tóstər/ *n.* an electrical device for making toast.

toast·mas·ter /tóstmastər/ *n.* (*fem.* **toast·mis·tress** /–mistris/) an official responsible for announcing toasts at a public occasion.

to·bac·co /təbákō/ *n.* (*pl.* **–cos**) **1** any plant of the genus *Nicotiana*, of American origin, with narcotic leaves used for smoking, chewing, or snuff. **2** its leaves, esp. as prepared for smoking. [Sp. *tabaco*, perh. f. an Amer. Indian lang.]

to·bac·co mo·sa·ic vi·rus *n.* a virus that causes mosaic disease in tobacco, much used in biochemical research.

to·bac·co·nist /təbákənist/ *n.* a retail dealer in tobacco and cigarettes, etc.

to·bog·gan /təbógən/ *n. & v.* ● *n.* a long light narrow sled curled up at the front for sliding downhill, esp. over compacted snow or ice. ● *v.intr.* ride on a toboggan. □□ **to·bog·gan·er** *n.* **to·bog·gan·ing** *n.* **to·bog·gan·ist** *n.* [Can. F *tabaganne* f. Algonquian]

to·by jug /tóbee/ *n.* (also **to·by, To·by**) a pitcher or mug for ale, etc., usu. in the form of a stout old man wearing a three-cornered hat. [familiar form of the name *Tobias*]

toc·ca·ta /təkaátə/ *n.* a musical composition for a keyboard instrument designed to exhibit the performer's touch and technique. [It., fem. past part. of *toccare* touch]

To·char·i·an /təkáireeən/ *n. & adj.* ● *n.* **1** an extinct Indo-european language of a central Asian people in the first millennium AD. **2** a member of the people speaking this language. ● *adj.* of or in this language. [F *tocharien* f. L *Tochari* f. Gk *Tokharoi* a Scythian tribe]

to·coph·er·ol /tōkófərawl, –rol/ *n.* any of several closely related vitamins, found in wheat germ oil, egg yolk, and leafy vegetables, and important in the stabilization of cell membranes, etc. Also called **vitamin E**. [Gk *tokos* offspring + *pherō* bear + –OL¹]

toc·sin /tóksin/ *n.* an alarm bell or signal. [F f. OF *touquesain, toquassen* f. Prov. *tocasenh* f. *tocar* TOUCH + *senh* signal bell]

to·day /tədáy/ *n. & adv.* ● *adv.* **1** on or in the course of this present day (*shall we go today?*). **2** nowadays; in modern times. ● *n.* **1** this present day (*today is my birthday*). **2** modern times. □ **today week** (or **fortnight, etc.**) *Brit.* a week (or fortnight, etc.) from today. [OE *tō dæg* on (this) day (as TO, DAY)]

tod·dle /tód'l/ *v. & n.* ● *v.intr.* **1** walk with short unsteady steps like those of a small child. **2** *colloq.* **a** (often foll. by *around, to,* etc.) take a casual or leisurely walk. **b** (usu. foll. by *off*) depart. ● *n.* **1** a toddling walk. **2** *colloq.* a stroll or short walk. [16th-c. *todle* (Sc. & No. of Engl.), of unkn. orig.]

tod·dler /tódlər/ *n.* a child who is just beginning to walk. □□ **tod·dler·hood** *n.*

tod·dy /tódee/ *n.* (*pl.* **–dies**) **1** a drink of liquor with hot water and sugar or spices. **2** the sap of some kinds of palm, fermented to produce arrack. [Hind. *tāṛī* f. *tāṛ* palm f. Skr. *tāla* palmyra]

to-do /tədōō/ *n.* a commotion or fuss. [*to do* as in *what's to do* (= to be done)]

to·dy /tódee/ *n.* (*pl.* **–dies**) any small insectivorous West Indian bird of the genus *Todus*, related to the kingfisher. [F *todier* f. L *todus*, a small bird]

toe /tō/ *n. & v.* ● *n.* **1** any of the five terminal projections of the foot. **2** the corresponding part of an animal. **3** the part of an item of footwear that covers the toes. **4** the lower end or tip of an implement, etc. **5** *Archit.* a projection from the foot of a buttress, etc., to give stability. **6** *Austral. & NZ sl.* speed; energy. ● *v.* (**toes, toed, toe·ing**)

1 *tr.* touch (a starting line, etc.) with the toes before starting a race. **2** *tr.* **a** mend the toe of (a sock, etc.). **b** provide with a toe. **3** *intr.* (foll. by *in*, *out*) **a** walk with the toes pointed in (or out). **b** (of a pair of wheels) converge (or diverge) slightly at the front. **4** *tr.* Golf strike (the ball) with a part of the club too near the toe. □ **on one's toes** alert; eager. **toe the line** conform to a general policy or principle, esp. unwillingly or under pressure. **turn up one's toes** colloq. die. □□ **toed** adj. (also in *comb.*). **toe·less** adj. [OE *tā* f. Gmc]

toe·cap /tṓkap/ n. the (usu. strengthened) outer covering of the toe of a boot or shoe.

toe clip n. a clip on a bicycle pedal to prevent the foot from slipping.

toe·nail /tṓnayl/ n. **1** the nail at the tip of each toe. **2** a nail driven obliquely through the end of a board, etc.

toe·rag /tṓrag/ n. Brit. sl. a term of contempt for a person. [earlier = tramp, vagrant, f. the rag wrapped round the foot in place of a sock]

toe·y /tṓee/ adj. Austral. sl. restless; nervous; touchy.

toff /tof/ n. & v. Brit. sl. • n. a distinguished or well-dressed person; a dandy. • v.tr. (foll. by *up*) dress up smartly. [perh. a perversion of *tuft* = titled undergraduate (from the gold tassel formerly worn on the cap)]

tof·fee /táwfee, tóf–/ n. (also **tof·fy**) (pl. **tof·fees** or **tof·fies**) **1** a kind of firm or hard candy softening when sucked or chewed, made by boiling sugar, butter, etc. **2** a small piece of this. □ **for toffee** Brit. sl. (prec. by *can't*, etc.) (denoting incompetence) at all (*they couldn't sing for toffee*). [earlier TAFFY]

tof·fee-nosed adj. esp. Brit. sl. snobbish; pretentious.

toft /toft/ n. Brit. **1** a homestead. **2** land once occupied by this. [OE f. ON *topt*]

to·fu /tṓfōō/ n. a curd made from mashed soybeans. [Jap. *tōfu* f. Chin., = curdled beans]

tog¹ /tog/ n. & v. colloq. • n. (usu. in pl.) **1** an item of clothing. **2** Austral. & NZ colloq. a bathing suit. • v.tr. & intr. (**togged**, **tog·ging**) (foll. by *out*, *up*) dress, esp. elaborately. [app. abbr. of 16th-c. cant *togeman* (s), *togman*, f. F *toge* or L *toga*: see TOGA]

to·ga /tṓgə/ n. hist. an ancient Roman citizen's loose flowing outer garment. □□ **to·gaed** adj. [L, rel. to *tegere* cover]

to·geth·er /təgéthər/ adv. & adj. • adv. **1** in company or conjunction (*walking together; built it together; were at school together*). **2** simultaneously; at the same time (*both shouted together*). **3** one with another (*were talking together*). **4** into conjunction; so as to unite (*tied them together; put two and two together*). **5** into union or companionship (*came together in friendship*). **6** uninterruptedly (*could talk for hours together*). • adj. colloq. well organized or controlled. □ **together with** as well as; and also. [OE *tōgedere* f. TO + *gædre* together: cf. GATHER]

to·geth·er·ness /təgéthərnis/ n. **1** the condition of being together. **2** a feeling of comfort from being together.

tog·ger·y /tógəree/ n. colloq. clothes; togs.

tog·gle /tógəl/ n. & v. • n. **1** a device for fastening (esp. a garment), consisting of a crosspiece which can pass through a hole or loop in one position but not in another. **2** a pin or other crosspiece put through the eye of a rope, a link of a chain, etc., to keep it in place. **3** a pivoted barb on a harpoon. **4** Computing a switch action that is operated the same way but with opposite effect on successive occasions. • v.tr. provide or fasten with a toggle. [18th-c. Naut.: orig. unkn.]

tog·gle switch n. an electric switch with a projecting lever to be moved usu. up and down.

To·go·lese /tṓgəleéz/ adj. & n. • adj. of or relating to Togo in W. Africa. • n. (pl. same) **1** a native or inhabitant of Togo. **2** a person of Togolese descent.

toil /toyl/ v. & n. • v.intr. **1** work laboriously or incessantly. **2** make slow painful progress (*toiled along the path*). • n. prolonged or intensive labor; drudgery. □□ **toil·er** n.

toile /twaal/ n. **1** a type of sheer fabric. **2** a garment reproduced in muslin or other cheap material for fitting or for making copies. [F *toile* cloth f. L *tela* web]

toi·let /tóylit/ n. **1 a** a fixture, as in a bathroom, etc., for defecating and urinating. **b** a bathroom or lavatory. **2** the process of washing

oneself, dressing, etc. (*make one's toilet*). **3** the cleansing of part of the body after an operation or at the time of childbirth.

WORD HISTORY toilet

Mid-16th century: from French *toilette* 'cloth, wrapper,' diminutive of *toile*. The word originally denoted a cloth used as a wrapper for clothes, or occasionally a cloth placed around the shoulders during hairdressing; hence, the articles needed for washing and dressing or the process involved (sense 2). In the US the word came to denote a dressing-room, especially one with washing facilities, hence, a bathroom (early 20th century).

toi·let pa·per n. (also **toi·let tis·sue**) paper for cleaning oneself after excreting.

toi·let roll n. a roll of toilet paper.

toi·let·ry /tóylitree/ n. (pl. **–ries**) (usu. in pl.) any of various articles or cosmetics used in washing, dressing, etc.

toi·let set n. a set of hairbrushes, combs, etc.

toi·let soap n. mild soap for washing oneself.

toi·let ta·ble n. a dressing table usu. with a mirror.

toi·lette /twaalét/ n. = TOILET 2. [F: see TOILET]

toi·let train·ing n. the training of a young child to use a toilet. □□ **toi·let train** v.tr.

toi·let wa·ter n. a diluted form of perfume used esp. after washing.

toils /toylz/ n.pl. a net or snare. [pl. of *toil* f. OF *toile* cloth f. L *tela* web]

toil·some /tóylsəm/ adj. involving toil; laborious. □□ **toil·some·ly** adv. **toil·some·ness** n.

to-ing and fro-ing /tṓing ənd frṓing/ n. constant movement to and fro; bustle; dispersed activity. [TO adv. + FRO + –ING¹]

To·kay /tōkáy/ n. **1** a sweet aromatic wine made near Tokaj in Hungary. **2** a similar wine produced elsewhere.

to·ken /tṓkən/ n. **1** a thing serving as a symbol, reminder, or distinctive mark of something (*as a token of affection; in token of my esteem*). **2** a thing serving as evidence of authenticity or as a guarantee. **3** a voucher exchangeable for goods (often of a specified kind), given as a gift. **4** anything used to represent something else, esp. a metal disk, etc., used instead of money in coin-operated machines, as subway fare, etc. **5** (*attrib.*) **a** nominal or perfunctory (*token effort*). **b** conducted briefly to demonstrate strength of feeling (*token resistance; token strike*). **c** serving to acknowledge a principle only (*token payment*). **d** chosen by way of tokenism to represent a particular group (*the token woman on the committee*). □ **by the same** (or **this**) **token** **1** similarly. **2** moreover. [OE *tāc(e)n* f. Gmc, rel. to TEACH]

to·ken·ism /tṓkənizəm/ n. **1** esp. Polit. the principle or practice of granting minimum concessions, esp. to appease radical demands, etc. (cf. TOKEN 5d). **2** making only a token effort.

to·ken mon·ey n. coins having a higher face value than their worth as metal.

to·ken vote n. (in the UK) a parliamentary vote of money, the stipulated amount of which is not meant to be binding.

tol·booth var. of TOLLBOOTH 2, 3.

told past and past part. of TELL¹.

To·le·do /təleédó/ n. (pl. **–dos**) a fine sword or sword blade made in Toledo in Spain.

tol·er·a·ble /tólərəbəl/ adj. **1** able to be endured. **2** fairly good; mediocre. □□ **tol·er·a·bil·i·ty** /–bílitee/ n. **tol·er·a·ble·ness** n. **tol·er·a·bly** adv. [ME f. OF f. L *tolerabilis* (as TOLERATE)]

tol·er·ance /tólərəns/ n **1** a willingness or ability to tolerate; forbearance. **2** the capacity to tolerate. **3** an allowable variation in any measurable property. **4** the ability to tolerate the effects of a drug, etc., after continued use. [ME f. OF f. L *tolerantia* (as TOLERATE)]

tol·er·ant /tólərənt/ adj. **1** disposed or accustomed to tolerate others or their acts or opinions. **2** (foll. by *of*) enduring or patient. **3** exhibiting tolerance of a drug, etc. □□ **tol·er·ant·ly** adv. [F *tolérant* f. L *tolerare* (as TOLERATE)]

tol·er·ate /tólərayt/ v.tr. **1** allow the existence or occurrence of without authoritative interference. **2** leave unmolested. **3** endure or permit, esp. with forbearance. **4** sustain or endure (suffering, etc.). **5** be capable of continued subjection to (a drug, radiation, etc.) without harm. **6** find or treat as endurable. □□ **tol·er·a·tor** n. [L *tolerare tolerat-* endure]

tol·er·a·tion /tóləráyshən/ n. the process or practice of tolerating, esp. the allowing of differences in religious opinion without discrimination. [F *tolération* f. L *toleratio* (as TOLERATE)]

WORD HISTORY toil

Middle English (in the senses 'strife' and 'contend verbally'): from Old French *tooillier* (verb), *tooil* (noun) 'confusion,' from Latin *tudiculare* 'stir about,' from *tudicula* 'machine for crushing olives,' related to *tundere* 'crush.'

toga

toggle 1

toll[1] /tōl/ *n.* **1** a charge payable for permission to pass a barrier or use a bridge or road, etc. **2** the cost or damage caused by a disaster, battle, etc., or incurred in an achievement (*death toll*). **3** a charge for a long distance telephone call. □ **take its toll** be accompanied by loss or injury, etc. [OE f. med.L *toloneum* f. LL *teloneum* f. Gk *telōnion* tollhouse f. *telos* tax]

toll[2] /tōl/ *v. & n.* • *v.* **1** *intr.* (of a bell) sound with a slow uniform succession of strokes. **b** *tr.* ring (a bell) in this way. **c** *tr.* (of a bell) announce or mark (a death, etc.) in this way. **2** *tr.* strike (the hour). • *n.* **1** the act of tolling. **2** a stroke of a bell. [ME, special use of (now dial.) *toll* entice, pull, f. an OE root *–tyllan* (recorded in *fortyllan* seduce)]

toll·booth /tōlbōōth/ *n.* **1** a booth on a toll road or toll bridge, etc., from which tolls are collected. **2** (also **tol·booth**) *Sc. archaic* a town hall. **3** (also **tol·booth**) *Sc. archaic* a town jail.

toll bridge *n.* a bridge at which a toll is charged.

toll·gate /tōlgayt/ *n.* a gate preventing passage until a toll is paid.

toll·house /tōlhows/ *n.* a house at a tollgate or toll bridge, used by a toll collector.

toll road *n.* a road maintained by the tolls collected on it.

Tol·tec /tōltek, tól–/ *n.* **1** a member of a Native American people that flourished in Mexico before the Aztecs. **2** the language of this people. □□ **Tol·tec·an** *adj.*

to·lu /tōlōō, tōlōō/ *n.* a fragrant brown balsam obtained from either of two South American trees, *Myroxylon balsamum* or *M. toluifera*, and used in perfumery and medicine. [Santiago de *Tolu* in Colombia]

tol·u·ene /tólyōō-een/ *n.* a colorless aromatic liquid hydrocarbon derivative of benzene, orig. obtained from tolu, used in the manufacture of explosives, etc. Also called **methyl benzene**. □□ **to·lu·ic** *adj.* **tol·u·ol** *n.* [TOLU + –ENE]

tom /tom/ *n.* a male of various animals, esp. (in full **tomcat**) a male cat. [abbr. of the name *Thomas*]

tom·a·hawk /tóməhawk/ *n. & v.* • *n.* **1** a Native American war ax with a stone or iron head. **2** *Austral.* a hatchet. • *v.tr.* strike, cut, or kill with a tomahawk. [Renape *tämähāk* f. *tämäham* he, etc., cuts]

tomahawk

to·ma·to /tə máytō, –maá–/ *n.* (*pl.* **–toes**) **1** a glossy red or yellow pulpy edible fruit. **2** a solanaceous plant, *Lycopersicon esculentum*, bearing this. □□ **to·ma·to·ey** *adj.* [17th-c. *tomate*, = F or Sp. & Port., f. Mex. *tomatl*]

PRONUNCIATION TIP   **tomato**

"You say tomato, I say to-MAH-to." The lyrics to this song by George and Ira Gershwin highlight the difference between the British (and regional American) pronunciation ("ta-MAH-toe") and the usual American "ta-MAY-toe." Both are considered acceptable, although the British variant seems affected in some parts of the U.S.

tomb /tōōm/ *n.* **1** a large, esp. underground, vault for the burial of the dead. **2** an enclosure cut in the earth or in rock to receive a dead body. **3** a sepulchral monument. **4** (prec. by *the*) the state of death. [ME *t(o)umbe* f. AF *tumbe*, OF *tombe* f. LL *tumba* f. Gk *tumbos*]

tom·bac /tómbak/ *n.* an alloy of copper and zinc used esp. as material for cheap jewelry. [F f. Malay *tambāga* copper]

tom·bo·lo /tómbəlō/ *n.* (*pl.* **–los**) a spit joining an island to the mainland. [It., = sand dune]

tom·boy /tómboy/ *n.* a girl who behaves in a boisterous boyish way. □□ **tom·boy·ish** *adj.* **tom·boy·ish·ness** *n.*

tomb·stone /tōōmstōn/ *n.* a stone standing or laid over a grave, usu. with an epitaph.

Tom Col·lins /tom kólinz/ *n.* a tall iced drink of gin with soda, lemon or lime juice, and sugar. [20th c.: orig. unkn.]

Tom, Dick, and Har·ry /tóm dik ənd háree/ *n.* (usu. prec. by *any*, *every*) ordinary people taken at random; anyone.

tome /tōm/ *n.* a large heavy book or volume. [F f. L *tomus* f. Gk *tomos* section, volume f. *temnō* cut]

-tome /tōm/ *comb. form* forming nouns meaning: **1** an instrument for cutting (*microtome*). **2** a section or segment. [Gk *tomē* a cutting, *–tomos* –cutting, f. *temnō* cut]

to·men·tum /tōméntəm/ *n.* (*pl.* **to·men·ta** /–tə/) **1** *Bot.* matted woolly down on stems and leaves. **2** *Anat.* the tufted inner surface of the pia mater in the brain. □□ **to·men·tose** /–tōs/ *adj.* **to·men·tous** *adj.* [L, = cushion stuffing]

tom·fool /tómfōōl/ *n.* **1** a foolish person. **2** (*attrib.*) silly; foolish (*a tomfool idea*).

tom·fool·er·y /tómfōōləree/ *n.* (*pl.* **–ies**) **1** foolish behavior; nonsense. **2** an instance of this.

Tom·my /tómee/ *n.* (*pl.* **–mies**) *colloq.* a British enlisted soldier. [*Tommy* (*Thomas*) *Atkins*, a name used in specimens of completed official forms]

tom·my bar /tómee/ *n.* a short bar adding leverage when used with a wrench, etc.

tom·my gun /tómee/ *n.* a type of submachine gun. [J. T. *Thompson*, US Army officer d. 1940, its co-inventor]

tom·my·rot /tómeerot/ *n. sl.* nonsense.

to·mo·gram /tóməgram/ *n.* a record obtained by tomography.

to·mog·ra·phy /təmógrəfee/ *n.* a method of radiography displaying details in a selected plane within the body. [Gk *tomē* a cutting + –GRAPHY]

to·mor·row /təmáwrō, –mór–/ *adv. & n.* • *adv.* **1** on the day after today. **2** at some future time. • *n.* **1** the day after today. **2** the near future. □ **tomorrow morning** (or **afternoon**, etc.) in the morning (or afternoon, etc.) of tomorrow. **tomorrow week** *Brit.* a week from tomorrow. [TO + MORROW: cf. TODAY]

tom·pi·on var. of TAMPION.

Tom Thumb /tom thúm/ *n.* **1** a dwarf or midget. **2** a dwarf variety of various plants. [the name of a tiny person in fairy tales]

tom·tit /tómtit/ *n.* any of various tit birds, esp. a blue tit.

tom-tom /tómtom/ *n.* **1** an early drum beaten with the hands. **2** a tall drum beaten with the hands and used in jazz bands, etc. [Hindi *tamtam*, imit.]

-tomy /təmee/ *comb. form* forming nouns denoting cutting, esp. in surgery (*laparotomy*). [Gk *–tomia* cutting f. *temnō* cut]

ton[1] /tun/ *n.* **1** (in full **short ton**) a unit of weight equal to 2,000 lb. (907.19 kg). **2** (in full **long ton**) a unit of weight equal to 2,240 lb. (1016.05 kg). **3** = *metric ton*. **4 a** (in full **displacement ton**) a unit of measurement of a ship's weight or volume in terms of its displacement of water with the loadline just immersed, equal to 2,240 lb. or 35 cu ft. (0.99 cubic meters). **b** (in full **freight ton**) a unit of weight or volume of cargo, equal to a metric ton (1,000 kg) or 40 cu. ft. **5 a** (in full **gross ton**) a unit of gross internal capacity, equal to 100 cu. ft. (2.83 cubic meters). **b** (in full **net** or register ton) an equivalent unit of net internal capacity. **6** a unit of refrigerating power able to freeze 2,000 lb. of ice at 0°C in 24 hours. **7** a measure of capacity for various materials, esp. 40 cu. ft. of lumber. **8** (usu. in *pl.*) *colloq.* a large number or amount (*tons of money*). **9** esp. *Brit. sl.* **a** a speed of 100 m.p.h. **b** a sum of £100. **c** a score of 100. □ **weigh a ton** *colloq.* be very heavy. [orig. the same word as TUN: differentiated in the 17th c.]

ton[2] /toN/ *n.* **1** a prevailing mode or fashion. **2** fashionable society. [F]

ton·al /tónəl/ *adj.* **1** of or relating to tone or tonality. **2** (of a fugue, etc.) having repetitions of the subject at different pitches in the same key. □□ *tonalis* (as TONE)]

to·nal·i·ty /tōnálitee/ *n.* (*pl.* **–ties**) **1** *Mus.* **a** the relationship between the tones of a musical scale. **b** the observance of a single tonic key as the basis of a composition. **2** the tone or color scheme of a picture. **3** *Linguistics* the differentiation of words, syllables, etc., by a change of vocal pitch.

ton·do /tóndō/ *n.* (*pl.* **ton·di** /–dee/) a circular painting or relief. [It., = round (plate), f. L *rotondo* f. L *rotundus* round]

tone /tōn/ *n. & v.* • *n.* **1** a musical or vocal sound, esp. with reference to its pitch, quality, and strength. **2** (often in *pl.*) modulation of the voice expressing a particular feeling or mood (*a cheerful tone; suspicious tones*). **3** a manner of expression in writing. **4** *Mus.* **a** a musical sound, esp. of a definite pitch and character. **b** an interval of a major second, e.g., C– D. **5 a** the general effect of color or of light and shade in a picture. **b** the tint or shade of a color. **6 a** the prevailing character of the morals and sentiments, etc., in a group. **b** an attitude or sentiment expressed, esp. in a letter, etc. **7** the proper firmness of bodily organs. **8** a state of good or specified health or quality. **9** *Phonet.* **a** an accent on one syllable of a word. **b** the pitch of a word to distinguish it from others of a similar sound (*Mandarin has four tones*). • *v.* **1** *tr.* give the desired tone to. **2** *tr.* modify the tone of. **3** *intr.* (often foll. by *to*) attune. **4** *intr.* (foll. by *with*) be in harmony (esp. of color) (*does not tone with the wallpaper*). **5** *tr. Photog.* give (a monochrome picture) an altered color in finishing by means of a chemical solution. **6** *intr.* undergo a change in color by toning. □ **tone down 1** make or become less harsh in tone of sound or color. **2** make (a statement, etc.) less harsh or emphatic. **tone up 1** make or become stronger in tone of sound or color. **2** make (a statement, etc.) more emphatic. **3** make (muscles) firm by exercise, etc.; make or become fitter. □□ **tone·less** *adj.* **tone·less·ly** *adv.* **ton·er** *n.* [ME f. OF *ton* or L *tonus* f. Gk *tonos* tension, tone f. *teinō* stretch]

tone arm *n.* the movable arm supporting the pickup of a record player.

tone·burst /tónbərst/ *n.* an audio signal used in testing the transient response of audio components.

tone-deaf *adj.* unable to perceive differences of musical pitch accurately. □□ **tone deafness** *n.*

ton·eme /tóneem/ *n.* a phoneme distinguished from another only by its tone. □□ **tonemic** /–néemik/ *adj.* [TONE after *phoneme*]

tone po·em *n.* = SYMPHONIC POEM.

tone row *n. Mus.* a series of varying tones that recur in sequence throughout a composition.

tong /tawng, tong/ *n.* a Chinese guild, association, or secret society. [Chin. *tang* meeting place]

ton·ga /tónggə/ *n.* a light horse-drawn two-wheeled vehicle used in India. [Hindi *tāngā*]

tongs /tawngz, tongz/ *n.pl.* (also **pair of tongs** *sing.*) an instrument with two hinged or sprung arms for grasping and holding. [pl. of *tong* f. OE *tang(e)* f. Gmc]

tongue /tung/ *n. & v.* ● *n.* **1** the fleshy muscular organ in the mouth used in tasting, licking, and swallowing, and (in humans) for speech. **2** the tongue of an ox, etc., as food. **3** the faculty of or a tendency in speech (*a sharp tongue*). **4** a particular language (*the German tongue*). **5** a thing like a tongue in shape or position, esp.: **a** a long low promontory. **b** a strip of leather, etc., attached at one end only, under the laces in a shoe. **c** the clapper of a bell. **d** the pin of a buckle. **e** the projecting strip on a wooden, etc., board fitting into the groove of another. **f** a vibrating slip in the reed of some musical instruments. **g** a jet of flame. ● *v.* (**tongues, tongued, tongu·ing**) **1** *tr.* produce staccato, etc., effects with (a flute, etc.) by means of tonguing. **2** *intr.* use the tongue in this way. □ **find** (or **lose**) **one's tongue** be able (or unable) to express oneself after a shock, etc. **the gift of tongues** the power of speaking in unknown languages, regarded in some Christian denominations as one of the gifts of the Holy Spirit (Acts 2). **keep a civil tongue in one's head** avoid rudeness. **with one's tongue hanging out** eagerly or expectantly. □□ **tongued** *adj.* (also in *comb.*). **tongue·less** *adj.* [OE *tunge* f. Gmc, rel. to L *lingua*]

tongue and groove *n.* wooden planking in which adjacent boards are joined by means of interlocking ridges and hollows down their sides. □□ **tongued-and-grooved** *adj.*

tongue de·pres·sor *n.* a doctor's implement for holding the tongue in place while examining the throat or mouth.

tongue-in-cheek *adj. & adv.* ● *adj.* ironic; slyly humorous. ● *adv.* insincerely or ironically.

tongue-lash·ing *n.* a severe scolding or reprimand.

tongue-tie *n.* a speech impediment due to a malformation of the tongue.

tongue-tied *adj.* **1** too shy or embarrassed to speak. **2** having a tongue-tie.

tongue twist·er *n.* a sequence of words difficult to pronounce quickly and correctly.

tongu·ing /túnging/ *n. Mus.* the technique of playing a wind instrument using the tongue to articulate certain notes.

ton·ic /tónik/ *n. & adj.* ● *n.* **1** an invigorating medicine. **2** anything serving to invigorate. **3** = TONIC WATER. **4** *Mus.* the first degree of a scale, forming the keynote of a piece (see KEYNOTE 3). ● *adj.* **1** serving as a tonic; invigorating. **2** *Mus.* denoting the first degree of a scale. **3 a** producing tension, esp. of the muscles. **b** restoring normal tone to organs. □□ **ton·i·cal·ly** *adv.* [F *tonique* f. Gk *tonikos* (as TONE)]

ton·ic ac·cent *n.* an accent marked by a change of pitch within a syllable.

to·nic·i·ty /tōnísitee/ *n.* **1** the state of being tonic. **2** a healthy elasticity of muscles, etc. **3** *Linguistics* phonetic emphasis at a certain place in an intonation pattern.

ton·ic sol-fa *n. Mus.* a system of notation used esp. in teaching singing, with do as the keynote of all major keys and la as the keynote of all minor keys.

ton·ic spasm *n.* continuous muscular contraction (cf. CLONUS).

ton·ic wa·ter *n.* a carbonated mineral water containing quinine.

to·night /tənít/ *adv. & n.* ● *adv.* on the present or approaching evening or night. ● *n.* the evening or night of the present day. [TO + NIGHT: cf. TODAY]

ton·ka bean /tóngkə/ *n.* the black fragrant seed of a South American tree, *Dipteryx odorata*, used in perfumery, etc. [*tonka*, its name in Guyana, + BEAN]

ton-mile *n.* one ton of goods carried one mile, as a unit of traffic.

ton·nage /túnij/ *n.* **1** a ship's internal cubic capacity or freight-carrying capacity, measured in tons. **2** the total carrying capacity, esp. of a country's merchant marine. **3** a charge per ton on freight or cargo. [orig. in sense 'duty on a tun of wine': OF *tonnage* f. *tonne* TUN: later f. TON[1]]

tonne /tun/ *n.* = METRIC TON. [F: see TUN]

ton·neau /tənó, tōnó/ *n.* the part of an automobile occupied by the back seats, esp. in an open car. [F, lit. cask, tun]

ton·neau cov·er *n.* a removable flexible cover for the passenger seats in an open car, boat, etc., when they are not in use.

to·nom·e·ter /tōnómitər/ *n.* **1** a tuning fork or other instrument for measuring the pitch of tones. **2** an instrument for measuring the pressure of fluid. [formed as TONE + –METER]

ton·sil /tónsəl/ *n.* either of two small masses of lymphoid tissue on each side of the root of the tongue. □□ **ton·sil·lar** *adj.* [F *tonsilles* or L *tonsillae* (pl.)]

ton·sil·lec·to·my /tónsiléktəmee/ *n.* (*pl.* **–mies**) the surgical removal of the tonsils.

ton·sil·li·tis /tónsilítis/ *n.* inflammation of the tonsils.

ton·so·ri·al /tonsáwreeəl/ *adj.* usu. *joc.* of or relating to a hairdresser or barber or hairdressing. [L *tonsorius* f. *tonsor* barber f. *tondēre tons-* shave]

ton·sure /tónshər/ *n. & v.* ● *n.* **1** the shaving of the crown of the head or the entire head, esp. of a person entering a priesthood or monastic order. **2** a bare patch made in this way. ● *v.tr.* give a tonsure to. [ME f. OF *tonsure* or L *tonsura* (as TONSORIAL)]

ton·tine /tonteén/ *n.* an annuity shared by subscribers to a loan, the shares increasing as subscribers die until the last survivor gets all, or until a specified date when the remaining survivors share the proceeds. [F, f. the name of Lorenzo *Tonti* of Naples, originator of tontines in France *c.* 1653]

ton·y /tónee/ *adj.* (**ton·i·er, ton·i·est**) *colloq.* having 'tone'; stylish; fashionable.

too /too/ *adv.* **1** to a greater extent than is desirable, permissible, or possible for a specified or understood purpose (*too colorful for my taste; too large to fit*). **2** *colloq.* extremely (*you're too kind*). **3** in addition (*are they coming too?*). **4** moreover (*we must consider, too, the time of year*). □ **none too 1** somewhat less than (*feeling none too good*). **2** barely. **too bad** see BAD. **too much, too much for** see MUCH. **too right** see RIGHT. [stressed form of TO, f. 16th-c. spelling *too*]

tood·le-oo /tood'lóo/ *int.* (also *Brit.* **tood·le-pip**) *colloq.* goodbye. [20th c.: orig. unkn.: perh. alt. of F *à tout à l'heure* see you soon]

took *past of* TAKE.

tool /tool/ *n. & v.* ● *n.* **1** any device or implement used to carry out mechanical functions whether manually or by a machine. **2** a thing used in an occupation or pursuit (*the tools of one's trade; literary tools*). **3** a person used as a mere instrument by another. **4** *coarse sl.* the penis. **5 a** a distinct figure in the tooling of a book. **b** a small stamp or roller used to make this. ● *v.tr.* **1** dress (stone) with a chisel. **2** impress a design on (a leather book cover). **3** (foll. by *along, around*, etc.) *sl.* drive or ride, esp. in a casual or leisurely manner. **4** (often foll. by *up*) equip with tools. □ **tool up 1** *sl.* arm oneself. **2** equip oneself. □□ **tool·er** *n.* [OE *tōl* f. Gmc]

SYNONYM TIP tool

APPARATUS, APPLIANCE, IMPLEMENT, INSTRUMENT, UTENSIL. A wrench is a **tool**, meaning that it is a device held in and manipulated by the hand and used by a mechanic, plumber, carpenter, or other laborer to work, shape, move, or transform material (*He couldn't fix the drawer without the right tools*). An **implement** is a broader term referring to any *tool* or mechanical device used for a particular purpose (*agricultural implements*). A washing machine is an **appliance**, which refers to a mechanical or power-driven device, especially for household use (*The newly-married couple went shopping for appliances*). A **utensil** is also for domestic use (*eating utensils*), while an **instrument** is used for scientific or artistic purposes (*musical instrument, surgical instrument*). **Apparatus** refers to a collection of distinct *instruments, tools*, or devices that are used in connection or combination with one another for a certain purpose (*The gym was open, but the exercise apparatus had not been set up*).

tool·ing /tóoling/ *n.* **1** the process of dressing stone with a chisel. **2** the ornamentation of a book cover with designs impressed by heated tools.

tool·mak·er /tóolmaykər/ *n.* a person who makes precision tools, esp. tools used in a press. □□ **tool·mak·ing** *n.*

toot[1] /toot/ *n. & v.* ● *n.* **1** a short sharp sound as made by a horn, trumpet, or whistle. **2** *sl.* cocaine or a snort (see SNORT *n.* 4) of cocaine. **3** *sl.* a drinking session; a binge; a spree. ● *v.* **1** *tr.* sound (a horn, etc.) with a short sharp sound. **2** *intr.* give out such a sound. □□ **toot·er** *n.* [prob. f. MLG *tüten*, or imit.]

toot[2] /toot/ *n. Austral. sl.* a toilet. [20th c.: orig. unkn.]

tooth /tooth/ *n. & v.* ● *n.* (*pl.* **teeth** /teeth/) **1** each of a set of hard bony enamel-coated structures in the jaws of most vertebrates, used for biting and chewing. **2** a toothlike part or projection, e.g., the cog of a gearwheel, the point of a saw or comb, etc. **3** (often foll. by *for*) one's sense of taste; an appetite or liking. **4** (in *pl.*) force or effectiveness (*the penalties give the contract teeth*). ● *v.tr.* **1** provide with teeth. **2** *intr.* (of cogwheels) engage, interlock. □ **armed to the teeth** completely and elaborately armed or equipped. **fight tooth and nail** fight very fiercely. **get** (or **sink**) **one's teeth into** devote oneself seriously to. **in the teeth of 1** in spite of (opposition or difficulty, etc.). **2** contrary to (instructions, etc.). **3** directly against (the wind, etc.). **set a person's teeth on edge** see EDGE. □□ **toothed** *adj.* (also in *comb.*). **tooth·less** *adj.* **tooth·like** *adj.* [OE *tōth* (pl. *tēth*) f. Gmc]

tooth·ache /tóothayk/ *n.* a (usu. prolonged) pain in a tooth or teeth.

tooth-billed *adj.* (of a bird) having toothlike projections on the cutting edges of the bill.

tooth•brush /tóbthbrush/ *n.* a brush for cleaning the teeth.

tooth comb *n. Brit.* = FINE-TOOTH COMB.

tooth•ing /tóbthing/ *n.* projecting bricks or stones left at the end of a wall to allow its continuation.

tooth•paste /tóbthpayst/ *n.* a paste for cleaning the teeth.

tooth•pick /tóbthpik/ *n.* a small sharp instrument for removing small pieces of food lodged between the teeth.

tooth pow•der *n.* powder for cleaning the teeth.

tooth shell *n.* = TUSK SHELL.

tooth•some /tóbthsəm/ *adj.* **1** (of food) delicious; appetizing. **2** attractive; esp. sexually. □□ **tooth•some•ly** *adv.* **tooth•some•ness** *n.*

tooth•wort /tóbthwərt, –wawrt/ *n.* a parasitic plant, *Lathraea squamaria*, with toothlike root scales.

tooth•y /tóbthee/ *adj.* (**tooth•i•er, tooth•i•est**) having or showing large, numerous, or prominent teeth (*a toothy grin*). □□ **tooth•i•ly** *adv.*

too•tle /tóbt'l/ *v.intr.* **1** toot gently or repeatedly. **2** (usu. foll. by *along, around*, etc.) *colloq.* move casually or aimlessly. □□ **too•tler** *n.*

too•too *adj. & adv. colloq.* excessively annoying or fatiguing.

toot•sy /tóbtsee/ *n.* (also **toot•sie**) (*pl.* **–sies**) *sl.* usu. *joc.* a foot. [E joc. dimin.: cf. FOOTSIE]

top[1] /top/ *n., adj., & v.* ● *n.* **1** the highest point or part (*the top of the house*). **2 a** the highest rank or place (*at the top of the school*). **b** a person occupying this (*was top in spelling*). **c** esp. *Brit.* the upper end or head (*the top of the table*). **3** the upper surface of a thing, esp. of the ground, a table, etc. **4** the upper part of a thing, esp.: **a** a blouse, sweater, etc., for wearing with a skirt or pants. **b** the upper part of a shoe or boot. **c** the stopper of a bottle. **d** the lid of a jar, saucepan, etc. **e** the creamy part of unhomogenized milk. **f** the folding roof of a car, carriage, etc. **g** the upper edge or edges of a page or pages in a book (*gilt top*). **5** the utmost degree; height (*called at the top of his voice*). **6** (in *pl.*) *colloq.* a person or thing of the best quality (*he's tops at swimming*). **7** (esp. in *pl.*) the leaves, etc., of a plant grown esp. for its root (*turnip tops*). **8** (usu. in *pl.*) a bundle of long wool fibers prepared for spinning. **9** *Naut.* a platform around the head of the lower mast, serving to extend the topmost rigging or carry guns. **10** (in *pl.*) esp. Bridge the two or three highest cards of a suit. **11** *Baseball* the first half of an inning. **12** *Brit.* = TOP GEAR (*climbed the hill in top*). **13** = TOPSPIN. ● *adj.* **1** highest in position (*the top shelf*). **2** highest in degree or importance (*at top speed; the top job*). ● *v.tr.* (**topped, top•ping**) **1** provide with a top, cap, etc. (*cake topped with icing*). **2** remove the top of (a plant, fruit, etc.), esp. to improve growth, prepare for cooking, etc. **3** be higher or better than; surpass; be at the top of (*topped the list*). **4** *Brit. sl.* execute, esp. by hanging; kill. **b** (*refl.*) commit suicide. **5** reach the top of (a hill, etc.). **6 a** hit (a ball) above the center. **b** make (a hit or stroke) in this way. □ **come to the top** *colloq.* win distinction. **from top to toe** from head to foot; completely. **off the top of one's head** see HEAD. **on top 1** in a superior position; above. **2** on the upper part of the head (*bald on top*). **on top of 1** fully in command of. **2** in close proximity to. **3** in addition to. **4** above; over. **on top of the world** *colloq.* exuberant. **over the top 1** over the parapet of a trench (and into battle). **2** into a final or decisive state. **3** to excess; beyond reasonable limits (*that joke was over the top*). **top off 1** put an end or the finishing touch to (a thing). **2** fill up, esp. a container already partly full. **top out** put the highest stone on (a building). **top one's part** esp. Theatr. act or discharge one's part to perfection. **top up 1 a** esp. *Brit.* complete (an amount or number). **b** fill up (a glass, fuel tank, or other partly full container). **2** top up something for (a person) (*may I top you up with coffee?*). □□ **top•most** *adj.* [OE *topp*]

top[2] /top/ *n.* a wooden or metal toy, usu. conical, spherical, or pear-shaped, spinning on a point when set in motion by hand, string, etc. [OE, of uncert. orig.]

to•paz /tópaz/ *n.* **1** a transparent or translucent aluminum silicate mineral, usu. yellow, used as a gem. **2** any South American hummingbird of the genus *Topaza*. [ME f. OF *topace, topaze* f. L *topazos* f. Gk *topazos*]

to•paz•o•lite /təpázəlīt/ *n.* a yellow or green kind of garnet. [TOPAZ + –LITE]

top ba•na•na *n.* **1** *Theatr. sl.* a comedian who tops the bill of a show. **2** *sl.* a leader; the head of an organization, etc.

top boot *n.* esp. *hist.* a boot with a high top, esp. of a different material or color.

top brass *n.* esp. *Mil. colloq.* the highest ranking officers, heads of industries, etc.

top•coat /tópkōt/ *n.* **1** an overcoat. **2** an outer coat of paint, etc.

top cop•y *n.* the uppermost typed copy (cf. CARBON COPY).

top dog *n. colloq.* a victor or master.

top drawer *n. & adj.* ● *n.* **1** the uppermost drawer in a chest, desk, etc. **2** (**the top drawer**) *colloq.* high social position or class. ● *adj.* (**top-drawer**) of the highest quality or social class.

top-dress•ing *n.* an application of manure or fertilizer laid on top of the soil instead of being plowed in. □□ **top-dress** *v.tr.*

tope[1] /tōp/ *v.intr.* drink alcohol to excess, esp. habitually. □□ **top•er** *n.* [perh. f. obs. *top* quaff]

tope[2] /tōp/ *n. Ind.* a grove, esp. of mangoes. [Telugu *tōpu*, Tamil *tōppu*]

tope[3] /tōp/ *n.* = STUPA. [Punjab *tōp* f. Prakrit & Pali *thūpo* f. Skr. STU-PA]

tope[4] /tōp/ *n.* a small shark, *Galeorhinus galeus*. [perh. f. Corn.]

to•pee /tópee/ *n.* (also **to•pi**) (*pl.* **to•pees** or **to•pis**) *Anglo-Ind.* a lightweight hat or helmet, often made of pith. [Hindi *topī*]

top fruit *n. Brit.* fruit grown on trees, not bushes.

top•gal•lant /topgálənt, təgálənt/ *n. Naut.* the mast, sail, yard, or rigging immediately above the topmast and topsail.

top gear *n.* esp. *Brit.* the highest gear in a motor vehicle or bicycle.

top-ham•per *n.* an encumbrance on top, esp. the upper sails and rigging of a ship.

top hat *n.* a man's tall silk hat.

top-heav•y /tóphévee/ *adj.* **1** disproportionately heavy at the top so as to be in danger of toppling. **2 a** (of an organization, business, etc.) having a disproportionately large number of people in senior administrative positions. **b** overcapitalized. **3** *colloq.* (of a woman) having a disproportionately large bust. □□ **top-heav•i•ly** *adv.* **top-heav•i•ness** *n.*

To•phet /tófit, –fet/ *n. Bibl.* hell. [name of a place in the Valley of Hinnom near Jerusalem used for idolatrous worship and later for burning refuse: f. Heb. *tōpet*]

top-hole *adj. Brit. colloq.* first-rate.

to•phus /tófəs/ *n.* (*pl.* **to•phi** /–fī/) **1** *Med.* a gouty deposit of crystalline uric acid and other substances at the surface of joints. **2** *Geol.* = TUFA. [L, name of loose porous stones]

to•pi var. of TOPEE.

to•pi•ar•y /tópee-eree/ *adj. & n.* ● *adj.* concerned with or formed by clipping shrubs, trees, etc., into ornamental shapes. ● *n.* (*pl.* **–ies**) **1** topiary art. **2** an example of this. □□ **to•pi•ar•i•an** /–peeáireeən/ *adj.* **to•pi•a•rist** *n.* [F *topiaire* f. L *topiarius* landscape gardener f. *topia opera* fancy gardening f. Gk *topia* pl. dimin. of *topos* place]

top•ic /tópik/ *n.* **1** a theme for a book, discourse, essay, sermon, etc. **2** the subject of a conversation or argument. [L *topica* f. Gk (*ta*) *topika* topics, as title of a treatise by Aristotle f. *topos* a place, a commonplace]

top•i•cal /tópikəl/ *adj.* **1** dealing with the news, current affairs, etc. (*a topical song*). **2** dealing with a place; local. **3** *Med.* (of an ailment, medicine, etc.) affecting a part of the body. **4** of or concerning topics. □□ **top•i•cal•i•ty** /–kálitee/ *n.* **top•i•cal•ly** *adv.*

top•knot /tópnot/ *n.* a knot, tuft, crest, or bow worn or growing on the head.

top•less /tóplis/ *adj.* **1** without or seeming to be without a top. **2 a** (of clothes) having no upper part. **b** (of a person) wearing such clothes; barebreasted. **c** (of a place, esp. a beach, bar, etc.) where women go topless. □□ **top•less•ness** *n.*

top-lev•el *adj.* of the highest level of importance, prestige, etc.

top•loft•y /tópláwftee, –lóf–/ *adj. colloq.* haughty.

top•man /tópmən/ *n.* (*pl.* **–men**) *Naut.* a man doing duty in a top.

top•mast /tópməst, –mast/ *n. Naut.* the mast next above the lower

---

PRONUNCIATION TIP **topmast**

See note at GUNWALE.

---

top-notch *adj. colloq.* first rate.

to•pog•ra•phy /təpógrəfee/ *n.* **1 a** a detailed description, representation on a map, etc., of the natural and artificial features of a town, district, etc. **b** such features. **2** *Anat.* the mapping of the surface of the body with reference to the parts beneath. □□ **to•pog•ra•pher** *n.* **top•o•graph•ic** /tópəgráfik/ *adj.* **top•o•graph•i•cal** *adj.* **top•o•graph•i•cal•ly** *adv.* [ME f. LL *topographia* f. Gk f. *topos* place]

to•pol•o•gy /təpóləjee/ *n. Math.* the study of geometrical properties and spatial relations unaffected by the continuous change of shape or size of figures. □□ **top•o•log•i•cal** /tópəlójikəl/ *adj.* **top•o•log•i•cal•ly** *adv.* **to•pol•o•gist** *n.* [G *Topologie* f. Gk *topos* place]

top•o•nym /tópənim/ *n.* **1** a place-name. **2** a descriptive place-name, usu. derived from a topographical feature of the place. [TOPONYMY]

to•pon•y•my /təpónimee/ *n.* the study of the place-names of a region. □□ **top•o•nym•ic** /tópənímik/ *adj.* [Gk *topos* place + *onoma* name]

to•pos /tópōs, –pos/ *n.* (*pl.* **to•poi** /–poy/) a stock theme in literature, etc. [Gk, = commonplace]

top•per /tópər/ *n.* **1** a thing that tops. **2** *colloq.* = TOP HAT. **3** *Brit. colloq.* a good fellow; a good sort.

top•ping /tóping/ *adj. & n.* ● *adj.* **1** preeminent in position, rank, etc. **2** *Brit. archaic sl.* excellent. ● *n.* anything that tops something else, esp. icing, etc., on a cake.

top•ple /tópəl/ *v.intr. & tr.* (usu. foll. by *over, down*) **1 a** fall or cause to fall as if top-heavy. **b** fall or cause to fall from power. **2** totter or cause to totter and fall. [TOP[1] + –LE[4]]

top•sail /tópsəl, –sayl/ *n.* a square sail next above the lowest fore-and-aft sail on a gaff.

PRONUNCIATION TIP **topsail**

See note at GUNWALE.

top·saw·yer *n.* **1** a sawyer in the upper position in a sawmill. **2** *Brit.* a person who holds a superior position; a distinguished person.

top se·cret *n.* of the highest secrecy.

top·side /tópsīd/ *n.* **1** the side of a ship above the waterline. **2** *Brit.* the outer side of a round of beef.

top·soil /tópsoyl/ *n.* the top layer of soil (opp. SUBSOIL).

top·spin /tópspin/ *n.* a fast forward spinning motion imparted to a ball in tennis, etc., by hitting it forward and upward.

top·sy·tur·vy /tópseetórvee/ *adv., adj., & v.* ● *adv. & adj.* **1** upside down. **2** in utter confusion. ● *n.* utter confusion. □□ **top·sy·tur·vi·ly** *adv.* **top·sy·tur·vi·ness** *n.* [app. f. TOP¹ + obs. *terve* overturn]

top ten *n.* (also **twen·ty**, etc.) the first ten (or twenty, etc.) records, movies, etc., at a given time in terms of sales, popularity, etc.

top-up *n.* an addition; something that serves to top up (esp. a partly full glass).

toque /tōk/ *n.* **1** a woman's small brimless hat. **2** *hist.* a small cap or bonnet for a man or woman. [F, app. = It. *tocca*, Sp. *toca*, of unkn. orig.]

to·qui·lla /tǝkeéyǝ/ *n.* **1** a palmlike tree, *Carludovica palmata*, native to S. America. **2** a fiber produced from the leaves of this. [Sp., = small gauze headdress, dimin. of *toca* toque]

tor /tor/ *n.* a hill or rocky peak. [OE *torr*: cf. Gael. *tòrr* bulging hill]

To·rah /tórǝ, táwrǝ, tōráǝ/ *n.* **1** (usu. prec. by *the*) **a** the Pentateuch. **b** a scroll containing this. **2** the will of God as revealed in Mosaic law. [Heb. *tōrāh* instruction]

torc var. of TORQUE 1.

torch /tawrch/ *n. & v.* ● *n.* **1 a** a piece of wood, cloth, etc., soaked in tallow and lighted for illumination. **b** any similar lamp, e.g., an oil lamp on a pole. **2** a source of heat, illumination, or enlightenment (*bore aloft the torch of freedom*). **3** = BLOWTORCH. **4** *sl.* an arsonist. **5** (also **e·lec·tric torch**) *Brit.* = FLASHLIGHT. ● *v.tr. sl.* set alight with or as with a torch. □ **carry a torch for** suffer from unrequited love for. **put to the torch** destroy by burning. [ME f. OF *torche* f. L *torqua* f. *torquēre* twist]

tor·chère /tawrsháir/ *n.* **1** a tall stand with a small table for a candlestick, etc. **2** a tall floor lamp giving indirect light. [F (as TORCH)]

torch·light /táwrchlīt/ *n.* the light of a torch or torches.

tor·chon /táwrshon/ *n.* (in full **torchon lace**) coarse bobbin lace with geometrical designs. [F, = duster, dishcloth f. *torcher* wipe]

torch-race *n. Gk Antiq.* a festival performance of runners handing lighted torches to others in relays.

torch sing·er *n.* a singer, esp. a woman, who sings torch songs.

torch song *n.* a popular song of unrequited love.

tore¹ *past of* TEAR¹.

tore² /tawr/ *n.* = TORUS 1, 4. [F f. L *torus*: see TORUS]

to·re·a·dor /táwreeǝdor/ *n.* a bullfighter, esp. on horseback. [Sp. f. *torear* fight bulls f. *toro* bull f. L *taurus*]

to·re·a·dor pants *n.pl.* close-fitting calf-length women's slacks.

to·re·ro /tawráirō/ *n.* (*pl.* **–ros**) a bullfighter. [Sp. *toro*: see TOREADOR]

to·reu·tic /tǝróōtik/ *adj. & n.* ● *adj.* of or concerning the chasing, carving, and embossing of esp. metal. ● *n.* (in *pl.*) the art or practice of this. [Gk *toreutikos* f. *toreuō* work in relief]

to·ri *pl.* of TORUS.

tor·ic /táwrik/ *adj. Geom.* having the form of a torus or part of a torus.

to·ri·i /táwree-ee/ *n.* (*pl.* same) the gateway of a Shinto shrine, with two uprights and two crosspieces. [Jap.]

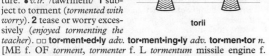

torii

tor·ment *n. & v.* ● *n.* /táwrment/ **1** severe physical or mental suffering (*was in torment*). **2** a cause of this. **3** *archaic* **a** torture. **b** an instrument of torture. ● *v.tr.* /tawrmént/ **1** subject to torment (*tormented with worry*). **2** tease or worry excessively (*enjoyed tormenting the teacher*). □□ **tor·ment·ed·ly** *adv.* **tor·ment·ing·ly** *adv.* **tor·men·tor** *n.* [ME f. OF *torment, tormenter* f. L *tormentum* missile engine f. *torquēre* to twist]

tor·men·til /táwrmǝntil/ *n.* a low-growing plant, *Potentilla erecta*, with bright yellow flowers and a highly astringent rootstock used in medicine. [ME f. OF *tormentille* f. med.L *tormentilla*, of unkn. orig.]

torn *past part.* of TEAR¹.

tor·na·do /tawrnáydō/ *n.* (*pl.* **–does**) **1** a violent storm of small extent with whirling winds, esp.: **a** over a narrow path often accompanied by a funnel-shaped cloud. **b** in West Africa at the beginning and end of the rainy season. **2** an outburst or volley of cheers, hisses, missiles, etc. □□ **tor·na·dic** /–nádik/ *adj.* [app. assim. of Sp. *tronada* thunderstorm (f. *tronar* to thunder) to Sp. *tornar* to turn]

to·roid /táwroyd/ *n.* a figure of toroidal shape.

to·roi·dal /tawróyd'l/ *adj. Geom.* of or resembling a torus. □□ **to·roi·dal·ly** *adv.*

to·rose /táwrōs/ *adj.* **1** *Bot.* (of plants, esp. their stalks) cylindrical

with bulges at intervals. **2** *Zool.* knobby; bulging. [L *torosus* f. *torus*: see TORUS]

tor·pe·do /tawrpeédō/ *n. & v.* ● *n.* (*pl.* **–does**) **1 a** a cigar-shaped self-propelled underwater missile that explodes on impact with a ship. **b** a similar device dropped from an aircraft. **2** *Zool.* an electric ray. **3** a type of explosive device or firework. ● *v.tr.* (**–does, –doed**) **1** destroy or attack with a torpedo. **2** make (a policy, institution, plan, etc.) ineffective or inoperative; destroy. □□ **tor·pe·do·like** *adj.* [L, = numbness, electric ray f. *torpēre* be numb]

tor·pe·do boat *n.* a small fast lightly armed warship for carrying or discharging torpedoes.

tor·pe·do net *n.* (also **tor·pe·do net·ting**) netting of steel wire hung around a ship to intercept torpedoes.

tor·pe·do tube *n.* a tube from which torpedoes are fired.

tor·pe·fy /táwrpifī/ *v.tr.* (**–fies, –fied**) make numb or torpid. [L *torpefacere* f. *torpēre* be numb]

tor·pid /táwrpid/ *adj.* **1** sluggish; inactive; dull; apathetic. **2** numb. **3** (of a hibernating animal) dormant. □□ **tor·pid·i·ty** /–píditee/ *n.* **tor·pid·ly** *adv.* **tor·pid·ness** *n.* [L *torpidus* (as TORPOR)]

tor·por /táwrpǝr/ *n.* torpidity. □□ **tor·por·if·ic** /–pǝrífik/ *adj.* [L f. *torpēre* be sluggish]

tor·quate /táwrkwayt/ *adj. Zool.* (of an animal) with a ring of distinctive color or texture of hair or plumage round the neck. [L *torquatus* (as TORQUE)]

torque /tawrk/ *n.* **1** (also **torc**) *hist.* a necklace of twisted metal, esp. of the ancient Gauls and Britons. **2** *Mech.* the moment of a system of forces tending to cause rotation. [(sense 1 F f. L *torques*) f. L *torquēre* to twist]

torque con·vert·er *n.* a device to transmit the correct torque from the engine to the axle in a motor vehicle.

torr /tawr/ *n.* (*pl.* same) a unit of pressure used in measuring partial vacuums, equal to 133.32 pascals. [E. *Torricelli*, It. physicist d. 1647]

tor·re·fy /táwrifī, tór–/ *v.tr.* (**–fies, –fied**) **1** roast or dry (metallic ore, a drug, etc.). **2** parch or scorch with heat. □□ **tor·re·fac·tion** /–fákshǝn/ *n.* [F *torréfier* f. L *torrefacere* f. *torrēre* scorch]

tor·rent /táwrǝnt, tór–/ *n.* **1** a rushing stream of water, lava, etc. **2** (usu. in *pl.*) a great downpour of rain (*came down in torrents*). **3** (usu. foll. by *of*) a violent or copious flow (*uttered a torrent of abuse*). □□ **tor·ren·tial** /tǝrénshǝl/ *adj.* **tor·ren·tial·ly** /tǝrénshǝlee/ *adv.* [F f. It. *torrente* f. L *torrens –entis* scorching, boiling, roaring f. *torrēre* scorch]

Torricellian vacuum /táwrichéleeǝn/ *n.* a vacuum formed when mercury in a long tube closed at one end is inverted with the open end in a reservoir of mercury (the principle on which a barometer is made). [*Torricelli*: see TORR]

tor·rid /táwrid, tór–/ *adj.* **1 a** (of the weather) very hot and dry. **b** (of land, etc.) parched by such weather. **2** (of language or actions) emotionally charged; passionate; intense. □□ **tor·rid·i·ty** /–ríditee/ *n.* **tor·rid·ly** *adv.* **tor·rid·ness** *n.* [F *torride* or L *torridus* f. *torrēre* parch]

tor·rid zone *n.* the central belt of the earth between the Tropics of Cancer and Capricorn.

torse /tawrs/ *n. Heraldry* a wreath. [obs. F *torse, torce* wreath ult. f. L *torta* fem. past part. (as TORT)]

tor·sel var. of TASSEL².

tor·sion /táwrshǝn/ *n.* **1** twisting, esp. of one end of a body while the other is held fixed. **2** *Math.* the extent to which a curve departs from being planar. **3** *Bot.* the state of being twisted into a spiral. **4** *Med.* the twisting of the cut end of an artery after surgery, etc., to impede bleeding. □□ **tor·sion·al** *adj.* **tor·sion·al·ly** *adv.* **tor·sion·less** *adj.* [ME f. OF f. LL *torsio –onis* f. L *tortio* (as TORT)]

tor·sion bal·ance *n.* an instrument for measuring very weak forces by their effect upon a system of fine twisted wire.

tor·sion bar *n.* a bar forming part of a vehicle suspension, twisting in response to the motion of the wheels, and absorbing their vertical movement.

tor·sion pen·du·lum *n.* a pendulum working by rotation rather than by swinging.

torsk /tawrsk/ *n.* a fish of the cod family, *Brosmius brosme*, abundant in northern waters and often dried for food. [Norw. *to(r)sk* f. ON *tho (r)skr* prob. rel. to *thurr* dry]

tor·so /táwrsō/ *n.* (*pl.* **–sos** or **–si**) **1** the trunk of the human body. **2** a statue of a human consisting of the trunk alone, without head or limbs. **3** an unfinished or mutilated work (esp. of art, literature, etc.). [It., = stalk, stump, torso, f. L *thyrsus*]

tort /tawrt/ *n. Law* a breach of duty (other than under contract) leading to liability for damages. [ME f. OF f. med.L *tortum* wrong, neut. past part. of *torquēre* twist]

torte /táwrt/ *n.* (*pl.* **tor·ten** /táwrt'n/ or **tortes**) an elaborate sweet cake. [G]

tort·fea·sor /táwrtfeezǝr/ *n. Law* a person guilty of tort. [OF *tortfesor, tort-faiseur*, etc. f. *tort* wrong, *–fesor, faiseur* doer]

tor·ti·col·lis /táwrtikólis/ n. Med. a rheumatic, etc., disease of the muscles of the neck, causing twisting and stiffness. [mod.L f. L tortus crooked + collum neck]

tor·til·la /tawrtéeyə/ n. a thin flat orig. Mexican corn or wheat bread eaten hot or cold with or without a filling. [Sp. dimin. of torta cake f. LL]

tor·tious /táwrshəs/ adj. Law constituting a tort; wrongful. □□ **tor·tious·ly** adv. [AF torcious f. torcion extortion f. LL tortio torture: see TORSION]

tor·toise /táwrtəs/ n. 1 any slow-moving, esp. land reptile of the family Testudinidae, encased in a scaly or leathery domed shell, and having a retractile head and elephantine legs. 2 Rom. Antiq. = TESTUDO. □□ **tor·toise·like** adj. & adv. [ME tortuce, OF tortue, f. med.L tortuca, of uncert. orig.]

tor·toise·shell /táwrtəs-shel/ n. & adj. ●n. 1 the yellowish brown mottled or clouded outer shell of some turtles, used for decorative combs, jewelry, etc. 2 a = TORTOISESHELL CAT. b = TORTOISESHELL BUTTERFLY. ●adj. having the coloring or appearance of tortoiseshell.

tor·toise·shell but·ter·fly n. any of various butterflies, esp. of the genus Nymphalis, with wings mottled like tortoiseshell.

tor·toise·shell cat n. a domestic cat with markings resembling tortoiseshell.

tor·trix /táwrtriks/ n. (also **tor·tri·cid**) any moth of the family Tortricidae, esp. Tortrix viridana, the larvae of which live inside rolled leaves. [mod.L, fem. of L tortor twister: see TORT]

tor·tu·ous /táwrchŏŏəs/ adj. 1 full of twists and turns (followed a tortuous route). 2 devious; circuitous; crooked (has a tortuous mind). □□ **tor·tu·os·i·ty** /-ósitee/ n. (pl. **-ties**). **tor·tu·ous·ly** adv. **tor·tu·ous·ness** n. [ME f. OF f. L tortuosus f. tortus a twist (as TORT)]

▶Tortuous means 'full of twists and turns' or 'devious, circuitous,' e.g., Both paths were tortuous and are strewn with boulders. **Torturous** is derived from torture and means 'involving torture, excruciating,' e.g., I found the concert torturous because of the music's volume.

tor·ture /táwrchər/ n. & v. ●n. 1 the infliction of severe bodily pain, esp. as a punishment or a means of persuasion. 2 severe physical or mental suffering (the torture of defeat). ●v.tr. 1 subject to torture (tortured by guilt). 2 force out of a natural position or state; deform; pervert. □□ **tor·tur·a·ble** adj. **tor·tur·er** n. **tor·tur·ous·ly** adv. [F f. LL tortura twisting (as TORT)]

tor·tur·ous /táwrchərəs/ adj. characterized by, involving, or caused by extreme physical pain or suffering.

▶See note at TORTUOUS.

tor·u·la /táwryŏŏlə, -əlŏ, tór-/ n. (pl. **tor·u·lae** /-lee/) 1 a yeast, Candida utilis, used medicinally as a food additive. 2 any yeastlike fungus of the genus Torula, growing on dead vegetation. [mod.L, dimin. of torus: see TORUS]

to·rus /táwrəs/ n. (pl. **to·ri** /-rī/) 1 Archit. a large convex molding, esp. as the lowest part of the base of a column. 2 Bot. the receptacle of a flower. 3 Anat. a smooth ridge of bone or muscle. 4 Geom. a surface or solid formed by rotating a closed curve, esp. a circle, about a line in its plane but not intersecting it. [L, = swelling, bulge, cushion, etc.]

To·ry /táwree/ n. & adj. ●n. (pl. **-ries**) 1 esp. Brit. colloq. = CONSERVATIVE n. 2 Brit. hist. a member of the party that opposed the exclusion of James II and later supported the established religious and political order and gave rise to the Conservative party (opp. WHIG). 3 a colonist loyal to the English during the American Revolution. ●adj. colloq. = CONSERVATIVE adj. 3. □□ **To·ry·ism** n. [orig. = Irish outlaw, prob. f. Ir. f. tóir pursue]

tosh /tosh/ n. esp. Brit. colloq. rubbish; nonsense. [19th c.: orig. unkn.]

toss /taws, tos/ v. & n. ●v. 1 tr. throw up (a ball, etc.) esp. with the hand. 2 tr. & intr. roll about, throw, or be thrown, restlessly or from side to side (the ship tossed on the ocean; was tossing and turning all night; tossed her head angrily). 3 tr. (usu. foll. by to, away, aside, out, etc.) throw (a thing) lightly or carelessly (tossed the letter away). 4 tr. **a** throw (a coin) into the air to decide a choice, etc., by the side on which it lands. **b** (also absol.; often foll. by for) settle a question or dispute with (a person) in this way (tossed him for the armchair; tossed for it). 5 tr. **a** (of a bull, etc.) throw (a person, etc.) up with the horns. **b** (of a horse, etc.) throw (a rider) off its back. 6 tr. coat (food) with dressing, etc., by mixing or shaking. 7 tr. bandy about in debate; discuss (tossed the question back and forth). ●n. 1 the act or an instance of tossing (a coin, the head, etc.). 2 a fall, esp. from a horse. □ **tossing the caber** the Scottish sport of throwing a tree trunk. **toss oars** Brit. raise oars to an upright position in salute. **toss off 1** drink off at one swallow. 2 dispatch (work) rapidly or without effort (tossed off an omelette). 3 Brit. coarse sl. masturbate. **toss up** toss a coin to decide a choice, etc. □□ **toss·er** n. [16th c.: orig. unkn.]

toss-up n. 1 a doubtful matter; a close thing (it's a toss-up whether he wins). 2 the tossing of a coin.

tos·ta·da /tōstaáadə/ n. a crisp fried tortilla, often topped with meat, cheese, etc. [Mex. Sp.]

tot¹ /tot/ n. 1 a small child (a tiny tot). 2 esp. Brit. a dram of liquor. [18th c., of dial. orig.]

tot² /tot/ v. & n. esp. Brit. ●v. (**tot·ted, tot·ting**) 1 tr. (usu. foll. by up) add (numbers, etc.). 2 intr. (foll. by up) (of items) mount up. ●n. Brit. archaic a set of figures to be added. □ **tot up to** amount to. [abbr. of TOTAL or of L totum the whole]

tot³ /tot/ v. & n. Brit. sl. ●v.intr. (**tot·ted, tot·ting**) collect salable items from refuse as an occupation. ●n. an article collected from refuse. [19th c.: orig. unkn.]

to·tal /tōt'l/ adj., n., & v. ●adj. 1 complete; comprising the whole (the total number of people). 2 absolute; unqualified (in total ignorance; total abstinence). ●n. a total number or amount. ●v. (**to·taled, to·tal·ing** or **to·talled, to·tal·ling**) 1 tr. amount in number to (they totaled 131). **b** find the total of (things, a set of numbers, etc.). 2 intr. (foll. by to, up to) amount to; mount up to. 3 tr. sl. wreck completely; demolish. □□ **to·tal·ly** adv. [ME f. OF f. med.L totalis f. totus entire]

to·tal ab·sti·nence n. abstaining completely from alcohol.

to·tal e·clipse n. an eclipse in which the whole disk (of the sun, moon, etc.) is obscured.

to·tal in·ter·nal re·flec·tion n. reflection without refraction of a light ray meeting the interface between two media at more than a certain critical angle to the normal.

to·tal·i·tar·i·an /tōtálitáireeən/ adj. & n. ●adj. of or relating to a centralized dictatorial form of government requiring complete subservience to the state. ●n. a person advocating such a system. □□ **to·tal·i·tar·i·an·ism** n.

to·tal·i·ty /tōtálitee/ n. 1 the complete amount or sum. 2 Astron. the time during which an eclipse is total.

to·tal·i·za·tor /tót'lizaytər/ n. (also **to·tal·i·sa·tor**) = PARI-MUTUEL 2.

to·tal·ize /tót'līz/ v.tr. collect into a total; find the total of. □□ **to·tal·i·za·tion** /-īzáyshən/ n.

to·tal·iz·er /tót'līzər/ n. = TOTALIZATOR.

to·tal re·call n. the ability to remember every detail of one's experience clearly.

to·tal war n. a war in which all available weapons and resources are employed.

tote¹ /tōt/ n. sl. 1 a totalizator. 2 a lottery. [abbr.]

tote² /tōt/ v.tr. colloq. carry or convey, esp. a heavy load (toting a gun). □□ **tot·er** n. (also in comb.). [17th-c. US, prob. of dial. orig.]

tote bag n. a large open-topped bag for shopping, etc.

tote box n. a small container for tools, etc.

to·tem /tōtəm/ n. 1 a natural object, esp. an animal, adopted by Native American people as an emblem of a clan or an individual. 2 an image of this. □□ **to·tem·ic** /-témik/ adj. **to·tem·ism** n. **to·tem·ist** n. **to·tem·is·tic** /-təmístik/ adj. [Algonquian]

to·tem pole n. 1 a pole on which totems are carved or hung. 2 a hierarchy.

toth·er /túthər/ adj. & pron. (also **t'oth·er**) dial. or joc. the other. □ **tell tother from which** Brit. joc. tell one from the other. [ME the tother, for earlier thet other 'that other'; now understood as = the other]

tot·ter /tótər/ v. & n. ●v.intr. 1 stand or walk unsteadily or feebly (tottered out of the bar). 2 a (of a building, etc.) shake or rock as if about to collapse. **b** (of a system of government, etc.) be about to fall. ●n. an unsteady or shaky movement or gait. □□ **tot·ter·er** n. **tot·ter·y** adj. [ME f. MDu. touteren to swing]

tot·ting-up n. 1 the adding of separate items. 2 Brit. the adding of convictions for driving offenses to cause disqualification.

tou·can /tŏŏkan/ n. any tropical American fruit-eating bird of the family Ramphastidae, with an immense beak and brightly colored plumage. [Tupi tucana, Guarani tucã]

touch /tuch/ v. & n. ●v. 1 tr. come into or be in physical contact with (another thing) at one or more points. 2 tr. (often foll. by with) bring the hand, etc., into contact with (touched her arm). 3 a intr. (of two things, etc.) be in or come into contact with one another (the balls were touching). **b** tr. bring (two things) into mutual contact (they touched hands). 4 tr. rouse tender or painful feelings in (was touched by his appeal). 5 tr. strike lightly (just touched the wall with the back bumper). 6 tr. (usu. with neg.) **a** disturb or harm (don't touch

totem pole

toucan

my things). **b** have any dealings with (*won't touch bricklaying*). **c** consume; use up; make use of (*dare not touch alcohol; has not touched her breakfast; need not touch your savings*). **d** cope with; affect; manage (*soap won't touch this dirt*). **7** *tr.* **a** deal with (a subject) lightly or in passing (*touched the matter of their expenses*). **b** concern (*it touches you closely*). **8** *tr.* **a** reach or rise as far as, esp. momentarily (*the thermometer touched 90 °*). **b** (usu. with *neg.*) approach in excellence, etc. (*can't touch him for style*). **9** *tr.* affect slightly; modify (*pity touched with fear*). **10** *tr.* (as **touched** *adj.*) slightly mad. **11** *tr.* esp. Art mark lightly; put in (features, etc.) with a brush, pencil, etc. **12** *tr.* **a** strike (the keys, strings, etc., of a musical instrument). **b** strike the keys or strings of (a piano, etc.). **13** *tr.* (usu. foll. by *for*) *sl.* ask for and get money, etc., from (a person) as a loan or gift (*touched him for $5*). **14** *tr.* injure slightly (*blossom touched by frost*). **15** *tr.* *Geom.* be tangent to (a curve). • *n.* **1** the act or an instance of touching, esp. with the body or hand (*felt a touch on my arm*). **2 a** the faculty of perception through physical contact, esp. with the fingers (*has no sense of touch in her right hand*). **b** the qualities of an object, etc., as perceived in this way (*the soft touch of silk*). **3** a small amount; a slight trace (*a touch of salt; a touch of irony*). **4 a** a musician's manner of playing keys or strings. **b** the manner in which the keys or strings respond to touch. **c** an artist's or writer's style of workmanship, writing, etc. (*has a delicate touch*). **5** a distinguishing quality or trait (*a professional touch*). **6** (esp. in *pl.*) **a** a light stroke with a pen, pencil, etc. **b** a slight alteration or improvement (*speech needs a few touches*). **7** = TAG². **8** (prec. by *a*) slightly (*is a touch too arrogant*). **9** *sl.* **a** the act of asking for and getting money, etc., from a person. **b** a person from whom money, etc., is so obtained. **10** *Soccer & Rugby* the part of the field outside the side limits. **11** *archaic* a test with or as if with a touchstone (*put it to the touch*). □ **at a touch** if touched, however lightly (*opened at a touch*). **get** (or **put**) **in** (or **into**) **touch with** come or cause to come into communication with; contact. **in touch** (often foll. by *with*) **1** in communication (*we're still in touch after all these years*). **2** up to date, esp. regarding news, etc. (*keeps in touch with events*). **3** aware; conscious; empathetic (*not in touch with her own feelings*). **keep in touch** (often foll. by *with*) **1** remain informed (*kept in touch with the latest developments*). **2** continue correspondence, a friendship, etc. **lose touch** (often foll. by *with*) **1** cease to be informed. **2** cease to correspond with or be in contact with another person. **lose one's touch** not show one's customary skill. **out of touch** (often foll. by *with*) **1** not in correspondence. **2** not up to date or modern. **3** lacking in awareness or sympathy (*out of touch with his son's beliefs*). **to the touch** when touched (*was cold to the touch*). **touch and go** uncertain regarding a result; risky (*it was touch and go whether we'd catch the train*). **touch at** (of a ship) call at (a port, etc.). **touch base** (**with**) make contact with; briefly communicate with. **touch bottom 1** reach the bottom of water with one's feet. **2** be at the lowest or worst point. **3** be in possession of the full facts. **touch down** (of an aircraft or spacecraft) make contact with the ground in landing. **touch off 1** represent exactly (in a portrait, etc.). **2** explode by touching with a match, etc. **3** initiate (a process) suddenly (*touched off a run on the peso*). **touch on** (or **upon**) **1** treat (a subject) briefly, refer to or mention casually. **2** verge on (*that touches on impudence*). **touch the spot** = **hit the spot. touch up 1** give finishing touches to or retouch (a picture, writing, etc.). **2** *Brit. sl.* **a** caress so as to excite sexually. **b** sexually molest. **3** strike (a horse) lightly with a whip. **touch wood** esp. *Brit.* touch something wooden with the hand to avert bad luck. **would not touch with a bargepole** see BARGEPOLE. □□ **touch•a•ble** *adj.* **touch•er** *n.* [ME f. OF *tochier, tuchier* (v.), *touche* (n.): prob. imit., imitating a knock]

touch-and-go *n.* an airplane landing and immediate takeoff done esp. as practice.

touch•back /túchbak/ *n. Football* a play in which the ball is downed behind the goal line after it has been caught there; the ball is put back in play at the 20-yard line of the team making the catch, who then take over on offense.

touch•down /túchdown/ *n.* **1** the act or an instance of an aircraft or spacecraft making contact with the ground during landing. **2** *Football* the act or an instance of scoring by crossing the goal line.

tou•ché /tōōsháy/ *int.* **1** the acknowledgment of a hit by a fencing opponent. **2** the acknowledgment of a justified accusation, a witticism, or a point made in reply to one's own. [F, past part. of *toucher* TOUCH]

touch foot•ball *n.* football with touching in place of tackling.

touch•ing /túching/ *adj. & prep.* • *adj.* moving; pathetic (*a touching incident; touching confidence*). • *prep.* concerning; about. □□ **touch•ing•ly** *adv.* **touch•ing•ness** *n.* [ME f. TOUCH: (prep.) f. OF *touchant* pres. part. (as TOUCH)]

touch-in-goal *n. Soccer* each of the four corners enclosed by continuations of the touchlines and goal lines.

touch•line /túchlīn/ *n.* (in various sports) either of the lines marking the side boundaries of the field.

touch•mark /túchmaark/ *n.* the maker's mark on pewter.

touch-me-not *n.* any of various plants of the genus *Impatiens*, with ripe seed capsules bursting open when touched.

touch-nee•dle *n.* a needle of gold or silver alloy of known composition used as a standard in testing other alloys on a touchstone.

touch of na•ture *n.* **1** a natural trait. **2** *colloq.* an exhibition of human feeling with which others sympathize (from a misinterpretation of Shakesp. *Troilus and Cressida* III. iii. 169).

touch of the sun *n.* **1** a slight attack of sunstroke. **2** a little sunlight.

touch pa•per *n.* paper impregnated with niter, for firing gunpowder, fireworks, etc.

touch•stone /túchstōn/ *n.* **1** a fine-grained dark schist or jasper used for testing alloys of gold, etc., by marking it with them and observing the color of the mark. **2** a standard or criterion.

touch-tone *adj. & n.* • *adj.* of or relating to a tone dialing telephone system. • *n.* **1** (**Touch-Tone**) *Trademark* a telephone that produces tones when buttons are pushed. **2** one of the set of tones generated by such a telephone.

touch-type *v.* type without looking at the keys. □□ **touch-typ•ing** *n.* **touch-typ•ist** *n.*

touch•wood /túchwŏŏd/ *n.* readily flammable wood, esp. when made soft by fungi, used as tinder.

touch•y /túchee/ *adj.* (**touch•i•er, touch•i•est**) **1** apt to take offense; overly sensitive. **2** not to be touched without danger; ticklish; risky; awkward. □□ **touch•i•ly** *adv.* **touch•i•ness** *n.* [perh. alt. of TETCHY after TOUCH]

tough /tuf/ *adj. & n.* • *adj.* **1** hard to break, cut, tear, or chew; durable; strong. **2** (of a person) able to endure hardship; hardy. **3** unyielding; stubborn; difficult (*it was a tough job; a tough customer*). **4** *colloq.* **a** acting sternly; hard (*get tough with*). **b** (of circumstances, luck, etc.) severe; unpleasant; hard; unjust. **5** *colloq.* criminal or violent (*tough guys*). • *n.* a tough person, esp. a gangster or criminal. □ **tough it out** *colloq.* endure or withstand difficult conditions. □□ **tough•en** *v.tr. & intr.* **tough•en•er** *n.* **tough•ish** *adj.* **tough•ly** *adv.* **tough•ness** *n.* [OE *tōh*]

tough guy *n. colloq.* **1** a hard unyielding person. **2** a violent aggressive person.

tough•ie (also **tough•y**) /túfee/ *n. colloq.* a tough person or problem.

tough-mind•ed *adj.* realistic; not sentimental. □□ **tough-mind•ed•ness** *n.*

tou•pee /tōōpáy/ *n.* a wig or artificial hairpiece to cover a bald spot. [F *toupet* hair tuft dimin. of OF *toup* tuft (as TOP¹)]

tour /tŏŏr/ *n. & v.* • *n.* **1 a** a journey from place to place as a vacation. **b** an excursion, ramble, or walk (*made a tour of the yard*). **2 a** a period of duty on military or diplomatic service. **b** the time to be spent at a particular post. **3** a series of performances, games, etc., at different places on a route through a country, etc. • *v.* **1** *intr.* (usu. foll. by *through*) make a tour (*toured through Italy*). **2** *tr.* make a tour of (a country, etc.). □ **on tour** (esp. of a team, theater company, etc.) touring. [ME f. OF *to(u)r* f. L *tornus* f. Gk *tornos* lathe]

tou•ra•co var. of TURACO.

tour de force /tŏŏr də fáwrs/ *n.* a feat of strength or skill. [F]

tour•er /tŏŏrər/ *n.* a vehicle, esp. a car, for touring. [TOUR]

tour•ing car *n.* a car with room for passengers and much luggage.

tour op•er•a•tor *n.* a travel agent specializing in package tours.

tour•ism /tŏŏrizəm/ *n.* the organization and operation of tours, esp. as a commercial enterprise.

tour•ist /tŏŏrist/ *n.* a person making a visit or tour as a vacation; a traveler. (often *attrib.*: *tourist accommodations*). □□ **tour•is•tic** *adj.* **tour•is•ti•cal•ly** *adv.*

tour•ist class *n.* the lowest class of passenger accommodations in a ship, aircraft, etc.

tour•ist•y /tŏŏristee/ *adj.* usu. *derog.* appealing to or visited by many tourists.

tour•ma•line /tŏŏrməlin, –leen/ *n.* a boron aluminum silicate mineral of various colors, possessing unusual electrical properties, and used in electrical and optical instruments and as a gemstone. [F f. Sinh. *toramalli* porcelain]

tour•na•ment /tŏŏrnəmənt, tór–/ *n.* **1** any contest of skill between a number of competitors, esp. played in heats or a series of games (*chess tournament; tennis tournament*). **2** (in the UK) a display of military exercises, etc. (*Royal Tournament*). **3** *hist.* **a** a pageant in which jousting with blunted weapons took place. **b** a meeting for jousting between single knights for a prize, etc. [ME f. OF *torneiement* f. *torneier* TOURNEY]

tour•ne•dos /tŏŏrnədō/ *n.* (*pl.* same /–dōz/) a small round thick cut from a tenderloin of beef. [F]

tour•ney /tŏŏrnee, tór–/ *n. & v.* • *n.* (*pl.* **–neys**) a tournament. • *v.intr.* (**–neys, –neyed**) take part in a tournament. [ME f. OF *tornei* (n.), *torneier* (v.), ult. f. L *tornus* a turn]

tour•ni•quet /tŏŏrnikit, tŏŏr–/ *n.* a device for stopping the flow of blood through

tourniquet

an artery by twisting a dowel, etc., in a ligature or bandage. [F prob. f. OF *tournicle* coat of mail, TUNICLE, infl. by *tourner* TURN]

tou•sle /tówzəl/ *v.tr.* **1** make (esp. the hair) untidy; rumple. **2** handle roughly or rudely. [frequent. of (now dial.) *touse*, ME f. OE rel. to OHG −*zuson*]

tous-les-mois /tŏŏlaymwaá/ *n.* **1** food starch obtained from tubers of a canna, *Canna indica*. **2** this plant. [F, lit. = every month, prob. corrupt. of W.Ind. *toloman*]

tout /towt/ *v. & n.* ● *v.* **1** *intr.* (usu. foll. by *for*) solicit patronage persistently; pester customers (*touting for business*). **2** *tr.* solicit the patronage of (a person) or for (a thing). **3** *intr.* **a** *Brit.* spy out the movements and condition of racehorses in training. **b** offer racing tips for a share of the resulting profit. ● *n.* a person employed in touting. □□ **tout•er** *n.*

WORD HISTORY **tout**

Old English *tȳtan* ' look out,' of Germanic origin; related to Dutch *tuit* ' spout, nozzle.' The Old English meaning gave rise to the sense ' be on the lookout,' hence 'be on the lookout for customers, solicit' (mid-18th century), also 'watch, spy on' (early 19th century).

tout de suite /tŏŏt swéet/ *adv.* at once, immediately. [F]

to•va•rich /təvaárish/ *n.* (also **to•va•rish**) (in esp. communist Russia) comrade (esp. as a form of address). [Russ. *tovarishch*]

tow[1] /tō/ *v. & n.* ● *v.tr.* **1** (of a motor vehicle, horse, or person controlling it) pull (a boat, another motor vehicle, a trailer, etc.) along by a rope, tow bar, etc. **2** pull (a person or thing) along behind one. ● *n.* the act or an instance of towing; the state of being towed. □ **have in** (or **on**) **tow 1** be towing. **2** be accompanied by and often in charge of (a person). □□ **tow•a•ble** *adj.* **tow•age** /tóij/ *n.* [OE *togian* f. Gmc, rel. to TUG]

tow[2] /tō/ *n.* **1** the coarse and broken part of flax or hemp prepared for spinning. **2** a loose bunch of rayon, etc., strands. □□ **tow•y** /tóee/ *adj.* [ME f. MLG *touw* f. OS *tou*, rel. to ON *tó* wool: cf. TOOL]

to•ward /tawrd, təwáwrd, twawrd/ *prep. & adj.* (also **towards** /tawrdz, təwáwrdz, twawrdz/) ● *prep.* **1** in the direction of (*set out toward town*). **2** as regards; in relation to (*his attitude toward death*). **3** as a contribution to; for (*put this toward your expenses*). **4** near (*toward the end of our journey*). ● *adj. archaic* **1** about to take place; in process. **2** docile; apt. **3** promising; auspicious. □□ **to•ward•ness** *n.* (in sense of *adj.*). [OE *tōweard* (adj.) f. TO, −WARD]

tow bar *n.* a bar for towing, esp. a trailer or camper.

tow-col•ored *adj.* (of hair) very light blonde.

tow•el /tówəl/ *n. & v.* ● *n.* **1 a** a piece of absorbent cloth used for drying oneself or a thing after washing. **b** absorbent paper used for this. **c** a cloth used for drying plates, dishes, etc.; a dish towel. **2** *Brit.* = SANITARY NAPKIN. ● *v.* (**tow•eled, tow•el•ing** or **tow•elled, tow•el•ling**) **1** *tr.* (often *refl.*) wipe or dry with a towel. **2** *intr.* wipe or dry oneself with a towel. **3** *tr. sl.* thrash. □□ **tow•el•ing** or **tow•el•ling** *n.* [ME f. OF *toail(l)e* f. Gmc]

tow•el rack *n.* (also **tow•el horse** or **tow•el rail**) a rail, esp. one attached to a wall, for hanging towels on.

tow•er /tówər/ *n. & v.* ● *n.* **1 a** a tall esp. square or circular structure, often part of a church, castle, etc. **b** a fortress, etc., comprising or including a tower. **c** a tall structure housing machinery, apparatus, operators, etc. (*cooling tower; control tower*). **2** a place of defense; a protection. ● *v.intr.* **1** (usu. foll. by *above, high*) reach or be high or above; be superior. **2** (of a bird) soar or hover. **3** (as **towering** *adj.*) **a** high, lofty (*towering intellect*). **b** violent (*towering rage*). □□ **tow•ered** /tówərd/ *adj.* **tow•er•y** *adj.* [OE *torr*, & ME *tūr*, AF & OF *tur*, etc., f. L *turris* f. Gk]

tow•er block *n. Brit.* a tall building containing offices or apartments.

tow•er of strength *n.* a person who gives strong and reliable support.

tow•head /tóhed/ *n.* **1** tow-colored or blond hair. **2** a person with such hair. □□ **tow•head•ed** *adj.*

town /town/ *n.* **1 a** an urban area with a name, defined boundaries, and local government, being larger than a village and usu. not incorporated as a city. **b** any densely populated area, esp. as opposed to the country or suburbs. **c** the people of a town (*the whole town knows of it*). **2 a** *Brit.* London or the chief city or town in an area (*went up to town*). **b** the central business or shopping area in a neighborhood (*just going into town*). **3** the permanent residents of a university town as distinct from the members of the university (cf. GOWN). □ **go to town** *colloq.* act or work with energy or enthusiasm. **on the town** *colloq.* enjoying the entertainments, esp. the nightlife, of a town; celebrating. □□ **town•ish** *adj.* **town•less** *adj.* **town•let** *n.* **town•ward** *adj. & adv.* **town•wards** *adv.* [OE *tūn* enclosure f. Gmc]

town clerk *n.* the officer of a town in charge of records, etc.

town coun•cil *n.* (esp. in the UK) the elective governing body in a municipality.

town coun•ci•lor *n.* (esp. in the UK) an elected member of this.

town cri•er *n. hist.* a person employed to make public announcements in the streets or marketplace of a town..

tow net *n.* (also **tow•ing net**) a net used for dragging through water to collect specimens.

town hall *n.* a building for the administration of local government, having public meeting rooms, etc.

town house *n.* **1** a town residence, esp. of a person with a house in the country. **2** a row house. **3** a house in a development. **4** *Brit.* a town hall.

town•ie /tównee/ *n.* (also *Brit.* **town•ee**) *colloq.* a person living in a town, esp. as opposed to a student, etc.

town meet•ing *n.* a meeting of the voters of a town for the transaction of public business.

town plan•ning *n.* the planning of the construction and growth of towns.

town•scape /tównskayp/ *n.* **1** the visual appearance of a town or towns. **2** a picture of a town.

towns•folk /tównzfōk/ *n.* the inhabitants of a particular town or towns.

town•ship /tównship/ *n.* **1** *S.Afr.* **a** an urban area formerly set aside for black residents. **b** a white urban area (esp. if new or about to be developed). **2** *US & Can.* **a** a division of a county in some states with some corporate powers. **b** a district six miles square in some states. **3** *Brit. hist.* **a** a community inhabiting a manor, parish, etc. **b** a manor or parish as a territorial division. **c** a small town or village forming part of a large parish. **4** *Austral. & NZ* a small town; a town site. [OE *tūnscipe* (as TOWN, −SHIP)]

towns•man /tównzmən/ *n.* (*pl.* −**men;** *fem.* **towns•wom•an,** *pl.* −**wom•en**) an inhabitant of a town; a fellow citizen.

towns•peo•ple /tównzpeepəl/ *n.pl.* the people of a town.

tow•y see TOW[2].

tox•e•mi•a /tokseémeeə/ *n.* (*Brit.* **tox•ae•mi•a**) **1** blood poisoning. **2** a condition in pregnancy characterized by increased blood pressure. □□ **tox•e•mic** *adj.* [as TOXI- + −EMIA]

toxi- /tóksee/ *comb. form* (also **toxico-** /tóksikō/, **toxo-** /tóksō/) poison; poisonous; toxic.

tox•ic /tóksik/ *adj.* **1** of or relating to poison (*toxic symptoms*). **2** poisonous (*toxic gas*). **3** caused by poison (*toxic anemia*). □□ **tox•i•cal•ly** *adv.* **tox•ic•i•ty** /−sísitee/ *n.* [med.L *toxicus* poisoned f. L *toxicum* f. Gk *toxikon* (*pharmakon*) (poison for) arrows f. *toxon* bow, *toxa* arrows]

tox•i•col•o•gy /tóksikóləjee/ *n.* the scientific study of poisons. □□ **tox•i•co•log•i•cal** /−kəlójikəl/ *adj.* **tox•i•col•o•gist** *n.*

tox•in /tóksin/ *n.* a poison produced by a living organism, esp. one formed in the body and stimulating the production of antibodies. [TOXIC + −IN]

tox•o•car•a /tóksōkaárə/ *n.* any nematode worm of the genus *Toxocara*, parasitic in the alimentary canal of dogs and cats. □□ **tox•o•ca•ri•a•sis** /−kəríəsis/ *n.* [*toxo-* (see TOXI-) + Gk *kara* head]

tox•oph•i•lite /toksófilīt/ *n. & adj.* ● *n.* a student or lover of archery. ● *adj.* of or concerning archery. □□ **tox•oph•i•ly** *n.* [Ascham's *Toxophilus* (1545) f. Gk *toxon* bow + −*philos* −PHILE]

toy /toy/ *n. & v.* ● *n.* **1 a** a plaything, esp. for a child. **b** (often *attrib.*) a model or miniature replica of a thing, esp. as a plaything (*toy gun*). **2 a** a thing, esp. a gadget or instrument, regarded as providing amusement or pleasure. **b** a task or undertaking regarded in an unserious way. **3** (usu. *attrib.*) a diminutive breed or variety of dog, etc. ● *v.intr.* (usu. foll. by *with*) **1** trifle; amuse oneself, esp. with a person's affections; flirt (*toyed with the idea of going to Africa*). **2 a** move a material object idly (*toyed with her necklace*). **b** nibble at food, etc., unenthusiastically (*toyed with a peach*). [16th c.: earlier = dallying, fun, jest, whim, trifle: orig. unkn.]

toy box *n.* a usu. wooden box for keeping toys in.

toy boy *n.* esp. *Brit.* a male lover who is much younger than his partner (see BOY 1).

toy sol•dier *n.* **1** a miniature figure of a soldier. **2** *sl.* a soldier in a peacetime army.

tp. *abbr.* **1** (also **t.p.**) title page. **2** township. **3** troop.

tpk. *abbr.* turnpike.

tra•be•a•tion /tráybeeáyshən/ *n.* the use of beams instead of arches or vaulting in construction. □□ **tra•be•ate** /tráybeeət, −ayt/ *adj.* [L *trabs trabis* beam]

tra•bec•u•la /trəbékyələ/ *n.* (*pl.* **tra•bec•u•lae** /−lee/) **1** *Anat.* a supporting band or bar of connective or bony tissue, esp. dividing an organ into chambers. **2** *Bot.* a beamlike projection or process within a hollow structure. □□ **tra•bec•u•lar** *adj.* **tra•bec•u•late** /−lət, −layt/ *adj.* [L, dimin. of *trabs* beam]

trace[1] /trays/ *v. & n.* ● *v.tr.* **1 a** observe, discover, or find vestiges or signs of by investigation. **b** (often foll. by *along, through, to,* etc.) follow or mark the track or position of (*traced their footprints in the mud; traced the outlines of a wall*). **c** (often foll. by *back*) follow to its origins (*can trace my family to the 12th century; the report has been traced back to you*). **2** (often foll. by *over*) copy (a drawing, etc.) by drawing over its lines on a superimposed piece of translucent paper, or by using carbon paper. **3** (often foll. by *out*) mark out, delineate, sketch, or write, often laboriously (*traced out a plan of the* *district; traced out his vision of the future*). **4** pursue one's way along (a path, etc.). ● *n.* **1 a** a sign or mark or other indication of something having existed; a vestige (*no trace remains of the castle; has the traces of a vanished beauty*). **b** a very small quantity. **c** an amount of rainfall, etc., too small to be measured. **2** a track or footprint left by a person or animal. **3** a track left by the moving pen of an instrument, etc. **4** a line on the screen of a cathode-ray tube showing the path of a moving spot. **5** a curve's projection on or intersection with a plane, etc. **6** a change in the brain caused by learning processes. □□ **trace·a·ble** *adj.* **trace·a·bil·i·ty** /tráysə bílitee/ *n.* **trace·less** *adj.* [ME f. OF *trace* (n.), *tracier* (v.) f. L *tractus* drawing: see TRACT[1]]

trace[2] /trays/ *n.* each of the two straps, chains, or ropes by which a horse draws a vehicle. □ **kick over the traces** become insubordinate or reckless. [ME f. OF *trais*, pl. of TRAIT]

trace el·e·ment *n.* **1** a chemical element occurring in minute amounts. **2** a chemical element required only in minute amounts by living organisms for normal growth.

trace fos·sil *n.* a fossil that represents a burrow, footprint, etc., of an organism.

trace horse *n.* a horse that draws in traces or by a single trace, esp. one hitched on to help draw uphill, etc.

trac·er /tráysər/ *n.* **1** a person or thing that traces. **2** *Mil.* a bullet, etc., that is visible in flight because of flames, etc., emitted. **3** an artificially produced radioactive isotope capable of being followed through the body by the radiation it produces.

trac·er·y /tráysəree/ *n.* (*pl.* –ies) **1** ornamental stone openwork, esp. in the upper part of a Gothic window. **2** a fine decorative pattern. **3** a natural object finely patterned. □□ **trac·er·ied** *adj.*

tra·che·a /tráykeeə/ *n.* (*pl.* **tra·che·ae** /–kee-ee/ or **tra·che·as**) **1** the passage, reinforced by rings of cartilage, through which air reaches the bronchial tubes from the larynx; the windpipe. **2** each of the air passages of the body of an insect, etc. **3** any duct or vessel in a plant. □□ **tra·che·al** /tráykeeəl/ *adj.* **tra·che·ate** /tráykeeayt/ *adj.* [ME f. med.L, = LL *trachia* f. Gk *trakheia (artēria)* rough (artery), f. *trakhus* rough]

tracheo- /tráykeeō/ *comb. form* of or relating to the trachea (*tracheotomy*).

tra·che·ot·o·my /traykeeótəmee/ *n.* (also **tra·che·os·to·my** /–óstəmee/) (*pl.* –mies) an incision made in the trachea to relieve an obstruction to breathing.

tra·che·ot·o·my tube *n.* a breathing tube inserted into a tracheotomy.

tra·cho·ma /trəkómə/ *n.* a contagious disease of the eye with inflamed granulation on the inner surface of the lids. □□ **tra·chom·a·tous** /–kómətəs, –kómətəs/ *adj.* [mod.L f. Gk *trakhōma* f. *trakhus* rough]

tra·chyte /trákit, trayk–/ *n.* a light-colored volcanic rock rough to the touch. □□ **tra·chyt·ic** /trə kítik/ *adj.* [F f. Gk *trakhutēs* roughness (as TRACHOMA)]

trac·ing /tráysing/ *n.* **1** a copy of a drawing, etc., made by tracing. **2** = TRACE[1] *n.* 3. **3** the act or an instance of tracing. □ **tracing paper** translucent paper used for making tracings.

track[1] /trak/ *n. & v.* ● *n.* **1 a** a mark or marks left by a person, animal, or thing in passing. **b** (in *pl.*) such marks, esp. footprints. **2 a** rough path, esp. one beaten by use. **3** a continuous railway line (*laid three miles of track*). **4 a** a course for racing horses, dogs, etc. **b** a prepared course for runners, etc. **c** various sports performed on a track, as running or hurdles. **5 a** a groove on a phonograph record. **b** a section of a phonograph record, compact disk, etc., containing one song, etc. (*this side has six tracks*). **c** a lengthwise strip of magnetic tape containing one sequence of signals. **6 a** a line of travel, passage, or motion (*followed the track of the hurricane; Canada followed in the same track*). **b** the path traveled by a ship, aircraft, etc. (cf.

COURSE *n.* 2c). **7** a continuous band around the wheels of a tank, tractor, etc. **8** the transverse distance between a vehicle's wheels. **9** = SOUNDTRACK. **10** a line of reasoning or thought (*this track proved fruitless*). **11** any of several levels of instruction to which students are assigned based on their abilities, interests, etc. **12** a course of action or planned future (*management track*) ● *v.* **1** *tr.* follow the track of (an animal, person, spacecraft, etc.). **2** in possession of a clue to a person's conduct, plans, etc.; trace by vestiges. **3** *intr.* (often foll. by *back, in,* etc.) (of a movie or television camera) move in relation to the subject being filmed. **4** *intr.* (of wheels) run so that the back ones are exactly in the track of the front ones. **5** *intr.* (of a record stylus) follow a groove. **6** *tr.* **a** make a track with (dirt, etc.) from the feet. **b** leave such a track on (a floor, etc.). □ **in one's tracks** *colloq.* where one stands; then and there (*stopped him in his tracks*). **keep** (or **lose**) **track of** follow (or fail to follow) the course or development of. **make tracks** *colloq.* go or run away. **make tracks for** *colloq.* go in pursuit of or toward. **off the track** away from the subject. **on a person's track 1** in pursuit of him or her. **2** in possession of a clue to a person's conduct, plans, etc. **on the wrong side of** (or **across**) **the tracks** *colloq.* in an inferior or dubious part of town. **on the wrong** (or **right**) **track** following the wrong (or right) line of inquiry. **track down** reach or capture by tracking. **track with** *Austral. sl.* associate with; court. □□ **track·age** *n.* [ME f. OF *trac*, perh. f. LG or Du. *tre (c)k* draft, etc.]

track[2] /trak/ *Brit. v.* **1** *tr.* tow (a boat) by rope, etc., from a bank. **2** *intr.* travel by being towed. [app. f. Du. *trekken* to draw, etc., assim. to TRACK[1]]

track·ball *n.* a small ball set in a holder that can be rotated by hand to move a cursor on a computer screen.

track·er /trákər/ *n.* **1** a person or thing that tracks. **2** a police dog tracking by scent. **3** a wooden connecting rod in the mechanism of an organ.

track e·vents *n.pl.* running races as opposed to jumping, etc. (cf. FIELD EVENTS).

track·ing /tráking/ *n.* **1** assignment of students in a track system. **2** *Electr.* the formation of a conducting path over the surface of an insulating material.

track·ing sta·tion *n.* an establishment set up to track objects in the sky.

track·lay·er /tráklayər/ *n.* **1** a person employed in laying or repairing railroad tracks. **2** a tractor or other vehicle equipped with continuous tracks (see TRACK[1] *n.* 7).

track·lay·ing *n. & adj.* ● *n.* the laying of railway track. ● *adj.* (of a vehicle) having a caterpillar tread.

track·less /tráklis/ *adj.* **1** without a track or tracks; untrodden. **2** leaving no track or trace. **3** not running on a track.

track·less trol·ley *n.* an electric bus running on the road, powered by a trolley wire.

track·man /trákmən/ *n.* (*pl.* –men) a tracklayer.

track rec·ord *n.* a person's past performance or achievements.

track shoe *n.* a spiked shoe worn by a runner.

track suit *n.* a loose warm suit worn by an athlete, etc., for exercising or jogging.

track sys·tem *n.* a system of grouping children of similar ability in education.

track·way /trákway/ *n.* a beaten path; an ancient roadway.

tract[1] /trakt/ *n.* **1** a region or area of indefinite, esp. large, extent (*pathless desert tracts*). **2** *Anat.* an area of an organ or system (*respiratory tract*). **3** *Brit. archaic* a period of time, etc. [L *tractus* drawing f. *trahere tract-* draw, pull]

tract[2] /trakt/ *n.* a short treatise in pamphlet form, esp. on a religious subject. [app. abbr. of L *tractatus* TRACTATE]

tract[3] /trakt/ *n. RC Ch. & Mus.* an anthem replacing the alleluia in some Masses. [med.L *tractus (cantus)* drawn out (song), past part. of L *trahere* draw]

trac·ta·ble /tráktəbəl/ *adj.* **1** (of a person) easily handled; manageable; docile. **2** (of material, etc.) pliant; malleable. □□ **trac·ta·bil·i·ty** /–bílitee/ *n.* **trac·ta·ble·ness** *n.* **trac·ta·bly** *adv.* [L *tractabilis* f. *tractare* handle, frequent. of *trahere tract-* draw]

Trac·tar·i·an·ism /tráktáireeənizəm/ *n. hist.* = OXFORD MOVEMENT. □□ **Trac·tar·i·an** *adj. & n.* [after *Tracts for the Times*, published in Oxford 1833 –41 and outlining the movement's principles]

trac·tate /tráktayt/ *n.* a treatise. [L *tractatus* f. *tractare*: see TRACTABLE]

trac·tion /trákshən/ *n.* **1** the act of drawing or pulling a thing over a surface, esp. a road or track (*steam traction*). **2 a** a sustained pulling on a limb, muscle, etc., by means of pulleys, weights, etc. **b** contraction, e.g., of a muscle. **3** the grip of a tire on a road, a wheel on a rail, etc. □□ **trac·tion·al** *adj.* **trac·tive** /tráktiv/ *adj.* [F *traction* or med.L *tractio* f. L *trahere tract-* draw]

trac·tion en·gine *n.* a steam or diesel engine for drawing heavy loads on roads, fields, etc.

trac·tion wheel *n.* the driving wheel of a locomotive, etc.

trac·tor /tráktər/ n. 1 a motor vehicle used for hauling, esp. farm machinery, heavy loads, etc. 2 a traction engine. [LL tractor (as TRACTION)]

trac·tor-trail·er n. a truck consisting of a tractor or cab unit attached to a trailer.

trad /trad/ n. & adj. esp. Brit. colloq. ● n. traditional jazz. ● adj. traditional. [abbr.]

trade /trayd/ n. & v. ● n. 1 a buying and selling. b buying and selling conducted between nations, etc. c business conducted for profit (esp. as distinct from a profession) (a butcher by trade). d business of a specified nature or time (Christmas trade; tourist trade). 2 a skilled craft, esp. requiring an apprenticeship (learned a trade; his trade is plumbing). 3 (usu. prec. by the) a the people engaged in a specific trade (the trade will never agree to it; trade inquiries only). b Brit. colloq. licensed victuallers. 4 a transaction, esp. a swap. 5 (usu. in pl.) a trade wind. ● v. 1 intr. (often foll. by in, with) engage in trade; buy and sell (trades in plastic novelties; we trade with Japan). 2 tr. a exchange in commerce; barter (goods). b exchange (insults, blows, etc.). 3 intr. (usu. foll. by with, for) have a transaction with a person for a thing. □ be in trade Brit. esp. derog. be in commerce, esp. keep a shop. trade in (often foll. by for) exchange (esp. a used car, etc.) in esp. part payment for another. trade off exchange, esp. as a compromise. trade on take advantage of (a person's credulity, one's reputation, etc.). □□ trad·a·ble, trade·a·ble adj. [ME f. MLG trade track f. OS trada, OHG trata: cf. TREAD]

Trade Board n. Brit. hist. a statutory body for settling disputes, etc., in certain industries.

trade book n.n. a book published by a commercial publisher and intended for general readership.

trade cy·cle n. Brit. recurring periods of boom and recession.

trade def·i·cit n. (also **trade gap**) the extent by which a country's imports exceed its exports.

trade-in n. a thing, esp. a car, exchanged in this way.

trade jour·nal n. a periodical containing news, etc., concerning a particular trade.

trade-last n. a compliment from a third person that is reported to the person complimented in exchange for one to the reporter.

trade·mark /tráydmaark/ n. 1 a device, word, or words, secured by legal registration or established by use as representing a company, product, etc. 2 a distinctive characteristic, etc.

trade name n. 1 a name by which a thing is called in a trade. 2 a name given to a product. 3 a name under which a business trades.

trade-off n. such an exchange.

trade pa·per n. = TRADE JOURNAL.

trade price n. a wholesale price charged to the dealer before goods are retailed.

trad·er /tráydər/ n. 1 a person engaged in trade. 2 a merchant ship.

tra·de·scan·tia /trádiskánteeə/ n. any usu. trailing plant of the genus Tradescantia, with large blue, white, or pink flowers. [mod.L f. J. Tradescant, Engl. naturalist d. 1638]

trade se·cret n. 1 a secret device or technique used esp. in a trade. 2 joc. any secret.

trades·man /tráydzmən/ n. (pl. –men; fem. **trades·wom·an**, pl. –wom·en) a person engaged in trading or a trade, as a skilled craftsman or Brit. a shopkeeper.

trades·peo·ple /tráydzpeepəl/ n.pl. people engaged in trade.

Trades Un·ion Con·gress n. Brit. the official representative body of British trade unions, meeting annually.

trade un·ion n. Brit. = LABOR UNION.

trade wind n. a wind blowing continually toward the equator and deflected westward, f. obs. blow trade = blow regularly.

trad·ing /tráyding/ n. the act of engaging in trade.

trad·ing es·tate n. esp. Brit. a specially designed industrial and commercial area.

trad·ing post n. a store, etc., established in a remote or unsettled region.

trad·ing stamp n. a stamp given to customers by some stores that is exchangeable in large numbers for various articles.

tra·di·tion /trədíshən/ n. 1 a a custom, opinion, or belief handed down to posterity, esp. orally or by practice. b this process of handing down. 2 esp. joc. an established practice or custom (it's a tradition to complain about the weather). 3 artistic, literary, etc, principles based on experience and practice; any one of these (stage tradition; traditions of the Dutch School). 4 Theol. doctrine or a particular doctrine, etc., claimed to have divine authority without documentary evidence, esp.: a the oral teaching of Christ and the Apostles. b the laws held by the Pharisees to have been delivered by God to Moses. c the words and deeds of Muhammad not in the Koran. 5 Law the formal delivery of property, etc. □□ **tra·di·tion·ar·y** adj. **tra·di·tion·ist** n. **tra·di·tion·less** adj. [ME f. OF tradicion or L traditio f. tradere hand on, betray (as TRANS-, dare give)]

tra·di·tion·al /trədíshənəl/ adj. 1 of, based on, or obtained by tradition. 2 (of jazz) in the style of the early 20th c. □□ **tra·di·tion·al·ly** adv.

tra·di·tion·al·ism /trədíshənəlizəm/ n. 1 respect, esp. excessive, for tradition, esp. in religion. 2 a philosophical system referring all religious knowledge to divine revelation and tradition. □□ **tra·di·tion·al·ist** n. **tra·di·tion·al·is·tic** adj.

tra·duce /trədoos, –dyoos/ v.tr. speak ill of; misrepresent. □□ **tra·duce·ment** n. **tra·duc·er** n. [L traducere disgrace (as TRANS-, ducere duct-lead)]

traf·fic /tráfik/ n. & v. ● n. 1 (often attrib.) a vehicles moving on a public highway, esp. of a specified kind, density, etc. (heavy traffic on the interstate; traffic cop). b such movement in the air or at sea. 2 (usu. foll. by in) trade, esp. illegal (the traffic in drugs). 3 a the transportation of goods; the coming and going of people or goods by road, rail, air, sea, etc. b the persons or goods so transported. 4 dealings or communication between people, etc. (had no traffic with them). 5 the messages, signals, etc., transmitted through a communications system; the flow or volume of such business. ● v. (traf·ficked, traf·fick·ing) 1 intr. (often foll. by in) deal in something, esp. illegally (trafficked in narcotics; traffics in innuendo). 2 tr. deal in; barter. □□ **traf·fick·er** n. **traf·fic·less** adj. [F traf(f)ique, Sp. tráfico, It. traffico, of unkn. orig.]

traf·fic cir·cle n. a road junction at which traffic moves in one direction around a central island.

traf·fic is·land n. a paved or grassy area in a road to divert traffic and provide a space for pedestrians.

traf·fic jam n. traffic at a standstill because of construction, an accident, or heavy congestion.

traf·fic light n. (also **traf·fic sig·nal**) a usu. automatic signal with colored lights to control road traffic, esp. at intersections.

traf·fic war·den n. Brit. a uniformed official employed to help control road traffic and esp. parking.

trag·a·canth /trágəkanth, tráj–/ n. a white or reddish gum from a plant, Astragalus gummifer, used in pharmaceuticals, calico printing, etc., as a vehicle for drugs, dye, etc. [F tragacante f. L tragacantha f. Gk tragakantha, name of a shrub, f. tragos goat + akantha thorn]

tra·ge·di·an /trəjéedeeən/ n. 1 a writer of tragedies. 2 an actor in tragedy. [ME f. OF tragediane (as TRAGEDY)]

tra·ge·di·enne /trəjéedee-én/ n. an actress in tragedy. [F fem. (as TRAGEDIAN)]

trag·e·dy /trájidee/ n. (pl. –dies) 1 a serious accident, crime, or natural catastrophe. 2 a sad event; a calamity (the team's defeat is a tragedy). 3 a a play in verse or prose dealing with tragic events and with an unhappy ending, esp. concerning the downfall of the protagonist. b tragic plays as a genre (cf. COMEDY). [ME f. OF tragedie f. L tragoedia f. Gk tragōidia f. tragos goat song + ōidē song]

trag·ic /trájik/ adj. 1 (also **trag·i·cal** /–kəl/) sad; calamitous; greatly distressing (a tragic tale). 2 of, or in the style of, tragedy (tragic drama; a tragic actor). ds>**trag·i·cal·ly** adv. [F tragique f. L tragicus f. Gk tragikos f. tragos goat: see TRAGEDY]

trag·i·com·e·dy /trájikómidee/ n. (pl. –dies) 1 a a play having a mixture of comedy and tragedy. b plays of this kind as a genre. 2 an event, etc., having tragic and comic elements. □□ **trag·i·com·ic** /–kómik/ adj. **trag·i·com·i·cal·ly** adv. [F tragicomédie or It. tragicomedia f. LL tragicomoedia f. L tragico-comoedia (as TRAGIC, COMEDY)]

trag·ic i·ro·ny n. a device, orig. in Greek tragedy, by which words carry a tragic, esp. prophetic, meaning to the audience, unknown to the character speaking.

trag·o·pan /trágəpan/ n. any Asian pheasant of the genus Tragopan, with erect fleshy horns on its head. [L f. Gk f. tragos goat + Pan the god Pan]

trail /trayl/ n. & v. ● n. 1 a a track left by a thing, person, etc., moving over a surface (left a trail of wreckage; a slug's slimy trail). b a track or scent followed in hunting, seeking, etc. (he's on the trail). 2 a beaten path or track, esp. through a wild region. 3 a part dragging behind a thing or person; an appendage (a trail of smoke; a condensation trail). 4 the rear end of a gun carriage stock. ● v. 1 tr. & intr. draw or be drawn along behind, esp. on the ground. 2 intr. (often foll. by behind) walk wearily; lag; straggle. 3 tr. follow the trail of; pursue (trailed him to his home). 4 intr. be losing in a game or other contest (trailing by three points). 5 intr. (usu. foll. by away, off) peter out; tail off. 6 intr. a (of a plant, etc.) grow or hang over a wall, along the ground, etc. b (of a garment, etc.) hang loosely. 7 tr. (often refl.) drag (oneself, one's limbs, etc.) along wearily, etc. 8 tr. advertise (a movie, a radio or television program, etc.) in advance by showing extracts, etc. 9 tr. apply (slip) through a nozzle or spout to decorate pottery. □ **trail one's coat** deliberately provoke a quarrel, fight, etc. [ME (earlier as verb) f. OF traillier to tow, or f. MLG treilen haul f. L tragula dragnet]

trail bike n. a light motorcycle for use in rough terrain.

trail·blaz·er /tráylblayzər/ n. 1 a person who marks a new track through wild country. 2 a pioneer; an innovator.

trail·blaz·ing /tráylblayzing/ n. & attrib.adj. ● n. the act or process of blazing a trail. ● attrib.adj. that blazes a trail; pioneering.

trail·er /tráylər/ n. 1 a person or thing that trails. 2 a series of brief extracts from a movie, etc., used to advertise it in advance. 3 a vehicle towed by another, esp.: a the rear section of a tractor-trailer.

b an open cart. **c** a platform for transporting a boat, etc. **d** a camper. **4** a mobile home. **5** a trailing plant.

trail•er park *n.* a place where trailers are parked as dwellings, often with special amenities.

trailing arbutus *n.* the mayflower, *Epigaea repens*, a creeping plant of the heath family with pink or white flowers.

trail•ing edge *n.* **1** the rear edge of an aircraft's wing, etc. **2** *Electronics* the part of a pulse in which the amplitude diminishes (opp. LEADING EDGE 2).

trail•ing wheel *n.* a wheel not given direct motive power.

train /trayn/ *v. & n.* • *v.* **1 a** *tr.* (often foll. by *to* + infin.) teach (a person, animal, oneself, etc.) a specified skill, esp. by practice (*trained the dog to beg; was trained in midwifery*). **b** *intr.* undergo this process (*trained as a teacher*). **2** *tr. & intr.* bring or come into a state of physical fitness by exercise, diet, etc.; undergo physical exercise, esp. for a specific purpose (*trained me for the high jump; the team trains every evening*). **3** *tr.* cause (a plant) to grow in a required shape (*trained the peach tree up the wall*). **4** (usu. as **trained** *adj.*) make (the mind, eye, etc.) sharp or discerning as a result of instruction, practice, etc. **5** *tr.* (often foll. by *on*) point or aim (a gun, camera, etc.) at an object, etc. **6** *colloq.* **a** *intr.* go by train. **b** *tr.* esp. *Brit.* (foll. by *it* as object) make a journey by train (*trained it to Aberdeen*). **7** *tr.* (usu. foll. by *away*) *archaic* entice; lure. • *n.* **1** a series of railroad cars drawn by an engine. **2** something dragged along behind or forming the back part of a dress, robe, etc. (*wore a dress with a long train; the train of the peacock*). **3** a succession or series of people, things, events, etc. (*a long train of camels; interrupted my train of thought; a train of ideas*). **4** a body of followers; a retinue (*a train of admirers*). **5** a succession of military vehicles, etc., including artillery, supplies, etc. (*baggage train*). **6** a line of gunpowder, etc., to fire an explosive charge. **7** a series of connected wheels or parts in machinery. □ **in train** properly arranged or directed. **in a person's train** following behind a person. **in the train of** as a sequel to. **train down** *Brit.* train with exercise or diet to lower one's weight. □□ **train•a•ble** *adj.* **train•a•bil•i•ty** /tráynəbílitee/ *n.* **train•ee** /-née/ *n.* **train•less** *adj.* [ME f. OF *traïner, trahiner*, ult. f. L *trahere* draw]

train•band /tráynband/ *n. hist.* any of several divisions of 16th or 17th c. citizen soldiers in England or America.

train•er /tráynər/ *n.* **1** a person who trains. **2** a person who trains or provides medical assistance, etc., to horses, athletes, etc., as a profession. **3** an aircraft or device simulating it used to train pilots. **4** *Brit.* a soft running shoe of leather, canvas, etc.

train•ing /tráyning/ *n.* the act or process of teaching or learning a skill, discipline, etc. (*physical training*). □ **go into training** begin physical training. **in training 1** undergoing physical training. **2** physically fit as a result of this. **out of training 1** no longer training. **2** physically unfit.

train•ing col•lege *n. Brit.* a college or school for training esp. prospective teachers.

train•ing ship *n.* a ship on which young people are taught seamanship, etc.

train•man /tráynmən/ *n.* (*pl.* **–men**) a railroad employee working on trains.

train oil *n.* oil obtained from the blubber of a whale (esp. of a right whale).

train•sick /tráynsik/ *adj.* affected with nausea by the motion of a train. □□ **train•sick•ness** *n.*

traipse /trayps/ *v. & n. colloq.* or *dial.* • *v.intr.* **1** tramp or trudge wearily. **2** esp. *Brit.* (often foll. by *about*) go on errands. • *n.* **1** a tedious journey on foot. **2** *archaic* a slattern. [16th-c. *trapes* (v.), of unkn. orig.]

trait /trayt/ *n.* a distinguishing feature or characteristic, esp. of a person.

WORD HISTORY trait

Late 15th century (as a rare usage denoting arrows or other missiles): from French, from Latin *tractus* 'drawing, draft.' An early sense was 'stroke of the pen or pencil,' giving rise to the notion of 'a trace,' hence the current sense 'a characteristic' (mid-18th century).

trai•tor /tráytər/ *n.* (*fem.* **trai•tress** /-tris/) (often foll. by *to*) a person who is treacherous or disloyal, esp. to his or her country. □□ **trai•tor•ous** *adj.* **trai•tor•ous•ly** *adv.* [ME f. OF *traït(o)ur* f. L *traditor –oris* f. *tradere*: see TRADITION]

tra•jec•to•ry /trəjéktəree/ *n.* (*pl.* **–ries**) **1** the path described by a projectile flying or an object moving under the action of given forces. **2** *Geom.* a curve or surface cutting a system of curves or surfaces at a constant angle. [(orig. adj.) f. med.L *trajectorius* f. L *traicere traject–* (as TRANS-, *jacere* throw)]

tra-la /traaláa/ *int.* an expression of joy or gaiety, esp. as in a song. [imit. of song]

tram[1] /tram/ *n.* **1** *Brit.* = STREETCAR. **2** a four-wheeled vehicle used in coal mines. [MLG & MDu. *trame* balk, beam, barrow shaft]

tram[2] /tram/ *n.* (in full **tram silk**) double silk thread used for the weft of some velvets and silks. [F *trame* f. L *trama* weft]

tram•car /trámkaar/ *n. Brit.* = TRAM[1].

tram•lines /trámlīnz/ *n.pl. Brit.* **1** rails for a streetcar. **2** *colloq.* **a** either pair of two sets of long parallel lines at the sides of a lawn tennis court. **b** similar lines at the side or back of a badminton court. **3** inflexible principles or courses of action, etc.

tram•mel /trámǝl/ *n. & v.* • *n.* **1** (usu. in *pl.*) an impediment to free movement; a hindrance (*the trammels of domesticity*). **2** a triple dragnet for fish, which are trapped in a pocket formed when they attempt to swim through. **3** an instrument for drawing ellipses, etc., with a bar sliding in upright grooves. **4** a beam compass. **5** a hook in a fireplace for a kettle, etc. • *v.tr.* (**tram•meled, tram•mel•ing** or **tram•melled, tram•mel•ling**) confine or hamper with or as if with trammels. [in sense 'net' ME f. OF *tramail* f. med.L *tramaculum, tremaculum*, perh. formed as TRI- + *macula* (MAIL[2]): later history uncert.]

tra•mon•ta•na /traamontáanǝ, –tánǝ/ *n.* a cold north wind in the Adriatic. [It.: see TRAMONTANE]

tra•mon•tane /trǝmóntayn, trámǝn–/ *adj. & n.* • *adj.* **1** situated or living on the other side of mountains, esp. the Alps as seen from Italy. **2** (from the Italian point of view) foreign; barbarous. • *n.* **1 a** tramontane person. **2** = TRAMONTANA. [ME f. It. *tramontano* f. L *transmontanus* beyond the mountains (as TRANS-, *mons montis* mountain)]

tramp /tramp/ *v. & n.* • *v.* **1** *intr.* **a** walk heavily and firmly (*tramping about upstairs*). **b** go on foot, esp. a distance. **2** *tr.* **a** cross on foot, esp. wearily or reluctantly. **b** cover (a distance) in this way (*tramped forty miles*). **3** *tr.* (often foll. by *down*) tread on; trample; stamp on. **4** *tr. Austral. colloq.* dismiss from employment; fire. **5** *intr.* live as a tramp. • *n.* **1** an itinerant vagrant or beggar. **2** the sound of a person, or esp. people, walking, marching, etc., or of horses' hooves. **3** a journey on foot, esp. protracted. **4 a** an iron plate protecting the sole of a boot used for digging. **b** the part of a spade that it strikes. **5** *sl. derog.* a promiscuous woman. **6** (also **tramp steam•er**) a merchant ship that takes on any cargo available. □□ **tramp•er** *n.* **tramp•ish** *adj.* [ME *trampe* f. Gmc]

tram•ple /trámpǝl/ *v. & n.* • *v.* **1** tread underfoot. **2** press down or crush in this way. • *n.* the sound or act of trampling. □ **trample on** (or **underfoot**) **1** tread heavily on. **2** treat roughly or with contempt; disregard (a person's feelings, etc.). □□ **tram•pler** *n.* [ME f. TRAMP + –LE[4]]

tram•po•line /trámpǝleen/ *n. & v.* • *n.* a strong fabric sheet connected by springs to a horizontal frame, used by gymnasts, etc., for somersaults, as a springboard, etc. • *v.intr.* use a trampoline. □□ **tram•po•lin•ist** *n.* [It. *trampolino* f. *trampoli* stilts]

tram•way /trámway/ *n. Brit.* **1** rails for a streetcar. **2** a streetcar system.

trance /trans/ *n. & v.* • *n.* **1 a** a sleeplike or half-conscious state without response to stimuli. **b** a hypnotic or cataleptic state. **2** such a state as entered into by a medium. **3** a state of extreme exaltation or rapture; ecstasy. • *v.tr. poet.* = ENTRANCE[2]. □□ **trance•like** *adj.* [ME f. OF *transe f. transir* depart, fall into trance f. L *transire*: see TRANSIT]

tranche /traansh/ *n.* a portion, esp. of income, or of a block of bonds or stocks. [F, = slice (as TRENCH)]

tran•ny /tránee/ *n.* (*pl.* **–nies**) **1** *sl.* a vehicle transmission. **2** esp. *Brit. colloq.* a transistor radio. [abbr.]

tran•quil /trángkwil/ *adj.* calm; serene; unruffled. □□ **tran•quil•li•ty** /–kwílitee/ *n.* **tran•quil•ly** *adv.* [F *tranquille* or L *tranquillus*]

tran•quil•ize /trángkwilīz/ *v.tr.* make tranquil, esp. by a drug, etc.

tran•quil•iz•er /trángkwilīzǝr/ *n.* a drug used to diminish anxiety.

trans- /trans, tranz/ *prefix* **1** across; beyond (*transcontinental; transgress*). **2** on or to the other side of (*transatlantic*) (opp. CIS-). **3** through (*transonic*). **4** into another state or place (*transform; transcribe*). **5** surpassing; transcending (*transfinite*). **6** *Chem.* **a** (of an isomer) having the same atom or group on opposite sides of a given plane in the molecule (cf. CIS- 4). **b** having a higher atomic number than (*transuranic*). [from or after L *trans* across]

trans. *abbr.* **1** transaction. **2** transfer. **3** transitive. **4** (also **transl.**) translated. **5** (also **transl.**) translation. **6** (also **transl.**) translator. **7** transmission. **8** transportation. **9** transpose. **10** transposition. **11** transverse.

trans•act /tranzákt, –sákt/ *v.tr.* perform or carry through (business). □□ **trans•ac•tor** *n.* [L *transigere transact–* (as TRANS-, *agere* do)]

trans•ac•tion /tranzákshǝn, –sák–/ *n.* **1 a** a piece of esp. commercial business done; a deal (*a profitable transaction*). **b** the management of business, etc. **2** (in *pl.*) published reports of discussions, papers read, etc., at the meetings of a learned society. □□ **trans•ac•tion•al** *adj.* **trans•ac•tion•al•ly** *adv.* [ME f. LL *transactio* (as TRANSACT)]

trans•al•pine /tránzálpīn, trans–/ *adj.* beyond the Alps, esp. from the Italian point of view. [L *transalpinus* (as TRANS-, *alpinus* ALPINE)]

trans•at•lan•tic /tránzǝtlántik, trans–/ *adj.* **1** beyond the Atlantic, esp.: **a** European. **b** *Brit.* American. **2** crossing the Atlantic (*a transatlantic flight*).

trans·ax·le /tranzáksəl/ *n.* a unit in front-wheel drive vehicles that combines the functions of the transmission and differential.

trans·ceiv·er /transéevər/ *n.* a combined radio transmitter and receiver.

tran·scend /transénd/ *v.tr.* **1** be beyond the range or grasp of (human experience, reason, belief, etc.). **2** excel; surpass. [ME f. OF *transcendre* or L *transcendere* (as TRANS-, *scandere* climb)]

tran·scend·ent /transéndənt/ *adj. & n.* ● *adj.* **1** excelling; surpassing (*transcendent merit*). **2** transcending human experience. **3** *Philos.* **a** higher than or not included in any of Aristotle's ten categories in scholastic philosophy. **b** not realizable in experience in Kantian philosophy. **4** (esp. of the supreme being) existing apart from, not subject to the limitations of, the material universe (opp. IMMANENT). ● *n. Philos.* a transcendent thing. □□ **tran·scend·ence** *n.* **tran·scend·en·cy** *n.* **tran·scend·ent·ly** *adv.*

tran·scen·den·tal /tránsendént'l/ *adj. & n.* ● *adj.* **1** = TRANSCENDENT. **2 a** (in Kantian philosophy) presupposed in and necessary to experience; a priori. **b** (in Schelling's philosophy) explaining matter and objective things as products of the subjective mind. **c** (esp. in Emerson's philosophy) regarding the divine as the guiding principle in man. **3 a** visionary; abstract. **b** vague; obscure. **4** *Math.* (of a function) not capable of being produced by the algebraical operations of addition, multiplication, and involution, or the inverse operations. ● *n.* a transcendental term, conception, etc. □□ **tran·scen·den·tal·ly** *adv.* [med.L *transcendentalis* (as TRANSCENDENT)]

tran·scen·den·tal·ism /tránsendént'lizəm/ *n.* **1** transcendental philosophy. **2** exalted or visionary language. □□ **tran·scen·den·tal·ist** *n.* **tran·scen·den·tal·ize** *v.tr.*

tran·scen·den·tal med·i·ta·tion *n.* a method of detaching oneself from problems, anxiety, etc., by silent meditation and repetition of a mantra.

trans·code /tranzkṓd, trans–/ *v.tr. & intr.* convert from one form of coded representation to another.

trans·con·ti·nen·tal /tránzkontinént'l, trans–/ *adj. & n.* ● *adj.* (of a railroad, etc.) extending across a continent. ● *n.* a transcontinental railroad or train. □□ **trans·con·ti·nen·tal·ly** *adv.*

tran·scribe /transkríb/ *v.tr.* **1** make a copy of, esp. in writing. **2** transliterate. **3** write out (shorthand, notes, etc.) in ordinary characters or continuous prose. **4 a** record for subsequent reproduction. **b** broadcast in this form. **5** arrange (music) for a different instrument, etc. □□ **tran·scrib·er** *n.* **tran·scrip·tion** /–skrípshən/ *n.* **tran·scrip·tion·al** *adj.* **tran·scrip·tive** /–skríptiv/ *adj.* [L *transcribere* *transcript-* (as TRANS-, *scribere* write)]

tran·script /tránskript/ *n.* **1** a written or recorded copy. **2** any copy. [ME f. OF *transcrit* f. L *transcriptum* neut. past part.: see TRANSCRIBE]

trans·duc·er /tranzdṓosər, –dyṓō–, trans–/ *n.* any device for converting a nonelectrical signal into an electrical one, e.g., pressure into voltage. [L *transducere* lead across (as TRANS-, *ducere* lead)]

tran·sect /transékt/ *v.tr.* cut across or transversely. □□ **tran·sec·tion** *n.* [TRANS- + L *secare sect-* cut]

tran·sept /tránsept/ *n.* **1** either arm of the transept of a cross-shaped church at right angles to the nave (*north transept; south transept*). **2** this part as a whole. □□ **tran·sep·tal** *adj.* [mod.L *transeptum* (as TRANS-, SEPTUM)]

trans·fer *v. & n.* ● *v.* /transfér/ (**trans·ferred, trans·fer·ring**) **1** *tr.* (often foll. by *to*) **a** convey, remove, or hand over (a thing, etc.) (*transferred the bag from the car to the station*). **b** make over the possession of (property, a ticket, rights, etc.) to a person (*transferred his membership to his son*). **2** *tr. & intr.* change or move to another group, club, department, school, etc. **3** *intr.* change from one station, route, etc., to another on a journey. **4** *tr.* **a** convey (a drawing, etc.) from one surface to another, esp. to a lithographic stone by means of transfer paper. **b** remove (a picture) from one surface to another, esp. from wood or a wall to canvas. **5** *tr.* change (the sense of a word, etc.) by extension or metaphor. ● *n.* /tránsfər/ **1** the act or an instance of transferring or being transferred. **2 a** a design, etc., conveyed or to be conveyed from one surface to another. **b** a small usu. colored picture or design on paper, which is transferable to another surface; a decal. **3** a student, etc., who is or is to be transferred. **4 a** the conveyance of property, a right, etc. **b** a document effecting this. **5** a ticket allowing a journey to be continued on another route, etc. □□ **trans·fer·ee** /–reé/ *n.* **trans·fer·or** /–fə́rər/ esp. Law *n.* **trans·fer·rer** /–fə́rər/ *n.* [ME f. F *transférer* or L *transferre* (as TRANS-, *ferre lat-* bear)]

trans·fer·a·ble /tránsfə́rəbəl/ *adj.* capable of being transferred. □□ **trans·fer·a·bil·i·ty** /–bílitee/ *n.*

trans·fer com·pa·ny *n.* a company conveying passengers or luggage between stations.

trans·fer·ence /transfə́rəns, tránsfər–/ *n.* **1** the act or an instance of transferring; the state of being transferred. **2** *Psychol.* the redirection of childhood emotions to a new object, esp. to a psychoanalyst.

trans·fer ink *n.* ink used for making designs on a lithographic stone or transfer paper.

trans·fer pa·per *n.* specially coated paper to receive the impression of transfer ink and transfer it to stone.

trans·fer·ral /transfə́rəl/ *n.* = TRANSFER *n.* 1.

trans·fer·rin /transférin/ *n.* a protein transporting iron in the blood serum. [TRANS- + L *ferrum* iron]

trans·fer RNA *n.* RNA conveying an amino acid molecule from the cytoplasm to a ribosome for use in protein synthesis, etc.

trans·fig·u·ra·tion /transfigyəráyshən/ *n.* **1** a change of form or appearance. **2 a** Christ's appearance in radiant glory to three of his disciples (Matt. 17:2, Mark 9:2–3). **b** (**Transfiguration**) the festival of Christ's transfiguration, Aug. 6. [ME f. OF *transfiguration* or L *transfiguratio* (as TRANSFIGURE)]

trans·fig·ure /transfígyər/ *v.tr.* change in form or appearance, esp. so as to elevate or idealize. [ME f. OF *transfigurer* or L *transfigurare* (as TRANS-, FIGURE)]

trans·fi·nite /tránsfínīt/ *adj.* **1** beyond or surpassing the finite. **2** *Math.* (of a number) exceeding all finite numbers.

trans·fix /transfiks/ *v.tr.* **1** pierce with a sharp implement or weapon. **2** root (a person) to the spot with horror or astonishment; paralyze the faculties of. □□ **trans·fix·ion** /–fíkshən/ *n.* [L *transfigere transfix-* (as TRANS-, FIX)]

trans·form *v. & n.* ● *v.* /transfáwrm/ **1 a** *tr.* make a thorough or dramatic change in the form, outward appearance, character, etc., of. **b** *intr.* (often foll. by *into, to*) undergo such a change. **2** *tr. Electr.* change the voltage, etc., of (a current). **3** *tr. Math.* change (a mathematical entity) by transformation. ● *n.* /tránsfawrm/ *Math. & Linguistics* the product of a transformation. □□ **trans·form·a·ble** *adj.* **trans·form·a·tive** *adj.* [ME f. OF *transformer* or L *transformare* (as TRANS-, FORM)]

trans·for·ma·tion /tránsfərmáyshən/ *n.* **1** the act or an instance of transforming; the state of being transformed. **2** *Zool.* a change of form at metamorphosis, esp. of insects, amphibians, etc. **3** the induced or spontaneous change of one element into another. **4** *Math.* a change from one geometrical figure, expression, or function to another of the same value, magnitude, etc. **5** *Biol.* the modification of a eukaryotic cell from its normal state to a malignant state. **6** *Linguistics* a process, with reference to particular rules, by which one grammatical pattern of sentence structure can be converted into another, or the underlying meaning of a sentence can be converted into a statement of syntax. [ME f. OF *transformation* or LL *transformatio* (as TRANSFORM)] □□ **trans·for·ma·tion·al** /tránsfərmáyshənəl/ *adj.* relating to or involving transformation. **trans·for·ma·tion·al·ly** *adv.*

trans·for·ma·tion·al gram·mar *n.* *Linguistics* a grammar that describes a language by means of transformation (see TRANSFORMATION 6).

trans·form·er /transfáwrmər/ *n.* **1** an apparatus for reducing or increasing the voltage of an alternating current. **2** a person or thing that transforms.

trans·fuse /transfyṓōz/ *v.tr.* **1 a** permeate (*purple dye transfused the water*) **b** instill (an influence, quality, etc.) into (*transfused enthusiasm into everyone*). **2 a** transfer (blood) from one person or animal to another. **b** inject (liquid) into a blood vessel to replace lost fluid. **3** cause (fluid, etc.) to pass from one vessel, etc., to another. □□ **trans·fu·sion** /–fyṓōzhən/ *n.* [ME f. L *transfundere transfus-* (as TRANS-, *fundere* pour)]

trans·gen·ic /tranzjénik/ *adj.* *Biol.* (of an animal or plant) having genetic material introduced from another species.

trans·gress /tranzgrés/ *v.tr.* (also *absol.*) **1** go beyond the bounds or limits set by (a commandment, law, etc.); violate; infringe. **2** *Geol.* (of the sea) spread over (the land). □□ **trans·gres·sion** /–gréshən/ *n.* **trans·gres·sive** *adj.* **trans·gres·sor** *n.* [F *transgresser* or L *transgredi transgress-* (as TRANS-, *gradi* go)]

trans·ship var. of TRANSSHIP.

trans·hu·mance /tranz-hyṓōməns/ *n.* the seasonal moving of livestock to a different region. [F f. *transhumer* f. L TRANS- + *humus* ground]

tran·sient /tránzhənt, –shənt, –zeeənt/ *adj. & n.* ● *adj.* **1** of short duration; momentary; passing; impermanent (*life is transient; of transient interest*). **2** *Mus.* serving only to connect; inessential (*a transient chord*). ● *n.* **1** a temporary visitor, worker, etc. **2** *Electr.* a brief current, etc. □□ **tran·sience** *n.* **tran·sien·cy** *n.* **tran·sient·ly** *adv.* [L *transire* (as TRANS-, *ire* go)]

trans·il·lu·mi·nate /tránzilṓōminayt/ *v.tr.* pass a strong light through for inspection, esp. for medical diagnosis. □□ **trans·il·lu·mi·na·tion** /–náyshən/ *n.*

trans·i·re /transír/ *n.* *Brit.* a customs permit for the passage of goods. [L *transire* go across (as TRANSIENT)]

tran·sis·tor /tranzístər/ *n.* **1** a semiconductor device with three connections, capable of amplification in addition to rectification. **2** (in full **transistor radio**) a portable radio with transistors. [portmanteau word, f. TRANSFER + RESISTOR]

tran·sit /tránzit, –sit/ *n. & v.* ● *n.* **1** the act or process of going, conveying, or being conveyed, esp. over a distance (*transit by rail; made* *a transit of the lake*). **2** a passage or route (*the overland transit*). **3 a** the apparent passage of a celestial body across the meridian of a place. **b** such an apparent passage across the sun or a planet. **4** the local conveyance of passengers on public transportation. **5** a surveying instrument consisting of a theodolite with a telescope mounted so it can be turned in a vertical plane. • *v.* (**tran·sit·ed, tran·sit·ing**) **1** *tr.* make a transit across. **2** *intr.* make a transit. □ **in transit** while going or being conveyed. [ME f. L *transitus* f. *transire* (as TRAN-SIENT)]

tran·sit camp *n.* a camp for the temporary accommodation of soldiers, refugees, etc.

tran·sit cir·cle *n.* (also **tran·sit in·stru·ment**) an instrument for observing the transit of a celestial body across the meridian.

tran·sit com·pass (also **the·od·o·lite**) a surveyor's instrument for measuring a horizontal angle.

tran·sit du·ty *n.* duty paid on goods passing through a country.

tran·si·tion /tranzíshǝn, –síshǝn/ *n.* **1** a passing or change from one place, state, condition, etc., to another (*an age of transition; a transition from plains to hills*). **2** *Mus.* a momentary modulation. **3** *Art* a change from one style to another, esp. *Archit.* from Norman to Early English. **4** *Physics* a change in an atomic nucleus or orbital electron with emission or absorption of radiation. □□ **tran·si·tion·al** *adj.* **tran·si·tion·al·ly** *adv.* **tran·si·tion·ar·y** *adj.* [F *transition* or L *transitio* (as TRANSIT)]

tran·si·tion met·al *n.* (also **tran·si·tion element**) *Chem.* any of a set of elements in the periodic table characterized by partly filled *d* or *f* orbitals and the ability to form colored complexes.

tran·si·tion point *n.* *Physics* the point at which different phases of the same substance can be in equilibrium.

tran·si·tive / tránzitiv, –si–/ *adj.* **1** *Gram.* (of a verb or sense of a verb) that takes a direct object (whether expressed or implied), e.g., *saw* in *saw the donkey, saw that she was ill* (opp. INTRANSITIVE). **2** *Logic* (of a relation) such as to be valid for any two members of a sequence if it is valid for every pair of successive members. □□ **tran·si·tive·ly** *adv.* **tran·si·tive·ness** *n.* **tran·si·tiv·i·ty** /–t ívitee/ *n.* [LL *transitivus* (as TRANSIT)]

GRAMMAR TIP transitive

Transitive vs. Intransitive Verbs. Verbs are classified as either *transitive* or *intransitive*, and their senses are labeled as such in this dictionary. A **transitive verb** takes a direct object; in other words, it shows an action affecting someone (*she* **hit** *me*) or something (*the car* **struck** *a concrete wall*). An **intransitive verb** does not take a direct object. There is no receiver of whatever action is expressed in the sentence (*the ground* **hardened** *from the drought; he* **writes** *beautifully*). Linking verbs, such as *be* and *become* , which express a state of being or show equality, are also intransitive (*fourteen* **is** *the right answer; we* **were** *unimpressed by his performance; she* **became** *the party's nominee for president*).

---

tran·sit lounge *n.* a lounge at an airport for passengers waiting between flights.

tran·si·to·ry /tránzitawree/ *adj.* not permanent; brief; transient. □□ **tran·si·to·ri·ly** /–táwrilee/ *adv.* **tran·si·to·ri·ness** /–táwreenis/ *n.* [ME f. AF *transitorie*, OF *transitoire* f. L *transitorius* (as TRANSIT)]

tran·sit vi·sa *n.* a visa allowing only passage through a country.

transl. *abbr.* **1** translated. **2** translation. **3** translator.

trans·late /tránzláyt, tráns–/ *v.* **1** *tr.* (also *absol.*) **a** (often foll. by *into*) express the sense of (a word, sentence, speech, book, etc.) in another language. **b** do this as a profession, etc. (*translates for the UN*). **2** *intr.* (of a literary work, etc.) be translatable; bear translation (*does not translate well*). **3** *tr.* express (an idea, book, etc.) in another, esp. simpler, form. **4** *tr.* interpret the significance of; infer as (*translated his silence as dissent*). **5** *tr.* move or change, esp. from one person, place, or condition, to another (*was translated by joy*). **6** *intr.* (foll. by *into*) result in; be converted into; manifest itself as. **7** *tr.* *Eccl.* **a** remove (a bishop) to another see. **b** remove (a saint's relics, etc.) to another place. **8** *tr.* *Bibl.* convey to heaven without death; transform. **9** *tr.* *Mech.* **a** cause (a body) to move so that all its parts travel in the same direction. **b** impart motion without rotation to. □□ **trans·lat·a·ble** *adj.* **trans·lat·a·bil·i·ty** /–laytǝbílitee/ *n.* [ME f. L *translatus*, past part. of *transferre*: see TRANSFER]

trans·la·tion /tranzláyshǝn, tráns–/ *n.* **1** the act or an instance of translating. **2** a written or spoken expression of the meaning of a word, speech, book, etc., in another language. □□ **trans·la·tion·al** *adj.* **trans·la·tion·al·ly** *adv.*

trans·la·tor /tránzláytǝr, tráns–/ *n.* **1** a person who translates from one language into another. **2** a television relay transmitter. **3** a program that translates from one (esp. programming) language into another.

trans·lit·er·ate /tranzlítǝrayt, tráns–/ *v.tr.* represent (a word, etc.) in the closest corresponding letters or characters of a different alphabet or language. □□ **trans·lit·er·a·tion** /–ráyshǝn/ *n.* **trans·lit·er·a·tor** *n.* [TRANS- + L *littera* letter]

trans·lo·cate /tranzlókayt, tráns–/ *v.tr.* **1** move from one place to

another. **2** (usu. in *passive*) *Bot.* move (substances in a plant) from one part to another. □□ **trans·lo·ca·tion** /–káyshǝn/ *n.*

trans·lu·cent /tranzlóosǝnt, tráns–/ *adj.* **1** allowing light to pass through diffusely; semitransparent. **2** transparent. □□ **trans·lu·cence** *n.* **trans·lu·cen·cy** *n.* **trans·lu·cent·ly** *adv.* [L *translucēre* (as TRANS-, *lucēre* shine)]

trans·lu·nar /tránzlóonǝr, tráns–/ *adj.* **1** lying beyond the moon. **2** of or relating to space travel or a trajectory toward the moon.

trans·ma·rine /tránzmǝréen, tráns–/ *adj.* situated or going beyond the sea. [L *transmarinus* f. *marinus* MARINE]

trans·mi·grant /tranzmígrǝnt, tráns–/ *adj. & n.* • *adj.* passing through, esp. a country on the way to another. • *n.* a migrant or alien passing through a country, etc. [L *transmigrant-*, part. stem of *transmigrare* (as TRANSMIGRATE)]

trans·mi·grate /tranzmígrayt, tráns–/ *v.intr.* **1** (of the soul) pass into a different body; undergo metempsychosis. **2** migrate. □□ **trans·mi·gra·tion** /–gráyshǝn/ *n.* **trans·mi·gra·tor** *n.* **trans·mi·gra·to·ry** /–mígrǝtawree/ *adj.* [ME f. L *transmigrare* (as TRANS-, MIGRATE)]

trans·mis·sion /tranzmíshǝn, tráns–/ *n.* **1** the act or an instance of transmitting; the state of being transmitted. **2** a broadcast radio or television program. **3** the mechanism by which power is transmitted from an engine to the axle in a motor vehicle. [L *transmissio* (as TRANS-, MISSION)]

trans·mis·sion line *n.* a conductor or conductors carrying electricity over large distances with minimum losses.

trans·mit /tranzmít, tráns–/ *v.tr.* (**trans·mit·ted, trans·mit·ting**) **1 a** pass or hand on; transfer (*transmitted the message; how diseases are transmitted*). **b** communicate (ideas, emotions, etc.). **2 a** allow (heat, light, sound, electricity, etc.) to pass through; be a medium for. **b** be a medium for (ideas, emotions, etc.) (*his message transmits hope*). **3** broadcast (a radio or television program). □□ **trans·mis·si·ble** /–mísǝbǝl/ *adj.* **trans·mis·sive** /–mísiv/ *adj.* **trans·mit·ta·ble** *adj.* **trans·mit·tal** *n.* [ME f. L *transmittere* (as TRANS-, *mittere* miss- send)]

trans·mit·ter /tránzmítǝr, tráns–/ *n.* **1** a person or thing that transmits. **2** a set of equipment used to generate and transmit electromagnetic waves carrying messages, signals, etc., esp. those of radio or television. **3** = NEUROTRANSMITTER.

trans·mog·ri·fy /tranzmógrifi, tráns–/ *v.tr.* (**–fies, –fied**) *joc.* transform, esp. in a magical or surprising manner. □□ **trans·mog·ri·fi·ca·tion** /–fikáyshǝn/ *n.* [17th c.: orig. unkn.]

trans·mon·tane /transmóntayn, tranz–/ *adj.* = TRAMONTANE. [L *transmontanus*: see TRAMONTANE]

trans·mu·ta·tion /tránzmyǒotáyshǝn, tráns–/ *n.* **1** the act or an instance of transmuting or changing into another form, etc. **2** *Alchemy hist.* the supposed process of changing base metals into gold. **3** *Physics* the changing of one element into another by nuclear bombardment, etc. **4** *Geom.* the changing of a figure or body into another of the same area or volume. **5** *Biol.* Lamarck's theory of the change of one species into another. □□ **trans·mu·ta·tion·al** *adj.* **trans·mu·ta·tion·ist** *n.* [ME f. OF *transmutation* or LL *transmutatio* (as TRANSMUTE)]

trans·mute /tranzmyǒot, tráns–/ *v.tr.* **1** change the form, nature, or substance of. **2** *Alchemy hist.* subject (base metals) to transmutation. □□ **trans·mut·a·ble** *adj.* **trans·mut·a·bil·i·ty** /–tǝbílitee/ *n.* **trans·mu·ta·tive** /–myǒotǝtiv/ *adj.* **trans·mut·er** *n.* [ME f. L *transmutare* (as TRANS-, *mutare* change)]

trans·na·tion·al /tránznáshǝnǝl, tráns–/ *adj.* extending beyond national boundaries.

trans·o·ce·an·ic /tránzóshiánik, tráns–/ *adj.* **1** situated beyond the ocean. **2** concerned with crossing the ocean (*transoceanic flight*).

tran·som /tránsǝm/ *n.* **1** a horizontal bar of wood or stone across a window or the top of a door (cf MULLION). **2** each of several beams fixed across the sternpost of a ship. **3** a beam across a saw pit to support a log. **4** a strengthening crossbar. **5** = TRANSOM WINDOW. □□ **tran·somed** *adj.* [ME *traversayn, transyn, –ing*, f. OF *traversin* f. *traverse* TRAVERSE]

tran·som win·dow *n.* **1** a window divided by a transom. **2** a window placed above the transom of a door or larger window; a fanlight.

tran·son·ic /transónik/ *adj.* (also **trans·son·ic**) relating to speeds close to that of sound. [TRANS- + SONIC, after *supersonic*, etc.]

trans·pa·cif·ic /tránzpǝsífik, tráns–/ *adj.* **1** beyond the Pacific. **2** crossing the Pacific.

trans·par·ence /tranzpárǝns, traanz–, –páirǝns/ *n.* = TRANSPARENCY 1.

trans·par·en·cy /tranzpárǝnsee, –páirǝnsee, tráns–/ *n.* (*pl.* **–cies**) **1** the condition of being transparent. **2** *Photog.* a positive transparent photograph on glass or in a frame to be viewed using a slide projector, etc. **3** a picture, inscription, etc., made visible by a light behind it. [med.L *transparentia* (as TRANSPARENT)]

trans·par·ent /tranzpáirǝnt, –párǝnt, tráns–/ *adj.* **1** allowing light to pass through so that bodies can be distinctly seen (cf. TRANSLU-CENT). **2 a** (of a disguise, pretext, etc.) easily seen through. **b** (of a motive, quality, etc.) easily discerned; evident; obvious. **3** (of a person, etc.) easily understood; frank; open. **4** *Physics* transmitting heat or other electromagnetic rays without distortion. □□ **trans•par•ent•ly** *adv.* **trans•par•ent•ness** *n.* [ME f. OF f. med.L *transparens* f. L *transparēre* shine through (as TRANS-, *parēre* appear)]

trans•pierce /tranzpéers, trans–/ *v.tr.* pierce through.

tran•spire /transpír/ *v.* **1** *intr.* (of a secret or something unknown) leak out; come to be known. **2** *intr. disp.* **a** (prec. by *it* as subject) turn out; prove to be the case (*it transpired he knew nothing about it*). **b** occur; happen. **3** *tr. & intr.* emit (vapor, sweat, etc.), or be emitted, through the skin or lungs; perspire. **4** *intr.* (of a plant or leaf) release water vapor. □□ **tran•spir•a•ble** *adj.* **tran•spi•ra•tion** /–spiráyshən/ *n.* **tran•spir•a•to•ry** /–spírətawree/ *adj.* [F *transpirer* or med.L *transpirare* (as TRANS-, L *spirare* breathe)]

trans•plant *v. & n.* ● *v.tr.* /tranzplánt, trans–/ **1 a** plant in another place (*transplanted the daffodils*). **b** move to another place (*whole nations were transplanted*). **2** *Surgery* transfer (living tissue or an organ) and implant in another part of the body or in another body. ● *n.* /tránzplant, trans–/ **1** *Surgery* **a** the transplanting of an organ or tissue. **b** such an organ, etc. **2** a thing, esp. a plant, transplanted. □□ **trans•plant•a•ble** *adj.* **trans•plan•ta•tion** /–táyshən/ *n.* **trans•plant•er** *n.* [ME f. LL *transplantare* (as TRANS-, PLANT)]

tran•spon•der /tranzpóndər, trans–/ *n.* a device for receiving a radio signal and automatically transmitting a different signal. [TRANSMIT + RESPOND]

trans•pon•tine /tránzpóntin, tráns–/ *adj.* on the other side of a bridge, esp. *Brit.* on the south side of the Thames. [TRANS- + L *pons pontis* bridge]

trans•port *v. & n.* ● *v.tr.* /tranzpáwrt, trans–/ **1** take or carry (a person, goods, troops, baggage, etc.) from one place to another. **2** *hist.* take (a criminal) to a penal colony; deport. **3** (as **transported** *adj.*) (usu. foll. by *with*) affected with strong emotion. ● *n.* /tránzpawrt, tráns–/ **1 a** a system of conveying people, goods, etc., from place to place. **b** esp. *Brit.* the means of this (*our transport has arrived*). **2** a ship, aircraft, etc., used to carry soldiers, stores, etc. **3** (esp. in *pl.*) vehement emotion (*transports of joy*). **4** *hist.* a transported convict. [ME f. OF *transporter* or L *transportare* (as TRANS-, *portare* carry)]

trans•port•a•ble /tranzpáwrtəbəl, trans–/ *adj.* **1** capable of being transported. **2** *hist.* (of an offender or an offense) punishable by transportation. □□ **trans•port•a•bil•i•ty** /–bílitee/ *n.*

trans•por•ta•tion /tránzpərtáyshən, tráns–/ *n.* **1** the act of conveying or the process of being conveyed. **2 a** a system of conveying. **b** the means of this. **3** *hist.* removal to a penal colony.

trans•port•er /tránzpáwrtər, trans–/ *n.* **1** a person or device that transports. **2** a vehicle used to transport other vehicles or large pieces of machinery, etc., by road.

trans•port•er bridge *n.* a bridge carrying vehicles, etc., across water on a suspended moving platform.

trans•pose /tranzpóz, trans–/ *v.tr.* **1 a** cause (two or more things) to change places. **b** change the position of (a thing) in a series. **2** change the order or position of (words or a word) in a sentence. **3** *Mus.* write or play in a different key. **4** *Algebra* transfer (a term) with a changed sign to the other side of an equation. □□ **trans•pos•a•ble** *adj.* **trans•pos•er** *n.* [ME, = transform f. OF *transposer* (as TRANS-, L *ponere* put)]

trans•po•si•tion /tránzpəzíshən, tráns–/ *n.* the act or an instance of transposing; the state of being transposed. □□ **trans•po•si•tion•al** *adj.* **trans•pos•i•tive** /–pózitiv/ *adj.* [F *transposition* or LL *transpositio* (as TRANS-, POSITION)]

trans•sex•u•al /tránséksho͞oəl/ *adj. & n.* ● *adj.* having the physical characteristics of one sex and the supposed psychological characteristics of the other. ● *n.* **1** a transsexual person. **2** a person whose sex has been changed by surgery. □□ **trans•sex•u•al•ism** *n.*

trans•ship /tranz-ship, trans–/ *v.tr.* (also **tran•ship**) *intr.* (**–shipped**, **–shipping**) transfer from one ship or form of transport to another. □□ **trans•ship•ment** *n.*

trans•son•ic var. of TRANSONIC.

tran•sub•stan•ti•a•tion /tránsəbstánsheeáyshən/ *n.* *Theol. & RC Ch.* the conversion of the Eucharistic elements wholly into the body and blood of Christ, only the appearance of bread and wine still remaining. [med.L (as TRANS-, SUBSTANCE)]

tran•sude /transo͞od/ *v.intr.* (of a fluid) pass through the pores or interstices of a membrane, etc. □□ **tran•su•da•tion** /–dáyshən/ *n.* **tran•su•da•to•ry** /–dətawree/ *adj.* [F *transsuder* f. OF *tressuer* (as TRANS-, L *sudare* sweat)]

trans•u•ran•ic /tránzyoͅoránik, trans–/ *adj.* *Chem.* (of an element) having a higher atomic number than uranium.

trans•ver•sal /tranzvórsəl, trans–/ *adj. & n.* ● *adj.* (of a line) cutting a system of lines. ● *n.* a transversal line. □□ **trans•ver•sal•i•ty** /–sálitee/ *n.* **trans•ver•sal•ly** *adv.* [ME f. med.L *transversalis* (as TRANSVERSE)]

trans•verse /tránzvórs, tráns–/ *adj.* situated, arranged, or acting in a crosswise direction. □□ **trans•verse•ly** *adv.* [L *transvertere transvers-* turn across (as TRANS-, *vertere* turn)]

trans•verse mag•net *n.* a magnet with poles at the sides and not the ends.

trans•verse wave *n.* *Physics* a wave in which the medium vibrates at right angles to the direction of its propagation.

trans•ves•tism /tranzvéstizəm, trans–/ *n.* (also **trans•ves•ti•tism** /–véstitizəm/) the practice of wearing the clothes of the opposite sex, esp. as a sexual stimulus. □□ **trans•ves•tist** *n.* [G *Transvestismus* f. TRANS- + L *vestire* clothe]

trans•ves•tite /tranzvéstīt, trans–/ *n.* a person given to transvestism.

trap[1] /trap/ *n. & v.* ● *n.* **1 a** an enclosure or device, often baited, for catching animals, usu. by affording a way in but not a way out. **b** a device with bait for killing vermin, esp. = MOUSETRAP. **2 a** trick betraying a person into speech or an act (*is this question a trap?*). **3** an arrangement to catch an unsuspecting person, e.g., a speeding motorist. **4** a device for hurling an object such as a clay pigeon into the air to be shot at. **5** a compartment from which a greyhound is released at the start of a race. **6** a shoe-shaped wooden device with a pivoted bar that sends a ball from its heel into the air on being struck at the other end with a bat. **7 a** a curve in a downpipe, etc., that fills with liquid and forms a seal against the upward passage of gases. **b** a device for preventing the passage of steam, etc. **8** *Golf* a bunker. **9** a device allowing pigeons to enter but not leave a loft. **10** a two-wheeled carriage (*a pony and trap*). **11** = TRAPDOOR. **12** *sl.* the mouth (esp. *shut one's trap*). **13** (esp. in *pl.*) *colloq.* a percussion instrument, esp. in a jazz band. ● *v.tr.* (**trapped**, **trap•ping**) **1** catch (an animal) in a trap. **2** catch (a person) by means of a trick, plan, etc. **3** stop and retain in or as in a trap. **4** provide (a place) with traps. □□ **trap•like** *adj.* [OE *treppe, treppe*, rel. to MDu. *trappe*, med.L *trappa*, of uncert. orig.]

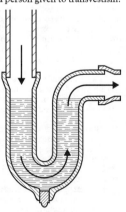

trap 7a

trap[2] /trap/ *v.tr.* (**trapped**, **trap•ping**) (often foll. by *out*) **1** provide with trappings. **2** adorn. [obs. *trap* (n.): ME f. OF *drap*: see DRAPE]

trap[3] /trap/ *n.* (in full **traprock**) any dark-colored igneous rock, fine-grained and columnar in structure, esp. basalt. [Sw. *trapp* f. *trappa* stair, f. the often stairlike appearance of its outcroppings]

trap•door /trápdáwr/ *n.* a door or hatch in a floor, ceiling, or roof, usu. made flush with the surface.

trap•door spi•der *n.* any of various spiders, esp. of the family Ctenizidae, that make a hinged trapdoor at the top of their nest.

tra•peze /trapéez/ *n.* a crossbar or set of crossbars suspended by ropes used as a swing for acrobatics, etc. [F *trapèze* f. LL *trapezium*: see TRAPEZIUM]

tra•pe•zi•um /trapéezeeəm/ *n.* (*pl.* **tra•pe•zi•a** /–zeeə/ or **tra•pe•zi•ums**) **1** a quadrilateral with no two sides parallel. **2** *Brit.* = TRAPEZOID 1. [LL f. Gk *trapezion* f. *trapeza* table]

trap•e•zoid /trápizoyd/ *n.* **1** a quadrilateral with only one pair of sides parallel. **2** *Brit.* = TRAPEZIUM 1. □□ **trap•e•zoi•dal** *adj.* [mod.L *trapezoides* f. Gk *trapezoeidēs* (as TRAPEZIUM)]

TRAPEZIUM

TRAPEZOID

trapezium and trapezoid

trap•per /trápər/ *n.* a person who traps wild animals, esp. to obtain furs.

trap•pings /trápingz/ *n.pl.* **1** ornamental accessories, esp. as an indication of status (*the trappings of office*). **2** the harness of a horse, esp. when ornamental. [ME (as TRAP[2])]

Trap•pist /trápist/ *n. & adj.* ● *n.* a member of a branch of the Cistercian order founded in 1664 at La Trappe in Normandy, France, and noted for an austere rule including a vow of silence. ● *adj.* of or relating to this order. [F *trappiste* f. *La Trappe*]

traps /traps/ *n.pl.* esp. *Brit. colloq.* personal belongings; baggage. [perh. contr. f. TRAPPINGS]

trash /trash/ *n. & v.* **1 a** worthless or poor quality stuff, esp. literature. **b** rubbish; refuse. **c** absurd talk or ideas; nonsense. **2 a** worthless person or persons. **3** a thing of poor workmanship or material. **4** (in full **cane trash**) *W.Ind.* the refuse of crushed sugarcanes and dried stripped leaves and tops of sugarcane used as fuel. ● *v.tr.* **1** *colloq.* wreck. **2** strip (sugarcanes) of their outer leaves to speed up the ripening process. **3** *colloq.* expose the worthless nature of; disparage. **4** *colloq.* throw away; discard. [16th c.: orig. unkn.]

trash·y /tráshee/ *adj.* (**trash·i·er, trash·i·est**) worthless; poorly made. □□ **trash·i·ly** *adv.* **trash·i·ness** *n.*

trat·to·ri·a /rátərēə/ *n.* an Italian restaurant. [It.]

trau·ma /tráwmə, trów–/ *n.* (*pl.* **trau·ma·ta** /–mətə/ or **trau·mas**) **1** any physical wound or injury. **2** physical shock following this, characterized by a drop in body temperature, mental confusion, etc. **3** *Psychol.* emotional shock following a stressful event, sometimes leading to long-term neurosis. □□ **trau·ma·tize** *v.tr.* **trau·ma·ti·za·tion** *n.* [Gk *trauma traumatos* wound]

PRONUNCIATION TIP | **trauma**

The first syllable of this word can be pronounced to rhyme with *jaw*, or it can be pronounced to rhyme with *cow*. Both are considered acceptable, although the latter may be less frequent.

---

trau·mat·ic /trəmátik, trow–, traw–/ *adj.* **1** of or causing trauma. **2** *colloq.* (in general use) distressing; emotionally disturbing (*a traumatic experience*). **3** of or for wounds. □□ **trau·mat·i·cal·ly** *adv.* [LL *traumaticus* f. Gk *traumatikos* (as TRAUMA)]

trau·ma·tism /tráwmətizəm, tráw–/ *n.* **1** the action of a trauma. **2** a condition produced by this.

trav. *abbr.* **1** travel. **2** traveler.

tra·vail /trəváyl, trávayl/ *n.* & *v.* ● *n.* **1** painful or laborious effort. **2** the pangs of childbirth. ● *v.intr.* undergo a painful effort, esp. in childbirth. [ME f. OF *travail, travailler* ult. f. med.L *trepalium* instrument of torture f. L *tres* three + *palus* stake]

trav·el /trávəl/ *v.* & *n.* ● *v.intr.* & *tr.* (**trav·eled, trav·el·ing** or **trav·elled, trav·el·ling**) **1** *intr.* go from one place to another; make a journey, esp. of some length or abroad. **2** *tr.* **a** journey along or through (a country). **b** cover (a distance) in traveling. **3** *intr. colloq.* withstand a long journey (*wines that do not travel*). **4** *intr.* go from place to place as a salesman. **5** *intr.* move or proceed in a specified manner or at a specified rate (*light travels faster than sound*). **6** *intr. colloq.* move quickly. **7** *intr.* pass esp. in a deliberate or systematic manner from point to point (*the photographer's eye traveled over the scene*). **8** *intr.* (of a machine or part) move or operate in a specified way. **9** *intr.* (of deer, etc.) move onward in feeding. ● *n.* **1 a** the act of traveling, esp. in foreign countries. **b** (often in *pl.*) a tour or occurrence of this (*have returned from their travels*). **2** the range, rate, or mode of motion of a part in machinery. □□ **trav·el·ing** *adj.* [ME, orig. = TRAVAIL]

trav·el a·gen·cy (also **trav·el bu·reau**) an agency that makes the necessary arrangements for travelers. □□ **trav·el a·gent** *n.* a person or business acting as a travel agency.

trav·eled /trávəld/ *adj.* experienced in traveling (also in *comb.*: *much traveled*).

trav·el·er /trávələr, trávlər/ *n.* **1** a person who travels or is traveling. **2** *Brit.* a traveling salesman. **3** a Gypsy. **4** *Austral.* an itinerant worker; a swagman. **5** a moving mechanism, such as an overhead crane.

trav·el·er's check *n.* a check for a fixed amount that may be cashed on signature, usu. internationally.

trav·el·ing rug *n. Brit.* = LAP ROBE.

trav·el·ing sales·man *n.* a person who travels to solicit orders as a representative of a company, etc.

trav·el·ing wave *n. Physics* a wave in which the medium moves in the direction of propagation.

trav·e·logue /trávəlog/ *n.* (also **trav·e·log**) a movie or illustrated lecture about travel. [TRAVEL after *monologue*, etc.]

trav·erse /trávərs, trəvárs/ *v.* & *n.* ● *v.* **1** travel or lie across (*traversed the country; a pit traversed by a beam*). **2** *tr.* consider or discuss the whole extent of (a subject). **3** *tr.* turn (a large gun) horizontally. **4** *tr. Law* deny (an allegation) in pleading. **5** *tr.* thwart, frustrate, or oppose (a plan or opinion). **6** *intr.* (of the needle of a compass, etc.) turn on or as on a pivot. **7** *intr.* (of a horse) walk obliquely. **8** *intr.* make a traverse in climbing. ● *n.* **1** a sideways movement. **2** an act of traversing. **3** a thing, esp. part of a structure, that crosses another. **4** a gallery extending from side to side of a church or other building. **5 a** a single line of survey, usu. plotted from compass bearings and with chained or paced distances between angular points. **b** a tract surveyed in this way. **6** *Naut.* a zigzag line taken by a ship because of contrary winds or currents. **7** a skier's similar movement on a slope. **8** the sideways movement of a part in a machine. **9 a** a sideways motion across a rock face from one practicable line of ascent or descent to another. **b** a place where this is necessary. **10** *Mil.* a pair of right-angle bends in a trench to avoid enfilading fire. **11** *Law* a denial, esp. of an allegation of a matter of fact. **12** the act of turning a large gun horizontally to the required direction. □□ **tra·vers·a·ble** *adj.* **tra·vers·al** *n.* **tra·vers·er** *n.* [OF *traverser* f. LL *traversare, transversare* (as TRANSVERSE)]

trav·er·tine /trávərteen/ *n.* a white or light-colored calcareous rock deposited from springs. [It. *travertino, tivertino* f. L *tiburtinus* of Tibur (Tivoli) near Rome]

trav·es·ty /trávistee/ *n.* & *v.* ● *n.* (*pl.* **–ties**) a grotesque misrepresen-

tation or imitation (*a travesty of justice*). ● *v.tr.* (**–ties, –tied**) make or be a travesty of. [(orig. adj.) f. F *travesti* past part. of *travestir* disguise, change the clothes of, f. It. *travestire* (as TRANS–, *vestire* clothe)]

tra·vois /trəvóy/ *n.* (*pl.* same /–vóyz/) a vehicle of two joined poles pulled by a horse, etc., for carrying a burden, orig. used by Native American people of the Plains. [earlier *travail* f. F, perh. the same word as TRAVAIL]

trawl /trawl/ *v.* & *n.* ● *v.* **1** *intr.* **a** fish with a trawl or seine. **b** seek a suitable candidate, etc., by sifting through a large number. **2** *tr.* **a** catch by trawling. **b** seek a suitable candidate, etc., from (a certain area or group, etc.) (*trawled the schools for new trainees*). ● *n.* **1** an act of trawling. **2** (in full **trawl net**) a large wide-mouthed fishing net dragged by a boat along the bottom. **3** (in full **trawl line**) a long sea fishing line buoyed and supporting short lines with baited hooks. [prob. f. MDu. *traghelen* to drag (cf. *traghel* drag-net), perh. f. L *tragula*]

trawl·er /tráwlər/ *n.* **1** a boat used for trawling. **2** a person who trawls.

tray /tray/ *n.* **1** a flat shallow vessel usu. with a raised rim for carrying dishes, etc., or containing small articles, papers, etc. **2** a shallow lidless box forming a compartment of a trunk. □□ **tray·ful** *n.* (*pl.* **–fuls**). [OE *trīg* f. Gmc, rel. to TREE]

treach·er·ous /tréchərəs/ *adj.* **1** guilty of or involving treachery. **2** (of the weather, ice, the memory, etc.) not to be relied on; likely to fail or give way. □□ **treach·er·ous·ly** *adv.* **treach·er·ous·ness** *n.* [ME f. OF *trecherous* f. *trecheor* a cheat f. *trechier, trichier*: see TRICK]

treach·er·y /tréchəree/ *n.* (*pl.* **–ies**) **1** violation of faith or trust; betrayal. **2** an instance of this.

trea·cle /treekəl/ *n.* **1** esp. *Brit.* **a** a syrup produced in refining sugar. **b** molasses. **2** cloying sentimentality or flattery. □□ **trea·cly** *adj.* [ME *triacle* f. OF f. L *theriaca* f. Gk *thēriakē* antidote against venom, fem. of *thēriakos* (adj.) f. *thērion* wild beast]

tread /tred/ *v.* & *n.* ● *v.* (**trod** /trod/; **trod·den** /tród'n/ or **trod**) **1** *intr.* (often foll. by *on*) **a** set down one's foot; walk or step (*do not tread on the grass; trod on a snail*). **b** (of the foot) be set down. **2** *tr.* **a** walk on. **b** (often foll. by *down*) press or crush with the feet. **3** *tr.* perform (steps, etc.) by walking (*trod a few paces*). **4** *tr.* make (a hole, etc.) by treading. **5** *intr.* (foll. by *on*) suppress; subdue mercilessly. **6** *tr.* make a track with (dirt, etc.) from the feet. **7** *tr.* (often foll. by *in, into*) press down into the ground with the feet (*trod dirt into the carpet*). **8** *tr.* (also *absol.*) (of a male bird) copulate with (a hen). ● *n.* **1** a manner or sound of walking (*recognized the heavy tread*). **2** the top surface of a step or stair. **3** the thick molded part of a vehicle tire for gripping the road. **4 a** the part of a wheel that touches the ground or rail. **b** the part of a rail that the wheels touch. **5** the part of the sole of a shoe that rests on the ground. **6** (of a male bird) copulation. □ **tread the boards** (or **stage**) be or become an actor; appear on the stage. **tread on air** see AIR. **tread on a person's toes** offend a person or encroach on a person's privileges, etc. **tread out** esp. *Brit.* **1** stamp out (a fire, etc.). **2** press out (wine or grain) with the feet. **tread water** maintain an upright position in the water by moving the feet with a walking movement and the hands with a downward circular motion. □□ **tread·er** *n.* [OE *tredan* f. WG]

trea·dle /tredəl/ *n.* & *v.* ● *n.* a lever worked by the foot and imparting motion to a machine. ● *v.intr.* work a treadle. [OE *tredel* stair (as TREAD)]

tread·mill /trédmil/ *n.* **1** a device for producing motion by the weight of persons or animals stepping on movable steps on the inner surface of a revolving upright wheel. **2** monotonous routine work.

tread wheel *n.* a treadmill or similar machine.

trea·son /treezən/ *n.* **1** violation by a subject of allegiance to the sovereign or to the nation, esp. by attempting to kill or overthrow the sovereign or to overthrow the government. **2** *hist.* murder of one's master or husband, regarded as a form of treason. □□ **trea·son·ous** *adj.* [ME f. AF *treisoun*, etc., OF *traïson*, f. L *traditio* handing over (as TRADITION)]

trea·son·a·ble /treezənəbəl/ *adj.* involving or guilty of treason. □□ **trea·son·a·bly** *adv.*

treas·ure /trézhər/ *n.* & *v.* ● *n.* **1 a** precious metals or gems. **b** a hoard of these. **c** accumulated wealth. **2** a thing valued for its rarity, workmanship, associations, etc. (*art treasures*). **3** *colloq.* a much loved or highly valued person. ● *v.tr.* **1** (often foll. by *up*) store up as valuable. **2** value (esp. a long-kept possession) highly. [ME f. OF *tresor*, ult. f. Gk *thēsauros*: see THESAURUS]

treas·ure hunt *n.* **1** a search for treasure. **2** a game in which players seek a hidden object from a series of clues.

treas·ure trove *n.* **1** *Law* treasure of unknown ownership found hidden. **2** a hidden store of valuables.

treas·ur·er /trézhərər/ *n.* **1** a person appointed to administer the funds of a society or municipality, etc. **2** an officer authorized to receive and disburse public revenues. □□ **treas·ur·er·ship** *n.* [ME

f. AF *tresoror*, OF *tresorier* f. *tresor* (see TREASURE) after LL *thesaurarius*]

treas•ur•y /tréezhəree/ *n.* (*pl.* **–ies**) **1** a place or building where treasure is stored. **2** the funds or revenue of a nation, institution, or society. **3** (**Treasury**) **a** the department managing the public revenue of a country. **b** the offices and officers of this. **c** the place where the public revenues are kept. [ME f. OF *tresorie* (as TREASURE)]

treas•ur•y bill *n.* a bill of exchange issued by the government to raise money for temporary needs. ¶ Abbr: **T bill**

treas•ur•y note *n.* a note issued by the Treasury for use as currency or as a bond.

treat /treet/ *v. & n.* • *v.* **1** *tr.* act or behave toward or deal with (a person or thing) in a certain way (*treated me kindly; treat it as a joke*). **2** *tr.* deal with or apply a process to; act upon to obtain a particular result (*treat it with acid*). **3** *tr.* apply medical care or attention to. **4** *tr.* present or deal with (a subject) in literature or art. **5** *tr.* (often foll. by *to*) provide with food or drink or entertainment, esp. at one's own expense (*treated us to dinner*). **6** *intr.* (often foll. by *with*) negotiate terms (with a person). **7** *intr.* (often foll. by *of*) give a spoken or written exposition. • *n.* **1** an event or circumstance (esp. when unexpected or unusual) that gives great pleasure. **2** a meal, entertainment, etc., provided by one person for the enjoyment of another or others. **3** *Brit.* (prec. by *a*) extremely good or well (*they looked a treat; has come on a treat*). □□ **treat•a•ble** *adj.* **treat•er** *n.* **treat•ing** *n.* [ME f. AF *treter*, OF *traitier* f. L *tractare* handle, frequent. of *trahere tract-* draw, pull]

trea•tise /treétis/ *n.* a written work dealing formally and systematically with a subject. [ME f. AF *tretis* f. OF *traitier* TREAT]

treat•ment /treétmənt/ *n.* **1** a process or manner of behaving toward or dealing with a person or thing (*received rough treatment*). **2** the application of medical care or attention to a patient. **3** a manner of treating a subject in literature or art. **4** (prec. by *the*) *colloq.* the customary way of dealing with a person, situation, etc. (*got the full treatment*).

trea•ty /treétee/ *n.* (*pl.* **–ties**) **1** a formally concluded and ratified agreement between nations. **2** an agreement between individuals or parties, esp. for the purchase of property. [ME f. AF *treté* f. L *tractatus* TRACTATE]

trea•ty port *n. hist.* a port that a country was bound by treaty to keep open to foreign trade.

tre•ble /trébəl/ *adj., n., & v.* • *adj.* **1 a** threefold. **b** triple. **c** three times as much or many (*treble the amount*). **2** (of a voice) high-pitched. **3** *Mus.* = SOPRANO (esp. of an instrument or with ref. to a boy's voice). • *n.* **1** a treble quantity or thing. **2** *Darts* a hit on the narrow ring enclosed by the two middle circles of a dartboard, scoring treble. **3 a** *Mus.* = SOPRANO (esp. a boy's voice or part, or an instrument). **b** a high-pitched voice. **4** the high-frequency output of a radio, record player, etc., corresponding to the treble in music. **5** *Brit.* a system of betting in which the winnings and stake from the first bet are transferred to a second and then (if successful) to a third. **6** *Brit. Sports* three victories or championships in the same game, sport, etc. • *v.* **1** *tr. & intr.* make or become three times as much or many; increase threefold; multiply by three. **2** *tr.* amount to three times as much as. □□ **tre•bly** *adv.* (in sense 1 of *adj.*). [ME f. OF f. L *triplus* TRIPLE]
▶See note at TRIPLE.

tre•ble clef *n.* a clef placing G above middle C on the second lowest line of the staff.

tre•ble rhyme *n.* a rhyme including three syllables.

treb•u•chet /trébyōshét/ *n.* (also **tre•buck•et** /trébəkít, trebyōōkét/) *hist.* **1** a military machine used in siege warfare for throwing stones, etc. **2** a tilting balance for accurately weighing light articles. [ME f. OF f. *trebucher* overthrow, ult. f. Frank.]

tre•cen•to /traychéntō/ *n.* the style of Italian art and literature of the 14th c. □□ **tre•cen•tist** *n.* [It., = 300 used with reference to the years 1300–99]

tree /tree/ *n. & v.* • *n.* **1 a** a perennial plant with a woody self-supporting main stem or trunk when mature and usu. unbranched for some distance above the ground (cf. SHRUB[1]). **b** any similar plant having a tall erect usu. single stem, e.g., palm tree. **2** a piece or frame of wood, etc., for various purposes (*shoe tree*). **3** *archaic* or *poet.* **a** a gibbet. **b** a cross, esp. the one used for Christ's crucifixion. **4** (in full **tree diagram**) *Math.* a diagram with a structure of branching connecting lines. **5** = FAMILY TREE. • *v.tr.* **1** force to take refuge in a tree. **2** put into a difficult position. **3** stretch on a shoe tree. □ **up a tree** cornered; nonplussed. □□ **tree•less** *adj.* **tree•less•ness** *n.* **tree•like** *adj.* [OE *trēow* f. Gmc]

tree ag•ate *n.* agate with treelike markings.

tree calf *n.* a calf binding for books stained with a treelike design.

tree•creep•er /treékreepər/ *n.* any small creeping bird, esp. of the family Certhiidae, feeding on insects in the bark of trees.

treen /treen/ *n.* (treated as *pl.*) small domestic wooden objects, esp. antiques. [*treen* (adj.) wooden f. OE *trēowen* (as TREE)]

tree fern *n.* a large fern, esp. of the family Cyatheaceae, with an upright trunklike stem.

tree frog *n.* any arboreal tailless amphibian, esp. of the family Hylidae, climbing by means of adhesive pads on its digits.

tree hop•per *n.* any insect of the family Membracidae, living in trees.

tree house *n.* a structure in a tree for children to play in.

tree line *n.* = TIMBERLINE.

tree•nail /treénayl/ *n.* (also **tre•nail**) a hard wooden pin for securing timbers, etc.

tree of heav•en *n.* an ornamental Asian tree, *Ailanthus altissima*, with foul-smelling flowers.

tree of life *n.* **1** (**Tree of Life**) (in the Bible) a tree in the Garden of Eden whose fruit imparts eternal life (Gen. 3:22-24). **2** = ARBOR VITAE.

tree ring *n.* a ring in a cross section of a tree, from one year's growth.

tree shrew *n.* any small insectivorous arboreal mammal of the family Tupaiidae having a pointed nose and bushy tail.

tree spar•row *n.* **1** a European sparrow, *Passer montanus*, inhabiting woodland areas. **2** a N. American finch, *Spizella arborea*, inhabiting grassland areas.

tree sur•geon *n.* a person who treats decayed trees in order to preserve them. □□ **tree sur•ger•y** *n.* the art or practice of such treatment.

tree toad *n.* = TREE FROG.

tree to•ma•to *n.* = TAMARILLO.

tree•top /treétop/ *n.* the topmost part of a tree.

tree trunk *n.* the trunk of a tree.

tref /tráyf/ *adj.* (also **trefa** /tráyfə/ and other variants) not kosher. [Heb. *ṭ*ə*rēpāh* the flesh of an animal torn f. *ṭāraṗ* rend]

tre•foil /treéfoyl, tréf–/ *n. & adj.* • *n.* **1** any leguminous plant of the genus *Trifolium*, with leaves of three leaflets and flowers of various colors, esp. clover. **2** any plant with similar leaves. **3** a three-lobed ornamentation, esp. in tracery windows. **4** a thing arranged in or with three lobes. • *adj.* of or concerning a three-lobed plant, window tracery, etc. □□ **tre•foiled** *adj.* (also in *comb.*). [ME f. AF *trifoil* f. L *trifolium* (as TRI-, *folium* leaf)]

trefoil 3

trek /trek/ *v. & n.* • *v.intr.* (**trekked, trek•king**) **1** travel or make one's way arduously (*trekking through the forest*). **2** esp. *S. Afr. hist.* migrate or journey with one's belongings by ox wagon. **3** (of an ox) draw a vehicle or pull a load. • *n.* **1 a** a journey or walk made by trekking (*it was a trek to the nearest laundromat*). **b** each stage of such a journey. **2** an organized migration of a body of persons. □□ **trek•ker** *n.* [S.Afr. Du. *trek* (n.), *trekken* (v.) draw, travel]

trel•lis /trélis/ *n. & v.* • *n.* (in full **trellis-work**) a lattice or grating of light wooden or metal bars used esp. as a support for fruit trees or creepers and often fastened against a wall. • *v.tr.* (**trel•lised, trel•lis•ing**) **1** provide with a trellis. **2** support (a vine, etc.) with a trellis. [ME f. OF *trelis, trelice* ult. f. L *trilix* three-ply (as TRI-, *licium* warp-thread)]

trellis

trem•a•tode /trémətōd, treé–/ *n.* any parasitic flatworm of the class Trematoda, esp. a fluke, equipped with hooks or suckers, e.g., a liver fluke. [mod.L *Trematoda* f. Gk *trēmatōdēs* perforated f. *trēma* hole]

trem•ble /trémbəl/ *v. & n.* • *v.intr.* **1** shake involuntarily from fear, excitement, weakness, etc. **2** be in a state of extreme apprehension (*trembled at the very thought of it*). **3** move in a quivering manner (*leaves trembled in the breeze*). • *n.* **1** a trembling state or movement; a quiver (*couldn't speak without a tremble*). **2** (in *pl.*) a disease (esp. of cattle) marked by trembling. □□ **trem•bling•ly** *adv.* [ME f. OF *trembler* f. med.L *tremulare* f. L *tremulus* TREMULOUS]

trem•bling pop•lar *n.* an aspen.

trem•bly /trémblee/ *adj.* (**trem•bli•er, trem•bli•est**) *colloq.* trembling; agitated.

tre•men•dous /triméndəs/ *adj.* **1** awe inspiring; fearful; overpowering. **2** *colloq.* remarkable; considerable; excellent (*a tremendous explosion; gave a tremendous performance*). □□ **tre•men•dous•ly** *adv.* **tre•men•dous•ness** *n.* [L *tremendus*, gerundive of *tremere* tremble]

trem•o•lo /trémolō/ *n. Mus.* **1** a tremulous effect in playing stringed and keyboard instruments or singing, esp. by rapid reiteration of a note; in other instruments, by rapid alternation between two notes (cf. VIBRATO). **2** a device in an organ producing a tremulous effect. [It. (as TREMULOUS)]

trem•or /trémər/ *n. & v.* • *n.* **1** a shaking or quivering. **2** a thrill (of fear or exultation, etc.). **3** a slight earthquake. • *v.intr.* undergo a tremor or tremors. [ME f. OF *tremour* & L *tremor* f. *tremere* tremble]

trem•u•lous /trémyələs/ *adj.* **1** trembling or quivering (*in a tremulous voice*). **2** (of a line, etc.) drawn by a tremulous hand. **3** timid or vacillating. □□ **trem•u•lous•ly** *adv.* **trem•u•lous•ness** *n.* [L *tremulus* f. *tremere* tremble]

tre•nail var of TREENAIL.

trench /trench/ *n. & v.* ● *n.* **1** a long narrow usu. deep depression or ditch. **2** *Mil.* **a** this dug by troops to stand in and be sheltered from enemy fire. **b** (in *pl.*) a defensive system of these. **3** a long narrow deep depression in the ocean bed. ● *v.* **1** *tr.* dig a trench or trenches in (the ground). **2** *tr.* turn over the earth of (a field, garden, etc.) by digging a succession of adjoining ditches. **3** *intr.* (foll. by *on, upon*) *archaic* **a** encroach. **b** verge or border closely. [ME f. OF *trenche* (n.) *trenchier* (v.), ult. f. L *truncare* TRUNCATE]

trench•ant /trénchənt/ *adj.* **1** (of a style or language, etc.) incisive; terse; vigorous. **2** *archaic* or *poet.* sharp; keen. □□ **trench•an•cy** *n.* **trench•ant•ly** *adv.* [ME f. OF, part. of *trenchier*: see TRENCH]

trench coat *n.* **1** a soldier's lined or padded waterproof coat. **2** a loose belted raincoat.

trench•er /trénchər/ *n.* **1** *hist.* a wooden or earthenware platter for serving food. **2** (in full **trencher cap**) a stiff square academic cap; a mortarboard. [ME f. AF *trenchour*, OF *trencheoir* f. *trenchier*: see TRENCH]

trench•er•man /trénchərmən/ *n.* (*pl.* **–men**) a person who eats well, or in a specified manner (*a good trencherman*).

trench fe•ver *n.* a highly infectious disease, transmitted by lice, that infested soldiers in the trenches in World War I.

trench mor•tar *n.* a light simple mortar throwing a bomb from one's own into the enemy trenches.

trench war•fare *n.* hostilities carried on from more or less permanent trenches.

trend /trend/ *n. & v.* ● *n.* a general direction and tendency (esp. of events, fashion, or opinion, etc.). ● *v.intr.* **1** bend or turn away in a specified direction. **2** be chiefly directed; have a general and continued tendency. [ME 'revolve,' etc., f. OE *trendan* f. Gmc: cf. TRUNDLE]

trend•set•ter /tréndsetər/ *n.* a person who leads the way in fashion, etc. □□ **trend•set•ting** *adj.*

trend•y /tréndee/ *adj. & n. colloq.* ● *adj.* (**trend•i•er, trend•i•est**) often *derog.* fashionable; following fashionable trends. ● *n.* (*pl.* **–ies**) a fashionable person. □□ **trend•i•ly** *adv.* **trend•i•ness** *n.*

tre•pan /trɪpán/ *n. & v.* ● *n.* **1** a cylindrical saw formerly used by surgeons for removing part of the bone of the skull. **2** a borer for sinking shafts. ● *v.tr.* (**tre•panned, tre•pan•ning**) perforate (the skull) with a trepan. □□ **trep•a•na•tion** /trépənáyshən/ *n.* **tre•pan•ning** *n.* [ME f. med.L *trepanum* f. Gk *trupanon* f. *trupaō* bore f. *trupē* hole]

tre•pang /trɪpáng/ *n.* a kind of sea cucumber eaten in China, usu. in long dried strips. [Malay *trīpang*]

tre•phine /trɪfín, –féen/ *n. & v.* ● *n.* an improved form of trepan with a guiding center pin. ● *v.tr.* operate on with this. □□ **treph•i•na•tion** /tréfináyshən/ *n.* [orig. *trafine*, f. L *tres fines* three ends, app. formed after TREPAN]

trep•i•da•tion /trépidáyshən/ *n.* **1** a feeling of fear or alarm; perturbation of the mind. **2** tremulous agitation. **3** the trembling of limbs, e.g., in paralysis. [L *trepidatio* f. *trepidare* be agitated, tremble, f. *trepidus* alarmed]

tres•pass /tréspəs, –pas/ *v. & n.* ● *v.intr.* **1** (usu. foll. by *on, upon*) make an unlawful or unwarrantable intrusion (esp. on land or property). **2** (foll. by *on*) make unwarrantable claims (*shall not trespass on your hospitality*). **3** (foll. by *against*) *literary* or *archaic* offend. ● *n.* **1** *Law* a voluntary wrongful act against the person or property of another, esp. unlawful entry to a person's land or property. **2** *archaic* a sin or offense. □□ **tres•pass•er** *n.* [ME f. OF *trespasser* pass over, trespass, *trespas* (n.), f. med.L *transpassare* (as TRANS-, PASS¹)]

tress /tres/ *n. & v.* ● *n.* **1** a long lock of human (esp. female) hair. **2** (in *pl.*) a woman's or girl's head of hair. ● *v.tr.* arrange (hair) in tresses. □□ **tressed** *adj.* (also in *comb.*). **tress•y** *adj.* [ME f. OF *tresse*, perh. ult. f. Gk *trikha* threefold]

tres•tle /trésəl/ *n.* **1** a supporting structure for a table, etc., consisting of two frames fixed at an angle or hinged or of a bar supported by two divergent pairs of legs. **2** (in full **trestle table**) a table consisting of a board or boards laid on trestles or other supports. **3** (also **trestlework**) an open braced framework to support a bridge, etc. **4** (also **trestletree**) *Naut.* each of a pair of horizontal pieces on a lower mast supporting the topmast, etc. [ME f. OF *trestel* ult. f. L *transtrum*]

tret /tret/ *n. hist.* an allowance of extra weight formerly made to purchasers of some goods for waste in transportation. [ME f. AF & OF, var. of *trait* draft: see TRAIT]

tre•val•ly /trɪválee/ *n.* (*pl.* **–lies**) any Australian fish of the genus *Caranx*, used as food. [prob. alt. f. *cavally*, a kind of fish, f. Sp. *caballo* horse f. L (as CAVALRY)]

trews /trōōz/ *n.pl. esp. Brit.* trousers, esp. close-fitting tartan trousers worn by women. [Ir. *trius*, Gael. *triubhas* (sing.): cf. TROUSERS]

trey /tray/ *n.* (*pl.* **treys**) the three on dice or cards. [ME f. OF *trei, treis* three f. L *tres*]

tri- /trī/ *comb. form* forming nouns and adjectives meaning: **1** three or three times. **2** *Chem.* (forming the names of compounds) containing three atoms or groups of a specified kind (*triacetate*). [L & Gk f. L *tres*, Gk *treis* three]

tri•a•ble /trī́əbəl/ *adj.* **1** liable to a judicial trial. **2** that may be tried or attempted. [ME f. AF (as TRY)]

tri•ac•e•tate /trīásitayt/ *n.* a cellulose derivative containing three acetate groups, esp. as a base for manmade fibers.

tri•ad /trī́ad/ *n.* **1** a group of three (esp. notes in a chord). **2** the number three. **3** a Chinese secret society, usu. criminal. **4** a Welsh form of literary composition with an arrangement of subjects or statements in groups of three. □□ **tri•ad•ic** *adj.* **tri•ad•i•cal•ly** *adv.* [F *triade* or LL *trias triad-* f. Gk *trias –ados* f. *treis* three]

tri•a•del•phous /trī́ədélfəs/ *adj. Bot.* having stamens united in three bundles. [TRI- + Gk *adelphos* brother]

tri•age /tree-aázh, treé-aazh/ *n.* **1** the act of sorting according to quality. **2** the assignment of degrees of urgency to decide the order of treatment of wounds, illnesses, etc. [F f. *trier*: cf. TRY]

tri•al /trī́əl/ *n.* **1** a judicial examination and determination of issues between parties by a judge with or without a jury (*stood trial for murder*). **2 a** a process or mode of testing qualities. **b** experimental treatment. **c** a test (*will give you a trial*). **d** an attempt. **e** (*attrib.*) experimental. **3** a trying thing or experience or person, esp. hardship or trouble (*the trials of old age*). **4** a preliminary contest to test the ability of players eligible for selection to a team, etc. **5** *Brit.* a test of individual ability on a motorcycle over rough ground or on a road. **6** any of various contests involving performance by horses, dogs, or other animals. □ **on trial 1** being tried in a court of law. **2** being tested; to be chosen or retained only if suitable. [AF *trial, triel* f. *trier* TRY]

tri•al and er•ror *n.* repeated (usu. varied and unsystematic) attempts or experiments continued until successful.

tri•al bal•ance *n.* (of a ledger in double-entry bookkeeping), a comparison of the totals on either side, the inequality of which reveals errors in posting.

tri•al by or•deal *n.* see ORDEAL 2.

tri•al ju•ry *n.* = *petit jury*.

tri•al run *n.* a preliminary test of a vehicle, vessel, machine, etc.

tri•an•drous /trīándrəs/ *adj. Bot.* having three stamens.

tri•an•gle /trī́anggəl/ *n.* **1** a plane figure with three sides and angles. **2** any three things not in a straight line, with imaginary lines joining them. **3** an implement of this shape. **4** a musical instrument consisting of a steel rod bent into a triangle and sounded by striking it with a smaller steel rod. **5** a situation, esp. an emotional relationship, involving three people. **6** a right-angled triangle of wood, etc., as a drawing implement. **7** *Naut.* a device of three spars for raising weights. **8** *hist.* a frame of three halberds joined at the top to which a soldier was bound for flogging. [ME f. OF *triangle* or L *triangulum* neut. of *triangulus* three-cornered (as TRI-, ANGLE¹)]

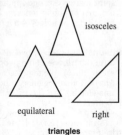

isosceles

equilateral   right

triangles

tri•an•gle of forc•es *n.* a triangle whose sides represent in magnitude and direction three forces in equilibrium.

tri•an•gu•lar /trīánggyələr/ *adj.* **1** triangle-shaped; three-cornered. **2** (of a contest or treaty, etc.) between three persons or parties. **3** (of a pyramid) having a three-sided base. □□ **tri•an•gu•lar•i•ty** /–láiritee/ *n.* **tri•an•gu•lar•ly** *adv.* [LL *triangularis* (as TRIANGLE)]

tri•an•gu•late *v. & adj.* ● *v.tr.* /trīánggyəlayt/ **1** divide (an area) into triangles for surveying purposes. **2 a** measure and map (an area) by the use of triangles with a known base length and base angles. **b** determine (a height, distance, etc.) in this way. ● *adj.* /trīángyələt/ *Zool.* marked with triangles. □□ **tri•an•gu•late•ly** /–lətlee/ *adv.* **tri•an•gu•la•tion** /–láyshən/ *n.* [L *triangulatus* triangular (as TRIANGLE)]

Tri•as•sic /trīásik/ *adj. & n. Geol.* ● *adj.* of or relating to the earliest period of the Mesozoic era with evidence of an abundance of reptiles (including the earliest dinosaurs) and the emergence of mammals. ● *n.* this period or system. [LL *trias* (as TRIAD), because the strata are divisible into three groups]

tri•ath•lon /trīáthlən, –lon/ *n.* an athletic contest consisting of three different events, esp. running, swimming, and bicycling. □□ **tri•ath•lete** /–leet/ *n.* [TRI- after DECATHLON]

tri•a•tom•ic /trī́ətómik/ *adj. Chem.* **1** having three atoms (of a specified kind) in the molecule. **2** having three replacement atoms or radicals.

tri·ax·i·al /triákseeəl/ *adj.* having three axes.

trib. *abbr.* **1** tribunal. **2** tribune. **3** tributary.

trib·ade /tríbəd/ *n.* a lesbian. □□ **trib·a·dism** *n.* [F *tribade* or L *tribas* f. Gk f. *tribō* rub]

trib·al /tríbəl/ *adj.* of, relating to, or characteristic of a tribe or tribes. □□ **trib·al·ly** *adv.*

trib·al·ism /tríbəlizəm/ *n.* **1** tribal organization. **2** strong loyalty to one's tribe, group, etc. □□ **trib·al·ist** *n.* **trib·al·is·tic** *adj.*

tri·ba·sic /tríbáysik/ *adj. Chem.* (of an acid) having three replaceable hydrogen atoms.

tribe /trīb/ *n.* **1** a group of (esp. primitive) families or communities, linked by social, economic, religious, or blood ties, and usu. having a common culture and dialect, and a recognized leader. **2** any similar natural or political division. **3** *Rom.Hist.* each of the political divisions of the Roman people. **4** each of the 12 divisions of the Israelites. **5** a set or number of persons, esp. of one profession, etc., or family (*the whole tribe of actors*). **6** *Biol.* a group of organisms usu. ranking between genus and the subfamily. **7** (in *pl.*) large numbers. [ME, orig. in pl. form *tribuz, tribus* f. OF or L *tribus* (sing. & pl.)]

tribes·man /tríbzmən/ *n.* (*pl.* **–men**) a member of a tribe or of one's own tribe.

tribo- /tríbō, trí–/ *comb. form* rubbing; friction. [Gk *tribos* rubbing]

tri·bo·e·lec·tric·i·ty /tríbō-ílektrísitee, trīb–/ *n.* the generation of an electric charge by friction.

tri·bol·o·gy /tríbóləjee/ *n.* the study of friction, wear, lubrication, and the design of bearings; the science of interacting surfaces in relative motion. □□ **tri·bol·o·gist** *n.*

tri·bo·lu·mi·nes·cence /tríbōlooōminésəns, trīb–/ *n.* the emission of light from a substance when rubbed, scratched, etc. □□ **tri·bo·lu·mi·nes·cent** *adj.*

tri·bom·e·ter /tríbómitər/ *n.* an instrument for measuring friction in sliding.

tri·brach /tríbrak, trīb–/ *n. Prosody* a foot of three short or unstressed syllables. □□ **tri·brach·ic** *adj.* [L *tribrachys* f. Gk *tribrakhus* (as TRI–, *brakhus* short)]

trib·u·la·tion /tríbyəláyshən/ *n.* **1** great affliction or oppression. **2** a cause of this (*was a real tribulation to me*). [ME f. OF f. eccl.L *tribulatio* –*onis* f. L *tribulare* press, oppress, f. *tribulum* sledge for threshing, f. *terere* trit– rub]

tri·bu·nal /tríbyoōnəl, trī–/ *n.* **1** a board appointed to adjudicate in some matter, esp. one appointed by the government to investigate a matter of public concern. **2** a court of justice. **3** a seat or bench for a judge or judges. **4 a** a place of judgment. **b** judicial authority (*the tribunal of public opinion*). [F *tribunal* or L *tribunus* (as TRIBUNE²)]

trib·une¹ /tríbyoōn, tribyoōn/ *n.* **1** a popular leader or demagogue. **2** (in full **tribune of the people**) an official in ancient Rome chosen by the people to protect their interests. **3** (in full **military tribune**) a Roman legionary officer. □□ **trib·u·nate** /–nət, –nayt/ *n.* **trib·une·ship** *n.* [ME f. L *tribunus*, prob. f. *tribus* tribe]

trib·une² /tríbyoōn, tribyoōn/ *n.* **1** *Eccl.* **a** a bishop's throne in a basilica. **b** an apse containing this. **2** a dais or rostrum. **3** a raised area with seats. [F f. It. f. med.L *tribuna* TRIBUNAL]

trib·u·tar·y /tríbyətəree/ *n. & adj.* • *n.* (*pl.* **–ies**) **1** a river or stream flowing into a larger river or lake. **2** *hist.* a person or nation paying or subject to tribute. • *adj.* **1** (of a river, etc.) that is a tributary. **2** *hist.* **a** paying tribute. **b** serving as tribute. □□ **trib·u·tar·i·ly** /–táirilee/ *adv.* **trib·u·tar·i·ness** /–táireenis/ *n.* [ME f. L *tributarius* (as TRIBUTE)]

trib·ute /tríbyoōt/ *n.* **1** a thing said or done or given as a mark of respect or affection, etc. (*paid tribute to their achievements; floral tributes*). **2** *hist.* **a** a payment made periodically by one nation or ruler to another, esp. as a sign of dependence. **b** an obligation to pay this (*was paid under tribute*). **3** (foll. by *to*) an indication of (some praiseworthy quality) (*their success is a tribute to their perseverance*). **4** a proportion of ore or its equivalent paid to a miner for his work, or to the owner of a mine. [ME f. L *tributum* neut. past part. of *tribuere* *tribut*– assign, orig. divide between tribes (*tribus*)]

trice /trīs/ *n.* □ **in a trice** in a moment; instantly. [ME *trice* (v.) pull, haul f. MDu. *trīsen*, MLG *trīssen*, rel. to MDu. *trīse* windlass, pulley]

tri·cen·ten·ar·y /trísenténəree/ *n.* (*pl.* **–ies**) = TERCENTENARY.

tri·ceps /tríseps/ *adj. & n.* • *adj.* (of a muscle) having three heads or points of attachment. • *n.* any triceps muscle, esp. the large muscle at the back of the upper arm. [L, = three-headed (as TRI–, –*ceps* f. *caput* head)]

tri·cer·a·tops /trísérətops/ *n.* an herbivorous dinosaur with three sharp horns on the forehead and a wavy-edged collar around the neck. [mod.L f. Gk *trikeratos* three-horned + *ōps* face]

tri·chi·a·sis /trísíkəsis/ *n. Med.* ingrowth or introversion of the eyelashes. [LL f. Gk *trikhiasis* f. *trikhiaō* be hairy]

tri·chi·na /trikínə/ *n.* (*pl.* **tri·chi·nae** /–nee/) any hairlike parasitic nematode worm of the genus *Trichinella*, esp. *T. spiralis*, the adults

of which live in the small intestine, and whose larvae become encysted in the muscle tissue of humans and carnivorous animals. □□ **trich·i·nous** *adj.* [mod.L f. Gk *trikhinos* of hair: see TRICHO–]

trich·i·no·sis /tríkinósis/ *n.* a disease caused by trichinae, usu. ingested in meat, and characterized by digestive disturbance, fever, and muscular rigidity.

tricho- /tríkō/ *comb. form* hair. [Gk *thrix trikhos* hair]

tri·chog·e·nous /trikójənəs/ *adj.* causing or promoting the growth of hair.

tri·chol·o·gy /trikóləjee/ *n.* the study of the structure, functions, and diseases of the hair. □□ **tri·chol·o·gist** *n.*

trich·ome /tríkōm/ *n. Bot.* a hair, scale, prickle, or other outgrowth from the epidermis of a plant. [Gk *trikhōma* f. *trikhoō* cover with hair (as TRICHO–)]

tri·cho·mon·ad /tríkəmónad, –mó–/ *n.* any flagellate protozoan of the genus *Trichomonas*, parasitic in humans, cattle, and fowls.

tri·cho·mo·ni·a·sis /tríkəmənίəsis/ *n.* any of various infections caused by trichomonads parasitic on the urinary tract, vagina, or digestive system.

tri·chop·a·thy /trikópəthee/ *n.* the treatment of diseases of the hair. □□ **trichopathic** /tríkəpáthik/ *adj.*

tri·chot·o·my /trikótəmee/ *n.* (*pl.* **–mies**) a division (esp. sharply defined) into three categories, esp. of human nature into body, soul, and spirit. □□ **trich·o·tom·ic** /–kətómik/ *adj.* [Gk *trikha* threefold f. *treis* three, after DICHOTOMY]

tri·chro·ic /tríkrόik/ *adj.* (esp. of a crystal viewed in different directions) showing three colors. □□ **tri·chro·ism** /tríkrō-izəm/ *n.* [Gk *trikhroos* (as TRI–, *khrōs* color)]

tri·chro·mat·ic /tríkrəmátik/ *adj.* **1** having or using three colors. **2** (of vision) having the normal three color sensations, i.e., red, green, and blue. □□ **tri·chro·ma·tism** /–krómətizəm/ *n.*

trick /trik/ *n., adj., & v.* • *n.* **1** an action or scheme undertaken to fool, outwit, or deceive. **2** an optical or other illusion (*a trick of the light*). **3** a special technique; a knack or special way of doing something. **4 a** a feat of skill or dexterity. **b** an unusual action (e.g., begging) learned by an animal. **5** a mischievous, foolish, or discreditable act; a practical joke (*a mean trick to play*). **6** a peculiar or characteristic habit or mannerism (*has a trick of repeating himself*). **7 a** the cards played in a single round of a card game, usu. one from each player. **b** such a round. **c** a point gained as a result of this. **8** (*attrib.*) done to deceive or mystify or to create an illusion (*trick photography; trick question*). **9** *Naut.* a sailor's turn at the helm, usu. two hours. **10 a** a prostitute's client. **b** a sexual act performed by a prostitute and a client. • *adj.* unreliable or inclined to weaken suddenly (*trick knee*). • *v.tr.* **1** deceive by a trick; outwit. **2** (often foll. by *out of*, or *into* + verbal noun) cheat; treat deceitfully so as to deprive (*were tricked into agreeing; were tricked out of their savings*). **3** (of a thing) foil or baffle; take by surprise; disappoint the calculations of. □ **do the trick** *colloq.* accomplish one's purpose; achieve the required result. **how's tricks?** *colloq.* how are you? **not miss a trick** see MISS¹. **trick of the trade** a special usu. ingenious technique or method of achieving a result in an industry or profession, etc. **trick or treat** a children's custom of calling at houses at Halloween with the threat of pranks if they are not given candy. **trick out** (or **up**) dress, decorate, or deck out, esp. showily. **turn tricks** engage in prostitution. **up to one's tricks** *colloq.* misbehaving. **up to a person's tricks** aware of what a person is likely to do by way of mischief. □□ **trick·er** *n.* **trick·ish** *adj.* **trick·less** *adj.* [ME f. OF dial. *trique*, OF *triche* f. *trichier* deceive, of unkn. orig.]

trick·er·y /tríkəree/ *n.* (*pl.* **–ies**) **1** the practice or an instance of deception. **2** the use of tricks.

trick·le /tríkəl/ *v. & n.* • *v.* **1** *intr. & tr.* flow or cause to flow in drops or a small stream (*water trickled through the crack*). **2** *intr.* come or go slowly or gradually (*information trickles out*). • *n.* a trickling flow. [ME *trekel, trikle*, prob. imit.]

trick·le charg·er *n.* an electrical charger for batteries that works at a steady slow rate.

trick·le-down *adj.* (of an economic system) in which the poorest gradually benefit as a result of the increasing wealth of the richest.

trick·ster /tríkstər/ *n.* a deceiver or rogue.

trick·sy /tríksee/ *adj.* (**trick·si·er, trick·si·est**) full of tricks; playful. □□ **trick·si·ly** *adv.* **trick·si·ness** *n.* [TRICK: for –*sy* cf. FLIMSY, TIPSY]

trick·y /tríkee/ *adj.* (**trick·i·er, trick·i·est**) **1** difficult or intricate; requiring care and adroitness (*a tricky job*). **2** crafty or deceitful. **3** resourceful or adroit. □□ **trick·i·ly** *adv.* **trick·i·ness** *n.*

tri·clin·ic /tríklínik/ *adj.* **1** (of a mineral) having three unequal oblique axes. **2** denoting the system classifying triclinic crystalline substances. [Gk TRI– + *klinō* incline]

tri·clin·i·um /tríklíneeəm/ *n.* (*pl.* **tri·clin·i·a** /–neeə/) *Rom. Antiq.* **1** a dining table with couches along three sides. **2** a room containing this. [L f. Gk *triklinion* (as TRI–, *klinē* couch)]

tri·col·or /tríkulər/ *n. & adj.* • *n.* a flag of three colors, esp. the French national flag of blue, white, and red. • *adj.* (also **tri·col·ored**) having three colors. [F *tricolore* f. LL *tricolor* (as TRI–, COLOR)]

tri·corn /tríkawrn/ *adj. & n.* (also **tri·corne**) • *adj.* **1** having three horns. **2** (of a hat) having a brim turned up on three sides. • *n.* **1** an

tri•cot /tréekō/ n. **1 a** a hand-knitted woolen fabric. **b** an imitation of this. **2** a ribbed woolen cloth. [F, = knitting f. *tricoter* knit, of unkn. orig.]

tri•crot•ic /trīkrótik/ adj. (of the pulse) having a triple beat. [TRI- after DICROTIC]

tri•cus•pid /trīkúspid/ n. & adj. • n. **1** a tooth with three cusps or points. **2** a heart valve formed of three triangular segments. • adj. (of a tooth) having three cusps or points.

tri•cy•cle /trísikəl/ n. & v. • n. **1** a vehicle having three wheels, two on an axle at the back and one at the front, driven by pedals in the same way as a bicycle. **2** a three-wheeled motor vehicle for a disabled driver. • v.intr. ride on a tricycle. □□ **tri•cy•clist** n.

tri•dac•tyl /trīdáktil/ adj. (also **tri•dac•tyl•ous** /–dáktiləs/) having three fingers or toes.

tri•dent /tríd'nt/ n. **1** a three-pronged spear, esp. as an attribute of Poseidon (Neptune) or Britannia. **2 (Trident)** a type of submarine-launched ballistic missile. [L *tridens tridant-* (as TRI-, *dens* tooth)]

tri•den•tate /trīdéntayt/ adj. having three teeth or prongs. [TRI- + L *dentatus* toothed]

Tri•den•tine /trīdéntin, –tīn, –teen/ adj. & n. • adj. of or relating to the Council of Trent, held at Trento in Italy 1545– 63, esp. as the basis of Roman Catholic doctrine. • n. a Roman Catholic adhering to this traditional doctrine. [med.L *Tridentinus* f. *Tridentum* Trent]

trident

Tri•den•tine mass n. the eucharistic liturgy used by the Roman Catholic Church from 1570 to 1964.

trid•u•um /tríjŏŏəm, trídyŏŏəm/ n. RC Ch. esp. hist. three days' prayer in preparation for a saint's day or other religious occasion. [L (as TRI-, *dies* day)]

trid•y•mite /trídimīt/ n. a crystallized form of silica, occurring in cavities of volcanic rocks. [G *Tridymit* f. Gk *tridumos* threefold (as TRI-, *didumos* twin), from its occurrence in groups of three crystals]

tried past and past part. of TRY.

tri•en•ni•al /trī-éneeəl/ adj. & n. • adj. **1** lasting three years. **2** recurring every three years. • n. a visitation of an Anglican diocese by its bishop every three years. □□ **tri•en•ni•al•ly** adv. [LL *triennis* (as TRI-, L *annus* year)]

tri•en•ni•um /trī-éneeəm/ n. (pl. **tri•en•ni•ums** or **tri•en•ni•a** /–neeə/) a period of three years. [L (as TRIENNIAL)]

tri•er /tríər/ n. **1** a person who perseveres (*is a real trier*). **2** a tester, esp. of foodstuffs. **3** Brit. Law a person appointed to decide whether a challenge to a juror is well founded.

tri•fa•cial nerve /trīfáyshəl/ n. = TRIGEMINAL NERVE.

tri•fect•a /trīféktə/ n. a form of betting in which the first three places in a race must be predicted in the correct order. [TRI- + PERFECTA]

tri•fid /trífid/ adj. Biol. partly or wholly split into three divisions or lobes. [L *trifidus* (as TRI-, *findere fid-* split)]

tri•fle /trífəl/ n. & v. • n. **1** a thing of slight value or importance. **2 a** a small amount of money (*was sold for a trifle*). **b** (prec. by a) somewhat (*seems a trifle annoyed*). **3** Brit. a confection of sponge cake with custard, jelly, fruit, cream, etc. • v. **1** intr. talk or act frivolously. **2** intr. (foll. by *with*) **a** a treat or deal with frivolously or derisively; flirt heartlessly with. **b** refuse to take seriously. **3** tr. (foll. by *away*) waste (time, energies, money, etc.) frivolously. □□ **tri•fler** n. [ME f. OF *truf(f)le* by-form of *trufe* deceit, of unkn. orig.]

tri•fling /trífling/ adj. **1** unimportant; petty. **2** frivolous. □□ **tri•fling•ly** adv.

tri•fo•cal /trīfókəl/ adj. & n. • adj. having three focuses, esp. of a lens with different focal lengths. • n. (in pl.) trifocal eyeglasses.

tri•fo•li•ate /trīfóleeət/ adj. **1** (of a compound leaf) having three leaflets. **2** (of a plant) having such leaves.

tri•fo•ri•um /trīfáwreeəm/ n. (pl. **tri•fo•ri•a** /–reeə/) a gallery or arcade above the arches of the nave, choir, and transepts of a church. [AL, of unkn. orig.]

tri•form /trífawrm/ adj. (also **tri•formed**) **1** formed of three parts. **2** having three forms or bodies.

tri•fur•cate v. & adj. • v.tr. & intr. /trífərkayt/ divide into three branches. • adj. /trífərkət/ divided into three branches.

trig¹ /trig/ n. colloq. trigonometry. [abbr.]

trig² /trig/ adj. & v. archaic or dial. • adj. trim or spruce. • v.tr. (**trigged, trig•ging**) make trim; neaten. [ME, = trusty, f. ON *tryggr*, rel. to TRUE]

trig•a•mous /trígəməs/ adj. **1 a** three times married. **b** having three wives or husbands at once. **2** Bot. having male, female, and hermaphroditic flowers in the same head. □□ **trig•a•mist** n. **trig•a•my** n. [Gk *trigamos* (as TRI-, *gamos* marriage)]

tri•gem•i•nal nerve /trījéminəl/ n. Anat. the largest cranial nerve, which divides into the ophthalmic, maxillary, and mandibular nerves. [as TRIGEMINUS]

tri•gem•i•nal neu•ral•gia n. Med. neuralgia involving one or more of these branches, and often causing severe pain.

tri•gem•i•nus /trījéminəs/ n. (pl. **tri•gem•i•ni** /–nī/) the trigeminal nerve. [L, = born as a triplet (as TRI-, *geminus* born at the same birth)]

trig•ger /trígər/ n. & v. • n. **1** a movable device for releasing a spring or catch and so setting off a mechanism (esp. that of a gun). **2** an event, occurrence, etc., that sets off a chain reaction. • v.tr. **1** (often foll. by *off*) set (an action or process) in motion; initiate; precipitate. **2** fire (a gun) by the use of a trigger. □ **quick on the trigger** quick to respond. □□ **trig•gered** adj. [17th-c. *tricker* f. Du. *trekker* f. *trekken* pull: cf. TREK]

trig•ger•fish n. any usu. tropical marine fish of the family Balistidae with a first dorsal fin spine that can be depressed by pressing on the second.

trig•ger-hap•py adj. apt to shoot without or with slight provocation.

tri•glyph /tríglif/ n. Archit. each of a series of tablets with three vertical grooves, alternating with metopes in a Doric frieze. □□ **tri•glyph•ic** /–glífik/ adj. **tri•glyph•i•cal** /–glífikəl/ adj. [L *triglyphus* f. Gk *trigluphos* (as TRI-, *gluphē* carving)]

tri•gon /trígon/ n. **1** a triangle. **2** an ancient triangular lyre or harp. **3** the cutting region of an upper molar tooth. [L *trigonum* f. Gk *trigōnon* neuter of *trigōnos* three-cornered (as TRI-, –GON)]

trig•o•nal /trígənəl/ adj. **1** triangular; of or relating to a triangle. **2** Biol. triangular in cross section. **3** (of a crystal, etc.) having an axis with threefold symmetry. □□ **trig•o•nal•ly** adv. [med.L *trigonalis* (as TRIGON)]

trig•o•nom•e•try /trígənómitree/ n. the branch of mathematics dealing with the relations of the sides and angles of triangles and with the relevant functions of any angles. □□ **trig•o•no•met•ric** /–nəmétrik/ adj. **trig•o•no•met•ri•cal** adj. [mod.L *trigonometria* (as TRIGON, –METRY)]

tri•graph /trígraf/ n. (also **tri•gram** /–gram/) **1** a group of three letters representing one sound. **2** a figure of three lines.

tri•gy•nous /tríjinəs/ adj. Bot. having three pistils.

tri•he•dral /trīheedrəl/ adj. having three surfaces.

tri•he•dron /trīheedrən/ n. a figure of three intersecting planes.

tri•hy•dric /trīhídrik/ adj. Chem. containing three hydroxyl groups.

trike /trīk/ n. & v.intr. colloq. tricycle. [abbr.]

tri•la•bi•ate /trīlábeeət/ adj. Bot. & Zool. three-lipped.

tri•lat•er•al /trīlátərəl/ adj. & n. • adj. **1** of, on, or with three sides. **2** shared by or involving three parties, countries, etc. (*trilateral negotiations*). • n. a figure having three sides.

tril•by /trílbee/ n. (pl. **–bies**) Brit. a soft felt hat with a narrow brim and indented crown. □□ **tril•bied** adj. [name of the heroine in G. du Maurier's novel *Trilby* (1894), in the stage version of which such a hat was worn]

tri•lin•e•ar /trílíneeər/ adj. of or having three lines.

tri•lin•gual /trílínggwəl/ adj. **1** able to speak three languages, esp. fluently. **2** spoken or written in three languages. □□ **tri•lin•gual•ism** n.

tri•lit•er•al /trílítərəl/ adj. **1** of three letters. **2** (of a Semitic language) having (most) roots with three consonants.

tri•lith /trílith/ n. (also **tri•lith•on** /–lithən/) a monument consisting of three stones, esp. of two uprights and a lintel. □□ **tri•lith•ic** adj. [Gk *trilithon* (as TRI-, *lithos* stone)]

trill /tril/ n. & v. • n. **1** a quavering or vibratory sound, esp. a rapid alternation of sung or played notes. **2** a bird's warbling sound. **3** the pronunciation of *r* with a vibration of the tongue. • v. **1** intr. produce a trill. **2** tr. warble (a song) or pronounce (*r*, etc.) with a trill. [It. *trillo* (n.), *trillare* (v.)]

tril•lion /trílyən/ n. (pl. same or (in sense 3) **tril•lions**) **1** a million million (1,000,000,000,000 or 10¹²). **2** esp. Brit. a million million million (1,000,000,000,000,000,000 or 10¹⁸). **3** (in pl.) colloq. a very large number (*trillions of times*). □□ **tril•lionth** adj. & n. [F *trillion* or It. *trilione* (as TRI-, MILLION), after *billion*]

tri•lo•bite /trílōbīt/ n. any fossil marine arthropod of the class Trilobita of Palaeozoic times, characterized by a three-lobed body. [mod.L *Trilobites* (as TRI-, Gk *lobos* lobe)]

tril•o•gy /tríləjee/ n. (pl. **–gies**) **1** a group of three related literary or operatic works. **2** Gk Antiq. a set of three tragedies performed as a group. [Gk *trilogia* (as TRI-, –LOGY)]

trim /trim/ v., n., & v. • v. (**trimmed, trim•ming**) **1** tr. **a** set in good order. **b** make neat or of the required size or form, esp. by cutting away irregular or unwanted parts. **2** tr. (foll. by *off*, *away*) remove by cutting off (such parts). **3** tr. **a** (often foll. by *up*) make (a person) neat in dress and appearance. **b** ornament or decorate (esp. clothing, a hat, etc.). by adding ribbons, lace, etc.). **4** tr. adjust the balance of (a ship or aircraft) by the arrangement of its cargo, etc. **5** tr. arrange (sails) to suit the wind. **6** intr. associate oneself with currently prevailing views, esp. to advance oneself. **b** hold a middle course in politics or opinion. **7** *tr. colloq.* **a** rebuke sharply. **b** thrash. **c** get the better of in a bargain, etc. • *n.* **1** the state or degree of readiness or fitness (*found everything in perfect trim*). **2** ornament or decorative material. **3** dress or equipment. **4** the act of trimming a person's hair. **5** the inclination of an aircraft to the horizontal. • *adj.* **1** neat, slim, or tidy. **2** in good condition or order; well arranged or equipped. □ **in trim 1** looking smart, healthy, etc. **2** *Naut.* in good order. □□ **trim·ly** *adv.* **trim·ness** *n.* [perh. f. OE *trymman, trymian* make firm, arrange: but there is no connecting evidence between OE and 1500]

tri·ma·ran /trímərən/ *n.* a vessel like a catamaran, with three hulls side by side. [TRI- + CATAMARAN]

tri·mer /trímər/ *n. Chem.* a polymer comprising three monomer units. □□ **tri·mer·ic** /–mérik/ *adj.* [TRI- + –MER]

trim·er·ous /trímərəs/ *adj.* having three parts.

tri·mes·ter /tríméstər/ *n.* a period of three months, esp. of human gestation or as a college or university term. □□ **tri·mes·tral** *adj.* **tri·mes·tri·al** *adj.* [F *trimestre* f. L *trimestris* (as TRI-, *–mestris* f. *mensis* month)]

trim·e·ter /trímitər/ *n. Prosody* a verse of three measures. □□ **tri·met·ric** /trímétrik/ *adj.* **tri·met·ri·cal** *adj.* [L *trimetrus* f. Gk *trimetros* (as TRI-, *metron* measure)]

trim·mer /trímər/ *n.* **1** a person who trims articles of dress. **2** a person who trims in politics, etc.; a person swayed by prevailing opinion. **3** an instrument for clipping, etc. **4** *Archit.* a short piece of lumber across an opening (e.g., for a hearth) to carry the ends of truncated joists. **5** a small capacitor, etc., used to tune a radio set. **6** *Austral. colloq.* a striking or outstanding person or thing.

trim·ming /tríming/ *n.* **1** ornamentation or decoration, esp. for clothing. **2** (in *pl.*) *colloq.* the usual accompaniments, esp. of the main course of a meal. **3** (in *pl.*) pieces cut off in trimming.

tri·mor·phism /trímáwrfizəm/ *n. Bot., Zool.,* & *Crystallog.* existence in three distinct forms. □□ **tri·mor·phic** *adj.* **tri·mor·phous** *adj.*

trine /trīn/ *adj.* & *n.* • *adj.* **1** threefold; triple; made up of three parts. **2** *Astrol.* denoting the aspect of two heavenly bodies 120° (one-third of the zodiac) apart. • *n. Astrol.* a trine aspect. □□ **tri·nal** *adj.* [ME f. OF *trin trine* f. L *trinus* threefold f. *tres* three]

Trin·i·tar·i·an /trínitáireeən/ *n.* & *adj.* • *n.* a person who believes in the doctrine of the Trinity. • *adj.* of or relating to this belief. □□ **Trin·i·tar·i·an·ism** *n.*

tri·ni·tro·tol·u·ene /trínítrōtólyóoeen/ *n.* (also **tri·ni·tro·tol·u·ol** /–tólyoo-awl, –ōl/) = TNT.

trin·i·ty /trínitee/ *n.* (*pl.* **–ties**) **1** the state of being three. **2** a group of three. **3** (**the Trinity** or Holy Trinity) *Theol.* the three persons of the Christian Godhead (Father, Son, and Holy Spirit). [ME f. OF *trinité* f. L *trinitas –tatis* triad (as TRINE)]

Trin·i·ty Sun·day *n.* the next Sunday after Pentecost.

Trin·i·ty term *n. Brit.* the university and law term beginning after Easter.

trin·ket /tríngkit/ *n.* a trifling ornament, jewel, etc., esp. one worn on the person. □□ **trin·ket·ry** *n.* [16th c.: orig. unkn.]

tri·no·mi·al /trīnómeeəl/ *adj.* & *n.* • *adj.* consisting of three terms. • *n.* a scientific name or algebraic expression of three terms. [TRI- after BINOMIAL]

tri·o /trée-ō/ *n.* (*pl.* **–os**) **1** a set or group of three. **2** *Mus.* **a** a composition for three performers. **b** a group of three performers. **c** the central, usu. contrastive, section of a minuet, scherzo, or march. **3** (in piquet) three aces, kings, queens, or jacks in one hand. [F & It. f. L *tres* three, after *duo*]

tri·ode /trí-ōd/ *n.* **1** a thermionic valve having three electrodes. **2** a semiconductor rectifier having three connections. [TRI- + ELECTRODE]

tri·oe·cious /trī-éeshəs/ *adj. Bot.* having male, female, and hermaphroditic organs each on separate plants. [TRI- + Gk *oikos* house]

tri·o·let /trée·əláy, trílit/ *n.* a poem of eight (usu. eight syllable) lines rhyming *abaaabab,* the first line recurring as the fourth and seventh and the second as the eighth. [F (as TRIO)]

tri·ox·ide /trīóksīd/ *n. Chem.* an oxide containing three oxygen atoms.

trip /trip/ *v.* & *n.* • *v.intr.* & *tr.* (**tripped, trip·ping**) **1** *intr.* **a** walk or dance with quick light steps. **b** (of a rhythm, etc.) run lightly. **2 a** *intr.* & *tr.* (often foll. by *up*) stumble or cause to stumble, esp. by catching or entangling the feet. **b** *intr.* & *tr.* (foll. by *up*) make or cause to make a slip or blunder. **3** *tr.* detect (a person) in a blunder. **4** *intr.* make an excursion to a place. **5** *tr.* release (part of a machine) suddenly by knocking aside a catch, etc. **6 a** release and raise (an anchor) from the bottom by means of a cable. **b** turn (a yard, etc.) from a horizontal to a vertical position for lowering. **7** *intr. colloq.* have a hallucinatory experience caused by a drug. • *n.* **1** a journey or excursion, esp. for pleasure. **2 a** a stumble or blunder. **b** the act of tripping or the state of being tripped up. **3** a nimble step. **4** *colloq.* a hallucinatory experience caused by a drug. **5** a contrivance for a tripping mechanism, etc. □ **trip the light fantastic** *joc.* dance. [ME f. OF *triper, tripper,* f. MDu. *trippen* skip, hop]

tri·par·tite /trīpaártīt/ *adj.* **1** consisting of three parts. **2** shared by or

involving three parties. **3** *Bot.* (of a leaf) divided into three segments almost to the base. □□ **tri·par·tite·ly** *adv.* **tri·par·ti·tion** /–tíshən/ *n.* [ME f. L *tripartitus* (as TRI-, *partitus* past part. of *partiri* divide)]

tripe /trīp/ *n.* **1** the first or second stomach of a ruminant, esp. an ox, as food. **2** *colloq.* nonsense; rubbish (*don't talk such tripe*). [ME f. OF, of unkn. orig.]

trip ham·mer *n.* a large, heavy pivoted hammer used in forging, raised by a cam or lever and allowed to drop on the metal being worked.

tri·phib·i·ous /trīfíbeeəs/ *adj.* (of military operations) on land, on sea, and in the air. [irreg. f. TRI- after *amphibious*]

triph·thong /tríf-thawng, –thong, tríp–/ *n.* **1** a union of three vowels (letters or sounds) pronounced in one syllable (as in *fire*). **2** three vowel characters representing the sound of a single vowel (as in b*eau*). □□ **triph·thong·al** /–thónggəl/ *adj.* [F *triphtongue* (as TRI-, DIPHTHONG)]

tri·plane /tríplayn/ *n.* an early type of airplane having three sets of wings, one above the other.

tri·ple /trípəl/ *adj., n.,* & *v.* • *adj.* **1** consisting of three usu. equal parts or things; threefold. **2** involving three parties. **3** three times as much or many (*triple the amount; triple thickness*). • *n.* **1** a threefold number or amount. **2** a set of three. **3** a base hit allowing a batter to safely reach third base. **4** (in *pl.*) a peal of changes on seven bells. • *v.intr.* & *tr.* **1** multiply or increase by three. **2** to hit a triple. □□ **trip·ly** *adv.* [OF *triple* or L *triplus* f. Gk *triplous*]

▶**Triple** and **treble** can be used interchangeably to mean 'threefold,' or ' consisting of three parts.' But in American English, **triple** is more common, both as a verb (*to triple your money in less than five years*) and as an adjective (*in his triple role as a father, a son, and the company's president*). **Treble** is more commonly heard in its musical sense (*a treble instrument*), and in British English.

tri·ple crown *n.* **1** *RC Ch.* the pope's tiara. **2** the act of winning all three of a group of important events in horse racing, etc.

tri·ple jump *n.* an athletic exercise or contest comprising a hop, a step, and a jump.

tri·ple play *n. Baseball* the act of making all three outs in a single play.

tri·ple rhyme *n.* a rhyme including three syllables.

trip·let /tríplit/ *n.* **1** each of three children or animals born at one birth. **2** a set of three things, esp. of equal notes played in the time of two or of verses rhyming together. [TRIPLE + –ET[1], after *doublet*]

tri·ple time *n. Mus.* that with three beats to the bar; waltz time.

tri·plex /trípleks, trí–/ *adj.* & *n.* • *adj.* triple or threefold. • *n.* (**Triplex**) *Brit.* Trademark toughened or laminated safety glass for car windows, etc. [L *triplex –plicis* (as TRI-, *plic-* fold)]

trip·li·cate *adj., n.,* & *v.* • *adj.* /tríplikət/ **1** existing in three examples or copies. **2** having three corresponding parts. **3** tripled. • *n.* /tríplikət/ each of a set of three copies or corresponding parts. • *v.tr.* /tríplikayt/ **1** make in three copies. **2** multiply by three. □ **in triplicate** consisting of three exact copies. □□ **trip·li·ca·tion** /–káyshən/ *n.* [ME f. L *triplicatus* past part. of *triplicare* (as TRIPLEX)]

tri·plic·i·ty /tríplísitee/ *n.* (*pl.* **–ties**) **1** the state of being triple. **2** a group of three things. **3** *Astrol.* a set of three zodiacal signs. [ME f. LL *triplicitas* f. L TRIPLEX]

trip·loid /tríployd/ *n.* & *adj. Biol.* • *n.* an organism or cell having three times the haploid set of chromosomes. • *adj.* of or being a triploid. [mod.L *triploides* f. Gk (as TRIPLE)]

trip·loi·dy /tríploydee/ *n.* the condition of being triploid.

trip·me·ter /trípmeetər/ *n.* a vehicle instrument that can be set to record the distance of individual journeys.

tri·pod /trípod/ *n.* **1** a three-legged stand for supporting a camera, etc. **2** a stool, table, or utensil resting on three feet or legs. **3** *Gk Antiq.* a bronze altar at Delphi on which a priestess sat to utter oracles. □□ **trip·o·dal** /trípəd'l/ *adj.* [L *tripus tripodis* f. Gk *tripous* (as TRI-, *pous podos* foot)]

trip·o·li /trípəlee/ *n.* = ROTTENSTONE. [F f. *Tripoli* in N. Africa or in Syria]

tri·pos /trípos/ *n. Brit.* (at Cambridge University) the honors examination for the BA degree. [as TRIPOD, with ref. to the stool on which graduates sat to deliver a satirical speech at the degree ceremony]

trip·per /trípər/ *n.* **1** *Brit.* a person who goes on a pleasure trip or excursion. **2** *colloq.* a person experiencing hallucinatory effects of a drug.

trip·tych /tríptik/ *n.* **1 a** a picture or relief carving on three panels, usu. hinged vertically together and often used as an altarpiece. **b** a set of three associated pictures placed in this way. **2** a set of three writing tablets hinged or tied together. **3** a set of three artistic works. [TRI-, after DIPTYCH]

trip wire *n.* a wire stretched close to the ground, operating an alarm, etc., when disturbed.

tri·que·tra /trikétrə/ *n.* (*pl.* **tri·que·trae** /–tree/) a symmetrical ornament of three interlaced arcs. [L, fem. of *triquetrus* three-cornered]

tri·reme /tríreem/ *n.* an ancient Greek warship, with three banks of oarsmen on each side. [F *trirè me* or L *triremis* (as TRI-, *remus* oar)]

tri·sac·cha·ride /trīsákərīd/ *n. Chem.* a sugar consisting of three linked monosaccharides.

tri·sect /trīsékt/ *v. tr.* cut or divide into three (usu. equal) parts. □□ **tri·sec·tion** /–sékshən/ *n.* **tri·sec·tor** *n.* [TRI- + L *secare sect-* cut]

tri·shaw /trīshaw/ *n.* a light three-wheeled pedaled vehicle used in Asia. [TRI- + RICKSHA]

tris·kel·i·on /triskéleeən, trī–/ *n.* a symbolic figure of three legs or lines from a common center. [Gk TRI- + *skelos* leg]

tris·mus /trízməs/ *n. Med.* a variety of tetanus with tonic spasm of the jaw muscles causing the mouth to remain tightly closed. [mod.L f. Gk *trismos* = *trigmos* a scream, grinding]

triste /treest/ *adj.* sad; melancholy; dreary [F f. L *tristis*]

tri·syl·la·ble /trísiləbəl, trī–/ *n.* a word or metrical foot of three syllables. □□ **tri·syl·lab·ic** /–silábik/ *adj.*

tri·tag·o·nist /trítágənist/ *n.* the third actor in a Greek play (cf. DEUTERAGONIST). [Gk *tritagōnistēs* (as TRITO-, *agōnistēs* actor)]

trite /trīt/ *adj.* (of a phrase, opinion, etc.) hackneyed; worn out by constant repetition. □□ **trite·ly** *adv.* **trite·ness** *n.* [L *tritus* past part. of *terere* rub]

trit·i·ate /tríteeayt/ *v. tr.* replace the ordinary hydrogen in (a substance) by tritium. □□ **tritiation** /–áyshən/ *n.*

trit·i·um /tríteeəm/ *n. Chem.* a radioactive isotope of hydrogen with a mass about three times that of ordinary hydrogen. ¶ Symb.: **T**. [mod.L f. Gk *tritos* third]

trito- /trítō, trítō/ *comb. form* third. [Gk *tritos* third]

Tri·ton /trít'n/ *n.* **1** (in Greek mythology) a minor sea god usu. represented as a man with a fish's tail and carrying a trident and shell trumpet. **2** (**triton**) any marine gastropod mollusk of the family Cymatiidae, with a long conical shell. **3** (**triton**) a newt. [L f. Gk *Tritōn*]

tri·ton /trít'n/ *n.* a nucleus of a tritium atom, consisting of a proton and two neutrons.

tri·tone /trítōn/ *n. Mus.* an interval of an augmented fourth, comprising three tones.

trit·u·rate /trícherayt/ *v. tr.* **1** grind to a fine powder. **2** masticate thoroughly. □□ **trit·u·ra·ble** *adj.* **trit·u·ra·tion** /–ráyshən/ *n.* **trit·u·ra·tor** *n.* [L *triturare* thresh wheat f. *tritura* rubbing (as TRITE)]

tri·umph /tríəmf, –umf/ *n. & v.* ● *n.* **1 a** the state of being victorious or successful (*returned home in triumph*). **b** a great success or achievement. **2** a supreme example (*a triumph of engineering*). **3** joy at success; exultation (*could see triumph in her face*). **4** the processional entry of a victorious general into ancient Rome. ● *v. intr.* **1** (often foll. by *over*) gain a victory; be successful; prevail. **2** ride in triumph. **3** (often foll. by *over*) exult. [ME f. OF *triumphe* (n.), *triumpher* (v.), f. L *triump(h)us* prob. f. Gk *thriambos* hymn to Bacchus]

tri·um·phal /tríúmfəl/ *adj.* of or used in or celebrating a triumph. [ME f. OF *triumphal* or L *triumphalis* (as TRIUMPH)]

tri·um·phant /tríúmfənt/ *adj.* **1** victorious or successful. **2** exultant. □□ **tri·um·phant·ly** *adv.* [ME f. OF *triumphant* or L *triumphare* (as TRIUMPH)]

▶Triumphal vs. Triumphant. Triumphant, the more common of these words, means 'victorious' or 'exultant,' e.g., *She led an arduous campaign to its triumphant conclusion* or *He returned triumphant with a patent for his device.* Triumphal means 'used in or celebrating a triumph,' e.g., *a triumphal arch; a triumphal parade.*

tri·um·vir /tríəmveer, –úmvər/ *n.* (*pl.* **tri·um·virs** or **tri·um·vi·ri** /–rī/) **1** each of three men holding a joint office. **2** a member of a triumvirate. □□ **tri·um·vi·ral** *adj.* [L, orig. in pl. *triumviri*, back-form. f. *trium virorum* genit. of *tres viri* three men]

tri·um·vi·rate /tríúmvirət/ *n.* **1** a board or ruling group of three men, esp. in ancient Rome. **2** the office of triumvir.

tri·une /tríyōōn/ *adj.* three in one, esp. with ref. to the Trinity. □□ **tri·u·ni·ty** /–yōōnitee/ *n.* (*pl.* **–ties**). [TRI- + L *unus* one]

tri·va·lent /trīváylənt/ *adj. Chem.* having a valence of three. □□ **tri·va·lence** *n.* **tri·va·len·cy** *n.*

triv·et /trívit/ *n.* **1** an iron tripod or bracket for a hot pot, kettle, or dish to stand on. **2** an iron bracket designed to hook on to bars of a grate for a similar purpose. □ **as right as a trivet** *colloq.* in a perfectly good state, esp. healthy. [ME *trevet*, app. f. L *tripes* (as TRI-, *pes pedis* foot)]

triv·et ta·ble *n.* a table with three feet.

triv·i·a /tríveeə/ *n. pl.* **1** insignificant factual details. **2** trifles or trivialities. [mod.L, pl. of TRIVIUM, infl. by TRIVIAL]

triv·i·al /tríveeəl/ *adj.* **1** of small value or importance; trifling (*raised trivial objections*). **2** (of a person) concerned only with trivial things. **3** *archaic* commonplace or humdrum (*the trivial round of daily life*). **4** *Biol. & Chem.* of a name: **a** popular; not scientific. **b** specific, as opposed to generic. **5** *Math.* giving rise to no difficulty or interest. □□ **triv·i·al·i·ty** /–veeálitee/ *n.* (*pl.* **–ties**). **triv·i·al·ly** *adv.* **triv·i·al·ness** *n.* [L *trivialis* commonplace f. *trivium*: see TRIVIUM]

triv·i·al·ize /tríveeəlīz/ *v. tr.* make trivial or apparently trivial; minimize. □□ **triv·i·al·i·za·tion** *n.*

triv·i·um /tríveeəm/ *n. hist.* the medieval university studies of grammar, rhetoric, and logic. [L, = place where three roads meet (as TRI-, *via* road)]

tri·week·ly /tríweeklee/ *adj.* produced or occurring three times a week or every three weeks.

-trix /triks/ *suffix* (*pl.* **–trices** /trisiz, tríseez/ or **–trixes**) forming feminine agent nouns corresponding to masculine nouns in *–tor*, esp. in Law (*executrix*). [L *–trix –tricis*]

tRNA *abbr.* transfer RNA.

tro·car /trōkaar/ *n.* an instrument used for withdrawing fluid from a body cavity, esp. in edema, etc. [F *trois-quarts, trocart* f. *trois* three + *carre* side, face of an instrument, after its triangular form]

tro·cha·ic /trōkáyik/ *adj. & n. Prosody* ● *adj.* of or using trochees. ● *n.* (usu. in *pl.*) trochaic verse. [L *trochaicus* f. Gk *trokhaikos* (as TROCHEE)]

tro·chal /trōkəl/ *adj. Zool.* wheel-shaped. □ **trochal disk** *Zool.* the retractable disk on the head of a rotifer bearing a crown of cilia, used for drawing in food or for propulsion. [Gk *trokhos* wheel]

tro·chan·ter /trōkántər/ *n.* **1** *Anat.* any of several bony protuberances by which muscles are attached to the upper part of the femur. **2** *Zool.* the second segment of the leg in insects. [F f. Gk *trokhantēr* f. *trekhō* run]

tro·che /trōkee/ *n.* a small usu. circular medicated tablet or lozenge. [obs. *trochisk* f. OF *trochisque* f. LL *trochiscus* f. Gk *trokhiskos* dimin. of *trokhos* wheel]

tro·chee /trōkee/ *n. Prosody* a foot consisting of one long or stressed syllable followed by one short or unstressed syllable. [L *trochaeus* f. Gk *trokhaios* (*pous*) running (foot) f. *trekhō* run]

troch·le·a /trókleeə/ *n.* (*pl.* **troch·le·ae** /–lee-ee/) *Anat.* a pulleylike structure or arrangement of parts, e.g., the groove at the lower end of the humerus. □□ **troch·le·ar** *adj.* [L, = pulley f. Gk *trokhilia*]

tro·choid /trōkoyd/ *adj. & n.* ● *adj.* **1** *Anat.* rotating on its own axis. **2** *Geom.* (of a curve) traced by a point on a radius of a circle rotating along a straight line or another circle. ● *n.* a trochoid joint or curve. □□ **tro·choi·dal** *adj.* [Gk *trokhoeidēs* wheel-like f. *trokhos* wheel]

trod *past* and *past part.* of TREAD.

trod·den *past part.* of TREAD.

trog /trog/ *n.* esp. *Brit. sl.* a term of contempt for a person; a boor or hooligan. [abbr. of TROGLODYTE]

trog·lo·dyte /tróglədīt/ *n.* **1** a cave dweller, esp. of prehistoric times. **2** a hermit. **3** *derog.* a willfully obscurantist or old-fashioned person. □□ **trog·lo·dyt·ic** /–dítik/ *adj.* **trog·lo·dyt·i·cal** /–dítikəl/ *adj.* **trog·lo·dyt·ism** *n.* [L *troglodyta* f. Gk *trōglodutēs* f. the name of an Ethiopian people, after *trōglē* hole]

tro·gon /trōgon/ *n.* any tropical bird of the family Trogonidae, with a long tail and brilliantly colored plumage. [mod.L f. Gk *trōgōn* f. *trōgō* gnaw]

troi·ka /tróykə/ *n.* **1 a** a Russian vehicle with a team of three horses abreast. **b** this team. **2** a group of three people, esp. as an administrative council. [Russ. f. *troe* three]

troil·ism /tróylizəm/ *n.* sexual activity involving three participants. [perh. f. F *trois* three]

Tro·jan /trójən/ *adj. & n.* ● *adj.* of or relating to ancient Troy in Asia Minor. ● *n.* **1** a native or inhabitant of Troy. **2** a person who works, fights, etc., courageously (*works like a Trojan*). [ME f. L *Troianus* f. *Troia* Troy]

Tro·jan Horse *n.* **1** a hollow wooden horse said to have been used by the Greeks to enter Troy. **2** a person or device secreted, intended to bring about ruin at a later time. **3** *Computing* a set of instructions hidden in a program that cause damage or mischief.

troll[1] /trōl/ *n.* (in Scandinavian folklore) a fabled being, esp. a giant or dwarf dwelling in a cave. [ON & Sw. *troll*, Da. *trold*]

troll[2] /trōl/ *v. & n.* ● *v.* **1** *intr.* sing out in a carefree jovial manner. **2** *tr. & intr.* fish by drawing bait along in the water. **3** *intr.* esp. *Brit.* walk; stroll. ● *n.* **1** the act of trolling for fish. **2** a line or bait used in this. □□ **troll·er** *n.* [ME 'stroll, roll': cf. OF *troller* quest, MHG *trollen* stroll]

trol·ley /trólee/ *n.* (*pl.* **–leys**) **1** esp. *Brit.* a table, stand, or basket on wheels or castors for serving food, transporting luggage or shopping, gathering purchases in a supermarket, etc. **2** esp. *Brit.* a low truck running on rails. **3** (in full **trolley wheel**) a wheel attached to a pole, etc., used to carry current from an overhead electric wire to drive a vehicle. **4 a** = TROLLEY CAR. **b** = TROLLEY BUS. □ **off one's trolley** *sl.* crazy. [of dial. orig., perh. f. TROLL[2]]

trol·ley bus *n.* a trackless trolley.

trol·ley car *n.* an electric streetcar using a trolley wheel.

trol·lop /trólop/ *n.* **1** a disreputable girl or woman. **2** a prostitute. □□ **trol·lop·ish** *adj.* **trol·lop·y** *adj.* [17th c.: perh. rel. to TRULL]

trom·bone /trombṓn/ *n.* **1 a** a large brass wind instrument with a sliding tube.

trombone

b its player. **2** an organ stop with the quality of a trombone. □□ **trom·bon·ist** *n.* [F or It. f. It. *tromba* TRUMPET]

trom·mel /trómǝl/ *n. Mining* a revolving cylindrical sieve for cleaning ore. [G, = drum]

tro·mom·e·ter /trǝmómitǝr/ *n.* an instrument for measuring very slight earthquake shocks. [Gk *tromos* trembling + –METER]

tromp /tromp, trawmp/ *v.* **1** *tr. & intr.* walk heavily; trample. **2** *tr.* defeat decisively; trounce. [prob. a var. of TRAMPLE]

trompe /tromp/ *n.* an apparatus for producing a blast in a furnace by using falling water to displace air. [F, = trumpet: see TRUMP[1]]

trompe-l'œil /tro Nplóyǝ, trámpláy, –loí/ *n.* a still life painting, etc., designed to give an illusion of reality. [F, lit. 'deceives the eye']

-tron /tron/ *suffix Physics* forming nouns denoting: **1** an elementary particle (*positron*). **2** a particle accelerator. **3** a thermionic valve. [after ELECTRON]

troop /tro͞op/ *n. & v.* ● *n.* **1** an assembled company; an assemblage of people or animals. **2** (in *pl.*) soldiers or armed forces. **3** a cavalry unit commanded by a captain. **4** a unit of artillery and armored formation. **5** a unit of Girl Scouts, Boy Scouts, etc. ● *v.* **1** *intr.* (foll. by *in, out, off,* etc.) come together or move in large numbers. **2** *tr.* form (a regiment) into troops. □ **troop the color** esp. *Brit.* transfer a flag ceremonially at a public mounting or changing of garrison guards. [F *troupe,* back-form. f. *troupeau* dimin. of med.L *troppus* flock, prob. of Gmc orig.]

troop·er /tro͞opǝr/ *n.* **1** a soldier in a cavalry or armored unit. **2 a** a mounted police officer. **b** a state police officer. **3** a cavalry horse. **4** esp. *Brit.* a troopship. □ **swear like a trooper** swear extensively or forcefully.

trop. *abbr.* **1** tropic. **2** tropical.

trope /trōp/ *n.* a figurative (e.g., metaphorical or ironical) use of a word. [L *tropus* f. Gk *tropos* turn, way, trope f. *trepō* turn]

troph·ic /trófik, trō–/ *adj.* of or concerned with nutrition (*trophic nerves*). [Gk *trophikos* f. *trophē* nourishment f. *trephō* nourish]

-trophic /trófik, trō–/ *comb. form* relating to nutrition.

tropho- /trófō, trō–/ *comb. form* nourishment. [Gk *trophē:* see TROPHIC]

troph·o·blast /trófōblast, trō–/ *n.* a layer of tissue on the outside of a mammalian blastula, providing nourishment to an embryo.

tro·phy /trófee/ *n.* (*pl.* **–phies**) **1** a cup or other decorative object awarded as a prize or memento of victory or success in a contest, etc. **2** a memento or souvenir, e.g., a deer's antlers, taken in hunting. **3** *Gk & Rom. Antiq.* the weapons, etc., of a defeated army set up as a memorial of victory. **4** an ornamental group of symbolic or typical objects arranged for display. □□ **tro·phied** *adj.* (also in *comb.*). [F *trophée* f. L *trophaeum* f. Gk *tropaion* f. *tropē* rout f. *trepō* turn]

trop·ic /trópik/ *n. & adj.* ● *n.* **1** the parallel of latitude 23°27′ north (**tropic of Cancer**) or south (**tropic of Capricorn**) of the Equator. **2** each of two corresponding circles on the celestial sphere where the sun appears to turn after reaching its greatest declination. **3** (**the Tropics**) the region between the tropics of Cancer and Capricorn. ● *adj.* **1** = TROPICAL 1. **2** of tropism. [ME f. L *tropicus* f. Gk *tropikos* f. *tropē* turning f. *trepō* turn]

-tropic /trópik/ *comb. form* **1** = –TROPHIC. **2** turning toward (*heliotropic*).

trop·i·cal /trópikǝl/ *adj.* **1** of, peculiar to, or suggesting the Tropics (*tropical fish; tropical diseases*). **2** very hot; passionate; luxuriant. **3** of or by way of a trope. □□ **trop·i·cal·ly** *adv.*

trop·i·cal year *n.* see YEAR 1.

trop·ic bird *n.* any sea bird of the family Phaethontidae, with very long central tail feathers.

tro·pism /trópizǝm/ *n. Biol.* the turning of all or part of an organism in a particular direction in response to an external stimulus. [Gk *tropos* turning f. *trepō* turn]

tro·pol·o·gy /trǝpólǝjee/ *n.* **1** the figurative use of words. **2** figurative interpretation, esp. of the Scriptures. □□ **trop·o·log·i·cal** /trópǝlójikǝl, trō–/ *adj.* [LL *tropologia* f. Gk *tropologia* (as TROPE)]

trop·o·pause /trópǝpawz, trō–/ *n.* the interface between the troposphere and the stratosphere. [TROPOSPHERE + PAUSE]

trop·o·sphere /trópǝsfeer, trō–/ *n.* a layer of atmospheric air extending upward from the earth's surface, in which the temperature falls with increasing height (cf. STRATOSPHERE, IONOSPHERE). □□ **trop·o·spher·ic** /–sférik, –sfeer–/ *adj.* [Gk *tropos* turning + SPHERE]

trop·po[1] /trópō, tráwpō/ *adv. Mus.* too much (qualifying a tempo indication). [It.]

trop·po[2] /trópō/ *adj. Austral. sl.* mentally ill from exposure to a tropical climate.

trot /trot/ *v. & n.* ● *v.* (**trot·ted, trot·ting**) **1** *intr.* (of a person) run at a moderate pace, esp. with short strides. **2** *intr.* (of a horse) proceed at a steady pace faster than a walk lifting each diagonal pair of legs alternately. **3** *intr. colloq.* walk or go. **4** *tr.* cause (a horse or person) to trot. **5** *tr.* traverse (a distance) at a trot. ● *n.* **1** the action or exercise of trotting (*proceed at a trot; went for a trot*). **2** (**the trots**) *sl.* an attack of diarrhea. **3** a brisk steady movement or occupation. **4** (in *pl.*) *Austral. colloq.* **a** trotting races. **b** a meeting for these. **5** *sl.*

a literal translation of a text used by students; a crib. □ **on the trot** *Brit. colloq.* **1** continually busy (*kept them on the trot*). **2** in succession (*five weeks on the trot*). **trot out 1** cause (a horse) to trot to show his paces. **2** produce or introduce (as if) for inspection and approval, esp. tediously or repeatedly. [ME f. OF *troter* f. Rmc & med.L *trottare,* of Gmc orig.]

troth /trawth, trōth/ *n. archaic* **1** faith; loyalty. **2** truth. □ **pledge** (or **plight**) **one's troth** pledge one's word esp. in marriage or betrothal. [ME *trowthe,* for OE *trēowth* TRUTH]

Trot·sky·ism /trótskeeizǝm/ *n.* the political or economic principles of L. Trotsky, Russian politician d. 1940, esp. as urging worldwide socialist revolution. □□ **Trot·sky·ist** *n.* **Trot·sky·ite** *n. derog.*

trot·ter /trótǝr/ *n.* **1** a horse bred or trained for trotting. **2** (usu. in *pl.*) **a** an animal's foot as food (*pig's trotters*). **b** *joc.* a human foot.

trot·ting /tróting/ *n.* racing for trotting horses pulling a two-wheeled vehicle and driver.

trou·ba·dour /tro͞obǝdawr/ *n.* **1** any of a number of French medieval lyric poets composing and singing in Provençal in the 11th–13th c. on the theme of courtly love. **2** a singer or poet. [F f. Prov. *trobador* f. *trobar* find, invent, compose in verse]

trou·ble /trúbǝl/ *n. & v.* ● *n.* **1** difficulty or distress; vexation; affliction (*am having trouble with my car*). **2 a** inconvenience; unpleasant exertion; bother (*went to a lot of trouble*). **b** a cause of this (*the child was no trouble*). **3** a cause of annoyance or concern (*the trouble with you is that you can't say no*). **4** a faulty condition or operation (*kidney trouble; engine trouble*). **5 a** fighting; disturbance (*crowd trouble; don't want any trouble*). **b** (in *pl.*) political or social unrest; public disturbances. **6** disagreement; strife (*is having trouble at home*). ● *v.* **1** *tr.* cause distress or anxiety to; disturb (*were much troubled by their debts*). **2** *intr.* be disturbed or worried (*don't trouble about it*). **3** *tr.* afflict; cause pain, etc., to (*am troubled with arthritis*). **4** *tr. & intr.* (often *refl.*) subject or be subjected to inconvenience or unpleasant exertion (*sorry to trouble you; don't trouble yourself*). □ **ask** (or **look**) **for trouble** *colloq.* invite trouble or difficulty by one's actions, behavior, etc.; behave rashly or indiscreetly. **be no trouble** cause no inconvenience, etc. **go to the trouble** (or **some trouble,** etc.) exert oneself to do something. **in trouble 1** involved in a matter likely to bring censure or punishment. **2** *colloq.* pregnant while unmarried. **take trouble** (or **the trouble**) exert oneself to do something. □□ **trou·bler** *n.* [ME f. OF *truble* (n.), *trubler, turbler* (v.) ult. f. L *turbidus* TURBID]

trou·ble and strife *n. rhyming sl.* wife.

trou·bled /trúbǝld/ *adj.* showing, experiencing, or reflecting trouble, anxiety, etc. (*a troubled mind; a troubled childhood*).

trou·ble·mak·er /trúbǝlmaykǝr/ *n.* a person who habitually causes trouble. □□ **trou·ble·mak·ing** *n.*

trou·ble·shoot·er /trúbǝlsho͞otǝr/ *n.* **1** a mediator in industrial or diplomatic, etc., disputes. **2** a person who traces and corrects faults in machinery, etc. □□ **trou·ble·shoot·ing** *n.*

trou·ble·some /trúbǝlsǝm/ *adj.* **1** causing trouble. **2** vexing; annoying. □□ **trou·ble·some·ly** *adv.* **trou·ble·some·ness** *n.*

trou·ble spot *n.* a place where difficulties regularly occur.

trou·blous /trúblǝs/ *adj. archaic* or *literary* full of troubles; agitated; disturbed (*troublous times*). [ME f. OF *troubleus* (as TROUBLE)]

trough /trawf, trof/ *n.* **1** a long narrow open receptacle for water, animal feed, etc. **2** a channel for conveying a liquid. **3** an elongated region of low barometric pressure. **4** a hollow between two wave crests. **5** the time of lowest economic performance, etc. **6** a region around the minimum on a curve of variation of a quantity. **7** a low point or depression. [OE *trog* f. Gmc]

trounce /trowns/ *v.tr.* **1** defeat heavily. **2** beat; thrash. **3** punish severely. □□ **trounc·er** *n.* **trounc·ing** *n.* [16th c.: = afflict: orig. unkn.]

troupe /tro͞op/ *n.* a company of actors or acrobats, etc. [F, = TROOP]

troup·er /tro͞opǝr/ *n.* **1** a member of a theatrical troupe. **2** a staunch reliable person, esp. during difficult times.

trou·sers /trówzǝrz/ *n.pl.* **1** = PANTS. **2** (**trouser**) (*attrib.*) designating parts of this (*trouser leg*). □□ **trou·sered** *adj.* **trou·ser·less** *adj.* [archaic *trouse* (sing.) f. Ir. & Gael. *triubhas* TREWS: pl. form after *drawers*]

trous·seau /tro͞osō, troosṓ/ *n.* (*pl.* **trous·seaus** or **trous·seaux** /–sṓz/) the clothes and other possessions collected by a bride for her marriage. [F, lit. bundle, dimin. of *trousse* TRUSS]

trout /trowt/ *n.* (*pl.* same or **trouts**) **1** any of various freshwater fish of the genus *Salmo* of the northern hemisphere, valued as food. **2** a similar fish of the family Salmonidae (see also *salmon trout*). **3** *Brit. sl. derog.* a woman, esp. an old or ill-tempered one (usu. *old trout*). □□ **trout·let** *n.* **trout·ling** *n.* **trout·y** *adj.* [OE *truht* f. LL *tructa*]

trout 1

trou·vère /tro͞ováir/ *n.* a medieval epic poet in northern France in the 11th–14th c. [OF *trovere* f. *trover* find: cf. TROUBADOUR]

trove /trōv/ *n.* = TREASURE TROVE. [AF *trové* f. *trover* find]

tro·ver /tróvǝr/ *n. Law* **1** finding and keeping personal property.

2 common law action to recover the value of personal property wrongfully taken, etc. [OF *trover* find]

trow /trow, trō/ *v.tr. archaic* think; believe. [OE *trūwian, trēowian*, rel. to TRUCE]

trow·el /trówəl/ *n. & v.* ● *n.* **1** a small hand tool with a flat pointed blade, used to apply and spread mortar, etc. **2** a similar tool with a curved scoop for lifting plants or earth. ● *v.tr.* (**trow·eled, trow·el·ing** *or* **trow·elled, trow·el·ling**) **1** apply (plaster, etc.). **2** plaster (a wall, etc.) with a trowel. [ME f. OF *truele* f. med.L *truella* f. L *trulla* scoop, dimin. of *trua* ladle, etc.]

troy /troy/ *n.* (in full **troy weight**) a system of weights used for precious metals and gems, with a pound of 12 ounces or 5,760 grains. [ME, prob. f. *Troyes* in France]

tru·ant /trōōənt/ *n., adj., & v.* ● *n.* **1** a child who stays away from school without leave or explanation. **2** a person missing from work, etc. ● *adj.* (of a person, conduct, thoughts, etc.) shirking; idle; wandering. ● *v.intr.* (also **play truant**) stay away as a truant. □□ **tru·an·cy** *n.* [ME f. OF, prob. ult. f. Celt.: cf. Welsh *truan*, Gael. *truaghan* wretched]

truce /trōōs/ *n.* **1** a temporary agreement to cease hostilities. **2** a suspension of private feuding or bickering. □□ **truce·less** *adj.* [ME *trew(e)s* (pl.) f. OE *trēow*, rel. to TRUE]

truck[1] /truk/ *n. & v.* ● *n.* **1** a vehicle for carrying heavy or bulky cargo, etc. **2** *Brit.* a railroad freight car. **3** a vehicle for transporting troops, supplies, etc. **4** a swiveling wheel frame of a railroad car. **5** a wheeled stand for transporting goods; a handcart. **6** a *Naut.* a wooden disk at the top of a mast with holes for halyards. **b** a small solid wheel. ● *v.* **1** *tr.* convey on or in a truck. **2** *intr.* drive a truck. **3** *intr. sl.* proceed; go. □□ **truck·age** *n.* [perh. short for TRUCKLE in sense 'wheel, pulley']

truck[2] /truk/ *n. & v.* ● *n.* **1** dealings; exchange; barter. **2** small wares. **3** small farm or garden produce (*truck farm*). **4** *colloq.* odds and ends. **5** *hist.* the payment of workers in kind. ● *v.tr. & intr. archaic* barter; exchange. □ **have no truck with** avoid dealing with. [ME f. OF *troquer* (unrecorded) = *trocare*, of unkn. orig.]

truck·er /trúkər/ *n.* **1** a long-distance truck driver. **2** a firm dealing in long-distance transportation of goods.

truck·ie /trúkee/ *n. Austral. colloq.* a truck driver; a trucker.

truck·ing /trúking/ *n.* transportation of goods by truck.

truck·le /trúkəl/ *n. & v.* ● *n.* **1** (in full **truckle bed**) = TRUNDLE BED. **2** *orig. dial.* a small barrel-shaped cheese. ● *v.intr.* (foll. by *to*) submit obsequiously. □□ **truck·ler** *n.* [orig. = wheel, pulley, f. AF *trocle* f. L *trochlea* pulley]

truck stop *n.* a facility, esp. for truck drivers, usu. by a major highway and including a gas station, restaurant, etc.

truc·u·lent /trúkyələnt/ *adj.* **1** aggressively defiant. **2** aggressive; pugnacious. **3** fierce; savage. □□ **truc·u·lence** *n.* **truc·u·len·cy** *n.* **truc·u·lent·ly** *adv.* [L *truculentus* f. *trux trucis* fierce]

▶ **Truculence vs. Truculency.** Truculency is the older of these two words, but since the 18th century, it has been used synonymously with truculence. In American English, *truculence* is the more widely used.

trudge /truj/ *v. & n.* ● *v.* **1** *intr.* go on foot, esp. laboriously. **2** *tr.* traverse (a distance) in this way. ● *n.* a trudging walk. □□ **trudg·er** *n.* [16th c.: orig. unkn.]

trudg·en /trújən/ *n.* a swimming stroke like the crawl with a scissors movement of the legs. [J. *Trudgen*, 19th-c. English swimmer]

true /trōō/ *adj., adv., & v.* ● *adj.* **1** in accordance with fact or reality (*a true story*). **2** genuine; rightly or strictly so called; not spurious or counterfeit (*a true friend; the true heir to the throne*). **3** (often foll. by *to*) loyal or faithful (*true to one's word*). **4** (foll. by *to*) accurately conforming (to a standard or expectation, etc.) (*true to form*). **5** correctly positioned or balanced; upright; level. **6** exact; accurate (*a true aim; a true copy*). **7** (*absol.*) (also **it is true**) certainly; admittedly (*true, it would cost more*). **8** (of a note) exactly in tune. **9** *archaic* honest; upright (*twelve good men and true*). ● *adv.* **1** truly (*tell me true*). **2** accurately (*aim true*). **3** without variation (*breed true*). ● *v.tr.* (**trues, trued, true·ing** *or* **tru·ing**) bring (a tool, wheel, frame, etc.) into the exact position or form required. □ **come true** actually happen or be the case. **out of true** (or **the true**) not in the correct or exact position. **true to form** (or **type**) being or behaving, etc., as expected. **true to life** accurately representing etc. □□ **true·ish** *adj.* **true·ness** *n.* [OE *trēowe, trŷwe*, f. the Gmc noun repr. by TRUCE]

true bill *n.* a bill of indictment endorsed by a grand jury as being sustained by evidence.

true-blue *adj.* extremely loyal or orthodox.

true blue *n.* a person who is true-blue.

true-heart·ed *adj.* faithful; loyal.

true lov·er's knot *n.* a kind of knot with interlacing bows on each side, symbolizing true love.

true north *n.* north according to the earth's axis, not magnetic north.

true rib *n.* a rib joined directly to the breastbone.

truf·fle /trúfəl/ *n.* **1** any strong-smelling underground fungus of the order Tuberales, used as a culinary delicacy and found esp. in France by trained dogs or pigs. **2** a usu. round candy made of choc-

olate mixture covered with cocoa, etc. [prob. f. Du. *truffel* f. obs. F *truffle* ult. f. L *tubera* pl. of TUBER]

trug /trug/ *n. Brit.* **1** a shallow oblong garden basket usu. of wood strips. **2** *archaic* a wooden milk pan. [perh. a dial. var. of TROUGH]

tru·ism /trōōizəm/ *n.* **1** an obviously true or hackneyed statement. **2** a proposition that states nothing beyond what is implied in any of its terms. □□ **tru·is·tic** /–ístik/ *adj.*

trull /trul/ *n. archaic* a prostitute. [16th c.: cf. G *Trulle*, TROLLOP]

tru·ly /trōōlee/ *adv.* **1** sincerely; genuinely (*am truly grateful*). **2** really; indeed (*truly, I do not know*). **3** faithfully; loyally (*served them truly*). **4** accurately; truthfully (*is not truly depicted; has been truly stated*). **5** rightly; properly (*well and truly*). [OE *trēowlice* (as TRUE, –LY[2])]

tru·meau /trōōmṓ/ *n.* (*pl.* **tru·meaux** /–mṓz/) a section of wall or a pillar between two openings, e.g., a pillar dividing a large doorway. [F]

trump[1] /trump/ *n. & v.* ● *n.* **1** a playing card of a suit ranking above the others. **2** an advantage, esp. involving surprise. **3** *colloq.* **a** a helpful or admired person. **b** *Austral. & NZ* a person in authority. ● *v.* **1** a *tr.* defeat (a card or its player) with a trump. **b** *intr.* play a trump card when another suit has been led. **2** *tr. colloq.* gain a surprising advantage over (a person, proposal, etc.). □ **trump up** fabricate or invent (an accusation, excuse, etc.) (*on a trumped-up charge*). **turn up trumps** *Brit. colloq.* **1** turn out better than expected. **2** be greatly successful or helpful. [corrupt. of TRIUMPH in the same (now obs.) sense]

trump[2] /trump/ *n. archaic* a trumpet blast. □ **the last trump** the trumpet blast to wake the dead on Judgment Day in Christian theology. [ME f. OF *trompe* f. Frank.: prob. imit.]

trump card *n.* **1** a card belonging to, or turned up to determine, a trump suit. **2** *colloq.* **a** a valuable resource. **b** a surprise move to gain an advantage.

trump·er·y /trúmpəree/ *n. & adj.* ● *n.* (*pl.* **–ies**) **1** a worthless finery. **b** a worthless article. **2** junk. ● *adj.* **1** showy but worthless (*trumpery jewels*). **2** delusive; shallow (*trumpery arguments*). [ME f. OF *tromperie* f. *tromper* deceive]

trum·pet /trúmpit/ *n. & v.* ● *n.* **1 a a** tubular or conical brass instrument with a flared bell and a bright penetrating tone. **b** its player. **c** an organ stop with a quality resembling a trumpet. **2 a** the tubular corona of a daffodil, etc. **b** a trumpet-shaped thing (*ear trumpet*). **3** a sound of or like a trumpet. ● *v.* (**trum·pet·ed, trum·pet·ing**) **1** *intr.* **a** blow a trumpet. **b** (of an enraged elephant, etc.) make a loud sound as of a trumpet. **2** *tr.* proclaim loudly (a person's or thing's merit). □□ **trum·pet·less** *adj.* [ME f. OF *trompette* dimin. (as TRUMP[2])]

trumpet 1a

trump·et call *n.* an urgent summons to action.

trum·pet·er /trúmpitər/ *n.* **1** a person who plays or sounds a trumpet, esp. a cavalry soldier giving signals. **2** a bird making a trumpetlike sound, esp.: **a** a variety of domestic pigeon. **b** a large black S. American cranelike bird of the genus *Psophia*.

trum·pet·er swan *n.* a large N. American wild swan, *Cygnus buccinator*.

trum·pet ma·jor *n.* the chief trumpeter of a cavalry regiment.

trun·cal /trúngkəl/ *adj.* of or relating to the trunk of a body or a tree.

trun·cate /trúngkayt/ *v. & adj.* ● *v.tr.* **1** cut the top or the end from (a tree, a body, a piece of writing, etc.). **2** *Crystallog.* replace (an edge or an angle) by a plane. ● *adj. Bot. & Zool.* (of a leaf or feather, etc.) ending abruptly as if cut off at the base or tip. □□ **trun·cate·ly** *adv.* **trun·ca·tion** /–káyshən/ *n.* [L *truncare truncat-* maim]

trun·cheon /trúnchən/ *n.* **1** a short club or cudgel, esp. carried by a policeman; a billy club. **2** a staff or baton as a symbol of authority, esp. (in the UK) that of the Earl Marshal. [ME f. OF *tronchon* stump ult. f. L *truncus* trunk]

trun·dle /trúnd'l/ *v.tr. & intr.* roll or move heavily or noisily, esp. on or as on wheels. [var. of obs. or dial. *trendle, trindle*, f. OE *trendel* circle (as TREND)]

trun·dle bed *n.* a low bed on wheels that can be stored under a larger bed.

trunk /trungk/ *n.* **1** the main stem of a tree as distinct from its branches and roots. **2** a person's or animal's body apart from the limbs and head. **3** the main part of any structure. **4** a large box with a hinged lid for transporting luggage, clothes, etc. **5** the luggage compartment of an automobile. **6** an elephant's elongated prehensile nose. **7** (in *pl.*) men's often close-fitting shorts worn for swimming, boxing, etc. **8** the main body of an artery, nerve, communications network, etc. **9** an enclosed shaft or conduit for cables, ventilation, etc □□ **trunk·ful** *n.* (*pl.* **–fuls**). **trunk·less** *adj.* [ME f. OF *tronc* f. L *truncus*]

trunk call *n.* esp. *Brit.* a long-distance telephone call.

trunk·ing /trúngking/ *n.* **1** a system of shafts or conduits for cables, ventilation, etc. **2** the use or arrangement of trunk lines.

trunk line *n.* a main line of a railway, telephone system, etc.

trunk road *n.* esp. *Brit.* an important main road.

trun·nion /trúnyən/ *n.* **1** a supporting cylindrical projection on each side of a cannon or mortar. **2** a hollow gudgeon supporting a cylinder in a steam engine and giving passage to the steam. [F *trognon* core, tree trunk, of unkn. orig.]

truss /trus/ *n. & v.* ● *n.* **1** a framework, e.g., of rafters and struts, supporting a roof or bridge, etc. **2** a surgical appliance worn to support a hernia. **3** *Brit.* a bundle of old hay (56 lb.) or new hay (60 lb.) or straw (36 lb.). **4** a compact terminal cluster of flowers or fruit. **5** a large corbel supporting a monument, etc. **6** *Naut.* a heavy iron ring securing the lower yards to a mast. ● *v.tr.* **1** tie up (a fowl) compactly for cooking. **2** (often foll. by *up*) tie (a person) up with the arms to the sides. **3** support (a roof or bridge, etc.) with a truss or trusses. □□ **truss·er** *n.* [ME f. OF *trusser* (v.), *trusse* (n.), of unkn. orig.]

truss 1

trust /trust/ *n. & v.* ● *n.* **1 a** a firm belief in the reliability or truth or strength, etc., of a person or thing. **b** the state of being relied on. **2** a confident expectation. **3 a** a thing or person committed to one's care. **b** the resulting obligation or responsibility (*am in a position of trust; have fulfilled my trust*). **4** a person or thing confided in (*is our sole trust*). **5** reliance on the truth of a statement, etc., without examination. **6** commercial credit (*obtained merchandise on trust*). **7** *Law* **a** confidence placed in a person by making that person the nominal owner of property to be used for another's benefit. **b** the right of the latter to benefit by such property. **c** the property so held. **d** the legal relation between the holder and the property so held. **8 a** a body of trustees. **b** an organization managed by trustees. **c** an organized association of several companies for the purpose of reducing or defeating competition, etc., esp. one in which all or most of the stock is transferred to a central committee and shareholders lose their voting power although remaining entitled to profits. ● *v.* **1** *tr.* place trust in; believe in; rely on the character or behavior of. **2** *tr.* (foll. by *with*) allow (a person) to have or use (a thing) from confidence in its proper use (*was reluctant to trust them with my books*). **3** *tr.* (often foll. by *that* + clause) have faith or confidence or hope that a thing will take place (*I trust you will not be late; I trust that she is recovering*). **4** *tr.* (foll. by *to*) consign (a thing) to (a person) with trust. **5** *tr.* (foll. by *for*) allow credit to (a customer) for (merchandise). **6** *intr.* (foll. by *in*) place reliance in (*we trust in you*). **7** *intr.* (foll. by *to*) place (esp. undue) reliance on (*shall have to trust to luck*). □ **in trust** *Law* held on the basis of trust (see sense 7 of *n.*). **on trust 1** on credit. **2** on the basis of trust or confidence. **take on trust** accept (an assertion, claim, etc.) without evidence or investigation. □□ **trust·a·ble** *adj.* **trust·er** *n.* [ME *troste, truste* (n.) f. ON *traust* f. *traustr* strong: (v.) f. ON *treysta*, assim. to the noun]

trust com·pa·ny *n.* a company formed to act as a trustee or to deal with trusts.

trust·ee /trustée/ *n.* **1** *Law* a person or member of a board given control or powers of administration of property in trust with a legal obligation to administer it solely for the purposes specified. **2** a nation made responsible for the government of an area. □□ **trust·ee·ship** *n.*

trust·ful /trústfool/ *adj.* **1** full of trust or confidence. **2** not feeling or showing suspicion. □□ **trust·ful·ly** *adv.* **trust·ful·ness** *n.*

trust fund *n.* a fund of money, etc., held in trust.

trust·ing /trústing/ *adj.* having trust (esp. characteristically); trustful. □□ **trust·ing·ly** *adv.* **trust·ing·ness** *n.*

trust ter·ri·to·ry *n.* a territory under the trusteeship of the United Nations or of a nation designated by them.

trust·wor·thy /trústwurthee/ *adj.* deserving of trust; reliable. □□ **trust·wor·thi·ly** *adv.* **trust·wor·thi·ness** *n.*

trust·y /trústee/ *adj. & n.* ● *adj.* (**trust·i·er, trust·i·est**) **1** *archaic* or *joc.* trustworthy (*a trusty steed*). **2** *archaic* loyal (to a sovereign) (*my trusty subjects*). ● *n.* (*pl.* **–ies**) a prisoner who is given special privileges for good behavior. □□ **trust·i·ly** *adv.* **trust·i·ness** *n.*

truth /trooth/ *n.* (*pl.* **truths** /troothz, trooths/) **1** the quality or a state of being true or truthful (*doubted the truth of the statement; there may be some truth in it*). **2 a** what is true (*tell us the whole truth; the truth is that I forgot*). **b** what is accepted as true (*one of the fundamental truths*). □ **in truth** truly; really. **to tell the truth** (or **truth to tell**) to be frank. □□ **truth·less** *adj.* [OE *trīewth, trēowth* (as TRUE)]

truth drug *n.* (also **truth se·rum**) any of various drugs supposedly able to induce a state in which a person answers questions truthfully.

truth·ful /troothfool/ *adj.* **1** habitually speaking the truth. **2** (of a story, etc.) true. **3** (of a likeness, etc.) corresponding to reality. □□ **truth·ful·ly** *adv.* **truth·ful·ness** *n.*

truth ta·ble *n.* a list indicating the truth or falsity of various propositions in logic, etc.

try /trī/ *v. & n.* ● *v.* (**–ies, –ied**) **1** *intr.* make an effort with a view to success (often foll. by *to* + infin.; *colloq.* foll. by *and* + infin.: *tried to be on time; try and be early; I shall try hard*). **2** *tr.* make an effort to achieve (*tried my best; had better try something easier*). **3** *tr.* **a** test (the quality of a thing) by use or experiment. **b** test the qualities of (a person or thing) (*try it before you buy*). **4** *tr.* make severe demands on (a person, quality, etc.) (*my patience has been sorely tried*). **5** *tr.* examine the effectiveness or usefulness of for a purpose (*try cold water; have you tried kicking it?*). **6** *tr.* ascertain the state of fastening of (a door, window, etc.) **7** *tr.* **a** investigate and decide (a case or issue) judicially. **b** subject (a person) to trial (*will be tried for murder*). **8** *tr.* make an experiment in order to find out (*let us try which takes longest*). **9** *intr.* (foll. by *for*) **a** apply or compete for. **b** seek to reach or attain (*am going to try for a gold medal*). **10** *tr.* (often foll. by *out*) **a** extract (oil) from fat by heating. **b** treat (fat) in this way. **11** *tr.* (often foll. by *up*) smooth (roughly planed wood) with a plane to give an accurately flat surface. ● *n.* (*pl.* **–ies**) **1** an effort to accomplish something; an attempt (*give it a try*). **2** *Rugby* the act of touching the ball down behind the opposing goal line, scoring points and entitling the scoring side to a kick at the goal. **3** *Football* an attempt to score one or two extra points after a touchdown. □ **tried and true** (or **tested**) proved reliable by experience; dependable. **try conclusions with** see CONCLUSION. **try a fall with** contend with. **try on for size** try out or test for suitability. **try one's hand** see how skillful one is, esp. at the first attempt. **try it on** *Brit. colloq.* **1** test another's patience. **2** attempt to outwit or deceive another person. **try on** put on (clothes, etc.) to see if they fit or suit the wearer. **try out 1** put to the test. **2** test thoroughly. [ME, = separate, distinguish, etc., f. OF *trier* sift, of unkn. orig.]

try·ing /trí-ing/ *adj.* annoying; vexatious; hard to endure. □□ **try·ing·ly** *adv.*

try·ing-plane *n.* a plane used in trying (see sense 11 of *v.*).

try-on *n. Brit. colloq.* **1** an act of trying it on. **2** an attempt to fool or deceive.

try·pan·o·some /trípənəsōm, tripánə–/ *n. Med.* any protozoan parasite of the genus *Trypanosoma* having a long trailing flagellum and infesting the blood, etc. [Gk *trupanon* borer + –SOME³]

try·pan·o·so·mi·a·sis /trípənəsōmíəsis, tripánə–/ *n.* any of several diseases caused by a trypanosome including sleeping sickness and Chagas' disease.

tryp·sin /trípsin/ *n.* a digestive enzyme acting on proteins and present in the pancreatic juice. □□ **tryp·tic** /tríptik/ *adj.* [Gk *tripsis* friction f. *tribō* rub (because it was first obtained by rubbing down the pancreas with glycerine)]

tryp·sin·o·gen /trípsínəjən/ *n.* a substance in the pancreas from which trypsin is formed.

tryp·to·phan /tríptəfan/ *n. Biochem.* an amino acid essential in the diet of vertebrates. [as TRYPSIN + –*phan* f. Gk *phainō* appear]

try square *n.* a carpenter's square, usu. with one wooden and one metal limb.

tryst /trist/ *n. & v. archaic* ● *n.* **1** a time and place for a meeting, esp. of lovers. **2** such a meeting (*keep a tryst; break one's tryst*). ● *v.intr.* (foll. by *with*) make a tryst. □□ **tryst·er** *n.* [ME, = obs. *trist* (= TRUST) f. OF *triste* an appointed station in hunting]

tsar var. of CZAR.

tsar·e·vich var. of CZAREVICH.

tsa·ri·na var. of CZARINA.

tset·se /tsétsee, tét–, tseétsee, teé–/ *n.* any fly of the genus *Glossina* native to Africa that feeds on human and animal blood with a needlelike proboscis and transmits trypanosomiasis. [Setswana]

TSH *abbr.* thyroid-stimulating hormone.

T-shirt /teéshərt/ *n.* (also **tee·shirt**) a short-sleeved collarless casual top, usu. of knitted cotton and having the form of a T when spread out.

tsp. *abbr.* (*pl.* **tsps.**) teaspoon; teaspoonful.

T square /teéskwair/ *n.* a T-shaped instrument for drawing or testing right angles.

tsu·na·mi /tsŏonaámee/ *n.* (*pl.* **tsu·na·mis**) a long high sea wave caused by underwater earthquakes or other disturbances; tidal wave. [Jap. f. *tsu* harbor + *nami* wave]

T square

Tswa•na /tsw áánə, swaá–/ *n.* (also **Setswana** /setswaánə/) **1** a southern African people living in Botswana and neighboring areas. **2** a member of this people. **3** the Bantu language of this people. [native name]

▶ *Setswana* is now the preferred form for the language.

Tu. *abbr.* Tuesday.

tu•a•ta•ra /toʊ̅ə̅taːrə/ *n.* a large lizardlike reptile, *Sphenodon punctatus*, unique to certain small islands of New Zealand, having a crest of soft spines extending along its back and a third eye on top of its head. [Maori f. *tua* on the back + *tara* spine]

tub /tub/ *n. & v. • n.* **1** an open flat-bottomed usu. round container for various purposes. **2** a tub-shaped (usu. plastic) carton. **3** the amount a tub will hold. **4** *Brit. colloq.* a bath. **5 a** *colloq.* a clumsy slow boat. **b** a stout roomy boat for rowing practice. **6** (in mining) a container for conveying ore, coal, etc. *• v.* (**tubbed, tub•bing**) **1** *tr. & intr. esp. Brit.* plant, bathe, or wash in a tub. **2** *tr.* enclose in a tub. **3** *tr.* line (a mine shaft) with a wooden or iron casing. □ **tub chair** a chair with solid arms continuous with a usu. semicircular back. □□ **tub•ba•ble** *adj.* **tub•bish** *adj.* **tub•ful** *n.* (*pl.* **–fuls**). [ME, prob. of LG or Du. orig.: cf. MLG, MDu. *tubbe*]

tu•ba /toʊ̅bə, tyoʊ̅–/ *n.* (*pl.* **tu•bas**) **1 a** a low-pitched brass wind instrument. **b** its player. **2** an organ stop with the quality of a tuba. [It. f. L, = trumpet]

tub•al /toʊ̅bəl, tyoʊ̅–/ *adj. Anat.* of or relating to a tube, esp. the bronchial or Fallopian tubes.

tub•by /túbee/ *adj.* (**tub•bi•er, tub•bi•est**) **1** (of a person) short and fat; tub-shaped. **2** (of a violin) dull-sounding, lacking resonance. □□ **tub•bi•ness** *n.*

tube /toʊ̅b, tyoʊ̅b/ *n. & v. • n.* **1** a long hollow rigid or flexible cylinder, esp. for holding or carrying air, liquids, etc. **2** a soft metal or plastic cylinder sealed at one end and having a screw cap at the other, for holding a semiliquid substance ready for use (*a tube of toothpaste*). **3** *Anat. & Zool.* a hollow cylindrical organ in the body (*bronchial tubes; Fallopian tubes*) **4** (often prec. by *the*) *colloq.* the London subway system. **5 a** a cathode-ray tube, esp. in a television set. **b** (prec. by *the*) *colloq.* television. **6** = VACUUM TUBE. **7** = INNER TUBE. **8** the cylindrical body of a wind instrument. **9** (in full **tube top**) an elasticized upper garment shaped like a tube. **10** *Austral. sl.* a can of beer. *• v.tr.* **1** equip with tubes. **2** enclose in a tube. □□ **tube•less** *adj.* (esp. in sense 7 of *n.*). **tube•like** *adj.* [F *tube* or L *tubus*]

tuba

tu•bec•to•my /toʊ̅béktəmee, tyoʊ̅–/ *n.* (*pl.* **–mies**) *Surgery* removal of a Fallopian tube.

tu•ber /toʊ̅bər, tyoʊ̅–/ *n.* **1 a** the short thick rounded part of a stem or rhizome, usu. found underground and covered with modified buds, e.g., a potato. **b** the similar root of a dahlia, etc. **2** *Anat.* a lump or swelling. [L, = hump, swelling]

tu•ber•cle /toʊ̅bərkəl, tyoʊ̅–/ *n.* **1** a small rounded protuberance, esp. on a bone. **2** a small rounded swelling on the body or in an organ, esp. a nodular lesion characteristic of tuberculosis in the lungs, etc. **3** a small tumor; a wartlike growth. □□ **tu•ber•cu•late** /–bə́rkyələt, –layt/ *adj.* **tu•ber•cu•lous** /–bə́rkyələs/ *adj.* [L *tuberculum*, dimin. of *tuber*: see TUBER]

tu•ber•cle ba•cil•lus *n.* a bacterium causing tuberculosis.

tu•ber•cu•lar /toʊ̅bə́rkyələr, tyoʊ̅–/ *adj. & n. • adj.* of or having tubercles or tuberculosis. *• n.* a person with tuberculosis. [f. L *tuberculum* (as TUBERCLE)]

tu•ber•cu•la•tion /toʊ̅bə́rkyəláyshən, tyoʊ̅–/ *n.* **1** the formation of tubercles. **2** a growth of tubercles. [f. L *tuberculum* (as TUBERCLE)]

tu•ber•cu•lin /toʊ̅bə́rkyəlin, tyoʊ̅–/ *n.* a sterile liquid from cultures of tubercle bacillus, used in the diagnosis and treatment of tuberculosis. [f. L *tuberculum* (as TUBERCLE)]

tu•ber•cu•lin test *n.* a hypodermic injection of tuberculin to detect a tubercular infection.

tu•ber•cu•lin-test•ed *adj.* (of milk) from cows giving a negative response to a tuberculin test.

tu•ber•cu•lo•sis /toʊ̅bə́rkyəlósis, tyoʊ̅–/ *n.* an infectious disease caused by the bacillus *Mycobacterium tuberculosis*, characterized by tubercles, esp. in the lungs.

tu•be•rose[1] /toʊ̅bərōs, tyoʊ̅–/ *adj.* **1** covered with tubers; knobby. **2** of or resembling a tuber. **3** bearing tubers. □□ **tu•ber•os•i•ty** /–rósitee/ *n.* [L *tuberosus* f. TUBER]

tu•ber•ose[2] /toʊ̅bərōz, tyoʊ̅–/ *n.* a plant, *Polianthes tuberosa*, native to Mexico, having heavily scented white funnel-like flowers and strap-shaped leaves. [L *tuberosa* fem. (as TUBEROSE[1])]

tu•ber•ous /toʊ̅bərəs, tyoʊ̅–/ *adj.* = TUBEROSE[1]. [F *tubéreux* or L *tuberosus* f. TUBER]

tu•ber•ous root *n.* a thick and fleshy root like a tuber but without buds.

tu•bi•fex /toʊ̅bifeks, tyoʊ̅–/ *n.* any red annelid worm of the genus *Tubifex*, found in mud at the bottom of rivers and lakes and used as food for aquarium fish. [mod.L f. L *tubus* tube + *–fex* f. *facere* make]

tu•bi•form /toʊ̅bifawrm, tyoʊ̅–/ *adj.* tube-shaped.

tub•ing /toʊ̅bing, tyoʊ̅–/ *n.* **1** a length of tube. **2** a quantity of tubes.

tub-thump•er *n. colloq.* a ranting preacher or orator. **tub-thump•ing** *adj. & n. colloq.* ranting oratory.

tu•bu•lar /toʊ̅byələr, tyoʊ̅–/ *adj.* **1** tube-shaped. **2** having or consisting of tubes. **3** (of furniture, etc.) made of tubular pieces.

tu•bu•lar bells *n.pl.* an orchestral instrument consisting of a row of vertically suspended brass tubes that are struck with a hammer.

tu•bule /toʊ̅byool, tyoʊ̅–/ *n.* a small tube in a plant or an animal body. [L *tubulus*, dimin. of *tubus* tube]

tu•bu•lous /toʊ̅byələs, tyoʊ̅–/ *adj.* = TUBULAR.

tuck /tuk/ *v. & n. • v.* **1** *tr.* (often foll. by *in, up*) **a** draw, fold, or turn the outer or end parts of (cloth or clothes, etc.) close together so as to be held; thrust in the edge of (a thing) so as to confine it (*tucked his shirt into his trousers; tucked the sheet under the mattress*). **b** thrust in the edges of bedclothes around (a person) (*came to tuck me in*). **2** *tr.* draw together into a small space (*tucked her legs under her; the bird tucked its head under its wing*). **3** *tr.* stow (a thing) away in a specified place or way (*tucked it in a corner; tucked it out of sight*). **4** *tr.* **a** make a stitched fold in (material, a garment, etc.). **b** shorten, tighten, or ornament with stitched folds. *• n.* **1** a flattened usu. stitched fold in material, a garment, etc., often one of several parallel folds for shortening, tightening, or ornament. **2** *Brit. colloq.* food, esp. cake and candy eaten by children (also *attrib.*: *tuck box*). **3** *Naut.* the part of a ship's hull where the planks meet under the stern. **4** (in full **tuck position**) (in diving, gymnastics, etc.) a position with the knees bent upward into the chest and the hands clasped around the shins. □ **tuck away** (or **into**) *colloq.* eat (food) heartily (*tucked into their dinner; could really tuck it away*). **tuck in** *Brit. colloq.* eat food heartily. [ME *tukke, tokke,* f. MDu., MLG *tucken*, = OHG *zucchen* pull, rel. to TUG]

tuck•er /túkər/ *n. & v. • n.* **1** a person or thing that tucks. **2** *hist.* a piece of lace or linen, etc., in or on a woman's bodice. **3** *Austral. colloq.* food. *• v.tr.* (esp. in *passive*; often foll. by *out*) *colloq.* tire; exhaust. □ **best bib and tucker** see BIB[1].

tuck•er-bag *n.* (also **truck•er box**) *Austral. colloq.* a container for food.

tuck•et /túkit/ *n. archaic* a flourish on a trumpet. [ONF *toquer* beat (a drum)]

tuck-in *n. Brit. colloq.* a large meal.

tuck•ing /túking/ *n.* a series of usu. stitched tucks in material or a garment.

tuck shop *n. Brit.* a small shop, esp. near or in a school, selling food to children.

-tude /tōōd, tyōōd/ *suffix* forming abstract nouns (*altitude; attitude; solitude*). [from or after F *–tude* f. L *–tudo –tudinis*]

Tu•dor /tōōdər, tyoʊ̅–/ *adj. & n. hist. • adj.* **1** of, characteristic of, or associated with the royal family of England ruling 1485–1603 or this period. **2** of or relating to the architectural style of this period, esp. with half-timbering and elaborately decorated houses. *• n.* a member of the Tudor royal family. [Owen *Tudor* of Wales, grandfather of Henry VII]

Tu•dor rose *n.* (in late Perpendicular decoration) a conventional five-lobed figure of a rose, esp. a red rose encircling a white one.

Tues. *abbr.* (also **Tue.**) Tuesday.

Tues•day /tōōzday, –dee, tyoʊ̅–/ *n. & adv. • n.* the third day of the week, following Monday. *• adv.* **1** *colloq.* on Tuesday. **2** (**Tuesdays**) on Tuesdays; each Tuesday. [OE *Tiwesdæg* f. *Tiw* the Gmc god identified with Roman Mars]

tu•fa /tōōfə, tyoʊ̅–/ *n.* **1** a porous rock composed of calcium carbonate and formed around mineral springs. **2** = TUFF. □□ **tu•fa•ceous** /–fáyshəs/ *adj.* [It., var. of *tufo*: see TUFF]

tuff /tuf/ *n.* rock formed by the consolidation of volcanic ash. □□ **tuff•a•ceous** /tufáyshəs/ *adj.* [F *tuf, tuffe* f. It. *tufo* f. LL *tofus*, L TOPHUS]

tuf•fet /túfit/ *n.* **1** = TUFT *n.* **2.** **2** a low seat. [var. of TUFT]

tuft /tuft/ *n. & v. • n.* **1** a bunch or collection of threads, grass, feathers, hair, etc., held or growing together at the base. **2** *Anat.* a bunch of small blood vessels. *• v.* **1** *tr.* provide with a tuft or tufts. **2** *tr.* make depressions at regular intervals in (a mattress, etc.) by passing a thread through. **3** *intr.* grow in tufts. □□ **tuft•y** *adj.* [ME, prob. f. OF *tofe, toffe*, of unkn. orig.: for *–t* cf. GRAFT[1]]

tuft•ed /túftid/ *adj.* **1** having or growing in a tuft or tufts. **2** (of a bird) having a tuft of feathers on the head.

tug /tug/ *v. & n. • v.* (**tugged, tug•ging**) **1** *tr. &* (foll. by *at*) *intr.* pull hard or violently; jerk (*tugged it from my grasp; tugged at my sleeve*). **2** *tr.* tow (a ship, etc.) by means of a tugboat. *• n.* **1** a hard, violent, or jerky pull (*gave a tug on the rope*). **2** a sudden strong emotional feeling (*felt a tug as I watched them go*). **3** a small powerful boat for towing larger boats and ships. **4** an aircraft towing a glider. **5** (of a horse's harness) a loop from a saddle supporting a shaft or trace. □□ **tug•ger** *n.* [ME *togge, tugge,* intensive f. Gmc: see TOW[1]]

tug-of-war *n.* **1** a trial of strength between two sides pulling against each other on a rope. **2** a decisive or severe contest.

tugboat

tug·boat /túgbōt/ *n.* = TUG *n.* 3.

tu·i /tŏŏ-ee/ *n. NZ* a large honeyeater, *Prosthemadera novaeseelandiae,* native to New Zealand and having a long protrusible bill and glossy bluish black plumage with two white tufts at the throat. [Maori]

tu·i·tion /tŏŏ-íshən, tyŏŏ–/ *n.* **1** teaching or instruction, esp. if paid for (*driving tuition; music tuition*). **2** a fee for this. □□ **tu·i·tion·al** *adj.* [ME f. OF f. L *tuitio –onis* f. *tuēri tuit-* watch, guard]

tu·la·re·mi·a /tŏŏləreéemeeə/ *n.* a severe infectious disease of animals transmissible to humans; caused by the bacterium *Pasteurella tularense* and characterized by ulcers at the site of infection, fever, and loss of weight. □□ **tu·la·re·mic** *adj.* [mod.L f. *Tulare* County in California, where it was first observed]

tu·lip /tŏŏlip, tyŏŏ–/ *n.* **1** any bulbous spring-flowering plant of the genus *Tulipa,* esp. one of the many cultivated forms with showy cup-shaped flowers of various colors and markings. **2** a flower of this plant. [orig. *tulipa(n)* f. mod.L *tulipa* f. Turk. *tul(i)band* f. Pers. *dulband* TURBAN (from the shape of the expanded flower)]

tu·lip tree *n.* any of various trees, esp. of the genus *Liriodendron,* producing tuliplike flowers.

tulle /tŏŏl/ *n.* a soft fine silk, etc., net for veils and dresses. [*Tulle* in SW France, where it was first made]

tum /tum/ *n. Brit. colloq.* stomach. [abbr. of TUMMY]

tum·ble /túmbəl/ *v. & n.* • *v.* **1** *intr. & tr.* fall or cause to fall suddenly, clumsily, or headlong. **2** *intr.* fall rapidly in amount, etc. (*prices tumbled*). **3** *intr.* (often foll. by *about, around*) roll or toss erratically or helplessly to and fro. **4** *intr.* move or rush in a headlong or blundering manner (*the children tumbled out of the car*). **5** *intr.* (often foll. by *to*) *colloq.* grasp the meaning or hidden implication of an idea, circumstance, etc. (*they quickly tumbled to our intentions*). **6** *tr.* overturn; fling or push roughly or carelessly. **7** *intr.* perform acrobatic feats, esp. somersaults. **8** *tr.* rumple or disarrange; disorder. **9** *tr.* dry (laundry) in a tumble dryer. **10** *tr.* clean (castings, gemstones, etc.) in a tumbling barrel. **11** *intr.* (of a pigeon) turn over backward in flight. • *n.* **1** a sudden or headlong fall. **2** an somersault or other acrobatic feat. **3** an untidy or confused state. □ **tumble dry** *v.tr. & intr.* (**dries, dried**) dry in a tumble dryer.

> **WORD HISTORY** tumble
>
> Middle English (also in the sense 'dance with contortions'): of Germanic origin; related to German *taumeln* 'be giddy, stagger,' Swedish *tumla* 'tumble down'; related to Old English *tumbian* 'to dance.' The sense was probably influenced by Old French *tomber* 'to fall.' The noun dates from the mid-17th century.

tum·ble·down /túmbəldown/ *adj.* falling or fallen into ruin; dilapidated.

tum·ble dry·er *n.* a machine for drying laundry in a heated rotating drum.

tum·bler /túmblər/ *n.* **1** a drinking glass with no handle or foot (formerly with a rounded bottom so as not to stand upright). **2** an acrobat, esp. one performing somersaults. **3** (in full **tumbler dryer**) = TUMBLE DRYER. **4 a** a pivoted piece in a lock that holds the bolt until lifted by a key. **b** a notched pivoted plate in a gunlock. **5** a kind of pigeon that turns over backward in flight. **6** an electrical switch worked by pushing a small sprung lever. **7** a toy figure that rocks when touched. **8** = TUMBLING BARREL. □□ **tum·bler·ful** *n.* (*pl.* **–fuls**)

tum·ble·weed /túmbəlweed/ *n.* a plant, *Amaranthus albus,* that forms a globular bush that breaks off in late summer and is tumbled about by the wind.

tum·bling bar·rel *n.* (also **tum·bling box,** etc.) a revolving device containing an abrasive substance, in which castings, gemstones, etc., are cleaned by friction.

tum·bling bay *n.* **1** the outfall from a river, reservoir, etc. **2** a pool into which this flows.

tum·brel /túmbrəl/ *n.* (also **tum·bril** /–ril/) *hist.* **1** an open cart in which condemned persons were conveyed to their execution, esp. to the guillotine during the French Revolution. **2** a two-wheeled covered cart for carrying tools, ammunition, etc. **3** a cart that tips to empty its load, esp. one carrying dung. [ME f. OF *tumberel, tomberel* f. *tomber* fall]

tu·me·fy /tŏŏmifī, tyŏŏ–/ *v.* (**–fies, –fied**) **1** *intr.* swell; inflate; be inflated. **2** *tr.* cause to do this. □□ **tu·me·fa·ci·ent** /–fáyshənt/ *adj.* **tu·me·fac·tion** /–fákshən/ *n.* [F *tuméfier* f. L *tumefacere* f. *tumēre* swell]

tu·mes·cent /tŏŏmésənt, tyŏŏ–/ *adj.* **1** becoming tumid; swelling. **2** swelling as a response to sexual stimulation. □□ **tu·mes·cence** *n.* **tu·mes·cent·ly** *adv.* [L *tumescere* (as TUMEFY)]

tu·mid /tŏŏmid, tyŏŏ–/ *adj.* **1** (of parts of the body, etc.) swollen; inflated. **2** (of a style, etc.) inflated; bombastic. □□ **tu·mid·i·ty** /–mídi-tee/ *n.* **tu·mid·ly** *adv.* **tu·mid·ness** *n.* [L *tumidus* f. *tumēre* swell]

tum·my /túmee/ *n.* (*pl.* **–mies**) *colloq.* the stomach. [childish pronunc. of STOMACH]

tum·my ache *n.* an abdominal pain; indigestion.

tu·mor /tŏŏmər, tyŏŏ–/ *n.* a swelling, esp. from an abnormal growth of tissue. □□ **tu·mor·ous** *adj.* [L *tumor* f. *tumēre* swell]

tump /tump/ *n.* esp. *dial.* a hillock; a mound; a tumulus. [16th c.; orig. unkn.]

tu·mult /tŏŏmult, tyŏŏ–/ *n.* **1** an uproar or din, esp. of a disorderly crowd. **2** an angry demonstration by a mob; a riot; a public disturbance. **3** a conflict of emotions in the mind. [ME f. OF *tumulte* or L *tumultus*]

tu·mul·tu·ous /tŏŏmúlchŏŏəs, tyŏŏ–/ *adj.* **1** noisily vehement; uproarious; making a tumult (*a tumultuous welcome*). **2** disorderly. **3** agitated. □□ **tu·mul·tu·ous·ly** *adv.* **tu·mul·tu·ous·ness** *n.* [OF *tumultuous* or L *tumultuosus* (as TUMULT)]

tu·mu·lus /tŏŏmyələs, tyŏŏ–/ *n.* (*pl.* **tu·mu·li** /–lī/) an ancient burial mound or barrow. □□ **tu·mu·lar** *adj.* [L f. *tumēre* swell]

tun /tun/ *n. & v.* • *n.* **1** a large beer or wine cask. **2** a brewer's fermenting vat. **3** a measure of capacity, equal to 252 gallons. • *v.tr.* (**tunned, tun·ning**) store (wine, etc.) in a tun. [OE *tunne* f. med.L *tunna,* prob. of Gaulish orig.]

tu·na¹ /tŏŏnə, tyŏŏ–/ *n.* (*pl.* same or **tu·nas**) **1** any marine fish of the family Scombridae native to tropical and warm waters, having a round body and pointed snout, and used for food. Also called (esp. *Brit.*) **tunny.** **2** (in full **tuna fish**) the flesh of the tuna, usu. preserved in oil or brine. [Amer. Sp., perh. f. Sp. *atún* tunny]

tu·na² /tŏŏnə, tyŏŏ–/ *n.* **1** a prickly pear, esp. *Opuntia tuna.* **2** the fruit of this. [Sp. f. Haitian]

tun·dish /túndish/ *n.* **1** a wooden funnel, esp. in brewing. **2** an intermediate reservoir in metal-founding.

tun·dra /túndrə/ *n.* a vast level treeless Arctic region usu. with a marshy surface and underlying permafrost. [Lappish]

tune /tŏŏn, tyŏŏn/ *n. & v.* • *n.* a melody with or without harmony. • *v.* **1** *tr.* put (a musical instrument) in tune. **2 a** *tr.* adjust (a radio receiver, etc.) to the particular frequency of the required signals. **b** *intr.* (foll. by *in*) adjust a radio receiver to the required signal (*tuned in to the news*). **3** *tr.* adjust (an engine, etc.) to run smoothly and efficiently. **4** *tr.* (foll. by *to*) adjust or adapt to a required or different purpose, situation, etc. **5** *intr.* (foll. by *with*) be in harmony with. □ **in tune 1** having the correct pitch or intonation (*sings in tune*). **2** (usu. foll. by *with*) harmonizing with one's associates, surroundings, etc. **out of tune 1** not having the correct pitch or intonation (*always plays out of tune*). **2** (usu. foll. by *with*) clashing with one's associates, etc. **to the tune of** *colloq.* to the considerable sum or amount of. **tuned in 1** (of a radio, etc.) adjusted to a particular frequency, station, etc. **2** (foll. by *on, to*) *sl.* in rapport or harmony with. **3** *colloq.* up to date; aware of what is going on. **tune up 1** (of an orchestra) bring the instruments to the proper or uniform pitch. **2** begin to play or sing. **3** bring to the most efficient condition. □□ **tun·a·ble** *adj.* (also **tune·a·ble**). [ME: unexpl. var. of TONE]

tune·ful /tŏŏnfŏŏl, tyŏŏn–/ *adj.* melodious; musical. □□ **tune·ful·ly** *adv.* **tune·ful·ness** *n.*

tune·less /tŏŏnlis, tyŏŏn–/ *adj.* **1** unmelodious; unmusical. **2** out of tune. □□ **tune·less·ly** *adv.* **tune·less·ness** *n.*

tun·er /tŏŏnər, tyŏŏn–/ *n.* **1** a person who tunes musical instruments, esp. pianos. **2** a device for tuning a radio receiver.

tung /tung/ *n.* (in full **tung tree**) a tree, *Aleurites fordii,* native to China, bearing poisonous fruits containing seeds that yield oil. [Chin. *tong*]

tung oil *n.* an oil obtained from the seeds of the tung tree, used as a drying agent in inks, paints, and varnishes.

tung·sten /túngstən/ *n. Chem.* a steel-gray dense metallic element with a very high melting point, occurring naturally in scheelite and used for the filaments of electric lamps and for alloying steel, etc. ¶ Symb.: **W.** □□ **tung·state** /–stayt/ *n.* **tung·stic** /–stik/ *adj.* **tung·stous** /–stəs/ *adj.* [Sw. f. *tung* heavy + *sten* stone]

tung·sten car·bide *n.* a very hard black substance used in making dies and cutting tools.

tu·nic /tŏŏnik, tyŏŏ–/ *n.* **1 a** a close-fitting short coat as part of a police or military, etc., uniform. **b** a loose, often sleeveless garment usu. reaching to about the knees, as worn in ancient Greece and Rome. **c** any of various loose, pleated dresses gathered at the waist with a belt or cord. **d** a tunicle. **2** *Zool.* the rubbery outer coat of an ascidian, etc. **3** *Bot.* **a** any of the concentric layers of a bulb. **b** the tough covering of a part of this. **4** *Anat.* a membrane enclosing or lining an organ. [F *tunique* or L *tunica*]

tu·ni·ca /tŏŏnikə, tyŏŏ–/ *n.* (*pl.* **tu·ni·cae** /–kee/) *Bot. & Anat.* = TUNIC 3, 4. [L]

tu·ni·cate /tŏŏnikət, –kayt, tyŏŏ–/ *n. & adj.* • *n.* any marine animal of the subphylum Urochordata having a rubbery or hard outer coat, including sea squirts. • *adj.* **1** *Zool.* of or relating to this subphylum. **2 a** *Zool.* enclosed in a tunic. **b** *Bot.* having concentric layers. [L *tunicatus* past part. of *tunicare* clothe with a tunic (as TUNICA)]

tu·ni·cle /tŏŏnikəl, tyŏŏ–/ *n.* a short vestment worn by a bishop or subdeacon at Mass, etc. [ME f. OF *tunicle* or L *tunicula* dimin. of TUNICA]

tun·ing /tōōning, tyōō–/ *n.* the process or a system of putting a musical instrument in tune.

tun·ing fork *n.* a two-pronged steel fork that gives a particular note when struck, used in tuning.

tun·ing peg *n.* (also **tun·ing pin**, etc.) a peg or pin, etc., attached to the strings of a stringed instrument and turned to alter their tension in tuning.

tun·nel /túnəl/ *n. & v.* • *n.* **1** an artificial underground passage through a hill or under a road or river, etc., esp. for a railroad or road to pass through, or in a mine. **2** an underground passage dug by a burrowing animal. **3** a prolonged period of difficulty or suffering (esp. in metaphors, e.g., the end of the tunnel). **4** a tube containing a propeller shaft, etc. • *v.* **(tun·neled, tun·nel·ing** or **tun·nelled, tun·nel·ling) 1** *intr.* (foll. by *through, into*, etc.) make a tunnel through (a hill, etc.). **2** *tr.* make (one's way) by tunneling. **3** *intr. Physics* pass through a potential barrier. □□ **tun·nel·er** *n.* [ME f. OF *tonel* dimin. of *tonne* TUN]

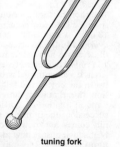

tuning fork

tun·nel di·ode *n. Electronics* a two-terminal semiconductor diode using tunneling electrons to perform high-speed switching operations.

tun·nel net *n.* a fishing net wide at the mouth and narrow at the other end.

tun·nel vi·sion *n.* **1** vision that is defective in not adequately including objects away from the center of the field of view. **2** *colloq.* inability to grasp the wider implications of a situation.

tun·ny /túnee/ *n.* (*pl.* same or **–nies**) esp. *Brit.* = TUNA[1]. [F *thon* f. Prov. *ton*, f. L *thunnus* f. Gk *thunnos*]

tup /tup/ *n. & v.* • *n.* **1** esp. *Brit.* a male sheep; a ram. **2** the striking head of a pile driver, etc. • *v.tr.* **(tupped, tup·ping)** esp. *Brit.* (of a ram) copulate with (a ewe). [ME *toje, tupe*, of unkn. orig.]

tu·pe·lo /tōōpilō, tyōō–/ *n.* (*pl.* **–los**) **1** any of various Asian and N. American deciduous trees of the genus *Nyssa*, with colorful foliage and growing in swampy conditions. **2** the wood of this tree. [Creek f. *ito* tree + *opilwa* swamp]

Tu·pi /tōōpee/ *n. & adj.* • *n.* (*pl.* same or **Tu·pis**) **1** a member of a Native American people native to the Amazon valley. **2** the language of this people. • *adj.* of or relating to this people or language. [native name]

tup·pence /túpəns/ *n. Brit.* = TWOPENCE. [phonet. spelling]

tup·pen·ny /túpənee/ *adj. Brit.* = TWOPENNY. [phonet. spelling]

Tup·per·ware /túpərwair/ *n. Trademark* a brand of plastic containers for storing food. [*Tupper*, name of the manufacturer, + WARE[1]]

tuque /tōōk/ *n.* a Canadian stocking cap. [Can. F form of TOQUE]

tu·ra·co /tōōrəkō/ *n.* (also **tou·ra·co**) (*pl.* **–cos**) any African bird of the family Musophagidae, with crimson and green plumage and a prominent crest. [F f. native W.Afr. name]

Tu·ra·ni·an /tōōráyneeən, tyōō–/ *n. & adj.* • *n.* the group of Asian languages that are neither Semitic nor Indo-European, esp. the Ural-Altaic family. • *adj.* of or relating to this group. [Pers. *Tūrān* region beyond the Oxus]

tur·ban /tɔ́rbən/ *n.* **1** a man's headdress of cotton or silk wound around a cap or the head, worn esp. by Muslims and Sikhs. **2** a woman's headdress or hat resembling this. □□ **tur·baned** *adj.* [16th c. (also *tulbant*, etc.), ult. f. Turk. *tülbent* f. Pers. *dulband*: cf. TULIP]

tur·ba·ry /tɔ́rbəree/ *n.* (*pl.* **–ries**) *Brit.* **1** the right of digging turf on common ground or on another's ground. **2** a place where turf or peat is dug. [ME f. AF *turberie*, OF *tourberie* f. *tourbe* TURF]

tur·bel·lar·i·an /tɔ́rbiláireeən/ *n. & adj.* • *n.* any usu. free-living flatworm of the class Turbellaria, having a ciliated surface. • *adj.* of or relating to this class. [mod.L *Turbellaria* f. L *turbella* dimin. of *turba* crowd: see TURBID]

turban 1

tur·bid /tɔ́rbid/ *adj.* **1** (of a liquid or color) muddy; thick; not clear. **2** (of a style, etc.) confused; disordered. □□ **tur·bid·i·ty** /–bíditee/ *n.* **tur·bid·ly** *adv.* **tur·bid·ness** *n.* [L *turbidus* f. *turba* a crowd, a disturbance]

▶**Turbid** is used of a liquid or color to mean 'muddy, not clear,' or of literary style, etc., to mean 'confused,' e.g., *the turbid utterances and twisted language of Carlyle.* **Turgid** means 'swollen, inflated, enlarged.' When used of literary style it means 'pompous, bombastic': *Communications from headquarters were largely turgid exercises in self-congratulation.*

tur·bi·nate /tɔ́rbinət/ *adj.* **1** shaped like a top or inverted cone. **2** (of a shell) with whorls decreasing rapidly in size. **3** *Anat.* (esp. of some nasal bones) shaped like a scroll. □□ **tur·bi·nal** *adj.* **tur·bi·na·tion** /–náyshən/ *n.* [L *turbinatus* (as TURBINE)]

tur·bine /tɔ́rbin, –bīn/ *n.* a rotary motor or engine driven by a flow of water, steam, gas, wind, etc., esp. to produce electrical power. [F f. L *turbo –binis* top, whirlwind]

tur·bit /tɔ́rbit/ *n.* a breed of domestic pigeon of stout build with a neck frill and short beak. [app. f. L *turbo* top, from its figure]

tur·bo /tɔ́rbō/ *n.* (*pl.* **–bos**) = TURBOCHARGER.

turbo- /tɔ́rbō/ *comb. form* turbine.

tur·bo·charg·er /tɔ́rbōchaarjər/ *n.* a supercharger driven by a turbine powered by the engine's exhaust gases.

tur·bo·fan /tɔ́rbōfan/ *n.* **1** a jet engine in which a turbine-driven fan provides additional thrust. **2** an aircraft powered by this.

tur·bo·jet /tɔ́rbōjet/ *n. Aeron.* **1** a jet engine in which the jet also operates a turbine-driven compressor for the air drawn into the engine. **2** an aircraft powered by this.

tur·bo·prop /tɔ́rbōprop/ *n. Aeron.* **1** a jet engine in which a turbine is used as in a turbojet and also to drive a propeller. **2** an aircraft powered by this.

tur·bo·shaft /tɔ́rbōshaft/ *n.* a gas turbine that powers a shaft for driving heavy vehicles, generators, pumps, etc.

tur·bo·su·per·charg·er /tɔ́rbōsōōpərchaarjər/ *n.* = TURBOCHARGER.

tur·bot /tɔ́rbət/ *n.* **1** a flatfish, *Psetta maxima*, having bony tubercles on the body and head and prized as food. **2** any of various similar fishes including halibut. [ME f. OF f. OSw. *törnbut* f. *törn* thorn + *but* BUTT[3]]

tur·bu·lence /tɔ́rbyələns/ *n.* **1** an irregularly fluctuating flow of air or fluid. **2** *Meteorol.* stormy conditions as a result of atmospheric disturbance. **3** a disturbance, commotion, or tumult.

tur·bu·lent /tɔ́rbyələnt/ *adj.* **1** disturbed; in commotion. **2** (of a flow of air, etc.) varying irregularly; causing disturbance. **3** tumultuous. **4** insubordinate; riotous. □□ **tur·bu·lent·ly** *adv.* [L *turbulentus* f. *turba* crowd]

Turco- /tɔ́rkō/ *comb. form* (also **Turko-**) Turkish; Turkish and. [med.L (as TURK)]

Tur·co·man var. of TURKOMAN.

turd /tərd/ *n. coarse sl.* **1** a lump of excrement. **2** a term of contempt for a person. [OE *tord* f. Gmc]

tur·doid /tɔ́rdoyd/ *adj.* thrushlike. [L *turdus* THRUSH[1]]

tu·reen /tōōréen, tyōō–/ *n.* a deep covered dish for serving soup, etc. [earlier *terrine*, *–ene* f. F *terrine* large circular earthenware dish, fem. of OF *terrin* earthen ult. f. L *terra* earth]

turf /tərf/ *n. & v.* • *n.* (*pl.* **turfs** or **turves**) **1 a** a layer of grass, etc., with earth and matted roots as the surface of grassland. **b** a piece of this cut from the ground. **c** an artificial ground covering, as on a playing field, etc. **2** a slab of peat for fuel. **3** (prec by *the*) **a** a horse racing generally. **b** a general term for racetracks. **4** *sl.* a person's territory or sphere of influence. • *v.tr.* **1** cover (ground) with turf. **2** (foll. by *out*) esp. *Brit. colloq.* expel or eject (a person or thing). [OE f. Gmc]

turf ac·count·ant *n. Brit.* a bookmaker.

turf·man /tɔ́rfmən/ *n.* (*pl.* **–men**) a devotee of horse racing.

turf·y /tɔ́rfee/ *adj.* (**turf·i·er, turf·i·est**) like turf; grassy.

tur·ges·cent /tərjésənt/ *adj.* becoming turgid; swelling. □□ **tur·ges·cence** *n.*

tur·gid /tɔ́rjid/ *adj.* **1** swollen; inflated; enlarged. **2** (of language) pompous; bombastic. □□ **tur·gid·i·ty** /–jíditee/ *n.* **tur·gid·ly** *adv.* **tur·gid·ness** *n.* [L *turgidus* f. *turgēre* swell]

▶See note at TURBID.

tur·gor /tɔ́rgər/ *n. Bot.* the rigidity of cells due to the absorption of water. [LL (as TURGID)]

tu·ri·on /tōōreeən, tyōō–/ *n. Bot.* **1** a young shoot or sucker arising from an underground bud. **2** a bud formed by certain aquatic plants. [F f. L *turio –onis* shoot]

Turk /tərk/ *n.* **1 a** a native or inhabitant of Turkey in SE Europe and Asia Minor. **b** a person of Turkish descent. **2 a** a member of a central Asian people from whom the Ottomans derived, speaking Turkic languages. **3** *offens.* a ferocious, wild, or unmanageable person. [ME, = F *Turc*, It., etc. *Turco*, med.L *Turcus*, Pers. & Arab. *Turk*, of unkn. orig.]

tur·key /tɔ́rkee/ *n.* (*pl.* **–keys**) **1** a large mainly domesticated game bird, *Meleagris gallopavo*, orig. of N. America, having dark plumage with a green or bronze sheen, prized as food, esp. on festive occasions including Christmas and Thanksgiving. **2** the flesh of the turkey as food.

turkey

3 *sl.* **a** a theatrical failure; a flop. **b** a stupid or inept person. □ **talk turkey** *colloq.* talk frankly and straightforwardly; get down to business. [16th c.: short for *turkeycock* or *turkeyhen*, orig. applied to the guinea-fowl, which was imported through Turkey, and then erron. to the Amer. bird]

tur·key cock *n.* **1** a male turkey. **2** a pompous or self-important person.

Tur·key red *n.* **1** a scarlet pigment obtained from the madder or alizarin. **2** a cotton cloth dyed with this.

tur·key vul·ture *n.* (also **tur·key buz·zard**) an American vulture, *Cathartes aura.*

Tur·ki /tórkee/ *adj. & n.* ● *adj.* of or relating to a group of Ural-Altaic languages (including Turkish) and the peoples speaking them. ● *n.* the Turki group of languages. □□ **Tur·kic** /–kik/ *adj.* [Pers. *turkī* (as TURK)]

Turk·ish /tórkish/ *adj. & n.* ● *adj.* of or relating to Turkey in SE Europe and Asia Minor, or to the Turks or their language. ● *n.* this language.

Turk·ish bath *n.* **1** a hot air or steam bath followed by washing, massage, etc. **2** (in *sing.* or *pl.*) a building for this

Turk·ish car·pet *n.* (also **Turk·ish rug**) a wool carpet with a thick pile and traditional bold design.

Turk·ish cof·fee *n.* a strong black coffee.

Turk·ish de·light *n.* a confection of lumps of flavored gelatin coated in powdered sugar.

Turk·ish tow·el *n.* a towel made of cotton terry cloth.

Turko- var. of TURCO-.

Tur·ko·man /tórkōmən/ *n.* (also **Tur·co·man**) (*pl.* **–mans**) **1** a member of any of various Turkic peoples in Turkmenistan in central Asia. **2** the language of these peoples. [Pers. *Turkumān* (as TURK, *mānistan* resemble)]

Tur·ko·man car·pet *n.* a traditional rich-colored carpet with a soft long nap.

Turk's-cap lil·y *n.* a lily with a nodding orange flower whose curled-back petals give the blossom a turbanlike appearance.

Turk's head *n.* a turbanlike ornamental knot.

tur·mer·ic /tórmərik/ *n.* **1** an E. Indian plant, *Curcuma longa*, of the ginger family, yielding aromatic rhizomes used as a spice and for yellow dye. **2** this powdered rhizome used as a spice, esp. in curry powder. [16th-c. forms *tarmaret*, etc., perh. f. F *terre mérite* and mod.L *terra merita*, of unkn. orig.]

tur·moil /tórmoyl/ *n.* **1** violent confusion; agitation. **2** din and bustle. [16th c.: orig. unkn.]

turn /tɔrn/ *v. & n.* ● *v.* **1** *tr. & intr.* move around a point or axis so that the point or axis remains in a central position; give a rotary motion to or receive a rotary motion (*turned the wheel; the wheel turns; the key turns in the lock*). **2** *tr. & intr.* change in position so that a different side, end, or part becomes outermost or uppermost, etc.; invert or reverse or cause to be inverted or reversed (*turned inside out; turned it upside down*). **3** *tr.* **a** give a new direction to (*turn your face this way*). **b** *intr.* take a new direction (*turn left here; my thoughts have often turned to you*). **4** *tr.* aim in a certain way (*turned the hose on them*). **5** *intr. & tr.* (foll. by *into*) change in nature, form, or condition to (*turned into a dragon; then turned him into a frog; turned the book into a play*). **6** *intr.* (foll. by *to*) **a** apply oneself to; set about (*turned to doing the ironing*). **b** have recourse to; begin to indulge in habitually (*turned to drink; turned to me for help*). **c** go on to consider next (*let us now turn to your report*). **7** *intr. & tr.* become or cause to become (*turned hostile; has turned informer*). **8 a** *tr. & intr.* (foll. by *against*) make or become hostile to (*has turned them against us*). **b** *intr.* (foll. by *on, upon*) become hostile to; attack (*suddenly turned on them*). **9** *intr.* (of hair or leaves) change color. **10** *intr.* (of milk) become sour. **11** *intr.* (of the stomach) be nauseated. **12** *intr.* (of the head) become giddy. **13** *tr.* cause (milk) to become sour, (the stomach) to be nauseated, or (the head) to become giddy. **14** *tr.* translate (*turn it into French*). **15** *tr.* move to the other side of; go around (*turned the corner*). **16** *tr.* pass the age or time of (*he has turned 40; it has now turned 4 o'clock*). **17** *intr.* (foll. by *on*) depend on; be determined by; c oncern (*it all turns on the weather tomorrow; the conversation turned on my motives*). **18** *tr.* send or put into a specified place or condition; cause to go (*was turned loose; turned the water out into a basin*). **19** *tr.* **a** perform (a somersault, etc.) with rotary motion. **b** twist (an ankle) out of position; sprain **20** *tr.* remake (a garment or a sheet) putting the worn outer side on the inside. **21** *tr.* make (a profit). **22** *tr.* (also foll. by *aside*) divert; deflect (something material or immaterial). **23** *tr.* blunt (the edge of a knife, slot of a screw, etc.). **24** *tr.* shape (an object) on a lathe. **25** *tr.* give an (esp. elegant) form to (*turn a compliment*). **26** *intr. Golf* begin the second half of a round. **27** *tr.* (esp. as **turned** *adj.*) *Printing* invert (type) to make it appear upside down (*a turned comma*). **28** *tr.* pass around (the flank, etc., of an army) so as to attack it from the side or rear. **29** *intr.* (of the tide) change from flood to ebb or vice versa. ● *n.* **1** the act or process or an instance of turning; rotary motion (*a single turn of the handle*). **2 a** a changed or a

change of direction or tendency (*took a sudden turn to the left*). **b** a deflection or deflected part (*full of twists and turns*). **3** a point at which a turning or change occurs. **4** a turning of a road. **5** a change of the tide from ebb to flow or from flow to ebb. **6** a change in the course of events. **7** a tendency or disposition (*is of a mechanical turn of mind*). **8** an opportunity or obligation, etc., that comes successively to each of several persons, etc. (*your turn will come; my turn to read*). **9** a short walk or ride (*shall take a turn around the block*). **10** a short performance on stage or in a circus, etc. **11** service of a specified kind (*did me a good turn*). **12** purpose (*served my turn*). **13** *colloq.* a momentary nervous shock or ill feeling (*gave me quite a turn*). **14** *Mus.* an ornament consisting of the principal note with those above and below it. **15** one round in a coil of rope, etc. **16** *Printing* **a** an inverted type as a temporary substitute for a missing letter. **b** a letter turned wrong side up. **17 a** *Brit.* the difference between the buying and selling price of stocks, etc. **b** a profit made from this. □ **at every turn** continually; at each new stage, etc. **by turns** in rotation of individuals or groups; alternately. **in turn** in succession; one by one. **in one's turn** when one's turn or opportunity comes. **not know which way** (or **where**) **to turn** be completely at a loss, unsure how to act, etc. **not turn a hair** see HAIR. **on the turn 1** changing. **2** (of milk) becoming sour. **3** at the turning point. **out of turn 1** at a time when it is not one's turn. **2** inappropriately; inadvisedly or tactlessly (*did I speak out of turn?*). **take turns** (or **take it in turns**) act or work alternately or in succession. **to a turn** (esp. cooked) to exactly the right degree, etc. **turn about** move so as to face in a new direction. **turn and turn about** esp. *Brit.* alternately. **turn around** (or *Brit.* **round**) **1** turn so as to face in a new direction. **2 a** *Commerce* unload and reload (a ship, vehicle, etc.). **b** receive, process, and send out again; cause to progress through a system. **3** adopt new opinions or policy. **turn aside** see TURN *v.* 22 above. **turn away 1** turn to face in another direction. **2** refuse to accept; reject. **3** send away. **turn back 1** begin or cause to retrace one's steps. **2** fold back. **turn one's back on** see BACK. **turn the corner 1** pass around it into another street. **2** pass the critical point in an illness, difficulty, etc. **turn a deaf ear** see DEAF. **turn down 1** reject (a proposal, application, etc.). **2** reduce the volume or strength of (sound, heat, etc.) by turning a knob, etc. **3** fold down. **4** place downward. **turn one's hand to** see HAND. **turn a person's head** see HEAD. **turn an honest penny** see HONEST. **turn in 1** hand in or over; deliver. **2** achieve or register (a performance, score, etc.). **3** *colloq.* go to bed in the evening. **4** fold inward. **5** incline inward (*his toes turn in*). **6** *colloq.* abandon (a plan, etc.). **turn in one's grave** see GRAVE[1]. **turn inside out** see INSIDE. **turn off 1 a** stop the flow or operation of (water, electricity, etc.) by means of a faucet, switch, etc. **b** operate (a faucet, switch, etc.) to achieve this. **2 a** enter a side road. **b** (of a side road) lead off from another road. **3** *colloq.* repel; cause to lose interest (*turned me right off with their complaining*). **4** *Brit.* dismiss from employment. **turn of speed** the ability to go fast when necessary. **turn on 1 a** start the flow or operation of (water, electricity, etc.) by means of a faucet, switch, etc. **b** operate (a faucet, switch, etc.) to achieve this. **2** *colloq.* excite; stimulate the interest of, esp. sexually. **3** *tr. & intr. colloq.* intoxicate or become intoxicated with drugs. **turn one's stomach** make one nauseous or disgusted. **turn on one's heel** see HEEL[1]. **turn out 1** expel. **2** extinguish (an electric light, etc.). **3** dress or equip (*well turned out*). **4** produce (manufactured goods, etc.). **5** esp. *Brit.* empty or clean out (a room, etc.). **6** empty (a pocket) to see the contents. **7** *colloq.* **a** get out of bed. **b** go out of doors. **8** *colloq.* assemble; attend a meeting, etc. **9** (often foll. by *to* + infin. or *that* + clause) prove to be the case; result (*turned out to be true; we shall see how things turn out*). **10** *Mil.* call (a guard) from the guardroom. **turn over 1** reverse or cause to reverse vertical position; bring the underside or reverse into view (*turn over the page*). **2** upset; fall or cause to fall over. **3 a** cause (an engine) to run. **b** (of an engine) start running. **4** consider thoroughly. **5** (foll. by *to*) transfer the care or conduct of (a person or thing) to (a person) (*shall turn it all over to my deputy; turned him over to the authorities*). **6** do business to the amount of (*turns over $5,000 a week*). **turn over a new leaf** improve one's conduct or performance. **turn the scales** see SCALE[2]. **turn the other cheek** respond meekly to insult or abuse. **turn the tables** see TABLE. **turn tail** turn one's back; run away. **turn the tide** reverse the trend of events. **turn to** set about one's work (*came home and immediately turned to*). **turn to account** see ACCOUNT. **turn turtle** see TURTLE. **turn up 1** increase the volume or strength of (sound, heat, etc.) by turning a knob, etc. **2** place upward. **3** discover or reveal. **4** be found, esp. by chance (*it turned up on a trash heap*). **5** happen or present itself; (of a person) put in an appearance (*a few people turned up late*). **6** *Brit. colloq.* cause to vomit (*the sight turned me up*). **7** shorten (a garment) by increasing the size of the hem. **turn up one's nose** (or **turn one's nose up**) react with disdain. [OE *tyrnan, turnian* f. L *tornare* f. *tornus* lathe f. Gk *tornos* lathe, circular movement: prob. reinforced in ME f. OF *turner, torner*]

turn·a·bout /tórnəbowt/ *n.* **1** an act of turning about. **2** an abrupt change of policy, etc.

turn·a·round /tórnərownd/ *n.* **1** time taken in a car's, plane's, etc., round trip. **2** a change in one's opinion; a reversal of a tendency (*that's a fairly dramatic turnaround considering your previous statement*). **3** space needed for a vehicle to turn around. **4 a** the process of loading and unloading. **b** the process of receiving, processing, and sending out again; progress through a system.

turn·buck·le /tórnbukəl/ *n.* a device for tightly connecting parts of a metal rod or wire.

turn·coat /tórnkōt/ *n.* a person who changes sides in a conflict, dispute, etc.

turn·down /tórndown/ *n. & adj.* ● *n.* a rejection, a refusal. ● *adj.* (of a collar) turned down.

turn·er /tórnər/ *n.* **1** a person or thing that turns. **2** a person who works with a lathe. [ME f. OF *tornere –eor* f. LL *tornator* (as TURN)]

turn·er·y /tórnəree/ *n.* **1** objects made on a lathe. **2** work with a lathe.

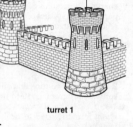
turnbuckle

turn·ing /tórning/ *n.* **1 a** a road that branches off another; a turn. **b** a place where this occurs. **2 a** use of the lathe. **b** (in *pl.*) chips or shavings from a lathe.

turn·ing cir·cle *n.* (or **turn·ing ra·di·us**) the smallest circle in which a vehicle can turn without reversing.

turn·ing point *n.* a point at which a decisive change occurs.

tur·nip /tórnip/ *n.* **1** a cruciferous plant, *Brassica rapa*, with a large white globular root and sprouting leaves. **2** this root used as a vegetable. **3** a large thick old-fashioned watch. □□ **tur·nip·y** *adj.* [earlier *turnep(e)* f. *neep* f. L *napus*: first element of uncert. orig.]

turn·key /tórnkee/ *n. & adj.* ● *n.* (*pl.* **–keys**) *archaic* a jailer. ● *adj.* (of a contract, etc.) providing for a supply of equipment in a state ready for operation.

turn·off /tórnof/ *n.* **1** a turning off a main road. **2** *colloq.* something that repels or causes a loss of interest.

turn·on *n. colloq.* a person or thing that causes (esp. sexual) arousal.

turn·out /tórnowt/ *n.* **1** the number of people attending a meeting, voting in an election, etc. (*rain reduced the turnout*). **2** the quantity of goods produced in a given time. **3** a set or display of equipment, clothes, etc. **4 a** a railroad siding. **b** a place where a highway widens so cars may park, pass, etc.

turn·o·ver /tórnōvər/ *n.* **1** the act or an instance of turning over. **2** the amount of money taken in a business. **3** the number of people entering and leaving employment, etc. **4** a small pastry made by folding a piece of pastry crust over a filling. **5** a change in a business's goods as items are sold, new merchandise arrives, etc. **6** *Sports* a change in possession of the ball from one team to the other usu. from fumbling, committing a foul, etc.

turn·pike /tórnpīk/ *n.* **1** a highway, esp. one on which a toll is charged. **2** *hist.* **a** a tollgate. **b** a road on which a toll was collected at a tollgate. **3** *hist.* a defensive frame of spikes.

turn sig·nal *n.* any of the flashing lights on the front or back of an automobile that are activated by a driver to indicate that the vehicle is about to turn or change lanes.

turn·sole /tórnsōl/ *n.* any of various plants supposed to turn with the sun. [OF *tournesole* f. Prov. *tournasol* f. L *tornare* TURN + *sol* sun]

turn·spit /tórnspit/ *n.* **1** *hist.* a person or small dog used to turn a spit. **2** a rotating spit.

turn·stile /tórnstīl/ *n.* a gate for admission or exit, with revolving arms allowing people through singly.

turn·stone /tórnstōn/ *n.* any wading bird of the genus *Arenaria*, related to the plover, that looks under stones for small animals to eat.

turn·ta·ble /tórntaybəl/ *n.* **1** a circular revolving plate supporting a phonograph record that is being played. **2** a circular revolving platform for turning a railroad locomotive or other vehicle.

turn·up *n. Brit.* (usu. **turn-ups**) **1** the lower turned up end of a trouser leg. **2** *colloq.* an unexpected (esp. welcome) happening; a surprise.

tur·pen·tine /tórpəntīn/ *n. & v.* ● *n.* an oleoresin secreted by several trees, esp. of the genus *Pinus, Pistacia, Syncarpia,* or *Copaifera*, and used in various commercial preparations. ● *v.tr.* apply turpentine to. [ME f. OF *ter(e)bentine* f. L *ter(e)binthina* (*resina* resin) (as TEREBINTH)]

tur·peth /tórpith/ *n.* (in full **turpeth root**) the root of an E. Indian plant, *Ipomoea turpethum*, used as a cathartic. [ME f. med.L *turbit(h)um* f. Arab. & Pers. *turbid*]

tur·pi·tude /tórpitōōd, –tyōōd/ *n. formal* baseness; depravity; wickedness. [F *turpitude* or L *turpitudo* f. *turpis* disgraceful, base]

turps /tórps/ *n. colloq.* oil of turpentine. [abbr]

tur·quoise /tórkwoyz, –koyz/ *n. & adj.* ● *n.* **1** a semiprecious stone, usu. opaque and greenish blue or blue, consisting of hydrated copper aluminum phosphate. **2** a greenish blue color. ● *adj.* of this color. [ME *turkeis*, etc. f. OF *turquoise* (later –*oise*) Turkish (stone)]

tur·ret /tórit, túr–/ *n.* **1** a small tower, usu. projecting from the wall of a building as a decorative addition. **2** a low flat usu. revolving armored tower for a gun and gunners in a ship, aircraft, fort, or tank. **3** a rotating holder for tools in a lathe, lenses in a microscope, etc. □□ **tur·ret·ed** *adj.* [ME f. OF *to(u)rete* dimin. of *to(u)r* TOWER]

turret 1

tur·tle /tórt'l/ *n.* **1** any of various terrestrial, marine, or freshwater reptiles of the order Chelonia, encased in a shell of bony plates, and having flippers or webbed toes used in swimming. **2** the flesh of the turtle, esp. used for soup. **3** *Computing* a directional cursor in a computer graphics system for children that can be instructed to move around a screen. □ **turn turtle** capsize. [app. alt. of *tortue*: see TORTOISE]

red-ear turtle

tur·tle·dove /tórt'lduv/ *n.* any wild dove of the genus *Streptopelia*, esp. *S. turtur*, noted for its soft cooing and its affection for its mate and young. [archaic *turtle* (in the same sense) f. OE *turtla*, *turtle* f. L *turtur*, of imit. orig.]

tur·tle·neck /tórt'lnek/ *n.* **1** a high close-fitting turned-over collar on a garment. **2** an upper garment with such a collar.

Tus·can /túskən/ *n. & adj.* ● *n.* **1** an inhabitant of Tuscany in central Italy. **2** the classical Italian language of Tuscany. ● *adj.* **1** of or relating to Tuscany or the Tuscans. **2** *Archit.* denoting the least ornamented of the classical orders. [ME f. F f. L *Tuscanus* f. *Tuscus* Etruscan]

turtleneck

Tus·can straw *n.* fine yellow wheat straw used for hats, etc.

Tus·ca·ro·ra /təskərórə, –ráwr–/ *n.* **1 a** a N. American people native to N. Carolina and later to New York. **b** a member of this people. **2** the language of this people.

tush[1] /tush/ *int. archaic* expressing strong disapproval or scorn. [ME: imit.]

tush[2] /tush/ *n.* **1** a long pointed tooth, esp. a canine tooth of a horse. **2** an elephant's short tusk. [OE *tusc* TUSK]

tush[3] /toosh/ *n. sl.* the buttocks. [20th c.: abbr. or dimin. of *tokus* f. Yiddish *tokhes*]

tusk /tusk/ *n. & v.* ● *n.* **1** a long pointed tooth, esp. protruding from a closed mouth, as in the elephant, walrus, etc. **2** a tusklike tooth or other object. ● *v.tr.* gore, thrust at, or tear up with a tusk or tusks. □□ **tusked** *adj.* (also in *comb.*). **tusk·y** *adj.* [ME alt. of OE *tux* var. of *tusc*: cf. TUSH[2]]

tusk·er /túskər/ *n.* an elephant or wild boar with well-developed tusks.

tusk shell *n.* **1** any of various mollusks of the class Scaphopoda. **2** its long tubular tusk-shaped shell.

tus·sah /túsə/ *n.* (also **tus·sore** /túsawr/, **tus·ser** /túsər/) **1** an E. Indian or Chinese silkworm, *Antheraea mylitta*, yielding strong but coarse brown silk. **2** (in full **tussah silk**) silk from this and some other silkworms. [Urdu f. Hindi *tasar* f. Skr. *tasara* shuttle]

tus·sive /túsiv/ *adj.* of or relating to a cough. [L *tussis* cough]

tus·sle /túsəl/ *n. & v.* ● *n.* a struggle or scuffle. ● *v.intr.* engage in a tussle. [orig. Sc. & N.Engl., perh. dimin. of *touse*: see TOUSLE]

tus·sock /túsək/ *n.* **1** a clump of grass, etc. **2** (in full **tussock moth**) any moth of the genus *Orgyia*, etc., with tufted larvae. □□ **tus·sock·y** *adj.* [16th c.: perh. alt. f. dial. *tusk* tuft]

tus·sock grass *n.* grass growing in tussocks, esp. *Poa flabellata* from Patagonia, etc.

tut var. of TUT-TUT.

tu·te·lage /tōōt'lij, tyōō–/ *n.* **1** guardianship. **2** the state or duration of being under this. **3** instruction. [L *tutela* f. *tuēri tuit-* or *tutlage*]

tu·te·lar·y /tōōt'lairee, tyōō–/ *adj.* (also **tu·te·lar** /–t'lər/) **1 a** serving as guardian. **b** relating to a guardian (*tutelary authority*). **2** giving protection (*tutelary saint*). [LL *tutelaris*, L *–arius* f. *tutela*: see TUTELAGE]

tu·te·nag /tōōt'nag/ *n.* **1** zinc imported from China and the E.

Indies. **2** a white alloy like German silver. [Marathi *tuttināg* perh. f. Skr. *tuttha* copper sulfate + *nāga* tin, lead]

tu·tor /tŏŏtər, tyŏŏ–/ *n. & v.* ● *n.* **1** a private teacher, esp. in general charge of a person's education. **2** esp. *Brit.* a university teacher supervising the studies or welfare of assigned undergraduates. **3** *Brit.* a book of instruction in a subject. ● *v.* **1** *tr.* act as a tutor to. **2** *intr.* work as a tutor. **3** *tr.* restrain; discipline. **4** *intr.* receive instruction. □□ **tu·tor·age** /–rij/ *n.* **tu·tor·ship** *n.* [ME f. AF, OF *tutour* or L *tutor* f. *tuēri tut–* watch]

tu·to·ri·al /tŏŏtáwreeəl, tyŏŏ–/ *adj. & n.* ● *adj.* of or relating to a tutor or tuition. ● *n.* **1** a period of individual instruction given by a tutor. **2** *Computing* a routine that allows one to instruct oneself in using a software program. □□ **tu·to·ri·al·ly** *adv.* [L *tutorius* (as TUTOR)]

tut·san /tútsən/ *n.* a species of St. John's wort, *Hypericum androsaemum,* formerly used to heal wounds, etc. [ME f. AF *tutsaine* all healthy]

tut·ti /tŏŏtee/ *adv. & n. Mus.* ● *adv.* with all voices or instruments together. ● *n.* (*pl.* **tut·tis**) a passage to be performed in this way. [It., *pl.* of *tutto* all]

tut·ti-frut·ti /tŏŏteefrŏŏtee/ *n.* (*pl.* **–frut·tis**) a confection, esp. ice cream, of or flavored with mixed fruits. [It., = all fruits]

tut-tut /tut-tút/ *int., n., & v.* (also **tut** /tut/) ● *int.* expressing rebuke, impatience, or contempt. ● *n.* such an exclamation. ● *v.intr.* (**–tut·ted, –tut·ting**) exclaim this. [imit. of a click of the tongue against the teeth]

tut·ty /tútee/ *n.* impure zinc oxide or carbonate used as a polishing powder. [ME f. OF *tutie* f. med.L *tutia* f. Arab. *tūtiyā*]

tu·tu[1] /tŏŏtōō/ *n.* a ballet dancer's short skirt of stiffened projecting frills. [F]

tu·tu[2] /tŏŏtōō/ *n. Bot.* a shrub, *Coriaria arborea,* native to New Zealand, bearing poisonous purplish black berries. [Maori]

tu-whit, tu-whoo /tŏŏwít tŏŏwŏŏ/ *n.* a representation of the cry of an owl. [imit.]

tux /tuks/ *n. colloq.* = TUXEDO.

tux·e·do /tukseédŏ/ *n.* (*pl.* **–dos** or **–does**) **1** a man's short black formal jacket. **2** a suit of clothes including this. [after a country club at *Tuxedo* Park, New York]

tu·yère /tweeyáir, tōō–/ *n.* (also **tu·yere, tw·yer**) a nozzle through which air is forced into a furnace, etc. [F f. *tuyau* pipe]

TV *abbr.* television.

TVA *abbr.* Tennessee Valley Authority.

TV din·ner *n.* a prepackaged frozen meal, usu. consisting of meat, potatoes, vegetable, and dessert.

TVP *abbr. Trademark* textured vegetable protein (in foods made from vegetable but given a meatlike texture).

twad·dle /twód'l/ *n. & v.* ● *n.* useless, senseless, or dull writing or talk. ● *v.intr.* indulge in this. □□ **twad·dler** *n.* [alt. of earlier *twattle,* alt. of TATTLE]

twain /twayn/ *adj. & n. archaic* two (usu. *in twain*). [OE *twegen,* masc. form of *twā* TWO]

twang /twang/ *n. & v.* ● *n.* **1** a strong ringing sound made by the plucked string of a musical instrument or bow. **2** the nasal quality of a voice compared to this. ● *v.* **1** *intr. & tr.* emit or cause to emit this sound. **2** *tr.* usu. *derog.* play (a tune or instrument) in this way. **3** *tr.* utter with a nasal twang. □□ **twang·y** *adj.* [imit.]

'twas /twuz, twoz/ *archaic* it was. [contr.]

twat /twot/ *n. coarse sl.* **1** the female genitals. **2** esp. *Brit.* a term of contempt for a person. [17th c.: orig. unkn.]
► Usually considered a taboo word.

tway·blade /twáyblayd/ *n.* any orchid of the genus *Listera,* etc., with green or purple flowers and a single pair of leaves. [*tway* var. of TWAIN + BLADE]

tweak /tweek/ *v. & n.* ● *v.tr.* **1** pinch and twist sharply; pull with a sharp jerk; twitch. **2** make small adjustments to (a mechanism). ● *n.* an instance of tweaking. [prob. alt. of dial. *twick* & TWITCH]

twee /twee/ *adj.* (**twe·er** /tweéər/; **twe·est** /tweé-ist/) *Brit.* usu. *derog.* affectedly dainty or quaint. □□ **twee·ly** *adv.* **twee·ness** *n.* [childish pronunc. of SWEET]

tweed /tweed/ *n.* **1** a rough-surfaced woolen cloth, usu. of mixed colors, orig. produced in Scotland. **2** (in *pl.*) clothes made of tweed. [orig. a misreading of *tweel,* Sc. form of TWILL, infl. by assoc. with the river *Tweed*]

Twee·dle·dum and Twee·dle·dee /tweéd'ldúm, tweéd'ldeé/ *n.* a pair of persons or things that are virtually indistinguishable. [after the stock names of rival musicians]

tweed·y /tweédee/ *adj.* (**tweed·i·er, tweed·i·est**) **1** of or relating to tweed cloth. **2** characteristic of the country gentry; heartily informal. □□ **tweed·i·ly** *adv.* **tweed·i·ness** *n.*

'tween /tween/ *prep. archaic* = BETWEEN. [contr.]

'tween-decks *n.pl. Naut.* the space between decks.

tweet /tweet/ *n. & v.* ● *n.* the chirp of a small bird. ● *v.intr.* make a chirping noise. [imit.]

tweet·er /tweétər/ *n.* a loudspeaker designed to reproduce high frequencies.

tweeze /tweez/ *v.tr.* pluck out with tweezers (*tweeze eyebrow hair*).

tweez·ers /tweézərz/ *n.pl.* a small pair of pincers for picking up small objects, plucking out hairs, etc. [extended form of *tweezes* (cf. *pincers,* etc.) pl. of obs. *tweeze* case for small instruments, f. *etweese* = *étuis,* pl. of ETUI]

twelfth /twelfth/ *n. & adj.* ● *n.* **1** the position in a sequence corresponding to the number 12 in the sequence 1–12. **2** something occupying this position. **3** each of twelve equal parts of a thing. **4** *Mus.* **a** an interval or chord spanning an octave and a fifth in the diatonic scale. **b** a note separated from another by this interval. ● *adj.* that is the twelfth. □□ **twelfth·ly** *adv.* [OE *twelfta* (as TWELVE)]

Twelfth Day *n.* Jan. 6, the twelfth day after Christmas, the festival of the Epiphany.

Twelfth Night *n.* the evening of Jan. 5, the eve of the Epiphany.

twelve /twelv/ *n. & adj.* ● *n.* **1** one more than eleven; the product of two units and six units. **2** a symbol for this (12, xii, XII). **3** a size, etc., denoted by twelve. **4** the time denoted by twelve o'clock (*is it twelve yet?*). **5** (**the Twelve**) the twelve apostles. ● *adj.* that amount to twelve. [OE *twelf(e)* f. Gmc, prob. rel. to TWO]

twelve·fold /twélvfōld/ *adj. & adv.* **1** twelve times as much or as many. **2** consisting of twelve parts.

twelve·mo /twélvmō/ *n.* = DUODECIMO.

twelve·month /twélvmunth/ *n. archaic* a year; a period of twelve months.

twelve-tone *adj. Mus.* using the twelve chromatic notes of the octave on an equal basis without dependence on a key system.

twen·ty /twéntee/ *n. & adj.* ● *n.* (*pl.* **–ties**) **1** the product of two and ten. **2** a symbol for this (20, xx, XX). **3** (in *pl.*) the numbers from 20 to 29, esp. the years of a century or of a person's life. **4** *colloq.* a large indefinite number (*have told you twenty times*). ● *adj.* that amount to twenty. □□ **twen·ti·eth** *adj. & n.* **twen·ty·fold** *adj. & adv.* [OE *twentig* (perh. as TWO, –TY[2])]

twen·ty-first *n.* (**twen·ty-second,** etc.) the ordinal numbers between twentieth and thirtieth.

24/7 *adv.* twenty-four hours a day and seven days a week (*we need a computer technician on call 24/7*).

twen·ty-one *n.* (**twen·ty-two,** etc.) the cardinal numbers between twenty and thirty.

twen·ty-one *n.* a card game in which players try to acquire cards with a face value totaling 21 points and no more.

twen·ty-twen·ty *adj.* (also **20/20**) **1** denoting vision of normal acuity. **2** *colloq.* denoting clear perception or hindsight.

'twere /twər/ *archaic* it were. [contr.]

twerp /twərp/ *n.* (also **twirp**) *sl.* a stupid or objectionable person. [20th c.: orig. unkn.]

twi·bill /twíbil/ *n.* a double-bladed battleax. [OE f. *twi-* double + BILL[3]]

twice /twīs/ *adv.* **1** two times (esp. of multiplication); on two occasions. **2** in double degree or quantity (*twice as good*). [ME *twiges* f. OE *twige* (as TWO, –S[3])]

twid·dle /twíd'l/ *v. & n.* ● *v.* **1** *tr. &* (foll. by *with,* etc.) intr. twirl, adjust, or play randomly or idly. **2** *intr.* move twirlingly. ● *n.* **1** an act of twiddling. **2** a twirled mark or sign. □ **twiddle one's thumbs 1** make them rotate around each other. **2** have nothing to do. □□ **twid·dler** *n.* **twid·dly** *adj.* [app. imit., after *twirl, twist,* and *fiddle, piddle*]

twig[1] /twig/ *n.* **1** a small branch or shoot of a tree or shrub. **2** *Anat.* a small branch of an artery, etc. □□ **twigged** *adj.* (also in *comb.*). **twig·gy** *adj.* [OE *twigge* f. a Gmc root *twi-* (unrecorded) as in TWICE, TWO]

twig[2] /twig/ *v.tr.* (**twigged, twig·ging**) *Brit. colloq.* **1** (also *absol.*) understand; grasp the meaning or nature of. **2** perceive; observe. [18th c.: orig. unkn.]

twi·light /twílīt/ *n.* **1** the soft glowing light from the sky when the sun is below the horizon, esp. in the evening. **2** the period of this. **3** a faint light. **4** a state of imperfect knowledge or understanding. **5** a period of decline or destruction. **6** *attrib.* of, resembling, or occurring at twilight. [ME f. OE *twi-* two (in uncert. sense) + LIGHT[1]]

twi·light sleep *n. Med.* a state of partial narcosis, esp. to ease the pain of childbirth.

twi·light zone *n.* **1** any physical or conceptual area that is undefined or intermediate, esp. one that is eerie or unreal. **2** *Brit.* an urban area that is becoming dilapidated.

twi·lit /twílit/ *adj.* (also **twi·light·ed** /–lītid/) dimly illuminated by or as by twilight. [past part. of *twilight* (v.) f. TWILIGHT]

twill /twil/ *n. & v.* ● *n.* a fabric so woven as to have a surface of diagonal parallel ridges. ● *v.tr.* (esp. as **twilled** *adj.*) weave (fabric) in this way. □□ **twilled** *adj.* [No. of Engl. var. of obs. *twilly,* OE *twili,* f. *twi-* double, after L *bilix* (as BI–, *licium* thread)]

'twill /twil/ *archaic* it will. [contr.]

tutu[1]

twin /twin/ *n., adj., & v.* ● *n.* **1** each of a closely related or associated pair, esp. of children or animals born at one birth. **2** the exact counterpart of a person or thing. **3** a compound crystal one part of which is in a reversed position with reference to the other. **4** (**the Twins**) the zodiacal sign or constellation Gemini. ● *adj.* **1** forming, or being one of, such a pair (*twin brothers*). **2** *Bot.* growing in pairs. **3** consisting of two closely connected and similar parts. ● *v.* (**twinned, twin•ning**) **1** *tr. & intr.* **a** join intimately together. **b** (foll. by *with*) pair. **2** *intr.* bear twins. **3** *intr.* grow as a twin crystal. □□ **twin•ning** *n.* [OE *twinn* double, f. *twi-* two: cf ON *tvinnr*]

twin bed *n.* each of a pair of single beds.

twine /twin/ *n. & v.* ● *n.* **1** a strong thread or string of two or more strands of hemp or cotton, etc., twisted together. **2** a coil or twist. **3** a tangle; an interlacing. ● *v.* **1** *tr.* form (a string or thread, etc.) by twisting strands together. **2** *tr.* form (a garland, etc.) of interwoven material. **3** *tr.* (often foll. by *with*) garland (a brow, etc.). **4** *intr.* (often foll. by *around, about*) coil or wind. **5** *intr. & refl.* (of a plant) grow in this way. □□ **twin•er** *n.* [OE *twin, twigin* linen, ult. f. the stem of *twi-* two]

twin-en•gine *adj.* having two engines.

twinge /twinj/ *n. & v.* ● *n.* a sharp momentary local pain or pang (*a twinge of toothache; a twinge of conscience*). ● *v.intr. & tr.* experience or cause to experience a twinge. [*twinge* (v.) pinch, wring f. OE *twengan* f. Gmc]

twin•kle /twíngkəl/ *v. & n.* ● *v.* **1** *intr.* (of a star or light, etc.) shine with rapidly intermittent gleams. **2** *intr.* (of the eyes) sparkle. **3** *intr.* (of the feet in dancing) move lightly and rapidly. **4** *tr.* emit (a light or signal) in quick gleams. **5** *tr.* blink or wink (one's eyes). ● *n.* **1 a** a sparkle or gleam of the eyes. **b** a blink or wink. **2** a slight flash of light; a glimmer. **3** a short rapid movement. □ **in a twinkle** (or **a twinkling** or **the twinkling of an eye**) in an instant. □□ **twin•kler** *n.* **twin•kly** *adj.* [OE *twinclian*]

twin-screw *adj.* (of a ship) having two propellers on separate shafts with opposite twists.

twirl /twərl/ *v & n.* ● *v.tr. & intr.* spin or swing or twist quickly and lightly around. ● *n.* **1** a twirling motion. **2** a form made by twirling, esp. a flourish made with a pen. □□ **twirl•er** *n.* **twirl•y** *adj.* [16th c.: prob. alt. (after *whirl*) of obs. *tirl* TRILL]

twirp var. of TWERP.

twist /twist/ *v. & n.* ● *v.* **1 a** *tr.* change the form of by rotating one end and not the other or the two ends in opposite directions. **b** *intr.* undergo such a change; take a twisted position (*twisted around in his seat*). **c** *tr.* wrench or pull out of shape with a twisting action (*twisted my ankle*). **2** *tr.* **a** wind (strands, etc.) around each other. **b** form (a rope, etc.) by winding the strands. **c** (foll. by *with, in with*) interweave. **d** form by interweaving or twining. **3 a** *tr.* give a spiral form to (a rod, column, cord, etc.) as by rotating the ends in opposite directions. **b** *intr.* take a spiral form. **4** *tr.* (foll. by *off*) break off or separate by twisting. **5** *tr.* distort or misrepresent the meaning of (words). **6 a** *intr.* take a winding course. **b** *tr.* make (one's way) in a winding manner. **7** *tr. Brit. colloq.* cheat (*twisted me out of my allowance*). **8** *tr.* cause (the ball, esp. in billiards) to rotate while following a curved path. **9** *tr.* (as **twisted** *adj.*) (of a person or mind) emotionally unbalanced. **10** *intr.* dance the twist. ● *n.* **1** the act or an instance of twisting. **2 a** a twisted state. **b** the manner or degree in which a thing is twisted. **3** a thing formed by or as by twisting, esp. a thread or rope, etc., made by winding strands together. **4** the point at which a thing twists or bends. **5** usu. *derog.* a peculiar tendency of mind or character, etc. **6 a** an unexpected development of events, esp. in a story, etc. **b** an unusual interpretation or variation. **c** a distortion or bias. **7** a fine strong silk thread used by tailors, etc. **8** a roll of bread, tobacco, etc., in the form of a twist. **9** *Brit.* a paper package with the ends twisted shut. **10** a curled piece of lemon, etc., peel to flavor a drink. **11** a spinning motion given to a ball in throwing, etc., to make it curve. **12 a** a twisting strain. **b** the amount of twisting of a rod, etc., or the angle showing this. **c** forward motion combined with rotation about an axis. **13** *Brit.* a drink made of two ingredients mixed together. **14** *Brit. colloq.* a swindle. **15** (prec. by *the*) a dance with a twisting movement of the body, popular in the 1960s. □ **round the twist** *Brit. sl.* crazy. **twist a person's arm** *colloq.* apply coercion, esp. by moral pressure. **twist around one's finger** see FIN-GER. □□ **twist•a•ble** *adj.* **twist•y** *adj.* (**twist•i•er, twist•i•est**). [ME, rel. to TWIN, TWINE]

twist•er /twístər/ *n.* **1** *colloq.* a tornado, waterspout, etc. **2** *Brit. colloq.* = *swindler* (SWINDLE). **3** a twisting ball in cricket or billiards, etc.

twit[1] /twit/ *n. sl.* a silly or foolish person. [orig. dial.: perh. f. TWIT[2]]

twit[2] /twit/ *v.tr.* (**twit•ted, twit•ting**) reproach or taunt, usu. good-humoredly. [16th-c. *twite* f. *atwite* f. OE *ætwītan* reproach with f. *æt* at + *wītan* blame]

twitch /twich/ *v. & n.* ● *v.* **1** *intr.* (of the features, muscles, limbs, etc.) move or contract spasmodically. **2** *tr.* give a short sharp pull at. ● *n.* **1** a sudden involuntary contraction or movement. **2** a sudden pull or jerk. **3** *colloq.* a state of nervousness. **4** a noose and stick for controlling a horse during a veterinary operation. □□ **twitch•y** *adj.*

(**twitch•i•er, twitch•i•est**) (in sense 3 of *n.*). [ME f. Gmc: cf. OE *twiccian*, dial. *twick*]

twitch•er /twíchər/ *n.* **1** *Brit. colloq.* a birdwatcher who tries to get sightings of rare birds. **2** a person or thing that twitches.

twitch grass /twich/ *n.* = COUCH[2]. [var. of QUITCH]

twite /twit/ *n.* a moorland finch, *Carduelis flavirostris*, resembling the linnet. [imit. of its cry]

twit•ter /twítər/ *v. & n.* ● *v.* **1** *intr.* (of or like a bird) emit a succession of light tremulous sounds. **2** *tr.* utter or express in this way. ● *n.* **1** the act or an instance of twittering. **2** *colloq.* a tremulously excited state. □□ **twit•ter•er** *n.* **twit•ter•y** *adj.* [ME, imit.: cf. –ER[4]]

'twixt /twikst/ *prep. archaic* = BETWIXT. [contr.]

two /too/ *n. & adj.* ● *n.* **1** one more than one; the sum of one unit and another unit. **2** a symbol for this (2, ii, II). **3** a size, etc., denoted by two. **4** the time of two o'clock (*is it two yet?*). **5** a set of two. **6** a card with two pips. **7** a two-dollar bill. ● *adj.* that amount to two. □ **in two** in or into two pieces. **in two shakes** (or **ticks**) see SHAKE, TICK[1]. **or two** denoting several (*a thing or two* = several things). **put two and two together** make (esp. an obvious) inference from what is known or evident. **that makes two of us** *colloq.* that is true of me also. **two by two** (or **two and two**) in pairs. **two can play at that game** *colloq.* another person's behavior can be copied to that person's disadvantage. [OE *twā* (fem. & neut.), *tū* (neut.), with Gmc cognates and rel. to Skr. *dvau, dve*, Gk & L *duo*]

two-bit *adj. colloq.* cheap; petty.

two-by-four *n.* a length of lumber with a rectangular cross section nominally 2 in. by 4 in.

two-di•men•sion•al *adj.* **1** having or appearing to have length and breadth but no depth. **2** lacking depth or substance; superficial.

two-edged *adj.* double-edged.

two-faced *adj.* **1** having two faces. **2** insincere; deceitful.

two•fold /toofold/ *adj. & adv.* **1** twice as much or as many. **2** consisting of two parts.

two-hand•ed *adj.* **1** having, using, or requiring the use of two hands. **2** (of a card game) for two players.

two•pence /túpəns/ *n. Brit.* **1** the sum of two pence, esp. before decimalization. **2** *colloq.* (esp. with *neg.*) a thing of little value (*don't care twopence*).

two•pen•ny /túpənee/ *adj. Brit.* **1** costing two pence, esp. before decimalization. **2** *colloq.* cheap; worthless.

two•pen•ny-half•pen•ny *adj.* /túpneeháypnee/ *Brit.* not worthy of consideration or respect; worthless and unimportant.

two-piece *adj.* (of a suit, etc.) consisting of two matching items. ● *n.* a two-piece suit, etc.

two-ply *adj.* of two strands, webs, or thicknesses. ● *n.* **1** two-ply wool. **2** two-ply wood made by gluing together two layers with the grain in different directions.

two-sid•ed *adj.* **1** having two sides. **2** having two aspects; controversial.

two•some /toosəm/ *n.* **1** two persons together. **2** a game, dance, etc., for two persons.

two-step *n.* a dance with a sliding step in march or polka time.

two-stroke *adj. & n.* (also **two-cy•cle**) ● *adj.* (of an internal combustion engine) having its power cycle completed in one up-and-down movement of the piston. ● *n.* a two-stroke engine or vehicle.

two-time *v.tr. colloq.* **1** deceive or be unfaithful to (esp. a partner or lover). **2** swindle; double-cross. □□ **two-tim•er** *n.*

two-tone *adj.* having two colors or sounds.

'twould /twood/ *archaic* it would. [contr.]

two-way *adj.* **1** involving two ways or participants. **2** (of a switch) permitting a current to be switched on or off from either of two points. **3** (of a radio) capable of transmitting and receiving signals. **4** (of a faucet, etc.) permitting fluid, etc., to flow in either of two channels or directions. **5** (of traffic, etc.) moving in two esp. opposite directions.

two-way mir•ror *n.* a panel of glass that can be seen through from one side and is a mirror on the other.

two-wheel•er *n.* a vehicle with two wheels.

twp. *abbr.* township.

TX *abbr.* Texas (in official postal use).

-ty[1] /tee/ *suffix* forming nouns denoting quality or condition (*cruelty; plenty*). [ME *-tie, -tee, -te* f. OF *-té, -tet* f. L *-tas -tatis*: cf. –ITY]

-ty[2] /tee/ *suffix* denoting tens (*twenty; thirty; ninety*). [OE *-tig*]

ty•chism /tíkizəm/ *n. Philos.* the theory that chance controls the universe. [Gk *tukhē* chance]

ty•coon /tikóon/ *n.* **1** a business magnate. **2** *hist.* a title applied by foreigners to the shogun of Japan 1854–68. [Jap. *taikun* great lord]

ty•ing *pres. part.* of TIE.

tyke /tik/ *n.* (also **tike**) **1** a small child. **2** a mongrel. **3** esp. *Brit.* an unpleasant or coarse man. **4** *Brit. sl.* a Yorkshireman. **5** *Austral. & NZ sl. offens.* a Roman Catholic. [ME f. ON *tík* bitch: sense 5 assim. from TAIG]

ty·lo·pod /tíləpod/ n. & adj. Zool. • n. any animal that bears its weight on the sole of the feet rather than on the hoofs, esp. the camel. • adj. (of an animal) bearing its weight in this way. □□ **tylopodous** /-lópədəs/ adj. [Gk tulos knob or tulē callus, cushion + pous podos foot]

tym·pan /tímpən/ n. 1 Printing an appliance in a printing press used to equalize pressure between the platen, etc., and a printing sheet. 2 Archit. = TYMPANUM. [F tympan or L tympanum: see TYMPANUM]

tym·pa·na pl. of TYMPANUM.

tym·pa·ni var. of TIMPANI.

tym·pan·ic /timpánik/ adj. 1 Anat. of, relating to, or having a tympanum. 2 resembling or acting like a drumhead.

tym·pan·ic bone n. Anat. the bone supporting the tympanic membrane.

tym·pan·ic mem·brane n. Anat. the membrane separating the outer ear and middle ear and transmitting vibrations resulting from sound waves to the inner ear.

tym·pa·ni·tes /tímpəníteez/ n. a swelling of the abdomen caused by gas in the intestine, etc. □□ **tym·pa·nit·ic** /-nítik/ adj. [LL f. Gk tumpanitēs of a drum (as TYMPANUM)]

tym·pa·num /tímpənəm/ n. (pl. **tym·pa·nums** or **tym·pa·na** /-nə/) 1 Anat. **a** the middle ear. **b** the tympanic membrane. 2 Zool. the membrane covering the hearing organ on the leg of an insect. 3 Archit. **a** a vertical triangular space forming the center of a pediment. **b** a similar space over a door between the lintel and the arch; a carving on this space. 4 a wheel, etc., for raising water from a stream. 5 the diaphragm in a telephone handset. [L f. Gk tumpanon drum f. tuptō strike]

Tyn·wald /tínwawld, -wəld/ n. the parliament of the UK's Isle of Man. [ON thing-völlr place of assembly f. thing assembly + völlr field]

type /tip/ n. & v. • n. 1 **a** a class of things or persons having common characteristics. **b** a kind or sort (would like a different type of car). 2 a person, thing, or event serving as an illustration, symbol, or characteristic specimen of another, or of a class. 3 (in comb.) made of, resembling, or functioning as (ceramic-type material; Cheddar-type cheese). 4 colloq. a person, esp. of a specified character (is rather a quiet type; is not really my type). 5 an object, conception, or work of art serving as a model for subsequent artists. 6 Printing **a** a piece of metal, etc., with a raised letter or character on its upper surface for use in printing. **b** a kind or size of such pieces (printed in large type). **c** a set or supply of these (ran short of type). 7 a device on either side of a medal or coin. 8 Theol. a foreshadowing in the Old Testament of a person or event of the New Testament. 9 Biol. an organism having or chosen as having the essential characteristics of its group and giving its name to the next highest group. • v. 1 tr. be a type or example of. 2 tr. & intr. write with a typewriter or keyboard. 3 tr. esp. Biol. & Med. assign to a type; classify. 4 tr. = TYPECAST. □ **in type** Printing composed and ready for printing. □□ **typ·al** adj. [ME f. F type or L typus f. Gk tupos impression, figure, type, f. tuptō strike]

a a *a*
roman   boldface   *italic*

type 6

type·cast /típkast/ v.tr. (past and past part. **–cast**) assign (an actor or actress) repeatedly to the same type of role.

type·face /típfays/ n. Printing 1 a set of type or characters in a particular design. 2 the inked part of type, or the impression made by this.

type found·er n. a designer and maker of metal types.

type found·ry n. a foundry where type is made.

type·script /típskript/ n. a typewritten document.

type·set·ter /típsetər/ n. Printing 1 a person who composes type. 2 a composing machine. □□ **type·set·ting** n.

type site n. Archaeol. a site where objects regarded as defining the characteristics of a period, etc., are found.

type spec·i·men n. Biol. the specimen used for naming and describing a new species.

type·write /típrit/ v.tr. & intr. (past **–wrote**; past part. **–writ·ten**) = TYPE v. 2.

type·writ·er /típritər/ n. a machine with keys for producing printlike characters one at a time on paper inserted around a roller.

type·writ·ten /típrit'n/ adj. produced with a typewriter.

typh·li·tis /tiflítis/ n. inflammation of the cecum. □□ **typh·lit·ic** /-lítik/ adj. [mod.L f. Gk tuphlon cecum or blind gut f. tuphlos blind + -ITIS]

ty·phoid /tífoyd/ n. & adj. • n. 1 (in full **typhoid fever**) an infectious bacterial fever with an eruption of red spots on the chest and abdomen and severe intestinal irritation. 2 a similar disease of animals. • adj like typhus. □□ **ty·phoi·dal** adj. [TYPHUS + -OID]

ty·phoid con·di·tion n. (also **ty·phoid state**) a state of depressed vitality occurring in many acute diseases.

ty·phoon /tifóon/ n. a violent hurricane in E. Asia. □□ **ty·phon·ic** /-fónik/ adj. [partly f. Port. tufão f. Arab. ṭūfān perh. f. Gk tuphōn whirlwind; partly f. Chin. dial. tai fung big wind]

ty·phus /tífəs/ n. an infectious fever caused by rickettsiae, characterized by a purple rash, headaches, fever, and usu. delirium. □□ **ty·phous** adj. [mod.L f. Gk tuphos smoke, stupor f. tuphō to smoke]

typ·i·cal /típikəl/ adj. 1 serving as a characteristic example; representative. 2 characteristic of or serving to distinguish a type. 3 (often foll. by of) conforming to expected behavior, attitudes, etc. (is typical of them to forget). 4 symbolic. □□ **typ·i·cal·i·ty** /-káli-tee/ n. **typ·i·cal·ly** adv. [med.L typicalis f. L typicus f. Gk tupikos (as TYPE)]

typ·i·fy /típifi/ v.tr. (**–fies, –fied**) 1 be a representative example of; embody the characteristics of. 2 represent by a type or symbol; serve as a type, figure, or emblem of; symbolize. □□ **typ·i·fi·ca·tion** /-fikáyshən/ n. **typ·i·fi·er** n. [L typus TYPE + -FY]

typ·ist /típist/ n. a person who types at a typewriter or keyboard.

ty·po /típō/ n. (pl. **–pos**) colloq. 1 a typographical error. 2 a typographer. [abbr.]

ty·pog·ra·pher /típógrəfər/ n. a person skilled in typography.

ty·pog·ra·phy /típógrəfee/ n. 1 printing as an art. 2 the style and appearance of printed matter. □□ **ty·po·graph·ic** /-pəgráfik/ adj. **ty·po·graph·i·cal** adj. **ty·po·graph·i·cal·ly** adv. [F typographie or mod.L typographia (as TYPE, -GRAPHY)]

ty·pol·o·gy /típóləjee/ n. the study and interpretation of (esp. biblical) types. □□ **ty·po·log·i·cal** /típəlójikəl/ adj. **ty·pol·o·gist** n. [Gk tupos TYPE + -LOGY]

ty·ran·ni·cal /tiránikəl/ adj. 1 acting like a tyrant; imperious; arbitrary. 2 given to or characteristic of tyranny. □□ **ty·ran·ni·cal·ly** adv. [OF tyrannique f. L tyrannicus f. Gk turannikos (as TYRANT)]

ty·ran·ni·cide /tiránisid/ n. 1 the act or an instance of killing a tyrant. 2 the killer of a tyrant. □□ **ty·ran·ni·cid·al** /-nisíd'l/ adj. [F f. L tyrannicida, -cidium (as TYRANT, -CIDE)]

tyr·an·nize /tírəniz/ v.tr. & (foll. by over) intr. behave like a tyrant toward; rule or treat despotically or cruelly. [F tyranniser (as TYRANT)]

ty·ran·no·sau·rus /tíránəsáwrəs/ n. (also **ty·ran·no·saur**) any bipedal carnivorous dinosaur of the genus Tyrannosaurus, esp. T. rex having powerful hind legs, small clawlike front legs, and a long well-developed tail. [Gk turannos TYRANT, after dinosaur]

tyr·an·ny /tírənee/ n. (pl. **–nies**) 1 the cruel and arbitrary use of authority. 2 a tyrannical act; tyrannical behavior. 3 **a** rule by a tyrant. **b** a period of this. **c** a nation ruled by a tyrant. □□ **tyr·an·nous** /-rənəs/ adj. **tyr·an·nous·ly** adv. [ME f. OF tyrannie f. med.L tyrannia f. Gk turannia (as TYRANT)]

ty·rant /tírənt/ n. 1 an oppressive or cruel ruler. 2 a person exercising power arbitrarily or cruelly. 3 Gk Hist. an absolute ruler who seized power without the legal right. [ME tyran, -ant, f. OF tiran, tyrant f. L tyrannus f. Gk turannos]

tyre Brit. var. of TIRE[2].

Tyr·i·an /tíreeən/ adj. & n. • adj. of or relating to ancient Tyre in Phoenicia. • n. a native or citizen of Tyre. [L Tyrius f. Tyrus Tyre]

Tyr·i·an pur·ple n. see PURPLE n. 2.

ty·ro /tírō/ n. (Brit. also **ti·ro**) (pl. **–ros**) a beginner or novice. [L tiro, med.L tyro, recruit]

Ty·ro·le·an /tíróleeən, ti-/ adj. of or characteristic of the Tyrol, an Alpine province of Austria. □□ **Ty·ro·lese** adj. & n.

Tyr·rhene /tíreen/ adj. & n. (also **Tyr·rhe·ni·an** /tiréeneeən/) archaic or poet. = ETRUSCAN. [L Tyrrhenus]

tzi·gane /tsigáan/ n. 1 a Hungarian gypsy. 2 (attrib.) characteristic of the tziganes or (esp.) their music. [F f. Magyar c(z)igány]

U

U¹ /yōo/ *n.* (also **u**) (*pl.* **Us** or **U's**) **1** the twenty-first letter of the alphabet. **2** a U-shaped object or curve (esp. in *comb.*: *U-bolt*).

U² /yōo/ *adj.* esp. *Brit. colloq.* **1** upper class. **2** supposedly characteristic of the upper class. [abbr.]

U³ /ōo/ *adj.* a Burmese title of respect before a man's name. [Burmese]

U⁴ *abbr.* (also **U.**) university.

U⁵ *symb. Chem.* the element uranium.

u *prefix* = MU 2 (μ).

UAE *abbr.* United Arab Emirates.

u·bi·e·ty /yōobíətee/ *n.* the fact or condition of being in a definite place; local relation. [med.L *ubietas* f. L *ubi* where]

-ubility /yōobílitee/ *suffix* forming nouns from, or corresponding to, adjectives in *–uble* (*solubility; volubility*). [L *–ubilitas*: cf. *–*ITY]

u·biq·ui·tar·i·an /yōobíkwitáireeən/ *adj. & n. Theol.* ● *adj.* relating to or believing in the doctrine of the omnipresence of Christ's body. ● *n.* a believer in this. □□ **u·biq·ui·tar·i·an·ism** *n.* [mod.L *ubiquitarius* (as UBIQUITOUS)]

u·biq·ui·tous /yōobíkwitəs/ *adj.* **1** present everywhere or in several places simultaneously. **2** often encountered. □□ **u·biq·ui·tous·ly** *adv.* **u·biq·ui·tous·ness** *n.* **u·biq·ui·ty** *n.* [mod.L *ubiquitas* f. L *ubique* everywhere f. *ubi* where]

-uble /yəbəl/ *suffix* forming adjectives meaning 'that may or must be' (see –ABLE) (*soluble; voluble*). [F f. L *–ubilis*]

-ubly /yəblee/ *suffix* forming adverbs corresponding to adjectives in *–uble.*

U-boat /yōobōt/ *n. hist.* a German submarine. [G *U-boot* = *Unterseeboot* undersea boat]

u.c. *abbr.* uppercase.

ud·der /údər/ *n.* the mammary gland of cattle, sheep, etc., hanging as a baglike organ with several teats. □□ **ud·dered** *adj.* (also in *comb.*). [OE *ūder* f. WG]

u·dom·e·ter /yōodómitər/ *n. formal* a rain gauge. [F *udomètre* f. L *udus* damp]

UFO /yōo-ef-ṓ, yōofṓ/ *n.* (also **ufo**) (*pl.* **UFOs** or **ufos**) unidentified flying object. [abbr.]

u·fol·o·gy /yōofóləjee/ *n.* the study of UFOs. □□ **u·fol·o·gist** *n.*

ugh /əkh, ug, ukh/ *int.* **1** expressing disgust or horror. **2** the sound of a cough or grunt. [imit.]

Ug·li /úglee/ *n.* (*pl.* **Ug·lis** or **Ug·lies**) *Trademark* a mottled green and yellow citrus fruit, a hybrid of a grapefruit and tangerine. [UGLY]

ug·li·fy /úglifī/ *v.tr.* (**-fies, -fied**) make ugly. □□ **ug·li·fi·ca·tion** /-fikáyshən/ *n.*

ug·ly /úglee/ *adj.* (**ug·li·er, ug·li·est**) **1** unpleasing or repulsive to see or hear (*an ugly scar; spoke with an ugly snarl*). **2** unpleasantly suggestive; discreditable (*ugly rumors are about*). **3** threatening; dangerous (*the sky has an ugly look; an ugly mood*). **4** morally repulsive; vile (*ugly vices*). □□ **ug·li·ly** *adv.* **ug·li·ness** *n.* [ME f. ON *uggligr* to be dreaded f. *ugga* to dread]

ug·ly duck·ling *n.* a person who turns out to be beautiful or talented, etc., against all expectations (with ref. to a cygnet in a brood of ducks in a tale by Hans Christian Andersen).

U·gri·an /ōogreeən/ *adj. & n.* (also **U·gric** /ōogrik/) ● *adj.* of or relating to the eastern branch of Finnic peoples, esp. the Finns and Magyars. ● *n.* **1** a member of this people. **2** the language of this people. [Russ. *Ugry* name of a race dwelling E. of the Urals]

UHF *abbr.* ultrahigh frequency.

uh-huh /úhú/ *int. colloq.* expressing assent. [imit.]

uh·lan /ōolaan, yōolaan/ *n. hist.* a cavalryman armed with a lance in some European armies, esp. the former German army. [F & G f. Pol. (*h*) *ulan* f. Turk. *oğlan* youth, servant]

UHT *abbr.* **1** ultrahigh temperature. **2** ultra-heat-treated (esp. of milk, for long keeping).

Uit·land·er /íttlandər, áy–, óyt–/ *n. S.Afr.* a foreigner or alien, esp. before the Boer War. [Afrik. f. Du. *uit* out + *land* land]

UK *abbr.* United Kingdom.

u·kase /yōokáys, –káyz/ *n.* **1** an arbitrary command. **2** *hist.* an edict of the czarist Russian government. [Russ. *ukaz* ordinance, edict f. *ukazat'* show, decree]

U·krain·i·an /yōokráyneeən/ *n. & adj.* ● *n.* **1** a native of Ukraine. **2** the language of Ukraine. ● *adj.* of or relating to Ukraine or its people or language. [*Ukraine* f. Russ. *ukraina* frontier region f. *u* at + *krai* edge]

u·ku·le·le /yōokəláylee/ *n.* a small, four-stringed Hawaiian (orig. Portuguese) guitar. [Hawaiian, = jumping flea]

-ular /yələr/ *suffix* forming adjectives, sometimes corresp. to nouns in *–ule* (*pustular*) but often without diminutive force (*angular, granular*). □□ **-ularity** /-láritee/ *suffix* forming nouns. [from or after L *–ularis* (as –ULE, –AR¹)]

ul·cer /úlsər/ *n.* **1** an open sore on an external or internal surface of the body, often forming pus. **2 a** a moral blemish. **b** a corroding or corrupting influence, etc. □□ **ul·cered** *adj.* **ul·cer·ous** *adj.* [ME f. L *ulcus –eris*, rel. to Gk *helkos*]

ul·cer·ate /úlsərayt/ *v.tr. & intr.* form into or affect with an ulcer. □□ **ul·cer·a·ble** *adj.* **ul·cer·a·tion** /-ráyshən/ *n.* **ul·cer·a·tive** *adj.* [ME f. L *ulcerare ulcerat-* (as ULCER)]

-ule /yōol, yōol/ *suffix* forming diminutive nouns (*capsule; globule*). [from or after L *–ulus, –ula, –ulum*]

u·le·ma /ōolimaa/ *n.* **1** a body of Muslim doctors of sacred law and theology. **2** a member of this. [Arab. *'ulamā* pl. of *'ālim* learned f. *'alama* know]

-ulent /yələnt/ *suffix* forming adjectives meaning 'abounding in; full of' (*fraudulent; turbulent*). □□ **-ulence** *suffix* forming nouns. [L *–ntus*]

u·lig·i·nose /yōolíjinōs/ *adj.* (also **u·lig·i·nous** /-nəs/) *Bot.* growing in wet or swampy places. [L *uliginosus* f. *uligo –ginis* moisture]

ul·lage /úlij/ *n.* **1** the amount by which a cask, etc., falls short of being full. **2** loss by evaporation or leakage. [ME f. AF *ulliage*, OF *ouillage* f. *ouiller* fill up, ult. f. L *oculus* eye, with ref. to the bunghole]

ul·na /úlnə/ *n.* (*pl.* **ul·nae** /-nee/) **1** the thinner and longer bone in the forearm, on the side opposite to the thumb (cf. RADIUS 3). **2** *Zool.* a corresponding bone in an animal's foreleg or a bird's wing. □□ **ul·nar** *adj.* [L, rel. to Gk *ōlenē* and ELL]

u·lot·ri·chan /yōolótrikən/ *adj. & n.* (also **u·lot·ri·chous** /-kəs/) having tightly curled hair, esp. denoting a human type. ● *n.* a person having such hair. [mod.L *Ulotrichi* f. Gk *oulos* woolly, crisp + *thrix trikhos* hair]

-ulous /yələs/ *suffix* forming adjectives (*fabulous; populous*). [L *–ulosus, –ulus*]

ul·ster /úlstər/ *n.* a man's long, loose overcoat of rough cloth. [*Ulster* in Ireland, where it was orig. sold]

Ul·ster·man /úlstərmən/ *n.* (*pl.* **–men**; *fem.* **Ul·ster·wom·an**; *pl.* **–wom·en**) a native of Ulster, the northern part of Ireland.

ult. *abbr.* **1** ultimo. **2** ultimate.

ul·te·ri·or /ultéereeər/ *adj.* **1** existing in the background, or beyond what is evident or admitted; hidden; secret (esp. ulterior motive). **2** situated beyond. **3** more remote; not immediate; in the future. □□ **ul·te·ri·or·ly** *adv.* [L, = further, more distant]

ul·ti·ma /últimə/ *n.* the last syllable of a word. [L *ultima* (*syllaba*), fem. of *ultimus* last]

ul·ti·ma·ta *pl.* of ULTIMATUM.

ul·ti·mate /últimət/ *adj. & n.* ● *adj.* **1** last; final. **2** beyond which no other exists or is possible (*the ultimate analysis*). **3** fundamental; primary; unanalyzable (*ultimate truths*). **4** maximum (*ultimate tensile strength*). ● *n.* **1** (prec. by *the*) the best achievable or imaginable. **2** a final or fundamental fact or principle. □□ **ul·ti·mate·ly** *adj.* **ul·ti·mate·ness** *n.* [LL *ultimatus* past part. of *ultimare* come to an end]

ul·ti·ma Thu·le /últimə thōolee, ōoltimaa tōolee/ *n.* a faraway, unknown region. [L, = furthest Thule, a remote northern region]

ul·ti·ma·tum /últimáytəm/ *n.* (*pl.* **ul·ti·ma·tums** or **ul·ti·ma·ta** /-tə/) a final demand or statement of terms by one party, the rejection of which by another could cause a breakdown in relations, war, or an end of cooperation, etc. [L neut. past part.: see ULTIMATE]

ul·ti·mo /últimō/ *adj. Commerce* of last month (*the 28th ultimo*). [L *ultimo mense* in the last month]

ul·ti·mo·gen·i·ture /últimōjénichər/ *n.* a system in which the youngest son has the right of inheritance (cf. PRIMOGENITURE 2). [L *ultimus* last, after PRIMOGENITURE]

ul·tra /últrə/ *adj. & n.* ● *adj.* favoring extreme views or measures, esp. in religion or politics. ● *n.* an extremist. [orig. as abbr. of F *ultra-royaliste*: see ULTRA-]

ultra- /últrə/ *comb. form* **1** beyond; on the other side of (opp. CIS-). **2** extreme(ly), excessive(ly) (*ultraconservative; ultramodern*). [L *ultra* beyond]

ul·tra·cen·tri·fuge /últrəséntrifyōoj/ *n.* a high-speed centrifuge used to separate small particles and large molecules by their rate of sedimentation from sols.

ul·tra·high /últrəhí/ *adj.* **1** (of a frequency) in the range 300 to 3,000 megahertz. **2** extremely high (*ultrahigh prices*; *ultrahigh suspension bridge*).

ul·tra·ist /últrəist/ *n.* the holder of extreme positions in politics, religion, etc. □□ **ul·tra·ism** *n.*

ul·tra·ma·rine /últrəməréen/ *n. & adj.* ●*n.* **1 a** a brilliant blue pigment orig. obtained from lapis lazuli. **b** an imitation of this from powdered fired clay, sodium carbonate, sulfur, and resin. **2** the color of this. ●*adj.* **1** of this color. **2** *archaic* situated beyond the sea. [obs. It. *oltramarino* & med.L *ultramarinus* beyond the sea (as ULTRA-, MARINE), because lapis lazuli was brought from beyond the sea]

ul·tra·mi·cro·scope /últrəmíkrəskōp/ *n.* an optical microscope used to reveal very small particles by means of light scattered by them.

ul·tra·mi·cro·scop·ic /últrəmíkrəskópik/ *adj.* **1** too small to be seen by an ordinary optical microscope. **2** of or relating to an ultramicroscope.

ul·tra·mon·tane /últrəmontáyn/ *adj. & n.* ●*adj.* **1** situated on the other side of the mountains (esp. the Alps) from the point of view of the speaker. **2** advocating supreme papal authority in matters of faith and discipline. ●*n.* **1** a person living on the other side of the mountains (esp. the Alps). **2** a person advocating supreme papal authority. [med.L *ultramontanus* (as ULTRA-, L *mons montis* mountain)]

ul·tra·mun·dane /últrəmúndayn/ *adj.* lying beyond the world or the solar system. [L *ultramundanus* (as ULTRA-, *mundanus* f. *mundus* world)]

ul·tra·son·ic /últrəsónik/ *adj.* of or involving sound waves with a frequency above the upper limit of human hearing. □□ **ul·tra·son·i·cal·ly** *adv.*

ul·tra·son·ics /últrəsóniks/ *n.pl.* (usu. treated as *sing.*) the science and application of ultrasonic waves.

ul·tra·sound /últrəsownd/ *n.* **1** sound having an ultrasonic frequency. **2** ultrasonic waves.

ul·tra·sound car·di·og·ra·phy *n.* = ECHOCARDIOGRAPHY.

ul·tra·struc·ture /últrəstrukchər/ *n. Biol.* fine structure not visible with an optical microscope.

ul·tra·vi·o·let /últrəvíələt/ *adj. Physics* **1** having a wavelength (just) beyond the violet end of the visible spectrum. **2** of or using such radiation.

ul·tra vi·res /últrə víreez, ōóltraa véerayz/ *adv. & predic.adj.* beyond one's legal power or authority. [L]

ul·u·late /úlyəlayt, yóōl–/ *v.intr.* howl; wail; make a hooting cry. □□ **ul·u·lant** *adj.* **ul·u·la·tion** /–láyshən/ *n.* [L *ululare ululat-* (imit.)]

um /um, əm/ *int.* expressing hesitation or a pause in speech. [imit.]

-um var. of –IUM 1.

um·bel /úmbəl/ *n. Bot.* a flower cluster in which stalks nearly equal in length spring from a common center and form a flat or curved surface, as in parsley. □□ **um·bel·lar** *adj.* **um·bel·late** /–bəlit, –layt, umbélit/ *adj.* **um·bel·lule** /úmbəlyōōl, –bélyōōl/ *adj.* [obs. F *umbelle* or L *umbella* sunshade, dimin. of UMBRA]

um·bel·lif·er /umbélifər/ *n.* any plant of the family Umbelliferae bearing umbels, including parsley and parsnip. □□ **um·bel·lif·er·ous** /–bəlifərəs/ *adj.* [obs. F *umbellifère* f. L (as UMBEL, –*fer* bearing)]

um·ber /úmbər/ *n. & adj.* ●*n.* **1** a natural pigment like ocher but darker and browner. **2** the color of this. ●*adj.* **1** of this color. **2** dark; dusky. [F *terre d'*)*ombre* or It. *(terra di) ombra* = shadow (earth), f. L UMBRA or *Umbra* fem. of *Umber* Umbrian]

um·bil·i·cal /umbílikəl/ *adj.* **1** of, situated near, or affecting the navel. **2** centrally placed. [obs. F *umbilical* f. L UMBILICUS]

um·bil·i·cal cord *n.* **1** a flexible, cordlike structure attaching a fetus to the placenta. **2** *Astronaut.* a supply cable linking a missile to its launcher, or an astronaut in space to a spacecraft.

um·bil·i·cate /umbílikət/ *adj.* **1** shaped like a navel. **2** having an umbilicus.

um·bil·i·cus /umbílikəs/ *n.* (*pl.* **um·bil·i·ci** /–bílisī/ or **um·bil·i·cus·es**) **1** *Anat.* the navel. **2** *Bot. & Zool.* a navellike formation. **3** *Geom.* a point in a surface through which all cross sections have the same curvature. [L, rel. to Gk *omphalos* and to NAVEL]

um·bles /úmbəlz/ *n.pl.* the edible offal of deer, etc. (cf. *eat humble pie*). [ME var. of NUMBLES]

um·bo /úmbō/ *n.* (*pl.* **–bos** or **um·bones** /–bóneez/) **1** the boss of a shield, esp. in the center. **2** *Bot. & Zool.* a rounded knob or protuberance. □□ **um·bo·nal** *adj.* **um·bo·nate** /–bónət/ *adj.* [L *umbo –onis*]

um·bra /úmbrə/ *n.* (*pl.* **um·bras** or **um·brae** /–bree/) *Astron.* **1** a total shadow usu. cast on the earth by the moon during a solar eclipse. **2** the dark central part of a sunspot (cf. PENUMBRA). □□ **um·bral** *adj.* [L, = shadow]

um·brage /úmbrij/ *n.* **1** offense; a sense of slight or injury (esp. give or take umbrage at). **2** *archaic* **a** a shade. **b** what gives shade. [ME f. OF ult. f. L *umbraticus* f. *umbra*: see UMBRA]

um·brel·la /umbrélə/ *n.* **1 a** a light, portable device for protection against rain, strong sun, etc., consisting of a usu. circular canopy of cloth mounted by means of a collapsible metal frame on a cen-

tral stick. **2** protection or patronage. **3** (often *attrib.*) a coordinating or unifying agency (*umbrella organization*). **4** a screen of fighter aircraft or a curtain of fire put up as a protection against enemy aircraft. **5** *Zool.* the gelatinous disk of a jellyfish, etc., which it contracts and expands to move through the water. □□ **um·brel·laed** /–ləd/ *adj.* **um·brel·la·like** *adj.* [It. *ombrella*, dimin. of *ombra* shade f. L *umbra*: see UMBRA]

um·brel·la bird *n.* any S. American bird of the genus *Cephalopterus*, with a black umbrella-like crest and long wattles.

um·brel·la pine *n.* **1** = STONE PINE. **2** a tall Japanese evergreen conifer, *Sciadopitys verticillata*, with leaves in umbrellalike whorls.

um·brel·la stand *n.* a stand for holding closed, upright umbrellas.

um·brel·la tree *n.* a small magnolia, *Magnolia tripetala*, with leaves in a whorl like an umbrella.

Um·bri·an /úmbreeən/ *adj. & n.* ●*adj.* of or relating to Umbria in central Italy. ●*n.* **1** the language of ancient Umbria, related to Latin. **2** an inhabitant of ancient Umbria.

Um·bri·an School *n.* a Renaissance school of Italian painting, to which Raphael and Perugino belonged.

um·brif·er·ous /umbrífərəs/ *adj. formal* providing shade. [L *umbrifer* f. *umbra* shade: see –FEROUS]

u·mi·ak /óōmeeak/ *n.* an Inuit skin-and-wood open boat propelled with paddles. [Eskimo *umiaq* women's boat]

um·laut /óōmlowt/ *n. & v.* ●*n.* **1** a mark (¨) used over a vowel, esp. in Germanic languages, to indicate a vowel change. **2** such a vowel change, e.g., German *Mann*, *Männer*, English *man*, *men*, due to *i*, *j*, etc. (now usu. lost or altered) in the following syllable. ●*v.tr.* modify (a form or a sound) by an umlaut. [G f. *um* about + *Laut* sound]

ump /ump/ *n. colloq.* an umpire. [abbr.]

um·pire /úmpīr/ *n. & v.* ●*n.* **1** a person chosen to enforce the rules and settle disputes in various sports. **2** a person chosen to arbitrate between disputants, or to see fair play. ●*v.* **1** *intr* (usu. foll. by *for*, *in*, etc.) act as umpire. **2** *tr.* act as umpire in (a game, etc.). □□ **um·pir·age** /–pīrij, –pərij/ *n.* **um·pire·ship** *n.* [ME, later form of *noumpere* f. OF *nonper* not equal (as NON-, PEER[2]): for loss of *n*- cf. ADDER]

ump·teen /úmpteen/ *adj. & pron. sl.* ●*adj.* indefinitely many; a lot of. ●*pron.* indefinitely many. □□ **ump·teenth** *adj.* [joc. form on –TEEN]

UN *abbr.* United Nations.

un-[1] /un/ *prefix* **1** added to adjectives and participles and their derivative nouns and adverbs, meaning: **a** not: denoting the absence of a quality or state (*unusable*; *uncalled-for*; *uneducated*; *unfailing*; *unofficially*; *unhappiness*). **b** the reverse of, usu. with an implication of approval or disapproval, or with some other special connotation (*unselfish*; *unsociable*; *unscientific*). **2** (less often) added to nouns, meaning 'a lack of' (*unrest*; *untruth*). [OE f. Gmc, rel. to L *in–*]

▶**1.** The number of words that can be formed with this prefix (and similarly with UN-[2]) is potentially as large as the number of adjectives in use; consequently only a selection, being considered the most current or semantically noteworthy, can be given here. **2.** Words formed as in sense 1 often have neutral counterparts in *non-* (see NON- 6) and counterparts in *in-* (see IN-[1]), e.g., *unadvisable*.

un-[2] /un/ *prefix* added to verbs and (less often) nouns, forming verbs denoting: **1** the reversal or cancellation of an action or state (*undress*; *unlock*; *unsettle*). **2** deprivation or separation (*unmask*). **3** release from (*unburden*; *uncage*). **4** causing to be no longer (*unman*). [OE *un-*, *on-* f. Gmc]

▶See the note at UN-[1].

'un /ən/ *pron. colloq.* one (*that's a good 'un*). [dial. var.]

un·a·bashed /únəbásht/ *adj.* not abashed. □□ **un·a·bash·ed·ly** /–shidlee/ *adv.*

un·a·bat·ed /únəbáytid/ *adj.* not abated; undiminished. □□ **un·a·bat·ed·ly** *adv.*

un·a·ble /únáybəl/ *adj.* (usu. foll. by *to* + infin.) not able; lacking ability.

un·a·bridged /únəbríjd/ *adj.* (of a text, etc.) complete; not abridged.

un·ab·sorbed /únəbsáwrbd, –sáwrbd/ *adj.* not absorbed.

un·ac·a·dem·ic /únakədémik/ *adj.* **1** not academic (esp. not scholarly or theoretical). **2** (of a person) not suited to academic study.

un·ac·cent·ed /únáksentid, –akséntid/ *adj.* not accented; not emphasized.

un·ac·cept·a·ble /únəkséptəbəl/ *adj.* not acceptable. □□ **un·ac·cept·a·ble·ness** *n.* **un·ac·cept·a·bly** *adv.*

un·ac·claimed /únəkláymd/ *adj.* not acclaimed.

un·ac·com·mo·dat·ing /únəkómədayting/ *adj.* not accommodating; disobliging.

un·ac·com·pa·nied /únəkúmpəneed/ *adj.* **1** not accompanied. **2** *Mus.* without accompaniment.

un·ac·com·plished /únəkómplisht/ *adj.* **1** not accomplished; uncompleted. **2** lacking accomplishments.

un·ac·count·a·ble /únəkówntəbəl/ *adj.* **1** unable to be explained. **2** unpredictable or strange in behavior. **3** not responsible. ●□□ **un·ac·count·a·bil·i·ty** /–bílitee/ *n.* **un·ac·count·a·ble·ness** *n.* **un·ac·count·a·bly** *adv.*

un·ac·count·ed /únəkówntid/ *adj.* of which no account is given. □ **unaccounted for** unexplained; not included in an account.

un·ac·cus·tomed /únəkústəmd/ *adj.* **1** (usu. foll. by *to*) not accustomed. **2** not customary; unusual (*his unaccustomed silence*). □□ **un·ac·cus·tomed·ly** *adv.*

un·a·chiev·a·ble /únəcheévəbəl/ *adj.* not achievable.

un·ac·knowl·edged /únəknólijd/ *adj.* not acknowledged.

un·ac·quaint·ed /únəkwáyntid/ *adj.* (usu. foll. by *with*) not acquainted.

un·a·dapt·a·ble /únədáptəbəl/ *adj.* not adaptable.

un·a·dapt·ed /únədáptid/ *adj.* not adapted.

un·ad·dressed /únədrést/ *adj.* (esp. of a letter, etc.) without an address.

un·ad·ja·cent /únəjáysənt/ *adj.* not adjacent.

un·a·dopt·ed /únədóptid/ *adj.* not adopted.

un·a·dorned /únədáwrnd/ *adj.* not adorned; plain.

un·a·dul·ter·at·ed /únədúltərəytid/ *adj.* **1** not adulterated; pure; concentrated. **2** sheer; complete; utter (*unadulterated nonsense*).

un·ad·ven·tur·ous /únədvénchərəs/ *adj.* not adventurous. □□ **un·ad·ven·tur·ous·ly** *adv.*

un·ad·ver·tised /únádvərtizd/ *adj.* not advertised.

un·ad·vis·a·ble /únədvízəbəl/ *adj.* **1** not open to advice. **2** (of a thing) inadvisable.

un·ad·vised /únədvízd/ *adj.* **1** indiscreet; rash. **2** not having had advice. □□ **un·ad·vis·ed·ly** /–zidlee/ *adv.* **un·ad·vis·ed·ness** *n.*

un·af·fect·ed /únəféktid/ *adj.* **1** (usu. foll. by *by*) not affected. **2** free from affectation; genuine; sincere. □□ **un·af·fect·ed·ly** *adv.* **un·af·fect·ed·ness** *n.*

un·af·fil·i·at·ed /únəfíleeaytid/ *adj.* not affiliated.

un·a·fraid /únəfráyd/ *adj.* not afraid.

un·aid·ed /únáydid/ *adj.* not aided; without help.

un·al·ien·a·ble /únáyleeənəbəl/ *adj. Law* = INALIENABLE.

un·a·ligned /únəlínd/ *adj.* **1** = NONALIGNED. **2** not physically aligned.

un·a·like /únəlík/ *adj.* not alike; different.

un·a·live /únəlív/ *adj.* **1** lacking in vitality. **2** (foll. by *to*) not fully susceptible or awake to.

un·al·le·vi·at·ed /únəleéveeaytid/ *adj.* not alleviated; relentless.

un·al·lied /únəlíd/ *adj.* not allied; having no allies.

un·al·low·a·ble /únəlówəbəl/ *adj.* not allowable.

un·al·loyed /únəlóyd/ *adj.* **1** not alloyed; pure. **2** complete; utter (*unalloyed joy*).

un·al·ter·a·ble /únáwltərəbl/ *adj.* not alterable. □□ **un·al·ter·a·ble·ness** *n.* **un·al·ter·a·bly** *adv.*

un·al·tered /únáwltərd/ *adj.* not altered; remaining the same.

un·a·mazed /únəmáyzd/ *adj.* not amazed.

un·am·big·u·ous /únəmbígyoóəs/ *adj.* not ambiguous; clear or definite in meaning. □□ **un·am·big·u·i·ty** /–gyoó-itee/ *n.* **un·am·big·u·ous·ly** *adv.*

un·am·bi·tious /únəmbíshəs/ *adj.* not ambitious; without ambition. □□ **un·am·bi·tious·ly** *adv.* **un·am·bi·tious·ness** *n.*

un·am·biv·a·lent /únəmbívələnt/ *adj.* (of feelings, etc.) not ambivalent; straightforward. □□ **un·am·biv·a·lent·ly** *adv.*

un-A·mer·i·can /únəmérikən/ *adj.* **1** not in accordance with American characteristics, etc. **2** contrary to the interests of the US; (in the US) treasonable. □□ **un-A·mer·i·can·ism** *n.*

un·a·mi·a·ble /únáymeeəbəl/ *adj.* not amiable.

un·am·pli·fied /únámplifīd/ *adj.* not amplified.

un·a·mused /únəmyoózd/ *adj.* not amused.

un·an·a·lyz·a·ble /únánəlízəbəl/ *adj.* not able to be analyzed.

un·an·a·lyzed /únánəlīzd/ *adj.* not analyzed.

un·a·neled /únəneéld/ *adj. archaic* not having received extreme unction.

u·nan·i·mous /yoónánimes/ *adj.* **1** all in agreement (*the committee was unanimous*). **2** (of an opinion, vote, etc.) held or given by general consent (*the unanimous choice*). □□ **u·na·nim·i·ty** /–nənímitee/ *n.* **u·nan·i·mous·ly** *adv.* **u·nan·i·mous·ness** *n.* [LL *unanimis*, L *unanimus* f. *unus* one + *animus* mind]

un·an·nounced /únənównst/ *adj.* not announced; without warning (of arrival, etc.).

un·an·swer·a·ble /únánsərəbəl/ *adj.* **1** unable to be refuted (*has an unanswerable case*). **2** unable to be answered (*an unanswerable question*). □□ **un·an·swer·a·ble·ness** *n.* **un·an·swer·a·bly** *adv.*

un·an·swered /únánsərd/ *adj.* not answered.

un·an·tic·i·pat·ed /únantísipaytid/ *adj.* not anticipated.

un·ap·par·ent /únəpárənt/ *adj.* not apparent.

un·ap·peal·a·ble /únəpeéləbəl/ *adj.* esp. *Law* not able to be appealed against.

un·ap·peal·ing /únəpeéling/ *adj.* not appealing; unattractive. □□ **un·ap·peal·ing·ly** *adv.*

un·ap·peas·a·ble /únəpeézəbəl/ *adj.* not appeasable.

un·ap·peased /únəpeézd/ *adj.* not appeased.

un·ap·pe·tiz·ing /únápitīzing/ *adj.* not appetizing. □□ **un·ap·pe·tiz·ing·ly** *adv.*

un·ap·plied /únəplíd/ *adj.* not applied.

un·ap·pre·ci·at·ed /únəpreésheeaytid/ *adj.* not appreciated.

un·ap·pre·ci·a·tive /únəpreéshətiv/ *adj.* not appreciative.

un·ap·proach·a·ble /únəpróchəbəl/ *adj.* **1** not approachable; remote; inaccessible. **2** (of a person) unfriendly. □□ **un·ap·proach·a·bil·i·ty** *n.* **un·ap·proach·a·ble·ness** *n.* **un·ap·proach·a·bly** *adv.*

un·ap·pro·pri·at·ed /únəprópreeaytid/ *adj.* **1** not allocated or assigned. **2** not taken into possession by anyone.

un·ap·proved /únəproóvd/ *adj.* not approved or sanctioned.

un·apt /únápt/ *adj.* **1** (usu. foll. by *for*) not suitable. **2** (usu. foll. by *to* + infin.) not apt. □□ **un·apt·ly** *adv.* **un·apt·ness** *n.*

un·ar·gu·a·ble /únaárgyoōəbəl/ *adj.* not arguable; certain.

un·arm /únaárm/ *v.tr.* deprive or free of arms or armor.

un·armed /únaármd/ *adj.* not armed; without weapons.

un·ar·rest·ing /únərésting/ *adj.* uninteresting; dull. □□ **un·ar·rest·ing·ly** *adv.*

un·ar·tic·u·lat·ed /únaartíkyəlaytid/ *adj.* not articulated or distinct.

un·ar·tis·tic /únaartístik/ *adj.* not artistic, esp. not concerned with art. □□ **un·ar·tis·ti·cal·ly** *adv.*

un·as·cer·tain·a·ble /únasərtáynəbəl/ *adj.* not ascertainable.

un·as·cer·tained /únasərtáynd/ *adj.* not ascertained; unknown.

un·a·shamed /únəsháymd/ *adj.* **1** feeling no guilt, shameless. **2** blatant; bold. □□ **un·a·sham·ed·ly** /–midlee/ *adv.* **un·a·sham·ed·ness** /–midnis/ *n.*

un·asked /únáskt/ *adj.* (often foll. by *for*) not asked, requested, or invited.

un·as·sail·a·ble /únəsáyləbəl/ *adj.* unable to be attacked or questioned; impregnable. □□ **un·as·sail·a·bil·i·ty** /–bílitee/ *n.* **un·as·sail·a·ble·ness** *n.* **un·as·sail·a·bly** *adv.*

un·as·ser·tive /únəsərtiv/ *adj.* (of a person) not assertive or forthcoming; reticent. □□ **un·as·ser·tive·ly** *adv.* **un·as·ser·tive·ness** *n.*

un·as·sign·a·ble /únəsínəbəl/ *adj.* not assignable.

un·as·signed /únəsínd/ *adj.* not assigned.

un·as·sim·i·lat·ed /únəsímiláytid/ *adj.* not assimilated. □□ **un·as·sim·i·la·ble** *adj.*

un·as·sist·ed /únəsístid/ *adj.* not assisted.

un·as·suaged /únəswáyjd/ *adj.* not assuaged. □□ **un·as·suage·a·ble** *adj.*

un·as·sum·ing /únəsoóming/ *adj.* not pretentious or arrogant; modest. □□ **un·as·sum·ing·ly** *adv.* **un·as·sum·ing·ness** *n.*

un·a·toned /únətónd/ *adj.* not atoned for.

un·at·tached /únətácht/ *adj.* **1** (often foll. by *to*) not attached, esp. to a particular body, organization, etc. **2** not engaged or married.

un·at·tack·a·ble /únətákəbəl/ *adj.* unable to be attacked or damaged.

un·at·tain·a·ble /únətáynəbəl/ *adj.* not attainable. □□ **un·at·tain·a·ble·ness** *n.* **un·at·tain·a·bly** *adv.*

un·at·tempt·ed /únətémptid/ *adj.* not attempted.

un·at·tend·ed /únəténdid/ *adj.* **1** (usu. foll. by *to*) not attended. **2** (of a person, vehicle, etc.) not accompanied; alone; uncared for.

un·at·trac·tive /únətráktiv/ *adj.* not attractive. □□ **un·at·trac·tive·ly** *adv.* **un·at·trac·tive·ness** *n.*

un·at·trib·ut·a·ble /únətríbyotəbəl/ *adj.* (esp. of information) that cannot or may not be attributed to a source, etc. □□ **un·at·trib·ut·a·bly** *adv.*

un·au·then·tic /únawthéntik/ *adj.* not authentic. □□ **un·au·then·ti·cal·ly** *adv.*

un·au·then·ti·cat·ed /únawthéntikaytid/ *adj.* not authenticated.

un·au·thor·ized /únáwthərīzd/ *adj.* not authorized.

un·a·vail·a·ble /únəváyləbəl/ *adj.* not available. □□ **un·a·vail·a·bil·i·ty** *n.* **un·a·vail·a·ble·ness** *n.*

un·a·vail·ing /únəváyling/ *adj.* not availing; achieving nothing; ineffectual. □□ **un·a·vail·ing·ly** *adv.*

un·a·void·a·ble /únəvóydəbəl/ *adj.* not avoidable; inevitable. □□ **un·a·void·a·bil·i·ty** *n.* **un·a·void·a·ble·ness** *n.* **un·a·void·a·bly** *adv.*

un·a·vowed /únəvówd/ *adj.* not avowed.

un·a·ware /únəwáir/ *adj. & adv.* **1** (usu. foll. by *of*, or *that* + clause) not aware; ignorant (*unaware of her presence*). **2** (of a person) insensitive; unperceptive. ● *adv.* = UNAWARES. □□ **un·a·ware·ness** *n.*

un·a·wares /únəwáirz/ *adv.* **1** unexpectedly (*met them unawares*). **2** inadvertently (*dropped it unawares*). [earlier *unware(s)* f. OE *unwær(es)*: see WARE[2]]

un·backed /únbákt/ *adj.* **1** not supported. **2** (of a horse, etc.) having no backers. **3** (of a chair, picture, etc.) having no back or backing.

un·bal·ance /únbáləns/ *v. & n.* ● *v.tr.* **1** upset the physical or mental balance of (*unbalanced by the blow*; *the shock unbalanced him*). **2** (as **unbalanced** *adj.*) **a** not balanced. **b** (of a mind or person) unstable or deranged. ● *n.* lack of balance; instability, esp. mental.

un·ban /únbán/ *v.tr.* (**un·banned**, **un·ban·ning**) cease to ban; remove a ban from.

un·bar /únbaár/ *v.tr.* (**un·barred**, **un·bar·ring**) **1** remove a bar or bars from (a gate, etc.). **2** unlock; open.

un·bear·a·ble /únbáirəbəl/ *adj.* not bearable. □□ **un·bear·a·ble·ness** *n.* **un·bear·a·bly** *adv.*

See page xx for the **Key to Pronunciation**.

un·beat·a·ble /únbeétəbəl/ *adj.* not beatable; excelling.

un·beat·en /únbeét'n/ *adj.* 1 not beaten. 2 (of a record, etc.) not surpassed.

un·beau·ti·ful /únbyóotifŏol/ *adj.* not beautiful; ugly. □□ **un·beau·ti·ful·ly** *adv.*

un·be·com·ing /únbikúming/ *adj.* 1 (esp. of clothing) not flattering or suiting a person. 2 (usu. foll. by *to, for*) not fitting; indecorous or unsuitable. □□ **un·be·com·ing·ly** *adv.* **un·be·com·ing·ness** *n.*

un·be·fit·ting /únbifíting/ *adj.* not befitting; unsuitable. □□ **un·be·fit·ting·ly** *adv.* **un·be·fit·ting·ness** *n.*

un·be·friend·ed /únbifréndid/ *adj.* not befriended.

un·be·got·ten /únbigót'n/ *adj.* not begotten.

un·be·hold·en /únbihóld'n/ *predic.adj.* (usu. foll. by *to*) under no obligation.

un·be·known /únbinón/ *adj.* (also **un·be·knownst** /–nónst/) (foll. by *to*) without the knowledge of (*was there all the time unbeknown to us*). [UN-¹ + *beknown* (archaic) = KNOWN]

un·be·lief /únbileéf/ *n.* lack of belief, esp. in religious matters. □□ **un·be·liev·er** *n.* **un·be·liev·ing** *adj.* **un·be·liev·ing·ly** *adv.* **un·be·liev·ing·ness** *n.*

un·be·liev·a·ble /únbileévəbəl/ *adj.* not believable; incredible. □□ **un·be·liev·a·bil·i·ty** *n.* **un·be·liev·a·ble·ness** *n.* **un·be·liev·a·bly** *adv.*

un·be·loved /únbilúvd/ *adj.* not beloved.

un·belt /únbélt/ *v.tr.* remove or undo the belt of (a garment, etc.).

un·bend /únbénd/ *v.* (*past* and *past part.* **un·bent**) 1 *tr. & intr.* change from a bent position; straighten. 2 *intr.* relax from strain or severity; become affable. 3 *tr. Naut.* **a** unfasten (sails) from yards and stays. **b** cast (a cable) loose. **c** untie (a rope).

un·bend·ing /únbénding/ *adj.* 1 not bending; inflexible. 2 firm; austere (*unbending rectitude*). 3 relaxing from strain, activity, or formality. □□ **un·bend·ing·ly** *adv.* **un·bend·ing·ness** *n.*

un·bi·ased /únbíəst/ *adj.* (also esp. *Brit.* **un·bi·assed**) not biased; impartial.

un·bib·li·cal /únbíblikəl/ *adj.* 1 not in or authorized by the Bible. 2 contrary to the Bible.

un·bid·da·ble /únbídəbəl/ *adj. Brit.* disobedient; not docile.

un·bid·den /únbíd'n/ *adj.* not commanded or invited (*arrived unbidden*).

un·bind /únbínd/ *v.tr.* (*past* and *past part.* **un·bound**) release from bonds or binding.

un·birth·day /únbɔ́rthday/ *n.* (often *attrib.*) *joc.* any day but one's birthday (*an unbirthday party*).

un·bleached /únbleécht/ *adj.* not bleached.

un·blem·ished /únblémisht/ *adj.* not blemished.

un·blessed /únblést/ *adj.* (also **un·blest**) not blessed.

un·blink·ing /únblíngking/ *adj.* 1 not blinking. 2 steadfast; not hesitating. 3 stolid; cool. □□ **un·blink·ing·ly** *adv.*

un·block /únblók/ *v.tr.* 1 remove an obstruction from (esp. a pipe, drain, etc.). 2 (also *absol.*) *Cards* allow the later unobstructed play of (a suit) by playing a high card.

un·blown /únblón/ *adj.* 1 not blown. 2 *archaic* (of a flower) not yet in bloom.

un·blush·ing /únblúshing/ *adj.* 1 not blushing. 2 unashamed; frank. □□ **un·blush·ing·ly** *adv.*

un·bolt /únbólt/ *v.tr.* release (a door, etc.) by drawing back the bolt.

un·bolt·ed /únbóltid/ *adj.* 1 not bolted. 2 (of flour, etc.) not sifted.

un·bon·net /únbónit/ *v.* (**un·bon·net·ed**, **un·bon·net·ing**) 1 *tr.* remove the bonnet from. 2 *intr. archaic* remove one's hat or bonnet esp. in respect.

un·book·ish /únbóokish/ *adj.* 1 not academic; not often inclined to read. 2 free from bookishness.

un·boot /únbóot/ *v.intr. & tr.* remove one's boots or the boots of (a person).

un·born /únbáwrn/ *adj.* 1 not yet born (*an unborn child*). 2 never to be brought into being (*unborn hopes*).

un·bos·om /únbóozəm/ *v.tr.* 1 disclose (thoughts, secrets, etc.). 2 (*refl.*) unburden (oneself) of one's thoughts, secrets, etc.

un·both·ered /únbóthərd/ *adj.* not bothered; unconcerned.

un·bound¹ /únbównd/ *adj.* 1 not bound or tied up. 2 unconstrained. 3 **a** (of a book) not having a binding. **b** having paper covers. 4 (of a substance or particle) in a loose or free state.

un·bound² *past* and *past part.* of UNBIND.

un·bound·ed /únbówndid/ *adj.* not bounded; infinite (*unbounded optimism*). □□ **un·bound·ed·ly** *adv.* **un·bound·ed·ness** *n.*

un·brace /únbráys/ *v.tr.* 1 (also *absol.*) free from tension; relax (the nerves, etc.). 2 remove a brace or braces from.

un·breach·a·ble /únbreéchəbəl/ *adj* not able to be breached.

un·break·a·ble /únbráykəbəl/ *adj.* not breakable.

un·breath·a·ble /únbreéthəbəl/ *adj.* not able to be breathed.

un·brib·a·ble /únbríbəbəl/ *adj.* not bribable.

un·bridge·a·ble /únbríjəbəl/ *adj.* unable to be bridged.

un·bri·dle /únbríd'l/ *v.tr.* 1 remove a bridle from (a horse). 2 remove constraints from (one's tongue, a person, etc.). 3 (as **unbridled** *adj.*) unconstrained (*unbridled insolence*).

un·bro·ken /únbrókən/ *adj.* 1 not broken. 2 not tamed (*an unbroken horse*). 3 not interrupted (*unbroken sleep*). 4 not surpassed (*an unbroken record*). □□ **un·bro·ken·ly** *adv.* **un·bro·ken·ness** /–ən-nis/ *n.*

un·bruised /únbróozd/ *adj.* not bruised.

un·buck·le /únbúkəl/ *v.tr.* release the buckle of (a strap, shoe, etc.).

un·build /únbíld/ *v.tr.* (*past* and *past part.* **un·built**) 1 demolish or destroy (a building, theory, system, etc.). 2 (as **unbuilt**.) not yet built or (of land, etc.) not yet built on.

un·bur·den /únbɔ́rd'n/ *v.tr.* 1 relieve of a burden. 2 (esp. *refl.*; often foll. by *to*) relieve (oneself, one's conscience, etc.) by confession, etc. □□ **un·bur·dened** *adj.*

un·bur·ied /únbéreed/ *adj.* not buried.

un·bur·y /únbéree/ *v.tr.* (**–ies, –ied**) 1 remove from the ground, etc., after burial. 2 unearth (a secret, etc.).

un·busi·ness·like /únbíznislīk/ *adj.* not businesslike.

un·but·ton /únbút'n/ *v.tr.* 1 **a** unfasten (a coat, etc.) by taking the buttons out of the buttonholes. **b** unbutton the clothes of (a person). 2 (*absol.*) *colloq.* relax from tension or formality, become communicative. 3 (as **unbuttoned** *adj.*) **a** not buttoned. **b** *colloq.* communicative; informal.

un·cage /únkáyj/ *v.tr.* 1 release from a cage. 2 release from constraint; liberate.

un·called /únkáwld/ *adj.* not summoned or invited.

un·called-for *adj.* (of an opinion, action, etc.) impertinent or unnecessary (*an uncalled-for remark*).

un·can·did /únkándid/ *adj.* not candid; disingenuous.

un·can·ny /únkáneé/ *adj.* (**un·can·ni·er, un·can·ni·est**) seemingly supernatural; mysterious. □□ **un·can·ni·ly** *adv.* **un·can·ni·ness** *n.* [(orig. Sc. & No. of Engl.) f. UN-¹ + CANNY]

un·ca·non·i·cal /únkənónikəl/ *adj.* not canonical. □□ **un·ca·non·i·cal·ly** *adv.*

un·cap /únkáp/ *v.tr.* (**un·capped, un·cap·ping**) 1 remove the cap from (a jar, bottle, etc.). 2 remove a cap from (the head or another person).

un·cared-for /únkáirdfawr/ *adj.* disregarded; neglected.

un·car·ing /únkáiring/ *adj.* lacking compassion or concern for others.

un·case /únkáys/ *v.tr.* remove from a cover or case.

un·cashed /únkásht/ *adj.* not cashed.

un·caught /únkáwt/ *adj.* not caught.

un·ceas·ing /únseésing/ *adj.* not ceasing; continuous (*unceasing effort*). □□ **un·ceas·ing·ly** *adv.*

un·cen·sored /únsénsərd/ *adj.* not censored.

un·cen·sured /únsénshərd/ *adj.* not censured.

un·cer·e·mo·ni·ous /únserimóneeəs/ *adj.* 1 lacking ceremony or formality. 2 abrupt; discourteous. □□ **un·cer·e·mo·ni·ous·ly** *adv.* **un·cer·e·mo·ni·ous·ness** *n.*

un·cer·tain /únsɔ́rt'n/ *adj.* 1 not certainly knowing or known (*uncertain what it means; the result is uncertain*). 2 unreliable (*his aim is uncertain*). 3 changeable; erratic (*uncertain weather*). □ **in no uncertain terms** clearly and forcefully. □□ **un·cer·tain·ly** *adv.*

un·cer·tain·ty /únsɔ́rt'ntee/ *n.* (*pl.* **–ties**) 1 the fact or condition of being uncertain. 2 an uncertain matter or circumstance.

SYNONYM TIP uncertainty

DOUBT, DUBIETY, DUBIOSITY, SKEPTICISM. If you're not sure about something, you're probably experiencing a degree of **uncertainty**, which is a general term covering everything from a mere lack of absolute certainty (*uncertainty about the time of the dinner party*) to an almost complete lack of knowledge that makes it impossible to do more than guess at the result or outcome (*uncertainty about the country's future*). **Doubt** implies both *uncertainty* and an inability to make a decision because the evidence is insufficient (*considerable doubt as to her innocence*), although *doubt* can also refer to a lack of religious faith (*doubts concerning the existence of God*). **Dubiety** comes closer in meaning to *uncertainty* than to *doubt*, because it stresses a lack of sureness rather than an inability to reach a decision; but unlike *uncertainty*, it connotes wavering or fluctuating between one conclusion and another (*no one would fail to notice the dubiety in his voice*). **Dubiosity**, often confused with *dubiety*, is *uncertainty* characterized by vagueness or confusion (*to state an opinion without a hint of dubiosity*). If you exhibit **skepticism**, you are not so much uncertain as unwilling to believe. It usually refers to a habitual state of mind or to a customary reaction (*she always listened to his excuses with skepticism*).

un·cer·tain·ty prin·ci·ple *n.* (in full **Heisenberg uncertainty principle** after W. Heisenberg, Ger. physicist d. 1976) *Physics* the principle that the momentum and position of a particle cannot both be precisely determined at the same time.

un·cer·ti·fied /únsɔ́rtifīd/ *adj.* 1 not attested as certain. 2 not guaranteed by a certificate of competence, etc. 3 not certified as insane.

un·chain /úncháyn/ *v.tr.* 1 remove the chains from. 2 release; liberate.

un·chal·lenge·a·ble /únchálinjəbəl/ *adj.* not challengeable; unassailable. □□ **un·chal·lenge·a·bly** *adv.*

un·chal·lenged /únchálinjd/ adj. not challenged.

un·change·a·ble /úncháynjəbəl/ adj. not changeable; immutable; invariable. □□ **un·change·a·bil·i·ty** n. **un·change·a·ble·ness** n. **un·change·a·bly** adv.

un·changed /úncháynjd/ adj. not changed; unaltered.

un·chang·ing /úncháynjing/ adj. not changing; remaining the same. □□ **un·chang·ing·ly** adv. **un·chang·ing·ness** n.

un·chap·er·oned /únshápərónd/ adj. without a chaperon.

un·char·ac·ter·is·tic /únkariktərístik/ adj. not characteristic. □□ **un·char·ac·ter·is·ti·cal·ly** adv.

un·charged /únchaárjd/ adj. not charged (esp. in senses 3, 7, 8 of CHARGE v.).

un·char·i·ta·ble /úncháritəbəl/ adj. censorious; severe in judgment. □□ **un·char·i·ta·ble·ness** n. **un·char·i·ta·bly** adv.

un·chart·ed /únchaártid/ adj. not charted, mapped, or surveyed.

un·char·tered /únchaártərd/ adj. **1** not furnished with a charter; not formally privileged or constituted. **2** unauthorized; illegal.

un·chaste /úncháyst/ adj. not chaste. □□ **un·chaste·ly** adv. **un·chaste·ness** n. **un·chas·ti·ty** /–chástitee/ n.

un·checked /únchékt/ adj. **1** not checked. **2** freely allowed; unrestrained (unchecked violence).

un·chiv·al·rous /únshívəlrəs/ adj. not chivalrous; rude. □□ **un·chiv·al·rous·ly** adv.

un·cho·sen /únchózən/ adj. not chosen.

un·chris·tian /únkríschən/ adj. **1 a** contrary to Christian principles, esp. uncaring or selfish. **b** not Christian. **2** colloq. outrageous. □□ **un·chris·tian·ly** adv.

un·church /únchŕch/ v.tr. **1** excommunicate. **2** deprive (a building) of its status as a church.

un·ci·al /únsheeəl, únshəl/ adj. & n.
• adj. **1** of or written in majuscule writing with rounded, unjoined letters found in manuscripts of the 4th–8th c., from which modern capitals are derived. **2** of or relating to an inch or an ounce. • n. **1** an uncial letter. **2** an uncial style or manuscript. [L uncialis f. uncia inch: sense 1 in LL sense of unciales litterae, the orig. application of which is unclear]

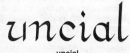
uncial

un·ci·form /únsifawrm/ n. = UNCINATE.

un·ci·nate /únsinət, –nayt/ adj. esp. Anat. hooked; crooked. [L uncinatus f. uncinus hook]

un·cir·cum·cised /únsŕkəmsīzd/ adj. **1** not circumcised. **2** spiritually impure; heathen. □□ **un·cir·cum·ci·sion** /–sízhən/ n.

un·civ·il /únsívil/ adj. **1** ill-mannered; impolite. **2** not public-spirited. □□ **un·civ·il·ly** adv.

un·civ·i·lized /únsívilizd/ adj. **1** not civilized. **2** rough; uncultured.

un·clad /únklád/ adj. not clad; naked.

un·claimed /únkláymd/ adj. not claimed.

un·clasp /únklásp/ v.tr. **1** loosen the clasp or clasps of. **2** release the grip of (a hand, etc.).

un·clas·si·fi·a·ble /únklásifíəbəl/ adj. not classifiable.

un·clas·si·fied /únklásifid/ adj. **1** not classified. **2** (of government information) not secret.

un·cle /úngkəl/ n. **1 a** the brother of one's father or mother. **b** an aunt's husband. **2** colloq. a name given by children to a male family friend. **3** sl. esp. hist. a pawnbroker. [ME f. AF uncle, OF oncle f. LL auunculus f. L avunculus maternal uncle: see AVUNCULAR]

-uncle /úngkəl/ suffix forming nouns, usu. diminutives (carbuncle). [OF –uncle, –oncle or L –unculus, –la, a special form of –ulus –ULE]

un·clean /únkléen/ adj. **1** not clean. **2** unchaste. **3** unfit to be eaten; ceremonially impure. **4** Bibl. (of a spirit) wicked. □□ **un·clean·ly** adv. **un·clean·ly** /–klénlee/ adv. **un·clean·li·ness** /–klénleenis/ n. **un·clean·ness** n. [OE unclǽne (as UN-1, CLEAN)]

un·clear /únkléer/ adj. **1** not clear or easy to understand; obscure; uncertain. **2** (of a person) doubtful; uncertain (I'm unclear as to what you mean). □□ **un·clear·ly** adv. **un·clear·ness** n.

un·clench /únklénch/ v. **1** tr. release (clenched hands, features, teeth, etc.). **2** intr. (of clenched hands, etc.) become relaxed or open.

Un·cle Sam n. colloq. the federal government or citizens of the US (will fight for Uncle Sam).

Un·cle Tom n. derog. a black man considered to be servile, cringing, etc. (from the hero of H. B. Stowe's Uncle Tom's Cabin, 1852).

un·clinch /únklínch/ v.tr. & intr. release or become released from a clinch.

un·cloak /únklók/ v.tr. **1** expose; reveal. **2** remove a cloak from.

un·clog /únklóg/ v.tr. (**un·clogged**, **un·clog·ging**) unblock (a drain, pipe, etc.).

un·close /únklóz/ v. **1** tr. & intr. open. **2** tr. reveal; disclose.

un·clothe /únklóth/ v.tr. **1** remove the clothes from. **2** strip of leaves or vegetation (trees unclothed by the wind). **3** expose; reveal. □□ **un·clothed** adj.

un·cloud·ed /únklówdid/ adj. **1** not clouded; clear; bright. **2** untroubled (unclouded serenity).

un·clut·tered /únklútərd/ adj. not cluttered; austere; simple.

un·co /úngkō/ adj., adv., & n. Sc. • adj. strange; unusual; notable.

• adv. remarkably; very. • n. (pl. –cos) **1** a stranger. **2** (in pl.) news. [ME, var. of UNCOUTH]

un·coil /únkóyl/ v.tr. & intr. unwind.

un·col·ored /únkúlərd/ adj. **1** having no color. **2** not influenced; impartial. **3** not exaggerated.

un·combed /únkómd/ adj. (of hair or a person) not combed.

un·come·ly /únkúmlee/ adj. **1** improper; unseemly. **2** ugly.

un·com·fort·a·ble /únkúmftəbəl, –kúmfortə–/ adj. **1** not comfortable. **2** uneasy; causing or feeling disquiet (an uncomfortable silence). □□ **un·com·fort·a·ble·ness** n. **un·com·fort·a·bly** adv.

un·com·mer·cial /únkəmŕshəl/ adj. **1** not commercial. **2** contrary to commercial principles.

un·com·mit·ted /únkəmítid/ adj. **1** not committed. **2** unattached to any specific political cause or group.

un·com·mon /únkómən/ adj. & adv. • adj. **1** not common; unusual; remarkable. **2** remarkably great, etc. (an uncommon fear of spiders). • adv. archaic uncommonly (he was uncommon fat). □□ **un·com·mon·ly** adv. **un·com·mon·ness** /–mən-nis/ n.

un·com·mu·ni·ca·tive /únkəmyóonikətiv/ adj. not wanting to communicate; taciturn. □□ **un·com·mu·ni·ca·tive·ly** adv. **un·com·mu·ni·ca·tive·ness** n.

un·com·pan·ion·a·ble /únkəmpányənəbəl/ adj. unsociable.

un·com·pen·sat·ed /únkómpənsaytid/ adj. not compensated.

un·com·pet·i·tive /únkəmpétitiv/ adj. not competitive.

un·com·plain·ing /únkəmpláyning/ adj. not complaining; resigned. □□ **un·com·plain·ing·ly** adv.

un·com·plet·ed /únkəmpléetid/ adj. not completed; incomplete.

un·com·pli·cat·ed /únkómplikaytid/ adj. not complicated; simple; straightforward.

un·com·pli·men·ta·ry /únkompliméntəree/ adj. not complimentary; insulting.

un·com·pound·ed /únkəmpówndid/ adj. not compounded; unmixed.

un·com·pre·hend·ing /únkomprihénding/ adj. not comprehending. □□ **un·com·pre·hend·ing·ly** adv. **un·com·pre·hen·sion** /–hénshən/ n.

un·com·pro·mis·ing /únkómprəmizing/ adj. unwilling to compromise; stubborn; unyielding. □□ **un·com·pro·mis·ing·ly** adv. **un·com·pro·mis·ing·ness** n.

un·con·cealed /únkənséeld/ adj. not concealed; obvious.

un·con·cern /únkənsŕn/ n. lack of concern; indifference; apathy. □□ **un·con·cerned** adj. **un·con·cern·ed·ly** /–nidlee/ adv.

un·con·clud·ed /únkənklóodid/ adj. not concluded.

un·con·di·tion·al /únkəndíshənəl/ adj. not subject to conditions; complete (unconditional surrender). □□ **un·con·di·tion·al·i·ty** /–nálitee/ n. **un·con·di·tion·al·ly** adv.

un·con·di·tioned /únkəndíshənd/ adj. **1** not subject to conditions or to an antecedent condition. **2** (of behavior, etc.) not determined by conditioning; natural.

un·con·di·tioned re·flex n. an instinctive response to a stimulus.

un·con·fined /únkənfínd/ adj. not confined; boundless.

un·con·firmed /únkənfŕmd/ adj. not confirmed.

un·con·form·a·ble /únkənfáwrməbəl/ adj. **1** not conformable or conforming. **2** (of rock strata) not having the same direction of stratification. **3** hist. not conforming to the provisions of the Act of Uniformity. □□ **un·con·form·a·ble·ness** n. **un·con·form·a·bly** adv. **un·con·form·i·ty** n.

un·con·gen·ial /únkənjéenyəl/ adj. not congenial.

un·con·jec·tur·a·ble /únkənjékchərəbəl/ adj. not conjecturable.

un·con·nect·ed /únkənéktid/ adj. **1** not physically joined. **2** not connected or associated. **3** (of speech, etc.) disconnected; not joined in order or sequence (unconnected ideas). **4** not related by family ties. □□ **un·con·nect·ed·ly** adv. **un·con·nect·ed·ness** n.

un·con·quer·a·ble /únkóngkərəbəl/ adj. not conquerable. □□ **un·con·quer·a·ble·ness** n. **un·con·quer·a·bly** adv.

un·con·quered /únkóngkərd/ adj. not conquered or defeated.

un·con·scion·a·ble /únkónshənəbəl/ adj. **1 a** having no conscience. **b** contrary to conscience. **2 a** unreasonably excessive (an unconscionable length of time). **b** not right or reasonable. □□ **un·con·scion·a·ble·ness** n. **un·con·scion·a·bly** adv. [UN-1 + obs. conscionable f. conscions obs. var. of CONSCIENCE]

un·con·scious /únkónshəs/ adj. & n. • adj. not conscious (unconscious of any change; fell unconscious on the floor; an unconscious prejudice). • n. that part of the mind which is inaccessible to the conscious mind but which affects behavior, emotions, etc. (cf. COLLECTIVE UNCONSCIOUS). □□ **un·con·scious·ly** adv. **un·con·scious·ness** n.

un·con·se·crat·ed /únkónsikraytid/ adj. not consecrated.

un·con·sent·ing /únkənsénting/ adj. not consenting.

un·con·sid·ered /únkənsídərd/ adj. **1** not considered; disregarded. **2** (of a response, etc.) immediate; not premeditated.

un·con·sol·a·ble /únkənsóləbəl/ adj. unable to be consoled; inconsolable. □□ **un·con·sol·a·bly** adv.

un·con·sti·tu·tion·al /únkonstitŏōshənəl, –tyŏō–/ *adj.* not in accordance with the political constitution or with procedural rules. □□ **un·con·sti·tu·tion·al·i·ty** /–nálitee/ *n.* **un·con·sti·tu·tion·al·ly** *adv.*

un·con·strained /únkənstráynd/ *adj.* not constrained or compelled. □□ **un·con·strain·ed·ly** /–nidlee/ *adv.*

un·con·straint /únkənstráynt/ *n.* freedom from constraint.

un·con·strict·ed /únkənstríktid/ *adj.* not constricted.

un·con·sumed /únkənsŏōmd/ *adj.* not consumed.

un·con·sum·mat·ed /únkónsəmaytid/ *adj.* not consummated.

un·con·tain·a·ble /únkəntáynəbəl/ *adj.* not containable.

un·con·tam·i·nat·ed /únkəntáminaytid/ *adj.* not contaminated.

un·con·test·ed /únkəntéstid/ *adj.* not contested. □□ **un·con·test·ed·ly** *adv.*

un·con·tra·dict·ed /únkontrədíktid/ *adj.* not contradicted.

un·con·trol·la·ble /únkəntróləbəl/ *adj.* not controllable. □□ **un·con·trol·la·ble·ness** *n.* **un·con·trol·la·bly** *adv.*

un·con·trolled /únkəntróld/ *adj.* not controlled; unrestrained; unchecked.

un·con·tro·ver·sial /únkontrəvérshəl/ *adj.* not controversial. □□ **un·con·tro·ver·sial·ly** *adv.*

un·con·tro·vert·ed /únkóntrəvórtid/ *adj.* not controverted. □□ **un·con·tro·vert·i·ble** *adj.*

un·con·ven·tion·al /únkənvénshənəl/ *adj.* not bound by convention or custom; unusual; unorthodox. □□ **un·con·ven·tion·al·ism** *n.* **un·con·ven·tion·al·i·ty** /–nálitee/ *n.* **un·con·ven·tion·al·ly** *adv.*

un·con·vert·ed /únkənvórtid/ *adj.* not converted.

un·con·vinced /únkənvínst/ *adj.* not convinced.

un·con·vinc·ing /únkənvínsing/ *adj.* not convincing. □□ **un·con·vinc·ing·ly** *adv.*

un·cooked /únkŏōkt/ *adj.* not cooked; raw.

un·cool /únkŏōl/ *adj. sl.* **1** unrelaxed; unpleasant. **2** (of jazz) not cool.

un·co·op·er·a·tive /únkō-ópərətiv, –óprətiv/ *adj.* not cooperative. □□ **un·co·op·er·a·tive·ly** *adv.*

un·co·or·di·nat·ed /únkō-áwrd'naytid/ *adj.* **1** not coordinated. **2** (of a person's movements, etc.) clumsy.

un·cop·i·able /únkópeeəbəl/ *adj.* not able to be copied.

un·cord /únkáwrd/ *v.tr.* remove the cord from.

un·cor·dial /únkáwrjəl/ *adj.* not congenial; unfriendly.

un·cork /únkáwrk/ *v.tr.* **1** draw the cork from (a bottle). **2** allow (feelings, etc.) to be vented.

un·cor·rob·o·rat·ed /únkəróbəraytid/ *adj.* (esp. of evidence, etc.) not corroborated.

un·cor·rupt·ed /únkərúptid/ *adj.* not corrupted.

un·count·a·ble /únkówntəbəl/ *adj.* **1** inestimable; immense (*uncountable wealth*). **2** *Gram.* (of a noun) that cannot form a plural or be used with the indefinite article (e.g., *happiness*). □□ **un·count·a·bil·i·ty** /–bilitee/ *n.* **un·count·a·bly** *adv.*

un·count·ed /únkówntid/ *adj.* **1** not counted. **2** very many; innumerable.

un·cou·ple /únkúpəl/ *v.tr.* **1** release (wagons) from couplings. **2** release (dogs, etc.) from couples. □□ **un·cou·pled** *adj.*

un·court·ly /únkáwrtlee/ *adj.* not courteous; ill-mannered.

un·couth /únkŏōth/ *adj.* **1** (of a person, manners, appearance, etc.) lacking in ease and polish; uncultured; rough (*uncouth voices; behavior was uncouth*). **2** *archaic* not known; desolate; wild; uncivilized (*an uncouth place*). □□ **un·couth·ly** *adv.* **un·couth·ness** *n.* [OE *uncūth* unknown (as UN-¹ + *c ūth* past part. of *cunnan* know, CAN¹)]

un·cov·e·nant·ed /únkúvənəntid/ *adj.* **1** not bound by a covenant. **2** not promised by or based on a covenant, esp. God's covenant.

un·cov·er /únkúvər/ *v.* **1** *tr.* **a** remove a cover or covering from. **b** make known; disclose (*uncovered the truth at last*). **2** *intr. archaic* remove one's hat, cap, etc. **3** *tr.* (as **uncovered** *adj.*) **a** not covered by a roof, clothing, etc. **b** not wearing a hat.

un·cre·ate /únkree-áyt/ *v.tr. literary* annihilate.

un·cre·at·ed /únkree-áytid/ *adj.* existing without having been created; not created. [UN-¹ + obs. *create* f. L *creatus* past part. of *creare*: see CREATE]

un·cre·a·tive /únkree-áytiv/ *adj.* not creative.

un·crit·i·cal /únkrítikəl/ *adj.* **1** not critical; complacently accepting. **2** not in accordance with the principles of criticism. □□ **un·crit·i·cal·ly** *adv.*

un·cropped /únkrópt/ *adj.* not cropped.

un·cross /únkráws, –krós/ *v.tr.* **1** remove (the limbs, knives, etc.) from a crossed position. **2** (as **uncrossed** *adj.*) **a** (of a letter or symbol, etc.) not crossed (*I recognize his writing by the uncrossed t's*). **b** not thwarted or challenged. **c** not wearing a cross.

un·crown /únkrówn/ *v.tr.* **1** deprive (a monarch, etc.) of a crown. **2** deprive (a person) of a position. **3** (as **uncrowned** *adj.*) **a** not crowned. **b** having the status but not the name of (*the uncrowned king of boxing*).

un·crush·a·ble /únkrúshəbəl/ *adj.* not crushable.

un·crushed /únkrúsht/ *adj.* not crushed.

unc·tion /úngkshən/ *n.* **1 a** the act of anointing with oil, etc., as a religious rite. **b** the oil, etc., so used. **2 a** soothing words or thought.

b excessive or insincere flattery. **3 a** the act of anointing for medical purposes. **b** an ointment so used. **4 a** a fervent or sympathetic quality in words or tone caused by or causing deep emotion. **b** a pretense of this. [ME f. L *unctio* f. *ung(u)ere unct-* anoint]

unc·tu·ous /úngkchŏōəs/ *adj.* **1** (of behavior, speech, etc.) unpleasantly flattering; oily. **2** (esp. of minerals) having a greasy or soapy feel; oily. □□ **unc·tu·ous·ly** *adv.* **unc·tu·ous·ness** *n.* [ME f. med.L *unctuosus* f. L *unctus* anointing (as UNCTION)]

un·culled /únkúld/ *adj.* not culled.

un·cul·ti·vat·ed /únkúltivaytid/ *adj.* (esp. of land) not cultivated.

un·cul·tured /únkúlchərd/ *adj.* **1** not cultured; unrefined. **2** (of soil or plants) not cultivated.

un·curb /únkárb/ *v.tr.* remove a curb or curbs from. □□ **un·curbed** *adj*

un·cured /únkyŏōrd/ *adj.* **1** not cured. **2** (of pork, etc.) not salted or smoked.

un·curl /únkárl/ *v.intr. & tr.* relax from a curled position; untwist.

un·cur·tailed /únkərtáyld/ *adj.* not curtailed.

un·cur·tained /únkárt'nd/ *adj.* not curtained.

un·cut /únkút/ *adj.* **1** not cut. **2** (of a book) with the pages not cut open or with untrimmed margins. **3** (of a book, film, etc.) complete; uncensored. **4** (of a stone, esp. a diamond) not shaped by cutting. **5** (of fabric) having its pile loops intact (*uncut moquette*).

un·dam·aged /úndámijd/ *adj.* not damaged; intact.

un·dat·ed /úndáytid/ *adj.* not provided or marked with a date.

un·daunt·ed /úndáwntid/ *adj.* not daunted. □□ **un·daunt·ed·ly** *adv.* **un·daunt·ed·ness** *n.*

un·dec·a·gon /undékəgon/ *n.* = HENDECAGON. [L *undecim* eleven, after *decagon*]

un·de·ceive /úndiseév/ *v.tr.* (often foll. by *of*) free (a person) from a misconception, deception, or error.

un·de·cid·ed /úndisídid/ *adj.* **1** not settled or certain (*the question is undecided*). **2** hesitating; irresolute (*undecided about their relative merits*). □□ **un·de·cid·ed·ly** *adv.*

un·de·ci·pher·a·ble /úndisífərəbəl/ *adj.* not decipherable.

un·de·clared /úndikláird/ *adj.* not declared.

un·de·feat·ed /úndifeétid/ *adj.* not defeated.

un·de·fend·ed /úndiféndid/ *adj.* (esp. of a lawsuit) not defended.

un·de·filed /úndifíld/ *adj.* not defiled; pure.

un·de·fined /úndifínd/ *adj.* **1** not defined. **2** not clearly marked; vague; indefinite. □□ **un·de·fin·a·ble** *adj.* **un·de·fin·a·bly** *adv.*

un·de·liv·ered /úndilívərd/ *adj.* **1** not delivered or handed over. **2** not set free or released. **3 a** (of a pregnant woman) not yet having given birth. **b** (of a child) not yet born.

un·de·mand·ing /úndimánding/ *adj.* not demanding; easily satisfied. □□ **un·de·mand·ing·ness** *n.*

un·dem·o·crat·ic /úndeməkrátik/ *adj.* not democratic. □□ **un·dem·o·crat·i·cal·ly** *adv.*

un·dem·on·strat·ed /úndémənstráytid/ *adj.* not demonstrated.

un·de·mon·stra·tive /úndimónstrətiv/ *adj.* not expressing feelings, etc., outwardly; reserved. □□ **un·de·mon·stra·tive·ly** *adv.* **un·de·mon·stra·tive·ness** *n.*

un·de·ni·a·ble /úndiníəbəl/ *adj.* **1** unable to be denied or disputed; certain. **2** excellent (*was of undeniable character*). □□ **un·de·ni·a·ble·ness** *n.* **un·de·ni·a·bly** *adv.*

un·de·nied /úndiníd/ *adj.* not denied.

un·de·pend·a·ble /úndipéndəbəl/ *adj.* not to be depended upon; unreliable.

un·der /úndər/ *prep., adv., & adj.* ● *prep.* **1 a** in or to a position lower than; below; beneath (*fell under the table; under the left eye*). **b** within; on the inside of (a surface, etc.) (*wore a vest under his jacket*). **2 a** inferior to; less than (*a captain is under a major; is under 18*). **b** at or for a lower cost than (*was under $20*). **3 a** subject or liable to; controlled or bound by (*lives under oppression; under pain of death; born under Saturn; the country prospered under him*). **b** undergoing (*is under repair*). **c** classified or subsumed in (*that book goes under biology; goes under many names*). **4** at the foot of or sheltered by (*hid under the wall; under the cliff*). **5** planted with (a crop). **6** powered by (sail, steam, etc.). **7** following (another player in a card game). **8** *archaic* attested by (esp. under one's hand and seal = signature). ● *adv.* **1** in or to a lower position or condition (*kept him under*). **2** *colloq.* in or into a state of unconsciousness (*put her under for the operation*). ● *adj.* lower (*the under jaw*). □ **under one's arm** see ARM¹. **under arms** see ARM². **under one's belt** see BELT. **under one's breath** see BREATH. **under canvas** see CANVAS. **under a cloud** see CLOUD. **under control** see CONTROL. **under the counter** see COUNTER¹. **under cover** see COVER *n.* 4. **under fire** see FIRE. **under hatches** see HATCH¹. **under a person's nose** see NOSE. **under the rose** see ROSE¹. **under separate cover** in another envelope. **under the sun** anywhere in the world. **under way** in motion; in progress. **under the weather** see WEATHER. □□ **un·der·most** *adj.* [OE f. Gmc]

under- /úndər/ *prefix* in senses of UNDER: **1** below; beneath (*undercarriage; underground*). **2** lower in status; subordinate (*undersecretary*). **3** insufficiently; incompletely (*undercook; underdeveloped*). [OE (as UNDER)]

un·der·a·chieve /úndərəcheév/ *v.intr.* do less well than might be expected (esp. scholastically). □□ **un·der·a·chieve·ment** *n.* **un·der·a·chiev·er** *n.*

un·der·act /úndərákt/ *v.* **1** *tr.* act (a part, etc.) with insufficient force. **2** *intr.* act a part in this way.

un·der·age /úndəráyj/ *adj.* **1** not old enough, esp. not yet of adult status. **2** involving underage persons (*underage smoking and drinking*).

un·der·arm /úndəraarm/ *adj., adv., & n.* ● *adj. & adv.* **1** *Sports* with the arm below shoulder level. **2** under the arm. **3** in the armpit. ● *n.* the armpit.

un·der·bel·ly /úndərbélee/ *n.* (*pl.* **–lies**) the underside of an animal, vehicle, etc., esp. as an area vulnerable to attack.

un·der·bid *v. & n.* ● *v.tr.* /úndərbíd/ (**–bid·ding**; *past* and *past part.* **–bid**) **1** make a lower bid than (a person). **2** (also *absol.*) *Bridge*, etc., bid less on (one's hand) than its strength warrants. ● *n.* /úndərbid/ **1** such a bid. **2** the act or an instance of underbidding.

un·der·bid·der /úndərbídər/ *n.* **1** the person who makes the bid next below the highest. **2** *Bridge*, etc., a player who underbids.

un·der·bod·y /úndərbódee/ *n.* (*pl.* **–ies**) the underside of the body of an animal, vehicle, etc.

un·der·bred /úndərbréd/ *adj.* **1** ill-bred; vulgar. **2** not of pure breeding.

un·der·brush /úndərbrúsh/ *n.* undergrowth in a forest.

un·der·car·riage /úndərkárij/ *n.* **1** a wheeled structure beneath an aircraft, usu. retracted when not in use, to receive the impact on landing and support the aircraft on the ground, etc. **2** the supporting frame of a vehicle.

un·der·charge /úndərchaarj/ *v.tr.* **1** charge too little for (a thing) or to (a person). **2** give less than the proper charge to (a gun, an electric battery, etc.).

un·der·class /úndərklas/ *n.* a subordinate social class.

un·der·clay /úndərklay/ *n.* a clay bed under a coal seam.

un·der·cliff /úndərklif/ *n.* a terrace or lower cliff formed by a landslide.

un·der·clothes /úndərklōz, –klōthz/ *n.pl.* clothes worn under others, esp. next to the skin.

un·der·cloth·ing /úndərklṓthing/ *n.* underclothes collectively.

un·der·coat /úndərkōt/ *n. & v.* **1 a** a preliminary layer of paint under the finishing coat. **b** the paint used for this. **2** an animal's under layer of hair or down. **3** a coat worn under another. ● *v.tr.* seal the underpart of (esp. a motor vehicle against rust, etc.) with an undercoat. □□ **un·der·coat·ing** *n.*

un·der·cov·er /úndərkúvər/ *adj.* (usu. *attrib.*) **1** surreptitious. **2** engaged in spying, esp. by working with or among those to be observed (*undercover agent*).

un·der·croft /úndərkrawft, –kroft/ *n.* a crypt. [ME f. UNDER- + *croft* crypt f. MDu. *crofte* cave f. med.L *crupta* for L *crypta*: see CRYPT]

un·der·cur·rent /úndərkárənt, –kur–/ *n.* **1** a current below the surface. **2** an underlying, often contrary, feeling, activity, or influence (*an undercurrent of protest*).

un·der·cut *v. & n.* ● *v.tr.* /úndərkút/ (**–cut·ting**; *past* and *past part.* **–cut**) **1** sell or work at a lower price or lower wages than. **2** *Golf* strike (a ball) so as to make it rise high. **3 a** cut away the part below or under (a thing). **b** cut away material to show (a carved design, etc.) in relief. **4** render unstable or less firm; undermine. ● *n.* /úndərkut/ **1** a notch cut in a tree trunk to guide its fall when felled. **2** any space formed by the removal or absence of material from the lower part of something. **3** *Brit.* the underside of a sirloin.

un·der·de·vel·oped /úndərdivéləpt/ *adj.* **1** not fully developed; immature. **2** (of a country, etc.) below its potential economic level. **3** *Photog.* not developed sufficiently to give a normal image. □□ **un·der·de·vel·op·ment** *n.*

un·der·dog /úndərdawg, –dog/ *n.* **1** a dog, or usu. a person, losing a fight. **2** a person whose loss in a contest, etc., is expected. **3** a person who is in a state of inferiority or subjection.

un·der·done /úndərdún/ *adj.* **1** not thoroughly done. **2** (of food) lightly or insufficiently cooked.

un·der·dress /úndərdrés/ *v.tr. & intr.* dress with too little formality or too lightly.

un·der·em·pha·sis /úndərémfəsis/ *n.* (*pl.* **–em·pha·ses** /–seez/) an insufficient degree of emphasis. □□ **un·der·em·pha·size** /–sīz/ *v.tr.*

un·der·em·ployed /úndərimplóyd/ *adj.* **1** not fully employed. **2** having employment inadequate to one's abilities, education, etc. □□ **un·der·em·ploy·ment** *n.*

un·der·es·ti·mate *v. & n.* ● *v.tr.* /úndəréstimayt/ form too low an estimate of. ● *n.* /úndəréstimət/ an estimate that is too low. □□ **un·der·es·ti·ma·tion** /–máyshən/ *n.*

un·der·ex·pose /úndərikspṓz/ *v.tr. Photog.* expose (film) for too short a time or with insufficient light. □□ **un·der·ex·po·sure** /–pṓzhər/ *n.*

un·der·fed /úndərféd/ *adj.* insufficiently fed.

un·der·floor /úndərflawr/ *attrib.adj. Brit.* situated or operating beneath the floor (*underfloor heating*).

un·der·flow /úndərflō/ *n.* esp. *Brit.* an undercurrent.

un·der·foot /úndərfŏŏt/ *adv.* **1** under one's feet. **2** on the ground. **3** in a state of subjection. **4** so as to obstruct or inconvenience.

un·der·gar·ment /úndərgaarmənt/ *n.* a piece of underclothing.

un·der·gird /úndərgírd/ *v.tr.* **1** make secure underneath. **2** strengthen; support.

un·der·glaze /úndərglayz/ *adj. & n.* ● *adj.* **1** (of painting on porcelain, etc.) done before the glaze is applied. **2** (of colors) used in such painting. ● *n.* underglaze painting.

un·der·go /úndərgṓ/ *v.tr.* (*3rd sing. present* **–goes**; *past* **–went**; *past part.* **–gone**) be subjected to; suffer; endure. [OE *undergān* (as UNDER-, GO¹)]

un·der·grad /úndərgrád/ *n. colloq.* = UNDERGRADUATE. [abbr.]

un·der·grad·u·ate /úndərgrájŏŏət/ *n.* a student at a college or university who has not yet taken a degree.

un·der·ground *adv., adj., n., & v.* ● *adv.* /úndərgrównd/ **1** beneath the surface of the ground. **2** in or into secrecy or hiding. ● *adj.* /úndərgrownd/ **1** situated underground. **2** secret, hidden, esp. working secretly to subvert a ruling power. **3** unconventional; experimental (*underground press*). ● *n.* /úndərgrownd/ **1** a secret group or activity, esp. aiming to subvert the established order. **2** *Brit.* subway system. ● *v.tr.* /úndərgrownd/ lay (cables) below ground level.

Un·der·ground Rail·road *n. US Hist.* a covert system of escape through which abolitionists helped fugitive slaves reach safe destinations, before 1863.

un·der·growth /úndərgrōth/ *n.* a dense growth of shrubs, etc., esp. under large trees.

un·der·hand *adj. & adv.* ● *adj.* /úndərhand/ **1** secret; clandestine; not aboveboard. **2** deceptive; crafty. **3** *Sports* underarm. ● *adv.* /úndərhánd/ in an underhand manner. [OE (as UNDER-, HAND)]

un·der·hand·ed /úndərhándid/ *adj. & adv.* = UNDERHAND.

un·der·hung /úndərhúng/ *adj.* **1** (of the lower jaw) projecting beyond the upper jaw. **2** having an underhung jaw.

un·der·lay¹ *v. & n.* ● *v.tr.* /úndərláy/ (*past* and *past part.* **–laid**) lay something under (a thing) to support or raise it. ● *n.* /úndərlay/ a thing laid under another, esp. material laid under a carpet or mattress as protection or support. [OE *underlecgan* (as UNDER-, LAY¹)]

un·der·lay² *past* of UNDERLIE.

un·der·lay·ment /úndərláymənt/ *n.* an underlay.

un·der·lease *n.* /úndərlees/ *v.tr.* /úndərlee's/ = SUBLEASE.

un·der·let /úndərlét/ *v.tr.* (**–let·ting**; *past* and *past part.* **–let**) **1** sublet. **2** let at less than the true value.

un·der·lie /úndərlí/ *v.tr.* (**–ly·ing**; *past* **–lay**; *past part.* **–lain**) **1** (also *absol.*) lie or be situated under (a stratum, etc.). **2** (also *absol.*) (esp. as **underlying** *adj.*) (of a principle, reason, etc.) be the basis of (a doctrine, law, conduct, etc.). **3** exist beneath the superficial aspect of. [OE *underlicgan* (as UNDER-, LIE¹)]

un·der·line *v. & n.* ● *v.tr.* /úndərlín/ **1** draw a line under (a word, etc.) to give emphasis or draw attention or indicate italic or other special type. **2** emphasize; stress. ● *n.* /úndərlin/ **1** a line drawn under a word, etc. **2** a caption below an illustration.

PUNCTUATION TIP underlining

In handwritten text, the names of books, magazines, newspapers, long poems, well-known speeches, movies, plays, musicals, operas, television shows, works of art, ships, and aircraft should be underlined, as an indicator of text that would be printed in italics (e.g., *Profiles in Courage, Life, USA Today,* the *Iliad, I Have a Dream, Gone with the Wind, Hamlet, My Fair Lady, Rigoletto, I Love Lucy,* the *Mona Lisa, Titanic, Air Force One*). If you are working on a computer and have an italic font, these sorts of names should be italicized rather than underlined.

---

un·der·lin·en /úndərlinin/ *n.* esp. *Brit.* underclothes, esp. of linen.

un·der·ling /úndərling/ *n.* usu. *derog.* a subordinate.

un·der·ly·ing *pres. part.* of UNDERLIE.

un·der·manned /úndərmánd/ *adj.* having too few people as crew or staff.

un·der·men·tioned /úndərménshənd/ *adj. Brit.* mentioned at a later place in a book, etc.

un·der·mine /úndərmín/ *v.tr.* **1** injure (a person, reputation, influence, etc.) by secret or insidious means. **2** weaken, injure, or wear out (health, etc.) imperceptibly or insidiously. **3** wear away the base or foundation of (*rivers undermine their banks*). **4** make a mine or excavation under. □□ **un·der·min·er** *n.* **un·der·min·ing·ly** *adv.* [ME f. UNDER- + MINE²]

un·der·neath /úndərneéth/ *prep., adv., n., & adj.* ● *prep.* **1** at or to a lower place than, below. **2** on the inside of, within. ● *adv.* **1** at or to a lower place. **2** inside. ● *n.* the lower surface or part. ● *adj.* lower. [OE *underneothan* (as UNDER + *neothan*: cf. BENEATH)]

un·der·nour·ished /úndərnṓrisht, –núr–/ *adj.* insufficiently nourished. □□ **un·der·nour·ish·ment** *n.*

un·der·paid *past* and *past part.* of UNDERPAY.

un·der·pants /úndərpants/ *n.pl.* an undergarment, esp. men's, covering the lower part of the body and part of the legs.

un·der·part /úndərpaart/ n. 1 a lower part, esp. of an animal. 2 a subordinate part in a play, etc.

un·der·pass /úndərpas/ n. 1 a road, etc., passing under another. 2 a crossing of this form.

un·der·pay /úndərpáy/ v.tr. (past and past part. –paid) pay too little to (a person) or for (a thing). □□ **un·der·pay·ment** n.

un·der·pin /úndərpín/ v.tr. (–pinned, –pin·ning) 1 support from below with masonry, etc. 2 support; strengthen.

un·der·pin·ning /úndərpíning/ n. 1 a physical or metaphorical foundation. 2 the action or process of supporting from below.

un·der·plant /úndərplánt/ v.tr. (usu. foll. by with) plant or cultivate the ground about (a tall plant) with smaller ones.

un·der·play /úndərpláy/ v. 1 tr. play down the importance of. 2 intr. & tr. Theatr. a perform with deliberate restraint. b underact.

un·der·plot /úndərplot/ n. a subordinate plot in a play, etc.

un·der·pop·u·lat·ed /úndərpópyəláytid/ adj. having an insufficient or very small population.

un·der·price /úndərprís/ v.tr. price lower than what is usual or appropriate.

un·der·priv·i·leged /úndərprívilijd, –prívlijd/ adj. 1 less privileged than others. 2 not enjoying the normal standard of living or rights in a society.

un·der·pro·duc·tion /úndərprəd úkshən/ n. production of less than is usual or required.

un·der·proof /úndərproof/ adj. containing less alcohol than proof spirit does.

un·der·prop /úndərpróp/ v.tr. (–propped, –prop·ping) 1 support with a prop. 2 support; sustain.

un·der·quote /úndərkwót/ v.tr. 1 quote a lower price than (a person). 2 quote a lower price than others for (goods, etc.).

un·der·rate /úndəráyt/ v.tr. have too low an opinion of.

un·der·score v. & n. ● v.tr. /úndərskáwr/ = UNDERLINE v. ● n. /úndərskawr/ = UNDERLINE n. 1.

un·der·sea /úndərsee/ adj. below the sea or the surface of the sea; submarine.

un·der·sec·re·tar·y /úndərsékrəteree/ n. (pl. –ies) a subordinate official, esp. a junior minister or senior civil servant.

un·der·sell /úndərsél/ v.tr. (past and past part. –sold) 1 sell at a lower price than (another seller). 2 sell at less than the true value.

un·der·set v. & n. ● v.tr. /úndərsét/ (–set·ting; past and past part. –set) place something under (a thing). ● n. /úndərset/ Naut. an undercurrent.

un·der·sexed /úndərsékst/ adj. having unusually weak sexual desires.

un·der·sher·iff /úndərsherif/ n. a deputy sheriff.

un·der·shirt /úndərshərt/ n. an undergarment worn under a shirt.

un·der·shoot v. & n. ● v.tr. /úndərshóot/ (past and past part. –shot) 1 (of an aircraft) land short of (a runway, etc.). 2 shoot short of or below. ● n. /úndərshoot/ the act or an instance of undershooting.

un·der·shorts /úndərsháwrts/ n. short underpants; trunks.

un·der·shot /úndərshót/ adj. 1 (of a waterwheel) turned by water flowing under it. 2 = UNDERHUNG.

un·der·shrub /úndərshrub/ n. = SUBSHRUB.

un·der·side /úndərsíd/ n. the lower or under side or surface.

un·der·signed /úndərsínd/ adj. whose signature is appended (we, the undersigned, wish to state . . .).

un·der·sized /úndərsízd/ adj. of less than the usual size.

un·der·skirt /úndərskərt/ n. a skirt worn under another; a petticoat.

un·der·slung /úndərslúng/ adj. 1 supported from above. 2 (of a vehicle chassis) hanging lower than the axles.

un·der·sold past and past part. of UNDERSELL.

un·der·sow /úndərsó/ v.tr. (past part. –sown) 1 sow (a later-growing crop) on land already seeded with another crop. 2 (foll. by with) sow land already seeded with (a crop) with a later-growing crop.

un·der·spend /úndərspénd/ v. (past and past part. –spent) 1 tr. spend less than (a specified amount). 2 intr. & refl. spend too little.

un·der·staffed /úndərstáft/ adj. having too few staff.

un·der·stand /úndərstánd/ v. (past and past part. –stood /–stood/) 1 tr. perceive the meaning of (words, a person, a language, etc.) (does not understand what you say; understood you perfectly; cannot understand French). 2 tr. perceive the significance or explanation or cause of (do not understand why he came; could not understand what the noise was about; do not understand the point of his remark). 3 tr. be sympathetically aware of the character or nature of, know how to deal with (quite understand your difficulty; cannot understand him at all; could never understand algebra). 4 tr. a (often foll. by that + clause) infer esp. from information received; take as implied; take for granted (I understand that it begins at noon; I understand him to be a distant relation; am I to understand that you refuse?). b (absol.) believe or assume from knowledge or inference (he is coming tomorrow, I understand). 5 tr. supply (a word) mentally (the verb may be either expressed or understood). 6 tr. accept (terms, conditions, etc.) as part of an agreement. 7 intr. have understanding (in general or

in particular). □ **understand each other** 1 know each other's views or feelings. 2 be in agreement or collusion. □□ **un·der·stand·a·ble** adj. **un·der·stand·a·bly** adv. **un·der·stand·er** n. [OE understandan (as UNDER-, STAND)]

un·der·stand·ing /úndərstánding/ n. & adj. ● n. 1 a the ability to understand or think; intelligence. b the power of apprehension; the power of abstract thought. 2 an individual's perception or judgment of a situation, etc. 3 an agreement; a thing agreed upon, esp. informally (had an understanding with the rival company; consented only on this understanding). 4 harmony in opinion or feeling (disturbed the good understanding between them). 5 sympathetic awareness or tolerance. ● adj. 1 having understanding or insight or good judgment. 2 sympathetic to others' feelings. □□ **un·der·stand·ing·ly** adv. [OE (as UNDERSTAND)]

un·der·state /úndərstáyt/ v.tr. (often as **understated** adj.) 1 express in greatly or unduly restrained terms. 2 represent as being less than it actually is. □□ **un·der·state·ment** /úndərstáytmənt/ n. **un·der·stat·er** n.

un·der·steer n. & v. ● n. /úndərsteer/ a tendency of a motor vehicle to turn less sharply than was intended. ● v.intr. /úndərsteér/ have such a tendency.

un·der·stood past and past part. of UNDERSTAND.

un·der·sto·ry /úndərstáwree/ n. (pl. –ries) 1 a layer of vegetation beneath the main canopy of a forest. 2 the plants forming this.

un·der·stud·y /úndərstúdee/ n. & v. esp. Theatr. ● n. (pl. –ies) a person who studies another's role or duties in order to act at short notice in the absence of the other. ● v.tr. (–ies, –ied) 1 study (a role, etc.) as an understudy. 2 act as an understudy to (a person).

un·der·sub·scribed /úndərsəbskríbd/ adj. without sufficient subscribers, participants, etc.

un·der·sur·face /úndərsórfis/ n. esp. Brit. = UNDERSIDE.

un·der·take /úndərtáyk/ v.tr. (past –took; past part. –tak·en) 1 bind oneself to perform; make oneself responsible for; engage in; enter upon (work, an enterprise, a responsibility). 2 (usu. foll. by to + infin.) accept an obligation; promise. 3 guarantee; affirm (I will undertake that he has not heard a word).

un·der·tak·er /úndərtaykər/ n. 1 a person whose business is to make arrangements for funerals. 2 (also /–táykər/) a person who undertakes to do something. 3 hist. an influential person in 17th-century England who undertook to procure particular legislation, esp. to obtain supplies from the House of Commons if the king would grant some concession.

un·der·tak·ing /úndərtáyking/ n. 1 work, etc., undertaken, an enterprise (a serious undertaking). 2 a pledge or promise. 3 /úndərtayking/ the management of funerals as a profession.

un·der·ten·ant /úndərtenənt/ n. a subtenant. □□ **un·der·ten·an·cy** n. (pl. –cies).

un·der·things /úndərthingz/ n.pl. colloq. underclothes.

un·der·tint /úndərtint/ n. a subdued tint.

un·der·tone /úndərtōn/ n. 1 a subdued tone of sound or color. 2 an underlying quality. 3 an undercurrent of feeling.

un·der·took past of UNDERTAKE.

un·der·tow /úndərtō/ n. a current below the surface of the sea moving in the opposite direction to the surface current.

un·der·trick /úndərtrik/ n. Bridge a trick by which the declarer falls short of his or her contract.

un·der·val·ue /úndərvályoo/ v.tr. (–val·ues, –val·ued, –val·u·ing) 1 value insufficiently. 2 underestimate. □□ **un·der·val·u·a·tion** n.

un·der·vest /úndərvest/ n. Brit. an undershirt.

un·der·wa·ter /úndərwáwtər, –wótər/ adj. & adv. ● adj. situated or done under water. ● adv. in and covered by water.

un·der·way /úndərwáy/ adj. occurring while in progress or in motion (the ship's underway food service was excellent).

un·der·wear /úndərwair/ n. underclothes.

un·der·weight adj. & n. ● adj. /úndərwáyt/ weighing less than is normal or desirable. ● n. /úndərwayt/ insufficient weight.

un·der·went past of UNDERGO.

un·der·whelm /úndərhwelm, –wélm/ v.tr. joc. fail to impress. [after OVERWHELM]

un·der·wing /úndərwing/ n. a wing placed under or partly covered by another.

un·der·wood /úndərwood/ n. undergrowth.

un·der·work /úndərwórk/ v. 1 tr. impose too little work on. 2 intr. do too little work.

un·der·world /úndərwərld/ n. 1 the part of society comprising those who live by organized crime and immorality. 2 the mythical abode of the dead under the earth. 3 the antipodes.

un·der·write /úndər-rít/ v. (past –wrote; past part. –writ·ten) 1 a tr. sign, and accept liability under (an insurance policy, esp. on shipping, etc.). b tr. accept (liability) in this way. c intr. practice (marine) insurance. 2 tr. undertake to finance or support. 3 tr. engage to buy all the stock in (a company, etc.) not bought by the public. 4 tr. write below (the underwritten names). □□ **un·der·writ·er** /ún–/ n.

un·de·scend·ed /úndiséndid/ adj. Med. (of a testicle) remaining in the abdomen instead of descending normally into the scrotum.

un·de·served /úndizə́rvd/ *adj.* not deserved (as reward or punishment). □□ **un·de·serv·ed·ly** /–vidlee/ *adv.*

un·de·serv·ing /úndizə́rving/ *adj.* not deserving. □□ **un·de·serv·ing·ly** *adv.*

un·de·signed /úndizínd/ *adj.* unintentional. □□ **un·de·sign·ed·ly** /–nidlee/ *adv.*

un·de·sir·a·ble /úndizírəbəl/ *adj. & n.* ● *adj.* not desirable; objectionable; unpleasant. ● *n.* an undesirable person. □□ **un·de·sir·a·bil·i·ty** /–bílitee/ *n.* **un·de·sir·a·ble·ness** *n.* **un·de·sir·a·bly** *adv.*

un·de·sired /úndizírd/ *adj.* not desired.

un·de·sir·ous /úndizírəs/ *adj.* not desirous.

un·de·tect·a·ble /únditéktəbəl/ *adj.* not detectable. □□ **un·de·tect·a·bil·i·ty** /–bílitee/ *n.* **un·de·tect·a·bly** *adv.*

un·de·tect·ed /únditéktid/ *adj.* not detected.

un·de·ter·mined /únditə́rmind/ *adj.* = UNDECIDED.

un·de·terred /únditə́rd/ *adj.* not deterred.

un·de·vel·oped /úndivéləpt/ *adj.* not developed.

un·de·vi·at·ing /úndeéveeayting/ *adj.* not deviating; steady; constant. □□ **un·de·vi·at·ing·ly** *adv.*

un·di·ag·nosed /úndíəgnōst, –nōzd/ *adj.* not diagnosed.

un·did *past of* UNDO.

un·dies /úndeez/ *n.pl. colloq.* (esp. women's) underclothes. [abbr.]

un·dif·fer·en·ti·at·ed /úndifərénsheeaytid/ *adj.* not differentiated; amorphous.

un·di·gest·ed /úndijéstid, úndī–/ *adj.* **1** not digested. **2** (esp. of information, facts, etc.) not properly arranged or considered.

un·dig·ni·fied /úndígnifid/ *adj.* lacking dignity.

un·di·lut·ed /úndilốotid/ *adj.* not diluted.

un·di·min·ished /úndimínisht/ *adj.* not diminished or lessened.

un·dine /úndeén, ún–/ *n.* a female water spirit. [mod.L *undina* (word invented by Paracelsus) f. L *unda* wave]

un·dip·lo·mat·ic /úndiplōmátik/ *adj.* tactless. □□ **un·dip·lo·mat·i·cal·ly** *adv.*

un·dis·charged /úndischaárjd/ *adj.* (esp. of a bankrupt or a debt) not discharged.

un·dis·ci·pline /úndísiplin/ *n.* lack of discipline.

un·dis·ci·plined /úndísiplind/ *adj.* lacking discipline; not disciplined.

un·dis·closed /úndisklốzd/ *adj.* not revealed or made known.

un·dis·cov·er·a·ble /úndiskúvərəbəl/ *adj.* that cannot be discovered.

un·dis·cov·ered /úndiskúvərd/ *adj.* not discovered.

un·dis·crim·i·nat·ing /úndiskríminayting/ *adj.* not showing good judgment.

un·dis·guised /úndisgízd/ *adj.* not disguised. □□ **un·dis·guis·ed·ly** /–zidlee/ *adv.*

un·dis·mayed /úndismáyd/ *adj.* not dismayed.

un·dis·put·ed /úndispyốotid/ *adj.* not disputed or called in question.

un·dis·solved /úndizólvd/ *adj.* not dissolved.

un·dis·tin·guish·a·ble /úndistínggwishəbəl/ *adj.* (often foll. by *from*) indistinguishable.

un·dis·tin·guished /úndistínggwisht/ *adj.* not distinguished; mediocre.

un·dis·trib·ut·ed /úndistríbyətid/ *adj.* not distributed.

un·dis·trib·ut·ed mid·dle *n. Logic* a fallacy resulting from the failure of the middle term of a syllogism to refer to all the members of a class.

un·dis·turbed /úndistə́rbd/ *adj.* not disturbed or interfered with.

un·di·vid·ed /úndivídid/ *adj.* not divided or shared; whole, entire (*gave him my undivided attention*).

un·do /úndốo/ *v.tr.* (*3rd sing. present* **–does**; *past* **–did**; *past part.* **–done**) **1 a** unfasten or untie (a coat, button, package, etc.). **b** unfasten the clothing of (a person). **2** annul; cancel (*cannot undo the past*). **3** ruin the prospects, reputation, or morals of. [OE *undōn* (as UN-², DO¹)]

un·dock /úndók/ *v.tr.* **1** (also *absol.*) separate (a spacecraft) from another in space. **2** take (a ship) out of a dock.

un·do·cu·ment·ed /úndókyəmentid/ *adj.* **1** not having the appropriate document. **2** not proved by or recorded in documents.

un·do·ing /úndốoing/ *n.* **1** ruin or a cause of ruin. **2** the process of reversing what has been done. **3** the action of opening or unfastening.

un·do·mes·ti·cat·ed /úndəméstikaytid/ *adj.* not domesticated.

un·done /úndún/ *adj.* **1** not done; incomplete (*left the job undone*). **2** not fastened (*left the buttons undone*). **3** *archaic* ruined.

un·doubt·a·ble /úndówtəbəl/ *adj.* that cannot be doubted; indubitable.

un·doubt·ed /úndówtid/ *adj.* certain; not questioned; not regarded as doubtful. □□ **un·doubt·ed·ly** *adv.*

un·drained /úndráynd/ *adj.* not drained.

un·draped /úndráypt/ *adj.* **1** not covered with drapery. **2** naked.

un·dreamed /úndreémd, úndrémt/ *adj.* (also **un·dreamt** /úndrémt/) (often foll. by *of*) not dreamed or thought of or imagined.

un·dress /úndrés/ *v. & n.* ● *v.* **1** take off one's clothes. **2** *tr.* take the clothes off (a person). ● *n.* **1** ordinary dress as opposed to full dress or uniform. **2** casual or informal dress.

un·dressed /úndrést/ *adj.* **1** not or no longer dressed; partly or whol-

ly naked. **2** (of leather, etc.) not treated. **3** (of food) **a** not having a dressing (*undressed salad*). **b** prepared simply, with no sauce, stuffing, etc. (*undressed turkey*).

un·drink·a·ble /úndríngkəbəl/ *adj.* unfit for drinking.

un·due /úndốo, –dyốo/ *adj.* **1** excessive; disproportionate. **2** not suitable. **3** not owed. □□ **un·du·ly** *adv.*

un·due in·flu·ence *n. Law* influence by which a person is induced to act otherwise than by his or her own free will, or without adequate attention to the consequences.

un·du·lant /únjələnt, –dyə–, –də–/ *adj.* moving like waves; fluctuating. [L *undulare* (as UNDULATE)]

un·du·lant fe·ver *n.* brucellosis in humans.

un·du·late *v. & adj.* ● *v.* /únjəlayt, –dyə–, –də–/ *intr. & tr.* have or cause to have a wavy motion or look. ● *adj.* /únjələt, –dyə–, –də–/ wavy; going alternately up and down or in and out (*leaves with undulate margins*). □□ **un·du·late·ly** *adv.* [LL *undulatus* f. L *unda* wave]

un·du·la·tion /únjəláyshən, –dyə–, –də–/ *n.* **1** a wavy motion or form; a gentle rise and fall. **2** each wave of this. **3** a set of wavy lines.

un·du·la·to·ry /únjələtawree, –dyə–, –də–/ *adj.* **1** undulating; wavy. **2** of or due to undulation.

un·du·ti·ful /úndốotifốol, –dyốo–/ *adj.* not dutiful. □□ **un·du·ti·ful·ly** *adv.* **un·du·ti·ful·ness** *n.*

un·dyed /úndíd/ *adj.* not dyed.

un·dy·ing /úndí-ing/ *adj.* **1** immortal. **2** never-ending (*undying love*). □□ **un·dy·ing·ly** *adv.*

un·earned /únə́rnd/ *adj.* not earned.

un·earned in·come *n.* income from interest payments, etc., as opposed to salary, wages, or fees.

un·earth /únə́rth/ *v.tr.* **1 a** discover by searching or in the course of digging or rummaging. **b** dig out of the earth. **2** drive (a fox, etc.) from its earth.

un·earth·ly /únə́rthlee/ *adj.* **1** supernatural; mysterious. **2** *colloq.* absurdly early or inconvenient (*an unearthly hour*). **3** not earthly. □□ **un·earth·li·ness** *n.*

un·ease /únéez/ *n.* lack of ease; discomfort; distress.

un·eas·y /únéezee/ *adj.* (**un·eas·i·er**, **un·eas·i·est**) **1** disturbed or uncomfortable in mind or body (*passed an uneasy night*). **2** disturbing (*had an uneasy suspicion*). □□ **un·eas·i·ly** *adv.* **un·eas·i·ness** *n.*

un·eat·a·ble /únéetəbəl/ *adj.* not able to be eaten, esp. because of its condition (cf. INEDIBLE).

un·eat·en /únéet'n/ *adj.* not eaten; left undevoured.

un·ec·o·nom·ic /únekənómik, –eekə–/ *adj.* not economic; incapable of being profitably operated, etc. □□ **un·ec·o·nom·i·cal·ly** *adv.*

un·ec·o·nom·i·cal /únekənómikəl, –eekə–/ *adj.* not economical; wasteful.

un·ed·i·fy·ing /únédifi-ing/ *adj.* not edifying, esp. uninstructive or degrading. □□ **un·ed·i·fy·ing·ly** *adv.*

un·ed·it·ed /únéditid/ *adj.* not edited.

un·ed·u·cat·ed /únéjəkaytid/ *adj.* not educated. □□ **un·ed·u·ca·ble** /–kəbəl/ *adj.*

un·e·lect·a·ble /úniléktəbəl/ *adj.* (of a candidate, party, etc.) associated with or holding views likely to bring defeat at an election.

un·em·bel·lished /únembélisht/ *adj.* not embellished or decorated.

un·e·mo·tion·al /únimóshənəl/ *adj.* not emotional; lacking emotion. □□ **un·e·mo·tion·al·ly** *adv.*

un·em·phat·ic /únimfátik/ *adj.* not emphatic. □□ **un·em·phat·i·cal·ly** *adv.*

un·em·ploy·a·ble /únimplóyəbəl/ *adj. & n.* ● *adj.* unfitted for paid employment. ● *n.* an unemployable person. □□ **un·em·ploy·a·bil·i·ty** /–bílitee/ *n.*

un·em·ployed /únimplóyd/ *adj.* **1** not having paid employment; out of work. **2** not in use.

un·em·ploy·ment /únimplóymənt/ *n.* **1** the state of being unemployed. **2** the condition or extent of this in a country or region, etc. (*the Northeast has higher unemployment*).

un·em·ploy·ment ben·e·fit *n.* a payment made by the government or a labor union to an unemployed person.

un·en·closed /úninklốzd/ *adj.* not enclosed.

un·en·cum·bered /úninkúmbərd/ *adj.* **1** (of an estate) not having any liabilities (e.g., a mortgage) on it. **2** having no encumbrance; free.

un·end·ing /únénding/ *adj.* having or apparently having no end. □□ **un·end·ing·ly** *adv.* **un·end·ing·ness** *n.*

un·en·dowed /únindówd/ *adj.* not endowed.

un·en·dur·a·ble /únindốorəbəl, –dyốor–/ *adj.* that cannot be endured. □□ **un·en·dur·a·bly** *adv.*

un·en·gaged /úningáyjd/ *adj.* not engaged; uncommitted.

un-En·glish /únéngglish/ *adj.* **1** not characteristic of the English. **2** not English.

un·en·joy·a·ble /úninjóyəbəl/ *adj.* not enjoyable.

un·en·light·ened /úninlít'nd/ *adj.* not enlightened.

un·en·ter·pris·ing /únéntərprizing/ *adj.* not enterprising.

See page xx for the **Key to Pronunciation.**

un·en·thu·si·as·tic /úninthőozeeástik/ *adj.* not enthusiastic. □□ **un·en·thu·si·as·ti·cal·ly** *adv.*

un·en·vi·a·ble /únénveeəbəl/ *adj.* not enviable. □□ **un·en·vi·a·bly** *adv.*

un·en·vied /únénveed/ *adj.* not envied.

un·e·qual /úneekwəl/ *adj.* **1** (often foll. by *to*) not equal. **2** of varying quality. **3** lacking equal advantage to both sides (*an unequal bargain*). □□ **un·e·qual·ly** *adv.*
▶Use **unequal**, usually followed by the preposition *to*, if you mean 'inadequate in ability, resources, etc.' (*he was unequal to the task of taking over the meeting himself*). There is no such word as *inequal*, although **inequality** is the noun that means 'the condition of being unequal.'

un·e·qualed /úneekwəld/ *adj.* (also esp. *Brit.* **un·e·qualled**) superior to all others.

un·e·qual·ize /úneekwəlīz/ *v.tr.* make unequal.

un·e·quipped /únikwípt/ *adj.* not equipped.

un·e·quiv·o·cal /únikwívəkəl/ *adj.* not ambiguous; plain; unmistakable. □□ **un·e·quiv·o·cal·ly** *adv.* **un·e·quiv·o·cal·ness** *n.*
▶The adverb that corresponds to *unequivocal* is **unequivocally**. There is no such word as *unequivocably*.

un·err·ing /únéring/ *adj.* not erring, failing, or missing the mark; true; certain. □□ **un·err·ing·ly** *adv.* **un·err·ing·ness** *n.*

un·es·cap·a·ble /úniskáypəbəl/ *adj.* inescapable.

UNESCO /yoonéskō/ *abbr.* United Nations Educational, Scientific, and Cultural Organization.

un·es·cort·ed /úniskáwrtid/ *adj.* not escorted.

un·es·sen·tial /únisénshəl/ *adj. & n.* ● *adj.* **1** not essential (cf. INESSENTIAL). **2** not of the first importance. ● *n.* an unessential part or thing.

un·es·tab·lished /únistáblisht/ *adj.* not established.

un·eth·i·cal /únéthikəl/ *adj.* not ethical, esp. unscrupulous in business or professional conduct. □□ **un·eth·i·cal·ly** *adv.*

un·e·van·gel·i·cal /úneevanjélikəl/ *adj.* not evangelical.

un·e·ven /úneevən/ *adj.* **1** not level or smooth. **2** not uniform or equable. **3** (of a contest) unequal. □□ **un·e·ven·ly** *adv.* **un·e·ven·ness** *n.* [OE *unefen* (as UN-¹, EVEN¹)]

un·e·vent·ful /únivéntfool/ *adj.* not eventful. □□ **un·e·vent·ful·ly** *adv.* **un·e·vent·ful·ness** *n.*

un·ex·am·ined /únigzámind/ *adj.* not examined.

un·ex·am·pled /únigzámpəld/ *adj.* having no precedent or parallel.

un·ex·cep·tion·a·ble /úniksépshənəbəl/ *adj.* with which no fault can be found; entirely satisfactory. □□ **un·ex·cep·tion·a·ble·ness** *n.* **un·ex·cep·tion·a·bly** *adv.*

un·ex·cep·tion·al /úniksépshənəl/ *adj.* not out of the ordinary; usual; normal. □□ **un·ex·cep·tion·al·ly** *adv.*

un·ex·cit·a·ble /úniksítəbəl/ *adj.* not easily excited. □□ **un·ex·cit·a·bil·i·ty** *n.*

un·ex·cit·ing /úniksíting/ *adj.* not exciting; dull.

un·ex·e·cut·ed /únéksikyóotid/ *adj.* not carried out or put into effect.

un·ex·haust·ed /únigzáwstid/ *adj.* **1** not used up, expended, or brought to an end. **2** not emptied.

un·ex·pect·ed /únikspéktid/ *adj.* not expected; surprising. □□ **un·ex·pect·ed·ly** *adv.* **un·ex·pect·ed·ness** *n.*

un·ex·pired /únikspírd/ *adj.* that has not yet expired.

un·ex·plain·a·ble /únikspláynəbəl/ *adj.* inexplicable. □□ **un·ex·plain·a·bly** *adv.*

un·ex·plained /úniksplaynd/ *adj* not explained.

un·ex·ploit·ed /úniksplóytid/ *adj.* (of resources, etc.) not exploited.

un·ex·plored /úniksplawrd/ *adj.* not explored.

un·ex·posed /únikspózd/ *adj.* not exposed.

un·ex·pressed /úniksprést/ *adj.* not expressed or made known (*unexpressed fears*).

un·ex·pur·gat·ed /únékspərgaytid/ *adj.* (esp. of a text, etc.) not expurgated; complete.

un·face·a·ble /únfáysəbəl/ *adj.* that cannot be faced or confronted.

un·fad·ing /únfáyding/ *adj.* that never fades. □□ **un·fad·ing·ly** *adv.*

un·fail·ing /únfáyling/ *adj.* **1** not failing. **2** not running short. **3** constant. **4** reliable. □□ **un·fail·ing·ly** *adv.* **un·fail·ing·ness** *n.*

un·fair /únfáir/ *adj.* **1** not equitable or honest (*obtained by unfair means*). **2** not impartial or according to the rules (*unfair play*). □□ **un·fair·ly** *adv.* **un·fair·ness** *n.* [OE *unfæger* (as UN-¹, FAIR¹)]

un·faith·ful /únfáythfool/ *adj.* **1** not faithful, esp. adulterous. **2** not loyal. **3** treacherous. □□ **un·faith·ful·ly** *adv.* **un·faith·ful·ness** *n.*

un·fal·ter·ing /únfáwltəring/ *adj.* not faltering; steady; resolute. □□ **un·fal·ter·ing·ly** *adv.*

un·fa·mil·iar /únfəmílyər/ *adj.* not familiar. □□ **un·fa·mil·i·ar·i·ty** /–leeáritee/ *n.*

un·fash·ion·a·ble /únfáshənəbəl/ *adj.* not fashionable. □□ **un·fash·ion·a·ble·ness** *n.* **un·fash·ion·a·bly** *adv.*

un·fash·ioned /únfáshənd/ *adj.* not made into its proper shape.

un·fas·ten /únfásən/ *v.* **1** *tr. & intr.* make or become loose. **2** *tr.* open the fastening(s) of. **3** *tr.* detach.

un·fas·tened /únfásənd/ *adj.* **1** that has not been fastened. **2** that has been loosened, opened, or detached.

un·fa·thered /únfaáthərd/ *adj.* **1** having no known or acknowledged father; illegitimate. **2** of unknown origin (*unfathered rumors*).

un·fa·ther·ly /únfaáthərlee/ *adj.* not befitting a father. □□ **un·fa·ther·li·ness** *n.*

un·fath·om·a·ble /únfáthəməbəl/ *adj.* incapable of being fathomed. □□ **un·fath·om·a·ble·ness** *n.* **un·fath·om·a·bly** *adv.*

un·fath·omed /únfáthəmd/ *adj.* **1** of unascertained depth. **2** not fully explored or known.

un·fa·vor·a·ble /únfáyvərəbəl/ *adj.* not favorable; adverse; hostile. □□ **un·fa·vor·a·ble·ness** *n.* **un·fa·vor·a·bly** *adv.*

un·fa·vor·ite /únfáyvərit, –fáyvrit/ *adj. colloq.* least favorite; most disliked.

un·fazed /únfáyzd/ *adj. colloq.* untroubled; not disconcerted.

un·feas·i·ble /únfeezibəl/ *adj.* not feasible; impractical. □□ **un·feas·i·bil·i·ty** /–bílitee/ *n.* **un·feas·i·bly** *adv.*

un·fed /únféd/ *adj.* not fed.

un·feel·ing /únfeeling/ *adj.* **1** unsympathetic; harsh; not caring about others' feelings. **2** lacking sensation or sensitivity. □□ **un·feel·ing·ly** *adv.* **un·feel·ing·ness** *n.* [OE *unfelende* (as UN-¹, FEELING)]

un·feigned /únfáynd/ *adj.* genuine; sincere. □□ **un·feign·ed·ly** /–fáynidlee/ *adv.*

un·felt /únfélt/ *adj.* not felt.

un·fem·i·nine /únféminin/ *adj.* not in accordance with, or appropriate to, female character. □□ **un·fem·i·nin·i·ty** /–nínitee/ *n.*

un·fenced /únfénst/ *adj.* **1** not provided with fences. **2** unprotected.

un·fer·ment·ed /únfərméntid/ *adj.* not fermented.

un·fer·ti·lized /únfórt'lizd/ *adj.* not fertilized.

un·fet·ter /únfétər/ *v.tr.* release from fetters.

un·fet·tered /únfétərd/ *adj.* unrestrained; unrestricted.

un·fil·i·al /únfileeəl/ *adj.* not befitting a son or daughter. □□ **un·fil·i·al·ly** *adv.*

un·filled /únfild/ *adj.* not filled.

un·fil·tered /únfíltərd/ *adj.* **1** not filtered. **2** (of a cigarette) not provided with a filter.

un·fin·ished /únfínisht/ *adj.* not finished; incomplete.

un·fit /únfit/ *adj. & v.* ● *adj.* (often foll. by *for*, or *to* + infin.) not fit. ● *v.tr.* (**un·fit·ted**, **un·fit·ting**) (usu. foll. by *for*) make unsuitable. □□ **un·fit·ly** *adv.* **un·fit·ness** *n.*

un·fit·ted /únfítid/ *adj.* **1** not fit. **2** not fitted or suited. **3** not provided with fittings.

un·fit·ting /únfíting/ *adj.* not fitting or suitable; unbecoming. □□ **un·fit·ting·ly** *adv.*

un·fix /únfíks/ *v.tr.* **1** release or loosen from a fixed state. **2** detach.

un·fixed /únfíkst/ *adj.* not fixed.

un·flag·ging /únfláging/ *adj.* tireless; persistent. □□ **un·flag·ging·ly** *adv.*

un·flap·pa·ble /únfláppəbəl/ *adj. colloq.* imperturbable; remaining calm in a crisis. □□ **un·flap·pa·bil·i·ty** /–bílitee/ *n.* **un·flap·pa·bly** *adv.*

un·flat·ter·ing /únflátəring/ *adj.* not flattering. □□ **un·flat·ter·ing·ly** *adv.*

un·fla·vored /únfláyvərd/ *adj.* not flavored.

un·fledged /únfléjd/ *adj.* **1** (of a person) inexperienced. **2** (of a bird) not yet fledged.

un·fleshed /únflésht/ *adj.* **1** not covered with flesh. **2** stripped of flesh.

un·flinch·ing /únflínching/ *adj.* not flinching. □□ **un·flinch·ing·ly** *adv.*

un·fo·cused /únfókəst/ *adj.* (also esp. *Brit.* **un·fo·cussed**) not focused.

un·fold /únfóld/ *v.* **1** *tr.* open the fold or folds of; spread out. **2** *tr.* reveal (thoughts, etc.). **3** *intr.* become opened out. **4** *intr.* develop. □□ **un·fold·ment** *n.* [OE *unfealdan* (as UN-², FOLD¹)]

un·forced /únfáwrst/ *adj.* **1** not produced by effort; easy; natural. **2** not compelled or constrained. □□ **un·forc·ed·ly** /–fáwrsidlee/ *adv.*

un·ford·a·ble /únfáwrdəbəl/ *adj.* that cannot be forded.

un·fore·see·a·ble /únfawrseéəbəl/ *adj.* not foreseeable.

un·fore·seen /únfawrseén/ *adj.* not foreseen.

un·fore·told /únfawrtóld/ *adj.* not foretold; unpredicted.

un·for·get·ta·ble /únfərgétəbəl/ *adj.* that cannot be forgotten; memorable; wonderful (*an unforgettable experience*). □□ **un·for·get·ta·bly** *adv.*

un·for·giv·a·ble /únfərgívəbəl/ *adj.* that cannot be forgiven. □□ **un·for·giv·a·bly** *adv.*

un·for·giv·en /únfərgívən/ *adj.* not forgiven.

un·for·giv·ing /únfərgíving/ *adj.* not forgiving. □□ **un·for·giv·ing·ly** *adv.* **un·for·giv·ing·ness** *n.*

un·for·got·ten /únfərgót'n/ *adj.* not forgotten.

un·formed /únfáwrmd/ *adj.* **1** not formed. **2** shapeless. **3** not developed.

un·for·mu·lat·ed /únfáwrmyəlaytid/ *adj.* not formulated.

un·forth·com·ing /únfawrthkúming/ *adj.* not forthcoming.

un·for·ti·fied /únfáwrtifíd/ *adj.* not fortified.

un·for·tu·nate /únfáwrchənət/ *adj. & n.* ● *adj.* **1** having bad fortune; unlucky. **2** unhappy. **3** regrettable. **4** disastrous. ● *n.* an unfortunate person.

un•for•tu•nate•ly /únfáwrchənətlee/ *adv.* **1** (qualifying a whole sentence) it is unfortunate that. **2** in an unfortunate manner.

un•found•ed /únfówndid/ *adj.* having no foundation (*unfounded hopes; unfounded rumor*). □□ **un•found•ed•ly** *adv.* **un•found•ed•ness** *n.*

un•framed /únfráymd/ *adj.* (esp. of a picture) not framed.

un•freeze /únfréez/ *v.* (*past* **un•froze**; *past part.* **un•fro•zen**) **1** *tr.* cause to thaw. **2** *intr.* thaw. **3** *tr.* remove restrictions from; make (assets, credits, etc.) realizable.

un•fre•quent•ed /únfreékwentid, –fríkwen–/ *adj.* not frequented.

un•friend•ed /únfréndid/ *adj.* *literary* without friends.

un•friend•ly /únfréndlee/ *adj.* (**un•friend•li•er**, **un•friend•li•est**) not friendly. □□ **un•friend•li•ness** *n.*

un•frock /únfrók/ *v.tr.* = DEFROCK.

un•froze *past* of UNFREEZE.

un•fro•zen *past part.* of UNFREEZE.

un•fruit•ful /únfroötfool/ *adj.* **1** not producing good results; unprofitable. **2** not producing fruit or crops. □□ **un•fruit•ful•ly** *adv.* **un•fruit•ful•ness** *n.*

un•ful•filled /únfoolfild/ *adj.* not fulfilled. □□ **un•ful•fill•a•ble** *adj.*

un•fund•ed /únfúndid/ *adj.* (of a debt) not funded.

un•fun•ny /únfúnee/ *adj.* (**un•fun•ni•er**, **un•fun•ni•est**) not amusing (though meant to be). □□ **un•fun•ni•ly** *adv.* **un•fun•ni•ness** *n.*

un•furl /únfárl/ *v.* **1** *tr.* spread out (a sail, umbrella, etc.). **2** *intr.* become spread out.

un•fur•nished /únfárnisht/ *adj.* **1** (usu. foll. by *with*) not supplied. **2** without furniture.

un•gain•ly /úngáynlee/ *adj.* (of a person, animal, or movement) awkward; clumsy. □□ **un•gain•li•ness** *n.* [UN-¹ + obs. *gainly* graceful ult. f. ON *gegn* straight]

un•gal•lant /úngálənt/ *adj.* not gallant. □□ **un•gal•lant•ly** *adv.*

un•gen•er•ous /únjénərəs/ *adj.* not generous; mean. □□ **un•gen•er•ous•ly** *adv.* **un•gen•er•ous•ness** *n.*

un•gen•ial /únjeényəl, –jeéneeəl/ *adj.* not genial.

un•gen•tle /únjént'l/ *adj.* not gentle. □□ **un•gen•tle•ness** *n.* **un•gen•tly** *adv.*

un•gen•tle•man•ly /únjéntəlmənlee/ *adj.* not gentlemanly. □□ **un•gen•tle•man•li•ness** *n.*

un•gift•ed /úngíftid/ *adj.* not gifted or talented.

un•gird /úngárd/ *v.tr.* **1** release the girdle, belt, or girth of. **2** release or take off by undoing a belt or girth.

un•glazed /úngláyzd/ *adj.* not glazed.

un•gloved /únglúvd/ *adj.* not wearing a glove or gloves.

un•god•ly /úngódlee/ *adj.* **1** impious; wicked. **2** *colloq.* outrageous (*an ungodly hour to arrive*). □□ **un•god•li•ness** *n.*

un•gov•ern•a•ble /úngúvərnəbəl/ *adj.* uncontrollable; violent. □□ **un•gov•ern•a•bil•i•ty** /–bílitee/ *n.* **un•gov•ern•a•bly** *adv.*

un•grace•ful /úngráysfool/ *adj.* not graceful. □□ **un•grace•ful•ly** *adv.* **un•grace•ful•ness** *n.*

un•gra•cious /úngrávshəs/ *adj.* **1** not kindly or courteous; unkind. **2** unattractive. □□ **un•gra•cious•ly** *adv.* **un•gra•cious•ness** *n.*

un•gram•mat•i•cal /úngrəmátikəl/ *adj.* contrary to the rules of grammar. □□ **un•gram•mat•i•cal•i•ty** /–kálitee/ *n.* **un•gram•mat•i•cal•ly** *adv.* **un•gram•mat•i•cal•ness** *n.*

un•grasp•a•ble /úngráspəbəl/ *adj.* that cannot be grasped or comprehended.

un•grate•ful /úngráytfool/ *adj.* **1** not feeling or showing gratitude. **2** not pleasant or acceptable. □□ **un•grate•ful•ly** *adv.* **un•grate•ful•ness** *n.*

un•ground•ed /úngrówndid/ *adj.* **1** having no basis or justification; unfounded. **2** *Electr.* not earthed. **3** (foll. by *in*) not properly instructed (in a subject). **4** (of an aircraft, ship, etc.) no longer grounded.

un•grudg•ing /úngrújing/ *adj.* not grudging. □□ **un•grudg•ing•ly** *adv.*

un•gual /únggwəl/ *adj.* of, like, or bearing a nail, hoof, or claw. [L UNGUIS]

un•guard /úngaàrd/ *v.tr.* *Cards* discard a low card that was protecting (a high card) from capture.

un•guard•ed /úngaárdid/ *adj.* **1** incautious; thoughtless (*an unguarded remark*). **2** not guarded; without a guard. □ **in an unguarded moment** unawares. □□ **un•guard•ed•ly** *adv.* **un•guard•ed•ness** *n.*

un•guent /únggwənt/ *n.* a soft substance used as ointment or for lubrication. [L *unguentum* f. *unguere* anoint]

un•guess•a•ble /úngésəbəl/ *adj.* that cannot be guessed or imagined.

un•guic•u•late /unggwíkyələt, –layt/ *adj.* **1** *Zool.* having one or more nails or claws. **2** *Bot.* (of petals) having an unguis. [mod.L *unguiculatus* f. *unguiculus* dimin. of UNGUIS]

un•guid•ed /úngídid/ *adj.* not guided in a particular path or direction; left to take its own course.

un•guis /únggwis/ *n.* (*pl.* **un•gues** /–weez/) **1** *Bot.* the narrow base of a petal. **2** *Zool.* a nail or claw. [L]

un•gu•la /úngyələ/ *n.* (*pl.* **un•gu•lae** /–lee/) a hoof or claw. [L, dimin. of UNGUIS]

un•gu•late /úngyələt, –layt/ *adj.* & *n.* ●*adj.* hoofed. ●*n.* a hoofed mammal. [LL *ungulatus* f. UNGULA]

un•hal•lowed /únhálōd/ *adj.* **1** not consecrated. **2** not sacred; unholy; wicked.

un•ham•pered /únhámpərd/ *adj.* not hampered.

un•hand /únhánd/ *v.tr.* *rhet.* or *joc.* **1** take one's hands off (a person). **2** release from one's grasp.

un•hand•some /únhánsəm/ *adj.* not handsome.

un•hand•y /únhándee/ *adj.* **1** not easy to handle or manage; awkward. **2** not skillful in using the hands. □□ **un•hand•i•ly** *adv.* **un•hand•i•ness** *n.*

un•hang /únháng/ *v.tr.* (*past* and *past part.* **un•hung**) take down from a hanging position.

un•hap•py /únhápee/ *adj.* (**un•hap•pi•er**, **un•hap•pi•est**) **1** not happy; miserable. **2** unsuccessful; unfortunate. **3** causing misfortune. **4** disastrous. **5** inauspicious. □□ **un•hap•pi•ly** *adv.* **un•hap•pi•ness** *n.*

un•harmed /únhaàrmd/ *adj.* not harmed.

un•harm•ful /únhaàrmfool/ *adj.* not harmful.

un•har•mo•ni•ous /únhaarmóneeəs/ *adj.* not harmonious.

un•har•ness /únhaárnis/ *v.tr.* remove a harness from.

un•hasp /únhásp/ *v.tr.* free from a hasp or catch; unfasten.

un•hatched /únhácht/ *adj.* (of an egg, etc.) not hatched.

un•health•ful /únhélthfool/ *adj.* harmful to health; unwholesome. □□ **un•health•ful•ness** *n.*

un•health•y /únhélthee/ *adj.* (**un•health•i•er**, **un•health•i•est**) **1** not in good health. **2 a** (of a place, etc.) harmful to health. **b** unwholesome. **c** *sl.* dangerous to life. □□ **un•health•i•ly** *adv.* **un•health•i•ness** *n.*

un•heard /únhárd/ *adj.* **1** not heard. **2** (usu. **unheard-of**) unprecedented; unknown.

un•heat•ed /únheétid/ *adj.* not heated.

un•heed•ed /únheédid/ *adj.* not heeded; disregarded.

un•heed•ful /únheédfool/ *adj.* heedless; taking no notice.

un•heed•ing /únheéding/ *adj.* not giving heed; heedless. □□ **un•heed•ing•ly** *adv.*

un•help•ful /únhélpfool/ *adj.* not helpful. □□ **un•help•ful•ly** *adv.* **un•help•ful•ness** *n.*

un•her•ald•ed /únhérəldid/ *adj.* not heralded; unannounced.

un•he•ro•ic /únhiróik/ *adj.* not heroic. □□ **un•he•ro•i•cal•ly** *adv.*

un•hes•i•tat•ing /únhézitayting/ *adj.* without hesitation. □□ **un•hes•i•tat•ing•ly** *adv.* **un•hes•i•tat•ing•ness** *n.*

un•hin•dered /únhíndərd/ *adj.* not hindered.

un•hinge /únhínj/ *v.tr.* **1** take (a door, etc.) off its hinges. **2** (esp. as **unhinged** *adj.*) unsettle or disorder (a person's mind, etc.), make (a person) crazy.

un•hip /únhíp/ *adj.* *sl.* unaware of current fashions.

un•his•tor•ic /únhistáwrik, –histórik/ *adj.* not historic or historical.

un•his•tor•i•cal /únhistáwrikl, –histór–/ *adj.* not historical. □□ **un•his•tor•i•cal•ly** *adv.*

un•hitch /únhích/ *v.tr.* **1** release from a hitched state. **2** unhook; unfasten.

un•ho•ly /únhólee/ *adj.* (**un•ho•li•er**, **un•ho•li•est**) **1** impious; profane; wicked. **2** *colloq.* dreadful; outrageous (*made an unholy ordeal out of nothing*). **3** not holy. □□ **un•ho•li•ness** *n.* [OE *unhālig* (as UN-¹, HOLY)]

un•hon•ored /únónərd/ *adj.* not honored.

un•hook /únhoök/ *v.tr.* **1** remove from a hook or hooks. **2** unfasten by releasing a hook or hooks.

un•hoped /únhópt/ *adj.* (foll. by *for*) not hoped for or expected.

un•horse /únháwrs/ *v.tr.* **1** throw or drag from a horse. **2** (of a horse) throw (a rider). **3** dislodge; overthrow.

un•house /únhówz/ *v.tr.* deprive of shelter; turn out of a house.

un•hu•man /únhyoōmən/ *adj.* **1** not human. **2** superhuman. **3** inhuman; brutal.

un•hung¹ /únhúng/ *adj.* **1** not (yet) executed by hanging. **2** not hung up (for exhibition).

un•hung² *past* and *past part.* of UNHANG.

un•hur•ried /únhúrid, –húr–/ *adj.* not hurried. □□ **un•hur•ried•ly** *adv.*

un•hurt /únhórt/ *adj.* not hurt.

un•husk /únhúsk/ *v.tr.* remove a husk or shell from.

un•hy•gi•en•ic /únhijénik, –jee-én–/ *adj.* not hygienic. □□ **un•hy•gi•en•i•cal•ly** *adv.*

un•hy•phen•at•ed /únhífənaytid/ *adj.* not hyphenated.

u•ni /yoönee/ *n.* (*pl.* **u•nis**) esp. *Brit.*, *Austral.*, & *NZ colloq.* a university. [abbr.]

uni- /yoönee/ *comb. form* one; having or consisting of one. [L f. *unus* one]

U•ni•ate /yoöneeit, –áyt/ *adj.* & *n.* (also **U•ni•at** /–at/) ●*adj.* of or relating to any community of Christians in E. Europe or the Near East that acknowledges papal supremacy but retains its own liturgy, etc. ●*n.* a member of such a community. [Russ. *uniyat* f. *uniya* f. L *unio* UNION]

u•ni•ax•i•al /yoöneeákseeəl/ *adj.* having a single axis. □□ **u•ni•ax•i•al•ly** *adv.*

u·ni·cam·er·al /yŏŏnikámərəl/ *adj.* with a single legislative chamber.

UNICEF /yŏŏnisef/ *abbr.* United Nations Children's (orig. International Children's Emergency) Fund.

u·ni·cel·lu·lar /yŏŏnisélyələr/ *adj.* (of an organism, organ, tissue, etc.) consisting of a single cell.

u·ni·col·or /yŏŏnikulər/ *adj.* (also **u·ni·col·ored**) of one color.

u·ni·corn /yŏŏnikawrn/ *n.* **1 a** a mythical animal with a horse's body and a single straight horn. **b** a heraldic representation of this, with a twisted horn, a deer's feet, a goat's beard, and a lion's tail. **c** used in old translations of the Old Testament for the Hebrew *r⁾em*, a two-horned animal, probably a wild ox. **2 a** a pair of horses and a third horse in front. **b** an equipage with these. [ME f. OF *unicorne* f. L *unicornis* f. UNI- + *cornu* horn, transl. Gk *monoceros*]

unicorn 1

u·ni·cus·pid /yŏŏnikúspid/ *adj. & n.* ● *adj.* with one cusp. ● *n.* a unicuspid tooth.

u·ni·cy·cle /yŏŏnisīkəl/ *n.* a single-wheeled cycle, esp. as used by acrobats. □□ **u·ni·cy·clist** *n.*

un·i·deal /únīdéeəl/ *adj.* not ideal.

un·i·den·ti·fi·a·ble /únīdéntifīəbəl/ *adj.* unable to be identified.

un·i·den·ti·fied /únīdéntifīd/ *adj.* not identified.

u·ni·di·men·sion·al /yŏŏnidiménshənəl, –dī–/ *adj.* having (only) one dimension.

u·ni·di·rec·tion·al /yŏŏnidirékshənəl, –dī–/ *adj.* having only one direction of motion, operation, etc. □□ **u·ni·di·rec·tion·al·i·ty** /–nálitee/ *n.* **u·ni·di·rec·tion·al·ly** *adv.*

u·ni·fi·ca·tion /yŏŏnifikáyshən/ *n.* the act or an instance of unifying; the state of being unified.

U·ni·fi·ca·tion Church *n.* a religious organization founded in 1954 in Korea by Sun Myung Moon (cf. MOONIE).

u·ni·fied field the·o·ry *n. Physics* a theory that seeks to explain all the field phenomena (e.g., gravitation and electromagnetism: see FIELD *n.* 9) formerly treated by separate theories.

u·ni·flow /yŏŏniflō/ *adj.* involving flow (esp. of steam or waste gases) in one direction only.

u·ni·form /yŏŏnifawrm/ *adj., n., & v.* ● *adj.* **1** not changing in form or character; the same; unvarying (*present a uniform appearance*; *all of uniform size and shape*). **2** conforming to the same standard, rules, or pattern. **3** constant in the course of time (*uniform acceleration*). **4** (of a tax, law, etc.) not varying with time or place. ● *n.* uniform distinctive clothing worn by members of the same body, e.g., by soldiers, police, and schoolchildren. ● *v.tr.* **1** clothe in uniform (*a uniformed officer*). **2** make uniform. □□ **u·ni·form·ly** *adv.* [F *uniforme* or L *uniformis* (as UNI-, FORM)]

u·ni·form·i·tar·i·an /yŏŏnifáwrmitáireeən/ *adj. & n.* ● *adj.* of the theory that geological processes are always due to continuously and uniformly operating forces. ● *n.* a holder of this theory. □□ **u·ni·form·i·tar·i·an·ism** *n.*

u·ni·form·i·ty /yŏŏnifáwrmitee/ *n.* (*pl.* **–ties**) **1** being uniform; sameness; consistency. **2** an instance of this. [ME f. OF *uniformité* or LL *uniformitas* (as UNIFORM)]

u·ni·fy /yŏŏnifī/ *v.tr.* (also *absol.*) (**–fies, –fied**) reduce to unity or uniformity. □□ **u·ni·fi·er** *n.* [F *unifier* or LL *unificare* (as UNI-, –FY)]

u·ni·lat·er·al /yŏŏnilátərəl/ *adj.* **1** performed by or affecting only one person or party (*unilateral disarmament*; *unilateral declaration of independence*). **2** one-sided. **3** (of the parking of vehicles) restricted to one side of the street. **4** (of leaves) all on the same side of the stem. **5** (of a line of descent) through ancestors of one sex only. □□ **u·ni·lat·er·al·ly** *adv.*

u·ni·lat·er·al·ism /yŏŏnilátərəlizəm/ *n.* **1** unilateral disarmament. **2** the pursuit of a foreign policy without allies. □□ **u·ni·lat·er·al·ist** *n. & adj.*

u·ni·lin·gual /yŏŏnilínggwəl/ *adj.* of or in only one language. □□ **u·ni·lin·gual·ly** *adv.*

u·ni·lit·er·al /yŏŏnilítərəl/ *adj.* consisting of one letter.

un·il·lu·min·at·ed /únilŏŏminaytid/ *adj.* not illuminated.

un·il·lus·trat·ed /úníləstraytid/ *adj.* (esp. of a book) without illustrations.

u·ni·loc·u·lar /yŏŏnilókyələr/ *adj. Bot. & Zool.* single-chambered.

un·im·ag·i·na·ble /únimájinəbəl/ *adj.* impossible to imagine. □□ **un·im·ag·i·na·bly** *adv.*

un·im·ag·i·na·tive /únimájinətiv/ *adj.* lacking imagination; stolid; dull. □□ **un·im·ag·i·na·tive·ly** *adv.* **un·im·ag·i·na·tive·ness** *n.*

un·im·paired /únimpáird/ *adj.* not impaired.

un·im·pas·sioned /únimpáshənd/ *adj.* not impassioned.

un·im·peach·a·ble /únimpéechəbəl/ *adj.* giving no opportunity for censure; beyond reproach or question. □□ **un·im·peach·a·bly** *adv.*

un·im·ped·ed /únimpéedid/ *adj.* not impeded. □□ **un·im·ped·ed·ly** *adv.*

un·im·por·tance /únimpáwrt'ns/ *n.* lack of importance.

un·im·por·tant /únimpáwrt'nt/ *adj.* not important.

un·im·pos·ing /únimpózing/ *adj.* unimpressive. □□ **un·im·pos·ing·ly** *adv.*

un·im·pressed /únimprést/ *adj.* not impressed.

un·im·pres·sion·a·ble /únimpréshənəbəl/ *adj.* not impressionable.

un·im·pres·sive /únimprésiv/ *adj.* not impressive. □□ **un·im·pres·sive·ly** *adv.* **un·im·pres·sive·ness** *n.*

un·im·proved /únimprŏŏvd/ *adj.* **1** not made better. **2** not made use of. **3** (of land) not used for agriculture or building; not developed.

un·in·cor·po·rat·ed /úninkáwrpəraytid/ *adj.* **1** not incorporated or united. **2** not formed into a corporation.

un·in·fect·ed /úninféktid/ *adj.* not infected.

un·in·flamed /úninfláymd/ *adj.* not inflamed.

un·in·flam·ma·ble /úninflámməbəl/ *adj.* not flammable.

un·in·flect·ed /úninfléktid/ *adj.* **1** *Gram.* (of a language) not having inflections. **2** not changing or varying. **3** not bent or deflected.

un·in·flu·enced /úninflŏŏinst/ *adj.* (often foll. by *by*) not influenced.

un·in·flu·en·tial /úninflŏŏ-énshəl/ *adj.* having little or no influence.

un·in·form·a·tive /úninfáwrmətiv/ *adj.* not informative; giving little information.

un·in·formed /úninfáwrmd/ *adj.* **1** not informed or instructed. **2** ignorant, uneducated.

un·in·hab·it·a·ble /úninhábitəbəl/ *adj.* that cannot be inhabited. □□ **un·in·hab·it·a·ble·ness** *n.*

un·in·hab·it·ed /úninhábitid/ *adj.* not inhabited.

un·in·hib·it·ed /úninhíbitid/ *adj.* not inhibited. □□ **un·in·hib·it·ed·ly** *adv.* **un·in·hib·it·ed·ness** *n.*

un·in·i·ti·at·ed /únínisheeaytid/ *adj.* not initiated; not admitted or instructed.

un·in·jured /únínjərd/ *adj.* not injured.

un·in·spired /úninspírd/ *adj.* **1** not inspired. **2** (of oratory, etc.) commonplace.

un·in·spir·ing /úninspíring/ *adj.* not inspiring. □□ **un·in·spir·ing·ly** *adv.*

un·in·struct·ed /úninstrúktid/ *adj.* not instructed or informed.

un·in·sur·a·ble /úninshŏŏrəbəl/ *adj.* that cannot be insured.

un·in·sured /úninshŏŏrd/ *adj.* not insured.

un·in·tel·li·gent /únintélijənt/ *adj.* not intelligent. □□ **un·in·tel·li·gent·ly** *adv.*

un·in·tel·li·gi·ble /únintélijibəl/ *adj.* not intelligible. □□ **un·in·tel·li·gi·bil·i·ty** *n.* **un·in·tel·li·gi·ble·ness** *n.* **un·in·tel·li·gi·bly** *adv.*

un·in·tend·ed /úninténdid/ *adj.* not intended.

un·in·ten·tion·al /úninténshənəl/ *adj.* not intentional. □□ **un·in·ten·tion·al·ly** *adv.*

un·in·ter·est·ed /úníntrəstid, –təristid, –təres–/ *adj.* **1** not interested. **2** unconcerned; indifferent. □□ **un·in·ter·est·ed·ly** *adv.* **un·in·ter·est·ed·ness** *n.*

▶See note at DISINTERESTED.

un·in·ter·est·ing /úníntrəsting, –təristing, –təres–/ *adj.* not interesting. □□ **un·in·ter·est·ing·ly** *adv.* **un·in·ter·est·ing·ness** *n.*

un·in·ter·pret·a·ble /únintərpritəbəl/ *adj.* that cannot be interpreted.

un·in·ter·rupt·a·ble /únintərúptəbəl/ *adj.* that cannot be interrupted.

un·in·ter·rupt·ed /únintərúptid/ *adj.* not interrupted. □□ **un·in·ter·rupt·ed·ly** *adv.* **un·in·ter·rupt·ed·ness** *n.*

u·ni·nu·cle·ate /yŏŏninŏŏkleeət, –ayt, –nyŏŏ–/ *adj. Biol.* having a single nucleus.

un·in·vent·ive /úninvéntiv/ *adj.* not inventive. □□ **un·in·vent·ive·ly** *adv.* **un·in·vent·ive·ness** *n.*

un·in·ves·ti·gat·ed /úninvéstigaytid/ *adj.* not investigated.

un·in·vit·ed /úninvítid/ *adj.* not invited. □□ **un·in·vit·ed·ly** *adv.*

un·in·vit·ing /úninvíting/ *adj.* not inviting; unattractive; repellent. □□ **un·in·vit·ing·ly** *adv.*

un·in·voked /úninvókt/ *adj.* not invoked.

un·in·volved /úninvólvd/ *adj.* not involved.

un·ion /yŏŏnyən/ *n.* **1** the act or an instance of uniting; the state of being united. **2 a** a whole resulting from the combination of parts or members. **b** a political unit formed in this way, esp. (**Union**) the US (esp. as distinct from the Confederacy during the Civil War), the UK, or South Africa. **3** = LABOR UNION. **4** marriage; matrimony. **5** concord; agreement (*lived together in perfect union*). **6** (**Union**) (in the UK) **a** a general social club and debating society at some universities and colleges. **b** the buildings or accommodation of such a society. **7** *Math.* the totality of the members of two or more sets. **8** a part of a flag with a device emblematic of union, normally occupying the upper corner next to the staff. **9** a joint or coupling for pipes, etc. **10** a fabric of mixed materials, e.g., cotton with linen or silk. [ME f. OF *union* or eccl. L *unio* unity f. L *unus* one]

un·ion-bash·ing *n. Brit. colloq.* active or vocal opposition to labor unions and their rights.

un·ion cat·a·log *n.* a catalog of the combined holdings of several libraries.

un•ion down *adj.* (of a flag) hoisted with the union below as a signal of distress.

un•ion•ist /yōōnyənist/ *n.* **1 a** a member of a labor union. **b** an advocate of labor unions. **2** (usu. **Unionist**) an advocate of union, esp.: **a** a person opposed to the rupture of the parliamentary union between Great Britain and Northern Ireland (formerly between Great Britain and Ireland). **b** *hist.* a person who opposed secession during the US Civil War. □□ **un•ion•ism** *n.* **un•ion•is•tic** /-nístik/ *adj.*

un•ion•ize /yōōnyəniz/ *v.tr. & intr.* bring or come under labor-union organization or rules. □□ **un•ion•i•za•tion** *n.*

un-i-on-ized /únionizd/ *adj.* not ionized.

Un•ion Jack *n.* (also **Un•ion flag**) the national ensign of the United Kingdom formed by the union of the crosses of St. George, St. Andrew, and St. Patrick.

un•ion jack *n.* a jack consisting of the union from a national flag.

un•ion shop *n.* a shop, factory, trade, etc., in which employees must belong to a labor union or join one within an agreed time.

un•ion suit *n.* a single undergarment for the body and legs; combinations.

u•nip•ar•ous /yōōnípərəs/ *adj.* **1** producing one offspring at a birth. **2** *Bot.* having one axis or branch.

u•ni•ped /yōōniped/ *n. & adj.* ● *n.* a person having only one foot or leg. ● *adj.* one-footed; one-legged. [UNI- + *pes pedis* foot]

u•ni•per•son•al /yōōnipə́rsənəl/ *adj.* (of the Deity) existing only as one person.

u•ni•pla•nar /yōōnipláynər/ *adj.* lying in one plane.

u•ni•pod /yōōnipod/ *n.* a one-legged support for a camera, etc. [UNI-, after TRIPOD]

u•ni•po•lar /yōōnipólər/ *adj.* **1** (esp. of an electric or magnetic apparatus) showing only one kind of polarity. **2** *Biol.* (of a nerve cell, etc.) having only one pole. □□ **u•ni•po•lar•i•ty** /-láritee/ *n.*

u•nique /yōōnéek/ *adj. & n.* ● *adj.* **1** of which there is only one; unequaled; having no like, equal, or parallel (*his position was unique; this vase is considered unique*). **2** *disp.* unusual; remarkable (*the most unique man I ever met*). ● *n.* a unique thing or person. □□ **u•nique•ly** *adv.* **u•nique•ness** *n.* [F f. L *unicus* f. *unus* one]
▶See note at PERFECT.

un•i•roned /únírnd/ *adj.* (esp. of clothing, linen, etc.) not ironed.

u•ni•se•ri•al /yōōniséereeəl/ *adj.* *Bot. & Zool.* arranged in one row.

u•ni•sex /yōōniseks/ *adj.* (of clothing, hairstyles, etc.) designed to be suitable for both sexes.

u•ni•sex•u•al /yōōnisékshōōəl/ *adj.* **1 a** of one sex. **b** *Bot.* having stamens or pistils but not both. **2** unisex. □□ **u•ni•sex•u•al•i•ty** /-shōōálitee/ *n.* **u•ni•sex•u•al•ly** *adv.*

u•ni•son /yōōnisən/ *n. & adj.* ● *n.* **1** *Mus.* **a** a coincidence in pitch of sounds or notes. **b** this regarded as an interval. **2** *Mus.* a combination of voices or instruments at the same pitch or at pitches differing by one or more octaves (*sang in unison*). **3** agreement; concord (*acted in perfect unison*). ● *adj.* *Mus.* coinciding in pitch. □□ **u•nis•o•nant** /yoonísənənt/ *adj.* **u•nis•o•nous** /yoonísənəs/ *adj.* [OF *unison* or LL *unisonus* (as UNI-, *sonus* SOUND[1])]

u•ni•son string *n.* a string tuned in unison with another string and meant to be sounded with it.

un•is•sued /únishōōd/ *adj.* not issued.

u•nit /yōōnit/ *n.* **1 a** an individual thing, person, or group regarded as single and complete, esp. for purposes of calculation. **b** each of the (smallest) separate individuals or groups into which a complex whole may be analyzed (*the family as the unit of society*). **2** a quantity chosen as a standard in terms of which other quantities may be expressed (*unit of heat; SI unit; mass per unit volume*). **3** the smallest share in a unit trust. **4** a device with a specified function forming part of a complex mechanism. **5** a piece of furniture for fitting with others like it or made of complementary parts. **6** a group with a special function in an organization. **7** a group of buildings, wards, etc., in a hospital. **8** the number 'one.' [L *unus*, prob. after DIGIT]

u•ni•tard /yōōnitaard/ *n.* a one-piece leotard that covers the legs as well as the torso.

U•ni•tar•i•an /yōōnitáireeən/ *n. & adj.* ● *n.* **1** a person who believes that God is not a Trinity but one being. **2** a member of a religious body maintaining this and advocating freedom from formal dogma or doctrine. ● *adj.* of or relating to the Unitarians. □□ **U•ni•tar•i•an•ism** *n.* [mod.L *unitarius* f. L *unitas* UNITY]

u•ni•tar•y /yōōnitéree/ *adj.* **1** of a unit or units. **2** marked by unity or uniformity. □□ **u•ni•tar•i•ly** *adv.* **u•ni•tar•i•ty** /-téritee/ *n.*

u•nit cell *n.* *Crystallog.* the smallest repeating group of atoms, ions, or molecules in a crystal.

u•nit cost *n.* the cost of producing one item of manufacture.

u•nite /yōōnít/ *v.* **1** *tr. & intr.* join together; make or become one; combine. **2** *tr. & intr.* join together for a common purpose or action (*united in their struggle against injustice*). **3** *tr. & intr.* join in marriage. **4** *tr.* possess (qualities, features, etc.) in combination (*united anger with mercy*). **5** *intr. & tr.* form or cause to form a physical or chemical whole (*oil will not unite with water*). □□ **u•ni•tive** /yōōnitiv/ *adj.* **u•ni•tive•ly** *adv.* [ME f. L *unire* unit- f. *unus* one]

u•nit•ed /yōōnítid/ *adj.* **1** that has united or been united. **2 a** of or produced by two or more persons or things in union; joint. **b** resulting

---

from the union of two or more parts (esp. in the names of churches, societies, and athletic clubs). **3** in agreement; of like mind. □□ **u•nit•ed•ly** *adv.*

U•nit•ed Breth•ren *n.* *Eccl.* the Moravians.

U•nit•ed King•dom *n.* Great Britain and Northern Ireland (until 1922, Great Britain and Ireland).

U•nit•ed Na•tions *n.* (orig., in 1942) those united against the Axis powers in the war of 1939–45, (later) a supranational peace-seeking organization of these and many other nations.

U•nit•ed States (in full **United States of America**) a federal republic of 50 states, mostly in N. America and including Alaska and Hawaii.

u•nit price *n.* the price charged for each unit of goods supplied.

u•nit trust *n.* *Brit.* = MUTUAL FUND.

u•ni•ty /yōōnitee/ *n.* (*pl.* **-ties**) **1** oneness; being one, single, or individual; being formed of parts that constitute a whole; due interconnection and coherence of parts (*disturbs the unity of the idea; the pictures lack unity; national unity*). **2** harmony or concord between persons, etc. (*lived together in unity*). **3** a thing forming a complex whole (*a person regarded as a unity*). **4** *Math.* the number 'one,' the factor that leaves unchanged the quantity on which it operates. **5** *Theatr.* each of the three dramatic principles requiring limitation of the supposed time of a drama to that occupied in acting it or to a single day (**unity of time**), use of one scene throughout (**unity of place**), and concentration on the development of a single plot (**unity of action**). [ME f. OF *unité* f. L *unitas -tatis* f. *unus* one]

Univ. *abbr.* University.

u•ni•va•lent *adj. & n.* ● *adj.* **1** /yōōniváylənt/ *Chem.* having a valence of one. **2** /yōōnívələnt/ *Biol.* (of a chromosome) remaining unpaired during meiosis. ● *n.* /yoonívələnt/ *Biol.* a univalent chromosome. [UNI- + *valent-* pres. part. stem (as VALENCE[1])]

u•ni•valve /yōōnivalv/ *adj. & n.* *Zool.* ● *adj.* having one valve. ● *n.* a univalve mollusk.

u•ni•ver•sal /yōōnivə́rsəl/ *adj. & n.* ● *adj.* **1** of, belonging to, or done, etc., by all persons or things in the world or in the class concerned; applicable to all cases (*the feeling was universal; met with universal approval*). **2** *Logic* (of a proposition) in which something is asserted of all of a class (opp. PARTICULAR 5). ● *n.* **1** *Logic* a universal proposition. **2** *Philos.* **a** a term or concept of general application. **b** a nature or essence signified by a general term. □□ **u•ni•ver•sal•i•ty** /-sálitee/ *n.* **u•ni•ver•sal•ize** *v.tr.* **u•ni•ver•sal•i•za•tion** /-lizáyshən/ *n.* **u•ni•ver•sal•ly** *adv.* [ME f. OF *universal* or L *universalis* (as UNIVERSE)]

u•ni•ver•sal a•gent *n.* an agent empowered to do all that can be delegated.

u•ni•ver•sal com•pass *n.* a compass with legs that may be extended for large circles.

u•ni•ver•sal•ist /yōōnivə́rsəlist/ *n.* *Theol.* **1** a person who holds that all mankind will eventually be saved. **2** a member of an organized body of Christians who hold this. □□ **u•ni•ver•sal•ism** *n.* **u•ni•ver•sal•is•tic** /-listik/ *adj.*

u•ni•ver•sal joint *n.* (also **u•ni•ver•sal cou•pling**) a joint or coupling which can transmit rotary power by a shaft at any selected angle.

u•ni•ver•sal lan•guage *n.* an artificial language intended for use by all nations.

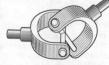

universal joint

U•ni•ver•sal Prod•uct Code *n.* a bar code on products that can be read by an electronic scanner, usu. providing price and product identification.

u·ni·ver·sal suf·frage *n.* a suffrage extending to all adults with minor exceptions.

u·ni·ver·sal time *n.* = GREENWICH MEAN TIME.

u·ni·verse /yo͞onivərs/ *n.* **1 a** all existing things; the whole creation; the cosmos. **b** a sphere of existence, influence, activity, etc. **2** all mankind. **3** *Statistics & Logic* all the objects under consideration. [F *univers* f. L *universum* neut. of *universus* combined into one, whole f. UNI- + *versus* past part. of *vertere* turn]

u·ni·verse of dis·course *n.* *Logic* = UNIVERSE sense 3.

u·ni·ver·si·ty /yo͞onivə́rsitee/ *n.* (*pl.* **–ties**) **1** an educational institution designed for instruction, examination, or both, of students in many branches of advanced learning, conferring degrees in various faculties, and often embodying colleges and similar institutions. **2** the members of this collectively. **3** *Brit.* a team, crew, etc., representing a university. □ **at university** esp. *Brit.* studying at a university. [ME f. OF *université* f. L *universitas –tatis* the whole (world), in LL college, guild (as UNIVERSE)]

u·niv·o·cal /yo͞onívəkəl, yo͞onivŏkəl/ *adj. & n.* ● *adj.* (of a word, etc.) having only one proper meaning. ● *n.* a univocal word. □□ **u·niv·o·cal·i·ty** /yo͞onivŏkálitee/ *n.* **u·niv·o·cal·ly** *adv.*

un·join /únjóyn/ *v.tr.* detach from being joined; separate.

un·joined /únjóynd/ *adj.* not joined.

un·joint /únjóynt/ *v.tr.* **1** separate the joints of. **2** disunite.

un·just /únjúst/ *adj.* not just; contrary to justice or fairness. □□ **un·just·ly** *adv.* **un·just·ness** *n.*

un·jus·ti·fi·a·ble /únjústifíəbəl/ *adj.* not justifiable. □□ **un·jus·ti·fi·a·bly** *adv.*

un·jus·ti·fied /únjústifīd/ *adj.* not justified.

un·kempt /únkémpt/ *adj.* **1** untidy; of neglected appearance. **2** uncombed; disheveled. □□ **un·kempt·ly** *adv.* **un·kempt·ness** *n.* [UN-¹ + archaic *kempt* past part. of *kemb* comb f. OE *cemban*]

un·kept /únképt/ *adj.* **1** (of a promise, law, etc.) not observed; disregarded. **2** not tended; neglected.

un·kill·a·ble /únkíləbəl/ *adj.* that cannot be killed.

un·kind /únkínd/ *adj.* **1** not kind. **2** harsh; cruel. **3** unpleasant. □□ **un·kind·ly** *adv.* **un·kind·ness** *n.*

un·king /únkíng/ *v.tr.* **1** deprive of the position of king; dethrone. **2** deprive (a country) of a king.

un·kink /únkíngk/ *v.* **1** *tr.* remove the kinks from; straighten. **2** *intr.* lose kinks; become straight.

un·knit /ún-nít/ *v.tr.* (**un·knit·ted, un·knit·ting**) separate (things joined, knotted, or interlocked).

un·knot /ún-nót/ *v.tr.* (**un·knot·ted, un·knot·ting**) release the knot or knots of; untie.

un·know·a·ble /ún-nóəbəl/ *adj. & n.* ● *adj.* that cannot be known. ● *n.* **1** an unknowable thing. **2** (**the Unknowable**) the postulated absolute or ultimate reality.

un·know·ing /ún-nóing/ *adj. & n.* ● *adj.* (often foll. by *of*) not knowing; ignorant; unconscious. ● *n.* ignorance (*cloud of unknowing*). □□ **un·know·ing·ly** *adv.* **un·know·ing·ness** *n.*

un·known /ún-nón/ *adj. & n.* ● *adj.* (often foll. by *to*) not known; unfamiliar (*his purpose was unknown to me*). ● *n.* **1** an unknown thing or person. **2** an unknown quantity (*equation in two unknowns*). □ **unknown to** without the knowledge of (*did it unknown to me*). □□ **un·known·ness** *n.*

un·known coun·try *n.* see COUNTRY.

un·known quan·ti·ty *n.* a person or thing whose nature, significance, etc., cannot be determined.

Un·known Sol·dier *n.* an unidentified representative member of a country's armed forces killed in war, given burial with special honors in a national memorial.

Un·known War·ri·or *n.* = UNKNOWN SOLDIER.

un·la·beled /únláybəld/ *adj.* not labeled; without a label.

un·la·bored /únláybərd/ *adj.* not labored.

un·lace /únláys/ *v.tr.* **1** undo the lace or laces of. **2** unfasten or loosen in this way.

un·lade /únláyd/ *v.tr.* **1** take the cargo out of (a ship). **2** discharge (a cargo, etc.) from a ship.

un·lad·en /únláyd'n/ *adj.* not laden.

un·lad·en weight *n.* the weight of a vehicle, etc., when not loaded with goods, etc.

un·la·dy·like /únláydeelík/ *adj.* not ladylike.

un·laid¹ /únláyd/ *adj.* not laid.

un·laid² *past* and *past part.* of UNLAY.

un·la·ment·ed /únləméntid/ *adj.* not lamented.

un·lash /únlásh/ *v.tr.* unfasten (a thing lashed down, etc.).

un·latch /únlách/ *v.* **1** *tr.* release the latch of. **2** *tr. & intr.* open or be opened in this way.

un·law·ful /únláwfŏŏl/ *adj.* not lawful; illegal; not permissible. □□ **un·law·ful·ly** *adv.* **un·law·ful·ness** *n.*

un·lay /únláy/ *v.tr.* (*past* and *past part.* **un·laid**) *Naut.* untwist (a rope). [UN-² + LAY¹]

un·lead·ed /únlédid/ *adj.* **1** (of gasoline, etc.) without added lead. **2** not covered, weighted, or framed with lead. **3** *Printing* not spaced with leads.

un·learn /únlórn/ *v.tr.* (*past* and *past part.* **un·learned** or **un·learnt**) **1** discard from one's memory. **2** rid oneself of (a habit, false information, etc.).

un·learn·ed¹ /únlórnid/ *adj.* not well educated; untaught; ignorant. □□ **un·learn·ed·ly** *adv.*

un·learned² /únlórnd/ *adj.* (also **un·learnt** /–lérnt/) that has not been learned.

un·leash /únleésh/ *v.tr.* **1** release from a leash or restraint. **2** set free to engage in pursuit or attack.

un·leav·ened /únlévənd/ *adj.* not leavened; made without yeast or other raising agent.

un·less /únlés, ən–/ *conj.* if not; except when (*shall go unless I hear from you; always walked unless I had a bicycle*). [ON or IN + LESS, assim. to UN-¹]

un·let·tered /únlétərd/ *adj.* **1** illiterate. **2** not well educated.

un·lib·er·at·ed /únlíbəraytid/ *adj.* not liberated.

un·li·censed /únlísənst/ *adj.* not licensed, esp. (in the UK) without a license to sell alcoholic drink.

un·light·ed /únlítid/ *adj.* **1** not provided with light. **2** not set burning.

un·lik·a·ble /únlíkəbəl/ *adj.* (also **un·like·a·ble**) not easy to like; unpleasant.

un·like /únlík/ *adj. & prep.* ● *adj.* **1** not like; different from (*is unlike both his parents*). **2** uncharacteristic of (*such behavior is unlike him*). **3** dissimilar; different. ● *prep.* differently from (*acts quite unlike anyone else*). □□ **un·like·ness** *n.* [perh. f. ON *ulíkr*, OE *ungelic*: see LIKE¹]

un·like·ly /únlíklee/ *adj.* (**un·like·li·er, un·like·li·est**) **1** improbable (*unlikely tale*). **2** (foll. by *to* + infin.) not to be expected to do something (*he's unlikely to be available*). **3** unpromising (*an unlikely candidate*). □□ **un·like·li·hood** *n.* **un·like·li·ness** *n.*

un·like signs *n.* *Math.* plus and minus.

un·lim·it·ed /únlímitid/ *adj.* without limit; unrestricted; very great in number or quantity (*has unlimited possibilities; an unlimited expanse of sea*). □□ **un·lim·it·ed·ly** *adv.* **un·lim·it·ed·ness** *n.*

un·lined¹ /únlínd/ *adj.* **1** (of paper, etc.) without lines. **2** (of a face, etc.) without wrinkles.

un·lined² /únlínd/ *adj.* (of a garment, etc.) without lining.

un·link /únlíngk/ *v.tr.* **1** undo the links of (a chain, etc.). **2** detach or set free by undoing or unfastening a link or chain.

un·liq·ui·dat·ed /únlíkwidaytid/ *adj.* not liquidated.

un·list·ed /únlístid/ *adj.* not included in a published list, esp. of stock exchange prices or of telephone numbers.

un·lit /únlít/ *adj.* not lit.

un·liv·a·ble /únlívəbəl/ *adj.* that cannot be lived or lived in.

un·lived-in /únlívdin/ *adj.* **1** appearing to be uninhabited. **2** unused by the inhabitants.

un·load /únlód/ *v.tr.* **1** (also *absol.*) remove a load from (a vehicle, etc.). **2** remove (a load) from a vehicle, etc. **3** remove the charge from (a firearm, etc.). **4** *colloq.* get rid of. **5** (often foll. by *on*) *colloq.* **a** divulge (information). **b** (also *absol.*) give vent to (feelings). □□ **un·load·er** *n.*

un·lock /únlók/ *v.tr.* **1 a** release the lock of (a door, box, etc.). **b** release or disclose by unlocking. **2** release thoughts, feelings, etc., from (one's mind, etc.).

un·locked /únlókt/ *adj.* not locked.

un·looked-for /únlŏŏktfawr/ *adj.* unexpected; unforeseen.

un·loose /únlóōs/ *v.tr.* (also **un·loos·en**) loose; set free.

un·lov·a·ble /únlúvəbəl/ *adj.* not lovable.

un·loved /únlúvd/ *adj.* not loved.

un·love·ly /únlúvlee/ *adj.* not attractive; unpleasant; ugly. □□ **un·love·li·ness** *n.*

un·lov·ing /únlúving/ *adj.* not loving. □□ **un·lov·ing·ly** *adv.* **un·lov·ing·ness** *n.*

un·luck·y /únlúkee/ *adj.* (**un·luck·i·er, un·luck·i·est**) **1** not fortunate or successful. **2** wretched. **3** bringing bad luck. **4** ill-judged. □□ **un·luck·i·ly** *adv.* **un·luck·i·ness** *n.*

un·made /únmáyd/ *adj.* **1** not made. **2** destroyed; annulled.

un·make /únmáyk/ *v.tr.* (*past* and *past part.* **un·made**) undo the making of; destroy; depose; annul.

un·mal·le·a·ble /únmáleeəbəl/ *adj.* not malleable.

un·man /únmán/ *v.tr.* (**un·manned, un·man·ning**) **1** deprive of supposed manly qualities (e.g., self-control, courage); cause to weep, etc.; discourage. **2** deprive (a ship, etc.) of men.

un·man·age·a·ble /únmánijəbəl/ *adj.* not (easily) managed, manipulated, or controlled. □□ **un·man·age·a·ble·ness** *n.* **un·man·age·a·bly** *adv.*

un·man·ly /únmánlee/ *adj.* not manly. □□ **un·man·li·ness** *n.*

un·manned /únmánd/ *adj.* **1** not manned. **2** esp. *Brit.* overcome by emotion, etc.

un·man·ner·ly /únmánərlee/ *adj.* **1** without good manners. **2** (of actions, speech, etc.) showing a lack of good manners. □□ **un·man·ner·li·ness** *n.*

un·marked /únmaárkt/ *adj.* **1** not marked. **2** not noticed.

un·mar·ket·a·ble /únmaárkitəbəl/ *adj.* not marketable.

un·mar·ried /únmáreed/ *adj.* not married; single.

un·mask /únmásk/ *v.* **1** *tr.* **a** remove the mask from. **b** expose the true character of. **2** *intr.* remove one's mask. □□ **un·mask·er** *n.*

un·match·a·ble /únmáchəbəl/ *adj.* that cannot be matched. □□ **un·match·a·bly** *adv.*

un·matched /únmácht/ *adj.* not matched or equaled.

un·ma·tured /únmətyoórd, –toórd, –choórd/ *adj.* not yet matured.

un·mean·ing /únmeéning/ *adj.* having no meaning or significance; meaningless. □□ **un·mean·ing·ly** *adv.* **un·mean·ing·ness** *n.*

un·meant /únmént/ *adj.* not meant or intended.

un·meas·ur·a·ble /únmézhərəbəl/ *adj.* that cannot be measured. □□ **un·meas·ur·a·bly** *adv.*

un·meas·ured /únmézhərd/ *adj.* **1** not measured. **2** limitless.

un·me·lo·di·ous /únmilódeeəs/ *adj.* not melodious; discordant. □□ **un·me·lo·di·ous·ly** *adv.*

un·melt·ed /únméltid/ *adj.* not melted.

un·mem·o·ra·ble /únmémərəbəl/ *adj.* not memorable. □□ **un·mem·o·ra·bly** *adv.*

un·men·tion·a·ble /únménshənəbəl/ *adj. & n.* ● *adj.* that cannot (properly) be mentioned. ● *n.* **1** (in *pl.*) *joc.* **a** undergarments. **b** *archaic* trousers. **2** a person or thing not to be mentioned. □□ **un·men·tion·a·bil·i·ty** /–bílitee/ *n.* **un·men·tion·a·ble·ness** *n.* **un·men·tion·a·bly** *adv.*

un·men·tioned /únménshənd/ *adj.* not mentioned.

un·mer·chant·a·ble /únmérchəntəbəl/ *adj.* not merchantable.

un·mer·ci·ful /únmérsifool/ *adj.* merciless. □□ **un·mer·ci·ful·ly** *adv.* **un·mer·ci·ful·ness** *n.*

un·mer·it·ed /únméritid/ *adj.* not merited.

un·met /únmét/ *adj.* (of a quota, demand, goal, etc.) not achieved or fulfilled.

un·met·aled /únmét'ld/ *adj. Brit.* (of a road, etc.) not made with road metal.

un·me·thod·i·cal /únmithódikəl/ *adj.* not methodical. □□ **un·me·thod·i·cal·ly** *adv.*

un·met·ri·cal /únmétrikəl/ *adj.* not metrical.

un·mil·i·tar·y /únmíliteree/ *adj.* not military.

un·mind·ful /únmíndfool/ *adj.* (often foll. by *of*) not mindful. □□ **un·mind·ful·ly** *adv.* **un·mind·ful·ness** *n.*

un·miss·a·ble /únmísəbəl/ *adj.* that cannot or should not be missed.

un·mis·tak·a·ble /únmistáykəbəl/ *adj.* that cannot be mistaken or doubted; clear. □□ **un·mis·tak·a·bil·i·ty** /–bílitee/ *n.* **un·mis·tak·a·ble·ness** *n.* **un·mis·tak·a·bly** *adv.*

un·mis·tak·en /únmistáykən/ *adj.* not mistaken; right; correct.

un·mit·i·gat·ed /únmítigaytid/ *adj.* **1** not mitigated or modified. **2** absolute; unqualified (*an unmitigated disaster*). □□ **un·mit·i·gat·ed·ly** *adv.*

un·mixed /únmíkst/ *adj.* not mixed.

un·mixed bless·ing *n.* a thing having advantages and no disadvantages.

un·mod·i·fied /únmódifīd/ *adj.* not modified.

un·mod·u·lat·ed /únmójələytid/ *adj.* not modulated.

un·mo·lest·ed /únməléstid/ *adj.* not molested.

un·moor /únmoőr/ *v.tr.* **1** (also *absol.*) release the moorings of (a vessel). **2** weigh all but one anchor of (a vessel).

un·mor·al /únmáwrəl, –mór–/ *adj.* not concerned with morality (cf. IMMORAL). □□ **un·mor·al·i·ty** /–rálitee/ *n.* **un·mor·al·ly** *adv.*

un·moth·er·ly /únmúthərlee/ *adj.* not motherly.

un·mo·ti·vat·ed /únmótivaytid/ *adj.* without motivation; without a motive.

un·mount·ed /únmówntid/ *adj.* not mounted.

un·mourned /únmáwrnd/ *adj.* not mourned.

un·moved /únmoővd/ *adj.* **1** not moved. **2** not changed in one's purpose. **3** not affected by emotion. □□ **un·mov·a·ble** *adj.* (also **un·move·a·ble**).

un·mown /únmón/ *adj.* not mown.

un·muf·fle /únmúfəl/ *v.tr.* **1** remove a muffler from (a face, bell, etc.). **2** free of something that muffles or conceals.

un·mur·mur·ing /únmúrməring/ *adj.* not complaining. □□ **un·mur·mur·ing·ly** *adv.*

un·mu·si·cal /únmyoőzikəl/ *adj.* **1** not pleasing to the ear. **2** unskilled in or indifferent to music. □□ **un·mu·si·cal·i·ty** /–kálitee/ *n.* **un·mu·si·cal·ly** *adv.* **un·mu·si·cal·ness** *n.*

un·mu·ti·la·ted /únmyoőt'laytid/ *adj.* not mutilated.

un·muz·zle /únmúzəl/ *v.tr.* **1** remove a muzzle from. **2** relieve of an obligation to remain silent.

un·nail /ún-náyl/ *v.tr.* unfasten by the removal of nails.

un·name·a·ble /ún-náyməbəl/ *adj.* that cannot be named, esp. too bad to be named.

un·named /ún-náymd/ *adj.* not named.

un·nat·u·ral /ún-náchərəl/ *adj.* **1** contrary to nature or the usual course of nature; not normal. **2 a** lacking natural feelings. **b** extremely cruel or wicked. **3** artificial. **4** affected. □□ **un·nat·u·ral·ly** *adv.* **un·nat·u·ral·ness** *n.*

un·nav·i·ga·ble /ún-návigəbəl/ *adj.* not navigable. □□ **un·nav·i·ga·bil·i·ty** /–bílitee/ *n.*

un·nec·es·sar·y /ún-nésəseree/ *adj. & n.* ● *adj.* **1** not necessary. **2** more than is necessary (*with unnecessary care*). ● *n.* (*pl.* –**ies**) (usu. in *pl.*) an unnecessary thing. □□ **un·nec·es·sar·i·ly** *adv.* **un·nec·es·sar·i·ness** *n.*

un·need·ed /ún-neédid/ *adj.* not needed.

un·neigh·bor·ly /ún-náybərlee/ *adj.* not neighborly. □□ **un·neigh·bor·li·ness** *n.*

un·nerve /ún-nórv/ *v.tr.* deprive of strength or resolution. □□ **un·nerv·ing·ly** *adv.*

un·no·tice·a·ble /ún-nótisəbəl/ *adj.* not easily seen or noticed. □□ **un·no·tice·a·bly** *adv.*

un·no·ticed /ún-nótist/ *adj.* not noticed.

un·num·bered /ún-númbərd/ *adj.* **1** not marked with a number. **2** not counted. **3** countless.

un·ob·jec·tion·a·ble /únəbjékshənəbəl/ *adj.* not objectionable; acceptable. □□ **un·ob·jec·tion·a·ble·ness** *n.* **un·ob·jec·tion·a·bly** *adv.*

un·o·blig·ing /únəblíjing/ *adj.* not obliging; unhelpful; uncooperative.

un·ob·scured /únəbskyoőrd/ *adj.* not obscured.

un·ob·serv·a·ble /únəbzórvəbəl/ *adj.* not observable; imperceptible.

un·ob·serv·ant /únəbzórvənt/ *adj.* not observant. □□ **un·ob·serv·ant·ly** *adv.*

un·ob·served /únəbzórvd/ *adj.* not observed. □□ **un·ob·serv·ed·ly** /–vidlee/ *adv.*

un·ob·struct·ed /únəbstrúktid/ *adj.* not obstructed.

un·ob·tain·a·ble /únəbtáynəbəl/ *adj.* that cannot be obtained.

un·ob·tru·sive /únəbtroősiv/ *adj.* not making oneself or itself noticed. □□ **un·ob·tru·sive·ly** *adv.* **un·ob·tru·sive·ness** *n.*

un·oc·cu·pied /únókyəpīd/ *adj.* not occupied.

un·of·fend·ing /únəfénding/ *adj.* not offending; harmless; innocent. □□ **un·of·fend·ed** *adj.*

un·of·fi·cial /únəfíshəl/ *adj.* **1** not officially authorized or confirmed. **2** not characteristic of officials. □□ **un·of·fi·cial·ly** *adv.*

un·oiled /únóyld/ *adj.* not oiled.

un·o·pened /únópənd/ *adj.* not opened.

un·op·posed /únəpózd/ *adj.* not opposed, esp. in an election.

un·or·dained /únawrdáynd/ *adj.* not ordained.

un·or·di·nar·y /únáwrd'neree/ *adj.* not ordinary.

un·or·gan·ized /únáwrgənīzd/ *adj.* not organized (cf. DISORGANIZE).

un·o·rig·i·nal /únəríjinəl/ *adj.* lacking originality; derivative. □□ **un·o·rig·i·nal·i·ty** /–nálitee/ *n.* **un·o·rig·i·nal·ly** *adv.*

un·or·na·men·tal /únawrnəmént'l/ *adj.* not ornamental; plain.

un·or·na·ment·ed /únáwrnəmentid/ *adj.* not ornamented.

un·or·tho·dox /únáwrthədoks/ *adj.* not orthodox. □□ **un·or·tho·dox·ly** *adv.* **un·or·tho·dox·y** *n.*

un·os·ten·ta·tious /únostentáyshəs/ *adj.* not ostentatious. □□ **un·os·ten·ta·tious·ly** *adv.* **un·os·ten·ta·tious·ness** *n.*

un·owned /únónd/ *adj.* **1** unacknowledged. **2** having no owner.

un·pack /únpák/ *v.tr.* **1** (also *absol.*) open and remove the contents of (a package, luggage, etc.). **2** take (a thing) out from a package, etc. □□ **un·pack·er** *n.*

un·paged /únpáyjd/ *adj.* with pages not numbered.

un·paid /únpáyd/ *adj.* (of a debt or a person) not paid.

un·paint·ed /únpáyntid/ *adj.* not painted.

un·paired /únpáird/ *adj.* **1** not arranged in pairs. **2** not forming one of a pair.

un·pal·at·a·ble /únpálətəbəl/ *adj.* **1** not pleasant to taste. **2** (of an idea, suggestion, etc.) disagreeable; distasteful. □□ **un·pal·at·a·bil·i·ty** *n.* **un·pal·at·a·ble·ness** *n.*

un·par·al·leled /únpárəleld/ *adj.* having no parallel or equal.

SPELLING TIP **unparalleled**

See note at PARALLEL.

un·par·don·a·ble /únpaárd'nəbəl/ *adj.* that cannot be pardoned. □□ **un·par·don·a·ble·ness** *n.* **un·par·don·a·bly** *adv.*

un·par·lia·men·ta·ry /únpaarləméntəree/ *adj.* contrary to proper parliamentary usage.

un·par·lia·men·ta·ry lan·guage *n.* oaths or abuse.

un·pas·teur·ized /únpáschərizd, –pástə–/ *adj.* not pasteurized.

un·pat·ent·ed /únpát'ntid/ *adj.* not patented.

un·pa·tri·ot·ic /únpaytreeótik/ *adj.* not patriotic. □□ **un·pa·tri·ot·i·cal·ly** *adv.*

un·paved /únpáyvd/ *adj.* not paved.

un·peeled /únpeéld/ *adj.* not peeled.

un·peg /únpég/ *v.tr.* (**un·pegged**, **un·peg·ging**) **1** unfasten by the removal of pegs. **2** cease to maintain or stabilize (prices, etc.).

un·peo·ple *v. & n.* ● *v.tr.* /únpeépəl/ depopulate. ● *n.pl.* /únpeepəl/ unpersons.

un·per·ceived /únpərseévd/ *adj.* not perceived; unobserved.

un·per·cep·tive /únpərséptiv/ *adj.* not perceptive. □□ **un·per·cep·tive·ly** *adv.* **un·per·cep·tive·ness** *n.*

un·per·fect·ed /únpərféktid/ *adj.* not perfected.

un·per·fo·rat·ed /únpərfərraytid/ *adj.* not perforated.

un·per·formed /únpərfáwrmd/ *adj.* not performed.

un·per·fumed /únpərfyōōmd/ *adj.* not perfumed.

un·per·son /únpərsən/ *n.* a person whose name or existence is denied or ignored.

un·per·suad·a·ble /únpərswáydəbəl/ *adj.* not able to be persuaded; obstinate.

un·per·suad·ed /únpərswáydid/ *adj.* not persuaded.

un·per·sua·sive /únpərswáysiv, –ziv/ *adj.* not persuasive. □□ **un·per·sua·sive·ly** *adv.*

un·per·turbed /únpərtúrbd/ *adj.* not perturbed. □□ **un·per·turbed·ly** /–bidlee/ *adv.*

un·phil·o·soph·i·cal /únfiləsófikəl/ *adj.* (also **un·phil·o·soph·ic**) **1** not according to philosophical principles. **2** lacking philosophy. □□ **un·phil·o·soph·i·cal·ly** *adv.*

un·phys·i·o·log·i·cal /únfizeeəlójikəl/ *adj.* (also **un·phys·i·o·log·ic**) not in accordance with normal physiological functioning. □□ **un·phys·i·o·log·i·cal·ly** *adv.*

un·pick /únpík/ *v.tr.* undo the sewing of (stitches, a garment, etc.).

un·picked /únpíkt/ *adj.* **1** not selected. **2** (of a flower) not plucked.

un·pic·tur·esque /únpikchərésk/ *adj.* not picturesque.

un·pin /únpín/ *v.tr.* (**un·pinned, un·pin·ning**) **1** unfasten or detach by removing a pin or pins. **2** *Chess* release (a piece that has been pinned).

un·pit·ied /únpíteed/ *adj.* not pitied.

un·pit·y·ing /únpíteeing/ *adj.* not pitying. □□ **un·pit·y·ing·ly** *adv.*

un·place·a·ble /únpláysəbəl/ *adj.* that cannot be placed or classified (*his accent was unplaceable*).

un·placed /únpláyst/ *adj.* not placed, esp. not placed as one of the first three finishing in a race, etc.

un·planned /únplánd/ *adj.* not planned.

un·plant·ed /únplántid/ *adj.* not planted.

un·plau·si·ble /únpláwzibəl/ *adj.* not plausible.

un·play·a·ble /únpláyəbəl/ *adj.* **1** *Sports* (of a ball) that cannot be struck or returned. **2** that cannot be played. □□ **un·play·a·bly** *adv.*

un·pleas·ant /únplézənt/ *adj.* not pleasant; displeasing; disagreeable. □□ **un·pleas·ant·ly** *adv.* **un·pleas·ant·ness** *n.*

un·pleas·ing /únpleézing/ *adj.* not pleasing. □□ **un·pleas·ing·ly** *adv.*

un·plowed /únplówd/ *adj.* not plowed.

un·plucked /únplúkt/ *adj.* not plucked.

un·plug /únplúg/ *v.tr.* (**un·plugged, un·plug·ging**) **1** disconnect (an electrical device) by removing its plug from the socket. **2** unstop.

un·plumbed /únplúmd/ *adj.* **1** not plumbed. **2** not fully explored or understood. □□ **un·plumb·a·ble** *adj.*

un·po·et·ic /únpō-étik/ *adj.* (also **un·po·et·i·cal**) not poetic.

un·point·ed /únpóyntid/ *adj.* **1** having no point or points. **2 a** not punctuated. **b** (of written Hebrew, etc.) without vowel points. **3** (of masonry or brickwork) not pointed.

un·pol·ished /únpólisht/ *adj.* **1** not polished; rough. **2** without refinement; crude.

un·po·lit·ic /únpólitik/ *adj.* impolitic; unwise.

un·po·lit·i·cal /únpəlítikəl/ *adj.* not concerned with politics. □□ **un·po·lit·i·cal·ly** *adv.*

un·polled /únpóld/ *adj.* **1** not having voted at an election. **2** not included in an opinion poll.

un·pol·lut·ed /únpəlốotid/ *adj.* not polluted.

un·pop·u·lar /únpópyələr/ *adj.* not popular; not liked by the public or by people in general. □□ **un·pop·u·lar·i·ty** /–láritee/ *n.* **un·pop·u·lar·ly** *adv.*

un·pop·u·lat·ed /únpópyəlaytid/ *adj.* not populated.

un·pos·sessed /únpəzést/ *adj.* **1** (foll. by *of*) not in possession of. **2** not possessed.

un·prac·ti·cal /únpráktikəl/ *adj.* **1** not practical. **2** (of a person) not having practical skill. □□ **un·prac·ti·cal·i·ty** /–kálitee/ *n.* **un·prac·ti·cal·ly** *adv.*

un·prac·ticed /únpráktist/ *adj.* **1** not experienced or skilled. **2** not put into practice.

un·prec·e·dent·ed /únprésidentid/ *adj.* **1** having no precedent; unparalleled. **2** novel. □□ **un·prec·e·dent·ed·ly** *adv.*

un·pre·dict·a·ble /únpridíktəbəl/ *adj.* that cannot be predicted. □□ **un·pre·dict·a·bil·i·ty** *n.* **un·pre·dict·a·ble·ness** *n.* **un·pre·dict·a·bly** *adv.*

un·pre·dict·ed /únpridíktid/ *adj.* not predicted or foretold.

un·prej·u·diced /únpréjədist/ *adj.* not prejudiced.

un·pre·med·i·tat·ed /únpriméditaytid/ *adj.* not previously thought over; not deliberately planned; unintentional. □□ **un·pre·med·i·tat·ed·ly** *adv.*

un·pre·pared /únpripáird/ *adj.* not prepared (in advance); not ready. □□ **un·pre·par·ed·ly** *adv.* **un·pre·par·ed·ness** *n.*

un·pre·pos·ses·sing /únpreepəzésing/ *adj.* not prepossessing; unattractive.

un·pre·scribed /únpriskríbd/ *adj.* (esp. of drugs) not prescribed.

un·pre·sent·a·ble /únprizéntəbəl/ *adj.* not presentable.

un·pressed /únprést/ *adj.* not pressed, esp. (of clothing) unironed.

un·pre·sum·ing /únprizooming/ *adj.* not presuming; modest.

un·pre·sump·tu·ous /únprizúmpchooəs/ *adj.* not presumptuous.

un·pre·tend·ing /únpriténding/ *adj.* unpretentious. □□ **un·pre·tend·ing·ly** *adv.* **un·pre·tend·ing·ness** *n.*

un·pre·ten·tious /únpriténshəs/ *adj.* not making a great display; simple; modest. □□ **un·pre·ten·tious·ly** *adv.* **un·pre·ten·tious·ness** *n.*

un·priced /únpríst/ *adj.* not having a price or prices fixed, marked, or stated.

un·primed /únprímd/ *adj.* not primed.

un·prin·ci·pled /únprínsipəld/ *adj.* lacking or not based on good moral principles. □□ **un·prin·ci·pled·ness** *n.*

un·print·a·ble /únpríntəbəl/ *adj.* that cannot be printed, esp. because too indecent or libelous or blasphemous. □□ **un·print·a·bly** *adv.*

un·print·ed /únpríntid/ *adj.* not printed.

un·priv·i·leged /únprívilijd, –prívlijd/ *adj.* not privileged.

un·prob·lem·at·ic /únprobləmátik/ *adj.* causing no difficulty. □□ **un·prob·lem·at·i·cal·ly** *adv.*

un·pro·claimed /únprōkláymd, –prə–/ *adj.* not proclaimed.

un·pro·cur·a·ble /únprōkyŏŏrəbəl, –prə–/ *adj.* that cannot be procured.

un·pro·duc·tive /únprədúktiv/ *adj.* not productive. □□ **un·pro·duc·tive·ly** *adv.* **un·pro·duc·tive·ness** *n.*

un·pro·fes·sion·al /únprəféshənəl/ *adj.* **1** contrary to professional standards of behavior, etc. **2** not belonging to a profession; amateur. □□ **un·pro·fes·sion·al·ly** *adv.*

un·prof·it·a·ble /únprófitəbəl/ *adj.* not profitable. □□ **un·prof·it·a·ble·ness** *n.* **un·prof·it·a·bly** *adv.*

un·pro·gres·sive /únprəgrésiv/ *adj.* not progressive.

un·prom·is·ing /únprómising/ *adj.* not likely to turn out well. □□ **un·prom·is·ing·ly** *adv.*

un·prompt·ed /únprómptid/ *adj.* spontaneous.

un·pro·nounce·a·ble /únprənównsəbəl/ *adj.* that cannot be pronounced. □□ **un·pro·nounce·a·bly** *adv.*

un·pro·pi·tious /únprəpíshəs/ *adj.* not propitious. □□ **un·pro·pi·tious·ly** *adv.*

un·pros·per·ous /únpróspərəs/ *adj.* not prosperous. □□ **un·pros·per·ous·ly** *adv.*

un·pro·tect·ed /únprətéktid/ *adj.* not protected. □□ **un·pro·tect·ed·ness** *n.*

un·pro·test·ing /únprətésting/ *adj.* not protesting. □□ **un·pro·test·ing·ly** *adv.*

un·prov·a·ble /únprōōvəbəl/ *adj.* that cannot be proved. □□ **un·prov·a·bil·i·ty** *n.* **un·prov·a·ble·ness** *n.*

un·proved /únprōōvd/ *adj.* (also **un·prov·en** /–vən/) not proved.

un·pro·vid·ed /únprəvídid/ *adj.* (usu. foll. by *with*) not furnished, supplied, or equipped.

un·pro·voked /únprəvōkt/ *adj.* (of a person or act) without provocation.

un·pub·lished /únpúblisht/ *adj.* not published. □□ **un·pub·lish·a·ble** *adj.*

un·punc·tu·al /únpúngkchooəl/ *adj.* not punctual. □□ **un·punc·tu·al·i·ty** /–chōōálitee/ *n.*

un·punc·tu·at·ed /únpúngkchooaytid/ *adj.* not punctuated.

un·pun·ish·a·ble /únpúnishəbəl/ *adj.* that cannot be punished.

un·pun·ished /únpúnisht/ *adj.* not punished.

un·pu·ri·fied /únpyŏŏrifid/ *adj.* not purified.

un·put·down·a·ble /únpootdównəbəl/ *adj. colloq.* (of a book) so engrossing that one has to go on reading it.

un·qual·i·fied /únkwólifid/ *adj.* **1** not competent (*unqualified to give an answer*). **2** not legally or officially qualified (*an unqualified practitioner*). **3** not modified or restricted; complete (*unqualified assent; unqualified success*).

un·quench·a·ble /únkwénchəbəl/ *adj.* that cannot be quenched. □□ **un·quench·a·bly** *adv.*

un·quenched /únkwéncht/ *adj.* not quenched.

un·ques·tion·a·ble /únkwéschənəbəl/ *adj.* that cannot be disputed or doubted. □□ **un·ques·tion·a·bil·i·ty** *n.* **un·ques·tion·a·ble·ness** *n.* **un·ques·tion·a·bly** *adv.*

un·ques·tioned /únkwéschənd/ *adj.* **1** not disputed or doubted; definite; certain. **2** not interrogated.

un·ques·tion·ing /únkwéschəning/ *adj.* **1** asking no questions. **2** done, etc., without asking questions. □□ **un·ques·tion·ing·ly** *adv.*

un·qui·et /únkwíət/ *adj.* **1** restless; agitated; stirring. **2** perturbed, anxious. □□ **un·qui·et·ly** *adv.* **un·qui·et·ness** *n.*

un·quot·a·ble /únkwót/ *adj.* that cannot be quoted.

un·quote /únkwót/ *v.tr.* (as *int.*) (in dictation, reading aloud, etc.) indicate the presence of closing quotation marks (cf. QUOTE *v.* 5 b).

un·quot·ed /únkwótid/ *adj.* not quoted, esp. on a stock exchange.

un·rav·el /únrávəl/ *v.* **1** *tr.* cause to be no longer raveled, tangled, or intertwined. **2** *tr.* probe and solve (a mystery, etc.). **3** *tr.* undo (a fabric, esp. a knitted one). **4** *intr.* become disentangled or unknitted.

un·reach·a·ble /únreéchəbəl/ *adj.* that cannot be reached. □□ **un·reach·a·ble·ness** *n.* **un·reach·a·bly** *adv.*

un·read /únréd/ *adj.* **1** (of a book, etc.) not read. **2** (of a person) not well-read.

un·read·a·ble /únreédəbəl/ *adj.* **1** too dull or too difficult to be worth reading. **2** illegible. □□ **un·read·a·bil·i·ty** /–bílitee/ *n.* **un·read·a·bly** *adv.*

un·read·y[1] /únrédee/ *adj.* **1** not ready. **2** not prompt in action. □□ **un·read·i·ly** *adv.* **un·read·i·ness** *n.*

un·read·y[2] /únrédee/ *adj. archaic* lacking good advice; rash (*Ethelred the Unready*). [UN-[1] + REDE, assim. to UNREADY[1]]

un·re·al /únreéəl/ *adj.* **1** not real. **2** imaginary; illusory. **3** *sl.* incredible, amazing. □□ **un·re·al·i·ty** /–reeálitee/ *n.* **un·re·al·ly** *adv.*

un·re·al·is·tic /únreeəlístik/ *adj.* not realistic. □□ **un·re·al·is·ti·cal·ly** *adv.*

un·re·al·iz·a·ble /unreéəlízəbəl/ *adj.* that cannot be realized.

un·re·al·ized /únreéəlizd/ *adj.* not realized.

un·rea·son /únreézən/ *n.* lack of reasonable thought or action. [ME, = injustice, f. UN-[1] + REASON]

un·rea·son·a·ble /únreézənəbəl/ *adj.* **1** going beyond the limits of what is reasonable or equitable (*unreasonable demands*). **2** not guided by or listening to reason. □□ **un·rea·son·a·ble·ness** *n.* **un·rea·son·a·bly** *adv.*

un·rea·soned /únreézənd/ *adj.* not reasoned.

un·rea·son·ing /únreézəning/ *adj.* not reasoning. □□ **un·rea·son·ing·ly** *adv.*

un·re·cep·tive /únriséptiv/ *adj.* not receptive.

un·re·cip·ro·cat·ed /únrisíprəkaytid/ *adj.* not reciprocated.

un·reck·oned /únrékənd/ *adj.* not calculated or taken into account.

un·re·claimed /únrikláymd/ *adj.* not reclaimed.

un·rec·og·niz·a·ble /unrékəgnízəbəl/ *adj.* that cannot be recognized. □□ **un·rec·og·niz·a·ble·ness** *n.* **un·rec·og·niz·a·bly** *adv.*

un·rec·og·nized /únrékəgnízd/ *adj.* not recognized.

un·rec·om·pensed /únrékəmpenst/ *adj.* not recompensed.

un·rec·on·ciled /únrékənsild/ *adj.* not reconciled.

un·re·con·struct·ed /únreekənstr úktid/ *adj.* **1** not reconciled or converted to the current political orthodoxy. **2** not rebuilt.

un·re·cord·ed /únrikáwrdid/ *adj.* not recorded. □□ **un·re·cord·a·ble** *adj.*

un·rec·ti·fied /únréktifid/ *adj.* not rectified.

un·re·deem·a·ble /únrideéməbəl/ *adj.* that cannot be redeemed. □□ **un·re·deem·a·bly** *adv.*

un·re·deemed /únrideémd/ *adj.* not redeemed.

un·re·dressed /únridrést/ *adj.* not redressed.

un·reel /únreél/ *v.tr. & intr.* unwind from a reel.

un·reeve /únreév/ *v.tr.* (*past* **un·rove**) withdraw (a rope, etc.) from being reeved.

un·re·fined /únrifínd/ *adj.* not refined.

un·re·flect·ing /únriflékting/ *adj.* not thoughtful. □□ **un·re·flect·ing·ly** *adv.* **un·re·flect·ing·ness** *n.*

un·re·formed /únrifáwrmd/ *adj.* not reformed.

un·re·gard·ed /únrigaárdid/ *adj.* not regarded.

un·re·gen·er·ate /únrijénərət/ *adj.* not regenerate; obstinately wrong or bad. □□ **un·re·gen·er·a·cy** *n.* **un·re·gen·er·ate·ly** *adv.*

un·reg·is·tered /únréjistərd/ *adj.* not registered.

un·reg·u·lat·ed /únrégyəlaytid/ *adj.* not regulated.

un·re·hearsed /únrihə́rst/ *adj.* not rehearsed.

un·re·lat·ed /únriláytid/ *adj.* not related. □□ **un·re·lat·ed·ness** *n.*

un·re·laxed /únrilákst/ *adj.* not relaxed.

un·re·lent·ing /únrilénting/ *adj.* **1** not relenting or yielding. **2** unmerciful. **3** not abating or relaxing. □□ **un·re·lent·ing·ly** *adv.* **un·re·lent·ing·ness** *n.*

un·re·li·a·ble /únrilíəbəl/ *adj.* not reliable; erratic. □□ **un·re·li·a·bil·i·ty** *n.* **un·re·li·a·ble·ness** *n.* **un·re·li·a·bly** *adv.*

un·re·lieved /únrileévd/ *adj.* **1** lacking the relief given by contrast or variation. **2** not aided or assisted. □□ **un·re·liev·ed·ly** /–vidlee/ *adv.*

un·re·li·gious /únrilíjəs/ *adj.* **1** not concerned with religion. **2** irreligious.

un·re·mark·a·ble /únrimaárkəbəl/ *adj.* not remarkable; uninteresting. □□ **un·re·mark·a·bly** *adv.*

un·re·mem·bered /únrimémbərd/ *adj.* not remembered; forgotten.

un·re·mit·ting /únrimíting/ *adj.* never relaxing or slackening; incessant. □□ **un·re·mit·ting·ly** *adv.* **un·re·mit·ting·ness** *n.*

un·re·morse·ful /únrimáwrsfŏŏl/ *adj.* lacking remorse. □□ **un·re·morse·ful·ly** *adv.*

un·re·mov·a·ble /únrimŏŏvəbəl/ *adj.* that cannot be removed.

un·re·mu·ner·a·tive /únrimyŏŏnərətiv, –raytiv/ *adj.* bringing no, or not enough, profit or income. □□ **un·re·mu·ner·a·tive·ly** *adv.* **un·re·mu·ner·a·tive·ness** *n.*

un·re·new·a·ble /únrinŏŏəbəl, –nyŏŏ–/ *adj.* that cannot be renewed. □□ **un·re·newed** *adj.*

un·re·pealed /únripeéld/ *adj.* not repealed.

un·re·peat·a·ble /únripeétəbəl/ *adj.* **1** that cannot be done, made,

or said again. **2** too indecent to be said again. □□ **un·re·peat·a·bil·i·ty** *n.*

un·re·pent·ant /únripéntənt/ *adj.* not repentant; impenitent. □□ **un·re·pent·ant·ly** *adv.*

un·re·port·ed /únripáwrtid/ *adj.* not reported.

un·rep·re·sent·a·tive /únreprizéntətiv/ *adj.* not representative. □□ **un·rep·re·sent·a·tive·ness** *n.*

un·rep·re·sent·ed /únreprizéntid/ *adj.* not represented.

un·re·proved /únripróövd/ *adj.* not reproved.

un·re·quest·ed /únrikwéstid/ *adj.* not requested or asked for.

un·re·quit·ed /únrikwítid/ *adj.* (of love, etc.) not returned. □□ **un·re·quit·ed·ly** *adv.* **un·re·quit·ed·ness** *n.*

un·re·serve /únrizórv/ *n.* lack of reserve; frankness.

un·re·served /únrizórvd/ *adj.* **1** not reserved (*unreserved seats*). **2** without reservations; absolute (*unreserved confidence*). **3** free from reserve (*an unreserved nature*). □□ **un·re·serv·ed·ly** /–vidlee/ *adv.* **un·re·serv·ed·ness** *n.*

un·re·sist·ed /únrizístid/ *adj.* not resisted. □□ **un·re·sist·ed·ly** *adv.*

un·re·sist·ing /únrizísting/ *adj.* not resisting. □□ **un·re·sist·ing·ly** *adv.* **un·re·sist·ing·ness** *n.*

un·re·solv·a·ble /únrizólvəbəl/ *adj.* (of a problem, conflict, etc.) that cannot be resolved.

un·re·solved /únrizólvd/ *adj.* **1 a** uncertain how to act; irresolute. **b** uncertain in opinion; undecided. **2** (of questions, etc.) undetermined; undecided; unsolved. **3** not broken up or dissolved. □□ **un·re·sol·ved·ly** /–vidlee/ *adv.* **un·re·sol·ved·ness** *n.*

un·re·spon·sive /únrispónsiv/ *adj.* not responsive. □□ **un·re·spon·sive·ly** *adv.* **un·re·spon·sive·ness** *n.*

un·rest /únrést/ *n.* **1** lack of rest. **2** restlessness; disturbance; agitation.

un·rest·ed /únréstid/ *adj.* not refreshed by rest.

un·rest·ful /únréstfŏŏl/ *adj.* not restful. □□ **un·rest·ful·ly** *adv.*

un·rest·ing /únrésting/ *adj.* not resting. □□ **un·rest·ing·ly** *adv.*

un·re·stored /únristáwrd/ *adj.* not restored.

un·re·strain·a·ble /únristráynəbəl/ *adj.* that cannot be restrained; irrepressible; ungovernable.

un·re·strained /únristráynd/ *adj.* not restrained. □□ **un·re·strain·ed·ly** /–nidlee/ *adv.* **un·re·strain·ed·ness** *n.*

un·re·straint /únristráynt/ *n.* lack of restraint.

un·re·strict·ed /únristríktid/ *adj.* not restricted. □□ **un·re·strict·ed·ly** *adv.* **un·re·strict·ed·ness** *n.*

un·re·turned /únritórnd/ *adj.* **1** not reciprocated or responded to. **2** not having returned or been returned.

un·re·vealed /únriveéld/ *adj.* not revealed; secret.

un·re·versed /únrivórst/ *adj.* (esp. of a decision, etc.) not reversed.

un·re·vised /únrivízd/ *adj.* not revised; in an original form.

un·re·voked /únrivókt/ *adj.* not revoked or annulled; still in force.

un·re·ward·ed /únriwáwrdid/ *adj.* not rewarded.

un·re·ward·ing /únriwáwrding/ *adj.* not rewarding or satisfying.

un·rhymed /únrímd/ *adj.* not rhymed.

un·rhyth·mi·cal /únríthmikəl/ *adj.* not rhythmical. □□ **un·rhyth·mi·cal·ly** *adv.*

un·rid·a·ble /únrídəbəl/ *adj.* that cannot be ridden.

un·rid·den /únríd'n/ *adj.* not ridden.

un·rid·dle /únríd'l/ *v.tr.* solve or explain (a mystery, etc.). □□ **un·rid·dler** *n.*

un·rig /únríg/ *v.tr.* (**un·rigged**, **un·rig·ging**) **1** remove the rigging from (a ship). **2** *dial.* undress.

un·right·eous /únríchəs/ *adj.* not righteous; unjust; wicked; dishonest. □□ **un·right·eous·ly** *adv.* **un·right·eous·ness** *n.* [OE *unrihtwīs* (as UN-[1], RIGHTEOUS)]

un·rip /únríp/ *v.tr.* (**un·ripped**, **un·rip·ping**) open by ripping.

un·ripe /únríp/ *adj.* not ripe. □□ **un·ripe·ness** *n.*

un·ris·en /únrízən/ *adj.* that has not risen.

un·ri·valed /únrívəld/ *adj.* having no equal; peerless.

un·riv·et /únrívit/ *v.tr.* **1** undo, unfasten, or detach by the removal of rivets. **2** loosen; relax; undo; detach.

un·robe /únrób/ *v.tr. & intr.* **1** disrobe. **2** undress.

un·roll /únról/ *v.tr. & intr.* **1** open out from a rolled-up state. **2** display or be displayed in this form.

un·ro·man·tic /únrəmántik/ *adj.* not romantic. □□ **un·ro·man·ti·cal·ly** *adv.*

un·roof /únrŏŏf, –rŏŏf/ *v.tr.* remove the roof of.

un·roofed /únrŏŏft, –rŏŏft/ *adj.* not provided with a roof.

un·root /únrŏŏt, –rŏŏt/ *v.tr.* **1** uproot. **2** eradicate.

un·rope /únróp/ *v.* **1** *tr.* detach by undoing a rope. **2** *intr. Mountaineering* detach oneself from a rope.

un·round·ed /únrówndid/ *adj.* not rounded.

un·rove *past* of UNREEVE.

un·ruf·fled /únrúfəld/ *adj.* **1** not agitated or disturbed; calm. **2** not physically ruffled.

un·ruled /únrōōld/ *adj.* **1** not ruled or governed. **2** not having ruled lines.

un·ru·ly /únrōōlee/ *adj.* (**un·ru·li·er, un·ru·li·est**) not easily controlled or disciplined; disorderly. □□ **un·ru·li·ness** *n.* [ME f. UN-¹ + *ruly* f. RULE]

UNRWA *abbr.* United Nations Relief and Works Agency.

un·sad·dle /únsád'l/ *v.tr.* **1** remove the saddle from (a horse, etc.). **2** dislodge from a saddle.

un·safe /únsáyf/ *adj.* not safe. □□ **un·safe·ly** *adv.* **un·safe·ness** *n.*

un·said¹ /únséd/ *adj.* not said or uttered.

un·said² *past* and *past part.* of UNSAY.

un·sal·a·ble /únsáyləbəl/ *adj.* (also **un·sale·a·ble**) not salable. □□ **un·sal·a·bil·i·ty** *n.*

un·sal·a·ried /únsáləreed/ *adj.* not salaried.

un·salt·ed /únsáwltid/ *adj.* not salted.

un·sanc·ti·fied /únsángktifīd/ *adj.* not sanctified.

un·sanc·tioned /únsángkshənd/ *adj.* not sanctioned.

un·san·i·tar·y /únsániteree/ *adj.* not sanitary.

un·sat·is·fac·to·ry /únsatisfáktəree/ *adj.* not satisfactory; poor; unacceptable. □□ **un·sat·is·fac·to·ri·ly** *adv.* **un·sat·is·fac·to·ri·ness** *n.*

un·sat·is·fied /únsátisfīd/ *adj.* not satisfied. □□ **un·sat·is·fied·ness** *n.*

un·sat·is·fy·ing /únsátisfī-ing/ *adj.* not satisfying. □□ **un·sat·is·fy·ing·ly** *adv.*

un·sat·u·rat·ed /únsáchəraytid/ *adj.* **1** *Chem.* (of a compound, esp. a fat or oil) having double or triple bonds in its molecule and therefore capable of further reaction. **2** not saturated. □□ **un·sat·u·ra·tion** /-ráyshən/ *n.*

un·saved /únsáyvd/ *adj.* not saved.

un·sa·vor·y /únsáyvəree/ *adj.* **1** disagreeable to the taste, smell, or feelings; disgusting. **2** disagreeable; unpleasant (*an unsavory character*). **3** morally offensive. □□ **un·sa·vor·i·ly** *adv.* **un·sa·vor·i·ness** *n.*

un·say /únsáy/ *v.tr.* (*past* and *past part.* **un·said**) retract (a statement).

un·say·a·ble /únsáyəbəl/ *adj.* that cannot be said.

un·scal·a·ble /únskáyləbəl/ *adj.* that cannot be scaled.

un·scarred /únskáard/ *adj.* not scarred or damaged.

un·scathed /únskáythd/ *adj.* without suffering any injury.

un·scent·ed /únséntid/ *adj.* not scented.

un·sched·uled /únskéjōōld/ *adj.* not scheduled.

un·schol·ar·ly /únskólərlee/ *adj.* not scholarly. □□ **un·schol·ar·li·ness** *n.*

un·schooled /únskōōld/ *adj.* **1** uneducated; untaught. **2** not sent to school. **3** untrained; undisciplined. **4** not made artificial by education.

un·sci·en·tif·ic /únsīəntífik/ *adj.* **1** not in accordance with scientific principles. **2** not familiar with science. □□ **un·sci·en·tif·i·cal·ly** *adv.*

un·scram·ble /únskrámbəl/ *v.tr.* restore from a scrambled state, esp. interpret (a scrambled transmission, etc.). □□ **un·scram·bler** *n.*

un·screened /únskreénd/ *adj.* **1 a** (esp. of coal) not passed through a screen or sieve. **b** not investigated or checked, esp. for security or medical problems. **2** not provided with a screen. **3** not shown on a screen.

un·screw /únskrōō/ *v.* **1** *tr.* & *intr.* unfasten or be unfastened by turning or removing a screw or screws or by twisting like a screw. **2** *tr.* loosen (a screw).

un·script·ed /únskríptid/ *adj.* (of a speech, etc.) delivered without a prepared script.

un·scrip·tur·al /únskrípchərəl/ *adj.* against or not in accordance with Scripture. □□ **un·scrip·tur·al·ly** *adv.*

un·scru·pu·lous /únskrōōpyələs/ *adj.* having no scruples; unprincipled. □□ **un·scru·pu·lous·ly** *adv.* **un·scru·pu·lous·ness** *n.*

un·seal /únseél/ *v.tr.* break the seal of; open (a letter, receptacle, etc.).

un·sealed /únseéld/ *adj.* not sealed.

un·search·a·ble /únsérchəbəl/ *adj.* inscrutable. □□ **un·search·a·ble·ness** *n.* **un·search·a·bly** *adv.*

un·searched /únsércht/ *adj.* not searched.

un·sea·son·a·ble /únseézənəbəl/ *adj.* **1** not appropriate to the season. **2** untimely; inopportune. □□ **un·sea·son·a·ble·ness** *n.* **un·sea·son·a·bly** *adv.*

un·sea·soned /únseézənd/ *adj.* **1** not flavored with salt, herbs, etc. **2** (esp. of timber) not matured. **3** not habituated.

un·seat /únseét/ *v.tr.* **1** remove from a seat, esp. in an election. **2** dislodge from a seat, esp. on horseback.

un·sea·wor·thy /únseéwúrthee/ *adj.* not seaworthy.

un·se·cured /únsikyóord/ *adj.* not secured.

un·see·a·ble /únseéəbəl/ *adj.* that cannot be seen.

un·seed·ed /únseédid/ *adj. Sports* (of a player) not seeded.

un·see·ing /únseé·ing/ *adj.* **1** unobservant. **2** blind. □□ **un·see·ing·ly** *adv.*

un·seem·ly /únseémlee/ *adj.* (**un·seem·li·er, un·seem·li·est**) **1** indecent. **2** unbecoming. □□ **un·seem·li·ness** *n.*

un·seen /únseén/ *adj.* & *n.* • *adj.* **1** not seen. **2** invisible. **3** esp. *Brit.* (of a translation) to be done without preparation. • *n. Brit.* an unseen translation.

un·seg·re·gat·ed /únségrigaytid/ *adj.* not segregated.

un·se·lect /únsilékt/ *adj.* not select.

un·se·lec·tive /únsiléktiv/ *adj.* not selective.

un·self-con·scious /únselfkónshəs/ *adj.* not self-conscious. □□ **un·self-con·scious·ly** *adv.* **un·self-con·scious·ness** *n.*

un·sel·fish /únsélfish/ *adj.* mindful of others' interests. □□ **un·sel·fish·ly** *adv.* **un·sel·fish·ness** *n.*

un·sen·sa·tion·al /únsensáyshənəl/ *adj.* not sensational. □□ **un·sen·sa·tion·al·ly** *adv.*

un·sen·ti·men·tal /únsentimént'l/ *adj.* not sentimental. □□ **un·sen·ti·men·tal·i·ty** /-tálitee/ *n.* **un·sen·ti·men·tal·ly** *adv.*

un·sep·a·rat·ed /únsépəraytid/ *adj.* not separated.

un·ser·vice·a·ble /únsérvisəbəl/ *adj.* not serviceable; unfit for use. □□ **un·ser·vice·a·bil·i·ty** *n.*

un·set·tle /únsét'l/ *v.* **1** *tr.* disturb the settled state or arrangement of; discompose. **2** *tr.* derange. **3** *intr.* become unsettled. □□ **un·set·tle·ment** *n.* **un·set·tling** *adv.*

un·set·tled /únsét'ld/ *adj.* **1** not (yet) settled. **2** liable or open to change or further discussion. **3** (of a bill, etc.) unpaid. □□ **un·set·tled·ness** *n.*

un·sewn /únsón/ *adj.* not sewn.

un·sewn bind·ing *n. Brit.* = *perfect binding.*

un·sex /únséks/ *v.tr.* deprive (a person, esp. a woman) of the qualities of her or his sex.

un·sexed /únsékst/ *adj.* having no sexual characteristics.

un·shack·le /únshákəl/ *v.tr.* **1** release from shackles. **2** set free.

un·shad·ed /únsháydid/ *adj.* not shaded.

un·shak·a·ble /únsháykəbəl/ *adj.* (also **un·shake·a·ble**) that cannot be shaken; firm; obstinate. □□ **un·shak·a·bil·i·ty** *n.* **un·shak·a·bly** *adv.*

un·shak·en /únsháykən/ *adj.* not shaken. □□ **un·shak·en·ly** *adv.*

un·shape·ly /únsháyplee/ *adj.* not shapely. □□ **un·shape·li·ness** *n.*

un·sharp /únsháarp/ *adj. Photog.* not sharp. □□ **un·sharp·ness** *n.*

un·shaved /únsháyvd/ *adj.* not shaved.

un·shav·en /únsháyvən/ *adj.* not shaved.

un·sheathe /únsheéth/ *v.tr.* remove (a knife, etc.) from a sheath.

un·shed /únshéd/ *adj.* not shed.

un·shell /únshél/ *v.tr.* (usu. as **unshelled** *adj.*) extract from its shell.

un·shel·tered /únshéltərd/ *adj.* not sheltered.

un·shield·ed /únsheéldid/ *adj.* not shielded or protected.

un·ship /únshíp/ *v.tr.* (**un·shipped, un·ship·ping**) **1** remove or discharge (a cargo or passenger) from a ship. **2** esp. *Naut.* remove (an object, esp. a mast or oar) from a fixed position.

un·shock·a·ble /únshókəbəl/ *adj.* that cannot be shocked. □□ **un·shock·a·bil·i·ty** /-bílitee/ *n.* **un·shock·a·bly** *adv.*

un·shod /únshód/ *adj.* not wearing shoes.

un·shorn /únsháwrn/ *adj.* not shorn.

un·shrink·a·ble /únshríngkəbəl/ *adj.* (of fabric, etc.) not liable to shrink. □□ **un·shrink·a·bil·i·ty** /-bílitee/ *n.*

un·shrink·ing /únshríngking/ *adj.* unhesitating; fearless. □□ **un·shrink·ing·ly** *adv.*

un·sight·ed /únsítid/ *adj.* **1** not sighted or seen. **2** prevented from seeing, esp. by an obstruction.

un·sight·ly /únsítlee/ *adj.* unpleasant to look at; ugly. □□ **un·sight·li·ness** *n.*

un·signed /únsínd/ *adj.* not signed.

un·sink·a·ble /únsíngkəbəl/ *adj.* unable to be sunk. □□ **un·sink·a·bil·i·ty** *n.*

un·sized¹ /únsízd/ *adj.* **1** not made to a size. **2** not sorted by size.

un·sized² /únsízd/ *adj.* not treated with size.

un·skill·ful /únskílfŏol/ *adj.* not skillful. □□ **un·skill·ful·ly** *adv.* **un·skill·ful·ness** *n.*

un·skilled /únskíld/ *adj.* lacking or not needing special skill or training.

un·skimmed /únskímd/ *adj.* (of milk) not skimmed.

un·slak·a·ble /únsláykəbəl/ *adj.* (also **un·slake·a·ble**) that cannot be slaked or quenched.

un·sleep·ing /únsleéping/ *adj.* not or never sleeping. □□ **un·sleep·ing·ly** *adv.*

un·sliced /únslíst/ *adj.* (esp. of a loaf of bread when it is bought) not having been cut into slices.

un·sling /únsling/ *v.tr.* (*past* and *past part.* **un·slung**) free from being slung or suspended.

un·smil·ing /únsmíling/ *adj.* not smiling. □□ **un·smil·ing·ly** *adv.* **un·smil·ing·ness** *n.*

un·smoked /únsmókt/ *adj.* **1** not cured by smoking (*unsmoked bacon*). **2** not consumed by smoking (*an unsmoked cigar*).

un·snarl /únsnáarl/ *v.tr.* disentangle. [UN-² + SNARL²]

un·so·cia·ble /únsóshəbəl/ *adj.* not sociable; disliking the company of others. □□ **un·so·cia·bil·i·ty** /-bílitee/ *n.* **un·so·cia·ble·ness** *n.* **un·so·cia·bly** *adv.*

un·so·cial /únsóshəl/ *adj.* **1** not social; not suitable for, seeking, or conforming to society. **2** *Brit.* outside the normal working day (*unsocial hours*). **3** antisocial. □□ **un·so·cial·ly** *adv.*

un·soiled /únsóyld/ *adj.* not soiled or dirtied.

un·sold /únsóld/ *adj.* not sold.

un•sol•der /únsódər/ *v.tr.* undo the soldering of.

un•sol•dier•ly /únsóljərlee/ *adj.* not soldierly.

un•so•lic•it•ed /únsəlísitid/ *adj.* not asked for; given or done voluntarily. □□ **un•so•lic•it•ed•ly** *adv.*

un•solv•a•ble /únsólvəbəl/ *adj.* that cannot be solved; insoluble. □□ **un•solv•a•bil•i•ty** /–bílitee/ *n.* **un•solv•a•ble•ness** *n.*

un•solved /únsólvd/ *adj.* not solved.

un•so•phis•ti•cat•ed /únsəfístikaytid/ *adj.* **1** artless; simple; natural; ingenuous. **2** not adulterated or artificial. □□ **un•so•phis•ti•cat•ed•ly** *adv.* **un•so•phis•ti•cat•ed•ness** *n.* **un•so•phis•ti•ca•tion** /–káyshən/ *n.*

un•sort•ed /únsáwrtid/ *adj.* not sorted.

un•sought /únsáwt/ *adj.* **1** not searched out or sought for. **2** unasked; without being requested.

un•sound /únsównd/ *adj.* **1** unhealthy; diseased. **2** rotten; weak. **3 a** ill-founded; fallacious. **b** unorthodox; heretical. **4** unreliable. **5** wicked. □ **of unsound mind** insane. □□ **un•sound•ly** *adv.* **un•sound•ness** *n.*

un•sound•ed[1] /únsówndid/ *adj.* **1** not uttered or pronounced. **2** not made to sound.

un•sound•ed[2] /únsówndid/ *adj.* unfathomed.

un•soured /únsówrd/ *adj.* not soured.

un•sown /únsốn/ *adj.* not sown.

un•spar•ing /únspáiring/ *adj.* **1** lavish; profuse. **2** merciless. □□ **un•spar•ing•ly** *adv.* **un•spar•ing•ness** *n.*

un•speak•a•ble /únspeékəbəl/ *adj.* **1** that cannot be expressed in words. **2** indescribably bad or objectionable. □□ **un•speak•a•ble•ness** *n.* **un•speak•a•bly** *adv.*

un•spe•cial•ized /únspéshəlīzd/ *adj.* not specialized.

un•spec•i•fied /únspésifid/ *adj.* not specified.

un•spec•tac•u•lar /únspektákyələr/ *adj.* not spectacular; dull. □□ **un•spec•tac•u•lar•ly** *adv.*

un•spent /únspént/ *adj.* **1** not expended or used. **2** not exhausted or used up.

un•spilled /únspíld/ *adj.* not spilled.

un•spilt /únspílt/ *adj.* not spilled.

un•spir•i•tu•al /únspírichŏŏəl/ *adj.* not spiritual; earthly; worldly. □□ **un•spir•i•tu•al•i•ty** /–chŏŏ-álitee/ *n.* **un•spir•i•tu•al•ly** *adv.* **un•spir•i•tu•al•ness** *n.*

un•spoiled /únspóyld/ *adj.* **1** not spoiled. **2** not plundered.

un•spoilt /únspóylt/ *adj.* not spoiled.

un•spo•ken /únspốkən/ *adj.* **1** not expressed in speech. **2** not uttered as speech.

un•sport•ing /únspáwrting/ *adj.* not sportsmanlike; not fair or generous. □□ **un•sport•ing•ly** *adv.* **un•sport•ing•ness** *n.*

un•sports•man•like /únspáwrtsmənlík/ *adj.* unsporting.

un•spot•ted /únspótid/ *adj.* **1 a** not marked with a spot or spots. **b** morally pure. **2** unnoticed.

un•sprung /únsprúng/ *adj.* not provided with a spring or springs; not resilient.

un•sta•ble /únstáybəl/ *adj.* (**un•sta•bler, un•sta•blest**) **1** not stable. **2** changeable. **3** showing a tendency to sudden mental or emotional changes. □□ **un•sta•ble•ness** *n.* **un•sta•bly** *adv.*

un•sta•ble e•qui•lib•ri•um *n.* a state in which a body when disturbed tends to move farther from equilibrium.

un•stained /únstáynd/ *adj.* not stained.

un•stamped /únstámpt/ *adj.* **1** not marked by stamping. **2** not having a stamp affixed.

un•starched /únstaárcht/ *adj.* not starched.

un•stat•ed /únstáytid/ *adj.* not stated or declared.

un•states•man•like /únstáytsmənlík/ *adj.* not statesmanlike.

un•stat•u•ta•ble /únstáchŏŏ təbəl/ *adj.* contrary to a statute or statutes. □□ **un•stat•u•ta•bly** *adv.*

un•stead•fast /únstédfast/ *adj.* not steadfast.

un•stead•y /únstédee/ *adj.* (**un•stead•i•er, un•stead•i•est**) **1** not steady or firm. **2** changeable; fluctuating. **3** not uniform or regular. □□ **un•stead•i•ly** *adv.* **un•stead•i•ness** *n.*

un•stick *v. & n.* ● *v.* /únstík/ (*past and past part.* **un•stuck** /–stúk/) **1** *tr.* separate (a thing stuck to another). **2** *Aeron. colloq.* **a** *intr.* take off. **b** *tr.* cause (an aircraft) to take off. ● *n.* /únstík/ *Aeron. colloq.* the moment of takeoff. □ **come unstuck** *colloq.* come to grief; fail.

un•stint•ed /únstíntid/ *adj.* not stinted. □□ **un•stint•ed•ly** *adv.*

un•stint•ing /únstínting/ *adj.* ungrudging; lavish. □□ **un•stint•ing•ly** *adv.*

un•stirred /únstárd/ *adj.* not stirred.

un•stitch /únstích/ *v.tr.* undo the stitches of.

un•stop /únstóp/ *v.tr.* (**un•stopped, un•stop•ping**) **1** free from obstruction. **2** remove the stopper from.

un•stop•pa•ble /únstópəbəl/ *adj.* that cannot be stopped or prevented. □□ **un•stop•pa•bil•i•ty** /–bílitee/ *n.* **un•stop•pa•bly** *adv.*

un•stop•per /únstópər/ *v.tr.* remove the stopper from.

un•strained /únstráynd/ *adj.* **1** not subjected to straining or stretching. **2** not injured by overuse or excessive demands. **3** not forced or produced by effort. **4** not passed through a strainer.

un•strap /únstráp/ *v.tr.* (**un•strapped, un•strap•ping**) undo the strap or straps of.

un•stressed /únstrést/ *adj.* **1** (of a word, syllable, etc.) not pronounced with stress. **2** not subjected to stress.

un•string /únstríng/ *v.tr.* (*past and past part.* **un•strung**) **1** remove or relax the string or strings of (a bow, harp, etc.). **2** remove from a string. **3** (esp. as **unstrung** *adj.*) unnerve.

un•struc•tured /únstrúkchərd/ *adj.* **1** not structured. **2** informal.

un•stuck *past and past part.* of UNSTICK.

un•stud•ied /únstúdeed/ *adj.* easy; natural; spontaneous. □□ **un•stud•ied•ly** *adv.*

un•stuffed /únstúft/ *adj.* not stuffed.

un•stuff•y /únstúfee/ *adj.* **1** informal; casual. **2** not stuffy.

un•sub•dued /únsəbdŏŏd, –dyŏŏd/ *adj.* not subdued.

un•sub•ju•gat•ed /únsúbjəgaytid/ *adj.* not subjugated.

un•sub•stan•tial /únsəbstánshəl/ *adj.* having little or no solidity, reality, or factual basis. □□ **un•sub•stan•ti•al•i•ty** /–sheeálitee/ *n.* **un•sub•stan•tial•ly** *adv.*

un•sub•stan•ti•at•ed /únsəbstánsheeaytid/ *adj.* not substantiated.

un•suc•cess /únsəksés/ *n.* **1** lack of success; failure. **2** an instance of this.

un•suc•cess•ful /únsəksésfŏŏl/ *adj.* not successful. □□ **un•suc•cess•ful•ly** *adv.* **un•suc•cess•ful•ness** *n.*

un•sug•ared /únshŏŏgərd/ *adj.* not sugared.

un•sug•gest•ive /únsəgjéstiv, –səjés–/ *adj.* not suggestive.

un•suit•a•ble /únsŏŏtəbəl/ *adj.* not suitable. □□ **un•suit•a•bil•i•ty** *n.* **un•suit•a•ble•ness** *n.* **un•suit•a•bly** *adv.*

un•suit•ed /únsŏŏtid/ *adj.* **1** (usu. foll. by *for*) not fit for a purpose. **2** (usu. foll. by *to*) not adapted.

un•sul•lied /únsúleed/ *adj.* not sullied.

un•sum•moned /únsúmənd/ *adj.* not summoned.

un•sung /únsúng/ *adj.* **1** not celebrated in song; unknown. **2** not sung.

un•su•per•vised /únsŏŏpərvīzd/ *adj.* not supervised.

un•sup•port•a•ble /únsəpáwrtəbəl/ *adj.* **1** that cannot be endured. **2** indefensible. □□ **un•sup•port•a•bly** *adv.*

un•sup•port•ed /únsəpáwrtid/ *adj.* not supported. □□ **un•sup•port•ed•ly** *adv.*

un•sure /únshŏŏr/ *adj.* not sure. □□ **un•sure•ly** *adv.* **un•sure•ness** *n.*

un•sur•pass•a•ble /únsərpásəbəl/ *adj.* that cannot be surpassed. □□ **un•sur•pass•a•bly** *adv.*

un•sur•passed /únsərpást/ *adj.* not surpassed.

un•sur•pris•ing /únsərprízing/ *adj.* not surprising. □□ **un•sur•pris•ing•ly** *adv.*

un•sus•cep•ti•ble /únsəséptibəl/ *adj.* not susceptible. □□ **un•sus•cep•ti•bil•i•ty** *n.*

un•sus•pect•ed /únsəspéktid/ *adj.* not suspected. □□ **un•sus•pect•ed•ly** *adv.*

un•sus•pect•ing /únsəspékting/ *adj.* not suspecting. □□ **un•sus•pect•ing•ly** *adv.* **un•sus•pect•ing•ness** *n.*

un•sus•pi•cious /únsəspíshəs/ *adj.* not suspicious. □□ **un•sus•pi•cious•ly** *adv.* **un•sus•pi•cious•ness** *n.*

un•sus•tained /únsəstáynd/ *adj.* not sustained.

un•swathe /unswoth, –swáyth/ *v.tr.* free from being swathed.

un•swayed /únswáyd/ *adj.* uninfluenced; unaffected.

un•sweet•ened /únsweét'nd/ *adj.* not sweetened.

un•swept /únswépt/ *adj.* not swept.

un•swerv•ing /únswárving/ *adj.* **1** steady; constant. **2** not turning aside. □□ **un•swerv•ing•ly** *adv.*

un•sworn /únswáwrn/ *adj.* **1** (of a person) not subjected to or bound by an oath. **2** not confirmed by an oath.

un•sym•met•ri•cal /únsimétrikəl/ *adj.* not symmetrical. □□ **un•sym•met•ri•cal•ly** *adv.*

un•sym•pa•thet•ic /únsimpəthétik/ *adj.* not sympathetic. □□ **un•sym•pa•thet•i•cal•ly** *adv.*

un•sys•tem•at•ic /únsistəmátik/ *adj.* not systematic. □□ **un•sys•tem•at•i•cal•ly** *adv.*

un•tack /únták/ *v.tr.* detach, esp. by removing tacks.

un•taint•ed /úntáyntid/ *adj.* not tainted.

un•tal•ent•ed /úntáləntid/ *adj.* not talented.

un•tam•a•ble /úntáyməbəl/ *adj.* (also **un•tame•a•ble**) that cannot be tamed.

un•tamed /úntáymd/ *adj.* not tamed; wild.

un•tan•gle /úntánggəl/ *v.tr.* **1** free from a tangled state. **2** free from entanglement.

un•tanned /úntánd/ *adj.* not tanned.

un•tapped /úntápt/ *adj.* not (yet) tapped or wired (*untapped resources*).

un•tar•nished /úntaárnisht/ *adj.* not tarnished.

un•tast•ed /úntáystid/ *adj.* not tasted.

un•taught /úntáwt/ *adj.* **1** not instructed by teaching; ignorant. **2** not acquired by teaching; natural; spontaneous.

un•taxed /úntákst/ *adj.* not required to pay or not attracting taxes.

un•teach /únteéch/ *v.tr.* (*past and past part.* **un•taught**) **1** cause (a person) to forget or discard previous knowledge. **2** remove from the mind (something known or taught) by different teaching.

un·teach·a·ble /úntéechəbəl/ *adj.* **1** incapable of being instructed. **2** that cannot be imparted by teaching.

un·tear·a·ble /úntáirəbəl/ *adj.* that cannot be torn.

un·tech·ni·cal /úntéknikəl/ *adj.* not technical. □□ **un·tech·ni·cal·ly** *adv.*

un·tem·pered /úntémpərd/ *adj.* (of metal, etc.) not brought to the proper hardness or consistency.

un·ten·a·ble /únténəbəl/ *adj.* not tenable; that cannot be defended. □□ **un·ten·a·bil·i·ty** *n.* **un·ten·a·ble·ness** *n.* **un·ten·a·bly** *adv.*

un·tend·ed /únténdid/ *adj.* not tended; neglected.

un·test·ed /úntéstid/ *adj.* not tested or proved.

un·teth·er /úntéthər/ *v.tr.* release (an animal) from a tether.

un·teth·ered /úntéthərd/ *adj.* not tethered.

un·thanked /únthángkt/ *adj.* not thanked.

un·thank·ful /únthángkfŏŏl/ *adj.* not thankful. □□ **un·thank·ful·ly** *adv.* **un·thank·ful·ness** *n.*

un·think·a·ble /únthíngkəbəl/ *adj.* **1** that cannot be imagined or grasped by the mind. **2** *colloq.* highly unlikely or undesirable. □□ **un·think·a·bil·i·ty** /–bílitee/ *n.* **un·think·a·ble·ness** *n.* **un·think·a·bly** *adv.*

un·think·ing /únthíngking/ *adj.* **1** thoughtless. **2** unintentional; inadvertent. □□ **un·think·ing·ly** *adv.* **un·think·ing·ness** *n.*

un·thought /úntháwt/ *adj.* (often foll. by *of*) not thought of.

un·thought·ful /úntháwtfŏŏl/ *adj.* unthinking; unmindful; thoughtless. □□ **un·thought·ful·ly** *adv.* **un·thought·ful·ness** *n.*

un·thread /únthréd/ *v.tr.* **1** take the thread out of (a needle, etc.). **2** find one's way out of (a maze).

un·thrift·y /únthríftee/ *adj.* **1** wasteful; extravagant; prodigal. **2** not thriving or flourishing. □□ **un·thrift·i·ly** *adv.* **un·thrift·i·ness** *n.*

un·throne /únthrṓn/ *v.tr.* dethrone.

un·ti·dy /úntídee/ *adj.* (**un·ti·di·er**, **un·ti·di·est**) not neat or orderly. □□ **un·ti·di·ly** *adv.* **un·ti·di·ness** *n.*

un·tie /úntí/ *v.tr.* (*pres. part.* **un·ty·ing**) **1** undo (a knot, etc.). **2** unfasten the cords, etc., of (a package, etc.). **3** release from bonds or attachment. [OE *untīgan* (as UN-[2], TIE)]

un·tied /úntíd/ *adj.* not tied.

un·til /əntíl, un–/ *prep. & conj.* = TILL[1]. [orig. northern ME *untill* f. ON *und* as far as + TILL[1]]

▶**Until** is more formal than **till**, and is more usual at the beginning of a sentence, e.g., *Until the 1920s it was quite unusual for women to wear short hair.* **'Til** is considered incorrect in standard English and should be avoided.

un·tilled /úntíld/ *adj.* not tilled.

un·time·ly /úntímlee/ *adj. & adv.* ● *adj.* **1** inopportune. **2** (of death) premature. ● *adv. archaic* **1** inopportunely. **2** prematurely. □□ **un·time·li·ness** *n.*

un·tinged /úntínjd/ *adj.* not tinged.

un·tir·ing /úntíring/ *adj.* tireless. □□ **un·tir·ing·ly** *adv.*

un·ti·tled /úntít'ld/ *adj.* having no title.

un·to /úntŏŏ, úntə/ *prep. archaic* = TO *prep.* (in all uses except as the sign of the infinitive): (*do unto others*; *faithful unto death*; *take unto oneself*). [ME f. UNTIL, with TO replacing northern TILL[1]]

un·told /úntṓld/ *adj.* **1** not told. **2** not (able to be) counted or measured (*untold misery*). [OE *untēald* (as UN-[1], TOLD)]

un·touch·a·ble /úntúchəbəl/ *adj. & n.* ● *adj.* that may not or cannot be touched. ● *n.* a member of a hereditary Hindu group held to defile members of higher castes on contact. □□ **un·touch·a·bil·i·ty** *n.* **un·touch·a·ble·ness** *n.*

▶Use of the term, and social restrictions accompanying it, were declared illegal under the Indian constitution in 1949.

un·touched /úntúcht/ *adj.* **1** not touched. **2** not affected physically; not harmed, modified, used, or tasted. **3** not affected by emotion. **4** not discussed.

un·to·ward /úntáwrd, –təwáwrd/ *adj.* **1** inconvenient; unlucky. **2** awkward. **3** perverse, refractory. **4** unseemly. □□ **un·to·ward·ly** *adv.* **un·to·ward·ness** *n.*

un·trace·a·ble /úntráysəbəl/ *adj.* that cannot be traced. □□ **un·trace·a·bly** *adv.*

un·traced /úntráyst/ *adj.* not traced.

un·trained /úntráynd/ *adj.* not trained.

un·tram·meled /úntrámǝld/ *adj.* not trammeled, unhampered.

un·trans·fer·a·ble /úntransfǝ́rǝbǝl, –tránsfǝr–/ *adj.* not transferable.

un·trans·lat·a·ble /úntranzláytəbəl, –trans–, –tránzlayt–, –tráns–/ *adj.* that cannot be translated satisfactorily. □□ **un·trans·lat·a·bil·i·ty** *n.* **un·trans·lat·a·bly** *adv.*

un·trans·port·a·ble /úntranzpáwrtəbəl, –trans–/ *adj.* that cannot be transported.

un·trav·eled /úntrávəld/ *adj.* **1** that has not traveled. **2** that has not been traveled over or through.

un·treat·a·ble /úntréetəbəl/ *adj.* (of a disease, etc.) that cannot be treated.

un·treat·ed /úntréetid/ *adj.* not treated.

un·tried /úntríd/ *adj.* **1** not tried or tested. **2** inexperienced. **3** not yet tried by a judge.

un·trod·den /úntród'n/ *adj.* not trodden, stepped on, or traversed.

un·trou·bled /úntrúbəld/ *adj.* not troubled; calm; tranquil.

un·true /úntrŏŏ/ *adj.* **1** not true; contrary to what is the fact. **2** (often foll. by *to*) not faithful or loyal. **3** deviating from an accepted standard. □□ **un·tru·ly** *adv.* [OE *untrēowe*, etc. (as UN-[1], TRUE)]

un·truss /úntrús/ *v.tr.* unfasten (a trussed fowl).

un·trust·wor·thy /úntrústwúrthee/ *adj.* not trustworthy. □□ **un·trust·wor·thi·ness** *n.*

un·truth /úntrŏŏth/ *n.* (*pl.* **un·truths** /–trŏŏthz, –trŏŏths/) **1** the state of being untrue; falsehood. **2** a false statement (*told me an untruth*). [OE *untrēowth*, etc. (as UN-[1], TRUTH)]

un·truth·ful /úntrŏŏthfŏŏl/ *adj.* not truthful. □□ **un·truth·ful·ly** *adv.* **un·truth·ful·ness** *n.*

un·tuck /úntúk/ *v.tr.* free (bedclothes, etc.) from being tucked in or up.

un·tun·a·ble /úntŏŏnəbəl, –tyŏŏ–/ *adj.* (of a piano, etc.) that cannot be tuned.

un·tuned /úntŏŏnd, –tyŏŏnd/ *adj.* **1** not in tune; not made tuneful. **2** (of a radio receiver, etc.) not tuned to any one frequency. **3** not in harmony or concord; disordered.

un·tune·ful /úntŏŏnfŏŏl, –tyŏŏn–/ *adj.* not tuneful. □□ **un·tune·ful·ly** *adv.* **un·tune·ful·ness** *n.*

un·turned /úntúrnd/ *adj.* **1** not turned over, around, away, etc. **2** not shaped by turning.

un·tu·tored /úntŏŏtərd, –tyŏŏ–/ *adj.* uneducated; untaught.

un·twine /úntwín/ *v.tr. & intr.* untwist; unwind.

un·twist /úntwíst/ *v.tr. & intr.* open from a twisted or spiraled state.

un·ty·ing *pres. part.* of UNTIE.

un·typ·i·cal /úntípikəl/ *adj.* not typical; unusual.

un·us·a·ble /únyŏŏzəbəl/ *adj.* (also **un·use·a·ble**) not usable.

un·used *adj.* **1** /únyŏŏzd/ **a** not in use. **b** never having been used. **2** /únyŏŏst/ (foll. by *to*) not accustomed.

un·u·su·al /únyŏŏzhŏŏəl/ *adj.* **1** not usual. **2** exceptional; remarkable. □□ **un·u·su·al·ly** *adv.* **un·u·su·al·ness** *n.*

un·ut·ter·a·ble /únútərəbəl/ *adj.* inexpressible; beyond description (*unutterable torment*; *an unutterable fool*). □□ **un·ut·ter·a·ble·ness** *n.* **un·ut·ter·a·bly** *adv.*

un·ut·tered /únútərd/ *adj.* not uttered or expressed.

un·vac·ci·nat·ed /únváksinaytid/ *adj* not vaccinated.

un·val·ued /únvályŏŏd/ *adj.* **1** not regarded as valuable. **2** not having been valued.

un·van·quished /únvángkwisht/ *adj.* not vanquished.

un·var·ied /únváirid/ *adj.* not varied.

un·var·nished /únvaárnisht/ *adj.* **1** not varnished. **2** (of a statement or person) plain and straightforward (*the unvarnished truth*).

un·var·y·ing /únváireeing/ *adj.* not varying. □□ **un·var·y·ing·ly** *adv.* **un·var·y·ing·ness** *n.*

un·veil /únváyl/ *v.* **1** *tr.* remove a veil from. **2** *tr.* remove a covering from (a statue, plaque, etc.) as part of the ceremony of the first public display. **3** *tr.* disclose; reveal; make publicly known. **4** *intr.* remove one's veil.

un·ven·ti·lat·ed /únvént'laytid/ *adj.* **1** not provided with a means of ventilation. **2** not discussed.

un·ver·i·fi·able /únvérəfīəbəl/ *adj.* that cannot be verified.

un·ver·i·fied /únvérifīd/ *adj.* not verified.

un·versed /únvúrst/ *adj.* (usu. foll. by *in*) not experienced or skilled.

un·vi·a·ble /únvíəbəl/ *adj.* not viable. □□ **un·vi·a·bil·i·ty** /–bílitee/ *n.*

un·vi·o·lat·ed /únvíəlaytid/ *adj.* not violated.

un·vis·it·ed /únvízitid/ *adj.* not visited.

un·vi·ti·at·ed /únvísheeaytid/ *adj.* not vitiated.

un·voiced /únvóyst/ *adj.* **1** not spoken. **2** *Phonet.* not voiced.

un·waged /únwáyjd/ *adj.* not receiving a wage; out of work.

un·want·ed /únwóntid/ *adj.* not wanted.

un·war·like /únwáwrlik/ *adj.* not warlike.

un·warmed /únwáwrmd/ *adj.* not warmed.

un·warned /únwáwrnd/ *adj.* not warned or forewarned.

un·war·rant·a·ble /únwáwrəntəbəl, –wór–/ *adj.* indefensible; unjustifiable. □□ **un·war·rant·a·ble·ness** *n.* **un·war·rant·a·bly** *adv.*

un·war·rant·ed /únwáwrəntid, –wór–/ *adj.* **1** unauthorized. **2** unjustified.

un·war·y /únwáiree/ *adj.* **1** not cautious. **2** (often foll. by *of*) not aware of possible danger, etc. □□ **un·war·i·ly** *adv.* **un·war·i·ness** *n.*

un·washed /únwósht, –wáwsht/ *adj.* **1** not washed. **2** not usually washed or clean. □ **the great unwashed** *colloq.* the rabble.

un·watched /únwócht/ *adj.* not watched.

un·watch·ful /únwóchfŏŏl/ *adj.* not watchful.

un·wa·tered /únwáwtərd, –wótərd/ *adj.* not watered.

un·wa·ver·ing /únwáyvəring/ *adj.* not wavering. □□ **un·wa·ver·ing·ly** *adv.*

un·weaned /únwéend/ *adj.* not weaned.

un·wear·a·ble /únwáirəbəl/ *adj.* that cannot be worn.

un·wea·ried /únwéereed/ *adj.* **1** not wearied or tired. **2** never becoming weary; indefatigable. **3** unremitting. □□ **un·wea·ried·ly** *adv.* **un·wea·ried·ness** *n.*

un·wea·ry /únwéeree/ adj. not weary.

un·wea·ry·ing /únwéereeing/ adj. **1** persistent. **2** not causing or producing weariness. □□ **un·wea·ry·ing·ly** adv.

un·wed /únwéd/ adj. unmarried.

un·wed·ded /únwédid/ adj. unmarried. □□ **un·wed·ded·ness** n.

un·weed·ed /únwéedid/ adj. not cleared of weeds.

un·weighed /únwáyd/ adj. **1** not considered; hasty. **2** (of goods) not weighed.

un·wel·come /únwélkəm/ adj. not welcome or acceptable. □□ **un·wel·come·ly** adv. **un·wel·come·ness** n.

un·well /únwél/ adj. **1** not in good health; (somewhat) ill. **2** indisposed.

un·wept /únwépt/ adj. **1** not wept for. **2** (of tears) not wept.

un·wet·ted /únwétid/ adj. not wetted.

un·whipped /únhwípt, –wípt/ adj. **1** not punished by or as by whipping. **2** Brit. not subject to a party whip.

un·whole·some /únhólsəm/ adj. **1** not promoting, or detrimental to, physical or moral health. **2** unhealthy; insalubrious. **3** unhealthy-looking. □□ **un·whole·some·ly** adv. **un·whole·some·ness** n.

un·wield·y /únwéeldee/ adj. (**un·wield·i·er**, **un·wield·i·est**) cumbersome, clumsy, or hard to manage, owing to size, shape, or weight. □□ **un·wield·i·ly** adv. **un·wield·i·ness** n. [ME f. UN-¹ + wieldy active (now dial.) f. WIELD]

un·will·ing /únwíling/ adj. not willing or inclined; reluctant. □□ **un·will·ing·ly** adv. **un·will·ing·ness** n. [OE unwillende (as UN-¹, WILLING)]

un·wind /únwínd/ v. (past and past part. **un·wound** /–wównd/) **1 a** tr. draw out (a thing that has been wound). **b** intr. become drawn out after having been wound. **2** intr. & tr. colloq. relax.

un·wink·ing /únwíngking/ adj. **1** not winking. **2** watchful; vigilant. □□ **un·wink·ing·ly** adv.

un·win·na·ble /únwínəbəl/ adj. that cannot be won.

un·wis·dom /únwízdəm/ n. lack of wisdom; folly; imprudence. [OE unwísdōm (as UN-¹, WISDOM)]

un·wise /únwíz/ adj. **1** foolish; imprudent. **2** injudicious. □□ **un·wise·ly** adv. [OE unwís (as UN-¹, WISE¹)]

un·wished /únwísht/ adj. (usu. foll by for) not wished for.

un·with·ered /únwíthərd/ adj. not withered; still vigorous or fresh.

un·wit·nessed /únwítnist/ adj. not witnessed.

un·wit·ting /únwíting/ adj. **1** unaware of the state of the case (an unwitting offender). **2** unintentional. □□ **un·wit·ting·ly** adv. **un·wit·ting·ness** n. [OE unwitende (as UN-¹, WIT²)]

un·wom·an·ly /únwŏŏmənlee/ adj. not womanly; not befitting a woman. □□ **un·wom·an·li·ness** n.

un·wont·ed /únwáwntid, –wón–, –wún–/ adj. not customary or usual. □□ **un·wont·ed·ly** adv. **un·wont·ed·ness** n.

un·wood·ed /únwŏŏdid/ adj. not wooded; treeless.

un·work·a·ble /únwórkəbəl/ adj. not workable; impracticable. □□ **un·work·a·bil·i·ty** n. **un·work·a·ble·ness** n. **un·work·a·bly** adv.

un·worked /únwórkt/ adj. **1** not wrought into shape. **2** not exploited or turned to account.

un·work·man·like /únwórkmənlīk/ adj. badly done or made.

un·world·ly /únwórldlee/ adj. **1** spiritually minded. **2** spiritual. □□ **un·world·li·ness** n.

un·worn /únwáwrn/ adj. not worn or impaired by wear.

un·wor·ried /únwóreed, –wúr–/ adj. not worried; calm.

un·wor·thy /únwúrthee/ adj. (**un·wor·thi·er**, **un·wor·thi·est**) **1** (often foll. by of) not worthy or befitting the character of a person, etc. **2** discreditable; unseemly. **3** contemptible; base. □□ **un·wor·thi·ly** adv. **un·wor·thi·ness** n.

un·wound¹ /únwównd/ adj. not wound or wound up.

un·wound² past and past part. of UNWIND.

un·wound·ed /únwŏŏndid/ adj. not wounded; unhurt.

un·wo·ven /únwóvən/ adj. not woven.

un·wrap /únráp/ v. (**un·wrapped**, **un·wrap·ping**) **1** tr. remove the wrapping from. **2** tr. open or unfold. **3** intr. become unwrapped.

un·wrin·kled /únríngkəld/ adj. free from wrinkles; smooth.

un·writ·a·ble /únrítəbəl/ adj. that cannot be written.

un·writ·ten /únrít'n/ adj. **1** not written. **2** (of a law, etc.) resting originally on custom or judicial decision, not on statute.

un·wrought /únráwt/ adj. (of metals) not hammered into shape or worked into a finished condition.

un·yield·ing /únyéelding/ adj. **1** not yielding to pressure, etc. **2** firm; obstinate. □□ **un·yield·ing·ly** adv. **un·yield·ing·ness** n.

un·yoke /únyók/ v. **1** tr. release from a yoke. **2** intr. cease work.

un·zip /únzíp/ v.tr. (**un·zipped**, **un·zip·ping**) unfasten the zipper of.

up /up/ adv., prep., adj., n., & v. ● adv. **1** at, in, or toward a higher place or position (jumped up in the air; what are they doing up there?). **2** to or in a place regarded as higher, esp.: **a** northward (up north in New England). **b** Brit. toward a major city or a university (went up to London). **3** colloq. ahead, etc., as indicated (went up front). **4 a** to or in an erect position or condition (stood it up). **b** to or in a prepared or required position (wound up the watch). **c** in or into a condition of efficiency, activity, or progress (stirred up trouble; the house is up

for sale; the hunt is up). **5** in a stronger or winning position or condition (our team was three goals up; am $10 up on the transaction). **6** (of a computer) running and available for use. **7** to the place or time in question or where the speaker, etc., is (a child came up to me; went straight up to the door; has been fine up till now). **8** at or to a higher price or value (our costs are up; shares are up). **9 a** completely or effectually (burn up; eat up; tear up; use up). **b** more loudly or clearly (speak up). **10** in a state of completion; denoting the end of availability, supply, etc. (time is up). **11** into a compact, accumulated, or secure state (pack up; save up; tie up). **12 a** awake. **b** out of bed (are you up yet?). **13** (of the sun, etc.) having risen. **14** happening, esp. unusually or unexpectedly (something is up). **15** esp. Brit. (usu. foll. by on or in) taught or informed (is well up in French). **16** (usu. foll. by before) appearing for trial, etc. (was up before the judge). **17** Brit. (of a road, etc.) being repaired. **18** (of a jockey) in the saddle. **19** toward the source of a river. **20** inland. **21** (of the points, etc., in a game): **a** registered on the scoreboard. **b** forming the total score for the time being. **22** upstairs, esp. to bed (are you going up yet?). **23** (of a theater curtain) raised, etc., to reveal the stage. **24** (as int.) get up. **25** (of a ship's helm) with rudder to leeward. **26** in rebellion. **27** Baseball at bat (he struck out his last time up). ● prep. **1** upward along, through, or into (climbed up the ladder). **2** from the bottom to the top of. **3** along (walked up the road). **4 a** at or in a higher part of (is situated up the street). **b** toward the source of (a river). ● adj. **1** (often in comb.) directed upward (upstroke). **2** Brit. of travel toward a capital or center (the up train; the up platform). **3** Brit. (of beer, etc.) effervescent; frothy. ● n. a spell of good fortune. ● v. (**upped**, **up·ping**) **1** intr. colloq. start up; begin abruptly to say or do something (upped and hit him). **2** intr. (foll. by with) raise; pick up (upped with his stick). **3** tr. increase or raise, esp. abruptly (upped all their prices). □ **be all up with** be disastrous or hopeless for (a person). **on the up and up** colloq. **1** honest(ly); on the level. **2** Brit. steadily improving. **something is up** colloq. something unusual or undesirable is afoot or happening. **up against 1** close to. **2** in or into contact with. **3** colloq. confronted with (up against a problem). **up against it** colloq. in great difficulties. **up and about** (or doing) having risen from bed; active. **up and down 1** to and fro (along). **2** in every direction. **3** colloq. in varying health or spirits. **up for** available for or being considered for (office, etc.). **up hill and down dale** up and down hills on an arduous journey. **up in arms** see ARM². **up the pole** see POLE¹. **up to 1** until (up to the present). **2** not more than (you can have up to five). **3** less than or equal to (adds up to $10). **4** incumbent on (it is up to you to say). **5** capable of or fit for (am not up to a long walk). **6** occupied or busy with (what have you been up to?). **up to the mark** see MARK¹. **up to snuff** see SNUFF². **up to one's tricks** see TRICK. **up to a person's tricks** see TRICK. **up with** int. expressing support for a stated person or thing. **what's up?** colloq. **1** what is going on? **2** what is the matter? [OE up(p), uppe, rel. to OHG ūf]

up- /up/ prefix in senses of UP, added: **1** as an adverb to verbs and verbal derivations, = 'upward' (upcurved; update). **2** as a preposition to nouns forming adverbs and adjectives (up-country; uphill). **3** as an adjective to nouns (upland; upstroke). [OE up(p)-, = UP]

up·an·chor v.intr. Naut. (of a ship) weigh anchor.

up-and-com·ing adj. colloq. (of a person) making good progress and likely to succeed.

U·pan·i·shad /ŏŏpánishad, ŏŏpáanishaad/ n. each of a series of philosophical compositions concluding the exposition of the Vedas. [Skr. f. upa near + ni-ṣad sit down]

u·pas /yŏŏpəs/ n. **1** (in full **upas tree**) **a** a Javanese tree, Antiaris toxicaria, yielding a milky sap used as arrow poison. **b** Mythol. a Javanese tree thought to be fatal to whatever came near it. **c** a pernicious influence, practice, etc. **2** the poisonous sap of upas and other trees. [Malay ūpas poison]

up·beat /úpbeet/ n. & adj. ● n. an unaccented beat in music. ● adj. colloq. optimistic or cheerful.

up·braid /upbráyd/ v.tr. (often foll. by with, for) chide or reproach (a person). □□ **up·braid·ing** n. [OE upbrēdan (as UP-, brēdan = bregdan BRAID in obs. sense 'brandish ')]

up·bring·ing /úpbringing/ n. the bringing up of a child; education. [obs. upbring to rear (as UP-, BRING)]

UPC abbr. = Universal Product Code.

up·cast n. & v. ● n. /úpkast/ **1** the act of casting up; an upward throw. **2** Mining a shaft through which air leaves a mine. **3** Geol. = UPTHROW. ● v.tr. /úpkást/ (past and past part. **up·cast**) cast up.

up·chuck /úpchuk/ v.tr. & intr. sl. vomit.

up·com·ing /úpkúming/ adj. forthcoming; about to happen.

up·coun·try /úpkúntree/ adv. & adj. inland; toward the interior of a country.

up·date v. & n. ● v.tr. /úpdáyt/ bring up to date. ● n. /úpdayt/ **1** the act or an instance of updating. **2** an updated version; a set of updated information. □□ **up·dat·er** n.

up·draft /úpdraft/ *n.* an upward draft of gas, esp. smoke in a chimney.

up·end /úpénd/ *v.tr. & intr.* set or rise up on end.

up·field /úpfeeld/ *adv.* in or to a position nearer to the opponents' end of a football, etc., field.

up·fold /úpfóld/ *n. Geol.* an anticline.

up-front *adv. & adj.* ● *adv.* (usu. **up front**) **1** at the front; in front. **2** (of payments) in advance. ● *adj.* **1** honest, open, frank. **2** (of payments) made in advance. **3** at the front or most prominent.

up·grade *v. & n.* ● *v.tr.* /úpgráyd/ **1** raise in rank, etc. **2** improve (equipment, machinery, etc.) esp. by replacing components. ● *n.* /úpgrayd/ **1** the act or an instance of upgrading. **2** an upgraded piece of equipment, etc. **3** an upward slope. □ **on the upgrade 1** improving in health, etc. **2** advancing; progressing. □□ **up·grad·er** *n.*

up·growth /úpgróth/ *n.* the process or result of growing upward.

up·heav·al /úpheeévəl/ *n.* **1** a violent or sudden change or disruption. **2** *Geol.* an upward displacement of part of the earth's crust. **3** the act or an instance of heaving up.

up·heave /úpheév/ *v.* **1** *tr.* heave or lift up, esp. forcibly. **2** *intr.* rise up.

up·hill *adv., adj., & n.* ● *adv.* /úphíl/ in an ascending direction up a hill, slope, etc. ● *adj.* /úphíl/ **1** sloping up; ascending. **2** arduous; difficult (*an uphill task*). ● *n.* /úphíl/ an upward slope.

up·hold /úphóld/ *v.tr.* (*past* and *past part.* **up·held** /–held/) **1** confirm or maintain (a decision, etc., esp. of another). **2** give support or countenance to (a person, practice, etc.). □□ **up·hold·er** *n.*

up·hol·ster /úphólstər, əpól–/ *v.tr.* **1** provide (furniture) with upholstery. **2** furnish (a room, etc.) with furniture, carpets, etc. □ **well-upholstered** *joc.* (of a person) fat. [back-form. f. UPHOLSTERER]

up·hol·ster·er /úphólstərər, əpól–/ *n.* a person who upholsters furniture, esp. professionally. [obs. *upholster* (n.) f. UPHOLD (in obs. sense 'keep in repair') + –STER]

up·hol·ster·y /úphólstəree, əpól–/ *n.* **1** textile covering, padding, springs, etc., for furniture. **2** an upholsterer's work.

up·keep /úpkeep/ *n.* **1** maintenance in good condition. **2** the cost or means of this.

up·land /úplənd/ *n. & adj.* ● *n.* the higher or inland parts of a country. ● *adj.* of or relating to these parts.

up·lift *v. & n.* ● *v.tr.* /úplíft/ **1** esp. *Brit.* raise; lift up. **2** elevate or stimulate morally or spiritually. ● *n.* /úplift/ **1** the act or an instance of being raised. **2** *Geol.* the raising of part of the earth's surface. **3** *colloq.* a morally or spiritually elevating influence. **4** support for the bust, etc., from a garment. □□ **up·lift·er** *n.* **up·lift·ing** *adj.* (esp. in sense 2 of *v.*).

up·mar·ket /úpmáarkit/ *adj. & adv.* = UPSCALE.

up·most var. of UPPERMOST.

up·on /əpón, əpáwn/ *prep.* = ON. [ME f. UP + ON *prep.*, after ON *uppá*]

▶Upon is sometimes more formal than **on**, and is preferred in the phrases *once upon a time* and *upon my word*, and in uses such as *row upon row of seats* and *Christmas is almost upon us*.

up·per[1] /úpər/ *adj. & n.* ● *adj.* **1 a** higher in place; situated above another part (*the upper atmosphere; the upper lip*). **b** *Geol.* designating a younger (and usually shallower) part of a stratigraphic division, or the period of its formation (*the Upper Jurassic*). **2** higher in rank or dignity, etc. (*the upper class*). **3** situated on higher ground, further to the north, or further inland (*Upper Egypt*). ● *n.* the part of a boot or shoe above the sole. □ **on one's uppers** *colloq.* extremely short of money. [ME f. UP + –ER[2]]

up·per[2] /úpər/ *n. sl.* a stimulant drug, esp. an amphetamine. [UP *v.* + –ER[1]]

up·per·case /úpərkáys/ *adj., n., & v.* ● *adj.* (of letters) capital. ● *n.* capital letters. ● *v.tr.* set or print in uppercase.

up·per class *n. & adj.* **1** the highest class of society, esp. (in the UK) the aristocracy. ● *adj.* (**upper-class**) of, relating to, or characteristic of such a group.

up·per crust *n. colloq.* (in the U.K.) the aristocracy. □□ **up·per-crust** *adj.*

up·per·cut /úpərkut/ *n. & v.* ● *n.* an upward blow delivered with the arm bent. ● *v.tr.* hit with an uppercut.

up·per hand *n.* dominance or control.

up·per house *n.* the higher house in a legislature, e.g., the U.S. Senate.

up·per·most /úpərmōst/ *adj. & adv.* ● *adj.* (also **up·most** /úpmōst/) **1** highest in place, rank, or importance. **2** predominant. ● *adv.* at or to the highest or most prominent position.

up·per re·gions *n.pl.* **1** the sky. **2** heaven.

up·per works *n.* the part of a ship that is above the water when fully laden.

up·pish /úpish/ *adj.* esp. *Brit. colloq.* self-assertive or arrogant; uppity. □□ **up·pish·ly** *adv.* **up·pish·ness** *n.*

up·pi·ty /úpitee/ *adj. colloq.* arrogant; snobbish. [fanciful f. UP]

up·raise /úpráyz/ *v.tr.* raise to a higher level.

up·right /úprit/ *adj., adv., & n.* ● *adj.* **1** erect; vertical (*an upright pos-*

ture; stood upright). **2** (of a piano) with vertical strings. **3** (of a person or behavior) righteous; strictly honorable or honest. **4** (of a picture, book, etc.) greater in height than breadth. ● *adv.* in a vertical direction; vertically upward; into an upright position. ● *n.* **1** a post or rod fixed upright, esp. as a structural support. **2** an upright piano. □□ **up·right·ly** *adv.* **up·right·ness** *n.* [OE *upriht* (as UP, RIGHT)]

up·rise /úpríz/ *v.intr.* (**up·rose, up·ris·en**) rise (to a standing position, etc.).

up·ris·ing /úprīzing/ *n.* a rebellion or revolt.

SYNONYM TIP   **uprising**

INSURGENCY, INSURRECTION, MUTINY, PUTSCH, REBELLION, REVOLUTION. There are a number of ways to defy the established order or overthrow a government. You can stage an **uprising**, which is a broad term referring to a small and usually unsuccessful act of popular resistance (*uprisings among angry workers all over the country*). An *uprising* is often the first sign of a general or widespread **rebellion**, which is an act of armed resistance against a government or authority; this term is usually applied after the fact to describe an act of resistance that has failed (*a rebellion against the landowners*). If it is successful, however, a *rebellion* may become a **revolution**, which often implies a war or an outbreak of violence (*the American Revolution*). Although a *revolution* usually involves the overthrow of a government or political system by the people, it can also be used to describe any drastic change in ideas, economic institutions, or moral values (*the sexual revolution*). An **insurrection** is an organized effort to seize power, especially political power, while an *insurgency* is usually aided by foreign powers. If you're on a ship, you can stage a **mutiny**, which is an *insurrection* against military or naval authority. But if you're relying on speed and surprise to catch the authorities off guard, you'll want to stage a **putsch**, which is a small, popular *uprising* or planned attempt to seize power.

---

up·roar /úprawr/ *n.* a tumult; a violent disturbance. [Du. *oproer* f. *op* up + *roer* confusion, assoc. with ROAR]

up·roar·i·ous /upráwreeəs/ *adj* **1** very noisy; tumultuous. **2** provoking loud laughter. □□ **up·roar·i·ous·ly** *adv.* **up·roar·i·ous·ness** *n.*

up·root /úpróot, róŏt/ *v.tr.* **1** pull (a plant, etc.) up from the ground. **2** displace (a person) from an accustomed location. **3** eradicate; destroy. □□ **up·root·er** *n.*

up·rose *past* of UPRISE.

up·rush /úprush/ *n.* an upward rush, esp. *Psychol.* from the subconscious.

up·sa-dai·sy var. of UPSY-DAISY.

ups and downs *n.pl.* **1** rises and falls. **2** alternate good and bad fortune.

up·scale /úpskáyl/ *adj., v., & n.* ● *adj.* toward or relating to the more affluent or upper sector of society or the market. ● *v.tr.* improve the quality or value of. ● *n.* (as *pl.*) upscale persons collectively (*apartments built for the upscale*).

up·set *v., n., & adj.* ● *v.* /úpsét/ (**up·set·ting;** *past* and *past part.* **up·set**) **1 a** *tr. & intr.* overturn or be overturned. **b** *tr.* overcome; defeat. **2** *tr.* disturb the composure or digestion of (*was very upset by the news; ate something that upset me*). **3** *tr.* disrupt. **4** *tr.* shorten and thicken (metal, esp. a tire) by hammering or pressure. ● *n.* /úpset/ **1** a condition of upsetting or being upset (*a stomach upset*). **2** a surprising result in a game, etc. ● *adj.* /úpsét/ disturbed (*an upset stomach*). □□ **up·set·ter** *n.* **up·set·ting·ly** *adv.*

up·set price *n.* the lowest acceptable selling price of a property in an auction, etc.; a reserve price.

up·shot /úpshot/ *n.* the final or eventual outcome or conclusion.

up·side down /úpsíd dówn/ *adv. & adj.* ● *adv.* **1** with the upper part where the lower part should be; in an inverted position. **2** in or into total disorder (*everything was turned upside down*). ● *adj.* (also **up·side-down** *attrib.*) that is positioned upside down; inverted. [ME, orig. *up so down*, perh. = 'up as if down']

up·side-down cake *n.* a cake baked with fruit in a syrup at the bottom, and inverted for serving.

up·sides /úpsídz/ *adv. Brit. colloq.* (foll. by *with*) equal with (a person) by revenge, retaliation, etc. [*upside* = top part]

up·si·lon /úpsilon, yŏŏp–/ *n.* the twentieth letter of the Greek alphabet (Υ, υ). [Gk, = slender U f. *psilos* slender, with ref. to its later coincidence in sound with Gk *oi*]

up·stage /úpstáyj/ *adj., adv., v., & n.* ● *adj. & adv.* **1** nearer the back of a theater stage. **2** snobbish(ly). ● *v.tr.* **1** (of an actor) move upstage to make (another actor) face away from the audience. **2** divert attention from (a person) to oneself; outshine. ● *n.* the part of the stage farthest from the audience.

up·stairs /úpstáyrz/ *adv., adj., & n.* ● *adv.* to or on an upper floor. ● *adj.* (also **up·stair**) situated upstairs. ● *n.* an upper floor.

up·stand·ing /úpstánding/ *adj.* **1** standing up. **2** strong and healthy. **3** honest or straightforward.

up·start /úpstaart/ *n. & adj.* ● *n.* a person who has risen suddenly to prominence, esp. one who behaves arrogantly. ● *adj.* **1** that is an upstart. **2** of or characteristic of an upstart.

up·state /úpstáyt/ *n., adj., & adv.* • *n.* part of a state remote from its large cities, esp. the northern part (*upstate New York*). • *adj.* of or relating to this part. □□ **up·stat·er** *n.*

up·stream /úpstreém/ *adv. & adj.* • *adv.* against the flow of a stream, etc. • *adj.* moving upstream.

up·stroke /úpstrōk/ *n.* a stroke made or written upward.

up·surge /úptayk/ *n.* an upward surge; a rise (esp. in feelings, etc.).

up·swept /úpswept/ *adj* **1** (of the hair) combed to the top of the head. **2** curved or sloped upward.

up·swing /úpswing/ *n.* an upward movement or trend.

up·sy-dai·sy /úpseedáyzee/ *int.* (also **up·sa·dai·sy**) expressing encouragement to a child who is being lifted or has fallen. [earlier *up-a-daisy*: cf. LACKADAISICAL]

up·take /úptayk/ *n. colloq.* understanding; comprehension (esp. *quick* or *slow on the uptake*). **2** the act or an instance of taking up.

up·throw /úpthrō/ *n.* **1** the act or an instance of throwing upward. **2** *Geol.* an upward dislocation of strata.

up·thrust /úpthrust/ *n.* **1** upward thrust, e.g., of a fluid on an immersed body. **2** *Geol.* = UPHEAVAL.

up·tight /úptít/ *adj. colloq.* **1** nervously tense or angry. **2** rigidly conventional.

up to date *adj.* (*attrib.* **up-to-date**) meeting or according to the latest information, ideas, knowledge, or fashion; modern.

up-to-the-min·ute *adj.* completely up to date.

up·town /úptówn/ *adj., adv., & n.* • *adj.* **1** of or in the residential part of a town or city. **2** characteristic of or suitable to affluent or sophisticated people. • *adv.* in or into this part. • *n.* this part. □□ **up·town·er** *n.*

up·turn *n. & v.* • *n.* /úptərn/ **1** an upward trend; an improvement. **2** an upheaval. • *v.tr.* /úptúrn/ turn up or upside down.

UPU *abbr.* Universal Postal Union.

up·ward /úpwərd/ *adv. & adj.* • *adv.* (also **up·wards**) toward what is higher, superior, larger in amount, more important, or earlier. • *adj.* moving, extending, pointing, or leading upward. □ **upwards of** more than (*found upwards of forty specimens*). [OE *upweard(es)* (as UP, –WARD)]

up·ward·ly /úpwərdlee/ *adv.* in an upward direction.

up·ward·ly mo·bile *adj.* able or aspiring to advance socially or professionally.

up·warp /úpwawrp/ *n. Geol.* a broad surface elevation; an anticline.

up·wind /úpwínd/ *adj. & adv.* against the direction of the wind.

ur- /oŏr/ *comb. form* primitive; original; earliest. [G]

u·ra·cil /yoŏrəsil/ *n. Biochem.* a pyrimidine derivative found in living tissue as a component base of RNA. [UREA + ACETIC]

u·rae·mi·a *Brit.* var. of UREMIA.

u·rae·us /yoŏrée·əs/ *n.* the sacred serpent as an emblem of power represented on the headdress of Egyptian divinities and sovereigns. [mod.L f. Gk *ouraios*, repr. the Egypt. word for 'cobra']

U·ral-Al·ta·ic /yoŏrəlaltáyik/ *n. & adj.* • *n. Philol.* a family of Finno-Ugric, Turkic, Mongolian, and other agglutinative languages of N. Europe and Asia. • *adj.* **1** of or relating to this family of languages. **2** of or relating to the Ural and Altai mountain ranges in west and central Asia.

u·ra·ni·um /yoŏráynee·əm/ *n. Chem.* a radioactive, gray, dense metallic element occurring naturally in pitchblende, and capable of nuclear fission and therefore used as a source of nuclear energy. ¶ Symb.: **U**. □□ **u·ran·ic** /–ránik/ *adj.* [mod.L, f. URANUS: cf. *tellurium*]

urano-[1] /yoŏrənō, yoŏráynō/ *comb. form* the heavens. [Gk *ouranos* heaven(s)]

urano-[2] /yoŏrənō/ *comb. form* uranium.

u·ra·nog·ra·phy /yoŏrənógrəfee/ *n.* the branch of astronomy concerned with describing and mapping the stars, planets, etc. □□ **u·ra·nog·ra·pher** *n.* **u·ra·no·graph·ic** /–nəgráfik/ *adj.*

U·ran·us /yoŏrənəs, yoŏráynəs/ *n.* **1** a planet discovered by Herschel in 1781, the outermost of the solar system except Neptune and Pluto. [L f. Gk *Ouranos* heaven, Uranus, in Gk Mythol. the son of Gaea (Earth) and father of Kronos (Saturn), the Titans, etc.]

ur·ban /órbən/ *adj.* of, living in, or situated in a town or city (*an urban population*) (opp. RURAL). [L *urbanus* f. *urbs urbis* city]

ur·bane /ərbáyn/ *adj.* courteous; suave; elegant and refined in manner. □□ **ur·bane·ly** *adv.* **ur·bane·ness** *n.* [F *urbain* or L *urbanus*: see URBAN]

ur·ban·ism /órbənizəm/ *n.* **1** urban character or way of life. **2** a study of urban life. □□ **ur·ban·ist** *n.*

ur·ban·ite /órbənīt/ *n.* a dweller in a city or town.

ur·ban·i·ty /ərbánitee/ *n.* **1** an urbane quality; refinement of manner. **2** urban life. [F *urbanité* or L *urbanitas* (as URBAN)]

ur·ban·ize /órbəniz/ *v.tr.* **1** make urban. **2** destroy the rural quality of (a district). □□ **ur·ban·i·za·tion** /–záyshən/ *n.* [F *urbaniser* (as URBAN)]

ur·ban re·new·al *n.* slum clearance and redevelopment in a city or town.

ur·ban sprawl *n.* the uncontrolled expansion of urban areas.

ur·ce·o·late /órseeələt, órseeəlayt/ *adj. Bot.* having the shape of a pitcher, with a large body and small mouth. [L *urceolus* dimin. of *urceus* pitcher]

ur·chin /órchin/ *n.* **1** a mischievous child, esp. young and raggedly dressed. **2** = SEA URCHIN. **3** *archaic* **a** a hedgehog. **b** a goblin. [ME *hirchon, urcheon* f. ONF *herichon*, OF *heriçon* ult. f. L (*h*)*ericius* hedgehog]

Ur·du /oŏrdoŏ, ór–/ *n.* a language related to Hindi but with many Persian words, an official language of Pakistan and also used in India. [Hind. (*zabān ī*) *urdū* (language of the) camp, f. Pers. *urdū* f. Turki *ordū*: see HORDE]

-ure /ər/ *suffix* forming: **1** nouns of action or process (*censure; closure; seizure*). **2** nouns of result (*creature; scripture*). **3** collective nouns (*legislature; nature*). **4** nouns of function (*judicature; ligature*). [from or after OF *–ure* f. L *–ura*]

u·re·a /yoŏrée·ə/ *n. Biochem.* a soluble, colorless, crystalline, nitrogenous compound contained esp. in the urine of mammals. □□ **u·re·al** *adj.* [mod.L f. F *urée* f. Gk *ouron* urine]

u·re·mi·a /yoŏrée·mee·ə/ *n.* (*Brit.* **u·rae·mi·a**) *Med.* a morbid condition due to the presence in the blood of urinary matter normally eliminated by the kidneys. □□ **u·re·mic** /–mik/ *adj.* [Gk *ouron* urine + *haima* blood]

u·re·ter /yoŏrée·tər/ *n.* the duct by which urine passes from the kidney to the bladder or cloaca. □□ **u·re·ter·al** *adj.* **u·re·ter·ic** /yoŏritérik/ *adj.* **u·re·ter·i·tis** /–rítis/ *n.* [F *uretère* or mod.L *ureter* f. Gk *ourētēr* f. *oureō* urinate]

u·re·thane /yoŏríthayn/ *n. Chem.* a crystalline amide, ethyl carbamate, used in plastics and paints. [F *uréthane* (as UREA, ETHANE)]

u·re·thra /yoŏrée·thrə/ *n.* (*pl.* **u·re·thras** or **u·re·thrae** /–ree/) the duct by which urine is discharged from the bladder. □□ **u·re·thral** *adj.* **u·re·thri·tis** /–rithrítis/ *n.* [LL f. Gk *ourēthra* (as URETER)]

urge /órj/ *v. & n.* • *v.tr.* **1** (often foll. by *on*) drive forcibly; impel; hasten (*urged them on; urged the horses forward*). **2** (often foll. by *to* + infin. or *that* + clause) encourage or entreat earnestly or persistently (*urged them to go; urged them to action; urged that they should go*). **3** (often foll. by *on, upon*) advocate (an action or argument, etc.) pressingly or emphatically (to a person). **4** adduce forcefully as a reason or justification (*urged the seriousness of the problem*). **5** ply (a person, etc.) hard with argument or entreaty. • *n.* **1** an urging impulse or tendency. **2** a strong desire. [L *urgēre* press, drive]

ur·gent /órjənt/ *adj.* **1** requiring immediate action or attention (*an urgent need for help*). **2** importunate; earnest and persistent in demand. □□ **ur·gen·cy** *n.* **ur·gent·ly** *adv.* [ME f. F (as URGE)]

urg·er /órjər/ *n.* **1** a person who urges or incites. **2** *Austral. sl.* a person who obtains money dishonestly, esp. as a racing tipster.

-uria /yoŏree·ə/ *comb. form* forming nouns denoting that a substance is (esp. excessively) present in the urine. [mod.L f. Gk *–ouria* (as URINE)]

u·ric /yoŏrik/ *adj.* of or relating to urine. [F *urique* (as URINE)]

u·ric ac·id *n.* a crystalline acid forming a constituent of urine.

u·ri·nal /yoŏrinəl/ *n.* **1** a sanitary fitting, usu. against a wall, for men to urinate into. **2** a place or receptacle for urination. [ME f. OF f. LL *urinal* neut. of *urinalis* (as URINE)]

u·ri·nal·y·sis /yoŏrinálisis/ *n.* (*pl.* **u·ri·nal·y·ses** /–seez/) the chemical analysis of urine, esp. for diagnostic purposes.

u·ri·nar·y /yoŏrineree/ *adj.* **1** of or relating to urine. **2** affecting or occurring in the urinary system (*urinary diseases*).

u·ri·nate /yoŏrinayt/ *v.intr.* discharge urine. □□ **u·ri·na·tion** /–náyshən/ *n.* [med.L *urinare* (as URINE)]

u·rine /yoŏrin/ *n.* a pale-yellow fluid secreted as waste from the blood by the kidneys, stored in the bladder, and discharged through the urethra. □□ **u·ri·nous** *adj.* [ME f. OF f. L *urina*]

urn /órn/ *n. & v.* • *n.* **1** a vase with a foot and usu. a rounded body, esp. for storing the ashes of the cremated dead or as a vessel or

---

SYNONYM TIP *urbane*

COSMOPOLITAN, GENTEEL, SOPHISTICATED, SUAVE. In his long career as a film star, Cary Grant was known for playing **urbane, sophisticated** roles. *Urbane* in this context suggests the social poise and polished manner of someone who is well-traveled and well-bred, while *sophisticated* means worldly-wise as opposed to naïve (*a sophisticated young girl who had spent her childhood in Paris and London*). **Cosmopolitan** describes someone who is at home anywhere in the world and is free from provincial attitudes (*a cosmopolitan man who could charm women of all ages and nationalities*), while **suave** suggests the gracious social behavior of *urbane* combined with a certain glibness or superficial politeness (*She was taken in by his expensive clothes and suave manner*). At one time **genteel** meant well-bred or refined, but nowadays it has connotations of self-consciousness or pretentiousness (*too genteel to drink wine from a juice glass*).

measure. **2** a large vessel with a tap, in which tea or coffee, etc., is made or kept hot. **3** *poet.* anything in which a dead body or its remains are preserved, e.g., a grave. ● *v. tr.* enclose in an urn. □□ **urn·ful** n. (*pl.* **–fuls**). [ME f. L *urna*, rel. to *urceus* pitcher]

uro-[1] /yŏŏrō/ *comb. form* urine. [Gk *ouron* urine]

uro-[2] /yŏŏrō/ *comb. form* tail. [Gk *oura* tail]

u·ro·chord /yŏŏrōkawrd/ n. the notochord of a tunicate.

ur·o·dele /yŏŏrōdeel/ n. any amphibian of the order Urodela, having a tail when in the adult form, including newts and salamanders. [URO-[2] + Gk *dēlos* evident]

u·ro·gen·i·tal /yŏŏrōjénit'l/ *adj.* of or relating to urinary and genital products or organs.

u·rol·o·gy /yŏŏróləjee/ n. the scientific study of the urinary system. □□ **u·ro·log·ic** /–rəlójik/ *adj.* **u·rol·o·gist** n.

u·ro·pyg·i·um /yŏŏrōpíjeeəm/ n. the rump of a bird. [med.L f. Gk *ouropugion*]

u·ros·co·py /yŏŏróskəpee/ n. *Med. hist.* the examination of urine, esp. in diagnosis.

Ur·sa Ma·jor /órsə máyjər/ n. = BIG DIPPER. [L, = greater bear]

Ur·sa Mi·nor /órsə mínər/ n. = LITTLE DIPPER. [L, = lesser bear]

ur·sine /órsīn/ *adj.* of or like a bear. [L *ursinus* f. *ursus* bear]

Ur·su·line /órsəlin, –lĭn, –leen, órsyə–/ n. & *adj.* ● n. a nun of an order founded by St. Angela in 1535 for nursing the sick and teaching girls. ● *adj.* of or relating to this order. [St. *Ursula*, the founder's patron saint]

ur·ti·car·i·a /órtikáireeə/ n. *Med.* skin rash, usu. from an allergic reaction; hives. [mod.L f. L *urtica* nettle f. *urere* burn]

ur·ti·cate /órtikayt/ *v. tr.* sting like a nettle. □□ **ur·ti·ca·tion** /–káyshən/ n. [med.L *urticare* f. L *urtica*: see URTICARIA]

u·rus /yŏŏrəs/ n. = AUROCHS. [L f. Gmc]

US *abbr.* **1** United States (of America). **2** *Brit.* undersecretary.

us /us, əs/ *pron.* **1** *objective case* of WE (*they saw us*). **2** *colloq.* = WE (*it's us again*). **3** *colloq.* = ME[1] (*give us a kiss*). [OE *ūs* f. Gmc]

USA *abbr.* **1** United States of America. **2** United States Army.

us·a·ble /yŏŏzəbəl/ *adj.* (also **use·a·ble**) that can be used. □□ **us·a·bil·i·ty** /–bílitee/ n **us·a·ble·ness** n.

USAF *abbr.* United States Air Force.

us·age /yŏŏsij/ n. **1** a manner of using or treating; treatment (*damaged by rough usage*). **2** habitual or customary practice, esp. as creating a right, obligation, or standard. [ME f. OF f. *us* USE n.]

▶**Usage** means 'manner of use; practice,' while **use** means 'the act of employing.' In discussions of writing, **usage** is the term for normal or prescribed practice: *Standard usage calls for a plural.* In describing particular examples, however, employ **use**: *The use of the plural with this noun is incorrect.*

us·ance /yŏŏzəns/ n. the time allowed by commercial usage for the payment of foreign bills of exchange. [ME f. OF (as USE)]

U.S.C. *abbr. Law* United States Code.

USCG *abbr.* United States Coast Guard.

use *v. & n.* ● *v. tr.* /yŏŏz/ **1 a** cause to act or serve for a purpose; bring into service; avail oneself of (*rarely uses the car; use your discretion*). **b** consume by eating or drinking; take (alcohol, a drug, etc.), esp. habitually. **2** treat (a person) in a specified manner (*they used him shamefully*). **3** exploit for one's own ends (*they are just using you; used his position*). **4** (in *past* /yŏŏst/; foll. by *to* + infin.) did or had in the past (but no longer) as a customary practice or state (*I used to be an archaeologist; it used not (or did not use) to rain so often*). **5** (as **used** *adj.*) secondhand. **6** (as **used** /yŏŏst/ *predic. adj.*) (foll. by *to*) familiar by habit; accustomed (*not used to hard work*). **7** apply (a name or title, etc.) to oneself. ● n. /yŏŏs/ **1** the act of using or the state of being used; application to a purpose (*put it to good use; is in daily use; worn and polished with use*). **2** the right or power of using (*lost the use of my right arm*). **3 a** the ability to be used (*a flashlight would be of use*). **b** the purpose for which a thing can be used (*it's no use talking*). **4** custom or usage (*long use has reconciled me to it*). **5** the characteristic ritual and liturgy of a church or diocese, etc. **6** *Law hist.* the benefit or profit of lands, esp. in the possession of another who holds them solely for the beneficiary. □ **could use** *colloq.* would be glad to have; would be improved by having. **have no use for 1** be unable to find a use for. **2** dislike or be impatient with. **make use of 1** employ; apply. **2** benefit from. **use a person's name** quote a person as an authority or reference, etc. **use up 1** consume completely; use the whole of. **2** find a use for (something remaining). **3** exhaust or wear out, e.g., with overwork. [ME f. OF *us, user*, ult. f. L *uti us-* use]

▶**1**. See note at USAGE. **2**. See note at UTILIZE.

use·ful /yŏŏsfŏŏl/ *adj.* **1 a** of use; serviceable. **b** producing or able to produce good results (*gave me some useful hints*). **2** *colloq.* highly creditable or efficient (*a useful performance*). □ **make oneself useful** perform useful services. □□ **use·ful·ly** *adv.* **use·ful·ness** n.

use·less /yŏŏslis/ *adj.* **1** serving no purpose; unavailing (*the contents were made useless by moisture; protest is useless*). **2** *colloq.* feeble or ineffectual (*am useless at swimming; a useless gadget*). □□ **use·less·ly** *adv.* **use·less·ness** n.

us·er /yŏŏzər/ n. **1** a person who uses (esp. a particular commodity or service, or a computer). **2** *colloq.* a drug addict. **3** *Law* the continued use or enjoyment of a right, etc.

us·er-friend·ly *adj.* esp. Computing (of a machine or system) designed to be easy to use.

ush·er /úshər/ n. & v. ● n. **1** a person who shows people to their seats in an auditorium or theater, etc. **2** a doorkeeper at a court, etc. **3** *Brit.* an officer walking before a person of rank. **4** *archaic* or *joc.* an assistant teacher. ● *v. tr.* **1** act as usher to. **2** (usu. foll. by *in*) announce or show in, or usher in (*ushered us into the room; ushered in a new era*). □□ **ush·er·ship** n. [ME f. AF *usser*, OF *uissier*, var. of *huissier* f. med.L *ustiarius* for L *ostiarius* f. *ostium* door]

ush·er·ette /úshərét/ n. a female usher, esp. in a movie theater.

USIA *abbr.* (also **U.S.I.A.**) United States Information Agency.

USM *abbr.* **1** United States Marines. **2** United States Mint.

USMC *abbr.* United States Marine Corps.

USN *abbr.* United States Navy.

USO *abbr.* (also **U.S.O.**) United Service Organizations.

USPS *abbr.* (also **U.S.P.S.**) United States Postal Service.

us·que·baugh /úskwibaw/ n. esp. *Ir. & Sc.* whiskey. [Ir. & Sc. Gael. *uisge beatha* water of life: cf. WHISKEY]

USS *abbr.* United States Ship.

USSR *abbr. hist.* Union of Soviet Socialist Republics.

usu. *abbr.* **1** usual. **2** usually.

u·su·al /yŏŏzhŏŏəl/ *adj.* **1** such as commonly occurs, or is observed or done; customary; habitual (*the usual formalities; it is usual to tip them; forgot my keys as usual*). **2** (prec. by *the, my*, etc.) *colloq.* a person's usual drink, etc. □□ **u·su·al·ly** *adv.* **u·su·al·ness** n. [ME f. OF *usual, usuel* or LL *usualis* (as USE)]

u·su·cap·tion /yŏŏzəkápshən/ n. (also **u·su·ca·pi·on** /–káypeeən/) (in Roman and Scots law) the acquisition of a title or right to property by uninterrupted and undisputed possession for a prescribed term. [OF *usucap(t)ion* or L *usucap(t)io* f. *usucapere* acquire by prescription f. *usu* by use + *capere capt-* take]

u·su·fruct /yŏŏzəfrukt, –sə–/ n. & v. ● n. (in Roman and Scots law) the right of enjoying the use and advantages of another's property short of the destruction or waste of its substance. ● *v. tr.* hold in usufruct. □□ **u·su·fruc·tu·ar·y** /–frúkchŏŏeree/ *adj. & n.* [med.L *usufructus* f. L *usus (et) fructus* f. *usus* USE + *fructus* FRUIT]

u·su·rer /yŏŏzhərər/ n. a person who practices usury. [ME f. AF *usurer*, OF *usureor* f. *usure* f. L *usura*: see USURY]

u·su·ri·ous /yoozhŏŏreeəs/ *adj.* of, involving, or practicing usury. □□ **u·su·ri·ous·ly** *adv.*

u·surp /yŏŏzórp, –sórp/ v. **1** *tr.* seize or assume (a throne or power, etc.) wrongfully. **2** *intr.* (foll. by *on, upon*) encroach. □□ **u·sur·pa·tion** /yŏŏzərpáyshən, –sər–/ n. **u·surp·er** n. [ME f. OF *usurper* f. L *usurpare* seize for use]

u·su·ry /yŏŏzhəree/ n. **1** the act or practice of lending money at interest, esp. *Law* at an exorbitant rate. **2** interest at this rate. □ **with usury** *rhet.* or *poet.* with increased force, etc. [ME f. med.L *usuria* f. L *usura* (as USE)]

UT *abbr.* **1** Utah (in official postal use). **2** universal time.

Ute /yŏŏt/ n. (*pl.* **Ute** or **Utes**) **1** a member of a N. American people native to the area that is now Colorado, New Mexico, Utah, and Arizona. **2** the language of these people.

u·ten·sil /yŏŏténsəl/ n. an implement or vessel, esp. for domestic use (*cooking utensils*). [ME f. OF *utensile* f. med.L, neut. of L *utensilis* usable (as USE)]

u·ter·ine /yŏŏtərin, –rīn/ *adj.* **1** of or relating to the uterus. **2** born of the same mother but not the same father (*sister uterine*). [ME f. LL *uterinus* (as UTERUS)]

u·ter·us /yŏŏtərəs/ n. (*pl.* **u·ter·i** /–rī/) the womb. □□ **u·ter·i·tis** /–rítis/ n. [L]

u·tile /yŏŏtil, –tīl/ *adj.* useful; having utility. [ME f. OF f. L *utilis* f. *uti* use]

u·til·i·tar·i·an /yŏŏtílitáireeən/ *adj. & n.* ● *adj.* **1** designed to be useful for a purpose rather than attractive; severely practical. **2** of utilitarianism. ● n. an adherent of utilitarianism.

u·til·i·tar·i·an·ism /yŏŏtílitáireeənizəm/ n. **1** the doctrine that actions are right if they are useful or for the benefit of a majority. **2** the doctrine that the greatest happiness of the greatest number should be the guiding principle of conduct.

u·til·i·ty /yŏŏtílitee/ n. (*pl.* **–ties**) **1** the condition of being useful or profitable. **2** a useful thing. **3** = PUBLIC UTILITY. **4** (*attrib.*) **a** severely practical and standardized (*utility furniture*). **b** made or serving for utility. [ME f. OF *utilité* f. L *utilitas –tatis* (as UTILE)]

u·til·i·ty room n. a room equipped with appliances for washing, ironing, and other domestic work.

u·til·i·ty ve·hi·cle n. (also **u·til·i·ty truck**, etc.) a vehicle capable of serving various functions.

u·ti·lize /yŏŏt'līz/ *v. tr.* make practical use of; turn to account; use ef-

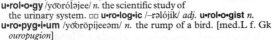

urn 1

fectively. □□ **u•ti•liz•a•ble** *adj.* **u•ti•li•za•tion** *n.* **u•ti•liz•er** *n.* [F *utiliser* f. It. *utilizzare* (as UTILE)]

▶Many people complain that **utilize** is nothing more than a pretentious substitute for **use**. While it's true that *use* is often just as good as *utilize* and less pompous (*the administrators hoped that most students would use public transportation instead of bringing cars on campus*), there are some contexts in which *utilize* is preferable. If you say "The teachers had no idea how to use the new video camera," you're implying that the teachers didn't know how to operate the camera. If you say *utilize*, however, you're implying that the teachers did not know how to best employ the video camera to teach their students.

-ution /ōõshən/ *suffix* forming nouns, = –ATION (*solution*). [F f. L –*utio*]

ut•most /útmōst/ *adj. & n.* ● *adj.* furthest, extreme, or greatest (*the utmost limits*; *showed the utmost reluctance*). ● *n.* (prec. by *the*) the utmost point or degree, etc. □ **do one's utmost** do all that one can. [OE *ūt(e)mest* (as OUT, –MOST)]

U•to•pi•a /yōōtṓpeeə/ *n.* an imagined perfect place or state of things. [title of a book (1516) by Thomas More: mod.L f. Gk *ou* not + *topos* place]

U•to•pi•an /yōōtṓpeeən/ *adj. & n.* (also **utopian**) ● *adj.* characteristic of Utopia; idealistic. ● *n.* an idealistic reformer. □□ **U•to•pi•an•ism** *n.*

u•tri•cle /yōōtrikəl/ *n.* a small cell or sac in an animal or plant, esp. one in the inner ear. □□ **u•tric•u•lar** /–tríkyələr/ *adj.* [F *utricule* or L *utriculus* dimin. of *uter* leather bag]

ut•ter[1] /útər/ *attrib.adj.* complete; total; absolute (*utter misery*; *saw the utter absurdity of it*). □□ **ut•ter•ly** *adv.* **ut•ter•ness** *n.* [OE *ūtera, ūttra*, compar. adj. f. *ūt* OUT: cf. OUTER]

ut•ter[2] /útər/ *v.tr.* **1** emit audibly (*uttered a startled cry*). **2** express in spoken or written words. **3** *Law* put (esp. forged money) into cir-

culation. □□ **ut•ter•a•ble** *adj.* **ut•ter•er** *n.* [ME f. MDu. *ūteren* make known, assim. to UTTER[1]]

ut•ter•ance /útərəns/ *n.* **1** the act or an instance of uttering. **2** a thing spoken. **3 a** the power of speaking. **b** a manner of speaking. **4** *Linguistics* an uninterrupted chain of spoken or written words not necessarily corresponding to a single or complete grammatical unit.

ut•ter•most /útərmōst/ *adj.* furthest; extreme.

U-turn /yōōtərn/ *n.* **1** the turning of a vehicle in a U-shaped course so as to face in the opposite direction. **2** a reversal of policy.

UV *abbr.* ultraviolet.

u•ve•a /yōōveeə/ *n.* the pigmented layer of the eye, lying beneath the outer layer. [med.L f. L *uva* grape]

u•vu•la /yōōvyələ/ *n.* (*pl.* **u•vu•las** or **u•vu•lae** /–lee/) **1** a fleshy extension of the soft palate hanging above the throat. **2** a similar process in the bladder or cerebellum. [ME f. LL, dimin. of L *uva* grape]

u•vu•lar /yōōvyələr/ *adj. & n.* ● *adj.* **1** of or relating to the uvula. **2** articulated with the back of the tongue and the uvula, as in *r* in French. ● *n.* a uvular consonant.

ux•o•ri•al /uksáwreeəl, ugzáwr–/ *adj.* of or relating to a wife.

ux•o•ri•cide /uksáwrisíd, ugzáwr–/ *n.* **1** the killing of one's wife. **2** a person who does this. □□ **ux•o•ri•cid•al** *adj.* [L *uxor* wife + –CIDE]

ux•o•ri•ous /uksáwreeəs, ugzáwr–/ *adj.* **1** greatly or excessively fond of one's wife. **2** (of behavior, etc.) showing such fondness. □□ **ux•o•ri•ous•ly** *adv.* **ux•o•ri•ous•ness** *n.* [L *uxoriosus* f. *uxor* wife]

Uz•bek /oŏzbek–, úz–/ *n.* (also **Uz•beg** /–beg/) **1** a member of a Turkic people living mainly in Uzbekistan, a country of south central Asia. **2** the language of this people. [Uzbek]

V

V¹ /vee/ *n.* (also **v**) (*pl.* **Vs** or **V's**) **1** the twenty-second letter of the alphabet. **2** a V-shaped thing. **3** (as a Roman numeral) five.

V² *abbr.* (also **V.**) volt(s).

V³ *symb. Chem.* the element vanadium.

v. *abbr.* **1** verse. **2** verso. **3** versus. **4** very. **5** *vide.*

VA *abbr.* **1** Veterans Administration. **2** Virginia (in official postal use). **3** vice admiral. **4** vicar apostolic. **5** (in the UK) Order of Victoria and Albert.

Va. *abbr.* Virginia.

vac /vak/ *n. colloq.* **1** vacuum cleaner. **2** *Brit.* vacation (esp. of universities). [abbr.]

va·can·cy /váykənsee/ *n.* (*pl.* **–cies**) **1 a** the state of being vacant or empty. **b** an instance of this; empty space. **2** an unoccupied position or job (*there are three vacancies for computer specialists*). **3** an available room in a hotel, etc. **4** emptiness of mind; idleness; listlessness.

va·cant /váykənt/ *adj.* **1** not filled nor occupied; empty. **2** not mentally active; showing no interest (*had a vacant stare*). □□ **va·cant·ly** *adv.* [ME f. OF *vacant* or L *vacare* (as VACATE)]

va·cant pos·ses·sion *n. Brit.* ownership of a house, etc., with any previous occupant having moved out.

va·cate /váykayt, vaykáyt/ *v.tr.* **1** leave vacant or cease to occupy (a house, room, etc.). **2** give up tenure of (a post, etc.). **3** *Law* annul (a judgment or contract, etc.). □□ **va·cat·a·ble** *adj.* [L *vacare vacat-* be empty]

va·ca·tion /vaykáyshən, və–/ *n. & v.* ● *n.* **1** a time of rest, recreation, etc., esp. spent away from home or in traveling, during which regular activities (esp. work or schooling) are suspended. **2** a fixed period of cessation from work, esp. in legislatures and courts of law. **3** the act of vacating (a house or post, etc.). ● *v.intr.* take a vacation, esp. away from home for pleasure and recreation. □□ **va·ca·tion·er** *n.* **va·ca·tion·ist** *n.* [ME f. OF *vacation* or L *vacatio* (as VACATE)]

va·ca·tion·land /vaykáyshənland, və–/ *n.* an area providing attractions for vacationers.

vac·ci·nate /váksinayt/ *v.tr.* inoculate with a vaccine to procure immunity from a disease; immunize. □□ **vac·ci·na·tion** /–náyshən/ *n.* **vac·ci·na·tor** *n.*

vac·cine /vakseén/ *n. & adj.* ● *n.* **1** an antigenic preparation used to stimulate the production of antibodies and procure immunity from one or several diseases. **2** *hist.* the cowpox virus used in vaccination against smallpox. ● *adj.* of or relating to cowpox or vaccination. □□ **vac·ci·nal** /–sinəl/ *adj.* [L *vaccinus* f. *vacca* cow]

SPELLING TIP vaccine

To remember the double *c* in *vaccine*, use the mnemonic: "Most vaccines are measured in *c*ubic *c*entimeters."

---

vac·cin·i·a /vaksíneeə/ *n. Med.* a virus used as a vaccine against smallpox. [mod.L (as VACCINE)]

vac·il·late /vásilayt/ *v.intr.* **1** fluctuate in opinion or resolution. **2** move from side to side; oscillate; waver. □□ **vac·il·la·tion** /–láyshən/ *n.* **vac·il·la·tor** *n.* [L *vacillare vacillat-* sway]

vac·u·a *pl.* of VACUUM.

va·cu·i·ty /vakyóoətee, və–/ *n.* **1** the condition, state, or quality of being vacuous. **2** complete lack of intelligence or thought; inanity. **3** something, such as a comment, that is senseless or inane. **4** an empty space.

vac·u·ole /vákyoo-ól/ *n. Biol.* a tiny space within the cytoplasm of a cell containing air, fluid, food particles, etc. □□ **vac·u·o·lar** /vakyoo-ólər, vákyoooələr/ *adj.* **vac·u·o·la·tion** /–láyshən/ *n.* [F, dimin. of L *vacuus* empty]

vac·u·ous /vákyooəs/ *adj.* **1** lacking expression (*a vacuous stare*). **2** unintelligent (*a vacuous remark*). **3** empty. □□ **va·cu·i·ty** /vəkyóo-itee/ *n.* **vac·u·ous·ly** *adv.* **vac·u·ous·ness** *n.* [L *vacuus* empty (as VACATE)]

vac·u·um /vákyōoəm, –yōom, –yəm/ *n. & v.* ● *n.* (*pl.* **vac·u·ums** or **vac·u·a** /–yōoə/) **1** a space entirely devoid of matter. **2** a space or vessel from which the air has been completely or partly removed by a pump, etc. **3 a** the absence of the normal or previous content of a place, environment, etc. **b** the absence of former circumstances, activities, etc. **4** (*pl.* **vac·u·ums**) *colloq.* a vacuum cleaner. **5** a decrease of pressure below the normal atmospheric value. ● *v. colloq.* **1** *tr.* clean with a vacuum cleaner. **2** *intr.* use a vacuum cleaner. [mod.L, neut. of L *vacuus* empty]

vac·u·um brake *n.* a brake in which pressure is caused by the exhaustion of air.

vac·u·um clean·er *n.* an apparatus for removing dust, etc., by suction.

vac·u·um flask *n. Brit.* = THERMOS.

vac·u·um gauge *n.* a gauge for testing the pressure after the production of a vacuum.

vac·u·um-packed *adj.* sealed after the partial removal of air.

vac·u·um pump *n.* a pump for producing a vacuum.

vac·u·um tube *n. Electronics* an evacuated glass tube that regulates the flow of thermionic electrons in one direction, used esp. in the rectification of a current and in radio reception.

va·de me·cum /váadee máykəm, váydee meékəm/ *n.* a handbook, etc., carried constantly for use. [F f. mod.L, = go with me]

vag·a·bond /vágəbond/ *n., adj., & v.* ● *n.* **1** a wanderer or vagrant, esp. an idle one. **2** *colloq.* a scamp or rascal. ● *adj.* having no fixed habitation; wandering. ● *v.intr.* wander about as a vagabond. □□ **vag·a·bond·age** *n.* [ME f. OF *vagabond* or L *vagabundus* f. *vagari* wander]

va·gal see VAGUS.

va·gar·y /váygəree, vəgáaree/ *n.* (*pl.* **–ies**) a caprice; an eccentric idea or act (*the vagaries of Fortune*). □□ **va·gar·i·ous** /vəgáireeəs/ *adj.* [L *vagari* wander]

va·gi *pl.* of VAGUS.

va·gi·na /vəjínə/ *n.* (*pl.* **va·gi·nas** or **va·gi·nae** /–nee/) **1** the canal between the uterus and vulva of a woman or other female mammal. **2** a sheath formed around a stem by the base of a leaf. □□ **vag·i·nal** /vájin'l/ *adj.* **vag·i·ni·tis** /vájinítis/ *n.* [L, = sheath, scabbard]

vag·i·nis·mus /vájinízməs/ *n.* a painful spasmodic contraction of the vagina, usu. in response to pressure. [mod.L (as VAGINA)]

va·grant /váygrənt/ *n. & adj.* ● *n.* **1** a person without a settled home or regular work. **2** a wanderer or vagabond. ● *adj.* **1** wandering or roving (*a vagrant musician*). **2** being a vagrant. □□ **va·gran·cy** /–grənsee/ *n.* **va·grant·ly** *adv.* [ME f. AF *vag(a)raunt*, perh. alt. f. AF *wakerant*, etc., by assoc. with L *vagari* wander]

vague /vayg/ *adj.* **1** of uncertain or ill-defined meaning or character (*gave a vague answer; has some vague idea of emigrating*). **2** (of a person or mind) imprecise; inexact in thought, expression, or understanding. □□ **vague·ly** *adv.* **vague·ness** *n.* **va·guish** *adj.* [F *vague* or L *vagus* wandering, uncertain]

va·gus /váygəs/ *n.* (*pl.* **va·gi** /–gī, –jī/) *Anat.* either of the tenth pair of cranial nerves with branches to the heart, lungs, and viscera. □□ **va·gal** *adj.* [L: see VAGUE]

vail /vayl/ *v. archaic* **1** *tr.* lower or doff (one's plumes, pride, crown, etc.), esp. in token of submission. **2** *intr.* yield; give place; remove one's hat as a sign of respect, etc. [ME f. obs. *avale* f. OF *avaler* to lower f. *a val* down f. *val* VALE¹]

vain /vayn/ *adj.* **1** excessively proud or conceited, esp. about one's own attributes. **2** empty; trivial; unsubstantial (*vain boasts; vain triumphs*). **3** useless; followed by no good result (*in the vain hope of dissuading them*). ● **in vain** without result or success (*it was in vain that we protested*). **take a person's name in vain** use it lightly or profanely. □□ **vain·ly** *adv.* **vain·ness** *n.* [ME f. OF f. L *vanus* empty, without substance]

SPELLING TIP vain/vane

To keep the distinction between *vain* and *vane*, use the mnemonic: "A va*i*n person is *I*-oriented."

---

vain·glo·ry /vayngláwree/ *n. literary* boastfulness; extreme vanity. □□ **vain·glo·ri·ous** *adj.* **vain·glo·ri·ous·ly** *adv.* **vain·glo·ri·ous·ness** *n.* [ME, after OF *vaine gloire*, L *vana gloria*]

vair /vair/ *n.* **1** *archaic* or *hist.* a squirrel fur widely used for medieval linings and trimmings. **2** *Heraldry* fur represented by small shield-shaped or bell-shaped figures usu. alternately azure and argent. [ME f. OF f. L (as VARIOUS)]

Vaish·na·va /víshnəvə/ *n. Hinduism* a devotee of Vishnu. [Skr. *vaiṣṇavá*]

Vais·ya /vísyə/ *n.* **1** the third of the four great Hindu castes, comprising the merchants and agriculturalists. **2** a member of this caste. [Skr. *vaiśya* peasant, laborer]

val·ance /váləns, váyl–/ *n.* (also **val·ence**) a short curtain around the

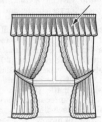

valance

frame or canopy of a bed, above a window, or under a shelf. □□ **val‧anced** adj. [ME ult. f. OF avaler descend: see VAIL]

vale[1] /vayl/ n. archaic or poet. (except in place-names) a valley (Vale of the White Horse). [ME f. OF val f. L vallis, valles]

vale[2] /vaalee, waalay/ int. & n. esp. Brit. • int. farewell. • n. a farewell. [L, imper. of valēre be well or strong]

val‧e‧dic‧tion /válidíkshən/ n. **1** the act or an instance of bidding farewell. **2** the words used in this. [L valedicere valedict- (as VALE[2], dicere say), after benediction]

val‧e‧dic‧to‧ri‧an /válidiktáwreeən/ n. a person who gives a valedictory, esp. the highest-ranking member of a graduating class.

val‧e‧dic‧to‧ry /válidíktəree/ adj. & n. • adj. serving as a farewell. • n. (pl. –ries) a farewell address.

va‧lence[1] /váyləns/ n. Chem. the combining power of an atom measured by the number of hydrogen atoms it can displace or combine with. [LL valentia power, competence f. valēre be well or strong]

val‧ence[2] var. of VALANCE.

val‧ence e‧lec‧tron n. an electron in the outermost shell of an atom involved in forming a chemical bond.

Va‧len‧ci‧ennes /vəlénsee–énz, valoNsyén/ n. a rich kind of lace. [Valenciennes in NE France, where it was made in the 17th and 18th c.]

va‧len‧cy /váylənsee/ n. (pl. –cies) Chem. Brit. = VALENCE[1].

val‧en‧tine /váləntin/ n. **1** a card or gift sent, often anonymously, as a mark of love or affection on St. Valentine's Day (Feb. 14). **2** a sweetheart chosen on this day. [ME f. OF Valentin f. L Valentinus, name of two saints]

vale of tears n. literary the world as a scene of life, trouble, etc.

va‧le‧ri‧an /vəleéreeən/ n. **1** any of various flowering plants of the family Valerianaceae. **2** the root of any of these used as a medicinal sedative. [ME f. OF valeriane f. med.L valeriana (herba), app. fem. of Valerianus of Valerius]

va‧ler‧ic ac‧id /vəlérik, –leérik/ n. Chem. a colorless liquid carboxylic acid used in making perfumes, esp. that derived from valerian root. [VALERIAN + –IC]

val‧et /valáy, válay, –lit/ n. & v. • n. **1** a gentleman's personal attendant who looks after his clothes, etc. **2** a hotel, etc., employee with similar duties. **3** a standing rack for holding one's suit, coat, etc. • v. (**val‧et‧ed, val‧et‧ing**) **1** intr. work as a valet. **2** tr. act as a valet to. **3** tr. clean or clean out (a car). [F, = OF valet, vaslet, VARLET: rel. to VASSAL]

PRONUNCIATION TIP   valet

Americans have a tendency to give this word a French pronunciation, either "VAL-ay" or "va-LAY." Pronouncing it "VAL-it" is more common in British English.

val‧e‧tu‧di‧nar‧i‧an /válitŏŏd΄náireeən, –tyŏŏd–/ n. & adj. • n. a person of poor health or unduly anxious about health. • adj. **1** of or being a valetudinarian. **2** of poor health. **3** seeking to recover one's health. □□ **val‧e‧tu‧di‧nar‧i‧an‧ism** n. [L valetudinarius in ill health f. valetudo –dinis health f. valēre be well]

val‧e‧tu‧di‧nar‧y /válitŏŏd΄neree/ adj. & n. (pl. –ies) = VALETUDINARIAN.

val‧gus /válgəs/ n. a deformity involving the outward displacement of the foot or hand from the midline. [L, = knock-kneed]

Val‧hal‧la /valhálə, vaalhaálə/ n. **1** (in Norse mythology) a palace in which the souls of slain heroes feasted for eternity. **2** a building used for honoring the illustrious. [mod.L f. ON Valhöll f. valr the slain + höll HALL]

val‧iant /vályənt/ adj. (of a person or conduct) brave; courageous. □□ **val‧iant‧ly** adv. [ME f. AF valiaunt, OF vailant ult. f. L valēre be strong]

val‧id /válid/ adj. **1** (of a reason, objection, etc.) sound or defensible; well-grounded. **2 a** executed with the proper formalities (a valid contract). **b** legally acceptable (a valid passport). **c** not having reached its expiration date. □□ **va‧lid‧i‧ty** /–líditee/ n. **val‧id‧ly** adv. [F valide or L validus strong (as VALIANT)]

val‧i‧date /válidayt/ v.tr. make valid; ratify; confirm. □□ **val‧i‧da‧tion** /–dáyshən/ n. [med.L validare f. L (as VALID)]

va‧line /váyleen/ n. Biochem. an amino acid that is an essential nutrient for vertebrates and a general constituent of proteins. [VALERIC (ACID) + –INE[4]]

va‧lise /vəleés/ n. **1** a small suitcase; traveling bag. **2** a knapsack. [F f. It. valigia corresp. to med.L valisia, f. unkn. orig.]

Val‧i‧um /váleeəm/ n. Trademark the drug diazepam used as a tranquilizer and relaxant. [20th c.: orig. uncert.]

Val‧kyr‧ie /valkeéree, válkiree/ n. (in Norse mythology) each of Odin's twelve handmaidens who selected heroes destined to be slain in battle. [ON Valkyrja, lit. 'chooser of the slain' f. valr the slain + (unrecorded) kur-, kuz- rel. to CHOOSE]

val‧lec‧u‧la /vəlékyələ/ n. (pl. **val‧lec‧u‧lae** /–lee/) Anat. & Bot. a groove or furrow. □□ **val‧lec‧u‧lar** adj. **val‧lec‧u‧late** /–layt/ adj. [LL, dimin. of L vallis valley]

val‧ley /válee/ n. (pl. **–leys**) **1** a low area more or less enclosed by hills and usu. with a stream flowing through it. **2** any depression compared to this. **3** Archit. an internal angle formed by the intersecting planes of a roof. [ME f. AF valey, OF valee ult. f. L vallis, valles: cf. VALE[1]]

val‧lum /váləm/ n. Rom. Antiq. a rampart and stockade as a defense. [L, collect. f. vallus stake]

va‧lo‧ni‧a /vəlóneeə/ n. acorn cups of an evergreen oak, Quercus macrolepis, used in tanning, dyeing, and making ink. [It. vallonia ult. f. Gk balanos acorn]

val‧or /válər/ n. (Brit. **val‧our**) personal courage, esp. in battle. □□ **val‧or‧ous** adj. [ME f. OF f. LL valor –oris f. valēre be strong]

val‧or‧ize /váləriz/ v.tr. raise or fix the price of (a commodity, etc.) by artificial means, esp. by government action. □□ **val‧or‧i‧za‧tion** n. [back-form. f. valorization f. F valorisation (as VALOR)]

val‧our Brit. var. of VALOR.

valse /vaals/ n. a waltz. [F f. G (as WALTZ)]

val‧u‧a‧ble /vályŏŏbəl, vályə–/ adj. & n. • adj. of great value, price, or worth (a valuable property; valuable information). • n. (usu. in pl.) a valuable thing, esp. a small article of personal property. □□ **val‧u‧a‧bly** adv.

val‧u‧a‧tion /vályŏŏ–áyshən/ n. **1 a** an estimation (esp. by a professional appraiser) of a thing's worth. **b** the worth estimated. **2** the price set on a thing. □□ **val‧u‧ate** v.tr.

val‧u‧a‧tor /vályoo–aytər/ n. a person who makes valuations; an appraiser.

val‧ue /vályŏŏ/ n. & v. • n. **1** the worth, desirability, or utility of a thing, or the qualities on which these depend (the value of regular exercise). **2** worth as estimated; valuation (set a high value on my time). **3** the amount of money or goods for which a thing can be exchanged in the open market; purchasing power. **4** the equivalent of a thing; what represents or is represented by or may be substituted for a thing (paid them the value of their lost property). **5** (in full **value for money**) something well worth the money spent. **6** the ability of a thing to serve a purpose or cause an effect (news value; nuisance value). **7** (in pl.) one's principles or standards; one's judgment of what is valuable or important in life. **8** Mus. the duration of the sound signified by a note. **9** Math. the amount denoted by an algebraic term or expression. **10** (foll. by of) **a** a meaning (of a word, etc.). **b** the quality (of a spoken sound). **11** the relative rank or importance of a playing card, chess piece, etc., according to the rules of the game. **12** the relation of one part of a picture to others in respect of light and shade; the part being characterized by a particular tone. **13** Physics & Chem. the numerical measure of a quantity or a number denoting magnitude on some conventional scale (the value of gravity at the equator). • v.tr. (**val‧ues, val‧ued, val‧u‧ing**) **1** estimate the value of; appraise (esp. professionally) (valued the property at $200,000). **2** have a high or specified opinion of; attach importance to (a valued friend). [ME f. OF, fem. past part. of valoir be worth f. L valēre]

val‧ue-add‧ed tax n. a tax on the amount by which the value of an article has been increased at each stage of its production.

val‧ue judg‧ment n. a subjective estimate of quality, etc.

val‧ue‧less /vályŏŏlis/ adj. having no value. □□ **val‧ue‧less‧ness** n.

val‧u‧er /vályŏŏər/ n. Brit. a person who estimates or assesses values, esp. professionally; an appraiser.

val‧ue re‧ceived n. money or its equivalent given for a bill of exchange.

va‧lu‧ta /vəlóŏtə/ n. **1** the value of one currency with respect to another. **2** a currency considered in this way. [It., = VALUE]

valve /valv/ n. **1** a device for controlling the passage of fluid through a pipe, etc., esp. an automatic device allowing movement in one direction only. **2** Anat. & Zool. a membranous part of an organ, etc., allowing a flow of blood, etc., in one direction only. **3** Brit. = VACUUM TUBE. **4** a device to vary the effective length of the tube in a brass musical instrument. **5** each of the two shells of an oyster, mussel, etc. **6** Bot. each of the segments into which a capsule or dry fruit dehisces. **7** archaic a leaf of a folding door. □□ **val‧vate** /–vayt/ adj. **valved** adj. (also in comb.). **valve‧less** adj. **val‧vule** n. [ME f. L valva leaf of a folding door]

valve 1

val‧vu‧lar /vályvŏŏlar/ adj. **1** having a valve or valves. **2** having the form or function of a valve. [mod.L valvula, dimin. of L valva]

val‧vu‧li‧tis /vályvŏŏlítis/ n. inflammation of the valves of the heart.

vam‧brace /vámbrays/ n. hist. defensive armor for the forearm. [ME f. AF vaunt-bras, OF avant-bras f. avant before (see AVAUNT) + bras arm]

va‧moose /vamóŏs, və–/ v.intr. (esp. as int.) sl. depart hurriedly. [Sp. vamos let us go]

vamp[1] /vamp/ n. & v. • n. **1** the upper front part of a boot or shoe. **2** a patched-up article. **3** an improvised musical accompaniment.

• *v.* **1** *tr.* (often foll. by *up*) repair or furbish. **2** *tr.* (foll. by *up*) make by patching or from odds and ends. **3** *a tr. & intr.* improvise a musical accompaniment (to). **b** *tr.* improvise (a musical accompaniment). **4** *tr.* put a new vamp to (a boot or shoe). [ME f. OF *avant-pié* f. *avant* before (see AVAUNT) + *pied* foot]

vamp² /vamp/ *n. & v. colloq.* • *n.* **1** an unscrupulous flirt. **2** a woman who uses sexual attraction to exploit men. • *v.* **1** *tr.* allure or exploit (a man). **2** *intr.* act as a vamp. [abbr. of VAMPIRE]

vam·pire /vámpīr/ *n.* **1** a ghost or reanimated corpse supposed to leave its grave at night to suck the blood of persons sleeping. **2** a person who preys ruthlessly on others. **3** (in full **vampire bat**) any tropical (esp. South American) bat of the family Desmodontidae, with incisors for piercing flesh and feeding on blood. **4** *Theatr.* a small spring trapdoor used for sudden disappearances. □□ **vam·pir·ic** /-pírik/ *adj.* [F *vampire* or G *Vampir* f. Magyar *vampir* perh. f. Turk. *uber* witch]

vam·pir·ism /vámpīrizəm/ *n.* **1** belief in the existence of vampires. **2** the practices of a vampire.

vam·plate /vámplayt/ *n. hist.* an iron plate on a lance protecting the hand when the lance was couched. [ME f. AF *vauntplate* (as VAMBRACE, PLATE)]

van¹ /van/ *n.* **1** a covered vehicle for conveying goods, etc., esp. a large truck or trailer (*moving van*). **2** a smaller such vehicle, similar to a panel truck and used esp. for carrying passengers, traveling gear, etc. **3** *Brit.* a railroad car for luggage or for the use of the guard. **4** *Brit.* a gypsy trailer. [abbr. of CARAVAN]

van² /van/ *n.* **1** a vanguard. **2** the forefront (*in the van of progress*). [abbr. of VANGUARD]

van³ /van/ *n.* **1** the testing of ore quality by washing on a shovel or by machine. **2** *archaic* a winnowing fan. **3** *archaic* or *poet.* a wing. [ME, southern & western var. of FAN¹, perh. partly f. OF *van* or L *vannus*]

van⁴ /van/ *n. Brit. Tennis colloq.* = ADVANTAGE. [abbr.]

va·na·di·um /vənáydeeəm/ *n. Chem.* a hard, gray, metallic transition element occurring naturally in several ores and used in small quantities for strengthening some steels. ¶ Symb.: **V**. □□ **van·a·date** /vánədayt/ *n.* **va·nad·ic** /-nádik/ *adj.* **van·a·dous** /vánədəs/ *adj.* [mod.L f. ON *Vanadís* name of the Scand. goddess Freyja + –IUM]

Van Al·len belt /van álən/ *n.* (also **Van Al·len lay·er**) each of two regions of intense radiation partly surrounding the earth at heights of several thousand miles. [J. A. *Van Allen*, US physicist b. 1914]

van·dal /vánd'l/ *n. & adj.* • *n.* **1** a person who willfully or maliciously destroys or damages property. **2** (**Vandal**) a member of a Germanic people that ravaged Gaul, Spain, N. Africa, and Rome in the 4th–5th c., destroying many books and works of art. • *adj.* of or relating to the Vandals. □□ **Van·dal·ic** /-álik/ *adj.* (in sense 2 of *n.*). [L *Vandalus* f. Gmc]

van·dal·ism /vánd'lizəm/ *n.* willful or malicious destruction or damage to works of art or other property. □□ **van·dal·is·tic** *adj.* **van·dal·is·ti·cal·ly** *adv.*

van·dal·ize /vánd'līz/ *v.tr.* destroy or damage willfully or maliciously.

Van de Graaff generator /ván də gráf/ *n. Electr.* a machine devised to generate electrostatic charge by means of a vertical endless belt collecting charge from a voltage source and transferring it to a large insulated metal dome, where a high voltage is produced. [R. J. *Van de Graaff*, US physicist d. 1967]

van der Waals forces /ván dər wáwlz, waálz/ *n.pl. Chem.* short-range attractive forces between uncharged molecules arising from the interaction of dipole moments. [J. *van der Waals*, Dutch physicist d. 1923]

Van·dyke /vandík/ *n. & adj.* • *n.* **1** each of a series of large points forming a border to lace or cloth, etc. **2** a cape or collar, etc., with these. • *adj.* in the style of dress, esp. with pointed borders, common in portraits by Van Dyck. [Sir A. *Van Dyck*, Anglicized *Vandyke*, Flem. painter d. 1641]

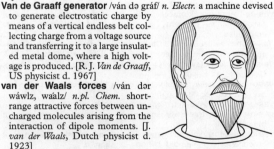

Vandyke beard

Van·dyke beard *n.* a neat, pointed beard.

Van·dyke brown *n.* a deep rich brown.

vane /vayn/ *n.* **1** (in full **weather vane**) a revolving pointer mounted on a church spire or other high place to show the direction of the wind (cf. WEATHERCOCK). **2** a blade of a screw propeller or a windmill, etc. **3** the sight of surveying instruments, a quadrant, etc. **4** the flat part of a bird's feather formed by the barbs.

vane 1

□□ **vaned** *adj.* **vane·less** *adj.* [ME, southern & western var. of obs. *fane* f. OE *fana* banner f. Gmc]

SPELLING TIP **vane**

See note at VAIN.

va·nes·sa /vənésə/ *n.* any butterfly of the genus *Vanessa*, including the red admiral and the painted lady. [mod.L]

vang /vang/ *n. Naut.* each of two guy ropes running from the end of a gaff to the deck. [earlier *fang* = gripping device: OE f. ON *fang* grasp f. Gmc]

van·guard /vángaard/ *n.* **1** the foremost part of an army or fleet advancing or ready to advance. **2** the leaders of a movement or of opinion, etc. [earlier *vandgard*, *(a)vantgard*, f. OF *avan(t)garde* f. *avant* before (see AVAUNT) + *garde* GUARD]

va·nil·la /vəníllə/ *n.* **1 a** any tropical climbing orchid of the genus *Vanilla*, esp *V. planifolia*, with fragrant flowers. **b** (in full **vanilla bean**) the fruit of these. **2** a substance obtained from the vanilla bean or synthesized and used to flavor ice cream, chocolate, etc. [Sp. *vainilla* pod, dimin. of *vaina* sheath, pod, f. L VAGINA]

va·nil·lin /vənílin/ *n.* **1** the fragrant principle of vanilla. **2** a synthetic preparation with a vanillalike fragrance or flavoring.

van·ish /vánish/ *v.* **1** *intr.* **a** disappear suddenly. **b** disappear gradually; fade away. **2** *intr.* cease to exist. **3** *intr. Math.* become zero. **4** *tr.* cause to disappear. [ME f. OF *e(s)vaniss-* stem of *e(s)vanir* ult. f. L *evanescere* (as EX-¹, *vanus* empty)]

van·ish·ing cream *n.* an ointment that leaves no visible trace when rubbed into the skin.

van·ish·ing point *n.* **1** the point at which receding parallel lines viewed in perspective appear to meet. **2** the state of complete disappearance of something.

van·i·ty /vánitee/ *n.* (*pl.* **-ties**) **1** conceit and desire for admiration of one's personal attainments or attractions. **2 a** futility or unsubstantiality (*the vanity of human achievement*). **b** an unreal thing. **3** ostentatious display. **4** a dressing table. **5** a unit consisting of a washbowl set into a flat top with cupboards beneath. [ME f. OF *vanité* f. L *vanitas* –*tatis* (as VAIN)]

van·i·ty bag *n.* (also **van·i·ty case**) a bag or case for carrying a small mirror, makeup, etc.

van·i·ty (also **Van·i·ty Fair**) the world (allegorized in Bunyan's *Pilgrim's Progress*) as a scene of vanity.

van·quish /vángkwish/ *v.tr. literary* conquer or overcome. □□ **van·quish·a·ble** *adj.* **van·quish·er** *n.* [ME *venkus*, *–quis*, etc., f. OF *vencus* past part. and *venquis* past tenses of *veintre* f. L *vincere*: assim. to –ISH²]

van·tage /vántij/ *n.* **1** (also **van·tage point** or **ground**) a place affording a good view or prospect. **2** *Tennis* = ADVANTAGE. **3** *archaic* advantage or gain. [ME f. AF f. OF *avantage* ADVANTAGE]

vap·id /vápid/ *adj.* insipid; lacking interest; flat; dull (*vapid moralizing*). □□ **va·pid·i·ty** /–píditee/ *n.* **vap·id·ly** *adv.* **vap·id·ness** *n.* [L *vapidus*]

va·por /váypər/ *n. & v.* (*Brit.* **va·pour**) • *n.* **1** moisture or another substance diffused or suspended in air, e.g., mist or smoke. **2** *Physics* a gaseous form of a normally liquid or solid substance (cf. GAS). **3** a medicinal agent for inhaling. **4** (in *pl.*) *archaic* a state of depression or melancholy thought to be caused by exhalations of vapor from the stomach. • *v.intr.* **1** rise as vapor. **2** make idle boasts or empty talk. □□ **va·por·ous** *adj.* **va·por·ous·ly** *adv.* **va·por·ous·ness** *n.* **va·por·er** *n.* **va·por·ing** *n.* **va·por·ish** *adj.* **va·por·y** *adj.* [ME f. OF *vapor* or L *vapor* steam, heat]

va·por den·si·ty *n.* the density of a gas or vapor relative to hydrogen, etc.

va·por·if·ic /váypərífik/ *adj.* concerned with or causing vapor or vaporization.

va·por·im·e·ter /váypərímitər/ *n.* an instrument for measuring the amount of vapor.

va·por·ize /váypərīz/ *v.tr. & intr.* convert or be converted into vapor. □□ **va·por·iz·a·ble** *adj.* (also **va·por·a·ble**). **va·por·i·za·tion** *n.*

va·por·iz·er /váypərīzər/ *n.* a device that vaporizes substances, esp. for medicinal inhalation.

va·por pres·sure *n.* the pressure of a vapor in contact with its liquid or solid form.

va·por trail *n.* a trail of condensed water from an aircraft or rocket at high altitude, seen as a white streak against the sky.

va·pour *Brit.* var. of VAPOR.

var. *abbr.* **1** variant. **2** variety.

va·rac·tor /vəráktər/ *n.* a semiconductor diode with a capacitance dependent on the applied voltage. [*varying* *reactor*]

var·ec /várek/ *n.* **1** seaweed. **2** = KELP. [F *varec(h)* f. ON: rel. to WRECK]

var·i·a·ble /váireeəbəl/ *adj. & n.* • *adj.* **1 a** that can be varied or adapted (*a rod of variable length; the pressure is variable*). **b** (of a gear) designed to give varying speeds. **2** apt to vary; not constant; unsteady (*a variable mood*; *variable fortunes*). **3** *Math.* (of a quantity) indeterminate; able to assume different numerical values. **4** (of wind or currents) tending to change direction. **5** *Astron.* (of a star) periodically varying in brightness. **6** *Bot. & Zool.* (of a species) including individuals or groups that depart from the type. **7** *Biol.* (of an organism or part of it) tending to change in structure or function. • *n.* **1** a variable thing or quantity. **2** *Math.* a variable quantity. **3** *Naut.* **a** a shifting wind. **b** (in *pl.*) the region between the NE and SE trade winds. □□ **var•i•a•bil•i•ty** /–bílitee/ *n.* **var•i•a•ble•ness** *n.* **var•i•a•bly** *adv.* [ME f. OF f. L *variabilis* (as VARY)]

var•i•ance /váireeəns/ *n.* **1** difference of opinion; dispute; disagreement; lack of harmony (*at variance among ourselves*; *a theory at variance with all known facts*). **2** *Law* a discrepancy between statements or documents. **3** *Statistics* a quantity equal to the square of the standard deviation. [ME f. OF f. L *variantia* difference (as VARY)]

var•i•ant /váireeənt/ *adj. & n.* • *adj.* **1** differing in form or details from the main one (*a variant spelling*). **2** having different forms (*forty variant types of pigeon*). **3** variable or changing. • *n.* a variant form, spelling, type, reading, etc. [ME f. OF (as VARY)]

var•i•ate /váireeət/ *n. Statistics* **1** a quantity having a numerical value for each member of a group. **2** a variable quantity, esp. one whose values occur according to a frequency distribution. [past part. of L *variare* (as VARY)]

var•i•a•tion /váireeáyshən/ *n.* **1** the act or an instance of varying. **2** departure from a former or normal condition, action, or amount, or from a standard or type (*prices are subject to variation*). **3** the extent of this. **4** a thing that varies from a type. **5** *Mus.* a repetition (usu. one of several) of a theme in a changed or elaborated form. **6** *Astron.* a deviation of a heavenly body from its mean orbit or motion. **7** *Math.* a change in a function, etc., due to small changes in the values of constants, etc. **8** *Ballet* a solo dance. □□ **var•i•a•tion•al** *adj.* [ME f. OF *variation* or L *variatio* (as VARY)]

var•i•cel•la /várisélə/ *n. Med.* = CHICKEN POX. [mod.L, irreg. dimin. of VARIOLA]

var•i•ces *pl.* of VARIX.

var•i•co•cele /várikōseel/ *n.* a mass of varicose veins in the spermatic cord. [formed as VARIX + –CELE]

var•i•col•ored /váirikúlərd, vári–/ *adj.* (*Brit.* **var•i•col•oured**) **1** variegated in color. **2** of various or different colors. [L *varius* VARIOUS + COLORED]

var•i•cose /várikōs/ *adj.* (esp. of the veins of the legs) affected by a condition causing them to become dilated and swollen. □□ **var•i•cos•i•ty** /–kósitee/ *n.* [L *varicosus* f. VARIX]

var•ied /váireed/ *adj.* showing variety; diverse. □□ **var•ied•ly** *adv.*

var•i•e•gate /váirigayt, váireeə–, vár–/ *v.tr.* **1** (often as **variegated** *adj.*) mark with irregular patches of different colors. **2** diversify in appearance, esp. in color. **3** (as **variegated** *adj.*) *Bot.* (of plants) having leaves containing two or more colors. □□ **var•i•e•ga•tion** /–gáyshən/ *n.* [L *variegare variegat*- f. *varius* various]

va•ri•e•tal /vəríət'l/ *adj.* **1** esp. *Bot. & Zool.* of, forming, or designating a variety. **2** (of wine) made from a single designated variety of grape. □□ **va•ri•e•tal•ly** *adv.*

va•ri•e•tist /vəríətist/ *n.* a person whose habits, etc., differ from what is normal.

va•ri•e•ty /vəríətee/ *n.* (*pl.* **–ties**) **1** diversity; absence of uniformity; many-sidedness; the condition of being various (*not enough variety in our lives*). **2** a quantity or collection of different things (*for a variety of reasons*). **3 a** a class of things different in some common qualities from the rest of a larger class to which they belong. **b** a specimen or member of such a class. **4** (foll. by *of*) a different form of a thing, quality, etc. **5** *Biol.* a subspecies. **a** a cultivar. **c** an individual or group usually fertile within the species to which it belongs but differing from the species type in some qualities capable of perpetuation. **6** a mixed sequence of dances, songs, comedy acts, etc. (usu. *attrib.*: *a variety show*). [F *variété* or L *varietas* (as VARIOUS)]

va•ri•e•ty store *n.* a retail store selling many kinds of small items.

var•i•fo•cal /váirifókəl/ *adj. & n.* • *adj.* having a focal length that can be varied, esp. of a lens that allows an infinite number of focusing distances for near, intermediate, and far vision. • *n.* (in *pl.*) varifocal spectacles.

var•i•form /váirifawrm/ *adj.* having various forms. [L *varius* + –FORM]

var•i•o•la /vəríələ/ *n. Med.* smallpox. □□ **va•ri•o•lar** *adj.* **va•ri•o•loid** /váireeəloyd/ *adj.* **va•ri•o•lous** /vəríələs/ *adj.* [med.L, = pustule, pock (as VARIOUS)]

var•i•ole /váireeōl/ *n.* **1** a shallow pit like a smallpox mark. **2** a small spherical mass in variolite. [med.L *variola*: see VARIOLA]

var•i•o•lite /váireeəlit/ *n.* a rock with embedded small spherical masses causing on its surface an appearance like smallpox pustules. □□ **var•i•o•lit•ic** /–lítik/ *adj.* [as VARIOLE + –ITE[1]]

var•i•om•e•ter /váireeómitər/ *n.* **1** a device for varying the inductance in an electric circuit. **2** a device for indicating an aircraft's rate of change of altitude. [as VARIOUS + –METER]

var•i•o•rum /váiree-áwrəm/ *adj. & n.* • *adj.* **1** (of an edition of a text)

having notes by various editors or commentators. **2** (of an edition of an author's works) including variant readings. • *n.* a variorum edition. [L f. *editio cum notis variorum* edition with notes by various (commentators): genit. pl. of *varius* VARIOUS]

var•i•ous /váireeəs/ *adj.* **1** different; diverse (*too various to form a group*). **2** more than one; several (*for various reasons*). □□ **var•i•ous•ly** *adv.* **var•i•ous•ness** *n.* [L *varius* changing, diverse]

var•is•tor /vərístər/ *n.* a semiconductor diode with resistance dependent on the applied voltage. [*varying* res*istor*]

var•ix /váireeks/ *n.* (*pl.* **var•i•ces** /váirəseez/) **1** *Med.* **a** a permanent abnormal dilation of a vein or artery. **b** a vein, etc., dilated in this way. **2** each of the ridges across the whorls of a univalve shell. [ME f. L *varix* –*icis*]

var•let /vaárlit/ *n.* **1** *archaic* or *joc.* a menial or rascal. **2** *hist.* a knight's attendant. □□ **var•let•ry** *n.* [ME f. OF, var. of *vaslet*: see VALET]

var•mint /vaármint/ *n. dial.* a mischievous or discreditable person or animal. [var. of *varmin*, VERMIN]

var•na /vaárnə/ *n.* each of the four Hindu castes. [Skr., = color, class]

var•nish /vaárnish/ *n. & v.* • *n.* **1** a resinous solution used to give a hard shiny transparent coating to wood, metal, paintings, etc. **2** any other preparation for a similar purpose (*nail varnish*). **3** external appearance or display without an underlying reality. **4** artificial or natural glossiness. **5** a superficial polish of manner. • *v.tr.* **1** apply varnish to. **2** gloss over (a fact). □□ **var•nish•er** *n.* [ME f. OF *vernis* f. med.L *veronix* fragrant resin, sandarac or med.Gk *berenikē* prob. f. *Berenice* in Cyrenaica]

var•si•ty /vaársitee/ *n.* (*pl.* **–ties**) **1** a high school, college, etc., first team in a sport. **2** *Brit. colloq.* (esp. with ref. to sports) university. [abbr.]

var•us /váirəs/ *n.* a deformity involving the inward displacement of the foot or hand from the midline. [L, = bent, crooked]

varve /vaarv/ *n.* annually deposited layers of clay and silt in a lake used to determine the chronology of glacial sediments. □□ **varved** *adj.* [Sw. *varv* layer]

var•y /váiree/ *v.* (**–ies, –ied**) **1** *tr.* make different; modify; diversify (*seldom varies the routine*; *the style is not sufficiently varied*). **2** *intr.* **a** undergo change; become or be different (*the temperature varies from 30° to 70°*). **b** be of different kinds (*his mood varies*). **3** *intr.* (foll. by *as*) be in proportion to. □□ **var•y•ing•ly** *adv.* [ME f. OF *varier* or L *variare* (as VARIOUS)]

vas /vas/ *n.* (*pl.* **va•sa** /váysə/) *Anat.* a vessel or duct. □□ **va•sal** /váysəl/ *adj.* [L, = vessel]

vas•cu•lar /váskyələr/ *adj.* of, made up of, or containing vessels for conveying blood or sap, etc. (*vascular functions*; *vascular tissue*). □□ **vas•cu•lar•i•ty** /–láritee/ *n.* **vas•cu•lar•ize** *v.tr.* **vas•cu•lar•ly** *adv.* [mod.L *vascularis* f. L VASCULUM]

vas•cu•lar plant *n.* a plant with conducting tissue.

vas•cu•lum /váskyələm/ *n.* (*pl.* **vas•cu•la** /–lə/) a botanist's (usu. metal) collecting case with a lengthwise opening. [L, dimin. of VAS]

vas de•fe•rens /défərenz/ *n.* (*pl.* **va•sa de•fe•ren•ti•a** /défərénsheeə/) *Anat.* the spermatic duct from the testicle to the urethra.

vase /vays, vayz, vaaz/ *n.* a vessel, usu. tall and circular, used as an ornament or container, esp. for flowers. □□ **vase•ful** *n.* (*pl.* **–fuls**). [F f. L VAS]

vas•ec•to•my /vəséktəmee/ *n.* (*pl.* **–mies**) the surgical removal of part of each vas deferens, esp. as a means of sterilization. □□ **vas•ec•to•mize** *v.tr.*

Vas•e•line /vásileen/ *n. Trademark* a type of petroleum jelly used as an ointment, lubricant, etc. [irreg. f. G *Wasser* + Gk *elaion* oil]

va•si•form /váyzifawrm, váso–/ *adj.* **1** duct-shaped. **2** vase-shaped. [L *vasi*- f. VAS + –FORM]

vaso- /váyzō/ *comb. form* a vessel, esp. a blood vessel (*vasoconstrictive*). [L *vaso*: see VAS]

vas•o•ac•tive /váyzō-áktiv/ *adj.* = VASOMOTOR.

vas•o•con•stric•tive /váyzōkənstríktiv/ *adj.* causing constriction of blood vessels.

vas•o•di•lat•ing /váyzōdílayting, –dílay–/ *adj.* causing dilatation of blood vessels. □□ **vas•o•di•la•tion** /–láyshən/ *n.*

vas•o•mo•tor /váyzōmótər/ *adj.* causing constriction or dilatation of blood vessels.

vas•o•pres•sin /váyzōprésin/ *n.* a pituitary hormone acting to reduce diuresis and increase blood pressure. Also called **antidiuretic hormone**.

vas•sal /vásəl/ *n.* **1** *hist.* a holder of land by feudal tenure on conditions of homage and allegiance. **2** *rhet.* a humble dependent. □□ **vas•sal•age** *n.* [ME f. OF f. med.L *vassallus* retainer, of Celt. orig.: cf. the root *vassus* corresp. to Bret. *gwaz*, Welsh *gwas*, Ir. *foss*: cf. VAVASOR]

vast /vast/ *adj. & n.* • *adj.* **1** immense; huge; very great (*a vast expanse of water*; *a vast crowd*). **2** *colloq.* great; considerable (*makes a vast difference*). **3** *rhet.* or *poet.* a vast space (*the vast of heaven*). □□ **vast•ly** *adv.* **vast•ness** *n.* [L *vastus* void, immense]

VAT /vat, vee-aytée/ *abbr.* value-added tax.

vat /vat/ *n. & v.* • *n.* **1** a large tank or other vessel, esp. for holding liquids or something in the process of brewing, tanning, dyeing, etc. **2** a dyeing liquor in which a textile is soaked to take up a colorless, soluble dye afterward colored by oxidation in air.

● *v.tr.* (**vat·ted, vat·ting**) place or treat in a vat. □□ **vat·ful** *n.* (*pl.* **–fuls**). [ME, southern & western var. of *fat*, OE *fæt* f. Gmc]

vat·ic /vátik/ *adj. formal* prophetic or inspired. [L *vates* prophet]

Vat·i·can /vátikən/ *n.* **1** the palace and official residence of the Pope in Rome. **2** papal government. □□ **Vat·i·can·ism** *n.* **Vat·i·can·ist** *n.* [F *Vatican* or L *Vaticanus* name of a hill in Rome]

Vat·i·can Cit·y an independent Papal State in Rome, instituted in 1929.

Vat·i·can Coun·cil *n.* an ecumenical council of the Roman Catholic Church, esp. that held in 1869–70 or that held in 1962–65.

va·tic·i·nate /vatísinayt/ *v.tr. & intr. formal* prophesy. □□ **va·tic·i·nal** *adj.* **va·tic·i·na·tion** /–náyshən/ *n.* **va·tic·i·na·tor** *n.* [L *vaticinari* f. *vates* prophet]

vaude·ville /váwdvil, váwdə–/ *n.* **1** variety entertainment. **2** a stage play on a trivial theme with interspersed songs. **3** a satirical or topical song with a refrain. □□ **vaude·vil·lian** /–vílyən/ *adj. & n.* [F, orig. of convivial song esp. any of those composed by O. Basselin, 15th-c. poet born at *Vau de Vire* in Normandy]

Vau·dois[1] /vṓdwaá/ *n. & adj.* ● *n.* (*pl.* same) **1** a native of Vaud in W. Switzerland. **2** the French dialect spoken in Vaud. ● *adj.* of or relating to Vaud or its dialect. [F]

Vau·dois[2] /vṓdwaá/ *n. & adj.* ● *n.* (*pl.* same) a member of the Waldenses. ● *adj.* of or relating to the Waldenses. [F, repr. med.L *Valdensis*: see WALDENSES]

vault /vawlt/ *n. & v.* ● *n.* **1 a** an arched roof. **b** a continuous arch. **c** a set or series of arches whose joints radiate from a central point or line. **2** a vaultlike covering (*the vault of heaven*). **3** an esp. underground chamber: **a** as a place of storage (*bank vaults*). **b** as a place of interment beneath a church or in a cemetery, etc. (*family vault*). **4** an act of vaulting. **5** *Anat.* the arched roof of a cavity. ● *v.* **1** *intr.* leap or spring, esp. while resting on one or both hands or with the help of a pole. **2** *tr.* spring over (a gate, etc.) in this way. **3** *tr.* (esp. as **vaulted**) **a** make in the form of a vault. **b** provide with a vault or vaults. □□ **vault·er** *n.* [OF *voute, vaute*, ult. f. L *volvere* roll]

vault·ing /váwlting/ *n.* **1** arched work in a vaulted roof or ceiling. **2** a gymnastic or athletic exercise in which participants vault over obstacles.

vault·ing horse *n.* a padded wooden block to be vaulted over by gymnasts.

vaunt /vawnt/ *v. & n. literary* ● *v.* **1** *intr.* boast; brag. **2** *tr.* boast of; extol boastfully. ● *n.* a boast. □□ **vaunt·er** *n.* **vaunt·ing·ly** *adv.* [ME f. AF *vaunter*, OF *vanter* f. LL *vantare* f. L *vanus* VAIN: partly obs. *avaunt* (v.) f. *avanter* f. *a-* intensive + *vanter*]

vav·a·sor /vávəsawr, –sōor/ *n. hist.* (also **vav·a·sour**) a vassal owing allegiance to a great lord and having other vassals under him. [ME f. OF *vavas(s)our* f. med.L *vavassor*, perh. f. *vassus vassorum* VASSAL of vassals]

vav·a·so·ry /vávəsawree/ *n.* (*pl.* **–ries**) *hist.* the estate of a vavasor. [OF *vavasorie* or med.L *vavasoria* (as VAVASOR)]

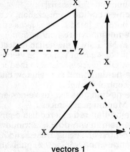
vaulting horse

VC *abbr.* **1** vice-chairman. **2** vice-chancellor. **3** vice-consul. **4** victoria Cross. **5** Vietcong.

VCR *abbr.* videocassette recorder.

VD *abbr.* venereal disease.

VDT *abbr.* video display terminal.

V-E *abbr.* Victory in Europe (in 1945).

V-E Day *n.* May 8, the day marking the Allied victory in Europe in 1945.

've *abbr.* (chiefly after pronouns) = HAVE (*I've; they've*).

veal /veel/ *n.* calf's flesh as food. □□ **veal·y** *adj.* [ME f. AF *ve(e) l*, OF *veiaus veel* f. L *vitellus* dimin. of *vitulus* calf]

vec·tor /véktər/ *n. & v.* ● *n.* **1** *Math. & Physics* a quantity having direction as well as magnitude, esp. as determining the position of one point in space relative to another (*radius vector*). **2** a carrier of disease. **3** a course to be taken by an aircraft. ● *v.tr.* direct (an aircraft in flight) to a desired point. □□ **vec·to·ri·al** /–táwreeəl/ *adj.* **vec·tor·ize** *v.tr.* (in sense 1 of *n.*). **vec·tor·i·za·tion** /–tərīzáyshən/ *n.* [L, = carrier, f. *vehere vect-* convey]

vec·tor sum *n. Math.* a force, etc., equivalent to two or more acting in different directions at the same point.

Ve·da /váydə, vée–/ *n.* (in *sing.* or *pl.*) the most ancient Hindu scrip-

tures, esp. four collections called Rig-Veda, Sāma-veda, Yajur-Veda, and Atharva-Veda. [Skr. *vēda*, lit. (sacred) knowledge]

Ve·dan·ta /vidáəntə, vedán–/ *n.* **1** the Upanishads. **2** the Hindu philosophy based on these, esp. in its monistic form. □□ **Ve·dan·tic** *adj.* **Ve·dan·tist** *n.* [Skr. *ved ānta* (as VEDA, *anta* end)]

Ved·da /védə/ *n.* (also **Ved·dah**) a Sri Lankan aboriginal. [Sinh. *veddā* hunter]

ve·dette /videt/ *n.* a mounted sentry positioned beyond an army's outposts to observe the movements of the enemy. [F, = scout, f. It. *vedetta, veletta* f. Sp. *vela(r)* watch f. L *vigilare*]

Ve·dic /váydik, vée–/ *adj. & n.* ● *adj.* of or relating to the Veda or Vedas. ● *n.* the language of the Vedas, an older form of Sanskrit. [F *Védique* or G *Vedisch* (as VEDA)]

vee /vee/ *n.* **1** the letter V. **2** a thing shaped like a V. [name of the letter]

vee·jay /véejay/ *n.* VIDEO JOCKEY.

veer[1] /veer/ *v. & n.* ● *v.intr.* **1** change direction, esp. (of the wind) clockwise (cf. BACK *v.* 5). **2** change in course, opinion, conduct, emotions, etc. **3** *Naut.* = WEAR[2]. ● *n.* a change of course or direction. [F *virer* f. Rmc, perh. alt. f. L *gyrare* GYRATE]

veer[2] /veer/ *v.tr. Naut.* slacken or let out (a rope, cable, etc.). [ME f. MDu. *vieren*]

veg /vej/ *n. & v.* ● *n. Brit. colloq.* a vegetable or vegetables. ● *v.* = VEGETATE 1. [abbr.]

Ve·ga /véegə, váy–/ *n. Astron.* a brilliant blue star in the constellation of the Lyra. [Sp. or med.L *Vega* f. Arab., = the falling vulture]

veg·an /véjən, véegən/ *n. & adj.* ● *n.* a person who does not eat or use animal products. ● *adj.* using or containing no animal products. [VEG(ETABLE) + –AN]

veg·e·ta·ble /véjtəbəl, véjitəbəl/ *n. & adj.* ● *n.* **1** *Bot.* any of various plants, esp. a herbaceous plant used wholly or partly for food, e.g., a cabbage, potato, turnip, or bean. **2** *colloq.* **a** a person who is incapable of normal intellectual activity, esp. through brain injury, etc. **b** a person lacking in animation or living a monotonous life. ● *adj.* **1** of, derived from, relating to, or comprising plants or plant life, esp. as distinct from animal life or mineral substances. **2** of or relating to vegetables as food. **3 a** unresponsive to stimulus (*vegetable behavior*). **b** uneventful; monotonous (*a vegetable existence*). [ME f. OF *vegetable* or LL *vegetabilis* animating (as VEGETATE)]

veg·e·ta·ble i·vo·ry *n.* a hard, white material obtained from the endosperm of the ivory nut.

veg·e·ta·ble mar·row *n.* see MARROW 3.

veg·e·ta·ble oys·ter *n.* = SALSIFY.

veg·e·ta·ble parch·ment *n.* see PARCHMENT 2.

veg·e·ta·ble sponge *n.* = LOOFAH.

veg·e·ta·ble tal·low *n.* a vegetable fat used as tallow.

veg·e·ta·ble wax *n.* an exudation of certain plants such as sumac.

veg·e·tal /véjit'l/ *adj.* **1** of or having the nature of plants (*vegetal growth*). **2** vegetative. [med.L *vegetalis* f. L *vegetare* animate]

veg·e·tar·i·an /véjitáireeən/ *n. & adj.* ● *n.* a person who abstains from animal food, esp. that from slaughtered animals, though often not eggs and dairy products. ● *adj.* excluding animal food, esp. meat (*a vegetarian diet*). □□ **veg·e·tar·i·an·ism** *n.* [irreg. f. VEGETABLE + –ARIAN]

veg·e·tate /véjitayt/ *v.intr.* **1 a** live an uneventful or monotonous life. **b** spend time lazily or passively, exerting oneself neither mentally nor physically. **2** grow as plants do; fulfill vegetal functions. [L *vegetare* animate f. *vegetus* f. *vegēre* be active]

veg·e·ta·tion /véjitáyshən/ *n.* **1** plants collectively; plant life (*luxuriant vegetation; no sign of vegetation*). **2** the process of vegetating. □□ **veg·e·ta·tion·al** *adj.* [med.L *vegetatio* growth (as VEGETATE)]

veg·e·ta·tive /véjitaytiv/ *adj.* **1** concerned with growth and development as distinct from sexual reproduction. **2** of or relating to vegetation or plant life. □□ **veg·e·ta·tive·ly** *adv.* **vegetativeness** *n.* [ME f. OF *vegetatif –ive* or med.L *vegetativus* (as VEGETATE)]

veg·gie /véjee/ *n.* (also **veg·ie**) *colloq.* **1** a vegetable. **2** a vegetarian. [abbr.]

ve·he·ment /véeəmənt/ *adj.* showing or caused by strong feeling; forceful; ardent (*a vehement protest; vehement desire*). □□ **ve·he·mence** /–məns/ *n.* **ve·he·ment·ly** *adv.* [ME f. F *véhément* or L *vehemens –entis*, perh. f. *vemens* (unrecorded) deprived of mind, assoc. with *vehere* carry]

ve·hi·cle /véeikəl, véehikəl/ *n.* **1** any conveyance for transporting people, goods, etc., esp. on land. **2** a medium for thought, feeling, or action (*the stage is the best vehicle for their talents*). **3** a liquid, etc., as a medium for suspending pigments, drugs, etc. **4** the literal meaning of a word or words used metaphorically (opp. TENOR 6).

□□ **ve•hic•u•lar** /veehíkyələr/ adj. [F véhicule or L vehiculum f. vehere carry]

It is common in American English not to pronounce the h in *vehicle* ("VEE-i-kul"), but the h is always pronounced in *vehicular* ("vee-HIK-ye-ler").

ve•hi•cle i•den•ti•fi•ca•tion num•ber n. a combination of letters and numbers used to identify vehicles for insurance, registration, etc.

veil /vayl/ n. & v. • n. **1** a piece of usu. more or less transparent fabric attached to a woman's hat, etc., esp. to conceal the face or protect against the sun, dust, etc. **2** a piece of linen, etc., as part of a nun's headdress, resting on the head and shoulders. **3** a curtain, esp. that separating the sanctuary in the Jewish temple. **4** a disguise; a pretext; a thing that conceals (*under the veil of friendship; a veil of mist*). **5** *Photog.* slight fogging. **6** huskiness of the voice. **7** = VELUM. • *v.tr.* **1** cover with a veil. **2** (esp. as **veiled** adj.) partly conceal (*veiled threats*). □ **beyond the veil** in the unknown state of life after death. **draw a veil over** avoid discussing or calling attention to. **take the veil** become a nun. □□ **veil•less** adj. [ME f. AF veil(e), OF voil(e) f. L vela f. of VELUM]

veil•ing /váyling/ n. light fabric used for veils, etc.

vein /vayn/ n. & v. • n. **1 a** any of the tubes by which blood is conveyed to the heart (cf. ARTERY). **b** (in general use) any blood vessel (*has royal blood in his veins*). **2** a nervure of an insect's wing. **3** a slender bundle of tissue forming a rib in the framework of a leaf. **4** a streak or stripe of a different color in wood, marble, cheese, etc. **5** a fissure in rock filled with ore or other deposited material. **6** a source of a particular characteristic (*a rich vein of humor*). **7** a distinctive character or tendency; a cast of mind or disposition; a mood (*spoke in a sarcastic vein*). • *v.tr.* fill or cover with or as with veins. □□ **vein•less** n. **vein•let** n. **vein•like** adj. **vein•y** adj. (**vein•i•er**, **vein•i•est**). [ME f. OF veine f. L vena]

vein•ing /váyning/ n. a pattern of streaks or veins.

ve•la pl. of VELUM.

ve•la•men /veláymən/ n. (pl. **ve•lam•i•na** /–minə/) an enveloping membrane, esp. of an aerial root of an orchid. [L f. velare cover]

ve•lar /véelər/ adj. **1** of a veil or velum. **2** *Phonet.* (of a sound) pronounced with the back of the tongue near the soft palate. [L velaris f. velum: see VELUM]

Vel•cro /vélkrō/ n. *Trademark* a fastener for clothes, etc., consisting of two strips of nylon fabric, one looped and one burred, which adhere when pressed together. □□ **Vel•croed** adj. [F velours croché hooked velvet]

veld /velt, felt/ n. (also **veldt**) *S.Afr.* open country; grassland. [Afrik. f. Du., = FIELD]

vel•i•ta•tion /vélitáyshən/ n. *archaic* a slight skirmish or controversy. [L velitatio f. velitari skirmish f. veles velitis light-armed skirmisher]

vel•le•i•ty /veléeitee/ n. *literary* **1** a low degree of volition not conducive to action. **2** a slight wish or inclination. [med.L velleitas f. L velle to wish]

vel•lum /véləm/ n. **1 a** fine parchment orig. from the skin of a calf. **b** a manuscript written on this. **2** smooth writing paper imitating vellum. [ME f. OF velin (as VEAL)]

ve•lo•cim•e•ter /véelōsímitər, vélō–/ n. an instrument for measuring velocity.

ve•loc•i•pede /vilósipeed/ n. **1** *hist.* an early form of bicycle propelled by pressure from the rider's feet on the ground. **2** a child's tricycle. □□ **ve•loc•i•ped•ist** n. [F vélocipède f. L velox –ocis swift + pes pedis foot]

ve•loc•i•ty /vilósitee/ n. (pl. **–ties**) **1** the measure of the rate of movement of a usu. inanimate object in a given direction. **2** speed in a given direction. **3** (in general use) speed. [F vélocité or L velocitas f. velox –ocis swift]

ve•loc•i•ty of escape n. = ESCAPE VELOCITY.

ve•lo•drome /véledrōm/ n. a special place or building with a track for cycling. [F vélodrome f. vélo bicycle (as VELOCITY, –DROME)]

ve•lour /vəloőr/ n. (also **ve•lours**) **1** a plushlike woven fabric or felt. **2** *archaic* a hat of this felt. [F velours velvet f. OF velour, velous f. L villosus hairy f. villus: see VELVET]

ve•lou•té /vəlootáy/ n. a sauce made from a roux of butter and flour with chicken, veal, or fish stock. [F, = velvety]

ve•lum /véeləm/ n. (pl. **ve•la** /–lə/) a membrane, membranous covering, or flap. [L, = sail, curtain, covering, veil]

ve•lu•ti•nous /vilőőt'nəs/ adj. covered with soft fine hairs. [perh. f. It. vellutino f. velluto VELVET]

vel•vet /vélvit/ n. & adj. • n. **1** a closely woven fabric of silk, cotton, etc., with a thick short pile on one side. **2** the furry skin on a deer's growing antler. **3** anything smooth and soft like velvet. • adj. of, like, or soft as velvet. □ **on** (or **in**) **velvet** in an advantageous or prosperous position. □□ **vel•vet•ed** adj. **vel•vet•y** adj. [ME f. OF veluotte f. velu velvety f. med.L villutus f. L villus tuft, down]

vel•vet•een /vélviteéen/ n. **1** a cotton fabric with a pile like velvet. **2** (in pl.) garments made of this.

vel•vet glove n. outward gentleness, esp. cloaking firmness or strength (cf. IRON HAND).

Ven. abbr. Venerable (as the title of an archdeacon).

ve•na ca•va /véenə káyvə/ n. (pl. **ve•nae ca•vae** /–nee –vee/) each of usu. two veins carrying blood into the heart. [L, = hollow vein]

ve•nal /véenəl/ adj. **1** (of a person) able to be bribed or corrupted. **2** (of conduct, etc.) characteristic of a venal person. □□ **ve•nal•i•ty** /–nálitee/ n. **ve•nal•ly** adv. [L venalis f. venum thing for sale]

▶Venal and venial are sometimes confused. **Venal** means 'corrupt, able to be bribed, or involving bribery,' e.g., *Local customs officials are notoriously venal, and smuggling thrives.* **Venial** is used among Christians to describe a certain type of sin and means 'pardonable, excusable, not mortal,' e.g., *purgatory, to Catholics, was an intermediate stage in which those who had committed venial sins might earn their way into heaven.*

ve•na•tion /vináyshən/ n. the arrangement of veins in a leaf or an insect's wing, etc., or the system of venous blood vessels in an organism. □□ **ve•na•tion•al** adj. [L vena vein]

vend /vend/ v.tr. **1** offer (small wares) for sale. **2** *Law* sell. □□ **vend•er** n. (usu. in comb.). **vend•i•ble** adj. [F vendre or L vendere sell (as VENAL, dare give)]

ven•dace /véndays/ n. a small delicate fish, *Coregonus albula*, found in some British lakes. [OF vendese, –oise f. Gaulish]

vend•ee /vendée/ n. *Law* the buying party in a sale, esp. of property.

ven•det•ta /vendétə/ n. **1 a** blood feud in which the family of a murdered person seeks vengeance on the murderer or the murderer's family. **b** this practice as prevalent in Corsica and Sicily. **2** a prolonged bitter quarrel. [It. f. L vindicta (as VINDICTIVE)]

ven•deuse /vo NDőz/ n. a saleswoman, esp. in a fashionable dress shop. [F]

vend•ing ma•chine n. a machine that dispenses small articles for sale when a coin or token is inserted.

ven•dor /véndər/ n. **1** *Law* the seller in a sale, esp. of property. **2** = VENDING MACHINE. [AF vendour (as VEND)]

ven•due /véndoo –dyōo, vendōo, –dyōo/ n. a public auction. [Du. vendu(e) f. F vendue sale f. vendre VEND]

ve•neer /vinéer/ n. & v. • n. **1 a** a thin covering of fine wood or other surface material applied to a coarser wood. **b** a layer in plywood. **2** (often foll. by of) a deceptive outward appearance of a good quality, etc. • v.tr. **1** apply a veneer to (wood, furniture, etc.). **2** disguise (an unattractive character, etc.) with a more attractive manner, etc. [earlier fineer. G furni(e)ren f. OF fournir FURNISH]

ve•neer•ing /vinéering/ n. material used as veneer.

ven•e•punc•ture var. of VENIPUNCTURE.

ven•er•a•ble /vénərəbəl/ adj. **1** entitled to veneration on account of character, age, associations, etc. (*a venerable priest; venerable relics*). **2** as the title of an archdeacon in the Church of England. **3** *RC Ch.* as the title of a deceased person who has attained a certain degree of sanctity but has not been fully beatified or canonized. □□ **ven•er•a•bil•i•ty** n. **ven•er•a•ble•ness** n. **ven•er•a•bly** adv. [ME f. OF venerable or L venerabilis (as VENERATE)]

ven•er•ate /vénərayt/ v.tr. **1** regard with deep respect. **2** revere on account of sanctity, etc. □□ **ven•er•a•tion** /–ráyshən/ n. **ven•er•a•tor** n. [L venerari adore, revere]

ve•ne•re•al /vinéereeəl/ adj. **1** of or relating to sexual desire or intercourse. **2** relating to venereal disease. □□ **ve•ne•re•al•ly** adv. [ME f. L venereus f. venus veneris sexual love]

ve•ne•re•al dis•ease n. any of various diseases contracted chiefly by sexual intercourse with a person already infected.

ve•ne•re•ol•o•gy /vinéereeóləjee/ n. the scientific study of venereal diseases. □□ **ve•ne•re•ol•o•gist** n.

ven•er•y[1] /vénəree/ n. *archaic* sexual indulgence. [med.L veneria (as VENEREAL)]

ven•er•y[2] /vénəree/ n. *archaic* hunting. [ME f. OF venerie f. vener to hunt ult. f. L venari]

ven•e•sec•tion /vénisekshən, véenə–/ n. (also **ven•i•sec•tion**) phlebotomy. [med.L venae sectio cutting of a vein (as VEIN, SECTION)]

Ve•ne•tian /vinéeshən/ n. & adj. • n. **1** a native or citizen of Venice in NE Italy. **2** the Italian dialect of Venice. **3** (**venetian**) = VENETIAN BLIND. • adj. of Venice. □□ **ve•ne•tianed** adj. (in sense 3 of n.). [ME f. OF Venicien, assim. to med.L Venetianus f. Venetia Venice]

ve•ne•tian blind n. a window blind of adjustable horizontal slats to control the light.

ve•ne•tian glass n. (or **Ve•ne•tian glass**) delicate glassware made at Murano near Venice.

Ve•ne•tian red n. a reddish pigment of ferric oxides.

Ve•ne•tian win•dow n. a window with three separate openings, the central one being arched and highest.

venge•ance /vénjəns/ n. punishment inflicted or retribution exacted for wrong to oneself or to a person, etc., whose cause one supports. □ **with a vengeance** in a higher degree than was expected or desired; in the fullest sense (*punctuality with a vengeance*). [ME f. OF f. venger avenge f. L (as VINDICATE)]

venge·ful /vénjfŏol/ adj. vindictive; seeking vengeance. □□ **venge·ful·ly** adv. **venge·ful·ness** n. [obs. *venge* avenge (as VENGEANCE)]

ve·ni·al /véeneeəl/ adj. (of a sin or fault) pardonable; excusable; not mortal. □□ **ve·ni·al·i·ty** /–neeálitee/ n. **ve·ni·al·ly** adv. **ve·ni·al·ness** n. [ME f. OF f. LL *venialis* f. *venia* forgiveness]
▶See note at VENAL.

ven·i·punc·ture /vénipungkchər, véenə–/ n. (also **ven·e·punc·ture**) *Med.* the puncture of a vein, esp. with a hypodermic needle, to withdraw blood or for an intravenous injection. [L *vena* vein + PUNCTURE]

ven·i·sec·tion var. of VENESECTION.

ven·i·son /vénisən, –zən/ n. a deer's flesh as food. [ME f. OF *veneso(u)n* f. L *venatio* –*onis* hunting f. *venari* to hunt]

Ve·ni·te /vinítee, venéetay/ n. **1** a canticle consisting of Psalm 95. **2** a musical setting of this. [ME f. L, = 'come ye,' its first word]

Venn di·a·gram /ven/ n. a diagram of usu. circular areas representing mathematical sets, the areas intersecting where they have elements in common. [J. *Venn*, Engl logician d. 1923]

ven·om /vénəm/ n. **1** a poisonous fluid secreted by snakes, scorpions, etc., usu. transmitted by a bite or sting. **2** malignity; virulence of feeling, language, or conduct. □□ **ven·omed** adj. [ME f. OF *venim*, var. of *venin* ult. f. L *venenum* poison]

ven·om·ous /vénəməs/ adj. **1 a** containing, secreting, or injecting venom. **b** (of a snake, etc.) inflicting poisonous wounds by this means. **2** (of a person, etc.) virulent; spiteful; malignant. □□ **ven·om·ous·ly** adv. **ven·om·ous·ness** n. [ME f. OF *venimeux* f. *venim*: see VENOM]

ve·nose /véenōs/ adj. having many or very marked veins. [L *venosus* f. *vena* vein]

ve·nous /véenəs/ adj. of, full of, or contained in veins. □□ **ve·nos·i·ty** /vinósitee/ n. **ve·nous·ly** adv. [L *venosus* VENOSE or L *vena* vein + –OUS]

vent¹ /vent/ n. & v. • n **1** a hole or opening allowing motion of air, etc., out of or into a confined space. **2** an outlet; free passage or play (*gave vent to their indignation*). **3** the anus esp. of a lower animal, serving for both excretion and reproduction. **4** the venting of an otter, beaver, etc. **5** an aperture or outlet through which volcanic products are discharged at the earth's surface. **6** a small hole in early firearms through which the charge is ignited. Also called **touchhole**. **7** a finger hole in a musical instrument. **8** a flue of a chimney. • v. **1** tr. **a** make a vent in (a cask, etc.). **b** provide (a machine) with a vent. **2** tr. give vent or free expression to (*vented my anger on the cat*). **3** *intr.* (of an otter or beaver) come to the surface for breath. **4** tr. & intr. discharge. ▪ **vent one's spleen on** scold or ill-treat without cause. □□ **vent·less** adj. [partly F *vent* f. L *ventus* wind, partly F *évent* f. *éventer* expose to air f. OF *esventer* ult. f. L *ventus* wind]

vent² /vent/ n. a slit in a garment, esp. in the lower edge of the back of a coat. [ME, var. of *fent* f. OF *fente* slip ult. f. L *findere* cleave]

ven·ti·duct /véntidukt/ n. *Archit.* an air passage, esp. for ventilation. [L *ventus* wind + *ductus* DUCT]

ven·ti·fact /véntifakt/ n. a stone shaped by windblown sand. [L *ventus* wind + *factum* neut. past part. of *facere* make]

ven·til /véntil/ n. *Mus.* **1** a valve in a wind instrument. **2** a shutter for regulating the airflow in an organ. [G f. It. *ventile* f. med.L *ventile* sluice f. L *ventus* wind]

ven·ti·late /vént'layt/ v.tr. **1** cause air to circulate freely in (a room, etc.). **2** submit (a question, grievance, etc.) to public consideration and discussion. **3** *Med.* **a** oxygenate (the blood). **b** admit or force air into (the lungs). □□ **ven·ti·la·tion** /–láyshən/ n. **ven·ti·la·tive** /–láytiv/ adj. [L *ventilare ventilat*- blow, winnow, f. *ventus* wind]

ven·ti·la·tor /véntilaytər/ n. **1** an appliance or aperture for ventilating a room, etc. **2** *Med.* = RESPIRATOR 2.

ven·tral /véntrəl/ adj. **1** *Anat.* & *Zool.* of or on the abdomen (cf. DORSAL). **2** *Bot.* of the front or lower surface. □□ **ven·tral·ly** adv. [obs. *venter* abdomen f. L *venter ventr*-]

ven·tral fin n. either of the ventrally placed fins on a fish.

ven·tri·cle /véntrikəl/ n. *Anat.* **1** a cavity in the body. **2** a hollow part of an organ, esp. in the brain or heart. □□ **ven·tric·u·lar** /–tríkyələr/ adj. [ME f. L *ventriculus* dimin. of *venter* belly]

ven·tri·cose /véntrikōs/ adj. **1** having a protruding belly. **2** *Bot.* distended; inflated. [irreg. f. VENTRICLE + –OSE¹]

ven·tril·o·quism /ventríləkwizəm/ n. the skill of speaking or uttering sounds so that they seem to come from the speaker's dummy or a source other than the speaker. □□ **ven·tril·o·quial** /véntrilŏkweeəl/ adj. **ven·tril·o·quist** n. **ven·tril·o·quize** v.intr. [ult. f. L *ventriloquus* ventriloquist f. *venter* belly + *loqui* speak]

ven·tril·o·quy /ventríləkwee/ n. = VENTRILOQUISM.

ven·ture /vénchər/ n. & v. • n **1 a** an undertaking of a risk. **b** a risky undertaking. **2** a commercial speculation. • v. **1** intr. dare; not be afraid (*did not venture to stop them*). **2** intr. (usu. foll. by *out*, etc.) dare to go (out), esp. outdoors. **3** tr. dare to put forward (an opinion, suggestion, etc.). **4 a** tr. expose to risk; stake (a bet, etc.). **b** intr. take risks. **5** intr. (foll. by *on, upon*) dare to engage in, etc. (*ventured on a longer journey*). ▪ **at a venture** at random; without previous consideration. [*aventure* = ADVENTURE]

ven·ture cap·i·tal n. money put up for speculative business investment.

ven·tur·er /vénchərər/ n. *hist.* a person who undertakes or shares in a trading venture.

ven·ture·some /vénchərsəm/ adj. **1** disposed to take risks. **2** risky. □□ **ven·ture·some·ly** adv. **ven·ture·some·ness** n.

ven·tu·ri /ventŏoree/ n. (pl. **ven·tu·ris**) a short piece of narrow tube between wider sections for measuring flow rate or exerting suction. [G. B. *Venturi*, It. physicist d. 1822]

ven·ue /vényŏo/ n. **1 a** an appointed meeting place, esp. for a sports event, meeting, concert, etc. **b** a rendezvous. **2** *Law hist.* the county or other place within which a jury must be gathered and a cause tried (orig. the neighborhood of the crime, etc.). [F, = a coming, fem. past part. of *venir* come f. L *venire*]

ven·ule /vényŏol/ n. *Anat.* a small vein adjoining the capillaries. [L *venula* dimin. of *vena* vein]

Ve·nus /véenəs/ n. (pl. **Ve·nus·es**) **1** the planet second from the sun in the solar system. **2** *poet.* **a** a beautiful woman. **b** sexual love; amorous influences or desires. □□ **Ve·nu·si·an** /vinŏoshən, –sheeən, –zeeən, –nyŏo–/ adj. & n. [OE f. L *Venus Veneris*, the goddess of love]

Ve·nus fly·trap n. (also **Ve·nus's fly·trap**) a carnivorous plant, *Dionaea muscipula*, with leaves that close on insects, etc.

ve·ra·cious /vəráyshəs/ adj. *formal* **1** speaking or disposed to speak the truth. **2** (of a statement, etc.) true or meant to be true. □□ **ve·ra·cious·ly** adv. **ve·ra·cious·ness** n. [L *verax veracis* f. *verus* true]

ve·rac·i·ty /vərásitee/ n. **1** truthfulness; honesty. **2** accuracy (of a statement, etc.). [F *veracité* or med.L *veracitas* (as VERACIOUS)]

Venus flytrap

ve·ran·da /vərándə/ n. (also **ve·ran·dah**) **1** a roofed platform along the outside of a house, level with the ground floor. **2** *Austral.* & *NZ* a roof over a pavement in front of a store. [Hindi *varandā* f. Port. *varanda*]

ve·ra·trine /vérətreen, –trin/ n. a poisonous compound obtained from sabadilla, etc., and used esp. as a local irritant in the treatment of neuralgia and rheumatism. [F *vératrine* f. L *veratrum* hellebore]

verb /vərb/ n. *Gram.* a word used to indicate an action, state, or occurrence, and forming the main part of the predicate of a sentence (e.g., *hear, become, happen*). [ME f. OF *verbe* or L *verbum* word, verb]

GRAMMAR TIP verb

For explanation of the grammar and function of verbs, see the following: *auxiliary verbs, gerund, infinitive, irregular, linking verbs, mood, perfect tenses, tense, transitive,* and *voice.*

ver·bal /vɜ́rbəl/ adj., n., & v. • adj. **1** of or concerned with words (*made a verbal distinction; verbal reasoning*). **2** oral; not written (*gave a verbal statement*). **3** *Gram.* of or in the nature of a verb (*verbal inflections*). **4** literal (*a verbal translation*). **5** talkative; articulate. • n. **1** *Gram.* **a** a verbal noun. **b** a word or words functioning as a verb. **2** *Brit. sl.* a verbal statement, esp. one made to the police. **3** *Brit. sl.* an insult; abuse (*gave them the verbal*). • v.tr. *Brit. sl.* attribute a damaging statement to (a suspect). □□ **ver·bal·ly** adv. [ME f. F *verbal* or LL *verbalis* (as VERB)]

ver·bal·ism /vɜ́rbəlizəm/ n. **1** minute attention to words; verbal criticism. **2** merely verbal expression. □□ **ver·bal·ist** n. **ver·bal·is·tic** /–lístik/ adj.

ver·bal·ize /vɜ́rbəliz/ v. **1** tr. express in words. **2** intr. be verbose. **3** tr. make (a noun, etc.) into a verb. □□ **ver·bal·iz·a·ble** adj. **ver·bal·i·za·tion** n. **ver·bal·iz·er** n.

ver·bal noun n. *Gram.* a noun formed as an inflection of a verb and partly sharing its constructions (e.g., *smoking* in *smoking is forbidden*: see –ING¹).

ver·ba·tim /vərbáytim/ adv. & adj. in exactly the same words; word for word (*copied it verbatim; a verbatim report*). [ME f. med.L (adv.), f. L *verbum* word: cf. LITERATIM]

ver·be·na /vərbéenə/ n. any plant of the genus *Verbena*, bearing clusters of fragrant flowers. [L, = sacred bough of olive, etc., in med.L *vervain*]

ver·bi·age /vɜ́rbeeij/ n. needless accumulation of words; verbosity. [F f. obs. *verbeier* chatter f. *verbe* word: see VERB]

ver·bose /vərbōs/ adj. using or expressed in more words than are needed. □□ **ver·bose·ly** adv. **ver·bose·ness** n. **ver·bos·i·ty** /–bósitee/ n. [L *verbosus* f. *verbum* word]

ver·bo·ten /ferbṓt'n/ adj. forbidden, esp. by an authority. [G]

verb sap /vərb/ int. expressing the absence of the need for a further explicit statement. [abbr. of L *verbum sapienti sat est* a word is enough for the wise person]

ver·dant /vә́rd'nt/ *adj.* **1** (of grass, etc.) green, fresh-colored. **2** (of a field, etc.) covered with green grass, etc. **3** (of a person) unsophisticated; raw; green. □□ **ver·dan·cy** /-d'nsee/ *n.* **ver·dant·ly** *adv.* [perh. f. OF *verdeant* part. of *verdoier* be green ult. f. L *viridis* green]

verd an·tique /vә́rd/ *n.* (also **verde an·tique**) **1** ornamental usu. green serpentine. **2** a green incrustation on ancient bronze. **3** green porphyry. [obs. F, = antique green]

ver·der·er /vә́rdәrәr/ *n. Brit.* a judicial officer of royal forests. [AF (earlier *verder*), OF *verdier* ult. f. L *viridis* green]

ver·dict /vә́rdikt/ *n.* **1** a decision on an issue of fact in a civil or criminal cause or an inquest. **2** a decision; a judgment. [ME f. AF *verdit*, OF *voirdit* f. *voir, veir* true f. L *verus* + *dit* f. L DICTUM saying]

ver·di·gris /vә́rdigrees, -gris, -gree/ *n.* **1 a** a green crystallized substance formed on copper by the action of acetic acid. **b** this used as a medicine or pigment. **2** green rust on copper or brass. [ME f. OF *verte-gres, vert de Grece* green of Greece]

ver·dure /vә́rjәr/ *n.* **1** green vegetation. **2** the greenness of this. **3** *poet.* freshness. □□ **ver·dured** *adj.* **ver·dur·ous** *adj.* [ME f. OF f. *verd* green f. L *viridis*]

verge[1] /vәrj/ *n.* **1** an edge or border. **2** an extreme limit beyond which something happens (*on the verge of tears*). **3** *Brit.* a grass edging of a road, flower bed, etc. **4** *Archit.* an edge of tiles projecting over a gable. **5** a wand or rod carried before a bishop, dean, etc., as an emblem of office. [ME f. OF f. L *virga* rod]

verge[2] /vәrj/ *v.intr.* **1** incline downward or in a specified direction (*the now verging sun; verge to a close*). **2** (foll. by *on*) border on; approach closely (*verging on the ridiculous*). [L *vergere* bend, incline]

verg·er /vә́rjәr/ *n.* **1** esp. *Brit.* an official in a church who acts as caretaker and attendant. **2** *Brit.* an officer who bears the staff before a bishop, etc. □□ **verg·er·ship** *n.* [ME f. AF (as VERGE[1])]

ver·glas /váirglaä/ *n.* a thin coating of ice or frozen rain. [F]

ve·rid·i·cal /viridikәl/ *adj.* **1** *formal* truthful. **2** *Psychol.* (of visions, etc.) coinciding with reality. □□ **ve·rid·i·cal·i·ty** /-kálitee/ *n.* **ve·rid·i·cal·ly** *adv.* [L *veridicus* f. *verus* true + *dicere* say]

ver·i·est /véreeist/ *adj.* (*superl.* of VERY). *archaic* real; extreme (*the veriest fool knows that*).

ver·i·fi·ca·tion /vérifikáyshәn/ *n.* **1** the process or an instance of establishing the truth or validity of something. **2** *Philos.* the establishment of the validity of a proposition empirically. **3** the process of verifying procedures laid down in weapons agreements.

ver·i·fy /vérifī/ *v.tr.* (**-fies, -fied**) **1** establish the truth or correctness of by examination or demonstration (*must verify the statement; verified my figures*). **2** (of an event, etc.) bear out or fulfill (a prediction or promise). **3** *Law* append an affidavit to (pleadings); support (a statement) by testimony or proofs. □□ **ver·i·fi·a·ble** *adj.* **ver·i·fi·a·bly** *adv.* **ver·i·fi·er** *n.* [ME f. OF *verifier* f. med.L *verificare* f. *verus* true]

ver·i·ly /vérilee/ *adv. archaic* really; truly. [ME f. VERY + -LY[2], after OF & AF]

ver·i·si·mil·i·tude /vérisimílitōōd, -tyōōd/ *n.* **1** the appearance or semblance of being true or real. **2** a statement, etc., that seems true. □□ **ver·i·sim·i·lar** /-símilәr/ *adj.* [L *verisimilitudo* f. *verisimilis* probable f. *veri* genit. of *verus* true + *similis* like]

ver·ism /véerizәm/ *n.* realism in literature or art. □□ **ver·ist** *n.* **ve·ris·tic** /-rístik/ *adj.* [L *verus* or It. *vero* true + -ISM]

ve·ris·mo /verízmō/ *n.* (esp. of opera) realism. [It. (as VERISM)]

ver·i·ta·ble /véritәbәl/ *adj.* real; rightly so called (*a veritable feast*). □□ **ver·i·ta·bly** *adv.* [OF (as VERITY)]

ver·i·ty /véritee/ *n.* (*pl.* **-ties**) **1** a true statement, esp. one of fundamental import. **2** truth. **3** a really existent thing. [ME f. OF *verité*, *verté* f. L *veritas -tatis* f. *verus* true]

ver·juice /vә́rjōōs/ *n.* **1** an acid liquor obtained from crab apples, sour grapes, etc., and formerly used in cooking and medicine. **2** bitter feelings, thoughts, etc. [ME f. OF *vertjus* f. VERT green + *jus* JUICE]

ver·meil /vә́rmil, vәrmáyl/ *n.* **1** (/vәrmáy/) silver gilt. **2** an orange-red garnet. **3** *poet.* vermilion. [ME f. OF: see VERMILION]

vermi- /vә́rmee/ *comb. form* worm. [L *vermi* worm]

ver·mi·an /vә́rmeeәn/ *adj.* of worms; wormlike. [L *vermis* worm]

ver·mi·cel·li /vә́rmichélee/ *n.* **1** pasta made in long slender threads. **2** *Brit.* shreds of chocolate used as cake decoration, etc. [It., pl. of *vermicello* dimin. of *verme* f. L *vermis* worm]

ver·mi·cide /vә́rmisīd/ *n.* a substance that kills worms.

ver·mic·u·lar /vәrmíkyәlәr/ *adj.* **1** like a worm in form or movement; vermiform. **2** *Med.* of or caused by intestinal worms. **3** marked with close wavy lines. [med.L *vermicularis* f. L *vermiculus* dimin. of *vermis* worm]

ver·mic·u·late /vәrmíkyәlәt/ *adj.* **1** = VERMICULAR. **2** worm-eaten. [L *vermiculatus* past part. of *vermiculari* be full of worms (as VERMICULAR)]

ver·mic·u·la·tion /vәrmíkyәláyshәn/ *n.* **1** the state or process of be-

ing eaten or infested by or converted into worms. **2** a vermicular marking. **3** a worm-eaten state. [L *vermiculatio* (as VERMICULATE)]

ver·mic·u·lite /vәrmíkyәlīt/ *n.* a hydrous silicate mineral usu. resulting from alteration of mica, and expandable into sponge by heating, used as an insulation material. [as VERMICULATE + -ITE[1]]

ver·mi·form /vә́rmifawrm/ *adj.* worm-shaped.

ver·mi·form ap·pen·dix *n.* see APPENDIX 1.

ver·mi·fuge /vә́rmifyōōj/ *adj. & n.* ● *adj.* that expels intestinal worms. ● *n.* a drug that does this.

ver·mil·ion /vәrmílyәn/ *n. & adj.* ● *n.* **1** cinnabar. **2 a** a brilliant red pigment made by grinding this or artificially. **b** the color of this. ● *adj.* of this color. [ME f. OF *vermeillon* f. *vermeil* f. L *vermiculus* dimin. of *vermis* worm]

ver·min /vә́rmin/ *n.* (usu. treated as *pl.*) **1** mammals and birds injurious to game, crops, etc., e.g., foxes, rodents, and noxious insects. **2** parasitic worms or insects. **3** vile persons. □□ **ver·min·ous** *adj.* [ME f. OF *vermin, -ine* ult. f. L *vermis* worm]

ver·mi·nate /vә́rminayt/ *v.intr.* **1** breed vermin. **2** become infested with parasites. □□ **ver·mi·na·tion** /-náyshәn/ *n.* [L *verminare verminat-* f. *vermis* worm]

ver·miv·o·rous /vәrmívәrәs/ *adj.* feeding on worms.

ver·mouth /vәrmōōth/ *n.* a wine flavored with aromatic herbs. [F *vermout* f. G *Wermut* WORMWOOD]

ver·nac·u·lar /vәrnákyәlәr/ *n. & adj.* ● *n.* **1** the language or dialect of a particular country (*Latin gave place to the vernacular*). **2** the language of a particular clan or group. **3** plain, direct speech. ● *adj.* **1** (of language) of one's native country; not of foreign origin or of learned formation. **2** (of architecture) concerned with ordinary rather than monumental buildings. □□ **ver·nac·u·lar·ism** *n.* **ver·nac·u·lar·i·ty** /-láritee/ *n.* **ver·nac·u·lar·ize** *v.tr.* **ver·nac·u·lar·ly** *adv.* [L *vernaculus* domestic, native f. *verna* home-born slave]

ver·nal /vә́rnәl/ *adj.* of, in, or appropriate to spring (*vernal equinox; vernal breezes*). □□ **ver·nal·ly** *adv.* [L *vernalis* f. *vernus* f. *ver* spring]

vernal equinox see EQUINOX.

ver·nal·i·za·tion /vә́rnәlīzáyshәn/ *n.* the cooling of seed before planting, in order to accelerate flowering. □□ **ver·nal·ize** /vә́rnәlīz/ *v.tr.* [(transl. of Russ. *yarovizatsiya*) f. VERNAL]

vernal grass *n.* a sweet-scented European grass, *Anthoxanthum odoratum*, grown for hay.

ver·na·tion /vәrnáyshәn/ *n. Bot.* the arrangement of leaves in a leaf bud (cf. ESTIVATION). [mod.L *vernatio* f. L *vernare* bloom (as VERNAL)]

ver·ni·cle /vә́rnikәl/ *n.* = VERONICA 2. [ME f. OF (earlier *ver(o)nique*), f. med.L VERONICA]

ver·nier /vә́rneeәr/ *n.* a small, movable graduated scale for obtaining fractional parts of subdivisions on a fixed main scale of a barometer, sextant, etc. [P. *Vernier*, Fr. mathematician d. 1637]

ver·nier en·gine *n.* an auxiliary engine for slight changes in the motion of a space rocket, etc.

Ve·ro·nal /vérәnol/ *n. Trademark* a sedative drug, a derivative of barbituric acid. [G, f. *Verona* in Italy]

ve·ron·i·ca /vәrónikә/ *n.* **1** any plant of the genus *Veronica* or *Hebe*, esp. speedwell. **2 a** a cloth supposedly impressed with an image of Christ's face. **b** any similar picture of Christ's face. **3** *Bullfighting* the movement of a matador's cape away from a charging bull. [med.L f. the name *Veronica*: in sense 2 from the association with St. Veronica]

ver·ru·ca /vәrōōkә/ *n.* (*pl.* **ver·ru·cae** /-rōōscc/ or **ver·ru·cas**) a wart or similar growth. □□ **ver·ru·cose** /véerookōz/ *adj.* **ver·ru·cous** /vérookәs/ *adj.* [L]

ver·sant /vә́rsәnt/ *n.* **1** the extent of land sloping in one direction. **2** the general slope of land. [F f. *verser* f. L *versare* frequent. of *vertere* vers- turn]

ver·sa·tile /vә́rsәt'l, -tīl/ *adj.* **1** turning easily or readily from one subject or occupation to another; capable of dealing with many subjects (*a versatile mind*). **2** (of a device, etc.) having many uses. **3** *Bot. & Zool.* moving freely about or up and down on a support (*versatile antenna*). **4** *archaic* changeable; inconstant. □□ **ver·sa·tile·ly** *adv.* **ver·sa·til·i·ty** /-tilitee/ *n.* [F *versatile* or L *versatilis* (as VERSANT)]

verse /vәrs/ *n. & v.* ● *n.* **1 a** a metrical composition in general (*wrote pages of verse*). **b** a particular type of this (*English verse*). **2 a** a metrical line in accordance with the rules of prosody. **b** a group of a definite number of such lines. **c** a stanza of a poem or song with or without refrain. **3** each of the short numbered divisions of a chapter in the Bible or other scripture. **4 a** a versicle. **b** a passage (of an anthem, etc.) for solo voice. ● *v.tr.* **1** express in verse. **2** (usu. *refl.*; foll. by *in*) instruct; make knowledgeable. □□ **verse·let** *n.* [OE *fers* f. L *versus* a turn of the plow, a furrow, a line of writing f. *vertere* vers- turn: in ME reinforced by OF *vers* f. L *versus*]

versed[1] /vәrst/ *predic.adj.* (foll. by *in*) experienced or skilled in; knowledgeable about. [F *versé* or L *versatus* past part. of *versari* be engaged in (as VERSANT)]

versed[2] /vәrst/ *adj. Math.* reversed. [mod.L (*sinus*) *versus* turned (sine), formed as VERSE]

versed sine *n.* one minus cosine.

vers·et /vŏrsit/ n. Mus. a short prelude or interlude for organ. [F: dimin. of vers VERSE]

ver·si·cle /vŏrsikəl/ n. each of the short sentences in a liturgy said or sung by a priest, etc., and alternating with responses. □□ **ver·sic·u·lar** /–síkyōōlər/ adj. [ME f. OF versicule or L versiculus dimin. of versus: see VERSE]

ver·si·col·ored /vŏrsikúlərd/ adj. (Brit. **ver·si·col·oured**) 1 changing from one color to another in different lights. 2 variegated. [L versicolor f. versus past part. of vertere turn + color color]

ver·si·fy /vŏrsifī/ v. (–fies, –fied) 1 tr. turn into or express in verse. 2 intr. compose verses. □□ **ver·si·fi·ca·tion** /–fikáyshən/ n. **ver·si·fi·er** n. [ME f. OF versifier f. L versificare (as VERSE)]

ver·sine /vŏrsīn/ n. (also **ver·sin**) Math. = VERSED SINE.

ver·sion /vŏrzhən, –shən/ n. 1 an account of a matter from a particular person's point of view (told them my version of the incident). 2 a book or work, etc., in a particular edition or translation (Authorized Version). 3 a form or variant of a thing as performed, adapted, etc. 4 a piece of translation, esp. as a school exercise. 5 Med. the manual turning of a fetus in the womb to improve presentation. □□ **ver·sion·al** adj. [F version or med.L versio f. L vertere vers- turn]

vers li·bre /vair leébrə/ = FREE VERSE. [F, = free verse]

ver·so /vŏrsō/ n. (pl. **–sos**) 1 a the left-hand page of an open book. b the back of a printed leaf of paper or manuscript (opp. RECTO). 2 the reverse of a coin. [L verso (folio) on the turned (leaf)]

verst /vŏrst/ n. a Russian measure of length, about 0.66 mile (1.1 km). [Russ. versta]

ver·sus /vŏrsəs, –səz/ prep. against (esp. in legal and sports use). ¶ Abbr.: **v.**, **vs.** [L, = toward, in med.L against]

vert /vŏrt/ n. & (usu. placed after noun) adj. Heraldry green. [ME f. OF f. L viridis green]

ver·te·bra /vŏrtibrə/ n. (pl. **ver·te·brae** /–bray, –bree/) 1 each segment of the backbone. 2 (in pl.) the backbone. □□ **ver·te·bral** adj. [L f. vertere turn]

ver·te·brate /vŏrtibrət, –brayt/ n. & adj. • n. any animal of the subphylum Vertebrata, having a spinal column, including mammals, birds, reptiles, amphibians, and fishes. • adj. of or relating to the vertebrates. [L vertebratus jointed (as VERTEBRA)]

ver·te·bra·tion /vŏrtibráyshən/ n. division into vertebrae or similar segments.

ver·tex /vŏrteks/ n. (pl. **ver·ti·ces** /–tiseez/ or **ver·tex·es**) 1 the highest point; the top or apex. 2 Geom. a each angular point of a polygon, polyhedron, etc. b a meeting point of two lines that form an angle. c the point at which an axis meets a curve or surface. d the point opposite the base of a figure. 3 Anat. the crown of the head. [L vertex –ticis whirlpool, crown of a head, vertex, f. vertere turn]

ver·ti·cal /vŏrtikəl/ adj. & n. • adj. 1 at right angles to a horizontal plane; perpendicular. 2 in a direction from top to bottom of a picture, etc. 3 of or at the vertex or highest point. 4 at, or passing through, the zenith. 5 Anat. of or relating to the crown of the head. 6 involving all the levels in an organizational hierarchy or stages in the production of a class of goods (vertical integration). • n. a vertical line or plane. □ **out of the vertical** not vertical. □□ **ver·ti·cal·i·ty** /–kálitee/ n. **ver·ti·cal·ize** v.tr. **ver·ti·cal·ly** adv. [F vertical or LL verticalis (as VERTEX)]

ver·ti·cal an·gles n.pl. Math. each pair of opposite angles made by two intersecting lines.

ver·ti·cal fin n. Zool. a dorsal, anal, or caudal fin.

ver·ti·cal plane n. a plane at right angles to the horizontal.

ver·ti·cal take·off n. the takeoff of an aircraft directly upward.

ver·ti·cil /vŏrtisil/ n. Bot. & Zool. a whorl; a set of parts arranged in a circle around an axis. □□ **ver·ti·cil·late** /–tísilət, –layt/ adj. [L verticillus whorl of a spindle, dimin. of VERTEX]

ver·tig·i·nous /vərtíjinəs/ adj. of or causing vertigo. □□ **ver·tig·i·nous·ly** adv. [L vertiginosus (as VERTIGO)]

ver·ti·go /vŏrtigō/ n. a condition with a sensation of whirling and a tendency to lose balance; dizziness; giddiness. [L vertigo –ginis whirling f. vertere turn]

ver·tu var. of VIRTU.

ver·vain /vŏrvayn/ n. Bot. any of various herbaceous plants of the genus Verbena, esp. V. officinalis with small blue, white, or purple flowers. [ME f. OF verveine f. L VERBENA]

verve /vŏrv/ n. enthusiasm; vigor; spirit, esp. in artistic or literary work. [F, earlier = a form of expression, f. L verba words]

ver·vet /vŏrvit/ n. a small, gray African monkey, Cercopithecus aethiops. [F]

ver·y /véree/ adv. & adj. • adv. 1 in a high degree (did it very easily; had a very bad cough; am very much better). 2 in the fullest sense (foll. by own or superl. adj.) (at the very latest; do your very best; my very own room). • adj. 1 (usu. prec. by the, this, his, etc.) a real; true; actual; truly such (emphasizing identity, significance, or extreme degree) (the very thing we need; those were his very words). b mere; sheer (the very idea of it was horrible). 2 archaic real; genuine (very God). □ **not very 1** in a low degree. **2** far from being. **the very same** see SAME. [ME f. OF verai ult. f. L verus true]

ver·y high fre·quen·cy n. radio frequency in the range 30–300 megahertz.

Ver·y light /véree, veĕree/ n. a flare projected from a pistol for signaling or temporarily illuminating the surroundings. [E. W. Very, Amer. inventor d. 1910]

Ver·y pis·tol n. a gun for firing a Very light.

Ver·y Rev·er·end n. the title of a religious officer below the rank of bishop or abbot.

ve·si·ca /vesíkə, vésikə/ n. 1 Anat. & Zool. a bladder, esp. the urinary bladder. 2 (in full **vesica piscis** /písis/ or **piscium** /píseeəm/) Art a pointed oval used as an aureole in medieval sculpture and painting. □□ **ve·si·cal** adj. [L]

ves·i·cate /vésikayt/ v.tr. raise blisters on. □□ **ves·i·cant** /–kənt/ adj. & n. **ves·i·ca·tion** /–káyshən/ n. **ves·i·ca·to·ry** /–kətawree/ adj. & n. [LL vesicare vesicat- (as VESICA)]

ve·si·cle /vésikəl/ n. 1 Anat., Zool., & Bot. a small bladder, bubble, or hollow structure. 2 Geol. a small cavity in volcanic rock produced by gas bubbles. 3 Med. a blister. □□ **ve·sic·u·lar** /–síkyələr/ adj. **ve·sic·u·late** /–síkyəlayt/ adj. **ve·sic·u·la·tion** /–láyshən/ n. [F vésicule or L vesicula dimin. of VESICA]

ves·per /véspər/ n. 1 Venus as the evening star. 2 poet. evening. 3 (in pl.) a the sixth of the canonical hours of prayer. b evensong. [L vesper evening (star): sense 3 partly f. OF vespres f. eccl.L vesperas f. L vespera evening]

ves·per·tine /véspərtīn, –tin/ adj. 1 Bot. (of a flower) opening in the evening. 2 Zool. active in the evening. 3 Astron. setting near the time of sunset. 4 of or occurring in the evening. [L vespertinus f. vesper evening]

ves·pi·ar·y /véspee-eree/ n. (pl. **–ies**) a nest of wasps. [irreg. f. L vespa wasp, after apiary]

ves·pine /véspīn/ adj. of or relating to wasps. [L vespa wasp]

ves·sel /vésəl/ n. 1 a hollow receptacle esp. for liquid, e.g., a cask, cup, pot, bottle, or dish. 2 a ship or boat, esp. a large one. 3 a Anat. a duct or canal, etc., holding or conveying blood or other fluid, esp. = BLOOD VESSEL. b Bot. a woody duct carrying or containing sap, etc. 4 Bibl. or joc. a person regarded as the recipient or exponent of a quality (a weak vessel). [ME f. AF vessel(e), OF vaissel(le) f. LL vascellum dimin. of vas vessel]

vest /vest/ n. & v. • n. 1 a waist-length close-fitting, sleeveless garment, often worn under a suit jacket, etc. 2 Brit. an undershirt. 3 a usu. V-shaped piece of material to fill the opening at the neck of a woman's dress. • v. 1 tr. (esp. in passive; foll. by with) bestow or confer (powers, authority, etc.) on (a person). 2 tr. (foll. by in) confer (property or power) on (a person) with an immediate fixed right of immediate or future possession. 3 intr (foll. by in) (of property, a right, etc.) come into the possession of (a person). 4 a tr. poet. clothe. b intr. Eccl. put on vestments. [(n.) F veste f. It. veste f. L vestis garment: (v.) ME, orig. past part. f. OF vestu f. vestir f. L vestire vestit- clothe]

ves·ta /véstə/ n. hist. a short wooden or wax match. [Vesta, Roman goddess of the hearth and household]

ves·tal /vést'l/ adj. & n. • adj. 1 chaste; pure. 2 of or relating to the Roman goddess Vesta. • n. 1 a chaste woman, esp. a nun. 2 Rom. Antiq. a vestal virgin. [ME f. L vestalis (adj. & n.) (as VESTA)]

ves·tal vir·gin n. Rom.Antiq. a virgin consecrated to Vesta and vowed to chastity, who shared the charge of maintaining the sacred fire burning on the goddess's altar.

ves·tee /vestée/ n. = VEST n. 3.

vest·ed in·ter·est n. Law an interest (usu. in land or money held in trust) recognized as belonging to a person. 2 a personal interest in a state of affairs, usu. with an expectation of gain.

ves·ti·ar·y /véstee-eree, –chee–/ n. & adj. • n. (pl. **–ies**) 1 a vestry. 2 cloakroom. • adj. of or relating to clothes or dress. [ME f. OF vestiarie, vestiaire: see VESTRY]

ves·ti·bule /véstibyōōl/ n. 1 a an antechamber, hall, or lobby next to the outer door of a building. b a porch of a church, etc. 2 an enclosed entrance to a railroad car. 3 Anat. a a chamber or channel communicating with others. b part of the mouth outside the teeth. c the central cavity of the labyrinth of the inner ear. □□ **ves·tib·u·lar** /–stíbyoolər/ adj. [F vestibule or L vestibulum entrance court]

ves·tige /véstij/ n. 1 a trace or piece of evidence; a sign (vestiges of an earlier civilization; found no vestige of their presence). 2 a slight amount; a particle (without a vestige of clothing; showed not a vestige of decency). 3 Biol. a part or organ of an organism that is reduced or functionless but was well developed in its ancestors. [F f. L vestigium footprint]

ves·tig·i·al /vestíjeeəl, –jəl/ adj. 1 being a vestige or trace. 2 Biol. (of an organ) atrophied or functionless from the process of evolution (a vestigial wing). □□ **ves·tig·i·al·ly** adv.

ves·ti·ture /véstichər/ n. 1 Zool. hair, scales, etc., covering a surface. 2 archaic a clothing. b investiture. [ME f. med.L vestitura f. L vestire: see VEST]

vest·ment /véstmənt/ n. 1 any of the official robes of clergy, choristers, etc., worn during divine service, esp. a chasuble. 2 a garment, esp. an official or state robe. [ME f. OF *vestiment, vestement* f. L *vestimentum* (as VEST)]

vest-pock-et *adj.* **1** small enough to fit into the pocket of a vest. **2** very small.

ves-try /véstree/ *n.* (*pl.* **-tries**) **1** a room or building attached to a church for keeping vestments in. **2** *hist.* **a** a meeting of parishioners usu. in a vestry for parochial business. **b** a body of parishioners meeting in this way. □□ **ves-tral** *adj.* [ME f. OF *vestiaire, vestiarie,* f. L *vestiarium* (as VEST)]

ves-try-man /véstreemən/ *n.* (*pl.* **-men**) a member of a vestry.

ves-ture /véschər/ *n. & v.* • *n. poet.* **1** garments; dress. **2** a covering. • *v.tr.* clothe. [ME f. OF f. med.L *vestitura* (as VEST)]

vet[1] /vet/ *n. & v.* • *n. colloq.* a veterinary surgeon. • *v.tr.* (**vet-ted, vet-ting**) **1** make a careful and critical examination of (a scheme, work, candidate, etc.). **2** examine or treat (an animal). [abbr.]

vet[2] /vet/ *n. colloq.* a veteran. [abbr.]

vetch /vech/ *n.* any plant of the genus *Vicia,* esp. *V. sativa,* largely used for silage or fodder. □□ **vetch-y** *adj.* [ME f. AF & ONF *veche* f. L *vicia*]

vetch-ling /véchling/ *n.* any of various plants of the genus *Lathyrus,* related to vetch.

vet-er-an /vétərən, vétrən/ *n.* **1** a person who has grown old in or had long experience of esp. military service or an occupation (*a war veteran; a veteran of the theater; a veteran marksman*). **2** an exserviceman or ex-servicewoman. [F *vétéran* or L *veteranus* (adj. & n.) f. *vetus -eris* old]

vet-er-an car *n. Brit.* a car made before 1916, or (strictly) before 1905.

Vet-er-ans Day *n.* November 11, a legal holiday in the US, commemorating the end of World War I and of World War II, and honoring all veterans.

vet-er-i-nar-i-an /vétərináreeən, vétrə-/ *n.* a doctor who practices veterinary medicine or surgery. [L *veterinarius* (as VETERINARY)]

vet-er-i-nar-y /vétərineree, vétrə-/ *adj. & n.* • *adj.* of or for diseases and injuries of farm and domestic animals, or their treatment. • *n.* (*pl.* **-ies**) a veterinary surgeon. [L *veterinarius* f. *veterinae* cattle]

vet-er-i-nar-y sur-geon *n. Brit.* a person qualified to treat diseased or injured animals.

vet-i-ver /vétivər/ *n.* = CUSCUS[1]. [F *vétiver* f. Tamil *veṭṭivēru* f. *vēr* root]

ve-to /véetō/ *n. & v.* • *n.* (*pl.* **-toes**) **1 a** a constitutional right to reject a legislative enactment. **b** the right of a permanent member of the UN Security Council to reject a resolution. **c** such a rejection. **d** an official message conveying this. **2** a prohibition (*put one's veto on a proposal*). • *v.tr.* (**-toes, -toed**) **1** exercise a veto against (a measure, etc.). **2** forbid authoritatively. □□ **ve-to-er** *n.* [L, = I forbid, with ref. to its use by Roman tribunes of the people in opposing measures of the Senate]

vex /veks/ *v.tr.* **1** anger by a slight or a petty annoyance; irritate. **2** *archaic* grieve; afflict. □□ **vex-er** *n.* **vex-ing** *adj.* **vex-ing-ly** *adv.* [ME f. OF *vexer* f. L *vexare* shake, disturb]

vex-a-tion /veksáyshən/ *n.* **1** the act or an instance of vexing; the state of being vexed. **2** an annoying or distressing thing. [ME f. OF *vexation* or L *vexatio -onis* (as VEX)]

vex-a-tious /veksáyshəs/ *adj.* **1** such as to cause vexation. **2** *Law* not having sufficient grounds for action and seeking only to annoy the defendant. □□ **vex-a-tious-ly** *adv.* **vex-a-tious-ness** *n.*

vexed /vekst/ *adj.* **1** irritated; angered. **2** (of a problem, issue, etc.) difficult and much discussed; problematic. □□ **vex-ed-ly** /véksidlee/ *adv.*

vex-il-lol-o-gy /véksilóləjee/ *n.* the study of flags. □□ **vex-il-lo-log-i-cal** *adj.* **vex-il-lol-o-gist** *n.* [VEXILLUM & -LOGY]

vex-il-lum /veksíləm/ *n.* (*pl.* **vex-il-la** /-lə/) **1** *Rom. Antiq.* **a** a military standard, esp. of a maniple. **b** a body of troops under this. **2** *Bot.* the large upper petal of a papilionaceous flower. **3** *Zool.* the vane of a feather. **4** *Eccl.* **a** a flag attached to a bishop's staff. **b** a processional banner or cross. [L = flag f. *vehere vect-* carry]

VF *abbr.* (also **V.F.**) **1** video frequency. **2** visual field.

VG *abbr.* **1** very good. **2** vicar-general.

VHF *abbr.* very high frequency.

VI *abbr.* Virgin Islands.

vi-a /víeə, víə/ *prep.* by way of; through (*New York to Washington via Philadelphia; send it via your secretary*). [L, ablat. of *via* way, road]

vi-a-ble /víəbəl/ *adj.* **1** (of a plan, etc.) feasible; practicable esp. from an economic standpoint. **2 a** (of a plant, animal, etc.) capable of living or existing in a particular climate, etc. **b** (of a fetus or newborn child) capable of maintaining life. **3** (of a seed or spore) able to germinate. □□ **vi-a-bil-i-ty** /-bílitee/ *n.* **vi-a-bly** *adv.* [F f. *vie* life f. L *vita*]

vi-a-duct /víədukt/ *n.* **1** a long, bridgelike structure, esp. a series of arches, carrying a road or railroad across a valley or dip in the ground. **2** such a road or railroad. [L *via* way, after AQUEDUCT]

vi-al /víəl/ *n.* a small (usu. cylindrical glass) vessel esp. for holding liquid medicines. □□ **vi-al-ful** *n.* (*pl.* **-fuls**). [ME, var. of *fiole,* etc.: see VIAL]

vi-a me-di-a /víə méedeeə, veéə médeeə/ *n. literary* a middle way or compromise between extremes. [L]

vi-and /víənd/ *n. formal* **1** an article of food. **2** (in *pl.*) provisions; victuals. [ME f. OF *viande* food, ult. f. L *vivenda,* neut. pl. gerundive of *vivere* to live]

vi-at-i-cum /víátikəm/ *n.* (*pl.* **vi-at-i-cums** or **vi-at-i-ca** /-kə/) **1** the Eucharist as given to a person near or in danger of death. **2** provisions or an official allowance of money for a journey. [L, neut. of *viaticus* f. *via* road]

vibes /víbz/ *n.pl. colloq.* **1** vibrations, esp. in the sense of feelings or atmosphere communicated (*the house had bad vibes*). **2** = VIBRA-PHONE. [abbr.]

vi-brac-u-lum /víbrákyələm/ *n.* (*pl.* **vi-brac-u-la** /-lə/) *Zool.* a whip-like structure of bryozoans used to bring food within reach by lashing movements. □□ **vi-brac-u-lar** *adj.* [mod.L (as VIBRATE)]

vi-brant /víbrənt/ *adj.* **1** vibrating. **2** (often foll. by *with*) (of a person or thing) thrilling; quivering (*vibrant with emotion*). **3** (of sound) resonant. **4** (of color) bright and vivid. □□ **vi-bran-cy** /-rənsee/ *n.* **vi-brant-ly** *adv.* [L *vibrare:* see VIBRATE]

vi-bra-phone /víbrəfōn/ *n.* a percussion instrument of tuned metal bars with motor-driven resonators and metal tubes giving a vibrato effect. □□ **vi-bra-phon-ist** *n.* [VIBRATO + -PHONE]

vi-brate /víbráyt/ *v.* **1** *intr. & tr.* move or cause to move continuously and rapidly to and fro; oscillate. **2** *intr. Physics* move unceasingly to and fro, esp. rapidly. **3** *intr.* (of a sound) throb; continue to be heard. **4** *intr.* (foll. by *with*) quiver; thrill (*vibrating with passion*). **5** *intr.* (of a pendulum) swing to and fro. □□ **vi-bra-tive** /-rətiv/ *adj.* [L *vibrare vibrat-* shake, swing]

vi-bra-tile /víbrətil, -tíl/ *adj.* **1** capable of vibrating. **2** *Biol.* (of cilia, etc.) used in vibratory motion. [VIBRATORY, after *pulsatile,* etc.]

vi-bra-tion /víbráyshən/ *n.* **1** the act or an instance of vibrating; oscillation. **2** *Physics* (esp. rapid) motion to and fro, esp. of the parts of a fluid or an elastic solid whose equilibrium has been disturbed or of an electromagnetic wave. **3** (in *pl.*) **a** a mental (esp. occult) influence. **b** a characteristic atmosphere or feeling in a place, regarded as communicable to people present in it. □□ **vi-bra-tion-al** *adj.* [L *vibratio* (as VIBRATE)]

vi-bra-to /víbráátō/ *n. Mus.* a rapid slight variation in pitch in singing or playing a stringed or wind instrument, producing a tremulous effect (cf. TREMOLO). [It., past part. of *vibrare* VIBRATE]

vi-bra-tor /víbráytər/ *n.* **1** a device that vibrates or causes vibration, esp. an electric or other instrument used in massage or for sexual stimulation. **2** *Mus.* a reed in a reed organ.

vi-bra-to-ry /víbrətawree/ *adj.* causing vibration.

vi-bris-sae /víbrísee/ *n.pl.* **1** stiff coarse hairs near the mouth of most mammals (e.g., a cat's whiskers) and in the human nostrils. **2** bristlelike feathers near the mouth of insect-eating birds. [L (as VIBRATE)]

vi-bur-num /víbárnəm, vee-/ *n. Bot.* any shrub of the genus *Viburnum,* usu. with white flowers, e.g., the guelder rose and snowball bush. [L, = wayfaring tree]

Vic. *abbr.* Victoria.

vic-ar /víkər/ *n.* **1 a** (in the Church of England) an incumbent of a parish where tithes formerly passed to a chapter or religious house or layman (cf. RECTOR). **b** (in an Episcopal Church) a member of the clergy deputizing for another. **2** *RC Ch.* a representative or deputy of a bishop. □□ **vic-ar-i-ate** /-káireeət/ *n.* **vic-ar-ship** *n.* [ME f. AF *viker(e),* OF *vicaire* f. L *vicarius* substitute f. *vicis:* see VICE[3]]

vic-ar-age /víkərij/ *n.* the residence or benefice of a vicar.

vic-ar ap-os-tol-ic *n. RC Ch.* a Roman Catholic missionary or titular bishop.

vic-ar-gen-er-al *n.* (*pl.* **vic-ars-gen-er-al**) **1** an Anglican official assisting or representing a bishop, esp. in administrative matters. **2** *RC Ch.* a bishop's assistant in matters of jurisdiction, etc.

vi-car-i-al /vikáireeəl/ *adj.* of or serving as a vicar.

vi-car-i-ous /vikáireeəs/ *adj.* **1** experienced in the imagination through another person (*vicarious pleasure*). **2** acting or done for another (*vicarious suffering*). **3** deputed; delegated (*vicarious authority*). □□ **vi-car-i-ous-ly** *adv.* **vi-car-i-ous-ness** *n.* [L *vicarius:* see VICAR]

Vic-ar of Christ *n.* the pope.

vice[1] /vís/ *n.* **1 a** evil or grossly immoral conduct. **b** a particular form of this, esp. involving prostitution, drugs, etc. **2 a** depravity; evil. **b** an evil habit; a particular form of depravity (*has the vice of gluttony*). **3** a defect of character or behavior (*drunkenness was not among his vices*). **4** a fault or bad habit in a horse, etc. □□ **vice-less** *adj.* [ME f. OF f. L *vitium*]

vice[2] *esp. Brit.* var. of VISE.

vice[3] /vísee, -sə/ *prep.* in the place of; in succession to. [L, ablat. of *vix* (recorded in oblique forms in *vic-*) change]

vice[4] /vís/ *n. colloq.* = VICE PRESIDENT, VICE ADMIRAL, etc. [abbr.]

vice- /vís/ *comb. form* forming nouns meaning: **1** acting as a substitute or deputy for (*vice-chancellor*). **2** next in rank to (*vice admiral*). [as VICE[4]]

vice ad-mi-ral /vís/ *n.* a naval officer ranking below admiral and above rear admiral. □□ **vice ad-mi-ral-ty** *n.* (*pl.* **-ties**).

vice-chan·cel·lor /vís-chánsələr/ n. a deputy chancellor, esp. of a university, discharging most of the administrative duties.

vice·ge·rent /vísjérənt/ adj. & n. • adj. exercising delegated power. • n. a vicegerent person; a deputy. □□ **vice·ge·ren·cy** /–rənsee/ n. (pl. –cies). [med.L vicegerens (as VICE³, L gerere carry on)]

vi·cen·ni·al /vīséneeəl/ adj. lasting for or occurring every twenty years. [LL vicennium period of 20 years f. vicies 20 times f. viginti 20 + annus year]

vice pres·i·dent /vís-prézidənt, –dent/ n. an official ranking below and deputizing for a president. □□ **vice pres·i·den·cy** n. (pl. –cies). **vice pres·i·den·tial** /–dénshəl/ adj.

vice·re·gal /vísreégəl/ adj. of or relating to a viceroy. □□ **vice·re·gal·ly** adv.

vice·reine /vísrayn/ n. **1** the wife of a viceroy. **2** a woman viceroy. [F (as VICE-, reine queen)]

vice ring n. a group of criminals involved in organizing illegal prostitution.

vice·roy /vísroy/ n. a ruler exercising authority on behalf of a sovereign in a colony, province, etc. □□ **vice·roy·al** adj. **vice·roy·al·ty** n. **vice·roy·ship** n. [F (as VICE-, roy king)]

vice squad n. a police department enforcing laws against prostitution, drug abuse, etc.

vice ver·sa /vísə vórsə, vīs/ adv. with the order of the terms or conditions changed; the other way around; conversely (could go from left to right or vice versa). [L, = the position being reversed (as VICE³, versa ablat. fem. past part. of vertere turn)]

PRONUNCIATION TIP vice versa

The first part of this Latin phrase may be pronounced either like vice or as "VY-sah."

---

vi·chys·soise /vísheeswaáz, vee–/ n. a creamy soup of pureed leeks and potatoes, usu. served chilled. [F vichyssois –oise of Vichy (in France)]

Vi·chy wa·ter /víshee, vee–/ n. an effervescent mineral water from Vichy in France.

vic·i·nage /vísinij/ n. **1** a neighborhood; a surrounding district. **2** relation in terms of nearness, etc., to neighbors. [ME f. OF vis(e)nage ult. f. L vicinus neighbor]

vic·i·nal /vísinəl/ adj. **1** neighboring; adjacent. **2** of a neighborhood; local. [F vicinal or L vicinalis f. vicinus neighbor]

vi·cin·i·ty /vísínitee/ n. (pl. –ties) **1** a surrounding district. **2** (foll. by to) nearness or closeness of place or relationship. □ **in the vicinity** (often foll. by of) near (to). [L vicinitas (as VICINAL)]

vi·cious /víshəs/ adj. **1** bad-tempered; spiteful (a vicious dog; vicious remarks). **2** violent; severe (a vicious attack). **3** of the nature of or addicted to vice. **4** (of language or reasoning, etc.) faulty or unsound. □□ **vi·cious·ly** adv. **vi·cious·ness** n. [ME f. OF vicious or L vitiosus f. vitium VICE¹]

vi·cious cir·cle n. see CIRCLE n. 10.

vi·cious spi·ral n. continual harmful interaction of causes and effects, esp. as causing repeated rises in both prices and wages.

vi·cis·si·tude /visísitōōd, –tyōōd/ n. **1** a change of circumstances, esp. variation of fortune. **2** archaic or poet. regular change; alternation. □□ **vi·cis·si·tu·di·nous** /F vicissitude or L vicissitudo –dinis f. vicissim by turns (as VICE³)]

vic·tim /víktim/ n. **1** a person injured or killed as a result of an event or circumstance (a road victim; the victims of war). **2** a person or thing injured or destroyed in pursuit of an object or in gratification of a passion, etc. (the victim of their ruthless ambition). **3** a prey; a dupe (fell victim to a confidence scam). **4** a living creature sacrificed to a deity or in a religious rite. [L victima]

vic·tim·ize /víktimīz/ v.tr. **1** single out (a person) for punishment or unfair treatment, esp. dismissal from employment. **2** make (a person, etc.) a victim. □□ **vic·tim·i·za·tion** /–izáyshən/ n. **vic·tim·iz·er** n.

vic·tor /víktər/ n. a winner in battle or in a contest. [ME f. AF victo(u)r or L victor f. vincere vict- conquer]

vic·to·ri·a /viktáwreeə/ n. **1** a low, light, four-wheeled carriage with a collapsible top, seats for two passengers, and a raised driver's seat. **2** a gigantic S. American water lily, Victoria amazonica. **3 a** a species of crowned pigeon. **b** a variety of domestic pigeon. **4** (also **vic·to·ri·a plum**) Brit. a large, red, luscious variety of plum. [Queen Victoria, d. 1901]

Vic·to·ri·a Cross /viktáwreeə/ n. a UK decoration awarded for conspicuous bravery in the armed services, instituted by Queen Victoria in 1856.

Vic·to·ri·an /viktáwreeən/ adj. & n. • adj. **1** of or characteristic of the time of Queen Victoria. **2** associated with attitudes attributed to this time, esp. of prudery and moral strictness. • n. a person, esp. a writer, of this time. □□ **Vic·to·ri·an·ism** n.

Vic·to·ri·an·a /viktáwreeánə, –áánə/ n.pl. **1** articles, esp. collectors' items, of the Victorian period. **2** attitudes characteristic of this period.

vic·to·ri·ous /viktáwreeəs/ adj. **1** having won a victory; conquering; triumphant. **2** marked by victory (victorious day). □□ **vic·to·ri·ous·**

---

ly adv. **vic·to·ri·ous·ness** n. [ME f. AF victorious, OF victorieux, f. L victoriosus (as VICTORY)]

vic·to·ry /víktəree/ n. (pl. –ries) **1** the process of defeating an enemy in battle or war or an opponent in a contest. **2** an instance of this; a triumph. [ME f. AF victorie, OF victoire, f. L victoria (as VICTOR)]

vict·ual /vít'l/ n. & v. • n. (usu. in pl.) food, provisions, esp. as prepared for use. • v. **1** tr. supply with victuals. **2** intr. obtain stores. **3** intr. eat victuals. □□ **vict·ual·less** adj. [ME f. OF vitaille f. LL victualia, neut. pl. of L victualis f. victus food, rel. to vivere live]

PRONUNCIATION TIP victual

The pronunciation of this word, which properly rhymes with whittle, is based on an Anglicized version of the Old French vitaille. The modern spelling reflects the word's etymological origin in an older spelling, which is the Late Latin victualia, meaning 'provisions.'

---

vict·ual·ler /vítlər/ n. (also **vict·ual·er**) **1 a** a person, etc., who supplies victuals. **b** (in full **licensed victualler**) Brit. a pub owner, etc., licensed to sell liquor. **2** a ship carrying stores for other ships. [ME f. OF vitaill(i) er, vitaillour (as VICTUAL)]

vi·cu·ña /vīkōōnə, –nyə, –kyōō–, vi–/ n. (also **vi·cu·na**) **1** a S. American mammal, Vicugna vicugna, related to the llama, with fine silky wool. **2 a** cloth made from this wool. **b** an imitation of this. [Sp. f. Quechua]

vi·de /vídee, veéday/ v.tr. (as an instruction in a reference to a passage in a book, etc.) see; consult. [L, imper. of videre see]

vi·de·li·cet /vídéliset, vī–/ adv. = VIZ. [ME f. L f. videre see + licet it is permissible]

vid·e·o /vídeeō/ adj., n., & v. • adj. **1** relating to the recording, reproducing, or broadcasting of visual images on magnetic tape. **2** relating to the broadcasting of television pictures. • n. (pl. –os) **1** the process of recording, reproducing, or broadcasting visual images on magnetic tape. **2** the visual element of television broadcasts. **3** colloq. = VIDEOCASSETTE RECORDER. **4** a movie, etc., recorded on a videotape. • v.tr. (–oes, –oed) make a video recording of. [L videre see, after AUDIO]

vid·e·o·cas·sette /vídeeōkasét, –kəsét/ n. a cassette of videotape.

vid·e·o·cas·sette re·cord·er n. ¶ Abbr: **VCR** an apparatus for recording and playing videotapes.

vid·e·o·disc /vídeeōdisk/ n. (also **vid·e·o·disk**) a metal-coated disk on which visual material is recorded for reproduction on a television screen.

vid·e·o dis·play ter·mi·nal n. ¶ Abbr: **VDT** Computing a device displaying data as characters on a screen and usu. incorporating a keyboard.

vid·e·o fre·quen·cy n. a frequency in the range used for video signals in television.

vid·e·o game n. a game played by electronically manipulating images produced by a computer program on a television screen.

vid·e·o jock·ey n. ¶ Abbr: **VJ** & **veejay** a person who introduces music videos, as on television.

vid·e·o·phone /vídeeōfōn/ n. a telephone device transmitting a visual image as well as sound.

vid·e·o re·cord·er n. = VIDEOCASSETTE RECORDER.

vid·e·o sig·nal n. a signal containing information for producing a television image.

vid·e·o·tape /vídeeōtayp/ n. & v. • n. magnetic tape for recording television pictures and sound. • v.tr. make a recording of (broadcast material, etc.) with this.

vid·e·o·tape re·cord·er n. = VIDEOCASSETTE RECORDER.

vid·e·o·tex /vídeeōteks/ n. (also **vid·e·o·text** /–tekst/) any electronic information system, esp. teletext or viewdata.

vie /vī/ v.intr. (vy·ing) (often foll. by with) compete; strive for superiority (vied with each other for recognition). [prob. f. ME (as EN-VY)]

Vi·en·nese /veéeneéz/ adj. & n. • adj. of, relating to, or associated with Vienna in Austria. • n. (pl. same) a native or citizen of Vienna.

Vi·et·nam·ese /vee-étnəmeéz/ adj. & n. • adj. of or relating to Vietnam in SE Asia. • n. (pl. same) **1** a native or national of Vietnam. **2** the language of Vietnam.

vieux jeu /vyőzhő/ adj. old-fashioned; hackneyed. [F, lit. old game]

view /vyōō/ n. & v. • n. **1** range of vision; extent of visibility (came into view; in full view of the crowd). **2 a** what is seen from a particular point; a scene or prospect (a fine view of the mountains; a room with a view). **b** a picture, etc., representing this. **3** an inspection by the eye or mind; a visual or mental survey. **4** an opportunity for visual inspection; a viewing (a private view of the exhibition). **5 a** an opinion (holds strong views on morality). **b** a mental attitude (took a favorable view of the matter). **c** a manner of considering a thing (took a long-term view of it). • v. **1** tr. look at; survey visually; inspect (we *are going to view the house*). **2** *tr.* examine; survey mentally (*different ways of viewing a subject*). **3** *tr.* form a mental impression or opinion of; consider (*does not view the matter in the same light*). **4** *intr.* watch television. **5** *tr.* see (a fox) break cover. □ **have in view 1** have as one's object. **2** bear (a circumstance) in mind in forming a judgment, etc. **in view of** having regard to; considering. **on view** being shown (for observation or inspection); being exhibited. **with a view to 1** with the hope or intention of. **2** with the aim of attaining (*with a view to marriage*). □□ **view•a•ble** *adj.* [ME f. AF *v(i)ewe*, OF *vēue* fem. past part. f. *vēoir* see f. L *vidēre*]

view•da•ta /vyoódaytə, –data/ *n.* a news and information service from a computer source to which a television screen is connected by telephone link.

view•er /vyoóər/ *n.* **1** a person who views. **2** a person watching television. **3** a device for looking at film transparencies, etc.

view•er•ship /vyoóərship/ *n.* a viewing audience, especially of a television program.

view•find•er /vyoófindər/ *n.* a device on a camera showing the area covered by the lens in taking a photograph.

view hal•loo *n. Hunting* a shout on seeing a fox break cover.

view•ing /vyoóing/ *n.* **1** an opportunity or occasion to view; an exhibition. **2** the act or practice of watching television.

view•less /vyoólis/ *adj.* **1** not having or affording a view. **2** lacking opinions.

view•point /vyoópoynt/ *n.* a point of view; a standpoint.

vi•ges•i•mal /vijésiməl/ *adj.* **1** of twentieths or twenty. **2** reckoning or reckoned by twenties. □□ **vi•ges•i•mal•ly** *adv.* [L *vigesimus* f. *viginti* twenty]

vig•il /víjil/ *n.* **1 a** keeping awake during the time usually given to sleep, esp. to keep watch or pray (*keep vigil*). **b** a period of this. **2** *Eccl.* the eve of a festival or holy day. **3** (in *pl.*) nocturnal devotions. [ME f. OF *vigile* f. L *vigilia* f. *vigil* awake]

vig•i•lance /víjiləns/ *n.* watchfulness; caution; circumspection. [F *vigilance* or L *vigilantia* f. *vigilare* keep awake (as VIGIL)]

vig•i•lance com•mit•tee *n.* a self-appointed body for the maintenance of order, etc.

vig•i•lant /víjilənt/ *adj.* watchful against danger, difficulty, etc. □□ **vig•i•lant•ly** *adv.* [L *vigilans –antis* (as VIGILANCE)]

SYNONYM TIP vigilant

CAREFUL, CAUTIOUS, CIRCUMSPECT, WARY, WATCHFUL, ALERT. All of these adjectives connote being on the lookout for danger or opportunity. **Watchful** is the most general term, meaning closely observant (*a watchful young man who noticed everything*). If you're **vigilant**, you are *watchful* for a purpose (*to be vigilant in the presence of one's enemies*), and **wary** suggests being on the lookout for treachery or trickery (*wary of his neighbor's motives in offering to move the fence*). If you're **alert**, you are quick to apprehend a danger, an opportunity, or an emergency (*she was much more alert after a good night's sleep*), and if you're **careful**, you may be able to avoid danger or error altogether. **Cautious** and **circumspect** also emphasize the avoidance of danger or unpleasant situations. To be *circumspect* is to be *watchful* in all directions and with regard to all possible consequences; to be *cautious* is to guard against contingencies (*a cautious approach*).

---

vig•i•lan•te /víjilántee/ *n.* a member of a vigilance committee or similar body. [Sp., = vigilant]

vigne•ron /véenyəráwN/ *n.* a winegrower. [F f. *vigne* VINE]

vi•gnette /vinyét/ *n. & v.* ●*n.* **1** a short descriptive essay or character sketch. **2** an illustration or decorative design, esp. on the title page of a book, not enclosed in a definite border. **3** a photograph or portrait showing only the head and shoulders with the background gradually shaded off. **4** a brief scene in a movie, etc. ●*v.tr.* **1** make a portrait of (a person) in vignette style. **2** shade off (a photograph or portrait). □□ **vi•gnet•tist** *n.* [F, dimin. of *vigne* VINE]

vig•or /vígər/ *n.* (*Brit.* **vig•our**) **1** active physical strength or energy. **2** a flourishing physical condition. **3** healthy growth; vitality; vital force. **4 a** mental strength or activity shown in thought or speech or in literary style. **b** forcefulness; trenchancy; animation. □□ **vig•or•less** *adj.* [ME f. OF *vigor* f. L *vigor –oris* f. *vigēre* be lively]

vig•or•ish /vígərish/ *n. sl.* **1** the percentage deducted by the organizers of a game from a gambler's winnings. **2** an excessive rate of interest on a loan. [prob. f. Yiddish f. Russ. *vȳigr ȳsh* gain, winnings]

vi•go•ro /vígərō/ *n. Austral.* a team ball game combining elements of cricket and baseball. [app. f. VIGOROUS]

vig•or•ous /vígərəs/ *adj.* **1** strong and active; robust. **2** (of a plant) growing strongly. **3** forceful; acting or done with physical or mental vigor; energetic. **4** full of vigor; showing or requiring physical strength or activity. □□ **vig•or•ous•ly** *adv.* **vig•or•ous•ness** *n.* [ME f. OF f. med.L *vigorosus* f. L *vigor* (as VIGOR)]

vig•our *Brit.* var. of VIGOR.

vi•ha•ra /vihaárə/ *n.* a Buddhist temple or monastery. [Skr.]

Vi•king /víking/ *n. & adj.* ●*n.* any of the Scandinavian seafaring pirates and traders who raided and settled in parts of NW Europe in the 8th–11th c. ●*adj.* of or relating to the Vikings or their time. [ON *víkingr*, perh. f. OE *wīcing* f. *wīc* camp]

vile /vīl/ *adj.* **1** disgusting. **2** morally base; depraved; shameful. **3** *colloq.* abominably bad (*vile weather*). **4** *archaic* worthless. □□ **vile•ly** *adv.* **vile•ness** *n.* [ME f. OF *vil* *vile* f. L *vilis* cheap, base]

vil•i•fy /vílifī/ *v.tr.* (**–fies**, **–fied**) defame; speak evil of. □□ **vil•i•fi•ca•tion** /–fikáyshən/ *n.* **vil•i•fi•er** *n.* [ME in sense 'lower in value,' f. LL *vilificare* (as VILE)]

vill /vil/ *n. hist.* a feudal township. [AF f. OF *vile*, *ville* farm f. L (as VILLA)]

vil•la /vílə/ *n.* **1** *Rom. Antiq.* a large country house with an estate. **2** a country residence. **3** *Brit.* a detached or semidetached house in a residential district. **4** a rented holiday home, esp. abroad. [It. & L]

vil•lage /vílij/ *n.* **1 a** a group of houses and associated buildings, larger than a hamlet and smaller than a town, esp. in a rural area. **b** the inhabitants of a village regarded as a community. **2** *Brit.* a self-contained district or community within a town or city, regarded as having features characteristic of village life. **3** a small municipality with limited corporate powers. □□ **vil•lag•er** *n.* **vil•lage•y** *adj.* [ME f. OF f. L *villa*]

vil•lain /vílən/ *n* **1** a person guilty or capable of great wickedness. **2** *colloq.* usu. *joc.* a rascal or rogue. **3** (also **vil•lain of the piece**) (in a play, etc.) a character whose evil actions or motives are important in the plot. **4** *Brit. colloq.* a professional criminal. **5** *archaic* a rustic; a boor. [ME f. OF *vilein* *vilain* ult. f. L *villa*: see VILLA]

vil•lain•ous /vílənəs/ *adj.* **1** characteristic of a villain; wicked. **2** *colloq.* abominably bad; vile (*villainous weather*). □□ **vil•lain•ous•ly** *adv.* **vil•lain•ous•ness** *n.*

vil•lain•y /vílənee/ *n.* (*pl.* **–ies**) **1** villainous behavior. **2** a wicked act. [OF *vilenie* (as VILLAIN)]

vil•la•nelle /vílənél/ *n.* a usu. pastoral or lyrical poem of 19 lines, with only two rhymes throughout, and some lines repeated. [F f. It. *villanella* fem. of *villanello* rural, dimin. of *villano* (as VILLAIN)]

-ville /vil/ *comb. form colloq.* forming the names of fictitious places with ref. to a particular quality, etc. (*dragsville*; *squaresville*). [F *ville* town, as in many town names]

vil•lein /vílin, –ayn, viláyn/ *n. hist.* a feudal tenant entirely subject to a lord or attached to a manor. [ME, var. of VILLAIN]

vil•lein•age /vílinij/ *n. hist.* the tenure or status of a villein.

vil•lus /víləs/ *n.* (*pl.* **vil•li** /–lī/) **1** *Anat.* each of the short, fingerlike processes on some membranes, esp. on the mucous membrane of the small intestine. **2** *Bot.* (in *pl.*) long, soft hairs covering fruit, flowers, etc. □□ **vil•li•form** /vílofawrm/ *adj.* **vil•lose** /vílōs/ *adj.* **vil•los•i•ty** /–lósitee/ *n.* **vil•lous** /–əs/ *adj.* [L, = shaggy hair]

vim /vim/ *n. colloq.* vigor. [perh. f. L, accus. of *vis* energy]

vi•min•e•ous /vimíneeəs/ *adj. Bot.* of or producing twigs or shoots. [L *vimineus* f. *vimen viminis* osier]

VIN *abbr.* = VEHICLE IDENTIFICATION NUMBER.

vi•na /véenə/ *n.* an Indian four-stringed musical instrument with a fretted fingerboard and a gourd at each end. [Skr. & Hindi *vīṇā*]

vi•na•ceous /vīnáyshəs, vi–/ *adj.* wine-red. [L *vinaceus* f. *vinum* wine]

vin•ai•grette /vínigrét/ *n.* **1** (in full **vinaigrette sauce**) a salad dressing of oil, vinegar, and seasoning. **2** a small ornamental bottle for holding smelling salts. [F, dimin. of *vinaigre* VINEGAR]

vin•ci•ble /vínsibəl/ *adj. literary* that can be overcome or conquered. □□ **vin•ci•bil•i•ty** *n.* [L *vincibilis* f. *vincere* overcome]

vin•cu•lum /víngkyələm/ *n.* (*pl.* **vin•cu•la** /–lə/) **1** *Algebra* a horizontal line drawn over a group of terms to show they have a common relation to what follows or precedes (e.g., $a + \overline{b} \times c = ac + bc$, but $a + \overline{b \times c} = a + bc$). **2** *Anat.* a ligament; a frenum. [L, = bond, f. *vincire* bind]

vin•di•cate /víndikayt/ *v.tr.* **1** clear of blame or suspicion. **2** establish the existence, merits, or justice of (one's courage, conduct, assertion, etc.). **3** justify (a person, oneself, etc.) by evidence or argument. □□ **vin•di•ca•ble** /–kəbəl/ *adj.* **vin•di•ca•tion** /–káyshən/ *n.* **vin•di•ca•tive** /víndíkətiv, víndikaytiv/ *adj.* **vin•di•ca•tor** *n.* [L *vindicare* claim, avenge f. *vindex –dicis* claimant, avenger]

vin•di•ca•to•ry /víndikətawree/ *adj.* **1** tending to vindicate. **2** (of laws) punitive.

vin•dic•tive /vindíktiv/ *adj.* **1** tending to seek revenge. **2** spiteful. □□ **vin•dic•tive•ly** *adv.* **vin•dic•tive•ness** *n.* [L *vindicta* vengeance (as VINDICATE)]

vin•dic•tive dam•ag•es *n.pl. Brit. Law* = PUNITIVE DAMAGES.

vine /vīn/ *n.* **1** any climbing or trailing woody-stemmed plant, esp. of the genus *Vitis*, bearing grapes. **2** a slender trailing or climbing stem. □□ **vin•y** *adj.* [ME f. OF *vi(g)ne* f. L *vinea* vineyard f. *vinum* wine]

vine•dress•er /víndréssər/ *n.* a person who prunes, trains, and cultivates vines, esp. grapevines.

vin•e•gar /vínigər/ *n.* **1** a sour liquid obtained from wine, cider, etc., by fermentation and used as a condiment or for pickling. **2** sour behavior or character. □□ **vin•e•gar•ish** *adj.* **vin•e•gar•y** *adj.* [ME f. OF *vyn egre* ult. f. L *vinum* wine + *acer*, *acre* sour]

vin•er•y /vínəree/ n. (pl. **–ies**) 1 a greenhouse for grapevines. 2 a vineyard.

vine•yard /vínyərd/ n. 1 a plantation of grapevines, esp. for winemaking. 2 *Bibl.* a sphere of action or labor (see Matt. 20:1). [ME f. VINE + YARD²]

vingt-et-un /vántayón/ n. = BLACKJACK¹. [F, = twenty-one]

vini- /vínee/ comb. form wine. [L vinum]

vin•i•cul•ture /vínikulchər/ n. the cultivation of grapevines. □□ **vin•i•cul•tur•al** adj. **vin•i•cul•tur•ist** n.

vin•i•fi•ca•tion /vínifikáyshən/ n. the conversion of grape juice, etc., into wine.

vin•ing /víning/ n. the separation of leguminous crops from their vines and pods.

vi•no /véenō/ n. sl. wine, esp. a red Italian wine. [Sp. & It., = wine]

vin ordinaire /ván awrdináir/ n. inexpensive (usu. red) table wine. [F, = ordinary wine]

vi•nous /vínəs/ adj. 1 of, like, or associated with wine. 2 addicted to wine. □□ **vi•nos•i•ty** /–nósitee/ n. [L vinum wine]

vin rosé /ván rōzáy/ n. = ROSÉ. [F]

vint¹ /vint/ v.tr. make (wine). [back-form. f. VINTAGE]

vint² /vint/ n. a Russian card game like auction bridge. [Russ., = screw]

vin•tage /víntij/ n. & adj. • n. 1 a a season's produce of grapes. b the wine made from this. 2 a the gathering of grapes for wine making. b the season of this. 3 a wine of high quality from a single identified year and district. 4 a the year, etc., when a thing was made, etc. b a thing made, etc., in a particular year, etc. 5 poet. or rhet. wine. • adj. 1 of high quality, esp. from the past or characteristic of the best period of a person's work. 2 of a past season. [alt. (after VINTNER) of ME vendage, vindage f. OF vendange f. L vindemia f. vinum wine + demere remove]

vin•tage car n. an automobile made in the early part of the twentieth century.

vin•tag•er /víntijər/ n. a grape gatherer.

vint•ner /víntnər/ n. a wine merchant. [ME f. AL vintenarius, vinetarius f. AF vineter, OF vinetier f. med.L vinetarius f. L vinetum vineyard f. vinum wine]

vin•y /víni/ see VINE.

vi•nyl /vínəl/ n. any plastic made by polymerizing a compound containing the vinyl group, esp. polyvinyl chloride. □ **vinyl group** the organic radical or group CH_2CH. [L vinum wine + –YL]

vi•ol /víəl/ n. a medieval stringed musical instrument, played with a bow and held vertically on the knees or between the legs. [ME viel, etc., f. OF viel(l) e, alt. of viole f. Prov. viola, viula, prob. ult. f. L vitulari be joyful: cf. FIDDLE]

vi•o•la¹ /vee-ṓlə/ n. 1 a an instrument of the violin family, larger than the violin and of lower pitch. b a viola player. 2 a viol. [It. & Sp., prob. f. Prov.: see VIOL]

vi•o•la² /vī-ṓlə, vee–, víələ/ n. 1 any plant of the genus *Viola*, including the pansy and violet. 2 a cultivated hybrid of this genus. [L, = violet]

vi•o•la•ceous /víəláyshəs/ adj. 1 of a violet color. 2 *Bot.* of the violet family Violaceae. [L violaceus (as VIOLA²)]

vi•o•la da brac•cio /də braáchō/ n. a viol corresponding to the modern viola.

vi•o•la da gam•ba /də gámbə/ n. (also **vi•ol da gam•ba**) a viol held between the player's legs, esp one corresponding to the modern cello.

vi•o•la d'a•more /damóray/ n. a sweet-toned tenor viol.

vi•o•late /víəlayt/ v.tr. 1 disregard; fail to comply with (an oath, treaty, law, etc.). 2 treat (a sanctuary, etc.) profanely or with disrespect. 3 break in upon; disturb (a person's privacy, etc.). 4 assault sexually; rape. □□ **vi•o•la•ble** adj. **vi•o•la•tion** /–láyshən/ n. **vi•o•la•tor** n. [ME f. L violare treat violently]

vi•o•lence /víələns/ n. 1 the quality of being violent. 2 violent conduct or treatment; outrage; injury. 3 *Law* the unlawful exercise of physical force. b intimidation by the exhibition of this. □ **do violence to 1** act contrary to; outrage. 2 distort. [ME f. OF f. L violentia (as VIOLENT)]

vi•o•lent /víələnt/ adj. 1 involving or using great physical force (*a violent person; a violent storm; came into violent collision*). 2 a intense; vehement; passionate; furious (*a violent contrast; violent dislike*). b vivid (*violent colors*). 3 (of death) resulting from external force or from poison (cf. NATURAL adj. 2). 4 involving an unlawful exercise of force (*laid violent hands on him*). □□ **vi•o•lent•ly** adv. [ME f. OF f. L violentus]

vi•o•let /víələt/ n. & adj. • n. 1 a any plant of the genus *Viola*, esp. the sweet violet, with usu. purple, blue, or white flowers. b any of various plants resembling the sweet violet. 2 the bluish-purple color or seen at the end of the spectrum opposite red. 3 a pigment of this color. b clothes or material of this color. • adj. of this color. [ME f. OF violet(te) dimin. of viole f. L VIOLA²]

vi•o•lin /víəlín/ n. 1 a musical instrument with four strings of treble pitch played with a bow. 2 a violin player. □□ **vi•o•lin•ist** n. [It. violino dimin. of VIOLA¹]

vi•ol•ist¹ /víəlist/ n. a viol player.

vi•o•list² /vee-ṓlist/ n. a viola player.

vi•o•lon•cel•lo /véeələnchélō, ví–/ n. (pl. **–los**) formal = CELLO. □□ **vi•o•lon•cel•list** n. [It., dimin. of VIOLONE]

vi•o•lo•ne /veeəlṓnay/ n. a double-bass viol. [It., augment. of VIOLA¹]

VIP abbr. very important person.

vi•per /vípər/ n. 1 any venomous snake of the family Viperidae, esp. the common viper (see ADDER). 2 a malignant or treacherous person. □□ **vi•per•ine** /–in, –rín/ adj. **vi•per•ish** adj. **vi•per•like** adj. **vi•per•ous** adj. [F vipère or L vipera f. vivus alive + parere bring forth]

vi•per's bu•gloss n. a stiff, bristly blue-flowered plant, *Echium vulgare*.

vi•per's grass n. scorzonera.

vi•ra•go /viraágō, –ráygō/ n. (pl. **–gos**) 1 a fierce or abusive woman. 2 archaic a woman of masculine strength or spirit. [OE f. L, = female warrior, f. vir man]

vi•ral /vírəl/ adj. of or caused by a virus. □□ **vi•ral•ly** adv.

vi•re•lay /virilay/ n. a short (esp. old French) lyric poem with two rhymes to a stanza variously arranged. [ME f. OF virelai]

vi•re•o /víreeō/ n. (pl. **–os**) any small American songbird of the family Vireonidae. [L, perh. = greenfinch]

vi•res•cence /virésəns/ n. 1 greenness. 2 *Bot.* abnormal greenness in petals, etc., normally of some bright color. □□ **vi•res•cent** adj. [L virescere, incept. of virēre be green]

vir•gate¹ /vórgayt/ adj. Bot. & Zool. slim, straight, and erect. [L virgatus f. virga rod]

vir•gate² /vórgət/ n. Brit. hist. a varying measure of land, esp. 30 acres. [med.L virgata (rendering OE gierd-land yard-land) f. L virga rod]

virg•er var. of VERGER.

Vir•gil•i•an /vərjíleeən/ adj. of, or in the style of, the Roman poet Virgil (d. 19 BC). [L Vergilianus f. P. Vergilius Maro, Virgil]

vir•gin /vórjin/ n. & adj. • n. 1 a person (esp. a woman) who has never had sexual intercourse. 2 a (**the Virgin**) Christ's mother the Blessed Virgin Mary. b a picture or statue of the Virgin. 3 (**the Virgin**) the zodiacal sign or constellation Virgo. 4 colloq. a naïve, innocent, or inexperienced person (*a political virgin*). 5 a member of any order of women under a vow to remain virgins. 6 a female insect producing eggs without impregnation. • adj. 1 that is a virgin. 2 of or befitting a virgin (*virgin modesty*). 3 not yet used, penetrated, or tried (*virgin soil*). 4 undefiled; spotless. 5 (of clay) not fired. 6 (of metal) made from ore by smelting. 7 (of wool) not yet, or only once, spun or woven. 8 (of an insect) producing eggs without impregnation. □□ **vir•gin•hood** n. [ME f. AF & OF virgine f. L virgo –ginis]

vir•gin•al /vórjinəl/ adj. & n. • adj. that is or befits or belongs to a virgin. • n. (usu. in pl.) (in full **pair of virginals**) an early form of spinet in a box, used in the sixteenth and seventeenth centuries. □□ **vir•gin•al•ist** n. **vir•gin•al•ly** adv. [ME f. OF virginal or L virginalis (as VIRGIN): name of the instrument perh. from its use by young women]

virgin birth n. 1 the doctrine of Christ's birth without a human father. 2 parthenogenesis.

virgin for•est n. a forest in its untouched natural state.

virgin hon•ey n. honey taken from a virgin comb, or drained from the comb without heat or pressure.

Vir•gin•ia /vərjínyə/ n. 1 tobacco from Virginia. 2 a cigarette made of this. □□ **Vir•gin•ian** n. & adj. [Virginia in US, orig. the first English settlement (1607), f. Virgin Queen]

Vir·gin·ia creep·er *n.* a N. American vine, *Parthenocissus quinquefolia*, cultivated for ornament.

Vir·gin·ia reel *n.* a country dance.

Vir·gin·ia stock *n.* (or **Vir·gin·ian stock**) a cruciferous plant, *Malcolmia maritima*, with white or pink flowers.

vir·gin·i·ty /vərjínitee/ *n.* the state of being a virgin. [OF *virginité* f. L *virginitas* (as VIRGIN)]

vir·gin queen *n.* an unfertilized queen bee.

Vir·gin Queen *n.* Queen Elizabeth I of England.

vir·gin's bow·er *n.* a clematis, *Clematis viticella*.

Vir·go /várgō/ *n.* (*pl.* **–gos**) **1** a constellation, traditionally regarded as contained in the figure of a woman. **2 a** the sixth sign of the zodiac (the Virgin). **b** a person born when the sun is in this sign. □□ **Vir·go·an** *n. & adj.* [OE f. L, = virgin]

vir·gule /várgyool/ *n.* **1** a slanting line used to mark division of words or lines. **2** = SOLIDUS 1. [F, = comma, f. L *virgula* dimin. of *virga* rod]

PUNCTUATION TIP virgule

See note at SLASH.

vir·i·des·cent /víridésənt/ *adj.* greenish, tending to become green. □□ **vir·i·des·cence** /–səns/ *n.* [LL *viridescere* f. L *viridis*: see VIRIDIAN]

vir·id·i·an /virídeeən/ *n. & adj.* ● *n.* **1** a bluish-green chromium oxide pigment. **2** the color of this. ● *adj.* bluish-green. [L *viridis* green f. *virēre* be green]

vir·id·i·ty /viríditee/ *n. literary* greenness; verdancy. [ME f. OF *viridité* or L *viriditas* f. *viridis*: see VIRIDIAN]

vir·ile /víral, –īl/ *adj.* **1** of or characteristic of a man; having masculine (esp. sexual) vigor or strength. **2** of or having procreative power. **3** of a man as distinct from a woman or child. □□ **vi·ril·i·ty** /virílitee/ *n.* [ME f. F *viril* or L *virilis* f. *vir* man]

vir·il·ism /vírilizəm/ *n. Med.* the development of secondary male characteristics in a female or precociously in a male.

vir·oid /víroyd/ *n.* an infectious entity affecting plants, similar to a virus but smaller and consisting only of nucleic acid without a protein coat.

vi·rol·o·gy /vīróləjee/ *n.* the scientific study of viruses. □□ **vi·ro·log·i·cal** /–rəlójikəl/ *adj.* **vi·ro·log·i·cal·ly** *adv.* **vi·rol·o·gist** *n.*

vir·tu /vərtóo/ *n.* (also **ver·tu**) **1** a knowledge of or expertise in the fine arts. **2** virtuosity. [It. *virtù* VIRTUE, virtu]

vir·tu·al /várchooəl/ *adj.* **1** that is such for practical purposes though not in name or according to strict definition (*is the virtual manager of the business*; *take this as a virtual promise*). **2** *Optics* relating to the points at which rays would meet if produced backward (*virtual focus*; *virtual image*). **3** *Mech.* relating to an infinitesimal displacement of a point in a system. **4** *Computing* not physically existing as such but made by software to appear to do so (*virtual memory*). □□ **vir·tu·al·i·ty** /–álitee/ *n.* **vir·tu·al·ly** *adv.* [ME f. med.L *virtualis* f. L *virtus* after LL *virtuosus*]

vir·tu·al re·al·i·ty *n.* the generation by computer software of an image or environment that appears real to the senses.

vir·tue /várchoo/ *n.* **1** moral excellence; uprightness; goodness. **2** a particular form of this (*patience is a virtue*). **3** chastity, esp. of a woman. **4** a good quality (*has the virtue of being adjustable*). **5** efficacy; inherent power (*no virtue in such drugs*). **6** an angelic being of the seventh order of the celestial hierarchy (see ORDER *n.* 19). □ **by** (or **in**) **virtue of** on the strength or ground of (*got the job by virtue of his experience*). **make a virtue of necessity** derive some credit or benefit from an unwelcome obligation. □□ **vir·tue·less** *adj.* [ME f. OF *vertu* f. L *virtus –tutis* f. *vir* man]

vir·tu·o·so /várchoo-ósō, –zō/ *n.* (*pl.* **vir·tu·o·si** /–see, –zee/ or **–sos**) **1 a** a person highly skilled in the technique of a fine art, esp. music. **b** (*attrib.*) displaying the skills of a virtuoso. **2** a person with a special knowledge of or taste for works of art or virtu. □□ **vir·tu·os·ic** /–ósik/ *adj.* **vir·tu·os·i·ty** /–ósitee/ *n.* **vir·tu·o·so·ship** *n.* [It., = learned, skillful, f. LL (as VIRTUOUS)]

vir·tu·ous /várchooəs/ *adj.* **1** possessing or showing moral rectitude. **2** chaste. □□ **vir·tu·ous·ly** *adv.* **vir·tu·ous·ness** *n.* [ME f. OF *vertuous* f. LL *virtuosus* (as VIRTUE)]

vir·tu·ous cir·cle *n.* a beneficial recurring cycle of cause and effect (cf. VICIOUS CIRCLE).

vir·u·lent /víryələnt, víra–/ *adj.* **1** strongly poisonous. **2** (of a disease) violent or malignant. **3** bitterly hostile (*virulent animosity*; *virulent abuse*). □□ **vir·u·lence** /–ləns/ *n.* **vir·u·lent·ly** *adv.* [ME, orig. of a poisoned wound, f. L *virulentus* (as VIRUS)]

vi·rus /vírəs/ *n.* **1** a microscopic organism consisting mainly of nucleic acid in a protein coat, multiplying only in living cells and often causing diseases. **2** *Computing* = COMPUTER VIRUS. **3** *archaic* a poison; a source of disease. **4** a harmful or corrupting influence. [L, = slimy liquid, poison]

Vis. *abbr.* **1** Viscount. **2** Viscountess.

vi·sa /véezə/ *n. & v.* ● *n.* an endorsement on a passport, etc., showing that it has been found correct, esp. as allowing the holder to enter or leave a country. ● *v.tr.* (**vi·sas, vi·saed** /–zəd/, **vi·sa·ing**) mark with a visa. [F f. L *visa* neut. pl. past part. of *vidēre* see]

vis·age /vízij/ *n. literary* a face; a countenance. □□ **vis·aged** *adj.* (also so in *comb.*). [ME f. OF f. L *visus* sight (as VISA)]

vis-à-vis /véezaavée/ *prep., adv., & n.* ● *prep.* **1** in relation to. **2** opposite to. ● *adv.* facing one another. ● *n.* (*pl.* same) **1** a person or thing facing another, esp. in some dances. **2** a person occupying a corresponding position in another group. **3** a social partner. [F, = face to face, f. *vis* face f. L (as VISAGE)]

▶This expression means 'face to face.' Avoid using it to mean 'about, concerning,' e.g., *he wanted to talk to me vis-à-vis next weekend*. In the sense 'in contrast, comparison, or relation to,' however, **vis-à-vis** is generally acceptable: *let us consider government regulations vis-à-vis employment rates*.

Visc. *abbr.* **1** Viscount. **2** Viscountess.

vis·ca·cha /viskáachə/ *n.* (also **viz·ca·cha** /viz–/) any S. American burrowing rodent of the genus *Lagidium*, having valuable fur. [Sp. f. Quechua (*h*)*uiscacha*]

vis·cer·a /vísərə/ *n.pl.* the interior organs in the great cavities of the body (e.g., brain, heart, liver), esp. in the abdomen (e.g., the intestines). [L, pl. of *viscus*: see VISCUS]

vis·cer·al /vísərəl/ *adj.* **1** of the viscera. **2** relating to inward feelings rather than conscious reasoning. □□ **vis·cer·al·ly** *adv.*

vis·cer·al nerve *n.* a sympathetic nerve (see SYMPATHETIC *adj.* 9).

vis·cid /vísid/ *adj.* **1** glutinous; sticky. **2** semifluid. □□ **vis·cid·i·ty** /–síditee/ *n.* [LL *viscidus* f. L *viscum* birdlime]

vis·com·e·ter /viskómitər/ *n.* an instrument for measuring the viscosity of liquids. □□ **vis·co·met·ric** /vískəmétrik/ *adj.* **vis·co·met·ri·cal·ly** /vískəmétrikəlee/ *adv.* **vis·com·e·try** *n.* [var. of *viscosimeter* (as VISCOSITY)]

vis·cose /vískōs/ *n.* **1** a form of cellulose in a highly viscous state suitable for drawing into yarn. **2** rayon made from this. [LL *viscosus* (as VISCID)]

vis·cos·i·ty /viskósitee/ *n.* (*pl.* **–ties**) **1** the quality or degree of being viscous. **2** *Physics* **a** (of a fluid) internal friction; the resistance to flow. **b** a quantity expressing this. □□ **vis·co·sim·e·ter** /–kəsímitər/ *n.* [ME f. OF *viscosité* or med.L *viscositas* (as VISCOUS)]

vis·count /víkownt/ *n.* a British nobleman ranking between an earl and a baron. □□ **vis·count·cy** /–kówntsee/ *n.* (*pl.* **–cies**). **vis·count·ship** *n.* **vis·count·y** *n.* (*pl.* **–ies**). [ME f. AF *viscounte*, OF *vi(s)conte* f. med.L *vicecomes –mitis* (as VICE, COUNT²)]

vis·count·ess /víkowntis/ *n.* **1** a viscount's wife or widow. **2** a woman holding the rank of viscount in her own right.

vis·cous /vískəs/ *adj.* **1** glutinous; sticky. **2** semifluid. **3** *Physics* having a high viscosity; not flowing freely. □□ **vis·cous·ly** *adv.* **vis·cous·ness** *n.* [ME f. AF *viscous* or LL *viscosus* (as VISCID)]

vis·cus /vískəs/ *n.* (*pl.* **vis·cer·a** /vísərə/) (usu. in *pl.*) any of the soft internal organs of the body. [L]

vise /vīs/ *n. & v.* ● *n.* (esp. *Brit.* **vice**) an instrument, esp. attached to a workbench, with two movable jaws between which an object may be clamped so as to leave the hands free to work on it. ● *v.tr.* secure in a vise. □□ **vise·like** *adj.* [ME, = winding stair, screw, f. OF *vis* f. L *vitis* vine]

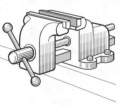

vise

Vish·nu /víshnoo/ *n.* a Hindu god regarded by his worshipers as the supreme deity and savior, by others as the second member of a triad with Brahma and Siva. □□ **Vish·nu·ism** *n.* **Vish·nu·ite** *n. & adj.* [Skr. *Vishṇu*]

vis·i·bil·i·ty /vízibílitee/ *n.* **1** the state of being visible. **2** the range or possibility of vision as determined by the conditions of light and atmosphere (*visibility was down to 50 yards*). [F *visibilité* or LL *visibilitas* f. L *visibilis*: see VISIBLE]

vis·i·ble /vízibəl/ *adj.* **1 a** that can be seen by the eye. **b** (of light) within the range of wavelengths to which the eye is sensitive. **2** that can be perceived or ascertained; apparent; open (*has no visible means of support*; *spoke with visible impatience*). **3** (of exports, etc.) consisting of actual goods (cf. INVISIBLE EXPORTS). □□ **vis·i·ble·ness** *n.* **vis·i·bly** *adv.* [ME f. OF *visible* or L *visibilis* f. *vidēre* vis– see]

Vis·i·goth /vízigoth/ *n.* a West Goth, a member of the branch of the Goths who settled in France and Spain in the 5th c. and ruled much of Spain until 711. [LL *Visigothus*]

vi·sion /vízhən/ *n. & v.* ● *n.* **1** the act or faculty of seeing; sight (*has impaired his vision*). **2 a** a thing or person seen in a dream or trance. **b** a supernatural or prophetic apparition. **3** a thing or idea perceived vividly in the imagination (*the romantic visions of youth*; *had visions of warm sandy beaches*). **4** imaginative insight. **5** statesmanlike foresight; sagacity in planning. **6** a person, etc., of unusual beauty. **7** what is seen on a television screen; television images collectively. ● *v.tr.* see or present in or as in a vision. □□ **vi·sion·al** *adj.* **vi·sion·less** *adj.* [ME f. OF f. L *visio –onis* (as VISIBLE)]

vi·sion·ar·y /vízhəneree/ *adj. & n.* ● *adj.* **1** informed or inspired by visions; indulging in fanciful theories. **2** existing in or characteristic of a vision or the imagination. **3** not practicable. ● *n.* (*pl.* **-ies**) a visionary person. □□ **vi·sion·ar·i·ness** *n.*

vis·it /vízit/ *v. & n.* ● *v.* (**vis·it·ed, vis·it·ing**) **1 a** *tr.* (also *absol.*) go or come to see (a person, place, etc.) as an act of friendship or ceremony, on business or for a purpose, or from interest. **b** *tr.* go or come to see for the purpose of official inspection, supervision, consultation, or correction. **2** *tr.* reside temporarily with (a person) or at (a place). **3** *intr.* be a visitor. **4** *tr.* (of a disease, calamity, etc.) come upon; attack. **5** *tr. Bibl.* **a** (foll. by *with*) punish (a person). **b** (often foll. by *upon*) inflict punishment for (a sin). **6** *intr.* **a** (foll. by *with*) go to see (a person) esp. socially. **b** (usu. foll. by *with*) converse; chat. **7** *tr. archaic* (often foll. by *with*) comfort; bless (with salvation, etc.). ● *n.* **1 a** an act of visiting; a call on a person or at a place (*was on a visit to some friends; paid him a long visit*). **b** temporary residence with a person or at a place. **2** (foll. by *to*) an occasion of going to a doctor, dentist, etc. **3** a formal or official call for the purpose of inspection, etc. **4** a chat. □□ **vis·it·a·ble** *adj.* [ME f. OF *visiter* or L *visitare* go to see, frequent. of *visare* view f. *vidēre* *vis-* see: (t.) perh. f. F *visite*]

vis·it·ant /vízit'nt/ *n. & adj.* ● *n.* **1** a visitor, esp. a supposedly supernatural one. **2** = VISITOR 2. ● *adj. archaic* or *poet.* visiting. [F *visitant* or L *visitare* (as VISIT)]

vis·it·a·tion /vizitáyshən/ *n.* **1** an official visit of inspection, esp. a bishop's examination of a church in his diocese. **2** trouble or difficulty regarded as a divine punishment. **3** (**Visitation**) **a** the visit of the Virgin Mary to Elizabeth related in Luke 1:39–56. **b** the festival commemorating this on July 2. **4** *Brit. colloq.* an unduly protracted visit or social call. **5** the boarding of a vessel belonging to another nation to learn its character and purpose. **6** the instance of a parent using his or her visitation rights. [ME f. OF *visitation* or LL *visitatio* (as VISIT)]

vis·it·a·tion rights *n.pl.* legal right of a noncustodial parent to visit or have temporary custody of his or her child.

vis·it·a·to·ri·al /vízitətáwreeəl/ *adj.* of an official visitor or visitation. [ult. f. L *visitare* (see VISIT)]

vis·it·ing /víziting/ *n. & adj.* ● *n.* paying a visit or visits. ● *attrib.adj.* (of an academic) spending some time at another institution (*a visiting professor*).

vis·it·ing card *n.* a card with a person's name, etc., sent or left in lieu of a formal visit; calling card.

vis·it·ing fire·man *n.* (*pl.* **-men**) *sl.* a visitor given especially cordial treatment.

visiting nurse *n.* a nurse, often employed by a public health agency, who visits the sick at home.

vis·i·tor /vízitər/ *n.* **1** a person who visits a person or place. **2** a migratory bird present in a locality for part of the year (*winter visitor*). **3** *Brit.* (in a college, etc.) an official with the right or duty of occasionally inspecting and reporting. [ME f. AF *visitour*, OF *visiteur* (as VISIT)]

vis·i·to·ri·al /vízitáwreeəl/ *adj.* of an official visitor or visitation.

vis·i·tors' book *n.* a book in which visitors to a hotel, church, embassy, etc., write their names and addresses and sometimes remarks.

vi·sor /vízər/ *n.* (also esp. *Brit.* **vi·zor**) **1 a** a movable part of a helmet covering the face. **b** *hist.* a mask. **c** the projecting front part of a cap. **2** a shield (fixed or movable) to protect the eyes from unwanted light, esp. one at the top of a vehicle windshield. □□ **vi·sored** *adj.* **vi·sor·less** *adj.* [ME f. AF *viser*, OF *visiere* f. *vis* face f. L *visus*: see VISAGE]

VISTA /vístə/ *abbr.* Volunteers in Service to America.

vis·ta /vístə/ *n.* **1** a long, narrow view as between rows of trees. **2** a mental view of a long succession of remembered or anticipated events (*opened up new vistas to his ambition*). □□ **vis·taed** *adj.* [It., = view, f. *visto* seen, past part. of *vedere* see f. L *vidēre*]

vis·u·al /vízhōōəl/ *adj. & n.* ● *adj.* of, concerned with, or used in seeing. ● *n.* (usu. in *pl.*) a visual image or display; a picture. □□ **vis·u·al·i·ty** /vízhoo-álitee/ *n.* **vis·u·al·ly** *adv.* [ME f. LL *visualis* f. L *visus* sight f. *vidēre* see]

vis·u·al aid *n.* a movie, model, etc., as an aid to learning.

vis·u·al an·gle *n.* the angle formed at the eye by rays from the extremities of an object viewed.

vis·u·al dis·play u·nit *n.* esp. *Brit.* = VIDEO DISPLAY TERMINAL.

vis·u·al field *n.* field of vision.

vis·u·al·ize /vízhōōəlíz/ *v.tr.* **1** make visible, esp. to one's mind (a thing not visible to the eye). **2** make visible to the eye. □□ **vis·u·al·iz·a·ble** *adj.* **vis·u·al·i·za·tion** /-izáyshən/ *n.*

vis·u·al pur·ple *n.* = RHODOPSIN.

vis·u·al ray *n. Optics* a line extended from an object to the eye.

vi·tal /vít'l/ *adj. & n.* ● *adj.* **1** of, concerned with, or essential to organic life (*vital functions*). **2** essential to the existence of a thing or to the matter in hand (*a vital question; secrecy is vital*). **3** full of life or activity. **4** affecting life. **5** fatal to the life of; essential to, etc. (*a vital error*). **6** *disp.* important. *n.* (in *pl.*) the body's vital organs, e.g., the heart and brain. □□ **vi·tal·ly** *adv.* [ME f. OF f. L *vitalis* f. *vita* life]

vi·tal ca·pac·i·ty *n.* the volume of air that can be expelled from the lungs after taking the deepest possible breath.

vi·tal force *n.* **1** (in Bergson's philosophy) life force. **2** any mysterious vital principle.

vi·tal·ism /vít'lizəm/ *n. Biol.* the doctrine that life originates in a vital principle distinct from chemical and other physical forces. □□ **vi·tal·ist** *n.* **vi·tal·is·tic** *adj.* [F *vitalisme* or f. VITAL]

vi·tal·i·ty /vītálitee/ *n.* **1** liveliness; animation. **2** the ability to sustain life; vital power. **3** (of an institution, language, etc.) the ability to endure and to perform its functions. [L *vitalitas* (as VITAL)]

vi·tal·ize /vít'líz/ *v.tr.* **1** endow with life. **2** infuse with vigor. □□ **vi·tal·i·za·tion** *n.*

vi·tal·ly /vít'lee/ *adv.* essentially; indispensably.

vi·tal pow·er *n.* the power to sustain life.

vi·tal signs *n.pl.* pulse rate, rate of respiration, and body temperature considered as signs of life.

vi·tal sta·tis·tics *n.pl.* **1** the number of births, marriages, deaths, etc. **2** *colloq.* the measurements of a woman's bust, waist, and hips.

vi·ta·min /vítəmin/ *n.* any of a group of organic compounds essential in small amounts for many living organisms to maintain normal health and development. [orig. *vitamine* f. L *vita* life + AMINE, because orig. thought to contain an amino acid]

vi·ta·min A *n.* = RETINOL.

vi·ta·min B com·plex *n.* (or **B vi·ta·mins**) any of a group of vitamins which, although not chemically related, are often found together in the same foods.

vi·ta·min B$_1$ *n.* = THIAMINE.

vi·ta·min B$_2$ *n.* = RIBOFLAVIN.

vi·ta·min B$_6$ *n.* = PYRIDOXINE.

vi·ta·min B$_{12}$ *n.* = CYANOCOBALAMIN.

vi·ta·min C *n.* = ASCORBIC ACID.

vi·ta·min D *n.* any of a group of vitamins found in liver and fish oils, essential for the absorption of calcium and the prevention of rickets in children and osteomalacia in adults.

vi·ta·min D$_2$ *n.* = CALCIFEROL.

vi·ta·min D$_3$ *n.* = CHOLECALCIFEROL.

vi·ta·min E *n.* = TOCOPHEROL.

vi·ta·min·ize /vítəminíz/ *v.tr.* add vitamins to.

vi·ta·min K *n.* any of a group of vitamins found mainly in green leaves and essential for the blood-clotting process.

vi·ta·min M *n.* = FOLIC ACID.

vi·tel·la·ry /vitélləree, vī–/ *adj.* of or relating to the vitellus.

vi·tel·li *pl.* of VITELLUS.

vi·tel·lin /vitélin, vī–/ *n. Chem.* the chief protein constituent of the yolk of egg. [VITELLUS + –IN]

vi·tel·line /vitélin, –leen, vī–/ *adj.* of the vitellus. [med.L *vitellinus* (as VITELLUS)]

vi·tel·line mem·brane *n.* the yolk sac.

vi·tel·lus /vitéləs, vī–/ *n.* (*pl.* **vi·tel·li** /–lī/) **1** the yolk of an egg. **2** the contents of the ovum. [L, = yolk]

vi·ti·ate /vísheeayt/ *v.tr.* **1** impair the quality or efficiency of; corrupt; debase; contaminate. **2** make invalid or ineffectual. □□ **vi·ti·a·tion** /–sheeáyshən/ *n.* **vi·ti·a·tor** *n.* [L *vitiare* f. *vitium* VICE¹]

vit·i·cul·ture /vítikulchər/ *n.* the cultivation of grapevines; the science or study of this. □□ **vit·i·cul·tur·al** *adj.* **vit·i·cul·tur·ist** *n.* [L *vitis* vine + CULTURE]

vit·re·ous /vítreeəs/ *adj.* **1** of, or of the nature of, glass. **2** like glass in hardness, brittleness, transparency, structure, etc. (*vitreous enamel*). □□ **vit·re·ous·ness** *n.* [L *vitreus* f. *vitrum* glass]

vit·re·ous hu·mor *n. Anat.* a transparent jellylike tissue filling the eyeball.

vi·tres·cent /vitrésənt/ *adj.* tending to become glass. □□ **vi·tres·cence** *n.*

vit·ri·form /vítrifawrm/ *adj.* having the form or appearance of glass.

vit·ri·fy /vítrifí/ *v.tr. & intr.* (**–fies, –fied**) convert or be converted into glass or a glasslike substance, esp. by heat. □□ **vit·ri·fac·tion** /–fákshən/ *n.* **vit·ri·fi·a·ble** *adj.* **vit·ri·fi·ca·tion** /–fikáyshən/ *n.* [F *vitrifier* or med.L *vitrificare* (as VITREOUS)]

vit·ri·ol /vítreeōl, –əl/ *n.* **1** sulfuric acid or a sulfate, orig. one of glassy appearance. **2** caustic or hostile speech, criticism, or feeling. [ME f. OF *vitriol* or med.L *vitriolum* f. L *vitrum* glass]

vit·ri·ol·ic /vítreeólik/ *adj.* (of speech or criticism) caustic or hostile.

vit·ta /vítə/ *n.* (*pl.* **vit·tae** /vítee/) **1** *Bot.* an oil tube in the fruit of some plants. **2** *Zool.* a stripe of color. □□ **vit·tate** *adj.* [L, = band, chaplet]

vi·tu·per·ate /vītōōpərayt, –tyōō–, vi–/ *v.tr. & intr.* revile; abuse. □□ **vi·tu·per·a·tion** /–ráyshən/ *n.* **vi·tu·per·a·tive** /–rətiv, –ráytiv/ *adj.* **vi·tu·per·a·tor** *n.* [L *vituperare* f. *vitium* VICE¹]

vi·va¹ /vívə, vee–/ *n. & v. Brit. colloq.* ● *n.* = VIVA VOCE *n.* ● *v.tr.* (**vi·vas, vi·vaed** /–vəd/, **vi·va·ing**) = VIVA VOCE *v.* [abbr.]

vi·va² /véevə/ *int. & n.* ● *int.* long live. ● *n.* a cry of this as a salute, etc. [It., 3rd sing. pres. subj. of *vivere* live f. L]

vi•va•ce /viváachay/ *adv. Mus.* in a lively brisk manner. [It. f. L (as VIVACIOUS)]

vi•va•cious /viváyshəs/ *adj.* lively; sprightly; animated. □□ **vi•va•cious•ly** *adv.* **vi•va•cious•ness** *n.* **vi•vac•i•ty** /vivásitee/ *n.* [L *vivax –acis* f. *vivere* live]

vi•var•i•um /vīváireeəm, vi–/ *n.* (*pl.* **vi•var•i•a** /–reeə/) a place artificially prepared for keeping animals in (nearly) their natural state. [L, = warren, fishpond, f. *vivus* living f. *vivere* live]

vi•vat /vívat, veévat/ *int. & n.* = VIVA[2]. [L, 3rd sing. pres. subj. of *vivere* live]

vi•va vo•ce /vívə vósee, vóchee, veévə/ *adj., adv., n., & v.* ● *adj.* oral. ● *adv.* orally. ● *n. Brit.* an oral examination for an academic qualification. ● *v.tr. Brit.* (**viva-voce**) (**–voces**, **–voced**, **–voc•ing**) examine orally. [med.L, = with the living voice]

vi•ver•rid /vivérid, vi–/ *n. & adj.* ● *n.* any mammal of the family Viverridae, including civets, mongooses, and genets. ● *adj.* of or relating to this family. [L *viverra* ferret + –ID[3]]

viv•id /vívid/ *adj.* **1** (of light or color) strong; intense; glaring (*a vivid flash of lightning; of a vivid green*). **2** (of a mental faculty, impression, or description) clear; lively; graphic (*has a vivid imagination; have a vivid recollection of the scene*). **3** (of a person) lively; vigorous. □□ **viv•id•ly** *adv.* **viv•id•ness** *n.* [L *vividus* f. *vivere* live]

viv•i•fy /vívifī/ *v.tr.* (**–fies**, **–fied**) enliven; animate; make lively or living. □□ **viv•i•fi•ca•tion** /–fikáyshən/ *n.* [F *vivifier* f. LL *vivificare* f. L *vivus* living f. *vivere* live]

vi•vip•a•rous /vīvípərəs, vi–/ *adj.* **1** *Zool.* bringing forth young alive, not hatching them by means of eggs (cf. OVIPAROUS). **2** *Bot.* producing bulbs or seeds that germinate while still attached to the parent plant. □□ **vi•vip•a•ri•ty** /vívipáritee/ *n.* **vi•vip•a•rous•ly** *adv.* **vi•vip•a•rous•ness** *n.* [L *viviparus* f. *vivus*: see VIVIFY]

viv•i•sect /vívisekt/ *v.tr.* perform vivisection on. [back-form. f. VIVISECTION]

viv•i•sec•tion /vívisékshən/ *n.* **1** dissection or other painful treatment of living animals for purposes of scientific research. **2** unduly detailed or ruthless criticism. □□ **viv•i•sec•tion•al** *adj.* **viv•i•sec•tion•ist** *n.* **viv•i•sec•tor** /–sektər/ *n.* [L *vivus* living (see VIVIFY), after *dissection* (as DISSECT)]

vix•en /víksən/ *n.* **1** a female fox. **2** a spiteful or quarrelsome woman. □□ **vix•en•ish** *adj.* **vix•en•ly** *adj.* [ME *fixen* f. OE, fem. of FOX]

viz. /viz, or by substitution náymlee/ *adv.* (usu. introducing a gloss or explanation) namely; that is to say; in other words (*came to a firm conclusion, viz. that we were right*). [abbr. of VIDELICET, *z* being med.L symbol for abbr. of *–et*]

▶This abbreviation for *videlicet* should be used to introduce a set of listed items (*I turned the nomination down for three reasons, viz., 1..., 2..., 3....*) or a more specific statement of what has been described only vaguely (*her sole means of support, viz., her writing*). Don't confuse *viz.* with *i.e.* (meaning 'that is') or *e.g.* (meaning 'such as' or 'for example').

viz•ard /vízərd/ *n. archaic* a mask or disguise. [VISOR + –ARD]

viz•ca•cha var. of VISCACHA.

vi•zier /vizéer, víziər/ *n. hist.* a high official in some Muslim countries, esp. in Turkey under Ottoman rule. □□ **vi•zier•ate** /–rət/ *n.* **vi•zier•i•al** /vizéereeəl/ *adj.* **vi•zier•ship** *n.* [ult. f. Arab. *wazīr* caliph's chief counselor]

vi•zor var. of VISOR.

VJ *abbr.* VIDEO JOCKEY.

Vlach /vlaak, vlak/ *n. & adj.* ● *n.* a member of a people chiefly inhabiting Romania and Moldova. ● *adj.* of or relating to this people. [Bulg. f. OSlav. *Vlach ŭ* Romanian, etc., f. Gmc, = foreigner]

V.M.D. *abbr.* doctor of veterinary medicine. [L *Veterinariae Medicinae Doctor*]

V neck /veénék/ *n.* (often *attrib.*) **1** a neck of a sweater, etc., with straight sides meeting at an angle in the front to form a V. **2** a garment with this.

VO *abbr.* **1** very old (as an indication of a whiskey's or brandy's age). **2** (in the UK) Royal Victorian Order.

voc. *abbr.* **1** vocational. **2** vocative.

vocab. *abbr.* vocabulary.

vo•ca•ble /vókəbəl/ *n.* a word, esp. with reference to form rather than meaning. [F *vocable* or L *vocabulum* f. *vocare* call]

vo•cab•u•lar•y /vōkábyəleree/ *n.* (*pl.* **–ies**) **1** the (principal) words used in a language or a particular book or branch of science, etc., or by a particular author (*scientific vocabulary; the vocabulary of Shakespeare*). **2** a list of these, arranged alphabetically with definitions or translations. **3** the range of words known to an individual (*his vocabulary is limited*). **4** a set of artistic or stylistic forms or techniques, esp. a range of set movements in ballet, etc. [med.L *vocabularius, –um* (as VOCABLE)]

vo•cal /vókəl/ *adj. & n.* ● *adj.* **1** of or concerned with or uttered by the voice (*a vocal communication*). **2** expressing one's feelings freely in speech (*was very vocal about her rights*). **3** *Phonet.* voiced. **4** *poet.* (of trees, water, etc.) endowed with a voice or a similar faculty. **5** (of music) written for or produced by the voice with or without

accompaniment (cf. INSTRUMENTAL). ● *n.* **1** (in *sing.* or *pl.*) the sung part of a musical composition. **2** a musical performance with singing. □□ **vo•cal•i•ty** /vəkálitee/ *n.* **vo•cal•ly** *adv.* [ME f. L *vocalis* (as VOICE)]

vocal cords *n.pl.* folds of the lining membrane of the larynx near the opening of the glottis, with edges vibrating in the air stream to produce the voice.

vo•cal•ic /vōkálik/ *adj.* of or consisting of a vowel or vowels.

vo•cal•ism /vókəlizəm/ *n.* **1** the use of the voice in speaking or singing. **2** a vowel sound or system.

vo•cal•ist /vókəlist/ *n.* a singer, esp. of jazz or popular songs.

vo•cal•ize /vókəlīz/ *v.* **1** *tr.* **a** form (a sound) or utter (a word) with the voice. **b** make sonant (*f is vocalized into v*). **2** *intr.* utter a vocal sound. **3** *tr.* write (Hebrew, etc.) with vowel points. **4** *intr. Mus.* sing with several notes to one vowel. □□ **vo•cal•i•za•tion** *n.* **vo•cal•iz•er** *n.*

vocal score *n.* a musical score showing the voice parts in full.

vo•ca•tion /vōkáyshən/ *n.* **1** a strong feeling of fitness for a particular career or occupation (in religious contexts regarded as a divine call). **2 a** a person's employment, esp. regarded as requiring dedication. **b** a trade or profession. [ME f. OF *vocation* or L *vocatio* f. *vocare* call]

vo•ca•tion•al /vōkáyshənəl/ *adj.* **1** of or relating to an occupation or employment. **2** (of education or training) directed at a particular occupation and its skills. □□ **vo•ca•tion•al•ism** *n.* **vo•ca•tion•al•ize** *v.tr.* **vo•ca•tion•al•ly** *adv.*

voc•a•tive /vókətiv/ *n. & adj. Gram.* ● *n.* the case of nouns, pronouns, and adjectives used in addressing or invoking a person or thing. ● *adj.* of or in this case. [ME f. OF *vocatif –ive* or L *vocativus* f. *vocare* call]

vo•cif•er•ate /vōsífərayt/ *v.* **1** *tr.* utter (words, etc.) noisily. **2** *intr.* shout; bawl. □□ **vo•cif•er•ance** /–rəns/ *n.* **vo•cif•er•ant** /–rənt/ *adj. & n.* **vo•cif•er•a•tion** /–ráyshən/ *n.* **vo•cif•er•a•tor** *n.* [L *vociferari* f. *vox* voice + *ferre* bear]

vo•cif•er•ous /vōsífərəs/ *adj.* **1** (of a person, speech, etc.) noisy; clamorous. **2** insistently and forcibly expressing one's views. □□ **vo•cif•er•ous•ly** *adv.* **vo•cif•er•ous•ness** *n.*

SYNONYM TIP vociferous

BLATANT, BOISTEROUS, CLAMOROUS, OBSTREPEROUS, STRIDENT. An angry crowd might be **vociferous**, which implies loud and unrestrained shouting or crying out. A happy crowd might be **boisterous**, which implies noisy exuberance or high-spirited rowdiness (*a boisterous celebration of spring*). A crowd that wants something is likely to be **clamorous**, which suggests an urgent or insistent *vociferousness* in demanding or protesting something. If their demands are not met, they might become **obstreperous**, which means noisy in an unruly and aggressive way, usually in defiance of authority (*an obstreperous child*). **Blatant** implies a tendency to be conspicuously, offensively noisy, while **strident** suggests a harsh, grating loudness that is particularly distressing to the ear (*her strident voice could be heard throughout the building*).

vo•cod•er /vōkódər/ *n.* a synthesizer that produces sounds from an analysis of speech input. [VOICE + CODE]

vod•ka /vódkə/ *n.* an alcoholic spirit made orig. in Russia by distillation of rye, etc. [Russ., dimin. of *voda* water]

vogue /vōg/ *n.* **1** (prec. by *the*) the prevailing fashion. **2** popular use or currency (*has had a great vogue*). □ **in vogue** in fashion, generally current. □□ **vogu•ish** *adj.* [F f. It. *voga* rowing, fashion f. *vogare* row, go well]

vogue word *n.* a word currently fashionable.

voice /voys/ *n. & v.* ● *n.* **1 a** sound formed in the larynx, etc., and uttered by the mouth, esp. human utterance in speaking, shouting, singing, etc. (*heard a voice; spoke in a low voice*). **b** the ability to produce this (*has lost her voice*). **2 a** the use of the voice; utterance, esp. in spoken or written words (esp. *give voice*). **b** an opinion so expressed. **c** the right to express an opinion (*I have no voice

GRAMMAR TIP voice

Active vs. Passive Voice. Voice expresses the relationship between the subject of a sentence and the action of the verb. When the subject performs the action, the verb is said to be in the **active voice** (*I drove* the car today). Verbs are said to be in the **passive voice** when the subject receives the action (*I was driven* home). Passive verbs normally consist of a form of the verb *to be* followed by a past participle. The active voice is usually simpler and makes a more powerful impression on the reader than the passive voice, but there are certain situations in which the passive voice is preferred: (1) when you want to avoid mentioning the performer of the action (*a terrible mistake was made*), or when the performer is not known (*the car was stolen*); (2) when you want to avoid using a vague pronoun as your subject (*the cars are built here in the U.S.* is more direct than *they build the cars here in the U.S.*); and (3) when the result of the action is more important than the person performing it (*the man was arrested for breaking and entering*).

in the matter). **d** an agency by which an opinion is expressed. **3** *Gram.* a form or set of forms of a verb showing the relation of the subject to the action (*active voice; passive voice*). **4** *Mus.* **a** a vocal part in a composition. **b** a constituent part in a fugue. **5** *Phonet.* sound uttered with resonance of the vocal cords, not with mere breath. **6** (usu. in *pl.*) the supposed utterance of an invisible guiding or directing spirit. • *v.tr.* **1** give utterance to; express (*the letter voices our opinion*). **2** (esp. as **voiced** *adj.*) *Phonet.* utter with vibration of the vocal cords (e.g., *b, d, g, v, z*). **3** *Mus.* regulate the tone quality of (organ pipes). □ **in voice** (or **good voice**) in proper vocal condition for singing or speaking. **with one voice** unanimously. □□ **–voiced** *adj.* **voic•er** *n.* (in sense 3 of v.). [ME f. AF *voiz*, OF *vois* f. L *vox vocis*]

voice box *n.* the larynx.

voice•ful /vóysfŏŏl/ *adj.* poet. or *rhet.* **1** vocal. **2** sonorous.

voice•less /vóyslis/ *adj.* **1** dumb; mute; speechless. **2** *Phonet.* uttered without vibration of the vocal cords (e.g., *f, k, p, s, t*). □□ **voice•less•ly** *adv.* **voice•less•ness** *n.*

voice mail *n.* an automatic telephone answering system that records messages from callers.

voice-o•ver *n.* narration in a movie, etc., not accompanied by a picture of the speaker.

voice•print /vóysprint/ *n.* a visual record of speech, analyzed with respect to frequency, duration, and amplitude.

voice vote *n.* a vote taken by noting the relative strength of calls of *aye* and *no*.

void /voyd/ *adj., n., & v.* • *adj.* **1 a** empty, vacant. **b** (foll. by *of*) lacking; free from (*a style void of affectation*). **2** esp. Law (of a contract, deed, promise, etc.) invalid; not binding (*null and void*). **3** useless; ineffectual. **4** (often foll. by *in*) *Cards* (of a hand) having no cards in a given suit. **5** (of an office) vacant (esp. *fall void*). • *n.* **1** an empty space; a vacuum (*vanished into the void; cannot fill the void made by death*). **2** an unfilled space in a wall or building. **3** (often foll. by *in*) *Cards* the absence of cards in a particular suit. • *v.tr.* **1** render invalid. **2** (also *absol.*) excrete. □□ **void•a•ble** *adj.* **void•ness** *n.* [ME f. OF dial. *voide*, OF *vuide, vuit*, rel. to L *vacare* VACATE: v. partly f. AVOID, partly f. OF *voider*]

void•ance /vóyd'ns/ *n.* **1** *Eccl.* a vacancy in a benefice. **2** the act or an instance of voiding; the state of being voided. [ME f. OF (as VOID)]

void•ed /vóydid/ *adj. Heraldry* (of a bearing) having the central area cut away so as to show the field.

voile /voyl, vwaal/ *n.* a thin, semitransparent dress material of cotton, wool, or silk. [F, = VEIL]

vol. *abbr.* **1** volume. **2** volcano. **3** volunteer.

vo•lant /vólənt/ *adj.* **1** *Zool.* flying; able to fly. **2** *Heraldry* represented as flying. **3** *literary* nimble; rapid. [F f. *voler* f. L *volare* fly]

vo•lar /vólər/ *adj. Anat.* of the palm or sole. [L *vola* hollow of hand or foot]

vol•a•tile /vólət'l, –til/ *adj. & n.* • *adj.* **1** evaporating rapidly (*volatile salts*). **2** changeable; fickle. **3** lively; lighthearted. **4** apt to break out into violence. **5** transient. • *n.* a volatile substance. □□ **vol•a•tile•ness** *n.* **vol•a•til•i•ty** /–tílitee/ *n.* [OF *volatil* or L *volatilis* f. *volare volat–* fly]

vol•a•tile oil *n.* = ESSENTIAL OIL.

vol•a•til•ize /vólət'līz/ *v.* **1** *tr.* cause to evaporate. **2** *intr.* evaporate. □□ **vol•a•til•iz•a•ble** *adj.* **vol•a•til•i•za•tion** *n.*

vol-au-vent /váwlōvoN/ *n.* a (usu. small) round case of puff pastry filled with meat, fish, etc., and sauce. [F, lit. 'flight in the wind']

vol•can•ic /volkánik/ *adj.* (also **vul•can•ic** /vul–/) of, like, or produced by a volcano. □□ **vol•can•i•cal•ly** *adv.* **vol•can•ic•i•ty** /vólkənísitee/ *n.* [F *volcanique* f. *volcan* VOLCANO]

vol•can•ic bomb *n.* a mass of ejected lava usu. rounded and sometimes hollow.

vol•can•ic glass *n.* obsidian.

vol•ca•no /volkáynō/ *n.* (*pl.* **–noes**) **1** a mountain or hill having an opening or openings in the earth's crust through which lava, cinders, steam, gases, etc., are or have been expelled continuously or

SYNONYM TIP *void*

ABROGATE, ANNUL, INVALIDATE, NEGATE, NULLIFY. To **void** a check, to **invalidate** a claim, to **abrogate** a law, and to **annul** a marriage all refer to the same basic activity, which is putting an end to something or depriving it of validity, force, or authority. But these verbs are not always interchangeable. *Annul* is the most general term, meaning to end something that exists or to declare that it never really existed (*the charter was annulled before it could be challenged*). *Abrogate* implies the exercise of legal authority (*Congress abrogated the treaty between the two warring factions*), while **nullify** means to deprive something of its value or effectiveness (*to nullify the enemy's attempt to establish communications*). *Void* and *invalidate* are often used interchangeably (*to void a legal document by tearing it up; to invalidate a check by putting the wrong date on it*), as they both mean to make null or worthless. **Negate** means to prove an assertion false (*her version of the story negated everything her brother had said*) or to *nullify* or make something ineffective (*the study's findings were negated by its author's arrest for fraud*).

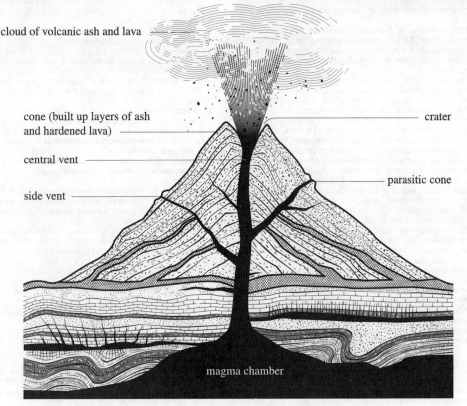

cloud of volcanic ash and lava

cone (built up layers of ash and hardened lava)

crater

central vent

parasitic cone

side vent

magma chamber

volcano

at intervals. **2 a** a state of things likely to cause a violent outburst. **b** a violent esp. suppressed feeling. [It. f. L *Volcanus* Vulcan, Roman god of fire]

vol·can·ol·o·gy /vólkənóləjee/ n. (also **vul·can·ol·o·gy** /vúl–/) the scientific study of volcanoes. □□ **vol·can·o·log·i·cal** /–nəlójikəl/ adj. **vol·can·ol·o·gist** n.

vole[1] /vōl/ n. any small ratlike or mouselike plant-eating rodent of the family Cricetidae. [orig. *vole-mouse* f. Norw. f. *voll* field + *mus* mouse]

vole[2] /vōl/ n. archaic the winning of all tricks at cards. [F f. *voler* fly f. L *volare*]

vo·let /vólay/ n. a panel or wing of a triptych. [F f. *voler* fly f. L *volare*]

vol·i·tant /vólit'nt/ adj. Zool. volant. [L *volitare* frequent. of *volare* fly]

vo·li·tion /vəlíshən/ n. **1** the exercise of the will. **2** the power of willing. □ **of** (or **by**) **one's own volition** voluntarily. □□ **vo·li·tion·al** adj. **vo·li·tion·al·ly** adv. **vol·i·tive** /vólitiv/ adj. [F *volition* or med.L *volitio* f. *volo* I wish]

vol·ley /vólee/ n. & v. • n. (pl. **–leys**) **1 a** the simultaneous discharge of a number of weapons. **b** the bullets, etc., discharged in a volley. **2** (usu. foll. by *of*) a noisy emission of oaths, etc., in quick succession. **3** *Tennis* the return of a ball in play before it touches the ground. **4** *Soccer* the kicking of a ball in play before it touches the ground. • v. (**–leys, –leyed**) **1** tr. (also absol.) *Tennis* & *Soccer* return or send (a ball) by a volley. **2** tr. & absol. discharge (bullets, abuse, etc.) in a volley. **3** intr. (of bullets, etc.) fly in a volley. **4** intr. (of guns, etc.) sound together. **5** intr. make a sound like a volley of artillery. □□ **vol·ley·er** n. [F *volée* ult. f. L *volare* fly]

vol·ley·ball /vóleebawl/ n. a game for two teams of six hitting a large ball by hand over a net.

volplane /vólplayn/ n. & v. Aeron. • n. a glide. • v.intr. glide. [F *vol plané* f. *vol* flight + *plané* past part. of *planer* hover, rel. to PLANE[1]]

vols. abbr. volumes.

volt[1] /vōlt/ n. the SI unit of electromotive force, the difference of potential that would carry one ampere of current against one ohm resistance. ¶ Abbr.: **V.** [A. *Volta*, It. physicist d. 1827]

volt[2] /vawlt, vōlt/ n. & v. • n. **1** *Fencing* a quick movement to escape a thrust. **2** a sideways circular movement of a horse. • v.intr. *Fencing* make a volt. [F f. It. *volta* turn, fem. past part. of *volgere* turn f. L *volvere* roll]

volt·age /vóltij/ n. electromotive force or potential difference expressed in volts.

volt·a·ic /vóltáyik/ adj. archaic of electricity from a primary battery; galvanic (*voltaic battery*).

volt·am·e·ter /vóltámitər/ n. an instrument for measuring an electric charge.

volte-face /vawltfaás/ n. **1** a complete reversal of position in argument or opinion. **2** the act or an instance of turning around. [F f. It. *voltafaccia*, ult. f. L *volvere* roll + *facies* appearance, face]

volt·me·ter /vóltmeetər/ n. an instrument for measuring electric potential in volts.

vol·u·ble /vólyəbəl/ adj. **1** speaking or spoken vehemently, incessantly, or fluently (*voluble spokesman*; *voluble excuses*). **2** *Bot.* twisting around a support; twining. □□ **vol·u·bil·i·ty** n. **vol·u·ble·ness** n. **vol·u·bly** adv. [F *voluble* or L *volubilis* f. *volvere* roll]

vol·ume /vólyoom/ n. **1 a** a set of sheets of paper, usu. printed, bound together and forming part or the whole of a work or comprising several works (*issued in three volumes*; *a library of 12,000 volumes*). **b** hist. a scroll of papyrus, etc., an ancient form of book. **2 a** a solid content; bulk. **b** the space occupied by a gas or liquid. **c** (foll. by *of*) an amount or quantity (*large volume of business*). **3 a** a quantity or power of sound. **b** fullness of tone. **4** (foll. by *of*) **a** a moving mass of water, etc. **b** (usu. in *pl.*) a wreath or coil or rounded mass of smoke, etc. □□ **vol·umed** adj. (also in comb.). [ME f. OF *volum(e)* f. L *volumen –minis* roll f. *volvere* to roll]

vol·u·met·ric /vólyoométrik/ adj. of or relating to measurement by volume. □□ **vol·u·met·ri·cal·ly** adv. [VOLUME + METRIC]

vo·lu·mi·nous /vəloominəs/ adj. **1** large in volume; flowing. **2** (of drapery, etc.) loose and ample. **3** consisting of many volumes. **4** (of a writer) producing many books. □□ **vo·lu·mi·nos·i·ty** /–nósitee/ n. **vo·lu·mi·nous·ly** adv. **vo·lu·mi·nous·ness** n. [LL *voluminosus* (as VOLUME)]

vol·un·ta·rism /vóləntərizəm/ n. **1** the principle of relying on voluntary action rather than compulsion. **2** *Philos.* the doctrine that the will is a fundamental or dominant factor in the individual or the universe. **3** hist. the doctrine that the church or schools should be independent of the government and supported by voluntary contributions. □□ **vol·un·ta·rist** n. [irreg. f. VOLUNTARY]

vol·un·tar·y /vóləntəree/ adj. & n. • adj. **1** done, acting, or able to act of one's own free will; not constrained or compulsory; intentional (*a voluntary gift*). **2** unpaid (*voluntary work*). **3** (of an institution) supported by voluntary contributions. **4** *Brit.* (of a school) built by a voluntary institution but maintained by a local education authority. **5** brought about, produced, etc., by voluntary action. **6** (of a movement, muscle, or limb) controlled by the will.

7 (of a confession by a criminal) not prompted by a promise or threat. **8** *Law* (of a conveyance or disposition) made without return in money or other consideration. • n. (pl. **–ies**) **1 a** an organ solo played before, during, or after a church service. **b** the music for this. **c** archaic an extempore performance esp. as a prelude to other music. **2** (in competitions) a special performance left to the performer's choice. **3** hist. a person who holds that the church or schools should be independent of the government and supported by voluntary contributions. □□ **vol·un·tar·i·ly** adv. **vol·un·tar·i·ness** n. [ME f. OF *volontaire* or L *voluntarius* f. *voluntas* will]

vol·un·tar·y·ism /vóləntereeizəm/ n. hist. = VOLUNTARISM 1, 3. □□ **vol·un·tar·y·ist** n.

vol·un·teer /vólənteér/ n. & v. • n. **1** a person who voluntarily undertakes a task or enters military or other service. **2** (usu. attrib.) a self-sown plant. • v. **1** tr. (often foll. by *to* + infin.) undertake or offer (one's services, a remark or explanation, etc.) voluntarily. **2** intr. (often foll. by *for*) make a voluntary offer of one's services; be a volunteer. [F *volontaire* (as VOLUNTARY), assim. to –EER]

vo·lup·tu·ar·y /vəlúpchooeree/ n. & adj. • n. (pl. **–ies**) a person given up to luxury and sensual pleasure. • adj. concerned with luxury and sensual pleasure. [L *volupt(u)arius* (as VOLUPTUOUS)]

vo·lup·tu·ous /vəlúpchooəs/ adj. **1** of, tending to, occupied with, or derived from, sensuous or sensual pleasure. **2** full of sexual promise, esp. through shapeliness or fullness. □□ **vo·lup·tu·ous·ly** adv. **vo·lup·tu·ous·ness** n. [ME f. OF *voluptueux* or L *voluptuosus* f. *voluptas* pleasure]

vo·lute /vəloōt/ n. & adj. • n. **1** *Archit.* a spiral scroll characteristic of Ionic capitals and also used in Corinthian and composite capitals. **2 a** any marine gastropod mollusk of the genus *Voluta*. **b** the spiral shell of this. • adj. esp. *Bot.* rolled up. □□ **vo·lut·ed** adj. [F *volute* or L *voluta* fem. past part. of *volvere* roll]

vo·lu·tion /vəlooshən/ n. **1** a rolling motion. **2** a spiral turn. **3** a whorl of a spiral shell. **4** *Anat.* a convolution. [as VOLUTE, after REVOLUTION, etc.]

volute

volute 1

vo·mer /vómər/ n. *Anat.* the small thin bone separating the nostrils in humans and most vertebrates. [L, = plowshare]

vom·it /vómit/ v. & n. • v.tr. **1** (also absol.) eject (matter) from the stomach through the mouth. **2** (of a volcano, chimney, etc.) eject (lava, smoke, etc.); belch (forth). • n. **1** matter vomited from the stomach. **2** archaic an emetic. □□ **vom·it·er** n. [ME ult. f. L *vomere* vomit- or frequent. L *vomitare*]

vom·i·to·ri·um /vómitáwreeəm/ n. (pl. **vom·i·to·ri·a** /–reeə/) *Rom. Antiq.* a vomitory. [L; see VOMITORY]

vom·i·to·ry /vómitawree/ adj. & n. • adj. emetic. • n. (pl. **–ries**) *Rom. Antiq.* each of a series of passages for entrance and exit in an amphitheater or theater. [L *vomitorius* (adj.), *–um* (n.) (as VOMIT)]

V-1 /veéwún/ n. hist. a type of German flying bomb used in World War II, esp. against England. [abbr. of G *Vergeltungswaffe* reprisal weapon]

voo·doo /voódoo/ n. & v. • n. **1** use of or belief in religious witchcraft, esp. as practiced in the W. Indies. **2** a person skilled in this. **3** a voodoo spell. • v.tr. (**voo·doos, voo·dooed**) affect by voodoo; bewitch. □□ **voo·doo·ism** n. **voo·doo·ist** n. [Dahomey *vodu*]

vo·ra·cious /vawráyshəs, və–/ adj. **1** greedy in eating; ravenous. **2** very eager in some activity (*a voracious reader*). □□ **vo·ra·cious·ly** adv. **vo·ra·cious·ness** n. **vo·rac·i·ty** /vərásitee/ n. [L *vorax* f. *vorare* devour]

-vorous /vərəs/ comb. form forming adjectives meaning 'feeding on' (*carnivorous*). □□ **–vora** /vərə/ comb. form forming names of groups. **–vore** /vawr/ comb. form forming names of individuals. [L *–vorus* f. *vorare* devour]

vor·tex /váwrteks/ n. (pl. **vor·ti·ces** /–tiseez/ or **vor·tex·es**) **1** a mass of whirling fluid, esp. a whirlpool or whirlwind. **2** any whirling motion or mass. **3** a system, occupation, pursuit, etc., viewed as swallowing up or engrossing those who approach it (*the vortex of society*). **4** *Physics* a portion of fluid whose particles have rotatory motion. □□ **vor·ti·cal** /–tikəl/ adj. **vor·ti·cal·ly** adv. **vor·tic·i·ty** /vawrtísitee/ n. **vor·ti·cose** /–tikōs/ adj. **vor·tic·u·lar** /vawrtíkyələr/ adj. [L *vortex –icis* eddy, var. of VERTEX]

vor·tex ring n. a vortex whose axis is a closed curve, e.g., a smoke ring.

vor·ti·cel·la /váwrtisélə/ n. any sedentary protozoan of the family Vorticellidae, consisting of a tubular stalk with a bell-shaped ciliated opening. [mod.L, dimin. of VORTEX]

vor·ti·cist /váwrtisist/ n. **1** *Art* a painter, writer, etc., of a school influenced by futurism and using the 'vortices' of modern civilization as a basis. **2** *Metaphysics* a person regarding the universe, with Descartes, as a plenum in which motion propagates itself in circles. □□ **vor·ti·cism** n.

vo·ta·ry /vótəree/ n. (pl. **–ries**; fem. **vo·ta·ress**) (usu. foll. by *of*) a person vowed to the service of God or a god or cult. **2** a devoted follower, adherent, or advocate of a person, system, occupation, etc. □□ **vo•ta•rist** *n.* [L *vot-*: see VOTE]

vote /vōt/ *n. & v. • n.* **1** a formal expression of choice or opinion by means of a ballot, show of hands, etc., concerning a choice of candidate, approval of a motion or resolution, etc. (*let us take a vote on it; gave my vote to the independent candidate*). **2** (usu. prec. by *the*) the right to vote, esp. in a government election. **3 a** an opinion expressed by a majority of votes. **b** *Brit.* money granted by a majority of votes. **4** the collective votes that are or may be given by or for a particular group (*will lose the Southern vote; the Conservative vote increased*). **5** a ticket, etc., used for recording a vote. *• v.* **1** *intr.* (often foll. by *for, against,* or *to* + infin.) give a vote. **2** *tr.* **a** (often foll. by *that* + clause) enact or resolve by a majority of votes. **b** grant (a sum of money) by a majority of votes. **c** cause to be in a specified position by a majority of votes (*was voted off the committee*). **3** *tr. colloq.* pronounce or declare by general consent (*was voted a failure*). **4** *tr.* (often foll. by *that* + clause) *colloq.* announce one's proposal (*I vote that we all go home*). **5** *tr.* cast a ballot in accordance with (*vote your conscience*). □ **put to a** (or **the**) **vote** submit to a decision by voting. **vote down** defeat (a proposal, etc.) in a vote. **vote in** elect by votes. **vote with one's feet** *colloq.* indicate an opinion by one's presence or absence. □□ **vot•a•ble** *adj.* **vote•less** *adj.* [ME f. past part. stem *vot-* of L *vovēre* vow]

vote of cen•sure *n.* = *vote of no confidence.*

vote of con•fi•dence *n.* (or **vote of no confidence**) a vote showing that the majority support (or do not support) the policy of the governing body, etc.

vot•er /vṓtər/ *n.* **1** a person with the right to vote at an election. **2** a person voting.

vot•ing ma•chine *n.* a machine for the automatic registering of votes.

vot•ing stock *n.* stock entitling the holder to a vote.

vo•tive /vṓtiv/ *adj.* offered or consecrated in fulfillment of a vow (*votive offering; votive picture*). [L *votivus* (as VOTE)]

vo•tive Mass *n. Eccl.* a Mass celebrated for a special purpose or occasion.

vouch /vowch/ *v.* **1** *intr.* (foll. by *for*) answer for; be surety for (*will vouch for the truth of this; can vouch for him; could not vouch for his honesty*). **2** *tr. archaic* cite as an authority. **3** *tr. archaic* confirm or uphold (a statement) by evidence or assertion. [ME f. OF *vo*(*u*)*cher* summon, etc., ult. f. L *vocare* call]

vouch•er /vówchər/ *n.* **1** a document which can be exchanged for goods or services as a token of payment made or promised by the holder or another. **2** a document establishing the payment of money or the truth of accounts. **3** a person who vouches for a person, statement, etc. [AF *voucher* (as VOUCH) or f. VOUCH]

vouch•safe /vówchsáyf/ *v.tr. formal* **1** condescend to give or grant (*vouchsafed me no answer*). **2** (foll. by *to* + infin.) condescend. [ME f. VOUCH in sense 'warrant' + SAFE]

vous•soir /vōōswaár/ *n.* each of the wedge-shaped or tapered stones forming an arch. [OF *vossoir,* etc. f. pop.L *volsorium* ult. f. L *volvere* roll]

vow /vow/ *n. & v. • n.* **1** *Relig.* a solemn promise, esp. in the form of an oath to God or another deity or to a saint. **2** (in *pl.*) the promises by which a monk or nun is bound to poverty, chastity, and obedience. **3** a promise of fidelity (*lovers' vows; marriage vows*). **4** (usu. as **baptismal vows**) the promises given at baptism by the baptized person or by sponsors. *• v.tr.* **1** promise solemnly (*vowed obedience*). **2** dedicate to a deity (also *absol.*) *archaic* declare solemnly. □ **under a vow** having made a vow. [ME f. AF *vo*(*o*)*u,* OF *vo*(*u*), f. L (as VOTE): (v.) f. OF *vouer,* in sense 2 partly f. AVOW]

vow•el /vówəl/ *n.* **1** a speech sound made with vibration of the vocal cords but without audible friction, more open than a consonant and capable of forming a syllable. **2** a letter or letters representing this, as *a, e, i, o, u, aw, ah.* □□ **vow•eled** *adj.* (also in *comb.*). **vow•el•less** *adj.* **vow•el•y** or **vow•el•ly** *adv.* [ME f. OF *vouel, voiel* f. L *vocalis* (*littera*) VOCAL (letter)]

vow•el gra•da•tion *n.* = ABLAUT.

vow•el•ize /vówəlīz/ *v.tr.* insert the vowels in (shorthand, Hebrew, etc.).

vow•el mu•ta•tion *n.* = UMLAUT 2.

vow•el point *n.* each of a set of marks indicating vowels in Hebrew, etc.

vox angelica /vóks anjélikə/ *n.* an organ stop with a soft tremulous tone. [LL, = angelic voice]

vox humana /vóks hyōōmáynə–, –máanə, –manə/ *n.* an organ stop with a tone supposed to resemble a human voice. [L, = human voice]

vox pop /vóks póp/ *n.* esp. *Brit.* Broadcasting *colloq.* popular opinion as represented by informal comments from members of the public; statements or interviews of this kind. [abbr. of VOX POPULI]

vox po•pu•li /vókspópyəlee, –lī/ *n.* public opinion, the general verdict, popular belief or rumor. [L, = the people's voice]

voy•age /vóyij/ *n. & v. • n.* **1** a journey, esp. a long one by water, air, or in space. **2** an account of this. *• v.* **1** *intr.* make a voyage. **2** *tr.* traverse, esp. by water or air. □□ **voy•age•a•ble** *adj.* **voy•ag•er** *n.* [ME f. AF & OF *veiage, voiage* f. L *viaticum*]

voy•a•geur /vwaáyaazhŕ/ *n.* a Canadian boatman, esp. (*hist.*) one

employed in transporting goods and passengers between trading posts. [F, = voyager (as VOYAGE)]

vo•yeur /vwaayŕr/ *n.* a person who obtains sexual gratification from observing others' sexual actions or organs. □□ **vo•yeur•ism** *n.* **vo•yeur•is•tic** /–rístik/ *adj.* **vo•yeur•is•ti•cal•ly** /–rístikəlee/ *adv.* [F f. *voir* see]

VP *abbr.* **1** vice president. **2** variable pitch. **3** verb phrase.

VR *abbr.* **1** Queen Victoria. **2** voltage regulator. [sense 1 f. L *Victoria Regina*]

VS *abbr.* veterinary surgeon.

vs. *abbr.* **1** versus. **2** verse.

V sign /vée sín/ *n.* **1** a sign of the letter V made with the first two fingers pointing up and the palm of the hand facing outward, as a symbol of victory. **2** *Brit.* a similar sign made with the back of the hand facing outward as a gesture of abuse, contempt, etc.

VSOP *abbr.* very special old pale (brandy).

VT *abbr.* Vermont (in official postal use).

Vt. *abbr.* Vermont.

VTO *abbr.* vertical takeoff.

VTOL /vée•tol/ *abbr.* vertical takeoff and landing.

V-2 /vée•tōō/ *n.* a type of German rocket-powered missile used in late World War II, esp. against England. [abbr. of G *Vergeltungswaffe* reprisal weapon]

vug /vug/ *n.* a rock cavity lined with crystals. □□ **vug•gy** *adj.* **vug•u•lar** *adj.* [Corn. *vooga*]

vul•can•ic var. of VOLCANIC.

vul•can•ite /vúlkənīt/ *n.* a hard, black, vulcanized rubber, ebonite. [as VULCANIZE]

vul•can•ize /vúlkənīz/ *v.tr.* treat (rubber or rubberlike material) with sulfur, etc., esp. at a high temperature to increase its strength. □□ **vul•can•iz•a•ble** *adj.* **vul•can•i•za•tion** *n.* **vul•can•iz•er** *n.* [*Vulcan,* Roman god of fire and metal-working]

vul•can•ol•o•gy var. of VOLCANOLOGY.

Vulg. *abbr.* Vulgate.

vul•gar /vúlgər/ *adj.* **1 a** of or characteristic of the common people; plebeian. **b** coarse in manners; low (*vulgar expressions; vulgar tastes*). **2** in common use; generally prevalent (*vulgar errors*). □□ **vul•gar•ly** *adv.* [ME f. L *vulgaris* f. *vulgus* common people]

vul•gar frac•tion *n. Brit.* = COMMON FRACTION.

vul•gar•i•an /vulgáireeən/ *n.* a vulgar (esp. rich) person.

vul•gar•ism /vúlgərizəm/ *n.* **1** a word or expression in coarse or uneducated use. **2** an instance of coarse or uneducated behavior.

vul•gar•i•ty /vulgáritee/ *n.* (*pl.* **–ties**) **1** the quality of being vulgar. **2** an instance of this.

vul•gar•ize /vúlgərīz/ *v.tr.* **1** make (a person, manners, etc.) vulgar; infect with vulgarity. **2** spoil (a scene, sentiment, etc.) by making it too common, frequented, or well known. **3** popularize. □□ **vul•gar•i•za•tion** *n.*

Vul•gar Lat•in *n.* informal Latin of classical times.

vul•gar tongue *n.* esp. *Brit.* the national or vernacular language, esp. formerly as opposed to Latin.

Vul•gate /vúlgayt, –gət/ *n.* **1 a** the Latin version of the Bible prepared mainly by St. Jerome in the late fourth century. **b** the official Roman Catholic Latin text as revised in 1592. **2** (**vulgate**) the traditionally accepted text of any author. **3** (**vulgate**) common or colloquial speech. [L *vulgata* (*editio* edition), fem. past part. of *vulgare* make public f. *vulgus:* see VULGAR]

vul•ner•a•ble /vúlnərəbəl/ *adj.* **1** that may be wounded or harmed. **2** (foll. by *to*) exposed to damage by a weapon, criticism, etc. **3** *Bridge* having won one game toward a rubber and therefore liable to higher penalties. □□ **vul•ner•a•bil•i•ty** *n.* **vul•ner•a•ble•ness** *n.* **vul•ner•a•bly** *adv.* [LL *vulnerabilis* f. L *vulnerare* to wound f. *vulnus –eris* wound]

vul•ner•ar•y /vúlnəreree/ *adj. & n. • adj.* useful or used for the healing of wounds. *• n.* (*pl.* **–ies**) a vulnerary drug, plant, etc. [L *vulnerarius* f. *vulnus:* see VULNERABLE]

vul•pine /vúlpīn/ *adj.* **1** of or like a fox. **2** crafty; cunning. [L *vulpinus* f. *vulpes* fox]

vul•ture /vúlchər/ *n.* **1** any of various large birds of prey of the family Cathartidae or Accipitridae, with the head and neck more or less bare of feathers, feeding chiefly on carrion and reputed to gather with others in anticipation of a death. **2 a** rapacious person. □□ **vul•tur•ine** /–rīn/ *adj.* **vul•tur•ish** *adj.* **vul•tur•ous** *adj.* [ME f. AF *vultur,* OF *voltour,* etc., f. L *vulturius*]

vul•va /vúlvə/ *n.* (*pl.* **vul•vas**) *Anat.* the external female genitals, esp. the external opening of the vagina. □□ **vul•var** *adj.* **vul•vi•tis** /–vítis/ *n.* [L, = womb]

vv. *abbr.* **1** verses. **2** volumes. **3** violins.

vy•ing *pres. part.* of VIE.

turkey vulture

W

W¹ /dúbəlyoō/ *n.* (also **w**) (*pl.* **Ws** or **W's**) the twenty-third letter of the alphabet.

W² *abbr.* (also **W.**) **1** watt(s). **2** West; Western. **3** women's (size). **4** Welsh.

W³ *symb. Chem.* the element tungsten.

w. *abbr.* **1** warden. **2** wide(s). **3** with. **4** wife. **5** watt(s).

WA *abbr.* **1** Washington (state) (in official postal use). **2** Western Australia.

WAAC /wak/ *n. hist.* a member of the Women's Army Auxiliary Corps (*US* 1942–48 or *Brit.* 1917–19). [initials *WAAC*]

Wac /wak/ *n.* a member of the US Army's Women's Army Corps.

wack¹ /wak/ *n. sl.* a crazy person. [prob. back-form. f. WACKY]

wack² /wak/ *n. Brit. dial.* a familiar term of address. [perh. f. *wacker* Liverpudlian]

wack·e /wákə/ *n. hist.* a grayish-green or brownish rock resulting from the decomposition of basaltic rock. [G f. MHG *wacke* large stone, OHG *wacko* pebble]

wack·o /wákō/ *adj. & n.* (also **whack·o**) *sl.* ● *adj.* crazy. ● *n.* (*pl.* **-os** or **-oes**) a crazy person. [WACKY + -O]

wack·y /wákee/ *adj. & n.* (also **whack·y**) *sl.* ● *adj.* (**-i·er**, **-i·est**) crazy. ● *n.* (*pl.* **-ies**) a crazy person. □□ **wack·i·ly** *adv.* **wack·i·ness** *n.* [orig. dial., = left-handed, f. WHACK]

wad /wod/ *n. & v.* ● *n.* **1** a lump or bundle of soft material used esp. to keep things apart or in place or to stuff up an opening. **2** a disk of felt, etc., keeping powder or shot in place in a gun. **3** a number of bills of currency or documents placed together. **4** *Brit. sl.* a bun, sandwich, etc. **5** (in *sing.* or *pl.*) a large quantity, esp. of money. ● *v.tr.* (**wad·ded**, **wad·ding**) **1** stop up (an aperture or a gun barrel) with a wad. **2** keep (powder, etc.) in place with a wad. **3** line or stuff (a garment or quilt, etc.) with wadding. **4** protect (a person, walls, etc.) with wadding. **5** press (cotton, etc.) into a wad or wadding. [perh. rel. to Du. *watten*, F *ouate* padding, cotton wool]

wad·ding /wóding/ *n.* **1** soft, pliable material of cotton or wool, etc., used to line or stuff garments, quilts, etc., or to pack fragile articles. **2** any material from which gun wads are made.

wad·dle /wód'l/ *v. & n.* ● *v.intr.* walk with short steps and a swaying motion, like a stout, short-legged person or a bird with short legs set far apart (e.g., a duck or goose). ● *n.* a waddling gait. □□ **wad·dler** *n.* [perh. frequent. of WADE]

wad·dy /wódee/ *n.* (*pl.* **-dies**) **1** an Australian Aboriginal war club. **2** *Austral. & NZ* any club or stick. [Aboriginal, perh. f. WOOD]

wade /wayd/ *v. & n.* ● *v.* **1** *intr.* walk through water or some impeding medium, e.g., snow, mud, or sand. **2** *intr.* make one's way with difficulty or by force. **3** *intr.* (foll. by *through*) read (a book, etc.) in spite of its dullness, etc. **4** *intr.* (foll. by *into*) *colloq.* attack (a person or task) vigorously. **5** *tr.* ford (a stream, etc.) on foot. ● *n.* a spell of wading. □ **wade in** *colloq.* make a vigorous attack or intervention. □□ **wad·a·ble** *adj.* (also **wade·a·ble**). [OE *wadan* f. Gmc, = go (through)]

wad·ing bird *n.* any long-legged waterbird that wades.

wad·er /wáydər/ *n.* **1 a** a person who wades. **b** a wading bird, esp. any of various birds of the order Charadriiformes. **2** (in *pl.*) high waterproof boots, or a waterproof garment for the legs and body, worn in fishing, etc.

wa·di /wáadee/ *n.* (also **wa·dy**) (*pl.* **wa·dis** or **wa·dies**) a rocky watercourse in N. Africa, etc., dry except in the rainy season. [Arab. *wādī*]

Waf /waf/ *n.* (in the US) a member of the Women in the Air Force.

wa·fer /wáyfər/ *n. & v.* ● *n.* **1** a very thin, light, crisp sweet cake, cookie, or biscuit. **2** a thin disk of unleavened bread used in the Eucharist. **3** *Brit.* a disk of red paper stuck on a legal document instead of a seal. **4** *Electronics* a very thin slice of a semiconductor crystal used as the substrate for solid-state circuitry. **5** *hist.* a small disk of dried paste formerly used for fastening letters, holding papers together, etc. ● *v.tr.* fasten or seal with a wafer. □□ **wa·fer·y** *adj.* [ME f. AF *wafre*, ONF *waufre*, OF *gaufre* (cf. GOFFER) f. MLG *wāfel* waffle: cf. WAFFLE²]

wa·fer-thin *adj.* very thin.

waf·fle¹ /wófəl/ *n. & v. colloq.* ● *n.* verbose but aimless, misleading, or ignorant talk or writing. ● *v.intr.* indulge in waffle. □□ **waf·fler** *n.* **waf·fly** *adj.* [orig. dial., frequent. of *waff* = yelp, yap (imit.)]

waf·fle² /wófəl/ *n.* a small, crisp batter cake with an indented lattice pattern. [Du. *wafel*, *waefel* f. MLG *wāfel*: cf. WAFER]

waf·fle i·ron *n.* a utensil, usu. of two shallow metal pans hinged together, for cooking waffles.

waft /woft, waft/ *v. & n.* ● *v.tr. & intr.* convey or travel easily as through air or over water; sweep smoothly and lightly along. ● *n.* **1** (usu. foll. by *of*) a whiff or scent. **2** a transient sensation of peace, joy, etc. **3** (also **wait** /wayf/) *Naut.* a distress signal, e.g., an ensign rolled or knotted or a garment flown in the rigging. [orig. 'convoy (ship, etc.),' back-form. f. obs. *waughter, wafter* armed convoy ship, f. Du. or LG *wachter* f. *wachten* to guard]

wag¹ /wag/ *v. & n.* ● *v.* (**wagged, wag·ging**) **1** *tr. & intr.* shake or wave rapidly or energetically to and fro. **2** *intr. archaic* (of the world, times, etc.) go along with varied fortune or characteristics. ● *n.* a single wagging motion (*with a wag of his tail*). □ **the tail wags the dog** the less or least important member of a society, section of a party, or part of a structure has control. **tongues** (or **beards** or **chins** or **jaws**) **wag** there is talk. [ME *waggen* f. root of OE *wagian* sway]

wag² /wag/ *n.* **1** a facetious person; a joker. **2** *Brit. sl.* a truant (*play the wag*). [prob. f. obs. *waghalter* one likely to be hanged (as WAG¹, HALTER)]

wage /wayj/ *n. & v.* ● *n.* **1** (in *sing.* or *pl.*) a fixed regular payment, usu. daily or weekly, made by an employer to an employee, esp. to a manual or unskilled worker (cf. SALARY). **2** (in *sing.* or *pl.*) requital (*the wages of sin is death*). **3** (in *pl.*) *Econ.* the part of total production that rewards labor rather than remunerating capital. ● *v.tr.* carry on (a war, conflict, or contest). [ME f. AF & ONF *wage*, OF *g(u)age*, f. Gmc, rel. to GAGE¹, WED]

wage earn·er *n.* a person who works for wages.

wa·ger /wáyjər/ *n. & v.tr. & intr.* = BET. [ME f. AF *wageure* f. *wager* (as WAGE)]

wa·ger of bat·tle *n. hist.* an ancient form of trial by personal combat between the parties or their champions.

wa·ger of law *n. hist.* a form of trial in which the defendant was required to produce witnesses who would swear to his or her innocence.

wage slave *n.* a person dependent on income from labor in conditions like slavery.

wag·ger·y /wágəree/ *n.* (*pl.* **-ies**) **1** waggish behavior, joking. **2** a waggish action or remark; a joke.

wag·gish /wágish/ *adj.* playful; facetious. □□ **wag·gish·ly** *adv.* **wag·gish·ness** *n.*

wag·gle /wágəl/ *v. & n. colloq.* ● *v.* **1** *intr. & tr.* wag. **2** *intr. Golf* swing the club head to and fro over the ball before playing a shot. ● *n.* a waggling motion. [WAG¹ + -LE⁴]

wag·gly /wáglee/ *adj.* unsteady.

Wag·ne·ri·an /vaagnéereeən/ *adj. & n.* ● *adj.* of, relating to, or characteristic of the music dramas of Richard Wagner, German composer d. 1883, esp. with reference to their large scale. ● *n.* an admirer of Wagner or his music.

wag·on /wágən/ *n.* (also *Brit.* **wag·gon**) **1 a** a four-wheeled vehicle for heavy loads, often with a removable tilt or cover. **b** a truck. **2** *Brit.* a railroad vehicle for goods, esp. a flatcar. **3** *Brit.* a cart for conveying tea, etc. **4** (in full **water wagon**) a vehicle for carrying water. **5** a light horse-drawn vehicle. **6** *colloq.* an automobile, esp. a station wagon. □ **on the wagon** (or *Brit.* **water wagon**) *sl.* teetotal. [earlier *wagon, wag(h)en*, f. Du. *wag(h)en*, rel. to OE *wægn* WAIN]

wag·on·er /wágənər/ *n.* (also *Brit.* **wag·gon·er**) the driver of a wagon. [Du. *wagenaar* (as WAGON)]

wag·on·ette /wágənét/ *n.* (also *Brit.* **wag·gon·ette**) a four-wheeled, horse-drawn pleasure vehicle, usu. open, with facing side seats.

wag·on-lit /vágawnlée/ *n.* (*pl.* **wag·ons-lits** *pronunc.* same) a railroad sleeping car, esp. in continental Europe. [F]

wag·on roof *n.* (also **wag·on vault**) = BARREL VAULT.

wag·tail /wágtayl/ *n.* any small bird of the genus *Motacilla* with a long tail in frequent motion.

Wah·ha·bi /wəhaábee/ *n.* (also **Wa·ha·bi**) (*pl.* **-bis**) a member of a sect of Muslim puritans following strictly the original words of the Koran. [Muhammad ibn Abd-el-*Wahhab*, founder in the 18th c.]

wa·hi·ne /waaheénee/ *n.* **1** (in Polynesia and Hawaii) a woman or wife. **2** *sl.* a female surfer. [Maori]

wa·hoo¹ /wóhoō, wáw-/ *n.* any of several N. American shrubs or trees, as *Ulmus alata*, an elm tree.

wa·hoo² /wóhoō, wáw-/ *n.* a shrubby N. American tree, *Euonymus atropurpurea.*

wa·hoo³ /wóhoō, wáw-/ *n.* a large mackerel, *Acanthocybium solanderi*, found in warm seas.

wa·hoo⁴ /wóhoō, wáw-/ *int. & n.* an expression of exhilaration or enthusiasm.

wah•wah var. of WA-WA.

waif /wayf/ *n.* **1** a homeless and helpless person, esp. an abandoned child. **2** an ownerless object or animal; a thing cast up by or drifting in the sea or brought by an unknown agency. **3** var. of WAFT *n.* 3. □□ **waif•ish** *adj.* [ME f. AF *waif, weif*, ONF *gaif*, prob. of Scand. orig.]

waifs and strays *n. Brit.* **1** homeless or neglected children. **2** odds and ends.

wail /wayl/ *n. & v.* • *n.* **1** a prolonged and plaintive loud, high-pitched cry of pain, grief, etc. **2** a sound like or suggestive of this. • *v.* **1** *intr.* utter a wail. **2** *intr.* lament or complain persistently or bitterly. **3** *intr.* (of the wind, etc.) make a sound like a person wailing. **4** *tr. poet.* or *rhet.* bewail; wail over. □□ **wail•er** *n.* **wail•ful** *adj. poet.* **wail•ing•ly** *adv.* [ME f. ON, rel. to WOE]

Wail•ing Wall *n.* a high wall in Jerusalem said to stand on the site of Herod's temple, where Jews traditionally pray and lament on Fridays.

wain /wayn/ *n. archaic* **1** a wagon. **2** (prec. by *the*) = CHARLES'S WAIN. [OE *wæg(e)n, wæn*, f. Gmc, rel. to WAY, WEIGH[1]]

wain•scot /wáynskət, –skot, –skōt/ *n. & v.* • *n.* **1** boarding or wooden paneling on the lower part of an interior wall. **2** *Brit. hist.* imported oak of fine quality. • *v.tr.* line with wainscot. [ME f. MLG *wagenschot*, app. f. *wagen* WAGON + *schot* of uncert. meaning]

wain•scot•ing /wáynskōting, –skot–, –skə–/ *n.* **1** a wainscot. **2** material for this.

wain•wright /wáynrīt/ *n.* a wagon builder.

waist /wayst/ *n.* **1 a** the part of the human body below the ribs and above the hips, usu. of smaller circumference than these; the narrower middle part of the normal human figure. **b** the circumference of this. **2** a similar narrow part in the middle of a violin, hourglass, wasp, etc. **3 a** the part of a garment encircling or covering the waist. **b** the narrow middle part of a woman's dress, etc. **c** a blouse or bodice. **4** the middle part of a ship, between the forecastle and the quarterdeck. □□ **waist•ed** *adj.* (also in *comb.*). **waist•less** *adj.* [ME *wast*, perh. f. OE f. the root of WAX[2]]

waist•band /wáystband/ *n.* a strip of cloth forming the waist of a garment.

waist•cloth /wáystklawth/ *n.* a loincloth.

waist•coat /wéskət, wáystkōt/ *n.* a close-fitting waist-length garment, without sleeves or collar but usu. buttoned, worn usu. over a shirt and often under a jacket; a vest.

waist-deep *adj.* (also **waist-high**) up to the waist (*waist-deep in water*).

waist•line /wáystlīn/ *n.* the outline or the size of a person's body at the waist.

wait /wayt/ *v. & n.* • *v.* **1** *intr.* **a** defer action or departure for a specified time or until some expected event occurs (*wait a minute; wait till I come; wait for a fine day*). **b** be expectant or on the watch (*waited to see what would happen*). **c** (foll. by *for*) refrain from going so fast that (a person) is left behind (*wait for me!*). **2** *tr.* await (an opportunity, one's turn, etc.). **3** *tr.* defer (an activity) until a person's arrival or until some expected event occurs. **4** *intr.* (usu. as **waiting** *n.*) *Brit.* park a vehicle for a short time at the side of a road, etc. (*no waiting*). **5** *intr.* **a** (in full **wait at** or **on table**) act as a waiter or as a servant with similar functions. **b** act as an attendant. **6** *intr.* (foll. by *on, upon*) **a** await the convenience of. **b** serve as an attendant to. **c** pay a respectful visit to. • *n.* **1** a period of waiting (*had a long wait for the train*). **2** (usu. foll. by *for*) watching for an enemy; ambush (*lie in wait; lay wait*). **3** (in *pl.*) *Brit.* **a** *archaic* street singers of Christmas carols. **b** *hist.* official bands of musicians maintained by a city or town. □ **wait and see** await the progress of events. **wait for it!** *Brit. colloq.* **1** do not begin before the proper moment. **2** used to create an interval of suspense before saying something unexpected or amusing. **wait on** **1** act as a waiter, etc. **2** be patient; wait. **wait up** (often foll. by *for*) **1** not go to bed until a person arrives or an event happens. **2** slow down until a person catches up, etc. (*wait up, I'm coming with you*). **you wait!** used to imply a threat, warning, or promise. [ME f. ONF *waitier* f. Gmc, rel. to WAKE[1]]

wait-a-bit *n.* a plant with hooked thorns, etc., that catch the clothing.

wait•er /wáytər/ *n.* **1** a person who serves at table in a hotel or restaurant, etc. **2** a person who waits for a time, event, or opportunity. **3** a tray or salver.

wait•ing /wáyting/ *n.* **1** in senses of WAIT *v.* **2 a** official attendance at court. **b** one's period of this.

wait•ing game *n.* abstention from early action in a contest, etc., so as to act more effectively later.

wait•ing list *n.* a list of people waiting for a thing not immediately available.

wait•ing room *n.* a room provided for people to wait in, esp. by a doctor, dentist, etc., or at a railroad or bus station.

wait•per•son /wáytpərson/ *n.* a waiter or waitress.

wait•ress /wáytris/ *n.* a woman who serves at table in a hotel or restaurant, etc.

wait-staff *n.* people who serve food to diners, as at a restaurant.

waive /wayv/ *v.tr.* refrain from insisting on or using (a right, claim, opportunity, legitimate plea, rule, etc.). [ME f. AF *weyver*, OF *gaiver* allow to become a WAIF, abandon]

▶**Waive**, meaning 'surrender,' and the related noun, *waiver*, should not be confused with **wave**, 'a back-and-forth or up-and-down motion,' or with **waver** 'to go back and forth, vacillate': *He waived potential rights in the case by by signing the waiver; She waved the papers at her friends across the room; Just as we were all ready to go, he wavered and said he wasn't sure whether he should go.*

waiv•er /wáyvər/ *n. Law* **1** the act or an instance of waiving. **2** a document recording a waiving of a right or claim. [as WAIVE]

wake[1] /wayk/ *v. & n.* • *v.* (*past* **woke** /wōk/ or **waked**; *past part.* **wok•en** /wōkən/ or **waked**) **1** *intr. & tr.* (often foll. by *up*) cease or cause to cease to sleep. **2** *intr. & tr.* (often foll. by *up*) become or cause to become alert, attentive, or active (*needs something to wake him up*). **3** *intr.* (*archaic* except as **waking** *adj. & n.*) be awake (*in her waking hours; waking or sleeping*). **4** *tr.* disturb (silence or a place) with noise; make reecho. **5** *tr.* evoke (an echo). **6** *intr. & tr.* rise or raise from the dead. • *n.* **1** a watch beside a corpse before burial; lamentation and (less often) merrymaking in connection with this. **2** (usu. in *pl.*) an annual holiday in (industrial) northern England. **3** *Brit. hist.* **a** a vigil commemorating the dedication of a church. **b** a fair or merrymaking on this occasion. □ **be a wake-up** (often foll. by *to*) *Austral. sl.* be alert or aware. □□ **wak•er** *n.* [OE *wacan* (recorded only in past *woc*), *wacian* (weak form), rel. to WATCH: sense 'vigil' perh. f. ON]

wake[2] /wayk/ *n.* **1** the track left on the water's surface by a moving ship. **2** turbulent air left behind a moving aircraft, etc. □ **in the wake of** behind; following; as a result of; in imitation of. [prob. f. MLG f. ON *vök* hole or opening in ice]

wake•ful /wáykfŏŏl/ *adj.* **1** unable to sleep. **2** (of a night, etc.) passed with little or no sleep. **3** vigilant. □□ **wake•ful•ly** *adv.* **wake•ful•ness** *n.*

wak•en /wáykən/ *v.tr. & intr.* make or become awake. [ON *vakna* f. Gmc, rel. to WAKE[1]]

wake-rob•in *n.* **1** an arum, esp. the cuckoopint. **2** any plant of the genus *Trillium*.

Wa•la•chi•an var. of WALLACHIAN.

Wal•den•ses /woldénseez/ *n.pl.* a puritan religious sect orig. in S. France, now chiefly in Italy, the United States, and Uruguay, founded *c.*1170 and much persecuted. □□ **Wal•den•si•an** *adj. & n.* [med.L f. Peter *Waldo* of Lyons, founder]

wale /wayl/ *n. & v.* • *n.* **1** = WEAL[1]. **2** a ridge on a woven fabric, e.g., corduroy. **3** *Naut.* a broad, thick timber along a ship's side. **4** a specially woven strong band around a woven basket. • *v.tr.* provide or mark with wales; thrash; whip. [OE *walu* stripe, ridge]

wale knot *n.* a knot made at the end of a rope by intertwining strands to prevent unraveling or act as a stopper.

walk /wawk/ *v. & n.* • *v.* **1** *intr.* **a** (of a person or other biped) progress by lifting and setting down each foot in turn, never having both feet off the ground at once. **b** progress with similar movements (*walked on his hands*). **c** go with the gait usual except when speed is desired. **d** (of a quadruped) go with the slowest gait, always having at least two feet on the ground at once. **2** *intr.* travel or go on foot. **b** take exercise in this way (*walks for two hours each day*). **3** *tr.* **a** perambulate; traverse on foot at walking speed; tread the floor or surface of. **b** traverse or cover (a specified distance) on foot (*walks five miles a day*). **4** *tr.* **a** cause to walk with one. **b** accompany in walking. **c** ride or lead (a horse, dog, etc.) at walking pace. **d** *Brit.* take charge of (a puppy) at walk (see sense 4 of *n.*). **5** *intr.* (of a ghost) appear. **6** *intr. Cricket* leave the wicket on being out. **7** *Baseball* **a** *intr.* reach first base on a count of four balls. **b** *tr.* allow to do this. **8** *intr. archaic* live in a specified manner; conduct oneself (*walk humbly; walk with God*). **9** *intr. sl.* be released from suspicion or from a charge. • *n.* **1 a** an act of walking, the ordinary human gait (*go at a walk*). **b** the slowest gait of an animal. **c** a person's manner of walking (*know him by his walk*). **2 a** a taking a (usu. specified) time to walk a distance (*is only ten minutes' walk from here; it's quite a walk to the bus stop*). **b** an excursion on foot; a stroll or constitutional (*go for a walk*). **c** a journey on foot completed to earn money promised for a charity, etc. **3 a** a place, track, or route intended or suitable for walking; a promenade, colonnade, or footpath. **b** a person's favorite place or route for walking. **c** *esp. Brit.* the round of a mail carrier, peddler, etc. **4** *esp. Brit.* a farm, etc., where a hound puppy is sent to accustom it to various surroundings. **5** the place where a gamecock is kept. **6** a part of a forest under one keeper. □ **in a walk** without effort (*won in a walk*). **walk about** stroll. **walk all over** *colloq.* **1** defeat easily **2** take advantage of. **walk away from** **1** easily outdistance. **2** refuse to become involved with; fail to deal with. **3** survive (an accident, etc.) without serious injury. **walk away with** *colloq.* = *walk off with*. **walk the boards** = *tread the boards* (see TREAD). **walk in** (often foll. by *on*) enter or arrive, esp. unexpectedly or easily. **walk into 1** *colloq.* encounter through unwariness (*walked into the trap*). **2** *sl. archaic* attack forcefully. **3** *sl. archaic* eat heartily. **walk it 1** make a journey on foot; not ride. **2** *colloq.* achieve something (esp. a victory) easily. **walk off 1** depart (esp. abruptly). **2** get rid of the effects of (a meal, ailment, etc.) by walking (*walked off his anger*). **walk a person off his** (or **her**) **feet** (or **legs**) exhaust a person with walking. **walk off with** *colloq.* **1** steal. **2** win easily. **walk of life** an occupation, profession, or calling. **walk on air** see AIR. **walk out 1** depart suddenly or angrily. **2** (usu. foll. by *with*) *Brit. archaic* go for walks in courtship. **3** cease work, esp. to go on strike. **walk out on** desert; abandon. **walk over 1** *colloq.* = *walk all over*. **2** (often *absol.*) traverse (a racecourse) without needing to hurry, because one has no opponents or only inferior ones. **walk the plank** see PLANK. **walk the streets 1** be a prostitute. **2** traverse the streets, esp. in search of work, etc. **walk tall** *colloq.* feel justifiable pride. **walk up!** *Brit.* a showman's invitation to a circus, etc. **walk up to** approach (a person) for a talk, etc. **walk the wards** *Brit.* be a medical student. □□ **walk•a•ble** *adj.* [OE *wealcan* roll, toss, wander, f. Gmc]

walk•a•bout /wáwkəbowt/ *n.* **1** esp. *Brit.* an informal stroll among a crowd by a visiting dignitary. **2** a period of wandering in the bush by an Australian Aboriginal.

walk•a•thon /wáwkəthon/ *n.* an organized fund-raising walk. [WALK, after MARATHON]

walk•er /wáwkər/ *n.* **1** a person or animal that walks. **2 a** a wheeled or footed framework in which a baby can learn to walk. **b** a usu. tubular metal frame with rubberized ferrules, used by disabled or elderly people to help them walk.

walk•ie-talk•ie /wáwkeetáwkee/ *n.* a two-way radio carried on the person, esp. by police officers, etc.

walk•ing del•e•gate *n.* a labor union official who visits members and their employers for discussions.

walk•ing dic•tion•ar•y *n.* (also **walk•ing en•cy•clo•pe•di•a**) *colloq.* a person having a wide general knowledge.

walk•ing fern *n.* any American evergreen fern of the genus *Camptosorus*, with fronds that root at the ends.

walk•ing leaf *n.* = WALKING FERN.

walk•ing pa•pers *n. colloq.* dismissal (*gave him his walking papers*).

walk•ing stick *n.* **1** a stick carried when walking, esp. for extra support. **2** (also **walk•ing•stick**) a stick insect, esp. *Diapheromera femorata*.

walk•ing tour *n.* esp. *Brit.* a pleasure journey on foot, esp. of several days.

walk•ing wound•ed *n.* **1** (of soldiers, etc.) able to walk despite injuries; not bedridden. **2** *colloq.* a person or people having esp. mental or emotional difficulties.

walking stick 2

Walk•man /wáwkmən/ *n.* (*pl.* **–mans**) *Trademark* a type of small portable stereo equipment with headphones.

walk-on *n.* **1** (in full **walk-on part**) a minor, esp. nonspeaking, dramatic role. **2** the player of this.

walk•out /wáwkowt/ *n.* a sudden angry departure, esp. as a protest or strike.

walk•o•ver /wáwkōvər/ *n.* an easy victory or achievement.

walk-up /wáwkup/ *adj. & n.* ● *adj.* (of a building) allowing access to the upper floors only by stairs. ● *n.* a walk-up building.

walk•way /wáwkway/ *n.* a passage or path for walking along, esp.: **1** a raised passageway connecting different sections of a building. **2** a wide path in a garden, etc.

wall /wawl/ *n. & v.* ● *n.* **1 a** a continuous and usu. vertical structure of usu. brick or stone, having little width in proportion to its length and height and esp. enclosing, protecting, or dividing a space or supporting a roof. **b** the surface of a wall, esp. inside a room (*hung the picture on the wall*). **2** anything like a wall in appearance or effect, esp.: **a** the steep side of a mountain. **b** a protection or obstacle (*a wall of steel bayonets; a wall of indifference*). **c** *Anat.* the outermost layer or enclosing membrane, etc., of an organ, structure, etc. **d** the outermost part of a hollow structure (*stomach wall*). **e** *Mining* rock enclosing a lode or seam. ● *v.tr.* **1** (esp. as **walled** *adj.*) surround or protect with a wall (*walled garden*). **2 a** (usu. foll. by *up, off*) block or seal (a space, etc.) with a wall. **b** (foll. by *up*) enclose (a person) within a sealed space (*walled them up in the dungeon*). □ **drive a person up the wall** *colloq.* **1** make a person angry; infuriate. **2** drive a person mad. **go to the wall** be defeated or ruined. **off the wall** *sl.* unorthodox; unconventional; crazy; outlandish. **up the wall** *colloq.* crazy or furious (*went up the wall when he heard*). **walls have ears** it is unsafe to speak openly, as there may be eavesdroppers. □□ **wall•ing** *n.* **wall-less** *adj.* [OE f. L *vallum* rampart f. *vallus* stake]

wal•la•by /wólləbee/ *n.* (*pl.* **–bies**) any of various marsupials of the family Macropodidae, smaller than kangaroos, having large hind feet and long tails. □ **on the wallaby** (or **wallaby track**) *Austral.* vagrant; unemployed. [Aboriginal *wolabā*]

Wal•la•chi•an /woláykeeən/ *adj. & n.* (also **Wa•la•chi•an**) ● *adj.* of the former Principality of Wallachia, now part of Romania. ● *n.* a native of Wallachia. [*Wallachia* (as VLACH)]

wal•lah /wólə/ *n. orig. Anglo-Ind.*, now esp. *Brit. sl.* **1** a person con-

cerned with or in charge of a usu. specified thing, business, etc. (*asked the ticket wallah*). **2** a person doing a routine administrative job; a bureaucrat. [Hindi *–wālā* suffix = –ER¹]

wal•la•roo /wólərōō/ *n.* a large, brownish-black kangaroo, *Macropus robustus*. [Aboriginal *wolarū*]

wall bar *n.* one of a set of parallel bars, attached to the wall of a gymnasium, on which exercises are performed.

wall•board /wáwlbawrd/ *n.* a type of wall covering made from wood pulp, plaster, etc.

wal•let /wólit/ *n.* **1** a small flat esp. leather case for holding paper money, etc. **2** *archaic* a bag for carrying food, etc., on a journey, esp. as used by a pilgrim or beggar. [ME *walet*, prob. f. AF *walet* (unrecorded), perh. f. Gmc]

wall•eye /wáwli/ *n.* **1 a** an eye with a streaked or opaque white iris. **b** an eye squinting outwards. **2** (also **wall-eyed pike**) an American perch, *Stizostedion vitreum*, with large prominent eyes. □□ **wall•eyed** *adj.* [back-form. f. *wall-eyed*: ME f. ON *vagleygr* f. *vagl* (unrecorded: cf. Icel. *vagl* film over the eye) + *auga* EYE]

wall fern *n.* an evergreen polypody, *Polypodium vulgare*, with very large leaves.

wall•flow•er /wáwlflowr/ *n.* **1 a** a fragrant spring garden plant, *Cheiranthus cheiri*, with esp. brown, yellow, or dark-red clustered flowers. **b** any of various flowering plants of the genus *Cheiranthus* or *Erysimum*, growing wild on old walls. **2** *colloq.* a neglected or socially awkward person, esp. a woman sitting out at a dance for lack of partners.

Wal•loon /wolóōn/ *n. & adj.* ● *n.* **1** a member of a French-speaking people inhabiting S. and E. Belgium and neighboring France (see also FLEMING). **2** the French dialect spoken by this people. ● *adj.* of or concerning the Walloons or their language. [F *Wallon* f. med.L *Wallo –onis* f. Gmc: cf. WELSH]

wal•lop /wóləp/ *v. & n. sl.* ● *v.tr.* **1 a** thrash; beat. **b** hit hard. **2** (as **walloping** *adj.*) big; strapping; thumping (*a walloping profit*). ● *n.* **1** a heavy blow; a thump. **2** *Brit.* beer or any alcoholic drink. □□ **wal•lop•ing** *n.* [earlier senses 'gallop', 'boil,' f. ONF (*walop* n. f.) *waloper*, OF *galoper*: cf. GALLOP]

wal•lop•er /wóləpər/ *n.* **1** a person or thing that wallops. **2** *Austral. sl.* a policeman.

wal•low /wólō/ *v. & n.* ● *v.intr.* **1** (esp. of an animal) roll about in mud, sand, water, etc. **2** (usu. foll. by *in*) indulge in unrestrained sensuality, pleasure, misery, etc. (*wallows in nostalgia*). ● *n.* **1** the act or an instance of wallowing. **2 a** a place used by buffalo, etc., for wallowing. **b** the depression in the ground caused by this. □□ **wal•low•er** *n.* [OE *walwian* roll f. Gmc]

wall paint•ing *n.* a mural or fresco.

wall•pa•per /wáwlpaypər/ *n. & v.* ● *n.* **1** paper sold in rolls for pasting on to interior walls as decoration. **2** esp. *Brit.* an unobtrusive background, esp. (usu. *derog.*) with ref. to sound, music, etc. ● *v.tr.* (often *absol.*) decorate with wallpaper.

wall pep•per *n.* a succulent stonecrop, *Sedum acre*, with a pungent taste.

wall plate *n.* timber laid in or on a wall to distribute the pressure of a girder, etc.

wall rocket *n.* a yellow-flowered weed, *Diplotaxis muralis*, emitting a foul smell when crushed.

wall rue *n.* a small fern, *Asplenium ruta-muraria*, with leaves like rue, growing on walls and rocks.

Wall Street *n.* the U.S. financial world and investment market. [street in New York City where banks, the stock exchanges, etc., are situated]

wall-to-wall *adj.* **1** (of a carpet) fitted to cover a whole room, etc. **2** *colloq.* profuse; ubiquitous (*wall-to-wall pop music*).

wal•ly /wólee/ *n.* (*pl.* **–lies**) *Brit. sl.* a foolish or inept person. [orig. uncert., perh. shortened form of *Walter*]

wal•nut /wáwlnut/ *n.* **1** any tree of the genus *Juglans*, having aromatic leaves and drooping catkins. **2** the nut of this tree containing an edible kernel in two half shells shaped like boats. **3** the timber of the walnut tree used in cabinetmaking. [OE *walh-hnutu* f. Gmc NUT]

Wal•pur•gis Night /valpóorgis/ *n.* the eve of May 1, when witches are alleged to meet on the Brocken mountain in Germany and hold revels with the Devil. [G *Walpurgisnacht* f. *Walpurgis* genit. of *Walpurga* Engl. woman saint (8th c.) + *Nacht* NIGHT]

wal•rus /wáwlrəs, wól–/ *n.* a large, amphibious, long-tusked arctic mammal, *Odobenus rosmarus*, related to the seal and sea lion. [prob. f. Du. *walrus, –ros*, perh. by metath. after *walvisch* 'whale-fish' f. word repr. by OE *horschwæl* 'horse-whale']

walrus

wal·rus mus·tache *n.* a long thick drooping mustache.

waltz /wawlts, wawls/ *n. & v.* ●*n.* **1** a dance in triple time performed by couples who rotate and progress around the floor. **2** the usu. flowing and melodious music for this. ●*v.* **1** *intr.* dance a waltz. **2** *intr.* (often foll. by *in, out, round,* etc.) *colloq.* move lightly, casually, with deceptive ease, etc. (*waltzed in and took first prize*). **3** *tr.* move (a person) in or as if in a waltz, with ease (*was waltzed off to Paris*). □□ **waltz·er** *n.* [G *Walzer* f. *walzen* revolve]

wam·pum /wómpəm/ *n.* beads made from shells and strung together for use as money, decoration, or as aids to memory by N. American Indians. [Algonquian *wampumpeag* f. *wap* white + *umpe* string + *-ag* pl. suffix]

wan /won/ *adj.* **1** (of a person's complexion or appearance) pale; exhausted, weak; worn. **2** (of a star, etc., or its light) partly obscured; faint. **3** *archaic* (of night, water, etc.) dark; black. □□ **wan·ly** *adv.* **wan·ness** *n.* [OE *wann* dark, black, of unkn. orig.]

wand /wond/ *n.* **1 a** a supposedly magic stick used in casting spells by a fairy, magician, etc. **b** a stick used by a magician for effect. **2** a slender rod carried or used as a marker in the ground. **3** a staff symbolizing some officials' authority. **4** *colloq.* a conductor's baton. **5** a handheld electronic device which can be passed over a bar code to read the data this represents. [ME prob. f. Gmc: cf. WEND, WIND²]

wan·der /wóndər/ *v. & n.* ●*v.* **1** *intr.* (often foll. by *in, off,* etc.) go about from place to place aimlessly. **2** *intr.* **a** (of a person, river, road, etc.) wind about; diverge; meander. **b** (of esp. a person) get lost; leave home; stray from a path, etc. **3** *intr.* talk or think incoherently; be inattentive or delirious. **4** *tr.* cover while wandering (*wanders the world*). ●*n.* the act or an instance of wandering (*went for a wander around the garden*). □□ **wan·der·er** *n.* **wan·der·ing** *n.* (esp. in *pl.*). [OE *wandrian* (as WEND)]

Wan·der·ing Jew *n.* **1 a** a legendary person said to have been condemned by Christ to wander the earth until the second advent. **b** a person who never settles down. **2 a** a climbing plant, *Tradescantia albiflora*, with stemless variegated leaves. **b** a trailing plant, *Zebrina pendula*, with pink flowers.

wan·der·ing sail·or *n.* the moneywort.

wan·der·lust /wóndərlust/ *n.* an eagerness for traveling or wandering. [G]

wan·der·oo /wondəróō/ *n.* a langur, *Semnopithecus vetulus*, of Sri Lanka. [Sinh. *wanderu* monkey]

wane /wayn/ *v. & n.* ●*v.intr.* **1** (of the moon) decrease in apparent size after the full moon (cf. WAX²). **2** decrease in power, vigor, importance, brilliance, size, etc.; decline. ●*n.* **1** the process of waning. **2** a defect of a plank, etc., that lacks square corners. □ **on the wane** waning; declining. □□ **wane·y** *adj.* (in sense 2 of *n.*). [OE *wanian* lessen f. Gmc]

wan·gle /wánggəl/ *v. & n. colloq.* ●*v.tr.* **1** (often *refl.*) to obtain (a favor, etc.) by scheming, etc. (*wangled himself a free trip*). **2** alter or fake (a report, etc.) to appear more favorable. ●*n.* the act or an instance of wangling. □□ **wan·gler** *n.* [19th-c. printers' sl.: orig. unkn.]

wank /wangk/ *v. & n. esp. Brit. coarse sl.* ●*v.intr. & tr.* masturbate. ●*n.* an act of masturbating. [20th c.: orig. unkn.] ▶This word is usually considered taboo.

Wan·kel en·gine /wángkəl, váng–/ *n.* a rotary internal-combustion engine with a continuously rotated and eccentrically pivoted, nearly triangular shaft. [F. Wankel, Ger. engineer d. 1988]

wank·er /wángkər/ *n. Brit. coarse sl.* **1** a contemptible or ineffectual person. **2** a person who masturbates. ▶This word is usually considered taboo.

wan·na·be /wónəbee/ *n. sl.* **1** an avid fan who tries to emulate the person he or she admires. **2** anyone who would like to be someone or something else.

want /wont, wawnt/ *v. & n.* ●*v.* **1** *tr.* **a** (often foll. by *to* + infin.) desire; wish for possession of; need (*wants a toy train; wants it done immediately; wanted to leave; wanted him to leave*). **b** need or desire (a person, esp. sexually). **c** *esp. Brit.* require to be attended to in esp. a specified way (*the garden wants weeding*). **d** (foll. by *to* + infin. *colloq.* ought; should; need (*you want to pull yourself together; you don't want to overdo it*). **2** *intr.* (usu. foll. by *for*) lack; be deficient (*wants for nothing*). **3** *tr.* be without or fall short by (esp. a specified amount or thing) (*the drawer wants a handle*). **4** *intr.* (foll. by *in, out*) *colloq.* desire to be in, out, etc. (*wants in on the deal*). **5** *tr.* (as **wanted** *adj.*) (of a suspected criminal, etc.) sought by the police. ●*n.* **1** (often foll. by *of*) **a** a lack, absence, or deficiency (*could not go for want of time; shows great want of judgment*). **b** poverty; need (*living in great want; in want of necessities*). **2 a** a desire for a thing, etc.

(*meets a long-felt want*). **b** a thing so desired (*can supply your wants*). □ **do not want to** am unwilling to. □□ **want·er** *n.*

want ad *n.* a classified newspaper advertisement, esp. for something sought.

want·ing /wónting, wáwn–/ *adj.* **1** lacking (in quality or quantity); deficient; not equal to requirements (*wanting in judgment; the standard is sadly wanting*). **2** absent; not supplied nor provided. □ **be found wanting** fail to meet requirements.

wan·ton /wóntən/ *adj., n., & v.* ●*adj.* **1** licentious; lewd; sexually promiscuous. **2** capricious; random; arbitrary; motiveless (*wanton destruction*). **3** luxuriant; unrestrained; unruly (*wanton extravagance; wanton behavior*). **4** *archaic* playful; sportive (*a wanton child*). ●*n.* *literary* an immoral or licentious person, esp. a woman. ●*v.intr. literary* **1** gambol; sport; move capriciously. **2** (foll. by *with*) behave licentiously. □□ **wan·ton·ly** *adv.* **wan·ton·ness** *n.* [ME *wantowen* (*wan–* UN-¹ + *towen* f. OE *togen* past part. of *tēon* discipline, rel. to TEAM)]

wap·en·take /wópəntayk, wáp–/ *n. Brit. hist.* (in areas of England with a large Danish population) a division of a shire; a hundred. [OE *w æpen(ge)tæc* f. ON *vápnatak* f. *vápn* weapon + *tak* taking f. *taka* TAKE: perh. with ref. to voting in assembly by show of weapons]

wap·i·ti /wópitee/ *n.* (*pl.* **wap·i·tis**) a N. American deer, *Cervus canadensis*. [Cree *wapitik* white deer]

war. *abbr.* warrent.

war /wawr/ *n. & v.* ●*n.* **1 a** armed hostilities esp. between nations; conflict (*war broke out; war zone*). **b** a specific conflict or the period of time during which such conflict exists (*was before the war*). **c** the suspension of international law, etc., during such a conflict. **2** (as **the war**) a war in progress or recently ended; the most recent major war. **3 a** hostility or contention between people, groups, etc. (*war of words*). **b** (often foll. by *on*) a sustained campaign against crime, disease, poverty, etc. ●*v.intr.* (**warred**, **war·ring**) **1** (as **war·ring** *adj.*) **a** rival; fighting (*warring factions*). **b** conflicting (*warring principles*). **2** make war. □ **at war** (often foll. by *with*) engaged in a war. **go to war** declare or begin a war. **go to the wars** *archaic* serve as a soldier. **have been in the wars** *colloq.* appear injured, bruised, unkempt, etc.

warb /wawrb/ *n. Austral. sl.* an idle, unkempt, or disreputable person. [20th c.: orig. unkn.]

war ba·by *n.* a child, esp. illegitimate, born in wartime, esp. of a soldier father.

war·ble¹ /wáwrbəl/ *v. & n.* ●*v.* **1** *intr. & tr.* sing in a gentle, trilling manner. **2** *tr.* speak or utter in a warbling manner. **b** express in a song or verse (*warbled his love*). ●*n.* a warbled song or utterance. [ME f. ONF *werble* (*r*) f. Frank. *hwirbilōn* whirl, trill]

war·ble² /wáwrbəl/ *n.* **1** a hard lump on a horse's back caused by the galling of a saddle. **2 a** the larva of a warble fly beneath the skin of cattle, etc. **b** a tumor produced by this. [16th c.: orig. uncert.]

war·ble fly *n.* any of various flies of the genus *Hypoderma,* infesting the skin of cattle and horses.

war·bler /wáwrblər/ *n.* **1** any small, insect-eating songbird of the family Sylviidae, including the black cap, or, in N. America, Parulidae, including the wood warbler, whitethroat, and chiffchaff, not always remarkable for their song. **2** a person, bird, etc., that warbles.

war bride *n.* a woman who marries a serviceman met during a war.

war chest *n.* funds for a war or any other campaign.

war cloud *n.* a threatening international situation; an indication of impending conflict.

war cor·res·pond·ent *n.* a correspondent reporting from a scene of war.

war crime *n.* a crime violating the international laws of war. □□ **war crim·i·nal** *n.*

war cry *n.* **1** a phrase or name shouted to rally one's troops. **2** a party slogan, etc.

ward /wawrd/ *n. & v.* ●*n.* **1** a separate room or division of a hospital, prison, etc. (*men's surgical ward*). **2 a** *Brit.* an administrative division of a constituency, usu. electing a councilor or councilors, etc. **b** a similar administrative division. **3 a** a minor under the care of a guardian appointed by the parents or a court. **b** (in full **ward of the court**) a minor or mentally deficient person placed under the protection of a court. **4** (in *pl.*) the corresponding notches and projections in a key and a lock. **5** *archaic* **a** the act of guarding or defending a place, etc. **b** the bailey of a castle. **c** a guardian's control; confinement; custody. ●*v.tr. archaic* guard; protect. □ **ward off 1** parry (a blow). **2** avert (danger, poverty, etc.). [OE *weard, weardian* f. Gmc: cf. GUARD]

-ward /wərd/ *suffix* (also **–wards**) added to nouns of place or destination and to adverbs of direction and forming: **1** adverbs (usu. –**wards**) meaning 'toward the place, etc.' (*moving backward*; *set off homeward*). **2** adjectives (usu. –**ward**) meaning 'turned or tending toward' (*a downward look*; *an onward rush*). **3** (less commonly) nouns meaning 'the region toward or about' (*look to the eastward*). [from or after OE *–weard* f. a Gmc root meaning 'turn']

war dance *n.* a dance performed by primitive peoples, etc., before a battle or to celebrate victory.

war·den /wáwrd'n/ *n.* **1** (usu. in *comb.*) a supervising official (*churchwarden*; *game warden*). **2 a** chief administrator of a prison. **b** *Brit.* a president or governor of a college, school, hospital, youth hostel, etc. □□ **war·den·ship** *n.* [ME f. AF & ONF *wardein* var. of OF *g(u)arden* GUARDIAN]

war de·part·ment *n.* a government office in charge of the army, etc.

ward·er /wáwrdər/ *n.* **1** *Brit.* (*fem.* **ward·ress**) a prison officer. **2** a guard. [ME f. AF *wardere*, –*our* f. ONF *warder*, OF *garder* to GUARD]

ward heel·er *n.* a party worker in elections, etc.

ward·robe /wáwrdrōb/ *n.* **1** a large movable or built-in case with rails, shelves, hooks, etc., for storing clothes. **2** a person's entire stock of clothes. **3** the costume department or costumes of a theater, a movie company, etc. **4** a department of a royal household in charge of clothing. [ME f. ONF *warderobe*, OF *garderobe* (as GUARD, ROBE)]

ward·robe mis·tress *n.* (also **ward·robe mas·ter**) a person in charge of a theatrical or movie wardrobe.

ward·robe trunk *n.* a trunk fitted with rails, shelves, etc., for use as a traveling wardrobe.

ward·room /wáwrdrōōm, –rŏŏm/ *n.* a room in a warship for the use of commissioned officers.

-wards var. of –WARD.

ward·ship /wáwrdship/ *n.* **1** a guardian's care or tutelage (*under his wardship*). **2** the condition of being a ward.

ware[1] /wair/ *n.* **1** (esp. in *comb.*) things of the same kind, esp. ceramics, made usu. for sale (*chinaware*; *hardware*). **2** (usu. in *pl.*) **a** articles for sale (*displayed his wares*). **b** a person's skills, talents, etc. **3** ceramics, etc., of a specified material, factory, or kind (*Wedgwood ware*; *delftware*). [OE *waru* f. Gmc, perh. orig. = 'object of care,' rel. to WARE[3]]

ware[2] /wair/ *v.tr.* (also esp. *Brit.* '**ware**) (esp. in hunting) look out for; avoid (usu. in *imper.*: *ware hounds!*). [OE *warian* f. Gmc (as WARE[3]), & f. ONF *warer*]

ware[3] /wair/ *predic.adj. poet.* aware. [OE *wær* f. Gmc: cf. WARD]

ware·house /wáirhows/ *n. & v.* ● *n.* **1** a building in which esp. retail goods are stored; a repository. **2** a wholesale or large retail store. ● *v.tr.* (also /–howz/) store (esp. furniture or bonded goods) temporarily in a repository. □□ **ware·house·man** *n.* (*pl.* –**men**).

war·fare /wáwrfair/ *n.* a state of war; campaigning or engaging in war (*chemical warfare*).

war·fa·rin /wáwrfərin/ *n.* a water-soluble anticoagulant used esp. as a rat poison. [*Wisconsin Alumni Research Foundation* + –*arin*, after COUMARIN]

war game *n.* **1** a military exercise testing or improving tactical knowledge, etc. **2** a battle, etc., conducted with toy soldiers.

war-gam·ing *n.* the playing of war games.

war grave *n.* the grave of a serviceman who died on active service, esp. one in a special cemetery, etc.

war·head /wáwrhed/ *n.* the explosive head of a missile, torpedo, or similar weapon.

war·horse /wáwrhawrs/ *n.* **1** *hist.* a knight's or soldier's powerful horse. **2** *colloq.* a veteran soldier, politician, etc. **3** a song, play, etc., that has been performed to the point of triteness.

war·like /wáwrlīk/ *adj.* **1** threatening war; hostile. **2** martial; soldierly. **3** of or for war; military (*warlike preparations*).

war·lock /wáwrlok/ *n.* *archaic* a sorcerer or wizard. [OE *wǣr-loga* traitor f. *wǣr* covenant: *loga* rel. to LIE[2]]

war·lord /wáwrlawrd/ *n.* a military commander or commander in chief.

warm /wawrm/ *adj., v., & n.* ● *adj.* **1** of or at a fairly or comfortably high temperature. **2** (of clothes, etc.) affording warmth (*needs warm gloves*). **3 a** (of a person, action, feelings, etc.) sympathetic; cordial; friendly; loving (*a warm welcome*; *has a warm heart*). **b** enthusiastic; hearty (*was warm in her praise*). **4** animated; heated; excited; indignant (*the dispute grew warm*). **5** *colloq. iron.* dangerous; difficult; or hostile (*met a warm reception*). **6** *colloq.* **a** (of a participant in esp. a children's game of seeking) close to the object, etc., sought. **b** near to guessing or finding out a secret. **7** (of a color, light, etc.) reddish, pink, or yellowish, etc., suggestive of warmth. **8** *Hunting* (of a scent) fresh and strong. **9 a** (of a person's temperament) amorous; sexually demanding. **b** erotic; arousing. ● *v.* **1** *tr.* **a** make warm (*fire warms the room*). **b** excite; make cheerful (*warms the heart*). **2** *intr.* **a** (often foll. by *up*) warm oneself at a fire, etc. (*warmed himself up*). **b** (often foll. by *to*) become animated, enthusiastic, or sympathetic (*warmed to his subject*). ● *n.* **1** the act of warming; the state of being warmed (*gave it a warm*; *had a nice warm by the fire*). **2** the warmth of the atmosphere, etc. **3** *Brit. archaic* a warm garment, esp. an army greatcoat. □ **warm up 1** (of an athlete, performer, etc.)

prepare for a contest, performance, etc., by practicing. **2** (of a room, etc.) become warmer. **3** (of a person) become enthusiastic, etc. **4** (of an engine, etc.) reach a temperature for efficient working. **5** reheat (food). □□ **warm·er** *n.* (also in *comb.*). **warm·ish** *adj.* **warm·ly** *adv.* **warm·ness** *n.* **warmth** *n.* [OE *wearm* f. Gmc]

warm-blood·ed *adj.* **1** (of an organism) having warm blood; mammalian (see HOMEOTHERM). **2** ardent; passionate.

warmed-o·ver *adj.* (or **–up**) **1** (of food, etc.) reheated. **2** stale; secondhand.

warm front *n.* an advancing mass of warm air.

warm-heart·ed /wáwrmhaártid/ *adj.* having a warm heart; kind; friendly. □□ **warm-heart·ed·ly** *adv.* **warm-heart·ed·ness** *n.*

warm·ing pan *n.* *hist.* a usu. brass container for live coals with a flat body and a long handle, used for warming a bed.

war·mon·ger /wáwrmunggər, –mong–/ *n.* a person who seeks to bring about or promote war. □□ **war·mon·ger·ing** *n. & adj.*

warm-up *n.* a period of preparatory exercise for a contest or performance.

warm work *n.* *Brit.* **1** work, etc., that makes one warm through exertion. **2** dangerous conflict, etc.

warn /wawrn/ *v.tr.* **1** (also *absol.*) **a** (often foll. by *of*, or *that* + clause, or *to* + infin.) inform of danger, unknown circumstances, etc. (*warned them of the danger*; *warned her that she was being watched*; *warned him to expect a visit*). **b** (often foll. by *against*) inform (a person, etc.) about a specific danger, hostile person, etc. (*warned her against trusting him*). **2** (usu. with *neg.*) admonish; tell forcefully (*has been warned not to go*). **3** give (a person) cautionary notice regarding conduct, etc. (*shall not warn you again*). □ **warn off** esp. *Brit.* **1** tell (a person) to keep away (from). **2** prohibit from attending races, esp. at a specified course. □□ **warn·er** *n.* [OE *war(e)nian*, *wearnian* ult. f. Gmc: cf. WARE[3]]

warn·ing /wáwrning/ *n.* **1** in senses of WARN *v.* **2** anything that serves to warn; a hint or indication of difficulty, danger, etc. **3** *archaic* = NOTICE *n.* 3b. □□ **warn·ing·ly** *adv.* [OE *war(e)nung*, etc. (as WARN, –ING[1])]

warn·ing col·or·a·tion *n.* *Biol.* conspicuous coloring that warns a predator, etc., against attacking.

warn·ing track *n.* (also **warn·ing path**) *Baseball* dirt strip that borders the outfield just inside the fence.

war of at·tri·tion *n.* a war in which one side wins by gradually wearing the other down with repeated attacks, etc.

war of the el·e·ments *n.* *poet.* storms or natural catastrophes.

war of nerves *n.* an attempt to wear down an opponent by psychological means.

warp /wawrp/ *v. & n.* ● *v.* **1** *tr. & intr.* **a** make or become bent or twisted out of shape, esp. by the action of heat, damp, etc. **b** make or become perverted, bitter, or strange (*a warped sense of humor*). **2 a** *tr.* haul (a ship) by a rope attached to a fixed point. **b** *intr.* progress in this way. **3** *tr.* fertilize by flooding with warp. **4** *tr.* (foll. by *up*) choke (a channel) with an alluvial deposit, etc. **5** *tr.* arrange (threads) as a warp. ● *n.* **1 a** a state of being warped, esp. of shrunken or expanded lumber. **b** perversion, bitterness, etc., of the mind or character. **2** the threads stretched lengthwise in a loom to be crossed by the weft. **3** a rope used in towing or warping, or attached to a trawl net. **4** sediment, etc., left esp. on poor land by standing water. □□ **warp·age** *n.* (esp. in sense 1a of *v.*). **warp·er** *n.* (in sense 5 of *v.*). [OE *weorpan* throw, *wearp* f. Gmc]

war·paint /wáwrpaynt/ *n.* **1** paint used to adorn the body before battle, esp. by N. American Indians. **2** *colloq.* elaborate make-up.

war·path /wáwrpath/ *n.* **1** a warlike expedition of N. American Indians. **2** *colloq.* any hostile course or attitude (*is on the warpath again*).

war·plane /wáwrplayn/ *n.* a military aircraft, esp. one armed for warfare.

war po·et *n.* a poet writing on war themes, esp. of the two world wars.

war·ra·gal var. of WARRIGAL.

war·rant /wáwrənt, wór–/ *n. & v.* ● *n.* **1 a** anything that authorizes a person or an action (*have no warrant for this*). **b** a person so authorizing (*I will be your warrant*). **2 a** a written authorization, money voucher, travel document, etc. (*a dividend warrant*). **b** a written authorization allowing police to search premises, arrest a suspect, etc. **3** a document authorizing counsel to represent the principal in a lawsuit (*warrant of attorney*). **4** a certificate of service rank held by a warrant officer. ● *v.tr.* **1** serve as a warrant for; justify (*nothing can warrant his behavior*). **2** guarantee or attest to esp. the genuineness of an article, the worth of a person, etc. □ **I** (or **I'll**) **warrant** I am certain; no doubt (*She'll be sorry, I'll warrant*). □□ **war·rant·er** *n.* **war·ran·tor** *n.* [ME f. ONF *warant*, var. of OF *guarant*, –*and* f. Frank. *werēnd* (unrecorded) f. *giwerēn* be surety for]

war·rant·a·ble /wáwrəntəbəl, wór–/ *adj.* **1** able to be warranted. **2** (of a deer) old enough to be hunted (5 or 6 years). □□ **war·rant·a·ble·ness** *n.* **war·rant·a·bly** *adv.*

war·ran·tee /wáwrəntee, wór–/ *n.* a person to whom a warranty is given.

war·rant of·fi·cer *n.* an officer ranking between commissioned officers and NCOs.

war·ran·ty /wáwrəntee, wór–/ *n.* (*pl.* **–ties**) **1** an undertaking as to the ownership or quality of a thing sold, leased, etc., often accepting responsibility for defects or liability for repairs needed over a specified period. **2** (usu. foll. by *for* + verbal noun) an authority or justification. **3** an undertaking by an insured person of the truth of a statement or fulfillment of a condition. [ME f. AF *warantie*, var. of *garantie* (as WARRANT)]

war·ren /wáwrən, wór–/ *n.* **1 a** a network of interconnecting rabbit burrows. **b** a piece of ground occupied by this. **2** a densely populated or labyrinthine building or district. **3** *hist.* an area of land on which game is preserved. [ME f. AF & ONF *warenne*, OF *garenne* game park f. Gmc]

war·ri·gal /wáwrigəl/ *n. & adj.* (also **war·ra·gal**) *Austral.* • *n.* **1** a dingo dog. **2** an untamed horse. • *adj.* wild, untamed. [Aboriginal]

war·ring /wáwring/ *adj.* rival; antagonistic.

war·ri·or /wáwreeər, wór–/ *n.* **1** a person experienced or distinguished in fighting. **2** a fighting person, esp. a man, esp. of primitive peoples. **3** (*attrib.*) martial (*a warrior nation*). [ME f. ONF *werreior*, etc., OF *guerreior*, etc., f. *werreier, guerreier* make WAR]

war·ship /wáwrship/ *n.* an armored ship used in war.

Wars of the Ros·es *n. hist.* the 15th-c. civil wars in England between the houses of York and Lancaster, represented by white and red roses.

wart /wawrt/ *n.* **1** a small, hardish, roundish growth on the skin caused by a virus-induced abnormal growth of papillae and thickening of the epidermis. **2** a protuberance on the skin of an animal, surface of a plant, etc. **3** *colloq.* an objectionable person. □ **warts and all** *colloq.* with no attempt to conceal blemishes or inadequacies. □□ **wart·y** *adj.* [OE *wearte* f. Gmc]

wart·hog /wáwrt-hog/ *n.* an African wild pig of the genus *Phacochoerus*, with a large head and warty lumps on its face, and large curved tusks.

war·time /wáwrtīm/ *n.* the period during which a war is waged.

war-wea·ry *adj.* (esp. of a population) exhausted and dispirited by war.

war wid·ow *n.* a woman whose husband has been killed in war.

war·y /wáiree/ *adj.* (**war·i·er, war·i·est**) **1** on one's guard; given to caution; circumspect. **2** (foll. by *of*) cautious; suspicious (*am wary of using elevators*). **3** showing or done with caution or suspicion (*a wary expression*). □□ **war·i·ly** *adv.* **war·i·ness** *n.* [WARE² + –Y¹]

war zone *n.* an area in which a war takes place.

was *1st & 3rd sing. past* of BE.

Wash. *abbr.* Washington.

wash /wosh, wawsh/ *v. & n.* • *v.* **1** *tr.* cleanse (oneself or a part of oneself, clothes, etc.) with liquid, esp. water. **2** *tr.* (foll. by *out, off, away*, etc.) remove (a stain or dirt, a surface, or some physical feature of the surface) in this way; eradicate all traces of. **3** *intr.* wash oneself or esp. one's hands and face. **4** *intr.* wash clothes, etc. **5** *intr.* (of fabric or dye) bear washing without damage. **6** *intr.* (foll. by *off, out*) (of a stain, etc.) be removed by washing. **7** *tr. poet.* moisten; water (*tear-washed eyes; a rose washed with dew*). **8** *tr.* (of a river, sea, etc.) touch (a country, coast, etc.) with its waters. **9** *tr.* (of moving liquid) carry along in a specified direction (*a wave washed him overboard; was washed up on the shore*). **10** *tr.* (also foll. by *away, out*) **a** scoop out (*the water had washed a channel*). **b** erode; denude (*sea-washed cliffs*). **11** *intr.* (foll. by *over, along*, etc.) sweep, move, or splash **12** *tr.* sift (ore) by the action of water. **13** *tr.* **a** brush a thin coat of watery paint or ink over (paper in watercolor painting, etc., or a wall). **b** (foll. by *with*) coat (inferior metal) with gold, etc. • *n.* **1 a** the act or an instance of washing; the process of being washed (*give them a good wash; only needed one wash*). **b** (prec. by *the*) treatment at a laundry, etc. (*sent them to the wash*). **2** a quantity of clothes for washing or just washed. **3** the visible or audible motion of agitated water or air, esp. due to the passage of a ship, etc., or aircraft. **4 a** soil swept off by water; alluvium. **b** a sandbank exposed only at low tide. **5** kitchen slops and scraps given to pigs. **6 a** thin, weak, or inferior liquid food. **b** liquid food for animals. **7** a liquid to spread over a surface to cleanse, heal, or color. **8** a thin coating of watercolor, wall paint, or metal. **9** malt, etc., fermenting before distillation. **10** a lotion or cosmetic. □ **come out in the wash** *colloq.* be clarified, or (of contingent difficulties) be resolved or removed, in the course of time. **wash one's dirty laundry in public** discuss one's personal affairs in public. **wash down 1** wash completely (esp. a large surface or object). **2** (usu. foll. by *with*) accompany or follow (food) with a drink. **washed out 1** faded by washing. **2** pale. **3** *colloq.* limp; enfeebled. **washed up** *sl.* defeated, having failed. **wash one's hands** *euphem.* go to the lavatory. **wash one's hands of** renounce responsibility for. **wash out 1** clean the inside of (a thing) by washing. **2** clean (a garment, etc.) by brief washing. **3 a** rain out (an event, etc.). **b** *colloq.* cancel. **4** (of a flood,

downpour, etc.) make a breach in (a road, etc.). **wash up** wash one's face and hands. **won't** (or **doesn't**) **wash** *colloq.* (of an argument, etc.) will not be (or is not) believed or accepted. [OE *w æscan*, etc., f. Gmc, rel. to WATER]

wash·a·ble /wóshəbəl, wáwsh–/ *adj.* that can be washed, esp. without damage. □□ **wash·a·bil·i·ty** /–bílitee/ *n.*

wash-and-wear *adj.* (of a fabric or garment) easily and quickly laundered.

wash·a·te·ri·a var. of WASHETERIA.

wash·ba·sin /wóshbaysin, wáwsh–/ *n.* = WASHBOWL.

wash·board /wóshbawrd, wáwsh–/ *n.* **1** a board of ribbed wood or a sheet of corrugated zinc on which clothes are scrubbed in washing. **2** this used as a percussion instrument, played with the fingers.

wash·bowl /wóshbōl, wáwsh–/ *n.* a bowl for washing one's hands, face, etc.

wash·cloth /wóshkloth, wáwsh–/ *n.* a cloth for washing the face or body.

wash·day /wóshday, wáwsh–/ *n.* a day on which clothes, etc., are washed.

wash·er /wóshər, wáwsh–/ *n.* **1 a** a person or thing that washes. **b** a washing machine. **2** a flat ring of rubber, metal, leather, etc., inserted at a joint to tighten it and prevent leakage. **3** a similar ring placed under the head of a screw, bolt, etc., or under a nut, to disperse its pressure. **4** *Austral.* a washcloth.

wash·er-up *n.* (*pl.* **wash·ers-up**) *Brit.* a person who washes dishes, etc.

wash·er·wom·an /wóshərwŏŏmən, wáwsh–/ *n.* (*pl.* **–wom·en**) (also **wash·wom·an**) a woman whose occupation is washing clothes; a laundress.

wash·e·te·ri·a /wóshətéereeə, wáwsh–/ *n.* (also **wash·a·te·ri·a**) = LAUNDROMAT.

wash·house /wóshhowss, wáwsh–/ *n.* a building where clothes, etc., are washed.

wash·ing /wóshing, wáwsh–/ *n.* a quantity of clothes for washing or just washed. □ **washing-up** *Brit.* **1** the process of washing dishes, etc., after use. **2** used dishes, etc., for washing.

wash·ing ma·chine *n.* a machine for washing clothes and linen, etc.

wash·ing so·da *n.* sodium carbonate, used dissolved in water for washing and cleaning.

wash·land /wóshland, wáwsh–/ *n. Brit.* land periodically flooded by a stream.

wash·out /wóshowt, wáwsh–/ *n. Geol.* a narrow river channel that cuts into preexisting sediments.

wash-out *n.* **1** *colloq.* a fiasco; a complete failure. **2** a breach in a road, railroad track, etc., caused by flooding.

wash·room /wóshrŏŏm, –rŏŏm, wáwsh–/ *n.* a room with washing and toilet facilities.

wash·stand /wóshstand, wáwsh–/ *n.* a piece of furniture to hold a washbowl, pitcher, soap, etc.

wash·tub /wóshtub, wáwsh–/ *n.* a tub or vessel for washing or soaking clothes, etc.

wash·y /wóshee, wáwsh–/ *adj.* (**wash·i·er, wash·i·est**) **1** (of liquid food) too watery or weak; insipid. **2** (of color) faded-looking; thin; faint. **3** (of a style, sentiment, etc.) lacking vigor or intensity. □□ **wash·i·ly** *adv.* **wash·i·ness** *n.*

was·n't /wúzənt, wóz/ *contr.* was not.

WASP /wosp/ *n.* (also **Wasp**) usu. *derog.* a middle-class American white Protestant descended from early English settlers. □□ **Wasp·y** *adj.* [*White Anglo-Saxon Protestant*]

wasp /wosp/ *n.* **1** a stinging, often flesh-eating insect of the order Hymenoptera, esp. the common social wasp *Vespa vulgaris*, with black and yellow stripes and a very thin waist. **2** (in *comb.*) any of various insects resembling a wasp in some way (*wasp beetle*). □□ **wasp·like** *adj.* [OE *wæfs, wæps, wæsp*, f. WG: perh. rel. to WEAVE¹ (from the weblike form of its nest)]

wasp·ish /wóspish/ *adj.* irritable; petulant; sharp in retort. □□ **wasp·ish·ly** *adv.* **wasp·ish·ness** *n.*

wasp waist *n.* a very slender waist. □□ **wasp-waist·ed** *adj.*

was·sail /wósəl, wósayl, wosáyl/ *n. & v. archaic* • *n.* **1** a festive occasion; a drinking bout. **2** a kind of liquor drunk on such an occasion. • *v. intr.* make merry; celebrate with drinking, etc. □□ **was·sail·er** *n.*

was·sail bowl *n.* (also **was·sail cup**) a bowl or cup from which healths were drunk, esp. on Christmas Eve and Twelfth Night.

WORD HISTORY   **wassail**

Middle English (as a salutation): from Old Norse *ves heill*, corresponding to the Old English greeting *wæs hæil* 'be in (good) health!' (source of HAIL²). No trace has been found of the use of drinking formulas in Old English, Old Norse or other Teutonic languages; *wassail* (and the reply *drinkhail* 'drink good health') were probably introduced by Danish-speaking inhabitants of England, the use then spreading to the native population. By the 12th century, the usage was considered, by the Normans, characteristic of Englishmen.

Was·ser·mann test /wáasərmən/ n. a test for syphilis using the reaction of the patient's blood serum. [A. von *Wassermann*, Ger. pathologist d. 1925]

wast /wost, wəst/ *archaic* or *dial*. 2nd sing. past of BE.

wast·age /wáystij/ n. 1 an amount wasted. 2 loss by use, wear, or leakage. 3 *Commerce* loss of employees other than by layoffs.

waste /wayst/ v., adj., & n. ● v. 1 tr. use to no purpose or for inadequate result or extravagantly (*waste time*). 2 tr. fail to use (esp. an opportunity). 3 tr. (often foll. by *on*) give (advice, etc.), utter (words, etc.), without effect. 4 tr. & intr. wear gradually away; make or become weak; wither. 5 tr. **a** ravage; devastate. **b** sl. murder; kill. 6 tr. treat as wasted or valueless. 7 intr. be expended without useful effect. ● adj. 1 superfluous; no longer serving a purpose. 2 (of a district, etc.) not inhabited nor cultivated; desolate (*waste ground*). 3 presenting no features of interest. ● n. 1 the act or an instance of wasting; extravagant or ineffectual use of an asset, of time, etc. 2 waste material or food; refuse; useless remains or by-products. 3 a waste region; a desert, etc. 4 the state of being used up; diminution by wear and tear. 5 *Law* damage to an estate caused by an act or by neglect, esp. by a tenant. 6 = WASTE PIPE. □ **go** (or **run**) **to waste** be wasted. **lay waste** ravage; devastate. **waste one's breath** see BREATH. **waste not, want not** extravagance leads to poverty. **waste words** see WORD. □□ **wast·a·ble** adj. **waste·less** adj. [ME f. ONF *wast(e)*, var. of OF *g(u)ast(e)*, f. L *vastus*]

waste·bas·ket /wáystbaskit/ n. a receptacle for wastepaper, etc.

waste·ful /wáystfʊl/ adj. 1 extravagant. 2 causing or showing waste. □□ **waste·ful·ly** adv. **waste·ful·ness** n.

waste·land /wáystland/ n. 1 an unproductive or useless area of land. 2 a place or time considered spiritually or intellectually barren.

waste·pa·per /wáystpaypər/ n. spoiled, valueless, or discarded paper.

waste·pa·per bas·ket n. = WASTEBASKET.

waste pipe n. a pipe to carry off waste material, e.g., from a sink.

waste prod·ucts n. useless by-products of manufacture or of an organism or organisms.

wast·er /wáystər/ n. 1 a wasteful person. 2 *colloq*. a wastrel.

wast·rel /wáystrəl/ n. 1 a wasteful or good-for-nothing person. 2 a waif; a neglected child.

watch /woch/ v. & n. ● v. 1 tr. keep the eyes fixed on; look at attentively. 2 tr. **a** keep under observation; follow observantly. **b** monitor or consider carefully; pay attention to (*have to watch my weight; watched their progress with interest*). 3 intr. (often foll. by *for*) be in an alert state; be vigilant; take heed (*watch for the holes in the road; watch for an opportunity*). 4 intr. (foll. by *over*) look after; take care of. 5 intr. *archaic* remain awake for devotions, etc. ● n. 1 a small portable timepiece for carrying on one's person. 2 a state of alert or constant observation or attention. 3 *Naut*. **a** a four-hour period of duty. **b** (in full **starboard** or **port watch**) each of the halves, divided according to the position of the bunks, into which a ship's crew is divided to take alternate watches. 4 *hist*. a watchman or group of watchmen, esp. patrolling the streets at night. 5 a former division of the night. 6 a period of wakefulness at night. 7 *Sc. hist*. irregular Highland troops in the 18th c. □ **on the watch** waiting for an expected or feared occurrence. **set the watch** *Naut*. station sentinels, etc. **watch it** (or **oneself**) *colloq*. be careful. **watch one's step** proceed cautiously. **watch out** 1 (often foll. by *for*) be on one's guard. 2 as a warning of immediate danger. □□ **watch·a·ble** adj. **watch·er** n. (also in *comb*.). [OE *wæcce* (n.), rel. to WAKE[1]]

watch·band /wóchband/ n. a strap or bracelet for fastening a watch on the wrist.

watch·case /wóchkays/ n. the outer, usu. metal case enclosing the works of a watch.

watch chain n. a metal chain for securing a pocket watch.

watch crys·tal n. a glass disk covering the dial of a watch.

watch·dog /wóchdawg, dog/ n. & v. ● n. 1 a dog kept to guard property, etc. 2 a person or body monitoring others' rights, behavior, etc. ● v.tr. (**-dogged**, **-dog·ging**) maintain surveillance over.

watch·ful /wóchfʊl/ adj. 1 accustomed to watching. 2 on the watch. 3 showing vigilance. 4 *archaic* wakeful. □□ **watch·ful·ly** adv. **watch·ful·ness** n.

watch glass n. *Brit*. a glass disk used in a laboratory, etc., to hold material for use in experiments.

watch·ing brief n. *Brit*. 1 a brief held by a barrister following a case for a client not directly involved. 2 a state of interest maintained in a proceeding not directly or immediately concerning one.

watch·mak·er /wóchmaykər/ n. a person who makes and repairs watches and clocks. □□ **watch·mak·ing** n.

watch·man /wóchmən/ n. (pl. **-men**) 1 a person employed to look after an empty building, etc., at night. 2 *archaic* or *hist*. a member of a night watch.

watch night n. 1 the last night of the year. 2 a religious service held on this night.

watch spring n. the mainspring of a watch.

watch strap n. esp. *Brit*. = WATCHBAND.

watch·tow·er /wóchtower/ n. a tower from which observation can be kept.

watch·word /wóchwərd/ n. 1 a phrase summarizing a guiding principle; a slogan. 2 *hist*. a military password.

wa·ter /wáwtər, wót-/ n. & v. ● n. 1 a colorless, transparent, odorless, tasteless liquid compound of oxygen and hydrogen. ¶ *Chem*. formula: H_2O. 2 a liquid consisting chiefly of this and found in seas, lakes, and rivers, in rain, and in secretions of organisms. 3 an expanse of water; a sea, lake, river, etc. 4 (in *pl*.) part of a sea or river (*in Icelandic waters*). 5 (often as **the waters**) mineral water at a spa, etc. 6 the state of a tide (*high water*). 7 a solution of a specified substance in water (*lavender water*). 8 the quality of the transparency and brilliance of a gem, esp. a diamond. 9 *Finance* an amount of nominal capital added by watering (see sense 10 of *v*.). 10 (*attrib*.) **a** found in or near water. **b** of, for, or worked by water. **c** involving, using, or yielding water. ● v. 1 tr. sprinkle or soak with water. 2 tr. supply (a plant) with water. 3 tr. give water to (an animal) to drink. 4 intr. (of the mouth or eyes) secrete water as saliva or tears. 5 tr. (as **watered** adj.) (of silk, etc.) having irregular wavy glossy markings. 6 tr. adulterate (milk, beer, etc.) with water. 7 tr. (of a river, etc.) supply (a place) with water. 8 intr. (of an animal) go to a pool, etc., to drink. 9 intr. (of a ship, engine, etc., or the person in charge of it) take in a supply of water. 10 tr. *Finance* increase (a company's debt, or nominal capital) by the issue of new shares without a corresponding addition to assets. □ **by water** using a ship, etc., for travel or transport. **cast one's bread upon the waters** see BREAD. **like water** lavishly; profusely. **like water off a duck's back** see DUCK[1]. **make one's mouth water** cause one's saliva to flow; stimulate one's appetite or anticipation. **of the first water** 1 (of a diamond) of the greatest brilliance and transparency. 2 of the finest quality or extreme degree. **on the water** on a ship, etc. **on the water wagon** *Brit*. see WAGON. **water down** 1 dilute with water. 2 make less vivid, forceful, or horrifying. **water under the bridge** past events accepted as past and irrevocable. □□ **wa·ter·er** n. **wa·ter·less** adj. [OE *wæter* f. Gmc, rel. to WET]

wa·ter bag n. a bag of leather, canvas, etc., for holding water.

wa·ter bear n. = TARDIGRADE n.

Wa·ter Bear·er n. (or esp. *Brit*. **Wa·ter Car·ri·er**) the zodiacal sign or constellation Aquarius.

wa·ter bed n. a mattress of rubber or plastic, etc., filled with water.

wa·ter bis·cuit n. (also **wa·ter crack·er**) an unsweetened cracker made from flour and water.

wa·ter blis·ter n. a blister containing a colorless fluid, not blood nor pus.

water bloom n. scum formed by algae on the surface of standing water.

wa·ter boat·man n. any aquatic bug of the family Notonectidae or Corixidae, swimming with oarlike hind legs.

wa·ter·borne /wáwtərbawrn, wótər-/ adj. 1 (of goods, etc.) conveyed by or traveling on water. 2 (of a disease) communicated or propagated by contaminated water.

wa·ter brash n. heartburn.

wa·ter·buck /wáwtərbuk, wótər-/ n. (pl. same or **wa·ter·bucks**) any of various African antelopes of the genus *Kobus*, frequenting riverbanks.

wa·ter buf·fa·lo n. the common domestic E. Indian buffalo, *Bubalus arnee*.

water buffalo

wa·ter·bus /wáwtərbus, wótər-/ n. (pl. **-bus·es** or **-bus·ses**) a boat carrying passengers on a regular run on a river, lake, etc.

wa·ter butt n. a barrel used to catch rainwater.

wa·ter can·non n. a device giving a powerful jet of water to disperse a crowd, etc.

wa·ter chest·nut n. 1 an aquatic plant, *Trapa natans*, bearing an edible seed. 2 **a** (in full **Chinese water chestnut**) a sedge, *Eleocharis tuberosa*, with rushlike leaves arising from a corm. **b** this corm used as food.

wa·ter clock n. a clock measuring time by the flow of water.

wa·ter clos·et n. a room or compartment equipped with a toilet bowl.

wa·ter·col·or /wáwtərkúlər, wótər-/ n. (*Brit*. **wa·ter·col·our**) 1 artists' paint made of pigment to be diluted with water and not oil. 2 a picture painted with this. 3 the art of painting with watercolors. □□ **wa·ter·col·or·ist** n.

wa·ter-cooled adj. cooled by the circulation of water.

wa·ter·cool·er /wáwtərkoolər, wótər-/ n. a tank of cooled drinking water.

wa·ter·course /wáwtərkawrs, wótər-/ n. 1 a brook, stream, or artificial water channel. 2 the bed along which this flows.

wa·ter·cress /wáwtərkres, wótər–/ *n.* a hardy perennial cress, *Nasturtium officinale*, growing in running water, with pungent leaves used in salad.

wa·ter cure *n.* = HYDROPATHY.

wa·ter di·vin·er *n.* esp. *Brit.* a person who dowses (see DOWSE¹) for water.

wa·ter·fall /wáwtərfawl, wótər–/ *n.* a stream or river flowing over a precipice or down a steep hillside.

Wa·ter·ford glass /wáwtərfərd, wótər–/ *n.* a clear, colorless flint glass. [*Waterford* in Ireland]

wa·ter·fowl /wáwtərfowl, wótər–/ *n.* (usu. collect. as *pl.*) birds frequenting water, esp. swimming game birds.

wa·ter·front /wáwtərfrunt, wótər–/ *n.* the part of a town or city adjoining a river, lake, harbor, etc.

Wa·ter·gate /wáwtərgayt, wótər–/ *n.* a political or commercial scandal on a large scale. [a building in Washington, DC, that in 1972 housed the national headquarters of the Democratic Party, the bugging and burglary of which by people connected with the Republican administration led to a national scandal and the resignation of President R. M. Nixon]

wa·ter gate *n.* **1** a floodgate. **2** a gate giving access to a river, etc.

wa·ter gauge *n.* **1** a glass tube, etc., indicating the height of water in a reservoir, boiler, etc. **2** pressure expressed in terms of a head of water.

wa·ter glass *n.* **1** a solution of sodium or potassium silicate used for preserving eggs, as a vehicle for fresco painting, and for hardening artificial stone. **2** a tube with a glass bottom enabling objects under water to be observed. **3** a drinking glass.

wa·ter ham·mer *n.* a knocking noise in a water pipe when a faucet is suddenly turned off.

wa·ter heat·er *n.* a device for heating (esp. domestic) water.

wa·ter hem·lock *n.* a poisonous plant, *Cicuta maculata*, found in marshes, etc. Also called **cowbane**.

wa·ter hole *n.* a shallow depression in which water collects (esp. in the bed of a river otherwise dry).

wa·ter hy·a·cinth *n.* a tropical river weed, *Eichhornia crassipes*.

wa·ter ice *n.* = SORBET.

wa·ter·ing /wáwtəring, wótər–/ *n.* the act or an instance of supplying water or (of an animal) obtaining water. [OE *wæterung* (as WATER, –ING¹)]

wa·ter·ing can *n.* a portable container with a long spout usu. ending in a perforated sprinkler, for watering plants.

wa·ter·ing hole *n.* **1** a pool of water from which animals regularly drink; = WATER HOLE. **2** *sl.* a bar.

wa·ter·ing place *n.* **1** = WATERING HOLE. **2** a spa or seaside resort. **3** a place where water is obtained.

wa·ter jump *n.* a place where a horse in a steeplechase, etc., must jump over water.

wa·ter lev·el **1 a** the surface of the water in a reservoir, etc. **b** the height of this. **2** *Brit.* = WATER TABLE. **3** a level using water to determine the horizontal.

wa·ter lil·y *n.* any aquatic plant of the family Nymphaeaceae, with broad flat floating leaves and large usu. cup-shaped floating flowers.

wa·ter·line /wáwtərlin, wótər–/ *n.* **1** the line along which the surface of water touches a ship's side (marked on a ship for use in loading). **2** a linear watermark.

wa·ter·logged /wáwtərlawgd, –logd, wótər–/ *adj.* **1** saturated with water. **2** (of a boat, etc.) hardly able to float from being saturated or filled with water. **3** (of ground) made useless by being saturated with water. [*waterlog* (v.), f. WATER + LOG¹, prob. orig. = 'reduce (a ship) to the condition of a log']

Wa·ter·loo /wáwtərloo, wótər–/ *n.* a decisive defeat or contest (*meet one's Waterloo*). [*Waterloo* in Belgium, where Napoleon was finally defeated in 1815]

wa·ter main *n.* the main pipe in a water-supply system.

wa·ter·man /wáwtərmən, wótər–/ *n.* (*pl.* –**men**) **1** a boatman plying for hire. **2** an oarsman as regards skill in keeping the boat balanced.

wa·ter·mark /wáwtərmaark, wótər–/ *n. & v.* ● *n.* a faint design made in some paper during manufacture, visible when held against the light, identifying the maker, etc. ● *v.tr.* mark with this.

wa·ter mead·ow *n.* a meadow periodically flooded by a stream.

wa·ter·mel·on /wáwtərmelən, wótər–/ *n.* a large, smooth, green melon, *Citrullus lanatus*, with red pulp and watery juice.

wa·ter me·ter *n.* a device for measuring and recording the amount of water supplied to a house, etc.

wa·ter mill *n.* a mill worked by a waterwheel.

wa·ter moc·ca·sin *n.* **1** a venomous snake, *Agkistrodon piscivorus*,

water lily

found in wet or marshy areas of the southern US; a cottonmouth. **2** any of various harmless water snakes.

wa·ter nymph *n.* a nymph regarded as inhabiting or presiding over water.

wa·ter of crys·tal·li·za·tion *n.* water forming an essential part of the structure of some crystals.

wa·ter of life *n. rhet.* spiritual enlightenment.

wa·ter ou·zel *n.* = DIPPER 1.

wa·ter pep·per *n.* an aquatic herb, *Polygonum hydropiper*. Also called **smartweed**.

wa·ter pipe *n.* **1** a pipe for conveying water. **2** a hookah.

wa·ter pis·tol *n.* a toy pistol shooting a jet of water.

wa·ter plan·tain *n.* any marsh plant of the genus *Alisma*, with plantainlike leaves.

wa·ter po·lo *n.* a game played by swimmers, with a ball like a soccer ball.

wa·ter·pow·er /wáwtərpowr, wótər–/ *n.* **1** mechanical force derived from the weight or motion of water. **2** a fall in the level of a river, as a source of this force.

wa·ter·proof /wáwtərproof, wótər–/ *adj., n., & v.* ● *adj.* impervious to water. ● *n. Brit.* a waterproof garment or material. ● *v.tr.* make waterproof.

wa·ter purs·lane *n.* a creeping plant, *Lythrum portula*, growing in damp places.

wa·ter rail *n.* a wading bird, *Rallus aquaticus*, frequenting marshes, etc.

wa·ter rat *n.* **1** any rodent of aquatic habits. **2** a muskrat. **3** *sl.* a waterfront vagrant or thug.

wa·ter-re·pel·lent *adj.* not easily penetrated by water.

wa·ter scor·pi·on *n.* any aquatic bug of the family Nepidae, living submerged and breathing through a bristlelike tubular tail.

wa·ter·shed /wáwtərshed, wótər–/ *n.* **1** a line of separation between waters flowing to different rivers, basins, or seas. **2** a turning point in affairs. [WATER + *shed* ridge of high ground (rel. to SHED²), after G *Wasserscheide*]

wa·ter·side /wáwtərsid, wótər–/ *n.* the margin of a sea, lake, or river.

wa·ter ski *n.* (*pl.* –**skis**) each of a pair of skis worn on the feet and used for skimming the surface of the water when towed by a motorboat.

wa·ter-ski /wáwtərskee, wótər–/ *v.intr.* (–**skis**, –**skied** /–skeed/; –**ski·ing**) travel on water skis. □□ **wa·ter-ski·er** *n.*

wa·ter sof·ten·er *n.* an apparatus or substance for softening hard water.

wa·ter-sol·u·ble *adj.* soluble in water.

wa·ter·spout /wáwtərspowt, wótər–/ *n.* a gyrating column of water and spray formed by a whirlwind between sea and cloud.

wa·ter sup·ply *n.* the provision and storage of water, or the amount of water stored, for the use of a town, house, etc.

wa·ter ta·ble *n.* a level below which the ground is saturated with water.

wa·ter·tight /wáwtərtit, wótər–/ *adj.* **1** (of a joint, container, vessel, etc.) closely fastened or fitted or made so as to prevent the passage of water. **2** (of an argument, etc.) unassailable.

wa·ter tor·ture *n.* a form of torture in which the victim is exposed to the incessant dripping of water on the head, or the sound of dripping.

wa·ter tow·er *n.* a tower with an elevated tank to give pressure for distributing water.

wa·ter vole *n.* an aquatic vole, esp. *Arvicola amphibius*; a water rat.

wa·ter·way /wáwtərway, wótər–/ *n.* **1** a navigable channel. **2** a route for travel by water. **3** a thick plank at the outer edge of a deck along which a channel is hollowed for water to run off by.

wa·ter·weed /wáwtərweed, wótər–/ *n.* any of various aquatic plants, esp. of the genus *Elodea*.

wa·ter·wheel /wáwtərhweel, wótər–, –weel/ *n.* a wheel driven by water to work machinery, or to raise water.

wa·ter wings *n.* inflated floats fixed on the arms of a person learning to swim.

wa·ter·works /wáwtərwərks, wótər–/ *n.* **1** an establishment for managing a water supply. **2** *colloq.* the shedding of tears. **3** *Brit. colloq.* the urinary system.

wa·ter·y /wáwtəree, wótər–/ *adj.* **1** containing too much water. **2** too thin in consistency. **3** of or consisting of water. **4** (of the eyes) suffused or running with water. **5** (of conversation, style, etc.) vapid; uninteresting. **6** (of color) pale. **7** (of the sun, moon, or sky) rainy-looking. □□ **wa·ter·i·ness** *n.* [OE *wæterig* (as WATER, –Y¹)]

wa·ter·y grave *n.* the bottom of the sea as a place where a person lies drowned.

waterwheel

WATS /wots/ *abbr.* Wide-Area Telecommunications Service.

watt /wot/ *n.* the SI unit of power, equivalent to one joule per second, corresponding to the rate of energy in an electric circuit where the potential difference is one volt and the current one ampere. ¶ Symb.: W. [J. *Watt,* Sc. engineer d. 1819]

watt·age /wótij/ *n.* an amount of electrical power expressed in watts.

watt-hour *n.* the energy used when one watt is applied for one hour.

wat·tle¹ /wót'l/ *n. & v.* • *n.* **1 a** interlaced rods and split rods as a material for making fences, walls, etc. **b** (in *sing.* or *pl.*) rods and twigs for this use. **2** an Australian acacia with long pliant branches, with bark used in tanning and golden flowers used as the national emblem. **3** *Brit. dial.* a wicker hurdle. • *v.tr.* **1** make of wattle. **2** enclose or fill up with wattles. [OE *watul,* of unkn. orig.]

wat·tle² /wót'l/ *n.* **1** a loose fleshy appendage on the head or throat of a turkey or other birds. **2** = BARB *n.* 3. □□ **wat·tled** *adj.* [16th c.: orig. unkn.]

wat·tle and daub *n.* a network of rods and twigs plastered with mud or clay as a building material.

watt·me·ter /wótmeetər/ *n.* a meter for measuring the amount of electricity in watts.

wattle²

wave /wayv/ *v. & n.* • *v.* **1 a** *intr.* (often foll. by *to*) move a hand, etc., back and forth in greeting or as a signal (*waved to me across the street*). **b** *tr.* move (a hand, etc.) in this way. **2 a** *intr.* show a sinuous or sweeping motion as of a flag, tree, or a wheat field in the wind; flutter; undulate. **b** *tr.* impart a waving motion to. **3** *tr.* brandish (a sword, etc.) as an encouragement to followers, etc. **4** *tr.* tell or direct (a person) by waving (*waved them away; waved them to follow*). **5** *tr.* express (a greeting, etc.) by waving (*waved good-bye to them*). **6** *tr.* give an undulating form to (hair, drawn lines, etc.); make wavy. **7** *intr.* (of hair, etc.) have such a form; be wavy. • *n.* **1** a ridge of water between two depressions. **2** a long body of water curling into an arched form and breaking on the shore. **3** a thing compared to this, e.g., a body of persons in one of successive advancing groups. **4** a gesture of waving. **5 a** the process of waving the hair. **b** an undulating form produced in the hair by waving. **6 a** a temporary occurrence or increase of a condition, emotion, or influence (*a wave of enthusiasm*). **b** a specified period of widespread weather (*heat wave*). **7** *Physics* **a** the disturbance of the particles of a fluid medium to form ridges and troughs for the propagation or direction of motion, heat, light, sound, etc., without the advance of the particles. **b** a single curve in the course of this motion (see also STANDING WAVE, TRAVELING WAVE). **8** *Electr.* a similar variation of an electromagnetic field in the propagation of radiation through a medium or vacuum. **9** (in *pl.*; prec. by *the*) *poet.* the sea; water. □ **make waves** *colloq.* cause trouble. **wave aside** dismiss as intrusive or irrelevant. □□ **wave·less** *adj.* **wave·like** *adj. & adv.* [OE *wafian* (v.) f. Gmc (n.) also alt. of ME *wawe, wage*] ▶ See note at WAIVE.

wave·band /wáyvband/ *n.* a range of (esp. radio) wavelengths between certain limits.

wave e·qua·tion *n.* a differential equation expressing the properties of motion in waves.

wave·form /wáyvfawrm/ *n.* *Physics* a curve showing the shape of a wave at a given time.

wave front *n.* *Physics* a surface containing points affected in the same way by a wave at a given time.

wave func·tion *n.* a function satisfying a wave equation and describing the properties of a wave.

wave·guide /wáyvgyd/ *n.* *Electr.* a metal tube, etc., confining and conveying microwaves.

wave·length /wáyvlengkth, –length, –lenth/ *n.* **1** the distance between successive crests of a wave, esp. points in a sound wave or electromagnetic wave. ¶ Symb.: λ. **2** this as a distinctive feature of radio waves from a transmitter. **3** *colloq.* a particular mode or range of thinking and communicating (*we don't seem to be on the same wavelength*).

wave·let /wáyvlit/ *n.* a small wave on water.

wave me·chan·ics *n.* a method of analysis of the behavior esp. of atomic phenomena with particles represented by wave equations (see QUANTUM MECHANICS).

wave num·ber *n.* *Physics* the number of waves in a unit distance.

wa·ver /wáyvər/ *v.intr.* **1** be or become unsteady; falter; begin to give way. **2** be irresolute or undecided between different courses or opinions; be shaken in resolution or belief. **3** (of a light) flicker. □□ **wa·ver·er** *n.* **wa·ver·ing·ly** *adv.* [ME f. ON *vafra* flicker f. Gmc, rel. to WAVE] ▶ See note at WAIVE.

wave the·o·ry *n.* *hist.* the theory that light is propagated through the ether by a wave motion imparted to the ether by the molecular vibrations of the radiant body

wav·y /wáyvee/ *adj.* (**wav·i·er, wav·i·est**) (of a line or surface) having waves or alternate contrary curves (*wavy hair*). □□ **wav·i·ly** *adv.* **wav·i·ness** *n.*

wa-wa /wáawaa/ *n.* (also **wah-wah**) *Mus.* an effect achieved on brass instruments by alternately applying and removing a mute and on an electric guitar by controlling the output from the amplifier with a pedal. [imit.]

wax¹ /waks/ *n. & v.* • *n.* **1** a sticky, plastic, yellowish substance secreted by bees as the material of honeycomb cells; beeswax. **2** a white translucent material obtained from this by bleaching and purifying and used for candles, in modeling, as a basis of polishes, and for other purposes. **3** any similar substance, e.g., earwax. **4** *colloq.* **a** a phonograph record. **b** material for the manufacture of this. **5** (*attrib.*) made of wax. • *v.tr.* **1** cover or treat with wax. **2** *colloq.* record for the phonograph. □□ **wax·er** *n.* [OE *wæx, weax* f. Gmc]

wax² /waks/ *v.intr.* **1** (of the moon between new and full) have a progressively larger part of its visible surface illuminated, increasing in apparent size. **2** become larger or stronger. **3** pass into a specified state or mood (*wax lyrical*). □ **wax and wane** undergo alternate increases and decreases. [OE *weaxan* f. Gmc]

wax³ /waks/ *n.* *Brit. sl.* a fit of anger. [19th c.: orig. uncert.: perh. f. WAX² *wroth,* etc.]

wax bean *n.* a yellow-podded snap bean.

wax·ber·ry /wáksbəree/ *n.* (*pl.* **–ries**) **1** a wax myrtle. **2** the fruit of this.

wax·bill /wáksbil/ *n.* any of various birds esp. of the family Estrildidae, with usu. red bills resembling the color of sealing wax.

wax·cloth /wáksklawth, –kloth/ *n.* *Brit.* oilcloth.

wax·en /wáksən/ *adj.* **1** having a smooth pale translucent surface as of wax. **2** able to receive impressions like wax; plastic. **3** *archaic* made of wax.

wax light *n.* a taper or candle of wax.

wax myr·tle *n.* a tree, *Myrtus cerifera,* yielding wax and oil used for candles.

wax palm *n.* **1** a South American palm, *Ceroxylon alpinum,* with its stem coated in a mixture of resin and wax. **2** a carnauba.

wax pa·per *n.* (also **waxed pa·per**) paper waterproofed with a layer of wax.

wax·wing /wákswing/ *n.* any bird of the genus *Bombycilla,* with small tips like red sealing wax to some wing feathers.

wax·work /wákswərk/ *n.* **1 a** an object, esp. a lifelike dummy, modeled in wax. **b** the making of waxworks. **2** (in *pl.*) an exhibition of wax dummies.

wax·y¹ /wáksee/ *adj.* (**wax·i·er, wax·i·est**) resembling wax in consistency or in its surface. □□ **wax·i·ly** *adv.* **wax·i·ness** *n.* [WAX¹ + –Y¹]

wax·y² /wáksee/ *adj.* (**wax·i·er, wax·i·est**) *Brit. sl.* angry; quick-tempered. [WAX³ + –Y¹]

way /way/ *n. & adv.* • *n.* **1** a road, track, path, etc., for passing along. **2** a course or route for reaching a place, esp. the best one (*asked the way to Rockefeller Center*). **3** a place of passage into a building, through a door, etc. (*could not find the way out*). **4** a method or plan for attaining an object (*that is not the way to do it*). **b** the ability to obtain one's object (*has a way with him*). **5 a** a person's desired or chosen course of action. **b** a custom or manner of behaving; a personal peculiarity (*has a way of forgetting things; things had a way of going badly*). **6** a specific manner of life or procedure (*soon got into the way of it*). **7** the normal course of events (*that is always the way*). **8** a traveling distance; a length traversed or to be traversed (*is a long way away*). **9** an unimpeded opportunity of advance. **b** a space free of obstacles. **10** a region or ground over which advance is desired or natural. **11** advance in some direction; impetus; progress (*pushed my way through*). **12** movement of a ship, etc. (*gather way; lose way*). **13** the state of being engaged in movement from place to place; time spent in this (*met them on the way home; with songs to speed them on their way*). **14** a specified direction (*step this way; which way are you going?*). **15** (in *pl.*) parts into which a thing is divided (*split it three ways*). **16** *Brit. colloq.* the scope or range of something (*want a few things in the stationery way*). **17** a person's line of occupation or business. **18** a specified condition or state (*things are in a bad way*). **19** a respect (*is useful in some ways*). **20 a** (in *pl.*) a structure of lumber, etc., down which a new ship is launched. **b** parallel rails, etc., as a track for the movement of a machine. • *adv. colloq.* to a considerable extent; far (*you're way off the mark*). □ **across** (or **over**) **the way** opposite. **any way** = ANYWAY. **be on one's way** set off; depart. **by the way 1** incidentally; as a more or less irrelevant comment. **2** during a journey. **by way of 1** through; by means of. **2** as a substitute for or as a form of (*did it by way of apology*). **3** with the intention of (*asked by way of discovering the truth*). **come one's way** become available to one; become one's lot. **find a way** discover a means of obtaining one's object. **get** (or **have**) **one's way** (or **have it one's own way,** etc.) get what one wants; ensure one's wishes are met. **give way 1 a** make concessions. **b** fail to resist; yield. **2** (often foll. by *to*) concede precedence (to). **3** (of a structure, etc.) be dislodged or broken under a load; collapse. **4** (foll. by *to*) be superseded by. **5** (foll. by *to*) be overcome by (an emotion, etc.). **6** (of rowers) row hard. **go out of one's way** (often foll. by *to* + infin.) make a special effort; act gratuitously or without compulsion (*went out of their way to help*). **go on one's own way** act independently, esp. against contrary advice. **go one's way** **1** leave; depart. **2** (of events, circumstances, etc.) be favorable to one. **go a person's way** accompany a person (*are you going my way?*). **have it both ways** see BOTH. **in its way** if regarded from a particular standpoint appropriate to it. **in no way** not at all; by no means. **in a way** in a certain respect but not altogether or completely. **in the** (or **one's**) **way** forming an obstacle or hindrance. **lead the way** **1** act as guide or leader. **2** show how to do something. **look the other way** **1** ignore what one should notice. **2** disregard an acquaintance, etc., whom one sees. **one way and another** taking various considerations into account. **one way or another** by some means. **on the** (or **one's**) **way** **1** in the course of a journey, etc. **2** having progressed (*is well on the way to completion*); in the pipeline. **3** *colloq.* (of a child) conceived but not yet born. **on the way out** *colloq.* going down in status, estimation, or favor; going out of fashion. **the other way around** (or **about**) in an inverted or reversed position or direction. **out of the way** **1** no longer an obstacle or hindrance. **2** disposed of; settled. **3** (of a person) imprisoned or killed. **4** uncommon; remarkable; seldom met with (*nothing out of the way*). **5** (of a place) remote; inaccessible. **out of one's way** not on one's intended route. **put a person in the way of** give a person the opportunity of. **way back** *colloq.* long ago. **way of life** the principles or habits governing all one's actions, etc. **way of thinking** one's customary opinion of matters. **way of the world** conduct no worse than is customary. [OE *weg* f. Gmc: (adv.) f. AWAY]

-way /way/ *suffix* = –WAYS.

way•back /wáybak/ *n.* esp. *Austral.* = OUTBACK.

way•bill /wáybil/ *n.* a list of goods being shipped on a vehicle.

way•far•er /wáyfairǝr/ *n.* a traveler, esp. on foot.

way•far•ing /wáyfairing/ *n.* traveling, esp. on foot.

way•far•ing tree *n.* a white-flowered European and Asian shrub, *Viburnum lantana*, common along roadsides, with berries turning from green through red to black.

way•lay /waylay/ *v.tr.* (*past* and *past part.* **way•laid**) **1** lie in wait for. **2** stop to rob or interview. □□ **way•lay•er** *n.*

way•leave /wáyleev/ *n.* a right of way granted over another's property.

way•mark /wáymaark/ *n. Brit.* a natural or artificial object as a guide to travelers, esp. walkers.

Way of the Cross *n.* the series of stations of the cross (see STATION).

way-out *adj. colloq.* **1** unusual; eccentric. **2** avant-garde; progressive. **3** excellent; exciting.

-ways /wayz/ *suffix* forming adjectives and adverbs of direction or manner (*sideways*) (cf. –WISE). [WAY + –'s]

ways and means *n.* **1** methods of achieving something. **2** methods of raising government revenue.

way•side /wáysīd/ *n.* **1** the side or margin of a road. **2** the land at the side of a road. □ **fall by the wayside** fail to continue in an endeavor or undertaking (after Luke 8:5).

way sta•tion *n.* **1** a minor station on a railroad. **2** a point marking progress in a certain course of action, etc.

way•ward /wáywǝrd/ *adj.* **1** childishly self-willed or perverse; capricious. **2** unaccountable or freakish. □□ **way•ward•ly** *adv.* **way•ward•ness** *n.* [ME f. obs. *awayward* turned away f. AWAY + –WARD: cf. FROWARD]

way•worn /wáywawrn/ *adj.* tired with travel.

Wb *abbr.* weber(s).

WC *abbr.* **1** *Brit.* water closet. **2** West Central (London postal district). **3** without charge.

we /wee/ *pron.* (*obj.* **us**; *poss.* **our, ours**) **1** (*pl.* of I[2]) used by and with reference to more than one person speaking or writing, or one such person and one or more associated persons. **2** used for or by a royal person in a proclamation, etc., and by a writer or editor in a formal context. **3** people in general (cf. ONE *pron.* 2). **4** *colloq.* = I[2] (*give us a chance*). **5** *colloq.* (often implying condescension) you (*how are we feeling today?*). [OE f. Gmc]

weak /week/ *adj.* **1** deficient in strength, power, or number; fragile; easily broken or bent or defeated. **2** deficient in vigor; sickly; feeble (*weak health; a weak imagination*). **3 a** deficient in resolution; easily led (*a weak character*). **b** (of an action or features) indicating a lack of resolution (*a weak surrender; a weak chin*). **4** unconvincing or logically deficient (*weak evidence; a weak argument*). **5** (of a mixed liquid or solution) watery; thin; dilute (*weak tea*). **6** (of a style, etc.) not vigorous nor well-knit; diffuse; slipshod. **7** (of a crew) short-handed. **8** (of a syllable, etc.) unstressed. **9** *Gram.* in Germanic languages: **a** (of a verb) forming inflections by the addition of a suffix to the stem. **b** (of a noun or adjective) belonging to a declension in which the stem originally ended in –*n* (opp. STRONG *adj.* 22). □□ **weak•ish** *adj.* [ME f. ON *veikr* f. Gmc]

weak•en /weékǝn/ *v.* **1** *tr. & intr.* make or become weak or weaker. **2** *intr.* relent; give way; succumb to temptation, etc. □□ **weak•en•er** *n.*

weak end•ing *n.* an unstressed syllable in a normally stressed place at the end of a verse line.

weak•er sex *n. derog.* women.

weak•fish /weékfish/ *n.* (*pl.* same or **–fish•es**) a marine fish of the genus *Cynoscion*, used as food. [obs. Du. *weekvisch* f. *week* soft (formed as WEAK) + *visch* FISH[1]]

weak grade *n. Gram.* an unstressed ablaut form.

weak•ling /weékling/ *n.* a feeble person or animal.

weak in•ter•ac•tion *n. Physics* the weakest form of interaction between elementary particles.

weak-kneed *adj. colloq.* lacking resolution.

weak•ly /weéklee/ *adv. & adj.* ● *adv.* in a weak manner. ● *adj.* (**weak•li•er, weak•li•est**) sickly; not robust. □□ **weak•li•ness** *n.*

weak-mind•ed *adj.* **1** mentally deficient. **2** lacking in resolution. □□ **weak-mind•ed•ness** *n.* the state of being weak-minded.

weak mo•ment *n.* a time when one is unusually compliant or temptable.

weak•ness /weéknis/ *n.* **1** the state or condition of being weak. **2** a weak point; a defect. **3** the inability to resist a particular temptation. **4** (foll. by *for*) a self-indulgent liking (*have a weakness for chocolate*).

weak point *n.* (also **weak spot**) **1** a place where defenses are assailable. **2** a flaw in an argument or character or in resistance to temptation.

weal[1] /weel/ *n. & v.* ● *n.* a ridge raised on the flesh by a stroke of a rod or whip. ● *v.tr.* mark with a weal. [var. of WALE, infl. by obs. *wheal* suppurate]

weal[2] /weel/ *n. literary* welfare; prosperity; good fortune. [OE *wela* f. WG (as WELL[1])]

Weald /weeld/ *n.* (also **weald**) (prec. by *the*) *Brit.* a formerly wooded district including parts of Kent, Surrey, and East Sussex. [OE, = *wald* WOLD]

weald clay *n.* beds of clay, sandstone, limestone, and ironstone, forming the top of Wealden strata, with abundant fossil remains.

wealth /welth/ *n.* **1** riches; abundant possessions; opulence. **2** the state of being rich. **3** (foll. by *of*) an abundance or profusion (*a wealth of new material*). **4** *archaic* welfare or prosperity. [ME *welthe*, f. WELL[1] or WEAL[2] + –TH[2], after *health*]

wealth•y /wélthee/ *adj.* (**wealth•i•er, wealth•i•est**) having an abundance esp. of money. □□ **wealth•i•ly** *adv.* **wealth•i•ness** *n.*

SYNONYM TIP **wealthy**

AFFLUENT, FLUSH, OPULENT, PROSPEROUS, RICH, WELL-TO-DO. If you have more money, possessions, or property than is necessary to satisfy normal needs, you are **rich**. If you're *rich* and are also an established and prominent member of the community whose lifestyle is in keeping with your income, you are **wealthy** (*a wealthy family whose influence on public opinion could not be ignored*). **Affluent** comes from the Latin word meaning to flow, and it connotes a generous income (*an affluent neighborhood*), while **opulent** suggests lavish spending or an ostentatious display of wealth (*an opulent mansion with every luxury*). One may come from an *affluent* family, in other words, and not have a particularly *opulent* lifestyle. If you're **prosperous**, you are thriving or flourishing (*a prosperous merchant; a prosperous business*). While *prosperous* suggests an economic situation that is on the rise, **flush** means having plenty of money on hand at a particular time (*she was feeling flush after receiving her first paycheck*). **Well-to-do** implies a comfortable income, enough to support easy living but not necessarily enough to be considered *rich* (*they were known as a well-to-do family with a strong commitment to educating their children*).

wean[1] /ween/ *v.tr.* **1** accustom (an infant or other young mammal) to food other than (esp. its mother's) milk. **2** (often foll. by *from, away from*) disengage (from a habit, etc.) by enforced discontinuance. [OE *wenian* accustom f. Gmc: cf. WONT]

SYNONYM TIP **weak**

DEBILITATED, DECREPIT, FEEBLE, ● FRAIL, INFIRM. Someone who is **weak** lacks physical, mental, or moral strength (*a weak heart; a weak excuse; too weak to resist temptation*). But there's nothing to suggest what the cause of this lack of strength might be. Someone who is **frail**, on the other hand, is *weak* because he or she has a slight build or delicate constitution (*a small, frail man*). Calling someone **feeble** implies that his or her weakness is pitiable (*too feeble to get out of bed*); when applied to things, *feeble* means faint or inadequate (*a feeble light*). **Infirm** suggests a loss of strength or soundness, as from aging or illness (*poverty and illness had made him infirm*). **Debilitated** and **decrepit** also suggest that strength once present has been lost. But while someone who is young may be *debilitated* by disease, *decrepit* specifically refers to a loss of strength due to advanced age or long use (*a decrepit old woman who seldom left her house; a decrepit building that would soon be torn down*).

wean[2] /ween/ *n. Sc.* a young child. [contr. of *wee ane* little one]

wean•er /weenər/ *n.* a young animal recently weaned.

wean•ling /weenling/ *n.* a newly weaned child, etc.

weap•on /wépən/ *n.* **1** a thing designed or used or usable for inflicting bodily harm (e.g., a gun or a knife). **2** a means employed for trying to gain the advantage in a conflict (*irony is a double-edged weapon*). □□ **weap•oned** *adj.* (also in *comb.*). **weap•on•less** *adj.* [OE *wǣp(e)n* f. Gmc]

weap•on•ry /wépənree/ *n.* weapons collectively.

wear[1] /wair/ *v. & n.* • *v.* (*past wore* /wawr/; *past part.* **worn** /wawrn/) **1** *tr.* have on one's person as clothing or an ornament, etc. (*is wearing shorts; wears earrings*). **2** *tr.* be dressed habitually in (*wears green*). **3** *tr.* exhibit or present (a facial expression or appearance) (*wore a frown; the day wore a different aspect*). **4** *tr. Brit. colloq.* (usu. with *neg.*) tolerate; accept (*they won't wear that excuse*). **5** (often foll. by *away, down*) **a** *tr.* injure the surface of, or partly obliterate or alter, by rubbing, stress, or use. **b** *intr.* undergo such injury or change. **6** *tr. & intr.* (foll. by *off, away*) rub or be rubbed off. **7** *tr.* make (a hole, etc.) by constant rubbing or dripping, etc. **8** *tr. & intr.* (often foll. by *out*) exhaust; tire or be tired. **9** *tr.* (foll. by *down*) overcome by persistence. **10** *intr.* **a** remain for a specified time in working order or a presentable state; last long. **b** (foll. by *well, badly*, etc.) endure continued use or life. **11 a** *intr.* (of time) pass, esp. tediously. **b** *tr.* pass (time) gradually away. **12** *tr.* (of a ship) fly (a flag). • *n.* **1** the act of wearing or the state of being worn (*suitable for informal wear*). **2** things worn; fashionable or suitable clothing (*sportswear; footwear*). **3** (in full **wear and tear**) damage sustained from continuous use. **4** the capacity for resisting wear and tear (*still a great deal of wear left in it*). □ **in wear** being regularly worn. **wear one's heart on one's sleeve** see HEART. **wear off** lose effectiveness or intensity. **wear out 1** use or be used until no longer usable. **2** tire or be tired out. **wear the pants** see PANTS. **wear thin** of patience, excuses, etc.) begin to fail. **wear (or wear one's years) well** *colloq.* remain young-looking. □□ **wear•a•ble** *adj.* **wear•a•bil•i•ty** /wáirəbilteeʾ/ *n.* **wear•er** *n.* **wear•ing** *adj.* **wear•ing•ly** *adv.* [OE *werian* f. Gmc]

wear[2] /wair/ *v.* (*past* and *past part.* **wore** /wawr/) **1** *tr.* bring (a ship) about by turning its head away from the wind. **2** *intr.* (of a ship) come about in this way (cf. TACK[1] *v.* 4a). [17th c.: orig. unkn.]

wea•ri•some /weereesəm/ *adj.* tedious; tiring by monotony or length. □□ **wea•ri•some•ly** *adv.* **wea•ri•some•ness** *n.*

wea•ry /weeree/ *adj. & v.* • *adj.* (**wea•ri•er**, **wea•ri•est**) **1** unequal to or disinclined for further exertion or endurance; tired. **2** (foll. by *of*) dismayed at the continuing of; impatient of. **3** tiring or tedious. • *v.* (**–ries**, **–ried**) **1** *tr. & intr.* make or grow weary. **2** *intr. esp. Sc.* long. □□ **wea•ri•less** *adj.* **wea•ri•ly** *adv.* **wea•ri•ness** *n.* **wea•ry•ing•ly** *adv.* [OE *wērig, wǣrig* f. WG]

wea•sel /weezəl/ *n. & v.* • *n.* **1** a small, reddish-brown, flesh-eating mammal, *Mustela nivalis*, with a slender body, related to the stoat and ferret. **2** a stoat. **3** *colloq.* a deceitful or treacherous person. • *v.intr.* **1** equivocate or quibble. **2** (foll. by *on, out*) default on an obligation. □□ **wea•sel•ly** *adj.* [OE *wesle, wesule* f. WG]

wea•sel-faced *adj.* having thin sharp features.

wea•sel word *n.* (usu. in *pl.*) a word that is intentionally ambiguous or misleading.

weath•er /wéthər/ *n. & v.* • *n.* **1** the state of the atmosphere at a place and time as regards heat, cloudiness, dryness, sunshine, wind, and rain, etc. **2** (*attrib.*) *Naut.* windward (*on the weather side*). • *v.* **1** *tr.* expose to or affect by atmospheric changes, esp. deliberately to dry, season, etc. (*weathered shingles*). **2 a** *tr.* (usu. in *passive*) discolor or partly disintegrate (rock or stones) by exposure to air. **b** *intr.* be discolored or worn in this way. **3** *tr.* make (boards or tiles) overlap downward to keep out rain, etc. **4** *tr.* **a** come safely through (a storm). **b** survive (a difficult period, etc.). **5** *tr.* (of a ship or its crew) get to the windward of (a cape, etc.). □ **keep a** (or **one's**) **weather eye open** be watchful. **make good** (or **bad**) **weather of it** *Naut.* (of a ship) behave well (or badly) in a storm. **make heavy weather of** *colloq.* exaggerate the difficulty or burden presented by (a problem, course of action, etc.). **under the weather** *colloq.* indisposed or out of sorts; drunk. [OE *weder* f. Gmc]

weath•er-beat•en *adj.* affected by exposure to the weather.

weath•er•board /wéthərbawrd/ *n. & v.* • *n. Brit.* clapboard; siding. • *v.tr.* fit or supply with weatherboards. □□ **weath•er•board•ing** *n.* **weath•er•board•ed** *adj.*

weath•er-bound *adj.* unable to proceed owing to bad weather.

weath•er•cock /wéthərkok/ *n.* **1** a weather vane (see VANE) in the form of a cock. **2** an inconstant person.

weath•er fore•cast *n.* an analysis of the state of the weather with an assessment of likely developments over a certain time.

weath•er•glass /wéthərglas/ *n.* a simple barometer or hygroscope.

weath•er•ing /wéthəring/ *n.* **1** the action of the weather on materials, etc., exposed to it. **2** exposure to adverse weather conditions (see WEATHER *v.* 1).

weath•er•ly /wéthərlee/ *adj. Naut.* **1** (of a ship) making little leeway. **2** capable of keeping close to the wind. □□ **weath•er•li•ness** *n.*

weath•er•man /wéthərman/ *n.* (*pl.* **–men**) a meteorologist, esp. one who broadcasts a weather forecast.

weath•er map *n.* a diagram showing the state of the weather over a large area.

weath•er•proof /wéthərproof/ *adj. & v.* • *adj.* resistant to the effects of bad weather, esp. rain. • *v.tr.* make weatherproof. □□ **weath•er•proofed** *adj.*

weath•er side *n.* the side from which the wind is blowing (opp. *lee side*).

weath•er sta•tion *n.* an observation post for recording meteorological data.

weath•er strip *n.* (also **weath•er strip•ping**) a piece of material used to make a door or window proof against rain or wind. □□ **weath•er-strip** *v.*

weath•er vane see VANE.

weath•er-worn /wéthərwawrn/ *adj.* damaged by exposure to weather.

weave[1] /weev/ *v. & n.* • *v.* (*past wove* /wōv/; *past part.* **wo•ven** /wóvən/ or **wove**) **1** *tr.* **a** form (fabric) by interlacing long threads in two directions. **b** form (thread) into fabric in this way. **2** *intr.* **a** make fabric in this way. **b** work at a loom. **3** *tr.* make (a basket or wreath, etc.) by interlacing rushes or flowers, etc. **4** *tr.* **a** (foll. by *into*) make (facts, etc.) into a story or connected whole. **b** make (a story) in this way. • *n.* a style of weaving. [OE *wefan* f. Gmc]

weave[2] /weev/ *v.intr.* **1** move repeatedly from side to side; take an intricate course to avoid obstructions. **2** *colloq.* maneuver an aircraft in this way; take evasive action. □ **get weaving** *Brit. sl.* begin action; hurry. [prob. f. ME *weve*, var. of *waive* f. ON *veifa* WAVE]

weav•er /weevər/ *n.* **1** a person whose occupation is weaving. **2** = WEAVERBIRD.

weav•er•bird /weevərbərd/ *n.* any tropical bird of the family Ploceidae, building elaborately woven nests.

weav•er's knot *n.* (also **weav•er's hitch**) a sheet bend (see SHEET[2]) used in weaving.

web /web/ *n. & v.* • *n.* **1 a** a woven fabric. **b** an amount woven in one piece. **2** a complete structure or connected series (*a web of lies*). **3** a cobweb, gossamer, or a similar product of a spinning creature. **4 a** a membrane between the toes of a swimming animal or bird. **b** the vane of a bird's feather. **5 a** a large roll of paper used in a continuous printing process. **b** an endless wire mesh on rollers, on which this is made. **6** a thin, flat part connecting thicker or more solid parts in machinery, etc. • *v.* (**webbed, web•bing**) **1** *tr.* weave a web on. **2** *intr.* weave a web. □□ **webbed** *adj.* [OE *web, webb* f. Gmc]

web•bing /wébing/ *n.* strong, narrow, closely woven fabric used for supporting upholstery, for belts, etc.

web•er /wébər, váybər/ *n.* the SI unit of magnetic flux, causing the electromotive force of one volt in a circuit of one turn when generated or removed in one second. ¶ Abbr.: **Wb**. [W. E. *Weber*, Ger. physicist d. 1891]

web-foot•ed *adj.* having the toes connected by webs.

web-off•set *n.* offset printing on a web of paper.

web•worm /wébwərm/ *n.* a gregarious caterpillar spinning a large web in which to sleep or to feed on enclosed foliage.

Wed. *abbr.* Wednesday.

wed /wed/ *v.* (**wed•ding**; *past* and *past part.* **wed•ded** or **wed**) **1** usu. *formal* or *literary* **a** *tr. & intr.* marry. **b** *tr.* join in marriage. **2** *tr.* unite (*wed efficiency to economy*). **3** *tr.* (as **wedded** *adj.*) of or in marriage (*wedded bliss*). **4** *tr.* (as **wedded** *adj.*) (foll. by *to*) obstinately attached or devoted (to a pursuit, etc.). [OE *weddian* to pledge f. Gmc]

we'd /weed/ *contr.* **1** we had. **2** we should; we would.

wed•ding /wéding/ *n.* a marriage ceremony (considered by itself or with the associated celebrations). [OE *weddung* (as WED, –ING[1])]

wed•ding cake *n.* a rich iced cake served at a wedding reception.

wed•ding day *n.* the day or anniversary of a wedding.

wed•ding march *n.* a march played at the entrance of the bride or the exit of the couple at a wedding.

wed•ding night *n.* the night after a wedding (esp. with ref. to its consummation).

wed•ding ring *n.* (also **wed•ding band**) a ring worn by a married person.

wedge[1] /wej/ *n. & v.* • *n.* **1** a piece of wood or metal, etc., tapering to a sharp edge, that is driven between two objects or parts of an object to secure or separate them; a thing separating two people or groups of people. **2** anything resembling a wedge (*a wedge of cheese; troops formed a wedge*). **3** a golf club with a wedge-shaped head. **4 a** a wedge-shaped heel. **b** a shoe with this. • *v.tr.* **1** tighten, secure, or fasten by means of a wedge (*wedged the door open*). **2** force open or apart with a wedge. **3** (foll. by *in, into*) pack or thrust (a thing or oneself) tightly in or into. □ **thin end of the wedge** esp. *Brit. colloq.* an action or procedure of little importance in itself, but likely to lead to more serious developments. □□ **wedge•like** *adj.* **wedge•wise** *adv.* [OE *wecg* f. Gmc]

wedge² /wej/ *v.tr.* *Pottery* prepare (clay) for use by cutting, kneading, and throwing down. [17th c.: orig. uncert.]

wedge-shaped *adj.* **1** shaped like a solid wedge. **2** V-shaped.

wedg·ie /wéjee/ *n.* *colloq.* **1** a shoe with an extended wedge-shaped heel. **2** the condition of having one's underwear, etc., wedged between one's buttocks.

Wedg·wood /wéjwŏŏd/ *n.* *Trademark* **1** ceramic ware made by J. Wedgwood, Engl. potter d. 1795, and his successors, esp. a kind of fine stoneware usu. with a white cameo design. **2** the characteristic blue color of this stoneware.

wed·lock /wédlok/ *n.* the married state. □ **born in** (or **out of**) **wedlock** born of married (or unmarried) parents. [OE *wedlāc* marriage vow f. *wed* pledge (rel. to WED) + *-lāc* suffix denoting action]

Wednes·day /wénzday, –dee/ *n. & adv.* ● *n.* the fourth day of the week, following Tuesday. ● *adv. colloq.* **1** on Wednesday. **2** (**Wednesdays**) on Wednesdays; each Wednesday. [ME *wednesdei*, OE *wōdnesdæg* day of (the god) Odin]

Weds. *abbr.* Wednesday.

wee¹ /wee/ *adj.* (**we·er** /weéər/; **we·est** /weéist/) **1** esp. *Sc.* little; very small. **2** *colloq.* tiny; extremely small (*a wee bit*). [orig. Sc. noun, f. north.ME *wei* (small) quantity f. Anglian *wēg*: cf. WEY]

wee² /wee/ *n.* esp. *Brit. sl.* = WEEWEE.

weed /weed/ *n. & v.* ● *n.* **1** a wild plant growing where it is not wanted. **2** a thin, weak-looking person or horse. **3** (*prec. by the*) *sl.* **a** marijuana. **b** tobacco. ● *v.* **1** *tr.* **a** clear (an area) of weeds. **b** remove unwanted parts from. **2** *tr.* (foll. by *out*) sort out (inferior or unwanted parts, etc.) for removal. **b** rid (a quantity or company) of inferior or unwanted members, etc. **3** *intr.* cut off or uproot weeds. □□ **weed·er** *n.* **weed·less** *adj.* [OE *wēod*, of unkn. orig.]

weed-kill·er *n.* a substance used to destroy weeds; herbicide.

weeds /weedz/ *n.pl.* (in full **widow's weeds**) *Brit. archaic* deep mourning worn by a widow. [OE *wǣd(e)* garment f. Gmc]

weed·y /weédee/ *adj.* (**weed·i·er**, **weed·i·est**) **1** having many weeds. **2** (esp. of a person) **a** weak; feeble; of poor stature. **b** very thin; lanky. □□ **weed·i·ness** *n.*

week /week/ *n.* **1** a period of seven days reckoned usu. from midnight on Saturday to midnight on Sunday. **2** a period of seven days reckoned from any point (*would like to stay for a week*). **3** the six days between Sundays. **4 a** the five days Monday to Friday. **b** a normal amount of work done in this period (*a 35-hour week*). **5** (in *pl.*) a long time; several weeks (*have not seen you for weeks*; *did it weeks ago*). **6** esp. *Brit.* (prec. by a specified day) a week after (that day) (*Tuesday week*; *tomorrow week*). [OE *wice* f. Gmc, prob. orig. = sequence]

week·day /weékday/ *n.* a day other than Sunday or other than at a weekend (often *attrib.*: *a weekday afternoon*).

week·end /weékénd/ *n. & v.* ● *n.* **1** the end of a week, esp. Saturday and Sunday. **2** this period extended slightly esp. for a vacation or visit, etc. (*going away for the weekend*; *a weekend cottage*). ● *v.intr.* spend a weekend (*decided to weekend in the country*).

week·end·er /weékéndər/ *n.* **1** a person who spends weekends away from home. **2** a weekend traveling bag.

week·long /weéklawng, lóng/ *adj.* lasting for a week.

week·ly /weéklee/ *adj., adv., & n.* ● *adj.* done, produced, or occurring once a week. ● *adv.* once a week; from week to week. ● *n.* (*pl.* **–lies**) a weekly newspaper or periodical.

ween /ween/ *v.tr. archaic* be of the opinion; think; suppose. [OE *wēnan* f. Gmc]

wee·ny /weénee/ *adj.* (**wee·ni·er**, **wee·ni·est**) *colloq.* tiny. □ **weeny-bopper** esp. *Brit.* a girl like a teenybopper but younger. [WEE¹ after *tiny*, *teeny*]

weep /weep/ *v. & n.* ● *v.* (*past* and *past part.* **wept** /wept/) **1** *intr.* shed tears. **2 a** *tr. &* (foll. by *for*) *intr.* shed tears for; bewail; lament over. **b** *tr.* utter or express with tears (*"Don't go," he wept; wept her thanks*). **3 a** *intr.* be covered with or send forth drops. **b** *intr. & tr.* come or send forth in drops; exude liquid (*weeping sore*). **4** *intr.* (as **weeping** *adj.*) (of a tree) having drooping branches (*weeping willow*). ● *n.* a fit or spell of weeping. □ **weep out** esp. *Brit.* utter with tears. □□ **weep·ing·ly** *adv.* [OE *wēpan* f. Gmc (prob. imit.)]

weep·er /weépər/ *n.* **1** a person who weeps, esp. *hist.* a hired mourner at a funeral. **2** a small image of a mourner on a monument. **3** (in *pl.*) **a** a man's crepe hatband for funerals. **b** a widow's black crepe veil or white cuffs.

weep·ie /weépee/ *n.* (also **weep·y**) (*pl.* **–ies**) *colloq.* a sentimental or emotional motion picture, play, etc; tearjerker.

weep·y /weépee/ *adj.* (**weep·i·er**, **weep·i·est**) *colloq.* inclined to weep; tearful. □□ **weep·i·ly** *adv.* **weep·i·ness** *n.*

wee·ver /weévər/ *n.* any marine fish of the genus *Trachinus*, with sharp venomous dorsal spines. [perh. f. OF *wivre*, *guivre*, serpent, dragon, f. L *vipera* VIPER]

wee·vil /weévil/ *n.* **1** any destructive beetle of the family Curculionidae, with its head extended into a beak or rostrum and feeding upon or on grain. **2** any insect damaging stored grain. □□ **wee·vil·y** *adj.* [ME f. MLG *wevel* f. Gmc]

wee-wee /weéwee/ *n. & v.* ● *n.* **1** the act or an instance of urinating. **2** urine. ● *v.intr.* (**–wees**, **–weed**, **–wee·ing**) urinate. [20th c.: orig. unkn.]

weft /weft/ *n.* **1 a** the threads woven across a warp to make fabric. **b** yarn for these. **c** a thing woven. **2** filling strips in basket weaving. [OE *weft(a)* f. Gmc: rel. to WEAVE¹]

Wehr·macht /váirmaakht/ *n. hist.* the German armed forces, esp. the army, from 1921 to 1945. [G, = defensive force]

weigh¹ /way/ *v.* **1** *tr.* find the weight of. **2** *tr.* balance in the hands to guess or as if to guess the weight of. **3** *tr.* (often foll. by *out*) **a** take a definite weight of; take a specified weight from a larger quantity. **b** distribute in exact amounts by weight. **4** *tr.* **a** estimate the relative value, importance, or desirability of; consider with a view to choice, rejection, or preference (*weighed the consequences*; *weighed the merits of the candidates*). **b** (foll. by *with*, *against*) compare (one consideration with another). **5** *tr.* be equal to (a specified weight) (*weighs three pounds*). **6** *intr.* **a** have (esp. a specified) importance; exert an influence. **b** (foll. by *with*) be regarded as important by (*the point that weighs with me*). **7** *intr.* (often foll. by *on*) be heavy or burdensome (to); be depressing (to). □ **weigh anchor** see ANCHOR. **weigh down 1** bring or keep down by exerting weight. **2** be oppressive or burdensome to (*weighed down with worries*). **weigh in** (of a boxer before a contest, or a jockey after a race) be weighed. **weigh into** *colloq.* attack (physically or verbally). **weigh in with** *colloq.* advance (an argument, etc.) assertively or boldly. **weigh up** *colloq.* form an estimate of; consider carefully. **weigh one's words** carefully choose the way one expresses something. □□ **weigh·a·ble** *adj.* **weigh·er** *n.*

WORD HISTORY weigh¹

Old English *wegan*, of Germanic origin; related to Dutch *wegen* 'weigh,' German *bewegen* 'move,' from an Indo-European root shared by Latin *vehere* 'convey.' Early senses included 'transport from one place to another' and 'raise up' (as in *weigh anchor*).

---

weigh² /way/ *n.* □ **under weigh** *disp.* = *under way.* [18th c.: from an erron. assoc. with *weigh anchor*]

weigh·bridge /wáybrij/ *n.* a platform scale for weighing vehicles, usu. having a plate set into the road for vehicles to drive on to.

weigh-in *n.* the weighing of a boxer, etc., before a fight.

weight /wayt/ *n. & v.* ● *n.* **1** *Physics* **a** the force experienced by a body as a result of the earth's gravitation (cf. MASS¹ n. 8). **b** any similar force with which a body tends to a center of attraction. **2** the heaviness of a body regarded as a property of it; its relative mass or the quantity of matter contained by it giving rise to a downward force (*is twice your weight*; *kept in position by its weight*). **3 a** the quantitative expression of a body's weight (*has a weight of three pounds*). **b** a scale of such weights (*troy weight*). **4** a body of a known weight for use in weighing. **5** a heavy body esp. used in a mechanism, etc. (*a clock worked by weights*). **6** a load or burden (*a weight off my mind*). **7 a** influence; importance (*carried weight with the public*). **b** preponderance (*the weight of evidence was against them*). **8** a heavy object thrown as an athletic exercise; = SHOT¹ 7. **9** the surface density of cloth, etc., as a measure of its suitability. ● *v.tr.* **1 a** attach a weight to. **b** hold down with a weight or weights. **2** (foll. by *with*) impede or burden. **3** *Statistics* multiply the components of (an average) by factors to take account of their importance. **4** assign a handicap weight to (a horse). **5** treat (a fabric) with a mineral, etc., to make it seem stouter. □ **put on weight 1** increase one's weight. **2** get fat. **throw one's weight about** (or **around**) *colloq.* be unpleasantly self-assertive. **worth one's weight in gold** (of a person) exceedingly useful or helpful. [OE (*ge*)*wiht* f. Gmc: cf. WEIGH¹]

weight·less /wáytlis/ *adj.* (of a body, esp. in an orbiting spacecraft, etc.) not apparently acted on by gravity. □□ **weight·less·ly** *adv.* **weight·less·ness** *n.*

weight·lift·ing /wáytlifting/ *n.* the sport or exercise of lifting a heavy weight, esp. a barbell. □□ **weight·lift·er** *n.*

weight·y /wáytee/ *adj.* (**weight·i·er**, **weight·i·est**) **1** weighing much; heavy. **2** momentous; important. **3** (of utterances, etc.) deserving consideration; careful and serious. **4** influential; authoritative. □□ **weight·i·ly** *adv.* **weight·i·ness** *n.*

Wei·mar·an·er /wíməraanər, ví–/ *n.* a usu. gray dog of a variety of pointer used as a hunting dog. [G, f. *Weimar* in Germany, where it was developed]

weir /weer/ *n.* **1** a dam built across a river to raise the level of water upstream or regulate its flow. **2** an enclosure of stakes, etc., set in a stream as a trap for fish. [OE *wer* f. *werian* dam up]

weird /weerd/ *adj. & n.* ● *adj.* **1** uncanny; supernatural. **2** *colloq.* strange; queer; incomprehensible. **3** *archaic* connected with fate. ● *n.* esp. *Sc. archaic* fate; destiny. □□ **weird·ly** *adv.* **weird·ness** *n.* [(earlier as noun) f. OE *wyrd* destiny f. Gmc]

weird·ie /weérdee/ *n.* (also **weird·y**) (*pl.* **–ies**) *colloq.* = WEIRDO.

weird·o /weérdō/ *n.* (*pl.* **–os**) *colloq.* an odd or eccentric person.

Weird Sis·ters *n.pl.* **1** the Fates. **2** witches.

Weis·mann·ism /vísmaanizəm/ *n.* the theory of heredity assuming continuity of germ plasm and nontransmission of acquired characteristics. [A. *Weismann*, Ger. biologist d. 1914]

we·ka /wékə/ *n.* any flightless New Zealand rail of the genus *Gallirallus*. [Maori: imit. of its cry]

Welch /welch, welsh/ var. of WELSH.

welch var. of WELSH.

wel·come /wélkəm/ *n., int., v., & adj.* ● *n.* the act or an instance of greeting or receiving (a person, idea, etc.) gladly; a kind or glad reception (*gave them a warm welcome*). ● *int.* expressing such a greeting (*welcome!*; *welcome home!*). ● *v.tr.* receive with a welcome (*welcomed them home*; *would welcome the opportunity*). ● *adj.* 1 that one receives with pleasure (*a welcome guest*; *welcome news*). 2 (foll. by *to*, or *to* + infin.) a cordially allowed or invited; released of obligation (*you are welcome to use my car*). b iron. gladly given (an unwelcome task, thing, etc.) (*here's my work and you are welcome to it*). □ **make welcome** receive hospitably. **overstay one's welcome** stay as a visitor longer than one is wanted. **you're** (or **you are**) **welcome** there is no need for thanks; your thanks are accepted. □□ **wel·come·ly** *adv.* **wel·come·ness** *n.* **wel·com·er** *n.* **wel·com·ing·ly** *adv.* [orig. OE *wilcuma* one whose coming is pleasing f. *wil-* desire, pleasure + *cuma* comer, with later change to *wel-* WELL[1] after OF *bien venu* or ON *velkominn*]

weld[1] /weld/ *v. & n.* ● *v.tr.* 1 a hammer or press (pieces of iron or other metal usu. heated but not melted) into one piece. b join by fusion with an electric arc, etc. c form by welding into some article. 2 fashion (arguments, members of a group, etc.) into an effectual or homogeneous whole. ● *n.* a welded joint. □□ **weld·a·ble** *adj.* **weld·a·bil·i·ty** /wéldəbílitee/ *n.* **weld·er** *n.* [alt. of WELL[2] *v.* in obs. sense 'melt or weld (heated metal),' prob. infl. by past part.]

weld[2] /weld/ *n.* 1 a plant, *Reseda luteola*, yielding a yellow dye. 2 *hist.* this dye. [ME f. OE *w(e)alde* (unrecorded): cf. MDu. *woude*, MLG *walde*]

wel·fare /wélfair/ *n.* 1 well-being; happiness; health and prosperity (of a person or a community, etc.). 2 a the maintenance of persons in such a condition esp. by statutory procedure or social effort. b financial support given for this purpose. [ME f. WELL[1] + FARE]

wel·fare state *n.* 1 a system whereby the government undertakes to protect the health and well-being of its citizens, esp. those in financial or social need, by means of grants, pensions, etc. 2 a country practicing this system.

wel·far·ism /wélfairizəm/ *n.* principles characteristic of a welfare state. □□ **wel·far·ist** *n.*

wel·kin /wélkin/ *n. poet.* sky; the upper air. [OE *wolcen* cloud, sky]

well[1] /wel/ *adv., adj., & int.* ● *adv.* (**bet·ter**, **best**) 1 in a satisfactory way (*you have worked well*). 2 in the right way (*well said*; *you did well to tell me*). 3 with some talent or distinction (*plays the piano well*). 4 in a kind way (*treated me well*). 5 a thoroughly; carefully (*polish it well*). b intimately; closely (*knew them well*). 6 with heartiness or approval; favorably (*speak well of*; *the book was well reviewed*). 7 probably; reasonably; advisably (*you may well be right*; *you may well ask*; *we might well take the risk*). 8 to a considerable extent (*is well over forty*). 9 successfully; fortunately (*it turned out well*). 10 luckily; opportunely (*well met!*). 11 with a fortunate outcome; without disaster (*were well rid of them*). 12 profitably (*did well for themselves*). 13 comfortably; abundantly; liberally (*we live well here*; *the job pays well*). ● *adj.* (**bet·ter**, **best**) 1 (usu. *predic.*) in good health (*are you well?*; *was not a well person*). 2 (*predic.*) a in a satisfactory state or position (*all is well*). b advisable (*it would be well to inquire*). ● *int.* expressing surprise, resignation, insistence, etc., or resumption or continuation of talk, used esp. after a pause in speaking (*well, I never!*; *well, I suppose so*; *well, who was it?*). □ **as well** 1 in addition; to an equal extent. 2 (also **just as well**) with equal reason; with no loss of advantage or need for regret (*may as well give up*; *it would be just as well to stop now*). **as well as** in addition to. **leave** (or **let**) **well enough alone** avoid needless change or disturbance. **take well** react calmly to (a thing, esp. bad news). **well and good** expressing dispassionate acceptance of a decision, etc. **well and truly** esp. *Brit.* decisively; completely. **well aware** certainly aware (*well aware of the danger*). **well away** 1 having made considerable progress. 2 *Brit. colloq.* fast asleep or drunk. **well worth** certainly worth (*well worth a visit*; *well worth visiting*). [OE *wel*, *well* prob. f. the same stem as WILL[1]]

▶1. A hyphen is normally used in combinations of *well-* when used attributively, but not when used predicatively, e.g., *a well-made coat* but *the coat is well made*. 2. See note at GOOD.

well[2] /wel/ *n. & v.* ● *n.* 1 a shaft sunk into the ground to obtain water, oil, etc. 2 an enclosed space like a well shaft, e.g., in the middle of a building for stairs or an elevator, or for light or ventilation. 3 (foll. by *of*) a source, esp. a copious one (*a well of information*). 4 a a mineral spring. b (in *pl.*) a spa. 5 = INKWELL. 6 *archaic* a water spring or fountain. 7 *Brit.* a railed space for lawyers, etc., in a court of law. 8 a depression for gravy, etc., in a dish or tray, or for a mat in the floor. 9 *Physics* a region of minimum potential, etc. ● *v.intr.* (foll. by *out*, *up*) spring as from a fountain; flow copiously. [OE *wella* (= OHG *wella* wave, ON *vella* boiling heat), *wellan* boil, melt f. Gmc]

we'll /weel, wil/ *contr.* we shall; we will.

well-ac·quaint·ed *adj.* (usu. foll. by *with*) familiar.

well-ad·just·ed *adj.* 1 in a good state of adjustment. 2 *Psychol.* mentally and emotionally stable.

well-ad·vised *adj.* (usu. foll. by *to* + infin.) (of a person) prudent (*would be well-advised to wait*).

well-af·fect·ed *adj.* (often foll. by *to*, *toward*) favorably disposed.

well-ap·point·ed *adj.* having all the necessary equipment.

well-bal·anced *adj.* 1 sane; sensible. 2 equally matched. 3 having a symmetrical or orderly arrangement of parts.

well-behaved *adj.* having good manners or conduct.

well-be·ing *n.* a state of being well, healthy, contented, etc.

well-be·loved *adj. & n.* ● *adj.* dearly loved. ● *n.* (*pl.* same) a dearly loved person.

well-born /wélbáwrn/ *adj.* of wealthy or noble lineage.

well-bred *adj.* having or showing good breeding or manners.

well-built *adj.* 1 of good construction. 2 (of a person) big and strong and well-proportioned.

well-cho·sen *adj.* (of words, etc.) carefully selected for effect.

well-con·di·tioned *adj.* in good physical or moral condition.

well-con·duct·ed *adj.* (of a meeting, etc.) properly organized and controlled.

well-con·nect·ed see CONNECTED.

well-cov·ered *adj. Brit. colloq.* plump; corpulent.

well-de·fined *adj.* clearly indicated or determined.

well-de·served *adj.* rightfully merited or earned.

well-dis·posed *adj.* (often foll. by *toward*) having a good disposition or friendly feeling (for).

well-done *adj.* 1 (of meat, etc.) thoroughly cooked. 2 (of a task, etc.) performed well (also as *int.*).

well-dressed *adj.* fashionably smart.

well-earned *adj.* fully deserved.

well-en·dowed *adj.* 1 well provided with talent, etc. 2 *colloq.* sexually potent or attractive; having large sexual organs.

well-es·tab·lished *adj.* long-standing; familiar; traditional.

well-fa·vored *adj.* good-looking.

well-fed *adj.* having or having had plenty to eat.

well-found *adj.* = WELL-APPOINTED.

well-found·ed *adj.* (of suspicions, etc.) based on good evidence; having a foundation in fact or reason.

well-groomed *adj.* (of a person) with carefully tended hair, clothes, etc.

well-ground·ed *adj.* 1 = WELL-FOUNDED. 2 having a good training in or knowledge of the groundwork of a subject.

well·head /wélhed/ *n.* a source esp. of a spring or stream; a fountainhead.

well-heeled *adj. colloq.* wealthy.

well-hung *adj. colloq.* (of a man) having large genitals.

well-in·formed *adj.* having much knowledge or information about a subject.

Wel·ling·ton /wélingtən/ *n.* (in full **Wellington boot**) *Brit.* a waterproof rubber or plastic boot usu. reaching the knee. [after the 1st Duke of *Wellington*, Brit. general and statesman d. 1852]

well-in·ten·tioned *adj.* having or showing good intentions.

well-judged *adj.* esp. *Brit.* opportunely, skillfully, or discreetly done.

well-kept *adj.* kept in good order or condition.

well-knit *adj.* closely related; compact; not loosely constructed nor sprawling (*a well-knit family*; *a well-knit physique*).

well-known *adj.* 1 known to many. 2 known thoroughly.

well-made *adj.* 1 strongly or skillfully manufactured. 2 (of a person or animal) having a good build.

well-man·nered *adj.* having good manners.

well-marked *adj.* distinct; easy to detect.

well-matched *adj.* fit to contend with each other, live together, etc., on equal terms.

well-mean·ing *adj.* (also **well-meant**) well-intentioned (but ineffective or unwise).

well·ness /wélnəs/ *n.* the state or condition of being in good physical and mental health.

well-nigh /wélní/ *adv. archaic* or *rhet.* almost (*well-nigh impossible*).

well-off *adj.* 1 having plenty of money. 2 in a fortunate situation or circumstance.

well-oiled *adj. colloq.* 1 drunk. 2 operating efficiently (*a well-oiled committee*); 3 esp. *Brit.* (of a compliment, etc.) easily expressed through habitual use.

well-or·dered *adj.* arranged in an orderly manner.

well-paid *adj.* 1 (of a job) that pays well. 2 (of a person) amply rewarded for a job.

well-pre·served *adj.* showing little sign of aging.

well-read *adj.* knowledgeable through much reading.

well-re·ceived *adj.* welcomed; favorably received.

well-round•ed adj. **1** complete and symmetrical. **2** (of a phrase, etc.) complete and well expressed. **3** (of a person) having or showing a fully developed personality, ability, etc. **4** fleshy; plump.

well-spent adj. (esp. of money or time) used profitably.

well-spo•ken adj. articulate or refined in speech.

well-thought-of adj. having a good reputation; esteemed; respected.

well-thought-out adj. carefully devised.

well-thumbed adj. esp. Brit. bearing marks of frequent handling.

well-timed adj. opportune; timely.

well-to-do adj. prosperous.

well-tried adj. often tested with good results.

well-trod•den adj. much frequented.

well-turned adj. **1** (of a compliment, phrase, or verse) elegantly expressed. **2** (of a leg, ankle, etc.) elegantly shaped or displayed.

well-wish•er n. a person who wishes one well.

well-worn adj. **1** much worn by use. **2** (of a phrase, etc.) trite; hackneyed.

Welsh /welsh/ adj. & n. ● adj. of or relating to Wales or its people or language. ● n. **1** the Celtic language of Wales. **2** (prec. by the; treated as pl.) the people of Wales. [OE Welisc, Wælisc, etc., f. Gmc f. L Volcae, the name of a Celtic people]

welsh /welsh/ v.intr. (also **welch** /welch/) **1** (of a loser of a bet, esp. a bookmaker) decamp without paying. **2** evade an obligation. **3** (foll. by on) **a** fail to carry out a promise to (a person). **b** fail to honor (an obligation). □□ **welsh•er** n. [19th c.: orig. unkn.]

Welsh cor•gi see CORGI.

Welsh dress•er n. a type of dresser with open shelves above a cupboard.

Welsh harp n. a harp with three rows of strings.

Welsh•man /wélshmən/ n. (pl. –men) a person who is Welsh by birth or descent; a resident of Wales.

Welsh on•ion n. a species of onion, Allium fistulosum, forming clusters of bulbs.

Welsh corgi

Welsh rab•bit n. (also **Welsh rare•bit** by folk etymology) a dish of melted cheese, etc., on toast.

Welsh•wom•an /wélshwŏŏmən/ n. (pl. –wom•en) a woman who is Welsh by birth or descent; a woman resident of Wales.

welt /welt/ n. & v. ● n. **1** a leather rim sewn around the edge of a shoe upper for the sole to be attached to. **2** = WEAL¹. **3** a ribbed or reinforced border of a garment; a trimming. **4** a heavy blow. ● v.tr. **1** provide with a welt. **2** strike (someone or something) hard and heavily; thrash. [ME welte, walt, of unkn. orig.]

Welt•an•schau•ung /véltaanshówŏŏng/ n. a particular philosophy or view of life; a conception of the world. [G f. Welt world + Anschauung perception]

wel•ter¹ /wéltər/ v. & n. ● v.intr. **1** roll; wallow; be washed about. **2** (foll. by in) lie prostrate or be soaked or steeped in blood, etc. ● n. **1** a state of general confusion. **2** (foll. by of) a disorderly mixture or contrast of beliefs, policies, etc. [ME f. MDu., MLG welteren]

wel•ter² /wéltər/ n. **1** a heavy rider or boxer. **2** colloq. a heavy blow. **3** colloq. a big person or thing. [19th c.: orig. unkn.]

wel•ter•weight /wéltərwayt/ n. **1** a weight in certain sports intermediate between lightweight and middleweight. **2** an athlete of this weight.

welt•schmerz /véltshmairts/ n. a feeling of pessimism; an apathetic or vaguely yearning outlook on life. [G f. Welt world + Schmerz pain]

wen¹ /wen/ n. **1** a benign tumor on the skin, esp. of the scalp. **2** Brit. an outstandingly large or congested city. □ **the great wen** Brit. London. [OE wen, wenn, of unkn. orig.: cf. Du. wen, MLG wene, LG wehne tumor, wart]

wen² var. of WYNN.

wench /wench/ n. & v. ● n. **1** joc. a girl or young woman. **2** archaic a prostitute. ● v.intr. archaic (of a man) consort with prostitutes. □□ **wench•er** n. [ME wenche, wenchel f. OE wencel child: cf. OE wancol weak, tottering]

Wend /wend/ n. a member of a Slavic people of N. Germany, now inhabiting E. Saxony. □□ **Wend•ic** adj. **Wend•ish** adj. [G Wende f. OHG Winida, of unkn. orig.]

wend /wend/ v.tr. & intr. literary or archaic go. □ **wend one's way** make one's way. [OE wendan turn f. Gmc, rel. to WIND²]

Wens•ley•dale /wénzleedayl/ n. **1** a variety of white or blue cheese. **2 a** a sheep of a breed with long wool. **b** this breed. [Wensleydale in Yorkshire]

went past of GO¹.

wen•tle•trap /wént'ltrap/ n. any marine snail of the genus Clathrus, with a spiral shell of many whorls. [Du. wenteltrap winding stair, spiral shell]

wept past of WEEP.

were 2nd sing. past, pl. past, and past subj. of BE.

we're /weer/ contr. we are.

were•n't /wərnt, wórənt/ contr. were not.

were•wolf /weerwŏŏlf, wáir–/ n. (also **wer•wolf** /wór–/) (pl. –wolves) a mythical being who at times changes from a person to a wolf. [OE werewulf: first element perh. f. OE wer man = L vir]

wert archaic 2nd sing. past of BE.

Wes•ley•an /wézleeən/ adj. & n. ● adj. of or relating to a Protestant denomination founded by the English evangelist John Wesley (d. 1791) (cf. METHODIST). ● n. a member of this denomination. □□ **Wes•ley•an•ism** n.

west /west/ n., adj., & adv. ● n. **1 a** the point of the horizon where the sun sets at the equinoxes (cardinal point 90° to the left of north). **b** the compass point corresponding to this. **c** the direction in which this lies. **2** (usu. **the West**) **a** European in contrast to Asian civilization. **b** the non-Communist nations of Europe and N. America. **c** the western part of the late Roman Empire. **d** the western part of a country, town, etc., esp. the American West. **3** Bridge a player occupying the position designated "west." ● adj. **1** toward, at, near, or facing west. **2** coming from the west (west wind). ● adv. **1** toward, at, or near the west. **2** (foll. by of) further west than. □ **go west** sl. be killed or destroyed, etc.; die. [OE f. Gmc]

west•bound /wéstbownd/ adj. traveling or leading westward.

West Bank n. a region west of the Jordan River assigned to Jordan in 1948 and occupied by Israel since 1967.

west•er•ing /wéstəring/ adj. (of the sun) nearing the west. [wester (v.) ME f. WEST]

west•er•ly /wéstərlee/ adj., adv., & n. ● adj. & adv. **1** in a western position or direction. **2** (of a wind) blowing from the west. ● n. (pl. –lies) a wind blowing from the west. [wester (adj.) f. OE westra f. WEST]

west•ern /wéstərn/ adj. & n. ● adj. **1** of or in the west; inhabiting the west. **2** lying or directed toward the west. **3** (**Western**) of or relating to the West (see WEST n. 2). ● n. a motion picture or novel about cowboys in western North America. □□ **west•ern•most** adj. [OE westerne (as WEST, –ERN)]

West•ern Church n. the part of Christendom that has continued to derive its authority, doctrine, and ritual from the popes in Rome.

west•ern hem•i•sphere n. the half of the earth containing the Americas.

West•ern•er /wéstərnər/ n. a native or inhabitant of the West.

west•ern•ize /wéstərnīz/ v.tr. (also **West•ern•ize**) influence with or convert to the ideas and customs, etc., of the West. □□ **west•ern•i•za•tion** n. **west•ern•iz•er** n.

West Ger•man•ic n. a group of languages including High and Low German, English, Frisian, and Dutch.

West In•di•an n. **1** a native or national of any island of the West Indies. **2** a person of West Indian descent.

West In•dies n. the islands of Central America, including Cuba and the Bahamas.

west•ing /wésting/ n. Naut. the distance traveled or the angle of longitude measured westward from either a defined north–south grid line or a meridian.

West•min•ster /wéstminstər/ n. the Parliament at Westminster in London.

west-north•west n. the direction or compass point midway between west and northwest.

West Side n. the western part of Manhattan in New York City.

west-south•west n. the direction or compass point midway between west and southwest.

west•ward /wéstwərd/ adj., adv., & n. ● adj. & adv. (also **west•wards**) toward the west. ● n. a westward direction or region.

wet /wet/ adj., v., & n. ● adj. (**wet•ter, wet•test**) **1** soaked, covered, or dampened with water or other liquid (a wet sponge; a wet surface; got my feet wet). **2** (of the weather, etc.) rainy (a wet day). **3** (of paint, ink, etc.) not yet dried. **4** used with water (wet shampoo). **5** Brit. colloq. feeble; inept. **6** Brit. Polit. colloq. Conservative with liberal tendencies, esp. as regarded by right-wing Conservatives. **7** sl. (of a country, of legislation, etc.) allowing the free sale of alcoholic drink. **8** (of a baby or young child) incontinent (is still wet at night). ● v.tr. (**wet•ting**; past and past part. **wet** or **wet•ted**) **1** make wet. **2 a** urinate in or on (wet the bed). **b** refl. urinate involuntarily. ● n. **1** moisture; liquid that wets something. **2** rainy weather; a time of rain. **3** Brit. colloq. a feeble or inept person. **4** Brit. Polit. colloq. a Conservative with liberal tendencies (see sense 6 of adj.). **5** Brit. colloq. a drink. □ **wet the baby's head** Brit. colloq. celebrate its birth with a (usu. alcoholic) drink. **wet behind the ears** immature; inexperienced. **wet through** (or **to the skin**) with one's clothes soaked. **wet one's whistle** colloq. drink. □□ **wet•ly** adv. **wet•ness** n. **wet•ta•ble** adj. **wet•ting** n. **wet•tish** adj. [OE wēt (adj. & n.), wǣtan (v.), rel. to WATER: in ME replaced by past part. of the verb]

wet•back /wétbak/ n. offens. an illegal immigrant from Mexico to the US. [WET + BACK: from the practice of swimming the Rio Grande to reach the US]

wet blan•ket n. colloq. a gloomy person preventing the enjoyment of others.

wet dock n. a dock in which a ship can float.

wet dream *n.* an erotic dream with involuntary ejaculation of semen.

wet fly *n.* an artificial fly used under water by an angler.

weth·er /wéthər/ *n.* a castrated ram. [OE f. Gmc]

wet·lands /wétləndz/ *n.pl.* swamps and other damp areas of land.

wet look *n.* a shiny surface given to clothing materials or hair.

wet nurse *n.* a woman employed to suckle another's child.

wet-nurse *v.tr.* **1** act as a wet nurse to. **2** *colloq.* treat as if helpless.

wet pack *n.* the therapeutic wrapping of the body in wet cloths, etc.

wet suit *n.* a close-fitting rubber garment worn by skin divers, etc., to keep warm.

wet·ting a·gent *n.* a substance that helps water, etc., to spread or penetrate.

we've /weev/ *contr.* we have.

wey /way/ *n. Brit.* a former unit of weight or volume varying with different kinds of goods, often 256 pounds or 40 bushels. [OE *wǣg(e)* balance, weight f. Gmc, rel. to WEIGH¹]

w.f. *abbr. Printing* wrong font.

whack /hwak, wak/ *v. & n. colloq.* • *v.tr.* **1** strike or beat forcefully with a sharp blow. **2** (as **whacked** *adj.*) esp. *Brit.* = WHACKED-OUT • *n.* **1** a sharp or resounding blow. **2** *Brit. sl.* a share. □ **have a whack at** *sl.* attempt. **out of whack** *sl.* out of order; malfunctioning. □□ **whack·er** *n.* **whack·ing** *n.* [imit., or alt. of THWACK]

whacked-out *adj.* **1** tired out; exhausted. **2** under the influence of narcotics or alcohol.

whack·ing /hwáking, wák-/ *adj. & adv. Brit. colloq.* • *adj.* very large. • *adv.* very (*a whacking great skyscraper*).

whack·o /hwákō, wák-/ *int., adj., & n.* • *int. Brit. sl.* expressing delight or enjoyment. • *adj. & n.* var. of WACKO.

whack·y var. of WACKY.

whale¹ /hwayl, wayl/ *n.* (*pl.* same or **whales**) any of the larger marine mammals of the order Cetacea, having a streamlined body and horizontal tail, and breathing through a blowhole on the head. See illustration, page 1152. □ **a whale of a** *colloq.* an exceedingly good or fine, etc. [OE *hwæl*]

whale² /hwayl, wayl/ *v.tr. colloq.* beat; thrash. [var. of WALE]

whale·back /hwáylbak, wáyl-/ *n.* anything shaped like a whale's back.

whale·boat /hwáylbōt, wáyl-/ *n.* a double-bowed boat of a kind used in whaling.

whale·bone /hwáylbōn, wáyl-/ *n.* an elastic horny substance growing in thin parallel plates in the upper jaw of some whales, used as stiffening, etc.

whale·bone whale *n.* a baleen whale.

whale oil *n.* oil from the blubber of whales.

whal·er /hwáylər, wáyl-/ *n.* **1** a whaling ship or a seaman engaged in whaling. **2** an Australian shark of the genus *Carcharhinus.* **3** *Austral. sl.* a tramp.

whale shark *n.* a large tropical whalelike shark, *Rhincodon typus,* feeding close to the surface.

whal·ing /hwáyling, wáyl-/ *n.* the practice or industry of hunting and killing whales, esp. for their oil or whalebone.

whal·ing mas·ter *n.* the captain of a whaler.

wham /hwam, wam/ *int., n., & v. colloq.* • *int.* expressing the sound of a forcible impact. • *n.* such a sound. • *v.* (**whammed, wham·ming**) **1** *intr.* make such a sound or impact. **2** *tr.* strike forcibly. [imit.]

wham·my /hwámee, wám-/ *n.* (*pl.* **–mies**) *colloq.* an evil or unlucky influence. [20th c.: orig. unkn.]

whang /hwang, wang/ *v. & n. colloq.* • *v.* **1** *tr.* strike heavily and loudly; whack. **2** *intr.* (of a drum, etc.) sound under or as under a blow. • *n.* a whanging sound or blow. [imit.]

whang·ee /hwanggée, wang-/ *n.* **1** a Chinese or Japanese bamboo of the genus *Phyllostachys.* **2** a cane made from this. [Chin. *huang* old bamboo sprouts]

wharf /hwawrf, wawrf/ *n. & v.* • *n.* (*pl.* **wharves** /wawrvz/ or **wharfs**) a level quayside area to which a ship may be moved to load and unload. • *v.tr.* **1** moor (a ship) at a wharf. **2** store (goods) on a wharf. [OE *hwearf*]

wharf·age /hwáwrfij, wáwr-/ *n.* **1** accommodation at a wharf. **2** a fee for this.

wharf·in·ger /hwáwrfinjər, wáwr-/ *n.* an owner or keeper of a wharf. [prob. ult. f. WHARFAGE]

wharves *pl.* of WHARF.

what /hwot, wot, hwut, wut/ *adj., pron., & adv.* • *interrog.adj.* **1** asking for a choice from an indefinite number or for a statement of amount, number, or kind (*what books have you read?; what news have you?*). **2** *colloq.* = WHICH *interrog.adj.* (*what book have you chosen?*). • *adj.* (usu. in exclam.) how great or remarkable (*what luck!*). • *rel.adj.* the or any…that (*will give you what help I can*). • *pron.* (corresp. to the functions of the *adj.*) **1** what thing or things? (*what is your name?; I don't know what you mean*). **2** (asking for a remark to be repeated) = what did you say? **3** asking for confirmation or agreement of something not completely understood (*you did what?; what, you really mean it?*). **4** how much (*what you must have suffered!*). **5** (as *rel.pron.*) that or those which; a or the any thing which (*what followed was worse; tell me what you think*). • *adv.* to what extent (*what does it matter?*). □ **what about** what is the news or position or your opinion of (*what about me?; what about a game of tennis?*). **what-d'-you-call-it** (or **whatchamacallit** or **what's-its-name**) *colloq.* a substitute for a name not recalled. **what for** *colloq.* **1** for what reason? **2** a severe reprimand (esp. give a person what for). **what have you** *colloq.* (prec. by *or*) anything else similar. **what if?** **1** what would result, etc., if. **2** what would it matter if. **what is more** and as an additional point; moreover. **what next?** *colloq.* what more absurd, shocking, or surprising thing is possible? **what not** (prec. by *and*) other similar things. **what of?** what is the news concerning? **what of it?** why should that be considered significant? **what's-his** (or **-its**) **-name** = what-d'you-call-it. **what's what** *colloq.* what is useful or important, etc. **what with** *colloq.* because of (usu. several things). [OE *hwæt* f. Gmc]

what·e'er /hwotáir, wot–, hwut–, wut–/ *poet.* var. of WHATEVER.

what·ev·er /hwotévər, wot–, hwut, wut–/ *adj. & pron.* **1** = WHAT (in relative uses) with the emphasis on indefiniteness (*lend me whatever you can; whatever money you have*). **2** though anything (*we are safe whatever happens*). **3** (with *neg.* or *interrog.*) at all; of any kind (*there is no doubt whatever*). **4** *colloq.* what at all or in any way (*whatever do you mean?*). □ **or whatever** *colloq.* or anything similar.

what·not /hwótnot, wót–, hw út–, wút–/ *n.* **1** an indefinite or trivial thing. **2** a stand with shelves for small objects.

whats·it /hwótsit, wót–, hw út–, wút–/ *n. colloq.* a person or thing whose name one cannot recall or does not know.

what·so /hwótsō, wót–, hw út–, wút–/ *adj. & pron. archaic* = WHATEVER 1, 2. [ME, f. WHAT + SO, f. OE *swā hwæt swā*]

what·so·e'er /hwótsō-áir, wót–, hwút–, w út–/ *poet.* var. of WHATSOEVER.

what·so·ev·er /hwótsō-évər, wót–, hwút–, wút–/ *adj. & pron.* = WHATEVER 1–3.

whaup /hwawp, wawp/ *n.* esp. *Sc.* a curlew. [imit. of its cry]

wheal var. of WEAL¹.

wheat /hweet, weet/ *n.* **1** any cereal plant of the genus *Triticum,* bearing dense four-sided seed spikes. **2** its grain, used in making flour, etc. □ **separate the wheat from the chaff** see CHAFF. [OE *hwǣte* f. Gmc, rel. to WHITE]

wheat belt *n.* a region where wheat is the chief agricultural product.

wheat·ear /hweéteer, weét–/ *n.* any small migratory bird of the genus *Oenanthe,* esp. with a white belly and rump. [app. f. *wheatears* (WHITE + ARSE)]

wheat·en /hweétən, weét–/ *adj.* made of wheat.

wheat germ *n.* the embryo of the wheat grain, extracted as a source of vitamins.

wheat·grass /hweétgras, weét–/ *n.* a couch grass grown esp. as forage.

Wheat·stone bridge /hweétstōn, weét–/ *n.* an apparatus for measuring electrical resistances by equalizing the potential at two points of a circuit. [C. *Wheatstone,* Engl. physicist d. 1875]

whee /hwee, wee/ *int.* expressing delight or excitement. [imit.]

whee·dle /hweédəl, weédəl/ *v.tr.* **1** coax by flattery or endearments. **2** (foll. by *out*) **a** get (a thing) out of a person by wheedling. **b** cheat (a person) out of a thing by wheedling. □□ **whee·dler** *n.* **whee·dling** *adj.* **whee·dling·ly** *adv.* [perh. f. G *wedeln* fawn, cringe f. *Wedel* tail]

wheel /hweel, weel/ *n. & v.* • *n.* **1** a circular frame or disk arranged to revolve on an axle and used to facilitate the motion of a vehicle or for various mechanical purposes. **2** a wheellike thing (*Catherine wheel; potter's wheel; steering wheel*). **3** motion as of a wheel, esp. the movement of a line of people with one end as a pivot. **4** a machine, etc., of which a wheel is an essential part. **5** (in *pl.*) *sl.* a car. **6** *sl.* = BIG WHEEL 2. **7** a set of short lines concluding a stanza. • *v.* **1** *intr. & tr.* **a** turn on an axis or pivot. **b** swing around in line with one end as a pivot. **2 a** *intr.* (often foll. by *about, around, round*) change direction or face another way. **b** *tr.* cause to do this. **3** *tr.* push or pull (a wheeled thing esp. a wheelbarrow, bicycle, wheelchair, or stroller, or its load or occupant). **4** *intr.* go in circles or curves (*seagulls wheeling overhead*). □ **at the wheel 1** driving a vehicle. **2** directing a ship. **3** in control of affairs. **on wheels** (or **oiled wheels**) *Brit.* smoothly. **wheel and deal** engage in political or commercial scheming. **wheels within wheels** *Brit.* **1** intricate machinery. **2** *colloq.* indirect or secret agencies. □□ **wheeled** *adj.* (also in *comb.*). **wheel·less** *adj.* [OE *hwēol, hwēogol* f. Gmc]

wheel-back *adj.* (of a chair) with a back shaped like or containing the design of a wheel.

wheel·bar·row /hweélbarō, weél–/ *n.* a small cart with one wheel and two shafts for carrying garden loads, etc.

wheelbarrow

sperm whale: up to 60 feet

humpback whale: 30–60 feet

orca: up to 30 feet

narwhal: up to 14 feet

bottlenose dolphin: 8–12 feet

harbor porpoise: 4–6 feet

whales

wheel•base /hweélbays, weél–/ *n.* the distance between the front and rear axles of a vehicle.

wheel•chair /hweélchair, weél–/ *n.* a chair on wheels for an invalid or disabled person.

wheel•er /hweélər, weé–/ *n.* **1** (in *comb.*) a vehicle having a specified number of wheels. **2** a wheelwright. **3** a horse harnessed next to the wheels and behind another.

wheel•er-deal•er *n. colloq.* a person who wheels and deals.

wheel•house /hweélhows, weél–/ *n.* = PILOTHOUSE.

wheel•ie /hweé–/ *n. sl.* the stunt of riding a bicycle or motor cycle for a short distance with the front wheel off the ground.

wheel lock *n. hist.* **1** a kind of gunlock having a steel wheel to rub against flint, etc. **2** a gun with this.

wheel•man /hweélmən, weél–/ *n.* **1** a driver of a wheeled vehicle, esp. a gataway car. **2** a helmsman.

wheel of for•tune *n.* **1** luck. **2** a gambling device that is spun and allowed to stop at random to indicate the winner or the prize.

wheels•man /hweélzmən, weél–/ *n.* (*pl.* **–men**) a helmsman.

wheel•spin /hweélspin, weél–/ *n.* rotation of a vehicle's wheels without traction.

wheel•wright /hweélrit, weél–/ *n.* a person who makes or repairs esp. wooden wheels.

wheeze /hweez, weez/ *v. & n.* • *v.* **1** *intr.* breathe with an audible chesty whistling sound. **2** *tr.* (often foll. by *out*) utter in this way. • *n.* **1** a sound of wheezing. **2** *colloq.* **a** *Brit.* a clever scheme. **b** an actor's interpolated joke, etc. **c** a catchphrase. □□ **wheez•er** *n.* **wheez•ing•ly** *adv.* **wheez•y** *adj.* (**wheez•i•er, wheez•i•est**). **wheez•i•ly** *adv.* **wheez•i•ness** *n.* [prob. f. ON *hvǽsa* to hiss]

whelk[1] /hwelk, welk/ *n.* any predatory marine gastropod mollusk of the family Buccinidae, esp. the edible kind of the genus *Baccinum*, having a spiral shell. [OE *wioloc, weoloc,* of unkn. orig.: perh. infl. by WHELK[2]]

whelk[2] /hwelk, welk/ *n.* a pimple. [OE *hwylca* f. *hwelian* suppurate]

whelm /hwelm, welm/ *v.tr. poet.* **1** engulf; submerge. **2** crush with weight; overwhelm. [OE *hwelman* (unrecorded) = *hwylfan* overturn]

whelk[1]

whelp /hwelp, welp/ *n. & v.* • *n.* **1** a young dog; a puppy. **2** *archaic* a cub. **3** an ill-mannered child or youth. **4** (esp. in *pl.*) a projection on the barrel of a capstan or windlass. • *v.tr.* (also *absol.*) **1** bring forth (a whelp or whelps). **2** *derog.* (of a human mother) give birth to. **3** originate (an evil scheme, etc.). [OE *hwelp*]

when /hwen, wen/ *adv., conj., pron., & n.* • *interrog.adv.* **1** at what time? **2** on what occasion? **3** how soon? **4** how long ago? • *rel.adv.* (prec. by *time,* etc.) at or on which (*there are times when I could cry*). • *conj.* **1** at the or any time that; as soon as (*come when you like; come when ready; when I was your age*). **2** although; considering that (*why stand up when you could sit down?*). **3** after which; and then; but just then (*was nearly asleep when the bell rang*). • *pron.* what time? (*till when can you stay?; since when it has been better*). • *n.* time, occasion, date (*have finally decided on the where and when*). [OE *hwanne, hwenne*]

whence /hwens, wens/ *adv. & conj. formal* • *adv.* from what place? (*whence did they come?*). • *conj.* **1** to the place from which (*return whence you came*). **2** (often prec. by *place,* etc.) from which (*the source whence these errors arise*). **3** and thence (*whence it follows that*). [ME *whannes, whennes* f. *whanne, whenne* f. OE *hwanon(e)* whence, formed as WHEN + –*s*[3]: cf. THENCE]

▶The redundant expression *from whence* (as in *the place from whence they came*), though common, is best avoided.

whence•so•ev•er /hwéns-sō-évər, wéns–/ *adv. & conj. formal* from whatever place or source.

when•e'er /hwenáir, wen–/ *poet.* var. of WHENEVER.

when•ev•er /hwenévər, wen–/ *conj. & adv.* **1** at whatever time; on whatever occasion. **2** every time that. □ **or whenever** *colloq.* or at any similar time.

when•so•e'er /hwénsō-áir, wén–/ *poet.* var. of WHENSOEVER.

when•so•ev•er /hwénsō-évər, wén–/ *conj. & adv. formal* = WHENEVER.

where /hwair, wair/ *adv., conj., pron., & n.* • *interrog.adv.* **1** in or to what place or position? (*where is the milk?; where are you going?*). **2** in what direction or respect? (*where does the argument lead?; where does it concern us?*). **3** in what book, etc.?; from whom? (*where did you read that?; where did you hear that?*). **4** in what situation or condition? (*where does that leave us?*). • *rel.adv.* (prec. by *place,* etc.) in or to which (*places where they meet*). • *conj.* **1** in or to the or any place, direction, or respect in which (*go where you like; that is where you are wrong; delete where applicable*). **2** and there (*reached Albuquerque, where the car broke down*). • *pron.* what place? (*where do you come from?; where are you going to?*). • *n.* place; scene of something (see WHEN *n.*). [OE *hwǽr, hwār*]

▶**Where** should refer only to a physical location, but people often use *where* when they should use **in which.** It is formally incorrect, for example, to say, "We have a situation where one person is unhappy and soon everyone is complaining." Say "We have a situation in which one person is unhappy…." Similarly, avoid such uses of *where* as in: "Freshman orientation week is where all the students come to campus a few days early." Rather, say "Freshman orientation week is (the time) when…."

where•a•bouts *adv. & n.* • *adv.* /hwáirəbówts, wáir–/ where or approximately where? (*whereabouts are they?; show me whereabouts to look*). • *n.* /hwáirəbowts, wáir–/ (as *sing.* or *pl.*) a person's or thing's location roughly defined.

where•af•ter /hwairáftər, wair/ *conj. formal* after which.

where•as /hwairáz, wair–/ *conj.* **1** in contrast or comparison with the fact that. **2** (esp. in legal preambles) taking into consideration the fact that.

where•at /hwairát, wair–/ *conj. archaic* **1** at which place or point. **2** for which reason.

where•by /hwairbí, wair–/ *conj.* by what or which means.

wher•e'er /hwairáir, wair–/ *poet.* var. of WHEREVER.

where•fore /hwáirfawr, wáir–/ *adv. & n.* • *adv. archaic* **1** for what reason? **2** for which reason. • *n.* a reason (*the whys and wherefores*).

where•from /hwairfrúm, –fróm, wair–/ *conj. archaic* from which; from where.

where•in /hwairín, wair–/ *conj. & adv. formal* • *conj.* in what or which place or respect. • *adv.* in what place or respect?

where•of /hwair úv, –óv, wair–/ *conj. & adv. formal* • *conj.* of what or which (*the means whereof*). • *adv.* of what?

where•on /hwairón, –áwn, wair–/ *conj. & adv. archaic* • *conj.* on what or which. • *adv.* on what?

where•so•e'er /hwáirsōáir, wáir–/ *poet.* var. of WHERESOEVER.

where•so•ev•er /hwáirsō-évər, wáir–/ *conj. & adv. formal* or *literary* = WHEREVER.

where•to /hwairtoō, wair–/ *conj. & adv. formal* • *conj.* to what or which. • *adv.* to what?

where•up•on /hwáirəpón, –páwn, wáir–/ *conj.* immediately after which.

wher•ev•er /hwairévər, wair–/ *adv. & conj.* • *adv.* in or to whatever place. • *conj.* in every place that. □ **or wherever** *colloq.* or in any similar place.

where•with•al /hwáirwithawl, –with–, wáir–/ *n. colloq.* money, etc., needed for a purpose (*has not the wherewithal to do it*).

wher•ry /hwéree, wéree/ *n.* (*pl.* **–ries**) **1** a light row boat usu. for carrying passengers. **2** *Brit.* a large, light barge. [ME: orig. unkn.]

wher•ry•man /hwéreemən, wér–/ *n.* (*pl.* **–men**) a person employed on a wherry.

whet /hwet, wet/ *v. & n.* • *v.tr.* (**whet•ted, whet•ting**) **1** sharpen (a scythe or other tool) by grinding. **2** stimulate (the appetite or a desire, interest, etc.). • *n.* **1** the act or an instance of whetting. **2** a small quantity stimulating one's appetite for more. □□ **whet•ter** *n.* (also in *comb.*). [OE *hwettan* f. Gmc]

wheth•er /hwéthər, wéth–/ *conj.* introducing the first or both of alternative possibilities (*I doubt whether it matters; I do not know whether they have arrived or not*). □ **whether or no** (or **not**) see NO[2]. [OE *hw æther, hwether* f. Gmc]

▶See note at IF.

whet•stone /hwétstōn, wét–/ *n.* **1** a tapered stone used with water to sharpen curved tools, e.g., sickles, hooks (cf. OILSTONE). **2** a thing that sharpens the senses, etc.

whew /hwyoō/ *int.* expressing surprise, consternation, or relief. [imit.: cf. PHEW]

whey /hway, way/ *n.* the watery liquid left when milk forms curds. [OE *hwæg, hweg* f. LG]

whey-faced *adj.* pale esp. with fear.

which /hwich, wich/ *adj. & pron.* • *interrog.adj.* asking for choice from a definite set of alternatives (*which John do you mean?; say which book you prefer; which way shall we go?*). • *rel.adj.* being the one just referred to; and this or these (*ten years, during which time they admitted nothing; a word of advice, which action is within your power, will set things straight*). • *interrog.pron.* **1** which person or persons (*which of you is responsible?*). **2** which thing or things (*say which you prefer*). • *rel.pron.* (poss. **of which, whose** /hoōz/) **1** which thing or things, usu. introducing a clause not essential for identification (cf. THAT *pron.* 7) (*the house, which is empty, has been damaged*). **2** used in place of *that* after *in* or *that* (*the house in which I was born; that which you have just seen*). □ **which is which** a phrase used when two or more persons or things are difficult to distinguish from each other. [OE *hwilc* f. Gmc]

▶**1. Which** should be employed only for nonrestrictive (or nonessential) clauses: The horse, which is in the paddock, is six years old (the *which* clause contains a nonessential fact, noted in passing; the horse would be six years old wherever it was). A *that* clause is restrictive (or essential), as it identifies a particular thing: *The horse that is in the paddock is six years old* (not any horse, but the one in the paddock). **2.** For use of **in which**, see note at WHERE.

which·ev·er /hwichévər, wích–/ *adj. & pron.* **1** any which (*take whichever you like; whichever one you like*). **2** no matter which (*whichever one wins, they both get a prize*).

which·so·ev·er /hwíchsō-évər, wích–/ *adj. & pron. archaic* = WHICHEVER.

whid·ah var. of WHYDAH.

whiff /hwif, wif/ *n. & v.* • *n.* **1** a puff or breath of air, smoke, etc. (*went outside for a whiff of fresh air*). **2** a smell (*caught the whiff of a cigar*). **3** (foll. by *of*) a trace or suggestion of scandal, etc. **4** *Brit.* a small cigar. **5** a minor discharge (of grapeshot, etc.). **6** *Brit.* a light, narrow outrigged scull. • *v.* **1** *tr. & intr.* blow or puff lightly. **2** *intr. Brit.* smell (esp. unpleasant). **3** *tr.* get a slight smell of. **4** *intr. Baseball* strike out by swinging and missing on the third strike. **5** *tr. Baseball* strike out a batter in this way. [imit.]

whif·fle /hwifəl, wíf–/ *v. & n.* • *v.* **1** *intr. & tr.* (of the wind) blow lightly, shift about. **2** *intr.* be variable or evasive. **3** *intr.* (of a flame, leaves, etc.) flicker; flutter. **4** *intr.* make the sound of a light wind in breathing, etc. • *n.* a slight movement of air. □□ **whif·fler** *n.* [WHIFF + –LE⁴]

whif·fle·tree /hwifəltree, wíf–/ *n.* a crossbar pivoted in the middle, to which the traces are attached in a cart, plow, etc. [var. of WHIPPLETREE]

whiff·y /hwifee, wíf–/ *adj. Brit. colloq.* (**whiff·i·er, whiff·fi·est**) having an unpleasant smell.

Whig /hwig, wig/ *n. hist.* **1** *Polit.* a member of the British reforming and constitutional party that after 1688 sought the supremacy of Parliament and was eventually succeeded in the 19th c. by the Liberal Party (opp. TORY *n.* 2). **2** a 17th-c. Scottish Presbyterian. **3 a** a supporter of the American Revolution. **b** a member of an American political party in the 19th c., succeeded by the Republicans. □□ **Whig·ger·y** *n.* **Whig·gish** *adj.* **Whig·gism** *n.* [prob. a shortening of Sc. *whiggamer, –more*, nickname of 17th-c. Sc. rebels, f. *whig* to drive + MARE¹]

while /hwīl, wīl/ *n., conj., v., & adv.* • *n.* **1** a space of time, time spent in some action (*a long while ago; waited a while; all this while*). **2** (prec. by *the*) **a** during some other process. **b** *poet.* during the time that. **3** (prec. by *a*) for some time (*have not seen you a while*). • *conj.* **1** during the time that; for as long as; at the same time as (*while I was away, the house was burglarized; fell asleep while reading*). **2** in spite of the fact that; although; whereas (*while I want to believe it, I cannot*). • *v.tr.* (foll. by *away*) pass (time, etc.) in a leisurely or interesting manner. • *rel.adv.* during which (*the summer while I was abroad*). □ **all the while** during the whole time (that). **for a long while** for a long time past. **for a while** for some time. **a good** (or **great**) **while** a considerable time. **in a while** (or **little while**) soon; shortly. **worth while** (or **one's while**) worth the time or effort spent. [OE *hwīl* f. Gmc: (conj.) abbr. of OE *thā hw;amile the*, ME *the while that*]

▶ **Worth While.** See note at WORTHWHILE.

whiles /hwīlz, wīlz/ *conj. archaic* = WHILE. [orig. in the adverbs *somewhiles, otherwhiles*]

whi·lom /hwílom, wí–/ *adv. & adj. archaic* • *adv.* formerly; once. • *adj.* former; erstwhile (*my whilom friend*). [OE *hwīlum* dative pl. of *hwīl* WHILE]

whilst /hwīlst, wīlst/ *adv. & conj.* esp. *Brit.* while. [ME f. WHILES: cf. AGAINST]

whim /hwim, wim/ *n.* **1 a** a sudden fancy; a caprice. **b** capriciousness. **2** *archaic* a kind of windlass for raising ore or water from a mine. [17th c.: orig. unkn.]

whim·brel /hwímbrəl, wím–/ *n.* a small curlew, esp. *Numenius phaeopus*. [WHIMPER (imit.): cf. *dotterel*]

whim·per /hwímpər, wím–/ *v. & n.* • *v.* **1** *intr.* make feeble, querulous, or frightened sounds; cry and whine softly. **2** *tr.* utter whimperingly. • *n.* **1** a whimpering sound. **2** a feeble note or tone (*the conference ended on a whimper*). □□ **whim·per·er** *n.* **whim·per·ing·ly** *adv.* [imit., f. dial. *whimp*]

whim·si·cal /hwímzikəl, wím–/ *adj.* **1** capricious. **2** fantastic. **3** odd or quaint; fanciful; humorous. □□ **whim·si·cal·i·ty** /–kálitee/ *n.* **whim·si·cal·ly** *adv.* **whim·si·cal·ness** *n.*

whim·sy /hwímzee, wím–/ *n.* (also **whim·sey**) (*pl.* **–sies** or **–seys**) **1** a whim; a capricious notion or fancy. **2** capricious or quaint humor. [rel. to WHIM-WHAM: cf. *flimsy*]

whim-wham /hwímhwam, wímwham/ *n. archaic* **1** a toy or plaything. **2** = WHIM 1. [redupl.: orig. uncert.]

whin¹ /hwin, win/ *n.* esp. *Brit.* (in *sing.* or *pl.*) furze; gorse. [prob. Scand.: cf. Norw. *hvine*, Sw. *hven*]

whin² /hwin, win/ *n. Brit.* **1** hard dark esp. basaltic rock or stone. **2** a piece of this. [ME: orig. unkn.]

whin·chat /hwínchat, wín–/ *n.* a small, brownish European songbird, *Saxicola rubetra*. [WHIN¹ + CHAT²]

whine /hwīn, wīn/ *n. & v.* • *n.* **1** a complaining, long-drawn wail as of a dog. **2** a similar shrill, prolonged sound. **3 a** a querulous tone.

b an instance of feeble or undignified complaining. • *v.* **1** *intr.* emit or utter a whine. **2** *intr.* complain in a querulous tone or in a feeble or undignified way. **3** *tr.* utter in a whining tone. □□ **whin·er** *n.* **whin·ing·ly** *adv.* **whin·y** *adj.* (**whin·i·er, whin·i·est**) [OE *hwīnan*]

whinge /hwinj, winj/ *v. & n. Brit. & Austral. colloq.* • *v.intr.* whine; grumble peevishly. • *n.* a whining complaint; a peevish grumbling. □□ **whing·er** *n.* **whing·ing·ly** *adv.* **whing·y** *adj.* [OE *hwinsian* f. Gmc]

whin·ny /hwínee, wín–/ *n. & v.* • *n.* (*pl.* **–nies**) a gentle or joyful neigh. • *v.intr.* (**–nies, –nied**) give a whinny. [imit.: cf. WHINE]

whin·stone /hwínstōn, wín–/ *n. Brit.* = WHIN².

whip /hwip, wip/ *n. & v.* • *n.* **1** a lash attached to a stick for urging on animals or punishing, etc. **2 a** a member of a political party in a legislative body appointed to control its party discipline and tactics, esp. ensuring attendance and voting in debates. **b** *Brit.* the whips' written notice requesting or requiring attendance for voting at a division, etc., variously underlined according to the degree of urgency (*three-line whip*). **c** (prec. by *the*) *Brit.* party discipline and instructions (*asked for the Labour whip*). **3** a dessert made with whipped cream, etc. **4** the action of beating cream, eggs, etc., into a froth. **5** = WHIPPER-IN. **6** a rope-and-pulley hoisting apparatus. • *v.* (**whipped, whip·ping**) **1** *tr.* beat or urge on with a whip. **2** *tr.* beat (cream or eggs, etc.) into a froth. **3** *tr. & intr.* take or move suddenly, unexpectedly, or rapidly (*whipped away the tablecloth; whipped out a knife; whip off your coat; whipped behind the door*). **4** *tr. Brit. sl.* steal (*who's whipped my pen?*). **5** *tr. sl.* **a** excel. **b** defeat. **6** *tr.* bind with spirally wound twine. **7** *tr.* sew with overcast stitches. **whip in** bring (hounds) together. **whip on** urge into action. **whip up 1** excite or stir up (feeling, etc.). **2** gather; summon up. **3** prepare (a meal, etc.) hurriedly. □□ **whip·less** *adj.* **whip·like** *adj.* **whip·per** *n.* [ME (*h*)*wippen* (v.), prob. f. MLG & MDu. *wippen* swing, leap, dance]

whip·cord /hwípkawrd, wíp–/ *n.* **1** a tightly twisted cord such as is used for making whiplashes. **2** a close-woven worsted fabric.

whip graft *n. Hort.* a graft with the tongue of the scion in a slot in the stock and vice versa.

whip hand *n.* **1** a hand that holds the whip (in riding, etc.). **2** (usu. prec. by *the*) the advantage or control in any situation.

whip·lash /hwíplash, wíp–/ *n.* **1** the flexible end of a whip. **2** a blow with a whip. **3** = WHIPLASH INJURY.

whip·lash in·ju·ry *n.* an injury to the neck caused by a jerk of the head, esp. as in a motor vehicle accident.

whip·per-in /hwípərin, wíp–/ *n.* a huntsman's assistant who manages the hounds.

whip·per·snap·per /hwípərsnapər, wíp–/ *n.* **1** a small child. **2** an insignificant but presumptuous or intrusive (esp. young) person. [perh. for *whipsnapper*, implying noise and unimportance]

whip·pet /hwípit, wíp–/ *n.* a crossbred dog of the greyhound type used for racing. [prob. f. obs. *whippet* move briskly, f. *whip it*]

whip·ping /hwíping, wíp–/ *n.* **1** a beating, esp. with a whip. **2** cord wound around in binding.

whip·ping boy *n.* **1** a scapegoat. **2** *hist.* a boy educated with a young prince and punished instead of him.

whip·ping cream *n.* cream suitable for whipping.

whip·ping post *n. hist.* a post used for public whippings.

whip·ple·tree /hwípəltree, wíp–/ *n.* = WHIFFLETREE. [app. f. WHIP + TREE]

whip·poor·will /hwípərwil, wíp–/ *n.* an American nightjar, *Caprimulgus vociferus*. [imit. of its cry]

whip·py /hwípee, wípee/ *adj.* (**whip·pi·er, whip·pi·est**) flexible; springy. □□ **whip·pi·ness** *n.*

whip·saw /hwípsaw, wíp–/ *n. & v.* • *n.* a saw with a narrow blade held at each end by a frame. • *v.* (*past part.* **–sawn** or **–sawed**) **1** *tr.* cut with a whipsaw. **2** *sl.* **a** *tr.* cheat by joint action on two others. **b** *intr.* be cheated in this way.

whip scor·pi·on *n.* any arachnid of the order Uropygi, with a long, slender, taillike appendage, which secretes an irritating vapor.

whip snake *n.* any of various long slender snakes of the family Colubridae.

whip·stitch /hwípstich, wíp–/ *v. & n.* • *v.tr.* sew with overcast stitches. • *n.* a stitch made this way.

whip·stock /hwípstok, wíp–/ *n.* the handle of a whip.

whir /hwər, wər/ *n. & v.* (also **whirr**) • *n.* a continuous rapid buzzing or softly clicking sound as of a bird's wings or of cogwheels in constant motion. • *v.intr.* (**whirred, whir·ring**) make this sound. [ME, prob. Scand.: cf. Da. *hvirre*, Norw. *kvirra*, perh. rel. to WHIRL]

whirl /hwərl, wərl/ *v. & n.* • *v.* **1** *tr. & intr.* swing around and around; revolve rapidly. **2** *tr. & intr.* (foll. by *away*) convey or go rapidly in a vehicle, etc. **3** *tr. & intr.* send or travel swiftly in an orbit or a curve. **4** *intr.* **a** (of the brain, senses, etc.) seem to spin around. **b** (of thoughts, etc.) be confused; follow each other in bewildering succession. • *n.* **1** a whirling movement (*vanished in a whirl of dust*). **2** a state of intense activity (*the social whirl*). **3** a state of confusion (*my mind is in a whirl*). **4** *colloq.* an attempt (*give it a whirl*). □□ **whirl·er** *n.* **whirl·ing·ly** *adv.* [ME: (v.) f. ON *hvirfla*: (n.) f. MLG & MDu. *wervel* spindle & ON *hvirfill* circle f. Gmc]

whirl·i·gig /hwórligig, wórl–/ *n.* **1** a spinning or whirling toy. **2 a**

merry-go-round. **3** a revolving motion. **4** anything regarded as hectic or constantly changing (*the whirligig of time*). **5** any freshwater beetle of the family Gyrinidae that circles about on the surface. [ME f. WHIRL + obs. *gig* whipping-top]

whirl·ing der·vish *n.* (also **danc·ing der·vish** or **howl·ing der·vish**) a dervish performing a wild dance, or howling, as a religious observance.

whirl·pool /hwórlpōōl, wórl–/ *n.* a powerful circular eddy in the sea, etc., often causing suction to its center.

whirl·wind /hwórlwind, wórl–/ *n.* **1** a mass or column of air whirling rapidly around and around in a cylindrical or funnel shape over land or water. **2** a confused tumultuous process. **3** (*attrib.*) very rapid (*a whirlwind romance*). □ **reap the whirlwind** suffer worse results of a bad action.

whirl·y·bird /hwórleebərd, wór–/ *n. colloq.* a helicopter.

whirr var. of WHIR.

whisht /hwisht/ *v.* (also **whist** /hwist/) esp. *Sc. & Ir. dial.* **1** *intr.* (esp. as *int.*) be quiet; hush. **2** *tr.* quieten. [imit.]

whisk /hwisk, wisk/ *v. & n.* ● *v.* **1** *tr.* (foll. by *away, off*) **a** brush with a sweeping movement. **b** take with a sudden motion (*whisked the plate away*). **2** *tr.* whip (cream, eggs, etc.). **3** *tr. & intr.* convey or go (esp. out of sight) lightly or quickly (*whisked me off to the doctor; the mouse whisked into its hole*). **4** *tr.* wave or lightly brandish. ● *n.* **1** a whisking action or motion. **2** a utensil for whisking eggs or cream, etc. **3** a bunch of grass, twigs, bristles, etc., for removing dust or flies. [ME *wisk*, prob. Scand.: cf. ON *visk* wisp]

whisk 2

whisk·er /hwískər, wís–/ *n.* **1** (usu. in *pl.*) the hair growing on a man's face, esp. on the cheek. **2** each of the bristles on the face of a cat, etc. **3** *colloq.* a small distance (*within a whisker of; won by a whisker*). **4** a strong, hairlike crystal of metal, etc. □ **have** (or **have grown**) **whiskers** *colloq.* (esp. of a story, etc.) be very old. □□ **whisk·ered** *adj.* **whisk·er·y** *adj.* [WHISK + –ER[1]]

whis·key /hwískee, wis–/ *n.* (also **whis·ky**) (*pl.* **–keys** or **–kies**) **1** an alcoholic liquor distilled esp. from grain, such as corn or malted barley. **2** a drink of this. [abbr. of obs. *whiskybae*, var. of USQUE-BAUGH]

whis·per /hwispər, wís–/ *v. & n.* ● *v.* **1 a** *intr.* speak very softly without vibration of the vocal cords. **b** *intr. & tr.* talk or say in a barely audible tone or in a secret or confidential way. **2** *intr.* speak privately or conspiratorially. **3** *intr.* (of leaves, wind, or water) rustle or murmur. ● *n.* **1** whispering speech (*talking in whispers*). **2** a whispering sound. **3** a thing whispered. **4** a rumor or piece of gossip. **5** a brief mention; a hint or suggestion. □ **it is whispered** there is a rumor. □□ **whis·per·er** *n.* **whis·per·ing** *n.* [OE *hwisprian* f. Gmc]

whis·per·ing gal·ler·y *n.* a gallery esp. under a dome with acoustic properties such that a whisper may be heard around its entire circumference.

whist[1] /hwist, wist/ *n.* a card game usu. for four players, with the winning of tricks. [earlier *whisk*, perh. f. WHISK (with ref. to whisking away the tricks): perh. assoc. with WHIST[2]]

whist[2] var. of WHISHT.

whist drive *n. Brit.* a social occasion with the playing of progressive whist.

whis·tle /hwisəl, wís–/ *n. & v.* ● *n.* **1** a clear shrill sound made by forcing breath through a small hole between nearly closed lips. **2** a similar sound made by a bird, the wind, a missile, etc. **3** an instrument used to produce such a sound. ● *v.* **1** *intr.* emit a whistle. **2 a** *intr.* give a signal or express surprise or derision by whistling. **b** *tr.* (often foll. by *up*) summon or give a signal to (a dog, etc.) by whistling. **3** *tr.* (also *absol.*) produce (a tune) by whistling. **4** *intr.* (foll. by *for*) vainly seek or desire. □ **as clean** (or **clear** or **dry**) **as a**

whistle very clean or clear or dry. **blow the whistle on** *colloq.* bring (an activity) to an end; inform on (those responsible). **whistle in the dark** pretend to be unafraid. [OE *(h)wistlian* (v.), *(h)wistle* (n.) of imit. orig.: cf. ON *hvísla* whisper, MSw. *hvísla* whistle]

whis·tle·blow·er /hwísəlblōər, wi–/ *n. colloq.* one who reports wrongdoing in a workplace or organization to authorities, the news media, etc.

whis·tler /hwíslər, wís–/ *n.* **1** any bird of the genus *Pachycephala*, with a whistling cry. **2** a kind of marmot.

whis·tle-stop *n.* **1** a small, unimportant town on a railroad line. **2** a politician's brief pause for a campaign speech on tour. **3** (*attrib.*) with brief pauses (*a whistle-stop tour*).

Whit /hwit, wit/ *adj.* connected with, belonging to, or following Whitsunday.

whit /hwit, wit/ *n.* a particle; a least possible amount (*not a whit better*). □ **every whit** the whole; wholly. **no** (or **never a** or **not a**) **whit** not at all. [earlier *w(h)yt* app. alt. f. WIGHT in phr. *no wight*, etc.]

white /hwīt, wīt/ *adj., n., & v.* ● *adj.* **1** resembling a surface reflecting sunlight without absorbing any of the visible rays; of the color of milk or fresh snow. **2** approaching such a color; pale esp. in the face (*turned as white as a sheet*). **3** less dark than other things of the same kind. **4 a** of the human group having light-colored skin. **b** of or relating to white people. **5** albino (*white mouse*). **6 a** (of hair) having lost its color esp. in old age. **b** (of a person) white-haired. **7** *colloq.* innocent; untainted. **8** (in *comb.*) (of esp. animals) having some white on the body (*white-throated*). **9 a** (of a plant) having white flowers or pale-colored fruit, etc. (*white hyacinth; white cauliflower*). **b** (of a tree) having light-colored bark, etc. (*white ash; white poplar*). **10** (of wine) made from white grapes or dark grapes with the skins removed. **11** *Brit.* (of coffee) with milk or cream added. **12** transparent; colorless (*white glass*). **13** *hist.* counterrevolutionary or reactionary (*white guard; white army*). ● *n.* **1** a white color or pigment. **2 a** a white clothes or material (*dressed in white*). **b** (in *pl.*) white garments as worn in tennis, etc. **3 a** (in a game or sport) a white piece, ball, etc. **b** the player using such pieces. **4** the white part or albumen around the yolk of an egg. **5** the visible part of the eyeball around the iris. **6** a member of a light-skinned race. **7** a white butterfly. **8** a blank space in printing. ● *v.tr.* *archaic* make white. □ **bleed white** drain (a person, country, etc.) of wealth, etc. □□ **white·ly** *adv.* **white·ness** *n.* **whit·ish** *adj.* [OE *hwīt* f. Gmc]

white ad·mir·al *n.* a butterfly, *Limenitis camilla*, with a white band across its wings.

white ant *n.* a termite.

white·bait /hwítbayt, wít–/ *n.* (*pl.* same) (usu. *pl.*) the small, silvery-white young of herrings and sprats esp. as food.

white·beam /hwítbeem, wít–/ *n.* a rosaceous tree, *Sorbus aria*, having red berries and leaves with a white, downy underside.

white·cap /hwítkap, wít–/ *n.* a white-crested wave at sea.

white cell *n.* (also **white blood cell** or **white cor·pus·cle**) a leukocyte.

white Christ·mas *n.* Christmas with snow on the ground.

white coal *n.* water as a source of power.

white-col·lar *adj.* (of a worker) engaged in clerical or administrative rather than manual work.

white cur·rant *n.* a cultivar of red currant with pale edible berries.

whit·ed sep·ul·cher *n.* a hypocrite (with ref. to Matt. 23:27).

white dwarf *n.* a small, very dense star.

white el·e·phant *n.* a useless and troublesome possession or thing.

white en·sign *n. Brit.* the ensign of the Royal Navy and the Royal Yacht Squadron.

white·face /hwítfays, wít–/ *n.* the white makeup of an actor, etc.

white feath·er *n.* a symbol of cowardice (a white feather in the tail of a game bird being a mark of bad breeding).

white·fish /hwítfish, wít–/ *n.* (*pl.* same or **–fish·es**) **1** any freshwater fish of the genus *Coregonus*, etc., of the trout family, and used esp. for food. **2** a marine fish, *Caulolatilus princeps*, of California used esp. for food. **3** *Brit.* any nonoily, pale-fleshed fish, e.g., plaice, cod, etc.

white flag *n.* a symbol of surrender or a period of truce.

white·fly /hwítflī, wít–/ *n.* (*pl.* **–flies**) any small insect of the family Aleyrodidae, having wings covered with white powder and feeding on the sap of shrubs, crops, etc.

white fri·ar *n.* (also **White Fri·ar**) a Carmelite.

white frost see FROST.

white goods *n.* **1** domestic linen. **2** large domestic electrical appliances.

White·hall /hwít-hawl, wít–/ *n.* **1** the British Government. **2** its offices or policy. [a street in London on which government offices are situated]

white·head /hwít-hed, wít–/ *n. colloq.* a white or white-topped skin pustule.

white heat *n.* **1** the temperature at which metal emits white light. **2** a state of intense passion or activity.

white hope n. **1** a person expected to achieve much for a group, organization, etc. **2** a white athlete, esp. a boxer that supporters hope or expect will defeat a black champion.

white hors·es n. whitecaps.

white-hot adj. at white heat.

White House n. the official residence of the US president and offices of the executive branch of government in Washington.

white lead n. a mixture of lead carbonate and hydrated lead oxide used as pigment.

white lie n. a harmless or trivial untruth.

white light n. colorless light, e.g., ordinary daylight.

white mag·ic n. magic used only for beneficent purposes.

white mat·ter n. the part of the brain and spinal cord consisting mainly of nerve fibers (see also GRAY MATTER).

white meat n. poultry, veal, rabbit, and pork.

white met·al n. a white or silvery alloy.

whit·en /hwítɘn, wít–/ v. tr. & intr. make or become white. □□ **whit·en·er** n. **whit·en·ing** n.

white night n. Brit. a sleepless night.

white noise n. noise containing many frequencies with equal intensities.

whiteout n. a dense blizzard esp. in polar regions.

white pa·per n. a government report giving information or proposals on an issue.

white pep·per n. the ripe or husked ground or whole berries of Piper nigrum as a condiment.

white pop·lar n. = ABELE.

white rose n. the emblem of Yorkshire, England or the House of York.

White Rus·sian n. **1** a Belorussian. **2** a cocktail of vodka, coffee liqueur, and cream or milk.

white sale n. a sale of household linen.

white sauce n. a sauce of flour, melted butter, and milk or cream.

white slave n. a woman tricked or forced into prostitution, usu. abroad. □□ **white slav·er·y** n. traffic in white slaves.

white·smith /hwítsmith, wít–/ n. **1** a worker in tin. **2** a polisher or finisher of metal goods.

white sock n. = STOCKING 3.

white sug·ar n. purified sugar.

white·thorn /hwít-thawrn, wít–/ n. the hawthorn.

white·throat /hwít-thrōt, wít–/ n. any of several birds with a white patch on the throat, esp. the warbler Sylvia communis or the finch Zonotrichia albicollis.

white tie n. a man's white bow tie as part of full evening dress.

white vit·ri·ol n. Chem. zinc sulfate.

white·wall /hwítwawl, wít–/ n. a tire having a white band encircling the outer sidewall.

white·wash /hwítwosh, –wawsh, wít–/ n. & v. ● n. **1** a solution of lime or of whiting and size for whitening walls, etc. **2** a means employed to conceal mistakes or faults in order to clear a person or institution of imputations. ● v.tr. **1** cover with whitewash. **2** attempt by concealment to clear the reputation of. **3** Brit. (in passive) (of an insolvent) get a fresh start by passage through a bankruptcy court. **4** defeat (an opponent) without allowing any opposing score. □□ **white·wash·er** n.

white wa·ter n. a shallow or foamy stretch of water.

white wed·ding n. Brit. a wedding at which the bride wears a formal white wedding dress.

white whale n. a northern cetacean, Delphinapterus leucas, white when adult. Also called **beluga**.

white·wood /hwítwŏŏd, wít–/ n. **1** any of several trees with white or light-colored wood, esp. the tulip tree. **2** the wood from such trees.

whit·ey /hwítee, wí–/ n. (also **White·y**) (pl. **-eys**) sl. offens. **1** a white person. **2** white people collectively.

whith·er /hwíthɘr, wíth–/ adv. & conj. archaic ● adv. **1** to what place, position, or state? **2** (prec. by place, etc.) to which (the house whither we were walking). ● conj. **1** to the or any place to which (go whither you will). **2** and thither (we saw a house, whither we walked). [OE hwider f. Gmc: cf. WHICH, HITHER, THITHER]

whith·er·so·ev·er /hwíthɘrsō-évɘr, wíth–/ adv. & conj. archaic to any place to which.

whit·ing[1] /hwíting, wí–/ n. a small, white-fleshed fish, Merlangus merlangus, used as food. [ME f. MDu. wijting, app. formed as WHITE + –ING[3]]

whit·ing[2] /hwíting, wí–/ n. ground chalk used in whitewashing, etc.

whit·leath·er /hwítlethɘr, wít–/ n. tawed leather. [ME f. WHITE + LEATHER]

whit·low /hwítlō, wít–/ n. an inflammation near a fingernail or toenail. [ME whitflaw, –flow, app. = WHITE + FLAW[1] in the sense 'crack,' but perh. of LG orig.: cf. Du. fijt, LG fīt whitlow]

Whit·sun /hwítsɘn, wít–/ n. & adj. ● n. = WHITSUNTIDE. ● adj. = WHIT. [ME, f. Whitsun Day = Whitsunday]

Whit·sun·day /hwítsúnday, wít–/ the seventh Sunday after Easter, commemorating the descent of the Holy Spirit at Pentecost (Acts 2). [OE Hwīta Sunnandæg, lit. white Sunday, prob. f. the white robes of the newly baptized at Pentecost]

Whit·sun·tide /hwítsɘntīd, wít–/ n. the weekend or week including Whitsunday.

whit·tle /hwítɘl, wítɘl/ v. **1** tr. & (foll. by at) intr. pare (wood, etc.) with repeated slicing with a knife. **2** tr. (often foll. by away, down) reduce by repeated subtractions. [var. of ME thwitel long knife f. OE thwītan to cut off]

whit·y /hwítee, wí–/ adj. (also **white·y**) whitish; rather white (usu. in comb.: whity-brown) (cf. WHITEY).

whiz /hwiz, wiz/ n. & v. (also **whizz**) colloq. ● n. (pl. **whiz·zes**) **1** the sound made by the friction of a body moving through the air at great speed. **2** (also **wiz**) colloq. a person who is remarkable or skillful in some respect (is a whiz at chess). ● v.intr. (**whizzed**, **whiz·zing**) move with or make a whiz. [imit.: in sense 2 infl. by WIZARD]

whiz·bang /hwízbang, wíz–/ n. & adj. ● n. colloq. **1** a high-velocity shell fired from a small-caliber gun, whose passage is heard before the gun's report. **2** a jumping kind of firework. ● adj. **1** very rapid, rushed, etc. **2** extremely effective and successful.

whiz kid n. colloq. a brilliant or highly successful young person.

WHO abbr. World Health Organization.

who /hŏŏ/ pron. (obj. **whom** /hŏŏm/ or colloq. **who**; poss. **whose** /hŏŏz/) **1 a** what or which person or persons? (who called?; you know who it was). **b** what sort of person or persons? (who am I to object?). **2** (a person) that (anyone who wishes can come; the woman whom you met; the man who you saw). **3** and or but he, she, they, etc. (gave it to Tom, who sold it to Jim). **4** archaic the or any person or persons that (whom the gods love die young). □ **as who should say** like a person who said; as though one said. **who-does-what** (of a dispute, etc.) about which group of workers should do a particular job. **who goes there?** see GO[1]. **who's who 1** who or what each person is (know who's who). **2** a list or directory with facts about notable persons. [OE hwā f. Gmc: whom f. OE dative hw ām, hwǣm : whose f. genit. hwæs]

▶ **Whom**, the objective case of **who**, is properly used where the word functions as an object: Our mayor is the one whom you mean; To whom is the package addressed? In informal usage, **who** often serves in all cases ("Who did you see?"), but in formal writing it is best to maintain the distinction.

whoa /wō/ int. used as a command to stop or slow a horse, etc. [var. of HO]

who'd /hŏŏd/ contr. **1** who had. **2** who would.

who·dun·it /hŏŏdúnit/ n. (also **who·dun·nit**) colloq. a story or play about the detection of a crime, etc., esp. murder. [= who done (illiterate for did) it?]

who·e'er /hŏŏ-áir/ poet. var. of WHOEVER.

who·ev·er /hŏŏ-évɘr/ pron. (obj. **whom·ev·er** /hŏŏm–/ or colloq. **who·ev·er**; poss. **whos·ev·er** /hŏŏz–/) **1** the or any person or persons who (whoever comes is welcome). **2** though anyone (whoever else objects, I do not; whosever it is, I want it). **3** colloq. (as an intensive) who ever; who at all (whoever heard of such a thing?).

whole /hōl/ adj. & n. ● adj. **1** in an uninjured, unbroken, intact, or undiminished state (swallowed it whole; there is not a plate left whole). **2** not less than; all there is of; entire; complete (waited a whole year; tell the whole truth; the whole school knows). **3** (of blood or milk, etc.) with no part removed. **4** (of a person) healthy; recovered from illness or injury. ● n. **1** a thing complete in itself. **2** all there is of a thing (spent the whole of the summer by the ocean). **3** (foll. by of) all members, inhabitants, etc., of (the whole of Congress knows it). □ **as a whole** as a unity; not as separate parts. **go (the) whole hog** see HOG. **on the whole** taking everything relevant into account; in general (it was, on the whole, a good report; they behaved well on the whole). **out of whole cloth** without fact; entirely fictitious. □□ **whole·ness** n. [OE hāl f. Gmc]

whole·food /hōlfŏŏd/ n. Brit. food which has not been unnecessarily processed nor refined.

whole-grain adj. made with or containing whole grains (whole-grain bread).

whole·heart·ed /hōlhaÌartid/ adj. **1** (of a person) completely devoted or committed. **2** (of an action, etc.) done with all possible effort, attention, or sincerity; thorough. □□ **whole·heart·ed·ly** adv. **whole·heart·ed·ness** n.

whole-life in·sur·ance n. life insurance for which premiums are payable throughout the remaining life of the person insured.

whole lot see LOT.

whole·meal /hōlmeel/ adj. Brit. = WHOLE-WHEAT.

whole note n. esp. Mus. a note having the time value of four quarter notes, and represented by a ring with no stem.

whole num·ber n. a number without fractions; an integer.

whole·sale /hōlsayl/ n., adj., adv., & v. ● n. the selling of things in large quantities to be retailed by others (cf. RETAIL). ● adj. & adv. **1** by wholesale; at a wholesale price (can get it for you wholesale). **2** on a large scale (wholesale destruction occurred; was handing out samples wholesale). ● v.tr. sell wholesale. □□ **whole·sal·er** n. [ME: orig. by whole sale]

whole·some /hōlsɘm/ adj. **1** promoting or indicating physical, mental, or moral health (wholesome pursuits; a wholesome appearance).

2 prudent (*wholesome respect*). □□ **whole•some•ly** *adv.* **whole•some•ness** *n.* [ME, prob. f. OE (unrecorded) *hālsum* (as WHOLE, –SOME¹)]

whole-tone scale *n. Mus.* a scale consisting entirely of tones, with no semitones.

whole-wheat *adj.* made of wheat with none of the bran or germ removed.

who•lism var. of HOLISM.

whol•ly /hólee/ *adv.* **1** entirely; without limitation nor diminution (*I am wholly at a loss*). **2** purely; exclusively (*a wholly bad example*). [ME, f. OE (unrecorded) *hāllīce* (as WHOLE, –LY²)]

whom *objective case* of WHO.
▶See note at WHO.

whom•ev•er *objective case* of WHOEVER.

whom•so *archaic objective case* of WHOSO.

whom•so•ev•er *objective case* of WHOSOEVER.

whoop /hoop, hwoop, woop/ *n. & v.* (also **hoop**) • *n.* **1** a loud cry of or as of excitement, etc. **2** a long, rasping, indrawn breath in whooping cough. • *v.intr.* utter a whoop. **whoop it up** *colloq.* **1** engage in revelry. **2** make a stir. [ME: imit.]

whoop•ee /hwoópee, woóp–, hwoó–, woó–/ *int. & n. colloq.* • *int.* expressing exuberant joy. • *n.* exuberant enjoyment or revelry. □ **make whoopee** *colloq.* **1** rejoice noisily or hilariously **2** engage in sexual play.

whoop•ee cush•ion *n.* a rubber cushion that when sat on makes a sound like the breaking of wind.

whoop•er /hoópər, hwoó–, woó–/ *n.* **1** one that whoops. **2** a whooping crane. **3** a whooper swan.

whoop•er swan *n.* a swan, *Cygnus cygnus*, with a characteristic whooping sound in flight.

whoop•ing cough *n.* an infectious bacterial disease, esp. of children, with a series of short, violent coughs followed by a whoop.

whoop•ing crane *n.* a white N. American crane with a loud, whooping cry.

whoops /hwoops, woops/ *int. colloq.* expressing surprise or apology, esp. on making an obvious mistake. [var. of OOPS]

whoosh /hwoosh, woosh/ *v., n., & int.* (also **woosh**) • *v.intr. & tr.* move or cause to move with a rushing sound. • *n.* a sudden movement accompanied by a rushing sound. • *int.* an exclamation imitating this. [imit.]

whop /hwop, wop/ *v.tr.* (**whopped, whop•ping**) *sl.* **1** thrash. **2** defeat; overcome. [ME: var. of dial. *wap*, of unkn. orig.]

whop•per /hwópər, wóp–/ *n. sl.* **1** something big of its kind. **2** a great lie.

whop•ping /hwóping, wóp–/ *adj. sl.* very big (*a whopping lie; a whopping fish*).

whore /hawr/ *n. & v.* • *n.* **1** a prostitute. **2** *derog.* a promiscuous woman. • *v.intr.* **1** (of a man) seek or chase after whores. **2** *archaic* (foll. by *after*) commit idolatry or iniquity. □□ **whore•dom** *n.* **whor•er** *n.* [OE *hōre* f. Gmc]

whore•house /hawrhows/ *n.* a brothel.

whore•mas•ter /háwrmastər/ *n. archaic* = WHOREMONGER.

whore•mon•ger /háwrmunggər, –mong–/ *n. archaic* a sexually promiscuous man; a lecher.

whore•son /háwrsən/ *n. archaic* **1** a disliked person. **2** (*attrib.*) (of a person or thing) vile.

whor•ish /háwrish/ *adj.* of or like a whore. □□ **whor•ish•ly** *adv.* **whor•ish•ness** *n.*

whorl /hwawrl, wawrl, hwərl, wərl/ *n.* **1** a ring of leaves or other organs around a stem of a plant. **2** one turn of a spiral, esp. on a shell. **3** a complete circle in a fingerprint. **4** *archaic* a small wheel on a spindle steadying its motion. □□ **whorled** *adj.* [ME *wharwyl, whorwil*, app. var. of WHIRL: infl. by *wharve* (n.) = whorl of a spindle]

whor•tle•ber•ry /hwórtəlberee, wərt–/ *n.* (*pl.* **–ries**) a bilberry. [16th c.: dial. form of *hurtleberry*, ME, of unkn. orig.]

whose /hooz/ *pron. & adj.* • *pron.* of or belonging to which person (*whose is this book?*). • *adj.* of whom or which (*whose book is this?; the man, whose name was Tim; the house whose roof was damaged*). ▶It is not necessary to avoid using **whose** in referring to things rather than people. *I admired the houses, whose windows glowed in the sunset* is perfectly acceptable. To say *I admired the houses, the windows of which glowed in the sunset* is more awkward.

whose•so *archaic poss.* of WHOSO.

whose•so•ev•er *poss.* of WHOSOEVER.

whos•ev•er /hoozévər/ *poss.* of WHOEVER.

who•so /hoósō/ *pron.* (*obj.* **whom•so** /hoóm–/; *poss.* **whose•so** /hoóz–/) *archaic* = WHOEVER. [ME, f. WHO + SO¹, f. OE *swā hwā swā*]

who•so•ev•er /hoósō-évər/ *pron.* (*obj.* **whom•so•ev•er** /hoóm–/; *poss.* **whose•so•ev•er** /hoóz–/) *archaic* = WHOEVER.

why /hwī, wī/ *adv., int., & n.* • *adv.* **1 a** for what reason or purpose (*why did you do it?; I do not know why you came*). **b** on what grounds (*why do you say that?*). **2** (*prec. by reason*, etc.) for which (*the reasons why I did it*). • *int.* expressing: **1** surprised discovery or recognition (*why, it's you!*). **2** impatience (*why, of course I do!*). **3** reflection (*why, yes, I think so*). **4** objection (*why, what is wrong with it?*). • *n.* (*pl.* **whys**) a reason or explanation (*esp.* whys and wherefores).

□ **why so?** on what grounds?; for what reason or purpose? [OE *hwī, hwȳ* instr. of *hwæt* WHAT f. Gmc]

whyd•ah /hwída, wid–/ *n.* (also **whid•ah**) any small African weaverbird of the genus *Vidua*, the male having mainly black plumage and tail feathers of great length. [orig. *widow bird*, altered f. assoc. with *Whidah* (now Ouidah) in Benin]

WI *abbr.* **1** West Indies. **2** West Indian. **3** Wisconsin (in official postal use).

wich- var. of WYCH-.

Wich•i•ta /wíchitaw/ *n.* **1 a** a N. American people native to Kansas. **b** a member of this people. **2** the language of this people.

wick¹ /wik/ *n. & v.* • *n.* **1** a strip or thread of fibrous or spongy material feeding a flame with fuel in a candle, lamp, etc. **2** *Surgery* a gauze strip inserted in a wound to drain it. • *v.tr.* draw (moisture) away by capillary action. □ **dip one's wick** *coarse sl.* (of a man) have sexual intercourse. **get on a person's wick** *Brit. colloq.* annoy a person. [OE *wēoce, –wēoc* (cf. MDu. *wiecke*, MLG *wēke*), of unkn. orig.]

wick² /wik/ *n. Brit. dial. exc.* in compounds, e.g., *bailiwick*, and in place names, e.g., *Hampton Wick, Warwick* **1** *archaic* a town, hamlet, or district. **2** *Brit.* a dairy farm. [OE *wīc*, prob. f. Gmc f. L *vicus* street, village]

wick•ed /wíkid/ *adj.* (**wick•ed•er, wick•ed•est**) **1** sinful; iniquitous; given to or involving immorality. **2** spiteful; ill-tempered; intending or intended to give pain. **3** playfully malicious. **4** *colloq.* foul; very bad; formidable (*wicked weather, a wicked cough*). **5** *sl.* excellent; remarkable. □□ **wick•ed•ly** *adv.* **wick•ed•ness** *n.* [ME f. obs. *wick* (perh. adj. use of OE *wicca* wizard) + –ED¹ as in *wretched*]

wick•er /wíkər/ *n.* plaited twigs or osiers, etc., as material for chairs, baskets, mats, etc. [ME, f. E.Scand.: cf. Sw. *viker* willow, rel. to *vika* bend]

wick•er•work /wíkərwərk/ *n.* **1** wicker. **2** things made of wicker.

wick•et /wíkit/ *n.* **1** (in full **wicket door** or **gate**) a small door or gate esp. beside or in a larger one or closing the lower part only of a doorway. **2** an aperture in a door or wall usu. closed with a sliding panel. **3** a croquet hoop. **4** *Cricket* **a** a set of three stumps with the bails in position defended by a batsman. **b** the ground between two wickets. **c** the state of this (*a slow wicket*). **d** an instance of a batsman being got out (*bowler has taken four wickets*). **e** a pair of batsmen batting at the same time (*a third-wicket partnership*). □ **on a good** (or **sticky**) **wicket** *Brit. colloq.* in a favorable (or unfavorable) position. [ME f. AF & ONF *wiket*, OF *guichet*, of uncert. orig.]

wick•et•keep•er /wíkitkeépər/ *n. Cricket* the fielder stationed close behind a batsman's wicket.

wick•i•up /wíkeeup/ *n.* a Native American hut of a frame covered with grass, etc. [Fox *wikiyap*]

wid•er•shins var. of WITHERSHINS.

wide /wīd/ *adj., adv., & n.* • *adj.* **1 a** measuring much or more than other things of the same kind across or from side to side. **b** considerable; more than is needed (*a wide margin*). **2** (following a measurement) in width (*a foot wide*). **3** extending far; embracing much; of great extent (*a wide range; has wide experience; reached a wide public*). **4** not tight nor close nor restricted; loose. **5 a** free; liberal; unprejudiced (*takes wide views*). **b** not specialized; general. **6** open to the full extent (*staring with wide eyes*). **7 a** (foll. by *of*) not within a reasonable distance of. **b** at a considerable distance from a point or mark. **8** *Brit. sl.* shrewd; skilled in sharp practice (*wide boy*). **9** (in *comb.*) extending over the whole of (*nationwide*). • *adv.* **1** widely. **2** to the full extent (*wide awake*). **3** far from the target, etc. (*is shooting wide*). • *n.* **1** *Cricket* a ball judged to pass the wicket beyond the batsman's reach and so scoring a run. **2** (prec. by *the*) the wide world. □ **give a wide berth to** see BERTH. **wide awake 1** fully awake. **2** *colloq.* wary; knowing. **wide of the mark** see MARK¹. □□ **wide•ness** *n.* **wid•ish** *adj.* [OE *wīd* (adj.), *wīde* (adv.) f. Gmc]

wide-an•gle *adj.* (of a lens) having a short focal length and hence a field covering a wide angle.

wide•a•wake /wídəwáyk/ *n.* a soft felt hat with a low crown and wide brim.

wide-eyed *adj.* surprised or naive.

wide•ly /wídlee/ *adv.* **1** to a wide extent; far apart. **2** extensively (*widely read; widely distributed*). **3** by many people (*it is widely thought that*). **4** considerably; to a large degree (*holds a widely different view*).

wid•en /wíd'n/ *v.tr. & intr.* make or become wider. □□ **wid•en•er** *n.*

wide o•pen *adj.* (often foll. by *to*) exposed or vulnerable (to attack, etc.).

wide-rang•ing *adj.* covering an extensive range.

wide•spread /wídspréd/ *adj.* widely distributed or disseminated.

wide world *n.* all the world great as it is.

widg•eon /wíjən/ *n.* (also **wig•eon**) a species of dabbling duck, esp. *Anas penelope* or *Anas americana*. [16th c.: orig. uncert.]

widg•et /wíjit/ *n. colloq.* any gadget or device. [perh. alt. of GADGET]

wid•ow /wídō/ *n. & v.* • *n.* **1** a woman who has lost her husband by death and has not married again. **2** a woman whose husband is often away on or preoccupied with a specified activity (*golf widow; football widow*). **3** extra cards dealt separately and taken by the highest bidder. **4** *Printing* the short last line of a paragraph, esp. at the top of a page or column. ● *v.tr.* **1** make into a widow or widower. **2** (as **widowed** *adj.*) bereft by the death of a spouse (*my widowed mother*). **3** (foll. by *of*) deprive of.

Old English *widewe, widuwe*, from an Indo-European root meaning 'be empty, be separated'; related to Sanskrit *vidh* 'be destitute,' Latin *viduus* 'bereft, widowed,' and Greek *ēitheos* ' unmarried man.'

wid·ow bird *n.* a whydah.

wid·ow's cruse *n.* an apparently small supply that proves or seems inexhaustible (see 1 Kgs. 17: 10–16).

wid·ow·er /wídōər/ *n.* a man who has lost his wife by death and has not married again.

wid·ow·hood /wídōhŏŏd/ *n.* the state or period of being a widow or widower.

wid·ow's mite *n.* a small money contribution, esp. by one who is quite poor (see Mark 12:42).

wid·ow's peak *n.* a V-shaped growth of hair toward the center of the forehead.

wid·ow's weeds see WEEDS.

width /width, with, with/ *n.* **1** measurement or distance from side to side. **2** a large extent. **3** breadth or liberality of thought, views, etc. **4** a strip of material of full width as woven. □□ **width·ways** *adv.* **width·wise** *adv.* [17th c. (as WIDE, –TH²) replacing *wideness*]

wield /weeld/ *v.tr.* **1** hold and use (a weapon or tool). **2** exert or command (power or authority, etc.). □□ **wield·er** *n.* [OE *wealdan, wieldan* f. Gmc]

wield·y /weeldee/ *adj.* (**wield·i·er, wield·i·est**) easily wielded, controlled, or handled.

wie·ner /weenər/ *n.* a frankfurter. [Ger. *Wiener wurst* Viennese sausage]

Wie·ner schnit·zel /veenər shnítsəl/ *n.* a veal cutlet breaded, fried, and garnished. [G, = Viennese slice]

wife /wīf/ *n.* (*pl.* **wives** /wīvz/) **1** a married woman esp. in relation to her husband. **2** *archaic* a woman, esp. an old or uneducated one. **3** (in *comb.*) a woman engaged in a specified activity (*fishwife; housewife; midwife*). □ **have** (or **take**) **to wife** *archaic* marry (a woman). □□ **wife·hood** *n.* **wife·less** *adj.* **wife·like** *adj.* **wife·ly** *adj.* **wife·li·ness** *n.* **wif·ish** *adj.* [OE *wīf* woman: ult. orig. unkn.]

wife swap·ping *n. colloq.* exchanging wives for sexual relations.

wig¹ /wig/ *n.* an artificial head of hair esp. to conceal baldness or as a disguise, or worn by a judge or barrister or as period dress. □□ **wigged** *adj.* (also in *comb.*). **wig·less** *adj.* [abbr. of PERIWIG: cf. WINKLE]

wig² /wig/ *v.tr.* (**wigged, wig·ging**) *Brit. colloq.* rebuke sharply; rate. [app. f. WIG¹ in sl. or colloq. sense 'rebuk ' (19th c.)]

wig·eon var. of WIDGEON.

wig·ging /wíging/ *n. Brit. colloq.* a reprimand.

wig·gle /wígəl/ *v. & n. intr. & tr.* move or cause to move quickly from side to side, etc. ● *n.* an act of wiggling. □□ **wig·gler** *n.* [ME f. MLG & MDu. *wiggelen*: cf. WAG¹, WAGGLE]

wig·gly /wíglee/ *adj.* (**wig·gli·er, wig·gli·est**) *colloq.* **1** showing wiggles. **2** having small irregular undulations.

wight /wīt/ *n. archaic* a person (*wretched wight*). [OE *wiht* = thing, creature, of unkn. orig.]

wig·wag /wígwag/ *v.intr.* (**wig·wagged, wig·wag·ging**) *colloq.* **1** move lightly to and fro. **2** wave flags in this way in signaling. [redupl. f. WAG¹]

wig·wam /wígwom/ *n.* **1** a Native American hut or tent of skins, mats, or bark on poles. **2** a similar structure for children, etc. [Ojibwa *wigwaum*, Algonquian *wikiwam* their house]

wil·co /wílkō/ *int. colloq.* expressing compliance or agreement, esp. acceptance of instructions received by radio. [abbr. of *will comply*]

wild /wīld/ *adj., adv., & n.* ● *adj.* **1** (of an animal or plant) in its original

wigwam

natural state; not domesticated nor cultivated (esp. of species or varieties allied to others that are not wild). **2** not civilized; barbarous. **3** (of scenery, etc.) having a conspicuously desolate appearance. **4** unrestrained; disorderly; uncontrolled (*a wild youth; wild hair*). **5** tempestuous; violent (*a wild night*). **6 a** intensely eager; excited; frantic (*wild with excitement; wild delight*). **b** (of looks, appearance, etc.) indicating distraction. **c** (foll. by *about*) *colloq.* enthusiastically devoted to (a person or subject). **7** *colloq.* infuriated; angry (*makes me wild*). **8** haphazard; ill-aimed; rash (*a wild guess; a*

wild shot; a wild venture). **9** (of a horse, game bird, etc.) shy; easily startled. **10** *colloq.* exciting; delightful. **11** (of a card) having any rank chosen by the player holding it (*the joker is wild*). ● *adv.* in a wild manner (*shooting wild*). ● *n.* **1** a wild tract. **2** a desert. □ **in the wild** in an uncultivated, etc., state. **in** (or **out in**) **the wilds** *colloq.* far from normal habitation. **run wild** grow or stray unchecked or undisciplined. **sow one's wild oats** see OAT. □□ **wild·ish** *adj.* **wild·ly** *adv.* **wild·ness** *n.* [OE *wilde* f. Gmc]

wild-and-wool·ly *adj.* uncouth; lacking refinement.

wild boar see BOAR.

wild card *n.* **1** a playing card that has any rank chosen by the player holding it. **2** *Computing* a character that will match any character or sequence of characters in a file name, etc. **3** *Sports* an extra player or team chosen to enter a competition at the selectors' discretion.

wild·cat /wíldkat/ *n. & adj.* ● *n.* **1** a hot-tempered or violent person. **2** any of various smallish cats, esp. the European *Felis sylvestris* or the N. American bobcat. **3** an exploratory oil well. ● *adj.* (*attrib.*) **1** reckless; financially unsound. **2** (of a strike) sudden and unofficial.

wild·cat strike *n.* an unauthorized strike by esp. union laborers.

wil·de·beest /wíldəbeest, víl–/ *n.* = GNU. [Afrik. (as WILD, BEAST)]

wil·der /wíldər/ *v.tr. archaic* **1** lead astray. **2** bewilder. [perh. based on WILDERNESS]

wil·der·ness /wíldərnis/ *n.* **1** a desert; an uncultivated and uninhabited region. **2** part of a garden left with an uncultivated appearance. **3** (foll. by *of*) a confused assemblage of things. □ **in the wilderness** *Brit.* out of political office. [OE *wildēornes* f. *wild dēor* wild deer]

wild·fire /wíldfīr/ *n. hist.* **1** a combustible liquid, esp. Greek fire, formerly used in warfare. **2** = WILL-O'-THE-WISP. □ **spread like wildfire** spread with great speed.

wild·flow·er /wíldflowər, wíold–, –flowr/ *n.* **1** any wild or uncultivated flowering plant. **2** the flower of such a plant.

wild·fowl /wíldfowl/ *n.* (*pl.* same) a game bird, esp. an aquatic one.

wild-goose chase *n.* a foolish or hopeless and unproductive quest.

wild horse *n.* **1** a horse not domesticated nor broken in. **2** (in *pl.*) *colloq.* even the most powerful influence, etc. (*wild horses would not drag the secret from me*).

wild hy·a·cinth *n.* = BLUEBELL 1.

wild·ing /wílding/ *n.* (also **wild·ling** /–ling/) **1** a plant sown by natural agency, esp. a wild crab apple. **2** the fruit of such a plant. [WILD + –ING³]

wild·life /wíldlīf/ *n.* wild animals collectively.

wild rice *n.* any tall grass of the genus *Zizania*, yielding edible grains.

wild silk *n.* **1** silk from wild silkworms. **2** an imitation of this from short silk fibers.

Wild West *n.* the western US in a time of lawlessness in its early history.

wild·wood /wíldwŏŏd/ *n. poet.* uncultivated woodland.

wile /wīl/ *n. & v.* ● *n.* (usu. in *pl.*) a stratagem; a trick or cunning procedure. ● *v.tr.* (foll. by *away, into*, etc.) lure or entice. [ME *wīl*, perh. f. Scand. (ON *vél* craft)]

wil·ful *Brit.* var. of WILLFUL.

will¹ /wil/ *v.aux. & tr.* (3rd sing. present **will**; past **would** /wŏŏd/) (foll. by infin. without *to*, or *absol.*; present and past only in use) **1** (in the 2nd and 3rd persons, and often in the 1st: see SHALL) expressing the future tense in statements, commands, or questions (*you will regret this; they will leave at once; will you go to the party?*). **2** (in the 1st person) expressing a wish or intention (*I will return soon*). **3** expressing desire, consent, or inclination (*will you have a sandwich?; come when you will; the door will not open*). **4** expressing ability or capacity (*the jar will hold a quart*). **5** expressing habitual or inevitable tendency (*accidents will happen; will sit there for hours*). **6** expressing probability or expectation (*that will be my wife*). □ **will do** *colloq.* expressing willingness to carry out a request. [OE *wyllan*, (unrecorded) *willan* f. Gmc: rel. to L *volo*]

▶See note at SHALL.

will² /wil/ *n. & v.* ● *n.* **1** the faculty by which a person decides or is regarded as deciding on and initiating action (*the mind consists of the understanding and the will*). **2** control exercised by deliberate purpose over impulse; self-control; willpower (*has a strong will*). **3** a deliberate or fixed desire or intention (*a will to live*). **4** energy of intention; the power of effecting one's intentions or dominating others. **5** directions (usu. written) in legal form for the disposition of one's property after death (*make one's will*). **6** disposition toward others (*good will*). **7** *archaic* what one desires or ordains (*thy will be done*). ● *v.tr.* **1** have as the object of one's will; intend unconditionally (*what God wills; willed that we should succeed*). **2** (*absol.*) exercise willpower. **3** instigate or impel or compel by the exercise of willpower (*you can will yourself into contentment*). **4** bequeath by the terms of a will (*shall will my money to charity*). □ **at will 1** whenever one pleases. **2** *Law* able to be evicted without notice (*tenant at will*). **have one's will** obtain what one wants. **what is your will?** what do you wish done? **where there's a will there's a way** determination will overcome any obstacle. **a will of one's own** obstinacy; willfulness of character. **with the best will in the world** esp. *Brit.* however good one's intentions. **with a will** energetically or resolutely. □□ **willed** *adj.* (also in *comb.*). **will•er** *n.* **will•less** *adj.* [OE *willa* f. Gmc]

wil•let /wílit/ *n.* (*pl.* same) a large N. American wader, *Catoptrophorus semipalmatus.* [*pill-will-willet,* imit. of its cry]

will•ful /wílfool/ *adj.* (*Brit.* **wil•ful**) **1** (of an action or state) intentional, deliberate (*willful murder; willful neglect; willful disobedience*). **2** (of a person) obstinate, headstrong. □□ **will•ful•ly** *adv.* **will•ful•ness** *n.* [ME f. WILL² + -FUL]

wil•lies /wíleez/ *n.pl. colloq.* nervous discomfort (esp. *give* or *get the willies*). [19th c.: orig. unkn.]

will•ing /wíling/ *adj. & n.* ● *adj.* **1** ready to consent or undertake (*a willing ally; am willing to do it*). **2** given or done, etc., by a willing person (*willing hands; willing help*). ● *n.* cheerful intention (*show willing*). □□ **will•ing•ly** *adv.* **will•ing•ness** *n.*

will-o'-the-wisp /wíləthəwísp/ *n.* **1** a phosphorescent light seen on marshy ground, perhaps resulting from the combustion of gases; ignis fatuus. **2** an elusive person. **3** a delusive hope or plan. [orig. *Will with the wisp: wisp* = handful of (lighted) hay, etc.]

wil•low /wílō/ *n.* **1** a tree or shrub of the genus *Salix,* growing usu. near water in temperate climates, with small flowers borne on catkins, and pliant branches yielding osiers and wood for cricket bats, baskets, etc. **2** an item made of willow wood, esp. a cricket bat. [OE *welig*]

wil•low herb *n.* any plant of the genus *Epilobium,* etc., esp. one with leaves like a willow and pale purple flowers.

wil•low pat•tern *n.* a conventional design representing a Chinese scene, often with a willow tree, of blue on white porcelain, stoneware, or earthenware.

wil•low war•bler *n.* (also **wil•low wren**) a small woodland bird, *Phylloscopus trochilus,* with a tuneful song.

wil•low•y /wílō-ee/ *adj.* **1** having or bordered by willows. **2** lithe and slender.

will•pow•er /wílpowr/ *n.* control exercised by deliberate purpose over impulse; self-control (*overcame his shyness by willpower*).

wil•ly-nil•ly /wíleenílee/ *adv. & adj.* ● *adv.* whether one likes it or not. ● *adj.* existing or occurring willy-nilly. [later spelling of *will I, nill I* I am willing, I am unwilling]

wil•ly-wil•ly /wíleewílee/ *n.* (*pl.* **–lies**) *Austral.* a cyclone or dust storm. [Aboriginal]

wilt¹ /wilt/ *v. & n.* ● *v.* **1** *intr.* (of a plant, leaf, or flower) wither; droop. **2** *intr.* (of a person) lose one's energy; flag; tire; droop. **3** *tr.* cause to wilt. ● *n.* a plant disease causing wilting. [orig. dial.: perh. alt. f. *wilk, welk,* of LG or Du. orig.]

wilt² /wilt/ *archaic 2nd person sing.* of WILL¹.

Wil•ton /wíltən/ *n.* a kind of woven carpet with a thick pile. [*Wilton* in S. England]

wil•y /wílee/ *adj.* (**wil•i•er, wil•i•est**) full of wiles; crafty; cunning. □□ **wil•i•ly** *adv.* **wil•i•ness** *n.*

wimp /wimp/ *n. colloq.* a feeble or ineffectual person. □□ **wimp•ish** *adj.* **wimp•ish•ly** *adv.* **wimp•ish•ness** *n.* **wimp•y** *adj.* [20th c.: orig. uncert.]

wim•ple /wímpəl/ *n. & v.* ● *n.* a linen or silk headdress covering the neck and the sides of the face, formerly worn by women and still worn by some nuns. ● *v.tr. & intr.* arrange or fall in folds. [OE *wimpel*]

Wims•hurst ma•chine /wímzhərst/ *n.* a device for generating an electric charge by turning glass disks in opposite directions. [J. *Wimshurst,* Engl. engineer d. 1903]

wimple

win /win/ *v. & n.* ● *v.* (**win•ning;** *past* and *past part.* **won** /wun/) **1** *tr.* acquire or secure as a result of a fight, contest, bet, litigation, or some other effort (*won some money; won my admiration*). **2** *tr.* be victorious in (a fight, game, race, etc.). **3** *intr.* **a** be the victor; win a race or contest, etc. (*who won?; persevere, and you will win*). **b** (foll. by *through, free,* etc.) make one's way or become by successful effort. **4** *tr.* reach by effort (*win the summit; win the shore*). **5** *tr.* obtain (ore) from a mine. **6** *tr.* dry (hay, etc.) by exposure to the air. ● *n.* victory in a game or bet, etc. □ **win the day** be victorious in battle, argument, etc. **win over** persuade; gain the support of. **win one's spurs 1** *colloq.* gain distinction or fame. **2** *Brit. hist.* gain a knighthood. **win through** (or **out**) overcome obstacles. **you can't win** *colloq.* there is no way to succeed. **you can't win them** (or **'em**) **all** *colloq.* a resigned expression of consolation on failure. □□ **win•na•ble** *adj.* [OE *winnan* toil, endure: cf. OHG *winnan,* ON *vinna*]

wince¹ /wins/ *n. & v.* ● *n.* a start or involuntary shrinking movement showing pain or distress. ● *v.intr.* give a wince. □□ **winc•er** *n.* **winc•ing•ly** *adv.* [ME f. OF *guenchir* turn aside: cf. WINCH, WINK]

wince² /wins/ *n. Brit.* var. of WINCH 4.

winch /winch/ *n. & v.* ● *n.* **1** the crank of a wheel or axle. **2** a windlass. **3** *Brit.* the reel of a fishing rod. **4** a roller for moving textile

fabric through a dyeing vat. ● *v.tr.* lift with a winch. □□ **winch•er** *n.* [OE *wince* f. Gmc: cf. WINCE¹]

Win•ches•ter /wínchestər/ *n.* **1** *Trademark* a breech-loading repeating rifle. **2** (in full **Winchester disk**) *Computing* a hermetically sealed data-storage device (so called because its original numerical designation corresponded to that of the rifle's caliber). [O. F. *Winchester* d. 1880, US manufacturer of the rifle]

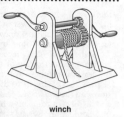

winch

wind¹ /wind/ *n. & v.* ● *n.* **1 a** air in more or less rapid natural motion, esp. from an area of high pressure to one of low pressure. **b** a current of wind blowing from a specified direction or otherwise defined (*north wind; opposing wind*). **2 a** breath as needed in physical exertion or in speech. **b** the power of breathing without difficulty while running or making a similar continuous effort (*let me recover my wind*). **c** a spot below the center of the chest where a blow temporarily paralyzes breathing. **3** mere empty words; meaningless rhetoric. **4** gas generated in the bowels, etc., by indigestion; flatulence. **5 a** an artificially produced current of air, esp. for sounding an organ or other wind instrument. **b** air stored for use or used as a current. **c** the wind instruments of an orchestra collectively (*poor balance between wind and strings*). **6** a scent carried by the wind, indicating the presence or proximity of an animal, etc. ● *v.tr.* **1** exhaust the wind of by exertion or a blow. **2** renew the wind of by rest (*stopped to wind the horses*). **3** make breathe quickly and deeply by exercise. **4** *Brit.* make (a baby) bring up wind after feeding; burp. **5** detect the presence of by a scent. **6** /wind/ (*past* and *past part.* **wind•ed** or **wound** /wownd/) *poet.* sound (a bugle or call) by blowing. □ **before the wind** helped by the wind's force. **between wind and water** at a vulnerable point. **close to** (or **near**) **the wind 1** sailing as nearly against the wind as is consistent with using its force. **2** *colloq.* verging on indecency or dishonesty. **get wind of 1** smell out. **2** begin to suspect; hear a rumor of. **get** (or **have**) **the wind up** *Brit. colloq.* be alarmed or frightened. **how** (or **which way**) **the wind blows** (or **lies**) **1** what is the state of opinion. **2** what developments are likely. **in the wind** happening or about to happen. **in the wind's eye** directly against the wind. **like the wind** swiftly. **off the wind** *Naut.* with the wind on the quarter. **on a wind** *Naut.* against a wind on either bow. **on the wind** (of a sound or scent) carried by the wind. **put the wind up** *Brit. colloq.* alarm or frighten. **take wind** *Brit.* be rumored; become known. **take the wind out of a person's sails** frustrate a person by anticipating an action or remark, etc. **throw caution to the wind** (or **winds**) not worry about taking risks; be reckless. **to the winds** (or **four winds**) **1** in all directions. **2** into a state of abandonment or neglect. **wind and weather** exposure to the effects of the elements. □□ **wind•less** *adj.* [OE f. Gmc]

wind² /wind/ *v. & n.* ● *v.* (*past* and *past part.* **wound** /wownd/) **1** *intr.* go in a circular, spiral, curved, or crooked course (*a winding staircase; the path winds up the hill*). **2** *tr.* make (one's way) by such a course (*wind your way up to bed; wound their way into our affections*). **3** *tr.* wrap closely; surround with or as with a coil (*wound the blanket around me; wound my arms around the child; wound the child in my arms*). **4 a** *tr.* coil; provide with a coiled thread, etc. (*wind the ribbon onto the reel; wound cotton on a reel; winding yarn into a ball*). **b** *intr.* coil; (of yarn, etc.) coil into a ball (*the vine winds around the pole; the yarn wound into a ball*). **5** *tr.* wind up (a clock, etc.). **6** *tr.* hoist or draw with a windlass, etc. (*wound the cable car up the moun-*

tain). ● *n.* **1** a bend or turn in a course. **2** a single turn when winding. □ **wind down 1** lower by winding. **2** (of a mechanism) unwind. **3** (of a person) relax. **4** draw gradually to a close. **wind off** unwind (string, wool, etc.). **wind around one's finger** see FINGER. **wind up 1** coil the whole of (a piece of string, etc.). **2** esp. *Brit.* tighten the coiling or coiled spring of (esp. a clock, etc.). **3 a** *colloq.* increase the tension or intensity of (*wound myself up to fever pitch*). **b** irritate or provoke (a person) to the point of anger. **4** bring to a conclusion; end (*wound up his speech*). **5** *Commerce* **a** arrange the affairs of and dissolve (a company). **b** (of a company) cease business and go into liquidation. **6** *colloq.* arrive finally; end in a specified state or circumstance (*you'll wind up in prison; wound up owing $100*). **7** *Baseball* (of a pitcher) carry out a windup. [OE *windan* f. Gmc, rel. to WANDER, WEND]

wind·age /wíndij/ *n.* **1** the friction of air against the moving part of a machine. **2 a** the effect of the wind in deflecting a missile. **b** an allowance for this. **3** the difference between the diameter of a gun's bore and its projectile, allowing the escape of gas.

wind·bag /wíndbag/ *n. colloq.* a person who talks a lot but says little of any value.

wind band *n.* a group of wind instruments as a band or section of an orchestra.

wind·blown /wíndblōn/ *adj.* exposed to or blown about by the wind.

wind·bound /wíndbownd/ *adj.* unable to sail because of opposing winds.

wind·break /wíndbrayk/ *n.* a row of trees or a fence or wall, etc., serving to break the force of the winds.

wind·break·er /wíndbraykər/ *n.* a kind of wind-resistant outer jacket with close-fitting neck, cuffs, and lower edge.

wind·burn /wíndbərn/ *n.* inflammation of the skin caused by exposure to the wind.

wind·cheat·er /wíndcheetər/ *n. Brit.* = WINDBREAKER.

wind·chill /wíndchil/ *n.* the cooling effect of wind blowing on a surface.

wind cone *n.* = WIND SOCK.

wind·er /wíndər/ *n.* a winding mechanism esp. of a clock or watch.

wind·down *n. colloq.* a gradual lessening of excitement or reduction of activity.

wind·fall /wíndfawl/ *n.* **1** an apple or other fruit blown to the ground by the wind. **2** a piece of unexpected good fortune, esp. a legacy.

wind·flow·er /wíndflowr/ *n.* an anemone.

wind force *n.* the force of the wind esp. as measured on the Beaufort, etc., scale.

wind gap *n.* a dried-up former river valley through ridges or hills.

wind gauge *n.* **1** an anemometer. **2** an apparatus attached to the sights of a gun enabling allowance to be made for the wind in shooting. **3** a device showing the amount of wind in an organ.

wind·hov·er /wíndhuvər/ *n. Brit.* a kestrel.

wind·ing /wínding/ *n.* **1** in senses of WIND² *v.* **2** curved or sinuous motion or movement. **3 a** a thing that is wound around or coiled. **b** *Electr.* coils of wire as a conductor around an armature, etc.

wind·ing sheet *n.* a sheet in which a corpse is wrapped for burial.

wind in·stru·ment *n.* a musical instrument in which sound is produced by a current of air, esp. the breath.

wind·jam·mer /wíndjamər/ *n.* **1** a merchant sailing ship. **2** a member of its crew.

wind·lass /wíndləs/ *n. & v.* ● *n.* a machine with a horizontal axle for hauling or hoisting. ● *v.tr.* hoist or haul with a windlass. [alt. (perh. by assoc. with dial. *windle* to wind) of obs. *windas* f. OF *guindas* f. ON *vindáss* f. *vinda* WIND² + *áss* pole]

windlass

win·dle·straw /wínd'lstraw/ *n. archaic* an old dry stalk of grass. [OE *windelstréaw* grass for plaiting f. *windel* basket (as WIND², −LE¹) + *stréaw* STRAW]

wind ma·chine *n.* a device for producing a blast of air or the sound of wind.

wind·mill /wíndmil/ *n.* **1** a mill worked by the action of the wind on its sails. **2** *Brit.* = PINWHEEL 2. □ **throw one's cap** (or **bonnet**) **over the windmill** esp. *Brit.* act recklessly or unconventionally. **tilt at** (or **fight**) **windmills** attack an imaginary enemy or grievance.

wind of change *n.* (also **winds of change**) a force or influence for reform.

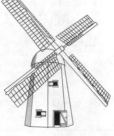

windmill

win·dow /wíndō/ *n.* **1 a** an opening in a wall, roof, or vehicle, etc., usu. with glass in fixed, sliding, or hinged frames, to admit light or air, etc., and allow the occupants to see out. **b** the glass filling this opening (*have broken the window*). **2** a space for display behind the front window of a shop. **3** an aperture in a wall, etc., through which customers are served in a bank, ticket office, etc. **4** an opportunity to observe or learn. **5** an opening or transparent part in an envelope to show an address. **6** a part of a computer monitor display selected to show a particular category or part of the data. **7 a** an interval during which atmospheric and astronomical circumstances are suitable for the launch of a spacecraft. **b** any interval or opportunity for action. **8** strips of metal foil dispersed in the air to obstruct radar detection. **9** a range of electromagnetic wavelengths for which a medium is transparent. □ **out of the window** *Brit. colloq.* no longer taken into account. □□ **win·dowed** *adj.* (also in *comb.*). **win·dow·less** *adj.* [ME f. ON *vindauga* (as WIND¹, EYE)]

win·dow box *n.* a box placed on an outside windowsill for growing flowers.

win·dow dress·ing *n.* **1** the art of arranging a display in a store window, etc. **2** an adroit presentation of facts, etc., to give a deceptively favorable impression.

win·dow·ing /wíndōing/ *n. Computing* the selection of part of a stored image for display or enlargement.

win·dow ledge *n.* = WINDOWSILL.

win·dow·pane /wíndōpayn/ *n.* **1** a pane of glass in a window. **2** a tattersall.

win·dow seat *n.* **1** a seat below a window, esp. in a bay or alcove. **2** a seat next to a window in an aircraft, train, etc.

win·dow-shop *v.tr.* (**-shopped, -shop·ping**) look at goods displayed in store windows, usu. without buying anything. □□ **win·dow-shop·per** *n.*

win·dow·sill /wíndōsil/ *n.* a sill below a window.

win·dow tax *n. Brit. hist.* a tax on windows or similar openings (abolished in 1851).

win·dow wash·er *n.* a person who is employed to clean windows.

wind·pipe /wíndpīp/ *n.* the air passage from the throat to the lungs; the trachea.

wind rose *n.* a diagram of the relative frequency of wind directions at a place.

wind·row /wíndrō/ *n.* a line of raked hay, sheaves of grain, etc., for drying by the wind.

wind sail *n.* a canvas funnel conveying air to the lower parts of a ship.

wind·screen /wíndskreen/ *n. Brit.* = WINDSHIELD.

wind shear *n.* a variation in wind velocity at right angles to the wind's direction.

wind·shield /wíndsheeld/ *n.* a shield of glass at the front of a motor vehicle.

wind·shield wip·er *n.* a device consisting of a rubber blade on an arm, moving in an arc, for keeping a windshield clear of rain, etc.

wind sock *n.* a canvas cylinder or cone on a mast to show the direction of the wind at an airfield, etc.

Wind·sor /wínzər/ *n.* (usu. *attrib.*) denoting or relating to the British royal family since 1917. [*Windsor* in S. England, site of the royal residence at Windsor Castle]

Wind·sor chair *n.* a wooden dining chair with a semicircular back supported by upright rods.

wind·surf·ing /wíndsərfing/ *n.* the sport of riding on water on a sailboard. □□ **wind·surf** *v.intr.* **wind·surf·er** *n.*

wind·swept /wíndswept/ *adj.* exposed to or swept back by the wind.

wind tun·nel *n.* a tunnellike device to produce an air stream past models of aircraft, etc., for the study of wind effects on them.

wind·up /wíndup/ *n.* **1** a conclusion; a finish. **2** *Brit.* a state of anxiety; the provocation of this. **3** *Baseball* the motions made by a pitcher, esp. arm swinging, in preparation for releasing a pitch.

wind·ward /wíndwərd/ *adj., adv., & n.* ● *adj. & adv.* on the side from which the wind is blowing (opp. LEEWARD). ● *n.* the windward region, side, or direction (*to windward; on the windward of*). □ **get to windward of 1** place oneself there to avoid the smell of. **2** gain an advantage over.

wind·y /wíndee/ *adj.* (**wind·i·er, wind·i·est**) **1** stormy with wind (*a windy night*). **2** exposed to the wind; windswept (*a windy plain*). **3** generating or characterized by flatulence. **4** *colloq.* wordy; verbose; empty (*a windy speech*). **5** *Brit. colloq.* nervous; frightened. □□ **wind·i·ly** *adv.* **wind·i·ness** *n.* [OE *windig* (as WIND¹, −Y¹)]

wine /wīn/ *n. & v.* ● *n.* **1** fermented grape juice as an alcoholic drink. **2** a fermented drink resembling this made from other fruits, etc., as specified (*elderberry wine; ginger wine*). **3** the dark-red color of red wine. ● *v.* **1** *intr.* drink wine. **2** *tr.* entertain with wine. □ **wine and dine** entertain to or have a meal with wine. □□ **wine·less** *adj.* [OE *wín* f. Gmc f. L *vinum*]

wine bar *n.* a bar or small restaurant where wine is the main drink available.

wine·ber·ry /wínberee/ *n.* (*pl.* **−ries**) **1 a** a deciduous bristly shrub, *Rubus phoenicolasius*, from China and Japan, producing scarlet berries used in cookery. **b** this berry. **2** = MAKO².

wine·bib·ber /wínbibər/ n. a tippler or drunkard. □□ **wine·bib·bing** n. & adj. [WINE + bib to tipple]

wine bot·tle n. a glass bottle for wine, the standard size holding 26²/₃ fl. oz. or 75 cl.

wine box n. a square carton of wine with a dispensing tap.

wine cel·lar n. **1** a cellar for storing wine. **2** the contents of this.

wine·glass /wínglas/ n. **1** a glass for wine, usu. with a stem and foot. **2** the contents of this, a wineglassful.

wine·glass·ful /wínglasfool/ n. (pl. **–fuls**) **1** the capacity of a wineglass, esp. of the size used for sherry, as a measure of liquid, about four tablespoons. **2** the contents of a wineglass.

wine·grow·er /wíngrōər/ n. a cultivator of grapes for wine.

wine list n. a list of wines available in a restaurant, etc.

wine·press /wínpres/ n. a press in which grapes are squeezed in making wine.

win·er·y /wínəree/ n. (pl. **–ies**) an establishment where wine is made.

wine·skin /wínskin/ n. a whole skin of a goat, etc., sewn up and used to hold wine.

wine stew·ard n. a waiter responsible for serving wine; sommelier.

wine·tast·ing /wíntaysting/ n. **1** judging the quality of wine by tasting it. **2** an occasion for this.

wine vin·e·gar n. vinegar made from wine as distinct from malt.

wing /wing/ n. & v. ● n. **1** each of the limbs or organs by which a bird, bat, or insect is able to fly. **2** a rigid horizontal winglike structure forming a supporting part of an aircraft. **3** part of a building, etc., which projects or is extended in a certain direction (lived in the north wing). **4 a** a forward player at either end of a line in soccer, hockey, etc. **b** the side part of a playing area. **5** (in pl.) the sides of a theater stage out of view of the audience. **6** a section of a political party in terms of the extremity of its views. **7** a flank of a battle array (the cavalry were massed on the left wing). **8** Brit. the fender of a motor vehicle. **9** a an air-force unit of several squadrons or groups. **b** (in pl.) a pilot's badge in the air force, etc. (get one's wings). **10** Anat. & Bot. a lateral part or projection of an organ or structure. ● v. **1** intr. & tr. travel or traverse on wings or in an aircraft (winging through the air; am winging my way home). **2** tr. wound in a wing or an arm. **3** tr. equip with wings. **4** tr. enable to fly; send in flight (fear winged my steps; winged an arrow toward them). □ **give** (or **lend**) **wings** to speed up (a person or a thing). **on the wing** flying or in flight. **on a wing and a prayer** with only the slightest chance of success. **spread** (or **stretch**) **one's wings** develop one's powers fully. **take under one's wing** treat as a protégé. **take wing** fly away; soar. **waiting in the wings** holding oneself in readiness. □□ **winged** adj. (also in comb.). **wing·less** adj. **wing·let** n. **wing·like** adj. [ME pl. wenge, –en, –es f. ON væingir, pl. of væingr]

wing beat n. one complete set of motions with a wing in flying.

wing case n. the horny cover of an insect's wing.

wing chair n. a chair with side pieces projecting forward at the top of a high back.

wing col·lar n. a man's high, stiff collar with turned-down corners.

wing·ding /wíngding/ n. sl. **1** a wild party. **2** a drug addict's real or feigned seizure. [20th c.: orig. unkn.]

winged words n. highly apposite or significant words.

wing game n. Brit. game birds.

wing·er /wíngər/ n. **1** a player on a wing in soccer, hockey, etc. **2** (in comb.) a member of a specified political wing (left-winger).

wing chair

wing nut n. a nut with projections for the fingers to turn it on a screw.

wing·span /wíngspan/ n. measurement right across the wings of a bird or aircraft.

wing·spread /wíngspred/ n. = WINGSPAN.

wing tip n. **1** the outer end of an aircraft's or a bird's wing. **2** a style of shoe with a pattern of perforations on the toe resembling extended bird wings.

wink /wingk/ v. & n. ● v. **1** a tr. close and open (one eye or both eyes) quickly. **b** intr. close and open an eye. **2** intr. (often foll. by at) wink one eye as a signal of friendship or greeting or to convey a message to a person. **3** intr. (of a light, etc.) twinkle; shine or flash intermittently. ● n. **1** the act or an instance of winking, esp. as a signal, etc. **2** colloq. a brief moment of sleep (didn't sleep a wink). □ **as easy as winking** esp. Brit. colloq. very easy. **in a wink** very quickly. **wink at 1** purposely avoid seeing; pretend not to notice. **2** connive at (a wrongdoing, etc.). [OE wincian f. Gmc: cf. WINCE¹, WINCH]

wink·er /wíngkər/ n. **1** Brit. colloq. a flashing indicator light on a motor vehicle. **2** (usu. in pl.) a horse's blinker.

win·kle /wíngkəl/ n. & v. ● n. see PERIWINKLE². ● v.tr. (foll. by out) esp. Brit. extract or eject (winkled the information out of them). □□ **win·kler** n. [abbr. of PERIWINKLE²: cf. WIG¹]

Win·ne·ba·go /winəbágō/ n. **1** a a N. American people native to Wisconsin. **b** a member of this people. **2** the language of this people.

win·ner /wínər/ n. **1** a person, racehorse, etc., that wins. **2** colloq. a successful or highly promising idea, enterprise, etc. (the new scheme seemed a winner).

win·ning /wíning/ adj. & n. ● adj. **1** having or bringing victory or an advantage (the winning entry; a winning basket). **2** attractive; persuasive (a winning smile; winning ways). ● n. (in pl.) money won esp. in betting, etc. □□ **win·ning·ly** adv. **win·ning·ness** n.

win·ning post n. a post marking the end of a race.

win·now /wínō/ v.tr. **1** blow (grain) free of chaff, etc., by an air current. **2** (foll. by out, away, from, etc.) get rid of (chaff, etc.) from grain. **3** a sift; separate; clear of refuse or inferior specimens. **b** sift or examine (evidence for falsehood, etc.). **c** clear, sort, or weed out (rubbish, etc.). **4** poet. **a** fan (the air with wings). **b** flap (wings). **c** stir (the hair, etc.). □□ **win·now·er** n. (in senses 1, 2). [OE windwian (as WIND¹)]

win·o /wínō/ n. (pl. **–os**) sl. a habitual excessive drinker of cheap wine; an alcoholic.

win·some /wínsəm/ adj. (of a person, looks, or manner) winning; attractive; engaging. □□ **win·some·ly** adv. **win·some·ness** n. [OE wynsum f. wyn JOY + –SOME¹]

win·ter /wíntər/ n. & v. ● n. **1** the coldest season of the year, in the N. hemisphere from December to February and in the S. hemisphere from June to August. **2** Astron. the period from the winter solstice to the vernal equinox. **3** a bleak or lifeless period or region, etc. (nuclear winter). **4** poet. a year (esp. of a person's age) (a man of fifty winters). **5** (attrib.) **a** characteristic of or suitable for winter (winter light; winter clothes). **b** (of fruit) ripening late or keeping until or during winter. **c** (of wheat or other crops) sown in autumn for harvesting the following year. ● v. **1** intr. (usu. foll. by at, in) pass the winter (likes to winter in Florida). **2** tr. keep or feed (plants, cattle) during winter. □□ **win·ter·er** n. **win·ter·less** adj. **win·ter·ly** adj. [OE f. Gmc, prob. rel. to WET]

win·ter ac·o·nite n. see ACONITE 2.

win·ter cress n. any bitter-tasting cress of the genus Barbarea, esp. B. vulgaris.

win·ter gar·den n. a garden or conservatory of plants flourishing in winter.

win·ter·green /wíntərgreen/ n. any of several plants esp. of the genus Pyrola or Gaultheria remaining green through the winter.

win·ter·ize /wíntəriz/ v.tr. adapt for operation or use in cold weather. □□ **win·ter·i·za·tion** n.

win·ter jas·mine n. a jasmine, Jasminum nudiflorum, with yellow flowers.

win·ter quar·ters n. a place where soldiers spend the winter.

win·ter sleep n. hibernation.

win·ter sol·stice n. the time at which the sun is farthest south from the equator, about Dec. 22 in the northern hemisphere.

win·ter sports n. sports performed on snow or ice esp. in winter (e.g., skiing, hockey, and ice skating).

win·ter·tide /wíntərtid/ n. poet. = WINTERTIME.

win·ter·time /wíntərtim/ n. the season of winter.

win·try /wíntree/ adj. (also **win·ter·y** /–təree/) (**win·tri·er**, **win·tri·est**) **1** characteristic of winter (wintry weather; a wintry sun; a wintry landscape). **2** (of a smile, greeting, etc.) lacking warmth or enthusiasm. □□ **win·tri·ly** adv. **win·tri·ness** n. [OE wintrig, or f. WINTER]

win·y /wínee/ adj. (**win·i·er**, **win·i·est**) resembling wine in taste or appearance. □□ **win·i·ness** n.

wipe /wip/ v. & n. ● v.tr. **1** clean or dry the surface of by rubbing with the hands or a cloth, etc. **2** rub (a cloth) over a surface. **3** spread (a liquid, etc.) over a surface by rubbing. **4** (often foll. by away, off, etc.) **a** clear or remove by wiping (wiped the mess off the table; wipe away your tears). **b** remove or eliminate completely (the village was wiped off the map). **5** a erase (data, a recording, etc., from a magnetic medium). **b** erase data from (the medium). **6** Austral. & NZ sl. reject or dismiss (a person or idea). ● n. **1** an act of wiping (give the floor a wipe). **2** a piece of disposable absorbent cloth, usu. treated with a cleansing agent, for wiping something clean (antiseptic wipes). □ **wipe down** clean (esp. a vertical surface) by wiping. **wipe a person's eye** Brit. colloq. get the better of a person. **wipe the floor with** colloq. inflict a humiliating defeat on. **wipe out 1 a** destroy; annihilate (the whole population was wiped out). **b** obliterate (wiped it out of my memory). **2** sl. murder. **3** clean the inside of. **4** Brit. avenge (an insult, etc.). **wiped out** adj. sl. tired out, exhausted. **wipe the slate clean** see SLATE. **wipe up 1** take up (a liquid, etc.) by wiping. **2** Brit. dry (dishes, etc.). [OE wipian: cf. OHG wī fan wind around, Goth. weipan crown: rel. to WHIP]

wipe·out /wípowt/ n. **1** the obliteration of one radio signal by another. **2** an instance of destruction or annihilation. **3** sl. a fall from a surfboard.

wip·er /wípər/ n. **1** = WINDSHIELD WIPER. **2** Electr. a moving contact. **3** a cam or tappet.

wire /wir/ n. & v. ● n. **1** a metal drawn out into the form of a thread or thin flexible rod. **b** a piece of this. **c** (*attrib.*) made of wire. **2 a** length or quantity of wire used for fencing or to carry an electric current, etc. **3** a telegram or cablegram. ● *v.tr.* **1** provide, fasten, strengthen, etc., with wire. **2** (often foll. by *up*) *Electr.* install electrical circuits in (a building, piece of equipment, etc.). **3** *colloq.* telegraph (*wired me that they were coming*). **4** snare (an animal, etc.) with wire. **5** (usu. in *passive*) *Croquet* obstruct (a ball, shot, or player) by a hoop. □ **by wire** by telegraph. **get one's wires crossed** become confused and misunderstood. □□ **wir•er** *n.* [OE *wīr*]

wire brush *n.* **1** a brush with tough wire bristles for cleaning hard surfaces, esp. metal. **2** a brush with wire strands brushed against cymbals to produce a soft metallic sound.

wire cloth *n.* cloth woven from wire.

wire cut•ter *n.* a tool for cutting wire.

wire•draw /wírdraw/ *v.tr.* (*past* **–drew** /–drōō/; *past part.* **–drawn** /–drawn/) **1** draw (metal) out into wire. **2** elongate; protract unduly. **3** (esp. as **wiredrawn** *adj.*) refine or apply or press (an argument, etc.) with idle or excessive subtlety.

wire gauge *n.* **1** a gauge for measuring the diameter of wire, etc. **2** a standard series of sizes in which wire, etc., is made.

wire gauze *n.* a stiff gauze woven from wire.

wire grass *n.* any of various grasses with tough wiry stems.

wire•haired /wírhaird/ *adj.* (esp. of a dog) having stiff or wiry hair.

wire•less /wírlis/ *n. & adj.* ● *n.* **1** esp. *Brit.* **a** (in full **wireless set**) a radio receiving set. **b** the transmission and reception of radio signals. **2** = WIRELESS TELEGRAPHY. ● *adj.* lacking or not requiring wires. ▶Now old-fashioned, esp. with ref. to broadcasting, and superseded by *radio*.

wire•less te•leg•ra•phy *n.* telegraphy using radio transmission.

wire•man /wírmən/ *n.* (*pl.* **–men**) **1** an installer or repairer of electric wires. **2** a journalist working for a telegraphic news agency. **3** a wiretapper.

wire net•ting *n.* netting of wire twisted into meshes.

wire-pull•er *n.* a politician, etc., who exerts a hidden influence. □□ **wire-pull•ing** *n.*

wire rope *n.* rope made by twisting wires together as strands.

wire serv•ice *n.* a business that gathers news and distributes it to subscribers, usu. newspapers.

wire•tap /wírtap/ *v.* (**–tapped**, **–tap•ping**) **1** *intr.* connect a listening device to (a telephone or telegraph line, etc.) to listen to a call or transmission. **2** *tr.* obtain (information, etc.) by wiretapping. □□ **wire•tap•per** *n.* **wire•tap•ping** *n.*

wire-walk•er *n.* = tightrope walker (see TIGHTROPE).

wire wheel *n.* a vehicle wheel with spokes of wire.

wire wool *n. Brit.* = STEEL WOOL.

wire•worm /wírwərm/ *n.* the larva of the click beetle causing damage to crop plants.

wir•ing /wíring/ *n.* **1** a system of wires providing electrical circuits. **2** the installation of this (*came to do the wiring*).

wir•y /wíree/ *adj.* (**wir•i•er**, **wir•i•est**) **1** tough and flexible as wire. **2** (of a person) thin and sinewy; untiring. **3** made of wire. □□ **wir•i•ly** *adv.* **wir•i•ness** *n.*

Wis. *abbr.* Wisconsin.

wis /wis/ *v.intr. archaic* know well. [orig. *I wis* = obs. *iwis* 'certainly' f. OE *gewis*, erron. taken as 'I know' and as pres. tense of *wist* (WIT[2])]

Wisd. *abbr.* Wisdom of Solomon (Apocrypha).

wis•dom /wízdəm/ *n.* **1** the state of being wise. **2** experience and knowledge together with the power of applying them critically or practically. **3** sagacity; prudence; common sense. **4** wise sayings, thoughts, etc., regarded collectively. □ **in his** (or **her**, etc.) **wisdom** usu. *iron.* thinking it would be best (*the committee in its wisdom decided to abandon the project*). [OE *wīsdōm* (as WISE[1], –DOM)]

wis•dom tooth *n.* each of four hindmost molars not usu. cut before 20 years of age.

wise[1] /wīz/ *adj. & v.* ● *adj.* **1 a** having experience and knowledge and judiciously applying them. **b** (of an action, behavior, etc.) determined by or showing or in harmony with such experience and knowledge. **2** sagacious; prudent; sensible; discreet. **3** having knowledge. **4** suggestive of wisdom (*with a wise nod of the head*). **5** *colloq.* **a** alert; crafty. **b** (often foll. by *to*) having (usu. confidential) information (about). ● *v.tr. & intr.* (foll. by *up*) *colloq.* put or get wise. □ **be** (or **get**) **wise to** *colloq.* become aware of. **no** (or **none the** or **not much**) **wiser** knowing no more than before. **put a person wise** (often foll. by *to*) *colloq.* inform a person (about). **without anyone's being the wiser** undetected. □□ **wise•ly** *adv.* [OE *wīs* f. Gmc: see WIT[2]]

wise[2] /wīz/ *n. archaic* way, manner, or degree (*in solemn wise; on this wise*). □ **in no wise** not at all. [OE *wīse* f. Gmc f. WIT[2]]

-wise /wīz/ *suffix* forming adjectives and adverbs of manner (*crosswise*; *clockwise*; *lengthwise*) or respect (*moneywise*) (cf. –WAYS). [as WISE[2]]

▶More fanciful phrase-based combinations, such as *employment-wise* (= as regards employment) are *colloq.*, and restricted to informal contexts.

wise•a•cre /wízaykər/ *n.* a person who affects a wise manner; a wise guy. [MDu. *wijssegger* soothsayer, prob. f. OHG *wīssago*, *wīzago*, assim. to WISE[1], ACRE]

wise•crack /wízkrak/ *n. & v. colloq.* ● *n.* a smart pithy remark. ● *v.intr.* make a wisecrack. □□ **wise•crack•er** *n.*

wise guy *n.* **1** *colloq.* a know-it-all. **2** *sl.* a member of organized crime.

wise man *n.* a wizard, esp. one of the Magi.

wi•sent /wéezənt/ *n.* the European bison, *Bison bonasus.* [G: cf. BISON]

wish /wish/ *v. & n.* ● *v.* **1** *intr.* (often foll. by *for*) have or express a desire or aspiration for (*wish for happiness*). **2** *tr.* (often foll. by *that* + clause, usu. with *that* omitted) have as a desire or aspiration (*I wish I could sing; I wished that I was dead*). **3** *tr.* want or demand, usu. so as to bring about what is wanted (*I wish to go; I wish you to do it; I wish it done*). **4** *tr.* express one's hopes for (*we wish you well; wish them no harm; wished us a pleasant journey*). **5** *tr.* (foll. by *on*, *upon*) *colloq.* foist on a person. ● *n.* **1 a** a desire, request, or aspiration. **b** an expression of this. **2** a thing desired (*got my wish*). □ **best** (or **good**) **wishes** hopes felt or expressed for another's happiness, etc. □□ **wish•er** *n.* (in sense 4 of *v.*); (also in *comb.*). [OE *wȳscan*, OHG *wunsken* f. Gmc, ult. rel. to WEEN, WONT]

wish•bone /wíshbōn/ *n.* **1** a forked bone between the neck and breast of a cooked bird: when broken between two people the longer portion entitles the holder to make a wish. **2** an object of similar shape.

wish•ful /wíshfŏŏl/ *adj.* **1** (often foll. by *to* + infin.) desiring; wishing. **2** having or expressing a wish. □ **wishful thinking** belief founded on wishes rather than facts. □□ **wish•ful•ly** *adv.* **wish•ful•ness** *n.*

wish ful•fill•ment *n.* a tendency for subconscious desire to be satisfied in fantasy.

wish•ing well *n.* a well into which coins are dropped and a wish is made.

wish-wash /wíshwosh, –wawsh/ *n.* **1** a weak or watery drink. **2** insipid talk or writing. [redupl. of WASH]

wish•y-wash•y /wísheewóshee, –wáwshee/ *adj.* **1** feeble, insipid, or indecisive in quality or character. **2** (of tea, soup, etc.) weak; watery; sloppy. [redupl. of WASHY]

wisp /wisp/ *n.* **1** a small bundle or twist of straw, etc. **2** a small separate quantity of smoke, hair, etc. **3** a small, thin person, etc. **4** a flock (of snipe). □□ **wisp•y** *adj.* (**wisp•i•er**, **wisp•i•est**). **wisp•i•ly** *adv.* **wisp•i•ness** *n.* [ME: orig. uncert.: cf. WFris. *wisp*, and WHISK]

wist *past* and *past part.* of WIT[2].

wis•te•ri•a /wisteéreeə/ *n.* (also **wis•tar•i•a** /–stáiriə/) any climbing plant of the genus *Wisteria*, with hanging racemes of blue, purple, or white flowers. [C. *Wistar* (or *Wister*), Amer. anatomist d. 1818]

wist•ful /wístfŏŏl/ *adj.* (of a person, looks, etc.) yearningly or mournfully expectant, thoughtful, or wishful. □□ **wist•ful•ly** *adv.* **wist•ful•ness** *n.* [app. assim. of obs. *wistly* (adv.) intently (cf. WHISHT) to *wishful*, with corresp. change of sense]

wit[1] /wit/ *n.* **1** (in *sing.* or *pl.*) intelligence; quick understanding (*has quick wits; a nimble wit*). **2 a** the unexpected, quick, and humorous combining or contrasting of ideas or expressions (*conversation sparkling with wit*). **b** the power of giving intellectual pleasure by this. **3** a person possessing such a power, esp. a cleverly humorous person. □ **at one's wit's** (or **wits'**) **end** utterly at a loss or in despair. **have** (or **keep**) **one's wits about one** be alert or vigilant or of lively intelligence. **live by one's wits** live by ingenious or crafty expedients, without a settled occupation. **out of one's wits** mad; distracted. **set one's wits to** esp. *Brit.* argue with. □□ **wit•ted** *adj.* (in sense 1); (also in *comb.*). [OE *wit(t)*, *gewit(t)* f. Gmc]

SYNONYM TIP wit[1]

HUMOR, IRONY, REPARTEE, SARCASM, SATIRE. If you're good at perceiving analogies between things that are dissimilar and at expressing them in quick, sharp, spontaneous observations or remarks, you have **wit**. **Humor**, on the other hand, is the ability to perceive and express what is comical, ridiculous, or ludicrous in a situation or character, and to do so in a way that makes others see or feel the same thing. It suggests more sympathy, more tolerance, and more kindliness than *wit* (*to have a sense of humor in the midst of trying circumstances*). **Irony** is the *humor* that is implicit in the contradiction between what is meant and what is expressed, or in the discrepancy between appearance and reality. An example would be to say, in the midst of a hurricane, "What a perfect day for a wedding!" Although **sarcasm** may take the form of *irony*, it is less subtle and is often used harshly or bitterly to wound or ridicule someone. Unlike *irony*, however, *sarcasm* depends on tone of voice for its effect ("*A fine friend you turned out to be!*" he said, *with obvious sarcasm*). **Satire** usually implies the use of *sarcasm* or *irony* for the purpose of ridicule or criticism, often directed at institutions or political figures (*to write a satire exposing government corruption*). If you are good at making quick, witty replies, you will be known for your **repartee**, which is the art of responding pointedly and skillfully, with *wit* or *humor*, in a conversational exchange (*No one could compete with her witty repartee*).

wit[2] /wit/ *v.tr. & intr.* (*1st & 3rd sing. present* **wot** /wot/; *past and past part.* **wist**) (often foll. by *of*) *archaic* know. □ **to wit** that is to say; namely. [OE *witan* f. Gmc]

witch /wich/ *n. & v.* ● *n.* **1** a sorceress, esp. a woman supposed to have dealings with the devil or evil spirits. **2** an ugly old woman; a hag. **3** a fascinating girl or woman. ● *v.tr. archaic* **1** bewitch. **2** fascinate; charm; lure. □□ **witch•ing** *adj.* **witch•like** *adj.* [OE *wicca* (masc.), *wicce* (fem.), rel. to *wiccian* (v.) practice magic arts]

witch- var. of WYCH-.

witch•craft /wíchkraft/ *n.* the use of magic; sorcery.

witch doc•tor *n.* a tribal magician of primitive people.

witch•er•y /wíchəree/ *n.* **1** witchcraft. **2** power exercised by beauty or eloquence or the like.

witch•et•ty /wíchətee/ *n.* (*pl.* **–ties**) *Austral.* a large white larva of a beetle or moth, eaten as food by Aborigines. [Aboriginal]

witch ha•zel *n.* **1** any American shrub of the genus *Hamamelis*, with bark yielding an astringent lotion. **2** this lotion, esp. from the leaves of *H. virginiana*.

witch•es' Sab•bath *n.* a supposed general midnight meeting of witches with the Devil.

witch-hunt *n.* **1** *hist.* a search for and persecution of supposed witches. **2** a campaign directed against a particular group of those holding unpopular or unorthodox views, esp. communists.

witch•ing hour *n.* midnight, when witches are supposedly active (after Shakesp. *Hamlet* III. ii. 377 *the witching time of night*).

wit•e•na•ge•mot /wít'nəgəmót/ *n. hist.* an Anglo-Saxon national council or parliament. [OE f. *witena* genit. pl. of *wita* wise man (as WIT[2]) + *gemōt* meeting: cf. MOOT]

with /with, with/ *prep.* expressing: **1** an instrument or means used (*cut with a knife; can walk with assistance*). **2** association or company (*lives with his mother; works with Shell; lamb with mint sauce*). **3** cause or origin (*shiver with fear; in bed with measles*). **4** possession; attribution (*the woman with dark hair; a vase with handles*). **5** circumstances; accompanying conditions (*sleep with the window open; a vacation with all expenses paid*). **6** manner adopted or displayed (*behaved with dignity; spoke with vehemence; handle with care; won with ease*). **7** agreement or harmony (*sympathize with; I believe with you that it can be done*). **8** disagreement; antagonism; competition (*incompatible with; stop arguing with me*). **9** responsibility or care for (*the decision rests with you; leave the child with me*). **10** material (*made with gold*). **11** addition or supply; possession of as a material, attribute, circumstance, etc. (*fill it with water; threaten with dismissal; decorate with flowers*). **12** reference or regard (*be patient with them; how are things with you?; what do you want with me?; there's nothing wrong with expressing one's opinion*). **13** relation or causative association (*changes with the weather; keeps pace with the cost of living*). **14** an accepted circumstance or consideration (*with all your faults, we like you*). □ **away** (or **in** or **out**, etc.) **with** (as *int.*) take, send, or put (a person or thing) away, in, out, etc. **be with a person 1** agree with and support a person. **2** *colloq.* follow a person's meaning (*are you with me?*). **one** with part of the same whole as. **with child** (or **young**) *literary* pregnant. **with it** *colloq.* **1** up to date; conversant with modern ideas, etc. **2** alert and comprehending. **with that** thereupon. [OE, prob. shortened f. a Gmc prep. corresp. to OE *wither*, OHG *widar* against]

with•al /witháwl, with–/ *adv. & prep. archaic* ● *adv.* moreover; as well; at the same time. ● *prep.* (placed after its expressed or omitted object) with (*what shall he fill his belly withal?*). [ME f. WITH + ALL]

with•draw /wi thdráw, with–/ *v.* (*past* **with•drew** /–dróo/; *past part.* **with•drawn** /–dráwn/) **1** *tr.* pull or take aside or back (*withdrew my hand*). **2** *tr.* discontinue; cancel; retract (*withdrew my support; the promise was later withdrawn*). **3** *tr.* remove; take away (*withdrew the child from school; withdrew their troops*). **4** *tr.* take (money) out of an account. **5** *intr.* retire or go away; move away or back. **6** *intr.* (as **withdrawn** *adj.*) abnormally shy and unsociable; mentally detached. □□ **with•draw•er** *n.* [ME f. *with-* away (as WITH) + DRAW]

with•draw•al /withdráwəl, with–/ *n.* **1** the act or an instance of withdrawing or being withdrawn. **2** a process of ceasing to take addictive drugs, often with an unpleasant physical reaction (*withdrawal symptoms*). **3** = COITUS INTERRUPTUS.

with•draw•ing room *n. archaic* = DRAWING ROOM 1.

withe /with, with, with/ *n.* a tough, flexible shoot esp. of willow or osier used for tying a bundle of wood, etc. [OE *withthe, withig* f. Gmc, rel. to WIRE]

with•er /wíthər/ *v.* **1** *tr. & intr.* (often foll. by *up*) make or become dry and shriveled (*withered flowers*). **2** *tr. & intr.* (often foll. by *away*) deprive of or lose vigor, vitality, freshness, or importance. **3** *intr.* decay; decline. **4** *tr.* **a** blight with scorn, etc. **b** (as **withering** *adj.*) scornful (*a withering look*). □□ **with•er•ing•ly** *adv.* [ME, app. var. of WEATHER differentiated for certain senses]

with•ers /wíthərz/ *n.pl.* the ridge between a horse's shoulder blades. [shortening of (16th-c.) *widersome* (or *–sone*) f. *wider-, wither-* against (cf. WITH), as the part that resists the strain of the collar: second element obscure]

with•er•shins /wíthərshinz/ *adv.* (also **wid•der•shins** /wíd–/) esp. *Sc.* **1** in a direction contrary to the sun's course (considered as un-

lucky). **2** counterclockwise. [MLG *weddersins* f. MHG *widersinnes* f. *wider* against + *sin* direction]

with•hold /wi th-hóld, with–/ *v.tr.* (*past and past part.* **–held** /–héld/) **1** (often foll. by *from*) hold back; restrain. **2** refuse to give, grant, or allow (*withhold one's consent; withhold the truth*). □□ **with•hold•er** *n.* [ME f. *with-* away (as WITH) + HOLD[1]]

with•in /within, with–/ *adv., prep., & n.* ● *adv. archaic* or *literary* **1** inside; to, at, or on the inside; internally. **2** indoors (*is anyone within?*). **3** in spirit (*make me pure within*). ● *prep.* **1** inside; enclosed or contained by. **2 a** not beyond or exceeding (*within one's means*). **b** not transgressing (*within the law; within reason*). **3** not further off than (*within three miles of a station; within shouting distance; within ten days*). ● *n.* the inside part of a place, building, etc. □ **within doors** esp. *Brit.* in or into a house. **within one's grasp** see GRASP. **within reach** (or **sight**) **of** near enough to be reached or seen. [OE *withinnan* on the inside (as WITH, *innan* (adv. & prep.) within, formed as IN)]

with-it *adj. colloq.* in step with the times, fashion, etc.

with•out /wi thówt, with–/ *prep., adv., n., & conj.* ● *prep.* **1** not having, feeling, or showing (*came without any money; without hesitation; without any emotion*). **2** with freedom from (*without fear; without embarrassment*). **3** in the absence of (*cannot live without you; the train left without us*). **4** with neglect or avoidance of (*do not leave without telling me*). **5** *archaic* outside (*without the city wall*). ● *adv. archaic* or *literary* **1** outside (*seen from without*). **2** out of doors (*remained shivering without*). **3** in outward appearance (*rough without but kind within*). ● *n.* the outside part of a place, building, etc. ● *conj. dial.* unless (*the dog won't eat without you give him some meat*) □ **without end** infinite; eternal. [OE *with ūtan* (as WITH, *ūtan* from outside, formed as OUT)]

▶ Use as a conjunction, as in *do not leave without you tell me*, is dialectal and should be avoided in formal use.

with•stand /wi thstánd, with–/ *v.* (*past and past part.* **–stood** /–stóod/) **1** *tr.* oppose; resist; hold out against (a person, force, etc.). **2** *intr.* make opposition; offer resistance. □□ **with•stand•er** *n.* [OE *withstandan* f. *with-* against (as WITH) + STAND]

with•y /withee/ *n.* (*pl.* **–ies**) esp. *Brit.* **1** a willow of any species. **2** a withe.

wit•less /wítlis/ *adj.* **1** lacking wits; foolish; stupid. **2** crazy. □□ **wit•less•ly** *adv.* **wit•less•ness** *n.* [OE *witlēas* (as WIT[1], –LESS)]

wit•ling /wítling/ *n. archaic* usu. *derog.* a person who fancies himself or herself as a wit.

wit•ness /wítnis/ *n. & v.* ● *n.* **1** a person present at some event and able to give information about it (cf. EYEWITNESS). **2 a** a person giving sworn testimony. **b** a person attesting another's signature to a document. **3** (foll. by *to, of*) a person or thing whose existence, condition, etc., attests or proves something (*is a living witness to their generosity*). **4** testimony; evidence; confirmation. ● *v.* **1** *tr.* be a witness of (an event, etc.) (*did you witness the accident?*). **2** *tr.* be witness to the authenticity of (a document or signature). **3** *tr.* serve as evidence or an indication of. **4** *intr.* (foll. by *against, for, to*) give or serve as evidence. □ **bear witness to** (or **of**) **1** attest the truth of. **2** state one's belief in. **call to witness** appeal to for confirmation, etc. [OE *witnes* (as WIT[1], –NESS)]

wit•ness-box *n. Brit.* = WITNESS STAND.

wit•ness stand *n.* an enclosure in a court of law from which witnesses give evidence.

wit•ter /wítər/ *v.intr.* (often foll. by *on*) *Brit. colloq.* speak tediously on trivial matters. [20th c.: prob. imit.]

wit•ti•cism /wítisizəm/ *n.* a witty remark. [coined by Dryden (1677) f. WITTY, after *criticism*]

wit•ting /wíting/ *adj.* **1** aware. **2** intentional. □□ **wit•ting•ly** *adv.* [ME f. WIT[2] + –ING[2]]

wit•ty /wítee/ *adj.* (**wit•ti•er, wit•ti•est**) **1** showing verbal wit. **2** characterized by wit or humor. □□ **wit•ti•ly** *adv.* **wit•ti•ness** *n.* [OE *witig, wittig* (as WIT[1], –Y[1])]

wi•vern var. of WYVERN.

wives *pl.* of WIFE.

wiz var. of WHIZ *n.* 2.

wiz•ard /wízərd/ *n. & adj.* ● *n.* **1** a sorcerer; a magician. **2** a person of remarkable powers; a genius. **3** a conjuror. ● *adj. sl. Brit.* wonderful; excellent. □□ **wiz•ard•ly** *adj.* **wiz•ard•ry** *n.* [ME f. WISE[1] + –ARD]

wiz•ened /wízənd/ *adj.* (also **wiz•en**) (of a person or face, etc.) shriveled-looking. [past part. of *wizen* shrivel f. OE *wisnian* f. Gmc]

wk. *abbr.* **1** week. **2** work. **3** weak.

wks. *abbr.* weeks.

Wm. *abbr.* William.

WMO *abbr.* World Meteorological Organization.

WNW *abbr.* west-northwest.

WO *abbr.* warrant officer.

woad /wōd/ *n. hist.* **1** a cruciferous plant, *Isatis tinctoria*, yielding a blue dye now superseded by indigo. **2** the dye obtained from this. [OE *wād* f. Gmc]

wob·be·gong /wóbigong/ *n.* an Australian brown shark, *Orectolobus maculatus*, with buff patterned markings. [Aboriginal]

wob·ble /wóbəl/ *v. & n. • v.* **1 a** *intr.* sway or vibrate unsteadily from side to side. **b** *tr.* cause to do this. **2** *intr.* stand or go unsteadily; stagger. **3** *intr.* waver; vacillate; act inconsistently. **4** *intr.* (of the voice or sound) quaver; pulsate. • *n.* **1** a wobbling movement. **2** an instance of vacillation or pulsation. □□ **wob·bler** *n.* [earlier *wabble*, corresp. to LG *wabbeln*, ON *vafla* waver f. Gmc: cf. WAVE, WAVER, –LE⁴]

wob·bly /wóblee/ *adj.* (**wob·bli·er, wob·bli·est**) **1** wobbling or tending to wobble. **2** wavy; undulating (*a wobbly line*). **3** unsteady; weak after illness (*feeling wobbly*). **4** wavering; vacillating; insecure (*the economy was wobbly*). □ **throw a wobbly** *Brit. sl.* have a fit of nerves. □□ **wob·bli·ness** *n.*

wodge /woj/ *n. Brit. colloq.* a chunk or lump. [alt. of WEDGE¹]

woe /wō/ *n. archaic* or *literary* **1** affliction; bitter grief; distress. **2** (in *pl.*) calamities; troubles. **3** *joc.* problems (*told me a tale of woe*). □ **woe betide** *Brit.* there will be unfortunate consequences for (*woe betide you if you are late*). **woe is me** an exclamation of distress. [OE *wā*, *wǣ* f. Gmc, a natural exclam. of lament]

woe·be·gone /wóbigon, –gawn/ *adj.* dismal-looking. [WOE + *begone* = surrounded f. OE *bēgān* (as BE-, GO¹)]

woe·ful /wófŏŏl/ *adj.* **1** sorrowful; afflicted with distress (*a woeful expression*). **2** causing sorrow or affliction. **3** very bad; wretched (*woeful ignorance*). □□ **woe·ful·ly** *adv.* **woe·ful·ness** *n.*

wog¹ /wog/ *n. sl. offens.* a foreigner, esp. a nonwhite one. [20th c.: orig. unkn.]

wog² /wog/ *n. Austral. sl.* an illness or infection. [20th c.: orig. unkn.]

wok /wok/ *n.* a bowl-shaped metal pan used in esp. Chinese cooking. [Cantonese]

woke *past* of WAKE¹.

wok·en *past part.* of WAKE¹.

wold /wōld/ *n.* a piece of high, open, uncultivated land. [OE *wald* f. Gmc, perh. rel. to WILD: cf. WEALD]

wolf /wŏŏlf/ *n. & v. • n.* (*pl.* **wolves** /wŏŏlvz/) **1** a wild, flesh-eating, tawny-gray mammal related to the dog, esp. *Canis lupus*, preying on rodents, mammals, etc., and hunting in packs. **2** *sl.* a man given to seducing women. **3** a rapacious or greedy person. **4** *Mus.* **a** a jarring sound from some notes in a bowed instrument. **b** an out-of-tune effect when playing certain chords on old organs (before the present 'equal temperament' was in use). • *v.tr.* (often foll. by *down*) devour (food) greedily. □ **cry wolf** raise repeated false alarms (so that a genuine one is disregarded). **have** (or **hold**) **a wolf by the ears** esp. *Brit.* be in a precarious position. **keep the wolf from the door** avert hunger or starvation. **throw to the wolves** sacrifice without compunction. **wolf in sheep's clothing** a hostile person who pretends friendship. □□ **wolf·ish** *adj.* **wolf·ish·ly** *adv.* **wolf·like** *adj. & adv.* [OE *wulf* f. Gmc]

wolf cub *n.* **1** a young wolf. **2** *Brit.* the former name for a Cub Scout.

wolf·fish /wŏŏlffish/ *n.* any large voracious blenny of the genus *Anarrhichas*.

wolf·hound /wŏŏlfhownd/ *n.* a borzoi or other dog of a kind used orig. to hunt wolves.

wolf pack *n.* an attacking group of submarines or aircraft.

wolf·ram /wŏŏlfrəm/ *n.* **1** tungsten. **2** tungsten ore; a native tungstate of iron and manganese. [G: perh. f. *Wolf* WOLF + *Rahm* cream, or MHG *rām* dirt, soot]

wolf·ram·ite /wŏŏlfrəmīt/ *n.* = WOLFRAM 2.

wolfs·bane /wŏŏlfsbayn/ *n.* an aconite, esp. *Aconitum lycoctonum*.

wolf·skin /wŏŏlfskin/ *n.* **1** the skin of a wolf. **2** a mat, cloak, etc., made from this.

wolf spi·der *n.* any ground-dwelling spider of the family Lycosidae, hunting instead of trapping its prey.

wolf whis·tle *n.* a sexually admiring whistle by a man to a woman.

wol·ver·ine /wŏŏlvəreen/ *n.* a voracious carnivorous mammal, *Gulo gulo*, of the weasel family. [16th-c. *wolvering*, somehow derived f. *wolv-*, stem of WOLF]

wolves *pl.* of WOLF.

wom·an /wŏŏmən/ *n.* (*pl.* **wom·en** /wímin/) **1** an adult human female. **2** the female sex; any or an average woman (*how does woman differ from man?*). **3** a wife or female sexual partner. **4** (prec. by *the*) emotions or characteristics traditionally associated with women (*brought out the woman in him*). **5** a man with characteristics traditionally associated with women. **6** (*attrib.*) female (*woman driver; women friends*). **7** (as second element in *comb.*) a woman of a specified nationality, profession, skill, etc. (*Englishwoman; horsewoman*). **8** *colloq.* a female domestic servant. **9** *archaic* or *hist.* a queen's, etc., female attendant ranking below lady (*woman of the bedchamber*).

wolverine

□□ **wom·an·less** *adj.* **wom·an·like** *adj.* [OE *wīfmon*, –*man* (as WIFE, MAN), a formation peculiar to English, the ancient word being WIFE]

wom·an·hood /wŏŏmənhŏŏd/ *n.* **1** female maturity. **2** womanly instinct. **3** womankind.

wom·an·ish /wŏŏmənish/ *adj. usu. derog.* **1** (of a man) effeminate; unmanly. **2** suitable to or characteristic of a woman. □□ **wom·an·ish·ly** *adv.* **wom·an·ish·ness** *n.*

wom·an·ize /wŏŏmənīz/ *v.* **1** *intr.* chase after women; philander. **2** *tr.* make womanish. □□ **wom·an·iz·er** *n.*

wom·an·kind /wŏŏmənkīnd/ *n.* (also **wom·en·kind** /wímin–/) women in general.

wom·an·ly /wŏŏmənlee/ *adj.* (of a woman) having or showing qualities traditionally associated with women; not masculine nor girlish. □□ **wom·an·li·ness** *n.*

wom·an of the streets *n.* a prostitute.

wom·en's lib *n. colloq.* = WOMEN'S LIBERATION. □□ **wom·en's lib·ber** *n.*

wom·en's lib·er·a·tion *n.* the liberation of women from inequalities and subservient status in relation to men, and from attitudes causing these.

Wom·en's Lib·er·a·tion *n.* (also **Wom·en's Move·ment**) a movement campaigning for women's liberation.

wo·men's rights *n.* rights that promote a position of legal and social equality of women with men.

womb /wŏŏm/ *n.* **1** the organ of conception and gestation in a woman and other female mammals; the uterus. **2** a place of origination and development. □□ **womb·like** *adj.* [OE *wamb*, *womb*]

wom·bat /wómbat/ *n.* any burrowing, plant-eating Australian marsupial of the family Vombatidae, resembling a small bear, with short legs. [Aboriginal]

wom·en *pl.* of WOMAN.

wom·en·folk /wíminfōk/ *n.* **1** women in general. **2** the women in a family.

wom·en·kind var. of WOMANKIND.

wombat

won *past* and *past part.* of WIN.

won·der /wúndər/ *n. & v. • n.* **1** an emotion excited by what is unexpected, unfamiliar, or inexplicable, esp. surprise mingled with admiration or curiosity, etc. **2** a strange or remarkable person or thing, specimen, event, etc. **3** (*attrib.*) having marvelous or amazing properties, etc. (*a wonder drug*). **4** a surprising thing (*it is a wonder you were not hurt*). • *v.* **1** *intr.* (often foll. by *at*, or *to* + infin.) be filled with wonder or great surprise. **2** *tr.* (foll. by *that* + clause) be surprised to find. **3** *tr.* desire or be curious to know (*I wonder what the time is*). **4** *tr.* expressing a tentative inquiry (*I wonder whether you would mind?*). **5** *intr.* (foll. by *about*) ask oneself with puzzlement or doubt about; question (*wondered about the sense of the decision*). □ **I shouldn't wonder** *colloq.* I think it likely. **I wonder** I very much doubt it. **no** (or **small**) **wonder** (often foll. by *that* + clause) one cannot be surprised; one might have guessed; it is natural. **wonders will** (or **will wonders**) **never cease** an exclamation of extreme (usu. agreeable) surprise. **work** (or **do**) **wonders 1** do miracles. **2** succeed remarkably. □□ **won·der·er** *n.* [OE *wundor*, *wundrian*, of unkn. orig.]

won·der·ful /wúndərfŏŏl/ *adj.* **1** very remarkable or admirable. **2** arousing wonder. □□ **won·der·ful·ly** *adv.* **won·der·ful·ness** *n.* [OE *wunderfull* (as WONDER, –FUL)]

won·der·ing /wúndəring/ *adj.* filled with wonder; marveling (*their wondering gaze*). □□ **won·der·ing·ly** *adv.*

won·der·land /wúndərlənd/ *n.* **1** a fairyland. **2** a land of surprises or marvels.

won·der·ment /wúndərmənt/ *n.* surprise; awe.

won·der·struck *adj.* (or –**strick·en**) reduced to silence by wonder.

won·der·work·er *n.* a person who performs wonders.

won·drous /wúndrəs/ *adj. & adv. poet. • adj.* wonderful. • *adv.* archaic or *literary* wonderfully (*wondrous kind*). □□ **won·drous·ly** *adv.* **won·drous·ness** *n.* [alt. of obs. *wonders* (adj. & adv.), = genit. of WONDER (cf. –S³) after *marvelous*]

won·ky /wóngkee/ *adj.* (**won·ki·er, won·ki·est**) *Brit. sl.* **1** crooked. **2** loose; unsteady. **3** unreliable. □□ **won·ki·ly** *adv.* **won·ki·ness** *n.* [fanciful formation]

wont /wónt, wawnt, wunt/ *adj., n., & v. • predic.adj.* archaic or literary (foll. by *to* + infin.) accustomed (*as we were wont to say*). • *n.* formal or *joc.* what is customary; one's habit (*as is my wont*). • *v.tr. & intr.* (*3rd sing. present* **wonts** or **wont**; *past* **wont** or **wont·ed**) archaic make or become accustomed. [OE *gewunod* past part. of *gewunian* f. *wunian* dwell]

won't /wōnt/ *contr.* will not.

wont·ed /wóntid, wáwn–, wún–/ *attrib.adj.* habitual; accustomed; usual.

woo /wŏŏ/ *v.tr.* (**woos, wooed**) **1** court; seek the hand or love of (a woman). **2** try to win (fame, fortune, etc.). **3** seek the favor or support of. **4** coax or importune. □□ **woo·a·ble** *adj.* **woo·er** *n.* [OE *wōgian* (intr.), *āwōgian* (tr.), of unkn. orig.]

wood /wŏŏd/ *n.* **1 a** a hard fibrous material that forms the main substance of the trunk or branches of a tree or shrub. **b** this cut for lumber or for fuel, or for use in crafts, manufacture, etc. **2** (in *sing.* or *pl.*) growing trees densely occupying a tract of land. **3** (prec. by *the*) wooden storage, esp. a cask, for wine, etc. (*poured straight from the wood*). **4** a wooden-headed golf club. **5** = BOWL² *n.* 1. □ **out of the woods** (or **wood**) out of danger or difficulty. □□ **wood•less** *adj.* [OE *wudu, wi(o)du* f. Gmc]

wood al•co•hol *n.* methanol.

wood a•nem•o•ne *n.* a wild spring-flowering anemone, *Anemone nemorosa*.

wood•bine /wŏŏdbīn/ *n.* **1** wild honeysuckle **2** Virginia creeper.

wood•block /wŏŏdblok/ *n.* a block from which woodcuts are made.

wood•chuck /wŏŏdchuk/ *n.* a reddish-brown and gray N. American marmot, *Marmota monax*. Also called **groundhog**. [Algonquian name: cf. Cree *wuchak, otchock*]

wood•cock /wŏŏdkok/ *n.* (*pl.* same) any game bird of the genus *Scolopax*, inhabiting woodland.

wood•craft /wŏŏdkraft/ *n.* **1** skill in woodwork. **2** knowledge of woodland esp. in camping, scouting, etc.

wood•cut /wŏŏdkut/ *n.* **1** a relief cut on a block of wood sawn along the grain. **2** a print made from this, esp. as an illustration in a book. **3** the technique of making such reliefs and prints.

wood•cut•ter /wŏŏdkutər/ *n.* **1** a person who cuts wood. **2** a maker of woodcuts.

wood•ed /wŏŏdid/ *adj.* having woods or many trees.

wood•en /wŏŏd'n/ *adj.* **1** made of wood. **2** like wood. **3 a** stiff, clumsy, or stilted; without animation or flexibility (*wooden movements; a wooden performance*). **b** expressionless (*a wooden stare*). □□ **wood•en•ly** *adv.* **wood•en•ness** *n.*

wood en•grav•er *n.* a maker of wood engravings.

wood en•grav•ing *n.* **1** a relief cut on a block of wood sawn across the grain. **2** a print made from this. **3** the technique of making such reliefs and prints.

wood•en•head /wŏŏd'nhed/ *n. colloq.* a stupid person.

wood•en•head•ed /wŏŏd'nhedid/ *adj. colloq.* stupid. □□ **wood•en•head•ed•ness** *n.*

wood•en horse *n.* = TROJAN HORSE.

wood•en spoon *n.* esp. *Brit.* a booby prize (orig. a spoon given to the candidate coming last in the Cambridge University mathematical tripos).

wood fi•ber *n.* fiber obtained from wood esp. as material for paper.

wood grouse *n.* = CAPERCAILLIE.

wood hy•a•cinth *n.* = BLUEBELL 1.

wood•land /wŏŏdlənd/ *n.* wooded country, woods (often *attrib.*: *woodland scenery*). □□ **wood•land•er** *n.*

wood•lark /wŏŏdlaark/ *n.* a lark, *Lullula arborea*.

wood louse *n.* any small terrestrial isopod crustacean of the genus *Oniscus*, etc., feeding on rotten wood, etc., and often able to roll into a ball.

wood•man /wŏŏdmən/ *n.* (*pl.* **–men**) **1** a forester. **2** a woodcutter.

wood mouse *n.* any of various forest-dwelling mice.

wood•note /wŏŏdnōt/ *n.* (often in *pl.*) a natural or spontaneous note of a bird, etc.

wood nymph *n.* a dryad or hamadryad.

wood•peck•er /wŏŏdpekər/ *n.* any bird of the family Picidae that climbs and taps tree trunks in search of insects.

wood pi•geon *n.* a dove, *Columba palumbus*, having white patches like a ring round its neck. Also called **ringdove**.

wood•pile /wŏŏdpīl/ *n.* a pile of wood, esp. for fuel.

wood pulp *n.* wood fiber reduced chemically or mechanically to pulp as raw material for paper.

wood•ruff /wŏŏdruf/ *n.* a white-flowered plant of the genus *Galium*, esp. *G. odoratum* grown for the fragrance of its whorled leaves when dried or crushed.

wood screw *n.* a metal male screw with a slotted head and sharp point.

wood•shed /wŏŏdshed/ *n.* a shed where wood for fuel is stored. □ **something nasty in the woodshed** esp. *Brit. colloq.* a shocking or distasteful thing kept secret.

woodpecker

woods•man /wŏŏdzmən/ *n.* (*pl.* **–men**) **1** a person who lives in or is familiar with woodland. **2** a person skilled in woodcraft.

wood sor•rel *n.* a small plant, *Oxalis acetosella*, with trifoliate leaves and white flowers streaked with purple.

wood spir•it *n.* crude methanol obtained from wood.

woods•y /wŏŏdzee/ *adj.* like or characteristic of woods. [irreg. f. WOOD + −Y¹]

wood war•bler *n.* **1** a European woodland bird, *Phylloscopus sibilatrix*, with a trilling song. **2** any American warbler of the family Parulidae.

wood•wind /wŏŏdwind/ *n.* (often *attrib.*) **1** (*collect.*) the wind instruments of the orchestra that were (mostly) orig. made of wood, e.g.,

the flute and clarinet. **2** (usu. in *pl.*) an individual instrument of this kind or its player (*the woodwinds are out of tune*).

wood-wool *n. Brit.* fine pine, etc., shavings used as a surgical dressing or for packing.

wood•work /wŏŏdwərk/ *n.* **1** the making of things in wood. **2** things made of wood, esp. the wooden parts of a building. □ **crawl** (or **come**) **out of the woodwork** *colloq.* (of something unwelcome) appear; become known. □□ **wood•work•er** *n.* **wood•work•ing** *n.*

wood•worm /wŏŏdwərm/ *n.* **1** the wood-boring larva of the furniture beetle. **2** the damaged condition of wood affected by this.

wood•y /wŏŏdee/ *adj.* (**wood•i•er, wood•i•est**) **1** (of a region) wooded; abounding in woods. **2** like or of wood (*woody tissue*). □□ **wood•i•ness** *n.*

wood•yard /wŏŏdyaard/ *n.* a yard where wood is used or stored.

wood•y night•shade see NIGHTSHADE.

woof¹ /wŏŏf/ *n. & v.* • *n.* the gruff bark of a dog. • *v.intr.* give a woof. [imit.]

woof² /wŏŏf, wōōf/ *n.* = WEFT. [OE *ōwef*, alt. of *ōwebb* (after *wefan* WEAVE¹), formed as A−², WEB: infl. by *warp*]

woof•er /wŏŏfər/ *n.* a loudspeaker designed to reproduce low frequencies (cf. TWEETER). [WOOF¹ + −ER¹]

wool /wŏŏl/ *n.* **1** fine, soft, wavy hair from the fleece of sheep, goats, etc. **2 a** yarn produced from this hair. **b** cloth or clothing made from it. **3** any of various woollike substances (*steel wool*). **4** soft, short, underfur or down. **5** *colloq.* a person's hair, esp. when short and curly. □ **pull the wool over a person's eyes** deceive a person. □□ **wool•like** *adj.* [OE *wull* f. Gmc]

wool•en /wŏŏlən/ *adj. & n.* (also **wool•len**) • *adj.* made wholly or partly of wool, esp. from short fibers. • *n.* **1** a fabric produced from wool. **2** (in *pl.*) woolen garments. [OE *wullen* (as WOOL, −EN²)]

wool fat *n.* lanolin.

wool•gath•er•ing /wŏŏlgathəring/ *n.* absentmindedness; dreamy inattention.

wool•grow•er /wŏŏlgrōər/ *n.* a breeder of sheep for wool. □□ **wool•grow•ing** *n.*

wool•ly /wŏŏlee/ *adj. & n.* (also **wool•y**) • *adj.* (**wool•li•er, wool•li•est**) **1** bearing or naturally covered with wool or woollike hair. **2** resembling or suggesting wool (*woolly clouds*). **3** (of a sound) indistinct. **4** (of thought) vague or confused. **5** *Bot.* downy. **6** lacking in definition, luminosity, or incisiveness. • *n.* (*pl.* **–lies**) esp. *Brit. colloq.* a woolen garment, esp. a knitted undergarment. □□ **wool•li•ness** *n.*

wool•ly bear *n.* a large hairy caterpillar, esp. of the tiger moth.

wool•sack /wŏŏlsak/ *n.* **1** (in the UK) the Lord Chancellor's wool-stuffed seat in the House of Lords. **2** the position of Lord Chancellor.

wool•skin /wŏŏlskin/ *n.* the skin of a sheep, etc., with the fleece still on.

wool sta•pler *n.* **1** a person who grades wool. **2** a wool dealer.

wool•sort•er's dis•ease /wŏŏlsawrtərz dizeéz/ *n.* anthrax.

wooz•y /wŏŏzee/ *adj.* (**wooz•i•er, wooz•i•est**) *colloq.* **1** dizzy or unsteady. **2** dazed or slightly drunk. **3** vague. □□ **wooz•i•ly** *adv.* **wooz•i•ness** *n.* [19th c.: orig. unkn.]

wop /wop/ *n. sl. offens.* an Italian or other S. European. [20th c.: orig. uncert.: perh. f. It. *guappo* bold, showy, f. Sp. *guapo* dandy]

Worces•ter•shire sauce /wŏŏstərsheer, –shər/ *n.* a pungent sauce first made in Worcester, England.

word /wərd/ *n. & v.* • *n.* **1** a sound or combination of sounds forming a meaningful element of speech, usu. shown with a space on either side of it when written or printed, used as part (or occas. as the whole) of a sentence. **2** speech, esp. as distinct from action (*bold in word only*). **3** one's promise or assurance (*gave us their word*). **4** (in *sing.* or *pl.*) a thing said, a remark or conversation. **5** (in *pl.*) the text of a song or an actor's part. **6** (in *pl.*) angry talk (*they had words*). **7** news; intelligence; a message. **8** a command, password, or motto (*gave the word to begin*). **9** a basic unit of the expression of data in a computer. • *v.tr.* put into words; select words to express (*how shall we word that?*). □ **at a word** as soon as requested. **be as good as** (or **better than**) **one's word** fulfill (or exceed) what one has promised. **break one's word** fail to do what one has promised. **have no words for** be unable to express. **have a word** (often foll. by *with*) speak briefly (to). **in other words** expressing the same thing differently. **in so many words** explicitly or bluntly. **in a word** briefly. **keep one's word** do what one has promised. **my word** an exclamation of surprise or consternation. **not the word for it** not an adequate or appropriate description. **of few words** taciturn. **of one's word** reliable in keeping promises (*a woman of her word*). **put into words** express in speech or writing. **take a person at his** (or **her**) **word** interpret a person's words literally or exactly. **take a person's word for it** believe a person's statement without investigation, etc. **waste words** talk in vain. **words fail me** an expression of disbelief, dismay, etc. **word for word** in exactly the same or (of translation) corresponding words. **a word to the wise** a hint or brief explanation is all that is required. □□ **word•age** n. **word•less** adj. **word•less•ly** adv. **word•less•ness** n. [OE f. Gmc]

word-blind adj. incapable of identifying written or printed words.

word•book /wɔ́rdbŏŏk/ n. a book with lists of words; a vocabulary or dictionary.

word-deaf adj. incapable of identifying spoken words.

word game n. a game involving the making or selection, etc., of words.

word•ing /wɔ́rding/ n. 1 a form of words used. 2 the way in which something is expressed.

word of hon•or n. an assurance given upon one's honor.

word of mouth n. speech (only).

word-of-mouth adj. verbal; unwritten.

word or•der n. the sequence of words in a sentence, esp. affecting meaning, etc.

word-per•fect adj. knowing one's part, etc., by heart.

word•play /wɔ́rdplay/ n. use of words to witty effect, esp. by punning.

word proc•es•sor n. a computer software program for electronically storing text entered from a keyboard, incorporating corrections, and providing a printout.

word•smith /wɔ́rdsmith/ n. a skilled user or maker of words.

word square n. a set of words of equal length written one under another to read the same down as across (e.g., *too old ode*).

word•y /wɔ́rdee/ adj. (**word•i•er**, **word•i•est**) 1 using or expressed in many or too many words; verbose. 2 consisting of words. □□ **word•i•ly** adv. **word•i•ness** n. [OE *wordig* (as WORD, -Y¹)]

wore¹ past of WEAR¹.

wore² past and past part. of WEAR².

work /wɔrk/ n. & v. ●n. 1 the application of mental or physical effort to a purpose; the use of energy. 2 **a** a task to be undertaken. **b** the materials for this. **c** (prec. by *the*; foll. by *of*) a task occupying (no more than) a specified time (*the work of a moment*). 3 a thing done or made by work; the result of an action; an achievement; a thing made. 4 a person's employment or occupation, etc., esp. as a means of earning income (*looked for work; is out of work*). 5 **a** a literary or musical composition. **b** (in pl.) all such by an author or composer, etc. 6 actions or experiences of a specified kind (*good work!; this is thirsty work*). 7 **a** (in comb.) things or parts made of a specified material or with specified tools, etc. (*ironwork; needlework*). **b** archaic needlework. 8 (in pl.) the operative part of a clock or machine. 9 Physics the exertion of force overcoming resistance or producing molecular change (*convert heat into work*). 10 (in pl.) colloq. all that is available; everything needed. 11 (in pl.) operations of building or repair (*road works*). 12 (in pl.; often treated as *sing.*) esp. Brit. a place where manufacturing is carried on. 13 (usu. in pl.) Theol. a meritorious act. 14 (usu. in pl. or in comb.) a defensive structure (*earthworks*). 15 (in comb.) **a** ornamentation of a specified kind (*scrollwork*). **b** articles having this. ●v. (past and past part. **worked** or (esp. as adj.) **wrought**) 1 intr. (often foll. by *at, on*) do work; be engaged in bodily or mental activity. 2 intr. **a** be employed in certain work (*works in industry; works as a secretary*). **b** (foll. by *with*) be the coworker of (a person). 3 intr. (often foll. by *for*) make efforts; conduct a campaign (*works for peace*). 4 intr. (foll. by *in*) be a craftsman (in a material). 5 intr. operate or function, esp. effectively (*how does this machine work?; your idea will not work*). 6 intr. (of a part of a machine) run; revolve; go through regular motions. 7 tr. carry on, manage, or control (*cannot work the machine*). 8 tr. **a** put or keep in operation or at work; cause to toil (*this mine is no longer worked; works the staff very hard*). **b** cultivate (land). 9 tr. bring about; produce as a result (*worked miracles*). 10 tr. knead; hammer; bring to a desired shape or consistency. 11 tr. do, or make by, needlework, etc. 12 tr. & intr. (cause to) progress or penetrate, or make (one's way), gradually or with difficulty in a specified way (*worked our way through the crowd; worked the peg into the hole*). 13 intr. (foll. by *loose*, etc.) gradually become (loose, etc.) by constant movement. 14 tr. artificially excite (*worked themselves into a rage*). 15 tr. solve (an equation, etc.) by mathematics. 16 tr. **a** purchase with one's labor instead of money (*work one's passage*). **b** obtain by labor the money for (one's way through college, etc.). 17 tr. (foll. by *on, upon*) have influence. 18 intr. be in motion or agitated; cause agitation; ferment (*his features worked violently; the yeast began to work*). 19 intr. Naut. sail against the wind. □ **at work** in action or engaged in work. **give a person the works** 1 colloq. give or tell a person everything. 2 colloq. treat a person harshly. 3 sl. kill a person. **have one's work cut out** be faced with a hard task. **in the works** colloq. in progress; in the pipeline. **out of work** unemployed. **set to work** begin or cause to begin operations. **work one's fingers to the bone** see BONE. **work in** find a place for. **work it** colloq. bring it about; achieve a desired result. **work off** get rid of by work or activity. **work out 1** solve (an equation, etc.) or find out (an amount) by calculation; resolve (a problem, etc.). **2** (foll. by *at*) be calculated (*the total works out at 230*). **3** give a definite result (*this sum will not work out*). **4** have a specified or satisfactory result (*the plan worked out*

well; glad the arrangement worked out). **5** provide for the details of (*has worked out a plan*). **6** accomplish or attain with difficulty (*work out one's salvation*). **7** exhaust with work (*the mine is worked out*). **8** engage in physical exercise or training. **work over 1** examine thoroughly. **2** colloq. treat with violence. **work up 1** bring gradually to an efficient state. **2** (foll. by *to*) advance gradually to a climax. **3** elaborate or excite by degrees; bring to a state of agitation. **4** mingle (ingredients) into a whole. **5** learn (a subject) by study. **work one's will** (foll. by *on, upon*) archaic accomplish one's purpose on (a person or thing). **work wonders** see WONDER. □□ **work•less** adj. [OE *weorc*, etc., f. Gmc]

work•a•ble /wɔ́rkəbəl/ adj. 1 that can be worked or will work. 2 that is worth working; practicable; feasible (*a workable plan*). □□ **work•a•bil•i•ty** (/-bilitee/) n. **work•a•ble•ness** n. **work•a•bly** adv.

work•a•day /wɔ́rkəday/ adj. 1 ordinary; everyday; practical. 2 fit for, used, or seen on workdays.

work•a•hol•ic /wɔ́rkəhólik/ n. & adj. colloq. (a person) addicted to working.

work•bench /wɔ́rkbench/ n. a bench for doing mechanical or practical work, esp. carpentry.

work•box /wɔ́rkboks/ n. a box for holding tools, materials for sewing, etc.

work camp n. 1 a camp at which community work is done esp. by young volunteers. 2 a prison camp.

work•day /wɔ́rkday/ n. a day on which work is usually done.

work•er /wɔ́rkər/ n. 1 a person who works, esp. a manual or industrial employee. 2 a neuter or undeveloped female of various social insects, esp. a bee or ant, that does the basic work of its colony.

work•force /wɔ́rkfawrs/ n. 1 the workers engaged or available in an industry, etc. 2 the number of such workers.

work•horse /wɔ́rk-hawrs/ n. a horse, person, or machine that performs hard work.

work•house /wɔ́rk-hows/ n. 1 a house of correction for petty offenders. 2 Brit. hist. a public institution in which the destitute of a parish received board and lodging in return for work done; poorhouse.

work•ing /wɔ́rking/ adj. & n. ●adj. 1 engaged in work, esp. in manual or industrial labor. 2 functioning or able to function. ●n. 1 the activity of work. 2 the act or manner of functioning of a thing. 3 **a** a mine or quarry. **b** the part of this in which work is being or has been done (*a disused working*).

work•ing cap•i•tal n. the capital actually used in a business.

work•ing class n. the class of people who are employed for wages, esp. in manual or industrial work. □□ **work•ing-class** adj.

work•ing draw•ing n. a drawing to scale, serving as a guide for construction or manufacture.

work•ing girl n. 1 a young woman who works for a living. 2 sl. a prostitute.

work•ing hy•poth•e•sis n. a hypothesis used as a basis for action.

work•ing knowl•edge n. knowledge adequate to work with.

work•ing lunch n. a midday meal at which business is conducted.

work•ing or•der n. the condition in which a machine works (satisfactorily or as specified).

work•ing pa•pers n. documents that authorize (a person, esp. an alien or a minor) to be employed.

work•load /wɔ́rklōd/ n. the amount of work to be done by an individual, etc.

work•man /wɔ́rkmən/ n. (pl. **–men**) 1 a person employed to do manual labor. 2 a person considered with regard to skill in a job (*a good workman*).

work•man•like /wɔ́rkmənlīk/ adj. characteristic of a good workman; showing practiced skill.

work•man•ship /wɔ́rkmənship/ n. 1 the degree of skill with which a product is made or a job is done. 2 a thing made or created by a specified person, etc.

work•mate /wɔ́rkmayt/ n. Brit. a coworker.

work of art n. a fine picture, poem, or building, etc.

work•out /wɔ́rkowt/ n. a session of physical exercise or training.

work•piece /wɔ́rkpees/ n. a thing worked on with a tool or machine.

work•place /wɔ́rkplays/ n. a place at which a person works; an office, factory, etc.

work•room /wɔ́rkrōōm, -rŏŏm/ n. a room for working in, esp. one equipped for a certain kind of work.

work sheet n. 1 a paper for recording work done or in progress. 2 a paper listing questions or activities for students, etc., to work through.

work•shop /wɔ́rkshop/ n. 1 a room or building in which goods are manufactured. 2 **a** a meeting for concerted discussion or activity (*a dance workshop*). **b** the members of such a meeting.

work•sta•tion /wɔ́rkstayshən/ n. 1 the location of a stage in a manufacturing process. 2 a computer terminal or the desk, etc., where this is located.

work-stud•y pro•gram n. a system of combining academic studies with related practical employment.

work•ta•ble /wɔ́rktayb'l/ n. a table for working at, esp. with a sewing machine.

work•top /wórktop/ n. esp. Brit. a flat surface for working on, esp. in a kitchen.

work•wom•an /wórkwoŏmən/ n. (pl. **–wom•en**) a female worker or operative.

world /wərld/ n. **1 a** the earth, or a planetary body like it. **b** its countries and their inhabitants. **c** all people; the earth as known or in some particular respect. **2 a** the universe or all that exists; everything. **b** everything that exists outside oneself (dead to the world). **3 a** the time, state, or scene of human existence. **b** (prec. by the, this) mortal life. **4** secular interests and affairs. **5** human affairs; their course and conditions; active life (how goes the world with you?). **6** average, respectable, or fashionable people or their customs or opinions. **7** all that concerns or all who belong to a specified class, time, domain, or sphere of activity (the medieval world; the world of baseball). **8** (foll. by of) a vast amount (that makes a world of difference). **9** (attrib.) affecting many nations, of all nations (world politics; a world champion). □ **be worlds apart** differ greatly, esp. in nature or opinion. **bring into the world** give birth to or attend at the birth of. **come into the world** be born. **for all the world** (foll. by like, as if) precisely (looked for all the world as if they were real). **get the best of both worlds** benefit from two incompatible sets of ideas, circumstances, etc. **in the world** of all; at all (used as an intensifier in questions) (what in the world is it?). **man** (or **woman**) **of the world** a person experienced and practical in human affairs. **the next** (or **other**) **world** life after death. **out of this world** colloq. extremely good, etc. (the food was out of this world). **see the world** travel widely; gain wide experience. **think the world of** have a very high regard for. **the** (or **all the**) **world over** throughout the world. [OE w(e)orold, world f. a Gmc root meaning 'age': rel. to OLD]

World Bank n. colloq. the International Bank for Reconstruction and Development, an organization administering economic aid among member nations.

world-class adj. of a quality or standard regarded as high throughout the world.

World Cup n. a competition among soccer or other sporting teams from various countries.

world-fa•mous adj. known throughout the world.

world lan•guage n. **1** an artificial language for international use. **2** a language spoken in many countries.

world•line /wórldlín/ n. Physics a curve in space-time joining the positions of a particle throughout its existence.

world•ly /wórldlee/ adj. (**world•li•er, world•li•est**) **1** temporal or earthly (worldly goods). **2** engrossed in temporal affairs, esp. the pursuit of wealth and pleasure. □□ **world•li•ness** n. [OE woruldlic (as WORLD, –LY[1])]

world•ly wis•dom n. prudence as regards one's own interests. □□ **world•ly-wise** adj.

world pow•er n. a nation having power in world affairs.

World Se•ries n. the championship for U.S. major-league baseball teams.

world•view /wórldvyōō/ n. = WELTANSCHAUUNG.

world war n. a war involving many important nations (First World War or World War I, 1914–18; Second World War or World War II, 1939–45).

world-wea•ri•ness n. being weary of the world and life in it. □□ **world-wea•ry** adj.

world•wide /wórldwíd/ adj. & adv. ● adj. affecting, occurring in, or known in all parts of the world. ● adv. throughout the world.

worm /wərm/ n. & v. ● n. **1** any of various types of creeping or burrowing invertebrate animals with long, slender bodies and no limbs, esp. segmented in rings or parasitic in the intestines or tissues. **2** the long, slender larva of an insect, esp. in fruit or wood. **3** (in pl.) intestinal or other internal parasites. **4** a blindworm or slowworm. **5** a maggot supposed to eat dead bodies in the grave. **6** an insignificant or contemptible person. **7 a** the spiral part of a screw. **b** a short screw working in a worm gear. **8** the spiral pipe of a still in which the vapor is cooled and condensed. **9** the ligament under a dog's tongue. ● v. **1** intr. & tr. (often refl.) move with a crawling motion (wormed through the bushes; wormed our way through the bushes). **2** intr. & refl. (foll. by into) insinuate oneself into a person's favor, confidence, etc. **3** tr. (foll. by out) obtain (a secret, etc.) by cunning persistence (managed to worm the truth out of them). **4** tr. cut the worm of (a dog's tongue). **5** tr. rid (a plant or dog, etc.) of worms. **6** tr. Naut. make (a rope, etc.) smooth by winding thread between the strands. □□ **worm•like** adj. [OE wyrm f. Gmc]

worm-eat•en adj. **1 a** eaten into by worms. **b** rotten; decayed. **2** old and dilapidated.

worm gear n. an arrangement of a toothed wheel worked by a revolving spiral.

worm•hole /wórmhōl/ n. **1** a hole left by the passage of a worm. **2** Physics a hypothetical connection between widely separated regions of space-time.

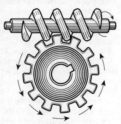

worm gear

worm•seed /wórmseed/ n. **1** seed used to expel intestinal worms. **2** a plant, e.g., santonica, bearing this seed.

worm•wood /wórmwoŏd/ n. **1** any woody shrub of the genus Artemisia, with a bitter aromatic taste, used in the preparation of vermouth and absinthe and in medicine. **2** bitter mortification or a source of this. [ME, alt. f. obs. wormod f. OE wormōd, wermōd, after worm, wood: cf. VERMOUTH]

worm•y /wórmee/ adj. (**worm•i•er, worm•i•est**) **1** full of worms. **2** wormeaten. □□ **worm•i•ness** n.

worn /wawrn/ past part. of WEAR[1]. ● adj. **1** damaged by use or wear. **2** looking tired and exhausted. **3** (in full **well-worn**) (of a joke, etc.) stale; often heard.

wor•ri•ment /wóreemənt, wúr–/ n. **1** the act of worrying or state of being worried. **2** a cause of worry.

wor•ri•some /wóreesəm, wúr–/ adj. causing or apt to cause worry or distress. □□ **wor•ri•some•ly** adv.

wor•ry /wóree, wúr–/ v. & n. ● v. (**–ries, –ried**) **1** intr. give way to anxiety or unease; allow one's mind to dwell on difficulty or troubles. **2** tr. harass; importune; be a trouble or anxiety to. **3** tr. **a** (of a dog, etc.) shake or pull about with the teeth. **b** attack repeatedly. **4** (as **worried** adj.) **a** uneasy; troubled in the mind. **b** suggesting worry (a worried look). ● n. (pl. **–ries**) **1** a thing that causes anxiety or disturbs a person's tranquillity. **2** a disturbed state of anxiety; anxiety; a worried state. **3** a dog's worrying of its quarry. □ **not to worry** colloq. there is no need to worry. **worry along** (or **through**) manage to advance by persistence in spite of obstacles. **worry oneself** (usu. in neg.) take needless trouble. **worry out** obtain (the solution to a problem, etc.) by dogged effort. □□ **wor•ried•ly** adv. **wor•ri•er** n. **wor•ry•ing•ly** adv. [OE wyrgan strangle f. WG]

wor•ry beads n. a string of beads manipulated with the fingers to occupy or calm oneself.

wor•ry•wart /wóreewawrt, wúr–/ n. colloq. a person who habitually worries unduly.

worse /wərs/ adj., adv., & n. ● adj. **1** more bad. **2** (predic.) in or into worse health or a worse condition (is getting worse; is none the worse for it). ● adv. more badly or more ill. ● n. **1** a worse thing or things (you might do worse than accept). **2** (prec. by the) a worse condition (a change for the worse). □ **none the worse** (often foll. by for) not adversely affected (by). **or worse** or as an even worse alternative. **the worse for drink** fairly drunk. **the worse for wear 1** damaged by use. **2** injured. **3** joc. drunk. **worse off** in a worse (esp. financial) position. [OE wyrsa, wiersa f. Gmc]

wors•en /wórsən/ v.tr. & intr. make or become worse.

wor•ship /wórship/ n. & v. ● n. **1 a** homage or reverence paid to a deity, esp. in a formal service. **b** the acts, rites, or ceremonies of worship. **2** adoration or devotion comparable to religious homage shown toward a person or principle (the worship of wealth; regarded them with worship in their eyes). **3** archaic worthiness; merit; recognition given or due to these; honor and respect. ● v. (**wor•shiped, wor•ship•ing** or **wor•shipped, wor•ship•ping**) **1** tr. adore as divine; honor with religious rites. **2** tr. idolize or regard with adoration (worships the ground she walks on). **3** intr. attend public worship. **4** intr. be full of adoration. □ **Your** (or **His** or **Her**) **Worship** esp. Brit. a title of respect used to or of a mayor, certain magistrates, etc. □□ **wor•ship•er** n. (or **wor•ship•per**). [OE weorthscipe (as WORTH, –SHIP)]

wor•ship•ful /wórshipfoŏl/ adj. **1** (usu. **Worshipful**) Brit. a title given to justices of the peace and to certain old companies or their officers, etc. **2** archaic entitled to honor or respect. **3** archaic imbued with a spirit of veneration. □□ **wor•ship•ful•ly** adv. **wor•ship•ful•ness** n.

worst /wərst/ adj., adv., n., & v. ● adj. most bad. ● adv most badly. ● n. the worst part, event, circumstance, or possibility (the worst of the storm is over; prepare for the worst). ● v.tr. get the better of; defeat; outdo. □ **at its**, etc., **worst** in the worst state. **at worst** (or **the worst**) in the worst possible case. **do your worst** an expression of defiance. **get** (or **have**) **the worst of it** be defeated. **if worst comes to worst** if the worst happens. [OE wierresta, wyrresta (adj.), wyrst, wyrrest (adv.), f. Gmc]

wor•sted /woŏstid, wór–/ n. **1** a fine smooth yarn spun from combed long, stapled wool. **2** fabric made from this. [Worste(a)d in S. England]

wort /wərt, wawrt/ n. **1** archaic (except in names) a plant or herb (liverwort; St. John's wort). **2** the infusion of malt which after fermentation becomes beer. [OE wyrt: rel. to ROOT[1]]

worth /wərth/ adj. & n. ● predic.adj. (governing a noun like a preposition) **1** of a value equivalent to (is worth $50; is worth very little). **2** such as to justify or repay; deserving; bringing compensation for (worth doing; not worth the trouble). **3** possessing or having property amounting to (is worth a million dollars). ● n. **1** what a person or thing is worth; the (usu. specified) merit of (*of great worth; persons of worth*). **2** the equivalent of money in a commodity (*ten dollars' worth of gasoline*). □ **for all one is worth** *colloq.* with one's utmost efforts; without reserve. **for what it is worth** without a guarantee of its truth or value. **worth it** *colloq.* worth the time or effort spent. **worth one's salt** see SALT. **worth while** (or **one's while**) see WHILE; also see note at WORTHWHILE. [OE *w* (*e*)*orth*]

worth·less /wórthlis/ *adj.* without value or merit. □□ **worth·less·ly** *adv.* **worth·less·ness** *n.*

worth·while /wórth–hwíl, wíl/ *adj.* that is worth the time or effort spent; of value or importance. □□ **worth·while·ness** *n.*

▶Worth while (two words) is used only in the predicate, e.g., *No-body thought it worth while to call the police,* and means 'worth the time or effort.' **Worthwhile** (one word) also has this meaning, but can be used both predicatively and attributively, e.g., *Would this investment be worthwhile?* (predicative), or *He was a worthwhile candidate for the office* (attributive).

wor·thy /wórthee/ *adj. & n.* ● *adj.* (**wor·thi·er, wor·thi·est**) **1** estimable; having some moral worth; deserving respect (*lived a worthy life*). **2** (of a person) entitled to (esp. condescending) recognition (*a worthy old couple*). **3 a** (foll. by *of* or *to* + infin.) deserving (*worthy of a mention; worthy to be remembered*). **b** (foll. by *of*) adequate or suitable to the dignity, etc., of (*in words worthy of the occasion*). ● *n.* (*pl.* **–thies**) **1** a worthy person. **2** a person of some distinction. **3** *joc.* a person. □□ **wor·thi·ly** *adv.* **wor·thi·ness** *n.* [ME *wurthi,* etc. f. WORTH]

-worthy /wərthee/ *comb. form* forming adjectives meaning: **1** deserving of (*blameworthy; noteworthy*). **2** suitable or fit for (*newsworthy; roadworthy*).

would /wŏŏd, when unstressed wəd/ *v. aux.* (*3rd sing.* **would**) *past* of WILL[1], used esp.: **1** (in the 2nd and 3rd persons, and often in the 1st: see SHOULD). **a** in reported speech (*he said he would be home by evening*). **b** to express the conditional mood (*they would have been killed if they had gone*). **2** to express habitual action (*would wait for her every evening*). **3** to express a question or polite request (*would they like it?; would you come in, please?*). **4** to express probability (*I guess she would be over fifty by now*). **5** (foll. by *that* + clause) *literary* to express a wish (*would that you were here*). **6** to express consent (*they would not help*). [OE *wolde,* past of *wyllan:* see WILL[1]]

▶See note at SHALL.

would-be *adj.* often *derog.* desiring or aspiring to be (*a would-be politician*).

would·n't /wŏŏd'nt/ *contr.* would not. □ **I wouldn't know** *colloq.* (as is to be expected) I do not know.

wouldst /wŏŏdst/ *archaic 2nd sing. past* of WOULD.

wound[1] /wŏŏnd/ *n. & v.* ● *n.* **1** an injury done to living tissue by a cut or blow, etc., esp. beyond the cutting or piercing of the skin. **2** an injury to a person's reputation or a pain inflicted on a person's feelings. **3** *poet.* the pangs of love. ● *v. tr.* inflict a wound on (*wounded soldiers; wounded feelings*). □□ **wound·ing·ly** *adv.* **wound·less** *adj.* [OE *wund* (n.), *wundian* (v.)]

wound[2] *past* and *past part.* of WIND[2] (cf. WIND[1] *v.* 6).

wound up *adj.* (of a person) excited or tense or angry.

wound·wort /wŏŏndwərt, –wawrt/ *n.* any of various plants esp. of the genus *Stachys,* formerly supposed to have healing properties.

wove[1] *past* of WEAVE[1].

wove[2] /wōv/ *adj.* (of paper) made on a wire-gauze mesh and so having a uniform unlined surface. [var. of *woven,* past part. of WEAVE[1]]

wo·ven *past part.* of WEAVE[1].

wow[1] /wow/ *int., n., & v.* ● *int.* expressing astonishment or admiration. ● *n. sl.* a sensational success. ● *v. tr. sl.* impress or excite greatly. [orig. Sc.: imit.]

wow[2] /wow/ *n.* a slow pitch fluctuation in sound reproduction, perceptible in long notes. [imit.]

WP *abbr.* word processor; word processing.

w.p. *abbr.* **1** weather permitting. **2** *Baseball* wild pitch(es).

w.p.m. *abbr.* words per minute.

wrack /rak/ *n.* **1** seaweed cast up or growing on the shore. **2** destruction. **3** a wreck or wreckage. **4** = RACK[2]. **5** = RACK[5]. [ME f. MDu. *wrak* or MLG *wra(c) k,* a parallel formation to OE *wræc,* rel. to *wrecan* WREAK: cf. WRECK, RACK[5]]

wraith /rayth/ *n.* **1** a ghost or apparition. **2** the spectral appearance of a living person supposed to portend that person's death. □□ **wraith·like** *adj.* [16th-c. Sc.: orig. unkn.]

wran·gle /ránggəl/ *n. & v.* ● *n.* a noisy argument, altercation, or dispute. ● *v.* **1** *intr.* engage in a wrangle. **2** *tr.* herd (cattle). [ME, prob. f. LG or Du.: cf. LG *wrangelen,* frequent. of *wrangen* to struggle, rel. to WRING]

wran·gler /ránglər/ *n.* **1** a person who wrangles. **2** a cowboy. **3** (at Cambridge University) a person placed in the first class of the mathematical tripos.

wrap /rap/ *v. & n.* ● *v. tr.* (**wrapped, wrap·ping**) **1** (often foll. by *up*) envelop in folded or soft encircling material (*wrap it up in paper; wrap up a package*). **2** (foll. by *around, about*) arrange or draw (a

pliant covering) around (a person) (*wrapped the coat closer around me*). **3** (foll. by *around*) *sl.* crash (a vehicle) into a stationary object. ● *n.* **1** a shawl or scarf or other such addition to clothing; a wrapper. **2** material used for wrapping. □ **take the wraps off** disclose. **under wraps** in secrecy. **wrapped up** in engrossed or absorbed in. **wrap up 1** finish off; bring to completion (*wrapped up the deal in two days*). **2** put on warm clothes (*mind you wrap up well*). **3** (in *imper.*) *Brit. sl.* be quiet. [ME: orig. unkn.]

wrap·a·round /rápərownd/ *adj. & n.* ● *adj.* **1** (esp. of clothing) designed to wrap around. **2** curving or extending around at the edges. ● *n.* anything that wraps around.

wrap·page /rápij/ *n.* a wrapping or wrappings.

wrap·per /rápər/ *n.* **1** a cover for a candy, chocolate, etc. **2** a cover enclosing a newspaper or similar packet for mailing. **3** a paper cover of a book, usu. detachable. **4** a loose enveloping robe or gown. **5** a tobacco leaf of superior quality enclosing a cigar.

wrap·ping /ráping/ *n.* (esp. in *pl.*) material used to wrap; wraps; wrappers.

wrap·ping pa·per *n.* strong or decorative paper for wrapping packages.

wrasse /ras/ *n.* any bright-colored marine fish of the family Labridae with thick lips and strong teeth. [Corn. *wrach,* var. of *gwrach,* = Welsh *gwrach,* lit. 'old woman']

wrath /rath, roth, rawth/ *n. literary* extreme anger. [OE *wrǣththu* f. *wrǣth* WROTH]

wrath·ful /ráthfŏŏl, róth–, ráwth–/ *adj. literary* extremely angry. □□ **wrath·ful·ly** *adv.* **wrath·ful·ness** *n.*

wreak /reek/ *v. tr.* **1** (usu. foll. by *upon*) give play or satisfaction to; put in operation (vengeance or one's anger, etc.). **2** cause (damage, etc.) (*the hurricane wreaked havoc on the crops*). **3** *archaic* avenge (a wrong or wronged person). □□ **wreak·er** *n.* [OE *wrecan* drive, avenge, etc., f. Gmc: cf. WRACK, WRECK, WRETCH]

wreath /reeth/ *n.* (*pl.* **wreaths** /reethz, reeths/) **1** flowers or leaves fastened in a ring esp. as an ornament for a person's head or a building or for laying on a grave, etc., as a mark of honor or respect. **2 a** a similar ring of soft twisted material such as silk. **b** *Heraldry* a representation of this below a crest. **3** a carved representation of a wreath. **4** (foll. by *of*) a curl or ring of smoke or cloud. **5** a light drifting mass of snow, etc. [OE *writha* f. weak grade of *wrīthan* WRITHE]

wreathe /reeth/ *v.* **1** *tr.* encircle as, with, or like a wreath. **2** *tr.* (foll. by *around*) put (one's arms, etc.) around (a person, etc.). **3** *intr.* (of smoke, etc.) move in the shape of wreaths. **4** *tr.* form (flowers, silk, etc.) into a wreath. **5** *tr.* make (a garland). [partly back-form. f. archaic *wrethen* past part. of WRITHE; partly f. WREATH]

wreck /rek/ *n. & v.* ● *n.* **1** the destruction or disablement esp. of a ship. **2** a ship that has suffered a wreck (*the shores are strewn with wrecks*). **3** a greatly damaged or disabled building, thing, or person (*had become a physical and mental wreck*). **4** (foll. by *of*) a wretched remnant or disorganized set of remains. **5** *Law* goods, etc., cast up by the sea. ● *v.* **1** *tr.* cause the wreck of (a ship, etc.). **2** *tr.* completely ruin (hopes, chances, etc.). **3** *intr.* suffer a wreck **4** *tr.* (as **wrecked** *adj.*) involved in a shipwreck (*wrecked sailors*). **5** *intr.* deal with wrecked vehicles, etc. [ME f. AF *wrec,* etc. (cf. VAREC) f. a Gmc root meaning 'to drive': cf. WREAK]

wreck·age /rékij/ *n.* **1** wrecked material. **2** the remnants of a wreck. **3** the action or process of wrecking.

wreck·er /rékər/ *n.* **1** a person or thing that wrecks or destroys. **2** esp. *hist.* a person on the shore who tries to bring about a shipwreck in order to plunder or profit by the wreckage. **3** a person employed in demolition, or in recovering a wrecked ship or its contents. **4** a person who breaks up damaged vehicles for spares and scrap. **5** a vehicle or train used in recovering a damaged one.

wren /ren/ *n.* any small, usu. brown, short-winged songbird of the family Troglodytidae, esp. *Troglodytes troglodytes* of Europe, having an erect tail. [OE *wrenna,* rel. to OHG *wrendo, wrendilo,* Icel. *rindill*]

wrench /rench/ *n. & v.* ● *n.* **1** a violent twist or oblique pull or act of tearing off. **2** an adjustable tool for gripping and turning nuts, etc. **3** an instance of painful uprooting or parting (*leaving home was a great wrench*). **4** *Physics* a combination of a couple with the force along its axis. ● *v. tr.* **1 a** twist or pull violently around or sideways. **b** injure (a limb, etc.) by undue straining; sprain. **2** (often foll. by *off, away,* etc.) pull off with a wrench. **3** seize or take forcibly. **4** distort (facts) to suit a theory, etc. [(earlier as verb:) OE *wrencan* twist]

wrest /rest/ *v. & n.* ● *v. tr.* **1** force or wrench away from a person's grasp. **2** (foll. by *from*) obtain by effort or with difficulty. **3** distort into accordance with one's interests or views (*wrest the law to suit themselves*). ● *n. archaic* a key for tuning a harp or piano, etc. [OE *wrǣstan* f. Gmc, rel. to WRIST]

wrest block *n.* the part of a piano or harpsichord holding the wrest pins.

wres·tle /résəl/ *n. & v.* ● *n.* **1** a contest in which two opponents grapple and try to throw each other to the ground, esp. as an athletic sport under a code of rules. **2** a hard struggle. ● *v.* **1** *intr.* (often foll. by *with*) take part in a wrestle. **2** *tr.* fight (a person) in a wrestle (*wrestled his opponent to the ground*). **3** *intr.* **a** (foll. by *with, against*) struggle; contend. **b** (foll. by *with*) do one's utmost to deal with (a task, difficulty, etc.). **4** *tr.* move with effort as if wrestling. □□ **wres•tler** *n.* **wres•tling** *n.* [OE (unrecorded) *wr æstlian*: cf. MLG *wrostelen*, OE *wraxlian*]

wrest pin *n.* each of the pins to which the strings of a piano or harpsichord are attached.

wretch /rech/ *n.* **1** an unfortunate or pitiable person. **2** (often as a playful term of depreciation) a reprehensible or contemptible person. [OE *wrecca* f. Gmc]

wretch•ed /réchid/ *adj.* (**wretch•ed•er**, **wretch•ed•est**) **1** unhappy or miserable. **2** of bad quality or no merit; contemptible. **3** unsatisfactory or displeasing. □ **feel wretched 1** be unwell. **2** be much embarrassed. □□ **wretch•ed•ly** *adv.* **wretch•ed•ness** *n.* [ME, irreg. f. WRETCH + -ED ¹: cf. WICKED]

wrig•gle /rígəl/ *v. & n.* •*v.* **1** *intr.* (of a worm, etc.) twist or turn its body with short, writhing movements. **2** *intr.* (of a person or animal) make wriggling motions. **3** *tr. & intr.* (foll. by *along*, etc.) move or go in this way (*wriggled into the corner; wriggled his hand into the hole*). **4** *tr.* make (one's way) by wriggling. **5** *intr.* practice evasion. •*n.* an act of wriggling. □ **wriggle out of** *colloq.* avoid on a contrived pretext. □□ **wrig•gler** *n.* **wrig•gly** *adj.* [ME f. MLG *wriggelen* frequent. of *wriggen*]

wright /rīt/ *n.* a maker or builder (usu. in *comb.*: *playwright; shipwright*). [OE *wryhta, wyrhta* f. WG: cf. WORK]

wring /ring/ *v. & n.* •*v.tr.* (*past* and *past part.* **wrung** /rung/) **1 a** squeeze tightly. **b** (often foll. by *out*) squeeze and twist esp. to remove liquid. **2** twist forcibly; break by twisting. **3** distress or torture. **4** extract by squeezing. **5** (foll. by *out, from*) obtain by pressure or importunity; extort. •*n.* an act of wringing; a squeeze. □ **wring a person's hand** clasp it forcibly or press it with emotion. **wring one's hands** clasp them as a gesture of great distress. **wring the neck of** kill (a chicken, etc.) by twisting its neck. [OE *wringan*, rel. to WRONG]

wring•er /ríngər/ *n.* **1** a device for wringing water from washed clothes, etc. **2** a difficult ordeal (*that exam put me through the wringer*).

wring•ing /rínging/ *adj.* (in full **wringing wet**) so wet that water can be wrung out.

wrin•kle /ríngkəl/ *n. & v.* •*n.* **1** a slight crease or depression in the skin such as is produced by age. **2** a similar mark in another flexible surface. **3** *colloq.* a useful tip or clever expedient. •*v.* **1** *tr.* make wrinkles in. **2** *intr.* form wrinkles; become marked with wrinkles. [orig. repr. OE *gewrinclod* sinuous]

wrin•kly /ríngklee/ *adj. & n.* •*adj.* (**wrin•kli•er**, **wrink•li•est**) having many wrinkles. •*n.* (also **wrin•klie**) (*pl.* **–klies**) *sl. offens.* an old or middle-aged person.

wrist /rist/ *n.* **1** the part connecting the hand with the forearm. **2** the corresponding part in an animal. **3** the part of a garment covering the wrist. **4 a** (in full **wrist-work**) the act or practice of working the hand without moving the arm. **b** the effect got in fencing, ball games, sleight of hand, etc., by this. **5** (in full **wrist pin**) *Mech.* a stud projecting from a crank, etc., as an attachment for a connecting rod. [OE f. Gmc, prob. f. a root rel. to WRITHE]

wrist•band /rístband/ *n.* a band forming or concealing the end of a shirt sleeve; a cuff.

wrist-drop *n.* the inability to extend the hand through paralysis of the forearm muscles.

wrist•let /rístlit/ *n.* a band or ring worn on the wrist to strengthen or guard it or as an ornament, bracelet, handcuff, etc.

wrist•watch /rístwoch/ *n.* a small watch worn on a strap around the wrist.

wrist•y /rístee/ *adj.* (esp. of a shot in tennis, etc.) involving or characterized by movement of the wrist.

writ¹ /rit/ *n.* **1** a form of written command in the name of a sovereign, court, government, etc., to act or abstain from acting in some way. **2** (in the UK) a Crown document summoning a peer to Parliament or ordering the election of a member or members of Parliament. □ **serve a writ on** deliver a writ to (a person). [OE (as WRITE)]

writ² /rit/ *archaic past part.* of WRITE. □ **writ large** in magnified or emphasized form.

write /rīt/ *v.* (*past* **wrote** /rōt/; *past part.* **writ•ten** /rít'n/) **1** *intr.* mark paper or some other surface by means of a pen, pencil, etc., with symbols, letters, or words. **2** *tr.* form or mark (such symbols, etc.). **3** *tr.* form or mark the symbols that represent or constitute (a word or sentence, or a document, etc.). **4** *tr.* fill or complete (a form, check, etc.) with writing. **5** *tr.* put (data) into a computer store. **6** *tr.* (esp. in *passive*) indicate (a quality or condition) by one's or its appearance (*guilt was written on his face*). **7** *tr.* compose (a text, article, novel, etc.) for written or printed reproduction or publication; put into literary, etc., form and set down in writing. **8** *intr.* be engaged in composing a text, article, etc. (*writes for the local newspaper*). **9** *intr.* (foll. by *to*) write and send a letter (to a recipient). **10** *tr. colloq.* write and send a letter to (a person) (*wrote him last week*). **11** *tr.* convey (news, information, etc.) by letter (*wrote that they would arrive next Friday*). **12** *tr.* state in written or printed form (*it is written that*). **13** *tr.* cause to be recorded. **14** *tr.* underwrite (an insurance policy). **15** *tr.* (foll. by *into, out of*) include or exclude (a character or episode) in a story by suitable changes of the text. **16** *tr. archaic* describe in writing. □ **nothing to write home about** *colloq.* of little interest or value. **write down 1** record or take note of in writing. **2** write as if for those considered inferior. **3** disparage in writing. **write in 1** send a suggestion, query, etc., in writing to an organization, esp. a broadcasting station. **2** add (an extra name) on a list of candidates when voting. **write off 1** write and send a letter. **2** cancel the record of (a bad debt, etc.); acknowledge the loss of or failure to recover (an asset). **3** damage (a vehicle, etc.) so badly that it cannot be repaired. **4** compose with facility. **5** dismiss as insignificant. **write out 1** write in full or in finished form. **2** exhaust (oneself) by writing (*have written myself out*). **write up 1** write a full account of. **2** praise in writing. **3** make a report (of a person) esp. to cite a violation of rules, etc. □□ **writ•a•ble** *adj.* [OE *wrītan* scratch, score, write, f. Gmc: orig. used of symbols inscribed with sharp tools on stone or wood]

write-down *n.* a reduction of the book value of (an asset, etc.).

write-in *n.* **1** a vote cast for an unlisted candidate by writing the candidate's name on a ballot paper. **2** a candidate for whom votes are cast in such a way.

write-off *n.* a thing written off, esp. a vehicle too badly damaged to be repaired.

writ•er /rítər/ *n.* **1** a person who writes or has written something. **2** a person who writes books; an author. **3** *Brit.* a clerk, esp. in the navy or in government offices. **4** *Brit.* a scribe. [OE *wrītere* (as WRITE)]

writ•er's block *n.* (of a writer) a temporary inability to proceed with the composition of a novel, play, etc.

writ•er's cramp *n.* a muscular spasm due to excessive writing.

write-up *n. colloq.* a written or published account; a review.

writhe /rīth/ *v. & n.* •*v.* **1** *intr.* twist or roll oneself about in or as if in acute pain. **2** *intr.* suffer severe mental discomfort or embarrassment (*writhed with shame; writhed at the thought of it*). **3** *tr.* twist (one's body, etc.) about. •*n.* an act of writhing. [OE *wrīthan*, rel. to WREATHE]

writ•ing /ríting/ *n.* **1** a group or sequence of letters or symbols. **2** = HANDWRITING. **3** the art or profession of literary composition. **4** (usu. in *pl.*) a piece of literary work done; a book, article, etc. **5** (**Writings**) the Hagiographa. □ **in writing** in written form. **the writing on the wall** an ominously significant event, etc. (see Dan. 5:5, 25-8).

writ•ten *past part.* of WRITE.

wrong /rawng, rong/ *adj., adv., n., & v.* •*adj.* **1** mistaken; not true; in error (*gave a wrong answer; we were wrong to think that*). **2** unsuitable; less or least desirable (*the wrong road; a wrong decision*). **3** contrary to law or morality (*it is wrong to steal*). **4** amiss; out of order; in or into a bad or abnormal condition (*something wrong with my heart; my watch has gone wrong*). •*adv.* (usually placed last) in a wrong manner or direction; with an incorrect result (*guessed wrong; told them wrong*). •*n.* **1** what is morally wrong; a wrong action. **2** injustice; unjust action or treatment (*suffer wrong*). •*v.tr.* **1** treat unjustly; do wrong to. **2** mistakenly attribute bad motives to; discredit. □ **do wrong** commit sin; transgress; offend. **do wrong to** malign or mistreat (a person). **get in wrong with** incur the dislike or disapproval of (a person). **get on the wrong side of** fall into disfavor with. **get wrong 1** misunderstand (a person, statement, etc.). **2** obtain an incorrect answer to. **get** (or **get hold of**) **the wrong end of**

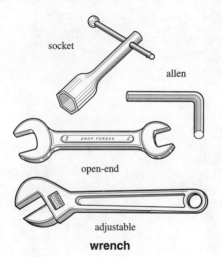

socket

allen

open-end

adjustable

wrench

the stick misunderstand completely. **go down the wrong way** (of food) enter the windpipe instead of the esophagus. **go wrong 1** take the wrong path. **2** stop functioning properly. **3** depart from virtuous or suitable behavior. **in the wrong** responsible for a quarrel, mistake, or offense. **on the wrong side of 1** out of favor with (a person). **2** somewhat more than (a stated age). □□ **wrong•er** *n.* **wrong•ly** *adv.* **wrong•ness** *n.* [OE *wrang* f. ON *rangr* awry, unjust, rel. to WRING]

wrong•do•er /ráwngdōōər, róng–/ *n.* a person who behaves immorally or illegally. □□ **wrong•do•ing** *n.*

wrong•ful /ráwngfŏŏl, róng–/ *adj.* **1** characterized by unfairness or injustice. **2** contrary to law. **3** (of a person) not entitled to the position, etc., occupied. □□ **wrong•ful•ly** *adv.* **wrong•ful•ness** *n.*

wrong•head•ed /ráwnghedid, róng–/ *adj.* perverse and obstinate. □□ **wrong•head•ed•ly** *adv.* **wrong•head•ed•ness** *n.*

wrong side *n.* the worse or undesired or unusable side of something, esp. fabric.

wrote *past* of WRITE.

wroth /rawth, roth, rōth/ *predic.adj. archaic* angry. [OE *wrāth* f. Gmc]

wrought /rawt/ *archaic past* and *past part.* of WORK.● *adj.* (of metals) beaten out or shaped by hammering.

wrought i•ron *n.* a tough malleable form of iron suitable for forging or rolling, not cast.

wrung *past* and *past part.* of WRING.

wry /rī/ *adj.* (**wry•er**, **wry•est** or **wri•er**, **wri•est**) **1** distorted or turned to one side. **2** (of a face or smile, etc.) contorted in disgust, disappointment, or mockery. **3** (of humor) dry and mocking. □□ **wry•ly** *adv.* **wry•ness** *n.* [*wry* (v.) f. OE *wrīgian* tend, incline, in ME deviate, swerve, contort]

wry•neck /rínek/ *n.* **1** = TORTICOLLIS. **2** any bird of the genus *Jynx* of the woodpecker family, able to turn its head over its shoulder.

WSW *abbr.* west-southwest.

wt. *abbr.* weight.

Wu /wōō/ *n.* a dialect of Chinese spoken in the Kiangsu and Chekiang Provinces. [Chin.]

wun•der•kind /vŏŏndərkind/ *n. colloq.* a person who achieves great success while relatively young. [G f. *Wunder* wonder + *Kind* child]

wurst /wərst, wŏŏrst/ *n.* German or Austrian sausage. [G]

wuss /wŏŏs/ *n. colloq.* a person seen as a coward or weakling. □□ **wuss•y** *adj.*

WV *abbr.* West Virginia (in official postal use).

W.Va. *abbr.* West Virginia.

WW *abbr.* World War (I, II).

WY *abbr.* Wyoming (in official postal use).

wych- /wich/ *comb. form* (also **wich-**, **witch-**) in names of trees with pliant branches. [OE *wic(e)* app. f. a Gmc root meaning 'bend': rel. to WEAK]

wynd /wīnd/ *n. Sc.* a narrow street or alley. [ME, app. f. the stem of WIND²]

wynn /win/ *n.* (also **wyn** or **wen** /wen/) a runic letter in Old and Middle English, later replaced by *w*. [OE, var. of *wyn* joy (see WINSOME), used because it begins with this letter: cf. THORN 3]

Wyo. *abbr.* Wyoming.

WYSIWYG /wízeewig/ *adj.* (also **wysiwyg**) *Computing* denoting the representation of text onscreen in a form exactly corresponding to its appearance on a printout. [acronym of *what you see is what you get*]

wy•vern /wívərn/ *n.* (also **wi•vern**) *Heraldry* a winged two-legged dragon with a barbed tail. [ME *wyver* f. OF *wivre*, *guivre* f. L *vipera*: for –*n* cf. BITTERN]

wyvern

X

X¹ /eks/ *n.* (also **x**) (*pl.* **xs** or **X's**) **1** the twenty-fourth letter of the alphabet. **2** (as a Roman numeral) ten. **3** (usu. **x**) *Algebra* the first unknown quantity. **4** *Geom.* the first coordinate. **5** an unknown or unspecified number or person, etc. **6** a cross-shaped symbol esp. used to indicate position (*X marks the spot*) or incorrectness or to symbolize a kiss or a vote, or as the signature of a person who cannot write.

X² *symb.* = X-RATED.

-x /z/ *suffix* forming the plural of many nouns ending in *–u* taken from French (*beaux*; *tableaux*). [F]

xan·thate /zánthayt/ *n.* any salt or ester of xanthic acid.

xan·thic /zánthik/ *adj.* yellowish. [Gk *xanthos* yellow]

xan·thic ac·id *n.* any colorless unstable acid containing the –OCS₂H group.

Xan·thip·pe /zanthípee, –típ–/ *n.* (also **Xan·tip·pe** /–típee/) a shrewish or ill-tempered woman or wife. [name of Socrates' wife]

xan·tho·ma /zanthṓmə/ *n.* (*pl.* **xan·tho·mas** or **xan·tho·ma·ta** /–mətə/) *Med.* **1** a skin disease characterized by irregular yellow patches. **2** such a patch. [as XANTHIC + –OMA]

xan·tho·phyll /zánthəfil/ *n.* any of various oxygen-containing carotenoids associated with chlorophyll, some of which cause the yellow color of leaves in the autumn. [as XANTHIC + Gk *phullon* leaf]

X chro·mo·some /éks krṓməsōm/ *n.* a sex chromosome of which the number in female cells is twice that in male cells. [*X* as an arbitrary label + CHROMOSOME]

x.d. *abbr.* ex dividend.

Xe *symb. Chem.* the element xenon.

xe·bec /zeébek/ *n.* (also **ze·bec, ze·beck**) a small, three-masted Mediterranean vessel with lateen and usu. some square sails. [alt. (after Sp. *xabeque*) of F *chebec* f. It. *sciabecco* f. Arab. *šabāk*]

xeno- /zénō, zeé–/ *comb. form* **1 a** foreign. **b** a foreigner. **2** other. [Gk *xenos* strange, foreign, stranger]

xe·nog·a·my /zənógəmee/ *n. Bot.* cross-fertilization. □□ **xe·nog·a·mous** *adj.*

xen·o·lith /zénəlith, zeénə–/ *n. Geol.* an inclusion within an igneous rock mass, usu. derived from the immediately surrounding rock.

xe·non /zénon, zeé–/ *n. Chem.* a heavy, colorless, odorless inert gaseous element occurring in traces in the atmosphere and used in fluorescent lamps. ¶ Symb.: **Xe**. [Gk, neut. of *xenos* strange]

xen·o·phobe /zénəfōb, zeénə–/ *n.* a person given to xenophobia.

xen·o·pho·bi·a /zénəfṓbeeə, zeénə–/ *n.* a deep dislike of foreigners. □□ **xen·o·pho·bic** *adj.*

xe·ran·the·mum /zeeránthiməm/ *n.* a composite plant of the genus *Xeranthemum*, with dry everlasting composite flowers. [mod.L f. Gk *xēros* dry + *anthemon* flower]

xe·ric /zérik, zeé–/ *adj. Ecol.* having or characterized by dry conditions. [as XERO– + –IC]

xero- /zeérō/ *comb. form* dry. [Gk *xēros* dry]

xe·ro·der·ma /zeérədórmə/ *n.* any of various diseases characterized by extreme dryness of the skin, esp. ichthyosis. [mod.L (as XERO–, Gk *derma* skin)]

xe·rog·ra·phy /zeerógrəfee/ *n.* a dry copying process in which black or colored powder adheres to parts of a surface remaining electrically charged after exposure of the surface to light from an image of the document to be copied. □□ **xe·ro·graph·ic** /–rəgráfik/ *adj.* **xe·ro·graph·i·cal·ly** *adv.*

xe·roph·i·lous /zeerófiləs/ *adj.* (of a plant) adapted to extremely dry conditions

xe·ro·phyte /zeérəfīt/ *n.* (also **xe·ro·phile** /–fīl/) a plant able to grow in very dry conditions, e.g., in a desert.

Xe·rox /zeéroks/ *n. & v. • n. Trademark* **1** a machine for copying by xerography. **2** a copy made using this machine. • *v.tr.* (**xerox**) reproduce by this process. [invented f. XEROGRAPHY]

Xho·sa /kṓsə, –zə, káw–/ *n. & adj.* • *n.* **1** (*pl.* same or **Xho·sas**) a member of a Bantu people of Cape Province, South Africa. **2** the Bantu language of this people, similar to Zulu. • *adj.* of or relating to this people or language. [native name]

xi /zī, sī, ksee/ *n.* the fourteenth letter of the Greek alphabet (Ξ, ξ). [Gk]

-xion /kshən/ *suffix* forming nouns (see –ION) from Latin participial stems ending in *–x-* (*fluxion*).

xiph·i·ster·num /zífistórnəm/ *n. Anat.* = XIPHOID PROCESS. [as XIPHOID + STERNUM]

xiph·oid /zífoyd/ *adj. Biol.* sword-shaped. [Gk *xiphoeidēs* f. *xiphos* sword]

xiph·oid proc·ess *n.* the cartilaginous process at the lower end of the sternum.

Xmas /krísməs, éksməs/ *n. colloq.* = CHRISTMAS. [abbr., with X for the initial chi of Gk *Khristos* Christ]

xo·a·non /zṓənon/ *n.* (*pl.* **xo·a·na** /–nə/) *Gk Antiq.* a primitive usu. wooden image of a deity supposed to have fallen from heaven. [Gk f. *xeō* carve]

X-rat·ed *adj.* (of motion pictures, etc.) classified as suitable for adults only.

X ray /éksray/ *n. & adj.* (also **X-ray, x-ray**) • *n.* **1** (in *pl.*) electromagnetic radiation of short wavelength, able to pass through opaque bodies. **2** an image made by the effect of X rays on a photographic plate, esp. showing the position of bones, etc., by their greater absorption of the rays. • *adj.* (**X-ray** or **x-ray**) of, relating to, or made by X ray. [transl. of G *x-Strahlen* (pl.) f. *Strahl* ray, so called because when discovered in 1895 the nature of the rays was unknown]

x-ray /éksray/ *v.tr.* (also **X-ray**) photograph, examine, or treat with X rays.

X-ray as·tron·o·my *n.* the branch of astronomy concerned with the X-ray emissions of celestial bodies.

X-ray crys·tal·log·ra·phy *n.* the study of crystals and their structure by means of the diffraction of X rays by the regularly spaced atoms of a crystalline material.

X-ray tube *n.* a device for generating X rays by accelerating electrons to high energies and causing them to strike a metal target from which the X rays are emitted.

xy·lem /zíləm/ *n. Bot.* woody tissue (cf. PHLOEM). [Gk *xulon* wood]

xy·lene /zíleen/ *n. Chem.* one of three isomeric hydrocarbons formed from benzene by the substitution of two methyl groups, obtained from wood, etc. [formed as XYLEM + –ENE]

xylo- /zílō/ *comb. form* wood. [Gk *xulon* wood]

xy·lo·carp /zíləkaarp/ *n.* a hard woody fruit. □□ **xy·lo·carp·ous** *adj.*

xy·lo·graph /zíləgraf/ *n.* a woodcut or wood engraving (esp. an early one).

xy·log·ra·phy /zīlógrəfee/ *n.* **1** the (esp. early or primitive) practice of making woodcuts or wood engravings. **2** the use of woodblocks in printing.

xy·loph·a·gous /zīlófəgəs/ *adj.* (of an insect or mollusk) eating, or boring into, wood.

xy·lo·phone /zíləfōn/ *n.* a musical instrument of wooden or metal bars graduated in length and struck with a small wooden hammer or hammers. □□ **xy·lo·phon·ic** /–fónik/ *adj.* **xy·lo·phon·ist** *n.* [Gk *xulon* wood + –PHONE]

xylophone

xys·tus /zístəs/ *n.* (*pl.* **xys·ti** /–tī/) **1** a covered portico used by athletes in ancient Greece for exercise. **2** *Rom. Antiq.* a garden walk or terrace. [L f. Gk *xustos* smooth f. *xuō* scrape]

Y

Y¹ /wī/ n. (also **y**) (pl. **Ys** or **Y's**) **1** the twenty-fifth letter of the alphabet. **2** (usu. **y**) *Algebra* the second unknown quantity. **3** *Geom.* the second coordinate. **4 a** a Y-shaped thing, esp. an arrangement of lines, piping, roads, etc. **b** a forked clamp or support.

Y² abbr. (also **Y.**) **1** yen. **2** yeomanry. **3** = YMCA, YWCA.

Y³ symb. Chem. the element yttrium.

y. abbr. year(s).

y- /ee/ prefix archaic forming past participles, collective nouns, etc. (*yclept*). [OE *ge-* f. Gmc]

-y¹ /ee/ suffix forming adjectives: **1** from nouns and adjectives, meaning: **a** full of; having the quality of (*messy; icy; horsy*). **b** addicted to (*boozy*). **2** from verbs, meaning 'inclined to', 'apt to' (*runny; sticky*). [from or after OE *-ig* f. Gmc]

-y² /ee/ suffix (also **-ey, -ie**) forming diminutive nouns, pet names, etc. (*granny; Sally; nightie; Mickey*). [ME (orig. Sc.)]

-y³ /ee/ suffix forming nouns denoting: **1** state, condition, or quality (*courtesy; orthodoxy; modesty*). **2** an action or its result (*colloquy; remedy; subsidy*). [from or after F *-ie* f. L *-ia, -ium*, Gk *-eia, -ia*: cf. -ACY, -ERY, -GRAPHY, and others]

yab·ber /yábər/ v. & n. Austral. & NZ colloq. • v.intr. & tr. talk. • n. talk; conversation; language. [perh. f. an Aboriginal language]

yab·by /yábee/ n. (pl. **-bies**) Austral. **1** a small freshwater crayfish, esp. of the genus *Cherax*. **2** a marine prawn, *Callianassa australiensis*, often used as bait. [Aboriginal]

yacht /yot/ n. & v. • n. **1** a light sailing vessel, esp. equipped for racing. **2** a larger usu. power-driven vessel equipped for cruising. • v.intr. race or cruise in a yacht. □□ **yacht·ing** n. [early mod.Du. *jaghte* = *jaghtschip* fast pirate ship f. *jag(h)t* chase f. *jagen* to hunt + *schip* SHIP]

yacht club n. a club for yachtsmen and yachtswomen organized to promote yachting and boating.

yachts·man /yótsmən/ n. (pl. **-men**; *fem.* **yachts·wom·an**, pl. **-wom·en**) a person who sails yachts.

yack /yak/ n. & v. (also **yack·e·ty-yack** /yákəteeyák/, **yak**) sl. derog. • n. trivial or unduly persistent conversation. • v.intr. engage in this. [imit.]

ya·ger var. of JAEGER.

yah /yaa/ int. expressing derision or defiance. [imit.]

ya·hoo /yaáhoo/ n. a coarse, bestial person. [name of an imaginary race of brutish creatures in Swift's *Gulliver's Travels* (1726)]

Yah·weh /yaáway, -we/ n. (also **Yah·veh** /-vay, -ve/) the Hebrew name of God in the Old Testament. [Heb. *YHVH* with added vowels: see JEHOVAH]

Yah·wist /yaáwist/ n. (also **Yah·vist** /-vist/) the postulated author or authors of parts of the Hexateuch in which God is regularly named *Yahweh*.

yak /yak/ n. a long-haired, humped Tibetan ox, *Bos grunniens*. [Tibetan *gyag*]

y'all var. of YOU-ALL.

yam /yam/ n. **1 a** any tropical or subtropical climbing plant of the genus *Dioscorea*. **b** the edible starchy tuber of this. **2** a sweet potato. [Port. *inhame* or Sp. *iñame*, of unkn. orig.]

yak

yam·mer /yámər/ n. & v. colloq. or dial. • n. **1** a lament, wail, or grumble. **2** voluble talk. • v.intr. **1** utter a yammer. **2** talk volubly. □□ **yam·mer·er** n. [OE *geōmrian* f. *geōmor* sorrowful]

yang /yang/ n. (in Chinese philosophy) the active male principle of the universe (cf. YIN). [Chin.]

Yank /yangk/ n. esp. Brit. colloq. often derog. an inhabitant of the US; an American. [abbr.]

yank /yangk/ v. & n. colloq. • v.tr. pull with a jerk. • n. a sudden hard pull. [19th c.: orig. unkn.]

Yan·kee /yángkee/ n. colloq. **1** often derog. = YANK. **2** an inhabitant of New England or one of the northern states. **3** hist. a federal Union soldier in the Civil War. **4** Brit. a type of bet on four or more horses to win (or be placed) in different races. **5** (attrib.) of or as of the Yankees. [18th c.: orig. uncert.: perh. f. Du. *Janke* dimin. of *Jan* John attested (17th c.) as a nickname]

Yan·kee Doo·dle n. **1** an American tune and song popularized during the American Revolution. **2** = YANKEE.

yap /yap/ v. & n. • v.intr. (**yapped, yap·ping**) **1** bark shrilly or fussily. **2** colloq. talk noisily, foolishly, or complainingly. **3** sl. the mouth. □□ **yap·per** n. [imit.]

ya·pok /yápok/ n. = POSSUM 2. [*Oyapok, Oiapoque*, N. Brazilian river]

yapp /yap/ n. Brit. a form of bookbinding with a limp leather cover projecting to fold over the edges of the leaves. [name of a London bookseller c.1860, for whom it was first made]

Yar·bor·ough /yaárbərō, -burō, -bərə/ n. a whist or bridge hand with no card above a 9. [Earl of *Yarborough* (d. 1897), said to have betted against its occurrence]

yard¹ /yaard/ n. **1** a unit of linear measure equal to 3 feet (0.9144 meter). **2** this length of material (*a yard and a half of fabric*). **3** a square or cubic yard esp. (in building) of sand, etc. **4** a cylindrical spar tapering to each end slung across a mast for a sail to hang from. **5** (in pl.; foll. by of) colloq. a great length (*yards of spare wallpaper*). □ **by the yard** esp. Brit. at great length. [OE *gerd* f.WG]

yard² /yaard/ n. & v. • n. **1** a piece of ground esp. attached to a building or used for a particular purpose. **2** the lawn and garden area of a house. • v.tr. put (cattle) into a stockyard. [OE *geard* enclosure, region, f Gmc: cf. GARDEN]

yard·age /yaárdij/ n. **1** a number of yards of material, etc. **2 a** the use of a stockyard, etc. **b** payment for this.

yard·arm /yaárdaarm/ n. the outer extremity of a ship's yard.

yard·bird /yaárdbərd/ n. sl. **1** a new military recruit. **2** a convict.

yard goods n.pl. = PIECE GOODS.

yard·man /yaárdmən/ n. (pl. **-men**) n. **1** a person working in a railroad yard or lumberyard. **2** a gardener or a person who does various outdoor jobs.

yard·mas·ter /yaárdmastər/ n. the manager of a railroad yard.

yard-of-ale n. Brit. **1** a deep, slender beer glass, about a yard long and holding two to three pints. **2** the contents of this.

yard·stick /yaárdstik/ n. **1** a standard used for comparison. **2** a measuring rod a yard long, usu. divided into inches, etc.

yar·mul·ke /yaárməlkə, yaáməl-/ n. (also **yar·mul·ka**) a skullcap worn by Jewish men. [Yiddish]

yarn /yaarn/ n. & v. • n. **1** any spun thread, esp. for knitting, weaving, rope making, etc. **2** colloq. a long or rambling story or discourse. • v.intr. colloq. tell yarns. [OE *gearn*]

yar·row /yárō/ n. any perennial herb of the genus *Achillea*, esp. milfoil. [OE *gearwe*, of unkn. orig.]

yash·mak /yaáshmaak, yáshmak/ n. a veil concealing the face except the eyes, worn by some Muslim women when in public. [Arab. *yasmak*, Turk. *yasmak*]

yat·a·ghan /yátəgan/ n. a sword without a guard and often with a double-curved blade, used in Muslim countries. [Turk. *yātāǧan*]

yat·ter /yátər/ v. & n. colloq. or dial. • v.intr. (often foll. by on) talk idly or incessantly; chatter. • n. idle talk; incessant chatter. □□ **yat·ter·ing** n. & adj.

yaw /yaw/ v. & n. • v.intr. (of a ship or aircraft, etc.) move on the vertical axis; fail to hold a straight course; fall off; go unsteadily (esp. turning from side to side). • n. the yawing of a ship, etc., from its course. [16th c.: orig. unkn.]

yawl /yawl/ n. **1** a two-masted, fore-and-aft sailing vessel with the mizzenmast stepped far aft. **2** a small kind of fishing boat. **3** hist. a ship's jolly boat with four or six oars. [MLG *jolle* or Du. *jol*, of unkn. orig.: cf. JOLLY²]

yawn /yawn/ v. & n. • v. **1** intr. (as a reflex) open the mouth wide and inhale esp. when sleepy or bored. **2** intr. (of a chasm, etc.) gape; be wide open. **3** tr. utter or say with a yawn. • n. **1** an act of yawning. **2** colloq. a boring or tedious idea, activity, etc. □□ **yawn·er** n. **yawn·ing·ly** adv. [OE *ginian, geonian*]

yawp /yawp/ n. & v. • n. **1** a harsh or hoarse cry. **2** foolish talk. • v.intr. utter these. □□ **yawp·er** n. [ME (imit.)]

yaws /yawz/ n.pl. (usu. treated as sing.) a contagious tropical skin disease with large skin swellings. [17th c.: orig. unkn.]

Yb symb. Chem. the element ytterbium.

Y chro·mo·some /wí-krómməsōm/ n. a sex chromosome occurring only in male cells. [*Y* as an arbitrary label + CHROMOSOME]

y·clept /iklépt/ adj. archaic or joc. called (by the name of). [OE *gecleopod* past part. of *cleopian* call f. Gmc]

yd. abbr. yard (measure).

yds. abbr. yards (measure).

ye¹ /yee/ pron. archaic pl. of THOU¹. □ **ye gods!** joc. an exclamation of astonishment. [OE *ge* f. Gmc]

ye² /yee/ adj. pseudo-archaic = THE (*ye olde tea shoppe*). [var. spelling f. the *y*-shaped letter THORN (representing *th*) in the 14th c.]

yea /yay/ *adv. & n. formal* ● *adv.* **1** yes. **2** indeed (*ready, yea eager*). ● *n.* an affirmative vote. □ **yea and nay** shilly-shally. [OE *gea, ge* f. Gmc]

yeas and nays *n.pl.* affirmative and negative votes.

yeah /yeə/ *adv. colloq.* yes. □ **oh yeah?** expressing incredulity. [casual pronunc. of YES]

yean /yeen/ *v.tr. & intr. archaic* bring forth (a lamb or kid). [perh. f. OE *geēanian* (unrecorded, as Y-, *ēanian* to lamb)]

yean·ling /yeenling/ *n. archaic* a young lamb or kid.

year /yeer/ *n.* **1** (also **as·tro·nom·i·cal year, e·qui·noc·tial year, nat·u·ral year, sol·ar year, trop·i·cal year**) the time occupied by the earth in one revolution around the sun, 365 days, 5 hours, 48 minutes, and 46 seconds in length (cf. SIDEREAL YEAR). **2** (also **calendar year, civil year**) the period of 365 days (**common year**) or 366 days (see LEAP YEAR) from Jan. 1 to Dec. 31, used for reckoning time in ordinary affairs. **3 a** a period of the same length as this starting at any point (*four years ago*). **b** such a period in terms of a particular activity, etc., occupying its duration (*school year; tax year*). **4** (in *pl.*) age or time of life (*young for his years*). **5** (usu. in *pl.*) *colloq.* a very long time (*it took years to get served*). **6** a group of students entering college, etc., in the same academic year; a class. □ **in the year of Our Lord** (foll. by the year) in a specified year AD. **of the year** chosen as outstanding in a particular year (*sportsman of the year*). **a year and a day** the period specified in some legal matters to ensure the completion of a full year. **year in, year out** continually over a period of years. [OE *gē(a)r* f. Gmc]

year·book /yeerbŏŏk/ *n.* **1** an annual publication dealing with events or aspects of the (usu. preceding) year. **2** such a publication, usu. produced by a school's graduating class and featuring students, activities, sports, etc.

year·ling /yeerling/ *n. & adj.* ● *n.* **1** an animal between one and two years old. **2** a racehorse in the calendar year after the year of foaling. ● *adj.* **1** a year old; having existed or been such for a year (*a yearling heifer*). **2** esp. *Brit.* intended to terminate after one year (*yearling bonds*).

year·long /yeerlông/ *adj.* lasting a year or the whole year.

year·ly /yeerlee/ *adj. & adv.* ● *adj.* **1** done, produced, or occurring once a year. **2** of or lasting a year. ● *adv.* once a year; from year to year. [OE *gēarlic, –lice* (as YEAR)]

yearn /yərn/ *v.intr.* **1** (usu. foll. by *for, after,* or *to* + infin.) have a strong emotional longing. **2** (usu. foll. by *to, toward*) be filled with compassion or tenderness. □□ **yearn·er** *n.* **yearn·ing** *n. & adj.* **yearn·ing·ly** *adv.* [OE *giernan* f. a Gmc root meaning 'eager']

year of grace *n.* the year AD.

year-round *adj.* existing, etc., throughout the year.

yeast /yeest/ *n.* **1** a grayish-yellow fungous substance obtained esp. from fermenting malt liquors and used as a fermenting agent, to raise bread, etc. **2** any of various unicellular fungi in which vegetative reproduction takes place by budding or fission. □□ **yeast·less** *adj.* **yeast·like** *adj.* [OE *gist, giest* (unrecorded): cf. MDu. *ghist,* MHG *jist,* ON *jöstr*]

yeast·y /yeestee/ *adj.* (**yeast·i·er, yeast·i·est**) **1** frothy or tasting like yeast. **2** in a ferment. **3** working like yeast. **4** (of talk, etc.) light and superficial. □□ **yeast·i·ly** *adv.* **yeast·i·ness** *n.*

yegg /yeg/ *n. sl.* a traveling burglar or safecracker. [20th c.: perh. a surname]

yell /yel/ *n. & v.* ● *n.* **1** a loud sharp cry of pain, anger, fright, encouragement, delight, etc. **2** a shout. **3** an organized cry, used esp. to support a sports team. **4** *Brit. sl.* an amusing person or thing. ● *v.tr. & intr.* utter with or make a yell. [OE *g(i)ellan* f. Gmc]

yel·low /yélō/ *adj., n., & v.* ● *adj.* **1** of the color between green and orange in the spectrum, of buttercups, lemons, egg yolks, or gold. **2** of the color of faded leaves, ripe wheat, etc. **3** having a yellow skin or complexion. **4** *colloq.* cowardly. **5** (of looks, feelings, etc.) jealous, envious, or suspicious. **6** (of newspapers, etc.) unscrupulously sensational. ● *n.* **1** a yellow color or pigment. **2** yellow clothes or material (*dressed in yellow*). **3 a** a yellow ball, piece, etc., in a game or sport. **b** the player using such pieces. **4** (usu. in *comb.*) a yellow moth or butterfly. **5** (in *pl.*) jaundice of horses, etc. **6** a peach disease with yellowed leaves. ● *v.tr. & intr.* make or become yellow. □□ **yel·low·ish** *adj.* **yel·low·ly** *adv.* **yel·low·ness** *n.* **yel·low·y** *adj.* [OE *geolu, geolo* f.WG, rel. to GOLD]

yel·low·back /yélōbak/ *n.* a cheap novel, etc., in a yellow cover.

yel·low-bel·lied *adj.* **1** *colloq.* cowardly. **2** (of a fish, bird, etc.) having yellow underparts.

yel·low-bel·ly /yélōbélee/ *n.* **1** *colloq.* a coward. **2** any of various fish with yellow underparts.

yellow card *n. Soccer* a card shown by the referee to a player being cautioned.

yellow fe·ver *n.* a tropical virus disease with fever and jaundice.

yellow flag *n.* **1** a flag displayed by a ship in quarantine. **2** an iridaceous plant, *Iris pseudacorus,* with slender sword-shaped leaves and yellow flowers.

yel·low·ham·mer /yélōhamər/ *n.* a bunting, *Emberiza citrinella,* of which the male has a yellow head, neck, and breast. [16th c.: orig. of *hammer* uncert.]

yel·low jack *n.* **1** = YELLOW FEVER. **2** = YELLOW FLAG..

yel·low jack·et *n.* **1** any of various wasps of the family Vespidae with yellow and black bands. **2** sl. a capsule of phenobarbital.

yel·low met·al *n.* brass of 60 parts copper and 40 parts zinc.

Yel·low Pag·es *n.pl.* (also **yel·low pag·es**) a section of a telephone directory on yellow paper and listing business subscribers according to the goods or services they offer.

yel·low per·il *n. derog.* the political or military threat regarded as emanating from Asian peoples, esp. the Chinese.

yel·low spot *n.* the point of acutest vision in the retina.

yel·low streak *n. colloq.* a trait of cowardice.

yelp /yelp/ *n. & v.* ● *n.* a sharp, shrill cry of or as of a dog in pain or excitement. ● *v.intr.* utter a yelp. □□ **yelp·er** *n.* [OE *gielp(an)* boast (imit.): cf. YAWP]

yen¹ /yen/ *n.* (*pl.* same) the chief monetary unit of Japan. [Jap. f. Chin. *yuan* round, dollar]

yen² /yen/ *n. & v. colloq.* ● *n.* a longing or yearning. ● *v.intr.* (**yenned, yen·ning**) feel a longing. [Chin. dial.]

yeo·man /yómən/ *n.* (*pl.* **–men**) **1** esp. *hist.* a man holding and cultivating a small landed estate. **2** *Brit. hist.* a person qualified by possessing free land of an annual value of 40 shillings to serve on juries, vote for the knight of the shire, etc. **3** *Brit.* a member of the yeomanry force. **4** *hist.* a servant in a royal or noble household. **5** *Brit.* (in full **yeoman of signals**) a petty officer in the navy, concerned with visual signaling. **6** in the US Navy, a petty officer performing clerical duties on board ship. □ **yeoman** (or **yeoman's**) **service** efficient or useful help in need. [ME *yoman, yeman,* etc., prob. f. YOUNG + MAN]

yeo·man·ly /yómənlee/ *adj.* **1** of the rank of yeoman. **2** characteristic of or befitting a yeoman; sturdy; reliable.

yeo·man of the guard *n.* **1** a member of the British sovereign's bodyguard. **2** (in general use) a warder in the Tower of London.

yeo·man·ry /yómənree/ *n.* (*pl.* **–ries**) **1** a body of yeomen. **2** *Brit. hist.* a volunteer cavalry force raised from the yeoman class (1794–1908).

yep /yep/ *adv. & n.* (also **yup** /yup/) *colloq.* = YES. [corrupt.]

-yer /yər/ *suffix* var. of –IER esp. after *w* (*bowyer, lawyer*).

yer·ba ma·té /yérbə mátay/ *n.* = MATÉ. [Sp., = herb maté]

yes /yes/ *adv. & n.* ● *adv.* **1** equivalent to an affirmative sentence: the answer to your question is affirmative; it is as you say or as I have said; the statement, etc., made is correct; the request or command will be complied with; the negative statement, etc., made is not correct. **2** (in answer to a summons or address) an acknowledgment of one's presence. ● *n.* an utterance of the word *yes.* □ **say yes** grant a request or confirm a statement. **yes?** **1** indeed? is that so? **2** what do you want? **yes and no** that is partly true and partly untrue. [OE *gēse, gīse,* prob. f. *gīa sīe* may it be (*gīa* is unrecorded)]

yes-man *n.* (*pl.* **–men**) *colloq.* a weakly acquiescent person.

yester- /yéstər/ *comb. form poet.* or *archaic* of yesterday; that is the last past (*yester-eve*). [OE *geostran*]

yes·ter·day /yéstərday/ *adv. & n.* ● *adv.* **1** on the day before today. **2** in the recent past. ● *n.* **1** the day before today. **2** the recent past. [OE *giestran dæg* (as YESTER-, DAY)]

yes·ter·day morn·ing *n.* (also **yes·ter·day af·ter·noon,** etc.) in the morning (or afternoon, etc.) of yesterday.

yes·ter·year /yéstəryeer/ *n. literary* **1** last year. **2** the recent past.

yet /yet/ *adv & conj.* ● *adv.* **1** as late as, or until, now or then (*there is yet time; your best work yet*). **2** (with *neg.* or *interrog.*) so soon as, or by, now or then (*it is not time yet; have you finished yet?*). **3** again; in addition (*more and yet more*). **4** in the remaining time available; before all is over (*I will do it yet*). **5** (foll. by *compar.*) even (*a yet more difficult task*). **6** nevertheless; and in spite of that; but for all that (*it is strange, and yet it is true*). ● *conj.* but at the same time; but nevertheless (*I won, yet what good has it done?*). □ **nor yet** esp. *Brit.* and also not (*won't listen to me nor yet to you*). [OE *gīet(a),* = OFris. *iēta,* of unkn. orig.]

yet·i /yétee/ *n.* = ABOMINABLE SNOWMAN. [Tibetan]

yew /yōō/ *n.* **1** any dark-leaved evergreen coniferous tree of the genus *Taxus,* having seeds enclosed in a fleshy red aril, and often planted in landscaped settings. **2** its wood, used formerly as a material for bows and still in cabinetmaking. [OE *īw, ēow* f. Gmc]

Ygg·dra·sil /ígdrəsil/ *n.* (in Scandinavian mythology) an ash tree whose roots and branches join heaven, earth, and hell. [ON *yg(g)drasill* f. *Yggr* Odin + *drasill* horse]

YHA *abbr.* Youth Hostels Association.

Yid /yid/ *n. sl. offens.* a Jew. [back-form. f. YIDDISH]

Yid·dish /yidish/ *n. & adj.* ● *n.* a vernacular used by Jews in or from central and eastern Europe, orig. a German dialect with words from Hebrew and several modern languages. ● *adj.* of or relating to this language. [G *jüdisch* Jewish]

yield /yeeld/ *v. & n.* ● *v.* **1** *tr.* (also *absol.*) produce or return as a fruit, profit, or result (*the land yields crops; the land yields poorly; the investment yields 15%*). **2** *tr.* give up; surrender; concede; comply with a demand for (*yielded the fortress; yielded themselves prisoners*). **3** *intr.*

(often foll. by *to*) **a** surrender; make submission. **b** give consent or change one's course of action in deference to; respond as required to (*yielded to persuasion*). **4** *intr.* (foll. by *to*) be inferior or confess inferiority to (*I yield to none in understanding the problem*). **5** *intr.* (foll. by *to*) give right of way to other traffic. **6** *intr.* allow another the right to speak in a debate, etc. ● *n.* an amount yielded or produced; an output or return. □□ **yield•er** *n.* [OE *g(i) eldan* pay f. Gmc]

yield•ing /yéelding/ *adj.* **1** compliant, submissive. **2** (of a substance) able to bend; not stiff or rigid. □□ **yield•ing•ly** *adv.* **yield•ing•ness** *n.*

yield point *n.* *Physics* the stress beyond which a material becomes plastic.

yin /yin/ *n.* (in Chinese philosophy) the passive female principle of the universe (cf. YANG). [Chin.]

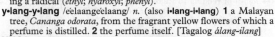

yip /yip/ *v. & n.* ● *v.intr.* (**yipped, yip•ping**) = YELP *v.* ● *n.* = YELP *n.* [imit.]

yip•pee /yípee/ *int.* expressing delight or excitement. [natural excl.]

yip•pie /yípee/ *n.* a hippie associated with political activism, esp. as a member of a radical organization. [*Y*outh *I*nternational *P*arty]

yin and yang

-yl /əl/ *suffix* *Chem.* forming nouns denoting a radical (*ethyl*; *hydroxyl*; *phenyl*).

y•lang-y•lang /éelaangéelaang/ *n.* (also **i•lang-i•lang**) **1** a Malayan tree, *Cananga odorata*, from the fragrant yellow flowers of which a perfume is distilled. **2** the perfume itself. [Tagalog *álang-ilang*]

YMCA *abbr.* Young Men's Christian Association.

YMHA *abbr.* Young Men's Hebrew Association.

-yne /īn/ *suffix* *Chem.* forming names of unsaturated compounds containing a triple bond (*ethyne* = acetylene).

yo /yō/ *int.* used to call attention, express affirmation, or greet informally.

yob /yob/ *n.* *Brit. sl.* a lout or hooligan. □□ **yob•bish** *adj.* **yob•bish•ly** *adv.* **yob•bish•ness** *n.* [back sl. for BOY]

yob•bo /yóbó/ *n.* (*pl.* **-bos**) *Brit. sl.* = YOB.

yod /yood, yod/ *n.* **1** the tenth and smallest letter of the Hebrew alphabet. **2** its semivowel sound /y/. [Heb. *yōd* f. *yad* hand]

yo•del /yód'l/ *v. & n.* ● *v.tr. & intr.* sing with melodious inarticulate sounds and frequent changes between falsetto and the normal voice in the manner of the Swiss mountain-dwellers. ● *n.* a yodeling cry. □□ **yo•del•er** *n.* [G *jodeln*]

yo•ga /yógə/ *n.* **1** a Hindu system of philosophic meditation and asceticism designed to effect reunion with the universal spirit. **2** = HATHA YOGA. □□ **yo•gic** /yógik/ *adj.* [Hind. f. Skr., = union]

yogh /yog/ *n.* a Middle English letter used for certain values of *g* and *y.* [ME]

yo•gi /yógee/ *n.* a person proficient in yoga. □□ **yo•gism** *n.* [Hind. f. YOGA]

yo•gurt /yógərt/ *n.* (also **yo•ghurt**) a semisolid sourish food prepared from milk fermented by added bacteria. [Turk. *yoğurt*]

yo-heave-ho *int.* = HEAVE-HO.

yo-ho /yōhó/ *int.* (also **yo-ho-ho** /yóhōhó/) **1** used to attract attention. **2** = YO-HEAVE-HO. [cf. YO-HEAVE-HO & HO]

yoicks /yoyks/ *int.* a cry used by foxhunters to urge on the hounds. [orig. unkn.: cf. *hyke* call to hounds, HEY[1]]

yoke /yōk/ *n. & v.* ● *n.* **1** a wooden crosspiece fastened over the necks of two oxen, etc., and attached to the plow or wagon to be drawn. **2** (*pl.* same or **yokes**) a pair (of oxen, etc.). **3** an object like a yoke in form or function, e.g., a wooden shoulderpiece for carrying a pair of pails, the top section of a dress or skirt, etc., from which the rest hangs. **4** sway, dominion, or servitude, esp. when oppressive. **5** a bond of union, esp. that of marriage. **6** *Rom. Hist.* an uplifted yoke, or an arch of three spears symbolizing it, under which a defeated army was made to march. **7** *archaic* the amount of land that one yoke of oxen could plow in a day. **8** a crossbar on which a bell swings. **9** the crossbar of a rudder to whose ends ropes are fastened. **10** a bar of soft iron between the poles of an electromagnet. ● *v.* **1** *tr.* put a yoke on. **2** *tr.* couple or unite (a pair). **3** *tr.* (foll. by *to*) link (one thing) to (another). **4** *intr.* match or work together. [OE *geoc* f. Gmc]

yoke 1

yo•kel /yókəl/ *n.* a rustic; a country bumpkin. [perh. f. dial. *yokel* green woodpecker]

yolk[1] /yōk/ *n.* **1** the yellow internal part of an egg that nourishes the young before it hatches. **2** *Biol.* the corresponding part of any animal ovum. □□ **yolked** *adj.* (also in *comb.*). **yolk•less** *adj.* **yolk•y** *adj.* [OE *geol(o)ca* f. *geolu* YELLOW]

yolk[2] /yōk/ *n.* = SUINT. [OE *eowoca* (unrecorded)]

yolk sac *n.* a membrane enclosing the yolk of an egg.

Yom Kip•pur /yawm kípər, keepóor, yōm, yom/ *n.* = Day of Atonement (see ATONEMENT). [Heb.]

yon /yon/ *adj., adv., & pron. literary & dial.* ● *adj. & adv.* yonder. ● *pron.* yonder person or thing. [OE *geon*]

yon•der /yóndər/ *adv. & adj.* ● *adv.* over there; at some distance in that direction; in the place indicated by pointing, etc. ● *adj.* situated yonder. [ME: cf. OS *gendra*, Goth. *jaindrē*]

yo•ni /yónee/ *n.* a symbol of the female genitals, venerated by Hindus, etc. [Skr., = source, womb, female genitals]

yoo-hoo /yóohóo/ *int.* used to attract a person's attention. [natural excl.]

yore /yawr/ *n. literary* □ **of yore** formerly; in or of old days. [OE *geāra*, *geāre*, etc., adv. forms of uncert. orig.]

York•ist /yáwrkist/ *n. & adj.* ● *n. hist.* a follower of the House of York or of the White Rose party supporting it in England's Wars of the Roses (cf. LANCASTRIAN). ● *adj.* of or concerning the House of York.

York•shire pud•ding /yáwrksheer/ *n.* a pudding of baked unsweetened batter usu. eaten with roast beef. [*Yorkshire* in the No. of England]

York•shire ter•ri•er /yáwrksheer/ *n.* a small, long-haired, blue-gray and tan kind of terrier.

Yo•ru•ba /yáwrəbə/ *n.* **1** a member of a black African people inhabiting the west coast, esp. Nigeria. **2** the language of this people. [native name]

you /yoo/ *pron.* (*obj.* **you**; *poss.* **your, yours**) **1** used with reference to the person or persons addressed or one such person and one or more associated persons. **2** (as *int.* with a noun) in an exclamatory statement (*you fools!*). **3** (in general statements) one, a person, anyone, or everyone (*it's bad at first, but you get used to it*). □ **you and yours** you together with your family, property, etc. [OE *ēow* accus. & dative of *gē* YE[1] f. WG: supplanting *ye* because of the more frequent use of the obj. case, and *thou* and *thee* as the more courteous form]

you-all *n.* (often **y'all**) esp. *Southern US colloq.* you (usu. more than one person).

you'd /yood/ *contr.* **1** you had. **2** you would.

you-know-what *n.* (also **you-know-who**) something or someone unspecified but understood.

you'll /yool, yool/ *contr.* you will; you shall.

young /yung/ *adj. & n.* ● *adj.* (**young•er** /yúnggər/; **young•est** /yúng-gist/) **1** not far advanced in life, development, or existence; not yet old. **2** immature or inexperienced. **3** felt in or characteristic of youth (*young love*; *young ambition*). **4** representing young people (*Young Republicans*; *young America*). **5** distinguishing a son from his father (*young Jones*). **6** (**younger**) **a** distinguishing one person from another of the same name (*the younger Davis*). **b** *Sc.* the heir of a landed commoner. ● *n.* (*collect.*) offspring, esp. of animals before or soon after birth. □ **with young** (of an animal) pregnant. □□ **young•ish** *adj.* **young•ling** *n.* [OE *g(e)ong* f. Gmc]

young blood *n.* see BLOOD.

young fustic *n.* a sumac, *Cotinus coggyria*, native to Europe. Also called **Venetian sumac**. **2** the wood of this tree.

young i•de•a *n.* the child's mind.

young la•dy *n.* **1** a young, usu. unmarried woman. **2** a girlfriend or sweetheart.

young man *n.* **1** a young adult male. **2** a boyfriend or sweetheart.

Young Pre•tend•er *n.* Charles Stuart (1720–80), grandson of James II and claimant to the British throne.

young•ster /yúngstər/ *n.* a child or young person.

young thing *n.* *archaic* or *colloq.* an indulgent term for a young person.

Young Turk *n.* **1** a member of a revolutionary party in Turkey in 1908. **2** a young person eager for radical change to the established order.

young 'un *n.* *colloq.* a youngster.

youn•ker /yúngkər/ *n. archaic* = YOUNGSTER. [MDu. *jonckher* f. *jonc* YOUNG + *hēre* lord: cf. JUNKER]

your /yŏŏr, yawr/ *poss.pron.* (*attrib.*) **1** of or belonging to or used by or for yourself or yourselves (*your house*; *your own business*). **2** *colloq.* usu. *derog.* much talked of; well known (*none so fallible as your self-styled expert*). [OE *ēower* genit. of *gē* YE[1]]

you're /yŏŏr, yawr/ *contr.* you are.

yours /yŏŏrz, yawrz/ *poss.pron.* **1** the one or ones belonging to or associated with you (*it is yours*; *yours are over there*). **2** your letter (*yours of the 10th*). **3** introducing a formula ending a letter (*yours ever*; *yours truly*). □ **of yours** of or belonging to you (*a friend of yours*).

your•self /yŏŏrsélf, yawr-/ *pron.* (*pl.* **your•selves** /-sélvz/) **1 a** *emphat. form* of YOU. **b** *refl. form* of YOU. **2** in your normal state of body or mind (*are quite yourself again*). □ **be yourself** act in your normal, unconstrained manner. **how's yourself?** *sl.* how are you? (esp. after answering a similar inquiry).

youth /yŏoth/ *n.* (*pl.* **youths** /yŏothz/) **1** the state of being young; the period between childhood and adult age. **2** the vigor or enthusiasm, inexperience, or other characteristic of this period. **3** an early stage of development, etc. **4** a young person (esp. male). **5** (*pl.*) young people collectively (*the youth of the country*). [OE *geoguth* f. Gmc, rel. to YOUNG]

youth cen•ter *n.* (also **youth club**) a place or organization provided for young people's leisure activities.

youth•ful /yŏothfŏol/ *adj.* **1** young, esp. in appearance or manner. **2** having the characteristics of youth (*youthful impatience*). **3** having the freshness or vigor of youth (*a youthful complexion*). □□ **youth•ful•ly** *adv.* **youth•ful•ness** *n.*

youth hos•tel *n.* a place where (esp. young) travelers can put up cheaply for the night. □□ **youth hos•tel•er** *n.*

you've /yŏov, yŏov/ *contr.* you have.

yowl /yowl/ *n. & v.* •*n.* a loud, wailing cry of or as of a cat or dog in pain or distress. •*v.intr.* utter a yowl. [imit.]

yo-yo /yóyō/ *n. & v.* •*n.* (*pl.* **yo-yos**) **1** *Trademark* a toy consisting of a pair of disks with a deep groove between them in which string is attached and wound, and which can be spun alternately downward and upward by its weight and momentum as the string unwinds and rewinds. **2** a thing that repeatedly falls and rises again. •*v.intr.*

(**yo-yoes, yo-yoed, yo-yo•ing**) **1** play with a yo-yo. **2** move up and down; fluctuate. [20th c.: orig. unkn.]

yr. *abbr.* **1** year(s). **2** your. **3** younger.

yrs. *abbr.* **1** years. **2** yours.

yt•ter•bi•um /itárbeeəm/ *n. Chem.* a silvery metallic element of the lanthanide series occurring naturally as various isotopes. ¶ Symb.: **Yb**. [mod.L f. *Ytterby* in Sweden]

yt•tri•um /itreeəm/ *n. Chem.* a grayish metallic element resembling the lanthanides, occurring naturally in uranium ores and used in making superconductors. ¶ Symb.: **Y**. [formed as YTTERBIUM]

yu•an /yŏo-aán, yŏ–/ *n.* (*pl.* same) the chief monetary unit of China. [Chin.: see YEN[1]]

yuc•ca /yúkə/ *n.* any American white-flowered liliaceous plant of the genus *Yucca*, with swordlike leaves. [Carib]

yuck /yuk/ *int. & n. sl.* •*int.* an expression of strong distaste or disgust. •*n.* something messy or repellent. [imit.]

yuck•y /yúkee/ *adj.* (**–i•er, –i•est**) *sl.* **1** messy; repellent. **2** sickly; sentimental.

Yu•go•slav /yŏógəslaav/ *n. & adj.* (also **Ju•go•slav**) *hist.* •*n.* **1** a native or national of the former republic of Yugoslavia. **2** a person of Yugoslav descent. •*adj.* of or relating to Yugoslavia or its people. □□ **Yu•go•sla•vi•an** *adj. & n.* [Austrian G *Jugoslav* f. Serb. *jugo-* f. *jug* south + SLAV]

yule /yŏol/ *n.* (in full **yuletide**) *archaic* the Christmas festival. [OE *gēol(a)*: cf. ON *jól*]

yucca

Yule log *n.* **1** a large log burned in the hearth on Christmas Eve. **2** a log-shaped cake eaten at Christmas.

Yu•ma /yŏomə/ *n.* **1 a** a N. American people native to Arizona. **b** a member of this people. **2** the language of this people.

yum•my /yúmee/ *adj.* (**yum•mi•er, yum•mi•est**) *colloq.* tasty; delicious. [YUM-YUM + –Y[1]]

yum-yum /yúmy úm/ *int.* expressing pleasure from eating or the prospect of eating. [natural excl.]

yup var. of YEP.

yup•pie /yúpee/ *n. & adj.* (also **yup•py**; *pl.* **–pies**) *colloq.*, usu. *derog.* •*n.* a young, middle-class professional person working in a city. •*adj.* characteristic of a yuppie or yuppies. [*young urban profes-sional*]

YWCA *abbr.* Young Women's Christian Association.

YWHA *abbr.* Young Women's Hebrew Association.

Z

Z /zee/ *n.* (also **z**) (*pl.* **Zs** or **Z's**) **1** the twenty-sixth letter of the alphabet. **2** (usu. **z**) *Algebra* the third unknown quantity. **3** *Geom.* the third coordinate. **4** *Chem.* atomic number.

za·ba·glio·ne /zàabaalyónee, –yáwne/ *n.* an Italian dessert of whipped and heated egg yolks, sugar, and (esp. Marsala) wine. [It.]

zaf·fer /záfər/ *n. Brit.* (**zaf·fre**) an impure cobalt oxide used as a blue pigment. [It. *zaffera* or F *safre*]

zag /zag/ *n. & v.* ● *n.* a sharp change of direction in a zigzag course. ● *v.intr.* (**zagged, zag·ging**) move in one of the two directions in a zigzag course. [ZIGZAG]

za·ny /záynee/ *adj. & n.* ● *adj.* (**za·ni·er, za·ni·est**) comically idiotic; crazily ridiculous. ● *n.* **1** a buffoon or jester. **2** *hist.* an attendant clown awkwardly mimicking a chief clown in shows. □□ **za·ni·ly** *adv.* **za·ni·ness** *n.* [F *zani* or It. *zan* (*n*)*i*, Venetian form of *Gianni, Giovanni* John]

zap /zap/ *v., n., & int. sl.* ● *v.* (**zapped, zap·ping**) **1** *tr.* **a** kill or destroy; deal a sudden blow to. **b** hit forcibly (*zapped the ball over the net*). **c** send an electric current, radiation, etc., through (someone or something). **2** *intr.* move quickly and vigorously. **3** *tr.* overwhelm emotionally. **4** *tr. Computing* erase or change (an item in a program). **5** *intr.* (foll. by *through*) fast-forward a videotape to skip a section. **6** *tr.* heat or cook (food) by microwave. **7** *tr.* change (television channels) by remote control. ● *n.* **1** energy; vigor. **2** a strong emotional effect. ● *int.* expressing the sound or impact of a bullet, ray gun, etc., or any sudden event. [imit.]

za·pa·te·a·do /zàapətayaádō, thàapaatayaátho, saá–/ *n.* (*pl.* **–dos**) **1** a flamenco dance with rhythmic stamping of the feet. **2** this technique or action. [Sp. f. *zapato* shoe]

zap·per /zápər/ *n. colloq.* a hand-held remote-control device for changing television channels, adjusting volume, etc.

zap·py /zápee/ *adj.* (**zap·pi·er, zap·pi·est**) *colloq.* **1** lively; energetic. **2** striking.

za·ra·pe var. of SERAPE.

Zar·a·thus·tri·an var. of ZOROASTRIAN.

za·re·ba /zəréebə/ *n.* (also **za·ri·ba**) **1** a hedged or palisaded enclosure for the protection of a camp or village in the Sudan, etc. **2** a restricting or confining influence. [Arab. *zarība* cattle pen]

zar·zue·la /zaarzwáylə, thaarthwáylə, saarswáy–/ *n.* a Spanish traditional form of musical comedy. [Sp.: app. f. a place-name]

zeal /zeel/ *n.* **1** earnestness or fervor in advancing a cause or rendering service. **2** hearty and persistent endeavor. [ME *zele* f. eccl.L *zelus* f. Gk *zēlos*]

zeal·ot /zélət/ *n.* **1** an uncompromising or extreme partisan; a fanatic. **2** (**Zealot**) *hist.* a member of an ancient Jewish sect aiming at a world Jewish theocracy and resisting the Romans until AD 70. □□ **zeal·ot·ry** *n.* [eccl.L *zelotes* f. Gk *zēlōtēs* (as ZEAL)]

zeal·ous /zéləs/ *adj.* full of zeal; enthusiastic. □□ **zeal·ous·ly** *adv.* **zeal·ous·ness** *n.*

ze·bec (also **ze·beck**) var. of XEBEC.

ze·bra /zéebrə/ *n.* **1** any of various African quadrupeds, esp. *Equus burchelli*, related to the ass and horse, with black and white stripes. **2** (*attrib.*) with alternate dark and pale stripes. □□ **ze·brine** /–brīn/ *adj.* [It. or Port. f. Congolese]

ze·bra cross·ing *n. Brit.* a striped crosswalk where pedestrians have precedence over vehicles.

ze·bu /zéebōo/ *n.* a humped ox, *Bos indicus*, of India, E. Asia, and Africa. [F *zébu*, of unkn. orig.]

Zech. *abbr.* Zechariah (Old Testament).

zed /zed/ *n. Brit.* the letter Z. [F *zède* f. LL *zeta* f. Gk ZETA]

zed·o·a·ry /zédōeree/ *n.* an aromatic, gingerlike substance made from the rootstock of E. Indian plants of the genus *Curcuma* and used in medicine, perfumery, and dyeing. [ME f. med.L *zedoarium* f. Pers. *zidw ār*]

zee /zee/ *n.* the letter Z. [17th c.: var. of ZED]

Zee·man effect /záymən/ *n. Physics* the splitting of the spectrum line into several components by a magnetic field. [P. *Zeeman*, Du. physicist d. 1943]

ze·in /zée-in/ *n. Biochem.* the principal protein of corn. [*Zea* the generic name of corn + –IN]

Zeit·geist /tsítgist, zít–/ *n.* **1** the spirit of the times. **2** the trend of thought and feeling in a period. [G f. *Zeit* time + *Geist* spirit]

Zen /zen/ *n.* a form of Mahayana Buddhism emphasizing the value of meditation and intuition. □□ **Zen·ist** *n.* (also **Zen·nist**). [Jap., = meditation]

ze·na·na /zináanə/ *n.* the part of a house for the seclusion of women of high-caste families in India and Iran. [Hind. *zenāna* f. Pers. *zanāna* f. *zan* woman]

Zend /zend/ *n.* an interpretation of the Avesta, each Zend being part of the Zend-Avesta. [Pers. *zand* interpretation]

Zend-A·ves·ta *n.* the Zoroastrian sacred writings of the Avesta or text and Zend or commentary.

Ze·ner cards /zéenər/ *n.* a set of 25 cards each with one of five different symbols, used in ESP research. [K. E. *Zener*, Amer. psychologist b. 1903]

ze·nith /zéenith/ *n.* **1** the part of the celestial sphere directly above an observer (opp. NADIR). **2** the highest point in one's fortunes; a time of great prosperity, etc. [ME f. OF *cenit* or med.L *cenit* ult. f. Arab. *samt* (*ar-ra's*) path (over the head)]

ze·nith·al /zéenithəl/ *adj.* of or relating to a zenith.

ze·nith·al pro·jec·tion *n.* a projection of part of a globe on to a plane tangential to the center of the part, showing the correct directions of all points from the center.

ze·nith dis·tance *n.* an arc intercepted between a celestial body and its zenith; the complement of a body's altitude.

ze·o·lite /zéeəlīt/ *n.* each of a number of minerals consisting mainly of hydrous silicates of calcium, sodium, and aluminum, able to act as cation exchangers. □□ **ze·o·lit·ic** /–lítik/ *adj.* [Sw. & G *zeolit* f. Gk *zeō* boil + –LITE (from their characteristic swelling and fusing under the blowpipe)]

Zeph. *abbr.* Zephaniah (Old Testament).

zeph·yr /zéfər/ *n.* **1** *literary* a mild gentle wind or breeze. **2** a fine cotton fabric. **3** an athlete's thin gauzy jersey. [F *zéphyr* or L *zephyrus* f. Gk *zephuros* (god of the) west wind]

zep·pe·lin /zépəlin/ *n. hist.* a German large dirigible airship of the early 20th c., orig. for military use. [Count F. von *Zeppelin*, Ger. airman d. 1917, its first constructor]

ze·ro /zeérō/ *n. & v.* ● *n.* (*pl.* **–ros**) **1 a** the figure 0; naught. **b** no quantity or number; nil. **2** a point on the scale of an instrument from which a positive or negative quantity is reckoned. **3** (*attrib.*) having a value of zero; no; not any (*zero population growth*). **4** (in full **zero hour**) **a** the hour at which a planned, esp. military, operation is timed to begin. **b** a crucial moment. **5** the lowest point; a nullity or nonentity. ● *v.tr.* (**–roes, –roed**) **1** adjust (an instrument, etc.) to zero point. **2** set the sights of (a gun) for firing. □ **zero in on 1** take aim at. **2** focus one's attention on. [F *zéro* or It. *zero* f. OSp. f. Arab. *ṣifr* CIPHER]

zebra

ze•ro op•tion *n.* a disarmament proposal for the total removal of certain types of weapons on both sides.

ze•ro-sum *adj.* (of a game, political situation, etc.) in which whatever is gained by one side is lost by the other so that the net change is always zero.

ze•roth /zéeróth/ *adj.* immediately preceding what is regarded as 'first' in a series.

zest /zest/ *n.* **1** piquancy; a stimulating flavor or quality. **2 a** keen enjoyment or interest. **b** (often foll. by *for*) relish. **c** gusto (*entered into it with zest*). **3** a scraping of orange or lemon peel as flavoring. □□ **zest•ful** *adj.* **zest•ful•ly** *adv.* **zest•ful•ness** *n.* **zest•i•ness** *n.* **zest•y** *adj.* (**zest•i•er, zest•i•est**). [F *zeste* orange or lemon peel, of unkn. orig.]

ze•ta /záytə, zée–/ *n.* the sixth letter of the Greek alphabet (Z, ζ). [Gk *zēta*]

zeug•ma /zóogmə/ *n.* a figure of speech using a verb or adjective with two nouns, to one of which it is strictly applicable while the word appropriate to the other is not used (e.g., *with weeping eyes and* [*grieving*] *hearts*) (cf. SYLLEPSIS). □□ **zeug•mat•ic** /–mátik/ *adj.* [L f. Gk *zeugma –atos* f. *zeugnumi* to yoke, *zugon* yoke]

zib•et /zíbit/ *n.* **1** an Asian or Indian civet, *Viverra zibetha.* **2** its scent. [med.L *zibethum:* see CIVET]

zi•do•vu•dine /zidóvyōōdeén/ *n.* = AZT. [chem. name *azidothymidine*]

ziff /zif/ *n. Austral. sl.* a beard. [20th c.: orig. unkn.]

zig•gu•rat /zígərat/ *n.* a rectangular stepped tower in ancient Mesopotamia, surmounted by a temple. [Assyr. *ziqquratu* pinnacle]

zig•zag /zígzag/ *n., adj., adv., & v.* ● *n.* **1** a line or course having abrupt alternate right and left turns. **2** (often in *pl.*) each of these turns. ● *adj.* having the form of a zigzag; alternating right and left. ● *adv.* with a zigzag course. ● *v.intr.* (**zig•zagged, zig•zag•ging**) move in a zigzag course. □□ **zig•zag•ged•ly** *adv.* [F f. G *zickzack*]

zilch /zilch/ *n. sl.* nothing. [20th c.: orig. uncert.]

zil•lah /zílə/ *n.* an administrative district in India, containing several parganas. [Hind. *ḍilah* division]

zil•lion /zílyən/ *n. colloq.* an indefinite large number. □□ **zil•lionth** *adj. & n.* [Z (perh. = unknown quantity) + MILLION]

zinc /zingk/ *n. Chem.* a white metallic element occurring naturally as zinc blende, and used as a component of brass, in galvanizing sheet iron, in electric batteries, and in printing plates. ¶ Symb.: **Zn.** □□ **zinced** *adj.* [G *Zink,* of unkn. orig.]

zinc blende *n.* = SPHALERITE.

zinc chlo•ride *n.* a white crystalline deliquescent solid used as a preservative and flux.

zin•co /zíngkō/ *n. & v.* ● *n.* (*pl.* **–cos**) = ZINCOGRAPH. ● *v.tr. & intr.* (**–coes, –coed**) = ZINCOGRAPH. [abbr.]

zin•co•graph /zíngkəgraf/ *n. & v.* ● *n.* **1** a zinc plate with a design etched in relief on it for printing from. **2** a print taken from this. ● *v.* **1** *tr.* etch on zinc. **2** *tr.* reproduce (a design) in this way. □□ **zin•cog•ra•phy** /–kógrəfee/ *n.*

zinc ox•ide *n.* a powder used as a white pigment and in medicinal ointments.

zinc•co•type /zíngkətīp/ *n.* = ZINCOGRAPH.

zinc sul•fate *n.* a white, water-soluble compound used as a mordant.

zing /zing/ *n. & v. colloq.* ● *n.* vigor; energy. ● *v.intr.* move swiftly or with a shrill sound. □□ **zing•y** *adj.* (**zing•i•er, zing•i•est**). [imit.]

zingaro /tséenggaarō/ *n.* (*pl.* **zingari** /–ree/; *fem.* **zingara** /–raa/) a gypsy. [It.]

zing•er /zíngər/ *n. sl.* **1** a witty retort. **2** an unexpected or startling announcement, etc. **3** an outstanding person or thing.

zin•ni•a /zíneeə/ *n.* a composite plant of the genus *Zinnia,* with showy rayed flowers of deep red and other colors. [J. G. *Zinn,* Ger. physician and botanist d. 1759]

Zi•on /zíən/ *n.* (also **Si•on** /síən/) **1** the hill of Jerusalem on which the city of David was built. **2 a** the Jewish people or religion. **b** the Christian church. **3** (in Christian thought) the kingdom of God in heaven. [OE f. eccl.L *Sion* f. Heb. *ṣiyôn*]

Zi•on•ism /zíənizəm/ *n.* a movement (orig.) for the reestablishment and (now) the development of a Jewish nation in what is now Israel. □□ **Zi•on•ist** *n.*

zip /zip/ *n. & v.* ● *n.* **1** a light fast sound, as of a bullet passing through air. **2** energy; vigor. **3** *Brit.* **a** (in full **zip fastener**) = ZIPPER. **b** (*attrib.*) having a zipper (*zip bag*). ● *v.* (**zipped, zip•ping**) **1** *tr. & intr.* (often foll. by *up*) fasten with a zipper. **2** *intr.* move with zip or at high speed. [imit.]

zip code /zip/ *n.* (also **ZIP code**) a US system of postal codes consisting of five-digit or nine-digit numbers. [*zone improvement plan*]

zip•per /zípər/ *n. & v.* ● *n.* a fastening device of two flexible strips with interlocking projections closed or opened by pulling a slide along them. ● *v.tr.* (often foll. by *up*) fasten with a zipper. □□ **zip•pered** *adj.*

zip•py /zípee/ *adj.* (**zip•pi•er, zip•pi•est**) *colloq.* **1** bright; fresh; lively. **2** fast; speedy. □□ **zip•pi•ly** *adv.* **zip•pi•ness** *n.*

zir•con /zórkon/ *n.* a zirconium silicate of which some translucent

varieties are cut into gems (see HYACINTH 4, JARGON²). [G *Zirkon:* cf. JARGON²]

zir•co•ni•um /zərkóneeəm/ *n. Chem.* a gray metallic element occurring naturally in zircon and used in various industrial applications. ¶ Symb.: **Zr.** [mod.L f. ZIRCON + –IUM]

zit /zit/ *n. sl.* a pimple. [20th c.: orig. unkn.]

zith•er /zíthər/ *n.* a musical instrument consisting of a flat wooden sound box with numerous strings stretched across it, placed horizontally and played with the fingers and a plectrum. □□ **zith•er•ist** *n.* [G (as CITTERN)]

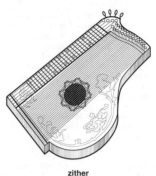

zither

zizz /ziz/ *n. & v. Brit. colloq.* ● *n.* **1** a whizzing or buzzing sound. **2** a short sleep. ● *v.intr.* **1** make a whizzing sound. **2** doze or sleep. [imit.]

zlo•ty /zláwtee/ *n.* (*pl.* same or **zlo•tys**) the chief monetary unit of Poland. [Pol., lit. 'golden']

Zn *symb. Chem.* the element zinc.

zo•di•ac /zódeeak/ *n.* **1 a** a belt of the heavens limited by lines about 8° from the ecliptic on each side, including all apparent positions of the sun, moon, and planets as known to ancient astronomers, and divided into twelve equal parts (**signs of the zodiac**), each formerly containing the similarly named constellation but now by precession of the equinoxes coinciding with the constellation that bears the name of the preceding sign: Aries, Taurus, Gemini, Cancer, Leo, Virgo, Libra, Scorpio, Sagittarius, Capricorn(us), Aquarius, Pisces. **b** a diagram of these signs. **2** a complete cycle, circuit, or compass. [ME f. OF *zodiaque* f. L *zodiacus* f. Gk *zōidiakos* f. *zōidion* sculptured animal figure, dimin. of *zōion* animal]

zo•di•a•cal /zədíəkəl/ *adj.* of or in the zodiac. [F (as ZODIAC)]

zo•di•a•cal light *n.* a luminous area of sky shaped like a tail triangle occasionally seen in the east before sunrise or in the west after sunset, esp. in the tropics.

zo•e•trope /zóeetrōp/ *n. hist.* an optical toy in the form of a cylinder with a series of pictures on the inner surface which give an impression of continuous motion when viewed through slits with the cylinder rotating. [irreg. f. Gk *zōē* life + *–tropos* turning]

-zoic */* comb. form **1** of or relating to animals. **2** *Geol.* (of rock, etc.) containing fossils; with traces of animal or plant life. [prob. back-form. f. AZOIC]

Zoll•ner illusion /tsólnər/ *n.* parallel lines made to appear not parallel by short oblique intersecting lines. [J. K. F. *Zöllner,* Ger. physicist d. 1882]

Zoll•ver•ein /tsáwlfərīn/ *n. hist.* a customs union, esp. of German states in the 19th c. [G]

zom•bie /zómbee/ *n.* **1** *colloq.* a dull or apathetic person. **2** a corpse said to be revived by witchcraft. [W.Afr. *zumbi* fetish]

zo•na•tion /zōnáyshən/ *n.* distribution in zones, esp. (*Ecol.*) of plants into zones characterized by the dominant species.

zon•da /zóndə/ *n.* a hot, dusty north wind in Argentina. [Amer. Sp.]

zone /zōn/ *n. & v.* ● *n.* **1** an area having particular features, properties, purpose, or use (*danger zone; erogenous zone; smokeless zone*). **2** any well-defined region of more or less beltlike form. **3 a** an area between two exact or approximate concentric circles. **b** a part of the surface of a sphere enclosed between two parallel planes, or of a cone or cylinder, etc., between such planes cutting it perpendicularly to the axis. **4** (in full **time zone**) a range of longitudes where a common standard time is used. **5** *Geol.,* etc., a range between specified limits of depth, height, etc., esp. a section of strata distinguished by characteristic fossils. **6** *Geog.* any of five divisions of the earth bounded by circles parallel to the equator (see FRIGID, TEMPERATE, TORRID). **7** an encircling band or stripe distinguishable in color, texture, or character from the rest of the object encircled. **8** *archaic* a belt or girdle worn around the body. ● *v.tr.* **1** encircle as or with a zone. **2** arrange or distribute by zones. **3** assign as or to a particular area. □□ **zon•al** *adj.* **zon•ing** *n.* (in sense 3 of *v.*). [F *zone* or L *zona* girdle f. Gk *zōnē*]

zonk /zongk/ *v. & n. sl.* ● *v.* **1** *tr.* hit or strike. **2** (foll. by *out*) **a** *tr.* overcome with sleep; intoxicate. **b** *intr.* fall heavily asleep. ● *n.* (often as *int.*) the sound of a blow or heavy impact. [imit.]

zonked /zongkt/ *adj. sl.* (often foll. by *out*) exhausted; intoxicated.

zoo /zoō/ *n.* a zoological garden. [abbr.]

zoo- /zóə/ *comb. form* of animals or animal life. [Gk *zōio-* f. *zōion* animal]

zo·o·ge·og·ra·phy /zóəjee-ógrəfee/ *n.* the branch of zoology dealing with the geographical distribution of animals. □□ **zo·o·ge·o·graph·ic** /–jeeəgráfik/ *adj.* **zo·o·ge·o·graph·i·cal** *adj.* **zo·o·ge·o·graph·i·cal·ly** *adv.*

zo·og·ra·phy /zō-ógrəfee/ *n.* descriptive zoology.

zo·oid /zố-oyd/ *n.* **1** a more or less independent invertebrate organism arising by budding or fission. **2** a distinct member of an invertebrate colony. □□ **zo·oi·dal** /–óyd'l/ *adj.* [formed as ZOO- + –OID]

zool. *abbr.* **1** zoological. **2** zoology.

zo·o·la·try /zō-ólətree/ *n.* the worship of animals.

zo·o·log·i·cal /zóəlójikəl/ *adj.* of or relating to zoology. □□ **zo·o·log·i·cal·ly** *adv.*

zo·o·log·i·cal gar·den *n.* (also **zo·o·log·i·cal gar·dens**) a public garden or park with a collection of animals for exhibition and study.

zo·ol·o·gy /zō-óləjee/ *n.* the scientific study of animals, esp. with reference to their structure, physiology, classification, and distribution. □□ **zo·ol·o·gist** *n.* [mod.L *zoologia* (as ZOO-, –LOGY)]

zoom /zoōm/ *v. & n.* ● *v.* **1** *intr.* move quickly, esp. with a buzzing sound. **2 a** *intr.* cause an airplane to mount at high speed and a steep angle. **b** *tr.* cause (an airplane) to do this. **3 a** *intr.* (of a camera) close up rapidly from a long shot to a close-up. **b** *tr.* cause (a lens or camera) to do this. ● *n.* **1** an airplane's steep climb. **2** a zooming camera shot. [imit.]

zo·om·an·cy /zóəmansee/ *n.* divination from the appearances or behavior of animals.

zoom lens *n.* a lens allowing a camera to zoom by varying the focal length.

zo·o·mor·phic /zóəmáwrfik/ *adj.* **1** dealing with or represented in animal forms. **2** having gods of animal form. □□ **zo·o·mor·phism** *n.*

zo·on·o·sis /zóənósis/ *n.* any of various diseases which can be transmitted to humans from animals. [ZOO- + Gk *nosos* disease]

zo·o·phyte /zóəfīt/ *n.* a plantlike animal, esp. a coral, sea anemone, or sponge. □□ **zo·o·phyt·ic** /–fítik/ *adj.* [Gk *zōophuton* (as ZOO-, –PHYTE)]

zo·o·plank·ton /zóəplángktən/ *n.* plankton consisting of animals.

zo·o·spore /zóəspawr/ *n.* a spore of fungi, algae, etc. capable of motion. □□ **zo·o·spor·ic** /–spáwrik/ *adj.*

zo·ot·o·my /zō-ótəmee/ *n.* the dissection or anatomy of animals.

zoot suit /zoōt/ *n. colloq.* a man's suit with a long, loose jacket and high-waisted, tapering pants. [rhyming on SUIT]

zo·ri /záwree/ *n.* (*pl.* same or **zo·ris**) a Japanese straw or rubber, etc., sandal held on the foot by a thong between the first two toes. [Jap.]

zor·il /záwril, zór–/ *n.* (also **zor·ille**) a flesh-eating African mammal, *Ictonyx striatus*, of the skunk and the weasel family. [F *zorille* f. Sp. *zorrilla* dimin. of *zorro* fox]

Zo·ro·as·tri·an /záwrō-ástreeən/ *adj. & n.* (also **Za·ra·thus·tri·an** /zárəthōóstreeən/) ● *adj.* of or relating to Zoroaster (or Zarathustra) or the dualistic religious system taught by him or his followers in the Zend-Avesta, based on the concept of a conflict between a spirit of light and good and a spirit of darkness and evil. ● *n.* a follower of Zoroaster. □□ **Zo·ro·as·tri·an·ism** *n.* [L *Zoroastres* f. Gk *Zōroastrēs* f. Avestan *Zarathustra*, Persian founder of the religion in the 6th c. BC]

Zou·ave /zoō-áav, zwaav/ *n.* a member of a French light-infantry corps originally formed of Algerians and retaining their oriental uniform. [F f. *Zouaoua*, name of a tribe]

zounds /zowndz/ *int. archaic* expressing surprise or indignation. [(*God*)'s *wounds* (i.e., those of Christ on the cross)]

ZPG *abbr.* zero population growth.

Zr *symb. Chem.* the element zirconium.

zuc·chet·to /zoōkétō, tsoōkétō/ *n.* (*pl.* **-tos**) a Roman Catholic ecclesiastic's skullcap, black for a priest, purple for a bishop, red for a cardinal, and white for a pope. [It. *zucchetta* dimin. of *zucca* gourd, head]

zuc·chi·ni /zoōkeénee/ *n.* (*pl.* same or **zuc·chi·nis**) a green variety of smooth-skinned summer suash. [It., pl. of *zucchino* dimin. of *zucca* gourd]

zug·zwang /tsoōktsvaang/ *n. Chess* an obligation to move in one's turn even when this must be disadvantageous. [G f. *Zug* move + *Zwang* compulsion]

Zu·lu /zoōloō/ *n. & adj.* ● *n.* **1** a member of a black South African people orig. inhabiting Zululand and Natal. **2** the language of this people. ● *adj.* of or relating to this people or language. [native name]

Zu·ni /zoōnee/ *n.* (also **Zu·ñi** /zoónyee/) **1 a** a N. American people native to New Mexico. **b** a member of this people. **2** the language of this people.

zwie·back /zwíbak, –baak, zweé–, swí–, sweé–/ *n.* a kind of rusk or sweet cake toasted in slices. [G, = twice baked]

Zwing·li·an /zwíngleeən, tsvíng–/ *n. & adj.* ● *n.* a follower of the Swiss religious reformer U. Zwingli (d. 1531). ● *adj.* of or relating to Zwingli or his reforms.

zwit·ter·i·on /tsvítəriən, zwít–/ *n.* a molecule or ion having separate positively and negatively charged groups. [G f. *Zwitter* a hybrid]

zygo- /zígō, zígə/ *comb. form* joining; pairing. [Gk *zugo-* f. *zugon* yoke]

zy·go·dac·tyl /zígōdáktil, zígə–/ *adj. & n.* ● *adj.* (of a bird) having two toes pointing forward and two backward. ● *n.* such a bird. □□ **zy·go·dac·ty·lous** *adj.*

zy·go·ma /zígómə, zee–/ *n.* (*pl.* **zy·go·ma·ta** /–tə/) the bony arch of the cheek formed by connection of the zygomatic and temporal bones. [Gk *zugōma –atos* f. *zugon* yoke]

zy·go·mat·ic /zígəmátik, zígə–/ *adj.* of or relating to the zygoma.

zy·go·mat·ic arch *n.* = ZYGOMA.

zy·go·mat·ic bone *n.* the bone that forms the prominent part of the cheek.

zy·go·mor·phic /zígəmáwrfik, zígə–/ *adj.* (also **zy·go·mor·phous** /–máwrfəs/) (of a flower) divisible into similar halves only by one plane of symmetry.

zy·go·spore /zígəspawr, zígə–/ *n.* a thick-walled spore formed by certain fungi.

zy·gote /zígōt, zíg–/ *n. Biol.* a cell formed by the union of two gametes. □□ **zy·got·ic** /–gótik/ *adj.* **zy·got·i·cal·ly** /–gótikəlee/ *adv.* [Gk *zugōtos* yoked f. *zugoō* to yoke]

zy·mase /zímays/ *n.* the enzyme fraction in yeast that catalyzes the alcoholic fermentation of glucose. [F f. Gk *zumē* leaven]

zy·mol·o·gy /zímóləjee/ *n. Chem.* the scientific study of fermentation. □□ **zy·mo·log·i·cal** /–məlójikəl/ *adj.* **zy·mol·o·gist** *n.* [as ZYMASE + –LOGY]

zy·mo·sis /zīmósis, zi–/ *n. archaic* fermentation. [mod.L f. Gk *zumōsis* (as ZYMASE)]

zy·mot·ic /zīmótik, zi–/ *adj. archaic* of or relating to fermentation. [Gk *zumōtikos* (as ZYMOSIS)]

zy·mot·ic dis·ease *n. archaic* an epidemic, endemic, contagious, infectious, or sporadic disease regarded as caused by the multiplication of germs introduced from outside.

zy·mur·gy /zímərjee/ *n.* the branch of applied chemistry dealing with the use of fermentation in brewing, etc. [Gk *zumē* leaven, after *metallurgy*]

Biographical Entries

Biographical Entries

Aar·on /áirən/, **Hank (Henry Louis)** 1934– ; U.S. baseball player.

Ab·e·lard /ábəlaard/, **Peter** 1079–1142; French theologian and philosopher.

A·bra·ham /áybrəham/ Hebrew patriarch.

A·che·be /aacháybay/, **Chinua** (born **Albert Chinualumgu**) 1930– ; Nigerian author.

Ach·e·son /áchəsən/, **Dean Gooderham** 1893–1971; U.S. secretary of state (1949–53).

Ad·ams /ádəmz/, **Ansel Easton** 1902–84; U.S. photographer.

Ad·ams family of U.S. politicians, including: **1** John 1735–1826; 2nd president of the U.S. (1797–1801); father of: **2** John Quincy 1767–1848; 6th president of the U.S. (1825–29).

Ad·ams, Samuel 1722–1803; U.S. patriot.

Ad·dams /ádəmz/, **Jane** 1860–1935; U.S. social worker.

Ad·di·son /ádəsən/, **Joseph** 1672–1719; English author.

A·de·nau·er /aád-nowər, ád–/, **Konrad** 1876–1967; chancellor of West Germany (1949–63).

Ad·ler /ádlər/, **Alfred** 1870–1937; Austrian psychiatrist.

Ael·fric /álfrik/ c. 955–c. 1020; English abbot, author, and grammarian.

Aes·chy·lus /éskələs/ c. 525–c. 456 B.C.; Greek playwright.

Ae·sop /éesaap, –səp/ 6th cent. B.C.; Greek writer of fables.

Ag·as·siz /ágəsee/, **(Jean) Louis** 1807–73; U.S. naturalist, born in Switzerland.

Ag·new /ágnoo/, **Spiro Theodore** 1918–96; U.S. vice president (1969–73); resigned.

Ai·ken /áykən/, **Conrad Potter** 1889–1973; U.S. poet.

Ak·bar /ákbər, –baar/, **Jalaludin Muhammad** 1542–1605; Mogul emperor of India (1556–1605).

Akh·na·ton /aaknaátən/ see **Amenhotep IV** (AMENHOTEP).

A·ki·hi·to /aakiheétō/ 1933– ; emperor of Japan (1989–).

Al·a·ric /álərik/ c. 370–410; king of the Visigoths (395–410); captured Rome (410).

Al·bee /áwlbee, ál–/, **Edward** 1928– ; U.S. playwright.

Al·bright /áwlbrīt/, **Madeleine** 1937– ; U.S. secretary of state (1997–), born in Czechoslovakia.

Al·ci·bi·a·des /alsəbíədeez/ c. 450–404 B.C.; Athenian general and statesman.

Al·cott /áwlkət, ál–, –kaat/, **Louisa May** 1832–88; U.S. novelist.

Al·cuin /álkwin/ c. 735–804; English theologian.

Al·ex·an·der /aligzándər/ (called **"the Great"**) 356–323 B.C.; king of Macedonia (336–323 B.C.); conqueror of the Persian Empire.

Al·ex·an·der name of three czars of Russia: **1** Alexander I 1777–1825; reigned 1801–25. **2** Alexander II (called **"the Liberator"**) 1818–81; reigned 1855–81; father of: **3** Alexander III 1845–94; reigned 1881–94.

Al·fred /álfrəd/ (called **"the Great"**) 849–899; Anglo-Saxon king (871–899).

A·li /aalée, alée/, **Muhammad** (born **Cassius Marcellus Clay, Jr.**) 1942– ; U.S. boxer.

A·li·ghie·ri /aləgyéree/, **Dante** see DANTE.

Al·len /álən/, **Ethan** 1738–89; American Revolutionary War soldier.

Al·len, Woody (born **Allen Stewart Konigsberg**) 1935– ; U.S. film director, author, and actor.

All·en·de Gos·sens /aayénday gáwsens/, **Salvador** 1908–73; Chilean political leader.

A·ma·ti /əmaátee, aa–/ family of Italian violin-makers, including: **1** Andrea c. 1520–c. 1580; grandfather of: **2** Nicolò 1596–1684.

A·men·ho·tep /aamənhótep/ (also **Am·e·no'phis**) name of four kings of Egypt: **1** Amenhotep I reigned 1546–1526 B.C. **2** Amenhotep II reigned 1450–1425 B.C. **3** Amenhotep III reigned 1417–1379 B.C.; built capital city of Thebes. **4** Amenhotep IV (also **Akh·na'ton; Ikh·na'ton**) reigned 1379–1362 B.C.

A·min /aameén/, **Idi** 1925– ; president of Uganda (1971–79); exiled (1979).

An·ax·ag·o·ras /anakságərəs/ c. 500–c. 428 B.C.; Greek philosopher.

An·der·sen /ándərsən, aán–/, **Hans Christian** 1805–75; Danish author.

An·der·son /ándərsən/, **Marian** 1902–93; U.S. contralto.

An·der·son, Maxwell 1888–1959; U.S. playwright.

An·der·son, Sherwood 1876–1941; U.S. author.

An·drew /ándrōō/, **St.** died c. 60; apostle of Jesus; patron saint of Scotland.

An·dro·pov /andrópawf/, **Yuri** 1914–84; Soviet politician.

An·ge·lou /aánjəlōō, –lō/, **Maya** 1928– ; U.S. novelist and poet.

An·nan /aánaan/, **Kofi** 1938– ; Ghanaian secretary-general of the United Nations (1997–).

Anne /an/ 1665–1714; queen of England (1702–14).

Anne Bol·eyn see BOLEYN, ANNE.

Anne of Cleves /kleevz/ 1515–57; 4th wife of Henry VIII.

An·nen·berg /ánənbərg/, **Walter** 1908– ; U.S. publisher and philanthropist.

A·nou·ilh /aanóōee/, **Jean** 1910–87; French playwright.

An·selm /ánselm/, **St.** c. 1033–1109; English theologian.

An·tho·ny /ánthənee/, **Susan B(rownell)** 1820–1906; U.S. suffragist.

An·to·ni·nus Pi·us /antənínəs píəs/ 86–161; Roman emperor (137–161).

An·to·ny /ántənee/, **Mark** (Latin name **Mar'cus An·to'ni·us**) c. 83–30 B.C.; Roman general and political leader.

Ap·ol·lo·ni·us /apəlóneeəs/ **of Rhodes** /rōdz/ 3rd cent. B.C.; Greek poet.

A·pu·lei·us /apyəláyəs/ 2nd cent.; Roman author.

A·qui·nas /əkwínəs/, **St. Thomas** 1225–74; Italian philosopher and theologian.

Ar·a·fat /árəfat/, **Yasser** 1929– ; Palestinian political leader.

A·ri·os·to /aaree-aástō, –óstō/, **Ludovico** 1474–1533; Italian poet.

Ar·is·ti·des /arəstídeez/ (called **"the Just"**) fl. 5th cent. B.C.; Athenian statesman and general.

Ar·is·toph·a·nes /arəstaáfəneez/ c. 450–c. 385 B.C.; Greek comic playwright.

Ar·is·tot·le /árəstaat'l, arəstaát'l/ 384–322 B.C.; Greek philosopher.

Arm·strong /aármstrawng/, **(Daniel) Louis** (called **"Satchmo"**) 1900–71; U.S. jazz trumpeter and bandleader.

Arm·strong, Neil Alden 1930– ; U.S. astronaut; first to walk on the moon (1969).

Ar·nold /aárnəld/, **Benedict** 1741–1801; American Revolutionary War general; turned traitor (1779).

Ar·nold, Matthew 1822–88; English poet and essayist.

Arou·et /áawə/, **François-Marie** see VOLTAIRE.

Ar·ta·xerx·es /aartəzórkseez/ name of three kings of Persia: **1** Artaxerxes I reigned 464–424 B.C.; son of Xerxes I. **2** Artaxerxes II reigned 404–358 B.C.; father of: **3** Artaxerxes III reigned 358–338 B.C.

Ar·thur /aárthər/ 5th cent. or 6th cent.; legendary king of Britain. □□ **Ar·thu'ri·an** adj.

Ar·thur, Chester Alan 1830–86; 21st president of the U.S. (1881–85).

Ashe /ash/, **Arthur Robert** 1943–93; U.S. tennis player.

As·i·mov /ázəmawf, –mawv/, **Isaac** 1920–92; U.S. scientist and author, born in Russia.

As·sad /aasáad/, **Hafiz al-** 1928– ; president of Syria (1971–).

A·staire /əstáir/, **Fred** (born **Frederick Austerlitz**) 1899–1987; U.S. dancer, singer, and actor.

As·tor /ástər/, **John Jacob** 1763–1848; U.S. capitalist, born in Germany.

As·tu·ri·as /aastóōreeəs, –tyoo-/, **Miguel Angel** 1899–1974; Guatemalan author.

A·ta·türk /átətərk/, **Kemal** (born **Mustafa Kemal**) 1881–1938; president of Turkey (1923–38).

At·ti·la /ətílə, át'lə/ 406–453; king of the Huns (434–453).

Att·lee /átlee/, **Clement Richard** 1883–1967; prime minister of Great Britain (1945–51).

At·tucks /átəks/, **Crispus** c. 1723–70; American patriot; killed in the Boston Massacre.

At·wood /átwŏod/, **Margaret** 1939– ; Canadian author and critic.

Au·den /áwd'n/, **W(ystan) H(ugh)** 1907–73; U.S. poet, born in England.

Au·du·bon /áwdəbaan, –bən/, **John James** 1785–1851; U.S. naturalist and artist.

Au·gus·tine /áwgusteen, awgústən/ name of two saints: **1** (called **St. Augustine of Hippo**) 354–430; early Christian author. **2** (also known as **Aus′tin**) died c. 604; first archbishop of Canterbury. □□ **Au·gus·tin′i·an** adj.

Au·gus·tus /awgústəs/ (also known as **Oc·ta′vi·an**) 63 B.C.–A.D. 14; first Roman emperor.

Aung San Suu Kyi /ówng saán sŏŏ chee/ 1945– ; Burmese political leader.

Au·re·li·us, Marcus see MARCUS AURELIUS.

Aus·ten /áwstən/, **Jane** 1775–1817; English novelist.

Aus·tin /áwstən/, **Stephen Fuller** 1793–1836; Texas pioneer and colonizer.

A·ver·ro·ës /əvéró-eez, avəró–/ c. 1126–98; Islamic philosopher, born in Spain.

A·vi·cen·na /avəsénə/ 980–1037; Islamic philosopher and physician, born in Persia.

Ayer /áyər/, **A(lfred) J(ules)** 1910–89; British philosopher.

Ba·ber /baábər/ (also **Ba′bar; Ba′bur**) 1483–1530; founder of the Mogul Empire.

Bach /baakh, baak/ family of German composers, including: **1** Johann Sebastian 1685–1750; father of: **2** Wilhelm Friedemann 1710–84; **3** C(arl) P(hilipp) E(manuel) 1714–88; **4** Johann Christoph Friedrich 1732–95; and **5** Johann Christian 1735–82.

Ba·con /báykən/, **Francis** 1561–1626; English statesman and philosopher.

Ba·con, Roger c. 1214–94; English scientist and philosopher.

Ba·den-Pow·ell /bayd'n pŏəl, pówəl/, **(Lord) Robert Stephenson Smyth** 1857–1941; English general; founder of the Boy Scouts (1908).

Bal·an·chine /bálənsheen/, **George** 1904–83; U.S. choreographer and ballet dancer, born in Russia.

Bal·boa /balbŏə/, **Vasco Núñez de** 1475–1517; Spanish explorer of America.

Bald·win /báwldwin/, **James** 1924–87; U.S. author.

Bald·win, Stanley 1867–1947; prime minister of Great Britain (1923–29; 1935–37).

Bal·four /bálfər, –fawr/, **Arthur James** 1848–1930; British statesman.

Ball /bawl/, **Lucille Désirée** 1911–1989; U.S. comedienne.

Bal·ti·more, Lord see CALVERT, GEORGE.

Bal·zac /báwlzak, bál–/, **Honoré de** 1799–1850; French novelist.

Bar·ba·ros·sa /baarbərŏsə/ see FREDERICK I.

Bar·nard /baárnərd/, **Christiaan Neethling** 1922– ; South African physician; performed first human heart transplant (1967).

Bar·num /baárnəm/, **P(hineas) T(aylor)** 1810–91; U.S. showman.

Bar·rett /bárit/, **Elizabeth** see BROWNING, ELIZABETH BARRETT.

Bar·rie /báree/, **(Sir) J(ames) M(atthew)** 1860–1937; Scottish author.

Bar·ry·more /bárimawr/ family of U.S. actors, including three siblings: **1** Lionel 1878–1954; **2** Ethel 1879–1959; and **3** John 1882–1942.

Barth /baarth/, **John** 1930– ; U.S. author.

Barth /baart/, **Karl** 1886–1968; Swiss Protestant theologian.

Barthes /baart/, **Roland** 1915–80; French author and critic.

Bar·tók /baártaak, –tawk/, **Béla** 1881–1945; Hungarian composer.

Bar·ton /baárt'n/, **Clara** 1821–1912; U.S. health worker; founded the American Red Cross (1881).

Ba·rysh·ni·kov /bəríshnikawf/, **Mikhail** 1948– ; U.S. ballet dancer and choreographer, born in Latvia.

Ba·sie /báysee/, **Count (William)** 1904–84; U.S. jazz pianist, bandleader, and composer.

Ba·tis·ta /bəteéstə/, **Fulgencio** 1901–73; president of Cuba (1940–44; 1954–59).

Bau·de·laire /bōd'lair/, **Charles** 1821–67; French poet and critic.

Beards·ley /beérdzlee/, **Aubrey Vincent** 1872–98; English artist.

Be·a·trix /báyətriks/ 1938– ; queen of the Netherlands (1980–).

Beau·mar·chais /bōmaarsháy/, **Pierre Augustin Caron de** 1732–99; French playwright.

Beau·mont /bómaant/, **Francis** 1584–1616; English playwright.

Beauvoir, Simone de see DE BEAUVOIR, SIMONE.

Beck·et /békit/, **St. Thomas à** c. 1118–70; archbishop of Canterbury; murdered for opposing King Henry II.

Beck·ett /békit/, **Samuel Barclay** 1906–89; Irish author.

Bede /beed/, **St.** (called **"the Venerable Bede"**) c. 673–735; English theologian and historian.

Bee·cher /beéchər/, **Henry Ward** 1813–87; U.S. abolitionist.

Beer·bohm /beérbōm/, **(Sir) Max (Henry Maximilian)** 1872–1956; English caricaturist and critic.

Bee·tho·ven /báytōvən/, **Ludwig van** 1770–1827; German composer.

Be·gin /bəgeén, báygin/, **Menachem** 1913–92; Israeli political leader.

Be·han /beéən/, **Brendan** 1923–64; Irish playwright and poet.

Bell /bel/, **Alexander Graham** 1847–1922; U.S. inventor of the telephone, born in Scotland.

Bel·li·ni /beleénee/ family of Italian artists, including: **1** Jacopo c. 1400–70; father of: **2** Gentile c. 1429–1507; and **3** Giovanni c. 1430–1516.

Bel·low /bélō/, **Saul** 1915– ; U.S. novelist, born in Canada.

Ben·e·dict /bénədikt/, **St.** c. 480–c. 550; Italian monk; founded Western monasticism.

Be·nét /bənáy/, **Stephen Vincent** 1898–1943; U.S. poet.

Ben-Gu·ri·on /ben gŏoreeən/, **David** (born **David Gruen** 1886–1973; prime minister of Israel (1948–53; 1955–63), born in Poland.

Ben·ny /bénee/, **Jack** (born **Benjamin Kubelsky**) 1894–1974; U.S. comedian.

Ben·tham /bénthəm/, **Jeremy** 1748–1832; English philosopher and jurist.

Ben·ton /bént'n/ **1** Thomas Hart 1782–1858; U.S. politician; great-uncle of: **2** Thomas Hart 1889–1975; U.S. artist.

Bent·sen /béntsən/, **Lloyd Millard** 1921– ; U.S. politician.

Benz /benz, bents/, **Karl Friedrich** 1844–1929; German automotive engineer.

Berg·son /bérgsən/, **Henri** 1859–1941; French philosopher.

Ber·ing /beéring, bér–/, **Vitus Jonassen** 1681–1741; Danish explorer.

Berke·ley /baárklee, bər–/, **George** 1685–1753; Irish philosopher and bishop.

Ber·lin /bərlín/, **Irving** (born **Israel Isidore Baline**) 1888–1989; U.S. composer, born in Russia.

Ber·li·oz /bérlee-ōz/, **Hector Louis** 1803–69; French composer.

Ber·na·dette /bərnədét/, **St.** (born **Marie-Bernarde Soubirous**) 1844–79; French peasant girl who had visions of the Virgin Mary at Lourdes.

Ber·nard /bərnaárd/ **of Clair·vaux** /klairvó/ 1090–1153; French theologian.

Bern·hardt /bérnhaart/, **Sarah** (born **Henriette Rosine Bernard**) 1844–1923; French actress.

Ber·ni·ni /bərneénee/, **Gianlorenzo** 1598–1680; Italian artist and architect.

Bern·stein /bérnstīn, –steen/, **Leonard** 1918–90; U.S. composer and conductor.

Ber·ry /béree/, **Chuck (Charles Edward)** 1931– ; U.S. rock and roll musician.

Bes·se·mer /bésimər/, **(Sir) Henry** 1813–98; English engineer and inventor.

Be·thune /bəthŏon, –yŏon/, **Mary McLeod** 1875–1955; U.S. educator.

Bet·je·man /béchəmən/, **(Sir) John** 1906–84; English poet.

Beyle /bel/, **Marie Henri** see STENDHAL.

Bhut·to /bŏotō/ **1** Zulfikar Ali 1928–79; president (1971–73) and prime minister (1973–77) of Pakistan; father of: **2** Benazir 1953– ; prime minister of Pakistan (1988–91; 1993–96).

Bierce /beers/, **Ambrose Gwinnett** 1842–c. 1914; U.S. author.

Bi·ko /beékō/, **Stephen** 1946–77; South African civil rights activist.

Bis·marck /bízmaark/, **Otto Eduard Leopold von** (called **"the**

Bi·zet /beezáy/, **Georges Alexandre César Léopold** 1838–75; French composer.

Black /blak/, **Shirley Temple** 1928– ; U.S. actress and diplomat.

Blair /blair/, **Tony (Anthony Charles Lynton)** 1953– ; prime minister of Great Britain (1997–).

Blake /blayk/, **William** 1757–1827; English artist and poet.

Bligh /blī/, **William** 1754–1817; British naval officer.

Bo·ad·i·ce·a /bōədəseeə/ (also **Bou·dic'ca**) died 62; warrior queen of the ancient Britons.

Boc·cac·ci·o /bəkaácheeō, –chō/, **Giovanni** 1313–75; Italian poet.

Bo·e·thi·us /bō-eétheeəs/, **Anicius Manlius Severinus** c. 480–524; Roman philosopher.

Bo·gart /bốgaart/, **Humphrey De Forest** 1899–1957; U.S. actor.

Bohr /bawr/, **Niels Henrik David** 1885–1962; Danish nuclear physicist.

Bol·eyn /boolín, boólən/, **Anne** 1507–36; 2nd wife of King Henry VIII of England; mother of Queen Elizabeth I; beheaded.

Bol·í·var /bōleévaar, baáləvər/, **Simón** (called **"the Liberator"**) 1783–1830; Venezuelan patriot and liberator of South America.

Bo·na·parte /bốnəpaart/ see NAPOLEON I; NAPOLEON III.

Boone /boon/, **Daniel** c. 1735–1820; American pioneer.

Boor·stin /boórstin/, **Daniel J(oseph)** 1914– ; U.S. author.

Booth /booth/, **John Wilkes** 1838–65; U.S. actor; assassin of President Abraham Lincoln (1865).

Bor·ges /báwrhays/, **Jorge Luis** 1899–1986; Argentine author.

Bor·gi·a /báwrjə, –zhə/ **1** Cesare 1476–1507; Italian cardinal and militarist; brother of: **2** Lucrezia 1480–1519; Italian patron of the arts.

Born /bawrn/, **Max** 1882–1970; German physicist.

Bosch /baash, bawsh/, **Hieronymus** c. 1450–1516; Dutch artist.

Bos·well /baázwel, –wəl/, **James** 1740–95; Scottish author; biographer of Samuel Johnson.

Bot·ti·cel·li /baatəchélee/, **Sandro** 1445–1510; Italian artist.

Bou·dic·ca /boodíkə/ see BOADICEA.

Bou·lez /boóléz/, **Pierre** 1925– ; French conductor and composer.

Bourke-White /boórk wīt/, **Margaret** 1906–71; U.S. photojournalist.

Bou·tros-Gha·li /boótrōs gaalee/, **Boutros** 1922– ; Egyptian statesman; secretary-general of the United Nations (1992–96).

Brad·bur·y /brádberee, –bəree/, **Ray(mond Douglas)** 1920– ; U.S. science-fiction author.

Brad·ford /brádfərd/, **William** 1590–1657; English Puritan governor of Plymouth colony in Massachusetts.

Brad·ley /brádlee/, **Omar Nelson** 1893–1981; U.S. general.

Bra·dy /bráydee/, **Mathew B.** 1823–96; U.S. Civil War photographer.

Brahe /braa, braáhee/, **Tycho** 1546–1601; Danish astronomer.

Brahms /braamz/, **Johannes** 1833–97; German composer.

Bran·deis /brándīs/, **Louis Dembitz** 1856–1941; U.S. Supreme Court justice (1916–39).

Bran·do /brándō/, **Marlon** 1924– ; U.S. actor.

Brandt /braant, brant/, **Willy** (born **Karl Herbert Frahm**) 1913–92; German politician.

Braun /brown/, **Wernher von** 1912–77; U.S. rocket scientist, born in Germany.

Brecht /brekht, brekt/, **Bertolt** 1898–1956; German playwright and poet.

Breu·ghel see BRUEGEL, PIETER.

Brey·er /bríər/, **Stephen Gerald** 1938– ; U.S. Supreme Court justice (1994–).

Brezh·nev /brézhnef, –nyəf/, **Leonid** 1906–83; Soviet political leader.

Bridg·es /bríjiz/, **Robert** 1844–1930; English poet and critic.

Brit·ten /brít'n/, **(Edward) Benjamin** 1913–76; English composer.

Brod·sky /braádskee, braát–/, **Joseph** 1940–1996; U.S. poet, born in Russia.

Bron·të /braántee, braántay/ family of English novelists; three sisters: **1** Charlotte 1816–55; **2** Emily Jane 1818–48; and **3** Anne 1820–49.

Brown /brown/, **John** 1800–59; U.S. radical abolitionist.

Brown·ing /brówning/ two English poets: **1** Elizabeth Barrett 1806–61; wife of: **2** Robert 1812–89.

Bruce /broos/, **Robert the** see ROBERT I.

Brue·gel /broýgəl/ (also **Breu'ghel**; **Brue'ghel**), **Pieter** c. 1525–69; Flemish artist.

Bru·nel·les·chi /broón'léskee/ (also **Bru·nel·les'co**), **Filippo** 1377–1446; Italian architect.

Bru·tus /broótəs/, **Marcus Junius** 85–42 B.C.; Roman senator; an assassin of Julius Caesar.

Bry·an /bríən/, **William Jennings** 1860–1925; U.S. lawyer, politician, and orator.

Bry·ant /bríənt/, **William Cullen** 1794–1878; U.S. poet.

Bryn·ner /brínər/, **Yul** 1915–85; U.S. actor, born in Russia.

Bu·ber /boóbər/, **Martin** 1878–1965; Israeli philosopher, born in Austria.

Bu·chan·an /byookánən/, **James** 1791–1868; 15th president of the U.S. (1857–61).

Buck /buk/, **Pearl S(ydenstricker)** 1892–1973; U.S. author.

Buck·ley /búklee/, **William F(rank)** 1925– ; U.S. political commentator and author.

Bud·dha /boódə, boódə/ (born **Siddhartha Gautama**) c. 563–c. 483 B.C.; Indian philosopher; founder of Buddhism.

Bult·mann /boóltmaan, –mən/, **Rudolf Karl** 1884–1976; German theologian.

Bunche /bunch/, **Ralph Johnson** 1904–71; U.S. diplomat.

Bu·nin /boónyeen/, **Ivan Alekseyevich** 1870–1953; Russian author and poet.

Bun·yan /búnyən/, **John** 1628–88; English author.

Bur·bank /bárbangk/, **Luther** 1849–1926; U.S. horticulturist.

Bur·ger /bárgər/, **Warren Earl** 1907–95; Chief Justice of the U.S. (1969–86).

Burke /bərk/, **Edmund** 1729–97; British author and politician.

Bur·nett /bərnét, bárnət/, **Frances (Eliza) Hodgson** 1849–1924; U.S. novelist, born in England.

Burns /bərnz/, **George** 1895–1996; U.S. entertainer.

Burns, **Robert** 1759–96; Scottish poet.

Burn·side /bárnsīd/, **Ambrose Everett** 1824–81; Union general in the American Civil War.

Burr /bər/, **Aaron** 1756–1836; vice president of the U.S. (1801–05).

Bur·roughs /bárōz/, **Edgar Rice** 1875–1950; U.S. author.

Bur·ton /bárt'n/, **Richard** (born **Richard Jenkins**) 1925–84; Welsh actor.

Bur·ton, **(Sir) Richard Francis** 1821–90; English explorer and anthropologist.

Bush /boósh/, **George Herbert Walker** 1924– ; 41st president of the U.S. (1989–93).

But·ler /bútlər/, **Samuel** 1612–80; English poet.

But·ler, **Samuel** 1835–1902; English novelist.

Byrd /bərd/, **Richard Evelyn** 1888–1957; U.S. polar explorer.

By·ron /bírən/, **(Lord) George Gordon** 1788–1824; English poet.

Cab·ot /kábət/, **John** (Italian name **Giovanni Caboto**) 1425–c. 1498; Italian explorer.

Ca·bri·ni /kəbreénee/, **St. Frances Xavier** (called **"Mother Cabrini"**) 1850–1917; U.S. nun, born in Italy.

Cad·il·lac /kád'l-ak, kaadeeyaák/, **Antoine de la Mothe** c. 1656–1730; French explorer.

Cae·sar /seézər/, **(Gaius) Julius** 100–44 B.C.; Roman general and statesman; assassinated.

Cag·ney /kágnee/, **James** 1904–86; U.S. actor.

Cal·der /káwldər/, **Alexander Milne** 1898–1976; U.S. sculptor, born in Scotland.

Cal·houn /kalhoón/, **John C(aldwell)** 1782–1850; U.S. politician.

Ca·lig·u·la /kəlígyələ/ (born **Gaius Caesar**) 12–41; Roman emperor (37–41).

Cal·las /káləs, kaál–/, **Maria** (born **Maria Anna Sofia Cecilia Kalogeropoulos**) 1923–77; U.S. operatic soprano.

Cal·vert /kálvərt/ family of English colonial administrators of Maryland, including: **1** (Lord) George (**1st Baron Baltimore**) c. 1580–1632; father of: **2** Cecilius (**2nd Baron Baltimore**) 1605–75; established Maryland colony; **3** Leonard 1606–47; and **4** Charles (**3rd Baron Baltimore**) 1637–1715; son of Cecilius Calvert.

Cal·vin /kálvən/, **John** 1509–64; French Protestant theologian.

Ca·mus /kamőő, kaamý/, **Albert** 1913–60; French author.

Ca·na·let·to /kan'létō/ (born **Giovanni Antonio Canale**) 1697–1768; Italian artist.

Ca·no·va /kənōvə/, **Antonio** 1757–1822; Italian sculptor.

Ca·nute /kənőőt, –nyőőt/ (also **Cnut; Knut**) died 1035; Danish king of England (1017–35), Denmark (1018–35), and Norway (1028–35).

Ca·pet /kaapáy, káypət/, **Hugh (Hugo)** 938–996; king of France (987–996).

Ca·pone /kəpōn/, **Al(phonse)** (called **"Scarface"**) 1899–1947; U.S. gangster, born in Italy.

Ca·po·te /kəpōtee/, **Truman** 1924–84; U.S. author.

Ca·ra·vag·gio /kaarəvaàjō, –jeeō/, **Michelangelo Merisi da** 1573–1610; Italian artist.

Car·lyle /kaarlíl, kaár–/, **Thomas** 1795–1881; Scottish historian and political philosopher.

Car·mi·chael /kaármikəl/, **Hoagy (Hoagland Howard)** 1899–1981; U.S. jazz pianist, singer, and composer.

Car·ne·gie /kaárnəgee, kaarnégee/, **Andrew** 1835–1919; U.S. industrialist and philanthropist, born in Scotland.

Car·o·lus Mag·nus /kárələs mágnəs/ see CHARLEMAGNE.

Car·rac·ci /kaaraáchee/ family of Italian artists, including: **1** Ludovico 1555–1619; cousin of two brothers: **2** Agostino 1557–1602; and **3** Annibale 1560–1609.

Car·re·ras /kəréraas/, **José** 1946– ; Spanish operatic tenor.

Car·roll /kárəl/, **Lewis** (pseudonym of **Charles Lutwidge Dodgson**) 1832–98; English author and logician.

Car·son /kaársən/, **Kit (Christopher)** 1809–68; U.S. frontiersman.

Car·son, **Rachel Louise** 1907–64; U.S. zoologist and ecologist.

Car·ter /kaártər/, **Jimmy (James Earl)** 1924– ; 39th president of the U.S. (1977–81).

Car·tier /kaartyáy, kaártee–ay/, **Jacques** 1491–1557; French explorer.

Ca·ru·so /kərőősō, –zō/, **Enrico** 1873–1921; Italian operatic tenor.

Car·ver /kaárvər/, **George Washington** 1864–1943; U.S. botanist and educator.

Ca·sals /kəsaálz/, **Pablo** 1876–1973; Spanish cellist and composer.

Cas·a·no·va /kasənōvə, kaz–/, **Giovanni Jacopo** 1725–98; Italian adventurer.

Cash /kash/, **Johnny** 1932– ; U.S. country music singer and songwriter.

Cas·satt /kəsát/, **Mary Stevenson** 1845–1926; U.S. artist.

Cas·sius /káshəs/, **Gaius** died 42 B.C.; Roman general; an assassin of Julius Caesar.

Cas·tro /kástrō/, **Fidel** 1927– ; Cuban revolutionary; president of Cuba (1976–).

Cath·er /káthər/, **Willa Sibert** 1876–1974; U.S. novelist.

Cath·er·ine II /káthərən, káthrən/ (called **"the Great"**) 1729–96; empress of Russia (1762–96), born in Germany.

Ca·the·rine de Méd·i·cis /maydeeséés, méd–/ (Italian name **Ca·te·ri·na de' Med·i·ci** /kaatayreénaa də médəchee, mədeéchee/) 1519–89; queen of Henry II of France, born in Florence.

Cath·er·ine of Ar·a·gon /áirəgon/ 1485–1536; 1st wife of Henry VIII; mother of Mary I.

Ca·to /káytō/, **Marcus Porcius** (called **"the Elder"** and **"the Censor"**) 234–149 B.C.; Roman statesman, orator, and author.

Catt /kat/, **Carrie Chapman Lane** 1859–1947; U.S. suffragist.

Ca·tul·lus /kətúləs/, **Gaius Valerius** c. 84–c. 54 B.C.; Roman poet.

Ca·vour /kəvőőr/, **Camillo Benso** 1810–61; Italian statesman.

Ceau·ses·cu /chowshéshkőő/, **Nicolae** 1918–89; president of Romania (1967–89); executed.

Cel·li·ni /chəleénee/, **Benvenuto** 1500–71; Italian artisan.

Cer·van·tes /sərvánteez, servaántays/ (**Saa·ve'dra**), **Miguel de** 1547–1616; Spanish author.

Cé·zanne /sayzáan/, **Paul** 1839–1906; French artist.

Cha·gall /shəgaál/, **Marc** 1887–1985; French artist, born in Russia.

Chal·lans /chálənz/ **Mary** see RENAULT, MARY.

Cham·ber·lain /cháymbərlən/, **(Arthur) Neville** 1869–1940; prime minister of Great Britain (1937–40).

Cham·plain /shampláyn/, **Samuel de** 1567–1635; French explorer and colonial statesman in Canada.

Chan·dler /chándlər/, **Raymond Thornton** 1888–1959; U.S. novelist.

Cha·nel /shənél/, **Coco (Gabrielle Bonheur)** 1883–1971; French fashion designer.

Chap·lin /cháplən/, **Charlie (Sir Charles Spencer)** 1889–1977; English film actor and director.

Char·le·magne /shaárləmayn/, (called **Carolus Magnus** or **Charles the Great**) 742–814; king of the Franks (768–814); Holy Roman Emperor (800–814).

Charles[1] /chaarlz/ name of two British kings: **1** Charles I 1600–49; reigned 1625–49. **2** Charles II 1630–85; reigned 1660–85.

Charles[2] name of four kings of Spain, including: **1** Charles I 1500–58; reigned 1516–56; (as **Charles V**) Holy Roman Emperor (1519–56). **2** Charles II 1661–1700; reigned 1665–1700.

Charles **(Prince of Wales)** 1948– ; heir apparent to the throne of the United Kingdom.

Charles Mar·tel /maartél/ c. 688–741; ruler of the Franks (714–741).

Chase /chays/, **Salmon P(ortland)** 1808–73; Chief Justice of the U.S. (1864–73).

Cha·teau·bri·and /shaatōbree–aáN/, **François-René (Vicomte de)** 1768–1848; French author and diplomat.

Chau·cer /cháwsər/, **Geoffrey** c. 1342–1400; English poet.

Chee·ver /cheévər/, **John** 1912–82; U.S. author.

Che·khov /chékawf, –awv/, **Anton Pavlovich** 1860–1904; Russian author.

Che·ops /keéaaps/ (also **Khu'fu**) fl. early 26th cent. B.C.; Egyptian king; built the pyramid at Giza.

Ches·ter·ton /chéstərtən/, **G(ilbert) K(eith)** 1874–1936; English author and critic.

Chiang Kai-shek /cháng kíshék/ 1887–1975; president of China (1928–31; 1943–49) and Taiwan (1950–75).

Chi·rac /shiraák, –rák/, **Jacques** 1932– ; prime minister (1974–76; 1986–88) and president (1995–) of France.

Chi·ri·co /keérikō, kír–/, **Giorgio de** 1888–1978; Italian artist, born in Greece.

Chom·sky /chaámskee/, **(Avram) Noam** 1928– ; U.S. linguist.

Cho·pin /shōpan, shōpáN/, **Frédéric François** 1810–49; French composer, born in Poland.

Chou En-lai /jō énlí/ (also **Zhou En-lai'**) 1898–1976; Chinese political leader.

Chré·tien de Troyes /kraytyáN də trwaá/ 12th cent.; French poet.

Chris·tie /krístee/, **(Dame) Agatha Mary Clarissa Miller** 1890–1976; English author.

Church /chərch/, **Frederick Edwin** 1826–1900; U.S. artist.

Church·ill /chérchil/, **John (1st Duke of Marlborough)** 1650–1722; British military commander.

Church·ill, **(Sir) Winston Leonard Spencer** 1874–1965; British statesman; prime minister of Great Britain (1940–45; 1951–55).

Cic·e·ro /sísərō/, **Marcus Tullius** 106–43 B.C.; Roman statesman and author.

Cid /sid/, **El** (born **Rodrigo Diaz de Vivar**) c. 1043–99; Spanish military hero.

Clap·ton /kláptən/, **Eric** 1945– ; British guitarist and composer.

Clark /klaark/, **1 George Rogers** 1752–1818; U.S. frontiersman and soldier; brother of: **2** William 1770–1838; U.S. explorer (with Meriwether Lewis) of the North American continent (1804–06).

Clarke /klaark/, **Arthur C(harles)** 1917– ; English science-fiction author.

Claude Lor·rain /klōd lawrén/ (born **Claude Gellée**) 1600–82; French landscape artist.

Clau·di·us /kláwdeeəs/ 10 B.C.–A.D. 54; Roman emperor (41–54).

Clau·se·witz /klówzəvits/, **Karl von** 1780–1831; Prussian military theorist.

Cla·vell /kləvél/, **James** 1924–94; U.S. author.

Clay /klay/, **Henry** 1777–1852; U.S. politician.

Clay, **Cassius** see ALI, MUHAMMAD.

Cle·men·ceau /klemənső/, **Georges Eugène Benjamin** 1841–1929; French political leader.

Clem·ens /klémənz/, **Samuel Langhorne** see TWAIN, MARK.

Cle·o·pat·ra /kleeōpátrə/ **(Cleopatra VII)** 69–30 B.C.; queen of Egypt (47–30 B.C.).

Cleve·land /kleévlənd/, **(Stephen) Grover** 1837–1908; 22nd and 24th president of the U.S. (1885–89; 1893–97).

Clin·ton /klínt'n/, **1** Bill (William Jefferson) 1946– ; 42nd president of the U.S. (1993–); husband of: **2** Hillary Rodham 1947– ; U.S. lawyer.

Clin·ton, DeWitt 1769–1828; governor of New York (1817–23; 1825–28); promoter of the Erie Canal.

Clo·vis /klóvəs/ 465–511; king of the Franks (481–511).

Cnut /kənoŏt, –nyoŏt/ see CANUTE.

Co·chise /kōcheés/ c. 1812–74; Apache Indian chief.

Coc·teau /kaaktó/, **Jean** 1889–1963; French playwright and film director.

Co·dy /kódee/, **William Frederick** (called "Buffalo Bill") 1846–1917; U.S. army scout and showman.

Co·han /kóhan/, **George M(ichael)** 1878–1942; U.S. songwriter and theatrical producer.

Cole /cōl/, **Nat King** (born Nathaniel Adams Coles) 1919–65; U.S. popular singer and pianist.

Cole, Thomas 1801–48; U.S. artist.

Cole·ridge /kólrij, kólərij/, **Samuel Taylor** 1772–1834; English poet, critic, and philosopher.

Co·lette /kəlét/ (born **Sidonie Gabrielle Claudine Colette**) 1873–1954; French novelist.

Colt /kōlt/, **Samuel** 1814–62; U.S. inventor; patented the Colt revolver (1836).

Co·lum·ba /kəlúmbə/, **St.** c. 521–597; Irish abbot and missionary.

Co·lum·bus /kəlúmbəs/, **Christopher** 1451–1506; Spanish explorer, born in Italy; initiated colonization of America by Europeans (1492).

Comte /kōNt/, **Auguste** 1798–1857; French philosopher.

Con·fu·cius /kənfyóoshəs/ (also **K'ung Fu-tzu**) 551–479 B.C.; Chinese philosopher. □□ **Con·fu′cian** *adj.*

Con·greve /kaán-greev, kaáng–/, **William** 1670–1729; English playwright.

Con·ner·y /kaánəree/, **Sean** (born **Thomas Connery**) 1930– ; Scottish actor.

Con·rad /kaánrad/, **Joseph** 1857–1924; British novelist, born in Poland.

Con·sta·ble /kaánstəbəl/, **John** 1776–1837; English artist.

Con·stan·tine /kaánstənteen, –tīn/ (called "the Great") c. 274–337; Roman emperor (306–337); adopted and sanctioned Christianity.

Cook /kook/, **(Captain) James** 1728–79; English explorer of the Pacific.

Cool·idge /koólij/, **(John) Calvin** 1872–1933; 30th president of the U.S. (1923–29).

Coop·er /koópər, koópər/, **James Fenimore** 1789–1851; U.S. novelist.

Co·per·ni·cus /kəpérnikəs/, **Nicolaus** 1473–1543; Polish astronomer; set forth the heliocentric theory of the solar system.

Cop·land /kóplənd/, **Aaron** 1900–90; U.S. composer.

Cop·ley /kaáplee/, **John Singleton** 1738–1815; U.S. artist.

Cor·day d'Ar·mont /kawrdáy daarmóN/, **(Marie-Anne) Charlotte** 1768–93; French patriot and political assassin.

Cor·i·o·la·nus /kawreeəláynəs/, **Gaius** (or **Gnaeus**) **Marcius** 6th cent.–5th cent. B.C.; legendary Roman general.

Cor·neille /kawrnáy/, **Pierre** 1606–84; French playwright.

Corn·wal·lis /kawrnwáwləs/, **Charles (1st Marquis)** 1738–1805; British general; surrendered at Yorktown (1781), ending American Revolutionary War.

Co·ro·na·do /kawrənaádō/, **Francisco Vásquez de** 1510–54; Spanish explorer in North America.

Co·rot /kawró/, **(Jean-Baptiste) Camille** 1796–1875; French artist.

Cor·reg·gio /kəréjō, –jeeō/, **Antonio Allegri da** c. 1489–1534; Italian artist.

Cor·tés /kawrtéz, kawrtés/ (also **Cor·tez′**), **Hernando** 1485–1547; Spanish conquistador; conqueror of Mexico.

Cos·by /kózbee/, **Bill (William Henry)** 1937– ; U.S. entertainer.

Cou·pe·rin /koóp(ə)ráN/, **François** 1668–1733; French composer.

Cow·ard /kówərd/, **(Sir) Noel Peirce** 1899–1973; English playwright, actor, and composer.

Cow·per /koópər, ków–/, **William** 1731–1800; English poet.

Crane /krayn/, **Stephen** 1871–1900; U.S. author.

Cran·mer /kránmər/, **Thomas** 1489–1556; English leader of Protestant Reformation.

Cras·sus /krásəs/, **Marcus Licinius** c. 115–53 B.C.; Roman politician; financier of First Triumvirate.

Cra·zy Horse /kráyzee hawrs/ c. 1849–77; Sioux chief of Oglala tribe; led Sioux uprising (1876–77).

Crick /krik/, **Francis Harry Compton** 1916– ; English biophysicist.

Crock·ett /kraákit/, **Davy (David)** 1786–1836; U.S. frontiersman.

Croe·sus /kreésəs/ died 546 B.C.; Lydian king of legendary wealth.

Crom·well /kraámwel, –wəl/, **Oliver** 1599–1658; English soldier and political leader.

Cro·nin /krónən/, **A(rchibald) J(oseph)** 1896–1981; Scottish novelist.

Cron·kite /krónkīt/, **Walter Leland, Jr.** 1916– ; U.S. broadcast journalist.

Cum·mings /kúmingz/, **Edward Estlin** (known as "e e cummings") 1894–1962; U.S. poet.

Cu·rie /kyooreé, kyoóree/ two French physicists and chemists: **1** Pierre 1859–1906; codiscovered radium and polonium with his wife: **2** Marie (born **Maria Sklowdowska**) 1867–1934; born in Poland.

Cur·tiss /kártəs/, **Glenn Hammond** 1878–1930; U.S. inventor and aviation pioneer.

Cus·ter /kústər/, **George Armstrong** 1839–76; U.S. cavalry commander.

Cym·be·line /símbəleen/ died c. 42; British chieftain of Catuvellauni tribe.

Cyr·a·no de Ber·ge·rac /seérənō də bérzhərak/, **Savinien de** 1619–55; French soldier and author.

Cyr·il /seérəl/, **St.** (called "the Apostle of the Slavs") 826–869; Greek missionary; inventor of the Cyrillic alphabet.

Cy·rus the Great /sírəs/ died 529 B.C.; king of Persia (559–529 B.C.).

Dahl /daal/, **Roald** 1916–90; British author.

Da·lai La·ma /daáli laamə, –lee/ title of the leader of Tibetan Buddhism.

Da·li /daálee/, **Salvador** 1904–89; Spanish surrealist artist.

Da·na /dáynə/, **Richard Henry** 1815–82; U.S. adventurer, author, and lawyer.

d'An·nun·zio /daanoóntsee-ō/, **Gabriele** 1863–1938; Italian novelist, playwright, and poet.

Dan·te /daántay, dántee/ (surname **Alighieri**) 1265–1321; Italian poet.

Dan·ton /daaNtóN/, **Georges-Jacques** 1759–94; French revolutionary leader.

Dare /dar, der/, **Virginia** 1587–?; first child born in W hemisphere of European parents.

Da·ri·us I /dəríəs/ (called "the Great") c. 550–486 B.C.; king of Persia (521–486 B.C.).

Dar·row /dáró/, **Clarence Seward** 1857–1938; U.S. lawyer.

Dar·win /daárwin/, **Charles Robert** 1809–82; English naturalist; promulgated theory of evolution.

Dau·det /dōdáy/, **Alphonse** 1840–97; French author.

Dau·mier /dōmyáy/, **Honoré** 1808–78; French artist.

Da·vid /dáyvid/ died c. 970 B.C.; biblical king of Israel.

Da·vid /daaveéd/, **Jacques-Louis** 1748–1825; French artist.

da Vin·ci, Leonardo see LEONARDO DA VINCI.

Da·vis /dáyvəs/, **Jefferson** 1808–89; president of the Confederate States of America (1861–65).

Da·yan /dī-aán, daa-yaán/, **Moshe** 1915–81; Israeli politician and military commander.

de Beau·voir /də bōvwaár/, **Simone** 1908–86; French playwright and novelist.

Debs /debz/, **Eugene Victor** 1855–1926; U.S. labor leader.

De·bus·sy /debyoóseé, dáybyoō–/, **(Achille) Claude** 1862–1918; French composer.

de Fal·la, Manuel see FALLA, MANUEL DE.

De·foe /difó/, **Daniel** 1660–1731; English novelist and journalist.

De·gas /daygaá/, **(Hilaire-Germain) Edgar** 1834–1917; French artist.

de Gaulle /də gól, gáwl/, **Charles André Joseph Marie** 1890–1970; French general and statesman.

de Klerk /də klérk, klárk/, **F(rederik) W(illem)** 1936– ; president of South Africa (1989–94).

de Koo·ning /də kŏŏning/, **Willem** 1904–97; U.S. artist, born in the Netherlands.

De·la·croix /deləkrwaá/, **(Ferdinand Victor) Eugène** 1798–1863; French artist.

de la Mare /del ə már, mér/, **Walter John** 1873–1956; English poet and novelist.

De·li·us /deéleeəs/, **Frederick Theodore Albert** 1862–1934; English composer.

De·moc·ri·tus /dimaákrətəs/ c. 460–c. 370 B.C.; Greek philosopher.

De·mos·the·nes /dimaásthəneez/ 384–322 B.C.; Athenian orator and statesman.

Demp·sey /démpsee/, **Jack (William Harrison)** (called "**the Manassa Mauler**") 1895–1983; U.S. boxer.

Deng Xiao·ping /dúng shówping/ (also **Teng Hsiao-p'ing**) 1904–97; Chinese political leader.

De Quin·cey /də kwínsee/, **Thomas** 1785–1859; English essayist and critic.

de Sade /də saád/, **Marquis** see SADE, DONATIEN.

Des·cartes /daykaárt/, **René** 1596–1650; French philosopher and mathematician.

de So·to /də sŏ́tō/, **Hernando** 1496–1542; Spanish explorer in Central and North America.

De Va·le·ra /devəlérə, –lírə/, **Eamon** 1882–1975; Irish political leader, born in U.S.

Dew·ey /dŏ́oee, d(y)ŏ́o–/, **John** 1859–1952; U.S. philosopher and educator.

Dew·ey, **Melvil** 1851–1931; U.S. librarian; developed decimal system for book classification (1876).

Di·a·ghi·lev /dee-aágəlef/, **Sergei Pavlovich** 1872–1929; Russian ballet impresario.

Di·an·a /diánə/ **(Princess of Wales)** (born **Diana Frances Spencer**) 1961–97; divorced wife of Charles, Prince of Wales.

Di·as /deéəs, deéaash/ (also **Di'az**), **Bartolomeu** c. 1450–1500; Portuguese explorer.

Dick·ens /díkənz/, **Charles John Huffam** 1812–70; English novelist.

Dick·in·son /díkinsən/, **Emily Elizabeth** 1830–86; U.S. poet.

Di·de·rot /deédərō/, **Denis** 1713–84; French philosopher, encyclopedist, and critic.

Di·Mag·gi·o /dimájeeō/, **Joe (Joseph Paul)** 1914–99; U.S. baseball player.

Di·o·cle·tian /dīəkleéshən/ 245–313; Roman emperor (284–305).

Di·og·e·nes /dī-aájəneez/ c. 400–c. 325 B.C.; Greek philosopher.

Di·o·ny·si·us I /dīənísheeəs, –níseeəs/ (called "**the Elder**") c. 430–367 B.C.; tyrant of Syracuse.

Dis·ney /díznee/, **Walt (Walter Elias)** 1901–66; U.S. animator, film producer, and theme-park creator.

Dis·rae·li /dizráylee/, **Benjamin (1st Earl of Beaconsfield)** 1804–81; prime minister of Great Britain (1868; 1874–80).

Dodg·son /daájsən/, **Charles Lutwidge** see CARROLL, LEWIS.

Dole /dōl/ **1 Robert Joseph** 1923– ; U.S. politician; husband of: **2 Elizabeth Hanford** 1936– ; U.S. public official.

Do·min·go /dəming-gō/, **Placido** 1941– ; Spanish operatic tenor.

Dom·i·nic /daáminik/, **St.** c. 1170–1221; Spanish cleric; founder of Dominican religious order.

Do·mi·tian /dəmíshən/ 51–96; Roman emperor (81–96).

Don·a·tel·lo /daanətélō/ (born **Donato de Betto di Bardi**) 1386–1466; Italian sculptor.

Don·i·zet·ti /donizétee, dōnə(d)zétee/, **Gaetano** 1797–1848; Italian composer.

Donne /dún/, **John** 1572–1631; English poet and priest.

Dos Pas·sos /dəs pásəs/, **John** 1896–1970; U.S. novelist.

Do·sto·ev·sky /daastəyéfskee, –yév–/ (also **Do·sto·yev·sky**), **Fyodor Mikhailovich** 1821–81; Russian author.

Doug·las /dúgləs/, **Stephen A(rnold)** 1813–61; U.S. political leader and orator.

Doug·lass /dúgləs/, **Frederick** (born **Frederick Augustus Washington Bailey**) c. 1817–95; U.S. abolitionist, author, and orator.

Doyle /doyl/, **(Sir) Arthur Conan** 1859–1930; Scottish author.

Dra·co /dráykō/ 7th cent. B.C.; Athenian lawgiver.

Drake /drayk/, **(Sir) Francis** c. 1540–96; English explorer; circumnavigated the world (1577–80).

Drei·ser /drízər/, **Theodore** 1871–1945; U.S. novelist.

Drey·fus /drífəs/, **Alfred** 1859–1935; French army officer; falsely convicted of treason.

Dry·den /dríd'n/, **John** 1631–1700; English poet.

Dub·ček /dŏŏbchek/, **Alexander** 1921–92; Czech political leader.

Du Bois /dŏŏ bóys/, **W(illiam) E(dward) B(urghardt)** 1868–1963; U.S. sociologist and educator.

Du·champ /dy shaáN/, **Marcel** 1887–1968; U.S. artist, born in France.

Du·de·vant /dŏŏdəvaaN/, **Amandine-Aurore-Lucile Dupin** see SAND, GEORGE.

Du·fy /dyfeé/, **Raoul** 1877–1953; French artist.

Dul·les /dúləs/, **John Foster** 1888–1959; U.S. secretary of state (1953–59).

Dumas /d(y)ŏŏmaá/ two French playwrights and novelists: **1** Alexandre (called "**Dumas père**") 1802–70; father of: **2** Alexandre (called "**Dumas fils**") 1824–95.

Du Mau·ri·er /də máwree-ay, dyŏŏ–/, two English literary figures: **1** George Louis Palmella Busson 1834–96; novelist and illustrator, born in France; grandfather of: **2** (Dame) Daphne 1907–89; novelist.

Dun·can /dúngkən/, **Isadora** 1878–1927; U.S. dancer.

Duns Sco·tus /duns skŏ́təs/, **John** c. 1265–1308; Scottish theologian.

du Pont /dŏŏpónt/, **Eleuthère Irénée** 1771–1834; U.S. industrialist, born in France.

Du·rant /dəránt/ two U.S. historians: **1** Will(iam James) 1885–1981; husband of: **2** Ariel (born **Ida Kaufman**) 1898–1981.

Dü·rer /dŏŏrər, dyŏŏ–/, **Albrecht** 1471–1528; German artist.

Durey /dyré/, **Louis-Edmond** 1888–1979; French composer.

Durk·heim /dyrkém, dárkhīm/, **Émile** 1858–1917; French sociologist.

Du·va·lier /dŏŏvaalyáy/, **François** (called "**Papa Doc**") 1907–71; president of Haiti (1957–71).

Dvo·řák /dváwrzhaak/, **Antonin Leopold** 1841–1904; Czech composer.

Dyl·an /dílən/, **Bob** (born **Robert Allen Zimmerman**) 1941– ; U.S. folk-rock singer and songwriter.

Ear·hart /érhaart, eér–/, **Amelia Mary** 1898–1937?; U.S. aviator.

East·man /eéstmən/, **George** 1854–1932; U.S. inventor and philanthropist; invented Kodak box camera (1888).

Eco /ékō/, **Umberto** 1932– ; Italian novelist and scholar.

Ed·dy /édee/, **Mary (Morse) Baker** 1821–1910; U.S. founder of the Christian Science Church.

E·den /eéd'n/, **(Sir) (Robert) Anthony** 1897–1977; prime minister of Great Britain (1955–57).

Ed·i·son /édisən/, **Thomas Alva** 1847–1931; U.S. inventor.

Ed·ward /édwərd/ name of eight British kings, including: **1** Edward I 1239–1307; reigned 1272–1307. **2** Edward VII 1841–1910; eldest son of Queen Victoria; reigned 1901–10. **3** Edward VIII 1894–1972; reigned 1936; abdicated, became Duke of Windsor.

Ed·wards /édwərdz/, **Jonathan** 1703–58; American theologian and clergyman.

Eich·mann /íkmən, íkhmaan/, **(Karl) Adolf** 1906–62; German Nazi officer; executed as a war criminal.

Eif·fel /ífəl/, **Alexandre Gustave** 1832–1923; French engineer; designer of the Eiffel Tower.

Ein·stein /ínstīn/, **Albert** 1879–1955; U.S. physicist, born in Germany; promulgated theory of relativity.

Ei·sen·how·er /ízənhowər/, **Dwight David** (called "**Ike**") 1890–1969; U.S. general and 34th president of the U.S. (1953–61).

Ei·sen·staedt /ízənstat/, **Alfred** 1898–1995; U.S. photojournalist, born in Germany.

El Cid see CID, EL.

El·ea·nor /élənər, –nawr/ **of Aq·ui·taine** /ákwitayn/ c. 1122–1204; queen of France (1137–52) and England (1154–89).

El·gar /élgaar, –gər/, **(Sir) Edward William** 1857–1934; English composer.

El Gre·co see GRECO, EL.

E·li·a /eéleeə/ see LAMB, CHARLES.

El·i·ot /éleeət/, **George** (pseudonym of **Mary Ann Evans**) 1819–80; English novelist.

El·i·ot, **T(homas) S(tearns)** 1888–1965; British poet and critic, born in U.S.

E·liz·a·beth /ilízəbəth/ name of two British monarchs: **1** Elizabeth I 1533–1603; reigned 1558–1603; **2** Elizabeth II 1926– ; reigned 1952– .

El·ling·ton /élingtən/, **Duke (Edward Kennedy)** 1899–1974; U.S. jazz pianist, bandleader, and composer.

El·lis /éləs/, **(Henry) Havelock** 1859–1939; English psychologist.

Em·er·son /émərsən/, **Ralph Waldo** 1803–82; U.S. essayist and poet.

Em·ped·o·cles /empédəkleez/ c. 493–c. 433 B.C.; Greek philosopher.

En·gels /éng-gəlz/, **Friedrich** 1820–95; German political philosopher in England.

En·ni·us /éneeəs/, **Quintus** 239–169 B.C.; Roman poet and playwright.

En·ver Pa·sha /énver paáshə, pəshaá/ 1881–1922; Turkish statesman and military leader.

E·pi·cu·rus /epikyōórəs/ 341–270 B.C.; Greek philosopher.

E·ras·mus /irázməs/, **Desiderius** c. 1469–1536; Dutch theologian and humanist.

Er·ic /érik/ (called **"the Red"**) c. 940–c. 1010; Norse explorer.

Er·ic·son /ériksən/ (also **Er′ics·son**; **Er′iks·son**), **Leif** early 11th cent.; Norse explorer.

Ernst /ernst/, **Max** 1891–1976; German artist.

Eth·el·red II /éthəlred/, (called **"the Unready"**) c. 969–1016; king of England (978–1016).

Eu·clid /yōóklid/ 3rd cent. B.C.; Greek mathematician.

Eu·gé·nie /yōōjənee, yōōjáynee/ 1826–1920; empress of France (1853–71), born in Spain; wife of Napoleon III.

Eu·rip·i·des /yōōrípideez/ 480–c. 406 B.C.; Greek playwright.

Ev·ans /évənz/, **(Sir) Arthur John** 1851–1941; British archaeologist.

Ev·ans, (Dame) Edith 1888–1976; English actress.

Ev·ans, Mary Ann see ELIOT, GEORGE.

Fa·ber·gé /fabərzháy/, **Peter Carl** 1846–1920; Russian goldsmith and jeweler.

Fahd /faad/ 1922– ; king of Saudi Arabia (1982–).

Fair·field /fáirfeeld/, **Cicily Isabel** see WEST, REBECCA.

Fal·la /faáyə/, **Manuel de** 1876–1946; Spanish composer.

Far·a·day /fárədee, –day/, **Michael** 1791–1867; British chemist and physicist.

Fa·rouk /fərōók/ 1920–65; king of Egypt (1936–52).

Far·ra·gut /fárəgət/, **David Glasgow** (born **James Glasgow Farragut**) 1801–70; U.S. naval commander.

Faulk·ner /fáwknər/, **William Cuthbert** 1897–1962; U.S. novelist.

Fau·ré /fawráy/, **Gabriel** 1845–1924; French composer.

Faust /fowst/ (also **Faus·tus**) died c. 1540; German astronomer and necromancer.

Fer·ber /főrbər/, **Edna** 1885–1968; U.S. author.

Fer·di·nand II /főrd'nand/ (called **"the Catholic"**) 1452–1516; W European king who founded the Spanish monarchy; husband of Isabella I.

Fer·mi /férmee/, **Enrico** 1901–54; U.S. nuclear physicist, born in Italy.

Fied·ler /féedlər/, **Arthur** 1894–1979; U.S. conductor.

Field·ing /féelding/, **Henry** 1707–54; English novelist.

Fields /feeldz/, **W. C.** (born **William Claude Dukenfield**) 1880–1946; U.S. vaudevillian and comedic actor.

Fill·more /fílmawr, –mōr/, **Millard** 1800–74; 13th president of the U.S. (1850–53).

Fitz·ger·ald /fitsjérəld/, **Ella** 1918–96; U.S. jazz singer.

Fitz·ger·ald, F(rancis) Scott Key 1896–1940; U.S. author.

Flau·bert /flōbér/, **Gustave** 1821–80; French author.

Flem·ing /fléming/, **(Sir) Alexander** 1881–1955; Scottish bacteriologist; discovered and developed penicillin.

Flem·ing, Ian Lancaster 1908–64; English novelist.

Fletch·er /fléchər/, **John** 1579–1625; English playwright.

Foch /fawsh/, **Ferdinand** 1851–1929; French general.

Fon·da /faándə/ family of U.S. actors, including: **1 Henry** 1905–82; father of: **2 Jane** 1937– .

Fon·teyn /faantáyn/, **(Dame) Margot** (born **Margaret Hookham**) 1919–91; English prima ballerina.

Ford /fawrd/, **Ford Madox** (born **Ford Hermann Hueffer**) 1873–1939; English novelist.

Ford, Gerald Rudolph, Jr. (born **Leslie Lynch King, Jr.**) 1913– ; 38th president of the U.S. (1974–77).

Ford, Henry 1863–1947; U.S. automobile manufacturer.

For·ster /fáwrstər/, **E(dward) M(organ)** 1879–1970; English novelist.

For·syth /fáwrsīth, fawrsíth/, **Frederick** 1938– ; English novelist.

Fos·ter /fáwstər, faástər/, **Stephen Collins** 1826–64; U.S. songwriter.

Fou·cault /fōōkó/, **Michel** 1929–84; French philosopher.

Fowles /fowlz/, **John** 1926– ; English novelist.

Fox /faaks/, **George** 1624–91; English founder of the Society of Friends (Quakers).

Fra·go·nard /fragənaár/, **Jean-Honoré** 1732–1806; French artist.

France /frans/, **Anatole** (pseudonym of **Jacques Anatole Thibault**) 1844–1924; French author.

Fran·cis /fránsis/ **of As·si·si** /əsísee, əseézee/, **St.** c. 1181–1226; Italian monk; founder of Franciscan religious order.

Franck /fraangk/, **César** 1822–90; French composer, born in Belgium.

Fran·co /frángkō, fraáng–/, **Francisco** 1892–1975; Spanish general; dictator of Spain (1939–75).

Frank /frangk/, **Anne** 1929–45; Jewish diarist, born in Germany; wrote diary while in hiding from the Nazis.

Frank·furt·er /frángkfərtər/, **Felix** 1882–1965; U.S. Supreme Court justice (1939–62), born in Austria.

Frank·lin /frángklən/, **Aretha** 1943– ; U.S. soul and gospel singer.

Frank·lin, Benjamin 1706–90; U.S. statesman, author, and inventor.

Franz Jo·sef I /fraanz yőzəf/ 1830–1916; emperor of Austria (1848–1916).

Fra·zer /fráyzər/, **(Sir) James George** 1854–1941; Scottish anthropologist.

Fred·er·ick I /fréd(ə)rik/ (called **"Barbarossa"**) c. 1123–90; Holy Roman emperor (1152–90).

Fred·er·ick II (called **"the Great"**) 1712–86; king of Prussia (1740–86).

Fred·er·ick Wil·liam /wílyəm/ (called **"the Great Elector"**) 1620–88; elector of Brandenburg (1640–88).

Fré·mont /fréemaant/, **John Charles** 1813–90; U.S. explorer and politician.

Freud /froyd/, **Lucian** 1922– ; British artist, born in Germany.

Freud, Sigmund 1856–1939; Austrian neurologist; founder of psychoanalysis.

Frie·dan /freedán/, **Betty** (born **Naomi Goldstein**) 1921– ; U.S. feminist and author.

Fried·man /fréedmən/, **Milton** 1912– ; U.S. economist.

Frost /frawst/, **Robert Lee** 1874–1963; U.S. poet.

Frye /frī/, **(Herman) Northrop** 1912–91; Canadian literary critic.

Fu·ad /fōō-aád/ two kings of Egypt: **1** Fuad I 1868–1936; reigned 1922–36. **2** Fuad II 1952– ; reigned 1952–53.

Fuen·tes /fwéntays/, **Carlos** 1928– ; Mexican author.

Ful·bright /fōōlbrīt/, **(James) William** 1905–95; U.S. senator.

Ful·ler /fōōlər/, **R(ichard) Buckminster** 1895–1983; U.S. engineer and architect.

Ful·ler, (Sarah) Margaret 1810–50; U.S. critic and social reformer.

Ful·ton /fōōlt'n/, **Robert** 1765–1815; U.S. engineer; developed first commercially successful steamboat.

Ga·ble /gáybəl/, **(William) Clark** 1901–60; U.S. actor.

Gad·da·fi /gədaáfee/ see QADHAFI, MUAMMAR.

Ga·ga·rin /gəgaárən/, **Yuri** 1934–68; Soviet cosmonaut; first human in space.

Gage /gayj/, **Thomas** 1721–87; British general.

Gains·bor·ough /gáynzbrō, –bərə/, **Thomas** 1727–88; English artist.

Gal·braith /gálbrayth/, **John Kenneth** 1908– ; U.S. economist, born in Canada.

Ga·len /gáylən/ c. 130–c. 201; Greek physician.

Gal·i·le·o /galəláyō, –leéō/ 1564–1642; Italian astronomer.

Gals·wor·thy /gáwlzwərthee/, **John** 1867–1933; English novelist and playwright.

Ga·ma /gaámə/, **Vasco da** c. 1469–1524; Portuguese navigator.

Gan·dhi /gaándee/ two Indian prime ministers: **1** Indira Priyadarshini Nehru 1917–84; in office 1966–77; 1980–84; assassinated; mother of: **2** Rajiv 1944–91; in office 1984–89; assassinated.

Gan·dhi, Mahatma (born **Mohandes Karamchand**) 1869–1948; Indian nationalist and spiritual leader.

Gar·bo /gaárbō/, Greta (born Greta Louisa Gustafsson) 1905–90; U.S. actress, born in Sweden.

Gar·cí·a Lor·ca /gaarseéə láwrkə/, Federico 1899–1936; Spanish poet and playwright.

Gar·cí·a Már·quez /gaarseéə maárkays/, Gabriel 1928– ; Colombian author.

Gard·ner /gaárdnər/, Erle Stanley 1899–1970; U.S. author.

Gar·field /gaárfeeld/, James Abram 1831–81; 20th president of the U.S. (1881); assassinated.

Gar·i·bal·di /garəbáwldee/, Giuseppe 1807–82; Italian nationalist.

Gar·land /gárlənd/, Judy (born Frances Gumm) 1922–69; U.S. singer and actress.

Gar·ri·son /gárəsən/, William Lloyd 1805–79; U.S. editor and abolitionist.

Gar·vey /gaárvee/, Marcus Mosiah 1887–1940; Jamaican black nationalist.

Gates /gayts/, Bill (William Henry) 1955– ; U.S. computer executive.

Gates, Horatio c. 1728–1806; American Revolutionary War general, born in England.

Gau·guin /gōgán/, (Eugène) Paul 1848–1903; French artist.

Gaulle see DE GAULLE.

Gau·ta·ma /gówtəmə, gáw–/ see BUDDHA.

Geh·rig /gérig/, Lou (Henry Louis) (called "the Iron Horse") 1903–41; U.S. baseball player.

Gei·sel /gízəl/, Theodor Seuss see SEUSS, DR.

Gen·ghis Khan /géng-gəs, jeng-gəs kaán/ c. 1162–1227; ruler of the Mongols; conquered most of Asia.

George III /jawrj/ 1738–1820; king of England (1760–1820); reigned during American Revolution.

George, St. died c. 337; patron saint of England.

Ge·ron·i·mo /jəraánəmō/ c. 1829–1909; Apache Indian leader.

Gersh·win /gérshwən/ 1 Ira 1896–1983; U.S. lyricist; brother of: 2 George 1898–1937; U.S. composer.

Get·ty /gétee/, J(ean) Paul 1892–1976; U.S. industrialist.

Gib·bon /gíbən/, Edward 1737–94; English historian.

Gib·ran /jibraán/, Kahlil 1883–1931; Lebanese author and artist.

Gide /zheed/, André 1869–1951; French author.

Giel·gud /geélgŏŏd/, (Sir) (Arthur) John 1904– ; English actor and director.

Gil·bert /gílbərt/, (Sir) W(illiam) S(chwenck) 1836–1911; English playwright and librettist; collaborated with composer (Sir) Arthur Sullivan.

Gil·les·pie /gəléspee/, Dizzy (John Birks) 1917–93; U.S. jazz musician.

Ging·rich /gíngrich/, Newt(on Leroy) 1943– ; U.S. politician.

Gins·berg /gínzbərg/, Allen 1926–97; U.S. poet.

Gins·berg, Ruth Bader 1933– ; U.S. Supreme Court justice (1993–).

Gior·gio·ne /jawrjṓnay/ c. 1478–1511; Italian artist.

Giot·to /jaátō, jee-aátō/ c. 1267–1337; Florentine artist.

Gis·card d'Es·taing /zheeskaár destáN/, Valéry 1926– ; president of France (1974–81).

Gish /gish/, Lillian 1896–1993; U.S. actress.

Glad·stone /gládstōn, –stən/, William Ewart 1809–98; prime minister of Great Britain (1868–74; 1880–85; 1886; 1892–94).

Glea·son /gleésən/, Jackie 1916–87; U.S. entertainer.

Glen·dow·er /glendówər/ (also Glyn-dwr′) /glindŏŏr/, Owen c. 1355–c. 1417; legendary Welsh rebel.

Glenn /glen/, John Herschel, Jr. 1921– ; U.S. astronaut and politician; first American to orbit the earth (1962).

God·dard /gaádərd/, Robert Hutchings 1882–1945; U.S. rocket scientist.

Go·di·va /gədívə/, Lady died 1080; legendary English noblewoman.

Go·du·nov /gŏd'n-awf, gáwd–/, Boris 1550–1605; czar of Russia (1598–1605).

Goeb·bels /gŏbəlz, gár–/, (Paul) Joseph 1897–1945; German director of Nazi propaganda.

Goe·ring /gŏring, gár–/, Hermann Wilhelm 1893–1946; German Nazi leader; directed the air force.

Goe·the /gŏtə, gár–/, Johann Wolfgang von 1749–1832; German poet and statesman.

Go·gol /gŏgawl, gáwgəl/, Nikolai Vasilievich 1809–52; Russian novelist and playwright.

Gol·ding /gólding/, (Sir) William 1911–93; English author.

Gold·smith /góldsmith/, Oliver 1728–74; Irish author.

Go·li·ath /gəlíəth/ biblical giant killed by David.

Gom·pers /gaámpərz/, Samuel 1850–1924; U.S. labor leader, born in England.

Good·man /gŏŏdmən/, Benny (Benjamin David) (called "the King of Swing") 1909–86; U.S. jazz clarinetist and bandleader.

Good·year /gŏŏdyeer/, Charles 1800–60; U.S. inventor; developed vulcanized rubber.

Gor·ba·chev /gáwrbəchawf, –chawv/, Mikhail Sergeyevich 1931– ; president of the Soviet Union (1988–91).

Gordimer /gáwrdimər/, Nadine 1923– ; South African novelist.

Gor·don /gáwrd'n/, Charles George 1833–85; British general and colonial administrator.

Gore /gawr/, Albert, Jr. 1948– ; U.S. vice president (1993–).

Gor·ky /gáwrkee/, Maxim (pseudonym of Aleksei Maksimovich Peshkov) 1868–1936; Russian author and revolutionary.

Gou·nod /gŏŏnṓ/, Charles François 1818–93; French composer.

Go·ya /góyə/, Francisco 1746–1828; Spanish artist.

Gra·ham /gráyəm, gram/, Billy (William Franklin) 1918– ; U.S. evangelical preacher.

Gra·ham, Katherine 1917– ; U.S. newspaper executive.

Gra·ham, Martha 1893–1991; U.S. dancer and choreographer.

Gra·hame /gráyəm/, Kenneth 1859–1932; Scottish author.

Grant /grant/, Cary (born Archibald Alexander Leach) 1904–86; U.S. actor, born in England.

Grant, Ulysses S(impson) (born Hiram Ulysses Grant) 1822–85; Union general in the American Civil War; 18th president of the U.S. (1869–77).

Grass /graas/, Günter 1927– ; German novelist and playwright.

Graves /grayvz/, Robert 1895–1985; English poet, novelist, and critic.

Gray /gray/, Thomas 1716–71; English poet.

Gre·co /grékō/, El (born Domenikos Theotokopoulos) 1541–1614; Spanish artist, born in Crete.

Gree·ley /greélee/, Horace 1811–72; U.S. journalist and politician.

Greene /green/, (Henry) Graham 1904–91; English novelist.

Greene, Nathanael 1742–86; American Revolutionary War general.

Green·span /greénspan/, Alan 1926– ; U.S. economist.

Greer /greer/, Germaine 1939– ; Australian feminist and author.

Greg·o·ry /grégəree/ name of sixteen popes, including: 1 Gregory I, St. (called "the Great") c. 540–604; pope (590–604); developed the Gregorian chant. 2 Gregory XIII 1502–85; pope (1572–85); introduced the modern calendar.

Gren·ville /grénvil/, George 1712–70; prime minister of Great Britain (1763–65).

Grey /gray/, (Lady) Jane 1537–54; queen of England (1553); executed by Mary I.

Grey, Zane 1875–1939; U.S. author.

Grieg /greeg/, Edvard 1843–1907; Norwegian composer.

Grif·fith /grífith/, D(avid Lewelyn) W(ark) 1875–1948; U.S. film director.

Grimm /grim/ two German philologists and folklorists: 1 Jacob Ludwig Karl 1785–1863; brother of: 2 Wilhelm Karl 1786–1859.

Gro·my·ko /grəmeékō/, Andrei 1909–89; Russian diplomat.

Gro·pi·us /grṓpeeəs/, Walter 1883–1969; U.S. architect, born in Germany.

Gue·va·ra /g(w)əvaárə, gay–/, Che (Ernesto) 1928–67; Cuban revolutionary, born in Argentina.

Guin·ness /gínəs/, (Sir) Alec 1914– ; British actor.

Gus·tav·us A·dol·phus /gustaávəs ədáwlfəs/ 1594–1632; king of Sweden (1611–32).

Gut·en·berg /gŏŏt'n-bərg/, Johannes c. 1400–68; German inventor of printing with movable type.

Guth·rie /gúthree/, Woody (Woodrow Wilson) 1912–67; U.S. folk musician, singer, and songwriter.

Hai·le Se·las·sie /hílee səlaásee, –lás–/ (born Tafari Makonnen) 1892–1975; emperor of Ethiopia (1930–74).

Hak·luyt /háklōōt, háklit/, Richard c. 1552–1616; English geographer.

Hale /hayl/, Nathan 1755–76; American Revolutionary hero; hanged as a spy by British.

Ha·ley /háylee/, **Alex Palmer** 1921–92; U.S. author.

Hal·ley /hálee, háylee/, **Edmund** 1656–1742; English astronomer.

Hals /haals/, **Frans** c. 1580–1666; Dutch artist.

Hal·sey /háwlzee/, **William Frederick** (called "Bull") 1882–1959; U.S. admiral.

Ham·il·ton /hámiltən/, **Alexander** 1755–1804; first U.S. secretary of the treasury (1789–95).

Ham·mar·skjold /haámərshəld, hám–/, **Dag** 1905–61; Swedish statesman; secretary-general of the United Nations (1953–61).

Ham·mer·stein /hámərstīn/, **Oscar, II** 1895–1960; U.S. lyricist and librettist.

Ham·mett /hámit/, **(Samuel) Dashiell** 1894–1961; U.S. author.

Ham·mu·ra·bi /haməraábee, haam–/ fl. 18th cent. B.C.; king of Babylon (1792–1750 B.C.); instituted early code of laws.

Ham·sun /haámsən/, **Knut** (pseudonym of **Knut Pedersen**) 1859–1952; Norwegian novelist.

Han·cock /hánkaak/, **John** 1737–93; American politician; first signer of the U.S. Declaration of Independence.

Han·del /hándəl/, **George Frederick** 1685–1759; British composer, born in Germany.

Han·dy /hándee/, **W(illiam) C(hristopher)** 1873–1958; U.S. blues musician and composer.

Hanks /hangks/, **Tom (Thomas J.)** 1956– ; U.S. actor.

Han·ni·bal /hánibəl/ 247–182 B.C.; Carthaginian general.

Har·ding /haárding/, **Warren Gamaliel** 1865–1923; 29th president of the U.S. (1921–23).

Har·dy /haárdee/, **Thomas** 1840–1928; English author.

Harms·worth /haármzwərth/, **Alfred (Viscount Northcliffe)** 1865–1922; English publisher and politician.

Har·ris /háris/, **Joel Chandler** 1848–1908; U.S. author.

Har·ri·son /hárisən/, **George** 1943– ; British pop and rock guitarist, singer, and songwriter.

Har·ri·son, (Sir) Rex 1908–90; English actor.

Har·ri·son, family of U.S. politicians, including: **1** William Henry 1773–1841; 9th president of the U.S. (1841); grandfather of: **2** Benjamin 1833–1901; 23rd president of the U.S. (1889–93).

Hart /haart/, **Lorenz** 1895–1943; U.S. lyricist.

Harte /haart/, **(Francis) Bret** 1836–1902; U.S. author.

Har·vey /haárvee/, **William** 1578–1657; English physician and anatomist.

Hath·a·way /háthəway/, **Anne** c. 1557–1623; wife of William Shakespeare.

Haupt·mann /hówptmaan/, **Gerhart** 1862–1946; German playwright.

Ha·vel /haávəl/, **Václav** 1936– ; Czech author and politician.

Hawke /hawk/, **Bob (Robert James Lee)** 1929– ; prime minister of Australia (1983–91).

Hawk·ing /háwking/, **Stephen William** 1942– ; British scientist.

Haw·thorne /háwthawrn/, **Nathaniel** 1804–64; U.S. author.

Hay /hay/, **John Milton** 1838–1905; U.S. statesman.

Hay·dn /híd'n/, **Franz Joseph** 1732–1809; Austrian composer.

Hayes /hayz/, **Helen** (born **Helen Hayes Brown**) 1900–93; U.S. actress.

Hayes, Rutherford B(irchard) 1822–93; 19th president of the U.S. (1877–81).

Hearst /hərst/, **William Randolph** 1863–1951; U.S. newspaper publisher.

Heath /heeth/, **(Sir) Edward** 1916– ; prime minister of Great Britain (1970–74).

He·gel /háygəl/, **Georg Wilhelm Friedrich** 1770–1831; German philosopher.

Hei·deg·ger /hídigər/, **Martin** 1889–1976; German philosopher.

Hei·fetz /hífəts/, **Jascha** 1901–87; U.S. violinist, born in Lithuania.

Hei·ne /hínə/, **(Christian) Heinrich** 1797–1856; German poet.

Heinz /hinz/, **Henry John** 1844–1919; U.S. manufacturer of processed foods.

Hel·ler /hélər/, **Joseph** 1923– ; U.S. author.

Hell·man /hélmən/, **Lillian Florence** 1905–84; U.S. playwright.

Hem·ing·way /hémingway/, **Ernest Miller** 1899–1961; U.S. author.

Hen·drix /héndriks/, **Jimi** 1942–70; U.S. rock guitarist, singer, and songwriter.

Hen·ry /hénree/ (called "the Navigator") 1394–1460; prince of Portugal; sponsor of geographic expeditions.

Hen·ry VIII 1491–1547; king of England (1509–47).

Hen·ry, O. (pseudonym of **William Sydney Porter**) 1862–1910; U.S. author.

Hen·ry, Patrick 1736–99; American patriot and orator.

Hen·son /hénsən/, **Jim (James Maury)** 1936–90; U.S. puppeteer; creator of the Muppets.

Hep·burn /hépbərn/, **Audrey** 1929–93; U.S. actress, born in Belgium.

Hep·burn, Katharine 1909– ; U.S. actress.

Her·a·cli·tus /herəklítəs/ c. 500 B.C.; Greek philosopher.

Her·od /hérəd/ several rulers of ancient Palestine, including: **1** Herod I (called "the Great") c. 74–4 B.C.; king of Judea (37–4 B.C.); father of: **2** Herod Antipas 22 B.C.–A.D. c. 40; ruler of Galilee (4 B.C.–A.D. 40). **3** Herod Agrippa I 10 B.C.–A.D. 44; king of Judea (41–44); grandson of Herod I.

He·rod·o·tus /həraádətəs/ (called "the Father of History") fl. 5th cent. B.C.; Greek historian.

Her·rick /hérik/, **Robert** 1591–1674; English poet.

Her·zl /hértsəl/, **Theodor** 1860–1904; Austrian founder of the Zionist movement, born in Hungary.

He·si·od /héeseeəd, hésee–/ fl. 8th cent. B.C.; Greek poet.

Hess /hes/, **(Walter Richard) Rudolf** 1894–1987; German Nazi official, born in Egypt.

Hes·se /hésə/, **Hermann** 1877–1962; Swiss author, born in Germany.

Hey·er·dahl /híərdaal/, **Thor** 1914– ; Norwegian explorer and ethnologist.

Hick·ok /híkaak/, **James Butler** (called "Wild Bill Hickock") 1837–76; U.S. frontiersman.

Hil·la·ry /híləree/, **(Sir) Edmund Percival** 1919– ; New Zealand mountaineer; climbed Mt. Everest (1953).

Hil·ton /hílt'n/, **James** 1900–54; English novelist.

Himm·ler /hímlər/, **Heinrich** 1900–45; German head of the Nazi secret police.

Hin·de·mith /híndəmit/, **Paul** 1895–1963; German composer.

Hin·den·burg /híndinbərg/, **Paul von** 1847–1934; German field marshal; 2nd president of Germany (1925–32).

Hip·poc·ra·tes /hipaákrəteez/ (called "the Father of Medicine") c. 460–c. 377 B.C.; Greek physician.

Hi·ro·hi·to /heerōheétō/ (also known as **Sho'wa**) 1901–89; emperor of Japan (1926–89).

Hitch·cock /híchkaak/, **(Sir) Alfred Joseph** 1899–1980; British film director.

Hit·ler /hítlər/, **Adolf** (born **Adolf Schicklgruber**) (called "Der Führer") 1889–1945; dictator of Nazi Germany (1934–45), born in Austria.

Ho Chi Minh /hố cheé mín/ (born **Nguyen That Thanh**) 1890–1969; Vietnamese revolutionary; president of North Vietnam (1954–1969).

Hobbes /haabz/, **Thomas** 1588–1679; English philosopher.

Ho·garth /hốgaarth/, **William** 1697–1764; English artist and engraver.

Hol·bein /hốlbīn, háwl–/ name of two German artists: **1** Hans (called "the Elder") c. 1465–1524; father of: **2** Hans (called "the Younger") c. 1497–1543; worked in England.

Hol·ins·hed /haálins-hed, –inshed/, **Raphael** died c. 1580; English chronicler.

Holmes /hōlmz, hōmz/ **1** Oliver Wendell 1809–94; U.S. author and physician; father of: **2** Oliver Wendell 1841–1935; U.S. Supreme Court justice (1902–32).

Holst /hōlst/, **Gustav** 1874–1934; English composer.

Ho·mer /hốmər/ 8th cent. B.C.; Greek epic poet.

Ho·mer, Winslow 1836–1910; U.S. artist.

Ho·neck·er /hốnəkər/, **Erich** 1912–94; head of state of East Germany (1976–89).

Hoo·ver /hốŏvər/, **Herbert Clark** 1874–1964; 31st president of the U.S. (1929–33).

Hoo·ver, J(ohn) Edgar 1895–1972; director of the Federal Bureau of Investigation (1924–72).

Hope /hōp/, **Bob** (born **Leslie Townes Hope**) 1903– ; U.S. comedian and actor, born in England.

Hop·kins /haápkinz/, **Gerard Manley** 1844–89; English poet.

Hop·per /haápər/, **Edward** 1882–1967; U.S. artist.

Hor·ace /háwrəs/, **(Quintus Horatius Flaccus)** 65–8 B.C.; Roman poet.

Hor·o·witz /háwrəwits, haár–/, **Vladimir** 1904–89; U.S. pianist, born in Russia.

Hou·di·ni /hoodeéenee/, **Harry** (born **Ehrich Weiss**) 1874–1926; U.S. magician and escape artist, born in Hungary.

Hous·man /hówsmən/, **A(lfred) E(dward)** 1859–1936; English poet.

Hous·ton /hyooóstən/, **Samuel** 1793–1863; U.S. general and president of the Republic of Texas (1836–38).

Howe /how/, **Elias** 1819–67; U.S. inventor of the sewing machine.

Howe, **Julia Ward** 1819–1910; U.S. social reformer and author.

How·ells /hówəlz/, **William Dean** 1837–1920; U.S. author and editor.

Hox·ha /háwjə/, **Enver** 1908–85; Albanian Communist political leader.

Hud·son /húdsən/, **Henry** died 1611?; English explorer.

Hughes /hyooz, yooz/, **Howard Robard** 1905–76; U.S. aviator and industrialist.

Hughes, **(James) Langston** 1902–67; U.S. author.

Hughes, **Ted** 1930–98; English poet.

Hu·go /hyoógo/, **Victor** 1802–85; French author.

Hume /hyoom, yoom/, **David** 1711–76; Scottish philosopher and historian.

Hum·per·dinck /húmpərdingk/, **Engelbert** 1854–1921; German composer.

Hus·sein I /hoo'sayn/ (also **Hu'sain**) 1935–99; king of Jordan (1953–99).

Hus·sein, **Saddam** 1937– ; political leader of Iraq.

Hus·serl /húsərl/, **Edmund** 1859–1938; German philosopher.

Hutch·in·son /húchinsən/, **Anne** 1591–1643; American religious leader, born in England.

Hux·ley /húkslee/, **Aldous Leonard** 1894–1963; English novelist.

Ibn Sa·ud /íbən saa-oód/, **Abdul-Aziz** c. 1880–1953; king of Saudi Arabia (1932–53).

Ib·sen /íbsən/, **Henrik** 1828–1906; Norwegian playwright.

Ig·na·tius /ignáyshəs/ **of Loy·o·la** /loyólə/, **St.** 1491–1556; Spanish founder of the Jesuit religious order.

Ikh·na·ton /iknaátən/ see *Amenhotep IV* (AMENHOTEP).

Inge /inj/, **William Motter** 1913–73; U.S. playwright.

In·gres /aNgr/, **Jean** 1780–1867; French artist.

Io·nes·co /yənéskō, eeə–/, **Eugène** 1912–94; French playwright, born in Romania.

Ir·ving /ə́rving/, **Washington** 1783–1859; U.S. author.

I·sa·bel·la I /izəbélə/ 1474–1504; queen of Castile and Aragon; sponsor of Christopher Columbus.

Ish·er·wood /íshərwood/, **Christopher William Bradshaw** 1904–86; U.S. novelist, born in England.

I·van IV /ívən/ (called **"Ivan the Terrible"**) 1530–84; first czar of Russia (1547–84).

Ives /īvz/, **Charles Edward** 1874–1954; U.S. composer.

Jack·son /jáksən/, **Andrew** (called **"Old Hickory"**) 1767–1845; U.S. general; 7th president of the U.S. (1828–37).

Jack·son, **Jesse Louis** 1941– ; U.S. clergyman and civil-rights activist.

Jack·son, **Michael** 1958– ; U.S. pop singer and songwriter.

Jack·son, **Shirley** 1919–65; U.S. author.

Jack·son, **Thomas Jonathan** (called **"Stonewall Jackson"**) 1824–63; Confederate general in the American Civil War.

Jag·ger /jágər/, **Mick (Michael Philip)** 1944– ; English rock singer.

James I /jaymz/, 1566–1625; king of England and Ireland (1603–25). □□ **Ja·co·be'an** *adj. & n.*

James, **Henry** 1843–1916; British novelist and critic, born in the U.S.

James, **Jesse Woodson** 1847–82; U.S. outlaw.

James, **P(hyliss) D(orothy)** 1920– ; British author.

James, **William** 1842–1910; U.S. philosopher and psychologist.

Jef·fer·son /jéfərsən/, **Thomas** 1743–1826; U.S. patriot and statesman; 3rd president of the U.S. (1801–09). □□ **Jef·fer·so'ni·an** /–sóneeən/ *adj.*

Je·rome /jəróm/, **St.** c. 342–420; early Christian scholar; translated the Vulgate Bible.

Je·sus /jeézəs, –zəz/ (also known as **Je'sus Christ'** or **Je'sus of Naz'a·reth**) c. 4 B.C.–c. A.D. 30; source of the Christian religion.

Joan /jōn/ **of Arc, St.** (called **"the Maid of Orleans"**) c. 1412–31; French national heroine and Christian martyr.

John /jaan/ (called **"John Lackland"**) 1165–1216; king of England (1199–1216); signed the Magna Carta (1215).

John Paul II /jaan páwl/ (born **Karol Jozef Wojtyla**) 1920– ; pope (1978–), born in Poland.

Johns /jaanz/, **Jasper** 1930– ; U.S. artist.

John·son /jaánsən/, **Andrew** 1808–75; 17th president of the U.S. (1865–69).

John·son, **Lyndon Baines** (called **"L.B.J."**) 1908–73; 36th president of the U.S. (1963–69).

John·son, **Samuel** 1709–84; English lexicographer and author.

Jo·li·et /zhawlyáy/, **Louis** 1645–1700; French-Canadian explorer.

Jones /jōnz/, **Inigo** 1573–1652; English architect.

Jones, **John Paul** (born **John Paul**) 1747–92; American naval hero, born in Scotland.

Jong /jong/, **Erica** 1942– ; U.S. author.

Jon·son /jaánsən/, **Ben(jamin)** 1572–1637; English playwright and poet.

Jordan /jáwrd'n/, **Michael Jeffrey** 1963– ; U.S. basketball player.

Jo·se·phus /jōseéfəs/, **Flavius** c. 37–c. 100; Jewish historian and general.

Joyce /joys/, **James** 1882–1941; Irish author.

Juan Car·los /waan kaárlōs, hwaan/ 1938– ; king of Spain (1975–).

Ju·das Is·car·i·ot /joódəs iskáireeət/ died c. 30; apostle who betrayed Jesus.

Jul·ius /joólyəs/, **Caesar** see CAESAR, (GAIUS) JULIUS.

Jung /yoong/, **Carl Gustav** 1875–1961; Swiss psychologist. □□ **Jung'i·an** /–eeən/ *adj.*

Jus·tin·i·an /justíneeən/ 483–565; Byzantine emperor (527–565); codified Roman law.

Ju·ve·nal /joóvən'l/ c. 60–c. 140; Roman satirist.

Kaf·ka /kaáfkə/, **Franz** 1883–1924; Czech author.

Ka·me·ha·me·ha I /kəmayəmáyhə/ c. 1758–1819; king of Hawaii (1810–19).

Kan·din·sky /kandínskee/, **Wassily** 1866–1944; Russian artist.

Kant /kaant, kant/, **Immanuel** 1724–1804; German philosopher.

Ka·wa·ba·ta /kaawəbaátə, kawaábətə/, **Yasunari** 1899–1972; Japanese author.

Keats /keets/, **John** 1795–1821; English poet.

Kel·ler /kélər/, **Helen Adams** 1880–1968; U.S. author, educator, and social reformer; deaf and blind from infancy.

Kel·ly /kélee/, **Grace** 1928–82; U.S. actress; princess of Monaco (1956–82).

Kem·pis /kémpis/, **Thomas à** (born **Thomas Hemerken**) c. 1379–1471; German monk and author.

Ken·ne·dy U.S. political family, including three brothers: **1** John Fitzgerald (called **"J.F.K."**) 1917–63; 35th president of the U.S. (1961–63); assassinated; **2** Robert Francis 1925–68; U.S. politician; assassinated; and **3** Ted (Edward Moore) 1932– ; U.S. politician.

Ken·ne·dy /kénədee/, **Anthony Mcleod** 1936– ; U.S. Supreme Court justice (1988–).

Ken·yat·ta /kenyaátə/, **Jomo** c. 1891–1978; Kenyan political leader.

Kep·ler /képlər/, **Johannes** 1571–1630; German astronomer.

Kern /kərn/, **Jerome** 1885–1945; U.S. composer.

Ker·ou·ac /kéroo-ak/, **Jack** 1922–69; U.S. author.

Key /kee/, **Francis Scott** 1779–1843; U.S. lawyer; wrote lyrics to "The Star-Spangled Banner."

Keynes /kaynz/, **John Maynard** 1883–1946; English economist. □□ **Keynes·i·an** /káynzeeən/ *adj. & n.*

Kho·mei·ni /khōmáynee, kō–/, **(Ayatollah) Ruhollah** c. 1900–89; Islamic head of state of Iran (1979–89).

Khrush·chev /krooóshchef, –chawf/, **Nikita Sergeyevich** 1894–1971; Russian politician; premier of the Soviet Union (1958–64).

Kidd /kid/, **William** (called **"Captain Kidd"**) 1645–1701; Scottish pirate.

Kier·ke·gaard /keérkəgaard, –gawr/, **Sören** 1813–55; Danish philosopher.

Kil·mer /kílmər/, **(Alfred) Joyce** 1886–1918; U.S. poet.

Kim Il Sung /kim il soong/ 1912–94; premier (1948–72) and president (1972–94) of North Korea.

King /king/, **Martin Luther, Jr.** 1929–68; U.S. civil-rights leader; assassinated.

King, **Stephen** 1947– ; U.S. author.

Kip·ling /kípling/, **(Joseph) Rudyard** 1865–1936; English author, born in India.

Kis·sin·ger /kísinjər/, **Henry Alfred** 1923– ; U.S. statesman, born in Germany.

Kitch·e·ner /kíchənər/, **(Horatio) Herbert (1st Earl Kitchener of Khartoum)** 1850–1916; British soldier and statesman.

Klee /klay/, **Paul** 1879–1940; Swiss artist.

Knox /naaks/, **Henry** 1750–1806; first U.S. secretary of war (1785–94).

Knox, John 1505–72; Scottish religious leader.

Knut, /kanóot, –nyóot/, see CANUTE.

Kohl /kōl/, **Helmut** 1930– ; German political leader.

Kos·ci·us·ko /kawshchóoshkō, kaasee-óoskō, kaaz–/, **Thaddeus** 1746–1817; Polish patriot; American Revolutionary War general in the Continental army.

Kos·suth /káasōoth, kaasóoth/, **Lajos** 1802–94; Hungarian patriot and statesman.

Kroc /kraak/, **Ray(mond Albert)** 1902–1984; U.S. entrepreneur; founder of McDonald's restaurant chain.

Ku·blai Khan /kóoblə káan, kóoblī/ c. 1215–94; founder of the Mongol dynasty in China.

K'ung Fu·tzu /kóongfóodzə/ see CONFUCIUS.

La·fa·yette (also **La Fa·yette**) /laafee-ét, laf–/, **Marie Joseph (Marquis de)** 1757–1834; French statesman; American Revolutionary War general in the Continental army.

La·Fol·lette /ləfaálit/, **Robert Marion** 1855–1925; U.S. politician.

La Fon·taine /laa fawNtén/, **Jean de** 1621–95; French author.

Lamb /lam/, **Charles** (pseudonym **"Elia"**) 1775–1834; English critic and essayist.

Lang·land /lángländ/, **William** c. 1330–c. 1400; English poet.

Lao·tse /lówdzóo/ (also **Lao·tsze, Lao·tsu**) c. 604–c. 531 B.C.; Chinese philosopher.

La Roche·fou·cauld /laa rawshfōokó/, **François (Duc de)** 1613–80; French author.

La·rousse /laaróos, lə–/, **Pierre** 1817–75; French lexicographer and encyclopedist.

La Salle /laa saál, lə sál/, **René Robert Cavalier (Sieur de)** 1643–87; French explorer.

Law·rence /láwrəns, laár–/, **D(avid) H(erbert)** 1885–1930; English author.

Law·rence, T(homas) E(dward) (called **"Lawrence of Arabia"**) 1888–1935; British soldier and author.

Lay·a·mon /líəmən, láy–/ late 12th cent.; English poet.

Lea·key /leékee/ **1** Louis Seymour Bazett 1903–72; British archaeologist and anthropologist; husband of: **2** Mary Douglas 1913–96; British archaeologist; their son: **3** Richard Erskine Frere Kenyan paleontologist.

Lear /leer/, **Edward** 1812–88; English artist and writer of humorous verse.

Lee /lee/, **Henry** (called **"Light-horse Harry"**) 1756–1818; American Revolutionary War cavalry commander.

Lee, Robert E(dward) 1807–70; Confederate commander in the American Civil War.

Leib·niz /lípnits, líbnəts/, **Gottfried Wilhelm** 1646–1716; German philosopher and mathematician.

L'En·fant /laaNfáaN/, **Pierre Charles** 1754–1825; American soldier and engineer, born in France; designed Washington, D.C.

Le·nin /lénin/ (born **Vladimir Ilich Ulyanov**) 1870–1924; Russian Communist leader.

Len·non /lénən/, **John Winston** 1940–80; English pop and rock musician, singer, and songwriter.

Le·o·nar·do da Vin·ci /leeənáardō də vínchee/ 1452–1519; Italian artist, inventor, and engineer.

Ler·ner /lórnər/, **Alan Jay** 1918–86; U.S. lyricist and librettist.

Les·seps /léseps, leséps/, **Ferdinand (Vicomte de)** 1805–94; French diplomat; promoter of the Suez Canal.

Lew·is /lóois/, **C(ecil) Day** 1904–72; English poet and critic.

Lew·is, C(live) S(taples) 1898–1963; English author.

Lew·is, (Harry) Sinclair 1885–1951; U.S. author.

Lew·is, Meriwether 1774–1809; U.S. explorer (with William Clark) of the North American continent (1804–06).

Lin·coln /língkən/, **Abraham** 1809–65; 16th president of the U.S. (1861–65); assassinated.

Lind·bergh /líndbərg, lín–/, **Charles Augustus** 1902–74; U.S. aviator; made first solo transatlantic flight (1927).

Lind·say /líndzee, lín–/, **(Nicholas) Vachel** 1879–1931; U.S. poet.

Lin·nae·us /ləneéəs, –náy–/, **Carolus** 1707–78; Swedish botanist.

Lis·ter /lístər/, **Joseph** 1827–1912; English surgeon; developed antiseptic surgery.

Liszt /list/, **Franz** 1811–86; Hungarian composer.

Liv·ing·stone /lívingstən/, **David** 1813–73; Scottish missionary and explorer.

Liv·y /lívee/ (Latin name **Titus Livius**) 59 B.C.–A.D. 17; Roman historian.

Lloyd George /loyd jáwrj/, **David** 1863–1945; prime minister of Great Britain (1916–22).

Lloyd Web·ber /loyd wébər/, **(Sir) Andrew** 1948– ; English composer.

Locke /laak/, **John** 1632–1704; English philosopher.

Loewe /lō/, **Frederick** 1904–88; U.S. composer, born in Austria.

Lon·don /lúndən/, **Jack (John Griffith)** 1876–1916; U.S. author.

Long /lawng/, **Huey Pierce** (called **"the Kingfish"**) 1893–1935; U.S. politician; assassinated.

Long·fel·low /láwngfelō/, **Henry Wadsworth** 1807–82; U.S. poet.

Lor·rain, Claude see CLAUDE LORRAIN.

Lou·is /lóoee, lweé/ name of eighteen kings of France, including: **1** Louis XIV (called **"the Sun King"**) 1638–1715; reigned 1643–1715. **2** Louis XVI 1754–93; reigned 1774–92.

Lou·is /lóoəs/, **Joe** (born **Joseph Louis Barrow**) (called **"the Brown Bomber"**) 1914–81; U.S. boxer.

Lou·is Phi·lippe /lweé fileép, lóoee/ 1773–1850; king of France (1830–48).

Low·ell /lóəl/, **Amy** 1874–1925; U.S. poet.

Low·ell, James Russell 1819–91; U.S. poet and critic.

Low·ell, Robert 1917–77; U.S. poet.

Lu·cre·tius /lōokreéshəs/ **(Titus Lucretius Carus)** c. 94–c. 55 B.C.; Roman poet and philosopher.

Lu·ther /lóothər/, **Martin** 1483–1546; German theologian; key figure of the Protestant Reformation.

Ly·cur·gus /likórgəs/ fl. 9th cent. B.C.; Spartan lawgiver.

Lyl·y /lílee/, **John** c. 1554–1606; English author.

Ly·on /líən/, **Mary** 1797–1849; U.S. educator.

Mac·Ar·thur /məkáarthər/, **Douglas** 1880–1964; U.S. general.

Ma·cau·lay /məkáwlee/, **Thomas Babington** 1800–59; English author and historian.

Mac·beth /məkbéth, mak–/ c. 1005–57; king of Scotland (1040–57); Shakespearean tragic hero.

Mac·ca·be·us /makəbeéəs/, **Judas** died 160 B.C.; Jewish patriot.

Mac·Don·ald /məkdáanld/, **(James) Ramsay** 1866–1937; prime minister of Great Britain (1924; 1929–35).

Mach /maakh, maak/, **Ernst** 1836–1916; Austrian physicist.

Mach·i·a·vel·li /makeeəvélee/, **Niccolò di Bernardo** 1469–1527; Italian political theorist.

Mac·ken·zie /məkénzee/, **Alexander** 1822–92; prime minister of Canada (1873–78).

Mac·ken·zie, (Sir) Alexander 1764–1820; Scottish explorer of Canada.

Mac·Leish /makleésh/, **Archibald** 1892–1982; U.S. poet and playwright.

Mac·mil·lan /məkmílən/, **(Maurice) Harold** 1895–1987; prime minister of Great Britain (1957–63).

Mad·i·son /mádisən/, **James** 1751–1836; 4th president of the U.S. (1809–17).

Mae·ter·linck /máytərlingk, met–/, **(Count) Maurice** 1862–1947; Belgian poet and playwright.

Ma·gel·lan /məjélən/, **Ferdinand** c. 1480–1521; Portuguese navigator.

Ma·gritte /maagreét/, **René** 1898–1967; Belgian artist.

Mahfouz /maafóoz/, **Naguib** 1911– ; Egyptian author.

Mah·ler /máalər/, **Gustav** 1860–1911; Austrian composer.

Mail·er /máylər/, **Norman** 1923– ; U.S. author.

Mai·mon·i·des /mīmaánideez/, **Moses** (born **Moses ben Maimon**) 1135–1204; Jewish theologian and scholastic philosopher, born in Spain.

Ma·jor /máyjər/, **John** 1943– ; prime minister of Great Britain (1990–97).

Mal·a·mud /máləməd/, **Bernard** 1914–86; U.S. author.

Mal·colm X /málkəm éks/ (born **Malcolm Little**) 1925–65; U.S. civil-rights activist; assassinated.

Ma·li·now·ski /malináwfskee/, **Bronislaw** 1884–1942; U.S. anthropologist, born in Poland.

Mal·lar·mé /maalaarmáy/, **Stéphane** 1842–98; French poet.

Mal·o·ry /máləree/, **(Sir) Thomas** died 1471; English author.

Mal·raux /malrṍ/, **André** 1901–76; French statesman and author.

Mal·thus /málthəs, máwl–/, **Thomas Robert** 1766–1834; English economist.

Man·de·la /mandélə/, **Nelson** 1918–   ; president of South Africa (1994–   ).

Man·et /manáy, maa–/, **Édouard** 1832–83; French artist.

Mann /man/, **Horace** 1796–1859; U.S. educator.

Mann /maan/, **Thomas** 1875–1955; German author.

Man Ray see RAY, MAN.

Mans·field /mánsfeeld/, **Katherine** (born **Kathleen Beauchamp**) 1888–1923; British author, born in New Zealand.

Man·son /mánsən/, **Charles** 1934–   ; U.S. cult leader and criminal.

Mao Ze·dong /mów dzədŏ́ng/ (also **Mao Tse-tung**) 1893–1976; Chinese Communist leader.

Ma·rat /maaraá/, **Jean Paul** 1743–93; French revolutionary leader, born in Switzerland; assassinated.

Mar·ci·a·no /maarsee-ánō, –shee–, –aánō/, **Rocky** (born **Rocco Francis Marchegiano**) 1923–69; U.S. boxer.

Mar·co Po·lo see POLO, MARCO.

Mar·co·ni /maarkṍnee/, **Guglielmo** 1874–1937; Italian inventor; pioneered wireless telegraphy.

Mar·cos /maárkōs/, **Ferdinand** 1917–89; president of the Philippines (1965–86).

Mar·cus Au·re·li·us /maárkəs awreéleeəs/ 121–180; Roman emperor and Stoic philosopher.

Mar·cuse /maarkŏ́ōzə/, **Herbert** 1898–1979; U.S. philosopher, born in Germany.

Mare, Walter de la see DE LA MARE, WALTER.

Mar·gre·the II /maargrétə/ 1940–   ; queen of Denmark (1972–   ).

Ma·rie An·toi·nette /mərée antwənét/ 1755–93; queen of France (1774–92), wife of Louis XVI.

Ma·rie de Mé·di·cis /mərée də maydeeseés/ (Italian name **Ma·ri·a de' Med·i·ci** /máydəchee/) 1573–1642; queen of France (1610–17).

Mark An·to·ny see ANTONY, MARK.

Mark·ham /maárkəm/, **(Charles) Edwin** 1852–1940; U.S. poet.

Marl·bor·ough /márlbərō, máwlbrə/, **1st Duke of** see CHURCHILL, JOHN.

Mar·lowe /maárlō/, **Christopher** 1564–93; English playwright and poet.

Mar·quand /maarkwaánd/, **J(ohn) P(hillips)** 1893–1960; U.S. author.

Mar·quette /maarkét/, **Jacques** 1637–75; Jesuit missionary and explorer of North America, born in France.

Már·quez, Gabriel García see GARCÍA MÁRQUEZ, GABRIEL.

Mar·shall /maárshəl/, **George C(atlett)** 1880–1959; U.S. general and statesman.

Mar·shall, John 1755–1835; Chief Justice of the U.S. (1801–35).

Mar·shall, Thurgood 1908–93; U.S. Supreme Court justice (1967–91).

Mar·tel, Charles see CHARLES MARTEL.

Mar·tial /maárshəl/ 1st cent. A.D.; Roman writer of epigrams, born in Spain.

Marx /maarks/, **Karl Heinrich** 1818–83; German political philosopher.

Mar·y /máiree/ (called "**the Virgin Mary**" or "**Blessed Virgin Mary**") 1st cent. B.C.–A.D. 1st cent.; mother of Jesus.

Mar·y I (also known as **Mary Tu·dor**) (called "**Bloody Mary**") 1516–58; queen of England (1553–58).

Mar·y, Queen of Scots (also known as **Mary Stu·art**) 1542–87; queen of Scotland (1542–67).

Ma·sa·ryk /maásaarik/, **Tomáš** 1850–1937; president of Czechoslovakia (1918–35).

Mase·field /máysfeeld/, **John Edward** 1878–1967; English poet, playwright, and novelist.

Mas·ters /mástərz/, **Edgar Lee** 1869–1950; U.S. poet.

Ma·tisse /maateés/, **Henri** 1869–1954; French artist.

Maugham /mawm/, **(William) Somerset** 1874–1965; English author.

Mau·pas·sant /mōpaasaáɴ/, **(Henri) Guy de** 1850–93; French author.

Mau·riac /mawr-yaák/, **François** 1885–1970; French author.

Max·i·mil·ian /maksimílyən/ 1832–67; emperor of Mexico (1864–67).

Maz·a·rin /maazaaráɴ/, **Jules** 1602–61; French cardinal and statesman, born in Italy.

Mboy·a /embóyə/, **Tom (Thomas Joseph)** 1930–69; Kenyan political leader; assassinated.

Mc·Car·thy /məkaárthee/, **Joseph Raymond** 1908–57; U.S. politician.

Mc·Car·thy, Mary 1912–89; U.S. author.

Mc·Cart·ney /məkaártnee/, **(James) Paul** 1942–   ; English pop and rock musician, singer, and songwriter.

Mc·Clel·lan /məklélən/, **George Brinton** 1826–85; Union general in the American Civil War.

Mc·Cor·mick /məkáwrmik/, **Cyrus Hall** 1809–84; U.S. developer of the mechanical reaper.

Mc·Kin·ley /məkínlee/, **William** 1843–1901; 25th president of the U.S. (1897–1901); assassinated.

Mc·Lu·han /məklŏ́ōən/, **(Herbert) Marshall** 1911–80; Canadian communications theorist.

Mead /meed/, **Margaret** 1901–78; U.S. anthropologist.

Meade /meed/, **George Gordon** 1815–72; Union general in the American Civil War.

Med·i·ci /médichee, médeechee/ powerful Italian family, including: **1** Cosimo de' (called "**the Elder**") 1389–1464; Florentine ruler, banker, and art patron. **2** Lorenzo de' (called "**the Magnificent**") 1449–92; Florentine ruler and art patron. **3** see CATHERINE DE MÉDICIS. **4** Cosimo de' (called "**the Great**") 1519–74; duke of Florence (1537–74). **5** Maria de' **see** MARIE DE MÉDICIS.

Mei·ji Ten·no /máyjee ténnō/ (born **Mutsuhito**) 1852–1912; emperor of Japan (1867–1912).

Me·ir /me-eér/, **Golda** (born **Goldie Mabovitch**) 1898–1978; prime minister of Israel (1969–74), born in Russia.

Mel·ba /mélbə/, **(Dame) Nellie** (born **Helen Porter Mitchell**) 1861–1931; Australian operatic soprano.

Mel·lon /mélən/, **Andrew William** 1855–1937; U.S. financier and art patron; U.S. secretary of the treasury (1921–32).

Mel·ville /mélvil/, **Herman** 1819–91; U.S. author.

Me·nan·der /mənándər/ c. 342–292 B.C.; Greek playwright.

Men·ci·us /méncheeəs/ (Latinized name of **Meng-tzu'** or **Meng·zi'**) c. 371–c. 289 B.C.; Chinese philosopher.

Menck·en /méngkən/, **H(enry) L(ouis)** 1880–1956; U.S. journalist and critic.

Men·del /méndəl/, **Gregor Johann** 1822–84; Austrian monk and botanist.

Men·dels·sohn /méndəlsən/, **Felix** 1809–47; German composer.

Me·nes /meéneez/ king of Egypt (c. 3100 B.C.).

Meng-tzu /múng dzŏ́ō/ (also **Meng·zi'**) see MENCIUS.

Me·not·ti /mənáwtee/, **Gian Carlo** 1911–   ; U.S. composer, born in Italy.

Men·u·hin /ményŏ́ōhin/, **Yehudi** 1916–99; U.S. violinist.

Mer·ca·tor /mərkáytər/, **Gerardus** 1512–94; Flemish cartographer.

Mer·e·dith /mérədith/, **George** 1828–1909; English novelist and poet.

Met·ter·nich /métərnik, –nikh/, **(Prince) Klemens** 1773–1859; Austrian statesman.

Mi·chel·an·ge·lo /mīkəlánjəlō, mikəl–/ (surname **Buonarroti**) 1475–1564; Italian artist and architect.

Mich·en·er /míchənər, míchnər/, **James A(lbert)** 1907–97; U.S. author.

Mies van der Rohe /mees vaan də rṍə/, **Ludwig** 1886–1969; U.S. architect and designer, born in Germany.

Mill /mil/, **J(ohn) S(tuart)** 1806–73; English philosopher and economist.

Mil·lay /məláy/, **Edna St. Vincent** 1892–1950; U.S. poet.

Mil·ler /mílər/, **Arthur** 1915–   ; U.S. playwright.

Mil·ler, (Alton) Glenn 1904–44; U.S. jazz trombonist and bandleader.

Mil·ler, Henry 1891–1980; U.S. author.

Mil·let /meeláy/, **Jean François** 1814–75; French artist.

Milne /miln/, **A(lan) A(lexander)** 1882–1956; English author.

Mil·ton /mílt'n/, **John** 1608–74; English poet.

Min·u·it /mínyŏ̄oit/, **Peter** 1580–1638; Dutch colonial administrator in America.

Mi·ró /mee-rṍ/, **Joan** 1893–1983; Spanish artist.

Mitch·ell /míchəl/, **Margaret** 1900–49; U.S. author.

Mit·ford /mítfərd/ **1** Nancy 1904–73; English author; sister of: **2** Jessica 1917–96; U.S. author, born in England.

Mith·ri·da·tes VI /mithrədáyteez/ (called **"the Great"**) c. 132–63 B.C.; king of Pontus (120–63 B.C.).

Mit·ter·rand /meeteráaN/, **François** 1916–96; president of France (1981–95).

Mo·bu·tu Se·se Se·ko /məbŏōtŏō sésay sékō/ 1930–97; president of (the former) Zaire (1965–97).

Mo·di·glia·ni /mōdeel-yaánee/, **Amedeo** 1884–1920; Italian artist.

Mo·ham·med /mōháamid/ see MUHAMMAD.

Mo·lière /mōlyér/ (pseudonym of **Jean-Baptiste Poquelin**) 1622–73; French playwright.

Mol·nár /mōlnaár/, **Ferenc** 1878–1952; Hungarian author.

Momm·sen /mŏmsən/, **Theodor** 1817–1903; German historian.

Mon·dale /móndayl/, **Walter Frederick** 1928– ; vice president of the U.S. (1977–81).

Mon·dri·an /máwndree-aan/, **Piet** 1872–1944; Dutch artist.

Mo·net /mawnáy/, **Claude** 1840–1926; French artist.

Mon·roe /mənrŏ/, **James** 1758–1831; 5th president of the U.S. (1817–25).

Mon·roe, **Marilyn** 1926–62; U.S. actress.

Mon·taigne /mawNtén, –tényə/, **Michel de** 1533–92; French essayist.

Mont·calm /mōNkáalm/, **Louis Joseph** 1712–59; French general.

Mon·tes·quieu /maantəskyŏ́ō/ 1689–1755; French political philosopher.

Mon·tes·so·ri /maantəsáwree/, **Maria** 1870–1952; Italian educator.

Mon·te·ver·di /maantəvérdee/, **Claudio** 1567–1643; Italian composer.

Mon·te·zu·ma II /maantəzŏ́ōmə/ 1466–1520; Aztec emperor (1502–20).

Moon /mŏōn/, **Sun Myung** 1920– ; Korean religious leader.

Moore /mawr, mŏōr/, **G(eorge) E(dward)** 1873–1958; English philosopher.

Moore, **Henry** 1898–1986; English sculptor.

Moore, **Marianne** 1887–1972; U.S. poet.

More /mawr/, **(Sir) Thomas** 1478–1535; English scholar and statesman.

Mor·gan /máwrgən/, **J(ohn) P(ierpont)** 1837–1913; U.S. financier and philanthropist.

Mor·i·son /máwrisən/, **Samuel Eliot** 1887–1976; U.S. historian.

Mo·ri·sot /mawrisŏ́/, **Berthe** 1841–95; French artist.

Mor·ris /máwrəs, maár–/, **Gouverneur** 1752–1816; U.S. statesman.

Mor·ris /máwrəs, maár–/, **Robert** 1734–1806; U.S. statesman and financier, born in England.

Mor·ri·son /máwrisən, maár–/, **Jim** 1943–1971; U.S. singer and songwriter.

Mor·ri·son, **Toni** 1931– ; U.S. novelist.

Morse /mawrs/, **Samuel F(inley) B(reese)** 1791–1872; U.S. artist and inventor; devised telegraphic code.

Mo·ses /mŏziz/ c. 14th cent. B.C.; Hebrew prophet and lawgiver.

Mo·ses /mŏziz/, **Anna Mary** (called **"Grandma Moses"**) 1860–1961; U.S. artist.

Mo·ses ben Mai·mon see MAIMONIDES.

Mo·ther Te·re·sa see TERESA, MOTHER.

Mott /maat/, **Lucretia Coffin** 1793–1880; U.S. social reformer.

Mount·bat·ten /mowntbát'n/, **Louis (1st Earl Mountbatten of Burma)** 1900–79; British admiral and statesman.

Mous·sorg·sky /mŏōsáwrgskee/ (also **Mus·sorg'sky**), **Modest** 1839–81; Russian composer.

Mo·zart /mŏtsaart/, **Wolfgang Amadeus** 1756–91; Austrian composer.

Mu·ga·be /mŏōgáabee/, **Robert** 1924– ; prime minister (1980–87) and president (1987–) of Zimbabwe.

Mu·ham·mad A·li see ALI, MUHAMMAD.

Mu·ham·mad /mŏōháaməd, mō–/ (also **Mo·ham'med; Ma·hom'et**) c. 570–632; Arab prophet, founder of Islam.

Muir /myŏōr/, **John** 1838–1914; U.S. naturalist and explorer, born in Scotland.

Mun·ro /mənrŏ/, **H(ector) H(ugh)** (pseudonym **"Saki"**) 1870–1916; Scottish author, born in Burma.

Mu·rat /myŏōraá/, **Joachim** c. 1767–1815; French general and king of Naples (1808–15).

Mur·doch /mə́rdaak/, **Rupert** 1931– ; Australian media executive.

Mur·ray /mə́ree/, **(Sir) James Augustus Henry** 1837–1915; British philologist and lexicographer.

Mus·so·li·ni /mŏōsəleénee, mŏ́osə–/, **Benito** (called **"Il Duce"**) 1883–1945; Fascist dictator of Italy (1922–43).

Mus·sorg·sky see MOUSSORGSKY.

My·ron /míən/ fl. c. 480–440 B.C.; Greek sculptor.

Na·bo·kov /nábəkawf, nəbáwkəf/, **Vladimir** 1899–1977; U.S. novelist, born in Russia.

Na·der /náydər/, **Ralph** 1934– ; U.S. consumer advocate.

Na·po·le·on I /nəpŏ́leeən/ (surname **Bonaparte**) 1769–1821; French general, born in Corsica; emperor of France (1804–15). ▫▫ **Na·po·le·on'ic** /–leeáanək/ adj.

Na·po·le·on III (**Louis Napoleon Bonaparte**) 1808–73; president (1848–52) and emperor (1852–70) of France.

Nash /nash/, **Ogden** 1902–71; U.S. writer of humorous verse.

Nas·ser /násər/, **Gamal Abdel** 1918–70; president of Egypt (1956–58).

Na·tion /náyshən/, **Carry Amelia Moore** 1846–1911; U.S. temperance activist.

Neb·u·chad·nez·zar /nebəkədnézər/ king of Babylon (605–562 B.C.).

Neh·ru /nérŏō, náyrŏō/, **Jawaharlal** 1889–1964; prime minister of India (1947–64).

Nel·son /nélsən/, **Horatio** 1758–1805; British admiral.

Ne·ro /neérŏ/ 37–68; Roman emperor (54–68).

Net·an·ya·hu /netaanyaáhŏō/, **Benjamin** 1949–99; prime minister of Israel (1996–).

Neu·mann /nóymaan/, **John von** 1903–57; U.S. mathematician, born in Hungary.

New·man /nŏ́ōmən, nyŏ́ō–/, **John Henry** 1801–91; English theologian.

New·ton /nŏ́ōt'n, nyŏ́ō–/, **(Sir) Isaac** 1642–1727; English mathematician and physicist.

Ngo Dinh Di·em /nŏ́ dín dee-ém/ 1901–63; president of South Vietnam (1956–63).

Nich·o·las II /níkələs, niklэs/ 1868–1918; last Russian czar (1894–1917); assassinated.

Nich·o·las, St. fl. 4th cent.; Christian bishop in Asia Minor.

Nick·laus /nikləs/, **Jack (William)** (called **"the Golden Bear"**) 1940– ; U.S. golfer.

Nie·buhr /neébŏōr/, **Reinhold** 1892–1971; U.S. theologian.

Nie·tzsche /neéchə, –chee/, **Friedrich Wilhelm** 1844–1900; German philosopher.

Night·in·gale /nít'n-gayl/, **Florence** 1820–1910; English nurse.

Ni·jin·sky /nəzhínskee, –jín–/, **Vaslav** 1890–1950; Russian ballet dancer and choreographer.

Nim·itz /nímits/, **Chester William** 1885–1966; U.S. admiral.

Nix·on /níksən/, **Richard Milhous** 1913–94; 37th president of the U.S. (1969–74); resigned.

Nkru·mah /enkrŏ́ōmə/, **Kwame** 1909–72; Ghanaian political leader.

No·bel /nōbél/, **Alfred Bernhard** 1833–96; Swedish inventor; endowed Nobel Prizes.

North /nawrth/, **Frederick** (called **"Lord North"**) 1732–92; prime minister of Great Britain (1770–82).

Nos·tra·da·mus /naastrədáyməs, naws–, –daáməs/ 1503–66; French astrologer and prophet.

Noyes /noyz/, **Alfred** 1880–1958; English poet and critic.

Nu·re·yev /nŏōráyəf, nŏōree-ef/, **Rudolf Hametovich** 1939–93; Russian ballet dancer.

O'Ca·sey /ōkáysee/, **Sean** 1880–1964; Irish playwright.

O'Con·nell /ōkaánl/, **Daniel** 1775–1847; Irish nationalist leader.

O'Con·nor /ōkaánər/, **(Mary) Flannery** 1925–1964; U.S. author.

O'Con·nor, **Sandra Day** 1930– ; U.S. Supreme Court justice (1981–); first woman appointed to Court.

Oc·ta·vi·an /oktávee-ən/ see AUGUSTUS.

O·dets /ōdéts/, **Clifford** 1906–63; U.S. playwright.

Of·fen·bach /áwfənbaakh, –baak/, **Jacques** 1819–80; French composer, born in Germany.

O·gle·thorpe /ŏ́gəlthawrp/, **James Edward** 1696–1785; English colonizer of Georgia.

O'Hig·gins /ōhíginz/, **Bernardo** (called **"the Liberator of Chile"**) c. 1778–1842; Chilean revolutionary; dictator of Chile (1817–23).

O'Keeffe /ōkéef/, **Georgia** 1887–1986; U.S. artist.

O·liv·i·er /əlívee-ay, ō–/, **(Sir) Laurence Kerr** 1907–89; English actor.

Olm·sted /ṓmstid/, **Frederick Law** 1822–1903; U.S. landscape architect.

O·mar Khay·yám /ōmaar kī-aám, kī-ám/ died 1123; Persian poet and astronomer.

O·nas·sis /ōnásis/ **1** Aristotle (Socrates) c. 1900–75; Greek shipping tycoon, born in Turkey; husband of: **2** Jacqueline Lee Bouvier Kennedy 1929–94; wife of John F. Kennedy (1953–63) and Aristotle Onassis (1968–75).

O'Neill /ōnéel/, **Eugene Gladstone** 1888–1953; U.S. playwright.

Op·pen·heim·er /aápənhīmər/, **J(ulius) Robert** 1904–67; U.S. nuclear physicist.

Or·well /áwrwel, –wəl/, **George** (pseudonym of **Eric Arthur Blair**) 1903–50; English author, born in India.

Os·man I /aázmən, aás–/ (also **Oth′man**) 1259–1326; Turkish ruler; founder of the Ottoman Empire.

Os·wald /aázwawld, –wəld/, **Lee Harvey** 1939–63; accused assassin of U.S. president John F. Kennedy.

O·tis /ṓtis/, **James** 1725–83; American Revolutionary War patriot.

Ov·id /aávid/ (born **Publius Ovidius Naso**) 43 B.C.–c. A.D. 17; Roman poet.

Ow·en /ṓən/, **David** 1938– ; British politician.

Ow·en, **Wilfred** 1893–1918; English poet.

Ow·ens /ṓənz/, **Jesse** (born **James Cleveland Owens**) 1913–80; U.S. Olympic athlete.

Pa·de·rew·ski /padəréfskee, –rév–/, **Ignace** 1860–1941; Polish pianist, composer, and statesman.

Pa·ga·ni·ni /pagənéenee/, **Nicolò** 1782–1840; Italian violinist and composer.

Pah·la·vi /paáləvee/, **Mohammed Reza** 1919–80; shah of Iran (1941–79); exiled.

Paine /payn/, **Thomas** 1737–1809; American patriot and political philosopher, born in England.

Pal·la·dio /pəláadee-ō/, **Andrea** 1508–80; Italian architect.

Pal·mer /paámər, paálmər/, **Arnold** 1929– ; U.S. golfer.

Pank·hurst /pángkhərst/, **Emmeline Goulden** 1858–1928; English suffragist.

Pa·pan·dre·ou /paapaandráyoō/, **George** 1888–1968; premier of Greece (1963; 1964–65).

Par·ker /paárkər/, **Dorothy Rothschild** 1893–1967; U.S. author and critic.

Park·man /paárkmən/, **Francis** 1823–93; U.S. historian.

Par·men·i·des /paarménideez/ early 5th cent. B.C.; Greek philosopher.

Par·nell /paarnél, paárn'l/, **Charles Stewart** 1846–91; Irish nationalist.

Pas·cal /paskál/, **Blaise** 1623–62; French mathematician and philosopher.

Pas·ter·nak /pástərnak/, **Boris** 1890–1960; Russian poet and novelist.

Pas·teur /pastṓr/, **Louis** 1822–95; French chemist and microbiologist.

Pat·rick /pátrik/, **St.** 5th cent.; patron saint of Ireland.

Pat·ton /pát'n/, **George S(mith)** 1885–1945; U.S. general.

Paul /pawl/, **St.** died c. 67; early Christian missionary.

Paul·ing /páwling/, **Linus Carl** 1901–94; U.S. chemist.

Pa·va·rot·ti /paavəráatee, pav–/, **Luciano** 1935– ; Italian operatic tenor.

Pav·lov /paávlawf, páv–, –lawv/, **Ivan** 1849–1936; Russian physiologist.

Pav·lo·va /pávləvə, pavlóvə/, **Anna** 1881–1931; Russian prima ballerina.

Peale /peel/, **Charles Willson** 1741–1827; U.S. artist.

Peale, **Norman Vincent** 1898–1994; U.S. religious leader.

Pea·ry /péeree/, **Robert Edwin** 1856–1920; U.S. Arctic explorer.

Pe·der·sen /páydərsən/, **Knut** see HAMSUN, KNUT.

Peel /peel/, **(Sir) Robert** 1788–1850; prime minister of Great Britain (1834–35; 1841–46).

Pei /pay/, **I(eoh) M(ing)** 1917– ; U.S. architect, born in China.

Penn /pen/, **William** 1644–1718; English Quaker and founder of Pennsylvania (1682).

Pep·in III /pépin/ (called **"the Short"**) c. 714–768; king of the Franks (751–768); father of Charlemagne.

Pepys /peeps/, **Samuel** 1633–1703; English diarist.

Pé·rez de Cué·llar /pérez de kwáyyaar/, **Javier** 1920– ; Peruvian diplomat; secretary-general of the United Nations (1982–92).

Per·i·cles /périkleez/ c. 495–429 B.C.; Athenian statesman and general.

Per·kins /pórkinz/, **Frances** 1882–1965; U.S. secretary of labor (1933–45); first woman cabinet member.

Pe·rón /pərṓn, pay–/ **1** Juan Domingo 1895–1974; president of Argentina (1946–55; 1973–74); husband of: **2** (Maria) Evita Duarte Ibarguren (called **"Evita"**) 1919–52; Argentine political figure.

Pe·rot /pərṓ/, **H(enry) Ross** 1930– ; U.S. business executive and politician.

Per·ry /péree/ **1** Oliver Hazard 1785–1819; U.S. naval officer; brother of: **2** Matthew Calbraith 1794–1858; U.S. commodore.

Per·shing /pórshing, –zhing/, **John J(oseph)** (called **"Black Jack"**) 1860–1948; U.S. commander of American forces during World War I.

Pesh·kov /pyáyshkəf/, **Aleksei Maksimovich** see GORKY, MAXIM.

Pé·tain /paytáN/, **Henri Philippe** 1856–1951; premier of Fascist Vichy France (1940–44).

Pe·ter I /péetər/ (called **the Great**) 1672–1725; emperor of Russia (1682–1725).

Pe·ter, St. (also known as Si′mon Pe′ter) died c. 67; apostle of Jesus.

Pe·ter·son /péetərsən/, **Roger Tory** 1908–1996; U.S. ornithologist, artist, and author.

Pe·trarch /péetraark, pé–/ 1304–74; Italian poet. □□ Pe·trarch·an /pətraárkən/ adj.

Phid·i·as /fídeeəs/ fl. 5th cent. B.C.; Athenian sculptor.

Phil·ip II /fíləp/ c. 382–336 B.C.; king of Macedonia; father of Alexander the Great.

Pi·af /pee-aáf/, **Edith** (born **Edith Giovanna Gassion**) 1915–63; French singer.

Pia·get /pyaazháy/, **Jean** 1897–1980; Swiss psychologist.

Pi·cas·so /pikaásō, –kás–/, **Pablo** 1881–1973; Spanish artist.

Pick·ett /píkət/, **George Edward** 1825–75; Confederate general in the American Civil War.

Pierce /peers/, **Franklin** 1804–69; 14th president of the U.S. (1853–57).

Pi·late /pílət/, **Pontius** 1st cent. A.D.; Roman procurator of Judea (26–c. 36).

Pin·dar /píndər, –daar/ 518–438 B.C.; Greek lyric poet.

Pink·er·ton /píngkərtən/, **Allan** 1819–84; U.S. detective, born in Scotland.

Pi·no·chet U·gar·te /peenōchét oōgaártay/, **Augusto** 1915– ; president of Chile (1973–89).

Pin·ter /píntər/, **Harold** 1930– ; English playwright.

Pi·ran·del·lo /peerəndélō/, **Luigi** 1867–1936; Italian author.

Pi·sis·tra·tus /pisístrətəs/ died c. 527 B.C.; Athenian ruler.

Pis·sar·ro /pisaárō/, **Camille** 1830–1903; French artist.

Pitt /pit/ **1** William (**1st Earl of Chatham**) (called **"the Elder Pitt"** and **"the Great Commoner"**) 1708–78; British political leader; father of: **2** William (called **"the Younger Pitt"**) 1759–1806; prime minister of Great Britain (1783–1801; 1804–06).

Pi·zar·ro /pizaárō/, **Francisco** c. 1478–1541; Spanish conquistador; conqueror of Peru.

Planck /plaangk, plangk/, **Max** 1858–1947; German physicist.

Plan·tag·e·net /plantájinit/ British ruling dynasty (1154–1485).

Plath /plath/, **Sylvia** 1932–63; U.S. poet and novelist.

Pla·to /pláytō/ 429–347 B.C.; Greek philosopher.

Plau·tus /pláwtəs/, **Titus Maccius** c. 250–184 B.C.; Roman comic playwright.

Plin·y /plínee/ **1** (called **"the Elder"**) c. 23–79; Roman scholar; uncle of: **2** (called **"the Younger"**) c. 61–c. 112; Roman author.

Plu·tarch /plṓtaark/ c. 46–c. 120; Greek biographer.

Po·ca·hon·tas /pōkəhaántəs/ (English name **Rebecca Rolfe**) c. 1595–1617; Native American princess; daughter of Powhatan.

Poe /pō/, **Edgar Allan** 1809–49; U.S. short-story author and poet.

Pol Pot /paal paát, pōl/ c. 1925–98; prime minister of Cambodia (1976–79).

Polk /pōk/, **James Knox** 1795–1849; 11th president of the U.S. (1845–49).

Pol·lock /paálək/, (Paul) Jackson 1912–56; U.S. artist.

Po·lo /pṓlō/, Marco 1254–1324; Venetian traveler in E Asia.

Pom·pey /paámpee/ (called "the Great") 106–48 B.C.; Roman general and politician.

Pom·pi·dou /pōNpeedṓ/, Georges 1911–74; president of France (1969–74).

Ponce de Le·ón /paans də léeən, pṓnsə day lee-ṓn, paants, pṓntsə/, Juan c. 1460–1521; Spanish explorer; discovered Florida (1513).

Pon·ti·ac /paántee-ak/ c. 1720–69; Ottawa Indian chief.

Pope /pōp/, Alexander 1688–1744; English poet.

Po·que·lin /pōklắN/, Jean-Baptiste see MOLIÈRE.

Porsche /páwrshə/, Ferdinand 1875–1952; Austrian car designer.

Por·ter /páwrtər, pṓr–/, Cole Albert 1891–1964; U.S. composer.

Por·ter, Katherine Anne Maria Veronica Callista Russell 1890–1980; U.S. author.

Por·ter, William Sydney see HENRY, O.

Pot·ter /paátər/, (Helen) Beatrix 1866–1943; English author.

Pound /pownd/, Ezra (Loomis) 1885–1972; U.S. poet and critic.

Pow·ell /pṓw'l/, Colin 1937– ; U.S. general.

Pow·ha·tan /powətán, pow-hát'n/ c. 1550–1618; Native American chief in early colonial Virginia.

Prax·it·e·les /praksít'l-eez/ fl. 370–330 B.C.; Athenian sculptor.

Pres·ley /prézlee, prés–/, Elvis Aron (called "the King of Rock and Roll") 1935–77; U.S. pop and rock singer.

Pre·vin /prévin/, André (born Andreas Priwin) 1929– ; U.S. composer and conductor, born in Germany.

Price /prīs/, (Mary) Leontyne 1927– ; U.S. operatic soprano.

Priest·ley /preéstlee/, J(ohn) B(oynton) 1894–1984; English author.

Priest·ley, Joseph 1733–1804; English scientist and theologian.

Pro·ko·fiev /prəkáwfyev, –yef, –yəf/, Sergei 1891–1953; Russian composer.

Prou·dhon /prōōdṓN/, Pierre Joseph 1809–65; French author.

Proust /prōōst/, Marcel 1871–1922; French author and critic.

Ptol·e·my /taálimee/ fl. 127–151; ancient astronomer and geographer in Alexandria.

Puc·ci·ni /pōōcheénee/, Giacomo 1858–1924; Italian opera composer.

Pu·las·ki /pəláskee, pyōō–/, (Count) Casimir c. 1748–79; Polish patriot; American RevolutionaryWar general in Continental army.

Pu·litz·er /pōōlitsər, pyōō–/, Joseph 1847–1911; U.S. newspaper publisher, born in Hungary.

Push·kin /pōōshkin/, Alexander 1799–1837; Russian author.

Py·thag·o·ras /pəthág(ə)rəs, pī–/ fl. late 6th cent. B.C.; Greek philosopher.

Qa·dha·fi /kədaáfee, –dáf–/ (also Gad·da'fi), Muammar (Muhammad) al- 1942– ; chief of state of Libya (1969–).

Rab·e·lais /rabəláy/, François c. 1494–1553; French satirical author.

Ra·bin /raabeén/, Yitzhak 1922–95; prime minister of Israel (1974–77; 1992–95); assassinated.

Rach·ma·ni·noff /raakmaáninawf/, Sergei 1873–1943; Russian composer.

Ra·leigh /ráwlee, raálee/ (also Ra'legh), (Sir) Walter c. 1552–1618; English courtier, explorer, and poet.

Ram·ses /rámseez/ (also Ram'e·ses) name of eleven pharaohs of Egypt, including: 1 Ramses I reigned 1320–1318 B.C.; grandfather of: 2 Ramses II reigned 1304–1237 B.C. 3 Ramses III reigned 1198–1166 B.C.

Rand /rand/, Ayn 1905–82; U.S. author, born in Russia.

Raph·a·el /ráfeeəl, ráyfee–, raáfee–/ (surname Sanzio) 1483–1520; Italian artist.

Ra·spu·tin /raspyṓōt'n/, Grigori 1871–1916; Russian mystic; influential in the court of Czar Nicholas II.

Ra·vel /rəvél/, Maurice 1875–1937; French composer.

Ray /ray/, Man (born Emmanuel Rudnitsky) 1890–1976; U.S. artist and photographer.

Rea·gan /ráygən/, Ronald Wilson 1911– ; 40th president of the U.S. (1981–89).

Reed /reed/, Walter C. 1851–1902; U.S. army physician.

Rehn·quist /rénkwist/, William H(ubbs) 1924– ; Chief Justice of the U.S. (1986–).

Re·marque /rəmaárk/, Erich Maria 1898–1970; U.S. author, born in Germany.

Rem·brandt /rémbrant/ (surname Harmensz van Rijn) 1606–69; Dutch artist.

Re·nault /rənáwlt/, Mary (pseudonym of Mary Challans) 1905–83; British novelist.

Re·no /reénō/, Janet 1938– ; U.S. attorney general (1993–).

Re·noir /rənwaár/, Pierre Auguste 1841–1919; French artist.

Re·vere /rəveér/, Paul 1735–1818; American patriot and silversmith.

Reyn·olds /rén'ldz/, (Sir) Joshua 1723–92; English artist.

Rhee /ree/, Syngman 1875–1965; president of South Korea (1948–60).

Rhodes /rōdz/, Cecil John 1853–1902; British colonial administrator in S Africa.

Ri·chard /ríchərd/ name of three kings of England: 1 Richard I (called "the Lionheart") 1157–99; reigned 1189–99. 2 Richard II 1367–1400; reigned 1377–99. 3 Richard III 1452–85; reigned 1483–85.

Rich·ard·son /ríchərdsən/, Samuel 1689–1761; English author.

Rich·e·lieu /ríshəlōō, –lyōō/, Armand Jean du Plessis (Duc de) 1585–1642; French cardinal and statesman.

Rick·o·ver /ríkōvər/, Hyman George 1900–86; U.S. admiral.

Ride /rīd/, Sally Kristen 1951– ; U.S. astronaut.

Rim·sky-Kor·sa·kov /rimskee káwrsəkawf/, Nikolai 1844–1908; Russian composer.

Ri·ve·ra /rivérə/, Diego 1886–1957; Mexican artist.

Rob·bins /raábinz/, Jerome 1918– ; U.S. ballet dancer and choreographer.

Robert I /róbərt/ (called "Robert the Bruce") 1274–1329; king of Scotland (1306–29).

Robe·son /róbsən/, Paul 1898–1976; U.S. actor and singer.

Robes·pierre /róbzpeer, –pyer/, Maximilien 1758–94; French revolutionary leader.

Rob·in·son /raábinsən/, Edwin Arlington 1869–1935; U.S. poet.

Rob·in·son, Jackie (John Roosevelt) 1919–72; U.S. baseball player.

Rock·e·fel·ler /rókəfelər/ U.S. family prominent in industry, philanthropy, and politics, including: 1 John D(avison) 1839–1937; oil magnate; father of: 2 John D(avison), Jr. 1874–1960; philanthropist; father of: 3 Nelson 1908–79; politician.

Rock·well /rókwel/, Norman 1894–1978; U.S. artist.

Rodg·ers /rójərz/, Richard 1902–79; U.S. composer.

Ro·din /rōdáN/, (François) Auguste 1840–1917; French sculptor.

Roent·gen see RÖNTGEN, WILHELM CONRAD.

Rog·ers /rójərz/, Will(iam Penn Adair) 1879–1935; U.S. humorist.

Röl·vaag /rólvaag/, Ole Edvart 1876–1931; U.S. author, born in Norway.

Rom·berg /rómbərg/, Sigmund 1887–1951; U.S. composer, born in Hungary.

Rom·mel /róməl/, Erwin Johannes Eugen (called "the Desert Fox") 1891–1944; German general.

Rönt·gen /réntgən, rénchən/ (also Roent'gen), Wilhelm Conrad 1845–1923; German physicist; discovered X rays.

Roo·se·velt /rózəvelt, –vəlt, rōō–/ 1 Franklin Delano 1882–1945; 32nd president of the U.S. (1933–45); husband of: 2 (Anna) Eleanor 1884–1962; U.S. diplomat and author.

Roo·se·velt, Theodore 1858–1919; 26th president of the U.S. (1901–08).

Ross /raws/, Betsy (Elizabeth Griscom) 1752–1836; reported maker of the first American flag (1776).

Ros·set·ti /rōzétee, –sét–/ 1 Dante Gabriel 1828–82; English poet and artist; brother of: 2 Christina Georgina 1830–94; English poet.

Ros·si·ni /rəseénee, raw–/, Gioachino 1792–1868; Italian composer.

Ros·tand /rawstaáN, rostánd/, Edmond 1868–1918; French playwright.

Roth /rawth/, Philip 1933– ; U.S. novelist.

Roth·schild /ráwth-child, ráwths–/ European-based family prominent in banking and finance, including: 1 Mayer Amschel 1743–1812; German financier. 2 Lionel Nathan, Baron de 1809–79; British financier.

Rous·seau /roōsó/, **Jean-Jacques** 1712–78; French philosopher and author, born in Switzerland.

Ru·bens /roōbənz/, **Peter Paul** 1577–1640; Flemish artist.

Ru·bin·stein /roōbinstīn/, **Arthur** (also **Artur**) 1886–1982; U.S. concert pianist, born in Poland.

Rush·die /roōshdee, rúsh–/, **(Ahmed) Salman** 1947– ; British novelist, born in India.

Rus·kin /rúskin/, **John** 1819–1900; English art and social critic.

Rus·sell /rúsəl/, **Bertrand** 1873–1970; British philosopher, mathematician, and social reformer.

Ruth /roōth/, **Babe (George Herman)** 1895–1948; U.S. baseball player.

Ruth·er·ford /rúthərfərd, –əfərd/, **(Sir) Ernest** 1871–1937; British nuclear physicist, born in New Zealand.

Ryle /rīl/, **Gilbert** 1900–76; English philosopher.

Saa·ri·nen /saárənən/ two U.S. architects, born in Finland: **1** (Gottlieb) Eliel 1873–1950; father of: **2** Eero 1910–61.

Sa·bin /sáybin/, **Albert Bruce** 1906–93; U.S. microbiologist, born in Russia; developed oral vaccine for polio.

Sac·a·ja·we·a /sakəjəweeə, –wáyə/ (also **Sa·ca·ga·we′a**) c. 1788–1812; Shoshone Indian guide for the Lewis and Clark expedition.

Sa·dat /sədaát, –dát/, **Anwar el-** 1918–81; president of Egypt (1970–81); assassinated.

Sade /saad/, **Donatien (Comte de)** (called **"Marquis de Sade"**) 1740–1814; French novelist and notorious sexual deviant.

Sa·gan /sáygən/, **Carl Edward** 1934–96; U.S. astronomer and author.

Saint-Gau·dens /saynt gáwdnz/, **Augustus** 1848–1907; U.S. sculptor, born in Ireland.

Saint-Saëns /saN saáNs/, **(Charles) Camille** 1835–1921; French composer.

Sa·kha·rov /saákhərawf, sák–/, **Andrei Dmitrievich** 1921–89; Russian nuclear physicist.

Sa·ki /saakee/ see MUNRO, H(ECTOR) H(UGH).

Sal·a·din /sálədeen, –ədin/ 1137–93; sultan of Egypt and Syria (1175–93).

Sa·la·zar /sáləzaar/, **António de Oliveira** 1899–1970; premier of Portugal (1932–68).

Sal·in·ger /sálinjər/, **J(erome) D(avid)** 1919– ; U.S. author.

Salk /saw(l)k/, **Jonas** 1914–95; U.S. physician and microbiologist; developed first polio vaccine (1955).

Sal·lust /sáləst/, (Latin name **Gaius Sallustius Crispus**) 86–34 B.C.; Roman historian and politician.

Sand /sand, saaNd/, **George** (pseudonym of **Amandine-Aurore-Lucile Dupin Dudevant**) 1804–76; French novelist.

Sand·burg /sánbərg, sánd–/, **Carl** 1878–1967; U.S. poet and biographer.

Sang·er /sángər/, **Margaret Louise Higgins** 1883–1966; U.S. reformer; proponent of birth control.

San·ta An·na /sántə ánə/ (also **San′ta An′a**), **Antonio López de** c. 1795–1876; Mexican military and political leader.

San·ta·ya·na /santəyáánə/, **George** 1863–1952; U.S. philosopher and poet, born in Spain.

Sap·pho /sáfō/ fl. 7th cent.–6th cent. B.C.; Greek lyric poet.

Sar·gent /saárjənt/, **John Singer** 1856–1925; U.S. portrait artist.

Sa·roy·an /səróyən/, **William** 1908–81; U.S. author.

Sar·tre /saártrə, saart/, **Jean-Paul** 1905–80; French philosopher and author.

Saus·sure /sōsoōr/, **Ferdinand de** 1857–1913; Swiss linguist.

Sav·o·na·ro·la /savənərōlə/, **Girolamo** 1452–98; Italian religious reformer.

Sca·li·a /skəleeə/, **Antonin** 1936– ; U.S. Supreme Court justice (1986–).

Scar·lat·ti /skaarlaátee/ two Italian composers: **1** Alessandro 1659–1725; father of: **2** (Giuseppe) Domenico 1685–1757.

Schles·in·ger /shlésinjər/ two U.S. historians: **1** Arthur Meier 1888–1965; father of: **2** Arthur Meier, Jr. 1917– .

Schil·ler /shílər/, **Johann Christoph Friedrich von** 1759–1805; German playwright and poet.

Schlie·mann /shleémaan/, **Heinrich** 1822–90; German archaeologist.

Schön·berg /shárnbərg/, **Arnold Franz Walter** 1874–1951; U.S. composer, born in Austria.

Scho·pen·hau·er /shōpənhowər/, **Arthur** 1788–1860; German philosopher.

Schrö·ding·er /shráydingər, shrốd–/, **Erwin** 1887–1961; German theoretical physicist.

Schu·bert /shoōbərt/, **Franz** 1797–1828; Austrian composer.

Schulz /shoōlts/, **Charles M(onroe)** 1922– ; U.S. cartoonist.

Schu·mann /shoōmaan, –mən/, **Robert** 1810–56; German composer.

Schwarz·kopf /shwáwrtskawf/, **H. Norman** 1934– ; U.S. general.

Schweit·zer /shwítsər/, **Albert** 1875–1965; French theologian, organist, and medical missionary in Africa.

Scip·i·o /sípee-ō, skíp–/ name of two Roman generals: **1** Publius Cornelius Scipio Africanus Major 236–c. 184 B.C.; defeated Hannibal; adoptive grandfather of: **2** Publius Cornelius Scipio Aemilianus Africanus 185–129 B.C.; destroyed Carthage.

Scott /skot/, **Dred** c. 1795–1858; U.S. slave; subject of a controversial U.S. Supreme Court proslavery decision (1857).

Scott, (Sir) Walter 1771–1832; Scottish novelist and poet.

Scott, Winfield (called **"Old Fuss and Feathers"**) 1786–1866; U.S. general.

Sea·borg /seébawrg/, **Glenn Theodor** 1912–99; U.S. chemist.

Se·go·vi·a /səgóveeə/, **Andrés** 1893–1987; Spanish classical guitarist.

Se·leu·cus I /səloōkəs/ c. 358–280 B.C.; Macedonian general; founded Seleucid Empire of Syria and Asia Minor.

Sen·e·ca /sénikə/, **Lucius Annaeus** c. 4 B.C.–A.D. 65; Roman philosopher and author.

Sen·nach·er·ib /sənakərib/ died 681 B.C.; king of Assyria (704–681 B.C.).

Se·quoy·a /sikwóyə/ c. 1770–1843; Cherokee Indian scholar.

Se·ton /seét'n/, **St. Elizabeth Ann Bayley** (called **"Mother Seton"**) 1774–1821; U.S. religious leader and educator.

Seu·rat /səraá/, **Georges** 1859–91; French artist.

Seuss /soōs/, **Dr.** (pseudonym of **Theodor Seuss Geisel**) 1904–91; U.S. children's author and illustrator.

Sew·ard /soōərd/, **William Henry** 1801–72; U.S. politician; advocated U.S. purchase of Alaska.

Shake·speare /sháykspeer/, **William** 1564–1616; English poet and playwright. □□ **Shake·spear′e·an** adj. **Shake·spear′i·an** adj.

Sha·li·kash·vi·li /shaaleekaashveélee/, **John Malchase** 1936– ; U.S. general, born in Poland; chairman of the Joint Chiefs of Staff (1993–97).

Shan·kar /shaángkaar/, **Ravi** 1920– ; Indian sitar player.

Shaw /shaw/, **George Bernard** 1856–1950; Irish playwright, novelist, and critic.

Shel·ley /shélee/ **1** Percy Bysshe 1792–1822; English poet; husband of: **2** Mary Wollstonecraft 1797–1851; English novelist.

Sher·i·dan /shérid'n/, **Phillip Henry** 1831–88; Union general in the American Civil War.

Sher·i·dan, Richard Brinsley 1751–1816; Irish playwright.

Sher·man /shérmən/, **Roger** 1721–93; American statesman and patriot.

Sher·man, William Tecumseh 1820–91; Union general in the American Civil War.

Shev·ard·na·dze /shevərdnaádzə/, **Eduard** 1928– ; president of the Georgian Republic (1992–).

Sho·sta·ko·vich /shostəkôvich/, **Dmitri** 1906–75; Russian composer.

Sho·wa /shốwə/ see HIROHITO.

Si·be·li·us /sibáyleeəs/, **Jean** 1865–1957; Finnish composer.

Sid·dhart·ha Gau·ta·ma /sidaártə, –thə; gówtəmə/ see BUDDHA.

Sie·mens /seémənz, zee–/, **(Ernst) Werner von** 1816–92; German electrical engineer and inventor.

Si·kor·sky /sikáwrskee/, **Igor** 1889–1972; U.S. aircraft designer, born in Russia.

Sills /silz/, **Beverly** (born **Belle Silverman**) 1929– ; U.S. operatic soprano.

Si·mon Pe·ter see PETER, ST.

Si·mon /símən/, **(Marvin) Neil** 1927– ; U.S. playwright.

Simp·son /símpsən/, **O(renthal) J(ames)** 1947– ; U.S. football player and actor.

Si·na·tra /sinaátrə/, **Frank (Francis Albert)** 1915–98; U.S. singer and actor.

Sin·clair /sínklair, –kláir/, **Upton** 1878–1968; U.S. novelist.

Sing·er /síng-ər/, **Isaac Bashevis** 1904–91; U.S. author, born in Poland.

Sing·er, Isaac Merritt 1811–75; U.S. inventor.

Sit·ting Bull /síting boŏl/ c. 1831–90; Sioux Indian leader.

Skin·ner /skínər/, **B(urrhus) F(rederic)** 1904–90; U.S. psychologist.

Sme·ta·na /smét'nə/, **Bedřich** 1824–84; Czech composer.

Smith /smith/, **Adam** 1723–90; Scottish philosopher and economist.

Smith, **John** 1580–1631; English colonist of Virginia.

Smith, **Joseph** 1805–44; founder of the Mormon Church (1830).

Smol·lett /smólit/, **Tobias George** 1721–71; English novelist.

Smuts /smʏts, smuts/, **Jan Christiaan** 1870–1950; prime minister of South Africa (1919–24; 1939–48).

Soc·ra·tes /sókrəteez/ 469–399 B.C.; Greek philosopher. □□ **So·crat·ic** /səkrátik/ *adj.*

So·lon /sólən/ c. 638–559 B.C.; Athenian lawgiver.

Sol·zhe·ni·tsyn /sōlzhəneétsin, sawl–/, **Alexander** 1918– ; Russian novelist.

Sond·heim /sóndhīm/, **Stephen Joshua** 1930– ; U.S. songwriter.

Son·tag /sóntag/, **Susan** 1933– ; U.S. author and critic.

Soph·o·cles /sófəkleez/ c. 496–406 B.C.; Greek tragedian.

Sou·sa /sốozə/, **John Philip** 1854–1932; U.S. bandmaster and composer.

Sou·ter /sốotər/, **David Hackett** 1939– ; U.S. Supreme Court justice (1990–).

Sou·they /súthee, sówthee/, **Robert** 1774–1843; English author.

So·yin·ka /shaw-yíngkə/, **Wole** 1934– ; Nigerian author.

Spar·ta·cus /spaártəkəs/ died 71 B.C.; Thracian gladiator; leader of a slave revolt against Rome.

Spen·ser /spénsər/, **Edmund** c. 1552–99; English poet.

Spiel·berg /spéelbərg/, **Steven** 1947– ; U.S. film director, writer, and producer.

Spi·no·za /spinōzə/, **Baruch (Benedict de)** 1632–77; Dutch philosopher.

Spock /spok/, **Benjamin** 1903–98; U.S. pediatrician and author.

Squan·to /skwaántō/ died 1622; Pawtuxet Indian who befriended Pilgrims at Plymouth Colony in Massachusetts.

Sta·lin /staálən, stál–/, **Joseph** (born **Iosif Vissarionovich Dzhugashvili**) 1879–1953; Soviet political leader.

Stan·dish /stándish/, **Myles** (or **Miles**) c. 1584–1656; English colonist in New England.

Stan·i·slav·sky /stanislaávskee/, **Konstantin** 1863–1938; Russian director and teacher of acting.

Stan·ley /stánlee/, **(Sir) Henry Morton** (born **John Rowlands**) 1841–1904; U.S. explorer and author, born in Wales.

Stan·ton /stánt'n/, **Elizabeth Cady** 1815–1902; U.S. social reformer.

Starr /staar/, **Ringo** (born **Richard Starkey**) 1940– ; British pop and rock drummer and singer.

Stein /stīn/, **Gertrude** 1874–1946; U.S. author.

Stein·beck /stínbek/, **John Ernst** 1902–68; U.S. author.

Stein·em /stínəm/, **Gloria** 1934– ; U.S. journalist, editor, and women's rights activist.

Sten·dhal /stendaál, staNdaál/ (pseudonym of **Henri Beyle**) 1783–1842; French novelist.

Sterne /stərn/, **Laurence** 1713–68; British novelist.

Steu·ben /styốbən, stōō–, shtóy–/, **(Baron) Friedrich von** 1730–94; Prussian military leader; American Revolutionary War general in the Continental army.

Ste·vens /steévənz/, **John Paul** 1920– ; U.S. Supreme Court justice (1975–).

Ste·vens, **Wallace** 1878–1955; U.S. poet.

Ste·ven·son /steévənsən/, **Adlai Ewing** 1900–65; U.S. politician and statesman.

Ste·ven·son, **Robert Louis Balfour** 1850–94; British novelist.

Stone /stōn/, **Lucy** 1818–93; U.S. suffragist.

Stop·pard /stópaard, –ərd/, **Tom** (born **Thomas Straussler**) 1937– ; English playwright, born in Czechoslovakia.

Stowe /stō/, **Harriet Beecher** 1811–96; U.S. author.

Stra·di·va·ri /stradəvaáree, –vár–/, **Antonio** c. 1644–1737; Italian violin-maker.

Strauss /strows, shtrows/, **Johann** (called "**the Waltz King**") 1825–99; Austrian composer.

Strauss, **Richard Georg** 1864–1949; German composer.

Stra·vin·sky /strəvínskee/, **Igor** 1882–1971; U.S. composer, born in Russia.

Strind·berg /strín(d)bərg/, **(Johan) August** 1849–1912; Swedish author.

Stu·art /stốoərt/, **Gilbert Charles** 1755–1828; U.S. portrait artist.

Stu·art, **Jeb (James Ewell Brown)** 1833–64; Confederate general in the American Civil War.

Stuy·ve·sant /stívəsənt/, **Peter** 1592–1672; Dutch colonial administrator in America.

Sue·to·ni·us /sweetốneeəs/ 75–150; Roman historian.

Su·kar·no /sŏokaárnō/, **Achmed** 1901–70; president of Indonesia (1949–67).

Su·har·to /sŏohaártō/, **Raden** 1921– ; president of Indonesia (1968–).

Su·lei·man I /sŏolaymaan, –li–/ (called "**the Magnificent**") c. 1495–1566; sultan of the Ottoman Empire.

Sul·la /súlə/, **Lucius Cornelius** c. 138–78 B.C.; Roman general and political leader.

Sun Yat-sen /sŏon yaátsén/ (also **Sun Yi-xian**) 1866–1925; Chinese political leader.

Suth·er·land /súthərlənd/, **Joan** 1926– ; Australian operatic soprano.

Swift /swift/, **Jonathan** 1667–1745; English clergyman and satirist, born in Ireland.

Swin·burne /swínbərn/, **Algernon Charles** 1837–1909; English poet and critic.

Synge /sing/, **(Edmund) John Millington** 1871–1909; Irish playwright.

Tac·i·tus /tásitəs/, **Cornelius** c. 55–c. 120; Roman historian.

Taft /taft/ **1 William Howard** 1857–1930; 27th president of the U.S. (1909–13); Chief Justice of the U.S. (1921–30); father of: **2 Robert A(lphonse)** 1889–1953; U.S. politician.

Ta·gore /təgáwr, –gốr/, **(Sir) Rabindranath** 1861–1941; Indian poet.

Tal·ley·rand-Pé·ri·gord /táleerand perəgáwr/, **Charles Maurice de (Prince de Bénévent)** 1754–1838; French diplomat.

Tam·er·lane /támərlayn/ c. 1336–1405; Mongol ruler.

Tar·king·ton /taárkingtən/, **(Newton) Booth** 1869–1946; U.S. author.

Tay·lor /táylər/, **Elizabeth** 1932– ; U.S. actress, born in England.

Tay·lor, **Zachary** 1784–1850; 12th president of the U.S. (1849–50).

Tchai·kov·sky /chīkáwfskee, –káwv–/, **Peter Ilyich** 1840–93; Russian composer.

Te Ka·na·wa /tay kaánəwə/, **Kiri** 1944– ; New Zealand operatic soprano.

Te·cum·seh /təkúmsə/ c. 1768–1813; Shawnee Indian leader.

Teil·hard de Char·din /tay-yaár də shaardáN/, **Pierre** 1881–1955; French Jesuit philosopher.

Tel·ler /télər/, **Edward** 1908– ; U.S. nuclear physicist, born in Hungary.

Tem·ple /témpəl/, **Shirley** see Black, Shirley Temple.

Teng Hsiao-p'ing /dúng shyówpíng/ see Deng Xiaoping.

Ten·ny·son /ténəsən/, **Alfred, Lord** 1809–92; English poet.

Te·re·sa /təreésə, –ráyzə/, **Mother** (born **Agnes Gonxha Bojaxhiu**) 1910–97; Roman Catholic missionary nun, born in Albania.

Tes·la /téslə/, **Nikola** 1856–1943; U.S. engineer and inventor.

Thack·er·ay /thákəree/, **William Makepeace** 1811–63; English author.

Tha·les /tháyleez/ fl. early 6th cent. B.C.; Greek philosopher.

Thant /t(h)aant, t(h)ánt/, **U** 1909–74; Burmese diplomat; secretary-general of the United Nations (1962–71).

Thatch·er /tháchər/, **(Lady) Margaret Hilda Roberts** (called "**the Iron Lady**") 1925– ; prime minister of Great Britain (1979–90).

Thi·bault /teebō/, **Jacques Anatole** see France, Anatole.

Thom·as à Kem·pis see Kempis, Thomas à.

Thom·as /taáməs/, **Clarence** 1948– ; U.S. Supreme Court justice (1991–).

Thom·as, **Dylan** 1914–53; Welsh poet.

Tho·reau /thərố, tháwrō/, **Henry David** (born **David Henry Thoreau**) 1817–62; U.S. author.

Thu·cyd·i·des /thŏoosídədeez, thyŏo–/ c. 455–c. 400 B.C.; Greek historian.

Thur·ber /thərbər/, **James Grover** 1894–1961; U.S. cartoonist and author.

Ti·be·ri·us /tībeéreeəs/ 42 B.C.–A.D. 37; Roman emperor (A.D. 14–37).

Til·lich /tílik/, **Paul Johannes** 1886–1965; U.S. theologian, born in Germany.

Tin·to·ret·to /tintərétō/ 1518–94; Italian artist.

See page xx for the **Key to Pronunciation.**

Ti·tian /tíshən/ c. 1488–1576; Italian artist.

Ti·to /teetō/, (born **Josip Broz**) 1892–1980; president of Yugoslavia (1953–80).

Tocque·ville /tŏkvil/, **Alexis de** 1805–59; French statesman and author.

Tof·fler /táwflər/, **Alvin** 1928– ; U.S. author.

To·jo /tōjō/, **Hideki** 1885–1948; war minister (1940–41) and prime minister (1941–44) of Japan; executed.

Tol·kien /taálkeen, tōl–/, **J(ohn) R(onald) R(euel)** 1892–1973; English author.

Tol·stoy /táwlstoy, tōl–, taál–/, (**Count**) **Leo** (or **Lev**) **Nikolaevich** 1828–1910; Russian author.

Tor·que·ma·da /tawrkəmaádə/, **Tomás de** c. 1420–98; Spanish cleric; led Spanish Inquisition.

Tos·ca·ni·ni /toskəneénee/, **Arturo** 1867–1975; Italian conductor.

Tou·louse-Lau·trec /toolōōs lōtrék/, **Henri de** 1864–1901; French artist.

Toyn·bee /tóynbee/, **Arnold Joseph** 1889–1975; English historian.

Tra·cy /tráysee/, **Spencer** 1900–67; U.S. actor.

Trev·i·thick /trévəthik/, **Richard** 1771–1833; British engineer.

Trol·lope /tróləp/, **Anthony** 1815–82; English novelist.

Trot·sky /trótskee/, **Leon** (born **Lev Davidovich Bronstein**) 1879–1940; Russian revolutionary.

Tru·deau /troodṓ/, **Pierre Elliott** 1919– ; prime minister of Canada (1968–79; 1980–84).

Tru·man /troōmən/ **1** Harry S 1884–1972; 33rd president of the U.S. (1945–53); father of: **2** Margaret 1924– ; U.S. author.

Trump /trump/, **Donald** 1946– ; U.S. business executive.

Tub·man /túbmən/, **Harriet** 1820–1913; U.S. abolitionist.

Tuch·man /túkmən/, **Barbara** 1912–89; U.S. historian.

Tur·ge·nev /toorgáynyəf, –gén–/, **Ivan** 1818–83; Russian novelist.

Tur·ner /tórnər/, **Joseph Mallord William** 1775–1851; English landscape artist.

Tur·ner, Nat 1800–31; U.S. slave insurrectionist.

Tur·ner, Ted (**Robert Edward**) 1938– ; U.S. media executive.

Tut·ankh·a·men /tootaangkaámən, –tang–/ 14th cent. B.C.; Egyptian king.

Tu·tu /tootoo/, **Desmond** (born **Mpilo**) 1931– ; South African archbishop and civil-rights leader.

Twain /twayn/, **Mark** (pseudonym of **Samuel Langhorne Clemens**) 1835–1910; U.S. author.

Tweed /tweed/, **Boss** (**William Marcy**) 1823–78; U.S. politician.

Ty·ler /tílər/, **John** 1790–1862; 10th president of the U.S. (1841–45).

Tyn·dale /tíndəl, –dayl/, **William** c. 1494–1536; English translator of the Bible.

Up·dike /úpdīk/, **John Hoyer** 1932– ; U.S. novelist.

Va·lé·ry /valəree/, **Paul Ambroise** 1871–1945; French poet and philosopher.

Van Bu·ren /van byoórən/, **Martin** (called "**Old Kinderhook**") 1782–1862; 8th president of the U.S. (1837–41).

Van·der·bilt /vándərbilt/, **Cornelius** 1794–1877; U.S. industrialist.

Van Dyck /van dík/, (**Sir**) **Anthony** 1599–1641; Flemish artist.

Van Eyck /van ík/, **Jan** died 1441; Flemish artist.

Van Gogh /van gṓ, gaákh/, **Vincent** 1853–90; Dutch artist.

Vaughan /vawn/, **Sarah** 1924–90; U.S. jazz singer.

Vaughan Wil·liams /vawn wílyəmz/, **Ralph** 1872–1958; English composer.

Ve·láz·quez /vəláskəs, –kwez/, **Diego** 1599–1660; Spanish artist.

Ver·di /vérdee/, **Giuseppe** 1813–1901; Italian opera composer.

Ver·gil /vórjəl/ see VIRGIL.

Ver·meer /vərmeér/, **Jan** 1632–75; Dutch artist.

Verne /vərn/, **Jules** 1828–1905; French author.

Ves·puc·ci /vespoŏchee/, **Amerigo** 1451–1512; Italian explorer.

Vic·to·ri·a /viktáwreeə/ 1819–1901; queen of Great Britain (1837–1901).

Vi·dal /vidaál, –dáwl/, **Gore** (born **Eugene Luther Vidal**) 1925– ; U.S. author.

Vil·la /veé-ə/, **Pancho** (**Francisco**) 1877–1923; Mexican revolutionary.

Vil·lon /vee-yṓN/, **François** 1431–c. 1463; French poet.

Vir·gil /vórjəl/ (also **Ver'gil**) 70–19 B.C.; Roman poet.

Vir·gin Mar·y see MARY.

Vi·val·di /vivaáldee/, **Antonio** 1678–1741; Italian composer.

Vol·ta /vṓwltə/, (**Count**) **Alessandro** 1745–1827; Italian physicist.

Vol·taire /vōltáir, vawl–, –tér/, (pseudonym of **François-Marie Arouet**) 1694–1778; French author.

Von·ne·gut /vónigət/, **Kurt** 1922– ; U.S. author.

Wag·ner /vaágnər/, **Richard** 1813–83; German composer.

Wald·heim /vaáldhīm/, **Kurt** 1918– ; Austrian political leader and diplomat; secretary-general of the United Nations (1972–82).

Wa·le·sa /vəlénsə, vəwénsə/, **Lech** 1943– ; Polish labor and political leader.

Wal·lace /waáləs/, **Alfred Russel** 1823–1913; British naturalist.

Wal·lace, George Corley 1919–98; U.S. politician.

Wal·pole /wáwlpōl/, **Horace (4th Earl of Orford)** 1717–97; English author.

Wal·ton /wáwlt'n/, **Izaak** 1593–1683; English author.

Wan·kel /vaángkəl/, **Felix** 1902–88; German engineer.

War·hol /wáwrhawl, –hōl/, **Andy** (born **Andrew Warhola**) c. 1930–87; U.S. artist and filmmaker.

War·ren /wáwrən, waár–/, **Earl** 1891–1974; Chief Justice of the U.S. (1953–69).

Wash·ing·ton /waáshingtən, wáwsh–/, **Booker T(aliaferro)** 1856–1915; U.S. educator and reformer.

Wash·ing·ton, George 1732–99; American patriot and Revolutionary War general; 1st president of the U.S. (1789–97).

Wat·son /waátson/, **James Dewey** 1928– ; U.S. biologist.

Watt /waat/, **James** 1736–1819; Scottish inventor.

Wat·teau /vaatṓ, waa–/, **Jean Antoine** 1684–1721; French artist.

Waugh /waw/, **Evelyn** 1903–66; English novelist.

Wayne /wayn/, **Anthony** (called "**Mad Anthony**") 1745–96; American Revolutionary War general.

Wayne, John (born **Marion Michael Morrison**) 1907–79; U.S. actor.

We·ber /váybər/, **Max** 1864–1920; German sociologist.

We·ber /wébər/, **Max** 1881–1961; U.S. artist, born in Russia.

Web·ster /wébstər/, **Daniel** 1782–1852; U.S. politician and orator.

Web·ster, Noah 1758–1843; U.S. lexicographer.

Wedg·wood /wéjwŏod/, **Josiah** 1730–95; English potter.

Weill /vīl/, **Kurt** 1900–50; German composer.

Weiz·mann /vítsmən/, **Chaim** 1874–1952; president of Israel (1949–52).

Wel·ling·ton /wélingtən/, **1st Duke of (Arthur Wellesley)** (called "**the Iron Duke**") 1769–1852; British general and statesman; prime minister of Great Britain (1828–30).

Wells /welz/, **H(erbert) G(eorge)** 1866–1946; English author.

Wel·ty /wéltee/, **Eudora** 1909– ; U.S. author.

Wes·ley /wéslee, wéz–/, **John** 1703–91; English evangelical leader; founder of Methodism.

West /west/, **Benjamin** 1738–1820; U.S. artist.

West, Rebecca (pseudonym of **Cicily Isabel Fairfield**) 1892–1983; English author.

Whar·ton /(h)wáwrt'n/, **Edith Newbold Jones** 1862–1937; U.S. novelist.

Wheat·ley /(h)weétlee/, **Phillis** c. 1753–84; American poet, probably born in Senegal.

Wheat·stone /(h)weétstōn/, (**Sir**) **Charles** 1802–75; English physicist and inventor.

Whis·tler /(h)wíslər/, **James Abbott McNeill** 1834–1903; U.S. artist.

White·head /(h)wít-hed/, **Alfred North** 1861–1947; English mathematician and philosopher.

Whit·man /(h)wítmən/, **Walt(er)** 1819–92; U.S. poet.

Whit·ney /(h)wítnee/, **Eli** 1765–1825; U.S. inventor and manufacturer.

Whit·tier /(h)wíteeər/, **John Greenleaf** 1807–92; U.S. poet.

Wie·sel /veezél, wizél/, **Elie** 1928– ; U.S. author and educator, born in Romania.

Wilde /wīld/, **Oscar** 1854–1900; Irish poet and playwright.

Wil·der /wíldər/, **Thornton Niven** 1897–1975; U.S. author.

Wil·lard /wílərd/, **Emma Hart** 1787–1870; U.S. educational reformer.

Wil·liam /wílyəm/ name of four kings of England, including: **1** William I (called "**the Conqueror**") c. 1027–87; reigned 1066–87. **2** William III 1650–1702; reigned 1689–1702 with his wife, Mary II.

Wil·liams /wílyəmz/, **Roger** c. 1603–83; English clergyman; established Rhode Island colony (1636).

Wil·liams, Tennessee (born **Thomas Lanier Williams**) 1911–83; U.S. playwright.

Wil·liams, William Carlos 1883–1963; U.S. poet.

Wil·son /wílsən/, **Edmund** 1895–1972; U.S. critic and author.

Wil·son, (Lord) (James) Harold 1916–95; prime minister of Great Britain (1964–70; 1974–76).

Wil·son, (Thomas) Woodrow 1856–1924; 28th president of the U.S. (1913–21).

Win·frey /wínfree/, **Oprah** 1954– ; U.S. television personality and actress.

Witt·gen·stein /vítgənshtīn, –stīn/, **Ludwig** 1889–1951; British philosopher, born in Austria.

Wode·house /wo͝odhows/, **(Sir) P(elham) G(renville)** 1881–1975; English author.

Wolfe /wo͝olf/, **Thomas** 1900–38; U.S. author.

Wol·las·ton /wo͝oləstən/, **William Hyde** 1766–1828; English scientist.

Wol·sey /wo͝olzee/, **Thomas** c. 1474–1530; English cleric and statesman.

Won·der /wúndər/, **Stevie** (born **Stephen Judkins**) 1950– ; U.S. pop singer and songwriter.

Wood /wo͝od/, **Grant** 1892–1942; U.S. artist.

Woods /wo͝odz/, **Tiger (Eldrick)** 1975– ; U.S. golfer.

Woolf /wo͝olf/, **(Adeline) Virginia** 1882–1941; English author.

Words·worth /wə́rdzwərth/, **William** 1770–1850; English poet.

Wouk /wōk/, **Herman** 1915– ; U.S. author.

Wren /ren/, **(Sir) Christopher** 1632–1723; English architect.

Wright /rīt/, **Frank Lloyd** 1869–1959; U.S. architect.

Wright, Richard 1908–60; U.S. author.

Wright two U.S. aviation pioneers: **1** Wilbur 1867–1912; brother of: **2** Orville 1871–1948.

Wy·eth /wíəth/ family of U.S. artists, including: **1** N(ewell) C(onvers) 1882–1945; father of: **2** Andrew Newell 1917– ; father of: **3** Jamie (James Browning) 1946– .

Xa·vi·er /záyvyər, igzáy–/, **St. Francis (Francisco Javier)** 1506–52; Spanish Jesuit missionary of the Far East.

Xen·o·phon /zénəfən, –fon/ c. 428–c. 354 B.C.; Greek author.

Xerx·es I /zə́rkseez/ c. 519–465 B.C.; king of Persia (486–465 B.C.).

Yeats /yayts/, **William Butler** 1865–1939; Irish poet and playwright.

Yelt·sin /yéltsin/, **Boris** 1931– ; president of the Russian federation (1991–).

Young /yung/, **Brigham** 1801–77; U.S. Mormon leader.

Za·pa·ta /zəpáátə/, **Emiliano** c. 1877–1919; Mexican revolutionary.

Zar·a·thus·tra /zaarətho͞ostrə/ see ZOROASTER.

Zep·pe·lin /zépəlin/, **(Count) Ferdinand von** 1838–1917; German airship developer.

Zhou En·lai /jő enlí/ see CHOU EN-LAI.

Zhu·kov /zho͝okawf, –kawv/, **Georgi Konstantinovich** 1896–1974; Soviet military leader in World War II.

Zieg·feld /zígfeld, zeég–/, **Flo(renz)** 1867–1932; U.S. theater producer.

Zo·la /zőlə, zōlaá/, **Émile** 1840–1902; French author.

Zo·ro·as·ter /záwrō-astər, zőr–/ (also **Zar·at·hus'tra**) c. 628–551 B.C.; Persian prophet; founder of Zoroastrianism.

Geographical Entries
and Maps

Geographical Entries and Maps

Aa·chen /áakhən/ *n.* city in W Germany. Pop. 241,900.

Ab·er·deen /abərdeén/ *n.* port city in E Scotland, United Kingdom. Pop. 218,200.

Ab·i·djan /abijáan/ *n.* port city and commercial capital of Ivory Coast. Pop. 2,797,000.

Ab·i·lene /ábəleen/ *n.* city in central Texas. Pop. 106,654.

A·bu Dha·bi /áaboō daábee/ *n.* capital of the United Arab Emirates. Pop. 363,400.

A·bu·ja /aabōójaa/ *n.* capital of Nigeria, in the central part. Pop. 339,100.

A·ca·di·a /akáydeeə/ **Na·tion·al Park** *n.* scenic area on the coast of Maine; includes parts of Mount Desert Island, Schoodic Peninsula, and Isle au Haut.

A·ca·pul·co /akəpoólkō, aak–, –poól–/ *n.* port city in S Mexico. Pop. 515,400.

Ac·cra /áakraá/ *n.* port city and capital of Ghana. Pop. 1,781,100.

A·con·ca·gua /aakənkáagwə/ *n.* mountain in the Andes range, in W Argentina; highest in W hemisphere: 22,831 ft.

Ad·dis A·ba·ba /ádis ábəbə/ *n.* capital of Ethiopia, in the central part. Pop. 2,200,200.

Ad·e·laide /ád'layd/ *n.* capital of South Australia, Australia, in the SE part. Pop. 1,023,600.

A·den /áad'n, áyd'n/ *n.* port city and economic capital of Yemen. Pop. 318,000.

A·den, Gulf of *n.* arm of the Arabian Sea, S of Yemen.

Ad·i·ron·dack /adəráandak/ **Moun·tains** *n.* mountain range in NE New York; part of the Appalachian range.

A·dri·at·ic /aydree-átik/ **Sea** *n.* arm of the Mediterranean Sea, between Italy and the Balkan Peninsula.

Ae·ge·an /ijeéən, ee–/ **Sea** *n.* arm of the Mediterranean Sea, between Greece and Turkey.

Af·ghan·i·stan /afgánistan/ *n.* republic in central Asia. Pop. 22,664,000. Capital: Kabul.

Afghanistan

Af·ri·ca /áfrikə/ *n.* continent between the Atlantic and Indian oceans, S of Europe. □□ **Af'ri·can** *n. & adj.*

A·gra /áagrə/ *n.* city in N central India; site of the Taj Mahal. Pop. 899,200.

A·guas·ca·lien·tes /aagwaaskaalyéntays/ *n.* state in central Mexico. Pop. 719,700. Capital: Aguascalientes.

Ah·mad·a·bad /áamədəbaad/ *n.* city in W India. Pop. 2,872,900.

Aix-en-Pro·vence /ayks aaN prōvaáNs, eks/*n.* city in SE France. Pop. 126,900.

Ak·ron /ákrən/ *n.* city in N Ohio. Pop. 223,019.

Al·a·bam·a /aləbámə/ *n.* state in SE U.S. Pop. 4,040,587. Capital: Montgomery. Abbr. **AL; Ala.** □□ **Al·a·bam'i·an, Al·a·bam'an** *n. & adj.*

A·las·ka /əláskə/ *n.* state in NW U.S. Pop. 550,043. Capital: Juneau. Abbr. **AK** □□ **A·las'kan** *n. & adj.*

A·las·ka, Gulf of *n.* arm of the N Pacific, on the S coast of Alaska.

Al·ba·ni·a /albáyneeə, awl–/ *n.* republic in S Europe, on the Balkan Peninsula. Pop. 3,249,000. Capital: Tiranë. □□ **Al·ba'ni·an** *n. & adj.*

Al·ba·ny /áwlbənee/ *n.* capital of New York, in the E part. Pop. 101,082.

Al·ber·ta /albúrtə/ *n.* province in W Canada. Pop. 2,662,000. Capital: Edmonton. □□ **Al·ber'tan** *n. & adj.*

Al·bu·quer·que /álbəkərkee/ *n.* city in central New Mexico. Pop. 384,736.

Al·ca·traz /álkətraz/ *n.* island in in San Francisco Bay; site of a former federal penitentiary.

A·lep·po /əlépō/ *n.* city in N Syria. Pop. 1,591,400.

A·leu·tian /əloóshən/ **Is·lands** *n.* (also called **the A·leu'tians**) island chain in Alaska, between the Bering Sea and the Pacific.

Al·ex·an·dri·a /aligzándreeə/ *n.* **1** port city in N Egypt. Pop. 3,382,000. **2** city in NE Virginia; Pop. 111,183.

Al·ge·ri·a /aljeéreeə/ *n.* republic in NW Africa. Pop. 29,183,000. Capital: Algiers. □□ **Al·ge'ri·an** *n. & adj.*

Algeria

Al·giers /aljeérz/ *n.* port city and capital of Algeria. Pop. 1,507,200.

Al·lah·a·bad /álahəbad, –baad/ *n.* city in N India. Pop. 806,400.

Al·le·ghe·ny /aləgáynee/ **Moun·tains** *n.* mountain range in E U.S., extending from Pennsylvania to Virginia; part of the Appalachian range.

Al·len·town /áləntown/ *n.* city in E Pennsylvania. Pop. 105,090.

al-Ma·nam·ah /al mənámə/ *n.* see MANAMA.

Al·ma·ty /aalmaateé/ *n.* (formerly **Alma-Ata** /aalmaá aataá/) former capital of Kazakhstan, in the SE part. Pop. 1,164,000.

Alps /alps/ *n.* mountain range in S Europe, extending from France through Switzerland and to the Balkan Peninsula.

Am·a·ril·lo /amərílō/ *n.* city in NW Texas. Pop. 157,615.

Am·a·zon /áməzaan, –zən/ **Riv·er** *n.* river in N South America, flowing 3,900 mi. from the Andes to the Atlantic; largest river in the world.

A·mer·i·ca /əmérikə, –már–/ *n.* **1** popular term for the United States of America. **2** (also called **the A·mer'i·cas**) the continents of North and South America, considered together. □□ **A·mer'i·can** *n. & adj.*

A·mer·i·can Sa·mo·a /səmóə/ *n.* (also **East'ern Sa·mo'a**) island group in the S Pacific, comprising the E islands of Samoa; a U.S. territory. Pop. 60,000. Capital: Pago Pago. See also WESTERN SAMOA. □□ **Sa·mo'an** *n. & adj.*

American Samoa

Am·i·ens /áamyaN, aamyáN/ *n.* city in N France. Pop. 136,200.

Am·man /aamaán/ *n.* capital of Jordan. Pop. 963,500.

Am·rit·sar /əmrítsər/ *n.* city in NW India. Pop. 709,500.

Am·ster·dam /ámstərdam/ *n.* port city and capital of the Netherlands. Pop. 724,100.

An·a·heim /ánəhīm/ *n.* city in SW California. Pop. 266,406.

An·chor·age /ángkərij/ *n.* port city in S Alaska. Pop. 226,338.

An·da·man /ándəmən, –man/ **Is·lands** *n.* island group in the Bay of Bengal, W of the Malay Peninsula.

Albania

An·des /ándeez/ *n.* mountain range in W South America, extending from Colombia to Cape Horn. □□ **An'de·an** *n. & adj.*

An·dor·ra /andáwrə/ *n.* republic in W Europe, on the border between France and Spain. Pop. 73,000. Capital: Andorra la Vella.

Andorra

An·gel /áynjəl/ **Falls** *n.* waterfall in SE Venezuela; highest in the world: 3,212 ft.

An·go·la /ang-gólə, an–/ *n.* republic in SW Africa. Pop. 10,343,000. Capital: Luanda. □□ **An·go'lan** *n. & adj.*

Angola

An·guil·la /anggwílə/ *n.* island in the E West Indies; dependent territory of the United Kingdom. Pop. 8,700.

An·ka·ra /áangkərə, áng–/ *n.* capital of Turkey, in the central part. Pop. 2,720,000.

An·nap·o·lis /ənápələs/ *n.* capital of Maryland, in the central part; site of U.S. Naval Academy. Pop. 33,187.

Ann Ar·bor /an aárbər/ *n.* city in SE Michigan. Pop. 109,592.

An·ta·na·na·ri·vo /antənanəreévō/ *n.* capital of Madagascar, in the E central part. Pop. 1,052,800.

Ant·arc·ti·ca /antaárktikə, –aártikə/ *n.* **1** largely ice-covered continent surrounding the South Pole. **2 (the Antarctic)** region of Antarctica and surrounding oceans. □□ **ant·arc'tic** *adj.*

Antarctica

An·ti·gua /anteégwə/ **and Bar·bu·da** /baarbóodə/ *n.* island state in the E West Indies. Pop. 66,000. Capital: St. John's.

Antigua and Barbuda

An·til·les /antíleez/ *n.* island chain in the West Indies, comprising the Greater Antilles and the Lesser Antilles.

An·tip·o·des /antípədeez/ *n.* **1** collective term for Australia and New Zealand. **2** island group in the S Pacific, SE of New Zealand.

Ant·werp /ántwərp/ *n.* port city in N Belgium. Pop. 462,900.

Ap·en·nines /ápəninz/ *n.* mountain range extending the length of the Italian peninsula.

A·pi·a /əpeéə/ *n.* port city and capital of Western Samoa. Pop. 32,900.

Ap·pa·la·chi·an /apəláychən, –lách–, –cheeən/ **Moun·tains** *n.* mountain range in E North America, extending from Quebec to Alabama.

Ap·po·mat·tox /apəmátəks/ **Court·house** *n. hist.* former town in central Virginia, at present-day Appomattox; site of Lee's surrender to Grant ending the American Civil War (1865).

A·ra·bi·an /əráybeeən/ **Pen·in·su·la** *n.* (also called **A·ra'bi·a**) peninsula in SW Asia, bounded by the Red Sea and the Persian Gulf, and comprising Kuwait, Oman, Qatar, Saudi Arabia, United Arab Emirates, and Yemen.

A·ra·bi·an Sea *n.* part of the Indian Ocean, between the Arabian Peninsula and India.

Ar·al /árəl/ **Sea** *n.* inland sea in W Asia.

Ar·a·rat /árərat/, **Mount** *n.* mountain in E Turkey; traditional landing site of Noah's Ark.

Arch·an·gel *n.* see ARKHANGELSK.

Arc·tic /aárktik, aártik/ *n.* region delimited by the Arctic Circle.

Arc·tic Cir·cle *n.* imaginary line at latitude 66° 32′ N, delimiting the Arctic region.

Arc·tic O·cean *n.* ocean N of North America, Asia, and Europe. Area 5,540,000 sq. mi.

Ar·gen·ti·na /aarjənteénə/ *n.* republic in SE South America. Pop. 34,673,000. Capital: Buenos Aires. □□ **Ar·gen·tine** /aárjənteen, –tīn/ *n. & adj.* **Ar·gen·tin·e·an** /aarjəntíneeən/ *n. & adj.*

Argentina

Ar·i·zo·na /arəzónə/ *n.* state in SW U.S. Pop. 3,665,118. Capital: Phoenix. Abbr. **Ariz.; AZ** □□ **Ar·i·zo'nan, Ar·i·zo'ni·an** *n. & adj.*

Ar·kan·sas /aárkənsaw/ *n.* state in S central U.S. Pop. 2,350,725. Capital: Little Rock. Abbr. **AR; Ark.** □□ **Ar·kan·san** /aarkánsən/ *n. & adj.*

Ar·khan·gelsk /aarkangélsk/ *n.* (also **Arch·an'gel**) port city in NW Russia. Pop. 407,100.

Ar·ling·ton /aárlingtən/ *n.* **1** city in N Texas. Pop. 261,721. **2** city in NE Virginia. Pop. 170,936.

Ar·me·ni·a /aarmeéneeə/ *n.* republic in W Asia. Pop. 3,464,000. Capital: Yerevan. □□ **Ar·me'ni·an** *n. & adj.*

Armenia

A·ru·ba /aaróobaa/ *n.* self-governing Caribbean island, NW of Venezuela. Pop. 68,000.

Aruba

Ash·ga·bat /áshkəbat/ *n.* (also **Ashkh'a·bad**) capital of Turkmenistan, in the S part. Pop. 518,000.

A·sia /áyzhə/ *n.* continent bounded by Europe, the Mediterranean and Red seas, and the Indian, Pacific, and Arctic oceans. □□ **A'sian** *n. & adj.*

A·sia Mi·nor *n. hist.* peninsula in W Asia, bounded by the Black and Mediterranean seas; roughly equivalent to present-day Turkey.

As·ma·ra /aasmaárə/ *n.* (also **As·me'ra**) capital of Eritrea, in the central part. Pop. 367,300.

As·ta·na /aastaánaa/ *n.* (formerly **Aqmola**) capital (since 1998) of Kazakhstan, in the central part. Pop. 130,000.

A·sun·ción /aasoōnsee-ón/ *n.* capital of Paraguay, in the SW part. Pop. 502,400.

As·wan /áswaan, –waán/ *n.* city in SE Egypt. Pop. 220,000.

A·syut /aasyoōt/ *n.* city in E central Egypt. Pop. 321,000.

A·ta·ca·ma /aatəkaámə, at–/ **Des·ert** *n.* arid region in N Chile.

Ath·a·bas·ka /athəbáskə/, **Lake** *n.* lake in W Canada.

Ath·ens /áthənz/ *n.* capital of Greece, in the E part. Pop. 748,100. □□ **A·the·ni·an** /əthéeneeən/ *n. & adj.*

At·lan·ta /ətlántə, at–/ *n.* capital of Georgia, in the NW central part. Pop. 394,017.

At·lan·tic /ətlántik, at–/ **In·tra·coast·al Wa·ter·way** *n.* system of sheltered waterways along the E seaboard of the U.S.

At·lan·tic O·cean *n.* ocean separating the Americas from Europe and Africa. Area 31,530,000 sq. mi.

At·las /átləs/ **Moun·tains** *n.* mountain range in NW Africa, extending from SW Morocco to NE Tunisia.

Auck·land /áwklənd/ *n.* port city in N New Zealand. Pop. 336,500.

Augs·burg /ówksboōrk, áwgzbərg/ *n.* city in S Germany. Pop. 264,800.

Au·gus·ta /əgústə/ *n.* capital of Maine, in the SW part. Pop. 21,325.

Au·ro·ra /əráwrə, –ŕŕrə/ *n.* **1** city in NE central Colorado. Pop. 222,103. **2** city in NE Illinois. Pop. 99,581.

Aus·tin /áwstən/ *n.* capital of Texas, in the E central part. Pop. 465,622.

Aus·tral·a·sia /awstrəláyzhə, aas–, –shə/ *n.* region including Australia, New Zealand, and neighboring islands in the S Pacific.

Aus·tral·ia /awstráylyə, aas–/ *n.* **1** continent SE of Asia, bounded by the Indian and Pacific oceans. **2** commonwealth of the states and territories of Australia and Tasmania. Pop. 18,261,000. Capital: Canberra. □□ **Aus·tral'i·an** *n. & adj.* See map p. 1208.

Aus·tri·a /áwstreeə, aás–/ *n.* republic in central Europe. Pop. 8,023,000. Capital: Vienna. □□ **Aus'tri·an** *n. & adj.* See map p. 1208

Austria

Az·er·bai·jan /azərbīzhaán, –jaán/ *n.* republic in SW Asia; formerly part of the USSR. Pop. 7,677,000. Capital: Baku. □□ **Az·er·bai·ja'ni** *n. & adj.*

Azerbaijan

A·zores /áyzawrz/ *n.* island group in the Atlantic, W of Portugal; autonomous region of Portugal.

A·zov /ázawf, áyzawf/, **Sea of** *n.* N arm of the Black Sea.

Bad·lands /bádlanz, –landz/ *n.* barren region in SW South Dakota and NW Nebraska.

Baf·fin /báfin/ **Bay** *n.* inlet of the Arctic Ocean, between Baffin Island and Greenland.

Baf·fin Is·land *n.* island in NE Canada, W of Greenland.

Bagh·dad /bágdad, bagdád/ *n.* (also **Bag'dad**) capital of Iraq, in the E central part. Pop. 4,044,000.

Ba·ha·mas /bəhaáməz/ *n.* island nation in the N West Indies, SE of Florida. Pop. 259,000. Capital: Nassau. □□ **Ba·ha·mi·an** /bəháymeeən/ *n. & adj.*

Bah·rain /baaráyn, baakhráyn/ *n.* sheikdom consisting of islands in the Persian Gulf. Pop. 590,000. Capital: Manama.

Bai·kal /bīkaál, ; n-káwl/, **Lake** *n.* lake in S Russia; deepest in the world: 5,700 ft.

Ba·ja Ca·li·for·nia /baáhaa kalifáwrnyə/ *n.* **1** peninsula in NW Mexico, bounded by the Pacific and the Gulf of California. **2** (formerly

Ba'ja Ca·li·for'nia Nor·te /náwrtay/) state in NW Mexico; N part of Baja California peninsula. Pop. 1,886,000. Capital: Mexicali.

Ba·ja Ca·li·for·nia Sur /soōr/ *n.* state in NW Mexico; S part of Baja California peninsula. Pop. 317,800. Capital: La Paz.

Ba·kers·field /báykərzfeeld/ *n.* city in S California. Pop. 174,820.

Ba·ku /baakoō/ *n.* port city and capital of Azerbaijan. Pop. 1,080,500.

Bal·e·ar·ic /balee-árik/ **Is·lands** *n.* island group in the W Mediterranean Sea; province of Spain.

Ba·li /baálee, bálee/ *n.* island in Indonesia, E of Java.

Bal·kan /báwlkən/ **Pen·in·su·la** *n.* peninsula in S Europe, bounded by the Adriatic and Black seas, and comprising the Balkan States.

Bal·kan States *n.* (also called **the Bal'kans**) countries of the Balkan Peninsula: Albania, Bulgaria, Greece, Romania, Croatia, Bosnia and Herzegovina, Yugoslavia (including Serbia), Macedonia, and European Turkey.

Bal·tic /báwltik/ **Sea** *n.* sea in N Europe, S of Scandinavian Peninsula.

Bal·ti·more /báwltəmawr/ *n.* port city in N central Maryland. Pop. 736,014.

Ba·ma·ko /báməkō/ *n.* capital of Mali, in the SW part. Pop. 745,800.

Ban·dung /baándoōng/ *n.* city in Indonesia, on Java. Pop. 2,026,900.

Ban·ga·lore /baánggəlawr/ *n.* city in SW India. Pop. 2,650,700.

Bang·kok /bángkaak/ *n.* port city and capital of Thailand. Pop. 5,572,700.

Ban·gla·desh /bbangglədésh, baang–/ *n.* republic in S Asia. Pop. 123,063,000. Capital: Dhaka. □□ **Ban·gla·desh'i** *n. & adj.*

Bangladesh

Ban·gui /baang-geé/ *n.* capital of Central African Republic, in the SW part. Pop. 524,000.

Ban·jul /baánjoōl/ *n.* port city and capital of Gambia. Pop. 44,200.

Bar·ba·dos /baarbáydōs, –öz/ *n.* island nation in the E West Indies. Pop. 257,000. Capital: Bridgetown. □□ **Bar·ba'di·an** *n. & adj.*

Barbados

Bahamas

Bahrain

AUSTRALIA

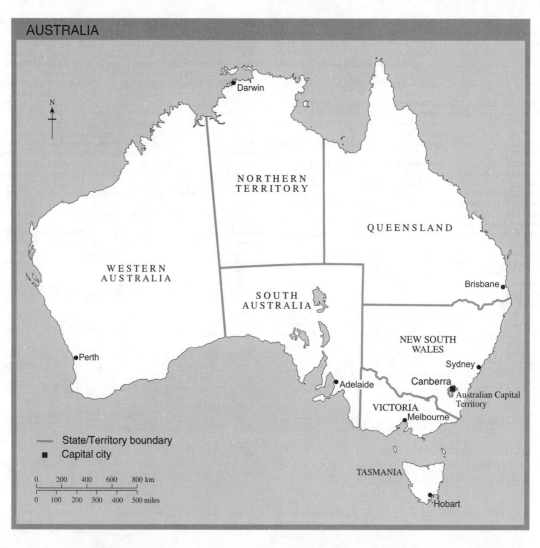

N

NORTHERN
TERRITORY

QUEENSLAND

WESTERN
AUSTRALIA

SOUTH
AUSTRALIA

• Perth

• Darwin

• Brisbane

NEW SOUTH
WALES

Sydney •

Canberra ■

Adelaide •

VICTORIA

Australian Capital
Territory

■ Melbourne

TASMANIA

— State/Territory boundary
■ Capital city

| 0 | 200 | 400 | 600 | 800 km |

| 0 | 100 | 200 | 300 | 400 | 500 miles |

Hobart •

AUSTRIA

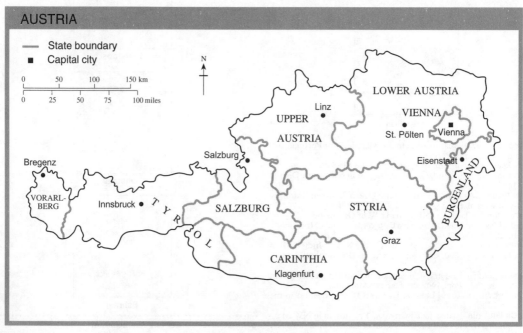

— State boundary
■ Capital city

| 0 | 50 | 100 | 150 km |

| 0 | 25 | 50 | 75 | 100 miles |

N

LOWER AUSTRIA

UPPER
AUSTRIA

Linz •

VIENNA

St. Pölten •   Vienna ■

Bregenz
•

Salzburg •

Eisenstadt •

VORARL-
BERG

Innsbruck •   T Y R O L

SALZBURG

STYRIA

BURGENLAND

Graz •

CARINTHIA

Klagenfurt •

Bar·ba·ry /báarbəree/ **Coast** n. Mediterranean coast of the former Barbary States, in N Africa.

Bar·ba·ry States n. hist. Morocco, Algiers, Tunis, and Tripoli; refuge for pirates between 1520 and 1830.

Bar·ce·lo·na /baarsəlónə/ n. port city in NE Spain. Pop. 1,630,900.

Ba·ri /báaree/ n. (also called **Ba'ri del·le Pu·glie** /delə poólyee/) port city in SE Italy. Pop. 339,000.

Ba·ro·da /bərốdə/ n. city in W India. Pop. 1,021,100.

Bar·ran·qui·lla /baaraankeéyə, –keélyə/ n. port city in N Colombia. Pop. 1,064,300.

Ba·sel /báazəl/ n. city in W Switzerland. Pop. 176,200.

Bas·ra /báasrə, baáz–/ n. city in SE Iraq. Pop. 616,700.

Basse·terre /baastér/ n. port city and capital of St. Kitts and Nevis. Pop. 15,000.

Basse-Terre /baas tér/ n. port city and capital of Guadeloupe. Pop. 14,100.

Ba·su·to·land /bəsoótoōland, –tōland/ n. see LESOTHO.

Bat·on Rouge /bat'n roózh/ n. capital of Louisiana, in the SE central part. Pop. 219,531.

Bat·tle /bát'l/ **Creek** n. city in S Michigan. Pop. 53,540.

Ba·ya·món /bīəmón/ n. city in N Puerto Rico. Pop. 202,100.

Beau·fort /bófərt/ **Sea** n. part of the Arctic Ocean, NE of Alaska.

Beau·mont /bómaant/ n. city in SE Texas. Pop. 114,323.

Bea·ver·ton /beévərtən/ n. city in NW Oregon. Pop. 53,310.

Beer·she·ba /beersheébə/ n. city in S Israel. Pop. 141,400.

Bei·jing /bayjíng, –zhíng/ n. (formerly **Peking**) capital of China, in the NE part. Pop. 5,769,600.

Bei·rut /bayroót/ n. capital of Lebanon, in the W part. Pop. 1,100,000.

Bel·a·rus /beləroós/ n. republic in E Europe; formerly, as Byelorussia, part of the USSR. Pop. 10,416,000. Capital: Minsk.

Belarus

Bel·fast /bélfast, belfást/ n. port city and capital of Northern Ireland, United Kingdom. Pop. 296,700.

Bel·gium /béljəm/ n. kingdom in W Europe. Pop. 10,170,000. Capital: Brussels. □□ **Bel'gian** n. & adj.

Belgium

Bel·go·rod /bélgəraad, byél–/ n. city in W Russia. Pop. 317,900.

Bel·grade /bélgrayd, –graad/ n. capital of Serbia, in the N part; capital of former Yugoslavia. Pop. 1,168,500.

Be·lize /bəleéz/ n. country in N Central America. Pop. 219,000. Capital: Belmopan.

Belize

Belle·vue /bélvyoō/ n. city in W central Washington. Pop. 86,874.

Bel·mo·pan /belmōpán/ n. capital of Belize, in the central part. Pop. 3,900.

Be·lo Ho·ri·zon·te /báylō hawrizaántee/ n. city in SE Brazil. Pop. 1,529,600.

Be·na·res /bənáaris, –eez/ n. see VARANASI.

Ben·e·lux /bén'ləks/ n. collective term for Belgium, the Netherlands, and Luxembourg.

Ben·gal /ben-gáwl, beng; n–/, **Bay of** n. inlet of the Indian Ocean, between India and Burma.

Ben·gha·zi /ben-gaázee/ n. port city in N Libya. Pop. 446,300.

Be·nin /bəneén, –nín/ n. republic in W Africa. Pop. 5,710,000. Capital: Porto-Novo.

Benin

Ber·gen /bérgən/ n. port city in SW Norway. Pop. 221,700.

Ber·ing /beéring, bér–/ **Sea** n. extension of the N Pacific, between Russia and Alaska.

Ber·ing Strait n. body of water separating Asia (Russia) from North America (Alaska).

Berke·ley /búrklee/ n. city in W California. Pop. 102,724.

Ber·lin /bərlín/ n. capital of Germany, in the NE part. Pop. 3,475,400. □□ **Ber·lin'er** n.

Ber·mu·da /bərmyoódə/ n. (also called **the Ber·mu'das**) island group in the Atlantic, E of North Carolina; British colony. Pop. 62,000. Capital: Hamilton. □□ **Ber·mu'dan, Ber·mu'di·an** n. & adj.

Bermuda

Ber·mu·da Tri·an·gle n. area in the Atlantic bounded by Puerto Rico, Bermuda, and Florida, where many ships and planes are said to have disappeared mysteriously.

Bern /bərn, bern/ n. (also **Berne**) capital of Switzerland, in the W central part. Pop. 134,600. □□ **Ber·nese** /bərneéz, –neés/ n. & adj.

Be·thes·da /bəthézdə/ n. city in central Maryland. Pop. 62,936.

Bho·pal /bōpaál/ n. city in central India. Pop. 1,063,700.

Bhu·tan /bootán, –taán/ n. monarchy in the Himalayas, NE of India. Pop. 1,823,000. Capital: Thimphu.

Bhutan

Bia·ly·stok /bee-aáleestawk/ n. city in E Poland. Pop. 276,100.

Bie·le·feld /beéləfelt/ n. city in W central Germany. Pop. 324,700.

Big Sur /big sər/ n. Pacific coastal region of California, from Carmel to San Simeon.

Bil·ba·o /bilbów, –báyō/ n. port city in N Spain. Pop. 371,800.

Bil·lings /bílingz/ n. city in S central Montana. Pop. 81,151.

Bir·ming·ham n. **1** /búrmingham/ city in N central Alabama. Pop. 265,968. **2** /búrmingəm/ city in central England. Pop. 1,024,100.

Bis·cay /biskáy/, **Bay of** n. inlet of the Atlantic, between France and Spain.

Bish·kek /bishkék/ n. capital of Kyrgyzstan, in the N part. Pop. 597,000.

Bis·marck /bízmaark/ n. capital of North Dakota, in the S central part. Pop. 49,256.

See page xx for the **Key to Pronunciation**.

Bis·sau /bisów/ *n.* port city and capital of Guinea-Bissau. Pop. 200,000.

Black /blak/ **Hills** *n.* mountains in NE Wyoming and W South Dakota.

Black·pool /blákpōōl/ *n.* city in NW England. Pop. 146,100.

Black /blak/ **Sea** *n.* sea enclosed by Turkey, the Balkan Peninsula, Ukraine, SW Russia, and Georgia.

Blanc /blaaN/, **Mont** /mawn/ *n.* mountain on the France-Italy-Switzerland border; highest in the Alps: 15,771 ft.

Bloem·fon·tein /blōōfaanten/ *n.* judicial capital of South Africa, in the central part. Pop. 126,900.

Bloo·ming·ton /blōōmingtən/ *n.* **1** city in SE central Minnesota. Pop. 86,335. **2** city in S central Indiana. Pop. 60,633.

Blue·grass /blōōgras/ **Re·gion** *n.* area of central Kentucky noted for thoroughbred horse breeding.

Blue Ridge /blōō rij/ **Moun·tains** *n.* mountain range in E U.S., extending from West Virginia to N Georgia; part of the Appalachian range.

Bo·go·tá /bōgətaá/ *n.* capital of Colombia, in the central part. Pop. 5,237,600.

Boi·se /bóysee, –zee/ *n.* capital of Idaho, in the SW part. Pop. 125,738.

Bo·liv·i·a /bəlíveeə/ *n.* republic in W South America. Pop. 7,165,000. Capitals: La Paz; Sucre. □□ **Bo·liv′i·an** *n. & adj.*

Bolivia

Bo·lo·gna /bəlónyə/ *n.* city in N Italy. Pop. 395,000. □□ **Bo·lo·gnese** /bōlənéez/ *n. & adj.*

Bom·bay /baambáy/ *n.* port city in W India. Pop. 14,496,000.

Bonn /baan, bawn/ *n.* city in W Germany; seat of government. Pop. 296,900.

Bon·ne·ville /baánivil/ **Salt Flats** *n.* barren salt flatland in NW Utah.

Bor·deaux /bawrdó/ *n.* city in SW France. Pop. 213,300.

Bor·ne·o /báwrnee-ō/ *n.* island in the Malay Archipelago.

Bos·ni·a /baázneeə/ **and Her·ze·go·vi·na** /hərtsəgōveénə, –góvinə/ *n.* (also called **Bos′ni·a-Her·ze·go·vi′na**) republic in S Europe, on the Balkan Peninsula; formerly part of Yugoslavia. Pop. 2,656,000. Capital: Sarajevo.

Bosnia

Bos·po·rus /baáspərəs/ *n.* strait connecting the Sea of Marmara and the Black Sea.

Bos·ton /báwstən/ *n.* capital of Massachusetts, in the E part. Pop. 574,283. □□ **Bos·ton′i·an** /bawstóneeən/ *n. & adj.*

Both·ni·a /baáthneeə/, **Gulf of** *n.* arm of the Baltic Sea, between Finland and Sweden.

Bot·swa·na /baatswaánə/ *n.* republic in S Africa. Pop. 1,478,000. Capital: Gaborone.

Botswana

Boul·der /bóldər/ *n.* city in N central Colorado. Pop. 83,312.

Bourne·mouth /báwrnməth/ *n.* city in S England. Pop. 151,300.

Bramp·ton /brámtən, brámp–/ *n.* city in SE Ontario, Canada. Pop. 234,400.

Bra·sil·ia /brəzílyə/ *n.* capital of Brazil, in the S central part. Pop. 411,300.

Bra·ti·sla·va /braatislaávə/ *n.* capital of Slovakia, in the W part. Pop. 446,700.

Bra·zil /brəzíl/ *n.* republic in E South America. Pop. 162,661,000. Capital: Brasilia. □□ **Bra·zil′ian** *n. & adj.* See map p. 1212.

Braz·za·ville /brázəvil/ *n.* capital of the Republic of the Congo, in the SE part. Pop. 937,600.

Brem·en /brémən/ *n.* port city in NW Germany. Pop. 551,600.

Brem·er·ha·ven /brémərhaavən/ *n.* port city in NW Germany. Pop. 131,500.

Bre·scia /bráyshə/ *n.* city in N Italy. Pop. 191,900.

Brest /brest/ *n.* **1** port city in W France. Pop. 153,100. **2** city in SW Belarus. Pop. 284,000.

Brid·al·veil /bríd′lvayl/ *n.* waterfall in Yosemite National Park, California: 620 ft. high.

Bridge·port /bríjpawrt, –pōrt/ *n.* city in SW Connecticut. Pop. 141,686.

Bridge·town /bríjtown/ *n.* port city and capital of Barbados. Pop. 6,100.

Brigh·ton /brít′n/ *n.* city in SE England. Pop. 143,600.

Bris·bane /brízbən, –bayn/ *n.* port city and capital of Queensland, Australia. Pop. 786,400.

Bris·tol /brístəl/ *n.* port city in SW England. Pop. 399,200.

Brit·ain /brít′n/ *n.* see GREAT BRITAIN.

Brit·ish Co·lum·bi·a /brítish kəlúmbeeə/ *n.* province in W Canada. Pop. 3,535,000. Capital: Victoria. □□ **Brit′ish Co·lum′bi·an** *n. & adj.*

Brit·ish Em·pire *n. hist.* countries under the control or leadership of the British Crown.

Brit·ish Vir·gin /várjin/ **Is·lands** *n.* island group in the E West Indies; British possession.

Br·no /búrnō/ *n.* city in E Czech Republic. Pop. 388,000.

Brock·ton /braáktən/ *n.* city in SE Massachusetts. Pop. 92,788.

Bronx /braangks/ *n.* (also **the Bronx**) one of the five boroughs of New York City. Pop. 1,203,789.

Brook·lyn /brōōklən/ *n.* one of the five boroughs of New York City. Pop. 2,300,664.

Browns·ville /brównzvil/ *n.* city in S Texas. Pop. 98,962.

Bruges /brōōzh, brVzh/ *n.* (also called **Brug·ge** /brúgə/) city in NW Belgium. Pop. 116,800.

Bru·nei /brōōní/ *n.* sultanate on the NW coast of Borneo. Pop. 300,000. Capital: Bandar Seri Begawan.

Brunei

Brus·sels /brúsəlz/ *n.* capital of Belgium, in the central part; site of European parliament. Pop. 949,100.

Bry·ansk /bree-aánsk/ *n.* city in W Russia. Pop. 460,900.

Bryce /brīs/ **Can·yon Na·tion·al Park** *n.* area in S Utah noted for its extensive natural rock formations.

Bu·cha·rest /bōōkərest/ *n.* capital of Romania, in the S part. Pop. 2,064,500.

Bu·da·pest /bōōdəpest/ *n.* capital of Hungary, in the N central part. Pop. 1,996,000.

Bue·nos Ai·res /bwaynəs éreez/ *n.* port city and capital of Argentina. Pop. 2,961,000.

Buf·fa·lo /búfəlō/ *n.* port city in W New York. Pop. 328,123.

Bu·jum·bu·ra /bōōjəmbŏŏrə/ *n.* capital of Burundi, in the E part. Pop. 300,000.

Bul·gar·i·a /bəlgáreeə, bul–/ *n.* republic in SE Europe. Pop. 8,613,000. Capital: Sofia. □□ **Bul·gar′i·an** *n. & adj.*

Bur·bank /búrbangk/ *n.* city in SW California. Pop. 93,643.

Bur·gos /bŏŏrgōs/ *n.* city in N Spain. Pop. 166,300.

Bur·ki·na Fa·so /bŏŏrkeénə faásó/ *n.* republic in W Africa. Pop. 10,623,000. Capital: Ouagadougou.

Bur·ma /búrmə/ *n.* (also called **My·an′mar**) republic in SE Asia. Pop. 45,976,000. Capital: Rangoon. □□ **Bur·mese** /bərmeéz/ *n. & adj.*

Bur·sa /bŏŏrsaá/ *n.* city in NW Turkey. Pop. 996,600.

Bu·run·di /bərŏŏndee/ *n.* republic in central Africa. Pop. 5,943,000. Capital: Bujumbura.

Bulgaria

Burkina Faso

Burma

Burundi

Bye·lo·rus·sia /byelōrúshə/ *n.* see BELARUS.

Byz·an·tine /bízanteen, ; n-tīn/ **Em·pire** *n. hist.* term for the Eastern Roman Empire from the fall of the Western Empire (476) to the fall of Constantinople (1453).

By·zan·ti·um /bizánshee-əm, –tee-əm/ *n.* see ISTANBUL.

Cá·diz /kədíz/ *n.* port city in SW Spain. Pop. 155,400.

Caen /kaaN/ *n.* city in NW France. Pop. 115,600.

Ca·guas /kaáwaas, –gwaas/ *n.* city in E central Puerto Rico. Pop. 139,800.

Cai·ro /kírō/ *n.* capital of Egypt, in the N part. Pop. 6,849,000.

Cal·cut·ta /kalkútə/ *n.* port city in E India. Pop. 4,399,800.

Cal·ga·ry /kálgəree/ *n.* city in S Alberta, Canada. Pop. 710,700.

Ca·li /kaálee/ *n.* city in SW Colombia. Pop. 1,718,900.

Cal·i·for·nia /kalifáwrnyə/ *n.* state in W U.S. Pop. 29,760,021. Capital: Sacramento. Abbr. **CA; Cal.; Calif.** □□ **Cal·i·for'ni·an** *n. & adj.*

Cal·i·for·nia, Gulf of *n.* arm of the Pacific, enclosed by Baja California.

Ca·ma·güey /kaaməgwáy/ *n.* city in central Cuba. Pop. 279,000.

Cam·bo·di·a /cambódeeə/ *n.* (also called **Kam·pu·che'a**) republic in SE Asia. Pop. 10,861,000. Capital: Phnom Penh. □□ **Cam·bo'di·an** *n. & adj.*

Cambodia

Cam·bridge /káymbrij/ *n.* **1** city in NE Massachusetts. Pop. 95,802. **2** city in SE England. Pop. 113,800.

Cam·den /kámdən/ *n.* city in SW New Jersey. Pop. 87,492.

Cam·e·roon /kamərŏŏn/ *n.* republic in W Africa. Pop. 14,262,000. Capital: Yaoundé.

Cameroon

Camp Da·vid /dáyvid/ *n.* U.S. presidential retreat in Catoctin Mountains of Maryland, NW of Washington, D.C.

Cam·pe·che /kampáychay, –peéchee/ *n.* state in SE Mexico. Pop. 535,200. Capital: Campeche.

Cam·pi·nas /kampeénəs/ *n.* city in SE Brazil. Pop. 748,100.

Can·a·da /kánədə/ *n.* country in N North America. Pop. 28,821,900. Capital: Ottawa. □□ **Ca·na·di·an** /kənáydee-ən/ *n. & adj.* See map p. 1212.

Ca·nar·y /kənáiree/ **Is·lands** *n.* island group in the Atlantic, off the NW coast of Africa.

Can·ber·ra /kánbərə, –brə/ *n.* capital of Australia, in the SE part. Pop. 303,700.

Can·ter·bur·y /kántərberee, –bree/ *n.* city in SE England; seat of the archbishop who heads the Anglican Church. Pop. 132,400.

Can·ton /kánt'n/ *n.* city in NE Ohio. Pop. 84,161.

Cape Ca·nav·er·al /kənávrəl, –návər–/ *n.* cape on the E central coast of Florida; site of Kennedy Space Center.

Cape Cod /kaad/ *n.* peninsula in SE Massachusetts, bounded by Cape Cod Bay, the Atlantic, and Nantucket Sound.

Cape Hat·ter·as /hátərəs/ *n.* cape on the North Carolina coast.

Cape Horn /hawrn/ *n.* headland of a S Chilean island; the southernmost tip of South America.

Cape of Good Hope /gŏŏd hōp/ *n.* cape at the SW tip of South Africa.

Cape Town *n.* port city and legislative capital of South Africa, in the SW part. Pop. 854,600.

Cape Verde /vərd/ *n.* republic in NW Africa, comprising an island group W of Senegal. Pop. 449,000. Capital: Praia.

Cape Verde

Ca·ra·cas /kərákəs, –raák–/ *n.* capital of Venezuela, in the N part. Pop. 1,822,500.

Car·diff /kaárdif/ *n.* port city and capital of Wales, United Kingdom. Pop. 300,000.

Car·ib·be·an /karəbeéən, kəríbeeən/ **Sea** *n.* arm of the Atlantic, enclosed by the West Indies, N South America, and Central America.

Carls·bad /kaárlzbad/ **Cav·erns** *n.* network of subterranean limestone caves in SE New Mexico.

Car·o·li·na /karəlínə/ *n.* **1** (also called **the Car·o·li·nas**) North and South Carolina. **2** /kaarəleénə/ city in NE Puerto Rico. Pop. 187,100.

Car·o·line /kárəlīn, kér–, –lin/ **Is·lands** *n.* island group in the Pacific, E of the Philippines; U.S. trusteeship.

Car·pa·thi·an /kaarpáytheeən/ **Moun·tains** *n.* mountain range in central Europe.

Car·son /kaársən/ **Cit·y** *n.* capital of Nevada, in the W part. Pop. 40,443.

Car·ta·ge·na /kaartəjeénə, –háynə/ *n.* port city in N Colombia. Pop. 745,700.

Car·thage /kaárthij/ *n. hist.* ancient city-state near present-day Tunis, in N Africa. □□ **Car·tha·gin'i·an** *n. & adj.*□□

Cas·a·blan·ca /kasəblángkə, kaz–/ *n.* port city in NW Morocco. Pop. 2,943,000.

BRAZIL

- State/Territory boundary
- ■ Capital city

0 500 1000 km
0 250 500 750 miles

N

RORAIMA
- Boa Vista
AMAPA
- Macapá
- Belém
- São Luis
MARANHÃO
- Fortaleza
CEARÁ
RÍO GRANDE DO NORTE
- Natal
PARAIBA
- João Pessoa
PERNAMBUCO
- Recife
- Teresina
PIAUI
- Maceió
ALAGOAS
- Aracajú
SERGIPE
- Manaus
AMAZONAS
PARÁ
ACRE
- Rio Branco
- Porto Velho
RONDÔNIA
TOCANTINS
- Palmas
BAHIA
- Salvador
MATO GROSSO
- Cuiabá
GOIÁS
FD
- Brasília
- Goiânia
MINAS GERAIS
- Belo Horizonte
ESPÍRITO SANTO
- Vitória
MATO GROSSO DO SUL
- Campo Grande
SÃO-PAULO
- São Paulo
RIO DE JANEIRO
- Rio de Janeiro
PARANÁ
- Curitiba
SANTA CATARINA
- Florianópolis
RIO GRANDE DO SUL
- Põrto Alegre

FD   FEDERAL DISTRICT

CANADA

- Province boundary
- ■ Capital city

0 500 1000 km
0 250 500 750 miles

N

YUKON
- Whitehorse
NORTHWEST TERRITORIES
- Yellowknife
BRITISH COLUMBIA
- Victoria
ALBERTA
- Edmonton
SASKATCHEWAN
- Regina
MANITOBA
- Winnipeg
ONTARIO
- Ottawa
- Toronto
QUEBEC
- Quebec
NEWFOUNDLAND AND LABRADOR
- St John's
NEW BRUNSWICK
- Fredericton
PRINCE EDWARD IS.
- Charlottetown
NOVA SCOTIA
- Halifax

Cas·cade /kaskáyd/ **Range** *n.* mountain range in W U.S., extending from N California into Canada.

Cas·pi·an /káspeeən/ **Sea** *n.* inland salt lake between Europe and Asia, N of Iran.

Cas·tries /kastreé, kaástrees/ *n.* port city and capital of St. Lucia. Pop. 11,100.

Cat·a·li·na /kat'l-eénə/ **Is·land** *n.* see SANTA CATALINA ISLAND.

Ca·ta·nia /kətaányə, –táyn–/ *n.* port city in E Sicily, Italy. Pop. 327,200.

Cats·kill /kátskil/ **Moun·tains** *n.* mountain range in SE New York; part of the Appalachian range.

Cau·ca·sus /káwkəsəs/ **Moun·tains** *n.* mountain range dividing Russia from Georgia and Azerbaijan; traditional division between Europe and Asia.

Cay·enne /kī-én, kay–/ *n.* port city and capital of French Guiana. Pop. 41,700.

Cay·man /káymən/ **Is·lands** *n.* island group in the NW Caribbean; dependent territory of the United Kingdom. Pop. 35,000.

Cayman Islands

Ce·dar /seédər/ **Rap·ids** *n.* city in E Iowa. Pop. 108,751.

Cel·e·bes /séləbeez/ *n.* see SULAWESI.

Cen·tral Af·ri·can Re·pub·lic *n.* republic in central Africa. Pop. 3,274,000. Capital: Bangui.

Central African Republic

Cen·tral A·mer·i·ca *n.* portion of continental North America between Mexico and South America.

Cen·tral Val·ley *n.* valley in W central California, between the San Joaquin and Sacramento rivers.

Cey·lon /silón, say–/ *n.* see SRI LANKA.

Chad /chad/ *n.* republic in N central Africa. Pop. 6,977,000. Capital: N'Djamena. **Chad'i·an** *n. & adj.*

Chad

Cham·paign /shampáyn/ *n.* city in E central Illinois. Pop. 63,502.

Cham·plain /shampláyn/, **Lake** *n.* lake in NE U.S., between New York and Vermont.

Chang /chang/ **Riv·er** *n.* (formerly **Yangtze River**) river in central China, flowing 3,400 mi. from Tibet to the East China Sea; longest river in China.

Chan·nel /chánəl/ **Is·lands** *n.* group of British islands in the English Channel, near the coast of France; includes Guernsey and Jersey.

Charles·ton /chaárlstən/ *n.* **1** capital of West Virginia, in the W central part. Pop. 57,287. **2** port city in SE South Carolina. Pop. 80,414.

Char·lotte /shaárlət/ *n.* city in S North Carolina. Pop. 395,934.

Char·lotte·town /shaárlət-town/ *n.* capital of Prince Edward Island, Canada, in the central part. Pop. 15,400.

Chat·ta·hoo·chee /chatəhoóchee/ **Riv·er** *n.* river in SE U.S., flowing 440 mi. from NE Georgia to the Gulf of Mexico.

Chat·ta·noo·ga /chatənoógə/ *n.* city in S Tennessee. Pop. 152,466.

Chel·ya·binsk /chelyaábinsk/ *n.* city in S Russia. Pop. 1,086,000.

Chem·nitz /khémnits/ *n.* (formerly **Karl-Marx-Stadt**) city in E central Germany. Pop. 274,200.

Ches·a·peake /chésəpeek/ *n.* city in SE Virginia. Pop. 151,976.

Ches·a·peake Bay *n.* inlet of the Atlantic, on the E coast of the U.S.

Che·tu·mal /chaytoomaál/ *n.* capital of Quintana Roo, Mexico, in the S part. Pop. 111,400.

Chey·enne /shīán, –én/ *n.* capital of Wyoming, in the SE part. Pop. 50,008.

Chi·a·pas /chee-aápəs, chaápəs/ *n.* state in S Mexico. Pop. 3,210,500. Capital: Tuxtla.

Chi·ba /cheébə/ *n.* city in Japan, on Honshu. Pop. 856,900.

Chi·ca·go /shikaágō, –káwgō/ *n.* city in NE Illinois. Pop. 2,783,726. □□ **Chi·ca'go·an** *n.*

Chi·hua·hua /chəwaáwaa, –wə/ *n.* state in N central Mexico. Pop. 2,441,900. Capital: Chihuahua.

Chil·e /chílee, cheélay/ *n.* republic in W South America. Pop. 14,333,000. Capital: Santiago. □□ **Chil'e·an** *n. & adj.*

Chile

Chil·pan·cin·go /chilpənsínggō/ *n.* capital of Guerrero, Mexico, in the E central part. Pop. 136,200.

Chi·lung /jeéloong/ *n.* (formerly **Keelung**) port city in N Taiwan. Pop. 352,900.

Chi·na /chínə/ *n.* (official name **People's Republic of China**; abbr. **PRC**) republic in E and central Asia. Pop. 1,210,005,000. Capital: Beijing. See map p. 1214.

Chi·nan /jénán/ *n.* see JINAN.

Chis·holm /chízəm/ **Trail** *n. hist.* cattle trail from San Antonio, Texas, to Abilene, Kansas, used after the Civil War.

Chi·și·nă·u /keesheenúoo/ *n.* see KISHINEV.

Chit·ta·gong /chítəgaang, –gawng/ *n.* port city in SE Bangladesh. Pop. 1,599,000.

Chong·qing /chúngchíng, –kíng/ *n.* (formerly **Chungking**) city in S central China. Pop. 2,980,000.

Chon·ju /júnjoŏ/ *n.* city in SW South Korea. Pop. 563,400.

Christ·church /krískərch, críst–/ *n.* city in E central New Zealand. Pop. 314,000.

Chuk·chi /chúkchee, choŏk–/ **Sea** *n.* arm of the Arctic Ocean, N of the Bering Strait.

Chu·la Vis·ta /choŏlə vístə/ *n.* city in SW California. Pop. 135,163.

Chung·king /chúngkíng, chón–/ *n.* see CHONGQING.

Cin·cin·nat·i /sinsinátee/ *n.* port city in SW Ohio. Pop. 364,040.

Cit·rus /sítrəs/ **Heights** *n.* city in central California. Pop. 107,439.

Ciu·dad Gua·ya·na /seeoodaád gwaayaánaa, seeyoō–/ *n.* see SANTO TOMÉ DE GUAYANA.

Ciu·dad Juá·rez /waáres, hwaáres/ *n.* city in N Mexico. Pop. 544,500.

Ciu·dad Vic·to·ria /veektáwree-ə/ *n.* capital of Tamaulipas, Mexico, in the W central part. Pop. 195,000.

Clear·wa·ter /kleérwawtər, –waatər/ *n.* city in W Florida. Pop. 98,784.

Cleve·land /kleévlənd/ *n.* city in N Ohio. Pop. 505,616.

Co·a·hui·la /kōəweélə, kwaaweélə/ *n.* state in N Mexico. Pop. 1,972,300. Capital: Saltillo.

Co·blenz /kóblens/ *n.* (also **Ko'blenz**) city in W Germany. Pop. 109,600.

Channel Islands

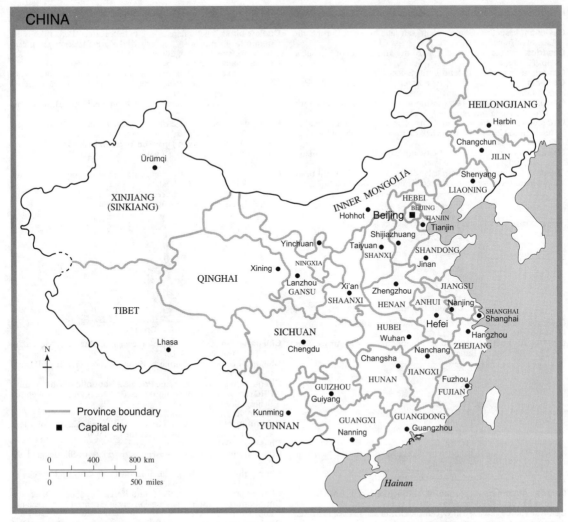

CHINA

Ürümqi

XINJIANG
(SINKIANG)

HEILONGJIANG

Harbin

Changchun

JILIN

Shenyang

LIAONING

INNER MONGOLIA

HEBEI

BEIJING
Hohhot   ■ Beijing
              TIANJIN
              ■ Tianjin

Yinchuan

Shijiazhuang

Taiyuan
SHANXI

SHANDONG

Jinan

QINGHAI

Xining ●

NINGXIA

Lanzhou
GANSU

Xi'an
SHAANXI

Zhengzhou

HENAN

JIANGSU

Nanjing

ANHUI

SHANGHAI
Shanghai

TIBET

Lhasa ●

SICHUAN

Chengdu ●

HUBEI

Wuhan ●

Hefei ●

Hangzhou

ZHEJIANG

Changsha ●

Nanchang ●

N

GUIZHOU

Guiyang ●

HUNAN

JIANGXI

Fuzhou

FUJIAN

Kunming ●
YUNNAN

Nanning ●

GUANGXI

GUANGDONG

Guangzhou ■

Province boundary

■ Capital city

0   400   800 km

0   500 miles

Hainan

Co·li·ma /kəleémə/ *n.* state in W Mexico. Pop. 428,500. Capital: Colima.

Co·logne /kəlón/ *n.* (German name **Köln**) city in W Germany. Pop. 963,800.

Co·lom·bi·a /kəlúmbeeə/ *n.* republic in NW South America. Pop. 36,813,000. Capital: Bogotá. □□ **Co·lom'bi·an** *n. & adj.*

Colombia

Co·lom·bo /kəlúmbō/ *n.* port city and capital of Sri Lanka. Pop. 615,000.

Col·o·ra·do /kaalərádō, –raádō/ *n.* state in W U.S. Pop. 3,294,394. Capital: Denver. Abbr. **Colo.**; **CO** □□ **Col·o·ra'dan, Col·o·ra'do·an** *n. & adj.*

Col·o·rad·o Riv·er *n.* river in W U.S., flowing 1,450 mi. from Colorado through the Grand Canyon and into the Gulf of California.

Col·o·rad·o Springs *n.* city in E central Colorado. Pop. 281,140.

Co·lum·bi·a /kəlúmbeeə/ *n.* **1** capital of South Carolina, in the central part. Pop. 98,052. **2** city in central Missouri. Pop. 69,101.

Co·lum·bi·a Riv·er *n.* river in W North America, flowing 1,200 mi. from W Canada through Washington and Oregon and into the Pacific.

Co·lum·bus /kəlúmbəs/ *n.* capital of Ohio, in the central part. Pop. 632,910.

Com·o·ros /kaámərōz, kəmáwrōz/ *n.* island republic in the Indian Ocean, between Africa and Madagascar. Pop. 569,000. Capital: Moroni. □□ **Com'o·ran, Co·mo'ri·an** *n. & adj.*

Comoros

Co·na·kry /kaánəkree/ *n.* port city and capital of Guinea. Pop. 1,508,000.

Con·cep·ción /kənsepsee-ốn/ *n.* city in S central Chile. Pop. 350,300.

Con·cord /kaángkərd, –kawrd/ *n.* **1** capital of New Hampshire, in the S part. Pop. 36,006. **2** city in W California. Pop. 111,348.

Con·go /kaánggō/ *n.* **1** (formerly **Zaire**) republic in central Africa. Pop. 41,151,000. Capital: Kinshasa. **2** (official name **Re·pub'lic of the Con'go**) republic in central Africa. Pop. 2,528,000. Capital: Brazzaville. □□ **Con·go·lese** /kaanggəleéz, –leés/ *n. & adj.*

Con·go Riv·er *n.* river in central Africa, flowing 3,000 mi. from SE Congo (formerly Zaire) to the Atlantic.

Con·nect·i·cut /kənétikət/ *n.* state in NE U.S. Pop. 3,287,116. Capital: Hartford. Abbr. **Conn.**; **CT**; **Ct.** □□ **Con·nect'i·cut·ter** *n.*

Con·nect·i·cut Riv·er *n.* river in New England, flowing 400 mi. from N New Hampshire to Long Island Sound.

Con·stan·tine /kaánstənteen, kawNstaaNteén/ *n.* city in NE Algeria. Pop. 440,900.

Con·stan·ti·no·ple /kaanstantənópəl/ *n.* see ISTANBUL.

Con·ti·nen·tal Di·vide *n.* (also called **Great Di·vide**) High ridge of the Rocky Mountains; watershed of the North American continent, separating the river systems flowing either W or E and S.

Cook /kʊ̄ok/ **Is·lands** *n.* island group in the S Pacific, belonging to New Zealand. Pop. 20,000.

Co·pen·ha·gen /kópənhaygən, –haagən/ *n.* port city and capital of Denmark. Pop. 1,353,300.

Cor·al /káwrəl/ **Sea** *n.* arm of the S Pacific, NE of Australia.

Cór·do·ba /káwrdəbə, –əvə/ *n.* **1** (also **Cor'do·va**) city in S Spain. Pop. 315,900. **2** city in central Argentina. Pop. 1,208,700.

Cor·fu /kawrfʊ̄o/ *n.* island in Greece, SW of Albania.

Cork /kawrk/ *n.* port city in S Ireland. Pop. 127,000.

Cor·pus Chris·ti /káwrpəs krístee/ *n.* port city in S Texas. Pop. 257,453.

Cor·si·ca /káwrsikə/ *n.* island in the Mediterranean Sea, W of Italy; a department of France. Capital: Ajaccio □□ **Cor'si·can** *n. & adj.*

Cos·ta Bra·va /kʊ̂ostə braávə/ *n.* region on the NE coast of Spain.

Cos·ta del Sol /del sʊ̂ol/ *n.* region on the S coast of Spain.

Cos·ta Me·sa /kʊ̂ostə máysə, káwstə/ *n.* city in SW California. Pop. 96,357.

Cos·ta Ri·ca /kʊ̂ostə reékə, káws–/ *n.* republic in S Central America. Pop. 3,463,000. Capital: San José. □□ **Cos'ta Ric'an** *n. & adj.*

Costa Rica

Côte d'A·zur /kōt dəzʊ̂or/ *n.* region on the SE coast of France.

Côte d'I·voire /kōt deevwaár/ *n.* see IVORY COAST.

Co·to·nou /kōt'n-ʊ̂ó/ *n.* port city and government center of Benin. Pop. 533,200.

Cov·en·try /kaávəntree, kúv–/ *n.* city in central England. Pop. 302,500.

Crac·ow /krákow, kraákʊ̄of/ *n.* (also **Kra'ków**) city in S central Poland. Pop. 746,000.

Cra·ter /kráytər/ **Lake** *n.* lake in S Oregon formed by an ancient volcanic crater.

Crete /kreet/ *n.* (also called **Can'di·a**) Greek island in the Mediterranean Sea, SE of the mainland.

Cri·me·a /krīmeéə/ *n.* peninsula in S Ukraine, bounded by the Black Sea and the Sea of Azov. □□ **Cri·me'an** *adj.*

Cro·a·tia /krōáyshə/ *n.* republic in S Europe, on the Balkan Peninsula; formerly part of Yugoslavia. Pop. 5,004,000. Capital: Zagreb.

Croatia

Cu·ba /kyʊ̄obə, kʊ̄obə/ *n.* island republic in the W West Indies. Pop. 10,951,000. Capital: Havana. □□ **Cu'ban** *n. & adj.*

Cuer·na·va·ca /kwernəvaákə/ *n.* capital of Morelos, Mexico, in the N part. Pop. 279,200.

Cu·lia·cán /kʊ̄olyəkaán/ *n.* capital of Sinaloa, Mexico, in the central part. Pop. 415,000.

Congo 2

Cum·ber·land /kúmbərlənd/ **Gap** *n.* natural pass through the Appalachian Mountains in Kentucky and Virginia.

Cum·ber·land Road *n.* see NATIONAL ROAD.

Cu·ra·çao /kʊ̄oorəsów, –sów, kyʊ̄oorə–/ *n.* largest island of the Netherlands Antilles, NW of Venezuela. Capital: Willemstad.

Cy·prus /síprəs/ *n.* island republic in the E Mediterranean Sea. Pop. 745,000. Capital: Nicosia.

Cyprus

Czech·o·slo·va·ki·a /chekəsləvaákeeə/ *n.* former republic of central Europe (1918–93); divided into Czech Republic and Slovakia.

Czechoslovakia

Czech /chek/ **Re·pub·lic** *n.* republic in central Europe; formerly the W part of Czechoslovakia. Pop. 10,321,000. Capital: Prague.

Czech Republic

Cze·sto·cho·wa /cheNstəkóvə/ *n.* city in S Poland. Pop. 259,800.

Da·kar /dəkaár, dákaar/ *n.* port city and capital of Senegal. Pop. 785,100.

Da·lian /daályén/ *n.* (formerly **Talien; Lüda**) port city in NE China. Pop. 2,400,300.

Dal·las /dáləs/ *n.* city in NE Texas. Pop. 1,006,877. □□ **Dal'las·ite** *n.*

Da·mas·cus /dəmáskəs/ *n.* capital of Syria, in the SW part. Pop. 1,550,000.

Da·nang /daanáang, dənáng/ *n.* port city in central Vietnam. Pop. 382,700.

Dan·ube /dányʊ̄ob/ **Riv·er** *n.* river in central Europe, flowing 1,720 mi. from SW Germany to the Black Sea.

Dar·da·nelles /daard'nélz/ *n.* strait in Turkey, connecting the Aegean Sea with the Sea of Marmara.

Dar es Sa·laam /daar es sələáam/ *n.* port city and capital of Tanzania. Pop. 1,360,900.

Dav·en·port /dávənpawrt/ *n.* city in E Iowa. Pop. 95,333.

Day·ton /dáyt'n/ *n.* city in SW Ohio. Pop. 182,044.

Cuba

D.C. *abbr.* (also **DC**) District of Columbia. See also Washington, D.C.

Dead /ded/ **Sea** *n.* inland salt lake, between Israel and Jordan.

Dear·born /deérbawrn, –bərn/ *n.* city in SE Michigan. Pop. 89,286.

Death /deth/ **Val·ley** *n.* desert basin in E California; lowest point is 282 ft. below sea level.

De·ca·tur /dikáytər/ *n.* city in central Illinois. Pop. 83,885.

Del·a·ware /déləwair, –wer/ *n.* state in E U.S. Pop. 666,168. Capital: Dover. Abbr. **DE**; **Del.** □□ **Del·a·war′e·an** *n. & adj.*

Del·a·ware Bay *n.* inlet of the Atlantic, between Delaware and New Jersey.

Del·a·ware Riv·er *n.* river in E U.S., flowing 280 mi. from S New York to Delaware Bay.

Del·hi /délee/ *n.* city in N India. Pop. 7,206,700.

Del·mar·va /delmaárvə/ **Pen·in·su·la** *n.* peninsula in E U.S., bounded by the Atlantic and Chesapeake Bay, and comprising parts of Delaware, Maryland, and Virginia.

De·na·li /denaálee/ **Na·tion·al Park** U.S. national park in S central Alaska; contains North America's highest peak, Mount McKinley.

Den·mark /dénmaark/ *n.* kingdom in N Europe. Pop. 5,250,000. Capital: Copenhagen.

Denmark

Den·ver /dénvər/ *n.* capital of Colorado, in the central part. Pop. 467,610.

Der·by /daárbee/ *n.* city in central England. Pop. 230,500.

Des Moines /di moín/ *n.* capital of Iowa, in the central part. Pop. 193,187.

De·troit /ditróyt, deétroyt/ *n.* city in SE Michigan. Pop. 1,027,974.

Dha·ka /daákə/ *n.* capital of Bangladesh, in the central part. Pop. 3,839,000.

Di·a·mond /dímənd, díə–/ **Head** *n.* extinct volcano on SE coast of Oahu, Hawaii.

Di·jon /dee-zháwN, –zhaán/ *n.* city in E France. Pop. 151,600.

Dis·trict of Co·lum·bi·a /kəlúmbeeə/ *n.* federal district in E U.S., on the Potomac River; coextensive with the national capital, Washington. Abbr. **DC**; **D.C.**

Dji·bou·ti /jibóotee/ *n.* **1** republic in E Africa. Pop. 428,000. Capital: Djibouti. **2** capital of Djibouti, in the E part. Pop. 290,000.

Djibouti

Dni·pro·pe·trovsk /neprōpətráwfsk, dənyeprō–/ *n.* city in E central Ukraine. Pop. 1,147,000.

Do·ha /dóhə/ *n.* port city and capital of Qatar. Pop. 313,600.

Dom·i·ni·ca /daamineékə, dəmínikə/ *n.* island republic in the E West Indies. Pop. 83,000. Capital: Roseau.

Dominica

Dom·i·ni·can /dəmínikən/ **Re·pub·lic** *n.* republic in the central West Indies, comprising the E part of Hispaniola. Pop. 8,089,000. Capital: Santo Domingo.

Do·netsk /dənétsk, –nyétsk/ *n.* city in E Ukraine. Pop. 1,088,000.

Don /daan/ **Riv·er** *n.* river in SW Russia, flowing 1,200 mi. from Tula to the Sea of Azov.

Dort·mund /dáwrtmoont,–mənd/ *n.* city in W Germany. Pop. 600,900.

Do·ver /dóvər/ *n.* **1** capital of Delaware, in the central part. Pop. 27,630. **2** port city in SE England. Pop. 32,800.

Dres·den /drézdən/ *n.* city in SE Germany. Pop. 474,400.

Du·bai /dōobí/ *n.* port city in N United Arab Emirates. Pop. 585,200.

Dub·lin /dúblin/ *n.* capital of the Republic of Ireland, in the E part. Pop. 478,400. □□ **Dub′lin·er** *n. & adj.*

Du·buque /dəbyóok/ *n.* city in E Iowa. Pop. 57,546.

Duis·burg /dóosboork, dyóos–, –bərg/ *n.* port city in W Germany. Pop. 536,100.

Du·luth /dəlóoth/ *n.* city in NE Minnesota. Pop. 85,493.

Dun·dee /dəndeé/ *n.* port city in E Scotland, United Kingdom. Pop. 167,600.

Du·ran·go /dooránggō, dyoorráng–/ *n.* state in N central Mexico. Pop. 1,349,400. Capital: Durango.

Dur·ban /dúrbən/ *n.* port city in SE South Africa. Pop. 715,700.

Dur·ham /dúrəm, dóor–/ *n.* city in NE central North Carolina. Pop. 136,600.

Du·shan·be /dooshaánbay, dyoo–, –sham–/ *n.* capital of Tadzhikistan, in the W part. Pop. 524,000.

Düs·sel·dorf /dóosəldawrf, dyóos–/ *n.* port city in W Germany. Pop. 572,600.

Dust Bowl agricultural region of about 50 million acres in central U.S.; site of great dust storms 1935–38.

East Chi·na Sea *n.* arm of the N Pacific, E of mainland China and N of Taiwan.

East Ger·ma·ny *n.* (also called **German Democratic Republic**) German state created in 1949, under Communist government; unified with West Germany in 1990.

East Los An·ge·les /laws ánjələs, –leez/ *n.* city in SW California. Pop. 126,379.

Ec·ua·dor /ékwədawr/ *n.* republic in NW South America. Pop. 11,466,000. Capital: Quito. □□ **Ec·ua·dor′an, Ec·ua·do′ri·an** /–reeən/ *n. & adj.*

Ecuador

Ed·in·burgh /éd′nbərə, –brə/ *n.* capital of Scotland, in the United Kingdom. Pop. 447,600.

Ed·mon·ton /édməntən/ *n.* capital of Alberta, Canada, in the central part. Pop. 616,700.

E·gypt /eéjipt/ *n.* republic in NE Africa. Pop. 63,575,000. Capital: Cairo.

Egypt

Eir·e /érə, írə/ *n.* see Ireland 2.

El·ba /élbə/ *n.* Italian island in the Mediterranean Sea, E of Corsica.

El·brus /elbróoz/, **Mount** *n.* mountain in the Caucasus range, on the

Dominican Republic

border between Russia and Georgia; highest peak in Europe: 18,481 ft.

El Gi·za / n./ see GIZA.

E·liz·a·beth /ilízəbəth/ /n./ city in NE New Jersey. Pop. 110,002.

El·lis /él·əs/ Is·land /n./ island in New York Harbor; former arrival point for European immigrants.

El Mon·te /el máantee/ /n./ city in SW California. Pop. 106,209.

El Ni·ño /neényō/ /n./ periodic occasional warm Pacific current that alters climate patterns.

El Pas·o /pásō/ /n./ city in W Texas. Pop. 515,342.

El Sal·va·dor /sálvədawr/ /n./ republic in NW Central America. Pop.

5,829,000. Capital: San Salvador. □□ **Sal·va·do′ran, Sal·va·do′ri·an** /-reeən/ /n. & adj./ See map p. 1218.

Eng·land /íngg|ənd/ /n./ largest division of the United Kingdom. Pop. 44,876,000. Capital: London. ¶ See note at GREAT BRITAIN.

Eng·lish /íngg|ish/ **Chan·nel** /n./ strait between S England and N France, connecting the Atlantic and the North Sea.

En·sche·de /énskədə/ /n./ city in the E Netherlands. Pop. 147,900.

E·qua·to·ri·al Guin·ea /ekwətóree-əl gínee/ /n./ mainland and island republic in W Africa. Pop. 431,000. Capital: Malabo. See map p. 1218.

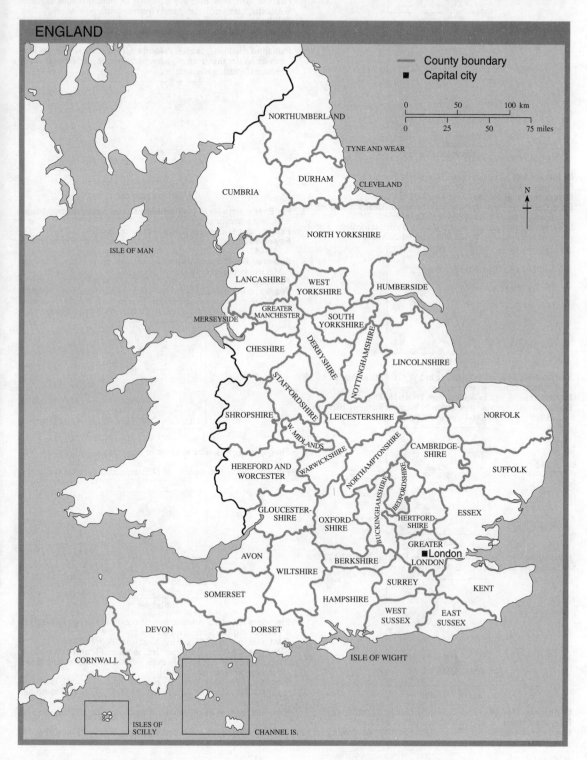

El Salvador

Equatorial Guinea

Er·furt /érfoort/ n. city in central Germany. Pop. 213,500.
E·rie /éeree/ n. city in NW Pennsylvania. Pop. 108,718.
E·rie, Lake n. one of the Great Lakes, N of Ohio.
E·rie Ca·nal n. canal in New York between Albany and Buffalo, connecting the Hudson River with Lake Erie.
Er·i·tre·a /eritreéə, –tráyə/ n. republic in E Africa; formerly a province of Ethiopia. Pop. 3,428,000. Capital: Asmara.

Eritrea

Es·con·di·do /eskəndeédō/ n. city in SW California. Pop. 108,635.
Es·fa·han /ésfəhaan/ n. see ISFAHAN.
Es·sen /ésən/ n. city in W Germany. Pop. 618,000.
Es·to·ni·a /estóneeə/ n. republic in N Europe; formerly part of the USSR. Pop. 1,459,000. Capital: Tallinn.

Estonia

E·thi·o·pi·a /eethee-ópeeə/ n. republic in E Africa. Pop. 57,172,000. Capital: Addis Ababa. □□ **E·thi·o′pi·an** n. & adj.

Ethiopia

Et·na /étnə/, **Mount** n. active volcano in Sicily: 11,122 ft. high.
Eu·gene /yoōjeén/ n. city in W Oregon. Pop. 112,669.
Eu·phra·tes /yoōfráyteez/ **Riv·er** n. river in SW Asia, flowing 1,700 mi. from central Turkey to the Persian Gulf.

Eu·rope /yoorəp/ n. continent bounded by the Arctic and Atlantic oceans, Asia, the Caucasus Mountains, and the Black, Mediterranean, Baltic, and North seas.
Eu·ro·pe·an /yoorəpeéən/ **Un·ion** n. (formerly **Eu·ro·pe′an Com·mu′ni·ty**) official name of a confederation of independent European countries.
Ev·ans·ton /évənstən/ n. city in NE Illinois. Pop. 73,233.
Ev·ans·ville /évənzvil/ n. city in SW Indiana. Pop. 126,272.
Ev·er·est /évrəst, évərəst/, **Mount** n. mountain in the Himalayas, on the Tibet-Nepal border; highest in the world: 29,028 ft.
Ev·er·glades /évərglaydz/ n. large area of swampland in S Florida.
Faer·oe /fárō, férō/ **Is·lands** n. cluster of Danish islands in the N Atlantic, between Iceland and Great Britain.
Fair·banks /fáirbangks, fér–/ n. city in central Alaska. Pop. 30,843.
Fai·sa·la·bad /físaaləbaád/ n. (formerly **Lyallpur**) city in E Pakistan. Pop. 1,104,200.
Falk·land /fáwkland, fáwlk–/ **Is·lands** n. (Spanish name **Is·las Mal·vin·as** /eéeslas maalveénəs/) island group in the Atlantic, E of Argentina; British possession.

Falkland Islands

Far East n. term for E Asia, including China, Japan, Korea, Mongolia, and adjacent areas.
Far·go /faárgō/ n. city in E North Dakota. Pop. 74,111.
Fay·ette·ville /fáyətvəl, –vil/ n. city in S central North Carolina. Pop. 75,695.
Fed·er·al Dis·trict of Mex·i·co n. national government district in Mexico, in the central part.
Fer·ra·ra /fəraárə/ n. city in NE Italy. Pop. 137,400.
Fez /fez, fes/ n. (also **Fès**) city in N central Morocco. Pop. 564,800.
Fi·ji /feéjee/ n. independent archipelago in the S Pacific, N of New Zealand. Pop. 782,000. Capital: Suva. □□ **Fi′ji·an** n. & adj.

Fiji

Fin·ger /fínggər/ **Lakes** n. chain of long, thin lakes in central New York.
Fin·land /fínlənd/ n. republic in N Europe. Pop. 5,105,000. Capital: Helsinki.

Finland

Flan·ders /flándərz/ Atlantic coastal region of Europe in Belgium, France, and the Netherlands.
Flint /flint/ n. city in SE central Michigan. Pop. 140,761.
Flor·ence /fláwrəns, flaár–/ n. (Italian name **Fi·ren·ze** /feeréntsay, fərénzə/) city in central Italy. Pop. 392,900. □□ **Flor·en·tine** /fláwrənteen, –tīn/ n. & adj.
Flor·i·da /fláwrədə, flaár–/ n. peninsular state in SE U.S. Pop. 12,937,926. Capital: Tallahassee. Abbr. **FL; Fla.** □□ **Flo·rid·i·an** /flərídeeən/ n. & adj.
Flor·i·da Keys n. island chain in Florida, extending from the S tip of Florida into the Gulf of Mexico.
Flor·i·da, Straits of n. channel separating Florida from Cuba.
For·mo·sa /fawrmósə/ n. see TAIWAN.

Fort Col·lins /kaálinz/ *n.* city in N Colorado. Pop. 87,758.
Fort Lau·der·dale /láwdərdayl/ *n.* city in SE Florida. Pop. 149,377.
Fort Wayne /wayn/ *n.* city in NE Indiana. Pop. 173,072.
Fort Worth /wúrth/ *n.* city in N Texas. Pop. 447,619.
France /frans/ *n.* republic in W Europe. Pop. 58,041,000. Capital: Paris. See map p. 1220.
Frank·fort /frángkfərt/ *n.* capital of Kentucky, in the N central part. Pop. 25,968.
Frank·furt /frángkfərt/ *n.* **1** (also called **Frank'furt am Main** /aam mín/) city in W Germany. Pop. 652,400. **2** (also called **Frank'furt an der O·der** /aan dər ódər/) city in E Germany. Pop. 70,000.
Fred·er·ic·ton /frédriktən/ *n.* capital of New Brunswick, Canada, in the S part. Pop. 46,500.
Free·town /fréetown/ *n.* port city and capital of Sierra Leone. Pop. 469,800.
Fre·mont /fréemaant/ *n.* city in W California. Pop. 173,339.
French Gui·an·a /geeaánə/ *n.* overseas department of France, on the NE coast of South America. Pop. 151,180. Capital: Cayenne.

French Guiana

French Pol·y·ne·sia /paalənéezhə, –shə/ *n.* island group in the S Pacific; territory of France. Pop. 225,000. Capital: Papeete.
Fres·no /fréznō/ *n.* city in central California. Pop. 354,202.
Fu·ji /foójee/, **Mount** *n.* dormant volcano in central Japan: 12,388 ft. high.
Fu·ku·o·ka /foókoo–ókə/ *n.* city in Japan, on Kyushu. Pop. 1,284,700.
Ful·ler·ton /foólərtən/ *n.* city in SW California. Pop. 114,144.
Fu·na·fu·ti /foónəfoótee, fyoónəfyoótee/ *n.* capital of Tuvalu, in the central part. Pop. 3,800.
Fun·dy /fúndee/, **Bay of** *n.* inlet of the Atlantic, between New Brunswick and Nova Scotia.
Fu·shun /foóshoon/ *n.* city in NE China. Pop. 1,350,000.
Ga·bon /gabáwɴ/ *n.* republic in W Africa. Pop. 1,253,000. Capital: Libreville. □□ **Gab·o·nese** /gabənéez, –nées/ *n. & adj.*

Gabon

Ga·bo·ro·ne /gaabərónee/ *n.* capital of Botswana, in the SE part. Pop. 156,800.
Gaines·ville /gáynzvəl, –vil/ *n.* city in N Florida. Pop. 84,770.
Ga·lá·pa·gos /gəláapəgəs/ **Is·lands** *n.* archipelago in the Pacific, W of Ecuador; province of Ecuador.
Gal·i·lee /gálilee/, **Sea of** *n.* lake in NE Israel.
Gal·ves·ton /gálvəstən/ **Bay** *n.* inlet of the Gulf of Mexico, SE of Houston, Texas.
Gam·bi·a /gámbeeə, gaám–/ *n.* (also **the Gambia**) republic in W Africa. Pop. 1,205,000. Capital: Banjul.

Gambia

Gan·ges /gánjeez/ **Riv·er** *n.* river in India, flowing 1,560 mi. from the Himalayas to the Bay of Bengal at Calcutta.
Gar·den Grove /gaárdən grōv/ *n.* city in SW California. Pop. 143,050.
Gar·land *n.* city in SW Texas. Pop. 180,650.

Gar·y /géree/ *n.* city in NW Indiana. Pop. 116,646.
Ga·tun /gətóón/ **Lake** *n.* artificial lake forming part of the Panama Canal.
Gaul /gawl/ *n. hist.* province of the ancient Roman Empire, in W Europe.
Ga·za Strip /gaázə/ area of land along the Mediterranean Sea, between Egypt and Israel.
Gdansk /gədaánsk, –dánsk/ *n.* port city in N Poland. Pop. 463,100.
Gdy·nia /gədíneeə/ *n.* port city in N Poland. Pop. 251,500.
Ge·ne·va /jənéevə/ *n.* city in SW Switzerland. Pop. 172,700.
Ge·ne·va, Lake *n.* (also called **Lake Le'man**) lake between Switzerland and France.
Gen·o·a /jénəwə/ *n.* port city in N Italy. Pop. 659,800.
George·town /jáwrjtown/ *n.* port city and capital of Guyana. Pop. 248,500.
Geor·gia /jáwrjə/ *n.* **1** state in SE U.S. Pop. 6,478,216. Capital: Atlanta. Abbr. **GA; Ga. 2** republic in E Europe; formerly part of the USSR. Pop. 5,220,000. Capital: Tbilisi. □□ **Geor'gian** *n. & adj.*

Georgia

Ger·ma·ny /júrmənee/ *n.* republic in W Europe. Pop. 83,536,000. Capital: Berlin. See map p. 1221.
Get·tys·burg /géteezbərg/ *n.* borough in S central Pennsylvania; site of a Civil War battle. Pop. 7,025.
Gha·na /gaánə/ *n.* republic in W Africa. Pop. 17,698,000. Capital: Accra. □□ **Gha'na·ian, Ghan'i·an** *n. & adj.*

Ghana

Ghent /gent/ *n.* port city in NW central Belgium. Pop. 227,500.
Gi·bral·tar /jibráwltər/ *n.* British crown colony near the S tip of Spain. Pop. 29,000.

Gibraltar

Gi·bral·tar, Strait of strait between Europe and Africa, at the Atlantic entrance to the Mediterranean Sea.
Gi·jón /heehón/ *n.* port city in N Spain, on the Bay of Biscay. Pop. 269,600.
Gi·za /géezə/ *n.* (also called **El Gi'za**) city in N Egypt. Pop. 2,144,000.
Glas·gow /gláskō, glázgō/ *n.* port city in SW Scotland, United Kingdom. Pop. 674,800. □□ **Glas·we·gian** /glasweéjən, -jeeən/ *n. & adj.*
Glen·dale /gléndayl/ *n.* **1** city in SW California. Pop. 180,038. **2** city in SW central Arizona. Pop. 148,134.
Glouces·ter /gláastər, gláws–/ *n.* port city in SW central England. Pop. 104,800.
Go·bi /góbee/ *n.* desert in E Asia, mostly in Mongolia.
Gö·te·borg /yótəbawr, –bawryə/ *n.* (also **Go·then·burg** /gaáthənberg/) port city in SW Sweden. Pop. 449,200.
Got·land /gaátlənd/ *n.* island province in SE Sweden, in the Baltic Sea.

FRANCE

0   50   100   150   200 km

0   25   50   75   100 miles

N

PAS-DE-CALAIS   •Lille
(13)

PICARDY

NORD

SOMME

Amiens•   (17)   ARDENNES

SEINE-
MARITIME
Rouen•   Chalons-
s-Marne•   (7)   Metz•   MOSELLE   BAS-
                                        RHIN

(15)   AISNE   MEUSE   Strasbourg•

OISE   MARNE   (11)   MEURTHE-   ALSACE
                                        ET-MOSELLE
Caen•   VAL-D'-OISE   (1)
CALVADOS   EURE   Paris   AUBE   HAUTE-   VOSGES   HAUT-
NORMANDY   PARIS   MARNE   RHIN
MANCHE   YVELINES   SEINE-ET-   HAUTE-
(14)   ORNE   MARNE   SAÔNE   FRANCHE-COMTÉ
                                        (8)   TERRITOIRE
FINISTÈRE   CÔTES-D'ARMOR   EURE-   ESSONNE   DOUBS   DE BELFORT
                              ET-LOIR   (21)
BRITTANY   ANJOU   YONNE   Besançon•
        Rennes•   MAYENNE   CÔTE-D'OR   JURA
(5)   ILLE-ET-   Orléans•   Dijon•
MORBIHAN   VILAINE   SARTHE   LOIRET   BURGUNDY
        MAINE-   NIÈVRE   SAÔNE-
(16)   ET-LOIRE   LOIR-   ET-LOIRE
LOIRE-   TOURAINE   ET-CHER   CHER   AIN   HAUTE-SAVOIE
ATLANTIQUE   INDRE-   RHÔNE
Nantes•   ET-LOIRE   INDRE   ALLIER   Lyon•   SAVOIE
        POITOU   VIENNE   (3)   LOIRE   (20)   ISÈRE
VENDÉE   DEUX-   Clermont-
        SÈVRES   Poitiers•   Ferrand•
(18)   LIMOUSIN   HAUTE-   CREUSE   PUY-DE-DÔME   DAUPHINY
CHARENTE-   VIENNE   Limoges•   (10)   HAUTES-
MARITIME   Limoges•   CORRÈZE   AUVERGNE   HAUTE-LOIRE   ALPES
        CHARENTE   PERIGORD   CANTAL   ARDÈCHE   DRÔME   (19)
Bordeaux•   DORDOGNE   ALPES-DE-
GIRONDE   GUYENNE   LOT   LOZÈRE   HTE-PROV.   ALPES-
(2)   LOT-ET-   AVEYRON   GARD   VAUCLUSE   MARITIMES
GASCONY   GARONNE   TARN-ET-   PROVENCE
LANDES   GARONNE   (12)   LANGUEDOC   Montpellier•   BOUCHES-
        GERS   Toulouse•   TARN   HÉRAULT   DU-RHÔNE   VAR
PYRÉNÉES-   Marseille•
ATLANTIQUES   HAUTE-GARONNE   AUDE   (9)
HAUTES-   ARIÈGE   PYRÉNÉES-
PYRÉNÉES   ORIENTALES

—— Regional boundary
······ Department boundary
■ Capital City
● Regional capital

Bastia•
CORSE
Ajaccio•

Departments of the Paris Region

VAL-D'-OISE

HAUTS-DE-SEINE   SEINE-SAINT-DENIS
        Paris
YVELINES   VAL-DE-MARNE

        SEINE-ET-MARNE

ESSONNE

Regions

(1)	Alsace	(12)	Midi-Pyrénées
(2)	Aquitaine	(13)	Nord-Pas-de-Calais
(3)	Auvergne	(14)	Basse Normandie
(4)	Bourgogne	(15)	Haute Normandie
(5)	Bretagne	(16)	Pays de La Loire
(6)	Centre	(17)	Picardie
(7)	Champagne-Ardenne	(18)	Poitou-Charentes
(8)	Franche-Comté	(19)	Provence-Alpes-Côte d'Azur
(9)	Languedoc-Roussillon		
(10)	Limousin	(20)	Rhône-Alpes
(11)	Lorraine	(21)	Ile-de-France

GERMANY

State boundary (Länder)

■ Capital city

0 50 100 150 km

0 25 50 75 100 miles

N

BREMEN

Kiel ●

SCHLESWIG-
HOLSTEIN

MECKLENBURG-WEST
POMERANIA

Hamburg ●

Schwerin ●

HAMBURG

Bremen ●

BRANDENBURG

LOWER SAXONY

Berlin ●

Potsdam ●

BERLIN

Hanover ●

Magdeburg ●

SAXONY-ANHALT

NORTH RHINE-WESTPHALIA

Düsseldorf ●

S A X O N Y

Dresden ●

Erfurt ●

T H U R I N G I A

H E S S E

RHINELAND-
PALATINATE

Wiesbaden ●

Mainz ●

Saarbrücken ●

SAARLAND

Stuttgart ●

B A V A R I A

BADEN-
WÜRTTEMBERG

Munich ●

Gra·na·da /grənáːdə/ *n.* city in S Spain. Pop. 271,200.

Grand Banks *n.* extensive shoal and fishing grounds SE of Newfoundland.

Grand Can·yon *n.* extensive gorge of the Colorado River, in NW Arizona.

Grand Cou·lee /kóolee/ **Dam** *n.* dam on the Columbia River, in NE central Washington; largest concrete dam in U.S.

Grand Rap·ids *n.* city in W Michigan. Pop. 189,126.

Grand Te·ton /teéton/ highest peak in the Teton range: 13,770 ft.

Graz /graats/ *n.* city in SE Austria. Pop. 237,800.

Great Ba·sin *n.* extensive desert region in W U.S.

Great Brit·ain /brít'n/ *n.* **1** island of NW Europe, comprising England, Scotland, and Wales. **2** popular term for the United Kingdom. ¶ *Great Britain* is the overall name given to the island that comprises *England, Scotland, Wales*; the *United Kingdom* includes the preceding and *Northern Ireland*; the *British Isles* include the *United Kingdom* together with the *Channel Islands* and all the other surrounding islands—the *Isles of Scilly*, the *Isle of Man*, and the *Orkney* and *Shetland* islands. The all-encompassing adjective is *British*, which is unlikely to offend anyone. *Welsh, Scottish,* and *English* should be used with care; it is safest to use *British* if unsure.

Great Di·vide *n.* see CONTINENTAL DIVIDE.

Great·er An·til·les /antíleez/ *n.* term for the larger islands of the West Indies: Cuba, Hispaniola, Jamaica, and Puerto Rico. See also LESSER ANTILLES.

Great·er Sun·da /súndə, sóondə/ **Is·lands** *n.* island chain in the Malay Archipelago; includes Borneo, Java, and Sumatra.

Great Lakes *n.* series of five freshwater lakes between the U.S. and Canada: Superior, Michigan, Huron, Erie, and Ontario.

Great Plains *n.* dry, grassy region E of the Rocky Mountains, in Canada and the U.S.

Great Salt Lake *n.* inland salt sea in NW Utah.

Great Salt Lake Des·ert *n.* arid region in NW Utah.

Great Slave Lake *n.* lake in S central Northwest Territories, Canada.

Great Smo·ky /smókee/ **Moun·tains** *n.* mountain range in E U.S., between Tennessee and North Carolina; part of the Appalachian range.

Greece /grees/ *n.* republic in S Europe, on the Balkan Peninsula. Pop. 10,539,000. Capital: Athens.

Greece

Green /green/ **Bay** *n.* city in E Wisconsin. Pop. 96,466.

Green·land /greénlənd, –land/ *n.* island territory of Denmark, NE of Canada; largest island in the world. Pop. 58,000. □□ **Green′·land·er** *n.* **Green·land′ic** *adj.*

Greenland

Green·land Sea *n.* arm of the Arctic Ocean, NE of Greenland.

Green /green/ **Moun·tains** *n.* mountain range in E North America, extending from S Quebec through Vermont into W Massachusetts; part of the Appalachian range.

Greens·bo·ro /greénzbərə/ *n.* city in N central North Carolina. Pop. 183,521.

Gre·na·da /grənáydə/ *n.* island country in the E West Indies. Pop. 95,000. Capital: St. George's.

Gre·no·ble /grənóbəl/ *n.* city in SE France. Pop. 154,000.

Gro·ning·en /gróningən/ *n.* city in the N Netherlands. Pop. 170,700.

Groz·ny /gráwznee, graáz−/ *n.* city in S Russia. Pop. 364,000.

Gua·da·la·ja·ra /gwaad'ləháárə/ *n.* capital of Jalisco, Mexico, in the N central part. Pop. 1,650,042.

Gua·dal·ca·nal /gwaad'lkənál/ *n.* island in the W Pacific; largest of the Solomon Islands; site of a World War II battle.

Gua·da·lu·pe /gwaad'lóopay/ *n.* city in NE Mexico. Pop. 535,300.

Gua·de·loupe /gwaad'lóop/ *n.* island in the E West Indies; dependency of France. Pop. 408,000. Capital: Basse-Terre.

Guadeloupe

Guam /gwaam/ *n.* island in the W Pacific; largest of the Mariana Islands; territory of the U.S. Pop. 157,000. □□ **Gua·ma′·ni·an** /–máyneeən/ *n. & adj.*

Guam

Gua·na·jua·to /gwaanəwaátō, –nəhwaá–/ *n.* state in central Mexico. Pop. 3,982,600. Capital: Guanajuato.

Guan·tá·na·mo /gwaantaánəmō/ *n.* city in SE Cuba; site of a U.S. naval base. Pop. 207,800.

Gua·te·ma·la /gwaatəmaálə/ *n.* republic in N Central America. Pop. 11,278,000. Capital: Guatemala City. □□ **Gua·te·ma′lan** *n. & adj.*

Guatemala

Gua·te·ma·la Cit·y *n.* capital of Guatemala, in the S central part. Pop. 823,300.

Guay·a·quil /gwīəkeél/ *n.* port city in Ecuador. Pop. 1,508,400.

Guern·sey /gúrnzee/ island in the English Channel; British crown dependency. Pop. 63,000. Capital: St. Peter Port.

Guer·re·ro /ger-rérō/ *n.* state in S Mexico. Pop. 2,620,600. Capital: Chilpancingo.

Guin·ea /gínee/ *n.* republic in W Africa. Pop. 7,412,000. Capital: Conakry.

Guin·ea-Bis·sau /bisów/ *n.* republic in W Africa. Pop. 1,151,000. Capital: Bissau.

Guin·ea, Gulf of *n.* arm of the Atlantic, on the W coast of Africa.

Gui·yang /gwáyyaáng/ *n.* (formerly **Kuei-yang**) city in S China. Pop. 1,018,600.

Gulf Stream *n.* warm Atlantic current flowing from Gulf of Mexico along the E coast of North America toward Europe.

Guy·a·na /gī-aánə, –ánə/ *n.* republic in NE South America. Pop. 712,000. Capital: Georgetown.

Gyan·dzha /gyaánjə/ *n.* city in W Azerbaijan. Pop. 282,200.

Haar·lem /haárləm/ *n.* city in the W Netherlands. Pop. 149,000.

Grenada

Hague /hayg/, **The** *n.* city in the SW Netherlands; seat of government. Pop. 444,200.

Hai·fa /hífə/ *n.* port city in NW Israel. Pop. 252,300.

Hai·phong /hífáwng/ *n.* port city in N Vietnam. Pop. 456,000.

Hai·ti /háytee/ *n.* republic in the central West Indies, comprising the W part of Hispaniola. Pop. 6,732,000. Capital: Port-au-Prince. □□ **Hai·tian** /háyshən/ *n. & adj.*

Haiti

Hal·i·fax /hálifaks/ *n.* capital of Nova Scotia, Canada, in the E part. Pop. 320,500.

Hal·le /haálə/ *n.* city in E central Germany. Pop. 290,100.

Ham·a·dan /hamədaán, -dán/ *n.* city in W Iran. Pop. 349,700.

Ham·burg /haámbərg/ *n.* port city in N Germany. Pop. 1,705,900.

Hamp·ton /hámptən/ *n.* city in SE Virginia. Pop. 133,793.

Ha·noi /hanóy/ *n.* capital of Vietnam, in the N part. Pop. 2,154,900.

Han·o·ver /hánōvər/ *n.* city in N central Germany. Pop. 525,800.

Ha·ra·re /həraárray/ *n.* capital of Zimbabwe, in the N part. Pop. 1,184,200.

Har·bin /haarbín/ *n.* city in NE China. Pop. 2,830,000.

Har·ris·burg /hárəsbərg/ *n.* capital of Pennsylvania, in the SE central part. Pop. 52,376.

Hart·ford /haártfərd/ *n.* capital of Connecticut, in the N central part. Pop. 139,739.

Ha·van·a /həvánə/ *n.* port city and capital of Cuba. Pop. 2,241,000.

Ha·wai·i /həwaáee, –wíee, –waáwee/ *n.* **1** state in the U.S. comprising eight Pacific islands. Pop. 1,108,229. Capital: Honolulu. Abbr. **HI 2** largest island of the state of Hawaii. □□ **Ha·wai'ian** /-waáyən, -wíən/ *n. & adj.*

Hay·ward /háywərd/ *n.* city in W California. Pop. 111,498.

Heb·ri·des /hébrədeez/ *n.* island group in the Atlantic, off the W coast of Scotland.

Hei·del·berg /híd'lbərg/ *n.* city in SW Germany. Pop. 139,000.

Hel·e·na /hélənə/ *n.* capital of Montana, in the W central part. Pop. 24,569.

Guinea

Guinea-Bissau

Guyana

Hel·sin·ki /hélsingkee/ *n.* port city and capital of Finland. Pop. 525,000.

Hē·rá·klei·on /herákleeaan/ *n.* see IRÁKLION.

Her·mo·si·llo /ermōseéyō/ *n.* capital of Sonora, Mexico, in the central part. Pop. 406,417.

Hi·a·le·ah /hīəleéə/ *n.* city in SE Florida. Pop. 188,004.

Hi·dal·go /hidálgō/ *n.* state in E central Mexico. Pop. 1,888,400. Capital: Pachuca.

Him·a·la·yas /himəláyəz, himaályəz, –ləyəz/ *n.* mountain range in S Asia, along the border between India and Tibet.

Hin·du Kush /híndoo koósh/ *n.* mountain range in central Asia, extending W from the Himalayas.

Hi·ro·shi·ma /heerəsheémə, heeróshimə/ *n.* port city in Japan, on Honshu; target of first atomic bomb. Pop. 1,108,900.

His·pan·io·la /hispənyólə/ *n.* island in the central West Indies, comprising the republic of Haiti and the Dominican Republic.

Ho·bart /hōbaart/ *n.* capital of Tasmania, Australia, in the SE part. Pop. 129,000.

Ho Chi Minh /hō chee mín/ **City** *n.* (formerly **Saigon**) city in S Vietnam. Pop. 4,322,300.

Hok·kai·do /haakídō/ *n.* (formerly **Yezo**) island in N Japan.

Hol·land /haálənd/ *n.* see NETHERLANDS, THE.

Hol·ly·wood /haáleewŏŏd/ *n.* **1** city in SE Florida. Pop. 121,697. **2** section of Los Angeles, California; center of U.S. motion-picture industry.

Ho·ly /hólee/ **Land** *n.* see PALESTINE.

Ho·ly Ro·man Em·pire *n. hist.* empire of W central Europe from 800 to 1806.

Hon·du·ras /haandŏŏrəs, –dyŏŏ–/ *n.* republic in N Central America. Pop. 5,605,000. Capital: Tegucigalpa. □□ **Hon·du'ran** *n. & adj.*

Hong Kong /haáng kaáng, háwng káwng/ *n.* city and commercial center of SE China; formerly (to 1997) a British crown colony. Pop. 6,305,000. Capital: Victoria.

Hong Kong

Ho·ni·a·ra /hōnee-aárə/ *n.* capital of the Solomon Islands, on Guadalcanal. Pop. 43,600.

Hon·o·lu·lu /haanəlŏŏlŏŏ, hōn-/ *n.* capital of Hawaii, on the S coast of Oahu. Pop. 365,272.

Hon·shu /haánshŏŏ/ *n.* largest island in Japan, in the central part.

Hood /hŏŏd/, **Mount** *n.* inactive volcanic peak in NW Oregon, in the Cascade range.

Hoo·ver /hŏŏvər/ **Dam** dam on the Colorado River, along the Arizona-Nevada border.

Hous·ton /hyŏŏstən, yŏŏs–/ *n.* city in SE Texas. Pop. 1,630,553.

Huang /hwaang/ **Riv·er** *n.* (also called **Yel'low Riv'er**) river in China, flowing 2,800 mi. from Qinghai to the Yellow Sea.

Hud·son /hədsən/ **Bay** *n.* inland sea in NE Canada; an arm of the Atlantic.

Hud·son Riv·er *n.* river in E New York, flowing 300 mi. from the Adirondacks to New York Bay.

Hull /həl/ *n.* (official name **Kings'ton up·on' Hull**) port city on the Humber River in England. Pop. 269,100.

Hun·ga·ry /húnggəree/ *n.* republic in central Europe. Pop. 10,003,000. Capital: Budapest.

Hungary

Hun·ting·ton /húntingtən/ *n.* city in SE New York. Pop. 191,474.

Hun·ting·ton Beach *n.* city in SW California. Pop. 181,519.

Hunts·ville /húntsvəl, –vil/ *n.* city in N Alabama. Pop. 159,789.

Hu·ron /hyŏoraan, yŏoraan, –ən/, **Lake** *n.* one of the Great Lakes, W of Michigan.

Hy·der·a·bad /hídərəbaad/ *n.* **1** city in W India. Pop. 3,145,900. **2** city in S Pakistan. Pop. 751,500.

I·ba·dan /ibaád'n/ *n.* city in SW Nigeria. Pop. 1,365,000.

I·be·ri·an /ibéereeən/ **Pen·in·su·la** *n.* (also called **I·be′ri·a**) peninsula in SW Europe, bounded by the Bay of Biscay, the Atlantic, and the Mediterranean Sea, and comprising Portugal and Spain.

Ice·land /íslənd/ *n.* island republic in the N Atlantic, between Scandinavia and Greenland. Pop. 270,000. Capital: Reykjavik.

Iceland

I·da·ho /ídəhō/ *n.* state in NW U.S. Pop. 1,006,749. Capital: Boise. Abbr. **ID; Ida.** □□ **I′da·ho·an** *n. & adj.*

I·guas·sú /eegwaasóo/ **Falls** *n.* waterfall on the Argentina-Brazil border: 210 ft. high.

Il·li·nois /ilənóy, –nóyz/ *n.* state in central U.S. Pop. 11,430,602. Capital: Springfield. Abbr. **IL; Ill.** □□ **Il·li·nois′an, Il·li·noi′an** /–nóyən/ *n. & adj.*

Im·pe·ri·al /impéereeəl/ **Val·ley** *n.* valley in S central California.

In·chon /ínchaan/ *n.* port city in NW South Korea. Pop. 2,307,600.

In·de·pend·ence /indipéndəns/ *n.* city in W Missouri. Pop. 112,301.

In·di·a /índeeə/ *n.* republic in S Asia. Pop. 952,108,000. Capital: New Delhi. See map p. 1225.

In·di·an·a /indee-ánə/ *n.* state in central U.S. Pop. 5,544,159. Capital: Indianapolis. Abbr. **IN; Ind.** □□ **In·di·an′an** *n. & adj.*

In·di·an·ap·o·lis /indeeənápələs/ *n.* capital of Indiana, in the central part. Pop. 731,327.

In·di·an /índeeən/ **O·cean** *n.* ocean between Africa and Australia, S of Asia. Area 28,350,500 sq. mi.

In·do·chi·na /índōchínə/ *n.* peninsula in SE Asia, bounded by the Bay of Bengal and the S China Sea, and comprising Burma, W Malaysia, Thailand, Cambodia, Laos, and Vietnam.

In·do·ne·sia /indəneéezhə/ republic of the Malay Archipelago in SE Asia. Pop. 206,612,000. Capital: Jakarta. □□ **In·do·ne′sian** *n. & adj.*

Indonesia

In·dus /índəs/ **Riv·er** *n.* river in Asia, flowing 1,900 mi. from Tibet through Pakistan and into the Arabian Sea.

Inglewood /ínggəlwŏod/ *n.* city in SW California. Pop. 109,602.

Inns·bruck /ínzbrŏok/ *n.* city in W Austria. Pop. 118,100.

I·o·ni·an /ī-óneeən/ **Sea** *n.* arm of the Mediterranean Sea, between Greece and Italy.

I·o·wa /íəwə/ *n.* state in central U.S. Pop. 2,776,755. Capital: Des Moines. Abbr. **IA; Ia.** □□ **I′o·wan** *n. & adj.*

I·o·wa Cit·y *n.* city in E Iowa. Pop. 59,738.

Ips·wich /ípswich/ *n.* city in E England. Pop. 114,800.

I·rá·kli·on /irákleeon/ (also **Hē·rá′klei·on**) port city and capital of Crete. Pop. 117,200.

I·ran /irán, iraán, irán/ *n.* (formerly **Persia**) republic in SW Asia. Pop. 66,094,000. Capital: Teheran. □□ **I·ra·ni·an** /iráyneeən/ *n. & adj.*

I·raq /irák, iraák, írák/ *n.* republic in SW Asia. Pop. 21,422,000. Capital: Baghdad. □□ **I·ra·qi** /irákee/ *n. & adj.*

Ir·bid /éerbid/ *n.* city in N Jordan. Pop. 314,700.

Ire·land /írlənd/ *n.* **1** island in the N Atlantic, W of England. **2** (official name **Re·pub′lic of Ire′land;** also called **Eir′e**) republic in NW Europe; occupies most of the island of Ireland. Pop. 3,567,000. Capital: Dublin. See also NORTHERN IRELAND. See map p. 1226.

I·rish /írish/ **Sea** *n.* arm of the Atlantic, between England and Ireland.

Ir·kutsk /eerkŏotsk/ *n.* city in S Russia. Pop. 654,000.

Ir·vine /úrvīn/ *n.* city in SW California. Pop. 110,330.

Ir·ving /úrving/ *n.* city in NE Texas. Pop. 155,037.

Is·fa·han /isfəhaán/ *n.* (also **Esfahan** or **Ispahan**) city in central Iran; former capital of Persia. Pop. 1,127,000.

Is·lam·a·bad /islaáməbaad/ *n.* capital of Pakistan, in the NE part. Pop. 204,400.

Is·ra·el /ízreeəl, –rayel/ *n.* **1** republic in SW Asia; formed in 1948 as a Jewish state. Pop. 5,422,000 (excluding territory occupied after 1967). Capital: Jerusalem. **2** *hist.* ancient biblical country of the Hebrews. □□ **Is·rae·li** /izráylee/ *n. & adj.*

Israel

Is·tan·bul /istaanbŏol/ *n.* (formerly **Constantinople**; ancient name **Byzantium**) port city in NW Turkey. Pop. 7,615,500.

It·a·ly /ít'lee/ *n.* republic in S Europe. Pop. 57,460,000. Capital: Rome. See map. p. 1227.

I·vo·ry /ívəree, ; n-vree/ **Coast** *n.* (official name **Côte d'I·voire′**) republic in W Africa. Pop. 14,762,000. Capital: Abidjan. □□ **I·vo·ri·an** /iváwreeən/ *n. & adj.*

I·wo Ji·ma /eewə jeémə, eewō/ *n.* island S of Japan; site of World War II battle.

Iz·mir /izmeér/ *n.* (formerly **Smyrna**) port city in E Turkey. Pop. 1,985,300.

Jack·son /jáksən/ *n.* capital of Mississippi, in the central part. Pop. 196,637.

Ja·kar·ta /jəkaártə/ *n.* capital of Indonesia, on NW coast of Java. Pop. 6,503,400.

Ja·la·pa /həlaápə/ *n.* capital of Veracruz, Mexico, in the central part. Pop. 111,800.

Ja·lis·co /həlískō/ *n.* state in W Mexico. Pop. 5,302,700. Capital: Guadalajara.

Ja·mai·ca /jəmáykə/ *n.* island republic in the W West Indies, S of Cuba. Pop. 2,595,000. Capital: Kingston.

Jamaica

Iran

Iraq

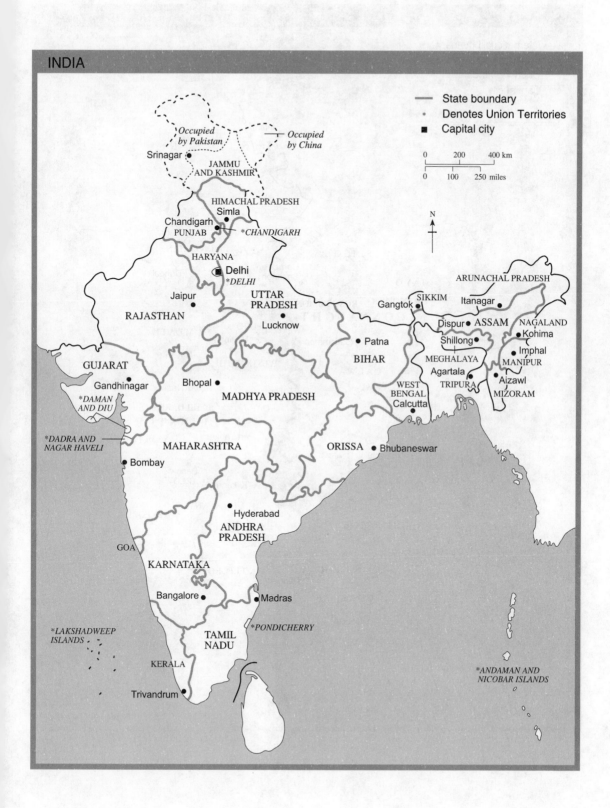

INDIA

State boundary
* Denotes Union Territories
■ Capital city

0   200   400 km
0   100   250 miles

N

Occupied by Pakistan
Occupied by China

Srinagar
JAMMU AND KASHMIR

HIMACHAL PRADESH
Simla
Chandigarh
PUNJAB   *CHANDIGARH

HARYANA
Delhi
*DELHI

ARUNACHAL PRADESH

Jaipur   UTTAR PRADESH   Gangtok   SIKKIM   Itanagar

RAJASTHAN   Lucknow   Dispur   ASSAM   NAGALAND
Kohima

Patna   Shillong   Imphal
MANIPUR
BIHAR   MEGHALAYA
GUJARAT   Agartala   Aizawl
Gandhinagar   Bhopal   TRIPURA   MIZORAM
*DAMAN AND DIU   MADHYA PRADESH   WEST BENGAL
Calcutta
*DADRA AND NAGAR HAVELI   MAHARASHTRA   ORISSA   Bhubaneswar

Bombay

Hyderabad
ANDHRA PRADESH

GOA

KARNATAKA

Bangalore   Madras

*LAKSHADWEEP ISLANDS   TAMIL NADU   *PONDICHERRY

KERALA   *ANDAMAN AND NICOBAR ISLANDS

Trivandrum

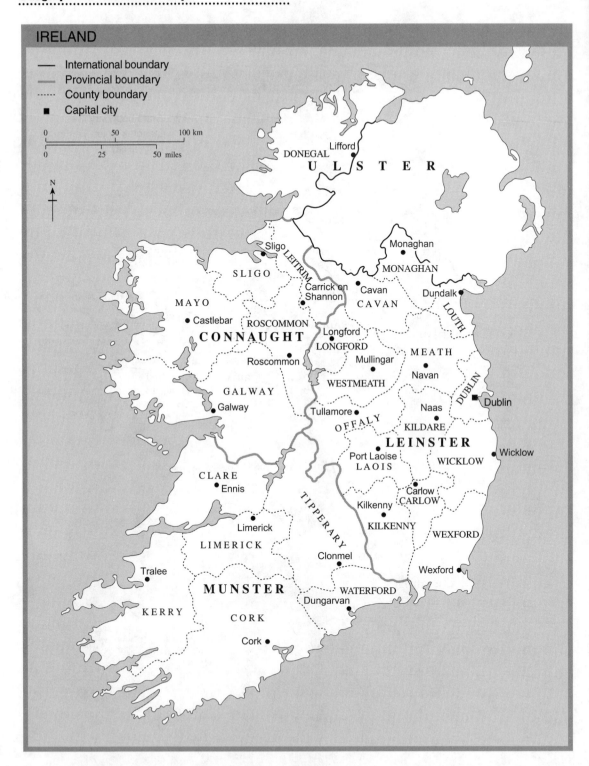

IRELAND

— International boundary
— Provincial boundary
····· County boundary
■ Capital city

0   50   100 km
0   25   50 miles

N

DONEGAL Lifford
U L S T E R

Sligo Monaghan
MONAGHAN
Carrick on Cavan
SLIGO Shannon Dundalk
MAYO CAVAN
Castlebar ROSCOMMON Longford LOUTH
CONNAUGHT LONGFORD
Roscommon MEATH
Mullingar Navan
GALWAY WESTMEATH
Galway Tullamore DUBLIN
OFFALY Naas Dublin
KILDARE
Port Laoise **LEINSTER** Wicklow
CLARE LAOIS WICKLOW
Ennis
Carlow
TIPPERARY Kilkenny CARLOW
Limerick KILKENNY
LIMERICK WEXFORD
Clonmel
Tralee Wexford
MUNSTER WATERFORD
Dungarvan
KERRY CORK

Cork

ITALY

Region boundary
■ Capital city

0 50 100 150 200 km
0 25 50 75 100 miles

N

TRENTINO-ALTO ADIGE

Trento

FRIULI-VENEZIA GIULIA

Aosta
VALLE D'AOSTA

LOMBARDY

VENETIA

Turin

Milan

Venice

Trieste

PIEDMONT

EMILIA-ROMAGNA

LIGURIA

Genoa

Bologna

Florence

Ancona

TUSCANY

THE MARCHES

Perugia

UMBRIA

L'Aquila

Rome

ABRUZZI

LATIUM

MOLISE

Campobasso

SARDINIA

Naples

CAMPANIA

Bari

APULIA

Potenza

BASILICATA

Cagliari

CALABRIA

Palermo

Reggio

SICILY

Ja·pan /jəpán/ *n.* island nation E of mainland Asia. Pop. 125,450,000. Capital: Tokyo.

Japan

Ja·pan, Sea of *n.* arm of the Pacific, between Japan and mainland Asia.

Ja·va /jaávə, jávə/ *n.* main island of Indonesia, SE of Sumatra.

Jef·fer·son /jéfərsən/ **City** *n.* capital of Missouri, in the central part. Pop. 35,481.

Je·na /yáynə/ *n.* city in E central Germany. Pop. 102,200.

Jer·sey /júrzee/ island in the English Channel; British crown dependency. Pop. 88,000. Capital: St. Helier.

Jer·sey City *n.* city in NE New Jersey. Pop. 228,537.

Je·ru·sa·lem /jərōōsələm, –sləm/ *n.* capital of Israel, in the E central part. Pop. 504,100.

Jid·da /jídə/ *n.* port city in W Saudi Arabia. Pop. 1,800,000.

Ji·nan /jeenaan/ (also **Chi·nan**) city in NE China. Pop. 1,100,000.

Jodh·pur /jaádpōōr/ *n.* city in NW India. Pop. 666,300.

Jo·han·nes·burg /jōhánəsbərg/ *n.* city in NE South Africa. Pop. 712,500.

Jo·li·et /jōlee-ét/ *n.* city in NE Illinois. Pop. 76,836.

Jor·dan /jáwrd'n/ *n.* kingdom in SW Asia, E of Israel. Pop. 4,212,000. Capital: Amman. ▫▫ **Jor·da·ni·an** /jawrdáyneeən/ *n. & adj.*

Jordan

Jor·dan Riv·er river in SW Asia, flowing 200 mi. from S Lebanon to the Dead Sea.

Juan de Fu·ca /waan də fōōkə, fyōō–/, **Strait of** *n.* channel separating Vancouver Island, Canada, from U.S.

Ju·neau /jōōnō/ *n.* capital of Alaska, in the SE part. Pop. 26,751.

Jung·frau /yōōngfrow/ *n.* mountain in the Alps, in S Switzerland: 13,642 ft. high.

Ka·bul /kaabōōl, kaábəl/ *n.* capital of Afghanistan, in the E part. Pop. 700,000.

Ka·go·shi·ma /kaagōsheémə, kaagósheemə/ *n.* port city in S Japan, on Kyushu. Pop. 546,300.

Ka·la·ha·ri /kaláhaáree, kaal–/ *n.* desert in SW Africa, mainly in Botswana.

Kal·a·ma·zoo /kaləməzōō/ *n.* city in SW Michigan. Pop. 80,277.

Ka·li·nin /kəleénin, –nyin/ *n.* (formerly **Tver**) city in W Russia. Pop. 455,000.

Ka·li·nin·grad /kəleéningrad, –nyingrad/ *n.* port city in W Russia. Pop. 419,000.

Kam·chat·ka /kamchaátkə/ *n.* peninsula in E Russia, bounded by the Sea of Okhotsk and the Bering Sea.

Kam·pa·la /kaampaálə/ *n.* capital of Uganda, in the SE part. Pop. 773,500.

Kam·pu·che·a /kampōōcheéə/ *n.* see CAMBODIA.

Ka·no /kaánō/ *n.* city in N central Nigeria. Pop. 657,300.

Kan·pur /kaánpōōr/ *n.* city in N India. Pop. 1,874,400.

Kan·sas /kánzəs/ *n.* state in central U.S. Pop. 2,477,574. Capital: Topeka. Abbr. **KS; Kan.; Kans.** ▫▫ **Kan'san** *n. & adj.*

Kan·sas City *n.* **1** city in W Missouri. Pop. 435,146. **2** city in E Kansas. Pop. 149,767.

Kao·hsiung /gówshee-ŏŏng/ *n.* port city in SW Taiwan. Pop. 1,426,518.

Ka·ra·chi /kəraáchee/ *n.* port city in S Pakistan. Pop. 5,208,100.

Karl-Marx-Stadt /kaarl maárks shtaat/ *n.* see CHEMNITZ.

Karls·ruh·e /kaárlzrōōə/ *n.* city in SW Germany. Pop. 277,000.

Kath·man·du /katmandōō/ *n.* (also **Kat·man·du'**) capital of Nepal, in the central part. Pop. 235,200.

Ka·to·wi·ce /kaatəveétsə/ *n.* city in S Poland. Pop. 355,100.

Kau·nas /kównəs/ *n.* city in S central Lithuania. Pop. 429,000.

Ka·wa·sa·ki /kaawəsaákee/ *n.* port city in Japan, on Honshu. Pop. 1,202,800.

Kay·se·ri /kīzəree/ *n.* city in central Turkey. Pop. 454,000.

Ka·zakh·stan /kəzaakstaán/ *n.* republic in central Asia; formerly part of the USSR. Pop. 16,916,000. Capital: Astana. ▫▫ **Ka·zakh'** *n.*

Kazakhstan

Kee·lung /keéelŏŏng/ *n.* see CHILUNG.

Ken·tuck·y /kəntúkee/ *n.* state in E central U.S. Pop. 3,685,296. Capital: Frankfort. Abbr. **KY; Ky.** ▫▫ **Ken·tuck'i·an** *n. & adj.*

Ken·ya /kényə, keén–/ *n.* republic in E Africa. Pop. 28,177,000. Capital: Nairobi.

Kenya

Khar·kiv /kaárkif/ *n.* (formerly **Khar'kov**) city in NE Ukraine. Pop. 1,555,000.

Khar·toum /kaartōōm/ *n.* capital of Sudan, in the E central part. Pop. 476,200.

Ki·ev /keé-ef, –ev/ *n.* capital of Ukraine, in the N central part. Pop. 2,630,000.

Ki·ga·li /kigaálee/ *n.* capital of Rwanda, in the central part. Pop. 232,700.

Ki·lau·e·a /kiləwáyə/ *n.* active volcano on the island of Hawaii.

Kil·i·man·ja·ro /kilimənjaárō/, **Mount** *n.* volcanic mountain in N Tanzania; highest peak in Africa: 19,340 ft.

Kings·ton /kíngstən/ *n.* port city and capital of Jamaica. Pop. 103,800.

Kings·ton up·on Hull *n.* see HULL.

Kings·town /kíngztown/ *n.* port city and capital of St. Vincent and the Grenadines. Pop. 15,500.

Kin·sha·sa /kinshaásə/ *n.* capital of the Congo (formerly Zaire), in the W part. Pop. 4,655,300.

Ki·ri·ba·ti /keereebaátee, kíribas/ *n.* island republic in the W Pacific, along the equator, comprising thirty-three islands. Pop. 81,000. Capital: Tarawa.

Kiribati

Kir·kuk /keerkŏŏk/ *n.* city in N Iraq. Pop. 570,000.

Ki·shi·nev /kíshinef/ *n.* (also called **Chi·și·nă'u**) capital of Moldova, in the central part. Pop. 662,000.

Ki·ta·kyu·shu /keetaakee-ŏŏshŏŏ/ *n.* port city in Japan, on Kyushu. Pop. 1,019,600.

Kitch·e·ner /kíchənər, kíchnər/ *n.* city in SE Ontario, Canada. Pop. 168,300.

Knox·ville /naáksvil/ *n.* city in E Tennessee. Pop. 165,121.

Ko·be /kóbay, –bee/ *n.* port city in Japan, on Honshu. Pop. 1,488,600.

Ko·blenz /kóblents/ *n.* see COBLENZ.

Ko·di·ak /kódee-ak/ **Is·land** *n.* island in Alaska, in the NW Gulf of Alaska.

Köln /köln/ *n.* see COLOGNE.

Kol·we·zi /kōlwáyzee/ *n.* city in S Congo (formerly Zaire). Pop. 417,800.

Kon·ya /kawnyaa/ *n.* city in SW central Turkey. Pop. 576,000.

Ko·re·a /kəreéə/ *n.* peninsula in E Asia, bounded by the Yellow Sea and the Sea of Japan; divided into two countries: **1 North Korea** Pop. 23,904,000. Capital: Pyongyang. See map p. 1236. **2 South Korea** Pop. 45,482,000. Capital: Seoul. See map p. 1243. ☐☐ **Ko·re'an** *n. & adj.*

Ko·so·vo /kaásəvō/ *n.* region of S Serbia. Pop. 2,000,000. ☐☐ **Ko'so·var** *n. & adj.*

Kra·ka·to·a /krakətóə/ *n.* (also **Kra·ka·tau** /krákətow/) island volcano in Indonesia; noted for its violent eruption in 1883.

Kra·ków /krákow, kraákoof/ *n.* see CRACOW.

Kras·no·yarsk /kraasnəyaársk/ *n.* city in central Russia. Pop. 869,400.

K2 *n.* (also called **God·win Aus·ten** /gaádwin áwstən/) mountain in N Kashmir; second highest in the world: 28,250 ft.

Kua·la Lum·pur /kwaálə ləmpoŏr/ *n.* capital of Malaysia, on the SW Malay Peninsula. Pop. 1,100,000.

Kuei·yang /gwáy-yáng/ (also **Kwei·yang**) see GUIYANG.

Kui·by·shev /kweébəshef, –shev/ see SAMARA.

Ku·ma·mo·to /koŏməmótō/ *n.* city in Japan, on Kyushu. Pop. 650,300.

Ku·ma·si /koŏmaásee/ *n.* city in S central Ghana. Pop. 385,200.

Ku·wait /kəwáyt/ *n.* **1** monarchy in W Asia, on the Persian Gulf. Pop. 1,950,000. **2** (also called **Ku·wait' Cit'y**) port city and capital of Kuwait. Pop. 44,200. ☐☐ **Ku·wai'ti** /–tee/ *n. & adj.*

Kuwait

Kwang·ju /gwaángjoŏ/ *n.* city in SW South Korea. Pop. 1,257,500.

Kyo·to /kee-ótō/ *n.* city in Japan, on Honshu. Pop. 1,463,600.

Kyr·gyz·stan /kirgistaán, –stán/ *n.* republic in W central Asia; formerly part of the USSR. Pop. 4,530,000. Capital: Bishkek.

Kyrgyzstan

Kyu·shu /kyoŏshoō/ *n.* island in SW Japan.

La·do·ga /laádəgə, lád–/, **Lake** *n.* lake N of St. Petersburg, Russia; largest lake in Europe.

La·hore /ləháwr, –hór/ *n.* city in E Pakistan. Pop. 2,952,700.

Lake Dis·trict *n.* noted scenic region in NW England.

Lake·wood /láykwoŏd/ *n.* city in central Colorado. Pop. 126,481.

La Ma·tan·za /laa mətaánsə/ *n.* city in E Argentina. Pop. 1,111,800.

Lan·sing /lánsing/ *n.* capital of Michigan, in the S part. Pop. 127,321.

La·os /laáōs/ *n.* country in SE Asia, between Thailand and Vietnam. Pop. 4,976,000. Capital: Vientiane. ☐☐ **La·o·tian** /lay-óshən/ *n. & adj.*

Laos

La Paz /lə paáz, paás/ *n.* **1** administrative capital of Bolivia, in the W part. Pop. 785,000 **2** capital of Baja California Sur, Mexico, in the S part. Pop. 161,000.

La Pla·ta /plaátə/ *n.* port city in E Argentina. Pop. 643,000.

La·re·do /ləráydō/ *n.* city in S Texas. Pop. 122,899.

Las Cru·ces /laas kroŏsəs/ *n.* city in S New Mexico. Pop. 62,126.

Las Pal·mas /paálməs/ *n.* port city of the Canary Islands, off the coast of Morocco. Pop. 342,000.

Las Ve·gas /váygəs/ *n.* city in SE Nevada. Pop. 258,295.

Lat·a·ki·a /latəkeéə/ *n.* port city in W Syria. Pop. 306,500.

Lat·vi·a /látveeə/ *n.* republic in N Europe; formerly part of the USSR. Pop. 2,469,000. Capital: Riga. ☐☐ **Lat'vi·an** *n. & adj.*

Latvia

Lau·sanne /lōzaán, –zán/ *n.* city in W Switzerland. Pop. 116,800.

La·val /laavaál, ləvál/ *n.* city in S Quebec, Canada. Pop. 314,400.

Leb·a·non /lébənaan, –nən/ *n.* republic in SW Asia. Pop. 3,776,000. Capital: Beirut. ☐☐ **Leb·a·nese** /–neéz/ *n. & adj.*

Lebanon

Leeds /leedz/ *n.* city in N England. Pop. 724,400.

Lee·ward /leéwərd, loŏərd/ **Is·lands** *n.* island group in the E West Indies, extending from Dominica NW to the U.S. Virgin Islands.

Leg·horn /léghawrn/ *n.* (Italian name **Li·vor'no**) port city in W Italy. Pop. 165,500.

Le Ha·vre /lə haáv, haávrə/ *n.* port city in N France. Pop. 197,200.

Leices·ter /léstər/ *n.* city in central England. Pop. 293,400.

Lei·den /líd'n/ city in the SW Netherlands. Pop. 115,500.

Leip·zig /lípsig, –sik/ *n.* city in E Germany. Pop. 481,100.

Le·man /leémən/, **Lake** *n.* see GENEVA, LAKE.

Le Mans /lə maaN/ *n.* city in NW France. Pop. 148,500.

Le·nin·grad /léningrad/ *n.* see SAINT PETERSBURG 1.

Le·ón /lay-áwn/ *n.* **1** city in NW Spain. Pop. 147,300. **2** city in central Mexico. Pop. 758,300.

Le·so·tho /ləsótō, –soōtoō/ *n.* (formerly **Basutoland**) monarchy in S Africa. Pop. 1,971,000. Capital: Maseru.

Lesotho

Less·er An·til·les /antíleez/ *n.* term for the smaller islands of the West Indies, comprising the Leeward and Windward islands, SE of Puerto Rico. See also GREATER ANTILLES.

Le·vant /ləvánt/ *n.* term for the countries on the E coast of the Mediterranean Sea; includes Israel, Syria, and Lebanon.

Lev·it·town /lévit-town/ *n.* city in SE New York, on Long Island. Pop. 53,286.

Lex·ing·ton /léksingtən/ *n.* **1** city in NE central Kentucky. Pop. 225,366. **2** town in NE Massachusetts; site of the first battle of the American Revolution (1775). Pop. 29,000.

Li·be·ri·a /libeéreeə/ *n.* republic in W Africa. Pop. 2,110,000. Capital: Monrovia. ☐☐ **Li·ber'i·an** *n. & adj.* See map p. 1230.

Li·bre·ville /leébrəvil/ *n.* port city and capital of Gabon. Pop. 362,400.

Lib·y·a /líbeeə/ *n.* republic in N Africa. Pop. 5,445,000. Capital: Tripoli. ☐☐ **Lib'y·an** *n. & adj.* See map p. 1226.

Liech·ten·stein /líkhtənshtin, líktənstin/ *n.* principality in central

Liberia

Libya

Liechtenstein

Europe. Pop. 31,000. Capital: Vaduz. ▫▫ **Liech′ten·stein·er** *n. & adj.*

Li·ège /lee-ézh/ *n.* city in E Belgium. Pop. 192,400.

Lille /leel/ *n.* city in N France. Pop. 178,300.

Li·long·we /liláwngway/ *n.* administrative capital of Malawi, in the central part. Pop. 395,500.

Li·ma /leémə/ *n.* capital of Peru, in the W part. Pop. 421,600.

Li·moges /leemózh/ *n.* city in central France. Pop. 136,400.

Lin·coln /língkən/ *n.* capital of Nebraska, in the E part. Pop. 191,972.

Linz /lins/ *n.* port city in NW Austria. Pop. 203,000.

Lis·bon /lízbən/ *n.* port city and capital of Portugal. Pop. 677,800.

Lith·u·a·ni·a /lithəwáyneeə/ *n.* republic in N Europe; formerly part of the USSR. Pop. 3,646,000. Capital: Vilnius.

Lithuania

Lit·tle Rock /lítəl raak/ *n.* capital of Arkansas, in the central part. Pop. 175,795.

Liv·er·pool /lívərpool/ *n.* port city in W England. Pop. 474,000. ▫▫ **Liv·er·pud·li·an** /livərpúdleeən/ *n. & adj.*

Li·vo·ni·a /livóneeə/ *n.* city in SE Michigan. Pop. 100,850.

Li·vor·no /leeváwrnaw/ *n.* see Leghorn.

Lju·blja·na /looblee-aánə, lyoo–/ *n.* capital of Slovenia. Pop. 276,100.

Lla·no Es·ta·ca·do /laanó estəkaádō/ *n.* (also called **Staked Plain**) extensive plateau in Texas and New Mexico.

Loch Ness /laak nes/ *n.* lake in NW Scotland.

Lódz /looj/ city in central Poland. Pop. 828,500.

Lo·mas de Za·mo·ra /lómaas də zəmáwrə/ *n.* city in E Argentina. Pop. 572,800.

Lo·mé /lómáy/ *n.* port city and capital of Togo. Pop. 366,500.

Lon·don /lúndən/ *n.* **1** capital of England and of the United Kingdom, in the S part of England. Pop. 6,967,500. **2** city in SE Ontario, Canada. Pop. 303,200.

Long /lawng/ **Beach** *n.* city in SW California. Pop. 429,433.

Long Is·land *n.* island in SE New York; includes portions of New York City.

Long Is·land Sound *n.* arm of the Atlantic, separating Connecticut from Long Island, New York.

Look·out /lóokowt/ **Moun·tain** *n.* ridge near Chattanooga in SE Tennessee; site of Civil War battle.

Los An·ge·les /laws ánjələs, –leez/ *n.* city in S California. Pop. 3,485,398. ▫▫ **An·ge·le·no** /anjəleénō/, **Los An·ge·le·no, Los An·ge·le·an** /anjəleéən/ *n.*

Lou·ise /loo-eéz, loo–/, **Lake** *n.* glacial lake in SW Alberta, Canada, in the Canadian Rocky Mountains.

Lou·i·si·an·a /loo-eezee-ánə/ *n.* state in S U.S. Pop. 4,219,973. Capital: Baton Rouge. Abbr. **LA; La.** ▫▫ **Lou·i·si·an′an, Lou·i·si·an′i·an** /–áneeən/ *n. & adj.*

Lou·is·ville /lóoeevil, –əvəl/ *n.* city in N central Kentucky. Pop. 269,063. ▫▫ **Lou·is·vill·ian** /lóoivilyən/ *n.*

Lourdes /loordz, loord/ *n.* town in SW France; site of a Roman Catholic shrine noted for miraculous cures. Pop. 18,100.

Lou·ren·ço Mar·ques /lərénsō maarkés, maárkəs/ *n.* see Maputo.

Low Coun·tries *n.* term for low-lying countries along the North Sea; includes Belgium, Luxembourg, and the Netherlands.

Low·ell /lóəl/ *n.* city in NE Massachusetts. Pop. 103,439.

Lu·an·da /loo-aándə/ *n.* port city and capital of Angola. Pop. 2,000,000.

Lub·bock /lúbək/ *n.* city in NW Texas. Pop. 186,206.

Lü·beck /lýbek/ *n.* port city in N Germany. Pop. 216,900.

Lu·blin /lóoblin/ *n.* city in E Poland. Pop. 352,500.

Lu·bum·ba·shi /loobóombaáshee/ *n.* city in S Congo (formerly Zaire). Pop. 851,400.

Luck·now /lúknow/ *n.* city in N India. Pop. 1,619,100.

Lü·da /lóodaá/ see Dalian.

Lu·gansk /loogaánsk/ *n.* (formerly **Voroshilovgrad**) city in E Ukraine. Pop. 487,000.

Lu·sa·ka /loosaákə/ *n.* capital of Zambia, in the SE part. Pop. 982,400.

Lux·em·bourg /lúksəmbərg/ *n.* **1** country and grand duchy in W Europe. Pop. 416,000. **2** capital of Luxembourg, in the S part. Pop. 76,400. **3** province in SE Belgium. ▫▫ **Lux′em·bourg·er** *n.* **Lux′em·bourg·i·an** /–bərgeeən/ *n. & adj.*

Luxembourg

Lviv /ləveéf/ *n.* (also **Lvov**) city in W Ukraine. Pop. 802,000.

Ly·all·pur /líəlpoor/ *n.* see Faisalabad.

Lyd·i·a /lídeeə/ *n. hist.* ancient kingdom of W Asia Minor. ▫▫ **Lyd′i·an** *n. & adj.*

Lynn /lin/ *n.* city in NE Massachusetts. Pop. 81,245.

Ly·ons /lee-áwn/ *n.* (also **Lyon**) city in E France. Pop. 422,400.

Maas·tricht /maástrikht/ *n.* city in the SE Netherlands. Pop. 118,300.

Ma·cau /məków/ *n.* overseas territory of Portugal (to 1999), consisting of a peninsula and two islands off the S coast of China. Pop. 497,000. Capital: Macau City.

Macau

Mac·e·do·ni·a /masədóneeə/ *n.* **1** *hist.* ancient country on the Balkan Peninsula, N of Greece. **2** independent state N of Greece; formerly part of Yugoslavia. Pop. 2,104,000. Capital: Skopje. ▫▫ **Mac·e·do′ni·an** /–neeən/ *n. & adj.*

Mac·ken·zie /məkénzee/ **Riv·er** *n.* river in NW Canada, flowing 1,120 mi. from Great Slave Lake to the Beaufort Sea.

Ma·con /máykən/ *n.* city in central Georgia. Pop. 106,612.

Mad·a·gas·car /madəgáskər/ *n.* (formerly **Malagasy Republic**) island country in the Indian Ocean, E of Mozambique. Pop. 13,671,000. Capital: Antananarivo. ▫▫ **Ma·da·gas′can** *n. & adj.*

Ma·dei·ra /mədéerə, –dérə/ *n.* **1** island group off the NW coast of Africa; part of Portugal. **2** the major island of this group.

Mad·i·son /mádisən/ *n.* capital of Wisconsin, in the S part. Pop. 191,262.

Ma·dras /mədrás, –dráas/ *n.* port city in SE India. Pop. 3,841,400.

Ma·drid /mədríd/ *n.* capital of Spain, in the central part. Pop. 3,041,100. □□ **Mad·ri·le·ni·an** /madrileéneeən/ *n. & adj.*

Mag·de·burg /mágdəbərg/ *n.* city in E central Germany. Pop. 265,400.

Ma·hal·la al-Ku·bra /məhálə al kóobrə/ *n.* city in N Egypt. Pop. 408,000.

Maine /mayn/ *n.* state in NE U.S. Pop. 1,227,928. Capital: Augusta. Abbr. **ME; Me.** □□ **Main'er** *n.*

Mainz /mīnts/ *n.* port city in W Germany. Pop. 184,600.

Ma·ju·ro /məjóorō/ *n.* capital of the Marshall Islands, in the SE part. Pop. 20,000.

Ma·la·bo /məláabō/ *n.* capital of Equatorial Guinea, on the island of Bioko. Pop. 58,000.

Má·la·ga /máləgə/ *n.* port city in S Spain. Pop. 531,400.

Mal·a·gas·y /máləgásee/ **Re·pub·lic** *n.* see MADAGASCAR.

Ma·lang /məláang/ *n.* city in Indonesia, on Java. Pop. 650,300.

Ma·la·wi /məláawee/ *n.* republic in SE Africa. Pop. 9,453,000. Capitals: Lilongwe; Zomba.

Malawi

Ma·la·wi, Lake *n.* see NYASA, LAKE.

Ma·lay·a /məláyə/ *n.* **1** see MALAY PENINSULA. **2** former federation of eleven states on the Malay Peninsula; now part of Malaysia.

Ma·lay /máylay/ **Ar·chi·pel·a·go** *n.* (formerly **Malaysia**) extensive group of islands between Australia and mainland Asia; includes the Philippines and Indonesia.

Ma·lay Pen·in·su·la *n.* (also called **Ma·lay'a**) peninsula in SE Asia, bounded by the South China Sea and the Strait of Malacca, and comprising parts of Burma, Malaysia, and Thailand.

Ma·lay·sia /məláyzhə/ **1** constitutional monarchy in SE Asia. Pop. 19,963,000 Capital: Kuala Lumpur. **2** see MALAY ARCHIPELAGO. □□ **Ma·lay'sian** *n. & adj.* See map p. 1232.

Mal·dives /máwldeevz, –dīvz/ *n.* republic comprising about 2,000 islands in the Indian Ocean, SW of India. Pop. 271,000. Capital: Male. □□ **Mal·div'i·an** /–díveeən/ *n. & adj.*

Ma·le /máalee/ *n.* capital of the Maldives, in the central part. Pop. 63,000.

Ma·li /máalee/ *n.* republic in W Africa. Pop. 9,653,000. Capital: Bamako. □□ **Ma'li·an** *n. & adj.*

Mali

Mal·mö /máalmə, –mər/ *n.* port city in S Sweden. Pop. 245,700.

Mal·ta /máwltə/ *n.* island state in the Mediterranean Sea, S of Sicily. Pop. 376,000. Capital: Valletta.

Malta

Mal·vi·nas, Is·las *n.* see FALKLAND ISLANDS.

Mam·moth /máməth/ **Cave** *n.* series of limestone caverns in central Kentucky; longest cave system in the world: more than 300 mi. of passages.

Man /man/, **Isle of** *n.* British island in the Irish Sea, between Britain and Ireland. Pop. 74,000. Capital: Douglas. □□ **Manx** /mangks/ *n. & adj.*

Ma·na·gua /mənáagwə/ *n.* capital of Nicaragua, in the W part. Pop. 682,100.

Ma·na·ma /mənámə/ *n.* (also called **al-Ma·nam'ah**) capital of Bahrain. Pop. 140,400.

Ma·náos /maanóws/ *n.* (also **Ma·naus'**) port city in W Brazil. Pop. 613,000.

Man·ches·ter /mánchestər/ *n.* **1** city in S New Hampshire. Pop. 99,600. **2** city in NW England. Pop. 431,100.

Man·da·lay /mandəláy/ *n.* city in N Burma. Pop. 532,900.

Man·hat·tan /manhát'n/ *n.* one of the five boroughs of New York City. Pop. 1,487,536.

Ma·nil·a /mənílə/ *n.* port city and capital of the Philippines. Pop. 1,894,700.

Man·i·to·ba /manitóbə/ *n.* province in central Canada. Pop. 1,116,000. Capital: Winnipeg. □□ **Man·i·to'ban** *n. & adj.*

Mann·heim /máanhīm/ *n.* city in SW Germany. Pop. 316,200.

Ma·pu·to /maapóotō/ *n.* (formerly **Lourenço Marques**) port city and capital of Mozambique. Pop. 931,600.

Mar·a·cai·bo /marəkíbō/ *n.* port city in NW Venezuela. Pop. 1,249,700.

Ma·ra·cay /maarakí/ *n.* city in NE Venezuela. Pop. 354,200.

Mar·i·an·a /maree-ánə, mer–/ **Trench** *n.* Pacific depression SW of the Mariana Islands and E of the Philippines; greatest known ocean depth: 36,201 ft.

Mar·i·time /máritīm/ **Prov·in·ces** *n.* Canadian provinces of New Brunswick, Nova Scotia, and Prince Edward Island.

Ma·ri·u·pol /maaree-óopawl/ *n.* (formerly **Zhdanov**) city in S Ukraine. Pop. 510,000.

Mar·ma·ra /máarmərə/, **Sea of** *n.* sea in W Turkey, between the Black and Mediterranean seas.

Mar·ra·kesh /márəkesh/ *n.* city in W central Morocco. Pop. 602,000.

Mar·seilles /maarsáy/ *n.* port city in SE France. Pop. 807,700.

Mar·shall /máarshəl/ **Is·lands** *n.* republic comprising a group of islands in the Pacific, NE of New Guinea. Pop. 58,000. Capital: Majuro. See map p. 1232.

Mar·tha's /máarthəz/ **Vine·yard** island in Massachusetts, S of Cape Cod.

Mar·ti·nique /maart'n-eék/ *n.* island in the E West Indies; department of France. Pop. 399,000. Capital: Fort-de-France. See map p. 1232.

Maldives

Macedonia

Madagascar

See page xx for the **Key to Pronunciation.**

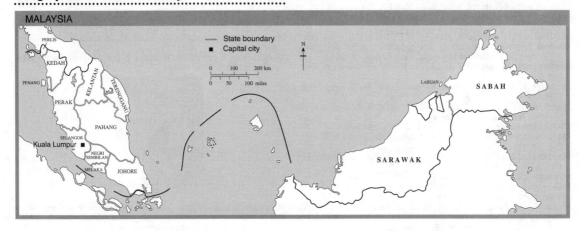

MALAYSIA

Marshall Islands

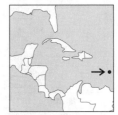

Martinique

Mar·y·land /mérələnd/ *n.* state in E central U.S. Pop. 4,781,468. Capital: Annapolis. Abbr. **MD; Md.** ▫▫ **Mar′y·land·er** *n.*

Ma·se·ru /maázərōō/ *n.* capital of Lesotho, in the W part. Pop. 109,400.

Ma·son-Dix·on /máysən díksən/ **Line** *n.* boundary between Pennsylvania and Maryland; traditional division between the North and the South.

Mas·sa·chu·setts /masəchóōsits/ *n.* state in NE U.S. Pop. 6,016,425. Capital: Boston. Abbr. **MA; Mass.**

Mat·a·mo·ros /matəmáwrəs/ *n.* city in NE Mexico. Pop. 266,100.

Mat·ter·horn /mátərhawrn/ *n.* mountain in the Alps, on the border of Switzerland and Italy: 14,692 ft. high.

Mau·i /mówee/ *n.* island of central Hawaii.

Mau·na Lo·a /mownə lóə/ *n.* mountain on the island of Hawaii; includes Kilauea volcano.

Mau·ri·ta·ni·a /mawritáyneeə/ *n.* republic in W Africa. Pop. 2,336,000. Capital: Nouakchott.

Mauritania

Mau·ri·tius /mawríshəs/ *n.* island republic in the Indian Ocean, E of Madagascar. Pop. 1,140,000. Capital: Port Louis.

Mauritius

Ma·ya·güez /mīəgwáys/ *n.* port city in W Puerto Rico. Pop. 100,400.

Ma·za·tlán /maazətlaán/ port city in W Mexico. Pop. 262,700.

Mba·bane /m-bəbaán, em-/ *n.* capital of Swaziland, in the W central part. Pop. 47,000.

Mc·Al·len /məkálən/ *n.* city in S Texas. Pop. 84,000.

Mc·Kin·ley /məkínlee/, **Mount** *n.* mountain in central Alaska; highest in North America: 20,320 ft.

Mead /meed/, **Lake** *n.* largest artificial lake in U.S.; formed by Hoover Dam.

Mec·ca /mékə/ *n.* city in W Saudi Arabia; holy site in Islam. Pop. 550,000.

Me·dan /maydaán/ *n.* city in Indonesia, on Sumatra. Pop. 1,686,000.

Me·del·lín /medəyéen/ *n.* city in NW Colombia. Pop. 1,621,400.

Me·di·na /mədeénə/ *n.* city in W Saudi Arabia. Pop. 290,000.

Med·i·ter·ra·ne·an /meditəráyneeən/ **Sea** *adj.* sea with coastlines along Europe, Asia, and Africa.

Mek·nès /meknés/ *n.* city in NE Morocco. Pop. 401,000.

Me·kong /máykáwng/ **Riv·er** *n.* river in SE Asia, flowing 2,600 mi. from S China to the South China Sea.

Mel·a·ne·sia /melənéezhə, –shə/ *n.* island region in the Pacific, NE of Australia.

Melanesia

Mel·bourne /mélbərn, –bawrn/ *n.* port city and capital of Victoria, Australia. Pop. 3,218,100.

Mem·phis /mémfis/ *n.* city in SW Tennessee. Pop. 610,337.

Mé·ri·da /méridə/ *n.* capital of Yucatán, Mexico, in the NW part. Pop. 523,400.

Mer·sin /merseén/ *n.* port city in S Turkey. Pop. 523,000.

Me·sa /máysə/ *n.* city in central Arizona. Pop. 288,091.

Me·shed /məshéd/ *n.* city in NE Iran. Pop. 1,759,200.

Mes·o·po·ta·mi·a /mesəpətáymeeə/ *n.* region in SW Asia, between the Tigris and Euphrates rivers; part of present-day Iraq.

Mes·quite /məskeét/ *n.* city in NE Texas. Pop. 101,484.

Mes·si·na /məseénə/ *n.* port city in NE Sicily. Pop. 233,800.

Met·air·ie /métəree/ *n.* city in SE Louisiana. Pop. 149,428.

Metz /mets/ *n.* city in NE France. Pop. 123,900.

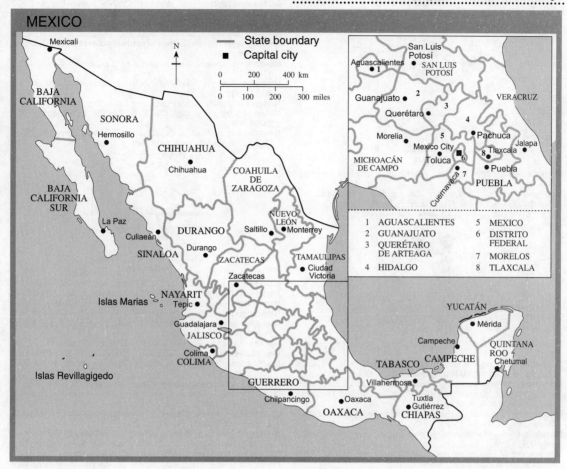

MEXICO

State boundary
■ Capital city

0   200   400 km
0   100   200   300 miles

1	AGUASCALIENTES	5	MEXICO
2	GUANAJUATO	6	DISTRITO FEDERAL
3	QUERÉTARO DE ARTEAGA	7	MORELOS
4	HIDALGO	8	TLAXCALA

Mex·i·cal·i /meksikálee/ *n.* capital of Baja California, Mexico, in the NE part. Pop. 438,400.

Mex·i·co /méksikō/ *n.* country in S North America. Pop. 95,772,000. Capital: Mexico City. □□ **Mex′i·can** *n. & adj.*

Mex·i·co, Gulf of *n.* arm of the Atlantic, S of the U.S. and E of Mexico.

Mex·i·co Cit·y *n.* capital of Mexico, in the central part. Pop. 9,815,800.

Mi·am·i /mī-ámee/ *n.* city in SE Florida. Pop. 358,548.

Mi·am·i Beach *n.* city in SE Florida. Pop. 92,639.

Mich·i·gan /míshigən/ *n.* peninsular state in N central U.S. Pop. 9,295,297. Capital: Lansing. Abbr. **MI**; **Mich.** □□ **Mich·i·gan·der** /mishigándər/, **Mich′i·gan·ite** /–gənīt/ *n.*

Mich·i·gan, Lake *n.* one of the Great Lakes, between Wisconsin and the lower peninsula of Michigan.

Mi·cho·a·cán /mèecho-aakaán/ *n.* state in SW Mexico. Pop. 3,548,200. Capital: Morelia.

Mi·cro·ne·sia /mikrəneézhə, –shə/ *n.* **1** region of Pacific islands E of the Philippines and N of the equator. **2** (official name **Federated States of Micronesia**) federation of islands in the S Pacific. Pop. 125,000. Capital: Palikir.

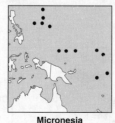

Micronesia

Mid·dle East *n.* (also **Near East**) region of SW Asia and N Africa, roughly from Afghanistan to Libya.

Mid·land /mídlənd/ *n.* city in W Texas. Pop. 89,443.

Mid·west /mídwést/ *n.* (also called **Mid′dle West**) region of N central U.S., from the Great Plains to the Allegheny Mountains.

Mi·lan /milán, –laán/ *n.* city in N Italy. Pop. 1,334,200. □□ **Mil·an·ese** /miləneéz/ *n. & adj.*

Mil·wau·kee /milwáwkee/ *n.* city in SE Wisconsin. Pop. 628,088.

Min·ne·ap·o·lis /minee-ápələs/ *n.* city in E Minnesota. Pop. 368,383.

Min·ne·so·ta /minəsótə/ *n.* state in N central U.S. Pop. 4,375,099. Capital: St. Paul. Abbr. **Minn.**; **MN** □□ **Min·ne·so′tan** *n. & adj.*

Minsk /minsk/ *n.* capital of Belarus. Pop. 1,700,600.

Mis·sis·sau·ga /misisáwgə/ *n.* city in Ontario, Canada. Pop. 463,400.

Mis·sis·sip·pi /misisípee/ *n.* state in S U.S. Pop. 2,573,216. Capital: Jackson. Abbr. **Miss.**; **MS** □□ **Mis·sis·sip′pi·an** *n. & adj.*

Mis·sis·sip·pi Riv·er *n.* river in central U.S., flowing 2,470 mi. from Minnesota to the Gulf of Mexico; largest river in U.S.

Mis·sour·i /mizóoree, –ə/ *n.* state in central U.S. Pop. 5,117,073. Capital: Jefferson City. Abbr. **MO**; **Mo.** □□ **Mis·sour′i·an** *n. & adj.*

Mis·sour·i Riv·er *n.* river in central U.S., flowing 2,700 mi. from Montana to the Mississippi River near St. Louis, Missouri.

Mo·bile /mōbeél, móbeel/ *n.* port city in SW Alabama. Pop. 196,278.

Mo·bile Bay *n.* arm of the Gulf of Mexico, S of Alabama.

Mo·de·na /máwd'nə/ *n.* city in N Italy. Pop. 176,600.

Mo·des·to /mədéstō/ *n.* city in central California. Pop. 164,730.

Mo·ga·di·shu /mōgədíshoo, –deéshoo/ *n.* port city and capital of Somalia. Pop. 900,000.

Mo·ja·ve /mōhaávee, mō–/ **Des·ert** *n.* arid basin in SE California.

Mol·do·va /məldóvə/ *n.* (formerly **Mol·da′vi·an** /mawldáyvee-ən/ **Soviet Socialist Republic**) republic in SE Europe; formerly part of the USSR. Pop. 4,464,000. Capital: Kishinev.

Mo·lo·kai /maaləkí, mō–/ *n.* island in central Hawaii.

Mo·luc·cas /məlúkəz/ *n.* (also called **Spice Is′lands**) island group in the S Pacific, in the Malay Archipelago, between New Guinea and Sulawesi.

Mom·ba·sa /maambaásə/ *n.* port city in SE Kenya. Pop. 600,000.

See page xx for the **Key to Pronunciation**.

Mon·a·co /maánəkō/ n. principality on the Mediterranean Sea, near Nice, France. Pop. 32,300. Capital: Monaco. □□ **Mon'a·can, Mon·e·gasque'** n. & adj.

Monaco

Mön·chen·glad·bach /mönkhən-gláátbaakh/ n. city in W Germany. Pop. 266,100.

Mon·go·li·a /maan-góleeə, maang–/ n. republic in E central Asia. Pop. 2,497,000. Capital: Ulan Bator. □□ **Mon·go'li·an** n.

Mongolia

Mon·ro·vi·a /mənróveeə/ n. port city and capital of Liberia. Pop. 421,100.

Mon·tan·a /maantánə/ n. state in NW U.S. Pop. 799,065. Capital: Helena. Abbr. **Mont.; MT.** □□ **Mon·tan'an** n. & adj.

Mon·te·ne·gro /məntəneˊegrō, –negrō/ n. republic in SE Europe; formerly part of Yugoslavia. Pop. 635,000. Capital: Podgorica. □□ **Mon·te·ne'gran** n. & adj.

Mon·ter·rey /maantəráy/ n. capital of Nuevo León, Mexico, in the W part. Pop. 1,069,000.

Mon·te·vi·de·o /maantəvidáyō/ n. port city and capital of Uruguay. Pop. 1,378,700.

Mont·gom·er·y /məntgúməree, maant–, –gúmree/ capital of Alabama, in the E central part. Pop. 187,106.

Mont·pel·ier 1 (/maantpeˊelyər/) n. capital of Vermont, in the N central part. Pop. 8,247. **2** (/mawṇpelyáy/) n. city in S France. Pop. 210,900.

Mont·re·al /maantree-áwl/ n. city in S Quebec, Canada. Pop. 1,017,700.

Mont·ser·rat /montsəráát/ n. island in the E West Indies; dependent territory of the United Kingdom. Pop. 13,000. Capital: Plymouth.

Montserrat

Mo·re·lia /məráylyə/ n. capital of Michoacán, Mexico, in the N part. Pop. 428,500.

Mo·re·los /məráyləs/ n. state in S central Mexico. Pop. 1,195,100. Capital: Cuernavaca.

Mo·re·no /məreˊenō/ **Val·ley** n. city in SW California. Pop. 118,779.

Mo·roc·co /məraˊakō/ n. kingdom in NW Africa. Pop. 29,779,000. Capital: Rabat. □□ **Mo·roc'can** /–kən/ n. & adj.

Mo·rón /mawrˊón/ n. city in E Argentina. Pop. 641,500.

Mo·ro·ni /mawrˊónee/ n. capital of Comoros, on Grande Comore Island. Pop. 30,000.

Mos·cow /maˊaskow, –kō/ n. capital of Russia, in the W part; former capital of the USSR. Pop. 8,717,000.

Mo·sul /mōsoˊol/ n. city in W Iraq. Pop. 664,200.

Mo·zam·bique /mōzambeˊek/ n. republic in SE Africa. Pop. 17,878,000. Capital: Maputo. □□ **Mo·zam·bi'can** n. & adj.

Mul·tan /moˊoltaán/ n. city in central Pakistan. Pop. 730,100.

Mu·nich /myoˊonik, –nikh/ n. city in SW Germany. Pop. 1,244,700.

Mün·ster /mýnstər, mún–/ n. city in NW Germany. Pop. 264,900.

Mur·cia /múrshə, –sheeə/ n. city in SE Spain. Pop. 341,500.

Mur·mansk /moormánsk/ n. port city in NW Russia. Pop. 407,000.

Mus·cat /múskaat, –kət/ n. port city and capital of Oman. Pop. 52,000.

My·an·mar /myaánmaar/ n. see BURMA.

My·sore /mīsáwr/ n. city in S India. Pop. 480,700.

Myu·ko·la·yiv /myoˊokəlíif/ n. (formerly **Nikolayev**) city in Ukraine. Pop. 508,000.

Na·ga·sa·ki /naagəsaákee/ n. port city in Japan, on Kyushu. Pop. 438,700.

Na·go·ya /nəgóyə, naágəyaa/ n. city in Japan, on Honshu. Pop. 2,152,300.

Nag·pur /naágpoor/ n. city in central India. Pop. 1,624,800.

Nai·ro·bi /nīróbee/ n. capital of Kenya, in the S central part. Pop. 2,000,000.

Na·mib·i·a /nəmíbeeə/ n. republic in SW Africa. Pop. 1,677,000. Capital: Windhoek. □□ **Na·mib'i·an** n. & adj.

Namibia

Nam·p'o /námpˊó/ n. city in SW North Korea. Pop. 370,000.

Nam·pu·la /nampoˊolə/ n. city in E Mozambique. Pop. 250,500.

Nan·chang /naánchaáng/ n. city in SE China. Pop. 1,350,000.

Nan·cy /naaṇseˊe, nánsee/ n. city in NE France. Pop. 102,400.

Nan·jing /naánjíng/ n. (formerly **Nan·king**) port city in E China. Pop. 2,500,000.

Nantes /naaṇt/ n. port city in W France. Pop. 252,000.

Nan·tuck·et /nantúkit/ n. island in Massachusetts, S of Cape Cod.

Na·ples /náypəlz/ n. (Italian name **Na'po·li**) port city in SW Italy. Pop. 1,061,600.

Nash·u·a /náshoˊoə/ n. city in S New Hampshire. Pop. 79,662.

Nash·ville /náshvil, –vəl/ n. capital of Tennessee, in the N central part. Pop. 487,969.

Nas·sau /násaw/ n. capital of the Bahamas, on New Providence Island. Pop. 172,200.

Na·tion·al /náshənəl/ **Road** n. (also called **National Old Trail Road**; **Cumberland Road**) first federal road in U.S., extending from Cumberland, Maryland, W to St. Louis, Missouri.

Na·u·ru /naa–oˊoroˊo/ n. island republic in the Pacific, W of Kiribati. Pop. 10,000.

Nauru

Mozambique

Morocco

Na·ya·rit /níərēét/ *n.* state in W Mexico. Pop. 824,600. Capital: Tepic.

N'Dja·me·na /enjəmáynə, –méenə/ *n.* capital of Chad, in the W part. Pop. 531,000.

Ndo·la /en-dólə/ *n.* city in N Zambia. Pop. 376,300.

Near East *n.* see MIDDLE EAST.

Ne·bras·ka /nəbráskə/ *n.* state in central U.S. Pop. 1,578,385. Capital: Lincoln. Abbr. **NE; Nebr.** □□ **Ne·bras′kan** *n. & adj.*

Neg·ev /négev/ **Des·ert** *n.* arid region in S Israel.

Ne·pal /nipáwl, –pál/ *n.* constitutional monarchy in S Asia. Pop. 22,094,000. Capital: Kathmandu. □□ **Ne·pa·lese** /nepəléez, –léés/ *n. & adj.*

Nepal

Neth·er·lands /néthərləndz/ *n.* (also called **Hol′land**) kingdom in W Europe. Capital: Amsterdam. Seat of government: The Hague. Pop. 15,568,000. □□ **Neth′er·land·er** *n.*

Netherlands

Neth·er·lands An·til·les /antíleez/ *n.* island group in the West Indies, comprised of islands off the NW coast of Venezuela and islands among the NW Leeward Islands; territory of the Netherlands. Pop. 209,000. Capital: Willemstad.

Netherlands Antilles

Ne·tza·hual·có·yotl /netsaawaalkóyōt'l/ *n.* city in central Mexico. Pop. 1,255,500.

Ne·vad·a /nəvádə, –vaádə/ *n.* state in W U.S. Pop. 1,201,833. Capital: Carson City. Abbr. **Nev.; NV** □□ **Ne·vad′an, Ne·vad′i·an** /–deeən/ *n. & adj.*

New·ark /nóoərk, nyóo–/ *n.* city in N New Jersey. Pop. 275,221.

New Bed·ford /nōō bédfərd, nyōo/ *n.* city in SE Massachusetts. Pop. 99,922.

New Bruns·wick /brúnzwik/ *n.* province in SE Canada. Pop. 751,000. Capital: Fredericton.

New Cal·e·do·ni·a /kalidóneeə, –dónyə/ *n.* island group in the S Pacific; territory of France. Pop. 188,000. Capital: Nouméa.

New Caledonia

New·cas·tle /nóokasəl, nookás–, nyóo–, nyoo–/ *n.* port city in SE Australia. Pop. 427,700.

New·cas·tle up·on Tyne /tīn/ *n.* port city in N England. Pop. 283,600.

New Del·hi /délee/ *n.* capital of India, in the N central part. Pop. 301,300.

New Eng·land /íngglənd/ *n.* region of the NE U.S.; includes Connecticut, Maine, Massachusetts, New Hampshire, Rhode Island, and Vermont.

New·found·land /nōofənlánd, nōófənlənd, nyōo–, nyóo–, –fənd–/ *n.* **1** island off the Atlantic coast of Canada. **2** province in E Canada, comprising Labrador and the island of Newfoundland. Pop. 581,000. Capital: St. John's. □□ **New′found·land·er** *n.*

New Guin·ea /gínee/ *n.* island in the East Indies, N of Australia; comprises parts of Papua New Guinea and Indonesia.

New Hamp·shire /hámpshər/ *n.* state in NE U.S. Pop. 1,109,252. Capital: Concord. Abbr. **NH; N.H.; N. Hamp.** □□ **New Hamp′shir·ite, New Hamp′shire·man** /–mən/ *n.*

New Ha·ven /háyvən/ *n.* city in S Connecticut. Pop. 130,474.

New Jer·sey /júrzee/ *n.* state in E U.S. Pop. 7,730,188. Capital: Trenton. Abbr. **NJ; N.J.** □□ **New Jer′sey·ite, New Jer′sey·an** *n.*

New Mex·i·co /méksikō/ *n.* state in SW U.S. Pop. 1,515,069. Capital: Santa Fe. Abbr. **NM; N. Mex.** □□ **New Mex′i·can** *n. & adj.*

New Or·le·ans /áwrleeənz, áwrlənz, awrléenz/ *n.* port city in SE Louisiana. Pop. 496,938. □□ **New Or·lea′ni·an** /awrlíneeən/ *n.*

New·port News /nōopawrt nōoz, –pərt, nyōo–/ *n.* city in SE Virginia. Pop. 170,045.

New South Wales /waylz/ *n.* state in SE Australia. Pop. 5,426,200. Capital: Sydney.

New York /yáwrk/ *n.* **1** state in NE U.S. Pop. 17,990,455. Capital: Albany. Abbr. **NY; N.Y. 2** (also **New York Cit′y**) city in SE New York. Pop. 7,322,564. Abbr. **NYC.** □□ **New York′er** *n.*

New Zea·land /zéelənd/ *n.* island country in the S Pacific, SE of Australia. Pop. 3,548,000. Capital: Wellington. □□ **New Zea′land·er** *n.*

New Zealand

Ni·ag·a·ra /nī-ágrə, ;n-ágərə/ **Falls** *n.* falls of the Niagara River, along the U.S.-Canada border.

Nia·mey /nee-aámay/ *n.* capital of Niger, in the SW part. Pop. 391,900.

Nic·a·ra·gua /nikəraágwə/ *n.* republic in central Central America. Pop. 4,272,000. Capital: Managua. □□ **Nic·a·ra′guan** *n. & adj.*

Nicaragua

Nice /nees/ *n.* port city in SE France. Pop. 345,700.

Nic·o·si·a /nikəséeə/ *n.* capital of Cyprus, in the central part. Pop. 186,400.

Ni·ger /níjər, neezhér/ *n.* republic in NW Africa. Pop. 9,113,000. Capital: Niamey. □□ **Ni·ge·ri·en** /nijéereeən/ *n. & adj.*

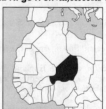

Niger

Ni·ge·ri·a /nījéereeə/ *n.* republic in W Africa. Pop. 103,912,000. Capital: Abuja. ▫▫ **Ni·ge'ri·an** *n. & adj.*

Nigeria

Ni·ger /níjər/ **Riv·er** *n.* river in W Africa, flowing 2,600 mi. from S Guinea to the Gulf of Guinea.

Ni·ko·la·yev /nikəláəyəf/ *n.* see Mʏᴜᴋᴏʟᴀʏɪᴠ.

Nile /nīl/ **Riv·er** *n.* river in E Africa, flowing 3,470 mi. from Lake Victoria to the Mediterranean Sea; longest river in the world.

Nîmes /neem/ *n.* city in S France. Pop. 133,600.

Nome /nōm/ *n.* city in W Alaska. Pop. 3,500.

Nor·folk /náwrfək, –fawk/ *n.* city in SE Virginia. Pop. 261,229.

Nor·man /náwrmən/ *n.* city in central Oklahoma. Pop. 80,071.

North Af·ri·ca *n.* term for region of Africa N of the Sahara Desert.

North A·mer·i·ca *n.* continent in the W hemisphere, comprising Canada, the United States, Mexico, and Central America. ▫▫ **North A·mer'i·can** *n. & adj.*

North·amp·ton /nawrthámtən, –hámptən/ *n.* city in central England. Pop. 187,200.

North Car·o·li·na /karəlínə/ *n.* state in SE U.S. Pop. 6,628,637. Capital: Raleigh. Abbr. **NC; N.C.; N. Car.** ▫▫ **North Car·o·lin'i·an** /–líneeən/ *n.*

North Da·ko·ta /dəkótə/ *n.* state in N central U.S. Pop. 638,800. Capital: Bismarck. Abbr. **ND; N.D.; N. Dak.** ▫▫ **North Da·ko'tan** /–kót'n/ *n.*

North·ern Ire·land /írlənd/ *n.* the NE part of the island of Ireland; part of the United Kingdom. Pop. 1,583,000. Capital: Belfast. ¶ See note at Gʀᴇᴀᴛ Bʀɪᴛᴀɪɴ.

North·ern Mar·i·an·a /maree-ánə, mer–/ **Is·lands** *n.* island group in the Pacific, N of Guam; U.S. possession. Pop. 52,000.

North Ko·re·a *n.* see Kᴏʀᴇᴀ.

North Korea

North Pole N end of the earth's axis, in the Arctic Ocean.

North Sea *n.* arm of the Atlantic, between Britain and N Europe.

North·west Ter·ri·to·ries *n.* territory of Canada, in the NW part. Pop. 63,000. Capital: Yellowknife.

Nor·way /náwrway/ *n.* kingdom of N Europe. Pop. 4,384,000. Capital: Oslo.

Norway

Nor·we·gian /nawrweéjən/ **Sea** *n.* arm of the Arctic Ocean, between Greenland and Norway.

Nor·wich /náwrij, –ich/ *n.* city in E England. Pop. 128,100.

Not·ting·ham /náatingəm/ *n.* city in central England. Pop. 282,400.

Nou·ak·chott /nōō–aákshaat/ *n.* capital of Mauritania, in the SW part. Pop. 393,300.

No·va Sco·tia /nóvə skóshə/ *n.* province in E Canada. Pop. 923,000. Capital: Halifax. ▫▫ **No'va Sco'tian** *n. & adj.*

Nov·go·rod /náavgəraad/ *n.* city in W Russia. Pop. 233,000.

No·vo·si·birsk /nōvōsibeérsk/ *n.* city in SW Russia. Pop. 1,369,000.

Nu·bi·an /nóōbeeən, nyóō–/ Des·ert *n.* arid region in NE Sudan.

Nue·vo La·re·do /nōō–áyvō ləráydō/ *n.* city in E Mexico, across the Rio Grande from Laredo, Texas. Pop. 218,400.

Nue·vo Le·ón /lay–ón/ *n.* state in NE Mexico. Pop. 3,098,700. Capital: Monterrey.

Nu·ku·a·lo·fa /nōōkōōəláwfə, –lófə/ *n.* port city and capital of Tonga. Pop. 34,000.

Nu·rem·berg /nóōrəmbərg/ *n.* (German name **Nürnberg** /nʏ́rnbərk/) city in S Germany. Pop. 495,800.

Nya·sa /nī–ásə/, **Lake** *n.* (also called **Lake Malawi**) freshwater lake in SE Africa, E of Malawi.

O·a·hu /ō–aáhōō/ *n.* Hawaiian island; includes Honolulu.

Oak·land /óklənd/ *n.* city in W California. Pop. 372,242.

Oa·xa·ca /waahaákə/ *n.* state in S Mexico. Pop. 3,019,600. Capital: Oaxaca.

O·ce·an·i·a /ōshee-áneeə/ *n.* collective term for Australia and the Pacific islands.

O·cean·side /óshənsīd/ *n.* city in SW California. Pop. 128,398.

O·den·se /ód'n–sə/ *n.* port city in S Denmark. Pop. 182,600.

O·der /ódər/ Riv·er *n.* river in central Europe, flowing 570 mi. from E Czech Republic to the Baltic Sea.

O·des·sa /ō·désə/ *n.* port city in S Ukraine. Pop. 1,046,000.

Og·bo·mo·sho /aagbəmóshō/ *n.* city in SW Nigeria. Pop. 711,900.

O·hi·o /ōhíō/ *n.* state in E central U.S. Pop. 10,847,115. Capital: Columbus. Abbr. **O.; OH** ▫▫ **O·hi'o·an** *n. & adj.*

O·hi·o Riv·er *n.* river in E central U.S., flowing 980 mi. from W Pennsylvania into the Mississippi River at Cairo, Illinois.

O·ka·ya·ma /ōkəyaámə/ *n.* city in Japan, on Honshu. Pop. 616,100.

O·kee·cho·bee /ōkəchóbee/, **Lake** *n.* lake in S Florida, in the N part of the Everglades.

O·ke·fe·no·kee /ōkeefənókee/ **Swamp** *n.* extensive wooded swamp area in S Georgia.

O·khotsk /əkháwtsk, ōkaátsk/, **Sea of** *n.* arm of the N Pacific, enclosed by the Kamchatka Peninsula and the Kuril Islands.

O·ki·na·wa /ōkinaáwə/ *n.* Japanese island between the East China Sea and the Pacific; largest of the Ryukyu Islands.

O·kla·ho·ma /ōkləhómə/ *n.* state in S central U.S. Pop. 3,145,585. Capital: Oklahoma City. Abbr. **OK; Okla.** ▫▫ **O·kla·ho'man** *n. & adj.*

O·kla·ho·ma Cit·y *n.* capital of Oklahoma, in the central part. Pop. 444,719.

Old Faith·ful /fáythfōōl/ *n.* regularly erupting geyser in Yellowstone National Park, Wyoming.

O·lym·pi·a /ōlímpeeə/ *n.* **1** capital of Washington, in the W part. Pop. 33,840. **2** *hist.* ancient Greek city; site of the ancient Olympic games.

O·lym·pus /ōlímpəs/ *n.* mountain in N Greece; home of the gods in Greek mythology.

O·ma·ha /ómahaa, –haw/ *n.* city in E Nebraska. Pop. 335,795.

O·man /ōmaán, ōmán/ *n.* independent sultanate on the SE Arabian Peninsula. Pop. 2,187,000. Capital: Muscat.

Oman

O·man, Gulf of *n.* arm of the Arabian Sea, at the entrance to the Persian Gulf.

Om·dur·man /aamdərmán/ *n.* city in NE central Sudan. Pop. 526,300.

Omsk /awmsk, aamsk/ *n.* city in SW Russia. Pop. 1,163,000.

On·tar·i·o /aantéreeō, –tár–/ *n.* province in S Canada. Pop. 10,746,000. Capital: Toronto. ▫▫ **On·tar'i·an** *n. & adj.*

On·tar·i·o, Lake *n.* easternmost and smallest of the Great Lakes, N of W New York.

O·por·to /ōpáwrtō/ *n.* (also **Pôr'to**) port city in NW Portugal. Pop. 310,600.

O·ran /ōraán/ *n.* port city in NW Algeria. Pop. 609,800.

Or·ange /áwrinj, ór–/ *n.* city in SW California. Pop. 110,658.

Or·an·je·stad /awraányəstaad, –jəstad/ *n.* city in W Aruba. Pop. 20,000.

Or·e·gon /áwrigən, aár–, –gaan/ *n.* state in NW U.S. Pop. 2,842,321. Capital: Salem. Abbr. **OR; Ore.** ▫▫ **Or·e·go·ni·an** /awrigóneeən, aar–/ *n. & adj.*

Or·e·gon Trail *n.* 19th-century pioneer route extending W 2,000 mi. from Independence, Missouri, to Oregon.

Ork·ney /áwrknee/ **Is·lands** *n.* island group in the N Atlantic, off the NE tip of Scotland.

Or·lan·do /awrlándō/ n. city in central Florida. Pop. 164,693.
Or·lé·ans /awrlayaáɴ/ n. city in central France. Pop. 108,000.
O·sa·ka /ōsáakə/ n. city in Japan, on Honshu. Pop. 2,602,400.
Osh·kosh /áashkaash/ n. city in E Wisconsin. Pop. 55,006.
Os·lo /áazlō, áas–/ n. capital of Norway, in the SE part. Pop. 487,900.
O·stra·va /áwstrəvə/ n. city in E Czech Republic. Pop. 325,800.
Ot·ta·wa /áátəwə, –waa, –waw/ n. capital of Canada, in the SE part of Ontario. Pop. 314,000.
Oua·ga·dou·gou /waagədōōgōō/ n. capital of Burkina Faso, in the central part. Pop. 690,000.
O·ver·land /ōvərland, –lənd/ Park n. city in NE Kansas. Pop. 111,790.
O·vi·e·do /ōvee-áydō/ n. city in N Spain. Pop. 201,700.
Ox·ford /áaksfərd/ n. city in S England. Pop. 132,000.
Ox·nard /áaksnaard/ n. city in SW California. Pop. 142,216.
O·zark /ōzaark/ Moun·tains n. mountain range in S central U.S.
Pa·chu·ca /pəchōōkə/ n. capital of Hidalgo, Mexico, in the central part. Pop. 314,000.
Pa·cif·ic /pəsifik/ O·cean n. ocean separating Asia and Australia from the Americas. Area 70,000,000 sq. mi.
Pa·cif·ic Rim n. the Pacific coastal regions of Asia, Australia, North America, and South America.
Pa·dang /páadaang/ n. port city in Indonesia, on Sumatra. Pop. 477,300.
Pad·u·a /pájəwə/ n. city in NE Italy. Pop. 212,600.
Pa·go Pa·go /paanggō paánggō/ n. capital of American Samoa, on Tutuila Island. Pop. 3,500.
Paint·ed /páyntəd/ Des·ert n. arid region in N central Arizona featuring multicolored rock surfaces.
Pa·ki·stan /pákistan, paakistaán/ n. republic in central Asia. Pop. 129,276,000. Capital: Islamabad. ◻◻ Pa·ki·stan′i n. & adj.

Pakistan

Pa·lat·i·nate /pəlát′nayt/ n. district in Germany, W of the Rhine.
Pa·lem·bang /paaləmbaáng/ n. port city in Indonesia, on Sumatra. Pop. 1,084,500.
Pa·ler·mo /pəlérmō/ n. port city in W Sicily. Pop. 694,700.
Pal·es·tine /pálɔstin, –steen/ n. 1 hist. ancient country on the E coast of the Mediterranean Sea. 2 (also called Ho′ly Land) area controlled by British 1923–48; now divided among Egypt, Israel, and Jordan. ◻◻ Pal·es·tin′i·an /–stineeən/ n. & adj.
Pal·ma /páalmə/ n. (also Pal′ma de Ma·llor·ca /day maayáwrkə, maalyáwrkə/) port city on island of Majorca, Spain. Pop. 296,754.
Pal·o Al·to /palō áltō/ n. city in W California. Pop. 55,900.
Pam·plo·na /pamplóⁿə/ n. city in N Spain. Pop. 182,500.
Pan·a·ma /pánəmaa, –maw/ n. 1 republic in S Central America. Pop. 2,655,000. 2 (also Pan′a·ma Cit′y) port city and capital of Panama. Pop. 411,500. ◻◻ Pa·na·ma·ni·an /panəmáyneeən/ n. & adj.

Panama

Pan·a·ma Ca·nal n. canal through the Isthmus of Panama, connecting the Pacific and Atlantic oceans.
Pan·chi·ao /paánchee-ów/ n. city in N Taiwan. Pop. 539,100.
Pa·pe·e·te /paapayáytay, paapétee/ port city and capital of French Polynesia, on Tahiti. Pop. 23,600.
Pap·u·a New Guin·ea /páapōōə nōō gínee, nyōō/ n. republic in the W Pacific, comprising the E part of New Guinea and nearby islands. Pop. 4,395,000. Capital: Port Moresby.
Par·a·dise /párədīs/ n. city in N California. Pop. 124,682.
Par·a·guay /párəgwī, –gway/ n. republic in central South America. Pop. 5,504,000. Capital: Asunción. ◻◻ Par·a·guay′an n. & adj.
Par·a·mar·i·bo /parəmáribō/ n. port city and capital of Suriname. Pop. 77,600.

Par·is /páris, paareé/ n. port city and capital of France. Pop. 2,175,200. ◻◻ Pa·ri·sian /pəreézhən/ n. & adj.
Par·ma /paármə/ n. city in N Italy. Pop. 169,300.
Pas·a·de·na /pásədeenə/ n. city in S California. Pop. 131,591.
Pat·er·son /pátərsən/ n. city in N New Jersey. Pop. 140,891.
Pat·na /pútnə/ n. city in NE India. Pop. 917,200.
Pearl /pərl/ Har·bor n. inlet on the S coast of Oahu, Hawaii.
Pe·king /payking, pee–/ n. see BEIJING.
Penn·syl·va·nia /pensəlváynyə/ n. state in NE U.S. Pop. 11,881,643. Capital: Harrisburg. Abbr. PA; Pa.; Penn.; Penna. ◻◻ Penn·syl·va′nian n. & adj.
Pen·sa·co·la /pensəkólə/ n. city in NW Florida. Pop. 58,165.
Pe·o·ri·a /pee-áwreeə, –ór–/ n. city in NW central Illinois. Pop. 113,504.
Perm /perm/ n. city in W Russia. Pop. 1,032,000.
Per·nam·bu·co /pərnambōōkō/ see RECIFE.
Per·sia /púrzhə/ n. 1 hist. ancient empire in W Asia. 2 official name (until 1935) of Iran.
Per·sian Gulf n. arm of the Arabian Sea, between the Arabian Peninsula and Iran.
Perth /pərth/ n. port city and capital of Western Australia, Australia. Pop. 809,000.
Pe·ru /pərōō/ n. republic in W South America. Pop. 24,523,000. Capital: Lima. ◻◻ Pe·ru′vi·an /–veeən/ n. & adj.

Peru

Pe·sha·war /pəshaáwər/ n. city in N Pakistan. Pop. 566,300.
Pet·ri·fied /pétrifīd/ For·est n. part of the Painted Desert in E Arizona; contains prehistoric fossilized tree trunks.
Phil·a·del·phi·a /filədélfeeə/ n. city in SE Pennsylvania. Pop. 1,585,577.
Phil·ip·pines /filipeenz, filipeénz/ n. republic consisting of about 7,100 islands in the Pacific, SE of China. Pop. 63,609,000. Capital: Manila.

Philippines

Papua New Guinea

Paraguay

Phnom Penh /pənaam pén/ *n.* port city and capital of Cambodia. Pop. 920,000.

Phoe·nix /féeniks/ *n.* capital of Arizona, in the central part. Pop. 983,403.

Pierre /peer/ *n.* capital of South Dakota, in the central part. Pop. 12,906.

Pikes /piks/ **Peak** *n.* mountain in the Rocky Mountains, in E central Colorado.

Pi·rae·us /pīréeəs, piráy–/ *n.* port city in E Greece. Pop. 169,600.

Pi·sa /péezə/ *n.* city in W Italy. Pop. 101,500.

Pitts·burgh /pítsbərg/ *n.* city in W Pennsylvania. Pop. 369,879.

Piu·ra /pyóoraa/ *n.* city in N Peru. Pop. 278,000.

Pla·no /pláynō/ *n.* city in NE Texas. Pop. 128,713.

Plo·es·ti /plaw-yéshtee, –yésht/ *n.* (also **Plo·ies'ti**) city in SE central Romania. Pop. 254,300.

Plym·outh /plíməth/ *n.* **1** port city in SW England. Pop. 255,800. **2** city in SE Massachusetts. Pop. 45,608.

Pod·go·ri·ca /páwdgawreetsaa/ *n.* capital of Montenegro, in the SE part. Pop. 54,500.

Point Bar·row /báró/ *n.* the N tip of Alaska; the northernmost point of the U.S.

Pointe-Noire /pwaant nwaár, nəwaár/ *n.* port city in the SW Republic of the Congo. Pop. 576,200.

Po·land /pólənd/ *n.* republic in central Europe. Pop. 38,643,000. Capital: Warsaw.

Poland

Pol·y·ne·sia /paaləneézhə, –shə/ *n.* islands in the central Pacific, from New Zealand N to the Hawaiian Islands; a subdivision of Oceania. □□ **Pol·y·ne'sian** *n. & adj.*

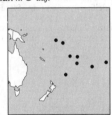

Polynesia

Po·mo·na /pəmónə/ *n.* city in S California. Pop. 131,723.

Pom·pa·no /páampənō/ **Beach** *n.* city in SE Florida. Pop. 72,411.

Pon·ce /páwnsay/ *n.* port city in S Puerto Rico. Pop. 190,500.

Pont·char·train /paánchərtrayn, paanchərtráyn/, **Lake** *n.* shallow inlet of the Gulf of Mexico, N of New Orleans, Louisiana.

Poo·na /póonə/ *n.* city in W India. Pop. 1,559,600.

Po·po·cat·e·petl /pópəkaatépit'l/ *n.* volcanic peak in SW Mexico: 17,887 ft. high.

Port-au-Prince /pawrt ō príns, práNs/ *n.* port city and capital of Haiti. Pop. 846,200.

Port E·liz·a·beth /ilízəbəth/ *n.* port city in S South Africa. Pop. 303,400.

Port·land /páwrtlənd/ *n.* **1** city in NW Oregon. Pop. 437,319. **2** city in SW Maine. Pop. 64,358.

Port Lou·is /lóois, loo-ée/ *n.* port city and capital of Mauritius. Pop. 144,800.

Port Mores·by /máwrzbee/ *n.* port city and capital of Papua New Guinea. Pop. 193,200.

Pôr·to /páwrtōō/ *n.* see Oporto.

Pôr·to A·le·gre /ələ́grə/ *n.* port city in S Brazil. Pop. 1,237,200.

Port-of-Spain /spayn/ *n.* port city and capital of Trinidad and Tobago. Pop. 52,500.

Por·to-No·vo /pawrtō nóvō/ *n.* port city and capital of Benin. Pop. 177,700.

Port Sa·id /saa-eéd/ *n.* port city in NE Egypt. Pop. 460,000.

Ports·mouth /páwrtsməth/ *n.* **1** port city in SE Virginia. Pop. 103,907. **2** city in S England. Pop. 189,100.

Por·tu·gal /páwrchəgəl/ *n.* republic in SW Europe, on the Iberian Peninsula. Pop. 9,865,000. Capital: Lisbon.

Port-Vi·la /pawrt veélə/ (also **Vi'la**) port city and capital of Vanuatu.

Po·to·mac /pətómik/ **Riv·er** *n.* river in E U.S., flowing 290 mi. from West Virginia to Chesapeake Bay.

Pots·dam /páatsdam/ *n.* city in NE Germany. Pop. 138,300.

Poz·nan /póznan, –nanyə/ *n.* city in W central Poland. Pop. 582,300.

Prague /praag/ *n.* capital of the Czech Republic, in the W central part. Pop. 1,213,300.

Prai·a /príə/ *n.* capital of Cape Verde, on São Tiago Island. Pop. 61,600.

Prai·rie /práiree/ **Prov·in·ces** *n.* term for the Canadian provinces of Alberta, Manitoba, and Saskatchewan.

Pres·i·den·tial Range *n.* mountain range in N New Hampshire; part of the White Mountain range.

Pre·to·ri·a /pritáwreeə/ *n.* administrative capital of South Africa, in the N part. Pop. 525,600.

Prince Ed·ward Is·land /prins édwərd/ *n.* island province in E Canada, in the Gulf of St. Lawrence. Pop. 132,000. Capital: Charlottetown.

Prince Wil·liam Sound /wílyəm/ *n.* arm of the Gulf of Alaska, off the S coast of Alaska.

Prov·i·dence /práavədəns/ *n.* capital of Rhode Island, in the NE part. Pop. 160,728.

Pro·vo /próvō/ *n.* city in N central Utah. Pop. 86,835.

Pue·bla /pwéblaa/ *n.* state in E central Mexico. Pop. 4,126,100. Capital: Puebla.

Pueb·lo /pwéblō, pŏō-éblō/ *n.* city in SE central Colorado. Pop. 98,640.

Puer·to Ri·co /páwrtə reékō, pwértō/ *n.* island in the E central West Indies; self-governing commonwealth of the U.S. Pop. 3,819,000. Capital: San Juan. □□ **Puer'to Ri'can** /–kən/ *n. & adj.*

Puerto Rico

Puer·to Ri·co Trench *n.* Atlantic depression N of Puerto Rico; deepest part of the Atlantic: 28,374 ft.

Pu·get /pyóŏjit/ **Sound** *n.* arm of the Pacific, in NW Washington.

Pu·san /póosaán/ *n.* port city in SE South Korea. Pop. 3,813,800.

Pyong·yang /pyáwng-yaáng/ *n.* capital of North Korea, in the W part. Pop. 2,355,000.

Pyr·e·nees /péerəneez/ *n.* mountain range in SW Europe, between France and Spain.

Qa·tar /káatər, gútər/ *n.* peninsular emirate on the Persian Gulf. Pop. 548,000. Capital: Doha. □□ **Qa·tar'i** *n. & adj.*

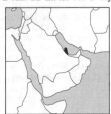

Qatar

Qing·dao /chíngdów/ *n.* (also **Tsing'tao'**) port city in E China. Pop. 1,459,200.

Qom /kōm/ *n.* city in NW Iran; Islamic holy site. Pop. 681,300.

Que·bec /kwibék, kibék/ *n.* **1** principally French-speaking province in E Canada. Pop. 7,209,000. **2** (also **Que·bec' Cit'y**) capital of Quebec, in the S part. Pop. 645,600. □□ **Que·beck'er, Que·bec·ois** /kaybekwaá/ *n.*

Queens /kweenz/ *n.* one of the five boroughs of New York City. Pop. 1,951,598.

Portugal

Queens·land /kweēnzlənd, –land/ *n.* state in NE Australia. Pop. 2,395,100. Capital: Brisbane.

Que·ré·ta·ro /kəráytərō/ *n.* state in central Mexico. Pop. 1,051,200. Capital: Querétaro.

Que·zon /kaysón/ **Cit·y** *n.* city in the Philippines, on Luzon. Pop. 1,676,600.

Quil·mes /keélmays/ *n.* city in E Argentina. Pop. 509,400.

Quin·ta·na Ro·o /keentáanə rō-ō/ *n.* state in E Mexico. Pop. 493,300. Capital: Chetumal.

Qui·to /keétō/ *n.* capital of Ecuador, in the N central part. Pop. 1,444,400.

Ra·bat /rəbáat/ *n.* port city and capital of Morocco. Pop. 518,600.

Ra·cine /rəseén, ray–/ *n.* city in SE Wisconsin. Pop. 84,298.

Rai·nier /rəneér, ray; n–/, **Mount** *n.* inactive volcano in W central Washington.

Ra·leigh /ráwlee, ráalee/ *n.* capital of North Carolina, in the central part. Pop. 207,951.

Ran·cho Cu·ca·mon·ga /ránchō kōōkəmáanggə/ *n.* city in SW California. Pop. 101,409.

Ran·goon /ranggōón/ *n.* (also **Yan'gon**) port city and capital of Burma. Pop. 3,851,000.

Rap·id /rápíd/ **Cit·y** *n.* city in SW South Dakota. Pop. 54,523.

Ra·ven·na /rəvénə/ *n.* city in NE Italy. Pop. 133,600.

Ra·wal·pin·di /raawəlpíndee/ *n.* city in N Pakistan. Pop. 794,800.

Read·ing /réding/ *n.* **1** city in SE Pennsylvania. Pop. 78,380. **2** city in S England. Pop. 137,700.

Re·ci·fe /rəseéfə/ *n.* (formerly **Pernambuco**) port city in NE Brazil. Pop. 1,297,000.

Red /red/ **Riv·er** *n.* **1** river in S central U.S., flowing 1,300 mi. from E New Mexico through Texas and into the Mississippi River in Louisiana. **2** (also called **Red Riv'er of the North**) river in N central U.S., flowing 530 mi. along the Minnesota–North Dakota border into Lake Winnipeg in Canada.

Red Sea *n.* arm of the Indian Ocean, between the Arabian Peninsula and Africa.

Re·gi·na /rijínə/ *n.* capital of Saskatchewan, Canada, in the S part. Pop. 179,200.

Reims /reNs, reemz/ *n.* city in NE France. Pop. 185,200.

Rennes /ren/ *n.* city in NW France. Pop. 203,500.

Re·no /reénō/ *n.* city in W Nevada. Pop. 133,850.

Ré·u·nion /ree-yōónyən/ *n.* island in the Indian Ocean; overseas department of France. Pop. 679,000. Capital: Saint-Denis.

Rey·kja·vik /ráykyəvik/ *n.* port city and capital of Iceland. Pop. 104,300.

Rhine /rin/ **Riv·er** *n.* river in W Europe, flowing 820 mi. from Switzerland to the North Sea.

Rhode /rōd/ **Is·land** *n.* (official name **Rhode Island and Providence Plantations**) state in NE U.S. Pop. 1,003,464. Capital: Providence. Abbr. **RI**, **R.I.** □□ **Rhode Is'land·er** *n.*

Rhodes /rōdz/ Greek island in the Aegean Sea, off the SW coast of Turkey.

Rho·de·sia /rōdeézhə, –shə/ *n.* former region of S Africa under British control; in 1965 became independent countries of Southern Rhodesia (now Zimbabwe) and Northern Rhodesia (now Zambia).

Rhone /rōn/ **Riv·er** *n.* river in W Europe, flowing 500 mi. from Switzerland to the Mediterranean Sea.

Rich·mond /ríchmənd/ *n.* capital of Virginia, in the E part. Pop. 203,056.

Ri·ga /reégə/ *n.* port city and capital of Latvia. Pop. 839,700.

Rim·i·ni /ríminee/ *n.* port city in N Italy. Pop. 130,000.

Ri·o de Ja·nei·ro /reéō day zhənérō/ *n.* port city in SE Brazil. Pop. 5,473,900.

Ri·o Gran·de /gránd, grándee/ *n.* river in North America, flowing 1,800 mi. from Colorado to the Gulf of Mexico; forms the border between Texas and Mexico.

Riv·er·side /rívərsīd/ *n.* city in SW California. Pop. 226,505.

Ri·yadh /reeáad, reeyáad/ *n.* capital of Saudi Arabia, in the E central part. Pop. 1,800,000.

Ro·a·noke /rōənōk/ *n.* city in W Virginia. Pop. 96,397.

Roch·es·ter /ráachestər, –əstər/ *n.* city in W New York. Pop. 231,636.

Rock·ford /ráakfərd/ *n.* city in N Illinois. Pop. 173,645.

Rock·y /ráakee/ **Moun·tains** *n.* (also called **the Rock'ies**) mountain range in W North America, extending from New Mexico to Alaska.

Ro·ma·ni·a /rōmáyneeə, rōō–/ *n.* (also **Ru·ma'ni·a**) republic in SE Europe. Pop. 21,657,000. Capital: Bucharest.

Rome /rōm/ *n.* capital of Italy, in the W central part. Pop. 2,687,900.

Ro·sa·ri·o /rōsáareeō, –zaár–/ *n.* port city in E central Argentina. Pop. 875,700.

Ro·seau /rōzō/ *n.* port city and capital of Dominica. Pop. 15,900.

Ross /raws, raas/ **Sea** *n.* arm of the S Pacific, extending into Antarctica, S of New Zealand.

Ros·tock /ráastaak, –tawk/ *n.* city in N Germany. Pop. 232,600.

Ros·tov /rəstáwf/ *n.* port city in SW Russia. Pop. 1,026,000.

Rot·ter·dam /ráatərdam/ *n.* port city in the W Netherlands. Pop. 599,400.

Rou·en /rōō–áaN/ *n.* city in NW France. Pop. 105,500.

Ru·ma·ni·a /rōōmáyneeə/ *n.* var. of ROMANIA.

Rush·more /rúshmawr/, **Mount** *n.* peak in the Black Hills of South Dakota, with carving of the faces of four U.S. presidents: Washington, Jefferson, T. Roosevelt, and Lincoln.

Rus·sia /rúshə/ *n.* republic in E Europe and Asia; chief republic of the former USSR. Pop. 148,178,000. Capital: Moscow.

Russia

Rwan·da /rōō-áandə/ *n.* republic in central Africa. Pop. 6,853,000. Capital: Kigali. □□ **Rwan'dan** *n. & adj.*

Rwanda

Sac·ra·men·to /sakrəméntō/ *n.* capital of California, in the N central part. Pop. 369,365.

Sa·har·a /səhárə, –háarə/ **Des·ert** *n.* extensive arid region in N Africa.

Sa·hel /səháyl, –heél/ *n.* arid region extending S from Senegal to Chad, S of the Sahara Desert.

Sai·gon /sīgáan, sígaan/ *n.* see HO CHI MINH CITY.

Saint Cath·a·rines /káthərinz, káthrinz/ *n.* city in S Ontario, Canada. Pop. 129,300.

St. Chris·to·pher /krístəfər/ **and Nevis** /neévis/ *n.* see ST. KITTS AND NEVIS.

Saint Geor·ge's /jórjəz/ *n.* capital of Grenada, on Grenada Island. Pop. 4,600.

St. Hel·ens /hélənz/, **Mount** *n.* active volcano in the Cascade Mountains of Washington.

St. John's /jaánz/ *n.* **1** capital of Antigua and Barbuda, on NW Antigua. Pop. 21,500. **2** capital of Newfoundland, Canada, in the NE part. Pop. 171,900.

St. Jo·seph /jōsəf, –zəf/ *n.* city in NW Missouri. Pop. 71,852.

St. Kitts /kits/ **and Ne·vis** /neévis/ *n.* (formerly **St. Christopher and Nevis**) two-island state in the E West Indies. Pop. 41,000. Capital: Basseterre.

St. Kitts and Nevis

Romania

See page xx for the **Key to Pronunciation**.

St. Law·rence /láwrəns, laár–/ **Riv·er** *n.* river in SE Canada, flowing 760 mi. from Lake Ontario to the Atlantic.

St. Law·rence Sea·way *n.* international waterway for oceangoing ships, connecting the Great Lakes to the Atlantic.

St. Lou·is /loŏis/ *n.* city in E Missouri. Pop. 396,685.

St. Lu·cia /looŏshə/ *n.* island country in the E West Indies. Pop. 158,000. Capital: Castries.

St. Lucia

St. Paul /pawl/ *n.* capital of Minnesota, in the E part. Pop. 272,235.

St. Pe·ters·burg /peétərzbərg/ *n.* **1** (formerly **Leningrad** 1924–91) port city in NW Russia. Pop. 4,838,000. **2** city in W central Florida. Pop. 238,629.

St. Vin·cent /vínsənt/ **and the Gren·a·dines** /grénədeenz/ *n.* island state in the SE West Indies. Pop. 118,000. Capital: Kingstown.

St. Vincent and the Grenadines

Sa·kai /saáki/ *n.* port city in Japan, on Honshu. Pop. 808,100.

Sa·kha·lin /sakəleén/ **Is·land** *n.* island in SE Russia, N of Japan.

Sa·la·man·ca /saaləmaángkə/ *n.* city in W Spain. Pop. 167,400.

Sa·lem /sáyləm/ *n.* capital of Oregon, in the NW part. Pop. 107,786.

Sa·ler·no /səlérnō/ *n.* port city in W Italy. Pop. 146,500.

Sa·li·nas /səleénəs/ *n.* city in W California. Pop. 108,777.

Sa·lon·i·ka /səlaánikə/ *n.* see THESSALONIKE.

Sal·ti·llo /saalteéō, –teéyō/ *n.* capital of Coahuila, Mexico, in the SW part. Pop. 420,900.

Salt Lake Cit·y *n.* capital of Utah, in the N central part. Pop. 159,936.

Sal·ton /sáwlt'n/ **Sea** *n.* shallow salt lake in S California; 240 ft. below sea level.

Sal·va·dor /sálvədawr, salvədáwr/ *n.* port city in E Brazil. Pop. 2,070,300.

Salz·burg /sáwlzbərg, saálz–, zaálts–/ *n.* city in central Austria. Pop. 144,000.

Sa·ma·ra /səmaárə/ *n.* (formerly **Kuibyshev** 1935–91) port city in E Russia. Pop. 1,239,000.

Sam·ar·kand /sámərkand/ *n.* city in E Uzbekistan. Pop. 368,000.

Sa·mo·a /səmóə/ *n.* (also **Sa·mo′a Is′lands**) see AMERICAN SAMOA; WESTERN SAMOA.

Sa·naa /sanaá/ *n.* political capital of Yemen, in the W part. Pop. 503,600.

San An·dre·as /san andráyəs/ **Fault** *n.* earthquake zone extending S to N along the California coast.

San An·to·ni·o /san antóneeō, əntō–/ *n.* city in S central Texas. Pop. 935,933.

San Ber·nar·di·no /san bərnədeénō, –nər–/ *n.* city in SE California. Pop. 164,164.

San Bue·na·ven·tu·ra /san bwenəventoŏrə, –ventyoŏ–/ *n.* (also **Ven·tura**) port city in SW California. Pop. 92,575.

San Di·e·go /san dee-áygō/ *n.* city in S California. Pop. 1,110,549.

San Fran·cis·co /san frənsískō, fran–/ *n.* port city in W California. Pop. 723,959. □□ **San Fran·cis′can** *n.*

San Fran·cis·co Bay *n.* inlet of the Pacific, in W central California.

San Joa·quin /san waakeén/ **Val·ley** *n.* rich agricultural area in the S part of California's Central Valley.

San Jo·sé /saan hōzáy/ *n.* capital of Costa Rica, in the central part. Pop. 299,500.

San Jo·se /san hōzáy, əzáy/ *n.* city in W California. Pop. 782,248.

San Juan /san waán, hwaán/ *n.* port city and capital of Puerto Rico. Pop. 438,100.

San Jus·to /saan hoŏstō/ *n.* city in E Argentina. Pop. 946,700.

San Lu·is Po·to·sí /saan looŏees pōtəseé/ *n.* state in central Mexico. Pop. 2,003,200. Capital: San Luis Potosí.

San Ma·ri·no /san məreénō/ *n.* republic in S Europe, surrounded by Italy; oldest independent country in Europe. Pop. 25,000. □□ **San Mar·i·nese′** /marəneéz, –neés/ *n. & adj.*

San Marino

San Ni·co·lás de los Gar·zas /saan neekōlaás de laws gaársaas/ *n.* city in NE Mexico. Pop. 436,600.

San Pe·dro Su·la /saan páydrō soŏlaa/ *n.* city in NW Honduras. Pop. 368,500.

San Sal·va·dor /san sálvədawr/ *n.* capital of El Salvador, in the S central part. Pop. 422,600.

San·ta An·a /santə ánə/ *n.* city in SW California. Pop. 293,742.

San·ta Bar·ba·ra /baárbərə, –brə/ *n.* city in SW California. Pop. 85,571.

San·ta Cat·a·li·na /kat'leénə/ **Is·land** *n.* (also **Cat·a·li′na Island**) island in SW California.

San·ta Cla·ra /klárə, klérə/ *n.* city in W California. Pop. 93,613.

San·ta Cla·ri·ta /kləreétə/ *n.* city in S California. Pop. 110,642.

San·ta Cruz /saántaa krōŏz/ *n.* city in central Bolivia. Pop. 767,300.

San·ta Cruz de Te·ne·rife /day tenəreéf, –ríf, –reéfay/ *n.* port city on Tenerife Island, Spain. Pop. 203,900.

San·ta Fe /santə fáy/ *n.* capital of New Mexico, in the N central part. Pop. 55,859.

San·ta Mon·i·ca /maánikə/ *n.* city in SW California. Pop. 86,905.

San·ta Ro·sa /rōzə/ *n.* city in W California. Pop. 113,313.

San·ti·a·go /saantee–aágō, sant–/ *n.* capital of Chile, in the central part. Pop. 5,076,800.

San·ti·a·go de Cu·ba /saantyaágō day koŏbaa, kyoŏ–/ *n.* port city in SE Cuba. Pop. 440,100.

San·to Do·min·go /sáantō dəmínggō/ *n.* port city and capital of the Dominican Republic. Pop. 1,600,000.

San·to To·mé de Gua·ya·na /tōmáy day gwaayaánə/ *n.* (also **Ciu·dad′ Gua·ya′na** /seeoŏdaad, seeyoŏ–/) city in NE Venezuela. Pop. 453,000.

São Pau·lo /sow pówlō/ *n.* city in SE Brazil. Pop. 9,393,800.

São To·mé /təmáy/ *capital* of São Tomé and Principe, on NE São Tomé Island. Pop. 35,000.

São Tomé and Principe

São To·mé and Prin·ci·pe /prínsəpə/ *n.* island republic in W Africa, in the Gulf of Guinea. Pop. 144,000. Capital: São Tomé.

Sap·po·ro /saapōrō, –páwrō/ *n.* city in Japan, on Hokkaido. Pop. 1,757,000.

Sar·a·gos·sa /sarəgósə/ *n.* (also **Za·ra·go′za**) city in NE Spain. Pop. 606,600.

Sa·ra·je·vo /sarəyáyvō, saar–/ *n.* capital of Bosnia and Herzegovina, in the E central part. Pop. 526,000.

Sar·a·so·ta /sarəsōtə/ *n.* city in W central Florida. Pop. 50,961.

Sar·din·i·a /saardíneeə/ *n.* Italian island in the Mediterranean Sea, W of Italy. Pop. 1,645,192. Capital: Cagliari.

Sas·katch·e·wan /səskáchəwən, sas–, –waan/ *n.* province in central Canada. Pop. 1,003,000. Capital: Regina.

Sas·ka·toon /saskətoŏn/ *n.* city in S central Saskatchewan, Canada. Pop. 186,100.

Sau·di A·ra·bi·a /sówdee əráybeeə, sáwdee/ *n.* kingdom in SW Asia, on the Arabian Peninsula. Pop. 19,409,000. Capital: Riyadh. □□ **Sau′di, Sau·di A·ra′bi·an** *n. & adj.*

Sa·van·nah /səvánə/ *n.* city in E Georgia. Pop. 137,560.

Sa·van·nah Riv·er *n.* river in S U.S., flowing 300 mi. from NW South Carolina to the Atlantic; forms the boundary between South Carolina and Georgia.

Say·da /sídə/ see SIDON.

Scan·di·na·vi·a /skandináyveeə/ *n.* **1** region of N Europe; includes Denmark, Norway, Sweden, and sometimes Finland, Iceland, and the Faeroe Islands. **2** (also called **Scan·di·na'vi·an Pen·in'su·la**) peninsula in N Europe, bounded by the Norwegian, North, and Baltic seas and the Gulf of Bothnia, and comprising Norway and Sweden. □□ **Scan·di·na'vi·an** *n. & adj.*

Scar·bor·ough /skaárbərō, –brə/ *n.* city in SE Ontario, Canada. Pop. 524,600.

Sche·nec·ta·dy /skənéktədee/ *n.* city in E New York. Pop. 65,566.

Schuyl·kill /skoolkil, skoókəl, skoólkəl/ **Riv·er** *n.* river in Pennsylvania, flowing 130 mi. from E central Pennsylvania into the Delaware River at Philadelphia.

Scil·ly /sílee/, **Isles of** *n.* island group in the Atlantic, off the SW coast of England.

Scot·land /skaátlənd/ *n.* division of the United Kingdom, N of England. Pop. 4,770,600. Capital: Edinburgh.

Scotts·dale /skaátsdayl/ *n.* city in SW central Arizona. Pop. 130,069.

Scran·ton /skránt'n/ *n.* city in NE Pennsylvania. Pop. 81,805.

Se·at·tle /seeát'l/ *n.* port city in W central Washington. Pop. 516,259.

Seine /sayn, sen/ **Riv·er** *n.* river in France, flowing 480 mi. from E France through Paris and into the English Channel.

Se·ma·rang /səmaáraang/ *n.* port city in Indonesia, on Java. Pop. 1,005,300.

Sen·dai /séndī/ *n.* city in Japan, on Honshu. Pop. 971,300.

Sen·e·gal /senəgáwl/ *n.* republic in W Africa. Pop. 9,093,000. Capital: Dakar. □□ **Sen·e·gal·ese** /–eéz/ *n. & adj.*

Senegal

Seoul /sōl/ *n.* capital of South Korea, in the NW part. Pop. 10,229,300.

Ser·bi·a /súrbeeə/ *n.* republic in SE Europe; formerly part of Yugoslavia. Pop. 9,979,000. Capital: Belgrade. □□ **Serb** *n. & adj.*

Se·vas·to·pol /səvástəpōl, –pawl/ *n.* port city in S Ukraine. Pop. 365,000.

Se·ville /səvíl/ *n.* port city in SW Spain. Pop. 714,100.

Sey·chelles /sayshél, –shélz/ *n.* island republic in the Indian Ocean, NE of Madagascar. Pop. 78,000. Capital: Victoria.

Seychelles

Shang·hai /shanghí, shánghī/ *n.* port city in E China. Pop. 7,830,000.

Shef·field /shéfeeld/ *n.* city in N England. Pop. 530,100.

Shen·yang /shúnyaáng/ *n.* city in NE China. Pop. 4,540,000.

Shet·land /shétlənd/ **Is·lands** *n.* island group in the N Atlantic, off the NE coast of Scotland.

Shi·ko·ku /shikókoo/ *n.* island in Japan, S of Honshu.

Shi·raz /shiraáz/ *n.* city in SW Iran. Pop. 965,100.

Shreve·port /shreévpawrt, –pōrt/ *n.* city in NW Louisiana. Pop. 198,525.

Shub·ra al-Khay·mah /shoobraá al kīmaá, –maákh/ *n.* city in N Egypt. Pop. 834,000.

Si·am /sī-ám/ *n.* see THAILAND.

Si·an /sheéaán/ *n.* see XIAN.

Saudi Arabia

Sic·i·ly /sísəlee/ *n.* Italian island in the Mediterranean Sea, off the SW tip of Italy. Pop. 4,910,000. Capital: Palermo.

Si·don /sīd'n/ *n.* (also **Say'da**) port city in SW Lebanon. Pop. 100,000.

Si·er·ra Le·one /see-érə lee-ón/ *n.* republic in W Africa. Pop. 4,793,000. Capital: Freetown. □□ **Si·er'ra Le·o'ne·an** /–neeən/ *n. & adj.*

Sierra Leone

Si·er·ra Ne·va·da /nəvádə, –vaádə/ **1** mountain range in E California. **2** mountain range in S Spain.

Sil·i·con Val·ley *n.* area in W California, from San Jose to Palo Alto.

Si·mi /simeé, seémee/ **Val·ley** *n.* city in SW California. Pop. 100,217.

Si·nai /sínī/ **Pen·in·su·la** peninsula in NE Egypt, bounded by the gulfs of Suez and Aqaba and the Red Sea.

Si·na·lo·a /seenəlóə/ *n.* state in NW Mexico. Pop. 2,204,100. Capital: Culiacán.

Sin·ga·pore /síngəpawr, síngə–/ *n.* republic in SE Asia, at the S tip of the Malay Peninsula. Pop. 3,397,000. Capital: Singapore. □□ **Sin·ga·po're·an** /–reeən/ *n.*

Singapore

Sioux /soo/ **Cit·y** *n.* city in W Iowa. Pop. 80,505.

Sioux Falls *n.* city in SE South Dakota. Pop. 100,814.

Skop·je /skáwpye, –yay/ *n.* capital of Macedonia, in the N part. Pop. 541,300.

Skye /skī/ *n.* island in the Hebrides, off the NW coast of Scotland.

Slo·va·ki·a /slōvaákeeə, slō–/ *n.* (also called **Slo'vak Re·pub'lic**) republic in central Europe; formerly part of Czechoslovakia. Pop. 5,374,000. Capital: Bratislava.

Slo·ve·ni·a /slōveéneeə, slō–/ *n.* republic in S Europe; formerly part of Yugoslavia. Pop. 1,951,000. Capital: Ljubljana. □□ **Slo·ve'ni·an** *n. & adj.*

Slovakia

Slovenia

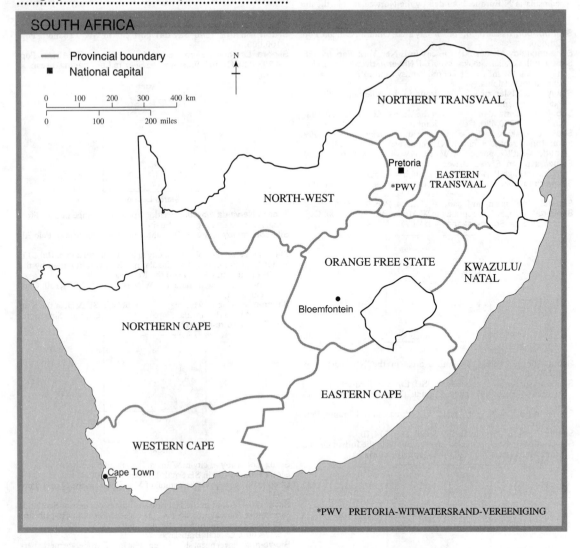

SOUTH AFRICA

— Provincial boundary
■ National capital

N

0 100 200 300 400 km

0 100 200 miles

NORTHERN TRANSVAAL

Pretoria ■

*PWV

EASTERN TRANSVAAL

NORTH-WEST

ORANGE FREE STATE

KWAZULU/ NATAL

NORTHERN CAPE

Bloemfontein ●

EASTERN CAPE

WESTERN CAPE

Cape Town ●

*PWV PRETORIA-WITWATERSRAND-VEREENIGING

Smo·lensk /sməlénsk/ *n.* city in W Russia. Pop. 355,000.

Smyr·na /smúrnə/ *n.* see IZMIR.

Snake /snayk/ **Riv·er** *n.* river in NW U.S., flowing 1,040 mi. from Yellowstone National Park, Wyoming, to the Columbia River in Washington.

So·ci·e·ty /səsíetee/ **Is·lands** *n.* island group in the S Pacific, forming part of French Polynesia.

So·fi·a /səféeə, sō–/ *n.* capital of Bulgaria, in the W part. Pop. 1,116,800.

Sol·o·mon /saáləmən/ **Is·lands** *n.* island country, in the Pacific, E of New Guinea. Pop. 413,000. Capital: Honiara.

Solomon Islands

So·ma·li·a /səmaályə, –eeə/ *n.* republic in E Africa. Pop. 9,639,000. Capital: Mogadishu. □□ **So·ma'li** *n.* **So·ma'li·an** *adj.*

So·no·ra /sənáwrə/ *n.* state in NW Mexico. Pop. 1,823,600. Capital: Hermosillo.

So·no·ran /sənáwrən/ **Des·ert** *n.* arid region in SW Arizona, SE California, and NW Mexico.

South Af·ri·ca *n.* republic in S Africa. Capitals: Bloemfontein; Cape Town; Pretoria. Pop. 41,743,000. □□ **South' Af'ri·can** *n. & adj.*

South A·mer·i·ca *n.* continent in the W hemisphere, S of Panama. □□ **South' A·mer'i·can** *n. & adj.*

South·amp·ton /sowthámtən, sowth-hámp–/ *n.* port city in S England. Pop. 211,700.

South Aus·tral·ia *n.* state in S central Australia. Pop. 1,285,000. Capital: Adelaide.

South Bend /bend/ *n.* city in N Indiana. Pop. 105,511.

South Car·o·li·na /karəlínə/ *n.* state in SE U.S. Pop. 3,486,703. Capital: Columbia. Abbr. **SC; S.C.; S. Car.** □□ **South Car·o·lin·i·an** /–líneeən/ *n. & adj.*

South Chi·na Sea *n.* arm of the W Pacific, enclosed by Borneo and the Philippines.

Somalia

SPAIN

Region boundary
Province boundary
■ Capital city

CANARY ISLANDS

South Da·ko·ta /dəkṓtə/ *n.* state in N central U.S. Pop. 696,004. Capital: Pierre. Abbr. **SD**; **S.D.**; **S. Dak.** □□ **South′ Da·ko′tan** *n. & adj.*

South Ko·re·a *n.* see KOREA.

South Korea

South Pole *n.* S end of the earth's axis, on Antarctica.

So·vi·et /sṓvee-ət/ **Un·ion** see UNION OF SOVIET SOCIALIST REPUBLICS.

So·we·to /səwétō, –wáytō/ *n.* group of townships in N South Africa. Pop. 596,600.

Spain /spayn/ *n.* monarchy in SW Europe, on the Iberian Peninsula. Pop. 39,181,000. Capital: Madrid.

Spice /spīs/ **Is·lands** *n.* see MOLUCCAS.

Spo·kane /spōkán/ *n.* city in E Washington. Pop. 177,196.

Spring·field /spríngfeeld/ *n.* **1** capital of Illinois, in the central part. Pop. 105,227. **2** city in SW Massachusetts. Pop. 156,983. **3** city in SW Missouri. Pop. 140,494.

Sri Lan·ka /sree laángkə, shree/ *n.* (formerly **Ceylon**) island republic in the Indian Ocean, off the S tip of India. Pop. 18,553,000. Capital: Colombo. □□ **Sri Lank′an** *n. & adj.*

Staked /staykt/ **Plain** *n.* see LLANO ESTACADO.

Sta·lin·grad /staálingrad/ *n.* see VOLGOGRAD.

Stam·ford /stámfərd/ *n.* city in SW Connecticut. Pop. 108,056.

Stat·en /stát'n/ **Is·land** *n.* island in New York Bay; one of the five boroughs of New York City. Pop. 378,977.

Stav·ro·pol /staavráwpəl, –rṓ–/ *n.* city in S Russia. Pop. 342,000.

Stock·holm /staákhōlm, –hōm/ *n.* port city and capital of Sweden. Pop. 711,100.

Stock·ton /staáktən/ *n.* city in central California. Pop. 210,943.

Stoke-on-Trent /stōk aan trént/ *n.* city in W central England. Pop. 254,200.

Stras·bourg /straasbŏŏrg, straásbərg/ *n.* city in NE France. Pop. 255,900.

Stutt·gart /shtŏŏtgaart/ *n.* city in SW Germany. Pop. 588,500.

Su·cre /sŏŏkray/ *n.* legislative capital of Bolivia, in the S part. Pop. 145,000.

Su·dan /sŏŏdán, –daán/ *n.* republic in NE Africa. Pop. 31,548,000. Capital: Khartoum.

Sudan

Su·ez /sŏŏ-éz, sŏŏez/ *n.* port city in NE Egypt. Pop. 388,000.

Su·ez Ca·nal *n.* canal in NE Egypt, connecting the Mediterranean and Red seas.

Su·la·we·si /sŏŏlaawáysee/ *n.* (formerly **Celebes**) island in central Indonesia, in the Malay Archipelago.

See page xx for the **Key to Pronunciation.**

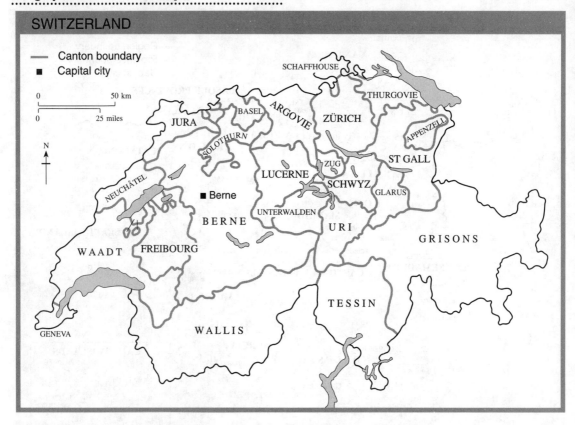

SWITZERLAND

— Canton boundary
■ Capital city

0   50 km
0   25 miles

N

SCHAFFHOUSE
THURGOVIE
JURA
BASEL
ARGOVIE
ZÜRICH
SOLOTHURN
APPENZELL
ST GALL
ZUG
LUCERNE
NEUCHÂTEL
SCHWYZ
GLARUS
■ Berne
UNTERWALDEN
BERNE
URI
GRISONS
WAADT
FREIBOURG
TESSIN
GENEVA
WALLIS

Su·ma·tra /soomaátrə/ *n.* island in W Indonesia.

Sum·ga·it /soomgaa-eét/ *n.* city in E Azerbaijan. Pop. 236,200.

Sun·chon /soónchávn/ *n.* city in S South Korea. Pop. 136,000.

Sun·da /sə́ndə, soóndaa/ **Is·lands** *n.* island chain in the Malay Archipelago; includes Borneo, Java, Sumatra, and smaller islands.

Sun·ny·vale /sóneevayl/ *n.* city in W California. Pop. 117,229.

Su·pe·ri·or /soopeéreeər/, **Lake** *n.* northernmost and largest of the Great Lakes, N of Michigan.

Su·ra·ba·ya /soorəbíə/ *n.* port city in Indonesia, on Java. Pop. 2,421,000.

Su·rat /soórət, sooraát/ *n.* port city in W India. Pop. 1,498,800.

Su·ri·na·me /soórinaám, –nám/ *n.* republic in N South America. Pop. 436,000. Capital: Paramaribo. □□ **Su·ri·na·mese** /soórənəmeéz, –meés/ *n. & adj.*

Suriname

Su·va /soóvə/ *n.* port city and capital of Fiji. Pop. 69,700.

Su·won /soówən/ *n.* city in NW South Korea. Pop. 755,500.

Sverd·lovsk /sferdláwfsk/ *n.* (also called **Ye·ka·te·rin·burg**) city in W Russia. Pop. 1,280,000.

Swan·sea /swaánzee/ *n.* port city in S Wales, United Kingdom. Pop. 189,300.

Swa·zi·land /swaázeeland/ *n.* kingdom in S Africa. Pop. 999,000. Capital: Mbabane.

Swe·den /sweéd'n/ *n.* kingdom in N Europe. Pop. 8,901,000. Capital: Stockholm. □□ **Swede** /sweed/ *n.* **Swed'ish** *adj.*

Switz·er·land /switsərlənd/ *n.* republic in central Europe. Pop. 6,779,000. Capital: Bern.

Syd·ney /sídnee/ *n.* port city and capital of New South Wales, Australia. Pop. 3,772,700.

Syr·a·cuse /seérəkyoos, sér–, –kyooz/ *n.* city in central New York. Pop. 163,860.

Syr·i·a /seéreeə/ *n.* republic in SW Asia. Pop. 15,609,000. Capital: Damascus. □□ **Syr'i·an** *n. & adj.*

Syria

Swaziland

Sweden

Szcze·cin /shchétseen/ *n.* port city in NW Poland. Pop. 419,600.

Ta·bas·co /təbáskō/ *n.* state in SE Mexico. Capital: Villahermosa. Pop. 1,501,700.

Ta·briz /təbreéz/ *n.* city in NW Iran. Pop. 1,089,000.

Ta·co·ma /təkṓmə/ *n.* port city in W central Washington. Pop. 176,664.

Ta·dzhik·i·stan /taajeékistán, –staán/ *n.* republic in central Asia; formerly part of the USSR. Pop. 5,916,000. Capital: Dushanbe. □□ **Ta·dzhik'** *n.*

Tae·gu /tágṓ/ *n.* city in SE South Korea. Pop. 2,449,100.

Tae·jon /tájáwn/ *n.* city in central South Korea. Pop. 1,272,100.

Ta·gus /táygəs/ **Riv·er** *n.* river on the Iberian Peninsula, flowing 570 mi. from E central Spain through Portugal and into the Atlantic.

Ta·hi·ti /təheétee/ *n.* island in the S Pacific; one of the Society Islands. □□ **Ta·hi'tian** /–shən/ *n. & adj.*

Ta·hoe /taáhō/, **Lake** *n.* glacial lake in the Sierra Nevada range, on the California-Nevada border: 6,228 ft. above sea level.

Tai·chung /tíchóng/ *n.* city in W central Taiwan. Pop. 761,800.

Ta·if /taáif/ *n.* city in W Saudi Arabia. Pop. 300,000.

Tai·nan /tínaán/ *n.* city in SW Taiwan. Pop. 683,300.

Tai·pei /típáy, –báy/ *n.* capital of Taiwan, in the N part. Pop. 2,626,100.

Tai·wan /tīwaán/ *n.* (also called **For·mo'sa**) island nation in SE China. Pop. 21,466,000. Capital: Taipei. □□ **Tai·wan·ese** /tīwəneéz/ *n. & adj.*

Taiwan

Tai·yuan /tíyōo-aán/ *n.* city in N China. Pop. 1,533,900.

Ta·lien /daálee-én/ *n.* see DALIAN.

Tal·la·has·see /taləhásee/ *n.* capital of Florida, in the NW part. Pop. 124,773.

Tal·linn /taályin, tál–, –lin/ *n.* port city and capital of Estonia. Pop. 434,800.

Ta·mau·li·pas /taamowleépaas/ *n.* state in NE Mexico. Pop. 2,249,600. Capital: Ciudad Victoria.

Tam·pa /támpə/ *n.* city in W central Florida. Pop. 280,015.

Tam·pi·co /tampeékō/ *n.* port city in E Mexico. Pop. 272,700.

Tan·gan·yi·ka /tangənyeékə, tanggən–/, **Lake** *n.* freshwater lake in central Africa, between Tanzania and Congo (formerly Zaire).

Tan·gier /tanjeér/ *n.* (also **Tan·giers** /–jeérz/) port city in N Morocco. Pop. 307,000.

Tang·shan /taángshaán/ *n.* city in NE China. Pop. 1,500,000.

Tan·za·ni·a /tanzəneéə/ *n.* republic in E Africa, formed by the merger of Tanganyika and Zanzibar. Pop. 29,058,000. Capital: Dar es Salaam. □□ **Tan·za·ni'an** *n. & adj.*

Tanzania

Tash·kent /tashként/ *n.* capital of Uzbekistan, in the E part. Pop. 2,106,000.

Tas·ma·ni·a /tazmáyneeə/ *n.* island state in SE Australia, S of Victoria. Pop. 452,800. Capital: Hobart.

Tbi·li·si /təbəleésee/ *n.* capital of the republic of Georgia, in the SE part. Pop. 1,279,000.

Te·gu·ci·gal·pa /təgōōsigálpə, –gaál–/ *n.* capital of Honduras, in the S part. Pop. 608,100.

Teh·ran /tayrán, –raán, tayə–/ *n.* (also **Te·he·ran**) capital of Iran, in the NW central part. Pop. 6,042,600.

Tel A·viv-Jaf·fa /tel əveev jaáfə/ *n.* (also called **Tel A·viv'**) city in W central Israel. Pop. 321,700.

Tem·pe /témpee/ *n.* city in central Arizona. Pop. 141,865.

Ten·nes·see /tenəseé/ *n.* state in S central U.S. Pop. 4,877,185. Capital: Nashville. Abbr. **Tenn.**; **TN** □□ **Ten·nes·see'an** *n. & adj.*

Ten·nes·see Riv·er *n.* river in E central U.S., flowing 650 mi. from

E Tennessee through Alabama and W Tennessee and Kentucky and into the Ohio River.

Te·pic /taypeék/ *n.* capital of Nayarit, Mexico, in the W part. Pop. 207,000.

Ter·re Haute /terə hốt, hə́t/ *n.* city in W Indiana. Pop. 57,483.

Te·ton /teéton/ **Range** *n.* mountain range in W Wyoming, part of the Rocky Mountain range.

Tex·as /téksəs/ *n.* state in S U.S. Pop. 16,986,510. Capital: Austin. Abbr. **Tex.**; **TX** □□ **Tex'an** *n. & adj.*

Thai·land /tílənd, –land/ *n.* (formerly **Siam**) kingdom in SE Asia. Pop. 58,851,000. Capital: Bangkok.

Thailand

Thai·land, Gulf of arm of the South China Sea, S and W of Thailand.

Thames /temz/ **Riv·er** *n.* river in S England, flowing 210 mi. from Gloucestershire through London and into the North Sea.

Thana /taánə/ *n.* city in W India. Pop. 803,400.

Thes·sa·lo·ni·ke /thesəlawneékee/ *n.* (also called **Salon'ika**) port city in NE Greece. Pop. 378,000.

Thim·phu /thimpōo̅/ *n.* official capital of Bhutan. Pop. 30,300.

Thou·sand /thówzənd/ **Is·lands** *n.* group of about 1,700 islands in the St. Lawrence River, between Ontario, Canada, and New York.

Thou·sand Oaks /ōks/ *n.* city in SW California. Pop. 104,352.

Tian·jin /tee-aánjín, tee-én–/ *n.* (formerly **Tientsin**) port city in NE China. Pop. 5,770,000.

Ti·bet /tibét/ *n.* autonomous region of W China. Capital: Lhasa.

Tien·tsin /tíntsín/ *n.* see TIANJIN.

Ti·er·ra del Fue·go /tee-érə del fwáygō/ *n.* island group at the S tip of South America; divided between Chile and Argentina.

Ti·gris /tígris/ **Riv·er** *n.* river in SW Asia, flowing 1,150 mi. from Turkey to the Euphrates River in Iraq.

Ti·jua·na /tihwaánə, teeəwaánə/ *n.* city in NW Mexico. Pop. 698,800.

Til·burg /tilbərg/ *n.* city in the S Netherlands. Pop. 164,100.

Ti·mi·soa·ra /teemishwaárə/ *n.* city in W Romania. Pop. 325,400.

Ti·ra·në /tiraánə/ *n.* capital of Albania, in the central part. Pop. 300,000.

Ti·ti·ca·ca /titeekaákə, tərlaa–/, **Lake** *n.* lake on the Bolivia-Peru border: 12,508 ft. above sea level.

Tlax·ca·la /tlaaskaálə, tərlaa–/ *n.* state in central Mexico. Pop. 761,300. Capital: Tlaxcala.

To·go /tṓgō/ *n.* country in W Africa. Pop. 4,571,000. Capital: Lomé.

Togo

To·ky·o /tṓkeeō/ *n.* capital of Japan, on Honshu. Pop. 7,966,200.

To·le·do /təleédō/ *n.* city in NW Ohio. Pop. 332,943.

To·lu·ca /təlōōkə/ *n.* capital of Mexico, Mexico, in the S part. Pop. 827,300.

Ton·ga /taánggə, táwng–/ *n.* island kingdom in the S Pacific, NE of New Zealand. Pop. 106,000. Capital: Nukualofa. □□ **Ton'gan** *n. & adj.* See map p. 1246.

To·pe·ka /təpeékə/ *n.* capital of Kansas, in the NE part. Pop. 119,883.

To·ri·no /təreénō/ *n.* see TURIN.

To·ron·to /təraántō/ *n.* capital of Ontario, Canada, in the SE part. Pop. 3,893,000.

Tor·rance /táwrəns, taár–/ *n.* city in SW California. Pop. 133,107.

Tor·re·ón /tawray-ón/ *n.* city in N Mexico. Pop. 328,100.

Tou·lon /tōōláwn/ *n.* port city in SE France. Pop. 170,200.

Tou·louse /tōōlōōz/ *n.* city in S France. Pop. 365,900.

Tours /tōōr/ *n.* city in NW central France. Pop. 133,400.

Tonga

Trans·vaal /tranzvaál/ *n.* province in NE South Africa.
Tran·syl·va·nia /transilváyneeə/ *n.* a region and former province of central Romania.
Tren·ton /trént'n/ *n.* capital of New Jersey, in the W central part. Pop. 88,675.
Tri·este /tree-ést/ *n.* port city in NE Italy. Pop. 226,700.
Trin·i·dad /trínidad/ **and To·ba·go** /təbáygō/ *n.* island republic in the SE West Indies. Pop. 1,272,000. Capital: Port-of-Spain.

Trinidad and Tobago

Trip·o·li /trípəlee/ *n.* **1** capital of Libya, in the NW part. Pop. 591,100. **2** port city in NW Lebanon. Pop. 240,000.
Trond·heim /trȧanhaym/ *n.* port city in central Norway. Pop. 143,700.
Troy /troy/ *n.* **1** *hist.* ancient city in NW Asia Minor (present-day Turkey). **2** city in E New York. Pop. 72,884. □□ **Tro·jan** /trṓjən/ *adj.*
Tru·ji·llo /trōōhéeyō/ *n.* port city in NW Peru. Pop. 509,300.
Tsing·tao /tsíngtów/ *n.* see QINGDAO.
Tuc·son /tōṓsaan/ *n.* city in S central Arizona. Pop. 405,390.
Tul·sa /túlsə/ *n.* city in NE Oklahoma. Pop. 367,302.
Tu·nis /tōṓnis, tyōō–/ *n.* port city and capital of Tunisia. Pop. 674,100.
Tu·ni·sia /tōōnéezhə, tyōō–, –nízhə/ *n.* republic in N Africa. Pop. 9,020,000. Capital: Tunis. □□ **Tu·ni'sian** *n. & adj.*

Tunisia

Tu·rin /tōṓrin, tōōrín, tyōō–, tyōō–/ *n.* (Italian name **To·ri'no**) city in NW Italy. Pop. 945,600.
Tur·key /tɔ́rkee/ *n.* republic in W Asia and SE Europe. Pop. 62,484,000. Capital: Ankara.

Turkey

Turk·me·ni·stan /tərkménistan/ *n.* republic in S Asia; formerly part of the USSR. Pop. 4,149,000. Capital: Ashgabat. □□ **Turk·men** *n.*
Turks /túrks/ **and Cai·cos** /kíkōs, káykōs/ **Is·lands** *n.* two island groups in the N Atlantic, SE of the Bahamas; dependent territory of the United Kingdom. Pop. 14,000. Capital: Grand Turk.

Tus·ca·loo·sa /təskəlōṓsə/ *n.* city in W Alabama. Pop. 77,759.
Tu·va·lu /tōōvaáloō, tyōō–, –vaár–/ *n.* island nation in the S Pacific, N of Fiji. Pop. 10,000. Capital: Funafuti.

Tuvalu

Tux·tla /tōṓstlaa/ *n.* (official name **Tux'tla Gu·ti·ér·rez** /gōōtyérays/) capital of Chiapas, Mexico, in the W central part. Pop. 289,600.
Tver /tver/ *n.* see KALININ.
U·fa /ōōfaá/ *n.* city in W Russia. Pop. 1,094,000.
U·gan·da /ōōgándə, yōō–/ *n.* republic in E Africa. Pop. 20,158,000. Capital: Kampala. □□ **U·gan'dan** *n. & adj.*

Uganda

U·jung Pan·dang /ōṓjōōng paadaáng/ *n.* port city in Indonesia, on Sulawesi. Pop. 913,200.
U·kraine /yōōkráyn/ *n.* republic in E Europe; formerly part of the USSR. Pop. 50,864,000. Capital: Kiev.

Ukraine

U·lan Ba·tor /ōṓlaan baátawr/ *n.* (also **U·laan·baa'tar**) capital of Mongolia, in the N central part. Pop. 619,000.
Ulm /ōōlm/ *n.* city in S Germany. Pop. 115,100.
Ul·san /ōṓlsaán/ *n.* city in SE South Korea. Pop. 967,400.
Un·ion of So·vi·et So·cial·ist Re·pub·lics *n.* (also called **So'vi·et Un'ion**) former union of fifteen constituent republics under Soviet direction, in E Europe and Asia; dissolved in 1991. Abbr. **USSR** □□ **So'vi·et** *n. & adj.*

Turkmenistan

Turks and Caicos Islands

U·nit·ed Ar·ab E·mir·ates /árəb émərəts, –rayts/ *n.* independent federation of seven emirates on the Persian Gulf. Pop. 3,057,000. Capital: Abu Dhabi.

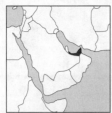

United Arab Emirates

U·nit·ed King·dom *n.* monarchy in NW Europe; includes England, Northern Ireland, Scotland, and Wales. Pop. 58,490,000. Capital: London. Abbr. **UK; U.K.**

United Kingdom

U·nit·ed States of A·mer·i·ca *n.* federal republic of 50 states: 49 states in North America and the island state of Hawaii in the N Pacific. Pop. 265,563,000. Capital: Washington, D.C. Abbr. **US; U.S.; USA; U.S.A.** See map p. 1248.

Upp·sa·la /ə́psəlaa, –saalə/ *n.* city in E Sweden. Pop. 183,500.

U·ral /yoo͝órəl/ **Moun·tains** *n.* mountain range in W Russia; considered part of the boundary between Europe and Asia.

Ur·fa /oo͝órfaa/ *n.* city in SE Turkey. Pop. 357,900.

U·ru·guay /oo͝órəgwī, yoo͝ó–, –gway/ *n.* republic in SE South America. Pop. 3,239,000. Capital: Montevideo. □□ **U·ru·guay′an** *n. & adj.*

Uruguay

Ü·rüm·qi /oo͝óroo͝óm-chee/ *n.* city in W China. Pop. 1,160,000.

USSR *abbr.* see UNION OF SOVIET SOCIALIST REPUBLICS.

U·tah /yoo͝ótaa, –taw/ *n.* state in W U.S. Pop. 1,722,850. Capital: Salt Lake City. Abbr. **UT; Ut.** □□ **U·tah·an** /yoo͝ótáaən, –táwən, yoo͝ótaan, –tawn/ *n. & adj.*

U·trecht /oo͝ótrekt, yoo͝ó–/ *n.* city in the central Netherlands. Pop. 235,400.

Uz·bek·i·stan /oo͝ozbékistaan, –stan/ *n.* republic in S central Asia; formerly part of the USSR. Pop. 23,418,000. Capital: Tashkent. □□ **Uz′bek** *n.*

Uzbekistan

Va·duz /faadoo͝óts/ *n.* capital of Liechtenstein, in the W part. Pop. 5,100.

Va·len·ci·a /vaalénseeə, –thyaa/ *n.* **1** port city in E Spain. Pop. 752,900. **2** city in N Venezuela. Pop. 903,100.

Va·lla·do·lid /valədəlíd, –leéd/ *n.* city in NW central Spain. Pop. 336,900.

Val·le·jo /vəláyō/ *n.* city in central California. Pop. 109,199.

Val·let·ta /vəlétə/ *n.* port city and capital of Malta. Pop. 9,100.

Val·pa·raí·so /valpərízō/ *n.* port city in central Chile. Pop. 282,200.

Van·cou·ver /vankoo͝óvər/ *n.* **1** island in SW Canada, off the SW coast of British Columbia. **2** port city in S British Columbia. Pop. 471,800.

Va·nu·a·tu /vaánəwaátoo͝ó, vaányə–/ *n.* island republic in the Pacific, NE of Australia. Pop. 178,000. Capital: Port-Vila.

Vanuatu

Va·ra·na·si /vəraánəsee/ *n.* (formerly **Benares**) city in NE India. Pop. 929,300.

Var·na /vaárnə/ *n.* port city in E Bulgaria. Pop. 301,400.

Vat·i·can Cit·y /vátikən/ *n.* independent seat of the Roman Catholic Church, within the city of Rome, Italy.

Ve·ne·zia /vənétseeə/ *n.* see VENICE.

Ven·e·zue·la /venəzəwáylə, –zwáylə/ *n.* republic in N South America. Pop. 21,983,000. Capital: Caracas. □□ **Ven·e·zue′lan** *n. & adj.*

Venezuela

Ven·ice /vénis/ *n.* (Italian name **Ve·ne·zia** /vənétseeə/) port city in NE Italy. Pop. 306,400. □□ **Ve·ne·tian** /neéshən/ *n. & adj.*

Ven·tu·ra /ventyoo͝órə, –choo͝ór–/ *n.* See SAN BUENAVENTURA.

Ve·ra·cruz /verəkroo͝ós, –kroo͝óz/ *n.* **1** state in E central Mexico. Pop. 6,228,200. Capital: Jalapa. **2** port city in E Veracruz, Mexico. Pop. 438,800.

Ver·mont /vərmaánt/ *n.* state in NE U.S. Pop. 562,758. Capital: Montpelier. Abbr. **VT; Vt.** □□ **Ver·mont′er** *n.*

Ve·ro·na /vərónə/ *n.* city in N Italy. Pop. 256,800.

Ve·su·vi·us /vəsoo͝óveeəs/ *n.* active volcano near Naples, Italy.

Vic·to·ri·a /viktáwreeə/ *n.* **1** capital of British Columbia, Canada, on Vancouver Island. Pop. 71,200. **2** state in SE Australia. Pop. 3,832,400. Capital: Melbourne. **3** port city and capital of Seychelles. Pop. 25,000.

Vic·to·ri·a, Lake *n.* freshwater lake in E central Africa; main source of the Nile River.

Vic·to·ri·a Falls *n.* waterfall in S Africa, on the Zambezi River: 420 ft. high.

Vi·en·na /vee-énə/ *n.* capital of Austria, in the NE part. Pop. 1,533,200. □□ **Vi·en·nese** /veeoneéz/ *n. & adj.*

Vien·tiane /vyentyaán/ *n.* capital of Laos, in the NW part. Pop. 178,200.

Vi·et·nam /vee-étnaám, veeət–, –nám/ *n.* republic in SE Asia, on the S China Sea. Pop. 73,977,000. Capital: Hanoi.

Vietnam

Vi·go /veégō/ *n.* port city in NW Spain. Pop. 288,600.

Vi·la /veélə/ *n.* see PORT-VILA.

Vi·lla·her·mo·sa /veeyə-ermósə, veelyə–/ *n.* capital of Tabasco, Mexico, in the S central part. Pop. 261,200.

See page xx for the **Key to Pronunciation**.

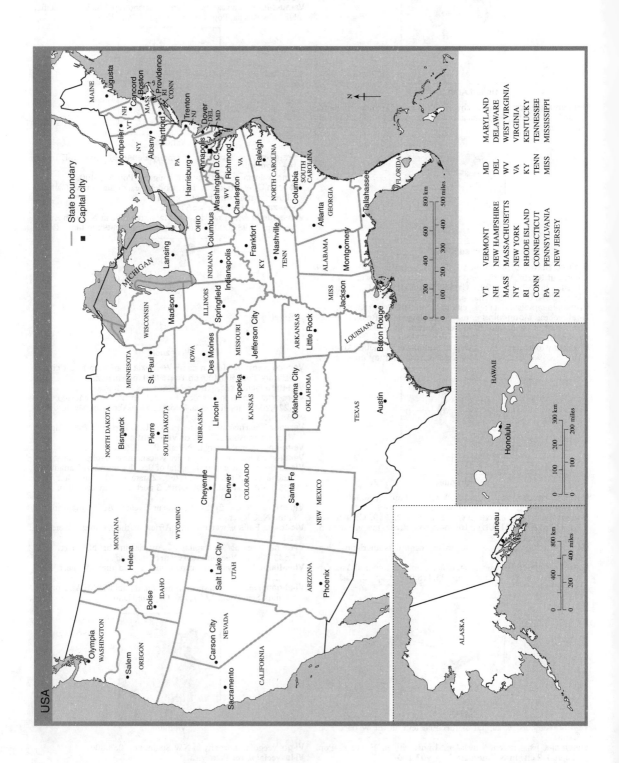

Vil·ni·us /vílneeəs/ *n.* capital of Lithuania, in the SE part. Pop. 590,100.

Vir·gin·ia /vərjínyə/ *n.* state in E U.S. Pop. 6,187,358. Capital: Richmond. Abbr. **VA; Va.** □□ **Vir·gin′ian** *n. & adj.*

Vir·gin·ia Beach *n.* city in SE Virginia. Pop. 393,069.

Vir·gin /vərjin/ **Is·lands of the U·nit·ed States** *n.* island group in the E West Indies; U.S. possession. Pop. 101,800. Capital: Charlotte Amalie.

Virgin Islands of the United States

Vi·sa·kha·pat·nam /visaakəpátnəm/ *n.* port city in E India. Pop. 752,000.

Vla·di·kav·kaz /vlaadəkaáfkaaz/ *n.* city in S Russia. Pop. 325,000.

Vla·di·vos·tok /vladivaástaak, –vəstaák/ *n.* port city in SE Russia. Pop. 632,000.

Vol·ga /vaálgə, váwl–, vól–/ **Riv·er** *n.* river in E Europe, flowing 2,320 mi. from W Russia to the Caspian Sea; longest river in Europe.

Vol·go·grad /vaálgəgrad, vól–/ *n.* (formerly **Stalingrad**) city in SW Russia. Pop. 1,003,000.

Vo·ro·shi·lov·grad /vərawsheélfgraad/ *n.* see LUGANSK.

Wa·bash /wáwbash/ **Riv·er** *n.* river in central U.S., flowing 475 mi. from W Ohio through Indiana and into the Ohio River; forms S Indiana-Illinois border.

Wa·co /wáykō/ *n.* city in central Texas. Pop. 103,590.

Wales /waylz/ *n.* division of the United Kingdom, W of England. Capital: Cardiff. Pop. 2,719,200. ¶ See note at GREAT BRITAIN.

War·ren /wáwrən, waár–/ *n.* city in SE Michigan. Pop. 144,864.

War·saw /wáwrsaw/ *n.* capital of Poland, in the E central part. Pop. 1,640,700.

Wash·ing·ton /waáshingtən, wáwsh–/ *n.* state in NW U.S. Pop. 4,866,692. Capital: Olympia. Abbr. **WA; Wash.** □□ **Wash·ing·ton·i·an** /–tŏneeən/ *n. & adj.*

Wash·ing·ton, D.C. *n.* capital of the U.S.; coextensive with the District of Columbia, between Virginia and Maryland. Pop. 606,900.

Wash·ing·ton, Mount *n.* mountain in the White Mountains in N New Hampshire; highest peak in NE U.S.: 6,288 ft.

Wa·ter·bur·y /wáwtərberee, waát–/ *n.* city in W Connecticut. Pop. 108,961.

Wed·dell /wədél, wéd'l/ **Sea** *n.* arm of the Atlantic, E of the Antarctic Peninsula.

Wel·ling·ton *n.* /wélingtən/ *n.* capital of New Zealand, on S North Island. Pop. 158,600.

West Bank *n.* disputed area in the Middle East, W of the Jordan River and the Dead Sea. Pop. 1,428,000.

West·ern Aus·tral·ia *n.* state in W Australia. Pop. 1,273,600. Capital: Perth.

West·ern Sa·mo·a /səmóə/ *n.* island country in the S Pacific, comprising the W islands of Samoa. Pop. 214,000. Capital: Apia. See also AMERICAN SAMOA. □□ **Sa·mo′an** *n. & adj.*

Western Samoa

West Ger·man·y /júrmənee/ *n.* (also called **Federal Republic of Germany**) German state created in 1949, under parliamentary government; unified with East Germany in 1990.

West In·dies /índeez/ *n.* island group off the E coast of North and South America, between the Atlantic and the Caribbean Sea; includes the Greater Antilles, the Lesser Antilles, and the Bahamas.

West Palm /paam, paw(l)m/ **Beach** *n.* city in SE Florida. Pop. 67,643.

West Vir·gin·ia /vərjínyə/ *n.* state in E central U.S. Pop. 1,793,477. Capital: Charleston. Abbr. **WV; W. Va.** □□ **West Vir·gin′ian** *n. & adj.*

Whee·ling /weéling, hweé–/ *n.* city in N West Virginia. Pop. 148,641.

White·horse /wít-hawrs, hwít–/ *n.* capital of Yukon Territory, Canada, in the S part. Pop. 17,900.

White /wīt/ **Moun·tains** *n.* mountain range in N New Hampshire; part of the Appalachian range. Highest peak: Mount Washington.

Whit·ney /wítnee, hwit–/ **Mount** *n.* mountain in the Sierra Nevada range, in central California; highest peak in conterminous U.S.: 14,495 ft.

Whit·ti·er /wíteeər, hwítee–/ *n.* city in SW California. Pop. 77,671.

Wich·i·ta /wíchətaw, –taa/ *n.* city in S central Kansas. Pop. 304,011.

Wies·ba·den /veésbaad'n/ *n.* city in W Germany. Pop. 266,100.

Wight /wīt/, **Isle of** *n.* island in S England, in the English Channel.

Wil·ming·ton /wílmingtən/ *n.* city in N Delaware. Pop. 71,529.

Wind·hoek /vínthook/ *n.* capital of Namibia, in the central part. Pop. 161,000.

Wind·sor /wínzər/ *n.* city in S Ontario, Canada. Pop. 191,400.

Wind·ward /wíndwərd/ **Is·lands** island group in the E West Indies, extending from Grenada N to Martinique.

Win·ni·peg /wínipeg/ *n.* capital of Manitoba, Canada, in the S part. Pop. 616,800.

Win·ston-Sa·lem /wínstən sáyləm/ *n.* city in N central North Carolina. Pop. 143,485.

Wis·con·sin /wiskaánsən/ *n.* state in N central U.S. Pop. 4,891,769. Capital: Madison. Abbr. **WI; Wis.** □□ **Wis·con′sin·ite** *n.*

Wol·ver·hamp·ton /woólvərhamptən, –vəramptən, –amtən/ *n.* city in W England. Pop. 245,100.

Worces·ter /woòstər/ *n.* city in central Massachusetts. Pop. 169,759.

Wroc·law /vráwtslaaf/ *n.* city in SW Poland. Pop. 642,900.

Wu·han /woōhaán/ *n.* city in E China. Pop. 3,750,000.

Wup·per·tal /voŏpərtaal/ *n.* city in W Germany. Pop. 383,800.

Wy·o·ming /wīóming/ *n.* state in W U.S. Pop. 453,588. Capital: Cheyenne. Abbr. **WY; Wyo.** □□ **Wy·o′ming·ite** *n.*

Xi·an /sheéaán/ *n.* (also **Si·an**) city in central China. Pop. 2,760,000.

Ya·mous·sou·kro /yaamoŏsoōkrō/ *n.* capital of Ivory Coast, in the S central part. Pop. 106,800.

Yan·gon /yaángoōn/ *n.* see RANGOON.

Yang·tze /yangtseé, –seé/ **Riv·er** *n.* see CHANG.

Ya·oun·dé /yowndáy/ *n.* capital of Cameroon, in the S part. Pop. 800,000.

Ya·ren /yaárən/ *n.* district in SW Nauru; seat of government. Pop. 600.

Ye·ka·te·rin·burg /yikaátərinboórg/ *n.* see SVERDLOVSK.

Yel·low·knife /yélōnif/ *n.* capital of Northwest Territories, Canada, in the S part. Pop. 15,200.

Yel·low /yélō/ **Riv·er** *n.* see HUANG RIVER.

Yel·low Sea *n.* arm of the N Pacific, between Korea and China.

Yel·low·stone /yéləstōn/ **Falls** *n.* waterfall of the Yellowstone River, in NW Wyoming.

Yem·en /yémən, yáymən/ *n.* republic on the SW Arabian Peninsula. Capitals: Aden; Sanaa. Pop. 13,483,000. □□ **Yem′en·ite, Yem′en·i** *n. & adj.*

Yemen

Ye·re·van /yerəvaán/ *n.* capital of Armenia, in the W part. Pop. 1,226,000.

Ye·zo /yeézaw/ *n.* see HOKKAIDO.

Yo·ko·ha·ma /yōkəhaámə/ *n.* port city in Japan, on Honshu. Pop. 3,307,400.

Yo·ko·su·ka /yōkəsoŏkə/ *n.* port city in Japan, on Honshu. Pop. 432,200.

Yon·kers /yaángkərz/ *n.* city in SE New York. Pop. 188,082.

York /yawrk/ *n.* **1** city in NE England. Pop. 104,000. **2** city in SE Ontario, Canada. Pop. 140,500.

York·town /yáwrktown/ *n.* village in E Virginia; site of British surrender to Washington (1781).

Yo·sem·i·te /yōsémitee/ **Na·tion·al Park** *n.* scenic mountain region in E California.

Youngs·town /yóngstown/ *n.* city in NE Ohio. Pop. 95,732.

Yu·ca·tán /yoōkətán, –taán/ *n.* state in SE Mexico. Pop. 1,362,900. Capital: Mérida.

See page xx for the **Key to Pronunciation.**

Yu·go·sla·vi·a /yōōgōslaáveeə/ *n.* federation (1918–92) in SE Europe that included Serbia, Croatia, Bosnia and Herzegovina, Montenegro, Macedonia, and Slovenia.

Yu·kon /yoókaan/ **Riv·er** *n.* river in NW North America, flowing 2,000 mi. from Yukon Territory, Canada, through Alaska and into the Bering Sea.

Yu·kon Ter·ri·to·ry *n.* territory in NW Canada, bordering Alaska. Pop. 32,000. Capital: Whitehorse.

Za·ca·te·cas /zaakətáykəs/ *n.* state in N central Mexico. Pop. 1,276,300. Capital: Zacatecas.

Za·greb /záagreb/ *n.* capital of Croatia, in the N part. Pop. 867,700.

Za·ire /zaa-ée r/ *n.* see CONGO 1.

Zam·be·zi /zambeéezee/ **Riv·er** *n.* river in S Africa, flowing 1,650 mi. from NW Zambia to the Indian Ocean.

Zam·bi·a /zámbeeə/ *n.* republic in S central Africa. Pop. 9,159,000. Capital: Lusaka. □□ **Zam′bi·an** *n. & adj.*

Zan·zi·bar /zánzibaar/ *n.* island in the Indian Ocean, off the E coast of Tanzania; part of Tanzania.

Za·ra·go·za /saaraagáwsaa/ *n.* see SARAGOSSA.

Zhdan·ov /zhdaánəf/ *n.* see MARIUPOL.

Zim·bab·we /zimbaábway/ *n.* republic in S central Africa. Pop. 11,271,000. Capital: Harare.

Zom·ba /záambə/ *n.* legislative capital of Malawi, in the S part. Pop. 62,700.

Zu·rich /zoórik/ *n.* city in N Switzerland. Pop. 342,900.

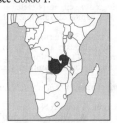

Zambia

Zimbabwe

Ready Reference Contents

STANDARD
WEIGHTS AND MEASURES
WITH METRIC EQUIVALENTS

Linear Measure

1 inch	= 2.54 centimeters
1 foot = 12 inches	= 0.3048 meter
1 yard = 3 feet	= 0.9144 meter = 36 inches
1 (statute) mile = 1,760 yards	= 1.609 kilometers
= 5,280 feet	

Square Measure

1 sq. inch	= 6.45 sq. centimeters
1 sq. foot = 144 sq. inches	= 9.29 sq. decimeters
1 sq. yard = 9 sq. feet	= 0.836 sq. meter
1 acre = 4,840 sq. yards	= 0.405 hectare
1 sq. mile = 640 acres	= 259 hectares

Cubic Measure

1 cu. inch	= 16.4 cu. centimeters
1 cu. foot = 1,728 cu. inches	= 0.0283 cu. meter
1 cu. yard = 27 cu. feet	= 0.765 cu. meter

Capacity Measure

DRY MEASURE

1 pint 33.60 cu. inches	= 0.550 liter
1 quart = 2 pints	= 1.101 liters
1 peck = 8 quarts	= 8.81 liters
1 bushel = 4 pecks	= 35.3 liters

LIQUID MEASURE

1 fluid ounce	= 29.573 milliliters
1 gill = 4 fluid ounces	= 118.294 milliliters
1 pint = 16 fluid ounces	= 0.473 liter = 28.88 cu. inches
1 quart = 2 pints	= 0.946 liter
1 gallon = 4 quarts	= 3.785 liters

Avoirdupois Weight

1 grain	= 0.065 gram
1 dram	= 1.772 grams
1 ounce = 16 drams	= 28.35 grams
1 pound = 16 ounces	= 0.4536 kilograms
= 7,000 grains	(0.45359237 exactly)
1 stone (British) = 14 pounds	= 6.35 kilograms
1 ton	= 2,000 pounds
1 hundred weight (US)	= 100 pounds
20 hundredweight (US)	= 2,000 pounds

CONVERSION FROM STANDARD TO METRIC MEASUREMENTS

Standard	Multiply By	To Get Metric
Length:		
inches	2.5	centimeters
feet	30	centimeters
yards	0.9	meters
miles	1.6	kilometers
Area:		
square inches	6.5	square centimeters
square feet	0.09	square meters
square yards	0.8	square meters
square miles	2.6	square kilometers
acres	0.4	hectares
Weight:		
ounces	28	grams
pounds	0.45	kilograms
short tons	0.9	metric tons
Volume:		
teaspoons	5	milliliters
tablespoons	15	milliliters
cubic inches	16	milliliters
fluid ounces	30	milliliters
cups	0.24	liters
pints	0.47	liters
quarts	0.95	liters
gallons	3.8	liters
cubic feet	0.03	cubic meters
cubic yards	0.76	cubic meters
Temperature:		
degrees Fahrenheit	subtract 32, then multiply by 5/9	degrees Celsius

METRIC WEIGHTS AND MEASURES WITH STANDARD EQUIVALENTS

Linear Measure

1 millimeter (mm)	= 0.039 inch
1 centimeter (cm) 10 millimeters	= 0.394 inch
1 decimeter (dm) 10 centimeters	= 3.94 inches
1 meter (m) 10 decimeters	= 1.094 yards
1 decameter 10 meters	= 10.94 yards
1 hectometer 100 meters	= 109.4 yards
1 kilometer (km) 1,000 meters	= 0.6214 mile

Square Measure

1 sq. centimeter	= 0.155 sq. inch
1 sq. meter 10,000 sq. centimeters	= 1.196 sq. yards
1 are 100 sq. meters	= 119.6 sq. yards
1 hectare 100 ares	= 2.471 acres
1 sq. kilometer 100 hectares	= 0.386 sq. mile

Cubic Measure

1 cu. centimeter	= 0.061 cu. inch
1 cu. meter 1,000,000 cu. centimeters	= 1.308 cu. yards

Capacity Measure

1 milliliter (ml)	= 0.034 fluid ounce
1 centiliter (cl) 10 milliliters	= 0.34 fluid ounce
1 deciliter (dl) 10 centiliters	= 3.38 fluid ounces
1 liter (l) 10 deciliters	= 1.06 quarts
1 decaliter 10 liters	= 2.20 gallons
1 hectoliter 100 liters	= 2.75 bushels

Weight

1 milligram (mg)	= 0.015 grain
1 centigram 10 milligrams	= 0.154 grain
1 decigram (dg) 10 centigrams	= 1.543 grains
1 gram (g) 10 decigrams	= 15.43 grains
1 decagram 10 grams	= 5.64 drams
1 hectogram 100 grams	= 3.527 ounces
1 kilogram (kg) 1,000 grams	= 2.205 pounds
1 ton (metric ton) 1,000 kilograms	= 0.984 (long) ton

CONVERSION FROM METRIC TO STANDARD MEASUREMENTS

Metric	Multiply By	To Get Standard
Length:		
millimeters	0.04	inches
centimeters	0.4	inches
meters	3.3	feet
meters	1.1	yards
kilometers	0.6	miles
Area:		
square centimeters	0.16	square inches
square meters	1.2	square yards
square kilometers	0.4	square miles
hectares	2.5	acres
Weight:		
grams	0.035	ounces
kilograms	2.2	pounds
metric tons	1.1	short tons
Volume:		
milliliters	0.03	fluid ounces
milliliters	0.06	cubic inches
liters	2.1	pints
liters	1.06	quarts
liters	0.26	gallons
cubic meters	35	cubic feet
cubic meters	1.3	cubic yards
Temperature:		
degrees Celsius	9/5, then add 32	degrees Fahrenheit

Mathematical Notation

Mathematical Power	Name	Prefix (symbol)
10^{18} or 1,000,000,000,000,000,000	one quintillion	exa- (E)
10^{15} or 1,000,000,000,000,000	one quadrillion	peta- (P)
10^{12} or 1,000,000,000,000	one trillion	tera- (T)
10^9 or 1,000,000,000	one billion	giga- (G)
10^6 or 1,000,000	one million	mega- (M)
10^3 or 1,000	one thousand	kilo- (K, k)
10^2 or 100	one hundred	hecto- (H, h)
10^1 or 10	ten	—
1	one	—
10^{-1} or 0.1	one tenth	deci- (d)
10^{-2} or 0.01	one hundredth	centi- (c)
10^{-3} or 0.001	one thousandth	milli- (m)
10^{-6} or 0.000 001	one millionth	micro- (µ)
10^{-9} or 0.000 000 001	one billionth	nano- (n)
10^{-12} or 0.000 000 000 001	one trillionth	pico- (p)
10^{-15} or 0.000 000 000 000 001	one quadrillionth	femto- (f)
10^{-18} or 0.000 000 000 000 000 001	one quintillionth	atto- (a)

Multiplication Tables

x	1	2	3	4	5	6	7	8	9	10	11	12
1	1	2	3	4	5	6	7	8	9	10	11	12
2	2	4	6	8	10	12	14	16	18	20	22	24
3	3	6	9	12	15	18	21	24	27	30	33	36
4	4	8	12	16	20	24	28	32	36	40	44	48
5	5	10	15	20	25	30	35	40	45	50	55	60
6	6	12	18	24	30	36	42	48	54	60	66	72
7	7	14	21	28	35	42	49	56	63	70	77	84
8	8	16	24	32	40	48	56	64	72	80	88	96
9	9	18	27	36	45	54	63	72	81	90	99	108
10	10	20	30	40	50	60	70	80	90	100	110	120
11	11	22	33	44	55	66	77	88	99	110	121	132
12	12	24	36	48	60	72	84	96	108	120	132	144

Multiplication Tables

×12				×13				×14		
1	12	13	156	1	13	13	169	1	14	13	182
2	24	14	168	2	26	14	182	2	28	14	196
3	36	15	180	3	39	15	195	3	42	15	210
4	48	16	192	4	52	16	208	4	56	16	224
5	60	17	204	5	65	17	221	5	70	17	238
6	72	18	216	6	78	18	238	6	84	18	252
7	84	19	228	7	91	19	247	7	98	19	266
8	96	25	300	8	104	25	325	8	112	25	350
9	108	35	420	9	117	35	455	9	126	35	490
10	120	45	540	10	130	45	585	10	140	45	630
11	132	55	660	11	143	55	715	11	154	55	770
12	144	65	780	12	156	65	845	12	168	65	910
		75	900			75	975			75	1050
		85	1020			85	1105			85	1190
		95	1140			95	1235			95	1330

×15		×16		×17		×18		×19	
1	15	1	16	1	17	1	18	1	19
2	30	2	32	2	34	2	36	2	38
3	45	3	48	3	51	3	54	3	57
4	60	4	64	4	68	4	72	4	76
5	75	5	80	5	85	5	90	5	95
6	90	6	96	6	102	6	108	6	114
7	105	7	112	7	119	7	126	7	133
8	120	8	128	8	136	8	144	8	152
9	135	9	144	9	153	9	162	9	171
10	150	10	160	10	170	10	180	10	190
11	165	11	176	11	187	11	198	11	209
12	180	12	192	12	204	12	216	12	228
13	195	13	208	13	221	13	234	13	247
14	210	14	224	14	238	14	252	14	266
15	225	15	240	15	255	15	270	15	285
16	240	16	256	16	272	16	288	16	304
17	255	17	272	17	289	17	306	17	323
18	270	18	288	18	306	18	324	18	342
19	285	19	304	19	323	19	342	19	361
25	375	25	400	25	425	25	450	25	475
35	525	35	560	35	595	35	630	35	665
45	675	45	720	45	765	45	810	45	855
55	825	55	880	55	935	55	990	55	1045
65	975	65	1040	65	1105	65	1170	65	1235
75	1125	75	1200	75	1275	75	1350	75	1425
85	1275	85	1360	85	1445	85	1530	85	1615
95	1425	95	1520	95	1615	95	1710	95	1805

Temperature

Fahrenheit: Water boils (under standard conditions) at 212° and freezes at 32°.

Celsius or Centigrade: Water boils at 100° and freezes at 0°.

Kelvin: Water boils at 373.15 K and freezes at 273.15 K.

Celsius	Fahrenheit	Fahrenheit	Celsius
−17.8°	0°	0°	−17.8°
−10°	14°	10°	−12.2°
0°	32°	20°	−6.6°
10°	50°	32°	0.0°
20°	68°	40°	3.5°
30°	86°	50°	10.0°
40°	104°	60°	15.5°
50°	122°	70°	21.1°
60°	140°	80°	26.6°
70°	158°	90°	32.2°
80°	176°	100°	37.6°
90°	194°	212°	100.0°
100°	212°		

To convert Celsius into Fahrenheit: multiply by 9, divide by 5, and add 32.

To convert Fahrenheit into Celcius: subtract 32, multiply by 5, and divide by 9.

Wind Chill Temperatures

The chart below illustrates the effect of wind speed on perceived air temperature. "Wind chill," or the perceived feeling of coldness of the air, increases with higher wind speed.

Air temperature (°F)	Wind speed in miles per hour								
	0	5	10	15	20	25	30	35	40
	Equivalent wind chill temperatures								
35	35	32	22	16	12	8	6	4	3
30	30	27	16	9	4	1	−2	−4	−5
25	25	22	10	2	−3	−7	−10	−12	−13
20	20	16	3	−5	−10	−15	−18	−20	−21
15	15	11	−3	−11	−17	−22	−25	−27	−29
10	10	6	−9	−18	−24	−29	−33	−35	−37
5	5	0	−15	−25	−31	−36	−41	−43	−45
0	0	−5	−22	−31	−39	−44	−49	−52	−53
−5	−5	−10	−27	−38	−46	−51	−56	−58	−60
−10	−10	−15	−34	−45	−53	−59	−64	−67	−69
−15	−15	−21	−40	−51	−60	−66	−71	−74	−76
−20	−20	−26	−46	−58	−67	−74	−79	−82	−84
−25	−25	−31	−52	−65	−74	−81	−86	−89	−92

Heat Index

As humidity increases, the air at a given temperature feels warmer. The combination of heat and high humidity reduces the body's natural ability to cool itself. For example, when the actual temperature is 85 degrees Fahrenheit with a relative humidity of 80 percent, the air feels like dry air at 97 degrees.

Humidity (%)	Temperature (°F)										
	70	75	80	85	90	95	100	105	110	115	120
	Equivalent Temperature (°F)										
0	64	69	73	78	83	87	91	95	99	103	107
10	65	70	75	80	85	90	95	100	105	111	116
20	66	72	77	82	87	93	99	105	112	120	130
30	67	73	78	84	90	96	104	113	123	120	148
40	68	74	79	86	93	101	110	123	137	135	
50	69	75	81	88	96	107	120	135	150		
60	70	76	82	90	100	114	132	149			
70	70	77	85	93	106	124	144				
80	71	78	86	97	113	136					
90	71	79	88	102	122						
100	72	80	91	108							

CHEMICAL ELEMENTS

Element	Symbol	Atomic Number	Element	Symbol	Atomic Number
actinium	Ac	89	neptunium	Np	93
aluminum	Al	13	nickel	Ni	28
americium	Am	95	nielsbohrium*	Ns	107
antimony	Sb	51	niobium	Nb	41
argon	Ar	18	nitrogen	N	7
arsenic	As	33	nobelium	No	102
astatine	At	85	osmium	Os	76
barium	Ba	56	oxygen	O	8
berkelium	Bk	97	palladium	Pd	46
beryllium	Be	4	phosphorus	P	15
bismuth	Bi	83	platinum	Pt	78
boron	B	5	plutonium	Pu	94
bromine	Br	35	polonium	Po	84
cadmium	Cd	48	potassium	K	19
calcium	Ca	20	praseodymium	Pr	59
californium	Cf	98	promethium	Pm	61
carbon	C	6	protactinium	Pa	91
cerium	Ce	58	radium	Ra	88
cesium	Cs	55	radon	Rn	86
chlorine	Cl	17	rhenium	Re	75
chromium	Cr	24	rhodium	Rh	45
cobalt	Co	27	rubidium	Rb	37
copper	Cu	29	ruthenium	Ru	44
curium	Cm	96	rutherfordium*	Rf	104
dysprosium	Dy	66	samarium	Sm	62
einsteinium	Es	99	scandium	Sc	21
erbium	Er	68	seaborgium*	Sg	106
europium	Eu	63	selenium	Se	34
fermium	Fm	100	silicon	Si	14
fluorine	F	9	silver	Ag	47
francium	Fr	87	sodium	Na	11
gadolinium	Gd	64	strontium	Sr	38
gallium	Ga	31	sulfur	S	16
germanium	Ge	32	tantalum	Ta	73
gold	Au	79	technetium	Tc	43
hafnium	Hf	72	tellurium	Te	52
hahnium*	Ha	105	terbium	Tb	65
hassium*	Hs	108	thallium	Tl	81
helium	He	2	thorium	Th	90
holmium	Ho	67	thulium	Tm	69
hydrogen	H	1	tin	Sn	50
indium	In	49	titanium	Ti	22
iodine	I	53	tungsten (wolfram)	W	74
iridium	Ir	77	uranium	U	92
iron	Fe	26	vanadium	V	23
krypton	Kr	36	xenon	Xe	54
lanthanum	La	57	ytterbium	Yb	70
lawrencium	Lr	103	yttrium	Y	39
lead	Pb	82	zinc	Zn	30
lithium	Li	3	zirconium	Zr	40
lutetium	Lu	71			
magnesium	Mg	12			
manganese	Mn	25			
meitnerium*	Mt	109			
mendelevium	Md	101			
mercury	Hg	80			
molybdenum	Mo	42			
neodymium	Nd	60			
neon	Ne	10			

*Names formed systematically based on atomic numbers are preferred by the International Union of Pure and Applied Chemistry (IUPAC) for numbers from 104 onward. These names are formed on the numerical roots *nil* (= 0), *un* (= 1), *bi* (= 2), etc. (e.g., *unnilquadium* = 104, *unnilpentium* = 105, *unnilhexium* = 106, *unnilseptium* = 107, *unniloctium* = 108, *unnilnovium* = 109, etc.).

SIGNS AND SYMBOLS

General

&	and
&c.	et cetera (and so forth)
©	copyright(ed)
®	registered; of a trademark or service mark
†	death; died
℞	take (Latin *recipe*); used on prescriptions
#	1. number (before a figure)
	2. pound(s) (after a figure)
	3. space (in printing)
×	by, as in *an 8' × 12" room*
w/	with
w/o	without
§	section (of a text)
"	ditto marks; repeat the word or sign located in the line above
☠	poison
☢	radioactive; radiation

Science and Mathematics

♂	male
♀	female
+	1. plus
	2. positive (number or charge)
−	1. minus
	2. negative (number or charge)
±	plus or minus
× or · or ⋆	multiplied by
÷	divided by
=	equal to
≠	not equal to
>	greater than
<	less than
≥	greater than or equal to
≤	less than or equal to
≡	identical with
≈	approximately equal to
≅	congruent to (in geometry)
:	is to; the ratio of
!	factorial of
Σ	sum
π	pi; the ratio of the circumference of a circle to its diameter (3.14159265+)
∞	infinity
∴	therefore
∵	since
∥	parallel to
⊥	perpendicular to
√	radical sign; root
°	degree
'	1. minute(s) of arc
	2. foot, feet
"	1. second(s) of arc
	2. inch(es)
∅	empty set

Commerce and Finance

$	dollar(s)
¢	cent(s)
£	pound(s) sterling (UK)
p	(new) pence (UK)
¥	yen (Japan)
@	at the rate of
%	percent
DM	Deutsche mark (Germany)
F	franc (France)

Proofreading Marks

¶	new paragraph
∧	insert here (caret mark)
ℐ	delete
◠	close up space
ℛ	delete and close up
#	leave space
=	insert hyphen
tr	transpose

Signs of the Zodiac

Spring

♈	Aries, the Ram
♉	Taurus, the Bull
♊	Gemini, the Twins

Summer

♋	Cancer, the Crab
♌	Leo, the Lion
♍	Virgo, the Virgin

Autumn

♎	Libra, the Balance
♏	Scorpio, the Scorpion
♐	Sagittarius, the Archer

Winter

♑	Capricorn, the Goat
♒	Aquarius, the Water Bearer
♓	Pisces, the Fishes

Diacritical Marks
(to distinguish sounds or values of letters)

´	acute (as in the French word *née*)
`	grave (as in the French word *père*)
~	tilde (as in the Spanish word *piñata*)
^	circumflex (as in the word *fête*
¯	macron (as used in pronunciation: *āge, īce*)
˘	breve (as used in pronunciation: *tăp, rĭp*)
¨	dieresis (as in the word *naïve*)
¸	cedilla (as in the word *façade*)

Alphabets

Braille

A B C D E

F G H I J

K L M N O

P Q R S T

U V W X Y

Z and for of the

Morse code

A ·— B —··· C —·—· D —·· E ·

F ··—· G ——· H ···· I ··

J ·——— K —·— L ·—·· M —— N —·

O ——— P ·——· Q ——·— R ·—·

S ··· T — U ··— V ···— W ·——

X —··— Y —·—— Z ——··

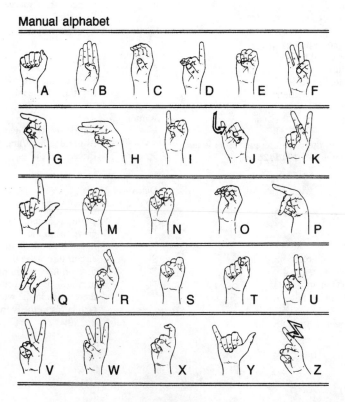

Manual alphabet

A B C D E F
G H I J K
L M N O P
Q R S T U
V W X Y Z

Arabic

Forms	Name	Translit.
ا ا	'alif	'
ب ب بـ بـ	bā'	b
ت ت تـ تـ	tā'	t
ث ث ثـ ثـ	thā'	th
ج ج جـ جـ	jīm	j
ح ح حـ حـ	ḥā'	ḥ
خ خ خـ خـ	khā'	kh
د د	dāl	d
ذ ذ	dhāl	dh
ر ر	rā'	r
ز ز	zay	z
س س سـ سـ	sīn	s
ش ش شـ شـ	shīn	sh
ص ص صـ صـ	ṣād	ṣ
ض ض ضـ ضـ	ḍād	ḍ
ط ط طـ طـ	ṭā'	ṭ
ظ ظ ظـ ظـ	ẓā'	ẓ
ع ع عـ عـ	'ayn	'
غ غ غـ غـ	ghayn	gh
ف ف فـ فـ	fā'	f
ق ق قـ قـ	qāf	q
ك ك كـ كـ	kāf	k
ل ل لـ لـ	lām	l
م م مـ مـ	mīm	m
ن ن نـ نـ	nūn	n
ه ه هـ هـ	hā'	h
و و	wāw	w
ي ي يـ يـ	yā'	y

Hebrew

Letter	Name	Translit.
א	aleph	'
ב	beth	b, bh
ג	gimel	g, gh
ד	daleth	d, dh
ה	he	h
ו	waw	w
ז	zayin	z
ח	ḥeth	ḥ
ט	ṭeth	ṭ
י	yodh	y
כ ך	kaph	k, kh
ל	lamedh	l
מ ם	mem	m
נ ן	nun	n
ס	samekh	s
ע	'ayin	'
פ ף	pe	p, ph
צ ץ	ṣadhe	ṣ
ק	qoph	q
ר	resh	r
שׂ	śin	ś
שׁ	shin	sh
ת	taw	t, th

Greek

Letter	Name	Translit.
$A\ \alpha$	alpha	a
$B\ \beta$	beta	b
$\Gamma\ \gamma$	gamma	g
$\Delta\ \delta$	delta	d
$E\ \epsilon$	epsilon	e
$Z\ \zeta$	zeta	z
$H\ \eta$	eta	ē
$\Theta\ \theta$	theta	th
$I\ \iota$	iota	i
$K\ \kappa$	kappa	k
$\Lambda\ \lambda$	lambda	l
$M\ \mu$	mu	m
$N\ \nu$	nu	n
$\Xi\ \xi$	xi	x
$O\ o$	omicron	o
$\Pi\ \pi$	pi	p
$P\ \rho$	rho	r, rh
$\Sigma\ \sigma\ \varsigma$	sigma	s
$T\ \tau$	tau	t
$\Upsilon\ \upsilon$	upsilon	u
$\Phi\ \phi$	phi	ph
$X\ \chi$	chi	kh
$\Psi\ \psi$	psi	ps
$\Omega\ \omega$	omega	ō

Russian

Letter	Translit.
А а	a
Б б	b
В в	v
Г г	g
Д д	d
Е е	e
Ё ё	ё
Ж ж	zh
З з	z
И и	i
Й й	ĭ
К к	k
Л л	l
М м	m
Н н	n
О о	o
П п	p
Р р	r
С с	s
Т т	t
У у	u
Ф ф	f
Х х	kh
Ц ц	ts
Ч ч	ch
Ш ш	sh
Щ щ	shch
Ъ ъ	" ('hard sign')
Ы ы	y
Ь ь	' ('soft sign')
Э э	é
Ю ю	yu
Я я	ya

Time Periods

Name	Period
bicentennial	200 years
biennial	2 years
century	100 years
day	24 hours
decade	10 years
centennial	100 years
decennial	10 years
duodecennial	12 years
half-century	50 years
half-decade	5 years
half-millennium	500 years
hour	60 minutes
leap year	366 days
millennium	1,000 years
minute	60 seconds
month	28-31 days
novennial	9 years
octennial	8 years
olympiad	4 years
quadrennial	4 years
quadricentennial	400 years
quincentennial	500 years
quindecennial	15 years
quinquennial	5 years
semicentennial	50 years
septennial	7 years
sesquicentennial	150 years
sexennial	6 years
tricennial	30 years
triennial	3 years
undecennial	11 years
vicennial	20 years
week	7 days
year	365 days
year	12 months
year	52 weeks

Wedding Anniversary Gifts

Year	Traditional	Modern (alternative)
1st	Paper	Clocks
2nd	Cotton	China
3rd	Leather	Crystal, glass
4th	Linen (silk)	Electrical appliances
5th	Wood	Silverware
6th	Iron	Wood
7th	Wool (copper)	Desk sets
8th	Bronze	Linen, lace
9th	Pottery (china)	Leather
10th	Tin (aluminum)	Diamond, jewelry
11th	Steel	Fashion, jewelry, accessories
12th	Silk	Pearls or colored gems
13th	Lace	Textile, furs
14th	Ivory	Gold jewelry
15th	Crystal	Watches
20th	China	Platinum
25th	Silver	Sterling silver jubilee
30th	Pearl	Diamond
35th	Coral (jade)	Jade
40th	Ruby	Ruby
45th	Sapphire	Sapphire
50th	Gold	Gold
55th	Emerald	Emerald
60th	Diamond	Diamond

Terms for Groups of Animals, etc.

Terms marked † belong to 15th-c. lists of "proper terms," notably that in the *Book of St. Albans* attributed to Dame Juliana Barnes (1486). Many of these are fanciful or humorous terms which probably never had any real currency, but have been taken up by Joseph Strutt in *Sports and Pastimes of England* (1801) and by other antiquarian writers.

a †shrewdness of apes
a herd or †pace of asses
a †cete of badgers
a †sloth or †sleuth of bears
a hive of bees; a swarm, drift, or bike of bees
a flock, flight (*dial.*) parcel, pod (small flock), †fleet, or †dissimulation of (small) birds; a volary of birds in an aviary
a sounder of wild boar
a †blush of boys
a herd or gang of buffalo
a †clowder or †glaring of cats; a †dowt or †destruction of wild cats
a herd, drove, (*dial.*) drift, or (*Austral.*) mob of cattle
a brood, (*dial.*) cletch or clutch, or †peep of chickens
a †chattering or †clattering of choughs
a †drunkship of cobblers
a †rag or †rake of colts
a †hastiness of cooks
a †covert of coots
a herd of cranes
a litter of cubs
a herd of curlew
a †cowardice of curs
a herd or mob of deer
a pack or kennel of dogs
a trip of dotterel
a flight, †dole, or †piteousness of doves
a raft, bunch, or †paddling of ducks on water; a team of wild ducks in flight
a fling of dunlins
a herd of elephants
a herd or gang of elk
a †business of ferrets
a charm or †chirm of finches
a shoal of fish; a run of fish in motion
a cloud of flies
a †stalk of foresters
a †skulk of foxes
a gaggle or (in the air) a skein, team, or wedge of geese
a herd of giraffes
a flock, herd, or (*dial.*) trip of goats
a pack or covey of grouse
a †husk or †down of hares
a cast of hawks let fly
an †observance of hermits
a †siege of herons
a stud or †haras of (breeding) horses; (*dial.*) a team of horses
a kennel, pack, cry, or †mute of hounds
a flight or swarm of insects
a mob or troop of kangaroos
a kindle of kittens
a bevy of ladies
a †desert of lapwing

an †exultation or bevy of larks
a †leap of leopards
a pride of lions
a †tiding of magpies
a †sord or †sute (suit) of mallard
a richesse of martens
a †faith of merchants
a †labor of moles
a troop of monkeys
a †barren of mules
a †watch of nightingales
a †superfluity of nuns
a covey of partridges
a †muster of peacocks
a †malapertness (impertinence) of peddlers
a rookery of penguins
a head or (*dial.*) nye of pheasants
a kit of pigeons flying together
a herd of pigs
a stand, wing, or †congregation of plovers
a rush or flight of pochards
a herd, pod, or school or porpoises
a †pity of prisoners
a covey of ptarmigan
a litter of pups
a bevy or drift of quail
a string of racehorses
an †unkindness of ravens
a bevy of roes
a parliament or †building of rooks
a hill of ruffs
a herd or rookery of seals; a pod (small herd) of seals
a flock, herd, (*dial.*) drift or trip, or (*Austral.*) mob of sheep
a †dopping of sheldrake
a wisp or †walk of snipe
a †host of sparrows
a †murmuration of starlings
a flight of swallows
a game or herd of swans; a wedge of swans in the air
a herd of swine; a †sounder of tame swine, a †drift of wild swine
a †glozing (fawning) of taverners
a †spring of teal
a bunch or knob of waterfowl
a school, herd, or gam of whales; a pod (small school) of whales; a grind of bottle-nosed whales
a company or trip of widgeon
a bunch, trip or plump of wildfowl; a knob (less than 30) of wildfowl
a pack or rout of wolves
a gaggle of women (*derisive*)
a †fall of woodcock
a herd of wrens

Selected Proverbs

A

ABSENCE makes the heart grow fonder
He who is ABSENT is always in the wrong
ACCIDENTS will happen
There is no ACCOUNTING for tastes
ACTIONS speak louder than words
When ADAM delved and Eve span, who was then the gentleman?
ADVENTURES are to the adventurous
ADVERSITY makes strange bedfellows
AFTER a storm comes a calm
AFTER dinner rest a while, after supper walk a mile
ALL good things must come to an end
It takes ALL sorts to make a world
ALL things are possible with God
ALL things come to those who wait
ALL would live long, but none would be old
Good AMERICANS when they die go to Paris
ANY port in a storm
If ANYTHING can go wrong, it will
APPEARANCES are deceptive
APPETITE comes with eating
An APPLE a day keeps the doctor away
The APPLE never falls far from the tree
One bad APPLE spoils the barrel (or bunch)
April showers bring May flowers
An ARMY marches on its stomach
ART is long and life is short
ASK a silly question and you get a silly answer
ASK no questions and hear no lies

B

A BAD excuse is better than none
BAD money drives out good
BAD news travels fast
A BAD penny always turns up
A BAD workman blames his tools
A BARKING dog never bites
BE what you would seem to be
BEAR and forbear
If you can't BEAT 'em, join 'em
BEAUTY is in the eye of the beholder
BEAUTY is only skin-deep
Where BEES are, there is honey
Set a BEGGAR on horseback, and he'll ride to the Devil
BEGGARS can't be choosers
BELIEVE nothing of what you hear, and only half of what you see
All's for the BEST in the best of all possible worlds
The BEST-laid schemes of mice and men gang aft agley
The BEST of friends must part
The BEST of men are but men at best
The BEST things come in small packages
The BEST things in life are free
It is BEST to be on the safe side
BETTER be an old man's darling, than a young man's slave
BETTER be envied than pitied
BETTER safe than sorry
BETTER late than never
The BETTER the day, the better the deed
The devil you know is BETTER than the devil you don't know
It is BETTER to be born lucky than rich
It is BETTER to give than to receive
'Tis BETTER to have loved and lost, than never to have loved at all
It is BETTER to travel hopefully than to arrive
BETTER to wear out than to rust out
BEWARE Greeks bearing gifts

BIG fish eat little fish
BIG fleas have little fleas upon their back to bite them, and little fleas have lesser fleas, and so *ad infinitum*
The BIGGER they are, the harder they fall
A BIRD in the hand is worth two in the bush
BIRDS in their little nests agree
BIRDS of a feather flock together
Little BIRDS that can sing and won't sing must be made to sing
BLESSED is he who expects nothing, for he shall never be disappointed
There's none so BLIND as those who will not see
When the BLIND lead the blind, both shall fall into the ditch
You can't get BLOOD from a stone
BLOOD is thicker than water
BLOOD will have blood
BLOOD will tell
BLUE are the hills that are far away
You can't tell (*or* judge) a BOOK by its cover
If you're BORN to be hanged then you'll never be drowned
Neither a BORROWER nor a lender be
You can take the BOY out of the country but you can't take the country out of the boy
Never send a BOY to do a man's job
BOYS will be boys
None but the BRAVE deserve the fair
BRAVE men lived before Agamemnon
The BREAD never falls but on its buttered side
What's BRED in the bone will come out in the flesh
BREVITY is the soul of wit
You cannot make BRICKS without straw
Happy is the BRIDE that the sun shines on
Always a BRIDESMAID, never a bride
If it ain't BROKE, don't fix it
A BULLY is always a coward
A BURNT child dreads the fire
The BUSIEST men have the most leisure
BUSINESS before pleasure
BUY in the cheapest market and sell in the dearest
Let the BUYER beware
The BUYER has need of a hundred eyes, the seller of but one

C

CAESAR's wife must be above suspicion
He who CAN, does; he who cannot, teaches
Where the CARCASS is, there shall the eagles be gathered together
A CARPENTER is known by his chips
A CAT in gloves catches no mice
A CAT may look at a king
When the CAT's away, the mice will play
The CAT would eat fish, but would not wet her feet
It is easier to CATCH flies with honey than with vinegar
At night all CATS are gray
A CHAIN is no stronger than its weakest link
Don't CHANGE horses in mid-stream
A CHANGE is as good as a rest
CHARITY begins at home
CHARITY covers a multitude of sins
CHEATERS never prosper
Monday's CHILD is fair of face
The CHILD is the father of the man
CHILDREN and fools tell the truth
CHILDREN are certain cares, but uncertain comforts
CHILDREN should be seen and not heard
CIRCUMSTANCES alter cases
A CIVIL question deserves a civil answer

CIVILITY costs nothing
CLEANLINESS is next to godliness
Hasty CLIMBERS have sudden falls
A CLOSED mouth catches no flies
CLOTHES make the man
Every CLOUD has a silver lining
Every COCK will crow upon his own dunghill
COLD hands, warm heart
COMING events cast their shadows before
A man is known by the COMPANY he keeps
The COMPANY makes the feast
COMPARISONS are odious
He that COMPLIES against his will is of his own opinion still
CONFESS and be hanged
CONFESSION is good for the soul
CONSCIENCE makes cowards of us all
CONSTANT dropping wears away a stone
CORPORATIONS have neither bodies to be punished nor souls to be damned
COUNCILS of war never fight
Don't COUNT your chickens before they are hatched
In the COUNTRY of the blind, the one-eyed man is king
Happy is the COUNTRY which has no history
The COURSE of true love never did run smooth
Why buy a COW when milk is so cheap?
COWARDS die many times before their death
Give CREDIT where credit is due
Don't CROSS the bridge till you come to it
CROSSES are ladders that lead to heaven
Don't CRY before you're hurt
It is no use CRYING over spilled milk
What can't be CURED must be endured
CURIOSITY killed the cat
CURSES, like chickens, come home to roost
The CUSTOMER is always right
Don't CUT off your nose to spite your face
CUT your coat according to your cloth

D

They that DANCE must pay the fiddler
The DARKEST hour is just before the dawn
Let the DEAD bury the dead
DEAD men don't bite
DEAD men tell no tales
Blessed are the DEAD that the rain rains on
There's none so DEAF as those who will not hear
A DEAF husband and a blind wife are always a happy couple
DEATH is the great leveler
DEATH pays all debts
The best DEFENSE is a good offense
DELAYS are dangerous
DESPERATE diseases must have desperate remedies
The DEVIL can quote Scripture for his own ends
The DEVIL finds work for idle hands to do
Why should the DEVIL have all the best tunes?
The DEVIL is not so black as he is painted
The DEVIL's children have the Devil's luck
DEVIL take the hindmost
The DEVIL was sick, the Devil a saint would be; the Devil was well, the devil a saint was he!
DIAMOND cuts diamond
You can only DIE once
DIFFERENT strokes for different folks
The DIFFICULT is done at once, the impossible takes a little longer
DILIGENCE is the mother of good luck
Throw DIRT enough, and some will stick
DIRTY water will quench fire
DISCRETION is the better part of valor
DISTANCE lends enchantment to the view
DIVIDE and conquer

DO as I say, not as I do
DO as you would be done by
DO right and fear no man
DO not that which you would not have known
DO unto others as you would they should do unto you
DOG does not eat dog
Every DOG has his day
Every DOG is allowed one bite
A DOG that will fetch a bone will carry a bone
DOGS bark, but the caravan goes on
What's DONE cannot be undone
A DOOR must either be shut or open
Whosoever DRAWS his sword against the prince must throw the scabbard away
DREAM of a funeral and you hear of a marriage
DREAMS go by contraries
He that DRINKS beer, thinks beer
A DRIPPING June sets all in tune
You can DRIVE out Nature with a pitchfork, but she keeps on coming back
A DROWNING man will clutch at a straw

E

EAGLES don't catch flies
The EARLY bird catches the worm
The EARLY man never borrows from the late man
EARLY to bed and early to rise, makes a man healthy, wealthy and wise
EAST, west, home's best
EASY come, easy go
EASY does it
You are what you EAT
We must EAT a peck (or pound) of dirt before we die
He that would EAT the fruit must climb the tree
EAT to live, not live to eat
An EGG today is better than a hen tomorrow
Don't put all your EGGS in one basket
EMPTY sacks will never stand upright
EMPTY vessels make the most sound
The END crowns the work
The END justifies the means
ENGLAND is the paradise of women, the hell of horses, and the purgatory of servants
ENGLAND's difficulty is Ireland's opportunity
The ENGLISH are a nation of shopkeepers
One ENGLISHMAN can beat three Frenchmen
An ENGLISHMAN's home is his castle
An ENGLISHMAN's word is his bond
ENOUGH is as good as a feast
To ERR is human (to forgive divine)
EVERY little (bit) helps
EVERY man for himself
EVERY man for himself, and God for us all
EVERY man for himself, and the Devil take the hindmost
EVERY man has his price
EVERY man is the architect of his own fortune
EVERY man to his taste
What EVERYBODY says must be true
EVERYBODY's business is nobody's business
EVERYTHING has an end
Never do EVIL that good may come of it
Of two EVILS choose the less(er)
EXAMPLE is better than precept
The EXCEPTION proves the rule
There is an EXCEPTION to every rule
A fair EXCHANGE is no robbery
He who EXCUSES, accuses himself
What can you EXPECT from a pig but a grunt?
EXPERIENCE is the best teacher
EXPERIENCE is the father of wisdom
EXPERIENCE keeps a dear school (yet fools will learn in no other)
EXTREMES meet
What the EYE doesn't see, the heart doesn't grieve over
The EYES are the window of the soul

F

FACT is stranger than fiction
FACTS are stubborn things
FAINT heart never won fair lady
All's FAIR in love and war
FAIR play's a jewel
FAITH will move mountains
FAMILIARITY breeds contempt
The FAMILY that prays together stays together
Like FATHER, like son
A FAULT confessed is half redressed
FEED a cold and starve a fever
The FEMALE of the species is more deadly than the male
FIELDS have eyes, and woods have ears
FIGHT fire with fire
He who FIGHTS and runs away, may live to fight another day
FINDERS keepers (losers weepers)
FINE feathers make fine birds
FINGERS were made before forks
FIRE is a good servant but a bad master
FIRST come, first served
The FIRST duty of a soldier is obedience
FIRST impressions are the most lasting
It is the FIRST step that is difficult
FIRST things first
There is always a FIRST time
The FISH always stinks from the head downwards
FISH and guests stink after three days
There are as good FISH in the sea as ever came out of it
A FOOL and his money are soon parted
A FOOL at forty is a fool indeed
There's no FOOL like an old fool
A FOOL may give a wise man counsel
You can FOOL all the people some of the time and some of the people all the time, but you cannot fool all the people all the time
FOOLS ask questions that wise men cannot answer
FOOLS build houses and wise men live in them
FOOLS for luck
FOOLS rush in where angels fear to tread
FOREWARNED is forearmed
FORTUNE favors the brave
FOUR eyes see more than two
There's no such thing as a FREE lunch
FULL cup, steady hand
Out of the FULLNESS of the heart the mouth speaks
One FUNERAL makes many

G

GARBAGE in, garbage out
It takes three GENERATIONS to make a gentleman
GENIUS is an infinite capacity for taking pains
Never look a GIFT horse in the mouth
GIVE and take is fair play
GIVE the Devil his due
He GIVES twice who gives quickly
Those who live in GLASS houses shouldn't throw stones
All that GLITTERS is not gold
GO abroad and you'll hear news of home
GO further and fare worse
You cannot serve GOD and Mammon
GOD helps them that help themselves
GOD made the country, and man made the town
GOD makes the back to the burden
GOD never sends mouths but He sends meat
GOD sends meat, but the Devil sends cooks
GOD's in his heaven; all's right with the world
GOD tempers the wind to the shorn lamb
Whom the GODS love die young
He that GOES a-borrowing, goes a-sorrowing
What GOES around comes around
When the GOING gets tough, the tough get going
GOLD may be bought too dear

A GOLDEN key can open any door
If you can't be GOOD, be careful
A GOOD beginning makes a good ending
The GOOD die young
He is a GOOD dog who goes to church
GOOD fences make good neighbors
The GOOD is the enemy of the best
A GOOD Jack makes a good Jill
GOOD men are scarce
There's many a GOOD tune played on an old fiddle
One GOOD turn deserves another
What is GOT over the Devil's back is spent under his belly
While the GRASS grows, the steed starves
The GRASS is always greener on the other side of the fence
A GREAT book is a great evil
GREAT minds think alike
GREAT oaks from little acorns grow
The GREATER the sinner, the greater the saint
The GREATER the truth, the greater the libel
When GREEK meets Greek, then comes the tug of war
All is GRIST that comes to the mill
A GUILTY conscience needs no accuser

H

What you've never HAD you never miss
HALF a loaf is better than none (or no bread)
The HALF is better than the whole
One HALF of the world does not know how the other half lives
HALF the truth is often a whole lie
When all you have is a HAMMER, everything looks like a nail
One HAND for oneself and one for the ship
One HAND washes the other
HANDSOME is as handsome does
One might as well be HANGED for a sheep as a lamb
HAPPY families are all alike
If you would be HAPPY for a week take a wife; if you would be happy for a month kill a pig; but if you would be happy all your life plant a garden
Call no man HAPPY till he dies
HARD words break no bones
HASTE is from the Devil
More HASTE, less speed
HASTE makes waste
Make HASTE slowly
What you HAVE, hold
You can't HAVE your cake and eat it too
If you don't like the HEAT, get out of the kitchen
HEAVEN helps those who help themselves
HEAVEN protects children, sailors, and drunken men
HELL hath no fury like a woman scorned
He who HESITATES is lost
Those who HIDE can find
HISTORY repeats itself
HOME is home though it's never so homely
HOME is where the heart is
(Be it ever so humble,) There's no place like HOME
HOMER sometimes nods
HONESTY is the best policy
HONEY catches more flies than vinegar
There is HONOR among thieves
HOPE deferred makes the heart sick
HOPE for the best and prepare for (or expect) the worst
HOPE is a good breakfast but a bad supper
HOPE springs eternal
If it were not for HOPE, the heart would break
You can take a HORSE to water, but you can't make him drink
HORSES for courses
One HOUR's sleep before midnight is worth two after
When HOUSE and land are gone and spent, then learning is most excellent
A HOUSE divided cannot stand
HUNGER drives the wolf out of the wood

HUNGER is the best sauce
The HUSBAND is always the last to know

I

An IDLE brain is the Devil's workshop
IDLE people have the least leisure
IDLENESS is the root of all evil
Where IGNORANCE is bliss, 'tis folly to be wise
IGNORANCE of the law is no excuse (for breaking it)
It's an ILL bird that fouls its own nest
ILL gotten goods never thrive
It's ILL waiting for dead men's shoes
ILL weeds grow apace
It's an ILL wind that blows nobody any good
IMITATION is the sincerest form of flattery
IN for a penny, in for a pound

J

Every JACK has his Jill
JACK is as good as his master
JAM tomorrow and jam yesterday, but never jam today
JOVE but laughs at lovers' perjury
No one should be JUDGE in his own cause
JUDGE not, that ye be not judged
Be JUST before you're generous

K

Why KEEP a dog and bark yourself?
KEEP a thing seven years and you'll always find a use for
    it
KEEP no more cats than will catch mice
KEEP your shop and your shop will keep you
The KING can do no wrong
KINGS have long arms
KISSING goes by favor
To KNOW all is to forgive all
What you don't KNOW can't hurt you
KNOW thyself
You never KNOW what you can do till you try
KNOWLEDGE is power

L

The LABORER is worthy of his hire
Every LAND has its own law
The LAST drop makes the cup run over
It is the LAST straw that breaks the camel's back
LAUGH and the world laughs with you; weep and you weep
    alone
Let them LAUGH that win
He LAUGHS best who laughs last
He who LAUGHS last, laughs best (or longest)
One LAW for the rich and another for the poor
A man who is his own LAWYER has a fool for his client
LEAST said, soonest mended
There is nothing like LEATHER
LEND your money and lose your friend
The LEOPARD does not change his spots
LESS is more
LET well (enough) alone
A LIAR ought to have a good memory
If you LIE down with dogs, you will get up with fleas
LIFE begins at forty
LIFE isn't all beer and skittles
While (or Where) there's LIFE there's hope
LIGHTNING never strikes the same place twice
LIKE breeds like
LIKE will to like
Loose LIPS sink ships
LISTENERS never hear any good of themselves
There is no LITTLE enemy
A LITTLE knowledge is a dangerous thing
LITTLE leaks sink the ship

LITTLE pitchers have large (or big) ears
A LITTLE pot is soon hot
LITTLE strokes fell great oaks
LITTLE thieves are hanged, but great ones escape
LITTLE things please little minds
LIVE and learn
LIVE and let live
If you want to LIVE and thrive, let the spider run alive
A LIVE dog is better than a dead lion
They that LIVE longest, see most
He who LIVES by the sword dies by the sword
He that LIVES in hope dances to an ill tune
He LIVES long who lives well
The LONGEST way around is the shortest way home
LOOK before you leap
You cannot LOSE what you never had
One man's LOSS is another man's gain
There's no great LOSS without some gain
LOVE and a cough cannot be hid
He that falls in LOVE with himself will have no rivals
One cannot LOVE and be wise
LOVE begets love
LOVE is blind
LOVE laughs at locksmiths
LOVE makes the world go round
LOVE me, love my dog
LOVE will find a way
LOVE your neighbor, yet don't pull down your hedge
There is LUCK in leisure
There is LUCK in odd numbers
LUCKY at cards, unlucky at love

M

Don't get MAD, get even
MAKE hay while the sun shines
As you MAKE your bed, so you must lie upon it
MAN cannot live by bread alone
Whatever MAN has done, man may do
A MAN is as old as he feels, and a woman as old as she
    looks
MAN is the measure of all things
MAN proposes, God disposes
MAN's extremity is God's opportunity
The same MAN cannot be both a friend and a flatterer
MANNERS maketh man
There's MANY a slip 'twixt cup and lip
MANY are called but few are chosen
MANY complain of their memory, few of their judgment
MANY hands make light work
MARCH comes in like a lion, and goes out like a lamb
MARRIAGE is a lottery
There goes more to MARRIAGE than four bare legs in a bed
MARRIAGES are made in heaven
Never MARRY for money, but marry where money is
MARRY in haste and repent at leisure
Like MASTER, like man
There is MEASURE in all things
One man's MEAT is another man's poison
Do not MEET troubles half-way
MIGHT makes right
The MILLS of God grind slowly, yet they grind exceeding
    small
The age of MIRACLES is past
MISERY loves company
MISFORTUNES never come singly
A MISS is as good as a mile
You never MISS the water till the well runs dry
If you don't make MISTAKES you don't make anything
MODERATION in all things
MONEY has no smell
MONEY isn't everything
MONEY is power
(The love of) MONEY is the root of all evil
MONEY makes a man
MONEY makes money

MONEY talks
MORE people know Tom Fool than Tom Fool knows
The MORE the merrier
The MORE you get, the more you want
MORNING dreams come true
Like MOTHER, like daughter
If the MOUNTAIN will not come to Mahomet, Mahomet must go to the mountain
A MOUSE may help a lion
Out of the MOUTHS of babes
MUCH cry and little wool
MUCH would have more
MURDER will out
What MUST be, must be

N

NATURE abhors a vacuum
The NEARER the bone, the sweeter the meat
The NEARER the church, the farther from God
NECESSITY is the mother of invention
NECESSITY knows no law
NECESSITY never made a good bargain
NEEDS must when the Devil drives
NEVER is a long time
NEVER say never
It is NEVER too late to learn
It is NEVER too late to mend
NEVER too old to learn
A NEW broom sweeps clean
You can't put NEW wine in old bottles
NIGHT brings counsel
NINE tailors make a man
No man can serve two masters
No man is a hero to his valet
No news is good news
No pain, no gain
A NOD's as good as a wink to a blind horse
NOTHING comes of nothing
NOTHING for nothing
NOTHING is certain but death and taxes
NOTHING is certain but the unforeseen
There is NOTHING new under the sun
NOTHING is so popular as goodness
NOTHING so bad but it might have been worse
There is NOTHING so good for the inside of a man as the outside of a horse
NOTHING succeeds like success
NOTHING venture(d) nothing gain(ed)

O

Beware of an OAK, it draws the stroke; avoid an ash, it counts the flash; creep under the thorn, it can save you from harm
He that cannot OBEY cannot command
It is best to be OFF with the old love before you are on with the new
OFFENDERS never pardon
OLD habits die hard
You cannot put an OLD head on young shoulders
OLD sins cast long shadows
OLD soldiers never die, they just fade away
You cannot make an OMELET without breaking eggs
ONCE a —, always a —
ONCE bitten, twice shy
When ONE door shuts, another opens
ONE nail drives out another
ONE year's seeding makes seven years' weeding
The OPERA isn't over till the fat lady sings
OPPORTUNITY makes a thief
OPPORTUNITY never knocks twice at any man's door
OTHER times, other manners
An OUNCE of prevention is worth a pound of cure
OUT of sight, out of mind

P

It is the PACE that kills
Things PAST cannot be recalled
PATIENCE is a virtue
If you PAY peanuts, you get monkeys
He who PAYS the piper calls the tune
You PAYS your money and you takes your choice
You get what you PAY for
If you want PEACE, you must prepare for war
Do not throw PEARLS to swine
The PEN is mightier than the sword
Take care of the PENNIES and the dollars will take care of themselves
A PENNY saved is a penny earned
PENNY wise and pound foolish
PHYSICIAN, heal thyself
One PICTURE is worth ten thousand words
Every PICTURE tells a story
See a PIN (or penny) and pick it up, all the day you'll have good luck; see a pin (or penny) and let it lie, bad luck you'll have all the day
The PITCHER will go to the well once too often
PITY is akin to love
A PLACE for everything, and everything in its place
There's no PLACE like home
If you PLAY with fire you get burned
You can't PLEASE everyone
POLITICS makes strange bedfellows
It is a POOR dog that's not worth whistling for
It is a POOR heart that never rejoices
POSSESSION is nine points of the law
When POVERTY comes in at the door, love flies out of the window
POVERTY is no disgrace, but it is a great inconvenience
POVERTY is not a crime
POWER corrupts; absolute power corrupts absolutely
PRACTICE makes perfect
PRACTICE what you preach
PRIDE feels no pain
PRIDE goes before a fall
PROCRASTINATION is the thief of time
PROMISES, like piecrust, are made to be broken
The PROOF of the pudding is in the eating
A PROPHET is not without honor save in his own country
PROVIDENCE is always on the side of the big battalions
Any PUBLICITY is good publicity
It is easier to PULL down than to build up
PUNCTUALITY is the politeness of princes
To the PURE all things are pure
Never PUT off till tomorrow what you can do today

Q

QUITTERS never win and winners never quit
The QUARREL of lovers is the renewal of love

R

The RACE is not to the swift, nor the battle to the strong
RAIN before seven, fine before eleven
It never RAINS but it pours
It is easier to RAISE the Devil than to lay him
The heart has its REASONS that reason knows nothing of
RED sky at night, shepherd's (or sailor's) delight; red sky in the morning, shepherd's (or sailor's) warning
A REED before the wind lives on, while mighty oaks do fall
There is a REMEDY for everything except death
REVENGE is a dish best eaten cold
REVENGE is sweet
The RICH man has his ice in the summer and the poor man gets his in the winter
If you can't RIDE two horses at once, you shouldn't be in the circus
He who RIDES a tiger is afraid to dismount
A RISING tide lifts all boats

The ROAD to hell is paved with good intentions
All ROADS lead to Rome
A ROLLING stone gathers no moss
When in ROME, do as the Romans do
ROME was not built in a day
There is always ROOM at the top
Give a man ROPE enough and he will hang himself
The ROTTEN apple injures its neighbor
There is no ROYAL road to learning
You cannot RUN with the hare and hunt with the hounds

S

SAFE bind, safe find
There is SAFETY in numbers
Help you to SALT, help you to sorrow
What's SAUCE for the goose is sauce for the gander
SAVE us from our friend
SCRATCH a Russian and you find a Tartar
He that would go to SEA for pleasure, would go to hell for
    a pastime
The SEA refuses no river
SECOND thoughts are best
What you SEE is what you get
SEE no evil, hear no evil, speak no evil
Good SEED makes a good crop
SEEING is believing
SEEK and ye shall find
SELF-PRESERVATION is the first law of nature
If you would be well SERVED, serve yourself
From SHIRTSLEEVES to shirtsleeves in three generations
If the SHOE fits, wear it
The SHOEMAKER's child always goes barefoot
SHROUDS have no pockets
A SHUT mouth catches no flies
SILENCE is golden
SILENCE means consent
You can't make a SILK purse out of a sow's ear
SING before breakfast, cry before night
SIX hours' sleep for a man, seven for a woman, and eight
    for a fool
Let SLEEPING dogs lie
SLOW but sure
SMALL choice in rotten apples
SMALL is beautiful
Where there's SMOKE there's fire
A SOFT answer turneth away wrath
SOFTLY, softly, catchee monkey
If you're not part of the SOLUTION, you're part of the prob-
    lem
You don't get SOMETHING for nothing
SOMETHING is better than nothing
SOMETHING old, something new, something borrowed,
    something blue
My SON is my son till he gets him a wife, but my daughter's
    my daughter all the days of her life
SOON ripe, soon rotten
The SOONER begun, the sooner done
A SOW may whistle, though it has an ill mouth for it
As you SOW, so you reap
They that SOW the wind shall reap the whirlwind
SPARE the rod and spoil the child
Never SPEAK ill of the dead
Everyone SPEAKS well of the bridge which carries him over
If you don't SPECULATE, you can't accumulate
SPEECH is silver, but silence is golden
What you SPEND, you have
It is not SPRING until you can plant your foot upon twelve
    daisies
The SQUEAKING wheel gets the grease
It is too late to shut the STABLE-door after the horse has
    bolted
One STEP at a time
It is easy to find a STICK to beat a dog
STICKS and stones may break my bones, but words (or
    names) will never hurt me

A STILL tongue makes a wise head
STILL waters run deep
A STITCH in time saves nine
STOLEN fruit is sweet
One STORY is good till another is told
STRAWS tell which way the wind blows
A STREAM cannot rise above its source
STRETCH your arm no further than your sleeve will reach
STRIKE while the iron is hot
The STYLE is the man
From the SUBLIME to the ridiculous is only a step
If at first you don't SUCCEED, try, try again
SUCCESS has many fathers, while failure is an orphan
Never give a SUCKER an even break
SUFFICIENT unto the day is the evil thereof
Never let the SUN go down on your anger
The SUN loses nothing by shining into a puddle
He who SUPS with the Devil should have a long spoon
One SWALLOW does not make a summer
From the SWEETEST wine, the tartest vinegar

T

TAKE the goods the gods provide
A TALE never loses in the telling
Never tell TALES out of school
TALK is cheap
TALK of the Devil, and he is bound to appear
TASTES differ
You can't TEACH an old dog new tricks
Don't TEACH your grandmother to suck eggs
TELL the truth and shame the Devil
Set (or It takes) a THIEF to catch a thief
When THIEVES fall out, honest men come by their own
If a THING's worth doing, it's worth doing well
When THINGS are at the worst they begin to mend
THINK first and speak afterwards
The THIRD time pays for all
The THIRD time's the charm
THOUGHT is free
THREATENED men live long
THREE may keep a secret, if two of them are dead
THRIFT is a great revenue
Don't THROW out your dirty water until you get in fresh
Don't THROW the baby out with the bathwater
There is a TIME and place for everything
TIME and tide wait for no man
TIME flies
Do not squander TIME, for that is the stuff life is made of
There is a TIME for everything
TIME is a great healer
TIME is money
No TIME like the present
TIME will tell
TIME works wonders
TIMES change and we with time
You may delay, but TIME will not
TOMORROW is another day
TOMORROW never comes
The TONGUE always returns to the sore tooth
TOO many cooks spoil the broth
You can have TOO much of a good thing
TRADE follows the flag
TRAVEL broadens the mind
He TRAVELS fastest who travels alone
As a TREE falls, so shall it lie
The TREE is known by its fruit
There are TRICKS in every trade
A TROUBLE shared is a trouble halved
Never TROUBLE trouble till trouble troubles you
Many a TRUE word is spoken in jest
Put your TRUST in God, and keep your powder dry
There is TRUTH in wine
TRUTH is stranger than fiction
TRUTH lies at the bottom of a well
TRUTH will out

TURNABOUT is fair play
As the TWIG is bent, so is the tree inclined
While TWO dogs are fighting for a bone, a third runs away
with it
Two heads are better than one
Two is company, but three's a crowd
Two of a trade never agree
If TWO ride on a horse, one must ride behind
There are TWO sides to every question
It takes TWO to make a bargain
It takes TWO to make a quarrel
It takes TWO to tango
Two wrongs don't make a right

U

The UNEXPECTED always happens
UNION is strength
UNITED we stand, divided we fall
What goes UP must come down

V

VARIETY is the spice of life
VIRTUE is its own reward
The VOICE of the people is the voice of God

W

We must learn to WALK before we can run
WALLS have ears
WALNUTS and pears you plant for your heirs
If you WANT a thing done well, do it yourself
For WANT of a nail the shoe was lost; for want of a shoe
the horse was lost; and for want of a horse the man was
lost
One does not WASH one's dirty linen in public
WASTE not, want not
A WATCHED pot never boils
Don't go near the WATER until you learn how to swim
The WAY to a man's heart is through his stomach
There are more WAYS of killing a cat than choking it with
cream

There are more WAYS of killing a dog than hanging it
The WEAKEST go to the wall
One WEDDING brings another
WEDLOCK is a padlock
WELL begun is half done
WELL done is better than well said
All's WELL that ends well
When the WELL is dry we know the worth of water
A WILFUL man must have his way
WILFUL waste makes woeful want
Where there's a WILL, there's a way
He who WILLS the end, wills the means
You WIN a few, you lose a few
You can't WIN them all
When the WIND is in the east, 'tis neither good for man
nor beast
In WINE there is truth
When the WINE is in, the wit is out
It is easy to be WISE after the event
It is a WISE child that knows its own father
The WISH is father to the thought
If WISHES were horses, beggars would ride
A WOMAN's place is in the home
A WOMAN's work is never done
WONDERS will never cease
Happy's the WOOING that is not long a-doing
Many go out for WOOL and come home shorn
A WORD to the wise is sufficient
All WORK and no play makes Jack a dull boy
WORK expands so as to fill the time available
It is not WORK that kills, but worry
If you won't WORK you shan't eat
Even a WORM will turn
The WORTH of a thing is what it will bring

Y

YOUNG folks think old folks to be fools, but old folks know
young folks to be fools
A YOUNG man married is a young man marred
YOUNG men may die, but old men must die
YOUNG saint, old devil
YOUTH must be served

THE BIBLE

The Bible is the sacred book in the Judeo-Christian tradition, where it is regarded as the Word of God, that is, inspired by God. It actually consists of many separate short books, poems or songs, and letters, compiled over several centuries. Tradition has it that the earliest books of the Bible were composed in about 1300 B.C. (the time of Moses, the Hebrew prophet and leader) as oral narratives, but the earliest actual manuscripts known to modern scholars date to about 250 B.C. The Dead Sea Scrolls are the oldest still-surviving manuscripts, and some of these date to the early first century B.C.

The Bible is also referred to as the Holy Bible, the Scriptures, the Holy Scriptures, and (especially in the Christian tradition) the Good Book. Bible is from the Greek biblia, which means 'books.' The Old Testament, also known as the Hebrew Bible, comprises the books that recount the earliest history and traditions of the origins of the Jewish faith and the covenant of God with man ("Testament" refers to the account of this covenant). This is also the underpinning of the Christian religion. Other books deal with the history of Israel and with God's relationship to the Jewish people.

The first five books of the Old Testament are called the Pentateuch (from Greek pentateuchos 'five scroll cases,' the containers in which ancient scroll manuscripts were stored) or, in the Jewish tradition, the Torah (from the Hebrew for 'instruction, law'). These books discuss the Jewish beliefs of the origins of the world, the early history of the Jewish people, and the fundamental elements of Mosaic law and tradition.

Books of the Old Testament (Hebrew Bible):

Genesis (Gen.)
Exodus (Exod.)
Leviticus (Lev.)
Numbers (Num.)
Deuteronomy (Deut.)
Joshua (Josh.)
Judges (Judg.)
Ruth
1st Book of Samuel (1 Sam.)
2nd Book of Samuel (2 Sam.)
1st Book of Kings (1 Kgs.)
2nd Book of Kings (2 Kgs.)

1st Book of Chronicles (1 Chr.)
2nd Book of Chronicles (2 Chr.)
Ezra
Nehemiah (Neh.)
Esther
Job
Psalms (Ps.)
Proverbs (Prov.)
Ecclesiastes (Eccles.)
Song of Songs or of Solomon, or Canticles (S. of S., Cant.)
Isaiah (Isa.)
Jeremiah (Jer.)

Lamentations (Lam.)
Ezekiel (Ezek.)
Daniel (Dan.)
Hosea (Hos.)
Joel
Amos
Obadiah (Obad.)
Jonah
Micah (Mic.)
Nahum (Nah.)
Habakkuk (Hab.)
Zephaniah (Zeph.)
Haggai (Hag.)
Zechariah (Zech.)
Malachi (Mal.)

The Apocrypha ('unknown, spurious'; perhaps referring to disputed authenticity) is a group of 14 or 15 books that are regarded as canonical or "biblical" only in the Roman Catholic and Greek Orthodox traditions. Some were written in Hebrew, some in Greek, and some in Aramaic, the Semitic language commonly used in ancient Palestine, Syria, and Mesopotamia.

1st Book of Esdras (1 Esd.)
2nd Book of Esdras (2 Esd.)
Tobit
Judith Rest of Esther (Rest of Esth.)
Wisdom of Solomon (Wisd.)

Ecclesiasticus or Wisdom of Jesus the Son of Sirach (Ecclus., Sir.)
Baruch
Song of the Three Children (S. of III Ch.)
Susanna (Sus.)

Bel and the Dragon (Bel & Dr.)
Prayer of Manasseh (Pr. of Man.)
1st Book of Maccabees (1 Macc.)
2nd Book of Maccabees (2 Macc.)

The New Testament comprises the books that recount the origin and early history of Christianity. The four Gospels are accounts of the life and death of Jesus Christ, and they recount the resurrection of Jesus from the dead, the key tenet of the Christian faith. The Acts of the Apostles tells of the early, formative days of Christianity. The Epistles, most written by the greatest early Christian missionary, St. Paul, are letters of counsel and encouragement to various Christian communities in the Mediterranean world of the mid-first century A.D. The last book, the Apocalypse, or Revelation (also Revelations), is a highly symbolic narrative touching on such Christian doctrines as the end of the world, the Second Coming of Christ, and Judgment Day.

Books of the New Testament:

Gospel of Matthew
(Matt.)
Gospel of Mark (Mark)
Gospel of Luke (Luke)
Gospel of John (John)
Acts of the Apostles
(Acts)
Epistle to the Romans
(Rom.)
1st Epistle to the
Corinthians (1 Cor.)
2nd Epistle to the
Corinthians (2 Cor.)
Epistle to the Galatians
(Gal.)
Epistle to the Ephesians
(Eph.)

Epistle to the
Philippians (Phil.)
Epistle to the Colossians
(Col.)
1st Epistle to the
Thessalonians (1
Thess.)
2nd Epistle to the
Thessalonians (2
Thess.)
1st Epistle to Timothy
(1 Tim.)
2nd Epistle to Timothy
(2 Tim.)
Epistle to Titus (Tit.)
Epistle to Philemon
(Philem.)

Epistle to the Hebrews
(Heb.)
Epistle of James (Jas.)
1st Epistle of Peter (1
Pet.)
2nd Epistle of Peter (2
Pet.)
1st Epistle of John (1
John)
2nd Epistle of John (2
John)
Third Epistle of John (3
John)
Epistle of Jude (Jude)
Revelation(s) or
Apocalypse (Rev.,
Apoc.)

Translations and Versions of the Bible

Hebrew Bible. The Old Testament was written in Hebrew, the Semitic language of the ancient Jewish people. But over time, Jews living in various parts of the Mediterranean world adopted the native languages of the countries they inhabited.

As a result, the Hebrew Bible came to be readable only by rabbis and scholars, and most of the Jewish community could no longer read it by the time of the Hellenistic Age (third century B.C.), when Greek was the language of most of the eastern Mediterranean world.

Septuagint. Hebrew scholars in Alexandria (an important city and center of learning at the time), in northern Egypt, set out to translate the Hebrew Bible into Greek. This translation came to be called the Septuagint ('seventy'), referring to the tradition that 70 Hebrew scholars worked on it. At least the Pentateuch was translated as early as the third century B.C.; other books may have been completed later. As centuries passed and the earliest manuscripts of Hebrew biblical texts were lost, destroyed, or simply deteriorated, the widely used Septuagint, available in multiple copies throughout the Judeo-Christian world, often became the earliest source for some biblical tracts. Hence, though a Greek translation, the Septuagint became an important source for biblical studies.

Vulgate. In the Roman world, especially in the western Mediterranean and areas that were controlled by the Romans by the time of Christ (including modern-day Italy, France, and Spain), Latin was the language of the people. The Latin word for 'common people' is vulgus, and it is from this that we have the term "Vulgar Latin," referring to the vernacular, informal Latin of the streets and of everyday conversation. Many aspects of this form of Latin were considered by scholars to be "low class" (hence the English sense of the word vulgar) when compared to the highly polished and formal classical Latin of the best authors. Nevertheless, Vulgar Latin was the native language of many people in the western Mediterranean area, including many early Christians, and was also the lingua franca of the ancient Roman empire, which stretched from Britain, through western Europe, and across the Mediterranean basin to parts of western Asia.

St. Jerome (ca. 340–420), the greatest scholar of the early Christian world, prepared the bulk of the Latin translation of the Bible called the Vulgate. Jerome was probably the only person in the western Mediterranean world of his day who knew Hebrew, which he had learned from rabbis during his years in the Holy Lands. Thus Jerome was able to prepare a translation that was based on Hebrew and Greek sources, and that gained authority for its careful philological scholarship as well as its convenience to the common people as a Latin translation. The Vulgate Bible remains the principal reference in the Roman Catholic tradition.

Notable English Translations of the Bible

Wycliffe. The earliest complete translation of the Bible into English was prepared by the English priest John Wycliffe and his followers in the 1380s.

Tyndale. William Tyndale translated the New Testament and much of the Old Testament into English, relying in part on the German translation of Martin Luther. It was published in the 1520s and 1530s.

Coverdale. The first complete English translation of the Bible to be printed was that of Miles Coverdale, an English bishop. It was printed in Germany in 1535.

Roman Catholic (Douay-Rheims). Roman Catholic refugees from England translated the Bible into English in France. The New Testament was published in 1582 in Rheims, and the Old Testament appeared in 1609 and 1610, in Douay. It came to be known as the Douay-Rheims or Douay Bible.

King James Bible. James I of England authorized a new translation in 1604. A committee of scholars prepared this most literary and influential of all English Bible translations, which was published in 1611. Also referred to as the Authorized Version, this translation is still widely in use in Christian churches, and usually is the source of the definitive English wording of famous Bible passages.

Modern versions. Various modern versions have attempted to incorporate the latest findings of biblical scholars in translations that reflect the English of today. The most notable and widely used versions (dates refer to the time of publication, often separate for the two testaments) include the Revised Version (1881; 1885), the Revised Standard Version (1946; 1952), the New English Bible (1961; 1970), the New American Standard Bible (1963; 1971), the Good News Bible (1966; 1976), the Jerusalem Bible (1966), the New American Bible (1970), the New Revised Standard Version (1973), and the New International Version (1973; 1976).

BILL OF RIGHTS

To Americans, the "Bill of Rights" normally refers to the first ten amendments to the U.S. Constitution. But in fact, there have been several bills of rights through history, each an influence on the U.S. Bill of Rights. These documents enumerate specific rights or freedoms that are guaranteed to the people by a system of law or government.

Magna Carta. The English royal charter of 1215 in which King John granted specific liberties, among them that "no free man shall be arrested or imprisoned . . . or exiled . . . or attack[ed] . . . except by the lawful judgment of his peers or by the law of the land."

Petition of Right. An Act of Parliament in 1628, agreed to reluctantly by King Charles I, declaring the "rights and liberties of the subject," and limiting royal prerogatives. It stated that freemen were protected against seizure of their property or imprisonment, outlawed the forced billeting of soldiers in private homes, and abolished martial law.

English Bill of Rights. In 1689, in the period of English history called "the Glorious Revolution," King William III and Queen Mary received a declaration from Parliament listing certain rights, including frequent Parliaments and free elections, and revoking the monarch's power to suspend laws. These were deemed the "true, ancient, and indubitable rights and liberties of the people."

Virginia's Declaration or Rights. Written by George Mason in 1776, this document was influential in Thomas Jefferson's drafting of the Declaration of Independence, and was later the basis for the U.S. Bill of Rights. Mason was active in the Constitutional Convention of 1789, but finally refused to sign the Constitution without a Bill of Rights and provision for a stronger judiciary. Both of his objections were finally met by the first eleven amendments.

Declaration of Independence. The document ratified on July 4, 1776, by the Continental Congress at Philadelphia stated "that all Men are created equal," and "that they are endowed by their Creator with certain unalienable Rights, that among these are Life, Liberty, and the Pursuit of Happiness." These were taken as justification for the American colonists declaring their independence from English rule.

French Bill of Rights. In 1789, at the time of the French Revolution, with the overthrow of the French monarchy and aristocracy amid popular cries for "Liberty, Equality, Brotherhood," the French adopted the Declaration of the Rights of Man and of the Citizen. This guaranteed freedom of religion, freedom of speech, freedom of the press, and right to personal security.

United States Bill of Rights. The U.S. Constitution as ratified in 1789 did not guarantee specific rights and freedoms to individuals. The states of North Carolina and Rhode Island refused to ratify it as such, and the first ten amendments to the Constitution, drawn up by James Madison (who had proposed fifteen), were adopted in 1791. These amendments came to be called the Bill of Rights, as they enumerate the fundamental rights and freedoms of every American citizen.

Rights and Freedoms, by amendment, in the U.S. Bill of Rights:

1. Freedom of religion, of speech, of the press; right of the people peaceably to assemble; right to petition the government for a redress of grievances.

2. Right to keep and bear arms.

3. Freedom from quartering of soldiers in time of peace in any house without consent of the owner.

4. Right of people to be secure in their persons, houses, papers, and effects against unreasonable searches and seizures; no warrants issued without probable cause supported by oath or affirmation.

5. Freedom from capital or other serious criminal charges unless indicted by a grand jury; "double jeopardy" provision (one cannot be tried twice for the same capital offense); freedom from having to testify against oneself in a criminal case; "due process" provision (one cannot be deprived of life, liberty, or property without proper legal procedure); freedom from seizure of property without just compensation.

6. Right of the accused to a speedy and public trial by jury in criminal cases; right to be informed of the nature and cause of the accusation; right to be confronted by the witnesses against the accuser; right to compulsory process for obtaining favorable witnesses; right to assistance of defense counsel.

7. Right to trial by jury in civil suits, with appeal according to the rules of common law.

8. Freedom from excessive bail or fines, or from cruel and unusual punishments.

9. Other rights not enumerated in the Constitution are not denied.

10. Powers not delegated by the Constitution are reserved for the States or the people.

PRESIDENTS OF THE UNITED STATES OF AMERICA

Name and life dates	Party (term in office)
1. George Washington 1732-99	Federalist (1789-97)
2. John Adams 1735-1826	Federalist (1797-1801)
3. Thomas Jefferson 1743-1826	Democratic-Republican (1801-09)
4. James Madison 1751-1836	Democratic-Republican (1809-17)
5. James Monroe 1758-1831	Democratic-Republican (1817-25)
6. John Quincy Adams 1767-1848	Independent (1825-29)
7 Andrew Jackson 1767-1845	Democrat (1829-37)
8. Martin Van Buren 1782-1862	Democrat (1837-41)
9. William H. Harrison 1773-1841	Whig (1841)
10. John Tyler 1790-1862	Whig, then Democrat (1841-45)
11. James K. Polk 1795-1849	Democrat (1845-49)
12. Zachary Taylor 1784-1850	Whig (1849-50)
13. Millard Fillmore 1800-74	Whig (1850-53)
14. Franklin Pierce 1804-69	Democrat (1853-57)
15. James Buchanan 1791-1868	Democrat (1857-61)
16. Abraham Lincoln 1809-65	Republican (1861-65)
17. Andrew Johnson 1808-75	Democrat (1865-69)
18. Ulysses S. Grant 1822-85	Republican (1869-77)
19. Rutherford B. Hayes 1822-93	Republican (1877-81)
20. James A. Garfield 1831-81	Republican (1881)
21. Chester A. Arthur 1830-86	Republican (1881-85)
22. Grover Cleveland 1837-1908	Democrat (1885-89)
23. Benjamin Harrison 1833-1901	Republican (1889-93)
24. Grover Cleveland (see above)	Democrat (1893-97)
25. William McKinley 1843-1901	Republican (1897-1901)
26. Theodore Roosevelt 1858-1919	Republican (1901-09)
27. William H. Taft 1857-1930	Republican (1909-13)
28. Woodrow Wilson 1856-1924	Democrat (1913-21)
29. Warren G. Harding 1865-1923	Republican (1921-23)
30. Calvin Coolidge 1872-1933	Republican (1923-29)
31. Herbert Hoover 1874-1964	Republican (1929-33)
32. Franklin D. Roosevelt 1882-1945	Democrat (1933-45)
33. Harry S Truman 1884-1972	Democrat (1945-53)
34. Dwight D. Eisenhower 1890-1969	Republican (1953-61)
35. John F. Kennedy 1917-63	Democrat (1961-63)
36. Lyndon B. Johnson 1908-73	Democrat (1963-69)
37. Richard M. Nixon 1913-94	Republican (1969-74)
38. Gerald R. Ford 1913-	Republican (1974-77)
39. James Earl Carter 1924-	Democrat (1977-81)
40. Ronald W. Reagan 1911-	Republican (1981-89)
41. George H.W. Bush 1924-	Republican (1989-93)
42. William J. Clinton 1946-	Democrat (1993-)

MONARCHS OF ENGLAND AND BRITAIN

House	Monarch	Reign
Wessex (West Saxon)	Egbert	802-839
	Ethelwulf	839-856
	Ethelbald	856-860
	Ethelbert	860-866
	Ethelred I	866-871
	Alfred the Great	871-899
	Edward the Elder	899-924
	Athelstan	925-939
	Edmund I	939-946
	Edred	946-955
	Edwy	955-957
	Edgar	959-975
	Edward the Martyr	975-978
	Ethelred II (the Unready)	978-1016
	Edmund II (Ironside)	1016
Danish	Canute (Cnut)	1016-1035
	Harold I	1035-1040
	Hardecanute	1040-1042
West Saxon (restored)	Edward II (the Confessor)	1042-1066
	Harold II	1066
Normandy	William I (the Conqueror)	1066-1087
	William II	1087-1100
	Henry I	1100-1135
	Stephen	1135-1154
Plantagenet (Anjou)	Henry II	1154-1189
	Richard I (the Lion-heart)	1189-1199
	John	1199-1216
	Henry III	1216-1272
	Edward I	1272-1307
	Edward II	1307-1327
	Edward III	1327-1377
	Richard II	1377-1399
Lancaster	Henry IV	1399-1413
	Henry V	1413-1422
	Henry VI	1422-1461
York	Edward IV	1461-1483
	Edward V	1483
	Richard III	1483-1485
Tudor	Henry VII	1485-1509
	Henry VIII	1509-1547
	Edward VI	1547-1553
	Jane (Lady Jane Grey)	1553

House	Monarch	Reign
	Mary I (Bloody Mary)	1553-1558
	Elizabeth I	1558-1603
(monarchs of Britain)		
Stuart	James I	1603-1625
	Charles I	1625-1649
Commonwealth	Long Parliament	1649-1660
Protectorate	Oliver Cromwell	1653-1658
	Richard Cromwell	1658-1660
Stuart	Charles II	1660-1685
	James II	1685-1688
interregnum		1688-1689
	William III and Mary II	1689-1694
	Anne	1702-1714
Hanover	George I	1714-1727
	George II	1727-1760
	George III	1760-1820
	George IV	1820-1830
	William IV	1830-1837
Saxe-Coburg-Gotha	Victoria	1837-1901
	Edward VII	1901-1910
Windsor	George V	1910-1936
	Edward VIII	1936
	George VI	1936-1952
	Elizabeth II	1952-

PRIME MINISTERS OF GREAT BRITAIN AND THE UNITED KINGDOM

Name	Party	Dates in Power
Sir Robert Walpole	Whig	1721-1742
Earl of Wilmington	Whig	1742-1743
Henry Pelham	Whig	1743-1754
Duke of Newcastle	Whig	1754-1756; 1757-1762
Earl of Bute	Tory	1762-1763
George Grenville	Whig	1763-1765
Marquis of Rockingham	Whig	1765-1766
Earl of Chatham	Whig	1766-1768
Duke of Grafton	Whig	1768-1770
Lord North	Tory	1770-1782
Marquis of Rockingham	Whig	1782
Earl of Shelburne	Whig	1782-1783
Duke of Portland	coalition	1783
William Pitt	Tory	1783-1801
Henry Addington	Tory	1801-1804
William Pitt	Tory	1804-1806

Name	Party	Dates in Power
Lord William Grenville	Whig	1806-1807
Duke of Portland	Tory	1807-1808
Spencer Perceval	Tory	1809-1812
Earl of Liverpool	Tory	1812-1827
George Canning	Tory	1827
Viscount Goderich	Tory	1827-1828
Duke of Wellington	Tory	1828-1830
Earl Grey	Whig	1830-1834
Viscount Melbourne	Whig	1834
Duke of Wellington	Tory	1834
Sir Robert Peel	Conservative	1834-1835
Viscount Melbourne	Whig	1835-1841
Sir Robert Peel	Conservative	1841-1846
Lord John Russell	Whig	1846-1852
Earl of Derby	Conservative	1852
Earl of Aberdeen	coalition	1852-1855
Viscount Palmerston	Liberal	1855-1858
Earl of Derby	Conservative	1858-1859
Viscount Palmerston	Liberal	1859-1865
Earl Russell	Liberal	1865-1866
Earl of Derby	Conservative	1866-1868
Benjamin Disraeli	Conservative	1868
William Ewart Gladstone	Liberal	1868-1874
Benjamin Disraeli	Conservative	1874-1880
William Ewart Gladstone	Liberal	1880-1885
Marquis of Salisbury	Conservative	1885-1892
William Ewart Gladstone	Liberal	1892-1894
Earl of Rosebery	Liberal	1894-1895
Marquis of Salisbury	Conservative	1895-1902
Arthur James Balfour	Conservative	1902-1905
Sir Henry Campbell-Bannerman	Liberal	1905-1908
Herbert Henry Asquith	Liberal	1908-1916
David Lloyd George	coalition	1916-1922
Andrew Bonar Law	Conservative	1922-1923
Stanley Baldwin	Conservative	1923-1924
James Ramsay MacDonald	Labour	1924
Stanley Baldwin	Conservative	1924-1929
James Ramsay MacDonald	coalition	1929-1935
Stanley Baldwin	coalition	1935-1937
Neville Chamberlain	coalition	1937-1940
Sir Winston Spencer Churchill	coalition	1940-1945
Clement Attlee	Labour	1945-1951
Sir Winston Spencer Churchill	Conservative	1951-1955
Sir Anthony Eden	Conservative	1955-1957
Harold Macmillan	Conservative	1957-1963
Sir Alec Douglas-Home	Conservative	1963-1964
Harold Wilson	Labour	1964-1970
Edward Heath	Conservative	1970-1974
Harold Wilson	Labour	1974-1976
James Callaghan	Labour	1976-1979
Margaret Thatcher	Conservative	1979-1990
John Major	Conservative	1990-1997
Anthony Blair	Labour	1997-

ACADEMY AWARD WINNERS

Note: The movie for which the award was given follows the individual's name, in parentheses.

1928

Best actor: Charles Chaplin (*The Circus*)
Best actress: Janet Gaynor (*Seventh Heaven*)
Best director (drama): Frank Borzage (*Seventh Heaven*)
Best director (comedy): Lewis Milestone (*Two Arabian Knights*)

1929

Best actor: Warner Baxter (*In Old Arizona*)
Best actress: Mary Pickford (*Coquette*)
Best director: Frank Lloyd (*The Divine Lady*)

1930

Best actor: George Arliss (*Disraeli*)
Best actress: Norma Shearer (*The Divorceé*)
Best director: Lewis Milestone (*All Quiet on the Western Front*)

1931

Best actor: Lionel Barrymore (*A Free Soul*)
Best actress: Marie Dressler (*Min and Bill*)
Best director: Norman Taurog (*Skippy*)

1932

Best actors: Wallace Berry (*The Champ*), Frederic March (*Dr. Jekyll and Mr. Hyde*)
Best actress: Helen Hayes (*The Sin of Madelon Claudet*)
Best director: Frank Borzage (*Bad Girl*)

1933

Best actor: Charles Laughton (*The Private Life of Henry VIII*)
Best actress: Katharine Hepburn (*Morning Glory*)
Best director: Frank Lloyd (*Cavalcade*)

1934

Best actor: Clark Gable (*It Happened One Night*)
Best actress: Claudette Colbert (*It Happened One Night*)
Best director: Frank Capra (*It Happened One Night*)

1935

Best actor: Victor McLaglen (*The Informer*)
Best actress: Bette Davis (*Dangerous*)
Best director: John Ford (*The Informer*)

1936

Best actor: Paul Muni (*The Story of Louis Pasteur*)
Best actress: Luise Rainer (*The Great Ziegfeld*)
Best director: Frank Capra (*Mr. Deeds Goes to Town*)

1937

Best actor: Spencer Tracy (*Captains Courageous*)
Best actress: Luise Rainer (*The Good Earth*)
Best director: Leo McCarey (*The Awful Truth*)

1938

Best actor: Spencer Tracy (*Boys Town*)
Best actress: Bette Davis (*Jezebel*)
Best director: Frank Capra (*You Can't Take It With You*)

1939

Best actor: Robert Donat (*Goodbye Mr. Chips*)

Best actress: Vivien Leigh (*Gone with the Wind*)

Best director: Victor Fleming (*Gone with the Wind*)

1940

Best actor: James Stewart (*The Philadelphia Story*)

Best actress: Ginger Rogers (*Kitty Foyle*)

Best director: John Ford (*The Grapes of Wrath*)

1941

Best actor: Gary Cooper (*Sergeant York*)

Best actress: Joan Fontaine (*Suspicion*)

Best director: John Ford (*How Green Was My Valley*)

1942

Best actor: James Cagney (*Yankee Doodle Dandy*)

Best actress: Greer Garson (*Mrs. Miniver*)

Best director: William Wyler (*Mrs. Miniver*)

1943

Best actor: Paul Lukas (*Watch on the Rhine*)

Best actress: Jennifer Jones (*The Song of Bernadette*)

Best director: Michael Curtiz (*Casablanca*)

1944

Best actor: Bing Crosby (*Going My Way*)

Best actress: Ingrid Bergman (*Gaslight*)

Best director: Leo McCarey (*Going My Way*)

1945

Best actor: Ray Milland (*The Lost Weekend*)

Best actress: Joan Crawford (*Love Letters*)

Best director: Billy Wilder (*The Lost Weekend*)

1946

Best actor: Frederic March (*The Best Years of Our Lives*)

Best actress: Olivia De Havilland (*To Each His Own*)

Best director: William Wyler (*The Best Years of Our Lives*)

1947

Best actor: Ronald Colman (*A Double Life*)

Best actress: Loretta Young (*The Farmer's Daughter*)

Best director: Elia Kazan (*Gentleman's Agreement*)

1948

Best actor: Laurence Olivier (*Hamlet*)

Best actress: Jane Wyman (*Johnny Belinda*)

Best director: John Huston (*The Treasure of the Sierra Madre*)

1949

Best actor: Broderick Crawford (*All the King's Men*)

Best actress: Olivia De Havilland (*The Heiress*)

Best director: Joseph L. Mankiewicz (*A Letter to Three Wives*)

1950

Best actor: Jose Ferrer (*Cyrano De Bergerac*)

Best actress: Judy Holliday (*Born Yesterday*)

Best director: Joseph L. Mankiewicz (*All About Eve*)

1951

Best actor: Humphrey Bogart (*The African Queen*)

Best actress: Vivien Leigh (*A Streetcar Named Desire*)

Best director: George Stevens (*A Place in the Sun*)

1952

Best actor: Gary Cooper (*High Noon*)

Best actress: Shirley Booth (*Come Back, Little Sheba*)

Best director: John Ford (*The Quiet Man*)

1953

Best actor: William Holden (*Stalag 17*)

Best actress: Audrey Hepburn (*Roman Holiday*)

Best director: Fred Zinnemann (*From Here to Eternity*)

1954

Best actor: Marlon Brando (*On the Waterfront*)

Best actress: Grace Kelly (*The Country Girl*)

Best director: Elia Kazan (*On the Waterfront*)

1955

Best actor: Ernest Borgnine (*Marty*)

Best actress: Anna Magnani (*The Rose Tattoo*)

Best director: Delbert Mann (*Marty*)

1956

Best actor: Yul Brynner (*The King and I*)

Best actress: Ingrid Bergman (*Anastasia*)

Best director: George Stevens (*Giant*)

1957

Best actor: Alec Guinness (*The Bridge on the River Kwai*)

Best actress: Joanne Woodward (*The Three Faces of Eve*)

Best director: David Lean (*The Bridge on the River Kwai*)

1958

Best actor: David Niven (*Separate Tables*)

Best actress: Susan Hayward (*I Want to Live!*)

Best director: Vincente Minnelli (*The Defiant Ones*)

1959

Best actor: Charlton Heston (*Ben-Hur*)

Best actress: Simone Signoret (*Room at the Top*)

Best director: William Wyler (*Ben-Hur*)

1960

Best actor: Burt Lancaster (*Elmer Gantry*)

Best actress: Elizabeth Taylor (*Butterfield 8*)

Best director: Billy Wilder (*The Apartment*)

1961

Best actor: Maximilian Schell (*Judgment at Nuremberg*)

Best actress: Sophia Loren (*Two Women*)

Best director: Jerome Robbins, Robert Wise (*West Side Story*)

1962

Best actor: Gregory Peck (*To Kill a Mockingbird*)

Best actress: Anne Bancroft (*The Miracle Worker*)

Best director: David Lean (*Lawrence of Arabia*)

1963

Best actor: Sydney Poitier (*Lilies of the Field*)
Best actress: Patricia Neal (*Hud*)
Best director: Tony Richardson (*Tom Jones*)

1964

Best actor: Rex Harrison (*My Fair Lady*)
Best actress: Julie Andrews (*Mary Poppins*)
Best director: George Cukor (*Mary Poppins*)

1965

Best actor: Lee Marvin (*Cat Ballou*)
Best actress: Julie Christie (*Darling*)
Best director: Robert Wise (*The Sound of Music*)

1966

Best actor: Paul Scofield (*A Man for All Seasons*)
Best actress: Elizabeth Taylor (*Who's Afraid of Virginia Woolf?*)
Best director: Fred Zinnemann (*A Man for All Seasons*)

1967

Best actor: Rod Steiger (*In the Heat of the Night*)
Best actress: Katharine Hepburn (*Guess Who's Coming to Dinner*)
Best director: Mike Nichols (*The Graduate*)

1968

Best actor: Cliff Robertson (*Charly*)
Best actress: Barbra Streisand (*Funny Girl*)
Best director: Carol Reed (*Oliver!*)

1969

Best actor: John Wayne (*True Grit*)
Best actress: Maggie Smith (*The Prime of Miss Jean Brodie*)
Best director: John Schlesinger (*Midnight Cowboy*)

1970

Best actor: George C. Scott (*Patton*)
Best actress: Glenda Jackson (*Women in Love*)
Best director: Franklin J. Schaffner (*Patton*)

1971

Best actor: Gene Hackman (*The French Connection*)
Best actress: Jane Fonda (*Klute*)
Best director: William Friedkin (*The French Connection*)

1972

Best actor: Marlon Brando (*The Godfather*)
Best actress: Liza Minnelli (*Cabaret*)
Best director: Bob Fosse (*Cabaret*)

1973

Best actor: Jack Lemmon (*Save the Tiger*)
Best actress: Glenda Jackson (*A Touch of Class*)
Best director: George Roy Hill (*The Sting*)

1974

Best actor: Art Carney (*Harry and Tonto*)
Best actress: Ellen Burstyn (*Alice Doesn't Live Here Anymore*)
Best director: Francis Ford Coppola (*The Godfather, Part II*)

1975

Best actor: Jack Nicholson (*One Flew Over the Cuckoo's Nest*)
Best actress: Louise Fletcher (*One Flew Over the Cuckoo's Nest*)
Best director: Milos Forman (*One Flew Over the Cuckoo's Nest*)

1976

Best actor: Peter Finch (*Network*)
Best actress: Faye Dunaway (*Network*)
Best director: John G. Avildsen (*Rocky*)

1977

Best actor: Richard Dreyfuss (*The Goodbye Girl*)
Best actress: Diane Keaton (*Annie Hall*)
Best director: Woody Allen (*Annie Hall*)

1978

Best actor: Jon Voight (*Coming Home*)
Best actress: Jane Fonda (*Coming Home*)
Best director: Michael Cimino (*The Deer Hunter*)

1979

Best actor: Dustin Hoffman (*Kramer vs. Kramer*)
Best actress: Sally Field (*Norma Rae*)
Best director: Robert Benton (*Kramer vs. Kramer*)

1980

Best actor: Robert De Niro (*Raging Bull*)
Best actress: Sissy Spacek (*Coal Miner's Daughter*)
Best director: Robert Redford (*Ordinary People*)

1981

Best actor: Henry Fonda (*On Golden Pond*)
Best actress: Katharine Hepburn (*On Golden Pond*)
Best director: Warren Beatty (*Reds*)

1982

Best actor: Ben Kingsley (*Gandhi*)
Best actress: Meryl Streep (*Sophie's Choice*)
Best director: Richard Attenborough (*Gandhi*)

1983

Best actor: Robert Duvall (*Tender Mercies*)
Best actress: Shirley MacLaine (*Terms of Endearment*)
Best director: James L. Brooks (*Terms of Endearment*)

1984

Best actor: F. Murray Abraham (*Amadeus*)
Best actress: Sally Field (*Places in the Heart*)
Best director: Milos Forman (*Amadeus*)

1985

Best actor: William Hurt (*Kiss of the Spider Woman*)
Best actress: Geraldine Page (*The Trip to Bountiful*)
Best director: Sydney Pollack (*Out of Africa*)

1986

Best actor: Paul Newman (*The Color of Money*)
Best actress: Marlee Matlin (*Children of a Lesser God*)
Best director: Oliver Stone (*Platoon*)

1987

Best actor: Michael Douglas (*Wall Street*)
Best actress: Cher (*Moonstruck*)
Best director: Bernardo Bertolucci (*The Last Emperor*)

1988

Best actor: Dustin Hoffman (*Rain Man*)
Best actress: Jodie Foster (*The Accused*)
Best director: Barry Levinson (*Rain Man*)

1989

Best actor: Daniel Day-Lewis (*My Left Foot*)
Best actress: Jessica Tandy (*Driving Miss Daisy*)
Best director: Oliver Stone (*Born on the Fourth of July*)

1990

Best actor: Jeremy Irons (*Reversal of Fortune*)
Best actress: Kathy Bates (*Misery*)
Best director: Kevin Costner (*Dances with Wolves*)

1991

Best actor: Anthony Hopkins (*The Silence of the Lambs*)
Best actress: Jodie Foster (*The Silence of the Lambs*)
Best director: Jonathan Demme (*The Silence of the Lambs*)

1992

Best actor: Al Pacino (*Scent of a Woman*)
Best actress: Emma Thompson (*Howards End*)
Best director: Clint Eastwood (*Unforgiven*)

1993

Best actor: Tom Hanks (*Philadelphia*)
Best actress: Holly Hunter (*The Piano*)
Best director: Steven Spielberg (*Schindler's List*)

1994

Best actor: Tom Hanks (*Forrest Gump*)
Best actress: Jessica Lange (*Blue Sky*)
Best director: Robert Zemeckis (*Forrest Gump*)

1995

Best actor: Nicolas Cage (*Leaving Las Vegas*)
Best actress: Susan Sarandon (*Dead Man Walking*)
Best director: Mel Gibson (*Braveheart*)

1996

Best actor: Geoffrey Rush (*Shine*)
Best actress: Frances McDormand (*Fargo*)
Best director: Anthony Minghella (*The English Patient*)

1997

Best actor: Jack Nicholson (*As Good As It Gets*)
Best actress: Helen Hunt (*As Good As It Gets*)
Best director: James Cameron (*Titanic*)

1998

Best actor: Robert Benigni (*Life is Beautiful* [*La Vita è Bella*])
Best actress: Gwyneth Paltrow (*Shakespeare in Love*)
Best director: Steven Spielberg (*Saving Private Ryan*)

Baseball Hall of Fame Inductees

Year of Induction	Player
1999	George Brett
	Nolan Ryan
	Robin Yount
1998	Don Sutton
1997	Phil Niekro
1995	Mike Schmidt
1994	Steve Carlton
1993	Reggie Jackson
1992	Rollie Fingers
	Tom Seaver
1991	Rod Carew
	Ferguson Jenkins
	Gaylord Perry
1990	Jim Palmer
	Joe Morgan
1989	Johnny Bench
	Carl Yastrzemski
1988	Willie Stargell
1987	Billy Williams
	Catfish Hunter
1986	Willie McCovey
1985	Lou Brock
	Hoyt Wilhelm
1983	Juan Marichal
	Brooks Robinson
1982	Hank Aaron
	Frank Robinson
1981	Bob Gibson
1980	Al Kaline
	Duke Snider
1979	Willie Mays
1978	Eddie Mathews
1977	Ernie Banks
1976	Bob Lemon
	Robin Roberts
1975	Ralph Kiner
1974	Whitey Ford
	Mickey Mantle
1973	Warren Spahn
	Roberto Clemente
1972	Yogi Berra
	Sandy Koufax
	Early Wynn
1970	Lou Boudreau
1969	Roy Campanella
	Stan Musial

Year of Induction	Player
1968	Joe Medwick
1967	Red Ruffing
	Ted Williams
1964	Luke Appling
1962	Bob Feller
	Jackie Robinson
1956	Joe Cronin
	Hank Greenberg
1955	Joe DiMaggio
	Gabby Hartnett
	Ted Lyons
	Dazzy Vance
1954	Bill Dickey
	Rabbit Maranville
	Bill Terry
1953	Dizzy Dean
	Al Simmons
1952	Harry Heilmann
	Paul Waner
1951	Jimmie Foxx
	Mel Ott
1949	Charlie Gehringer
1948	Herb Pennock
	Pie Traynor
1947	Michey Cochrane
	Frank Frisch
	Lefty Grove
	Carl Hubbell
1942	Rogers Hornsby
1939	Eddie Collins
	Lou Gehrig
	Willie Keeler
	George Sisler
1938	Grover Alexander
1937	Nap Lajoie
	Tris Speaker
	Cy Young
1936	Ty Cobb
	Walter Johnson
	Christy Mathewson
	Babe Ruth
	Honus Wagner

Year of Induction	Player
1998	George Davis
	Larry Doby
	Lee MacPhail
	Wilbur Rogan

Year of Induction	Player
1997	Tommy Lasorda
	Nellie Fox
	Willie J. Wells, Sr.
1996	Jim Bunning
	Earl Weaver
	Ned Hanlon
	Bill Foster
1995	Richie Ashburn
	Leon Day
	William Hulbert
	Vic Willis
1994	Leo Durocher
	Phil Rizzuto
1992	Hal Newhouser
	Bill McGowen
1991	Bill Veeck
	Tony Lazzeri
1989	Al Barlick
	Red Schoendienst
1987	Ray Dandridge
1986	Bobby Doerr
	Ernie Lombardi
1985	Enos Slaughter
	Arky Vaughan
1984	Rick Ferrell
	Pee Wee Reese
1983	Walter Alston
	George Kell
1982	Happy Chandler
	Travis Jackson
1981	Johnny Mize
	Rube Foster
1980	Chuck Klein
	Tom Yawkey
1979	Hack Wilson
	Warren Giles
1978	Larry MacPhail
	Addie Joss
1977	Al Lopez
	Amos Rusie
	Joe Sewell
1976	Roger Connor
	Cal Hubbard
	Fred Lindstrom
1975	Earl Averill
	Bucky Harris
	Billy Herman
1974	Jim Bottomley
	Jocko Conlan
	Sam Thompson
1973	Billy Evans
	George Kelly
	Mickey Welch
1972	Lefty Gomez
	William Harridge
	Ross Youngs
1971	Dave Bancroft
	Jake Beckley
	Chick Hafey
	Harry Hopper
	Joe Kelley
	Rube Marquard
	George Weiss
1970	Earle Combs
	Ford Frick
	Jesse Haines
1969	Stan Coveleski
	Waite Hoyt
1968	Kiki Cuyler
	Goose Goslin
1967	Branch Rickey
	Lloyd Waner
1966	Casey Stengel
1965	Pud Galvin
1964	Red Faber
	Burleigh Grimes
	Miller Huggins
	Tim Keefe
	Heine Manush
	John Ward
1963	John Clarkson
	Elmer Flick
	Sam Rice
	Eppa Rixey
1962	Bill McKechnie
	Edd Roush
1961	Max Carey
	Billy Hamilton
1959	Zack Wheat
1957	Sam Crawford
	Joe McCarthy
1955	Frank Baker
	Ray Schalk
1953	Ed Barrow
	Chief Bender
	Thomas Connolly
	Bill Klem
	Bobby Wallace
	Harry Wright
1949	Mordecai Brown
	Kid Nichols
1946	Jesse Burkett
	Frank Chance
	Jack Chesbro
	Johnny Evers
	Clark Griffith
	Tommy McCarthy
	Joe McGinnity

	Eddie Plank	1938	Alexander Cartwright, Jr.
	Joe Tinker		Henry Chadwick
	Rube Waddell	1936	Morgan Bulkeley
	Ed Walsh		Ban Johnson
1945	Roger Bresnahan		John McGraw
	Dan Brouthers		Connie Mack
	Fred Clarke		George Wright
	Jimmy Collins		
	Ed Delahanty	(elected by the Negro League
	Hugh Duffy	Committee)
	Hugh Jennings	

		Year of	
	Michael Kelly	Induction	Player
	Jim O'Rourke	1977	Pop Lloyd
	Wilbert Robinson		Martin Dihigo
1944	Kenesaw Mountain	1976	Oscar Charleston
	Landis	1975	Judy Johnson
1939	Cap Anson	1974	Cool Papa Bell
	Charles Comiskey	1973	Monte Irvin
	Candy Cummings	1972	Josh Gibson
	Buck Ewing		Buck Leonard
	Hoss Radbourn	1971	Satchel Paige
	Al Spalding		

PRO FOOTBALL HALL OF FAME INDUCTEES

1999
Eric Dickerson
Tom Mack
Ozzie Newsome
Billy Shaw
Lawrence Taylor

1998
Paul Krause
Tommy McDonald
Anthony Munoz
Mike Singletary
Dwight Stephenson

1997
Mike Haynes
Wellington Mara
Don Shula
Mike Webster

1996
Lou Creekmur
Dan Dierdorf
Joe Gibbs
Charlie Joiner
Mel Renfro

1995
Jim Finks
Henry Jordan
Steve Largent
Lee Roy Selmon
Kellen Winslow

1994
Tony Dorsett
Harry (Bud) Grant
Jimmy Johnson
Leroy Kelly
Jackie Smith
Randy White

1993
Dan Fouts
Larry Little
Chuck Noll
Walter Payton
Bill Walsh

1992
Lem Barney
Al Davis
John Mackey
John Riggins

1991
Earl Campbell
John Hannah
Stan Jones
Tex Schramm
Jan Stenerud

1990
Junious (Buck) Buchanan
Bob Griese
Franco Harris
Ted Hendricks
Jack Lambert
Tom Landry
Bob St. Clair

1989
Mel Blount
Terry Bradshaw
Art Shell
Willie Wood

1988
Fred Bilentnikoff
Mike Ditka
Jack Ham
Alan Page

1987
Larry Csonka
Len Dawson
Joe Greene
John Henry Johnson
Jim Langer
Don Maynard
Gene Upshaw

1986
Paul Hornung
Ken Houston
Willie Lanier
Frank Tarkenton
Doak Walter

1985
Frank Gatski
Joe Namath
Pete Rozelle
O.J. Simpson
Roger Stauback

1984
Willie Brown
Mike McCormack
Charley Taylor
Arnie Weinmeister

1983
Bobby Bell
Sid Gillman
Sonny Jurgensen
Bobby Mitchell
Paul Warfield

1982
Doug Atkins
Sam Huff
George Musso
Merlin Olsen

1981
Morris (Red) Badgro
George Blanda
Willie Davis
Jim Ringo

1980
Herb Adderley
David (Deacon) Jones
Bob Lilly
Jim Otto

1979
Dick Butkus
Yale Lary
Ron Mix
Johnny Unitas

1978
Lance Alworth
Weeb Ewbank
Alphonse (Tuffy) Leemans
Ray Nitschke
Larry Wilson

1977
Frank Gifford
Forrest Gregg
Gale Sayers
Bart Starr
Bill Willis

1976
Ray Flaherty
Len Ford
Jim Taylor

1975
Roosevelt Brown
George Connor
Dante Lavelli
Lenny Moore

1974
Tony Canadeo
Bill George
Lou Groza
Dick (Night Train) Lane

1973
Raymond Berry
Jim Parker
Joe Schmidt

1972
Lamar Hunt
Gino Marchetti
Ollie Matson
Clarence (Ace) Parker

1971
Jim Brown
Bill Hewitt
Frank (Bruiser) Kinard
Vince Lombardi
Andy Robustelli

Y.A. Tittle
Norm Van Brocklin

1970
Jack Christiansen
Tom Fears
Hugh McElhenny
Pete Pihos

1969
Glen (Turk) Edwards
Earle (Greasy) Neale
Leo Nomellini
Joe Perry
Ernie Stautner

1968
Cliff Battles
Art Donovan
Elroy (Crazylegs) Hirsch
Wayne Millner
Marion Motley
Charley Trippi
Alex Wojciechowicz

1967
Chuck Bednarik
Charles Bidwill
Paul Brown
Bobby Layne
Dan Reeves
Ken Strong
Joe Stydahar
Emlen Tunnell

1966
Bill Dudley
Joy Guyon
Arnie Herber
Walt Kiesling
George McAfee
Steve Owen
Hugh (Shorty) Ray
Clyde (Bulldog) Turner

1965
Guy Chamberlin
John (Paddy) Driscoll
Dan Fortmann
Otto Graham
Sid Luckman
Steve Van Buren
Bob Waterfield

1964
Jimmy Conzelman
Ed Healey
Clark Hinkle
Roy (Link) Lyman
August (Mike) Michaelske
Art Rooney
George Trafton

1963
Sammy Baugh
Bert Bell
Joe Carr
Earl (Dutch) Clark
Red Grange
George Halas
Mel Hein
Wilbur (Pete) Henry

Cal Hubbard
Don Hutson
Earl (Curly) Lambeau
Tim Mara
George Preston Marshall
Johnny Blood (McNally)
Bronko Nagurski
Ernie Nevers
Jim Thorpe

BASKETBALL HALL OF FAME INDUCTEES

Year of Induction	Player
1998	Larry Bird
	Arnie Risen
1996	Alex English
	Bailey Howell
1995	George Gervin
	Gail Goodrich
	David Thompson
	George Yardley
1994	Kareem Abdul-Jabbar
	Vern Mikkelsen
1993	Harold E. "Buddy" Jeanette
1992	Walt Bellamy
	Julius "Dr. J" Erving
	Dan Issel
	Dick McGuire
	Calvin Murphy
	Bill Walton
1991	Connie Hawkins
	Bob Lanier
1990	Nate "Tiny" Archibald
	Dave Cowens
	Harry "The Horse" Gallatin
1989	Dave Bing
	Elvin "The Big E" Hayes
	Neil Johnston
	Earl "The Pearl" Monroe
1988	William "Pop" Gates
	K.C. Jones
	Lenny Wilkens
1987	Clyde Lovellette
	Wes Unseld
1986	Rick Barry
	Walt "Clyde" Frazier
	Robert Houbregs
	Pete Maravich
	Bobby Wanzer
1985	Billy Cunningham
	Tom Heinsohn
1984	Al Cervi
	Nate Thurmond

Year of Induction	Player
1983	John Havlicek
	Sam Jones
1982	Bill Bradley
	Dave DeBusschere
	Jack Twyman
1981	Hal Greer
	Slater Martin
	Frank Ramsey
	Willis Reed
1979	Jerry Lucas
	Oscar Robertson
	Jerry West
1978	Wilt Chamberlain
1977	Paul Arizin
	Joe Fulks
	Cliff Hagan
	Jim Pollard
1976	Elgin Baylor
1975	Tom Gola
	Bill Sharman
1974	Bill Russell
1972	Dolph Schayes
1970	Bob Cousy
	Bob Pettit
1969	Bob Davies
1966	Joe Lapchick
1964	John "Honey" Russell
1961	Andy Phillip
1960	Edward "Easy Ed" Macauley
1959	George Mikan

Year of Induction	Coach
1998	Alex Hannum
	Lenny Wilkens
1996	Pete Carril
1993	Charles J. "Chuck" Daly
1991	Al McGuire
	Jack Ramsay
1985	William "Red" Holzman
1976	Frank McGuire
1975	Harry Litwack

1968	Arnold "Red" Auerbach	1965	Walter Brown
1967	Alvin "Doggie" Julian		Bill Mokray
1964	Ken Loeffler	1964	Edward "Ned" Irish
		1959	Harold Olsen

Year of Induction	**Contributor**	**Year of Induction**	**Referee**
1990	Larry Fleisher	1994	Earl Strom
	Larry O'Brien	1979	J. Dallas Shirley
1980	J. Walter Kennedy	1978	Jim Enright
1979	Lester Harrison	1977	John Nucatola
1978	Pete Newell	1959	Matthew "Pat" Kennedy
1973	Maurice Podoloff		
1971	Eddie Gottlieb		

ROCK AND ROLL HALL OF FAME INDUCTEES

1999
Billy Joel
Curtis Mayfield
Paul McCartney
Del Shannon
Dusty Springfield
Bruce Springsteen
Staple Singers

Non-Performer
George Martin

Early Influences
Charles Brown
Bob Wills and His Texas Playboys

1998
Eagles
Fleetwood Mac
Mamas and Papas
Lloyd Price
Santana
Gene Vincent

Non-Performer
Allen Toussaint

Early Influence
Jelly Roll Morton

1997
Bee Gees
Buffalo Springfield
Crosby, Stills and Nash
Jackson Five
Joni Mitchell
Parliament-Funkadelic
(Young) Rascals

Non-Performer
Syd Nathan

Early Influences
Mahalia Jackson
Bill Monroe

1996
David Bowie
Jefferson Airplane
Little Willie John
Gladys Knight and the Pips
Pink Floyd
Shirelles
Velvet Underground

Non-Performer
Tom Donahue

Early Influence
Pete Seeger

1995
The Allman Brothers Band
Al Green
Janis Joplin
Led Zeppelin
Martha and the Vandellas
Neil Young
Frank Zappa

Non-Performer
Paul Ackerman
Early Influence
Orioles

1994
Animals
The Band
Duane Eddy
Grateful Dead
Elton John
John Lennon
Bob Marley
Rod Stewart

Non-Performer
Johnny Otis

Early Influence
Willie Dixon

1993
Ruth Brown
Cream
Creedence Clearwater Revival
Doors
Etta James
Frankie Lymon and the Teenagers
Van Morrison
Sly and the Family Stone

Non-Performers
Dick Clark
Milt Gabler

Early Influence
Dinah Washington

1992
Bobby "Blue" Bland
Booker T. and the M.G.'s
Johnny Cash
Jimi Hendrix
Isley Brothers
Sam and Dave
Yardbirds

Non-Performers
Leo Fender
Bill Graham
Doc Pomus

Early Influences
Elmore James
Professor Longhair

1991
La Vern Baker
Byrds
John Lee Hooker
Impressions
Wilson Pickett
Jimmy Reed
Ike and Tina Turner

Non-Performers
Dave Bartholomew
Ralph Bass

Early Influence
Howlin' Wolf

Lifetime Achievement
Nesuhi Ertegun

1990
Hank Ballard
Bobby Darin
Four Seasons
Four Tops
Kinks
Platters
Simon and Garfunkel
The Who

Non-Performers
Gerry Goffin and Carole King
Holland, Dozier, and Holland

Early Influences
Louis Armstrong
Charlie Christian
Ma Rainey

1989
Dion
Otis Redding
Rolling Stones
Temptations
Stevie Wonder

Non-Performer
Phil Spector

Early Influences
The Ink Spots
Bessie Smith
Soul Stirrers

1988
Beach Boys
Beatles
Drifters
Bob Dylan
Supremes

Non-Performer
Berry Gordy, Jr.

Early Influences
Woody Guthrie
Lead Belly
Les Paul

1987
Coasters
Eddie Cochran
Bo Diddley
Aretha Franklin
Marvin Gaye
Bill Haley
B. B. King
Clyde McPhatter
Ricky Nelson
Roy Orbison
Carl Perkins
Smokey Robinson
Big Joe Turner
Muddy Waters
Jackie Wilson

Non-Performers
Leonard Chess

Ahmet Ertegun
Jerry Leiber and Mike Stoller
Jerry Wexler

Early Influences
Louis Jordan
T-Bone Walker
Hank Williams

1986
Chuck Berry
James Brown
Ray Charles
Sam Cooke
Fats Domino
Everly Brothers
Buddy Holly
Jerry Lee Lewis
Elvis Presley
Little Richard

Non-Performers
Alan Freed
Sam Phillips

Early-Influences
Robert Johnson
Jimmie Rodgers
Jimmy Yancey

Lifetime Achievement
John Hammond

COUNTRIES OF THE WORLD

Country	Capital	Continent/Area	Nationality
Afghanistan	Kabul	Asia	Afghan
Albania	Tirane	Europe	Albanian
Algeria	Algiers	Africa	Algerian
Andorra	Andorra la Vella	Europe	Andorran
Angola	Luanda	Africa	Angolan
Antigua and Barbuda	Saint John's	North America	Antiguan, Barbudan
Argentina	Buenos Aires	South America	Argentine
Armenia	Yerevan	Asia	Armenian
Australia	Canberra	Australia	Australian
Austria	Vienna	Europe	Austrian
Azerbaijan	Baku	Asia	Azerbaijani
Bahamas, The	Nassau	North America	Bahamian
Bahrain	Manama	Asia	Bahraini
Bangladesh	Dhaka	Asia	Bangaldeshi
Barbados	Bridgetown	North America	Barbadian
Belarus	Minsk	Europe	Belorussian, Belarussian, or Belarusian
Belgium	Brussels	Europe	Belgian
Belize	Belmopan	North America	Belizean
Benin	Porto-Novo	Africa	Beninese
Bhutan	Thimphu	Asia	Bhutanese
Bolivia	La Paz; Sucre	South America	Bolivian
Bosnia and Herzegovina	Sarajevo	Europe	Bosnian, Herzegovinian
Botswana	Gaborone	Africa	Motswana, sing., Batswana, pl.
Brazil	Brasilia	South America	Brazilian
Brunei	Bandar Seri Begawan	Asia	Bruneian
Bulgaria	Sofia	Europe	Bulgarian
Burkina	Ouagadougou	Africa	Burkinabe
Burma (Myanmar)	Rangoon	Asia	Burmese
Burundi	Bujumbura	Africa	Burundian, n.; Burundi, adj.
Cambodia	Phnom Penh	Asia	Cambodian
Cameroon	Yaound	Africa	Cameroonian
Canada	Ottawa	North America	Canadian
Cape Verde	Praia	Africa	Cape Verdean
Central African Republic	Bangui	Africa	Central African
Chad	N'Djamena	Africa	Chadian
Chile	Santiago	South America	Chilean
China	Beijing	Asia	Chinese
Colombia	Bogot	South America	Colombian
Comoros	Moroni	Africa	Comoran
Congo, Republic of the	Brazzaville	Africa	Congolese, n.; Congolese or Congo, adj.
Congo (formerly Zaire)	Kinshasa	Africa	Congolese
Costa Rica	San Jos	North America	Costa Rican
Côte d'Ivoire (Ivory Coast)	Yamoussoukro	Africa	Ivorian
Croatia	Zagreb	Europe	Croat, n.; Croatian, adj.
Cuba	Havana	North America	Cuban
Cyprus	Nicosia	Europe	Cypriot
Czech Republic	Prague	Europe	Czech
Denmark	Copenhagen	Europe	Dane, n.; Danish, adj.
Djibouti	Djibouti	Africa	Djiboutian
Dominica	Roseau	North America	Dominican
Dominican Republic	Santo Domingo	North America	Dominican
Ecuador	Quito	South America	Ecuadorian
Egypt	Cairo	Africa	Egyptian
El Salvador	San Salvador	North America	Salvadoran Equatorial
Guinea	Malabo	Africa	Equatorial Guinean or Equatoguinean
Eritrea	Asmara	Africa	Eritrean
Estonia	Tallinn	Europe	Estonian
Ethiopia	Addis Ababa	Africa	Ethiopian
Fiji	Suva	Oceania	Fijian
Finland	Helsinki	Europe	Finn, n.; Finnish, adj.
France	Paris	Europe	French
Gabon	Libreville	Africa	Gabonese
Gambia, The	Banjul	Africa	Gambian
Georgia	T'bilisi	Asia	Georgian
Germany	Berlin	Europe	German
Ghana	Accra	Africa	Ghanaian
Greece	Athens	Europe	Greek
Grenada	Saint George's	North America	Grenadian
Guatemala	Guatemala	North America	Guatemalan

Guinea	Conakry	Africa	Guinean
Guinea-Bissau	Bissau	Africa	Guinea-Bissauan
Guyana	Georgetown	South America	Guyanese
Haiti	Port-au-Prince	North America	Haitian
Holy See	Vatican City	Europe	
Honduras	Tegucigalpa	North America	Honduran
Hungary	Budapest	Europe	Hungarian
Iceland	Reykjavik	Europe	Icelander, n.; Icelandic, adj.
India	New Delhi	Asia	Indian
Indonesia	Jakarta	Asia	Indonesian
Iran	Tehran	Asia	Iranian
Iraq	Baghdad	Asia	Iraqi
Ireland	Dublin	Europe	Irish
Israel	Jerusalem	Asia	Israeli
Italy	Rome	Europe	Italian
Ivory Coast (see Côte d'Ivoire)			
Jamaica	Kingston	North America	Jamaican
Japan	Tokyo	Asia	Japanese
Jordan	Amman	Asia	Jordanian
Kazakhstan	Astana	Asia	Kazakhstani
Kenya	Nairobi	Africa	Kenyan
Kiribati	Tarawa	Oceania	I-Kiribati
Korea, North	P'yongyang	Asia	North Korean
Korea, South	Seoul	Asia	South Korean
Kuwait	Kuwait	Asia	Kuwaiti
Kyrgyzstan	Bishkek	Asia	Kyrgyz
Laos	Vientiane	Asia	Lao or Laotian
Latvia	Riga	Europe	Latvian
Lebanon	Beirut	Asia	Lebanese
Lesotho	Maseru	Africa	Mosotho, sing.; Basotho, pl.; Basotho, adj.
Liberia	Monrovia	Africa	Liberian
Libya	Tripoli	Africa	Libyan
Liechtenstein	Vaduz	Europe	Liechtensteiner, n.; Liechtenstein, adj.
Lithuania	Vilnius	Europe	Lithuanian
Luxembourg	Luxembourg	Europe	Luxembourger, n.; Luxembourg, adj.
Macedonia, The Former Yugoslav Republic of	Skopje	Europe	Macedonian
Madagascar	Antananarivo	Africa	Malagasy
Malawi	Lilongwe	Africa	Malawian
Malaysia	Kuala Lumpur	Asia	Malaysian
Maldives	Male	Asia	Maldivian
Mali	Bamako	Africa	Malian
Malta	Valletta	Europe	Maltese
Marshall Islands	Majuro	Oceania	Marshallese
Mauritania	Nouakchott	Africa	Mauritanian
Mauritius	Port Louis	Africa	Mauritian
Mexico	Mexico	North America	Mexican
Micronesia, Federated States of	Kolonia	Oceania	Micronesian
Moldova	Chisinau	Europe	Moldovan
Monaco	Monaco	Europe	Monacan or Monegasque
Mongolia	Ulaanbaatar	Asia	Mongolian
Morocco	Rabat	Africa	Moroccan
Mozambique	Maputo	Africa	Mozambican Myanmar (see Burma)
Namibia	Windhoek	Africa	Namibian
Nauru	Yaren District	Oceania	Nauruan
Nepal	Kathmandu	Asia	Nepalese
Netherlands	Amsterdam; The Hague	Europe	Dutchman or Dutchwoman, n.; Dutch, adj.
New Zealand	Wellington	Oceania	New Zealander, n.; New Zealand, adj.
Nicaragua	Managua	North America	Nicaraguan
Niger	Niamey	Africa	Nigerien
Nigeria	Abuja	Africa	Nigerian
Norway	Oslo	Europe	Norwegian
Oman	Muscat	Asia	Omani
Pakistan	Islamabad	Asia	Pakistani
Palau	Koror	Oceania	Palauan
Panama	Panama	North America	Panamanian Papua
New Guinea	Port Moresby	Oceania	Papua New Guinean
Paraguay	Asuncin	South America	Paraguayan
Peru	Lima	South America	Peruvian
Philippines	Manila	Asia	Filipino, n.; Philippine, adj.
Poland	Warsaw	Europe	Pole, n.; Polish, adj.
Portugal	Lisbon	Europe	Portuguese

Qatar	Doha	Asia	Quatari
Romania	Bucharest	Europe	Romanian
Russia	Moscow	Europe & Asia	Russian
Rwanda	Kigali	Africa	Rwandan
Saint Kitts and Nevis	Basseterre	North America	Kittsian; Nevisian
Saint Lucia	Castries	North America	St. Lucian
Saint Vincent and the Grenadines	Kingstown	North America	St. Vincentian or Vincentian
San Marino	San Marino	Europe	Sammarinese
Sao Tome and Principe	Sao Tome	Africa	Sao Tomean
Saudi Arabia	Riyadh	Asia	Saudi or Saudi Arabian
Senegal	Dakar	Africa	Senegalese
Seychelles	Victoria	Indian Ocean	Seychellois, n.; Seychelles, adj.
Sierra Leone	Freetown	Africa	Sierra Leonean
Singapore	Singapore	Asia	Singaporean, n.; Singapore, adj.
Slovakia	Bratislava	Europe	Slovak
Slovenia	Ljubljana	Europe	Slovene, n.; Slovenian, adj.
Solomon Islands	Honiara	Oceania	Solomon Islander
Somalia	Mogadishu	Africa	Somali
South Africa	Pretoria; Cape Town; Bloem-fontein	Africa	South African
Spain	Madrid	Europe	Spanish
Sri Lanka	Colombo	Asia	Sri Lankan
Sudan	Khartoum	Africa	Sudanese
Suriname	Paramaribo	South America	Surinamer, n.; Surinamese, adj.
Swaziland	Mbabane	Africa	Swazi
Sweden	Stockholm	Europe	Swede, n.; Swedish, adj.
Switzerland	Bern	Europe	Swiss
Syria	Damascus	Asia	Syrian
Tajikistan	Dushanbe	Asia	Tajik
Tanzania	Dar es Salaam	Africa	Tanzanian
Thailand	Bangkok	Asia	Thai
Togo	Lome	Africa	Togolese
Tonga	Nuku'alofa	Oceania	Tongan
Trinidad and Tobago	Port-of-Spain	South America	Trinidadian; Tobagonian
Tunisia	Tunis	Africa	Tunisian
Turkey	Ankara	Asia & Europe	Turk, n.; Turkish, adj.
Turkmenistan	Ashgabat	Asia	Turkmen
Tuvalu	Funafuti	Oceania	Tuvaluan
Uganda	Kampala	Africa	Ugandan
Ukraine	Kiev	Europe	Ukrainian
United Arab Emirates	Abu Dhabi	Africa	Emirian
United Kingdom	London	Europe	Briton, n.; British, collective pl. & adj.
United States of America	Washington, DC	North America	American
Uruguay	Montevideo	South America	Uruguayan
Uzbekistan	Tashkent	Asia	Uzbek
Vanuatu	Port-Vila	Oceania	Ni-Vanuatu
Venezuela	Caracas	South America	Venezuelan
Vietnam	Hanoi	Asia	Vietnamese
Western Samoa	Apia	Oceania	Western Samoan
Yemen	Sanaa	Asia	Yemeni
Yugoslavia (Serbia and Montenegro)	Belgrade	Europe	Yugoslav Serb, n.; Serbian, adj; Montenegran Zaire (see Congo)
Zambia	Lusaka	Africa	Zambian
Zimbabwe	Harare	Africa	Zimbabwean

STATES OF THE UNITED
STATES OF AMERICA

State	Traditional & Postal abbreviations	Capital
Alabama	Ala.; AL	Montgomery
Alaska	Alas.; AK	Juneau
Arizona	Ariz.; AZ	Phoenix
Arkansas	Ark.; AR	Little Rock
California	Calif.; CA	Sacramento
Colorado	Col.; CO	Denver
Connecticut	Conn.; CT	Hartford
Delaware	Del.; DE	Dover
Florida	Fla.; FL	Tallahassee
Georgia	Ga.; GA	Atlanta
Hawaii	Haw.; HI	Honolulu
Idaho	Id.; ID	Boise
Illinois	Ill.; IL	Springfield
Indiana	Ind.; IN	Indianapolis
Iowa	Ia.; IA	Des Moines
Kansas	Kan.; KS	Topeka
Kentucky	Ky.; KY	Frankfort
Louisiana	La.; LA	Baton Rouge
Maine	Me.; ME	Augusta
Maryland	Md.; MD	Annapolis
Massachusetts	Mass.; MA	Boston
Michigan	Mich.; MI	Lansing
Minnesota	Minn.; MN	St. Paul
Mississippi	Miss.; MS	Jackson
Missouri	Mo.; MO	Jefferson City
Montana	Mont.; MT	Helena
Nebraska	Nebr.; NE	Lincoln
Nevada	Nev.; NV	Carson City
New Hampshire	N.H.; NH	Concord
New Jersey	N.J.; NJ	Trenton
New Mexico	N. Mex.; NM	Santa Fe
New York	N.Y.; NY	Albany
North Carolina	N.C.; NC	Raleigh
North Dakota	N. Dak.; ND	Bismarck
Ohio	O.; OH	Columbus
Oklahoma	Okla.; OK	Oklahoma City
Oregon	Ore.; OR	Salem
Pennsylvania	Pa.; PA	Harrisburg
Rhode Island	R.I.; RI	Providence
South Carolina	S.C.; SC	Columbia
South Dakota	S. Dak.; SD	Pierre
Tennessee	Tenn.; TN	Nashville
Texas	Tex.; TX	Austin
Utah	Ut.; UT	Salt Lake City
Vermont	Vt.; VT	Montpelier
Virginia	Va.; VA	Richmond
Washington	Wash.; WA	Olympia
West Virginia	W. Va.; WV	Charleston
Wisconsin	Wis.; WI	Madison
Wyoming	Wyo.; WY	Cheyenne

LARGEST METROPOLITAN AREAS
OF THE WORLD

Metropolitan Area	Country	Pop. (1990) in millions
Mexico City	Mexico	20.2
Tokyo	Japan	18.1
São Paulo	Brazil	17.4
New York City	USA	16.2
Shanghai	China	13.4
Bombay (Mumbai)	India	12.6
Los Angeles	USA	11.9
Calcutta	India	11.8
Buenos Aires	Argentina	11.5
Seoul	Korea	11.0
Beijing	China	10.8
Rio de Janeiro	Brazil	10.7
Tianjin	China	9.4
Jakarta	Indonesia	9.3
Cairo	Egypt	9.0
Delhi	India	8.8
Moscow	Russia	8.8
Manila	Philippines	8.5
Osaka	Japan	8.5
Paris	France	8.5

WORLD LAND AREA BY CONTINENT

| | Area | | Percent of the |
	Sq. miles	Sq. km.	world's land
Asia	17,100,000	44,350,000	29.6
Africa	11,700,000	30,300,000	20.2
North America	9,350,000	24,250,000	16.2
South America	6,900,000	17,800,000	11.8
Antarctica	5,500,000	14,250,000	9.5
Europe	4,050,000	10,500,000	7.0
Oceania (incl. Australia and New Zealand	3,300,000	8,500,000	5.7
TOTAL	57,900,000	149,950,000	100.0

WORLD POPULATION BY CONTINENT

	Pop. (1990)	Pop. density (people/sq. mile)
Asia	3,112,700,000	293
Africa	642,111,000	54
Europe	498,371,000	249
North America	427,226,000	34
South America	296,716,000	44
Oceania	26,481,000	8
TOTAL	5,292,200,000	101

OCEANS AND SEAS OF THE WORLD

	Area		Maximum depth	
	Sq. miles	Sq. km.	Feet	Meters
Oceans				
Pacific Ocean	63,800	165,250	36,200	11,034
Atlantic Ocean	31,830	82,440	30,246	9,219
Indian Ocean	28,360	73,440	24,442	7,450
Arctic Ocean	5,400	14,090	17,881	5,450
Seas				
South China Sea	1,331	3,447	18,241	5,560
Caribbean Sea	1,063	2,754	25,197	7,680
Mediterranean Sea	967	2,505	16,470	5,020
Sea of Okhotsk	610	1,580	11,063	3,372
Gulf of Mexico	596	1,544	14,370	4,380
Hudson Bay	475	1,230	850	259
Sea of Japan	389	1,007	12,280	3,733
East China Sea	290	752	9,126	2,782
North Sea	222	575	2,170	659
Black Sea	178	461	7,360	2,237
Red Sea	169	438	7,370	2,240
Baltic Sea	163	422	1,440	437
Yellow Sea	161	417	300	91

MAJOR RIVERS OF THE WORLD

River	Length Miles	Km.
Nile	4,160	6,695
Amazon	4,150	6,683
Yangtze (Chiang Jiang)	3,964	6,380
Mississippi-Missouri-Red Rock	3,741	6,019
Ob-Irtysh	3,481	5,410
Yenesei-Angara	3,100	4,989
Yellow (Huang He)	3,000	4,830
Congo	2,800	4,630
Lena	2,750	4,400
Amur-Shilka	2,744	4,390
Mackenzie-Peace-Finlay	2,635	4,241
Mekong	2,600	4,180
Missouri-Red Rock	2,564	4,125
Niger	2,550	4,100
Mississippi	2,470	3,975
Plate-Paranà	2,450	3,943
Murray-Darling	2,331	3,751
Missouri	2,315	3,736
Volga	2,292	3,688
Purus	2,100	3,400
São Francisco	1,990	3,200
Rio Grande	1,880	3,030
Yukon	1,870	3,020
Tunguska, Lower	1,861	2,995
Brahmaputra	1,800	2,900
Indus	1,800	2,900
Japurà	1,750	2,815
Danube	1,700	2,736
Euphrates	1,700	2,736
Ganges	1,678	2,700
Para-Tocantins	1,640	2,640
Nelson-S. Saskatchewan-Bow	1,600	2,560
Zambezi	1,600	2,560
Paraguay	1,584	2,549
Ural	1,575	2,534
Amu Darya	1,500	2,400
Kolyma	1,500	2,400
Salween	1,500	2,400
Colorado	1,468	2,333
Arkansas	1,450	2,320
Dnieper	1,370	2,200
Syr Darya	1,370	2,200
Orange	1,155	1,859
St. Lawrence	750	1,200

MAJOR NATURAL LAKES OF THE WORLD

	Area	
	Sq. miles	Sq. km.
Caspian Sea	143,240	370,992
Lake Superior	32,526	84,243
Lake Victoria	26,820	69,464
Aral Sea	24,904	64,501
Lake Huron	24,361	63,096
Lake Michigan	22,300	57,757
Lake Tanganyika	12,650	32,764
Lake Baikal	12,160	31,494
Great Bear Lake	12,095	31,328
Lake Nyasa	11,150	28,879
Great Slave Lake	11,030	28,568
Lake Erie	9,966	25,812
Lake Winnipeg	9,416	24,387
Lake Ontario	7,336	19,001
Lake Balkhash	7,115	18,428
Lake Ladoga	6,835	17,703
Lake Chad*	6,300	16,317
Lake Maracaibo	5,120	13,261
Patos	3,920	10,153
Lake Onega	3,710	9,609
Lake Eyre*	3,600	9,320
Lake Titicaca	3,200	8,288
Lake Nicaragua	3,100	8,029
Lake Mai-Ndombe*	3,100	8,029
Lake Athabasca	3,064	7,935

*indicates large seasonal variations

MAJOR MOUNTAINS OF THE WORLD

Mountain	Location	Height Feet	Meters
Everest	Nepal-China	29,028	8,848
K2	Kashmir	28,250	8,611
Kanchenjunga	Nepal-India	28,209	8,598
Annapurna	Nepal	26,503	8,078
Communism Peak	Tajikstan	24,590	7,495
Aconcagua	Argentina-Chile	22,834	6,960
Ojos del Salado	Argentina-Chile	22,664	6,908
Bonete	Argentina	22,546	6,872
McKinley	Alaska, USA	20,110	6,194
Logan	Yukon, Canada	19,850	6,054
Kilimanjaro	Tanzania	19,340	5,895
Elbrus	Caucasus, Russia	18,481	5,642
Citlaltépetl	Mexico	18,503	5,699
Kenya	Kenya	17,058	5,200
Ararat	Turkey	16,946	5,165
Vinson Massif	Antarctica	16,863	5,140
Margherita Peak	Uganda-Zaire	16,763	5,109
Mont Blanc	France-Italy	15,771	4,807
Wilhelm	Papua New Guinea	14,739	4,509
Whitney	California, USA	14,495	4,418
Matterhorn	Italy-Switzerland	14,688	4,477
Elbert	Colorado, USA	14,431	4,399
Pikes Peak	Colorado, USA	14,110	4,300
Jungfrau	Switzerland	13,642	4,158
Cook	New Zealand	12,349	3,764
Hood	Oregon, USA	11,239	3,426
Olympus	Greece	9,570	2,917
Kosciusko	Australia	7,234	2,228

MAJOR VOLCANOES OF THE WORLD

Volcano	Location	Height (feet)	Last eruption (other notable eruptions)
Cameroon	Cameroon	13,354	1982
El Chichon	Mexico	7,300	1982
Erebus	Ross Is., Antarctica	12,450	1998
Etna	Italy	10,990	1998
Fuji	Honshu, Japan	12,368	1708
Kelud	Java, Indonesia	5,679	1990
Kilauea	Hawaii, USA	4,090	1998
Krakatau (Krakatoa)	Indonesia	2,667	1995 (1883)
Mauna Loa	Hawaii, USA	13,678	1984
Nevado del Ruiz	Colombia	17,457	1991 (1985)
Pelée	Martinique	4,583	1932 (1902)
Pinatubo	Luzon, Philippines	5,249	1995
Rainier	Washington, USA	14,410	1894
St. Helens	Washington, USA	8,312	1991 (1980)
Santa Maria	Guatemala	12,375	1998 (1902)
Santorini	Greece	1,850	1950 (c. 1500 B.C.)
Shasta	California, USA	14,162	1786
Stromboli	Italy	3,038	1998
Taal	Luzon, Philippines	984	1977 (1911)
Unzen	Japan	4,462	1996 (1792)
Vesuvius	Italy	4,190	1944 (A.D. 79)
Wrangell	Alaska, USA	14,269	1907